Chitty on Contracts

VOLUMES IN THE COMMON LAW LIBRARY

Arlidge, Eady & Smith on Contempt
Benjamin's Sale of Goods
Bowstead & Reynolds on Agency
Bullen & Leake & Jacob's Precedents of Pleadings
Charlesworth and Percy on Negligence
Chitty on Contracts
Clerk & Lindsell on Torts
Gatley on Libel and Slander
Goff & Jones, The Law of Restitution
Jackson & Powell on Professional Negligence
McGregor on Damages
Phipson on Evidence

COMMON LAW LIBRARY

CHITTY ON CONTRACTS

THIRY-THIRD EDITION

VOLUME II: SPECIFIC CONTRACTS

SWEET & MAXWELL  THOMSON REUTERS

Published in 2018 by Thomson Reuters,
trading as Sweet & Maxwell. Thomson Reuters is registered in England &
Wales, Company No. 1679046.
Registered office and address for service: 5 Canada Square, Canary Wharf,
London E14 5AQ.

For further information on our products and services, visit *http://
www.sweetandmaxwell.co.uk.*

Computerset by Sweet & Maxwell.
Printed and bound by CPI Group (UK) Ltd Croydon, CR0 4YY.
No natural forests were destroyed to make this product; only farmed timber
was used and re-planted.
A CIP catalogue record of this book is available from the British Library.

ISBN Volume II: 9780414065123

First edition	1826	By Joseph Chitty, Junior
Second edition	1834	By Joseph Chitty, Junior
Third edition	1841	By Thompson Chitty
Fourth edition	1850	By His Hon. Judge J. A. Russell, Q.C.
Fifth edition	1853	By His Hon. Judge J. A. Russell, Q.C.
Sixth edition	1857	By His Hon. Judge J. A. Russell, Q.C.
Seventh edition	1863	By His Hon. Judge J. A. Russell, Q.C.
Eighth edition	1868	By His Hon. Judge J. A. Russell, Q.C.
Ninth edition	1871	By His Hon. Judge J. A. Russell, Q.C.
Tenth edition	1876	By His Hon. Judge J. A. Russell, Q.C.
Eleventh edition	1881	By His Hon. Judge J. A. Russell, Q.C.
Twelfth edition	1890	By J. M. Lely and Sir William Geary
Thirteenth edition	1896	By J. M. Lely
Fourteenth edition	1904	By J. M. Lely
Fifteenth edition	1909	By W. Wyatt Paine
Sixteenth edition	1912	By W. Wyatt Paine
Seventeenth edition	1921	By W. Wyatt Paine
Eighteenth edition	1930	By W. A. MacFarlane and G. W. Wrangham
Nineteenth edition	1937	General Editor: Harold Potter
Twentieth edition	1947	General Editor: Harold Potter
Twenty-first edition	1955	Under the General Editorship of John Burke and Peter Allsop
Twenty-second edition	1961	General Editor: John Morris
Twenty-third edition	1968	General Editor: A. G. Guest
Second Impression	1972	General Editor: A. G. Guest
Twenty-fourth edition	1977	General Editor: A. G. Guest
Second Impression	1979	General Editor: A. G. Guest
Third Impression	1980	General Editor: A. G. Guest
Twenty-fifth edition	1983	General Editor: A. G. Guest
Twenty-sixth edition	1989	General Editor: A. G. Guest
Second Impression	1990	General Editor: A. G. Guest
Third Impression	1991	General Editor: A. G. Guest
Twenty-seventh edition	1994	General Editor: A. G. Guest
Second Impression	1995	General Editor: A. G. Guest
Third Impression	1997	General Editor: A. G. Guest
Fourth Impression	1998	General Editor: A. G. Guest
Twenty-eighth edition	1999	General Editor: H. G. Beale
Second Impression	2001	General Editor: H. G. Beale

Twenty-ninth edition	2004	General Editor: H. G. Beale
Thirtieth edition	2008	General Editor: H. G. Beale
Thirty-first edition	2012	General Editor: H. G. Beale
Thirty-second edition	2015	General Editor: H. G. Beale
Thirty-third edition	2018	General Editor: H. G. Beale

[vii]

G. J. VIRGO, Q.C. (Hon.), M.A. (Cantab.), B.C.L. (Oxon)
Bencher of Lincoln's Inn; Fellow of Downing College, Senior Pro-Vice-Chancellor (Education) and Professor of English Private Law, University of Cambridge

WILLIAM WEBB, B.A. (Cantab.), LL.M. (Virginia), B.C.L. (Oxon)
of Lincoln's Inn, Barrister

R. P. WHISH, Q.C. (Hon.), B.A., B.C.L. (Oxon)
Solicitor of the Supreme Court of Judicature; Emeritus Professor of Law, King's College London

SIMON WHITTAKER, D.Phil., D.C.L. (Oxon)
of Lincoln's Inn, Barrister; Fellow of St John's College and Professor of European Comparative Law, University of Oxford

NOTE TO READERS

Chitty on Contracts, 33rd edition, consists of two volumes. Volume I is the *General Principles* text and Volume II deals with *Specific Contracts*. Customers may choose to purchase either Volume I alone or both Volumes together.

Please note that Volume I contains Chapters 1 to 30 and an Index which relates to Volume I only.

Volume II contains Chapters 31 to 45 and an Index which relates to both Volumes I and II.

TABLE OF CONTENTS

VOLUME 1

PART ONE: INTRODUCTION

PART TWO: FORMATION OF CONTRACT

PART THREE: CAPACITY OF PARTIES

PART FOUR: THE TERMS OF CONTRACT

PART FIVE: ILLEGALITY AND PUBLIC POLICY

PART SIX: JOINT OBLIGATIONS, THIRD PARTIES AND ASSIGNMENT

PART SEVEN: PERFORMANCE AND DISCHARGE

PART EIGHT: REMEDIES FOR BREACH OF CONTRACT

PART NINE: RESTITUTION

PART TEN: CONFLICT OF LAWS

VOLUME 2

F. M. B. Reynolds

32   ARBITRATION

P. J. S. MacDonald Eggers

33   BAILMENT

E. G. McKendrick

34   BILLS OF EXCHANGE AND BANKING

R. J. A. Hooley

35   CARRIAGE BY AIR

D. McClean

36   CARRIAGE BY LAND

P. J. S. MacDonald Eggers

37 CONSTRUCTION CONTRACTS

V. Moran and W. Webb

38 CONSUMER CONTRACTS

S. Whittaker

39 CREDIT AND SECURITY

E. Lomnicka

40 EMPLOYMENT

M. R. Freedland and J. Prassl

41 GAMBLING CONTRACTS

G. H. Treitel

42 INSURANCE

P. J. S. MacDonald Eggers

43 RESTRICTIVE AGREEMENTS AND COMPETITION

R. Whish

44 SALE OF GOODS

L. Merrett

45 SURETYSHIP

S. Whittaker

CONTENTS

TABLE OF STATUTES

Where a reference indicates significant discussion of the statute in the text, it is in **bold**. Where a reference is to a footnote, it is *italic*.

[xvii]

TABLE OF STATUTORY INSTRUMENTS

Where a reference indicates significant discussion of the statutory instrument in the text, it is in **bold**. Where a reference is to a footnote, it is *italic*.

TABLE OF INTERNATIONAL STATUTORY MATERIAL

Where a reference indicates significant discussion of the legislation in the text, it is in **bold**. Where a reference is to a footnote, it is *italic*.

TABLE OF CASES

Where a reference indicates significant discussion of the case in the text, it is in **bold**. Where a reference is to a footnote, it is *italic*.

TABLE OF CASES

TABLE OF EUROPEAN CASES

Where a reference indicates significant discussion of the case in the text, it is in
bold. Where a reference is to a footnote, it is *italic*.

CHAPTER 31

AGENCY

F. M. B. Reynolds

[1]

1.   AGENCY IN GENERAL[1]

31-001   Scope of this chapter   Despite the fact that this chapter appears in Vol.II of the present work, which is entitled "Specific Contracts", agency is a much wider topic than a specific named contract. At common law the word "agency" can be said to represent a body of general rules under which one person, the agent, has the power to change the legal relations of another, the principal.[2] It is sometimes indeed said that prima facie what a person can do himself he can do by an agent; but this is not always so.[3] The main areas in which this power is analysed are the law of contract, where an agent may have power to bind and entitle his principal by contract and by acts connected with the performance of a contract, and the law of property, where he may have power to receive property for his principal or make a valid disposition of his principal's property; and these are dealt with in this chapter. Similar reasoning may appear in other areas (e.g. torts, evidence); but the doctrines of agency are not always so well worked out beyond the main spheres of their operation, and the context in which the reasoning is used and the extent of its use may therefore require careful consideration in each case. Agency reasoning may also be deployed in contexts far from the original paradigm. In such cases the use of the paradigm is often incomplete, but the general reasoning is usually recognisable.[4] The central doctrines which have been developed stress the generality of the agent's power to bind and entitle his principal, while himself dropping out of the transaction and incurring neither rights nor liabilities, though sometimes the agent may

---

[1]   The writer of this chapter is much indebted to discussions with Professor Peter Watts Q.C. of the University of Auckland.

[2]   *Restatement, Third, Agency*, paras 1.01, 2.01 (action that has "legal consequences for the principal").

[3]   The power to act by an agent is sometimes expressly recognised by statute: e.g. Bills of Exchange Act 1882 ss.22–26, 91; Limitation Act 1939 s.24 (now s.30 of the Limitation Act 1980) (see *Wright v Pepin* [1954] 1 W.L.R. 635; *Re Transplanters (Holding Co) Ltd* [1958] 1 W.L.R. 822). The power of trustees to delegate to others is regulated by Trustee Delegation Act 1999; Trustee Act 2000 ss.11–23. As to rights to conduct litigation for another see *Gregory v Turner* [2003] EWCA Civ 183, [2003] 1 W.L.R. 1149; as to verification of documents for another by affidavit see *Clauss v Pir* [1988] Ch. 267. Where a statute is silent, the normal implication is that, in the absence of other indications, the basic rule permitting acts by an agent applies: see *R. v Kent Justices* (1873) L.R. 8 Q.B. 305; *Re Whitley Partners Ltd* (1886) 32 Ch. D. 337; *R. v Assessment Committee of St Mary Abbot's, Kensington* [1891] 1 Q.B. 378; *LCC v Agricultural Food Products Ltd* [1955] 2 Q.B. 218; *McRae v Coulton* (1986) 7 N.S.W.L.R. 644 (containing illuminating discussion as to forms of signature); *General Legal Council (on the application of Whitter) v Frankson* [2006] UKPC 42, [2006] 1 W.L.R. 2803. The Statute of Frauds Amendment Act 1828 s.6 (as to which, see Vol.I, para.7-043) has been held to require personal signature, which has caused difficulties as to signature by agents of companies: see *Hirst v West Riding Union Banking Co* [1901] 2 K.B. 560; *UBAF Ltd v European American Banking Corp (The Pacific Colocotronis)* [1984] Q.B. 713 (noted [1984] J.B.L. 248); and see *McRae v Coulton*, above. A signature may be in electronic form: *Lindsay v O'Loughnane* [2010] EWHC 529 (QB) at [95]; in the context of the Statute of Frauds and guarantees: *Golden Ocean Group Ltd v Salgaocar Mining Industries Pvt Ltd* [2011] EWHC 56 (Comm), [2011] 1 W.L.R. 2575 at [95] (discussing different possible meanings of "electronic signature"); on appeal [2012] EWCA Civ 265, [2012] 1 Lloyd's Rep. 542 at [31] et seq. See also *Ramsay v Love* [2015] EWHC 65 (Ch) (writing machine operated by person with general authority).

[4]   For example, in the context of liquidators and receivers: see Tan and Wee, Ch.8 in *Agency Law in Commercial Practice*, Busch, Macgregor and Watts (eds) (2016). For an extreme use of the analogy see, e.g. *The Global Santosh* [2016] UKSC 20, [2016] 1 W.L.R. 1853, where it is used to allocate responsibility among subcontractors in the unloading of ships.

himself be liable and entitled in addition.[5] These may be said to concern the external aspect of agency. There are also certain typical rules concerning the rights and liabilities of principal and agent inter se. These usually, but not always, involve contractual relations between principal and agent, which can sometimes be appropriately called a contract of agency but are more likely to operate as special rules against the background of some other contract, such as a contract of employment or of hire of services. In particular, they deal with the agent's duties (normally of reasonable care), impose fiduciary duties on the agent,[6] and regulate his rights to remuneration (typically by commission) and to indemnity.[7] These, which alone fit the idea of agency as a specific contract, are usually said to concern the internal aspect of agency.

Incomplete agency: canvassing agents There are other persons who, because 31-002
they represent others in certain respects, may in common speech be called agents, yet who cannot be said to come within the full scope of the law of agency as defined in the previous paragraph These are agents whose function is to introduce business, such as (in England at least) real estate agents,[8] and insurance agents[9]: they are sometimes referred to as "canvassing agents". In the terminology of the previous paragraph, they have an internal relationship with their principals, but their external power to change their principal's legal relations may be very limited indeed[10] or even non-existent. It can indeed be said that persons acting in such a capacity are not agents at all[11]; yet, apart from the fact that the term agent is commonly used of them, most of the typical rules regulating the internal relation between principal and agent, especially those relating to fiduciary obligations,[12] may be applicable. Hence they are normally, and, it is submitted, correctly, subsumed under the law of agency, though its full consequences do not apply: they may be called examples of "incomplete agency".

Distributors and franchisees A third group to which the term "agent" may be 31-003
applied in common speech is that of distributors of particular products. Though it is possible that such a person is an agent in the sense that his obligation to his principal is that of an agent even though he deals with the outside world in his own

---

5   See below, paras 31-083, 3 084.
6   In *UBS AG v Kommunale Wasserwerke Leipzig GmbH* [2017] EWCA Civ 1567, [2017] 2 Lloyd's Rep. 621 at [92] it is said by the majority of the Court of Appeal that "there are no doubt many forms of non-fiduciary agency". This, with respect, may be doubted.
7   See below, paras 31-136 et seq. *Restatement, Third*, adds a requirement of control by the principal: see para.1.01. It is submitted in *Bowstead and Reynolds on Agency*, 21st edn (2018) at para.1-018 that this is of limited significance; but it is alluded to by Hamblen L.J. in *London Borough of Haringey v Ahmed* [2017] EWCA Civ 1861, [2018] 1 P.&C.R. DG12 at [28].
8   See below, para.31-012.
9   See below, para.31-015.
10   For example, they might make their principals liable for their misrepresentations.
11   See *Vogel v R & A Konstam Ltd* [1973] Q.B. 133, 136–137, 147. But cf. *Freehold Land Investments Ltd v Queensland Estates Pty Ltd* (1970) 123 C.L.R. 418, and it seems likely that some such persons involved in the sale of goods can be commercial agents: below, para.31-017.
12   Below, paras 31-118 et seq. *Premium Real Estate Ltd v Stevens* [2009] 2 N.Z.L.R. 384 (real estate agent); *McWilliam v Norton Finance (UK) Ltd* [2015] EWCA Civ 186, [2015] 1 All E.R. (Comm) 1026 (credit broker); *Tigris International BV v China Southern Airlines Co Ltd* [2014] EWCA Civ 1649.

name,[13] it is in fact more likely that the common law will classify such persons as purchasers for resale[14]; and as such no attempt has been made to extend any principles of agency law to them—an extension which would necessarily be by analogy only.[15]

31-004 **Foreign law** Civil law systems may tend to stress the unity of the (internal) notion of representation described above, sometimes deriving the agent's external power from a separate source.[16] They may in consequence classify, sometimes elaborately, different types of representative, developing special rules for the powers, rights and duties of each; and the term "agent" or its translation may carry a specific rather than a general meaning. Also, a distinction is often (but not universally) taken in civil law between "direct representation" and "indirect representation", the latter connoting a method of dealing whereby the "agent" deals personally, but remains on an agency basis with his principal internally.[17] While there can be no objection to a party acting in such a way, such a taxonomic distinction is not recognised by the common law.[18] A further feature of foreign agency law which has surprised some English lawyers is that certain agents may be protected

---

[13] See, e.g. *Bolus & Co Ltd v Inglis Bros Ltd* [1924] N.Z.L.R. 164, 175; *Fraser v Equitorial Shipping Co Ltd (The Ijaola)* [1979] 1 Lloyd's Rep. 103. Such an arrangement may be called "indirect agency" and would be similar to the contract of *commission* in civil law systems: see below, n.18. There could also be true agency functions as regards guarantees, servicing, repairs and the like.

[14] See below, para.31-022.

[15] But the use of "Romalpa" clauses in sale contracts raises problems which can be related to agency, for it may appear that the buyer under reservation of title resells as agent for the seller: see *Aluminium Industrie Vaassen BV v Romalpa Aluminium Ltd* [1976] 1 W.L.R. 676; *Caterpillar (NI) Ltd v John Holt & Co (Liverpool) Ltd* [2013] EWCA Civ 1232, [2014] 1 W.L.R. 2365, disapproved, but in respect of a different point, in *The Res Cogitans* [2016] UKSC 23, [2016] A.C. 1034; below, paras 44-169 et seq.; *Michelin Tyre Co Ltd v Macfarlane (Glasgow) Ltd* (1916) 55 Sc.L.Rep. 35, HL. And it may sometimes be arguable that distributors, and also franchisees, are subject to fiduciary duties: see *Feuer Leather Corp v Frank Johnstone & Sons* [1981] Com. L.R. 251; also *Artifakts Design Group Ltd v NP Rigg Ltd* [1993] 1 N.Z.L.R. 196 (sale of competing goods); cf. *Lothian v Jenolite Ltd*, 1969 S.C. 111; *Hospital Products Ltd v US Surgical Corp* (1985) 156 C.L.R. 41, especially at 92; *Jani-King (GB) Ltd v Pula Enterprises Ltd* [2007] EWHC 2433 (QB), [2008] 1 All E.R. (Comm) 451. In *Toycorp v Milton Bradley Australia Pty Ltd* [1992] 2 V.R. 572 a franchisor was held to have ordered goods as agent for its franchisee.

[16] See Schmitthoff, 1980 I Hague *Recueil des Cours* 115.

[17] This forms a basic division in the *Principles of European Contract Law* (2000). It appears also in the *Draft Common Frame of Reference* (2010) but is avoided in the UNIDROIT *Principles of International Commercial Contracts* (2004).

[18] In civil law countries such a party may sometimes be referred to as a commission agent or *commissionnaire*, to whom it is said that the common law undisclosed principal (below, para.31-063) offers a parallel. The similarity is limited: the doctrine of the undisclosed principal requires that the principal authorise the agent to bind him by contract, which is not true of *commissionnaires*. Such a figure occasionally appears in the English cases: e.g. *Ireland v Livingston* (1872) L.R. 5 H.L. 395, 407–408; *Armstrong v Stokes* (1872) L.R. 7 Q.B. 598, 605; *Robinson v Mollett* (1875) L.R. 7 H.L. 802, 809–810 (three expositions by Blackburn J.); *Maspons y Hermano v Mildred, Goyeneche & Co* (1882) 9 Q.B.D. 530; affirmed (1883) 8 App. Cas. 874; *R & J Bow Ltd v Hill* (1930) 37 Ll.L. Rep. 46, 47–48; *Triffit Nurseries v Salads Etcetera Ltd* [1999] 1 Lloyd's Rep. 697, 700; *Brandeis Brokers Ltd v Black* [2001] 2 Lloyd's Rep. 359; *Royal & Sun Alliance Insurance Plc v MK Digital FZE (Cyprus) Ltd* [2006] EWCA Civ 629, [2006] 2 Lloyd's Rep. 110; *OMV Petrom SA v Glencore International AG* [2015] EWHC 666 (Comm); cf. *Anglo-African Shipping Co Ltd v J. Mortner Ltd* [1962] 1 Lloyd's Rep 610, CA. It seems that such a mode of operation is sometimes artificially adopted for tax reasons. In that respect it risks being caught by the undisclosed principal rules: see especially below, paras 31-063, 31-065. See Hill (1968) 31 M.L.R. 623; *Bowstead and Reynolds on Agency*, 21st edn (2018), paras 1-021, 1-022, 12-029.

against what is thought to be the unfair termination of authority by means of a statutory right to indemnity or compensation for loss of goodwill built up.[19] In some countries these typical rules may be extended to franchise holders and distributors. Some intermediaries may also be entitled to the protections of employment law. Since under English law agents are not necessarily independent and may be employees, this last proposition may be true in England also, but would not normally be considered under the head of agency.

Use of the terms "agent", "agency" It follows from the indications given earlier **31-005** of the ways in which the notion of the agency can be employed, and the terms "agent" and "agency" used, that when it falls to be considered whether a person is an agent, and if so of which party to a transaction, it is often true that no simple answer can be given.[20] Some persons who describe themselves or are described by others as agents are not really such in any legal sense of the word, but rather independent merchants, dealers, consultants or intermediaries. Others may be agents in the sense that they owe the internal duties of the agent to his principal (mainly the fiduciary duties)[21] and are paid by commission, but have no or few external powers (for example, estate agents). Others may be agents in the full sense that they have power to bind and entitle their principals contractually or by disposition of property: but it does not follow from this that they may not be parties to any contract made also.[22] Some persons, again, may be parties to what is in the previous paragraph referred to as an "indirect representation" situation. The substance of the matter prevails over the form[23] and the use of the words "agent" or "agency", or even a denial that they are applicable, is not conclusive that any particular type of relationship exists. It has however been said that where the term "agent" is used in a formal document (to which English principles of interpretation are to be applied), it may be presumed that the word is used in its proper legal connotation (viz of a person having power to bind his principal) unless there are strong indications to the contrary[24]; and though this was said in a dissenting judgment it may well be a reasonable guide.

---

[19]   This is now part of UK Law. See below, para.31-153.

[20]   See, e.g. *Wong Mee Wan v Kwan Kin Travel Services Ltd* [1996] 1 W.L.R. 38 (tour operator held principal and so liable for negligence of sub-contractor); *Titshall Ltd v Qwerty Travel Ltd* [2011] EWCA Civ 1569; cf. *Shepperd v Crystal Holidays Ltd* [1997] C.L. 500 (holiday company agent to make contract with skiing instructor); *IRC v SecretHotels2 Ltd* [2014] UKSC 16, [2014] 2 All E.R. 685 (intermediary making hotel bookings: context, VAT). The Package Travel, Package Holidays and Package Tours Regulations 1992 (SI 1992/3288, as amended) place certain obligations on package tour organisers or retailers: see reg.15, discussed above, Vol.I, para.14-051. See also below, para.31-022.

[21]   Below, paras 31-118 et seq.

[22]   Below, para.31-084.

[23]   *Kennedy v De Trafford* [1897] A.C. 180, 188; below, para.31-022. See an informative discussion of agency in the context of commercial lenders, "originators" and "introducers" in *Tonto Home Loans Australia Pty Ltd v Tavares* [2011] NSWCA 389; also discussion in the context of collateralised debt in *AG v Kommunale Wasserwerke Leipzig GmbH* [2017] EWCA Civ 1567, [2017] 2 Lloyd's Rep. 621 at [79] et seq.

[24]   *Shell Co of Australia Ltd v Nat Shipping Bagging Services Ltd (The Kilmun)* [1988] 2 Lloyd's Rep. 1, 16, per Sir Denys Buckley. This problem may occur, for example, in the case of legislative or contractual provisions forbidding the use of "agents" and/or requiring disclosure of "commission" paid to "agents". If a tenderer for a contract uses the services of a local person or company to assist in the preparation of the tender and promises a commission, is he using the services of an "agent"? Not of an agent in the full legal sense. See also *Plevin v Paragon Personal Finance Ltd* [2014] UKSC

31-006   Relationship of principal and agent   On the orthodox and accepted common law analysis, the full paradigm relationship of principal and agent arises where one party, the principal, consents that another party, the agent, shall act on his behalf, and the agent consents so to act. This double consent is said to confer "authority" on the agent; and from this authority stems his power to affect the principal's legal position. The relationship between principal and agent need not be contractual: an agent can act gratuitously,[25] as many do under powers of attorney. There will usually however be a contract accompanying the grant of authority, but the grant itself is conceptually separate.[26] An extension of this reasoning is that the consent may also be given subsequently, by ratification.[27] Except perhaps in the case of agency of necessity,[28] such consent is however essential for the full agency relationship.[29] But under the doctrine of apparent authority, a further extension, a third party may be entitled to rely on the appearance of authority and hold the principal liable as if there had been such consent. This, since it only benefits the third party, is expounded in this chapter under a different head.[30] It will often be easier to prove than actual authority. The consent of the principal, which is regarded as the basic justification for the agent's power to affect his principal's legal relations, may of course be implied from his conduct or from his position with regard to the agent, and vice versa.[31] It has been suggested that "some wider conception of vicarious responsibility other than that of agency, as normally understood, may have to be recognised in order to accommodate some of the more elaborate cases which arise where there are two persons who become mutually involved or associated in one side of a transaction".[32] At present, however, this remains no more than a suggestion by a distinguished judge which has not been developed; and the trend of subsequent cases remains consistent with the traditional formulations of agency principle.[33]

31-007   General and special agents   For the purpose of determining the authority of any particular one, agents were sometimes in the past classified as general or special. A general agent has authority to act in all matters of a particular nature or concern-

---

61, [2014] 1 W.L.R. 4222 ("on behalf of" indicates agency reasoning).

[25] See below, para.31-117.

[26] See *Bowstead and Reynolds on Agency*, 21st edn (2018), para.1-006. A recent illustration is *Blankley v Central Manchester Children's University Hospitals NHS Trust* [2015] EWCA Civ 18, [2015] 1 W.L.R. 4307, where the authority might have at some points not existed by reason of mental incapacity, but the accompanying solicitor's retainer remained valid and was not frustrated. The existence of authority (often referred to in civil law systems as "representation") and the accompanying internal relationship (which may be referred to as mandate) are separate for the purposes of the conflict of laws. See e.g. Rome I Regulation [2008] O.J. L177/6 art.1(g).

[27] See below, paras 31-027 et seq.

[28] See below, para.31-035.

[29] *Pole v Leask* (1863) 33 L.J. Ch. 155, 161–162; *Garnac Grain Co Inc v HMF Faure & Fairclough Ltd* [1968] A.C. 1130n, 1137; Fridman (1968) 84 L.Q.R. 224.

[30] Below, paras 31-056 et seq.

[31] *Branwhite v Worcester Works Finance Ltd* [1969] 1 A.C. 552, 587; *Hely-Hutchinson v Brayhead Ltd* [1968] 1 Q.B. 549, 583; and see below, paras 31-027 et seq. as to ratification.

[32] *Branwhite v Worcester Works Finance Ltd*, above, at 587, per Lord Wilberforce.

[33] The agency cases plainly assert orthodox principles: *Sorrell v Finch* [1977] A.C. 728; *Moorgate Mercantile Co v Twitchings* [1977] A.C. 890; *Kooragang Investments Pty Ltd v Richardson & Wrench Ltd* [1982] A.C. 462; *British Bank of the Middle East v Sun Life Assurance Co of Canada (UK) Ltd* [1983] 2 Lloyd's Rep. 9. But cf. *First Energy (UK) Ltd v Hungarian International Bank Ltd* [1993] 2 Lloyd's Rep. 194; below, para.31-056. But as to vicarious liability in tort, see below, para.31-075.

ing a particular trade or business; or to act in the ordinary course of a business or profession, e.g. as a solicitor, broker or factor.[34] A special agent has authority only to do some particular act or act in some particular transaction which is not in the ordinary course of his business or profession as an agent. But the matter is one of degree, and it is doubtful whether the distinction (which was formerly significant in the emergence of the doctrine of apparent authority[35]) is nowadays of much utility.[36]

Servant (employee) and independent contractor The traditional formulation is **31-008** that a servant (or employee) is under the control of his master (or employer) not only as to what he does but also as to the manner in which he executes his work[37]; the independent contractor, on the other hand, undertakes to produce, or to endeavour to produce, a given result and is not under the orders or control of the principal in his manner of execution.[38] This distinction is principally used in the law of tort, where it retains some validity despite considerable recent modifications of the test for vicarious liability in general[39] and extensions of the law relating to breach of non-delegable duties.[40] Much energy has been devoted to attempts to systematise the relations between these figures and the agent. Though there are interconnections between tort and contract, the use of tort terminology is not usually appropriate in pure contract cases, and such attempts are probably of little practical value for the law as it stands at present. Some employees have agency powers, some not; the same is true of independent contractors. Some owe fiduciary duties, some not. Some agents fall into neither group (e.g. gratuitous agents).[41]

2. EXAMPLES OF TYPES OF AGENT

Factors and brokers[42] The distinction between these was important in **31-009** nineteenth-century commerce and is still important for the understanding of old cases. A factor was:

"… a person to whom goods are consigned for sale by a merchant residing abroad or at a distance from the place of sale; and he usually sells in his own name without disclosing that of his principal."[43]

---

34 As to factors and brokers see below, para.31-009.

35 See *Smith v M'Guire* (1853) 3 Hurl. & N. 554; *Brady v Todd* (1861) 9 C.B.(N.S.) 592; and *Barrett v Irvine* [1907] 2 I.R. 462. But cf. Brown [2004] J.B.L. 391.

36 But the notion was invoked (unsuccessfully) in the context of a company said to be general agent for its wholly owned subsidiary: *Dun & Bradstreet Software Services (England) Ltd v Provident Mutual Life Assn* [1998] 2 E.G.L.R. 175, CA.

37 *Mersey Docks & Harbour Board v Coggins & Griffiths (Liverpool) Ltd* [1947] A.C. 1; *Hewitt v Bonvin* [1940] 1 K.B. 188, 191.

38 For a standard formulation see *Honeywill & Stein Ltd v Larkin* [1934] 1 K.B. 191, 196.

39 See *Lister v Hesley Hall Ltd* [2001] UKHL 22, [2002] 1 A.C. 215; *Various Claimants v Catholic Child Welfare Society* [2012] UKSC 56, [2013] 2 A.C. 1. See further below, para.31-075.

40 *Woodland v Essex CC* [2013] UKSC 66, [2014] A.C. 537.

41 Below, para.31-117.

42 See Munday (1977) 6 Anglo-Am.L.Rev. 221 (a valuable survey). As to the converse situation of *buying* for another, see *Feise v Wray* (1802) 3 East 93; below, para.31-165.

43 *Baring v Corrie* (1818) 2 B. & Ald. 137, 143 per Abbott C.J.; see also *Stevens v Biller* (1883) 25 Ch. D. 31, 37. The definition of mercantile agent in the Factors Act 1889 has no relevance to the definition of a factor at common law: *Rolls Razor Ltd v Cox* [1967] 1 Q.B. 552, 568. See further below, paras 31-079 et seq.

A factor was therefore entitled to contract in his own name[44] and to receive payment,[45] and his possession of the goods and lien over them for his charges and expenses gave him the right to sue the third party on the contract of sale of them which he had made.[46] He might instead sometimes sell goods which he had bought from the person consigning the goods and were thus his own, and the third party might not always know which the factor was doing. These propositions were not normally true of brokers, who negotiated and often concluded contracts in respect of goods which they did not hold at all, and might be assumed to be dealing for others.[47] The factor is central to the development of the doctrine of the undisclosed principal,[48] under which the principal can sue or be sued directly on a contract with a person authorised to make it, who does not indicate at the time of contracting that he is acting for another—but subject to safeguards. This wider doctrine made it unnecessary to resolve all of the puzzles about the factor's position vis-à-vis the agent and third party, which was in effect superseded by a theory based in general agency law. The term "factor" is however not used in this sense in England nowadays, and the term "broker" has subsequently been applied to a much wider range of occupations, starting with stockbrokers but extending much further.

31-010   **Del credere agents**   An agent for the sale of goods sometimes acts under a del credere commission; that is, for a special commission,[49] he becomes responsible to his principal for the solvency of a buyer; or, in other words, he guarantees to his principal, in cases of sale, the payment by the buyer of the price of the goods sold for his principal, when ascertained and due.[50] His liability is however limited to ascertained sums which become due as debts: the principal may not litigate with a del credere agent disputes arising out of contracts made by the agent.[51] Such an agent does not become responsible to the buyer for due performance by his principal,[52] nor can he sue the buyer on the contract.[53] A del credere agency may be implied, or inferred from a course of conduct,[54] and does not need to be evidenced in writing because, being merely incidental to another transaction, it is not a promise to answer for the debt, default or miscarriage of another within s.4 of the Statute of Frauds, i.e. not a guarantee.[55] In modern commerce, such agency

---

44   *Baring v Corrie*, above.
45   *Drinkwater v Goodwin* (1775) 1 Cowp. 251.
46   *Drinkwater v Goodwin*, above; see *Bowstead and Reynolds on Agency*, 21st edn (2018), para.9-009; Reynolds in Lomnicka and Morse (eds), *Contemporary Issues in Commercial Law* (1997), p.161; below, para.31-099.
47   *Baring v Corrie* (1818) 2 B. & Ald. 137; *Linck, Moeller & Co v Jameson & Co* (1885) 2 T.L.R. 206.
48   See Goodhart and Hamson (1932) 4 C.L.J. 320; below, paras 31-063 et seq.
49   See *JM Weatherspoon & Co Ltd v Henry Agency House* (1961) 28 Malaya L.J. 86.
50   *Morris v Cleasby* (1816) 4 M. & S. 566, 574; *Hornby v Lacy* (1817) 6 M. & S. 166. See Chorley (1929) 45 L.Q.R. 221; (1930) 46 L.Q.R. 11.
51   *Thomas Gabriel & Sons v Churchill & Sim* [1914] 3 K.B. 1272; cf. *Rusholme & Bolton & Roberts Hadfield v SG Read & Co* [1955] 1 W.L.R. 146 (confirming house).
52   *Churchill & Sim v Goddard* [1937] 1 K.B. 92.
53   *Bramwell v Spiller* (1871) 21 L.T. 672.
54   *Shaw v Woodcock* (1827) 7 B. & C. 73. But this would be rare nowadays: cf. *Nouvelles Huileries Anversoises SA v HC Mann & Co* (1924) 40 T.L.R. 804.
55   *Couturier v Hastie* (1852) 8 Ex. 40; reversed on another point (1856) 5 H.L. Cas. 673. See below, para.45-050

could involve enormous liabilities, and it has largely been superseded by credit guarantees, confirmations[56] and other business methods.

Auctioneers The auctioneer has a lien over the goods which he sells and an inter- **31-011** est in their proceeds which is nowadays explained as a collateral contract, separate from that between vendor and purchaser, entitling him not only to receive the price but also to sue for it.[57]

> "The auctioneer sues for the price by virtue of his special property and his lien, and also, in most cases, by virtue of his contract with the buyer that the price shall be paid into his hands."[58]

An auctioneer is agent to sell at an open sale, but it has been held that he has no authority to give warranties as to the property auctioned unless he has been expressly authorised to do so[59]; authority to receive a contract deposit may be implied.[60] Although the auctioneer is primarily an agent for the vendor, he was also the agent of a purchaser to sign a contemporary memorandum sufficient to satisfy s.40 of the Law of Property Act 1925[61]; and it may be that the same reasoning applies now that the actual contract has to be in writing under the Law of Property (Miscellaneous Provisions) Act 1989 s.2.[62] The authority of the auctioneer to sign was held to arise directly the contract is concluded, and, at any rate on the part of the vendor, was said to be irrevocable.[63] The authority did not extend to the auctioneer's clerk unless the purchaser assented to the clerk's signing for him.[64]

Real estate agents[65] In England and Wales, an agent employed by the vendor to **31-012** find a purchaser is an agent in a limited sense only.[66] He has authority to describe

---

[56] As to confirming houses, see *Bowstead and Reynolds on Agency*. 21st edn (2018), para.9-021.

[57] *Chelmsford Auctions Ltd v Poole* [1973] Q.B. 542. See below, para.31-099; Reynolds, n.46 above, pp.265–266. In general the third party cannot avoid his liability by paying the vendor directly: *Robinson v Rutter* (1855) 4 E & B. 954, as explained in the *Chelmsford Auctions* case. The implication is more restricted in the case of land. The existence of the right does not mean that the auctioneer is liable to the vendor for not exercising it: *Fordham v Christie, Manson & Woods Ltd* [1977] E.G.D. 94.

[58] *Benton v Campbell, Parker & Co Ltd* [1925] 2 K.B. 410, 416.

[59] *Payne v Lord Leconfield* (1882) 51 L.J. Q.B. 642. See also *Overbrooke Estates Ltd v Glencombe Properties Ltd* [1974] 1 W.L.R. 1335; *Collins v Howell-Jones* [1981] E.G.D. 207.

[60] See *Mynn v Joliffe* (1834) 1 Mood & R. 326.

[61] *Chaney v Maclow* [1929] 1 Ch. 461. But not where he was himself plaintiff: see *Farebrother v Simmons* (1822) 5 B. & Ald. 333; cf. *Wilson & Sons v Pike* [1949] 1 K.B. 176; below, para.31-055; Vol.I, paras 5-036 et seq.

[62] But the section does not apply to sales by "public auction": so that in such cases a written contract is not normally required.

[63] *Phillips v Butler* [1945] Ch. 358 (highest bidder allowed to send deposit next day and in the meantime vendor withdraws auctioneer's authority—withdrawal ineffective). In principle authority is revocable: below, para 31-166. The reason given here is that a different rule "would be opening a wide door to fraud": *Van Praagh v Everidge* [1902] 2 Ch. 266, 270; but it is difficult to square with theory. See Reynolds in Cranston (ed.), *Making Commercial Law* (1997), pp.265–266.

[64] *Bell v Balls* [1897] 1 Ch. 66   See in general Murdoch, *Law of Estate Agency*, 5th edn (2009).

[65] See above, para.31-002; below, paras 31-115, 31-140 et seq. The qualifications and activities of estate agents are affected by the Estate Agents Act 1979: see Murdoch, *Law of Estate Agency*, 5th edn (2009), Ch.7. See also Consumers, Estate Agents and Redress Act 2007 Pt 3, as amended; Consumer Protection from Unfair Trading Regulations 2008 (SI 2008/1277).

[66] It should be noted that practice may differ in other jurisdictions.

the property and perhaps make statements as to its value so as to bind his principal,[67] but he has no implied authority to receive a pre-contract deposit on such terms as to make the prospective vendor liable[68] and no power, without express authority, to conclude a contract for a lease[69] or a sale.[70] He therefore provides an example of what has been called above "incomplete" or "canvassing agency".[71] It has been held that if he is instructed to sell, he is impliedly authorised to sign on behalf of his principal an open contract of sale, but not a contract containing special conditions.[72] It is his duty to communicate to his principal the best offer received by him at any time before a binding contract for the sale of the property has been actually signed by the principal,[73] unless, of course, he has been informed by his principal that such an offer is not acceptable[74]; and in general he owes fiduciary duties to his principal.[75]

31-013 **Solicitors**[76] Solicitors provide professional services for a fee, but may also have agency functions. In litigation, there are decisions that a solicitor, acting under a general retainer, has implied authority to accept service of process and appear for the client, but has no authority to commence an action.[77] As between client and opponent, the former is in general bound by the acts of his solicitor done in the ordinary course of practice. Solicitors and counsel were said to have a general implied authority to effect a reasonable compromise (unless forbidden) in all matters connected with the suit in question and not merely collateral to it. They would therefore have *apparent* authority[78] to do so even if forbidden by the client, against a third party without notice of the limitation[79]; though if the consent was given under

---

67   *Mullens v Miller* (1882) 22 Ch. D. 194; *Sorrell v Finch* [1977] A.C. 728, 753. But he has no authority to warrant that it may lawfully be used for a particular purpose: *Hill v Harris* [1965] 2 Q.B. 601; and the possibility of warranty may be expressly excluded: *Overbrooke Estates v Glencombe Properties Ltd* [1974] 1 W.L.R. 1335; *Collins v Howell-Jones* [1981] E.G.D. 207.
68   *Sorrell v Finch*, above, explaining *Ryan v Pilkington* [1959] 1 W.L.R. 403 and overruling *Goding v Frazer* [1967] 1 W.L.R. 286; *Burt v Claude Cousins & Co Ltd* [1971] 2 Q.B. 426 and (in part) *Barrington v Lee* [1972] 1 Q.B. 326. Nor payment: *Petersen v Moloney* (1951) 84 C.L.R. 91. As to deposits, see further below, para.31-109.
69   *Thuman v Best* (1907) L.T. 239; cf. *Walsh v Griffiths-Jones* (1980) 259 E.G. 331.
70   *Hamer v Sharp* (1874) L.R. 19 Eq. 108; *Chadburn v Moore* (1892) 61 L.J. Ch. 674; cf. *Keen v Mear* [1920] 2 Ch. 574; *Rosenbaum v Belson* [1900] 2 Ch. 267; *Wragg v Lovett* [1948] 2 All E.R. 968; *Law v Robert Roberts & Co* [1964] I.R. 292 (authorities reviewed). cf. *Spiro v Lintern* [1973] 1 W.L.R. 1002; and *Jawara v Gambian Airways* [1992] C.L.Y. 95, where there was authority on the facts.
71   Above, para.31-002.
72   *Keen v Mear*, above.
73   *Keppel v Wheeler* [1927] 1 K.B. 577.
74   See *Burchell v Gowrie & Blockhouse Collieries* [1910] A.C. 614, 625.
75   e.g. *Regier v Campbell-Stuart* [1939] Ch. 766; see below, paras 31-118 et seq.
76   See *Cordery on Legal Services*, 9th edn (looseleaf). But note in general *United Bank of Kuwait Ltd v Hammoud* [1988] 1 W.L.R. 1051, 1063, per Staughton L.J.: "I prefer to have regard to the expert evidence of today in deciding what is the ordinary authority of a solicitor". See further a useful summary in *Pavlovic v Universal Music Australia Pty Ltd* [2015] NSWCA 313, (2015) 90 N.S.W.L.R. 605; below, para.31-131.
77   *Wright v Castle* (1817) 3 Mer. 12.
78   See below, paras 31-056 et seq.
79   *Strauss v Francis* (1866) L.R. 1 Q.B. 379; *Re Newen* [1903] 1 Ch. 812; *Little v Spreadbury* [1910] 2 K.B. 658; *Welsh v Roe* (1918) 87 L.J. K.B. 520; *Thompson v Howley* [1977] 1 N.Z.L.R. 16; *Waugh v HB Clifford & Sons Ltd* [1982] Ch. 374 (authorities reviewed); *Penman v Parker* [1986] 1 W.L.R. 882 (notice under Road Traffic Act); *Marsden v Marsden* [1972] Fam. 280 (barrister). As to the authority of a representative from a Citizens' Advice Bureau see *Freeman v Sovereign Chicken Ltd*

a misapprehension it may be withdrawn before a consent order is drawn up.[80] But it is not at all clear that such authority would be easily inferred today. By s.69 of the Law of Property Act 925, the production of a deed containing a receipt for consideration money is authority for payment of that money in cash to the solicitor. Beyond this, solicitors may acquire confidential information, and owe fiduciary duties not necessarily attributable to their agency functions, but rather to confidential relationships with their clients. They may also hold money on trust for clients.

Partners The law of partnership raises many questions of agency law. The authority of partners is primarily[81] set out in s.5 of the Partnership Act 1890, which provides that: **31-014**

> "Every partner is an agent of the firm[82] and his other partners for the purpose of the business of the partnership; and the acts of every partner who does any act for carrying on in the usual way business of the kind carried on by the firm of which he is a member bind the firm and his partners, unless the partner so acting has in fact no authority to act for the firm in the particular matter, and the person with whom he is dealing either knows that he has no authority, or does not know or believe him to be a partner."[83]

This section sets out the principles of actual and apparent authority as applicable to partners. As a consequence of this general rule, the firm will prima facie be liable for any act done by a partner on behalf of the firm[84] if it was done for the purpose of carrying on the partnership business in the usual way, even though it was not in fact authorised by the other partners. The wording of the section, which dates from a time when the distinction between actual and apparent authority, and between them and vicarious liability in tort, was less well understood than it is now, has been held wide enough to make a partner liable for the fraud of another partner outside the scope not only of actual or apparent authority, but sufficiently connected with the acts he was asked to do to be regarded as done in the course of the firm's business.[85]

[1991] I.R.L.R. 408. See below, para.31-056 (apparent authority).

[80] *Shepherd v Robinson* [1919] 1 K.B. 474. See Foskett, *Law and Practice of Compromise*, 8th edn (2015).

[81] See also ss.6, 7, 8, 9, 14, 17, 36, 38; and in general *Lindley and Banks on Partnership*, 20th edn (2017).

[82] As to the meaning of "firm", see s.4.

[83] But a "limited partner" has no power to bind his firm: Limited Partnerships Act 1907 s.6 (though a member of a limited liability partnership has: Limited Liability Partnerships Act 2000 s.6); and joint adventurers are not necessarily partners with power to bind each other: *Heaps v Dobson* (1863) 15 C.B.(N.S.) 460; cf. *United Dominions Corp Ltd v Brian Pty Ltd* (1985) 157 C.L.R. 1. The last 11 words of s.5 are notoriously ambiguous: see Montrose (1939) 17 Can. Bar Rev. 700–701; Thomas (1971) 6 Victoria U. of Wellington L.R. 1.

[84] But not if done on his own account, or as trustee for the firm: *Construction Engineering (Aust) Pty Ltd v Hexyl Pty Ltd* (1985) 155 C.L.R. 541.

[85] *Dubai Aluminium Co Ltd v Salaam* [2002] UKHL 48, [2003] 2 A.C. 366 (dishonest assistance in fraudulent scheme); *Bank of Scotland v Henry Butcher & Co* [2003] EWCA 67, [2003] 2 All E.R. (Comm) 557; *JJ Coughlan Ltd v Ruparella* [2003] EWCA Civ 1057, [2004] P.N.L.R. 4; *Northampton Regional Livestock Centre Co Ltd v Cowling* [2015] EWCA Civ 651, [2016] 1 B.C.L.C. 431. See also the cases on solicitors, above, para.31-013.

31-015 **Insurance agents and brokers**[86]   The agent of an insurance company, working on commission or as an employee, normally acts for the company,[87] though his authority may not extend far beyond the submission of proposals.[88] It has however been held that he may sometimes become the agent of the proposer if he assists in the completion of the proposal form.[89] An insurance *broker*, on the other hand, is prima facie an agent of the prospective assured or assured, and not of the underwriter[90]: though he may also act as the underwriter's agent in certain respects, e.g. the handling of claims—a situation which has been construed as giving rise to a conflict of interests.[91] He may also act on behalf of reinsurers required by the insuring underwriter.[92]

31-016 **Deemed agency in credit transactions**   A dealer may be deemed to be the agent of the creditor if he negotiates a regulated consumer credit agreement, e.g. a loan, hire-purchase, credit-sale or conditional sale agreement, as regards representations made to the debtor, and for the purpose of receiving notice of cancellation, revocation of offer and rescission.[93] He may also at common law be its agent in other respects[94]; but there is no general agency relationship, and he acts primarily on his own behalf.[95]

3.   COMMERCIAL AGENTS

31-017 **Commercial agents**   An EC Directive, the most conspicuous effect of which is to confer special rights for certain agents, designated "commercial agents", in the event of termination of authority[96] has fairly recently been brought into effect in Great Britain by regulation,[97] and although the notion is unfamiliar in Great

---

[86] See Hodgin, *Insurance Intermediaries: Law and Regulation* (1992) (looseleaf).

[87] See above, para.31-002. See *Bawden v London, Edinburgh and Glasgow Assurance Co* [1892] 2 Q.B. 534; *Stone v Reliance Mutual Insurance Society Ltd* [1972] 1 Lloyd's Rep. 469 (noted (1972) 88 L.Q.R. 462); *Blackley v National Mutual Life Assn of Australasia Ltd* [1972] N.Z.L.R. 1038.

[88] See *British Bank of the Middle East v Sun Life Assurance Co of Canada Ltd* [1983] 2 Lloyd's Rep. 9.

[89] *Biggar v Rock Life Assurance Co* [1902] 1 K.B. 516; *Newsholme Bros v Road Transport and General Insurance Co Ltd* [1929] 2 K.B. 356; contrast the cases cited above, n.87.

[90] *Rozanes v Bowen* (1929) 32 Ll.L. Rep. 98, 101; *Con-Stan Industries of Australia Pty Ltd v Norwich Winterthur (Australia) Ltd* (1986) 160 C.L.R. 226; *Callaghan and Hedges v Thompson* [2000] Lloyd's Rep. I.R. 125. But cf. *Stockton v Mason* [1978] 2 Lloyd's Rep. 430, a puzzling case.

[91] *Anglo-African Merchants Ltd v Bayley* [1970] 1 Q.B. 311; *North and South Trust Co v Berkeley* [1971] 1 W.L.R. 470. But see *Goshawk Dedicated Ltd v Tyser & Co Ltd* [2006] EWCA Civ 54, [2006] 1 Lloyd's Rep. 566 (brokers must produce documents to underwriters).

[92] See *General Accident Fire and Life Assurance Corp Ltd v Tanter (The Zephyr)* [1984] 1 W.L.R. 100; [1985] 2 Lloyd's Rep. 529.

[93] Consumer Credit Act 1974 ss.56(2), 57(3), 69(6), 102(1). See *Powell v Lloyd's Bowmaker Ltd* 1996 S.L.T. 117 Sh Ct (agency as regards property sold or to be sold by dealer only; not as regards car traded in); *CF Asset Finance Ltd v Okonji* [2014] EWCA Civ 870, [2014] E.C.C. 23 (agency to receive notice of revocation of offer). See below, para.39-075.

[94] See *Financings Ltd v Stimson* [1962] 1 W.L.R. 1184; cf. *Campbell Discount v Gall* [1961] 1 Q.B. 431; *Northgran Finance v Ashley* [1963] 1 Q.B. 476; *Car & Universal Finance Co Ltd v Caldwell* [1965] 1 Q.B. 525; *Mercantile Credit Co Ltd v Hamblin* [1965] 2 Q.B. 242.

[95] *Branwhite v Worcester Works Finance Ltd* [1969] 1 A.C. 552 (but Lord Reid and Lord Wilberforce took a different view); *Shogun Finance Ltd v Hudson* [2003] UKHL 62, [2004] 1 A.C. 919 at [51], [52].

[96] Commercial Agents Directive 86/153 [1986] O.J. L382/17.

[97] By the Commercial Agents (Council Directive) Regulations 1993 (SI 1993/3053) as amended by SI

Britain,[98] cases in which agents have argued that they are entitled to the benefit of the regulations are now appearing. They "govern the relations between commercial agents and their principals".[99] "Commercial agent" is defined as "a self-employed intermediary[100] who has continuing authority[101] to negotiate[102] the sale or purchase of goods[103] on behalf of another person (the 'principal'), or to negotiate and conclude the sale or purchase of goods on behalf of and in the name of[104] that principal".[105] There are specific exceptions for officers of companies or associa-

---

1993/3173 and SI 1998/2868 Northern Ireland is covered by the Commercial Agents (Council Directive) Regulations (Northern Ireland) 1993 (SI 1993/483), effective from January 14, 1994. There is a full discussion in *Bowstead and Reynolds on Agency*, 21st edn (2018), Ch.11. For specialised works see Saintier and Scholes, *Commercial Agents and the Law* (2005); Randolph and Davey, *The European Law of Commercial Agency*, 3rd edn (2010); Singleton. *Commercial Agency Agreements: Law and Practice*, 4th edn (2015).

[98] A useful analysis of the functions of a commercial agent is given by A.G. Trstenjak in *Wood Floor Solutions Andreas Domberger GmbH v Silva Trade SA* (C-19/09) EU:C:2010:137, [2010] I.L.Pr. 21 at AG53 et seq.

[99] Commercial Agents Regulations reg.1(2). In *Wood Floor Solutions Andreas Domberger GmbH v Silva Trade SA* (C-19/09) EU:C:2010:137, [2010] 1 W.L.R. 900 the CJEU treated such a contract as one for the provisions of services for the purposes of Council Regulation 44/2001 on jurisdiction and the enforcement of judgments. (This report does not include the opinion of A.G. Trstenjak, above.)

[100] Such agency is not confined to natural persons: *Bell Electric Ltd v Aweco Appliance Systems GmbH & Co* [2002] EWHC 872, [2002] Eu. L.R. 443. The intermediary may have several principals: *Rossetti Marketing Ltd v Diamond Sofa Co Ltd* [2011] EWHC 2482 (QB), [2011] E.C.C. 28; point not referred to on appeal [2012] EWCA Civ 1021, [2013] 1 All E.R. (Comm) 308.

[101] The word "authority" could be taken to exclude some agents whose functions were purely canvassing (above, para.31-002), i.e. introducing business in some limited way. But in many cases there is an appointment of an agent whose main or even sole function is to introduce business over a period, and several cases accept such persons as coming within the definition: e.g. the cases cited below, n.102 and *Fern Computer Consultancy Ltd v Intergraph Cadworx & Analysis Solutions Inc* [2014] EWHC 2908 (Ch), [2014] Bus. L.R. 1397. Authority may be "continuing" if there is authority to conclude a single contract plus authority to negotiate extensions: *Poseidon Chartering BV v Marianne Zeeschip VO* (C-3/04) EU:C:2006:176, [2006] 2 Lloyd's Rep. 105. The nature and scope of an agent's retainer is to be judged by reference to his contract but at the time relief is determined: *W Nagel v Pluczenik Diamond Co NV* [2017] EWHC 1750 (Comm), [2017] 2 Lloyd's Rep. 215 at [33]–[34].

[102] "Negotiate" does not require that the agent have authority to agree terms: *PJ Pipe & Valve Co Ltd v Audco India Ltd* [2005] EWHC 1904 (QB), [2006] Eu. L.R. 368; *Nigel Fryer Joinery Services Ltd v Ian Firth Hardware Ltd* [2008] 2 Lloyd's Rep. 1080; *Invicta UK v International Brands Ltd* [2013] EWHC 1564 (QB), [2013] E.C.C. 30; *W Nagel v Pluczenik Diamond Co NV* [2017] EWHC 1750 (Comm), [2017] 2 Lloyd's Rep. 215 ("foster relationship of trust and promote goodwill").

[103] As to which see *Tamarind International Ltd v Eastern Natural Gas (Retail) Ltd* [2000] Eu. L.R. 708 (gas). In *Computer Associates UK Ltd v Software Incubator Ltd* [2018] EWCA Civ 518 it is decided that computer software supplied as a download does not rank as "goods" for the purposes of the regulation. Whether a licence to use it would rank as a sale is therefore not decided, though the question had been considered (or the basis that "goods" were involved) in *Fern Computer Consultancy Ltd v Intergraph Cadworx & Analysis Solutions Inc* [2014] EWHC 2908 (Ch), [2014] Bus. L.R. 1397. The question of software supplied on a disk, on which there is sale of goods authority, is not determined. See further *Benjamin's Sale of Goods*, 10th edn (2017), para.1-086.

[104] This would appear to include situations where the principal is unidentified: see below, para.31-089. But it does not include indirect agents (*commissionnaires*, above. para.31-004): *Mavrona & Sia OE v Delta Etaireia Symettochor AE* (C-85/03) EU:C:2004:83, [2004] O.J. C94/17; or in general agents who contract in their own name, which would cover agents for undisclosed principals: *Sagal v Atelier Bunz GmbH* [2009] EWCA Civ 700, [2009] 2 Lloyd's Rep. 303.

[105] Commercial Agents Regulations reg.2(1). A national law requiring such agents to register cannot prevent the application of the Directive: *Bellone v Yokohama SpA* (C-215/97) EU:C:1998:189, [1998] E.C.R. I-2191.

[13]

tions, partners, insolvency practitioners,[106] gratuitous agents, agents operating on commodity exchanges or in commodity markets,[107] the Crown Agents,[108] and persons whose activities as commercial agents are to be considered secondary.[109] This latter must be assessed by reference to the particular arrangement rather than the general balance of the agent's activities.[110]

31-018   The main effects of the regulations are referred to at appropriate points in this chapter. They cover the duties of agent to principal and principal to agent,[111] remuneration and commission,[112] termination of the contract,[113] (most conspicuously) rights to indemnity and compensation on such termination,[114] and restraint of trade clauses.[115] They do not supplant English law or any other governing law: rather, they are superimposed when inconsistent with that law.[116] Except in the case of sums payable on termination of agency, the rules do not differ much from the common law, though it is necessary to watch for differences of detail that may arise because of the specific wording of the regulations (e.g. in the case of entitlement to commission) when they apply, and because the regulations are to be interpreted as a European instrument. It should be noted also that under the regulations each party is entitled to a signed written document setting out the terms of the agency contract, including any terms subsequently agreed.[117]

31-019   The notion of a "commercial agent" is not known to the common law. It has fairly narrow limits. Apart from the specific exceptions, in the United Kingdom it only

---

[106]   As defined in s.388 of the Insolvency Act 1986 (as amended).

[107]   As to which see *W Nagel v Pluczenik Diamond Co NV* [2017] EWHC 1750 (Comm), [2017] 2 Lloyd's Rep. 215 (diamond market).

[108]   Commercial Agents Regulations reg.2(1), (2).

[109]   Commercial Agents Regulations reg.2(3). This provision is then defined specifically for the UK by a (rather unsatisfactory) Schedule. The vires of this part of the regulations was unsuccessfully challenged in *Crane v Sky In-Home Services Ltd* [2007] EWHC 66 (Ch), [2007] 2 All E.R. (Comm) 599.

[110]   See *AMB Imballaggi Plastics SRL v Pacflex Ltd* [1999] 2 All E.R. (Comm) 249, 254; *Tamarind International Ltd v Eastern Natural Gas (Retail) Ltd* [2000] Eu. L.R. 708; *Edwards v International Connection (UK) Ltd* [2006] EWCA Civ 662; *Crane v Sky In-Home Services Ltd* [2007] EWHC 66 (Ch), [2007] 2 All E.R. (Comm) 599 (extended discussion). UK courts, interpreting the extremely obscure definition contained in the Schedule to the regulations (described as "an almost impenetrable piece of drafting" in *AMB Imballaggi v Pacflex Ltd* [1999] 2 All E.R. (Comm) 249, 254), have used the restriction to impose quite strict limits on when the regulations apply, seeking to confine them to what may be called "goodwill-generating" functions even when some other agency function is more prominent. See *Gailey v Environmental Waste Controls* 2004 Scot SC 300 (OH), [2004] Eu.L.R.423; *McAdam v Boxpak Ltd* [2006] CSIH 9, 2006 S.L.T. 217. See a careful discussion of the genesis of the provision by Saintier [2012] J.B.L. 128; *Bowstead and Reynolds on Agency*, 21st edn (2018), paras 11-020 et seq. On a smaller scale, an argument, based on *Crane v Sky In-Home*, above, that where software is sold linked to hardware, the hardware constitutes the goods and the software only secondary was rejected in *Fern Computer Consultancy Ltd v Intergraph Cadworx & Analysis Solutions Inc* [2014] EWHC 2908 (Ch), [2014] Bus. L.R. 1397. But where the main function was excluded because in a commodity market, a lesser function was also excluded as secondary in *W Nagel v Pluczenik Diamond Co NV* [2017] EWHC 1750 (Comm), [2017] 2 Lloyd's Rep. 215.

[111]   Below, paras 31-112—31-115, 31-136.

[112]   Below, para.31-149.

[113]   Below, para.31-152.

[114]   Below, paras 31-153 et seq.

[115]   Below, para.31-159.

[116]   See *Fern Computer Consultancy Ltd v Intergraph Cadworx & Analysis Solutions Inc* [2014] EWHC 2908 (Ch), [2014] Bus. L.R. 1397 at [38].

[117]   Commercial Agents Regulations reg.13(1); a purported waiver is void: reg.13(2). The consequences of non-compliance are not stated.

applies to agents acting in respect of sales of goods and does not cover agents acting in regard to land, nor to those arranging services; it does not cover distributors who purchase for resale[118]; it only applies to self-employed agents, and only to those with *continuing* authority. It is uncertain to what extent markets in the United Kingdom are penetrated by agents of the sort referred to. It seems likely that when the Regulations do apply, t is still sometimes by accident.

The Commercial Agents Regulations: applicability[119] By virtue of reg.1(2) the **31-020** regulations apply "in relation to the activities of commercial agents in Great Britain". This does not of i self require that the contract between principal and commercial agent is subject to English law. It is not clear how this is to be interpreted where the agent also conducts activities elsewhere,[120] nor to what extent the word "conduct" requires the agent's presence.[121] But a further provision, reg.1(3)(a), a modification introduced in 1998,[122] provides that where the parties have agreed[123] that the agency contract is to be governed by the law of another Member State,[124] the law of that State (wh ch is of course likely to be to similar effect) is to be applied. Assuming that the limitation in reg.1(2) continues to be valid in the absence of other indications, this rule is presumably still confined to activities in Great Britain. However, a second provision, reg.1(3)(b), introduced at the same time and in response to representations from the EC Commission, then provides that the regulations are to be applied where the law of another Member State corresponding to the regulations enables the parties to agree that the agency contract is to be governed by the law of a different Member State and the parties have agreed that it is to be governed by the law of England and Wales or Scotland. It would appear that this is directed at activities outside Great Britain, but in another Member State, where the law referred to has been chosen. The meaning and purport of these changes is extremely obscure. In particular, there is no indication of which Member State would be relevant to its application, nor of where the activities are envisaged as being conducted.[125] It has been held that the Regulations are overriding and hence apply where an agent acts in Great Britain but under a contract governed by the law of a non-Member State, e.g. California.[126]

---

118 *AMB Imballaggi Plastics SRL v Pacflex Ltd* [1999] 2 All E.R. (Comm) 249; *Crane v Sky In-Home Service Ltd* [2007] EWHC 66 (Ch), [2007] Eu. L.R. 549; *Sagal v Atelier Bunz GmbH* [2009] EWCA Civ 700, [2009] 2 Lloyd's Lep. 303. But a commercial agent may be remunerated by markup: *Mercantile International Group Plc v Chuan Soon Huat Industrial Group Plc* [2002] EWCA Civ 288, [2002] 1 All E.R. (Comm) 788.
119 See *Dicey, Morris and Collins on the Conflict of Laws*, 15th edn (2012), paras 33-420 et seq.
120 See discussion in *Fern Computer Consultancy Ltd v Intergraph Cadworx & Analysis Solutions Inc* [2014] EWHC 2908 (Ch), [2014] Bus. L.R. 1397 at [108] et seq.
121 See *Dicey, Morris and Collins on the Conflict of Laws*, 15th edn (2012), para.33-422.
122 By the Commercial Agents (Council Directive) (Amendment) Regulations 1998 (SI 1998/2868).
123 A commercial agency contract was held subject to Spanish law in *Lawlor v Sandrik Mining & Construction, etc., Co* [2012] EWHC 1188 (QB), [2012] 2 Lloyd's Rep 25, apparently on the basis of art.4(2) of the Rome Convention (operative at the relevant time). A point is that some of the activities appear to have taken place outside Great Britain.
124 This includes a state which is a party to the Oporto EEA agreement of 1992 as adjusted by the Brussels Protocol of 1993: reg.2 of SI 1993/3173 as amended by reg.2 of SI 1998/2868, above.
125 The meaning of this amendment is considered in *Fern Computer Consultancy Ltd v Intergraph Cadworx & Analysis Solutions Inc* [2014] EWHC 2908 (Ch), [2014] Bus. L.R. 1397 at [114]–[115]. See also *Dicey, Morris and Collins on the Conflict of Laws*, 15th edn (2012), para.33-423.
126 *Ingmar GB Ltd v Leonard Technologies Inc* [2001] 1 All E.R. (Comm) 329, ECJ. See this case criticised by Verhagen (2002) 51 I.C.L.Q. 135; Roth (2002) 3 C.M.L.Rev. 369. See further *Accentu-*

4. CREATION OF AGENCY

31-021 **Creation of agency** As already stated, the relationship of principal and agent in the full sense is created by an express or implied agreement conferring authority on the agent, which usually is but need not be accompanied by a contract. Authority can also be conferred retrospectively by ratification, and may perhaps arise by operation of law where the ancient doctrine of agency of necessity applies. Furthermore, the principal may be bound to the third party under the doctrine of apparent authority or in some cases under the general doctrine of estoppel: this is dealt with in the section on the principal's relations with third parties.[127]

(a) Express Agreement

31-022 **How agency constituted** The appointment of an agent must be by the principal or by someone else with authority (actual or apparent) to act for him. An agent may of course be appointed in formal words, as by a power of attorney or a specific letter of appointment. But a grant of authority may be informal. In all situations, the substance of the matter is more important than the form. A retailer who describes himself as agent for a manufacturer is in fact more likely to buy from the manufacturer and sell to the customer,[128] and a person who agrees to procure goods may do so as agent, but may equally purport to do no more than buy them and offer or resell them to his principal.[129] A contract describing the parties respectively

---

ate Ltd v Asigra Inc [2009] EWHC 2655 (QB), [2009] 2 Lloyd's Rep. 599, where an arbitration clause in a commercial agency contract governed by the law of Ontario was held void even though the arbitration had already taken place. In that case service on the principal on a contract basis out of the jurisdiction was permitted, though the contractual justification for this was later rejected in *Fern Computer Consultancy Ltd v Intergraph Cadworx & Analysis Solutions Inc* [2014] EWHC 2908 (Ch), [2014] Bus. L.R.1397 at [114]–[115], on the basis that the claim for compensation under the regulations, was statutory, or at best tortious. Where no ground for service out on the principal can be found, it seems that the regulations can thus be evaded by choice of a foreign law and (preferably) jurisdiction: see the *Fern* case, above, at [54]. See discussion in *Bowstead and Reynolds on Agency*, 21st edn (2018), para.11-006; Carruthers, Ch.13 in *Agency Law in Commercial Practice*, Busch and Macgregor (eds) (2016).

[127] Below, para.31-056.
[128] See, e.g. *WT Lamb & Sons v Goring Brick Co Ltd* [1932] 1 K.B. 710; *Michelin Tyre Co Ltd v MacFarlane (Glasgow) Ltd* (1917) 55 Sc.L.Rep. 35, HL; *Sproule v Triumph Motor Cycle Co* [1927] N.I. 83; *International Harvester Co of Australia Pty Ltd v Carrigan's Hazeldene Pastoral Co* (1958) 100 C.L.R. 644. See also above, para.31-003. The distinction turns largely but not entirely on whether he takes the profit on resale or is remunerated by commission: see *Benjamin's Sale of Goods*, 10th edn (2017), paras 1-048, 1-049. The question has arisen in the context of the Commercial Agents Regulations, above, para.31-017; also in the specialised context of Value Added Tax. See *Commissioners of Customs and Excise v Johnson* [1980] S.T.C. 624 (provision of educational courses); *Potter v Commissioners of Customs and Excise* [1985] S.T.C. 45 ("Tupperware" sold at specially convened functions); *Hill v Commissioners of Customs and Excise* [1988] S.T.C. 424 (craft pottery); *Commissioners of Customs and Excise v Paget* [1989] S.T.C. 773 (school photographs sold to parents); *Cornhill Management Ltd v Commissioners of Customs and Excise* [1991] 1 V.A.T.T.R. 1 (fund managers); *Commissioners of Customs and Excise v Music and Video Exchange Ltd* [1992] S.T.C. 220 (profit on resale as commission). See also *Welsh Development Agency v Export Finance Co Ltd* [1992] B.C.L.C. 148. As to the distinction between agent and borrower in the context of subsidiary companies, see *Atlas Maritime Co SA v Avalon Maritime Co Ltd (The Coral Rose) (No.1)* [1994] 4 All E.R. 769.
[129] See, e.g. *Ireland v Livingston* (1871) L.R. 5 H.L. 395; *Brown & Gracie Ltd v FW Green & Co Pty Ltd* [1960] 1 Lloyd's Rep. 289; *Anglo-African Shipping Co of New York Inc v J Mortner Ltd* [1962] 1 Lloyd's Rep. 610.

from his acting on behalf of the principal[152]; but the mere fact that he does what was requested by the principal does not necessarily mean that he does it on the principal's behalf.[153]

(c) Ratification

General rule An act done for another by a person not assuming to act for himself, **31-027** but for such other person, though without any precedent authority, may rank as the act of the principal if subsequently ratified by him.[154] This can be regarded as a retrospective conferring of authority and much of its reasoning proceeds on the basis of that analogy. Although it is here classified as a method of creation of agency, it applies more frequently to persons already agents who are not authorised in the relevant respect. It operates on the act ratified only and does not confer any future authority, though a series of ratifications might give rise to apparent authority.[155] A purported ratification in advance can be no more than a promise to ratify, enforceable if supported by consideration. At common law, ratification is in principle to be confined to situations where the third party did not at the time of contracting know that the agent was unauthorised. Situations where the third party did have such knowledge at the time of contracting would require a different analysis in common law.[156] Views vary as to whether or not the doctrine is anomalous. It is certainly often convenient; but it requires safeguards to prevent unfair results. The merits of a case may vary in accordance with whether the principal seeks to ratify against an unwilling third party, or the third party claims ratification against an unwilling principal. The second is probably more common.

Proof of ratification Ratification will be implied from any act showing an inten- **31-028** tion to adopt the transaction, including commencement of or pleading in an action at law on the transaction in question.[157] No action in reliance is required. It may be inferred in appropriate cases even from silence or mere acquiescence[158]; and it seems clear that, like the grant of authority, it need not be communicated to the third party.[159] But if an act is adopted at all, it will be held to have been adopted

---

[152] *Roberts v Ogilby* (1821) 9 Price 269; *Moore v Peachey* (1891) 7 T.L.R. 748.

[153] *Kennedy v De Trafford* [1897] A.C. 180; *Garnac Grain Co Inc v HMF Faure & Fairclough Ltd*, above.

[154] *Wilson v Tumman* (1843) 6 M. & G. 236, 242; *Bird v Brown* (1850) 4 Ex. 786; *Firth v Staines* [1897] 2 Q.B. 70. For more modern formulations see *Suncorp Insurance and Finance Co Ltd v Milano Assicurazioni SpA* [1993] 2 Lloyd's Rep. 225; *Yona International Ltd v La Réunion Française Société Anonyme d'Assurances et de Réassurances* [1996] 2 Lloyd's Rep. 84, 103, 106.

[155] See below, para.31-056.

[156] Normally, as a contract "subject to ratification". See below, n.189; *Watson v Davies* [1931] 1 Ch. 455; *Warehousing and Forwarding Co of East Africa v Jafferali & Sons* [1964] A.C. 1; *Bowstead and Reynolds on Agency*, 21st edn (2018), paras 2-050–2-052.

[157] *Celthene Pty Ltd v WKJ Hauliers Pty Ltd* [1981] 1 N.S.W.L.R. 606, 614. But this must perhaps occur within a reasonable time: see below, para.31-034.

[158] *Bank Melli Iran v Barclays Bank (DCO)* [1951] 2 T.L.R. 1057, 1063; see also *Lyell v Kennedy* (1889) 14 App. Cas. 437. Ratification by acquiescence may be more difficult to establish in the case of an executory contract than in the case of an executed one, for in the latter there may be no choice but *to take the benefit of the transaction. See, e.g. Foreman & Co Pty Ltd v The Liddesdale* [1900] A.C. 190. But a person who did not intend to ratify may in appropriate cases be estopped from proving that he did not do so.

[159] See *Bowstead and Reynolds on Agency*, 21st edn (2018), para.2-078; accepted in *Pagnan SpA v Feed Products Ltd* [1987] 2 Lloyd's Rep. 601, 613; *Shell Co of Australia Ltd v Nat Shipping Bagging*

throughout.[160] Ratification of a contract required to be in writing need not be in writing,[161] but ratification of a contract required to be made by deed must be by deed.[162]

31-029 **Who can ratify** A contract can only be ratified by the person on whose behalf it was purportedly made: an undisclosed principal cannot ratify.[163] But if the contract was purportedly made on behalf of a principal, the fact that the agent actually intended to act for himself is irrelevant.[164] Despite difficulties in earlier cases, it has been held in the context of insurance that an unidentified principal[165] may ratify, and there seems no reason why this should not be true in all contexts, despite difficulties in ascertaining the actual party for whom the agent acted.[166] But a person who was not in existence and contemplated at the time a contract was made, e.g. a person who might in the future come within a particular class, cannot do so, though he can be the beneficiary of a trust,[167] a third party beneficiary of a contract[168] or perhaps the offeree of a unilateral contract.[169] It is not clear whether the personal representatives of a deceased person may ratify contracts made on his or her behalf, but they can plainly ratify contracts made for the estate.[170]

Services Ltd (The Kilmun) [1988] 2 Lloyd's Rep. 1, 8, 11, 14; *AMB Generali Holding AG v SEB Trygg Holding Aktiebolaget* [2005] EWCA Civ 1237, [2006] 1 Lloyd's Rep. 318 at [37].

[160] *Union Bank of Australia v McClintock* [1922] 1 A.C. 240; *Bank Melli Iran v Barclays Bank (DCO)*, above; *Commercial Banking Co of Sydney v Mann* [1961] A.C. 1. But where particular matters can be separated out, the operation of this principle can give rise to difficulty: cf. *Harrisons & Crossfield Ltd v LNWR* [1917] 2 K.B. 755; *Hughes v Hughes* (1971) 115 S.J. 911 (ratification of sale of house does not cover contract with estate agent); *Accidia Foundation Ltd v Simon C. Dickinson Ltd* [2010] EWHC 3058 (Ch) (ratification of sale does not involve ratification of commission agreement); and see *Canadian Laboratory Supplies Ltd v Engelhard Industries of Canada Ltd* [1979] 2 S.C.R. 787, 801 et seq.; (1979) 97 D.L.R. (3d) 1, 11 et seq.

[161] *Maclean v Dunn* (1828) 4 Bing. 722; *Soames v Spencer* (1822) 1 D. & R. 32; *Sheridan v Higgins* [1971] I.R. 291.

[162] *Hunter v Parker* (1840) 7 M. & W. 322; *Kidderminster Corp v Hardwick* (1873) L.R. 9 Ex. 13 (unless a deed was not necessary in any case). But see *Tupper v Foulkes* (1861) 9 C.B.(N.S.) 797 (ratification treated as redelivery). As to ratification by companies see *Bowstead and Reynolds on Agency*, 21st edn (2018), para.2-069.

[163] *Keighley, Maxsted & Co v Durant* [1901] A.C. 240. As to undisclosed principals see below, paras 31-063 et seq. It is surprising that this rule applies, as here, even though the agent is clearly such (but has exceeded his authority) and the case is one where it is sought to hold the ratifying principal liable, as opposed to one where he seeks to intervene or the person whose act is purportedly ratified is not an agent of the ratifier at all.

[164] *Re Tiedemann & Ledermann Frères* [1899] 2 Q.B. 66 (where the agent thought that the third party would not deal with him personally so purported to act for another, who could sue on ratifying).

[165] Below, paras 31-054, 31-089.

[166] *National Oilwell (UK) Ltd v Davy Offshore Ltd* [1993] 2 Lloyd's Rep. 582, 592–597; see Reynolds in Rose (ed.), *Consensus ad Idem* (1996), p.77. Indications of the agent's subjective intention to act for the person concerned may be required. cf. below, para.31-054.

[167] See *Trident General Ins Co Ltd v McNiece Bros Pty Ltd* (1987) 8 N.S.W.L.R. 270, 276–277 (insurance for "all contractors and subcontractors and/or suppliers": plaintiffs not appointed at time of insurance). But cf. *Celthene Pty Ltd v WKJ Hauliers Pty Ltd* [1981] 1 N.S.W.L.R. 606, 615. As to trust in this context, see *A Tomlinson (Hauliers) Ltd v Hepburn* [1966] A.C. 451 (bailee). See in general *Bowstead and Reynolds on Agency*, 21st edn (2018), para.2-061. In the *Trident* case the contractor was held entitled to sue as third party beneficiary of a contract. The actual decision was affirmed by the High Court of Australia without deciding on the agency points: (1988) 165 C.L.R. 107.

[168] Contracts (Rights of Third Parties) Act 1999 s.1(3).

[169] cf. *AM Satterthwaite Ltd v New Zealand Shipping Co Ltd (The Eurymedon)* [1975] A.C. 154; and see *Haberdasher Aske's Federation Trust Ltd v Lewisham LBC* [2018] EWHC 558 (TCC).

[170] See *Foster v Bates* (1843) 12 M. & W. 226; Powell, *Law of Agency*, 2nd edn (1961), p.388.

Knowledge of circumstances   It is often said that a person ratifying a contract **31-030**
must, at least in order to be bound, know fully of all the material circumstances in
which the act is done[171]; so a principal does not ratify a wrongful distress by receiving the proceeds of it unless he has full knowledge of the wrongful act,[172] and will
not be deemed to have ratified a voidable transaction if he did not know that it was
voidable.[173] But the principal will obviously be bound if he intends to ratify the act
in any event; thus where an agent had wrongfully signed a distress warrant and
levied distress, and the principal, when informed, had said that he would leave the
matter in the agent's hands, the principal was held to have ratified the agent's act
and to be responsible for irregularities in the levying of the distress.[174] And the
principal may be liable even though he has no knowledge of the legal effect of the
act ratified[175] or of collateral matters affecting its nature, e.g. that a purchase
amounted to a conversion.[176] It seems that this is correctly analysed as an internal
principle, i.e. one referable to the position between principal and agent. Where a
third party is involved, a lower degree of knowledge by the principal may entitle
the third party to rely on ratification: thus it has been said that he might do so despite
the fact that the principal in fact was unaware that the act was unauthorised, and
hence that there was anything to ratify.[177] Although it has been said that in such a
situation what occurs is still ratification,[178] it is close to estoppel. In general however
the very broad nature of the internal rules as to ratification by conduct will make
estoppel, or similar reasoning directed only to the third party, unnecessary.

Capacity: void and voidable acts   The doctrine of ratification presupposes that **31-031**
the principal could validly have done the act at the time it was done. Thus a
company not formed at the time of the act, but formed before the time of purported
ratification, cannot ratify[179]; and a person in some other way lacking capacity at the
time of the original act[180] cannot ratify. Beyond this, it is sometimes said that
whereas a voidable act can be ratified, a void one cannot, and this idea can be used
to justify the proposition that a forgery cannot be ratified.[181] But the word "void"
is not helpful: almost any unauthorised act on behalf of another could be called void,
yet it is precisely such acts which are the subject matter of the doctrine of

---

[171] *De Bussche v Alt* (1878) 8 Ch. D. 286, 313; cf. *Brennan v O'Connell* [1980] I.R. 13.
[172] *Lewis v Read* (1845) 14 L.J. Ex. 295.
[173] *Savery v King* (1856) 5 H.L.C. 627.
[174] *Haseler v Lemoyne* (1858) 28 L.J. C.P. 103.
[175] *Powell v Smith* (1872) L.R. 14 Eq. 85; *AMB Generali Holding AG v SEB Liv Holding Aktiebolaget*
      [2005] EWCA Civ 1237, [2006] 1 Lloyd's Rep. 318 at [34]–[47].
[176] *Hilberry v Hatton* (1864) 2 Hurl. & C. 822. See also *Brennan v O'Connell* [1980] I.R. 13 (ratifica-
      tion of contract by estate agent).
[177] This is suggested in *ING Re (UK) Ltd v R&V Versicherung AG* [2006] EWHC 1544 (Comm), [2006]
      2 All E.R. (Comm) 870 at [155]–[156], though the reliance was in fact held unjustified.
[178] *Suncorp Insurance and Finance v Milano Assecurazioni SpA* [1993] 2 Lloyd's Rep. 225, 243–235;
      and see *Great Atlantic Insurance Co v Home Insurance Co* [1981] 2 Lloyd's Rep. 219, 227.
[179] *Kelner v Baxter* (1866) L.R. 2 C.P. 174. This result is in some countries changed by statute. Capac-
      ity at the time of ratification is obviously required: *Firth v Staines* [1987] 2 Q.B. 70, 75.
[180] *Boston Deep Sea Fishing and Ice Co v Farnham* [1957] 1 W.L.R. 1051; *Kuenigl v Donnersmarck*
      [1955] 1 Q.B. 515 (alien enemies).
[181] *Brook v Hook* (1871) L.R. 6 Ex. 89. See also *Bedford Ins Co v Instituto de Resseguros do Brasil*
      [1985] Q.B. 966, 986–987 ("life cannot be given by ratification to prohibited transactions"). There
      may have been some connection with problems regarding marriage settlements by infants, which
      do not of course involve agency at all: see *Edwards v Carter* [1893] A.C. 360.

ratification.[182] The capacity cases can be explained as a separate category, and in the central case of forgery the forger does not profess to act *for* but *as* another.[183]

31-032 **Effect of ratification between principal and agent** It is often said that the effect of ratification is to put all parties in the position in which they would have been had the transaction been authorised. This is not entirely correct. The third party is entitled to take advantage of the ratification with such a result against the principal, and the principal against the third party: but it does not follow that the agent is freed from liability to the principal for exceeding his authority. The principal might have ratified out of commercial necessity, to preserve his reputation, or might have been held to have ratified as against the third party despite not being fully aware of the circumstances.[184] It may therefore be necessary to determine whether the principal's ratification as regards the third party was a waiver or exoneration as regards the agent or not.[185]

31-033 **Third parties** As stated above, as regards the third party a ratified transaction is valid as if authorised. Thus if an action is commenced without authority and is not properly constituted, the plaintiff can ratify his solicitor's act, so that it is not open to the defendant to object that the action is not properly brought.[186] Ratification is effective notwithstanding that the person ratifying at first repudiated the act.[187] More surprisingly it has been held that the retrospective effect of ratification may be such that a ratified contract is valid even though the third party has between formation and ratification purported to withdraw from it[188] unless it was made subject to ratification[189] or has been rescinded.[190] This rule, often referred to as the rule in

---

[182] See *Danish Mercantile Co v Beaumont* [1951] Ch. 680 (unauthorised institution of proceedings held not a nullity and ratifiable); *Hooper v Kerr, Stuart & Co Ltd* (1901) 83 L.T. 729 (unauthorised summoning of company meeting); *Bamford v Bamford* [1970] Ch. 212; *Winthrop Investments Ltd v Winns Ltd* [1975] 2 N.S.W.L.R. 666 (voidable issue of shares); *Alexander Ward & Co Ltd v Samyang Navigation Co Ltd* [1975] 1 W.L.R. 673 (arrest of ship); *Presentaciones Musicales SA v Secunda* [1994] Ch. 271 (issue of writ); applied in *Adams v Ford* [2012] EWCA Civ 544, [2012] 1 W.L.R. 3211.

[183] This principle may have been lost sight of in *English v English* [2010] EWHC 2058 (Ch). But unauthorised signature or affixing of a seal may also amount to forgery, and in this case there probably can be ratification: see Campbell (1960) 76 L.Q.R. at 130 et seq.; *M'Kenzie v British Linen Co* (1881) 6 App. Cas. 82, 99–100; *Northside Developments Pty Ltd v Registrar-General* (1990) 170 C.L.R. 146, especially at 199–200. And a person may be estopped from setting up forgery or want of authority: see *Greenwood v Martins Bank Ltd* [1933] A.C. 51; *Fung Kai Sing v Chang Fui Hing* [1951] A.C. 489; *Welch v Bank of England* [1955] Ch. 508.

[184] See above, para.31-030. See also below, para.31-112.

[185] *Suncorp Insurance and Finance v Milano Assecurazioni SpA* [1993] 2 Lloyd's Rep. 225, 243–235; also *Great Atlantic Insurance Co v Home Insurance Co* [1981] 2 Lloyd's Rep. 219, 227.

[186] *Danish Mercantile Co v Beaumont* [1951] Ch. 680.

[187] *Soames v Spencer* (1822) 1 D. & R. 32. Unless there is prejudice to the third party, which might give rise to estoppel: *McEvoy v Belfast Banking Co* [1935] A.C. 24, 45.

[188] *Bolton Partners v Lambert* (1889) 41 Ch. D. 295 (but note that the case is often misunderstood: at the time of withdrawal the third party did not know that the contract was unauthorised, but appears to have thought that the stage of contract formation had not been reached); cf. *Kidderminster Corp v Hardwick* (1873) L.R. 9 Ex. 13; *Athy Guardians v Murphy* [1896] 1 I.R. 65; *Fleming v Bank of New Zealand* [1900] A.C. 577.

[189] *Watson v Davies* [1931] 1 Ch. 455; *Warehousing & Forwarding Co v Jafferali* [1964] A.C. 1. In such a case, of course, there would be no contract from which to withdraw: cf. above, n.156. The "ratification" would be an acceptance and would require notice: *Jafferali's* case, at 9.

[190] *Walter v James* (1871) L.R. 6 Ex. 124; *London Borough of Haringey v Ahmed* [2016] EWHC 1257 (Ch), [2018] 1 P. & C.R. DG12.

Bolton Partners v Lambert[191] is controversial, and is subject to various limits, as appears from what follows.

Limits on ratification   It is plain that there must be some limits on the applicability of ratification, which is a sensible and practical idea in many situations, but could give rise to obviously unfair results in others. There has been little agreement, however, on what technique is to be used for this purpose. In the famous case of *Bird v Brown*[192] it was held that stoppage *in transitu* could not be ratified after the *transitus* had ended. This can be explained on the basis that to allow ratification would have been to divest a property interest, that of the consignee; or more generally that it would allow a time limit to be extended by ratification. The notion that a property interest cannot be divested by a ratification must certainly, if confined to the strict sense of property rights and their validity against third parties,[193] be correct, and may explain this case and another holding that the unauthorised exercise of an option could not be ratified (by the solicitor of the person entitled) after the expiry of the relevant period.[194] But the *contractual* aspect of the second situation can be considered separately, and in general a time limit rule is too narrow to provide a solution. There are in fact other situations where it is thought that ratification should be permitted even though the effect is to extend a time limit. It has been held that ratification of an act which if authorised would have prevented the limitation period from running is effective though it takes place after the expiry of the period.[195] It has been said that ratification must be within a reasonable time "which cannot extend after the time at which the contract is to commence".[196] But although it has been suggested that such a reasonable time rule should be the main control[197] there are numerous dicta against the existence of such a rule.[198] The question is elaborately discussed in this case (where many different lines of reasoning are deployed) and in two more recent decisions, one not allowing ratification,[199] the other permitting it.[200] What emerges from these three cases is that the matter can only be solved by a general principle, of which even the property cases are perhaps to be treated as examples, that ratification is not effective where to allow it would be unfairly prejudicial to the other party.[201] On this basis, a ratification on which the ratifier does not rely against the third party might, in some circumstances, be effective against the ratifier.

31-034

---

[191] Above, n.188.

[192] (1850) 4 Ex. 786. See *The Borvigilant* [2003] EWCA Civ 935, [2003] 2 Lloyd's Rep. 520 at [79] et seq.

[193] And hence not taking in notions operating only between the parties such as an accrued cause of action (see *The Borvigilant*, above at [89]) or an accrued defence (see *Smith v Henniker-Major & Co* [2002] EWCA Civ 762, [2003] Ch. 182 at [71]).

[194] *Dibbins v Dibbins* [1996] 2 Ch. 348. See also *Re Construction Forestry Mining and Energy Union* (1994) 181 C.L.R. 539, 545 (act must be valid and effective when done).

[195] *Presentaciones Musicales SA v Secunda* [1994] Ch. 271 (issue of writ).

[196] *Metropolitan Asylums Board v Kingham & Sons* (1890) 9 T.L.R. 217, 218, per Fry L.J.

[197] C.-H. Tan (2001) 117 L.Q.R. 626.

[198] See *Celthene Pty Ltd v WJK Hauliers Ltd* [1981] 1 N.S.W.L.R. 606, 615; *Bedford Ins Co Ltd v Instituto de Resseguros do Brasil* [1985] Q.B. 966, 986–987.

[199] *Smith v Henniker-Major & Co* [2002] EWCA Civ 762, [2003] Ch. 182 (no ratification of deed of assignment three years after execution).

[200] *The Borvigilant* [2003] EWCA Civ 935, [2003] 2 Lloyd's Rep. 520 (ratification by sub-contractor of clause conferring immunity from liability in tort).

[201] See *Smith v Henniker-Major & Co*, above, at [71]; *The Borvigilant*, above, at [70], [78], [79], [88].

(d) Agency of Necessity

31-035 Agency of necessity A number of decisions establish a doctrine whereby one person may in circumstances of emergency be regarded as empowered to act for another without prior authorisation. The traditional examples are those of the shipmaster, who has (or had) wide powers to contract on behalf of the shipowner[202] (or demise charterer) and also in some cases on behalf of the cargo owner[203]; and of the person who accepts a bill of exchange for the honour of the drawer.[204] Strict rules of quite ancient origin are usually attributed to this type of agency, though they are really relevant only to the shipmaster and not to the acceptor for honour. It must be impracticable for the agent to communicate with the principal[205]; the steps taken must be necessary for the benefit of the principal[206]; and the agent must act bona fide in the interests of the principal.[207] The requirement of impracticability of communication suggests that the authority does not exist if the principal had forbidden the act in advance.[208]

31-036 First type of case As will be seen from the two main examples, the cases are in fact of two different types. The first type involves an agent who purports to bind his principal by contract. It has been suggested that the term "agency of necessity" should be restricted to such situations, and that it is in such cases only that the strict requirements mentioned above are applicable.[209] Where the person concerned is already an agent, it may be possible to say that there is a general implied authority to act appropriately in an emergency,[210] regardless of the rather rigid ancient requirements for agency of necessity.[211] It was however fairly recently held that a master can only bind the *cargo owner* (as opposed to shipowner) by signing a salvage agreement when the requirements of the ancient rules are satisfied: thus the contract was not binding on that person where he could have been consulted.[212] The law on this point was determined by statute in 1994, under which the master has authority

---

[202] See *The Australia* (1859) 13 Moo. P.C. 132 (sale of ship); *The Renpor* (1883) 8 P.D. 115 (salvage). As to hypothecation see *The Karnak* (1869) L.R. 2 P.C. 505.

[203] *Australasian SN Co v Morse* (1872) L.R. 4 P.C. 222 (sale of cargo). As to hypothecation see *The Karnak*, above. As to salvage see *The Renpor*, above; Merchant Shipping Act 1995 s.224(1) and Sch.11 art.6. And see in general *Scrutton on Charterparties*, 23rd edn (2015), arts 146–148.

[204] Bills of Exchange Act 1882 s.65; below, para.34-142. See *Hawtayne v Bourne* (1841) 7 M. & W. 595, 599.

[205] *Springer v GW Ry* [1921] 1 K.B. 257, 265; cf. *Prager v Blatspiel, Stamp and Heacock Ltd* [1924] 1 K.B. 566, 571. See also *John Koch Ltd v C & H Products Ltd* [1956] 2 Lloyd's Rep. 59. Modern communications make such impracticability less common. But even where modern methods are available, it may be impracticable to communicate with, say, 250 holders of bills of lading.

[206] *Prager v Blatspiel, Stamp and Heacock Ltd*, above, at 571–572. It is enough if a reasonable man would think that there was a necessity: *Tetley & Co v British Trade Corp* (1922) 10 Ll.L. Rep. 678.

[207] *Prager v Blatspiel, Stamp and Heacock Ltd*, above, at 572–573.

[208] But see *Graanhandel T Vink BV v European Grain and Shipping Ltd* [1989] 2 Lloyd's Rep. 531, 533.

[209] *China Pacific SA v Food Corp of India (The Winson)* [1982] A.C. 939, 958, per Lord Diplock.

[210] e.g. *De Bussche v Alt* (1878) 8 Ch. D. 286 (subdelegation); *Montaignac v Shitta* (1890) 15 App. Cas. 357 (unusual terms); *Gokal Chand-Jagan Nath v Nand Ram Das-Atma Ram* [1939] A.C. 106 (giving credit); cf. *John Koch Ltd v C & H Products Ltd* [1956] 2 Lloyd's Rep. 59 (no authority to cancel contract).

[211] See the reasoning employed in *The Unique Mariner* [1978] 1 Lloyd's Rep. 438 (authority to sign salvage contract).

[212] *The Choko Star* [1990] 1 Lloyd's Rep. 516; *The Pa Mar* [1999] 1 Lloyd's Rep. 338, 341–342.

to sign a salvage agreement for cargo.[213] But the reasoning of the case suggests that where the person acting does not already have an agency relationship, authority of an abnormal sort only arises by operation of law under the old agency of necessity rules. It is however doubtful whether this should be so: the rules antedate the development of the modern principles of apparent and even implied authority, and if it is correct that they do not apply if the principal has forbidden the act, they should on more modern analysis be based on some form of implied, and hence apparent, authority. Further, though the master may have no relationship with the cargo owner, he is employed by the shipowner, who is bailee of the cargo: and the powers of a bailee have been established in the second type of case, as appears below. The difference between the traditional strict and a more general approach in such cases would not normally be great.[214] But it could be significant where one of the rather specific requirements is not fulfilled but the third party has no way of knowing that. If such a case arose the whole doctrine might merit reconsideration at the highest level.[215]

Second type of case The second type of case covers situations where one party 31-037 deals in some way on another's behalf and claims protection against an action for interference with the other's property, or goes further and seeks reimbursement for the cost of so acting. This type of situation raises restitutionary issues and is similar to the *negotiorum gestio* of Roman law. It seems that here the conduct will be more easily justified if there is already a pre-existing relationship between the parties, whether of agency or of some other sort such as that of bailor and bailee.[216] Thus it has been held that a salvor was entitled to reimbursement from the cargo owner for warehousing cargo after the termination of the salvage services, although it had not been impracticable to communicate with the cargo owner and it was at least arguable that the salvor had acted partly in his own interest, to preserve his lien.[217] So also carriers have been held entitled to reimbursement for expenses incurred in stabling uncollected horses,[218] and it has been implied that they would have a defence to an action of conversion if they disposed of perishable goods in circumstances of necessity.[219] It can also be said that there may in such cases be an actual duty on the bailee to act in the bailor's interests,[220] which justifies his action and entitles him to reimbursement.[221] In the absence of such an existing relationship, however, there is at present no general principle (outside the specialised area

---

[213] Merchant Shipping Act 1995 s.224(1) and Sch.11, implementing a Convention of 1989; applied in *The Altair* [2008] EWHC 612 (Comm), [2008] 2 All E.R. (Comm) 805.

[214] Some but not all of the problems could be solved by reasoning such as that used in *United Bank of Kuwait v Hammoud* [1988] 1 W.L.R. 145; below, para.31-056, n.342.

[215] See *Bowstead and Reynolds on Agency*, 21st edn (2018), para.4-008.

[216] *China Pacific SA v Food Corp of India (The Winson)* [1982] A.C. 939 at 960–961. See *Jebara v Ottoman Bank* [1927] 2 K.B. 254, 270–271; reversed on other grounds [1928] A.C. 269.

[217] *China Pacific SA v Food Corp of India*, above: see at 964–966.

[218] *GN Ry v Swaffield* (1874) L.R. 9 Ex. 132.

[219] *Sims & Co v Midland Ry Co* [1913] 1 K.B. 103; cf. *Springer v GW Ry* [1921] 1 K.B. 257 (no necessity). A bailee may now have power to sell under s.12 of the Torts (Interference with Goods) Act 1977, but this would not always be adequate in emergencies.

[220] *Notara v Henderson* (1872) L.R. 7 Q.B. 225; *GN Ry v Swaffield*, above.

[221] *Petroleo Brasileiro SA v ENE 1 Kos Ltd* [2012] UKSC 17, [2012] 2 A.C. 164 at [18] et seq. (carrier in possession of cargo after ship withdrawn from charterparty); *Cargo ex Argos* (1873) L.R. 5 P.C. 134; *Garriock v Walker* (1873) 1 Rettie 100 (where the cargo owner knew what was being done and did not acquiesce). See also as to agency of bailees *Tappenden v Artus* [1964] 2 Q.B. 185.

of marine salvage[222]) entitling a person who protects or benefits the property of another to reimbursement or even to a lien.[223] Whether the cases on the acceptor for honour should be extended, with certain other miscellaneous cases, or some other line of reasoning employed to give such a right is a question for the law of restitution.[224] But it is true that in some of the cases in which the existence of such a general right was denied, the matter was not really in issue, since any necessity concerned the interests of the agent rather than the principal.[225]

(e) Capacity

31-038 **Capacity to act as principal** As a general rule a person has capacity to authorise an agent, or to ratify the acts of one purporting to act as an agent, where the act can be done by an agent and the principal would have capacity to make the contract or to do the act himself. Thus a corporation could not in former times appoint an agent to act outside the scope of its charter or memorandum of association,[226] and an alien enemy may not normally appoint an agent at all.[227] A minor may appoint an agent: it has been said that "whenever a minor can lawfully do an action on his own behalf, so as to bind himself, he can instead appoint an agent to do it for him".[228] It was sometimes said that he cannot execute a power of attorney[229]: but the true position may be rather that any deed disposing of property executed by an agent so appointed is voidable by the minor as if he had executed it himself[230]—"An infant cannot appoint an agent so as to bind him irrevocably".[231] There is support for the view that a mentally disordered person incapable of understanding what he is doing, on the other hand, can neither execute a power of attorney[232] nor (perhaps) appoint an

---

[222] See Goff and Jones, *Law of Unjust Enrichment*, 9th edn (2016), Ch.18.

[223] *Nicholson v Chapman* (1793) 2 Hy.Bl. 254; *Falcke v Scottish Imperial Insurance Co* (1886) 34 Ch. D. 234; but see Vol.I, para.29-142. However, limited powers are conferred by the Mental Capacity Act 2005 s.9, which may enable a person acting for the benefit of a mentally incapable person to pledge his credit (relevant to the first type of agency of necessity) and to obtain reimbursement (relevant to the second).

[224] See Goff and Jones, *Law of Unjust Enrichment*, 9th edn (2016), Ch.17; Burrows, *Law of Restitution*, 3rd edn (2011), pp.470 et seq.; Vol.I, paras 29-136 et seq.

[225] *Falcke v Scottish Imperial Insurance Co*, above; *Sachs v Miklos* [1948] 2 K.B. 23, 26. See also *Munro v Wilmott* [1949] 1 K.B. 295; *Coldman v Hill* [1919] 1 K.B. 443; *Ridyard v Roberts* Unreported May 16, 1980, CA.

[226] *Montreal Assurance Co v M'Gillivray* (1859) 8 Moo. P.C. 87; *Ashbury Railway Carriage Co Ltd v Riche* (1875) L.R. 7 H.L. 653. And see *Re Banque des* Marchands de Moscou [1952] 1 All E.R. 1269 (dissolved foreign corporation can have no agent of necessity). But this principle is modified in its operation by s.39 of the Companies Act 2006: below, para.31-059.

[227] *Sovfracht, etc. v Van Udens, etc.* [1943] A.C. 203; *Boston Deep Sea Fishing & Ice Co v Farnham* [1957] 1 W.L.R. 1051. But cf. *Lepage v San Paulo Copper Estates Ltd* (1917) 33 T.L.R. 457 (agent appointed by foreign court); *Hangkam Kwingtong Woo v Liu Lan Fong* [1951] A.C. 707.

[228] *G(A) v G(T)* [1970] 2 Q.B. 643, 652, per Lord Denning M.R., limiting earlier dicta of his own in *Shephard v Cartwright* [1953] Ch. 728, 735.

[229] Cases sometimes cited are *Zouch d Abbott and Hallett v Parsons* (1765) 3 Burr. 1794; *Oliver v Woodroffe* (1839) 4 M. & W. 650. See also *Gibbons v Wright* (1954) 91 C.L.R. 423, 447 et seq. But a person under the age of 18 cannot create a lasting power of attorney: Mental Capacity Act 2005 s.9(2)(c).

[230] See *Edwards v Carter* [1893] A.C. 360. The position as to dispositions not by deed is unclear: see *Chaplin v Leslie Frewin (Publishers) Ltd* [1966] Ch. 71, 90, 93–94, 97.

[231] *G(A) v G(T)* [1970] 2 Q.B. 643 at 652, per Lord Denning M.R.

[232] *Daily Telegraph Co Ltd v McLaughlin* (1904) 1 C.L.R. 243; affirmed [1904] A.C. 776 (but based on non est factum doctrine); *Gibbons v Wright* (1954) 91 C.L.R. 423, especially at 444 et seq.

agent at all,[233] even though the contract made by the agent would, if made by the principal himself, have been voidable only.[234] But it is not clear that this is the best solution, and the whole area may require reconsideration.[235]

Capacity to act as agent   A contract made by an agent as such, is, in law, the   **31-039**
contract of the principal. The agent is considered merely as the medium by which the contract is effected; and his assent is merely the assent of his principal. He need not, therefore, be a person himself having full contractual capacity so long as he can understand what he is doing.[236] But any liability to his principal in contract would depend on his contractual capacity: so, probably, should his contractual liability to the third party.[237] A party to a contract may not be able to act as agent for the other party: thus it was held that one party to the contract cannot sign the agreement or memorandum as agent for the other so as to bind the other for the purposes of s.40 of the Law of Property Act 1925.[238] This rule presumably survives the Law of Property (Miscellaneous Provisions) Act 1989, under which the contract must itself be in writing, signed by or on behalf of each party to it.[239] This is not however a rule of capacity but of statutory interpretation.

Acting for both parties   As a matter of the general law on capacity, however, an   **31-040**
agent for one party may act as agent of the other party also, provided he acts within his obligations to his principal.[240] There is no formal incapacity so to act. There are however many judicial warnings as to the danger of the practice,[241] for such an agent may be the subject of a conflict of interests, and hence potentially at least in breach

---

[233] *Gibbons v Wright* (1954) 91 C.L.R. 423, especially at 444 et seq. See *Yonge v Toynbee* [1910] 1 K.B. 215 (agent liable for breach of warranty of authority); but cf. *Taylor v Walker* [1958] 1 Lloyd's Rep. 490, 514; *Gibbons v Wright*, above. See Watts, below, arguing that the initial manifestation is valid except against a third party with notice. Where the principal becomes incapable after granting authority he may be liable under the doctrine of apparent authority: *Drew v Nunn* (1879) 4 Q.B.D. 661. As to supervening incapacity of the *agent* see below, para.31-166.

[234] *Imperial Loan Co v Stone* [1892] 1 Q.B. 599.

[235] See in general *Bowstead and Reynolds on Agency*, 21st edn (2018), para.2-009; Watts [2015] C.L.J. 140, suggesting that actual authority can exist if the agent did not know of the principal's incapacity (including supervening incapacity). This approach receives a measure of approval in *Blankley v Central Manchester Children's University Hospitals NHS Trust* [2015] EWCA Civ 18, [2015] 1 W.L.R. 4307 at [34], [36]. The case holds that an accompanying contract (a solicitor's retainer) need not be frustrated by supervening incapacity of the donor.

[236] Co.Litt. 54a; *Foreman v GW Ry* (1878) 38 L T. 851 (the principal of an illiterate agent is in the same position as if he and not the agent had signed a document); *Re D'Angibau* (1880) 15 Ch. D. 228, 246 (minor). A person under the age of 18 cannot be an attorney under a Lasting Power of Attorney (below, para.31-172): Mental Capacity Act 2005 s.10(1)(a). As to the defence of non est factum when the agent does not understand the transaction, see *Norwich and Peterborough BS v Steed* [1993] Ch. 116.

[237] The contrary result was reached in *Commonwealth Trust Co v De Witt* (1974) 40 D.L.R. (3d) 113 (contract ultra vires company, but agency not: company liable as agent for undisclosed principal). See Weinrib (1975) 21 McGill L.J. 298; (1976) 40 Sask.L.Rev. 291.

[238] *Sharman v Brandt* (1871) L.R. 6 Q.B. 720.

[239] s.2. See Vol.I, paras 5-032 et seq.

[240] *Durrell v Evans* (1862) 31 L.J. Ex. 337 (factor); *Chaney v Maclow* [1929] 1 Ch. 461; *Wilson & Son v Pike* [1949] 1 K.B. 176 (auctioneer); *Gavaghan v Edwards* [1961] 2 Q.B. 220 (solicitor); *Briess v Woolley* [1954] A.C. 333 (director); *Newcastle United Plc v Revenue & Customs Commissioners* [2007] EWHC 612 (Ch), [2007] S.T.C. 1330 (football agent).

[241] See *Moody v Cox and Hatt* [1917] 2 Ch. 71, 91; *Spector v Ageda* [1973] 1 Ch. 30, 47; *Eagle Star Insurance Co Ltd v Spratt* [1971] 2 Lloyd's Rep. 116, 133 (insurance).

of his fiduciary duty to one of his principals.[242] Hence a transaction entered into may sometimes be voidable at the instance of that principal[243]; though sometimes an act done by the agent may be valid though wrongful.[244]

(f) Delegation

31-041 **When delegation permissible** An agent cannot, except with the express or implied assent of the principal, delegate his authority, and the principal will not be bound by the act or contract of a sub-agent whose appointment is not thus sanctioned. This is often expressed in the maxim *delegatus non potest delegare*, and especially applies where the personal skill of the agent is essential; or where there is a trust, confidence, or discretionary power reposed in the agent.[245] But the assent of the principal may and ought to be implied wherever, from the conduct of the parties to the original contract of agency, or from the usage of trade, or from the nature of the particular business which is the subject of the agency, it may reasonably be presumed that the parties originally intended that the agent should have such authority, or where, in the course of the employment, unforeseen emergencies arise which impose upon the agent the necessity of employing a substitute.[246] Thus, while solicitors may not normally delegate,[247] in former times a country solicitor was impliedly authorised by his client to delegate to his London agent where this was appropriate in the ordinary course of his business as a solicitor.[248] And the performance of purely ministerial acts may be delegated.[249]

31-042 **Effect of delegation** The normal effect of valid delegation is that the sub-agent is responsible to the agent; there is no privity of contract between a principal and a sub-agent merely because delegation has been authorised.[250] This may be so even

---

[242] *Fullwood v Hurley* [1928] 1 K.B. 498, 502 (hotel broker); *Anglo African Merchants Ltd v Bayley* [1970] 1 Q.B. 311 (insurance broker: above, para.31-015); *Imageview Management Ltd v Jack* [2009] EWCA Civ 63, [2009] 1 Lloyd's Rep.436. On which of two principals he is acting for in a particular respect, see *UBS v Kommunale Wasserwerke Leipzig GmbH* [2014] EWHC 3615 (Comm) at [615]–[620] (on appeal [2017] EWCA Civ 1567, [2017] 2 Lloyd's Rep. 621). See in general below, paras 31-118 et seq. The situation must be distinguished from that where a professional has knowledge from *previous* dealings with the other party. Here the question is likely to be one of confidential information. See *Prince Jefri Bolkiah v KPMG* [1999] 2 A.C. 222, 234–235.

[243] *North & South Trust Co v Berkeley* [1971] 1 W.L.R. 470, 485. It may sometimes even be void for lack of authority: see below, paras 31-044, 31-074.

[244] *North & South Trust Co v Berkeley*, above. See also *Gamba Holdings UK Ltd v Minories Finance Ltd* [1988] 1 W.L.R. 1231 (receivership: ownership of documents).

[245] *De Bussche v Alt* (1878) 8 Ch. D. 286, 310–311. For a more recent example see *John McCann & Co v Pow* [1974] 1 W.L.R. 1643 (estate agent). As to delegation by trustees, see Trustee Act 2000 s.5.

[246] *De Bussche v Alt* (1878) 8 Ch. D. 286, 310 (merchants authorised to sell ship wherever it might be); *Quebec & Richmond Railroad v Quinn* (1858) 12 Moo. P.C. 232, 265; *Harris v Fiat Motors* (1906) 22 T.L.R. 556; *Gwilliam v Twist* [1895] 2 Q.B. 84. As to apparent authority to delegate, see below, para.31-060.

[247] *Re Becket* [1918] 2 Ch. 72.

[248] *Re Newen* [1903] 1 Ch. 812. But he cannot make the London agent the client's solicitor: *Wray v Kemp* (1884) 26 Ch. D. 169; *Re Becket*, above.

[249] *Ex p. Sutton* (1788) 2 Cox 84; *Lord v Hall* (1848) 2 Car. & K. 698; *Ex p. Birmingham Banking Co* (1868) L.R. 3 Ch. App. 651; *Allam & Co v Europa Poster Services Ltd* [1968] 1 W.L.R. 638; *The Berkshire* [1974] 1 Lloyd's Rep. 185, 188; *Parkin v Williams* [1986] 1 N.Z.L.R. 294.

[250] *Calico Printers' Association v Barclays Bank* (1931) 145 L.T. 51 (HL; a leading case); *New Zealand and Australian Land Co v Watson* (1881) 7 Q.B.D. 374; *Kahler v Midland Bank Ltd* [1950] A.C.

where the sub-agent is authorised to make contracts binding the principal.[251] Privity may be created if the agent has clear authority (which could be apparent[252]) to create such privity, i.e. to appoint another agent to the principal[253] or his act in doing so is ratified;[254] but the principal's knowledge of or consent to the employment of a sub-agent is not in itself sufficient to imply authority to create privity.[255] In the normal case the agent is liable to the principal for money received by the sub-agent for the principal[256] and he is liable for the sub-agent's breaches of duty,[257] whether the sub-agent is appointed with[258] or without, the principal's knowledge. However, this might not be so in all situations, especially if he was authorised to establish privity between principal and sub-agent and had taken reasonable care in selection.[259] Where there is no privity between the principal and the sub-agent, it is generally thought that the principal cannot sue the sub-agent for money received by the sub-agent in the course of his agency[260] unless, perhaps, the sub-agent acknowledges to the principal that he holds the money on the principal's behalf.[261] It has also been held that the sub-agent is entitled to commission from the agent notwithstanding that the agent has not received his own commission from the principal.[262] But outside the field of pure contract, other techniques may apply. The sub-agent may be liable to repay secret profits to the principal[263] and may have a lien against the principal.[264] And there are cases where he is liable to the principal in tort, whether as sub-bailee[265] or where more generally there can be said to have

---

24; *Prentis Donegan & Partners Ltd v Leeds & Leeds Co Inc* [1998] 2 Lloyd's Rep. 326, suggesting (in the context of producing and placing brokers) that "since *Calico Printers the influence of De Bussche v Alt* would seem to have waned"(at 331); *Grosvenor Casinos Ltd v National Bank of Abu Dhabi* [2008] EWHC 511 (Comm), [2008] 2 Lloyd's Rep. 1 (customer of remitting bank and collecting bank); cf. *Velos Group Ltd v Harbour Insurance Services Ltd* [1997] 2 Lloyd's Rep. 461. It is possible, but unlikely, that such authorisation would confer on the sub-agent a right to sue the principal under s.1 of the Contracts (Rights of Third Parties) Act 1999.

[251] See *Temple Legal Protection Ltd v QBE Insurance (Europe) Ltd* [2009] EWCA Civ 453, [2010] 1 All E.R.(Comm) 703 at [21].

[252] See *AJU Remicon Co Ltd v Alida Shipping Co Ltd* [2007] EWHC 2246 (Comm).

[253] *De Bussche v Alt* (1878) 8 Ch. D. 286; *Powell & Thomas v Evan Jones & Co* [1905] 1 K.B. 11.

[254] *Keay v Fenwick* (1876) 1 C.P.D. 745.

[255] *New Zealand and Australian Land Co v Watson* (1881) 7 Q.B.D. 374.

[256] *Matthews v Haydon* (1796) 2 Esp. 509; *National Employers', etc. Assn v Elphinstone* [1929] W.N. 135; *Trading & General Investment Corp v Gault (The Okeanis)* [1986] 1 Lloyd's Rep. 195, 201.

[257] *Meyerstein v Eastern Agency Co* (1885) 1 T.L.R. 595; *Re Mitchell* (1884) 54 L.J. Ch. 342; *Ecossaise SS Co Ltd v Lloyd, Low & Co* (1890) 7 T.L.R. 76; *Stewart v Reavell's Garage* [1952] 2 Q.B. 545. This result is attributed to the notion of non-delegable duty in *Involnert Management Inc v Aprilgrange Ltd* [2015] EWHC 2225 (Comm) at [280].

[258] *Mackersy v Ramsays, Bonars & Co* (1843) 9 Cl. & F. 818; *Trading & General Investment Corp v Gault Armstrong & Kemble Ltd (The Okeanis)*, above.

[259] *Thomas Cheshire & Co v Vaughan Bros & Co* [1920] 3 K.B. 240, 259; *Involnert Management Inc v Aprilgrange Ltd* [2015] EWHC 2225 (Comm), [2016] 1 All E.R. (Comm) 913 at [280].

[260] *Robbins v Fennell* (1847) 11 Q.B. 248; *Cobb v Becke* (1845) 6 Q.B. 930; *New Zealand and Australian Land Co v Watson* (1881) 7 Q.B.D. 374. But this is doubted by Tettenborn (1999) 115 L.Q.R. 655.

[261] See *Shamia v Joory* [1958] 1 Q.B. 448; Davies (1959) 75 L.Q.R. 220.

[262] *Crema v Cenkos Securities Plc* [2010] EWCA Civ 1444, [2011] 1 W.L.R. 2066, denying the existence of a custom to the contrary.

[263] *Powell & Thomas v Evan Jones & Co* [1905] 1 K.B. 11; *Markel International Insurance Co Ltd v Surety Guarantee Consultants Ltd* [2008] EWHC 1135 (Comm), [2009] Lloyd's Rep. I.R. 77.

[264] *Fisher v Smith* (1878) 4 App. Cas. 1; *Lawrence v Fletcher* (1879) 12 Ch. D. 858. See further *Bowstead and Reynolds on Agency*, 21st edn (2018), art.68.

[265] See *Lee Cooper v CH Jeakins & Sons* [1967] 2 Q.B. 1; *The Pioneer Container* [1994] 2 A.C. 324.

been an assumption of responsibility by him.[266] Other tort actions are possible.[267] Hence it may be that the special position of a sub-agent could be further developed.[268]

5. AUTHORITY

31-043 **Distinction between actual and apparent authority** An agent's power to affect the legal position of his principal rests upon his authority: it may in fact be said that his authority *is* a power to affect his principal's position by doing acts on his behalf, though the ideas are slightly different inasmuch as authority is regarded as a fact, while power is a legal relation. Authority may be actual or apparent.[269] Actual authority is "a legal relationship between principal and agent created by a consensual agreement to which they alone are parties".[270] Apparent, or ostensible, authority is "the authority of an agent as it *appears* to others"[271]: under the doctrine of apparent authority the principal may be bound to third parties because the agent appeared to have authority, though as between principal and agent there was in fact no such authority granted and the normal consequences of such authority did not arise. This section deals primarily with actual authority only, apparent authority being dealt with in the section on the relationship between principal and third parties.[272] But the basis of the doctrine of apparent authority is that a third party is in many situations entitled to assume that an agent has such authority as he appears to have or would normally have, whether or not the principal has in fact granted such authority: decisions as to what authority agents do in fact normally possess as between themselves and their principals are obviously, therefore, relevant to the doctrine. Indeed, actual and apparent authority generally co-exist and coincide,[273] and it is often simpler to rely on apparent authority rather than seek to prove actual authority. It is in fact only comparatively recently that a clear analytical distinction has been made.[274]

---

[266] *Henderson v Merrett Syndicates Ltd* [1995] 2 A.C. 145 ("managing agents" held liable to Lloyd's "names"); and see *Riyad Bank v Ahli United Bank (UK) Plc* [2005] EWHC 279 (Comm), [2005] 2 Lloyd's Rep. 409 at [64]; *BP Plc v AON Ltd (No.2)* [2006] EWHC 424 (Comm), [2006] Lloyd's Rep I.R. 577. But the matter turns on the closeness of the relationship, bearing in mind the possible presence of an agreed contractual structure: cf. *Balsamo v Medici* [1984] 1 W.L.R. 951; *Pangood Ltd v Barclay Brown & Co Ltd* [1999] P.N.L.R. 678; *Involnert Management Inc v Aprilgrange Ltd* [2015] EWHC 2225 (Comm), [2016] 1 All E.R. (Comm) 913 at [291].

[267] e.g. *Markel International Insurance Co Ltd v Surety Guarantee Consultants Ltd* [2008] EWHC 1135 (Comm), [2009] Lloyd's Rep. I.R. 77 (procuring breach of contract, conspiracy, dishonest assistance).

[268] See Tettenborn, above, n.260; *Bowstead and Reynolds on Agency*, 21st edn (2018), paras 5-011, 5-012. It seems that a sub-agent who has no privity with the principal cannot be a commercial agent under the Commercial Agents Regulations (above, para.31-017) because these are geared to a contractual relationship between principal and agent: *Light v Ty Europe Ltd* [2003] EWCA Civ 1238, [2004] 1 Lloyd's Rep. 693.

[269] See *Freeman & Lockyer v Buckhurst Park Properties (Mangal) Ltd* [1964] 2 Q.B. 480, 502.

[270] See *Freeman & Lockyer v Buckhurst Park Properties (Mangal) Ltd* [1964] 2 Q.B. 480, 502.

[271] *Hely-Hutchinson v Brayhead Ltd* [1968] 1 Q.B. 549, 583.

[272] See below, para.31-056.

[273] *Hely-Hutchinson v Brayhead Ltd*, above, at 583, 588; *Freeman & Lockyer v Buckhurst Park Properties (Mangal) Ltd* [1964] 2 Q.B. 480 at 502.

[274] See *Burt v Claude Cousins & Co Ltd* [1971] 2 Q.B. 426, 454; *Barrington v Lee* [1972] 1 Q.B. 326, 336.

Express and implied authority These are types of actual authority. Express **31-044** authority is that "given by express words": implied authority is that "inferred from the conduct of the parties and the circumstances of the case".[275] This distinction, though useful, cannot always be definitively applied, since (apart from anything else) the meaning of express words may require interpretation. Implied authority may for convenience be divided into four types: incidental authority, usual authority, customary authority, and authority derived from the circumstances of the case. A general limit on all types of implied (but not apparent) authority is the fairly obvious proposition that there is no such authority to act other than honestly and in pursuit of the principal's interests,[276] and this may be taken into account in interpretation also. Of course, the principal may expressly authorise or even require actions which the agent thinks contrary to the principal's interests[277]; and where the agent does exactly what was authorised it may be possible to say that his motives for doing so were irrelevant.[278] However, equity sometimes, especially in the context of trustees and company directors, also gives relief on a more sensitive basis where a fiduciary does something that is authorised but for inappropriate motives, describable as a "fraud on a power" or exercise of power for an "improper purpose".[279]

Express authority: construction of documents Normally speaking, the usual **31-045** principles apply in the construction of documents conferring authority "including any proper implications from the express words used, the usages of the trade, or the course of business between the parties".[280] And where the authority is conferred in ambiguous terms, acts done by an agent in good faith upon a reasonable interpretation of the instructions will usually be regarded as authorised.[281] It is a well-established rule that *powers of attorney* must be strictly construed,[282] though it has recently been argued that there is no, or no longer, justification for a special rule applicable to a particular type of instrument.[283]

Implied authority: incidental authority An agent has implied authority to do **31-046**

---

[275] *Hely-Hutchinson v Brayhead Ltd* [1968] 1 Q.B. 549, 583.

[276] See *Lysaght v Falk Bros & Co Ltd* (1905) 2 C.L.R. 421, 430, 439; *Tobin v Broadbent* (1947) 75 C.L.R. 378 (power of attorney); *Heinl v Jyske Bank (Gibraltar) Ltd* [1999] Lloyd's Rep. Bank. 511, 521; *Hopkins v TL Dallas Group Ltd* [2004] EWHC 1379, [2005] 1 B.C.L.C. 543 at [89]; also *Criterion Properties Plc v Stratford UK Properties LLC* [2004] UKHL 28, [2004] 1 W.L.R. 1846; Watts [2017] J.B.L. 269 (explaining or rebutting dicta and arguments to the contrary); *Bowstead and Reynolds on Agency*, 21st edn (2018), art.23. As to authority to act illegally, see *Bowstead and Reynolds on Agency*, 21st edn (2018), para.2-025.

[277] See *Volkers v Midland Doherty* (1985) 17 D.L.R. (4th) 343 (instructions to stockbroker).

[278] See *Macmillan Inc v Bishopsgate Investment Trust Plc* [1995] 1 W.L.R. 978, 984; affirmed on other grounds [1996] 1 W.L.R. 387.

[279] See also below, para.31-118; *Bowstead and Reynolds on Agency*, 21st edn (2018), para.8-220.

[280] *Freeman & Lockyer v Buckhurst Park Properties (Mangal) Ltd* [1964] 2 Q.B. 480, 502; *Pole v Leask* (1860) 28 Beav. 562, 574; affirmed (1863) 33 L.J. Ch. 155.

[281] *Ireland v Livingston* (1872) L.R. 5 H.L. 395; *Loring v Davies* (1886) 32 Ch. D. 625; *Weigall & Co v Runciman & Co* (1916) 85 L.J. K.B. 1187. But for more modern discussion see *European Asian Bank AG v Punjab and Sind Bank (No.2)* [1983] 1 W.L.R. 642, 656; *Veljkovic v Vrybergen* [1985] V.R. 419; *Patel v Standard Chartered Bank* [2001] Lloyd's Rep. Bank. 229, 234. With modern communications it may be the agent's duty to seek clarification: *Woodhouse AC Israel Cocoa Ltd SA v Nigerian Produce Marketing Co Ltd* [1972] A.C. 741, 772.

[282] *Bryant v Banque du Peuple* [1893] A.C. 170, 177; *Jonmenjoy Coondoo v Watson* (1884) 9 App. Cas. 561; *Re Dowson & Jenkins' Contract* [1904] 2 Ch. 219. And see *Jacobs v Morris* [1902] 1 Ch. 816; *Danby v Coutts & Co* (1885) 29 Ch. D. 500; *Reckitt v Barnett, Pembroke & Slater* [1929] A.C. 176.

[283] See Dal Pont, in Busch and McGregor (eds), *Agency Law and Commercial Practice* (2015), Ch.12.

whatever is ordinarily or necessarily incidental to the due performance of his express authority.[284] Thus a person authorised to sell land for another had authority to sign a memorandum of the transaction sufficient to satisfy s.40 of the Law of Property Act 1925[285] and presumably now also the written contract required by s.2 of the Law of Property (Miscellaneous Provisions) Act 1989; and estate agents employed to find purchasers have authority to do various subordinate acts in connection with the property to be sold.[286] But an agent authorised to negotiate contracts may well have no authority to receive payment[287]; and persons authorised to sign bills of lading will usually have no authority to settle claims under them.[288]

31-047 **Usual authority**[289]   Agents appointed to positions involving the conduct of particular trades or businesses normally have implied authority to do whatever is usually done by persons occupying such positions[290]; and agents whose occupation involves acting in certain ways (e.g. solicitors, auctioneers, insurance brokers) have the authority usually possessed by persons in such occupations.[291] Both of these are regularly referred to as "usual authority".[292] Some old cases refer to those having usual authority, as above described, as general agents[293]; but, as has been said above,[294] it is doubtful whether the distinction between general and special agents is of much utility.

31-048 **Customary authority**   Agents are sometimes found to have implied authority to act in accordance with the established customs and usages of the places where they act, provided that such customs and usages are reasonable,[295] even where the

---

[284] *Pole v Leask* (1860) 28 Beav. 562, 574–575; affirmed (1863) 33 L.J. Ch. 155; *Howard v Baillie* (1796) 2 H. Bl. 618; *Collen v Gardner* (1856) 21 Beav. 540; *SMC Electronics v Akhtar Computers Ltd* [2001] 1 B.C.L.C. 433.

[285] *Rosenbaum v Belson* [1900] 2 Ch. 267.

[286] See above, para.31-012.

[287] Below, para.31-050.

[288] *Kenya Rys v Antares Co Pte Ltd (The Antares) (Nos 1 and 2)* [1987] 1 Lloyd's Rep. 424.

[289] See further as to this term *Bowstead and Reynolds on Agency*, 21st edn (2018), para.3-005.

[290] *Hely-Hutchinson v Brayhead Ltd* [1968] 1 Q.B. 549, 583; see, e.g. *Re Pearson* [1899] 2 Q.B. 618 (estate manager); *The Huntsman* [1894] P. 214 (managing owner of vessel); *Smith v Hull Glass Co* (1852) 11 C.B. 897 (company manager); *Linford v Provincial Insurance Co* (1864) 34 Beav. 291 (insurance agent); *Walker v GW Ry* (1867) L.R. 2 Ex. 228 (general manager of railway ordering medical attendance: cf. *Cox v Midland Ry* (1849) 3 Ex. 268). See also *Crabb v Arun DC* [1976] Ch. 179, 188, 193 (authority to negotiate).

[291] e.g. *Hatch v Hale* (1850) 15 Q.B. 10 (bailiff); *Richardson v Anderson* (1805) 1 Camp. 43n. (insurance broker); *Howard v Sheward* (1866) L.R. 2 C.P. 148 (horse dealer). And see above, paras 31-011, 31-012, as to estate agents and auctioneers.

[292] This phrase can also be invoked to refer to a possible development of the undisclosed principal doctrine: see below, para.31-064.

[293] In particular the 19th-century cases distinguishing between the powers of the agents of horse dealers, or the dealers themselves, and persons selling horses on behalf of private individuals: see *Howard v Sheward*, above; *Brady v Todd* (1861) 9 C.B.(N.S.) 592; *Brooks v Hassall* (1883) 49 L.T. 569; *Baldry v Bates* (1885) 52 L.T. 620; *Barrett v Irvine* [1907] 2 I.R. 462.

[294] See above, para.31-007.

[295] *Robinson v Mollett* (1875) L.R. 7 H.L. 802, 817–818; *Anglo Overseas Transport Ltd v Titan Industrial Corp* [1959] 2 Lloyd's Rep. 152, 160. Most of the cases concern the Stock Exchange as it then operated: see, e.g. *Coles v Bristowe* (1868) L.R. 4 Ch. App. 3. As to officially determined rules (as opposed to customs) see *Benjamin v Barnett* (1903) 19 T.L.R. 564; *Harker v Edwards* (1887) 57 L.J. Q.B. 147; *Cunliffe-Owen v Teather and Greenwood* [1967] 1 W.L.R. 1421; *Doyle v White City Stadium* [1935] 1 K.B. 110. Rules cannot confer the power on an official body to alter a contract: *Benjamin v Barnett*, above. In the present context "customs" means more than "what is customar-

principal had no notice of the custom[296]: but they have no authority to act in accordance with an unreasonable custom unless the principal had notice of it, in which case he may sometimes be regarded as having assented to it.[297] "Unreasonable" here seems to bear a special meaning: it does not mean harsh or oppressive, but rather inconsistent with the nature of the transaction which the agent was employed to carry out, or with the contract of agency itself.[298] Thus a usage whereby an agent buying for a principal becomes in effect a seller to his principal has been held unreasonable in this context; for the relationship of principal and agent is inconsistent with that of buyer and seller and specific consent to the adoption of a position within the latter relationship would be required.[299] The same applies to a usage whereby the agent can receive payment by way of set-off.[300]

Authority derived from the circumstances of the case   It is obvious that these categories cannot be exhaustive: there must also be a residual category of authority derived from the circumstances of the case.[301]   **31-049**

Authority to receive payment   It was said in 1860 that: **31-050**

> "An agent employed to negotiate and conclude contracts is not thereby authorised to ... receive money which may become due under such contracts, but the course of employment may justify the agent in so ... receiving money if known to the principal and not objected to by him."[302]

This must still be a reasonable starting point. Whether an agent who has authority to sell goods has authority to receive payment for them depends on the circumstances and the relevant business practices and understandings.[303] Even if the agent is authorised to receive payment, he may in some situations have prima facie no authority to receive it otherwise than in cash[304] (though a cheque that was honoured

---

ily done" and may be extremely difficult to establish: see, e.g. *Re North Western Rubber Co Ltd and Hüttenbach & Co* [1908] 2 K.B. 907, 919; *Stag Line v Board of Trade* (1950) 83 Ll.L. Rep. 356, 359, 360; *Cunliffe-Owen v Teather and Greenwood*, above, at 1438–1439; *Bell Group Ltd v Herald & Weekly Times Ltd* [1985] V.R. 613 (Stock Exchange dispute procedure).

296 *Robinson v Mollett* (1875) L.R. 7 H.L. 802, 817–818; *Pollock v Stables* (1848) 12 Q.B. 765.

297 *Robinson v Mollett*, above. For an example of assent see *Limako BV v Hentz & Co Inc* [1978] 1 Lloyd's Rep. 400.

298 *Robinson v Mollett*, above; *Limako BV v Hentz & Co Inc* [1978] 1 Lloyd's Rep. 400.

299 *Robinson v Mollett*, above (tallow trade); *Limako BV v Hentz & Co Inc* [1978] 1 Lloyd's Rep. 400. See also *Anglo-African Merchants Ltd v Bayley* [1970] 1 Q.B. 311; *North & South Trust Co v Berkeley* [1971] 1 W.L.R. 470 (insurance brokers acting for both parties); cf. *Scott and Horton v Godfrey* [1901] 2 K.B. 726; *Jones v Canavan* [1972] 2 N.S.W.L.R. 236 (stockbroker).

300 *Sweeting v Pearce* (1859) 7 C.B.(N.S.) 449 (insurance); *Pearson v Scott* (1878) 9 Ch. D. 198 (Stock Exchange).

301 *Hely-Hutchinson v Brayhead Ltd* [1968] 1 Q.B. 549, 583; and in the context of apparent authority, see *Gurtner v Beaton* [1993] 2 Lloyd's Rep. 369, 379. The word "necessarily", even if relevant to implied terms, is too strict to be a determinant of implied authority: *Targe Towing Ltd v Marine Blast Ltd* [2004] EWCA Civ 346, [2004] 1 Lloyd's Rep. 721 at [22].

302 *Pole v Leask* (1860) 28 Beav. 562, 575, per Romilly M.R.; affirmed (1863) 33 L.J. Ch. 155. For a more recent example in connection with apparent authority, see *Cleveland Mfg Co Ltd v Muslim Commercial Bank Ltd* [1981] 2 Lloyd's Rep. 646.

303 *Butwick v Grant* [1924] 2 K.B. 483 (authorities reviewed); *International Sponge Importers Ltd v Andrew Watt & Sons* [1911] A.C. 279. This being a matter of implied authorisation, it is not necessary to prove an actual custom or usage: proof of what is usually done will normally suffice to confer usual authority (above, para.31-047). See Vol.I, para.21-044.

304 *Sweeting v Pearce* (1859) 7 C.B.(N.S.) 449, 480, 484; affirmed (1861) 9 C.B.(N.S.) 534; *Papé v*

was held equivalent to cash[305]), or on different terms,[306] or in a different manner,[307] from that authorised by the contract. But the decline in the use of cash and the different methods of payment now available make generalisations beyond that in the first sentence of this paragraph unprofitable.[308] There is authority that emergencies may arise where the agent discharges his duty by getting what cash he can and giving credit for the rest.[309]

31-051 **Waiver or repudiation by agent** Questions of authority are not confined to the formation of contract. An agent may sometimes have authority to waive or vary terms of his principal's contract.[310] Whether he can evince an intention to repudiate a contract on behalf of his principal must again depend on his authority. If an agent is to deliver goods on behalf of his principal, and because of a mistake refuses to do so, it must depend on the particular circumstances of each case whether the agent's conduct shows, on behalf of the principal, an intention not to be further bound by the contract.[311]

31-052 **Presumed authority: married women** Until 1970 married women were normally treated as a separate topic in the law of agency, for special rules applied to them. These rules stemmed from two factors: the husband's obligation to support his wife, and the wife's inability until the late nineteenth century to own separate property and thus to be liable on contracts. They also reflect a method of buying on informal credit which does not correspond with modern trading patterns in England. Under the rules there was a presumption of authority in a wife arising from cohabitation; a special agency, sometimes referred to as an agency of necessity, in a wife who had been deserted; and a sizeable amount of case law, the true basis of which was not in all respects clear, on the position of a wife living apart from her husband by agreement.[312] The special powers of a deserted wife were however abolished by statute in 1970,[313] and any implied or apparent authority of a wife, since it must clearly stem only from normal principles, is no longer appropri-

---

Westacott [1894] 1 Q.B. 272; *Blumberg v Life Interests Corp* [1898] 1 Ch. 27; cf. *Australia & New Zealand Bank Ltd v Ateliers de Constructions Electriques de Charleroi* [1967] 1 A.C. 86. And see *Lloyds & Scottish Finance Ltd v Williamson* [1965] 1 W.L.R. 404, 408–409; Vol.I, para.21-045.

[305] *Bridges v Garrett* (1870) L.R. 5 C.P. 451; *Bradford & Sons v Price Bros* (1923) 92 L.J. K.B. 871; *Clay Hill Brick & Tile Co Ltd v Rawlings* [1938] 4 All E.R. 100.

[306] *Campbell v Hassel* (1816) 1 Stark. 233.

[307] *Sweeting v Pearce* (1859) 7 C.B.(N.S.) 449 (set-off); *Underwood v Nicholls* (1855) 17 C.B. 239.

[308] Further cases are collected in *Bowstead and Reynolds on Agency*, 21st edn (2018), art.28.

[309] *Gokal Chand-Jagan Nath v Nand Ram Das-Atma Ram* [1939] A.C. 106.

[310] See authorities discussed in *Surrey Shipping Co v Cie Continentale (France) SA (The Shackleford)* [1978] 1 W.L.R. 1080; see also *Toepfer v Warinco AG* [1978] 2 Lloyd's Rep. 569. It has been held that an agent who has not such authority may have authority to make representations as to the manner in which a general contractual provision will be enforced: *State Rail Authority of NSW v Heath Outdoor Pty Ltd* (1986) 7 N.S.W.L.R. 170.

[311] *Peter Dumenil & Co v James Ruddin Ltd* [1953] 1 W.L.R. 815. *Misperformance* by an agent would of course simply rank as the principal's misperformance. There are recent cases concerning the question whether notice of arbitration is validly served on an agent: *Sino Channel Asia Ltd v Dana Shipping and Trading Pte Singapore* [2017] EWCA Civ 1703, [2018] 1 Lloyd's Rep. 17; *Glencore Agriculture BV v Conqueror Holdings Ltd* [2017] EWHC 2893 (Comm), [2018] 1 Lloyd's Rep. 233.

[312] A full account of the whole topic was given in *Bowstead on Agency*, 13th edn (1968), arts 37–41. On both topics see Hardingham (1980) 54 A.L.J. 661 (discussing the cases here cited and additional Commonwealth authorities).

[313] Matrimonial Proceedings and Property Act 1970 s.41(1): the wife is now protected by the powers of the court.

ate for separate treatment.[314] All that remains therefore is a presumption of authority from cohabitation, which in fact need not be confined to wives (or indeed women) at all. In contemporary English conditions it is doubtful whether the topic any longer has much relevance as such.[315]

Joint and several authority Where authority is given to two or more persons 31-053 jointly without any provision as to action by a quorum, they must all join together in exercising it, or the principal will not be bound.[316] But this rule does not apply where an authority is given to two or more persons severally or jointly and severally.[317]

6. PRINCIPAL'S RELATIONS WITH THIRD PARTIES

(a) General Rule

General rule: identified and unidentified principal The general rule is that a 31-054 principal is bound by, and entitled to the benefit of, the contract of his agent made on his behalf within the scope of such agent's actual authority. This is so whether the agent at the time of acting named or identified his principal ("identified principal"[318]) or merely indicated that he was acting for a principal but did not identify him ("unidentified principal")—e.g. "bought for our principals". It is also true where the agent at that time gave no indication that he was acting for a principal at all, was not thought to do so, but in fact was. In such a case the principal is said to be undisclosed. Both of these are manifestations of a principle enunciated by Diplock L.J. in 1968:

> "Where an agent has such actual authority and enters into a contract with another party intending to do so on behalf of his principal, *it matters not whether he discloses to the other party the identity of his principal, or even that he is contracting on behalf of a principal at all*, if the other party is willing or leads the agent to believe that he is willing to treat as a party to the contract anyone on whose behalf the agent may have been authorised to contract. *In the case of an ordinary commercial contract such willingness of the other party may be assumed* by the agent unless either the other party manifests his unwillingness or there are other circumstances which should lead the agent to realise that the other party was not so willing."[319]

Both situations can, if disputes arise, raise serious problems of ascertaining the

---

314 For examples of implied authority see *Waithman v Wakefield* (1807) 1 Camp. 120; *Millard v Harvey* (1864) 34 Beav. 237; of apparent authority, *Ryan v Sams* (1848) 12 Q.B. 460; *Jetley v Hiil* (1884) Cab. & El. 239; *Drew v Nunn* (1879) 4 Q.B.D. 661. See also *Miss Gray Ltd v Earl Cathcart* (1922) 38 T.L.R. 562, 565.

315 An account of presumed authority was given in *Bowstead and Reynolds on Agency*, 16th edn (1996), paras 3-039—3-051.

316 *Re Liverpool Household Stores* (1890) 59 L.J. Ch. 616; *Brown v Andrew* (1849) 18 L.J. Q.B. 153; *Bell v Nixon* (1832) 9 Bing. 393. The Mental Capacity Act 2005 (below, para.31-172) contains special provisions for joint and several holders of Lasting Powers of Attorney: see s.10.

317 *Guthrie v Armstrong* (1822) 5 B. & Ald. 628.

318 This would include a principal described but not named, e.g. the heirs of property, whoever they may be: *Lyell v Kennedy* (1899) 14 App. Cas. 437.

319 *Teheran-Europe Co Ltd v S.T. Belton (Tractors) Ltd* [1968] 2 Q.B. 545, 555 (italics supplied) (described as "the beneficial assumption" by Lord Lloyd of Berwick in *Siu Yin Kwan v Eastern Assurance Co Ltd* [1994] 2 A.C. 199, 221).

subjective intention of the agent, which may determine for whom he was acting[320]; and it may also be found difficult to avoid permitting an agent in practice to allocate contracts between several principals which the agent has for the same or a similar transaction—a situation which at least in theory requires a different analysis.[321] But, even though the two are sometimes confused or run together,[322] the rules as to completely undisclosed principals are different from those relating to disclosed principals and require separate treatment.[323]

31-055   Cases where contract required to be in writing   The Statute of Frauds 1677, as re-enacted in respect of land contracts by s.40 of the Law of Property Act 1925, required in respect of certain contracts a note or memorandum "signed by the party to be charged or by some other person thereunto by him lawfully authorised". Under this it was held that so long as the writing identified two parties liable to each other, an undisclosed principal could intervene to sue,[324] in effect because there was no requirement of signature by the party suing, and could be sued, because signature by the authorised agent was all that was required: there was no requirement mentioned that the agent should also state for whom he acted.[325] The Law of Property (Miscellaneous Provisions) Act 1989 s.2, now requires that such a contract actually be in writing, "signed by or on behalf of each party to the contract". The reasoning by virtue of which an unexplained signature by an agent who undertook personal liability sufficed does not seem available in respect of this wording, and it is not clear to what extent the previous law survives, and to what extent unidentified and undisclosed principals can sue or be sued on contracts signed by their agents. Juridically, it appears that both types of principal are normally in such cases a party to the same, not a different, contract and hence should sign or be signed for.[326] If the purpose of the Act was to prevent disputes over the existence and terms of an agreement[327] it seems therefore that the principal, as a party to the contract,

---

[320] See (but in the context of insurance of construction projects) *National Oilwell (UK) Ltd v Davy Offshore Ltd* [1993] 2 Lloyd's Rep. 582, 596–597, per Colman J. This passage from the *National Oilwell* case, in the context of construction insurance, was doubted by Leggatt J. in the context of undisclosed principal (below, para.31-064) in *Magellan Spirit ApS v Vitol SA* [2016] EWHC 454 (Comm), [2016] 2 Lloyd's Rep. 1 at [19], apparently on the basis that objective criteria should be applied to the ascertainment of a principal. It was accepted in a different context in *Sackville UK Property Select II (GP) No.1 Ltd v Robertson Taylor Insurance Brokers Ltd* [2018] EWHC 122 (Ch) at [46] (on the question of on whose behalf a notice under a lease was served), and the dictum of Colman J. were explained in another construction insurance case, *Haberdasher Aske's Federation Trust Ltd v Lewisham LBC* [2018] EWHC 558 (TCC) at [39], [42]–[43], [50], [52]. Obviously, where objective evidence is available, for example in a contract between principal and agent, as often in construction cases, an objective ascertainment of intention is obviously much easier to require. In an agency context it is doubtful whether this will always be practicable.

[321] See e.g. *Scott and Horton v Godfrey* [1901] 2 K.B. 726 (practice on the London Stock Exchange as it operated at the time: see in particular the arguments of counsel). See in general Reynolds, in Busch and McGregor (eds), *Agency Law and Commercial Practice* (2015), Ch.3.

[322] For an example see *Teheran-Europe Co Ltd v S.T. Belton (Tractors) Ltd* [1968] 2 Q.B. 545, 552, 561.

[323] See below, paras 31-063 et seq.

[324] *Basma v Weekes* [1950] A.C. 441 (a case on an unidentified principal).

[325] *Davies v Sweet* [1962] 2 Q.B. 300. See a recent discussion in the context of guarantees in *Golden Ocean Group Ltd v Salgaocar Mining Industries PVT Ltd* [2012] EWCA Civ 265, [2012] 1 W.L.R. 674. See also *Rabiu v Marlbray Ltd* [2016] EWCA Civ 476, [2016] 1 W.L.R. 547.

[326] Below, paras 31-084, 31-099.

[327] See *Spiro v Glencrown Properties Ltd* [1991] Ch. 537, 541. The Law Commission papers give no guidance: W.P. No.92 (1985), para.5.16 simply indicates a wish to "let the ordinary principles of agency operate". See further Vol.I, para.5-038 (doubting this proposition and citing further author-

ought to be mentioned in it; and that the words "on behalf of" require that the principal be identified. This, if correct, would not permit intervention by an undisclosed principal.

(b) Apparent Authority

Apparent authority Where a person by words or conduct represents to a third **31-056** party that another has authority to act on his behalf, he may be bound by the acts of that other as if he had in fact authorised them.[328] This doctrine, called the doctrine of apparent or ostensible authority,[329] applies to cases where a person allows another who is not his agent at all to appear as his agent,[330] to cases where a principal allows his agent to appear to have more authority than he actually has,[331] to cases where a principal makes reservations in his agent's authority that limit the authority which such agent would normally have, but fails to indicate this to third parties,[332] and to cases where a principal allows it to appear that an agent has authority when such authority has in fact been reduced or terminated.[333] The doctrine is said to be an application of the estoppel principle,[334] but it is a somewhat weak one, the normal rules being leniently applied, particularly in the contractual context as regards reliance on the representation.[335] What is clear, however, is that, as in most legal systems, the liability ultimately springs from the conduct of the principal rather than the position of the third party.[336] The words "represent", and "representation", though regularly used in this context (and below), probably carry too specific connotations.[337] The rules as traditionally stated may however be divided as follows.

(i)   A representation must be made by words or conduct. But though such representation may be express, it may also be implied from acts of a quite general nature, e.g. putting the agent in a position carrying with it a usual

---

ity); *Bowstead and Reynolds on Agency*, 21st edn (2018), para.8-004.

[328] *Pickering v Busk* (1812) 15 East 38; *Pickard v Sears* (1837) 6 A. & E. 469; *Freeman v Cooke* (1848) 2 Exch. 654; *Smith v M'Guire* (1858) 3 Hurl. & N. 554; *Pole v Leask* (1863) 33 L.J. Ch. 155, 162; *Freeman & Lockyer v Buckhurst Park Properties (Mangal) Ltd* [1964] 2 Q.B. 480, 503 (the leading definition); *Hely-Hutchinson v Brayhead Ltd* [1968] 1 Q.B. 549.

[329] But often referred to in nineteenth-century cases as implied authority.

[330] e.g. *Barrett v Deere* (1828) Moo. & M. 200; *F Mildner & Sons v Noble* [1956] C.L.Y. 32; *Povey v Taylor* (1966) 116 New L.J. 1656. Such cases are rare. Much useful American material is referred to in *Hoddesdon v Koos Bros* 135 A. 2d 702 (1957) (bogus shop salesman).

[331] e.g. *Todd v Robinson* (1825) Ry. & M. 217. A possible modern example is *Pacific Carriers Ltd v BNP Paribas* (2004) 215 C.L.R. 451.

[332] e.g. *Montaignac v Shitta* (1890) 15 App. Cas. 357; *Manchester Trust v Furness* [1895] 2 Q.B. 539; *Waugh v HB Clifford & Sons Ltd* [1982] Ch. 374.

[333] e.g. *Summers v Solomon* (1857) 7 E. & B. 879; *Drew v Nunn* (1879) 4 Q.B.D. 661; *Rockland Industries Inc v Amerada Minerals Corp* [1980] 2 S.C.R. 2; (1980) 108 D.L.R. (3d) 513; *AMB Generali Holding AG v SEB Trygg Liv Holding Aktiebolaget* [2005] EWCA Civ 1237, [2006] 1 Lloyd's Rep. 318 at [37]; below, para.31-169.

[334] *Freeman & Lockyer v Buckhurst Park Properties (Mangal) Ltd* [1964] 2 Q.B. 480, 503; *Rama Corp v Proved Tin & General Investments* [1952] 2 Q.B. 147, 149–150; *Pole v Leask* (1863) 33 L.J. Ch. 155, 162. The initial burden of proof is on the person alleging authority: *PEC Asia Ltd v Golden Rice Co Ltd* [2014] EWHC 1583 (Comm).

[335] "Each form of estoppel has its own elements, although some are common. The similarities warrant their recognition as a form of estoppel but the differences make each a distinct form with its own history and requirements": Handley, *Estoppel by Conduct and Election*, 2nd edn (2016), p.30.

[336] See Watts [2015] L.M.C.L.Q. 36, 39. For a recent example see *Fielden v Christie-Miller* [2015] EWHC 87 (Ch), [2015] 2 P. & C.R. DG5.

[337] *Restatement, Third, Agency* uses the better word "manifestation": paras 1.03, 2.03.

authority.[338] Such a representation may arise from a course of dealing (especially one involving regular ratification), though it has been said that authority will not readily be inferred from this.[339]

(ii) The representation must be made by the principal, or someone authorised in accordance with the law of agency to act for him.[340] A representation by the agent as to his authority cannot of itself create apparent authority.[341] But the conduct of the principal may make it more reasonable for the agent's representation as to facts upon which his authority depends to be relied on[342]; and in a well-known decision the principal was held bound on the basis that the agent, known to have limited authority to contract, nevertheless had authority to communicate the principal's approval to the transaction in question.[343] The facts of the case were somewhat marginal, in that the communication of assent was said to be implicit in an actual contractual offer. But it has recently been affirmed that there are common situations, particularly in organisations, where a subordinate has no authority, actual or apparent, to perform an act, but may have actual or apparent authority to report the decisions of a superior or group of superiors in respect of which action has been or will be taken.[344]

---

[338] *Freeman & Lockyer v Buckhurst Park Properties (Mangal) Ltd*, above, at 503 (managing director); *Panorama Developments (Guildford) Ltd v Fidelis Furnishing Fabrics Ltd* [1971] 2 Q.B. 711 (company secretary); *Waugh v HB Clifford & Sons Ltd* [1982] Ch. 374 (solicitor); *Egyptian Intl Foreign Trade Co v Soplex Wholesale Supplies Ltd (The Raffaella)* [1985] 2 Lloyd's Rep. 36 (documentary credits manager); *Shearson Lehman Bros Inc v Maclaine, Watson & Co Ltd (No.2)* [1988] 1 W.L.R. 16, 28; *Pharmed Medicare Private Ltd v Univar Ltd* [2002] EWCA Civ 1569, [2003] 1 All E.R. (Comm) 321. As to usual authority see, above, para.31-047. For the view that deeds constitute an exception to the need for a representation by the principal see Watts (2002) 2 O.U.C.L.J. 93.

[339] See *PEC Asia Ltd v Golden Rice Co Ltd* [2014] EWHC 1583 (Comm), citing *Slingsby v District Bank Ltd* [1932] 1 K.B. 544, 566; but cf. Watts [2015] L.M.C.L.Q. 36, 57–60.

[340] *Freeman & Lockyer v Buckhurst Park Properties (Mangal) Ltd*, above, at 506; *British Bank of the Middle East v Sun Life Assurance Co of Canada (UK) Ltd* [1983] 2 Lloyd's Rep. 9, HL (no authority to answer queries as to authority of another agent); cf. *Canadian Laboratory Supplies Ltd v Engelhard Industries of Canada Ltd* [1979] 2 S.C.R. 787; (1979) 97 D.L.R. (3d) 1; *ING Re (UK) Ltd v R & V Versicherungs AG* [2006] EWHC (Comm) 1544, [2006] 2 All E.R. (Comm) 870; *PEC Asia Ltd v Golden Rice Co Ltd* [2014] EWHC 1583 (Comm) at [623]. In *Crabtree-Vickers Pty Ltd v Australian Direct Mail Advertising and Addressing Co Pty Ltd* (1975) 133 C.L.R. 72 it was held that an agent with apparent authority cannot by his conduct give rise to apparent authority in a sub-agent. Sed quaere: see below, para.31-060, n.377.

[341] *Freeman & Lockyer v Buckhurst Park Properties (Mangal) Ltd* [1964] 2 Q.B. 480 at 505; *Att-Gen for Ceylon v Silva* [1953] A.C. 461, 479; *Armagas Ltd v Mundogas SA (The Ocean Frost)* [1986] A.C. 717; *Savill v Chase Holdings (Wellington) Ltd* [1989] 1 N.Z.L.R. 257.

[342] *Colonial Bank v Cady and Williams* (1890) 15 App. Cas. 267, 273; and see *Canadian Laboratory Supplies Ltd v Englehard Industries of Canada Ltd*, above. An example is where an agent has usual authority to conduct a particular item of business: see *Egyptian Intl Foreign Trade Co v Soplex Wholesale Supplies Ltd (The Raffaella)*, above (documentary credits manager); *United Bank of Kuwait Ltd v Hammoud* [1988] 1 W.L.R. 1051 (solicitor); *Gurtner v Beaton* [1993] 2 Lloyd's Rep. 369 (aviation manager); but cf. *Hirst v Etherington* [1999] Lloyd's Rep. P.N. 938 (solicitor).

[343] *First Energy (UK) Ltd v Hungarian Intl Bank Ltd* [1993] 2 Lloyd's Rep. 194, an important case. But cf. *Armagas Ltd v Mundogas SA (The Ocean Frost)* [1986] A.C. 717; and *Hirst v Etherington*, above, in each of which there was little beyond an avowal by the agent that he had or had obtained authority.

[344] *Kelly v Fraser* [2012] UKPC 25, [2013] 1 A.C. 450 (Vice-President of company responsible for Employee Benefits Division reporting decision of and action taken for Trustees of Pension Fund). The *First Energy* case is perceptively considered at some length, but not favoured, by the Court of Appeal of Singapore in *Skandinaviska Enskilda Banken SA v Asia Pacific Breweries (Singapore) Pte Ltd* [2011] 3 S.L.R. 540. See also Watts [2015] L.M.C.L.Q. 36, 40 et seq.

(iii)   On general principles the representation must be of fact and not of law.[345] But propositions as to mistake of law may now need reconsideration in view of the decision of the House of Lords in *Kleinwort Benson Ltd v Lincoln CC*.[346]

(iv)   The third party must act on the representation.[347] If he does not know of any representation, express or implied, but deals with the agent as a principal, it is obvious that he cannot rely on the doctrine.[348] But the requirement that there must be a representation which is relied on is not interpreted strictly. Thus though a person cannot be held out as agent to the world,[349] the representation need not be to a specific person: it has been said that "the holding out must be to the particular individual who says he relied on it, or under such circumstances of publicity as to justify the inference that he knew of it and acted upon it".[350] Sometimes negligent conduct is relied on as constituting a holding out: this is principally so in the case of property transactions, to which indeed the passage quoted above refers. In that context it has sometimes been said that there must be a duty of care towards the third party, but here again it appears that such a duty can be owed to quite a wide class of persons.[351] It does not seem that the third party's reliance need have been to his detriment: although it is clear that if he did not rely on the representation at all,[352] or ignored a clear opportunity of ascertaining the agent's authority,[353] or was put on inquiry by the facts of the transaction,[354] he cannot hold the principal liable, it is probably sufficient reliance merely to enter into a transaction on the faith of the representation.[355]

(v)   The doctrine applies though the agent effects a forgery,[356] if the act in the course of which the forgery occurred was within his apparent authority and

---

[345]   See *Chapleo v Brunswick PBBS* (1881) 6 Q.B.D. 696.

[346]   [1999] 2 A.C. 349. See above, Vol.I, paras 29-044 et seq.

[347]   *Freeman & Lockyer v Buckhurst Park Properties (Mangal) Ltd*, above, at 503; *Nationwide BS v Lewis* [1998] Ch. 482 (partnership).

[348]   *Freeman & Lockyer v Buckhurst Park Properties (Mangal) Ltd*, above, at 503; *Underwood v Bank of Liverpool* [1924] 1 K.B. 775; *Farquharson Bros & Co v King & Co* [1902] A.C. 325.

[349]   *Dickinson v Valpy* (1829) 10 B. & C. 128, 140.

[350]   *Farquharson Bros & Co v King & Co*, above, at 341, per Lord Lindley (quoting Parke B.).

[351]   *Swan v North British Australasian Co* (1863) 2 H. & C. 175, 182; *Mercantile Bank of India v Central Bank of India Ltd* [1938] A.C. 287; *Mercantile Credit Co Ltd v Hamblin* [1965] 2 Q.B. 242, 271; *Moorgate Mercantile Co Ltd v Twitchings* [1977] A.C. 890 and see below, para.31-076.

[352]   *Swan v North British Australasian Co*, above; *Mac Fisheries Ltd v Harrison* (1924) 53 L.J. K.B. 811.

[353]   *Jacobs v Morris* [1902] 1 Ch. 816 (power of attorney); *Australian Bank of Commerce v Perel* [1926] A.C. 737. A fortiori if he knew or must be taken to have known of the lack of authority: *Morris v Kanssen* [1946] A.C. 459.

[354]   See (vii) below.

[355]   cf. *Silver v Ocean SS Co* [1930] 1 K.B. 416; *PEC Asia Ltd v Golden Rice Co Ltd* [2014] EWHC 1583 (Comm) at [73]. Where there is no obligation to be enforced the requirement may be even looser: see *Shearson Lehman Bros Inc v Maclaine, Watson & Co Ltd (No.2)* [1988] 1 W.L.R. 16, 29, HL. But cf. *Nationwide BS v Lewis* [1998] Ch. 482, where in the context of s.14 of the Partnership Act 1890 it was held that reliance on a holding-out as partner must be affirmatively proved.

[356]   *Uxbridge Permanent Benefit Building Society v Pickard* [1939] 2 K.B. 248; assuming always that he is purporting to act as agent. But a *counterfeit* signature or seal is simply a nullity and involves of itself no representation that the forger purports to act as agent: see *Northside Development Pty Ltd v Registrar-General* (1990) 170 C.L.R. 146 especially at 199–200.

the third party was unaware of the forgery.[357] The same is true where the agent is fraudulent, or acts illegally in some other way.[358]

(vi) The doctrine, being based on estoppel, does not of itself entitle a principal to sue on the contract[359]: but he will normally be able to ratify right up to the moment of trial.

(vii) The authority will be that which the agent reasonably appeared to have to the third party, taking into account the manifestations of the principal, the implied authority normally applicable in the circumstances or to a person in the agent's position, or both.[360] It has often been said that there is no constructive notice in commercial transactions and there is quite extensively argued recent authority[361] that the third party can rely on an appearance of authority unless its belief that there was authority was "dishonest or irrational", which would include turning a blind eye. But though there is also authority that "nothing short of bad faith will do"[362] such an approach may perhaps go too far in protecting third parties, and may not accord with all the existing authority cited here, always bearing in mind that the nature of reasonable inquiries may need to vary with the situation involved.[363]

31-057 **"True" estoppel** Although it seems that apparent authority should be attributed to a weak form of estoppel, there are some situations where a more orthodox form of estoppel, where there is more recognisable reliance, is employed in an agency context. This can be so where the agent cannot be said to have had actual or apparent authority, and nor has there been ratification, but nevertheless the "principal" caused the belief that the transaction in question was within the supposed agent's authority, or had been authorised, or, knowing that such a belief was held, took no

[357] See *Ruben v Great Fingall Consolidated* [1906] A.C. 439 where this was not so.

[358] *Navarro v Moregrand* [1951] 2 T.L.R. 674; cf. *Barker v Levinson* [1951] 1 K.B. 342.

[359] *Restatement, Third, Agency* allows the principal to sue: see para.2.03 and Reporter's Notes, p.136, citing *Equitable Variable Life Assurance Co v Wood* 362 S.E.2d 741 (Va., 1987). But the reasoning is unconvincing.

[360] See above, paras 31-046 et seq. as to implied authority; and for examples *Waugh v HB Clifford & Sons Ltd* [1982] Ch. 374; *United Bank of Kuwait Ltd v Hammoud* [1988] 1 W.L.R. 1051; *Hirst v Etherington* [1999] Lloyd's Rep. P.N. 938 (solicitors); *Egyptian Intl Foreign Trade Co v Soplex Wholesale Supplies Ltd (The Raffaella)* [1985] 2 Lloyd's Rep. 36 (documentary credits manager); *Gurtner v Beaton* [1993] 2 Lloyd's Rep. 369 (aviation manager). Where evidence as to what is usual in the particular occupation is relied on, this may be prejudicial to a third party who did not know of the practice, as in the harsh case of *British Bank of the Middle East v Sun Life Assurance Co of Canada (UK) Ltd* [1983] 2 Lloyd's Rep. 9, HL (levels of manager within company); cf. however *Cleveland Mfg Co Ltd v Muslim Commercial Bank Ltd* [1981] 2 Lloyd's Rep. 646.

[361] In the judgment of Lord Neuberger in the Hong Kong Court of Final Appeal in *Thanakhorn Kasikorn Thai Chamchat v Akai Holdings Ltd* (2010) 13 H.K.C.F.A.R. 479 at [51].

[362] *Lexi Holdings v Pannone & Partners* [2009] EWHC 2590 (Ch) at [61] et seq., per Briggs J. The Hong Kong case was followed by the Court of Appeal in *Quinn v CC Automotive Group Ltd* [2010] EWCA Civ 1412, [2011] 2 All E.R. (Comm) 584, where it is said that the reasonableness of the third party's belief was "neither here nor there"; see also *Newcastle International Airport Ltd v Eversheds LLP* [2012] EWHC 2648 (Ch), [2013] P.N.L.R. 5; *Acute Property Developments Ltd v Apostolou* [2013] EWHC 200 (Ch), [2013] Bus. L.R. D22; *LNOC Ltd v Watford Association Football Club Ltd* [2013] EWHC 3615 (Comm).

[363] See *Bowstead and Reynolds on Agency*, 21st edn (2018), art.73; Watts [2015] L.M.C.L.Q. 36. In particular it does not accord well with recent discussion in the context, admittedly different, of the inquiries to be made by bona fide purchaser in an equitable but commercial (banking) context: see *Papadimitriou v Crédit Agricole Corp* [2015] UKPC 13; see also *Gray v Smith* [2013] EWHC 4136 (Comm), [2014] 2 All E.R. (Comm) 359.

steps to correct it.[364] In some cases of this type the appearance of authority can perhaps sometimes be attributed also to the principal's negligence in operating a system under which an unauthorised person can appear to be authorised.[365]

Agents of companies[366] Special considerations arise in the case of agents of **31-058** companies, because companies can only act through agents, yet are limited in their permissible activities by their memoranda of association and have public documents indicating the distribution of powers within their constitution, which can be inspected. These features modify the application of the law of agency to agents of companies; but they have themselves been modified by statute. The law should be sought in specialised works[367]: what follows is only intended to draw attention to the impact of these special features on agency law.

Ultra vires First, if a contract made by the agent of a company was ultra vires **31-059** the company's memorandum of association, the company could not be bound. This doctrine was held not to apply to the exercise of powers of a type which the company undoubtedly possesses but where those powers have been used for purposes outside the memorandum or articles of association, or for improper motives.[368] But it is largely abolished in relation to external relations by s.39 of the Companies Act 2006,[369] which provides that "The validity of an act done by a company shall not be called in question on the ground of lack of capacity by reason of anything in the company's constitution". The doctrine continues to have some effect as regards a company's internal regulation, and in dealings with a director, or a person associated with a director.[370]

Notice of public documents Secondly, the operation of the doctrine of apparent **31-060** authority was affected by another doctrine, that a person dealing with a company was deemed to have constructive notice of its public documents, and hence of restrictions on the authority of the particular agent. This was to some extent balanced by the "indoor management" rule under which, where the person acting for the company *could* have been authorised, and either was specifically held out as authorised, or acted within the usual authority of company agents of that type,[371] the third party might be entitled to assume that procedures for authorisation had

---

[364] e.g. *Spiro v Lintern* [1973] 1 W.L.R.1002; *Worboys v Carter* [1987] 2 E.G.L.R. 1. For another example see *Geniki Investments International Ltd v Ellis Stockbrokers Ltd* [2008] EWHC 549 (QB), [2008] 1 B.C.L.C. 662. See also *City Bank of Sydney v McLaughlin* (1909) 9 C.L.R. 615, 625. The idea that this estoppel is different from that generally applicable in connection with apparent authority is rejected by the Singapore Court of Appeal in *The Bunga Melati 5* [2015] 2 S.L.R. 114.

[365] *Pacific Carriers Ltd v BNP Paribas* (2004) 218 C.L.R. 451 (documentary credits manager armed with rubber stamp). See also *Martin v Britannia Life Ltd* [2000] Lloyd's Rep. P.N. 412, 5.3.4 (supply of business cards); cf. *Kooragang Investments Pty v Richardson & Wrench Ltd* [1982] A.C. 462 (use of letterhead); *Smith v Prosser* [1907] 2 K.B. 735 (promissory note signed in blank).

[366] The leading recent common law cases are still *Freeman & Lockyer v Buckhurst Park Properties (Mangal) Ltd* [1964] 2 Q.B. 480 and *Hely-Hutchinson v Brayhead Ltd* [1968] 1 Q.B. 549. They should however be read subject to what follows.

[367] See also Vol.I, paras 10-020 et seq.; *Gower and Davies' Modern Company Law*, 10th edn (2016), Ch.7.

[368] *Rolled Steel Products (Holdings) Ltd v British Steel Corp* [1986] Ch. 246 (principle is one of capacity).

[369] Deriving from s.108 of the Companies Act 1989, giving effect to the EC First Directive on Company Law, and replacing earlier legislation which had been found inadequate for this purpose.

[370] Companies Act 2006 ss.40, 41.

[371] Above, para.31-047.

been complied with.[372] This constructive notice doctrine is also abolished by the Companies Act 2006,[373] under which the power of the directors to bind the company, or to authorise others to do so, is in favour of a person "dealing"[374] with the company "in good faith",[375] "deemed to be free of any limitation under the company's constitution".[376] In the overall result, a person dealing with the board of directors or a person authorised by it is well protected. But in the case of other agents, including particular directors, although the third party may now be entitled to assume that the company has full power to delegate, he can only assume that that power has been exercised if there has been a holding-out by the company,[377] whether specific or general, as under the indoor management rule. There are various cases on the authority of company officials, but practices change and in case of doubt it will be best to rely on contemporary evidence of practice.[378] The reasoning would not apply to a forgery in the sense of a counterfeit (as opposed to unauthorised) signature.[379]

31-061 **Agent acting in fraud of principal**   The fact that the agent acted in his own interests and in fraud of his principal will not relieve the principal of liability if in fact the agent's act was in other respects within the scope of his apparent authority.[380] This rule is not confined to the case of a contract made by an agent. A principal is bound by acts done by an agent in the scope of his apparent authority, whether in contract or tort or otherwise.[381]

"A third party, dealing in good faith with an agent acting within his ostensible authority,

---

[372] The so-called rule in *Royal British Bank v Turquand* (1856) 6 El. & Bl. 327.

[373] Companies Act 2006 s.40(1).

[374] Defined in Companies Act 2006 s.40(2)(b).

[375] Defined in s.40(2)(b). See *Barclays Bank Ltd v TOSG Trust Fund Ltd* [1984] B.C.L.C. 1, 18.

[376] See *Smith v Henniker-Major & Co* [2002] EWCA Civ 762, [2003] Ch. 182, considering (a) whether a quorum requirement is a "limitation"; (b) whether a director can be a third party for the purposes of this provision. See also *EIC Services Ltd v Phipps* [2003] EWHC 1507, [2003] 1 W.L.R. 2360.

[377] In *Crabtree-Vickers Pty Ltd v Australian Direct Mail Advertising and Addressing Co Pty Ltd* (1975) 133 C.L.R. 72 the High Court of Australia, following dicta of Diplock L.J. in the *Freeman & Lockyer* case, above, n.366, held that the holding-out must be by a person with actual authority within the company. This seems doubtful: provided the authority *finally* traces back to a person with actual authority, it is submitted that the person whose representation of authority is relied on may have apparent authority only to make it: *ING Re (UK) Ltd v R & V Versicherung AG* [2006] EWHC 1544 (Comm), [2006] 2 All E.R. (Comm) 870.

[378] See *Panorama Developments (Guildford) Ltd v Fidelis Furnishing Fabrics Ltd* [1971] 2 Q.B. 711 (changed role of company secretary); *United Bank of Kuwait Ltd v Hammoud* [1988] 1 W.L.R. 1051, 1063, per Staughton L.J.; *First Energy (UK) Ltd v Hungarian International Bank Ltd* [1993] 2 Lloyd's Rep. 194.

[379] *Northside Developments Pty Ltd v Registrar-General* (1990) 170 C.L.R. 146: see Prentice (1991) 107 L.Q.R. 14; Watts (2002) 2 O.U.C.L.J. 93 (arguing for special rules for deeds in general). But a party may be estopped by subsequent conduct from setting up the forgery: *Greenwood v Martins Bank Ltd* [1933] A.C. 51. See also the possible operation of s.44 of the Companies Act 2006 in the context of forgeries, discussed in *Lovett v Carson Country Homes Ltd* [2009] EWHC 1143 (Ch), [2009] 2 B.C.L.C. 196 at [99]. See further *Bowstead and Reynolds on Agency*, 21st edn (2018), para.8-041.

[380] *Hambro v Burnand* [1904] 2 K.B. 10 (sometimes however said to be a case on actual authority and indeed apparently argued as such); *Navarro v Moregrand Ltd* [1951] 2 T.L.R. 674; *Briess v Woolley* [1954] A.C. 233 and many other cases.

[381] *Lloyd v Grace, Smith & Co* [1912] A.C. 716; *Polkinghorne v Holland* (1934) 51 C.L.R. 143; *Uxbridge Permanent Benefit Building Society v Pickard* [1939] 2 K.B. 248; *Navarro v Moregrand* [1951] 2 T.L.R. 674; *Morris v CW Martin & Sons Ltd* [1966] 1 Q.B. 716; *United Bank of Kuwait v Hammoud* [1988] 1 W.L.R. 1051; and see below, para.31-075.

is not prejudiced by the fact that as between the principal and his agent the agent is using his authority in such a way that the principal can rightly complain that the agent is using his authority for his own benefit and not for that of his principal."[382]

But where the third party has notice from the nature of the transaction that he is or may be dealing with an agent who is exceeding his authority, the principal is not bound,[383] and the fact that the agent's acts are manifestly for his own benefit may amount to such notice.[384] And it is a standard proposition that a principal is not liable merely because by appointing the agent he gives him the opportunity to behave fraudulently.[385]

Apparent authority of Crown agents   Special considerations apply to the Crown   **31-062** and public authorities, since it is plain that no official can be given the power to validate ultra vires acts, and the freedom of action of the Crown or a public authority to do its public duty should not easily be fettered.[386] It has been said that "no public officer, unless he possesses some special power, can hold out on behalf of the Crown that he or some other public officer has the right to enter into a contract in respect of the property of the Crown when in fact no such right exists",[387] and though this may be overstated, apparent authority in such an agent is not easy to establish.[388] In general estoppel reasoning has to some extent been superseded in the area by the notions of legitimate expectations and abuse of power,[389] but where agents of a foreign government are in question there is room for the application of agency reasoning.[390]

(c)   Undisclosed Principal

Doctrine of the undisclosed principal   It has long been established that a   **31-063** principal who was at the time of contracting completely undisclosed as such can

---

[382] *Lloyds Bank Ltd v Chartered Bank of India* [1929] 1 K.B. 40, 56, per Scrutton L.J.; see also *Corporation Agencies Ltd v Home Bank of Canada* [1927] A.C. 318.

[383] *John v Dodwell* [1918] A.C. 563; and see above, para.31-056.

[384] e.g. *Reckitt v Barnett, Pembroke & Slater Ltd* [1929] A.C. 176 (attorney drew cheques for private debts); *Midland Bank Ltd v Reckitt* [1933] A.C. 1; cf. *Reckitt v Nunburnholme* (1929) 45 T.L.R. 629. See also *Lysaght Bros & Co Ltd v Falk* (1905) 2 C.L.R. 421.

[385] *Farquharson Bros & Co v King & Co* [1902] A.C. 325; *Morris v CW Martin & Sons Ltd* [1966] 1 Q.B. 716; *Leesh River Tea Co v British India SN Co* [1967] 2 Q.B. 250; *Canadian Laboratory Supplies Ltd v Engelhard Industries of Canada Ltd* [1979] 2 S.C.R. 787, (1979) 97 D.L.R. (3d) 1; *Kooragang Investments Pty Ltd v Richardson & Wrench Ltd* [1982] A.C. 462; *Crédit Lyonnais Bank Nederland NV v ECGD* [2000] 1 A.C. 486 (agent assisted in tort of deceit but did not commit it); *Frederick v Positive Solutions (Financial Services) Ltd* [2018] EWCA Civ 431. As to exclusion of liability for fraud of an agent see *HIH Casualty & General Insurance Ltd v Chase Manhattan Bank* [2003] UKHL 6, [2003] 2 Lloyd's Rep. 61.

[386] See *Southend-on-Sea Corp v Hodgson (Wickford) Ltd* [1962] 1 Q.B. 416.

[387] *Att-Gen for Ceylon v Silva* [1953] A.C. 461, 479. But cf. 480. See Vol.I, para.11-013. See also *JE Verreault et Fils v Att-Gen for Quebec* [1977] 1 S.C.R. 41, (1975) 57 D.L.R. (3rd) 403.

[388] As to constitutional limitations on the agent of a foreign state see *Donegal International Ltd v Republic of Zambia* [2007] EWHC 197 (Comm), [2007] 1 Lloyd's Rep. 397; *Law Debenture Trust Corp Plc v Ukraine* [2017] EWHC 655 (Comm), [2017] Q.B. 1249.

[389] See Vol.I, paras 11-034 et seq.

[390] See *Bowstead and Reynolds on Agency*, 21st edn (2018), para.12-022; *PEC Asia Ltd v Golden Rice Co Ltd* [2014] EWHC 1583 (Comm), [2014] B.C.C. 628, where evidence from distinguished Indian lawyers was considered.

sue or be sued on the contract of his agent,[391] though the juristic basis of this rule, and therefore the full scope of its application, is still uncertain. Indeed, many points as to its application have never been thought through.[392] It has been said that the contract is that of the principal[393]; but in fact the law in many respects treats the contract as that of the agent, for the third party cannot be deprived of the agent's liability should he desire it,[394] and can usually plead against the principal all defences that were available against the agent before notice of the principal's existence.[395] The agent can also sue, presumably subject to the superior right of the principal.[396] It has sometimes been explained as intervention on the analogy of assignment[397]; but it involves transfer of liability as well as rights, there is in fact no event that can be regarded as an assignment and it has in any case been held that an undisclosed principal can intervene on an unassignable contract (of insurance).[398] It does however seem accepted that the situation is to be regarded as one of intervention on the contract of another.[399] The origin of the principal's right to sue is said to be explained on the basis of his property in goods sold by his factor, and hence his right to their proceeds, rather than on the extension of a contract.[400] The liability to be sued and indeed the acceptance of what appears as a general agency doctrine may have been no more than a casually accepted consequence. In 1872 Blackburn J. said that it had "often been doubted whether it was originally right so to hold; but doubts of this kind come now too late".[401] Though long established, the principal's liability may be less desirable than his right to intervene, for it can be

---

[391] *Duke of Norfolk v Worthy* (1808) 1 Camp. 337; *Browning v Provincial Insurance Co of Canada* (1873) L.R. 5 P.C. 263, 272; *Siu Yin Kwan v Eastern Insurance Co Ltd* [1994] 2 A.C. 199, giving (at 376) a useful statement of the rules. The doctrine was applied to a breach under s.14(5) of the Sale of Goods Act 1979 in *Boyter v Thomson* [1995] 2 A.C. 628; see Brown (1996) 112 L.Q.R. 49.

[392] See, e.g. *Maynegrain v Compafina Bank* [1982] 2 N.S.W.L.R. 141 (attornment), discussed in *Bowstead and Reynolds on Agency*, 21st edn (2018), paras 8-172, 8-173.

[393] *Keighley, Maxsted & Co v Durant* [1901] A.C. 240, 261; above, para.31-029.

[394] *O'Herlihy v Hedges* (1803) 1 Sch. & Lef. 123; and see *Higgins v Senior* (1841) 8 M. & W. 834. See also *Public Trustee v Taylor* [1978] V.R. 289 (signature "for himself or as agent for an undisclosed principal": signatory liable). This is usually said, but *Cooke & Sons v Eshelby* (1887) 12 App. Cas. 271 does not accord with it. See below, para.31-069.

[395] *Browning v Provincial Insurance Co of Canada* (1873) L.R. 5 P.C. 263, 272; *Montgomerie v UK Mutual Steamship Association* [1891] 1 Q.B. 370, 372; *Sims v Bond* (1833) 5 B. & Ad. 389, 393.

[396] See below, para.31-088; *Bowstead and Reynolds on Agency*, 21st edn (2018), para.9-012.

[397] Goodhart and Hamson (1932) 4 C.L.J. 320. In *Pople v Evans* [1969] 2 Ch. 255 it was held in the context of res judicata that the principal's right was independent of that of the agent and did not arise out of any trust relationship.

[398] *Siu Yin Kwan v Eastern Insurance Co Ltd* [1994] 2 A.C. 199; citing *Browning v Provincial Insurance Co of Canada* (1873) L.R. 5 P.C. 263, 273, and rejecting the assignment analogy: see below, para.31-067.

[399] *Welsh Development Agency v Export Finance Co* [1992] B.C.L.C. 148, 173, 182. It was held in connection with s.40 of the Law of Property Act 1925 (now repealed: see Law of Property (Miscellaneous Provisions) Act 1989) that the effect of the intervention of the principal was to add rather than substitute a liability. See *Higgins v Senior* (1841) 8 M. & W. 834; *Calder v Dobell* (1871) L.R. 6 C.P. 486; *Basma v Weekes* [1950] A.C. 441; *Davies v Sweet* [1962] 2 Q.B. 300.

[400] See Goodhart and Hamson (1932) 4 C.L.J. 320. As to factors, see above, para.31-009.

[401] *Armstrong v Stokes* (1872) L.R. 7 Q.B. 598, 604.

argued to give rise to unfair results.[402] The doctrine is in fact, doubtless for such reasons, effectively cut down by other rules.[403]

Acts in respect of which the doctrine of undisclosed principal applies The **31-064** doctrine is well summarised in the judgment of Lord Lloyd of Berwick in the Privy Council case of *Siu Yin Kwan v Eastern Insurance Co Ltd*[404]:

"(1) An undisclosed principal may sue and be sued on a contract made by an agent on his behalf within the scope of his actual authority. (2) In entering into the contract, the agent must have intended to act on the principal's behalf. (3) The agent of an undisclosed principal may also sue and be sued on the contract. (4) Any defence which the third party may have against the agent is available against his principal. (5) The terms of the contract may, expressly or by implication, exclude the principal's right to sue and his liability to be sued. The contract itself, or the circumstances surrounding the contract, may show that the agent is the true and only principal."

As to (1), apparent authority is obviously not relevant, since the third party cannot rely on representations by a person of whose existence he is ignorant; and it has been decided that an undisclosed principal cannot ratify.[405] As to (2), it has been said that it is unacceptable to apply subjective techniques to the ascertainment of this and that objective criteria must be applied.[406] But it is submitted that while desirable this cannot always be practicable, and in so far as the statement is correct it is only so as regards the initial creation of the relationship of agency rather than the question whether the agent was on the particular occasion acting under his actual authority from the principal.[407] As to (5) the problem is considered below.[408] There are, however, a few cases simply holding an undisclosed principal liable on contracts made by his agent:

"... within the authority usually confided to an agent of that character, notwithstanding limitations, as between the principal and the agent, put upon that authority."[409]

The phrase "usual authority", which has other meanings also,[410] is sometimes deployed here, as if by way of explanation. In that they depart from the requirement of actual authority, these cases are open to serious criticism; and although they have been distinguished[411] they must be regarded as extremely doubtful.[412] Many

---

[402] See Zweigert and Kötz, *Introduction to Comparative Law*, 3rd edn (1998), p.440, arguing that the third party should bear the cost of the middleman's insolvency. On the other hand the principal's liability can be treated as a form of vicarious liability.

[403] Above, para.31-029; below, paras 31-066, 31-070 et seq.

[404] [1994] 2 A.C. 199, 207.

[405] *Keighley, Maxsted & Co v Durant* [1901] 1 A.C. 240; above, para.31-029.

[406] By Leggatt J. in *Magellan Spirit ApS v Vitol SA* [2016] EWHC 454 (Comm), [2016] 2 Lloyd's Rep. 1.

[407] The problem arises also in the context of unidentified principal, and of insurance. For further material relevant in both contexts see above, para.31-054.

[408] paras 31-066 et seq.

[409] *Watteau v Fenwick* [1893] 1 Q.B. 346, 348–349, a celebrated decision discussed in law schools throughout the common-law world; the other cases are *Edmunds v Bushell* (1865) L.R. 1 Q.B. 97; and *Kinahan v Parry* [1910] 2 K.B. 389 (reversed [1911] 1 K.B. 459). But cf. *Daun v Simmins* (1879) 41 L.T. 783; *Mac Fisheries Ltd v Harrison* (1924) 93 L.J. K.B. 811.

[410] Above, para.31-047.

[411] *Johnston v Reading* (1893) 9 T.L.R. 200; *Lloyds Bank v Swiss Bankverein* (1912) 107 L.T. 309 (affirmed (1913) 108 L.T. 143); *Jerome v Bentley* [1952] 2 All E.R. 114.

explanations have been attempted without obvious success.[413]

31-065 **Meaning of "undisclosed principal"** The cases do not define the term, but it seems to mean in general a principal who is not known by the third party to be connected with the particular transaction. On general principle, principal and agent must have consented to the existence of an agency relationship. It seems clear also that in entering into the contract, the agent must intend to do so on the principal's behalf.[414] Thus the mere fact that a company is operated by an individual for his own benefit does not make him the undisclosed principal of that company in a particular transaction.[415] But there are difficulties in going beyond this.[416] Two possibilities present themselves. One is that the undisclosed principal must be a person who has authorised the agent to bring him into contractual privity with the third party, but whose connection with the transaction is not disclosed, whether by his own wish or by the wish of the agent. The second is that an undisclosed principal is anyone who uses the services of another on an agency basis, viz the agent is remunerated by commission and undertakes only to use best endeavours, but nevertheless expects the agent to deal on his own account (sometimes called by some civil lawyers "indirect representation").[417] There is authority for both meanings.[418] The first seems clearly correct; but it gives the doctrine a somewhat limited scope. Those legal systems which identify a category of indirect representation usually permit or require the involvement of the principal, at any rate as claimant in some circumstances (usually insolvency of the agent), and writers familiar with such systems sometimes, but not entirely correctly, treat the common law undisclosed principal doctrine as a different approach to the same problem.[419]

31-066 **Exclusion of undisclosed principals** Where an agent makes a contract in writ-

---

[412] See *Rhodian River Shipping Co SA v Holla Maritime Corp (The Rhodian River)* [1984] 1 Lloyd's Rep. 373, 379, per Bingham J. *Watteau v Fenwick* has also been doubted in Commonwealth jurisdictions: e.g. *International Paper Co v Spicer* (1906) 4 C.L.R. 739, 763; *McLaughlin v Gentles*, 51 D.L.R. 383 (1919); *Sign-o-Lite Plastics Ltd v Metropolitan Life Insurance Co*, 73 D.L.R. (4th) 541 (1990). Such reasoning is however accepted in *Restatement, Third, Agency*, para.2.06; and, surprisingly, in the UNIDROIT *Principles of International Commercial Contracts* (2004), para.2.2.4(2).

[413] Montrose (1939) 17 Can.Bar Rev. 693; Hornby [1961] C.L.J. 239; Higgins (1965) 28 M.L.R. 167; Bester (1972) 89 S.A.L.J. 49; Tettenborn [1998] C.L.J. 274.

[414] *Siu Yin Kwan v Eastern Insurance Co Ltd* [1994] 2 A.C. 199, 207, above, para.31-064; and as to proof of intention see further above, para.31-054.

[415] *Yukong Lines Ltd v Rendsburg Investments Corp (The Rialto) (No.2)* [1998] 1 Lloyd's Rep. 322; and see *Atlas Maritime Co SA v Avalon Maritime Ltd (The Coral Rose)* [1991] 1 Lloyd's Rep. 563. For other attempts to fix the liability on the individual behind the company by means of agency reasoning see *The Swan* [1968] 1 Lloyd's Rep. 5 (liable concurrently in contract), below, para.31-084; *Williams v Natural Life Health Foods Ltd* [1998] 1 W.L.R. 830 (on the facts, director did not undertake duty); *Salim v Ingham Enterprises Pty Ltd* (1998) 55 N.S.W.L.R. 7 (director of company held the real principal); *Peterson Farms Inc v C & M Farming Ltd* [2004] EWHC 121 (Comm), [2004] 1 Lloyd's Rep. 603 (company not agent for others in group); below, para.31-075.

[416] See dicta in *Teheran-Europe Co Ltd v ST Belton (Tractors) Ltd* [1968] 2 Q.B. 545, 552, 561; *Bowstead and Reynolds on Agency*, 21st edn (2018), para.8-073.

[417] See above, para.31-004.

[418] For the first: *Hutton v Bulloch* (1874) L.R. 9 Q.B. 572; *Anglo-African Shipping Co of New York Inc v J Mortner Ltd* [1962] 1 Lloyd's Rep. 610; and see *Armstrong v Stokes* (1872) L.R. 7 Q.B. 598. For the second: *Maspons y Hermano v Mildred, Goyeneche & Co* (1882) 9 Q.B.D. 530; affirmed on other grounds (1883) 8 App. Cas. 874.

[419] See Kortmann and Kortmann, Ch.6 in *Agency Law in Practice*, Busch and Macgregor (eds) (2016). *A reference to this point in Bowstead and Reynolds on Agency* appears to have been misunderstood by counsel (but not by the judge) in *Kaefer Aislamientos SA v AMS Drilling Mexico SA* [2017]

ing in his own name, parol evidence is generally admissible to show that another person was the real principal, so that that principal can sue, for, as stated above, its effect is to add a party rather than to vary the contract.[420] But an undisclosed principal cannot intervene where such intervention would be inconsistent with the terms of the contract itself.[421] Sometimes such exclusion is an express term of the contract[422]; thus when an agent contracts for a named principal, no other principal can intervene.[423] But sometimes the exclusion is derived from words in the contract descriptive of the agent: thus it has been held, in the context of the parol evidence rule, that no intervention is permissible where the agent is described as "owner"[424] or "proprietor",[425] though a different solution has been reached in similar, more recent cases.[426] It seems that not too much should be derived from the use of particular words: the question is whether on the full interpretation of the situation, personality is a term of the contract.[427] The normal assumption has been said to be that in the case of ordinary commercial contracts the third party is willing to deal with anyone by whom the counterparty was authorised.[428]

There may nevertheless be other situations where the personality of the agent is **31-067** so important that no one else can intervene; but the true applicable rule for such situations is still uncertain. Thus in *Said v Butt*[429] it was held that an undisclosed principal (a theatre critic) could not intervene and take the benefit of a contract for admission to a theatre on a first night; but the judgment is reasoned on the assumption that the contract is between the principal and the third party, which is probably not so. There are dicta suggesting simply that an undisclosed principal can-

---

EWHC 2598 (Comm), [2017] 2 Lloyd's Rep. 575.
[420] *Fred Drughorn Ltd v Rederiaktiebolaget Transatlantic* [1919] A.C. 203.
[421] See *Teheran-Europe Co Ltd v ST Belton (Tractors) Ltd* [1968] 2 Q.B. 545, 552.
[422] *UK Mutual Steamship Association v Nevill* (1887) 19 Q.B.D. 110.
[423] See *Phillips v Duke of Bucks* (1683) 1 Vern. 227; *J.H. Rayner (Mincing Lane) Ltd v Department of Trade and Industry* [1990] 2 A.C. 418, 516.
[424] *Humble v Hunter* (1848) 12 Q.B. 310. See also *Davis v Capel* [1959] N.Z.L.R. 825.
[425] *Formby v Formby* (1910) 102 L.T. 116 (though the point was not actually decided); *Fawcett v Star Car Sales Ltd* [1960] N.Z.L.R. 406; *JH Rayner (Mincing Lane) Ltd v Department of Trade and Industry* [1989] Ch. 72, 190–191 ("as principals").
[426] *Fred Drughorn Ltd v Rederiaktiebolaget Transatlantic* [1919] A.C. 203 ("charterer"); *Killick & Co v Price & Co* (1896) 12 T.L.R. 263; *Danziger v Thompson* [1944] K.B. 654; *Hanstown Properties Ltd v Green* (1977) 246 E.G. 917, CA ("tenant"); *Epps v Rothnie* [1945] K.B. 562 ("landlord"); *O/Y Wasa SS Co v Newspaper Pulp & Wood Exports* (1949) 82 Ll.L. Rep. 936 ("disponent owner": authorities reviewed); *Finzel Berry & Co v Eastcheap Dried Fruit Co* [1962] 1 Lloyd's Rep. 370, 375; affirmed [1962] 2 Lloyd's Rep. 11; *Murphy v Rae* [1967] N.Z.L.R. 103; *Asty Maritime Co Ltd v Rocco Giuseppe & Figli (The Astyanax)* [1985] 2 Lloyd's Rep. 109.
[427] McLauchlan, *The Parol Evidence Rule* (Wellington, NZ, 1976), Ch.13.
[428] *Teheran-Europe Co Ltd v ST Belton (Tractors) Ltd* [1968] 2 Q.B. 545, 555, quoted above, para.31-054; applied in *Novasen SA v Alimenta SA* [2011] EWHC 49 (Comm), [2011] 1 Lloyd's Rep. 390. For a case where this did not apply see *Rolls Royce Power Engineering Plc v Ricardo Consulting Engineers Ltd* [2003] EWHC 2871, [2004] 2 All E.R. (Comm) 129. An undisclosed principal was held to be excluded by the wording of an insurance contract in *Talbot Underwriting Ltd v Nausch, Hogan & Murray Inc (The Jascon 5)* [2006] EWCA Civ 889, [2006] 2 Lloyd's Rep. 195. Contrast *Ferryways NV v Associated British Ports* [2008] EWHC 225 (Comm), [2008] 1 Lloyd's Rep. 639, where intervention on an employment contract was permitted; *White v Baycorp Advantage Business Information Services Ltd* (2006) 200 F.L.R. 125 (rental agreement and assignment); *Diamond Stud Ltd v New Zealand Bloodstock Finance Ltd* [2010] NZCA 423 (terms of auction did not exclude undisclosed principal).
[429] [1920] 3 K.B. 497 (the action brought was actually for inducement of breach of contract). See also *Smith v Wheatcroft* (1878) 9 Ch. D. 223, discussed by Goodhart and Hamson, below, n.431 at 344.

not intervene where the personality of the agent is relevant,[430] but one of the cases can be explained on the grounds that an undisclosed principal intervenes subject to defences available against the agent, and the other on the grounds that only the agent to whom it was made could rescind for misrepresentation. It was suggested[431] that there was a rule that the undisclosed principal cannot intervene where the benefit of the contract is unassignable or its burden cannot be vicariously performed.[432] It is clear that if the burden of the contract cannot be performed vicariously the undisclosed principal cannot intervene on the performer's side to enforce it, since his intervention would itself be a breach of the contract.[433] But the assignment analogy has been rejected by the Privy Council in a case concerning a policy of liability insurance, which was unassignable, but where in the circumstances the identity of the employer insured was admitted to be a matter of indifference to the insurer.[434] It seems therefore that the basic exclusionary rule must be no more than the general proposition, that the undisclosed principal cannot intervene where the terms of the contract, express or implied, exclude his right to sue and his liability to be sued.[435] It is however a rule that does not give much guidance. If the agent represents that he does not act for a, or for a particular, principal, and this is incorrect, this is a misrepresentation: the third party has a defence to an action on the contract and may take proceedings to rescind it.[436] But mere non-disclosure that the agent acts for a principal does not of itself amount to misrepresentation.[437]

(d) Principals and Third Parties: Further Rules

31-068 **Deeds, bills, notes and cheques**   There are exceptions to the general rules in the case of deeds, bills, notes and cheques. No one can sue or be sued on any deed inter partes unless he is described as a party thereto and the deed is executed in his name.[438] But when the agent is a trustee of his rights for his principal, the principal may enforce his rights under the deed in the name of the agent, joining the agent as co-plaintiff or as co-defendant.[439] And by virtue of the Powers of Attorney Act

---

[430] *Greer v Downs Supply Co* [1927] 2 K.B. 28; *Collins v Associated Greyhound Racecourses Ltd* [1930] 1 Ch. 1.

[431] Goodhart and Hamson (1932) 4 C.L.J. 320. There was some support in *Dyster v Randall & Sons* [1926] Ch. 932, where an undisclosed principal was held entitled to enforce a contract where he knew that the third party would not have sold to him, and one of the reasons given was that the benefit of the contract could have been assigned. See also *Nash v Dix* (1898) 78 L.T. 445, where the "agent" was held to have bought for resale to his principal. See also above para.31-063.

[432] See Vol.I, paras 19-055 et seq., 19-082 et seq.

[433] Goodhart and Hamson (1932) 4 C.L.J. 320 at 341.

[434] *Siu Yin Kwan v Eastern Insurance Co Ltd* [1994] 2 A.C. 199; citing *Browning v Provincial Insurance Co of Canada* (1876) L.R. 5 P.C. 263, especially at 273; above paras 31-063, 31-064. See Reynolds [1994] J.B.L. 260.

[435] *Siu Yin Kwan v Eastern Insurance Co Ltd*, above, at 207. But the case is in fact very close to being one of unidentified principal: see Reynolds, in Rose (ed.), *Consensus ad Idem* (1996), pp.92–95.

[436] *Archer v Stone* (1898) 79 L.T. 34.

[437] *Dyster v Randall* [1926] Ch. 932.

[438] *Schack v Anthony* (1813) 1 M. & S. 573; *Berkeley v Hardy* (1826) 3 B. & C. 355. But the principal may be able to sue by virtue of s.56 of the Law of Property Act 1925 if the deed purports to grant something to him: see *Beswick v Beswick* [1968] A.C. 58. And if the deed is not inter partes, he can sue if he is a covenantee: see *Cooker v Child* (1673) 2 Lev. 74; *Sunderland Marine Insurance Co v Kearney* (1851) 16 Q.B. 925. For the view that properly executed deeds bind the principal even if they are not authorised see Watts (2002) 2 O.U.C.L.J. 93.

[439] *Harmer v Armstrong* [1934] Ch. 65.

1971 s.7(1),[440] if the donee of a power of attorney is an individual, he may, if he thinks fit, execute any instrument with his own signature, and, where sealing is required, with his own seal, by the authority of the donor of the power.[441] It would seem, however, that the principal should be mentioned in the deed, and that the section does not permit intervention by an undisclosed principal.[442] As regards bills, notes and cheques, no one can be liable on any such instrument unless his signature is upon it,[443] and no one can be liable as acceptor of a bill except the person on whom it was drawn,[444] except where it is accepted for honour. But signature of a principal's name by an authorised agent suffices in these cases.[445]

Settlement with and set-off against agent[446]   The general rule here is that settle-   **31-069**
ment with the agent does not discharge the third party unless the agent has actual or apparent authority to receive such settlement[447]; and that the third party has no right to set off against the principal claims that he may have against the agent.[448] But where the principal is undisclosed, the position may be different in both cases. Where the third party reasonably believes that the person with whom he is dealing acts as principal, the principal will be bound by settlement with[449] and set-offs against[450] the agent accruing before notice of the principal's existence. It might be expected that the rationale of the rule would be simply that the undisclosed principal intervenes, like an assignee, subject to equities already accrued.[451] The leading case[452] suggests however that the rule rests on estoppel, i.e. on the principal having induced the third party to believe that the agent acted for himself.[453] It is difficult to see how a principal who is undisclosed can (except by conduct unknown to the third party) be regarded as doing this; and such an explanation is contrary to the normal assumption that the third party cannot be deprived of the agent's liability should he desire it.[454] It may be said that such reasoning gives undue weight to the notion that the contract is that of the principal, rather than that of the agent

---

[440] Superseding Law of Property Act 1925 s.123(1); and as modified by s.1(8) of and Sch.1 to the Law of Property (Miscellaneous Provisions) Act 1989 in respect of "sealing".

[441] As to the meaning of this see above, para.31-025.

[442] See *Harmer v Armstrong*, above, where it was assumed that such intervention was not in general possible.

[443] Bills of Exchange Act 1882 s.23, 89.

[444] s.17(1); *Polhill v Walter* (1832) 3 B. & Ad. 114; *Steele v M'Kinlay* (1880) 5 App. Cas. 754.

[445] s.91(1).

[446] See Derham, *Law of Set-Off*, 4th edn (2010); Wood, *English and International Set-Off* (1989).

[447] As to authority to receive payment, see above, para.31-050. Settlement with and set-off against the agent may sometimes however be operative to the extent of the agent's lien: see *Drinkwater v Goodwin* (1775) Cowp. 251; *Hudson v Granger* (1821) 5 B. & Ald. 27; cf. above, para.31-009; below, para.31-099.

[448] *Fish v Kempton* (1849) 7 C.B. 687; *Mildren v Maspons* (1883) 8 App. Cas. 874. But the principal may authorise settlement in this way: *Barker v Greenwood* (1837) 2 Y. & C. Ex. 414; *Stewart v Aberdein* (1838) 4 M. & W. 211, 228. A custom that a third party may so settle is unreasonable and does not bind a principal who had no knowledge of it: *Sweeting v Pearce* (1859) 7 C.B.(N.S.) 449; *Pearson v Scott* (1879) 9 Ch. D. 198.

[449] *Coates v Lewes* (1808) 1 Camp. 444; *Curlewis v Birkbeck* (1863) 3 F. & F. 894. The agent may vary the contract: *Blackburn v Scholes* (1810) 2 Camp. 341.

[450] *George v Clagett* (1797) 7 T.R. 359; *Montagu v Forwood* [1893] 2 Q.B. 350.

[451] *Rabone v Williams* (1797) 7 Term Rep. 360n; *Turner v Thomas* (1871) L.R. 6 C.P. 610, 613; Powell, *Law of Agency*, 2nd edn (1961), pp.174–178. But as to this analogy, see above, paras 31-063, 31-067.

[452] *Cooke & Sons v Eshelby* (1887) 12 App. Cas. 271. But cf. *Montagu v Forwood*, above.

[453] *Cooke & Sons v Eshelby*, above, at 278.

[454] See above, para.31-063.

on which the principal intervenes. In the case itself the third party admitted that he had no views as to whether the agent (a broker) dealt on his own account or as agent (a very common situation); so he should not have been surprised by the presence of a principal. The agent was in fact a broker, who might be assumed to have a principal.[455] However, if this is the correct approach in general, such a principal is only bound by settlement with or set-off against the agent, occurring before notice[456] of his involvement, and where the belief that the agent was principal can be said to have been induced by him. In this part of the law it seems however that the mere entrusting of goods to the agent is treated as giving reasonable grounds for such belief.[457]

31-070 **Effect of judgment against agent**   Where the agent, having made a contract in such terms that he is personally liable,[458] has been sued on it to judgment, it appears that no action is maintainable against the principal on the same contract. This rule is said to be based on the notion that there cannot be two judgments on the same debt,[459] though it is open to criticism as being an unnecessary extension of the rules for joint debts,[460] which have in any case in this respect been altered by statute.[461] It certainly applies where the principal is undisclosed[462]; but it seems that it may apply also where he is disclosed, though the authority and rationale here are distinctly less compelling.[463] The rule has been applied though the first judgment was a summary one under Ord.14 of the then Rules of the Supreme Court,[464] or a default judgment,[465] or in an action in which principal and agent were sued jointly,[466] or was obtained for part only of the amount claimed,[467] or was wholly unsatisfied.[468] It has been applied notwithstanding that judgment was set aside by consent,[469] but not where it was set aside on the merits.[470] But it cannot, of course, apply where

---

[455] See *Baring v Corrie* (1818) 2 B. & Ald. 137, 143; *Armstrong v Stokes* (1872) L.R. 7 Q.B. 598, 610.

[456] It is often said that constructive notice is not sufficient in commercial transactions. But the validity of this proposition has been considerably modified over recent years: see e.g. material cited above; para.31-056(vii); and for the present context, e.g. *Dresser v Norwood* (1864) 17 C.B.(N.S.) 466.

[457] *Borries v Imperial Ottoman Bank* (1873) L.R. 9 C.P. 38. Yet this is not so where the passing of property is in issue: *Weiner v Gill* [1905] 2 K.B. 172, 182; below, paras 31-076—31-077.

[458] i.e. when his principal is undisclosed and in certain other circumstances, as to which see below, paras 31-084 et seq.

[459] See *Kendall v Hamilton* (1879) 4 App. Cas. 504, 515; *Moore v Flanagan* [1920] 1 K.B. 919, 926.

[460] See *Bowstead and Reynolds on Agency*, 21st edn (2018), art.82.

[461] Civil Liability Contribution Act 1978 s.3. But the obtaining of such a judgment might still rank as an election: below, para.31-071.

[462] *Priestly v Fernie* (1865) 3 H. & C. 977; *Kendall v Hamilton* (1879) 4 App. Cas. 504 at 514–515; *Marginson v Ian Potter & Co* (1976) 136 C.L.R. 161, 169.

[463] See *Morel Bros & Co Ltd v Earl of Westmorland* [1904] A.C. 11; *Sullivan v Sullivan* [1912] 2 I.R. 116, 127–128; *Moore v Flanagan*, above; *RMKRM (A Firm) v MRMVL (A Firm)* [1926] A.C. 761; *Debenham's Ltd v Perkins* (1925) 133 L.T. 252, 254; *Barrington v Lee* [1972] 1 Q.B. 326 (all cases of disclosed but unidentified principals).

[464] *Morel Bros & Co Ltd v Earl of Westmorland*, above.

[465] *Cross & Co v Mattews and Wallace* (1904) 91 L.T. 500.

[466] *Moore v Flanagan* [1920] 1 K.B. 919.

[467] *French v Howie* [1906] 2 K.B. 674.

[468] *Kendall v Hamilton* (1879) 4 App. Cas. 504, 514; *London General Omnibus Co Ltd v Pope* (1922) 38 T.L.R. 270.

[469] *Hammond v Schofield* [1891] 1 Q.B. 453; and see *Cross & Co v Matthews and Wallace* (1904) 91 L.T. 500; *Cyril Lord (Carpet Sales) v Browne* (1966) 111 S.J. 51; cf. *Longman v Hill* (1891) 7 T.L.R. 639.

[470] *Hammond v Schofield*, above; *Partington v Hawthorne* (1888) 55 J.P. 807; *Goodey v Garriock* [1972]

there are completely separate causes of action.[471] And even if it is in general correct, it is difficult to justify in the case of summary or default judgments, where the interpretation of the facts may in effect be settled by accidents of how litigation arises, and an undefended judgment against a party who is in fact not liable at all (and perhaps cannot pay either) could bar an action against the party who is liable. Two fairly recent Commonwealth cases refuse to accept the doctrine in such a situation.[472]

Election Where principal and agent are both liable, it is further said that the third **31-071** party may lose his right to sue one by an unequivocal election to sue the other[473]; this is again because the two rights are said to be inconsistent.[474] This doctrine is even more open to question than that regarding judgment[475]: it is difficult to see any reason for it (though an *estoppel* would be a different matter). The vast majority of cases invoke it only to hold that there has been no election. Those suggesting that there has been election in cases of undisclosed principals[476] can be explained on the basis of estoppel, whereby the third party induced the principal to settle with the agent[477]: those cited for the proposition in connection with disclosed principals can be explained as cases on formation of contract, dealing with the question "With whom was the contract made"?[478] If election does apply here, however, on general grounds before a party can be held to have elected he must have had knowledge of the facts[479]: but once the facts are discovered he must make his election within a reasonable time, at least if principal or agent would be prejudiced by the delay.[480] The question whether an election has been made is one of fact to be decided in all the circumstances of the case.[481] Debiting one party may[482] or may not[483] constitute such election. The institution of legal proceedings against one party provides a prima facie case of election,[484] but is not conclusive evidence: nor is filing a

---

2 Lloyd's Rep. 369; *Petersen v Moloney* (1951) 84 C.L.R. 91.

[471] See *Debenham's Ltd v Perkins* (1933) 125 L.T. 252 (two sales); *BO Morris Ltd v Perrott and Bolton* [1945] 1 All E.R. 567 (cheque). See also *Isaacs v Salbstein* [1916] 2 K.B. 139 (first party sued not liable). See below, para.31-084.

[472] *LC Fowler & Sons v St Stephen's College Board of Governors* [1991] 3 N.Z.L.R. 304; *Lang Transport Ltd v Plus Factor International Trucking Ltd* (1997) 143 D.L.R.(4th) 672.

[473] *Clarkson Booker v Andjel* [1964] 2 Q.B. 775; *Calder v Dobell* (1871) L.R. 6 C.P. 486, 499; *Curtis v Williamson* (1874) L.R. 10 Q.B. 57; dicta in *Chestertons v Barone* [1987] 1 E.G.L.R. 15; *Banca Nazionale di Lavoro v Playboy Club London Ltd* [2018] UKSC 43 at [12].

[474] Citing *Scarf v Jardine* (1882) 7 App. Cas. 345, 360; *Clarkson Booker v Andjel*, above, at 794.

[475] See *Bowstead and Reynolds on Agency*, 21st edn (2018), art.82. In the United States "election" is used to cover both aspects of the doctrine, and leading cases (rightly) reject the notion: e.g. *Grinder v Bryans Road Building and Supply Co*, 423 1 2d 453 Ct App Md 1981 ("the foregoing reasoning is unassailable on any other ground than its lack of strict adherence to the precedents").

[476] *MacClure v Schemeil* (1871) 20 W.R. 168; *Smethurst v Mitchell* (1859) 1 E. & E. 622.

[477] See below, para.31-072.

[478] See *Addison v Gandasequi* (1812) 4 Taunt. 574 *Paterson v Gandasequi* (1812) 15 East 62; *Thomson v Davenport* (1829) 9 B. & C. 78. There is a further confusion with cases on taking bills in satisfaction: see, e.g. *Robinson v Read* (1829) 9 B. & C. 449; *The Huntsman* [1949] P. 214.

[479] *Dunn v Newton* (1884) Cab. & El. 278; *Clarkson Booker v Andjel* [1964] 2 Q.B. 775, 792.

[480] *Smethurst v Mitchell* (1859) 1 E. & E. 622; but see explanation of this case in *Davison v Donaldson* (1882) 9 Q.B. 623, 628.

[481] *Calder v Dobell* (1871) L.R. 6 C.P. 486; *Clarkson Booker v Andjel*, above, at 792.

[482] *Addison v Gandassequi* (1812) 4 Taunt. 547 (but see explanation of this case above).

[483] *Thomson v Davenport* (1829) 9 B. & C. 78; *Eastman v Harry* (1875) 33 L.T. 800.

[484] *Clarkson Booker v Andjel* [1964] 2 Q.B. 775; *Cyril Lord (Carpet Sales) v Browne* (1966) 111 S.J. 51; *Chestertons Ltd v Barone* [1987] 1 E.G.L.R. 15; cf. *Blake v Melrose* [1950] N.Z.L.R. 781 (third-

winding-up[485] petition and obtaining an order, nor proving in one party's bankruptcy,[486] nor obtaining leave to sign judgment against one party,[487] nor appointing an arbitrator.[488]

31-072 **Where principal is discharged by settling with agent**   Normally speaking a disclosed principal is not discharged from liability to the third party by settling with his agent.[489] But he may be so discharged where the third party by his conduct leads the principal to believe that the agent has paid,[490] or gives the agent more time to pay, or otherwise indicates that he intends to rely on the agent alone for payment.[491] Where a seller gave credit to an agent supposing him to be the principal (i.e. to an agent acting for an *undisclosed* principal), however, and, before the seller discovered the truth, the principal settled the account with his agent, it was held by Blackburn J. in *Armstrong v Stokes*[492] that the settlement with the agent released the principal from liability to the seller on the ground that any other conclusion would give rise to "intolerable hardship". This case was subsequently doubted by the Court of Appeal in *Irvine & Co v Watson & Sons*[493] on the basis of reasoning seeking fault in the third party, similar to that accepted as regards fault of the principal in *Cooke & Sons v Eshelby*.[494] On the facts however it seems to be based on the fact that it concerned commission agents, who dealt in their own name and were intended to do so, a situation rather like that of the indirect representation known to some civil law jurisdictions.[495]

(e)   Agent Bribed

31-073 **Effect of bribery of agent**

> "For the purposes of the civil law a bribe means the payment of a secret commission, which only means (i) that the person making the payment makes it to the agent of the other person with whom he is dealing; (ii) that he makes it to that person knowing that that person is acting as the agent of the other person with whom he is dealing; (iii) that he fails

---

party notice).

[485] *Con-Stan Industries of Australia Pty Ltd v Norwich Winterthur Insurance (Australia) Ltd* (1986) 160 C.L.R. 226.

[486] *Curtis v Williamson* (1874) L.R. 10 Q.B. 57. But cf. *Fell v Parkin* (1882) 52 L.J. Q.B. 99; *MacClure v Schemeil* (1871) 20 W.R. 168.

[487] *C Christopher (Hove) Ltd v Williams* [1936] 3 All E.R. 68.

[488] *Pyxis Special Shipping Co Ltd v Dritsas & Kaglis Bros Ltd (The Scaplake)* [1978] 2 Lloyd's Rep. 380.

[489] *Kymer v Suwercropp* (1807) 1 Camp. 109; *Heald v Kenworthy* (1855) 10 Exch. 739; *Irvine & Co v Watson & Sons* (1880) 5 Q.B.D. 414.

[490] *MacClure v Schemeil* (1871) 20 W.R. 168; *Wyatt v Hertford* (1802) 3 East 147; *Horsfall v Fauntleroy* (1830) 10 B. & C. 755.

[491] *Smith v Ferrand* (1827) 7 B. & C. 19; *Kymer v Suwercropp*, above; see also *Macfarlane v Giannacopulo* (1858) 3 H. & N. 86; *Smethurst v Mitchell* (1855) 1 E. & E. 622 as explained in *Davison v Donaldson* (1882) 9 Q.B.D. 623; *Sopwith Aviation and Engineering Co Ltd v Magnus Motors Ltd* [1928] N.Z.L.R. 433.

[492] (1872) L.R. 7 Q.B. 598.

[493] (1880) 5 Q.B.D. 414 (but a case on unidentified principal), and *Davison v Donaldson* (1882) 9 Q.B.D. 623 (but a pre-1890 case on partnership).

[494] (1887) 12 App. Cas. 271, above, para.31-069.

[495] See above, para.31-004, n.18. It was in *Armstrong v Stokes* that Blackburn J. (who understood the notion of commission agent (see para.31-004, n.18)) made the famous remark about the undisclosed principal doctrine reported above, para.31-063, text to n.401.

to disclose to the other person with whom he is dealing that he has made that payment to the person whom he knows to be the other person's agent."[496]

Once the bribe is established it is conclusively presumed against the donor of the bribe that his motive was corrupt and against the agent that he was affected and influenced by the payment.[497] Practices permitting undisclosed commissions will not be upheld.[498] It is not necessary that the bribe induce a contract.[499] A principal whose agent has accepted a secret commission is therefore not obliged to prove that the agent's mind was actually influenced by the receipt of the commission.[500] The third party is regarded as a party to the breach of duty where he knows that he is depriving the principal of the disinterested advice of the agent, or is wilfully blind to that,[501] and the principal may rescind a transaction entered into with him[502]; and when the principal has repudiated a contract on an insufficient ground he may subsequently justify the repudiation on the ground of the bribe, even though ignorant of it at the time of repudiation.[503] If he rescinds, he is not required to account for the bribe, which he may recover from the agent or retain and treat as a gift to himself.[504] Besides his right to rescind, a principal whose agent has been bribed may recover from the third party the amount of the bribe in an action said to lie in money had and received[505]; or he may sue the third party in tort[506] for loss

---

[496] *Industries & General Mortgage Co v Lewis* [1949] 2 All E.R. 573, 575, per Slade J.; followed in *Taylor v Walker* [1958] 1 Lloyd's Rep. 490. An excellent and more recent exposition of the rules is to be found in the first instance judgment of Christopher Clarke J. in *Novoship (UK) Ltd v Michayluk* [2012] EWHC 3586 (Comm) at [108]–[109] (partly reversed [2014] EWCA Civ 908, [2015] Q.B. 499). It may sometimes be appropriate to disclose the actual amount of the commission: see Scrutton L.J. in *Fullwood v Hurley* [1928] 1 K.B. 498; *Hurstanger Ltd v Wilson* [2007] EWCA Civ 299, [2007] 1 W.L.R. 2351. For bribery by an agent of the third party, see *Armagas Ltd v Mundogas SA (The Ocean Frost)* [1986] A.C. 717, 743–745, 755, CA. The first instance decision also contains discussion of the effect of a bribe paid, agreed or adopted after the conclusion of the contract: see [1985] 1 Lloyd's Rep. 1, 18–22. Where the bribed agent acted in some respects for both parties the question will be whether in paying the bribe the agent was acting within the scope of its agency for the party seeing to enforce the contract: *UBS v Kommunale Wasserwerke Leipzig GmbH* [2014] EWHC 3615 (Comm) at [615] et seq. In the case of a company, disclosure to one director is insufficient: *Ross River Ltd v Cambridge City Football Club* [2007] EWHC 2115 (Ch), [2008] 1 All E.R. 1004. See also Vol.I, para.29-164; Berg [2001] L.M.C.L.Q. 27 (a valuable article). Bribery can be a criminal offence under the Bribery Act 2010.

[497] *Industries and General Mortgage Co v Lewis*, above; *Hovenden v Milhoff* (1900) 83 L.T. 41; *Harrington v Victoria Graving Dock Co* (1878) 3 Q.B.D. 549.

[498] *Fullwood v Hurley* [1928] 1 K.B. 498.

[499] *Petrotrade Inc v Smith* [2000] 1 Lloyd's Rep. 486.

[500] *Shipway v Broadwood* [1899] 1 Q.B. 369; *Smith v Sorby* (1875) 3 Q.B.D. 552n.

[501] *Tigris International NV v China Southern Airlines Co Ltd* [2014] EWCA Civ 1649 at [79].

[502] *Panama & South Pacific Telegraph Co v India Rubber, etc. Co* (1875) L.R. 10 Ch. App. 515, 526; *Re a Debtor* [1927] 2 Ch. 367, 376–377; *Taylor v Walker* [1958] 1 Lloyd's Rep. 490, 509–513; *North & South Trust Co v Berkeley* [1971] 1 W.L.R. 470, 485. But not a transaction entered into before the bribery: *Ross River Ltd v Cambridge City Football Club* [2007] EWHC 2115 (Ch), [2008] 1 All E.R. 1004.

[503] *Alexander v Webber* [1922] 1 K.B. 642; *Boston Deep Sea Fishing & Ice Co v Ansell* (1888) 39 Ch. D. 339.

[504] *Logicrose Ltd v Southend United Football Club* [1988] 1 W.L.R. 1256.

[505] The action is in personam but is difficult to justify in terms of restitution since the third party pays rather than receives the bribe. For discussion see *Bowstead and Reynolds on Agency*, 21st edn (2018), para.8-223; and see below. Compare the action against the agent: below, para.31-132.

[506] Said to be not deceit but a "special form of fraud": see *ING Re (UK) Ltd v R & V Versicherungs AG* [2006] EWHC (Comm) 1344, [2006] 2 All E.R. (Comm) 870 at [19].

suffered.[507] Only the entry of judgment on one or the other cause of action will constitute a final election between the two.[508] He may likewise sue the agent on the same two causes of action, subject again to election.[509] But he may not obtain double recovery in such proceedings, and if he sues both, satisfaction of judgment against one will bar an action against the other except for any excess.[510] Where the loss suffered is less than the amount of the bribe, the (restitutionary) action in money had and received will obviously be preferable.

31-074   The above is a statement of the traditional rules concerning bribery, on which there is a cluster of cases mostly around the turn of the nineteenth and twentieth centuries. They now require to be assessed taking into account other considerations which have more recently come into focus. First, it seems that at common law a contract obtained by bribery is likely to be unauthorised because dishonestly made contrary to the principal's interests; hence it may sometimes actually be void as opposed to voidable in equity.[511] Secondly, the first main nineteenth-century case on the right to rescind[512] did not concern bribery in the strict sense, though it can be said that such cases "concern a form of fraudulent activity amounting to a bribe".[513] It can also be said that the decision applied the typical rules, and also a variety of remedies, to what may in wider terms be described as being dishonest assistance to a breach of fiduciary duty by the agent.[514] Hence with more modern developments it may be appropriate to think of flexible equitable remedies being available against the briber in that more general context. It has been held that an account of profits may be available in such a case[515] and it seems likely that equitable

---

[507] *Mahesan v Malaysia Government Officers' Co-operative Housing Society Ltd* [1979] A.C. 374, explaining *Hovenden & Sons v Millhoff* (1900) 83 L.T. 41; *Arab Monetary Fund v Hashim* [1996] 1 Lloyd's Rep. 589. Both causes of action are difficult to classify, and it is therefore possible that the leading case of *Mahesan*, a Privy Council decision, may at some time need reconsideration.

[508] *Mahesan v Malaysia Government Officers' Co-operative Housing Society Ltd*, above, applying *United Australia Ltd v Barclays Bank Ltd* [1941] A.C. 1.

[509] *Mahesan v Malaysia Government Officers' Co-operative Housing Society Ltd*, above, para.31-043.

[510] *Mahesan v Malaysia Government Officers' Co-operative Housing Society Ltd*, above, at 382–383, applying *United Australia Ltd v Barclays Bank Ltd*, above. But see Tettenborn (1979) 95 L.Q.R. 68; Needham (1979) 95 L.Q.R. 536.

[511] See *Heinl v Jyske Bank (Gibraltar) Ltd* [1999] Lloyd's Rep. Bank. 511, 521; *Bowstead and Reynolds on Agency*, 21st edn (2018), art.23; above, paras 31-039, 31-043. But it appears that an arbitration clause remains effective even in such a case: see *Premium Nafta Products Ltd v Fiji Shipping Co Ltd* [2007] UKHL 40, [2007] Bus. L.R. 1719: Rushworth (2008) 124 L.Q.R. 195; Briggs [2008] L.M.C.L.Q. 1.

[512] *Panama & South Pacific Telegraph Co v India Rubber, etc. Telegraph Works Co* (1875) L.R. 10 Ch. App. 515. The remedies awarded vary: see *Bowstead and Reynolds on Agency*, above, paras 6-087, 8-221, 8-223. Some cases, including this, can be explained on the basis of discharge of contract by breach: see *Ross River Ltd v Cambridge City Football Club* [2007] EWHC 2815 (Ch), [2008] 1 All E.R. 1004. See also an elaborate discussion of rescission in *Conway v Prince Eze* [2018] EWHC 29 (Ch), in which however it was held that the sum involved was not a bribe.

[513] *Tigris International NV v China Southern Airlines Co Ltd* [2014] EWCA Civ 1649 at [176]. In the case itself it is referred to as "surreptitious dealing": (1875) 10 Ch. App. 515, 526.

[514] *Logicrose v Southend United FC* [1988] 1 W.L.R. 1256, 1261; *UBS AG v Kommunale Wasserwerke Leipzig GmbH* [2017] EWCA Civ 1567, [2017] 2 Lloyd's Rep. 621. cf. *Chancery Client Partners Ltd v MRC 1957 Ltd* [2016] EWHC 2142 (Ch), [2016] Lloyd's Rep. F.C. 578.

[515] *Novoship (UK) Ltd v Mikhaylyuk* [2014] EWCA Civ 908, [2015] Q.B. 499: see also *Logicrose v Southend United FC* [1988] 1 W.L.R. 1256, 1261, per Millett J.; *Fyffes Group Ltd v Templeman* [2000] 2 Lloyd's Rep. 643; *Ultraframe (UK) Ltd v Fielding* [2005] EWHC 1638 (Ch), [2006] F.S.R. 17 at [1594]; but cf. *Petrotrade Inc v Smith* [2000] 1 Lloyd's Rep. 486.

compensation will be available in appropriate cases.[516] It is now established that where it is identifiable, an agent holds a bribe on constructive trust.[517]

(f) Agent's Torts

Agent's torts A principal is liable for the torts of his agent in accordance with the normal principles of vicarious liability in tort. Thus he is liable for the acts of an employee agent acting in the course of his employment, and also where the agent is an independent contractor in the (uncertain) circumstances in which the duty is held non-delegable.[518] The criteria for connection with the employer have however over recent years been the subject of considerable relaxation in connection with physical assault[519] and persons whose positions can be regarded as analogous to those of employees.[520] From the point of view of agency law, the significant question is whether in view of this relaxation the agency-based notion of authority has any longer a role to play in determining tort liability for representations, which constitute an area in which it might still be expected to do so. In *Armagas Ltd v Mundogas SA (The Ocean Frost)*[521] it was held by the House of Lords that a principal was not liable for the deceit of an employee agent where the agent was acting outside his actual and apparent authority, and that in such circumstances the contractual agency rules applied rather than the tortious vicarious liability rules, which might have imposed liability. More recently however the current looser vicarious liability criteria have been applied to make a bank liable for a misrepresentation by a junior employee that was not actually or apparently authorised, and it was said that the reasoning in *The Ocean Frost* was confined to deceit.[522] It is difficult to see why a principal should be more readily liable for his agent's negligent misrepresentation than for his fraud, and a significant Privy Council case in which a principal was held not liable for the unauthorised act of an agent[523] was not cited. It has fairly recently been clarified that liability for

31-075

---

[516] Such an award was made in *Hurstanger Ltd v Wilson* [2007] EWCA Civ 299, [2007] 1 W.L.R. 2351, on the basis that the commission was not secret so as to attract the "full armoury of remedies" (principally rescission) but that non-disclosure of the sum involved gave rise to equitable relief for the amount of the commission.

[517] *FHR European Ventures Ltd v Cedar Capital Partners LLC* [2014] UKSC 45, [2015] A.C. 250, which however only concerns a claim against the agent: see below, para.31-132. But the reasoning would not be operative in the context of limitation: *Williams v Central Bank of Nigeria* [2014] UKSC 10, [2014] A.C. 1189.

[518] This category has been rationalised and to some extent expanded of late: see *Woodland v Essex CC* [2013] UKSC 66, [2014] A.C. 357. See *Clerk & Lindsell on Torts*, 22nd edn (2018), Ch.6. For discussion of a recent case in the Singapore Court of Appeal comparing the two techniques see David Tan (2018) 134 L.Q.R. 193.

[519] *Lister v Hesley Hall Ltd* [2001] UKHL 22, [2001] 1 A.C. 215 (warden of school boarding house); for a more recent example see *Mohamud v Wm Morrison Supermarkets Plc* [2016] UKSC 11, [2016] A.C. 677 (supermarket petrol station attendant).

[520] e.g. *Dubai Aluminium Co Ltd v Salaam* [2002] UKHL 48, [2002] 2 A.C. 366 (partner: dishonest assistance in breach of trust) (see esp. at [23]–[36], [123]–[131]); *Various Claimants v Institute of Brothers of the Christian Schools* [2012] UKSC 56, [2013] 2 A.C. 1 (monks involved in education); *Cox v Ministry of Justice* [2016] UKSC 10, [2016] A.C. 660 (prisoner working in prison kitchen). See *Clerk and Lindsell on Torts*, 21st edn (2014), paras 6-28 et seq.

[521] [1986] A.C. 717.

[522] *So v HSBC Bank Plc* [2009] EWCA Civ 296, [2009] 1 C.L.C. 503. See Watts (2012) 128 L.Q.R. 260; [2015] L.M.C.L.Q. 36.

[523] *Kooragang Investments Pty v Richardson & Wrench Ltd* [1982] A.C. 462 (valuation by employee

misrepresentations is based on an assumption of responsibility,[524] with the result that a company director who did not assume responsibility for a negligently prepared report was held not liable. It follows from this that an agent who is actually or apparently authorised but does not assume personal responsibility can create an assumption of responsibility by his principal.

> "Just as an agent can contract on behalf of another without assuming personal liability, so an agent can assume responsibility on behalf of another for the purposes of the *Hedley Byrne* rule without assuming personal responsibility."[525]

Thus a vendor of land has been held liable, where appropriate reliance could be established, for misrepresentations by his estate agent,[526] or by his solicitor.[527] This indicates a rule whereby the principal of a *non-employee agent* will in appropriate cases be liable on a misrepresentation made by his agent within actual or apparent authority,[528] and there seems no reason why the same reasoning should not apply in respect of this tort to employee agents.[529] There are also a few cases holding a principal liable for wrongful statements of an independent contractor not involving representations, and hence not using any notion of authority, on reasoning which nevertheless appears to connect to their status as an agent but not to any idea of non-delegable duty.[530] Unless they can be limited to statements, they are presumably to be explained as examples, possibly unusual, justified by some more general notion of vicarious liability, going beyond employment and outside the sphere of representation, in respect of matters undertaken in order to achieve the principal's objectives.[531] Such a loose principle has little to commend it.

(g) Disposition of Property through Agent

31-076 **Disposition of property by agent** A disposition of property made by an agent acting within his actual authority obviously transfers the property, in accordance with

---

using letterhead to person to whom he had been prohibited from giving valuations).

[524] *Williams v Natural Life Health Foods Ltd* [1998] 1 W.L.R. 830.

[525] *Standard Chartered Bank v Pakistan National Shipping Corp (No.2)* [2002] UKHL 43, [2003] 1 A.C. 959 at [21] per Lord Hoffmann; see also *Williams v Natural Life Health Foods Ltd*, above, at 838; *Steel v NRAM Ltd* [2018] UKSC 13 at [24] ("this concept remains the foundation of the liability" per Lord Wilson of Culworth).

[526] *Richards v Norris Smith Real Estate Ltd* [1977] 1 N.Z.L.R. 152.

[527] *Cemp Properties (UK) Ltd v Dentsply Research and Development Corp* [1989] 2 E.G.L.R. 196 (Misrepresentation Act 1967 s.2(1)). See further *Steel v NRAM Ltd* [2018] UKSC 13 and below, para.31-111.

[528] See a useful discussion in *Ong Hang Ling v American International Assurance Co Ltd* [2017] SGHC 327 at [207] et seq.

[529] The question is instructively discussed by Flaux L.J. in *Frederick v Positive Solutions (Financial Services) Ltd* [2018] EWCA Civ 431, where however it was not necessary to reach a conclusion as the case was plainly one where the person concerned did no more than provide the opportunity for unauthorised wrongdoing by another, as in the *Kooragang* case above.

[530] See *Colonial Mutual Life Assurance Society Ltd v Producers' and Citizens' Cooperative Assurance Co Ltd* (1931) 46 C.L.R. 41, where an Australian company was held liable for defamation of another company by its independent agent while seeking business for it—though surely a fringe case: contrast *Colonial Mutual Life Assurance Society v Macdonald* [1931] A.D. 412 (same company in South Africa not liable for negligent driving of representative while on business). For a simpler example see *Gordon v Selico Co Ltd* [1986] 1 E.G.L.R. 71 (estate agent). For a wider rationale see Atiyah, *Vicarious Liability in the Law of Torts* (1967), Chs 9 and 10.

[531] See *Sweeney v Boylan Nominees Ltd* (2006) 226 C.L.R. 161 at [14] et seq. (equipment leasing company not liable for negligence of independent contractor used by it for repair services).

general principles.[532] And a disposition made by an agent acting within his apparent authority will likewise be effective: though if the doctrine of apparent authority is based on estoppel, the estoppel has here an unusually wide effect, for it operates as against all the world.[533] The principal must have made a representation as to the agent's authority to the third party or to a group of third parties, or have been negligent in circumstances in which he owed a duty of care.[534] It is, however, clear that the mere entrusting of the possession of goods does not confer apparent authority upon the receiver to dispose of them, for otherwise there would be no need for the Factors Acts.[535] There must be something more, e.g. the fact that the agent is a person having a usual authority[536] to dispose of goods,[537] or the transfer of additional indicia of title or power to sell.[538] But the rules are easier to state than to apply, and judgments sometimes fall back on the imprecise dictum that "wherever one of two innocent persons must suffer by the acts of a third, he who has enabled such third person to occasion the loss must sustain it".[539]

Apparent ownership   A similar principle, which is not strictly a principle of agency at all,[540] but rather a manifestation of more general rules as to estoppel by conduct, operates where the principal enables another person to appear as the owner of goods. Here again, the mere entrusting of goods to such person does not give him apparent ownership: there must be something more, e.g. putting the other person in possession of documents whereby the person who is in fact the owner offers to buy the goods,[541] or allowing the goods to stand in the name of another.[542]   **31-077**

---

[532]   But if the agent holds property on trust the principal's equitable interest will prevail except against a bona fide purchaser for value: *Gray v Smith* [2013] EWHC 4136 (Comm), [2014] 2 All E.R. (Comm) 359; see also *Feuer Leather Corp v Frank Johnstone & Sons* [1981] Com. L.R. 251.

[533]   *Eastern Distributors v Goldring* [1957] 2 Q.B. 600, 611 (stated without explanation). See also Sale of Goods Act 1979 s.21; *Moorgate Mercantile Co Ltd v Twitchings* [1977] A.C. 890; *Shearson Lehman Brothers Inc v Maclaine Watson & Co Ltd (No.2)* [1988] 1 W.L.R. 16, 28 (strong inference when acting in course of employment).

[534]   See above, para.31-056.

[535]   *Weiner v Gill* [1905] 2 K.B. 172, 182; *Central Newbury Car Auctions Ltd v Unity Finance Ltd* [1957] 1 Q.B. 371 at 388; *Jerome v Bentley & Co* [1952] 2 All E.R. 114. As to the Factors Acts, see below, para.31-079.

[536]   Above, para.31-047.

[537]   *Pickering v Busk* (1812) 15 East 38 (broker); *Rainbow v Howkins* [1904] 2 K.B. 322 (auctioneer); cf. *Tobin v Broadbent* (1947) 75 C.L.R. 378 (stockbroker).

[538]   See *Mercantile Credit Co Ltd v Hamblin* [1965] 2 Q.B. 242; *Eastern Distributors v Goldring* [1957] 2 Q.B. 600.

[539]   *Lickbarrow v Mason* (1787) 2 Term Rep. 63, 70; and see *Commonwealth Trust v Akotey* [1926] A.C. 72. But whether a person has "enabled" seems to turn on the existence of a duty: *Central Newbury Car Auctions Ltd v Unity Finance Ltd* [1957] 1 Q.B. 371, 389; *Jerome v Bentley & Co* [1952] 2 All E.R. 114, 118. See below, paras 44-196 et seq.

[540]   Though it has affinities with the supposed principle of *Watteau v Fenwick* [1893] 1 Q.B. 346, above, para.31-064.

[541]   *Eastern Distributors v Goldring* [1957] 2 Q.B. 500; *Stoneleigh Finance v Phillips* [1965] 2 Q.B. 537; *Snook v London & West Riding Investments Ltd* [1967] 2 Q.B. 786; cf. *Mercantile Credit Co Ltd v Hamblin* [1905] 2 Q.B. 242. A car registration document is not such indicium of title as to give rise to apparent ownership: *Central Newbury Car Auctions Ltd v Unity Finance Ltd* [1957] 1 Q.B. 371; *J Sargent (Garages) Ltd v Motor Auctions (West Bromwich) Ltd* [1977] R.T.R. 121; *Beverley Acceptances Ltd v Oakley* [1982] R.T.R. 417. See also below, paras 39-414, 39-415, 44-196 et seq.

[542]   *Henderson v Williams* [1895] 1 Q.B. 521. But cf. *Farquharson Bros & Co v King & Co* [1902] A.C. 325; *Motor Credits (Hire Finance) Ltd v Pacific Motor Auctions Pty Ltd* (1963) 109 C.L.R. 87; reversed on other grounds [1965] A.C. 867; *Moorgate Mercantile Co v Twitchings* [1977] A.C. 890.

31-078 Cases where the agent has some authority A small group of cases concern persons given the indicia of property and a limited authority, who perform an act or acts over the property which go beyond what was authorised.[543] It has recently been said that the principle is not based on actual authority given to the agent, but rather on a combination of factors: "... where the owner has furnished the agent with the means of holding himself out to a purchaser or lender as the owner of the asset or as having the full authority of the owner to deal with it; together with an omission by the owner to bring to the attention of the person dealing with the agent any limitation that exists as to the extent of the actual authority of the agent".[544] There seem to be two separate justifications behind this. The first is based on reasoning concerning priority of equities: "the man possessed of a prior equity cannot be deprived of his title unless he has been guilty of some negligence".[545] The second is the doctrine of apparent ownership, or something akin to it, which like apparent authority can be related to estoppel.[546] Whatever doctrine there is needs careful limitation to avoid conflicting with the general proposition stated above, that mere parting with property does not imperil ownership of it.

31-079 Mercantile agents The Factors Act 1889 extends the common law rules by protecting third parties in respect of dispositions of goods by mercantile agents permitted by the owner to be in possession thereof.[547] For the purposes of this statute a mercantile agent is defined (in almost circular fashion) as a mercantile agent having, in the customary course of his business as such agent, authority either to sell goods, or to consign goods for the purpose of sale, or to buy goods, or to raise money on the security of goods.[548] The Act was the last of several directed at problems concerning the operations of the nineteenth-century factor, who received the goods of others on consignment and might resell them without making clear whether he acted as agent or principal[549]; but trading patterns have changed and its modern relevance is to much more casual forms of agency. Thus these words have been held to include a retail jeweller to whom stock was sent for sale by a manufacturing jeweller,[550] and a dealer in pictures and furniture on commission,[551] but not a mere clerk,[552] a person who has been on a single occasion entrusted with a motor car for sale,[553] nor a person who normally buys and sells on his own

---

[543] The principal cases normally cited are *Brocklesby v Temperance Building Society* [1895] A.C. 173 (title deeds plus authority to pledge for limited sum); *Rimmer v Webster* [1902] 2 Ch. 163 (bond plus authority to sell); *Fry v Smellie* [1912] 3 K.B. 282 (share certificates accompanied by signed blank transfers). See Watts (2002) 2 O.U.C.L.J. 93, 99–100.

[544] *Wishart v Credit & Mercantile Plc* [2015] EWCA Civ 655 at [52] per Sales L.J. In this case the person concerned abstained entirely from involvement in the mechanics of purchase of land, thus leaving documents in the hands of a person acting on his behalf.

[545] *Rimmer v Webster* [1902] 2 Ch. 163, 172 per Farwell J. These cases thus link to cases on priority of mortgages. The principle is referred to by Millett J. as "the arming principle" in *Macmillan Inc v Bishopsgate Investment Trust Plc* [1995] 1 W.L.R. 978, 1012 (point not referred to on appeal [1996] 1 W.L.R. 387).

[546] *Rimmer v Webster*, above, at 173; *Thompson v Foy* [2009] EWHC 1076 (Ch), [2010] 1 P. & C.R. 16 at [42]; *Bank of Scotland v Hussain* [2010] EWHC 2812 (Ch) at [100] et seq.

[547] See below, para.31-080.

[548] Factors Act 1889 s.1(1).

[549] Above, para.31-009.

[550] *Weiner v Harris* [1910] 1 K.B. 285.

[551] *Lowther v Harris* [1927] 1 K.B. 393.

[552] *Lamb v Attenborough* (1862) 1 B. & S. 831.

[553] *Heap v Motorists' Advisory Agency Ltd* [1923] 1 K.B. 577; *Budberg v Jerwood* (1934) 51 T.L.R. 99;

account.[554] It is however possible for a person to be a mercantile agent although he has only one customer,[555] and it does not appear that the person concerned must carry on business as a mercantile agent of a recognised type.[556]

Dispositions by mercantile agents   Section 2(1) of the Act provides: **31-080**

"Where a mercantile agent is, with the consent of the owner, in possession[557] of goods or of the documents of title[558] to goods,[559] any sale, pledge,[560] or other disposition[561] of the goods made by him[562] when acting in the ordinary course of business of a mercantile agent shall, subject to the provisions of this Act, be as valid as if he were expressly authorised by the owner of the goods to make the same; provided that the person taking under the disposition acts in good faith, and has not at the time of the disposition notice that the person making the disposition has not authority to make the same."[563]

Although it is necessary that the disposition should be made by the agent when acting in the ordinary course of business of a mercantile agent,[564] the power to make a binding disposition which the statute confers upon the agent cannot be overridden by the custom of a particular trade that no such dispositions should be made by an agent.[565] It is probably not within the ordinary course of business in the United Kingdom to sell a car without its registration document.[566]

Consent of the owner   It is not clear what restriction these words impose on the   **31-081**
agent's possession. It seems that the goods must not merely be in his possession as a mercantile agent; they must have been entrusted to him as such and not, e.g. solely

---

Fairfax General Holdings Ltd v Capital Bank Plc [2006] EWHC 3439, [2007] 1 Lloyd's Rep. 171; reversed on other grounds [2007] EWCA Civ 1226, [2008] 1 Lloyd's Rep. 297.

554 *Belvoir Finance Co Ltd v Harold G Cole & Co Ltd* [1969] 1 W.L.R. 1877.

555 *Lowther v Harris* [1927] 1 K.B. 393.

556 See *Weiner v Harris* [1910] 1 K.B. 285, 289 (argument); *Mortgage Loan & Finance Co of Australia Ltd v Richards* (1931) 32 S.R.(N.S.W.) 50.

557 Possession is defined by s.1(2) as existing where the "goods or documents are in his actual custody or held by any other person, subject to his control, or for him or on his behalf". See *Beverley Acceptances Ltd v Oakley* [1982] R.T.R. 417; *Fairfax General Holdings Ltd v Capital Bank Plc* [2006] EWHC 3439, [2007] 1 Lloyd's Rep. 171, above.

558 As to the meaning of this phrase in this context see *Benjamin's Sale of Goods*, 10th edn (2017), para.7-036.

559 See note above.

560 See *Waddington & Sons v Neale & Sons* (1907) 96 L.T. 786.

561 As to this word see *Worcester Works Finance Ltd v Cooden Engineering Co Ltd* [1972] 1 Q.B. 210.

562 The possession and disposition must be simultaneous: *Beverley Acceptances Ltd v Oakley* [1982] R.T.R. 417.

563 As to good faith, see *Barclays Bank Ltd v TOSG Trust Fund Ltd* [1984] B.C.L.C. 1. See *Benjamin's Sale of Goods*, 10th edn (2017), paras 7-045 et seq. The onus of proving good faith and absence of notice is on the disponee: *Heap v Motorists' Advisory Agency Ltd* [1923] 1 K.B. 577; *Fairfax General Holdings Ltd v Capital Bank Plc* [2006] EWHC 3439. [2007] 1 Lloyd's Rep. 171; following *The Saetta* [1993] 2 Lloyd's Rep. 268. Various saving provisions are contained in ss.12 and 13.

564 See *Turner v Sampson* (1911) 27 T.L.R. 200. *Jamesich v Attenborough & Son* (1910) 102 L.T. 605; *De Gorter v Attenborough & Son* (1905) 21 T.L.R. 19; *Biggs v Evans* [1894] 1 Q.B. 88; *Newtons of Wembley Ltd v Williams* [1965] 1 Q.B. 560; *Lloyds & Scottish Finance Ltd v Williamson* [1965] 1 W.L.R. 404, 408. But it is not necessary that the third party should know that the person concerned is acting as a mercantile agent: *Oppenheimer v Attenborough & Son* [1908] 1 K.B. 221.

565 *Oppenheimer v Attenborough & Son*, above.

566 *Pearson v Rose and Young Ltd* [1951] 1 K.B. 275; *Lambert v G & C Finance Corp* (1963) 107 S.J. 666; *Stadium Finance Ltd v Robbins* [1962] 2 Q.B. 664. But cf. *Astley Industrial Trust Ltd v Miller* [1968] 2 All E.R. 36. The procedure nowadays is slightly different.

as a bailee,[567] and they must have been entrusted to him for a purpose which is in some way connected with his business as a mercantile agent; it may not actually be for sale—it may be for display or to get offers; but it must be something of that kind before the owner can be deprived of his goods.[568] Thus, if a person takes his car to a garage to be repaired, the proprietors of the garage cannot sell it with a good title, under s.2 of the Act, merely because they happen also to be dealers in second-hand cars. For the purposes of the statute the consent of the owner is to be presumed in the absence of evidence to the contrary.[569] Where the owner consents to possession, the operation of the Act is not defeated by the fact that the consent was obtained by deception or fraud[570] —unless the owner did not intend the agent to have possession at all.[571] It should be noted that this requirement makes relevant matters which the third party may have no means of knowing, and shows that the Act is not by modern standards merely a specific example of apparent authority reasoning.

31-082   **Disposition of property to agent**   The question of *acquisition* of property through agents can be of great conceptual difficulty.[572] It seems clear that a disposition of property to an agent known to be acting for a principal may, if the third party making the disposition and the agent so intend, and the agent has authority,[573] vest property in the principal. It is also arguable that where the agent intends to acquire for an undisclosed principal and is authorised to do so the property vests in the principal without the necessity for further transfer,[574] subject perhaps to the limits on the doctrine of undisclosed principal.[575] In both these cases it would seem that *possession* rests with the agent (until he makes a fresh transfer or attorns to the principal). It has however been held that an attornment to the agent of an undisclosed principal can create a pledge interest in the principal.[576] It is of course possible for the agent to acquire legal title but hold on trust for the principal.[577]

---

[567] *Staffs Motor Guarantee v British Wagon Co* [1934] 2 K.B. 305; *Pearson v Rose & Young Ltd* [1951] 1 K.B. 275, 288; *Astley Industrial Trust Ltd v Miller*, above.

[568] *Pearson v Rose & Young Ltd*, above; *Stadium Finance Ltd v Robbins*, above; and see *Turner v Sampson* (1911) 27 T.L.R. 200; *Moody v Pall Mall Deposit and Forwarding Co Ltd* (1917) 33 T.L.R. 306; *Henderson v Prosser* [1982] C.L.Y. 21 (car entrusted for valeting).

[569] Factors Act 1889 s.2(4).

[570] *Whitehorn Bros v Davison* [1911] 1 K.B. 463; *Folkes v King* [1923] 1 K.B. 282; *Du Jardin v Beadman Bros* [1952] 2 Q.B. 712; *Ingram v Little* [1961] 1 Q.B. 31, 70.

[571] *Pearson v Rose & Young Ltd* [1951] 1 K.B. 275; *Stadium Finance Ltd v Robbins* [1962] 2 Q.B. 664; *Du Jardin v Beadman Bros*, above, at 718. And see *Debs v Sibec Developments Ltd* [1990] R.T.R. 91 (car taken at gun point).

[572] See *Bowstead and Reynolds on Agency*, 21st edn (2018), art.89; Goode, *Proprietary Rights and Insolvency in Sales Transactions* (1985), pp.8–10.

[573] In appropriate cases it seems that the doctrine of apparent authority could apply.

[574] But see *Ireland v Livingston* (1872) L.R. 5 H.L. 395; *Cassaboglou v Gibb* (1883) 11 Q.B.D. 797, 804; below, para.31-165.

[575] Which are themselves controversial: above, para.31-067.

[576] *Maynegrain Pty Ltd v Compafina Bank* [1982] 2 N.S.W.L.R. 141 (decision reversed by the Privy Council on other grounds (1984) 58 A.L.J.R. 389). See also the cases cited below, para.31-165.

[577] *Gray v Smith* [2013] EWHC 4136 (Comm), [2014] 2 All E.R. (Comm) 359.

7. AGENT'S RELATIONS WITH THIRD PARTIES

(a) On the Main Contract

General rule   Upon the general principle that the contract of an agent is the   **31-083**
contract of the principal,[578] it is often said that an agent is prima facie neither liable upon any agreement into which he enters in a representative capacity nor able
to sue on it.[579] For example, in old cases it was held that a commodity broker, who
in that capacity sold goods, could not sue[580] or be sued[581] on the contract of sale,
and that a solicitor who retains or subpoenas witnesses was prima facie not personally liable for their expenses.[582] But such reasoning can be relied on too much. It
has been pointed out that:

> "It is not the law that, if a principal is liable, his agent cannot be. The true principal of
> law is that a person is liable for his engagements (as for his torts) even though he is acting for another, unless he can show that by the law of agency he is to be held to have
> expressly or impliedly negatived his personal liability."[583]

When agent liable and entitled   The fact that a person is an agent and is known   **31-084**
to be so does not therefore of itself necessarily prevent his incurring personal liability, and there are many examples of this.[584] Similarly he may be entitled to sue.[585]
Whether this is so is to be determined by the construction of the contract, if writ-

---

578   Above, para.31-054.
579   *Ex p. Hartop* (1806) 12 Ves. Jr. 349; *Spittle v Lavender* (1821) 2 Brod. & Bing. 452; *Thomas v
      Edwards* (1836) 2 M. & W. 215, 217; *Lewis v Nicholson* (1852) 18 Q.B. 503; *Montgomerie v UK
      Mutual SS Assn Ltd* [1891] 1 Q.B. 370, 371.
580   *Fawkes v Lamb* (1862) 31 L.J. Q.B. 98; and see *Sharman v Brandt* (1871) L.R. 6 Q.B. 720; *Fairlie
      v Fenton* (1870) L.R. 5 Ex. 169.
581   *Southwell v Bowditch* (1876) 1 C.P.D. 374; *Gadd v Houghton* (1876) 1 Ex. D. 357; cf. *Universal
      Steam Navigation Co Ltd v James McKelvie & Co* [1923] A.C. 492.
582   *Robins v Bridge* (1837) 7 L.J. Ex. 49; and see *Wakefield v Duckworth* [1915] 1 K.B. 218; cf. *Cocks
      v Bruce, Searl and Good* (1904) 21 T.L.R. 62.
583   *Yeung Kai Yung v Hong Kong and Shanghai Banking Corp* [1981] A.C. 787, 795, per Lord Scarman.
      Sometimes an agent's conduct may estop him from disputing his liability even though he acted as
      agent only: see *Pacol v Trade Lines Ltd (The Henrik Sif)* [1982] 1 Lloyd's Rep. 456; *Arctic Shipping Co Ltd v Mobilia AB (The Tatra)* [1990] 2 Lloyd's Rep. 51.
584   *Yeung Kai Yeung v Hong Kong and Shanghai Banking Corp* [1981] A.C. 787, 795; *Carminco Gold
      & Resources Ltd v Findlay & Co Stockbrokers (Underwriters) Pty Ltd* [2007] FCAFC 194 at [1]
      ("the law of agency clearly admits of this possibility") and [23]. See, e.g. *Hichens, Harrison,
      Woolston & Co v Jackson & Sons* [1943] A.C. 266; *Sobell Industries v Cory Bros & Co Ltd* [1955]
      2 Lloyd's Rep. 82; *The Swan* [1968] 1 Lloyd's Rep. 5 (this case contains the clearest application of
      such a possibility, though its context is the field of one-person companies); *Format International
      Security Printers Ltd v Mosden* [1975] 1 Lloyd's Rep. 37; *Salsi v Jetspeed Air Services Ltd* [1977]
      2 Lloyd's Rep. 57; *Sika Contracts Ltd v Gill* (1978) 9 B.L.R. 11; *Fraser v Equitorial Shipping Co
      Ltd (The Ijaola)* [1979] 1 Lloyd's Rep. 103; *Eas Biret Cie SA v Yukiteru Kaiun KK (The Sun Happiness)* [1984] 2 Lloyd's Rep. 381; cf. *N & J Vlessopulos Ltd v Ney Shipping Ltd (The Santa Carina)*
      [1977] 1 Lloyd's Rep. 478; *Foalquest Ltd v Roberts* [1990] 1 E.G.L.R. 50; *Petroleum Shipping Ltd
      v Vatis (The Riza and The Sun)* [1997] 2 Lloyd's Rep. 314; *Foxtons Ltd v Thesleff* [2005] EWCA
      Civ 514, [2005] 2 E.G.L.R. 29. The proposition is also supported by Statute of Frauds cases, which
      are discussed in *Basma v Weekes* [1950] A.C. 441.
585   *Short v Spackman* (1831) 2 B. & Ad. 962; *Clay v Southern* (1852) 7 Ex. 717; *Fairlie v Fenton* (1870)
      L.R. 5 Ex. 169, 171; *HO Brandt & Co v HN Morris & Co Ltd* [1917] 2 K.B. 784; *Lavan v Walsh*
      [1964] I.R. 87.

ten, and by its nature and the surrounding circumstances.[586] The fact that agents may often be of more substance than their principals suggests that such involvement in the contract may be more appropriate nowadays than in former times. When the agent does contract personally, the scope of the contract which he makes requires careful analysis. He may undertake sole liability to the exclusion of his principal[587]; he may undertake joint or joint and several liability on the main contract together with his principal.[588] He may act as surety for his principal,[589] or enter into a collateral contract with its own terms.[590] The possibilities shade into one another, and there is no general rule. An agent may undertake liability without being entitled to sue, but he cannot easily be entitled to sue if he is not liable, for there would usually be no consideration to support the liability of the other party.[591]

31-085 **Written documents** Written documents must be construed as a whole; but by their wording they may make an agent a party to the contract, whether alone or together with his principal. Again, most of the older cases concern whether a party is liable as principal or is not liable as agent.[592] To take an old example, where the defendant by a written agreement expressed to be made by himself "on behalf of A B of the one part", and the plaintiff of the other part, promised that "he, the defendant, would execute to the plaintiff a lease of certain premises", which, as it was proved, belonged to A B, it was held that the defendant was personally liable.[593] So also a solicitor who "personally" undertook in writing that a record should be withdrawn and costs paid in a cause which he was conducting, was held personally liable,[594] as were solicitors undertaking as such to pay a distraining landlord his rent.[595] The signatory of a charterparty was held personally liable despite a statement in the body of the document. "This vessel was chartered on behalf and for account of General Organisation for Supply Goods, Cairo".[596] On the other hand persons who signed a charterparty "as agents" were held not to have made themselves personally liable, notwithstanding that they were described in the body

---

[586] *Rusholme, etc. Ltd v SG Read & Co* [1955] 1 W.L.R. 146, 150; *Maritime Stores v HP Marshall & Co* [1963] 1 Lloyd's Rep. 602; *The Swan*, above; *Domsalla v Dyason* [2007] EWHC 1174 (TCC), [2007] B.L.R. 348 (insurer, building owner and builder); *Goei Tsusho Co Ltd v Leader Engineering and Construction Ltd* [2010] 2 H.K.L.R.D. 1084 (joint liability).

[587] See the *Carminco Gold & Resources Ltd* case above, n.584.

[588] *International Ry Co v Niagara Parks Commission* [1941] A.C. 328, 342; *Montgomerie v UK Mutual SS Assn* [1891] 1 Q.B. 370, 372; *The Swan* [1968] 1 Lloyd's Rep. 5; *Teheran-Europe Co Ltd v ST Belton (Tractors) Ltd* [1968] 2 Q.B. 53, 59–60, 558.

[589] *Imperial Bank v London & St Katharine Docks Co* (1877) 5 Ch. D. 195, 200; *Fleet v Murton* (1871) L.R. 7 Q.B. 126, 132; *Young v Schuler* (1883) 11 Q.B.D. 651.

[590] As in the case of auctioneers. See below, para.31-099.

[591] *Evans v Hooper* (1875) 1 Q.B.D. 45. But such a situation is possible: e.g. a third party in return for introduction to the principal might undertake liability to the agent.

[592] *Gadd v Houghton* (1876) 1 Ex. D. 357; *Universal Steam Navigation Co Ltd v James McKelvie & Co* [1923] A.C. 492, 499; *Lavan v Walsh* [1964] I.R. 87.

[593] *Norton v Herron* (1825) Ry. & M. 229; and see *Tanner v Christian* (1855) 4 El. & Bl. 591.

[594] *Iveson v Conington* (1823) 1 B. & C. 160; cf. *Allaway v Duncan* (1867) 16 L.T. 264. See also *Lavan v Walsh* [1964] I.R. 87.

[595] *Burrell v Jones* (1819) 3 B. & Ald. 47; see also *Harper v Williams* (1843) 4 Q.B. 219.

[596] *Tudor Marine Ltd v Tradax Export SA (The Virgo)* [1976] 2 Lloyd's Rep. 135; see also *HO Brandt & Co v HN Morris & Co Ltd* [1917] 2 K.B. 784; *The Swan* [1968] 1 Lloyd's Rep. 5; *Pyxis Special Shipping Co Ltd v Dritsas & Kaglis Bros Ltd (The Scaplake)* [1978] 2 Lloyd's Rep. 380; *Jugoslavenska Linijska Plovidba v Hulsman (The Primorje)* [1980] 2 Lloyd's Rep. 74; *Punjab National Bank v de Boinville* [1952] 1 W.L.R. 1138 ("P Bank, a/c E": bank liable); *Internaut Shipping GmbH v Fercometal SARL Elikon* [2003] 2 Lloyd's Rep. 430.

of the instrument as "charterers".[597] Similarly, where a broker on behalf of his principal, T, made a contract with the defendant, L, in the following terms "Mr. L—I have this day bought in my own name, for your account, of T, 259 puncheons of Cuba rum", signed "A F, broker", it was held that the broker could not sue the buyer in his own name for the price of the rum.[598] And where a shipmaster signed bills of lading covenanting to deliver cargo to the shippers or their assigns at the port of discharge upon their "paying freight as per charterparty", it was held, in an action by the master against the charterers for freight, that in signing the bills of lading he had done so merely as agent for the shipowner, and consequently was not entitled to maintain the action.[599] In all these cases the nature of the liability must be carefully analysed, as stated in the previous paragraph.[600] A signature merely to authenticate the signature of a corporate entity does not usually bind the signer personally.[601]

Custom and usage of trade   In certain cases, usually where the principal is   **31-086**
disclosed but not named, even an agent who contracts expressly "as agent" may, by usage of trade, be held nevertheless personally liable on the contract. Marine insurance brokers are generally liable to underwriters for all premiums payable on policies which they have effected with them[602] and can sometimes sue on such policies.[603] And there are many cases in which it has been held that brokers and the like are, by custom of the trade or market in which they act, personally liable on contracts made for a (usually unidentified) principal,[604] though it is again not always made clear whether they are liable instead of or in addition to the principal. Evidence of a custom making an agent personally liable on a contract is inadmissible under the parol evidence rule if the custom is actually inconsistent with the express terms of a written contract[605]; but even signature "as agents to merchants"

---

597 *Universal Steam Navigation Co Ltd v James McKelvie & Co* [1923] A.C. 492. See also *Deslandes v Gregory* (1860) 30 L.J. Q.B. 36; *Parker v Winlow* (1857) 7 E. & B. 942; *Electrosteel Castings Ltd v Scan Trans Shipping and Chartering Sdn Bhd* [2002] EWHC 1993 (Comm), [2002] 2 All E.R. (Comm) 1064.
598 *Fawkes v Lamb* (1862) 31 L.J. Q.B. 98; and see *Sharman v Brandt* (1871) L.R. 6 Q.B. 720; *Fairlie v Fenton* (1870) L.R. 5 Ex. 169; *Gadd v Houghton* (1876) 1 Ex. D. 357; *Southwell v Bowditch* (1876) 1 C.P.D. 374; *Lester v Balfour Williamson* [1953] 2 Q.B. 168.
599 *Repetto v Millar's Karri, etc. Forests Ltd* [1901] 2 K.B. 306.
600 For a recent example of both principal and agent being liable see *Savills (UK) Ltd v Blacker* [2017] EWCA Civ 68.
601 *Newborne v Sensolid (Great Britain) Ltd* [1954] 1 Q.B. 45; *Black v Smallwood* (1966) 117 C.L.R. 52; *Badgerhill Properties Ltd v Cottrell* [1991] B.C.L.C. 805.
602 Marine Insurance Act 1906 s.53(1).
603 *Provincial Insurance Co of Canada v Leduc* (1874) L.R. 6 P.C. 224.
604 *Dale v Humfrey* (1858) El. Bl. & El. 1004 (oil); *Cropper v Cook* (1868) L.R. 3 C.P. 194 (wool); *Fleet v Murton* (1871) L.R. 7 Q.B. 126 (fruit); *Hutchinson v Tatham* (1873) L.R. 8 C.P. 482 (charterparty); *Imperial Bank v London & St Katharine Docks Co* (1877) 5 Ch. D. 195 (fruit); *Bacmeister v Fenton, Levy & Co* (1883) C. & E. 121 (rice); *Pike v Ongley* (1887) 18 Q.B.D. 708 (hops); *Thornton v Fehr & Co* (1935) 51 Ll.L. Rep. 330 (tallow); *Anglo Overseas Transport Ltd v Titan Industrial Corp (United Kingdom) Ltd* [1959] 2 Lloyd's Rep. 152; *Perishables Transport Co v N Spyropoulos (London) Ltd* [1964] 2 Lloyd's Rep. 379 (forwarding agents); cf. *Wilson v Avec Audio-Visual Equipment Ltd* [1974] 1 Lloyd's Rep. 81 (no such custom as to insurance brokers)
605 See *Barrow & Bros v Dyster, Nalder & Co* (1884) 13 Q.B.D. 635; *Miller, Gibb & Co v Smith & Tyrer Ltd* [1917] 2 K.B. 141. But per contra if the agent signs as principal he may not thereafter prove that he acted as agent only: below, para.31-092. As to the parol evidence rule see Vol.I, paras 13-109 et seq.

may not necessarily be inconsistent with liability,[606] depending again on how the agent's liability is analysed.[607] And there is no doubt that in principle such custom can *add* to the agent's liability to that of the principal.

31-087 Agent for foreign principal It was long the case that where an agent contracted on behalf of a foreign principal, he was presumed to contract personally, unless a contrary intention appeared from the terms of the contract or the surrounding circumstances.[608] In 1968, however, the Court of Appeal held that the presumption no longer exists, for "the usages of the law merchant are not immutable".[609] It was however said that the fact that the principal is foreign is a matter to be taken into account in determining:

> "... whether or not the other party to the contract was willing, or led the agent to believe that he was willing, to treat as a party to the contract the agent's principal, and, if he was so willing, whether the mutual intention of the other party and the agent was that the agent should be personally entitled to sue and liable to be sued on the contract as well as his principal."[610]

31-088 Undisclosed principal An important exception to the rule that an agent is neither entitled to sue nor liable to be sued on a contract made by him in a purely representative capacity is to be found where an authorised agent makes the contract in his own name without disclosing the fact that he is acting on behalf of another. On such contracts he can sue and be sued in his own name because he is then to all appearances the real contracting party.[611] The intervention of the undisclosed principal may put an end to the agent's right of action,[612] but not necessarily to the third party's right of action against the agent.

---

[606] See *Hutchinson v Tatham* (1873) L.R. 8 C.P. 482.

[607] Above, para.31-084.

[608] See *Bowstead and Reynolds on Agency*, 21st edn (2018), para.9-020. This was originally based on the authority supposedly granted (or not granted) by the foreign principal himself, and not on the agent's dealings with the third party. It is at least in part connected with the likelihood that such an agent was operating by way of indirect representation (above, para.31-004) under which the agent deals in his own name: see *Elbinger Actiengesellschaft v Claye* (1873) L.R. 8 Q.B. 313. Both he disclosed and (more especially) the undisclosed principal rules would have given results unexpected to the foreign principal.

[609] *Teheran-Europe Co Ltd v ST Belton (Tractors) Ltd* [1968] 2 Q.B. 545, 562.

[610] At 558, per Diplock L.J.

[611] See *Allen v FW O'Hearn & Co* [1937] A.C. 213, 218. As to the undisclosed principal doctrine see above, paras 31-063 et seq. It seems likely that if the agent sues, he can recover his principal's performance interest (but probably not idiosyncratic loss), on the basis not of any special principle of agency law, but of the reasoning of Lord Goff and Lord Millett in *Alfred McAlpine Construction Ltd v Panatown Ltd* [2001] 1 A.C. 518 (see Vol.I, paras 18-060 et seq.) and *L/M International Construction Inc v The Circle Ltd Partnership* (1995) 49 Con. L.R. 12. This is an early example of the necessity for such reasoning: see *Bowstead and Reynolds on Agency*, 21st edn (2018), para.9-013. In *Garnac Grain Co Ltd v HMF Faure & Fairclough Ltd* [1966] 1 Q.B. 650 it was held at first instance that in an action by the agent it was a defence to prove that the contract was induced by the fraud of the principal. The decision was reversed on other grounds, but this view was accepted in the Court of Appeal: see [1966] 1 Q.B. 650 at 685–686. See also [1968] A.C. 1130n, HL.

[612] *Atkinson v Cotesworth* (1825) 3 B. & C. 647; *Sadler v Leigh* (1815) 4 Camp. 195; *Sargent v Merris* (1820) 3 B. & Ald. 277; *Gardiner v Davis* (1825) 2 Car. & P. 49; *Pople v Evans* [1969] 2 Ch. 255, 261–262. This rule also applies to disclosed principals: *Rogers v Hadley* (1863) 2 H. & C. 227. But the position may be different where there are circumstances creating a separate contract between agent and third party: see *Drinkwater v Goodwin* (1775) Cowp. 251; above, para.31-009, below, para.31-099.

Unidentified principal   An agent, while disclosing the fact that he is acting as an   **31-089**
agent, may do so without disclosing the name of his principal. Such a principal is
not undisclosed,[613] but may be called "unidentified".[614] Jessel M.R. said in *Southwell
v Bowditch*[615]:

> "No doubt it does not absolutely follow from the defendant's appearing on the contract
> to be broker that he is not liable as principal. There are two ways in which he might so
> be made liable: first, intention on the face of the contract making the agent liable as well
> as the principal: secondly, usage".

In written contracts it seems that non-disclosure of the principal's name makes it
more probable the agent will be treated as a party to it, whether alone or together
with his principal.[616] Certainly, trade usages imposing liability on the agent often
relate to situations where his principal is unidentified.[617] But it is a question of fact
or, in the case of a written contract, of construction, in each particular case whether
it was intended that the agent should or should not be personally liable and/or
entitled to sue. Thus where solicitors sold certain shares on behalf of a client, not
disclosing her name at the time when they instructed their stockbrokers, they were,
held liable as principals on the transaction.[618] In *Restatement, Third, Agency*, it is
provided that in the absence of other indications the agent for an unidentified
principal is a party to the contract together with the principal.[619] No such view can
be taken in England: the matter is simply one of interpretation of the dealings. This
it has been held that where brokers ordered fuel for a ship from other brokers
without saying for whom the fuel was intended, the broker placing the order, who
was known not to own ships, was not personally liable (and the owner would be).[620]

Deeds   It has been held that where an agent, by deed under his own hand and seal,   **31-090**
covenants "for himself, his heirs", etc. for the act of another, he is personally liable on his covenant, although he also describes himself in the deed as covenanting "for and on behalf of" another person.[621]

Bills of exchange   A bill of exchange promissory note or cheque[622] may be signed   **31-091**
by an agent.[623] The agent will not be personally liable on such an instrument un-

---

613   Above, paras 31-063, 31-065. But see *Tehran-Europe Co Ltd v ST Belton (Tractors) Ltd* [1968] 2
      Q.B. 545, 552, 556, 561.
614   There may be problems in identifying the principal. See above, para.31-054.
615   (1876) 1 C.P.D. 374, 377.
616   e.g. *Transcontinental Underwriting Agency SRL v Grand Union Ins Co Ltd* [1987] 2 Lloyd's Rep.
      409; *Seatrade Groningen BV v Geest Industries Ltd (The Frost Express)* [1996] 2 Lloyd's Rep. 375.
      See also the cases cited above, n.584.
617   Above, para.31-086.
618   *Hichens, Harrison, Woolston & Co v Jackson & Sons* [1943] A.C. 266.
619   *Restatement, Third, Agency*, para.6.02.
620   *N & J Vlassopulos Ltd v Ney Shipping Ltd (The Santa Carina)* [1977] 1 Lloyd's Rep. 478: see
      especially at 481–482 (Baltic Exchange).
621   *Appleton v Binks* (1804) 5 East 148; *Hancock v Hodgson* (1827) 12 Moore 504; *Chapman v Smith*
      [1907] 2 Ch. 97; *Plant Engineers (Sales) Ltd v Davis* (1969) 113 S.J. 484. It is not clear whether
      these cases are affected by s.7(1) of the Powers of Attorney Act 1971 (replacing Law of Property
      Act 1925 s.123) under which an agent having a power of attorney may execute a deed with his own
      signature and seal.
622   As to promissory notes and cheques, see Bills of Exchange Act 1882 s.89(1).
623   s.91(1). See below, para.34-041.

less his name appears on it,[624] and where a person signs such an instrument in his own name but adds words to his signature indicating that he signs for or on behalf of a principal, or in a representative character, he is not personally liable on it; but the mere addition to his signature of words describing him as an agent, or as filling a representative character, does not exempt him from personal liability.[625] An agent signing his name will therefore be personally liable "unless he states upon the face of the bill that he subscribes it for another, or by procuration of another".[626] In determining whether a signature on a bill is that of the principal or that of the agent by whose hand it is written, the construction most favourable to the validity of the instrument is to be adopted.[627]

31-092 **Agreement excluding or limiting agent's liability** If the terms of a written contract show that it was intended that the agent should be liable personally, parol evidence to the contrary is not admissible.[628] But there is some authority to the effect that the agent may show, by way of defence, that there was an agreement between himself and the plaintiff that he should not be made personally liable.[629] And it is obvious that an agent may expressly stipulate on the face of the agreement that, after a certain time, his liability under it is to cease.[630]

31-093 **Crown agents** An agent of the Crown (other than a public body incorporated by statute or the like)[631] will rarely be held to have contracted personally.[632]

31-094 **Judgment and election** Where principal and agent are both liable, there is some authority that the doctrines of merger and election may apply, and the third party may be debarred from suing one by obtaining judgment against,[633] or even perhaps electing to look to,[634] the other. But even if correct this can only be so where the two remedies available are inconsistent, and this may not be so in all cases. The nature of the liability assumed by the agent may thus be crucial.[635]

---

[624] s.23. The officer of a company signing a bill on which the company's name is not mentioned may be personally liable: below, para.34-045.

[625] s.26(1) (a useful statement of the general law). See *Chapman v Smethurst* [1909] 1 K.B. 927; *Bondina v Rollaway Shower Blinds Ltd* [1986] 1 W.L.R. 517. Parol evidence may be admissible in the case of ambiguity: *Rolfe Lubbell & Co v Keith* [1979] 1 All E.R. 860 (apparent indorsement by acceptor). See below, para.34-056.

[626] *Leadbitter v Farrow* (1816) 5 M. & S. 345, 349.

[627] s.26(2).

[628] *Higgins v Senior* (1841) 8 M. & W. 834; *Jones v Littledale* (1837) 6 Ad. & El. 486; *Magee v Atkinson* (1837) 2 M. & W. 440; *Sobell Industries v Cory Bros & Co Ltd* [1955] 2 Lloyd's Rep. 82; see also *Basma v Weekes* [1950] A.C. 441; and Vol.I, paras 13-109 et seq.

[629] *Wake v Harrop* (1862) 1 H. & C. 202; *Cowie v Witt* (1874) 23 W.R. 76; *Alliance Acceptance Co Ltd v Oakley* (1987) 47 S.A.S.R. 148; reversed on other grounds (1988) 48 S.A.S.R. 337. And see *Breslauer v Barwick* (1876) 36 L.T. 52; *Mostyn v West Mostyn Coal & Iron Co* (1876) 1 C.P.D. 145; Senior Courts Act 1981 s.49(2).

[630] *Oglesby v Yglesias* (1858) El. Bl. & El. 930; *Milvain v Perez* (1861) 3 E. & E. 495 (cases on the cesser clause in charterparties). But cf. *Schmaltz v Avery* (1851) 16 Q.B. 655.

[631] As to which see *Graham v Public Works Commissioners* [1901] 2 K.B. 781; *International Ry Co v Niagara Parks Commission* [1941] A.C. 328.

[632] *Macbeath v Haldimand* (1786) 1 T.R. 172. See Vol.I, paras 11-014, 11-015.

[633] *London General Omnibus Co v Pope* (1922) 38 T.L.R. 270. But not where the liability is joint: Civil Liability Contribution Act 1978 s.3.

[634] *Clarkson Booker v Andjel* [1964] 2 Q.B. 775; *Beigtheil & Young v Stewart* (1900) 16 T.L.R. 177. But these propositions are not unassailable: see above, paras 31-070, 31-071.

[635] See discussion above, para.31-084.

Where "agent" is in fact principal: his liabilities In some cases a party who   **31-095**
purports to act as agent has no principal but himself. There is authority that if the
other party can establish that fact, the apparent agent can be sued on the contract[636]
unless, perhaps, he has expressly contracted in such terms as to exclude his liability as a principal.[637] Likewise where an agent refuses to disclose the name of
his true principal,[638] or where his evidence on this question is disbelieved by the
court[639] he may be held personally liable on the contract. But in many and perhaps
all such cases it seems that liability on a collateral warranty would nowadays be
analytically more appropriate.[640]

Where "agent" is in fact principal: his rights It may also be that such a person   **31-096**
may in certain cases be allowed to sue as principal on the contract which he has thus
made. In a charterparty case there is authority for the proposition that he can do so
if he has not named anyone else as his true principal, on the ground that in such a
case the other party cannot, in entering into the contract, have been influenced by
the personal qualifications of the supposed principal.[641] Secondly, where such a
contract has been in part performed and that performance has been accepted by the
other contracting party with full knowledge that the party who was described as
agent in the contract was the real principal, it has been held that the latter may after
that sue for the completion of the contract.[642] But though it has recent judicial support,[643] this proposition is not beyond criticism[644]; and it is clear that an agent cannot sue as principal if the identity of the contracting party is material.[645]

Where principal is company not yet in existence At common law, if a contract   **31-097**
is made by an agent on behalf of a company not yet in existence, it has sometimes
been held that he intended to assume personal responsibility on the contract.[646] But
there is no general rule that where there is no principal, the agent contracts person-

---

[636] *Jenkins v Hutchinson* (1849) 13 Q.B. 744, 752; *Railton v Hodgson* (1804) 4 Taunt. 576n. But the
cases are by no means clear. The authority that the agent can sue is stronger, though still criticisable:
see below, para.31-096; *Bowstead and Reynolds on Agency*, 21st edn (2018), art.108.

[637] *Gardiner v Heading* [1928] 2 K.B. 284, 290; *Salim v Ingham Enterprises Pty Ltd* (1998) 55
N.S.W.L.R. 7; cf. *Newborne v Sensolid (Great Britain) Ltd* [1954] 1 Q.B. 45.

[638] *Owen v Gooch* (1797) 2 Esp. 567; and see *Hersom v Bernett* [1955] 1 Q.B. 98. As to inter-
rogatories, see also *Thöl v Leask* (1855) 10 Exch. 704; *Hancocks v Lablache* (1878) 3 C.P.D. 197;
Sebright v Hanbury [1916] 2 Ch. 245.

[639] *Hersom v Bernett*, above.

[640] See *Bowstead and Reynolds on Agency*, 21st edn (2018), para.9-066; below, para.31-092; Reynolds
[2012] L.M.C.L.Q. 189.

[641] *Schmaltz v Avery* (1851) 16 Q.B. 655 (a case on the cesser clause, a very specialised provision: see
above, para.31-092); *Harper & Co v Vigers Brothers* [1909] 2 K.B. 549. Some support can be
derived from the "beneficial assumption", above, para.31-054.

[642] *Rayner v Grote* (1846) 15 M. & W. 359; *Fellowes v Lord Gwydyr* (1829) 1 Russ. & M. 83; *Bickerton
v Burrell* (1816) 5 M. & S. 383. Perhaps this could be treated as a novation; or on the basis of
estoppel.

[643] See *Braymist Ltd v Wise Finance Ltd* [2002] EWCA Civ 127, [2002] Ch. 273, per Arden L.J.

[644] See *Hill SS Co v Stinnes*, 1941 S.C. 324; *Sharman v Brandt* (1871) L.R. 6 Q.B. 720. And consider
Hardman v Booth (1863) 1 H. & C. 803. See in general *Bowstead and Reynolds on Agency*, 21st
edn (2018), para.9-096.

[645] *Gewa Chartering BV v Remco Shipping Lines Ltd (The Remco)* [1984] 2 Lloyd's Rep. 205. But cf.
Leigh & Sillivan Ltd v Aliakmon Shipping Co Ltd [1983] 1 Lloyd's Rep. 203, 207; *Fraser v Thames
Television Ltd* [1984] Q.B. 44, 54–55.

[646] *Kelner v Baxter* (1866) L.R. 2 C.P. 174; *Wilson & Co v Baker, Lees & Co* (1901) 17 T.L.R. 473; *Rita
Joan Dairies Ltd v Thompson* [1974] 1 N.Z.L.R. 285; *Marblestone Industries Ltd v Fairchild* [1975]
1 N.Z.L.R. 529. But cf. *Wickberg v Shatsky* (1969) 4 D.L.R. (3d) 540; *Hawke's Bay Milk Corp Ltd*

ally or is his own principal.[647] Thus where a contract is, on the face of it, made solely with such a company, a person who has added his signature to that of the company in order merely to confirm it does not thereby entitle himself to sue or make himself liable to be sued on the contract, which is therefore wholly unenforceable.[648] And a person who clearly contracts as agent only cannot sue or be liable on that contract.[649] A person may perhaps estop himself by subsequent conduct from alleging that he is not party to such a contract.[650]

31-098   But statutory correction of these inconvenient results is common. In England, s.51(1) of the Companies Act 2006 provides:

> "A contract that purports to be made by or on behalf of a company at a time when the company has not been formed has effect, subject to any agreement to the contrary, as one made with the person purporting to act for the company or as agent for it, and he is personally liable on the contract accordingly."

It was held under the previous (effectively identical) legislation that this displaces the above rules whatever the form of signature, whether it indicates signature as the company or as agent for the company.[651] It does not however apply where the company exists but is wrongly named in the contract[652] nor to contracts with foreign companies.[653] It has been held in proceedings under the previous version of this enactment that the final words should not be read as limiting the consequences of the effectiveness of the contract and that the person concerned can sue as well as be sued.[654]

---

647   *v Watson* [1974] 1 N.Z.L.R. 236.
647   *Black v Smallwood* (1966) 117 C.L.R. 52; see also *Coral (UK) Ltd v Rechtman* [1996] 1 Lloyd's Rep. 235. Contrast *Restatement, Third, Agency*, para.6.02.
648   *Newborne v Sensolid (Great Britain) Ltd* [1954] 1 Q.B. 45; *Black & Smallwood*, above; *Miller Associates (Australia) Pty Ltd v Bennington Pty Ltd* [1975] 2 N.S.W.L.R. 506. As to the possibility of an action for breach of warranty of authority, see *Newborne v Sensolid* at 47; *Black v Smallwood* at 64–65; *Hawke's Bay Milk Corp Ltd v Watson*, above; *General Motors Acceptance Corp of Canada Ltd v Weisman* (1976) 96 D.L.R. (3d) 159. Such an action was allowed in *Delta Construction Co Ltd v Lidstone* (1979) 96 D.L.R. (3d) 457.
649   *Hollman v Pullin* (1884) Cab. & El. 254. As regards unincorporated associations, see *Overton v Hewett* (1886) 3 T.L.R. 246; *Steele v Gourley* (1887) 3 T.L.R. 772; *Bradley Egg Farm Ltd v Clifford* [1943] 2 All E.R. 378; *Peckham v Moore* [1975] 1 N.S.W.L.R. 353; *Keeler* (1971) 34 M.L.R. 615; *Fletcher* (1979) 11 U. Queensland L.J. 53. The problem is similar, but the third party is less likely to be protected, and the companies legislation is not applicable.
650   On the basis of the reasoning in *Pacol Ltd v Trade Lines Ltd (The Henrik Sif)* [1982] 1 Lloyd's Rep. 456; see also *Arctic Shipping Co Ltd v Mobilia AB (The Tatra)* [1990] 2 Lloyd's Rep. 51. An argument to this effect was however rejected in *Rover International Ltd v Cannon Film Sales Ltd* [1987] B.C.L.C. 540. The question was not pursued on appeal: [1989] 1 W.L.R. 912.
651   See *Phonogram Ltd v Lane* [1982] Q.B. 938. The exception for contrary agreement is considered in *Royal Mail Estates Ltd v Maple Teesdale* [2015] EWHC 1890 (Ch), [2016] 1 W.L.R. 942.
652   *Oshkosh B'Gosh Inc v Dan Marbel Inc Ltd* [1989] B.C.L.C. 507; *Badgerhill Properties Ltd v Cottrell* [1991] B.C.L.C. 805; *Cotronic (UK) Ltd v Dezonie* [1991] B.C.L.C. at 721 (company struck off); and see *Coral (UK) Ltd v Rechtman* [1996] 1 Lloyd's Rep. 235.
653   *Rover International Ltd v Cannon Film Sales Ltd* [1987] B.C.L.C. 540; decision varied on other grounds [1989] 1 W.L.R. 912. See in general *Gower & Davies' Principles of Modern Company Law*, 10th edn (2016), paras 5-25 et seq.
654   *Braymist Ltd v Wise Finance Ltd* [2002] EWCA Civ 127, [2002] Ch. 273 (a different basis for the decision from that referred to above, n.643).

(b) Collateral Contract with Agent

Collateral contracts   An agent may also be liable and entitled on a contract col- **31-099**
lateral to the main contract with his principal containing special terms. The position of an auctioneer provides the best example of this.[655] When an auctioneer sells
goods by auction the extent of his liability to a third party depends upon the conditions of the sale, the nature of the subject matter and other surrounding
circumstances.[656] Thus where his principal is undisclosed, an auctioneer may be
regarded as having contracted personally and be liable for non-delivery,[657] and in
some cases he may so be liable even where his principal is disclosed,[658] though not
where the contract is for sale of a specific chattel known not to be his property.[659]
He warrants that he knows of no defect in his principal's title, but does not normally
warrant the title itself in the case of specific goods sold for a disclosed principal,
identified or unidentified.[660] His right to commission gives him a lien over goods
and an interest in their proceeds which entitles him to sue for their price[661] even
when he has been paid a sum sufficient to cover his commission and charges[662]; but
he has no such interest over *land* entitling him to sue for the price[663] and any implied
contract on the sale of land would necessarily be of a more limited nature.[664]

(c) Breach of Warranty of Authority

Liability of agent acting without authority   One who expressly or impliedly **31-100**
indicates that he has the authority of another is liable in contract for breach of warranty of authority to any person to whom the indication is given and who suffers
damage by acting in the faith of it, if in fact he had no such authority.[665] This is a
specific type, in fact probably the original type, of collateral contract: the agent offers to warrant his authority in return for the third party's dealing with his principal,
or with another person,[666] or otherwise acting on the faith of the warranty. The liability is absolute and not based on negligence. The historical reason for this is that
no action in tort could be contemplated at the time (1857); but it is still true that if
strict liability is required, contract is the only way to secure it. It seems that a similar
liability is found in civil law countries. The rule is not confined to contracts; it covers other transactions into which a third party enters on the faith of a representa-

---

[655] Another example is the 19th-century factor: see *Drinkwater v Goodwin* (1775) Cowp. 251; above,
paras 31-009, 31-011.
[656] *Wood v Baxter* (1883) 49 L.T. 45.
[657] *Franklyn v Lamond* (1847) 4 C.B. 637 (principal possibly unidentified rather than undisclosed).
[658] *Woolfe v Horne* (1877) 2 Q.B.D. 355.
[659] *Benton v Campbell, Parker & Co* [1925] 2 K.B. 410.
[660] *Benton v Campbell, Parker & Co* [1925] 2 K.B. 410.
[661] *Williams v Millington* (1788) 1 H. Bl. 81. Even where he has in his capacity of agent for the vendor
misdescribed the goods: *Elder Smith Goldsbrough Mort Ltd v McBride* [1976] 2 N.S.W.L.R. 631.
[662] *Chelmsford Auctions Ltd v Poole* [1973] Q.B. 542. See also *Pollway Ltd v Abdullah* [1974] 1 W.L.R.
493 (right to sue on cheque).
[663] *Cherry v Anderson* (1876) I.R. 10 C.L. 204.
[664] cf. *Pollway Ltd v Abdullah*, above (warranty of authority to accept deposit). See in general Murdoch,
Law of Estate Agency, 5th edn (2009); Reynolds [2012] L.M.C.L.Q. 189.
[665] *Collen v Wright* (1857) 8 El. & Bl. 647 (land agent signing lease without authority liable for costs
of action against principal).
[666] *Penn v Bristol & West BS* [1997] 1 W.L.R. 1356 (warranty to mortgage lender). A solicitor acting
for both parties to a land transaction may owe a strict duty to one as regards his authority but merely
a duty of care to the other: see *Bristol & West BS v Fancy & Jackson* [1997] 4 All E.R. 582 at 613,
per Chadwick L.J. But see *Bowstead and Reynolds on Agency*, 21st edn (2018), para.9-065.

tion that the person with whom he is doing business has the authority of some other person.[667] It is also relevant to the court's jurisdiction to award costs against solicitors who take unauthorised steps in litigation.[668] Though wide, its limits are however uncertain: it is not, for example, clear whether or not it lies in respect of a signature purporting to authenticate that of an unformed company. This would require a different sort of warranty, that a company exists which the signer is authorised to bind.[669] But, provided that the authority does not in fact exist at the material time, it is immaterial that the agent originally had such authority and did not know and had no means of ascertaining that the authority had been terminated.[670] This is also true where the termination is by death or by supervening mental incapacity of the principal.[671]

31-101 **Implied representation of authority**   It is not necessary that the representation of authority should be made expressly: merely purporting to act as agent will normally constitute a representation. Thus a solicitor who institutes or takes steps in an action warrants that he has a principal and is properly authorised to do so, even though he makes no express statement to that effect.[672] In this context it has been held, however, that he does not warrant that his client has good cause of action, is solvent or even correctly named.[673] If, therefore, only a limited warranty of authority is given, no wider warranty can be implied. Thus where shipbrokers signed a charterparty "by telegraphic authority" "as agents", a form of words which was understood in the trade to warrant merely that the agents had such authority as a telegram, possibly erroneous, might confer on them, it was held that the shipbrokers were not liable for exceeding their authority owing to a mistake in the telegram,[674] and such reasoning could well be used in a wider sphere.

---

[667] *Firbank's Executors v Humphreys* (1886) 18 Q.B.D. 54; *Starkey v Bank of England* [1903] A.C. 114; *British Russian Gazette Ltd v Associated Newspapers Ltd* [1933] 2 K.B. 616. Examples are Penn's case, above, and *V/O Rasnoimport v Guthrie & Co Ltd* [1966] 1 Lloyd's Rep. 1 (warranty to bill of lading holder); *Bank of Scotland v Qutb* [2012] EWCA Civ 1661 (deliberate bringing of proceedings on behalf of person known to be deceased); *Adams v Ford* [2012] EWCA Civ 544, [2012] 1 W.L.R. 3211.

[668] See *Yonge v Toynbee* [1910] 1 K.B. 215; *SEB Trygg Liv Holding AB v Manches* [2005] EWCA Civ 1237, [2006] 1 W.L.R. 2276, 2298; *Re Sherlock Holmes International Society Ltd* [2016] EWHC 1392 (Ch), [2016] 4 W.L.R. 173 (affirmed without reference to this point [2017] EWCA Civ 1875, [2018] B.C.C. 110).

[669] See *Brownett v Newton* (1941) 64 C.L.R. 439; *Black v Smallwood* (1966) 117 C.L.R. 52, 64–65; *Delta Construction Co Ltd v Lidstone*, 96 D.L.R. (3d) 457 (1979). Such an argument was successful in *Lomax v Dankel* (1981) 29 S.A.S.R. 68. See *Bowstead and Reynolds on Agency*, 21st edn (2018), para.9-066; above, para.31-097.

[670] *Yonge v Toynbee* [1910] 1 K.B. 215 (mental incapacity of principal: solicitor ignorant of it liable for costs).

[671] *Yonge v Toynbee*, above; but see *Blankley v Central Manchester, etc NHS Trust* [2015] EWCA Civ 18, [2015] 1 W.L.R. 4307 at [36].

[672] *Fernée v Gorlitz* [1915] 1 Ch. 177; *Yonge v Toynbee*, above; *Simmons v Liberal Opinion* [1911] 1 K.B. 966; *Nelson v Nelson* [1997] 1 W.L.R. 233 (bankrupt could authorise action) (actually cases on the court's costs jurisdiction over solicitors). "A solicitor's warranty of authority imposes a no-fault liability and is therefore narrowly confined to being that a solicitor has a client against whom a costs order can be made": *Re Sherlock Holmes International Society Ltd* [2016] EWHC 1392 (Ch), [2016] 4 W.L.R. 173 at [52], per Mark Anderson Q.C.

[673] *Nelson v Nelson* [1997] 1 W.L.R. 233; *AMB Generali Holding AG v SEB Trygg Liv Holding AB* [2005] EWCA Civ 1237, [2006] W.L.R. 276. See also *Knight Frank LLP v Du Haney* [2011] EWCA Civ 404.

[674] *Lilly v Smales* [1892] 1 Q.B. 456; cf. *Stuart v Haigh* (1893) 9 T.L.R. 488. See also *Enterprise Plus Ltd v Wagenmann* [2003] EWHC 1827 (Comm) (facts did not support any such commitment).

Representation must be of fact and relied on It must be shown that the plaintiff **31-102**
accepted and relied upon the defendant's representation as a warranty. Therefore
where the plaintiff knew that the defendant had no authority he could not succeed.[675]
So where the facts were equally known to both parties and the representation
complained of was as to a matter of law only it has been held that the defendant
was not liable.[676] But propositions as to mistake of law may need reconsideration
in view of the decision of the House of Lords in *Kleinwort Benson Ltd v Lincoln
City Council*.[677]

Description of principal In the simple case, the agent promises that he has **31-103**
authority from a named person. But where an identity fraud has been practised on
an agent, for example where a solicitor is asked to convey land by an impostor and
is not negligent in failing to discover the deception, the situation can become more
complicated, for (absent fraud) professionals are not normally held liable for more
than negligence. One solution to the problem is to seek by interpretation appropriate to the facts to limit the scope of what is warranted, as by saying (to put it in
rather crude form) that the solicitor only warrants that he has a client about whom
reasonable inquiries have been made.[678] Support for such an approach can be
obtained from the cases concerning what is warranted in litigation referred to in the
previous paragraph, which indicate that a solicitor does not warrant that a name
given is correct. In a recent decision however it was held that where the principal's
name is given to a third party who relies entirely on the written name supplied by
the vendor's solicitor, and especially where the solicitor signs for that person, there
is a promise that the agent has authority from the actual person named.[679] The decision then goes on to hold that the third party did not rely on the warranty of authority but rather on the assumption that the normal checks had been performed.[680] If
this is possible on the facts, it provides another way of circumventing the strict
liability. It seems clear overall that the strict liability postulated in initial simple
examples, although it has been extended to other situations, may not always[681] be

---

[675] *Halbot v Lens* [1901] 1 Ch. 344. See further *P&P Property Ltd v Owen White and Catlin LLP* [2018]
EWCA Civ 1082, below, n.679. This may also be so where the third party is aware of uncertainty
as to the agent's authority, especially where this is or may be itself the subject of litigation: *Re
Sherlock Holmes International Society Ltd* [2016] EWHC 1392 (Ch), [2016] 4 W.L.R. 173; *Zoya
Ltd v Sheikh Nasir Ahmed* [2016] EWHC 2249 (Ch), [2016] 4 W.L.R. 174.
[676] *Beattie v Lord Ebury* (1872) L.R. 7 H.L. 102; cf. *Cherry and M'Dougall v Colonial Bank of
Australasia* (1869) 38 L.J.P.C. 49; *Weeks v Propert* (1873) L.R. 8 C.P. 427. See also *Eaglesfield v
Londonderry* (1876) 4 Ch. D. 693; affirmed 38 L.T. 303; *Rashdall v Ford* (1866) L.R. 2 Eq. 750;
Saffron Walden SBBS v Rayner (1880) 14 Ch. D. 406. The distinction is not an easy one: see
Bowstead and Reynolds on Agency, 21st edn (2018), para.9-069.
[677] [1999] 2 A.C. 249. See above, Vol.I, paras 29-044 et seq.
[678] *Excel Securities Plc v Masood* [2010] Lloyd's Rep. P.N. 165 ("authority to act on behalf of a person
going by the name of James Charles Whittaker Goulding and claiming to be the same individual as
a person of that name who appeared to be the registered proprietor of the property at 17 Richards
Place"). The same reasoning was accepted in *Cheshire Mortgage Corp Ltd v Grandison* [2012] CSIH
66, 2013 S.C. 160 ("an agent ... warranted merely that he had been instructed by the person for
whom he affected to act; he did not warrant that that person was the principal he purported to be");
see also *Stevenson v Singh* [2012] EWHC 2880 (QB).
[679] *P&P Property Ltd v Owen White and Catlin LLP* [2018] EWCA Civ 1082, [2018] P.N.L.R. 29.
[680] See at [61] ("What induced Mr Robinson to allow his client to exchange contracts was his belief
that the necessary due diligence had been carried out").
[681] See *Chu Said Thong v Vision Law LLC* [2014] 4 S.L.R. 375, where a different sort of fraud was
perpetrated and damages awarded.

appropriate when it is applied to more complicated scenarios involving professionals whose undertakings are only of due care in performance of their functions.[682]

31-104 **Crown agents** It was held in the late nineteenth century[683] that a Crown agent was not liable for breach of warranty of authority. The usual view is that a Crown agent cannot be so liable, on grounds of public policy, though possibly the matter cannot be regarded as conclusively settled.[684]

31-105 **Powers of attorney** By s.5(1) of the Powers of Attorney Act 1971 a donee of a power of attorney who acts in pursuance of the power at a time when it has been revoked shall not, by reason of the revocation, incur any liability (either to the donor or to any other person) if at that time he did not know that the power had been revoked.[685]

31-106 **Damages** The damages recoverable in these cases from the agent will be those which directly flow from the breach of warranty. Thus where an agent bought a ship without authority for £6,000, and, on the principal repudiating the contract, the seller had to resell for £5,500, the agent became liable for the £500[686]; brokers selling wool for repudiating principals became liable to the purchasers for the costs of an unsuccessful action by the purchasers against the principals[687]; and the same principle applies to a contract for a grant,[688] or for a renewal of a lease.[689] The rule applied is in general the normal rule for contractual damages, which seek to put the injured party in the position in which he would have been if the contract had been performed or (as in this situation) the statement as to authority true: damages in tort might be assessed differently.[690] There may be cases where no loss arising from lack of authority can be established. This will occur when the main contract with the principal is void[691]; or unenforceable for lack of writing,[692] or where the principal

---

[682] The decision goes on however to hold the vendor's solicitor strictly liable for breach of trust for paying the price over to his client when there was no genuine completion; and also in breach of an undertaking implied by the Law Society Code for Completion by Post (2011), which could possibly be regarded as giving rise to a different action in damages.

[683] *Dunn v Macdonald* [1897] 1 Q.B. 401; see Vol.I, para.11-015.

[684] See Street, *Governmental Liability* (1953), p.93. This might not apply to agents of foreign governments.

[685] This covers revocation by death, etc.: s.5(5); and applies to powers whenever created, but only to transactions after the commencement of the Act: s.5(7). It stems from 19th century legislation probably arising from concern about the decision in *Collen v Wright*.

[686] *Simons v Patchett* (1857) 7 E. & B. 568; see also *Re National Coffee Palace Co* (1883) 24 Ch. D. 367; *Richardson v Williamson* (1871) L.R. 6 Q.B. 276; *Weeks v Propert* (1873) L.R. 8 C.P. 427; *Meek v Wendt* (1888) 21 Q.B.D. 126; *Suleman v Shahsavari* [1988] 1 W.L.R. 1181; *Habton Farms v Nimmo* [2002] EWCA Civ 68, [2004] Q.B. 1 (seller of horse did not accept repudiation by buyer; horse died; unauthorised agent for buyer liable for whole price).

[687] *Hughes v Graeme* (1864) 33 L.J. Q.B. 335; *Greenglade Estates Ltd v Chana* [2012] EWHC 1913 (Ch), [2012] 3 E.G.L.R. 99 (where reasonable to sue both parties, damages to be assessed at time of breach of warranty proceedings). As to the cost of defending proceedings brought by an unauthorised agent, see *Yonge v Toynbee* [1910] 1 K.B. 215.

[688] *Collen v Wright* (1857) 8 El. & Bl. 647.

[689] *Spedding v Nevell* (1869) L.R. 4 C.P. 212. See also *Godwin v Francis* (1870) L.R. 5 C.P. 295.

[690] But see *Doyle v Olby (Ironmongers) Ltd* [1969] 2 Q.B. 158, 168; cf. *Salvesen & Co v Rederi A/B Nordstjernan* [1905] A.C. 302; Vol.I, paras 1-152 et seq., 1-168 et seq., 7-056 et seq.

[691] *Heskell v Continental Express Ltd* [1950] 1 All E.R. 1033; cf. *V/O Rasnoimport v Guthrie & Co* [1966] 1 Lloyd's Rep. 1.

[692] See *Fay v Miller* [1941] Ch. 360; the contract itself would now require to be in writing by virtue of

is insolvent.[693] Where the principal is liable under the doctrine of apparent authority it has been held that the correct approach is that the action for breach of warranty of authority will not lie where it would put the third party in a better position than if he had relied on apparent authority. But that if this would not have been so, for example because the apparent authority would have been negatived by incapacity, the action for breach of authority will lie.[694] Similar considerations apply where the principal ratifies.

Liability in tort[695]   The agent in this context will be liable in tort where he fraudulently represents that he has authority,[696] and perhaps sometimes where he is negligent in so doing.[697] But in the latter case a duty of care must be established. It has been held in New Zealand that there was no such duty of care in such a case; but the facts were rather special.[698]   **31-107**

Procedure   Where the authority of the agent is disputed by the person on whose behalf the contract is made, the person who made the contract may be joined with him as co-defendant and relief claimed against them alternatively.[699]   **31-108**

(d)   Restitution[700]

Repayment of money   If a person pays money to the agent of another and that other has in fact no right to it, or wrongfully induced the payment, the person who paid the money may recover it directly from the agent if the agent still has it in his possession.[701] But the agent cannot be sued in such a case if the person claiming the repayment could not successfully sue the principal, e.g. because the principal   **31-109**

---

the Law of Property (Miscellaneous Provisions) Act 1989 s.2.

693   *Simons v Patchett* (1857) 7 E. & B. 568, 574; *Re National Coffee Palace Co* (1883) 24 Ch. D. 367, 372; and see *Charan Singh v Sardar Investments Ltd* [2002] EWCA Civ 1706; *Skylight Maritime SA v Ascot Underwriting Ltd* [2005] EWHC 15 (Comm), [2005] P.N.L.R. 25 (solicitor's client would not have been able to meet costs order). But see *Firbank's Executors v Humphreys* (1886) 18 Q.B.D. 54, where the principal was insolvent but loss could be proved. And there may be loss in attempting to deliver goods to and/or suing the supposed principal: see *Farley Health Products v Babylon Trading Co, The Times,* July 29, 1987.

694   *Re Sherlock Holmes International Society Ltd* [2016] EWHC 1392 (Ch), [2016] 4 W.L.R. 173 at [40] et seq., considering *Rainbow v Howkins & Sons* [1904] 2 K.B. 322.

695   See also below, para.31-111.

696   *Polhill v Walter* (1832) 3 B. & Ad. 114; *Randell v Trimen* (1856) 18 C.B. 786; *West London Commercial Bank Ltd v Kitson* (1884) 13 Q.B.D. 360. Even probably, if the misrepresentation was one of law: but there is no clear authority.

697   But an action under s.2(1) of the Misrepresentation Act 1967 is excluded by the wording of the section: see *The Skopas,* below, para.31-111, n.724.

698   *Kavanagh v Continental Shelf Co (No.46) Ltd* [1993] 2 N.Z.L.R. 648. The tort was specifically pleaded as a representation of authority, whereas an agent's tort liability could be pleaded in other ways; and one purpose was to argue vicarious liability in the principal. Contrast a different decision in Singapore: *Fong Maun Yee v Yoong Weng Ho Robert* [1997] 1 S.L.R.(R.) 751.

699   See *Honduras Inter-Oceanic Ry Co v Lefevre & Tucker* (1877) 2 Ex. D. 301; *Massey v Heynes* (1888) 21 Q.B.D. 330; *Bennetts v McIlwraith* [1896] 2 Q.B. 464; *Sanderson v Blyth Theatre Co* [1903] 2 K.B. 533; CPR r.44.3.8.

700   The analysis of this area is controversial. See in general Burrows, *Law of Restitution*, 3rd edn (2011), pp.558 et seq.; Stevens [2005] L.M.C.L.Q. 101, *Bowstead and Reynolds on Agency*, 21st edn (2018), art.111.

701   *Kleinwort, Sons & Co v Dunlop Rubber Co* (1907) 97 L.T. 263; *Nizam of Hyderabad v Jung* [1957] Ch. 185 (but see n.702, below).

is a foreign sovereign.[702] Nor will the agent be liable if he has actually paid the money over to his principal without notice of the third person's claim,[703] unless the money was obtained by means of some wrongful act to which the agent was himself a party.[704] But an agent who is relying on the payment over defence must show that he has actually paid his principal or done something equivalent to payment, not merely that he has given him credit[705]; and this will be so even though he has altered his position for the worse by giving the principal further time for the payment of a debt in reliance upon the amount so credited.[706] The cases on this topic antedate the recognition of the defence of change of position in restitution cases[707] and their proper assessment for the present day remains uncertain.[708] Where, however, the agent deals as principal, he is personally liable, and it is no defence for him to prove that he has accounted for or transmitted the money to another.[709]

31-110   The above propositions are well established where the liability to repay arises immediately. But, in general, where money is received by an agent acting within his authority, it is received by the principal and it is the principal who is liable for it.[710] The interaction of these principles is unresolved. At least where the liability arises subsequently, as on a breach of contract, it would seem that the principal is the only defendant (e.g. in an action for the return of a deposit paid under a contract for the sale of land[711]) and the agent is not liable even though he still has the money. Where however the agent acts as pre- or post-contract stakeholder he will be personally liable for failure to comply with his obligations.[712] In a post-contract situation

---

[702] *Rahimtoola v Nizam of Hyderabad* [1958] A.C. 379, 401; reversing *Nizam of Hyderabad v Jung*, above. See now State Immunity Act 1978.

[703] *Buller v Harrison* (1777) Cowp. 565; *Gowers v Lloyds & National Provincial Foreign Bank Ltd* [1938] 1 All E.R. 766; *Australia and New Zealand Banking Group Ltd v Westpac Banking Corp* (1988) 164 C.L.R. 662. But if he recovers the money from his principal he is again liable: *British American Continental Bank v British Bank for Foreign Trade* [1926] 1 K.B. 328.

[704] *Snowdon v Davis* (1808) 1 Taunt. 359; *Sharland v Mildon* (1846) 5 Hare 469; *Keegan v Palmer* [1961] 2 Lloyd's Rep. 449. But not where he cannot be regarded as a party to the wrong: *Owen v Cronk* [1895] 1 Q.B. 265.

[705] *Buller v Harrison*, above; *Holland v Russell* (1863) 4 B. & S. 14; *Kleinwort, Sons & Co v Dunlop Rubber Co* (1907) 97 L.T. 263.

[706] *Scottish Metropolitan Assurance Co Ltd v P Samuel & Co Ltd* [1923] 1 K.B. 348.

[707] *Lipkin Gorman v Karpnale Ltd* [1991] 2 A.C. 548. See Vol.I, paras 29-186 et seq.

[708] See *Australia and New Zealand Banking Group Ltd v Westpac Banking Corp* (1988) 165 C.L.R. 662; *Agip (Africa) Ltd v Jackson* [1990] Ch. 265, 288–289; *Portman Building Society v Hamlyn Taylor Neck* [1998] 4 All E.R. 202, 207.

[709] *Gurney v Womersley* (1854) 4 E. & B. 133; *Royal Exchange Assurance v Moore* (1863) 8 L.T. 242; *Continental Caoutchouc & Gutta Percha Co v Kleinwort* (1904) 90 L.T. 474; *Baylis v Bishop of London* [1913] 1 Ch. 127.

[710] *Ellis v Goulton* [1893] 1 Q.B. 350; *Portman Building Society v Hamlyn Taylor Neck*, above, at 207; *Jones v Churcher* [2009] 2 Lloyd's Rep. 94; *Marsfield Automotive Inc v Siddiqui* [2017] EWHC 187 (Comm).

[711] *Ellis v Goulton*, above (solicitor); but cf. *Elizabeth Wolf v Hosier & Dickinson Ltd* [1981] Com. L.R. 89 (held stakeholder); *Goodey v Garriock* [1972] 2 Lloyd's Rep. 369 (ship broker); *Ojelay v Neosale Ltd* [1987] 2 E.G.L.R. 167. See Burrows, *Law of Restitution*, 3rd edn (2011), 558 et seq.

[712] *Burrough v Skinner* (1770) 5 Burr. 2639; *Edwards v Hodding* (1814) 5 Taunt. 815; *Furtado v Lumley* (1890) 6 T.L.R. 168 (auctioneers); *Eltham v Kingsman* (1818) 1 B. & Ald. 683; *Hampden v Walsh* (1876) 1 Q.B.D. 189 (wagers); *Burt v Claude Cousins & Co Ltd* [1971] 2 Q.B. 426, 435–436; *Potters (A Firm) v Loppert* [1973] Ch. 399, 406 (estate agents); below, para.31-134, n.864. As to the duties of a post-contract stakeholder, see *Rockeagle Ltd v Alsop Wilkinson* [1992] Ch. 47; *Hastingwood Property Ltd v Sanders Bearman Anselm* [1991] Ch. 114; as to a pre-contract stakeholder see *Gribbon v Lutton* [2001] EWCA Civ 1956, [2002] Q.B. 902.

the principal will be liable also[713]; in a pre-contract situation only the agent is liable, unless the principal authorised the receipt of the deposit.[714]

(e) Tort

Agent's liability in tort   In principle an agent is liable for torts which he commits whether or not the principal is liable also. To this extent he does not "drop out" of a transaction as it is often said that he does in a contractual situation. Thus although a principal can be liable for a fraud by an agent committed within the scope of his apparent authority, the agent is also liable.

31-111

"No one can escape liability for his fraud by saying 'I wish to make it clear that I am committing this fraud on behalf of someone else and I am not to be personally liable'."[715]

However, where tortious liability for negligent misrepresentation is involved, it has fairly recently become clear that the agent will only be liable if he can be regarded as having assumed responsibility towards the third party[716]: if he has not, he will not be liable, though if the misrepresentation is within his actual or apparent authority his principal will be, as having made the representation himself.[717] In this respect it can be said that the agent may "drop out", as in contract.[718] There certainly are situations in which an agent is liable to third parties: thus valuers have been held liable to buyers for misrepresentations,[719] and there are some situations in which solicitors acting for vendors have been held to do so,[720] though this is rarer,[721] and older cases may require to be reviewed in the light of the requirement of assumption of responsibility. A recent leading Supreme Court decision[722] concerns solicitors and stresses that for there to be liability under the assumption of responsibility test the agent must have reason to anticipate reliance on his statements, which would of course be true of other agents also and would be affected by the existence of a disclaimer.[723] Although tortious liability to another contracting party is undoubtedly possible, an agent is not liable under s.2 of the Misrepresentation Act

---

[713] See *Annesley v Muggridge* (1816) 1 Madd. 593; *Rowe v May* (1854) 18 Beav. 613 (auctioneers).

[714] *Sorrell v Finch* [1977] A.C. 728. In such a case, the agent must repay the deposit to the prospective purchaser on demand, which suggests that he is better regarded as agent of that party only.

[715] *Standard Chartered Bank v Pakistan National Shipping Corp* [2002] UKHL 43, [2003] 1 A.C. 959 at [22], per Lord Hoffmann (company director).

[716] *Williams v Natural Life Health Foods Ltd* [1998] 1 W.L.R. 830; and see *Fairline Shipping Corp v Adamson* [1975] Q.B. 180. In *Trevor Ivory Ltd v Anderson* [1992] 2 N.Z.L.R. 517 it was suggested that by virtue of the company's incorporation a director excluded personal responsibility, but this is unlikely now to be accepted except where circumstances actually indicate non-assumption of responsibility.

[717] *Williams v Natural Life Health Foods Ltd*, above, at 838; *Standard Chartered Bank v Pakistan National Shipping Corp*, above, at [21]. See above, para.31-075.

[718] But his liability may sometimes be affected by s.6 of the Statute of Frauds Amendment Act 1828 (Lord Tenterden's Act), which requires that representations as to the credit of a third party be in writing. See Vol.I, para.7-043; *Contex Drouzhba Ltd v Wiseman* [2007] EWCA Civ 1201, [2008] 1 B.C.L.C. 631 (signature by director ranked as his own signature as well as that of the company).

[719] e.g. *Merrett v Babb* [2001] EWCA Civ 214, [2001] Q.B. 1174.

[720] See the cases discussed by the Supreme Court in *Steel v NRAM*, below; also a further useful discussion in *P&P Property Ltd v Owen White and Catlin LLP* [2018] EWCA Civ 1082, [2018] P.N.L.R. 29.

[721] cf. e.g. *Gran Gelato Ltd v Richcliff (Group) Ltd* [1992] Ch. 560.

[722] *Steel v NRAM Ltd* [2018] UKSC 13, [2018] 1 W.L.R. 119.

[723] See *McCullagh v Lane Fox Partners Ltd* [1996] 1 E.G.L.R. 35 (estate agent misstating acreage of property).

1967, because he is not a party to the relevant contract.[724] Agents, particularly directors, have been held liable for procuring wrongs by others[725]; but it has been held that an agent is not liable for inducing a breach of contract by his principal.[726] The reasoning supporting this[727] is not convincing, but the rule is well established.[728] Some acts of an agent, at least in respect of property, may rank as ministerial only.[729] An agent may sometimes be able to take the benefit of exclusion and similar clauses in his principal's contract.[730]

8. OBLIGATIONS OF PRINCIPAL AND AGENT INTER SE

(a) Duties of Agents

(i) Common Law: Carrying out Instructions

31-112 **Carrying out instructions and not exceeding authority** If the agent acts under a bilateral contract (which may be of service or for services) he must do what he has undertaken to do[731]; he must, in performance of his duties, carry out any express instructions, whether positive or negative, given to him by his principal, even though he may reasonably believe that in departing from them he would be promoting his principal's interests.[732] If, however, his instructions are susceptible of two meanings, he often may incur no liability if he reasonably interprets them in the sense not intended by the principal.[733] An agent who fails to carry out his instructions also has no right to remuneration, because in such a case he has not earned it.[734] Where the act which the agent is employed to perform is one which by law is

---

[724] *Resolute Maritime Inc v Nippon Kaiji Kyokai (The Skopas)* [1983] 1 W.L.R. 857; *MCI WorldCom International Inc v Primus Telecommunications Inc* [2003] EWHC 2182 (Comm), [2004] 1 All E.R. (Comm) 138.

[725] See *Bowstead and Reynolds on Agency*, 21st edn (2018), para.9-120.

[726] *Said v Butt* [1920] 3 K.B. 497.

[727] Principally that the principal would be liable vicariously for the agent's tort, when what is in issue is his own breach of contract.

[728] *Welsh Development Agency v Export Finance Ltd* [1992] B.C.L.C. 148; cf. *The Leon* [1991] 2 Lloyd's Rep. 611, 623–625.

[729] See discussion in *Standard Chartered Bank v Pakistan National Shipping Corp* [1995] 2 Lloyd's Rep. 365 (signing of false bill of lading not ministerial); *Marcq v Christie, Manson & Woods Ltd* [2003] EWCA Civ 731 (QB), [2004] Q.B. 286.

[730] See Vol.II, paras 15-042 et seq.

[731] *Smith v Lascelles* (1788) 2 T.R. 187; *Barber v Taylor* (1839) 5 M. & W. 527; *Bertram Armstrong & Co v Godfrey* (1830) 1 Kn. 381; *Turpin v Bilton* (1843) 5 M. & G. 455; *LS Harris Trustees Ltd v Power Packing Services (Hermit Road) Ltd* [1970] 2 Lloyd's Rep. 65. But he has no duty to carry out instructions to do anything unlawful: *ABTA v British Airways Plc* [2000] 1 Lloyd's Rep. 169.

[732] *Overend & Gurney Co v Gibb* (1872) L.R. 5 H.L. 480; *Fray v Voules* (1859) 1 El. & El. 839; *The Hermione* [1922] P. 162; *Volkers v Midland Doherty Ltd* (1985) 17 D.L.R. (4th) 343; *RH Deacon & Co Ltd v Varga* (1972) 30 D.L.R. (3d) 653; affirmed (1973) 41 D.L.R. (3d) 767. Where the Commercial Agents (Council Directive) Regulations (above, para.31-017) apply, he must comply with reasonable instructions: reg.3(2)(c). The duty is unexcludable: reg.5. As to the notion of "right of control" see above, para.31-001, n.7.

[733] *Ireland v Livingston* (1872) L.R. 5 H.L. 395; *Weigall v Runciman* (1916) 85 L.J. K.B. 1187; *Larsen v Anglo American Oil Co Ltd* (1924) 20 Ll.L. Rep. 39, 67. See also above, para.31-045.

[734] See, e.g. *Toppin v Healey* (1863) 11 W.R. 466; below, paras 31-148 et seq. For an example of dismissal for abusive conduct towards the principal see *Gledhill v Bentley Designs (UK) Ltd* [2010] EWHC 1965 (QB), [2011] 1 Lloyd's Rep. 270; cf. *Crocs Europe BV v Anderson* [2012] EWCA Civ 1400, [2013] 1 Lloyd's Rep. 1.

void the principal cannot recover damages for the failure to perform it.[735] But an agent acting under a unilateral contract may have no duty to act at all.[736] And a *gratuitous* agent's liability is in tort only: he can only be liable for failure to act in those situations in which he can be regarded as having assumed responsibility.[737]

Authority Equally, an agent must not exceed his authority as described above: if he does so he is liable to his principal for loss caused.[738] This liability is strict as contrasted with the agent's liability in respect of services provided, which is usually for negligence only. Such loss may arise because the principal is unwillingly bound under the doctrine of apparent authority, or because the principal ratifies unwillingly, for example to preserve his commercial reputation. This can usually be explained on the basis of contractual relations between principal and agent, and this may even be so where the agent acts after his authority is terminated.[739] Where, however, one person purports to act for another in circumstances where no conferring of authority or even ratification can be detected, and causes loss to that other, there must presumably be liability to the purported principal in negligence, though such a situation would be rare.[740]   **31-113**

(ii) Common Law: Exercise of Care and Skill

Exercise of care and skill An agent acting under a bilateral contract must exhibit such a degree of skill and diligence as is appropriate to the performance of the duties that he has accepted.[741] In particular, a professional agent must show the degree of care to be expected of those in his profession.[742] But he does not normally   **31-114**

---

[735] *Thomas Cheshire & Co v Vaughan Bros & Co* [1920] 3 K.B. 240 (PPI policy). See further below, paras 31-160, 31-161, 31-163.
[736] Below, para.31-146.
[737] See *Henderson v Merrett Syndicates Ltd* [1995] 2 A.C. 145; *London Borough of Bromley v Ellis* [1971] 1 Lloyd's Rep. 97; *General Accident Fire and Life Insurance Corp v Tanter (The Zephyr)* [1984] 1 W.L.R. 100, [1985] 2 Lloyd's Rep. 529; *Youell v Bland Welch & Co Ltd (the Superhulls Cover Case) (No.2)* [1990] 2 Lloyd's Rep. 431; *Norwest Refrigeration Services Pty Ltd v Bain Dawes (WA) Pty Ltd* (1984) 157 C.L.R. 149. This could apply to the holder of a power of attorney.
[738] e.g. *Fray v Voules* (1859) 1 El. & El. 839.
[739] See *OBG Ltd v Allan* [2007] UKHL 21, [2008] 1 A.C.1 at [93], per Lord Hoffmann, rejecting a view put forward by Mance L.J. in the Court of Appeal that there should be liability in tort. Ratification may here provide the basis for the application of contractual reasoning. See also above, para.31-033.
[740] e.g. *Montrod GmbH v Grundkotter Fleischvertriebs GmbH* [2001] EWCA Civ 1954, [2002] 1 W.L.R. 1975, where an action in negligence was considered. If the person concerned makes a profit by unjustifiably purporting to act as agent he must account for it: *English v Dedham Vale Properties Ltd* [1978] 1 W.L.R. 93. See *Bowstead and Reynolds on Agency*, 21st edn (2018), para.6-003; Watts (2009) 17 Torts L.J. 100. The "agent" could be liable to *third party* for breach of warranty of authority; above, para.31-100.
[741] *Harmer v Cornelius* (1858) 5 C.B.(N.S.) 236; *Lee v Walker* (1872) L.R. 7 C.P. 121; *Commonwealth Portland Cement Co v Weber* [1905] A.C. 66; *Weld-Blundell v Stephens* [1920] A.C. 956; *Lage v Siemens Bros Co Ltd* (1932) 42 Ll.L. Rep. 252; *Cyril Andrade Ltd v Sotheby & Co* (1931) 47 T.L.R. 244. He may also be liable in tort: *Henderson v Merrett Syndicates Ltd*, above; *BP Plc v Aon Ltd (No.2)* [2006] EWHC 424 (Comm), [2006] 1 All E.R. (Comm) 789. But the duty is a general one and though it may diminish, does not expand to meet the particular contract duty: *Aiken v Stewart Wrightson Members Agency Ltd* [1995] 2 Lloyd's Rep. 618. See above, Vol.I, paras 1-184 et seq.
[742] *Lanphier v Phipos* (1838) 8 C. & P. 475; *Lee v Walker* (1872) L.R. 7 C.P. 121; *Simmons v Pennington & Son* [1955] 1 W.L.R. 183; *Lister v Romford Ice and Cold Storage Co Ltd* [1957] A.C. 555, 572–573; cf. *Luxmoore May v Messenger May Baverstock* [1990] 1 W.L.R. 1009, especially at 1020

guarantee results,[743] is not responsible to his principal for a mere mistake or error of judgment, not amounting to a failure to exercise proper care or skill,[744] and the mere fact that by a different course of action he might have averted a loss sustained by his principal is not of itself evidence of such a failure.[745]

31-115 Due care for principal's interests Where the agent has a discretion to exercise, he must exercise it honestly, with due care and in his principal's interests.[746] An agent must, in general, keep his principal fully informed[747] and must act with the necessary amount of speed and diligence.[748] If the agent cannot carry out his instructions he must normally inform the principal without delay.[749] Where an agent is employed to sell property, his duty does not cease when he has procured an offer of purchase which is accepted subject to contract; until final contracts have been signed he remains under a duty to inform the vendor of any better offer which he may receive.[750] He must also inform his principal of anything coming to his knowledge which is likely to influence the principal in the making of the contract.[751]

31-116 Disclosure of misdoing It is usually said that a failure by the agent to disclose his own misdoings is not in itself a breach of contract,[752] so that an employee negotiating for severance is not bound, in the absence of fraud, to disclose such breaches of duty as would have given the employer the opportunity of dismissing

---

(provincial auctioneer: suggestion that standard of London specialist auctioneer should be higher). Where the Commercial Agents (Council Directive) Regulations (above, para.31-017) apply, he must make proper efforts to negotiate and conclude transactions: reg.3(2)(a).

[743] See e.g. *Bieber v Teathers Ltd* [2012] EWHC 190 (Ch), [2012] B.C.L.C. 585 at [86] ("An investor cannot say that a stockbroker is authorised only to make successful investments"), affirmed [2012] EWCA Civ 1466, [2013] 1 B.C.L.C. 248; but strict liability is sometimes undertaken—cf. *Platform Funding Ltd v Bank of Scotland* [2008] EWCA Civ 930, [2009] Q.B. 426 (surveyor); *Martin v JRC Commercial Mortgages Plc* [2012] EWCA Civ 63, [2012] P.N.L.R. 8 (fixed fee mortgage broker); *Salkeld Investments v West 1 Loans Ltd* [2012] EWHC 2701 (QB) (arranger of packages and bridging finance).

[744] See *Comber v Anderson* (1808) 1 Camp. 523; *Nitrate Producers' Co v Wills* (1905) 21 T.L.R. 699; *Stafford v Conti Commodity Services Ltd* [1981] 1 Lloyd's Rep. 466; *Whitehouse v Jordan* [1981] 1 W.L.R. 246.

[745] *Commonwealth Portland Cement Co v Weber* [1905] A.C. 66.

[746] *Gokal Chand-Jagan Nath v Nand Ram Das-Atma Ram* [1939] A.C. 106; *Morten v Hilton* [1937] 2 K.B. 176n. This comes within the fringe of the agent's fiduciary liability or duty of loyalty: see below, para.31-118. See also above, para.31-036.

[747] *Sill v Thomas* (1839) 8 Car. & P. 762; *Johnson v Kearley* [1908] 2 K.B. 514; *Dunton Properties Ltd v Coles, Knapp v Kennedy* [1959] E.G.D. 221. Where the Commercial Agents (Council Directive) Regulations (above, para.31-017) apply, he must communicate "all the necessary information" to his principal: reg.3(2)(b). The duty is unexcludable: reg.5. See also *Fairstar Heavy Transport NV v Adkins* [2013] EWCA Civ 886, [2013] 2 C.L.C. 272 (order on termination of appointment of Chief Executive to give access to emails).

[748] *Callander v Oelrichs* (1838) 5 Bing. N.C. 58; *Barber v Taylor* (1839) 5 M. & W. 527; *Potter v Equitable Bank* (1921) 8 Ll.L. Rep. 291, 332; *World Transport Agency Ltd v Royte (England) Ltd* [1957] 1 Lloyd's Rep. 381.

[749] *Salvesen & Co v Rederi A/B Nordstjernan* [1905] A.C. 302; *Hood v West End Motor Car Packing Co* [1917] 2 K.B. 38, 47; *Youell v Bland Welch & Co (the Superhulls Cover Case) (No.2)* [1990] 2 Lloyd's Rep. 431, 446–447. This principle may sometimes apply to gratuitous agents.

[750] *Keppel v Wheeler* [1927] 1 K.B 577.

[751] *Heath v Parkinson* (1926) 42 T.L.R. 693.

[752] *Healey v Societe Anonyme Francaise Rubastic* [1917] 1 K.B. 946; *University of Nottingham v Fishel* [2000] I.C.R. 1462.

him.[753] But it has been held that an employee may sometimes be under a duty to disclose breaches of duty by *other* employees[754] and also that outside the above context a director, as a fiduciary owing a duty of loyalty, may come under a duty to disclose his own breaches that have ongoing relevance to the principal's business[755]: it may be that a senior employee would also.[756]

Gratuitous agents   It used to be said that a gratuitous agent (whose liability, as **31-117** stated above, lies only in tort) owes duties of a different type: he is only liable for the care which he exercises in his own affairs.[757] But such categorisation, even if the test is interpreted objectively,[758] has long seemed obsolete: and it has more recently been said that the appropriate standard is that which might reasonably be expected in the circumstances.[759] On this basis the difference between such an agent and one who is paid becomes one of degree only.

(iii)   Equity: Fiduciary Duties and Duties of Loyalty[760]

Fiduciary duties and duties of loyalty   An agent, where he undertakes to act for **31-118** another in circumstances giving rise to a relationship of trust and confidence, owes fiduciary duties derived from Equity to prefer his principal's interests to his own.[761] Although there are dicta which might appear to indicate that the fiduciary duties are

---

753 *Bell v Lever Bros Ltd* [1932] A.C. 161, 228.

754 *Sybron Corp v Rochem Ltd* [1984] Ch. 112.

755 *Item Software (UK) Ltd v Fassihi* [2004] EWCA Civ 1244, [2005] 2 B.C.L.C. 91 (not followed in Australia in *P & V Industries Pty Ltd v Porto* [2006] VSC 131 and said in *Stupples v Stupples & Co (High Wycombe) Ltd* [2012] EWHC 1226 (Ch), [2013] 1 B.C.L.C. 729 at [59] to concern directors).

756 This depends to some extent on whether the duty is fiduciary or specific to directors and perhaps certain employees. See *Bowstead and Reynolds on Agency*, 21st edn (2018), para.6-054; Berg (2005) 121 L.Q.R. 213; Flannigan [2006] Bus. L.Rev. 258 (Canada); Ho and Lee [2007] C.L.J. 348; Watts (2007) 123 L.Q.R. 21.

757 *Wilson v Brett* (1843) 11 M. & W. 113; *Beal v S Devon Ry* (1864) 3 Hurl. & C. 337; *Grill v General Iron Screw Collier Co* (1866) L.R. 1 C.P. 600, 612; *Giblin v McMullen* (1868) L.R. 2 P.C. 317, 336; *Moffat v Bateman* (1869) L.R. 3 P.C. 115.

758 As in *Gomer v Pitt & Scott* (1922) 12 Ll.L. Rep. 115.

759 *Chaudhry v Prabhakar* [1989] 1 W.L.R. 29, following dicta in *Houghland v RR Low (Luxury Coaches) Ltd* [1962] 1 Q.B. 694, 698 (which were also followed in *Avery v Salie* (1972) 25 D.L.R. (3d) 495). Quaere, however, if there should have been a duty of care in *Chaudry's* case at all: this was conceded. See pp.38–39.

760 See in general Goff and Jones, *Law of Restitution*, 7th edn (2007), Ch.33 (not in later editions); Finn, *Fiduciary Obligations* (1977, republ. 2016), Pt II; *Snell's Equity*, 33rd edn (2015), Ch.7; *Bowstead and Reynolds on Agency*, 21st edn (2018), arts 43–51. The fiduciary duties of directors are now prescribed by statute: see Companies Act 2006 Pt 10 Ch.2.

761 For an example where there was no relevant duty see *Halton International Inc (Holdings) SARL v Guernroy Ltd* [2005] EWHC 1968 (Ch), [2006] 1 B.C.L.C. 78 (power of attorney to vote shares); affirmed [2006] EWCA Civ 801, [2006] W.T.L.R. 1241; and *John Youngs Insurance Services Ltd v Aviva Insurance Service UK Ltd* [2011] EWHC 1515 (TCC) (claims handling and building repair services: agency services fiduciary but not other services in same contract). Where the Commercial Agents Regulations (above, para.31-017) apply the agent must act "dutifully and in good faith": reg.3(1). The duty is unexcludable: reg.5. Arguments on the basis of good faith were rejected in *Smith v Reliance Water Controls Ltd* [2003] Eu. L.R. 874 and *Monk v Largo Foods Ltd* [2016] EWHC 1837 (Comm) (on the power to terminate). There may be criminal liability under the Fraud Act 2006, especially s.4: see discussion in *Cavell USA Inc v Seaton Insurance Co* [2009] EWCA Civ 1363, [2009] 2 C.L.C. 991 at [25].

based entirely on the contract between principal and agent[762] it is fairly well established that they are separate[763] (though not without overlap) and to some extent counterbalance the stricter rules on implication of contract terms at common law. In any case, not all agents act under a contract.[764] These duties are sometimes subsumed into the wider phrase "duties of loyalty", some of which are positive duties, though taking in the two basic fiduciary duties imposed by equity and discussed below, that of avoiding conflicts of interest and that of not profiting from position, which are themselves negative only and thus can be said to be prophylactic in operation.[765] Breach of these duties generally entails deliberate, not negligent acts.[766] But the two basic duties referred to above and explained below operate strictly, without proof of intentional wrongdoing, or even fault.

31-119 The equitable duties can be regarded as a weaker extension to agents of some (but not all) the restrictions imposed on express trustees; but they can also be regarded as stemming from more central principles of equity, and were (and are) also applied to others in analogous positions such as partners, directors and company promoters. They therefore vary with the function involved; it has been said that "The precise scope of the obligation must be moulded according to the nature of the relationship".[767]

31-120 **Summary of fiduciary duties** It is relevant at this point to quote a useful summary concerning the duty of loyalty and the fiduciary:

> "The distinguishing obligation of a fiduciary is the obligation of loyalty. The principal is entitled to the single-minded loyalty of his fiduciary. This core liability has several facets. A fiduciary must act in good faith; he must not make a profit out of his trust; he must not place himself in a position where his duty and his interest may conflict; he may not act for his own benefit of the benefit of a third person without the informed consent of his principal. This is not intended to be an exhaustive list, but it is sufficient to indicate the nature of fiduciary obligations."[768]

31-121 **Conflict of interest** A general principle,[769] is that as a fiduciary, an agent must not, without first obtaining the informed consent of his principal, put himself in a position where his duty to his principal conflicts[770] or may conflict[771] with his own

---

[762] *Kelly v Cooper* [1993] A.C. 205, 213–214; and see *Clark Boyce v Mouat* [1994] 1 A.C. 428, 437.

[763] *Re Goldcorp Exchange Ltd* [1995] 1 A.C. 74, 98.

[764] Above, para.31-117; and see *Conway v Ratiu* [2005] EWCA Civ 1302, [2006] 1 All E.R. 571.

[765] This is the basis of a distinctive approach by Conaglen, *Fiduciary Loyalty* (2010); see also Flannigan (2006) 122 L.Q.R. 449. But for a different view see Heydon (2014) 20 *Trusts and Trustees* 1006. Analysis on the basis of positive duties is supported by the law concerning trustees; and it has the advantage of taking in certain duties, which can be described as relating to a "fraud on a power", which require fiduciaries undoubtedly acting within their authority nevertheless to take into account the interests of their principals in certain ways: see *Bowstead and Reynolds on Agency*, 21st edn (2018), para.8-220.

[766] *Bristol & West BS v Mothew* [1998] Ch. 1, 19.

[767] *New Zealand Netherlands Society "Oranje" Inc v Kuys* [1973] 1 W.L.R. 1126, 1130 per Lord Wilberforce.

[768] *Bristol & West BS v Mothew* [1998] Ch. 1, 18, per Millett L.J. This is (part of) a famous exposition, but not everyone agrees with the result of the case itself: see Heydon, above, n.765.

[769] See *Lewin on Trusts*, 19th edn (2014), para.20-001; *Bowstead and Reynolds on Agency*, 21st edn (2018), art.44; *Chan v Zacharia* (1984) 154 C.L.R. 178, 198–199.

[770] See below; and generally *Re Cape Breton Co* (1885) 29 Ch. D. 795, 811; affirmed on other grounds sub nom. *Cavendish-Bentinck v Fenn* (1887) 12 App. Cas. 652; *Aberdeen Ry v Blaikie Bros* (1854) 1 Macq. 461; *Bray v Ford* [1896] A.C. 44; *Phipps v Boardman* [1967] 2 A.C. 46; *Industrial Develop-*

interests or the interests of another principal.[772] An injunction may often be obtained against an agent who is or may be in such a position.[773] Any benefit or gain made in circumstances where a conflict or significant possibility of conflict existed must be accounted for to the principal.[774] A principal who has full knowledge of the facts may however assent to the agent's acts[775]; and sometimes his instructions may be so specific as to leave the agent with no discretion, and hence to exclude this rule.[776]

Secret profit[777]   A further consequence of the agent's fiduciary position is that un-   **31-122**
less he fully informs his principal and obtains his consent,[778] he may not use his position as agent,[779] including his principal's property[780] or confidential information,[781] to make a profit for himself. He must account to the principal for any profit so made.[782] Thus an auctioneer appointed to sell goods at a lump sum commission plus out-of-pocket expenses charged his principal with the gross cost of expenses without revealing that he had trade discounts. He was held liable to his principal

---

     ment Consultants Ltd v Cooley [1972] 1 W.L.R. 443; *Canadian Aero Services Ltd v O'Malley* [1974] S.C.R. 592, (1973) 40 D.L.R. (3d) 371; cf. *Peso Silver Mines Ltd v Cropper* [1966] S.C.R. 673, (1966) 58 D.L.R. (2d) 1. And see Estate Agents Act 1979 s.21.

[771] See *Anglo-African Merchants Ltd v Bayley* [1970] 1 Q.B. 311; *North & South Trust Co v Berkeley* [1971] 1 W.L.R. 470; *Farrington v Rowe McBride & Partners* [1985] 1 N.Z.L.R. 83; *Clark Boyce v Mouat* [1994] 1 A.C. 428. Requirements of disclosure are imposed on estate agents by the Estate Agents (Provision of Information) Regulations 1991 (SI 1991/859) reg.2. See also Estate Agents (Undesirable Practices) (No.2) Order 1991 (SI 1991/1032); Consumer Protection from Unfair Trading Regulations 2008 (SI 2008/277). Exemptions are made by s.70 of the Enterprise and Regulatory Reform Act 2013. See also Consumer Rights Act 2015 ss.83 et seq. (letting agents).

[772] cf. above, para.31-040 (no actual incapacity); see also below, para.31-125.

[773] The majority of the cases concern confidential information possessed by accountants and solicitors: see *Prince Jefri Bolkiah v KPMG* [1999] 2 A.C. 222; below, para.31-122, n.781.

[774] See below, para.31-130; *Chan v Zacharia* (1984) 154 C.L.R. 178, 198–199; *Imageview Management Ltd v Jack* [2009] EWCA Civ 63, [2009] 1 Lloyd's Rep. 436 (a strong application of the rule; see Watts (2009) 125 L.Q.R. 369 and below, para.31-161). The case is followed in *Rahme v Smith & Williamson Trust Corp Ltd* [2009] EWHC 911 (Ch). As to account of profits, see below, para.31-130.

[775] *Cavendish-Bentinck v Fenn* (1887) 12 App. Cas. 652: *Queensland Mines Ltd v Hudson* (1978) 52 A.L.J.R. 399, PC. But the knowledge must be full: see *Hurstanger Ltd v Wilson* [2007] EWCA Civ 299, [2007] 1 W.L.R. 235.

[776] See *Dalgety & Co Ltd v Gray* (1919) 26 C.L.R. 249, 256, PC (loan to principal); *RH Deacon & Co Ltd v Varga* (1972) 30 D.L.R. (3d) 653; affirmed (1973) 41 D.L.R. (3d) 767 (stockbroker); *Volkers v Midland Doherty Ltd* (1985) 17 D.L.R. (4th) 343.

[777] See *Bowstead and Reynolds on Agency*, 21st edn (2018), arts 46 and 47; Conaglen, *Fiduciary Loyalty*, Ch.5.

[778] *Re Haslam* [1902] 1 Ch. 765; *Queensland Mines Ltd v Hudson* (1978) 52 A.L.J.R. 399, PC.

[779] *Cook v Deeks* [1916] 1 A.C. 554; *Tarkwa Main Reef v Merton* (1903) 19 T.L.R. 367; *Regal (Hastings) Ltd v Gulliver* [1942] 1 All E.R. 378, [1967] 2 A.C. 134n.; *Reading v Att-Gen* [1951] A.C. 507; *Phipps v Boardman* [1967] 2 A.C. 46; cf. *NZ Netherlands Society "Oranje" Inc v Kuys* [1973] 1 W.L.R. 1126.

[780] *Shallcross v Oldham* (1862) 2 Johns. & H. 609; *Parker v McKenna* (1874) L.R. 10 Ch. App. 96; *Morison v Thompson* (1874) L.R. 9 Q.B. 480.

[781] *Regal (Hastings) Ltd v Gulliver*, above; *Seager v Copydex Ltd* [1967] 1 W.L.R. 923; *Phipps v Boardman*, above; *Schering Chemicals Ltd v Falkman Ltd* [1982] Q.B. 1; *Prince Jefri Bolkiah v KPMG* [1999] 2 A.C. 222. But this is really an application of a wider principle. See Millett (1998) 114 L.Q.R. 214, 220–221; Goff and Jones, *Law of Restitution*, 7th edn (2007), Ch.34 (not in later editions); *Bowstead and Reynolds on Agency*, 21st edn (2018), para.6-077; Gurry, *Breach of Confidence* 2nd edn (2012).

[782] See below, para.31-130.

for the amount of the discounts.[783] A more extreme case is *Reading v Att-Gen*,[784] where an army sergeant was held accountable to the Crown for sums which he had illegally made in the Egyptian black market by using his rank and uniform to ensure that the trucks on which he was travelling were not searched by military police. A secret commission can be in kind.[785]

31-123 It is not relevant that the principal has suffered no loss,[786] nor that the agent has himself been at risk.[787] Thus in the perhaps extreme case of *Phipps v Boardman*[788] self-appointed "agents"[789] to a trust used the trust's position as a shareholder in the company gradually to gain control of the company and ultimately to make a profit for themselves as well as the trust. They were held liable to account to the trust for their personal profit (though with an allowance for work done), notwithstanding that the trust had not been at risk, and that the persons concerned might have made a loss and had been acting bona fide throughout. It is no defence to the principal's claim that the profit was made by means of a fraud on a third party, nor that the agent may have rendered himself liable to a third party.[790] Although in general the fiduciary duties end when the relationship of agency ends,[791] the agent's duty not to misuse his position or the property or information of his principal may extend beyond the period of the agency.[792]

31-124 **Self-dealing**[793] There is also much authority that an agent employed to buy may not be the seller himself, even though he sells at the market price,[794] nor may an

---

[783] *Hippisley v Knee Brothers* [1905] 1 K.B. 1.

[784] [1951] A.C. 507.

[785] *Fiona Trust & Holding Corp v Privalov* [2010] EWHC 3199 (Comm) (free holiday); and *Towers v Premier Waste Management Ltd* [2011] EWCA Civ 923, [2012] 1 B.C.L.C. 67 (use of equipment).

[786] *Parker v McKenna* (1874) L.R. 10 Ch. App. 96; *De Bussche v Alt* (1878) 8 Ch. D. 286; *Reid-Newfoundland Co v Anglo-American Telegraph Co* [1912] A.C. 555; *Phipps v Boardman* [1967] 2 A.C. 46.

[787] *Burrell v Mossop* (1888) 4 T.L.R. 270; *Williams v Stevens* (1866) L.R. 1 P.C. 352.

[788] [1967] 2 A.C. 46; see also *O'Sullivan v Management Agency and Music Ltd* [1985] Q.B. 428. An extension of this principle, often called the "corporate opportunity" doctrine, is to be found in cases where agents whose functions include locating assets or business opportunities, or who have assumed management functions in the principal's business affairs, proceed to acquire them for themselves. A striking example is *Re Bhullar Bros* [2003] EWCA Civ 424, [2003] 3 B.C.L.C. 241. Much of the authority occurs in connection with corporations. See *Bowstead and Reynolds on Agency*, 21st edn (2018), paras 6-080, 6-081.

[789] For a clearer example of a person acting as an agent without any relevant preceding relationship see *English v Dedham Vale Properties Ltd* [1978] 1 W.L.R. 93 (though the case is on the fringes of ratification doctrine).

[790] *Jubilee Cotton Mills v Lewis* [1924] A.C. 958.

[791] See *Bowstead and Reynolds on Agency*, 21st edn (2018), para.6-038.

[792] *Carter v Palmer* (1842) 8 Cl. & F. 657; *Regier v Campbell-Stuart* [1939] Ch. 766; *Longstaff v Birtles* [2001] EWCA Civ 1219, [2002] 1 W.L.R. 470. See also *CMS Dolphin Ltd v Simonet* [2001] 2 B.C.L.C. 704. Compare the unusual case of *Nordisk Insulinlaboratorium v Gorgate Products Ltd* [1953] Ch. 430, where no information was acquired and the agents used their position only by virtue of special provisions relating to alien enemies. It will usually be in relation to confidential information that the agent's duty will continue after termination of the agency contract: see, e.g. *Lamb v Evans* [1893] 1 Ch. 218; *Robb v Green* [1895] 2 Q.B. 315; *Prince Jefri Bolkiah v KPMG* [1999] 2 A.C. 222.

[793] See *Bowstead and Reynolds on Agency*, 21st edn (2018), art.45; Conaglen, *Fiduciary Loyalty* (2010), pp.126–128; Goff and Jones, *Law of Unjust Enrichment*, 8th edn (2011), paras 8-102 et seq. This is referred to separately in *Bristol & West B.S. v Mothew* [1998] Ch. 1, 19.

[794] e.g. *Massey v Davies* (1794) 2 Ves. Jr. 317; *Bentley v Craven* (1853) 18 Beav. 75; *Armstrong v Jackson* [1917] 2 K.B. 822; *Headway Construction Co Ltd v Downham* (1974) 233 E.G. 675. The

agent appointed to sell buy the property himself.[795] However fair the transaction, it may be set aside by the principal,[796] unless the agent had made full disclosure of all the material facts and the nature and extent of his interest and obtained his principal's consent or unless the principal subsequently waives the breach of duty.[797] It is not sufficient that the agent has put his principal on inquiry; moreover the burden of proving full disclosure lies on the agent.[798] The agent's good faith is not material.[799] So, where a large trading company which carried on separately an estate agency and a building business was employed, through its estate agency, to sell property and subsequently, through its building department, inspected the drains on behalf of the purchaser, it was held that it had committed a breach of duty.[800] An orthodox view of the cases is to the effect that the basic remedy here is rescission, and that other remedies are not often available except incidentally. Thus it is said that an agent selling to his principal is only liable for a secret profit if he acquired the property in question while owing fiduciary duties, and so would be liable for it under general principles[801]; and there are comparatively few cases holding agents who buy from their principals liable to account for profits made, usually where rescission is impossible or inappropriate.[802] It can, however, be argued that the application of a more general right to equitable compensation is often as appropriate to breaches of these duties as it is to those of other fiduciary duties.[803]

Conflict of duty and duty[804]   Sometimes the agent finds himself in a position **31-125** where his duty to one principal actually conflicts with his duty to another. He may then be in breach of duty to one by acting with the intention of furthering the interest of the other at the expense of the first; or by failure to disclose to one information relevant to him—information which he would be in breach of duty to the other in disclosing without consent. Here he is unlikely to make a profit at the expense of either, but may well cause loss for which he may be liable at common law in tort or in breach of contract[805]; but sometimes an action may lie in equity.[806] He may also in appropriate cases be restrained by injunction. He must serve each as faithfully

---

remedies available differ in accordance with how the agent acquired the property: see *Walden Properties Ltd v Beaver Properties Pty Ltd* [1973] 2 N.S.W.L.R. 815, 835–837.

[795] e.g. *McPherson v Watt* (1877) 3 App. Cas. 254; *Dunne v English* (1874) L.R. 18 Eq. 524.

[796] *Aberdeen Ry v Blaikie Bros* (1854) 1 Macq. 461; *Transvaal Lands Co v New Belgium (Transvaal) Land & Development Co* [1914] 2 Ch. 488. cf. *Connolly v Brown* (2006) 207 S.L.T. 778. See below, para.31-128.

[797] The rule for express trustees is stricter.

[798] *Dunne v English* (1874) L.R. 18 Eq. 524; *JD Wetherspoon Plc v Van de Berg & Co Ltd* [2009] EWHC 639 (Ch).

[799] *Phipps v Boardman* [1967] 2 A.C. 46.

[800] *Harrods Ltd v Lemon* [1931] 2 K.B. 157. See also *Standard Investments Ltd v Canadian Imperial Bank of Commerce* (1988) 22 D.L.R. (4th) 410. cf. *John Youngs Insurance Services Ltd v Aviva Insurance Service UK Ltd* [2011] EWHC 1515 (TCC), [2012] 1 All E.R. (Comm) 1045 (principal aware of collateral services provided).

[801] The case usually cited is *Re Cape Breton Co* (1885) 29 Ch. D. 795; affirmed sub nom. *Cavendish-Bentinck v Fenn* (1887) 12 App. Cas. 652.

[802] e.g. *McKenzie v MacDonald* [1927] V.L.R. 134; and see *JJ Harrison (Properties) Ltd v Harrison* [2001] 1 B.C.L.C. 158.

[803] See Conaglen (2003) 119 L.Q.R. 246; below, para.31-131.

[804] See *Bowstead and Reynolds on Agency*, 21st edn (2018). paras 6-048 et seq.; Conaglen (2009) 125 L.Q.R. 111.

[805] See *Hilton v Barker-Booth and Eastwood* [2005] UKHL 8, [2005] 1 W.L.R. 567 (solicitor: irreconcilable duties to two clients: damages in contract); *Marks & Spencer Plc v Freshfields Bruckhaus Deringer* [2004] EWCA Civ 741, [2005] P.N.L.R. 4; affirming [2004] EWHC 1337, [2005] 1 W.L.R. 2331 (different transactions); *HIH Casualty and General Insurance Ltd v JLT Risk Solutions Ltd*

and loyally as if he were his only principal,[807] and if he cannot do this he may need to resign one or both of his commitments.

However, where the agent is of a type known to act for many parties (e.g. an estate agent) it may be held that the situation is impliedly assented to by his principals and that there is no breach of duty.[808] There has as yet been little judicial consideration of the conflicts that might arise from the prospect of an agent obtaining future business from the counterparty of his principal.[809]

31-126 **Exclusion of liability**[810] Especially in the financial world, clauses may be inserted in contracts with persons who would in normal speech be called agents, e.g. stockbrokers, whereby the "agent" indicates that he may act in ways which would normally be inconsistent with the fiduciary duties, e.g. that he may without disclosure sell to his principal shares which he owns. Such clauses may be valid as making disclosure to the principal and hence satisfying the fiduciary obligation, or as indicating a contractual variation of the contract terms which would normally be implied.[811] It is however submitted that where the clause is potentially inconsistent with the nature of the relationship apparently undertaken, it must very clearly show that the relationship is other than what would be expected, in such a way as to enable the principal to make an informed choice whether to use the services of the person concerned.[812] Such clauses may also be subject to the Unfair Contract Terms Act 1977[813] and subject to the requirement of reasonableness. It would seem that compliance with the requirements of a regulatory body should be evidence, but not (in the absence of a statutory provisions deciding the question) conclusive evidence, of reasonableness[814]: such bodies cannot be, unless expressly, empowered to dispense with the general law relating to fiduciaries.

[2007] EWCA Civ 710, [2007] 2 Lloyd's Rep. 278 (insurance broker not liable in negligence).

[806] e.g. an action for an account of profits, equitable compensation, or rescission. See *North & West Trust Co v Berkeley* [1971] 1 W.L.R. 470, 484–485.

[807] *Bristol & West BS v Mothew* [1998] Ch. 1, 19, per Millett L.J.

[808] *Kelly v Cooper* [1993] A.C. 205 (estate agent) as explained in *Prince Jefri Bolkiah v KPMG* [1999] 2 A.C. 222, 235; and see *Bristol & West BS v Mothew* [1998] Ch. 1. But it is submitted that some of the dicta in *Kelly v Cooper* are too wide. See above, para.31-118. As to solicitors, see above, para.31-013. The leading cases mostly concern single practitioners and small firms. For further developments of the problems arising in larger organisations see Finn in McKendrick (ed.), *Commercial Aspects of Trusts and Fiduciary Obligations* (1992), Ch.1, pp.15–36. It is certainly doubtful whether such reasoning could apply where the Commercial Agents Regulations (above, para.31-017) are operative: see regs 3(1), 5(1).

[809] See *Dennard v PricewaterhouseCoopers LLP* [2010] EWHC 812 (Ch) at [213]–[221]; *Premium Real Estate Ltd v Stevens* [2009] 2 N.Z.L.R. 384.

[810] See *Bowstead and Reynolds on Agency*, 21st edn (2018), para.6-056.

[811] Some extremely strong exclusions have been assumed to be valid unless statute intervenes. See *Spread Trustee Co Ltd v Hutcheson* [2011] UKPC 13, [2012] 2 A.C. 194, PC.

[812] See *Farrington v Rowe McBride & Partners* [1985] 1 N.Z.L.R. 83, 92–93. But cf. *Hayim v Citibank NA* [1987] A.C. 730 (clause reducing executor's liability to beneficiaries); *Armitage v Nurse* [1998] Ch. 241 (trustee); *Bogg v Raper* [1998] T.L.R. 249, CA (solicitor drafting will entitled to benefit of clause limiting liability); *Citibank NA v MBIA Assurance SA* [2006] EWHC 3215 (Ch), [2007] 1 All E.R. (Comm) 1219; noted by Trukhtanov (2007) 123 L.Q.R. 342; *Australian Securities and Investments Commission v Citigroup Global Markets Australia Pty Ltd* (2007) 62 A.C.S.R 427.

[813] s.3, especially s.3(2)(b)(i); and in consumer cases Consumer Rights Act 2015 Pt 2. See Vol.I, paras 15-084 et seq.

[814] In this connection, the extent of the wide powers conferred by Pt 9A of the Financial Services and Markets Act 2000 as amended by the Financial Services Act 2012 is open to question. The regulatory authority is at present the Financial Conduct Authority.

(iv) Remedies

Common law Breaches of the common law or equitable duties may justify   **31-127**
dismissal of the agent (where this is relevant), and also disentitle him to remuneration and/or indemnity.[815] Damages may be recoverable either for breach of contract
or in tort. A gratuitous agent cannot, of course, be liable in contract, but he may
sometimes be liable in tort.[816] The same may be true of an agent who simply
introduces business, for he may have no contractual liability towards his principal.[817]
Where there is a contractual relationship between principal and agent the agent's
breach of duty will generally sound in contract; but where there is a duty of care
there is also liability in tort.[818] If the equitable duties have been complied with, the
action is in effect a common law one, and no different results are obtained by
designating it as one for breach of fiduciary duty.[819] The contractual measure of
damages for breach of duty on the part of the agent is the loss sustained by the
principal which is within the contemplation of the parties at the time when the
contract was made.[820] An action in negligence would render the defendant liable for
foreseeable loss caused by the negligence.[821] The effects of limitation might be different, and the Law Reform (Contributory Negligence) Act 1945 would more easily apply. But even in a contract action the liability may sometimes be simply for
loss caused. Thus where agents incorrectly represented to their principals that they
had made a contract on their behalf, it was held that the principals could only
recover the loss actually sustained by them in consequence of the misrepresentation, and not the profits that they would have made if the representation had been
true.[822] A principal who is induced, by the negligence of his agent, to enter into an
adventure from which loss ensues is entitled to recover from the agent the amount
he has actually lost plus compensation for loss of time.[823] If estate agents, after
procuring an offer for their principal which he accepts subject to contract, fail to
inform him of a later higher offer, they may be liable for the difference between the
price agreed with the first offeror and the second offer.[824]

Equity: injunction and rescission An injunction may be available to restrain an   **31-128**
agent from acting contrary to his fiduciary duties. Conspicuous examples concern
accountants and solicitors who act for both parties to a transaction, or have
knowledge from an earlier transaction about a party against whom they are acting
or may act. Claims that such clashes are eliminated by the setting up of "Chinese
walls" within a firm are not always accepted.[825] Rescission is in principle available as between principal and fiduciary where the agent's fiduciary duties (for

---

[815] See above, para.31-073; below, paras 31-161, 31-163.
[816] Above, paras 31-112, 31-117.
[817] e.g. *Cherry Ltd v Allied Insurance Brokers Ltd* [1978] 1 Lloyd's Rep. 274 (insurance broker); but
cf. *Kenney v Hall, Pain & Foster* [1976] E.G.D. 629 (estate agent).
[818] *Henderson v Merrett Syndicates Ltd* [1995] 2 A.C. 145. See Vol.I, paras 1-162 et seq. This may be
relevant in the assessment of damages; as to limitation; as to jurisdiction, and other matters.
[819] *Bristol & West BS v Mothew* [1998] Ch. 1, 17. Contra, Heydon (2014) 20 *Trusts and Trustees* 1006.
[820] *C Czarnikow Ltd v Koufos (The Heron II)* [1969] 1 A.C. 350. See Vol.I, Ch.26.
[821] *The Wagon Mound* [1961] A.C. 388. See Vol.I, para.1-193.
[822] *Salvesen & Co v Rederi A/B Nordstjernan* [1905] A.C. 302 (ship brokers).
[823] *Johnston v Braham* [1917] 1 K.B. 586 (theatrical agent). It has been held that insurance brokers who
act negligently may be liable to a client in respect of damages not covered by insurance, and fines
for driving while uninsured: *Osman v J Ralph Moss Ltd* [1970] 1 Lloyd's Rep. 313.
[824] *Keppel v Wheeler* [1927] 1 K.B. 577.
[825] e.g. *Prince Jefri Bolkiah v KPMG* [1999] 2 A.C. 222; *Bowstead & Reynolds on Agency*, 21st edn

example as to self-dealing, accepting bribes or secret commissions, or acting also for the third party to a relevant transaction) have been broken; and between principal and third party where such duties have been broken and the third party is or should be aware of the position. The normal limits on the right to rescind apply.[826]

31-129 **Equity: duty to account and restitution of the trust estate**   Equity provides much of the reasoning in this area, substantive as well as remedial, and must be invoked when a claim is in respect of one of the equitable duties and is not simply a common law claim for breach of contract or negligence.[827] The remedy to which general reference is usually made is that of a duty to account, though some of the technical terminology within this is more relevant to the procedure accompanying the taking of an account against a trustee, and the modern approach is to look more to substantive general principles.[828] To the extent that an agent is in possession or control of the principal's money or funds as trustee and misapplies them, equity will both require the agent personally to restore the trust fund and will also give proprietary remedies to the extent that the moneys or their traceable substitutes are identifiable in the agent's or a third party's hands, subject to applicable defences that the third party may have.[829] Where such remedies are applicable, there would be consequences as regards limitation, for by virtue of s.21(1)(b) of the Limitation Act 1980 its provisions do not apply to actions by a beneficiary to recover trust property. Such reasoning when deployed in a commercial context may be used to facilitate attempts to avoid the consequences of, for example, a fall in property values. Although it seems that the normal rules for accounting by trustees do not in all circumstances call for the restitution of the entire trust fund,[830] recent English decisions concerning fact situations of this sort have invoked rules of equitable compensation to facilitate making an award for no more than the amount perceived as having been lost by reason of the trustee's actions, using some general notion of "but for" causation to assist in the process.[831] It is not clear that the somewhat ill-defined category of equitable compensation needed to be enlarged in this way to provide a way of dealing with inadmissible claims. There must also certainly be situations where an agent who holds as trustee, for example a solicitor in conveyancing matters whose power to pay out a fund is specifically limited, could be rightly made liable for wrongful disposal of the trust estate.[832]

31-130 **Account of profits and proprietary remedies**   It is well established that equity

---

(2018), paras 6-049 et seq.

[826] See *Snell's Equity*, 33rd edn (2015), paras 7-053 et seq.

[827] See *Bowstead and Reynolds on Agency*, 21st edn (2018), at paras 6-040 to 6-044; and Millett (1998) 114 L.Q.R. 214.

[828] See *Libertarian Investments v Hall* [2013] 16 H.K.C.F.A.R. 681 at [97]–[99], [166]–[172].

[829] See *Re Dawson* [1966] 2 N.S.W.L.R. 211; *Youyang Pty Ltd v Minter Ellison Morris Fletcher* (2003) 212 C.L.R. 484 (see Elliott and Edelman (2003) 119 L.Q.R. 545); *Bairstow v Queen's Moat House Plc* [2001] EWCA Civ 712, [2001] B.C.L.C. 531; *Lloyd's TSB Bank Plc v Markandan & Uddin* [2012] EWCA Civ 65, [2012] 2 All E.R. 884.

[830] See Lord Millett in *Libertarian Investments v Hall*, n.828 above, at [166]–[172]; (1998) 114 L.Q.R. 214, 227; *Lewin on Trusts*, 19th edn (2014), paras 39-001 et seq.

[831] *Target Holdings Ltd v Redferns* [1996] A.C. 421; *AIB Group (UK) Plc v Mark Redler & Co Solicitors* [2014] UKSC 58, [2015] A.C. 1503; Lee (2015) J. Eq. 94; but cf. Ho (2015) 131 L.Q.R. 213; Gummow (2015) 45 Aust. Bar Rev. 5; Millett [2015] *UK Supreme Court Yearbook* 193; Turner [2015] C.L.J. 188; Davies (2015) 78 M.L.R. 681.

[832] As in *Various Claimants v Giambrone & Law* [2017] EWCA Civ 1193, [2018] P.N.L.R. 2, where however common law damages are also considered.

will give an account of profits against an agent who makes an unauthorised profit from use of his position,[833] or by breaching his equitable duties to the principal[834]; the account being a somewhat pragmatic remedy in personam in this context.[835] However, the position whether a proprietary remedy, in the form of a constructive trust, should be awarded over identifiable profits solely on the basis that they could not have been obtained but for breach of fiduciary duty has been controversial. The main objection to such an approach is the priority in insolvency which it may carry. The position has now been settled for England and Wales by the acceptance, in the context of bribery, of a proprietary remedy by way of the imposition of a constructive trust, on the basis that this applies to all benefits received by a fiduciary in breach of his duties.[836] It is unlikely that this should be confined to bribery situations, which indeed have a weaker case for being brought within the rule than other benefits. It seems fairly clear that the trust is intended to be regarded as institutional rather than remedial, though this makes it difficult to avoid the insolvency consequences of such reasoning; but there are other matters to be settled, for example the operation of the Limitation Act 1980.[837] Other jurisdictions may take a more flexible view of such a constructive trust.[838]

Equitable compensation[839] The acceptance of a general notion of equitable **31-131** compensation is a fairly recent development, at any rate in England and Wales.[840] The phrase refers to a monetary award for loss caused by breach of fiduciary duty,[841] and is to be distinguished from "equitable damages", a phrase that can be used of an award of damages in lieu of specific performance under Lord Cairns' Act, which used to be regarded by some as the only occasion in which a court of Equity could give monetary judgments. Equitable compensation is plainly an appropriate remedy where an agent disloyally[842] or acts in breach of trust.[843] It is less clear whether a mere conflict of interest will support equitable compensation, unless the claim-

---

833 See, e.g. *Regal (Hastings) Ltd v Gulliver* [1942] 1 All E.R. 378, [1967] 2 A.C. 134n.; *Phipps v Boardman* [1967] 2 A.C. 46.

834 See *JJ Harrison (Properties) Ltd v Harrison* [2001] EWCA Civ 1295, [2002] 1 B.C.L.C. 162; and *Gwembe Valley Development Co Ltd v Koshy (No.3)* [2003] EWCA Civ 1048, [2004] 1 B.C.L.C. 131; *Hurstanger Ltd v Wilson* [2007] EWCA Civ 299, [2007] 1 W.L.R. 2351.

835 See the discussion in *Warman International Ltd v Dwyer* (1995) 182 C.L.R. 544. It may be necessary to elect between an account of profits and the common law claim to damages: *Tang Man Sit v Capacious Investments Ltd* [1996] 1 A.C. 514.

836 *FHR European Ventures LLP v Cedar Capital Partners LLC* [2014] UKSC 45, [2015] A.C. 250, following *Att-Gen of Hong Kong v Reid* [1994] 1 A.C. 324, PC; see Gummow (2015) 131 L.Q.R. 21. See also below, para.31-131.

837 As to which see discussion in *Gwembe Valley Development Co Ltd v Koshy* [2003] EWCA Civ 1048, [2004] 1 B.C.L.C. 131; see also *Williams v Central Bank of Nigeria* [2014] UKSC 10, [2014] A.C. 1189.

838 See by way of illustration only *LAC Minerals Ltd v International Corona Resources Ltd* [1989] 2 S.C.R. 574 (Canada); *Muschinski v Dodds* (1985) 160 C.L.R. 653; *Warman International Pty Ltd v Dwyer* (1995) 182 C.L.R. 544; *Grimaldi v Chameleon Mining NL* (2012) 287 A.L.R. 22 (Australia). A flexible (in effect remedial) approach may grant the proprietary remedy for appropriate situations, while avoiding its insolvency consequences. See, e.g. Barnett (2015) 35 L.S. 302.

839 See *Bowstead and Reynolds on Agency*, 21st edn (2018), para.6-043.

840 Trustees have always been liable for causing loss to the beneficiaries. The wider right now accepted is often traced back to *Nocton v Ashburton* [1914] A.C. 932, a case in which the reasoning is not completely clear.

841 See *Libertarian Investments Ltd v Hall* (2013) 16 H.K.C.F.A.R. 681 at [84] et seq., per Ribeiro P.J.; [166] et seq. per Lord Millett N.P.J.; *Interactive Technology Corp Ltd v Ferster* [2018] EWCA Civ 1594.

842 See, e.g. *Také Ltd v BSM Marketing Ltd* [2009] EWCA Civ 45 (agent for furniture); *Premium Real*

ant can establish that had the conflict been disclosed the principal would not have made the decision that caused the loss.[844] The conflict of interest may, however, help to support an allegation that the agent has acted in breach of his (contractual or tortious) duties of care.[845] Where equitable compensation is awarded, the common law principles for the assessment of damages and contributory negligence are in principle not relevant.[846] In general, questions of causation are more likely to be relevant in some form than matters of contemplation, foreseeability and scope of duty.[847] But where the duty broken is simply one of exercising care, the duty, even if historically remediable in equity as well as common law, is not a fiduciary one and common law principles apply.[848] This whole problem often arises in connection with the dual functions of professionals such as solicitors and accountants, who are primarily persons offering services on a commercial basis (for example, they have no duty to tell their clients that another person offering the same services would charge less), but may perform many functions in respect of which they are fiduciaries, often because of information known by or available to them, and if solicitors, may also hold property on trust, though frequently only for a short time and in support or implementation of a transaction for which their services are utilised. They may sometimes have agency powers, for example to make contracts or settle cases on behalf of their principals,[849] and their knowledge may sometimes be attributed to their principals. This conjunction of roles may require very careful analysis within legal categories, bearing in mind that a reasonable external observer might regard many of the disputes litigated as simply concerning inadequate performance by a solicitor of his contractual duties.

(v) An Illustration: Bribery

31-132 **Bribes and secret commissions** An important illustration of the remedies in respect of breach of the duty of loyalty, and of the conflict and no-profit rules within it, is provided by the law relating to the taking of bribes and the receipt of secret commissions.[850] Here we encounter an overlap between common law and equity. The breach will justify dismissal of an agent acting under a bilateral contract,[851] and negative any right to remuneration or indemnity on the transaction in question,[852]

Estate Ltd v Stevens [2009] 2 N.Z.L.R. 384 (estate agent).

[843] See *Bairstow v Queen's Moat House Plc* [2001] EWCA Civ 712, [2001] 2 B.C.L.C. 531.

[844] See *Gwembe Valley Development Co Ltd v Koshy (No.3)* [2003] EWCA Civ 1048, [2004] 1 B.C.L.C. 131 at [159] (held account of profits appropriate).

[845] See *Hilton v Barker Booth & Eastwood* [2005] UKHL 8, [2005] 1 W.L.R. 567 (conflict of interest between two principals, where damages on a common law basis appear to be envisaged).

[846] See *Canson Enterprises Ltd v Boughton & Co* [1991] 4 S.C.R. 534, (1997) 85 D.L.R. (4th) 129.

[847] See *Swindle v Harrison* [1997] 4 All E.R. 705; *Gwembe Valley Development Co Ltd v Koshy* [2003] EWCA Civ 1048, [2004] 1 B.C.L.C. 131.

[848] *Bristol & West BS v Mothew* [1998] Ch. 1 (oversight in conveyancing); and see *Bank of New Zealand v New Zealand Guardian Trust Co Ltd* [1999] 1 N.Z.L.R. 664. Contra, Heydon (2014) 20 *Trusts and Trustees* 1006.

[849] See above, paras 31-013, 31-083.

[850] An extended consideration of the position appears in *Bowstead & Reynolds on Agency*, 21st edn (2018), art.49; as to the position of third parties see above, para.31-073. As to the criminal law, see Bribery Act 2010.

[851] *Boston Deep Sea Fishing and Ice Co v Ansell* (1888) 39 Ch. D. 339; *Swale v Ipswich Tannery Ltd* (1906) 11 Com. Cas. 88.

[852] Below, paras 31-161, 31-163.

whether or not the principal has suffered loss as a consequence.[853] The agent will be liable in restitution for the bribe and incidental profits. There has been considerable controversy whether equity will require the agent to hold such gains on constructive trust for the principal, but it has recently been clarified that the bribe is so held.[854] A bribe-taker can also be liable in damages for deceit, subject to election between these remedies which becomes final on judgment.[855] The briber is similarly liable.[856] The principal is not, however, entitled to double recovery, but can only recover the amount of the bribe and any additional loss he can prove; satisfaction of judgment against one will bar an action against the other except for any excess.[857]

(vi)   Agent Holding Money for Principal

Trustee or debtor?   Where the agent holds money on account of his principal, **31-133** whether emanating from his principal or emanating from a third party and received on his principal's account, a question may arise as to whether it is the principal's money which he holds on trust or whether he is simply a debtor to his principal. Although it is possible to suggest indications as to when the property is held on trust (for example, where it is received in pursuance of a single transaction[858] as opposed to a group of transactions in respect of which a general account is to be rendered[859]) the present trend is to approach the matter functionally and ask whether the trust relationship is appropriate to the commercial relationship in which the parties find themselves, and whether the money was intended to be held separately, or used as part of the agent's normal cash flow and subject to a relationship of debtor and creditor only.[860]

---

[853] *Rhodes v Macalister* (1923) 29 Com. Cas. 19; and see *Shipway v Broadwood* [1899] 1 Q.B. 369. The agent cannot recover an unpaid bribe from a third party: *Harrington v Victoria Graving Docks* (1878) 3 Q.B.D. 549; but cf. *Meadow Schama & Co v C Mitchell & Co Ltd* [1973] E.G.D. 252 (sum promised after commission earned: not a bribe).

[854] *FHR European Ventures LLP v Cedar Capital Partners LLC* [2014] UKSC 45, [2015] A.C. 250: see above, para.31-130.

[855] *Mahesan v Malaysian Government Officers Co-operative Housing Society Ltd* [1979] A.C. 374.

[856] Above, para.31-073.

[857] *Mahesan's* case, above, at 383; above, para.31-073. But cf. *Logicrose Ltd v Southend United Football Club Ltd* [1988] 1 W.L.R. 1256 (rescission of contract with briber and recovery of bribe from agent).

[858] e.g. *Westpac Banking Corp v Savin* [1985] 2 N.Z.L.R. 41.

[859] See *Burdick v Garrick* (1870) L.R. 5 Ch. App. 233; *Kirkham v Peel* (1880) 43 L.T. 171; 44 L.T. 195; *Henry v Hammond* [1913] 2 K.B. 515; *Neste Oy v Lloyds Bank Plc* [1983] 2 Lloyd's Rep. 658 (ship's agents) (disapproved in respect of one transaction in respect of which a constructive trust was found, in *Angove's Pty Ltd v Bailey* [2016] UKSC 47, [2016] 1 W.L.R. 3179); *Kingscroft Insurance Co Ltd v HS Weavers (Underwriting) Agencies Ltd* [1993] 1 Lloyd's Rep. 187; *Canadian Pacific Air Lines Ltd v Canadian Imperial Bank of Commerce* (1987) 42 D.L.R. (4th) 375; *Stephens Travel Service Intl Pty Ltd v Qantas Airways Ltd* (1988) 13 N.S.W.L.R. 331 (travel agent). An agent may of course hold under a *Quistclose* trust: see *Lewin on Trusts*, 19th edn (2015), paras 8-040 et seq.

[860] See *Walker v Corboy* (1990) 19 N.S.W.L.R. 382 (a valuable survey); *Lord Napier and Ettrick v Hunter* [1993] A.C. 713, 744; *Re Fleet Disposal Services* [1995] 1 B.C.L.C. 345; *Style Financial Services Ltd v Bank of Scotland* 1997 S.C.L.R. 633; *Paragon Finance Plc v DB Thakerar & Co* [1999] 1 All E.R. 400, 415–416; *Re Japan Leasing (Europe) Plc* [1999] B.P.I.R. 911; *Triffit Nurseries v Salads Etcetera Ltd* [2000] 1 All E.R. (Comm) 737; *Pearson v Lehman Brothers Finance SA* [2011] EWCA Civ 1544 at [68] (trust sustained even though identification of varying beneficial ownership of assets would be complex); *Eieber v Teathers Ltd* [2012] EWHC 190 (Ch), [2012] B.C.L.C. 58 at [25] (on appeal [2012] EWCA Civ 1466, [2013] 1 B.C.L.C. 248).

31-134 **Interest** Under the Senior Courts Act 1981[861] the court has power in any proceedings before it to award interest on all or any part of a debt or damages for which judgment is given or payment made before judgment. This rendered many old cases on this topic obsolete. But where the agent is a trustee, it is fundamental that he is not allowed to make any profit from his trust without his principal's informed consent. Unless, therefore, he has been specifically permitted to retain interest, any interest earned on the trust property is itself trust property.[862] If the trust property does not earn interest the trustee does not have to pay interest. He may, however, be in breach of trust for failing to generate interest, and in this event he will be liable for his breach of trust.[863] It has been held that a stakeholder is not a trustee of the stake he holds and thus is not liable to account to either party for interest earned on the stake.[864]

(vii) Estoppel as to Principal's Title

31-135 **When agent estopped as to title** An agent cannot in general dispute the title of his principal[865] or set up the right of a third party to the property in the goods, or the documents of title to the goods, with which he is entrusted by his principal.[866] It was formerly the law that if he was a bailee he could not (subject to exceptions) set up a better title to the goods bailed than that of his bailor (*jus tertii*). But this rule was abolished by s.8(1) of the Torts (Interference with Goods) Act 1977.[867]

(b) Rights of Agents

31-136 **General** In general the common law itself confers few rights on agents: it has been assumed that it is the principal who requires protection against the agent rather than the reverse. Attempts to impose fiduciary liabilities on principals have been unsuccessful[868] though there seems no reason in principle why they should not succeed in appropriate cases. Where the Commercial Agents (Council Directive) Regulations[869] apply, however, reg.4, which in general requires the principal, no less than the agent, to act "dutifully and in good faith", imposes duties on the principal to provide necessary documentation, inform the agent of acceptance, refusal and non-execution of contracts procured by the agent, and, most important, notify the agent within a reasonable period once he anticipates that the volume of transactions will be significantly lower than the agent could normally have expected (e.g.

---

[861] s.35A, inserted by Administration of Justice Act 1982 s.15.

[862] *Brown v IRC* [1965] A.C. 244. Solicitors are subject to special rules relating to interest earned on clients' money (see Solicitors' Accounts Rules 2011, made under Solicitors' Act 1974 ss.32, 34).

[863] See *Lewin on Trusts*, 19th edn (2015), para.39-052.

[864] *Potters (A Firm) v Loppert* [1973] Ch. 399; following *Harrington v Hoggart* (1830) 1 B. & Ad. 577. The Estate Agents Act 1979 ss.12, 13 provides for money received in the course of estate agency work to be held on trust: but the Rules made as to interest (SI 1981/1520, as amended) do not apply to money held as stakeholder.

[865] *Lyell v Kennedy* (1889) 14 App. Cas. 437; and see *Williams v Pott* (1871) L.R. 12 Eq. 149.

[866] *Blaustein v Maltz, Mitchell & Co* [1937] 2 K.B. 142; *Tassell v Cooper* (1850) 9 C.B. 509, 533; *White v Bartlett* (1832) 9 Bing. 378.

[867] See *Clerk & Lindsell on Torts*, 22nd edn (2018), para.17-83. He may apply for the joinder of the third party: *De Franco v Commissioner of Police for the Metropolis*, *The Times*, May 8, 1987.

[868] See *Jirna Ltd v Mister Donut of Canada Ltd* (1973) 40 D.L.R. (3d) 303; *Jani-King (GB) Ltd v Pula Enterprises Ltd* [2007] EWHC 2433 (QB), [2008] 1 All E.R.(Comm) 451.

[869] Above, para.31-017.

by withdrawal of a manufactured line). These duties are unexcludable,[870] and at the very least provide an opportunity for arguments that might not be possible at common law.[871]

(i) Remuneration

Right to remuneration   It is the duty of the principal to pay his agent any com-   **31-137**
mission or other remuneration contractually agreed upon.[872] When there is an express term as to remuneration, the right to payment and the amount will depend on that term. Thus if the contract provides that the amount of commission is left to the discretion of the principal, the court cannot determine the basis and rate of commission, since to do so would be making a new agreement between the parties and transferring to the court the discretion vested in the principal.[873] There is an implied agreement to pay remuneration whenever a person is employed to act as an agent under circumstances which raise the presumption that he would, to the knowledge of the principal, have expected to be paid.[874] The amount of the payment and the conditions on which it is payable will depend on the circumstances. If there is a custom or usage of the particular trade regulating the payment of remuneration, it may be presumed, in the absence of any express agreement to the contrary, that the parties contracted for the payment of the remuneration in accordance with this custom or usage.[875] But if there is no proof of such custom and no express agreement, then a reasonable remuneration is payable.[876] In estimating what is a reasonable remuneration, evidence of the bargainings between the parties is admissible as showing the value put upon the agent's services by the parties.[877] The Commercial

---

[870] Commercial Agents Regulations reg.5(1).

[871] See discussion in *Simpson v Grant & Bowman Ltd* [2006] Eu. L.R. 933; McGee [2013] J.B.L. 534, 541–543; Tosato [2016] O.J.L.S.661. See also *Monk v Largo Foods Ltd* [2016] EWHC 1837 (Comm) (obligation of good faith does not constrain principal's absolute right to terminate).

[872] The Estate Agents Act 1979 s.18, requires the agent to give the client certain information as to "prospective liabilities", largely defined in terms of "remuneration", before entering into a contract under which he will "engage in estate agency work": otherwise the contract is not enforceable without the leave of the court (which may be granted subject to conditions). If however the contract is unilateral, viz formed on the introduction of a purchaser, it would seem that such a situation will not strictly arise. Further prescription as to information which must be supplied is made in the Estate Agents (Provision of Information) Regulations 1991 (SI 1991/859). It is considered in *Great Eastern Group Ltd v Digby* [2011] EWCA Civ 1120, where a majority of the Court of Appeal takes the view that "remuneration" includes damages for breach of a sole agency contract.

[873] *Obu v A Strauss & Co Ltd* [1951] A.C. 243. See also *Taylor v Brewer* (1813) 1 M. & S. 290; *Roberts v Smith* (1859) 4 H. & N. 315; *Re Richmond Gate Property Co Ltd* [1965] 1 W.L.R. 335.

[874] *Way v Latilla* [1937] 3 All E.R. 759; *L.J. Hooker Ltd v WJ Adams Estates Ltd* (1977) 138 C.L.R. 52, 74–75. See below, para.31-138.

[875] *Wilkie v Scottish Aviation*, 1956 S.C. 198. The existence of such a custom is not easily proved. A standard scale of charges will not apply unless it is expressly or impliedly incorporated. The mere fact that it is commonly used will not suffice: *Debenham v King's College, Cambridge* (1884) 1 T.L.R. 170; *Drew v Josolyne* (1888) 4 T.L.R. 717; *Faraday v Tamworth Union* (1916) 86 L.J. Ch. 436; but see *Re Wolfe, Heller v Wolfe* [1952] 2 All E.R. 545; *Hugh v Allen & Co Ltd v Holmes* [1968] 1 Lloyd's Rep. 348.

[876] *Brown v Nairne* (1839) 9 C. & P. 204, 205; *Berezovsky v Edmiston & Co Ltd (The Darius)* [2011] EWCA Civ 431, [2011] 1 C.L.C. 922 (2.5 per cent, £6m, on sale of yacht reasonable). See Murdoch [1981] Conv. 424, differentiating between cases where the agent is and is not remunerated by results, and suggesting that in the first a scale fee may be appropriate, but for the second a "time and trouble" calculation.

[877] *Way v Latilla* [1937] 3 All E.R. 759.

Agents (Council Directive) Regulations[878] provide similar rules for cases when there are no express contract provisions.[879]

31-138 **Claims on a restitutionary quantum meruit** Where services are not rendered under a contract but are freely accepted, the courts have sometimes awarded a reasonable sum on a restitutionary basis. For example, the original contract may have been made without authority, ratification being impossible[880]; or unenforceable because the terms were too vague; or subsequently rescinded.[881] The cases do not for the most part concern agency, but a recent leading case bases recovery on unjust enrichment.[882]

31-139 **Commission** The remuneration of the agent typically, but not always,[883] takes the form of a commission, being a percentage of the value of the transaction the agent is to bring about for the principal. In such cases the agent does not become entitled to his commission until the event has occurred upon which his entitlement arises. What this event is must be ascertained from the terms of the agency contract. In most cases where the agent is engaged to find a third party to enter into a contract with his principal there will be little difficulty because the event will occur when the principal and the third party enter into the contract which the agent was engaged to bring about. The agent's task is then successfully completed.

31-140 **Estate agents**[884] The majority of cases on commission concern that payable to estate agents.[885] Although the context is specialised, the principles are undoubtedly of general application, subject to differences of commercial background. The present somewhat detailed discussion is retained because of the large number of cases give good illustrations of the reasoning employed for commission disputes in general.[886] The decisions turn on the words used in the particular agreement. The difficulties have arisen in this context because estate agents have frequently considered that their task is completed and that they should therefore be entitled to commission when they introduce to their principal (the potential vendor) a person who shows a real interest in buying. This stage is normally reached when the potential purchaser makes an offer "subject to contract" or "subject to survey" or subject to some other condition. But in English common law such an offer, even if accepted, does not create a contract between the potential vendor and the potential

---

[878] Above, para.31-017.
[879] regs 6–9. The regulations do not apply to gratuitous agents: reg.2(2)(a).
[880] e.g. *Craven-Ellis v Canons Ltd* [1936] 2 K.B. 403.
[881] e.g. *Faraday v Tamworth Union* (1916) 86 L.J. Ch. 436. For a recent example see *Cooke v Hopper* [2012] EWCA Civ 175.
[882] *Benedetti v Sawiris* [2013] UKSC 50, [2014] A.C. 938. See Vol.I, paras 29-080 et seq.; *Bowstead and Reynolds on Agency*, 21st edn (2018), para.7-009; Goff and Jones, *Law of Unjust Enrichment*, 8th edn (2011), Ch.17. See also *MSM Consulting Ltd v United Republic of Tanzania* [2009] EWHC 121 (QB), 123 Con. L.R. 154; below, para.31-148. Contrast *Devani v Wells* [2016] EWCA Civ 1106, [2017] Q.B. 959, where no terms had been agreed before the party was introduced.
[883] For a case (in the context of the Commercial Agents Regulations) where an agent was remunerated by markup see *Mercantile International Group Plc v Chuan Soon Huat Industrial Group Plc* [2002] EWCA Civ 288, [2002] 1 All E.R. (Comm) 788.
[884] See also above, para.31-012.
[885] Murdoch, *Law of Estate Agency*, 5th edn (2009); Murdoch (1975) 91 L.Q.R. 357; Ash, *Willing to Purchase* (1963).
[886] But as to commercial agents (above, para.31-017) see below, para.31-149.

purchaser.[887] The contract is not made until the parties exchange contracts.[888] There is a third stage to the transaction, completion, at which the vendor hands the title deeds to the purchaser in exchange for the purchase price. The agent is engaged to bring about a sale, but he generally wants his commission before sale, i.e. at the "subject to contract" stage. He is free to stipulate whatever event he wishes in his agency contract, but it has been said that it is "the common understanding of men that the agent's commission is payable out of the purchase price",[889] and it requires fairly clear words to entitle the agent to commission if no sale is made.[890] In all cases however the question is whether the event upon which it is stipulated that commission is due has taken place.

Commission on the introduction of a purchaser It is not unusual for estate **31-141**
agents to stipulate for their commission on some such event as "the introduction of a purchaser",[891] or on "finding a purchaser"[892] or "finding someone to buy"[893]; in one case commission was payable "in the event of business resulting".[894] Two questions arise here: as to the meaning of "introduce" where that word is used, and as to the meaning of "purchaser". As to the first, it has recently been held by the Court of Appeal in *Foxtons Ltd v Bicknell*[895] that the introduction must be "to the purchase and not merely to the property"[896] and that the words used referred to "a person who becomes a purchaser as a result of the introduction"[897]: thus where the property was eventually sold to a person reintroduced by another agent, commission was not due to the first agent. This decision, which is becoming a leading case, certainly reduces the availability of commission, and the possibility of two commissions being due, and can be said to take a different course from that normally followed, which is to solve such questions by inquiring whether an introduction was the (or an) "effective cause" of the purchase.[898] The new reasoning may direct attention back to the idea that commission is normally to be paid out of the price, but it cannot avoid the consequences of clear wording designed to achieve a different object.[899] As to the second question, whenever the event is referable to a contract ultimately taking place, commission is not earned until that contract has been made.[900] Thus, if the

---

[887] *Chillingworth v Esche* [1924] 1 Ch. 97. The position is further affected by s.2 of the Law of Property (Miscellaneous Provisions) Act 1989: see Vol.I, paras 5-032 et seq.

[888] See *Chillingworth v Esche*, above, and *Eccles v Bryant* [1948] Ch. 93.

[889] *Dennis Reed Ltd v Goody* [1950] 2 K.B. 277, 284, per Denning L.J.

[890] *Luxor (Eastbourne) Ltd v Cooper* [1941] A.C. 108, 129; *Midgley Estates Ltd v Hand* [1952] 2 Q.B. 432, 435–436. See also *HW Liebig & Co Ltd v Leading Investments Ltd* (1986) 25 D.L.R. (4th) 161.

[891] *Jones v Lowe* [1945] K.B. 73.

[892] *Fowler v Bratt* [1950] 2 K.B. 96.

[893] *McCallum v Hicks* [1950] 2 K.B. 271.

[894] *Murdoch Lownie v Newman* [1949] 2 All E.R. 783.

[895] [2008] EWCA Civ 419, [2008] 2 E.G.L.R. 23 (sole agent); see Watts [2009] J.B.L. 268; followed in *Charania v Harbour Estates Ltd* [2009] EWCA Civ 1123. The wording used in the contract in question was not specifically drafted by or for the claimant firm but was actually taken, with a small addition, from the information required to be supplied to clients by the Estate Agents (Provision of Information) Regulations 1991 (SI 1991/859), with the result that the case is authority on the interpretation of that wording. *Dashwood v Fleurets Ltd* [2007] EWHC 1610 (QB), [2007] 2 E.G.L.R. 7 may be doubtful in view of this decision.

[896] *Foxtons Ltd v Bicknell* [2008] EWCA Civ 419 at [36].

[897] *Foxtons Ltd v Bicknell* [2008] EWCA Civ 419 at [22], per Lord Neuberger.

[898] See below, para.31-147.

[899] See below, para.31-144.

[900] A variant whereby commission was due to a mortgage broker in the event of an "offer of a

agent introduces[901] a person who makes an offer "subject to contract" which is accepted, he does not become entitled to commission, because such a transaction is not in law a contract at all.[902] The agent's entitlement cannot, in such a case, arise until the parties have entered into a contract of sale. For example, if the event is the introduction or finding of a "purchaser", the person introduced or found is not a "purchaser" until he actually purchases by entering into a contract. Moreover, if the person introduced withdraws after contract but before completion, whether rightfully or wrongfully vis-à-vis the vendor, the agent is no longer entitled to commission, because the person he introduced was not a "purchaser" since he never purchased.[903] But it seems that if the *vendor* wrongfully (vis-à-vis the purchaser) withdraws, the agent's entitlement to commission may not be lost[904]; though this must depend on the precise words used,[905] and his right may sometimes be one for damages for breach of an implied term.[906]

31-142 **Commission upon the introduction of a person "ready, willing and able to purchase"[907]** Because it is not possible for the agent to obtain commission before sale in the above cases, some estate agents drafted their contracts to provide that commission was due upon the introduction of a person "ready, willing and able to purchase" or something similar.[908] By this means it was hoped to define the event (viz the introduction) without reference to the ultimate contract of sale. The courts, however, applied a strict test and held that the agent will only be entitled to commission if the person introduced exactly fits the description of the person upon whose introduction the entitlement arises. For this purpose it does not matter what adjectives are used to describe the potential purchaser; the introduction must be of a person who fulfils the qualifications specified, for until this time the agent will not have brought about the event which entitles him to commission.

---

mortgage", was considered in *Mustafa v KG Palos* (1972) 116 S.J. 354. The court held that this meant an offer which actually led to a mortgage. Commission due on the introduction of "an intending buyer" was held not payable when the proposed buyer acquired the shares in the vendor company in *Estafnous v London & Leeds Business Centres Ltd* [2011] EWCA Civ 1157, [2012] 1 P. & C.R. DG4.

901 See above, n.895 and *DC Wylde & Co v Sparg* 1977 (2) S.A.L.R. 75; *John D Wood & Co v Dantata* [1987] 2 E.G.L.R. 23, 25; *Christie, Owen & Davis Plc v King* [1998] S.C.L.R. 786.

902 *James v Smith (1921)* [1931] 2 K.B. 317n; *Martin v Perry & Daw* [1931] 2 K.B. 310.

903 *James v Smith*, above; *Martin v Perry & Daw*, above; *John D. Wood (Residential & Agricultural) Ltd v Craze* [2007] EWHC 2658 (QB), [2008] 1 E.G.L.R. 17; *Foxtons Ltd v O'Reardon* [2011] EWHC 2946 (QB) (wrongful withdrawal: no term that purchaser had to be a cash purchaser).

904 *Luxor (Eastbourne) Ltd v Cooper* [1941] A.C. 108, 126, 142; *Dennis Reed Ltd v Goody* [1950] 2 K.B. 277, 285.

905 If the contract expressly or impliedly provides that commission shall be paid out of the purchase price when received, nothing is due if the price is not received: *Boots v E Christopher & Co* [1952] 1 K.B. 89. See also *Beningfield v Kynaston* (1887) 3 T.L.R. 279; *Knight, Frank & Rutley v Gordon* (1923) 39 T.L.R. 399; *Blake & Co v Sohn* [1969] 1 W.L.R. 1412.

906 *Alpha Trading Ltd v Dunnshaw-Patten Ltd* [1981] Q.B. 290; *John D Wood & Co v Craze* [2005] EWHC 2658 (QB) (implied term that seller will not imperil contract by making fraudulent representations); below, para.31-150.

907 The phrase "ready, willing and able purchaser" is defined in the Estate Agents' (Provision of Information) Regulations 1991 (SI 1991/859) and an estate agent using it must provide a written explanation in accordance with that definition: reg.5(1). Terms "having a similar purport or effect" must also be explained in writing: reg.5(2).

908 e.g. *Dennis Reed v Nicholls* [1948] 2 All E.R. 914; *Bennett & Partners v Millett* [1949] 1 K.B. 362; *E P Nelson v Rolfe* [1950] 1 K.B. 139; *Dennis Reed Ltd v Goody* [1950] 2 K.B. 277. Sometimes one or more of the adjectives are dropped (e.g. *Graham & Scott (Southgate) Ltd v Oxlade* [1950] 2 K.B. 257—"willing and able").

If the person introduced is to be "able" to purchase, he must be able to do so in **31-143** every way, and this includes having the financial ability.[909] It seems that he is not able to do so if at the relevant time the vendor has sold or contracted to sell the house to another.[910] If he is to be "willing", he shows that he is not willing if he withdraws before completion.[911] He does not show his willingness merely by entering into an agreement "subject to contract" or "subject to survey" or some other such condition, for he has in such a case reserved for himself a *locus poenitentiae* and is not, therefore, shown to be willing.[912] However, if the agent does introduce a person who is shown to fulfil the required description, he becomes entitled to commission although no contract of sale has been made. Thus, it has been said, an unqualified offer to purchase by the person introduced will normally entitle the agent to his commission under a "ready, willing and able" contract because the potential purchaser has thereby been shown to be "ready, willing and able".[913] The terms upon which he was willing and able to purchase must however have been terms upon which at the material time the vendor had expressed a willingness to sell.[914] The question whether the person introduced fulfils the contractual description is a question of fact.[915] Thus, in one case the contract provided for commission to be earned upon the introduction of a person who made an offer to purchase on terms to which the vendor might "assent". The majority of the Court of Appeal said that this assent did not need to be such assent as to make a legally binding contract of sale, and that it could be proved that the vendor did "assent", within the meaning of that word in the contract, without having communicated her assent to the potential purchaser so as to make a contract of sale. If she had assented, the event would have occurred and commission would have been earned.[916]

Other types of estate agent's agreement   The same principles apply to other **31-144** forms of wording. Thus, in *Midgley Estates Ltd v Hand*[917] and *Scheggia v Gradwell*[918] the agents stipulated for commission if a person introduced by them entered into a legally binding contract. Contracts were exchanged, and in each case

---

909 *Dellafiora v Lester* [1962] 1 W.L.R. 1208, where the potential purchaser of a lease was held not to be "able" to purchase because the potential vendor's landlord would not consent to the assignment of the lease to the potential purchaser.
910 *AA Dickson & Co v O'Leary* [1980] E.G.D. 265. But there may be cases where two agents are entitled to commission in respect of different prospective purchasers: see at 268; *Christie, Owen & Davies Ltd v Rapacioli* [1974] Q.B. 781, 790; *Lordsgate Properties Ltd v Balcombe* [1985] 1 E.G.L.R. 20.
911 *Dennis Reed Ltd v Goody* [1950] 2 K.B. 277. But he need not be willing at the point of introduction: *Knight, Frank & Rutley v Fraser*, 1964 S.L.T. 50, Ct of Sess.
912 *Graham & Scott (Southgate) Ltd v Oxlade* [1950] 2 K.B. 257; *Dennis Reed Ltd v Goody*, above; *Christie, Owen & Davies Ltd v Stockton* [1953] 1 W.L.R. 1353. So also the Court of Appeal held in *Bennett Walden & Co v Wood* [1950] 2 All E.R. 134 that an offer "subject to contract" did not entitle the agent to commission when the contract provided that commission was earned when the agents "secured an offer". These cases overruled a number of earlier authorities, such as *Giddy & Giddy v Horsfall* [1947] 1 All E.R. 460; *Bennett & Partners v Millett* [1949] 1 K.B. 362.
913 *AL Wilkinson Ltd v Brown* [1966] 1 W.L.R. 194, 203. Presumably it would still be open to the potential vendor to prove that, notwithstanding the offer, there was still some other flaw which would have prevented a sale taking place.
914 *Christie, Owen & Davies Ltd v Rapacioli* [1974] Q.B. 781; following *AL Wilkinson Ltd v O'Neil* [1962] E.G. D. 405; see also *Trinder & Partners v Haggis* [1951] W.N. 416. See, for further discussion of the first case, *Bowstead and Reynolds on Agency*, 21st edn (2018), para.7-019.
915 *Ackroyd & Sons v Hasan* [1960] 2 Q.B. 144, 156.
916 *Ackroyd & Sons v Hasan*, above. See also *Martin, Gale & Wright v Buswell* (1961) 105 S.J. 466.
917 [1952] 2 Q.B. 432.
918 [1963] 1 W.L.R. 1049. This type of contract was described by Salmon L.J. in *AL Wilkinson Ltd v*

the agents were held to be entitled to their commission although in the first case the purchaser withdrew before completion, and in the second the contract would not have been enforced by specific performance. On the other hand, in *Peter Long & Partners v Burns*[919] the contract was voidable, and the agent was not entitled to his commission because the person introduced had not signed a *legally binding* contract. In *Drewery & Drewery v Ware-Lane*[920] the agents stipulated for commission when the potential purchaser introduced by them signed their "purchaser's agreement" and the vendor signed their "vendor's agreement". Both these documents were "subject to contract", but the court held that, because both documents were signed, the stipulated for event had occurred, and commission was due, although no sale resulted. A contract may entitle an agent to commission for negotiating a sale to a person whom he did not introduce.[921]

31-145 **Summary of principles relating to estate agents** "First, when an agent claims that he has earned the right to commission, the test is whether upon the proper interpretation of the contract between the principal and the agent the event has happened upon which commission is to be paid. Secondly, there are no special principles of construction applicable to commission contracts with estate agents.[922] Thirdly, contracts under which a principal is bound to pay commission for an introduction which does not result in a sale must be expressed in clear language".[923] Similar principles will be applied in cases where other types of agent claim commission.[924]

31-146 **"Sole" and "exclusive" agencies** It seems that the estate agent's contract is prima facie a unilateral one, viz the agent earns his commission by doing an act but himself makes no promise.[925] The principal may before commission is earned sell the property himself[926] or through another agent; depending on the terms of his offer[927] he can reject persons introduced, and take his property "off the market" without liability.[928] But a sole agency contract is usually said to be bilateral, the agent promising to use his best endeavours to sell the property.[929] Such an arrange-

---

Brown [1966] 1 W.L.R. 194, 202 as a "ridiculous bargain". See, however, *Brian Cooper & Co v Fairview Estates (Investments) Ltd* [1987] 1 E.G.L.R. 18 (introduction of a person "with whom we have not been in prior communication and who subsequently completes a contract"). In *Foxtons Ltd v Bicknell* [2008] 2 E.G.L.R.23, discussed above, the provision as to multiple agency made commission payable in the case of "a purchaser to whose attention we brought the availability of property": see discussion of this at [27].

919 [1956] 1 W.L.R. 1083: *John D. Wood (Residential & Agricultural) Ltd v Craze* [2007] EWHC 2658 (QB), [2008] 1 E.G.L.R. 17.

920 [1960] 1 W.L.R. 1204. For another unusual form, see *Jaques v Lloyd D George & Partners Ltd* [1968] 1 W.L.R. 625 (but as to dicta in this case, see (1968) 31 M.L.R. 700).

921 *FP Rolfe & Co v George* [1969] E.G.D. 330; cf. *Hoddell v Smith* [1976] E.G.D. 217.

922 See also *Luxor (Eastbourne) Ltd v Cooper* [1941] A.C. 108, 124.

923 *Ackroyd & Sons v Hasan* [1960] 2 Q.B. 144, 154, per Upjohn L.J.

924 See above, para.31-140.

925 *Luxor (Eastbourne) Ltd v Cooper* [1941] A.C. 108; *LJ Hooker Ltd v WJ Adams Estates Pty Ltd* (1977) 138 C.L.R. 52, 73. For the effect of letters sent following engagement see Murdoch (1977) 242 E.G. 609; cf. McConnell (1983) 265 E.G. 547.

926 *Brinson v Davies* (1911) 27 T.L.R. 442.

927 Above, paras 31-140 et seq.

928 See below, para.31-151.

929 *E Christopher & Co v Essig* [1948] W.N. 461; *Mendoza & Co v Bell* [1952] E.G.D. 364. But see Murdoch (1975) 91 L.Q.R. 357.

ment does not normally mean that the principal is not entitled to sell himself[930] or perhaps (at any rate if he gives notice) to decide not to sell at all[931]; but a sale through another agent would be a breach of contract or sometimes entitle the agent to commission.[932] Similar analysis may be applied to other contracts with "canvassing agents".[933]

Agent must be effective cause of transaction It is traditional to say that, subject **31-147** to clear indications to the contrary,[934] where the agency contract provides that the agent earns his remuneration upon bringing about a certain transaction, he is not entitled to such remuneration unless he is the[935] effective cause of the transaction being brought about. This is often said to result from the implication of a term[936]: but the rules for such implication are not generous and an appropriate result must frequently be obtained by interpretation of the contract: any principle is certainly

---

930 *Bentall, Horsley & Baldry v Vicary* [1931] 1 K.B. 253; approved by the House of Lords in *Luxor (Eastbourne) Ltd v Cooper* [1941] A.C. 108; *Simpson v Lamb* (1856) 17 C.B. 603; *Sadler v Whittaker* (1953) 162 E.G. 404. In *WT Lamb & Sons v Goring Brick Co* [1932] 1 K.B. 710 a manufacturer appointed a merchant his "sole selling agent", and it was held that this prevented the manufacturer from himself selling. In this case, the relations between the parties were not those of principal and agent but those of buyer and seller. But this may also be correct for agents described in this way: see *Great Eastern Group Ltd v Digby* [2011] EWCA Civ 1120.

931 See below, para.31-150.

932 *Milsom v Bechstein* (1898) 14 T.L.R. 159. This matter is discussed in *Great Eastern Group Ltd v Digby*, above; see also *Harwood v Smith* [1998] 1 E.G.L.R. 5. The measure of damages is to be calculated with reference to the probability that the agent would earn his commission: *Hampton & Sons Ltd v George* [1939] 3 All E.R. 627

933 Above, para.31-002. For a discussion of types of "sole agency" and "sole selling agreements" see *Brodie Marshall & Co (Hotel Division) Ltd v Sharer* [1988] 1 E.G.L.R. 21; *GF Galvin (Estates) Ltd v Hedigan* [1985] I.L.R.M. 295. Where an estate agent uses the phrases "sole selling rights" or "sole agency", these are defined by statutory instrument and he must supply the prescribed definition in writing: Estate Agents (Provision of Information) Regulations 1991 (SI 1991/859) reg.5(1); *The Great Eastern Group Ltd v Digby*, above. Terms having "a similar purport or effect" must also be explained in writing: reg.5(2).

934 As in *Brian Cooper & Co v Fairview Estates (Investments) Ltd* [1987] 1 E.G.L.R. 18 (where such a requirement was not upheld); *Glentree Estates Ltd v Favermead Ltd* [2010] EWCA Civ 1473, [2011] 1 E.G.L.R. 23 (unusual facts); *County Homesearch (Thames & Chilterns) Ltd v Cowham* [2008] EWCA Civ 26, [2008] 1 W.L.R. 909 ("deemed introduction"); *Edmond de Rothschild Securities (UK) Ltd v Exilla Energy Plc* [2014] EWHC 2165 (Comm), [2014] 5 Costs L.Q. 749 ("success fee").

935 As to whether he should be "the" or "an" effective cause see *Brian Cooper Ltd v Fairview Estates Ltd*, above, at 20; *Nahum v Royal Holloway and Bedford New College* [1999] E.M.L.R. 252; *Harding Maughan Hambly Ltd v Cie Européenne de Courtage d'Assurances, etc.* [2000] 1 Lloyd's Rep. 316, 334–337 (preferring "an" in the context of a chain of Lloyd's brokers); and see *Egan Lawson Ltd v Standard Life Assurance Co* [2001] E.G.L R. 27. The search is usually for "the" cause: "that which had the greatest efficacy": *Tufton Associates Ltd v Dilmun Shipping* [1992] 1 Lloyd's Rep. 71, 78; see *Robert Drummond v Mangles* [1981] E.G.D. 264; *John D Wood & Co v Dantata* [1987] 2 E.G.L.R. 23; *Chesterfield & Co Ltc v Zahid* [1989] 2 E.G.L.R. 24. The rationale of the implication has been said to be to avoid the principal being liable for two commissions: see *County Homesearch Co (Thames & Chilterns) Ltd v Cowham* [2008] EWCA Civ 26, [2008] 1 W.L.R. 909 at [14] (suggesting that the situation with a purchasing agent might be different). For a different explanation see *Doyle v Mount Kidston Mining & Exploration Pty Ltd* [1984] 2 Qd R 386, 392. Cases may nevertheless arise where two agents are entitled to commission, particularly where they have contracted on different terms: see *Lordsgate Properties Ltd v Balcombe* [1985] 1 E.G.L.R. 20; *Bernard Marais & Co v Ashraf* [1983] 1 E.G.L.R. 7; *Peter Yates & Co v Bullock* [1990] 2 E.G.L.R. 24. For extended but finally inconclusive discussion in the High Court of Australia see *Moneywood Pty Ltd v Salamon Nominees Pty Ltd* (2001) 202 C.L.R. 351.

936 *Homesearch (Thames & Chilterns) Ltd v Cowham* [2008] EWCA Civ 26, [2008] 1 W.L.R. 909.

subject to contrary indications.[937] On this point there is a substantial body of case law, resulting from the use of words such as "find" or "introduce" a purchaser.[938] Thus in *Millar v Radford*[939] the plaintiff was retained by the defendant to find a purchaser of the defendant's property or, if that was not possible, a tenant. A tenant was found and the plaintiff was paid his commission. Over a year later the tenant bought the property from the defendants. The plaintiff claimed commission although he had not been in any way concerned with the sale. The Court of Appeal held that he was not entitled to commission, since he had not brought about a sale and was not the effective cause of it taking place. The agent need not, however, be the *immediate* cause of the transaction, provided that there is sufficient connection between his act and the ultimate transaction.[940] Thus, an auctioneer was instructed to sell the island of Herm by auction or otherwise, but the island failed to reach the reserve price at the auction. A potential buyer then asked the auctioneer for the name of the owner and, upon receiving it, purchased the island directly from him. It was held that the auctioneer was entitled to his commission.[941] If the transaction which results in a sale is different from that which the agent was engaged to bring about, it will be a matter of construction whether the parties intended remuneration to be payable in the changed circumstances.[942] If the agent was the effective cause of the ultimate transaction the court may make the necessary implication or may imply a new contract from the fact that the agent continued to act at the principal's request towards completion of the new transaction. But if the ultimate transaction was of a wholly different nature from that contemplated or worked towards, the agent may not be entitled to remuneration. Thus, where an agent employed to find a buyer introduced a government department which then compulsorily acquired the property, he was not entitled to commission.[943]

31-148   **No contractual quantum meruit where commission not earned**   Remuneration under a quantum meruit may be awarded where there is a contract but it does not provide for remuneration, or does not do so for the circumstances which have arisen.[944] But where the contract makes express provision for the agent to be remunerated only upon the happening of a certain event, he will not normally be

---

937 See discussion by Lord Neuberger in *Foxtons Ltd v Bicknell* [2008] EWCA Civ 419, [2008] 2 E.G.L.R. 23 at [18]–[20].

938 See discussion of the "effective cause" principle by Lord Neuberger in *Foxtons Ltd v Bicknell* [2008] EWCA Civ 419, [2008] 2 E.G.L.R. 23 at [18]–[20]; *Wilkinson v Martin* (1837) 8 C. & P. 1; *Green v Bartlett* (1863) 14 C.B.(N.S.) 681; *Rimmer v Knowles* (1874) 30 L.T. 496; *Toulmin v Millar* (1887) 58 L.T. 96; affirmed on another point (1887) 12 App. Cas. 746; *Mansell v Clements* (1874) L.R. 9 C.P. 139; *Tribe v Taylor* (1876) 1 C.P.D. 505; *Burchell v Gowrie* [1910] A.C. 614; *Jack Windle Ltd v Brierley* [1952] 1 All E.R. 398; *Allan v Leo Lines Ltd* [1957] 1 Lloyd's Rep. 127; *Bartlett v Cole* [1963] E.G.D. 452; *The 4You* [2014] EWHC 1098 (Comm), [2014] 2 Lloyd's Rep. 88.

939 (1903) 19 T.L.R. 575. See also *Toulmin v Millar* (1887) 58 L.T. 96; *Nightingale v Parsons* [1914] 2 K.B. 621.

940 e.g. *Re Beale* (1885) 5 Morr. 37; *Lumley v Nicholson* (1886) 34 W.R. 716; *Mansell v Clements* (1874) L.R. 9 C.P. 139; *Burton v Hughes* (1885) 1 T.L.R. 207; *Steere v Smith* (1886) 2 T.L.R. 131; *Barnett v Brown* (1890) 6 T.L.R. 463; *Thompson v Thomas* (1896) 11 T.L.R. 304; *Nahum v Royal Holloway and Bedford New College* [1999] E.M.L.R. 252.

941 *Green v Bartlett* (1863) 14 C.B.(N.S.) 681.

942 *Gunn v Showell's Brewery Co Ltd* (1902) 18 T.L.R. 659; *Burchell v Gowrie* [1910] A.C. 614; *Price Davies & Co v Smith* (1929) 141 L.T. 490; *Lord v Trippe* (1977) 51 A.L.J.R. 574; *LJ Hooker Ltd v WJ Adams Estates Pty Ltd* (1977) 138 C.L.R. 52. And see *Savills (UK) Ltd v Blacker* [2017] EWCA Civ 68 (commission due though property not marketed as proposed by agent).

943 *Hodges v Hackbridge Park Residential Hotel Ltd* [1940] 1 K.B. 404.

944 Above, para.31-138; e.g. *Reiff Diner & Co v Catalytic International Inc* (1978) 246 E.G. 743;

entitled to claim reasonable remuneration if it does not happen.[945] Such a claim would depend upon an implied promise to pay a reasonable sum if the event does not occur, and such an implication cannot normally be made because it would be inconsistent with the express terms of the contract.[946] Thus, an estate agent was held not to be entitled to payment on a quantum meruit when the principal sold the property elsewhere.[947] The implication of a term that a reasonable sum should be paid when the event upon which remuneration is due does not occur will therefore be rare.[948]

Commercial agents　For commercial agents, the Commercial Agents (Council Directive) Regulations[949] contain provisions as to when commission is due and payable. As some of these are specifically made non-excludable to the detriment of the agent, it seems likely that the rest may be excluded by contrary agreement.[950] Thus the agent is entitled to commission where a transaction has been concluded as a result of[951] his action; where a transaction is concluded with a third party whom he has previously acquired as a customer for transactions of the same kind; or where a transaction is concluded during the period covered by the agency contract where he has a right to a specific geographical area and the transaction is entered into with a customer belonging to that area or group.[952] There are provisions, some unexcludable, concerning the time at which commission is payable.[953] There is also an unexcludable provision that the right to commission can only be extinguished if and to the extent that it is established that the contract between the third party and the principal will not be executed,[954] and that fact is due to a reason for which the **31-149**

Sinclair Goldsmith v Minero Peru Comercial [1978] E.G.D. 194. But see as to these cases Murdoch [1981] Conv. 424, differentiating between cases where the agent is and is not paid by results.

[945] *Howard Houlder & Partners Ltd v Manx Isles SS Co Ltd* [1923] 1 K.B. 110; *Bentall, Horsley & Baldry v Vicary* [1931] 1 K.B. 253; *Fairvale Ltd v Sabharwal* [1992] 2 E.G.L.R. 27. See *MSM Consulting Ltd v United Republic of Tanzania* [2009] EWHC 121 (QB), 123 Con. L.R. 154; above, para.31-138.

[946] *Martin v Tucker* (1885) 1 T.L.R. 655; *Barnett v Isaacson* (1888) 4 T.L.R. 645; *Lott v Outhwaite* (1893) 10 T.L.R. 76.

[947] *Bentall, Horsley & Baldry v Vicary*, above.

[948] See, e.g. *Re Allison* [1904] 2 K.B. 327; *Firth v Hylane* [1959] E.G.D. 212.

[949] Above, para.31-017; McGee [2013] J.B.L. 543–545.

[950] See discussion in *Bowstead and Reynolds on Agency*, 21st edn (2018), para.11-033.

[951] This obviously has similarities with the notion of effective cause, above, para.31-147.

[952] SI 1993/3053 reg.7. It is not necessary, in the last case, that there has been an action by the agent to secure the transaction: *Kontogeorgas v Kartonpak AE* [1997] 1 C.M.L.R. 1093. But it is necessary that there should have been action by the principal: *Chevassus-Marché v Groupe Danone* (C-19/07) EU:C:2008:23, [2008] 1 Lloyd's Rep. 475.

[953] reg.10.

[954] This applies also to partial non-execution of the contract, as by non-compliance with the volume of transactions or the duration envisaged by the contract. If commission becomes due to the extent that the transactions are executed, the right to commission is extinguished to the extent of inexecution (subject to subpara.(b)): *ERGO Poist'ovna a.s. v Barlikova* (C-48/16) EU:C:2017:377, [2018] Bus. L.R. 41.

principal is not to blame.[955] The agent has a right to receive information as to commission, and extracts from the principal's books.[956]

31-150 **Opportunity to earn commission**[957]   At common law, the employment of an agent on the terms that his commission is to be payable on results does not deprive the principal of his freedom to take any step which results in the agent being deprived of his opportunity to earn commission, unless there is an express promise or trade custom to the contrary, or unless a promise to the contrary must be implied to give business efficacy to the contract or otherwise to effect the intention of the parties. Thus where a person was employed as sole agent to sell his principal's coal for seven years, it was held that there was no implied term that the principal would not sell the colliery within that period and so deprive the agent of the chance of earning commission.[958] Where a steamer was chartered for 18 months under a charterparty which provided for payment to a broker of commission on the hire paid and earned under the charterparty, it was held that on the sale by the owners of the ship during the currency of the charterparty, the broker was not entitled to any commission for the unexpired period of the charterparty.[959] Both these cases can perhaps be explained on the basis that "a person is entitled to deal with his property as he chooses, and a person is entitled either to carry on his business or give up carrying on his business as he wishes".[960] But in some cases there may be more room for the implication of a term. Thus an express promise is sometimes treated as giving a right to a "continuing benefit"[961] so that it is operative unless it can be shown that there is something to "qualify what on the face of it appears to be an absolute obligation".[962] Thus where a shirt manufacturer agreed to employ a traveller for five years on the terms that the traveller would do his utmost, for remuneration by commission, to obtain orders for goods manufactured or sold by the manufacturer or forwarded by sample to the traveller, it was held that the traveller could recover substantial damages from the manufacturer for not forwarding samples at the end of two years: and further that the manufacturer was not excused from fulfilling his

---

[955] reg.11. The notion of a contract party being "to blame" is unfamiliar to the common law. It has been held that this requires, not a legal reason leading directly to the termination, but an assessment of whether the principal is in common sense terms to blame for the inexecution, as where his behaviour caused customers to become dissatisfied and terminate their contracts: *ERGO Poist'ovna a.s. v Barlikova* (C-48/16) EU:C:2017:377, [2018] Bus. L.R. 41.

[956] reg.12. For a way in which this might be enforced at common law see *Yahuda Fire Insurance Co v Orion Marine Insurance Underwriting Agency* [1995] Q.B. 174 (not a case on the Regulations); *Fairstar Heavy Transport NV v Adkins* [2013] EWCA Civ 886, [2013] 2 C.L.C. 272 (order against CEO). See also *Equitas Ltd v Horace Holman & Co Ltd* [2007] EWHC 903 (Comm), [2007] Lloyd's Rep. I.R. 567.

[957] See further Burrows (1968) 31 M.L.R. 390; Powell, *Law of Agency*, 2nd edn (1961), pp.380–385; *Bowstead and Reynolds on Agency*, 21st edn (2018), para.10-042.

[958] *Rhodes v Forwood* (1876) 1 App. Cas. 256.

[959] *L French & Co Ltd v Leeston Shipping Co* [1922] 1 A.C. 451. See also *Ex p. Maclure* (1870) L.R. 5 Ch. App. 737; *Hamlyn & Co v Wood & Co* [1891] 2 Q.B. 488; *Northey v Trevillion* (1902) 7 Com. Cas. 201; *Re RS Newman Ltd* [1916] 2 Ch. 309; cf. *Orient Overseas Management and Finance Ltd v File Shipping Co Ltd (The Energy Progress)* [1993] 1 Lloyd's Rep. 355 (owner of ship liable to managers for loss of bonus).

[960] *Alpha Trading Ltd v Dunnshaw-Patten* [1981] Q.B. 290, 304. See also *Lazarus v Cairn Line Ltd* (1912) 106 L.T. 378, 380; *George Moundreas & Co SA v Navimpex Centrala Navala* [1985] 2 Lloyd's Rep. 515; *Sun Alliance Pensions Life and Investments Services Ltd v RJL* [1991] 2 Lloyd's Rep. 410.

[961] *Lazarus v Cairn Line Ltd*, above.

[962] *General Publicity Services v Best's Brewery Co Ltd* [1951] 2 T.L.R. 875, 879.

contract by the destruction of his factory by fire.[963] And where an agent's commission depended on matters occurring during the performance of a contract, and the principal decided for his own purposes to break the contract, a term was implied in the agent's favour.[964]

Termination of contract: common law   Where any contract between principal   **31-151**
and agent is unilateral the principal may be able to terminate it, i.e. revoke his offer, before the agent has earned commission,[965] except in those cases where a collateral contract not to revoke is appropriate.[966] Where the contract is bilateral, however, the termination may be a breach of contract, rendering the principal liable for accrued commission, or in damages for loss of the prospect of earning commission. Whether notice is required to terminate a continuing agency contract of indefinite duration depends also on its express or implied terms. No term will necessarily be implied to prevent either party terminating summarily, but such an implication may be made if it is appropriate, which it usually will be. This may be so where the contract is analogous to a contract of employment, or where the agent undertakes to use his best endeavours to carry out his principal's business, or has expended capital sums to carry out his duties. In such cases, for example, a term may be implied that either party must give the other reasonable notice of termination.[967] Such a contract can, of course, also be determined by the principal in consequence of the agent's repudiatory breach.[968] But if it is the principal whose breach is repudiatory, the agent likewise can accept the breach and determine the contract.[969] The question of termination of *contract* is not the same as that of termination of *authority*, which is dealt with below.[970]

---

[963] *Turner v Goldsmith* [1891] 1 Q.B. 544; see also *Mutzenbecher v La Aseguradora Española SA* [1906] 1 K.B. 254; *Reigate v Union Manufacturing Co (Ramsbottom) Ltd* [1918] 1 K.B. 592; *Warren & Co v Agdeshman* (1922) 38 T.L.R. 588; *Re Premier Products Ltd* [1965] N.Z.L.R. 50.

[964] *Alpha Trading Ltd v Dunnshaw-Patten* [1981] Q.B. 290; *George Moundreas & Co SA v Navimpex Centrala Navala* [1985] 2 Lloyd's Rep. 515; *Martin-Smith v Williams* [1999] E.M.L.R. 571; *C. Christo & Co Ltd v Marathon Advisory Service Ltd* [2015] EWHC 1971 (QB). cf. *Marcan Shipping (London) Ltd v Polish SS Co (The Manifest Lipkowy)* [1988] 2 Lloyd's Rep. 171. Sometimes the matter is expressly provided for: see *Christie & Vesey Ltd v Maatschappij &c. (The Helvetia-S)* [1960] 1 Lloyd's Rep. 540; *Micklefield v SAC Technology Ltd* [1990] 1 W.L.R. 1002.

[965] *Motion v Michaud* (1892) 8 T.L.R. 447; *Joynson v Hunt & Son* (1905) 93 L.T. 470; *Levy v Goldhill* [1917] 2 Ch. 297.

[966] The dictum of (Reginald) Goff L.J. in *Daulia Ltd v Four Millbank Nominees Ltd* [1978] Ch. 231, 239 is surely too wide.

[967] *Bauman v Hulton Press Ltd* [1952] 2 All E.R. 1121; *Martin-Baker Aircraft Co Ltd v Murison* [1955] 2 Q.B. 556; *Decro-Wall International SA v Practitioners in Marketing Ltd* [1971] 1 W.L.R. 361, 376–377; *Crawford Fitting Co v Sydney Valve and Fittings Pty Ltd* (1988) 14 N.S.W.L.R. 438; cited in *Alpha Lettings Ltd v Neptune Research and Development Ltd* [2003] EWCA Civ 704; *Paper Reclaim Ltd v Aoteasoa International Ltd* [2007] 3 N.Z.L.R. 169; *W Nagel v Pluczenik Diamond Co NV* [2017] EWHC 1750 (Comm), [2017] 2 Lloyd's Rep. 215. Reasonableness is judged at the time of termination: *Turner v Ogilvy & Mather (NZ) Ltd* [1996] 1 N.Z.L.R. 641, 646. See Carnegie (1969) 85 L.Q.R. 392; Vol.I, para.14-029.

[968] See below, para.31-161; Vol.I, Ch.24.

[969] e.g. *Decro-Wall International SA v Practitioners in Marketing Ltd*, above (where the agent (actually a distributor) was also granted an injunction: see also *Evans Marshall & Co Ltd v Bertola SA* [1973] 1 W.L.R. 349).

[970] Below, para.31-166.

31-152 **Termination: where Commercial Agents Regulations applicable** Where the Commercial Agents (Council Directive) Regulations[971] apply, special restrictions operate as between principal and agent on the "termination" of an agency contract; though these again cannot affect the principal's power to terminate summarily the *authority* of the agent to bind him. First, where the agency contract is concluded for an indefinite period, either party may terminate it by notice,[972] and minimum periods, which can be extended but not reduced by agreement, are specified for this.[973] Secondly, an agency contract for a fixed period which continues to be performed after the period has expired is converted into a contract for an indefinite period and so subject to the limits already referred to.[974] Thirdly, it is provided by reg.16 that the regulations do not affect:

"… the operation of any enactment or rule of law which provides for the immediate termination of the agency contract (a) because of the failure of one party to carry out all or part of his obligations under that contract; or (b) where exceptional circumstances arise".

This must refer to rules of domestic law, but is not well drafted for its purpose. For common law, the reference must be to the rule of (what a common lawyer would call) repudiatory breach of contract, and (something similar to, but not necessarily the same as) frustration. As regards breach, it has been said that it refers to "a provision of the applicable law that justifies immediate termination regardless of the terms of the contract".[975] This must cover repudiatory conduct, and presumably breach of condition, which likewise emanates from the general law, but excludes specific contract terms entitling termination.[976] However, it was held in the same case that even though notice was served under such a specific contract term, if the breach was in fact repudiatory and the principal could be regarded as acting "because of" it, the wording of reg.16 permitted reliance on it.[977] As regards frustration, this must be confined to forms of frustration relating to the contract obligation rather than the agent performing it, for death and incapacity are specifically mentioned in reg.18(a) as entitling indemnity or compensation. English law requires the innocent party to accept the breach, and it seems likely that this rule comes

---

971 Above, para.31-017. See in general *Bowstead and Reynolds on Agency*, 21st edn (2018), Ch.11; McGee [2013] J.B.L. 534, 545–551.

972 Commercial Agents Regulations reg.15(1). See discussion in McGee [2011] J.B.L. 782, 785.

973 Commercial Agents Regulations reg.15(2)–(5).

974 Commercial Agents Regulations reg.14.

975 *Crane v Sky In-Home Service Ltd* [2007] EWHC 66 (Ch), [2007] 2 All E.R. (Comm) 599 at [84]. "The terms of the contract" might be more clearly expressed "specific contract terms".

976 cf. *Spar Shipping AS v Grand China Logistics Holding (Group) Co Ltd* [2016] EWCA Civ 982, [2016] 2 Lloyd's Rep. 447 (on the withdrawal clause in a time charter).

977 *Crane v Sky In-Home Service Ltd*, above, at [91] (passing off warranties as agent's own); see also *Nigel Fryer Joinery Services Ltd v Ian Firth Hardware Ltd* [2008] 2 Lloyd's Rep. 108. But in *Volvo Car Germany GmbH v Autohof Weidensdorf GmbH* (C-203/09) EU:C:2010:647, [2011] 1 All E.R. (Comm) 906 it was held that it did not apply where the relevant conduct occurred after the giving of notice but before the contract expired but was not known to the principal at the time the contract ended. As to the applicability under the regulations of the common law rule that a termination on inadequate grounds can be justified on valid grounds existing at the time of termination see *Rossetti Marketing Ltd v Diamond Sofa Co Ltd* [2012] EWCA Civ 1021, [2013] 1 All E.R. (Comm) 308 at [55], [56], [59]. Contrast *Cooper v Pure Fishing (UK) Ltd* [2003] EWCA Civ 375, [2004] 2 Lloyd's Rep. 518, where the principal simply did not renew a contract, though he believed he had grounds for terminating it.

within the "provisions of the applicable law".[978] But beyond this, except where the contract is justifiably terminated by the principal for the agent's breach,[979] or is terminated by the agent without justification,[980] the agent is after the termination of the agency contract entitled to be indemnified or compensated for damage.[981] This entitlement to a payment on termination is absolute. It therefore applies not only when the agent is unjustifiably dismissed[982] or when he himself justifiably terminates the contract by reason of circumstances attributable to the principal,[983] but also when the contract is for a fixed term which expires,[984] or is subject to a review which entitles termination by the principal,[985] or where the agent dies,[986] retires,[987] becomes too old, infirm or ill to continue his activities,[988] or bankrupt.[989] It has been held that the entitlement does not apply to a termination of part of the agency contract only.[990] Although proceedings for wrongful termination and unpaid commission are contractual as regards EU jurisdiction[991] it has been held in the context of English jurisdiction to serve process in a non-EU country that proceedings for indemnity or compensation are not contractual but statutory.[992] Claims in respect of either must be notified within one year of the termination of the agency.[993]

Indemnity and compensation for commercial agents: indemnity An indemnity is a sum calculated on an equitable basis with regard to the extent to which the agent has brought the principal new customers or has significantly increased the volume **31-153**

---

978 *Bell Electric Ltd v Aweco Appliance Systems GmbH & Co* [2002] EWHC 872 (QB), [2002] Eu.L.R. 44 (principal's breach not accepted by agent); *Alan Ramsay Sales & Marketing Ltd v Typhoo Tea Ltd* [2016] EWHC 486 (Comm), [2016] 4 W.L.R. 59 (agent's breach not accepted by principal). But this is, at least as regards acceptance by the agent, criticised by Saintier and Scholes, above, para.31-017, n.97 as prejudicial to the protection of the agent.

979 Commercial Agents Regulations reg.18(a), invoking reg.16, discussed above. For a recent case where the agent's conduct was held not sufficiently serious see *Crocs Europe BV v Anderson* [2012] EWCA Civ 1400, [2013] 1 Lloyd's Rep 1 (dismissing some rather strange arguments).

980 Commercial Agents Regulations reg.18(b)(i). See above as to acceptance of the breach. These words do not cover failure to continue renewal negotiations: *Elsevier Masson v La Diffusion Sofradif* [2017] E.C.C. 30 (French Cour de Cassation). The rights also do not apply where the agent, with the principal's agreement, assigns his rights and duties under the contract: reg.18(c).

981 Commercial Agents Regulations reg.17. See McGee [2011] J.B.L. 782, 786 et seq.

982 Commercial Agents Regulations regs 16, 18(a).

983 Commercial Agents Regulations reg.18(b)(i).

984 *Frape v Emreco International Ltd*, 2002 S.L.T. 371 OH; following *Whitehead and Jenks v Cattell* [1995] Eu. L.R. 827; *Tigana Ltd v Decoro Ltd* [2003] EWHC 23 (QB), [2003] Eu. L.R. 189; *Light v Ty Europe Ltd* [2003] EWHC 174 (QB), [2003] 1 All E.R. (Comm) 568, reversed on other grounds [2003] EWCA Civ 1238, [2003] Eu. L.R. 858.

985 *Monk v Largo Foods Ltd* [2016] EWHC 1837 (Comm) ("subject to the completion of a successful review"); *Conseil et mise en relations (CMR) SARL v Demeures terre et tradition SARL* (C-645/16), [2018] Bus. L.R. 1164 (termination during trial period covered).

986 Commercial Agents Regulations reg.17(8).

987 Even if healthy enough to continue: *Abbott v Condici Ltd* [2005] 2 Lloyd's Rep. 450.

988 Commercial Agents Regulations reg 18(b)(ii).

989 See EC Report, below, n.998, at 2.

990 *Scottish Power Energy Retail Ltd v Taskforce Contracts Ltd* [2008] CSOH 110, [2009] Eu. L.R. 62.

991 *Arcado v Haviland* (C-9/87) EU:C:1988:127, [1988] E.C.R. 1539 (jurisdiction).

992 *Fern Computer Consultancy Ltd v Intergraph Cadworx & Analysis Solutions Inc* [2014] EWHC 2908 (Ch), [2014] Bus. L.R. 1397 at [34] et seq., especially [46].

993 Commercial Agents Regulations reg.17(9). As to the form of the notice required see *Hackett v Advanced Medical Computer Systems* [1999] C.L.C. 160. As to the timing of the notice in this connection see *Claramoda Ltd v Zoomphase Ltd* [2009] EWHC 2857 (Comm), [2010] E.C.C. 1.

of business[994] with existing customers and the principal continues to derive substantial benefits from such customers after the cessation of the contract. It must take into account the commission lost by the agent on business transacted with such customers.[995] But it relates principally therefore to benefits rather than losses, and should not be affected by notions of mitigation of damages.[996] It is limited to a "figure equivalent to an indemnity for one year calculated from the commercial agent's annual remuneration over the preceding five years and if the contract goes back less than five years the indemnity shall be calculated on the average for the period in question".[997] The indemnity is the principal remedy in German law, where there is a substantial body of authority as to how it is to be calculated.[998] Under the United Kingdom regulations it applies only where specifically provided for,[999] though its one-year limit makes it often less onerous to the principal than compensation. The right to damages (for wrongful termination under the general law) is not excluded, provided that there is no double recovery of commission.[1000]

31-154   **Compensation**   The other remedy is compensation, and under the United Kingdom Regulations this remedy applies unless the agency contract otherwise provides.[1001] The right cannot be derogated from to the detriment of the agent before the expiry of the contract (but may by a settlement afterwards).[1002] It covers "damage he suffers as a result of termination of his relations with his principal", and particularly when the termination takes place either in circumstances which deprive the agent of commission "which proper performance of the agency contract would have secured him" and provide benefits to the principal; or have not enabled the agent to amortise costs and expenses incurred in performance of his function.[1003] It seems therefore on the wording used to be based on loss rather than profit: but it

---

994 This covers customers brought in by the agent who may have had business relations with the supplier in relation to other goods: *Marchon Germany GmbH v Karaszkiewicz* (C-315/14) EU:C:2016:211, [2016] Bus. L.R. 694; and see *Re Sales of Spectacle Frames* [2017] E.C.C. 19 (German Bundesgerichtshof).

995 Commercial Agents Regulations reg.17(3). If the benefits exceed the lost commission the requirement that the award be equitable does not prevent the benefits being taken into account (contrary to a practice in the German courts): *Semen v Deutsche Tamoil GmbH* (C-348/07) EU:C:2009:195, [2009] 1 Lloyd's Rep. 653.

996 See *Moore v Piretta*, below, n.998.

997 Commercial Agents Regulations reg.17(4). This is a "cap": it is not the basis of calculation.

998 See the European Commission Report of July 23, 1998, *The Application of the Commercial Agents Directive* (COM 96/354 FINAL), which contains a careful exposition, with an example, of how an indemnity can be calculated. See also a valuable comment by O'Neill, 1997 S.L.T. 141. There is one useful decision on calculating indemnity under English law: *Moore v Piretta PTA Ltd* [1999] 1 All E.R. 174, discussed by Segal in (1998) 142 S.J. 376.

999 Commercial Agents Regulations reg.17(2). It seems likely that when it is chosen it must be taken in the form prescribed: reg.19. For a case where it was held that the contract provided for indemnity despite using the word "compensation" see *Hardie Polymers Ltd v Polymerland Ltd*, 2000 S.C.L.R. 64 OH.

1000 Commercial Agents Regulations reg.17(5); *Quenon K SPRL v Beobank SA* (C-338/14) EU:C:2015:795, [2016] Bus. L.R. 264.

1001 Commercial Agents Regulations reg.17(2). See the specialist books cited above, para.31-017, n.97; McGee [2011] J.B.L. 782, 791 et seq.

1002 Commercial Agents Regulations reg.19. For an example of a clause held invalid see *Shearman v Hunter Boot Ltd* [2013] EWHC 47 (QB), [2014] E.C.C. 12 (clause providing for indemnity, but compensation if the amount would be lower: default regime applied); cf. *Brand Studio v St John Knits Inc* [2015] EWHC 3143 (QB), [2015] Bus. L.R. 1421, where a similar clause was held severable.

1003 Commercial Agents Regulations reg.17(7).

again seems that principles of mitigation should not apply.[1004] It is usually regarded as representing the approach of French law to this problem,[1005] and for that reason some courts have had recourse to evidence of, or information concerning, French law, though such a method is not to be justified from EU law itself.[1006] Since it applies where the termination involves no breach of contract, it might seem to be a narrow form of indemnity; but as stated above it may in fact work out at a sum exceeding the indemnity by reason of the indemnity's one-year rule: French courts have awarded sums calculated by reference to two years' commission.[1007] It has been held that the right to damages at common law persists,[1008] though such a right is not preserved in the wording as it is for the indemnity[1009] and the proposition seems doubtful in view of the wide phraseology relating to compensation in it and the emphasis in that phraseology on loss. However, if the notion of compensation is in this context to be developed independently, there may be value in retaining the common law rules as to damages even though there is no specific reservation of the right to such damages.

Calculation of compensation   The method of assessment of compensation for the **31-155** United Kingdom[1010] was laid down by the House of Lords' decision in *Lonsdale v Howard & Hallam Ltd*,[1011] which superseded earlier authority, of which a considerable amount (of varied quality) had been accumulating.[1012] Such an idea of compensation has so far been unique to French law. The opinion of Lord Hoffmann accepts the French notion that the agent is regarded "as having had a share in the goodwill of the principal's business which he has helped to create".[1013] "This means, primarily, the right to future commissions 'which proper performance of the agency contract would have procured him.'"[1014] It appears that in its implementation French courts have regularly awarded, though not by way of applying a rule, a sum equivalent to twice the average annual gross commission over the previous three years. It is clear however that other countries are not under any obligation to follow any one state's method of calculation.[1015] The French practice appears to be based on the assumption that agencies in France change hands at the sort of valu-

---

[1004] See the European Commission Report cited above, n.998, at 6.

[1005] See European Commission Report at 5.

[1006] See *Nicolas Corman & Fils SA v Hauptzollamt Gronau* (C-64/81) EU:C:1982:5, [1982] E.C.R. 13; followed in Case 296/95 *R. v Customs and Excise Commissioners Ex p. EMU Tabac SARL* [1998] Q.B. 791; both cited in *Bell Electric L d v Aweco Appliance Systems GmbH & Co* [2002] EWHC 872 (QB), [2002] Eu. L.R. 443.

[1007] See the European Commission Report cited above, n.998, at 5; below, para.31-155.

[1008] *Duffen v Frabo SpA* [2000] 1 Lloyd's Rep. 180; *Alan Ramsay Sales & Marketing Ltd v Typhoo Tea Ltd* [2016] EWHC 486 (Comm), [2016] 4 W.L.R. 59; *Computer Associates Ltd v Software Incubator Ltd* [2016] EWHC 1587 (QB), revised on other grounds [2018] EWCA Civ 518 (QB), [2017] Bus. L.R. 245.

[1009] Commercial Agents Regulations reg.17(5).

[1010] The regulations apply in Scotland as well as England and Wales, and there are parallel regulations in Northern Ireland. The House of Lords is the final appellate tribunal for all three jurisdictions.

[1011] [2007] UKHL 32, [2007] 1 W.L.R. 2055, in substantial accord with the judgment of Moore-Bick L.J. in the Court of Appeal: [2006] EWCA 63, [2006] 1 W.L.R. 1281. Noted by Saintier (2008) 124 L.Q.R. 31.

[1012] Principally the decision of the Inner House of the Court of Session in *King v T Tunnock Ltd*, 2000 S.C. 424, which was not approved in the House of Lords, though it may be valid in Scotland. Other cases are also considered in the opinion of Lord Hoffmann.

[1013] at [9].

[1014] at [10].

[1015] *Honeyvem Informazioni Commerciali SrL v Mariella de Zotti* (C-465/04) EU:C:2006:199, [2006]

ation mentioned above, whereas there is no such market in the United Kingdom.[1016] The courts of the United Kingdom are entitled, therefore, to use their own methods of calculating the loss for which the compensation is payable. "What has to be valued is the income stream which the agency would have generated".[1017] This should be done "by reference to the value of the agency on the assumption that it continued: the amount which the agent could reasonably expect to receive for the right to stand in his shoes, continue to perform the duties of the agency and receive the commission which he would have received".[1018] If the agency was unassignable, it must be assumed that a purchaser would have been entitled to take it over, but not that he would thereby acquire an assignable asset.[1019] The court would require information about "the standard methodology for the valuation of such businesses", though there might be cases where courts could eventually take judicial notice of the "standard case".[1020] In the case in question the business concerned was declining, and the agency would not be likely to change hands at any considerable value. The court would therefore have been justified in awarding nothing, and this is a significant part of the decision.[1021] However, a small award made by the judge (much less than the amount claimed) was approved. By the same reasoning, the converse might have been the case had the business been increasing.

It was also said in the Court of Appeal that:

"... if the agency is terminated in circumstances where the agent has not been able to amortise expenses which he has incurred on the advice of the principal in setting up the agency, the value attaching to the business may or may not provide sufficient compensation ... the agent is entitled to recover whatever loss he can show he has suffered which in a case of this kind might consist in whole or in part of the amount of the unamortized expenses."[1022]

31-156   Commission after cessation of agency   The duration of an agent's common law right to remuneration depends on the construction of the terms of the agency agreement. These will frequently provide, expressly or by implication, that the right to remuneration is coterminous with his employment and ceases upon the termination of the agency.[1023] If this is so, a principal is not normally liable to pay commission upon orders sent by a customer originally introduced to the principal by an

---

E.C.R. I-02789; and for this reason the House declined to make a reference to the European Court of Justice.

[1016] at [18]. See also at [26]: "the French practice is of no evidential value whatever."

[1017] at [12].

[1018] at [21].

[1019] at [13].

[1020] at [35], [36].

[1021] An argument that an agency had no value was rejected in *Warren v Drukkerij Flach BV* [2014] EWCA Civ 993, [2015] 1 Lloyd's Rep. 111; but the court did not accept the view that Lord Hoffmann's opinion implied that it was to be assumed that the agency had a value—"the argument that the agency is in fact valueless does have to be addressed" (at [14]). See also *Monk v Largo Foods Ltd* [2016] EWHC 1837 (Comm).

[1022] [2006] EWCA 63, [2006] 1 W.L.R. 1281 at [29], per Moore-Bick L.J. Cases considering calculation of compensation since *Lonsdale* include *McQuillan v McCormick* [2010] EWHC 1112 (QB), [2011] E.C.C. 18 (jewellery); *Invicta UK Ltd v International Brands Ltd* [2013] EWCA Civ 1564 (QB), [2013] E.C.C. 30 (wine for supermarkets); *Alan Ramsay Sales & Marketing Ltd v Typhoo Tea Ltd* [2016] EWHC 486 (Comm), [2016] 4 W.L.R. 59 (food sector); *Monk v Largo Foods Ltd* [2016] EWHC 1837 (Comm) (consultant to food manufacturer) and *W Nagel v Pluczenik Diamond Co NV* [2017] EWHC 1750 (Comm), [2017] 2 Lloyd's Rep. 215 (diamond broker).

[1023] See *Bickley v Browning* (1913) 30 T.L.R. 388; *Weare v Brimsdown Lead Co* (1910) 103 L.T. 429.

agent after the latter has ceased to represent the principal.[1024] But the agency contract may provide that the *right* to commission accrues before the time when the commission becomes *payable*. In such cases, the commission must be paid after termination of the agency contract, because the agent's right to receive it arose when the contract subsisted. The agent has a vested right to the money, and termination of his contract does not deprive him of it. So, if the agreement is to pay commission on "repeat orders", commission will usually be payable on such orders even if the agency has meanwhile terminated[1025]; however, the term "repeats" may, on the proper construction of the contract, refer only to repeat orders received during the continuance of the agency.[1026] An undertaking "to cover you with an agreed commission on any other business transacted with your friends", in return for an introduction, was held to entitle the agent to commission on a subsequent transaction resulting from an advertisement in a newspaper; the condition was not too vague to be enforceable.[1027] And where commission was payable when advertisements secured by the agent were published and not when orders for them were obtained by him, it was held that the agent was entitled to commission on advertisements published after the termination of his contract, because the entitlement accrued as soon as the orders were obtained, regardless of the publication date.[1028] Again, if the agreement is to pay commission as long as the customer does business with the principal, commission will be payable even after the death of the agent.[1029] The appropriate remedy in such cases will normally be not an order for an account but an award of damages.[1030]

Commercial agents   For commercial agents, the Commercial Agents Regulations[1031] have specific provisions on this point. The agent is entitled to commission on a transaction concluded after the agency contract has been terminated if the transaction is mainly attributable to the agent's efforts and entered into within a reasonable time after termination, or the order reached the principal before the contract terminated.[1032] A subsequent commercial agent would not then be so entitled unless "it is equitable because of the circumstances for the commission to be shared between the commercial agents".[1033] There is also a provision on "repeat orders".[1034] These provisions operate only in the absence of other agreement.   **31-157**

[1024] *Marshall v Glanvill* [1917] 2 K.B. 87; *Bettany v Eastern Morning, etc. News Co* (1900) 16 T.L.R. 401; *Gerahty v Baines & Co* (1903) 19 T.L.R. 554; *Cramb v Goodwin* (1919) 35 T.L.R. 477.

[1025] *Levy v Goldhill* [1917] 2 Ch. 297.

[1026] *Crocker Horlock Ltd v B Lang & Co Ltd* [1949] 1 All E.R. 526.

[1027] *British Bank for Foreign Trade Ltd v Novinex Ltd* [1949] 1 K.B. 623.

[1028] *Sellers v London Counties Newspapers* [1951] 1 K.B. 784. See also *Gold v Life Assurance Co of Pennsylvania* [1971] 2 Lloyd's Rep. 164. The whole question is considered by Rix L.J. in *Explora Group Plc v Hesco Bastion Ltd* [2005] EWCA Civ 646 at [49] et seq.

[1029] *Wilson v Harper* [1908] 2 Ch. 370.

[1030] *Roberts v Elwells Engineers Ltd* [1972] 2 Q.B. 586.

[1031] Above, paras 31-017 et seq.

[1032] Commercial Agents Regulations reg.8. "Mainly attributable to" in reg.8 sets a more exacting test than "concluded as a result of" in reg.7(1)(a): *Monk v Largo Foods Ltd* [2016] EWHC 1837 (Comm). For an application see *Tigana Ltd v Decoro Ltd* [2003] EWHC 23 (QB), [2003] Eu. L.R. 189. See McGee [2013] J.B.L. 534, 543–545. For an example of a claim for compensation combined with a claim under reg.8 and at common law see *McQuillan v McCormick* [2010] EWHC 1112 (QB), [2011] E.C.C. 18.

[1033] Commercial Agents Regulations reg.9(1). It is provided that the principal is liable for the sum due and can recover an undue payment from the agent who has received it: reg.9(2).

[1034] Commercial Agents Regulations reg.7(1)(b); see above, para.31-156.

31-158   Overpayment of commission   If the agency contract provides for the payment of advances against commission and the agent's contract is properly terminated before he has earned sufficient commission to offset the payment, it is a question of interpretation whether or not the overpayment can be recovered.[1035] An action in restitution would seem to be the form of action most likely to succeed.[1036]

31-159   Restrictions on activity after cessation of agency   Agency contracts may contain restrictions on the agent's commercial activity after he has ceased to act for the principal concerned; this is especially so where the agent is an employee. The general validity of such restrictions is governed by the law relating to stipulations in restraint of trade[1037]; but when the Commercial Agents Regulations (Council Directive)[1038] are applicable (which would require the agent to be self-employed), they contain specific provisions of a similar nature, with a requirement of writing.[1039] In principle the restrictions should not apply where the principal wrongfully terminated the contract[1040]; but they would apply (insofar as valid and enforceable) if the agent wrongfully terminates it or is justifiably dismissed.[1041]

31-160   Illegality of service   An agent cannot recover commission where his acting as agent is illegal,[1042] or upon a transaction which is obviously or to his knowledge, illegal, e.g. where he effects a sale of shares in an illegal association,[1043] or an illegal policy of insurance.[1044] This is an application of the general rules as to illegal contracts.[1045]

31-161   Loss of commission at common law by default or misconduct   Where the agent commits a breach of his obligations, it may obviously sometimes be the case that thereby he does not perform the act or acts entitling him to remuneration, which he therefore cannot claim.[1046] However, a more serious breach may be regarded as going to the root of the contract and hence repudiatory, or creating a total failure of consideration. In such a case the agent's services may be terminated, damages may be due, and no further commission will be payable, and commission already received recoverable, beyond anything already earned.[1047] In a recent case, however,

---

[1035] See *Clayton Newbury Ltd v Findlay* [1953] 1 W.L.R. 1194n.; *Rivoli Hats Ltd v Gooch* [1953] 1 W.L.R. 1190; *Bronester Ltd v Priddle* [1961] 1 W.L.R. 1294; *Prudential Assurance Co Ltd v Rodrigues* [1982] 2 N.Z.L.R. 54.

[1036] See Vol.I, paras 29-065 et seq.; *DO Ferguson & Associates v Sohl* [1992] 62 B.L.R. 95, discussed by Birks in Rose (ed.) *Consensus ad Idem* (1996), 179, 199.

[1037] See Vol.I, paras 16-106 et seq.

[1038] Above, para.31-017.

[1039] Commercial Agents Regulations reg.20: the restriction cannot continue for more than two years after termination. See *BCM Group Plc v Visualmark Ltd* [2006] EWHC 1831 (QB) (length acceptable but coverage too wide).

[1040] See *Photo Production Ltd v Securicor Transport Ltd* [1980] A.C. 827, 848–850.

[1041] See *Thomas Marshall (Exports) Ltd v Guinlé* [1979] Ch. 227.

[1042] e.g. where he is an unqualified solicitor: Solicitors Act 1974 s.25(1); cf. *SCF Finance Co Ltd v Masri (No.2)* [1987] Q.B. 1002.

[1043] *Josephs v Pebrer* (1825) 3 B. & C. 639.

[1044] See *Alkins v Jupe* (1877) 2 C.P.D. 375.

[1045] On authority to act illegally see *Bowstead and Reynolds on Agency*, 21st edn (2018), para.2-025; and see in general Vol.I, Ch.16.

[1046] e.g. *Salomons v Pender* (1865) 3 Hurl. & C. 639 (also involving an element of self-dealing).

[1047] e.g. *Boston Deep Sea Fishing & Ice Co v Ansell* (1888) 39 Ch. D. 339. See also *Macnamara v Martin* (1908) 7 C.L.T. 699 (conduct contrary to fiduciary duties after commission earned).

Imageview Management Ltd v Jack,[1048] an agent acting on commission who had secured employment for a professional footballer also acted for the relevant club to procure an immigration permit for his client and charged the club a fee for doing so. The Court of Appeal held that there was a breach of fiduciary duty, and in consequence the commission was forfeit: no more commission need be paid and the footballer was entitled to repayment of the commission already paid.[1049] The sum paid for the permit was treated as a secret profit and to be paid to the agent without any allowance for the value of work done.[1050] The only exception that appears to be envisaged to such a forfeiture was one of "harmless collaterality".[1051] The decision as to the secret profit is less controversial, but as regards the greater forfeiture this is a harsh case and it is not clear that there is satisfactory authority in equity or common law for the notion of forfeiture in this context. Had there been a total failure of consideration as regards the agent's performance, the money paid would be refundable and no more money due. But the principal services required had here been uncontroversially performed and it is equally not clear that a non-dishonest breach of fiduciary obligation, as this seems to have been, should be treated under general contract law as of itself creating such a failure or as justifying forfeiture. The previous cases use various different lines of reasoning[1052] and cannot be said to be clear except in strong hostility to breach of fiduciary duty.[1053] The *Imageview* case has since been both followed[1054] and distinguished.[1055] It is possible that the introduction of the notion of forfeiture in this area may at some time require reconsideration. Apart from this, the principal can waive the breach,[1056] but waiver will not be implied merely from the principal's accepting the benefit of the transaction negotiated,[1057] or suing the agent for a bribe received.[1058] Where the breach does not go to the whole of the agent's obligation, he may be able to recover commission[1059]; and where the breach is in respect of a severable transaction he may be able to recover commission for services not affected by the breach.[1060]

[1048] [2009] EWCA Civ 63, [2009] Bus. L.R. 1034: see Watts (2009) 125 L.Q.R. 369; Oram [2010] L.M.C.L.Q. 95.

[1049] See at [51].

[1050] See at [59].

[1051] See at [30].

[1052] The strongest for the result obtained are *Andrews v Ramsay & Co* [1903] 2 K.B. 635 and *Rhodes v Macalister* (1923) 29 Com. Cas. 19.

[1053] See the brief but trenchant judgment of Mummery L.J. at [64].

[1054] *Rahme v Smith & Williamson* [2009] EWHC 911 (Ch); *Stupples v Stupples & Co (High Wycombe) Ltd* [2012] EWHC 1226 (Ch), [2013] 1 B.C.L.C. 729; *Avrahami v Biran* [2013] EWHC 1776 (Ch); *Hosking v Marathon Asset Management LLP* [2016] EWHC 2418 (Ch), [2017] Ch. 157 (forfeiture of share in partnership profits). See also *Premium Real Estate Ltd v Stevens* [2009] 2 N.Z.L.R. 384, decided very shortly after the *Imageview* case.

[1055] *Accidia Foundation v Simon C. Dickinson Ltd* [2010] EWHC 3058 (Ch); *Bank of Ireland v Jaffery* [2012] EWHC 1377 (Ch); *Wright Hassall LLP v Horton Jr* [2015] EWHC 3716 (QB); *Gamatronic (UK) Ltd v Hamilton* [2016] EWHC 2225 (QB)

[1056] *Harrods Ltd v Lemon* [1931] 2 K.B. 157; *Thornton Hall & Partners v Wembley Electrical Appliances Ltd* [1947] 2 All E.R. 630.

[1057] *Salomons v Pender* (1865) 3 H. & C 639; *Rhodes v Macalister* (1923) 29 Com. Cas. 19.

[1058] *Andrews v Ramsay* [1903] 2 K.B. 635.

[1059] *Keppel v Wheeler* [1927] 1 K.B. 577; and see *Robinson Scammell & Co v Ansell* [1985] 2 E.G.L.R. 41 (bona fide mistake); *Eric V Stansfield (A Firm) v South East Nursing Home Services Ltd* [1986] 1 E.G.L.R. 29; *The Peppy* [1997] 2 Lloyd's Rep. 722, 728–729.

[1060] *Hippisley v Knee Brothers* [1905] 1 K.B. 1; *Nitedals Taendstikfabrik v Bruster* [1906] 2 Ch. 671; *Stupples v Stupples & Co (High Wycombe) Ltd* [2012] EWHC 1226 (Ch), [2013] 1 B.C.L.C. 729 (commission still earned on work for another client). But cf. *Headway Construction Co Ltd v*

(ii) Indemnity at Common Law

31-162 Indemnity of agent[1061]   Unless otherwise agreed, the principal is under a common law duty to reimburse and indemnify the agent against all expenses and liabilities incurred in the execution of his authority.[1062] This may be enforced by action against the principal, by the exercise of any lien which the agent may have,[1063] or by way of set-off.[1064] Where the agency is contractual this duty can be regarded as contractual: but in some cases the agency may not be contractual, and the duty must be enforced by an action in restitution.[1065] At any rate where the agency is contractual, the liability is not confined to payments made in discharge of debts legally binding on the principal: the agent may recover indemnity for payments which he is bound to make though the principal is not,[1066] liabilities which he has not yet himself discharged,[1067] payments which may not have been necessary but which when they were made reasonably appeared to be necessary,[1068] and payments of debts which could not be legally enforced but non-payment of which would involve serious consequences.[1069] But the act of the agent must have been within the scope of his express or implied authority, as extended by custom operative in the market in which the agent deals, provided that such custom is reasonable or known to the principal[1070]; or else it must have been ratified.[1071]

31-163 Where no indemnity available   There is, however, no duty of indemnity in

---

Downham (1974) 233 E.G. 675.

[1061] This is not the same as the indemnity sometimes available to commercial agents on termination of their agency: above, para.31-154.

[1062] *Thacker v Hardy* (1878) 4 Q.B.D. 685, 687. For a modern example, see *Islamic Republic of Iran Shipping Lines v Zannis Cia Naviera SA (The Tzelepi)* [1991] 2 Lloyd's Rep. 265. In many cases, however, the right to indemnity is superseded by the remuneration payable, e.g. as to advertising expenses. Whether or not this is so depends on the interpretation of the contract and any relevant custom. See also below, para.40-113.

[1063] Below, para.31-164. The agent who is liable together with his principal may sometimes have a right to contribution under s.1 of the Civil Liability (Contribution) Act 1978.

[1064] *Cropper v Cook* (1868) L.R. 3 C.P. 194; *Curtis v Barclay* (1826) 5 B. & C. 141. But not where the money which the principal claims was deposited with the agent for a specific purpose which has failed: *Stumore v Campbell* [1892] 1 Q.B. 314; *Re Mid-Kent Fruit Factory* [1896] 1 Ch. 567.

[1065] This may be more limited: see *Brook's Wharf v Goodman* [1937] 1 K.B. 534. But the duty to indemnify is sometimes stated in very general terms: see *Dugdale v Lovering* (1875) L.R. 10 C.P. 196; *Sheffield Corp v Barclay* [1905] A.C. 392; *Secretary of State v Bank of India* [1938] 2 All E.R. 797; *Owen v Tate* [1976] Q.B. 402; *Yeung Kai Yung v Hong Kong and Shanghai Banking Corp* [1981] A.C. 787; cf. *Naviera Mogor SA v Soc Metallurgique de Normandie (The Nogar Marin)* [1988] 1 Lloyd's Rep. 412; Vol.I, paras 29-119 et seq.; Goff and Jones, *Law of Unjust Enrichment*, 8th edn (2010), paras 19-16 et seq.

[1066] *Adams v Morgan* [1924] 1 K.B. 751 (supertax); *Brittain v Lloyd* (1845) 14 M. & W. 762.

[1067] *Lacey v Hill, Crowley's Claim* (1874) L.R. 18 Eq. 182.

[1068] *Frixione v Tagliaferro* (1856) 10 Moo. P.C. 175; *Williams v Lister* (1913) 109 L.T. 699; *Pettman v Keble* (1850) 9 C.B. 701. And see *John Koch Ltd v C & H Products Ltd* [1956] 2 Lloyd's Rep. 59.

[1069] e.g. payment by solicitor of barrister's fees; *Rhodes v Fielder* (1919) 89 L.J. K.B. 15; payments made by stockbrokers in accordance with the rules and usages of the Stock Exchange: *Reynolds v Smith* (1893) 9 T.L.R. 494; *Taylor v Stray* (1857) 2 C.B.(N.S.) 175, 197; *Chapman v Shepherd* (1867) L.R. 2 C.P. 228; *Biederman v Stone* (1867) L.R. 2 C.P. 504. But cf. *Liberian Insurance Inc v Mosse* [1977] 2 Lloyd's Rep. 560.

[1070] Above, para.31-048. See also *Anglo Overseas Transport Co Ltd v Titan Industrial Corp* [1959] 2 Lloyd's Rep. 152; *Perishables Transport Co Ltd v N Spyropoulos (London) Ltd* [1964] 2 Lloyd's Rep. 379; cf. *Wilson v Avec Audio-Visual Equipment Ltd* [1974] 1 Lloyd's Rep. 81.

[1071] Above, paras 31-027 et seq.

respect of liability incurred solely by the agent's negligence or breach of duty,[1072] or through his insolvency[1073]; in respect of transactions which are obviously or to the agent's knowledge unlawful.[1074]

(iii) Lien

Lien It is usually said that an agent has a general or particular possessory lien on his principal's goods[1075] in respect of lawful claims arising in the course of the agency, though whether such a right really attaches to the notion of an "agent" is perhaps doubtful, and the support for such a right arises in specific contexts. Thus an auctioneer has a lien on goods he is employed to sell in respect of his charges and commission.[1076] The agent must be in lawful possession of the goods in the course of his agency[1077] and hold them in the same capacity as that in which he claims the lien.[1078] There must be no agreement inconsistent with a lien[1079] nor must the goods be delivered with directions or for a purpose inconsistent with a lien.[1080] An agent's lien is usually a particular lien unless by agreement or custom or usage he is given a general lien, e.g. factors, insurance brokers, stockbrokers, solicitors, bankers and wharfingers have general liens.[1081] A lien is lost by tender to the agent of the sum due,[1082] by the agent entering into an agreement or acting in a capacity inconsistent with it,[1083] or by loss of possession,[1084] or by waiver.[1085] Sub-agents may

31-164

[1072] *Thacker v Hardy* (1878) 4 Q.B.D. 685, 687; *Lewis v Samuel* (1846) 8 Q.B. 685; *Ellis v Pond* [1898] 1 Q.B.D. 426; *Lage v Siemens Bros & Co Ltd* (1932) 42 Ll.L. Rep. 252. An implied promise to indemnify can obviously not extend thus far: further, the agent cannot take advantage of his own wrong. But see *Linklaters v HSBC Bank Plc* [2003] 2 Lloyd's Rep. 545, 552–553 (limits on principle).

[1073] *Duncan v Hill* (1873) L.R. 8 Ex. 242. The insolvency was "entirely the result of [the agent's] own default".

[1074] *Ex p. Mather* (1797) 3 Ves. Jr. 373. This is an application of the general rules as to illegal contracts, where the agency is contractual: see Vol.I, Ch.16. Aliter where the illegality is not known or obvious: *Adamson v Jarvis* (1827) 4 Bing. 66; *WH Smith & Son v Clinton* (1908) 99 L.T. 840. And where principal and agent are joint tortfeasors, there may be a right of contribution under the Civil Liability (Contribution) Act 1978. See also Solicitors Act 1974 s.25 (no costs recoverable by unqualified person).

[1075] But he has no general right to retain money received for his principal: *Dyson v Peat* [1917] 1 Ch. 99. As to the availability of set-off to solicitors see *Heslop v Cousins* [2007] 3 N.Z.L.R. 679 at [190].

[1076] *Williams v Millington* (1788) 1 H. Bl. 81; above, para.31-011. As to whether the principal's conduct must be repudiatory before the lien is exercisable see *Cia. Financiera "Soleada" v Hamoor Tanker Corp Inc (The Borag)* [1980] 1 Lloyd's Rep. 111 (actual decision reversed [1981] 1 W.L.R. 274).

[1077] *Taylor v Robinson* (1818) 2 Moo. 730.

[1078] *Dixon v Stansfeld* (1850) 10 C.B. 398; *Houghton v Matthews* (1803) 3 Bos. & P. 485.

[1079] *Wolstenholm v Sheffield Union Banking Co* (1886) 54 L.T. 746; *Withers LLP v Langbar International Ltd* [2011] EWCA Civ 1419 (solicitor).

[1080] *Brandao v Barnett* (1846) 12 Cl. & F. 787; *Rolls Razor Ltd v Cox* [1967] 1 Q.B. 552.

[1081] See *Bowstead and Reynolds on Agency*, 21st edn (2018), art.65. See further *Woodworth v Conroy* [1976] Q.B. 884 (accountant). But the existence of liens turns on custom, which is difficult to establish: see, e.g. *Tellrite Ltd v London Confirmers Ltd* [1962] 1 Lloyd's Rep. 236 (confirming house); *Langley, Beldon & Gaunt Ltd v Morley* [1965] 1 Lloyd's Rep. 297 (forwarding agent).

[1082] See *Albemarle Supply Co Ltd v Hind* [1928] 1 K.B. 307.

[1083] *Fisher v Smith* (1878) 4 App. Cas. 1; *Re Lawrance* [1894] 1 Ch. 556.

[1084] *Sweet v Pym* (1800) 1 East 4. But not where the goods are unlawfully obtained from the agent: *Wallace v Woodgate* (1824) Ry. & M. 193; *Dicas v Stockley* (1836) 7 C. & P. 587. Nor where the agent gives the goods to another to hold on his behalf: *Wilson v Kymer* (1813) 1 M. & S. 157; or to his principal to deal with on his behalf under a trust receipt: *North Western Bank Ltd v Poynter, Son & Macdonalds* [1895] A.C. 56; nor where the agent delivers the goods with an express reservation of

have a lien when delegation to them is authorised or contemplated.[1086] A lien is not determined by the principal's bankruptcy.[1087]

(iv) Agent in Position of Unpaid Vendor

31-165   Stoppage in transit and vendors' lien   Where an agent is personally liable to a third party for the purchase price of goods which he has bought for his principal[1088] he may stand towards the principal in the position of an unpaid vendor, and enjoy the vendor's rights of stoppage in transit[1089] and lien.[1090]

9.   TERMINATION OF AUTHORITY

31-166   How authority terminated   An agent's authority may be terminated in the following ways.

(i)   By the express revocation of it by the principal; or by renunciation of the agency on the part of the agent himself.[1091] Such revocation or renunciation is effective notwithstanding that the agency was created by deed or for consideration,[1092] and may be oral even though the appointment was by deed.[1093] But though it terminates the authority it does so without prejudice to any right that either party may have against the other to damages or loss of rights under a contract[1094]; and as between the parties a

---

his lien to which objection is not taken: *Watson v Lyon* (1855) 7 De G.M. & G. 288; *Caldwell v Sumpters* [1972] Ch. 478; *Bentley v Gaisford* [1997] Q.B. 627.

[1085] *Jacobs v Latour* (1828) 5 Bing. 130; *Hewison v Guthrie* (1836) 2 Bing. N.C. 755; *Weeks v Goode* (1859) 6 C.B.(N.S.) 367; *Re Morris* [1908] 1 K.B. 473.

[1086] See *Bowstead and Reynolds on Agency*, 21st edn (2018), art.69; *Chellaram & Sons (London) Ltd v Butlers Warehousing and Distribution Ltd* [1978] 2 Lloyd's Rep. 412.

[1087] *Robson v Kemp* (1802) 4 Esp. 233; *Re Rapid Road Transit Co* [1909] 1 Ch. 96.

[1088] See above, paras 31-084 et seq.

[1089] *Feise v Wray* (1802) 3 East 93; *Jenkyns v Usborne* (1844) 7 M. & G. 678.

[1090] *Imperial Bank v London & St Katharine Docks* (1876) 5 Ch. D. 195; Sale of Goods Act 1979 s.39. He may also be able to rely on having the property in the goods in some cases. But he is not in all respects a seller to his principal, for the position of seller is inconsistent with that of agent: *Cassaboglou v Gibb* (1883) 11 Q.B.D. 797; *Tetley v Shand* (1872) 25 L.T. 658. There is a connection between these cases and the position of the *commissionnaire*, above, para.31-004. See below, paras 44-032, 44-309; *Bowstead and Reynolds on Agency*, 21st edn (2018), para.1-020 and art.69; cf. *Benjamin's Sale of Goods*, 10th edn (2017), paras 15-010, 15-011. See also Hill (1972) 3 J. Maritime Law and Commerce 307.

[1091] *Frith v Frith* [1906] A.C. 254, 259.

[1092] *Venning v Bray* (1862) 2 B. & S. 502; *Doward, Dickson & Co v Williams & Co* (1889) 6 T.L.R. 316. Thus a power of attorney is revocable: *Walsh v Whitcomb* (1797) 2 Esp. 565. But in some circumstances equity may restrain the revocation: see *Regent International Hotels (UK) Ltd v Pageguide Ltd, The Times,* May 10, 1985, CA; *Lauritzencool AB v Lady Navigation Inc* [2005] EWCA Civ 579, [2005] 1 W.L.R. 3686. And there are a few cases which simply appear to assume that authority can be made irrevocable, e.g. *Phillips v Butler* [1945] Ch. 358 (above, para.31-011); *Daly v Lime Street Underwriting Agencies Ltd* [1987] 2 F.T.L.R. 277 (Lloyd's: see below, n.1116).

[1093] *The Margaret Mitchell* (1858) Sw. 382.

[1094] As to damages, whether for breach of contract, or by way of compensation under the Commercial Agents Directive (above, paras 31-017, 31-154). As to loss of rights, this can occur, for example, in liability insurance, where the insurer wishes to control proceedings brought on behalf of the assured and the assured withdraws authority to do so. As to the effect of termination of a partnership, see *Hurst v Bryk* [2002] 1 A.C. 185.

repudiatory breach of contract, at any rate by the principal, is, in accordance with general rules, inoperative until accepted.[1095]

(ii) By the principal's death,[1096] or by his becoming bankrupt or insolvent[1097] or mentally disordered so as to be incapable of consenting to the agency, whether or not these facts are known to the agent[1098]; by the death of the agent, or his becoming similarly mentally incapable,[1099] or by his bankruptcy or insolvency, if this makes him unable to perform his duties.[1100]

(iii) By effluxion of time, where a specific period is fixed, either by express agreement or by the usage of trade, for the execution of the act to be done by the agent.[1101]

(iv) By the execution of his commission, whereby the agent becomes functus officio[1102]; by the destruction of the subject matter of the agency[1103]; or by the happening of an event which renders the continuance of the agency impossible[1104] or unlawful.[1105] Thus the retainer of a solicitor normally ceases when his client becomes an alien enemy,[1106] though not merely because he becomes an enemy alien.[1107]

Irrevocable authority   Though an agent's authority is, as stated above, normally **31-167**
revocable at will (without prejudice to his right, if any, to damages for breach of

---

[1095] *Atlantic Underwriting Agencies Ltd v Cia di Assicurazione di Milano SpA* [1979] 2 Lloyd's Rep. 240. See Vol.I, paras 24-003 et seq.

[1096] *Blades v Free* (1829) 9 B. & C. 167; *Campanari v Woodburn* (1854) 15 C.B. 400; *Pool v Pool* (1889) 58 L.J.P. 67. *Restatement, Third, Agency*, para.3.07 provides that actual authority should not terminate until the agent knows of the principal's death, which might be a better rule: see *Bowstead and Reynolds on Agency*, 21st edn (2018), para.10-016. The dissolution of a company has the same effect: *Salton v New Beeston Cycle Co* [1900] 1 Ch. 43. So does the dissolution of a partnership, as to which see Partnership Act 1890 ss.14, 17, 36(3), 38; *Tasker v Shepherd* (1861) 6 H. & N. 575; *Robson v Drummond* (1831) 2 B. & Ad. 303; *Brace v Calder* [1895] 2 Q.B. 253; *Friend v Young* [1897] 2 Ch. 421; *Bovine Ltd v Dent and Wilkinson* (1904) 21 T.L.R. 82; *Hurst v Bryk*, above.

[1097] *Drew v Nunn* (1879) 4 Q.B.D. 661, 665–666; *Kynaston v Crouch* (1845) 14 M. & W. 266, 274. But see *Nelson v Nelson* [1997] 1 W.L.R. 233 (authority not terminated in certain respects: bankrupt's power to bring actions). See Vol.I, Ch.20.

[1098] *Drew v Nunn* (1879) 4 Q.B.D. 661, 665–666; *Yonge v Toynbee* [1910] 1 K.B. 215. *Gibbons v Wright* (1954) 91 C.L.R. 423, 425 (power of attorney). But see Watts [2015] C.L.J. 140, arguing that in the case of mental disorder this should not be so unless the disorder is or should be known to the third party; also *Blankley v Central Manchester, etc, University Hospitals NHS Trust* [2015] EWCA Civ 18, [2015] 1 W.L.R. 4307.

[1099] This would appear to follow from the fact that the agent no longer has capacity, and it would be surprising if the principal was to be regarded as impliedly authorising the acts of an agent who had lost capacity. In any case, apparent authority persists. A Hong Kong case suggests however that actual authority persists: *Probus v Treble & Triple Ltd* [2010] HKCU 2485, affirmed without reference to this point, CACV270/2010.

[1100] *McCall v Australian Meat Co* (1870) 19 W.R. 188; *Hudson v Granger* (1821) 5 B. & Ald. 27, 33; *Phelps v Lyle* (1840) 10 A. & E. 113.

[1101] *Dickinson v Lilwall* (1815) 4 Camp. 279; *Lawford & Co v Harris* (1896) 12 T.L.R. 275. Where the Commercial Agents Directive (above, para 31-017) applies there may be a right to compensation even in such a case: see above, para.31-154.

[1102] *Blackburne v Scholes* (1810) 2 Camp. 341; *Bell v Balls* [1897] 1 Ch. 663 (auctioneer); *Gillow & Co v Lord Aberdare* (1893) 9 T.L.R. 12 (house agent).

[1103] *Rhodes v Forwood* (1876) 1 App. Cas. 256; above, para.31-150.

[1104] e.g. *Morgan v Manser* [1948] 1 K.B. 184 (military service).

[1105] *Hugh Stevenson & Sons Ltd v Aktiengesellschaft für Cartonnagen-Industrie* [1918] A.C. 239.

[1106] *Sovfracht v Van Udens, etc.* [1943] A.C. 203, 253–255.

[1107] i.e. the subject of an enemy state resident in the UK. See *Schostall v Johnson* (1919) 36 T.L.R. 75.

contract) there are some cases where this is not so. It is often said that if the authority is coupled with an interest, that is, if an agreement is entered into by deed or on a sufficient consideration, whereby an authority to sell goods is given for the purpose of providing a security, such an authority is irrevocable,[1108] even by death,[1109] mental disorder or bankruptcy.[1110] This is in fact hardly a case of agency at all, since the donee of the authority acts at least largely in *his own* interest, and the authority is in effect the security. The method may also be used to effect an assignment. Such doctrine dates back to reasoning used in the nineteenth century when many of the principles now accepted were not formulated: the objective of such arrangements can nowadays usually be achieved by other means, especially the statutory assignment and the floating charge. Its extent for the present day has recently been considered by the Supreme Court of the United Kingdom in *Angove's Pty Ltd v Bailey*.[1111] Here it was suggested by Lord Sumption that an explanation on the above lines might be too limited, in that it was possible for irrevocability to co-exist with the agent's duty to act on the principal's behalf: for example, although an agent could not have irrevocable authority to protect his interest in receiving commission on the transaction involved[1112] (the main point in issue in the case) he could be given it to secure a right to commission already accrued.[1113] It is submitted that such a security arrangement by employment of agency techniques could indeed be set up, but it would need to be specific and outside the general purpose of the agency[1114]; otherwise it would be contrary to the agent's fundamental duty to act in his principal's interest. There are also a number of other cases where somewhat different reasoning has been employed to justify authority being irrevocable. The principal ones concern undertakings to underwrite (or sub-underwrite) share issues by giving the relevant party authority to apply for a number of shares in the name of the party underwriting if they were not taken up on the market.[1115] If these undertakings were not complied with, an action in damages would normally be of little value to the person who set up the underwriting arrangement. In such cases the authority to achieve the object of the contract by applying for shares on behalf of the party underwriting has been held to be irrevocable, thus enabling the shares to be allotted and creating a new liability to the company. An alternative or cumulative line of reasoning is that the failure to comply with the undertaking may be prejudicial to other persons who have given the same undertaking. Such reasoning has also been used in connection with arrangements among Lloyd's underwriters.[1116] These cases are specifically not discussed in the *Angove* case, but they may provide at least another type of situation where an agent's authority can be irrevocable.

[1108] *Smart v Sandars* (1848) 5 C.B. 895, 917–918; *Frith v Frith* [1906] A.C. 254; *Despot v Registrar-General of NSW* [2013] NSWCA 313 (extended discussion on traditional basis); *Restatement, Third, Agency* (2006), para.3.12. See also Powers of Attorney Act 1971 s.4(1), below, para.31-168.

[1109] *Spooner v Sandilands* (1842) 1 Y. & C. Ch. 390.

[1110] *Alley v Hotson* (1815) 4 Camp. 325.

[1111] [2016] UKSC 17, [2016] 1 W.L.R. 3179 at [9]. See Watts (2017) 133 L.Q.R. 11.

[1112] *Doward, Dickson & Co v Williams & Co* (1890) 6 T.L.R. 316.

[1113] See at [9]. Lord Sumption cited (at [8] by way of example s.4 of the Powers of Attorney Act 1971); but this requires that the authority be actually expressed to be irrevocable, which does not seem to be true at common law.

[1114] See *Smart v Sandars* (1848) 5 C.B. 895, 917–918, per Wilde C.J.

[1115] *Re Hannan's Empress Gold Mining and Development Co* [1896] 2 Ch. 643; *Re Olympic Reinsurance Co* [1920] 2 Ch. 341.

[1116] *Society of Lloyd's v Leigh* [1997] C.L.C. 759, 773, per Colman J., affirmed on other grounds [1997] C.L.C. 1398 (Equitas rescue scheme). See also *Temple Legal Protection Ltd v QBE Insurance (Europe) Ltd* [2009] EWCA Civ 453, [2010] 1 All E.R. (Comm) 703 at [52]. For use of the technique

Powers of attorney A power of attorney is a formal authority to one person to **31-168**
act in the place of another, and the donor of such a power is liable to third parties
in respect of any acts of the donee within the scope of the power. A power of attorney must be created by deed.[1117] It is nevertheless revocable in accordance with
normal principles. But a statutory implementation of both the principles in the
preceding paragraph, s.4(1) of the Powers of Attorney Act 1971, provides that where
such a power is expressed to be irrevocable and is given to secure (a) a proprietary
interest of the donee of the power[1118]; or (b) the performance of an obligation owed
to the donee, then, so long as the donee has that interest or the obligation remains
undischarged, the power shall not be revoked (i) by the donor without the consent
of the donee; or (ii) by the death, incapacity or bankruptcy of the donor, or if the
donor is a body corporate, by its winding up or dissolution.[1119] This formulation does
not however completely accord with the common law position.[1120]

Apparent authority The mere happening of events terminating the agency will **31-169**
not necessarily prevent the principal from being bound by the agent's acts, for he
may be liable under the doctrine of apparent authority[1121]:

> "Where a person has given authority to another, the authority being such as would appar-
> ently continue, he is bound to those who act upon the faith of that authority, though he
> has revoked it, unless he has given the proper notice of the revocation ... The failure to
> give that notice precludes him from denying that he gave the authority against those who
> acted upon the faith that that authority continued."[1122]

This dictum comes from a partnership case, and refers to "proper notice of the
revocation", a matter later specifically dealt with in the Partnership Act 1890.[1123] In
a less formal context it may be more difficult for a principal to know how to indicate
to those who might justifiably rely on apparent authority that the actual authority
has been withdrawn or restricted; or how to formulate a rule determining for how
long a third party is under the doctrine of apparent authority entitled to assume that
authority survives. There may be a difference between cases where there has been
a specific representation of authority, and those where the agent has a usual authority, i.e. the authority normally going with a particular post or function.[1124] There may
also be a more obvious duty to notify where the authority of an agent is not

---

to preserve an advantage going with property (a liquor licence) see *Slatter v Railway Commissioners (NSW)* (1931) 45 C.L.R. 68.

[1117] Powers of Attorney Act 1971 s.1(1), as amended by Law of Property (Miscellaneous Provisions) Act
1989 s.1.

[1118] This plainly does not protect the power of attorney given to a receiver appointed by debenture holders, for it is their interests and not his that are protected. The common law rule however may do so.

[1119] A power given to secure a proprietary interest may be given to the person entitled to the interest and
persons deriving title under him: s.4(2).

[1120] The common law does not require that the power be expressed to be irrevocable, and the
circumstances here prescribed for which is must be given form a creative exercise on the common
law position. The words are however taken by Lord Sumption in *Angove's Pty Ltd v Bailey* as reflecting that position: see above, n.1113.

[1121] See above, para.31-056.

[1122] *Scarf v Jardine* (1882) 7 App. Cas. 345, 356–357, per Lord Blackburn.

[1123] s.36, requiring notice in the *London Gazette*.

[1124] See above, para.8-015; *AMB Generali Holding AG v SEB Trygg Liv Holding AG* [2005] EWCA Civ
1237, [2006] 1 Lloyd's Rep. 318 at [32].

withdrawn but restricted, for example as to value of transactions authorised.[1125] It may be best to go outside specific formulations and references to "notice" and simply follow the general principle formulated in *Restatement, Third, Agency*[1126] that:

"Apparent authority ends when it is no longer reasonable for the third party with whom the agent deals to believe that the agent continues to act with actual authority."

This doctrine should, arguably at least, not in principle apply where the revocation of authority is caused by the principal's incapacity, on the basis that the principal is (legally) removed from the scene. But though it is probably true that the doctrine does not apply in the case of the principal's death[1127] or bankruptcy,[1128] there is authority that he can be liable under the doctrine of apparent authority though he becomes mentally incapable,[1129] and this despite the fact that the agent is, it seems, also liable in such a case for breach of warranty of authority.[1130]

31-170 **Statutory protection where power of attorney revoked** There is again special statutory provision in the case of powers of attorney. By s.5(2) of the Powers of Attorney Act 1971, where a power of attorney has been revoked and a person, without knowledge of the revocation, deals with the donee of the power, the transaction between them shall, in favour of that person, be as valid as if the power had then been in existence. Similar protection is by s.5(3) given to a third party dealing with the donee of a power expressed to be given by way of security which was not in fact given by way of security; and where the interest of a purchaser depends on whether a transaction was valid by virtue of s.5(2) certain presumptions operate in favour of the purchaser by virtue of s.5(4).

31-171 **Enduring powers of attorney** The Enduring Powers of Attorney Act 1985[1131] sought to deal with the situation where a person who has granted a power of attorney becomes mentally incapable. In such a case the power is at common law automatically revoked subject to the statutory protections referred to above. This is in many cases extremely inconvenient, since the power may have been granted, for example by an elderly person, with this very contingency in mind. It appears that attorneys often continued to act in such circumstances, at risk to themselves and third parties; and use of the Court of Protection for all such situations would have placed an excessive strain on its resources. The Act therefore permitted a

---

[1125] See *Rockland Industries Inc v Amerada Minerals Corp* [1980] 2 S.C.R. 2 (specific requirement of consent for one particular contract). See also *Benourad v Compass Group Plc* [2010] EWHC 1882 (QB) at [113] (director moving from one company to another: apparent authority for former company may persist).

[1126] *Restatement, Third, Agency*, para.3.11.

[1127] *Blades v Free* (1829) 9 B. & C. 167. But the possibility of apparent authority may not have been clear at the time: see *Drew v Nunn* (1879) 4 Q.B.D. 661, 668 for a suggestion to the contrary.

[1128] *Drew v Nunn*, above, at 665–666.

[1129] *Drew v Nunn*, above.

[1130] *Yonge v Toynbee* [1910] 1 K.B. 215, a case on the court's jurisdiction over solicitors. It may be that apparent authority was not considered in this case. Otherwise, it would seem that there was no loss that the plaintiff could prove, in view of the fact that the principal might have been held bound: see above, para.31-106. See in general *Bowstead and Reynolds on Agency*, 21st edn (2018), para.10-032.

[1131] See *Cretney and Lush on Lasting and Enduring Powers of Attorney*, 8th edn (2017) and as to the purposes of the legislation Law Com. No.122 (1983). A recent case on the wording as applied to successive enduring powers is *Re J* [2009] EWHC 436 (Ch), [2009] 2 All E.R. 1051.

person to create, subject to restrictions, a power of attorney which survives such incapacity.[1132]

Lasting powers of attorney   The above type of Power of Attorney has now been **31-172** superseded by a new type of instrument, the Lasting Power of Attorney, provided by the Mental Capacity Act 2005,[1133] the relevant parts of which became effective on October 1, 2007.[1134] This is a wider type of power, under which the donee, or different donees, can be given authority to act in respect of the donor's personal welfare as well as his or her property and affairs,[1135] though limited powers can of course be conferred in either respect. Such powers require two separate documents, one for each power, in prescribed form.[1136] The Act begins with elaborate "principles" regarding what constitutes mental incapacity,[1137] and what constitutes the "best interests" of the incapacitated person.[1138] Even without such a document, a person may sometimes be justified in acting reasonably in the interests of another in respect of care or treatment,[1139] and may in other circumstances be entitled to pledge that other's credit, use that other's money and obtain reimbursement.[1140] These powers are not dissimilar from the more limited authority applicable in cases of agency of necessity and are referred to also under that head.[1141] Lasting Powers of Attorney require a "certificate of capacity" that the donor acts voluntarily and understands the purpose of the document.[1142] The power is invalid until registered,[1143] but registration can be effected before the onset of incapacity. It is revocable both before and after registration provided the donor has capacity to do so.[1144] The court may control the exercise of the power,[1145] or appoint a "deputy" to take decisions for the incapacitated person.[1146] The Court of Protection is reconstituted by the Act as part of the reforms. There are provisions protecting the donee and bona fide third parties where no power was created or the power has been revoked.[1147] Regulations supplement the provisions of Schs 1 and 4 to the Act regarding registration and revocation of powers of the new, and also of the former,

---

[1132] The Act is now repealed, but existing powers were not affected. For a recent case on it see *Day v Harris* [2013] EWCA Civ 191, [2014] Ch. 211.

[1133] ss.9–29; stemming from recommendations contained in Law Com No.231 (1995). Certain modifications largely connected with deprivation of liberty are made by the Mental Health Act 2007.

[1134] SI 2007/1897, amended by SIs 2007/2051, 2007/2161, 2009/1884, 2010/1063, 2011/2189. Some parts of the Act had already been brought into effect on April 1 by SI 2007/563. See in general Bartlett, *Blackstone's Guide to the Mental Capacity Act 2005*, 2nd edn (2008); Bryant (2007) No.84, Trusts and Estates Law & Tax Jo 5; Hopkins and Nichols (2006) 150 S.J. 632 (drawing attention to difficulties).

[1135] ss.9, 11, 12.

[1136] Lasting Powers of Attorney, Enduring Powers of Attorney and Public Guardian Regulations 2007 (SI 2007/1253) cl.5 (setting out forms for use) (as amended by SI 2013/506).

[1137] ss.1–3.

[1138] s.4 (specifying criteria for establishing reasonable belief).

[1139] ss.5, 6.

[1140] s.8 (the person lacking capacity is liable for necessaries supplied by virtue of s.7).

[1141] See above, annotation to para.31-037.

[1142] Sch.1 cl.2(1)(e).

[1143] s.9(2)(b).

[1144] s.13(1) (2). Bankruptcy of the donor need not always constitute revocation: see s.13(3) (4).

[1145] ss.22–23.

[1146] s.16.

[1147] s.14, in terms similar to s.9 of the Enduring Powers of Attorney Act 1985 and similarly modifying s.5 of the Powers of Attorney Act 1971.

types.[1148] The Act is supported by a Code of Practice issued by the Lord Chancellor.[1149]

Enduring Powers of Attorney created before the operative date above are still valid (as regards property and affairs),[1150] but the Act of 1985 is repealed and such powers may no longer be created.[1151]

[1148] See Lasting Powers of Attorney, Enduring Powers of Attorney and Public Guardian Regulations 2007 (SI 2007/1953).

[1149] In accordance with ss.42 and 43 of the Act, and published by TSO.

[1150] s.66(3); they are regulated by Sch.4 to the new Act, which in substance reproduces the 1985 Act. Quaere whether the "Principles" of ss.1 and 2 of the Act should be applied under Sch.4.

[1151] s.66(1) (2). Nor can they be converted.

CHAPTER 32

ARBITRATION[1]

P. J. S. MacDonald Eggers

Introductory References to arbitration are of two main kinds, conventional and **32-001** statutory. In the first, the parties agree to refer their present or future disputes to a tribunal of their own choosing, instead of to a court. In the second, such reference is imposed upon them by the terms of a particular statute.[2] This chapter is concerned only with the first kind of arbitration, and in particular with the validity and scope of arbitration agreements, the enforcement of such agreements by the court's power to stay an action brought in breach thereof, the appointment and removal of arbitrators, the conduct of the arbitral proceedings, the extent to which the court can assist the arbitral process, the arbitral award, the powers of the court in relation to the award and the enforcement of the award. These matters are for the most part regulated by statute.

---

[1] For a more detailed account of arbitration, and practice and procedure, the reader should consult: Merkin, *Arbitration Law* (2007); Merkin and Flannery, *Arbitration Act 1996*, 5th edn (2014); *Russell on Arbitration*, 24th edn (2015); Tweeddale and Tweeddale, *Arbitration of Commercial Disputes*, 2nd edn (2012); Harris, Planterose and Tecks, *Arbitration Act 1996*, 5th edn (2014); Mustill and Boyd, *Commercial Arbitration*, 2nd edn (1989) and Supplement (2001); Redfern and Hunter, *Law and Practice of International Arbitration*, 5th edn (2009); Park, *Arbitration of International Business Disputes*, 2nd edn (2012).

[2] See Arbitration Act 1996 ss.94–98. The County Courts Act 1984 s.64, enabled a county court in such cases as might be prescribed, to order any proceedings to be referred to arbitration. By s.92 of the 1996 Act, nothing in Pt I of that Act applies to such county court arbitration. The "small claims track" has now replaced small claims arbitration: CPR Pt 27.

1. STATUTORY REGULATION

32-002 **Arbitration Act 1996** The current principal statute is the Arbitration Act 1996. This Act reproduced, with very few changes, the provisions of a draft Bill formulated by a Departmental Advisory Committee on International Commercial Arbitration Law appointed by the Secretary of State for Trade and Industry and chaired by Saville L.J. The Committee produced a detailed Report on the Bill ("the DAC Report")[3] and this report has often been referred to in construing the provisions of the Act. To a limited extent the Act restated, in different language, the previous legislation on arbitration as set out in the Arbitration Acts 1950, 1975 and 1979, whilst at the same time codifying principles established by case law. But, more importantly, it introduced a number of substantial changes designed to clarify and improve the arbitral process. Its provisions reflect as far as possible those of the United Nations Commission on International Trade Law ("UNCITRAL") Model Law on International Commercial Arbitration.[4]

32-003 The Act is written in clear "user-friendly" language and this should lessen the need to have regard to the pre-1996 law where the provisions of the Act set out the law.[5] It is also unusual in that it sets out, in s.1, certain general principles on which Pt I of the Act—which contains its main substantive provisions—is stated to be founded and in accordance with which it is to be construed. These are that:

"(a) the object of arbitration is to obtain the fair resolution of disputes by an impartial tribunal without unnecessary delay or expense;

(b) the parties should be free to agree how their disputes are resolved, subject only to such safeguards as are necessary in the public interest;

(c) in matters governed by [Pt I] the court should not intervene except as provided in this Part".

Following these general principles, the Act allows considerable flexibility in the way arbitrations are conducted, recognises party autonomy and limits the role of the courts to supporting the arbitral process and intervening only in cases where there is, or is likely to be, a denial of justice. Certain provisions of Pt I are mandatory[6] and have effect notwithstanding any agreement to the contrary. But, for the most part, the provisions of Pt I are not mandatory: they permit the parties to make their own arrangements by written agreement[7] but provide rules which apply in the absence of such agreement. The parties may make such arrangements by agreeing to the application of institutional rules,[8] such as those of the International Chamber of Commerce, the London Court of International Arbitration or any other international or national institution.

32-004 **Commencement** The Act was brought into force (except for ss.85 to 87) on Janu-

---

3   February 1996. See also the 1997 Supplementary Report (January 1997).
4   *http://www.uncitral.org*. See Hacking (1997) 63 *Arbitration* 291. The Model Law was revised in 2006 (the "Revised Model Law").
5   *Seabridge Shipping AB v AC Orssleff's Eftf's A/S* [1999] 2 Lloyd's Rep. 685, 690; *Lesotho Highlands Development Authority v Impregilo SpA* [2005] UKHL 43, [2006] 1 A.C. 221 at [19]; *Bilta (UK) Ltd v Nazir* [2010] EWHC 1086 (Ch), [2010] 2 Lloyd's Rep. 29 at [22].
6   Arbitration Act 1996 s.4(1) and Sch.1. The sections are: ss.9–13, 24, 26(1), 28, 29, 31–33, 37(2), 40, 43, 56, 60, 66–68, 70–75.
7   s.4(2).
8   s.4(3).

ary 31, 1997,[9] and the provisions of Pt I apply to arbitral proceedings commenced on or after that date under an arbitration agreement whenever made. They do not apply to arbitral proceedings commenced before that date,[10] but they do apply to arbitration applications made on or after that date (except those relating to arbitration proceedings commenced before that date).[11]

Sections 85 to 87 of the Act,[12] which make special provision in relation to **32-005** domestic arbitration agreements, are unlikely to be brought into force, since there appears to be little support for the maintenance of a distinction between international and domestic agreements and it is arguable that to draw such a distinction is contrary to the provisions of the Treaty on the Functioning of the European Union.[13] Indeed, these sections are likely to be repealed by an order made under s.88(1).

As a result of the Civil Procedure (Amendment No.5) Rules 2001,[14] the rules **32-006** relating to the arbitration claims and arbitration enforcement proceedings are CPR Pt 62 rr.62.1 to 62.21, and there is also a practice direction CPR PD62 (in this chapter referred to as "PD62").

Scope of application of the Act: seat of arbitration in England[15] Section 2(1) **32-007** sets out the basic rule which governs the application of Pt I of the Act: it applies where the seat of the arbitration is in England.[16] The "seat of the arbitration" means "the juridical seat of the arbitration which is designated:

(a) by the parties to the arbitration agreement,[17] or
(b) by any arbitral or other institution or person vested by the parties with powers in that regard, or
(c) by the arbitral tribunal if so authorised by the parties,[18]

or which, in the absence of any such designation, has been determined having regard to the parties' agreement and all the relevant circumstances".[19] The "seat" is not necessarily the *place* where the arbitration is conducted, but usually the seat

---

9   Arbitration Act 1996 (Commencement No.1) Order 1996 (SI 1996/3146).
10   s.84(1), SI 1996/3146 art.4 and Sch.2(2)(a); *Great Ormond Street Hospital NHS Trust v Secretary of State for Health* [1998] C.L.Y. 250.
11   SI 1996/3146 art.4 and Sch.2.
12   DAC Report paras 317–331; Supplementary Report paras 47–49.
13   *Philip Alexander Securities & Futures Ltd v Bamberger, The Times,* July 22, 1996, CA.
14   SI 2001/4015.
15   The Act extends to England and Wales but not, in general. to Scotland: s.108.
16   References in this chapter to England include Wales and Northern Ireland.
17   *XL Insurance Ltd v Owens Corning* [2000] 2 Lloyd's Rep. 500, 508; *Shashoua v Sharma* [2009] EWHC 957 (Comm), [2009] 2 Lloyd's Rep. 376; *Enercon GmbH v Enercon (India) Ltd* [2012] EWHC 689 (Comm), [2012] 1 Lloyd's Rep. 519. Contrast *Braes of Doune Wind Farm (Scotland) Ltd v Alfred McAlpine Business Services Ltd* [2008] EWHC 426 (TCC), [2008] 1 Lloyd's Rep. 608 (contract provides that seat of arbitration to be Scotland but that English courts should have exclusive jurisdiction and Arbitration Act 1996 should apply: Akenhead J. held seat of arbitration was England).
18   *Arab National Bank v El Abdali* [2004] EWHC 2381 (Comm), [2005] 1 Lloyd's Rep. 541.
19   Arbitration Act 1996 s.3. See DAC Report paras 26, 27; *ABB Lummus Global Ltd v Keppel Fels Ltd* [1999] 2 Lloyd's Rep. 24 (LCIA rules); *Dubai Islamic Bank PJSC v Paymentech Merchant Services Inc* [2001] 1 Lloyd's Rep. 65, 74; *Arab National Bank v El Abdali*, above; and *Braes of Doune Wind Farm (Scotland) Ltd v Alfred McAlpine Business Services Ltd*, above (relevant circumstances); Petrodulos [2002] L.M.C.L.Q. 66. See also *Tonkstar Ltd v American Home Assurance Co* [2006] EWHC 1234 (Comm), [2005] 1 Lloyd's Rep. I.R. 32 (which court is to determine seat).

of the arbitration and that place will coincide. Once identified, the seat cannot move.[20]

32-008 **Applicants' arbitrations not seated in England**   This basic rule is, however, subject to a number of exceptions. The effect of these is to enable the English courts to recognise and enforce foreign arbitration agreements and awards and to support, in appropriate cases, foreign arbitral proceedings.[21] First, the provisions relating to a stay of legal proceedings (ss.9 to 11) and to the enforcement of arbitral awards (s.66) apply even if the seat of the arbitration is outside England or no seat has been designated or determined.[22] Secondly, the powers conferred by s.43 (securing the attendance of witnesses) and s.44 (court powers exercisable in support of arbitral proceedings) likewise apply even if the seat of the arbitration is outside England or no seat has been designated or determined, but the court may refuse to exercise the power if in its opinion the fact that the seat of the arbitration is or is likely to be elsewhere makes it inappropriate to do so.[23] Thirdly, the court may exercise any other power conferred on it by Pt I of the Act for the purpose of supporting the arbitral process where no seat of arbitration has been designated or determined and by reason of a connection with England it is satisfied that it is appropriate to do so.[24] Fourthly, the provisions of s.7 (separability of the arbitration agreement) and s.8 (death of a party) apply where the law applicable to the arbitration agreement is the law of England even if the seat of the arbitration is elsewhere or has not been designated or determined.[25] It is generally irrelevant that the law applicable to the substance of the dispute is a foreign law.

32-009 **Choice of foreign law**   The Act does not purport to set out any comprehensive regime concerning the conflict of laws issues that may arise in relation to arbitration.[26] It has been pointed out[27] that three potentially relevant systems of law may be involved:

(i)   the law governing the substance of the dispute[28];

(ii)   the law governing the agreement to arbitrate[29]; and

(iii)   the law governing the arbitral proceedings (the *lex arbitri*), which will normally be the law of the seat of the arbitration.[30]

These three laws may well be the same. But the law that governs the substance of

---

[20]   *Dubai Islamic Bank PJSC v Paymentech Merchant Services Inc*, above.

[21]   See Blackaby (1997) 3 *Arbitration International* 431.

[22]   s.2(2). See *A v B* [2006] EWHC 2006 (Comm), [2007] 1 Lloyd's Rep. 237 and below, paras 32-074, 32-186.

[23]   s.2(3); *Mobil Cerro Negro Ltd v Petroleos de Venezuela SA* [2008] EWHC 532 (Comm), [2008] 1 Lloyd's Rep. 684.

[24]   s.2(4); *Chalbury McCouat International Ltd v PG Foils Ltd* [2010] EWHC 2050 (TCC), [2011] 1 Lloyd's Rep. 23 (English law likely to be applied to substance of dispute).

[25]   s.2(5).

[26]   See *Dicey, Morris and Collins on the Conflict of Laws*, 15th edn, Ch.16.

[27]   *Black Clawson International Ltd v Papierwerke Wildhof Aschaffenburg AG* [1981] 2 Lloyd's Rep. 446, 453; *Naviera Amazonica Peruana SA v Compania Internacional de Seguros de Peru* [1988] 1 Lloyd's Rep. 116, 119; *C v D* [2007] EWCA Civ 1282, [2008] 1 Lloyd's Rep. 239 at [24].

[28]   See s.46; below, para.32-133; Dicey, Morris and Collins at paras 16-047—16-061. The rules of Regulation 593/2008 (Rome I) (see Vol.I, para.30-018) may apply. See also *Chalbury McCouat International Ltd v PG Foils Ltd* [2010] EWHC 2050 (TCC), [2011] 1 Lloyd's Rep. 23 at [26].

[29]   See Dicey, Morris and Collins at paras 16-011—16-028. The rules of Regulation 593/2008 (Rome I) do not apply: see Vol.I, para.30-051 and Parish (2010) 76 *Arbitration* 661.

[30]   See Dicey, Morris and Collins at paras 16-029—16-046.

the dispute may often differ from the *lex arbitri*[31] and the law governing the agreement to arbitrate may be different from that of the substantive contract out of which the dispute has arisen and of which it forms part.[32] Moreover, even if the seat of the arbitration is in England, the parties may choose a foreign law to govern any matter provided for in a non-mandatory provision of Pt I of the Act, such as, for example, the arbitration procedure, and effect must then be given to their choice.[33]

Prior legislation   The previous principal statute was the Arbitration Act 1950 (as **32-010** amended). Part I of that Act was repealed by the 1996 Act,[34] but Pt II, which deals with the enforcement of certain foreign awards and in particular with those to which the Geneva Protocol (1923) applies, remains unrepealed.[35]

The Arbitration Act 1975, which gave effect in the United Kingdom to the New **32-011** York Convention on the Recognition and Enforcement of Foreign Arbitral Awards (1958), and the Arbitration Act 1979, which abolished the much-criticised "case stated" procedure, established a new procedure for judicial review of an award and made other amendments to the 1950 Act, were entirely repealed by the 1996 Act.[36] Their provisions were incorporated, though not without changes, into the 1996 Act.

The 1996 Act also repealed[37] and reproduced[38] the provisions of the 1950 Act[39] **32-012** and of the Administration of Justice Act 1970[40] which allowed for the appointment of a judge of the Commercial Court or an official referee as sole arbitrator or umpire by or by virtue of an arbitration agreement.

Consumer arbitration agreements   It may be detrimental to the interests of **32-013** consumers to require them, by contract, to submit disputes to arbitration rather than to have resort to legal proceedings, in particular because of the increased expense involved. The Consumer Arbitration Agreements Act 1988 extended to consumers the right, in certain circumstances. not to be compelled to take a dispute to arbitration. This Act was repealed by the 1996 Act.[41] But the Unfair Terms in

---

[31]   e.g. because the parties have expressly chosen a different law to be applicable to the substance of the dispute: *Shagang South-Asia (Hong Kong) Trading Co Ltd v Daewoo Logistics* [2015] EWHC 194 (Comm), [2015] 1 Lloyd's Rep. 504.

[32]   *Deutsche Shachtbau v Shell International Petroleum Ltd* [1990] 1 A.C. 295, 310, CA (reversed on other grounds at 329); *XL Insurance Ltd v Owens Corning* [2000] 2 Lloyd's Rep. 500; *C v D* [2007] EWCA Civ 1282, [2008] 1 Lloyd's Rep. 239; *Tamil Nadu Electricity Board v ST-CMS Electric Co Private Ltd* [2007] EWHC 1713 (Comm), [2008] 1 Lloyd's Rep. 93; *Musawi v RE International (UK) Ltd* [2007] EWHC 2981 (Ch), [2008] 1 Lloyd's Rep. 326; *Sulamerica CIA Nacional de Seguros SA v Enesa Engenharia SA* [2012] EWCA Civ 638, [2012] 1 Lloyd's Rep. 671; *Abuja International Hotels Ltd v Meridien SAS* [2012] EWHC 87 (Comm), [2012] 1 Lloyd's Rep. 461; *Habas Sinai Ve Tibbi Gazlar Istihsal Endustrisi As v VSC Steel Co Ltd* [2013] EWHC 4071 (Comm), [2014] 1 Lloyd's Rep 479. cf. *Arsanovia Ltd v Cruz City 1 Mauritius Holdings* [2012] EWHC 3702 (Comm), [2013] 2 All E.R. (Comm) 1. See Vol.I, paras.30-051 and 32-029, below.

[33]   s.4(5). But see *Naviera Amazonica Peruana SA v Compania Internacional de Seguros de Peru* [1998] 1 Lloyd's Rep. 116; *Halpern v Halpern* [2006] EWHC 603 (Comm), [2006] 2 Lloyd's Rep. 83 at [62] (reversed in part [2007] EWCA Civ 291, [2007] 2 Lloyd's Rep. 56).

[34]   s.107(2) and Sch.4.

[35]   s.99. Its effect has been largely superseded by the New York Convention. See below, para.32-190.

[36]   s.107(2) and Sch.4.

[37]   s.107(2) and Sch.4.

[38]   s.93 and Sch.2.

[39]   s.11, as substituted by s.99 of the Courts and Legal Services Act 1990.

[40]   s.4 and Sch.3.

[41]   s.107(2) and Sch.4.

Consumer Contracts Regulations 1999[42] and the Consumer Rights Act 2015 Pt 2 (the scope and effect of which are discussed in Ch.38) includes in the "grey list" of the terms that may be regarded as unfair a term which has the object or effect of "excluding or hindering the consumer's right to take legal action or exercise any other legal remedy, in particular by requiring the consumer to take disputes exclusively to arbitration not covered by legal provisions".[43] Moreover, by s.89 of the 1996 Act,[44] ss.90 and 91 extend the application of the Regulations and Pt 2 of the 2015 Act in relation to a term which constitutes an arbitration agreement. Section 90[45] provides that the Regulations and Pt 2 of the 2015 Act apply where the consumer is a legal person (for example, a company) as they apply where the consumer is a natural person or (under the 2015 Act) an individual. And s.91[46] provides that a term which constitutes an arbitration agreement is unfair for the purposes of the Regulations and Pt 2 of the 2015 Act so far as it relates to a claim for a pecuniary remedy which does not exceed the amount specified by order for the purposes of this section. An amount of £5,000 has been so specified.[47] The result is that an arbitration agreement which is not individually negotiated is not binding on the consumer if it requires him to submit to arbitration a claim which does not exceed £5,000.[48] But even where a claim exceeds this limit, an arbitration clause may be held to be unfair and so not binding on the consumer.[49]

32-014 **ACAS arbitration** The Act has been amended with respect to ACAS arbitration by the ACAS Arbitration Scheme (England and Wales) Order 2001.[50]

32-015 **Human Rights Act 1998** The implications of the Human Rights Act 1998 for arbitration are by no means certain.[51] It is necessary to bear in mind that the European Convention on Human Rights, to which the Act gives effect, creates rights against states and not against private individuals. Article 6(1) of the Convention provides:

> "In the determination of his civil rights and obligations ... everyone is entitled to a fair and public hearing within a reasonable time by an independent and impartial tribunal established by law".

---

[42] SI 1999/2083; replaced by the Consumer Rights Act 2015 Pt 2 for contracts made on or after October 1, 2015. See below, para.38-390.

[43] 1999 Regulations Sch.2 para.1(q); Consumer Rights Act 2015 Sch.2 Pt 1 para.20.

[44] As amended by the 2015 Act Sch.4 para.31.

[45] As amended by the 2015 Act Sch.4 para.32.

[46] As amended by SI 1999/678 art.6 and the 2015 Act Sch.4 para.33.

[47] Unfair Arbitration Agreements (Specified Amount) Order 1999 (SI 1999/2167).

[48] This should not prevent the consumer from relying on the clause if the consumer wishes to do so.

[49] *Zealandair v Laing Homes Ltd* (2000) 2 T.C.L.R. 724; *Mylcrist Builders v Buck* [2008] EWHC 2172 (TCC), [2008] B.L.R 611. cf. *Heifer International Inc v Christiansen* [2007] EWHC 3015 (TCC), [2008] 2 All E.R. (Comm) 831 (Danish arbitration clause inserted by consumer's own lawyers); below, para.38-302. See also *Mostaza Claro v Centro Movil Milenium SL* (C-168/05) EU:C:2006:675, [2007] Bus. L.R. 60, ECJ (consumer's failure to raise unfairness in arbitral proceedings does not determine issue); but see *Asturcom Telecommunications SL v Rodriguez Nogueira* (C-40/08) EU:C:2009:615 on this point.

[50] SI 2001/1185. But ACAS deals only with employment relations and not with commercial disputes: *Flight Training International Inc v International Fire Training Equipment Ltd* [2004] EWHC 721, [2004] 2 All E.R. (Comm) 568.

[51] See Ambrose [2000] L.M.C.L.Q. 468; Nappert [2001] B.J.I.B. & F.L. 16(3), 108–113; Haydn-Williams (2001) 67 *Arbitration* 289; Robinson and Kasolowsky (2002) 18 *Arbitration International* 453; Sandy (2004) 20 *Arbitration International* 305; Berkovits (2005) 71 *Arbitration* 189; Qureshi (2007) 157 N.L.J. 46; Stothard (2008) 29 Bus. L.R. 2.

An arbitral tribunal established by voluntary agreement of the parties is not a "tribunal established by law" within the meaning of the article as it is not an emanation of the state.[52] It might therefore appear that to compel a person to resort to arbitration would be incompatible with his entitlement under the article to have his civil rights and obligations determined by a tribunal established by law, e.g. by a court. And, in any event, there would be a clear infringement of the "public hearing" requirement of the article, since an arbitral hearing will not be public unless all parties so agree. The way out of these difficulties has been to hold that a person who freely and unequivocally enters into a valid arbitration agreement thereby waives his right to have his dispute determined at a public hearing by a tribunal for which the state is responsible under the Convention.[53] But this may be the full extent of the waiver,[54] and it is probable that a party to an arbitration agreement does not thereby waive his right under the article to a fair hearing by an independent and impartial tribunal and within a reasonable time. The question then arises as to the remedies available to a person who claims that proceedings before an arbitral tribunal to which he was a party have not complied with art.6 of the Convention (except to the extent that his rights under the article have been validly waived). Section 6 of the 1998 Act provides that "it is unlawful for a public authority to act in a way that is incompatible with a Convention right" and s.7 gives a direct right of action to a person who claims that a public authority has acted (or proposes to act) in such a way. Despite the fact that a "public authority" is defined in s.6(3) to include "a court or tribunal", and "tribunal" is further defined in s.21(1) as "any tribunal in which legal proceedings may be brought", it is submitted that an arbitral tribunal to which the parties have agreed to submit their dispute for adjudication is not a "public authority" within the meaning of the Act, since its functions are not of a public nature. Any direct action against the arbitrators, based on the 1998 Act, is therefore ruled out.

The expression "public authority" in the Act does, however, include a court.[55] In **32-016**

---

[52] *Le Compte, Van Leuven and De Meyere v Belgium* Unreported May 27, 1981, EHR Court (not an arbitration case).

[53] *Deweer v Belgium* [1980] 2 E.H.R.R. 439 EHR Court, February 27, 1980; *KR v Switzerland*, E Com. H.R., Application No.10881/84, March 4, 1987; *Axelsson v Sweden*, E Com. H.R., Application No.11960/86, July 13, 1990; *Jakob Boss Sohne KG v Germany*, E Com. H.R., Application No.18479/91, December 2, 1991; *Molin v Turkey*, E Com. H.R., Application No.23173/94, October 22, 1996; *Nordstrom-Janzon v Netherlands*, E Com. H.R., Application No.2810/95, November 22, 1996; *Suovaniemi v Finland*, E Com. H.R., Application No.31737/96, February 23, 1999; *North Range Shipping Ltd v Seatrans Shipping Corp* [2002] EWCA Civ 405, [2002] 1 W.L.R. 2397 at [17]; *Welex AG v Rosa Maritima Ltd (The Epsilon Rosa)* [2002] EWHC 762 (Comm), [2002] 2 Lloyd's Rep. 81 at [31] (affirmed [2003] EWCA Civ 938, [2003] 2 Lloyd's Rep. 509); *BLCT (13096) Ltd v J Sainsbury Plc* [2003] EWCA Civ 884, [2004] 2 P. & C.R. 3; *Department of Economics, Policy and Development of the City of Moscow v Bankers Trust Co* [2004] EWCA Civ 314, [2005] Q.B. 207 at [27]; *Stretford v Football Association Ltd* [2007] EWCA Civ 238, [2007] 2 Lloyd's Rep. 31 at [45]; *Premium Nafta Products Ltd v Fili Shipping Co Ltd* [2007] UKHL 40, [2008] 1 Lloyd's Rep. 254 at [20]; *El Nasharty v J Sainsbury Plc* [2007] EWHC 2618 (Comm), [2008] 1 Lloyd's Rep. 360 at [25]; *Broda Agro Trade (Cyprus) Ltd v Alfred C Toepfer International GmbH* [2009] EWHC 3318 (Comm), [2010] 1 Lloyd's Rep. 533 at [37]–[43] (affirmed on other grounds [2010] EWCA Civ 1100, [2011] 1 Lloyd's Rep. 243). See also *Nishin Shipping Co Ltd v Cleaves & Co Ltd* [2003] EWHC 2602, [2004] 1 Lloyd's Rep. 38 at [52] (third parties). cf. *Shuttari v Solicitors' Indemnity Fund* [2007] EWCA Civ 244, [2007] 1 C.L.C. 303.

[54] cf. *Nordstrom-Janzon v Netherlands*, above; *Suovaniemi v Finland*, above; *Stretford v Football Association Ltd*, above, at [56].

[55] 1998 Act s.6(3).

KR v Switzerland[56] the European Commission on Human Rights expressed the opinion that "the State cannot be held responsible for the arbitrators' actions unless, and only in so far as, the national courts were required to intervene". This leaves open the question whether, if required to intervene, national courts must ensure that arbitral tribunals comply with the procedural safeguards of art.6(1) except insofar as these have been validly waived. To this question conflicting answers have been given. In *Nordstrom-Janzon v Netherlands* (1996)[57] the Commission stated that the Convention does not require national courts to ensure that arbitration proceedings have been conducted in conformity with art.6(1). But in the earlier case of *Jakob Boss Sohne KG v Germany* (1991)[58] the Commission decided that the courts did have the role of guaranteeing the fairness of arbitral proceedings and of ensuring that they were conducted in accordance with fundamental rights. It is submitted that the latter view is to be preferred and that courts, when exercising regulatory or enforcement functions in relation to arbitration, are under a duty to ensure that the arbitral proceedings have been conducted in conformity with art.6(1), except where validly waived. The provisions of the Arbitration Act 1996 confer sufficient powers on the English courts to enable them, if called upon to intervene, to ensure that proceedings before an arbitral tribunal seated in England have complied with the requirements of the Article.[59]

32-017   National courts must also, when exercising their regulatory or enforcement functions, themselves comply with art.6(1).[60] Thus in *North Range Shipping Ltd v Seatrans Shipping Corp*[61] the Court of Appeal held that art.6 requires that a judge of the High Court must, when dismissing an application for permission to appeal on a point of law from an arbitrator's award under s.69 of the 1996 Act, give adequate reasons for his decision, although the adequacy of those reasons is dependant on the circumstances of the particular case. However, it has been held that none of the following involved an infringement of art.6 rights: the absence of any right to an oral hearing on an application under s.69 of the 1996 Act,[62] an order that a judgment rendered on an application under s.68 should remain private and not be disclosed to the public,[63] the exclusion by mutual agreement of any right of appeal

---

56 E Com. H.R., Application No.10881/84, March 4, 1987.

57 E Com. H.R., Application No.2810/95, November 22, 1996.

58 E Com. H.R., Application No.18479/91, December 2, 1991.

59 See *Stretford v Football Association Ltd* [2007] EWCA Civ 238, [2007] 2 Lloyd's Rep. 31 at [36]; *Broda Agro Trade (Cyprus) Ltd v Alfred C Toepfer International GmbH* [2009] EWHC 3318 (Comm), [2010] 1 Lloyd's Rep. 533 at [46] (affirmed on other grounds [2010] EWCA Civ 1100, [2011] 1 Lloyd's Rep. 243); Haydn-Williams (2001) 67 *Arbitration* 289. However, s.24 of the 1996 Act (see below, para.32-096) only empowers the court to remove an arbitrator if circumstances exist which give rise to justifiable doubts as to his impartiality, and not his *independence*. But s.3(1) of the 1998 Act requires (so far as it is possible to do so) that statutes be read and given effect in a way compatible with convention rights so that the concept of independence may be imported from art.6(1): See *R. v A (No.2)* [2001] UKHL 25, [2002] A.C. 45 at [44]; *Ghaidan v Godin-Mendoza* [2004] UKHL 30, [2004] 2 A.C. 557 at [37]–[52]. See also *Stretford v Football Association Ltd*, above, at [39]–[40]; Sandy (2004) 20 *Arbitration International* 305.

60 *Axelsson v Sweden*, E Com. H.R., Application No.11960/86, July 13, 1990; *Stran Greek Refineries v Greece*, EHR Court, Application No.13427/87, December 9, 1994; *Molin v Turkey*, E Com. H.R., Application No.23173/94, October 22, 1996.

61 [2002] EWCA Civ 405, [2002] 1 W.L.R. 2397: see below, para.32-169.

62 *BLCT (13096) Ltd v J Sainsbury Ltd* [2003] EWCA Civ 884, [2004] 2 P. & C.R. 3; para.32-172, below.

63 *Department of Economics, Policy and Development of the City of Moscow v Banters Trust Co* [2004] EWCA Civ 314, [2005] Q.B. 207.

on a point of law under s.69,[64] and the absence of any right of appeal from a refusal of permission to appeal on a s.68 application,[65] from a refusal of permission to appeal under s.69(8),[66] and from a refusal of permission to appeal on a s.67 application.[67]

The broader question also arises whether an arbitral tribunal seated in England, **32-018** when applying English law to the substance of the dispute, is bound to decide the issues presented to it in a manner compatible with the parties' substantive rights under the Convention, for example, the right to protection of property conferred by art.1 of the first Protocol, and what remedies would be available if the tribunal decided in a way incompatible with those rights. Section 6 of the 1998 Act provides that it is illegal for a public authority to act in a way that is incompatible with a Convention right. If either of the parties to the arbitral proceedings is a public authority, it is arguable that the arbitral tribunal must take account of and, as appropriate,[68] give effect to this provision as part of English law in making its award. In the event that the tribunal fails to do so, then the award will be subject to appeal on a point of law under s.69 of the Arbitration Act 1996.[69] More tentatively perhaps, whether or not English law is the law applicable to the dispute, it might be argued that the award is open to challenge under s.68 of the 1996 Act (serious irregularity)[70] on the ground that the award or the way in which it was procured is contrary to public policy.[71] There is, however, considerably more doubt as to whether the same principle will apply if neither of the parties to the arbitral proceedings is a public authority.[72] In the first chapter of Vol.I of this book the view has been expressed that in certain circumstances a court in a similar situation will be under a duty to interpret and apply English substantive law in a way that is compatible with the convention.[73] If that is so, then to that extent, when applying English law, an arbitral tribunal ought to interpret it and apply it in the same manner. Failure to do so would constitute an error of law which, again, would render the award open to appeal under s.69.

Composition of arbitral tribunal It has also been held that there was no infringe- **32-019** ment of art.6 rights where an arbitration clause incorporated the rules of a trade association and the application of those rules might lead to the result that a majority of the tribunal would consist of arbitrators approved by the association, of which one party was a member but the other was not.[74] In *Jivraj v Hashwani*[75] the Supreme

---

[64] *Sumukan Ltd v Commonwealth Secretariat* [2007] EWCA Civ 243, [2007] 2 Lloyd's Rep. 87.
[65] *ASM Shipping Ltd of India v TTMI Ltd of England* [2006] EWCA Civ 1341, [2007] 1 Lloyd's Rep. 136; but see below, para.32-185.
[66] *CGU International Insurance Plc v Astrazenka Insurance Co Ltd* [2006] EWCA Civ 1340, [2007] 1 Lloyd's Rep. 142; but see below, para.32-185.
[67] *Republic of Kazakhstan v Istil Group Ltd* [2007] EWCA Civ 471, [2007] 2 Lloyd's Rep. 548; but see below, para.32-185. See also *Yegiazaryan v Smagin* [2016] EWCA Civ 1290, [2017] 1 Lloyd's Rep. 102 at [26].
[68] Depending on the issue involved, see Vol.I, para.1-080.
[69] See below, para.32-168.
[70] See below, para.32-163.
[71] s.68(2)(g), para.32-163, below.
[72] See Vol.I, para.1-089.
[73] See Vol.I, paras 1-094 et seq.
[74] *Capes Hatherden Ltd v Western Arable Services* [2009] EWHC 3065 (QB), [2010] 1 Lloyd's Rep. 477.
[75] [2011] UKSC 40, [2011] 1 W.L.R. 1872. See Style and Cleobury (2011) 27 *Arbitration International*

Court unanimously reversed a decision of the Court of Appeal[76] which had held an arbitration clause, which required that the tribunal should be composed of members of a particular religious community (the Ismaili community), was rendered void as a result of the Employment Equality (Religion or Belief) Regulations 2003.[77]

2. THE ARBITRATION AGREEMENT

32-020 **Definition of "arbitration agreement" and arbitrability** The Arbitration Act 1996 defines an arbitration agreement to mean "an agreement to submit to arbitration present or future disputes (whether they are contractual or not)"[78] and "dispute" is defined to include any difference.[79] It is clear, therefore, that a claim in tort or a dispute which involves a charge of fraud may be the subject matter of an arbitration agreement, although the Act expressly preserves any rule of law as to matters which are "not capable of settlement by arbitration".[80] Certain disputes will obviously not be arbitrable, for example, in family matters, disputes as to the marital status of the parties or the custody of children,[81] or disputes as to the existence or validity of an intellectual property right granted by the state, such as a patent or trade mark. But most commercial disputes will be arbitrable.[82] However, the question has arisen as to the arbitrability of commercial disputes which involve consideration of anti-trust or competition laws, having regard to the complexity of the issues raised and the public interest in ensuring compliance with and observance of those laws.[83] There is little doubt that, in English law, such disputes are arbitrable, although there may be doubts in a particular case whether the claim made falls

---

563.

[76] [2010] EWCA Civ 712, [2010] 2 Lloyd's Rep. 534.

[77] SI 2003/1660; see now the Equality Act 2010, para.40-039 below. But see the Arbitration and Mediation Services (Equality) Bill (HL) which prohibits any preference being given to the evidence, interests or property of a man over that of a woman.

[78] s.6(1). In *Yegiazaryan v Smagin* [2016] EWCA Civ 1290, [2017] 1 Lloyd's Rep. 102 at [43], the Court of Appeal held that the contractual provision under review was an arbitration agreement because it was a mechanism by which a contracting party could be compelled through arbitration to ensure that it complies with its obligations. By contrast, in *Berkeley Burke SIPP Administration LLP v Charlton* [2017] EWHC 2396 (Comm), [2018] 1 Lloyd's Rep. 337 at [15]–[22], it was held that an agreement pursuant to which a third party, such as the Financial Ombudsman, is asked to resolve a dispute but on terms which do not bind the complainant to accept the decision of the third party cannot be an arbitration agreement within the meaning of s.6(1).

[79] s.82(1).

[80] s.81(1)(a).

[81] But see *AI v MT* [2013] EWHC 100 (Fam), [2013] 2 F.L.R. 371 ("non-binding arbitration").

[82] But see *O'Callaghan v Coral Racing Ltd* [1998] C.L.Y. 854 (gaming contract); *Accentuate Ltd v Asigra Inc* [2009] EWHC 2655 (QB), [2009] 2 Lloyd's Rep. 599 at [62]–[89] (mandatory provisions of EU law); *Clyde & Co LLP v Bates van Winkelhof* [2011] I.R.L.R. 467 (sex discrimination in employment). See also *Interprods Ltd v De la Rue International Ltd* [2014] EWHC 68 (Comm), [2014] 1 Lloyd's Rep. 540; *London Steam Ship Owners Mutual Insurance Association Ltd v Spain (No.2)* [2013] EWHC 3188 (Comm), [2014] 1 Lloyd's Rep. 309 (allegations of criminality) and *Re Vocam Europe Ltd* [1998] B.C.C. 396; *Exeter City Association Football Club v Football Conference Ltd* [2004] EWHC 31 (Ch), [2004] 1 W.L.R. 2910; *Fulham Football Club (1987) Ltd v Richards* [2011] EWCA Civ 855, [2012] 1 All E.R. 414 (statutory rights of a member of a company). The arbitral tribunal may decide the issue: *Azov Shipping Co v Baltic Shipping Co* [1999] 2 Lloyd's Rep. 159, 178; *Republic of Serbia v Image Sat International* [2009] EWHC 2583 (Comm), [2010] 1 Lloyd's Rep. 324 at [114], [123]. Arbitrability and who should determine it is discussed by various authors in (1996) 12 *Arbitration International*, Issues 2 and 3.

[83] See *Mitsubishi Motors Corp v Soler Chrysler-Plymouth*, 473 U.S. 614 (1985); *Att-Gen of New Zealand v Mobil Oil New Zealand Ltd* [1989] 2 N.Z.L.R. 649; *IBM Australia Ltd v National Distribution Services Pty Ltd* (1991) 100 A.L.R. 361 Australia; Carbonneau (1986) 2 *Arbitration*

within the scope of the arbitration agreement on its true construction.[84] Further, the European Court of Justice has ruled[85] that the arbitral tribunal must address the issue and that a national court to which an application is made for the annulment of the award must grant the application if it considers that the award is in fact contrary to art.81 of the EU Treaty (now art.101 of the TFEU).

Form of agreement   The arbitration agreement need be in no particular form, and **32-021** an arbitration clause even in a most summary form, e.g. "arbitration to be settled in London",[86] "& arbitration ... in London",[87] "arbitration, if any, by ICC rules in London"[88] or "suitable arbitration clause"[89] may be sufficient to amount to an arbitration agreement. But a clause providing, first for arbitration and then, where no resolution is forthcoming for litigation, is not a valid arbitration agreement.[90] An agreement to submit a matter to the decision of a third party as valuer or expert will ordinarily not be an arbitration agreement,[91] but it will be an arbitration agreement if the intention of the parties was that he should hold an inquiry in the nature of a judicial inquiry and hear the respective cases of the parties and decide upon evidence laid before him.[92] There can be a valid arbitration agreement even though the agreement confers on one party alone the right to refer a matter to arbitration, and does not give mutual rights of reference.[93] A clause which provides that "either party may elect to have the dispute referred to arbitration" becomes a binding arbitration agreement once a valid election is made.[94]

The arbitration agreement may be an ad hoc agreement to refer a particular mat- **32-022** ter to arbitration or it may consist of an arbitration clause in a larger agreement

International 116; Lowenfeld (1986) 2 Arbitration International 178; Kühn (1987) 3 Arbitration International 226; Park (1989) 63 Tulane L.R. 648; Dalhuisen (1995) 11 Arbitration International 151; von Mehren (2003) 19 Arbitration International 465; Billiet (2010) 76 Arbitration (1) 86; Radicati Di Brozolo (2011) 27 Arbitration International 1.

84 ET Plus SA v Welter [2005] EWHC 2115 (Comm), [2006] 1 Lloyd's Rep. 251 at [51].
85 Eco Swiss China Time Ltd v Benetton International NV (C-126/97) EU:C:1999:269, [1999] 2 All E.R. (Comm) 44.
86 Tritonia Shipping Inc v South Nelson Products Corp [1966] 1 Lloyd's Rep. 114. See also Naviera Amazonica Peruana v Compañiá Internacional de Seguros de Peru [1988] 1 Lloyd's Rep. 116 ("arbitration under the conditions and laws of London"—seat of arbitration London).
87 Transamerican Ocean Contractors Inc v Transchemical Rotterdam BV [1978] 1 Lloyd's Rep. 238.
88 Mangistaumunaigaz Oil Production Association v United World Trade Inc [1995] 1 Lloyd's Rep. 617.
89 Hobbs Padgett & Co (Reinsurance) Ltd v Kirkland Ltd [1969] 2 Lloyd's Rep. 547.
90 Kruppa v Benedetti [2014] EWHC 1887 (Comm), [2014] 2 All E.R. (Comm) 617.
91 See below, para.32-197.
92 Re Carus-Wilson v Greene (1886) 18 Q.B.D. 7, 9. See David Wilson Homes Ltd v Survey Services Ltd [2000] EWCA Civ 34, [2001] 1 All E.R. (Comm) 449 (reference to Q.C. of English bar an arbitration agreement); Wilkinshaw v Diniz [2000] 2 All E.R. (Comm) 237 (reference to Contract Recognition Board, motor racing federation in part an arbitration agreement). cf. O'Callaghan v Coral Racing Ltd, The Times, November 26, 1998, CA (reference of disputes to the editor of Sporting Life, not an arbitration agreement); Wilky Property Holdings Plc v London & Surrey Investments Ltd [2011] EWHC 2226 (Ch) (reference to valuer not arbitration agreement).
93 Pittalis v Sherefettin [1986] Q.B. 868; RGE (Group Services) Ltd v Cleveland Offshore Ltd (1986) 11 Con. L.R. 77; NB Three Shipping Ltd v Harebell Shipping Ltd [2004] EWHC 2001, [2005] 1 Lloyd's Rep. 509. See Mulcahy (2004) 70 Arbitration 172; Nesbitt and Quinlan (2006) 22 Arbitration International 133. Such a provision may be valid in some countries but not in others, e.g. Russia, Sweden.
94 Westfal-Larsen & Co A/S v Ikerigi Compañiá Naviera SA [1983] 1 Lloyd's Rep. 424; Whiting v Halverson [2003] EWCA Civ 403.

between the parties.[95] It may also consist of, or be limited or extended by, the terms of reference agreed to by the parties, as in the case of ICC arbitrations.[96]

32-023 **Agreements to be in writing** The provisions of Pt I of the 1996 Act apply only where the arbitration agreement is in writing.[97] But the concept of an agreement in writing is widely defined.[98] There is an agreement in writing:

(a) if the agreement is made in writing (whether or not it is signed by the parties);

(b) if the agreement is made by the exchange of communications in writing; or

(c) if the agreement is evidenced in writing.[99]

An oral agreement made by reference to terms which are in writing, for example, to a standard form of salvage agreement such as Lloyd's Open Form which contains an arbitration clause, is an agreement "made in writing"[100]; and an oral agreement is "evidenced in writing" if it is recorded by one of the parties to the agreement, or by a third party, with the authority of the parties to the agreement.[101] Further, if in an exchange of written submissions in arbitral or legal proceedings the existence of an oral agreement is alleged by one party against another party and not denied by the latter in his response, this constitutes as between those parties an agreement in writing to the effect alleged.[102] In view of rapidly evolving means of recording, "writing" includes recording by any means.[103]

32-024 Any other agreement between the parties as to any matter provided for in Pt I of the 1996 Act is likewise effective only if in writing.[104] Thus any derogation by agreement from the non-mandatory provisions of Pt I must be in writing, subject to the broad definition mentioned above.

32-025 **Oral agreements** An oral agreement to arbitrate is not invalid, since the common law recognises such an agreement and it is expressly saved by s.81(1)(b). But the provisions of Pt I do not then apply, including, for example, the right to require a stay of legal proceedings[105] and the right to summary enforcement of the award.[106]

32-026 **Incorporation by reference** An arbitration clause may be incorporated in a contract by reference, e.g. to the standard terms of a trade association or other organisation,[107] or by course of dealing between the parties.[108] If this is disputed, the final decision rests with the court, since it goes to the substantive jurisdiction

---

95 But see below, para.32-028 (separability).

96 *Republic of Serbia v Image Sat International NV* [2009] EWHC 2853 (Comm), [2010] 1 Lloyd's Rep. 324 at [66], [95], [97]–[99].

97 s.5(1).

98 DAC Report, paras 31–40.

99 s.5(2); *TTMI SARL v Statoil ASA* [2011] EWHC 1150 (Comm), [2011] 2 Lloyd's Rep. 220; *Barrier Ltd v Redhall Marine Ltd* [2016] EWHC 381 (QB).

100 s.5(3). See also *Oceanografia SA De CV v DSND Subsea AS* [2006] EWHC (Comm), [2007] 1 All E.R. (Comm) 28 (waiver of condition precedent and estoppel by convention): above, Vol.I, paras 4-082, 4-086, 4-108.

101 1996 Act s.5(4).

102 s.5(5).

103 s.5(6). Quaere whether a voicemail message is included.

104 s.5(1). But see s.23(4) (termination of the arbitration agreement).

105 1996 Act s.9.

106 s.66.

107 *Stretford v Football Association Ltd* [2007] EWCA Civ 238, [2007] 2 Lloyd's Rep. 31; *Sumukan v Commonwealth Secretariat* [2007] EWCA Civ 243, [2007] 2 Lloyd's Rep. 87.

of the arbitral tribunal. By s.6(2) of the 1996 Act, the reference in an agreement to a written form of arbitration clause or to a document containing an arbitration clause constitutes an arbitration agreement if the reference is such as to make that clause part of the agreement. This sub-section does not, however, purport to decide what is required for the effective incorporation of an arbitration clause by reference, i.e. whether there must be a specific reference to the arbitration clause or whether a reference to a document containing an arbitration clause will suffice.[109] That is left to be decided by the common law. It has been pointed out[110] that the authorities recognise a distinction between cases in which the parties incorporate the terms of a contract between two other parties or between one of them and a third party (such as bills of lading, reinsurance contracts, excess insurance contracts and building or engineering sub-contracts) and those in which they incorporate standard terms. A restrictive approach is adopted to the incorporation of arbitration clauses in two-contract situations, whereas in a one-contract situation general words suffice. It is therefore a question of construction in each case whether words in a bill of lading which incorporate some or all of the terms of a charterparty into the bill will have the effect of incorporating into the bill an arbitration clause contained in the charterparty.[111] Where the parties enter into an agreement subsequent to an agreement which contains an arbitration clause, the clause may be incorporated into the

---

[108] See Vol.I, para.13-011.

[109] DAC Report para.42; *Trygg Hansa Insurance Co Ltd v Equitas Ltd* [1998] 2 Lloyd's Rep. 439, 446; *Trade Maritime Corp v Hellenic Mutual War Risks Assn (Bermuda) Ltd* [2006] EWHC 2530 (Comm), [2007] 1 Lloyd's Rep. 280 at [77].

[110] By Christopher Clarke J. in *Habas Sinai v Sibbi Gazlar Isthisal Endustri AS v Sometal SAL* [2010] EWHC 29 (Comm), [2010] 1 Lloyd's Rep. 661 at [12], [13], [34]. See also *Sea Trade Maritime Corp v Hellenic Mutual War Risks Association (Bermuda) Ltd* [2006] EWHC 2530 (Comm), [2007] 1 Lloyd's Rep. 280 at [65], [81] (Langley J.; Tweeddale and Tweeddale (2010) 76 *Arbitration* 656; Ahmed (2010) 26 *Arbitration International* 409; Allison and Dharmananda (2014) 30 *Arbitration International* (2) 265.

[111] The principles to be derived from previous cases were summarised by Brandon J. at first instance in *The Annefield* [1971] P. 168. See *Hamilton & Co v Mackie & Sons* (1889) 5 T.L.R. 677; *T W Thomas & Co Ltd v Portsea SS Co Ltd* [1912] A.C. 1; *The Njegos* [1936] P. 90; *The Merak* [1965] P. 223 (but see *Caresse Navigation Ltd v Zurich Assurances Maroc (The Channel Ranger)* [2014] EWCA Civ 1366, [2015] 1 Lloyd's Rep. 256 at [37]–[39]); *The Phonizien* [1966] 1 Lloyd's Rep. 150; *The Annefield*, above; *The Rena K* [.978] 1 Lloyd's Rep. 545, 550, [1979] Q.B. 377; *Astro Valiente Compania Naviera SA v Govt of Pakistan (No.2)* [1982] 1 W.L.R. 1096; *The Sevonia Team* [1983] 2 Lloyd's Rep. 640; *Miramar Maritime Corp v Holborn Oil Trading Ltd* [1984] A.C. 676; *Skips A/S Nordheim v Syrian Petroleum Co Ltd* [1984] Q.B. 599; *Navigazione Alta Italia SpA v Svenska Petroleum AB* [1988] 1 Lloyd's Rep. 452; *Federal Bulk Carriers Inc v C Itoh & Co Ltd* [1989] 1 Lloyd's Rep. 103; *Partenreederei m/s Heidberge and Vega Reederei Friedrich Dauber v Grosvenor Grain and Feed Co* [1994] 2 Lloyd's Rep. 287; *Daval Aciers d'Usinor et de Sacilor v Armare SRL* [1996] 1 Lloyd's Rep. 1; *The Delos* [2001] 1 Lloyd's Rep. 703; *Welex AG v Rosa Maritime Ltd* [2003] EWCA Civ 938, [2003] 2 Lloyd's Rep. 509; *Sotrade Denizcilik Sanayi ve Ticaret AS v Amadon Lo* [2008] EWHC 2762 (Comm), [2009] 1 Lloyd's Rep. 145; *Kallang Shipping SA Panama v AXA Assurances Senegal* [2008] EWHC 2761 (Comm), [2009] 1 Lloyd's Rep. 124; *Caresse Navigation Ltd v Zurich Assurances Maroc (The Channel Ranger)* [2014] EWCA Civ 1366, [2015] 1 Lloyd's Rep. 256; *Golden Endurance Shipping SA v RMA Watanya SA* [2014] EWHC 3917 (Comm), [2015] 1 Lloyd's Rep. 266. See also (in other contexts) *Modern Building Wales Ltd v Limmer & Trinidad Co Ltd* [1975] 1 W.L.R. 1281; *The St Raphael* [1985] 1 Lloyd's Rep. 403; *Pine Top Insurance Co Ltd v Unione Italiana Anglo Saxon Reinsurance Co Ltd* [1987] 1 Lloyd's Rep. 476; *Aughton v MF Kent Services* (1991) 57 B.L.R. 1; *Barrett v Henry Boot Management Ltd* [1995] C.I.L.L. 1026; *Co-operative Wholesale Soc v Saunders and Taylor* [1995] 11 Const. L.J. 118; *OK Petroleum AB v Vitol Energy SA* [1995] 2 Lloyd's Rep. 160; *Ceval Alimentos v Agrimpex Trading Co Ltd* [1996] 2 Lloyd's Rep. 319; *Extrudakerb (Maltby Engineering) Ltd v Whitemountain Quarries Ltd, The Times*, July 10, 1996; *Excess Insurance Co Ltd v Mander* [1997] 2 Lloyd's Rep. 119; *Roche Products Ltd v Freeman Process Systems Ltd* (1997) 80 Build. L.R. 802; *Trygg Hansa Insur-*

subsequent agreement only if that agreement is not a separate and independent contract.[112]

32-027 **Onerous or unusual clauses** An arbitration clause incorporated by reference may be challenged on the ground that it was an onerous or unusual term that ought to have been drawn specifically to the attention of the party alleged to be bound by it.[113]

32-028 **Separability of arbitration agreement**[114] Where parties enter into an ad hoc agreement to refer to arbitration an existing or future dispute between them relating to an alleged contract, it is clear that the arbitration agreement is an agreement distinct and separate from the contract in question. But an arbitration clause is often embedded in the substantive contract (the "matrix contract") to which it relates. Section 7 of the 1996 Act maintains the principle established by the common law[115] that, unless otherwise agreed,[116] the arbitration agreement is an agreement distinct from the contract of which it forms part and that its validity or existence or effectiveness is not affected by the fact that that contract is invalid, or did not come into existence or has become ineffective. Two consequences follow. First, since the arbitration clause must be treated as a "distinct agreement" it can be void or voidable only on grounds which relate directly to that agreement.[117] Thus the clause may be valid and binding even if, for example, the matrix contract is void, voidable for

ance Co Ltd v Equitas Ltd [1998] 2 Lloyd's Rep. 439; *Secretary of the State for Foreign and Commonwealth Office v Percy Thomas Partnership* (1998) 65 Con. L.R. 11; *Cigna Life Insurance Co of Europe SA NV v Intercaser SA de Seguros y Reaseguros* [2002] 1 All E.R. (Comm) 235; *Sea Trade Maritime Corp v Hellenic Mutual War Risks Assn (Bermuda) Ltd* [2006] EWHC 2530 (Comm), [2007] 1 Lloyd's Rep. 280; *Habas Sinai v Tibbi Gazlar Isthisal Endustri AS v Sometal SAL* [2101] EWHC 29 (Comm), [2010] 1 Lloyd's Rep. 661; *British American Insurance (Kenya) Ltd v Matelec SAL* [2013] EWHC 3278 (Comm), [2014] Lloyd's Rep.I.R. 287. See also the cases cited in n.112, below.

112 *Taylor v Warden Insurance Co Ltd* (1933) 45 Ll.L. Rep. 218; *Kianta Osakeytio v Britain & Overseas Trading Co Ltd* [1954] 1 Lloyd's Rep. 247; *Union of India v EB Aaby's Rederi A/S* [1975] A.C. 797; *Faghirzadeh v Rudolf Wolff (SA) Pty Ltd* [1977] 1 Lloyd's Rep. 630; *Fletamentos Maritimos SA v Effjohn International BV* [1996] 2 Lloyd's Rep. 304. See also *Viscous Global Investment Ltd v Palladium Navigation Corp* [2014] EWHC 2654 (Comm), [2014] 2 Lloyd's Rep. 600 (arbitration clause in letter of undertaking replacing charterparty arbitration clauses).

113 *Kaye v Nu Skin UK Ltd* [2009] EWHC 3509 (Ch), [2011] 1 Lloyd's Rep. 40 and para.13-015 above. But see *Sumukan v Commonwealth Secretariat* [2007] EWCA Civ 243, [2007] 2 Lloyd's Rep. 87; *Stretford v Football Association Ltd* [2007] EWCA Civ 238, [2007] 2 Lloyd's Rep. 31; *William McIlroy Swindon Ltd v Quinn Insurance Ltd* [2010] EWHC 2448 (TCC), [2011] B.L.R. 136.

114 See Schwebel, *International Arbitration: Three Salient Problems* (1987), pp.1–60; Rogers and Launders (1994) 10 *Arbitration International* 77; Samuel (2008) 24 *Arbitration International* 489. Under Regulation 593/2008 (Rome I) (Vol.I, para.30-018) arbitration agreements are excluded from the scope of the Regulation, although the contract in which the agreement is contained is subject to the Regulation: see below, para.32-055, n.231.

115 *Harbour Assurance Co (UK) Ltd v Kansa General International Insurance Co Ltd* [1993] Q.B. 701; *Lesotho Highlands Development Authority v Impregilo SA* [2005] UKHL 43, [2006] 1 A.C. 221 at [21]. See DAC Report paras 43–47.

116 In *National Iranian Oil Co v Crescent Petroleum Co International Ltd* [2016] EWHC 510 (Comm), [2016] 2 Lloyd's Rep. 146 at [7]–[14] the Court held that a contractual choice of law clause, on its own, will not operate as an agreement to the contrary for the purposes of s.7.

117 *Premium Nafta Products Ltd v Fili Shipping Co Ltd* [2007] UKHL 40, [2008] 1 Lloyd's Rep. 254 at [17] [19] [35]. See also *Harbour Assurance Co (UK) Ltd v Kansa General International Insurance Co Ltd*, above, at 724; *Vee Networks Ltd v Econet Wireless International Ltd* [2004] EWHC 2909 (Comm), [2005] 1 Lloyd's Rep. 192 at [20]; *DDT Trucks or North America Ltd v DDT Holdings Ltd* [2007] EWHC 1542 (Comm), [2007] 2 Lloyd's Rep. 213; *Comondate Marine Corp v Pan*

fraud or misrepresentation, or if it has been discharged by breach, frustration or supervening illegality. Of course, there may be cases in which a claim that no contract came into existence between the parties necessarily entails a denial that there was any agreement to arbitrate. Cases of non est factum, forgery and mistake as to the person may provide instances. But the initial invalidity or illegality of the matrix contract will not necessarily involve these consequences unless it is such as directly to impeach the arbitration agreement itself.[118] Also an arbitration agreement may be binding even though the matrix contract has not come into existence.[119] Secondly, if the arbitration agreement is valid and binding and is sufficiently wide in its terms,[120] issues relating to the validity, existence or effectiveness of the matrix contract are within the substantive jurisdiction of the arbitral tribunal and it can decide on those issues. So, for example, it can decide whether an initially valid but voidable contract has been or ought to be rescinded,[121] whether an allegedly illegal contract is unenforceable by one or both of the parties,[122] whether a breach of the contract by one party has brought the contract to an end,[123] whether the contract has been frustrated and the consequences of frustration,[124] and whether one party is entitled to terminate or invalidate the contract by virtue of a term contained in it.[125] Even if the arbitration agreement is directly impeached, the tribunal may rule on this issue, though not conclusively.[126] An appropriately worded

Australia Shipping Pty Ltd [2006] FCAFC 192, [2008] 1 Lloyd's Rep. 119 at [218]–[230]; *El Nasharty v J Sainsbury Plc* [2007] EWHC 2618 (Comm), [2008] 1 Lloyd's Rep. 360. See also *Associated British Ports v Tata Steel UK Ltd* [2017] EWHC 694 (Ch), [2017] 2 Lloyd's Rep. 11.

[118] *Harbour Assurance Co (UK) Ltd v Kansa General International Insurance Co Ltd*, above, at 712, 715, 724; *Westacre Investments Inc v Jugo-import-SPDR Holding Co Ltd* [2000] Q.B. 288; *FAI General Insurance Ltd v Ocean Marine Mutual Protection and Indemnity Assn (No.2)* [1998] Lloyd's Rep. IR 24. *Vee Networks Ltd v Econet Wireless International Ltd*, above, at [21]; *Premium Nafta Products Ltd v Fili Shipping Co Ltd*, above, at [17]–[19]; *Beijing Jianlong Heavy Industry Group v Golden Ocean Group Ltd* [2013] EWHC 1063 (Comm), [2013] 2 All E.R. (Comm) 436. cf. *Smith, Coney & Barrett v Becker, Gray & Co* [1916] 2 Ch. 86, 92 (war); *Soleimany v Soleimany* [1999] Q.B. 785 (public policy); *Credit Suisse First Boston (Europe) Ltd v Seagate Trading Co Ltd* [1999] 1 Lloyd's Rep. 784 (fraud and mistake); *Capital Structures Plc v Time & Tide Construction Ltd* [2006] B.L.R. 226 at [28], [29] (duress); *Albon v Naza Motor Trading Sdn Bhd (No.3)* [2007] EWHC 665 (Ch), [2007] 2 Lloyd's Rep. 1 (forgery).

[119] *Premium Nafta Products Ltd v Fili Shipping Co Ltd* [2007] UKHL 40, [2008] 1 Lloyd's Rep. at [18]; *UR Power GmbH v Kuok Oils and Grains Pte Ltd* [2009] EWHC 1940 (Comm), [2009] 2 Lloyd's Rep. 495 at [40]; *Novasen SA v Alimenta* [2011] EWHC 49 (Comm), [2011] 1 Lloyd's Rep. 390 at [52]. The wording of s.7 provides for this. cf. *Hyundai Merchant Marine Co Ltd v Americas Bulk Transport Ltd* [2013] EWHC 470 (Comm), [2013] 2 All E.R. (Comm) 649 at [35].

[120] See below, para.32-030.

[121] *Mackender v Feldia AG* [1967] 2 Q.B. 590; *Ashville Investments Ltd v Elmer Contractors Ltd* [1989] 1 Q.B. 488; *Premium Nafta Products Ltd v Fili Shipping Co Ltd*, above; *El Nasharty v J Sainsbury Plc*, above.

[122] *Harbour Assurance Co (UK) Ltd v Kansa General International Insurance Co Ltd*, above; *Westacre Investments Inc v Jugo-import-SDPR Holding Co Ltd*, above, at 129. See also *Prodexport State Company for Foreign Trade v ED & F Man Ltd* [1973] Q.B. 389 (supervening illegality); *Azov Shipping Co v Baltic Shipping Co* [1999] 2 Lloyd's Rep. 159, 178 (non-justiciability).

[123] *Heyman v Darwins Ltd* [1942] A.C. 356.

[124] *Heyman v Darwins Ltd*, above, at 366, 383, 400–401; *Kruse v Questier & Co Ltd* [1953] 1 Q.B. 669; *Government of Gibraltar v Kenney* [1956] 2 Q.B. 410.

[125] *Stebbing v Liverpool and London Globe Insurance Co Ltd* [1917] 2 K.B. 433; *Woodall v Pearl Assurance* [1919] 1 K.B. 593; *Freshwater v Western Australian Assurance Co* [1933] 1 K.B. 515; *Paul Smith Ltd v H & S International Holding Inc* [1991] 2 Lloyd's Rep. 127. See also *De la Garde v Workshop & Co* [1928] Ch. 17 (condition precedent).

[126] See below, para.32-101.

arbitration clause may also be held to confer upon the tribunal jurisdiction to rectify the contract in which the clause is contained.[127]

32-029 Section 7 applies where the law applicable to the arbitration agreement is the law of England even if the seat of the arbitration is elsewhere or has not been designated or determined.[128] The law applicable to the arbitration agreement may be different from that which is applicable to the matrix contract.[129] Where there is in the same contract an arbitration clause and a clause submitting disputes to the exclusive jurisdiction of a national court, the arbitration clause may be held to have priority over the jurisdiction clause on the ground that the parties must be taken to have agreed on a single tribunal for the resolution of their disputes.[130] Alternatively the arbitration clause might be construed as applying to all disputes relating to substantive issues and the jurisdiction clause as a submission to the supervisory or ancillary jurisdiction of the court in respect of the arbitration.[131]

32-030 **Scope of the arbitration agreement** The scope of an arbitration agreement is to be determined by reference to the precise wording of the agreement, construed according to its language and in the light of the circumstances in which it was made.[132] But the court will endeavour to give a sensible and effective interpretation to the words used,[133] and will start with the assumption that the parties, as rational businessmen, are likely to have intended any dispute arising out of the relationship into which they have entered or purported to enter to be decided by the same tribunal.[134] The words "all disputes or differences" or "all claims" are words of wide import, but must necessarily be controlled by the subject-matter to which they

---

127 *Ashville Investments Ltd v Elmer Contractors Ltd* [1989] Q.B. 488; *Overseas Union Insurance Co Ltd v AA Mutual Insurance Co Ltd* [1988] 2 Lloyd's Rep. 63; *Ethiopian Oil Seeds & Pulses Export Corp v Rio del Mar Foods Inc* [1990] 1 Lloyd's Rep. 86. Contrast *Printing Machinery Co Ltd v Linotype and Machinery Ltd* [1912] 1 Ch. 566; *Crane v Hegeman-Harris Co Inc* [1939] 3 All E.R. 68.

128 1996 Act s.2(5).

129 *C v D* [2007] EWCA Civ 1282, [2008] 1 Lloyd's Rep. 239 at [22]–[29]; *Sulamerica CIA Nacional de Seguros SA v Enesa Engenharia SA* [2012] EWCA Civ 638, [2012] 1 Lloyd's Rep. 671; *Abuja International Hotels Ltd v Meridien SAS* [2012] EWHC 87 (Comm), [2012] 1 Lloyd's Rep. 461; *Habors Sinai Ve Tibbi Gazlar Istihsal Endustrisi As v VSC Steel Co Ltd* [2013] EWHC 4071 (Comm), [2014] 1 Lloyd's Rep. 479 at [99]–[119]. cf. *Arsanovia Ltd v Cruz City 1 Mauritius Holdings* [2012] EWHC 3702 (Comm), [2013] 2 All E.R. (Comm) 1. See Haydn-Williams (2012) 78 *Arbitration* (4) 387; Pearson (2013) 29 *Arbitration International* (1) 115; Dundas (2013) 79 *Arbitration* (3) 325; Charles (2014) 80 *Arbitration* (1) 55; and see Vol.I, para.30-039; above, para.32-009.

130 *Sulamerica CIA Nacional de Seguros SA v Enesa Enghenharia SA* [2012] EWHC 42 at [48], [2012] EWCA Civ 638, [2012] 1 Lloyd's Rep. 671; *British American Insurance (Kenya) Ltd v Matelec SAL* [2013] EWHC 3278 (Comm), [2014] Lloyd's Rep.I.R. 287 at [51].

131 *Paul Smith Ltd v H & S International Holdings Inc* [1991] 2 Lloyd's Rep. 127; *Tri MG Intra Asia Airlines v Norse Air Charter Ltd* [2009] SGHC 13, [2009] 1 Lloyd's Rep. 258.

132 *Heyman v Darwins Ltd* [1942] A.C. 356, 366; *Lobb Partnership Ltd v Aintree Racecourse Ltd* [2000] B.L.R. 65.

133 *Star Shipping AS v China National Foreign Trade Transportation Corp* [1999] 2 Lloyd's Rep. 445, 452; *Benford Ltd v Lopecan SL* [2004] EWHC 1897 (Comm), [2004] 2 Lloyd's Rep. 618 at [26].

134 *Premium Nafta Products Ltd v Fili Shipping Co Ltd* [2007] UKHL 40, [2008] 1 Lloyd's Rep. 254 at [13]; *Comandate Marine Corp v Pan Australia Shopping Pty Ltd* [2006] FCAFC 192, [2008] 1 Lloyd's Rep. 119 at [165]; *Emmott v Michael Wilson & Partners Ltd (No.2)* [2009] EWHC 1 (Comm), [2009] 1 Lloyd's Rep. 233; *Bilta (UK) Ltd v Nazir* [2010] EWHC 1086 (Ch), [2010] 2 Lloyd's Rep. 29 at [18]. See also *CMA CGM SA v Hyundai Mipo Dockyard Co Ltd* [2008] EWHC 2791, [2009] 1 Lloyd's Rep. 213 ("if any dispute should arise in connection with the interpretation and fulfilment of this contract"). cf. *Secretary of State for Transport v Stagecoach South Western Trains Ltd* [2009] EWHC 2431 (Comm), [2010] 1 Lloyd's Rep. 175 at [29], [36].

relate.[135] The word "difference" is wide enough to embrace a difference between the parties, e.g. as to the price, where the contract provides for this to be determined by mutual agreement, and the parties fail to agree.[136] There can be a "dispute" between the parties if a claim is made by one party on the other, which is neither admitted nor disputed, but merely ignored.[137] There is also a "dispute" even if the claim made by one party on the other is indisputable, that is, one to which there is no arguable defence.[138] The words "in connection with" "in relation to" "in respect of" "concerning" or "with regard to" (a contract) are clearly wide in scope. A wide meaning will also be attributed to the words "arising out of".[139] Thus even a claim for damages in tort[140] or for contribution under the Civil Liability (Contribution) Act 1978[141] or for general average[142] may be within an arbitration clause if closely connected with the contract, but not a claim on a bill of exchange.[143] The words "arising under" a contract were at one time thought to have a narrower meaning[144]; but this distinction has now been rejected by the House of Lords.[145]

---

[135] *Re Hohenzollern Act für Locomotivbahn and the City of London Contract Corp* (1886) 54 L.T. 596.

[136] *F & G Sykes (Wessex) Ltd v Fine Fare Ltd* [1967] 1 Lloyd's Rep. 53; *Vosper Thorneycroft Ltd v Ministry of Defence* [1976] 1 Lloyd's Rep. 58; *Queensland Electricity Generating Board v New Hope Collieries Pty Ltd* [1989] 1 Lloyd's Rep. 205. The word "difference" is less hard-edged than "dispute": *Amec Civil Engineering Ltd v Secretary of State for Transport* [2005] EWCA Civ 291, [2005] 1 W.L.R. 2339 at [31].

[137] *Tradax Internacional SA v Cerrahogullari TAS* [1981] 3 All E.R. 344, 350; *Ellerine Bros (Pty) Ltd v Klinger* [1982] 1 W.L.R. 1375; *Secretary of State for Foreign and Commonwealth Office v Percy Thomas Partnership* (1998) 65 Con. L.R. 11; *Marc Rich Agriculture Trading SA v Agrimex Ltd* [2000] 1 All E.R. (Comm) 951; *Amec Civil Engineering Ltd v Secretary of State for Transport*, above, at [30]–[31]; *Collins (Contractors) Ltd v Baltic Quay Management (1994) Ltd* [2004] EWCA Civ 1757 at [63]. See also *Exfin Shipping Ltd v Tolani Shipping Co Ltd* [2006] EWHC 1090 (Comm), [2006] 2 Lloyd's Rep. 388 (liability admitted but refusal of immediate payment).

[138] *Halki Shipping Corp v Sopex Oils Ltd* [1998] 1 W.L.R. 726; *Wealands v CLC Contractors Ltd* [1999] 2 Lloyd's Rep. 739.

[139] *Ethiopian Oil Seeds & Pulses Export Corp v Rio del Mar Foods Inc* [1990] 1 Lloyd's Rep. 86; *Harbour Assurance Co (UK) Ltd v Kansa General International Insurance Co Ltd* [1993] Q.B. 701; Mustill and Boyd, *Commercial Arbitration*, 2nd edn, p.120. Collateral or even prior or subsequent contracts may, in certain circumstances, be covered: *Faghirzadeh v Rudolf Wolff (SA) Pty Ltd* [1977] 1 Lloyd's Rep. 630; *Overseas Union Insurance Ltd v AA Mutual International Insurance Ltd* [1988] 2 Lloyd's Rep. 63; *Norscot Rig Management Pvt Ltd v Essar Oilfields Services Ltd* [2010] EWHC 195 (Comm), [2010] 2 Lloyd's Rep. 209 at [16]; *Deutsche Bank AG v Tongkah Harbour Public Co Ltd* [2011] EWHC 2251 (QB), (2011) 108 (34) L.S.G. 20. cf. *X Ltd v Y Ltd* [2005] EWHC 769 (TCC), [2005] Build. L.R. 341.

[140] *Astro Vencedor Compañía Naviera SA of Panama v Mabanaft GmbH* [1971] 2 Q.B. 588; *Lonrho Ltd v Shell Petroleum Ltd, The Times,* February 1, 1978; *The Playa Larga* [1983] 2 Lloyd's Rep. 171; *Société Commerciale de Réassurance v Eras International Ltd* [1992] 1 Lloyd's Rep. 570; *Chimimport Plc v G D'Alesio SAS* [1994] 2 Lloyd's Rep. 366; *Abdullah M Fahem & Co v Mareb Yemen Insurance Co* [1997] 2 Lloyd's Rep. 738; *Wealands v CLC Contractors Ltd* [1999] 2 Lloyd's Rep. 739; *The Delos* [2001] 1 Lloyd's Rep. 703; *Capital Thrush Investments Ltd v Radio Design TJAB* [2002] EWCA Civ 135, [2002] 2 All E.R. 450; *Asghar v Legal Services Commission* [2004] EWHC 1803 (Ch); *ET Plus SA v Welter* [2005] EWHC 2115 (Comm), [2006] 1 Lloyd's Rep. 251; *CMA CGM SA v Hyundai Mipo Dockyard Co Ltd* [2008] EWHC 2791 (Comm), [2009] 1 Lloyd's Rep. 213 at [31]; *Bilta (UK) Ltd v Nazir* [2010] EWHC 1086 (Ch), [2010] 2 Lloyd's Rep. 29 at [17].

[141] *Wealands v CLC Contractors Ltd* [1999] 2 Lloyd's Rep. 739.

[142] *Union of India v EB Aaby's Rederi A/S* [1975] A.C. 797.

[143] *Nova (Jersey) Knit Ltd v Kammgarn Spinnerei GmbH* [1977] 1 W.L.R. 713. Contrast *Parharpur Cooling Towers Ltd v Paramount (WA) Ltd* [2007] WASC 234 (Australia).

[144] *Heyman v Darwins Ltd* [1942] A.C. 356, 399 (cf. at 393, 394); *Government of Gibraltar v Kenney* [1956] 2 Q.B. 410, 421; *Fillite (Runcorn) Ltd v Aqua-Lift* (1989) 45 Build. L.R. 27.

[145] *Premier Nafta Products Ltd v Fili Shipping Co Ltd* [2007] UKHL 40, approving the view of Longmore L.J. in the Court of Appeal sub nom. *Fiona Trust and Holding Corp v Privalov* [2007]

32-031   Under a clause submitting to arbitration any dispute arising out of a contract, an arbitrator has jurisdiction finally to determine the application of a trade custom affecting the rights and obligations of the parties,[146] provided that it is not inconsistent with the contract or unreasonable.[147]

32-032 Set-off and counterclaim   Subject to the terms of the arbitration clause, a counterclaim by way of set-off arising out of the same or a closely related contract will be within the scope of the clause but not a counterclaim by way of set-off arising out of a separate and unconnected contract.[148]

32-033 Substantive jurisdiction for court   Though the arbitral tribunal may (unless otherwise agreed) rule whether or not the dispute is within the scope of the arbitration agreement,[149] it cannot finally decide this issue: it goes to the substantive jurisdiction of the arbitral tribunal which, if challenged, is a matter for the court to determine.[150]

32-034   A dispute as to whether notices of appeal from an arbitrator's award to an appellate tribunal have been properly served does not arise out of the contract but out of the award and is therefore not within the scope of an arbitration clause.[151]

32-035 Pre-conditions   There will normally be no valid reference to arbitration if the arbitration agreement stipulates that certain facts or events shall be a pre-condition of a reference to arbitration and the pre-condition is not fulfilled.[152] Here, too, the arbitral tribunal may rule whether or not facts or events exist which found its jurisdiction,[153] but the final determination of this question rests with the court.[154] A stipulation that the parties should first strive to settle the dispute amicably, or that the dispute should, in the first place, be submitted for conciliation, is not normally

---

EWCA Civ 20, [2007] 2 Lloyd's Rep. 267 at [17]–[18]. See also *Comandate Marine Corp v Pan Australia Shipping Pty Ltd* [2006] FCAFC 192, [2008] 1 Lloyd's Rep. 119 at [162]–[187]; *Yegiazaryan v Smagin* [2016] EWCA Civ 1290, [2017] 1 Lloyd's Rep. 102 at [44]. cf. *Microsoft Mobile Oy (Ltd) v Sony Europe Ltd* [2017] EWHC 374 (Ch), [2017] 5 C.M.L.R. 5 at [43]–[54].

[146] *Produce Brokers Co Ltd v Olympia Oil and Cake Co Ltd* [1916] 1 A.C. 314.

[147] *Produce Brokers Co Ltd v Olympia Oil and Cake Co Ltd* [1916] 2 K.B. 296, [1917] 1 K.B. 320, described by Scrutton L.J. at 324 as "a terrible example of the disadvantages of combining a commercial arbitration with proceedings in the courts". See Vol.I, paras 13-137, 13-143, 14-033, 14-035.

[148] *Metal Distributors (UK) Ltd v ZCCM Investment Holdings Plc* [2005] EWHC 156 (Comm), [2005] 2 Lloyd's Rep. 37 at [18]. See also *ED&F Man v Société Anonyme Tripolitaine des Usines* [1970] 2 Lloyd's Rep. 416; *Aectra Refining and Manufacturing Inc v Exmar NV* [1994] 1 W.L.R 1634, 1650; *Ronly Holdings v JSC Zestafoni Nikoladze Ferroalloy Plant* [2004] EWHC 1354 (Comm), [2004] 1 C.L.C. 1168; *Benford Ltd v Lopecan SL* [2004] EWHC 1897 (Comm), [2004] 2 Lloyd's Rep. 618; *Prekons Insaat Sanayi AS v Rowlands Castle Contracting Group Ltd* [2006] EWHC 1367 (Comm), [2007] 1 Lloyd's Rep. 98; *Norscot Rig Management Pvt Ltd v Essar Oilfields Services Ltd* [2010] EWHC 195 (Comm), [2010] 2 Lloyd's Rep. 209 at [16]. Contrast *Econet Satellite Services Ltd v Vee Networks Ltd* [2006] EWHC 1664 (Comm), [2006] 2 Lloyd's Rep. 423 (UNCITRAL rules); *Emmott v Michael Wilson & Partners Ltd (No.2)* [2009] EWHC 1 (Comm), [2009] 1 Lloyd's Rep. 233.

[149] Arbitration Act 1996 ss.30, 31. See below, para.32-101.

[150] ss.32, 67, 72.

[151] *Getreide-import GmbH v Contimar SA Compañía Industrial Commercial y Maritima* [1953] 1 W.L.R. 793. Contrast *Gunter Henck v André et Cie SA* [1970] 1 Lloyd's Rep. 235.

[152] *Smith v Martin* [1925] 1 K.B. 745; *Mid-Glamorgan CC v Land Authority for Wales* (1990) 49 B.L.R. 61. See, e.g., *Ruby Roz Agricol LLP v Republic of Kazakhstan* [2017] EWHC 439 (Comm).

[153] Arbitration Act 1996 ss.30, 31.

[154] ss.32, 67, 72.

such a pre-condition and may not create an enforceable legal obligation.[155] Where parties agreed that arbitration would be held in London before two arbitrators and an umpire in accordance with ICC rules, the fact that the ICC declined jurisdiction did not frustrate the reference.[156]

Parties bound by arbitration agreement: minors   A minor is bound by an   **32-036** arbitration agreement in a contract of apprenticeship if the contract as a whole is for his benefit.[157]

Trustees in bankruptcy   Where a bankrupt has become party to a contract   **32-037** containing an arbitration agreement before the commencement of his bankruptcy, then, if the trustee in bankruptcy adopts the contract, the arbitration agreement is enforceable by or against the trustee in relation to matters arising from or connected with the contract.[158] Even if the trustee does not adopt the contract, the court has power, on the application either of the trustee with the consent of the creditors' committee established under s.301 of the Insolvency Act 1986, or of any other party to the arbitration agreement, to make an order that the matter be referred to arbitration.[159] A trustee in bankruptcy may, with the permission of the creditors' committee, refer any dispute to arbitration.[160] The making of a bankruptcy order does not terminate or operate as a stay of current arbitration proceedings unless the court so orders.[161]

Companies   A party must make an application to the court for permission to bring   **32-038** an arbitration against a company in compulsory liquidation[162] and the same applies to a party that wishes to commence or continue arbitration proceedings against a company in administration.[163] Where a company is being wound up, the liquidator may, with the sanction of the court or of the liquidation committee, bring or

---

[155] *Courtney & Fairbairn Ltd v Tolaini Bros (Hotels) Ltd* [1975] 1 W.L.R. 297; *Itex Shipping Pte Ltd v China Ocean Shipping Co* [1989] 2 Lloyd's Rep. 522, 525; *Paul Smith Ltd v H & S International Holding Inc* [1991] 2 Lloyd's Rep. 127, 131; *Sulamerica CIA Nacional de Seguros SA v Enesa Enghenharia SA* [2012] EWCA Civ 638, [2012] 1 Lloyd's Rep. 671 at [35], [36]; *Wah v Grant Thornton International Ltd* [2012] EWHC 3198 (Ch), [2013] 1 Lloyd's Rep. 11. But see *Charnel Tunnel Group Ltd v Balfour Beatty Construction Ltd* [1993] A.C. 334; *Halifax Financial Services Ltd v Intuitive Systems Ltd* [1999] 1 All E.R. (Comm) 303; *Cable & Wireless Plc v IBM United Kingdom Ltd* [2002] EWHC 2059 (Comm), [2002] 2 All E.R. (Comm) 1041; *Holloway v Chancery Mead Ltd* [2007] EWHC 2495 (TCC), [2008] 1 All E.R. (Comm) 653; *International Research Corp v Lufthansa Systems Asia Pacific Pte Ltd* [2012] SGHC 226, [2013] 1 Lloyd's Rep. 24 (Singapore); *Emirates Trading Agency LLC v Prime Mineral Exports Private Ltd* [2014] EWHC 2104 (Comm), [2014] 2 Lloyd's Rep. 457 (alternative dispute resolution procedure) and ss.9(2), 12(1)(b) of the 1996 Act. See also *Amec Civil Engineering Ltd v Secretary of State for Transport* [2005] EWCA Civ 291, [2005] 1 W.L.R. 2339 (reference to engineer under ICE Conditions of Contract); Dundas (2013) 79 *Arbitration* (2) 221.
[156] *Sumitomo Heavy Industries v Oil and Natural Gas Commission* [1994] 1 Lloyd's Rep. 45.
[157] *Slade v Metrodent* [1953] 2 Q.B. 112.
[158] Insolvency Act 1986 s.349A(2) (inserted by s.107(1) of and Sch.3 para.46 to the Arbitration Act 1996).
[159] Insolvency Act 1986 s.349A(3).
[160] Insolvency Act 1986 s.314 and Sch.5 para.6.
[161] Under Insolvency Act 1986 s.285(1). See also *Syska v Vivendi Universal SA* [2009] EWCA Civ 677, [2009] Bus. L.R. 1494 (foreign bankruptcy).
[162] Insolvency Act 1986 s.130(2).
[163] Insolvency Act 1986 Sch.B1 paras 43, 44 inserted by the Enterprise Act 2002 s.248 and Sch.16; *S. Straume (UK) Ltd v Bradlov Developments Ltd* [2000] B.C.C. 33.

defend proceedings in the name of and on behalf of the company.[164] But once a company in liquidation is struck off the register of companies it will be dissolved[165] and ceases to exist. Any arbitration to which the company was a party then comes to an end[166]: it cannot be revived unless the company is restored to the register.[167] If the rights and obligations of a party to the arbitration agreement are transferred to another company before or at the time of the original party's dissolution by a doctrine of universal succession or a similar mechanism, the successor may rely on and enforce the arbitration agreement.[168]

32-039   Group of companies   The "group of companies" doctrine which in some legal systems allows a claim to be made in arbitral proceedings by or against a company in the same group of companies as the company that entered into the arbitration agreement forms no part of English law.[169]

32-040   Personal representatives   Unless otherwise agreed by the parties, an arbitration agreement is not discharged by the death of a party and may be enforced by or against the personal representatives of that party.[170] Personal representatives may submit to arbitration any debt or claim relating to the deceased's estate.[171]

32-041   The Crown   Part I of the Arbitration Act 1996 binds the Crown.[172]

32-042   Assignees   An assignee of a contract is bound by and may take the benefit of an arbitration clause contained therein,[173] but he cannot continue an arbitration already commenced by the assignor unless and until he gives notice of the assignment to the other party to the dispute and submits to the jurisdiction of the arbitrator.[174] However, if the right to assign the contract in which the arbitration clause is

---

[164] Insolvency Act 1986 ss.165, 166, 167 and Sch.4 para.4.
[165] Companies Act 2006 s.1001. See also ss.1000, 1003. As to a case where there is an issue whether a foreign company has been dissolved, see *Silver Dry Bulk Co Ltd v Homer Hulbert Maritime Co Ltd* [2017] EWHC 44 (Comm), [2017] 1 Lloyd's Rep. 154 at [25]–[31].
[166] *Morris v Harris* [1927] A.C. 252; *Baytur SA v Finagro Holdings SA* [1992] 1 Lloyd's Rep. 134. cf. *Eurosteel Ltd v Stinnes AG* [2000] 1 All E.R. (Comm) 964 (assignment before dissolution).
[167] Companies Act 2006 ss.1024–1034; *Union Trans-Pacific Co Ltd v Orient Shipping Rotterdam VB* [2002] EWHC 1451 (Comm).
[168] *A v B* [2016] EWHC 3003 (Comm), [2017] 1 W.L.R. 2030.
[169] *Peterson Farms Inc v C & M Farming Ltd* [2004] EWHC 121 (Comm), [2004] 1 Lloyd's Rep. 602 at [59].
[170] Arbitration Act 1996 s.8. See also s.2(5) (conflict of laws).
[171] Trustee Act 1925 s.15.
[172] s.106.
[173] *Aspell v Seymour* [1929] W.N. 152; *Shayler v Woolf* [1946] 1 Ch. 320; *Rumput (Panama) SA v Islamic Republic of Iran Shipping Lines* [1984] 2 Lloyd's Rep. 259; *Court Line Ltd v Aktiebolaget Gotaverken* [1984] 1 Lloyd's Rep. 283, 289; *The Padre Island* [1984] 2 Lloyd's Rep. 408; *Kaukomarkkinat O/Y v "Elbe" Transport Union GmbH* [1985] 2 Lloyd's Rep. 85; *Montedipe SpA v JTP-Ro Jugotanker* [1990] 2 Lloyd's Rep. 11, 15; *Schiffahrtsgesellschaft Detlev von Appen GmbH v Voest Alpine Intertrading GmbH* [1997] 2 Lloyd's Rep. 279; *STX Pan Ocean Co Ltd v Woori Bank* [2012] EWHC 981 (Comm). Contrast *Cottage Club Estates Ltd v Woodside Estates Co Ltd* [1928] 2 K.B. 463; *London Steamship Owners Mutual Insurance Association Ltd v Bombay Trading Co Ltd* [1990] 2 Lloyd's Rep. 21, 25; Mustill and Boyd at pp.137–139. See [1992] 8 *Arbitration International* 121. An assignor under an equitable assignment, of which no notice has been given to the respondent, may still commence an arbitration: *Herkules Piling Ltd v Tilbury Construction Ltd* (1992) 61 Build. L.R. 107.
[174] *Montedipe SpA v JTP-Ro Jugotanker*, above; *Baytur SA v Finagro Holding SA* [1992] Q.B. 610; *Charles M Willie & Co (Shipping) Ltd v Ocean Laser Shipping Ltd* [1999] 1 Lloyd's Rep. 225, 241.

contained is taken away or restricted, then the right to claim arbitration will be similarly circumscribed.[175]

Novation   Where, as a result of a consensual novation[176] the claimant has replaced   **32-043**
the person originally named as a party, who therefore has ceased to have any rights or duties under the contract, the new party can and must enforce the arbitration clause, for his position is the same as if he had been a party from the outset.[177]

Third parties   The Contracts (Rights Against Third Parties) Act 1999 enables   **32-044**
third parties, that is to say, persons who are not parties to a contract, to enforce a substantive term contained in it in their own right in certain circumstances. Section 8(1) of the Act provides that, where a right to enforce such a term is subject to a term which provides in writing for the submission of disputes to arbitration, then the third party is to be treated for the purposes of the Arbitration Act 1996 as a party to the arbitration agreement as regards disputes between himself and the promisor relating to the enforcement of the substantive term by the third party.[178] Thus, a third party who is granted the right to enforce a term of the contract, takes it subject to any obligation imposed by the contract to resort to arbitration in order to exercise that right.[179] Section 8(2) of the 1999 Act further provides for the rare situation which may arise where a right is expressly conferred upon a third party (who does not fall within subs.(1)) to enforce a written arbitration agreement. In such a case. he is to be treated as a party to the agreement for the purposes of the 1996 Act.[180]

Subrogation   A person subrogated to the rights of an assured under a policy of   **32-045**
insurance by virtue of the Third Parties (Rights against Insurers) Act 1930 or otherwise is bound by an arbitration clause contained in the policy.[181]

See also *A v B* [2016] EWHC 3003 (Comm), [2017] 1 W.L.R. 2030.

[175] *Yeandle v Wynn Realisations Ltd* (1999) 47 Const. L.R. 1; Tackaberry [2001] Const. L.J. 17(4), 287.
[176] See Vol.I, para.19-087.
[177] Mustill and Boyd, *Commercial Arbitration*, 2nd edn (1989), p.137. See *Freshwater v Western Australian Assurance Co Ltd* [1933] 1 K.B. 315; *Dennehy v Bellamy* (1938) 60 LI. L. Rep. 259; *Smith v Pearl Assurance Co Ltd* (1939) 63 LI. L. Rep. 1; *Oakland Metal Co Ltd v Banairn & Co Ltd* [1953] 2 Lloyd's Rep. 192; *CMA CGM SA v Hyundai Mipo Dockyard Co Ltd* [2008] EWHC 2791 (Comm), [2009] 1 Lloyd's Rep. 213 at [23].
[178] *AES Ust-Kamenogorsk Hydropower Plant LLP v Ust-Kamenogorsk Hydropower Plant JSC* [2010] EWHC 772 (Comm), [2010] 2 Lloyd's Rep. 493 at [27], [28], [32] (affirmed [2011] EWCA Civ 647, [2011] 2 Lloyd's Rep. 233, [2013] UKSC 35); *Fortress Value Recovery Fund 1 LLC v Blue Skye Special Opportunities Fund LP* [2013] EWCA Civ 367, [2013] 1 Lloyd's Rep. 606; Tweeddale (2011) 27 *Arbitration International* 553.
[179] *Nisshin Shipping Co Ltd v Cleaves & Co Ltd* [2003] EWHC 2602 (Comm), [2004] 1 Lloyd's Rep. 38; Vol.I, para.18-101. In *Fortress Value Recovery Fund 1 LLC v Blue Skye Special Opportunities Fund LP* [2013] EWCA Civ 367, [2013] 1 Lloyd's Rep. 606 the Court of Appeal stated that a third party, which seeks to rely on the defence of an exclusion clause in the contract, may in some circumstances be entitled to invoke an arbitration clause in the contract.
[180] Wright (1999) 2 Int. Arb. L.R. 137; Diamond (2001) 17 *Arbitration International* 211; Ambrose [2001] J.B.L. 415. cf. *Fortress Value Recovery Fund 1 LLC v Blue Skye Special Opportunities Fund LP* [2013] EWCA Civ 367, [2013] 1 Lloyd's Rep. 606 at [31], [47].
[181] *Freshwater v Western Australia Insurance Co Ltd* [1933] 1 K.B. 515; *Dennehy v Bellamy* [1938] 2 All E.R. 262; *Smits v Pearl Assurance Co Ltd* [1939] 1 All E.R. 95; *Digby v General Accident Fire and Life Assurance Corp Ltd* [1940] 2 K.B. 226, 236; *The Padre Island* [1984] 2 Lloyd's Rep. 408, 414; *The Padre Island (No.2)* [1987] 2 Lloyd's Rep. 529, 533; *London Steamship Owners Mutual Insurance Association Ltd v Bombay Trading Co Ltd* [1990] 2 Lloyd's Rep. 21, 26; *Schiffahrtsgesellschaft Detler von Appen GmbH v Wiener Allianz Versicherungs AG* [1997] 2 Lloyd's Rep.

32-046   Guarantor   A guarantor may be held to have agreed to arbitration where it has specifically endorsed as surety the contract between the creditor and the principal debtor which contains an arbitration clause.[182]

32-047   Award a condition precedent to action   The parties to a contract can agree that the award of an arbitrator shall be a condition precedent to the right to bring any legal action in relation to the contract.[183] Such a provision is known as a *"Scott v Avery* clause". Its effect is that no action or other legal proceedings[184] may be brought until the matters in dispute have been submitted to arbitration,[185] unless the condition has been waived by the party relying on the clause,[186] or if his neglect or default has prevented the other party from obtaining an award.[187] However, if an application is made for a stay of legal proceedings under s.9 of the 1996 Act, and the court refuses a stay, the condition is of no effect in relation to those proceedings.[188]

32-048   Since the cause of action under such a clause does not arise until an arbitrator has made his award, it was formerly held that time under the Statutes of Limitation ran from the date of the award and not from the date of the breach.[189] But s.13(3) of the 1996 Act provides that, in determining for the purposes of the Limitation Acts when a cause of action accrued, any provision that an award is a condition precedent to the bringing of legal proceedings in respect of a matter to which an arbitration agreement relates is to be disregarded.[190]

32-049   If an accident insurance policy contains a *Scott v Avery* clause, and by reason of the insolvency of the insured his rights pass to the injured third party under the Third Parties (Rights against Insurers) Act 1930, the third party is bound by the clause, for he is merely subrogated by the statute to the rights of the insured.[191]

279; *West Tankers Inc v Ras Riunione Adriatica di Sicurta* [2005] EWHC 454 (Comm), [2005] 2 Lloyd's Rep. 257 (appealed to the House of Lords on another point: [2007] UKHL 4, [2007] 1 Lloyd's Rep. 391); *Through Transport Mutual Insurance Assn (Eurasia) Ltd v New India Assurance Co Ltd (No.2)* [2005] EWHC 455 (Comm), [2005] 2 Lloyd's Rep. 378; *Starlight Shipping Co v Tai Ping Insurance Co* [2007] EWHC 1893 (Comm), [2008] 1 Lloyd's Rep. 230 at [13]; *William McIlroy Swindon Ltd v Quinn Insurance Ltd* [2010] EWHC 2448 (TCC), [2011] B.L.R. 136. cf. *Markel International Co Ltd v Craft* [2006] EWHC 3150 (Comm), [2007] Lloyd's Rep. I.R. 403. See also *The Fanti and the Padre Island (No.2)* [1990] 2 Lloyd's Rep. 191. For the position where arbitration proceedings have already commenced, see *London Steamship Owners Mutual Insurance Association v Bombay Trading Co Ltd*, above. The 1930 Act will be repealed and replaced by the Third Parties (Rights against Insurers) Act 2010 when brought into force.

182   *Stellar Shipping Co LLC v Hudson Shipping Lines* [2010] EWHC 2985 (Comm), [2012] I.C.L.C. 476.

183   *Scott v Avery* (1856) 5 H.L.C. 811.

184   *B v S* [2011] EWHC 691 (Comm), [2011] 2 Lloyd's Rep. 18. cf. *Mantovani v Carapelli* [1978] 2 Lloyd's Rep. 63. See Tweeddale and Tweeddale (2011) 77 *Arbitration* 423.

185   A claim for damages may, in certain circumstances, lie for breach of the clause, which claim will be a dispute arising out of the contract and subject to the arbitration clause: *Mantovani v Carapelli SpA* [1980] 1 Lloyd's Rep. 375. See also *Glencore Grain Ltd v Argos Trading Ltd* [1999] 2 Lloyd's Rep. 410.

186   *Toronto Ry v National British, etc. Insurance Co* (1914) 20 Com. Cas. 1.

187   As to this, see *Hickman & Co v Roberts* [1913] A.C. 229; *Neale v Richardson* [1938] 1 All E.R. 753; cf. *Panamena Europea Navigacion Cia Lda v Frederick Leyland & Co Ltd* [1947] A.C. 428.

188   s.9(5). See also s.10(2) (interpleader).

189   *Board of Trade v Cayzer, Irvine & Co* [1927] A.C. 610.

190   See also s.71(4), para.32-181, below.

191   *Dennehy v Bellamy* [1938] 2 All E.R. 262; *Socony Mobil Oil Co Inc v West of England Shipowners Mutual Assurance (London) Ltd* [1984] 2 Lloyd's Rep. 408 (the 1930 Act will be repealed and

Confidentiality   Parties who arbitrate in England expect that the hearing will be   **32-050**
in private. But an essential corollary of the privacy of arbitral proceedings is that
they should be and remain confidential. The parties to an arbitration are therefore
under a duty to keep confidential information acquired by them in the course of the
arbitration.[192] The obligation of confidentiality has often been said to depend upon
an implied term in the arbitration agreement but the better view is that it is a rule
of law,[193] the existence and extent of which in a particular case is to be determined
by the court and not by the arbitral tribunal.[194] The duty extends not only to the
award[195] but also to pleadings, written submissions, proofs of witnesses as well as
transcripts and notes of the evidence given in the arbitration.[196] It is, however, not
absolute. It is subject to a number of exceptions, in particular if the other party
consents to disclosure, or if disclosure is by order or leave of the court or if it is
reasonably necessary for the establishment or protection of the legitimate interests
of the arbitrating party or if it is required in the interests of justice.[197] But there may
be further exceptions or qualifications: for example, the existence and details of an
arbitration claim may need to be disclosed to insurers, or to shareholders, or to
regulatory authorities.[198] The law in this area has still to be worked out[199] and there
is in any event a certain measure of discretion vested in the court to decide whether
an exception to confidentiality exists or applies.[200] In particular there is some doubt
whether the duty of confidence is subject to any broad "public interest" exception.[201]
Breach of the obligation of confidentiality will be restrained by injunction unless

---

[192] replaced when the Third Party (Rights against Insurers) Act 2010 is brought into force).
[192] *Emmott v Michael Wilson & Partners Ltd* [2008] EWCA Civ 184, [2008] 1 Lloyd's Rep. 616 at [79],
[105], [115] and [134]. See also *Dolling-Baker v Merrett* [1990] 1 W.L.R. 1205; *Hassneh Insurance Co v Stewart J Mew* [1993] 2 Lloyd's Rep. 243; *London & Leeds Estates Ltd v Paribas (No.2)*
[1995] 1 E.G.L.R. 102; *Ali Shipping Corp v Shipyard Trogir* [1999] 1 W.L.R. 314. Contrast *Esso
Australia Resources Ltd v Plowman* (1995) 183 C.L.R. 10 (High Court of Australia) (not followed
in *Secretary of State for Transport v Stagecoach South Western Trains Ltd* [2009] EWHC 2431
(Comm), [2010] 1 Lloyd's Rep. 175). See Neill (1996) 12 *Arbitration International* 287; Rogers and
Miller (1996) 12 *Arbitration International* 319; Fortier (1999) 15 *Arbitration International* 131;
Trakman (2002) 18 *Arbitration International* 1; Rawding and Seeger (2003) 19 *Arbitration
International* 483; Tweeddale (2005) 21 *Arbitration International* 59; Kovris (2005) 22 J. Int. Arb.
(2) 127; Seriki [2006] J.B.L. 300; Misra and Jordans (2006) 23 J. Int. Arb. (1) 39; Crookenden (2009)
25 *Arbitration International* 603. See also *Glidepath BV v Thomson* [2005] EWHC 818 (Comm),
[2005] 2 Lloyd's Rep. 548 (application by non-party for copies of documents on court record refused
on grounds of confidentiality).
[193] *Associated Electric and Gas Insurance Services Ltd v European Reinsurance Co of Zurich* [2003]
UKPC 11, [2003] 1 W.L.R. 1041 at [20]; *Emmott v Michael Wilson & Partners Ltd* [2008] EWCA
Civ 184, [2008] 1 Lloyd's Rep. 616 at [84].
[194] *Emmott v Michael Wilson & Partners Ltd* above, at [84]. But see Thomas L.J. at [119].
[195] See also *Department of Economics, Policy and Development of the City of Moscow v Bankers Trust
Co* [2004] EWCA Civ 314, [2005] Q.B. 307 (judgment on application to challenge award); CPR
r.62.10. Contrast *C v D* [2007] EWCA Civ 1282, [2008] 1 Lloyd's Rep. 239 at [34] (practice of Court
of Appeal).
[196] *Ali Shipping Corp v Shipyard Trogir*, above, at 327.
[197] *Ali Shipping Corp v Shipyard Trogir*, above, at 326; *Emmott v Michael Wilson & Partners Ltd* above,
at [93], [107]; *Westwood Shipping Lines Inc v Universal Schiffahrtsgesellschaft mbH* [2012] EWHC
3837 (Comm), [2013] 1 Lloyd's Rep. 670.
[198] *Emmott v Michael Wilson & Partners Ltd*, above, at [85].
[199] *Emmott v Michael Wilson & Partners Ltd*, above, at [107], [131].
[200] cf. *Emmott v Michael Wilson & Partners Ltd*, above, at [87].
[201] *Esso Australia Resources Ltd v Plowman* (1995) 183 C.L.R. 10; *Commonwealth of Australia v
Cockatoo Dockyard Pty Ltd* (1995) 36 N.S.W.L.R. 662; *London and Leeds Estates Ltd v Paribas
Ltd (No.2)* [1995] 1 E.G.L.R. 102, 109; *Ali Shipping Corp v Shipyard Trogir* [1999] 1 W.L.R. 314,
327–328; *Emmott v Michael Wilson & Partners Ltd*, above, at [96]–[100].

the objecting party can be shown to be fraudulent or the claim to relief is in the nature of an abuse of process.[202] An implied, or even express, confidentiality provision will not, however, prevent a party from enforcing or challenging the award by proceedings in open court, or from relying on the award to found a plea of issue estoppel[203] in subsequent arbitration proceedings between the same parties.[204]

3. STAY OF LEGAL PROCEEDINGS

32-051 **Resort to legal proceedings** If, contrary to an agreement to refer a matter to arbitration, one party resorts to legal proceedings in an English court in respect of that matter, the court has jurisdiction to hear the dispute.[205] The existence of the arbitration agreement, or even the fact that an arbitration is already in progress, affords no defence to the action. The appropriate course is for the other party to apply for a stay of the legal proceedings.[206] Conversely, there is no principle that requires arbitral proceedings to terminate if a party to the arbitration resorts to legal proceedings.[207] Nor does resort to legal proceedings of itself constitute a repudiation of the arbitration agreement,[208] However, where one party denies that he is bound by the arbitration agreement and thereby repudiates it, the issue of legal proceedings by the other party may amount to an acceptance of the repudiation and so bring the agreement to an end.[209] If there are concurrent or overlapping proceedings in respect of the same matter, both in arbitral and legal proceedings, the court may grant an injunction to restrain the continuance of the arbitral proceedings. But it will not necessarily do so and may allow them to continue.[210] Yet in such a case, it would seem that an award in concurrent proceedings without the consent of both parties would then have no effect.[211]

32-052 Damages may be awarded against a party who resorts to legal proceedings in breach of an arbitration agreement,[212] or an indemnity,[213] although damages may

---

[202] *Ali Shipping Corp v Shipyard Trogir*, above, at 329.

[203] See below, para.32-147.

[204] *Associated Electric and Gas Insurance Services Ltd v European Reinsurance Co of Zurich* [2003] UKPC 11, [2003] 1 W.L.R. 1041.

[205] See also s.43A of the Senior Courts Act 1981, inserted by s.100 of the Courts and Legal Services Act 1990 (specific powers of arbitrator exercisable by High Court).

[206] See below, paras 32-064—32-074.

[207] *Lloyd v Wright* [1983] Q.B. 1065.

[208] *Rederi Kommanditselskaabet Merc-Scandia IV v Couniniotis SA* [1980] 2 Lloyd's Rep. 183; *Lloyd v Wright*, above; *World Pride Shipping Ltd v Daiichi Chuo Kisen Kaisha* [1984] 2 Lloyd's Rep. 489; *BEA Hotels NV v Bellway LLC* [2007] EWHC 1363 (Comm), [2007] 2 Lloyd's Rep. 493; *Entico Corp Ltd v UNESCO* [2008] EWHC 531 (Comm), [2008] 1 Lloyd's Rep. 673 at [11]; *Tri-MG Asia Airlines v Noise Air Charter Ltd* [2009] SGHC 13, [2009] 1 Lloyd's Rep. 259 at [15]–[21]; *National Navigation Co v Endesa Generacion SA* [2009] EWHC 196 (Comm), [2009] 1 Lloyd's Rep. 666 at [113]–[117] (reversed on other grounds [2009] EWCA Civ 1397, [2010] 1 Lloyd's Rep. 193).

[209] *Downing v Al Tameer Establishment* [2002] EWCA Civ 721, [2002] 2 All E.R. (Comm) 545. Contrast *Hackwood Ltd v Areen Design Services Ltd* [2005] EWHC 2322 (TCC), (2006) 22 Const. L.J. 68 (unsuccessful application under s.72).

[210] *Northern Regional HA v Derek Crouch Construction Co Ltd* [1984] Q.B. 644; *Industrie Chimiche Italia Centrale v Alexander G Tsavliris & Sons* [1987] 1 Lloyd's Rep. 508. See also *Lloyd v Wright*, above. cf. *University of Reading v Miller Construction Ltd* (1995) 11 Const. L.J. 388; *National Navigation Co v Endesa Generacion SA*, above, at [113].

[211] *Doleman & Sons v Ossett Corp* [1912] 3 K.B. 257, as interpreted in *Lloyd v Wright*, above.

[212] *Mantovani v Carapelli SpA* [1980] 1 Lloyd's Rep. 375; *Sotrade Denizcilik Sanayi Ve Ticaret AS v Amadou Lo* [2008] EWHC 2762 (Comm), [2009] 1 Lloyd's Rep. 145 at [55]; *Kallang Shipping SA Panama v AXA Assurances Senegal* [2008] EWHC 2761 (Comm), [2009] 1 Lloyd's Rep. 124 at [79];

well be an inadequate remedy.[214] A third party who knowingly and intentionally induces or procures such a breach of contract may also be liable in damages in tort.[215]

Foreign proceedings outside the EU The court has power[216] to restrain by injunction the institution or continuance of proceedings in a foreign court (not being a court of a Member State of the European Union or of a Lugano Convention state) which are brought in breach of an agreement to arbitrate in England.[217] Such

32-053

West Tankers Inc v Allianz SpA [2012] EWHC 854 (Comm). See also *CMA CGH SA v Hyundai Mipo Dockyard Co Ltd* [2008] EWHC 2791 (Comm), [2009] 1 Lloyd's Rep. 213; Michaelson and Blanke (2008) 74 *Arbitration* 23.

[213] *West Tankers Inc v Allianz SpA* [2012] EWHC 854 (Comm), [2012] 2 All E.R. (Comm) 395.

[214] *Starlight Shipping Co v Tai Ping Insurance Co Ltd* [2007] EWHC 1893 (Comm), [2008] 1 Lloyd's Rep. 230 at [12]; *Sheffield United Football Club Ltd v West Ham United Football Club Plc* [2008] EWHC 2855 (Comm), [2009] 1 Lloyd's Rep. 167 at [22]. See Tan and Yao (2003) 4 L.M.C.L.Q. 435.

[215] *Sotrade Denizcilik Sanayi Ve Ticaret AS v Amadou Lo*, above; *Kallang Shipping SA Panama v AXA Assurances Senegal*, above.

[216] Under s.37 of the Senior Courts Act 1981 and s.44 of the Arbitration Act 1996; see *AES Ust-Kamenogorsk Hydropower Plant LLP v Us -Kamenogorsk Hydropower Plant JSC* [2013] UKSC 35, [2013] 1 W.L.R. 1889; *BNP Paribas SA v Open Joint Stock Company Russian Machines* [2011] EWHC 308 (Comm), [2012] 1 Lloyd's Rep. 61. For the view that the jurisdiction resides only in s.37, see *Southport Success SA v Tsingshen Holding Group Co Ltd* [2015] EWHC 1974 (Comm), [2015] 2 Lloyd's Rep. 578.

[217] *Pena Copper Mines Ltd v Rio Tinto Co Ld* (1912) 105 L.T. 846; *Gorthon Invest AB v Ford Motor Co Ltd* [1976] 2 Lloyd's Rep. 720; *Marazura Navegacion SA v Oceanus Mutual Underwriting Association* [1977] 1 Lloyd's Rep. 283; *Tracomin SA v Sudan Oil Seeds Co Ltd (No.2)* [1983] 1 W.L.R. 1026; *Sokana Industries Co Inc v Freyre & Co Inc* [1994] 2 Lloyd's Rep. 57; *Aggeliki Charis Compania Maritima SA v Pagnan SpA* [1995] 1 Lloyd's Rep. 87; *Schiffahrtsgesellschaft Detlev von Appen GmbH v Voest Alpine Intertrading GmbH* [1997] 1 Lloyd's Rep. 179; *Shell International Petroleum Co v Coral Oil Co Ltd* [1999] 1 Lloyd's Rep. 72; *Bankers Trust Co Ltd v PT Jakarta International Hotels and Development* [1999] 1 Lloyd's Rep. 910; *XL Insurance Ltd v Owens Corning* [2002] 2 Lloyd's Rep. 500; *The Epsilon Rosa (No.2)* [2002] EWHC 2033 (Comm), [2002] 2 Lloyd's Rep. 701; affirmed [2003] EWCA Civ 509, [2003] 2 Lloyd's Rep. 509; *Through Transport Mutual Insurance Association (Eurasia) Ltd v New India Assurance Co Ltd* [2004] EWCA Civ 1598, [2005] 1 Lloyd's Rep. 67; *Atlanska Plovibda v Consignaciones Asturianas SA* [2004] EWHC 1273 (Comm), [2004] 2 Lloyd's Rep. 109 at [25]; *Starlight Shipping Co v Tai Ping Insurance Co Ltd* [2007] EWHC 1893 (Comm), [2008] 1 Lloyd's Rep. 330; *Shashoua v Sharma* [2009] EWHC 957 (Comm), [2009] 2 Lloyd's Rep. 376; *Midgulf International Ltd v Groupe Chimicke Tunisien* [2010] EWCA Civ 66, [2010] 2 Lloyd's Rep. 543; *AES Ust-Kamenogorsk Hydropower Plant LLP v Ust-Kamenogorsk Hydropower Plant JSC* [2013] UKSC 35, [2013] 1 W.L.R. 1889; *REC Wafer Norway AS v Moser Baer Photo Voltaic Ltd* [2010] EWHC 2581 (Comm), [2011] 1 Lloyd's Rep. 410; *Tryggingarfelagio Foroyar P/F v CPT Empresas Maritimas SA* [2011] EWHC 589 (Admlty); *STX Pan Ocean Co Ltd v Woori Bank* [2012] EWHC 981 (Comm); *Joint Stock Asset Management Co Ingosstrakh-Investments v BNP Paribas SA* [2012] EWCA Civ 644, [2012] 1 Lloyd's Rep. 649; *Caresse Navigation Ltd v Zurich Assurances Maroc (The Channel Ranger)* [2014] EWCA Civ 1366, [2015] 1 Lloyd's Rep. 256; *Golden Endurance Shipping SA v RMA Watanya SA* [2014] EWHC 3917 (Comm), [2015] 1 Lloyd's Rep. 266. See also *Ecom Agroindustrial Corp Ltd v Mosharaf Composite Textile Mill Ltd* [2013] EWHC 1276 (Comm), [2013] 2 All E.R. (Comm) 983 (mandatory injunction); *Michael Wilson & Partners Ltd v Emmott* [2018] EWCA Civ 51, [2018] 1 Lloyd's Rep. 299. cf. *Louis Dreyfus Commodities Kenya Ltd v Bolster Shipping Co Ltd* [2010] EWHC 1732 (Comm), [2011] 1 Lloyd's Rep. 455; *Dicey, Morris and Collins on the Conflict of Laws*, 15th edn, para.16-088; Dunning (2008) 74 *Arbitration* 254, 259. For the test to be applied by an English court when invited to grant an anti-suit injunction, see *Donohue v Armco* [2001] UKHL 64, [2002] 1 Lloyd's Rep. 425; *Turner v Grovit* [2001] UKHL 654, [2002] 1 W.L.R. 107 at [22]–[29]; *Malhotra v Malhotra* [2012] EWHC 3020 (Comm), [2013] 1 Lloyd's Rep. 285; *AES Ust-Kamenogorsk Hydropower Plant LLP v Ust-Kamenogorsk Hydropower Plant JSC* [2013] UKSC 35, [2013] 1

an injunction will lie even when neither of the parties to the agreement has commenced or intends to commence arbitration proceedings.[218] It will also, where the parties have expressly chosen England as the seat of arbitration, restrain by injunction foreign legal proceedings seeking to challenge, vacate or review an English arbitral award[219] or if it is in the interests of justice to do so.[220] The courts now appear to be more willing to grant anti-suit injunctions than heretofore,[221] but it is arguable that the appropriate course for the aggrieved party to take should be to apply to the foreign court for a stay or similar relief.[222] A judgment given by a court of an overseas country in any proceedings will not be recognised or enforced in the United Kingdom if the bringing of proceedings in that court was contrary to a valid and effective agreement[223] under which the dispute in question was to be settled otherwise than by proceedings in the courts of that country, and those proceedings were not brought in that court by, or with the agreement of, the person against whom the judgment was given, and that person did not counterclaim or otherwise submit to the jurisdiction[224] of that court.[225]

32-054 Proceedings within the EU In *West Tankers Inc v RAS Riunione Adriatica di Sicurta*[226] the House of Lords referred to the European Court of Justice the following question:

"Is it consistent with EC Regulation 44/2001 for a court of a Member State to make an order to restrain a person from commencing or continuing proceedings in another Member State on the ground that such proceedings are in breach of an arbitration agreement?"

W.L.R. 1889.

[218] *AES Ust-Kamenogorsk Hydropower Plant LLP v Ust-Kamenogorsk Hydropower Plant JSC* [2013] UKSC 35, [2013] 1 W.L.R. 1889; *Bannai v Erez* [2013] EWHC 3689 (Comm), [2014] B.P.I.R. 4.

[219] *C v D* [2007] EWCA Civ 1282, [2008] 1 Lloyd's Rep. 239; *Noble Assurance Co v Gerling-Konzern General Insurance Co* [2007] EWHC 253 (Comm), [2007] 1 C.L.C. 85.

[220] *Midgulf International Ltd v Groupe Chimiche Tunisien* [2010] EWCA Civ 66, [2010] 2 Lloyd's Rep. 543 at [142]; *Terna Bahrain Holding Co WLL v Al Shamsi* [2012] EWHC 3283 (Comm), [2013] 1 All E.R. (Comm) 580 at [129]–[135].

[221] *Aggeliki Charis Compañía Maritima SA v Pagnan SpA* [1995] 1 Lloyd's Rep. 87; *Donohue v Armco*, above. But see *Airbus Industrie GIE v Patel* [1999] 1 A.C. 119; *Verity Shipping SA v NV Norexa* [2008] EWHC 213 (Comm), [2008] 1 Lloyd's Rep. 652. See also *Sheffield United Football Club Ltd v West Ham United Football Club Plc* [2008] EWHC 2855 (Comm), [2009] 1 Lloyd's Rep. 167; *Masri v Consolidated Contractors International SAL* [2008] EWCA Civ 625, [2008] 2 Lloyd's Rep. 301; *Malhotra v Malhotra* [2012] EWHC 3020 (Comm), [2013] 1 Lloyd's Rep. 285; *Crescendo Maritime Co v Bank of Communications Co Ltd* [2015] EWHC 3364 (Comm), [2016] 1 Lloyd's Rep. 414. In *ADM Asia-Pacific Trading Pte Ltd v PT Budi Semesta Satria* [2016] EWHC 1427 (Comm) the Court declined to grant an anti-suit injunction because of the delay in making the application. See also *Essar Shipping Ltd v Bank of China Ltd* [2015] EWHC 3266 (Comm), [2016] 1 Lloyd's Rep. 427; *Ecobank Transnational Inc v Tanoh* [2015] EWCA Civ 1309, [2016] 1 W.L.R. 2231 (anti-enforcement injunction). The court will not necessarily restrain an application brought in a foreign court for interim or conservatory measures with respect to an arbitration in England: *U&M Mining Zambia Ltd v Kankola Copper Mines Plc* [2013] EWHC 260 (Comm), [2013] 2 Lloyd's Rep. 218. Where a third party seeks to exercise rights under a contract containing an arbitration clause, see *Shipowners' Mutual Protection and Indemnity Association (Luxembourg) v Containerships Denizcilik Nakliyat ve Ticaret AS* [2016] EWCA Civ 386, [2016] 1 Lloyd's Rep. 641.

[222] *World Pride Shipping Ltd v Daiichi Chuo Kisen Kaisha* [1984] 2 Lloyd's Rep. 489, 498 (but see the observations on this case in *Aggeliki Charis Compania Maritima SA v Pagnan SpA*, above).

[223] Civil Jurisdiction and Judgments Act 1982 s.32(2). But see s.32(3) and n.217, above.

[224] Civil Jurisdiction and Judgments Act 1982 s.33.

[225] Civil Jurisdiction and Judgments Act 1982 s.32(1). See *Tracomin SA v Sudan Oil Seeds Co Ltd (No.2)* [1983] 1 W.L.R. 1026; *AES Ust-Kamenogorsk Hydropower Plant LLP v Ust-Kamenogorsk Hydropower Plant JSC* [2013] UKSC 35, [2013] 1 W.L.R. 1889.

[226] [2007] UKHL 4, [2007] 1 Lloyd's Rep. 391.

The Court, sub nom. *Allianz SpA v West Tankers Inc*,[227] answered that question in the negative. As a result of this ruling, it is clear that it was no longer open to an English court to issue an anti-suit injunction to restrain a party from commencing or continuing proceedings in another Member State (including a Lugano Convention State) in breach of an arbitration agreement, although it was equally clear that the ruling did not prevent the issue of an anti-suit injunction where the proceedings were in a non-Member State.[228]

The Revised Brussels Regulation   The *Allianz* decision attracted considerable   **32-055**
criticism because it appeared to create the opportunity to deploy what has been termed the "foreign torpedo",[229] that is to say, that a recalcitrant party could effectively torpedo the arbitral process by initiating proceedings in another Member State where it considered that a favourable decision on the merits and/or on the invalidity or inapplicability of the arbitration agreement was more probable. The further implications of the decision were subsequently considered by the Court of Appeal in *National Navigation Co v Endesa Generacion SA (The Wadi Sudr)*.[230] In that case a number of important questions were addressed with respect to the effect on an arbitration in England, and on English proceedings relating to arbitration, of legal proceedings in another Member State. These questions involved, in particular, the scope of the "arbitration exception" in art.1(2)(d) of Regulation 44/2001, which provided that the Regulation as a whole should "not apply to arbitration".[231] In the *Allianz* case, the European Court gave a narrow interpretation to that exception. Since that time, however, Regulation 44/2001 has been repealed and replaced (from January 10, 2015) by Regulation (EU) 1215/2012 of the European Parliament and the Council. This new regulation (the "revised Regulation" or "Brussels Regulation Recast" or "Brussels *bis*") explains and expands the meaning of the identical arbitration exception in its provisions. Certain aspects of the *National Navigation* case in consequence now require reconsideration in the light of this change.

Recital (12) of the revised Regulation provides: **32-056**

"This Regulation should not apply to arbitration. Nothing in this Regulation should prevent the courts of a Member State, when seised of an action in a matter in respect of which the parties have entered into an arbitration agreement, from referring the parties to arbitration, from staying or dismissing the proceedings, or from examining whether the arbitration agreement is null and void, inoperative or incapable of being performed, in accordance with their national law.

A ruling given by a court of a Member State as to whether or not an arbitration agreement is null and void, inoperative or incapable of being performed should not be subject to the rules of recognition and enforcement laid down in this Regulation, regardless of whether the court decided on this as a principal issue or as an incidental question.

On the other hand, where a court of a Member State, exercising jurisdiction under this

---

[227] C-185/07, EU:C:2009:69, [2009] 1 Lloyd's Rep. 413 (see also the opinion of Advocate-General Kokott in the reference: [2008] 2 Lloyd's Rep. 661).

[228] *Shashoua v Sharma* [2009] EWHC 957 (Comm) at [23] and [35]–[39]; *Midgulf International Ltd v Groupe Chimiche Tunisien* [2010] EWCA Civ 66, [2010] 2 Lloyd's Rep. 543 at [68].

[229] See Dutson and Howarth (2009) 75 *Arbitration* (3) 334; (2010) 76 *Arbitration* (2) 374. See also generally on the effect of the Revised Regulation: Camilleri (2013) 62 I.C.L.Q. 899–916.

[230] [2009] EWCA Civ 1397, [2010] 1 Lloyd's Rep. 175 (reversing a decision at first instance of Gloster J. [2009] EWHC 196 (Comm), [2009] 1 Lloyd's Rep. 666).

[231] See *Marc Rich & Co AG v Societa Italiana Impianti SpA (The Atlantic Emperor)* (C-190/89) EU:C:1991:319, [1991] E.C.R I-3855, [1992] 1 Lloyd's Rep. 342, ECJ.

Regulation or under national law, has determined that an arbitration agreement is null and void, inoperative or incapable of being performed, this should not preclude that court's judgment on the substance of the matter from being recognised or, as the case may be enforced in accordance with this Regulation. This should be without prejudice to the competence of the courts of the Member States to decide on the recognition and enforcement of arbitral awards in accordance with the Convention on the Recognition and Enforcement of Foreign Arbitral Awards, done at New York on 10 June 1958 ('the 1958 New York Convention'), which takes precedence over this Regulation.

This Regulation should not apply to any action or ancillary proceedings relating to, in particular, the establishment of an arbitral tribunal, the powers of arbitrators, the conduct of an arbitration procedure or any other aspects of such a procedure, nor to any action or judgment concerning the annulment, review, appeal, recognition or enforcement of an arbitral award."

The effect of Recital (12) is not entirely clear, but the following propositions can, it is submitted, be formulated as a result of the revised Regulation.

32-057   First, the revised Regulation does not revive the power of the English courts to issue an anti-suit injunction to restrain a party from commencing or continuing legal proceedings in another Member State in breach of an arbitration agreement since, as the European Court stated in the *Allianz* case, "an anti-suit injunction ... runs counter to the trust which the Member States accord to one another's legal systems and judicial Institutions".[232]

32-058   Secondly, where an arbitration is seated in England and one of the parties commences or continues proceedings in another Member State with respect to an identical or related matter either on the substantive claim, e.g. for damages for breach of contract or a declaration of non-liability, or as to the validity or applicability of the arbitration agreement, neither the arbitral tribunal nor an English court in proceedings ancillary to the arbitration is precluded from considering those matters by reason of the mere existence of the foreign proceedings.[233] There is nothing to prevent parallel proceedings in both jurisdictions.

32-059   Thirdly, neither the arbitral tribunal nor the court is bound to recognise or enforce the decision of a court of another Member State as to the validity or applicability of an arbitration agreement. The tribunal and the court are free to reach their own conclusion on this matter. This appears clearly from the first and second paragraphs of Recital (12). So, for example, in arbitral proceedings or on an application to the court under ss.32 or 67 of the Arbitration Act 1996 to determine the jurisdiction of the arbitral tribunal or under ss.66 or 101 to enforce the award, the tribunal and the court would not be bound to recognise the judgment of a court of another Member State which has held the arbitration agreement to be invalid or inapplicable. This effectively reverses the decision of the Court of Appeal in the *National Navigation* case where the court had held[234] that the judgment of a Spanish court that a London arbitration clause had never been effectively incorporated into the parties' contract had to be recognised under Regulation 44/2001.

32-060   Fourthly, it seems that an English court is (subject to certain exceptions) bound by arts 36 and 39 of the revised Regulation to recognise or, as the case may be, to enforce a judgment given in proceedings in another Member State on the *substance*

---

232 *Nori Holdings Ltd v Public Joint-Stock Co Bank Otkritie Financial Corp* [2018] EWHC 1343 (Comm). But see *Gazprom OAO* (C-536/13) EU:C:2015:316, [2015] 1 Lloyd's Rep. 610 (anti-suit injunction by arbitral tribunal).
233 *Toyota Tsusho Sugar Trading Ltd v Prolat SRL* [2014] EWHC 3649 (Comm) at [15]–[17].
234 [2009] EWCA Civ 1397, [2010] 1 Lloyd's Rep. 175.

of the matter where the foreign court has determined that the arbitration agreement is invalid or inapplicable. The third paragraph of Recital (12) indicates that the "arbitration exception" cannot then be invoked. An English court cannot refuse to recognise the judgment of a court of another Member State on the substance of the matter on the ground that the foreign court came to an erroneous decision on the applicability or enforceability of the arbitration agreement and wrongly assumed jurisdiction. Article 45(3) of the revised Regulation provides that the jurisdiction of a court of Member State cannot be reviewed by a court of another Member State. In any event, it has been held[235] that the mere fact that a claim is the subject of an arbitration agreement does not deprive a Member State's court, which could otherwise determine the substance of the claim, of its jurisdiction under Regulation 44/2001 and the same would apply in the case of the revised Regulation. Nevertheless, it might be argued that at least in certain circumstances, recognition of a judgment on the substance of the matter obtained in a court of a Member State in breach of an arbitration agreement might properly be refused by an English court on the ground that such recognition would be "manifestly contrary to public policy" (art.45(1)(a) of the revised Regulation): see Waller L.J. in *Phillip Alexander Securities Ltd v Bamberger*.[236] However, it has been held that a refusal to recognise a judgment under the identical provision (art.34) in Regulation 44/2001 could only be justified if recognition would be "at variance to an unacceptable degree with the legal order of the state in which enforcement is sought inasmuch as it infringes a fundamental principle".[237] In the *National Navigation* case the Court of Appeal[238] rejected the public policy argument: it could not be said that the judgment of the Spanish court in that case "would involve a manifest breach of a rule of law regarded as essential in the legal order of the United Kingdom or a right recognised as being fundamental within that legal order". It is therefore unlikely whether circumstances would ever exist (e.g. even a "blatant disregard" of the arbitration agreement) for the application of art.45(1)(a) to be successfully invoked.

The obligation of the court to recognise a judgment given on the substance of the **32-061** matter is, however, subject to two exceptions. The first is indicated in the third paragraph of Recital (12) itself. In the event of a conflict between the judgment of the Member State's court on the substance of the matter and an arbitral award, an English court would be at liberty to decide not to recognise the judgment but instead to enforce the award in accordance with the New York Convention,[239] which takes precedence over the Regulation. The second exception is that art.45(1)(c) of the revised Regulation requires recognition to be refused "if the judgment sought to be enforced is irreconcilable with a judgment given between the same parties in the Member State addressed". So, unless and until the foreign court gives judgment, it is open to the claimant to continue the arbitration, obtain an award[240] and then to

---

[235] *Youell v La Reunion Aerienne* [2009] EWCA Civ 175 at [34].
[236] [1997] I.L.Pr. 73 at [14] (referred to in *CMA CGM SA v Hyundai Mipo Dockyard Co Ltd*, above, at [35], and *DHL GBS (UK) Ltd v Fallimento Finmatica SpA*, above, at [21]).
[237] *Krombach v Bamerski* (C-7/98) EU:C:2000:164, [2000] E.C.R. I-1935 at [23]; *Gambazzi v Daimler-Chrysler Canada Inc* (C-394/07) EU:C:2009:219, [2009] 1 Lloyd's Rep. 647 at [27].
[238] [2009] EWCA Civ 1397 at [66], [131] (even by Waller L.J.).
[239] See below, para.32-190. But the New York Convention (art.1) applies essentially only to the recognition or enforcement in one state of an award made in another state and not to the recognition or enforcement of an award made in the state in which recognition or enforcement is sought.
[240] Including an award of damages for breach of the obligation to arbitrate or for an indemnity: *West Tankers Inc v Allianz SpA* [2012] EWHC 854 (Comm).

enforce that award as a judgment under s.66 of the 1996 Act.[241] Any subsequent judgment of the foreign court to the contrary on the substance of the matter would not then be required to be recognised in England.[242]

32-062 The final question relates to the effect (if any) on the arbitration itself where the arbitration is seated in England and one of the parties brings proceedings on the substantive claim in another Member State in breach of the arbitration agreement and obtains a judgment on that claim. It is clear that the revised Regulation does not oblige the arbitral tribunal to recognise a judgment given in parallel proceedings in another Member State (even if an English court would be so obliged) because the revised Regulation does not apply to an arbitral tribunal.[243] Where, however, English law applies to the substance of the matter, then, if English law requires the court to recognise the foreign court's judgment, it would seem that the arbitral tribunal in applying English law would have to recognise that judgment. An arbitral tribunal, in applying English law, would therefore have to consider whether, under ordinary common law principles, the foreign judgment gives rise to an issue estoppel. In the *National Navigation* case Moore-Bick L.J. said[244]:

> "A judgment of a foreign court which is regarded under English conflict of laws rules as having jurisdiction and which is final and conclusive on the merits is entitled to recognition at common law: see *Dicey, Morris and Collins on the Conflict of Laws*, 14th Edition, paragraphs 14-027—14-029.[245] It follows, therefore, that arbitrators applying English law are bound to give effect to that rule."

Nevertheless, despite this statement, it must be pointed out that, at common law, as a general rule (subject to certain exceptions) estoppel by res judicata cannot be raised against the party alleged to be estopped where that party has not submitted to the jurisdiction of the foreign court by voluntarily appearing in the foreign proceedings.[246]

32-063 The overall result of the changes made by the revised Regulation is to reduce the effectiveness of the "foreign torpedo" but to open up the possibility of conflicting Member State court decisions on the validity of the arbitration agreement and to accord a certain primacy to the judgment of that court which is the first to arrive at a decision on the substance of the matter. It would, perhaps, have been preferable if the revision had, instead, given to the courts of the seat, or putative seat, of arbitration the exclusive—or at least the primary—right to pronounce on the validity and applicability of the arbitration agreement and for that decision then to be recognised and enforceable in other Member States. Unfortunately, however, the concept of the seat is not favoured in certain Member States, nor is there unanimity as to how the seat is to be determined. Moreover, at present, even the English courts have not shown themselves averse to deciding questions on jurisdiction in respect of an al-

---

[241] *West Tankers Inc v Allianz SpA* [2012] EWCA Civ 27, [2012] 1 Lloyd's Rep. 398; *African Fertilizers and Chemicals NIG Ltd v BD Shipsnavo GmbH & Co Reederei KG* [2011] EWHC 2452 (Comm), [2011] 2 Lloyd's Rep. 531 (enforcement of declaratory awards).

[242] art.45(1)(c).

[243] *CMA CGM SA v Hyundai Mipo Dockyard Co Ltd* [2008] EWHC 2791 (Comm), [2009] 1 Lloyd's Rep. 213 at [43]–[46]; *National Navigation* case [2009] EWCA Civ 1397 at [118].

[244] [2009] EWCA Civ 1397, [2010] 1 Lloyd's Rep. 175 at [115], disapproving the view to the contrary taken by Burton J. in *CMA CGM SA v Hyundai Mipo Dockyard Ltd*, above, at [46].

[245] In the 15th edition, paras 14-054—14-096.

[246] Dicey, Morris and Collins on the Conflict of Laws, 15th edn, para.14-068.

leged arbitration agreement providing for arbitration in another Member State.[247] A more far-reaching revision is therefore unlikely to be achieved.

Stay of legal proceedings   Section 9 of the Arbitration Act 1996 provides for a   **32-064** stay of legal proceedings brought in an English court contrary to an arbitration agreement. It is a mandatory provision. By s.9(1):

"A party to an arbitration agreement against whom legal proceedings are brought ... in respect of a matter which under the agreement is to be referred to arbitration may (upon notice to the other parties to the proceedings) apply to the court in which the proceedings have been brought to stay the proceedings so far as they concern that matter".[248]

An application can only be made by a party against whom legal proceedings are brought (as opposed to any other party).[249] But "party" is defined to include any person claiming under or through a party to the arbitration agreement,[250] e.g. an assignee.[251] The claimant in the legal proceedings must also be a party[252] and the claim in those proceedings must be in respect of a matter which under the agreement is to be referred to arbitration.[253] What constitutes a "matter" is to be determined in a practical and commonsense manner without adopting an analysis which is unduly broad or narrow.[254] A stay can be sought of a counterclaim as well as of a claim,[255] or of part of the legal proceedings only, and an application may be made notwithstanding that the matter is to be referred to arbitration only after the exhaustion of other dispute resolution procedures.[256] Section 9 applies even if the seat of the arbitration is outside England or no seat has been designated or

---

[247] *Claxton Engineering Services Ltd v TXM Olaj-es Gazkutato Kft* [2010] EWHC 2567 (Comm), [2011] 1 Lloyd's Rep. 252; *Claxton Engineering Services Ltd v TXM Olaj-es Gazkutato Kft* [2011] EWHC 345 (Comm), [2011] 1 Lloyd's Rep. 510.

[248] For procedure, see CPR r.62.8, PD 62.2. Contrast *Exeter City Association Football Club Ltd v Football Conference Ltd* [2004] EWHC 831 (Ch), [2004] 1 W.L.R. 2910 (no stay of petition under s.459 of Companies Act 1985); *Best Beat Ltd v Rossall* [2006] EWHC 1494, [2006] B.P.I.R. 1357 (no stay of winding-up petition).

[249] *Excalibur Ventures LLC v Texas Keystone Inc* [2011] EWHC 1624 (Comm), [2011] 2 Lloyd's Rep. 289 at [74]. But see CPR r.3.1(2)(f).

[250] 1996 Act s.82(2). See *Roussel-Uclaf v GD Searle & Co Ltd* [1978] 1 Lloyd's Rep. 225 (overruled by the Court of Appeal in *City of London v Sancheti* [2008] EWCA Civ 1283, [2009] 1 Lloyd's Rep. 117); *Rumput (Panama) SA v Islamic Republic of Iran Shipping Lines* [1984] 2 Lloyd's Rep. 259. But not by a third party: *Etri Fans Ltd v NMB (UK) Ltd* [1987] 1 W.L.R. 110, or by the arbitrator: *A v B* [2006] EWHC 2006 (Comm), [2007] 1 Lloyd's Rep. 237. A guarantor of a party to a contract containing an arbitration clause is not such a person: *Alfred McAlpine Construction v Unex Corp* [1994] N.P.C. 16, but the court might stay an action against the guarantor under its inherent jurisdiction: as before and see *Roche Products Ltd v Freeman Process Systems Ltd* (1997) 80 Build. L.R. 802.

[251] See above, para.32-042.

[252] *City of London v Sancheti* [2008] EWCA Civ 1283, [2009] 1 Lloyd's Rep. 117; *J&W Sanderson Ltd v Fenox (UK) Ltd* [2014] EWHC 4322 (Ch).

[253] *Lombard North Central Plc v GATX Corp* [2012] EWHC 1067 (Comm), [2012] 1 Lloyd's Rep. 662. cf. *Sheffield United Football Club v West Ham United Football Club Plc* [2008] EWHC 2855 (Comm), [2009] 1 Lloyd's Rep. 157 (application for anti-suit injunction not such a matter). In *Sodzawiczny v Ruhan* [2018] EWHC 1908 (Comm), [43], it was held that a "matter" was any issue which is capable of constituting a dispute or difference which may fall within the scope of an arbitration agreement.

[254] *Autoridad del Canal de Panama v Sacyr SA* [2017] EWHC 2228 (Comm), [2017] 2 Lloyd's Rep. 351 at [123]–[129].

[255] 1996 Act s.9(1).

[256] s.9(2).

determined.[257] An appeal lies to the Court of Appeal against the grant or refusal of a stay.[258]

32-065 Costs of a successful application for a stay may be awarded on an indemnity basis.[259]

32-066 **Time for application to stay** By s.9(3), an application for a stay:

"... may not be made by a person before taking the appropriate procedural step (if any) to acknowledge the legal proceedings against him or after he has taken any step in those proceedings to answer the substantive claim."

These conditions reflect to some extent the language of s.4(1) of the Arbitration Act 1950 which stated that an application for a stay might be made "at any time after appearance, and before delivering any pleadings or taking any other steps in the proceedings". With respect to the 1950 Act it was said:

"The authorities show that a step in the proceedings means something in the nature of an application to the court, and not mere talk between solicitors and solicitors' clerks nor the writing of letters, but the taking of some step, such as taking out a summons or something of that kind, which is, in the technical sense, a step in the proceedings".[260]

But s.9(2) of the 1996 Act adds to the words "after he has taken any step in those proceedings" the words "to answer the substantive claim", which limits still further the types of procedural steps that may be held to bar an application for a stay.[261] Thus the following have been held not to constitute such a bar: an application for leave to defend and counterclaim,[262] an application for summary judgment in the event that an application for a stay should prove unsuccessful,[263] and filing a defence subject to a reservation of rights pending an application for permission to appeal from a decision refusing a stay.[264] Commencing an action in a foreign court not having jurisdiction to try the claim is not a step in the proceedings.[265] An application for a stay should nevertheless be made as soon as possible lest costs are unnecessarily incurred and thrown away by the delay in taking the arbitration point.[266] CPR Pt 11 is not applicable to applications under s.9.[267]

32-067 **Mandatory stay** On an application under s.9, s.9(4) provides that the court *shall*

---

[257] s.2(2); *ET Peus SA v Welter* [2005] EWHC 2115 (Comm), [2006] 1 Lloyd's Rep. 251 (ICC arbitration in Paris). Contrast *Abu Dhabi Investment Co v H Clarkson & Co Ltd* [2006] EWHC 1252 (Comm), [2006] 2 Lloyd's Rep. 381 (arbitration in UAR where not compulsory).

[258] *Inco Europe Ltd v First Choice Distribution* [2000] 1 W.L.R. 586 HL.

[259] *A v B (No.2)* [2007] EWHC 54 (Comm), [2007] 1 Lloyd's Rep. 358. See also *Kyrgyz Mobil Tel Ltd v Fellows International Holdings Ltd* [2005] EWHC 1329 (HC); and (damages) Michaelson and Blanke (2008) 74 *Arbitration* (1) 12. Contrast *C v D* [2007] EWCA Civ 1282, [2008] 1 Lloyd's Rep. 239 at [33].

[260] *Ives and Barker v Willans* [1894] 2 Ch. 478, 484. See also *Eagle Star Insurance Co Ltd v Yuval Insurance Co Ltd* [1978] 1 Lloyd's Rep. 357, 361; and the cases cited in Mustill and Boyd, *Commercial Arbitration*, pp.472–473.

[261] *Patel v Patel* [2002] Q.B. 551.

[262] *Patel v Patel* [2002] Q.B. 551. cf. *Baker Hughes Ltd v Steadfast Engineering Ltd* [2009] EWHC 3123 (QB); *Bilta (UK) Ltd v Nazir* [2010] EWHC 1086 (Ch), [2010] 2 Lloyd's Rep. 29 (application to extend time for defence).

[263] *Capital Trust Investments Ltd v Radio Design TJAB* [2002] EWCA Civ 1356, [2002] All E.R. 450.

[264] *Autoridad del Canal de Panama v Sacyr SA* [2017] EWHC 2337 (Comm) at [20]–[40].

[265] *Thyssen Inc v Calypso Shipping Corp SA* [2002] 2 Lloyd's Rep. 243.

[266] *Bovis Homes Ltd v Kendrick Construction Ltd* [2009] EWHC 1359 (TCC), [2009] T.C.L.R. 8.

[267] *Bilta (UK) Ltd v Nazir* [2010] EWHC 1086 (Ch), [2010] 2 Lloyd's Rep. 29.

grant a stay unless satisfied that the arbitration agreement is null and void,[268] inoperative,[269] or incapable of being performed.[270] This provision for a mandatory stay reflects the provisions of the UNCITRAL Model Law and the New York Convention on the Recognition and Enforcement of Foreign Arbitral Awards. It is in the same terms as that of s.1 of the Arbitration Act 1975 but with the significant omission of the further ground for refusing a stay contained in the 1975 Act that "there is not in fact any dispute between the parties with regard to the matter agreed to be referred". The onus of satisfying the court that one or more of the three statutory grounds exist for refusing a stay rests upon the party resisting the stay.[271] A cross-claim by way of legal set-off which is subject to a mandatory stay, cannot be set-off against a claim in legal proceedings for summary judgment.[272]

The court has power to decide, on an application for a stay, whether there was **32-068** an arbitration agreement and whether the dispute was within the agreement, even though the same question could be decided by the arbitral tribunal under s.30.[273] The court can:

(1) determine on affidavit evidence that there was an arbitration agreement in which case a stay must be granted;

---

[268] *Willcock v Pickfords Removals Ltd* [1979] 1 Lloyd's Rep. 244; *AB Bofors-UVA v AB Skandia* [1982] 1 Lloyd's Rep. 410; *Accentuate Ltd v As gra Inc* [2009] EWHC 2655 (QB), [2009] 2 Lloyd's Rep. 599 at [89]; cf. *Cia Maritima Zorroza SA v Sesostris* [1984] 1 Lloyd's Rep. 652; *JSC BTA Bank v Ablyazov* [2011] EWHC 587 (Comm), [2011] 2 Lloyd's Rep. 129; *Assaubayer v Michael Wilson and Partners Ltd* [2014] EWHC 821 (QB). See also *Associated British Ports v Tata Steel UK Ltd* [2017] EWHC 694 (Ch), [2017] 2 Lloyd's Rep. 11 at [20] (the issue in this case was whether the arbitration agreement was void for uncertainty).

[269] *Downing v Al Tameer Establishment* [2002] EWCA Civ 121, [2002] 2 All E.R. (Comm) 545; *Accentuate Ltd v Asigra Inc* [2009] EWHC 2655, [2009] 2 Lloyd's Rep. 599 at [89]; *Aeroflot-Russian Airlines v Berezovsky* [2012] EWHC 1610 (Ch) at [104]–[112]; cf. *Lonhro v Shell Petroleum Co, The Times*, February 1, 1978; *The Merak* [1965] P. 223, 229; *Ethiopian Oilseeds & Pulses Export Corp v Rio del Mar Foods Inc* [1990] 1 Lloyd's Rep. 86, 98; *JSC BTA Bank v Ablyazov* [2011] EWHC 587 (Comm), [2011] 2 Lloyd's Rep. 129; *Lombard North Central Plc v GATX Corp* [2012] EWHC 1067 (Comm), [2012] 1 Lloyd's Rep. 662; *Joint Stock Co Aeroflot Russian Airlines v Berezovsky* [2013] EWCA Civ 784, [2013] 2 Lloyd's Rep. 242; *BDM Ltd v Rafael Advance Defence Systems* [2014] EWHC 451 (Comm). An arbitration agreement may be inoperative if it has been abandoned or repudiated, or if a party to the agreement is estopped from relying on it: *Costain Ltd v Tarmac Holdings Ltd* [2017] EWHC 319 (TCC), [2017] 1 Lloyd's Rep. 331 at [81]–[127].

[270] cf. *The Rena K.* [1979] Q.B. 377 (ability to satisfy award irrelevant); *Paczy v Haendler & Natermann GmbH* [1981] 1 Lloyd's Rep. 302 (impecuniosity of claimant irrelevant).

[271] *Nova (Jersey) Knit Ltd v Kammgarn Spinnerei GmbH* [1977] 1 W.L.R. 713, 718. But cf. at 732. See also *Associated British Ports v Tata Steel UK Ltd* [2017] EWHC 694 (Ch), [2017] 2 Lloyd's Rep. 11 at [20].

[272] *Aectra Refining and Manufacturing Inc v Exmar NV* [1994] 1 W.L.R. 1634.

[273] See below, para.32-101. In *Fiona Trust & Holding Corp v Privalov* [2007] EWCA Civ 20, [2007] 2 Lloyd's Rep. 267 (affirmed sub nom. *Premier Nafta Products Ltd v Fili Shipping Co Ltd* [2007] UKHL 40) the Court of Appeal appears to have suggested (at [34]) that the arbitrators should be the first tribunal to consider jurisdiction. Contrast *Law Debenture Trust Corp v Elektrim Finance Debenture Trust Corp v Elektrim Finance BV* [2005] EWHC 1412 (Ch), [2005] 2 Lloyd's Rep. 755; *Albon Naza Motor Trading Sdn Bnd (No.3)* [2007] EWHC 327 (Ch), [2007] 2 Lloyd's Rep. 1; *JSC BTA Bank v Ablyazov* [2011] EWHC 587 (Comm), [2011] 2 Lloyd's Rep. 129; *AES Ust-Kamenogorsk Hydropower Plant LLP v Ust-Kamenogorsk Hydropower Plant JSC* [2011] EWCA Civ 647, [2011] 2 Lloyd's Rep. 233 at [81]–[85], [98]–[100], [2013] UKSC 35, [2013] 1 W.L.R. 1889; *Excalibur Ventures LLC v Texas Keystone Inc* [2011] EWHC 1624 (Comm), [2011] 2 Lloyd's Rep. 289 at [57]–[67].

(2)   stay the proceedings on the basis that the arbitral tribunal is to determine the jurisdictional question under s.30[274];

(3)   refuse to decide the question immediately and order an issue to be tried[275]; or

(4)   decide that there was no arbitration agreement and dismiss the application for a stay.[276]

If the answer to the question is clear, the court should resolve the matter itself rather than grant a stay of the proceedings. Indeed, the Court has said that referring the issue to the arbitral tribunal would be contrary to s.9.[277] The Court has held that in order to determine that there is an applicable arbitration agreement in accordance with s.9(1), the Court must be satisfied that such an agreement exists; it is not sufficient for the applicant to show merely that it has an arguable case that it is a party to an arbitration agreement.[278] If the respondent to the application for a stay wishes to rely on s.9(4) in order to prevent the stay, the Court must come to a clear conclusion that the agreement is null and void, inoperative or incapable of performance; a mere arguable case to the contrary would be sufficient for the Court to give effect to the arbitration agreement under s.9(4) because the respondent would not have discharged its burden of proof under that sub-section.[279]

32-069   **Discretionary stay**   Section 86 of the 1996 Act nevertheless provides that, in the case of a "domestic agreement" (as defined in s.85(1)), the court may refuse a stay on the further ground that "there are other sufficient grounds for not requiring the parties to abide by the arbitration agreement". This section, in effect, confers upon the court a wide discretion to refuse a stay similar to that previously conferred in the case of "domestic arbitration agreements" by s.4(1) of the Arbitration Act 1950.

---

274 In *Albon v Naza Motor Trading Sdn Bhd (No.3)*, above, at [16] it was suggested that this could only be done under the inherent jurisdiction (below, para.32-070) as s.9 requires the court to be satisfied that there is an arbitration agreement and that the dispute is within that agreement before granting a stay. See also *Capes (Hatherden) Ltd v Western Arable Services Ltd* [2009] EWHC 3065 (QB), [2010] 1 Lloyd's Rep. 477 at [22]; *Hashwani v OMV Maurice Energy Ltd* [2015] EWHC 1811 (Comm) at [26], [2015] EWCA Civ 1171, (2015) 163 Con. L.R. 259 at [31]–[34] (reversing the judge's decision in exercising his discretion to order a stay).

275 *Bilta (UK) Ltd v Nazir* [2010] EWHC 1086 (Ch), [2010] 2 Lloyd's Rep. 29; *Kaye v Nu Skin UK Ltd* [2009] EWHC 3509 (Ch), [2011] 1 Lloyd's Rep. 40. But see *JSC BTA Bank v Ablyazov* [2011] EWHC 587 (Comm), [2011] 2 Lloyd's Rep. 129 at [29], [50].

276 *Ahmad Al-Naimi (t/a Buildmaster Construction Services) v Islamic Press Agency Inc* [2000] 1 Lloyd's Rep. 522; approving the analysis in *Buise Construction Ltd v St David Ltd* [1999] B.L.R. 194; [2000] B.L.R. 57; *Capes (Hatherden) Ltd v Western Arable Services Ltd* [2009] EWHC 3065 (QB), [2010] 1 Lloyd's Rep. 477; *Dallah Real Estate & Tourism Co v Ministry of Religious Affairs of the Government of Pakistan* [2010] UKSC 46, [2011] 1 A.C. 763 at [97]; *JSC BTA Bank v Ablyozov* [2011] EWHC 587 (Comm), [2011] 2 Lloyd's Rep. 129 at [28]. But see the observations of the Court of Appeal in *Claxton Engineering Services Ltd v TXM Olaj-es Gazkutato Kft* [2011] EWCA Civ 410, [2011] Arb. L.R. 16.

277 *Joint Stock Company "Aeroflot Russian Airlines" v Berezovsky* [2013] EWCA Civ 784, [2013] 2 Lloyd's Rep. 242 at [76]–[79]; *Costain Ltd v Tarmac Holdings Ltd* [2017] EWHC 319 (TCC), [2017] 1 Lloyd's Rep. 331 at [80]; *Microsoft Mobile Oy (Ltd) v Sony Europe Ltd* [2017] EWHC 374 (Ch), [2017] 5 C.M.L.R. 5 at [41] and [82]–[84].

278 *Associated British Ports v Tata Steel UK Ltd* [2017] EWHC 694 (Ch), [2017] 2 Lloyd's Rep. 11 at [20].

279 *Golden Ocean Group Ltd v Humpuss Intermoda Transportasi TBK Ltd (The Barito)* [2013] EWHC 1240 (Comm), [2013] 2 Lloyd's Rep. 421 at [59].

But s.86 of the 1996 Act is unlikely to be brought into force[280] and in consequence a stay will be mandatory even in the case of a domestic agreement, subject to the exceptions set out in s.9.

The court also has power, under its inherent jurisdiction to grant a stay[281] and it has used this power, for example, to stay proceedings properly brought in England in order to await the outcome of an arbitration in a foreign country[282] or on case management grounds.[283] **32-070**

Claims indisputably due The additional words, referred to in para.32-067 above, which were contained in the 1975 Act but omitted from s.9(4), were a source of some confusion and possible misinterpretation. In particular, they had been held to justify the court, upon an application by a claimant for summary judgment under the former RSC Ord.14,[284] to refuse a stay and give judgment for the amount claimed where the court was satisfied that the claim was indisputably due, on the ground that the court had then decided that in reality there was not in fact any "dispute" between the parties.[285] The omission of the additional words has taken away from the court the power to refuse a stay and give summary judgment on an indisputable, though nevertheless disputed, claim.[286] Accordingly a claimant will only be entitled to summary judgment without a stay if his claim is admitted. Where part of the claim is admitted, then the court may, on an application for a stay, give summary judgment for that amount, but stay the action in respect of the balance or other matters in dispute.[287] Likewise if liability is admitted, but there is a dispute as to damages, it would seem that the court could grant a stay on the issue of damages only.[288] The power of the court to give summary judgment on an *admitted* claim appears to derive from the fact that an admission, in effect, amounts to an **32-071**

---

280 See above, para.32-005.
281 *Ahmad Al-Naimi (t/a Buildmaster Construction Services) v Islamic Press Agency* [2000] 1 Lloyd's Rep. 522, 525; *T&N Ltd v Royal & Sun A liance Plc* [2002] EWHC 2420, [2002] C.L.C. 1342; *Albon v Naza Motor Trading Sdn Bhd (No.3)* [2007] EWHC 327 (Ch), [2007] 2 Lloyd's Rep. 1 at [16]–[24]; *Turville Heath Inc v Chartis Insurance UK Ltd* [2012] EWHC 3019 (TCC), 145 Con. L.R. 163; *Assaubayer v Michael Wilson and Partners Ltd* [2014] EWHC 821 (QB); cf. *El Nasharty v J Sainsbury Plc* [2003] EWHC 2195 (Comm), [2004] 1 Lloyd's Rep. 309 at [29]; *City of London v Sancheti* [2008] EWCA Civ 1283, [2009] 1 Lloyd's Rep. 117; *Clyde & Co LLP v Bates van Winkelhof* [2011] EWHC 668 (QB), [2011] I.R.L.R. 467; *PT Thiess Contractors Indonesia v PT Kaltim Prima Coal* [2011] EWHC 1842 (Comm); *Deutsche Bank AG v Tongkah Harbour Public Co Ltd* [2011] EWHC 2251 (QB), [2012] 1 All E.R. (Comm) 194; *J&W Sanderson Ltd v Fenox (UK) Ltd* [2014] EWHC 4322 (Ch).
282 *Reichhold Norway ASA v Goldman Sachs International* [2002] 1 W.L.R. 173; *ET Plus SA v Welter* [2005] EWHC 2115 (Comm), [2006] 1 Lloyd's Rep. 251 at [91]; *Citigroup Global Markets Ltd v Amatra Leveraged Feeder Holdings Ltd* [2012] EWHC 1331 (Comm) at [73]–[82]. See also *A v B* [2006] EWHC 2006 (Comm), [2007] 1 Lloyd's Rep. 237 (application by arbitrator). cf. *Classic Maritime Inc v Lion Diversified Holdings Berhad* [2009] EWHC 1142 (Comm), [2010] 1 Lloyd's Rep. 59.
283 *JSC BTA Bank v Ablyazov* [2011] EWHC 587 (Comm), [2011] 2 Lloyd's Rep. 129; *Lombard North Central Plc v GATX Corp* [2012] EWHC 1067 (Comm), [2012] 1 Lloyd's Rep. 662.
284 Now CPR Pt 24.
285 See the discussion in *Hayter v Nelson and Home Insurance Co* [1990] 2 Lloyd's Rep. 265, CA; DAC Report para.55.
286 *Halki Shipping Corp v Sopex Oils Ltd* [1998] 1 W.L.R. 726; *Wealands v CLC Contractors Ltd* [1999] 2 Lloyd's Rep. 739; *Collins (Contractors) Ltd v Baltic Quay Management (1994) Ltd* [2004] EWCA Civ 1757, [2005] Build. L.R. 63.
287 *Ellis Mechanical Services Ltd v Wates Construction Ltd* [1978] 1 Lloyd's Rep. 33. Contrast *Associated Bulk Carriers Ltd v Koch Shipping Inc* [1978] 1 Lloyd's Rep. 24.
288 *Texaco Ltd v Eurogulf Shipping Ltd* [1987] 2 Lloyd's Rep. 541.

agreement to pay the claim, so that the legal proceedings are not brought "in respect of a matter which under the agreement is to be referred to arbitration".[289]

32-072   It is arguable that the court has lost a useful power in no longer being able to give summary judgment on an indisputable, but nevertheless disputed, claim, especially in relation to construction disputes where arbitrations may be long drawn out. But, when seised of such a claim, the arbitration tribunal itself could (under and subject to s.33 of the Act)[290] adopt a procedure equivalent to summary judgment to deal with the claim. If, however, it feels that this is too bold a step to take, it could give directions for an early trial of the issue on the merits.[291]

32-073   **Interpleader issues**   Section 10 of the 1996 Act provides[292] that where in legal proceedings relief by way of interpleader is granted and any issue between the claimants is one in respect of which there is an arbitration agreement between them, the court granting the relief is to direct that the issue be determined by arbitration. The court must so direct unless the circumstances are such that proceedings brought by a claimant in respect of the matter would not be stayed.[293]

32-074   **Admiralty proceedings**   Under s.11,[294] where Admiralty proceedings are stayed on the ground that the dispute in question should be submitted to arbitration, the court granting the stay may, if in those proceedings property has been arrested or bail or other security has been given to prevent or obtain release from arrest, either order that the property arrested be retained as security for the satisfaction of an enforceable[295] award given in the arbitration in respect of that dispute, or order that the stay of those proceedings be conditional on the provision of equivalent security for the satisfaction of any such award.

4.   COMMENCEMENT OF ARBITRAL PROCEEDINGS

32-075   **Conditions as to time**   The parties to a contract may lawfully agree that arbitral proceedings must be commenced, and the claimant's arbitrator appointed, within a shorter time than that allowed by the Limitation Act 1980, and that if this provision is not complied with the claim shall be deemed to be waived and absolutely barred.[296] Such a clause is not contrary to public policy as tending to oust the

---

[289]   But in *Glencore Trading Ltd v Agros Trading Ltd* [1999] 2 Lloyd's Rep. 410, Clarke L.J. said, 422, "I do not accept that a dispute cannot continue to be a dispute once the claim has been admitted". See also *Getwick Engineers Ltd v Pilecon Engineering Ltd* [2002] 1020 HKCV 1 at [23]; *Tri-MG Intra Asia Airlines v Norse Air Charters Ltd* [2009] SGHC 13, [2009] 1 Lloyd's Rep. 258 at [58] and above, para.32-030.

[290]   See below, para.32-106.

[291]   See (1997) 13 *Arbitration International* 403, 424; cf. (1998) 64 *Arbitration* (No.1, Supplement) 48.

[292]   This section is based on s.5 of the 1950 Act. It is mandatory.

[293]   subs.(2) deals with the effect of dismissal of the application on a "Scott v Avery" clause: see above, para.32-047.

[294]   This section re-enacted s.26 of the Civil Jurisdiction and Judgments Act 1982, but with the omission of subs.(2) of that section. It is mandatory.

[295]   i.e. enforceable in England.

[296]   *Atlantic Shipping Co Ltd v Louis Dreyfus & Co* [1922] 2 A.C. 250. See Mustill and Boyd *Commercial Arbitration*, at p.201. A claim may be barred even though the cause of action has not yet arisen when the time limit expired: *The Himmerland* [1965] 2 Lloyd's Rep. 353, 360; *Union of India v EB Aaby's Rederi A/S* [1975] A.C. 797, 810, 813, 817–818; *Comdel Commodities Ltd v Siporex Trade SA (No.2)* [1989] 2 Lloyd's Rep. 13 affirmed [1991] 1 A.C. 148; cf. *The M Eregli* [1981] 2 Lloyd's Rep. 169, 173. See (2009) 75 *Arbitration* (4) 481. Failure to observe a time limit for arbitra-

jurisdiction of the court, however short the time may be.[297] Yet a clause of this nature will be narrowly construed[298] and it may even be that a party who commits a fundamental breach of contract will be unable to take advantage of the clause when sued in the ordinary courts.[299] But if the other party claims arbitration in such a case, he cannot do so after the time has expired[300] unless the court exercises its statutory power to extend the time. A claim will be barred by an arbitrator's award deciding that the claim is out of time,[301] but not by an arbitrator declining jurisdiction.[302]

Power of court to extend time for beginning arbitral proceedings Section 12 **32-076** of the 1996 Act confers on the court power to extend a contractual time limit which would otherwise bar the claim. Where an arbitration agreement to refer future disputes to arbitration provides that a claim shall be barred, or the claimant's right extinguished, unless the claimant takes within a time fixed by the agreement some step to begin arbitral proceedings (or to begin other dispute resolution procedures which must be exhausted before arbitral proceedings can be begun), the court may by order extend the time for taking that step.[303] An application for such an order can be made only after a claim has arisen and after exhausting any available arbitral process for obtaining an extension of time.[304] Previously, under s.27 of the 1950 Act, the court had a wide discretion to extend time "if of opinion that in the circumstances of the case undue hardship would otherwise be caused". But, under s.12(3), a much narrower test is to be applied.[305] The court can make an order only if satisfied:

(a) that the circumstances are such as were outside the reasonable contemplation of the parties when they agreed the provision in question, and that it would be just to extend the time, or

(b) that the conduct of one party makes it unjust to hold the other party to the strict terms of the provision in question.

It is to be noted that subs.3(a) places no limit on the circumstances referred to and that all the circumstances in which the application for an extension arises are potentially relevant,[306] provided that they caused or at least significantly contributed to the failure to observe the time bar.[307] But the court can have regard only to such circumstances as were "outside the reasonable contemplation of the parties when they agreed the provision in question" and this may involve consideration of the

---

tion will bar litigation after the time limit has expired: *Wholecrop Marketing Ltd v Wolds Produce Ltd* [2013] EWHC 2079 (Ch).

[297] See n.296, above.

[298] *Board of Trade v Steel Bros & Co Ltd* [1952] 1 Lloyd's Rep. 87; *Alan v El Nasr Export and Import Co* [1972] 2 Q.B. 189, [1971] 1 Lloyd's Rep. 401; *Bunge SA v Deutsche Conti-Handelsgesellschaft mbH (No.2)* [1980] 1 Lloyd's Rep. 352; *Ch Daudruy van Cauwenberghe & Fils SA v Tropical Products Sales SA* [1986] 1 Lloyd s Rep. 535. cf. *Wholecrop Marketing Ltd v Wolds Produce Ltd* [2013] EWHC 2079 (Ch).

[299] *Ford & Co Ltd v Cie Furness* [1922] 2 K.B. 797, 802; *Smeaton Hanscomb & Co Ltd v Sassoon I. Setty, Son & Co (No.1)* [1953] 1 W.L.R. 1468, 1471. But contrast *Woolf v Collis Removal Service* [1948] 1 K.B. 11 and see above, Vol.I, para.15-011.

[300] *Ford & Co Ltd v Cie Furness*, above.

[301] *Ayscough v Sheed, Thomson & Co Ltd* (1924) 40 T.L.R. 707 HL.

[302] *Pinnock Brothers v Lewis and Peat Ltd* [1923] 1 K.B. 690.

[303] s.12(1).

[304] s.12(2). See PD 62.

[305] DAC Report paras 62–75.

[306] *Vosnoc Ltd v Trans Global Projects Ltd* [1998] 1 W.L.R. 101, 112.

[307] *Monella v Pizza Express (Restaurants) Ltd* [2003] EWHC 2966 (Ch), [2004] 12 E.G. 172.

relevant transaction, of ordinary practices within that type of transaction and with the reasonable expectation of parties involved in such a transaction.[308] It has also been said that the circumstances must be such that, if they had been drawn to the attention of the parties when they agreed the provision, they would at the very least have contemplated that the time-bar might not apply.[309] The fact that a party failed to read or comprehend the time limitation clause in the contract, or the fact that a party made a mistake as to the operation of the clause both in regard to making a claim and appointing an arbitrator, has been held not to be something which was outside the reasonable contemplation of the parties.[310] The ground set out in subs.3(b) would appear to require at least that the failure to comply with the time bar is attributable to the conduct of the party relying on the clause.[311]

32-077   An order extending time is therefore likely to be the exception rather than the rule. It is arguable that time limitation clauses are a beneficial feature in commercial contracts, since they enable the parties to draw a line beneath transactions at a much earlier stage than limitation statutes allow, and the underlying philosophy of the 1996 Act is to respect party autonomy. Nevertheless, a clause barring a claim unless arbitral proceedings or other dispute resolution procedures are begun within a short period of time can operate very harshly in some situations, for example, in "string" contracts where the buyer resells the goods and defects therein do not become apparent until time has expired. In consumer contracts, clauses imposing a time limit for the commencement of arbitral proceedings may well be regarded as unfair and so not binding on the consumer under the Unfair Terms in Consumer Contracts Regulations 1999[312] or (for contracts made after October 1, 2014) the Consumer Rights Act 2015 Pt 2.[313]

32-078   If the conditions are satisfied for the making of an order, the court may extend the period and on such terms as it thinks fit, and may do so whether or not the time previously fixed (by agreement or by a previous order) has expired.[314] The permission of the court is required for any appeal from a decision of the court under s.12.[315] The applicant will normally have to pay the costs of any s.12 application.

---

[308] *Cathiship SA v Allanasons Ltd* [1998] 2 Lloyd's Rep. 511.

[309] *Harbour & General Works Ltd v Environmental Agency* [2000] 1 W.L.R 950, 960; *Korbetis v Transgrain Shipping BV* [2005] EWHC 1345 (QB); *SOS Corporacion Alimentaria SA v Inerco Trade SA* [2010] EWHC 162 (Comm), [2010] 2 Lloyd's Rep. 345 at [54].

[310] *Harbour & General Works Ltd v Environmental Agency*, above. *Grimaldi Compāgnia di Navigazione Spa v Sekihyo Lines Ltd* [1999] 1 W.L.R. 708; *Fox & Widley v Guram* [1998] 3 E.G. 142; *Harbour & General Works Ltd v Environmental Agency*; *Thyssen Inc v Calypso Shipping Corp SA* [2002] 2 Lloyd's Rep. 243, 248; *Monella v Pizza Express (Restaurants) Ltd* [2003] EWHC 299 (Ch), [2004] E.G. 172; *SOS Corporacion Alimentaire SA V Inerco Trade SA* [2010] EWHC 162 (Comm), [2010] 2 Lloyd's Rep. 345 (extension refused). cf. *Vosnoc Ltd v Trans Global Projects Ltd* [1998] 1 W.L.R. 101; *Union Trans-Pacific Co Ltd v Orient Shipping Rotterdam BV* [2002] EWHC 1451 (Comm) (extension granted). See (2009) 75 *Arbitration* (4) 481, 483.

[311] *Fox & Widley v Guram*, above; *Grimaldi Compāgnia di Navigazione Spa v Sekihyo Lines Ltd*, above, at 725; *Cathiship SA v Allanasons Ltd* [1998] 2 Lloyd's Rep. 511 at 522; *Harbour & General Works Ltd v Environmental Agency* [2002] 1 Lloyd's Rep. 65, 72, [2000] I W.L.R. 950; *Thyssen Inc v Calypso Shipping Corp SA*, above, at 248; *Lantic Sugar Ltd v Baffin Investments Ltd* [2009] EWHC 3325 (Comm), [2010] 2 Lloyd's Rep. 141; *William McIlroy Swindon Ltd v Quinn Insurance Ltd* [2010] EWHC 2448 (TCC), [2011] B.L.R. 136 at [104], [108]; *Anglian Water Services Ltd v Laing O'Rourke Utilities Ltd* [2010] EWHC 1529 (TCC), [2011] 1 All E.R. (Comm) 1143; *Expofrut SA v Melville Services Inc* [2015] EWHC 1950 (Comm), [2015] 2 C.L.C. 218 at [12]–[14].

[312] SI 1999/2083.

[313] As to replacement of the Regulations by the 2015 Act, see below, para.38-006.

[314] s.12(4).

[315] s.12(6). But see below, para.32-185.

The court's power to extend time for beginning arbitral proceedings applies, not **32-079** only where the effect of a failure to comply with the stipulated time limit is merely to deprive a claimant of the right to go to arbitration, but also where non-compliance bars or extinguishes the claim itself.[316] But no such power exists if the clause provides that a claim is to be barred or extinguished unless notified to the other party within a limited period of time, except where such notification is a step to begin arbitral proceedings.[317] Nor can such a power be exercised where a statutory time bar applies, e.g. that provided for in the Hague-Visby Rules.[318]

Section 12 is a mandatory provision.[319] Under the corresponding provision in the **32-080** 1950 Act it was held that the power to extend time could be exercised where the law applicable to the contract containing the arbitration clause (including the time bar) was English law, even though some other law might govern the subsequent arbitration procedure.[320] The effect of the 1996 Act, however, is that the power to extend time can be exercised only where either (a) the seat of the arbitration is in England or (b) no seat has been designated or determined and the court is satisfied that it is appropriate to do so by reason of a connection with England (though such a connection could be that the arbitration agreement was governed by English law or that it is very likely that, once a seat is designated, the seat will be in England).[321]

Commencement of arbitral proceedings   The parties are free to agree when **32-081** arbitral proceedings are to be regarded as commenced for the purposes of Pt I of the 1996 Act and for the purpose of the Limitation Acts.[322] If there is no such agreement, then s.14[323] provides that arbitral proceedings are commenced in respect of a matter[324] as follows:

---

[316] *Consolidated Investment and Contracting Co v Saponaria Shipping Co Ltd* [1978] 2 Lloyd's Rep. 167; *Tradax Export SA v Italcarbo Societe di Navigazione SpA* [1983] 1 Lloyd's Rep. 514; *Jadranska Slobodna Plovidba v Oleagine SA* [1984] 1 W.L.R. 300; *The Medusa* [1986] 2 Lloyd's Rep. 328; *The Stephanos* [1989] 1 Lloyd's Rep. 506.

[317] *Smeaton Hanscomb & Co Ltd v Sassoon I Setty, Son & Co (No.1)* [1953] 1 W.L.R. 1468; *Metalimex Foreign Trade Corp v Eugenie Maritime Co Ltd* [1962] 1 Lloyd's Rep. 378; *Babanaft International Co SA v Avant Petroleum Inc* [1982] 1 W.L.R. 871; *Crown Estate Commissioners v John Mowlem & Co* [1994] 10 Const. L.J. 311; *Metalfe Corp v Pan Ocean Shipping Co Ltd* [1998] 2 Lloyd's Rep. 632.

[318] *Kenya Railways v Antares Co Pte Ltd* [1987] 1 Lloyd's Rep. 424. Contrast *Nea Agrex SA v Baltic Shipping Co Ltd* [1976] Q.B. 933; *Consolidated Investment & Contracting Co v Saponaria Shipping Co Ltd* [1978] 2 Lloyd's Rep. 167 (Hague Rules incorporated by contract). cf. *Freedom General Shipping SA v Tokai Shipping Co Ltd* [1982] 1 Lloyd's Rep. 73; *Government of Sierra Leone v Marmaro Shipping Co Ltd* [1989] 2 Lloyd's Rep. 130; Mann (1987) 103 L.Q.R. 523; Vol.I, para.28-116. See also s.12(5) of the 1996 Act.

[319] s.4(1) and Sch.1.

[320] *International Tank and Pipe SAK v Kuwait Aviation Fuelling Co KSC* [1975] Q.B. 224. Contrast *CM Van Stillevoldt BV v El Carriers Inc* [1983] 1 W.L.R. 207; *Mitsubishi Corp v Castletown Navigation Ltd* [1989] 2 Lloyd's Rep. 383 (foreign applicable law).

[321] s.2(4).

[322] s.14(1). See *Transpetrol Ltd v Ekali Shipping Co Ltd* [1989] 1 Lloyd's Rep. 62; *Taylor Woodrow Construction v RMD Kwikform Ltd* [2008] EWHC 825 (TCC), [2008] 2 Lloyd's Rep. 345; Vol.I, para.28-126.

[323] This section replaces s.34(3) of the Limitation Act 1980 and reflects to some extent art.21 of the Model law. Since the wording of subss.(3) and (4) is similar to that of s.34(3) of the 1980 Act, decisions on the latter may be relevant: see the 27th edn of this book, Vol.I, para.16-071, n.75. But In *Seabridge Shipping AB v AC Orssleff's Eftf's A/S* [1999] 2 Lloyd's Rep. 685, 690, Thomas J. expressed the view that s.14 should be interpreted "broadly and flexibly" and without reference to any pre-1996 Act decision. See also Moore-Bick J. in *Atlanska Plovidba v Consignaciones*

(i)   where the arbitrator is named or designated in the arbitration agreement, when one party serves on the other party or parties a notice in writing requiring him or them to submit that matter to the person so named or designated[325];

(ii) where the arbitrator or arbitrators are to be appointed by the parties, when one party serves on the other party or parties a notice in writing requiring him or them to appoint an arbitrator or to agree to the appointment of an arbitrator in respect of that matter[326];

(iii) where the arbitrator or arbitrators are to be appointed by a person other than a party to the proceedings, when one party gives notice in writing to that person requesting him to make the appointment in respect of that matter.[327]

32-082 Service of notices and other documents   The parties are free to agree on the manner of service of any notice or other document.[328] If and to the extent that there is no such agreement, s.76 deals with service.[329] In particular, subs.(3) of that section provides that a notice or other document may be served on a person "by any effective means". A notice may be sent by email, but it must be despatched to what is, in fact, the email address of the intended recipient and must not be rejected by the system.[330] Notice may be given to a party if it is sent to another person who is actually or ostensibly authorised to accept such service on behalf of that party.[331]

5.   THE ARBITRAL TRIBUNAL

32-083 The arbitral tribunal   The constitution of the arbitral tribunal is primarily a matter for the parties to decide. They are free to agree on the number of arbitrators to

---

Asturianas SA [2004] EWHC 1273 (Comm), [2004] 2 Lloyd's Rep. 109 at [17]; *Easybiz Investments v Sinograin* [2010] EWHC 2565 (Comm), [2011] 1 Lloyd's Rep. 688 at [11] (single notice in respect of disputes arising under 10 separate contracts); *Finmoon Ltd v Baltic Reefers Management Ltd* [2012] EWHC 920 (Comm); *Agarwal Coal Corporation (s) Pte Ltd v Harmony Innovation Shipping Pte Ltd* [2017] EWHC 3556 (Comm) (whether notice sent to two companies resulted in a single tripartite arbitration or two separate arbitrations); Tweeddale (2002) 68 *Arbitration* 238. But see *Lantic Sugar Ltd v Baffin Investments Ltd* [2009] EWHC 3325 (Comm), [2010] 2 Lloyd's Rep. 141.

[324] "Matter" include both disputes and claims: DAC Report para.76. cf. *Cruden Construction Ltd v Commission for New Towns* [1995] 2 Lloyd's Rep. 387.

[325] s.14(3).

[326] s.14(4). See *Seabridge Shipping AB v AC Orssleffs Eftf's A/S*, above (fax sent to proposed arbitrator and copied to respondents sufficed); *Bulk and Metal Transport UK LLP v Voc Bulk Ultra Handymax Pool LLC* [2009] EWHC 288 (Comm), [2009] 1 Lloyd's Rep. 418 (message stating that arbitration would be commenced failing payment sufficed). Contrast *Taylor Woodrow Construction v RMD Quikform Ltd* [2008] EWHC 825 (TCC), [2008] 2 Lloyd's Rep. 345 (notice threatening arbitration if demands not met did not suffice); *Glencore International AG v PT Tera Logistic Indonesia* [2016] EWHC 82 (Comm), [2016] 1 Lloyd's Rep. 527 (arbitral proceedings were held to have been commenced in respect of counterclaims by reason of the reference to "claims" and "all disputes arising under the contract" in the arbitration notices).

[327] s.14(5).

[328] s.76(1). See also s.77 (powers of court).

[329] ss.76(3)–(6). Contrast CPR Pt 6. See *Lantic Sugar Ltd v Baffin Investments Ltd* [2009] EWHC 3325 (Comm), [2010] 2 Lloyd's Rep. 141.

[330] *Bernuth Lines Ltd v High Seas Shipping Ltd* [2005] EWHC 3020 (Comm), [2006] 1 Lloyd's Rep. 537 at [28]–[29].

[331] *Glencore Agriculture BV v Conqueror Holdings Ltd* [2017] EWHC 2893 (Comm), [2018] 1 Lloyd's Rep. 233.

form the tribunal and whether there is to be a chairman or an umpire.[332] Unless otherwise agreed by the parties, an agreement that the number of arbitrators shall be two or any other even number is to be understood as requiring the appointment of an additional arbitrator as chairman of the tribunal.[333] If there is no agreement as to the number of arbitrators, the tribunal is to consist of a sole arbitrator.[334]

Appointment of arbitrators No particular form is required for the appointment **32-084** of an arbitrator, unless the arbitration agreement so requires. As a general rule, however, an arbitrator is fully "appointed" only when (a) the designated person is told of his nomination and is asked whether he is willing to act; (b) he consents so to act; and (c) his name and appointment are communicated to the other side.[335]

Procedures for appointment when parties do not agree The 1996 Act contains **32-085** provisions which, in the absence of agreement between the parties, establish procedures for the appointment of arbitrators and which are designed to ensure that the arbitration agreement will not be inoperative merely because one party refuses to make an appointment or if the procedure for the appointment of the arbitral tribunal fails. The parties are free to agree on the procedure for appointing the arbitrator or arbitrators, including the procedure for the appointment of any chairman or umpire.[336] If or to the extent that there is no such agreement, the following provisions apply[337]:

(i) if the tribunal is to consist of a sole arbitrator, the parties are jointly to appoint the arbitrator not later than 28 days after service of a request in writing by either party to do so[338];

(ii) if the tribunal is to consist of two arbitrators, each party is to appoint one arbitrator not later than 14 days after service of a request in writing by either party to do so[339];

(iii) if the tribunal is to consist of three arbitrators, each party is to appoint one arbitrator not later than 14 days after service of a request in writing by either party to do so, and the two so appointed are forthwith to appoint a third arbitrator as the chairman of the tribunal[340];

(iv) if the tribunal is to consist of two arbitrators and an umpire, each party is

---

[332] s.15(1).
[333] s.15(2). For the chairman, see s.20; below, para.32-090.
[334] s.15(3). See *Villa Denizcilik Sanayi Ve Ticaret AS v Longen SA* [1998] 1 Lloyd's Rep. 195.
[335] *Tradax SA v Volkswagenwerk AG* [1970] 1 Q.B. 537. See also *Toepfer v Cremer* [1975] 2 Lloyd's Rep. 118; *Carras Shipping Co Ltd v Food Corp of India* [1979] 2 Lloyd's Rep. 179; *Hannaford v Smallcombe, The Times,* December 30, 1993. cf. *Legumbres SACIFIA v Central de Cooperativas, etc. Ltda* [1986] 1 Lloyd's Rep. 401; *Petredec Ltd v Tokumaru Kaiun Co Ltd* [1994] 1 Lloyd's Rep. 162; *Robinson v Moody, The Times,* February 23, 1994; *Atlanska Plovidba v Consignaciones Asturianas SA* [2004] EWHC 1273 (Comm), [2004] 2 Lloyd's Rep. 109 at [17].
[336] s.16(1). Where there is a failure by one party to appoint an arbitrator and the arbitration agreement provides for the constitution of the arbitral tribunal in default of that appointment, the Court has no power to act under s.18: *Silver Dry Bulk Co Ltd v Homer Hulbert Maritime Co Ltd* [2017] EWHC 44 (Comm), [2017] 1 Lloyd's Rep. 154 at [32]–[33].
[337] s.16(2). For reckoning of periods of time, see s.78. The time limits may be extended by agreement, or by order of the court (s.79).
[338] s.16(3). See *Villa Denizcilik Sanayi Ve Ticaret AS v Longen SA* [1998] 1 Lloyd's Rep. 195. If one party refuses to appoint, an application must be made to the court under s.18, para.32-087, below: *Mylcrist Builders Ltd v Buck* [2008] EWHC 2172 (TCC), [2008] B.L.R. 611.
[339] s.16(4).
[340] s.16(5).

to appoint one arbitrator not later than 14 days after service of a request in writing by either party to do so, and the two so appointed may appoint an umpire at any time after they themselves are appointed and must do so before any substantive hearing or forthwith if they cannot agree on a matter relating to the arbitration.[341]

In any other case, resort is to be made to s.18 of the Act which provides for the case of a failure of the agreed appointment procedure.[342]

32-086 Power in case of default to appoint sole arbitrator The parties may, for example, have agreed that the reference is to be to two arbitrators, one to be appointed by each party, or that it shall be to three arbitrators, one to be appointed by each party and the third to be appointed by the two appointed by the parties or in some other manner specified in the agreement. Section 17 of the 1996 Act[343] provides a summary procedure which is available in case one party defaults in the appointment of his arbitrator. Unless the parties otherwise agree, where each of two parties to an arbitration agreement is to appoint an arbitrator and one party ("the party in default") refuses to do so, or fails to do so within the time specified,[344] the other party, having duly appointed his arbitrator, may give notice in writing to the party in default that he proposes to appoint his arbitrator to act as sole arbitrator.[345] If the party in default does not within seven clear days[346] of that notice being given (a) make the required appointment; and (b) notify the other party that he has done so, the other party may appoint his arbitrator as sole arbitrator, in which case his award is binding on both parties as if he had been appointed by agreement.[347] Where a sole arbitrator has been thus appointed, the party in default may (upon notice to the appointing party) apply to the court which may set aside the appointment.[348] The Act does not specify the grounds on which the court may so act, but no doubt the court would only set aside the appointment if satisfied that there was real likelihood that the person appointed could not, or would not, fairly determine the issues in the arbitration.

32-087 Failure of appointment procedure The parties are free to agree what is to happen in the event of a failure of the procedure for the appointment of the arbitral tribunal.[349] If and to the extent that there is no such agreement, the court may exercise the powers conferred upon it by s.18 of the Act upon the application of any

---

[341] s.16(6).
[342] s.16(7). See below, para.32-087.
[343] This replaces, with changes, s.7(b) of the 1950 Act: see the DAC Report paras 83–86. Section 17 does not apply where the tribunal is to consist of a sole arbitrator but one party refuses to make a joint appointment under s.16(3). Resort must then be had to s.18: *Mylcrist Builders Ltd v Buck* [2008] EWHC 2172 (TCC), [2008] Build. L.R. 611.
[344] There is no reference in s.17(1), as there was in s.10(3)(b) of the Arbitration Act 1950, to "or, if no time is specified, within a reasonable time". See s.16(4) (5).
[345] s.17(1). cf. *Minermet SpA Milan v Luckyfield Shipping Corp SA* [2004] EWHC 729 (Comm), [2004] 2 Lloyd's Rep. 348 (no need for notice where parties otherwise agree).
[346] s.78(4) (5) and see s.79 (extension of time).
[347] s.17(2). Each stage of the procedure under subss.(1) and (2) must be meticulously complied with.
[348] s.17(3). But all that is set aside is the appointment as *sole* arbitrator. Permission of the court is required for any appeal from a decision of the court under s.17(3): s.17(4); but see below, para.32-185.
[349] s.18(1). See *Medov Lines SpA v Traelandsfos A/S* [1969] 2 Lloyd's Rep. 225. There is no failure if an appointment is duly made under s.17 unless that appointment is set aside.

party to the arbitration agreement (and notice to the other parties).[350] The section does not, however, define what constitutes "a failure of the procedure for the appointment of the arbitral tribunal". But presumably this will embrace (inter alia) cases where a person designated as arbitrator or umpire refuses to act, or is incapable of acting, or dies[351]; where the parties or two arbitrators are required or at liberty to appoint an arbitrator or umpire and either cannot agree on the appointment or otherwise fail to appoint; and where an arbitrator or umpire is to be appointed by a third party (e.g. an arbitral institution) and the third party refuses or fails to make an appointment. The powers of the court under the section are[352]:

(a) to give directions as to the making of any necessary appointments[353];
(b) to direct that the tribunal shall be constituted by such appointments (or any one or more of them) as have been made;
(c) to revoke any appointments already made[354]; and
(d) to make any necessary appointments itself.

An appointment made by the court under this section has effect as if made with the agreement of the parties.[355]

The powers conferred upon the court by s.18 are discretionary.[356] If, for example, **32-088** an application is made for the court to appoint an arbitrator, then it would seem that the court could refuse to appoint on the ground of undue delay by the applicant if in the circumstances justice would not require the making of an appointment.[357] But the desirability of holding the parties to their agreement weighs strongly in favour

---

[350] s.18(2); PD 62. In *Vale do Rio Doce Navegacao SA v Shanghai Bao Steel Ocean Shipping Co Ltd* [2000] 2 Lloyd's Rep. 1 at [43]–[60], Thomas J. suggested that, on an application under s.18, the court could not intervene to determine whether or not there is an arbitration agreement. Contrast *Sinochem International Oil (London) Co Ltd v Fortune Oil Co Ltd* [2000] 1 Lloyd's Rep. 682; *Midgulf International Ltd v Groupe Chim ce Tunisien* [2009] EWHC 1684 (Comm). [2009] 1 C.L.C. 1000, [2010] EWCA Civ 66. In *Noble Denton Middle East v Noble Denton International Ltd* [2010] EWHC 2574 (Comm), [2011] 1 Lloyd's Rep. 387, Burton J. held that s.18 was "simply a gateway" and that it was for the arbitrators, and not the court, to decide on the validity of the arbitration clause if an arguable case was shown; *Man Enterprise SAL v Al-Waddam Hotel Ltd* [2013] EWHC 2356 (TCC), [2014] 1 Lloyd's Rep. 217; *Silver Dry Bulk Co Ltd v Homer Hulbert Maritime Co Ltd* [2017] EWHC 44 (Comm), [2017] 1 Lloyd's Rep. 154 at [25]–[29]. But cf. s.72. See also Aeberli (2005) 21 *Arbitration International* 253, 258 (on the use of s.72).
[351] i.e. cases previously falling under ss.7, 10 of the Arbitration Act 1950.
[352] s.18(3); *City & General (Holborn) Ltd v AYH Plc* [2005] EWHC 2494 (TCC), [2005] 2 Lloyd's Rep. 378.
[353] *Charlbury McCouat International Ltd v PG Foils Ltd* [2010] EWHC 2050 (TCC), [2011] 1 Lloyd's Rep. 23 (LCIA to appoint).
[354] See para.88 of the DAC Report.
[355] s.18(4). Permission of the court is required for any appeal from a decision of the court under this section: s.18(5); but see below, para.32-185; *Johann MK Blumenthal GmbH & Co KG v Itochu Corp* [2012] EWCA Civ 996, [2013] 1 All E.R. (Comm) 504.
[356] *Villa Denizcilik Sanayi Ve Ticaret AS v Longen SA* [1998] 1 Lloyd's Rep. 195; *Through Transport Mutual Insurance Assn (Euroasia) Ltd v New India Assurance Co Ltd (No.2)* [2005] EWHC 455 (Comm), [2005] 2 Lloyd's Rep. 378. See also *Enercon GmbH v Enercon (India) Ltd* [2012] EWHC 689 (Comm), [2012] 1 Lloyd's Rep. 519 (application stayed pending hearing by foreign court).
[357] *Petredec Ltd v Tokumaru Kaiun Co Ltd* [1994] 1 Lloyd's Rep. 162; *Frota Oceanica Brasiliera SA v Steamship Mutual Underwriting Association (Bermuda) Ltd* [1996] 2 Lloyd's Rep. 461; *Secretary of State for Foreign and Commonwealth Office v Percy Thomas Partnership* (1998) 65 Con. L.R. 11; *West of England Ship Owners Mutual Protection and Indemnity Assn v Hellenic Industrial Development Bank SA* [1999] 1 Lloyd's Rep. 93 (on s.10 of the 1950 Act). cf. *Durtnell (R) & Sons Ltd v Secretary of State For Trade and Industry* [2001] 1 Lloyd's Rep. 275.

of exercising the discretion.[358] The s.18 powers may be exercised not only where the seat of the arbitration is in England but also where no seat of the arbitration has been designated or determined and by reason of a connection with England the court is satisfied that it is appropriate to do so.[359]

32-089 Qualifications of arbitrators An arbitrator does not have to possess any or any particular qualifications to act as arbitrator, unless the arbitration agreement so requires. Where the appointed arbitrator does not possess the required qualifications, an objection that the arbitral tribunal is improperly constituted may be made under ss.31 and 32 of the 1996 Act.[360] The unqualified arbitrator may also be removed by the court under s.24,[361] or his award challenged under s.67.[362] In deciding whether to exercise, and in considering how to exercise, any of its powers under s.16 or s.18, the court is to have due regard to any agreement of the parties as to the qualifications required of the arbitrators.[363]

32-090 Chairman The Arbitration Act 1950 made no provision for the office of chairman. But s.20 of the 1996 Act provides for the role of chairman. The parties are free to agree what his functions shall be.[364] In the absence of agreement,[365] decisions, orders and awards are to be made by all or a majority of the arbitrators (including the chairman),[366] but the view of the chairman is to prevail in relation to a decision, order or award in respect of which there is neither unanimity nor a majority,[367] for example, if there are three arbitrators and each (including the chairman) has a different view on the amount of the award.

32-091 Umpire Traditionally, an umpire differs from a chairman in that he is not strictly one of the arbitrators but replaces the two party-appointed arbitrators in the event that they are unable to agree. Section 21 of the 1996 Act provides that, where the parties have agreed that there is to be an umpire, they are free to agree what his functions shall be, and in particular whether he is to attend the proceedings and when he is to replace the other arbitrators as the tribunal with power to make decisions, orders and awards.[368] If and to the extent that there is no agreement,[369] he is to attend the proceedings (though not take an active part in them) and be supplied

---

358 *Atlanska Plovidba v Consignaciones Asturianas SA* [2004] EWHC 1273 (Comm), [2004] 2 Lloyd's Rep. 109 at [24].

359 s.2(4). *Charlbury McCouat International Ltd v PG Foils Ltd* [2010] EWHC 2050 (TCC), [2011] 1 Lloyd's Rep. 23 (English law likely to apply to substance of dispute).

360 cf. *Pan Atlantic Group Inc v Hassneh Insurance Co of Israel Ltd* [1992] 2 Lloyd's Rep. 120.

361 1996 Act s.24(1)(b).

362 *Sumukan Ltd v Commonwealth Secretariat (No.2)* [2007] EWCA Civ 1148, [2008] 1 Lloyd's Rep. 40.

363 s.10. See *Villa Denizcilik Sanayi Ve Ticaret AS v Longen SA* [1998] 1 Lloyd's Rep. 195. In *Allianz Insurance Plc v Tonicstar Ltd* [2018] EWCA Civ 434, [2018] 1 Lloyd's Rep 389, where the arbitration agreement provided that "the arbitration tribunal shall consist of persons with not less than ten years' experience of insurance or reinsurance", it was held that a Queen's Counsel who has practised as a barrister specialising in the field of insurance and reinsurance for more than ten years satisfied this requirement.

364 s.20(1).

365 s.20(2).

366 s.20(3).

367 s.20(4).

368 s.21(1). Parties will have "agreed that there is to be an umpire" within the meaning of s.21(1) even though the umpire is to be appointed by the arbitrators, and even though his authority to act is contingent on disagreement: *Van der Giessen de-Noord Shipbuilding Division BV v Imtech Marine*

with the same documents and materials as are supplied to the other arbitrators.[370] If and when the arbitrators cannot agree on a matter relating to the arbitration, they must forthwith give notice in writing to the parties and to the umpire, and he then replaces them as the tribunal and with power to make decisions, orders and awards as if he were sole arbitrator.[371] Should one or both of the arbitrators fail to give the necessary notice, any party to the arbitral proceedings can apply to the court for an order that the umpire shall replace the other arbitrators.[372]

No chairman or umpire In the event that the parties agree not to have a chairman or umpire, they are free to agree how the tribunal is to make decisions, orders and awards. If there is no such agreement, they are to be made by all or a majority of the arbitrators.[373]   **32-092**

Revocation of arbitrator's authority The parties are free to agree in what   **32-093**
circumstances the authority of an arbitrator may be revoked.[374] If and to the extent that there is no such agreement,[375] s.23 of the 1996 Act confirms the long-established rule that it is impossible for one party unilaterally to revoke the authority of an arbitrator.[376] The parties acting jointly may nevertheless do so,[377] but this must be agreed in writing unless the parties also agree (whether or not in writing) to terminate the arbitration agreement.[378] An arbitrator's authority may also be revoked by an arbitral or other institution or person vested by the parties with powers in that regard.[379]

Death of arbitrator The authority of an arbitrator is personal and ceases on   **32-094**
death.[380] But, unless otherwise agreed by the parties, the death of a person by whom an arbitrator was appointed does not revoke the arbitrator's authority.[381]

Court's power to revoke appointment The power conferred on the court under   **32-095**
the 1950 Act[382] to revoke the authority of an arbitrator or umpire where the dispute involved a charge of fraud was not preserved by the 1996 Act. But the court may

---

& *Offshore BV* [2008] EWHC 2904 (Comm), [2009] 1 Lloyd's Rep. 273 at [106].
[369] s.21(2).
[370] s.21(3). cf. *Fletamentos Maritimos SA v Effjohn International BV* [1995] 1 Lloyd's Rep. 311; *Fletamentos Maritimos SA v Effjohn International BV (No.2)* [1997] 1 Lloyd's Rep. 295, [1997] 1 Lloyd's Rep. 644 (on 1950 Act).
[371] s.21(4).
[372] s.21(5). Permission of the court is required for any appeal from a decision of the court under this section: s.21(6). See PD 62; but see below, para.32-185.
[373] s.22(1) (2).
[374] s.23(1). Institutional rules may provide for challenges to and revocation of the appointment of an arbitrator, as, for example, art.10 of the LCIA rules: see Walsh and Teitelbaum (2011) 27 *Arbitration International* 283 (decisions of the LCIA Court).
[375] s.23(2).
[376] Arbitration Act 1950 s.1.
[377] s.23(3)(a).
[378] s.23(4).
[379] s.23(3)(b).
[380] s.26(1). This sub-section is mandatory.
[381] s.26(2).
[382] Arbitration Act 1950 s.24(2).

revoke an appointment under s.18 (powers exercisable in case of failure of appointment procedure)[383] and may remove an arbitrator on the grounds specified in s.24.[384]

32-096 **Removal of arbitrator** The court has in certain circumstances the power to remove an arbitrator. This may be done, under s.24 of the 1996 Act, upon the application of a party to the arbitral proceedings.[385] The grounds on which such an application may be made are any of the following:

> (a) that circumstances exist which give rise to justifiable doubts as to his impartiality[386];

---

[383] s.18(3)(c); see above, para.32-087.

[384] Below, para.32-096.

[385] Upon notice to the other parties, to the arbitrator concerned and to any other arbitrator: s.24(1). See PD 62. Permission of the court is required for any appeal from a decision of the court under this section: s.24(6); but see below, para.32-184.

[386] *Save and Prosper Pensions Ltd v Homebase Ltd* [2002] L. & T.R. 11 (arbitrator's firm instructed in substantial property matter by associated company of one of the parties); *Sphere Drake Insurance v American Reliable Insurance Company* [2004] EWHC 796 (Comm) (arbitrator involved as consultant to certain key players in the market at centre of dispute); *ASM Shipping Ltd of India v TTMI Ltd of England* [2005] EWHC 2238 (Comm), [2006] 1 Lloyd's Rep. 375, [2006] EWCA Civ 1341, [2007] 1 Lloyd's Rep. 136 (arbitrator instructed as counsel in previous case against one of the parties); *Sierra Fishing Co Ltd v Mohamed* [2015] EWHC 140 (Comm), [2015] 1 Lloyd's Rep. 514 (arbitrator's business connections, involvement in negotiations and drafting of agreement, conduct of reference). cf. (where application to remove failed) *Andrews (t/a BA Constructers) v Bradshaw* [2000] B.L.R. 6 (irritation on part of arbitrator and receiving payment of fee from one party where the other refused to pay); *Laker Airways Inc v FLS Aerospace Ltd* [2000] 1 W.L.R. 113 (arbitrator in same chambers as barrister representing one of parties, but see *Smith v Kvaerner Cementation Foundations Ltd* [2006] EWCA Civ 242, [2007] 1 W.L.R. 370 at [171]); *Rustal Trading Ltd v Gill & Duffus SA* [2000] 2 Lloyd's Rep. 14 (arbitrator involved in earlier dispute with party's consultant); *AT & T Corp v Saudi Arabian Cable Co* [2000] 1 Lloyd's Rep. 22, [2000] 2 Lloyd's Rep. 127, CA (arbitrator was non-executive director of rival bidder for project); *ASM Shipping Ltd v Harris* [2007] EWHC 1513 (Comm), [2008] 1 Lloyd's Rep. 61 (two arbitrators remain after recusal of third for alleged bias); *Goel v Amega Ltd* [2010] EWHC 2454 (Comm) (case management issues); *A v B* [2011] EWHC 2345 (Comm), [2011] 2 Lloyd's Rep. 591 (barrister arbitrator involved in case for solicitors for party); *Interprods Ltd v De La Rue International Ltd* [2014] EWHC 68 (Comm) (arbitrator after appointment was appointed arbitrator in two other cases where one party represented by solicitors for claimant: s.68(2)(a) application failed); *Cofely Ltd v Bingham* [2016] EWHC 240 (Comm), [2016] 2 All E.R. (Comm) 129 at [98]–[116] (arbitrator removed on the ground of apparent bias where 18 per cent of his appointments and 25 per cent of his arbitrator/adjudicator income over the previous three years had come from cases involving the defendant as a party or as a claims consultant and where the Chartered Institute of Arbitrators acceptance of nomination form calls for disclosure of "any involvement, however remote, with either party over the last five years"); *W Ltd v M Sdn Bhd* [2016] EWHC 422 (Comm), [2016] 1 Lloyd's Rep. 552 at [27]–[44] (the IBA Guidelines 2014 are of assistance to the Court, but they are not a statement of English law; the Court noted some "weaknesses" in the IBA Guidelines 2014); *Halliburton v Chubb Bermuda Insurance Ltd* [2018] EWCA Civ 817, [2018] 1 W.L.R. 3361 (arbitrator had accepted appointments in a number of references concerning the same or overlapping subject matter with only one common party). For the test to be applied in cases of alleged bias, see *Dimes v Proprietors of Grand Junction Canal* (1852) 3 H.L Cas. 759; *R. v Spencer* [1987] A.C. 128; *R. v Gough* [1993] A.C. 646; *R. v Bow Street Magistrate Ex. P Pinochet Ugarte (No.2)* [2002] 1 A.C. 119; *Laker Airways Inc v FLS Aerospace Ltd*, above; *Locobail (UK) Ltd v Bayfield Property Ltd* [2000] Q.B. 451; *AT & T Corp v Saudi Arabian Cable Co* above; *Re Medicaments and Related Classes of Goods (No.2)* [2001] 1 W.L.R. 700; *Porter v Magill* [2001] UKHL 67, [2002] 2 A.C. 357 at [103]; *ASM Shipping Ltd of India v TTMI Ltd of England*, above, at [39]; *Cofely Ltd v Bingham* [2016] EWHC 240 (Comm), [2016] 2 All E.R. (Comm) 129 at [72]; *H v L* [2017] EWHC 137 (Comm), [2017] 1 Lloyd's Rep. 553 at [16]. See IBA Guidelines on conflicts of interest in International Arbitration 2014; Chartered Institute of Arbitrators: Code of Professional and Ethical Conduct (2009); AAA/ABA Code of Ethics for Arbitra-

(b)   that he does not possess the qualifications required by the arbitration agreement[387];

(c)   that he is physically or mentally incapable of conducting the proceedings or there are justifiable doubts as to his capacity to do so;

(d)   that he has refused or failed:

　　(i)   properly to conduct the proceedings[388]; or

　　(ii)   to use all reasonable despatch in conducting the proceedings or making an award[389];

and that substantial injustice has been or will be caused to the applicant.

With respect to ground (a), s.24 omits the reference in the Model Law to "independence" as well as "impartiality": the Departmental Committee concluded that lack of independence, unless it gave rise to justifiable doubts about the impartiality of the arbitrator, was of no significance.[390] With respect to ground (d), the use by a party of this provision to delay or disrupt the arbitral proceedings is discouraged by the requirement that the conduct of the arbitrator must be such that "substantial injustice" has been or will be caused to the applicant,[391] and also by fact that the arbitral tribunal is further empowered to continue the arbitral proceedings while an application to the court is pending.[392] Moreover, s.73(1) provides that a party must object promptly to any impropriety or irregularity in the proceedings,[393] and subs.(2) of s.24 provides that if there is an arbitral or other institution or person vested with the authority to remove an arbitrator, the court is not to exercise its power of removal unless it is satisfied that the applicant has first

---

tors in Commercial Disputes (2004 revision); Chung (2011) 77 *Arbitration* 167; Park (2011) 27 *Arbitration International* 473. As to the validity of a rule in the Arbitrators' Code of Conduct of the International Cotton Association, see *Aldcroft v International Cotton Association Ltd* [2017] EWHC 642 (Comm), [2017] 1 Lloyd's Rep. 635.

[387]   See above, para.32-089.

[388]   See *Wicketts v Brine Builders* [2001] CILL 1805 (autonomous conduct by arbitrator); *Norbrook Laboratories Ltd v Tank* [2006] EWHC 1055 (Comm), [2006] 2 Lloyd's Rep. 485 (unilateral telephone contact with parties and direct contact with witnesses) and (on removal under s.23(1) of the 1950 Act): *Hagop Ardahalian v Unifert International SA* [1984] 2 Lloyd's Rep. 84, 89; and *Modern Engineering (Bristol) Ltd v C Miskin & Son Ltd* [1981] 1 Lloyd's Rep. 135 (issue of interim award without hearing submissions on raised point of law); *Town and City Properties (Development) Ltd v Wiltshier Southern Ltd* (1989) 44 B.L.R. 109 (procedure akin to valuation adopted rather than arbitration); *Lovell Partnerships (Northern) Ltd v AW Construction Plc* (1996) 81 Build. L.R. 83, 99 (test to be applied), cf. *Home of Homes Ltd v Hammersmith Fulham LBC* [2003] EWHC 807, [2003] 92 Const. L.R. 48 (arbitrator takes leading counsel's opinion on issues of costs and jurisdiction); *Norbrook Laboratories Ltd v Tank*, above (hearings curtailed). On the question of reliance of the arbitrator on his own knowledge and experience, see *Fox v Wellfair Ltd* [1981] 2 Lloyd's Rep. 514; *Warborough Investments Ltd v S Robinson & Sons (Holdings) Ltd* [2003] EWCA Civ 751, [2003] 2 E.G.L.R. 149; *Checkpoint Ltd v Strathclyde Pension Fund* [2003] EWCA 751, [2003] 2 E.G.L.R. 149; *St George's Investment Co Ltd v Gemini Consulting Ltd* [2004] EWHC 2353 (Ch); *Claire & Co Ltd v Thames Water Utilities Ltd* [2005] EWHC 1022, [2005] Build. L.R. 366; *JD Wetherspoon Plc v Jay Mar Estates* [2007] EWHC 856 (TCC), [2007] Build. L.R. 285.

[389]   See (on removal under s.13(3) of the 1950 Act): *Pratt v Swanmore Builders Ltd* [1980] 2 Lloyd's Rep. 504.

[390]   DAC Report paras 101–104. But see above para.32-016, n.59.

[391]   DAC Report para.105. See also below, para.32-164; *Norbrook Laboratories v Tank*, above.

[392]   s.24(3). See (1998) 64 *Arbitration* 188

[393]   See below, paras 32-165, 32-177; *Rustal Trading Ltd v Gill & Duffus SA* [2000] 1 Lloyd's Rep. 14; *Sinclair v Woods of Winchester Ltd* [2005] EWHC 1631 (QB), [2005] 102 Const. L.R. 127; *ASM Shipping Ltd of India v TTMI Ltd*, above; *ASM Shipping Ltd v Harris* [2007] EWHC 1513 (Comm), [2008] 1 Lloyd's Rep. 61. cf. *Sierra Fishing Co Ltd v Mohamed* [2015] EWHC 140 (Comm), [2015] 1 Lloyd's Rep. 514.

exhausted his right of recourse to that institution or person. The arbitrator concerned is entitled to appear and be heard by the court before any order is made.[394] If he is removed, this does not affect his immunity, but the court can adjust his entitlement to recover or retain fees or expenses.[395] The filling of the vacancy created is dealt with by s.27.[396] Section 24 is a mandatory provision.[397]

32-097   Resignation of arbitrator   An arbitrator will be liable[398] if he resigns in breach of the express or implied terms of his engagement unless the parties agree to release him from his engagement or from liability. Section 25 of the 1996 Act enables him to apply to the court for relief from liability and for an order as to the recovery or retention of his fees and expenses.

32-098   Filling of vacancy   Where an arbitrator ceases to hold office, the parties are free to agree whether and if so how the vacancy is to be filled, whether and if so to what extent the previous proceedings should stand, and what effect (if any) his ceasing to hold office has on any appointment made by him (alone or jointly).[399] If or to the extent that there is no such agreement,[400] then:

  (a)   the provisions of ss.16 and 18 apply in relation to the filling of the vacancy as in relation to an original appointment[401];

  (b)   the tribunal (when reconstituted) is to determine whether and if so to what extent the previous proceedings are to stand[402]; and

  (c)   his ceasing to hold office does not affect any appointment by him (alone or jointly) of another arbitrator, in particular any appointment of a chairman or umpire.[403]

In contrast with the Arbitration Act 1950,[404] the 1996 Act does not give to the court any initial power to fill a vacancy caused by its removal of an arbitrator: the original appointment procedure is to be used.[405]

32-099   Liability for arbitrators' fees and expenses   As a matter of general contract law, an arbitrator is entitled to be paid whatever has been agreed between him and any of the parties.[406] This is a several liability which is incurred by the party with whom the agreement was made. However, under s.28 of the Act, all parties are jointly and severally liable to an arbitrator for his fees and expenses, but this joint and several liability is limited to "such reasonable fees and expenses (if any) as are appropri-

---

[394]   s.24(5).
[395]   s.24(4).
[396]   See below, para.32-098.
[397]   s.4(1) and Sch.1.
[398]   He is not immune from such liability: s.29(3).
[399]   s.27(1).
[400]   s.27(2). See *Federal Insurance Co and Chubb Insurance Co of Europe SA v Transamerica Occidental Life Insurance Co* [1999] 2 Lloyd's Rep. 286.
[401]   s.27(3).
[402]   This does not affect any right of a party to challenge those proceedings on any ground which had arisen before the arbitrator ceased to hold office: s.27(4).
[403]   s.27(5).
[404]   Arbitration Act 1950 s.25(1).
[405]   DAC Report para.117. See above, para.32-085 (s.16).
[406]   See DAC Report para.120; Mustill and Boyd at pp.233; *Chartered Institute of Arbitrators: Guidelines for arbitrators as to how to formulate their terms of remuneration* (2011). For the difficulties that may arise, see *K/S Norjarl A/S v Hyundai Heavy Industries Ltd* [1992] Q.B. 863 (commitment fee demanded); *Turner v Stevenage BC* [1998] Ch. 28 (request for interim fee).

ate in the circumstances".[407] The section further enables a party to apply to the court to adjust fees and expenses before they are paid,[408] and, if it is reasonable in the circumstances to do so, to order repayment of fees and expenses after the arbitrator has been paid.[409] The section nevertheless makes it clear that this power to make adjustments and to order repayment does not affect any contractual right of the arbitrator to his fees and expenses.[410] Nor does the section deal with the question which of the parties (as between themselves) are to pay the costs and expenses of the arbitration.[411] It is to be noted that arbitrators' expenses in this section include the fees and expenses of an expert, legal adviser or assessor appointed by the tribunal for which the arbitrators are liable.[412] Section 28 is mandatory.[413]

Difficult problems may arise concerning the liability for fees and expenses of a **32-100** person who successfully objects to or challenges the substantive jurisdiction of the tribunal.[414] Section 28 refers to a liability of "the parties" to pay the arbitrators' fees and expenses. If a person has taken no part in the arbitral proceedings, and it is determined that the tribunal has no substantive jurisdiction, it is scarcely arguable that he should be liable for any part of those fees and expenses. But under s.30 the tribunal is empowered to rule on its own jurisdiction and a person may have participated in the proceedings, even though ultimately he establishes that the tribunal lacks jurisdiction. The Act does not answer the question whether such a person is to be considered a "party" for the purposes of liability under this section. If the tribunal rules that it has no jurisdiction, it is arguable that, in the absence of agreement,[415] the successful objector—even if he has participated—should not be liable to pay any part of the arbitrator's fees and expenses as the tribunal has itself declared that the objector was never a party to any valid arbitral proceedings brought against him. However, it could be said that, by participating, the objector has impliedly agreed to pay the reasonable fees and expenses of the arbitrator in ruling on jurisdiction and that an arbitrator can "give value"[416] by providing a ruling on jurisdiction. If the tribunal rules that it has jurisdiction, but its award on this issue is set aside by the court under s.67, it might be argued that the case is stronger still for the recovery by an arbitrator under s.28 of his reasonable fees and expenses from a participating "party" because the award is binding until set aside by the court.[417]

---

[407] s.28(1). See also s.28(6) (arbitrator who has ceased to act, and umpire).

[408] s.28(2). See CPR r.62.6, PD 62.4. For an example of reduction of fees, see *Hussman (Europe) Ltd v Al Ameen Developments & Trade Co* [2000] 2 Lloyd's Rep. 83; *Agrimex Ltd v Tradigrain* [2003] EWHC 1656 (Comm), [2003] 2 Lloyd's Rep. 537.

[409] s.28(3). See CPR r.62.6 PD 62.4.

[410] s.28(5).

[411] s.28(5). See ss.59–65; below, paras 32-148—32-155.

[412] s.37(2).

[413] s.4(1) and Sch.1.

[414] DAC Report para.126.

[415] *Commonwealth Development Corp (UK) v Montague* [2000] QCA 252 Queensland Court of Appeal; Greenberg and Secomb (2002) 18 *Arbitration International* 125.

[416] *Systech International Ltd v PC Harrington Contractors Ltd* [2012] EWCA Civ 1371, [2013] 1 All E.R. (Comm) 1074 at [36].

[417] *Systech International Ltd v PC Harrington Contractors Ltd* [2012] EWCA Civ 1371, [2013] 1 All E.R. (Comm) 1074 at [36].

6. JURISDICTION OF THE ARBITRAL TRIBUNAL

32-101 Tribunal can rule on its own jurisdiction English law has always taken the view that the arbitral tribunal cannot be the final adjudicator of its own jurisdiction. The final decision as to the substantive jurisdiction of the tribunal rests with the court.[418] However, there is no reason why the tribunal should not have the power, subject to review by the court, to rule on its own jurisdiction. Indeed, such a power (often referred to as the principle of "*kompetenz-kompetenz*") has been generally recognised in other legal systems. It had also been recognised by English law before the 1996 Act,[419] but s.30 of the Act puts this on a statutory basis. Unless otherwise agreed by the parties, the arbitral tribunal may rule on its own substantive jurisdiction, that is, as to (a) whether there is a valid arbitration agreement; (b) whether the tribunal is properly constituted; and (c) what matters have been submitted to arbitration in accordance with the arbitration agreement.[420] Any such ruling may be challenged by any arbitral process of appeal or review or in accordance with the provisions of Pt I of the Act,[421] notably by an application under s.32[422] or by a challenge to the award under s.67[423] or at the enforcement stage under ss.66 and 103(2)(b).[424]

32-102 Objection to substantive jurisdiction of tribunal[425] Section 31 of the 1996 Act (which is a mandatory provision[426]) limits the period within which an objection to the substantive jurisdiction of the arbitral tribunal can be raised and sets out the courses open to the tribunal if such an objection is made. An objection that the tribunal lacks jurisdiction at the outset of the proceedings must be raised by a party not later than the time he takes the first step in the proceedings to contest the merits

---

[418] *May v Mills* (1914) 30 T.L.R. 287; *Produce Brokers Co Ltd v Olympia Oil and Cake Co Ltd* [1916] 1 A.C. 314, 327; *Heyman v Darwins Ltd* [1942] A.C. 356, 393; *Brown v Genossenschaft Oesterreichischer Waldbesitzer R GmbH* [1954] 1 Q.B. 8; *Dalmia Dairy Industries Ltd v National Bank of Pakistan* [1978] 2 Lloyd's Rep. 223, 285–293; *Willcock v Pickfords Removals Ltd* [1979] 1 Lloyd's Rep. 244, 245; *Peoples Insurance Co of China v Vysanthi Shipping Co Ltd* [2003] EWHC 1655 (Comm), [2003] 2 Lloyd's Rep. 617 at [25]; *Dallah Real Estate & Tourism Co v Ministry of Religious Affairs of the Government of Pakistan* [2010] UKSC 46, [2011] 1 A.C. 763 at [26], [86], [96], [104], [148].

[419] *Golodetz v Schrier* (1947) 80 Ll.L. Rep. 647, 650; *Brown v Genossenschaft Oesterreichischer Waldbesitzer R GmbH*, above; *Lucanda Exportadora SARL v Wahbe Tamari & Sons* [1967] 2 Lloyd's Rep. 353, 364; *Dallah Real Estate & Tourism Co v Ministry of Religious Affairs of the Government of Pakistan* [2010] UKSC 46, [2011] 1 A.C. 763 at [25], [93].

[420] s.30(1). See the Chartered Institute of Arbitrators: Guidelines for Arbitrators dealing with Jurisdictional Problems (2011) 77 *Arbitration* 220; *Vee Networks Ltd v Econet Wireless International Ltd* [2004] EWHC 2909 (Comm), [2005] 1 Lloyd's Rep. 192 at [22]; *UR Power GmbH v Kuok Oils and Grains Pte Ltd* [2009] EWHC 1940 (Comm), [2009] 2 Lloyd's Rep. 495; *Dallah Real Estate & Tourism Co v Ministry of Religious Affairs of the Government of Pakistan* [2010] UKSC 46, [2011] 1 A.C. 763 at [25], [79], [93]–[95]; *Assaubayer v Michael Wilson and Partners Ltd* [2014] EWHC 821 (QB). But see the cases cited above, para.32-068, n.273 (court may nevertheless be the first to decide). In *C v D1* [2015] EWHC 2126 (Comm) at [135] the Court said that s.30 is likely to contain an exhaustive definition of jurisdictional matters.

[421] s.30(2).

[422] See below, para.32-104.

[423] See below, para.32-158.

[424] *Dallah Real Estate & Tourism Co v Ministry of Religious Affairs of the Government of Pakistan* [2010] UKSC 46, [2011] 1 A.C. 763.

[425] Aeberli (2005) 21 *Arbitration International* 253, 264.

[426] s.4(1) and Sch.1.

of any matter[427] in relation to which he challenges the tribunal's jurisdiction.[428] And any objection during the course of the arbitral proceedings that the tribunal is exceeding its jurisdiction must be made as soon as possible after the matter alleged to be beyond its jurisdiction is raised.[429] The tribunal may, however, admit an objection made later if it considers the delay justified.[430] If a party to arbitral proceedings takes part or continues to take part in the proceedings without duly objecting that the tribunal lacks substantive jurisdiction, he cannot raise that objection later, before the tribunal or the court, unless he shows that he did not then know and could not with reasonable diligence have discovered the grounds for the objection.[431] The prudent course for a party contemplating a jurisdictional challenge in a two-tier arbitration scheme is to advance such objections before the first tier arbitrators; if not, it may well be at risk of losing that right.[432]

Where an objection is duly taken to the tribunal's substantive jurisdiction and the **32-103** tribunal has power to rule on its own jurisdiction, s.31(4) states that the tribunal may adopt one of two courses: first, it may rule on the matter in an award on jurisdiction; secondly, it may deal with the objection in its award on the merits. It may be presumed that at least the first of these alternatives is open to the tribunal if it rules that it lacks jurisdiction as well as if it rules that it has jurisdiction, although it is somewhat peculiar to categorise the declining of jurisdiction as an "award". If the parties agree which of these two courses the tribunal should take, the tribunal is to proceed accordingly. In either case the award may be challenged in court under s.67 of the Act.[433] But a third way of proceeding is also contemplated, albeit in limited circumstances. This is for an application (under s.32) to be made to the court by a party before any award.[434] In this situation, the tribunal may (and, if the parties

---

[427] *Vee Networks Ltd v Econet Wireless International Ltd* [2004] EWHC 2909 (Comm), [2005] 1 Lloyd's Rep. 192 at [65]; cf. *Athletic Union of Constantinople v National Basketball Association* [2002] EWCA Civ 830, [2002] 1 Lloyd's Rep. 305, at [39]. *Gulf Import & Export Co v Bunge SA* [2007] EWHC 2667 (Comm), [2008] 1 Lloyd's Rep. 316 at [47]; *Republic of Serbia v Image Sat International NV* [2009] EWHC 2853 (Comm), [2010] 1 Lloyd's Rep. 324 at [107]–[110]. See Yang (2004) 70 *Arbitration* 279.

[428] s.31(1). A party is not precluded from raising such an objection by the fact that he has appointed or participated in the appointment of an arbitrator.

[429] s.31(2).

[430] s.31(3). cf. *Republic of Serbia v Image Sat International NV* [2009] EWHC 2583 (Comm), [2010] 1 Lloyd's Rep. 324 at [110].

[431] s.73(1); see below, para.32-177; *Hussman (Europe) Ltd v Al Amen Development & Trade Co* [2002] 2 Lloyd's Rep. 83, 91; *Athletic Union of Constantinople v National Basketball Association* [2002] EWCA Civ 830, [2002] 1 Lloyd's Rep. 305 at [20]–[27]; *JSC Zestafoni G Nikoladz Ferroalloy Plant v Ronly Holdings Ltd* [2004] EWHC 245 (Comm), [2004] 2 Lloyd's Rep. 335 at [64]; *Westland Helicopters Ltd v Sheikh Salah-al-Hejailan (No.1)* [2004] EWHC 1625 (Comm), [2004] 2 Lloyd's Rep. 523; *Vee Networks Ltd v Econet Wireless International Ltd* [2004] EWHC 2909 (Comm), [2005] 1 Lloyd's Rep. 192 at [66]; *Frontier Agriculture Ltd v Bratt Bros* [2015] EWCA Civ 611, [2015] 2 Lloyd's Rep. 500; *A v B* [2016] EWHC 3003 (Comm), [2017] 1 W.L.R. 2030 at [50]–[63]. But if the arbitrator determines that he lacks jurisdiction and a party challenges that determination, s.73 is inapplicable since that party is not making any of the objections to which s.73 applies; *LG Caltex Gas Co Ltd v China National Petroleum Corp* [2002] EWCA Civ 788, [2002] 1 W.L.R. 1892.

[432] *UK Power GmbH v Kuok Oils and Grains Pte Ltd* [2009] EWHC 1940 (Comm), [2009] 2 Lloyd's Rep. 495 at [32].

[433] See below, para.32-157. But cf. *Aoot Kalmneft v Glencore International AG* [2002] 1 Lloyd's Rep. 128, 138–139 (decision of tribunal on what course to take under s.31(4) cannot be challenged under s.67).

[434] See below, para.32-104.

agree, must) stay the arbitral proceedings whilst such an application is made.[435] It must, however, be borne in mind that a person who is alleged to be a party to arbitral proceedings but who takes no part in those proceedings because he considers that the tribunal lacks substantive jurisdiction cannot be required to take any positive steps to object to the jurisdiction of the tribunal. He may choose instead to challenge the jurisdiction of the tribunal by proceedings in court for a declaration or injunction or other appropriate relief under s.72[436] or to challenge any award made under s.67.[437] By contrast, a party asserting the existence of an arbitration agreement will not be able to seek a declaration from the Court that the arbitration exists other than pursuant to the procedures laid down in the Arbitration Act 1996 (unless the declaration is sought in support of other relief, such as an anti-suit injunction).[438]

32-104 **Determination of preliminary point of jurisdiction** Section 32 of the 1996 Act confers upon a party, in limited circumstances, the right to apply to the court to determine any question as to the substantive jurisdiction of the arbitral tribunal.[439] Such an application, if made at the outset of arbitral proceedings, may result in considerable savings of time and costs.[440] However, in view of the power given to the tribunal by s.30 to rule on its own jurisdiction, the Departmental Advisory Committee expressed the opinion that such an application was intended to be made in exceptional cases only.[441] The application cannot be considered unless either it is made with the agreement in writing of all the other parties to the proceedings, or it is made with the permission of the tribunal and the court is satisfied (a) that the determination of the question is likely to produce substantial savings in costs; (b) that the application was made without delay; and (c) that there is good reason why the matter should be decided by the court.[442] Unless otherwise agreed by the parties, the tribunal may continue the arbitral proceedings and make an award while an application to the court is pending.[443]

32-105 Restrictions are placed by subss.(5) and (6) of s.32 on the right of appeal. Un-

---

[435] s.31(5). See (1998) 64 *Arbitration* 188.

[436] See below, para.32-158; *Caparo Group Ltd v Fagor Arrasato Sociead Cooerativa* [2000] A.D.R.L.J. 24; *Law Debenture Trust Corp v Elekrim Finance BV* [2005] EWHC 1412 (Ch), [2005] 2 Lloyd's Rep. 755; *Broda Agro Trade (Cyprus) Ltd v Alfred C Toepfer International GmbH* [2010] EWCA Civ 110, [2011] 1 Lloyd's Rep. 243.

[437] See below, para.32-157.

[438] *HC Trading Malta Ltd v Tradeland Commodities SL* [2016] EWHC 1279 (Comm), [2016] 1 W.L.R. 3120 at [16]–[20], [40].

[439] s.32(1).

[440] *Azov Shipping Co v Baltic Shipping Co* [1999] 2 Lloyd's Rep. 159, 161. cf. Aeberli (2005) 21 *Arbitration International* 253, 273. An application cannot be made after the arbitrator has made his award: *Five Oceans Salvage Ltd v Wenzhou Timber Group Co* [2011] EWHC 3282 (Comm), [2012] 1 Lloyd's Rep. 289.

[441] DAC Report para.147. Yet the court has power to determine, without restriction, the same issue upon an application for a stay: see above, para.32-068.

[442] s.32(2); *Belgravia Property Co Ltd v S & R (London) Ltd* [2001] B.L.R. 424; *Esso Exploration & Production UK Ltd v Electricity Supply Board* [2004] EWHC 723 (Comm), [2004] 1 All E.R. (Comm) 926; *Film Finance Inc v Royal Bank of Scotland* [2007] EWHC 195 (Comm), [2007] 1 Lloyd's Rep. 382; *Viscous Global Investment Ltd v Palladium Navigation Corp* [2014] EWHC 2654 (Comm), [2014] 2 Lloyd's Rep. 600; *Toyota Tsusho Sugar Trading Ltd v Prolat SRL* [2014] EWHC 3649 (Comm), [2015] 1 Lloyd's Rep. 344. Unless made with the agreement of the parties, the application must also state the grounds on which it is said that the matter should be decided by the court: s.32(3). See *ABB Lummus Global Ltd v Keppel Fels Ltd* [1999] 2 Lloyd's Rep. 24; *Azov Shipping Co v Baltic Shipping Co*, above, at [161]; PD 62.9.

[443] s.32(4). See (1998) 64 *Arbitration* 188.

less the court gives permission, no appeal lies from a decision of the court whether the conditions referred to above have been met.[444] So far as the decision of the court on the question of jurisdiction is concerned, this is treated as a judgment of the court for the purposes of an appeal. But no appeal lies without the permission of the court which will not be given unless the court considers that the question involves a point of law which is one of general importance or is one which for some other special reason should be considered by the Court of Appeal.[445] It would appear that no appeal lies against a refusal to give permission. Section 32 is mandatory.[446]

7. THE ARBITRAL PROCEEDINGS

Conduct of the reference   Section 33 of the 1996 Act sets out the general duty   **32-106**
of the arbitral tribunal in the conduct of the reference. The tribunal is to act fairly and impartially as between the parties, giving each party a reasonable opportunity of putting his case and dealing with that of his opponent,[447] and is to adopt procedures suitable to the circumstances of the particular case, avoiding unnecessary delay or expense, so as to provide a fair means for the resolution of the matters falling to be determined.[448] The tribunal must comply with this general duty in conducting the arbitral proceedings, in its decisions on matters of procedure and evidence and in the exercise of all other powers conferred upon it.[449] This is a mandatory provision.[450] Subject to the overriding requirements of fairness, impartiality and even-handedness, it is intended to encourage the tribunal to adapt its procedures to suit the particular case and not slavishly to follow court or other set procedures if these are inappropriate.[451]

The generality of the wording of s.33 might, nevertheless, be thought likely to   **32-107**
tempt unsuccessful parties to challenge procedural decisions taken by the tribunal, or the award, on the ground that the tribunal has failed to observe one or more of the duties stipulated by the section, especially since the Departmental Advisory Committee suggested that a proceeding which departed from those duties could not "properly be described as an arbitration".[452] However, the sanctions for breach of duty are narrowly circumscribed. They are, first, that the court should remove the arbitrator under s.24 (but this is subject to the limitations imposed by that section)[453]; secondly, that the court should remit, set aside or invalidate the award under s.68 on the ground of "serious irregularity". But an irregularity is only "serious" if the court considers that it has caused or will cause substantial injustice to the

---

[444]   s.32(5).

[445]   s.32(6); but see para.32-185, below.

[446]   s.4(1) and Sch.1.

[447]   s.33(1)(a). In *Reliance Industries Ltd v Union of India* [2018] EWHC 822 (Comm), [2018] 1 Lloyd's Rep. 562 at [25] it was held that the requirement in the UNCITRAL Rules, art.15(1), that each party should have a "full" opportunity of presenting its case, rather than a "reasonable" opportunity as required by s.33(1)(a), did not impose a higher burden on the arbitral tribunal. It was observed that the different wording was introduced in s.33(1)(a) by the DAC (para.165) because the word "full" might have reflected a difference in timing.

[448]   s.33(1)(b).

[449]   s.33(2).

[450]   s.4(1) and Sch.1.

[451]   DAC Report para.151; *Margulead v Exide Technologies* [2004] EWHC 1019 (Comm), [2005] 1 Lloyd's Rep. 324 (claimant not allowed last word).

[452]   DAC Report para.150.

[453]   See above, para.32-096.

applicant.[454] Experience has shown that the courts will not uphold challenges based on breaches of s.33 which are insubstantial.[455]

32-108 **Procedural and evidential matters** The arbitral tribunal has a general power to control the manner in which proceedings are conducted. Section 34(1) of the 1996 Act makes this clear by providing that it is for the tribunal to decide all procedural and evidential matters, subject to the right of the parties to agree any matter. There could be a potential conflict between the mandatory duty of the tribunal under s.33 and the principle of party autonomy contained in s.34,[456] for example, if the parties agreed to adopt a procedure, e.g. extended disclosure, which involved unnecessary delay or expense contrary to s.33(1)(b). But such a conflict is likely to be more theoretical than real. In practice, the parties will be free to agree on any procedural or evidential matter, for example, by agreeing to apply the procedural rules of a particular arbitral institution. In the absence of any effective agreement between the parties in respect of such a matter, the tribunal decides how best to proceed in the circumstances of the case.[457]

32-109 Section 34(2) gives an illustrative and non-exhaustive list of the procedural and evidential matters referred to. These include:

    (a) "when and where any part of the proceedings is to be held"—so empowering the tribunal to decide, for example, when meetings are to be held, or that meetings are to be held elsewhere than at the seat of arbitration[458];

    (b) "the language or languages to be used in the proceedings and whether translations of any relevant documents are to be supplied"[459];

    (c) "whether any and if so what form of written statements of claim and defences are to be used, when these should be supplied and the extent to which such statements can be later amended"—so empowering the tribunal to determine the form of pleadings (if any), whether to order particulars, and to allow and disallow amendments[460];

    (d) "whether any and if so which documents or classes of documents should be disclosed between and produced by the parties and at what stage"—so empowering the tribunal to apply or depart from the rules relating to disclosure and inspection applied in court proceedings[461];

    (e) "whether any and if so what questions should be put to and answered by the respective parties and when and in what form this should be done"—so empowering the tribunal to control the oral and written questioning of the parties[462];

    (f) "whether to apply strict rules of evidence (or any other rules) as to the admissibility, relevance or weight of any material (oral, written or other) sought to be tendered on any matters of fact or opinion, and the time, manner and form in which such material should be exchanged and presented"—so empowering the tribunal to dispense with technical rules of

---

[454] See below, para.32-164.
[455] See below, paras 32-162—32-165, and DAC Report para.151.
[456] cf. DAC Report paras 154–163. See also DAC Report para.175 (s.40).
[457] For international arbitrations, see the IBA Evidence Rules 2010.
[458] See Hunter (1997) 13 *Arbitration International* 345 at 347.
[459] (1997) 13 *Arbitration International* 345 at 347.
[460] (1997) 13 *Arbitration International* 345 at 349.
[461] (1997) 13 *Arbitration International* 345.
[462] (1997) 13 *Arbitration International* 345 at 350.

evidence and, as an incidental result, to put an end to any arguments that it is a question of law whether there is material to support a finding of fact[463];

(g) "whether and to what extent the tribunal should itself take the initiative in ascertaining the facts and the law"—so empowering the tribunal to discard the rules applicable to an adversarial procedure and adopt an inquisitorial approach, by, for example, itself procuring evidence[464];

(h) "whether and to what extent there should be oral or written evidence or submissions"—so, for example, allowing the tribunal to decide the case on the basis of documents only or to render an award after a very short oral hearing.[465]

Subsection (3) of s.34 further allows the tribunal to fix time limits for any directions it gives and to extend time limits fixed.[466] It can fix the dates of hearings and does not necessarily act unfairly if it refuses an adjournment requested by one of the parties.[467] The tribunal has the power to change its mind about any order made (though it is not desirable for it to do so) and to revise or reverse an earlier decision.[468]

Consolidation of proceedings and concurrent hearings   The parties are free to **32-110** agree that their arbitral proceedings are to be consolidated with others or that concurrent hearings shall be held.[469] But all parties to all such proceedings must so agree. Unless the parties agree to confer such power on the tribunal, for example, by adopting forms of contract[470] or institutional rules which provide for consolidation or concurrent hearings,[471] neither the arbitral tribunal nor the court has that power.[472] This can constitute a considerable drawback to arbitration as a method of dispute resolution where a number of parties are involved, particularly in relation to construction and engineering projects.[473] But it seems to follow inevitably from the fact that, unless the parties otherwise agree, only their own disputes arising out

---

463 (1997) 13 *Arbitration International* 345 at 351.
464 (1997) 13 *Arbitration International* 345 at 354 (subject to allowing the parties to comment on the evidence).
465 (1997) 13 *Arbitration International* 345 at 357; *O'Donoghue v Enterprise Inns Plc* [2008] EWHC 815.
466 (1997) 13 *Arbitration International* 345.
467 *Konkola Copper Mines Plc v U&M Mining Zambia Ltd* [2014] EWHC 2374 (Comm), [2014] 2 Lloyd's Rep. 649 ("show cause" order).
468 *Charles McWillie & Co (Shipping) Ltd v Ocean Laser Shipping Ltd* [1999] 1 Lloyd's Rep. 225, 248.
469 s.35(1). See *Chartered Institute of Arbitrators: Guidelines for Arbitrators on how to approach issues relating to multi-party arbitrations*.
470 See *Redland Aggregates Ltd v Shepherd Hill Civil Engineering Ltd* [2002] 1 W.L.R. 1621 HL (FCEC Standard Form of Subcontract); *Dredging and Construction Ltd v Delta Civil Engineering Ltd* [2002] C.L.C. 213 (FCEC form of contract); *Belgravia Property Co Ltd v S & R (London) Ltd* [2001] B.L.R. 424 (JCT form of contract); *City and General (Holborn) Ltd v AYH Plc* [2006] B.L.R. 55 (JCT form of contract).
471 e.g. CIArb Rules art.73. See Knowles (1996) 62 *Arbitration* 191; Hanotiau (1998) 14 *Arbitration International* 369; Hardy (2000) 66 *Arbitration* 15; Platte (2002) 18 *Arbitration International* 67; Dillon and Limbert (2006) 9 Int. A.L. Rev. 53; Cremades and Madalena (2008) 24 *Arbitration International* 507.
472 s.35(2).
473 There may also be difficulties in the case of "string" or "back-to-back" contracts in other spheres. See also *Sacor Maritima SA v Repsol Petroleo SA* [1998] 1 Lloyd's Rep. 518; and *Aquator Shipping Ltd v Kleimar NV* [1998] 2 Lloyd's Rep. 379 (head charter and sub-charter).

of their own agreement can be referred to the agreed tribunal.[474] A fortiori there is no power in the tribunal or in the court to order that a person who has never agreed to arbitration should be joined as a party to the proceedings. However, a party who has never agreed to arbitration, but who seeks to enforce a substantive right conferred on him by the Contracts (Rights of Third Parties) Act 1999 will be treated as a party to an arbitration agreement to which the term conferring the right is subject.[475]

32-111   **Legal or other representation**   A party to arbitral proceedings may be represented in the proceedings by a lawyer or other person chosen by him.[476] This right is conferred by s.36 of the 1996 Act, but the parties are free to agree otherwise and the rules of some arbitral institutions preclude legal representation at first-tier hearings. The section does not entitle a party to insist that he be represented by a particular person and to delay the proceedings on the ground of the non-availability of that person.[477]

32-112   **Power to appoint experts, etc**[478]   The arbitral tribunal is empowered to appoint experts or legal advisers to report to it and the parties, or to appoint assessors to assist it on technical matters, and it may allow such persons to attend the proceedings.[479] The parties must be given a reasonable opportunity to comment on any information, opinion or advice offered by them.[480] This power does not require the positive agreement of the parties, but the parties may otherwise agree and it is in any event subject to the general duty of the tribunal set out in s.33. The fees and expenses of an expert, etc. appointed by the tribunal for which the arbitrators are liable are expenses of the arbitrators for which (assuming they are reasonable) the parties are jointly and severally liable.[481]

32-113   **General powers exercisable by tribunal**   One of the major objectives of the 1996 Act was to enlarge the powers of the arbitral tribunal in the conduct of the reference and to reduce the occasions on which a party would have to apply to the court to intervene in the proceedings. Section 38 of the Act provides that the parties are free to agree on the powers exercisable by the tribunal for the purposes of and in relation to the proceedings.[482] But it then sets out a number of powers which the tribunal has unless otherwise agreed.[483]

32-114   **Security for costs**   Subsection (3) empowers the tribunal to order a claimant to provide security for the costs of the arbitration.[484] This was a major change from the previous law where only the court could order security for costs. The power is

---

[474] DAC Report para.179. See also above, para.32-050 (confidentiality).

[475] See above, para.32-044.

[476] s.36. See *IBA Guidelines on Party Representation in International Arbitration* 2013; *Piper Double Glazing Ltd v DC Contracts* [1994] 1 All E.R. 177 (costs incurred by unqualified person).

[477] DAC Report para.184.

[478] See the Chartered Institute of Arbitrators: Guidelines on the use of tribunal appointed experts, legal advisers and assessors: 70 *Arbitration* 45–50.

[479] s.37(1)(a).

[480] s.37(1)(b); *Hussman (Europe) Ltd v Al Ameen Development and Trade Co* [2002] 2 Lloyd's Rep. 83, 94.

[481] s.37(2). See also s.28; above, para.32-099. This is a mandatory provision.

[482] s.38(1).

[483] s.38(2).

[484] See Chartered Institute of Arbitrators: Guideline on Security for Costs.

no longer vested in the court[485] but only in the tribunal. It is discretionary, as is the power conferred upon the court by the provisions of the CPR dealing with security for costs. But it does not seem that the tribunal is bound to exercise its discretion in the same manner as the court under the CPR[486] and, indeed, in contrast to the CPR, it is expressly provided that the residence or incorporation of the claimant outside the United Kingdom is not to be a ground for the exercise of the power.[487] When the power was vested in the court it was held that, where an arbitration takes place in England under the rules of the International Chamber of Commerce, an order should not ordinarily be made that the claimant give security for costs.[488] The mere fact, however, that an arbitration was international did not render inappropriate an order for security, especially if the arbitration was of a type regularly conducted in London and the contract was governed by English law.[489]

Other directions   The section[490] also empowers the tribunal to give directions in relation to property which is the subject of the proceedings owned by or in the possession of a party,[491] to direct that a party or witness shall be examined on oath or affirmation[492] and to give directions to a party for the preservation of any evidence in his custody or control.[493]

32-115

Provisional relief with agreement of parties   An arbitral tribunal is entitled under s.47 of the 1996 Act to make interim awards or awards on different issues in the course of the proceedings. Such awards, however, are to be distinguished from orders for provisional relief, for example, a provisional order for the payment of money[494] which is subject to reversal or adjustment when a decision has been reached on the underlying merits of the dispute. Section 39 provides that the parties are free to agree that the tribunal shall have power to order on a provisional basis any relief which it would have power to grant in a final award.[495] But, unless the parties agree to confer such a power on the tribunal, it has no such power.[496] Conferment of the power to order conservatory measures, for example, or to grant interim injunctive relief, will sometimes be found in institutional rules adopted by the parties in the arbitration agreement and so be available to the tribunal.[497]

32-116

Duties of parties   Section 40 of the 1996 Act imposes a general duty on the par-

32-117

---

485   But see s.70(6); below, para.32-178.
486   CPR 25.13. See (1997) 63 *Arbitration* 166 (guidelines); Reid (2002) 152 N.L.J. 1426; Altaras (2002) 69 *Arbitration* 81; (2007) 73 *Arbitration* 191; De Battista (2010) 76 *Arbitration* 421.
487   s.38(3).
488   *Bank Mellat v Helliniki Techniki SA* [1984] Q.B. 291. But contrast *SA Coppée Lavalin NV v Ken-Ren Chemicals and Fertilisers Ltd* [1995] 1 A.C. 38.
489   *K/S A/S Bani v Korea Shipbuilding and Engineering Corp* [1987] 2 Lloyd's Rep. 445; *Flender Werft AG v Aegean Maritime Ltd* [1990] 2 Lloyd's Rep. 27, 29; *Regia Autonoma de Electricitate Revel v Gulf Petroleum International Ltd* [1996] 1 Lloyd's Rep. 67.
490   s.38(4). See (1998) 64 *Arbitration* 84 (guidelines), 180; Oyre (1999) 65 *Arbitration* 113 (interim relief); CPR r.25.1; *Emmot v Michael Wilson & Partners Ltd (No.2)* [2009] EWHC 1 (Comm), [2009] 1 Lloyd's Rep. 233 at [63].
491   Under s.12(6)(g) of the Arbitration Act 1950, this power was previously reserved to the court.
492   This confirms s.12(1)–(3) of the 1950 Act.
493   Under s.12(6)(e), (g) of the 1950 Act, this power was previously reserved to the court.
494   s.39(2)(a).
495   s.39(1); cf. *Kastner v Jason* [2004] EWCA Civ 1599, [2005] 1 Lloyd's Rep. 397 at [14]–[19] (freezing order). See also s.39(3) (to be taken into account in the final award); and CPR Pt 25.
496   s.39(4).
497   Thomas (1997) 13 *Arbitration International* 405; (1998) 64 *Arbitration* 17 (guidelines).

ties to do all things necessary for the expeditious conduct of the arbitral proceedings. This includes prompt compliance with decisions, orders and directions of the arbitral tribunal and taking promptly any steps to obtain a decision of the court on a preliminary question of jurisdiction or law.[498] Section 40 is a mandatory provision.[499] It does not, however, create duties which are owed by the parties as implied terms of the arbitration agreement the breach of which has contractual consequences (e.g. repudiation of the agreement), nor does the 1996 Act give the court any express power to intervene with breaches of the duties imposed by the section, the remedies for such breaches being set out in ss.41, 42.[500]

32-118 Default It is open to the parties to agree what shall be the powers of the tribunal in the event of a party's failure to do something necessary for the proper and expeditious conduct of the arbitration.[501] The rules of arbitral institutions often contain provisions which empower the tribunal to take action in cases of default. But, unless otherwise agreed, s.41 of the 1996 Act confers upon the tribunal certain specific powers which may be exercised in case of a party's default.[502]

32-119 Want of prosecution An arbitrator has, at common law, no inherent power to dismiss a claim for want of prosecution,[503] nor had the court power to do so under the 1950 Act or otherwise.[504] However, subs.(3) of s.41 re-enacts[505] s.13A of the 1950 Act and enables the arbitral tribunal to make an award dismissing a claim on the ground of want of prosecution.[506] Unless otherwise agreed by the parties,[507] the conditions which must be satisfied for the making of such an award reflect the case law at the date of the Act[508] relating to the powers of a court to dismiss an action for want of prosecution. These conditions are that there has been inordinate and inexcusable delay on the part of the claimant in pursuing his claim and that the delay (a) gives rise, or is likely to give rise, to a substantial risk that it is not possible to have a fair resolution of the issues in that claim; or (b) has caused, or is likely to cause, serious prejudice to the respondent.[509] It is, however, an error of law for an

---

[498] ss.32, 45; above, para.32-104; below, para.32-126.

[499] s.4(1) and Sch.1. For a possible conflict with s.34(1), see DAC Report para.175.

[500] *Elektrim SA v Vivendi Universal SA* [2007] EWHC 11 (Comm), [2007] 1 Lloyd's Rep. 693 at [123]–[131].

[501] s.41(1).

[502] s.41(2).

[503] *Bremer Vulkan Schiffbau und Maschinenfabrik v South India Shipping Corp Ltd* [1981] A.C. 909.

[504] *Bremer Vulkan Schiffbau und Maschinenfabrik v South India Shipping Corp Ltd* [1981] A.C. 909.

[505] But with slight changes of language in s.41(3)(a).

[506] *Birkett v James* [1978] A.C. 297; *Department of Transport v Chris Smaller (Transport) Ltd* [1989] A.C. 1197; *L'Office Cherifien des Phosphates v Yamashita—Shinnihon Steamship Co* [1994] 1 A.C. 486. See also *Trill v Sacher* [1993] 1 W.L.R. 1379; *Roebuck v Mungovin* [1994] 2 A.C. 224; Davies (1997) 63 *Arbitration* 286; Chartered Institute of Arbitrators: Guidelines for Arbitrators on Proceeding and Making Awards in Default of Party Participation (2011).

[507] *Al Hadha Trading Co v Tradigrain SA* [2002] 2 Lloyd's Rep. 512, 522 (GAFTA arbitration).

[508] See the changes to case management subsequently brought about by the Civil Procedure Rules: *Securum Finance Ltd v Ashton* [2001] Ch. 291.

[509] *TAG Wealth Management v West* [2008] EWHC 1466 (Comm), [2008] 2 Lloyd's Rep. 699. However, if the parties have contracted for a shorter limitation period, the arbitral tribunal can exercise this power before the expiry of the limitation period under the Limitation Act 1980: *Dera Commercial Estate v Derya Inc* [2018] EWHC 1673 (Comm), [63]–[73].

arbitrator to dismiss a claim for want of prosecution before the expiration of the limitation period, save in exceptional circumstances.[510]

Absence of party or failure to submit evidence[511]   Subsection (4) of s.41 empowers the tribunal to proceed in the absence of a party at an oral hearing or if a party fails after due notice to submit written evidence or make written submissions.   **32-120**

Peremptory orders[512]   If without showing sufficient cause a party fails to comply with any order or directions of the arbitral tribunal, the tribunal may make a peremptory order to the same effect as the preceding order which was not complied with, prescribing a time limit for compliance.[513] It is advisable that any such order should expressly state that it is peremptory, the time limit for compliance and the intended sanction to be imposed. Subsections (6) and (7) of s.41 set out the various powers of the tribunal in the event of non-compliance by a party with that peremptory order.[514] These are that the tribunal may: exclude allegations or material which was the subject matter of the order[515]; draw adverse inferences from the non-compliance[516]; proceed to an award on the basis of the materials provided to the tribunal[517]; and make an order as to the costs of the arbitration incurred as a result of the non-compliance.[518] But the powers conferred do not include a power simply to make an award against the defaulting party. They do, however, include, in the case of non-compliance with a peremptory order to provide security for costs, the power to make an award dismissing the claim.[519]   **32-121**

Powers are also conferred upon the court by s.42 to enforce a peremptory order of the tribunal.[520] But this is envisaged to be a last resort.[521] An application to the court can only be made where the parties have so agreed or the tribunal permits a party to apply or makes the application itself.[522] The court must also be satisfied that there has been a default in complying with the peremptory order within the time prescribed in the order (or, if no time was prescribed, within a reasonable time)[523] and that the applicant has exhausted any available arbitral process in respect of   **32-122**

---

[510] *James Lazenby & Co v McNicholas Construction Co Ltd* [1995] 1 W.L.R. 615. But see *Securum Finance Ltd v Ashton*, above.

[511] See Chartered Institute of Arbitrators: Guidelines for Arbitrators on Proceeding and Making Awards in Default of Party Participation (2011).

[512] See Chartered Institute of Arbitrators: Guidelines for Arbitrators on how to approach an application for a Peremptory and "Unless" Orders and related matters.

[513] s.41(5); *Emmott v Michael Wilson & Partners Ltd (No.2)* [2009] EWHC 1 (Comm). [2009] 1 Lloyd's Rep. 233.

[514] There is no obligation on the arbitral tribunal to exercise these powers: *Enterprise Insurance Co Plc v U-Drive Solutions (Gibraltar) Ltd* [2016] EWHC 1301 (QB) at [47]–[59].

[515] s.41(7)(a).

[516] s.41(7)(b).

[517] s.41(7)(c).

[518] s.41(7)(d).

[519] s.41(6).

[520] Unless otherwise agreed by the parties: s.42(1); *Pearl Petroleum Co Ltd v Kurdistan Regional Government of Iraq* [2015] EWHC 3361 (Comm), [2016] 4 W.L.R. 2 at [17]–[27]. See also Sch.2 para.4 (exercise of powers by judge-arbitrator and the Scheme for Construction Contracts (England and Wales) Regulations 1998 (SI 1998/649); *Macob Civil Engineering Ltd v Morrison Construction Ltd* [1999] Build. L.R. 93; para.32-199, below.

[521] DAC Report para.212.

[522] s.42(2).

[523] s.42(4).

failure to comply with the order.[524] The power of the court is discretionary but the court is not required in every case to satisfy itself that the case is a proper one for the order which is sought by reviewing the decision made by the tribunal and considering whether the tribunal ought to have made the order in question.[525] There may, however, be circumstances where the court might decide not to make the order.[526]

8. POWERS OF THE COURT

32-123 **Court powers in support of arbitral proceedings** There is no inherent jurisdiction in the court to supervise arbitrations.[527] But the aid of the court may be invoked to assist the arbitral process. Section 43 of the 1996 Act[528] provides that a party to arbitral proceedings may use the same court procedures as are available in relation to legal proceedings[529] to secure the attendance before the tribunal of a witness in order to give oral testimony or to produce documents or other material evidence, i.e. to obtain a witness summons.[530] But this may only be done with the permission of the tribunal or the agreement of the other parties.[531] Moreover, these particular court procedures may only be used if the witness is in the United Kingdom and the arbitral proceedings are being conducted in England.[532]

32-124 Section 44 of the Act also confers upon the court, unless otherwise agreed between the parties,[533] the same powers on certain matters in relation to arbitral

---

[524] s.42(3). See also CPR Pt 62 PD 62. The permission of the court is required for any appeal from a decision of the court under this section: s.42(5); but see below, para.32-185.

[525] *Emmott v Michael Wilson & Partners Ltd (No.2)* [2009] EWHC 1 (Comm), [2009] 1 Lloyd's Rep. 233 at [59].

[526] See *Emmott v Michael Wilson & Partners Ltd (No.2)*, above, where Teare J. identified a number of such circumstances at [59]–[64]. cf. *Patley Wood Farm LLP v Brake & Brake* [2013] EWHC 4035 (Ch) at [52]. See Dundas (2013) 80 *Arbitration* (2) 196.

[527] *Exormisis Shipping SA v Oonsoo* [1975] 1 Lloyd's Rep. 432, 434; *Bremer Vulkan Schiffbau und Maschinenfabrik v South India Shipping Corp Ltd* [1981] A.C. 909, 979; *K/S A/S Bill Biakh v Hyundai Corp* [1988] 1 Lloyd's Rep. 187, 189; *Kirkawa Corp v Gatoil Overseas Inc* [1990] 1 Lloyd's Rep. 154, 157; *Charles McWillie & Co (Shipping) Ltd v Ocean Laser Shipping Ltd* [1999] 1 Lloyd's Rep. 225, 248. cf. *Japan Line Ltd v Aggeliki Charis Compañía Maritima SA* [1980] 1 Lloyd's Rep. 288, 292.

[528] s.43(1). Section 43 derives from s.12(4) and (5) of the Arbitration Act 1950. It is mandatory. See also Sch.2 para.4 (exercise of power by judge-arbitrator).

[529] CPR Pt 62 PD 62.

[530] For the need to identify the documents, see *Assimina Maritime Ltd v Pakistan Shipping Corp* [2004] EWHC 3005 (Comm), [2005] 1 Lloyd's Rep. 525; *Tajik Aluminium Plant v Hydro Aluminium AS* [2005] EWCA Civ 1218, [2006] 1 Lloyd's Rep. 155 (witness summons requiring production of documents); *Silver Dry Bulk Co Ltd v Homer Hulbert Maritime Co Ltd* [2017] EWHC 44 (Comm), [2017] 1 Lloyd's Rep. 154 at [39]–[46] (witness summons for production of documents). But see previous case and *BNP Paribas v Deloitte and Touche LLP* [2003] EWHC 2874 (Comm), [2004] 1 Lloyd's Rep. 233 (no power to order disclosure by non-party); *EDO Corp v Ultra Electronics Ltd* [2009] EWHC 682 (Ch), [2009] 2 Lloyd's Rep. 349 (no power to order pre-action disclosure).

[531] s.43(2).

[532] s.43(3), i.e. England and Wales, or (as the case may be) Northern Ireland.

[533] The arbitration clause may, on its true construction, exclude the power of the court to grant ancillary relief (*Mantovani v Carapelli* [1980] 1 Lloyd's Rep. 375), though such a construction will be rare: see *The Lisboa* [1980] 2 Lloyd's Rep. 546; *Petronin SA v Sechav Marine Ltd* [1995] 1 Lloyd's Rep. 603, 613; *Ultisol Transport Contractors Ltd v Bouygues Offshore SA (No.1)* [1996] 2 Lloyd's Rep. 140, 144, reversed on other grounds [1998] 2 Lloyd's Rep. 461; *Re Qs Estate* [1999] 1 Lloyd's Rep. 931; *SAB Miller Africa BV v East African Breweries Ltd* [2009] EWCA Civ 1564, [2010] 2 Lloyd's Rep. 422 at [8]. But see *B v S* [2011] EWHC 691, [2011] 2 Lloyd's Rep. 18 (FOSFA

proceedings as it has in relation to legal proceedings.[534] These are: the taking and preservation of evidence, making orders in relation to property, the sale of any goods, and the granting of an interim injunction or the appointment of a receiver.[535] However, these powers may only be used when the tribunal or arbitral institution is unable to act or to act effectively.[536] This limitation is entirely consistent with one of the aims of the Act, which is to restrict the power of the court to intervene in the

conditions).

[534] s.44(1). *Hiscox Underwriting Ltd v Dickson Manchester & Co Ltd* [2004] EWHC 479, [2004] 2 Lloyd's Rep. 438 (interim order for disclosure); *Assimina Maritime Ltd v Pakistan Shipping Corp* [2004] EWHC 3005 (Comm), [2005] 1 Lloyd's Rep. 525 (no power to order disclosure by non-party but power to order preservation of documents by non-party); *Lauritzencool AB v Lady Navigation Inc* [2005] EWCA Civ 579, [2005] 2 Lloyd's Rep. 63 (interim injunction restraining activity outside the contract pending arbitration); *Cetelem SA v Roust Holdings Ltd* [2005] EWCA Civ 618, [2005] 2 Lloyd's Rep. 494 (injunction to deliver contractual documentation before arbitration commenced); *SAB Miller Africa BV v East African Breweries Ltd* [2009] EWCA Civ 1564, [2010] 2 Lloyd's Rep. 442 (injunction to restrain breach of contract pending establishment of tribunal). See also s.44(6) Sch.2 para.4 (exercise of power by judge–arbitrator) and CPR Pt 62 PD 62. The permission of the court is required for any appeal under s.44: s.44(7) (but see below, para.32-185); *SAB Miller Africa BV v East African Breweries Ltd* 2009] EWCA Civ 1564, [2010] 2 Lloyd's Rep. 422.

[535] s.44(2). See Thomas (1997) 13 *Arbitration International* 105. cf. *Tsakos Shipping & Trading SA v Orizon Tanker Co Ltd* [1998] C.L.C. 1003 (order for inspection and tests set aside); *Commerce and Industry Co of Canada v Certain Underwriters of Lloyd's of London* [2002] 1 W.L.R. 1323 (application for examination of witnesses to provide depositions in New York arbitration refused); *Econet Wireless Ltd v Vee Networks Ltd* [2006] EWHC 1568 (Comm), [2006] 2 Lloyd's Rep. 428 (application for injunction to restrain sale of shares refused); *Permasteelisa Japan KK v Bouyguesstroi* [2007] EWHC 3508 (TCC) (application for injunction to restrain calls on performance bonds refused); *Travelers Insurance Co Ltd v Countrywide Surveyors Ltd* [2010] EWHC 2455 (TCC), [2011] 1 All E.R. (Comm) 631 (order for pre-action disclosure refused); *Silver Dry Bulk Co Ltd v Homer Hulbert Maritime Co Ltd* [2017] EWHC 44 (Comm), [2017] 1 Lloyd's Rep. 154 at [47]–[53] (order for letters of request to a foreign court refused); *Dainford Navigation Inc v PDVSA Petroleo SA* [2017] EWHC 2150 (Comm), [2017] 2 Lloyd's Rep 409 (order for sale of goods the subject of the proceedings). For the power of the court under s.37 of the Senior Courts Act 1981 to intervene outside the 1996 Act, see *Hiscox Underwriting Ltd v Dickson Manchester & Co*, above; *Cetelem SA v Roust Holdings Ltd*, above, at [74]; *Weissfisch v Julius* [2006] EWCA Civ 218, [2006] 1 Lloyd's Rep. 716 at [33]; *Elektrim SA v Vivendi Universal SA (No.2)* [2007] EWHC 571 (Comm), [2007] 2 Lloyd's Rep. 8; *Starlight Shipping Co v Tai P ng Insurance Co Ltd* [2007] EWHC 1893 (Comm), [2008] 1 Lloyd's Rep. 230; *Republic of Kazakhstan v Istil Group Inc (No.2)* [2007] EWHC 2729 (Comm), [2008] 1 Lloyd's Rep. 382; *Sheffield United Football Club Ltd v West Ham United Football Club Plc* [2008] EWHC 2855 (Comm), [2009] 1 Lloyd's Rep. 167 at [31]–[32]; *British Telecommunications Plc v SAE Group Inc* [2009] EWHC 252 (TCC), [2009] B.L.R. 231 (CPR Pt 8); *SAB Miller Africa BV v East African Breweries Ltd* [2009] EWCA Civ 1564, [2010] 2 Lloyd's Rep. 422; *REC Wafer Norway AS v Moser Baer Photo Voltaic Ltd* [2010] EWHC 2581 (Comm), [2011] 1 Lloyd's Rep. 410; *Enercon GmbH v Enercon (India) Ltd* [2012] EWHC 689 (Comm), [2012] 1 Lloyd's Rep. 519 at [68]; *AES Ust-Kamenogorsk Hydropower Plant LLP v Ust-Kamenogorsk Hydropower Plant JSC* [2013] UKSC 35, [2013] 1 W.L.R. 1889 at [48]; *Barnwell Enterprises Ltd v ECP Africa FII Investments LLC* [2013] EWHC 2517 (Comm), [2014] 1 Lloyd's Rep. 171. See also in relation to s.33(2) of the 1981 Act: *Travelers Insurance Co Ltd v Countrywide Surveyors Ltd* [2010] EWHC 2455 (TCC), [2011] 1 All E.R. (Comm) 631; *Mi-Space (UK) Ltd v Lend Lease Construction (EMEA) Ltd* [2013] EWHC 2001 (TCC), [2013] B.L.R. 600. For the power of the court under s.25(3) of the Civil Jurisdiction and Judgments Act 1982 and the restraints imposed by the ICSID Convention and sovereign immunity, see *ETI Euro Telecom International NV v Republic of Bolivia* [2008] EWCA Civ 800, [2008] 2 Lloyd's Rep. 421.

[536] s.44(5); *Pacific Maritime Asia Ltd v Holystone Overseas Ltd* [2007] EWHC 2319 (Comm), [2008] 1 Lloyd's Rep. 371 (arbitrator's order would not be sufficiently effective); *Hiscox Underwriting Ltd v Dickson Manchester & Co Ltd*, above (arbitrator newly appointed and unfamiliar with case and so, in effect, unable to act). Contrast *Econet Wireless Ltd v Vee Networks Ltd*, above (England not appropriate forum); *Patley Wood Farm LLP v Brake and Brake* [2014] EWHC 4192 (Ch) (arbitrator's directions not workable). See also *Sheffield United Football Club Ltd v West Ham United*

arbitral process. Exercise of the power should not usurp the function of the arbitrators.[537] If the case is one of urgency, the court may, on the application of a party or proposed party to the arbitral proceedings, make such orders as it considers necessary for the purpose of preserving evidence or assets,[538] for instance, it may make a search order or grant a freezing injunction.[539] It may also grant an anti-suit injunction[540] as the right to have disputes referred to arbitration is an "asset".[541] But if the case is not one of urgency or if the order sought is not necessary for the purpose of preserving evidence or assets,[542] then the court can act only upon an application of a party to the arbitral proceedings made with the permission of the tribunal or the agreement in writing of the other parties.[543] It has been held that orders under s.44 cannot be made against non-parties to the arbitration agreement.[544]

32-125   The powers of the court under ss.43 and 44 may be exercised even if the seat of the arbitration is outside England or no seat has been designated or determined, but the court may refuse to exercise any such power if, in its opinion, the fact that the seat is outside England, or that when designated or determined the seat is likely to be outside England, makes it inappropriate to do so.[545]

32-126 Determination of preliminary point of law by the court   Section 2 of the

---

Football Club Ltd, above (actions likely to be taken by parties would lead to an identical impasse).

[537] *ZIM Integrated Shipping Services Ltd v European Containers ICS* [2013] EWHC 3581 (Comm).

[538] s.44(3); *Cetelem SA v Roust Holdings Ltd,* above; *National Insurance and Guarantee Group Ltd v M Young Legal Services Ltd* [2004] EWHC 2972 (QB), [2005] 2 Lloyd's Rep. 46; *Starlight Shipping Co v Tai Ping Insurance Co Ltd,* above; *Pacific Maritime Asia Ltd v Holystone Overseas Ltd,* above; *Sheffield United Football Club Ltd v West Ham United Football Club Ltd,* above; *BNP Paribas SA v Open Joint Stock Company Russian Machines* [2011] EWHC 308 (Comm), [2012] 1 Lloyd's Rep. 61 (even against non-party); *Euroil Ltd v Cameroon Offshore Petroleum SARL* [2014] EWHC 52 (Comm). See also *Telenor East Holdings II AS v Altumo Holdings and Investments Ltd* [2011] EWHC 735 (Comm) (on meaning of "necessary" in s.44(3)). Unless there is an existing or intended arbitration there is no "party or proposed party": *AES Ust-Kamenogorsk Hydropower Plant LLP v Ust-Kamenogorsk Hydropower Plant JSC* [2010] EWHC 772 (Comm), [2010] 2 Lloyd's Rep. 493 at [20] (affirmed [2011] EWCA Civ 647).

[539] *Re Q's Estate* [1999] 1 Lloyd's Rep. 931; *Cogentra AG v Sixteen Thirteen Marine SA* [2008] EWHC 1615 (Comm), [2008] 2 Lloyd's Rep. 602; *Emmott v Michael Wilson & Partners Ltd (No.2)* [2009] EWHC 1 (Comm), [2009] 1 Lloyd's Rep. 233 at [83].

[540] See para.32-053, above.

[541] *Cetelem SA v Roust Holdings Ltd,* above, at [57]; *Starlight Shipping Co v Tai Ping Insurance Co Ltd,* above at [21]; *Sheffield United Football Club Ltd v West Ham United Football Club Ltd,* above at [32]; *BNP Paribas SA v Open Joint Stock Company Russian Machines,* above.

[542] *Cetelem SA v Roust Holdings Ltd,* above, at [47]; *Mobil Cerro Negro Ltd v Petroleos Venezuela SA* [2008] EWHC 532, [2008] 1 Lloyd's Rep. 684; *Travelers Insurance Co Ltd v Countrywide Surveyors Ltd* [2010] EWHC 2455 (TCC), [2011] 1 All E.R. (Comm) 631. In *Cetelem SA v Roust Holdings Ltd,* above, it was stated that a contractual right or chose in action was an "asset" (at [57], [62]); *Euroil Ltd v Cameroon Offshore Petroleum SARL* [2014] EWHC 52 (Comm). But discretion to make an order is more likely to be exercised where the asset is a conventional asset: *ZIM Integrated Shipping Serves Ltd v European Containers ICS* [2013] EWHC 3581 (Com); *Euroil Ltd v Cameroon Offshore Petroleum SARL,* above, at [18]–[20].

[543] s.44(4); *Petroleum Investigation Co Ltd v Kantupan Holdings Co Ltd* [2002] 1 All E.R. (Comm) 124; *Assimina Maritime Ltd v Pakistan Shipping Corp,* above.

[544] *DTEK Trading SA v Morozov* [2017] EWHC 94 (Comm), [2017] 1 Lloyd's Rep. 126.

[545] s.2(3); *Mobil Cerro Negro Ltd v Petroleos Venezuela SA* [2008] EWHC 532, [2008] 1 Lloyd's Rep. 684 (but see s.43(3)). cf. *Channel Tunnel Group Ltd v Balfour Beatty Construction Ltd* [1993] A.C. 334; *Econet Wireless Ltd v Vee Networks Ltd,* above. The court has power to order "provisional, including protective measures" under art.35 of Regulation (EU) 1215/2012 (Brussels *bis*) even though the courts of another contracting state have jurisdiction as to the substance of the matter. cf. *Van Uden Maritime BV v Kommanditgesellschaft in Firma Decoline* (C-391/95) EU:C:1998:543; [1999] Q.B. 1225, ECJ.

Arbitration Act 1979 enabled a party to an arbitration to apply to the court to determine a question of law arising in the course of the reference. This "Consultative Case" procedure was useful in certain instances since it enabled a definitive answer to be obtained from the court at an early stage of the arbitral proceedings. Section 45 of the 1996 Act confers a similar power on the court to determine any question of law[546] arising in the course of the proceedings, but the court must be satisfied that the question of law substantially affects the rights of one or more of the parties.[547] Further, in order not to interfere unduly in the arbitral process, the conditions subject to which the court is empowered to consider such an application are also limited: the application must be made with the agreement of all the other parties to the proceedings or with the permission of the tribunal, and, in the latter case, the court must be satisfied that the determination of the question is likely to produce substantial savings in costs[548] and that the application is made without delay.[549] Unless otherwise agreed by the parties, the arbitral tribunal may continue the arbitral proceedings and make an award while an application to the court is pending.[550]

It is open to the parties, by agreement, to exclude the court's jurisdiction under this section[551] and an agreement to dispense with reasons for the tribunal's award is to be considered as such an exclusion agreement.[552]   **32-127**

No appeal lies to the Court of Appeal from a decision as to whether or not the conditions have been met to enable the court to consider the application unless the court gives permission to appeal.[553] The decision of the court on the question of law itself is to be treated as a judgment of the court for the purposes of an appeal. But no appeal to the Court of Appeal lies without the permission of the court, which is not to be given unless the court considers that the question is one of general public importance or is one which for some other special reason ought to be considered by the Court of Appeal.[554] It would appear that no appeal lies against a refusal of the court to give permission to appeal.   **32-128**

Power of court to extend time limits   Section 79 of the 1996 Act confers upon the court a general power to extend any time limit agreed by the parties or specified in any provision of Pt I of the Act having effect in default of such agreement[555] (with the exception of the time limit for beginning arbitral proceedings dealt   **32-129**

---

546 See (on s.2 of the 1950 Act) *Chapman v Charlwood Alliance Properties* (1981) 260 E.G. 1041.
547 s.45(1). See (on ss.1, 2 of the 1950 Act) *Manders (Property) Estates v Magnet House Properties* (1989) 42 E.G. 111; *Urban Small Space v Burford Investments Co* (1990) 28 E.G. 116. For the form of the application, see s.45(3) and PD 62.9.
548 *Secretary of State for Defence v Turner Estate Solutions Ltd* [2015] EWHC 1150 (TCC), [2015] Build. L.R. 448.
549 1996 Act s.45(2). See *Taylor Woodrow Holdings Ltd v Barnes & Elliott Ltd* [2006] EWHC 1693 (TCC), [2006] Build. L.R. 376 (court retains discretion even though parties agree).
550 s.45(4).
551 s.45(1). See also s.69(1) and below, para.32-168. In the case of a domestic arbitration agreement, s.87 provides that any such exclusion agreement must be made after the commencement of arbitral proceedings. But s.87 is unlikely to be brought into force: see above, para.32-005. The specific exceptions listed in s.4 of the Arbitration Act 1950 were not retained.
552 s.45(1).
553 s.45(5). But see below, para.32-185.
554 s.45(6).
555 s.79 does not apply to a time limit specified in Pt 1 of the Act but not in default of agreement between the parties: *Aoot Kalmneft v Glencore International AG* [2002] 1 Lloyd's Rep. 128, 135.

with in s.12)[556] but only after any available arbitral process has been exhausted and only if a substantial injustice would otherwise be done.[557] An application for an extension should be made as soon as reasonably possible after the party seeking relief ought to appreciate that it is required.[558]

32-130 **Anti-arbitration injunction** The court has power under s.72(1) of the Act[559] and under s.37 of the Senior Courts Act 1981[560] to restrain by injunction a party, or an arbitrator, from pursuing an arbitration.[561] But it has been said that "Part I of the Act contemplates that once matters are referred to arbitration it is the arbitral tribunal that will generally deal with issues of their jurisdiction and the procedure in the arbitration up to the date of the award"[562] and it is therefore seldom—save in exceptional cases—that any injunction will be granted.[563] An unsuccessful applica-

---

[556] See above, para.32-076.

[557] s.79(3); *Minermet SpA Milan v Luckyfield Shipping Corp SA* [2004] EWHC 729 (Comm), [2004] 2 Lloyd's Rep. 348; *Pirtek (UK) Ltd v Deanswood Ltd* [2005] EWHC 2301 (Comm), [2005] 2 Lloyd's Rep. 728 at [44], [46]; *Gold Coast Ltd v Naval Gijon SA* [2006] EWHC 1044 (Comm), [2006] 2 Lloyd's Rep. 400; *Rotenberg v Sucafina SA* [2011] EWHC 901 (Comm), [2011] 2 Lloyd's Rep. 159; *Xstrata Coal Queensland Pty Ltd v Benxi Iron & Steel (Group) International Economic & Trading Co Ltd* [2016] EWHC 2022 (Comm), [2017] 1 All E.R. (Comm) 299. The application may be made a party or by the arbitral tribunal: s.79(2), PD62. On the extent of this power, see s.79(4), (5). The permission of the court is required for any appeal from a decision of the court under this section: s.79(6); but see below, para.32-184.

[558] *Equatorial Traders Ltd v Louis Dreyfus Trading Ltd* [2002] 2 Lloyd's Rep. 638, 642.

[559] See below, para.32-157.

[560] See above, para.32-124, n.535.

[561] *Zaporozhyve Production Society v Ashly Ltd* [2002] EWHC 1410 (Comm); *Arab National Bank v El-Abdali* [2004] EWHC 238 (Comm), [2005] 1 Lloyd's Rep. 541; *Weissfisch v Julius* [2006] EWCA Civ 218, [2006] 1 Lloyd's Rep. 716; *Intermet FZCO v Ansol Ltd* [2007] EWHC 226 (Comm); *Elektrim SA v Vivendi Universal SA (No.2)* [2007] EWHC 571 (Comm), [2007] 2 Lloyd's Rep. 8; *Albon v Naza Motor Trading Sdn Berhad (No.4)* [2007] EWCA Civ 1124, [2008] 1 Lloyd's Rep. 1; *Republic of Kazakhstan v Istil Group Inc (No.2)* [2007] EWHC 2729 (Comm), [2008] 1 Lloyd's Rep. 382; *Excalibur Ventures LLC v Texas Keystone Inc* [2011] EWHC 1624 (Comm), [2011] 2 Lloyd's Rep. 289; *Golden Ocean Group Ltd v Humpuss Intermodal Transportasi TBK Ltd* [2013] EWHC 1240 (Comm), [2013] 2 All E.R. (Comm) 1025; Dunning (2008) 74 *Arbitration* 254. See also *British Telecommunications Plc v SAE Group Inc* [2009] EWHC 252 (TCC), [2009] B.L.R. 231 (declaration). The court has power to injunct arbitral proceedings taking place in another Member State of the European Union: *Claxton Engineering Services Ltd v TXM Olaj-es Gazkutato KFT* [2010] EWHC 345 (Comm), [2011] 1 Lloyd's Rep. 510 (but see [2011] EWCA Civ 410); Seriki (2013) 16 Int. A.L.R. 2, 43.

[562] *Elektrim SA v Vivendi Universal SA (No.2)*, above, at [70]. See also *Fiona Trust and Holding Corp v Privalov* [2007] EWCA Civ 20, [2007] 2 Lloyd's Rep. 267 at [40] (affirmed sub nom. *Premium Nafta Products Ltd v Fili Shipping Co Ltd* [2007] UKHL 40, [2008] 1 Lloyd's Rep. 254). Contrast *British Telecommunications Plc v SAE Group Inc* [2009] EWHC 252 (TCC), [2009] B.L.R. 231; *Excalibur Ventures LLC v Texas Keystone Inc* [2011] EWHC 1624 (Comm), [2011] 2 Lloyd's Rep. 289.

[563] See also the limitations imposed by CPR 6.20 (5) and *Albon v Naza Motor Trading Sdn Berhad (No.4)*, above (at first instance) [2007] EWHC 1879 (Ch), [2007] 2 Lloyd's Rep. 420; *J Jarvis v Blue Circle Dartford Estates* [2007] EWHC 1262 (TCC), [2007] Build. L.R. 439 ("very sparingly"); *Claxton Engineering Services Ltd v TXM Olaj-es Gazkutato KFT* [2010] EWHC 345 (Comm), [2011] 1 Lloyd's Rep. 510 ("only … in exceptional circumstances"); *Excalibur Ventures LLC v Texas Keystone Inc* [2011] EWHC 1624 (Comm), [2011] 2 Lloyd's Rep. 289 at [54], [56] ("in exceptional circumstances and with caution"); *Nomihold Securities Inc v Mobile Telesystems Finance SA* [2012] EWHC 130 (Comm), [2012] 1 Lloyd's Rep. 442 at [55]; *Sabbagh v Khoury* [2018] EWHC 1330 (Comm). Contrast *British Telecommunications Plc v SAE Group Inc* [2009] EWHC 252 (TCC), [2009] B.L.R. 231 (declaration). See also *Golden Ocean Group Ltd v Humpuss Intermodal Transportasi TBK Ltd* [2013] EWHC 1240 (Comm), [2013] 2 All E.R. (Comm) 1025 (Singapore

tion under s.72 does not preclude a party from subsequently participating in the arbitration.[564]

<h2>9. THE AWARD[565]</h2>

Arbitrator's award: legal or other criteria Before the enactment of the 1996   **32-131**
Act, it was very doubtful whether an arbitration agreement which expressly authorised an arbitrator to decide *ex aequo et bono* or as *amiable compositeur* or otherwise free from the constraints of law[566] was a valid arbitration agreement in English law, or whether an award so made would be enforceable in England as a valid award.[567] But, if the parties so agree, s.46(1)(b) of the Act now authorises—and indeed requires—the arbitral tribunal to decide the dispute in accordance with such considerations as are agreed by the parties or determined by the tribunal. "Equity clauses" or arbitration *ex aequo et bono*, *amiable composition* or, indeed, any other type of clause which permits the tribunal to decide in accordance with general considerations of fairness and justice will, if so agreed by the parties, therefore be upheld, although it should be noted that the parties are then in effect excluding any right of appeal to the courts as there will be no "question of law" to appeal. The same provision in the Act will also give validity to clauses which stipulate, for example, that the tribunal is to apply a non-national system of law,[568] the *lex mercatoria* or "general principles of law".

In the absence of any such agreement, however, "the duty of an arbitrator is to   **32-132**
decide the questions submitted to him according to the legal rights of the parties, and not according to what he may consider fair and reasonable under the circumstances".[569] The arbitral tribunal must therefore apply some fixed and recognisable system of law, whether English or foreign.[570] It cannot make a new contract for the parties,[571] but it must give effect to the usages of the trade applicable to the transaction if so required by the law which governs the contract.[572] It has jurisdiction to decide and is bound to give effect to all legal and equitable defences, including the Statute of Limitations[573] and the fact that the contract was illegal.[574]

---

arbitration put on hold pending determination of jurisdiction issue by English court); *AmTrust Europe Ltd v Trust Risk Group SpA* [2015] EWHC 1927 (Comm), [2015] 2 Lloyd's Rep. 231.

[564] *Hackwood Ltd v Areen Design Services Ltd* [2005] EWHC 2322 (TCC), (2006) 22 Const. L.J. 68.

[565] See Chartered Institute of Arbitrators: Guidelines for Arbitrators on the Formalities for Drafting an Arbitral Award.

[566] cf. *Deutsche Shachtbau-und-Tiefbohr Gesellschaft mbH v R'As al-Khaimah National Oil Co* [1990] 1 A.C. 295.

[567] *Home and Overseas Insurance (UK) Ltd v Mentor Insurance Co (UK) Ltd* [1990] 1 W.L.R. 153, 161, 166. See also *Czarnikow v Roth Schmidt & Co* 1922] 2 K.B. 478; *Orion Compañía Espanola de Seguros v Belfort Maatschappij voor Algemeine Versekgrungen* [1962] 2 Lloyd's Rep. 257, 264; *Home Insurance Co v Administratia Asigurarilor de Stat* [1983] 2 Lloyd's Rep. 674, 677.

[568] *Halpern v Halpern* [2007] EWCA Civ 291, [2007] 2 Lloyd's Rep. 56 at [38]; *Musawi v RE International (UK) Ltd* [2007] EWHC 2981 (Ch), [2008] 1 Lloyd's Rep. 326 at [82].

[569] *David Taylor & Son Ltd v Barnett Trading Co* [1953] 1 W.L.R. 562, 568.

[570] *Orion Compañía Espanola de Seguros v Belfort Maatschappij voor Algemeine Versekgrungen*, above; *Musawi v RE International (UK) Ltd*, above, at [22], [23]. See the criticisms of Shackleton (1997) 13 *Arbitration International* 375.

[571] *Hooper & Co v Balfour, Williamson & Co* (1890) 62 L.T. 646; *Jager v Tolme and Runge* [1916] 1 K.B. 939, 953, 957, 961.

[572] DAC Report para.222.

[573] *Board of Trade v Cayzer, Irvine & Co* [1927] A.C. 610, 614; *Naamlooze, etc. Vulcaan v A/S Ludwig*

32-133 **Conflict of laws** The tribunal must decide the dispute in accordance with the law chosen by the parties as applicable to the substance of the dispute.[575] An express choice of law clause must therefore, unless the parties otherwise agree, be upheld. In the absence of any such choice or agreement, the tribunal is required to apply "the law determined by the conflict of laws rules which it considers applicable".[576] The arbitral tribunal therefore has a discretion as to which conflict of laws rules it will apply and, though the seat of the arbitration is in England, is not bound to apply English conflict rules.[577] It cannot, however, unless otherwise agreed,[578] proceed directly to apply whatever substantive law it considers appropriate, but must arrive at the appropriate law by the application of conflict of law rules.

32-134 **Interim awards** As in the case of the 1950 Act,[579] s.47 of the 1996 Act enables the arbitral tribunal to make an interim award unless otherwise agreed by the parties.[580] The expression "interim award" is, however, something of a misnomer,[581] since such an award is in fact final on the matters dealt with in the award. More accurately, therefore, s.47 states that the tribunal "may make more than one award at different times on different aspects of the matters to be determined"[582] and that it may, in particular, make an award relating to an issue affecting the whole claim or to a part only of the claims or cross-claims submitted to it for decision.[583] Under the 1950 Act it was held that an arbitrator had a complete discretion whether or not to make an interim reward as opposed to dealing with the matter in a final award and that he might impose any proper condition which he thought fit on the making of the interim award.[584] There is little doubt that the 1996 Act will be construed no less widely and that, in practice, arbitrators should feel encouraged to use the power

---

Mowinckels Rederi (1938) 43 Com. Cas. 252 HL; *Leif Hoegh & Co A/S v Petrolsea Inc* [1992] 1 Lloyd's Rep. 45.

[574] *David Taylor & Son Ltd v Barnett Trading Co* [1953] 1 W.L.R. 562. cf. *Harbour Assurance Co (UK) Ltd v Kansa General International Insurance Co Ltd* [1993] Q.B. 701.

[575] s.46(1)(a) and (2) (no renvoi); *Peterson Farms Inc v C & M Farming Ltd* [2004] EWHC 121 (Comm), [2004] 1 Lloyd's Rep. 603 at [46]. Contrast (invalid choice of law) *Accentuate Ltd v Asigra Inc* [2009] EWHC 2655 (QB), [2009] 2 Lloyd's Rep. 599. In *Hussman (Europe) Ltd v Al Ameen Development & Trade Co* [2000] 2 Lloyd's Rep. 83 at [42], Thomas J. stated that s.46(1)(a) does not require an arbitral tribunal sitting in London, where the applicable law is other than the law of England and Wales, to obtain general evidence and guidance in relation to that foreign law. If not raised by the parties, the tribunal is free to decide on the presumption that the applicable law is the same as the law of England and Wales. An error in the application of the chosen law does not involve a lack of substantive jurisdiction for the purposes of s.67; *B v A* [2010] EWHC 1626 (Comm), [2010] 2 Lloyd's Rep. 681 at [29].

[576] s.46(3). See Wortmann (1998) 14 *Arbitration International* 97.

[577] DAC Report para.225.

[578] Such an agreement may be made by the adoption of institutional rules, e.g. the ICC rules.

[579] s.14.

[580] cf. *Rotenberg v Sucafina SA* [2012] EWCA Civ 637 (rules of the Coffee Trade Federation not such an agreement).

[581] *Rotenberg v Sucafina SA* [2011] EWHC 901 (Comm), [2011] 2 Lloyd's Rep. 159 at [42] where Eder J. suggests instead "Partial Award pursuant to s.47 of the 1996 Act" (affirmed [2012] EWCA Civ 637).

[582] s.47(1); *Sea Trade Maritime Corp v Hellenic War Risks Assn (Bermuda) Ltd* [2006] EWHC 578 (Comm), [2006] 1 Lloyd's Rep. 397 (subsequent award on costs).

[583] s.47(2).

[584] See *Japan Line v Aggeliki Charis Compañía Maritime SA* [1980] 1 Lloyd's Rep. 288; *SL Sethia Liners v Naviagro Maritime Corp* [1981] 1 Lloyd's Rep. 18; *Leon Corp v Atlantic Lines and Navigation Co Inc* [1985] 2 Lloyd's Rep. 470, 476; *Exmar BV v National Iranian Tanker Co* [1992] 1 Lloyd's Rep. 169; *Modern Trading Co Ltd v Swale Building and Construction Ltd* (1990) 24 Con. L.R. 59. cf. *Minerals & Metals Trading Corp of India Ltd v Encounter Bay Shipping Co Ltd* [1988]

to make interim awards in order to separate out issues for early determination. However, if the tribunal makes an interim award, it must specify in its award the issue, or the claim or part of a claim, which is the subject matter of the award.[585] An interim award will (subject to any appeal or other proper challenge) constitute a permanent final decision as to the matters dealt with and determined by it.[586]

Remedies The parties are free to agree on the powers exercisable by the arbitral tribunal as regards remedies[587] and could therefore, by agreement, empower the tribunal to grant forms of relief that are not available to the courts.[588] They are also free to agree that the tribunal is not to have the power to grant certain forms of relief.[589] Unless otherwise agreed by the parties, the tribunal may order the payment of a sum of money in any currency,[590] whether the claim is for a debt or damages, and it should award damages in the currency which best expresses the claimant's loss.[591] It may also grant declaratory relief,[592] including a declaration that one party is entitled to be indemnified by the other. There is further conferred upon the tribunal the same powers as the court to grant injunctive relief,[593] to order specific performance of a contract (other than a contract relating to land),[594] and to order the rectification, setting aside or cancellation of a deed or other document.[595]   **32-135**

Interest The parties are free to agree on the powers of the tribunal as regards the award of interest.[596] Section 49 of the 1996 Act provides that, subject to the contrary agreement of the parties,[597] the tribunal may award simple or compound interest at such rates and with such rests as it considers meets the justice of the case in respect of periods both before and after the award.[598] But a party seeking award of "post-award" interest must ask for it.[599] Although the power to award interest is (unless excluded or modified by agreement) discretionary, interest should ordinarily be   **32-136**

---

1 Lloyd's Rep. 51.

[585] s.47(3).

[586] ss.47, 58; *Rotenberg v Sucafina SA* [2012] EWCA Civ 637.

[587] s.48(1), e.g. contribution (*Wealands v CLC Contractors Ltd* [1998] C.L.C. 808).

[588] DAC Report para.234. But these may be difficult to enforce: see below, para.32-186.

[589] *Vertex Data Science Ltd v Powergen Retail Ltd* [2006] EWHC 1340 (Comm), [2006] 2 Lloyd's Rep. 591.

[590] s.48(4). But in *Lesotho Highlands Development Authority v Impregilo SpA* [2005] UKHL 43, [2006] 1 A.C. 221, there was a difference of opinion as to the ambit of this subs. at paras [22]–[23], [42], [49], [55] and [56].

[591] *Services Europe Atlantique Sud (SEAS) v Stockholms Rederiaktiebolag* [1979] A.C. 685.

[592] s.48(3).

[593] s.48(5)(a); Senior Courts Act 1981 s.37; *Bath and North East Somerset DC v Mowlem* [2004] EWCA Civ 115, [2004] C.I.L.L. 2081; Debattista (2010) 76 *Arbitration* 421. But see *Kastner v Jason* [2004] EWCA Civ 1599, [2005] 1 Lloyd's Rep. 397 at [16]–[19] (freezing injunction).

[594] s.48(5)(b): CPR Pt 24 24PD-001. See *Tilia Sonera Ab v Hilcourt (Docklands) Ltd* [2003] EWHC 3540 (Ch); *McCaughan v Belwood Homes Ltd* [2011] Arb. L.R. 53 (N.I.) Gemmell (2010) 76 *Arbitration* 467.

[595] s.48(5)(c).

[596] s.49(1).

[597] s.49(2), e.g. in the principal contract: cf. *Lesotho Highlands Development Authority v Impregilo SpA* [2005] UKHL 43, [2006] 1 A.C. 221 (provisions of foreign law applicable to the contract not such an agreement).

[598] s.49(3), (4), (5). See Chartered Institute of Arbitrators: Guidelines for Arbitrators on how to approach the making of awards on interest; Altaras (2004) 70 *Arbitration* 108.

[599] *Walker v Rowe* [2000] 1 Lloyd's Rep. 116, 121; *Sonatrach v Statoil Natural Gas LLC* [2014] EWHC 875 (Comm), [2014] 2 Lloyd's Rep. 252. See also below, para.32-186, n.829.

awarded in a commercial arbitration.[600] The tribunal's powers to award interest include compound interest.[601] However, compound interest should only be ordered on a compensatory, and not on a punitive, basis.[602] If an arbitrator misdirects himself in his award as to the principles on which his discretion ought to be exercised, this would, it seems, be a question of law which could be made the subject of an appeal to the court.[603] But otherwise the exercise of his discretion will not be open to appeal or challenge.[604] These powers are in addition to any other power of the tribunal to award interest, e.g. under institutional rules or contract or statute.[605]

32-137 **Extension of time for making award** There is no statutory time limit placed on the arbitral tribunal within which it must make an award. But the arbitration agreement or institutional rules may impose such a time limit. Unless otherwise agreed by the parties, the court then has power to extend that time limit subject to two qualifications: first, arbitral procedures for obtaining an extension must be exhausted before recourse to the court, and, secondly, the court must be satisfied that substantial injustice would be done if the time were not extended.[606]

32-138 **Settlement in form of agreed award** Section 51 of the 1996 Act enables an agreed settlement of the dispute to be given the status of an arbitral award which can then be enforced as such. Unless the parties otherwise agree, such an award need not contain any reasons,[607] nor need it be stated in the award that it is an agreed award. However, the tribunal can refuse to make the award[608] and might well decline to do so if, for example, it was in terms which were designed to mislead third parties, such as HM Revenue and Customs, or if it dealt with matters not arbitrable under the applicable law. An arbitrator may still retain jurisdiction notwithstanding a settlement if there is a dispute as to how far the settlement extended.[609]

32-139 **Form of award** The parties are free to agree on the form of an award.[610] If or to

---

[600] *Re Badger* (1819) 2 B. & Ald. 691; *Edwards v GW Ry* (1851) 11 C.B. 588; *Chandris v Isbrandtsen Moller Co Inc* [1951] 1 K.B. 240; *Panchaud Frères SA v Pagnan & Fratelli* [1974] 1 Lloyd's Rep. 394; *P J Van der Zijden Wildhandel NV v Tucker & Cross Ltd* [1976] 1 Lloyd's Rep. 341; *Nea Tyhi Maritime Co Ltd v Compagnie Grainiere SA* [1978] 1 Lloyd's Rep. 16; *Thos P Gonzalez Corp v FR Waring (International) (Pty) Ltd* [1978] 1 Lloyd's Rep. 494, [1980] 2 Lloyd's Rep. 160; *Warinco AG v Andre et Cie SA* [1979] 2 Lloyd's Rep. 298; *Tehno-Impex v Gebr van Weelde-Scheepvaart Kantoor BV* [1981] Q.B. 648.
[601] See Vol.I, para.26-290.
[602] *National Bank of Greece SA v Pinios Shipping Co (No.1)* [1990] 1 A.C. 637.
[603] Under s.69; below, para.32-168.
[604] *Amec Building Ltd v Cadmus Investment Co Ltd* (1997) 51 Con. L.R. 105; *Lesotho Highlands Development Authority v Impregilo SpA* [2005] UKHL 43, [2006] 1 A.C. 221. Contrast *Westland Helicopters Ltd v Sheikh Salah' al-Hejailan (No.1)* [2004] EWHC 1625, [2004] 2 Lloyd's 523 (lack of jurisdiction).
[605] s.49(6); see Vol.I, para.26-272.
[606] s.50. See CPR Pt 62 PD 62. Permission of the court is required for any appeal under this section; s.50(5); but see below para.32-185.
[607] s.52(4).
[608] s.51(2).
[609] *Dawes v Treasure & Son Ltd* [2010] EWHC 3218 (TCC), [2011] Bus. L.R. 676; *Sun United Maritime Ltd v Kestell Marine Inc* [2014] EWHC 1476 (Comm), [2014] 2 Lloyd's Rep. 386; Ahmed (2011) 77 *Arbitration* 369.
[610] s.52(1).

the extent that there is no agreement,[611] the award must be in writing signed by all the arbitrators or all those assenting to the award[612]; it must contain the reasons for the award[613]; and it must state the seat of the arbitration and the date when the award is made.[614] Failure to comply with these requirements of form is a ground for challenge to the award,[615] but only if it has caused or will cause substantial injustice to the applicant.[616] Where there is a reference to the decision of three arbitrators, all the arbitrators, acting together, must fairly consider all the issues in the case prior to the award.[617] But they may sign the award separately[618] and, if it is a majority award, there is no need for the majority to meet with the dissenting arbitrator to discuss with him the re-drafting of their award.[619] The majority may allow a dissenting opinion to be attached to the reasons of the majority[620] but, unless the parties agree or institutional rules otherwise provide, a dissenting arbitrator has no right to insist on his opinion being incorporated in the award.[621]

Place of award   In *Hiscox v Outhwaite*[622] the House of Lords held that the place **32-140** of signature determined where an award was made. But s.53 of the 1996 Act reverses that decision in part[623] by providing that the award shall be treated as made at the seat of the arbitration (if in England) regardless of where it was signed despatched or delivered to the parties.

Date of award   The arbitral tribunal is to decide what is the date of the award.[624] **32-141** But, if it does not do so, the date of the award is to be taken to be the date on which it is signed by the arbitrator or, where more than one arbitrator signs, by the last of them. The date of the award is important in particular because the time limit for challenge or appeal runs from the date of the award.[625] Where the award is corrected[626] time runs from the date on which the correction is published.[627]

---

[611] s.52(2).

[612] s.52(3).

[613] s.52(4) (Unless it is an agreed award or the parties have agreed to dispense with reasons). See *Al Hadha Trading Co v Tradigrain SA* [2002] 2 Lloyd's Rep. 512 (GAFTA arbitration rules: absolute discretion conferred by rules to admit or refuse to admit a claim did not dispense with need to give reasons for exercise of discretion). cf. *Tame Shipping Ltd v Easy Navigation Ltd* [2004] EWHC 1862 (Comm), [2004] 2 Lloyd's Rep. 626 (reasons can be set out in separate "confidential" document: see below, para.32-166). See also *Bremer Handelsgesellschaft mbH v Westzucker GmbH (No.2)* [1981] 2 Lloyd's Rep. 130, 132–133 (sufficient for arbitrator to explain how he reached his conclusion). cf. *Compton Beauchamp Estates Ltd v Spence* [2013] EWHC 1101 (Ch), [2013] 20 E.G. 107 (C.S.) at [41]–[52], [79] (adequacy of reasons).

[614] s.52(5).

[615] s.68(2)(h).

[616] s.68(2); below, para.32-164.

[617] *European Grain & Shipping Ltd v R Johnston* [1983] Q.B. 520; *Bank Mellat v GAA Development and Construction Co* [1988] 2 Lloyd's Rep. 44.

[618] *European Grain & Shipping Ltd v R Johnston*, above.

[619] *Bank Mellat v GAA Development and Construction Co*, above.

[620] But see *F Ltd v M Ltd* [2009] EWHC 275 (TCC), [2009] 1 Lloyd's Rep. 537 (dissenting arbitrator's opinion not relevant to challenge under s.68).

[621] *Cargill International SA v Sociedad Iberica de Molturacion SA* [1998] 1 Lloyd's Rep. 489, 497, CA; cf. Rees and Rohn (2009) 25 *Arbitration International* 329.

[622] [1992] 1 A.C. 562.

[623] See also s.100(2)(b).

[624] s.54. Unless otherwise agreed by the parties.

[625] See below, paras 32-176, 32-188.

[626] See below, para.32-144.

32-142 **Notification of and power to withhold award** Subject to contrary agreement, the award must be notified to the parties without delay after the award is made by service on them of copies of the award.[628] However, the tribunal may refuse to deliver an award to the parties except upon full payment of the fees and expenses of the arbitrators.[629] If it refuses on that ground to deliver an award, then, in the absence of any available arbitral process for appeal or review of the amount demanded, a party may apply to the court for an order that the tribunal shall deliver the award pending determination by the court of the amount properly payable.[630] This is a mandatory provision.[631]

32-143 **Correction of award or additional award: the "slip rule"** Section 57 of the 1996 Act allows the arbitral tribunal to correct an award so as to remove any clerical mistake or error arising from an accidental slip or omission or clarify or remove any ambiguity in the award[632] or to make an additional award in respect of any claim (including a claim for interest or costs) which was presented to the tribunal but was not dealt with in the award.[633] This may be done by the tribunal on its own initiative or on the application of a party,[634] but only within certain time limits.[635] However, the arbitral tribunal is not permitted to exercise this power to correct an

---

[627] cf. *Al Hadha Trading Co v Tradigrain SA* [2002] 2 Lloyd's Rep. 512, 525.

[628] s.55.

[629] s.56. This is a mandatory provision.

[630] s.56(2). See CPR r.62.6 PD 62. Permission of the court is required for any appeal: s.56(7); but see below, para.32-185.

[631] s.4(1) and Sch.1.

[632] s.57(3)(a). See *Gannet Shipping Ltd v Eastrade Commodities Inc* [2002] 1 Lloyd's Rep. 712; *Torch Offshore LLC v Cable Shipping Inc* [2004] EWHC 787 (Comm), [2004] 2 Lloyd's Rep. 446; *Sinclair v Woods of Winchester Ltd* [2005] EWHC 1631 (QB), (2005) 102 Const. L.R. 127; *Gold Coast Ltd v Naval Gijon SA* [2006] EWHC 1044 (Comm), [2006] 2 Lloyd's Rep. 400; *Bulk Ship Union SA v Clipper Bulk Shipping Ltd* [2012] EWHC 2595 (Comm), [2012] 2 Lloyd's Rep. 533 at [30]–[31]; *Union Marine Classification Services LLC v Comoros* [2015] EWHC 508 (Comm), [2015] 2 Lloyd's Rep. 49. But see *World Trade Corp v C Czarnikow Sugar Ltd* [2004] EWHC 2332 (Comm), [2005] 1 Lloyd's Rep. 422 at [8]. The ambit of this provision is, perhaps unexpectedly, wide: *Groundshire v VHE Construction* [2001] Build. L.R. 395; *Al Hadha Trading Co v Tradigrain SA* [2002] 2 Lloyd's Rep. 512, 526–527; *Torch Offshore LLC v Cable Shipping Inc*, above, at [28] (request to supply missing reasons).

[633] s.57(3)(b). But see *Torch Offshore LLC v Cable Shipping Inc*, above, at [27] ("claim" only applies to a claim which has been presented to the tribunal but has not been dealt with as opposed to an issue which remains undetermined as part of a claim); *World Trade Corp v C Czarnikow Sugar Ltd*, above, at [14] ("claim" does not mean a submission in support of a relevant question of fact as opposed to a claim for relief such as would have to be pleaded); *Sea Trade Maritime Corp v Hellenic Mutual War Risks Assn (Bermuda) Ltd* [2006] EWHC 578 (Comm), [2006] 2 Lloyd's Rep. 147 (costs claim "dealt with" when costs reserved). See also *Pirtek (UK) Ltd v Deanswood Ltd* [2005] EWHC 2301 (Comm), [2005] 2 Lloyd's Rep. 728 (burden of proof); *Buyuk Camlica Shipping Trading and Industry Co Inc v Progress Bulk Carriers Ltd* [2010] EWHC 442 (Comm), [2011] B.L.R. 199; *Cadogan Maritime Inc v Turner Shipping Inc* [2013] EWHC 138 (Comm), [2013] 1 Lloyd's Rep. 630 at [42]–[50]; *Union Marine Classification Services LLC v Government of the Union of Comoros* [2016] EWCA Civ 239, [2016] 2 Lloyd's Rep. 193.

[634] s.57(3). For the effect of a failure to apply, see s.70(2)(b) and *Gbangbola v Smith & Sherriff Ltd* [1998] 3 All E.R. 730; *Groundshire v VHE Construction*; *Torch Offshore LLC v Cable Shipping Inc*, above at [28], para.32-176, below.

[635] These time limits are set out in subss.(4), (5), (6). See *Pirtek (UK) Ltd v Deanswood Ltd*, above, and (extension of time) s.79 and *Gold Coast Ltd v Naval Gijon SA*, above; *Xstrata Coal Queensland Pty Ltd v Benxi Iron & Steel (Group) International Economic & Trading Co Ltd* [2016] EWHC 2022 (Comm), [2017] 1 All E.R. (Comm) 299. But see *Surefire Systems Ltd v Guardian ECL Ltd* [2005] EWHC 1860 (TCC), [2005] B.L.R. 534; *Price v Carter I* [2010] EWHC 1451 (TCC), and para.32-176, n.793, below.

award as a result of oversights or errors in the production of evidence or argument before the tribunal or a misunderstanding of the evidence.[636] The parties are nevertheless free to agree that the tribunal shall have further or different powers to correct an award or make an additional award outside the terms of s.57.[637]

Effect of award   The rules of a trade association may, for example, provide for a   **32-144**
process of appeal or review from the award of an arbitrator to an appellate arbitral tribunal. But subject to this and to any other contrary agreement of the parties, and subject to the powers of the court in relation to the award which are set out in Pt I of the 1996 Act, an award made by the tribunal pursuant to an arbitration agreement is final and binding both on the parties and on any persons claiming through or under them.[638]

Award as a defence   Except where it is expressly provided to the contrary in the   **32-145**
arbitration agreement, or the award is an interim award only, a valid award of damages duly made in pursuance of a submission to arbitration operates between the parties as a bar to any further action in personam[639] by the claimant in respect of the matters referred.[640] This is so even though the damages payable under the award have not been paid,[641] the claimant's remedy being to enforce the award. In contrast an award for payment of a debt does not operate as a bar to further action for the original debt,[642] although the parties are bound by the award as to the amount due.[643]

An award will preclude a claimant from commencing a second arbitration against   **32-146**
the same party to recover further damages arising from the same cause of action which was the subject of the award.[644] The rule that damages resulting from one and the same cause of action must be assessed and recovered once for all in the same proceedings applies in principle to arbitration[645] as it does to actions.[646] But this rule may be displaced if there is an arbitral practice to the contrary in a particular trade[647] or if certain matters only have been included in the terms of reference in the first arbitration[648] or if the first award is merely declaratory of the claimant's rights.[649]

---

636 *Ases Havacilik Servis ve Destek Hizmetleri AS v Delkor UK Ltd* [2012] EWHC 3518 (Comm), [2013] 1 Lloyd's Rep. 254; *No Curfew Ltd v Feiges Properties Ltd* [2018] EWHC 744 (Ch).
637 *Pirtek (UK) Ltd v Deanswood Ltd* [2005] EWHC 2301 (Comm), [2005] 2 Lloyd's Rep. 728 at [35].
638 s.58 (replacing s.16 of the Arbitration Act 1950).
639 But not an action in rem, see *The Rena K* [1978] 1 Lloyd's Rep. 545, 560; *The Irina Zharkikh* [2001] 2 Lloyd's Rep. 319. But see *Republic of India v India Steamship Co Ltd* [1998] A.C. 878.
640 Unlike a judgment (see Vol.I, para.25-007), the cause of action does not technically merge in the award, but the effect is the same. cf. *Doleman & Sons v Ossett Corp* [1912] 3 K.B. 257 (award after action brought, where no application is made to stay the action or a stay is refused).
641 *Gascoyne v Edwards* (1826) 1 Y. & J. 19.
642 *Allen v Milner* (1831) 2 Cr. & J. 47; *Richard Adler v Soutos (Hellas) Maritime Corp* [1984] 1 Lloyd's Rep. 296.
643 *Cummings v Heard* (1869) L.R. 4 Q.B. 669, 673–674.
644 *Conquer v Boot* [1928] 2 K.B. 336.
645 *Dunn v Murray* (1829) 9 B. & C. 780; *Naamlooze, etc. Vulcaan v A/S Ludwig Mowinckels Rederi* (1938) 60 Ll.L. Rep. 217, 223; *HE Daniels Ltd v Carmel Exporters and Importers Ltd* [1953] 2 Q.B. 242, 255; *Compagnie Grainière SA v Fritz Kopp AG* [1978] 1 Lloyd's Rep. 511, 521; *Telfair Shipping Corp v Inersea Carriers SA* [1983] 2 Lloyd's Rep. 351, 353; *Ron Jones (Burton-on-Trent) Ltd v Hall* (2000) 2 T.C.L.R. 195.
646 See Vol.I, para.25-008.
647 *EE & Brian Smith (1928) Ltd v Wheatsheaf Mills Ltd* [1939] 2 K.B. 302; cf. *HE Daniel Ltd v Carmel Exporters and Importers Ltd*, above.
648 *Purser & Co (Hillingdon) Ltd v Jackson* [1977] Q.B. 166; *Compagnie Grainière SA v Fritz Kopp*

Successive arbitrations may, however, be commenced in respect of different causes of action, even though these arise out of the same contract.[650]

32-147   A party may be estopped from raising a second time a cause of action which has been conclusively determined by a valid award in previous arbitration proceedings between the same parties or their privies,[651] or an issue raised and determined in such proceedings which it was necessary to determine for the purpose of those proceedings.[652] Moreover the court has an inherent jurisdiction to strike out as an abuse of its process a claim based on factual issues which had been raised, or should with reasonable diligence have been raised, in previous arbitration proceedings that have been adjudicated upon by the arbitral tribunal in those proceedings,[653] and it is possible that a court could restrain a party from asserting such a claim in subsequent arbitration proceedings.[654]

10.   COSTS OF THE ARBITRATION

32-148   **Costs**   Sections 59 to 65 of the 1996 Act provide a code dealing with how the costs of the arbitration should be allocated as between the parties. The "costs of the arbitration" are defined as the arbitrators' fees and expenses, the fees and expenses of any arbitral institution concerned, and the legal or other costs of the parties.[655] Although it is open to the parties to provide how these costs are to be allocated, an agreement which has the effect that a party is to pay the whole or part of the costs of the arbitration in any event is only valid if made after the dispute in question has arisen.[656] This is a mandatory provision.[657] An agreement in the parties' submis-

---

AG [1978] 1 Lloyd's Rep. 351; *Excomm Ltd v Guan Guan Shipping (Pte) Ltd* [1987] 1 Lloyd's Rep. 330, 344.

[649] *FJ Bloemen Pty Ltd v City of Gold Coast Council* [1973] A.C. 115, 126; *Compagnie Grainière SA v Fritz Kopp AG*, above, at 522.

[650] *Brunsden v Humphrey* (1884) 14 Q.B.D. 141; *Telfair Shipping Corp v Inersea Carriers SA* [1983] 2 Lloyd's Rep. 351; *Siporex Trade SA v Comdel Commodities Ltd* [1986] 2 Lloyd's Rep. 428. But see *Dunn v Murray* (1829) 9 B. & C. 780 and the cases cited in n.653, below.

[651] *Ayscough v Sheed, Thomson & Co Ltd* (1924) 40 T.L.R. 707; *Aktiebolaget Legis v V Berg & Sons Ltd* [1964] 1 Lloyd's Rep. 203. Contrast *Sun Life Assurance Co of Canada v Lincoln National Life Insurance Co* [2004] EWCA Civ 1660, [2005] 1 Lloyd's Rep. 606 (no estoppel where arbitration between one of the parties and a stranger). cf. *Arts & Antiques Ltd v Richards* [2013] EWHC 336 (Comm), [2014] P.N.L.R. 10. In *Michael Wilson & Partners Ltd v Sinclair* [2017] EWCA Civ 3, [2017] 1 W.L.R. 2646 the Court of Appeal held that it would be a rare case where legal proceedings against a person who was not a party to an earlier arbitration would be struck out by reason of the award in that earlier arbitration.

[652] *Fidelitas Shipping Co Ltd v V/O Exportchleb* [1960] 1 Q.B. 630, 640, 643; discussed in *Carl Zeiss Stiftung v Rayner & Keeler Ltd (No.2)* [1967] 1 A.C. 853; *Associated Electric and Gas Insurance Services Ltd v European Reinsurance Co of Zurich* [2003] UKPC 11, [2003] 1 W.L.R. 1041. See Vol.I, para.25-011.

[653] *Henderson v Henderson* (1843) 3 Hare 100, 114; *Fidelitas Shipping Co Ltd v V/O Exportchleb*, above, at 640; *Yat Tung Investment Co Ltd v Dao Heng Bank Ltd* [1975] A.C. 581, 590; *Dallal v Bank Mellat* [1986] Q.B. 441. See also *Johnson v Gore Wood & Co* [2002] 2 A.C. 1 and Vol.I, para.25-013. Contrast *Sun Life Assurance Co of Canada v Lincoln National Life Insurance Co* [2004] EWCA Civ 1660, [2005] 1 Lloyd's Rep. 606 at [54] (only between parties to the proceedings).

[654] cf. *Associated Electric and Gas Insurance Services Ltd v European Reinsurance Co of Zurich*, above, at [16].

[655] s.59(1). See also s.59(2) (costs of taxation proceedings). In *Essar Oilfield Services Ltd v Norscot Rig Management Pvt Ltd* [2016] EWHC 2361 (Comm), [2016] 2 Lloyd's Rep. 481 at [68]–[72], the Court held that "other costs" in s.59 can include the costs of obtaining litigation funding.

[656] s.60. This is based on s.18(3) of the Arbitration Act 1950.

[657] s.4(1) and Sch.1.

sion letter that they will share equally the arbitrators' hourly charge does not imply that the costs of the arbitration between the parties are to be similarly allocated.[658]

The arbitral tribunal is empowered to make an award as to costs[659] and is required   **32-149** (unless the parties otherwise agree) to award costs on the principle that costs are to follow the event except where it appears to the tribunal that in the circumstances this is not appropriate.[660] The tribunal does not therefore have a complete and unfettered discretion over costs but must follow the general approach of the English courts.[661] The court will not interfere merely because it would have exercised that discretion differently.[662]. Under the previous law, if the tribunal failed to exercise judicially[663] its discretion over costs in making its award, the aggrieved party could apply to the court for an order that the award, or that part of the award that deals with costs, be varied, remitted or set aside. But, following cases on the Arbitration Act 1979,[664] it would appear that an award as to costs can now ordinarily be challenged only through the medium of appeal to the court on a point of law under s.69 of the 1996 Act.[665] As a result, if there is an effective exclusion agreement,[666] no such appeal will lie, so that a bona fide error on the part of the arbitral tribunal in the matter of costs will be irremediable.[667] An award will only be susceptible to challenge under s.67 or s.68 of the 1996 Act (which sections cannot be excluded)[668] where some other sufficient ground exists, such as a failure to deal at all with the issue of costs,[669] an excess of jurisdiction, or a serious irregularity in relation to

---

[658] *Carter v Harold Simpson Associates* [2004] UKPC 29, [2005] 1 W.L.R. 919.
[659] s.61(1) (subject to any agreement of the parties).
[660] s.61(2).
[661] CPR Pt 44. See the Chartered Institute of Arbitrators: Guideline for Arbitrators Making Orders Relating to the costs of the Arbitration. For statement of the principles involved, see *Malkinson v Trim* [2002] EWCA Civ 1273, [2003] 1 W.L.R. 463. See also Henchie (2004) 70 *Arbitration* 77.
[662] *Rosen & Co Ltd v Dowley and Selby* [1943] 2 All E.R. 172, 174; *Smeaton Hanscomb & Co Ltd v Sassoon I Setty, Son & Co (No.2)* [1953] 1 W.L.R. 1481, 1483; *The Erich Schroeder* [1974] 1 Lloyd's Rep. 192, 194; *Blue Horizon Shipping Co SA v ED & F Man Ltd* [1980] 1 Lloyd's Rep. 17; *W Wilhemsen v Canadian Transport Co* [1980] 2 Lloyd's Rep. 204, 209; *Eleftheria Niki Compañía Naviera SA v Eastern Mediterranean Marine Ltd* [1980] 2 Lloyd's Rep 252, 260; *President of India v Jadranska Slobodna Plovidba* [1992] 2 Lloyd's Rep. 274, 280; *Everglade Maritime Inc v Schiffahrtsgesellschaft Detlef Von Appen mbH* [1993] 1 W.L.R. 33, 39; affirmed [1993] Q.B. 780
[663] i.e. in the same manner as the High Court.
[664] *Blixen Ltd v G Percy Trentham Ltd* (1990) 42 E.G. 133, CA; *King v Thomas McKenna Ltd* [1991] 2 Q.B. 480, 499; *President of India v Jadranska Slobodna Plovidba* [1992] 2 Lloyd's Rep. 274, 276–280; *Everglade Maritime Inc v Schiffahrtsgesellschaft Detlef Von Appen mbH* [1993] Q.B. 780; *Cohen v Baram* [1994] 2 Lloyd's Rep. 138.
[665] *Sanghi Polyesters (India) v International Investor (KCFC) (Kuwait)* [2000] 1 Lloyd's Rep. 480, 485; *Transition Feeds LLP v Itochu Europe Plc* [2013] EWHC 3855 (Comm); *Sun United Maritime Ltd v Kasteli Marine Inc* [2014] EWHC 1476 (Comm). See below, para.32-168.
[666] Below, para.32-172.
[667] *King v Thomas McKenna Ltd* [1991] 2 Q.B. 480 at 499.
[668] Below, paras 32-157, 32-162.
[669] *Re Becker, Shillan & Co and Barry Brothers* [1921] 1 K.B. 391. But an application may be made under s.57(3)(b) (para.32-143, above); cf. *Sea Trade Maritime Corp v Hellenic Mutual War Risks Assn (Bermuda) Ltd* [2006] EWHC 578 (Comm), [2006] 2 Lloyd's Rep. 147 (costs reserved).

costs,[670] but not simply on the ground of an alleged unjudicial exercise of the tribunal's discretion.[671]

32-150 Section 63 of the 1996 Act provides that the parties may agree what costs of the arbitration are recoverable.[672] If they do not do so,[673] the tribunal may determine by award the recoverable costs of the arbitration (i.e. assess the amount) on such basis as it thinks fit, but in so doing must specify the basis on which it has acted and the items of recoverable costs and the amount referable to each.[674] If the tribunal does not determine the recoverable costs, any party may apply to the court.[675] The tribunal therefore has the power, but not the obligation, to deal with the costs of the arbitration.[676] The usual practice is for the tribunal to determine in its award the fees and expenses of the arbitrators.[677] The determination of the recoverable legal or other costs of the parties is better left to the court.

32-151 If the tribunal rules that it lacks substantive jurisdiction with respect to the matter referred to it, or if the court determines, on an application under s.32[678] or s.67[679] of the Act, that the tribunal does not have substantive jurisdiction, it would appear to follow that any award made by the tribunal as to costs is a nullity, unless there can be inferred an ad hoc agreement empowering the tribunal to make such an award,[680] or unless it can be said that the party who initiates arbitration impliedly consents to an order for costs being made against him if the tribunal rules that it has no jurisdiction.[681] The costs incurred by a party in relation to the abortive or invalid arbitration proceedings are irrecoverable.[682]

32-152 **Basis of costs** Unless the tribunal or the court determines otherwise, costs will be awarded on a standard basis.[683]

---

[670] *Harrison v Thompson* [1989] 1 W.L.R. 1325; *King v Thomas McKenna Ltd* [1991] 2 Q.B. 480; *President of India v Jadranska Slobodna Plovidba* [1992] 2 Lloyd's Rep. 274 at 279, 280; *Gbangbola v Smith & Sherriff Ltd* [1998] 3 All E.R. 730; *Newfield Construction Ltd v Tomlinson* [2004] EWHC 3051 (TCC), (2004) 97 Const. L.R. 148. See also *Danae Air Transport SA v Air Canada* [2000] 1 W.L.R. 395 (mathematical error).

[671] *Fence Gate Ltd v NEL Construction Ltd* (2002) 82 Const. L.R. 41; Dundas (2003) 69 *Arbitration* 90.

[672] s.63(1). But see s.62.

[673] s.63(2).

[674] s.63(3). See *Rotary Watches Ltd v Rotary Watches (USA) Inc* Unreported, noted (2005) 71 Arbitration 172 (interim payment). cf. s.62.

[675] s.63(4); PD.62. The court is defined in s.105 to mean the High Court or a county court. cf. Sch.2 para.9 (judge-arbitrator).

[676] As under s.18(1) of the Arbitration Act 1950. cf. *M/S Alghanim Industries Inc v Skandia International Insurance Corp* [2001] 2 All E.R. (Comm) 30 (ARIAS arbitration rules).

[677] Including fees and expenses of an expert, etc. under s.37(2). See *SN Kurkjian (Commodity Brokers) Ltd v Marketing Exchange for Africa Ltd* [1986] 2 Lloyd's Rep. 618 (taxation of fees of legal adviser), but cf. s.63(7).

[678] See above, para.32-104.

[679] See below, para.32-157.

[680] *Commonwealth Development Corp (UK) v Montague* [2000] QCA 252 Queensland Court of Appeal; Greenberg and Secomb (2002) 18 *Arbitration International* 125.

[681] This might also arguably be said to follow from s.30 of the Act: para.32-101, above.

[682] *Crest Nicholson (Eastern) Ltd v Western* [2008] EWHC 1325 (TCC), [2008] Build. L.R. 426.

[683] s.63(5); CPR r.44.4.

Fees and expenses   Only the reasonable fees and expenses of the arbitrators are   **32-153**
recoverable and what fees and expenses are "reasonable" may on the application
of any party, be determined by the court.684

Power to limit recoverable costs   Section 65 of the 1996 Act gives to the arbitral   **32-154**
tribunal a new power not found in previous legislation: the power to limit in
advance the amount of recoverable costs.685 The tribunal can put a ceiling on costs.
A party can incur costs in excess of this ceiling but the excess will then not be
recoverable from the other party. The Departmental Advisory Committee
considered that this power, properly used, could prove extremely valuable as an aid
to reducing expenditure and would discourage those who wished to employ their
financial muscle to intimidate their opponents.686 But the power appears to be little used in practice.

Sealed offers   A sealed offer by the respondent in arbitral proceedings is   **32-155**
analogous to, but not identical with,687 a Pt 36 payment.688 If the claimant in the end
has achieved no more than he would have achieved by accepting the offer, the
continuance of the arbitration after that date has been a waste of time and money.
Prima facie, the claimant should recover his costs up to the date of the offer and
should be ordered to pay the respondent's costs after that date. If he has achieved
more by going on, the respondent should pay the costs throughout.689

11.   POWERS OF THE COURT IN RELATION TO THE AWARD

Introduction   The Court's powers to review an arbitration award are set out in   **32-156**
ss.67–69 of the Arbitration Act 1996. An application under ss.67–69 must conform
to the requirements of those provisions and the procedural requirements set out in
s.70. The mere fact that the parties agree that the Court should hear a challenge or
appeal against an award will not confer jurisdiction on the Court unless the requirements of the Act are satisfied.690 In order that ss.67–69 may apply, there must have
been an "award" made by the arbitral tribunal.691 An "award" is a formal written
record of the arbitral tribunal's decision, in an arbitral reference made pursuant to
an arbitration agreement,692 which disposes of or resolves an issue or dispute
between the parties.693

Challenging the award: substantive jurisdiction   A party to arbitral proceed-   **32-157**

---

684   s.64, PD 62.
685   s.65. Unless otherwise agreed by the parties.
686   DAC Report para.272. See also Bange (2000) 11 Const. Law 23 and the *Controlled Cost Arbitration Rules of the Chartered Institute of Arbitrators*. cf. Miller (1999) 149 N.L.J. 530.
687   *Huron Liberian Co v Rheinoel GmbH* [1985] 2 Lloyd's Rep. 58n.
688   CPR Pt 36. See Wood (2008) 74 *Arbitration* 139.
689   *Tramountana Armadora SA v Atlantic Shipping Co SA* [1978] 1 Lloyd's Rep. 391, 398; *Everglade
Maritime Inc v Schiffahrtsgesellschaft Detlef Von Appen MbH* [1993] Q.B. 780; *Lindner Ceilings
Floors Partitions Plc v How Engineering Services Ltd* [2001] Build. L.R. 90. cf. *Cadmus Investment Ltd v Amec Building Ltd* [1997] C.L.Y. 270.
690   *Enterprise Insurance Co Plc v U-Drive Solutions (Gibraltar) Ltd* [2015] EWHC 1301 (QB) at [34].
691   In *Enterprise Insurance Co Plc v U-Drive Solutions (Gibraltar) Ltd* [2016] EWHC 1301 (QB) at
[39]–[40], [116] the Court held that an order refusing to strike out a claim and an order for security
for costs were not "awards" for the purposes of ss.68 and 69.
692   s.5 of the Arbitration Act 1996. A decision by the secretariat of the arbitral institution, as opposed
to the tribunal, will not be an award unless the arbitral institution's rules provide otherwise.
693   s.52 of the Arbitration Act 1996 makes provision for the form of the award. See above, para.32-

ings may apply[694] to the court under s.67 of the 1996 Act[695] challenging any award of the arbitral tribunal as to its substantive jurisdiction[696] or for an order declaring an award made by the tribunal on the merits to be of no effect, in whole or in part, because the tribunal did not have substantive jurisdiction.[697] Such an application must normally be made within the 28 day time limit prescribed by s.70(3)[698] and is subject to certain restrictions.[699] Where the arbitral tribunal rules that it has substantive jurisdiction and a party to arbitral proceedings who could have questioned that ruling by an arbitral process of appeal or review, or by challenging the award, does not do so within the time allowed by the arbitration agreement or any provisions of Pt I of the Act, or at all, he may not object later to the tribunal's substantive jurisdiction on any ground which was the subject of that ruling.[700] On the hearing of the application the court may by order confirm the award, vary the award or set aside the award in whole or in part.[701] The hearing is to be treated as a full rehearing (including oral evidence) and not merely as a review and new evidence may therefore be adduced (subject to the Court's control).[702] Pending the hearing of the application the arbitral tribunal may continue the arbitral proceed-

---

139.

694 See CPR Pt 62.

695 Having regard to s.1(c) of the Act, the question arises whether the court still retains in addition its inherent powers to rule on jurisdiction: see *ABB Lummus Global Ltd v Keppel Fils Ltd* [1999] 2 Lloyd's Rep. 24; *Vale do Rio Doce Navegacao SA v Shanghai Bao Steel Ocean Shipping Co Ltd* [2000] 2 Lloyd's Rep. 1; *J T Mackley & Co Ltd v Gosport Marina Ltd* [2002] EWHC 1315 (TCC), [2002] Build. L.R. 367. But see *British Telecommunications Plc v SAE Group Inc* [2009] EWHC 252 (TCC), [2009] B.L.R. 231 (declaration).

696 s.67(1)(a). See ss.30, 31, 82; above, paras 32-101, 32-102. A negative jurisdictional decision of the tribunal can be challenged under the provision: *LG Caltex Gas Co Ltd v China National Petroleum Corp* [2001] EWCA Civ 788, [2001] 1 W.L.R. 1892; *TTMI SARL v Statoil ASA* [2011] EWHC 1150 (Comm), [2011] 2 Lloyd's Rep. 220. For an instance of a decision not relating to the tribunal's substantive jurisdiction, see *Petroleum Company of Trinidad and Tobago Ltd v Samsung Engineering Trinidad Co Ltd* [2017] EWHC 3055 (TCC), [2018] 1 Lloyd's Rep. 242.

697 s.67(1)(b); *Republic of Kazakhstan v Istil Group Inc* [2006] EWHC 448 (Comm), [2006] 2 Lloyd's Rep. 370; (affirmed [2007] EWCA Civ 471, [2007] 2 Lloyd's Rep. 548); *Sumukan Ltd v Commonwealth Secretariat (No.2)* [2007] EWCA Civ 1148, [2008] 1 Lloyd's Rep. 40.

698 Below, para.32-176. See *Yegiazaryan v Smagin* [2016] EWCA Civ 1290, [2017] 1 Lloyd's Rep. 102 at [27]–[28].

699 s.70(2); below, para.32-176; CPR Pt 62.

700 s.73(2); *Emirates Trading Agency LLC v Sociedade de Fomento Industrial Private Ltd* [2015] EWHC 1452 (Comm), [2015] 2 Lloyd's Rep. 487.

701 s.67(3).

702 *Azov Shipping Co v Baltic Shipping Co* [1999] 1 Lloyd's Rep. 68; *Aoot Kalmneft v Glencore International AG* [2002] 1 Lloyd's Rep. 128, 141; *Electrosteel Castings Ltd v Scan-Transshipping and Chartering Sdn Bhd* [2002] EWHC 1993 (Comm), [2003] 1 Lloyd's Rep. 190 at [22]; *Zaporozhyve Production Society v Ashly Ltd* [2002] EWHC 1410 (Comm); *Peoples Insurance Co of China v Vysanthi Shipping Co Ltd* [2003] EWHC 1655 (Comm), [2003] 2 Lloyd's Rep. 617; *Peterson Farms Inc v C&M Farming Ltd* [2004] EWHC 121 (Comm), [2004] 1 Lloyd's Rep. 603 at [18]; *Metal Distributors UK Ltd v ZCCM Investments Holdings Plc* [2005] EWHC 156 (Comm), [2005] 2 Lloyd's Rep. 37 at [16]; *Republic of Ecuador v Occidental Exploration & Production Co (No.2)* [2006] EWHC 345 (Comm), [2006] 1 Lloyd's Rep. 773 at [7] (affirmed [2007] EWCA Civ 656, [2007] 2 Lloyd's Rep. 352); *Czech Republic v European Media Ventures SA* [2007] EWHC 2851 (Comm), [2008] 1 Lloyd's Rep. 186 at [13]; *Habas Sinai v Tibbi Gazlar Isthisal Endustri AS v Sometal SAL* [2101] EWHC 29 (Comm), [2010] 1 Lloyd's Rep. 661 at [1]; *Norscot Rig Management PVT Ltd v Essar Oilfields Services Ltd* [2010] EWHC 195 (Comm), [2010] 2 Lloyd's Rep. 209 at [1]; *Dallah Real Estate & Tourism Co v Ministry of Religious Affairs of the Government of Pakistan* [2010] UKSC 46, [2011] 1 A.C. 763 at [104], [160]; *A v B* [2010] EWHC 3302 (Comm), [2011] 1 Lloyd's Rep. 363 at [25]; *TTMI SARL v Statoil ASA* [2011] EWHC 1150 (Comm), [2011] 2 Lloyd's Rep. 220 at [16]; *Hyundai Merchant Marine Co Ltd v Americas Bulk Transport Ltd* [2013]

ings and make a further award if it wishes to do so.[703] Section 67 is a mandatory provision.[704]

The same right to challenge the award is given to a person alleged to be a party **32-158** to arbitral proceedings but who takes no part in the proceedings.[705] Alternatively such a person may question whether there is a valid arbitration agreement, or whether the tribunal is properly constituted, or what matters have been properly submitted to arbitration in accordance with the arbitration agreement, by proceedings in court for a declaration or injunction or other appropriate relief.[706]

A party to arbitral proceedings will lose the right to object that the tribunal lacks **32-159** substantive jurisdiction if he fails to object timeously and thereafter takes part, or continues to take part, in the proceedings, unless he did not know and could not with reasonable diligence have discovered the grounds for the objection.[707] But even where this is not the case, then at common law if the parties appoint or accept the appointment of an arbitrator and thereafter take part in the arbitral proceedings without objection on the mistaken assumption that the tribunal has jurisdiction with respect to the whole or a part of the subject matter of the dispute, they may be held to have entered into an ad hoc agreement to submit their dispute to the jurisdiction of the tribunal,[708] unless that agreement can be said to be vitiated by a fundamental

---

EWHC 470 (Comm), [2013] 2 All E.R. (Comm) 649 at [31]; *GPF GP SARL v Poland* [2018] EWHC 409 (Comm), [2018] 1 Lloyd's Rep 410 at [54]–[71]. cf. *Primetrade AG v Ythan Ltd* [2005] EWHC 2399 (Comm), [2006] 1 Lloyd's Rep. 457: *Central Trading Exports Ltd v Ficralba Shipping Co* [2014] EWHC 2397 (Comm), [2014] 2 Lloyd's Rep. 449 (in the circumstances new evidence not allowed to be introduced).

[703] s.67(2). See (1998) 64 *Arbitration* 188.
[704] s.4(1) and Sch.1.
[705] s.72(2)(a). Taking part in an arbitration on the merits or substance of the alleged claim amounts to taking part in the arbitration proceedings for the purposes of this sub-section; see *Broda Agro Trade (Cyprus) Ltd v Alfred C Toepfer International Ltd* [2010] EWCA Civ 1100, [2011] 1 Lloyd's Rep. 243, likewise making submissions to the tribunal as to its jurisdiction: at [42]–[49].
[706] s.72(1); *London Steam Ship Owners Mutual Insurance Association Ltd v Spain (The Prestige)* [2013] EWHC 2840 (Comm), [2014] All E.R. (Comm) 300 at [79]–[81]. cf. *Secretary of State for Transport v Stagecoach South Western Trains Ltd* [2009] EWHC 2431 (Comm), [2010] 1 Lloyd's Rep. 175. In *Sino Channel Asia Ltd v Dana Shipping and Trading Pte Singapore* [2016] EWHC 1118 (Comm), [2016] 2 Lloyd's Rep. 97 at [4]–[5] the Court said that there was no time limit applicable to proceedings under s.72 and such an action may be brought after the making of an arbitration award.
[707] s.73(1); *Hussman (Europe) Ltd v Al Ameer Development & Trade Co* [2000] 2 Lloyd's Rep. 83, 91; *Athletic Union of Constantinople v National Basketball Association* [2002] 1 Lloyd's Rep. 305, 310; *JSC Zestafoni G Nikoladz Ferroalloy Plant v Ronly Holdings Ltd* [2004] EWHC 245 (Comm), [2004] 2 Lloyd's Rep. 335; *Westland Helicopters Ltd v Sheikh Salah al-Hejailan (No.1)* [2004] EWHC 1625 (Comm), [2004] 2 Lloyd's Rep. 523; *Vee Networks Ltd v Econet Wireless International Ltd* [2004] EWHC 2909 (Comm), [2005] 1 Lloyd's Rep. 192; *Primetrade AG v Ythan Ltd* [2005] EWHC 2399 (Comm), [2006] 1 Lloyd's Rep. 457 at [56]; *Frontier Agriculture Ltd v Bratt Bros* [2015] EWCA Civ 611, [2015] 2 Lloyd's Rep. 500; *A v B* [2016] EWHC 3003 (Comm), [2017] 1 W.L.R. 2030 at [50]–[63]; *Stockman Interhold SA v Arricano Real Estate Plc* [2017] EWHC 2909 (Comm), [2018] 1 Lloyd's Rep. 135 at [144]–[151]; *Exportadora de Sal SA de CV v Corretaje Maritimo Sud-Americano Inc* [2018] EWHC 224 (Comm), [2018] 1 Lloyd's Rep 399. cf. *Sumukan Ltd v Commonwealth Secretarial (No.2)* [2007] EWCA Civ 1148, [2008] 1 Lloyd's Rep. 40; *Habas Sinai Ve Tibbi Gazlar Istihsal Endustrisi As v VSC Steel Co Ltd* [2013] EWHC 4071 (Comm), [2014] 1 Lloyd's Rep. 479; see above, para.32-102 and below, para.32-177, But if the tribunal determines that it lacks jurisdiction and a party challenges that determination, s.73(1) is inapplicable, since that party is not making any of the objections to which s.73(1) applies: *LG Caltex Gas Co Ltd v China National Petroleum Corp* [2001] EWCA Civ 788, [2001] 1 W.L.R. 1892. Section 73(1) is inapplicable to applications under s.72(1): *London Steam Ship Owners Mutual Insurance Association Ltd v Spain (The Prestige)* [2013] EWHC 2840 (Comm), [2014] 1 All E.R. (Comm) 300 at [82].
[708] *Westminster Chemicals & Produce Ltd v Eicholz & Loeser* [1954] 1 Lloyd's Rep. 99; *Luanda*

mistake.[709] In this latter situation, however, even if there is no or no valid ad hoc agreement, each may be estopped by convention[710] from alleging lack of jurisdiction on the part of the tribunal.[711]

32-160   The power conferred on the court by s.67 is exercisable only if the seat of arbitration is in England.[712] Where that is the case, the fact that the issue to be determined by the tribunal involves an investment dispute between an investor and a sovereign state under the provisions of a treaty will not deprive the court of its supervisory jurisdiction under the Act.[713]

32-161   If an award is successfully challenged and set aside by the court, this does not mean that the functions of the arbitral tribunal are necessarily at an end. The tribunal may be revivified and proceed to make a second, valid award which is within its jurisdiction to make.[714] Section 67 does not enable a challenge to be made to a procedural order not amounting to an award.[715]

32-162   Challenging the award: serious irregularity   Prior to the enactment of the 1996 Act the High Court had an unqualified power to remit an award for the reconsideration of the arbitrator,[716] and it could set aside an award where the arbitrator had misconducted himself or the proceedings or the arbitration or award had been improperly procured.[717] "Misconduct" did not necessarily imply any reflection on the competence or integrity of the arbitrator: it covered irregularities or procedural unfairness which was not proper in relation to quasi-judicial proceedings.[718] The concept of misconduct was not retained in the 1996 Act. Section 68 establishes a different regime which enables a party to arbitral proceedings to apply to the court challenging the award on the ground of serious irregularity affecting the tribunal, the proceedings or the award.[719] This is a mandatory provision.[720] The same right to challenge the award is given to a person alleged to be a party to arbitral proceed-

---

Exportadora SARL v Wahbe Tamari & Sons Ltd [1967] 2 Lloyd's Rep. 353; *Cia Maritima Zorroza SA v Sesostris SAE* [1984] 1 Lloyd's Rep. 652; *Almare Societa di Navigazione SpA v Derby & Co Ltd* [1989] 2 Lloyd's Rep. 376; *Furness Withy (Australia) Pty Ltd v Metal Distributors (UK) Ltd* [1990] 1 Lloyd's Rep. 236; *Athletic Union of Constantinople v National Basketball Association*, above, at 311. Contrast *LG Caltex Gas Co Ltd v China National Petroleum Corp*, above; *Republic of Kazakhstan v Istil Group Inc*, above, at [59]–[60].

[709] *Altco Ltd v Sutherland* [1971] 2 Lloyd's Rep. 515; *Furness Withy (Australia) Pty Ltd v Metal Distributors (UK) Ltd*, above.

[710] See Vol.I, para.4-108.

[711] *Furness Withy (Australia) Pty Ltd v Metal Distributors (UK) Ltd*, above. But see Vol.I, paras 4-114, 4-115.

[712] s.2(1).

[713] *Republic of Ecuador v Occidental Exploration and Production Co* [2005] EWCA Civ 1116, [2006] Q.B. 432. On the subsequent hearing of the challenge under ss.67, 68, the court upheld the award: *Republic of Ecuador v Occidental Exploration and Production Co (No.2)* [2006] EWHC 345 (Comm), [2006] 1 Lloyd's Rep. 773 (affirmed [2007] EWCA Civ 656, [2007] 2 Lloyd's Rep. 352).

[714] *Hussman (Europe) Ltd v Pharaon* [2003] EWCA Civ 266, [2003] 1 All E.R. (Comm) 879.

[715] *Michael Wilson & Partners Ltd v Emmott* [2008] EWHC 2684 (Comm), [2009] 1 Lloyd's Rep. 162.

[716] Arbitration Act 1950 s.22.

[717] Arbitration Act 1950 s.23(2).

[718] See the 27th edition of this book, Vol.I, para.15-042.

[719] s.68(1). See CPR Pt 62. The claim form must identify exactly what constitutes the alleged irregularity: *Orascom TMT Investments Sarl v Veon Ltd* [2018] EWHC 985 (Comm), at [2]; *T v V & W* [2018] EWHC 1492 (Comm), at [5].

[720] s.4(1) and Sch.1.

ings but who takes no part in the proceedings.[721] It has, however, been pointed out that the law places a "high hurdle" in the way of an applicant under s.68.[722]

For "serious irregularity" to have occurred there must, first, have been an ir- **32-163** regularity of one or more of the following kinds[723]:

(a) failure by the tribunal to comply with s.33 of the Act (general duty of the tribunal)[724];

---

[721] s.72(2)(b).
[722] *Lesotho Highlands Development Authority v Impregilo SpA* [2005] UKHL 43, [2006] 1 A.C. 221 at [28]; *ABB AG v Hochtief Airport GmbH* [2006] EWHC 388 (Comm), [2006] 2 Lloyd's Rep. 1 at [61]–[67]; *Bandwith Shipping Corp v Intaari* [2007] EWCA Civ 998, [2008] 1 Lloyd's Rep. 7 at [38]; *Gulf Import and Export Co v Bunge SA* [2007] EWHC 2667 (Comm), [2008] 1 Lloyd's Rep. 316 at [21]; *London Underground Ltd v Citylink Telecommunications Ltd* [2007] Build. L.R. 391 at [22]; *TAG Wealth Management v West* [2008] EWHC 1466 (Comm), [2008] 2 Lloyd's Rep. 699 at [29]; *Petrochemical Industries Co (KSC) v Dow Chemical Co* [2012] EWHC 2739 (Comm), [2012] 2 Lloyd's Rep. 691 at [16]; *Secretary of State for the Home Department v Raytheon Systems Ltd* [2014] EWHC 4375 (TCC) at [33]; *Lorand Shipping Ltd v Davof Trading (Africa) BV* [2014] EWHC 3521 (Comm), [2015] 1 Lloyd's Rep. 67; *Essar Oilfield Services Ltd v Norscot Rig Management Pvt Ltd* [2016] EWHC 2361 (Comm), [2016] 2 Lloyd's Rep. 481 at [8]–[11].
[723] s.68(2).
[724] *Weldon Plant Hire Ltd v Commission for the New Towns* [2000] B.L.R. 496; *Pacol Ltd v Joint Stock Co Rossakhar* [2000] 1 Lloyd's Rep. 109; *Rustal Trading Ltd v Gill & Duffus SA* [2000] 1 Lloyd's Rep. 14; *Sanghi Polyesters (India) v International Investor (KCFC) (Kuwait)* [2000] 1 Lloyd's Rep. 480; *Groundshire v VHE Construction* [2001] Build. L.R. 395; *RC Pillar & Sons v Edwards* [2001] C.I.L.L. 1799; *Aoot Kalmneft v Glencore International AG* [2002] 1 Lloyd's Rep. 128; *Al Hadha Trading Co v Tradigrain SA* [2002] 2 Lloyd's Rep. 512, 523–524; *Checkpoint Ltd v Strathclyde Pension Fund* [2003] EWCA Civ 84, [2003] E.G. 214; *Bulfracht (Cyprus) Ltd v Boneset Shipping Co Ltd* [2002] EWHC 2292 (Comm), [2002] 2 Lloyd's Rep. 681; *Warborough Investments Ltd v S Robinson & Sons (Holdings) Ltd* [2003] EWCA 751, [2003] 2 E.G.L.R. 149; *Minermet SpA Milan v Luckyfield Shipping Corp SA* [2004] EWHC 729 (Comm), [2004] 2 Lloyd's Rep. 348; *Westland Helicopters Ltd v Sheikh Salah al-Hejailan (No.1)* [2004] EWHC 1625 (Comm), [2004] 2 Lloyd's Rep. 523; *Tame Shipping Ltd v Easy Navigation Ltd* [2004] EWHC 1862 (Comm), [2004] 2 Lloyd's Rep. 626; *Newfield Construction Ltd v Tomlinson* [2004] EWHC 3051 (TCC), (2004) 97 Const. L.R. 98; *Alphapoint Shipping Ltd v Rotem Amfert Negev* [2004] EWHC 2232 (Comm), [2005] 1 Lloyd's Rep. 23; *Vee Networks Ltd v Econet Wireless International Ltd* [2004] EWHC 2909 (Comm), [2005] 1 Lloyd's Rep. 192; *Margulead Ltd v Exide Technologies* [2004] EWEC 1019 (Comm), [2005] 1 Lloyd's Rep. 324; *Home of Homes Ltd v Hammersmith & Fulham LBC* [2003] EWHC 807, (2003) 92 Const. L.R. 48; *Ronly Holdings Ltd v JSC Zestafoni G Nicoladze Ferroalloy Plant* [2004] EWHC 1354 (Comm), [2004] 1 C.L.C. 1168; *Omnibridge Consulting Ltd v Clearsprings Management Ltd* [2004] EWHC 2276 (Comm); *St George's Investment Co Ltd v Gemini Consulting Ltd* [2004] EWHC 2358 (Ch); *Bottiglieri di Navigazione SpA v Cosco Qingdao Ocean Shipping Co* [2005] EWHC 244 (Comm), [2005] 2 Lloyd's Rep. 1; *ASM Shipping Ltd of India v TTMI Ltd of England* [2005] EWHC 2238 (Comm), [2006] 1 Lloyd's Rep. 375, [2006] EWCA Civ 1341, [2007] 1 Lloyd's Rep. 136; *Bernuth Lines Ltd v High Seas Shipping Ltd* [2005] EWHC 3020 (Comm), [2006] 1 Lloyd's Rep. 536 at [53]; *Claire & Co Ltd v Thames Water Utilities Ltd* [2005] EWHC 1022 (TCC), [2005] Build. L.R. 366; *Cameroon Airlines v Transnet Ltd* [2004] EWHC 1829 (Comm), [2006] T.C.L.R. 1; *ABB AG v Hochtief Airport GmbH* [2006] EWHC 388 (Comm), [2006] 2 Lloyd's Rep. 1; *Norbrook Laboratories Ltd v Tank* [2006] EWHC 1055 (Comm), 2006] 2 Lloyd's Rep. 485; *Sumukan Ltd v Commonwealth Secretariat (No.2)* [2007] EWHC 188 (Comm), [2007] 1 Lloyd's Rep. 370 (reversed [2007] EWCA Civ); *HBC Hamburg Bulk Carriers GmbH & Co KG v Tangshan Haixing Shipping Co Ltd* [2006] EWHC 3250 (Comm), [2007] 2 Lloyd's Rep. 222; *OAO Northern Shipping Co v Remolcadores de Marin SL* [2007] EWHC 1821 (Comm), [2007] 2 Lloyd's Rep. 302; *JD Wetherspoon Plc v Jay Mar Estates* [2007] EWHC 856 (TCC), [2007] Build. L.R. 285; *Bandwith Shipping Corp v Intaari* [2007] EWCA Civ 998, [2008] 1 Lloyd's Rep. 7; *Stern Settlement Trustees v Levy* [2007] EWHC 1187 (TCC), (2007) 113 Const. L.R. 92; *TAG Wealth Management v West* [2008] EWHC 1466 (Comm), [2008] 2 Lloyd's Rep. 699; *Thomas O'Donoghue v Enterprise Inns Plc* [2008] EWHC 815 (Comm); *F Ltd v M Ltd* [2009] EWHC 275 (TCC), [2009] 2 Lloyd's Rep. 537 (irrelevance of dissenting arbitrator's opinion); *Van der Giessen de-Noord Shipbuilding Divi-*

(b) the tribunal exceeding its powers (otherwise than by exceeding its substantive jurisdiction: see s.67)[725];

(c) failure of the tribunal to conduct the proceedings in accordance with the procedure agreed by the parties[726];

(d) failure by the tribunal to deal with all the issues that were put to it[727];

---

sion BV v Imtech Marine & Offshore BV [2008] EWHC 2904 (Comm), [2009] 1 Lloyd's Rep. 273; *UR Power GmbH v Kuok Oils and Grains Pte Ltd* [2009] EWHC 1940 (Comm), [2009] 2 Lloyd's Rep. 495; *Compania Sud-Americana de Vapores SA V Nippon Yusen Kaisha* [2009] EWHC 1880 (Comm), [2010] 1 Lloyd's Rep. 436; *Double K Oil Products 1996 Ltd v Neste Oil OYJ* [2009] EWHC 3380 (Comm), [2010] 1 Lloyd's Rep. 141; *Michael Wilson & Partners Ltd v Emmott* [2011] EWHC 1441 (Comm); *Milan Nigeria Ltd v Angeliki B Maritime Co* [2011] EWHC 892 (Comm); *Ispat Industries Ltd v Western Bulk Pte Ltd* [2011] EWHC 93 (Comm); *AK Kablo Imalat San Ve Tic AS v Intamex SA* [2011] EWHC 2970 (Comm); *Microperi SrL v Shipowners Mutual P&I Association* [2011] EWHC 2686 (Comm); *EDF Man Sugar Ltd v Belmont Shipping Ltd* [2011] EWHC 2992 (Comm), [2012] 1 Lloyd's Rep. 206; *Abuja International Hotels Inc v Meridien SAS* [2012] EWHC 87 (Comm), [2012] 1 Lloyd's Rep. 461; *Petrochemical Industries Co (KSC) v Dow Chemical Co* [2012] EWHC 2739 (Comm), [2012] 2 Lloyd's Rep. 691; *Terna Bahrain Holding Co WLL v Al Shamsi* [2012] EWHC 3283 (Comm), [2013] 1 All E.R. (Comm) 580 at [85]; *Bulk Ship Union SA v Clipper Bulk Shipping Ltd* [2012] EWHC 2595 (Comm), [2012] 2 Lloyd's Rep. 533 at [11]–[18]; *Flame SA v Glory Wealth Shipping Pte Ltd* [2013] EWHC 3153 (Comm), [2013] 2 Lloyd's Rep. 653 at [101]–[107]; *Interprods Ltd v De La Rue International Ltd* [2014] EWHC 68 (Comm) at [18] (see above, para.32-096); *Secretary of State for Defence v Turner Estate Solutions Ltd* [2014] EWHC 244 (TCC); *Brockton Capital LLP v Atlantic-Pacific Capital Inc* [2014] EWHC 1459 (Comm), [2014] 2 Lloyd's Rep. 475; *Lorand Shipping Ltd v Davof Trading (Africa) BV* [2014] EWHC 3521 (Comm), [2015] 1 Lloyd's Rep. 67; *BV Scheepswerf Damen Gorinchem v Marine Institute* [2015] EWHC 1810 (Comm), [2015] 2 Lloyd's Rep. 351; *W Ltd v M Sdn Bhd* [2016] EWHC 422 (Comm), [2016] 1 Lloyd's Rep. 552. On the use by the arbitrator of his own knowledge and experience, see above, para.32-096, n.388.

[725] cf. *Equatorial Traders Ltd v Louis Dreyfus Trading Ltd* [2002] 2 Lloyd's Rep. 638; *Westland Helicopters Ltd v Sheikh Salah al-Hejailan*, above; *Newfield Construction Ltd v Tomlinson*, above; *Republic of Ecuador v Occidental Exploration & Production Co (No.2)* [2006] EWHC 345 (Comm), [2006] 1 Lloyd's Rep. 773; *ABB AG v Hochtief Airport GmbH*, above; *Gulf Import & Export Co v Bunge SA* [2007] EWHC 2667 (Comm), [2008] 1 Lloyd's Rep. 316 at [20]; *CNH Global NV v PGN Logistics Ltd* [2009] EWHC 977 (Comm), [2009] 1 C.L.C. 807; *Abuja International Hotels Inc v Meridien SAS* [2012] EWHC 87 (Comm), [2012] 1 Lloyd's Rep. 461; *New Age Alzarooni 2 Ltd v Range Energy Natural Resources Inc* [2014] EWHC 4358 (Comm). In *Lesotho Highlands Development Authority v Impregilo SpA* [2005] UKHL 43, [2006] 1 A.C. 221, the House of Lords held that a mere error of law by the arbitrators did not amount to an excess of power under s.68(2)(b), but at [29] Lord Steyn gave some examples of such an excess of power. See also *B v A* [2010] EWHC 1626 (Comm), [2010] 2 Lloyd's Rep. 681 (error in application of chosen law); *C v D1* [2015] EWHC 2126 (Comm) at [136]–[147]; *Essar Oilfield Services Ltd v Norscot Rig Management Pvt Ltd* [2016] EWHC 2361 (Comm), [2016] 2 Lloyd's Rep. 481 at [41]–[47]; *PT Transportasi Gas Indonesia v ConocoPhillips (Grissik) Ltd* [2016] EWHC 2834 (Comm), [2016] 2 Lloyd's Rep. 600 at [53]–[56].

[726] *Westland Helicopters v Sheikh Salah al-Hejailan*, above; *Newfield Construction Ltd v Tomlinson*, above; *Michael Wilson & Partners Ltd v Emmott* [2011] EWHC 1441 (Comm).

[727] *Weldon Plant Hire Ltd v Commission for the New Towns* [2000] B.L.R. 496; *Ascot Commodities NV v Olam International Ltd* [2001] EWHC 520 (Comm), [2002] C.L.C. 277; *Hussman (Europe) Ltd v Al Ameen Development & Trade Co* [2002] 2 Lloyd's Rep. 83; *Petroships Pte Ltd v Petec Trading and Investment Corp* [2001] 2 Lloyd's Rep. 348, 351, 355, 357; *Checkpoint Ltd v Strathclyde Pension Fund* [2003] EWCA Civ 84; *Torch Offshore LLS v Cable Shipping Inc* [2004] EWHC 787 (Comm), [2004] 2 Lloyd's Rep. 446; *Tame Shipping Ltd v Easy Navigation Ltd*, above; *Alphapoint Shipping Ltd v Rolem Amfert Negev Ltd*, above; *Margulead Ltd v Exide Technologies*, above; *World Trade Corp v C Czarnikow Sugar Ltd* [2004] EWHC 2332 (Comm), [2005] 1 Lloyd's Rep. 422; *Marklands Ltd v Virgin Retail Ltd* [2003] EWHC 3428, [2004] 27 E.G. 130; *Fidelity Management SA v Myriad International Holdings BV* [2005] EWHC 1193 (Comm), [2005] 2 Lloyd's Rep. 508; *Benaim (UK) Ltd v Davies Middleton & Davies Ltd (No.2)* [2005] EWHC 1370 (TCC), (2005) 102 Const. L.R. 1; *Protech Projects Constructions Pty Ltd v Al-Kharafi & Sons* [2005] EWHC 2165

(e)   any arbitral or other institution or person vested by the parties with powers relating to the proceedings or the award exceeding its powers;

(f)   uncertainty or ambiguity as to the effect of the award[728];

(g)   the award being obtained by fraud or the award or the way in which it was procured being contrary to public policy[729];

(Comm), [2005] 2 Lloyd's Rep. 779; *Sinclair v Woods of Winchester Ltd* [2005] EWHC 1631, (2005) 102 Const. L.R. 127; *ABB AG v Hochtief Airport GmbH*, above: *London Underground Ltd v Citylink Telecommunications Ltd* [2007] EWHC 1749 (TCC), [2007] Build. L.R. 391 at [41]; *TAG Wealth Management v West* [2008] EWHC 1466, [2008] 2 Lloyd's Rep. 699; *Van der Giessen de-Noord Shipbuilding Division BV v Imtech Marine & Offshore BV* [2008] EWHC 2904 (Comm), [2009] 1 Lloyd's Rep. 273 at [8]–[15]; *Metropolitan Property Realizations Ltd v Atmore Investments Ltd* [2008] EWHC 2925 (Ch) (criticised by Dundas (2009) 75 *Arbitration* 284); *Pace Shipping Co Ltd v Churchgate (Nigeria) Ltd* [2009] EWHC 1975 (Comm), [2010] 1 Lloyd's Rep. 183; *Double K Oil Products 1996 v Neste Oil OYJ* [2009] EWHC 3380 (Comm), [2010] 1 Lloyd's Rep. 141; *Shaw v MFP Foundation & Pilings Ltd* [2010] EWHC 1839 (TCC); *Buyuk Camiica Shipping Trading and Industry Co Inc v Progress Bulk Carriers Ltd* [2010] EWHC 442 (Comm), [2011] Bus. L.R. D99; *Michael Wilson & Partners Ltd v Emmott* [2011] EWHC 1441 (Comm); *Ispat Industries Ltd v Western Bulk Pte Ltd* [2011] EWHC 93 (Comm); *Soeximex SAS v Agrocorp International Pte Ltd* [2011] EWHC 2743 (Comm), [2012] 1 Lloyd's Rep. 52; *Latvian Shipping Co v Russian People's Insurance Co* [2012] EWHC 1412 (Comm); *Transition Feeds LLP v Itochu Europe LLP* [2013] EWHC 3629 (Comm); *Secretary of State for the Home Department v Raytheon Systems Ltd* [2014] EWHC 4375 (TCC) at [33]. A mere failure to set out in the award the tribunal's reasoning in relation to all the arguments advanced in the arbitration will not suffice: *Margulead Ltd v Exide Technologies*, above, at [29]–[35]; *Fidelity Management SA v Myriad International Holdings BV* [2005] EWHC 1193 (Comm), [2005] 2 Lloyd's Rep. 508 at [7]–[10]. In *Petrochemical Industries Co (KSC) v Dow Chemical Co* [2012] EWHC 2739 (Comm), [2012] 2 Lloyd's Rep. 691 at [16]–[21] Andrew Smith J. considered the distinction between "issues" on the one hand and "arguments", "points", "lines of reasoning" and "steps in an argument" on the other. See also *Atkins Ltd v Secretary of State for Transport* [2013] EWHC 139 (TCC), [2013] B.L.R. 193; *Primera Maritime (Hellas) Ltd v Jiangsu Eastern Heavy Industry Co Ltd* [2013] EWHC 3066 (Comm), [2014] 1 All E.R. (Comm) 813 at [8]; *Transition Feeds LLP v Itochu Europe Plc* [2013] EWHC 3629 (Comm) at [18]; *BV Scheepswerf Damen Gorinchem v Marine Institute* [2015] EWHC 1810 (Comm); *PT Transportasi Gas Indonesia v ConocoPhillips (Grissik) Ltd* [2016] EWHC 2834 (Comm), [2016] 2 Lloyd's Rep. 600 at [57]–[64]; *A v B* [2017] EWHC 596 (Comm), [2017] 2 Lloyd's Rep. 1 at [35]–[39].

728 *Gbangbola v Smith & Sherriff Ltd* [1998] 3 All E.R. 730. *Benaim (UK) Ltd v Davies Middleton & Davies Ltd (No.2)*, above; *Pace Shipping Co Ltd v Churchgate (Nigeria) Ltd* [2009] EWHC 1975 (Comm), [2010] 1 Lloyd's Rep. 183.

729 *Cuflet Chartering v Carousel Shipping Co Ltd* [2001] 1 Lloyd's Rep. 707; *Profilati Italia Srl v Painewebber Inc* [2001] 1 Lloyd's Rep. 715; *Thyssen Canada Ltd v Mariana Maritime SA* [2005] EWHC 219 (Comm), [2005] 1 Lloyd's Rep. 640; *Protech Projects Construction Pty Ltd v Al-Kharafi & Sons*, above; *Elektrim SA v Vivendi Universal SA* [2007] EWHC 11 (Comm), [2007] 1 Lloyd's Rep. 693, especially at [75]–[87]; *DDT Trucks of North America Ltd v DDT Holdings Ltd* [2007] EWHC 1542 (Comm), [2007] 2 Lloyd's Rep. 213 at [22]–[23]; *Colliers International Property Consultants v Colliers Jordan Lee Jafaar Sd Bhd* [2008] EWHC 1524 (Comm), [2008] 2 Lloyd's Rep. 368; *R v V* [2008] EWHC 1531 (Comm), [2009] 1 Lloyd's Rep. 97; *Michael Wilson & Partners Ltd v Emmott* [2011] EWHC 1441 (Comm); *Nestor Maritime SA v Sea Anchor Shipping Co Ltd* [2012] EWHC 996 (Comm); *Stockman Interhold SA v Arricano Real Estate Plc* [2017] EWHC 2909 (Comm), [2018] 1 Lloyd's Rep. 135 at [168]–[169]. In *Double K Oil Products 1996 Ltd v Neste Oil OYJ* [2009] EWHC 3380 (Comm), [2010] 1 Lloyd's Rep. 141, Blair J. stated that the court had to be satisfied that some form of reprehensible or unconscionable conduct had contributed in a substantial way to the obtaining of the award (allegation in the case was fraud in the production of evidence). See also *Chantiers de L'Atlantique SA v Gaztransport & Technigaz SAS* [2011] EWHC 3383 (Comm) at [53]–[62]; *Celtic Bioenergy Ltd v Knowles* [2017] EWHC 472 (TCC), [2017] 1 Lloyd's Rep. 495 (fraud in a party's deliberate failure to draw the tribunal's attention to relevant correspondence). As to relevance of the public policy of a foreign state, see *PT Transportasi Gas Indonesia v ConocoPhillips (Grissik) Ltd* [2016] EWHC 2834 (Comm), [2016] 2 Lloyd's Rep. 600 at [66]–[72].

(h) failure to comply with the requirements as to the form of the award[730]; or

(i) any irregularity in the conduct of the proceedings or in the award which is admitted by the tribunal or by any arbitral or other institution or person vested by the parties with powers in relation to the proceedings or the award.[731]

It will be noted that the list of irregularities is a closed one. Some of the listed elements nevertheless have their origins in the previous law relating to misconduct, "procedural mishaps" and mistakes admitted by the arbitrator.[732] However, the award cannot be challenged on the ground that the tribunal has come to an erroneous decision, whether of fact or law, and whether or not its findings of fact are supported by evidence.[733] In a two-tier arbitration, under which there is a right of appeal to an appeal board and the appeal board's award supersedes that of the first tier arbitrator, it is submitted that the award cannot be challenged on the ground of any irregularity in the conduct of the first tier proceedings if no irregularity is alleged in respect of the appeal.[734]

32-164 Secondly, the irregularity must be of a kind which the court considers has caused or will cause substantial injustice to the applicant.[735] In this respect, the DAC Report states that the section was:

---

[730] *Al Hadha Trading Co v Tradigrain SA* [2002] 2 Lloyd's Rep. 512, 521; *Benaim (UK) Ltd v Davies Middleton & Davies Ltd*, above.

[731] *Gannet Shipping Ltd v Eastrade Commodities Inc* [2002] 1 Lloyd's Rep. 713, 717–718. An admission by a member of the tribunal who is in the minority or who dissents would not be sufficient for this purpose: *A v B* [2017] EWHC 596 (Comm), [2017] 2 Lloyd's Rep. 1 at [53]–[56].

[732] See the 27th edition of this book, Vol.I, paras 15-040—15-042.

[733] *Lindner Ceilings Floors Partitions Plc v How Engineering Services Ltd* [2001] Build. L.R. 90; *Arduina Holdings BV v Celtic Resource Holdings Plc* [2006] EWHC 3155 (Comm); *Schwebel v Schwebel* [2010] EWHC 3280 (TCC), [2011] 2 All E.R. (Comm) 1048; *Flame SA v Glory Wealth Shipping Pte Ltd* [2013] EWHC 3153 (Comm), [2013] 2 Lloyd's Rep. 653; *Atkins Ltd v Secretary of State for Transport* [2013] EWHC 139 (TCC), [2013] B.L.R. 193; *Sonatrach v Statoil Natural Gas LLC* [2014] EWHC 875 (Comm), [2014] 2 Lloyd's Rep. 252 at [11]; *New Age Alzarooni 2 Ltd v Range Energy Natural Resources Inc* [2014] EWHC 4358 (Comm) at [13]; *Secretary of State for the Home Department v Raytheon Systems Ltd* [2014] EWHC 4375 (TCC) at [33]. See also *World Trade Corp v C Czarnikow Sugar Ltd* [2004] EWHC 2322 (Comm), [2005] 1 Lloyd's Rep. 422 (weight of evidence); *Lesotho Highlands Development Authority v Impregilo SpA* [2005] UKHL 43, [2006] 1 A.C. 221 at [28]. But it may be that a failure by the tribunal to take account of or consider evidence (as opposed to an alleged failure to evaluate the evidence correctly) could come within ss.33(2), 68(2)(a). *Arduina Holdings BV v Celtic Resources Holdings Plc* [2006] EWHC 3155 (comm) at [46]; *Schwebel v Schwebel* [2010] EWHC 3280 (TCC) at [27]; *Petrochemical Industries Co (KSC) v Dow Chemical Co* [2012] EWHC 2739 (Comm), [2012] 2 Lloyd's Rep. 691 at [36]; *Brockton Capital LLP v Atlantic-Pacific Capital Inc* [2014] EWHC 1459 (Comm), [2014] 2 Lloyd's Rep. 275. In *Elektrim SA v Vivendi Universal SA* [2007] EWHC 11 (Comm), [2007] 1 Lloyd's Rep. 693 at [75]–[76] Aikens J. said that the previous law was no longer applicable which gave to the court a power to remit the award where fresh evidence came to light after the award was made; cf. Gee (2006) 22 *Arbitration International* 337, 366.

[734] *Costa v British Indian Trading Co Ltd* [1963] 1 Q.B. 201.

[735] s.68(2); *Egmatra v Marco Trading Corp* [1999] 1 Lloyd's Rep. 862; *Conder Structures v Kvaerner Construction Ltd* [1999] A.D.R. L.J. 305; *Pacol Ltd v Joint Stock Co Rossakhar* [2000] 1 Lloyd's Rep. 109, 115; *Sanghi Polyesters Ltd (India) v International Investor (KCFC) (Kuwait)* [2000] 1 Lloyd's Rep. 480, 484; *Hussman (Europe) Ltd v Al Ameen Development & Trade Co* [2000] 2 Lloyd's Rep. 83, 95; *Profilati Italia Srl v Painewebber Inc* [2001] 1 Lloyd's Rep. 715, 720, 722; *Petroships Pte Ltd v Retec Trading and Investment Corp* [2001] 2 Lloyd's Rep. 348, 351; *Brandeis Brokers Ltd v Black* [2001] 2 Lloyd's Rep. 359, 370–371; *Groundshire v VHE Construction* [2001] Build. L.R. 395; *Al Hadha Trading Co v Tradigrain SA* [2002] 2 Lloyd's Rep. 512, 521–522; *Check Point Ltd v Strathclyde Pension Fund* [2003] EWCA Civ 84 [2003] E.G. 214; *Warborough Investments Ltd v S Robinson & Sons (Holdings) Ltd* [2003] EWCA Civ 751, [2003] 2 E.G.L.R. 145; *Torch*

"… really designed as a long stop, only available in extreme cases where the tribunal has gone so wrong in its conduct of the arbitration that justice calls out for it to be corrected".[736]

It has been said that "the element of substantial injustice does not depend on the arbitrator having come to the wrong conclusion as a matter of law or fact but whether he was caused by adopting inappropriate means to reach one conclusion whereas had he adopted appropriate means he might well have reached another conclusion favourable to the applicant".[737] On this view, it is necessary (and sufficient) for the applicant to show that, but for the irregularity, the tribunal might realistically have come to a significantly different conclusion[738] although it is possible that a less stringent test might be adopted where the applicant has effectively been denied a fair opportunity to state his case.[739] At any rate a substantial injustice will normally be inferred where it is shown that there was actual or apparent bias

---

[736] *Offshore LLS v Cable Shipping Inc* [2004] EWHC 787 (Comm), [2004] 2 Lloyd's Rep. 446; *Alphapoint Shipping Ltd v Rotem Amfert Negev Ltd* [2004] EWHC 2232 (Comm), [2005] 1 Lloyd's Rep. 23; *Newfield Construction Ltd v Tomlinson* [2004] EWHC 3051 (TCC), (2004) 97 Const. L.R. 148; *Fidelity Management SA v Myriad International Holdings BV* [2005] EWHC 1193 (Comm), [2005] 2 Lloyd's Rep. 508; *ASM Shipping Ltd of India v TTMI Ltd of England* [2005] EWHC 2238 (Comm), [2006] 1 Lloyd's Rep. 375, [2006] EWCA Civ 1341, [2007] 1 Lloyd's Rep. 136; *Bernuth Lines Ltd v High Seas Shipping Ltd* [2005] EWHC 3020 (Comm), [2006] 1 Lloyd's Rep. 537; *Cameroon Airlines v Transnet Ltd* [2004] EWHC 1829 (Comm), [2006] T.C.L.R. 1; *ABB AG v Hochtief Airport GmbH* [2006] EWHC 388 (Comm), [2006] 2 Lloyd's Rep. 1; *Norbrook Laboratories Ltd v Tank* [2006] EWHC 1055 (Comm), [2006] 2 Lloyd's Rep. 485; *CNH Global NV v PGN Logistics Ltd* [2009] EWHC 977 (Comm), [2009] 1 C.L.C. 807; *Compania Sud-Americana de Vapores SA V Nippon Yusen Kaisha* [2009] EWHC 1880 (Comm), [2010] 1 Lloyd's Rep. 436; *Double K Oil Products 1996 Ltd v Neste Oil OYJ* [2009] EWHC 3380 (Comm), [2010] 1 Lloyd's Rep. 141; *Michael Wilson & Partners Ltd v Emmott* [2011] EWHC 1441 (Comm); *E D & F Man Sugar Ltd v Belmont Shipping Ltd* [2011] EWHC 2992 (Comm), [2012] 1 Lloyd's Rep. 206 at [20]; *Petrochemical Industries Co (KSC) v Dow Chemical Co* [2012] EWHC 2739 (Comm), [2012] 2 Lloyd's Rep. 691; *Terna Bahrain Holding Co WLL v Al Shamsi* [2012] EWHC 3283 (Comm), [2013] 1 All E.R. (Comm) 580 at [121]; *Compton Beauchamp Estates Ltd v Spence* [2013] EWHC 1101 (Ch), [2013] 20 E.G. 107 (C.S.) at [36], [79]; *Transition Feeds LLP v Itochu Europe Plc* [2013] EWHC 3629 (Comm); *BV Scheepswerf Damen Gorinchem v Marine Institute* [2015] EWHC 1810 (Comm), [2015] 2 Lloyd's Rep. 351.

[736] para.280; *Petroships Pte Ltd v Retec Trading and Investment Corp*, above, at 351; *Bandwith Shipping Corp v Intaari*, above, at [46]; *Michael Wilson & Partners Ltd v Emmott* [2011] EWHC 1441 (Comm) at [18]; *Ispat Industries Ltd v Western Bulk Pte Ltd* [2011] EWHC 93 (Comm) at [17]; *Bulk Ship Union SA v Clipper Bulk Shipping Ltd* [2012] EWHC 2595 (Comm), [2012] 2 Lloyd's Rep. 533 at [18]; *Flame SA v Glory Wealth Shipping Pte Ltd* [2013] EWHC 3153 (Comm), [2013] 2 Lloyd's Rep. 653 at [101]–[107]; *Secretary of State for Defence v Turner Estate Solutions Ltd* [2014] EWHC 244 (TCC) at [69]; *Lorand Shipping Ltd v Davof Trading (Africa) BV* [2014] EWHC 3521 (Comm), [2015] 1 Lloyd's Rep. 67 at [18].

[737] *Vee Networks Ltd v Econet Wireless International Ltd* [2004] EWHC 2909 (Comm), [2005] 1 Lloyd's Rep. 192 at [88]–[90].

[738] *St George's Investment Co Ltd v Gemini Consulting Ltd* [2004] EWHC 2353 (Ch), *Newfield Construction Ltd v Tomlinson* [2004] EWHC 305 (TCC), (2004) 97 Const. L.R. 148; *BTC Bulk Transport Corp v Glencore International AG* [2006] EWHC 1857 (Comm); *JD Wetherspoon Plc v Jay Mar Estates* [2007] EWHC 856 (TCC) [2007] Build. L.R. 285; *OAO Northern Shipping Co v Remolcadores de Marin SL* [2007] EWHC 1821 (Comm), [2007] 2 Lloyd's Rep. 302; *London Underground Ltd v Citylink Communications Ltd* [2007] B.L.R. 391; *Michael Wilson & Partners Ltd v Emmott* [2011] EWHC 1441 (Comm) at [17]; *Brockton Capital LLP v Atlantic-Pacific Capital Inc* [2014] EWHC 1459 (Comm), [2014] 2 Lloyd's Rep. 275 at [27]–[31]; *Secretary of State for the Home Department v Raytheon Systems Ltd* [2014] EWHC 4375 (TCC) at [33]. cf. *Soeximex v Agrocorp International Pte Ltd* [2011] EWHC 2743 (Comm), [2012] 1 Lloyd's Rep. 52 at [25]; *Maass v Musion Events Ltd* [2015] EWHC 1346 (Comm), [2015] 2 Lloyd's Rep. 383 at [40]–[42].

[739] s.33(1)(a); *Checkpoint Ltd v Strathclyde Pension Fund* [2003] EWCA Civ 751, [2003] E.G.L.R. 149;

affecting the tribunal, on the ground that:

"... there can be no more serious or substantial injustice than having a tribunal which was not, *ex hypothesi*, impartial, determine the parties' rights."[740]

32-165 The application must normally be made within the 28 day time limit prescribed by s.70(3)[741] and is subject to certain restrictions.[742] A party may have lost the right to object to the irregularity if he failed to object timeously and thereafter took part, or continued to take part, in the proceedings, unless he did not know and could not with reasonable diligence have discovered the grounds for the objection.[743] If a serious irregularity is shown to have occurred, the court may remit the award to the arbitral tribunal for reconsideration, or it may set the award aside, or it may declare the award to be of no effect. It may exercise these powers in relation to the whole of the award or only part of it. The court is not to set the award aside or declare it to be of no effect unless it is satisfied that it would be inappropriate to remit the matters in question to the tribunal for reconsideration.[744] A party may be precluded from having an award remitted, set aside or declared to be of no effect if he has in fact taken the benefit of the award and so affirmed it.[745]

32-166 Where, by agreement of the parties,[746] the arbitral tribunal makes an award without stating its reasons for the award but sets out its reasons in a separate "confidential" document, this does not preclude the court from looking at those reasons for the purpose of an application under the section.[747]

32-167 The power conferred on the court by s.68 is exercisable only if the seat of arbitration is in England.[748] The section applies only to awards and not to interlocutory directions which are not made in the form of an award.[749]

Warborough Investment Ltd v S Robinson & Sons (Holdings) Ltd [2003] EWHC 787 (Comm), [2005] 1 Lloyd's Rep. 23. See also the European Convention on Human Rights, above, para.32-015. But see *JD Wetherspoon Plc v Jay Mar Estates*, above.

[740] *ASM Shipping Ltd of India v TTMI Ltd of England* (at first instance) [2005] EWHC 2238 (Comm), [2006] 1 Lloyd's Rep. 375, [2006] EWCA Civ 1341, [2007] 1 Lloyd's Rep. 136 at [39]; *Norbrook Laboratories v Tank* [2006] EWHC 1055 (Comm), [2006] 2 Lloyd's Rep. 485 at [144]–[145].

[741] Below, para.32-176. For extension of time, see s.79.

[742] s.70(2); below, para.32-176. See also CPR Pt 62.

[743] s.73(1); below, para.32-176. See *Rustal Trading Ltd v Gill & Duffus SA* [2000] 1 Lloyd's Rep. 14, 19–20, and below, para.32-177. See also *Essar Oilfield Services Ltd v Norscot Rig Management Pvt Ltd* [2016] EWHC 2361 (Comm), [2016] 2 Lloyd's Rep. 481 at [78]–[85].

[744] s.68(3). Remitting the award would be the normal remedy under s.68(2)(d), (f) and (h). But see *Pacol Ltd v Joint Stock Co Rossakhar* [2000] 1 Lloyd's Rep. 109, 115; *Secretary of State for the Home Department v Raytheon Systems Ltd (No.2)* [2015] EWHC 311 (TCC), [2015] 1 Lloyd's Rep. 493. cf. *Van der Giessen de-Noord Shipbuilding Division BV v Imtech Marine & Offshore BV* [2008] EWHC 2904 (Comm), [2009] 1 Lloyd's Rep. 273 (appointment of umpire). For remission in a case under s.68(2)(a), see *Brockton Capital LLP v Atlantic-Pacific Capital Inc* [2014] EWHC 1459 (Comm), [2014] 2 Lloyd's Rep. 275.

[745] *Dexters Ltd v Hill Crest Oil Co (Bradford) Ltd* [1926] 1 K.B. 348; *AA Amram Ltd v Bremar Co Ltd* [1966] 1 Lloyd's Rep. 494; *European Grain & Shipping Ltd v R Johnston* [1983] Q.B. 520; *ASM Shipping Ltd of India v TTMI Ltd of England* (at first instance) [2005] EWHC 2238 (Comm), [2006] 1 Lloyd's Rep. 375, [2006] EWCA Civ 1341, [2007] 1 Lloyd's Rep. 136 at [49]. Contrast *Lissenden v CAV Bosch Ltd* [1940] A.C. 412; *Sokratis Rokopoulos v Esperia SpA* [1978] 1 Lloyd's Rep. 456; *Banner Industrial and Commercial Properties v Clark Paterson* (1990) 47 E.G. 64.

[746] s.52(4).

[747] *Tame Shipping Ltd v Easy Navigation Ltd* [2004] EWHC 1862 (Comm), [2004] 2 Lloyd's Rep. 626.

[748] s.2(1).

[749] See (on s.22 of the Arbitration Act 1950) *Fletamentos Maritimos SA v Effjohn International BV (No.2)* [1997] 2 Lloyd's Rep. 302.

Appeal on point of law[750]   Section 69 of the 1996 Act restates in an amended form   **32-168**
s.1 of the Arbitration Act 1979 and provides that, unless otherwise agreed by the
parties, a party to arbitral proceedings may appeal to the court on a question of law
arising out of an award made in the proceedings.[751] It is to be emphasised that an
appeal lies under s.69 only on a question of law. There is no room for any appeal
under the section against the findings of fact in the award itself since these have to
be accepted for the purpose of the appeal.[752] By s.82(1), "question of law" means,
for a court in England and Wales a question of the law of England and Wales.[753]
Such an appeal lies only with the agreement of all other parties to the proceedings[754] or with permission of the court.[755] By subs.(3) of the section, permission to
appeal is not to be given unless the court is satisfied:

   (a)   that the determination of the question will substantially affect the rights of
        one or more of the parties[756];
   (b)   that the question is one which the tribunal was asked to determine[757];

---

[750] Needham (1999) 65 *Arbitration* 205; Holmes and O'Reilly (2003) 69 *Arbitration* 1; Dundas (2003)
69 *Arbitration* 172; (2006) 72 *Arbitration* 11 , 281; Esposito (2008) 74 *Arbitration* 429; Tweedale
and Tweedale (2013) 79 *Arbitration* (3) 265; Tweedale, Tweedale and Nguyen (2013) 80 *Arbitration* (2) 136.

[751] s.69(1); CPR Pt 62, PD 62.12.

[752] s.69(3)(c); *Demco Investments & Commercial SA v SE Banken Forsakring Holding Aktiebolag*
[2005] EWHC 154 (Comm), [2005] 2 Lloyd's Rep. 650 at [35]; *Benaim (UK) Ltd v Davies Mid-
dleton & Davies Ltd* (2005) EWHC 1370 (TCC), (2005) 102 Const. L.R. 1 (application of law to
fact); *CTI Group Inc v Transclear SA* [2008] EWCA Civ 856, [2008] 2 Lloyd's Rep. 526 at [11];
TAG Wealth Management v West [2008] EWHC 1466, [2008] 2 Lloyd's Rep. 699 at [46]–[52]; *ASM
Shipping Ltd of India v TTMI Ltd of England* [2009] 1 Lloyd's Rep. 293n; *Trustees of Edmond Stern
Settlement v Levy* [2009] EWHC 14 (TCC), [2009] 1 Lloyd's Rep. 345; *Dolphin Tanker SRL v
Westport Petroleum Inc* [2010] EWHC 2617 (Comm), [2011] 1 Lloyd's Rep. 550 at [29]; *Eitzen Bulk
A/S v TTMI SARL* [2012] EWHC 202 (Comm), [2012] 2 All E.R. 100 at [20]–[35]; *Wuhan Ocean
Economic & Technical Co-operation Co Ltd v Schiffahrts-Gesellschaft "Hansa Murcia" mbH & Co
KG* [2012] EWHC 3104 (Comm), [2013] 1 Lloyd's Rep. 273 at [15]–[18], [22]–[31]; *Latvian Ship-
ping Co v Russian People's Insurance Co* [2012] EWHC 1412 (Comm), [2012] 2 Lloyd's Rep. 181;
Sun United Maritime Ltd v Kastell Marine Inc [2014] EWHC 1476 (Comm), [2014] 2 Lloyd's Rep.
386. See also *Guangzhon Dockyards Co Ltd v ENE Aegiali I* [2010] EWHC 2826 (Comm), [2011]
1 Lloyd's Rep. 30 at [30]–[34] (doubtful whether court can hear appeal from arbitrators on questions of fact even if parties so agree).

[753] *Egmatra v Marco Trading Corp* [1999] 1 Lloyd's Rep. 862; *Sanghi Polyesters (India) v International
Investor (KCFC) Kuwait* [2000] 1 Lloyd's Rep. 480; *Reliance Industries Ltd v Enron Oil and Gas
Ltd* [2002] 1 Lloyd's Rep. 645; *Athletic Union of Constantinople v National Basketball Associa-
tion* [2002] 1 Lloyd's Rep. 305, 313; *Schwebel v Schwebel* [2010] EWHC 3280 (TCC), [2011] 2 All
E.R. (Comm) 1048. For a court in Northern Ireland, it means the law of Northern Ireland.

[754] *Poseidon Schiffahrt GmbH v Nomadic Navigation Co Ltd* [1998] 1 Lloyd's Rep. 57; and *Royal and
Sun Alliance Insurance Plc v BAE Systems (Operations) Ltd* [2008] EWHC 743 (Comm), [2008] 1
Lloyd's Rep. 712 (consent in advance); cf. *ST Shipping and Transport Pte Ltd v Space Shipping Ltd*
[2016] EWHC 880 (Comm), [2016] 2 Lloyd's Rep. 17. In this situation, the barriers set by subs.(3)
will not apply.

[755] s.69(2).

[756] *CMA CGMSA v KGMS "Northern Pioneer"* [2002] EWCA Civ 1878, [2003] 1 W.L.R. 1015; *Stern
Settlement Trustees v Levy* [2007] EWHC 187 (TCC), (2007) 113 Const. L.R. 92; *Shaw v MFP
Foundations Pilings Ltd* [2010] EWHC 1839 (TCC); *Corooba Holdings Ltd v Ballymore Proper-
ties Ltd* [2011] EWHC 1636 (Ch); *House of Fraser Ltd v Scottish Widows Plc* [2011] EWHC 2800
(Ch).

[757] *Marklands Ltd v Virgin Retail Ltd* [2003] EWHC 3428, [2004] 2 E.G.L.R. 43; *Pace Shipping Co
Ltd v Churchgate (Nigeria) Ltd* [2009] EWHC 1975 (Comm), [2010] 1 Lloyd's Rep. 183 at [43];
House of Fraser Ltd v Scottish Widows Plc [2011] EWHC 2800 (Ch); cf. *HOK Sport Ltd v Aintree
Racecourse Co Ltd* [2002] EWHC 3094 (TCC), [2003] Build. L.R. 155.

(c) that on the basis of the findings of fact in the award:
　　(i) the decision of the tribunal on the question is obviously wrong,[758] or
　　(ii) the question is one of general public importance and the decision of the tribunal is at least open to serious doubt[759]; and

(d) that, despite the agreement of the parties to resolve the matter by arbitration, it is just and proper in all the circumstances for the court to determine the question.[760]

The subsection reflects the limitations placed on the right of appeal under the 1979 Act by the House of Lords, notably in *Pioneer Shipping Ltd v BTP Tioxide Ltd (The Nema)*[761] and *Antaios Compânia Naviera SA v Salen Rederiana AB (The Antaios)*,[762] but further limits court intervention by requiring that it must be "just and proper in all the circumstances for the court to determine the question".[763]

32-169　The application for permission to appeal must identify the question of law to be

---

[758] *HMV UK Ltd v Propinvest Friar Ltd* [2011] EWCA Civ 1708, [2012] 1 Lloyd's Rep. 416 at [5], [6] (i.e. transparent and clear upon a mere perusal of the reasoned award itself); *Morris Homes (West Midlands) Ltd v Keay* [2013] EWHC 932 (TCC), [2013] B.L.R. 370 at [50]; *AMEC v Secretary of State for Defence* [2013] EWHC 110 (TCC), 146 Con. L.R. 152; *Transition Feeds LLP v Itochu Europe Plc* [2013] EWHC 3629 (Comm).

[759] See *CMA CGM SA v KGMS "Northern Pioneer"*, above; *Icon Navigation Corp v Sinochem International Petroleum (Bahamas) Co Ltd* [2002] EWHC 2812 (Comm), [2003] 1 All E.R. (Comm) 405. *HOK Sport Ltd v Aintree Racecourse Co Ltd*, above; *Keydon Estates Ltd v Western Power Distribution (South Wales) Ltd* [2004] EWHC 996 (Ch); *JSC Zestafoni G Nikoladz Ferroalley Plant v Ronly Holdings Ltd* [2004] EWHC 245 (Comm), [2004] 2 Lloyd's Rep. 335; *Vrinera Marine Co Ltd v Eastern Rich Operations Inc* [2004] EWHC 1752 (Comm), [2004] 2 Lloyd's Rep. 465; *Alphapoint Shipping Ltd v Rotem Amfert Negev Ltd* [2004] EWHC 2232 (Comm), [2005] 1 Lloyd's Rep. 23; *Newfield Construction Ltd v Tomlinson* [2004] EWHC 3051 (TCC), (2004) 97 Const. L.R. 148; *Bottiglieri di Navigazione SpA v Cosco Quindao Ocean Shipping Co* [2005] EWHC 244 (Comm), [2005] 2 Lloyd's Rep. 1; *Surefire Systems Ltd v Guardian ECL Ltd* [2005] EWHC 1860 (TCC), [2006] Build. L.R. 534; *Essex CC v Premier Recycling Ltd* [2007] Build. L.R. 233; *DDT Trucks of North America Ltd v DDT Holdings Ltd* [2007] EWHC 154 (Comm), [2007] 2 Lloyd's Rep. 213; *Stern Settlement Trustees v Levy* [2007] EWHC 1187 (TCC), [2007] 113 Const. L.R. 92; *Braes of Doune Wind Farm (Scotland) Ltd v Alfred McAlpine Business Services Ltd* [2008] EWHC 426 (TCC), [2008] 1 Lloyd's Rep. 608 at [26]–[32]; *Mayhaven Healthcare Ltd v Bothma* [2009] EWHC 2634 (TCC), 127 Con. L.R. 1; *UR Power GmbH v Kuok Oils and Grains Pte Ltd* [2009] EWHC 1940 (Comm), [2009] 2 Lloyd's Rep. 495; *National Trust v Fleming* [2009] EWHC 1789 (Ch), [2009] N.P.C. 97; *Pace Shipping Co Ltd v Churchgate (Nigeria) Ltd* [2009] EWHC 1975 (Comm), [2010] 1 Lloyd's Rep. 183; *Gas Natural Approvisionamientos SDG SA v Methane Services Ltd* [2009] EWHC 2298 (Comm), [2010] 1 Lloyd's Rep. 610; *SOS Corporacion Alimentaria SA v Inerco Trade SA* [2010] EWHC 162 (Comm), [2010] 2 Lloyd's Rep. 345; *Sylvia Shipping Co Ltd v Progress Bulk Carriers Ltd* [2010] EWHC 542 (Comm), [2010] 2 Lloyd's Rep. 81; *Dolphin Tanker SRL v Westport Petroleum Inc* [2010] EWHC 2617 (Comm), [2011] 1 Lloyd's Rep. 550; *Milan Nigeria Ltd v Angeliki B Maritime Co* [2011] EWHC 892 (Comm); *Ispat Industries Ltd v Western Bulk Pte Ltd* [2011] EWHC 93 (Comm); *Cordoba Holdings Ltd v Ballymore Properties Ltd* [2011] EWHC 1636 (Ch); *HMV UK Ltd v Propinvest Friar Ltd Partnership* [2011] EWCA Civ 1708; *House of Fraser Ltd v Scottish Widows Plc* [2011] EWHC 2800 (Ch); *MRI Trading AG v Erdenet Mining Corp LLC* [2012] EWHC 1988 (Comm), [2012] 2 Lloyd's Rep. 465; *Morris Homes (West Midlands) Ltd v Keay* [2013] EWHC 932 (TCC), [2013] B.L.R. 370.

[760] See n.763, below.

[761] [1982] A.C. 724.

[762] [1985] A.C. 191; *CMA CGM SA v KGMS "Northern Pioneer"*, above, at [11], [60].

[763] *Egmatra v Marco Trading Corp* [1999] 1 Lloyd's Rep. 862 (foreign law); *CMA CGM SA v KGMS "Northern Pioneer"*, above (question rendered academic); *HOK Sport Ltd v Aintree Racecourse Co Ltd* [2002] EWHC 3094 (TCC), [2003] Build. L.R. 155 (delay allegedly prejudicial); *Keydon Estates Ltd v Western Power Distribution (South Wales) Ltd*, above (expert tribunal); *Essex CC v Premier Recycling Ltd* [2007] Build. L.R. 534 ("final and binding" decision); *Stern Settlement Trustees v Levy* [2007] EWHC 1187 (TCC), [2007] 113 Con. L.R. 92, at [29] (waste of time, cost and resource in

determined and state the grounds on which it is alleged that permission to appeal should be granted.[764] The court will normally determine the application for permission without a hearing.[765] As a general rule, the appeal must be brought within the 28 day time limit prescribed by s.70(3)[766] and is subject to certain restrictions.[767] Appeals are only permitted on a question of law "arising out of an award" and not in respect of extrinsic matters arising in the course of the arbitral proceedings.[768] The court will no doubt, as under the previous law, continue to set its face against entertaining questions of law framed in the form of a question whether there was sufficient, or any, evidence to support a particular finding of fact.[769] The court may make any permission which it gives conditional upon the appellant complying with such conditions as it considers appropriate, and in particular may order security for costs or that money payable under the award is to be brought into court or otherwise secured.[770] If the application is unsuccessful, it will normally be sufficient for the applicant to be told which of the tests in subs.(3) he has failed, and the judge need not go further and explain why the relevant test has been failed. But whether the tribunal's decision was obviously wrong or open to serious doubt, if may be necessary, in a particular case, for the judge to give brief reasons to explain why the ap-

---

pursuing weak challenge in context of arbitration claim of modest proportions). See also (on s.1 of the Arbitration Act 1979) *Aden Refinery Co Ltd v Ugland Management Co Ltd* [1987] Q.B. 650; *Petraco (Bermuda) Ltd v Petromed International Ltd* [1988] 1 W.L.R. 896; *Ipswich BC v Fisons Plc* [1990] Ch. 709.

[764] s.69(4). CPR Pt 62.12; *Parbulk II A/S v Heritage Maritime SA* [2011] EWHC 2917 (Comm), [2012] 2 All E.R. (Comm) 418.

[765] s.69(5) (unless it appears to the court that a hearing is required). This is not contrary to art.6 of the European Convention on Human Rights: *BLCT (13096) Ltd v J Sainsbury Plc* [2003] EWCA Civ 884, [2004] 2 P & C.R. 3; above, para.32-017. See also *CMA CGM SA v KGMS "Northern Pioneer"*, above (brevity required in written submissions).

[766] See below, para.32-176.

[767] s.70(2); below, para.32-176. See also CPR P 62, PD 62.12.

[768] *Universal Petroleum Co Ltd v Handels und Transport GmbH* [1987] 1 W.L.R. 1178, 1189; *Foley's Ltd v City and East London Family and Community Services* [1997] A.D.R.L.J. 401; *HOK Sport Ltd v Aintree Racecourse Co Ltd* [2002] EWHC 3094 (TCC), [2003] B.L.R. 155; *Great Western Trains Co Ltd v Network Rail Infrastructure Ltd* [2010] EWHC 117 (Comm) at [89]; *Sylvia Shipping Co Ltd v Progress Bulk Carriers Ltd* [2010] EWHC 542 (Comm), [2010] 2 Lloyd's Rep. 81 at [88]; *Dolphin Tanker SRL v Westport Petroleum Inc* [2010] EWHC 2617 (Comm), [2011] 1 Lloyd's Rep. 550 at [29]–[30]. cf. *Kershaw Mechanical Services Ltd v Kendrick Construction Ltd* [2006] EWHC 727 (TCC), [2006] 4 All E.R. 79 at [45]; *White Young Green Consulting v Brooke House Sixth Form College* [2007] EWHC 2018 (TCC) at [25].

[769] *Demco Investments & Commercial SA v SE Banken Forsakring Holding Aktiebolag* [2005] EWHC 1542 (Comm), [2005] 2 Lloyd's Rep. 650 at [35]–[48]; *Surefire Systems Ltd v Guardian ECL Ltd* [2005] EWHC 1860 (TCC), [2006] Build. L.R. 534; *London Underground Ltd v Citylink Telecommunications Ltd* [2007] EWHC 1749 (TCC), [2007] 2 All E.R. (Comm) 694; *House of Fraser Ltd v Scottish Widows Plc* [2011] EWHC 2800 (Ch); *Guangzhou Dockyards Co Ltd v ENE Aegiali I* [2010] EWHC 2826 (Comm), [2011] 2 All E.R. (Comm) 595. See (before the Act) *Mondial Trading Co GmbH v Gill & Duffus Zuckerhandelsgesellschaft mbH* [1980] 2 Lloyd's Rep. 376, 379; *Hayn Roman & Co SA v Cominter (UK) Ltd* [1982] 2 Lloyd's Rep. 458, 462; *Bulk Oil (Zug) AG v Sun International Ltd* [1984] 1 Lloyd's Rep. 531, 533; *Athens Cape Naviera SA v Deutsche Dampfschiffahrtsgesellschaft Hansa AG* [1985] 1 Lloyd's Rep. 528, 531–532; *Universal Petroleum Co Ltd v Handels und Transport GmbH*, above; *Geogas SA v Trammo Gas Ltd* [1993] 1 Lloyd's Rep. 215, 217. But see (no evidence) *Edwards v Bairstow* [1956] A.C. 14; *Pioneer Shipping Ltd v BTP Tioxide Ltd (The Nema)* [1982] A.C. 724, 752; *Antaios Compania Naviera SA v Salen Rederiana AB (The Antaios)* [1985] A.C. 191, 205; *CMA CGM SA v KGMS "Northern Pioneer"* [2002] EWCA Civ 1878, [2003] 1 W.L.R. 1015, at [28]. cf. *Benaim (UK) Ltd v Davies Middleton & Davies Ltd* [2005] EWHC 1370 (TCC); *CTI Group Inc v Transclear SA* [2007] EWHC 2340 (Comm), [2007] 2 C.L.C. 530.

[770] s.70(6), (7), (8).

plicant has lost.[771] The court has jurisdiction under CPR r.3.1(7) or its inherent jurisdiction to set aside an order granting leave to appeal.[772]

32-170 On an appeal under s.69 the court may confirm, vary or set aside the award or remit the award to the tribunal for reconsideration in the light of the court's determination. It may exercise its powers of setting aside or remission as to the whole of the award or only part of it. The court cannot exercise its power to set aside an award unless it is satisfied that it would be inappropriate to remit the matters in question to the tribunal for reconsideration.[773]

32-171 **Combined applications** Applications under s.68 (challenge on the ground of serious irregularity) and s.69 (for leave to appeal on a point of law) may be combined in one hearing[774] but they involve two quite distinct processes of judicial analysis.[775] In many cases determination of the s.69 application before that of the s.68 application may be logically preferable, but in each case it is a matter for the court whether the application for leave to appeal should be tried first.[776]

32-172 **Right of appeal: exclusion agreements** Section 69, unlike ss.67 and 68, is not a mandatory provision and it is open to the parties by agreement to exclude the right of appeal.[777] In the case of a domestic arbitration agreement s.87 of the 1996 Act provides that any agreement to exclude the jurisdiction of the court under s.69 or under s.45 (determination of preliminary point of law) is not to be effective unless entered into after the commencement of the arbitral proceedings in which the award is made. But s.87 is not yet in force and is unlikely to be brought into force.[778] The special categories of disputes mentioned in s.4(1) of the 1979 Act where the efficacy of an exclusion agreement was limited have not been retained in the 1996 Act. The parties are therefore free to exclude the right of appeal either in the original arbitration agreement or by the adoption of institutional rules[779] which exclude that right. An agreement to dispense with reasons for the tribunal's award is to be

[771] *North Range Shipping Ltd v Seatrans Shipping Corp (The Western Triumph)* [2002] EWCA Civ 405, [2002] 1 W.L.R. 2397. cf. *Mousaka Inc v Golden Seagull Maritime Inc* [2002] 1 W.L.R. 295.

[772] *Latvian Shipping Co v Russian People's Insurance Co* [2012] EWHC 1412 (Comm), [2012] 2 Lloyd's Rep. 181.

[773] s.69(7). cf. *Loon Navigation Corp v Sinochern International Petroleum (Bahamas) Co Ltd* [2002] EWHC 2812, [2003] 1 All E.R. (Comm) 405; *Vrinera Marine Co Ltd v Eastern Rich Operations Inc* [2004] EWHC 1752 (Comm), [2004] 2 Lloyd's Rep. 465 at [15]. There is no reason why the judge who granted permission to appeal on a point of law cannot hear the substantive appeal: *L v A* [2016] EWHC 1789 (Comm) at [4]–[8].

[774] *Bulfracht (Cyprus) Ltd v Boneset Shipping Co Ltd* [2002] EWHC 2292 (Comm), [2002] 2 Lloyd's Rep. 681; *Newfield Construction Ltd v Tomlinson* [2004] EWHC 3051 (TCC), (2004) 97 Const. L.R. 148; *Alphapoint Shipping Ltd v Rotem Amfert Negev Ltd* [2004] EWHC 2232, [2005] 1 Lloyd's Rep. 23.

[775] *Alphapoint Shipping Ltd v Rotem Amfert Negev Ltd*, above, at [5]–[7].

[776] *Alphapoint Shipping Ltd v Rotem Amfert Negev Ltd*, above, at [7].

[777] s.69(1).

[778] See above, para.32-005.

[779] *Anglo African Energy Corp Ltd v Olieprodukten Nederland NV* [1983] 2 Lloyd's Rep. 419; *Marine Contractors Inc v Shell Petroleum Development Co of Nigeria* [1984] 2 Lloyd's Rep. 77; *Sanghi Polyesters (India) v International Investor (KCFC) (Kuwait)* [2000] 1 Lloyd's Rep. 480 (ICC rules); *Sumukan Ltd v Commonwealth Secretariat* [2006] EWHC 304 (Comm), [2007] EWCA Civ 243, [2007] 2 Lloyd's Rep. 87 (Com Sec rules). Contrast *Shell Egypt West Manzala GmbH v Dana Gas Egypt Ltd* [2009] EWHC 2097 (Comm), [2010] 1 Lloyd's Rep. 109 (UNCITRAL Arbitration Rules 1976).

considered an agreement to exclude the court's jurisdiction under s.69,[730] but not merely a provision that an award is to be "final and binding".[781] An exclusion agreement is not contrary to art.6 of the European Convention on Human Rights.[782]

Challenge or appeal: reasons for award   The arbitral tribunal is required to give **32-173** reasons for the award unless the award is an agreed award or the parties have agreed to dispense with reasons.[783] But, in order that the procedures for challenge or appeal may be effective, s.70(4) of the 1996 Act empowers the court to compel the tribunal to give reasons or further reasons for its award.[784] If on an application or appeal it appears to the court that the award does not contain the tribunal's reasons or does not set out the tribunal's reasons in sufficient detail to enable the court properly to consider the application or appeal, the court may order the tribunal to state the reasons for the award in sufficient detail for that purpose. In relation to the similar power conferred upon the court under s.1(5) of the 1979 Act, it was held that this power should be exercised sparingly[785] and the same applies to s.70(4).[786] It is not sufficient that it would be helpful to the court to have such reasons[787] and it is probable that the court will have to be satisfied that, if an order were made, the application or appeal would be likely to succeed.[788] Otherwise there would be no point in ordering reasons or further reasons to be stated.

Challenge or appeal: additional costs   Where the court makes the order, it may **32-174** make such further order as it thinks fit with respect to any additional costs of the arbitration resulting from the order.[789]

Challenge or appeal: facts on which decision based   The power to order the **32-175**

---

[780] s.69(1).
[781] *Essex CC v Premier Recycling Ltd* [2007] Build. L.R. 233; but see s.69(3)(d), above, para.32-168. See also *Shell Egypt West Manzala GmbH v Dana Gas Egypt Ltd* [2009] EWHC 2097 (Comm), [2010] 1 Lloyd's Rep. 109 ("final, conclusive and binding").
[782] *Sumukan Ltd v Commonwealth Secretariat* [2006] EWHC 304 (Comm). [2007] EWCA Civ 243, [2007] 2 Lloyd's Rep. 87; see above, para.32-017.
[783] s.52(4). In maritime and some other arbitrations reasons may, by agreement, be set out in a separate "confidential" document and not in the award: see above, para.32-166.
[784] This replaced s.1(5) of the Arbitration Act 1979. (Considered by the Court of Appeal in *Universal Petroleum Co Ltd v Handels und Transport GmbH* [1987] 1 W.L.R. 1178). But s.70(4) extended the courts' ability to order reasons beyond appeal on a point of law to applications under ss.67, 68. See *JFS (UK) Ltd v South West Water Services Ltd* (1998) 65 Con. L.R. 157; *Petroships Pte Ltd v Petec Trading and Investment Corp* [2001] 2 Lloyd's Rep. 348, 357; *Alphapoint Shipping Ltd v Rotem Amfert Negev Ltd* [2004] EWHC 2232 (Comm), [2005] 1 Lloyd's Rep. 23 at [5]; *Margulead Ltd v Exide Technologies* [2004] EWHC 1019 (Comm), [2005] 1 Lloyd's Rep. 324 at [41]–[42]; *Van der Giessen de-Noord Shipbuilding Division BV v Imtech Marine & Offshore BV* [2008] EWHC 2904 (Comm), [2009] 1 Lloyd's Rep. 273 at [14]. cf. *Navios International Inc v Sangamon Transportation Group* [2012] EWHC 166 (Comm), [2012] 1 Lloyd's Rep. 493 (order not necessary).
[785] *Universal Petroleum Co Ltd v Handels und Transport GmbH*, above, at 1194; *Granges Aluminium AB v The Cleveland Bridge and Engineering Co, The Times,* May 15, 1990, CA.
[786] *Navios International Inc v Sangamon Transportation Group*, above, at [26].
[787] *Navios International Inc v Sangamon Transportation Group*, above, at [24].
[788] *The Gay Fidelity* [1982] 1 Lloyd's Rep. 469, 470; *Warde v Feedex International Inc* [1984] 1 Lloyd's Rep. 310, 314, [1985] 2 Lloyd's Rep. 289; *Trave Schiffahrtsgesellschaft mbH v Ninemia Maritime Corp* [1986] Q.B. 802; *Universal Petroleum Co Ltd v Handels und Transport GmbH*, above, at 1194; *Gebr Van Weelde Scheepvaart Kantoor BV v Société Industrielle d'Acide, etc.* [1986] 1 Lloyd's Rep. 435; *Kansa General Insurance Co Ltd v Bishopsgate Insurance Plc* [1988] 1 Lloyd's Rep. 503, 511; *JFS (UK) Ltd v South West Water Services Ltd*, above.
[789] s.70(5).

tribunal to state reasons for the award extends not only to "reasoning" but also to the relevant facts upon which its decision is based.[790] But the power cannot or should not be used to order the tribunal to set out the evidence on which it relied in order to reach its conclusion.[791] There is no power in the court, before an award is made, to order the tribunal to state reasons for pre-award rulings.[792]

32-176 Challenge or appeal: restrictions and time limits An application or appeal may not be brought if the applicant or appellant has not first exhausted any available process of appeal or review and any available recourse under s.57 (correction of award or additional award).[793] Any application or appeal must be brought within 28 days of the date of the award or, if there has been any arbitral process of appeal or review, of the date when the applicant or appellant was notified of the result of that process.[794] This period may be extended by the court in accordance with rules of the court[795] (though the criteria applicable to applications for such an extension may differ from those applicable under the CPR).[796]

---

[790] *Schiffahrtsagentur Hamburg Middle East Line GmbH v Virtue Shipping Corp* [1981] 1 Lloyd's Rep. 533, 539; *Bulk Oil (Zug) AG v Sun International Ltd (No.2)* [1984] 1 Lloyd's Rep. 531, 533.

[791] *Interbulk Ltd v Aiden Shipping Co Ltd* [1983] 2 Lloyd's Rep. 424, 429, [1984] 2 Lloyd's Rep. 66; *Mafracht v Patries Shipping Co SA* [1986] 2 Lloyd's Rep. 405, 414; *Universal Petroleum Co Ltd v Handels und Transport GmbH* [1987] 1 W.L.R. 1178; Mustill and Boyd at p.541. See also *Hayn Roman & Co SA v Cominter (UK) Ltd* [1982] 2 Lloyd's Rep. 458, 462; *Bulk Oil (Zug) AG v Sun International Ltd (No.2)*, above, at 533; *Athens Cape Naviera SA v Deutsche Dampschiffahrtsgesellschaft Hansa AG* [1985] 1 Lloyd's Rep. 528.

[792] *Three Valleys Water Committee v Binnie and Partners* (1990) 52 B.L.R. 42.

[793] s.70(2); CPR Pt 62, PD 62.11; *Groundshire v VHE Construction* [2001] Build. L.R. 395; *Al Hadha Trading Co v Tradigrain SA* [2002] 2 Lloyd's Rep. 512; *Torch Offshore LLC v Cable Shipping Inc* [2004] EWHC 787 (Comm), [2004] 2 Lloyd's Rep. 446; *Sinclair v Woods of Winchester Ltd* [2005] EWHC 1631 (QB), (2005) 102 Const. L.R. 127; *Bulk Ship Union SA v Clipper Bulk Shipping Ltd* [2012] EWHC 2595 (Comm), [2012] 2 Lloyd's Rep. 533 at [31]–[32]; cf. *Gbangbola v Smith & Sherriff Ltd* [1998] 3 All E.R. 730; *World Trade Corp v C Czarnikow Sugar Ltd* [2004] EWHC 2332 (Comm), [2005] 1 Lloyd's Rep. 422; *Ases Havacilik Servis ve Destek Hizmetleri AS v Delkor UK Ltd* [2012] EWHC 3518 (Comm), [2013] 1 Lloyd's Rep. 254 at [19]–[24]; *A Ltd v B Ltd* [2014] EWHC 1870 (Comm). See above, para.32-143 and *Buyuk Camlica Shipping Trading and Industry Co Inc v Progress Bulk Carriers Ltd* [2010] EWHC 442 (Comm), [2011] Bus. L.R. D99.

[794] s.70(3); *Westland Helicopters Ltd v Sheikh Salah al-Hejailan (No.1)* [2004] EWHC 1625 (Comm), [2004] 2 Lloyd's Rep. 523; *Thyssen Canada Ltd v Mariana Maritime SA* [2005] EWHC 219 (Comm), [2005] 1 Lloyd's Rep. 640; *Sinclair v Woods of Winchester Ltd*, above; *UR Power GmbH v Kuok Oils and Grains Pte Ltd* [2009] EWHC 1940 (Comm), [2009] 2 Lloyd's Rep. 495 at [58] and *PEC Ltd v Asia Golden Rice Ltd* [2012] EWHC 846 (Comm), [2013] 1 Lloyd's Rep. 82 (two-tier arbitration). It is a moot point whether the extended time for appeal under s.70(2)(a) or applies to an application under s.57 as well: see *Surefire Systems Ltd v Guardian ECL Ltd* [2005] EWHC 1860 (TCC), [2005] B.L.R. 534; *Price v Carter* [2010] EWHC 1451 (TCC). In *Essar Oilfield Services Ltd v Norscot Rig Management Pvt Ltd* [2016] EWHC 2361 (Comm), [2016] 2 Lloyd's Rep. 481 at [90]–[93] the Court held that if the award is corrected pursuant to s.57, the 28-day time period runs from the date of the corrected award, provided that the application to correct is material to the issue being raised by the application to the Court. An application is material if it is necessary to enable the party to know whether he has grounds to challenge the award or not. It is unclear when time would start running if the application to correct the award is refused. See also *K v S* [2015] EWHC 1945 (Comm), [2015] 2 Lloyd's Rep. 363; *Daewoo Shipbuilding & Marine Engineering Co Ltd v Songa Offshore Equinox Ltd* [2018] EWHC 538 (Comm) at [52]–[65]. An application or appeal may also be struck out for want of prosecution: *Huyton SA v Jakil Spa* [1999] 2 Lloyd's Rep. 83.

[795] s.80(5), CPR rr.3.1, 3.9; *Dubai Islamic Bank PJSC v Paymentech Merchant Services Inc* [2001] 1 Lloyd's Rep. 65, 75; *Aoot Kalmneft v Glencore International AG* [2002] 1 Lloyd's Rep. 128, 134; *Peoples Insurance Co of China v Vysanthi Shipping Co Ltd* [2003] EWHC 1655 (Comm), [2003] 2 Lloyd's Rep. 616; *Thyssen Canada Ltd v Mariana Maritime SA*, above; *Sinclair v Woods of*

The right to object to the tribunal's substantive jurisdiction will be lost if the chal- **32-177**
lenge is not made timeously.[797] Also a party to arbitral proceedings will be held to
have lost the right to object that the tribunal lacks substantive jurisdiction, or that
the proceedings have been improperly conducted, or that there has been a failure
to comply with the arbitration agreement or any provision of Pt I of the Act, or that
there has been any other irregularity affecting the tribunal or the proceedings, if he
failed to object timeously[798] and thereafter took part or continued to take part in the
proceedings,[799] unless he shows that he did not then know and could not with
reasonable diligence have discovered the grounds for the objection.[800] It is clear that

---

Winchester Ltd, above; *Elektrim SA v Vivendi Universal SA* [2007] EWHC 11 (Comm), [2007] 1
Lloyd's Rep. 693 at [72]; *PEC Ltd v Asia Golden Rice Ltd* [2012] EWHC 846 (Comm), [2013] 1
Lloyd's Rep. 82; *Terna Bahrain Holding Co WLL v Al Shamsi* [2012] EWHC 3283 (Comm), [2013]
1 All E.R. (Comm) 580; *London Steam Ship Owners Mutual Insurance Association Ltd v Spain (The
Prestige)* [2013] EWHC 2840 (Comm), [2014] 1 All E.R. (Comm) 300.

796 In *Aoot Kalmneft v Glencore International AG*, above, Colman J. (at 137) set out six considerations which, in his judgment, were likely to be material to the exercise by the court of its power to
extend time (applied in *Nagusina Naviera v Allied Maritime Inc* [2002] EWCA Civ 1147, [2003] 2
C.L.C. 1; *Gold Coast Ltd v Naval Gijon SA* [2006] EWHC 1044 (Comm), [2006] 2 Lloyd's Rep.
400 (s.79 application); *DDT Trucks of North America Ltd v DDT Holdings Ltd* [2007] EWHC 1542
(Comm), [2007] 2 Lloyd's Rep. 213); *Colliers International Property Consultants v Colliers Jordan
Lee Jafaar Sdn Bhd* [2008] EWHC 1524 (Comm), [2008] 2 Lloyd's Rep. 396; *L Brown & Sons Ltd
v Crosby Homes (North West) Ltd* [2008] EWHC 817 (TCC), [2008] Build. L.R. 366; *ASM Ship-
ping Ltd of India v TTMI Ltd of England* [2009] 1 Lloyd's Rep. 293n; *UR Power GmbH v Kuok Oils
and Grains Pte Ltd* [2009] EWHC 1940 (Comm), [2009] 2 Lloyd's Rep. 495 at [62], [63]; *Broda
Agro Trade (Cyprus) Ltd v Alfred C Toepfer International Ltd* [2010] EWCA Civ 1100, [2011] 1
Lloyd's Rep. 243; *Chantiers de L'Atlantique SA v Gaztransport & Technigaz SAS* [2011] EWHC
3383 (Comm) at [63]; *Nestor Maritime SA v Sea Anchor Shipping Co Ltd* [2012] EWHC 996
(Comm); *PEC Ltd v Asia Golden Rice Ltd* [2012] EWHC 846 (Comm), [2013] 1 Lloyd's Rep. 82
at [21]; *Terna Bahrain Holding Co WLL v Al Shamsi* [2012] EWHC 3283 (Comm), [2013] 1 All E.R.
(Comm) 580 at [27]–[34]; *London Steam Ship Owners Mutual Insurance Association Ltd v Spain
(The Prestige)* [2013] EWHC 2840 (Comm), [2014] 1 All E.R. (Comm) 300; *K v S* [2015] EWHC
1945 (Comm); *Daewoo Shipbuilding & Marine Engineering Co Ltd v Songa Offshore Equinox Ltd*
[2018] EWHC 538 (Comm) at [70]–[77]; Dundas (2012) 78 *Arbitration* (3) 293. In *S v A* [2016]
EWHC 846 (Comm), [2016] 1 Lloyd's Rep. 604 at [26], the Court applied the test laid down in *Terna
Bahrain Holding Company WLL v Al Shamsi* because it was common ground that it should do so,
but questioned whether such a test should continue to apply in light of the Court's more recent decision in *Denton v TH White Ltd* [2014] EWCA Civ 906, [2014] 1 W.L.R. 3926.

797 s.73(2); see above, para.32-157.

798 *Wicketts v Brine Builders* [2001] C.I.L.L. 1805; *Essar Oilfield Services Ltd v Norscot Rig Management Pvt Ltd* [2016] EWHC 2361 (Comm), [2016] 2 Lloyd's Rep. 481 at [78]–[85].

799 *Gater Assets Ltd v NAK Naftogaz Ukrainiy* [2007] EWCA Civ 988, [2007] 2 Lloyd's Rep. 588 at
[79]; *Broda Agro Trade (Cyprus) Ltd v Alfred C Toepfer International GmbH* [2010] EWCA Civ
1100, [2011] 1 Lloyd's Rep. 243; *Sovarex SA v Romero Alvarez SA* [2011] EWHC 1661 (Comm),
[2011] 2 Lloyd's Rep. 320 at [12]–[15]; *Sierra Fishing Co Ltd v Mohamed* [2015] EWHC 140
(Comm) at [72]; *Frontier Agriculture Ltd v Bratt Bros (A Firm)* [2015] EWCA Civ 611, [2015] 2
Lloyd's Rep. 500, at [35]; *A v B* [2016] EWHC 3003 (Comm), [2017] 1 W.L.R. 2030 at [50]–[63].

800 s.73(1); *Rustal Trading Ltd v Gill & Duffus SA* [2000] 1 Lloyd's Rep. 14, 19; *Hussman (Europe)
Ltd v Al Ameen Development & Trade Co* [2000] 2 Lloyd's Rep. 83, 91; *Athletic Union of
Constantinople v National Basketball Association* [2002] 1 Lloyd's Rep. 305, 311; *Peterson Farms
Inc v C&M Farming Ltd* [2004] EWHC 121 (Comm), [2004] 1 Lloyd's Rep. 603; *JSC Zestafoni G
Nikoladz Ferroalloy Plant v Ronly Holdings Ltd* [2004] EWHC 245 (Comm) 2004, [2004] 2 Lloyd's
Rep. 335; *Westland Helicopters Ltd v Sheikh Salah al-Hejailan (No.1)* [2004] EWHC 1625 (Comm),
[2004] 2 Lloyd's Rep. 523; *Vee Networks Ltd v Econet Wireless International Ltd* [2004] EWHC
2909 (Comm), [2005] 1 Lloyd's Rep. 192; *Margulead Ltd v Exide Technologies* [2004] EWHC 1019
(Comm), [2005] 1 Lloyd's Rep. 324; *Thyssen Canada Ltd v Mariana Maritime SA* [2005] EWHC
219 (Comm), [2005] 1 Lloyd's Rep. 640; *ASM Shipping Ltd of India v TTMI Ltd of England* [2005]
EWHC 2238 (Comm), [2006] 1 Lloyd's Rep. 375, [2006] EWCA Civ 1341, [2007] 1 Lloyd's Rep.

it is unnecessary for him to have had actual knowledge of the grounds of objection in order for him to lose his right to challenge the award and in *Rustal Trading Ltd v Gill & Duffus SA*[801] Moore-Bick J. stated "If the respondent can show that the applicant took part or continued to take part in the proceedings without objection after the grounds of objection had arisen, the burden passes to the applicant to show that he did not know, and could not with reasonable diligence have discovered those grounds at the time". He further expressed the view that it was unnecessary for the applicant to have taken a positive step in the proceedings: "... unless a party makes it clear that he is withdrawing from the proceedings, he continues to take part in them until they reach their conclusion, normally in the publication of a final award".

32-178 **Challenge or appeal: supplementary orders** The court may order the applicant or appellant to provide security for the costs of the application or appeal[802] and may order that any money payable under the award shall be brought into court or otherwise secured.[803]

32-179 **Challenge or appeal: effect of order of the court** Where the award is varied by the court, the variation has effect as part of the tribunal's award.[804]

32-180 Where the award is remitted by the court to the tribunal for reconsideration, the tribunal must make a fresh award in respect of the matter remitted within three months of the date of the order or such longer or shorter period as the court

---

136; *Primetrade AG v Ythan Ltd* [2005] EWHC 2399 (Comm), [2006] 1 Lloyd's Rep. 457; *Sinclair v Woods of Winchester Ltd* [2005] EWHC 1631 (QB), [2005] 102 Const. L.R. 127; *Sumukan Ltd v Commonwealth Secretariat (No.2)* [2007] EWCA Civ 1148, [2008] 1 Lloyd's Rep. 40; *ASM Shipping Ltd v Harris* [2007] EWHC 1513 (Comm), [2008] 1 Lloyd's Rep. 61; *Stern Settlement Trustees v Levy* [2007] EWHC 1187 (TCC), (2007) 113 Const. L.R. 92; *Colliers International Property Consultants v Colliers Jordan Lee Jafaar Sdn Bhd* [2008] EWHC 1524 (Comm), [2008] 2 Lloyd's Rep. 396; *Nestor Maritime SA v Sea Anchor Shipping Co Ltd* [2012] EWHC 996 (Comm); *Habas Sinai Ve Tibbi Gazlav Istihsal Endustrisi AS v VSC Steel Co Ltd* [2013] EWHC 4071 (Comm), [2014] 1 Lloyd's Rep. 479 at [81]–[87]. See also above, paras 32-102, 32-159, 32-165, 32-169.

801 [2000] 1 Lloyd's Rep. 14, 19, 20. See also *JSC Zestafoni G Nikoladz Ferroalloy Plant v Ronly Holdings Ltd*, above, at [63]–[64]. But see *Sumukan Ltd v Commonwealth Secretariat (No.2)*, above, at [36]; *Ases Havacilik Servis ve Destek Hizmetleri AS v Delkor UK Ltd* [2012] EWHC 3518 (Comm), [2013] 1 Lloyd's Rep. 254.

802 s.70(5), (6); CPR Pt 25. *Azov Shipping Co v Baltic Shipping Co* [1999] 2 Lloyd's Rep. 39; *Republic of Kazakhstan v Istil Group Ltd* [2005] EWCA Civ 1468, [2006] 1 W.L.R. 596; *Peterson Farms Inc v C & M Farming Ltd* [2003] EWHC 2298 (QB), [2004] 1 Lloyd's Rep. 614; *Moondance Maritime Enterprises SA v Carbofer Maritime Trading APS* [2012] EWHC 3618 (Comm), [2013] 1 Lloyd's Rep. 269; *X v Y* [2013] EWHC 1104 (Comm), [2013] 2 Lloyd's Rep. 230; *Konkola Copper Mines Plc v U&M Mining Zambia Ltd* [2014] EWHC 2374 (Comm), [2014] 2 Lloyd's Rep. 649; *Progas Energy Ltd v Islamic Republic of Pakistan* [2018] EWHC 209 (Comm), [2018] 1 Lloyd's Rep. 252 at [18]–[46].

803 s.70(7); Merkin, *Arbitration Act 1996*, 5th edn, 346–348. cf. *Peterson Farms Inc v C & M Farming Ltd* [2003] EWHC 2298 (QB), [2004] 1 Lloyd's Rep. 614; *Tajik Aluminium Plant v Hydro Aluminium AS* [2006] EWHC 1135 (Comm); *Moondance Maritime Enterprises SA v Carbofer Maritime Trading APS* [2012] EWHC 3618 (Comm), [2013] 1 Lloyd's Rep. 269 at [9]; *X v Y* [2013] EWHC 1104 (Comm), [2013] 2 Lloyd's Rep. 230; *Konkola Copper Mines Plc v U&M Mining Zambia Ltd* [2014] EWHC 2374 (Comm), [2014] 2 Lloyd's Rep. 649; *Erdenet Mining Corp LLC v ICBC Standard Bank Plc* [2017] EWHC 1090 (Comm), [2017] 2 Lloyd's Rep. 25; *Progas Energy Ltd v Islamic Republic of Pakistan* [2018] EWHC 209 (Comm), [2018] 1 Lloyd's Rep. 252 at [47]–[68]. But see *A v B* [2010] EWHC 3302 (Comm), [2011] 1 Lloyd's Rep. 363 (differing requirements for s.70(7) with respect to applications under s.67 on the one hand and ss.68, 69 on the other).

804 s.71(2).

directs.[805] The effect of the order is to revive the jurisdiction of the tribunal, but only insofar as is necessary to deal with the matter remitted.[806] Following a remission, the first award is suspended: once a second award is published, the first award becomes null.[807]

Where the award is set aside by the court or declared to be of no effect, the court **32-181** may also order that any *Scott v Avery* clause[808] is to be of no effect.[809]

Challenge or appeal: appeals to the Court of Appeal[810]   An appeal lies to the **32-182** Court of Appeal from a decision of the court on an application under s.67 or s.68, but such an appeal lies only if the court gives permission.[811] Only the judge who hears that application can give permission to appeal: the Court of Appeal itself cannot do so.[812] Refusal by the court to give permission to appeal to the Court of Appeal is unappealable.[813]

The permission of the court is required for any appeal to the Court of Appeal **32-183** from a decision of the court under s.69 to grant or refuse permission to appeal.[814] It is probable that permission to appeal will only be granted in exceptional circumstances.[815] Refusal by the court to give permission to appeal to the Court of Appeal is unappealable.[816]

The decision of the court on an appeal under s.69 is to be treated as a judgment **32-184** of the court for the purposes of a further appeal.[817] But no such appeal lies without the permission of the court, which will not be given unless the court considers that the question is one of general importance or is one which for some other special

---

[805] s.71(3).
[806] *Interbulk Ltd v Aiden Shipping Co Ltd* [1983] 2 Lloyd's Rep. 410.
[807] *Huyton SA v Jakil SpA* [1999] 2 Lloyd's Rep. 83 (on s.22 of the 1950 Act).
[808] See above, para.32-048.
[809] s.71(4).
[810] See Senior Courts Act 1981 s.18(1)(g), as substituted by s.107(1) and Sch.3 para.37, of the Arbitration Act 1996.
[811] ss.67(4), 68(4).
[812] *Athletic Union of Constantinople v National Basketball Association (No.2)* [2002] EWCA Civ 830, [2002] 1 W.L.R. 2863; *ASM Shipping Ltd of India v TTMI Ltd of England* [2006] EWCA Civ 1341, [2007] 1 Lloyd's Rep. 136; *Republic of Kazakhstan v Istil Group Ltd* [2007] EWCA Civ 471, [2007] 2 Lloyd's Rep. 548; *Integral Petroleum Ltd v Melars Group Ltd* [2016] EWCA Civ 108, [2016] 2 Lloyd's Rep. 141. But the Court of Appeal could set aside permission to appeal under CPR r.52.18.
[813] This does not infringe art.6 of the European Convention on Human Rights: *ASM Shipping Ltd of India v TTMI Ltd of England*, above; *Republic of Kazakhstan v Istil Group Ltd*, above: see above, para.32-017.
[814] s.69(6). But a decision that the parties had entered into an exclusion agreement (para.32-172, above) is not within s.69(6); *Sumukan Ltd v Commonwealth Secretariat* [2007] EWCA Civ 243, [2007] 2 Lloyd's Rep. 87.
[815] *CMA CGM SA v KGMS "Northern Pioneer"* [2002] EWCA Civ 1878, [2003] 1 W.L.R. 1015 at [12]–[13], reflecting s.1(6A) of the Arbitration Act 1979: *The Antaios* [1985] A.C. 191, 205; *Petraco (Bermuda) Ltd v Petromed International Ltd* [1988] 1 W.L.R. 896, 899.
[816] *Aden Refinery Co Ltd v Ugland Management Co Ltd* [1987] Q.B. 650.
[817] s.69(8).

reason should be considered by the Court of Appeal.[818] No appeal lies to the Court of Appeal against a refusal by the court to give permission to appeal.[819]

32-185   In the circumstances referred to above, and in other cases[820] where the Act provides that no appeal lies to the Court of Appeal without permission of the first instance court, the Court of Appeal has held that it is nevertheless entitled in certain situations to entertain an appeal despite a refusal of permission to appeal. The first situation is where the first instance court has made an order which it was not within its jurisdiction or not empowered to make under the provision of the Act relied on.[821] The second is where the decision of that court is invalidated by misconduct[822] or by unfairness in the process of arriving at its decision.[823] This residuary appellate jurisdiction exists both apart from[824] and consistently with the European Convention on Human Rights.[825] It does not, however, enable an appeal to be brought without permission on the ground that the court's decision on the merits was erroneous or unfair.[826]

32-186   Enforcement of awards   By s.66 of the 1996 Act,[827] an award made by the tribunal pursuant to an arbitration agreement may, by permission of the court, be enforced in the same manner as a judgment or order of the court to the same effect,[828] and where permission is so given, judgment may be entered in terms of the

---

[818] s.69(8). But only the court (and not the Court of Appeal) can give leave. Section 69(8) is unaffected by s.55 of the Access to Justice Act 1999: *Henry Boot Construction (UK) Ltd v Malmaison Hotel (Manchester) Ltd* [2001] Q.B. 388, CA. A decision that the parties had entered into an exclusion agreement (para.32-172, above) is not within s.69(8): *Sumukan Ltd v Commonwealth Secretariat*, above.

[819] This does not infringe art.6 of the European Convention on Human Rights: *CGU International Insurance Plc v Astrazenica Insurance Co Ltd* [2006] EWCA Civ 1340, [2007] 1 Lloyd's Rep. 142; see above, para.32-017.

[820] ss.12(6), 17(4), 18(5), 21(6), 24(6), 25(5), 32(6), 42(5), 44(7), 45(5), 50(5), 56(7), 77(4), 79(6).

[821] *Cetelem SA v Roust Holdings Ltd* [2005] EWCA Civ 618, [2005] 2 Lloyd's Rep. 494 at [28]. cf. *Shuttari v Solicitors' Indemnity Fund* [2007] EWCA Civ 244, [2007] 1 C.L.C. 303.

[822] *Aden Refinery Co Ltd v Ugland Management Co Ltd*, above, at p.666.

[823] *North Range Shipping Ltd v Seatrans Shipping Corp* [2002] EWCA Civ 405, [2002] 1 W.L.R. 2397 at [44]; *CGU International Insurance Plc v Astrazeneca Insurance Co Ltd* [2006] EWCA Civ 1340, [2007] 1 Lloyd's Rep. 142 at [45]–[47]; *Republic of Kazakhstan v Istil Group Ltd* [2007] EWCA Civ 417, [2007] 2 Lloyd's Rep. 548 at [30]–[31]; *Bunge SA v Kyla Shipping Co Ltd* [2013] EWCA Civ 734, [2013] 3 All E.R. 1006. See also *BLCT (13096) Ltd v J Sainsbury Ltd* [2003] EWCA Civ 884, [2004] 2 P. & C.R. 3.

[824] Senior Courts Act 1981 s.16. In *Michael Wilson & Partners Ltd v Emmott* [2015] EWCA Civ 1285, [2016] 1 W.L.R. 857 the Court explained the nature of the Court's jurisdiction. See also *Integral Petroleum Ltd v Melars Group Ltd* [2016] EWCA Civ 108, [2016] 2 Lloyd's Rep. 141 at [25]–[31].

[825] arts 3, 6, 8; see above, para.32-017. See also *Yegiazaryan v Smagin* [2016] EWCA Civ 1290, [2017] 1 Lloyd's Rep. 102 at [26].

[826] *CGU International Insurance Plc v Astrazeneca Insurance Co Ltd*, above, at [58]–[63]; *Republic of Kazakhstan v Istil Group Ltd*, above, at [32].

[827] This section replaced s.26 of the Arbitration Act 1950. It is mandatory.

[828] s.66(1). See CPR r.62.18 and Sch.2 para.11 (judge-arbitrator); *Norwich Union v Whealing Horton & Toms* [2008] EWHC 370 (TCC); *African Fertilizers and Chemicals Nig Ltd v BD Shipsnavo GmbH & Co Reederi KG* [2011] EWHC 2452, [2011] 2 Lloyd's Rep. 53 (declaration); *West Tankers Inc v Allianz SpA* [2012] EWCA Civ 27, [2012] 1 Lloyd's Rep. 398 (negative declaration); *Mobile Telesystems Finance SA v Nomihold Securities Inc* [2011] EWCA Civ 140, [2012] 1 Lloyd's Rep. 6. Part of an award may be enforced where the remaining balance has been duly satisfied: *Continental Grain Co v Bremer Handelsgesellschaft mbH (No.2)* [1984] 2 Lloyd's Rep. 121, 124.

award.[829] These two steps are distinct[830]; the former permitting a party to use the court's enforcement mechanisms for the purpose of enforcing the award and the latter enabling a party to obtain a judgment of the court itself in terms of the award. Permission to enforce an award cannot be given where, or to the extent that, the person against whom it is sought to be enforced shows that the tribunal lacked substantive jurisdiction to make the award,[831] but any objection must be made timeously.[832] Otherwise, the court has a discretion whether or not to permit enforcement of the award. Permission should be given to enforce the award unless there is a real ground for doubting its validity.[833] But permission might be refused, for example, if the award dealt with matters which are not capable of settlement by arbitration,[834] or on the grounds of public policy,[835] or if it was not in a form in which it could be entered as a judgment.[836] An award made in a foreign currency may be enforced,[837] but not an award which specifically requires payment in a foreign country.[838] An award may be enforced under s.66 even though the seat of the arbitration is outside England or no seat has been designated or determined.[839] It would appear that the court will not make an order for security for costs against an award

---

[829] s.66(2). Judgment must be entered in the same terms as the award: *Norsk Hydro ASA v The State Property Fund of the Ukraine* [2002] EWHC 2120 (Comm). The court has no power to add interest under s.35A of the Senior Courts Act 1981 to a sum awarded by the arbitral tribunal which remains unpaid after the award: *Walker v Rowe* [2000] 1 Lloyd's Rep. 116; *Sonatrach v Statoil Natural Gas LLC* [2014] EWHC 875 (Comm), [2014] 2 Lloyd's Rep. 252; cf. *Yukos Capital SARL v OJSC Oil Co Rosneft* [2014] EWHC 2188 (Comm), [2014] 2 Lloyd's Rep. 435. But, where judgment is entered under s.66(2) or s.101(3) in terms of the award, the obligation to pay interest follows from the power of the court under s.17 of the Judgments Act 1838: *Gater Assets Ltd v Nak Naftogaz Ukrainiy (No.3)* [2008] EWHC 1108 (Comm), [2008] 2 Lloyd's Rep. 294; *Sonatrach v Statoil Natural Gas LLC* [2014] EWHC 875 (Comm), [2014] 2 Lloyd's Rep. 252 (s.66); *Nigerian National Petroleum Corp v IPCO (Nigeria) Ltd (No.2)* [2008] EWCA Civ 1157, [2009] 1 Lloyd's Rep. 89 (on s.101(3)).

[830] *ASM Shipping Ltd of India v TTMI Ltd of England (No.2)* [2007] EWHC 927 (Comm), [2007] 2 Lloyd's Rep. 155 at [26]. cf. *Mobile Telesystems Finance SA v Nomihold Securities Inc* [2011] EWHC Civ 1040, [2012] 1 Lloyd's Rep. 6 at [10]. See also *National Ability SA v Tinna Oils and Chemicals Ltd* [2009] EWCA Civ 1330, [2010] 1 Lloyd's Rep. 222 at [10], [14] (limitation).

[831] s.66(3). See *Sovarex SA V Romero Alvarez SA* [2011] EWHC 1661 (Comm), [2011] 2 Lloyd's Rep. 320 (power to determine disputed issues of fact).

[832] s.73; above, paras 32-102, 32-157, 32-176. But see *Dallah Real Estate & Tourism Co v Ministry of Religious Affairs of the Government of Pakistan* [2010] UKSC 46, [2010] 1 A.C. 763 at [98]; *London Steam Ship Owners Mutual Insurance Association Ltd v Spain (The Prestige)* [2013] EWHC 2840, [2014] 1 All E.R. 300 (defendant does not participate in the arbitration).

[833] *Middlemiss & Gould v Hartlepool Corp* [1972] 1 W.L.R. 1643 (not following *Re Boks & Co and Peters Rushton & Co Ltd* [1919] 1 K.B. 491, 497); *Curacao Trading Co BV v Harkisandas & Co* [1992] 2 Lloyd's Rep. 186, 192.

[834] See above, para.32-020.

[835] *Soleimany v Soleimany* [1999] Q.B. 785 (illegality). cf. *R v V* [2008] EWHC 1531 (Comm), [2009] 1 Lloyd's Rep. 97. See s.81(1)(c).

[836] *Margulies Brothers Ltd v Dafaris Thomside & Co (UK) Ltd* [1958] 1 W.L.R. 398, 404.

[837] *Jugoslovenska Oceanska Plovidba v Castle Investment Co Inc* [1974] Q.B. 292 (approved in *Miliangos v George Frank Textiles Ltd* [1976] A.C. 443). The date for conversion into sterling of the award was said in the former case to be the date of the award, but in the latter case (at 469) it was suggested that conversion could be made on the date that leave to enforce was given.

[838] *Dalmia Cement Ltd v National Bank of Pakistan* [1975] Q.B. 9. But see *Dalmia Dairy Industries Ltd v National Bank of Pakistan* [1978] 2 Lloyd's Rep. 223 (action for damages); and *Bank Mellat v GAA Development and Construction Co* [1988] 2 Lloyd's Rep. 44, 55 (requirement not part of award).

[839] s.2(2)(b).

creditor in respect of an application to enforce.[840] But the court has power to stay enforcement and order security.[841]

32-187 An award may also be enforced by bringing an action on the award.[842] This will be the only method of enforcement available where the arbitration agreement was not in writing[843] or permission to enforce the award under s.66 is refused. In an action on the award the defendant cannot plead as a defence that the findings of the arbitral tribunal were wrong[844] or that the arbitral proceedings leading to the award were unfair, irregular or unsatisfactory.[845] His remedy is to appeal to the court on a question of law arising out of the award[846] or to apply to the court to set aside the award on the ground of serious irregularity,[847] but in either case within the time limits and subject to the restrictions prescribed.[848] He can, however, raise the defence that the arbitral tribunal acted without jurisdiction or exceeded its jurisdiction.[849]

32-188 A claim on an award is a claim for damages for the breach of an implied term in the submission to arbitration that any award would be fulfilled.[850] Therefore, a claimant wishing to enforce an award in English proceedings has to prove, not only the award, but also the submission to arbitration which gave the arbitral tribunal the power to make its award and which contained the implied term that the parties would fulfil any award made pursuant to the submission.[851] There is, however, no need to plead and prove the underlying dispute arising under the contract between the parties.[852] A claim to enforce an award made in relation to a dispute arising out of a charterparty is not within the Admiralty Jurisdiction in rem as a claim "arising out of any agreement for the carriage of goods in a ship or to the use or hire of a ship" under s.20(2)(h) of the Senior Courts Act 1981.[853]

32-189 An order may be made under s.37(1) of the Senior Courts Act 1981 for the disclosure of assets in aid of execution to enforce an arbitration award where the arbitration is seated in England.[854] But the court has no jurisdiction to make a freezing order in aid of enforcement of an English arbitrator's award against subsidiar-

---

[840] *Gater Assets Ltd v NAK Naftogaz Ukrainiy* [2007] EWCA Civ 988, [2007] 2 Lloyd's Rep. 588. But see *Diag Human SE v Czech Republic* [2013] EWHC 3190 (Comm), [2014] 1 All E.R. (Comm) 605.

[841] *Apis AS v Fantazia Kereskedelmi KFT* [2001] 1 All E.R. (Comm) 348; *Socadec SA v Pan Afric Impex Co Ltd* [2003] EWHC 2086 (QB); *Broda Agro Trade (Cyprus) Ltd v Alfred C Toepfer International GmbH* [2009] EWHC 3318 (Comm), [2010] 1 Lloyd's Rep. 533 at [70] (affirmed [2010] EWCA Civ 1100, [2011] 1 Lloyd's Rep. 243). cf. *Y v S* [2015] EWHC 612 (Comm), [2015] 1 Lloyd's Rep. 703.

[842] See Mustill and Boyd at p.417.

[843] See above, para.32-025.

[844] *Walshaw v Brighouse Corp* [1899] 2 Q.B. 286.

[845] *Thorburn v Barnes* (1867) L.R. 2 C.P. 384; *Oppenhaim & Co v Majomed Janeef* [1922] 1 A.C. 482; *Scrimaglio v Thornett and Fehr* (1924) 131 L.T. 174.

[846] s.69; above, para.32-168.

[847] s.68; above, para.32-163.

[848] ss.70, 73; above, paras 32-165, 32-169, 32-176; *Birtley and District Co-operative Soc Ltd v Windy Nook and District Co-operative Soc Ltd (No.1)* [1959] 1 W.L.R. 142.

[849] *Brown v Genossenschaft Oesterreichischer Waldbesitzer R GmbH* [1954] 1 Q.B. 8.

[850] *Bremer Oeltransport GmbH v Drewry* [1993] 1 K.B. 753, 764; *FL Bloemen Pty Ltd v City of Gold Coast Council* [1973] A.C. 115, 126; *The Bumbesti* [2000] Q.B. 559, 566.

[851] *The Bumbesti*, above, at 566. See also CPR r.62.18(6) and *Colliers International Property Consultants v Colliers Jordan Lee Jafaar Sdn Bhd* [2008] EWHC 1524 (Comm), [2008] 2 Lloyd's Rep. 368 at [19].

[852] *The Bumbesti*, above, at 566.

[853] *The Beldis* [1936] P. 51; *The Bumbesti*, above (not following *The Santa Anna* [1983] 1 W.L.R. 895).

[854] *Cruz City 1 Mauritius Holdings v Unitech Ltd* [2013] EWHC 1323 (Comm), [2013] 2 All E.R. (Comm) 1137. See also below, para.32-194.

ies of the award debtor against whom nc substantial claim is asserted and who have no presence or assets within the jurisdiction.[855]

Foreign awards   A foreign award may be enforced in England in a number of   **32-190**
ways. First, it may likewise be enforced under s.66 of the Act or by action.[856] Secondly, an award made,[857] in pursuance of an arbitration agreement, in the territory of a state[858] which is a party to the New York Convention on the Recognition and Enforcement of Foreign Arbitral Awards (1958) may, by permission of the court, be enforced in the same manner as a judgment or order of the court to the same effect by virtue of s.101 of the 1995 Act.[859] Thirdly, except insofar as an award is a New York Convention award, by virtue of Pt II of the Arbitration Act 1950 a foreign award is enforceable in the same manner as an English award if it is made in pursuance of an arbitration agreement to which the Geneva Protocol (1923) applies,[860] and which is made between persons of whom one is subject to the jurisdiction of a state party to the Geneva Convention for the Execution of Foreign Arbitral Awards (1927),[861] and the award is made in such a state.[862] Fourthly, an arbitration award made in a Commonwealth country to which Pt II of the Administration of Justice Act 1920 or Pt I of the Foreign Judgments (Reciprocal Enforcement) Act 1933 has been extended[863] can be enforced in the same manner as a judgment of a court in that place, i.e. by registration under those Acts, provided that it has become enforceable in the same manner as a judgment given by a court in that country.[864] Fifthly, various other statutes permit the enforcement of certain awards upon

---

[855] *Cruz City 1 Mauritius Holdings v Unitech Ltd* [2014] EWHC 3704 (Comm), [2015] 1 Lloyd's Rep. 181. But see *Cruz City 1 Mauritius Holdings v Unitech Ltd* [2014] EWHC 3131 (Comm), [2015] 1 All E.R. (Comm) 336 (receiver).

[856] See ss.2(2)(b), 104 and *Dicey, Morris and Collins on the Conflict of Laws*, 15th edn, para.16-099.

[857] An award is to be treated as made at the seat of the arbitration (see above, para.32-140) regardless of where it was signed, despatched or delivered to any of the parties: s.100(2)(b).

[858] For a list of contracting states, see *http://www.newyorkconvention.org* and *http://www.uncitral.org*.

[859] See ss.66(4), 100–104 and *Government of the State of Kuwait v Sir Frederick Snow and Partners* [1984] A.C. 426; *Agromet Motoimport v Maulden Engineering (Beds) Ltd* [1985] 1 W.L.R. 762; *Bank Mellat v GAA Development and Construction Co* [1988] 2 Lloyd's Rep. 44. cf. *Deutsche Schachtbau-und Tiefbohrgesellschaft mbH v R'as al-Khaimah National Oil Co* [1990] 1 A.C. 295; *Soleh Boneh International Ltd v Government of Uganda* [1993] 2 Lloyd's Rep. 208; *Minmetals German GmbH v Ferco Steel Ltd* [1999] 1 All E.R. Comm. 315; *Norsk Hydro ASA v The State Property Fund of Ukraine* [2002] EWHC 2120 (Comm); *Dicey, Morris and Collins on the Conflict of Laws*, 15th edn, para.16-128; CPR r.62.18. In *Pencil Hill Ltd v US Citta Di Palermo SpA*, Unreported, January 19, 2016 at [30], the Court said that there is a strong leaning towards the enforcement of foreign arbitral awards and the circumstances in which the English Court may refuse enforcement are narrow. In this case, the Court allowed the enforcement of an award which included a penalty. For procedure, see *Lombard Knight v Rainstorm Pictures Inc* [2014] EWCA Civ 356, [2014] 2 Lloyd's Rep. 74. The court retains jurisdiction in relation to challenge to or appeal from an award (ss.67–69) if the seat of arbitration is in England (or, as the case may be Northern Ireland): s.2(1) and *Hiscox v Outhwaite* [1992] 1 A.C. 562. A judgment entered in terms of the award under s.101(3) carries interest under s.17 of the Judgments Act 1838; *Gater Assets Ltd v Nak Naftogaz Ukrainiy (No.3)* [2008] EWHC 1108 (Comm), [2008] 2 Lloyd's Rep. 295; *Sonatrach v Statoil Natural Gas LLC* [2014] EWHC 875 (Comm), [2014] 2 Lloyd's Rep. 252.

[860] Arbitration Act 1950 Sch.1.

[861] Arbitration Act 1950 Sch.2.

[862] Arbitration Act 1996 ss.66(4), 99; *Dicey, Morris and Collins on the Conflict of Laws*, 15th edn, para.16-100; CPR Pt 62; DAC Report para.346.

[863] For a list of such countries, see *http://www.lexisnexis.com/uk/lexispsl/disputeresolution/home*.

[864] Administration of Justice Act 1920 s.12(1); Foreign Judgments (Reciprocal Enforcement) Act 1933 s.10A (added by Civil Jurisdiction and Judgments Act 1982 Sch.10 para.4); *Dicey, Morris and Collins on the Conflict of Law*, 15th edn, para.16-161; CPR r.62.20. See also *LR Avionics Technologies*

registration.[865] The conditions for enforcement and the grounds on which enforcement of a foreign award may be refused must be ascertained by reference to the particular statute,[866] but neither at common law nor under the statutes concerned can the merits of the arbitrator's decision be impugned.

32-191   Once a foreign award has been converted into an English judgment, the judgment is subject to the same procedural rules and conditions as generally apply to such judgments. So, in principle, the court can grant a stay of execution of the

Ltd v Federal Republic of Nigeria [2016] EWHC 1761 (Comm), [2016] 4 W.L.R. 120 at [24]–[27].
[865] Arbitration (International Investment Disputes) Act 1966 ss.1, 2; Multilateral Investment Guarantee Agency Act 1988 s.4; Carriage of Goods by Road Act 1965 ss.4(1), 7(1) and Sch.; Arbitration Act 1996 s.66(4) and Sch.3 paras 21, 24, 49; *Dicey, Morris and Collins on the Conflict of Laws*, 15th edn, paras 16-161, 16-172; CPR r.62.21.
[866] For the closed list of cases in which recognition or enforcement of a New York Convention award may be refused, see s.103 of the 1996 Act and *Rosseel NV v Oriental Shipping (UK) Ltd* [1991] 2 Lloyd's Rep. 625; *China Agrebusiness Development Corp v Balli Trading* [1998] 2 Lloyd's Rep. 76; *Soinco Saci v Novokuznetsk Aluminium Plant* [1998] 2 Lloyd's Rep. 337; *Westacre Investments Ltd v Jugoimport-SPDR Holding Co Ltd* [2000] Q.B. 288; *Soleimany v Soleimany* [1999] Q.B. 785; *Minmetals German GmbH v Ferco Steel Ltd* [1999] 1 All E.R. (Comm) 315; *Omnium de Traitement SA v Hilmarton Ltd* [1999] 2 Lloyd's Rep. 222; *Eco Swiss China Time Ltd v Benetton International NV* [1999] 2 All E.R. (Comm) 44, ECJ; *Irvani v Irvani* [2000] 1 Lloyd's Rep. 412; *ABCI v Banque Franco-Tunisienne* [2002] 1 Lloyd's Rep. 511, 538; *Dardana Ltd v Yukos Oil Co* [2002] EWCA Civ 543, [2002] 2 Lloyd's Rep. 326; *Reeves v One World Challenge LLC* [2005] NZCA 314; *Svenska Petroleum Exploration AB v Government of the Republic of Lithuania* [2005] EWHC 9 (Comm), [2005] 1 Lloyd's Rep. 515; *Ipco (Nigeria) Ltd v Nigerian National Petroleum Ltd* [2005] EWHC 726 (Comm), [2005] 2 Lloyd's Rep. 326; *Kanoria v Guinness* [2006] EWCA Civ 222, [2006] 1 Lloyd's Rep. 701; *Tamil Nadu Electricity Board v ST-CMS Electric Co Private Ltd* [2007] EWHC 1713 (Comm), [2008] 1 Lloyd's Rep. 93; *Gater Assets Ltd v NAK Naftogaz Ukrainiy (No.2)* [2008] EWHC 237 (Comm), [2008] 1 Lloyd's Rep. 479; *AC Ward & Sons Ltd v Catlin (Five) Ltd* [2009] EWCA Civ 1098; *Dallah Real Estate & Tourism Co v Ministry of Religious Affairs of the Government of Pakistan* [2010] UKSC 46, [2011] 1 A.C. 763; *Norsk Hydro ASA v State Property Fund of Ukraine* [2002] EWHC 2120 (Admin), [2009] Bus. L.R. 558; *Nigerian National Petroleum Corp v IPCO (Nigeria) Ltd (No.2)* [2008] EWCA Civ 1157, [2009] 1 Lloyd's Rep. 89 (enforcement in part); *HJ Heinz Co Ltd v EFL Inc* [2010] EWHC 1203 (Comm), [2010] 2 Lloyd's Rep. 727; *Yukos Capital SARL v OJSC Rosneft Oil Co* [2012] EWCA Civ 855, [2013] 1 All E.R. 223; *Honeywell International Middle East Ltd v Meydan Group LLC* [2014] EWHC 1344 (TCC), [2014] 2 Lloyd's Rep. 133; *Diag Human SE v Czech Republic* [2014] EWHC 1639 (Comm), [2014] 2 Lloyd's Rep. 283; *IPCO (Nigeria) Ltd v Nigerian National Petroleum Corp* [2015] EWCA Civ 1144, [2016] 1 Lloyd's Rep. 5, [2015] EWCA Civ 1145, [2016] 1 Lloyd's Rep. 36; *Lombard Knight v Rainstorm Pictures Inc* [2014] EWCA Civ 356, [2014] 2 Lloyd's Rep. 74; *Travis Coal Restructured Holdings LLC v Essar Global Fund Ltd* [2014] EWHC 2510 (Comm), [2014] 2 Lloyd's Rep. 414; *Malicorp Ltd v Egypt* [2015] EWHC 361 (Comm), [2015] 1 Lloyd's Rep. 423; *Stati v Republic of Kazakhstan* [2017] EWHC 1348 (Comm), [2017] 2 Lloyd's Rep. 201; *RBRG Trading (UK) Ltd v Sinocore International Co Ltd* [2017] EWHC 251 (Comm), [2017] 2 Lloyd's Rep. 375; [2018] EWCA Civ 838. But the court has power under s.103(5) to adjourn the decision on enforcement and to order security: see *Soleh Boneh International Ltd v Government of Uganda* [1993] 2 Lloyd's Rep. 208; *Dardana Ltd v Yukos Oil Co*, above; *Apis AS v Fantazia Kereskedelmi* [2001] 1 All E.R. (Comm) 348; *Ipco (Nigeria) Ltd v Nigerian National Petroleum Ltd*, above; *Gater Assets Ltd v NAK Naftogaz Ukrainiy* [2007] EWHC 697 (Comm), [2007] 1 Lloyd's Rep. 522; *Nigerian National Petroleum Corp v IPCO (Nigeria) Ltd (No.2)*, above; *Dowans Holding SA v Tanzania Electric Supply Co Ltd* [2011] EWHC 1957 (Comm), [2011] 2 Lloyd's Rep. 474; *IPCO (Nigeria) Ltd v Nigerian National Petroleum Corp* [2015] EWCA Civ 1144, [2016] 1 Lloyd's Rep. 5, [2015] EWCA Civ 1145, [2016] 1 Lloyd's Rep. 36; *Travis Coal Restructured Holdings LLC v Essar Global Fund Ltd* [2014] EWHC 2510 (Comm), [2014] 2 Lloyd's Rep. 414. In *IPCO (Nigeria) Ltd v Nigerian National Petroleum Corp* [2017] UKSC 16, [2017] 1 W.L.R. 970 the Supreme Court held that there was nothing in s.103(2) or (3) which provided that an enforcing court could make the decision of an issue raised under that subsection conditional on the provision of security in respect of the award (unlike s.103(5)).

judgment. However, it would rarely be appropriate to order a stay in respect of a foreign award enforceable under the New York Convention when, by definition under the Convention, the time for enforcement had arrived.[867]

Where a State has agreed in writing to submit a dispute which has arisen, or may arise, to arbitration, the State is not immune as respects proceedings in the courts of the United Kingdom, except (a) where contrary provision is made in the arbitration agreement or (b) where the arbitration agreement is between States.[868] A State cannot, therefore, as a normal rule raise a defence of State immunity in respect of an application to enforce an award as a judgment, whether the award is an English or a foreign award.[869]   **32-192**

Civil Jurisdiction and Judgments Act 1982   The 1982 Act provides a sum-   **32-193** mary procedure for the enforcement by registration of an award which has become enforceable in the part of the United Kingdom in which it was given in the same manner as a judgment given by a court of law in that part.[870] But it has been held that a judgment in a foreign state party to the Brussels Convention by which a foreign arbitral award was made enforceable could not be registered as a judgment in England under the Act, since such a judgment fell within the exception in art.1(4) of that Convention relating to arbitration.[871]

Proceedings in aid of execution   A freezing order may be made in aid of execu-   **32-194** tion, whether the award is domestic or foreign,[872] and third party debt proceedings may be brought in appropriate circumstances.[873]

Limitation   An action to enforce an award, where the submission is not by deed,   **32-195** must be brought within six years of the date on which the cause of action ac-

---

[867] *Far Eastern Shipping Co v AKP Sovcomflot* [1995] 1 Lloyd's Rep. 520.
[868] State Immunity Act 1978 s.9. In challenging the jurisdiction of an arbitral tribunal under the State Immunity Act 1978, the parties are not bound by the constraints of the Arbitration Act 1996: *PAO Tatneft v Ukraine* [2018] EWHC 1797 (Comm), at [34]–[35].
[869] *Svenska Petroleum Exploration AB v Government of the Republic of Lithuania (No.2)* [2006] EWCA Civ 1529, [2007] Q.B. 886; *Norsk Hydro ASA v State Property Fund of Ukraine* [2002] EWHC 2120 (Admin), [2009] Bus. L.R. 558; *London Steam Ship Owners Mutual Insurance Association Ltd v Spain (No.2)* [2015] EWCA Civ 333, [2015] 2 Lloyd's Rep. 33; *Taurus Petroleum Ltd v State Oil Marketing Company of the Ministry of Oil, Republic of Iraq* [2013] EWHC 3494 (Comm), [2014] 1 All E.R. (Comm) 942; *Gold Reserve Inc v Bolivarian Republic of Venezuela* [2016] EWHC 153 (Comm), [2016] 1 W.L.R. 2829; *LR Avionics Technologies Ltd v Federal Republic of Nigeria* [2016] EWHC 1761 (Comm), [2016] 4 W.L.R. 120. This is a distinct question from that of immunity from execution: see *Dicey, Morris and Collins on the Conflict of Laws*, 15th edn, para.10-014. See above para.12-021.
[870] s.18(2)(e) (definition of "judgment") and Schs 6 or 7. See *Dicey, Morris and Collins on the Conflict of Laws*, 15th edn, para.16-157; Shone (2005) 71 *Arbitration* 46.
[871] *Arab Business Consortium International Finance and Investment Co v Banque Franco-Tunisienne* [1996] 1 Lloyd's Rep. 485; affirmed [1997] 1 Lloyd's Rep. 531. The same will now apply in the case of art.1(2)(d) of Regulation (EU) 1215/2012 which has replaced the Brussels Convention.
[872] *Ministry of Trade of the Republic of Iraq v Tsavliris Salvage (International) Ltd* [2008] EWHC 612 (Comm), [2008] 2 Lloyd's Rep. 90. But see *Posseel NV v Oriental Commercial Shipping (UK) Ltd* [1990] 1 W.L.R. 1387 (world-wide freezing order refused where award foreign). A freezing order ought ordinarily to contain an "ordinary course of business" exception: *Mobile Telesystems Finance SA v Nomihold Securities Inc* [2011] EWCA Civ 1040, [2012] 1 Lloyd's Rep. 6. See also above, para.32-189.
[873] cf. *Deutsche Schachtbau-und Tiefbohrgesellschaft mbH v R'as al-Khaimah National Oil Co* [1990] 1 A.C. 295.

crued,[874] i.e. from the date on which the claimant was entitled to enforce the award.[875] Alternatively, if the claim is regarded as being one for damages for breach of an implied promise to pay the award, then it accrues when a reasonable time to pay the award has elapsed.[876] However, an action may be brought within six years on a judgment obtained to enforce an award even though by then more than six years have passed since the accrual of the cause of action to enforce the award.[877]

12. MISCELLANEOUS

32-196 **Arbitration and exemption clauses compared** An arbitration clause differs from an exemption clause in that it is inserted as machinery for settling disputes and is not a term which excludes or restricts the liability of one or both parties.[878] Accordingly, it is not to be treated as an exemption clause at common law,[879] nor is an agreement in writing to submit present or future disputes to arbitration subject to the control of the Unfair Contract Terms Act 1977.[880] However, arbitration clauses may in some circumstances be detrimental to the interests of consumers in that legal aid is not available for arbitration proceedings, and such proceedings may involve greater expense than, e.g. proceedings in the county court. Moreover, the arbitration agreement may provide for the appointment of an arbitrator designated by the supplier of the goods or services to the consumer. In consequence, the application of the Unfair Terms in Consumer Contracts Regulations 1999 and (for contracts made on or after October 1, 2015) Pt 2 of the Consumer Rights Act 2015[881] is extended in relation to a term which constitutes an arbitration agreement.[882]

32-197 **Valuers, experts, etc** An agreement to refer a price to a valuer or a question to an expert for decision is, as a general rule,[883] not an arbitration agreement[884] and the provisions of the Arbitration Act 1996 do not apply.[885] A valuation or expert's

---

874 Limitation Act 1980 s.7. But see (extension of the period) Vol.I, Ch.28, and see the Foreign Limitation Periods Act 1984, Vol.I, para.30-348.

875 *International Bulk Shipping and Services Ltd v Minerals and Metals Trading Corp of India* [1996] 1 All E.R. 1017.

876 *International Bulk Shipping and Services Ltd v Minerals and Metals Trading Corp of India* [1996] 1 All E.R. 1017. But see *Agromet Motoimport v Maulden Engineering Co (Beds) Ltd* [1985] 1 W.L.R. 762 (date of defendant's failure to honour award when called upon to do so); *Good Challenger Navigante SA v Metalexportimport SA* [2003] EWCA Civ 1668, [2004] 1 Lloyd's Rep. 67 at [9] (date of defendant's breach of implied obligation to pay the award); *National Ability SA v Tinna Oils and Chemicals Ltd* [2009] EWCA Civ 1330, [2010] 1 Lloyd's Rep. 222 at [4] (date the award should have been paid).

877 *ED & F Man Sugar Ltd v Lendoudis* [2007] EWHC 2268 (Comm), [2007] 2 Lloyd's Rep. 579 at [53].

878 *Heyman v Darwins Ltd* [1942] A.C. 356, 373–375, 400; *Woolf v Collis Removal Service* [1948] 1 K.B. 11.

879 *Woolf v Collis Removal Service*, above. But see above, para.32-075, n.299.

880 s.13(2); *Kaye v Nu Skin UK Ltd* [2009] EWHC 3509 (Ch), [2011] 1 Lloyd's Rep. 40.

881 See below, para.38-302.

882 See above, para.32-013.

883 cf. *Re Carus-Wilson and Greene* (1886) 18 Q.B.D. 7, 9; *Leigh v English Property Corp Ltd* [1976] 2 Lloyd's Rep. 298 and above, para.32-021.

884 *Re Dawdy and Hartcup* (1885) 15 Q.B.D. 426; *Re Carus-Wilson and Greene*, above. See also *Leeds v Burrows* (1810) 12 East 1; *Goodyear v Simpson* (1845) 15 M. & W. 16; *Re Hammond and Waterton* (1890) 62 L.T. 808; *Campbell v Edwards* [1976] 1 W.L.R. 403; *Arenson v Arenson* [1977] A.C. 405; *Wilky Property Holdings Plc v London & Surrey Investments Ltd* [2011] EWHC 2226 (Ch).

885 *Collins v Collins* (1858) 26 Beav. 306; *Bos v Helsham* (1866) L.R. 2 Ex. 72; *Turner v Goulden* (1873)

certificate cannot be challenged or appealed as if it were an award[886] nor can it be enforced as if it were a judgment of a court. Nevertheless the court has, under its inherent jurisdiction, a discretionary power to stay an action brought contrary to a dispute resolution agreement which is nearly an effective agreement to arbitrate, but not quite,[887] or which submits the dispute to the decision of an expert.[888] The court also has jurisdiction to determine an issue of construction before the valuer or expert has made his decision,[889] but must be satisfied that the issue is a real one (and not hypothetical) and that it is in the interests of justice and convenience to determine the matter itself rather than allowing the expert to determine it first.[890]

The function of an architect in certifying payments due under a building contract from the employer to the contractor is not to be equated with that of an arbitrator.[891] **32-198**

A person appointed in an agreement as "sole judge" of matters of fact is not an arbitrator. His decision is binding and not reviewable, provided that he acts fairly and not perversely in making his determination.[892] **32-199**

L.R. 9 C.P. 57; *Re Dawdy and Hartcup*, above; *Re Hammond and Waterton*, above; *Cott (UK) Ltd v FE Barber Ltd* [1997] 3 All E.R. 540; *British Telecommunications Plc v SAE Group Inc* [2009] EWHC 252 (TCC), [2009] B.L.R. 231.

886 *Campbell v Edwards*, above; *Baber v Kenwood Manufacturing Co* [1978] 1 Lloyd's Rep. 175. For the limited grounds, and method of impeaching a valuation or expert's certificate, see, e.g. *Collier v Mason* (1858) 25 Beav. 200; *Finnegan v Allen* [1943] K.B. 425; *Dean v Prince* [1954] Ch. 409; *Frank H Wright (Construction) Ltd v Frodoor* [1967] 1 W.L.R. 506; *Jones (H) v Jones (RR)* [1971] 1 W.L.R. 840, 856; *Smith v Gale* [1974] 1 W.L.R. 9; *Campbell v Edwards*, above; *Baber v Kenwood Manufacturing Co*, above; *Burgess v Purchase & Sons (Farms) Ltd* [1983] Ch. 216; *Jones v Sherwood Computer Services Plc* [1992] 1 W.L.R. 277; *Nikko Hotels (UK) v MEPC* (1991) 28 E.G. 86; *Pontsarn Investments v Kasallis-Osako-Pankki* (1992) 22 E.G. 103; *Mercury Communications Ltd v Director General of Communications* [1996] 1 W.L.R. 48, 58; *British Shipbuilders v VSEL Consortium Plc* [1997] 1 Lloyd's Rep. 106, 109; *Shell UK Ltd v Enterprise Oil Plc* [1999] 2 Lloyd's Rep. 456, 469; *Galaxy Energy International Ltd (PVI) v Eurobunter SpA* [2001] 2 All E.R. (Comm) 912; *Veba Oil Supply and Trading GmbH v Petrotrade Inc* [2001] EWCA Civ 1832, [2002] 1 Lloyd's Rep. 295; *Invensys Plc v Automotive Sealing Systems Ltd* [2002] 1 All E.R. (Comm) 222; *Bernhard Schulte GmbH & Co KG v Nile Holdings Ltd* [2004] EWHC 977 (Comm), [2004] 2 Lloyd's Rep. 352; *Barclays Bank Plc v Nylon Capital LLP* [2011] EWCA Civ 826, [2011] 2 Lloyd's Rep. 347; see also below, para.44-053. But the court has power to order the expert to give further reasons for his determination: *Halifax Life Ltd v Equitable Life Assurance Society* [2007] EWHC 503 (Comm), [2007] 1 Lloyd's Rep. 528. See also *Homepace Ltd v SITA South East Ltd* [2008] EWCA Civ 1 (criticised by Dundas (2008) 74 *Arbitration* 185); *Owen Pell Ltd v Bindi (London) Ltd* [2008] EWHC 1420 (TCC), [2008] Build. L.R. 436.

887 *Channel Tunnel Group Ltd v Balfour Beatty Construction Ltd* [1993] A.C. 334. cf. *Halifax Financial Services Ltd v Intuitive Systems Ltd* Unreported, December 21, 1998.

888 *Cott (UK) Ltd v FE Barber Ltd* [1997] 3 All E.R. 540; *Thames Valley Power Ltd v Total Gas & Power Ltd* [2005] EWHC 2208 (Comm), [2005] 1 Lloyd's Rep. 441 at [43].

889 *Barclays Bank Plc v Nylon Capital LLP* [2011] EWCA Civ 826, [2011] 2 Lloyd's Rep. 347.

890 *Mercury Communications Ltd v Director General of Communications* [1994] C.L.C. 1125, 1140, CA, [1996] 1 W.L.R. 48 (HL); *Barclays Bank Plc v Nylon Capital LLP* above, at [42]; *Wilky Property Holdings Plc v London & Surrey Investments Ltd* [2011] EWHC 2226 (Ch). cf. *British Shipbuilders v VSEL Consortium Plc*, above, at 109.

891 *Sutcliffe v Thackrah* [1974] A.C. 727. cf. *John Barker Construction Ltd v London Portman Hotel Ltd* (1996) 12 Const. L.J. 277.

892 *West of England Ship Owners Mutual Insurance Assn (Luxembourg) v Cristal* [1996] 1 Lloyd's Rep. 370.

32-200 **Adjudication** The Housing Grants, Construction and Regeneration Act 1996[893] provides that a party to a construction contract[894] has the right to refer a dispute arising under the contract for adjudication under a procedure provided by the Act.[895] The purpose of this measure is to establish, in the construction industry, a procedure for the speedy and inexpensive resolution of disputes on a provisional interim basis, and for enabling the adjudicator's decisions to be enforced pending the final determination of such disputes.[896] But adjudication differs from arbitration in that it does not involve a final disposal of the dispute between the parties. The adjudicator does not perform an arbitral function[897] and does not make any final award definitive of the parties' rights. His decision is, however, binding until the dispute is finally determined by legal proceedings, by arbitration or by agreement.[898] But it cannot be enforced as if it were an arbitral award.[899] Adjudication is dealt with in Ch.37 of this book.[900]

32-201 **Mediation** Mediation (or conciliation) is distinct from arbitration. The role of the mediator or conciliator is to make proposals for a settlement and not to render an award. He assists the parties in their attempt to reach an amicable settlement of their dispute. It is inadvisable, if the mediation fails, for the mediator to become an arbitrator (a process known as "Med/Arb"). There are too many obstacles, with respect to the need for impartiality and a fair hearing, for a mediator to change roles and re-appear as an arbitrator.

32-202 **Immunity of arbitrators and arbitral institutions, etc** At common law, the extent of the immunity of an arbitrator was not free from doubt.[901] Section 29 of the 1996 Act resolved that uncertainty.[902] An arbitrator is not liable for anything done or omitted in the discharge or purported discharge of his functions as arbitrator unless the act or omission is shown to have been in bad faith, and the same im-

---

[893] As amended by the Local Democracy, Economic Development and Construction Act 2009 Pt 8: see SI 2011/1569 (c.58), SI 2011/1582 (c.59).

[894] Defined in s.104(1).

[895] ss.108 (as amended), 114; Scheme for Construction Contracts (England and Wales) Regulations 1998 (SI 1998/649). See below, para.37-264.

[896] *Macob Civil Engineering Ltd v Morrison Construction Ltd* [1999] Build. L.R. 93. See also *MBE Electrical Contractors Ltd v Honeywell Control Systems Ltd* [2010] EWHC 2244 (TCC), [2010] B.L.R. 561 (party seeking to refer jurisdictional issues concerning adjudicator to arbitration: stay refused). In *RMC Building & Civil Engineering Ltd v UK Construction Ltd* [2016] EWHC 241 (TCC), [2016] B.L.R. 264 at [56], the Court said that the provisions introduced by the 1996 Act and the Scheme are all about maintaining cash flow.

[897] *A Cameron Ltd v John Mowlem & Co Plc* (1990) 52 Build. L.R. 30; *Drake & Scull Engineering Ltd v McLaughlin & Harvey Plc* (1992) 60 B.L.R. 107. cf. *Cape Durasteel Ltd v Rosser & Russell Building Services Ltd* (1996) 46 Con. L.J. 75.

[898] Housing Grants, Construction and Regeneration Act 1996 s.108(3). But the parties may agree to accept the decision of the adjudicator as finally determining the dispute.

[899] *A Cameron Ltd v John Mowlem & Co Plc*, above. But it can be enforced by an application for summary judgment or possibly under s.42 of the 1996 Act: see para.24 of Sch. Pt I to the 1998 Regulations, above, and *Macob Civil Engineering Ltd v Morrison Construction Ltd*, above; see also below, para.37-265.

[900] See below, paras 37-262—37-268.

[901] *Arenson v Arenson* [1977] A.C. 405, 431, 432, 440, 442.

[902] It is a mandatory provision: s.4(1) and Sch.1.

munity attaches to his employees or agents.[903] This immunity does not affect any liability incurred by an arbitrator by reason of his resigning.[904]

A similar immunity attaches to an arbitral institution or person responsible for **32-203** the appointment or nomination of an arbitrator in the discharge or purported discharge of its function in that respect.[905] Nor is such an institution or person vicariously liable for the acts or omissions of the arbitrator nominated or appointed.[906]

On the other hand, a valuer, expert or adjudicator enjoys no statutory immunity. **32-204** A valuation or expert certification which is made negligently may give rise to an action in damages at the suit of the party injured thereby.[907] An adjudicator, however, is under the terms of the construction contract to have immunity (subject to an exception in case of bad faith) in the discharge or purported discharge of his functions.[908]

---

[903] s.29(1) (2). See (1996) 62 *Arbitration* 202.
[904] s.29(3). But see s.25; above, para.32-097.
[905] s.74(1), (3). This will, it is submitted, include a decision by an arbitral institution whether to accept or decline to administer an arbitration: see *Global Gold Mining LLC v Peter M Robinson* 533 F. Supp. 2d 442 (S.D.N.Y. 2008).
[906] s.74(2) (3).
[907] *Sutcliffe v Thackrah* [1974] A.C. 727; *Arenson v Arenson* [1977] A.C. 405.
[908] Housing Grants Construction and Regeneration Act 1996 s.108(4).

CHAPTER 33

BAILMENT

E. G. McKendrick

1. IN GENERAL[1]

Definition of bailment In many respects bailment "stands at the point at which **33-001** contract, property and tort converge".[2] It is a subject which it is difficult both to classify and to define. Indeed, it is easier to give examples of bailment than to define its scope. A simple example of a bailment is a contract of hire of goods. Possession of the goods is handed over to someone who is not their owner and that person ("the bailee") is subject to certain obligations in relation to the goods which obliga-

---

[1] On bailment in general, see *Palmer on Bailment*, 3rd edn (2009); N. Palmer, "Bailment", in A Burrows (ed.), *English Private Law*, 3rd edn (Oxford, 2013), Ch.16; Bell, *Modern Law of Personal Property in England and Ireland* (1989); Paton, *Bailment in the Common Law* (1952); *Jones on Bailments*, 4th edn (1833); *Story on Bailments*, 9th edn (1878); Wyatt Paine, *Bailments* (1901); Laidlaw (1930–1931) 16 Corn. L.Q. 286; Bell in Palmer and McKendrick (eds), *Interests in Goods*, 2nd edn (1998), p.461. For a more sceptical view of bailment, see McMeel [2003] L.M.C.L.Q. 169 where he concludes (at 199) that bailment is, at best, a "useful shorthand for all those situations where there is a transfer of possession of tangible personal property short of outright sale".

[2] *Palmer on Bailment* (hereafter, Palmer) at para.1-001.

tions are owed to their owner ("the bailor"). At a high level of abstraction, it can be said that bailment "denotes a separation of the actual possession of goods from some ultimate or reversionary possessory right".[3] Possession is therefore central to bailment[4]: its essence involves the transfer of possession of a chattel[5] to the bailee[6] (or the acquisition[7] of possession by him) so that the bailee becomes subject to certain obligations in relation to the goods and in turn is entitled to possessory remedies (such as trespass or conversion) against all strangers, and even, in many cases, against the bailor himself.[8]

33-002 **Bailment and contract** The relationship between bailment and contract is a close one, hence the inclusion of bailment within this volume. Many bailments arise out of, or are founded upon, a contract between the bailor and the bailee, as in the case of a contract of hire.[9] For many years it was believed that bailment was founded on contract so that the existence of a valid and enforceable contract was an essential pre-requisite to the creation of a bailment.[10] This view no longer holds good today. It is now clear that a contract is not essential for bailment.[11] The clearest illustration is a gratuitous bailment,[12] where it is clear that the bailment is independent of the law of contract.[13] Other illustrations can be found.[14] Thus a bailment created by contract is not necessarily terminated by the contract coming to an end[15] and, conversely, the withdrawal by the bailor of consent to the bailee continuing in possession of the goods does not necessarily operate to terminate the contractual

---

3   Palmer at para.1-001.
4   Palmer at para.1-001.
5   The law of bailment is confined to personal chattels. See Palmer at paras 1-006—1-009.
6   Winfield, *Province of the Law of Tort* (1931), pp.101–102; Tay (1966) 5 Sydney L. Rev. 239. See also *Fairline Shipping Corp v Adamson* [1975] Q.B. 180, 189–190 (defendant did not have exclusive possession of the goods at the relevant time and thus was not bailee of them) and *Kamidian v Holt* [2008] EWHC 1483 (Comm), [2009] Lloyd's Rep. I.R. 242 (physical custody by employee was only fleeting and for the purposes of handling; it did not amount to a transfer of possession so that the employee was not a bailee of the goods). On attornment, see below, para.33-030. cf. Stoljar (1958) 21 M.L.R. 27 and see below, para.44-241. A person may leave a chattel on another's premises without transferring possession to the latter: see below, para.33-061.
7   In some circumstances the bailee "acquires" possession without any "transfer" of possession, e.g. bailment by finding a lost chattel (below, para.33-037); involuntary bailment (below, para.33-036); or where a seller continues in possession pending delivery to the buyer (below, paras 44-214 et seq.). So the relationship of bailment may arise without the bailor having consented to the bailee having possession of the goods: *The Pioneer Container* [1994] 2 A.C. 324, 341–342. But the bailee must have had some knowledge of the existence of his bailor: *Marcq v Christie, Manson & Woods Ltd* [2003] EWCA Civ 731, [2004] Q.B. 286 at [49]–[50].
8   Holmes, *The Common Law* (1882), p.175. See below, paras 33-019, 33-024.
9   *Sandeman Coprimar SA v Transitos y Transportes Integrales SL* [2003] EWCA Civ 113, [2003] Q.B. 1270 at [63] ("the principles of the law of bailment have always overlapped with those of the law of contract, for bailment and contract often go hand in hand").
10 See, for example, *R. v Ashwell* (1885) 16 Q.B.D. 190, 223; *Banbury v Bank of Montreal* [1918] A.C. 626, 657; *Rosenthal v Alderton and Sons Ltd* [1946] 1 All E.R. 583, 584.
11 *East West Corp v DKBS 1912 and Akts Svendborg* [2003] EWCA Civ 83, [2003] 1 Lloyd's Rep. 239 at [24]; *Yearworth v North Bristol NHS Trust* [2009] EWCA Civ 37, [2010] Q.B. 1 at [48].
12 See below, paras 33-032 et seq.
13 See, for example, *Morris v CW Martin & Sons Ltd* [1966] 1 Q.B. 716, 731–732; *Hedley Byrne & Co Ltd v Heller & Partners Ltd* [1964] A.C. 465, 526.
14 See further Palmer at paras 1-027—1-035.
15 Laidlaw (1930–1931) 16 Corn. L.Q. 286, 292. See (1903) 19 T.L.R. 534 and below, paras 39-330— 39-341.

relationship which exists between bailor and bailee.[16] There may also be a valid bailment even though the contract from which it arises is invalid or voidable, as where the bailee is a minor,[17] or where the bailee obtains goods by false pretences.[18] Bailment cannot be explained entirely in contractual terms for the further reason that a bailment is more than a contract in that possession, a proprietary interest less than ownership, is transferred to, or acquired by, the bailee[19] and many remedies in tort and crime become available to the bailee because he enjoys possession.

Bailment and consent The contractual analysis of bailment was replaced by an **33-003** analysis of bailment which sought to explain it in what might be called consensual terms. Thus Pollock and Wright famously stated that:

"Any person is to be considered as a bailee who otherwise than as a servant[20] either receives possession of a thing from another or consents to receive or hold possession of a thing for another upon an understanding with the other person either to keep and return or deliver to him the specific thing or to (convey and) apply the specific thing according to the directions antecedent or future of the other person."[21]

While this statement continues to be cited in the courts,[22] the attempt to explain bailment entirely in consensual terms has "been overtaken by events"[23] because it now seems clear that the creation of a bailment does not require the consent of the bailor.[24] While it is true that in many, if not most cases, the bailor does consent to the bailee taking possession of the goods, cases can be found in which the bailor clearly does not consent to the bailee taking possession of the goods but a bailment is nevertheless found to exist (where, for example, the finder of a chattel is held to be a bailee notwithstanding the fact that the bailor was wholly unaware of the intervention of the bailee[25] or where the bailor does not consent to a sub-

16 *Perdana Properties Bhd v United Orient Leasing Co Sdn Bhd* [1981] 1 W.L.R. 1496.
17 *R. v McDonald* (1885) 15 Q.B.D. 323. See further Palmer at para.1-027. cf. *Mills v Graham* (1804) 1 Bos. & Pul. 140; *Fawcett v Smethurst* (1914) 31 T.L.R. 68; and *Ballett v Mingay* [1943] K.B. 281.
18 *London Jewellers Ltd v Attenborough* [1934] 2 K.B. 206.
19 *Bristol Airport Plc v Powdrill* [1990] Ch. 744 (the lessee's interest under a chattel lease was "property" within s.436 of the Insolvency Act 1986).
20 An employee obtains mere custody (not possession) of his employer's goods entrusted to his control: Pollock and Wright at pp.58–60; *Kamidian v Holt* [2008] EWHC 1483 (Comm), [2009] Lloyd's Rep. I.R. 242 at [77]. This exception in favour of a servant does not extend to agents, especially in the commercial sphere: *The Rigoletto* [2000] 2 Lloyd's Rep. 532, 539.
21 *Possession in the Common Law* (1888), p.163. The distinction between a consensual bailment and a contractual bailment was noted by Lord Sumption in *ENE Kos 1 Ltd v Petroleo Brasileiro SA (No.2)* [2012] UKSC 17, [2012] 2 A.C. 164 at [20].
22 See, for example, *Sutcliffe v Chief Constable of West Yorkshire* [1996] R.T.R. 86, 90.
23 Palmer at para.1-036. While it is correct to say that it has "been overtaken by events" it probably remains true to say that "bailment typically stems from the mutual consent of bailor and bailee": *Tongue v Royal Society for the Prevention of Cruelty to Animals* [2017] EWHC 2508 (Ch), [2018] B.P.I.R. 229 at [72].
24 *The Pioneer Container* [1994] 2 A.C. 324. The context of the decision of the Privy Council was whether or not it was necessary for the bailor to have consented to the terms on which the bailee was prepared to assume possession, but the reasoning seems equally applicable to the case where the issue is whether or not the bailor was prepared to allow the bailee to assume possession at all. However, it has been stated that it is the consent of the bailee, rather than the bailor, which is fundamental: *East West Corp v DKBS 1912 and Akts Svendborg* [2003] EWCA Civ 83, [2003] 1 Lloyd's Rep. 239 at [24]; *Kamidian v Holt* [2008] EWHC 1483 (Comm), [2009] Lloyd's Rep. I.R. 242 at [76].
25 Palmer at para.1-037.

bailment or the terms of a sub-bailment but is nevertheless held to be bound by it).[26]

33-004 **Bailment and tort** The demise of the consent theory of bailment may herald a move towards the law of tort and the eventual absorption of bailment into the mainstream of the law of tort. It is suggested that this is an unlikely development. Although liability in tort and in bailment may overlap[27] the two sources of liability are in fact independent and the "common law liabilities of a bailee ... appear both independent of, and significantly different from, those that would apply under the general law of tort".[28] The clearest example of this is the fact that the burden of proof in a negligence case rests upon the claimant, whereas in a bailment case the burden of proof is upon the bailee to show that he has discharged his duties.[29] Although liability in tort and in bailment are conceptually distinct, the failure of parliamentary draftsmen to recognise a distinct head of liability based on breach of bailment has meant that, in some contexts, the courts have construed a reference to "tort" as including a reference to "breach of bailment".[30] On the other hand, claims by a bailor against his bailee which are based on breach of bailment (e.g. breach of his common law duty of care)[31] may not fall within the overall category of "wrongful interference with goods" defined in s.1 of the Torts (Interference with Goods) Act 1977.[32] Each case turns on the construction of the particular statute and, while in some cases the courts have strained for instrumental reasons to encompass a bailment action within the fold of tort, the cases cannot be used to construct a more general argument in support of the assimilation of bailment to tort. They are authority only in relation to the particular statute under consideration.

33-005 **Bailment and property**[33] As has been noted, a transfer of possession to the bailee is an essential pre-requisite of a bailment and possession, of course, constitutes a proprietary interest. Thus it can be said that a bailment creates or gives rise to a property interest but it cannot be said that bailment lies in the law of property and not in the law of obligations. While a bailment gives rise to proprietary rights (viz possessory rights which may be vindicated against a third party or, indeed, against the bailor himself), it also creates personal rights and obligations and these rights and obligations cannot be located within the law of property. Although the language of the law of trusts is employed in many of the early definitions of bailment, there are in fact many distinctions between a bailment and a trust,[34] e.g. trusts may cover

---

26 *The Pioneer Container* [1994] 2 A.C. 324.
27 See below, paras 33-010—33-014.
28 Palmer at para.1-047. For example, in the case of a gratuitous bailment, it does not follow from the fact that the bailment is not contractual that the liability of the bailee must lie in tort. The liability of the bailee is best seen as being sui generis: *Yearworth v North Bristol NHS Trust* [2009] EWCA Civ 37, [2010] Q.B. 1 at [48].
29 See, e.g. *British Road Services Ltd v Arthur V Crutchley & Co Ltd* [1968] 1 All E.R. 811, 822. Further examples of the differences between an action in bailment and an action in tort are provided by Palmer at paras 1-048—1-071.
30 *American Express Co v British Airways Board* [1983] 1 W.L.R. 701 (s.29(1) of the Post Office Act 1969 which provided that "no proceedings in tort shall lie against the Post Office ..." in respect of loss or damage to mail): cf. *Chesworth v Farrar* [1967] 1 Q.B. 407 (see below, para.33-007, n.38).
31 See below, paras 33-032, 33-049. See also below, para.33-026 (text at n.127).
32 See Palmer (1978) 41 M.L.R. 629. cf. *Harold Stephen & Co Ltd v Post Office* [1977] 1 W.L.R. 1172, 1177–1178, 1179–1180.
33 See Palmer at paras 1-106—1-130.
34 e.g. Paton at pp.5–6; Palmer at paras 3-089 and 32-001—32-002. Although there are many differ-

realty as well as personalty; the beneficiary under a trust has an equitable interest only, whereas a bailee has a legal interest (viz various possessory rights); a trustee has the legal title or ownership, and so has power to convey a good title to a bona fide purchaser for value, whereas the bailee has only possessory rights.

No one unifying theory The reality of the matter is that there is no one theory which seems to be capable of providing a comprehensive definition of bailment. It consists of an amalgam of different ideas.[35] Thus, "the judicial analysis of bailment seems to have reached the stage at which any person who voluntarily assumed possession of goods belonging to another would be held to owe at least the principal duties of the bailee at common law".[36] Within this broad definition of bailment, certain key ideas can be identified. The first is that the bailee must be in possession of the goods. The second is that there must have been a "voluntary assumption" of possession; in other words, the consent of the bailee is necessary. The third is that the bailee must be aware of the existence of the bailor.[37] Finally, it would appear that it is no longer necessary that the bailor consent to the bailee taking possession of the goods; a bailment can exist even when the bailor is unaware of the fact that the bailee has possession of his goods.

33-006

Bailment and statute Notwithstanding the claim which bailment has to recognition as an independent source of obligations, statute has consistently refused to recognise the independence of bailment. One consequence of this has been that the courts have been compelled to squeeze bailment claims into legislation designed to regulate other categories of liability, principally contract and tort. A classic example of this phenomenon is provided by the law relating to limitation of actions. There is no limitation period prescribed for bailment claims and so the courts have applied the limitation periods for contract or tort. Whether the claim is brought in contract or in tort, the bailor cannot sue to recover the thing bailed more than six years after his cause of action accrued.[38] The regulation of the limitation period applicable to contractual claims is dealt with in Vol.I.[39] Where the claim is brought by the bailor in conversion, the cause of action accrues at the date of conversion,

33-007

---

ences between bailment and trust, the relationship between a bailor and bailee may nonetheless be fiduciary in nature; *Matthew v TM Sutton Ltd* [1994] 1 W.L.R. 1455 (see below, para.33-144, n.891).

[35] It is largely on this basis that bailment is attacked as a "redundant" concept by McMeel [2003] L.M.C.L.Q. 169. A more charitable view is that the law has simply become more complex as new variations on the basic model of bailment are developed. In *TRM Copy Centres (UK) Ltd v Lanwall Services Ltd* [2009] UKHL 35, [2009] 1 W.L.R. 1375 Lord Hope of Craighead (at [10]–[11]) noted the different ways in which bailments can be classified, and that many examples of bailments do not fit precisely into any particular category, but it was not necessary for him to resolve these classificatory issues in order to decide the case and he did not do so. The label which the parties have attached to their relationship is not decisive, so the fact that the parties have expressly stated that there is no bailment cannot in itself resolve the question of the existence or otherwise of a bailment.

[36] Palmer at para.1-041.

[37] *Marcq v Christie, Manson & Woods Ltd* [2003] EWCA Civ 731, [2004] Q.B. 286 at [49]–[50].

[38] Limitation Act 1980 ss.2, 5. The period may be extended in certain circumstances: ss.1(2), 28–33. See Vol.I, paras 28-072 et seq. The old rule that an "action in tort" lay against the estate of a deceased tortfeasor only if proceedings were brought not later than six months after his personal representatives took out representation was later repealed by s.1 of the Proceedings Against Estates Act 1970; under the former rule, it had been held that a claim against the estate of a deceased bailee in respect of his obligations as bailee at common law was (despite the existence of a contract giving rise to the bailment) in substance "a cause of action in tort": *Chesworth v Farrar* [1967] 1 Q.B. 407.

[39] See Ch.28, above.

irrespective of the bailor's knowledge of the conversion.[40] If there have been successive conversions (or wrongful detentions) of the same chattel, the period of limitation runs from the original conversion.[41] If the bailee has fraudulently concealed the bailor's right of action, the period of limitation runs from the time the fraud was discovered, or could by reasonable diligence have been discovered.[42] If the bailor fails to commence an action to recover the chattel before the expiration of the period of limitation, both his right of action and his title to the chattel are extinguished.[43]

33-008 **Classification of bailments** Roman law has had considerable influence on the English law of bailment[44] and in the leading authority of *Coggs v Bernard*[45] Holt C.J. classified bailments into six classes by analogy with Roman law. Other writers[46] have reduced the number of classes in their classifications, and in the present chapter a simple classification into two classes will be adopted: (a) gratuitous bailments; and (b) bailments for valuable consideration.[47] In the first category, some bailments are for the benefit of the bailor (e.g. deposit and mandate), while some are for the benefit of the bailee (e.g. gratuitous loan for use); similarly in the second category the valuable consideration may be received either by the bailee (e.g. custody) or by the bailor (e.g. hire for use). The Court of Appeal has held that there is no difference between these two classes of bailments as far as the standard of care required of the bailee is concerned: whether the bailment is gratuitous or for reward, the bailee must take reasonable care of the chattel according to the circumstances of the particular case.[48] (The fact that the bailment is gratuitous is, however, a relevant circumstance.[49]) The existence of the duty, and the standard of care required, are to be judged objectively.[50] The classification into the two classes is retained in this chapter because other aspects of the relationship between bailor and bailee vary from one type of bailment to the other, e.g. exemption clauses may oper-

40 *RB Policies at Lloyds v Butler* [1950] 1 K.B. 76. Before the abolition of detinue (see below, para.33-010) the action was held to accrue upon the refusal to return the chattel: *Miller v Dell* [1891] 1 Q.B. 468. See now below, paras 33-011, 33-014.
41 Limitation Act 1980 s.3(1) (reversing, on this point, *Spackman v Foster* (1883) 11 Q.B.D. 99, and *Miller v Dell*, above). The effect of s.3 is uncertain in regard to *Wilkinson v Verity* (1871) L.R. 6 C.P. 206; cf. *Beaman v ARTS Ltd* [1948] 2 All E.R. 89, 93; reversed on another point: [1949] 1 K.B. 550.
42 Limitation Act 1980 s.32; *Beaman v ARTS Ltd*, above.
43 Limitation Act 1980 s.3(2).
44 Paton at Ch.2 (*History of Bailment*).
45 (1703) 2 Ld. Raym. 909.
46 Palmer at Ch.3; Story at para.3; Jones, 1st edn, at pp.35, 36. The five-fold classification adopted in Jones and the six-fold classification adopted by Holt C.J. in *Coggs v Barnard* (1703) 2 Ld. Raym. 909 was referred to by Lord Hope of Craighead in *TRM Copy Centres (UK) Ltd v Lanwall Services Ltd* [2009] UKHL 35, [2009] 1 W.L.R. 1375 at [10]–[11]. However, it was not necessary for him to choose between the different classificatory schemes and he did not do so.
47 There may be bailment "for reward" without a special payment being made in respect of the bailment: see below, para.33-057.
48 *Houghland v RR Low (Luxury Coaches) Ltd* [1962] 1 Q.B. 694, 698; *Sutcliffe v Chief Constable of West Yorkshire* [1996] R.T.R. 86, 90. (A similar duty of care "that which may reasonably be expected of him in all the circumstances", applies in the analogous situation of a gratuitous agent: *Chaudhry v Prabhakar* [1989] 1 W.L.R. 29). cf. *Hunt & Winterbotham (West of England) Ltd v BRS (Parcels) Ltd* [1962] 1 Q.B. 617; *Morris v CW Martin & Sons Ltd* [1966] 1 Q.B. 716, 737. cf. also below, para.33-032 nn.158 and 166.
49 Paton at p.110.
50 *Chaudhry v Prabhakar*, above (an analogous case). If the defendant represents himself as possessing a particular skill or experience, on which the claimant reasonably relies, he will be held to it.

ate contractually if the bailment is for reward; and the Supply of Goods and Services Act 1982[51] applies to many contractual bailments, but not to gratuitous bailments. There appears to be no advantage in making a more complicated classification than that based on the twofold division proposed above. Bailment in contracts of carriage will be considered in Chs 35 and 36, below, and hire-purchase agreements in Ch.39, below. Before turning to a consideration of this twofold division, it is necessary to explore in more detail the significance of possession and related matters.

2. POSSESSION AND RELATED MATTERS

Possession, not ownership   A conveyance which transfers both possession and   **33-009** ownership to the transferee cannot be a bailment. The essence of bailment is the transfer of possession, not ownership. The fact that possession is transferred to the bailee is of significance both in terms of the relationship between the bailor and the bailee and in terms of its impact on the relationship between the bailor and third parties and between the bailee and third parties. The impact of the transfer of possession and not ownership on the various parties is considered in the following paragraphs.

The obligation to return the goods   In the first place, the fact that the bailee is   **33-010** given possession of the goods and not ownership means that he cannot keep the goods. They must be returned to the bailor at the end of the period of the bailment. The bailee is therefore normally[52] under an obligation to return the bailed chattel to the bailor at the end of the period of the bailment,[53] unless he can show good cause for not returning it.[54] Before the tort of detinue was abolished in 1977,[55] the bailee was liable in detinue at the suit of the bailor where the bailee had unequivocally[56] and wrongfully refused or failed to comply with the bailor's demand for the return of the chattel.[57] Detention by the bailee, after a demand by the bailor and a refusal to return on the part of the bailee, could also be evidence of a denial of the

---

[51] See below, para.33-044.
[52] If it is the obligation of the bailor to collect the chattel from the bailee, the latter may be entitled to the statutory remedy of sale when the bailor neglects to collect it: see below, paras 33-095—33-100. On the effect of delay by the bailor in collecting the goods, see Palmer [1987] L.M.C.L.Q. 43.
[53] *British Crane Hire Corp Ltd v Ipswich Plant Hire Ltd* [1975] Q.B. 303, 311, 313. (See also below, para.33-064.) On the termination of a bailment see below, para.33-014. cf. the cases on the termination of the hiring under a hire-purchase agreement, see below, paras 39-330—39-338; see also Vol.I, para.16-219. On the measure of damages in conversion (which now includes former cases of detinue: see below, this paragraph), see *Rosenthal v Alderton & Sons Ltd* [1946] K.B. 374; *Sachs v Miklos* [1948] 2 K.B. 23; *Munro v Willmott* [1949] 1 K.B. 295; *Strand Electric and Engineering Co Ltd v Brisford Entertainments Ltd* [1952] 2 Q.B. 246; *General and Finance Facilities Ltd v Cooks Cars (Romford) Ltd* [1963] 1 W.L.R. 644; *Hillesden Securities Ltd v Ryjak Ltd* [1983] 1 W.L.R. 959. See *McGregor on Damages*, 20th edn (2017), Ch.38 *Clerk & Lindsell on Torts*, 22nd edn (2017), paras 17-93 et seq.; and see for damages in similar hire-purchase cases, below, paras 39-341, 39-426.
[54] *British Crane Hire Corp Ltd v Ipswich Plant Hire Ltd*, above, at 311–312, 313. The possession of a bailee may change to possession as donee under an immediate gift or as donee under a *donatio mortis causa*: *Woodard v Woodard* [1995] 3 All E.R. 980.
[55] By s.2(1) of the Torts (Interference with Goods) Act 1977. (For its replacement, see below.)
[56] cf. a temporary refusal in order to clear up a doubt: *Clayton v Le Roy* [1911] 2 K.B. 1031; *Strand Electric and Engineering Co Ltd v Brisford Entertainments Ltd*, above, at 252, 253.
[57] *Miller v Dell* [1891] 1 Q.B. 468. In the absence of any specific contractual provision, the bailee is not bound to deliver the chattel to the bailor's address when the latter demands its return; the bailee's only obligation is not to prevent the bailor from taking it: *Capital Finance Co Ltd v Bray* [1964] 1 W.L.R. 323.

bailor's title, which would entitle the bailor to sue in conversion.[58] Since the 1977 Act, it has been held that a refusal to permit the bailor to enter the bailee's premises in order to collect the chattel is conversion.[59]

33-011 **Section 2(2) of the 1977 Act** Section 2(2) of the Torts (Interference with Goods) Act 1977 now provides that: "An action lies in conversion for loss or destruction of goods which a bailee has allowed to happen in breach of his duty to his bailor (that is to say it lies in a case which is not otherwise conversion, but would have been detinue before detinue was abolished)". Before this subsection, there was considerable overlap between the scope of detinue and that of conversion but that overlap was not complete; in particular, it was not clear that conversion could encompass all cases of wrongful detention of goods by the bailee. Section 2(2) now extends the scope of conversion to cover many of these cases. In order to establish liability for wrongful detention of goods, there must have been deliberate withholding of the goods or interference with them[60] and such conduct is commonly, but not invariably, found in a demand for the goods followed by their retention.[61] Although the demand and the refusal need not be express, they must be unequivocal[62]: for example, in an appropriate case, an unequivocal refusal may be inferred from a delay in responding to a demand beyond a reasonable time.[63] But it has been argued[64] persuasively that in many situations in which a bailor could previously have claimed in detinue, he could also have claimed in contract, or for breach of his common law rights as bailor, and that these claims fall outside the scope of s.2.

33-012 **Accidental loss of goods** If the bailee has wrongfully parted with the chattel[65] or lost it by negligence, it is no defence for him to show that he is unable to return it[66]; but the accidental loss or destruction of the chattel, without default on the part of the bailee, will excuse his failure to return it.[67] The loss of, or injury to, the chattel

---

58 *Pillot v Wilkinson* (1863) 2 H. & C. 72; (1864) 3 H. & C. 345; *Howard E Perry & Co Ltd v British Railways Board* [1980] 1 W.L.R. 1375. (cf. s.11(3) of the 1977 Act.) The bailor can sue in conversion without making a demand if the bailee commits a definite act of conversion: *Grainger v Hill* (1838) 4 Bing. N.C. 212.

59 *Howard E Perry & Co Ltd v British Railways Board*, above (fear of industrial action by the bailee's employees). See Palmer (1980) 9 An.-Am.L.R. 279.

60 *Clayton v Le Roy* [1911] 2 K.B. 1031; *R. (on the application of Atapattu) v Secretary of State for the Home Department* [2011] EWHC 1388 (Admin), [2011] All E.R. (D) 20 (Jun) at [89].

61 *Barclays Mercantile Business Finance Ltd v Sibec Developments Ltd* [1992] 1 W.L.R. 1253, 1257–1258. In the case where the goods have been lost by the bailee, there is no need for a refusal by the bailee. It suffices that there has been a demand for the return of the goods which has not been satisfied: *Mitchell v Ealing London BC* [1979] Q.B. 1.

62 *R. (on the application of Atapattu) v Secretary of State for the Home Department* [2011] EWHC 1388 (Admin), [2011] All E.R. (D) 20 (Jun) at [89].

63 However, the courts may be slow to draw such an inference, given that delay in many cases is likely to be equivocal: *Schwarzschild v Harrods Ltd* [2008] EWHC 521 (QB), [2008] All E.R. (D) 299 (Mar).

64 Palmer at para.1-089 (also in (1978) 41 M.L.R. 629, where other arguments on the scope of s.2 are deployed).

65 e.g. *Alexander v Railway Executive* [1951] 2 K.B. 882; and see below, para.33-052.

66 *Jones v Dowle* (1841) 9 M. & W. 19, 20; *Reeve v Palmer* (1858) 5 C.B.(N.S.) 84; *Genn v Winkel* (1912) 107 L.T. 434, 437. On exemption clauses, see Vol.I, Ch.15, especially para.15-037.

67 *Taylor v Caldwell* (1863) 3 B. & S. 826, 833; *British Crane Hire Corp Ltd v Ipswich Plant Hire Ltd* [1975] Q.B. 303, 311–312, 313. Accidental loss or destruction is, however, no defence if it occurred while the bailee was wrongfully detaining the chattel: *Shaw & Co v Symmons & Sons* [1917] 1 K.B. 799; *Mitchell v Ealing London B C* [1979] Q.B. 1 (see below, para.33-032, n.156). On frustra-

while it is in the bailee's possession places the onus of proof on the bailee to show that it occurred without his fault.[68]

Power of the court to order specific delivery   Although the bailor's claim against   **33-013**
the bailee who wrongfully detains the chattel cannot now be in detinue,[69] he may still be able to recover the chattel itself from the bailee. Section 3 of the Torts (Interference with Goods) Act 1977 provides that, in proceedings for wrongful interference against a person who is in possession or in control[70] of the goods, the court may make an order for delivery of the goods which does not give the defendant the alternative of retaining them on payment of their value as assessed by the court.[71] But the court has a discretion whether or not to make such an order,[72] and may impose conditions.[73] The court:

> "... in particular, where damages by reference to the value of the goods would not be the whole of the value of the goods, may require an allowance to be made by the claimant to reflect the difference. For example, a bailor's action against the bailee may be one in which the measure of damages is not the full value of the goods, and then the court may order delivery of the goods, but require the bailor to pay the bailee a sum reflecting the difference".[74]

Conversion of the chattel by the bailee   In addition to his obligation to return   **33-014**
the goods, the bailee is under a duty to his bailor not to convert the chattel, i.e. not to do intentionally in relation to the chattel an act inconsistent with the bailor's right of property in it and which excludes him from use and possession of the chattel[75];

---

tion, see *British Berna Motor Lorries Ltd v Inter-Transport Co Ltd* (1915) 31 T.L.R. 200; Vol.I, Ch.23, especially paras 23-041—23-046 (analogous cases on charterparties).

68   See below, para.33-050 and cases cited in nn.267 and 268 thereto; also *British Crane Hire Corp Ltd v Ipswich Plant Hire Ltd*, above, at 311–312, 313.

69   See above, para.33-010.

70   A bailee who had sub-bailed the goods may still be in "control" of them.

71   This section is based on the common law rules governing detinue: see *General and Finance Facilities v Cooks Cars (Romford)* [1963] 1 W.L.R. 644. (s.4 of the 1977 Act provides for interlocutory relief where goods are wrongfully detained.) See CPR Pt 25 r.25.1(1)(c). See also above, para.33-010.

72   1977 Act ss.3(3)(b) and 3(6). For an illustration, see *Howard E Perry & Co Ltd v British Railways Board* [1980] 1 W.L.R. 1375. By CPR Pt 40 r.40.14, a claimant who is only a partial owner of the goods, and who has no immediate right to the possession of them, is confined to a remedy in damages for the injury to his reversionary interest unless the claimant has the written authority of all other part-owners of the goods to make the claim on his behalf as well as for himself.

73   s.3(6). By ss.3(7) and 6(4), the court may also make an allowance under s.6(1) or (2) in respect of an improvement to the goods made by the defendant.

74   s.3(6).

75   *Caxton Publishing Co Ltd v Sutherland Publishing Co Ltd* [1939] A.C. 178, 202; *Morris v CW Martin & Sons Ltd* [1966] 1 Q.B. 716, 732; *Garnham, Harris & Elton Ltd v Alfred W Ellis (Transport) Ltd* [1967] 1 W.L.R. 940; *Kuwait Airways Corp v Iraqi Airways Co (Nos 4 and 5)* [2002] UKHL 19, [2002] 2 A.C. 833 at [39]–[42] (on which see Cane (2002) 118 L.Q.R. 544); *Sang Stone Hamoon Jonoub Co Ltd v Baoyue Shipping Co Ltd (The Bao Yue)* [2015] EWHC 2288 (Comm), [2016] 1 Lloyd's Rep. 320 (although goods may be converted by a person who creates a lien without the authority of the owner, an owner who authorises a bailee to deliver goods into storage must be taken to authorise the creation of a lien where that is a reasonable and foreseeable incident of the storage contract which the bailee is authorised to conclude). The requirement that there must be a sufficient encroachment on the rights of the owner as to exclude him from use and possession of the goods assumed importance in *Marcq v Christie, Manson & Woods Ltd* [2003] EWCA Civ 731, [2004] Q.B. 286, especially at [13]–[24]. See also s.2(2) of the Torts (Interference with Goods) Act

thus a sale,[76] pledge,[77] or offering for sale,[78] of the chattel terminates the bailment forthwith, and the immediate right to the possession of the chattel revests in the bailor.[79] The assessment of the bailor's damages is discussed below.[80]

33-015 **Jus tertii** Given that the bailor does not transfer ownership in the chattel to the bailee, he retains a proprietary interest in the chattel. He is said to retain the "general" property in the chattel, while the bailee obtains a "special" property in it. In litigation between the bailor and the bailee, the latter was, at common law, estopped from questioning the bailor's title to the chattel bailed to him, and the bailee could not set up the title of a third person in reply to the bailor's demand for redelivery of the chattel.[81] But s.8(1) of the Torts (Interference with Goods) Act 1977 abolished this rule (known as the *jus tertii*): "The defendant in an action for wrongful interference shall be entitled to show, in accordance with rules of court,[82] that a third party has a better right than the plaintiff as respects all or any part of the interest claimed by the plaintiff, or in right of which he sues, and any rule of law (sometimes called *jus tertii*) to the contrary is abolished".[83]

33-016 The main effect of s.8(1) will be where the bailor is suing the bailee: an illustration would be where a warehouseman could show that, since the goods were delivered to him by the bailor, a change in their ownership had taken place so that a third party now had acquired either a partial interest in them or had become their full owner.[84] If the bailee can prove that a third party has, at the time of the suit, a partial interest in the chattel, leaving the bailor with only a partial interest, the bailor's damages recoverable from the bailee for his failure to redeliver the chattel will be, not for its full value, but only in respect of the bailor's remaining interest in it.[85] It should be noted, however, that s.8 applies only to claims for wrongful interference with goods; if the bailor sues, not in tort, but in contract or for breach of the bailee's common law obligations arising from the bailment, it appears[86] that the bailee could not avail himself of the protection of the section.[87]

1977 (above, para.33-010); and s.11(3) (below, para.33-135, n.821).

[76] See the cases cited below, para.33-023, n.109.

[77] *Nyberg v Handelaar* [1892] 2 Q.B. 202.

[78] *North General Wagon & Finance Co Ltd v Graham* [1950] 2 K.B. 7.

[79] See below, paras 33-023, 39-333.

[80] See below, para.33-018.

[81] *Gosling v Birnie* (1831) 7 Bing. 337; *Biddle v Bond* (1865) 6 B. & S. 225; *Tongue v Royal Society for the Prevention of Cruelty to Animals* [2017] EWHC 2508 (Ch), [2018] B.P.I.R. 229 at [76]. The House of Lords has (obiter) referred to this common law rule, without adverting to the 1977 Act (see below): *China Pacific SA v Food Corp of India* [1982] A.C. 939, 959. The bailee could set up the *jus tertii* against his bailor only where he had been actually evicted by title paramount (*Biddle v Bond*, above, at 234), or where he defended on behalf of, and with the express authority of the third person (*Rogers, Sons & Co v Lambert & Co* [1891] 1 Q.B. 318, 325). Arguments which would have extended the scope of the bailee's estoppel were rejected by the Privy Council in *Re Goldcorp Exchange* [1995] 1 A.C. 74.

[82] The power to create rules of court is contained in s.8(2) of the Torts (Interference with Goods) Act 1977. The rules were formerly contained in RSC Ord.15 r.10A, which has not been retained in the current version of the CPR. The position therefore remains uncertain. The defendant's entitlement is stated clearly in s.8(1), but the rules which give effect to it are not readily apparent.

[83] Even before the 1977 Act, the bailee could interplead between the bailor and a third party claimant to the chattel: RSC Ord.17; CCR Ord.33 rr.6–12.

[84] The warehouseman would also be able to delay proceedings against him by requiring the third party to be made a party to the proceedings.

[85] This result is produced by s.7 of the 1977 Act (see below, para.33-017), in combination with s.8.

[86] One interpretation of the section might be that it covers a situation where the bailor *could* have sued

Avoidance of double liability As a result of s.7 of the Torts (Interference with **33-017** Goods) Act 1977, the bailee need no longer fear "double liability",[88] both to his bailor, and to a third party who can prove a better title (either full or partial) to the goods than the bailor. By s.7(2) of the Act, where two or more claimants are parties to proceedings for wrongful interference,[89] the court is to grant relief so as to avoid double liability of the wrongdoer. By s.7(3), on satisfaction of his claim, a claimant is liable to account over to another claimant to such extent as will avoid double liability; while by s.7(4), any claimant who is unjustly enriched to any extent (viz beyond the value of his own interest in the chattel) is liable to reimburse the wrongdoer to the extent of that unjust enrichment. Thus, if the bailee pays damages, first to his bailor, and then to the true owner, the bailor is unjustly enriched unless he accounts to the true owner under s.7(3); and the true owner then would be unjustly enriched and would be liable to reimburse the bailee under s.7(4).[90]

Bailor's damages against the bailee[91] The preceding paragraphs have dealt with **33-018** the bailor's damages when a third party has an interest in the chattel. But it could be the defendant bailee himself who has an outstanding interest in the chattel, which should be deducted from the full value of the chattel when the bailor's damages are assessed,[92] e.g. if the bailee had paid in advance for the contractual right to retain the chattel for a given period, but the bailor was entitled to terminate the bailment prematurely and to sue for damages, the assessment should allow for the value of the bailee's interest during the unexpired part of that period.[93] The bailor may also have remedies in restitution, e.g. to recover the proceeds of a wrongful sale by the bailee.[94]

The bailee's claim against his bailor The fact that the bailee has a possessory **33-019** interest in the chattel has an impact on the bailee's remedies against the bailor and against third parties. A bailee for a term (as distinct from a bailee at will) may maintain a possessory action against the bailor himself, if the bailor interferes with the bailee's possession of the chattel during the term.[95] If the bailor wrongfully

---

for wrongful interference, e.g. where there was overlapping liability in tort or in contract. But liability in contract could arise in circumstances in which no tort had been committed: Palmer at para.4-062.

87   Palmer at paras 4-057—4-063.

88   Defined in s.7(1).

89   On the question of joining in the action any third party who claims an interest in the chattel, see s.8 (see above, para.33-015). Section 9 provides machinery for allowing concurrent proceedings for wrongful interference with the same goods to be heard together, even where they originated in different courts.

90   This example is adapted from that given in s.7(4) itself.

91   Rules on the assessment of damages in conversion must be sought elsewhere e.g. *Cierk & Lindsell on Torts*, 22nd edn (2017), paras 17-93 et seq.; Tettenborn [1993] C.L.J. 128. For an example, see *IBL Ltd v Coussens* [1991] 2 All E.R. 133 (especially on the date at which damages are to be assessed).

92   cf. the analogous situation in s.3(6) of the 1977 Act (above, para.33-013). Similarly, where a pledgee is liable to the pledgor in damages for conversion, the amount of the debt should be deducted from the damages: below, para.33-136.

93   cf. the analogous situation in hire-purchase: below, paras 39-341, 39-426.

94   *Chesworth v Farrar* [1967] 1 Q.B. 407. (On the particular situation in this case, above, n.38.) On restitution in general, see Vol.I, Ch.29.

95   *Roberts v Wyatt* (1810) 2 Taunt. 268; *Turner v Hardcastle* (1862) 11 C.B.(N.S.) 683; *Johnson v Stear* (1863) 15 C.B.(N.S.) 330; *Halliday v Holgate* (1868) L.R. 3 Ex. 299, 301. cf. *Rose v Matt* [1951] 1

retakes possession of the chattel, the bailee may seek the exercise of the court's discretion to make an order for specific delivery of the chattel to him.[96] The bailee's damages for any wrongful interference of his possession by the bailor will reflect only the extent of the injury to the bailee's interest in the chattel.[97]

33-020 **The effect of bailment on third parties**[98] The impact of bailment on third parties is a complex issue. The remedies which the law makes available to protect the possessory interest of the bailee and the reversionary interest of the bailor have an obvious impact on third parties. Where the bailee himself bails the chattel to a third party, the sub-bailee, difficult issues have arisen in relation to the entitlement of the bailor to sue the third party and in relation to the entitlement of the sub-bailee to rely on the terms of the bailment between the bailor and the bailee by way of defence to the bailor's claim.

33-021 **Entitlement to sue** Where the bailment is for reward and for a period to be determined in accordance with the agreed terms (as in hire or pledge) the bailee enjoys both possession and the immediate right to possession during the period; hence the bailee can,[99] and the bailor cannot,[100] sue a third person for trespass or conversion during that period.[101] However, if a third person destroys or permanently injures the chattel while it is in the possession of the bailee, the bailor may have an action against the third party for the injury to his reversionary interest.[102] But attempts to extend the protection of the law of torts to other interests in chattels (viz those not based on possession, or the immediate or reversionary right to possess at the relevant time) have failed. So where a third person negligently causes loss or damage to a chattel in which a claimant has only a contractual interest[103] at the time

---

K.B. 810. See also the implied warranty of quiet possession in a contract for the hire of goods, below, para.33-067.

[96] See above, para.33-013.
[97] cf. s.3(6) of the Torts (Interference with Goods) Act 1977 (above, para.33-013).
[98] See also above, paras 33-015—33-017. On distress, see below, paras 39-427 et seq.
[99] *Lee v Atkinson & Brook* (1609) Yel. 172. See also the cases cited in, para.33-024, n.111 below.
[100] *Gordon v Harper* (1796) 7 Term Rep. 9; *Ferguson v Cristall* (1829) 5 Bing. 305. cf. the decision in *O'Sullivan v Williams* [1992] 3 All E.R. 385 which can only be justified on the ground that it was a bailment at will: see below, para.33-022. Apart from a special contractual term, the bailor cannot compel the bailee to sue a third party for loss of, or damage to the goods: *The Albazero* [1977] A.C. 774, 846. The proposition that the bailor cannot sue rests on the assumption that the bailor does not have the immediate right to possession of the goods. Where, however, the bailor can demonstrate that it does have an immediate right to possession of the goods, it can bring a claim in conversion. When determining whether or not someone has possession of goods, a court must have regard to all the facts and circumstances of the case. Thus it cannot universally be the case that a person who receives goods for storage for reward obtains possession of them: *Mainland Private Hire Ltd v Nolan* [2011] EWCA Civ 189, [2011] C.T.L.C. 145.
[101] The bailee may also sue a third party who has negligently damaged the chattel while it is in the possession of the bailee: *The Winkfield* [1902] P. 42. See also below, paras 33-026, 33-027.
[102] *Mears v LSW Ry* (1862) 11 C.B.(N.S.) 850; *Dee Trading Co Pty Ltd v Baldwin* [1938] V.L.R. 173; *Moukataff v BOAC* [1967] 1 Lloyd's Rep. 396, 415–416 (below, para.33-026); *HSBC Rail (UK) Ltd v Network Rail Infrastructure Ltd* [2005] EWCA Civ 1437, [2006] 1 Lloyd's Rep. 358. See Fleming (1958) 32 A.L.J. 267; Tettenborn [1994] C.L.J. 326. cf. *Meux v GE Ry* [1895] 2 Q.B. 387. See also Palmer at paras 4-066—4-076 and s.1(d) of the Torts (Interference with Goods) Act 1977.
[103] e.g. the goods being transported under a c.i.f. contract are at the risk of the buyer at a time when he has neither the possession of, nor any proprietary interest in the goods: *Leigh and Sillavan Ltd v Aliakmon Shipping Co Ltd* [1986] A.C. 785.

of the loss or damage, the claimant cannot sue the third person under the tort of negligence.[104]

Bailment at will   Where the bailment is at will (as in gratuitous bailments) the   **33-022**
bailor retains the immediate right to possession of the chattel, and may therefore bring an action for conversion against any stranger who wrongfully takes the chattel out of the possession of the bailee.[105] The bailor at will may demand the return of the chattel at any time, and so there is a tendency to attribute "possession" to him as well, so that he may exercise the possessory remedies which are available to the possessor.[106] If a bailor at will does recover damages from a tortfeasor for the loss of the chattel and for loss of its use, the bailee no longer has any claim against the tortfeasor[107] but if in this situation the bailee at will has some interest in the chattel enforceable against the bailor, the latter must account appropriately to the bailee.[108]

Effect of act inconsistent with bailment   The bailment may be determined   **33-023**
prematurely by the bailee dealing wrongfully with the chattel in a manner wholly inconsistent with the bailment; in this event, the immediate right to possession revests in the bailor, who may then bring an action for conversion against any person dealing with the chattel,[109] as well as against the bailee.[110]

The bailee's claim against a third party   Since a bailment always gives the   **33-024**
bailee possession of the chattel, he may maintain any possessory action against a stranger.[111] As against a mere stranger, possession always imparts a better right to

---

[104] *The Aliakmon* case, above; *Candlewood Navigation Corp Ltd v Mitsui OSK Lines Ltd* [1986] A.C. 1, PC.

[105] *Manders v Williams* (1849) 4 Exch. 339, 344. Alternatively, the bailee at will may sue, basing his claim to sue upon his possession: cf. *Nicolls v Bastard* (1835) 2 Cr. M. & R. 659, 660. For the assessment of damages in the bailee's claim against a third party, see below, para.33-024.

[106] *United States of America and Republic of France v Dollfus Mieg et Cie SA* [1952] A.C. 582, 605, 611. See also *Lotan v Cross* (1810) 2 Camp. 464; *Nicolls v Bastard*, above; *Wilson v Lombank Ltd* [1963] 1 W.L.R. 1294; *Perpetual Trustees and National Executors of Tasmania Ltd v Perkins* (1989) Aust. Tort Rep. 80–295. cf. *Towers & Co Ltd v Gray* [1961] 2 Q.B. 351. The decision in *O'Sullivan v Williams* [1992] 3 All E.R. 385, can be justified only on the ground that the bailment was at will: see at 388; and cf. the text at n.100, above.

[107] *O'Sullivan v Williams*, above. It is submitted that this decision cannot apply to a bailment for a term where it is the bailee who is in possession and is therefore entitled to sue the tortfeasor (see text at n.99 above): in such a bailment the bailor may sue the tortfeasor only in respect of any injury to his reversionary interest (see n.102 above; also CPR Pt 40 r.40.14).

[108] *O'Sullivan v Williams*, above. cf. *The Winkfield* [1902] P. 42 (below, para.33-024). See also above, paras 33-015—33-018.

[109] *Cooper v Willomatt* (1845) 1 C.B. 672 (sale); *Bryant v Wardell* (1848) 2 Exch. 479; *Fenn v Bittleson* (1851) 7 Ex. 152, 159 (sale); *Consolidated Co v Curtis & Son* [1892] 1 Q.B. 495; *North General Wagon & Finance Co Ltd v Graham* [1950] 2 K.B. 7 (giving auctioneer possession, with instructions to sell); *Moorgate Mercantile Co Ltd v Finch and Read* [1962] 1 Q.B. 701; *Union Transport Finance Ltd v British Car Auctions Ltd* [1978] 2 All E.R. 385. However, an auctioneer who receives goods from their apparent owner and simply redelivers them to him when they are unsold is not liable in conversion provided that he has acted in good faith and without knowledge of any adverse claim to them: *Marcq v Christie, Manson & Woods Ltd* [2003] EWCA Civ 731, [2004] Q.B. 286. See also above, para.33-014; and below, para.33-130, n.792. See also Pollock and Wright, *Possession in the Common Law* (1888), p.132. cf. *Rogers v Arnott* [1960] 2 Q.B. 244.

[110] cf. *Shell International Petroleum Co Ltd v Gibbs (The Salem)* [1982] 1 All E.R. 225, 240–241. See above, para.33-014.

[111] *The Winkfield* [1902] P. 42. See also *Rooth v Wilson* (1817) 1 B. & Ald. 59 (gratuitous bailee); *Swaffer v Mulcahy* [1934] 1 K.B. 608 (replevin by bailee).

possession[112]; hence, the bailee may also bring against such a stranger an action which is based on the immediate right to possession, such as conversion.[113] Under the common law, the bailee could recover from a stranger who destroyed or detained the chattel, damages assessed at its full value, as if he were its absolute owner.[114] But the third party can now avail himself of s.8(1) of the 1977 Act, and prove the outstanding interest of the bailor[115]; if the third party fails to do so, he will be liable to the bailee for damages assessed at the full value. But in the latter situation, the operation of s.7 of the Act will ultimately prevent double recovery if the bailor (or the true owner) later also recovers damages from the third party.[116]

33-025 **Insurable interest** A bailee has an insurable interest in the goods bailed to him, and is entitled to insure them for their full value[117]; if the insurers make a payment under such a policy, the bailee may retain so much as would cover his own interest, and is a trustee for the bailor in respect of the balance.[118]

33-026 **Sub-bailment** If, without the express or implied consent of the bailor, the bailee himself bails the chattel to a third person, the bailor might, in appropriate circumstances, have an action in tort for conversion against the third person,[119] as well as against the bailee[120]; if, through the negligence of the third person, the chattel is lost or damaged, the bailor may have an action in tort for negligence against the third person.[121] The bailor may, however, have given the bailee actual[122] or

---

[112] *Armory v Delamirie* (1722) 1 Str. 505; *Jeffries v GW Ry* (1856) 5 El. & Bl. 802, 806; *The Winkfield*, above, at 60; Pollock and Wright at pp.22, 91 et seq.

[113] *Rooth v Wilson*, above; *The Winkfield*, above. Hence, a pledgee (below, para.33-121) may sue a stranger who tortiously interferes with his rights to the chattel: *Chabbra Corp Pte Ltd v Jag Shakti (Owners)* [1986] A.C. 337. In such a claim, the bailee may seek an order for specific delivery of the chattel, which does not give the defendant the option of paying damages assessed at the value of the chattel: above, para.33-013. But the defendant is able to rely on ss.7 and 8 of the 1977 Act (above, paras 33-015, 33-017).

[114] *The Winkfield*, above; *The Jag Shakti*, above (below, para.33-133); *Obestain Inc v National Mineral Development Corp Ltd* [1987] 1 Lloyd's Rep. 465. The fact that the bailee may not be responsible to the bailor for loss of or damage to the chattel does not prevent the bailee recovering full damages from a stranger who causes such loss or damage: *The Winkfield*, above. The bailee is under an obligation to account to the bailor for the damages recovered beyond the bailee's own interest: *The Winkfield*, above, at 60–61; *Eastern Construction Co Ltd v National Trust Co Ltd* [1914] A.C. 197, 210; *The Joannis Vatis* [1922] P. 92; *The Albazero* [1977] A.C. 774, 846; *The Jag Shakti*, see above cf. *O'Sullivan v Williams* [1992] 3 All E.R. 385 (above, para.33-022, n.107).

[115] See above, para.33-015. Section 8 applies in cases of damage to the chattel, as well as its total loss.

[116] See above, para.33-017.

[117] The extent of the bailee's insurance cover is a question of construction of the particular policy and it is not the case that the bailee will in all cases be entitled to recover the full value of the goods lost or damaged. In particular, the policy may be held to cover only the legal liabilities of the bailee towards the bailor or a third party: see *Ramco (UK) Ltd v International Insurance Co of Hanover* [2004] EWCA Civ 675, [2004] 2 All E.R. (Comm) 866.

[118] *Hepburn v A Tomlinson (Hauliers) Ltd* [1966] A.C. 451 (below, paras 42-008—42-010; Vol.I, paras 18-133, 29-168. cf. the situation where the insurance policy expressly covers the respective interests of both the bailor and the bailee: *Amev Finance Ltd v Mercantile Mutual Insurance (Workers' Compensation) Ltd* [1988] 1 Qd. R. 487. See also above, n.114).

[119] See *Clerk & Lindsell on Torts*, 22nd edn (2017), paras 17-16 et seq. Palmer and Murdoch (1983) 46 M.L.R. 73.

[120] See above, para.33-014, for the bailor's right of action against the bailee in these circumstances.

[121] *Lee Cooper Ltd v CH Jeakins & Sons Ltd* [1967] 2 Q.B. 1. But the terms of the contract between the original bailor and bailee are relevant to the extent of any tortious duty owed by the sub-bailee to the original bailor: see *Mitsui & Co Ltd v Novorossiysk Shipping Co (The Gudermes)* [1993] 1

ostensible[123] authority to sub-bail the chattel to the third person, in which case the mere fact that the third person has taken possession of the chattel under the sub-bailment will not constitute a tort as against the original bailor, because the latter will be taken to have consented to the sub-bailment. Such authority to sub-bail may be inferred from the parties' knowledge of ordinary commercial practices, e.g. that a carrier who carries goods over a long distance may engage a sub-contractor as his local delivery agent[124]; or that the Post Office may engage an airline to carry airmail.[125] Where there is such actual or apparent consent to the sub-bailing, the relationship of bailment will arise directly between the original bailor and the sub-bailee[126]; hence, the original bailor may take advantage of rules of bailment against the sub-bailee,[127] instead of relying on the ordinary rules of the law of tort. The original bailor need not rely on any *contract* of sub-bailment: the relationship of bailment will arise between the original bailor and the sub-bailee where the latter voluntarily received the goods from the bailee, knowing that another person "is interested in the goods".[128] Thus, by relying on the fact that there is a sub-bailment, the original bailor need[129] not prove a duty of care owed by the sub-bailee under the ordinary tort of negligence, since the sub-bailee will owe him all the duties of a bailee,[130] including the duty to take reasonable care of the chattel[131]; again, when the chattel is lost or damaged while in the possession of the sub-

Lloyd's Rep. 311, 327–328. cf. *Bart v British West Indian Airways Ltd* [1967] 1 Lloyd's Rep. 239 (no liability on sub-bailee for delay). cf. also *Fairline Shipping Corp v Adamson* [1975] Q.B. 180, 190–191 (see para.33-027 below). cf. also *Balsamo v Medici* [1984] 1 W.L.R. 951 (no direct claim in tort for negligence against sub-agent).

122 *The Pioneer Container* [1994] 2 A.C. 324, PC; *Morris v CW Martin & Sons Ltd* [1966] 1 Q.B. 716.
123 "Ostensible authority" from the original bailor (in addition to actual or implied authority) is recognised by the Privy Council in *The Pioneer Container*, above, at 341, 342.
124 *Learoyd Bros & Co v Pope & Sons Ltd* [1966] 2 Lloyd's Rep. 142, 148 (the sub-bailees were treated as bailees of the original bailor although the latter did not know that his bailee, a carrier, might sub-bail by engaging another carrier as sub-contractor). See n.126 below. cf. *Garnham, Harris & Elton Ltd v Alfred W Ellis (Transport) Ltd* [1967] 1 W.L.R. 940.
125 *Moukataff v BOAC* [1967] 1 Lloyd's Rep. 396. See also below, para.33-052; see *American Express Co v British Airways Board* [1983] 1 W.L.R. 701 (above, para.33-004, n.30).
126 *The Pioneer Container*, above, at 336–338, 341, 342; *China Pacific SA v Food Corp of India* [1982] A.C. 939, 957–959; *Morris v CW Martin & Sons Ltd*, above, at 729, 732; *Gilchrist Watt & Sanderson Pty Ltd v York Products Pty Ltd* [1970] 1 W.L.R. 1262. See also Pollock and Wright at p.169; below, para.33-031 and cf. *Hooper v LNW Ry* (1880) 50 L.J. Q.B. 103 (below, para.36-044). It is, however, necessary to distinguish between consent to a sub-bailment and consent to the creation of a direct contractual relationship between the bailor and the sub-bailee. The two are "conceptually different": see *Targe Towing Ltd v Marine Blast Ltd* [2004] EWCA Civ 346, [2004] 1 Lloyd's Rep. 721 at [28].
127 *The Pioneer Container*, above. On the question of the sub-bailee denying the bailor's title to the goods, above, para.33-015.
128 *The Pioneer Container*, above, at 342 (at 340–341, the Privy Council overruled *Johnson Matthey & Co Ltd v Constantine Terminals Ltd* [1976] 2 Lloyd's Rep. 215). On the sub-bailee's knowledge, see Palmer and Murdoch (1983) 46 M.L.R. 73; also Carnegie, 3 Adelaide L.R. 7 (1967).
129 Although the original bailor seems to have assumed the onus of proving this in *Moukataff v BOAC*, above, at 416.
130 *Learoyd Bros & Co v Pope & Sons Ltd* [1966] 2 Lloyd's Rep. 142, 149 ("negligence ... attributable to the defendants in their character of bailees"); *Moukataff v BOAC*, above, at 414; *Gilchrist Watt & Sanderson Pty Ltd v York Products Pty Ltd*, above; *The Pioneer Container*, above, at 336–338 ("... if the sub-bailment is for reward, the obligation owed by the sub-bailee to the owner must likewise be that of a bailee for reward, notwithstanding that the reward is payable not by the owner but by the bailee" (at 338)).
131 *James Buchanan & Co Ltd v Hay's Transport Services Ltd* [1972] 2 Lloyd's Rep. 535; *Homburg Houtimport BV v Agrosin Private Ltd (The Starsin)* [2003] UKHL 12, [2004] 1 A.C. 705 at [136]. See also below, para.33-049.

bailee, the onus of proof may be on him to show that the loss or damage occurred without any failure on his part to take reasonable care[132]; similarly, if the original bailor sues the sub-bailee for conversion, he need prove only that the act of the sub-bailee was wholly inconsistent with the sub-bailee's duties qua bailee or with his contractual duties under the contract of sub-bailment,[133] i.e. he will not be obliged to prove conversion according to the ordinary principles of the law of tort. (But since the Supply of Goods and Services Act 1982[134] applies only where there is a contract for the supply of a service, no terms implied by that Act will affect the position of a sub-bailee vis-à-vis the head bailor, unless a contract between them is proved.)

33-027 **The sub-bailee and protective clauses** There may also be advantages from the point of view of the sub-bailee in relying, as against the original bailor, on the fact that the sub-bailment was made with the actual or ostensible authority of the original bailor. Thus, by the terms of the contract of sub-bailment the sub-bailee may be protected from certain liabilities towards the original bailor if the contract of sub-bailment was made by the bailee as agent of the bailor.[135] Even if there was no agency, so that the exempting terms do not bind the original bailor in contract (because of the lack of a contract between them),[136] he will be bound[137] where he has consented to them: where the original bailor consents (whether expressly, impliedly or under the principle of ostensible authority) to the bailee sub-bailing the goods,[138] the original bailor's "rights against the sub-bailee will only be subject to terms of the sub-bailment if he has consented to them, i.e., if he has authorised the bailee to entrust the goods to the sub-bailee on those terms ..."[139] [terms which

---

[132] *Nippon Yusen Kaisha v International Import and Export Co Ltd* [1978] 1 Lloyd's Rep. 206. See below, para.33-050. cf. *Thomas National Transport Ltd v May & Baker Ltd* [1966] 2 Lloyd's Rep. 347, 352, 365.

[133] *Morris v CW Martin & Sons Ltd*, above; *Moukataff v BOAC*, above, at 414.

[134] See below, paras 33-044 et seq.

[135] *Hall v NE Ry* (1875) L.R. 10 Q.B. 437; *Barratt v GN Ry* (1904) 20 T.L.R. 175. (The bailee might also be treated as the agent of the sub-bailee for the purpose of making a contract with the bailor.) cf. *New Zealand Shipping Co Ltd v AM Satterthwaite & Co Ltd* [1975] A.C. 154; *Port Jackson Stevedoring Pty Ltd v Salmond and Spraggon (Australia) Pty Ltd* [1981] 1 W.L.R. 138. cf. also *Junior Books Ltd v Veitchi Co Ltd* [1983] 1 A.C. 520, 546; *Leigh and Sillavan Ltd v Aliakmon Shipping Co Ltd* [1986] A.C. 785, 817 (in this case there was no bailment between the plaintiff and the defendant). Different principles apply when the sub-bailee seeks to take advantage of the terms of the head bailment. In such a case the ability of the sub-bailee to invoke the terms depends upon the scope of the agreement between the bailor and the sub-bailee, entered into by the bailee as agent for the sub-bailee: see *The Mahkutai* [1996] A.C. 650. The fact that there is a Himalaya clause in the contract between the goods owner and the bailee does not, however, oust the sub-bailee's right to rely upon the terms of the sub-bailment: *Homburg Houtimport BV v Agrosin Private Ltd (The Starsin)* [2003] UKHL 12, [2004] 1 A.C. 705 at [136].

[136] *Midland Silicones Ltd v Scruttons Ltd* [1962] A.C. 446. (But cf. the *New Zealand Shipping* case, above; the *Port Jackson* case, see above). The bailee has often been held to have made the contract of sub-bailment as principal: *L Harris (Harella) Ltd v Continental Express Ltd* [1961] 1 Lloyd's Rep. 251, 259; *Learoyd Bros & Co v Pope & Sons Ltd* [1966] 2 Lloyd's Rep. 142; *Lee Cooper Ltd v CH Jeakins & Sons Ltd* [1967] 2 Q.B. 1; *Moukataff v BOAC* [1967] 1 Lloyd's Rep. 396, 416–418.

[137] On the effect of the Unfair Contract Terms Act 1977, see Palmer (1978) 128 New L.J. 887, 915.

[138] See above, para.33-026.

[139] *The Pioneer Container* [1994] 2 A.C. 324, 341, discussed in more detail by Palmer and Merkin [1994] All E.R. Annual Review 28–35; and Phang (1995) 58 M.L.R. 422. For earlier authority, see *Morris v CW Martin & Sons Ltd*, above, at 729–730 (cf. at 731, 741); *Singer Co (UK) v Tees and Hartlepool Port Authority* [1988] 2 Lloyd's Rep. 164; *Hispanica de Petroleos SA v Veucedora*

the original bailor] has actually (expressly or impliedly) or even ostensibly authorised".[140] Similarly, where the original bailor consents to the bailee sub-bailing the goods on terms which include a term conferring a lien on the sub-bailee, the sub-bailee may be entitled to rely on the lien as against the original bailor.[141]

Imposing more onerous obligations on the sub-bailee   Sub-bailment may oper-   **33-028** ate to the disadvantage of the sub-bailee in the sense that some of the terms agreed between the bailee and the sub-bailee may increase the liability of the sub-bailee beyond that which would otherwise have arisen under the common law. The bailor may be entitled to enforce such conditions against the sub-bailee where the bailee has the consent, and thus the authority, of the bailor to enter into a sub-bailment on such terms. In such a case, "all the terms agreed between the bailee and the sub-bailee, in so far as these are applicable to the relationship of the bailor and the sub-bailee, apply as between the bailor and the sub-bailee".[142]

Duty of care apart from sub-bailment   Even in the absence of sub-bailment to   **33-029** a third person, the owner of the goods may be owed, under the tort of negligence, a duty of care by the person in actual control of the goods. Thus, where goods were agreed to be stored by a company but were in the actual control of the managing director in a store owned by him, he was held liable in tort for negligently allowing them to be damaged, despite the fact that he did not have exclusive possession of them and accordingly could not be treated as a bailee.[143]

Attornment[144]   If the bailor directs the bailee (e.g. a warehouseman) to hold the   **33-030** chattel[145] in his possession[146] on behalf of a third person (the claimant) and the bailee thereupon attorns to the claimant by accepting the bailor's direction,[147] or by

---

Oceanic Navegacion SA [1987] 2 Lloyd's Rep. 321, 336, 340; *Compania Portorafti Commerciale SA v Ultramar Panama Inc (The Captain Gregos) (No.2)* [1990] 2 Lloyd's Rep. 395; *Mitsui & Co Ltd v Novorossiysk Shipping Co (The Gudermes)* [1993] 1 Lloyd's Rep. 311, 327–328; *Spectra International Plc v Hayesoak Ltd* [1997] 1 Lloyd's Rep. 153, 155; Palmer and Murdoch (1983) 46 M.L.R. 73. The court may, in its discretion, stay the bailor's action against the sub-bailee, if it is brought in breach of the contract with the bailee: *Nippon Yusen Kaisha v International Import and Export Co Ltd* [1978] 1 Lloyd's Rep. 206.

[140] *The Pioneer Container*, above, at 342 (the original bailor, the owner of the goods, was bound by an "exclusive jurisdiction" clause in the contract between the bailee and the sub-bailee). *Homburg Houtimport BV v Agrosin Private Ltd (The Starsin)* [2003] UKHL 12, [2004] 1 A.C. 705 at [136]; *East West Corp v DKBS 1912 and Akts Svendborg* [2003] EWCA Civ 83, [2003] 1 Lloyd's Rep. 239 at [24].

[141] *Jarl Tra Ab v Convoys Ltd* [2003] EWHC 1488 (Comm), [2003] 2 Lloyd's Rep. 459.

[142] *Sandeman Coprimar SA v Transitos y Transportes Integrales SL* [2003] EWCA Civ 113, [2003] Q.B. 1270 at [62]. See also Palmer at para.23-038.

[143] *Fairline Shipping Corp v Adamson* [1975] Q.B. 180, 190–191.

[144] Palmer at Ch.25. See also Palmer and Merkin [1994] All E.R. Annual Review 23–25. Arguments which would have extended the scope of attornment were rejected by the Privy Council in *Re Goldcorp Exchange* [1995] 1 A.C. 74.

[145] For attornment to operate, the chattel must be specific, e.g. a specific appropriation may be necessary: *Unwin v Adams* (1858) 1 F. & F. 312; *Laurie and Morewood v Dudin & Sons* [1926] 1 K.B. 223. cf. *Re London Wine Co (Shippers) Ltd* [1986] P.C.C. 121.

[146] If the bailee agrees to attorn before the chattel comes into his possession, the attornment will take effect as soon as the chattel does come into his possession: *Holl v Griffin* (1833) 10 Bing. 246, 248.

[147] *Gosling v Birnie* (1831) 7 Bing. 337; *Laurie and Morewood v Dudin & Sons*, above (receipt, but not "acceptance", of the delivery order). cf. below, paras 33-123, 44-254.

acknowledging to the claimant that the claimant now has title to the chattel,[148] the bailee will become the bailee of the claimant.[149] At common law, the bailee was also estopped from denying the claimant's title, but by statute the bailee may now set up the title of a third person in reply to the bailor's demand for redelivery of the chattel.[150] However, a delivery order given by the bailor to a third person directing the bailee to deliver the goods to the third person is a mere authority to receive possession, and does not of itself imply an undertaking by the bailor that the bailee will deliver the goods.[151]

33-031 **Vicarious liability** The bailee is not normally the agent of the bailor, so as to render the bailor vicariously liable to a third person who is injured by the negligence or wrongful act of the bailee in the management of the thing bailed.[152] But the bailor may be so liable if the bailee is acting on behalf of the bailor as his agent and for his purposes, or the bailor retains some control over the management of the chattel.[153]

3.   GRATUITOUS BAILMENT

(a)   Deposit

33-032 **Deposit**[154] Deposit is the bailment of a chattel to be kept by the bailee without reward[155] and to be returned upon demand to the bailor or his nominee.[156] The obligation of the gratuitous bailee arises only upon actual delivery of the chattel to him and his acceptance of the deposit[157]; he then must take reasonable care of the

---

148 cf. *Re Savoy Estate Ltd* [1949] Ch. 622.
149 *Henderson & Co v Williams* [1895] 1 Q.B. 521; *Dublin City Distillery Ltd v Doherty* [1914] A.C. 823, 847–848. cf. below, para.33-058. The bailee apparently holds the chattel on the same terms as under the original bailment: *Leigh and Sillavan v Aliakmon Shipping Co Ltd* [1986] A.C. 785, 812; *Compania Portorafti Commerciale SA v Ultramar Panama Inc (The Captain Gregos) (No.2)* [1990] 2 Lloyd's Rep. 395, 404–405; *Mitsui & Co Ltd v Novorossiysk Shipping Co (The Gudermes)* [1993] 1 Lloyd's Rep. 311, 324. The claimant may be bound by an exemption clause in the contract between the bailee and the original bailor, if the claimant is treated as an assignee of the benefit of this contract: *HMF Humphrey Ltd v Baxter, Hoare & Co Ltd* (1933) 149 L.T. 603; *Britain & Overseas Trading (Bristles) Ltd v Brooks Wharf & Bull Wharf Ltd* [1967] 2 Lloyd's Rep. 51, 60.
150 See above, paras 33-015—33-017.
151 *Alicia Hosiery Ltd v Brown Shipley & Co Ltd* [1970] 1 Q.B. 195.
152 *Morgans v Launchbury* [1973] A.C. 127; *Smith v Bailey* [1891] 2 Q.B. 403; *Britt v Galmoye and Nevill* (1928) 44 T.L.R. 294; *Hewitt v Bonvin* [1940] 1 K.B. 188; *Klein v Caluori* [1971] 1 W.L.R. 619. See Atiyah, *Vicarious Liability* (1967), Ch.13.
153 *Sampson v Aitchison* [1912] A.C. 844; *Pratt v Patrick* [1924] 1 K.B. 488; *Ormrod v Crosville Motor Services Ltd* [1953] 1 W.L.R. 1120. cf. *Morgans v Launchbury*, above.
154 Palmer at Ch.10; also (1978) 128 New L.J. 791.
155 cf. Custody, below, para.33-049. Since there is no consideration in deposit, it is an instance of bailment without a contract. A bailment may be for reward, although no consideration moves from the bailor: *Andrews v Home Flats Ltd* [1945] 2 All E.R. 698. cf. *Oliver v Sadler & Co* [1929] A.C. 584, 596; *Collett v National Fur Co* (1945) 78 Ll.L. Rep. 1. As to the efforts of the courts to "invent" consideration so as to find a contract of bailment, see Vol.I, para.4-198.
156 If a gratuitous bailee fails to return the goods on demand, he may become an insurer and hold them at his peril: *Mitchell v Ealing London BC* [1979] Q.B. 1. (See Palmer (1978) 128 New L.J. 791.) It is not, however, necessary for the bailor expressly to reserve a right to require that the chattel ultimately be restored to his own possession or to his order, provided that it is established that what was intended was a bailment and not a donation: *Yearworth v North Bristol NHS Trust* [2009] EWCA Civ 37, [2010] Q.B. 1 at [48].
157 e.g. *Blount v War Office* [1953] 1 W.L.R. 736.

chattel, and the standard of care required of him will depend on all the circumstances of the particular case.[158] The onus of proof is on the bailee to show that he was not negligent in his care of the chattel.[159] The fact that the bailment is gratuitous is one of the circumstances affecting the standard of care required of the bailee[160]; other relevant circumstances would include the nature and value of the chattel,[161] and the manner in which the bailee keeps his own chattels[162]; but he cannot show that he took reasonable care of the chattel merely by showing that he kept the goods deposited with him in the same manner as he kept his own.[163] The liability of the gratuitous bailee is probably best classified as sui generis and it should not be assumed that it follows from the fact that the bailment is not contractual that the liability of the gratuitous bailee must lie in tort.[164] Indeed, where the gratuitous bailee has extended, and broken, a particular promise to his bailor, the measure of damages "may be more akin to that referable to breach of contract rather than to tort".[165]

Expenses The House of Lords has held that if the gratuitous bailee fulfils his duty of care, he has a correlative right to charge the bailor with the expenses reasonably incurred by him in doing so.[166]   **33-033**

---

[158] *Houghland v RR Low (Luxury Coaches) Ltd* [1962] 1 Q.B. 694 (above, para.33-008); *Graham v Voigt* (1989) 89 A.L.R. 11; *Sutcliffe v Chief Constable of West Yorkshire* [1996] R.T.R. 86; *City Television v Conference and Training Office Ltd* [2001] EWCA Civ 1770; *Grocutt v Khan* [2002] EWCA Civ 1945, [2003] R.T.R. 22 at [23]. But see the House of Lords in *China Pacific SA v Food Corp of India* [1982] A.C. 939 at 960, where (obiter) the older formulation of the test was referred to, viz that the bailee in gratuitous deposit must show that degree of diligence which men of common prudence generally exercise about their own affairs or would take for the preservation of their own property; *Giblin v McMullen* (1869) L.R. 2 P.C. 317, 337–338; *Bullen v Swan Electric Engraving Co* (1907) 23 T.L.R. 258; *Blount v War Office*, above, at 739. But the line between the two standards is very fine: *Port Swettenham Authority v TW Wu and Co (M) Sdn Bhd* [1979] A.C. 580, 589. See also Palmer at paras 10-005—10-021; Paton at pp.101–110; Story at para.62; *Coggs v Bernard* (1703) 2 Ld. Raym. 909, 913–915; *Mytton v Cock* (1738) 2 Str. 1099; *Martin v LCC* [1947] K.B. 628, 631. If a gratuitous bailee holds himself out to the bailor as able to deploy some special skill in relation to the chattel, his duty is to take such care of it as is reasonably to be expected of a person with such skill: *Wilson v Brett* (1843) 11 M. & W. 113; *Yearworth v North Bristol NHS Trust* [2009] EWCA Civ 37, [2010] Q.B. 1 at [48].

[159] *Houghland v RR Low (Luxury Coaches) Ltd*, above; *Port Swettenham Authority v TW Wu and Co (M) Sdn Bhd*, above; *Sutcliffe v Chief Constable of West Yorkshire*, above; *Pennington v De Wan* [2017] EWHC 4 (Ch) at [22]. See also *Coggs v Bernard*, above, at 913–915; *Doorman v Jenkins* (1834) 2 A. & E. 256; *Giblin v McMullen*, above, at 339; *Trefftz v Canelli* (1872) L.R. 4 P.C. 277, 284. And see below, para.33-050.

[160] Paton at p.110.

[161] *Sutcliffe v Chief Constable of West Yorkshire*, above; *Grocutt v Khan* [2002] EWCA Civ 1945, [2003] R.T.R. 22 at [23].

[162] *Giblin v McMullen*, above, at 339.

[163] *Giblin v McMullen*, above, at 339; *Coggs v Bernard*, above, at 914, 915. cf. *Doorman v Jenkins*, above. Some old authorities suggest that if the bailor knows that the bailee is a negligent or imprudent man, the latter may be liable only if he fails to take the same care as he usually does for his own chattels of a similar kind: *Coggs v Bernard*, above. at 914–915; *The William* (1806) 6 Ch. Rob. 316.

[164] *Yearworth v North Bristol NHS Trust* [2009] EWCA Civ 37, [2010] Q.B. 1 at [48].

[165] *Yearworth v North Bristol NHS Trust* [2009] EWCA Civ 37, [2010] Q.B. 1 at [48].

[166] *China Pacific SA v Food Corp of India*, above. (At 964, Lord Simon said that the bailee "incurred reasonable expenses in safeguarding and preserving the goods, to the benefit of the bailor"; in this case, the expenses were storage charges paid by the bailee.) The Supreme Court has left open the question whether the bailee can recover remuneration in respect of the services rendered: *ENE Kos 1 Ltd v Petroleo Brasileiro SA (No.2)* [2012] UKSC 17, [2012] 2 A.C. 164 at [29] and [35]. A similar doubt exists in relation to the recovery of storage charges, as opposed to storage expenses. The former may not be recoverable: *Garside v Black Horse Ltd* [2010] EWHC 190 (QB), [2010] All E.R.

33-034 **Use of the chattel by the bailee**   A gratuitous bailee is not permitted to use the chattel bailed for his own personal advantage in any way at all (without the express or implied consent of the bailor) unless such use is necessary for its preservation[167]; if he wrongfully makes use of the chattel he will be responsible for any loss or injury resulting from the use unless he can show that the loss or damage did not arise from his breach of duty.[168] If the bailee's act is wholly inconsistent with his obligations as bailee, as where the bailee, in the absence of any emergency or necessity, sells the chattel,[169] the bailment is terminated forthwith and the right to immediate possession reverts to the bailor, who may sue the bailee for conversion.[170]

33-035 **Deposits with bankers**   Where a customer deposits valuables or securities with a banker for safe custody and the banker makes no special charge, the bailment has sometimes been held to be gratuitous[171] and sometimes for reward.[172] It is submitted that the latter is the better opinion: it is based on the view that the banker might indirectly benefit from the bailment, in that it induces the customer to continue to keep his account with the banker.[173] It has been held, even on the basis that the bankers are gratuitous bailees, that where valuables or securities in a locked box or sealed parcel are deposited for safe custody with the bankers, they have no right to open the box or parcel, and its contents are not subject to any lien for previous or subsequent debts of the customer.[174]

(b)   Involuntary Bailees

33-036 **Involuntary bailees[175]**   Normally, "a man cannot without his knowledge and consent be considered as a bailee of property …",[176] but circumstances may arise

---

(D) 98 (Mar) at [122]. A shipowner in the exercise of his lien for general average contribution may be entitled to recover the costs involved in exercising that lien in terms of the continuing expense of looking after the cargo instead of being able to discharge it: *Metall Market OOO v Vitorio Shipping Co Ltd (The "Lehmann Timber")* [2013] EWCA Civ 650, [2014] Q.B. 760. However, a right to be reimbursed will not arise in every case: *Tongue v Royal Society for the Prevention of Cruelty to Animals* [2017] EWHC 2508 (Ch), [2018] B.P.I.R. 229 at [78]–[84] (where the relationship between the parties was not commercial and it was held not to be apparent to the alleged bailor that the bailee who was a charity would seek to charge for the services that it had provided).

167 Bac.Abr. Bailment A. cf. *Re Tidd* [1893] 3 Ch. 154.

168 *Lilley v Doubleday* (1881) 7 Q.B.D. 510, 511. cf. *Coldman v Hill* [1919] 1 K.B. 443.

169 *Sachs v Miklos* [1948] 2 K.B. 23, 36; *Munro v Willmott* [1949] 1 K.B. 295.

170 *Fenn v Bittleston* (1851) 7 Ex. 152, 159; *North General Wagon and Finance Co Ltd v Graham* [1950] 2 K.B. 7, 15. See above, para.33-014.

171 *Giblin v McMullen* (1869) L.R. 2 P.C. 317 (which was, however, "gravely doubted" by the Privy Council in *Port Swettenham Authority v TW Wu and Co (M) Sdn Bhd* [1979] A.C. 580, 589); *Bullen v Swan Electric Engraving Co* (1906) 22 T.L.R. 275; affirmed (1907) 23 T.L.R. 258.

172 *Re United Service Co* (1870) L.R. 6 Ch. App. 212. See below, paras 34-438—34-440; and Paget's *Law of Banking*, 14th edn (2014), para.7.2.

173 *Bullen v Swan Electric Engraving Co*, above, at 277 (affirmed; above); the *Port Swettenham* case, above, at 589. It has even been contended that the mere entrusting with the property is sufficient consideration: see *Banbury v Bank of Montreal* [1917] 1 K.B. 409, 439; affirmed [1918] A.C. 626.

174 *Leese v Martin* (1873) L.R. 17 Eq. 224 (following *Brandao v Barnett* (1846) 12 Cl. & F. 787); *R. v Robson* (1861) 31 L.J.M.C. 22. On a banker's lien, see below, paras 34-545—34-548.

175 Palmer at Ch.13 (also in (1978) 128 New L.J. 763). Bailment may arise without the bailor having consented to the bailee having possession of the goods: *The Pioneer Container* [1994] 2 A.C. 324, 341–342 (above, para.33-026).

176 Winfield, *Province of the Law of Tort*, p.100. See *Lethbridge v Phillips* (1819) 2 Stark. 544; *Neuwith v Over Darwen Industrial Co-operative Society* (1894) 63 L.J. Q.B. 290. cf. *R. v Ashwell* (1885) 16

where a person finds that, without any consent on his part, he has another's chattel in his control or on his premises.[177] The legal position of an involuntary bailee is by no means clear, but the balance of authority suggests that, although gross negligence or deliberate injury will make him liable,[178] mere negligence will not.[179] Thus, where an author sent a manuscript of a play to the defendant (the lessee of a theatre) who lost it, it was held that no duty of any kind was imposed on the defendant by receipt of something he had not asked for.[180] The ruling has, however, been questioned[181] in another case,[182] where a customer accidentally left her brooch behind in the defendants' shop, and it was handed by an assistant to a shopwalker, who put it in his desk instead of taking it to the lost property office; the brooch was then stolen from the desk, and the defendants were held liable because they had not exercised reasonable care. There was in this case, however, some assumption of control over the brooch by the defendants' employee.[183] In a further case,[184] the judge held that, "If persons were involuntary bailees *and had done everything reasonable* they were not liable to pay damages if something which they did resulted in the loss of the property".[185] Where an involuntary bailee wrote to the bailor saying that he was no longer willing to hold the goods and wanted them removed but the bailor did nothing even after receiving a second letter which stated that the goods would be sold unless removed, the court may infer that the bailor impliedly consented to the sale.[186] But this view is not without difficulty because of the principle, applicable at least to the analogous situation of offer and acceptance, that silence is not consent.[187] The involuntary bailee may now, however, be able to avail himself of the wide powers of sale conferred by ss.12 and 13 of the Torts (Interference with Goods) Act 1977.[188] The duty of an involuntary bailee in

---

Q.B.D. 190. In the case of sub-bailment, the Privy Council said that "They incline to the opinion that a sub-bailee can only be said for these purposes to have voluntarily taken into his possession the goods of another if he has sufficient notice that a person other than the bailee is interested in the goods …": *The Pioneer Container*, above, at 342.

[177] e.g. carriers may become involuntary bailees when the goods are not accepted at the consignee's address: *Heugh v LNW Ry* (1870) L.R. 5 Ex. 51 (at 56, Kelly C.B. apparently approved of the practice of the carrier to charge the consignee with the cost of keeping the goods thereafter).

[178] *Hiort v Bott* (1874) L.R. 9 Ex. 86, 90 (obiter, since this was a case of conversion and the defendant did not acquire possession of the goods).

[179] Paton at pp.113–117; Palmer at paras 13-005—13-021; *Winfield and Jolowicz on Tort*, 19th edn (2014) paras 18-017—18-018. But see *Houghland v RR Low (Luxury Coaches) Ltd* [1962] 1 Q.B. 694, 698 (see above, para.33-008). See also Burnett (1960) 76 L.Q.R. 364; Tay (1966) 5 Sydney L.Rev. 239.

[180] *Howard v Harris* (1884) Cab. & El. 253.

[181] cf. *Summer v Challenor* (1926) 70 S.J. 760, where an actor wrote acknowledging and promising to read a play and was held liable for its safe custody.

[182] *Newman v Bourne & Hollingsworth* (1915) 31 T.L.R. 209.

[183] *Gilchrist Watt and Sanderson Pty Ltd v York Products Pty Ltd* [1970] 1 W.L.R. 1262, 1268 ("the taking of possession in the circumstances involves an assumption of responsibility for the safe keeping of the goods").

[184] *Elvin & Powell Ltd v Plummer Roddis Ltd* (1933) 50 T.L.R. 158. cf. *Hiort v Bott* (1874) L.R. 9 Ex. 86.

[185] (1933) 50 T.L.R.158 at 159 (emphasis added); *Scotland v Solomon* [2002] EWHC 1886 (Ch); *Da Rocha-Afodu v Mortgage Express Ltd* [2014] EWCA Civ 454, [2014] All E.R. (D) 212 (Mar); *Campbell v Redstone Mortgages Ltd* [2014] EWHC 3081 (Ch), [2014] All E.R. (D) 193 (Oct).

[186] *Sachs v Miklos* [1948] 2 K.B. 23, 37.

[187] *Sachs v Miklos*, above.

[188] See below, paras 33-095—33-100. Since there is no definition of "bailment" or "bailee" in the Act, it is not clear whether involuntary bailees are included.

possession of goods will be enlarged, and he will become responsible for failure to take reasonable care, if he spontaneously and officiously proposes to keep the goods[189]; or if he changes his character as gratuitous bailee, by taking charge of the goods for reward.[190]

33-037 **Finding** The question whether a person who finds goods is a bailee of them is one which admits of no easy answer. It has been argued that "cases in finding give rise to a bailment, at least to the extent that the finder owes substantially the same common law duties in relation to the chattel as an ordinary consensual bailee".[191] While dicta can be found to support this proposition,[192] there are also dicta which are hostile to the equation of finding and bailment.[193] The equation of finding and bailment is acceptable provided that it is accepted that bailment rules cannot be translated wholesale into the law of finding.[194] The law on finding should be sought elsewhere.[195]

33-038 **Unsolicited goods** The Unsolicited Goods and Services Act 1971 was passed to deal with the problem of goods being delivered or sent by post to recipients who did not order them, but might be subjected by the sender to some pressure to pay for them. The Act has since been supplemented by reg.27M of the Consumer Protection from Unfair Trading Regulations 2008[196] as amended by the Consumer Contracts (Information, Cancellation and Additional Charges) Regulations 2013.[197]

33-039 It is an unfair commercial practice for a trader to demand immediate or deferred payment for or the return or safekeeping of products supplied by the trader, but not solicited by the consumer.[198] In such a case the consumer is exempted from any obligation to provide consideration for the product supplied by the trader[199] and the absence of a response from the consumer following the supply does not constitute consent to the provision of consideration for, or the return or safekeeping of, the products.[200] Further, in the case of an unsolicited supply of goods, the consumer may, as between the consumer and the trader, use, deal with or dispose of the goods as if they were an unconditional gift to the consumer.[201]

---

[189] Jones at p.48; see also *Nelson v Macintosh* (1816) 1 Stark. 237.
[190] Jones at p.49.
[191] Palmer at para.1-037.
[192] See, for example, *Morris v CW Martin & Sons Ltd* [1966] 1 Q.B. 716, 731–732; and *Gilchrist Watt and Sanderson Pty Ltd v York Products Pty Ltd* [1970] 3 All E.R. 825, 831–832.
[193] See, e.g. *Newman v Bourne and Hollingsworth Ltd* (1915) 31 T.L.R. 209.
[194] An obvious example is that the rule that the bailee is estopped from denying his bailor's title cannot apply to cases of finding.
[195] Pollock and Wright, *Possession in the Common Law*, pp.171–187; Palmer at Ch.26; Paton at pp.118–129. See *Parker v British Airways Board* [1982] Q.B. 1004; *Waverley Borough Council v Fletcher* [1996] Q.B. 334. See also the *Report of the Law Reform Committee on Conversion and Detinue*, Cmnd.4774 (1971), App.I.
[196] SI 2008/1277.
[197] SI 2013/3134 Pt 4. The 2008 Regulations (in Pt 2) superseded the Consumer Protection (Distance Selling) Regulations 2000 (SI 2000/2334) reg.24 of which dealt with inertia selling and made more complete provision than that to be found in the current Regulations.
[198] Consumer Protection from Unfair Trading Regulations 2008 (SI 2008/1277) Sch.1 para.29.
[199] SI 2008/1277 reg.27M(2).
[200] SI 2008/1277 reg.27M(3).
[201] SI 2008/1277 reg.27M(4).

(c) Mandate

Mandate   Mandate is the bailment of a specific chattel in respect of which the   **33-040**
bailee undertakes to perform a gratuitous act.[202] In deposit the main object is the safe
custody of the chattel, whereas in mandate it is some service or labour to be
performed by the bailee in connection with the chattel.[203] As in gratuitous deposit,
above, the bailor derives an advantage from the gratuitous exertions of the bailee;
but despite the absence of reward to the bailee, he must take reasonable care of the
chattel according to the circumstances of the case, once he begins his task.[204] In the
older cases, the absence of reward led the courts to hold that the mandatary was only
bound to exercise ordinary diligence, and was not liable unless gross negligence,
breach of orders, or fraud was proved against him.[205] In the present law, the fact that
the bailment is gratuitous is only one of the relevant circumstances affecting the
standard of care required of the mandatary.[206] Similarly, if the situation or profession of the gratuitous mandatary implies[207] special skill in the task he undertakes,
his omission to employ that skill will be treated as negligence on his part.[208] The
mandatary is liable to the bailor for the loss of, or damage to, the chattel bailed, arising from any breach of the mandatary's duty. He is, however, entitled to be
reimbursed by the bailor in respect of his expenses incurred in executing the
mandate.[209] If the mandatary does some act to or with the chattel which is
unauthorised by the terms of the bailment, he is responsible for any resulting loss
or damage.[210] If the bailor refuses or neglects to take redelivery of the chattel, the
mandatary will be able to avail himself of statutory powers of sale.[211]

(d) Gratuitous Loan for Use

Obligations of the borrower[212]   A gratuitous[213] bailment where the benefit is   **33-041**
conferred upon the bailee arises when a chattel is bailed to be used by the bailee

---

[202] Palmer at Ch.11; *Story on Bailments*, 9th edn, para.137.
[203] *Coggs v Bernard* (1703) 2 Ld. Raym. 909, 918.
[204] *Houghland v RR Low (Luxury Coaches) Ltd* [1962] 1 Q.B. 694, 698. The standard of care is to be
judged objectively: above, para.33-008.
[205] *Jones on Bailments*, p.120; *Mytton v Cock* (1738) 2 Str. 1099; *Shiells v Blackburne* (1789) 1 H. Bl.
158; *Dartnall v Howard* (1825) 4 B. & C. 345, 350; *Doorman v Jenkins* (1834) 2 A. & E. 256; *Parry
v Roberts* (1835) 3 A. & E. 118. See also *Moffat v Bateman* (1869) L.R. 3 P.C. 115, 122 (a case on
gratuitous carriage of a person, which is criticised by Paton at pp.140–144).
[206] cf. *Southcote's Case* (1600) 4 Co. Rep. 83b; *Beauchamp v Powley* (1831) 1 Moo. & R. 38; but see
Copland v Brogan, 1916 S.C. 277.
[207] The same position would hold where the mandatary represents to the bailor that he possesses
particular skill or experience, and the bailor reasonably relies on that representation: *Chaudhry v
Prabhakar* [1989] 1 W.L.R. 29, an analogous case of gratuitous agency.
[208] *Shiells v Blackburne*, above, at 162; *Wilson v Brett* (1843) 11 M. & W. 113; *O'Hanlon v Murray*
(1860) 12 Ir.C.L.R. 161; *Fish v Kelly* (1864) 17 C.B. N.S.) 194, 206; Story at para.182a. cf. *Harmer
v Cornelius* (1858) 5 C.B.(N.S.) 236; *Banbury v Bank of Montreal* [1918] A.C. 626, 657.
[209] Story at para.154. cf. the analogous case of gratuitous deposit: see above, para.33-032. cf. Vol.I, paras
29-119 et seq.
[210] *Nelson v Macintosh* (1816) 1 Stark. 237; *Miles v Castle* (1830) 4 Moo. & P. 630.
[211] Torts (Interference with Goods) Act 1977 ss.12 and 13 (see below, paras 33-095—33-100). But as
there is no definition of "bailment" or "bailee" in the Act, it is not certain that the mandatary is
included.
[212] Palmer at Ch.12.
[213] See above, para.33-032, n.155.

without charge, and without any advantage to the bailor (*commodatum*). Since the lender intends the borrower to use the chattel, the borrower is not liable for reasonable wear and tear.[214] But he is liable for negligence,[215] for fraud, for misuse and for his failure to exercise reasonable skill in using the chattel.[216] The standard of care required of the borrower will depend upon all the circumstances, including the nature of the chattel, and the occupation of the borrower; but since the bailment is gratuitous, the standard will usually be a high one (*exactissima diligentia* of Roman law). If the borrower represents to the lender that he possesses a particular skill in regard to the use of the chattel, and the lender reasonably relies on that representation, the borrower will be held to that standard.[217] The borrower, in the absence of agreement, must bear any usual or ordinary expense arising from his use of the chattel.[218] The borrower must also return the chattel to the lender at the appointed time and place: if the lender refuses or neglects to take redelivery, the borrower will be entitled to avail himself of statutory powers of sale.[219]

33-042 **Limits upon the borrower's right to use the chattel**   The borrower has no right to deviate from the conditions of the loan, and if the goods are used for a materially different purpose he becomes an insurer, liable for any loss of or injury to the chattel.[220] Thus, if a horse is lent to a person to ride, this will not entitle him to allow the horse to be ridden by his employee[221]; for the borrower has no right, without the consent of the lender, to lend the goods to a third person, since the lender grants a purely personal permission to the borrower. If the borrower lends the chattel to a third person, without the consent of the lender, the bailment is determined, and the borrower is liable for any loss suffered by the lender.[222] However, delegation may be permitted where in the ordinary course of business the custody would naturally devolve upon, or the act be performed by, some employee or agent of the bailee, and in such a case the bailee is not liable if loss or damage to the chattel occurs during the period of delegation, without any negligence on the part of his substitute.[223] For instance, where a horse was for sale and the vendor allowed the defendant to have the horse in order to try it, the defendant was entitled to allow a competent person to ride the horse for that purpose.[224]

---

[214] *Blakemore v Bristol and Exeter Ry* (1858) 8 El. & Bl. 1035, 1050. See also *Pomfret v Ricroft* (1669) 1 Saund. 321, 323; *Coggs v Bernard* (1704) 2 Ld. Raym. 909, 915; *Vaughan v Menlove* (1837) 3 Bing.N.C. 468, 475; Jones at pp.50, 65.

[215] *Houghland v RR Low (Luxury Coaches) Ltd* [1962] 1 Q.B. 694, 698 (above, para.33-008). The standard to be applied to the borrower is objective, depending on all the circumstances: *Chaudhry v Prabhakar* [1989] 1 W.L.R. 29 (the analogous situation of gratuitous agency).

[216] See the cases cited in n.214, above; also Palmer at paras 12-022 et seq.

[217] *Chaudhry v Prabhakar*, above.

[218] *Handford v Palmer* (1820) 2 Brod. & Bing. 359. (cf. below, para.33-082.) The legal position is doubtful when extraordinary expense, arising from circumstances beyond the borrower's control, is incurred to preserve the chattel: Story at paras 273–274. See also Vol.I, para.29-137.

[219] Torts (Interference with Goods) Act 1977 ss.12 and 13 (see below, paras 33-095—33-100). But the absence of a definition of "bailment" or "bailee" in the Act means that it is not certain that a borrower is included.

[220] *Coggs v Bernard*, above, at 915; *Wilson v Shepherd*, 1913 S.C. 300.

[221] *Bringloe v Morrice* (1676) 1 Mod. 210. cf. *Ballett v Mingay* [1943] K.B. 281 (minor borrower); *Gwilliam v Twist* [1895] 2 Q.B. 84.

[222] See cases in n.221.

[223] *Camoys v Scurr* (1840) 9 Car. & P. 383; Story at para.234. cf. above, paras 33-026—33-029.

[224] *Camoys v Scurr*, above.

Liability of the lender If the lender knows[225] of defects in the chattel which are 33-043
not apparent to the borrower and which make it unfit for the borrower's purpose,
he is under a duty to inform the borrower of the defects; if he fails to do so, and
the borrower suffers injury through such defects, the lender is liable.[226] Thus, if the
chattel has not been used for years, and is out of repair, a warning ought to be given
to the borrower.[227]

4. BAILMENTS FOR VALUABLE CONSIDERATION

(a) The Supply of Services: Statutory Provisions

The Supply of Goods and Services Act 1982 This Act, by Pt II, codified certain 33-044
terms[228] implied at common law into contracts[229] for the supply of services.[230] These
implied terms are not exhaustive, since Pt II has effect "subject to any other enactment which defines or restricts the rights, duties or liabilities" of the parties.[231] But
(subject to the provisions of the Unfair Contract Terms Act 1977)[232] the Act permits
the implied terms[233] to be negatived or varied by express agreement, by the course
of dealing between the parties or by "such usage as binds" them.[234] The term
"service" is not defined in the Act.[235] So far as bailment is concerned, it would seem
to cover all types of bailments for valuable consideration (where there is a contract).

---

[225] If the lender is unaware of the defect, he is not liable: *MacCarthy v Young* (1861) 6 H. & N. 329;
Coughlin v Gillison [1899] 1 Q.B. 145. cf. *Lor gmeid v Holliday* (1851) 6 Ex. 761, 767–768.
However, since *Donoghue v Stevenson* [1932] A.C. 562, the lender may now be liable in negligence:
see *Hawkins v Coulsdon and Purley UDC* [1954] 1 Q.B. 319, 333; *Clerk & Lindsell on Torts*, 22nd
edn (2017), para.11-08; Marsh (1950) 66 L.Q.R. 39.

[226] *Coughlin v Gillison*, above, at 147, approving *Blakemore v Bristol and Exeter Ry* (1858) 8 El. & Bl.
1035, 1051 (crane); *MacCarthy v Young*, above. For an extension of the principle, see *Oliver v Saddler & Co* [1929] A.C. 584, 596. The lender is not liable to a third person injured through the borrower's negligence in using the chattel: *Hewitt v Bonvin* [1940] 1 K.B. 188 (approved in *Launchbury
v Morgans* [1973] A.C. 127); *Norwood v Navan* [1981] R.T.R. 457. cf. *Ormrod v Crosville Motor
Services Ltd* [1953] 1 W.L.R. 1120.

[227] *Coughlin v Gillison*, above, at 148.

[228] The Act leaves it to the common law to determine the status of these "terms", viz whether the remedy
includes termination of the contract: see Vol.I, paras 13-019 et seq.

[229] It is a contract "whatever is the nature of the consideration ..." (s.12(3)). Sch.1 para.38 of the
Consumer Rights Act 2015 inserts the word "relevant" before the words "contract for the supply of
a service" in the Supply of Goods and Services Act 1982. Sch.1 para.51 further amends s.12(1) of
the 1982 Act by providing that a contract to which Ch.4 of Pt 1 of the Consumer Rights Act 2015
applies shall not fall within the scope of the 1982 Act. Thus a contract under which a trader agrees
to supply a service to a consumer will, if the contract was made on or after October 1, 2015, be
governed by the 2015 Act and not the 1982 Act.

[230] A review of the Act and its operation is found in the Law Commission's Report on "*Implied Terms
in Contracts for the Supply of Services*" (1986) Law Com. No.156. See also Palmer (1983) 46 M.L.R.
619, 627–631; Woodroffe, *Goods and Services—The New Law* (1982), Chs 6, 7. In the case of a
contract for a trader to supply a service to a consumer (as defined in the Consumer Rights Act 2015,
on which see below, paras 38-465 et seq.), the statutory rights of the consumer and the remedies
available to the consumer are to be found in ss.48–57 of the Act.

[231] s.16(4). By s.16(3)(b), other terms not inconsistent with Pt II of the Act may continue to be implied
into such contracts.

[232] See below, paras 33-054, 33-078.

[233] Those implied by ss.13 to 15 (below).

[234] s.16(1). On exclusion of liability, below, paras 33-053—33-054. Pt II of the Law Commission report
(n.230, above) reviews the power of the supplier to exclude his liability towards consumers.

[235] But a "contract of service or apprenticeship" is excluded (s.12(2)). The Secretary of State is

33-045   **The Consumer Rights Act 2015**   This Act, by Ch.4 of Pt 1, treats contracts under which a trader[236] agrees to supply a service to a consumer[237] (and which were made on or after October 1, 2015) as including a number of terms. These terms are also not exhaustive, since Ch.4 provides that it does not affect "any enactment or rule of law that imposes a stricter duty on the trader".[238] But the ability of a trader to exclude the operation of these terms is extremely limited.[239] The term "service" is not defined in the Act.[240] As is the case with the Supply of Goods and Services Act 1982, so far as bailment is concerned, Ch.4 would seem to cover all types of bailment between a trader and a consumer for valuable consideration (where there is a contract).

33-046   **Standard of workmanship and care of the chattel**   Section 13 of the Supply of Goods and Services Act 1982 provides that:

> "In a contract for the supply of a service where the supplier is acting in the course of a business,[241] there is an implied term that the supplier[242] will carry out the service with reasonable care and skill."[243]

The common law decisions before the Act will obviously be relevant in deciding the standard of care and skill to be expected of the bailee/supplier of services. The reference to skill will apply whenever the bailee holds himself out as professing a particular skill or expertise (in which case he will be held to the standard of the reasonably competent member of the class professing that skill or expertise).[244]

33-047   **The time for performance**   Where the bailee (supplier of a service) acts in the course of a business, s.14(1) of the Supply of Goods and Services Act 1982 provides[245] that where the contract does not fix or stipulate a method for determining the time for performance (and that time cannot be determined by a course of

---

empowered by Order to exempt specified services from any of ss.13–15 (s.12(4)) but no Orders affecting bailments have been made under this power.

[236] As defined in s.2(1) of the Act.

[237] As defined in s.2(3) of the Act.

[238] s.53(1).

[239] See s.57, on which see further para.38-586.

[240] But a "contract of employment or apprenticeship" is excluded (s.48(2)). The Secretary of State is empowered by Order to exempt specified services from Ch.4 (s.48(5)).

[241] Partly defined in s.18(1) as including a profession and the activities of government departments and of local or public authorities. It is submitted that the term "business" would extend to regular, part-time work conducted for profit. On the work of charities, see Law Com. Report No.156 (n.230, above), para.2.27.

[242] s.13 probably does not affect the common law rules as to when the bailee may delegate performance of his duty of care: para.2.25 of Law Com. Report No.156 (see n.230, above): cf. Palmer (1983) 46 M.L.R. 619, 628–629.

[243] *Wilson v Best Travel Ltd* [1993] 1 All E.R. 353 (duty of care of travel agent in inspecting foreign hotel). This implied term will obviously not prevent the implication of a term (in appropriate cases) that the supplier has undertaken to produce a stated result (which implies strict liability if that result is not produced). See s.16(3)(a) of the Act which preserves any rule of law which imposes on the supplier a duty stricter than that imposed by ss.13 or 14 (below), e.g. innkeepers (below, para.33-103). The equivalent term in a contract between a trader and a consumer to supply a service (if made on or after October 1, 2015) is to be found in s.49(1) of the Consumer Rights Act 2015.

[244] The standards generally practised by the class will normally apply, but it is possible for the court to find that such a standard fails to meet the statutory standard.

[245] See above, n.243 (on s.16(3)(a)).

dealing between the parties), there is an implied term that the service will be carried out within a reasonable time; and under s.14(2), what is a reasonable time is a question of fact.[246] Where, however, the bailee's obligation to perform depends on the cooperation of the bailor, the time implied at common law will be that each party will "use reasonable diligence in performing his part".[247]

Price for the service Under s.15(1) of the Supply of Goods and Services Act **33-048** 1982, where the consideration to be paid by the customer (bailor) is not provided for by the contract (or determined by a course of dealing between the parties) he must pay a reasonable charge[248] (which is "a question of fact").[249] Where the bailee refuses to return the chattel to the bailor unless he pays a charge which is unreasonably high (not being expressly provided for in the contract), the bailor who pays it under protest in order to obtain the release of the chattel may have a claim in restitution to recover the excess above a reasonable charge.[250]

(b) Custody for Reward

(i) In General

Custody for reward[251] Where goods are delivered to a bailee to be taken care of **33-049** by him in return for remuneration to be paid by the bailor, the contract is one of custody for reward.[252] Possession of the chattel must be transferred to the bailee.[253] By s.13 of the Supply of Goods and Services Act 1982[254] (covering bailments where the bailee acts in the course of a business), s 49(1) of the Consumer Rights Act 2015 (covering bailments between a trader and a consumer, where the contract is made on or after October 1, 2015[255]) and by the common law (applicable to other cases) the bailee must take reasonable care of the chattel, according to the circumstances of the particular case.[256] Thus, the bailee must take reasonable care to see that the

---

[246] The equivalent term in a contract between a trader and a consumer to supply a service (if made on or after October 1, 2015) is to be found in s.52 of the Consumer Rights Act 2015.

[247] *Ford v Cotesworth* (1868) L.R. 4 Q.B. 127, 134 (not a bailment case).

[248] This provision (unlike ss.13 and 14, above) is not confined to where the supplier acts in course of a business.

[249] s.15(2). The equivalent term in a contract between a trader and a consumer to supply a service (if made on or after October 1, 2015) is to be found in s.51 of the Consumer Rights Act 2015 cf. s.8 of the Sale of Goods Act 1979 (below, para.44-051).

[250] See Vol.I, paras 29-098 et seq. See also CPR Pt 25 r 25.1(1)(m).

[251] Palmer at Ch.14. See below for the special cases of warehousemen (para.33-058) agisters (para.33-059), garaging of vehicles (para.33-060), railway cloakrooms (para.33-062), innkeepers (paras 33-101 et seq.) and lodging-house keepers (para.33-120).

[252] In deposit (above, para.33-032) there is no reciprocal advantage enjoyed by the bailee. As to custody "for reward" where there is no special payment for the custody, see below, para.33-057.

[253] cf. *Ashby v Tolhurst* [1937] 2 K.B. 242; *Tinsley v Dudley* [1951] 2 K.B. 18. (See below, para.33-061.)

[254] See above, paras 33-044 and 33-046.

[255] See below, para.38-571.

[256] *Houghland v RR Low (Luxury Coaches) Ltd* [1962] 1 Q.B. 694; *Morris v CW Martin & Sons Ltd* [1966] 1 Q.B. 716, 726. (The older formulation of the standard was that the custodian for reward must exercise the care and diligence exercised by a careful man in the custody of his own chattels of a similar kind: see *Coggs v Bernard* (1703) 2 Ld. Raym. 909, 916; *Dean v Keate* (1811) 3 Camp. 4; Jones at pp.86, 87.) It is not a defence that the bailee treated the chattel with the same care as he treated his own chattels: *Re United Service Co* (1870) L.R. 6 Ch. App. 212.

place[257] where the chattel is kept is fit for the purpose of custody.[258] But there is no authority "to hold that a depositor of goods for safe custody, who, by himself or his servants, has had an opportunity of observing certain defects in the storehouse, must be taken to have agreed that any risk of injury to his goods which might possibly be occasioned by these defects should be borne by him, and not by his paid bailee ... the duty is incumbent on the latter, in the due fulfilment of his contract, of considering whether his premises can be safely used for the storage of [the goods bailed], and, if they cannot, to take immediate steps for placing the goods in a position of safety".[259] The bailee must also take reasonable care to protect the chattel against any imminent danger[260]; this may include a duty to take reasonable precautions against arson or vandalism by third parties.[261] He must take all proper measures to protect the bailor's interests when the chattel is stolen[262] or when claims adverse to the bailor are made to the chattel.[263] The bailee is not, however, an insurer and he will not be liable (apart from a special obligation undertaken in the contract)[264] where the loss or damage occurred without negligence on his part.[265]

33-050   **The onus of proof and the scope of the duty**   The loss of, or injury to, the chattel while in the bailee's possession places the onus of proof on the bailee to show that it was not caused[266] by any failure on his part to take reasonable care[267]; but he need not show exactly how the loss or injury occurred.[268] The bailee's duty to take

---

[257] The bailee must also take care that any equipment used in connection with the chattel (e.g. tackle) is adequate for the purpose: *Thomas v Day* (1803) 4 Esp. 262.

[258] *Searle v Laverick* (1874) L.R. 9 Q.B. 122; *Brabant & Co v King* [1895] A.C. 632; *Turner v Stallibrass* [1898] 1 Q.B. 56; *Martin v LCC* [1947] K.B. 628. But the bailee's duty is reduced if the bailor directs where the goods are to be placed: *Harper v Jones* (1879) 4 V.L.R. (L) 536.

[259] *Brabant & Co v King*, above, at 641 (on the facts the goods bailed were explosive goods).

[260] *Brabant & Co v King*, above, at 641 (flood).

[261] *Lockspeiser Aircraft Ltd v Brooklands Aircraft Co Ltd* [1990] C.L.Y. 250 (examined in detail by Palmer at para.14-032). But the duty is only one to take reasonable care: *Sutcliffe v Chief Constable of West Yorkshire* [1996] R.T.R. 86; *Rana v Tears of Sutton Bridge* [2015] EWHC 2597 (QB).

[262] *Coldman v Hill* [1919] 1 K.B. 443.

[263] *Ranson v Platt* [1911] 2 K.B. 291. See above, para.33-015.

[264] A contractual obligation upon the bailee to insure the goods may justify the implication of an implied term making the bailee fully liable for loss of, or damage to, the goods: Roberts (1973) 124 New L.J. 849. On an undertaking to insure, see *Lockspeiser Aircraft Ltd v Brooklands Aircraft Co Ltd*, above.

[265] *Searle v Laverick* (1874) L.R. 9 Q.B. 122; *Chapman v GW Ry* (1880) 5 Q.B.D. 278; *Fagan v Green and Edwards Ltd* [1926] 1 K.B. 102. The position is different where the bailee delivers the chattel to an unauthorised person: see below, para.33-052. It is not, however, necessary in order to avoid liability for a bailee to show what caused the loss: the bailee must show either that he took reasonable care of the goods or that his failure to do so did not contribute to the damage: *Coopers Payen Ltd v Southampton Container Terminal Ltd* [2003] EWCA Civ 1223, [2004] 1 Lloyd's Rep. 331 at [28].

[266] The onus is on the bailee to prove the absence of any causal connection between a negligent act on his part and the loss of or damage to the chattel: *Coldman v Hill*, above, at 458; *British Road Services Ltd v Arthur V Crutchley & Co Ltd* [1968] 1 All E.R. 811, 820, 824; *Piper v Hales* [2013] All E.R. (D) 257 (Jan) at [30].

[267] *Brook's Wharf and Bull Wharf Ltd v Goodman Bros* [1937] 1 K.B. 534, 538–539; *Gutter v Tait* (1947) 177 L.T. 1; *Houghland v RR Low (Luxury Coaches) Ltd* [1962] 1 Q.B. 694; *Global Dress Co Ltd v WH Boase & Co Ltd* [1966] 2 Lloyd's Rep. 72; *Transmotors Ltd v Robertson, Buckley & Co Ltd* [1970] 1 Lloyd's Rep. 224; *Port Swettenham Authority v TW Wu and Co (M) Sdn Bhd* [1979] A.C. 580, 590. See also above, paras 33-012, 33-032 (deposit); see below, para.33-064, 33-079 (hire), 35-059, 36-018 (carriage). cf. *Phipps v New Claridge's Hotel Ltd* (1905) 22 T.L.R. 49.

[268] *Bullen v Swan Electric Engraving Co* (1907) 23 T.L.R. 258. cf. *Phipps v New Claridge's Hotel Ltd*,

reasonable care may include the duty to prevent damage to the chattel by the deliberate act of a third party.[269] If the bailee relies on an exemption clause[270] he must prove facts which bring him within the exemption.[271] The bailee is liable to the bailor for loss of or injury to the chattel caused by the negligence of the bailee's employees or agents[272] acting within the course of their employment or the apparent scope of their authority.[273] If the bailee entrusts the performance of his duty to take reasonable care of the chattel to an employee, then the bailee is liable, not only for the employee's negligence which injures the chattel, but also for the employee's fraud or dishonesty in making away with the chattel.[274]

Damages   Where the bailee is liable for loss of the chattel, the bailor can recover **33-051** as damages the actual value of the chattel, but he can recover further damages for consequential loss only if it was within the reasonable contemplation of the parties at the time the bailment was made.[275] The bailee has an insurable interest in the chattel, and may insure it for its full value.[276]

Unauthorised dealings   The bailee must deal with the chattel in the manner **33-052** authorised by the bailor.[277] Thus, the bailee may not delegate the storage to a third

---

above; *Joseph Travers & Sons Ltd v Cooper* [1915] 1 K.B. 73. While it is not necessary as a matter of law for a bailee to show what the cause of the damage was, the identification of the cause may be a "significant pointer as to whether or not the bailee has exercised reasonable care": *Coopers Payne Ltd v Southampton Container Terminal Ltd* [2003] EWCA Civ 1223, [2004] 1 Lloyd's Rep. 331 at [29].

[269] *Lockspeiser Aircraft Ltd v Brooklands Aircraft Co Ltd*, above. cf. *Sutcliffe v Chief Constable of West Yorkshire* [1996] R.T.R. 86 and *Rana v Tears of Sutton Bridge* [2015] EWHC 2597 (QB).

[270] See below, para.33-053; also Vol.I, Ch.15.

[271] *LNW Ry v JP Ashton & Co* [1920] A.C. 84; *Levison v Patent Steam Carpet Cleaning Co Ltd* [1978] Q.B. 69, 82, 83, 85. cf. *Re S Davis & Co Ltd* [1945] Ch. 402; *Richmond Metal Co Ltd v J Coales & Son Ltd* [1970] 1 Lloyd's Rep. 423. *Euro Cellular (Distribution) Plc v Danzas Ltd t/a Danzas AEI Intercontinental* [2003] EWHC 3161 (Comm), [2004] 1 Lloyd's Rep. 521 at [60]–[66].

[272] The bailee may be vicariously liable for the negligence of his independent contractor to whom he has delegated part of his duty to take care of the chattel: *British Road Services Ltd v Arthur V Crutchley & Co Ltd* [1968] 1 All E.R. 811, 820, 824; *Bosman (Transport) Ltd v LKW Walter International Transportorganisation AG* [2002] EWCA Civ 850; *East West Corp v DKBS 1912 and Akts Svendborg* [2003] EWCA Civ 83, [2003] 1 Lloyd's Rep. 239 at [29].

[273] *Randleson v Murray* (1838) 8 A. & E. 109; *Beard v London General Omnibus Co* [1900] 2 Q.B. 530. The custodian may be personally liable for negligence in choosing the employee in question: *Williams v Curzon Syndicate Ltd* (1919) 35 T.L.R. 475; *John Carter (Fine Worsteds) Ltd v Hanson Haulage (Leeds) Ltd* [1965] 2 Q.B. 495.

[274] *Morris v CW Martin & Sons Ltd* [1966] 1 Q.B. 716 (approved by the House of Lords in *Photo Production Ltd v Securicor Transport Ltd* [1980] A.C. 827, 846, 852; and in *Lister v Hesley Hall Ltd* [2001] UKHL 22, [2002] 1 A.C. 215 at [19]–[20], [44]–[46], [55]–[60] and [71]–[76]; and by the Privy Council in the *Port Swettenham* case, above, at 591). cf. *Leesh River Tea Co Ltd v British India SN Co Ltd* [1967] 2 Q.B. 250. See also *Brink's Global Services Inc v Igrox Ltd* [2010] EWCA Civ 1207, [2011] I.R.L.R. 343 and Atiyah, *Vicarious Liability* (1967), pp.268–272.

[275] *Anderson v NE Ry* (1861) 4 L.T. 216. cf. *Strand Electric and Engineering Co Ltd v Brisford Entertainments Ltd* [1952] 2 Q.B. 246, 253–254. For the general principles of remoteness of damage in contract, see Vol.I, paras 26-117 et seq.

[276] *Hepburn v A Tomlinson (Hauliers) Ltd* [1966] A.C. 451 (see above, para.33-025). The extent of the bailee's insurance cover is a question of construction of the particular policy and it is not the case that the bailee will in all cases be entitled to recover the full value of the goods lost or damaged. In particular, the policy may be held to cover only the legal liabilities of the bailee towards the bailor or a third party: see *Ramco (UK) Ltd v International Insurance Company of Hanover* [2004] EWCA Civ 675, [2004] 2 All E.R. (Comm) 866.

[277] *Lilley v Doubleday* (1881) 7 Q.B.D. 510, 511. cf. *Davies v Collins* [1945] 1 All E.R. 247; *Tap-*

person without the bailor's permission, since personal considerations are involved in the bailor's choice of a bailee with whom to store his goods.[278] If the bailee deals with the chattel in an unauthorised manner, he takes upon himself the risk of loss and will be liable unless he shows that the loss occurred independently of his own acts.[279] So where the bailee delivers the chattel to a person not authorised by the bailor to receive it, he is liable in conversion for the misdelivery, and the question of reasonable care is irrelevant.[280]

33-053 **Exemptions from liability** Subject to the provisions of the Unfair Contract Terms Act 1977 and the Consumer Rights Act 2015,[281] the bailee may exempt himself from his common law liability by special conditions in the contract,[282] but the exempting words must be express, unambiguous and adequate in all the circumstances[283] since they are likely to be construed strictly against the bailee.[284] Although the scope of an exemption clause is a question of construction, depending on the intention of the parties,[285] the courts will generally be slow to infer that a bailee is entitled to rely on his exemption clause if he deals with the chattel in an unauthorised manner[286] and it will require clear words for an exemption clause to be construed as wide enough to cover a fundamental breach[287] of the contract of

---

penden v Artus [1964] 2 Q.B. 185 (see below, paras 33-079—33-080); see also above, paras 33-026—33-029.

[278] *Edwards v Newland & Co* [1950] 2 K.B. 534; *Metaalhandel JA Magnus BV v Ardfields Transport Ltd* [1987] 2 F.T.L.R. 319 (a "quasi-bailee" (who had contracted to collect and store goods) cannot avoid responsibility for their care by delegating their care to a sub-contractor). See Palmer (1978) 128 New L.J. 863.

[279] *James Morrison & Co Ltd v Shaw Savill and Albion Co Ltd* [1916] 2 K.B. 783, 795, 796, 800; *Lilley v Doubleday*, above; *Edwards v Newland & Co*, above.

[280] *Jackson v Cochrane* [1989] 2 Qd. R. 23. See also *Ashby v Tolhurst* [1937] 2 K.B. 242; *Hollins v Davy Ltd* [1963] 1 Q.B. 844.

[281] See below, para.33-054.

[282] See Vol.I, Ch.15 and see below, paras 39-390—39-391; Coote, *Exception Clauses* (1964), Ch.2; Laskin (1956) 11 Univ. of Toronto L.J. 202. See, in addition to the cases cited below, *Harris v GW Ry* (1876) 1 Q.B.D. 515; *Joseph Travers & Sons Ltd v Cooper* [1915] 1 K.B. 73; *Turner v Civil Service Supply Association* [1926] 1 K.B. 50; *British Traders and Shippers Ltd v Ubique Transport and Motor Engineering Co (London) Ltd* [1952] 2 Lloyd's Rep. 236; *Hollins v J Davy Ltd* [1963] 1 Q.B. 844.

[283] *Alderslade v Hendon Laundry Ltd* [1945] K.B. 189; *Olley v Marlborough Court Ltd* [1949] 1 K.B. 532; *Canada SS Lines Ltd v R* [1952] A.C. 192 (cf. *Gillespie Bros & Co Ltd v Roy Bowles Transport Ltd* [1973] Q.B. 400); *Hollier v Rambler Motors (AMC) Ltd* [1972] 2 Q.B. 71. cf. exemption clauses in hiring agreements, see below, para.33-078.

[284] cf. *Price & Co v Union Lighterage Co* [1904] 1 K.B. 412; *Rutter v Palmer* [1922] 2 K.B. 87, 94.

[285] *Photo Production Ltd v Securicor Transport Ltd* [1980] A.C. 827 (explaining *Suisse Atlantique Société d'Armement Maritime SA v NV Rotterdamsche Kolen Centrale* [1967] 1 A.C. 361). See Vol.I, paras 15-007 et seq.

[286] *Gibaud v GE Ry* [1921] 2 K.B. 426, 431, 435; *LNW Ry v Neilson* [1922] 2 A.C. 263, 273–274; *Cunard SS Co v Buerger* [1927] A.C. 1; *Alexander v Railway Executive* [1951] 2 K.B. 882; *Sydney City Council v West* (1965) 114 C.L.R. 481; *Mendelssohn v Normand Ltd* [1970] 1 Q.B. 177; cf. *J Evans & Son (Portsmouth) Ltd v Andrea Merzario Ltd* [1976] 1 W.L.R. 1078. See also above, para.33-052.

[287] The "doctrine" of fundamental breach was rejected by the House of Lords in the *Photo Production* case, above. For earlier cases on what amounts to a fundamental breach by the bailee, see *Kenyon, Son & Craven Ltd v Baxter Hoare & Co Ltd* [1971] 1 W.L.R. 519; *United Fresh Meat Co Ltd v Charterhouse Cold Storage Ltd* [1974] 2 Lloyd's Rep. 286. See now Vol.I, paras 15-023—15-027, 24-042.

bailment[288]; nor can the bailee rely on an exemption clause if he orally misrepresents the scope of the clause at the time when the contract is made.[289] A sub-bailee may rely on exempting conditions as against the original bailor but only if the latter has actually (expressly or impliedly) or ostensibly authorised the bailee to make a sub-bailment containing those conditions.[290]

Statutory control of exemption clauses   The main provisions of the Unfair   **33-054**
Contract Terms Act 1977 apply (inter alia) to contracts of bailment.[291] Thus, where one party is dealing on the other's written standard terms of business the other party cannot, by reference to any contract term,[292] when himself in breach of contract exclude or restrict any business[293] liability of his in respect of breach,[294] or claim to be entitled (inter alia) "to render a contractual performance substantially different from that which was reasonably expected of him, or, in respect of the whole or any part of his contractual obligation, to render no performance at all",[295] except insofar as the term satisfies the requirement of reasonableness.[296] Similarly, a contract term or notice[297] purporting to exclude or restrict business liability for loss or damage to property resulting from negligence must, to be effective, satisfy the requirement of reasonableness.[298] These provisions will therefore apply to the obligations of warehousemen, dry-cleaners and other business custodians for reward. In the case of bailments between a trader and a consumer, the Consumer Rights Act 2015 places substantial limits on the extent to which a trader can exclude liability to consumers in respect of a breach of the terms which the Act states are included in contracts of bailment.[299]

Lien of custodian   Normally, a custodian for reward has no lien for his charges   **33-055**
upon the chattel bailed with him[300] except where there is a special agreement grant-

---

[288] The following decisions on this point must now be read in the light of the more recent House of Lords decisions (see n.285, above): *Martin v N Negin Ltd* (1945) 172 L.T. 275; *Alexander v Railway Executive*, above; *Adams (Durham) Ltd and Day v Trust Houses Ltd* [1960] 1 Lloyd's Rep. 380. cf. *J Spurling Ltd v Bradshaw* [1956] 1 W.L.R. 461; and *John Carter (Fine Worsteds) Ltd v Hanson Haulage (Leeds) Ltd* [1965] 2 Q.B. 495; *Levison v Patent Steam Carpet Cleaning Co Ltd* [1978] Q.B. 69. See Vol.I, paras 15-037—15-041.

[289] *Curtis v Chemical Cleaning and Dyeing Co* [1951] 1 K.B. 805; *Mendelssohn v Normand Ltd*, above; *J Evans & Son (Portsmouth) Ltd v Andrea Merzario Ltd* [1976] 1 W.L.R. 1078.

[290] *The Pioneer Container* [1994] 2 A.C. 324, 341–342; *Morris v CW Martin & Sons Ltd* [1966] 1 Q.B. 716, 729–730 (cf. at 731, 741). See Vol.I, paras 15-037—15-041.

[291] For a fuller treatment of the Act, see Vol.I, paras 15-066 et seq. For the effect of the Act on exclusions of liability under non-contractual bailments, see Palmer (1978) 28 New L.J. 887, 915.

[292] It seems that gratuitous bailments are outside the protection of this section (s.3), as is a bailor's claim against a sub-bailee (above, para.33-026) which does not depend on a contract between the parties. cf. however, s.2(2) and n.297 below.

[293] s.1(3); see Vol.I, para.15-072.

[294] s.3(2)(a).

[295] s.3(2)(b).

[296] See Vol.I, para.15-096.

[297] Non-contractual bailments could be caught by this provision, e.g. even car park operators who operate under "licences" rather than bailments: see below, para.33-061.

[298] s.2(2).

[299] See below, para.38-586. The Act applies to contracts made on or after October 1, 2015, see below, para.38-465.

[300] *Hatton v Car Maintenance Co Ltd* [1915] 1 Ch. 621; *Gordon v Gordon* [2002] EWCA Civ 1884 at [8]. cf. the lien of a person who expends skill or labour upon the chattel (see below, para.33-093). See generally Palmer at paras 14-096—14-103.

ing him a lien.[301] Special categories of custodians, however, have, by custom, acquired such a lien.[302]

33-056 **Statutory power to sell uncollected goods**   Since 1977 there has been a wide statutory power conferred on bailees to sell the goods when the bailor is in breach of an obligation to take delivery of them.[303] These powers clearly extend to cases of custody of the goods.[304] The bailee, in appropriate circumstances, may follow the prescribed procedure and sell without the authority of the court[305]; but, in some circumstances, he must (and in others he may) apply to the court to authorise a sale of the goods.[306] The details of these powers are examined later in this chapter.[307]

33-057 **Custody without special reward**   Custody for reward may arise despite the absence of valuable consideration specifically allocated to the custody. For instance, where the wife of a tenant in a block of flats deposited a trunk in the room provided for storage by the landlords, it was held, notwithstanding that the rent was paid by the husband and that the wife made no special payment for the storage, that the relationship between the landlords and at least the families of tenants of the flats, if not also guests, was a business arrangement and not a gratuitous bailment.[308] Similarly, a hospital authority which is under a statutory duty to receive a patient, whose estate is liable for the cost of his maintenance, is a bailee for reward; therefore, when it takes possession of a patient's chattels upon his admission to the hospital, it must take reasonable care of them, e.g. it will be liable if valuable jewellery is lost through its failure to deposit the jewellery in a safe.[309] A banker who holds his customer's securities and valuables for safe custody may receive no special remuneration for doing so; but the better view, it is submitted, is that he should be treated as a bailee for reward.[310]

(ii)   Illustrations of Custody for Reward

33-058 **Warehousemen**   A warehouseman is liable[311] for any loss caused by want of reasonable care on his part or on the part of an agent or independent contractor to whom he has delegated performance of part of his duty to take reasonable care of

---

301 e.g. *Jowitt & Sons v Union Cold Storage Co* [1913] 3 K.B. 1.
302 See *Bock v Gorrissen* (1860) 2 De G.F. & J. 434, 443 (wharfingers); *Re Witt* (1876) 2 Ch. D. 489 (packers); *Re London and Globe Finance Corp* [1902] 2 Ch. 416 (factors, bankers and stockbrokers). cf. *Singer Manufacturing Co v LSW Ry* [1894] 1 Q.B. 833, 836, 837 (railway cloakrooms: see below, para.33-062).
303 Torts (Interference with Goods) Act 1977 ss.12 and 13 (see below, paras 33-095—33-100).
304 e.g. Sch.1 Pt I para.4(1) expressly covers the situation where "a bailee is in possession of goods which he has held as custodian ...".
305 s.12.
306 s.13.
307 See below, paras 33-095—33-100.
308 *Andrews v Home Flats* (1945) 173 L.T. 408. cf. *The Pioneer Container* [1994] 2 A.C. 324, 338. (See above, para.33-026, n.130.)
309 *Martin v LCC* [1947] K.B. 628.
310 See above, para.33-035, and below, paras 34-438—34-440.
311 Both under s.13 of the Supply of Goods and Services Act 1982 (covering cases where the warehouseman-bailee acts in the course of a business); and under the common law: *Cailiff v Danvers* (1792) Peake 155; *Chapman v GW Ry* (1880) 5 Q.B.D. 278; *Mitchell v Lancs & Yorks Ry* (1875) L.R. 10 Q.B. 256.

the chattel.[312] When the chattel is lost, the onus is on the warehouseman to acquit himself by showing that he was not in default.[313] He may, however (subject to statutory controls),[314] contract out of his liability.[315] It has been held that where a wharfinger negligently makes a representation to a third party as to certain goods being in his custody when, in fact, such goods have long since disappeared, he is estopped from denying that he has such goods in his possession, if, by reason of his negligence, the third party suffers damage.[316]

Agisters The common law duty of a bailee with whom cattle are left to be fed for reward on a contract called agistment is to take reasonable care of them.[317] Thus, an agister has been held to be in breach of his duty where the cattle are stolen through his negligence,[318] or where he put the animal in a field knowing that there was not a sufficient fence to keep out a bull kept on the adjoining land.[319] He does not discharge his duty as a bailee by proving that they were stolen without his default, if by using reasonable diligence he could have recovered them.[320] Further, if they are put in a place where by reason of their surroundings they are liable to suffer injury,[321] or if they escape through the negligence of the bailee or his employee and in consequence of the escape are injured,[322] the bailee will be liable. He has no lien, for he merely feeds without expending skill.[323] But if a lien is actually acquired by special agreement, and the owner for the purpose of defeating such lien gets the cattle away by fraud, the agister has a right to resume possession of the cattle and for so doing is not answerable in conversion.[324]

33-059

Stabling of horses and garaging of vehicles Where a horse is stabled or a vehicle is garaged in the bailee's building, he is obliged not only to take reason-

33-060

---

[312] *British Road Services Ltd v Arthur V Crutchley & Co Ltd* [1968] 1 All E.R. 811, 820, 824 (the obligation was placed on the bailee on the basis of an implied term in the contract of bailment).

[313] *Mackenzie v Cox* (1840) 9 C. & P. 632; *Reeve v Palmer* (1858) 5 C.B.(N.S.) 84; *Brooks Wharf Bull & Wharf Ltd v Goodman Bros* [1937] 1 K.B. 534. cf. see above, paras 33-032—33-050.

[314] See above, para.33-054.

[315] *Rosin and Turpentine Import Co v Jacobs* (1910) 15 Com. Cas. 111; *Gibaud v GE Ry* [1921] 2 K.B. 426; *Rutter v Palmer* [1922] 2 K.B. 87. See the approach to exemption clauses adopted by the House of Lords: see above, para.33-053; Vol.I, Ch.15, paras 15-024—15-027.

[316] *Seton v Lafone* (1887) 19 Q.B.D. 68. cf. *Laurie & Morewood v Dudin & Sons* [1926] 1 K.B. 223. On attornment, see above, para.33-030.

[317] *Smith v Cook* (1875) 1 Q.B.D. 79, 81; *Turner v Stallbrass* [1898] 1 Q.B. 56; *Coldman v Hill* [1919] 1 K.B. 443, 451. See also ss.12 and 13 of the Supply of Goods and Services Act 1982 (see above, paras 33-044—33-048) which cover cases where the bailee (supplier of services) acts in the course of a business and s.49(1) of the Consumer Rights Act 2015 which, for contracts made on or after October 1, 2015, covers cases where the bailee is a trader contracting with a consumer. cf. *Sheehy v Faughan* [1991] 1 I.R. 425 (mare left at defendant's stud: onus of proof lay on defendant to show that her death was not due to his neglect).

[318] *Coldman v Hill*, above.

[319] *Smith v Cook*, above.

[320] *Coldman v Hill*, above.

[321] *Turner v Stallibrass*, above; cf. *Reid v Calderwood* (1911) 45 Ir.L.T. 139 (owner aware of dangerous state of the field).

[322] *Halestrap v Gregory* [1895] 1 Q.B. 561.

[323] *Jackson v Cummins* (1839) 5 M. & W. 342; *Re Southern Livestock Producers Ltd* [1964] 1 W.L.R. 24; *Bell and Bell v Clare* (1989) 23 F.C.R. 274. See also *Ward v Fielden* [1985] C.L.Y. 2000 (racehorse trainer has no lien over horses being trained).

[324] *Wallace v Woodgate* (1824) 1 Car. & P. 575.

able care of the horse or vehicle itself, but also to take reasonable care to see that the building is reasonably safe for the purpose of stabling or garaging.[325]

33-061 Bailment distinguished from licence.[326] The circumstances of a particular case may show that, although one person permits another to leave his chattel on land in the possession of the former, there is no bailment. Thus, where the owner of a motorcar left it in an open car park and, upon payment of a shilling to the car park attendant, received a ticket on which were printed words negativing liability and stating that all cars were left at owners' risk, it was held that the relationship between the owners of the car park and the owner of the car was that of licensor and licensee and not that of bailor and bailee.[327] Similarly, where a motorbicycle was left in a covered yard forming part of the premises of a public house the publican was not liable for its loss through theft by a third party; he was not a bailee, since the motorbicycle had not been delivered into his possession and he was unaware that it was on his premises.[328] There was no duty at common law owed to the owner of the chattel in these circumstances to take reasonable care to protect him and his chattel from the risk of the chattel being stolen by some third party.[329] But under ss.12 and 13 of the Supply of Goods and Services Act 1982, there may be a duty on the defendant as a person who "agrees to carry out a service" in the course of a business[330] and a similar duty may arise when a trader contracts to supply a service to a consumer under s.49(1) of the Consumer Rights Act 2015.

33-062 Railway warehouses and cloakrooms *The National Rail Conditions of Travel*, published in March 2018, no longer indicate when transport begins and ends.[331] According to these Conditions, a train company or rail service provider will only be liable for any loss or damage to luggage, articles, animals or cycles in its trains or on its premises if the loss or damage was caused by the fault of a member of staff of the train company or rail service provider.[332] The maximum liability of a train company or rail service provider with regard to these matter is £1,500 per

---

325 *Searle v Laverick* (1874) L.R. 9 Q.B. 122 (a livery-stable keeper); see also above, paras 33-044—33-046. A livery-stable keeper has no lien on a horse for its keep: *Judson v Etheridge* (1833) 1 C. & M. 743; *Orchard v Rackstraw* (1850) 9 C.B. 698; *Re Southern Livestock Producers Ltd*, above. cf. *Bevan v Waters* (1828) 3 Car. & P. 520.

326 This paragraph was cited with approval and applied in *BG Transport Service Ltd v Marston Motor Co Ltd* [1970] 1 Lloyd's Rep. 371 (distinguishing *Sydney City Council v West* (1965) 114 C.L.R. 481). See Palmer at paras 5-001 et seq. The distinction between a bailment and a licence can, however, be a difficult one to draw on the facts of an individual case: see, for example, *The Rigoletto* [2000] 2 Lloyd's Rep. 532, 545–547 (but note the dissent of Chadwick L.J. at 548) and *Odone v Hawarden Services Ltd* [2014] EWHC 1694 (QB), [2014] All E.R. (D) 214 (May).

327 *Ashby v Tolhurst* [1937] 2 K.B. 242. See also *Halbauer v Brighton Corp* [1954] 1 W.L.R. 1161. cf. *Shorters Parking Station Ltd v Johnson* [1963] N.Z.L.R. 135; *James Buchanan & Co Ltd v Hay's Transport Services Ltd* [1972] 2 Lloyd's Rep. 535, 542.

328 *Tinsley v Dudley* [1951] 2 K.B. 18.

329 But to the extent that the law might impose a duty to take reasonable care in respect of *damage* to the chattel left on the premises of the defendant, the provisions of s.2(2) of the Unfair Contract Terms Act 1977 might apply see Vol.I, para.15-081.

330 See above, paras 33-044—33-046.

331 Previously, the conditions published by the British Railways Board stated that, after the "termination of the transit", the Board held goods carried by them as warehousemen, not as carriers, and the relevant conditions were those applicable to the former situation. The distinction between the beginning and the end of transit is discussed further below at para.36-077.

332 Cl.26. See further below para.36-076.

passenger.[333] Property found on a train or on a train company's or rail service provider's premises must be handed over as soon as possible to a member of staff of the train company or rail service provider and is not to be treated as the property of the finder.[334] In the case of such property, the train company may (i) open it and examine its contents before removing it to a secure place and (ii) without being liable, remove or dispose of any property which might in its opinion cause damage or injury or inconvenience to staff or passengers[335] and (iii) within prescribed limits, make a charge for retrieval of the property by the owner.[336] The Conditions further state that a train company or rail service provider will take reasonable care of any luggage, articles, animals or cycles which are taken into its safekeeping after being left in its trains or on its premises and will make a reasonable effort to contact the owner.[337] However, a train company or a rail service provider may limit access to retrieve any property left in its trains or on its premises but will, if necessary, make alternative arrangements for it to be recovered.[338] It has been held that a train company must redeliver the goods to the person producing the ticket on a reasonable request and within a reasonable time.[339]

The train company may vary their liabilities as bailees by special clauses in the contract[340] or in a ticket handed to the bailor.[341] The train company has a lien for its charges on goods deposited in a cloakroom, and the lien will prevail against the owner of the goods even where the person depositing them was only a hirer, e.g. under a hire-purchase agreement.[342]

33-063

(c) Hire

(i) Hire (Unregulated by the Consumer Credit Act)

Hire[343]   In the bailment termed "hire" the bailee receives both possession of the chattel and the right to use it,[344] in return for remuneration to be paid to the bailor or other reward provided to the bailor.[345] The bailee is under an obligation to return

33-064

---

[333] Cl 26.

[334] Cl.42.1.

[335] Cl.43.

[336] Cl.44.

[337] Cl.42.2. See further below para.36-076.

[338] Cl.42.3.

[339] *Stallard v GW Ry* (1862) 2 B. & S. 419.

[340] e.g. *Harris v GW Ry* (1876) 1 Q.B.D. 515, 529–530; *Pratt v SE Ry* [1897] 1 Q.B. 718. See above, para.33-050, and Vol.I, Ch.15.

[341] As to conditions in tickets being incorporated into the contract, see Vol.I, paras 13-008 et seq.

[342] *Singer Manufacturing Co v LSW Ry* [1894] 1 Q.B. 833 (this is an extension of the lien exercisable by a railway undertaking as a carrier).

[343] For an account of chattel-hiring, see the *Crowther Report on Consumer Credit*, Cmnd.4596 (1971), paras 2.4.56 et seq. The contract of hire-purchase is dealt with separately in Ch.39. below (many of the respective duties of the owner and hirer discussed in paras 39-311 et seq. apply to ordinary hire).

[344] e.g. *Beecham Foods Ltd v North Supplies (Edmonton) Ltd* [1959] 1 W.L.R. 643. Where a contract of hiring is specifically enforceable, the hirer may have an equitable interest in the chattel: *Bristol Airport Plc v Powdrill* [1990] Ch. 744, 759.

[345] *TRM Copy Centres (UK) Ltd v Lanwall Services Ltd* [2009] UKHL 35, [2009] 1 W.L.R. 1375 at [11]. The "remuneration" can be paid either in cash or in kind. On the facts of the case it was held that no remuneration was paid by the party who received the photocopier so that the bailment was not by way of hire but was a gratuitous bailment. This was a case in which the provider of the photocopier paid the other party for the privilege of locating its photocopier in a place where it might

the chattel to the owner (or his nominee) at the expiration of the fixed period of the hiring[346] and to pay the cost of returning it[347]; but in a hiring or lease of livestock, the progeny of the livestock born during the hiring belongs to the hirer (unless the contract provides to the contrary).[348] While the bailment continues to subsist, the bailee is entitled to possessory remedies, and can prevent anyone, including the owner,[349] from interfering with the chattel against his will.

33-065   This section will first examine the rules applicable to a hiring not falling within the definition of a "consumer hire agreement" regulated by the Consumer Credit Act 1974,[350] and will then consider that Act.

33-066   **Terms implied into a contract of hire**[351]   The Supply of Goods and Services Act 1982 has introduced[352] into contracts for the hire of goods a number of implied terms (broadly corresponding with those implied into contracts for the sale of goods).[353] The Consumer Rights Act 2015 has similarly included in contracts for the hire of goods between a trader and a consumer a number of terms which also broadly correspond with those implied into contracts for the sale of goods.[354] Although most problems may be solved by reference to the terms implied by these Acts,[355] the common law rules should also be examined, because, in the case of contracts of hire which fall within the scope of the Supply of Goods and Services Act 1982, the Act provides that it does not prejudice the operation of:

> "… any rule of law whereby any condition or warranty (other than one relating to quality or fitness[356]) is to be implied in … a contract for the hire of goods."[357]

It would, nevertheless, be true to say that the common law rules are now consider-

---

generate income for both parties. If it did not generate any income, the recipient was not obliged to make any payment to the provider.

[346] *Mills v Graham* (1804) 1 Bos. & P.N.R. 140, 145; *British Crane Hire Corp Ltd v Ipswich Plant Hire Ltd* [1975] Q.B. 303, 311, 313. (But the hirer might escape liability for failure to return the chattel if he can prove that the loss of the chattel was not due to his fault: *British Crane Hire Corp Ltd v Ipswich Plant Hire Ltd*, above, at 311–312, 313 (see below, para.33-079); or the terms of the hiring may oblige the bailee to deliver the chattel to a third person at the expiration of the period: see above, para.33-010.) cf. *Ballett v Mingay* [1943] K.B. 281. In the unlikely event of the bailor not accepting redelivery, the bailee may be able to sell the chattel under statutory powers: see below, paras 33-095—33-100.

[347] *British Crane Hire Corp Ltd v Ipswich Plant Hire Ltd*, above, at 312.

[348] *Tucker v Farm and General Investment Trust Ltd* [1966] 2 Q.B. 421.

[349] *Lee v Atkinson & Brook* (1609) Yel. 172; *Turner v Hardcastle* (1862) 11 C.B.(N.S.) 683. See above, para.33-019.

[350] See below, paras 33-085—33-090.

[351] Palmer at paras 21-016 et seq.; the Law Commission's report on *Law of Contract: Report on Implied Terms in Contracts for the Supply of Goods*, Law Com. No.95 (1979).

[352] In addition to ss.13–15 of the Act, which apply if the hiring is also part of "a contract for the supply of services" (see above, paras 33-044—33-048).

[353] See below, paras 44-074 et seq. The Act is noted by Palmer in (1983) 46 M.L.R. 619 and [1983] L.M.C.L.Q. 377; see also Woodroffe, *Goods and Services—The New Law* (1982), Ch.5.

[354] A contract for the hire of goods is defined in s.6(1) of the Act (which applies to contracts made on or after October 1, 2015) as one under which the trader gives or agrees to give the consumer possession of the goods with the right to use them, subject to the terms of the contract, for a period determined in accordance with the contract. A hire-purchase agreement is not, for this purpose, a contract of hire. See below paras 38-489 et seq.

[355] See below, paras 33-068, 33-071—33-072.

[356] s.9(1) (see below, para.33-071, n.393).

[357] s.11(3).

ably diminished in significance. The common law rules will therefore be set out briefly before turning to the terms implied by the 1982 and 2015 Acts.

Implied terms as to possession   At common law there was no authority which **33-067** expressly recognised the existence of an obligation on the part of the bailor that he had the right to transfer possession of the goods by way of hire. But the common law did recognise the existence of a warranty that the bailee would enjoy uninterrupted use and enjoyment of the goods for the period of the hire.[358] These terms have now been considerably strengthened by the Supply of Goods and Services Act 1982[359] which provides that certain terms[360] are to be implied in "a contract for the hire of goods"[361] (which is not restricted to hiring in the course of a business by either party): "there is an implied condition on the part of the bailor that in the case of a bailment he has a right to transfer possession of the goods by way of hire for the period of the bailment"[362]; "there is also an implied warranty that the bailee will enjoy quiet possession of the goods for the period of the bailment except so far as the possession may be disturbed by the owner or other person entitled to the benefit of any charge or encumbrance disclosed or known to the bailee before the contract is made".[363] Similar terms are to be treated as included in a contract of hire concluded between a trader and a consumer under the Consumer Rights Act 2015.[364] Thus a term is to be included that at the beginning of the period of hire the trader has the right to transfer possession of the goods by way of hire for that period[365] and that the consumer will enjoy quiet possession of the goods except so far as it may be disturbed by the owner or other person entitled to the benefit of any charge or encumbrance disclosed or known to the consumer before entering into the contract.[366]

Implied terms as to description and sample   The common law on hiring has lit-   **33-068** tle authority on correspondence with description or sample. But it is clear that the owner must supply a chattel which corresponds with the description of the chattel which, in the contract of hire, he undertook to supply.[367] The Supply of Goods and

---

[358] See, for example, *Lee v Atkinson & Brook* (1609) Yel. 172; *Turner v Hardcastle* (1862) 11 C.B.(N.S.) 683.

[359] See below, para.33-071. cf. the terms implied into contracts for the sale of goods (see below, paras 44-074 et seq.) or for hire-purchase (see below, paras 39-382 et seq.).

[360] Except by s.9(1) (see n.393, below), the Act does not prejudice other legislation or any rule of law about terms to be implied in a contract for the hire of goods: s.11(3).

[361] Defined to mean "a contract under which one person bails or agrees to bail goods to another by way of hire" (whether or not services are also provided, and whatever is the nature of the consideration); but the definition excludes hire-purchase agreements, and contracts under which goods are to be bailed in exchange for trading stamps on their redemption: s.6. (For definitions, see s.18(1).) Palmer [1983] L.M.C.L.Q. 377 discusses various types of contract covered by the Act. In a conditional sale or under a *Romalpa* clause (see below, paras 44-173—44-188), the provisions of the 1982 Act could apply to the period of bailment (i.e. before the passing of property to the bailee).

[362] And that "in the case of an agreement to bail he will have such a right at the time of the bailment": s.7(1). cf. below, paras 44-075 et seq.

[363] s.7(2). The right of the bailor to repossess the goods under an express or implied term of the contract is not affected: s.7(3) (but equitable relief against forfeiture (Vol.I, paras 26-245 et seq.) could prevent the bailor from repossessing). cf. below, paras 44-078 et seq.

[364] s.17. The Act applies to contracts made on or after October 1, 2015; see below, para.38-508.

[365] s.17(1).

[366] s.17(2)(c).

[367] *Astley Industrial Trust Ltd v Grimley* [1963] 1 W.L.R. 584; *Charterhouse Credit Co Ltd v Tolly*

Services Act 1982 also implies terms on hiring by description or by sample. Where, in a contract for the hire of goods (the definition is not restricted to hiring in the course of a business), the bailor bails or agrees to bail the goods by description,[368] there is an implied condition that the goods will correspond with the description[369]; where he bails or agrees to bail the goods by reference to a sample, "there is an implied condition—(a) that the bulk will correspond with the sample in quality; and (b) that the bailee will have a reasonable opportunity of comparing the bulk with the sample; and (c) that the goods will be free from any defect, making their quality unsatisfactory,[370] which would not be apparent on reasonable examination of the sample".[371] Contracts of hire which fall within the scope of Ch.2 of the Consumer Rights Act 2015 are also to be treated as including a term that the goods will match the description[372] and, in the case where the hire is by reference to a sample of goods, that the goods will match the sample except to the extent that any differences between the sample and the goods are brought to the consumer's attention before the contract is made and that the goods will be free from any defects that makes their quality unsatisfactory and that would not be apparent on a reasonable examination of the sample.[373]

33-069   **Common law as to quality and fitness**   The common law rules as to quality and fitness are not clearly formulated,[374] and they are now of very limited practical utility.[375] Subject to any express contractual provisions,[376] the normal rule is that the owner who lets out a chattel on hire must take reasonable care to see that it is in a reasonably fit condition for the purpose for which the bailee is to use it.[377] Thus, in

---

[1963] 2 Q.B. 683 (overruled on another point: *Photo Production Ltd v Securicor Transport Ltd* [1980] A.C. 827). On the consequences of the breach of this undertaking, see below, paras 39-387— 39-389.

368   The definition includes the situation where "being exposed for supply, the goods are selected by the bailee": s.8(4).

369   s.8(1) and (2). See, by way of example, *Brewer v Mann* [2012] EWCA Civ 246, [2012] R.T.R. 28. If the reference is to a sample as well as a description it is not sufficient that the bulk of the goods corresponds with the sample if the goods do not also correspond with the description: s.8(3). cf. below, para.44-086 (sale of goods).

370   "Satisfactory quality" is to be construed in accordance with s.9(2A), and s.18(3).

371   s.10(2). cf. below, paras 44-095 et seq.

372   s.11(1).

373   s.13(2). Similar terms are to be treated as included in a contract to hire goods by reference to a model of the goods that is seen or examined by the consumer before entering into the contract: s.14(2).

374   See Davies (1964) 38 Aust.L.J. 277; Turner (1972) 46 Aust.L.J. 560, 619; Palmer (1975) 4 An.– Am.L.R. 207; and the Law Commission Report cited in n.351, above.

375   It can be argued that the common law rules still apply to contracts where the bailor is not acting in the course of a business. The basis for this argument is that s.11(3) states that nothing in the preceding provisions of the Act "prejudices" the operation of any rule of law whereby any condition (other than one relating to quality or fitness) is to be implied into such contracts. However, the words in brackets, taken together with the wording of s.9(1), suggest that there is no longer any room for the common law implied term. The better view would therefore appear to be that the common law rules are practically redundant: see Palmer at para.21-026.

376   *Astley Industrial Trust Ltd v Grimley* [1963] 1 W.L.R. 584; *Charterhouse Credit Co Ltd v Tolly*, above; *Doobay v Mohabeer* [1967] 2 A.C. 278; *Hadley v Droitwich Construction Co Ltd* [1968] 1 W.L.R. 37. See, however, the provisions of the Unfair Contract Terms Act 1977 (see above, para.33-054; see below, para.33-078).

377   *Yeoman Credit Ltd v Apps* [1962] 2 Q.B. 508; *Oliver v Saddler & Co* [1929] A.C. 584 (in this case there was no actual hiring, but since the transaction was for the mutual convenience of bailor and bailee, the House of Lords did not treat it as a gratuitous bailment, but as analogous to a hiring); *Mowbray v Merryweather* [1895] 2 Q.B. 640; cf. *MacCarthy v Young* (1861) 6 H. & N. 329

an ordinary hiring contract, the owner impliedly assumes some contractual responsibility for the fitness of the chattel for the purpose for which the hirer requires it,[378] but the existence and extent of the obligation depends on the contractual intention of the parties,[379] which is to be ascertained from the provisions of the particular contract and the circumstances in which the contract was made.[380] The implied undertaking, however, is only to the effect that the chattel is as fit for the purpose as reasonable care and skill on the part of the owner can make it[381]; breach of the undertaking may lead to liability for consequential damage.[382] Although the undertaking implied at common law does not render the bailor liable where the immediate cause of the injury was a defect in the chattel not discoverable by reasonable care or skill,[383] the onus of proving such a defence is on the bailor.[384]

Illustrations of the terms implied at common law   Where a motor car is let on **33-070** hire, the owner (subject to the express terms of the contract) impliedly undertakes that it is "a functioning car which could be used on the roads", "a viable motorcar", "a roadworthy car".[385] Such an implied undertaking depends on the existence of a bailment for hire; it has been held, for instance, that the relationship of bailment may arise between a company owning taxi-cabs and the drivers of the cabs where the company receives a proportion of the fares earned by the drivers.[386] Many older cases on the undertaking as to fitness implied at common law concerned the hire of horses and carriages: e.g. the owner was liable if the horse was vicious,[387] or if the horse was not fit for the particular purpose for which it was hired.[388] The

---

(gratuitous loan); *The Moorcock* (1889) 14 P.D. 64; *Farnworth Finance Facilities Ltd v Attryde* [1970] 1 W.L.R. 1053, 1056 (hire-purchase: see below, para.39-385).

[378] *Fowler v Lock* (1872) L.R. 7 C.P. 272, 280, 282 (subsequent proceedings (1874) L.R. 10 C.P. 90). cf. *European and Australian Royal Mail Co Ltd v Royal Mail Steam Packet Co* (1861) 30 L.J. C.P. 247.

[379] The circumstances must show that the hirer is not relying solely on his own judgment of the chattel: *Yeoman Credit Ltd v Apps* [1962] 2 Q.B. 508; but a cursory inspection by the hirer does not preclude his relying on the implied warranty: *Jones v Page* (1867) 15 L.T. 619. cf. *Robertson v Amazon Tug and Lighterage Co* (1881) 7 Q.B.D. 598; *GM Shepherd Ltd v North West Securities Ltd*, 1991 S.L.T. 499.

[380] *Astley Industrial Trust Ltd v Grimley* [1963] 1 W.L.R. 584 (cf. below, para.39-385); *Charterhouse Credit Co Ltd v Tolly* [1963] 2 Q.B. 683. (This case also deals with the measure of damages when the implied undertaking as to fitness is broken: see below, para.39-389.)

[381] *Mowbray v Merryweather* [1895] 2 Q.B. 640; *Reed v Dean* [1949] 1 K.B. 188; *Yeoman Credit Ltd v Apps*, above; *Astley Industrial Trust Ltd v Grimley*, above, at 598. See also *Vogan & Co v Oulton* (1899) 81 L.T. 435, and see below, para.39-385. cf. the analogous sale of goods cases (see below, paras 44-105—44-112).

[382] *Mowbray v Merryweather*, see above.

[383] *Readhead v Midland Ry* (1869) L.R. 4 Q.B. 379 (contract for carriage of passengers for reward: obligation of carrier in regard to the condition of the vehicle).

[384] *Hyman v Nye* (1881) 6 Q.B.D. 685 (approved in *The West Cock* [1911] P. 208, 227, 231 (a contract for towage by a tug)).

[385] *Yeoman Credit Ltd v Apps* [1962] 2 Q.B. 508, 520, 523, 525. See also the cases cited in n.381, above. cf. the similar obligation to deliver a "reasonably fit" car under a contract of sale: Whincup (1975) 38 M.L.R. 660.

[386] *London General Cab Co Ltd v IRC* [1950] 2 All E.R. 566. See Paton at pp.287–289.

[387] *Jones v Page* (1867) 15 L.T. 619; *Chew v Jones* (1847) 10 L.T.(O.S.) 231; *Windle v Jordan* (1883) 75 Maine 149; *Hyman v Nye*, above. As to liability to third parties, see *White v Steadman* [1913] 3 K.B. 340.

[388] *Fowler v Lock* (1872) L.R. 7 C.P. 272 (subsequent proceedings (1874) L.R. 10 C.P. 90). cf. *Burnard v Haggis* (1863) 14 C.B.(N.S.) 45 (hirer expressly told horse not fit for jumping).

undertaking as to fitness implied at common law may extend to cover an employee of the bailor whose services are hired, together with the vehicle, in order to drive it[389]; although the undertaking is limited to those acts of the employee which are within the scope of his employment, under the doctrine of vicarious liability in tort the scope of employment may be wide enough to cover even fraudulent acts of the employee.[390]

33-071 **Implied terms as to quality: the 1982 Act**[391]   The Supply of Goods and Services Act 1982 also provides implied terms as to quality and fitness[392]: where under a contract for the hire of goods, "the bailor bails goods in the course of a business",[393] there is an implied condition[394] that the goods supplied under the contract are of satisfactory quality"[395]; but there is no such condition "(a) as regards defects specifically drawn to the bailee's attention before the contract is made; (b) if the bailee examines the goods before the contract is made, as regards defects which that examination ought to reveal; or (c) where the goods are bailed by reference to a sample, which would have been apparent on a reasonable examination of the sample".[396]

33-072 **Implied term as to fitness: the 1982 Act**   Finally, the Act implies a term about fitness for a particular purpose where "the bailor bails goods in the course of a business".[397] Where "the bailee, expressly or by implication, makes known [to the bailor or to a credit-broker[398]] … any particular purpose for which the goods are being bailed"[399] under a contract for hire, there is "an implied condition that the goods

---

[389] *Abraham v Bullock* (1902) 86 L.T. 796. cf. the cases cited in n.390, see below.

[390] *Morris v CW Martin & Sons Ltd* [1966] 1 Q.B. 716 (see above, para.33-050) (approved by the House of Lords in *Photo Production Ltd v Securicor Transport Ltd* [1980] A.C. 827, 846, 852; and in *Lister v Hesley Hall Ltd* [2001] UKHL 22, [2002] 1 A.C. 215 at [19]–[20], [44]–[46], [55]–[60] and [71]–[76]). cf. *Sanderson v Collins* [1904] 1 K.B. 628; *Adams (Durham) Ltd and Day v Trust Houses Ltd* [1960] 1 Lloyd's Rep. 380; *Leesh River Tea Co Ltd v British India SN Co Ltd* [1967] 2 Q.B. 250.

[391] Under s.46(1) of the Consumer Protection Act 1987, the bailor may commit an offence if he hires or offers to hire any consumer goods which fail to meet certain safety requirements; and by s.12, regulations may prohibit the hiring of specified goods.

[392] By s.9(1), no term is to be implied about the quality or fitness for any particular purpose of the goods, except as provided by ss.9 and 10 of the Act or by any other enactment. However, s.9(7) recognises that such a term "may be annexed by usage to a contract for the hire of goods". (The meaning of "quality" is extended by s.18(3).) cf. below, para.44-094.

[393] s.9(8) extends this provision to a person "who in the course of a business is acting as agent for another", except where the bailee knows (or ought to know) that the principal is not bailing in the course of a business. cf. below, paras 44-096, 44-097.

[394] cf. also *Karsales (Harrow) Ltd v Wallis* [1956] 1 W.L.R. 936, 940 (term implied that the goods should, at the time of delivery to the bailee, be in substantially the same condition as they were at the time the bailee had previously inspected them).

[395] s.9(2). Goods are declared to be of satisfactory quality if they meet the standard that a reasonable person would regard as satisfactory, taking account of any description of the goods, the consideration for the bailment (if any) and all the other relevant circumstances (s.9(2A)). The definition of "quality" is expanded by s.18(3) so that, in appropriate cases, it encompasses (a) fitness for all the purposes for which goods of the kind in question are commonly supplied, (b) appearance and finish, (c) freedom from minor defects, (d) safety and (e) durability.

[396] s.9(3). cf. see below, paras 44-101—44-102.

[397] s.9(4).

[398] Either "to the bailor in the course of negotiations conducted by him in relation to the making of the contract", or to a credit-broker who sold the goods to the bailor before they were bailed: s.9(4). (For definitions, see s.18(1).)

[399] s.9(4).

supplied under the contract are reasonably fit for that purpose, whether or not that is a purpose for which such goods are commonly supplied".[400] But this provision "does not apply where the circumstances show that the bailee does not rely, or that it is unreasonable for him to rely, on the skill or judgment of the bailor or credit-broker".[401]

Durability   The express reference to durability[402] in the list of factors which can   **33-073** be taken into account when deciding whether or not goods are of satisfactory quality, resolves a point which had been of some doubt at common law, namely whether the implied terms continue to apply to the hired goods for a period after the bailor has transferred possession to the bailee.[403] In the case of many contracts of hire the obligation of the hirer is not a continuing one, in the sense that the obligation of the bailor is to supply and then to permit the bailee to retain possession until the hire terminates but, in other contexts, the court may infer from the terms of the contract between the parties that the obligation to supply goods of satisfactory quality may be held to be continuing one.[404]

Implied terms as to quality and fitness: the 2015 Act   The Consumer Rights Act   **33-074** 2015 provides that contracts for the hire of goods from a trader to a consumer are to be treated as including a term that the quality of goods is satisfactory.[405] Where, before the contract is made, the consumer, either expressly or by implication, makes known to the trader any particular purpose for which the consumer is contracting for the goods, the contract is also to be treated as including a term that the goods are reasonably fit for that purpose, whether or not that is a purpose for which goods of that kind are usually supplied.[406] However, the latter term is not to be treated as included in the contract if the circumstances show that the consumer did not rely or it was unreasonable for the consumer to rely on the skill or judgment of the trader of credit-broker.[407]

Remedies: diminution of price and damages   If the owner supplies a defective   **33-075** chattel in breach of his warranty of fitness for purpose, the hirer can set up that breach in diminution or extinction of the rentals due under the contract. If the dam-

---

[400] s.9(5). cf. below, paras 44-105 et seq.

[401] s.9(6). cf. below, para.44-108. In the case of finance leasing, the bailee's reliance may be on the supplier's skill or judgment, rather than on that of the bailor who obtained the goods from the supplier.

[402] s.18(3)(e).

[403] There was some authority at common law for the proposition that there was a continuing element to the warranty of fitness for purpose: see *James Pty Ltd v Duncan* [1970] V.R. 705, 717; *Lambert v Lewis* [1982] A.C. 225, 276 (see below, para.44-104).

[404] See, for example, *Stoke-on-Trent College v Pelican Rouge Coffee Solutions Group Ltd* [2017] EWHC 2829 (TCC) at [131]–[133].

[405] s.9(1). The Act applies to contracts made on or after October 1, 2015. Goods are stated to be of satisfactory quality if they meet the standard that a reasonable person would consider satisfactory, taking account of any description of the goods, the price or other consideration for the goods (if any) and all the other relevant circumstances (s.9(2)). The definition of "quality" is expanded by s.9(3) so that, in appropriate cases, it encompasses (a) fitness for all the purposes for which goods of the kind in question are usually supplied, (b) appearance and finish, (c) freedom from minor defects, (d) safety and (e) durability. The relevant circumstances referred to in s.9(2) include any public statement about the specific characteristics of the goods made by the trader, the producer or any representative of the trader or the producer (s.9(5)–(7)).

[406] s.10(1) and (3).

[407] s.10(4).

ages are assessed on the basis of hiring a similar item on similar terms they are likely to equal the claim for rentals.[408] In the case of a contract of hire which falls within the Consumer Rights Act, the consumer is given a right to a price reduction in the circumstances prescribed in s.24 of the Act.[409]

33-076 **Remedies: termination** At common law the remedies for breach of an implied term turn on the nature of the term broken. Where the term broken is a condition, then the bailee is in principle entitled to terminate the contract of hire.[410] But where the term broken is a warranty, the bailee is not entitled to terminate the contract and is confined to a remedy in damages.[411] The Supply of Goods and Services Act 1982 makes no general provision for the consequences of breach and so the entitlement of the bailee to terminate will turn on whether the term broken has been classified by the Act as a condition or a warranty. The Act does, however, contain one restriction on the right of the bailee to terminate. Section 10A(1) of the Act states that where the bailee would, apart from this subsection, have the right to treat the contract as repudiated by reason of a breach on the part of the bailor of a term implied by ss.8, 9, 10(2)(a) or 10(2)(b) of the Act and the breach is so slight that it would be unreasonable for him to do so the breach is not to be treated as a breach of a condition but may be treated as a breach of warranty. In other words, termination is not an available remedy in these circumstances and the only remedy is damages. This provision has created an element of uncertainty in commercial transactions. It is for the bailor to show that the consequences of the breach are so slight that it would be unreasonable for the bailee to treat the contract as repudiated.[412] It is open to the parties to contract out of this provision, either actually or inferentially,[413] and thereby restore a greater element of certainty to their dealings. One restriction on the right to terminate which is not contained in the Act is that there is no provision which corresponds to s.11(4) of the Sale of Goods Act 1979 which states that where the buyer has accepted the goods the breach of a condition is generally only to be regarded as a breach of warranty. A court which wished to avoid the conclusion that the hirer had not lost his right to terminate where he continues to use the goods after becoming aware of the breach might find that he has lost his right to terminate as a result of his affirmation of the contract.[414]

33-077 **Remedies: the Consumer Rights Act** The remedies available to a consumer under the Consumer Rights Act 2015[415] where the trader has breached one of the terms treated as being included in a contract of hire concluded between a trader and consumer is more elaborate than that to be found at common law or in the Supply of Goods and Services Act 1982. These include a short-term right to reject the

---

[408] *UCB Leasing Ltd v Holtom* [1987] R.T.R. 362, CA (the claim for damages related to the period when the hirer had not terminated the contract on account of the breach). See also *Charterhouse Credit Co Ltd v Tolly* [1963] 2 Q.B. 683; *Doobay v Mohabeer* [1967] 2 A.C. 278, 288–289. A deduction from the damages should be made for the value of any use which the hirer has made of the chattel.
[409] On which see below, para.38-518. The Act applies to contracts made on or after October 1, 2015.
[410] See Vol.I, para.13-025.
[411] See Vol.I, para.13-031.
[412] s.10A(3).
[413] s.10A(2).
[414] See further on this point, Palmer (1983) 46 M.L.R. 619, 626–627.
[415] The Act applies to contracts made on or after October 1, 2015: see below, para.38-465.

goods,[416] a right of partial rejection,[417] a right to repair or replacement[418] and a right to a price reduction or final right to reject.[419]

Exemption clauses[420]   At common law, the liability of the bailor for breach of the   **33-078**
implied undertaking of fitness may be excluded by a special clause in the contract, provided the terms of the clause are made known to the hirer.[421] Subject to the provisions of the Unfair Contract Terms Act 1977 the terms implied by the 1982 Act may be negatived or varied by express agreement, by the course of dealing between the parties or by usage.[422] But the ability of a bailor to exclude or restrict his liability for breach of obligations or duties arising from things done or to be done by him in the course of a business[423] is curtailed by the provisions of the Unfair Contract Terms Act 1977.[424] In addition to the control imposed by s.2 of the Act (liability for death, personal injury or other loss or damage resulting from negligence)[425] and s.3 (exclusion or restriction of liability arising in contract where the person against whom the exemption clause is raised deals on the other's written standard terms of business),[426] s.7 applies specifically to contracts[427] of bailment ("where the possession ... of goods passes under ... a contract not governed by the law of sale of goods or hire-purchase ...")[428] and to terms in such contracts "excluding or restricting liability"[429] for breach of obligation arising by implication of law from the nature of the contract.[430] Section 7 thus applies to clauses which exclude or restrict a business liability under (inter alia) contracts of hire, or for work and labour. It does not specify the terms to be implied into the contract,[431] but it controls attempts to exclude or restrict liability arising under such terms. Section 7(1A)[432] provides:

"Liability in respect of the goods' correspondence with description or sample, of their quality or fitness for any particular purpose, cannot be excluded or restricted by reference to such a term except in so far as the term satisfies the requirement of reasonableness."

Section 7(4) further provides that:

---

[416] ss.20 and 22, on which see further para.38-513 and 38-516.
[417] s.21, on which see further para.38-515.
[418] s.23, on which see further para.38-517.
[419] s.24, on which see further paras 38-518—38-519.
[420] See Vol.I, Ch.15.
[421] e.g. *Astley Industrial Trust Ltd v Grimley* [1963] 1 W.L.R. 584; *Handley v Marston* (1962) 106 S.J. 327. Where a clause sought to be incorporated into a contract is particularly onerous or unusual, it must be fairly and reasonably brought to the attention of the party affected by it: *Interfoto Picture Library Ltd v Stiletto Visual Programmes Ltd* [1989] Q.B. 433; *AEG (UK) Ltd v Logic Resource Ltd* [1996] C.L.C. 265; *Goodlife Foods Ltd v Hall Fire Protection Ltd* [2018] EWCA Civ 1371.
[422] s.11(1). An express term does not negative one implied by the Act "unless inconsistent with it": s.11(2).
[423] s.1(3); and see Vol.I, para.15-072.
[424] For a fuller treatment of the Act, see Vol.I, paras 15-066 et seq.
[425] s.2.
[426] See above, para.33-054; Vol.I, para.15-085.
[427] See above, para.33-054, n.292.
[428] s.7(1).
[429] On the extended meaning of this phrase, see s.13 (Vol.I, paras 15-069—15-070).
[430] s.7(1). See also Vol.I, para.15-094.
[431] s.7 applies to terms implied into the contract by law or from the nature of the contract: see above, paras 33-066 et seq.; see below, para.33-092.
[432] Which for contracts made on or after October 1, 2015, replaces s.7(3).

"Liability in respect of—

    (a)   the right to transfer ownership of the goods, or give possession; or

    (b)   the assurance of quiet possession to a person taking goods in pursuance of the contract,

cannot[433] ... be excluded or restricted by reference to any such term except in so far as the term satisfies the requirement of reasonableness."

As far as the Consumer Rights Act 2015 is concerned, a term of a contract to hire goods from a trader to a consumer is not binding on the consumer to the extent that it would exclude or restrict the trader's liability arising under ss.9–16 of the Act.[434] Apart from the 1977 and 2015 Acts, the applicability of an exemption clause is a question of construction, depending on the intention of the parties[435]; it will require clear words for an exemption clause to be construed as wide enough to exempt the bailor from a fundamental breach of his undertaking.[436] The rules on incorporation[437] also apply. Thus the hirer will not be bound by an exemption clause printed on the back of a ticket which purports to be merely a receipt.[438]

33-079   **Obligations of the hirer**   The hirer is liable to pay the agreed hire,[439] to return the chattel at the expiration of the agreed period,[440] and to pay the cost of returning it.[441] The hirer may escape liability for failure to return the chattel if he can prove that the chattel was lost without the loss being due to his fault,[442] or that there was "good cause" for not returning it.[443] The hirer is bound to take reasonable care of the chattel hired, but he is not liable for damage to it if he can prove[444] that he or his employee (acting in the course of his employment) were not negligent in causing the damage.[445] A special clause in the contract may vary the hirer's liability at com-

---

[433] The excluded words refer to subs.(3A) which does not apply to contracts of hire.

[434] s.31, on which see further below, para.38-531. Note the extensions to the scope of s.31(1) to be found in s.31(2) and (3).

[435] *Photo Production Ltd v Securicor Transport Ltd* [1980] A.C. 827 (explaining *Suisse Atlantique Société d'Armement Maritime SA v NV Rotterdamsche Kolen Centrale* [1967] 1 A.C. 361 (Vol.I, paras 15-024 et seq.)).

[436] The *Photo Production* case, see above. cf. the earlier cases: *Karsales (Harrow) Ltd v Wallis* [1956] 1 W.L.R. 936; *Yeoman Credit Ltd v Apps* [1962] 2 Q.B. 508 (see below, para.39-392). See also *White v John Warwick & Co Ltd* [1953] 1 W.L.R. 1285 (construction of clause).

[437] See Vol.I, paras 13-008—13-018.

[438] *Chapelton v Barry UDC* [1940] 1 K.B. 532. On "ticket cases" generally, see Vol.I, paras 13-008 et seq.

[439] See above, para.33-048 (s.15 of the 1982 Act).

[440] *British Crane Hire Corp Ltd v Ipswich Plant Hire Ltd* [1975] Q.B. 303, 311–312, 313.

[441] [1975] Q.B. 303 at 312.

[442] [1975] Q.B. 303 at 311–312, 313.

[443] [1975] Q.B. 303 at 313 ("... if some great boulder descended on the vehicle and damaged it beyond repair, that might well be good cause for not returning it. As regards getting stuck in a snowdrift or a marsh, I would not think such a happening could normally constitute good cause", per Sir Eric Sachs). See the doctrine of frustration: *Taylor v Caldwell* (1863) 3 B. & S. 826, 838–839; Vol.I, Ch.23.

[444] On the onus of proof where the bailee has died, see *National Trust Co v Wong Aviation* [1969] 2 Lloyd's Rep. 340.

[445] *Sanderson v Collins* [1904] 1 K.B. 628 (liability for employee); *British Crane Hire Corp Ltd v Ipswich Plant Hire Ltd*, above, at 311–312, 313. See also *Dean v Keate* (1811) 3 Camp. 4; *Coupé Co v Maddick* [1891] 2 Q.B. 413.

mon law, and such a clause may be interpreted in the light of the condition of the chattel at the commencement of the hiring.[446]

Restrictions on use   The hirer may use the chattel only for the purpose for which it was let to him.[447] So, in early cases, if a horse was let for riding, the hirer was not permitted to use it for jumping[448]; if a horse was let for a particular journey, the hirer was not allowed to exceed that journey.[449] But the authority granted to the hirer to use the chattel will be construed as conferring on him implied authority to do in relation to the chattel anything reasonably incidental to its reasonable use, unless there is express provision to the contrary in the contract.[450] The hirer who uses a chattel for a purpose not contemplated by the contract of hiring will be liable both in contract and in tort for any loss caused by such use.[451]
33-080

Relief against forfeiture   Where the contract provides for forfeiture of amounts paid, or for premature termination of the hiring, upon a breach by the hirer, the doctrine of relief against forfeiture may apply.[452]
33-081

Repair and maintenance of the hired chattel   The terms of the contract may make the bailor liable for the repair of the chattel.[453] Apart from a special obligation undertaken in the contract, the hirer is not responsible for fair wear and tear,[454] nor is he under any obligation to do any repairs[455] except such as are naturally incidental to the due performance of his obligation to take reasonable care.[456] The hirer of a horse must provide it with suitable food, unless there is an agreement to the contrary.[457] Similarly, the hirer of a motorcar is obliged to pay for petrol and oil and other "running expenses". The mere fact of a bailment does not confer on the bailee any authority to deliver the chattel bailed to a third party for repair or otherwise so as to give that third party a lien for work done on the chattel: but where the circumstances show implied authority from the owner (e.g. where the bailee expressly agrees to keep the chattel in repair), a third party who repairs it at the
33-082

---

[446] *Schroder v Ward* (1863) 13 C.B.(N.S.) 410; *Brice & Sons v Christiani & Nielsen* (1928) 44 T.L.R. 335. But see the statutory controls over exemption clauses: see above, paras 33-054, 33-078.

[447] Palmer at paras 21-071—21-075; Story at para.413; Jones at pp.68, 69.

[448] *Burnard v Haggis* (1863) 14 C.B.(N.S.) 45.

[449] *Walley v Holt* (1876) 35 L.T. 631.

[450] *Tappenden v Artus* [1964] 2 Q.B. 185 (see below, para.33-094). cf. *Morris v CW Martin & Sons Ltd* [1966] 1 Q.B. 716, 729–720 (decision approved in the House of Lords: see above, para.33-070, n.390).

[451] *Burnard v Haggis*, above; *Walley v Holt*, above.

[452] See Vol.I, paras 26-245 et seq.; see below, para.39-343.

[453] Story at para.385. The assignee of the owner may, in some circumstances, discharge the latter's liability to repair: *British Waggon Co v Lea & Co* (1880) 5 Q.B.D. 149. (On such vicarious performance, see Vol.I, paras 19-082 et seq.) See also *Brady v St Margaret's Trust Ltd* [1963] 2 Q.B. 494.

[454] *Blakemore v Bristol and Exeter Ry* (1858) 8 El. & Bl. 1035 (a case of gratuitous loan, but the same principle would, it is submitted, apply to a hiring); *Coupé Co v Maddick* [1891] 2 Q.B. 413, 415.

[455] cf. *Sutton v Temple* (1843) 12 M. & W. 52, 60; *Hopkins v GE Ry* (1895) 12 T.L.R. 25; also, see above, para.33-041. A bailee who executes repairs to the chattel without the owner's consent probably cannot recover the expense from the bailor. cf. also Story at para.392.

[456] Story at para.393.

[457] *Handford v Palmer* (1820) 2 Brod. & Bing. 359; Story at para.393 (citing American cases, French and Roman law to the same effect).

request of the hirer may acquire, for the cost of the repairs, a lien effective against the owner as well as against the hirer.[458]

33-083 **Damages for wrongful detention by the hirer**   Where the hirer wrongfully detains a chattel hired to him by the claimant, and the chattel is one which the claimant, as part of his business, hires out to users, the normal measure of damages is the full market rate of hire for the whole period of the detention if the hirer has made beneficial use of the chattel during that period.[459]

(ii)   Equipment Leasing

33-084 **Finance leasing**   In the light of various tax advantages,[460] a form of long-term financing has developed, which is known as finance leasing. In a finance lease, the lessee selects the equipment to be supplied by a manufacturer or dealer, but the lessor (a finance company) provides the funds, acquires title to the equipment and allows the lessee to use it for all (or most) of its expected useful life. During the period of the lease the usual risks and rewards of ownership are substantially transferred to the lessee, who bears the risks of loss, destruction and depreciation of the leased equipment (fair wear and tear only excepted) and of its obsolescence or malfunctioning.[461] The lessee also bears the costs of maintenance, repairs and insurance. The regular rental payments during the primary period of the lease are calculated to enable the lessor to amortise its capital outlay and to make a profit from its finance charges.[462] At the end of the primary leasing period, there will frequently be a secondary leasing period during which the lessee may opt to continue the lease at a nominal rental, or the equipment may be sold and a proportion of the sale proceeds returned to the lessee as a rebate of rentals.[463] The lessee thus acquires any residual value in the equipment, after the lessor has recouped its investment and charges. If the lease is terminated prematurely, the lessor is entitled to recoup its capital investment (less the realisable value of the equipment at the time) and its expected finance charges (less an allowance to reflect the accelerated return of the capital). The bailment which underlies finance leasing is therefore only a device to provide the finance company with a security interest (its reversionary

---

[458] See the cases cited below, para.33-094 nn.558 and 559.

[459] *Strand Electric and Engineering Co Ltd v Brisford Entertainments Ltd* [1952] 2 Q.B. 246; *Hillesden Securities Ltd v Ryjak Ltd* [1983] 1 W.L.R. 959. cf. Vol.I, para.29-152.

[460] In finance leasing, tax writing-down allowances are claimed by the lessor, and the rentals payable by the lessee are reduced accordingly; the rentals are usually an expense allowed against the lessee's liability to corporation tax.

[461] Finance leases with non-consumers inevitably exclude the terms implied by the Supply of Goods and Services Act 1982 (see above, paras 33-044 et seq.). It is believed that in the case of most such finance leases the reasonableness requirement in s.7(1A) of the Unfair Contract Terms Act 1977 (see above, para.33-078) will be satisfied: see *R & B Customs Brokers Ltd v United Dominions Trust Ltd* [1988] 1 W.L.R. 321, 331–332.

[462] A lease of equipment which does not have the characteristics set out in this paragraph is known as an "operating lease"; in such a lease the lessee has the use of the chattel for only a relatively short time and the equipment will have a substantial residual value at the end of the lease.

[463] Unlike a hire-purchase transaction where, at the end of the hiring period, the hirer has the *option* of buying the chattel for a nominal sum (see below, para.39-306).

right)[464]; a finance lease is similar in function to outright purchase or hire purchase.[465] Details of finance leasing must be sought elsewhere.[466]

(iii) Statutory Control of Hiring

The Consumer Credit Act 1974 This Act imposes statutory controls, not only **33-085** upon consumer credit agreements, but also on "consumer hire agreements". A consumer hire agreement is defined[467] as an agreement made by a person with an individual[468] (the "hirer") for the bailment[469] of goods to the hirer, being an agreement which: (a) is not a hire-purchase agreement[470]; and (b) is capable of subsisting for more than three months.[471] The use of the term "hire" has been held to imply that there is a payment or reward for the hire so that a gratuitous bailment does not fall within the scope of the definition.[472] A consumer hire agreement is a regulated agreement[473] for the purposes of the Act if it is a regulated consumer hire agreement for the purposes of Ch.14B of Pt 2 of the Financial Services and Markets Act 2000 (Regulated Activities) Order 2001.[474] The general provisions of the Act, together with the Regulations implementing the Consumer Credit Directive 2008, are examined below in Ch.39[475]: these include the power to make regulations about the information to be disclosed to a hirer before a regulated agreement is made[476]; controls over the form and content of agreements[477]; the duty to supply copies of agreements[478]; the right of the hirer to cancel certain agreements within a "cooling-off period"[479]; the duty of the owner to give notice before taking certain actions to enforce a term of the agreement[480]; restrictions on the rights of the owner follow-

---

[464] GM Shepherd Ltd v North West Securities Ltd, 1991 S.L.T. 499, 511, 513–514.

[465] On Demand Information Plc v Michael Gerson (Finance) Plc [1999] 1 All E.R. (Comm) 512, 515–516, where reliance was placed by the court on this passage. See also On Demand Information Plc v Michael Gerson (Finance) Plc [2001] 1 W.L.R. 155, 158, CA. The point did not arise on the subsequent appeal to the House of Lords: [2002] UKHL 13, [2003] 1 A.C. 551.

[466] Adams, Commercial Hiring and Leasing (1989); Sadler, Reisbach and Thomas, Equipment Leasing (1993, looseleaf); Davies, Equipment and Motor Vehicle Leasing and Hiring (1997).

[467] s.15(1); see also below, para.39-035.

[468] Defined in s.189(1); see below, para.39-016.

[469] See Palmer and Yates [1979] C.L.J. 180.

[470] Defined in s.189(1); see below, para.39-356.

[471] There was at one time a further requirement, namely that the agreement did not require the hirer to make payments exceeding £25,000. The financial limit was removed by s.2 of the Consumer Credit Act 2006 in relation to non-business hire, which came into force on April 6, 2008 (see Consumer Credit Act 2006 (Commencement No.4 and Transitional Provisions) Order (SI 2008/831) Sch.2 para.1).

[472] TRM Copy Centres (UK) Ltd v Lanwell Services Ltd [2009] UKHL 35, [2009] 1 W.L.R. 1375 at [11].

[473] Defined in s.189(1); see below, paras 39-036, 39-038.

[474] SI 2001/544 art.60N (inserted by Financial Services and Markets Act 2000 (Regulated Activities) (Amendment) (No.2) Order 2016 (SI 2016/392) Pt 2 art.2). An exempt agreement is a consumer credit hire agreement which is an exempt agreement under arts 60O–60Q of SI 2001/544.

[475] See below, paras 39-002 et seq.

[476] s.55 (below, paras 39-076—39-077).

[477] ss.60–61 (below, paras 39-080—39-081); SI 1983/1553 (as amended) and, in the case of the Regulations implementing the Consumer Credit Directive 2008 (SI 2010/1014, as amended) (below, para.39-082).

[478] ss.62–64 (below, paras 39-088—39-089); SI 1983/1557 (as amended) and s.61A (below, para.39-092).

[479] ss.64, 67–73 (below, paras 39-091, 39-102 et seq.).

[480] s.76 (below, paras 39-164 et seq.); SI 1983/1561 (as amended).

ing the death of the hirer[481]; the duty of the owner to serve a "default notice" on the hirer before enforcing certain rights following breach by the hirer,[482] or to give notice of termination of the agreement in non-default cases[483]; provisions regulating securities[484] and the taking of negotiable instruments[485]; and the powers of the court when enforcement of the agreement is sought.[486] There are many Regulations made under the Act, details of which must be sought elsewhere.[487] In this section, only those provisions of the Act which are specifically applicable to hiring agreements will be examined.

33-086   Duties on the parties to give information   The owner[488] under a regulated consumer hire agreement,[489] within 12 working days[490] after receiving a request in writing to that effect from the hirer and payment of a fee of £1,[491] must give[492] to the hirer a copy[493] of the executed agreement,[494] together with a statement signed by or on behalf of the owner showing, according to the information to which it is practicable for him to refer, the total sum which has become payable under the agreement by the hirer but remains unpaid and the various amounts comprised in that total sum, with the date when each became due.[495] (This provision does not apply to a non-commercial agreement.[496]) If the owner fails to comply with this provision he is not entitled, while the default continues, to enforce the agreement.[497] The statement when given by the owner is binding on him.[498] A surety under a regulated consumer hire agreement may similarly request copies of the agreement, documents and the security instrument, and a similar financial statement.[499]

---

[481] s.86 (below, para.39-175).
[482] ss.87–89 (below, paras 39-166 et seq.); SI 1983/1561 (as amended).
[483] s.98 (below, para.39-172); SI 1983/1561 (as amended) and s.98A (below, para.39-173).
[484] ss.105–106, 110–113 (below, paras 39-180 et seq.); SI 1983/1556 (as amended).
[485] ss.123–125 (below, paras 39-196 et seq.). But see SI 1984/435.
[486] ss.127–132; 135–136. (Below, paras 39-200 et seq.).
[487] Guest, *Credit Law*; Goode, *Consumer Credit: Law and Practice*; Bennion, *Consumer Credit Control*, Vol.2; F. Philpott, W. Hibbert, S. Neville, S. Popplewell, B. Say, P. Sayer and J. Smith, *The Law of Consumer Credit and Hire* (2009).
[488] Defined in s.189(1) (together with a corresponding definition for "hirer"). See below, para.39-037.
[489] For the definition of this term (in s.15(2) of the Act) see below, paras 39-035, 39-036—39-043.
[490] SI 1983/1569 reg.2.
[491] SI 1998/997.
[492] "Give" means deliver or send by appropriate method to: s.189(1), as amended by SI 2004/3236 art.2(9).
[493] See s.180 and SI 1983/1557, as amended, made thereunder, for the form and content of copies.
[494] Defined in s.189(1). A copy must also be given of any other document referred to in the agreement: s.79(1).
[495] s.79(1). (The subsection does not apply to an agreement under which no sum is payable by the hirer, or to a request made less than one month after a previous request was complied with: s.79(2).)
[496] s.79(4). (For the definition of "a non-commercial agreement", see s.189(1) and see below, para.39-049).
[497] s.79(3)(a). Originally, if the default continued for one month, an offence was committed (s.79(3)(b)) but this provision was repealed by the Consumer Protection from Unfair Trading Regulations 2008 (SI 2008/1277) reg.30(1) and Sch.2.
[498] s.172(1). (But the court has a discretion to grant the owner relief if the statement is shown to be incorrect.)
[499] s.109. (See below, para.39-137.)

Whereabouts of goods   Where, under a regulated agreement, the hirer must keep   **33-087**
the goods in his possession or control, he must, within seven working days after he
has received a request in writing from the owner, tell him where the goods are.[500]

Right to terminate hire agreement   Irrespective of the terms of the agreement,   **33-088**
the Act gives the hirer under a regulated consumer hire agreement[501] the right to
terminate the agreement by giving notice to any person entitled or authorised to
receive the sums payable under the agreement.[502] Such notice must not expire earlier
than 18 months after the making of the agreement[503]; otherwise, the minimum
period of notice (unless the agreement provides for a shorter period) is as follows:
(1) if the agreement provides for the making of payments by the hirer at equal
intervals, the length of one interval or three months (whichever is less)[504]; (2) if the
agreement provides for such payments at differing intervals, the length of the shortest interval, or three months (whichever is less)[505]; (3) in any other case, three
months' notice.[506] The right to terminate under this provision[507] does not apply to:
(1) any agreement where the payments exceed in total £1,500 in any year[508]; or (2)
where the goods are bailed to the hirer for the purposes of a business carried on by
him[509] and the goods are selected by the hirer, and acquired by the owner for the
purposes of the agreement at the request of the hirer from any person other than the
owner's associate[510]; or (3) any agreement where the hirer requires[511] the goods for
the purpose of bailing or hiring them to other persons in the course of a business
carried on by him[512]; or (4) if the Financial Conduct Authority exempts a person
from the provision.[513]

Restrictions on the owner's rights   The owner is not entitled, without an order   **33-089**
of the court, to enter any premises to take possession of goods subject (inter alia)
to a regulated consumer hire agreement.[514] Special provision is made for the owner
to prove that the hirer is in adverse possession of the goods.[515] When the court

---

[500]   s.80 (which is examined see below, para.39-140).

[501]   For the definition, see below, paras 39-035, 39-036—39-043.

[502]   s.101(1). (But termination under this subsection does not affect any liability under the agreement
which has accrued before the termination: s.101(2).)

[503]   s.101(3). (In the case of a "modifying agreement" (see s.189(1)) this reads "after the making of the
original agreement": s.101(9).)

[504]   s.101(4).

[505]   s.101(5).

[506]   s.101(6). On the extent of the protection granted by s.101 see Palmer and Yates [1979] C.L.J. 180,
195–199.

[507]   s.101.

[508]   s.101(7)(a). (Payments under this subsection do not take account of breach of the agreement.) The
monetary limit may be amended: s.181. See SI 1998/997.

[509]   "or the hirer holds himself out as requiring the goods for those purposes": s.101(7)(b).

[510]   s.101(7)(b). This provision would cover many ordinary leasing agreements.

[511]   "or holds himself out as requiring": s.101(7)(c).

[512]   s.101(7)(c).

[513]   s.101(8). The exemption may be granted if "it appears ... to be in the interests of hirers to do so",
and may be made subject to conditions. In addition, the FCA may, subject to conditions, grant an
exemption of a more general nature to a consumer hire agreement which falls within a specified
description: s.101(8A).

[514]   s.92(1). (An entry in contravention of s.92(1) is actionable as a breach of statutory duty: s.92(3).)

[515]   s.134 (the same provision applies to other types of regulated agreements: see below, para.39-366).

makes an order under a regulated agreement it has wide power[516] to impose conditions on the parties, or to suspend the operation of any term of the order; but it may not extend the period for which the hirer, under the terms of a consumer hire agreement, is entitled to possession of the goods.[517]

33-090 Financial relief for the hirer   Where the owner under a regulated consumer hire agreement[518] recovers possession of the goods otherwise than by action, the Act entitles the hirer to apply to the court for an order that the whole or part of any sum paid by the hirer to the owner in respect of the goods shall be repaid, and that the obligation to pay the whole or part of any sum owed by the hirer to the owner shall cease.[519] The court is empowered to make such orders "if it appears to the court just to do so, having regard to the extent of the enjoyment of the goods by the hirer".[520] The terms of the enactment may be wide enough to cover payments under any heading of the agreement, e.g. for rental, for "depreciation", or as "liquidated damages".[521] If a court orders the hirer to deliver to the owner the goods covered by a regulated consumer hire agreement, an order may be made granting financial relief to the hirer in a similar way.[522]

(d)   Work and Labour

33-091 Bailment for hire of work and labour   Where a chattel is bailed to the bailee in order that he may perform work upon it for reward,[523] it is a bailment for hire of work and labour.[524] The duty of the bailor to pay the agreed price, or a reasonable remuneration upon a quantum meruit,[525] depends upon general principles of the law of contract,[526] or (where applicable) on s.15 of the Supply of Goods and Services Act 1982 or s.51 of the Consumer Rights Act 2015 (discussed above[527]); this type of contract is discussed here only insofar as it involves a bailment.

33-092 Duties and liabilities of the worker   Wherever the worker is acting in the course of a business, the standard of workmanship and of care of the chattel which he must achieve is laid down in the term implied by s.13 of the Supply of Goods and Services Act 1982[528] and where a trader is supplying a service to a consumer it is to be found in s.49(1) of the Consumer Rights Act 2015.[529] These standards merely

---

[516] s.135(1) (see below, para.39-208).

[517] s.135(3).

[518] For the definition, see below, paras 39-035, 39-036—39-043.

[519] s.132(1).

[520] s.132(1). For an illustration, see *Automotive Financial Services Ltd v Henderson*, 1992 S.L.T. (Sh. Ct.) 63.

[521] See Vol.I, paras 26-190 et seq.

[522] s.132(2).

[523] On voluntary service performed without request, see *Taylor v Laird* (1856) 25 L.J. Ex. 329, 332; also Vol.I, paras 4-026, 4-030, 29-071.

[524] Palmer at Ch.15; Paton at pp.331 et seq.

[525] e.g. payment for "extras": see *Wilmot v Smith* (1828) 3 C. & P. 453; Vol.I, paras 29-070—29-071 and 29-076.

[526] On substantial performance of an entire contract, see Vol.I, para.21-033; on waiver, see Vol.I, para.22-040; on frustration, see Vol.I, Ch.23.

[527] See above, para.33-048.

[528] See above, para.33-046.

[529] The Consumer Rights Act 2015 Act applies to contracts made on or after October 1, 2015: see below, para.38-465.

codify the common law rules[530] (which still apply to any such bailment not covered by the Acts): the reported cases will therefore still be relevant. Since the worker is to be remunerated, the common law required him to perform the work in an efficient manner,[531] showing reasonable competence in any art or craft which he publicly professes[532]; it also required him to take reasonable care of the chattel bailed to him[533] and to return it to the bailor at the expiration of the agreed[534] period.[535] This duty of care may require the bailee to take precautionary measures once the chattel is found to be in unexpected danger.[536] If the chattel is lost or injured during the bailment, the onus is on the bailee to show that the loss or injury was due to inevitable accident, inherent vice in the chattel, or some other cause not involving any failure on the part of himself or his employees[537] to take reasonable care.[538] Even after the work is completed, the liability of the bailee for negligence continues until the relationship of bailment terminates.[539] Subject to the provisions of the Unfair Contract Terms Act 1977 and the Consumer Rights Act 2015,[540] the bailee may exclude his liability by a special clause in the contract.[541] The scope of such an exemption clause is a question of construction, depending on the intention of the parties.[542] Normally, the worker may not delegate his task to another, but the nature of the work to be done may indicate the bailor's implied permission that the worker may delegate.[543] If the worker deals with the chattel in a way not contemplated by the contract, he acts at his peril [544]

---

[530] For a statement, see *Smith v Eric S Bush* [1990] 1 A.C. 83., 843.

[531] *Kimber v William Willett Ltd* [1947] K.B. 570.

[532] *Lamphier v Phipos* (1838) 8 Car. & P. 475, 479. See also *Duncan v Blundell* (1820) 3 Stark. 6; *Harmer v Cornelius* (1858) 5 C.B.(N.S.) 236, 246; Jones at p.99.

[533] *Morris v CW Martin & Sons Ltd* [1966] 1 Q.B. 716. See also *Leck v Maestaer* (1807) 1 Camp. 138; *Clark v Earnshaw* (1818) Gow. 30. cf. *Wilson v Powis* (1820) 3 Bing. 633; *Becker v Lavender Ltd* (1946) 62 T.L.R. 504 (misdelivery by bailee's negligence); *Houghland v RR Low (Luxury Coaches) Ltd* [1962] 1 Q.B. 694, 698 (see above, para.33-008). On special clauses limiting liability, see above, para.33-053, and Vol.I, Ch.15.

[534] On the time when performance is due, see s.14 of the Supply of Goods and Services Act 1982 (see above, para.33-047) which applies wherever the bailee is supplying services in the course of a business and s.52 of the Consumer Rights Act 2015 where a trader is supplying a service to a consumer.

[535] Or when demanded: wrongful detention beyond this period makes the worker liable in damages for the amount which a profit-earning chattel would have earned for the owner (*Re Trent and Humber Co* (1868) L.R. 4 Ch. App. 112, 117) and also liable as an insurer if the chattel is lost or destroyed (*Shaw & Co v Symmons Sons* [1917] 1 K.B. 799; *Mitchell v Ealing LBC* [1979] Q.B. 1).

[536] *Leck v Maestaer*, above.

[537] *Aitchison v Page Motors Ltd* (1935) 154 L.T. 128. cf. *Jobson v Palmer* [1893] 1 Ch. 71. See also above, text at para.33-070, n.390.

[538] Story at para.437; *Leck v Maestaer*, above; *Clarke v Earnshaw*, above. cf. *Joseph Travers & Sons Ltd v Cooper* [1915] 1 K.B. 73; *Mayne v Silvermere Cleaners Ltd* [1939] 1 All E.R. 693; *Levison v Patent Steam Carpet Cleaning Co Ltd* [1978] Q.B. 69, 82, 83, 85; *Sheehy v Faughan* [1991] 1 I.R. 425 (mare left at defendant's stud). cf. above, paras 33-010, 33-032. 33-049, 33-064, 33-079.

[539] *Mitchell v Davis* (1920) 37 T.L.R. 68. On the power of the bailee to terminate the bailment and to sell the chattel, see below, paras 33-095 et seq.

[540] See above, paras 33-054, 33-078.

[541] Exclusion is also permitted under Pt II of the 1982 Act (see above, para.33-044) but the ability to exclude liability under the Consumer Rights Act 2015 is more limited (see s.57, on which see further para.38-586).

[542] *Photo Production Ltd v Securicor Transport Ltd* [1980] A.C. 827. On exemption clauses generally, see Vol.I, Ch.15; see above, paras 33-053, 33-078.

[543] cf. *Davies v Collins* [1945] 1 All E.R. 247; *Martin v N Negin Ltd* (1945) 172 L.T. 275; *Morris v CW Martin & Sons Ltd* [1966] 1 Q.B. 716 (see above, para.33-092) (approved by the House of Lords in *Photo Production Ltd v Securicor Transport Ltd* [1980] A.C. 827, 846, 852). See further, on vicari-

33-093   **Lien of the worker**   Where a worker is to be paid[545] for work done on a chattel bailed to him[546] he has at common law, after completion of the work,[547] a lien[548] on the chattel for the remuneration due to him[549]; hence he may refuse to return the chattel until he is paid.[550] An express or implied term of the contract, especially one relating to credit, may, however, exclude such a lien.[551] The lien covers the sum due for materials supplied and work performed on the chattel,[552] but not charges for warehousing or storage, even during the period of the lien.[553] There is no lien at common law for the maintenance of the chattel in its original condition without improvement.[554] The lien is lost by waiver[555] or by the worker relinquishing possession of the chattel,[556] but the mere taking of security for the debt does not discharge the lien, unless it is inconsistent with the existence of the lien.[557]

---

ous performance, Vol.I, paras 19-082—19-085.

[544] *Doucette v Proud* [1940] 4 D.L.R. 111 (sed quaere whether the bailor had waived the breach in this case); cf. above, paras 33-042, 33-052.

[545] The statements of the rule assume that the lien arises although a precise price may not have been fixed beforehand: e.g. *Scarfe v Morgan* (1838) 4 M. & W. 270, 283.

[546] The worker must have possession of the chattel: *Forth v Simpson* (1849) 13 Q.B. 680; *James Bibby Ltd v Woods and Howard* [1949] 2 K.B. 449, 453.

[547] If the bailor countermands his order for the work before it is completed, the worker has a lien for the work actually done: *Lilley v Barnsley* (1844) 1 C. & K. 344, 346.

[548] A lien does not entitle the worker to exercise any remedy of self-help, e.g. by removing engine parts so as to disable a ship from moving: *The "Gregos"* [1985] 2 Lloyd's Rep. 347, 361–362. (The worker is simply entitled to retain the chattel in his possession.) A lien cannot be exercised if the worker fails to give the bailor proper details of the work done: *Thaper v Singh* [1987] F.L.R. 369 (accountant).

[549] Where the remuneration has not been agreed, but the worker claims an unreasonably high amount, the bailor who pays under protest may have a claim in restitution to recover the excess over a reasonable charge: see above, para.33-048; Vol.I, paras 29-098—29-103.

[550] Story at para.440; *Franklin v Hosier* (1821) 4 B. & Ald. 341; *Scarfe v Morgan* (1838) 4 M. & W. 270 (lien on mare for services of stallion); *Steadman v Hockley* (1846) 15 M. & W. 553, 556–557. cf. *R. v Wade* (1869) 11 Cox C.C. 549; *Woodworth v Conroy* [1976] 1 Q.B. 884 (accountants have a lien over the books of account, files and papers delivered to them in the course of their professional work); and the lien of an agent, see above, para.31-164.

[551] *Raitt v Mitchell* (1815) 4 Camp. 146 (custom excluding lien); *Chase v Westmore* (1816) 5 M. & S. 180, 186; *Scarfe v Morgan*, above, at 283; *Forth v Simpson* (1849) 13 Q.B. 680. See also the references in nn.558, 559, below.

[552] On a general lien, see Paton at pp.345–347.

[553] *Somes v British Empire Shipping Co Ltd* (1860) 8 H.L. Cas. 338 (distinguished by the House of Lords in *China Pacific SA v Food Corp of India* [1982] A.C. 939, 962–963 (owner benefited from the expenditure, which was made *before* he demanded redelivery of the goods: gratuitous bailment following salvage)). The principle laid down in *Somes* has since been restrictively interpreted (see *Metall Market OOO v Vitorio Shipping Co Ltd (The "Lehmann Timber")* [2013] EWCA Civ 650, [2014] Q.B. 760 at [70]) and it would now appear to stand for the proposition that the common law remedy of an artificer's lien does not attach to it, or contain within it, a right of claim to the expenses of enforcing it or exercising it and that there is no lien for such expenses unless the contract provides for one (at [90]). In any event, the principle in *Somes* is unlikely to apply outside the context of an artificer's lien, given that it has been stated to be of "doubtful status outside that context" (at [122]). See also *Hartley v Hitchcock* (1816) 1 Stark. 408.

[554] *Jackson v Cummins* (1839) 5 M. & W. 342 (mere agistment of an animal: see above, para.33-059; cf. charges for training an animal: *Bevan v Waters* (1828) Mood. & M. 235; *Forth v Simpson* (1849) 13 Q.B. 680); *Hatton v Car Maintenance Co Ltd* [1915] 1 Ch. 621. cf. *Steadman v Hockley* (1846) 15 M. & W. 553, 556.

[555] *White v Gainer* (1824) 2 Bing. 23.

[556] *Hartley v Hitchcock* (1816) 1 Stark. 408; *Jacobs v Latour* (1828) 5 Bing. 130; *Legg v Evans* (1840) 6 M. & W. 36, 42; *Pennington v Reliance Motor Works Ltd* [1923] 1 K.B. 127; *Hatton v Car Maintenance Co Ltd*, above. cf. *Albemarle Supply Co Ltd v Hind & Co* [1928] 1 K.B. 307 (lien

Lien in favour of third person   Where the circumstances show that a bailee has **33-094** actual or ostensible authority from the bailor to deliver the chattel to a third person for work to be performed upon it (e.g. when the bailee expressly undertakes to keep it in repair), the third party will obtain a lien which may be effective against the bailor as well as against the bailee.[558] Thus the hirer of a motor-vehicle will normally have implied authority to permit a garage to obtain a lien over it for repairs which it has carried out.[559]

Uncollected goods: statutory power of sale[560]   In the absence of agreement, the **33-095** right of lien does not, at common law, confer on the bailee the right to sell the chattel.[561] However, subject to the terms of the bailment,[562] the Torts (Interference with Goods) Act 1977 confers a power of sale on a bailee in possession of uncollected goods.[563] The Act does not define bailment[564] and therefore all types of bailment appear to be included.[565] The Act provides for two separate powers of sale, one with,[566] and one without the authority of the court. The non-judicial power of sale arises in any one of the following situations[567]: (a) where the bailor is in breach of an obligation to take delivery of the goods (or, if the terms of the bailment so provide, to give directions as to their delivery); (b) where the bailee could impose such an obligation by giving notice to the bailor, but is unable to trace or communicate with the bailor; or (c) where the bailee can reasonably expect to be relieved of any duty to safeguard the goods by giving notice to the bailor, but is unable to trace or communicate with the bailor.

Power to impose an obligation to take delivery   Because many bailments do not **33-096** impose a definite obligation on the bailor to collect the goods before a fixed time, the 1977 Act entitles[568] the bailee, by a notice in writing given to the bailor, to impose on him an obligation to take delivery of the goods (or, where relevant, to

---

continued despite temporary loss of possession); *Caldwell v Sumpters* [1972] Ch. 478 (solicitor's lien over documents not lost when they were sent to the client's present solicitors with the request to hold them to the order of the sender).

[557] *Angus v McLachlan* (1883) 23 Ch. D. 330. cf. *Ex p. Willoughby* (1881) 16 Ch. D. 604.

[558] *Keene v Thomas* [1905] 1 K.B. 136; *Green v All Motors Ltd* [1917] 1 K.B. 625; *Albemarle Supply Co Ltd v Hind & Co*, above; *Jarl Tra Ab v Convoys Ltd* [2003] EWHC 1488 (Comm), [2003] 2 Lloyd's Rep. 459. cf. *Cassils & Co and Sassoon & Co v Holden Wood Bleaching Co Ltd* (1914) 84 L.J. K.B. 834; *K Chellaram & Sons (London) Ltd v Butlers Warehousing and Distribution Ltd* [1977] 2 Lloyd's Rep. 192; *Pennington v Reliance Motor Works Ltd*, above; *Bowmaker Ltd v Wycombe Motors Ltd* [1946] K.B. 505 (no lien arose after owners had validly terminated a hire-purchase agreement). See below, para.39-423. See also Peden (1969) 18 I.C.L.Q. 129.

[559] *Tappenden v Artus* [1964] 2 Q.B. 185.

[560] On the right of innkeepers to sell, see below, para.33-118.

[561] *Thames Iron Works Co v Patent Derrick Co* (1860) 1 J. & H. 93. Perishable goods, however, may be sold by order of the court.

[562] s.12(8). See also Sch.1 Pt I para.1(6). Section 12 therefore cannot be read as a provision which excludes previously existing common law rules regarding contracts of bailment: *JJD SA v Avon Tyres Ltd, The Times,* January 25, 1999.

[563] ss.12 and 13.

[564] The words "bailor" and "bailee" in ss.12 and 13 include successors in title: s.12(7)(a).

[565] Sed quaere, in the case of involuntary bailment, sub-bailment, or bailment without the owner's consent. On the possible application of the sections to pledge, see below, para.33-132, to an innkeeper, see below, para.33-118.

[566] See below, para.33-100.

[567] s.12(1).

[568] For the purposes of s.12(1), see above: s.12(2) and Sch.1 Pt I.

give directions as to their delivery).[569] This power is without prejudice to the provisions of the contract[570] and is not confined to commercial bailments where the bailee is in business, so that gratuitous bailments (e.g. between friends) are included.[571] The notice must be in writing,[572] and must comply with the requirements of Sch.1 Pt I, which, in summary, are: the notice must specify the bailee's name and address; must give sufficient particulars of the goods and their location; must state that the goods are ready for delivery, or (where combined with a notice terminating the contract of bailment) will be ready for delivery when the contract is terminated; and must specify any amount payable to the bailee which became due before the notice.[573] There are further provisions[574] about *when* the notice must be given in various circumstances, according to the purpose of the bailment in question, e.g. at any time after "the repair or other treatment [of the goods] has been carried out"; or "after the bailee has carried out the valuation or appraisal"; or (in cases of storage or warehousing by a bailee who is not a mercantile agent)[575] after the bailee's "obligation as custodian has come to an end".

33-097 **Notice of intention to sell**[576] Once the power of sale arises under the above provisions, the bailee is entitled[577] to sell the goods, if he is reasonably satisfied that the bailor owns the goods and either (a) he has given notice to the bailor of his intention to sell the goods; or (b) he has failed to trace or communicate with the bailor with a view to giving him such a notice, after having taken reasonable steps for the purpose.[578] The notice of intention to sell must be in writing and be sent by registered letter or by the recorded delivery service,[579] and must specify the following information[580]: the bailee's name and address; particulars of the goods and of their location; the date on or after which their sale is proposed; and the amount, if any, payable by the bailor to the bailee in respect of the goods, and which became due before the giving of the notice.[581] The period between the notice and the proposed date of sale must afford the bailor "a reasonable opportunity of taking delivery of the goods", and, when any payment is due, must be not less than three months.[582]

33-098 **Disputes** The non-judicial procedure before sale cannot be used if there is a dispute between the bailor and the bailee. It is laid down that the notice of inten-

---

[569] Sch.1 Pt I paras 1(1) and (6).

[570] Sch.1 Pt I para.1(6). The power also arises whether or not the bailor has paid any amount due to the bailee in respect of the goods: Sch.1 Pt I para.5. The importance of the fact that s.12 does not remove the common law rules or prevent the implication of terms into the contract of bailment was demonstrated in *JJD SA v Avon Tyres Ltd*, *The Times*, January 25, 1999.

[571] Sch.1 Pt I para.5.

[572] Sch.1 Pt I para.1(2).

[573] Sch.1 Pt I para.1(3).

[574] Sch.1 Pt I paras 2–4.

[575] Sch.1 Pt I para.4(2).

[576] The notice required under Sch.1 Pt I (above, para.33-096), may be combined with this notice: Sch.1 Pt I para.1(4).

[577] As against the bailor: see below, para.33-099.

[578] s.12(3). If the bailee is in doubt whether the steps he has taken would be considered reasonable, it would be prudent to apply for the authority of the court: see below, para.33-100.

[579] Sch.1 Pt II para.6(4).

[580] Sch.1 Pt II para.6.

[581] Sch.1 Pt II para.6(1).

[582] Sch.1 Pt II para.6(2) and (3).

tion to sell may not be given, nor may the goods be sold pursuant to such a notice, at a time when the bailee "has notice that, because of a dispute concerning the goods, the bailor is questioning or refusing to pay all or any part of what the bailee claims to be due to him in respect of the goods".[583] In these circumstances, the goods may be sold only if the court authorises the sale.[584]

Effect of the sale   A sale duly made under the provisions of the 1977 Act gives a   **33-099**
good title to the purchaser as against the bailor, but not as against the true owner.[585] After the sale, the bailee must account to the bailor for the proceeds of sale, less any costs of sale; the account is to be taken on the footing that the bailee should have adopted the best method of sale reasonably available in the circumstances and any sum due to the bailee in respect of the goods before he gave notice of intention to sell may be deducted.[586] The bailor's rights against the goods are therefore divested, and replaced by a right to claim from the bailee the balance of the proceeds of sale.

Sale authorised by the court   There are some circumstances in which it would   **33-100**
not be prudent for the bailee to sell under the non-judicial power given by s.12 discussed in the preceding paragraphs, e.g. where the goods are of high value, or where the bailee is unable to notify the bailor, and considers that he might be at risk in selling on the basis that he had taken "reasonable steps" to trace him.[587] Section 13 therefore permits a sale with the authority of the court, which will preclude the bailor from later challenging the bailee's actions. In one situation, however, the bailee is expressly prevented from using the non-judicial power and can therefore sell only with the authority of the court, viz he cannot sell under s.12 if there is a dispute between him and the bailor over any payment claimed by the bailee.[588] Section 13 of the 1977 Act enables the bailee to sell under the authority of the court, and thereby to gain the protection of a decision which, subject to any right of appeal, is "conclusive, as against the bailor, of the bailee's entitlement to sell the goods".[589] The bailee must satisfy the court[590] that he is entitled (or would be entitled if he had given the required[591] notice) to sell under s.12.[592] The court may impose terms, may fix deductions from the proceeds of sale, and may direct that the net proceeds of sale be paid into court to be held to the bailor's credit.[593]

---

583   Sch.1 Pt II para.7(1).
584   Under s.13 (below, para.33-100).
585   s.12(4) and (6). A sale under the Act does not give a good title as against the true owner, nor against anyone claiming under the true owner: s.12(4).
586   s.12(5).
587   See s.12(3)(b) (see above, para.33-097).
588   Sch.1 Pt II para.7 (see above, para.33-098).
589   s.13(2). A sale under the authority of the court "gives a good title to the purchaser as against the bailor".
590   The "court" includes the county court: s.13(3).
591   See Sch.1 Pt II (above, para.33-097).
592   For the requirements of selling under this section, see above, paras 33-095—33-099.
593   s.13(1).

(e) Innkeepers[594]

33-101 **Definition of an inn** By the Hotel Proprietors Act 1956,[595] only a hotel within the definition contained in the Act is an inn. By the Act[596] an "'hotel' means an establishment held out[597] by the proprietor as offering food, drink and, if so required, sleeping accommodation, without special contract, to any traveller presenting himself who appears able and willing to pay a reasonable sum for the services and facilities provided and who is in a fit state to be received".[598] This definition excludes establishments which had at common law been held not to be inns e.g. lodging houses,[599] boarding houses,[600] private residential hotels,[601] alehouses (i.e. "public houses" where there is no obligation to receive and entertain guests),[602] houses of public entertainment,[603] or restaurants.[604] A "tavern" and a "coffeehouse" may, however, fall within the statutory definition of an hotel,[605] and so may a temperance hotel.[606] The name by which premises are designated is not conclusive: the important matter is the use to which they are applied.[607] By s.1(1) of the Act, the duties, liabilities and rights which immediately before the commencement of the Act (viz January 1, 1957) by law attached to an innkeeper as such attach, subject to the provisions of the Act, to the proprietor of an hotel within the statutory definition and do not attach to any other person. If a limited company is the proprietor of an hotel, the company is the innkeeper, even though a manager conducts the affairs of the hotel and holds the licence for the sale of intoxicating liquors in the hotel.[608]

---

[594] See Palmer at Ch.27. The Member States of the Council of Europe have agreed certain minimum rules relevant to the liability of hotel-keepers: see the convention on the liability of hotel-keepers concerning the property of their guests (December 17, 1962) ratified by the United Kingdom on July 12, 1963. The convention entered into force on February 15, 1967 (Cmnd.3205: *Treaty Series No.9*, 1967) but although its provisions bind the United Kingdom, they are not part of English municipal law.

[595] s.1(1). The Act implemented the *Law Reform Committee's Second Report (on Innkeepers' Liability)*, Cmnd.9161 (1954). The statutory definition supersedes many judicial statements attempting to define an inn.

[596] s.1(3).

[597] A sign is not essential for an inn: *R. v Collins* (1623) Palm. 373; *Parker v Flin* (1703) 12 Mod. 254.

[598] At common law the innkeeper was also bound to receive all travellers, and was not permitted to discriminate between them: *Browne v Brandt* [1902] 1 K.B. 696, 698. cf. *Lamond v Richard* [1897] 1 Q.B. 541, 545.

[599] *Parker v Flint*, above; *Thompson v Lacy* (1820) 3 B. & Ald. 283, 287.

[600] *Dansey v Richardson* (1854) 3 El. & Bl. 144. cf. *Holder v Soulby* (1860) 8 C.B.(N.S.) 254, 266; *Scarborough v Cosgrove* [1905] 2 K.B. 805. cf. also *R. v Jones* [1898] 1 Q.B. 119, 159.

[601] *Duke of Devonshire v Simmons* (1894) 11 T.L.R. 52, 53. cf. *Olley v Marlborough Court Ltd* [1949] 1 K.B. 532.

[602] *Pidgeon v Legge* (1857) 21 J.P. 743; *Sealey v Tandy* [1902] 1 K.B. 296, 299. A bar or shop for the sale of spirits is not an inn even where it is under the same roof as an inn, if it is separate from the inn and has a separate entrance: *R. v Rymer* (1877) 2 Q.B.D. 136.

[603] cf. *Webb v Fagotti Brothers* (1898) 79 L.T. 683, 684.

[604] cf. *Ultzen v Nicols* [1894] 1 Q.B. 92; *Orchard v Bush & Co* [1898] 2 Q.B. 284.

[605] *Thompson v Lacy* (1820) 3 B. & Ald. 283. cf. *Doe D Pitt v Laming* (1814) 4 Camp. 73, 77; *Fitz v Iles* [1893] 1 Ch. 77.

[606] *Cunningham v Philp* (1896) 12 T.L.R. 352.

[607] *Thompson v Lacy*, above, at 286.

[608] *Dixon v Birch* (1873) L.R. 8 Ex. 135.

Duty to receive guests At common law an innkeeper is obliged to receive and lodge in his inn all travellers who come to him, and to entertain them at reasonable prices, unless he has a reasonable ground for refusal.[609] **33-102**

Liability for goods of guests Subject to certain exceptions and limitations,[610] the proprietor of an hotel in his capacity as an innkeeper[611] is strictly liable to his guests for the loss of[612] or damage to[613] the property of the guest within the hospitium of the inn. The liability of the innkeeper is strict in that he is liable even in the absence of proof of negligence on his part or on the part of his employees[614]; nor does the fact that he was sick or insane at the time of the loss or damage exclude his liability.[615] The liability is only strict, however, and not absolute, since there are certain defences available to the innkeeper[616] and he may, subject to certain conditions, limit the amount of his liability.[617] This strict liability of the innkeeper depends on common law and the custom of the realm[618] as modified by statute; it does not necessarily depend upon contract, bailment or pledge.[619] The innkeeper is almost an insurer of the goods of his guest[620] in that, apart from the specified defences, he is liable even for unexplained loss of or damage to the goods.[621] An innkeeper cannot contract out of his strict liability by special agreement,[622] nor can he escape liability by informing the guest that he will not be responsible for goods not placed under lock and key,[623] or that there are persons in the inn whose character he does not know so that the guest should lock his goods in his room.[624] **33-103**

Extension of liability to cover damage to the goods The Hotel Proprietors Act 1956 extended the common law liability of the innkeeper for loss of his guests' **33-104**

---

[609] *Constantine v Imperial Hotels Ltd* [1944] K.B. 693. See also *Browne v Brandt* [1902] 1 K.B. 696; *Thompson v McKenzie* [1908] 1 K.B. 905; *R. v Higgins* [1948] 1 K.B. 165. For full details of the innkeeper's liability to receive guests, see *Halsbury's Laws of England*, 5th edn, Vol.68, paras 650–675. For more general duties applicable see s.29 of the Equality Act 2010 and Pt II of the Supply of Goods and Services Act 1982 (above, paras 33-044—33-048) will also apply.

[610] See below, paras 33-110—33-114.

[611] See above, para.33-101.

[612] *Resolution of Judges* (1624) Hut. 99; *Squire v Wheeler* (1867) 16 L.T. 93. "Loss" includes theft of the goods: *Reniger v Fogossa* (1552) Plowd. 1, 9; *Robins & Co v Gray* [1895] 2 Q.B. 501, 504. "Loss" does not include loss by accidental fire: *Williams v Owen* [1955] 1 W.L.R. 1293, 1297–1298 (applying the Fires Prevention (Metropolis) Act 1774 s.86, to limit the liability of an innkeeper).

[613] Hotel Proprietors Act 1956 s.1(2). See below, para.33-104.

[614] *Shacklock v Ethorpe Ltd* [1939] 3 All E.R. 372, HL. See also *Morgan v Ravey* (1861) 6 H. & N. 265; *Squire v Wheeler* (1867) 16 L.T. 93; *Cunningham v Philp* (1896) 12 T.L.R. 352; *Butler & Co Ltd v Quilter* (1900) 17 T.L.R. 159.

[615] *Cross v Andrews* (1597) Cro. Eliz. 622.

[616] See below, paras 33-109—33-114.

[617] See below, paras 33-110—33-111.

[618] *Calye's* case (1583) 8 Co. Rep. 32a; *Kent v Shuckard* (1831) 2 B. & Ad. 803, 804; *Robins & Co v Gray*, above, at 503–505; *Shacklock v Ethorpe Ltd*, above, at 373; 1 Smith's L.C., 13th edn, 120. See also Winfield, *Province of the Law of Tort*, pp.57, 59–62.

[619] See n.618 above.

[620] *Bather v Day* (1863) 32 L.J. Ex. 171, 173; *Squire v Wheeler*, above.

[621] *Morgan v Ravey*, above; *Winkworth v Raven* [1931] 1 K.B. 652, 657–659.

[622] *Williams v Linnitt* [1951] 1 K.B. 565, 584–585; *Burns v Royal Hotel (St Andrews) Ltd*, 1957 S.L.T. 53, 56.

[623] *Harland's Case* (1641) Clay. 97.

[624] *Anon.* (1566) Moore K.B. 78.

goods by providing[625] that he is under the same liability to make good to any guest of any damage to property brought to the hotel as he would be under to make good the loss of any such property. Before the Act, there was some doubt whether the innkeeper was liable for damage to goods as distinct from loss of the goods.[626]

33-105 **Conditions necessary for strict liability** For the innkeeper to come under strict liability for loss of or damage to his guests' property, six conditions must be satisfied:

(1) it must be an "inn" within the statutory definition[627];
(2) the guest must be a traveller who has been received at the inn[628];
(3) the guest must have engaged sleeping accommodation at the inn[629];
(4) the loss or damage must occur within a specified period of time[630];
(5) the property of the guest which is lost or damaged must fall within the category to which strict liability relates[631];
(6) the property must, at the time of the loss or damage, be within the hospitium of the inn.[632]

The first of these conditions has already been discussed[633]; the others will be discussed in the succeeding paragraphs.

33-106 **Who is a guest?** A traveller becomes a guest only when the innkeeper accepts him as such[634]; even if the traveller is wrongfully refused accommodation[635] he is still not a guest. For strict liability to arise, the traveller must engage sleeping accommodation,[636] but the term "traveller" or "guest" does not include everyone who sleeps at the inn, since it excludes the innkeeper's family, his employees, his private guests and his lodgers.[637] If a person is refused accommodation, and then, without the permission of the innkeeper, another guest permits him to share a bedroom, he is not a guest.[638] A guest continues to be a guest even if he remains at the hotel for some considerable time,[639] even for months,[640] provided nothing occurs to alter his

---

[625] s.1(2).

[626] *Winkworth v Raven*, above, at 657 (followed in *Williams v Owen* [1955] 1 W.L.R. 1293, 1297).

[627] See above, para.33-101.

[628] See below, para.33-106.

[629] See below, para.33-107.

[630] See below, para.33-107.

[631] See below, para.33-108.

[632] See below, para.33-109.

[633] See above, para.33-101.

[634] *White's case* (1557) 2 Dyer 158b. cf. *Grant v Cardiff Hotels Co Ltd* (1921) 37 T.L.R. 775 (some retrospective operation given to the acceptance of a guest: see the Hotel Proprietors Act 1956 s.2(1)(b)).

[635] See above, para.33-102.

[636] See below, para.33-107.

[637] *Williams v Linnitt* [1951] 1 K.B. 565, 579. See also *Calye's case* (1583) 8 Co. Rep. 32a.

[638] *White's case*, above.

[639] In old law, a traveller ceased to be a guest if he stayed more than three days: *Calye's case*, above (overruled on this point in *Harland's case* (1641) Clay. 97 (14 days)). See now *Thompson v Lacy* (1820) 3 B. & Ald. 283 (83 days); *Chesham Automobile Supply Co Ltd v Beresford Hotel (Birchington) Ltd* (1913) 29 T.L.R. 584.

[640] *Allen v Smith* (1862) 12 C.B.(N.S.) 638 (seven months); *Hanley v Bethell Hotels Ltd* (1917) 52 I.L.T. 10.

status as a guest.[641] The mere length of his stay is only one of the circumstances to be taken into consideration when deciding whether he is still a guest.[642] If the guest makes an agreement for board at the inn for a considerable period, such as three months, he will probably be held to be a boarder, and not a guest.[643] It is a question of fact when a person ceases to be a guest[644]; once a person ceases to be a guest he may be given reasonable notice to leave the inn.[645] The guest need not be physically within the inn at the time when his goods are lost or damaged,[646] but if he is away for several days, he will not be a guest during that period, even though his goods remain at the inn.[647] A person may be a guest although a third person is to pay the innkeeper[648]; thus, in some cases the innkeeper's liability does not depend on the existence of a contractual relationship with the guest.

Statutory conditions for strict liability   The Hotel Proprietors Act 1956 alters **33-107** the strict liability of the innkeeper at common law by excluding his liability towards a traveller who seeks only temporary refreshment and not sleeping accommodation[649] and by limiting his liability to loss or damage occurring during a specified period. It is provided by the Act[650] that without prejudice to any other liability[651] incurred by him with respect to any property brought to the hotel, the proprietor of an hotel shall not be liable as an innkeeper to make good to any traveller any loss of or damage to such property except where: (a) at the time of the loss or damage sleeping accommodation at the hotel had been engaged for the traveller[652]; and (b) the loss or damage occurred during the period commencing with the midnight immediately preceding, and ending with the midnight immediately following a period for which the traveller was a guest at the hotel and entitled to use the accommodation so engaged.

Property to which strict liability relates   The Hotel Proprietors Act 1956[653] **33-108** provides that without prejudice to any other liability[654] or right of his with respect thereto, the proprietor of an hotel is not as an innkeeper liable to make good to any

---

[641] (1917) 52 I.L.T. 10.

[642] *Lamond v Richard* [1897] 1 Q.B. 541, 546.

[643] *Drope v Thaire* (1626) Lat. 126.

[644] *Portmand v Griffin* (1913) 29 T.L.R. 225 (payment of bill terminated the relationship). See the Hotel Proprietors Act 1956 s.2(1) (below, para.33-107).

[645] *Lamond v Richard*, above.

[646] See the notes to *White's* case (1557) 2 Dyer 158b (goods stolen while guest away for the day).

[647] See the Hotel Proprietors Act 1956 s.2(1) (see below, para.33-107); *Gelley v Clerk* (1606) Cro. Jac. 188. cf. *Allen v Smith* (1862) 12 C.B.(N.S.) 638.

[648] *Wright v Anderton* [1909] 1 K.B. 209. cf. *Cryan v Hotel Rembrandt Ltd* (1925) 133 L.T. 395.

[649] For the position at common law, see *Calye's* case (1583) 8 Co. Rep. 32a; *Bennett v Mellor* (1793) 5 Term Rep. 273; *Orchard v Bush* [1898] 2 Q.B. 284; *Williams v Linnitt* [1951] 1 K.B. 565.

[650] s.2(1).

[651] e.g. for negligence, or as a bailee. (See on the latter, *Williams v Gesse* (1837) 3 Bing.N.C. 849; *Adams (Durham) Ltd and Day v Trust Houses Ltd* [1960] 1 Lloyd's Rep. 380.)

[652] cf. *Strauss v County Hotel and Wine Co* (1883) 12 Q.B.D. 27 (plaintiff intended to sleep at an inn, but after receiving a telegram waiting for him at the inn decided not to stay; he left his baggage with the porter, and went to the refreshment room which was under the same management as the inn: held, he was not a guest at the inn).

[653] s.2(2). The innkeeper has no lien in regard to the property mentioned in this subsection: s.2(2). On his lien, see below, paras 33-115—33-118.

[654] e.g. for negligence, or as a bailee. (See above, para.33-107, n.651.) See also Pt II of the Supply of Goods and Services Act 1982 (see above, paras 33-044—33-048).

guest[655] of his any loss of or damage to any vehicle or any property left therein, or any horse or other live animal or its harness or other equipment. Subject to this exception, the innkeeper is strictly liable for the safety of all movables and moneys[656] brought by the guest into the inn; the category includes charters, or evidences concerning freeholds and inheritances, or obligations or other deeds or specialties, being things in action.[657] Where, however, goods are deposited in an inn for the purpose of being forwarded by a carrier, the innkeeper is not strictly liable.[658]

33-109   Hospitium of the inn   The innkeeper is strictly liable only where the goods of the guest are within the hospitium of the inn.[659] The hospitium of the inn consists in the buildings of the inn and the precincts so intimately related to those buildings as to be treated as forming part of them.[660] If the innkeeper invites his guests, whether expressly or by implication, to place any of his goods outside the inn, he is treating that place as within the hospitium and so will be liable if the goods are lost or damaged there.[661] But mere permission, not amounting to an invitation, given by an innkeeper to leave a chattel in such a place will not extend the hospitium of the inn to it.[662] Stable buildings and garages attached to the inn, car parks, inner courts enclosed by the walls of the inn[663] and a yard alongside the inn,[664] have been treated as within the hospitium of the inn. But a place which is not obviously attached to the inn premises, e.g. a petrol station runway, is not within the hospitium.[665] The test is whether the place is intended and suitable for use in connection with the innkeeper's business.[666] The Hotel Proprietors Act 1956[667] excludes strict liability for the kind of property most likely to be left outside the inn (e.g. vehicles or any property left therein), but it may still be necessary to determine the extent of the hospitium in the case of other chattels.[668]

33-110   Limitation of liability by means of a notice   Provided he displays a statutory notice,[669] the proprietor of an hotel, in his capacity as innkeeper,[670] may limit his

---

[655] On the term "guest", see above, para.33-106.

[656] *Kent v Shuckard* (1831) 2 B. & Ad. 803; *Doorman v Jenkins* (1834) 2 A. & E. 256.

[657] *Calye's* case (1583) 8 Co. Rep. 32a; *Kent v Shuckard*, above, at 804, 805.

[658] *Williams v Gesse* (1837) 3 Bing.N.C. 849.

[659] *Williams v Linnitt* [1951] 1 K.B. 565, 580.

[660] [1951] 1 K.B. 565, 580.

[661] [1951] 1 K.B. 565 at 581. See also *Jones v Tyler* (1834) 1 A. & E. 522; *Aria v Bridge House Hotel (Staines) Ltd* (1927) 137 L.T. 299 (but see above, para.33-108 on vehicles); *Watson v People's Refreshment House Association Ltd* [1952] 1 K.B. 318, 322.

[662] *Watson v People's Refreshment House Association Ltd*, above, at 322. cf. *Gresham v Lyon* [1954] 1 W.L.R. 1100, 1104.

[663] *Williams v Linnitt*, above; *Gee, Walker and Slater Ltd v Friary Hotel (Derby) Ltd* (1949) 66 T.L.R. (Pt 1) 59.

[664] *Davies v Clarke* (1953) 103 L.J. 141.

[665] *Watson v People's Refreshment House Association Ltd*, above.

[666] *Williams v Linnitt*, above, at 580, 581; *Watson v People's Refreshment House Association Ltd*, above, at 323, 324.

[667] s.2(2). See above, para.33-108.

[668] If goods are lost or damaged outside the hospitium of the inn, the innkeeper may still be liable in negligence or under s.13 of the Supply of Goods and Services Act 1982 (see above, para.33-046) or possibly under s.49(1) of the Consumer Rights Act 2015.

[669] See below, para.33-111.

[670] See above, para.33-101.

liability to make good the loss of or damage to property brought to the hotel,[671] so that his liability to any one guest will not exceed £50 in respect of any one article, nor £100 in the aggregate, except where: (a) the property was stolen, lost or damaged through the default, neglect or wilful[672] act of the proprietor or some servant of his[673]; or (b) the property was deposited by or on behalf of the guest expressly for safe custody with the proprietor or some servant of his authorised, or appearing to be authorised, for the purpose[674] and, if so required by the proprietor or that servant, in a container fastened or sealed by the depositor; or (c) at a time after the guest had arrived at the hotel, the property in question was offered for deposit as aforesaid and the proprietor or his servant refused to receive it, or the guest or some other guest acting on his behalf wished so to offer the property in question but, through the default of the proprietor or a servant of his, was unable to do so.[675] The onus of proving the default, neglect or wilful act of the proprietor or his servant within exception (a) above, rests upon the guest.[676] For there to be an express deposit under exception (b) above, it must be shown that something was said or done to inform the innkeeper in a reasonable and intelligible manner that it was a deposit for safe custody[677]; it is insufficient merely to place a bag in the office without saying a word.[678]

Statutory notice   The limitation of liability under the statute does not apply to the   **33-111** proprietor of an hotel unless, at the time when the property in question was brought to the hotel, a copy of the notice set out in the Schedule to the Act printed in plain type was conspicuously displayed in a place where it could conveniently be read by his guests at or near the reception office or desk or, where there is no reception office or desk, at or near the main entrance to the hotel.[679] The innkeeper cannot rely on the statutory limitation of his liability unless the notice is properly exhibited[680]; an unintentional misprint, even the omission of one word, may exclude the limitation.[681]

Defences: negligence of the guest   The innkeeper is not liable for loss or dam-   **33-112**

---

[671] Hotel Proprietors Act 1956 s.2(3). The financial limits of £50 and £100 set in this subsection have *not* been increased in line with inflation.

[672] The word "wilful" does not qualify "default or neglect": *Behrens v Grenville Hotel (Bude) Ltd* (1925) 69 S.J. 346; *Belleville v Palatine Hotel and Buildings Co Ltd* (1944) 171 L.T. 363.

[673] See *Medawar v Grand Hotel Co* [1891] 2 Q.B. 11; *Belleville v Palatine Hotel and Buildings Co Ltd*, above; *Bonham-Carter v Hyde Park Hotel Ltd* (1948) 64 T.L.R. 177 *Olley v Marlborough Court Ltd* [1949] 1 K.B. 532. The reference to "servant" does not incorporate the common law doctrine of vicarious liability: *Kott v Gordon Hotels Ltd* [1968] 2 Lloyd's Rep. 228.

[674] *Behrens v Grenville Hotel (Bude) Ltd*, above. cf. *Moss v Russell* (1884) T.L.R. 13 ("boots" of hotel has no implied authority to receive goods for safe deposit).

[675] See n.671, above.

[676] *Whitehouse v Pickett* [1908] A.C. 357.

[677] [1908] A.C. 357 at 361. See also *Moss v Russell*, above; *O'Connor v Grand International Hotel Co* [1898] 2 Ir.R. 92. cf. *Cryan v Hotel Rembrandt Ltd* (1925) 133 L.T. 395.

[678] *Whitehouse v Pickett*, above.

[679] Hotel Proprietors Act 1956 s.2(3) proviso. On the sufficiency of notices under previous legislation (which was not identical with this proviso) see *Shacklock v Ethorpe Ltd* [1937] 4 All E.R. 672 (affirmed on another ground: [1939] 3 All E.R. 372); *Carey v Long's Hotel Co Ltd* (1891) 7 T.L.R. 213; affirming 6 T.L.R. 415.

[680] *Hodgson v Ford & Sons* (1892) 8 T.L.R. 722.

[681] *Spice v Bacon* (1877) 2 Ex. D. 463 (decided under the Innkeepers' Liability Act 1863 ss.1, 3 (now repealed); the notice to be exhibited under the 1956 Act is not identical with that which was required by the 1863 Act).

age to his guests' property if he can show that the loss or damage was due to the negligence or misconduct[682] of the guest or his employee.[683] Gross negligence need not be proved,[684] but the onus of proving negligence is upon the innkeeper.[685] Negligence in a guest has been defined for this purpose as the absence of "the ordinary care that a prudent man may be reasonably expected to take under the circumstances"[686]; the negligence must be such as to render likely the loss of the property.[687] The decisions seem to show that the mere fact of a guest omitting to lock the door of the bedroom or other apartment which he occupies at an inn or hotel is not necessarily enough, of itself, to raise a presumption of negligence sufficient to avoid the liability of the innkeeper,[688] even though there may have been a notice in the room requiring the occupant to lock the door.[689] But leaving open a window communicating with a balcony which gave access to several rooms, when coupled with a failure to lock the door and a prior display in a public room of a bag containing money, has been held sufficient to absolve an innkeeper from responsibility.[690] And it is carelessness conducing to the loss if a guest, after ostentatiously rolling up notes and letting people see him put them away in an ill-secured box, leaves the box in a public room.[691] In one case, even failure to act upon a notice in the room to the effect that "the proprietor will be happy to take charge of any valuables", was held to avoid the innkeeper's liability for loss.[692] A guest is not negligent in failing to discover whether a watch is kept to prevent strangers gaining access to bedrooms; he is entitled to assume that the innkeeper will take reasonable precautions in this regard.[693]

33-113 **Contributory negligence** It is an undecided point whether the negligence of the guest should be treated, in proper cases, as contributory negligence under the Law Reform (Contributory Negligence) Act 1945. Under the Act, "Where any person suffers damage as the result partly of his own fault and partly of the fault of any other person"[694] the damages recoverable may be reduced to such an extent as the court thinks just and equitable. It has been argued that the Act should apply to cases of strict liability upon the defendant, including innkeepers' liability.[695]

33-114 **Other defences** The innkeeper is not strictly liable when the guest chooses to

---

[682] e.g. theft by servant of the guest: *Calye's* case (1583) 8 Co. Rep. 32a; *Burgess v Clements* (1815) 4 M. & S. 306.

[683] *Calye's* case, above; *Cashill v Wright* (1856) 6 E. & B. 891; *Robins & Co v Gray* [1895] 2 Q.B. 501, 504. See also, in addition to the cases cited in nn.685–693, below, *Butler & Co v Quilter* (1900) 17 T.L.R. 159; *Hansen v Killick* [1925] Ir.R. 70.

[684] *Cashill v Wright*, above.

[685] *Cashill v Wright*, above; *Gee, Walker & Slater Ltd v Friary Hotel (Derby) Ltd* (1949) 66 T.L.R. (Pt 1) 59. cf. *Cross and Tapper on Evidence*, 12th edn (2010), p.127, n.54 (discussing *Medawar v Grand Hotel Co* [1891] 2 Q.B. 11).

[686] *Cashill v Wright*, above, at 900.

[687] *Armistead v Wilde* (1851) 17 Q.B. 261.

[688] *Filipowski v Merryweather* (1860) 2 F. & F. 285; *Shacklock v Ethorpe Ltd* [1939] 3 All E.R. 372; *Brewster v Drennan* [1945] 2 All E.R. 705. See also *Herbert v Markwell* (1881) 45 L.T. 649.

[689] *Morgan v Ravey* (1860) 2 F. & F. 283; *Carpenter v Haymarket Hotel Ltd* [1931] 1 K.B. 364.

[690] *Oppenheim v White Lion Hotel Co Ltd* (1871) L.R. 6 C.P. 515.

[691] *Armistead v Wilde*, above.

[692] *Jones v Jackson* (1873) 29 L.T. 399; but see *Huntly v Bedford Hotel Co* (1892) 56 J.P. 53; *Wright v Embassy Hotel* (1934) 39 S.J. 12.

[693] *Olley v Marlborough Court Ltd* [1949] 1 K.B. 532, 542, 548.

[694] s.1(1).

[695] Williams, *Joint Torts and Contributory Negligence* (1951), pp.207–209, 326, 327. Contributory negligence is available as a defence to a claim based on s.2(1) of the Misrepresentation Act 1967:

make himself exclusively responsible for the safety of his goods[696]; the guest must show an intention to relieve the innkeeper of all liability.[697] It depends on the facts whether the conduct of the guest indicates his assumption of entire responsibility for his own goods; thus the fact that a guest does not deposit an article at the office of the hotel, in accordance with a notice in his bedroom, does not amount to an exemption of the innkeeper's liability.[698] The common law also exempts the innkeeper from liability when the loss arises from an act of God or of alien enemies.[699] It has also been held that the Fires Prevention (Metropolis) Act 1774[700] limits the strict liability of an innkeeper, so that he is not liable for loss or damage caused to his guest's goods by an accidental fire, i.e. a fire which occurred without negligence on the part of the innkeeper or his employees.[701]

Lien of the innkeeper   An innkeeper[702] has at common law a general lien, for the unpaid amount of his bill, on all the chattels which the guest takes, in his capacity as guest,[703] into the hospitium of the inn.[704] The lien exists to cover the price of the guest's personal food and lodging while he is a guest[705]; it does not cover money lent to the guest by the innkeeper[706] nor money disbursed by the innkeeper on behalf of a guest.[707] The exercise of the lien is not limited to articles which the innkeeper receives in the inn as luggage,[708] but the lien has been held not to attach where the goods were merely sent to the guest for some particular purpose, as where a manufacturer sent in a piano to a professional pianist for him to play on during his stay.[709] The Hotel Proprietors Act 1956[710] provides that the proprietor of an hotel[711] has, as an innkeeper, no lien on any vehicle or any property left therein or any horse or other live animal or its harness or other equipment. This provision reverses, on their facts, many common law cases,[712] though they will remain authoritative on the general principles of an innkeeper's lien. As a result of this enactment, the lien now applies only to the property of the guest in respect of which the innkeeper is strictly

33-115

Gran Gelato v Richcliff (Group) Ltd [1992] Ch. 560; but not to a claim in deceit: *Standard Chartered Bank v Pakistan National Shipping Corp (Nos 2 and 4)* [2002] UKHL 43, [2003] 1 A.C. 959.

[696] *Farnworth v Packwood* (1816) 1 Stark. 249; *Richmond v Smith* (1828) 8 B. & C. 9.

[697] See n.696, above.

[698] *Carpenter v Haymarket Hotel Ltd* [1931] 1 K.B. 364. cf. the cases cited in n.689, above.

[699] *Morgan v Ravey* (1861) 6 H. & N. 265.

[700] s.86.

[701] *Williams v Owen* [1955] 1 W.L.R. 1293, 1297–1298.

[702] See above, para.33-101. The keeper of a lodging-house has no lien: *Aldis v Huxley* (1891) 12 S.R.(N.S.W.) 158; nor, in the absence of a special agreement, has the keeper of a livery-stable: *Wallace v Woodgate* (1824) Ry. & M. 193; or the trainer of a racehorse: *Ward v Fielden* [1985] C.L.Y. 2000.

[703] cf. *Binns v Pigot* (1840) 9 Car. & P. 208 (goods deposited at the inn by a person who was not a guest).

[704] See above, para.33-109.

[705] *Mulliner v Florence* (1878) 3 Q.B.D. 484. cf. *Smith v Dearlove* (1848) 6 C.B. 132.

[706] *Matsuda v Waldorf Hotel Co Ltd* (1911) 27 T.L.R. 153 (stolen railway tickets deposited as a security for money advanced by the innkeeper); *Chesham Automobile Supply Co Ltd v Beresford Hotel (Birchington) Ltd* (1913) 29 T.L.R. 584.

[707] *Chesham Automobile Supply Co Ltd v Beresford Hotel (Birchington) Ltd*, see above; cf. *Ferguson v Peterkin*, 1953 S.L.T. (Sh. Ct.) 91 (no lien for damage caused by the guest).

[708] *Marsh v Police Commissioner* [1945] K.B. 43.

[709] *Broadwood v Granara* (1854) 10 Ex. 417.

[710] s.2(2).

[711] See above, para.33-101.

[712] e.g. *Scarfe v Morgan* (1838) 4 M. & W. 270; *Chase v Westmore* (1816) 5 M. & S. 180; *Mulliner v Florence*, above, at 493; *Chesham Automobile Supply Co Ltd v Beresford Hotel (Birchington) Ltd*, above.

liable for loss or damage.[713] Even at common law, however, the innkeeper had no right to detain the person of his guest, or to strip off his clothes, to secure payment.[714] While the goods are detained under the lien, they are in the possession of the innkeeper as bailee, and he is no longer subject to the strict liability of an innkeeper[715]; according to the modern formulation of the bailee's liability, he will be required to take reasonable care of them.[716] In a nineteenth-century case,[717] where the innkeeper locked up the guest's clothes in a cupboard where his own goods of a similar character were kept, and the guest's clothes were damaged by moths and rats, the innkeeper was held to be not liable. The cost of storing the goods during the lien cannot be claimed by the innkeeper, since the detention is for his benefit.[718]

33-116 **Goods not owned by the guest**   The lien covers all the chattels brought in by the guest, provided the innkeeper accepts them as part of the guest's luggage, even though the chattels do not belong to the guest,[719] or the owner has not consented to their being taken into the inn.[720] The fact that the innkeeper knows that a third person owns the chattels does not prevent the lien, so long as the innkeeper accepted them as part of the chattels accompanying the guest.[721] The lien of the innkeeper prevails over the rights of the true owner in these circumstances, even if the goods were hired[722]; if the innkeeper did not know of the facts, the lien even covers goods which had been stolen or wrongfully obtained.[723] Where a husband and wife are guests, the lien for the food and lodging of both extends to the chattels of both which are brought into the inn, even though credit may be given solely to the husband, and the wife's luggage is her property.[724]

33-117 **Loss of lien**   The lien exists so long as the innkeeper retains possession of the goods.[725] If he allows the goods to be taken away before the guest pays his bill, and the guest returns on a subsequent occasion, the innkeeper cannot claim a lien in

---

713 See above, para.33-108.

714 *Sunbolf v Alford* (1838) 3 M. & W. 248. See also *R. v Stewart* (1895) 59 J.P. 650.

715 *Angus v McLachlan* (1883) 23 Ch. D. 330.

716 *Houghland v RR Low (Luxury Coaches) Ltd* [1962] 1 Q.B. 694, 698 (see above, para.33-008); see also s.13 of the Supply of Goods and Services Act 1982 and s.49(1) of the Consumer Rights Act 2015 (see above, paras 33-044—33-046).

717 See n.715, above.

718 *British Empire Shipping Co v Somes* (1858) E.B. & E. 353, 367; affirmed (1860) 8 H.L. Cas. 338. However it has since been held that the principle established in *Somes* is a "narrow one" which is of "doubtful status" outside of the context of artificer's liens and so on this basis it may not apply to an innkeeper, in which case an innkeeper may be entitled to recover the cost of storing the goods during the detention (*Metall Market OOO v Vitorio Shipping Co Ltd (The "Lehmann Timber")* [2013] EWCA Civ 650, [2014] Q.B. 760 at [122]). Where the innkeeper is held to be acting for his own benefit, then it is unlikely that the innkeeper will be entitled to make the charge, but the position may be otherwise where the guest has failed in breach of contract to remove his or her possessions from the inn.

719 *Robinson v Walter* (1617) 3 Bulst. 269; *Turrill v Crawley* (1849) 13 Q.B. 197; *Snead v Watkins* (1856) 26 L.J. C.P. 57. See also the cases cited in nn.720–722, below.

720 *Johnson v Hill* (1822) 3 Stark. 172.

721 *Robins & Co v Gray* [1895] 2 Q.B. 501 (sewing machines sent by employers to a commercial traveller for sale).

722 *Threfall v Borwick* (1875) L.R. 10 Q.B. 210; *Chesham Automobile Supply Co Ltd v Beresford Hotel (Birchington) Ltd* (1913) 29 T.L.R. 584.

723 *Mulliner v Florence* (1878) 3 Q.B.D. 484; *Gordon v Silber* (1890) 25 Q.B.D. 491; *Marsh v Police Commissioner* [1945] K.B. 43.

724 *Gordon v Silber*, above. cf. *Mulliner v Florence*, above, at 488.

725 *Jones v Thurloe* (1723) 8 Mod. 172; *Jacobs v Latour* (1828) 5 Bing. 130 (innkeeper allowed sheriff

regard to the former bill.[726] The relationship of innkeeper and guest has, however, been held to continue in some circumstances despite occasional absences of the guest,[727] so that the innkeeper's lien continues to apply in regard to the bill covering the whole period.[728] The innkeeper's lien is not necessarily waived by his taking security for the guest's bill, unless the taking of the security in the circumstances is inconsistent with the lien and destructive of it.[729]

Innkeeper's right of sale At common law an innkeeper has no right to sell the **33-118** property of a guest,[730] and this is so even where he is put to expense and inconvenience by keeping it,[731] but the Innkeepers Act 1878[732] allows the innkeeper[733] to sell by public auction any goods or chattels left or deposited with him by a guest indebted to him for board, lodging or keep of horses or other animals.[734] There is no power to sell until the goods have been left with him[735] for six weeks without the debt having been paid, nor until at least one month's notice of the intended sale has been given, in one London and one local newspaper, by an advertisement containing a description of the goods and the name of the owner if it is known.[736] Any surplus upon the sale, after payment of the debt, costs and expenses, must be paid to the guest upon demand.

It is not clear how far the powers of sale in ss.12 and 13 of the Torts (Interfer- **33-119** ence with Goods) Act 1977[737] would apply to an innkeeper. To the extent that he is holding the goods of his guest for safe-keeping, he would probably be a "bailee" within the terms of "goods in the possession or under the control of a bailee where—(a) the bailor is in breach of an obligation to take delivery of the goods"[738]; but if the innkeeper holds the goods under his lien,[739] it is very doubtful whether these words would apply to the situation.[740]

Liability of boarding-house keepers[741] Though strict liability for the safety of **33-120** a guest's property is imposed only in the case of an innkeeper who keeps an "inn"

---

[726] to seize the goods, and did not assert his lien); *Legg v Evans* (1840) 6 M. & W. 36; *Orchard v Rackstraw* (1850) 9 C.B. 698. cf. *Wallace v Woodgate* (1824) 1 Car. & P. 575 (goods fraudulently taken from innkeeper's custody, in order to destroy lien).

[726] *Jones v Thurloe*, above.

[727] See above, para.33-106.

[728] *Allen v Smith* (1862) 12 C.B.(N.S.) 638; affirmed (1863) 9 Jur.(N.S.) 1274.

[729] *Angus v McLachlan* (1883) 23 Ch. D. 330; *Matsuda v Waldorf Hotel Co Ltd* (1911) 27 T.L.R. 153.

[730] *Mulliner v Florence*, above, at 489.

[731] *Jones v Thurloe*, above.

[732] s.1.

[733] The Act refers to the landlord, proprietor, keeper or manager of any hotel, inn or licensed public-house, and so has a wider application than the "hotel proprietor" referred to in the Hotel Proprietors Act 1956 (above, para.33-101).

[734] The right of sale under this Act is unaffected by the statutory abolition of the innkeeper's lien in respect of certain property: see above, para.33-115.

[735] cf. *Chesham Automobile Supply Co Ltd v Beresford Hotel (Birchington) Ltd* (1913) 29 T.L.R. 584.

[736] s.1.

[737] Examined above, paras 33-095—33-100.

[738] s.12(1)(a). Sch.1 Pt I para.4(1) explicitly includes "possession of goods which he has held as custodian".

[739] See above, paras 33-115—33-117.

[740] ss.12 and 13 were particularly designed for goods not collected by their owners after repairs, valuations or appraisals, as well as custody, e.g. s.12(5)(b) entitles the bailee to deduct from the proceeds of sale "any sum payable *in respect of the goods*" (italics supplied), which is not relevant to the innkeeper's lien.

[741] See Palmer at Ch.28.

within the statutory definition,[742] a lodging-house or boarding-house keeper owes the lower duty of reasonable care[743]: he must take reasonable care of the property which his guests bring into his house.[744] In *Scarborough v Cosgrove*[745] a husband and wife took a room in the defendant's boarding-house. They told the defendant that they had property which they wished to keep under lock and key and asked for a second key to their room. This request was refused, and they were told that the key must be left in the door, to enable the defendant's employees to clean the room. They also asked for a key to the chest of drawers, but no key was given to them. Some of the plaintiff's jewellery was stolen by a fellow guest, and the Court of Appeal held that the defendant was liable since he had failed in his duty to take reasonable care. Romer L.J. said that the goods left in the room were not bailed to the defendant, but "seeing that the landlord carries on his business of a boarding-house keeper for reward, I think he is bound to carry on that business with reasonable care, having regard to the nature and normal conduct of the business as known to the guest or as represented to the guest by him".[746] Similarly, in *Olley v Marlborough Court Ltd*[747] the proprietors of a "residential" hotel were liable for their negligence in permitting the theft of articles from a guest's room. The custom was for residents to deposit the keys of their rooms on a keyboard when they went out. A stranger entered the hotel during the plaintiff's absence, took the key and stole the articles. It was held that the proprietors were negligent in permitting the keyboard to be unguarded.[748]

(f)   Pledge[749]

(i)   Pledge at Common Law

33-121   Definition of pledge   Although the Consumer Credit Act 1974 regulates many categories of pledge[750] the common law on pledges must first be examined, since it defines the concept of pledge or pawn used in the Act[751] and still applies to all pledges falling outside the Act. A pledge or pawn is "a bailment of goods[752] by a

---

[742] See above, para.33-101.

[743] At common law (see the following note) and under the term implied (in a contract to supply services in the course of a business) by s.13 of the Supply of Goods and Services Act 1982 and included in a contract between a trader and a consumer under s.49(1) of the Consumer Rights Act 2015 (see above, paras 33-044—33-046).

[744] *Scarborough v Cosgrove* [1905] 2 K.B. 805; *Paterson v Norris* (1914) 30 T.L.R. 393; *Caldecutt v Piesse* (1932) 49 T.L.R. 26; *Olley v Marlborough Court Ltd* [1949] 1 K.B. 532. A similar duty to take reasonable care lies upon the proprietors of a residential club: *Williams v Curzon Syndicate Ltd* (1919) 35 T.L.R. 475. On the distinction between a lodger and a tenant (to whom no such duty of care is owed) see *Appah v Parncliffe Investments Ltd* [1964] 1 W.L.R. 1064.

[745] See above.

[746] See n.743, above.

[747] See above.

[748] This case also concerned a notice purporting to exempt the proprietors from liability: see above, para.33-110.

[749] See generally Palmer and Hudson, "Pledge" in Palmer and McKendrick (eds), *Interests in Goods*, 2nd edn (1998), pp.621 et seq.

[750] See below, paras 33-137—33-144.

[751] See below, para.33-137, n.838.

[752] A pledge can be created only in respect of a chattel capable of delivery; thus there can be no pledge of a chose in action as such: *Harrold v Plenty* [1901] 2 Ch. 314, 316.

debtor to his creditor to be kept by him till the debt be discharged"[753]; the bailment is intended to be a security for some debt or engagement.[754] The general property in the goods pledged remains in the pledgor, but a special property in them passes to the pledgee in order that he may be able to sell the goods if his right to sell arises.[755] This "special property" is strictly only a right to possession of the goods[756] together with a power of sale upon default.[757] The special property is such that if a bailee accepts an object of value as security for a debt, the dishonest retaking of the object by the bailor is theft.[758]

Characteristics of pledge Sale upon default in payment of the debt is an incident   **33-122**
of pledge, whereas a lien gives merely a right to detain the goods until the debt is paid[759]; again, a pledge, unlike a lien,[760] is assignable, and may be taken in execution against the pledgee.[761] A mortgage of chattels or bill of sale differs from a pledge in that on a mortgage the property passes by assignment, subject to a right of redemption, while possession need not pass to the mortgagee.[762]

Delivery essential for pledge Delivery, either actual or constructive, of the   **33-123**
articles pledged in consideration of the debt or advance is essential for pledge.[763] Constructive delivery is sufficient where it is practically impossible to give physical possession (as in the case of bulky goods) or where the pledge remains in the possession of the pledgor for a special purpose[764]; the pledge may be legally delivered though it does not actually pass from the hands of the pledgor to those of the pledgee.[765] Delivery of a key of a warehouse in which goods are stored,[766] or the handing over of a delivery order directing a warehouseman to deliver goods

---

[753] Jones at p.118. See also *Coggs v Bernard* (1703) 2 Ld. Raym. 909, 913; *Donald v Suckling* (1866) L.R. 1 Q.B. 585, 594. The debt creates a personal liability to pay, irrespective of the pledge: *South Sea Co v Duncomb* (1731) 2 Str. 919; *Jones v Marshall* (1889) 24 Q.B.D. 269, 271.

[754] There must have been an intention to pledge the goods: *Marcq v Christie, Manson & Woods Ltd* [2003] EWCA Civ 731, [2004] Q.B. 286 at [41].

[755] *Ex p. Hubbard* (1886) 17 Q.B.D. 690, 698.

[756] Which entitles the pledgee to sue strangers who tortiously interfere with the goods: see below, para.33-133.

[757] *The Odessa* [1916] 1 A.C. 145, 158–159. See also *Halliday v Holgate* (1868) L.R. 3 Ex. 299, 302; *Attenborough & Son v Solomon* [1913] A.C. 76, 84. The pledgee may be under some fiduciary obligations towards the pledgor: see *Mathew v TM Sutton Ltd* [1994] 1 W.L.R. 1455 (see below, para.33-144, n.891; commented on by Palmer and Merkin [1994] All E.R. Annual Review 26–28).

[758] *Rose v Matt* [1951] 1 K.B. 810 (larceny under the law before the Theft Act 1968: see now ss.1 and 5(1) of that Act).

[759] *Yungraan v Briesemann* (1892) 67 L.T. 642. cf. above, paras 33-093, 33-115.

[760] *Donald v Suckling*, above, at 612.

[761] *Re Rollason* (1887) 34 Ch. D. 495. cf. Insolvency Act 1986 s.311(5).

[762] *Re Morritt* (1886) 18 Q.B.D. 222, 232, 234–235. A pledge is also distinguishable from an equitable mortgage (e.g. a pledgee has no right of foreclosure, since he has only a special property in the chattel): *Carter v Wake* (1877) 4 Ch. D. 605; *Re Richardson* (1885) 30 Ch. D. 396, 403.

[763] *Dublin City Distillery Ltd v Doherty* [1914] A.C. 823, 843; *Kum v Wah Tat Bank Ltd* [1971] 1 Lloyd's Rep. 439, PC. Thus there may be a pledge of bearer bonds (*Carter v Wake*, above), but not a chose in action such as shares (*Harrold v Plenty* [1901] 2 Ch. 314, 316). Apart from the Factors Act 1889 s.3, and the exceptional case of bills of lading (below, para.33-128) the delivery of a document of title to goods is insufficient for a pledge at common law, although a lien (without a power of sale) may arise.

[764] *Reeves v Capper* (1838) 5 Bing. N.C. 136; *Martin v Reid* (1862) 11 C.B.(N.S.) 730.

[765] *Barber v Meyerstein* (1866) L.R. 2 C.P. 38; (1870) L.R. 4 H.L. 317. On constructive delivery, see Stoljar (1958) 21 M.L.R. 27, 31 et seq.

[766] *Young v Lambert* (1870) L.R. 3 P.C. 142; *Hilton v Tucker* (1888) 39 Ch. D. 669. See also *Ward v Turner* (1752) 2 Ves. Sen. 431, 443. However, the delivery of a pin code may not suffice to constitute

to the pledgee (followed by the warehouseman's acknowledgment of the delivery order)[767] may be sufficient in law to form constructive delivery. But where the goods are in the possession of a third person, such as a warehouseman, the latter must attorn to the pledgee in order for possession to pass to the pledgee.[768]

33-124   In pledge, it is not essential that the advance and the delivery should be contemporaneous. It is sufficient if possession is delivered within a reasonable time of the advance, in pursuance of the contract to pledge.[769] Redelivery of the goods to the pledgor for a limited purpose and on the understanding that the pledge is to continue, does not destroy the pledge.[770]

33-125   **Bills of Sale Acts**   If a document is signed which gives the terms of the pledge, this is not a bill of sale under the Bills of Sale Acts 1878 and 1882, since the document is not a transfer of title nor a licence to take possession of goods; it is the delivery of possession which distinguishes the pledge from a mortgage or bill of sale.[771] Where, however, the document is essential to the proof of the creditor's right to possession of the goods, because there has been no delivery to complete a pledge, it is a bill of sale within the Acts, and requires registration.[772] In deciding whether a transaction is one to which the Acts apply the court should look not merely at the documents but at the real nature of the transaction.[773] A delivery order, addressed to a warehouseman who holds the goods, is not a bill of sale, since it is merely a step in the transfer of possession to the pledgee.[774]

33-126   **Pledge of negotiable instrument**   Where a pledgor pledges a negotiable instrument[775] to which he has no title or in which he has only a limited interest, but the pledgee receives it for value and in good faith, the pledgee becomes an innocent holder for value; the pledgee's right to the negotiable instrument will then prevail against the true owner despite the pledgor's lack of title.[776] Thus in *London Joint*

---

delivery: *MSC Mediterranean Shipping Co SA v Glencore International AG* [2017] EWCA Civ 365, [2017] 2 Lloyd's Rep. 186 at [25]–[42].

[767] *Grigg v National Guardian Assurance Co* [1891] 3 Ch. 206. But the goods must be ascertained: *Re London Wine Co (Shippers) Ltd* [1986] P.C.C. 121.

[768] *Madras Official Assignee v Mercantile Bank of India Ltd* [1935] A.C. 53, 58–59; *Impala Warehousing and Logistics (Shanghai) Co Ltd v Wanxiang Resources (Singapore) Pte Ltd* [2015] EWHC 811 (Comm), [2015] 2 All E.R. (Comm) 234 at [54]–[59]. But the Privy Council has held that delivery under a contract of pledge to a bank is completed when the goods are shipped under a mate's receipt naming the bank as consignee: *Kum v Wah Tat Bank Ltd* [1971] 1 Lloyd's Rep. 439. cf. above, para.33-030, see below, para.44-015, n.82, para.44-254.

[769] *Hilton v Tucker*, above; *Reeves v Capper*, above.

[770] *North Western Bank Ltd v John Poynter, Son & Macdonalds* [1895] A.C. 56; *Re David Allester Ltd* [1922] 2 Ch. 211; *Lloyds Bank Ltd v Bank of America National Trust and Savings Association* [1938] 2 K.B. 147 (see below, para.34-544). On "trust receipts", see below and *Benjamin's Sale of Goods*, 10th edn (2017), paras 7-033, 18-286—18-290.

[771] *Ex p. Hubbard* (1886) 17 Q.B.D. 690; *Charlesworth v Mills* [1892] A.C. 231. See also *Re David Allester Ltd*, above.

[772] *Dublin City Distillery Ltd v Doherty* [1914] A.C. 823; *Re David Allester Ltd*, above; *Madras Official Assignee v Mercantile Bank of India Ltd*, above. See also below, para.34-543; and Diamond (1960) 23 M.L.R. 399.

[773] *Dublin City Distillery Ltd v Doherty*, above, at 848; *Madras Official Assignee v Mercantile Bank of India Ltd*, above, at 58. See also below, paras 39-519—39-528.

[774] *Grigg v National Guardian Assurance Co* [1891] 3 Ch. 206. cf. s.29(4) of the Sale of Goods Act 1979 (below, para.44-254).

[775] See below, paras 34-001 et seq.

[776] *London Joint Stock Bank v Simmons* [1892] A.C. 201; followed in *Fuller v Glyn, Mills, Currie &*

for his debt, retaining the pledge as a security.[801] But if a time for payment has not been agreed upon, or if the time agreed upon has been extended indefinitely, the pledgee cannot sell the pledge until after demand for payment and notice of his intention to sell.[802] The pledgee must take care that it is a provident sale.[803] At common law, he sells by virtue of an implied authority from the pledgor and for the benefit of both parties; hence he must, after deducting his debt, account to the pledgor for any surplus of the proceeds of the sale.[804] If, however, the proceeds of the sale do not satisfy the debt, the pledgor is still personally liable for the deficit.[805]

Statutory powers of sale   The wide powers of sale conferred on bailees by ss.12 and 13 of the Torts (Interference with Goods) Act 1977 were not designed with pledges in mind,[806] but they could be construed as wide enough to include pledges.[807] The statutory powers were examined earlier in this chapter[808]; the procedure under s.13, which empowers a bailee to apply to the court to authorise a sale, may be especially useful to a pledgee.[809] There is a special statutory procedure for the sale of a pawn.[810]   **33-132**

Other powers of the pledgee   Until repayment, the pledgee is, by virtue of his possession and his immediate right to possession of the thing pledged, the only person who may sue a stranger for trespass or conversion[811]; where the pledgee is deprived of possession by the tortious act of a stranger, the measure of damages recoverable by the pledgee is the full market value of the thing at the time when and the place where he should have obtained possession.[812] (The tortfeasor cannot take advantage of the pledgee's liability, upon his receiving that value, to account to the pledgor (or another) for any amount exceeding the pledgee's interest.[813]) The pledgee may assign or sub-pledge to a third person his special property or interest in the thing pledged[814]; such a transfer is lawful only if it purports to transfer no   **33-133**

---

[801]   *South Sea Co v Duncomb* (1731) 2 Str. 919; *Lawton v Newland* (1817) 2 Stark. 72.

[802]   *Pigot v Cubley*, above; *France v Clark* (1883) 22 Ch. D. 830; 26 Ch. D. 257; *Burdick v Sewell* (1883) 10 Q.B.D. 363, 367; (1884) 10 App. Cas. 74; see *Re Morritt*, above; and *The Ningchow*, above. The pledgor may redeem at any time up to the actual sale: *Re Morritt*, above, at 232; *France v Clark*, above.

[803]   cf. s.121(6) and (7) of the Consumer Credit Act 1974 (below, para.33-144).

[804]   *The Odessa* [1916] 1 A.C. 145, 159. cf. s.121(3) of the Consumer Credit Act 1974 (below, para.33-144, especially n.891).

[805]   *Jones v Marshall* (1889) 24 Q.B.D. 269 (extending this principle to the former "special contract" of pawn). cf. now s.121(4) of the Consumer Credit Act 1974 (below, para.33-144).

[806]   e.g. the categories in Sch.1 Pt I paras 2–4, do not include pledges.

[807]   cf. the submission made above, para.33-119, in the case of the innkeeper's lien.

[808]   See above, paras 33-095—33-100.

[809]   See above, para.33-100.

[810]   See below, para.33-144.

[811]   *Martin v Reid* (1862) 11 C.B.(N.S.) 730; *Broadbent v Varley* (1862) 12 C.B.(N.S.) 214. Under the common law, the pledgor need not be joined as claimant: *Saville v Tankred* (1748) 1 Ves. Sen. 101; and the measure of damages is the full value of the thing: *Swire v Leach* (1865) 18 C.B.(N.S.) 479. But for the statutory rules, see above, paras 33-010—33-022.

[812]   *Chabbra Corp Pte Ltd v Jag Shakti (Owners)* [1986] A.C. 337 (following *Swire v Leach* (1865) 18 C.B.(N.S.) 479; and *The Winkfield* [1902] P. 42). See above, para.33-024, n.113.

[813]   *The Jag Shakti*, above cf. see below, para.33-144, n.891.

[814]   *Donald v Suckling* (1866) L.R. 1 Q.B. 585, 614; *Halliday v Holgate* (1868) L.R. 3 Ex. 299.

more than the pledgee's interest in the thing, and the pledgee continues to be liable for reasonable care being taken for its safe custody.[815]

33-134 The right of the pledgee to use the thing pledged will depend upon the agreed terms of the pledge; in the absence of any express or implied term, there is old authority to the effect that the pledgee may not use it if it is something which will be the worse for such use, such as clothes,[816] but that he may, at his own risk, use a thing which will not be the worse for use.[817] If the keeping of the thing is an expense to the pledgee, such as a cow or horse, he may milk the cow or ride the horse in recompense for the keeping.[818] If during the pledge there is any increase in the value of the thing pledged, the pledgee is entitled to the increase as part of his security.[819]

33-135 **Unlawful dealing by the pledgee** If the pledgee deals with the thing pledged in an unlawful manner, such as by sale before the time fixed for repayment of the debt,[820] or by wrongfully claiming to be absolute owner of the thing,[821] the contract of pledge is not determined[822] and the pledgor cannot, without payment or tender of the debt, sue the pledgee for conversion.[823] But if the pledgee "deals with it in a manner other than is allowed by law for the payment of his debt, then, in so far as by disposing of the reversionary interest of the pledgor he causes to the pledgor any difficulty in obtaining possession of the pledge on payment of the sum due, and thereby does him any real damage, he commits a legal wrong against the pledgor".[824]

33-136 **Termination of pledge** By a bailment in pledge the pledgee impliedly undertakes to return the chattel to the pledgor upon payment of the debt.[825] Upon repayment, the contract of pledge is extinguished, and the pledgee is divested of his special property in the chattel.[826] The pledgor (or his personal representative)[827] may, by virtue of his general property in the thing pledged, and upon tender of the debt,[828]

---

[815] *Donald v Suckling*, above, at 615, 616. cf. *Nicholson v Hooper* (1838) 4 My. & Cr. 179. On the pledgee's liability if the thing is damaged in the hands of the third person, or if the pledgor is prejudiced by delay in redelivery of the thing after tender of the debt, see *Donald v Suckling*, above, at 618.

[816] *Mores v Conham* (1609) Owen 123.

[817] *Anon.* (1693) 2 Salk. 522.

[818] *Coggs v Bernard* (1703) 2 Ld. Raym. 909, 916, 917; Story at paras 329–331; Jones at p.81, n.38; Paton at pp.369, 370. cf. *Cooke v Haddon* (1862) 3 F. & F. 229.

[819] Story at para.292.

[820] Or a sub-pledge for a sum greater than that owed by the pledgor: *Donald v Suckling* (1866) L.R. 1 Q.B. 585. On an alleged custom for moneylenders to repledge, see *Sheffield v London Joint Stock Bank* (1888) 13 App. Cas. 333 (see also above, para.33-133).

[821] *Yungmann v Briesemann* (1892) 67 L.T. 642. But note that "Denial of title is not of itself conversion": s.11(3) of the Torts (Interference with Goods) Act 1977. (There must in addition be some dealing with the thing pledged.)

[822] Unless some special personal confidence is reposed in the pledgee: *Donald v Suckling*, above, at 615.

[823] *Donald v Suckling*, above, at 610, 616, 618; *Halliday v Holgate* (1868) L.R. 3 Ex. 299. cf. *Pigot v Cubley* (1864) 15 C.B.(N.S.) 701. (The pledgor's claim for specific recovery must follow the rules in s.3 of the Torts (Interference with Goods) Act 1977: see above, para.33-013).

[824] *Halliday v Holgate*, above, at 302. See also *Donald v Suckling*, above, at 611, 612, 618.

[825] *Singer Manufacturing Co v Clark* (1879) 5 Ex. D. 37.

[826] *Babcock v Lawson* (1880) 5 Q.B.D. 284.

[827] Under the Law Reform (Miscellaneous Provisions) Act 1934 s.1. In view of this Act, it is submitted that the decision in *Ratcliff v Davis* (1610) Yel. 178 is no longer good law on this point.

[828] *Coggs v Bernard* (1703) 2 Ld. Raym. 909, 917.

redeem it at any time[829] until the pledge is lawfully sold by the pledgee. If the debtor tenders the debt to the pledgee, but the pledgee refuses to deliver up the pledge, the pledgee's special property therein is determined, and the pledgor becomes entitled to the immediate possession of the thing pledged; the pledgee thereupon becomes liable for conversion[830] at the suit of the pledgor, or his assignee.[831] But apparently, even in such a case, the pledgee is entitled to deduct from the damages he must pay the amount of the debt.[832] If, after tender of the debt, the pledgee retains the thing pledged, he is strictly liable for its safety.[833]

(ii)   Statutory Control of Pledges

The Consumer Credit Act 1974   This Act replaced previous legislation on **33-137** pawnbrokers by ss.114–122, under the heading of "Pledges".[834] The general provisions of the Act are discussed below in Ch.39[835]; if a pledge of goods is given as security for a regulated consumer credit agreement or a regulated consumer hire agreement,[836] the agreement and the security are governed by these general provisions, in addition to the sections dealing specifically with pledges. It should be noted that the sections on pledges cover a wider range of transactions than are associated with the popular concept of "pawnbroking". Under the Act,[837] a person who takes any article in pawn[838] under "a regulated agreement",[839] must give to the person from whom he receives it a "pawn-receipt" in the prescribed form.[840] However, the obligation to give a pawn-receipt[841] and the other provisions of the

---

[829] After the pledgee's death, his personal representative is liable to return the pledge upon redemption: *Ratcliff v Davis*, above.

[830] *Coggs v Bernard*, above, at 917; *Donald v Suckling* (1866) L.R. 1 Q.B. 585, 610; *Yungmann v Briesemann* (1892) 67 L.T. 642. In a claim for conversion, the pledgor may seek an order for specific delivery of the chattel: see above, para.33-013. If ownership of the thing pledged is in dispute, a temporary refusal to return it, pending investigation, is justified: *Vaughan v Watt* (1840) 6 M. & W. 492. cf. *Clayton v Le Roy* [1911] 2 K.B. 1031, 1051. On the statutory rules applicable where third parties claim an interest in the chattel, see above, paras 33-015—33-016.

[831] *Franklin v Neate* (1844) 13 M. & W. 481.

[832] *Johnson v Stear* (1863) 15 C.B.(N.S.) 330; see also *Halliday v Holgate* (1868) L.R. 3 Ex. 299; *Yungmann v Briesemann*, above. cf. above, para.33-017.

[833] *Anon.* (1693) 2 Salk. 522 (goods stolen). cf. his liability during the period he is lawfully in possession: see above, para.33-129.

[834] On these sections generally, see Bennion, *Consumer Credit Control*, paras 8-200 et seq.; Guest, Encyclopedia of Consumer Credit Law, paras 2-115 et seq. For the application of the Regulations implementing the Consumer Credit Directive 2008 to pledges, see below, para.39-195.

[835] See below, paras 39-002 et seq.

[836] For definitions of these terms, see below, paras 39-017, 39-018, 39-035, 39-036.

[837] s.114(1).

[838] "Pawn" is defined by s.189(1) as "any article subject to a pledge"; "pledge" is defined as "the pawnee's rights over an article taken in pawn". These definitions appear to leave the meaning of "pledge" and "pawn" to be elucidated by the common law on the subject. (The extended meaning of pledge in s.1(5) of the Factors Act 1889 would not apply.)

[839] The definition of "a regulated agreement" is found in s.189(1) which in turn refers to s.15(2) and which is examined below paras 39-017, 39-036.

[840] "Prescribed" means prescribed by Regulations to be made by the Secretary of State: s.189(1). See the Consumer Credit (Pawn-Receipts) Regulations 1983 (SI 1983/1566), as amended by SI 2004/3236. If the pawn-receipt is not separate from the document embodying the regulated agreement, reg.4 of the Consumer Credit (Agreements) Regulations 1983 (SI 1983/1553, as amended, especially by SI 2004/1482) applies.

[841] s.114(1).

Act on pledges (ss.114–122) do not apply to two categories[842]: (a) a pledge of documents of title or of bearer bonds[843]; or (b) a non-commercial agreement.[844] It is submitted in Ch.39[845] that these sections do not apply to choses in action nor to deeds or certificates of title to land deposited with a creditor as security.

33-138 Prohibited transactions It is an offence for a person to take any article in pawn from an individual whom he knows to be, or who appears to be and is, a minor.[846] There are still various statutory prohibitions against pledges of particular items, e.g. naval, military and air force equipment, arms and stores,[847] and other special articles.[848]

33-139 Redemption period The Act lays down several tests for the period within which the debtor may redeem the pawn. First (and irrespective of the terms of the agreement between the parties)[849] the Act provides that a pawn is redeemable at any time within six months after it was taken.[850] Subject to this provision, a pawn is redeemable (secondly) within the period fixed by the parties for the duration of the credit secured by the pledge, or (thirdly) within such longer period as they may agree.[851] The longest of these three periods is "the redemption period", but if the pawn has not been redeemed by the end of the redemption period, it nevertheless (subject to one exception) remains redeemable until it is realised by the pawnee under the statutory procedure set out below[852]; the exception is where the property in the pawn passes to the pawnee in accordance with the provision dealing with a pawn securing a credit not exceeding £75.[853]

33-140 Redemption procedure On surrender of the pawn receipt, and payment of the amount owing, at any time when the pawn is redeemable, the pawnee must deliver the pawn to the bearer of the pawn-receipt[854] (except in the special situation discussed below).[855] If the pawnee delivers the pawn to the bearer of the pawn-receipt in accordance with this provision, he is not liable to any person in tort[856]; nor is the pawnee liable to any person in tort if he refuses to deliver it where the person demanding delivery does not surrender the pawn-receipt[857] or pay the amount owing, or in the special situation where "the pawnee knows or has reason-

---

842 s.114(3) (as amended by the Banking Act 1979 s.38(2)).
843 Documents of title are not defined in the Act. The common law definition is examined in *Benjamin's Sale of Goods*, 10th edn (2017), paras 18-006—18-010.
844 A "non-commercial agreement" is defined by s.189(1) as a consumer credit agreement or a consumer hire agreement not made by the creditor or owner in the course of a business carried on by him: a "business" includes a profession or trade. See below, para.39-049.
845 See below, para.39-194.
846 s.114(2).
847 The specific prohibitions have now been repealed but actions of this kind may now be caught by s.24 of the Armed Forces Act 2006.
848 e.g. Firearms Act 1968 s.3(6).
849 It is not possible to contract out of the provisions of s.116: see s.173. See *Wilson v Robertson (London) Ltd* [2005] EWHC 1425 (Ch), [2005] C.C.L.R. 6.
850 s.116(1).
851 s.116(2).
852 s.121 (below, para.33-144).
853 s.120(1)(a) (set out below, para.33-143).
854 s.117(1).
855 s.117(2), see below.
856 s.117(3). (cf. the previous law: *Singer Manufacturing Co v Clark* (1879) 5 Ex. D. 37.)
857 See below, para.33-142, for the procedure to be adopted where a pawn-receipt has been lost or

able cause to suspect that the bearer of the pawn-receipt is neither the owner of the pawn nor authorised by the owner to redeem it".[858] The pawnee is granted immunity only "in tort" in this special situation, which means that he could still be liable in contract.

It is provided[859] that no special charge may be made for redemption of a pawn **33-141** after the end of the redemption period,[860] and that charges in respect of the safe keeping of the pawn shall not be at a higher rate after the end of the redemption period than before. It is a criminal offence if a person who has taken a pawn under a regulated agreement[861] refuses without reasonable cause[862] to allow the pawn to be redeemed[863]; although the debtor is entitled to a contractual remedy against the pawnee in these circumstances, the criminal remedy may be more efficient since the court, upon conviction of the pawnee, may make an order for restitution to the debtor.[864]

Loss of pawn-receipt   The Act prescribes[865] the procedure to be adopted by a **33-142** person who is not in possession of the pawn-receipt but claims to be the owner of the pawn or to be otherwise entitled or authorised to redeem it. Such a claimant may redeem the pawn (at any time when it is redeemable) by tendering in place of the pawn-receipt, either (a) a statutory declaration made by the claimant in the prescribed form[866]; or (b) (when the pawn is security for a credit not exceeding £75,[867] and the pawnee agrees) a statement in writing in the prescribed form[868] signed by the claimant.[869] Such a declaration or statement is to be treated for the purpose of the redemption procedure[870] as if it were the pawn-receipt, and the pawn-receipt itself then becomes inoperative for that purpose.[871]

---

destroyed.
[858] s.117(2).
[859] s.116(4).
[860] For the definition of "the redemption period", see above, para.33-139.
[861] For the definition of this term, see below, paras 39-017, 39-036.
[862] By s.171(6) the burden is on the pawnee to prove that he had reasonable cause to refuse to allow the pawn to be redeemed.
[863] s.119(1).
[864] By s.119(2), the court may, upon the conviction of a pawnee under subs.(1), make an order for restitution under s.148 of the Powers of Criminal Courts (Sentencing) Act 2000, as if he had been convicted of theft. Under s.148, the court may order restitution of the goods themselves, or of other goods which directly or indirectly represent them, or may order payment of the value of the goods. (s.122 of the Consumer Credit Act 1974 provides for a court order in Scotland for delivery up of the pawn following a relevant conviction.)
[865] s.118.
[866] Consumer Credit (Loss of Pawn-Receipt) Regulations 1983 (SI 1983/1567) (made under s.189(1) of the 1974 Act).
[867] "Where the pawn is security for fixed-sum credit not exceeding £75 or running-account credit on which the credit limit does not exceed £75". (For definitions of the terms used in this provision, see below, para.33-143 nn.876–878). By s.181(1), the monetary limits in this provision may be amended by statutory instrument: the figure of £75 was fixed by the Consumer Credit (Further Increase of Monetary Amounts) Order 1998 (SI 1998/997).
[868] To be prescribed by Regulations: s.189(1). See n.840, above.
[869] s.118(1).
[870] s.117 (see above, para.33-140). (But s.117(2) still applies.)
[871] s.118(2). cf. *Burslem v Attenborough* (1873) L.R. 8 C.P. 122 (decided on ss.15 and 16 of the Pawnbrokers Act 1800 (now repealed)).

33-143 **Consequence of failure to redeem**   If at the end of the redemption period[872] (or in some cases[873] after the expiry of five days following the end of the redemption period), the pawn has not been redeemed, it becomes (with one exception) realisable by the pawnee.[874] The exceptional case is where the redemption period is six months, the pawn is security for fixed-sum credit[875] not exceeding £75 or running-account credit[876] on which the credit limit[877] does not exceed £75, and the pawn was not immediately before the making of the regulated consumer credit agreement a pawn under another regulated consumer credit agreement in respect of which the debtor has discharged his indebtedness in part[878]: at the end of the redemption period, the property in such a pawn passes to the pawnee.[879] The redemption period is extended for these purposes where the debtor is entitled to apply to the court for a time order[880]: if he is so entitled, the pawn becomes realisable (or the property is automatically vested in the pawnee, as the case may be) if after the expiry of five days following the end of the redemption period the pawn has not been redeemed.[881]

33-144 **Realisation of pawn**   When the pawn has become realisable by him,[882] the pawnee may sell it, after giving to the pawnor[883] not less than the prescribed[884] period (14 days) of notice[885] of intention to sell, indicating in the notice the asking price and such other particulars as may be prescribed.[886] Within the prescribed period (20 working days)[887] after the sale takes place, the pawnee must give the pawnor the prescribed information in writing as to the sale, its proceeds and expenses.[888] Where the net proceeds of sale[889] are not less than the sum which would have been payable for its redemption,[890] the debt secured by the pawn is discharged and any

---

[872] For the definition of this period, see ss.116, 189(1) (examined above, para.33-139).
[873] See below (s.120(2)).
[874] s.120(1). The procedure for realisation of the pawn is laid down by s.121 (see below, para.33-144). The question whether a default notice under s.87 must be served on the debtor (in addition to a notice of intention to sell under s.121(1) (see below, para.33-144)) is discussed in Guest, *Encyclopedia of Consumer Credit Law*, para.2-122.
[875] Defined by ss.10(1)(b), 189(1); see below, para.39-026.
[876] Defined by ss.10(1)(a), 189(1); see below, para.39-024.
[877] Defined by ss.10(2), 189(1); see below, para.39-025.
[878] Under s.94(3)
[879] s.120(1)(a). (By s.181(1) these monetary limits may be amended by statutory instrument: see n.867, above): the figure of £75 was fixed by the Consumer Credit (Further Increase of Monetary Amounts) Order 1998 (SI 1998/997).
[880] s.129 (discussed below, paras 39-202—39-205).
[881] s.120(2).
[882] By virtue of the provisions of s.120 (see above, para.33-143).
[883] Except in such cases as may be prescribed: s.121(1). Agreements where the credit or credit limit is not more than £100 are exempted by the Consumer Credit (Realisation of Pawn) Regulations 1983 (SI 1983/1568), as amended by SI 2004/3236: these Regulations also fix the periods stated in the text, and prescribe the information to be given in the notices. The figure of £100 was fixed by the Consumer Credit (Realisation of Pawn) (Amendment) Regulations 1998 (SI 1998/998).
[884] viz "prescribed by regulations made by the Secretary of State": s.189(1). See SI 1983/1568, as amended by SI 2004/3236.
[885] A "notice" is defined by s.189(1) as "notice in writing".
[886] s.121(1).
[887] To be prescribed by Regulations: s.189(1). See SI 1983/1568, as amended by SI 2004/3236.
[888] s.121(2).
[889] Defined as "the amount realised (the 'gross amount') less the expenses (if any) of the sale": s.121(5).
[890] Calculated as "if the pawn had been redeemed on the date of the sale": s.121(3).

surplus must be paid by the pawnee to the pawnor.[891] If the net proceeds are less than the sum payable for redemption,[892] the debt shall be treated as from the date of sale as equal to the amount by which the net proceeds of sale fall short of the sum which would have been payable for the redemption of the pawn on that date.[893] If the pawnor alleges that the gross amount realised on the sale of the pawn is less than the true market value of the pawn on the date of sale, it is for the pawnee to prove that he and any agents employed by him in the sale used reasonable care to ensure that the true market value was obtained[894]; if the pawnee fails to prove this, the references above to "the net proceeds of sale"[895] shall have effect as if "the true market value" were substituted for the gross amount realised on the sale.[896] If the pawnor alleges that the expenses of the sale were unreasonably high, it is for the pawnee to prove that they were reasonable, and if he fails to do so, the calculation of "the net proceeds of sale"[897] in the provisions above[898] shall have effect as if "reasonable expenses" were substituted for "expenses".[899] (Unlike the former law, the 1974 Act does not require the sale of the pawn to take place by auction.)

---

[891] s.121(3). The relationship between the parties being fiduciary in nature, the pawnbroker holds the surplus upon trust for the pawnor: the pawnor may therefore claim an award of interest in equity: *Mathew v TM Sutton Ltd* [1994] 1 W.L.R. 1455. The limitation period for a claim by the pawnor to the surplus will be six years from the sale: see Vol.I, para.28-002.

[892] viz "Where subs.(3) does not apply": s.121(4).

[893] s.121(4). (See the decision of *Jones v Marshall* (1889) 24 Q.B.D. 269 (on the former law: the Pawnbrokers Act 1872 did not affect the right of the pawnbroker at common law to recover the deficit if the sale of the article pawned realised less than the amount advanced on it).)

[894] s.121(6).

[895] Defined in s.121(5): see above, n.889.

[896] s.121(6).

[897] Defined in s.121(5): see above, n.889.

[898] s.121(3) and (4), see above.

[899] s.121(7).

CHAPTER 34

BILLS OF EXCHANGE AND BANKING

R. J. A. Hooley

1. NEGOTIABLE INSTRUMENTS

(a) The Nature of Negotiable Instruments

34-001 **The meaning of negotiability** The essential feature of negotiable instruments (which include bills of exchange, cheques and promissory notes) is that they can be transferred from person to person. The principles governing negotiable instruments differ from some of the fundamental principles of the law of contract. First, in a simple contract, the persons entitled to enforce it are either parties to the contract when it is made or, in certain cases, assignees.[1] In the case of a negotiable instrument, any "holder" (i.e. the payee or indorsee who is in possession of it or the bearer) can bring an action to enforce it.[2] There is, thus, a fundamental difference in the concept of privity. In a simple contract a privy or party is either a person who enters into the contract when it is made or an assignee. In the case of negotiable instruments any holder becomes a party. Secondly, although most contracts may be assigned, an assignee cannot sue without joining the assignor as a party unless certain requirements of form are satisfied and, in particular, notice must be given to the debtor.[3] A negotiable instrument, on the other hand, may be transferred by the payee or by any subsequent holder to a third party either—insofar as the instrument is payable to order—by indorsement (i.e. the holder's signature on the back of the instrument) and delivery, or—insofar as the instrument is payable to bearer—by mere delivery of the instrument to the third party.[4] No notice of the transfer need be given. Thirdly, when a contract is assigned, the assignee's rights

---

[1] See Vol.I, paras 19-001 et seq.
[2] See below, paras 34-092 et seq.
[3] See Vol.I, paras 19-017 et seq.
[4] See below, paras 34-085 et seq.

are usually subject to the equities between the debtor and the assignor.[5] In the case of negotiable instruments, a transferee obtains a right to enforce payment of the instrument, despite any defects in the title of or equities available to the transferor, provided the transferee is a "holder in due course". A holder in due course is a person who takes a negotiable instrument which is:

(a)   complete and regular on its face;
(b)   for value (i.e. consideration); and
(c)   in good faith, i.e. without notice of any defect in the title of the transferor.[6]

Thus, the rule *nemo dat quod non habet* applies to negotiable instruments subject to considerable modifications.

Negotiable instruments as choses in action and in possession   There is a further **34-002** fundamental distinction between simple contracts and negotiable instruments. The formation of a contract confers upon the parties thereto certain rights. These rights are not dependent upon the physical possession of the instrument in which the terms of the contract are recorded. They arise from the creation of the contract itself and are enforceable by action. Negotiable instruments, likewise, confer certain rights on the payee and the transferees, i.e. the procedural right to sue on the instrument and, in certain cases, the right to enforce payment. To this extent negotiable instruments resemble contracts.[7] However, in the case of negotiable instruments possession of the instrument itself is of importance. Usually a person who obtains the possession of a negotiable instrument becomes a "holder" and has a right to sue on it. Moreover, a person can have a title to a negotiable instrument and the concept of ownership, thus, applies.[8] Negotiable instruments may, therefore, be regarded as a special type of personal property. They differ from most types of chattel in that their possession confers certain contractual rights on the holder. But they differ from contracts by reason of the existence of proprietary elements.[9]

Practical use of negotiable instruments   The widespread use of electronic pay- **34-003** ment systems has reduced the significance of negotiable instruments in modern commercial practice.[10] Nevertheless, negotiable instruments are still used in international sales as well as in domestic trade. Foremost in international transactions is the bill of exchange, which is primarily used to facilitate the payment of the price of goods. The practice is for the seller to draw a bill of exchange on the buyer, to attach it to the documents relating to the shipment of the goods and to arrange through banking channels for the presentation of this "documentary bill" for payment and for acceptance. Of particular advantage to the seller is that in many cases

---

5   See Vol.I, para.19-071.
6   See below, paras 34-075 et seq.
7   cf. *R. v Duru* [1974] 1 W.L.R. 2, 8 (overruled in relation to s.15(1) of the Theft Act 1968 by *R. v Preddy* [1996] A.C. 815, 836–837). For an analysis of the contractual rights conferred by a negotiable instrument, see *Pollway Ltd v Abdullah* [1974] 1 W.L.R. 493, 496.
8   See, e.g. s.80 of the Bills of Exchange Act 1882, which refers to the "true owner" of a cheque. See *Citibank NA v Brown, Shipley & Co* [1991] 1 Lloyd's Rep. 576 (Waller J.); *Dextra Bank and Trust Co Ltd v Bank of Jamaica* [2002] 1 All E.R. (Comm) 193, PC (indicating a bailee can confer title on the "true owner").
9   e.g. it is possible to bring an action for conversion of a cheque and, by a "legal fiction", damages are based on the face value of the cheque rather than the value of the cheque as paper; on the other hand, the House of Lords has held (by a majority) that the tort of conversion does not cover the appropriation of choses in action: see *OBG Ltd v Allan* [2007] UKHL 21, [2008] 1 A.C. 1.
10   See below, paras 34-377 et seq.

the bank, or other financial institution engaged by him, may agree to discount the documentary bill or to make an advance against it. In modern times this advantage has led to a noticeable increase in the volume of "commercial bills" drawn under "acceptance credits", which are facilities used by banks to assist their customers in obtaining finance from third parties. To this end the issuing bank undertakes in the acceptance credit to accept and to pay at maturity bills of exchange drawn on it by the customer at a usance which is usually of 90 or 180 days' sight. The customer acquires the funds needed by discounting these bills, which attain their currency mainly on the basis of the bank's signature. The customer promises to furnish the amounts of the bills to the bank before their maturity. If he requires further credit to do so, he is asked to draw a fresh set of bills which are, again, accepted by the bank and discounted on the bills market. This procedure is known as a "roll over" of bills. The amount of the new bills usually reflects the finance charges involved in the roll-over exercise.[11]

34-004 Promissory notes Promissory notes are used in international trade to a limited extent, their main function being to serve as security for instalments due under transactions involving medium or long-term credit.[12] The popularity of promissory notes is greater in domestic trade, where, basically, they serve two functions. In the first place, promissory notes made by the debtor (or by the "hirer" of a lease or of a hire-purchase agreement) constitute a useful security. The dates of payment of the notes are usually made to coincide with the dates of the instalments provided for by the main contract. If the debtor or hirer falls in arrears, the creditor is able to bring an action to enforce the corresponding promissory note or notes. The advantage of such an action over an action based on the main contract is that, even if an action on a note is maintained by the original creditor or lessor, the debtor cannot plead certain defences concerned with the main contract.[13] For this reason, the taking of promissory notes has been precluded in respect of regulated consumer credit and consumer hire agreements by the Consumer Credit Act 1974.[14] In the second place, promissory notes executed by the debtor facilitate the refinancing of the transaction: the creditor can discount the promissory notes with a financial institution and, in this way, obtain credit against them well before the date of maturity. From the discounter's point of view, the transfer to him of promissory notes is more attractive than a mere assignment of the main contract. While a simple contract is assigned subject to the equities available to the debtor against the assignor, a transferee of a negotiable instrument, who attains the status of a holder in due course, is entitled to enforce the instrument despite defects in the title of previous parties. Subject to the limitations imposed by the Consumer Credit Act 1974,[15] promissory notes are the main negotiable instruments used as security for inland transactions.[16] Bills of exchange (other than cheques) are not common in domestic trade. Cheques, of course, are used to effect payment.

---

[11] See generally Robertson (1976) 3 Auckland L. Rev. 1; Ellinger (1978) 20 Malaya L. Rev. 84; E.P. Ellinger, E. Lomnicka and C.V.M. Hare, *Ellinger's Modern Banking Law*, 5th edn (2011), Ch.10, s.10.

[12] See, e.g. *Banque Cantonale de Genève v Sanomi* [2016] EWHC 3353 (Comm). Promissory notes are used in some transactions covered by export credit guarantees; see *Benjamin's Sale of Goods*, 10th edn (2017), Ch.25.

[13] See below, paras 34-094 et seq.

[14] ss.123, 124; see below, paras 34-007, 34-081 and 39-196.

[15] s.123(3), (4); below, paras 34-007, 34-081 and 39-196.

[16] See below, paras 34-190 et seq. discussing also NIFs.

The sources of the law of negotiable instruments   When a person wants to create a negotiable instrument, he must choose one of the forms recognised by law. Persons cannot, at will, create novel types of negotiable instruments. The negotiability of an instrument may be established either by statute[17] or by mercantile usage.[18] Such a usage must be notorious,[19] certain[20] and reasonable[21] and must further be a general usage, i.e. one recognised and adopted by the commercial world in general.[22] The usage need not be of long standing, but it must have prevailed for a sufficiently long period in order to achieve certainty and notoriety. Thus, the courts may give effect to mercantile usages which establish the validity of new kinds of negotiable instruments.   **34-005**

The Bills of Exchange Act 1882   The most important source of the law of negotiable instruments is the Bills of Exchange Act 1882. The Act is not, however, exhaustive and, by s.97(2), the rules of the common law, including the law merchant, continue to apply to bills of exchange, cheques and promissory notes, save insofar as these rules are inconsistent with the Act. Cases decided before the Act are, thus, not without importance. However, in *Bank of England v Vagliano Bros*[23] the House of Lords indicated that such decisions should be used as a source of construction only when the sections of the Act are ambiguous or their language technical. When the language of the Act is clear, there is, indeed, no need to refer to decisions predating it. Apart from cases of ambiguities in the Act, such decisions are also of importance as regards problems on which the Act is silent.   **34-006**

Effect of Consumer Credit Act 1974   The use of negotiable instruments in inland transactions involving individuals (including unincorporated traders) has been affected by the coming into force of specific provisions of the Consumer Credit Act 1974.[24] Section 123 restricts the use of negotiable instruments[25] in "regulated" consumer credit agreements and consumer hire agreements, other than in the case of non-commercial agreements, i.e. those not concluded in the course of a business carried on by the creditor or the lessor ("owner").[26] Subsection (1) prohibits the taking of a negotiable instrument other than a cheque in discharge of amounts   **34-007**

---

17   e.g. promissory notes, the validity of which was for the first time established in 1704 in 3 & 4 Anne, c.8.
18   *Goodwin v Robarts* (1875) L.R. 10 Ex. 337; *London Joint Stock Bank v Simmons* [1892] A.C. 201; *Venables v Baring Bros* [1892] 3 Ch. 527; *Bechuanaland Exploration Co v London Trading Bank* [1898] 2 Q.B. 658; *Edelstein v Schuler & Co* [1902] 2 K.B. 144.
19   *Tucker v Linger* (1883) 8 App. Cas. 508.
20   *Sewell v Corp* (1824) 1 C. & P. 392, 393; *Devonald v Rosser & Sons* [1906] 2 K.B. 728, 743.
21   *Paxton v Courtnay* (1860) 2 F & F 131; *Tucker v Linger*, above; *Gibbon v Pease* [1905] 1 K.B. 810.
22   *Easton v London Joint Stock Bank* (1886) 34 Ch. D. 95, 113; reversed on a different point sub nom. *Sheffield v London Joint Stock Bank* (1888) 13 App. Cas. 333.
23   [1891] A.C. 107, 120, 127, 144–145.
24   See below, paras 34-081, 39-196 and see E.P. Ellinger, E. Lomnicka and C.V.M. Hare, *Ellinger's Modern Banking Law*, 5th edn (2011), Ch.10, s.11.
25   The term "negotiable instrument" is not defined in the Act. It is therefore questionable whether a bill of exchange, a cheque, or a promissory note, the negotiability of which has been restricted in the manner prescribed by s.8 of the Bills of Exchange Act 1882 (discussed below, paras 34-026, 34-163) falls within the scope of ss.123–125 of the Consumer Credit Act 1974. See also below, paras 34-081 et seq.; for an exemption by order under s.123(6) respecting certain hire agreements which have a connection with a country outside the UK, see the Consumer Credit (Negotiable Instruments) (Exemption) Order 1984 (SI 1984/435).
26   "Consumer credit agreement" is defined in s.8 of the 1974 Act and in art.60B(3) of the Financial Services and Markets Act 2000 (Regulated Activities) Order 2001 (SI 2001/544) ("RAO") (below,

payable by the debtor or hirer, or by a surety.[27] Subsection (3) prohibits the taking of any negotiable instrument (including a cheque) as security for an amount payable under such an agreement.[28] A person who takes an instrument in contravention of these provisions is not entitled to enforce it.[29] While the owner or creditor may take a cheque in payment of an amount due to him under a regulated agreement, he is not allowed to negotiate it except to a banker.[30] The object of this last provision is to preclude the negotiation of a cheque to an assignee of a regulated agreement, or to a stranger to the transaction, who may seek to enforce the cheque notwithstanding disputes relating to the regulated agreement. Negotiation to a banker is permitted so as to provide for the clearing of the cheque.[31]

(b) Bills of Exchange[32]

(i) Definitions and Requirements

34-008 **Important definitions: "bill of exchange"** According to s.3(1) of the Act, a bill of exchange is an unconditional order in writing, addressed by one person to another, signed by the person giving it, requiring the person to whom it is addressed to pay on demand or at a fixed or determinable future time a sum certain in money to, or to the order of, a specified person or to bearer.[33] According to s.3(2) an instrument which does not comply with these conditions, or which requires an additional act to be done,[34] is not a bill of exchange. However, s.3(4) provides that a bill is not invalid if it is not dated,[35] or fails to specify the value given for it or the place at which it has been drawn or is to be payable.

---

[27] para.39-016); "consumer hire agreement" in s.15 of the 1974 Act and in art.60N(3) of the RAO (below, para.39-035); as regards "regulated" agreements, see ss.8(3) and 15(2) of the 1974 Act, and arts 60B and 60N of the RAO. "Non-commercial" agreement is defined in s.189(1).

[27] Defined in s.189(1); below, para.39-183.

[28] As to when a negotiable instrument is considered to have been taken by way of security, see s.123(4). But note exemption where a transaction involves the extension of credit respecting the supply of goods or services outside the UK: the Financial Services and Markets Act 2000 (Regulated Activities) Order 2001 (SI 2001/544) art.60C(8).

[29] s.125(1) (see below, para.34-082). The bill may nevertheless be enforced by a transferee (see below, para.34-082); but the creditor or owner has to indemnify the hirer, debtor or surety in respect of this liability: s.125(3).

[30] s.123(2). The use of the word "negotiation" is puzzling. Negotiation involves the transfer of the instrument and of the right to enforce it (below, para.34-085) and is not required where a cheque is remitted by the payee to a banker for collection purposes (below, para.34-361). It would have been more consistent with the policy of the Act to prohibit negotiation altogether and, to avoid doubt, to permit transfer to a bank for collection.

[31] The position of a holder of an instrument, made or negotiated in contravention of s.123, is discussed in the part of the chapter concerning the holder's rights; below, para.34-092.

[32] For detailed works on the subject, see *Chalmers and Guest on Bills of Exchange and Cheques*, 18th edn (2017); for the special aspects respecting the use of bills of exchange in international trade, see *Benjamin's Sale of Goods*, 10th edn (2017), Ch.22.

[33] In *Weir v National Westminster Bank*, 1944 S.L.T. 1251 it was held that a withdrawal form did not constitute a bill of exchange.

[34] e.g. requires the drawee to employ staff and to pay their salary: *Dickie v Singh*, 1974 S.L.T. (Notes) 3.

[35] *Aspinall's Club Ltd v Al-Zayat* [2007] EWCA Civ 1001 at [27] (Lloyd L.J.: "The fact that it is not dated does not prevent the payee from presenting it for payment immediately"). However, banking practice indicates that an undated cheque is not a valid payment instruction such that the bank is entitled to ignore it: *Griffiths v Dalton* [1940] 2 K.B. 264, 265, and R. Cranston, E. Avgouleas, K. van Zwieten, C. Hare and T. van Sante, *Principles of Banking Law*, 3rd edn (2018), p.376.

"Drawer", "drawee", "acceptor", "payee", "indorsor" and "holder"   The ele-   **34-009**
ments of the definition of s.3(1) will have to be discussed in detail, but before doing so it will be convenient to define a few other terms used in connection with bills
of exchange. First, the person who draws the bill is known as "the drawer".
Secondly, the person on whom the bill is drawn, i.e. the person to whom the
drawer's order is directed, is known as "the drawee". If the drawee agrees to comply
with the instruction of the drawer he may "accept" the bill. By doing so he promises
to honour the bill and becomes an "acceptor". Thirdly, the person to whose order
the bill is payable is known as the "payee". Fourthly, the payee, or any subsequent
transferee, may warrant that the bill will be duly honoured by signing his name at
the back of the bill. Such a signature is known as an "indorsement" and the person
so signing becomes an "indorser". Finally, the payee of a bill, who has its physical
possession, and any other person, who subsequently obtains its possession either
under an indorsement completed by delivery or—in the case of a bearer bill—by
mere delivery, is known as "the holder". If the holder has given value, i.e. consideration for the bill, he is a "holder for value".[36] If, in addition, he satisfies the requirements of s.29 of the Act, he is a "holder in due course".[37] It is important to
emphasise that a person cannot become a holder—let alone a holder for value or a
holder in due course—except insofar as he acquires the possession of the bill as
payee, as indorsee or as bearer. A person does not become a holder merely because
the object of the bill is to discharge a debt due to him. Thus, where a bill drawn for
the payment of a deposit due under a contract of sale is made payable to the order
of auctioneers, the vendor is not a holder[38]; but he can, of course, become the holder
of the bill, if it is indorsed and delivered to him by the auctioneers. The payee of a
bill becomes its holder even if, in reality, it is made out to his order and delivered
to him in his capacity as another person's agent.[39]

Unconditional order in writing   A bill of exchange must be an unconditional   **34-010**
order in writing.[40] "Written" includes "printed"[41] and, presumably, typewritten. The
order given by the drawer to the drawee need not be in any specified form, and it
is sufficient that the words used by the drawer constitute an unqualified order. An

---

[36]   The Act occasionally used inconsistent terminology, e.g. by referring to a "holder for value" as a
"holder who has taken for value" or a "holder who has given value"; see *Barclays Bank Ltd v Astley
Industrial Trust Ltd* [1970] 2 Q.B. 527, 538–539.

[37]   As regards the position of the drawer, see below, paras 34-029, 34-031, 34-114; as regards the
drawee, see below, para.34-029 and as regards the acceptor and acceptance, see below, paras 34-
113, 34-116; as regards the payee, see below, para.34-021; as regards indorsers and indorsements,
see below, paras 34-090—34-091, 34-116; as regards the position of a holder, see below, para.34-
095 (holder for value), below, para.34-093 (holder in due course), and below, paras 34-092—34-
099 (rights of holders).

[38]   *Pollway Ltd v Abdullah* [1974] 1 W.L.R. 493, 495.

[39]   *Silk Bros v Security Pacific National Bank* (1987) 72 A.L.R. 535, 538–539 Aust.

[40]   s.3(1). In *Banque Cantonale de Genève v Sanomi* [2016] EWHC 3353 (Comm) at [32]–[36], Blair
J., having been referred to the requirement in s.83(1) of the Act that a promissory note must be in
writing, held that there is a principle (admittedly, of uncertain scope) to the effect that oral evidence
is not admissible to contradict the terms of the written instrument.

[41]   s.2. The Bills of Exchange Act 1882 has not yet been altered pursuant to s.8 of the Electronic Communications Act 2000 to allow for the creation of electronic bills of exchange. The 1882 Act includes
a number of paper-based concepts, and so there would be major difficulties to overcome before it
was possible to have an electronic bill of exchange (see Law Commission's Advice to Government, *Electronic Commerce: Formal Requirements in Commercial Transactions*, December 2001,
para.9.5). See also *Chalmers and Guest on Bills of Exchange and Cheques*, 18th edn (2017), para.2-
011.

instruction is considered an "order" even if it is phrased in polite language, provided it is imperative.[42] If, on the other hand, the drawer makes a precative request instead of issuing an order, the instrument is not a bill.[43]

34-011   If the order given by the drawer to the drawee is subject to any qualification,[44] it is not "unconditional" within the meaning of the definition and the instrument is not a bill of exchange. An order to pay out of a particular fund,[45] or "out of my rents in your hands"[46] or "out of S's money, as soon as you receive it"[47] is not unconditional. On the other hand, under s.3(3) of the Act, an order which is in itself unqualified is unconditional although it is coupled with (a) an indication of a particular fund out of which the drawee is to reimburse himself or a particular account to be debited with the amount, or (b) a statement of the transaction which gives rise to the bill. An order is conditional only when the qualification or limitation is directed to the drawee. Thus, an order of the drawer to the drawee, to pay the bill only if the payee signs a form of receipt printed at the back of the instrument, is conditional.[48] But if the drawer's instruction that a receipt need be signed is directed not to the drawee but to the payee, the order to the drawee remains unconditional, and the instrument is a bill of exchange.[49] Similarly, an undated cheque is not conditional where there is an agreement between the drawer and the payee that it would not be dated and presented for payment until a dispute between them had been resolved.[50] Whether such an instruction is directed to the drawee or the payee is a question of fact, but an important factor to be taken into account is the part of the bill in which the instruction appears. Where the instruction that a receipt must be signed appeared immediately after the amount of the bill and above the signature of the drawer, it was held that the order to the drawee was conditional.[51] Where the same instruction appeared at the foot of the bill, beneath the signature of the drawer, it was held that the order to the drawee remained unconditional.[52] Thus where the qualifying words appear beneath the drawer's signature, the courts are not inclined to treat them as forming part of the order addressed to the drawee.

34-012   Bill addressed to drawee   The drawee must be named or indicated in the bill with

---

[42]   *Ruff v Webb* (1794) 1 Esp. 129, in which "Mr. N will much oblige Mr. W by paying to the order of R 20 guineas in his account" was held to be imperative and thus a valid order, but it is to be doubted if such language would be considered imperative at present. cf. *R. v Ellor* (1784) 1 Leach C.C. 323.

[43]   *Little v Slackford* (1828) Mood. & M. 171, where an instrument reading "Please to let the bearer have seven pounds, and place it to my account, and you will oblige" was held not to be a bill of exchange. cf. *Hamilton v Spottiswoode* (1849) 4 Exch. 200, 210.

[44]   As regards a qualification concerning the time of payment, see below, para.34-014.

[45]   s.3(3).

[46]   *Jenney v Herle* (1723) 2 Ld. Raym. 1361.

[47]   *Dawkes v Lord De Loraine* (1771) 3 Wils. K.B. 207. See also *Buck v Robson* (1878) 3 Q.B.D. 686; *Fisher v Calvert* (1879) 27 W.R. 301.

[48]   *Bavins Jnr & Sims v London and South Western Bank Ltd* [1900] 1 Q.B. 270.

[49]   *Nathan v Ogdens Ltd* (1905) 93 L.T. 553 (affirmed (1905) 94 L.T. 126). As regards "claused bills", see *Chalmers and Guest on Bills of Exchange and Cheques*, 18th edn (2017), para.2-020.

[50]   *Aspinall's Club Ltd v Al-Zayat* [2007] EWHC 362 (Comm) at [10] (summary judgment), although the Court of Appeal, [2007] EWCA Civ 1001, allowed the defendant's appeal on the ground, inter alia, that the cheque might have been a sham because the parties did not have a common intention that it would be paid on first presentation within two banking days as required by s.16(3) of the Gaming Act 1968 (since repealed and replaced by the Gambling Act 2005); cf. *The Ritz Hotel Casino Ltd v Al-Daher* [2014] EWHC 2847 (QB), where the provision by a casino of a cheque cashing facility for members was held not to constitute the (prohibited) provision of "credit" for the purposes of the Gambling Act 2005.

[51]   *Bavins Jnr & Sims v London and South Western Bank Ltd*, above.

[52]   *Nathan v Ogdens Ltd*, above.

reasonable certainty.[53] The bill may be addressed to two or more drawees, whether they are partners or not, but an order addressed to two drawees in the alternative or to two or more drawees in succession is not a bill of exchange.[54] A bill of exchange must be drawn by one person on another.[55] It follows that if the drawer draws a bill on himself, the instrument is not a bill of exchange. A draft drawn by a branch of a bank on the main office or on another branch of the same bank is, therefore, not considered a bill of exchange.[56] However, according to s.5(2) of the Act, where in a bill the drawer and the drawee are the same person, or where the drawee is a fictitious person or a person not having capacity to contract, the holder may treat the instrument at his option either as a bill of exchange or as a promissory note. The holder of such an instrument is, therefore, for all purposes in as good a position as the holder of a valid bill. If he treats the instrument as a bill of exchange, he retains the rights which a holder usually has against the drawer. If he treats the instrument as a promissory note, he retains against the drawer the rights which a holder has against the maker of a promissory note, whose position is similar to that of an acceptor of a bill of exchange.[57]

When payable: on demand   According to s.3(1) a bill of exchange may be payable on demand or at a fixed or determinable future time. A bill is payable on demand (a) if it is expressed to be payable on demand, at sight or at presentation, or (b) if no time for payment is mentioned in it.[58] Moreover, where a bill is accepted or indorsed when it is overdue it is, as regards the acceptor or indorser, deemed to be a bill payable on demand.[59]   **34-013**

At a determinable future time   A bill is payable at a determinable future time within the meaning of the Act if it is expressed to be payable (a) at a fixed period after the date of its issue or after "sight", i.e. its presentation for acceptance, or (b) on or at a fixed period after the occurrence of a specified event which is certain to happen, though the time of its occurrence may be uncertain.[60] An instrument expressed to be payable on a contingency is not a bill and the happening of the event does not cure the defect.[61] Thus, an order to pay "ten days after the death of X",[62] or "on January 12, when X should come of age",[63] was held to be a valid bill of exchange. On the other hand, it was held that an order to pay "two months next after   **34-014**

---

53 s.6(1).
54 s.6(2).
55 s.3(1).
56 *Capital and Counties Bank v Gordon* [1903] A.C. 240, 250. The instrument is equivalent to a promissory note of a bank: *Commercial Banking Co of Sydney Ltd v Mann* [1961] A.C. 1, 7. In *Abbey National Plc v JSF Finance & Currency Exchange Ltd* [2006] EWCA Civ 328 at [12], Sir Andrew Morritt C. said that "the legal effect of such an instrument is identical to that of a bankers' draft". Generally as regards bankers' drafts, see *Chalmers and Guest on Bills of Exchange and Cheques*, 18th edn (2017), paras 2-003, 2-012 and 2-040.
57 s.89(2).
58 s.10(1).
59 s.10(2).
60 s.11.
61 s.11. To invalidate the bill, the contingency need be apparent on the face of the instrument. English courts are unlikely to follow the decision to the contrary of the Nova Scotia Supreme Court in *Eastern Elevator Services Ltd v Wolfe*, 119 D.L.R. (3rd) 643 (1981).
62 *Colehan v Cooke* (1742) Willes 393, 399. The following were held to be certain events: "12 months after notice"—*Clayton v Gosling* (1826) 5 B. & C. 360; "two months after demand in writing"—*Price v Taylor* (1860) 5 H. & N. 540.
63 *Goss v Nelson* (1757) 1 Burr. 226.

I marry X",[64] or "when my circumstances will admit without detriment to myself",[65] was not a bill of exchange, as the occurrence of such an event could not be considered a certainty. While the principle involved is clear, some authorities may be questioned. The words "when X comes of age" do not describe an event the occurrence of which is more certain than that denoted by the words "two months next after I marry X". A marriage arrangement may of course be cancelled, but the coming of age of a minor is, likewise, not a certainty as he may die before the relevant date. A strict test would, in fact, lead to treating most future events as mere contingencies. A bill is considered as payable on a contingency if the drawee is given an option concerning the date of payment. Thus, a promissory note payable "on or before December 31, 1956" has been held invalid because the maker's option concerning the date of payment created a contingency or uncertainty.[66] The same element of uncertainty was held to have been introduced into a note where it was made payable "by" a given date.[67] These principles should apply to a bill payable "on or before" or "by" a specified future date.

34-015 **Ambiguity in date** A bill is also invalid if there is an ambiguity as regards its date of payment. In *Korea Exchange Bank v Debenhams (Central Buying) Ltd*[68] the drawer used a standard form of a bill of exchange but struck out the word "sight" and inserted instead of it the letters "D/A". The completed bill read: "90 days D/A of this first of Exchange pay ...". The Court of Appeal held that these words were unclear as they did not indicate whether the designated period was to run from the date of the acceptance, the date of the drawing of the bill or from any other date. Megaw L.J. added that as the word "sight" had been expressly cancelled on the face of the bill it would have been bold to conclude that the bill was nonetheless payable 90 days after sight. It followed that as the bill was not expressed to be payable at a fixed period after date or after sight it failed to comply with s.11 and was, therefore, invalid.

34-016 **Tendency to uphold** Where possible, however, the courts uphold the negotiability of an instrument even if, on a strict construction, it is open to question. In *Hong Kong and Shanghai Banking Corp Ltd v GD Trade Co Ltd*[69] the drawers, who used blank forms of bills of exchange supplied by the bank, inserted the words "90 days after acceptance" in the blank space left between the printed words "At" and "sight". It was argued, inter alia, that this formulation rendered the instruments payable on a contingency because it was not certain at the outset whether the bills would be accepted or dishonoured by the drawee. Affirming Cresswell J.'s decision, the Court of Appeal rejected this argument. The bills were to be read as pay-

---

64 *Pearson v Garrett* (1693) 4 Mod. 242.
65 *Ex p. Tootell* (1798) 4 Ves. Jr. 372. The following were held to be contingencies: "30 days after the arrival of the ship P."—*Palmer v Pratt* (1824) 2 Bing. 185; "90 days after sight or when realised"— *Alexander v Thomas* (1851) 16 Q.B. 333.
66 *Williamson v Rider* [1963] 1 Q.B. 89, CA. See also (from South Africa) *Salot v Naidoo* 1981 (3) S.A. 959; *Standard Credit Corp Ltd v Kleyn* 1988 (4) S.A. 441. Contrast: *John Burrows Ltd v Subsurface Surveys Ltd* [1968] S.C.R. 607, 614 (Canada); *Creative Press Ltd v Harman* (1973) I.R. 313 (Ireland); *Emu Brewery Mezzanine Ltd v ASIC* [2006] WASCA 105 (Australia); *Re York Street Mezzanine Pty Ltd* [2007] FCA 922 (Australia); *Club Securities Ltd v Hurley* [2008] 1 N.Z.L.R. 711 (New Zealand).
67 *Claydon v Bradley* [1987] 1 W.L.R. 521.
68 [1979] 1 Lloyd's Rep. 100.
69 [1998] C.L.C. 238.

able "90 days after acceptance/sight". As "sight" referred to presentment for acceptance, the bills were payable 90 days following their presentment regardless of whether or not the drawee accepted them. The bills were, accordingly, not payable subject to a contingency. In reaching this conclusion, the Court accepted that as negotiability was the essence of a bill of exchange, a strict construction should be adopted. But their Lordships added:

"Nevertheless [a bill] is a document in use in hundreds of commercial transactions and, in the case of an instrument which has been drawn as a bill with the plain intention that it should take effect as such, the court should lean in favour of a construction which upholds its validity as a bill where that is reasonably possible."[70]

Moreover, it is arguable that the drawee's acceptance can remove doubts arising from the manner in which the bill is drawn. The English courts have yet to decide the issue. In *Novaknit Hellas SA v Kumar Bros International Ltd*[71] the drawer made the bill payable "on 60 days from shipment". The drawee accepted it as payable 60 days after the date of his acceptance. The Court of Appeal held that the instrument so drawn was valid on the ground that "shipment is certain to have taken place prior to presentation of documents including the [bill of exchange]".[72] Waller L.J. was also sympathetic to the argument that the drawee's qualified acceptance cured any defect as to time of payment, although it was not necessary to decide the issue.[73]

Date of bill and computation of time of payment Where a bill, acceptance or **34-017** indorsement is dated, that date is presumed to be the true one.[74] A bill is not invalid merely because it is post-dated, ante-dated or dated on a Sunday.[75] Where a bill is not payable on demand, the day on which it falls due is determined in accordance with s.14(1) of the Bills of Exchange Act 1882 as amended by s.3(2) of the Banking and Financial Dealings Act 1971. Such a bill is due and payable in all cases on the last day of the time of payment as fixed by the bill, or if that is a non-business day, on the succeeding business day. The 1971 Act repealed the provision for days of grace of the original s.14(1). The meaning of the phrase "non-business day" continues to be governed by s.92 of the 1882 Act,[76] but subject to amendments introduced by the 1971 Act. Non-business days are Bank Holidays,[77] Good Friday, Christmas Day, Sundays,[78] Saturdays,[79] and any day declared as such by the

---

70 [1998] C.L.C. 238 at 242.
71 [1998] Lloyd's Rep. Bank. 287, CA.
72 [1998] Lloyd's Rep. Bank. 287, 292, per Waller L.J., and also Chadwick L.J. at 295. See also *Credit Agricole Indosuez v Ecumet (UK) Ltd* Unreported March 29, 2001, where Tomlinson J. was uncertain as to whether this reasoning was part of the *ratio decidendi* in *Novaknit Hellas*.
73 [1998] Lloyd's Rep. Bank. 287, 292, following dicta in *Hong Kong and Shanghai Banking Corp Ltd v GD Trade Co Ltd* [1998] C.L.C. 238, 243, where it was also unnecessary to decide the issue. cf. *Credit Agricole Indosuez v Ecumet (UK) Ltd* Unreported March 29, 2001, where Tomlinson J. regarded the terms of the acceptance as the "critical element" in *Novaknit Hellas*. See also *Chalmers and Guest on Bills of Exchange and Cheques*, 18th edn (2017), para.2-089 (acceptor may be liable as the maker of a promissory note).
74 s.13(1).
75 s.13(2).
76 This section excludes non-business days when computing time where the Act requires something to be done in less than three days. See also s.1(4) of the 1971 Act.
77 s.92(b); see also s.4(1) of the 1971 Act.
78 s.92(a).
79 Added to s.92(a) by s.3(1) of the 1971 Act.

Treasury under s.2 of the 1971 Act.[80] Section 1(1) of the same Act determines which days are "Bank Holidays", providing for separate days for England and Wales, for Scotland and for Northern Ireland.[81] Additional Bank Holidays may be appointed by Royal proclamation[82]; in the same manner a Bank Holiday may be suspended in any given year.[83]

34-018 Where a bill is payable at a fixed period after date, after sight, or after the happening of a specified event, the time of payment is determined by excluding the day from which the time is to begin to run and by including the day of payment.[84] Where a bill is payable at a fixed period after sight, the time begins to run from the date of its acceptance, or if acceptance is refused from the date of noting or of protest.[85] As the term "month" in a bill means calendar month,[86] bills dated, for example, respectively November 28, 29 and 30, payable at three months after date, all fall due on February 28 in an ordinary year, but in a leap-year the first falls due on the 28th and the second and third on the 29th. It is assumed that none of these due dates is a non-business day.

34-019 **A sum certain in money** According to s.3(1) of the Act, a bill of exchange must be for a sum certain in money. An order[87] requiring the drawee to pay a sum of money and do some other act, e.g. deliver up goods to the payee,[88] is not a bill of exchange. A sum is certain within the meaning of the Act, although it is required to be paid:

(a) with interest;

(b) by stated instalments with or without a provision that upon default in payment of any instalment the whole shall become due[89]; and

(c) according to an indicated rate of exchange or according to a rate of exchange to be ascertained as directed by the bill.[90]

A Canadian authority, however, suggests that if interest on the bill is stated to run from the date of the making of the advance, the sum is uncertain as its calculation then depends on extrinsic facts.[91] For the same reason, the amount of the bill is uncertain if interest is to be charged at the rate applied to advances to "most creditworthy customers".[92] It remains to be seen whether a formula such as "interest at 2 per cent above prime" will be considered on the same basis. When the bill is payable with interest, it runs, in the absence of stipulation to the contrary, from the date

---

[80] s.92(d) of the 1882 Act, inserted by s.4(4) of the 1971 Act. Under s.92(c)—which is not affected by the 1971 Act—non-business days include any day appointed by Royal proclamation as public fast or thanksgiving.

[81] Sch.1.

[82] s.1(3) of the 1971 Act. New Year's Day is appointed a Bank Holiday by Royal proclamation under the said section of the Act.

[83] s.1(2).

[84] s.14(2).

[85] s.14(3).

[86] s.14(4).

[87] As to "order", see above, para.34-011.

[88] *Martin v Chauntry* (1747) 2 Str. 1271; cf. *Re Boyse* (1886) 33 Ch. D. 612, 621. See also *Dickie v Singh*, 1974 S.L.T. (Notes) 3 (instrument promising payment of a certain amount coupled with an undertaking to employ staff and to pay their salaries, held not to be a promissory note).

[89] For a Canadian case in point, see *Canada Permanent Trust Co v Kowal* (1981) 120 D.L.R. (3d) 760.

[90] s.9(1).

[91] *Macleod Savings and Credit Union Ltd v Perrett* (1981) 118 D.L.R. (3d) 193.

[92] *Bank of Montreal v Dezcam Industries Ltd* (1983) 147 D.L.R. (3d) 359.

of the bill or, if it is undated, from the date of issue.[93] Section 3(1) has been augmented by s.2(1) of the Decimal Currency Act 1969, according to which a bill, drawn on or after February 15, 1971, is invalid "if the sum payable is an amount of money wholly or partly in shillings or pence".[94] A bill covering a given amount "plus bank charges" has been held to be for an uncertain amount.[95]

Discrepancy between words and figures   Where the sum payable is expressed in words and also in figures, and there is a discrepancy between the two, the sum denoted by the words is the amount payable.[96] But if the words are unclear, e.g. "pay to my order twenty-five, fifty pence", the figures, e.g. £25.50 may be used to clarify the intention of the drawer.[97] In the case of a cheque in which the amount expressed in words differs from that expressed in figures, the banking practice is to return the cheque unpaid, with the remark "words and figures differ".

34-020

The payee   According to s.3(1) of the Act, a bill of exchange must be payable to a specified person or to bearer. A bill may be made payable to the order of the drawer or of the drawee.[98] An instrument which is made payable for a specified purpose, e.g. "cash or order", is not a bill of exchange, as it is not payable to a specified person or to bearer.[99] A bill payable to "cash or bearer" should, on the other hand, be considered valid, as it is payable to the bearer. Difficulties may arise when the drawer leaves the space meant for the name of the payee blank. In *Daun and Vallentin v Sherwood*[100] it was held that a promissory note, which did not specify the name of the payee, was payable to bearer "because that is the natural legal effect". It cannot be argued that a bill of exchange payable to "—or order" should be regarded as payable to bearer, as the words "or order" obviate such an interpretation. The drawer of such a bill has, however, the intention of creating a negotiable instrument, and one manner of giving effect to his intention is to treat the bill as payable to himself. Thus, in *Chamberlain v Young and Tower*[101] it was held that an instrument which read "pay—order" should be construed as meaning "pay my order" and be considered a bill of exchange. In *R. v Randall*[102] an instrument reading "pay—or order" was held not to be a bill. An attempt has been made to distinguish the cases on the ground that the addition of the word "my" to the phrase "pay—or order" would be meaningless. But the phrase could easily be read as "pay myself or order", a formula commonly used in bills payable to the drawer's own order which are transferable by his indorsement and delivery. It is to be doubted whether the decision in *R. v Randall* would be followed at present.

34-021

---

[93]   s.9(3).

[94]   But note saving in s.2(2), concerning a bill dated on or after February 15, 1971 but proved to have been drawn earlier.

[95]   *Dalgety Ltd v John J. Hilton Pty Ltd* [1981] 2 N.S.W.L.R. 169 Aust.

[96]   s.9(2). See *Saunderson v Piper* (1839) 5 Bing. N.C. 425; *Garrard v Lewis* (1882) 10 Q.B.D. 30, 34, 35.

[97]   *Phipps v Tanner* (1833) 5 Car. & P. 488.

[98]   s.5(1).

[99]   *North and South Insurance Corp Ltd v National Provincial Bank Ltd* [1936] 1 K.B. 328; *Cole v Milsome* [1951] 1 All E.R. 311; *Orbit Mining and Trading Co v Westminster Bank* [1963] 1 Q.B. 794.

[100]   (1895) 11 T.L.R. 211.

[101]   [1893] 2 Q.B. 206.

[102]   (1811) Russ. & Ry 195. Contrast the Scottish case of *Henderson, Sons & Co Ltd v Wallace and Pennell*, 1902 40 S.L.R. 70, in which an instrument in the form of a bill of exchange, reading "pay—or order", was treated as a promissory note.

34-022 **Bearer bills** A bill of exchange may be payable either to order or to bearer.[103] A bill is payable to bearer either if it is expressed to be so payable or if the last indorsement is in blank.[104] It is payable to order either if it is expressed to be so payable or if it is expressed to be payable to a particular person and does not contain words prohibiting transfer or indicating an intention that it should not be transferable.[105] The Act does not state explicitly whether a bill which is drawn as payable to bearer may be converted into an order bill by the execution of a special indorsement, i.e. an indorsement which specifies the name of the indorsee.[106] According to an Australian authority such a bill remains payable to bearer regardless of the indorsement.[107] But this view may be questioned as, under s.34, "any holder may convert [a] blank indorsement by writing above the indorser's signature a direction to pay the bill to or to the order of himself or some other person". Although this provision does not apply to a bill drawn payable to bearer but only where the bill has been indorsed in blank, it tends to reflect the policy of the Act. As a bill which has become payable to bearer by reason of the blank indorsement can be converted into an order bill, it is difficult to see why a bill which is originally drawn as payable to bearer may not be equally converted into an order bill by the execution of a special indorsement.

34-023 **Bills payable to order** Where the bill is payable to order it must specify with reasonable certainty the identity of the payee.[108] A bill may be made payable to two or more payees jointly or to one or more out of several payees in the alternative. It may also be made payable to the holder of an office for the time being.[109] Where there is difficulty in establishing the identity of the payee because of some ambiguity in his description in the bill, resort must be had to the intention of the drawer.[110] Extrinsic evidence is admissible to identify a misnamed payee or one designated by description only.[111] However, if it is impossible to ascertain the identity of the payee, e.g. due to the lack of evidence regarding the drawer's intention, the bill is invalid, unless it may be treated as payable to a fictitious or non-existing person.

34-024 **Fictitious or non-existing payee** According to s.7(3) of the Act, where a bill is made payable to a fictitious or non-existing person, it may be treated as payable to bearer. In *Bank of England v Vagliano Bros*[112] the plaintiffs, Vagliano Bros, were in the habit of accepting bills drawn on them by Vucina and payable to the order of P & Co. A clerk of the plaintiffs forged such a bill. The plaintiffs, who did not discover the forgery of Vucina's signature as drawer by the clerk, accepted the bill and made it payable at the defendant bank. The clerk then added an indorsement of P & Co to the bill, presented it to the bank and obtained payment. An action brought by the plaintiffs for a declaration that the bank was not entitled to debit their account with the amount of the bill was dismissed. The House of Lords held that

---

[103] s.8(2).
[104] s.8(3).
[105] s.8(4).
[106] Below, para.34-088.
[107] *Miller Associates (Australia) Pty Ltd v Bennington Pty Ltd* [1975] 7 A.L.R. 144; Chappenden (1981) 55 A.L.J. 135.
[108] s.7(1).
[109] s.7(2).
[110] *Bird & Co v Thomas Cook & Son Ltd* [1937] 2 All E.R. 227, 230–231.
[111] *Willis v Barrett* (1817) 2 Stark. 29; *Soares v Glyn* (1845) 8 Q.B. 24.
[112] [1891] A.C. 107.

the bill was payable to a fictitious or non-existing person and, therefore, to bearer. Although a firm by the name of P & Co did exist, the person who actually drew the bill—i.e. the clerk—had no intention that the bill should be paid to it. Thus a fictitious or non-existing person may be not only a creation of fiction (e.g. "Ivanhoe") or a person who does not exist at the time the bill is drawn (e.g. a dissolved company), but also a real payee whose name is written on the bill as a mere pretence. Whether a payee is fictitious or not depends, accordingly, on the intention of the drawer.

The principle of the *Vagliano Bros* case was applied in *Clutton & Co v Attenborough*,[113] where a clerk induced his employer to draw cheques payable to one John Brett by falsely representing that a person of that name was entitled to a remuneration for certain work done for the employer. It was held that the payee, John Brett, was a non-existing person. As the employer, the drawer, intended to make the cheques payable to a John Brett who had completed some work for him, and as there was in fact no such person in existence, this decision appears well founded. However, the position is different if the drawer is induced, by a fraudulent misrepresentation of another person, to draw a cheque payable to a designated real person. Such a cheque is not payable to a fictitious or non-existing person and, therefore, may not be treated as payable to bearer.[114] The reason for this is that, although the motive which induces the drawer to draw the bill is the misrepresentation, e.g. his being misled into believing that he owes money to the payee, the drawer has, nevertheless, the intention of creating an instrument payable to that designated person.[115] Conceptually, though, a person may be non-existing even if the drawer intends to make the bill payable to him. An example is a bill payable to a payee who passed away before the date of issue.[116] **34-025**

Destruction of negotiability On occasions a drawer may wish to create a bill of exchange, but without allowing for its transfer or negotiation. This can be achieved by including in the bill words prohibiting transfer. When a bill contains words prohibiting transfer, or indicating an intention that it should not be transferable, it is valid as between the parties thereto, but may not be transferred.[117] This effect can be achieved by drawing a bill payable to the order of a specified payee "only". There cannot be a holder, let alone a holder in due course, capable of suing on it.[118] The intention to prohibit negotiation or transfer must, however, appear clearly on **34-026**

---

[113] [1897] A.C. 90. See also (from Canada) *Royal Bank of Canada v Concrete Column Clamps* [1977] 2 S.C.R. 456; *Canada Trust Co v The Queen* [1982] 2 F.C. 722; *Fok Cheong Shing Investments Co Ltd v Bank of Nova Scotia* [1982] 2 S.C.R. 488; *Boma Manufacturing Ltd v CIBC* [1996] 3 S.C.R. 727; *Bank of Nova Scotia v Toronto-Dominion Bank* (2001) 145 O.A.C. 106; *Rouge Valley Health System v TD Canada Trust* [2012] ONCA 17; *Raza Kayani LLP v Toronto-Dominion Bank* [2014] ONCA 862.

[114] *Vinden v Hughes* [1905] 1 K.B. 795; *North and South Wales Bank Ltd v Macbeth* [1908] A.C. 137.

[115] It is doubtful whether the drawee may treat as payable to bearer a cheque whose payee is fictitious or non-existent, if the printed words "or bearer" following the payee's name have been struck out and a crossing accompanied by the words "not negotiable—a/c payee only" have been added thereto: *Rhostar (Pvt) Ltd v Netherlands Bank of Rhodesia Ltd* [1972] 2 S.A.L.R. 703, 709–711. As from 1992, such a cheque is, in any event, non-transferable and so, it is submitted, incapable of being payable to bearer under s.7(3): below, para.34-166.

[116] *Canada Trust Co v The Queen* [1982] 2 F.C. 722 Can.

[117] s.8(1). See, e.g. *Banque Cantonale de Genève v Sanomi* [2016] EWHC 3353 (Comm) at [29] (a promissory note case).

[118] See *Hibernian Bank Ltd v Gysin and Hanson* [1939] 1 K.B. 483. As regards the effect of words limiting negotiability written by the acceptor, see *Meyer & Co v Decroix, Verley et Cie* [1891] A.C. 520.

the face of the bill. If the drawer makes a bill payable to a particular person, without adding the words "or order", but does not add words prohibiting transfer, it is treated as payable to that person's order and is negotiable.[119]

34-027 **Cancellation of "or order" or "or bearer"** A problem which awaits a direct determination concerns the effect of the mere cancellation of the words "or order" or "or bearer" in a bill written on a standard form. If the drawer strikes out these words, it may be assumed that his purpose is to prohibit transfer. The bill, however, does not "contain *words* prohibiting transfer or indicating an intention that it should not be transferable". Section 8(1) of the Act governs only the effect of a bill containing such words. A strict interpretation of this section would probably lead to the conclusion that a mere cancellation of the words "or order" or "or bearer" does not destroy the negotiability of the bill, but renders it payable to the particular payee named therein. Under s.8(4), such a bill is, however, payable to that payee's order. Such an effect may be desirable where the drawer has cancelled the words "or bearer" in a bill executed on a standard form. The cancellation of the words "or bearer" would, on this interpretation, affect the bill's transferability; by becoming an order bill, it would cease to be transferable by mere delivery, and would require the payee's indorsement to effect transfer. But this line of argument produces a strange result where the standard form, used by the drawer, includes the printed words "or order". The cancellation of these words would, again, leave the bill payable to the named payee and hence to that payee's order. The cancellation would therefore be without any practical effect. This, however, may be an inescapable conclusion from a strict construction of s.8.

34-028 **"A/C payee only" on crossed cheques** Since 1992, one type of bill of exchange—namely, a cheque—can be rendered non-transferable by the execution of a crossing accompanied by the words "A/C payee only". The provision to this effect, in the Cheques Act 1992, reversed the law as decided in a series of late nineteenth and twentieth century cases,[120] which had held that the words in question did not have the effect of destroying the negotiability of a crossed cheque. Notably, the negotiability of other types of bills of exchange could always be destroyed by the addition to the instrument of the words "not negotiable".[121]

34-029 **Definition and requirements of acceptance** The drawee's assent to the order given to him by the drawer is known as "acceptance".[122] There are two requirements concerning the form of an acceptance. First, it must be written on the bill and signed by the drawee; the mere signature of the drawee without additional words is sufficient.[123] If the drawee writes "accepted" on the bill but does not sign, or writes an acceptance in a separate letter, this is insufficient.[124] An acceptance of the

---

The words "not negotiable" have a special meaning when written on a crossed cheque; as regards these and the addition of the words "a/c payee only" to a crossed cheque, see below, paras 34-163 et seq.

[119] s.8(4).
[120] And see below, para.34-163.
[121] *Hibernian Bank Ltd v Gysin and Hanson* [1939] 1 K.B. 483.
[122] s.17(1).
[123] s.17(2)(a).
[124] At common law an acceptance written on a separate paper was sufficient: *Pierson v Dunlop* (1777) 2 Cowp. 571; *Mason v Hunt* (1779) 1 Doug. 297; *Wynne v Raikes* (1804) 5 East 514.

drawee written on the back of the bill is, probably, valid.[125] Secondly, the accept-ance must not express that the drawee will perform his promise by any other means than payment of money.[126] Thus, if the drawee writes on a bill "payable in bills" or "payable in goods", this is not an acceptance.[127] At the same time, an accept-ance to pay out of funds standing to the credit of a special account, e.g. an external account, is a promise to pay money and constitutes a valid acceptance.[128] By ac-cepting the bill the drawee engages to pay it when it falls due,[129] and thus becomes primarily liable on the bill. As the bill is drawn on a specified drawee, the signature on the bill of any other person, even when accompanied by words indicating an intention to accept it, is not an acceptance,[130] and will probably be construed as an indorsement.[131] If a bill is addressed to no one, and a person writes an acceptance on it, he is not liable as acceptor of a bill, but may be liable as the maker of a promissory note.[132]

Time for acceptance   The drawee's acceptance gives the bill additional currency.   **34-030** In most cases a bill will be presented soon after it has been signed and delivered by the drawer and before it falls due.[133] But a bill may be accepted even before it has been signed by the drawer or while it is otherwise incomplete,[134] and likewise when it is overdue, or after it has been dishonoured previously by non-acceptance or by non-payment.[135] If a bill is accepted by the drawee when it is overdue, it becomes, as against him, payable on demand.[136] When a bill payable at a fixed date after sight is dishonoured by non-acceptance, and the drawee subsequently ac-cepts it, the holder is entitled to have the bill accepted as of the date of the first presentment for acceptance.[137] When the acceptance of a bill payable at a fixed period after sight is undated, the holder is entitled to insert the true date of acceptance.[138] When an acceptance is undated, there is a presumption that it has been given within a reasonable time after the date of issue of the bill and before it falls due.[139]

---

[125] *Young v Glover* (1857) 3 Jur.(N.S.) 637.
[126] s.17(2)(b).
[127] *Russell v Phillips* (1850) 14 Q.B. 891.
[128] *Banca Popolare di Novara v John Livanos & Sons Ltd* [1965] 2 Lloyd's Rep. 149.
[129] s.54(1); *Philpot v Briant* (1828) 4 Bing. 717, 720.
[130] *Jackson v Hudson* (1810) 2 Camp. 447; *Davis v Clarke* (1844) 6 Q.B. 16; *Steele v M'Kinlay* (1880) 5 App. Cas. 754, 770. As regards acceptance of bills drawn on a partnership, see *Re Barnard, Edwards v Barnard* (1886) 32 Ch. D. 447. As regards acceptance for honour, see below, para.34-142.
[131] s.56.
[132] *Fielder v Marshall* (1861) 30 L.J. C.P. 158; *Mason v Lack* (1929) 140 L.T. 696; *Haseldine v Winstanley* [1936] 2 K.B. 101.
[133] When a bill is payable on demand it is usual to present it simultaneously for acceptance and for payment. As to how far it is necessary to present a bill for payment, see below, paras 34-105—34-107.
[134] s.18(1); *London and South Western Bank Ltd v Wentworth* (1880) 5 Ex. D. 96.
[135] s.18(2).
[136] s.10(2).
[137] s.18(3).
[138] s.12. Similarly, he is entitled to add the date of issue of a bill payable at a fixed time after date.
[139] *Roberts v Bethell* (1852) 12 C.B. 778.

34-031 **General and unqualified acceptance** An acceptance may be either general or qualified.[140] It is general when the drawee assents, without any qualification, to the order of the drawer. It is qualified if the drawee varies in express terms the effect of the bill as drawn, i.e. modifies the order of the drawer. In particular an acceptance is qualified if it is:

(a) conditional, i.e. makes payment by the acceptor dependent on the fulfilment of a condition;

(b) partial, i.e. for less than the amount specified by the drawer;

(c) local, i.e. an acceptance to pay only at a particular specified place;

(d): qualified as to time; and

(e) if the bill is drawn on more than one drawee and is not accepted by all of them.[141]

An acceptance, however, is not qualified merely because it makes the bill payable at a particular place, provided it does not state that the bill is payable only there.[142]

34-032 **Delivery** According to s.21(1) of the Act, every contract on a bill, whether it be the drawer's, the acceptor's or an indorser's, is incomplete and revocable until the delivery of the bill; but where an acceptance is written on a bill and the drawee gives notice that he has accepted it, the acceptance then becomes complete. Thus, an acceptance becomes complete not at the time it is written, but when the acceptor gives notice of it.[143] Delivery of the accepted bill would, however, constitute notice of the acceptance.

34-033 **Constructive transfer of possession** Under s.2 of the Act, delivery means the transfer of possession, whether actual or constructive, from one person to another. In most cases possession is transferred by the physical delivery of the bill. A constructive transfer of the possession of a bill may occur in the following cases:

(a) when a person originally holds the bill for himself but subsequently holds it as an agent;

(b) when a bill is originally held by one person as the agent of a second person but subsequently as agent of a third person;

(c) when a person originally holds the bill as an agent of another person but subsequently holds it for himself.[144]

34-034 **Authorised delivery** As between immediate parties, and as regards a remote party other than a holder in due course, the delivery, in order to be effective, must be made by the party drawing, accepting or indorsing the bill, as the case may be. It may, of course, be effected by that party in person but it is also valid if effected

---

[140] s.19(1).

[141] s.19(2). See also *Banca Popolare di Novara v John Livanos & Sons Ltd* [1965] 2 Lloyd's Rep. 149, 155 (concerning an acceptance to pay out of a designated account); *Geo Thompson (Aust) Pty Ltd v Vittadello* [1978] V.R. 199, 207 (concerning an acceptance of a bill drawn on a partnership by only one of the partners who was acting in his personal capacity).

[142] s.19(2)(c), proviso. See *Halstead v Skelton* (1843) 5 Q.B. 86; *Ex p. Hayward* (1887) 3 T.L.R. 687; *Banku Polskiego v KJ Mulder & Co* [1941] 2 K.B. 266; affirmed [1942] 1 K.B. 497. As to what constitutes a particular place, see *Eimco Corp v Tutt Bryant Ltd* [1970] 2 N.S.W.R. 249. cf. *Day v Bate* (1979) 41 F.L.R. 222 Aust.

[143] *Cox v Troy* (1822) 5 B. & Ald. 474; *Bank of Van Diemen's Land v Bank of Victoria* (1871) L.R. 3 P.C. 526.

[144] See, e.g. *Bosanquet v Forster* (1841) 9 C. & P. 659; *Belcher v Campbell* (1845) 8 Q.B. 1.

by that party's agent, bailee or messenger.[145] Evidence may be called to show that the delivery has been conditional or for a special purpose only and not for the purpose of transferring the property in the bill.[146] However, evidence is not admissible to show that delivery of a bill by an acceptor was made conditionally, under an agreement to renew the bill at maturity, because the effect of such evidence would be to contradict the terms of a written instrument.[147] The position of a party to the bill who is not a holder in due course is, to a certain extent, strengthened by the rule that when a bill is no longer in the possession of the person who has signed it as drawer, a valid and unconditional delivery by him is presumed until the contrary is proved. The same presumption applies as regards the acceptor and indorsers.[148] If the bill is in the hands of a holder in due course, a valid delivery of the bill by all parties prior to him so as to make them liable is conclusively presumed.[149]

Inchoate instruments   According to s.20(1), where a simple signature on a blank   **34-035** paper is delivered by the signer in order that it may be converted into a bill, it oper ates as a prima facie authority to fill it up as a complete bill for any amount, using the signature for that of the drawer, or of the acceptor, or of an indorser; and, in like manner, when a bill is wanting in any material particular, the person in possession of it has a prima facie authority to fill up the omission in any way he thinks fit.[150] In order that any such instrument may, when completed, be enforceable against any person who became a party to it prior to its completion, it must be filled up within a reasonable time and strictly in accordance with the authority given. What amounts to a reasonable time is a question of fact.[151] If such a paper is not filled up within a reasonable time or in strict accordance with the authority given, a mere holder cannot enforce it.[152] However, under the proviso to s.20(2), if such an instrument is after completion negotiated to a holder in due course, it is valid and effectual for all

145 *Citibank NA v Brown, Shipley & Co* [1991] 1 Lloyd's Rep. 576; *Dextra Bank and Trust Co Ltd v Bank of Jamaica* [2002] 1 All E.R. (Comm) 193, PC; *Abbey National Plc v JSF Finance & Currency Exchange Co Ltd* [2006] EWCA Civ 328.

146 s.21(2). As regards conditional delivery, see *Bell v Viscount Ingestre* (1848) 12 Q.B. 317, 319; *Castrique v Buttigieg* (1855) 10 Moo. P.C. 94, 108.

147 *New London Credit Syndicate Ltd v Neale* [1898] 2 Q.B. 487; applied in *Banque Cantonale de Genève v Sanomi* [2016] EWHC 3353 (Comm) at [36].

148 s.21(3). See *Colin v Gibson* (1927) 27 S.R. (N.S.W.) 328, 331; *Equitable Securities Ltd v Neal* [1987] 1 N.Z.L.R. 233, 240; *Midland Bank Plc v Brown Shipley & Co Ltd* [1991] 1 Lloyd's Rep. 576, 583; *National Bank of Canada v Tardival Associates* (1994) 109 D.L.R. (4th) 126; *Surrey Asset Finance Ltd v National Westminster Bank, The Times,* November 30, 2000, permission to appeal refused [2001] EWCA Civ 60. The same presumption applies as regards the maker of a note; see s.89(2), *Yan v Post Office Bank Ltd* [1994] 1 N.Z.L.R. 154.

149 s.21(2); as to the application of this provision to a holder who takes the bill from a holder in due course, see *Insurance Corp of Ireland v Dunluce Meats* [1991] N.I. 286. As to who is a holder in due course, see s.29, discussed in para.34-072, below.

150 s.20(1). See generally *Crutchly v Mann* (1814) 5 Taunt. 529; *Schultz v Astley* (1836) 2 Bing. N.C. 544; *Scard v Jackson* (1875) 34 L.T. 65n.; *London and South Western Bank Ltd v Wentworth* (1880) 5 Ex. D. 96; *Carter v White* (1882) 20 Ch. D. 225 (affirmed (1883) 25 Ch. D. 666); *France v Clark* (1884) 26 Ch. D. 257, 262; *Dunn v Jefferson* (1925) 69 S.J. 725. See also s.12 concerning the position when a bill or acceptance is undated. As regards the application of this provision where a bill is indorsed for accommodation before it is signed by the drawer, see *Bank of Nova Scotia v Hogg*, 24 O.R. (2nd) 494 (1979) Can.

151 s.20(2).

152 *Herdman v Wheeler* [1902] 1 K.B. 361.

purposes in his hands, and he may enforce it as if it had been filled up within a reasonable time and strictly in accordance with the authority given.[153]

34-036   Section 20 applies only where the blank signed paper is delivered by the signer in order that it may be converted into a bill.[154] A blank signed paper may however be delivered for some other purpose, such as its retention by the signer's agent pending instructions. If this paper is fraudulently converted into a bill, it is probably not enforceable under s.20 even if it comes into the hands of a holder in due course. Section 20(2) provides that "if any *such instrument* after completion is negotiated to a holder in due course it shall be valid and effectual ...". It stands to reason that the words "such instrument" in this subsection refer to the type of paper described in s.20(1), i.e. to "a blank paper ... delivered by the signer in order that it may be converted into a bill". It appears to follow that if the signer does not deliver the paper with the intention of its being converted into a bill, s.20(2) does not apply.[155]

34-037   **Common law estoppel**   Where the blank instrument had been delivered with an intention of its being converted into a negotiable instrument, the drawer might be estopped at common law from alleging that it was completed in a different manner than that intended, even in situations where s.20 would not protect the holder. In *Lloyds Bank Ltd v Cooke*[156] the defendant signed his name on blank stamped paper, delivered it to C and authorised him to fill it up as a promissory note for £250 payable to the plaintiffs, and to deliver it to them as security for an advance to be made by them to C. C fraudulently filled up the form as a note for £1,000 and obtained an advance of that amount from the plaintiffs, who had no notice of the fraud. As the plaintiffs were the original payees of the bill they were not holders in due course and could not rely on the proviso to s.20(2). However, the defendant was held to be estopped at common law from denying the validity of the note as between himself and the plaintiffs. This principle applies only when the blank paper is intended by the drawer to be completed as a negotiable instrument. In *Wilson and Meeson v Pickering*[157] the plaintiff delivered a blank form of a cheque, crossed "not negotiable", to his servant and instructed him to insert the amount of £2 and make it payable to a certain firm. The servant filled in the amount of £54 4s. and made the cheque payable to the defendant, to whom he was indebted to this amount. It was held that the plaintiff was entitled to recover from the defendant the amount of £54 4s. paid by the drawee bank. Lord Greene M.R. said:

> "... the authority of *Cooke's* case cannot in my opinion be extended beyond the particular facts there in question ... [A]part, of course, from some specific representation of authority or some holding out or some special character of the agent from which his authority

[153] s.20(2), proviso. See *Montague v Perkins* (1853) 22 L.J. C.P. 187; *Barker v Sterne* (1854) 9 Ex. 684; *Garrard v Lewis* (1882) 10 Q.B.D. 30; *Dunn v Jefferson* (1925) 69 S.J. 725; *Guildford Trust Ltd v Goss* (1927) 43 T.L.R. 167. As to the definition of a holder in due course, see below, paras 34-072 et seq.

[154] However, if the proviso to s.20(2) does not apply, the holder may, nevertheless, succeed in an action on the bill if he can, on the facts, plead a common law estoppel precluding the drawer or acceptor from alleging the invalidity of the bill: *France v Clark* (1884) 26 Ch. D. 257, 262; *Lloyds Bank Ltd v Cooke* [1907] 1 K.B. 794; discussed below, in which the plaintiff, as original payee, could not claim to be a holder in due course.

[155] For this type of case, see *Baxendale v Bennett* (1878) 3 Q.B.D. 525; *Smith v Prosser* [1907] 2 K.B. 735 (in which, however, liability might have been based on the principle established subsequently in *Lloyd v Grace, Smith & Co* [1912] A.C. 716).

[156] [1907] 1 K.B. 794. cf. *RE Jones Ltd v Waring and Gillow Ltd* [1926] A.C. 670.

[157] [1946] K.B. 422.

would naturally be inferred, the rule that a person who signs an instrument in blank cannot be heard as against a person who has changed his position on the faith of it, to assert that the instrument as filled in is a forgery or that it was filled in in excess of the agent's authority, is confined to the case of negotiable instruments."[158]

The instrument in *Cooke's* case was such a negotiable instrument. In *Pickering's* case the cheque, crossed "not negotiable", was not a fully negotiable instrument.

Completion after security indorsement A bill drawn payable to the drawer's **34-038**
order is incomplete until indorsed by him. If the bill bears the indorsement of a third party, who has indorsed it with the intention of making himself liable as guarantor,[159] the drawer may, under s.20, complete the bill by indorsing it, and may recover against the third party.[160]

(ii) Capacity and Authority of Parties

Capacity to contract on a bill According to s.22(1) of the Act, capacity to incur **34-039**
liability as a party to a bill is co-extensive with capacity to contract. A drawer, acceptor or indorser who has no capacity to contract is not liable on the bill. However, the fact that one party to the bill has no capacity does not, in itself, release the other parties from their liability.[161] The section provides that nothing in it shall enable a corporation to make itself liable as a drawer, acceptor or indorser of a bill unless it is competent to do so under the law relating to corporations. At common law, a corporation incurred no liability in drawing, accepting or indorsing a bill of exchange, unless expressly or impliedly authorised by its memorandum to do so. In the case of a trading company the fact of its incorporation for trading purposes conferred on it, among other incidental powers, the capacity to draw, accept and indorse bills of exchange.[162] It appears that a non-trading company, on the other hand, had no capacity to draw, accept or indorse bills unless such powers were expressly or by clear implication conferred on it in its memorandum.[163] If a company entered into a contract which was beyond its capacity, the transaction was ultra vires and void.[164] However, so far as third parties are concerned, the ultra vires rule has been abolished for most companies by statute.[165] The current statutory provision is s.39(1) of the Companies Act 2006, which provides that "the validity of an act done by a company shall not be called into question on the ground of lack of capacity by reason of anything in the company's constitution". Beyond that, the

---

[158] [1946] K.B. 422 at 427. cf. *Mercantile Credit Co Ltd v Hamblin* [1965] 2 Q.B. 242, 274–275, 278–279.

[159] The so-called "security indorsement", provided for by s.56 of the Bills of Exchange Act, below, para.34-115.

[160] *Glenie v Bruce Smith* [1908] 1 K.B. 263; *Re Gooch* [1921] 2 K.B. 593; *Gerald McDonald & Co v Nash & Co* [1924] A.C. 625 (distinguishing *Steel v M'Kinlay* (1880) 5 App. Cas. 754); *National Sales Corp Ltd v Bernardi* [1931] 2 K.B. 188 (in which it was held that the drawer's indorsement may in such cases be either above or below that of the third party); *McCall Bros Ltd v Hargreaves* [1932] 2 K.B. 423 (in which it was held that although an indorsement, in these cases, is given by way of guarantee, there is no need for a separate memorandum to satisfy the Statute of Frauds). See also above, para.34-035.

[161] *Wauthier v Wilson* (1912) 28 T.L.R. 239 (father liable on note made jointly by himself and his minor son).

[162] *Re Peruvian Rys* (1867) L.R. 2 Ch. App. 617.

[163] *Bateman v Mid-Wales Ry* (1866) L.R. 1 C.P. 499.

[164] *Ashbury Railway Carriage & Iron Co v Riche* (1875) L.R. 7 H.L. 653.

[165] Companies that are charities remain subject to the rule (see Companies Act 2006 s.42).

Companies Act does not confer on companies a specific capacity to draw, accept or indorse bills of exchange, but merely regulates the exercise of the capacity where it exists.[166]

34-040 **Capable parties liable**   Section 22(2) provides that, where a bill is drawn or indorsed by a minor or a corporation having no capacity or power to incur liability on a bill, the drawing or indorsement entitles the holder to enforce the bill against other parties to it. Thus, a bill remains negotiable even though it has been drawn or indorsed by a party who has no capacity so to do. However, it remains unenforceable against the incapacitated party, even if the incapacity is subsequently removed. It has been held that, if a minor draws a post-dated cheque, dating it a few days after his coming of age, he is not liable on it.[167]

34-041 **Signature essential to liability**   Under s.23 of the Act, a person is liable as a drawer, acceptor or indorser of a bill only if he has signed it in such a capacity. However, s.91 of the Act provides that where any instrument is required to be signed by any person, it is not necessary that he should sign it with his own hand, and his signature may be written by some other person who acts under his authority. In such cases the signature must be in the name of the principal and not the agent. An agent who signs the name of his principal without authority is not liable on the bill personally, as he has not signed it in his own name.[168] But when an agent signs a bill in his own name, the agent alone is bound and not the principal, even if the payee is aware that the signer is an agent.[169]

34-042 **Sufficient signature**   The Act does not provide what amounts to a sufficient signature. It has been held that a signature written by pencil[170] is sufficient, and it appears that a lithographed or stamped signature would, too, suffice.[171] Where the maker of a promissory note, instead of signing underneath the undertaking, wrote

---

[166] Companies Act 2006 s.52.

[167] *Ex p. Kibble* (1875) L.R. 10 Ch. App. 373; *Hutley v Peacock* (1913) 30 T.L.R. 42. As to whether a bill made by a person after attaining majority for the satisfaction of a debt contracted during his minority can be enforced by a holder in due course, see *Belfast Banking Co v Doherty* (1879) 4 L.R.Ir. 124; *Smith v King* [1892] 2 Q.B. 543; *Hutley v Peacock*, above. See also Vol.I, para.9-050.

[168] The agent may, however, be sued for a false representation of authority: *Starkey v Bank of England* [1903] A.C. 114.

[169] *Leadbitter v Farrow* (1816) 5 M. & S. 345, 349; *Ex p. Rayner* (1868) 17 W.R. 64.

[170] *Geary v Physic* (1826) 5 B. & C. 234. And see *Chalmers and Guest on Bills of Exchange and Cheques*, 17th edn (2009), para.3-023.

[171] This appears from *Ex p. Birmingham Banking Co* (1868) L.R. 3 Ch. App. 651, 653–654; *Bird & Co v Thomas Cook & Son Ltd* [1937] 2 All E.R. 227. And see the observations of Lord Denning in *Goodman v J Eban Ltd* [1954] 1 Q.B. 550, which is inconsistent with his dictum in the later case of *Lazarus Estates Ltd v Beasley* [1956] 1 Q.B. 702, 710. cf. *Silk Bros v Security Pacific National Bank* (1987) 72 A.L.R. 535, 540 Aust. See also s.2, defining "writing". A bill of exchange or promissory note is not yet an electronic communication or electronic storage within the Electronic Communications Act 2000 (no order has been made under s.8), and so it is not possible to have an electronic signature of a bill or note: see above, para.34-010. If it becomes possible to have an electronic bill or note, an electronic signature may be valid: see *Lindsay v O'Loughnane* [2010] EWHC 529 (QB), [2012] B.C.C. 153 at [95] (Statute of Frauds Amendment Act 1828 s.6); *J. Pereira Fernandes SA v Mehta* [2006] EWHC 813 (Ch), [2006] 1 W.L.R. 1543 at [29] (Statute of Frauds 1677 s.4); *WS Tankship II BV v Kwangju Bank Ltd* [2011] EWHC 3103 (Comm) at [155] (Statute of Frauds 1677 s.4); *Golden Ocean Group Ltd v Salgaocar Mining Industries Pvt Ltd* [2012] EWCA Civ 265 (Statute of Frauds 1677 s.4); *Bassano v Toft* [2014] EWHC 377 (Ch), [2014] ECC 14 at [43] (Consumer Credit Act 1974 s.60(1)); and also *Chalmers and Guest on Bills of Exchange and Cheques*, 18th edn (2017), para.3-023A (considering, inter alia, EU Regulation No.910/2014 on electronic identifica-

"I William Smith promise to pay", it was held that the writing of the name constituted a valid signature.[172]

Trade or assumed name   Section 23(1) of the Act provides that where a person signs a bill in a trade or assumed name, he is liable as if he had signed it in his own name.

34-043

Partnerships   Section 23(2) makes special provisions for the liability of a partnership. It provides that the signature of the name of a firm is equivalent to the signature, by the person so signing, of the names of all the persons liable as partners in that firm. But this section has a limited scope of application. If a bill drawn on the partnership is accepted by one of the partners in his personal capacity by signing it in his own name, the other partners are not bound.[173]

34-044

Personal liability of company's director   Under s.349(4) of the Companies Act 1985, if a director or other officer of a company signed or authorised to be signed on behalf of the company any bill of exchange, promissory note, cheque or order for money or goods in which its name was not mentioned in legible characters, he was liable to a fine; and he was further personally liable to the holder of the bill, etc. unless the instrument was duly paid by the company. Where a bill was presented for payment and dishonoured, the bill was not "duly paid" for the purposes of s.349(4).[174] The courts applied this subsection strictly so that directors or other officers of the company were held liable where the company's name was misstated even to a relatively minor degree.[175] However, where the misstatement was attributable to the holder of the bill, etc. that holder was estopped from holding the company's signatory liable.[176] Nevertheless, s.349(4) could operate harshly, especially on junior employees of the company, and there were calls for its repeal. The Company Law Review took this view in its *Final Report*,[177] as did the government,[178] and, with effect from October 1, 2008, s.349(4) was repealed by the Companies Act 2006.[179] The Company, Limited Liability Partnership and Business (Names and Trading Disclosures) Regulations 2015[180] now require every company to disclose its registered name on (inter alia) its bills of exchange, promis-

34-045

---

tion and trust services for electronic transactions in the internal market).

[172] *Taylor v Dobbins* (1720) 1 Stra. 399; *Ruff v Webb* (1794) 1 Esp. 129.

[173] *Geo Thompson (Aust) Pty Ltd v Vittadello* [1978] V.R. 199, 206–208, 219–220.

[174] Personal liability under s.349(4) could occur even where the bill had not been presented for payment. A bill is dishonoured by non-payment when presentment is excused and the bill is overdue and unpaid (Bills of Exchange Act 1882 s.47(1)(b)). Presentment is excused where the drawee is not bound, as between himself and the drawer, to pay the bill and the drawer had no reason to believe that it would be paid if presented (Bills of Exchange Act 1882 s.46(2)(c), as applied in *Fiorentino Comm Giuseppe Srl v Farnesi* [2005] EWHC 160 (Ch), [2005] 1 W.L.R. 3718, where a director was held personally liable under s.349(4) despite the fact that the cheque had not been presented for payment).

[175] See, e.g. *Fiorentino Comm Giuseppe Srl v Farnesi*, above, where the company's name was stated as "Portofino Collections (London)" instead of "Portofino Collections (London) Ltd" on a cheque.

[176] *Durham Fancy Goods Ltd v Michael Jackson (Fancy Goods Ltd)* [1968] 2 Q.B. 839, CA.

[177] Company Law Review Steering Group, *Final Report* (2001), para.11.57.

[178] White Paper, *Modernising Company Law* (July 2002), Cm.5553-I and Cm.5553-II; White Paper, *Company Law Reform* (March 2005) Cm.6456.

[179] Companies Act 2006 s.1259 and Sch.6. Companies Act 2006 (Commencement No.5, Transitional Provisions and Savings) Order 2007 (SI 2007/3495) arts 8, 12 and Sch.4.

[180] SI 2015/17 (in force on January 31, 2015), made under the Companies Act 2006 s.82, and revoking the Companies (Trading Disclosures) Regulations 2008 (SI 2008/495).

sory notes, endorsements and order forms,[181] and also on cheques purporting to be signed by or on behalf of the company.[182] Under s.83 of the Companies Act 2006, if legal proceedings are brought by a company to enforce a contract made in the course of a business in respect of which the company was, at the time the contract was made, in breach of these regulations, the legal proceedings will be dismissed if the defendant shows (a) that he has a claim against the company arising out of the contract which he has been unable to pursue because of the breach of the regulations, or (b) that the company's breach of the regulations has caused him to suffer financial loss in connection with the contract, unless (in either case) the court is satisfied that it is just and equitable to permit the proceedings to continue. The company and any officer of the company may be subject to a criminal penalty for breach of the regulation.[183]

34-046   **Non est factum**   There is one important exception to the rule that a person is liable on a bill which he has signed. This exception relates to the defence of non est factum.[184] If the person signing the bill is induced by the fraud of another to believe that he is signing a document which is essentially or fundamentally different, e.g. if he believes himself to be signing a contract of guarantee[185] or merely to be witnessing another's signature,[186] the mistake will render his signature null and void. He will not be liable on the bill even at the suit of a holder in due course. The mistake, however, must occur without negligence. The person signing the bill is not entitled to disown his signature, unless he proves that he has exercised reasonable care.[187] Thus, in *Crédit Lyonnais v PT Barnard & Associates Ltd*[188] two bills of exchange were accepted on behalf of the defendants by their general manager who, being ignorant of the French language in which the bills were drawn, believed them to be mere receipts acknowledging the arrival of a consignment of watches in the United Kingdom. Mocatta J. held the defendants liable to a holder in due course of the bills as, in his Lordship's opinion, any prudent man would have subjected the instruments to an examination and on noticing such words as "bank" and "Lloyds", which appeared in the bills, would have been put on inquiry.

34-047   **Forged or unauthorised signature**   Section 24 of the Bills of Exchange Act provides that where a *signature* on a bill is forged or placed on it without the authority of the person whose signature it purports to be, the forged or unauthorised signature is wholly inoperative, and no right to retain the bill, enforce it or discharge it can be acquired through or under that signature unless the party against whom it is sought to retain it or enforce payment of the bill is precluded from setting up the forgery or want of authority. The word "signature" is not defined in the Act, but the language of s.24 indicates that it refers to any type of signature on a bill, i.e. that of the drawer, drawee or of an indorser.

34-048   **Meaning of forgery**   The word "forgery" is, likewise, not defined in the Act. Section 24 distinguishes between a "forged" signature on a bill and a signature "placed

---

181   reg.24(1)(b).
182   reg.24(1)(c).
183   reg.28(1), and Companies Act 2006 s.84.
184   See Vol.I, paras 3-049 et seq.
185   *Foster v Mackinnon* (1869) L.R. 4 C.P. 704.
186   *Lewis v Clay* (1897) 14 T.L.R. 149.
187   *Foster v Mckinnon*, above; *Saunders v Anglia Building Society [Gallie v Lee]* [1971] A.C. 1004.
188   [1976] 1 Lloyd's Rep. 557, especially at 561.

thereon without the authority of the person whose signature it purports to be". Under the Forgery Act 1861,[189] which was in force when the Bills of Exchange Act 1882 was passed, the placing of an unauthorised signature on a bill was not a forgery. The position was changed by s.1 of the Forgery Act 1913, which has been superseded in turn by s.9(1)(d) of the Forgery and Counterfeiting Act 1981, which is basically similar. Section 9(1)(d) treats a document as a forgery "if it purports to have been made … on the authority of a person who did not in fact authorise its making in those terms". This obvious departure from the 1861 Act, originally effected by the 1913 Act, has had an important implication regarding the analysis of the nature of a signature made by an agent who abuses the authority to sign his principal's name on bills. Before the coming into force of the 1913 Act, in *Morison v London County and Westminster Bank Ltd*,[190] where an agent had authority to draw cheques on his principal's account, it was held that the fraudulent misuse of that authority did not render the cheques forgeries. After 1913, in *Kreditbank Cassel v Schenkers Ltd*,[191] a manager of a company fraudulently drew and indorsed bills on the company's behalf for his own purposes. It was held that his signatures on these bills were forgeries within the meaning of the Forgery Act 1913 and that the bills were, thus, void. Obviously, the position ought to be the same under the 1981 Act.

Ratification of forged or unauthorised signature   In view of this, it is doubtful 34-049 whether such a fraudulent signature may be ratified by the principal. On the one hand, s.24 provides that nothing in it affects the ratification of an unauthorised signature not amounting to a forgery, and the section distinguishes between an unauthorised signature and a forged one. On the other hand, under the 1981 Act, an unauthorised fraudulent signature amounts to a forgery, and most authorities indicate that a forgery may not be ratified.[192] The basis of this doctrine is that as the forger does not act and does not purport to act under the authority of the person whose signature he forges, there is no room for the adoption of his act by way of ratification. However, in the case of a fraudulent unauthorised signature, although it is technically a forgery, the agent purports to sign the bill in the name of his principal. It may perhaps be argued that, for the purpose of ratification, the distinction between a forged and an unauthorised signature should continue to be recognised, especially as it is stressed in the proviso to s.24.

Estoppels: statutory   Section 24 is stated to be subject to the "provisions of this 34-050 Act". This refers to the provisions of ss.54 and 55. Under s.54(2) an acceptor is estopped from denying to a holder in due course the genuineness of the drawer's signature. According to s.55(2) an indorser is estopped from denying to a holder in

---

[189] s.22 concerned forgery of bills and notes.

[190] [1914] 3 K.B. 356, 366. Although the decision of the Court of Appeal was delivered after the coming into effect of the 1913 Act, this Act was not relied upon as it had not been in force at the time of the trial in the King's Bench Division.

[191] [1927] 1 K.B. 826.

[192] *Ex p. Edwards* (1841) 2 Mon. D. & D. 241; *Brook v Hook* (1871) L.R. 6 Ex. 89. See also *Williams v Bayley* (1866) L.R. 1 H.L. 200; *Imperial Bank of Canada v Begley* [1936] 2 All E.R. 367, 374; *Stoney Stanton Supplies (Coventry) Ltd v Midland Bank Ltd* [1966] 2 Lloyd's Rep. 373. Contrast *M'Kenzie v British Linen Co* (1881) 6 App. Cas. 82, 99 (which was a Scottish authority and in which the three first-cited English authorities were not mentioned).

due course the genuineness and regularity of the signatures of the drawer and all previous indorsers.[193]

34-051   Estoppel: common law   Apart from these statutory estoppels, a party may by his own conduct be precluded from pleading that his purported signature is a forgery. In *Leach v Buchanan*[194] the acceptance of a firm was forged on a bill. Before purchasing the bill, the holder inquired whether the acceptance was genuine and the firm assured him that it was. It was held that the firm was estopped from alleging subsequently that the acceptance was forged. In *Greenwood v Martins Bank*[195] a husband came to know that his wife had forged his signature upon several cheques, but did not inform the bank until the death of the wife, which occurred eight months after he became aware of the forgeries. It was held that as this delay had caused the bank the loss of its right of action against the wife, the husband was estopped from alleging that the signatures were not his own. The principle, though, is not as wide as might be anticipated at first glance. In the first place an estoppel can be pleaded only by a person who has relied on a statement of another person to his disadvantage. Secondly, the estoppel is bound to fail unless the customer has actual knowledge of the facts. Constructive notice is inadequate.[196]

34-052   Forged indorsement: bearer bills   The effect of a forged indorsement depends on whether the bill is payable to bearer or to order. A bearer bill is transferred by mere delivery[197] and the rights of the holder against the drawer and the indorsers do not depend on the transferor's indorsement. If he is a holder in due course, who is entitled to enforce the bill despite any defects in the title of prior parties,[198] the fact that an indorsement was forged would appear to be immaterial.

34-053   Forged indorsements: order bills   A bill payable to order is transferred by indorsement and delivery.[199] The rights of a holder of an order bill appear, thus, to depend on the validity of the indorsement. Whether a person may be a holder in due course of an order bill despite the forged indorsement is not altogether certain, but three arguments indicate a negative answer. The first argument against considering such a person a holder in due course follows from the definition, in s.2 of the Act, of the word "holder", i.e. "the payee or indorsee of a bill or note who is in possession of it, or the bearer thereof". A holder in due course, it is argued, must be a "holder"; when an indorsement is forged the person holding under it is not an indorsee and thus not a holder.[200] The difficulty with this argument is that the word "indorsee" is not defined in the Act and the presumption that a person who takes the bill under a defective indorsement is not an indorsee is not directly supported by authorities based on the Bills of Exchange Act 1882. The second argument is

---

[193]   Other sections which are covered by the proviso are ss.60, 64 and 80.
[194]   (1802) 4 Esp. 226. See also *Brook v Hook*, above; *M'Kenzie v British Linen Co*, above.
[195]   [1933] A.C. 51. See also *Brown v Westminster Bank* [1964] 2 Lloyd's Rep. 187. cf. *Ontario Woodsworth Memorial Foundation v Grozbord*, 48 D.L.R. (2d) 385 (1965); *Jervis B Webb Co v Bank of Nova Scotia*, 49 D.L.R. (2d) 692 (1965); *Walpole & Patterson Ltd v National Bank of New Zealand* [1975] 1 N.Z.L.R. 7.
[196]   *Price Meats Ltd v Barclays Bank Plc* [2000] 2 All E.R. (Comm) 346. cf. *Patel v Standard Chartered Bank* [2001] 1 Lloyd's Rep. Bank. 229, in which it was held that Nelsonian knowledge, i.e. wilful blindness, would have the same effect as express knowledge.
[197]   s.31(2).
[198]   s.38(2).
[199]   s.31(3).
[200]   See *Chalmers and Guest on Bills of Exchange and Cheques*, 18th edn (2017), para.3-066.

that, according to s.29 of the Act, a person can be a holder in due course only if he takes a bill which is complete and regular, and that a forged indorsement renders the bill irregular. However, s.29 refers to completeness and regularity *on the face of the bill*, and it is difficult to agree that a forgery necessarily renders the bill irregular on its face. The third argument is that s.38(2) of the Act extends to a holder in due course the right to enforce the bill despite any defect in the title of the transferor, but not if the transferor has no title at all. While it is true that a forger has no title to the bill, it is difficult to agree that the distinction between a defective title and the absence of title has any room within the law of negotiable instruments. If it had, then a person who took a bill from a thief—who could have no title to the bill—could never be a holder in due course. Such an interpretation would defeat the main object of the law of negotiable instruments: it would then be necessary for a transferee to trace the title of the transferor before taking a bill.[201]

Cases   There is no authority decided after the coming into force of the 1882 Act   **34-054**
in which the rights of a holder, who took in good faith and for value an order bill bearing a forged indorsement of the payee, constituted a main issue. Cases decided before the Bills of Exchange Act 1882 held that such a person could not get a good title.[202] In *Lacave & Co v Crédit Lyonnais*[203] Collins J., obiter, expressed his view that s.24 of the Act was only declaratory of pre-existing law and that a person who took an order bill with a forged indorsement could not obtain a good title. Authority thus supports the view that a person cannot obtain a good title under a forged indorsement on an order bill.[204]

Instruments signed by agents   The rights of the parties to a bill signed in   **34-055**
representative form are governed by ss.25 and 26 of the Act. Section 25 governs the position of a third party who takes a bill signed by an agent. It provides that a signature by procuration operates as a notice that the agent has limited authority to sign, and that the principal is bound only in so far as the agent has acted within the limits of his actual authority. The effect of this section is that a holder in due course of such a bill cannot enforce it against the principal if the agent has exceeded his authority.[205] Moreover, the fact that the bill purports to be signed by an agent constitutes a "red flag". A collecting banker who takes such a bill without inquiry may be considered as having acted negligently and thus may lose the protection against actions in conversion conferred on him by s.4 of the Cheques Act 1957.[206] This rule may, however, be less stringently applied in the case of bills signed by bodies corporate, as these can only act through their agents.[207]

Signature in representative form   Section 26(1) provides that a person who signs   **34-056**

---

[201] That this is not so, see *Chichester v Hill* (1882) 52 L.J. Q.B. 160.
[202] *Mead v Young* (1790) 4 Term Rep. 28; *Esdaile v La Nauze* (1835) 1 Y. & C. Ex. 394; *Johnson v Windle* (1836) 3 Bing. N.C. 225; *Bobbett v Pinkett* (1876) 1 Ex. D. 368.
[203] [1897] 1 Q.B. 148.
[204] cf. *Embiricos v Anglo-Austrian Bank* [1905] 1 K.B. 677 as regards problems of private international law concerning the validity of forged indorsements.
[205] *Morison v London County and Westminster Bank Ltd* [1914] 3 K.B. 356, especially at 367; *Sniderman v McGarry*, 60 D.L.R. (2d) 404, 408 (1966).
[206] *Midland Bank Ltd v Reckitt* [1933] A.C. 1 (decided under s.82 of the Bills of Exchange Act 1882, replaced and re-enacted by s.4 of the Cheques Act 1957).
[207] *Re Land Credit Co of Ireland* (1869) L.R. 4 Ch. App. 460, 468; *Alexander Stewart & Son v Westminster Bank Ltd* [1926] W.N. 126 (reversed on a different point [1926] W.N. 271). cf. *Kreditbank Cassel v Schenkers Ltd* [1927] 1 K.B. 826.

a bill (whether as drawer, acceptor or indorser) in representative form, i.e. by adding words indicating that he signs on behalf of his principal, does not incur liability on the bill. However, the mere addition to a signature of words describing
the signatory as an agent, or as acting in a representative character, does not, in
itself, exempt him from personal liability.[208] The determining factor is whether the
words, indicating the signatory's position as agent, are meant to describe his occupation, or whether they are meant to show that he signs the bill on behalf of his
principal. Thus, where a bill was drawn on a company and accepted by it, and, at
the drawer's request, the directors indorsed it as "B. Co Ltd, J.S. & E.D., Directors", it was held that they were personally liable.[209] Where a promissory note was
signed by "J. S., Managing Director" beneath a rubber stamp setting out the name
of the company, the managing director was held not to be personally liable on the
bill.[210] The best explanation of the provision is to be found in *Bondina v Rollaway
Shower Blinds Ltd*[211] in which the signatures of two directors of the company, on
whose account the cheques were drawn, was executed in ink beneath the company's
name, which was printed on the cheque. One of the directors, against whom the
payee sought to enforce payment, denied that he was personally liable on the
instrument. Dillon L.J. said that, when the director executed his signature on the
cheque, he adopted not only the writing designating the payee's name and the
amount but also the printing of the company's name and of the numbers which set
out the company's account. In this way, the director indicated that the cheque was
drawn on the company's account and that there was no intention to create an instrument imposing joint liability. The intention of the signatory is, thus, of importance,
and it may, it appears, be determined by extrinsic evidence.[212]

34-057 Construction to uphold validity According to s.26(2) in determining whether
a signature on a bill is that of the principal or that of an agent by whose hand it is
written, the construction most favourable to the validity of the instrument is to be
adopted. This provision was discussed in *Rolfe Lubell & Co v Keith*[213] in which the
plaintiff agreed to supply goods to a company provided that two of its directors
indorsed in their personal capacity bills of exchange drawn for the price. The
defendant, who was one of the directors, indorsed the bills but added to his signature
by means of a rubber stamp the words: "For and on behalf of the [company];
director". Kilner-Brown J. observed that as the company assumed liability as acceptor of the bills, an indorsement executed by it would be meaningless and of no
value. In view of this patent ambiguity in the bills it was permissible to call evidence
to clarify the intention of the parties. On the basis of the evidence, his Lordship
concluded that the words imprinted by means of the rubber stamp were of no
significance. He emphasised that the "only way in which validity [could] be given

---

[208] As regards signature of agent on a cheque form on which the principal's name is printed, see *Sniderman v McGarry*, 60 D.L.R. (2d) 404 (1966).

[209] *Elliott v Bax-Ironside* [1925] 2 K.B. 301; cf. *Kettle v Dunster and Wakefield* (1927) 43 T.L.R. 770.
See also above, para.31-091.

[210] *Chapman v Smethurst* [1909] 1 K.B. 927. See also *HB Etlin Co Ltd v Asselstyne*, 32 D.L.R. (2d) 489
(1962). cf. *Jones v John Barr & Co (Pty) Ltd* [1967] 3 S.A.L.R. 292, 301 et seq.

[211] [1986] 1 All E.R. 564. cf. *Holtz v G Parckdale Refrigeration Ltd*, 30 O.R. (2d) 513 (1980) Can;
Plascon Evans Paints (Tvl) Ltd v Ming [1980] 3 S.A. 378; *Bank of Nova Scotia v Radocsay*, 33 O.R.
(2d) 785 (1981) Can.

[212] *HB Etlin Co Ltd v Asselstyne*, above; *Rolfe Lubell & Co v Keith* [1979] 1 All E.R. 860; *Heller Factors Pty Ltd v Toy Corp Pty Ltd* [1984] 1 N.S.W.L.R. 121 (Aust).

[213] [1979] 1 All E.R. 860.

to this indorsement [was] by construing it to bind someone other than the acceptor".[214] This interpretation had the additional merit of giving currency and hence full validity to the bills.

End result   In the majority of cases the result of ss.25 and 26 is that, where an **34-058** agent exceeds his authority, neither he nor his principal are liable on the bill. However, although the agent is not liable on the bill, he can be sued either in deceit (if he committed a fraud) or in an action for breach of warranty of his authority to sign.[215]

(iii)   The Consideration for a Bill

Value and holder for value   Section 27(1) provides that valuable consideration **34-059** for a bill may be constituted by (a) any consideration sufficient to support a simple contract[216]; and (b) an antecedent debt or liability. Such debt or liability is deemed valuable consideration whether the bill is payable on demand or at a future time. Thus, while past consideration is insufficient to support a simple contract, it can, nevertheless, constitute good consideration for a bill. For example, if a person whose banking account is overdrawn negotiates to his bankers a cheque, drawn by a third party, to reduce the overdraft, the banker becomes a holder for value of the cheque.[217] The pre-existing debt of the overdraft is a sufficient consideration for the negotiation of the cheque to the banker.

Past consideration   The meaning of s.27(1)(b) was discussed in *Oliver v Davis*.[218] **34-060** The plaintiff lent the first defendant £350 and obtained from him a post-dated cheque for £400. Before the presentment of the cheque, the first defendant persuaded the second defendant to draw a cheque for £400 in favour of the plaintiff. The cheque was forwarded to the plaintiff but, before its presentment, was countermanded by the second defendant. The second defendant did not receive any consideration for the cheque from either the plaintiff or the first defendant, and the plaintiff did not change his position in reliance on the cheque. It was held that no valuable consideration within the meaning of s.27(1) was given for the cheque. Evershed M.R. pointed out that the alleged consideration in this case was not the debt of the drawer (the second defendant) but that of a third party (the first defendant). He explained that the main object of s.27(1)(b) is to establish that a past obligation of the drawer or acceptor of a cheque is valuable consideration. If the alleged consideration for the bill is not an antecedent debt or liability of the drawer or acceptor but of a third party, there must, at least, be some connection between

214 [1979] 1 All E.R. 860 at 863.
215 *Polhill v Walter* (1832) 3 B. & Ad. 114; *West London Commercial Bank Ltd v Kitson* (1884) 13 Q.B.D. 360; *Starkey v Bank of England* [1903] A.C. 114. cf. *Gowers v Lloyds and National Provincial Foreign Bank Ltd* [1938] 1 All E.R. 766.
216 As regards a situation in which the consideration is illegal, e.g. under the Gaming Act 1968 (since repealed and replaced by the Gambling Act 2005), see *Ladup v Shaik* [1983] Q.B. 225.
217 *McLean v Clydesdale Banking Co* (1883) 9 App. Cas. 95. See also *Ex p. Richdale* (1882) 19 Ch. D. 409; *Royal Bank of Scotland v Tottenham* [1894] 2 Q.B. 715; *Barclays Bank Ltd v Astley Industrial Trust Ltd* [1970] 2 Q.B. 527, 539. For a modern case concerning the meaning of "consideration sufficient to support a simple contract" within the meaning of s.27(1)(a), see *Sharp v Ellis* [1972] V.R. 137. As regards a consideration which fails *in toto*, see *Miller Associates (Australia) Pty Ltd v Bennington Pty Ltd* (1975) 7 A.L.R. 144 noted in (1981) 55 A.L.J. 135.
218 [1949] 2 K.B. 727.

the receipt of the bill and the antecedent debt or liability. His Lordship added that when a cheque or bill has been post-dated, the courts have, in the absence of express evidence, implied a promise of the payee (creditor) to forbear from claiming the debt from the drawer (debtor) until the date of the bill. In such cases the forbearance is valuable consideration. But even where there is an antecedent debt or liability on the part of the drawer or acceptor, it does not always follow that there is consideration for the bill, as there may be no connection between the past obligation and the giving of the bill. A fortiori, when the debt or liability is that of a third party, the matter is a question of evidence.

34-061 **Need to move from promisee** This analysis of Evershed M.R., it is submitted, overlooks one important aspect. Section 27(1) does not modify the well-known principle that consideration must move from the promisee. It is true that a consideration given for a bill by one *party* accrues, on occasions, for the benefit of other parties to the bill.[219] But it does not follow that an obligation, whether past or present, given by a *stranger* to the bill is valuable consideration for it. It is true that if, at the request of the drawer or the acceptor, the payee or holder of the bill forbears from claiming a debt due to him from a third party, there is valuable consideration for the bill.[220] But the consideration is the forbearance of the holder, not the antecedent obligation of the third party (debtor).[221] If, on the other hand, the drawer draws the bill in favour of the payee not in order to induce him to give time to the third party (debtor), but, for example, in order to pay a debt of this third party, there is no valuable consideration for the bill. This is not due to the fact that the obligation of the third party (debtor) is past, but because no consideration for the bill is given by the promisee, i.e. the holder or payee. It is submitted that an antecedent debt or liability of a stranger to the bill cannot, in itself, constitute consideration.[222] This submission has the weight of authority behind it.[223] However, it seems that there may be consideration to support a cheque drawn in respect of a third party's debt where there exists a commercial relationship between the drawer of the cheque and the third party debtor.[224]

34-062 **Pollway Ltd v Abdullah** Support for this submission is to be found in two cases.

[219] e.g. in the case of a person who, without giving consideration for it, obtains it from a holder in due course: s.29(3); and see below, respecting s.27(2).
[220] For a recent example, see *Banque Cantonale de Genève v Sanomi* [2016] EWHC 3353 (Comm) at [48]–[62].
[221] [2016] EWHC 3353 (Comm) at [47].
[222] In *Crears v Hunter* (1887) 19 Q.B.D. 341, cited by Evershed M.R., the holder of a promissory note forbore from claiming a debt due to him from a third party at the request of the maker of the note. Consideration moved from the maker. See also the decision of Somervell L.J. in *Oliver v Davis*, above, especially at 741. The view taken in cases decided in Australia and New Zealand is that past consideration furnished by a third party constitutes good consideration under s.27(1)(a) provided there is a close link between the issuing of the bill and the consideration provided in the underlying transaction: *Electrical Technologies Ltd v Auckland Electrical Services Ltd* [1995] 3 N.Z.L.R. 726 and cases there cited including *Walsh, Spriggs, Nolan and Finney v Hoag & Bosh Pty Ltd* (1976) 12 A.L.R. 411 Aust; *Bonior v Asiery Ltd* [1968] N.Z.L.R. 254; *Finch Motors Ltd v Quin* [1980] 2 N.Z.L.R. 513; *International Ore and Fertilizer Corp v East Coast Fertilizer Co Ltd* [1987] 1 N.Z.L.R. 9.
[223] *Oliver v Davis* [1949] 2 K.B. 727; *Hasan v Willson* [1977] 1 Lloyd's Rep. 431; *MK International Development Co Ltd v Housing Bank* [1991] 1 Bank. L.R. 74; *Lomax Leisure Ltd v Miller* [2008] 1 B.C.L.C. 262, [47]–[50]; *Confezioni v Rozenthal* [2011] EWHC 4105 (QB) at [19]–[27]. See generally, *Chalmers and Guest on Bills of Exchange and Cheques*, 18th edn (2017), paras 4-023 et seq.; *Byles on Bills of Exchange and Cheques*, 29th edn (2013), paras 19-011 et seq.
[224] *Autobiography Ltd v Byrne* [2005] EWHC 213 (Ch); distinguished in *Lomax Leisure Ltd v Miller*

The first is a dictum in *Pollway Ltd v Abdullah*.[225] The defendant purchased a property in an auction and gave the auctioneers a cheque payable to their order and covering the amount of the deposit due under the terms of the sale. Subsequently, the defendant refused to proceed with the sale and stopped payment of the cheque. He resisted the auctioneers' action to enforce the cheque on the ground that no consideration was furnished by them. Rejecting this argument, the Court of Appeal held that the consideration for the cheque was either the auctioneers' warranty to the defendant—as drawer of the cheque—of their authority to take the cheque as named payees in diminution of his obligation to pay the full price to the vendors or the auctioneers' acceptance of the cheque in the place of payment of the deposit in cash. Roskill L.J. emphasised that the vendors' undertaking to sell could not be regarded as consideration for the cheque, as this consideration did not move from the auctioneers, i.e. the payees.

Hasan v Wilson   The second case is *Hasan v Wilson*.[226] The plaintiff, a broker act-   **34-063**
ing on behalf of an unnamed government, was entitled to an amount of £50,000 by way of agreed damages for the breach of a contract for the sale of gold coins concluded through his efforts between his principals and S. To facilitate further negotiations and as the plaintiff was not prepared to take a cheque drawn by S, the latter induced the defendant, a respectable businessman, to draw one cheque payable to the plaintiff for £50,000 and another cheque payable to S's wife for £5,000. In exchange for these cheques, S gave the defendant a cheque for £55,000, drawn by S's wife on the account of a certain company. It was clear from the facts that the defendant agreed to furnish his cheques solely for the purpose of assisting one of his friends, who stood to make a profit from the deal negotiated between S and the plaintiff. To protect himself, the defendant arranged for the special clearance of the cheque drawn by S's wife. When this cheque was dishonoured for want of funds, the defendant promptly stopped his own two cheques. Dismissing the action brought by the plaintiff as holder of the defendant's cheque for £50,000, Goff J. held that "the antecedent debt or liability referred to in s.27(1)(b) must be an antecedent debt or liability of the promisor or drawer of the relevant bill of exchange and not of a stranger to the bill".[227] The amount of £50,000 owed by S to the plaintiff could, therefore, not constitute a consideration for the defendant's cheque payable to the plaintiff. The consideration furnished by means of the cheque drawn by S's wife had, of course, failed in toto when it was dishonoured.

Need not be adequate   Apart from the exception concerning past consideration,   **34-064**
and some other exceptions,[228] the doctrine of consideration remains unmodified in the case of negotiable instruments. An important general rule is that consideration need not be adequate.[229] However, the inadequacy of the consideration given by the

---

[2008] 1 B.C.L.C. 262, [47]–[50]. See further, E.P. Ellinger, E. Lomnicka and C.V.M. Hare, *Ellinger's Modern Banking Law*, 5th edn (2011), pp.400, 435–436.

[225] [1974] 1 W.L.R. 493, 497.
[226] [1977] 1 Lloyd's Rep. 431.
[227] [1977] 1 Lloyd's Rep. 431 at 440–441. See also *AEG (UK Ltd v Lewis* [1993] 1 C.L. 132, noted in [1993] J.B.L. 275. Contrast *Walsh, Spriggs, Nolan and Finney v Hoag & Bosh Pty Ltd* (1976) 12 A.L.R. 411 Aust. And see Geva (1981) 39 C.L.J. 360.
[228] As to which, see below.
[229] *Jones v Gordon* (1877) 2 App. Cas. 616; *Adib el Hinnawi v Yacoub Fahmi* [1936] 1 All E.R. 638.

holder for a bill may be evidence of bad faith or of knowledge of defects in the title of the transferor.[230]

34-065 **Effect of s.27(2)**   Section 27(2) provides that, where value has at any time been given for a bill, the holder is deemed to be a holder for value as regards the acceptor and all persons who became parties to the bill prior to such time. Thus, any party who takes the bill after consideration has been given for it is deemed a holder for value. This is, to a certain extent, a modification of the rule that consideration must move from the promisee. Two cases illustrate the effect of this provision. In *Scott v Lifford*[231] a debtor asked the creditor to give him time. It was agreed that the debtor would accept a bill drawn on him by his uncle, the defendant, in favour of the creditor. The bill was dishonoured by the acceptor and the creditor sued the defendant, as drawer. It was held that, as the creditor (holder) gave value for the bill to the debtor (acceptor), the creditor was a holder for value of the bill and was entitled to sue the defendant (drawer) although the latter received no value. However, as the creditor gave time to the debtor against this bill, it may be argued that the drawer in fact obtained consideration by the creditor's forbearance. In *Diamond v Graham*[232] H gave G his own cheque in return for G's cheque, which was payable to D's order and in reliance on which D gave H a loan. It was held that D was a holder for value of G's cheque. Consideration for G's cheque was given, in the first place, by H when he drew his own cheque in favour of D and, secondly, by D himself when he granted the loan to H on the basis of G's cheque. Emphasising that each one of these two considerations was adequate Danckwerts L.J. said:

> "There is nothing in the subsection which appears to require value to have been given by the holder as long as value has been given for the cheque ..."[233]

An important effect of s.27(2) is that a transferee of a bill, e.g. a banker, who gives value for it to the transferor becomes a holder for value and can sue previous parties to the bill even if these did not obtain any consideration for it.[234]

34-066 **Review by Court of Appeal**   The most recent analysis of s.27(1) and (2) is to be found in the Court of Appeal's decision in *MK International Development Co Ltd v Housing Bank*.[235] A relative of King Hussein of Jordan, one N, required office space and some financial accommodation during a few months spent in London in 1983 and 1984. K made the required arrangements through two companies controlled by him. The plaintiffs, MK, provided the necessary space against N's undertaking to reimburse an amount of £1,000 towards expenses and Y Ltd granted N a substantial loan. When N defaulted, K wrote directly to King Hussein, using MK's letterhead, asking that pressure be put on N to repay his debts. In due course, K received a letter from the Royal Court, enclosing a cheque for £50,965, drawn by the H Bank in Amman on the Arab Bank in London and made payable to MK or bearer. However, before MK had the time to clear the cheque, N contacted the King's staff and denied the existence of any indebtedness to K. The cheque was

---

[230] *Jones v Gordon*, above. See also *Allen v Davis* (1850) 20 L.J. Ch. 44; *Simons v Cridland* (1862) 5 L.T. 523.
[231] (1808) 1 Camp. 246.
[232] [1968] 1 W.L.R. 1061; cf. *Pollway Ltd v Abdullah* [1974] 1 W.L.R. 493, 497.
[233] [1968] 1 W.L.R. 1061, 1064.
[234] Below, paras 34-098 et seq.
[235] [1991] 1 Bank. L.R. 74.

thereupon countermanded and accordingly dishonoured by the Arab Bank by non-payment. The Court of Appeal held that leave to serve a summons outside the jurisdiction ought to be granted as the contract was made in England and was governed by English law. Their Lordships further concluded that, as there was an arguable case on the issue respecting the consideration given for the cheque, the H Bank was to be granted unconditional leave to defend. The issue in question arose, principally, as the cheque was payable to MK whilst the amount covered by it—except the £1,000 respecting the office expenses—was due to Y or to K. MK sought to overcome the apparent absence of consideration by raising four arguments.

Argument respecting subs.(1)(a)–(b) MK's first argument was that N's debts **34-067**
furnished past consideration which, under s.27(1)(b), was adequate to support an undertaking given in a negotiable instrument. MK's second and complementary plea was that there was a "consideration sufficient to support a simple contract", within the meaning of s.27(1)(a) as, in reliance on the cheque, K and MK forbore to enforce their respective claims against N. Mustill L.J. pointed out that[236]:

> "... the line between the two ways of putting the case seems vanishingly thin, for if the antecedent debt is to furnish any useful consideration this must be because it is regarded as nullified by the substitution of the new obligation; and the distinction between a contract which causes the old debt to cease to exist and one which requires the creditor not to enforce it appears of little practical significance."

However, as the authorities treated the pleas as distinct, his Lordship dealt with them separately. As regards s.27(1)(b), Mustill L.J. concluded that N's antecedent liabilities did not furnish a valid consideration for the cheque drawn by the H Bank in favour of MK. N was a stranger to the cheque and hence his past debts, due to Y or to K, did not constitute a valid consideration for the cheque drawn in favour of MK. Mustill L.J. then turned to subs.1(*a*) and the forbearance issue. Agreeing that such forbearance would usually constitute good consideration, his Lordship pointed out that only a small amount, from the total sum of the cheque, was owed by N to MK. Could MK's forbearance to enforce that minute claim furnish valuable consideration for the total amount of the cheque? Mustill L.J. took the view that the answer to this question did not depend on whether consideration had to be adequate rather than real, but on whether a partial absence of consideration provided a good defence to MK's action on the cheque. He pointed out that, although this question had not been the subject of a direct decision, it was established that "an ascertained cross-claim under the contract which formed the consideration for the bill [was] a good defence pro tanto as against an immediate party". His Lordship concluded:

> "There seems no logical reason why, if subsequent failure of an ascertained part of the consideration is a defence as between immediate parties, the same should not be so where, as to part, the consideration was never there in the first place."

This reasoning led Mustill L.J. to the conclusion that MK could have a good cause of action on the bill, albeit limited to the amount of the debt owed to it. His Lordship emphasised, however, that due to the dearth of direct authority, he did not feel the "confidence which one ought to be able to feel on a point so apparently

---

[236] [1991] 1 Bank. L.R. 74 at 78.

simple".[237]

34-068 Critique of decision respecting s.27(1) It is important to recall that the instant judgment was delivered in respect of issues raised in a preliminary hearing. A final answer would undoubtedly depend on the facts to be established at a trial. The issue would be whether MK's indulgence or forbearance was related to the issuing of the cheque and, further, on whether it was exercised in reliance on a request—express or implied—attributable to the H Bank. Thus, if, on the facts, the relevant forbearance constituted a consideration for the payment to be obtained from the King, would it, necessarily, be also a consideration for the H Bank's own undertaking in the cheque? From a purely commercial point of view, the H Bank issued its cheque at the instruction of the King's staff and the consideration obtained for it was the amount debited to the relevant account. It may be asserted, as against this point, that MK may still have forborne from exercising its rights against N when it received the cheque. The real issue is whether it could be shown on the facts that the claim against N could or would have been pursued but for MK's receipt of the cheque. A great deal might, for instance, depend on the length of time that had passed between the date on which the cheque was received by MK and the date on which it was dishonoured by the Arab Bank.

34-069 MK's case: s.27(2) The third attempt to establish the existence of a valid consideration centred on an argument based on s.27(2). It was argued that as the King had given value for the cheque, MK was deemed to be a holder for value. Mustill L.J. indicated that the authorities suggested that s.27(2) applied only where the instrument had been negotiated and not in favour of the original payee. He was, further, inclined to the view that, in any event, the consideration specified in s.27(2) would have to move from a promisee of the cheque and not from a stranger, such as the King. The fourth and final attempt to establish the presence of consideration was based on the fact that the cheque was payable to "MK or bearer". Mustill L.J. observed that, if the cheque was, accordingly, payable to bearer, then the King could well be considered its first holder. Under s.27(2), the consideration furnished by him would then support the claim of any subsequent holder, such as MK.

34-070 Lienee as holder for value under s.27(3) Section 27(1) and (2) define the type of consideration that is adequate in the context of the law of bills of exchange. Subsection (3) makes special provisions respecting the position of a lienee: where the holder of a bill has a lien on it, arising either from a contract or by implication of law, he is deemed to be a holder for value to the extent of the sum for which he has the lien.[238] A holder who has taken a bill against payment of part of its sum to the transferor is entitled to recover the whole amount of the bill, and on recovery

---

[237] [1991] 1 Bank. L.R. 74 at 79. Mustill L.J. referred to Robert Goff J.'s words in *Hasan v Wilson* [1977] 1 Lloyd's Rep. 431 at 440–441, cited above, para.34-063, and to *Oliver v Davis* [1949] 2 K.B. 727; *Diamond v Graham* [1968] 1 W.L.R. 1061; and *Pollway v Abdullah* [1974] 1 W.L.R. 493. But cf. *Walsh, Spriggs, Nolan and Finney v Hoag & Bosh Pty Ltd* (1976) 12 A.L.R. 411 Aust.

[238] s.27(3); and see *Redfern v Rosenthal* (1902) 18 T.L.R. 718; *Re Keever* [1967] Ch. 182; *Barclays Bank Ltd v Astley Industrial Trust Ltd* [1970] 2 Q.B. 527, 539 (showing that if, in addition, the requirements of s.29(1) are satisfied, such a lien would render the holder a holder in due course); *Bank of Credit and Commerce Int SA v Dawson* [1987] F.L.R. 342.

becomes trustee for the person entitled to the remainder of the money, after deducting the amount he has advanced.[239]

Accommodation bill or party   Accommodation bills are dealt with by s.28, which provides that an accommodation party to a bill is a person who has signed a bill as drawer, acceptor or indorser without receiving value therefor and for the purpose of lending his name to some other person. An accommodation party is liable on the bill to a holder for value; and it is immaterial whether, when such holder took the bill, he knew such party to be an accommodation party or not.[240] A bill which is signed by one or more accommodation parties is frequently spoken of as an accommodation bill, but this is incorrect. An accommodation bill is a bill in which the acceptor (i.e. the principal debtor according to the terms of the instrument) is in substance a mere surety for some other person who may or may not be a party thereto.[241] The bill is discharged when it is honoured by the accommodated party.[242]

34-071

Holder in due course   Section 29 provides that four requirements must be fulfilled before a person may be considered a holder in due course.[243] First, he must take the bill when it is complete and regular on its face. Secondly, he must take it before it is overdue[244] and without notice that it was previously dishonoured, if such was the fact. Knowledge that a bill is bound to be dishonoured may also be relevant. Thus, a Canadian authority suggests that a holder, who has taken a cheque with the knowledge of its having been countermanded, is not a holder in due course.[245] Thirdly, he must take it in good faith and without having notice of any defect in the title of the person who negotiates the bill to him. In particular the title of the person who negotiates the bill is defective when he obtained the bill or its acceptance by fraud, duress or other unlawful means, or for an illegal consideration, or when he negotiates it in breach of faith or under circumstances amounting to fraud.[246] Last, a holder in due course must take the bill for value, i.e. consideration.[247] Apart from these requirements, it follows from the language of s.29 that a holder in due course must be a "holder who has taken a bill …".[248] It has been held that these words refer to a holder to whom the bill has been negotiated and that the original payee of a

34-072

---

[239] *Reid v Furnival* (1833) 1 Cr. & M. 538. A stay of proceedings may in such a case be granted, if in an action on the bill, it turns out that the claimant is trustee of part of the sum and the defendant has a claim which could be pleaded by way of set-off against the beneficiary of the trust: *Barclays Bank Ltd v Aschaffenburger Zellstoffwerke AG* [1967] 1 Lloyd's Rep. 387.

[240] s.28. The person accommodated is not discharged if the bill is not duly presented for payment (s.46(2)), or by the absence of notice of dishonour (s.50(2)) or of protest (s.51(9)).

[241] *Chalmers and Guest on Bills of Exchange and Cheques*, 18th edn (2017), para.4-042.

[242] s.59(3).

[243] The rights of a holder in due course are stated in s.38(2).

[244] As to when a bill payable on demand becomes overdue, see s.36(3).

[245] *Galco Enterprises Ltd v Hatty* (1979) 27 N.B.R. (2d) 608.

[246] s.29(2).

[247] The orthodox view, which relies on the wording of s.29(1), is that a holder becomes a holder in due course only insofar as he acquires the bill for value or, in other words, furnishes consideration for it: *Chalmers and Guest on Bills of Exchange and Cheques*, 18th edn (2017), para.4-057. But see *Clifford Chance v Silver* [1992] N.P.C. 103 in which the Court of Appeal, on a summary judgment application, held that, under s.27(2), the holder in due course could, equally, attain his status in reliance on value provided by a previous party. For a critique, see Hitchens [1993] J.B.L. 571.

[248] But he may become a holder in due course by reason of his having a lien over the bill: s.27(3) and *Barclays Bank Ltd v Astley Industrial Trust Ltd* [1970] 2 Q.B. 527, 539.

bill cannot, therefore, be a holder in due course.[249] The second requirement specified in s.29 has not given rise to much litigation and the last has been discussed above in relation to a holder for value; but it will be useful to examine in detail the other two requirements.

34-073 **Regularity** Whether a bill is complete and regular on its *face* is a question of fact, and must be determined by looking only at the bill. However, an Australian authority suggests that in cases of doubt there is room for expert evidence and that regard may be had to banking practice.[250] The word "face" in s.29 includes the back of the bill.[251] A bill is not considered complete if any material detail is missing, e.g. the name of the payee, the amount payable or any necessary indorsement.[252] A bill is not incomplete merely because it has not been accepted.[253] When the blanks in a bill, which was incomplete when issued, are filled up before it comes into the hands of a holder in due course, he is entitled to enforce it even if it has not been completed strictly in accordance with the drawer's authority.[254]

34-074 A bill is considered irregular whenever anything on the face or the back of the bill can give rise to doubts or is out of the ordinary, e.g. if there is a discrepancy between the words and figures denoting the amount,[255] or if the bill is pasted together after having been torn.[256] But a bill is, in all probability, not irregular merely because it is post-dated.[257] The indorsement of the payee is irregular when it differs materially from the name written by the drawer on the front of the bill.[258] Thus, if a bill is indorsed "J. Williams" instead of "John Williams", the indorsement is not irregular. But where a payee is described on the face of the bill by the wrong name (e.g. W. Williams) and then indorses the bill in his true name (e.g. John Williams) the discrepancy between the front and the back of the bill renders the bill "irregular" within the meaning of s.29.[259] In order to achieve regularity the payee should in such cases add an indorsement in the misnomer by which he was described by the drawer. Titles and descriptions of the payee mentioned on the front of the bill, such as "Mr" or "Dr", may be omitted in the indorsement without impairing its regularity, but the omission of the word "company" may be of considerable significance and its omission, certainly on a foreign bill, renders an indorsement irregular.[260] If the indorsements on the back of the bill are not arranged in their correct sequence, the bill is not, necessarily, irregular. Thus, where the indorsement of

---

[249] *RE Jones Ltd v Waring and Gillow Ltd* [1926] A.C. 670, 680, HL; *Lloyds Bank Ltd v Chartered Bank of India, Australia and China* [1929] 1 K.B. 40, 57, 75, CA.

[250] *Heller Factors Pty Ltd v Toy Corp Pty Ltd* [1984] 1 N.S.W.L.R. 121, 140–142.

[251] *Arab Bank Ltd v Ross* [1952] 2 Q.B. 216, 226.

[252] *Whistler v Forster* (1863) 14 C.B.(N.S.) 248, 258 (indorsement of payee missing on a bill payable to order); *Slingsby v District Bank* [1931] 2 K.B. 588 (affirmed [1932] 1 K.B. 544); *Arab Bank Ltd v Ross*, above. Section 2 of the Cheques Act 1957, however, creates an exception as regards discounting bankers: see below, para.34-372.

[253] *National Park Bank of New York v Berggren & Co* (1914) 110 L.T. 907.

[254] s.20. And see above, para.34-035.

[255] For an extreme case, concerning a difference between the description of the currency accompanying the amount in words and its description preceding the amount in figures, see *Banco di Roma v Orru* [1973] 2 Lloyd's Rep. 505.

[256] See on this point *Scholey v Ramsbottom* (1810) 2 Camp. 485; *Ingham v Primrose* (1859) 7 C.B.(N.S.) 82; *Redmayne v Burton* (1860) 2 L.T. 324.

[257] *Hitchcock v Edwards* (1889) 60 L.T. 636 and see below, para.34-156.

[258] *Arab Bank Ltd v Ross* [1952] 2 Q.B. 216.

[259] Although the indorsement is valid for the purpose of transferring the title, provided there was an intention to make the bill payable to this payee: s.31(3) and *Arab Bank Ltd v Ross*, above.

[260] *Arab Bank Ltd v Ross*, above.

the payee was written beneath those of two directors of the company which drew the bill, evidence was admitted to show that they signed their names above the payee's indorsement in order to assume liability towards him as guarantors. The bill was, therefore, not irregular on its face.[261]

Good faith   As regards the requirement that the holder must take the bill in good faith and without knowledge of the defects in the title of the transferor, s.90 specifies that a thing is deemed to be done in good faith where it is in fact done honestly, whether it is done negligently or not. In *Jones v Gordon*[262] Lord Blackburn said that in order to establish that a holder did not take a bill in good faith:

> "... it is necessary to show that the person who gave value for the bill, whether the value given be great or small, was affected with notice that there was something wrong about it when he took it. I do not think it is necessary that he should have notice of what the particular wrong was".

34-075

The word "notice" which appears in this dictum, as well as in s.29, means actual though not formal notice, i.e. either knowledge of the facts, or a suspicion of something wrong combined with a wilful disregard of the means of knowledge. While the doctrine of constructive notice does not apply in the law of negotiable instruments, the holder is not entitled to disregard a "red flag" which has raised his suspicions.[263] The knowledge in question may be that of the holder himself or that of an executive in his employment, even if that person's involvement is contrary to the holder's interest.[264]

Notice of facts respecting underlying transaction   The defect of title or suspicious circumstance, knowledge of which precludes the holder or transferee from holding the bill in due course, may relate not only to a matter pertinent to the transferor's title to the bill but also to one concerning its negotiation or issuing. Thus, in a Canadian authority, *Williams and Glyn's Bank v Belkin Packaging Ltd*,[265] it was held that a bank's knowledge, that promissory notes discounted by it had been issued with a view to their being retained by the payee and replaced by a subsequent issue of notes if a certain commercial event took place, constituted notice of a defect which precluded the bank from becoming a holder in due course.[266] The rule is, however, subject to one limitation, which was defined in *Österreichische Länderbank v S'Elite Ltd*.[267] A bill of exchange was negotiated to the plaintiff bank by the drawer who, to the bank's knowledge, was insolvent. The acceptors dishonoured the bill and sought leave to defend an action to enforce it on the ground

34-076

---

261 *Lombard Banking Ltd v Central Garage and Engineering Co Ltd* [1963] 1 Q.B. 220. See also *Yeoman Credit Ltd v Gregory* [1963] 1 W.L.R. 343.

262 (1877) 2 App. Cas. 616, 628. See also *Bank of Cyprus (London) Ltd v Jones* (1984) 134 New L.J. 522. As to the distinction between negligence and lack of good faith, see *Raphael v Bank of England* (1855) 17 C.B. 161. See also *Baker v Barclays Bank Ltd* [1955] 1 W.L.R. 822.

263 *Raphael v Bank of England*, above.

264 *Bank of Credit and Commerce Int SA v Dawson and Wright* [1987] F.L.R. 342.

265 [1982] 6 W.W.R. 481, Can SC.

266 And see *Bank of Credit and Commerce Int SA v Dawson and Wright*, above. Note also that, where a defect of title was cured before that date on which delivery became unconditional, the transferee's status as a holder in due course is not impaired by notice of the original defect: *Clifford Chance v Silver* [1992] N.P.C. 103.

267 [1980] 2 All E.R. 651, overruling *Banca Popolare di Novara v John Livanos & Sons Ltd* [1965] 2 Lloyd's Rep. 149.

that the transfer of the bill involved an undue preference under s.44(1) of the Bankruptcy Act 1914.[268] Their argument was that, in view of these circumstances, the negotiation was tainted with fraud within the meaning of s.29 of the Bills of Exchange Act. Rejecting this argument, the Court of Appeal held that to vitiate the rights of a holder in due course the alleged circumstances had to involve a common law fraud.

34-077   An altogether different approach is taken by Canadian authorities, which have held that a finance company, which has a close business relationship with a dealer, may not claim to be a holder in due course of bills of customers of the dealer negotiated by him to the finance company in connection with purchases by the customers from the dealer, financed by the company.[269] However, it is difficult to agree that, if such a finance company has no "notice" within the meaning of s.29 of any irregularity or suspicious circumstance concerning a transaction financed by it, it may not be a holder in due course of bills negotiated to it by the dealer.

34-078   **Basic rights of holder in due course**   A holder in due course takes the bill free from any defects in the title of all prior parties as well as from any equities available to prior parties among themselves, and is entitled to enforce payment against all parties liable on the bill.[270] The same rights accrue to any holder (whether for value or not) who derives his title from a holder in due course, provided he is not himself a party to any fraud affecting the bill.[271] Mere knowledge of a fraud or illegality by a person who has derived his title from a holder in due course does not deprive him of these rights.[272] It is noteworthy that in certain circumstances the rights of a holder in due course may be enforced even by the drawer of the bill. This is the position where, after the dishonour of the bill by the acceptor, the drawer regains its possession by paying it to the holder in due course.[273]

34-079   **Presumption of good faith**   Every party whose signature appears on a bill is prima facie deemed to have become a party thereto for value.[274] Every holder of a bill is prima facie deemed to be a holder in due course; but if the acceptance, issue or subsequent negotiation of the bill was affected with fraud, duress or illegality, the burden of proof is shifted, and the holder must prove that, subsequent to the alleged fraud or illegality, value was in good faith given for the bill.[275] Thus, once a fraud is proved, the burden of proof is shifted to the holder who must then show not only that value has been given for the bill, but also that he took the bill in good

---

[268] Now the Insolvency Act 1986 ss.239, 340.

[269] *Rand Investments Ltd v Bertrand*, 58 D.L.R. (2d) 372 (1966); *Keelan v Norray Distributing Ltd*, 62 D.L.R. (2d) 466 (1967). See also *Stenning v Radio and Domestic Finance Ltd* [1961] N.Z.L.R. 7. Contrast *Automobile Finance of Australia Ltd v Henderson* (1928) 23 Tas.L.R. 9; *Scottish Loan Finance Co Ltd v Payne* (1935) 52 W.N.(N.S.W.) 175.

[270] s.38(2). But see para.34-070 above, and below, para.34-099.

[271] s.29(3).

[272] *May v Chapman* (1847) 16 M. & W. 355.

[273] *Jade International Steel Stahl und Eisen GmbH & Co Kg v Robert Nicholas (Steels) Ltd* [1978] Q.B. 917, 924, 926; *First Discount Ltd v Cranston* [2002] EWCA Civ 71 at [4] and [17].

[274] s.30(1).

[275] s.30(2), and see *Berrett v Smith* [1965] N.Z.L.R. 460. See also *Banque du Rhône SA v Fuerst Day Lawson Ltd* [1968] 2 Lloyd's Rep. 153, where it was held that if the holder, who seeks to enforce the bill, resides in a foreign jurisdiction and the drawee alleges that the acceptance was obtained by means of fraud, the court may—under RSC Ord.23 r.1, preserved by CPR—order the holder to give security for costs.

faith and without notice of the fraud.[276] If the holder can discharge this onus he is, again, in the position of a holder in due course. Thus, in *Bank für Gemeinwirtschaft AG v City of London Garages*,[277] where the holder proved that he had discounted bills in good faith and without any knowledge or suspicion of illegality connected with them, the court refused to grant the drawer, the acceptors and the indorsers leave to defend an action brought by the holder in summary procedure under RSC Ord.14 r.1 (see now CPR Pt 24).

Position of original payee   As the original payee of the bill is not a holder in due   **34-080**
course,[278] he cannot be deemed to be one under s.30(2). But there is authority for the view that, when the bill is in the hands of a payee who has taken it in good faith and for value, the drawer or acceptor can escape liability only if he is able to prove that the payee was aware of a defect. In *Talbot v Von Boris*[279] a husband forced his wife to become together with him the joint maker of a promissory note. It was held that the onus was on the wife, who had to prove that the payee was aware of the duress. This case was, however, decided before it was held by the House of Lords that the original payee of a bill could not be a holder in due course. As s.38(2) of the Act confers a right to enforce a bill despite defects in title of prior parties only on a holder in due course, it is to be doubted whether the rights of the original payee are not defeated by defects of this type.[280] On this basis, it could be questioned whether *Talbot v Von Boris* was rightly decided although, in *Hasan v Wilson*,[281] Goff J., who considered himself bound by this decision, said that a defect, such as duress or fraud committed by a third party, would constitute a defence only if the payee was proved to have had notice thereof. More recently, in *Dextra Bank & Trust Co Ltd v Bank of Jamaica*,[282] the Privy Council, applying *Talbot v Von Boris* and *Hasan v Willson*, stated that the payee of a cheque, obtained by a third party from the drawer in fraud of the drawer, would acquire good title to the cheque provided that the payee had no notice of that fraud.[283]

Effect of Consumer Credit Act 1974   It will be recollected that s.123(1) prohibits   **34-081**
the taking of bills of exchange and of promissory notes by an "owner" or "creditor" in discharge of sums payable under "regulated agreements" and that s.123(3) prohibits the taking of any negotiable instrument (including a cheque) as security for the payment of such sums.[284] Under s.123(2), cheques may be taken in discharge of payment of amounts due under regulated agreements, but negotiation is prohibited except to a banker. Significant exemptions from the restrictions imposed

---

[276] *Tatam v Haslar* (1889) 23 Q.B.D. 345; *Baker v Barclays Bank Ltd* [1955] 1 W.L.R. 822; *Bank of Cyprus (London) Ltd v Jones* (1984) 134 New L.J. 522.
[277] [1971] 1 W.L.R. 149. See also *Barclays Bank Ltd v Astley Industrial Trust Ltd* [1970] 2 Q.B. 527, 536–537; *Begley Industries Ltd v Cramp* [1977] 2 N.Z.L.R. 207.
[278] See above, para.34-072; *RE Jones Ltd v Waring and Gillow Ltd* [1926] A.C. 670.
[279] [1911] 1 K.B. 854. cf. *Herdman v Wheeler* [1902] 1 K.B. 361, 372, 375; *Lloyds Bank Ltd v Cooke* [1907] 1 K.B. 794, 807–808.
[280] *Ayres v Moore* [1940] 1 K.B. 278, 286 et seq.
[281] [1977] 1 Lloyd's Rep. 431, 441.
[282] [2002] 1 All E.R. (Comm) 193.
[283] At [22]. And see *Abbey National Plc v JSF Finance & Currency Exchange Co Ltd* [2006] EWCA Civ 328, where, for the purposes for an interlocutory application, the Court of Appeal held that the payee's knowledge should be assessed taking account of the wider circumstances in which the transaction took place, including the fact that there had been a number of similar, previous transactions which the payee knew to be fraudulent.
[284] See above, para.34-007. See also below, paras 39-196 et seq.

by s.123 are made in two Orders. The first exempts consumer hire agreements, which have a connection with a country outside the United Kingdom, provided the goods are hired in the course of the hirer's business.[285] The second exempts credit transactions financing international trade where credit is provided to the debtor in the course of his business.[286] Such agreements are not "regulated agreements" and hence fall outside the ambit of s.123.

34-082 **Bill taken in violation** What is the position of a person who takes a negotiable instrument in disregard of the Act and what are the rights of a transferee? According to s.125(1) a person who takes a negotiable instrument (other than a cheque) in payment in contravention of s.123(1) or who takes a negotiable instrument (including a cheque) as security in contravention of s.123(3) is not a holder in due course and is not entitled to enforce it. But the Act does not appear to affect the rights of a person to whom such an instrument is negotiated. Provided the transferee is not himself the owner or creditor of the regulated agreement within the meaning of the Act,[287] his taking the instrument by way of transfer is not prohibited by s.123. Moreover, under s.125(4), nothing in the Act affects the rights of a holder in due course of any negotiable instrument. It is therefore clear that the Act contemplates the enforcement by a transferee—who is a holder in due course—of an instrument extracted from the debtor or hirer in contravention of s.123. Another surmise—based on reading ss.123 and 125 together with ss.29 and 30 of the Bills of Exchange Act 1882—is that a person may be a holder in due course of an instrument although he discounts it with the knowledge of its having been taken by the transferor in violation of subss.(1) or (3) of s.123. This startling conclusion is based on the fact that neither the taking of the instrument by the owner or creditor nor its negotiation is deemed to be a defect of title for the purposes of s.29 of the 1882 Act.[288] Consistently, the taking and the negotiation of such an instrument have not been added to the list of factors which, under s.30(2) of the 1882 Act, shift on the transferee or holder the onus of proving good faith and the furnishing of value.

34-083 **Negotiation of cheque to non-banker** The effect of the negotiation of a cheque, taken for payment of an amount due under a regulated agreement, to a person other than a banker is governed by s.125(2):

"Where a person negotiates a cheque in contravention of s.123(2), his doing so constitutes a defect in his title within the meaning of the Bills of Exchange Act 1882."

The phrase "defect of title" occurs in s.29(1)(b), according to which a person, who takes a bill of exchange with notice of a defect in the transferor's title, is not a holder in due course. It follows that a person (other than a banker), who discounts a cheque with the knowledge of its having been drawn for payment of an amount due under a regulated agreement, is not a holder in due course. However, the burden of prov-

---

[285] Consumer Credit (Negotiable Instruments) (Exemption) Order 1984 (SI 1984/435).

[286] Financial Services and Markets Act 2000 (Regulated Activities) Order 2001/544 art.60C(8).

[287] Note that under s.189 the terms "creditor" and "owner" include assignees of a regulated agreement but do not include transferees of bills of exchange.

[288] The list of factors which constitute a defect of title, enumerated in s.29(2), is not exhaustive. But in view of the specific designation of a prohibited negotiation of a cheque to a non-banker as a defect of title within the meaning of the Act, it seems probable that the failure to equally include the negotiation of instruments taken in contravention of subss.(1) and (3), precludes its being treated as a defect of title on an ejusdem generis basis.

ing the discounter's knowledge of the relevant facts rests on the drawer of the cheque: the prohibited negotiation has not been added to the list of factors which, under s.30(2), shifts the onus of proof on the person seeking to enforce the bill.

Indemnity   It is important to emphasise that a person who at the suit of a holder   **34-084**
in due course is forced to pay a bill or note taken from him in contravention of s.123(1) or (3), or a cheque negotiated in contravention of s.123(2), is entitled to be indemnified by the creditor or owner. But this right—conferred by s.125(4) of the Consumer Credit Act 1974—is of little consolation to the consumer where the creditor or owner is insolvent.[289]

(iv)   Transfer of Bills

Negotiation of a bill   A bill is negotiated when it is transferred from one person   **34-085**
to another in such a manner as to constitute the transferee the holder of the bill.[290] A bill payable to bearer is negotiated by mere delivery.[291] A bill payable to the order of a specified payee is negotiated by the indorsement of the payee, or the holder to whom the bill has been specially indorsed, and delivery of it.[292] Section 31(4) provides that where the holder of a bill payable to his order transfers it for value without indorsing it, the transfer gives the transferee such title as the transferor had in the bill, and the transferee, in addition, acquires the right to have the indorsement of the transferor.[293] However, until this has been obtained the transferee is in the position of an assignee of a chose in action, and has no better title than the assignor.[294] He does not have a right to indorse the bill in the transferor's name and it has been suggested that he may not be able to sue on the bill without joining the transferor as a party to the action.[295]

Section 31(5) provides that where a person is under an obligation to indorse a bill in representative manner, he is entitled to indorse in terms negativing personal liability.[296]

Valid indorsement[297]   Section 32 explains when an indorsement is valid and ef-   **34-086**
fective to negotiate a bill:

---

[289] But note that the drawer may be able to base a defence on the *rationes* of the decisions cited above.
[290] s.31(1).
[291] s.31(2). "Delivery" is defined in s.2 as the "transfer of possession, actual or constructive, from one person to another". Contrast the narrower definition of delivery in s.61(1) of the Sale of Goods Act 1979: "*voluntary* transfer of possession from one person to another …". As to which bills are payable to bearer, see above, para.34-022.
[292] s.31(3). See *Standard Chartered Bank v Dorchester LNG (2) Ltd, The Erin Schulte* [2014] EWCA Civ 1382, where an analogy was made between indorsement of bills of lading under the Carriage of Goods by Sea Act 1992 s.5(2)(b), and the indorsement of bills of exchange: held (at [16]) that "[d]elivery therefore represents an essential element in a series of voluntary acts designed to give effect to the holder's intention to transfer the rights which it represents" and (at [28]) that "completion of an indorsement by delivery requires the voluntary and unconditional transfer of possession by the holder to the indorsee and an unconditional acceptance by the indorsee". As to which bills are payable to order, see above, para.34-023.
[293] *Walters v Neary* (1904) 21 T.L.R. 146.
[294] *Whistler v Forster* (1863) 14 C.B.(N.S.) 248. As regards the validity of the assignment of a chose in action conferred by a bill, see *Geo Thompson (Aust) Pty Ltd v Vittadello* [1978] V.R. 199, 208–212.
[295] *Cunliffe v Whitehead* (1837) 3 Bing. N.C. 828, 830; *Harrop v Fisher* (1861) 10 C.B.(N.S.) 196, 203.
[296] And see ss.16(1), 26.
[297] A valid indorsement may nevertheless be irregular, see above, para.34-074.

(a) According to s.32(1) it must be written on the bill itself and be signed by the indorser. The signature of the indorser on the bill, without additional words, is sufficient. An indorsement written on an *allonge* (i.e. an attached slip) or a "copy" of a bill, issued or negotiated in a country where such copies are recognised, is deemed to be written on the bill itself. Although it is usual to indorse a bill on its back it has been held that an indorsement on the front of the bill is valid.[298]

(b) According to s.32(2), the indorsement must transfer the entire bill. A partial indorsement, that is to say, an indorsement which purports to transfer to the indorsee a part only of the amount payable, or which purports to transfer the bill to two or more indorsees severally, does not operate as a negotiation of the bill.

(c) According to s.32(3), where a bill is payable to the order of two or more payees or indorsees who are not partners, all must indorse it, unless the one indorsing has authority to indorse for the others. But where the bill is payable to two payees in the alternative, the indorsement of either is sufficient.[299]

(d) According to s.32(4) where, in a bill payable to order, the payee or indorsee is wrongly designated, or his name is misspelt, he may indorse the bill as therein described, adding, if he thinks fit, his proper signature. This subsection is not imperative in terms. If, despite the misnomer, it is clear whom the drawer had in mind, then the indorsement of this person in his correct name is valid.[300] An indorsement of the payee by the name written in the bill is also valid.[301]

(e) According to s.32(5) where there are two or more indorsements on a bill, the indorsements are deemed to have been made in the order in which they appear on the bill, until the contrary is proved.

(f) According to s.32(6) an indorsement may be made in blank or special. It may also contain terms making it restrictive.[302]

34-087 Conditional indorsements According to s.33, where a bill purports to be indorsed conditionally, the condition may be disregarded by the payer, and payment to the indorsee is valid whether the condition has been fulfilled or not.

34-088 Indorsement in blank and special indorsement An indorsement in blank specifies no indorsee, and a bill so indorsed becomes payable to bearer. A special indorsement specifies the person to whom, or to whose order, the bill is to be payable. The provisions of the Act relating to a payee apply with the necessary modifications to an indorsee under a special indorsement. When a bill has been indorsed in blank, any holder may convert the blank indorsement into a special indorsement by writing above the indorser's signature a direction to pay the bill to or to the order of

---

[298] *Young v Glover* (1857) 3 Jur.(N.S.) 637; *Ex p. Yates* (1857) 2 De G. & J. 191.

[299] This appears to follow from *Watson v Evans* (1863) 32 L.J. Ex. 137. As to the possibility of having alternative payees, see s.7(2), discussed in para.34-023, above.

[300] *Bird & Co v Thomas Cook & Son Ltd* [1937] 2 All E.R. 227; *Arab Bank Ltd v Ross* [1952] 2 Q.B. 216. (But such an indorsement will be irregular and a holder of such a bill cannot be a holder in due course: see above, para.34-074.)

[301] *Willis v Barrett* (1817) 2 Stark. 29.

[302] As to restrictive indorsements, see below, para.34-089. As to the effect of a blank indorsement, see s.8(3).

himself or some other person.[303] A holder is, further, entitled to strike out an indorsement of a previous party. The indorser whose indorsement has been struck out and all subsequent indorsers are then discharged.[304] An indorser often strikes out his previous indorsement when he honours the bill after its dishonour by the acceptor or drawer, in order to avoid liability if the bill is lost. By doing so he does not lose his right of recourse against prior indorsers or the drawer.

Restrictive indorsement   The indorsement of a bill to a specified person without   **34-089**
the words "or order" is not restrictive and the bill, which remains negotiable, is to be treated as if these words were included.[305] An indorsement is restrictive if it either prohibits further transfers or if it specifies that it is not a transfer but a mere authority to the indorsee to deal with the bill as thereby directed, e.g. if it is indorsed "Pay D only", or "Pay D for the account of X", or "Pay D or order for collection".[306] The statement in an indorsement, that the consideration has been furnished by a third party, does not render it a restrictive indorsement.[307] A restrictive indorsement gives the indorsee the right to receive payment of the bill and to sue any party that his indorser could have sued, but gives him no power to transfer his rights as indorsee unless it expressly authorises him to do so.[308] However, the acceptor is not liable to the indorser if the indorsee, after obtaining payment of the bill under the restrictive indorsement, misappropriates the proceeds.[309] Where a restrictive indorsement authorises further transfer, all subsequent indorsees take the bill with the same rights and subject to the same liabilities as the first indorsee under the restrictive indorsement.[310] As an indorsee, who takes a bill bearing a restrictive indorsement, is aware of the limitation of the title of the transferor, he cannot be a holder in due course.

Overdue or dishonoured bill   A bill remains negotiable until it is either   **34-090**
restrictively indorsed or discharged. However, if an overdue bill is transferred, the transferee takes it subject to any equities available to the acceptor, drawer or indorser.[311] Such equities include an agreement not to transfer the bill,[312] and probably the illegality of the consideration,[313] but neither the absence of consideration[314] nor a personal right of set-off available to the acceptor against the drawer.[315] A bill payable on demand is deemed to be overdue when it appears on its face to have been in circulation for an unreasonably long time; what constitutes an unreasonably long time is a question of fact.[316] The holder of a bill is presumed to have taken it before it became overdue, provided the indorsement is not dated after

---

[303] s.34. And see above, para.34-022.
[304] *Wilkinson v Johnson* (1824) 3 B. & C. 428; *Mayer v Jadis* (1833) 1 M. & Rob. 247.
[305] s.8(4) which, in view of s.34(3), applies to indorsements.
[306] s.35(1).
[307] *Buckley v Jackson* (1868) L.R. 3 Ex. 135.
[308] s.35(2); *Lloyd v Sigourney* (1829) 5 Bing. 525.
[309] *Williams, Deacon & Co v Shadbolt* (1885) 1 Cab. & E. 529; (1885) 1 T.L.R. 417.
[310] s.35(3).
[311] s.36(1) and (2). That a party who takes an overdue bill cannot be a holder in due course, see s.29.
[312] *Parr v Jewell* (1855) 16 C.B. 684; *Redfern v Rosenthal* (1902) 86 L.T. 855.
[313] See *Chalmers and Guest on Bills of Exchange and Cheques*, 18th edn (2017), para.5-041.
[314] *Sturtevant v Ford* (1842) 4 M. & G. 101; *Ex p. Swan* (1868) L.R. 6 Eq. 344.
[315] *Oulds v Harrison* (1854) 10 Exch. 572; *Ex p. Swan*, above.
[316] s.36(3).

the date of maturity.[317] If a person takes a bill, knowing that it has been dishonoured, he is in the same position as if he took an overdue bill.[318]

34-091 **Negotiation to party already liable** Section 37 provides that where a bill is negotiated back to the drawer or to an indorser or to the acceptor such party may, subject to the provisions of ss.59 to 64 (respecting the discharge of the bill), reissue and further negotiate the bill; but he is not entitled to enforce payment of the bill against any party to whom he was previously liable. It has been held that, as against the acceptor, such a drawer or indorser would be in the position of a holder in due course, provided the person from whom he acquired the bill enjoyed such a status.[319]

34-092 **Rights of holder: generally** The rights of the holder depend primarily on whether he is a "mere holder", a "holder for value" or a "holder in due course". In certain cases it is also relevant whether a dispute is between "immediate parties" or "remote parties".[320] Immediate parties are those who, in addition to the privity created by the bill, have a direct legal relationship with each other. The drawer and the acceptor, the drawer and the payee and an indorser and his indorsee are usually parties who have entered into a contract with one another, such as an agreement to extend credit, a sale of goods or an arrangement for the discount of negotiable instruments; they are therefore predominantly immediate parties. But in certain circumstances even these parties may be remote parties, e.g. where the drawer makes the bill payable to the payee's order, or where the drawee executes his acceptance, at the request of a stranger to the bill. It is maintained by some writers that, generally, the defences which can be pleaded against a remote party are more restricted than those available against an immediate party.[321] It will be shown, however, that the distinction between remote and immediate parties is relevant mainly in respect of actions brought on a bill by a holder for value. The superior rights of a holder in due course are defined in s.38(2) of the Act, which does not draw a distinction between remote and immediate parties.[322] At the other end of the scale, a mere holder, who has not furnished value, appears to hold the bill subject to virtually all equities available against prior parties, including immediate parties.

---

[317] s.36(4). As to when this presumption is rebutted, see *Bounsall v Harrison* (1836) 1 M. & W. 611.

[318] s.36(5).

[319] *Jade International Steel Stahl und Eisen GmbH & Co Kg v Robert Nicholas (Steels) Ltd* [1978] Q.B. 917, 924, 926; *First Discount Ltd v Cranston* [2002] EWCA Civ 71 at [4] and [17].

[320] As regards the rights of the payee of a bill, see above, para.34-080. Note that the transferee of a holder in due course is in a position similar to that of his transferor: s.29(3), discussed above, para.34-078. As regards the effect of fraud and illegality on the position of immediate parties, see also *Universal Import Export v Bank of Scotland*, 1994 S.C.L.R. 944 OH.

[321] *Byles on Bills of Exchange and Cheques*, 29th edn (2013), paras 18-013 et seq.; Crawford, *Payment, Clearing and Settlement in Canada* (2002), Vol.II, pp.986 et seq.; Cowen & Gering, *Law of Negotiable Instruments in South Africa*, 5th edn, pp.103–109 et seq. The distinction is not fully worked out in decided cases, but see *Watson v Russell* (1864) 5 B. & S. 968; 34 L.J. Q.B. 93 (suggesting that the drawer and the drawee of a cheque are not always immediate parties). See also *Oscar Harris, Son & Co v Vallarman & Co* [1940] 1 All E.R. 185, CA; *Bank Lenmi Le-Israel v Coniplan (UK) Ltd* Unreported July 31, 1987; *Solo Industries UK Ltd v Canara Bank* [2001] 2 Lloyd's Rep. 578 at [39], CA; *GMAC Commercial Finance Ltd v Mint Apparel Ltd* [2010] EWHC 2452 (Comm) at [26]. For a detailed discussion, see *Chalmers and Guest on Bills of Exchange and Cheques*, 18th edn (2017), paras 4-005 et seq.

[322] Note that only an indorsee can be a holder in due course (above, para.34-080) and that only his transferor can be regarded an immediate party. From a practical point of view, the circumstances under which a transferee has to take the bill in order to attain the status of a holder in due course are such as to rule out the need to distinguish in his case between an action against an immediate

Rights of holder in due course   According to s.38(2) a holder in due course holds   **34-093**
the bill free from any defects in the title of previous parties as well as from any equities available to prior parties among themselves and may enforce payment against
all parties liable on the bill. Defects of title, which under s.29(2) include fraud,
duress, force and fear and illegality connected with the issuing, with the acceptance or with the negotiation of the bill,[323] are directly related to the bill itself and
before the passage of the Act were known as "equities attaching to the
instrument".[324] The term "equities available to prior parties among themselves",
employed in s.38(2), is not defined in this provision or indeed elsewhere in the Act.
In all probability it means personal defences, available to parties among themselves,
which do not stem from the bill. By way of illustration consider defences based on
an underlying contract of sale, such as the unsuitability of the goods or the failure
to ship them on time. By conferring on the holder in due course the right to enforce
the bill despite defects in the title of previous parties and regardless of personal
defences available against them, s.38(2) enables bankers and other financial institutions to discount commercial bills without assuming the risk of becoming involved
in disputes concerning the underlying business transaction.[325] Thus, where the
discounter is a holder in due course, he can enforce the bill of exchange against the
drawee even if the latter had accepted it in the mistaken belief that a forged bill of
lading attached to the bill of exchange was genuine.[326] The position of a holder in
due course is further safeguarded by the following sections of the Act: 12, 20(2)
(completion of inchoate instruments), 21(2) (delivery), 54(2), 55(2) and 64(2).[327]
In effect, to defeat an action by a holder in due course it is necessary to establish a
defect in his own title in which case, of course, he is not a holder in due course.[328]

Rights of mere holder   Section 38(1) prescribes that a holder (or "mere holder")   **34-094**
has the right to bring an action on the bill in his own name,[329] but does not indicate
what type of defence is available against him. From a comparison of the language

---

party and an action against a remote party.
[323] See also above, para.34-072. Cowen & Gering, *Law of Negotiable Instruments in South Africa*, 4th
edn, pp.271–274 (and see 5th edn, pp.103 et seq.) suggests that defects in title are defences in rem
whilst personal equities constitute defences in personam. See also Crawford, *Payment, Clearing and
Settlement in Canada* (2002), Vol.II, pp.986 et seq.; *Chalmers and Guest on Bills of Exchange and
Cheques*, 18th edn (2017), paras 4-062—4-069.
[324] *Re Overend, Gurney & Co Ex p. Swan* (1868) L.R. 6 Eq. 344, 359–362; *Alcock v Smith* [1892] 1
Ch. 238, 263. See also *Sturtevant v Ford* (1842) 4 M. & G. 101, 106.
[325] It will be shown subsequently that certain personal equities may not be pleaded against any holder,
including a mere holder.
[326] *Robinson v Reynolds* (1841) 2 Q.B. 196; *Guaranty Trust Co of New York v Hannay & Co* [1918] 2
K.B. 623, 652. cf. *Leather v Simpson* (1871) L.R. 11 Eq. 398.
[327] As regards ss.12 and 20(2), see above, para.34-035; as regards s.21, see above, para.34-032; as
regards s.54(2), see below, para.34-113; as regards s.55(2), see below, para.34-114; as regards s.64,
see below, para.34-141.
[328] This can, for example, be done by showing that he holds a bill payable to the order of a specific payee
under a forged indorsement: above, para.34-053.
[329] An action to enforce a negotiable instrument may be brought under Pt 24 of the CPR (previously
under RSC Ord.14) under which the claimant applies for summary judgment. As to when leave to
defend will be granted, see *Byles on Bills of Exchange and Cheques*, 29th edn (2013), paras 26-013
et seq.; and *James Lamont & Co Ltd v Hyland* [1950] 1 K.B. 585; *Brown Shipley & Co Ltd v Alicia
Hosiery Ltd* [1966] 1 Lloyd's Rep. 668; *Barclays Bank Ltd v Aschaffenburger Zellstoffwerke AG*
[1967] 1 Lloyd's Rep. 387 (below, para.34-102); *All Trades Distributors Ltd v Agencies Kaufman
Ltd* (1969) 113 S.J. 995; *Saga of Bond Street Ltd v Avalon Promotions Ltd* [1972] 2 Q.B. 325; *Cebora
SNC v SIP (Industrial Products) Ltd* [1976] 1 Lloyd's Rep. 271; *Montebianco Industrie Tessili SpA
v Carlyle Mills (London) Ltd* [1981] 1 Lloyd's Rep. 509. Although these cases were decided under

of this subsection with s.38(2) it emerges that, as against an action by a mere holder, the defendant is entitled to raise defences stemming from a defect in title of prior parties and at least some personal defences available against them. This view derives support from old authorities which, in view of the absence of explicit regulation of the question in the Act, remain good law. Thus, it has been held that absence of consideration[330] and total failure of consideration[331] are valid defences against a mere holder. Partial failure of consideration is a valid defence where a liquidated amount is involved,[332] but cannot be raised where the amount involved is an unascertained or unliquidated demand.[333] Thus, an acceptor does not have a valid defence to an action on the bill where arbitration proceedings are brought by him against the payee in respect of the underlying contract of sale. Neither can the claim involved be raised by way of a set-off or a counterclaim.[334] A fortiori, a right against a previous party which has no direct bearing on the bill or on the transaction related to it, such as an independent right of set-off, cannot be raised as a defence to the holder's action on the bill.[335]

34-095 **Rights of holder for value** The rights of a holder for value are not defined in the

---

RSC Ord.14, they are likely to remain good law (*Safa Ltd v Banque du Caire* [2000] 2 Lloyd's Rep. 600, 605–606, Waller L.J.). See, e.g. *Solo Industries UK Ltd v Canara Bank* [2001] 2 Lloyd's Rep. 578 at [22]–[28]; *Isovel Contracts Ltd (in administration) v ABB Building Technologies Ltd* [2002] 1 B.C.L.C. 390 at [15]–[22]; *Banque Saudi Fransi v Lear Siegler Services Inc* [2007] 2 Lloyd's Rep. 47 at [14]–[16]; *Enka Insaat Ve Sanayi AS v Banca Populare Dell'Alto Adige SpA* [2009] EWHC 2410 (Comm) at [19]–[25]; *National Infrastructure Development Co Ltd v Banco Santander SA* [2017] EWCA Civ 27 at [20]–[24].

330 *Forman v Wright* (1851) 11 C.B. 481, 492–494; cf. *Easton v Pratchett* (1835) 1 Cr. M. & R. 798, 808–809; *Milnes v Dawson* (1850) 5 Exch. 948, 950–951. Note that s.28(2) does not confer on a mere holder the right to enforce a bill against an accommodation party. As regards the authority of cases decided before the passing of the Act, see above, para.34-006.

331 See para.34-098, below, showing this defence as available even against a holder for value.

332 *Forman v Wright*, above; *Agra and Masterman's Bank v Leighton* (1866) L.R. 2 Ex. 56, 64, 65 (supply of ascertained portion of goods instead of delivery of quantity ordered); *Thoni GmbH v RTP Equipment Ltd* [1979] 2 Lloyd's Rep. 282.

333 *Day v Nix* (1824) 9 Moo. C.P. 159; 2 L.J. (O.S.) C.P. 133; *Sully v Frean* (1854) 10 Ex. 535; *Warwick v Nairn* (1855) 10 Exch. 762 (alleged inferiority of quality of goods).

334 *Nova (Jersey) Knit Ltd v Kammgarn Spinnerei GmbH* [1977] 1 W.L.R. 713, where the majority of the House of Lords further refused to grant a stay based on the arbitration agreement respecting the underlying contract. But much turns on the construction of the arbitration agreement: as to which, see *Fiona Trust & Holding Corp v Privalov* [2007] UKHL 40, [2008] 1 Lloyd's Rep. 254. See also *Piallo GmbH v Yafriro International Pte Ltd* [2013] SGHC 260, disapproved of by Sing CA in *Cassa di Risparmio di Parma e Piacenza SpA v Rals International Pte Ltd* [2016] SGCA 53. In *Uttam Galva Steels Ltd v Gunvor Singapore Pte Ltd* [2018] EWHC 1098 (Comm), where there was a challenge to the arbitrator's jurisdiction, Picken J. held, at [57], "that there is no rule of English law that an arbitration clause cannot extend to a claim under a bill of exchange, certainly anyway as between the immediate parties to the underlying sale contract and in circumstances where those parties remain the parties to the bill of exchange" (adding, at [61]–[62], that the reasoning of the Sing CA in the *Rals* case was flawed, having been overly influenced by the fact that the claimants in that case were (third party) indorsees of the relevant promissory notes). By contrast, in *China Export & Credit Insurance Corp v Emerald Energy Resources Ltd* [2018] EWHC 1503 (Comm), application for stay of English proceedings, commenced under non-exclusive jurisdiction clause in promissory note, was refused despite arbitration clause in underlying contract.

335 *Burrough v Moss* (1830) 10 B. & C. 558, 563; *Whitehead v Walker* (1842) 10 M. & W. 696; *Oulds v Harrison* (1854) 10 Exch. 572, 578–579; *Re Overend, Gurney & Co Ex p. Swan* (1868) L.R. 6 Eq. 344, 359–360. cf. *Re European Bank Ex p. Oriental Commercial Bank* (1870) L.R. 5 Ch. App. 358. But an agreement made at the time the bill is executed, which contemplates a future set-off, may be an equity affecting the bill: *Holmes v Kidd* (1858) 3 H. & N. 891.

Act. In most regards his position is similar to that of a mere holder.[336] Thus, his action on the bill would be defeated if the bill was obtained by means of fraud or of duress or where the consideration furnished was illegal.[337] This proposition derives support from the language of the Act. Under s.29(2) fraud, duress, force and fear and illegality of consideration are factors which render the transferor's title defective. Section 38(2) explicitly grants the right to enforce the bill despite such defects in the transferor's title to a holder in due course but does not purport to confer them on a holder for value. It follows that, subject to specific defences conferred on a holder for value by other provisions of the Act, his rights—like those of a mere holder—are governed by s.38(1) of the Act, which only confers on the holder a right to bring an action on the bill in his own name.

Total failure of consideration   Can a holder for value enforce the bill where there **34-096** has been a total or partial failure of the consideration furnished to the person who is sued on the bill or where no consideration has been furnished to him? As the holder for value has furnished consideration to the transferor, the absence of consideration between prior parties to the bill does not constitute a valid defence against him.[338] Moreover, when a person becomes a party to a bill without obtaining consideration, he usually acts as an accommodation party. Under s.28(2), such a party is liable to a holder for value who takes the bill with full knowledge of this fact.

Partial failure of consideration   In respect of partial failure of consideration, it **34-097** is important to recall the distinction between immediate parties and remote parties. An immediate party is entitled to plead partial failure of consideration as a defence to an action by a holder for value, provided the "partial failure" involves an ascertained and liquidated amount. Thus, if a seller supplies only one half of the goods, he cannot recover more than half the amount of the bill drawn for the price and accepted by the buyer.[339] But if the goods turn out to be of an inferior quality, this defect cannot be raised as a defence to the seller's action on the bill.[340] An illustration in point is the decision of the Court of Appeal in *Thoni GmbH v RTP*

---

336 *Whistler v Forster* (1863) 14 C.B.(N.S.) 248, 258.
337 But note that the list of defects, set out in s.29(2) is not exhaustive: see *Williams and Glyn's Bank Ltd v Belkin Packaging Ltd*, 123 D.L.R. (3rd) 612 (1981).
338 *Mills v Barber* (1836) 1 M. & W. 425, 430–431; *Barber v Richards* (1851) 6 Exch. 63. cf. *Forman v Wright* (1851) 11 C.B. 481, 492–494; see also s.27(2), considered in *MK International Development Co Ltd v Housing Bank* [1991] 1 Bank. L.R. 74; above, para.34-066. As to whether the holder can recover the full amount of the bill or only an amount equal to the value furnished by him, see *Darnell v Williams* (1817) 2 Stark. 166; *Jones v Hibbert* (1817) 2 Stark. 304; *Re Bunyard Ex p. Newton* (1880) 16 Ch. D. 330, 336.
339 *Agra and Masterman's Bank v Leighton* (1866) L.R. 2 Ex. 56, 64, 65. See also *Forman v Wright*, above, at 492.
340 *Glennie v Imri* (1839) 3 Y. & C. Ex. 436, 442–443; *Agra and Masterman's Bank v Leighton*, above; cf. *Hitchings and Coulthurst Co v Northern Leather Co* [1914] 3 K.B. 907. See also *Fielding and Platt Ltd v Najjar* [1969] 1 W.L.R. 357 (where the seller had performed part of the bargain before the buyer dishonoured the bill); *All Trades Distributors Ltd v Agencies Kaufman Ltd*, below (rejection of goods); *Montecchi v Shimco Ltd* [1979] 1 W.L.R. 1180; *Montebianco Industrie Tessili SpA v Carlyle Mills (London) Ltd* [1981] 1 Lloyd's Rep. 509 (the fact that the defect in the goods confers on the drawee a valid counterclaim is no defence to the action on the bill). But note that the buyer may counterclaim. As to whether a stay of proceedings would be granted pending the counterclaim, see *James Lamont & Co Ltd v Hyland Ltd* [1950] 1 K.B. 585; *All Trades Distributors Ltd v Agencies Kaufman Ltd* (1969) 113 S.J. 995; *Cebora SNC v SIP (Industrial Products) Ltd* [1976] 1 Lloyd's Rep. 271. For a recent example, see *Oxigen Environmental Ltd v Mullan* [2012] NIQB 17 (sum-

Equipment Ltd.[341] To settle an account related to the supply of hoses, the defendants agreed to accept the plaintiffs' bill of exchange for Ö.Sch. 1m. and to make, in addition, certain fixed periodic payments. When a subsequent shipment comprised defective hoses, the plaintiffs claimed to be entitled to a refund. They ceased to make the periodic payments and dishonoured the bill of exchange. Granting leave to defend an action on the bill, Buckley L.J. stressed that there was an arguable defence in respect of a substantial and defined part of the amount of the bill. His Lordship based this conclusion on the finding that it was established on the facts that the defendants' indebtedness was limited to Ö.Sch. 400,897. There was, therefore, a prima facie defence in respect of the balance of Ö.Sch. 599,103 as the consideration furnished for this amount had failed.

34-098 **As against remote party**   Partial failure of consideration does not appear to afford a defence against a remote party who is a holder for value even where the deficiency or loss is liquidated.[342] One authority suggests that total failure of consideration does not provide a defence to an action brought by a holder for value who is a remote party.[343] This view deserves support; as a remote party who is a holder for value has furnished consideration for the bill, it seems irrelevant that a consideration furnished by prior parties has failed. The position differs where an action is brought by an immediate party who furnished for the bill a consideration which, though valid at the time of transfer, has failed *in toto* at a subsequent point of time. In effect, such a party is not a holder for value *strictu sensu*, and the total failure of consideration is a good defence against him.[344]

34-099 **Holder suing for benefit of third party**   Normally the holder of a bill of exchange is entitled to judgment for the full sum represented by the bill. But when he sues as agent or trustee for another person, or when he sues wholly or in part for the benefit of another person, any defence or set-off available against that person is

---

mary judgment on promissory note but stay of execution pending hearing of counterclaim for breach of underlying contract). Note that the amount of a dishonoured bill can be set off against an amount of damages recoverable under the underlying contract: *Handley Page Ltd v Rockwell Machine Tool Co Ltd* [1970] 2 Lloyd's Rep. 459, 465 (affirmed [1971] 2 Lloyd's Rep. 298).

341 [1979] 2 Lloyd's Rep. 282.

342 *Archer v Bamford* (1822) 3 Stark. 175; cf. *Oscar Harris, Son & Co v Vallarman & Co* [1940] 1 All E.R. 185 (which regards the rule as insufficiently settled to justify on its basis the striking out of an action). See also *GMAC Commercial Finance Ltd v Mint Apparel Ltd* [2010] EWHC 2452 (Comm) at [26]–[33].

343 *Watson v Russell* (1864) 5 B. & S. 968; some indirect support for the proposition follows from *Misa v Currie* (1876) 1 App. Cas. 554, especially 566. But even a remote party could not sue if he knew at the time he took the bill that consideration had totally failed; *Lloyd v Davis* (1824) 3 L.J.(O.S.) K.B. 38; cf. *Fairclough v Pavia* (1854) 9 Exch. 690, 695 (where, however, the transferee may have taken the bill from a holder in due course). It is arguable to the contrary, that as s.38(2) precludes the raising of a defence based on defects in title and on personal equities solely as against a holder in due course, a holder for value's rights may be defeated by failure of consideration (which presumably constitutes a personal equity).

344 *Solly v Hinde* (1834) 2 Cr. & M. 516 (maker executed promissory note to induce payee to act as executor of maker's will; held that as maker outlived payee, the payee's estate could not enforce the instrument); *Astley and Williams v Johnson* (1860) 5 Hurl. & N. 137 (remote party was suing as agent of immediate party and hence was regarded as immediate party); *Fielding and Platt Ltd v Najjar* [1969] 1 W.L.R. 357. As to whether an injunction may be granted to restrain negotiation where there has been total failure of consideration, see *Patrick v Harrison* (1792) 3 Bro. C.C. 476; *Glennie v Imri* (1839) 3 Y. & C. Ex. 436; *Bainbrigge v Hemingway* (1865) 12 L.T. 74.

available pro tanto against the holder.[345] Thus, in *Barclays Bank v Aschaffenburger Zellstoffwerke AG*[346] A accepted bills drawn by B in payment for goods sold to him by B. C purchased the bills from B, paying 73 per cent of their face value and agreeing that when the bills were met on maturity the balance would be paid to B. Two of the bills were dishonoured, and, when sued by C, A sought to rely on a counterclaim in respect of the goods sold by B. It was held that C was a holder for value as to 73 per cent of the claim and trustee for the balance on behalf of B, so that there should be summary judgment for the whole amount of the bills, but with a stay of execution in respect of 27 per cent of that amount.

(v) General Duties of Holder

Outline Before the holder is entitled to claim payment of a bill from the drawer **34-100**
and indorsers he must perform several duties. In most cases the failure of the holder to perform these duties discharges the drawer and indorsers and there is authority for saying that the debt, for the payment of which the bill is transferred to holder, is likewise discharged.[347]

Necessity of presentment for acceptance Presentment of the bill for accept- **34-101**
ance is required in the following cases: (a) when the bill is payable after sight, in which case presentment is necessary to determine the maturity of the instrument; (b) when a bill expressly stipulates that it must be presented for acceptance; and (c) when it is drawn payable elsewhere than at the residence or business place of the drawee. In the last two cases it must be presented for acceptance before it can be presented for payment.[348] Where a bill is payable after sight the holder must either present it for acceptance or negotiate it within a reasonable time; otherwise the drawer and indorsers are discharged.[349] What constitutes reasonable time depends on the nature of the bill, the usage of trade with respect to similar bills, and the facts of the particular case.[350]

Rules as to presentment for acceptance Section 41(1) of the Act specifies the **34-102**
following rules for the presentment of a bill for acceptance:

(a) the presentment must be made by or on behalf of the holder to the drawee or to some person authorised to accept or refuse acceptance on his behalf at a reasonable hour on a business day and before the bill is overdue;

(b) where a bill is addressed to two or more drawees, who are not partners, presentment must be made to them all, unless one has authority to accept for all in which case presentment may be made to him only;

---

[345] *De La Chaumette v Bank of England* (1829) 9 B. & C. 208 (as explained in *Currie v Misa* (1875) L.R. 10 Ex. 153, 164; (1876) 1 App. Cas. 554, 570); *Thornton v Maynard* (1875) L.R. 10 C.P. 695.

[346] [1967] 1 Lloyd's Rep. 387. See also *Re Bunyard Ex p. Newton* (1880) 16 Ch. D. 330, 336. cf. *Nova (Jersey) Knit Ltd v Kammgarn Spinnerei GmbH* [1977] 1 W.L.R. 713. See also *GMAC Commercial Finance Ltd v Mint Apparel Ltd* [2010] EWHC 2452 (Comm) at [19]–[25].

[347] *Soward v Palmer* (1818) 8 Taunt. 277; *Peacock v Purssell* (1863) 32 L.J. C.P. 266.

[348] s.39(1), (2), (3). Subs.(4) makes special provisions applicable when a bill is payable elsewhere than at the residence or place of business of the drawee and the holder is unable to present it for acceptance before the day of maturity.

[349] s.40(1), (2).

[350] s.40(3). See, e.g. *Fry v Hill* (1817) 7 Taunt. 397; *Shute v Robins* (1828) 3 Car. & P. 80; *Mellish v Rawdon* (1832) 9 Bing. 416; *Straker v Graham* (1839) 4 M. & W. 721; *Ramchurn Mullick v Luchmeechund Radakissen* (1854) 9 Moo. P.C. 46; *Godfray v Coulman* (1859) 13 Moo. P.C. 11.

(c) where the drawee is dead, presentment may be made to his personal representative;

(d) where the drawee is bankrupt, presentment may be made to him or to his trustee in bankruptcy;

(e) where authorised by agreement or usage, presentment through the post office is sufficient.

According to s.41(2) presentment in accordance with the above rules is excused, and the bill may be treated as dishonoured by non-acceptance, in the following cases:

(a) where the drawee is dead or bankrupt, or is a fictitious person or a person not having capacity to contract;

(b) where, after the exercise of reasonable diligence, due presentment cannot be effected;

(c) where, although the presentment has been irregular, acceptance has been refused on some other ground.

The fact that the holder has reason to believe that the bill, on presentment, will be dishonoured does not excuse failure to present it.[351]

34-103 Dishonour by non-acceptance According to s.43(1) a bill is dishonoured by non-acceptance if:

(a) it is duly presented and acceptance is refused or cannot be obtained; and

(b) if presentment for acceptance is excused and the bill is not accepted.

Where a bill is duly presented for acceptance, and is not accepted within the customary time, the holder must treat it as dishonoured by non-acceptance, and if he fails so to treat it, he loses his immediate right of recourse against the drawer and indorsers.[352] This right of recourse accrues to the holder as soon as the bill is dishonoured by non-acceptance, and he need not present the bill for payment.[353] If after dishonour the drawee offers to accept the bill, it appears that the holder has the option of treating the bill as dishonoured or as accepted.[354]

34-104 Duties as to qualified acceptances The holder of a bill may refuse to take a qualified acceptance, and if he does not obtain an unqualified acceptance may treat the bill as dishonoured. Where a qualified acceptance is taken, and the drawer or an indorser has not expressly or impliedly authorised the holder to take it, or does not give his assent subsequently, the drawer or indorser is discharged from his liability on the bill. But this does not apply to a partial acceptance, of which due notice has been given. When the drawer or indorser of a bill receives notice of a qualified acceptance, and does not within a reasonable time express his dissent to the holder, he is deemed to have given his assent.[355]

34-105 Presentment for payment According to s.45 all bills of exchange must, subject

---

[351] s.41(3).

[352] s.42.

[353] s.43(2). This right is subject to the provisions of s.65 (acceptance for honour). Before exercising this right of recourse the holder must perform certain duties, i.e. the sending of notice of dishonour (s.48) and, in certain cases, protesting the bill (s.51).

[354] That a bill may be accepted after its initial dishonour follows from s.18(2), (3).

[355] s.44. This section also provides that where a foreign bill has been accepted as to part, it must be protested as to the balance.

to certain provisions of the Act,[356] be presented for payment and if the holder fails to do so the drawer and indorsers are discharged. There are several differences between presentment for acceptance and for payment. First, presentment for acceptance is, mainly, personal as its purpose is to obtain the drawee's undertaking to pay. The bill must, therefore, be presented for acceptance at the drawee's place. Presentment for payment is, on the other hand, for the purpose of obtaining actual payment and the bill must be presented at the place at which it has been made payable. Secondly, the date for presentment for payment is, except in the case of bills payable on demand, determinable from the bill. Presentment for acceptance, on the other hand, can be made whenever suitable to the holder, provided he does so within reasonable time.[357]

Due presentment   The rules as to what amounts to due presentment for payment   **34-106**
are specified in s.45 of the Act, and are as follows: if the bill is not payable on demand, it must be presented for payment when it falls due. If it is payable on demand it must be presented within a reasonable time after its issue in order to render the drawer liable, and within a reasonable time after its indorsement in order to render the indorser liable.[358] The bill must be presented at a reasonable hour on a business day by the holder or his agent, either to the person designated in the bill as payer or to his agent. It must also be presented either at the place specified in the bill, or, if no such place is specified, at the place of business of the drawee, or if this place is not known, at his residence.[359] If no person who is authorised to pay or refuse the bill can be found at the proper place, no further presentment is required. If the bill has been accepted by two or more persons who are not partners, and no place for presentment is specified, it must be presented to all of them. If the acceptor dies the bill must be presented to his personal representative. When authorised by agreement or usage, presentment through the post office is sufficient.

Excuses for delay or non-presentment for payment   According to s.46(1) delay   **34-107**
in presentment for payment is excused when it is caused by circumstances beyond the control of the holder and not imputable to his default, misconduct or negligence.[360] When the cause of the delay ceases to operate, the bill must be presented with reasonable diligence. According to s.46(2) presentment for payment is dispensed with in five cases. First, it is dispensed with where, after the exercise of reasonable diligence, presentment cannot be effected, e.g. where the bill is made "payable at Guildford" and the drawee neither resides nor has an office there.[361] Secondly, presentment is dispensed with where the drawee is a fictitious person. Thirdly, presentment is excused as regards the drawer, where the drawee is not bound towards the drawer to accept or pay the bill and the drawer has no reason to believe that it would be paid if presented. Thus, if the drawer's account

---

[356] i.e. ss.39(4), 46. For discharge of drawer of a cheque, see para.34-151, below; and see further special provisions for the truncation and imaging of cheques: below, paras 34-152 et seq.

[357] See *Chalmers and Guest on Bills of Exchange and Cheques*, 18th edn (2017), para.6-022.

[358] As regards the importance of due presentment for payment, see *Yeoman Credit Ltd v Gregory* [1963] 1 W.L.R. 343.

[359] If the bill cannot be so presented, it may be presented to the drawer or to the acceptor wherever he may be found or at his last place of business or residence: r.4(d).

[360] See, e.g. *Rouquette v Overmann* (1875) L.R. 10 Q.B. 525; *Re Francke and Rasch* [1918] 1 Ch. 470; *Hamilton Finance Co v Coverley Westray Walbaum & Tosetti Ltd* [1969] 1 Lloyd's Rep. 53, 72 (delay by post alleged but not proved).

[361] *Hardy v Woodroofe* (1818) 2 Stark. 319.

with his bank is overdrawn, and he has not been granted an overdraft, presentment of his cheque for payment is not necessary.[362] However, the mere fact that the holder has reason to believe that the bill will be dishonoured, does not excuse presentment. Thus, where the holder comes to know that the drawer has requested the acceptor to dishonour the bill, presentment is not excused.[363] Fourthly, as regards the indorser, presentment is excused if the bill has been made for his accommodation and he has no reason to expect that it will be honoured. Finally, presentment for payment may also be waived, either expressly or impliedly.[364]

34-108 **Dishonour by non-payment** According to s.47(1) a bill is dishonoured by non-payment either when not paid on presentation or, if presentment for payment is excused, when the bill is overdue and unpaid.[365] According to s.47(2) when a bill is dishonoured by non-payment, the holder obtains an immediate right of recourse against the drawer and indorsers.[366] An action to enforce this right can, however, be brought only if the holder gives notice of dishonour or protests the bill, if either is required.

34-109 **Notice of dishonour** According to s.48, when a bill is dishonoured by non-acceptance or non-payment,[367] the holder must send a notice of dishonour and any drawer or indorser to whom no such notice is given is discharged.[368] However, if a bill which is dishonoured by non-acceptance or non-payment comes subsequently into the hands of a holder in due course, his rights are not affected by the failure of a previous holder to send a notice of dishonour. If notice of dishonour is given when a bill is dishonoured by non-acceptance, there is no need for notice of dishonour for non-payment, unless the bill has been accepted after its original dishonour. The rules prescribing the requirements of a valid notice of dishonour are set out at length in s.49 of the Act.[369] It is clear from the language of s.48, that notice need not be given to the acceptor.

34-110 **Excuses for delay or failure to give notice** According to s.50(1), delay in sending notice of dishonour is excused under the same circumstances as delay in presentment for payment.[370] According to s.50(2) notice of dishonour is dispensed with in the following cases: first, notice is dispensed with when after exercise of reasonable diligence it cannot be given, e.g. if the drawer's place of business is

---

[362] *Wirth v Austin* (1875) L.R. 10 C.P. 689; *Re Bethell* (1887) 34 Ch. D. 561; *Fiorentino Comm Giuseppe Srl v Farnesi* [2005] EWHC 160 (Ch), [2005] 1 W.L.R. 3718.

[363] *Hill v Heap* (1823) Dow & Ry.N.P. 57. See also *Baker v Birch* (1811) 3 Camp. 107.

[364] As regards waiver of presentment of an accommodation bill, see *Reisler v Kulcsar*, 57 D.L.R. (2d) 730 (1966).

[365] In *Commissioner for Inland Revenue v Thomas Cook (NZ) Ltd* [2003] 2 N.Z.L.R. 296, the Court of Appeal of New Zealand held that a demand does not have to be made in order to cause a stale cheque, presentment of which is dispensed with, to be "overdue and unpaid"; although this was later doubted, without deciding the matter, by the Privy Council on appeal in the same case: [2004] UKPC 53 at [11].

[366] This right of recourse is subject to the provisions of ss.65 to 68.

[367] As regards notice sent before actual dishonour, see *Eaglehill Ltd v J Needham Builders Ltd* [1973] A.C. 992.

[368] If the holder presents the bill for payment through a collecting bank he is entitled to await its return before giving notice: *Lombard Banking Ltd v Central Garage and Engineering Co Ltd* [1963] 1 Q.B. 220.

[369] *Chalmers and Guest on Bills of Exchange and Cheques*, 18th edn (2017), paras 6-096 et seq.

[370] As to which, see para.34-107, above.

closed,[371] or if it fails to reach the drawer or indorser because it is lost in the post.[372] Secondly, notice may be waived, expressly or impliedly, both before and after it becomes due.[373] Thirdly, as regards the drawer, notice is dispensed with:

(a) where the drawer and drawee are the same person;
(b) where the drawee is either a fictitious person or does not have capacity to contract;
(c) where the drawer is the person to whom the bill is presented for payment;
(d) where the drawee or acceptor is as between the drawer and himself not bound to honour the bill[374]; and
(e) where the drawer has countermanded payment.[375]

Fourthly, notice is dispensed with as regards an indorser:

(a) where the indorser is aware that the drawee is a fictitious person or one without capacity to contract;
(b) where the indorser is the person to whom the bill is presented for payment;
(c) where the bill was accepted or made for the indorser's accommodation.

According to s.52(3) notice of dishonour is not necessary in order to render the acceptor liable.

Noting or protest of bill   Under s.51(1) protest is optional when the dishonoured   **34-111** instrument is an inland bill, i.e. one which is, or on the face of it purports to be, either both drawn and payable within the British Islands or drawn within the British Islands on a person resident therein.[376] Under s.51(2) protest is required when a bill which both is and appears on its face to be a foreign bill, i.e. any bill other than an inland bill, is dishonoured either by non-acceptance or, if not dishonoured previously by non-acceptance, by non-payment. Failure duly to protest such a bill discharges the drawer and indorsers but not the acceptor. A protest is carried out by the presentation of the bill for acceptance or payment, after the dishonour, by a notary public. If the bill is dishonoured when presented by the notary, he makes a copy of it in his register and "notes" on the bill the date of presentment, the answer given and the amount of his fee. After "noting" the bill, a copy of the protest must be sent to each drawer and indorser. The correct procedure for a protest is specified in s.51(3)–(8)[377] of the Act. According to s.93, it is sufficient if the noting of the bill is within the specified time and the formal protest may be extended subsequently. The provisions concerning both excuses for the delay in and dispensation of noting or protest, which are specified in s.51(9), are similar to those prevailing in the case of notice of dishonour. According to s.94 of the Act, when the services of a notary public cannot be obtained, a householder or substantial resident of the place may, in the presence of two witnesses, give a certificate attesting the dishonour of the bill.

Duties of holder towards the acceptor or drawee   The performance of the du-   **34-112**

---

[371] *Allen v Edmundson* (1848) 2 Exch. 719, 723; *Studdy v Beesty* (1889) 60 L.T. 647, 649.
[372] *Mackay v Judkins* (1858) 1 F. & F. 208.
[373] *Lombard Banking Ltd v Central Garage and Engineering Co Ltd* [1963] 1 Q.B. 220.
[374] See, e.g. *Lafitte v Slatter* (1830) 6 Bing. 623; *Wirth v Austin* (1875) L.R. 10 C.P. 689.
[375] And see *Barclays Bank Ltd v WJ Simms Son & Cooke (Southern) Ltd* [1980] 1 Q.B. 677, 702–703.
[376] s.4, which also defines the term British Islands. As regards this definition, see below, para.34-197.
[377] As amended by s.1 of the Bills of Exchange (Time of Noting) Act 1917. See *Chalmers and Guest on Bills of Exchange and Cheques*, 18th edn (2017), paras 6-143 et seq.

ties of the holder, discussed above, is a condition precedent to the liability of the drawer and indorsers. The only duty which the holder owes to the acceptor or drawee is to exhibit the bill when the holder demands payment and to deliver it against payment.[378] As the acceptor is the main obligee of the bill, his liability does not depend on the due sending of notice of dishonour or on the protest of the bill by the holder.[379] Presentment for payment is not necessary to render the acceptor liable if the bill is either accepted generally or if the terms of a qualified acceptance do not require it.[380] Moreover, even if the terms of a qualified acceptance require presentment for payment, the acceptor is not, in the absence of an express stipulation to that effect, discharged if the holder fails to present the bill for payment on the day it is due.[381] But if the acceptance requires presentment for payment, the bill must be so presented before the holder's right of action against the acceptor matures.[382]

(vi) Liabilities of Parties

34-113 **Liability of acceptor** A bill of exchange does not constitute an assignment of funds which the drawer has in the hands of the drawee, and the holder does not usually have a cause of action against a drawee who has not accepted the bill.[383] Thus, the holder of a cheque has no action for its dishonour against the drawee bank.[384] However, when the drawee accepts the bill, he undertakes to pay it according to the tenor of his acceptance.[385] The acceptor is estopped from denying to a holder in due course:

(a) the existence of the drawer, the genuineness of the drawer's signature and his capacity and authority to draw the bill;

(b) if the bill is payable to the drawer's order, the capacity of the drawer to indorse, but not the genuineness and validity of his indorsement;

(c) if the bill is payable to the order of a third party, the existence of the payee and his capacity to indorse the bill, but not the genuineness and validity of his indorsement.[386]

It should be stressed that these estoppels operate only in favour of a holder in due course, and a mere holder is not entitled to plead them.[387] As the provisions of the Act are not exhaustive, a holder may in certain cases be able to rely on a common law estoppel to preclude the acceptor from raising certain defences. Thus, if before discounting a bill, the holder were assured by the acceptor that a certain indorsement was genuine, the acceptor could not subsequently allege that it was a

---

[378] s.52(4).

[379] s.52(3).

[380] s.52(1), (2).

[381] s.52(2).

[382] *Halstead v Skelton* (1843) 5 Q.B. 86, 93–94.

[383] s.53(1). That the drawing of the bill does not constitute an equitable assignment follows from *Shand v Du Buisson* (1874) L.R. 18 Eq. 283, 288–289. The position is different in Scotland: s.53(2); as to which, see *Williams v Williams*, 1980 S.L.T. 25 Sh Ct holding that a countermanded cheque would not be effective to constitute an assignment; *Sutherland v Royal Bank of Scotland Plc* 1997 S.L.T. 329 OH.

[384] *Hopkinson v Forster* (1874) L.R. 19 Eq. 74; *Schroeder v Central Bank* (1876) 34 L.T. 735. But see s.74(3).

[385] s.54(1).

[386] s.54(2).

[387] *Ayres v Moore* [1940] 1 K.B. 278.

forgery.[388]

Liability of drawer and indorser By drawing the bill, the drawer engages that **34-114** it will be honoured by the drawee when duly presented, and that if it be dishonoured he will compensate the holder or any indorser who is compelled to pay it, provided the required proceedings on dishonour are taken.[389] A similar engagement is undertaken by each indorser to all subsequent indorsers and to the holder.[390] The drawer is precluded from denying to a holder in due course the existence of the payee and his capacity to indorse the bill, but not the genuineness of his indorsement.[391] The indorser is estopped from denying to a holder in due course the genuineness and regularity in all respects of the drawer's signature and of all previous indorsements.[392] As against an immediate or subsequent indorsee, the indorser is precluded from denying that, at the time of his indorsement, the bill was valid and subsisting and that he had a good title to it.[393] In effect, both the drawer and the indorser undertake that the bill will be honoured by the drawee and, for most purposes, are in a position similar to that of joint guarantors of a debt. Thus, when the bill is dishonoured, the holder is entitled to sue the acceptor, the drawer or the indorser, or all of them together. The drawer and indorser are entitled to the equities of a surety.[394]

Other signatures Where a person signs a bill otherwise than as drawer or accep- **34-115** tor, he incurs the liabilities of an indorser to a holder in due course.[395] His liability, though, is incurred only towards subsequent parties. Even if the indorsement is executed for security purposes, the indorser does not assume liability to any holder who, initially, became a party to the bill before him.[396] Furthermore, the indorser's liability is subject to the holder's due performance of the formalities prescribed by the Act in respect of dishonoured bills. On these two points, the position of an indorser differs from that of a guarantor, whose liability would be concurrent with the acceptor's.[397] But whilst a guarantee of a bill, which is known as an *aval*, is recognised in countries which have adopted the Uniform Law on Bills of the Geneva Convention as well as in the United States,[398] the prevailing view is that an

---

[388] *Brook v Hook* (1871) L.R. 6 Ex. 89, 99, and cases cited in para.34-053, above.

[389] s.55(1)(a). As regards a bill indorsed for accommodation before its having been signed by the drawer, see *Bank of Nova Scotia v Hogg*, 24 O.R. (2d) 494 (1979) Can.

[390] s.55(2)(a). But note that under s.16(1) the drawer or indorser may insert in the bill words negativing his liability.

[391] s.55(1)(b).

[392] s.55(2)(b).

[393] s.55(2)(c).

[394] *Duncan Fox & Co v North and South Wales Bank* (1880) 6 App. Cas. 1, especially at 19–20. See also *Rouquette v Overmann* (1875) L.R. 10 Q.B. 525, 537; *Double Diamond Bowling Supply Ltd v Eglington Bowling Ltd* [1963] 2 O.R. 222, 224–226; *Re Securitibank Ltd* [1978] 1 N.Z.L.R. 97, 212; *Guaranty Trust Co of Canada v Seller's Oil Field Service Ltd* (1984) 55 A.R. 348 at [13]–[15]; *Scholefield Goodman & Sons Ltd v Zyngier* [1984] V.R. 445, affirmed [1986] A.C. 562, PC. And see *Chalmers and Guest on Bills of Exchange and Cheques*, 18th edn (2017), para.7-021. See also below, paras 45-126 et seq.

[395] s.56.

[396] *Steele v M'Kinlay* (1880) 5 App. Cas. 745; *Stagg, Mantle & Co v Brodrick* (1895) 12 T.L.R. 12.

[397] *Stagg, Mantle & Co v Brodrick*, above; *Chalmers and Guest on Bills of Exchange and Cheques*, 18th edn (2017), paras 7-031 et seq.

[398] ULB, arts 30–32; Uniform Commercial Code (USA) s.3-419 (Revised Version), under which the *aval* is treated as a specie of accommodation signature and binding as such: Ellinger, "Negotiable

aval is not effective in English law.[399] However, in *G & H Montage GmbH v Irvani*[400] Saville J. held that English law would uphold the validity of an *aval*, if its validity was recognised by the foreign law system governing the instrument. His Lordship further observed that the words commonly used in an *aval*, e.g. "payment guaranteed", constituted an adequate memorandum within the meaning of the Statute of Frauds. His decision was affirmed, on the same grounds, by the Court of Appeal.[401] This important decision indicates that at least one of the objections traditionally raised against the recognition of an *aval* in English may not be of substance.

34-116 **Indorsement for collection** Not every signature appearing on the back of the bill has the effect of an indorsement. It may be executed for the purpose of facilitating the collection and not the negotiation of the instrument. A person who appends his signature for this purpose is not an indorser and does not assume liability on the bill. Usually he manifests his intention by adding to his signature words indicating that the bill is transmitted solely for collection.[402] In other cases the same intention may be inferred from the circumstances. Thus, it was held by an Australian authority that the signature of the payee on a cheque payable to himself "or bearer" was not to be regarded an indorsement as such a bill was transferable by mere delivery. The payee's signature was therefore not required to effect transfer and, by signing the bill on its back, he did not purport to assume the liability of an indorser.[403] But this decision may be questioned as, in such a case, the payee's signature may be executed at the transferee's request for the very purpose of rendering the payee liable to pay the bill in the event of its dishonour by the drawee. It is arguable that whether or not a particular signature constitutes an indorsement depends on the signer's intention. In the absence of proof to the contrary, s.56 leads to the conclusion that a signature executed by a person other than the drawer or the drawee constitutes an indorsement.

34-117 **Measure of damages for dishonour** The damages for the dishonour of a bill payable in the United Kingdom consist of:

(a) the amount of the bill;

(b) interest thereon either, if the bill is payable on demand, from the date of presentment, or in the case of any other bill, from the date of maturity; and

(c) the expenses of noting or of protest, when protest is required.[404]

Section 57 does not specify the rate of interest to be applied. When calculating the

---

Instruments", being Ch.4 of the *Encyclopedia of Comparative Law* (Hamburg, 2001), Vol.IX, para.389.

[399] *Jackson v Hudson* (1810) 2 Camp. 447, 448; *Steele v M'Kinlay* (1880) 5 App. Cas. 745 at 772.

[400] [1988] 1 W.L.R. 1285.

[401] [1990] 1 Lloyd's Rep. 14; see also, as regards *avals* on foreign bills, *Banco Atlantico SA v British Bank of the Middle East* [1990] 2 Lloyd's Rep. 504; and see *Chalmers and Guest on Bills of Exchange and Cheques*, 18th edn (2017), paras 7-039—7-041.

[402] *Keene v Beard* (1860) 8 C.B.(N.S.) 372, 382; *Gerald McDonald & Co v Nash* [1924] A.C. 625, 634.

[403] *Miller Associates (Australia) Pty Ltd v Bennington Pty Ltd* (1975) 7 A.L.R. 144; and see Chappenden (1981) 55 A.L.J. 135.

[404] s.57(1). The claim is in damages and not in debt (*Standard Chartered Bank v Dorchester LNG (2) Ltd* [2014] EWCA Civ 1382 at [40]). If the law which governs the party's contract on the instrument is part of the law of the UK, then the measure of damages will be determined in accordance with s.57, but if the law which governs that contract is the law of some foreign country, s.57 will not apply, and the measure of damages will be determined by that law: *Chalmers and Guest on Bills*

appropriate rate of interest for a period from the date of the cause of action to the date of the judgment, the rate payable on judgment debts is a convenient starting point.[405] However, the usual practice in the Commercial Court is to award interest at 1 per cent above base rate, unless such rate would be unfair to one or other of the parties or to be otherwise inappropriate.[406] For small claims, it is easier to claim interest at the judgment rate.[407]

Foreign currency bills   The rule prescribed by s.57 is adequate in respect of bills   **34-118** payable in pounds sterling. Problems arise in respect of bills payable in a foreign currency as, fundamentally, the conversion of the amount so expressed can be based on the rate of exchange prevailing on one of four possible dates:

(i)   the date on which the bill is payable;
(ii)   the date of commencement of proceedings to enforce the bill;
(iii)   the date of judgment; and
(iv)   the date on which payment is actually made.

Traditionally English law favoured the first alternative[408] and, until 1977, this was reflected in ss.57(2) and 72(4) of the Act. Under the former provision the holder of a bill dishonoured abroad was entitled to claim the amount of "re-exchange" of the bill with interest thereon until the actual time of payment. "Re-exchange" meant the amount for which a sight draft had to be drawn at the time and place of dishonour in order to realise the amount of the bill and the expenses resulting from dishonour taking into account the rate of exchange prevailing at that date.[409] Under the latter provision the amount of a bill expressed in foreign currency and drawn out of the United Kingdom but payable within the realm was, in the absence of stipulation to the contrary, to be calculated according to the rate of exchange for sight drafts at the place of payment on the date of maturity.[410]

New rule   Both ss.57(2) and 72(4) further reflected the principle under which the   **34-119** judgment of an English court for the payment of money had to be expressed in pounds sterling. This rule was, however, reversed by the House of Lords in *Miliangos v George Frank (Textiles) Ltd*[411] in which a foreign seller sued an English buyer for the payment of an amount which was expressed in the contract of sale in Swiss francs and in respect of which the buyer had accepted bills of exchange payable in Switzerland. It was held that the amount payable by the English buyer was to be determined on the basis of the rate of exchange prevailing at the date of actual

---

of Exchange, 18th edn (2017), para.7-052, applied by Blair J. in *Karafarin Bank v Dara (No.2)* [2009] EWHC 3265 (Comm), [2010] 1 Lloyd's Rep. 236 at [25]–[27].
[405] See the notes to the CPR 1998 in the *White Book 2017*, paras.7.0.13 et seq.
[406] There is no presumption to the effect that base rate plus 1 per cent is the appropriate measure and awards of 2 per cent above base rate are common: see the notes to the CPR 1988 in the *White Book 2017*, para.7.0.15—7.0.16.
[407] CPR Pt 12 r.12.6 (default judgments). On claims for interest generally, see *Chalmers and Guest on Bills of Exchange and Cheques*, 18th edn (2017), para.7-047.
[408] So explained by Lord Wright in *Salim Nasrallah Khoury (Syndic in Bankruptcy) v Khayat* [1943] A.C. 507, 512–513.
[409] *Re Commercial Bank of South Australia* (1887) 36 Ch. D. 522, 528. And see *Re Gillespie* (1886) 18 Q.B.D. 286.
[410] But note that it has been suggested that s.72(4) was not meant to cover cases of default: *Barclays Bank International Ltd v Levin Bros (Bradford) Ltd* [1977] Q.B. 270.
[411] [1976] A.C. 443, especially at 468–469.

payment, i.e. the date on which actual enforcement of the judgment was ordered. The judgment itself was expressed in Swiss francs.

34-120 Scope of application At one stage it was thought that this new rule, which enabled English courts to order the payment of an amount expressed in foreign currency, was applicable only in respect of contracts and bills of exchange governed by a foreign proper law. But in *Barclays Bank International Ltd v Levin Bros (Bradford) Ltd*,[412] Mocatta J. held that the same principle applied in respect of a bill of exchange drawn in US dollars for the price of goods supplied by an American exporter to an English purchaser. His Lordship reached this conclusion although the bill was payable in London, although the proper law governing the buyer's acceptance was that of England and although the currency of payment was, accordingly, the pound sterling. This decision has been reinforced by the repeal of ss.57(2) and 72(4) of the Act.[413]

34-121 Transferor by delivery Where the holder of a bill payable to bearer negotiates it by delivery without indorsing it, he is called a "transferor by delivery".[414] A transferor by delivery is not liable on the bill, and if it is dishonoured cannot be sued on it even by the immediate transferee.[415] However, by negotiating the bill, the transferor by delivery warrants to his immediate transferee (provided the latter is a holder for value), that the bill is what it purports to be, that he has a right to transfer it and that he is not aware of any fact which renders it valueless.[416] Thus, if it turns out that the bill is a forgery and hence worthless, the transferor by delivery is obliged to reimburse the transferee.[417] The holder of a bill who presents it for payment to the drawer is not a "transferor" and does not warrant its authenticity.[418]

(vii) Discharge of Bill

34-122 Discharge defined A bill is discharged:

(a) by payment in due course (s.59);
(b) when the acceptor becomes the holder of it at or after its maturity (s.61);
(c) by express waiver or renunciation (s.62);
(d) by cancellation (s.63); and
(e) to a certain extent, where a bill is materially altered without the assent of the parties liable on it (s.64).

The effect of the discharge of a bill is to extinguish all rights of action based thereon, as the bill ceases to be a negotiable instrument.[419] However, the position of a person who, in good faith and for valuable consideration takes a discharged bill that does not show on its face that it has been discharged, gives rise to difficulties. It has been suggested that such a person could claim to be a holder in due course and that he

---

[412] [1977] Q.B. 270.
[413] Administration of Justice Act 1977 s.4.
[414] s.58(1).
[415] s.58(2). But see s.2 of the Cheques Act 1957.
[416] s.58(3). Note that his liability is not incurred towards subsequent parties: *Miller Associates (Australia) Pty Ltd v Bennington Pty Ltd* (1975) 7 A.L.R. 144.
[417] *Gurney v Womersley* (1854) 4 E. & B. 133.
[418] *Guaranty Trust Co of New York v Hannay & Co* [1918] 2 K.B. 623, 631–632.
[419] *Harmer v Steele* (1849) 4 Exch. 1, 13; *Burchfield v Moore* (1854) 23 L.J. Q.B. 261.

may be entitled to enforce the bill.[420] It should, however, be recollected that a person is a holder in due course only if he takes a bill before it is overdue. The problem could, thus, arise only in the case of a bill payable on demand or, in the case of any other bill, if it was paid before maturity. In these cases it could, perhaps, be argued that an acceptor who failed to indicate on the bill that it had been discharged, should be estopped from pleading this.

Payment in due course   According to s.59(1), a bill is discharged by payment in due course, i.e. when the drawee pays it at or after maturity to a holder, and does this in good faith and without notice that the holder's title is defective. A holder is defined as the payee or indorsee of a bill who has its possession or the bearer.[421] It is, therefore, doubtful whether payment to a person who obtained the bill under a forged indorsement of the payee constitutes a discharge.[422] It has been held that payment by the acceptor in good faith to a thief, who had stolen a bill payable to bearer, constituted payment in due course.[423] Payment in good faith by the acceptor to an indorsee who has obtained the bill by fraud constitutes a discharge.[424]   **34-123**

Payment by drawer or indorser   When a bill (not being an accommodation bill)[425] is paid by the drawer or an indorser, it is not discharged. If a bill payable to a third party is paid by the drawer, he is entitled to enforce payment against the acceptor but may not re-issue the bill. If a bill payable to the drawer's own order is indorsed by him to another person but subsequently is paid by the drawer himself, he is restored to his former rights against the acceptor and antecedent parties; he is entitled to strike out his own indorsement and again negotiate the bill. This is also the position of an indorser who pays a bill.[426] When a drawer or indorser pays a bill to a holder, he becomes entitled to the benefit of securities given to the holder by the acceptor. The reason for this is that the drawer and indorsers are considered to be guarantors of the acceptor's debt to the holder, and thus are subrogated to the holder's (creditor's) security rights vis-à-vis the debtor.[427]   **34-124**

Claims for repayment by drawee or acceptor[428]   The position of a drawee or an acceptor who has paid a bill to a person not entitled to it, gives rise to problems. When such a drawee is a banker, he may be entitled to debit his customer's account despite his having paid the cheque or bill to an unauthorised person.[429] Where the drawee does not acquire such a right, he may attempt to claim repayment of the amount of the cheque or of the bill from the payee as money paid under a mistake of fact. Moreover, even where the drawee is entitled to debit the drawer's account with the amount paid on the bill, the drawee may be induced by commercial   **34-125**

---

[420] *Glasscock v Balls* (1889) 24 Q.B.D. 13, 15. See *Chalmers and Guest on Bills of Exchange and Cheques*, 18th edn (2017), para.8-003.

[421] s.2.

[422] See above, para.34-053. An exception applies in the case of cheques. See s.60 discussed below in paras 34-346 et seq.

[423] *Smith v Sheppard* (1776), cited in *Chitty on Bills*, 11th edn, p.278.

[424] *Robarts v Tucker* (1851) 16 Q.B. 560, 576–577, 579.

[425] Which is discharged by the party for whose accommodation it has been made: s.59(3).

[426] s.59(2).

[427] *Duncan Fox & Co v North and South Wales Bank* (1880) 6 App. Cas. 1. See also para.34-114 above.

[428] For a detailed discussion, see E.P Ellinger, E. Lomnicka and C.V.M. Hare, *Ellinger's Modern Banking Law*, 5th edn (2011), Ch.12. Note that the rights of the acceptor are also affected by s.54(2), as to which see above, para.34-113.

[429] s.60, discussed in paras 34-346 et seq., below.

considerations to seek a remedy against the payee. The drawee's right to demand repayment from the payee depends on the facts of each case; the principal factors to be taken into account are the nature of the mistake that induced the drawee to honour the instrument and the capacity in which the payee presented it. The drawee is not entitled to demand repayment from a payee who, having presented the bill as an agent, has remitted the proceeds to his principal.[430] The drawee stands a better chance of succeeding against a payee who has obtained payment for himself. It is well established that restitution will be ordered against a payee who obtains payment with the knowledge that the drawee is acting under a mistake as to the facts.[431] If the payee receives payment in good faith, the drawee or acceptor's rights depend on the nature of the mistake.

34-126 **Nature of mistake** To be operative, the mistake must be material. Some authorities suggest that, to be material, a mistake must have some direct bearing on the transaction between the drawee and the payee and that a mistake concerning an extraneous fact, affecting the legal relationship between the drawee and the drawer, is usually irrelevant.[432] But in *Barclays Bank Ltd v WJ Simms Son & Cooke (Southern) Ltd*[433] Robert Goff J. described this view as too narrow. His Lordship said that a mistake is material if it leads the bank to the erroneous conclusion that it has the customer's mandate to effect payment. A mistake which does not directly or indirectly mislead the bank as regards its mandate to pay is inoperative.[434] Goff J.'s analysis derives support from cases according to which the bank is not entitled to reclaim payment made as a result of a mistaken belief that the customer's account has an adequate balance for meeting the instrument.[435] In such a case the bank actually complies with the customer's order to pay on the basis of a mistake. In doing so, it remains within the scope of its authority. His Lordship's opinion derives further support from cases which hold that the bank is entitled to reclaim payment if it has overlooked the customer's countermand even if the payee too has been

---

[430] *Buller v Harrison* (1777) 2 Cowp. 565, 568; *Pollard v Bank of England* (1871) L.R. 6 Q.B. 623, 631; *Bank of Montreal v The King* (1906) 11 O.L.R. 595 (affirmed 38 S.C.R. 258 (1907) Can); *Gowers v Lloyds and National Provincial Bank* [1938] 1 All E.R. 766, 773; *National Westminster Bank Ltd v Barclays Bank International Ltd* [1975] Q.B. 654. This doctrine, originally protecting an agent who has changed his position by paying the money received to his principal, has been restated as a general defence to an action in restitution in *Lipkin Gorman v Karpnale Ltd* [1991] 2 A.C. 548. However, this is probably wrong as the defence of an agent who has paid money over to his principal is best regarded as a separate defence with its own rules (*Portman Building Society v Hamlyn Taylor Neck (a firm)* [1998] 4 All E.R. 202 at 207, per Millett L.J.; *Jones v Churcher* [2009] EWHC 722 (QB), [2009] 2 Lloyd's Rep. 94 at [77]–[78]; *Jeremy D Stone Consultants Ltd v National Westminster Bank Plc* [2013] EWHC 208 (Ch) at [244]). But note that the agent can be sued as long as the proceeds remain in his hands; the agent cannot defeat such an action by asserting a lien or right of set-off over the proceeds: *Kleinwort, Sons & Co v Dunlop Rubber Co* (1907) 97 L.T. 263; *Kerrison v Glyn, Mills Currie & Co* (1911) 81 L.J. K.B. 465; *RE Jones Ltd v Waring and Gillow Ltd* [1926] A.C. 670. See further, E Bant, "Payment over and change of position: lessons from agency law" [2007] L.M.C.L.Q. 225.
[431] *Kendal v Wood* (1871) L.R. 6 Ex. 243.
[432] *Aiken v Short* (1856) 1 H. & N. 210; *Barclay & Co Ltd v Malcolm & Co* (1925) 133 L.T. 512, 513.
[433] [1980] Q.B. 677, 694. As regards the question of materiality generally, see at 692.
[434] [1980] Q.B. 677 at 699–700.
[435] *Chambers v Miller* (1862) 32 L.J. C.P. 30; *Pollard v Bank of England* (1871) L.R. 6 Q.B. 623, 633; *Dominion Bank v Jacobs* [1951] 3 D.L.R. 233. And see Goff J. in *Barclays Bank* case, above, at 689; and *Lloyd's Bank Plc v Independent Insurance Co Ltd* [1999] 1 Lloyd's Rep. Bank. 1.

unaware of the stop order at the time of payment.[436] In such a case the bank makes payment without having its customer's mandate.

Mistake respecting instrument The drawee or acceptor is a fortiori entitled to recover payment where the mistake relates to the instrument itself, e.g. where the drawer's signature or a subsequent indorsement is forged or where the amount of the instrument has been fraudulently raised. There are, however, some cases which suggest that even in this type of case the drawee is unable to claim repayment of the amount paid, except where he notifies the payee of the fraud on the very day of payment.[437] But these cases have been questioned; it will be convenient to consider the reasoning in the authorities in point. **34-127**

Three reasons are canvassed in the cases which deny the drawee's right to demand restitution of an amount paid on the basis of a mistake of fact relating to a negotiable instrument presented by the payee. First, it is suggested that when the drawee pays the instrument he induces the payee to believe that it is valid; the drawee is therefore precluded from subsequently asserting a forgery or irregularity in the bill.[438] Secondly, at least one authority suggests that the drawee is unable to recover where he is negligent at the time of payment, e.g. where he fails to scrutinise the drawer's signature.[439] Obviously, this argument would enable the drawee to recover the amount paid where he had not acted negligently, e.g. where the forgery was executed so skilfully as to defy detection. Thirdly, it has been said that the drawee loses his right to recover when the payee changes his position in reliance on the payment of the instrument; it is further asserted in this context that, unless the payee is notified about the forgery without any delay, his position is automatically altered to his detriment because a lapse of time deprives him of the opportunity to serve due notice of dishonour on previous parties.[440] As delay in giving notice is, however, excused in cases of this type,[441] this reasoning is not plausible. It has been suggested that the most convincing argument in support of **34-128**

---

[436] *Barclays Bank Ltd v WJ Simms Son & Cooke (Southern) Ltd*, above. See also *Southland Savings Bank v Anderson* [1974] 1 N.Z.L.R. 118 (suggesting that if the payee was aware of the countermand, he could be sued in deceit). Contrast *Commonwealth Trading Bank v Reno Auto Sales Pty Ltd* [1967] V.R. 790 Aust.

[437] As regards the right of restitution where notice of the forgery is given on the day of payment, see *Wilkinson v Johnson* (1824) 3 B. & C. 428; *Cocks v Masterman* (1829) 9 B. & C. 902, 908–909.

[438] *Price v Neal* (1762) 3 Burr. 1354, 1357; *London and River Plate Bank Ltd v Bank of Liverpool Ltd* [1896] 1 Q.B. 7, 10–11; *Bank of Montreal v R.* (1906) 11 O.L.R. 595 (affirmed (1907) 38 S.C.R. 258 Can). See also dicta in *Hart v Frontino and Bolivia South American Gold Mining Co* (1870) L.R. 5 Ex. 111, 115; *Simm v Anglo-American Telegraph Co* (1879) 5 Q.B.D. 188, 196, per Lindley J. (the decision was reversed by the Court of Appeal, but the dictum in question remains unaffected). That a holder does not warrant the genuineness of a bill by presenting it for payment or for acceptance, see *Guaranty Trust Co of New York v Hannay & Co* [1918] 2 K.B. 623. In *BMP Global Distribution Inc v Bank of Nova Scotia* [2009] 1 S.C.R. 504 at [32], Deschamps J., delivering the judgment of the Supreme Court of Canada, said: "I do not accept that [*Price v Neal*] provides a basis for an unqualified rule that a drawee will never have any recourse against either the collecting bank or the payee where payment has been made on the forged signature of the drawer".

[439] *Smith v Mercer* (1815) 6 Taunt. 76, 81, 87. See also *Price v Neal*, above, but contrast *London and River Plate Bank Ltd v Bank of Liverpool Ltd*, above, which suggests that negligence is not the correct test.

[440] *Cocks v Masterman* (1829) 9 B. & C. 902, 908–909; and see below, paras 34-133 et seq. as regards the position in the light of *Lipkin Gorman's* case, above. See also *BMP Global Distribution Inc v Bank of Nova Scotia* [2009] 1 S.C.R. 504.

[441] Bills of Exchange Act 1882 s.50(1); above, para.34-110. And note that notice is altogether excused as regards the drawer if the cheque had been stopped: s.50(2); and see *Barclays Bank Ltd v WJ Simms Son & Cooke (Southern) Ltd* [1980] Q.B. 677, 700–703.

the cases in question is that the holder of a bill or of a cheque is entitled to know promptly upon presentation whether the instrument is to be honoured or not.[442] On this view, the cases in question establish an exception, concerning payment of amounts due on negotiable instruments, to the general rule that entitles the payer to claim repayment of an amount paid under a mistake of fact despite his having been negligent in failing to ascertain the correct position and regardless of a change to the detriment in the payee's position.[443] The existence of such an exception to the general rule has, however, been questioned in two cases.[444] It is there suggested that, even if the cases establishing the exception constitute good law, the exception, as based on these cases, is confined to the payment under a mistake of fact of genuine negotiable instruments and does not affect the payment of instruments which are forgeries *in toto* and hence not negotiable. One difficulty concerning this narrow interpretation is that in many cases the holder has no means of ascertaining whether the instrument concerned is a total forgery (such as a bill bearing a forged signature of the drawer) or a valid instrument.

34-129 **Attempt to reconcile** An attempt to reconcile the earlier authorities is to be found in Robert Goff J.'s decision in *Barclays Bank Ltd v WJ Simms Son & Cooke (Southern) Ltd.*[445] The drawer of a cheque stopped it when he was informed that a receiver was appointed under a mortgage debenture issued by the payee. Due to a clerical error, the bank paid the cheque to the receiver. When the bank discovered its mistake, it recredited the drawer's account and claimed repayment. Giving judgment for the bank, Goff J. said that, on the basis of the "formidable line of authority" certain simple principles could be deduced[446]:

> "(1) If a person pays money to another under a mistake of fact which causes him to make the payment, he is prima facie entitled to recover it as money paid under a mistake of fact. (2) His claim may however fail if (a) the payer intends that the payee shall have the money at all events, whether the fact be true or false, or is deemed in law so to intend; or (b) the payment is made for good consideration, in particular if the money is paid to discharge, and does discharge, a debt owed to the payee (or a principal on whose behalf he is authorised to receive the payment) by the payer or by a third party by whom he is authorised to discharge the debt; or (c) the payee has changed his position in good faith, or is deemed in law to have done so."

34-130 **Effect of mistake** These rules led his Lordship to certain conclusions concerning the effect of a mistake of fact resulting in the payment of a cheque. If, despite the existence of the mistake, the bank paid the cheque in compliance with its

---

[442] So in *Cocks v Masterman*, above, at 908–909. See also *Mather v Maidstone* (1856) 18 C.B. 273, 294 (where the acceptance itself was forged). See also *BMP Global Distribution Inc v Bank of Nova Scotia* [2009] 1 S.C.R. 504.

[443] See Vol.I, paras 29-186 et seq.

[444] *Imperial Bank of Canada v Bank of Hamilton* [1903] A.C. 49; *National Westminster Bank Ltd v Barclays Bank International Ltd* [1975] Q.B. 654. See also *Bank of India v Abeyesinghe* (1927) 29 N.L.R. (Ceylon) 257. See also *BMP Global Distribution Inc v Bank of Nova Scotia* [2009] 1 S.C.R. 504.

[445] [1980] Q.B. 677, discussed by Matthews (1980) 130 New L.J. 587; Goode (1981) 97 L.Q.R. 254, who argues that a payee, who receives payment of a stopped cheque without notice, is entitled to retain the amount to the extent that he is entitled to succeed against the drawer. The bank, on the basis of subrogation, is entitled to maintain the debit in the drawer's account to the same extent. See also *Bank of New South Wales v Murphett* [1983] 1 V.R. 489.

[446] [1980] Q.B. 677 at 695. For a recent example of Goff J.'s exception (2)(a), see *Leslie v Farrar Construction Ltd* [2016] EWCA Civ 1041 at [51]–[56].

customer's mandate, it would be entitled to debit his account. The payment involved would further discharge the customer's debt to the payee. Goff J. concluded that, accordingly, the bank would not be entitled to claim the amount back on the basis of its having been paid under a mistake of fact.[447] But if the bank paid the instrument without having a mandate to do so, it would not be entitled to debit the customer's account. Unless the customer ratified payment, the bank would be entitled to recover the amount paid from the payee.[448] In the case in question the balance standing to customer's account was adequate for meeting the cheque. But Goff J. intimated that his decision would have been the same even if, on the basis of its mistake, the bank had permitted the customer's account to become overdrawn.[449]

General recognition of defence of change in position   The two substantive defences for actions for the recovery of money paid under a mistake of fact, applicable respectively where a bank pays the funds received by it to its customer and the cases respecting payments of negotiable instruments, constitute special applications of the general doctrine under which money is not recoverable from a payee who has changed his position in good faith in reliance on the payment made to him. These two special defences were recognised although the general doctrine or defence was, for many years, held inapplicable in English law.[450] The law in point was, however, finally changed by the House of Lords in 1991 in *Lipkin Gorman v Karpnale Ltd.*[451] C, who was a junior partner in a firm of solicitors, misappropriated money from the firm's client account and used it for the purchase of gaming chips with which he gambled at the premises of the defendant club. Occasionally he won and paid part of his gains to the credit of the client account; but in most instances he lost. All in all, C lost £154,695 out of the total amount of £323,224 stolen by him from the firm. The firm brought an action to recover the money from the club. Reversing the decision of the majority of the Court of Appeal, the House of Lords held that the supply of the chips by the club's cashier to C did not constitute the furnishing of a separate lawful consideration by the club. C's transactions with the club involved gambling and, as the contracts so made were void, the club had not furnished value for the funds. The firm was, accordingly, entitled to recover. This finding gave rise to the question of whether the firm was entitled to recover the total amount stolen and placed by C on the betting table or only the net amount lost by him.   **34-131**

Decision in Lipkin Gorman   Finding that the club had changed its position to the extent of the amounts paid out to C, their Lordships held that only the net amount won by the club was recoverable. In reaching this conclusion, their Lordships expressly gave effect to the doctrine under which an action in restitution does not lie against a person who has in good faith changed his position in reliance on the funds received. In such a case: **34-132**

"... the injustice of requiring [the defendant] so to repay outweighs the injustice of deny-

---

[447] See also *Lloyds Bank Plc v Independent Insurance Co Ltd* [2000] Q.B. 110, CA.

[448] [1980] Q.B. 677 at 699–700.

[449] [1980] Q.B. 677 at 700. See also *National Westminster Bank Ltd v Barclays Bank International Ltd* [1975] Q.B. 654.

[450] For its final rejection in the 20th century, see *RE Jones & Co Ltd v Waring & Gillow Ltd* [1926] A.C. 670.

[451] [1991] 2 A.C. 548.

ing the plaintiff restitution. If the plaintiff pays money to the defendant under a mistake of fact, and the defendant then, acting in good faith, pays the money or part of it to charity, it is unjust to require the defendant to make restitution to the extent that he has so changed his position. Likewise, … if a thief steals … money and pays it to a third party, who gives it away to charity, that party should have a good defence to an action for money had and received. In other words, bona fide change of position should of itself be a good defence in cases such as these."[452]

34-133 **Present scope of doctrine** The House of Lords has, thus, introduced the defence of the payee's change in position as a general defence to restitutionary claims.[453] Their Lordship emphasised, at the same time, that not every change in a payee's position would, as a matter of course, entitle him to plead the defence in question. Lord Goff of Chieveley emphasised[454]:

"I am most anxious that, in recognising this defence to actions of restitution, nothing should be said at this stage to inhibit the development of the defence on a case to case basis, in the usual way. It is, of course, plain that the defence is not open to one who has changed his position in bad faith, as where the defendant has paid away the money with knowledge of the facts entitling the plaintiff to restitution; and it is commonly accepted that the defence should not be open to a wrongdoer."

Lord Goff added that the mere fact that the payee had spent the money did not, of itself, involve a change in his position that would bring the doctrine into operation. The "expenditure might in any event have been incurred by him in the ordinary course of things".[455] The payee must have incurred expense that he would otherwise not have incurred[456] or have acted in such a way as to render it unjust that he should now be compelled to refund the payment.[457] Where the payee still retains the benefit of goods or services that he purchased, he may still be held to have been unjustly enriched to their value as a result of the payment.[458]

34-134 **Assessment** It is to be expected that the principles governing the change of position defence will be refined and articulated in due course.[459] It will then be seen also whether the two specific applications of the doctrine, discussed earlier in respect

---

[452] [1991] 2 A.C. 548 at 579, per Lord Goff of Chieveley.

[453] But there remains uncertainty as to whether the defence extends to all restitutionary claims. The defence of change of position is available against restitutionary claims based on unjust enrichment, but even then it is not open to a wrongdoer (*Lipkin Gorman (a firm) v Karpnale Ltd* [1991] 2 A.C. 548 at 580). There is some doubt as to whether it is available against a restitutionary claim based on the vindication of property rights, where the action is subject to the bona fide purchaser for value defence (*Foskett v McKeown* [2001] 1 A.C. 102 at 129; *Papamichael v National Westminster Bank* [2003] 1 Lloyd's Rep. 341 at 376; *Armstrong DLW GmbH v Winnington Networks Ltd* [2012] EWHC 10 (Ch) at [103]). In *Haugesund Kommune v Depfa ACS Bank* [2010] EWCA Civ 579, [2012] 2 W.L.R. 199 at [122], where Aikens L.J. said that "the defence of change of position is a general defence to all restitution claims (for money or other property) based on unjust enrichment".

[454] [1991] 1 A.C. 548 at 580. That an anticipatory mistake may be operative, see *Dextra Bank and Trust Co Ltd v Bank of Jamaica* [2002] 1 All E.R. (Comm) 193, PC; *Commerzbank AG v Gareth Price-Jones* [2003] EWCA Civ 1663 (noted by Birks (2004) 120 L.Q.R. 373); cf. *South Tyneside Metropolitan Borough Council v Svenska International Plc* [1995] 1 All E.R. 545, Clarke J.

[455] [1991] 1 A.C. 548; and see *United Overseas Bank v Jiwani* [1976] 1 W.L.R. 964.

[456] *Test Claimants in the FII Group Litigation v HMRC (No.2)* [2014] EWHC 4302 (Ch) at [353] (Henderson J.).

[457] See *Commerzbank AG v Price-Jones* [2003] EWCA Civ 1663 at [39]–[40], [65]–[70].

[458] E.P. Ellinger, E. Lomnicka and C.V.M. Hare, *Ellinger's Modern Banking Law*, 5th edn (2011), p.530.

[459] Important recent cases on the availability of the change of position defence include: *Philip Collins Ltd v Davis* [2000] 3 All E.R. 808; *Scottish Equitable Plc v Derby* [2001] EWCA Civ 369, [2001]

of the payment of funds by a collecting bank to its customer and as regards payments of negotiable instruments, will be redefined in the light of the mainstream of future cases expounding the general doctrine. In the meantime, it is advisable to regard the existing cases, respecting the two specific applications of the doctrine, as basically unaffected.[460]

Tracing order   Where the payee of an amount, paid by a bank under a mistake   **34-135** of fact, is insolvent, the bank may wish to obtain a tracing order so as to enable it to recover the amount involved *in specie*. Thus, in *Chase Manhattan Bank NA v Israel-British Bank (London) Ltd*[461] the plaintiff, a New York bank, was asked by one of its correspondents to pay a certain amount to the M Bank, another New York bank, for the account of the defendant, an English bank. Due to an error, the plaintiff paid the amount twice. Before the plaintiff noticed its error, the defendant went into liquidation. Granting a tracing order, Goulding J. observed that such an order would be available both under the laws of New York and of England. His Lordship rejected the argument that an equitable tracing order would be granted only where a fiduciary relationship existed between the payer and the payee at the time payment took

2 All E.R. (Comm) 274; and *Crédit Suisse (Monaco) SA v Attar* [2004] EWHC 374 (Comm) (on the need for a causal connection between the mistaken receipt and the change of position); *Dextra Bank & Trust Co Ltd v Bank of Jamaica* [2002] 1 All E.R. (Comm) 193; and *Commerzbank AG v Gareth Price-Jones* [2003] EWCA Civ 1663 (on anticipatory change of position); *Niru Battery Manufacturing Co v Milestone Trading Ltd* [2002] EWHC 1425 (Comm), [2002] 2 All E.R. (Comm) 705, 741; approved [2003] EWCA Civ 1446, [2004] 4 All E.R. (Comm) 193 (on what constitutes "bad faith"); *Barros Mattos Junior v MacDaniels Ltd* [2004] EWHC 1188 (Ch), [2004] 3 All E.R. 299 (on change of position which constituted an illegal action); *Campden Hill Ltd v Chakrani* [2005] EWHC 911 (Ch) (on retention of benefit acquired as result of change of position); *Abou-Rahmah v Abacha* [2006] EWCA Civ 492, [2007] 1 Lloyd's Rep. 115 (on defendant's conduct at time of change of position); *Test Claimants in the FII Group Litigation v Commissioners for Revenue and Customs* [2008] EWHC 2893 (Ch), [2009] S.T.C. 254 at [320], [337] (wrongdoer bar to the defence of change of position); *Jones v Churcher* [2009] EWHC 722 (QB), [2009] 2 Lloyd's Rep. 94 (when good faith requires inquiry to be made before disposing of the mistaken payment); *Haugesund Kommune v Depfa ACS Bank* [2010] EWCA Civ 579, [2012] 2 W.L.R. 199 (recipient of payment made under void contract of loan took risk that money would have to be repaid); *Jeremy D Stone Consultants Ltd v National Westminster Bank Plc* [2013] EWHC 208 (Ch) (on whether defence barred by bank's alleged failure to monitor its relationship with customer, contrary to the Money Laundering Regulations 2007 reg.8(1), and its alleged failure to report criminal activity, contrary to the Proceeds of Crime Act 2002 s.330); *Bellis (a firm) v Challinor* [2015] EWCA Civ 59 at [115]–[120] (in circumstances failure to make diligent enquiry before disposing of mistaken payment did not constitute commercially unacceptable conduct); *T & L Sugars Ltd v Tate & Lyle Industries Ltd* [2015] EWHC 2696 (Comm) at [137] (on anticipatory reliance); *Dexia Crediop SpA v Comune di Prato* [2016] EWHC 2824 (Comm) at [75] (on need for "but for" causal connection between the receipt and any change of position)—but see also [2017] EWCA Civ 428, where the Court of Appeal reversed an earlier, related judgment on a key conflict of law issue in this case, and also held (at [213]) that there was no basis for restitutionary claims by either party. In *BMP Global Distribution Inc v Bank of Nova Scotia* [2009] 1 S.C.R. 504, [62]–[65], the Supreme Court of Canada held that (1) the general of change of position defence applies to mistaken payments made on forged cheques; and (2) neither the collecting bank nor the payee changed their position merely by allowing the proceeds of a cheque to be credited to the payee's account. For detailed coverage, see E. Bant, *The Change of Position Defence* (2009). See generally, Vol.I, paras 29-186 et seq.

460 For further discussion of the relationship between the payment over defence and the change of position defence, see E Bant, "Payment over and change of position: lessons from agency law" [2007] L.M.C.L.Q. 225. The separate nature of the two defences was stressed in *Jones v Churcher* [2009] EWHC 722 (QB), [2009] 2 Lloyd's Rep. 94 at [77]–[78], and also in *Jeremy D Stone Consultants Ltd v National Westminster Bank Plc* [2013] EWHC 208 (Ch) at [244], with both cases citing Millet L.J. in *Portman Building Society v Hamlyn Taylor Neck (a firm)* [1998] 4 All E.R. 202 at 207.

461 [1979] 3 All E.R. 1025.

place. It was "enough that … the payment into the wrong hands itself gave rise to a fiduciary relationship".[462] Such a relationship eventuated because a person who paid money to another under a factual mistake retained an equitable property in it and the payee's conscience would be subjected to a fiduciary duty to respect this proprietary right.[463]

34-136 Goulding J.'s reasoning has since been strongly criticised (obiter) by Lord Browne-Wilkinson in *Westdeutsche Landesbank Girozentrale v Islington LBC*.[464] *Chase Manhattan* seems no longer to represent good law.[465] There is no basis for the contention that, in the ordinary course, a person retains an equitable (or any) interest in money paid away. Nevertheless, Lord Browne-Wilkinson did concede that, despite Goulding J.'s faulty reasoning, *Chase Manhattan* may well have been rightly decided. The recipient bank had known of the mistake made by the paying bank within two days of the receipt of the money. Lord Browne-Wilkinson concluded (at 715):

> "Although the mere receipt of money, in ignorance of the mistake, gives rise to no trust, the retention of the moneys after the recipient bank learned of the mistake may well have given rise to a constructive trust."[466]

34-137 Acceptor holder at maturity If at or after maturity of a bill the acceptor becomes

---

462 [1979] 3 All E.R. 1025 at 1032.

463 For recent cases analysing the situations in which a court will grant a tracing order at law or in equity, see *Agip (Africa) Ltd v Jackson* [1991] Ch. 547 (affirming [1990] Ch. 265 (Millett J.)); *Polly Peck Plc v Nadir (No.2)* [1992] 4 All E.R. 769; *Abdul Ghani el Ajou v Dollar Land Holdings Plc* [1993] 3 All E.R. 717 (Millett J.); *Bank Tejarat v HKSB (CI) Ltd* [1995] 1 Lloyd's Rep. 239; *Re Goldcorp Exchange Ltd (in Receivership)* [1995] 1 A.C. 74; *Friends' Provident Life Office v Hillier Parker May & Rowden* [1997] Q.B. 85; *FHR European Ventures LLP v Mankarious* [2016] EWHC 359 (Ch); *Bainbridge v Bainbridge* [2016] EWHC 898 (Ch) and the decision of the Supreme Court of Singapore in *Re Untalan, Hongkong and Shanghai Banking Corp Ltd v United Overseas Bank Ltd* [1992] 2 S.L.R. 195 (Michael Hwang J.C.). See also *BMP Global Distribution Inc v Bank of Nova Scotia* [2009] 1 S.C.R. 504 at [80], [85], where the Supreme Court of Canada held that tracing at law was not defeated merely because the funds have passed through a mixed fund or a clearing system (noted by Ogilvie (2010) 25 B.F.L.R. 545; Fox [2010] C.L.J. 28; McInnes (2009) 125 L.Q.R. 552). As regards the issue of tracing funds paid into an overdrawn account, see *Style Financial Services Ltd v Bank of Scotland* [1986] 5 Bank. L.R. 15; *Bishopsgate Investment Management Ltd v Homan* [1995] Ch. 211, CA; *Box v Barclays Bank Plc* [1998] Lloyd's Rep. Bank 185 at 203; *Shalson v Russo* [2003] EWHC 1637 (Ch), [2005] Ch. 281 at [140]–[141]; *Cooper v PRG Powerhouse Ltd* [2008] EWHC 498 (Ch) at [28]–[33]; *Re BA Peters Plc* [2008] EWCA Civ 1604 at [13]–[24]; *Serious Fraud Office v Lexi Holdings Plc* [2008] EWCA Crim 1443 at [51]. See also Smith [1995] C.L.J. 290; Conaglen (2011) 127 L.Q.R. 432. The arguments of Smith and Conaglen were reviewed by the Judicial Board of the Privy Council in *Brazil v Durant International Corp* [2015] UKPC 35, which (at [40]) rejected the argument that there can never be "backward tracing", or that the court can never trace the value of an asset whose proceeds are paid into an overdrawn account. The relationship between tracing and unjust enrichment was explored by the Court of Appeal in *Relfo Ltd (In Liquidation) v Varsani* [2014] EWCA Civ 360, noted by Nolan (2015) 131 L.Q.R. 8.

464 [1996] A.C. 669 at 714–715 (a case where money was paid under a void contract). See also the criticisms of Lord Millett, writing extra-judicially, in "Restitution and Constructive Trusts", in W. Cornish et al (eds) *Restitution—Past, Present and Future* (1998), p.212.

465 Aikens J. refused to follow it in *Bank of America v Arnell* [1999] Lloyd's Rep. Bank 399 at 406.

466 This seems to require actual knowledge on the part of the recipient (*Papamichael v National Westminster Bank Plc* [2003] 1 Lloyd's Rep. 341, 372), but it has also been suggested that an objective test of unconscionability ought to be adopted (*Fitzalan-Howard (Norfolk) v Hibbert* [2009] EWHC 2855 (QB), [2010] P.N.L.R. 11 at [49]). See also *Commerzbank AG v IMB Morgan Plc* [2004] EWHC 2771 (Ch), [36]; *Bank of Ireland v Pexxnet Ltd* [2010] EWHC 1872 (Comm), [55].

its holder, *in his own right*, the bill is discharged.[467] Thus, if a bill is accepted jointly by three drawees, and is at maturity indorsed to one of them, it is discharged, and the remaining acceptors cannot be sued on the bill, although they may be liable to contribute as joint debtors.[468] If the acceptor of a bill becomes the executor of the holder, the bill is discharged.[469] However, this would probably not be the case if the acceptor became an administrator, as he would then not hold the bill "in his own right".[470]

Waiver   A bill is discharged if at or after its maturity the holder expressly and   **34-138**
absolutely renounces his rights against the acceptor either in writing or by delivering the bill to him.[471] The bill is likewise discharged if it is delivered to the acceptor's executors or administrators with an intention that it be discharged. In *Edwards v Walters*,[472] where the holder of a promissory note voluntarily delivered it up, after the death of the maker, to a devisee of his real estate, which he had charged with the payment of his debts, the delivery was held not to operate as a renunciation of the note. The court indicated, however, that if the devisee had been appointed executor or administrator the bill would have been discharged. In *Rimalt v Cartwright*[473] it was held that the acceptance by the holder of an offer by the acceptor to pay a composition was not a "renunciation in writing" of the holder's rights. The liabilities of any party to a bill may in like manner be renounced by the holder before, at, or after its maturity; but such renunciation does not affect the rights of a holder in due course.[474]

Cancellation   A bill is discharged by an apparent, intentional, cancellation of it   **34-139**
by the holder or his agent.[475] In like manner the holder or his agent may discharge any party liable on the bill by cancelling his signature. In such a case any indorser, who would have had a right of recourse against the party whose signature is cancelled, is also discharged.[476] A cancellation is effective only if it is obvious: where a bill, which had been torn into two pieces, was picked up and mended, a holder in due course, who took it subsequently, was allowed to enforce it against the acceptor.[477] A holder may prove that a cancellation was made unintentionally or under a mistake of fact or without his authority, and in that case it is inoperative.[478]

Alteration of bill   Where a bill or acceptance is materially altered without the as-   **34-140**
sent of all parties, the bill is, by the terms of s.64(1), avoided, except as against a party who has himself made, authorised or assented to the alteration and subsequent

---

[467] s.61.
[468] *Harmer v Steele* (1849) 4 Exch. 1. cf. *Foster, Hight & Co v Ward* (1883) 1 Cab. & E. 168.
[469] *Jenkins v Jenkins* [1928] 2 K.B. 501.
[470] For a detailed analysis see *Chalmers and Guest on Bills of Exchange and Cheques*, 18th edn (2017), para.8-058.
[471] s.62(1).
[472] [1896] 2 Ch. 157. cf. *D Gokal & Co (HK) Ltd v Rippleworth Ltd* [1998] 11 C.L. 370.
[473] (1924) 40 T.L.R. 803.
[474] s.62(2).
[475] s.63(1).
[476] s.63(2).
[477] *Ingham v Primrose* (1859) 7 C.B.(N.S.) 82. See also *Ralli v Dennistoun* (1851) 6 Exch. 483; *Bank of Scotland v Dominion Bank* [1891] A.C. 592.
[478] s.63(3). See *Warwick v Rogers* (1843) 5 M. & G. 340, approved in *Prince v Oriental Bank Corp* (1878) 3 App. Cas. 325.

indorsers.[479] The section provides that where a bill has been materially altered, but the alteration is not apparent, and the bill is in the hands of a holder in due course, he may avail himself of the bill as if it had not been altered, and may enforce payment of it according to its original tenor. An alteration is considered apparent, if it would be observed by a person who intends becoming a holder of it and who scrutinises it with reasonable care.[480] The effect of this section is that a holder in due course can enforce a bill according to its original terms. Thus, where a bill has been altered from £500 to £3,500, a holder in due course is entitled to enforce payment of £500.[481] If, before being aware of the alteration of the amount of a cheque, the drawee bank pays a holder in due course the amount as altered, it may be entitled to recover from him the difference between this amount and the original one.[482]

34-141   The following alterations are, by s.64(2), material: any alteration of the date,[483] the sum payable, the time of payment, the place of payment, and, where a bill has been accepted generally, the addition of a place of payment without the acceptor's assent. The list of alterations specified in this subsection is not, however, exhaustive and whether a specific alteration is material or not is a question of fact.[484] An alteration which is not deliberately made by any person, but is caused by accident, does not invalidate the bill.[485] An alteration made before a bill is completely issued, e.g. the alteration by the drawer of a purported place of drawing inserted by an acceptor, who has accepted a bill before its being signed by the drawer, is not a material alteration,[486] although the same alteration may be material if made after the bill is properly issued.[487]

(viii)   Acceptance and Payment for Honour

34-142   **Acceptance for honour**   Where the drawee of a bill dishonours it by non-acceptance, a person who is not a party to the bill may, before the bill is overdue, and provided the holder consents to his doing so, accept the bill supra protest for the honour of any party liable thereon.[488] The acceptor for honour undertakes to pay the bill himself if it is dishonoured by non-payment by the drawee, provided the bill is duly presented to the drawee and protested. He incurs liability towards the holder and all parties to the bill subsequent to the one for whose honour he has accepted it.[489] Where a bill has been accepted for honour supra protest, it must be protested for its non-payment by the drawee before it is presented for payment to the accep-

---

[479] s.64(1) has been explained as an application of the rule in *Pigot's* case (1614) 11 Co. Rep. 26b: *Habibsons Bank Ltd v Standard Chartered Bank (Hong Kong) Ltd* [2010] EWCA Civ 1335, [2011] Q.B. 943 at [28].

[480] *Woollatt v Stanley* (1928) 138 L.T. 620. See generally Hudson [1975] J.B.L. 108.

[481] *Scholfield v Londesborough* [1896] A.C. 514.

[482] *Imperial Bank of Canada v Bank of Hamilton* [1903] A.C. 49. See also above, paras 34-126 et seq.

[483] *Heller Factors Pty Ltd v Toy Corp Pty Ltd* [1984] 1 N.S.W.L.R. 121 Aust.

[484] See, e.g. *Smith v Lloyds TSB Group Plc* [2000] 2 All E.R. (Comm) 693, where the Court of Appeal held that altering the payee's name on a cheque was a "material" alteration.

[485] *Hong Kong and Shanghai Banking Corp v Lo Lee Shi* [1928] A.C. 181.

[486] *Foster v Driscoll* [1929] 1 K.B. 470, 494.

[487] *Koch v Dicks* [1933] 1 K.B. 307. See also *Raiffeisen Zentralbank Österreich AG v Crossseas Shipping Ltd* [2000] 1 W.L.R. 1135 at [19], CA.

[488] s.65.

[489] s.66.

tor for honour.[490] Where a bill is dishonoured by the acceptor for honour, it must be protested for non-payment.[491]

Payment for honour supra protest Where a bill has been protested for non- **34-143** payment, any person may intervene and pay it supra protest for the honour of any party liable thereon.[492] In order that it may operate as payment for honour and not as a mere voluntary payment, the payment must be attested by a notarial act in a specified form.[493] Where a bill has been paid for honour, all the parties subsequent to the party for whose honour it is paid are discharged; the payer for honour is subrogated to and succeeds to both the rights and duties of the holder as regards the party for whose honour he pays, and all parties liable to that party.[494] If the holder of the bill refuses to receive payment for honour supra protest, he loses his right of recourse against all the parties who would have been discharged by such payment.[495] If the holder receives such payment as well as payment of notarial expenses which he incurred due to the dishonour of the bill, he is obliged to deliver the bill and the protest to the payer for honour.[496]

Referee in case of need According to s.15 of the Act, the drawer or any indorser **34-144** may insert in the bill the name of a person to whom the holder may resort if the bill is dishonoured by non-acceptance or non-payment. Such a person is known as a "referee in case of need". The holder has the option to resort to the referee in case of need. A bill which contains a reference in case of need must, in the case of its dishonour by the drawee, be protested for non-payment before it is presented for payment to the referee in case of need.[497]

(ix) Lost Instruments

Holder's right to duplicate of lost bill According to s.69, where a bill has been **34-145** lost before it is overdue, the last holder is entitled to request another bill of the same tenor from the drawer, but must give him an indemnity against claims by any persons, arising in case the lost bill is found again. If the drawer refuses to give such duplicate bill, he may be compelled to do so. No power is given by this section to obtain an indorsement or acceptance over again.

Action on lost bill According to s.70, in any action or proceeding on a bill, the **34-146** court may order that the loss of the instrument shall not be set up, provided an indemnity be given against the claims of any other person. If the claimant wishes to secure an order for costs, he should offer the indemnity before bringing an action on the lost instrument.[498]

---

[490] s.67(1); even a bill payable after sight must be presented to the drawee after its acceptance for honour: *Williams v Germaine* (1827) 7 B. & C. 468. As regards the time and place for such present-ment, see s.67(2). As regards excuses for delay, see s.67(3).
[491] s.67(4). As to the computation of the maturity of such bills, see s.65(5).
[492] s.68(1), as regards the position if more than one person offers to pay a bill supra protest, see s.68(2).
[493] s.68(3), (4).
[494] s.68(5). He cannot, however, negotiate the bill: *Ex p. Swan* (1868) L.R. 6 Eq. 344.
[495] s.68(7).
[496] s.68(6).
[497] s.67(1).
[498] *King v Zimmerman* (1871) L.R. 6 C.P. 466, 469. Note that the section has been repealed as regards

(x) Bills in a Set

34-147   Rules as to sets   Where a bill is drawn in a set, each part of which is numbered[499] and contains a reference to the other parts, all these parts constitute one bill. Where the holder of a set indorses two or more parts to different persons, he is liable on every such part, and every indorser subsequent to him is liable on the part he has himself indorsed, as if the different parts were separate bills. Where two or more parts of a set are negotiated to different holders in due course, the holder whose title first accrues is, as between such holders, deemed the true owner of the bill; but this does not, in itself, affect the rights of a person who in due course accepts or pays the part first presented to him. The acceptance may be written on any part, and it must be written on one part only. If the drawee accepts more than one part, and such accepted parts get into the hands of different holders in due course, he is liable on every such part as if it were a separate bill. When the acceptor of a bill drawn in a set pays it without requiring the part bearing his acceptance to be delivered up to him, and that part is, at maturity, outstanding in the hands of a holder in due course, he is liable to this holder. Subject to the preceding rules, where any one part of a bill drawn in a set is discharged, the whole bill is discharged.[500]

(c) Cheques

(i) General Provisions

34-148   Cheques defined   According to s.73 of the Act, a cheque is a bill of exchange drawn on a banker, payable on demand.[501] It should be noted that the Act does not limit the definition to bills drawn on the bank *by a customer*. While it is customary to draw cheques on forms contained in a cheque book supplied by a bank, a cheque may be drawn on any paper. In *Roberts & Co v Marsh*[502] a person drew a cheque on a sheet of writing paper, wrote on it the words "to be retained" and promised the payee to substitute a cheque written on a form. It was held that, as the words "to be retained" were directed to the payee, this instrument was a valid cheque.[503]

34-149   Provisions on bills payable on demand apply   According to s.73, except as otherwise provided in the part of the Bills of Exchange Act 1882 relating to cheques (ss.73–81A), the provisions of the Act applicable to bills of exchange payable on demand apply to cheques.[504]

Northern Ireland: Judicature (Northern Ireland) Act 1978 s.122 and Sch.7 Pt I.

[499] The parts of the set are usually expressed to be the "First", "Second", etc. "of Exchange". Such a bill is rarely used except for overseas trade, when it may be convenient to send the various parts separately to ensure the early delivery of, at any rate, one part.

[500] s.71.

[501] As to which bills are payable on demand, see s.10 of the Act, discussed in para.34-013, above.

[502] [1915] 1 K.B. 42. cf. *Burnett v Westminster Bank Ltd* [1966] 1 Q.B. 742.

[503] As regards "cheques" drawn to "cash or order", see above, para.34-021.

[504] Note that a new Pt 4A (presentment of cheques and other instruments by electronic means) was introduced into the Bills of Exchange Act 1882 by the Small Business, Enterprise and Employment Act 2015 s.13: see below, paras 34-153—34-154.

Certifying or marking cheques A cheque is not intended to be (and in practice **34-150** never is) accepted.[505] In some Commonwealth countries bankers do, however, "mark" or "certify" cheques drawn on them by writing on the cheques the word "good" or "approved". At one time it was thought that such a certification constituted an acceptance,[506] but this view has been rejected in more recent cases, and it is at present clear that a certification does not, in itself, give the holder a right to sue the certifying banker.[507] However, a certification can have some effect if it is written by the drawee bank on a post-dated cheque. In such a case a banker may be estopped from pleading that the customer's account did not have a credit balance, sufficient to meet the cheque, at the date of the certification.[508] But it is to be doubted whether such an estoppel would assist the holder's case, because an estoppel cannot, in itself, constitute a cause of action. Moreover, the certification of a post-dated cheque does not entitle the banker to "earmark" any amount standing to the credit of the customer's account for the purpose of meeting this cheque, and the banker will be obliged to honour any cheque presented between the date of the certification of the post-dated cheque and the date of its presentation. Thus, even if there is a sufficient balance for meeting the post-dated cheque at the date of certification, there may not be sufficient funds at the date of presentation. The certification cannot, therefore, be regarded as constituting a promise of the drawee bank that the cheque will be paid when presented. This is particularly so as the customer can effectively countermand, i.e. "stop", the payment of a certified cheque.[509]

Presentment for payment While presentment of a cheque for payment is **34-151** required—except where excused by s.46—failure so to do does not necessarily discharge the drawer.[510] Section 74(1) of the Act provides that where a cheque is not presented for payment within a reasonable time[511] of its issue and the drawer had the right, at the time at which the cheque should have been presented, to have it paid by the banker, he is discharged to the extent of his actual loss, i.e. to the extent to which the drawer is the creditor of the banker to a larger amount than he

---

505 *Bellamy v Marjoribanks* (1852) 7 Exch. 389, 404; *Bank of Baroda Ltd v Punjab National Bank Ltd* [1944] A.C. 176, 188.
506 *Robson v Bennett* (1810) 2 Taunt. 388, 396.
507 *Gaden v Newfoundland Savings Bank* [1899] A.C. 281; *Bank of Baroda Ltd v Punjab National Bank Ltd*, above; *Southland Savings Bank v Anderson* [1974] 1 N.Z.L.R. 118. But note that where a cheque is marked by the drawee bank at the request of another bank for clearing purposes, that other bank is by mercantile usage entitled to payment: *Robson and Waugh v Bennett* (1810) 2 Taunt. 388; *Goodwin v Robarts* (1875) L.R. 10 Ex. 337, 351 (affirmed (1876) 1 App. Cas. 476). In *BMP Global Distribution Bank Ltd v Bank of Nova Scotia* [2009] 1 S.C.R. 504, [87]–[88], the Supreme Court of Canada held that certification by a bank does not prevent it from recovering the proceeds of a cheque paid by mistake.
508 *Bank of Baroda Ltd v Punjab National Bank Ltd* [1944] A.C. 176 at 191. It is to be doubted whether a certification could give rise to an action by the holder against the certifying banker for a negligent misrepresentation under the rule in *Hedley Byrne & Co v Heller & Partners* [1964] A.C. 465. The reason for this is that by certifying the cheque the banker does *not* warrant that it will be paid.
509 *Keyes v Royal Bank of Canada* [1947] 3 D.L.R. 161; *Southland Savings Bank v Anderson*, above, at 121; cf. *Gibson v Minet* (1824) 2 Bing. 7.
510 As to when a cheque is considered to have been "presented" through the clearing system, see *Barclays Bank Plc v Bank of England* [1985] 1 All E.R. 385. But for presentment of a cheque by electronic means, see para.34-154 below.
511 As to what constitutes "reasonable time", see s.74(2), which is similar to the relevant part of s.45(2); see also *King v Porter* [1925] N.I. 107. For cheques presented by electronic means, s.89A(5) preserves the requirement that presentation must be within a reasonable time.

would have been had the cheque been paid. The effect of this provision is that the drawer is discharged only if the banker becomes insolvent, and to the extent of his actual loss. Section 74(3) provides that when the drawer is so discharged, the holder becomes the banker's creditor in lieu of the drawer.

34-152 Cheque truncation Under the traditional banking procedure, as spelt out in the Clearing House Rules, cheques had to be presented for payment through the clearing house to the branch on which they were drawn.[512] This resulted in a cumbersome and prolonged clearing cycle for cheques. For many years the cheque clearing cycle took three working days after receipt of the cheque by the payee's bank.[513] In order to speed up the clearing process, the Bills of Exchange Act 1882 was amended in 1996 to allow for cheque truncation, i.e. the presentation of a cheque by means of an electronic message which sets out the serial number of the cheque, the code which identifies the drawee bank, the number of the account on which the cheque is drawn and its amount.[514] Under a fully truncated system only this essential information about the cheque is sent electronically from the collecting bank to the drawee bank and not the cheque itself, which remains with the collecting bank. But a fully truncated cheque clearing system was never developed in the UK. The declining use of cheques, and the high costs associated with the development of a fully truncated system, meant that UK banks adopted a system of partial truncation with code line information being transferred electronically through an Inter Bank Data Exchange system, but with the cheque still being physically presented through the clearing system to the drawee bank's clearing centre.[515] In fact those provisions introduced in 1996 to allow for cheque truncation (ss.74B and 74C of the Bills of Exchange Act 1882) have now been repealed by s.13 of the Small Business, Enterprise and Employment Act 2015, which introduces fresh amendments to the 1882 Act that allow for cheques to be cleared through presentation of an electronic image of the cheque (known as "cheque imaging") in place of presentation of the cheque itself.[516] However, one amendment introduced in 1996 remains

---

[512] *Barclays Bank v Bank of England* [1985] 1 All E.R. 385.

[513] Described by Bingham J. in *Barclays Bank v Bank of England* [1985] 1 All E.R. 385 at 387. However, since November 2007 the payee of a UK cheque has been entitled to interest (if the account bears interest) or credit, if overdrawn, on the proceeds after a maximum of two days from deposit of the cheque, to withdraw the proceeds after a maximum of four days and to know the fate of the cheque after a maximum of six days (known as "T+2-4-6"). This means that after six working days funds credited to his account cannot be reclaimed, e.g. if there are insufficient funds in the drawer's account. The speed of the cheque clearing process will be increased with full implementation of the UK's new image-based cheque clearing system expected in the summer of 2018. Cleared funds will be available at the latest by midnight of the working day following deposit (Cheque & Credit Clearing Company, *Cheque Imaging Explained*, October 30, 2017, pp.2–3). See further, para.34-153.

[514] Bills of Exchange Act 1882 ss.74B–C, inserted by the Deregulation (Bills of Exchange) Order 1996 (SI 1996/2993). See *Chalmers and Guest on Bills of Exchange and Cheques*, 18th edn (2017), paras 13-021—13-030; and, on cheque truncation generally, see also Vroegop [1990] L.M.C.L.Q. 244.

[515] In December 2009, the Payments Council announced that the cheque clearing system was to close in 2018, but reversed that decision in July 2012 following public pressure. For critique of reversal of Payment Council's decision to abolish cheque clearing, see S. Booysen [2018] J.B.L. 283.

[516] See Pt 4A of the Bills of Exchange Act 1882 (as inserted by s.13). Section 13 came into force on March 26, 2015 for the purposes of enabling the making of regulations under Pt 4A of the 1882 Act, and on July 31, 2016 for all other purposes: Small Business, Enterprise and Employment Act 2015 s.164(4).

in force. According to s.74A of the Bills of Exchange Act 1882,[517] a bank may by a notice published in the London, Edinburgh and Belfast Gazettes specify an address at which cheques drawn on it may be presented for payment. A cheque presented at such an address, for instance at the bank's own data processing centre, is, then, deemed to have been presented at the "proper address". Section 74A is not limited to presentation through the cheque truncation process set out in s.74B, and it remains relevant for cheques that fall outside the new cheque imaging clearing process.

Cheque imaging   In March 2014 the government consulted with a view to introducing legislation to allow for "cheque imaging", which will speed up the clearing process, reducing it from six to two days,[518] by sending a digital image of a cheque for clearing rather than the piece of paper itself.[519] For example, this would enable a customer to take a photograph of their cheque on their smartphone and pay it in to his bank electronically via the bank's mobile banking app. In June 2014, following the consultation exercise, the government announced its intention to legislate to facilitate cheque imaging.[520] The Small Business, Enterprise and Employment Act 2015 was enacted on March 26, 2015, and s.13 of that Act provides the legal framework for the introduction of cheque imaging by inserting a new Pt 4A (ss.89A–F) into the Bills of Exchange Act 1882.[521] It is anticipated that by the summer of 2018 all of the UK's banks and building societies will clear all cheques via a new image-based cheque clearing system.[522]   **34-153**

Summary of Pt 4A   The main effect of new Pt 4A of the Bills of Exchange Act 1882 is to remove the right of the paying bank to demand delivery of the original paper cheque. Section 89A(1) provides that a cheque, or other instrument to which the section applies, may be presented for payment by providing an electronic image of the front and back of the cheque, instead of by presenting the physical cheque, if the person to whom presentment is made accepts the cheque as effective.[523] The electronic image of the cheque will become equivalent to the original paper cheque,[524] but only for the purpose of presentation.[525] Cheques will still have to be written on paper. The new legislation also extends the benefits of   **34-154**

---

[517] Inserted by the Deregulation (Bills of Exchange) Order 1996 (SI 1996/2993).

[518] Cleared funds will be available at the latest by midnight of the working day following deposit (Cheque & Credit Clearing Company, *Cheque Imaging Explained*, October 30, 2017, p.2): compare para.34-152.

[519] HM Treasury Consultation, *Speeding up cheque payments: legislating for cheque imaging* (March 6, 2014).

[520] HM Treasury, *Speeding up cheque payments: legislating for cheque imaging* (June 25, 2014).

[521] s.13 came into force on March 26, 2015 for the purposes of enabling the making of regulations under Pt 4A of the Bills of Exchange Act 1882, and on July 31, 2016 for all other purposes: Small Business, Enterprise and Employment Act 2015 s.164(4).

[522] Cheque & Credit Clearing Company, *Cheque Imaging Explained*, October 30, 2017, p.3.

[523] subss.(2)–(3) enable the Treasury to make regulations to restrict the circumstances in which presentment by image is permissible. Furthermore, s.89C provides that the new method of presentation is not available where the bank imposes terms on a customer which require the customer to provide an image of the instrument for paying in, and prevent the customer from providing the instrument itself to the bank.

[524] reg.3 of the Electronic Presentment of Instruments (Evidence of Payments and Compensation for Loss) Regulations 2018 (SI 2018/832), made by the Treasury under s.89D of the Bills of Exchange Act 1882, requires a banker who has paid an instrument following presentation under s.89A of the 1882 Act to provide a copy of the instrument and certain prescribed accompanying information to the creator of the instrument (in the case of a cheque, this means the drawer) on request. Regula-

imaging to paper instruments other than cheques that are currently cleared using the same system, e.g. bankers' drafts, postal orders, government payable orders, warrants, travellers' cheques and bank giro credits.[520] The new legislation makes it clear that the banks involved in the clearing process are subject to the same duties in relation to collection and payment of the cheque (or other relevant instrument) as if the physical instrument had been presented. But the legislation also goes further and ensures that there are clear liabilities for banks involved in the clearing process. The government considered that the bank which collects the cheque/cheque image and introduces it into the clearing system (the collecting bank) is best placed to implement measures to make the system secure, detect security risks at the earliest stage and reduce fraud in the system. Therefore, the new legislation gives the Treasury power to make delegated legislation which provides, in effect, that the collecting bank,[527] and not the paying bank, should be liable for fraud or error.[528]

34-154A   Made pursuant the Treasury's power contained in s.89E(1) of the Bills of Exchange Act 1882, reg.5 of the Electronic Presentment of Instruments (Evidence of Payment and Compensation for Loss) Regulations 2018[529] ensures that if a customer of the bank which pays the cheque or the bank that pays the cheque ("the claimant") incurs a loss[530] in connection with the electronic presentment, or purported electronic presentment, of a cheque (and that loss did not result from gross negligence or fraudulent activity on their part), and they have not already received compensation, they can obtain compensation from the bank which

---

tion 4 provides for the copy and information provided to be evidence of receipt by the payee named in the instrument of the sum payable by the instrument (there being similar provision for paper cheques in s.3 of the Cheques Act 1957).

[525] s.89A(4) removes existing requirements that apply to the presentment of a cheque or similar instrument that would be inconsistent with presentment in an electronic system, such as the exhibition, presentment and delivery of the paper instrument itself, and a particular place and time of payment. But note that s.89A(5) saves any requirement as to the latest time for presentment (see above, para.34-151).

[526] s.89B. The key requirements, set out in s.89B(1)(b), are that (i) the instrument is one which enables a person to obtain payment from a banker, (ii) it is an instrument that must be presented for payment, and (iii) it could not otherwise be presented electronically. Banknotes are expressly excluded from the new regime (s.89B(2)).

[527] s.89F(5) extends the definition of "collecting bank" beyond that found in s.4 of the Cheques Act 1957 (see para.34-365) for the purposes of Pt 4A, and includes where the bank has credited the customer's account with some value other than money. See *Chalmers and Guest on Bills of Exchange and Cheques*, 18th edn (2017), para.15-078.

[528] s.89E. Under s.89E(1), the Treasury may by regulations make provision for the "responsible banker" to compensate any person for any loss of a kind specified by the regulations which that person incurs in connection with electronic presentation or purported electronic presentation of a cheque or other relevant instrument. The Explanatory Notes to the Small Business, Enterprise and Employment Act 2015 (para.160) explain that such regulations could, for example, provide for a claim by the drawer of the cheque or the bank that paid the cheque where the payment was made to the wrong account because of a defect in the image, or where the image had been created fraudulently. The term "responsible banker" is defined in subs.(3) to mean (a) the banker who is authorised to collect payment of the instrument on a customer's behalf, or (b) if the holder of the instrument is a banker, that banker. It should be noted that, under subs.(5), the regulations may make provision for (a) the responsible banker to be required to pay compensation irrespective of fault (i.e. strict liability); and (b) the amount of compensation to be reduced by virtue of anything done, or any failure to act, by the person to whom compensation is payable (i.e. contributory negligence). Subs.(6) makes it clear that if a bank has to pay compensation under the regulations, it is not prevented from making a claim against another party for a contribution towards compensation.

[529] SI 2018/832, made on July 10, 2018 and coming into force on the 21st day after that date (reg.1).

[530] Meaning loss arising directly from the debiting of funds from the claimant's account and not further consequential loss (reg.5(4)).

presented the cheque. The regulation sets out conditions to be met in order for compensation to be payable, including that the claimant has made a claim in accordance with reg.6, which sets out the procedure for such a claim. Importantly, a right to compensation can only arise where one of the following two criteria is met: (a) the electronic presentment or purported electronic presentment of the instrument was of a type described in s.89E(2)(c), (d) or (e) of the Bills of Exchange Act 1882[531]; (b) the cheque was collected for or paid to a person other than its true owner.[532] The claimant's right to compensation may also be affected by two additional factors. First, the claimant is not entitled to compensation if they are protected by s.80 of the Bills of Exchange Act 1882 (protection to banker and drawer where cheque is crossed).[533] Secondly, the amount of compensation to be paid will be reduced where any act or omission of the claimant contributed to the loss.[534]

Revocation of payment According to s.75, the duty and authority of a banker to   **34-155**
pay a cheque drawn on him by a customer are determined by countermand of payment and by notice of the customer's death.[535] Notice of the customer's bankruptcy[536] or that he has, due to a mental disorder, become incapable of managing his affairs[537] appear, likewise, to determine the banker's authority to pay.

Post-dated cheques[538] A practice has developed of writing on a cheque a date   **34-156**
later than that of the actual day of drawing. The purpose in drawing such a "post-dated cheque" is to prevent the payee or a holder from presenting it before the day written on it. It has been held that, in view of s.13(2) of the Act,[539] such a cheque is not invalid.[540] Moreover, a person who obtains such a cheque for value and in good faith becomes a holder in due course when he actually takes the cheque, and not only as from the date on which it purports to be made.[541] At the same time, a banker should not honour a cheque while it is post-dated.[542] If he does, and the cheque is countermanded by the customer before the purported date of issue, the

---

531 s.89E(2)(c) covers "purported presentment for payment by any means involving provision of an electronic image of an instrument that may not be presented for payment in that way"; (d) covers "provision, in purported presentment for payment, of (i) an electronic image that purports to be, but is not, an image of a physical instrument (including an image that has been altered electronically), or (ii) an electronic image of an instrument which has no legal effect"; (e) covers "provision, in presentment or purported presentment for payment of an electronic image which has been stolen".
532 reg.5(1)(e), (2).
533 reg.7. For Bills of Exchange Act 1882 s.80, see below, para.34-347.
534 reg.7.
535 As regards countermand, see further below, para.34-322.
536 Insolvency Act 1986 s.284.
537 *Imperial Loan Co Ltd v Stone* [1892] 1 Q.B. 599. But the position may be different where an order has been made under the Mental Capacity Act 2005 (replacing the Mental Health Act 1983 Pt VII): see *Chalmers and Guest on Bills of Exchange*, 18th edn (2017), para.13-047.
538 See *Chalmers and Guest on Bills of Exchange and Cheques*, 18th edn (2017), para.2-098.
539 Discussed in para.34-017, above.
540 *Hitchcock v Edwards* (1889) 60 L.T. 636; *Royal Bank of Scotland v Tottenham* [1894] 2 Q.B. 715. See also *Hodgson & Lee Pty Ltd v Mardonius Pty Ltd* (1986) 78 A.L.R. 573, 84 F.L.R. 323. (In Australia, s.16(3) of the Cheques Act 1986 (Cth) now provides that "[f]or the purpose of determining whether a post-dated instrument is a cheque, the fact that the instrument is post-dated shall be disregarded".) A cheque is not invalid by reason of the fact that it is not dated (Bills of Exchange Act 1882 s.3(4)(a)); *Aspinall's Club Ltd v Al-Zayat* [2007] EWCA Civ 1001.
541 *Hitchcock v Edwards*, above.
542 *Brien v Dwyer* (1979) 53 A.L.J.R. 123, in which it was held that the furnishing of a post-dated cheque did not comply with a contractual term permitting payment by cheque.

banker is not entitled to debit the customer's account.[543] It has been suggested that a post-dated cheque is a bill of exchange payable at a future date.[544]

34-157 **Use of cheque cards** Cheque cards used to be issued by banks in the UK for use with their customers' cheques. Through the card the bank undertook to the payee of the cheque that payment would be made (up to the limit indicated on the card itself) regardless of the state of the customer's account, provided that certain condition were met. Cheque cards are no longer in use in the UK.[545]

(ii) Crossed Cheques

34-158 **What constitutes a "crossing"** According to s.76(1) of the Act, a cheque is "crossed generally" if it bears across its face two transverse parallel lines to which may be added the words "and company" or "not negotiable" or both. According to s.76(2) a cheque is "crossed specially" to a designated banker, if it bears across its face the name of that banker either with or without the addition of the words "not negotiable". In practice a special crossing is, too, written between two transverse parallel lines. The provisions of the Act concerning crossed cheques are, by s.95, applied also to dividend warrants. By s.5 of the Cheques Act 1957 they are further extended to:

"(a) any document issued by a customer of any banker which, though not a bill of exchange, is intended to enable a person to obtain payment from that banker of the sum mentioned in the document[546];

(b) any document issued by a public officer which is intended to enable a person to obtain payment from the Paymaster General or the Queen's and Lord Treasurer's Remembrancer of the sum mentioned in the document

(c) any draft drawn by a banker on himself and payable on demand."

34-159 **Who is entitled to cross a cheque** According to s.77 of the Act, a cheque may be crossed generally or specially by the drawer and holder. The holder[547] is entitled to cross a cheque even if it has been uncrossed, may change a general crossing into a special one by adding the name of a banker, and is always entitled to add the words "not negotiable". Where a cheque is crossed specially, the banker to whom it is crossed may again cross it specially to another banker for collection. Where an uncrossed cheque, or a cheque crossed generally, is sent to a banker for collection, he may cross it specially to himself.

34-160 **Effect of crossing** A crossing is a material part of the cheque and, except where authorised by the Act, it is not lawful for any person to obliterate a crossing or to

---

[543] *Morley v Culverwell* (1840) 7 M. & W. 174, 178; *Pollock v Bank of New Zealand* (1901) 20 N.Z.L.R. 174; *Keyes v Royal Bank of Canada* [1947] 3 D.L.R. 161. Contrast *Magill v Bank of North Queensland* (1895) 6 Q.L.J. 262.

[544] *Brien v Dwyer* (1979) 53 A.L.J.R. 123, per Aickin J. at 134; contrast *Hodgson & Lee Pty Ltd v Mardonius* (1986) 78 A.L.R. 573, 84 F.L.R. 323; *Shapiro v Greenstein*, 10 D.L.R. (3rd) 746 (1970).

[545] The UK Domestic Cheque Card Scheme was closed on June 30, 2011. For discussion of cheque cards and, in particular, the law relating to the use of stolen cheque cards, see the 31st edition of this work, paras 34-156—34-158.

[546] This includes a cheque payable to "cash or order": *Orbit Mining and Trading Co v Westminster Bank* [1963] 1 Q.B. 794.

[547] For a definition of holder, see s.2 of the Act. "Holder" includes an agent for collection: *Akrokerri Mines v Economic Bank* [1904] 2 K.B. 465, 472; *Sutters v Briggs* [1922] 1 A.C. 1; *Baker v Barclays Bank Ltd* [1955] 1 W.L.R. 822.

add to it.[548] Any crossing affects the duties of the drawee bank. In the case of an uncrossed cheque the holder can obtain payment in two ways: first, he can send the cheque to his own bankers and request them to collect it on his behalf, i.e. present it on his behalf for payment to the drawee bank. Secondly, he may himself present the cheque for payment at the counter of the drawee bank. When a cheque bears either a general or a special crossing, this second mode of realisation is not available to the holder. If the cheque bears a general crossing, it must be presented for payment through a bank; if it bears a special crossing to a designated bank, it must be presented for payment through that bank.[549] If the drawee bank pays a generally crossed cheque over the counter, or to a person who is not a banker, it is liable to compensate the true owner of the cheque for any loss the latter may sustain owing to the cheque having been so paid.[550] The drawee bank incurs similar liability to the true owner if it pays a specially crossed cheque otherwise than to the banker to whom it is crossed or his agent for collection. It is, however, provided that when a cheque is presented for payment and does not, at that time, appear to be crossed or to have had a crossing which has been altered or obliterated, the drawee bank does not incur any liability to the true owner, provided it paid the cheque in good faith and without negligence.[551]

Protects true owner   Thus, one of the main effects of a crossing is to protect the rights of the true owner.[552] The phrase "true owner", which is not defined in the Act, has been held to include the holder in due course of a cheque.[553] But the true owner may be a person other than the holder. By way of illustration, take the case of a cheque payable to order, which is discounted by a financial institution at the request of a thief who has forged the payee's indorsement. As the indorsement is ineffective,[554] the true owner is the payee and not the financial institution. Another effect of a crossing is to protect the drawer. A banker, who pays a cheque in a manner prohibited by a crossing executed on it, exceeds the authority conferred on him by the cheque and is not entitled to debit the customer's (drawer's) account.[555] If a banker pays a cheque according to the tenor of the crossing he obtains a certain protection against the customer and the true owner of the cheque.[556]   **34-161**

Effect of the addition of the words "not negotiable" to a crossing   According   **34-162**
to s.81 of the Act, where the words "not negotiable" are added to a crossed cheque,

---

548   s.78.
549   According to s.79(1), if a cheque is crossed specially to more than one banker, the drawee bank must refuse payment. But see s.77(5).
550   s.79(2). See also *Law Society of Northern Ireland v The Governor & Company of the Bank of Ireland* [2013] N.I.Q.B. 130 at [73]–[74], [80].
551   s.79(2).
552   As to whether the true owner had a right at common law to sue the paying banker in conversion following the wrongful payment of the cheque, see *Smith v Union Bank* (1875) L.R. 10 Q.B. 291, 295–296; affirmed (1875) 1 Q.B.D. 31.
553   *Smith v Union Bank*, above. In most instances, the true owner is either the issuer or the payee of the cheque: *Marquess of Bute v Barclays Bank* [1955] 1 Q.B. 202 (applied in *Australian Guarantee Corp v State Bank of Victoria* [1989] V.R. 617, Vic Aus SC). But note that the issuer of a cheque loses his title, and ceases to be the true owner of the instrument, when he delivers it to a fraudster: *Citibank NA v Brown Shipley & Co* [1991] 1 Lloyd's Rep. 576 (Waller J.); see also *Abbey National Plc v JSF Finance & Currency Exchange Co Ltd* [2006] EWCA Civ 328.
554   See above, para.34-086.
555   *Bobbett v Pinkett* (1876) 1 Ex. D. 368, 372–373.
556   s.80 of the Act discussed in para.34-347, below.

a person taking it does not obtain a better title than that of the transferor, and cannot give a better title to a further transferee. Thus, while a cheque crossed "not negotiable" remains transferable, each transferee takes it subject to the defects in the title of all previous parties so that no person can become a holder in due course of the instrument. In *Great Western Railway Co v London and County Banking Corp* Lord Lindley said[557]: "Everyone who takes a cheque marked 'not negotiable' takes it at his own risk, and his title to the money got by its means is as defective as his title to the cheque itself".

34-163 **Cheques crossed "account payee only"** It is a well-established practice to add the words "account payee only" to a general crossing. Until 1992 the phrase "account payee only" was not given a statutory definition. Although, generally, customers added these words to a crossing in the belief that they rendered the cheque non-transferable, a long list of cases established that the phrase did not have this effect. It was held that the words in question constituted a warning to the collecting bank that the cheque should not be collected for a person other than the nominated payee[558] but that the transferability of the cheque was not, in itself, affected.[559] In essence, the courts took the view that, on a strict reading, the phrase "account payee only" did not comprise words prohibiting transfer or evidencing an intention that the instrument be non-transferable within the meaning of s.8(1) of the Bills of Exchange Act 1882.

34-164 **Recommendations for reform** A similar approach was advocated by the Review Committee on Banking Services Law (the "Jack Committee"),[560] which recommend that cheques should, indeed, remain transferable even if they bore a crossing accompanied by the phrase in question. But this recommendation was rejected in the White Paper presented to Parliament by the Chancellor of the Exchequer in March 1990.[561] Seeking to give effect to what was considered the natural meaning and common understanding of the words in question, the White Paper recommended that the addition to a crossed cheque of the words "account payee only" (or of certain similar words) should render the instrument non-transferable.

34-165 **The 1992 Act** The Cheques Act 1992, which amends certain provisions of the Bills of Exchange Act 1882 and of the Cheques Act 1957, gives effect to the recommendation made in the White Paper. The new s.81A of the Bills of Exchange Act 1882, inserted by the 1992 Act, reads:

---

[557] [1901] A.C. 414, 424. See also *Universal Guarantee Pty Ltd v National Bank of Australasia* [1965] 1 Lloyd's Rep. 525, 531. cf. *Miller Associates (Australia) Pty Ltd v Bennington Pty Ltd* (1975) 7 A.L.R. 144.

[558] *Akrokerri (Atlantic) Mines Ltd v Economic Bank* [1904] 2 K.B. 465, 472; *House Property Co of London Ltd v London County and Westminster Bank* (1915) 84 L.J. K.B. 1846; *Universal Guarantee Pty Ltd v National Bank of Australasia Ltd*, above; *New Zealand Law Society v ANZ Banking Group Ltd* [1985] 1 N.Z.L.R. 280, 287; *Algemene Bank Nederland NV v Happy Valley Restaurant Pte Ltd* [1991] 1 S.L.R. 708, 713. As to no negligence being involved if a suitable explanation was given, see *Souhrada v Bank of NSW* [1976] 2 Lloyd's Rep. 444, especially at 452.

[559] *National Bank v Silke* [1891] 1 Q.B. 435; *Importers Co Ltd v Westminster Bank Ltd* [1927] 2 K.B. 297; *Universal Guarantee Pty Ltd v National Bank of Australasia* [1965] 2 All E.R. 98; see also *Standard Bank of South Africa Ltd v Sham Magazine Centre* [1977] 1 S.A.L.R. 484 App Div.

[560] Cmnd.622 paras 7.18–7.20, submitted in February 1989 and adopting the approach of s.39(2) of the Australian Cheques and Payment Orders Act 1986, which became the Cheques Act 1986 s.39(2) following the enactment of the Cheques and Payment Orders Amendment Act 1998 (Cth).

[561] Cmnd.1026 Annex 5 para.5.6.

"(1)   Where a cheque is crossed and bears across its face the words 'account payee' or
       'a/c payee,' either with or without the word 'only,' the cheque shall not be transfer-
       able, but shall only be valid as between the parties.
 (2)   A banker is not to be treated for the purposes of s.80 above as having been negligent
       by reason only of his failure to concern himself with any purported indorsement of
       a cheque which under subs.(1) above or otherwise is not transferable."

Effect of s.81A(1)   Subsection (1), effectively, applies the provisions of s.8(1) to   **34-166**
cheques bearing a crossing accompanied by the words "a/c payee only". Such a
cheque now has the same effect as one in which the words "not transferable" appear on the face of the cheque or a cheque on which the word "only" is added after
the payee's name.[562] Under s.8(1) and the new s.81A, the title to an instrument bearing any of these formulae cannot be passed by its negotiation. Consequently, the
original payee, to whom the instrument has been issued, remains its owner
notwithstanding his attempt to transfer the instrument. The transferee, thus, does not
obtain a title to the cheque and cannot bring an action to enforce it in his own
name.[563]

Effect of s.81A(2)   Subsection (2) gives effect to another recommendation made   **34-167**
in the White Paper. It sets out to ensure that the drawee or paying bank, that pays a
crossed cheque bearing the words "a/c payee only", retains the defence available
under s.80 of the Bills of Exchange Act 1882 as augmented by s.1 of the Cheques
Act 1957.[564] A consequential amendment to s.80 itself—effected by s.2 of the 1992
Act—has the object of putting the matter beyond doubt.

Negligence issue   Section 81A(2) provides that a banker is not to be treated for   **34-168**
the purposes of s.80 as having been negligent *by reason only* of his failure to
concern himself with any purported indorsement of a cheque which under s.81A(1)
or otherwise is not transferable. This means that the paying bank can normally
ignore any purported indorsement on the cheque, as it is the responsibility of the
collecting bank to ensure that a non-transferable cheque is collected only for the account of the named payee. However, there may be other, additional circumstances,
for example where the paying bank is reliably informed that the cheque has been
stolen from the payee,[565] or where it is clear that the cheque has been collected on
behalf of a party other than the payee,[566] in which it might be negligent for a bank
to pay a non-transferable cheque bearing a purported indorsement without first
satisfying itself that it was in fact being paid to the person entitled to receive it.[567]

"A/c payee" on uncrossed cheques   A question which is not settled by the Act   **34-169**

---

[562] See above, para.34-026.

[563] As to the effect of a crossing accompanied by the words "A/C payee only" where a cheque is payable to bearer, see *Chalmers and Guest on Bills of Exchange and Cheques*, 18th edn (2017), para.14-
039.

[564] And note that, under s.3 of the 1992 Act, cheques bearing a crossing accompanied by the words "a/c
payee only" (or the recognised similar formulae) are specifically equated with other types of cheque
in respect of the defence conferred on the collecting bank (see *Honourable Society of the Middle
Temple v Lloyd's Bank Plc* [1999] 1 All E.R. (Comm) 193). Note further that the provisions respecting crossings, made under the 1882 Act, apply to such cheques in the same manner as to negotiable
cheques: Cheques Act 1957 s.5, read together with s.4 of that Act (as amended by s.3 of the 1992
Act).

[565] This assumes the drawer has not, or has not yet, countermanded payment.

[566] *Linklaters v HSBC Bank Plc* [2003] EWHC 1113 (Comm), [2003] 2 Lloyd's Rep. 545 at [65]–[74].

[567] *Chalmers and Guest on Bills of Exchange and Cheques*, 18th edn (2017), para.14-028.

concerns the effect of the words "a/c payee only" on an uncrossed cheque. The answer is, accordingly, provided by the authorities, decided prior to 1992, which treat the formula as falling outside the ambit of s.8(1) of the 1882 Act. On their basis, the addition of the words in question would leave the uncrossed cheque transferable. The problem, though, is academic. In practice, the words in question are either printed on the cheque as part of the crossing or are appended by means of a rubber stamp which includes the two transverse lines of the crossing. The only situation in which the problem is likely to arise is where the drawer opens a crossing but fails to cancel the words "a/c payee only". As already indicated, the cheque would, in all probability, remain transferable.

34-170 **Protection of collecting banker** The provisions giving a protection to a collecting banker were originally set out in s.82 of the Act. This section has been repealed but its provisions have been re-enacted and extended in s.4 of the Cheques Act 1957 which is applicable to all cheques, whether crossed or uncrossed, and to certain analogous instruments. The issues are discussed in the section dealing with the position of the collecting banker.[568]

(iii)   Travellers' Cheques[569]

34-171 **Description** Travellers' cheques are widely used by tourists and businessmen all over the world. Most travellers' cheques bear two blank spaces meant for the signature of the traveller who purchases them from the issuing bank or from its agents for sale. The first signature, known as "the signature", is written on the instrument by the traveller, at the time he purchases the instrument, in the presence of a clerk of the issuing bank. The second signature, known as "the countersignature", is affixed by the traveller when he cashes or negotiates the instrument. A traveller's cheque is treated as containing a promise of the issuing bank to pay the amount specified in the instrument to the traveller or a transferee, provided the signature and countersignature correspond.

While travellers' cheques appear in different forms the following three patterns are the most common ones: first, the instrument may assume the form of an order by the directors of the issuing bank, to that bank, to pay a certain amount to the order of the payee (whose name is left blank) provided the signature and countersignature correspond. Secondly, the instrument may assume the form of an order given by the traveller in the absence of stipulation to the contrary who acts as drawer, to the bank, to pay the amount to his own order, provided the instrument is duly countersigned by himself. The instrument bears the signature of the directors of the issuing bank, which, presumably, constitutes an acceptance. Thirdly, some instruments assume the form of a promise by the issuing bank to pay a certain amount of money to the payee (whose name is left blank) provided the signature and countersignature correspond.

34-172 **Legal nature** It will be noted that travellers' cheques drafted in the first two patterns mentioned above resemble bills of exchange while those following the third pattern resemble promissory notes. However, the order in the first two patterns as well as the promise in the third one are conditional, i.e. dependent on the cor-

---

[568] See below, paras 34-365 et seq.
[569] Hawkland (1966) 15 Buffalo L. Rev. 501; Ellinger (1969) 19 Univ. of Toronto L.J. 132; Stassen (1978) 95 S.A.L.J. 180; Frohlich (1980) 54 A.L.J. 388.

respondence between the signature and the countersignature. Thus, the instruments do not fall within the respective definitions of bills of exchange (s.3(1) of the Act) and promissory notes (s.83).[570] Treating the request for a countersignature as a demand for an indorsement does not render the instrument unconditional. While an indorsement is necessary for the *negotiation* of a bill or a note payable to order,[571] it is not a prerequisite of *payment*. In the case of travellers' cheques, however, a countersignature is needed before the drawee or maker may pay the instrument, even if it is presented by the original payee. A travellers' cheque cannot, therefore, be regarded as an unconditional order or promise to pay and does not constitute a bill or note.[572] But travellers' cheques are regarded as negotiable instruments by the mercantile community as well as by tourists all over the world. It is arguable that they ought to be treated as a novel species of negotiable instruments established as such by a universal mercantile usage.[573] It is well established that, if such a usage is proved, it will be recognised and acted upon by the courts.[574]

Application of 1882 Act   It stands to reason that the general principles of the law   **34-173**
of negotiable instruments (most of which are now codified in the Bills of Exchange Act 1882) apply, with the necessary modifications, to travellers' cheques. This view derives support from recent cases.[575] That travellers' cheques do not have greater currency than negotiable instruments and are not to be treated as the equivalent of banknotes has been decided by a South African authority.[576] To date, the detailed analysis of travellers' cheques remains the province of American authorities which, thus, merit discussion. There are only three English cases in point.

The position of the traveller   Usually the relationship of "traveller", i.e. the   **34-174**
person to whom the instrument is issued, and issuing banker does not give rise to problems. The issuing banker is obliged to pay the amount of the traveller's cheque to the traveller when it is presented and properly countersigned. Difficulties may, however, arise when the traveller loses the cheques. If the loss of the instruments occurs while they do not bear a countersignature, the traveller—in the absence of stipulation to the contrary—is entitled to obtain their face value from the issuing banker, provided he agrees to sign an indemnity.[577] Such an indemnity would protect the banker if it turned out that, despite the travellers' statement, the cheques had been countersigned before they were lost. In such cases the banker would have to

---

570   As to the meaning of "conditional", see above, para.34-010 (regarding bills of exchange) and below, para.34-180 (regarding promissory notes).

571   See s.31(3) which applies, mutatis mutandis, to notes: s.89(1).

572   Contrast Stassen (1978) 95 S.A.L.J. 180 at 182–183, who argues that the countersignature is only a means of identification. This point, which is to be doubted, does not overcome the fact that—on its face—the order to pay is conditional. Contrast also Uniform Commercial Code s.3-106(c); E. McKendrick (ed.), *Goode on Commercial Law*, 5th edn (2016), para.21.11.

573   So held in *Ashford v Thomas Cook & Son (Bankers) Ltd* (1970) 471 P. 2d 531, 532. See also *S. v Katsikaris* [1980] 3 S.A.L.R. 580, 592.

574   *Goodwin v Robarts* (1875) L.R. 10 Ex. 337 (affirmed (1876) 1 App. Cas. 476); *London Joint Stock Bank v Simmons* [1892] A.C. 201; *Venables v Baring Bros* [1892] 3 Ch. 527; *Bechuanaland Exploration Co v London Trading Bank* [1898] 2 Q.B. 658; *Edelstein v Schuler & Co* [1902] 2 K.B. 144.

575   *Fellus v National Westminster Bank Plc* (1983) 133 New L.J. 766; *Braithwaite v Thomas Cook Travellers Cheques Ltd* [1989] Q.B. 553; *El Awadi v Bank of Credit and Commerce International SA* [1990] Q.B. 606.

576   *S v Katsikaris* [1980] 3 S.A.L.R. 580 at 592–593.

577   This is usually provided for in the form signed by the traveller when making application for the travellers' cheques.

honour them when presented by a holder in due course,[578] and the indemnity would enable him to recover the amount so paid from the traveller. The indemnity does not, however, enable the banker to recover from the traveller an amount paid to a holder who was not entitled to payment.[579]

34-175 **Loss of uncountersigned cheque**   In the absence of an express term to the contrary, the traveller's right to claim the face value of lost uncountersigned travellers' cheques does not depend on his notifying the banker promptly of their loss. In *Sullivan v Knauth*[580] the plaintiff lost uncountersigned travellers' cheques issued by the defendants and, having forgotten the defendants' name and address, did not notify them of the loss for several weeks. In the meantime the travellers' cheques, bearing forged countersignatures, were paid by the defendants to a third party. The defendants refused to reimburse the plaintiff and relied on a clause, printed on the folder which contained the travellers' cheques, by which prompt report of a loss was made a prerequisite to the defendants' duty to refund the amount of the cheques. It was held that the defendants' payment against forged countersignatures did not discharge them from their liability to reimburse the plaintiff.[581] An English court, though, could be persuaded to follow this decision only if it concluded that the clauses printed on the folder were not made terms of the contract entered into between the parties.[582] As long as an express clause incorporated in the contract concluded between the issuer and the traveller at the time of the purchase of the instruments was reasonable and fair it would be hard to assail.[583]

34-176 **Effect of clauses**   The English courts will uphold express terms of a standard term contract respecting the purchase of travellers' cheques provided the terms are clear. In *Braithwaite v Thomas Cook Travellers' Cheques Ltd*,[584] the application signed by the traveller when he purchased the travellers' cheque rendered his right to obtain a refund subject to his having properly safeguarded each cheque against loss or theft. The traveller, who was allowed to leave the bank without signing the substantial bundle of cheques acquired by him, signed some of them whilst in the airport, others whilst in a coffee house and the remaining ones whilst travelling on the underground. Thereafter he spent an evening socialising, without making any arrangements to safeguard the instruments. It would appear that the paper bag in which he kept them after executing his signature was stolen when he fell asleep whilst travelling again on the underground. Dismissing his action for a refund, Schiemann J. held that the traveller had failed to safeguard the cheques properly

---

[578] See below, para.34-179.

[579] *Sullivan v Knauth* (1914) 146 N.Y.S. 583; affirmed (1915) 115 N.E. 460.

[580] Above. But see now Uniform Commercial Code, ss.3-106(c), 3-305(a)(2).

[581] The decision of the Court of Appeal in *Burnett v Westminster Bank Ltd* [1966] 1 Q.B. 742, indicates that a notice printed on a folder of a cheque book does not necessarily form a term of the contract of banker and customer.

[582] For an illustration, see below, para.34-322.

[583] For contracts made before October 1, 2015, the applicability of the Unfair Contract Terms Act 1977 and the Unfair Terms in Consumer Contracts Regulations 1999 (SI 1999/2083), will need to be considered in relation to any provision in the contract between issuer and the traveller. For such contracts made on or after October 1, 2015, Pt 2 of the Consumer Rights Act 2015 amends the Unfair Terms in Consumer Contracts Act 1977 so that it no longer applies to "consumer contracts" or "consumer notices" as defined by the new Act, and revokes and replaces the Unfair Terms in Consumer Contracts Regulations 1999. For detailed analysis of the impact of the 2015 Act on the 1977 Act and 1999 Regulations, see below, Ch.38.

[584] [1989] Q.B. 553. See also *Thomas Cook Ltd v Kumari* [2002] NSWCA 141.

and found he had, thus, acted carelessly. That such a finding would not, however, be made lightly is demonstrated by the slightly earlier decision in *Fellus v National Westminster Bank Plc*,[585] in which Stuart-Smith J. held that a traveller was not negligent in the handling of his travellers' cheques simply because he left them in the pocket of a blazer which he had taken off for a few moments in a department store whilst trying on a new jacket. His Lordship further held that, in cases of this type, the onus of proof rested on the issuer, who would, accordingly, have to establish the traveller's negligence.

Ambiguous terms That the courts strive to give clauses of the type under consideration a reasonable construction can be also gleaned from *El Awadi v Bank of Credit and Commerce International SA*.[586] In this case, the standard terms executed by the traveller provided that a refund was to be subject to the bank's "approval". Hutchinson J. concluded that this clause did not have the effect of conferring on the issuer an absolute discretion respecting refunds. A refusal would have to be based on a breach by the traveller of one of the contractual obligations undertaken by him. His Lordship refused to regard the clause under consideration as imposing on the issuer a right to refuse to make a refund on the basis of the traveller's carelessness in the handling of the cheques. As the cheques involved had been lost or stolen before they had been countersigned, he held the issuer liable to reimburse the traveller.[587] It is significant that, like Stuart-Smith J. in *Fellus'* case, Hutchinson J. referred to brochures published by financial institutions seeking to promote the sale of travellers' cheques, in which emphasis was placed on the safety provided by these instruments and on the provisions for refunds in cases of loss. An important additional argument in support of the decision in *El Awadi*'s case is that, as the cheques involved had not been countersigned at the time of their loss, the issuer was not under an obligation to pay them on presentment. Why, then, should the traveller be refused a refund? **34-177**

Loss after appending countersignature If travellers' cheques are lost after they have been countersigned, the traveller is not entitled to claim payment from the bank, even if the loss is promptly reported. In *Emerson v American Express Co*[588] it was held that the countersignature renders a traveller's cheque payable to bearer. As a result, the issuing banker becomes liable to honour the instrument when presented by a holder in due course. **34-178**

The rights of a holder A holder who obtains a properly countersigned cheque from the traveller or from a transferee is entitled to payment. Where a holder obtains a traveller's cheque from a person who does not have a good title, his rights depend, first, on the genuineness of the countersignature and, secondly, on his holding the cheque in due course. To be a holder in due course of a traveller's cheque the holder must be able to show that he took it in good faith, for valuable consideration and while it was complete and regular on its face.[589] A traveller's cheque is considered as being complete on its face even while some spaces, which are in practice left **34-179**

---

[585] (1983) 133 New L.J. 766.
[586] [1990] Q.B. 606.
[587] At 253–256, obiter, Hutchison J. said that if there had been no express term requiring the issuer to refund the value of the lost or stolen cheques such a term ought to be implied.
[588] (1952) 90 A. 2d 236.
[589] s.29 of the Act which provides the general definition of a holder in due course.

blank until the cheque is paid, are not filled up. Thus, if the space meant for the name of the payee is usually left blank in a traveller's cheque, then a person can be a holder in due course even if he takes it with such a blank space.[590] However, if the traveller's cheque does not bear a countersignature, or bears a forged one, a holder cannot hold it in due course and cannot enforce payment.[591]

(d) Promissory Notes

34-180 Definition A promissory note is an unconditional promise in writing made by one person to another, signed by the maker, engaging to pay on demand or at a fixed or determinable future time a sum certain in money, to, or to the order of, a specified person or to bearer. An instrument in the form of a note payable to the maker's order is not a promissory note unless and until it is indorsed by the maker. A note is not invalid by reason only that it contains also a pledge of collateral security with authority to sell or dispose thereof. But if a note is made to run concurrently with a charge in respect of which it is issued, the promise to pay may thereby be rendered conditional.[592] A note which is, or on the face of it, purports to be, both made and payable within the British Islands is an inland note. Any other note is a foreign note.[593]

34-181 In *Kirkwood v Carroll*[594] it was held that a joint and several note for the payment of £225 by instalments, the whole to become due on default in payment of any one instalment, and providing that no time given to either party should prejudice the rights of the holder to proceed against any other party, was a valid promissory note. In *Mason v Lack*[595] an instrument in the form of a bill, signed by a person as drawer and not addressed to anyone, but accepted by another person, was held to be a promissory note and not a bill. In *Haseldine v Winstanley*,[596] a similar instrument, which had been completed by the holder, with the drawer's consent, by adding the name of the acceptor as addressee, was held to be good as a bill if the alteration was justifiable, or good as a note if it was not. An IOU containing a promise to pay is—provided the promise is in the terms specified in s.83—a promissory note.[597]

34-182 Application of provisions regarding bills of exchange to promissory notes Ac-

---

[590] *Emerson v American Express Co*, above; cf. *Gray v American Express Co, 239 S.E. 2d 621* (1977), in which, however, *Emerson*'s case was not cited and where the holder observed the transferor's execution of both a signature and a countersignature. cf. *Chalmers and Guest on Bills of Exchange and Cheques*, 18th edn (2017), para.13-012: "it is doubtful whether [*Emerson v American Express Co*] would be followed in this country".

[591] *Samberg v American Express Co* (1904) 99 N.W. 879; *Sullivan v Knauth* (1914) 146 N.Y.S. 583. But see now Uniform Commercial Code ss.3-106 (c), 3-305(a)(2).

[592] *Bank of Montreal v Faulkner*, 127 A.P.R. 256 (1987) Can.

[593] s.83. For the meaning of the following words, see section quoted: "unconditional"—s.3(1) and see *Crouch v Crédit Foncier of England* (1873) L.R. 8 Q.B. 374; *Williamson v Rider* [1963] 1 Q.B. 89, 97–98, 101 (above, para.34-010); cf. *John Burrows Ltd v Subsurface Surveys Ltd* [1968] S.C.R. 607, 614 (Canada); *Creative Press Ltd v Harman* (1973) I.R. 313 (Ireland); *Emu Brewery Mezzanine Ltd v ASIC* [2006] WASCA 105 (Australia); *Re York Street Mezzanine Pty Ltd* [2007] FCA 922 (Australia); *Club Securities Ltd v Hurley* [2008] 1 N.Z.L.R. 711 (New Zealand); "on demand"—s.10 and "fixed or determinable future time"—s.11 (above, paras 34-013 et seq.); "sum certain"—s.9 (above, para.34-019); "British Islands"—s.4 (below, para.34-197).

[594] [1903] 1 K.B. 531.

[595] (1929) 45 T.L.R. 363.

[596] [1936] 2 K.B. 101.

[597] *Brooks v Elkins* (1836) 2 M. & W. 74; *Muir v Muir*, 1912 1 S.L.T. 304.

cording to s.89(1) of the Act, the provisions relating to bills of exchange apply, with the necessary modifications, to promissory notes.[598] According to s.89(2), in applying these provisions, the maker of the note is deemed to correspond with the acceptor of a bill, and the first indorser with the drawer of an accepted bill payable to his own order. Section 89(3) provides that the following provisions relating to bills of exchange do not apply to promissory notes:

(a)   those relating to presentment for acceptance (ss.39–44);
(b)   those relating to acceptance (ss.17–19);
(c)   those relating to acceptance supra protest (ss.65–67); and
(d)   those relating to bills in a set (s.71).

By s.89(4) protest is not required where a foreign note is dishonoured.[599] Further provisions, varying the law relating to promissory notes from that relating to bills of exchange, are set out in ss.84–88 of the Act, and will be discussed presently.

Delivery   According to s.84 a promissory note is inchoate and incomplete until   **34-183**
its delivery to the payee or bearer. It should be noted that, as regards bills of exchange, s.21 enacts that a party may revoke his contract on the bill until he delivers it, but the section does not provide that the bill itself is inchoate. The proviso to s.21(1) as well as subss.(2) and (3)[600] apply, mutatis mutandis, to promissory notes.

Joint and several notes   According to s.85 of the Act, a promissory note may be   **34-184**
made by two or more makers, and they may be liable thereon jointly and severally, according to its tenor. Where a note reads "I promise to pay" and is signed by two or more persons, it is deemed to be their joint and several note. When two or more persons are jointly liable, a judgment against one of them, even though unsatisfied, is a bar to proceedings against the other or others, but not if the liability is several as well as joint.[601] The fact that one of two joint makers of a note is not liable does not release the other. Thus, in *Wauthier v Wilson*[602] a father and his son, a minor, made a joint and several note in respect of a loan given to the son. It was held that the minor was not liable, but that the father was liable as principal debtor.

Note payable on demand   According to s.86, where a note payable on demand   **34-185**
has been indorsed, it must be presented within a reasonable time. If it is not so presented the indorser is discharged. What amounts to reasonable time depends on the nature of the instrument, the usage of trade and the facts of the particular case. However, the section provides that, where a note payable on demand is negotiated, it is not deemed to be overdue—so as to prevent a holder from being a holder in due course—by reason that it appears that a reasonable time for presenting it for payment has elapsed since its issue.

Note given to secure payment of debt   Where a promissory note payable on   **34-186**
demand is given to secure payment of a debt, the discharge of the debt does not, in

---

[598]   See, e.g. *Banque Cantonale de Genève v Sanomi* [2016] EWHC 3353 (Comm).
[599]   A fortiori protest will not be required where an inland note is dishonoured: s.51.
[600]   As to which, see above, para.34-034.
[601]   *Kendall v Hamilton* (1879) 4 App. Cas. 504.
[602]   (1912) 28 T.L.R. 239.

itself, discharge the note. In *Glasscock v Balls*[603] the payee of a note payable on demand, who had as further security obtained a mortgage from the maker, realised the mortgage, and thus obtained the amount of a debt. He retained the note, and negotiated it to the plaintiff, who took it in good faith and for value. It was held that the note had not been paid, and that the plaintiff could recover from the maker.

34-187 **Presentment for payment**[604]   Any promissory note must be presented for payment in order to render an indorser liable on it.[605] If the note is made payable at a particular place, it must be presented there. If the place of payment is indicated by way of memorandum only, the note may be presented at that place, but due presentment to the maker elsewhere suffices to render the indorser liable.[606] The maker's liability is subject to due presentment for payment only if the bill is made payable at a particular place.[607] A note is considered so payable only if the relevant words are imperative and constitute a part of the promise.[608] Thus, where a place of payment was indicated at the foot of the note, the maker was liable although the note was not presented for payment.[609]

34-188 **Limitation of action**   The period of limitation under the Limitation Act 1980 runs in favour of the maker of a note payable on demand from the date of the note or its issue, and not from the date of demand.[610]

34-189 **Liability of maker**   The maker of the note is the principal debtor and his position is similar to that of an acceptor of a bill of exchange.[611] Section 88(1) of the Act provides that the maker engages that he will pay the note according to its tenor. By s.88(2) the maker is precluded from denying to a holder in due course the existence of the payee and his capacity to indorse.[612]

34-190 **New forms of negotiable instruments**   New forms of negotiable instruments have been making their appearance in recent years. Usually, they assume a form similar to that of a promissory note but, due to special terms incorporated in their text, fall outside the ambit of the definition of s.83. Thus, the instruments used in many note issue facilities (NIFS) provide for maturity of the "note" before the designated date in the event of a default under the underlying agreement. Such an instrument is, of course, not payable at a designated future time and hence does not constitute a promissory note. Another popular instrument is the negotiable certificate of deposit (NCD), which uses a language similar to that of an ordinary deposit

---

[603] (1889) 24 Q.B.D. 13.
[604] The requirement of presentment of a promissory note for payment is to be found in s.87 of the Bills of Exchange Act 1882, and is summarised in this paragraph. However, s.87 is subject to Pt 4A of the 1882 Act (presentment by electronic means), inserted by s.13 of the Small Business, Enterprise and Employment Act 2015: see above, paras 34-153—34-154.
[605] s.87(2).
[606] s.87(3).
[607] s.87(1); as to what constitutes a "particular place", see *Eimco Corp v Tutt Bryant Ltd* [1970] 2 N.S.W.R. 249. cf. *Day v Bate* (1979) 41 F.L.R. 222 Aust.
[608] *Re British Trade Corp Ltd* [1932] 2 Ch. 1.
[609] *Masters v Baretto* (1849) 8 C.B. 433.
[610] *Norton v Ellam* (1837) 2 M. & W. 461.
[611] s.89(2), discussed in para.34-182, above.
[612] Compare the estoppels concerning the acceptor of a bill: s.54 of the Act, discussed in para.34-113, above.

receipt,[613] except that it is stated to be negotiable or transferable. However, many NCDs do not include an express promise of the issuer to repay the amount deposited either to the payee's order or to bearer. Such NCDs, therefore, do not constitute promissory notes.

Established by mercantile usage Can the negotiability of such novel instru- **34-191** ments be based on some other reasoning? It is true that the decision in *Customs and Excise Commissioners v Guy Butler (Int) Ltd*[614] suggests that NCDs constitute a novel form of negotiable instrument, established by a mercantile usage. The point, though, was not in issue in that case and the relevant passage is a mere observation. Cases concerning the recognition of modern mercantile usages establishing novel forms of negotiable instruments show that it is difficult to persuade courts to proclaim the validity of a new type of instrument. To be legally recognised, the usage has to be certain, reasonable, "notorious" and of a general standing.[615] Thus, although it is possible, perhaps even likely, that the courts would recognise the negotiability of NCDs if the point were argued and supported by forceful expert evidence, the outcome is not free from doubt.[616]

(e) Negotiable Instruments in the Conflict of Laws[617]

(i) General

Determining negotiability Whether an instrument is negotiable or not is **34-192** determined in an English court according to English law. Thus, if by a mercantile usage, prevailing in England, an instrument is treated as being negotiable, the courts will be prepared to treat it as such.[618] As the recognition in England of a usage establishing the negotiability of an instrument depends mainly on the prevalence of the usage in this country, it is possible that an instrument may not be considered as negotiable in England although it is so considered in the country of its issue.[619] Negotiable instruments, however, are usually of international standing and in most cases a usage establishing the negotiability of a class of instruments will prevail not only in the place of issue of such an instrument but also at the place of payment. Generally, if an instrument derives its negotiability from a general or universal mercantile usage, it is likely that the usage will be recognised as applying in England.[620]

Sources of law There are a number of express provisions in the Bills of Exchange **34-193** Act 1882 concerning conflict of laws. They constitute a basis, but not an exhaus-

---

[613] Which, unlike a promissory note, does not spell out a duty to pay.
[614] [1977] Q.B. 377, 382.
[615] See above, para.34-005.
[616] For endorsement of the view that NCDs are negotiable by mercantile usage, see E. McKendrick (ed.), *Goode on Commercial Law*, 5th edn (2017), para.21.18; S. Paterson and R. Zakrzewski (eds), *McKnight, Paterson and Zakrzewski on the Law of International Finance*, 2nd edn (2017), para.10.4.3.
[617] See Dicey, Morris and Collins on the Conflict of Laws, 15th edn (2012), para.33R–334 et seq.
[618] *Goodwin v Robarts* (1875) L.R. 10 Ex. 337 (affirmed (1876) 1 App. Cas. 476); *Edelstein v Schuler & Co* [1902] 2 K.B. 144. See also *Bechuanaland Exploration Co v London Trading Bank* [1898] 2 Q.B. 658.
[619] *Picker v London and County Banking Co* (1887) 18 Q.B.D. 515.
[620] See above, especially *Easton v London Joint Stock Bank* (1886) 34 Ch. D. 95, 113 (reversed on a different point sub nom. *Sheffield v London Joint Stock Bank* (1888) 13 App. Cas. 333).

tive[621] regulation, of the rules of private international law applicable to bills of exchange, cheques and promissory notes.[622] These are augmented by decisions applying general principles of the conflict of laws.

34-194   Article 1(2)(d) of the Rome I Regulation (EC) 593/2008 provides that "obligations arising under bills of exchange, cheques and promissory notes and other negotiable instruments to the extent that the obligations under such other negotiable instruments arise out of their negotiable character" are excluded from the scope of the Regulation.[623] A similar exclusion is contained in art.1(2)(c) of the Rome II Regulation (EC) 864/2007 on the law applicable to non-contractual obligations.

34-195 **International conventions**   It is perhaps unfortunate that the United Kingdom has not adopted the two treaties of the Geneva Convention of 1930 relating to the conflict of laws in respect of negotiable instruments.[624]

34-196 **Series of contracts**   It is essential for an examination of the conflict problems arising in connection with bills of exchange to remember that a bill of exchange does not represent a single contract but a series of different promises which, while closely interconnected because they are embodied in the same instrument, are nevertheless in many respects independent. This explains why the different promises contained in a bill of exchange may be subject to different legal systems.[625]

34-197   The sections of the Bills of Exchange Act 1882 dealing with conflict rules run as follows:

"**4.—**(1)   An inland bill is a bill which is or on the face of it purports to be (a) both drawn and payable within the British Islands or (b) drawn within the British Islands upon some person resident therein. Any other bill is a foreign bill.[626]

For the purposes of this Act "British Islands" mean any part of the United Kingdom of Great Britain and Ireland,[627] the Islands of Man, Guernsey, Jersey, Alderney, and Sark, and the islands adjacent to any of them being part of the dominions of Her Majesty.

(2)   Unless the contrary appear on the face of the bill the holder may treat it as an inland bill."

---

621   *Re Gillespie* (1886) 18 Q.B.D. 286, 293; *Embiricos v Anglo-Austrian Bank* [1905] 1 K.B. 677, 685; *Koechlin et Cie v Kestenbaum Bros* [1927] 1 K.B. 889, 895; *Zebrarise Ltd v De Nieffe* [2005] 1 Lloyd's Rep. 154 at [36].

622   While the provisions refer to bills of exchange they apply, mutatis mutandis, to cheques (s.73) and to promissory notes (s.89); and see *Embiricos v Anglo-Austrian Bank*, above.

623   An identical provision was previously set out in art.1(2)(c) of the 1980 Rome Convention on the Law applicable to Contractual Obligations (applied in the UK under the Contracts (Applicable Law) Act 1990), which was replaced, from December 17, 2009 by the Rome I Regulation. For analysis of the Rome I Regulation, see Vol.I, paras 30-019 et seq.

624   The Convention for the Settlement of Certain Conflicts of Laws in Connection with Bills of Exchange and Promissory Notes, signed on June 7, 1930, *League of Nations Treaty Series*, Vol.CXLII, p.319, No.3314 (hereinafter: Geneva Convention on Bills) and the Convention for the Settlement of Certain Conflicts of Laws in Connection with Cheques, signed on March 19, 1931, as before, p.409, No.3317 (hereinafter: Geneva Convention on Cheques).

625   Dicey, Morris and Collins on the Conflict of Laws, 15th edn (2012), paras 3-335 et seq.; see also *Lebel v Tucker* (1867) L.R. 3 Q.B. 77, 83; Geneva Convention on Bills arts 2, 3, 4; Geneva Convention on Cheques arts 2, 4, 5.

626   As regards the corresponding provisions regarding promissory notes, see s.83(4) referred to in para.34-184, above. And see *Canadian Life Assurance Co v Canadian Bank of Imperial Commerce*, 98 D.L.R. (3d) 670 (1979).

627   The Republic of Ireland is not included: see Irish Free State (Consequential Adaptation of Enactments) Order 1923 (SR & O 1923/405) r.2.

"**72.** Where a bill drawn in one country is negotiated, accepted or payable in another, the rights, duties, and liabilities of the parties thereto are determined as follows:

(1) The validity of a bill as regards requisites in form is determined by the law of the place of issue, and the validity as regards requisites in form of the supervening contracts, such as acceptance, or indorsement, or acceptance supra protest, is determined by the law of the place where such contract was made.

Provided that—

(a) Where a bill is issued out of the United Kingdom, it is not invalid by reason only that it is not stamped in accordance with the law of the place of issue.

(b) Where a bill, issued out of the United Kingdom, conforms, as regards requisites in form, to the law of the United Kingdom, it may, for the purpose of enforcing payment thereof, be treated as valid as between all persons who negotiate, hold, or become parties to it in the United Kingdom.

(2) Subject to the provisions of this Act, the interpretation of the drawing, indorsement, acceptance, or acceptance *suprà protest* of a bill, is determined by the law of the place where such contract is made.

Provided that where an inland bill is indorsed in a foreign country the indorsement shall as regards the payer be interpreted according to the law of the United Kingdom.

(3) The duties of the holder with respect to presentment for acceptance or payment and the necessity for or sufficiency of a protest or notice of dishonour, or otherwise, are determined by the law of the place where the act is done or the bill is dishonoured.

(4) ...[628]

(5) Where a bill is drawn in one country and is payable in another, the due date thereof is determined according to the law of the place where it is payable."

Summary It follows from s.4 that a foreign bill is one which is either (a) drawn **34-198**
by a person who is not resident in the British Isles; or (b) drawn by a person resident in the British Isles on a person abroad and payable abroad. It should be noted that, if a bill is drawn and payable in the British Isles, it is not a foreign bill, even if the payee resides abroad. Moreover, an inland bill does not become a foreign bill because of any subsequent contract embodied in it, as for instance by indorsements effected in foreign countries. The most important difference between an inland and a foreign bill is that a foreign bill must be protested if dishonoured, while a protest is not, usually, required in the case of an inland bill.[629]

Section 72 applies where an instrument "drawn in one country is negotiated, ac- **34-199**
cepted, or payable in another". Section 72 has no application where all matters connected with the instrument take place in one country.[630] As regards the reference in s.72 to "the place of issue" or "the place where the contract is made" it should be recollected that:

"... every contract on a bill, whether it be the drawer's, the acceptor's or an indorser's, is incomplete and revocable until delivery of the instrument."[631]

Thus, the bill must be considered as issued, and each contract as concluded, at the

---

[628] s.72(4) has been repealed by s.4 of the Administration of Justice Act 1977.

[629] s.51. Promissory notes need not be protested: s.89(4).

[630] *Karafarin Bank v Dara (No.2)* [2009] EWHC 3265 (Comm), [2010] 1 Lloyd's Rep. 236 at [10], Blair J.

[631] s.21. See *Aspinall's Club Ltd v Al-Zayat* [2007] EWHC 362 (Comm) at [16], reversed on other grounds [2007] EWCA Civ 1001. As regards promissory notes, see s.84, discussed in para.34-183, above. See *Zebrarise Ltd v De Nieffe* [2005] 1 Lloyd's Rep. 154 at [36].

place in which delivery takes place, and not at the place at which the promisor signs the document.[632]

(ii) Form

34-200 **Generally** Section 72(1) enacts as a general rule that every separate contract contained in a bill of exchange has to satisfy the formal requirements of the law of the place where the contract has been concluded. Compliance with the proper law of the contract, which in the case of simple contracts may be alternative to compliance of form with the *lex loci contractus*,[633] is thus excluded. The following issues have been regarded as questions of form, viz whether a bill of exchange contains an unconditional or conditional order,[634] or whether an undisclosed agent can execute an indorsement binding on his principal.[635] The Act provides two exceptions to the rule that the validity of form depends on the law of the place at which the contract is made, and these will be discussed presently.

34-201 **Foreign stamp law** Section 72(1)(a) lays down that a bill of exchange is not invalidated merely because it fails to comply with the stamp law in the place of issue. An English court will, thus, treat a bill as valid although a court in the place of issue may be obliged to treat it as void or unenforceable.

34-202 **Foreign bills** Another exception to the rule that the *lex loci contractus* prevails as regards the form of a bill of exchange, is to be found in s.72(1)(b) of the Act. It provides that if a bill, issued outside the United Kingdom, conforms, as regards requisites of form, to the law of the United Kingdom, it is to be treated as valid as between all the persons who have become parties to it in the United Kingdom. However, even as between these parties it is to be treated as being valid only for the purpose of enforcing payment.[636]

(iii) Essential Validity

34-203 **Essential validity** Section 72(2) of the Act provides that the "interpretation" of a contract contained in a bill is to be governed by the law of the country in which the contract is made. In this context, the term "interpretation" has to be construed liberally. The draftsman of the Act suggested that this term "clearly includes the obligations of the parties as deduced from such interpretation".[637] This view has been confirmed by judicial authority. In *Alcock v Smith*,[638] Romer J. observed that

---

[632] *Chapman v Cottrell* (1865) 3 Hurl. & C. 865.

[633] See Vol.I, paras 30-019 et seq. (Under art.3 of the Geneva Convention on Bills, the form must, subject to certain exceptions, comply with the requirements of the place in which each contract has been signed; the same principle applies under the Geneva Convention on Cheques art.4.)

[634] *Guaranty Trust Co of New York v Hannay & Co* [1918] 1 K.B. 43. The decision was reversed by the Court of Appeal on a different point: [1918] 2 K.B. 623.

[635] *Koechlin et Cie v Kestenbaum Bros* [1927] 1 K.B. 889, per Bankes L.J. at 896–897, Sargant L.J., *dubitante*, at 899.

[636] The following cases were decided before the Act, but appear to be good law: *Bradlaugh v De Rin* (1870) L.R. 5 C.P. 473; *Re Marseilles Extension Railway and Land Co* (1885) 30 Ch. D. 598, 603.

[637] Chalmers, *Bills of Exchange*, 9th edn, p.282 (and see currently 18th edn, 2017, para.12-015), cited with approval in *Nova (Jersey) Knit Ltd v Kammgarn Spinnerei GmbH* [1979] 1 W.L.R. 713, 718.

[638] [1892] 1 Ch. 238, 256. See also *Embiricos v Anglo-Austrian Bank* [1905] 1 K.B. 677. As regards illegality, see *Moulis v Owen* [1907] 1 K.B. 746; *Belize Bank Ltd v Association of Concerned*

"interpretation" in this subsection includes "the legal effect" of the contract. This subsection deals, therefore, with what is usually called the essential, as opposed to the formal, validity of the contract. The construction and interpretation of the document, the quality and import of the obligations arising from the agreement of the parties, the legality of the promises embodied in the document—these and similar questions all fall under the subsection. The Act admits, however, of an exception, which will be examined later,[639] to the rule applying the *lex loci contractus* to questions of essential validity.

The Act, thus, replaces the proper law doctrine by a rigid application of the *lex loci contractus*. The exclusion of the *lex loci solutionis* leads to a remarkable result. A bill drawn in England, on a drawee in New York but payable in Montreal, would—as regards matters of the essential validity of the bill, arising in a dispute concerning the drawee's contract—be governed by the law prevailing in New York and not Montreal. The proper law doctrine, on the other hand, might well lead to the application of the *lex loci solutionis*, i.e. the law of Montreal.[640] However, in most cases a bill would be payable at the place of acceptance.[641]

34-204

Embiricos   The operation of the principle laid down in subs.(2) of s.72 is illustrated by *Embiricos v Anglo-Austrian Bank*.[642] In this case, the validity of an indorsement was in issue. A Roumanian bank drew, in Roumania, a cheque on a London bank payable to the plaintiffs' order. The plaintiffs indorsed the cheque in Roumania to a London firm and posted it to them. A clerk of the plaintiffs stole the cheque, forged the indorsement of the London firm and negotiated the cheque to bankers in Vienna, who in good faith paid its value to the fraudulent clerk. The Vienna bank then indorsed the cheque to the defendants in London and the latter presented it to the drawees who honoured the cheque. By this action the plaintiffs claimed back the money from the defendants, alleging conversion of the cheque. The defence was that, according to Austrian law, the defendants had acquired a good title from their Austrian transferor, and that, according to Austrian law, a bona fide indorsee may acquire a title even under a forged indorsement. The plaintiffs replied that the title of the defendants had to be ascertained according to English law, which does not recognise a good title through a forged indorsement. The Court of Appeal held that the validity of the indorsement was governed by Austrian law and decided, therefore, in favour of the defendants. Vaughan Williams and Romer L.JJ. based their decision on the ground that Austrian law was the law governing the transfers of the cheque. Stirling L.J. and Walton J. who had decided the case in the King's Bench Division, attached more weight to the additional ground that the case was covered by s.72(2) of the Bills of Exchange Act 1882.[643]

34-205

Belizeans [2011] UKPC 35 at [45]. See also Dicey, Morris and Collins on the Conflict of Laws, 15th edn (2012), paras 33-350 et seq.

[639] See below, para.34-207.

[640] For a criticism of the provision, see Dicey, Morris and Collins on the Conflict of Laws, 15th edn (2012), para.33-350.

[641] Under art.4 of the Geneva Convention on Bills, the law of the place at which the bill is payable determines the effect of the acceptance; the effect of other signatures is determined by the law of the place at which they are affixed. See also the Geneva Convention on Cheques art.5, applying the *lex loci contractus*.

[642] [1905] 1 K.B. 677.

[643] As regards the construction of an *aval* (viz guarantee), see *G & H Montage GmbH v Irvani* [1988] 1 W.L.R. 1285 (affirmed [1990] 1 W.L.R. 667).

34-206 **Transfer** The reference in s.72(2) to the case of indorsements indicates that the *lex loci contractus* applies also to the negotiation of a bill. In *Koechlin et Cie v Kestenbaum Bros*[644] a bill of exchange was drawn in France by one E.V. on the defendants. The payee was one M.V. who was the father of the drawer and likewise resided in France. The bill was accepted by the defendants and was made payable at a bank in London. Subsequently, the bill was indorsed by the drawer E.V. in his own name to the plaintiffs, but it never showed an indorsement of the payee M.V. The defendants refused to pay the bill. The plaintiffs maintained that they were holders in due course and sued the defendants as acceptors. The defence was that the indorsement was irregular on its face because it did not emanate from the payee (as required by s.31(3) of the Act), and that, according to English law, no oral evidence was admissible to show that E.V. acted as agent for the payee. The plaintiffs replied that, as the validity of the indorsement was governed by French law, E.V.'s indorsement was good. The Court of Appeal held that the case was covered by s.72 of the Act and that the validity of the indorsement was to be determined according to French law. The court, therefore, gave judgment against the defendants. Sargent L.J. was inclined to consider the issue as a question of form governed by s.72(1), but explained that if it were not covered by that subsection, it was covered by subs.(2):

> "... in view of the very wide effect of the decision in *Embiricos v Anglo-Austrian Bank*.[645] ... If the indorsement in fact made is, according to the law of the place where it is made, sufficient to give a title to the indorsee, it appears to me that by the express terms of the Act the indorsee is entitled to sue. The effect is not to increase the liabilities of the acceptor, but merely to enlarge the methods by which the right to enforce those liabilities can be transferred from the person originally entitled to them to some subsequent indorsee."[646]

34-207 **Exception to the application of the lex loci contractus** It is now necessary to consider the exception admitted by the Act to the rule that the essential validity of a contract contained in a bill of exchange is determined by the law of the place where the contract is made. The proviso to subs.(2) enacts that, in the case of an inland bill indorsed in a foreign country, the indorsement is to be interpreted, as regards the payer, according to the law of the United Kingdom. It codifies the law as it stood before the Act.[647] Thus, where an inland bill was indorsed in France in a manner void according to French but valid according to English law, it was held that the obligation of the acceptor towards the indorsee was not affected thereby.[648] As a result, the purchaser of an inland bill is in a more favourable position than the purchaser of a foreign bill whose rights may be defeated by some infirmity imposed by foreign law. Conversely, the liability of the acceptor may be greater in the case of a foreign bill than in the case of an inland bill. The situation which existed prior to the Act and which the Act purported to adopt was described by Sargent L.J. as follows:

> "The result was that any one dealing with a foreign bill of exchange was in a less certain

---

[644] [1927] 1 K.B. 889. See also *Alcock v Smith* [1892] 1 Ch. 238.
[645] [1905] 1 K.B. 677.
[646] [1927] 1 K.B. at 899. The *lex loci contractus* applies likewise under the Geneva Convention on Bills art.4, and under the Geneva Convention on Cheques art.5; the latter however applies some special rules in art.7.
[647] *De la Chaumette v Bank of England* (1831) 2 B. & Ad. 385; *Lebel v Tucker* (1867) L.R. 3 Q.B. 77.
[648] *Lebel v Tucker*, above.

position than a person dealing with an inland bill, because in the case of an indorsement abroad on a foreign bill he might find substituted for the person to whom he was originally liable as acceptor not merely a person to whom the transfer would have been good if made in England, but a person to whom the transfer by indorsement would be good if made according to the law of the country in which it was made."[649]

(iv) Performance

Duties of holder   The rules relating to the performance of obligations arising from the bill are to be found in subss.(3) and (5) of s.72. The first of these enacts that the duties of the holder, as well as the sufficiency of the performance of his duties (e.g. presentment for acceptance and payment) are to be governed by the law of the place where the act is done or the bill is dishonoured.[650] These two places will usually coincide. It should be noted that the holder's performance of his duty to present the bill for payment, and his duty of sending a notice of dishonour and protesting the bill, are not usually prerequisites for charging the acceptor.[651] However, where any prerequisites exist before the holder may sue the acceptor, it is reasonable to assume that they should be governed by the law of the place of the acceptor.[652]   **34-208**

Effect of failure to perform   Greater difficulties arise as regards the effect which the failure of the holder to perform any of his duties has—once the bill is dishonoured—on his rights against the drawer and indorsers, and the rights of each indorser against antecedent parties. The problem in particular is whether a notice of dishonour, which is necessary to preserve the rights of a holder or indorser against antecedent parties, is sufficient and valid. Here two interpretations of subs.(3) are possible, viz that the mode and sufficiency of the notice of dishonour are governed by the law of the place where the acceptor has to pay the bill,[653] or that these incidents depend on the contract between indorser and indorsee, and consequently are governed by the law of the place where this contract is to be discharged.[654] Both interpretations are reconcilable with the words of the subsection, though the former view does not strain the words of the enactment as much as the latter.   **34-209**

Suggested construction   It is suggested that the true meaning of this subsection is that the mode and sufficiency of the notice of dishonour are, as between indorsers, governed by the same law that determines ancillary rules relating to payment by the acceptor, i.e. by the law of the place where the bill was made payable and   **34-210**

---

[649] *Koechlin et Cie v Kestenbaum Bros* [1927] 1 K.B. 889, 898.

[650] For a criticism of this section, see Dicey, Morris and Collins on the Conflict of Laws, 15th edn (2012), paras 33-367—33-372. See also the Geneva Convention on Bills art.8; Geneva Convention on Cheques art.8.

[651] See above, para.34-114.

[652] cf. Foote, *Private International Law*, 5th edn, pp.460–461, who thinks that it is "at least reasonable to presume that these incidents of non-payment will be governed by the same law that applies to all incidents of payment". As regards the question of the necessity for presentment, see *Banku Polskiego v K J Mulder & Co* [1941] 2 K.B. 266 (affirmed [1942] 1 K.B. 497); *Cornelius v Banque Franco-Serbe* [1941] 2 All E.R. 728, 732 (the case is also reported in [1942] 1 K.B. 29, where the relevant passage does not occur).

[653] *Rothschild v Currie* (1841) 1 Q.B. 43; *Hirschfeld v Smith* (1866) L.R. 1 C.P. 340.

[654] *Horne v Rouquette* (1878) 3 Q.B.D. 514; Westlake, *Private International Law*, 7th edn, para.232, pp.322–323.

dishonoured. Three reasons can be advanced in favour of this view: first, the indorser, when negotiating the bill, is fully aware where the bill has to be paid.

> "The indorser of a bill accepted payable in France, promises to pay in the event of dishonour in France, and notice thereof. By his contract he must be taken to know the law of France relating to the dishonour of bills; and notice of dishonour is a portion of that law."[655]

Secondly, on principle, it is preferable that questions extending to protest and notice of dishonour should, as far as the indorsers of a bill are concerned, be regulated by a single law rather than by several legal systems. Thirdly, it should be noted that the indorser's undertaking is, in the first place, that the bill will be honoured by the drawee, and only in the second place, that upon its dishonour, he will pay it himself.[656] The indorser's main promise is, thus, that the bill will be paid in the acceptor's place, where the holder has, under his contract with the indorser, to seek payment. The construction of s.72(3), which is supported in this book, gives effect to the intention of the parties.

34-211   The result is that all ancillary rules with respect to presentment for acceptance or payment, or with respect to protest or notice of dishonour, are, in principle, governed by a single law, i.e. the law prevailing at the place of the payment of the bill, no matter whether the dispute concerns the original promise of the acceptor or a subsequent contract between indorser and indorsee.

34-212   **Amount payable**   Until 1977 the position was governed by s.72(4) of the Act, based on the traditional common law rule under which a foreign debt was to be converted into sterling on the basis of the rate prevailing at the time at which payment was due. The introduction of the new rule, sanctioning the conversion of a foreign debt on the basis of the rate prevailing at the time at which payment is enforced by the court, has led to the repeal of s.72(4). Under the new doctrine, the holder is entitled to bring an action to enforce payment of the bill in the foreign currency in which it is expressed.[657]

34-213   **Date of payment**   Section 72(5) provides that where a bill is drawn in one country and payable in another, the date of payment is determined by the law of the place at which the bill is payable. Thus, in *Re Francke and Rasch*[658] an English bank purchased before the First World War bills payable in Germany and Austria. The war legislation of these countries postponed the maturity of the bills indefinitely. The English bank brought an action against the acceptor in the English courts but failed because the postponement of the dates of maturity by the German and Austrian decrees was effective against the holder.

---

[655] *Hirschfeld v Smith*, above, at 352. See also *Cornelius v Banque Franco-Serbe* [1941] 2 All E.R. 728, 732 (the relevant passage does not appear in the report of the case in [1942] 1 K.B. 29).

[656] See s.55(2)(a) of the Act.

[657] See above, para.34-118.

[658] [1918] 1 Ch. 470. See also *Rouquette v Overmann* (1875) L.R. 10 Q.B. 525. In *Banku Polskiego v K J Mulder & Co* [1941] 2 K.B. 266 (affirmed [1942] 1 K.B. 497), the bills were payable in London and not in Amsterdam, the acceptor being a firm in London and having accepted the bills generally.

2. ASPECTS OF BANKING LAW

Introduction   The treatment of banking law in this section of the chapter is   **34-214**
concerned with the relationship of banker and customer. In order to place that
relationship in its proper context, it is necessary to begin with an outline of the way
banking activities are controlled in the United Kingdom.

(a)   Bank Regulation

(i)   Overview

Financial Services and Markets Act 2000   Section 19 of the Financial Services   **34-215**
and Markets Act 2000 ("the FSMA 2000") provides that no person may carry on,
or purport to carry on, a regulated activity in the United Kingdom unless authorised
or exempt. Deposit-taking is included in the list of regulated activities contained in
Sch.2 to the Act.[659] Until mid-1998, the authorisation and supervision of deposit-
taking institutions was a function of the Bank of England. However, a series of high-
profile financial scandals in the 1990s raised doubts over whether the Bank of
England was an effective supervisor and led the government to introduce legislation transferring the Bank of England's banking supervision function to a new
super-regulatory body called the Financial Services Authority (FSA). The transfer
was effected by the Bank of England Act 1998, which came into force on June 1,
1998. From December 1, 2001, the FSA assumed full regulatory powers in relation to banking, insurance and investment business under the FSMA 2000.[660]

Financial Services Act 2012   The banking crisis of 2007–2008 led to widespread   **34-216**
criticism of the role and performance of the FSA. This resulted in the Government
proposing reform of the regulatory system.[661] The Financial Services Act 2012

---

[659]   FSMA 2000 Sch.2 Pt I para.4 defines "deposit taking" to mean "accepting deposits". See also the
Financial Services and Markets Act 2000 (Regulated Activities) Order 2001 (SI 2001/544, as
amended) Pt II Ch.II. See below, paras 34 230 et seq.

[660]   For a summary of the regulatory regime established by the FSMA 2000 in the context of deposit-
taking, see E.P. Ellinger, E. Lomnicka and C.V.M. Hare, *Ellinger's Modern Banking Law*, 5th edn
(2011), Ch.2. For detailed review, see E. Lomnicka and J. Powell, *Encyclopedia of Financial Services
Law* (looseleaf), Pt 2A.

[661]   The process of reform has been wide ranging. This has been achieved through primary legislation,
supported by a raft of statutory instruments. Three legislative developments stand out. First, the
Banking Act 2009 established (a) a permanent special resolution regime, which gave the Treasury,
Bank of England and FSA (now PRA/FCA) "stabilisation options" for dealing with banks that get
into financial difficulties; (b) a new bank insolvency procedure to facilitate the orderly winding up
of a failed bank; and (c) a new bank administration procedure for use where there has been a partial
transfer of business from a failing bank. Secondly, the Financial Services (Banking Reform) Act 2013
introduced a retail ringfence for banks; primary loss-absorbing capacity for systemically important
banks; a preference for certain depositors on insolvency; a "bail-in" tool as a new stabilisation option available to the Bank of England where a bank is failing; a new framework for the oversight of
individuals within banks, including a new criminal offence aimed at senior managers whose reckless decisions cause a bank to fail; a new payment systems regulator and a special administration
regime for operators of systemically important inter-bank payment systems and securities settlement systems in the event of insolvency. Thirdly, the Treasury published various statutory instruments to implement the Bank Recovery and Resolution Directive 2014/59/EU of 15 May 2014,
which establishes a common framework across the EU for the recovery and resolution of failing
credit institutions and investment firms (the main piece of legislation implementing the Directive

received Royal Assent on December 19, 2012. The new Act substantially amends the FSMA 2000 and introduces key structural changes to the structure of financial regulation in the UK. The FSA was dismantled and replaced by two new regulatory bodies. First, responsibility for significant prudential regulation was transferred from the FSA to a new Prudential Regulation Authority (PRA), originally established as a subsidiary of the Bank of England but, since March 2017, made part of the Bank of England as a result of the Bank of England and Financial Services Act 2016. The PRA's regulatory remit extends to deposit-taking, insurance business and dealing in investments as principal.[662] Secondly, the Financial Conduct Authority (FCA) was tasked with the regulation of the conduct of business of all financial firms, including retail conduct and market conduct. The FCA is also responsible for the prudential regulation of firms that are not regulated by the PRA and, since April 2014, for the regulation of consumer credit business.[663] Finally, the 2012 Act gave the Bank of England, acting through a new Financial Policy Committee, macro-prudential responsibility for oversight of the financial system.

34-217 **The Prudential Regulation Authority (PRA) and the Financial Conduct Authority (FCA)**   Since April 1, 2013, the PRA has been responsible for the prudential regulation of those firms considered by the Government to be systemically important, such as banks, insurers and significant investment firms.[664] These firms may be described as "dual-regulated" firms (or PRA-authorised firms) because they are also regulated by the FCA for conduct of business purposes. The FCA is responsible for the conduct of business regulation of all firms, including dual-regulated firms. The PRA and the FCA are under a statutory duty to coordinate their approach to the regulation of dual-regulated firms. The FCA is also responsible for the prudential regulation of firms not regulated by the PRA. The FCA has also taken over the majority of the FSA's market regulatory functions, including the FSA's role as the UK Listing Authority. The PRA has its own Rulebook[665] and the FCA its own handbook.[666]

34-218 **Demise of the Banking Codes**   Prior to November 1, 2009, in an attempt to ward off the threat of increased statutory control of banking activities, especially in the retail sector, the banking industry engaged in a series of measures based on voluntary self-regulation. The most notable of these measures was the introduction in 1992 of a voluntary code of best practice for banks and building societies when dealing with personal customers in the UK. The code, known as the *Banking Code*, was revised on a number of occasions. In March 2002 the banking industry introduced the *Business Banking Code*, a voluntary code of best practice for banks when dealing with small business customers (i.e. non-personal account

---

is the Bank Recovery and Resolution Order 2014 (SI 2014/3329)).

[662] Financial Services and Markets Act 2000 (PRA-Regulated Activities) Order 2013 (SI 2013/556). See also the PRA's policy statement on the designation of investment firms for prudential regulations (March 2013).

[663] On April 1, 2014, the FCA assumed responsibility for consumer credit regulation from the Office of Fair Trading.

[664] See para.34-216, above.

[665] Available via the Bank of England's website: *http://www.bankofengland.co.uk*.

[666] Available via the FCA's website: *http://www.fca.org.uk*. See, in particular, the following sections of the *FCA Handbook: Principles for Businesses* (PRIN); *Banking Conduct of Business Sourcebook* (BCOBS) and *Consumer Credit Sourcebook* (CONC).

holders with an annual turnover of less than £1 million or an income of under £1 million in the case of charities and clubs). On November 1, 2009, the Banking Code and the Business Banking Code were replaced by the FSA's (now FCA's) new *Banking Conduct of Business Sourcebook* (BCOBS) and the Payment Services Regulations 2009 ("PSRs 2009").[667] The PSRs 2009 have since been revoked and replaced by the Payment Services Regulations 2017.[668]

Banking Conduct of Business Sourcebook (BCOBS)   BCOBS applies to all   **34-219** banks, building societies and credit unions. The change coincided with the introduction of the new PSRs 2009 implementing the Payment Services Directive in the UK.[669] The PSRs 2009 have since been revoked and replaced by the Payment Services Regulations 2017,[670] which implement in part the EU's Revised Payment Services Directive in the UK.[671] The PSRs apply to most retail bank accounts and themselves supersede about 40 per cent of the provisions of the Banking Codes.[672] BCOBS and the PSRs together form what has been described as the new Banking and Payment Services conduct regime.[673] As originally envisaged, the FSA was central to the supervision and enforcement of this new regime, but that function shifted to the FCA on April 1, 2013.[674] Outside the new regime, there are also self-regulatory Standards of Lending Practice for both personal customers and small business customers.[675]

BCOBS is the *FCA's Handbook* module relating to retail banking conduct of   **34-220** business. It applies to firms[676] with respect to the regulated activity of accepting deposits from banking customers carried on from an establishment in the UK and activities connected with that activity (e.g. cheques and foreign exchange).[677] Except as provided for in BCOBS 1.1.4R, BCOBS does not apply to payment services where Pts 6 and 7 of the Payment Services Regulations 2017 apply. BCOBS 1.1.4R(1) provides that Chs 2, 2A, 5 and 6 of BCOBS (except BCOBS 5.1.10AR–5.1.19R) and BCOBS 4.3 apply to payment services where Pts 6 and 7 of the Payment Services Regulations 2017 apply.[678] But a firm is not subject to BCOBS to the extent that it would be contrary to the UK's obligations under an EU instrument.[679]

---

[667] SI 2009/209 (as amended). The background to, and reasons for, this shift away from industry self-regulation to FSA control is set out in FSA Consultation Paper CP 08/19, *Regulating retail banking conduct of business*.

[668] SI 2017/752, as amended. See para.34-224 below.

[669] SI 2009/209, as amended, implementing Directive 2007/64 of the European Parliament and of the Council on payment systems in the internal market ([2007] O.J. L319/1).

[670] SI 2017/752, as amended. See para.34-224 below.

[671] Revised Payment Services Directive 2015/2366/EU.

[672] FSA Consultation Paper CP 08/19 (November 2008), para.3.13.

[673] See G. McMeel [2010] L.M.C.L.Q. 431. It should also be noted that since April 1, 2014 a bank's consumer credit-related activities (e.g. overdrafts and credit cards) have been regulated by the FCA according to the conduct of business standards set out in the *FCA's Consumer Credit Sourcebook* (CONC).

[674] See para.34-216 above.

[675] See paras 34-222—34-223 below.

[676] Including UK authorised banks and building societies, as well as incoming EEA branches of credit institutions.

[677] BCOBS 1.1.1R.

[678] Ch.3 of BCOBS also applies (with modifications) where Pts 6 and 7 of the Payment Services Regulations 2017 apply (BCOBS 1.1.4R(2)).

[679] BCOBS 1.1.4R(3).

Banking customers are defined as consumers, micro-enterprises[680] and charities with an annual income of less than £1 million.[681]

34-221   BCOBS provides rules and guidance on the following areas of activity to the extent that this would not be contrary to the provisions of the Revised Payment Services Directive[682]: communications with banking customers and financial promotions[683]; optional additional products[684]; distance communications[685]; information to be communicated to banking customers, including appropriate information and statements of account[686]; post-sale requirements on prompt, efficient and fair service, moving accounts, and lost and dormant accounts[687]; and cancellation, including the right to cancel and the effects of cancellation.[688] Under the Financial Services and Markets Act 2000, s.138D(2), a "private person" who has suffered loss as the result of a breach of the BCOBS rules has a right of action, as if it were an actionable breach of statutory duty.[689]

34-222   **The Standards of Lending Practice** New voluntary Standards of Lending Practice for Personal Customers came into operation on October 1, 2016. They replaced the self-regulatory Lending Code, which had been introduced in November 2009. The Standards for Lending Practice apply to personal customers and set out standards of good practice in relation to credit (and charge) cards, overdrafts and loans. The Standards represent a move away from the Lending Code, which was focused more on compliance with provisions than customer outcomes.

34-223   New voluntary Standards of Lending Practice for Business Customers came into operation on July 1, 2017. They replace the micro-enterprise provisions of the Lending Code. The protections of the Standards of Lending Practice for Business Customers apply to businesses/organisations, which at the point of lending (a) have an annual turnover of up to £6.5 million and (b) do not have a complex ownership structure (e.g. businesses with overseas, multiple, or layered ownership structures). They set out standards of good practice in relation to credit (and charge) cards,

---

[680] A micro-enterprise is defined in the *FCA's Handbook* glossary as an enterprise which employs fewer than 10 persons and has a turnover or annual balance sheet that does not exceed €2 million, including self-employed persons, family businesses, partnerships and associations regularly engaged in economic activity.

[681] *FSA Handbook*, "Glossary of Definitions".

[682] 2015/2366/EU.

[683] BCOBS Ch.2.

[684] BCOBS Ch.2A.

[685] BCOBS Ch.3.

[686] BCOBS Ch.4.

[687] BCOBS Ch.5.

[688] BCOBS Ch.6.

[689] See, e.g. *Parmar v Barclays Bank Plc* [2018] EWHC 1027 (Ch) (unsuccessful swap mis-selling claim). The definition of a "private person" is to be found in FSMA 2000 (Rights of Action) Regulations 2001 (SI 2001/2256), as amended. The courts have interpreted the definition broadly so that a company carrying on business of any kind, irrespective of whether this related to financial services, is not a "private person" for these purposes. See *Titan Steel Wheels Ltd v Royal Bank of Scotland Plc* [2010] EWHC 211 (Comm), [2010] 2 Lloyd's Rep. 92 at [68]–[70]; *Camerata Property Inc v Credit Suisse Securities (Europe) Ltd* [2012] EWHC 7 (Comm), [2012] 1 C.L.C. 234 at [89]–[98]; *Bailey v Barclays Bank Plc* [2014] EWHC 2882 (QB) at [44]; *Thornbridge Ltd v Barclays Bank Plc* [2015] EWHC 3430 (QB) at [138]–[141] (appeal dismissed, Unreported January 9, 2018); *Sivagnanam v Barclays Bank Plc* [2015] EWHC 3985 (Comm) at [8]–[21]. A claim by a private person under s.138D(2) of the FSMA 2000 may be assigned: *Connaught Income Fund Series 1 v Capital Financial Management Ltd* [2014] EWHC 3619 (Comm), [2015] 1 All E.R. (Comm) 751 at [45]–[46]. Exceptions to right of action under s.138D(2) are found in subss.(3) and (5).

overdrafts and loans. From October 1, 2018, the Standards will apply to asset finance, namely hire purchase and leasing (excluding contract hire) products.[690]

Payment Services Regulations 2017   The Payment Services Regulations 2017   **34-224** ("PSRs 2017")[691] implement (in part) the EU's Revised Payment Services Directive in the UK.[692] The PSRs 2017 revoke and replace the PSRs 2009.[693] Payment services include the execution of payment transactions, card issuing, merchant acquiring, money remittance, certain services based on mobile phones or other electronic devices, and the operation of "payment accounts". Regulation 2(1) of the PSRs 2017 defines a "payment account" as "an account held in the name of one or more payment service users which is used for the execution of payment transactions", and a "payment transaction" as "an act, initiated by the payer or payee, or on behalf of the payer, of placing, transferring or withdrawing funds, irrespective of any underlying obligations between the payer and the payee". Thus, payment accounts include current accounts and easy access savings accounts. The PSRs 2017 focus only on electronic means of payment; they do not apply to cash-only transactions directly between payer and payee[694] or payments based on paper instruments, e.g. cheques.[695]

In the context of retail banking, the PSRs 2017 impose conduct of business   **34-225** requirements on payment services that are within scope.[696] The PSRs 2017 are of wider scope than the PSRs 2009. Pts 5 (informational requirements) and 6 (rights and obligations) of the PSRs 2009, with some exceptions, only applied if the service was provided from an establishment maintained by a payment service provider or its agent in the UK, the payment service providers of both the payer and the payee were within the EEA, and the transaction was in euros, sterling or another non-euro Member State currency.[697] This changed with the PSRs 2017. So long as the payment services are provided from an establishment maintained by a service provider or its agent in the UK,[698] Pts 6 (informational requirements) and 7 (rights and obligations) of the PSRs 2017 extend, with some exceptions, to (i) services relating to transactions in EEA currencies where the payment service providers of both the payer and the payee are located within the EEA, (ii) services relating to transactions in non-EEA currencies where the payment service providers of both the payer and the payee are located in EEA countries,[699] and (iii) services relating to transactions where the payment service provider of either the payer or the payee, but not both, is in the EEA.[700] In the case of (ii) and (iii), Pts 6 and 7 apply only in

---

[690] The Standards of Lending Practice for Business Customers—Asset Finance (June 2018, Lending Standards Board).

[691] SI 2017/752, as amended.

[692] Revised Payment Services Directive 2015/2366/EU ("PSD2").

[693] With certain exceptions as set out in reg.1, which include where the implementation period is linked to the coming into force of the secure communication and authentication requirements adopted under art.98 of PSD2, the PSRs 2017 came into force on January 13, 2018 (PSRs 2017 reg.1(6)).

[694] But the placement and withdrawal of cash to and from a payment account is within the scope of the PSRs 2017.

[695] PSRs 2017 Sch.1 Pt 2.

[696] For detailed discussion of PSRs 2017, see paras 34-402 et seq.

[697] PSRs 2009 regs 33(1), 51(1), (2): reg.73 (value date and availability of funds) applied whether or not the payment service providers of both the payer and the payee were located within the EEA.

[698] PSRs 2017 regs 40(1)(a), 63(1)(a).

[699] PSRs 2017 regs 40(1)(b)(ii), 63(1)(b)(ii).

[700] PSRs 2017 regs 40(1)(b)(iii), 63(1)(b)(iii).

respect of those parts of the transaction which are carried out in the EEA,[701] and when they apply they do so in a more restricted manner than in the case of (i).[702]

34-226 The conduct of business regulations mostly relate to providing information to payment services users, both before and after the execution of particular transactions.[703] There are separate provisions for single payment service contracts[704] and framework contracts.[705] There are also common provisions including a prohibition on charging for certain information.[706] Other information requirements extend to account information service providers, information on ATM withdrawals and provision of information leaflets.[707] The Regulations also set out the legal rights and obligations as between payment service providers and users. They provide for matters including consent to payment transactions,[708] unauthorised or incorrectly executed payment transactions, liability for unauthorised payment transactions,[709] refunds, execution of payment transactions, execution time and liability of payment service providers.[710] The 2017 version of the Regulations extend, for the first time, to the activities of "payment initiation services" and "account information services",[711] although in a much more limited way than with other payment services providers.[712]

34-227 As with reg.120(1) of the PSRs 2009, reg.148(1) of the PSRs 2017 makes any breach of the requirements of Pts 6 or 7 actionable by a "private person" who suffers loss as a result of the contravention, subject to defences and other incidents applying to actions for breach of statutory duty.[713] However, and new to the PSRs 2017, it is provided, in reg.148(4), that where there is a contravention of a requirement under regs 76(5)(b), 77(6), 93(4) or 95 for a payment service provider to compensate another service provider, the payment service provider to which

---

[701] PSRs 2017 regs 40(2)(a),(3)(a), 63(2)(a), (3)(a).

[702] PSRs 2017 regs 40(2)(b), (3)(b), 63(2)(b), (3)(b). Significantly, for a transfer in a non-EEA currency, regs 84 to 88 (amounts transferred and received and execution times) do not apply (reg.63(2)(b)).

[703] See *BAWAG PSK Bank für Arbeit und Wirtschaft und Österreichische Postsparkasse AG v Verein für Konsumenteninformation* (C-375/15) EU:C:2017:38, January 25, 2017, CJEU for meaning of requirement that payment service provider must "provide" information on a "durable medium" for purposes of arts 36(1) and 41(1) of the Payment Services Directive 2007/64/EC. See also Revised Payment Services Directive 2015/2366/EU arts 44(1) and 54(1).

[704] PSRs 2017 regs 43–47.

[705] PSRs 2017 regs 48–54.

[706] PSRs 2017 regs 55–58.

[707] PSRs 2017 regs 60–62.

[708] PSRs 2017 reg.67.

[709] PSRs 2017 regs 74–77.

[710] PSRs 2017 regs 79–96.

[711] PSRs 2017 Sch.1 Pt 1(g), (h).

[712] PSRs 2017 regs 40(4), 63(4): Pts 6 and 7 do not apply to registered account information service providers or EEA registered account information service providers, except for, in the case of Pt 6, regs 59 and 60, and, in the case of Pt 7, regs 70, 71(7) to (10), 72(3) and 98 to 100.

[713] In PSR 2017 reg.148, a "private person" means (a) any individual, except where the individual suffers the loss in question in the course of providing payment services; and (b) any person who is not an individual, except where that person suffers the loss in question in the course of carrying on business of any kind (reg.148(3)). A fiduciary or representative may also, generally, bring the action on behalf of a private person: reg.148(2). In the context of the similarly worded definition of "private person" in the FSMA 2000 (Rights of Action) Regulations 2001, "in the course of carrying on business of any kind" has been interpreted broadly by the courts so that a company carrying on business of any kind, irrespective of whether this related to financial services, falls outside the definition of "private person": for cases on the definition, see para.34-221 above.

compensation is required to be paid is to be treated for the purposes of reg.148 as if it were a "private person".

Payment service providers may contract out of certain obligations with custom- **34-228** ers who are not consumers, micro-enterprises or small charities for the purposes of the Regulations.[714] For these purposes a "consumer" is a natural person who, in payment service contracts, is acting for purposes other than his trade, business or profession. A "micro-enterprise" is an enterprise which employs fewer than 10 persons and has a turnover or annual balance sheet that does not exceed €2 million, including self-employed persons, family businesses, partnerships and associations regularly engaged in economic activity. A "charity" is one with an annual income of less than £1 million.

There are a number of exemptions to be found in Pt 2 of Sch.1 to the Regulations. **34-229** These activities do not constitute payment services. The exemptions mainly cover wholesale activities of financial institutions. There are no specific exemptions based on transaction size although low-value payment instruments are subject to fewer requirements.[715] Certain requirements of the PSRs (relating to information and rights and obligations) are disapplied where the Consumer Credit Act 1974 already contains similar requirements.[716]

(ii)   The Regulation of Deposit-taking

Financial Services and Markets Act 2000   The FSMA 2000 carries forward the **34-230** need for institutions to be authorised in order to carry on banking in the UK in the sense of "accepting deposits".[717] This is done by imposing a "general prohibition" on anyone carrying on, or purporting to carry on, a regulated activity "in the United Kingdom" unless he is an authorised person or an exempt person (FSMA 2000 s.19(1)). Regulated activities are listed in Sch.2 to the Act and are defined in detail in the Financial Services and Markets Act 2000 (Regulated Activities) Order 2001 (the "RAO").[718] One such regulated activity is "accepting deposits" by way of business (RAO art.5).[719] The FSMA 2000 has extraterritorial scope because of the extended meaning of "in the United Kingdom".[720] This means that an institution based in the United Kingdom will require authorisation even though it is offering deposit-taking services exclusively to customers outside the UK.

"Accepting deposits"   Article 5(1) of the RAO defines "accepting deposits" in **34-231** terms of two alternative categories of activity.[721] The first is where "money received by way of deposit is lent to others". The second is where "any other activity of the person accepting the deposit is financed wholly or to any material extent, out of the capital or of interest on money received on deposit". A "deposit" is defined in arts 5(2)–(3) to mean a sum of money paid on the basis that it will be repaid with or

---

[714] PSRs 2017 regs 40(7), 63(5).
[715] PSRs 2017 regs 42, 65.
[716] PSRs 2017 regs 41, 64.
[717] Deposit-taking is defined as "accepting deposits" in the FSMA 2000 Sch.2 Pt I para.4. Many banks will also have permission to engage in other regulated activities, e.g. investment business, regulated mortgage business and insurance mediation.
[718] SI 2001/544, as amended.
[719] See *Financial Services Authority v Anderson* [2010] EWHC 599 (Ch).
[720] FSMA 2000 s.418, as amended.
[721] See *Financial Services Authority v Anderson* [2010] EWHC 599 (Ch).

without interest or premium either on demand or as agreed. However, it does not include an arrangement for the payment of money on terms which are "referable to the provision of property (other than currency) or services or the giving of security". The wide definition of a "deposit" has led to specific exclusions: e.g. loans by banks and other institutions engaged in the lending business, loans between companies in the same group and transactions between relatives are all excluded from the definition.[722]

34-232   A construction of this elaborate definition is to be found in *SCF Finance Co v Masri (No.2)*,[723] decided in respect of a similar definition used in the Banking Act 1979. In that case it was argued that a firm of futures brokers, who obtained a deposit to secure its client's trading in commodities, carried on the business of deposit taking in contravention of s.1 of the 1979 Act. It was held that the payment involved did not constitute a "deposit". It fell outside the ambit of the relevant definition because its object was to secure a contract respecting a service provided by the brokers to the client.

34-233   **Accepting deposits "by way of business"**   A person does not accept deposits "by way of business" if he does not hold himself out as accepting deposits on a day-to-day basis, and any deposit which he accepts are accepted only on particular occasions, whether or not involving the issue of any securities.[724] In determining whether deposits are accepted only on particular occasions, "regard is to be had to the frequency of those occasions and to any characteristics distinguishing them from each other".[725] In *SCF Finance Co v Masri (No.2)*, discussed above, deposits were accepted from clients by a firm of brokers, commingled with the firm's general funds and, occasionally, lent on to other clients. In most cases the deposits were accepted as margin payments providing the brokers with security for orders placed on behalf of customers. Occasionally, the brokers also invested deposits at the request of specific clients. The Court of Appeal held that in neither case did the brokers act by way of business. It was held that the brokers had not held themselves out as running a deposit taking business and that the payments were received on particular occasions despite the frequency of those occasions.[726] Recent amendment of the Financial Services and Markets Act 2000 (Carrying on Regulated Activities by Way of Business) Order 2001 ensures that non-financial services businesses do not accept deposits "by way of business" when borrowing funds via peer-to-peer lending platforms.[727] This ensures that peer-to-peer lending platforms are not facilitating unlawful deposit taking in such circumstances.

---

[722] RAO arts 6–9AC. See *Re Kaupthing Singer & Friedlander Ltd (in administration)* [2010] EWCA Civ 561, [2010] 2 B.C.L.C. 259. See further, E.P. Ellinger, E. Lomnicka and C.V.M. Hare, *Ellinger's Modern Banking Law*, 5th edn (2011), p.37.

[723] [1987] Q.B. 1002.

[724] Financial Services and Markets Act 2000 (Carrying on Regulated Activities by Way of Business) Order 2001 (SI 2001/1177) art.2(1).

[725] SI 2001/1177 art.2(2). This amplification was added by the Banking Act 1987 s.6(4) and is repeated in the Order. See also *Financial Services Authority v Anderson* [2010] EWHC 599 (Ch).

[726] But now see the amplification of what is a "particular occasion" contained in SI 2001/1177 art.2(2), which was considered in *Financial Services Authority v Anderson* [2010] EWHC 599 (Ch) at [53]–[57], and see also *R. v Napoli* [2012] EWCA Crim 1129. Nevertheless, it is strongly arguable that the case would not be decided any differently today (see E.P. Ellinger, E. Lomnicka and C.V.M. Hare, *Ellinger's Modern Banking Law*, 5th edn (2011), p.36).

[727] SI 2001/1177 art.2(3)–(5) inserted by the Financial Services and Markets Act 2000 (Carrying on Regulated Activities by Way of Business) (Amendment) Order 2018 (SI 2018/394) in force on March

Exempt persons   Although persons accepting deposits in the UK by way of busi-   **34-234**
ness generally require authorisation, the FSMA 2000 gives power to the Treasury
to exempt institutions from this requirement.[728] Such persons are termed "exempt
persons" and include the Bank of England, other EEA central banks, the European
Central Bank, the EU and related international bodies, and certain development
banks.[729]

Authorised persons   Unless an exempt person, anyone accepting deposits in the   **34-235**
UK by way of business must be an "authorised person". This means that they must
either be a person who has obtained authorisation from the PRA, or a person
authorised in another EEA Member State and entitled, through the application of
the single European passport principle, to establish branches or provide cross-
border services in the UK.[730]

Part 4A permission   Since April 1, 2013, the PRA has been the body responsible   **34-236**
for the authorisation of "dual-registered" firms.[731] The PRA decides whether or not
to grant permission but must obtain the consent of the FCA before granting
permission.[732] The FCA is responsible for considering applications for authorisation by any person seeking to carry out regulated activities that do not include any
PRA-regulated activities.[733] Where the applicant is a member of a group which
includes a "dual-regulated" firm, the FCA must consult with the PRA before granting authorisation.[734] The new regime has made important changes to the threshold
conditions for authorisation to carry on regulated activities, including (a) the application of different threshold conditions to dual-regulated and FCA-regulated
firms; and (b) giving the PRA and the FCA the power to make "threshold condition codes".[735] There is a right of appeal to the Upper Tribunal for those aggrieved
by the PRA's or the FCA's exercise of their powers in relation to Pt 4A
permission.[736]

Powers to obtain information and documents   The FSMA 2000 gives the PRA   **34-237**
and the FCA wide powers to require the provision of information from and the
production of documents by an authorised person and any person connected with
the authorised person.[737] Both regulators also have power to require an authorised
person to provide a report by an accountant or other person with relevant professional skills.[738] Both regulators have the right of entry to obtain documents and
information on a magistrate's warrant.[739] Section 167 of the FSMA 2000 gives the

22, 2018.

[728]   s.38.
[729]   Financial Services and Markets Act 2000 (Exemption) Order 2001 (SI 2001/1201), as amended by
the Financial Services and Markets Act 2000 (Exemption) (Amendment) Order 2015 (SI 2015/
447).
[730]   See below, para.34-243.
[731]   FSMA 2000 s.55A(2)(a). For what is meant by a "dual-regulated" firm, see para.34-217 above.
[732]   FSMA 2000 s.55F(2).
[733]   FSMA 2000 s.55A(2)(b).
[734]   FSMA 2000 s.55E(3).
[735]   FSMA 2000 ss.55B, 137O and Sch.6.
[736]   FSMA 2000 s.55Z3.
[737]   s.165 and, for additional powers of the PRA, ss.165A–165C.
[738]   ss.166–166A.
[739]   s.176.

PRA and FCA (or Secretary of State) power to appoint investigators to conduct general investigations into authorised persons and appointed representatives.

34-238   Sanctions for unauthorised acceptance of deposits   A person who contravenes the "general prohibition" is guilty of a criminal offence.[740] Where a deposit is accepted in breach of the general prohibition, and the depositor is not entitled under the agreement between himself and the deposit-taker to recover without delay the money deposited by him, he may apply to the court for an order directing the deposit-taker to return the money to him.[741] The court "need not make such an order" if it is satisfied that it would not be "just and equitable" on the basis of a reasonable belief by the deposit-taker that he was not in breach of the general prohibition.[742] The FSMA 2000 also gives the appropriate regulator power to apply to court for injunctions and "disgorgement" orders both against the person acting in breach of the general prohibition and anyone else knowingly concerned in the breach.[743]

34-239   Liability of the PRA/FCA   The English courts have generally been reluctant to hold a bank regulator liable in damages to a depositor or investor of a failed bank. It has been repeatedly held by the courts that a bank regulator does not owe a duty of care to individual commercial banks,[744] nor to their depositors,[745] when carrying out its regulatory function. As Lord Millett stated in *Three Rivers DC v Bank of England*[746]:

> "... [u]nfortunately for the depositors, a regulatory authority cannot be held liable in English law for negligence, however gross, in the exercise of its supervisory functions."

34-240   Statutory immunity of the PRA/FCA   In any event, the FSMA 2000 affords the PRA and the FCA, and any person who is, or is acting as, a member, officer or member of staff of those Authorities, statutory immunity from liability in damages "for anything done or omitted in the discharge, or purported discharge, of the [Authority's] functions".[747] The immunity is not absolute: it does not apply to acts

---

[740] s.23(1). But subject to a due diligence defence (s.23(3)). An "authorised" (or "exempt") person cannot be in breach of the general prohibition. Authorised persons who exceed the limits of their permission to undertake a regulated activity are subject to disciplinary sanction and not the sanctions for breach of the general prohibition (s.20). But an authorised person is guilty of an offence if that person carries on a credit-related regulated activity in the UK, or purports to do so, otherwise than in accordance with permission given to that person under Pt 4A or resulting from any other provision of the FSMA 2000 (s.23(1A)). See also s.20(1) and (1A).

[741] s.29(2).

[742] s.29(3), (4).

[743] ss.380, 382. See *Financial Services Authority v Anderson* [2010] EWHC 599 (Ch). For the meaning of "knowingly concerned", see Lomnicka (2000) 21 *Company Lawyer* 210. The court has jurisdiction under the Senior Courts Act 1981 s.37 to make an order freezing the bank accounts of third parties over which the person who has contravened the authorisation requirements of the 2000 Act has control. See *Financial Services Authority v Fitt* [2004] EWHC 1669 (Ch).

[744] *Minories Finance Ltd v Arthur Young (a firm)* [1989] 2 All E.R. 105.

[745] *Yuen Kun Yeu v A-G of Hong Kong* [1988] A.C. 175, PC; *Davies v Radcliffe* [1990] 1 W.L.R. 821, PC.

[746] [2001] Lloyd's Rep. Bank. 125 at 169. See also *SRM Global Master Fund LP v Commissioners of Her Majesty's Treasury* [2009] EWCA Civ 788, [2010] B.C.C. 558 at [80].

[747] FSMA 2000 Sch.1ZA para.25 (FCA) and Sch.1ZB para.33 (PRA): note also the limited extension of immunity (to vicarious liability) in para.25(1)(c) and para.33(1)(c). Questions have been raised by some commentators as to whether this blanket immunity contravenes art.6 of the European

or omissions shown to have been in bad faith or in breach of the Human Rights Act 1998,[748] nor does it prevent judicial review of the regulator's decisions. The regulator could be liable to depositors for the tort of misfeasance in public office where the necessary elements of the tort are established.[749] The tort of misfeasance in public office entails bad faith and so falls outside the statutory immunity. But it will not be easy to prove that the PRA or FCA acted or failed to act because of bad faith, as opposed to negligence, and the claim is more likely to be struck out than to succeed.[750] In any event, it may also be difficult to show that the acts or omissions of the regulator were the effective cause of the depositors' loss.

Financial Services Compensation Scheme   For many years now the UK has had   **34-241** an industry funded depositor protection scheme. This has ensured that depositors receive (limited) compensation in the event of a bank failing. Depositor compensation is now provided for as part of the Financial Services Compensation Scheme (the FSCS), which was established under the FSMA 2000 Pt 15. Rules governing depositor compensation are made by the PRA, which is the competent authority and designated authority under the EU's Directive on deposit guarantee schemes.[751] Under the EU Directive, consumer and all business (not just SME) depositors are protected up to a maximum of €100,000, or its sterling equivalent (£85,000 as from January 30, 2017),[752] with additional protection available for "temporary high balances".

(iii)   EU Harmonisation Measures

EU single market in banking   A number of changes in UK bank regulation have   **34-242** resulted from the implementation of the EU single market in banking.[753] The EC Second Banking Coordination Directive 89/646 introduced the concept of a single banking licence enabling a bank (or "credit institution") incorporated in a Member State to enjoy mutual recognition throughout the Community by virtue of recognition in its home country. Once the appropriate licence or authorisation is granted by the home supervisor, the bank can establish and offer certain "listed" banking services (including deposit-taking, lending and most ordinary types of banking business) in any Community country without first having to obtain host country authorisation. The main burden of the continued supervision of the bank's activi-

---

Convention of Human Rights which guarantees the right to a fair and public hearing: see C. Proctor [2002] J.I.B.F.L. 15 and 71; M. Andenas and D. Fairgrieve (2002) 51 I.C.L.Q. 757.
[748] FSMA 2000 Sch.1ZA para.25(3) and Sch.1ZB para.33(3).
[749] *Three Rivers DC v Governor and Company of the Bank of England* [2000] 2 W.L.R. 1220, where the House of Lords also held that individual depositors were not given rights under relevant European legislation.
[750] See *Hall v Bank of England* [2000] Lloyd's Rep. Bank. 186, CA; although in *Three Rivers DC v Bank of England* [2001] Lloyd's Rep. Bank. 125, HL, a claim against the Bank of England was, somewhat surprisingly, allowed to proceed to trial. The claim was eventually abandoned at the trial itself: see [2006] EWHC 816 (Comm).
[751] See the Deposit Guarantee Scheme Regulations 2015 (SI 2015/486), which implement in part Directive 2014/49/EU of the European Parliament and of the Council of 16th April 2014 on deposit guarantee schemes (recast) repealing Directive 94/19/EC of 30th May 1994 on deposit-guarantee schemes.
[752] PRA Policy Statement PS1/17 Deposit Protection Limit.
[753] E.P. Ellinger, E. Lomnicka and C.V.M. Hare, *Ellinger's Modern Banking Law*, 5th edn (2011), pp.69–77.

ties is then placed on the home supervisor and not the host state. Through a series of banking directives, the EU has ensured similar standards of control across EU Member States. Until recently, the key directives were Directive 2006/48 relating to the taking up and pursuit of the business of credit institutions and Directive 2006/49 on the capital adequacy of investment firms and credit institutions. The Capital Requirements Directive IV package implements the Basel III global standards on bank capital in the EU through the Capital Requirements Directive 2013/36[754] (CRD) and the Capital Requirements Regulation[755] (CRR). Directive 2006/48 and Directive 2006/49 have been repealed and merged into the CRD and the CRR.

34-243 **Single European passport** The Second Banking Coordination Directive was given effect in the UK by the Banking Coordination (Second Council Directive) Regulations 1992,[756] which made substantial amendments to the Banking Act 1987. The Regulations were repealed by a Treasury order made under s.426 of the FSMA 2000. However, the principle of the single European passport has been carried through into the regulatory regime established under the FSMA 2000. Banks authorised to carry on regulated activities in other European Economic Area ("EEA") Member States are granted automatic authorisation to carry on those activities in the UK through branches or the provision of cross-border services, provided they comply with certain formalities.[757] These banks, referred to as "EEA firms" in the FSMA 2000, are subject to regulation as "authorised persons" by the PRA, but only in a manner that is consistent with EU law which provides for division of responsibility between "home" (i.e. other EEA Member State) and "host" (UK) regulators. UK authorised banks are also entitled to exercise their single European passport rights throughout the EEA.[758]

34-244 **Single payment market** Directive 2007/64 of the European Parliament and of the Council on payment services in the internal market (more commonly known as the "Payment Services Directive") was published in the Official Journal of the EU on December 5, 2007. It provided a legal foundation for the creation of a single market for payments in the EU, repealing previous legislation on cross-border credit transfers, and amending a number of existing Directives, including the Banking Consolidation Directive. The Directive established an authorisation regime for non-bank payment service providers, such as money remitters and non-bank credit card issuers (known as "payment institutions"), and it set out conduct of business rules (concerning information provision and liability) for all payment service providers, including banks, e-money institutions and payment institutions. The Directive also contained provisions stipulating that rules governing access to payment systems should be non-discriminatory so as to support competition amongst payment service providers. The Payment Services Directive was implemented in the UK thorough

---

[754] Directive 2013/36/EU of the European Parliament and of the Council on the access to the activity of credit institutions and the prudential supervision of credit institutions and investment firms.

[755] Regulation (EU) 575/2013 of the European Parliament and of the Council on prudential requirements for credit institutions and investment firms.

[756] SI 1992/3218.

[757] s.31(1)(b) and Sch.3. See also the Financial Services and Markets Act 2000 (EEA Passport Rights) Regulations 2001 (SI 2001/2511).

[758] Sch.3 Pt III, and see also Pt III of the EEA Passport Rights Regulations (above).

the Payment Service Regulations 2009, which came fully into force on November 1, 2009.[759]

The Payment Services Directive has been repealed and replaced by the EU's **34-245** Revised Payment Services Directive (known as "PSD2").[760] EU Member States had until January 13, 2018 to implement the requirements of PSD2. The PSRs 2017, implement in part PSD2 in the UK.[761] The PSRs 2017 revoke and replace the PSRs 2009. With certain exceptions as set out in reg.1, which include where the implementation period is linked to the coming into force of the secure communication and authentication requirements adopted under art.98 of PSD2, the PSRs 2017 came into force on January 13, 2018.[762] The PSRs 2017 are considered further in Sect.2(e) of the current chapter.

(b) The Relationship of Banker and Customer

(i) Definition of a Bank

Who is a banker: scope of problem The question of whether or not a given **34-246** financial institution constitutes a bank arises mainly where a statute confers certain privileges or rights or imposes given duties or controls on a "bank". In the majority of cases the statute in point includes a definition of the word "bank" or "banker". Basically, there are two types of definition. The first, which is the standard common law definition, defines a "bank" as a concern engaged in "banking business". The construction of the latter phrase has been left to the courts. This common law definition is still used in the Bills of Exchange Act 1882.[763] The second type of definition, which was utilised in a number of regulatory Acts, provided that a "bank" was a body holding a certificate to this effect issued by a specific authority. Until relatively recently, the term "bank" was usually defined in these statutes as "an institution authorised under the Banking Act 1987".[764] However, the Banking Act 1987 has since been repealed and replaced by the Financial Services and Markets Act 2000.[765] Those statutes which defined a "bank" in terms of authorisation under the 1987 Act have been amended to refer to an "authorised person" (granted permission to accept deposits by the Prudential Regulation Authority) and an "EEA firm" (exercising single European passport rights in the UK) as provided for in the 2000 Act.[766]

Who is a banker: common law definition "Banker" is defined in the Bills of **34-247** Exchange Act as "a body of persons, whether incorporated or not, who carry on the business of banking".[767] As the term "banking business" is not defined, and as it has

---

[759] SI 2009/209, as amended.

[760] Revised Payment Services Directive 2015/2366/EU.

[761] SI 2017/752, as amended.

[762] PSRs 2017 reg.1(6).

[763] s.2. For a detailed discussion, see E.P. Ellinger, E. Lomnicka and C.V.M. Hare, *Ellinger's Modern Banking Law*, 5th edn (2011), Ch.3.

[764] Banking Act 1987 s.108(1) and Sch.6.

[765] See para.34-230 above.

[766] For what is an "authorised person", see para.34-235 above; for what is an "EEA firm", see para.34-243 above. But the term "bank" has not been excised entirely from the "UK regulatory lexicon", see D.A. Sabalot [2016] J.I.B.F.L. 631.

[767] s.2.

been held that its meaning may vary from time to time,[768] it is not always easy to say with certainty whether or not an institution is a bank. Basically, following the established case law, the main types of "banking business" are the opening of current accounts operable by cheques[769] and deposit accounts, as well as the collection of cheques for customers.[770] Nevertheless, in recent years the use of cheques has declined and money is frequently transferred into and out of bank accounts using electronic means (e.g. by ATM and debit card transactions, or by mobile, internet and telephone banking). In the light of this modern practice, it is submitted that the common law definition of the terms "bank", "banking" and "banking business" should not turn on the precise mechanism by which money is paid into and out of bank accounts.[771]

34-248 **Reputation** It is uncertain whether an institution may be considered a bank merely because it is so regarded by the business community. This question came before the Court of Appeal in *United Dominions Trust Ltd v Kirkwood*.[772] A finance company brought an action to recover a loan from a dealer. The dealer pleaded that the company was an unregistered moneylender and that the contract was therefore illegal as it contravened the provisions of the Money-lenders Act 1900.[773] The finance company claimed that under s.6(d) of this Act it was exempted from the provisions concerning registration, because it carried on, bona fide, the business of banking. The main issue in the case was, thus, whether the finance company carried on the business of banking, or—in other words—was a banker. It was proved that the finance company was regarded as a banker in the City, enjoyed some privileges given solely to bankers and had a special clearing number. It was further established that in some cases the company furnished loans to clients by crediting the relevant amount to a current account opened in the respective client's name. The finance company did receive money on deposits, but these were invariably repayable on agreed dates of maturity and not on demand. There was no evidence to suggest that the company collected cheques on behalf of customers. On these facts, Lord Denning M.R. questioned whether the company carried on the "business of banking". Nevertheless, he held that the company was a bank on the basis of its established reputation as "banker" in the city. Diplock L.J. concurred in holding that the company was a bank, but based his opinion on different grounds, stressing that he considered the question of reputation to be of limited importance. Harman L.J. gave a dissenting judgment, as in his opinion the company was not a bank, regardless of its reputation.

---

[768] *Woods v Martins Bank Ltd* [1959] 1 Q.B. 55; *United Dominions Trust Ltd v Kirkwood* [1966] 2 Q.B. 431.

[769] *Commissioners of the State Savings Bank of Victoria v Permewan, Wright & Co Ltd* (1915) 19 C.L.R. 457, 470–471; *Bank of Chettinad Ltd v Commissioner of Income Tax, Colombo* [1948] A.C. 378, 383; *United Dominions Trust Ltd v Kirkwood*, above.

[770] *United Dominions Trust Ltd v Kirkwood*, above, approving the definition of banking business in Paget, *Law of Banking*, 9th edn, pp.5–7 (currently 14th edn, 2014, para.4.2).

[771] See further, E.P. Ellinger, E. Lomnicka and C.V.M. Hare, *Ellinger's Modern Banking Law*, 5th edn (2011), p.85.

[772] [1966] 2 Q.B. 431. See also *Re Birkbeck Permanent Benefit Building Society* [1912] 2 Ch. 183.

[773] Repealed by the Consumer Credit Act 1974 s.192(4) and Sch.5 Pt I, also repealing s.123 of the Companies Act 1967, which empowered the Board of Trade to declare an institution a bank for the purposes of the Money-lenders Act. Note that, in view of the similarity between the definition of banker in the Money-lenders Act and in the Bills of Exchange Act, *Kirkwood's* case remains of topical importance.

Banking as ancillary business   It is, thus, clear that in *Kirkwood*'s case Diplock   **34-249**
and Harman L.JJ. doubted that reputation was, in itself, a conclusive criterion for
establishing that a firm was a bank as defined at common law. Their judgments
indicate that the crucial point is whether or not the firm carries on banking business.
But it has been accepted that a firm may be a bank although its activities are not
confined to the carrying on of banking business. Some early cases suggest that, in
such a case, the firm's principal business must be that of banking business.[774] But
this requirement was relaxed in *Re Roe's Legal Charge*.[775] As in *Kirkwood*'s case,
the problem in *Roe's Legal Charge* arose in respect of the Money-lenders Act. It
was established that the lending institution opened current accounts for some
customers and collected cheques payable to them. The institution also provided
certain foreign currency facilities and arranged for the payment of customers' bills
by means of money transfer orders. There were, however, four main differences
between this institution's business and that of a regular bank. First, its entire banking services were furnished not at premises maintained in its own name but through
an agency bank. Secondly, the number of current and deposit accounts opened by
it was less than 200 and in the course of 1984 only 58 cheques had been cleared
for customers. Thirdly, about three-quarters of its existing deposits were made by
shareholders, by subsidiaries and by associated companies. Fourthly, the institution did not solicit deposits from the public by means of advertisements. Holding
that the institution was engaged in banking business, Lawton L.J., in the Court of
Appeal, said that it was immaterial that the size of the institution's banking business was negligible in comparison with that of a clearing bank. It was also irrelevant that the institution did not carry on all facets of banking business and that
its main activities were in another field. The only question was whether the
institution's banking business was real in terms of its entire business.

Use of "bank" in name   There were tight controls on the use of the terms "bank"   **34-250**
and "banker" in the Banking Act 1987. Section 67 of the 1987 Act provided that,
subject to certain exceptions, no person was entitled to use any banking name (i.e.
indicating that the person was a bank or a banker or as carrying on banking business) unless that person was an authorised institution under the Banking Act 1987.
Section 69 of the Act provided that no person was entitled to describe himself or
hold himself out as to indicate that he was a bank or a banker or was carrying on a
banking business unless authorised (or exempt) under the 1987 Act. These provisions have since been repealed by, and are not repeated in, the Financial Services
and Markets Act 2000. The relevant provision is now s.24 of the Financial Services
and Markets Act 2000, which makes it a criminal offence for anyone who is neither
an authorised person nor an exempt person in relation to the regulated activity in
question to describe himself as either authorised or exempt or who behaves or
otherwise holds himself out as being authorised or exempt under the 2000 Act. It
is submitted that this provision would catch an institution that called itself a "bank"
without proper authorisation as this implies such authorisation.

---

[774]   *Re Birkbeck Permanent Benefit Building Society*, above; *Bank of Chettinad Ltd v Commissioner of
Income Tax, Colombo* [1948] A.C. 378. Contrast *Stafford v Henry* (1850) 12 Ir.Eq.R. 400.
[775]   [1982] 2 Lloyd's Rep. 370. See also *Canadian Pioneer Management Ltd v Labour Relations Board*,
107 D.L.R. (3rd) 1 (1980); *Koh v Asia Commercial Banking Corp Ltd* [1984] 1 W.L.R. 850 JC.

(ii)   Definition of a Customer

34-251   **Who is a customer**   The word "customer" is not defined in any statute, but it appeared in s.82 of the Bills of Exchange Act 1882 (now replaced by s.4 of the Cheques Act 1957). It has been held, in this context, that a person becomes a customer either when the banker opens an account in his name[776] or when the banker accepts his instruction to open an account and receives a deposit to be credited to it.[777] The fact that a banker habitually performs a casual service for a person, e.g. cashes over the counter cheques obtained by that person from third parties, does not render that person a customer.[778] Duration is, thus, not the essence of the relationship of banker and customer.

34-252   **Intention of parties**   The relationship of banker and customer comes into existence only if both parties have an intention that it be established. Usually this intention is expressly manifested when the account is opened at the customer's request. There are, however, cases in which the customer's consent to the opening of the account is given tacitly. Thus, in *Rowlandson v National Westminster Bank Ltd*[779] a business woman made a cheque payable to a bank, at which she was known but with which she did not have an account, and explained that the proceeds were a gift to her grandchildren. The bank opened an account in the grandchildren's joint names and conferred the right to draw on their guardians. Although the guardians did not expressly approve this arrangement and were not even expressly notified of the opening of the account they did eventually learn of its existence and one of them drew a cheque on it. It was held that the bank owed a fiduciary duty to the grandchildren and, furthermore, that it had committed a breach of this duty when it permitted one of the guardians to draw on the account for the credit of his own personal account. It would appear to follow that a relationship of banker and customer came into existence between the bank and the grandchildren, presumably as a result of the tacit approval of the opening of the account by the guardians. The case may, however, rest on its exceptional facts.

34-253   **Account in nominee's name**   A relationship of banker and customer does not usually come into existence merely because an account in a person's name has been opened by the bank. Thus, where A forges B's signature and opens a bank account in B's name without his authority, no relationship of banker and customer exists between the bank and B, and so no question respecting the breach of a contractual duty owed to B can arise.[780] In effect, the bank's customer is the person who negotiates the making of the contract and not a third party such as a nominee. Thus, in *Thavorn v Bank of Credit and Commerce International SA*[781] the plaintiff, an elderly

---

[776] *Lacave & Co v Crédit Lyonnais* [1897] 1 Q.B. 148; *Great Western Ry v London and County Banking Co* [1901] A.C. 414; *Ladbroke v Todd* (1914) 30 T.L.R. 433; *Commissioners of Taxation v English, Scottish and Australian Bank* [1920] A.C. 683.

[777] *Ladbroke v Todd*, above; *Woods v Martins Bank Ltd* [1959] 1 Q.B. 55 (in which, however, the question was discussed not in relation to s.82).

[778] *Great Western Ry v London and County Banking Co*, above. See also *Commissioners of Taxation v English, Scottish and Australian Bank*, above, at 687. cf. *Matthews v Brown & Co* (1894) 10 T.L.R. 386.

[779] [1978] 1 W.L.R. 798.

[780] *Stoney Stanton Supplies (Coventry) Ltd v Midland Bank Ltd* [1966] 2 Lloyd's Rep. 373.

[781] [1985] 1 Lloyd's Rep. 259, especially at 263.

woman, opened an account with the bank in her nephew's name but stipulated that during her lifetime she was to be the only person authorised to draw on it. Lloyd J. held that it was an irresistible inference that the debt created by the opening of the account was due to the plaintiff and not to the nephew. It followed that the bank's customer was the plaintiff, who had arranged for the opening of the account and who intended to retain the control over it, and not the nephew, who was a mere nominee. The position would, undoubtedly, have differed if the drawing rights had been conferred on the nephew or his guardian. In such a situation—as demonstrated by *Rowlandson*'s case—the customer would have been the nephew.[782] In all cases it is important for the bank to know the identity of its customer. If a bank fails to have appropriate identification procedures in place, it risks committing an offence under the legislation designed to combat money laundering.[783]

(iii)   Nature of the Banker–Customer Relationship

Nature of relationship   As bankers perform different services for their custom-   **34-254** ers the nature of the relationship between the parties may vary from transaction to transaction. Thus, when the banker accepts the custody of documents or goods he acts as bailee[784] and when he agrees to hold moneys on trust he becomes a trustee. The basic relationship of banker and customer, however, is established, as has been shown, by the opening of an account. When a banker opens an account for the customer the relationship established is one of debtor and creditor.[785] When the account is in credit, the customer is the creditor and the banker the debtor. Consequently, funds deposited by the customer become the bank's money[786]; the customer acquires a debt or chose in action claimable from the bank. The position is reversed when the account is overdrawn. While the relationship of debtor and creditor prevails in all types of accounts opened by bankers, there are superadded obligations in some types of accounts, which will be discussed subsequently.

---

[782] But where an account is opened in the name of a company, it is the company and not the sole owner that is the bank's customer (*Diamantides v JP Morgan Chase Bank* [2005] EWHC 263 (Comm), upheld on different grounds [2005] EWCA Civ 1612).

[783] EU Member States had to implement the Fourth Money Laundering Directive 2015/849/EU by June 26, 2017. The UK did this through the Money Laundering, Terrorist Financing and Transfer of Funds (Information on the Payer) Regulations 2017 (SI 2017/692), which replace the Money Laundering Regulations 2007 (SI 2007/2157) and the Transfer of Funds (Information on the Payer) Regulations 2007 (SI 2007/3298). The Fifth Money Laundering Directive 2018/843/EU must be implemented in EU Member States by January 10, 2020. The Sanctions and Anti-Money Laundering Act 2018 comes into force on March 29, 2019 and, inter alia, enables the government to make regulations for the detection, investigation and prevention of money laundering or terrorist financing.

[784] See below, paras 34-438—34-440.

[785] *Foley v Hill* (1848) 2 H.L. Cas. 28; *Joachimson v Swiss Bank Corp* [1921] 3 K.B. 110; *Rowlandson v National Westminster Bank Ltd* [1978] 1 W.L.R. 798, 803–804; *Financial Services Authority v Anderson* [2010] EWHC 599 (Ch) at [44].

[786] Note that this is the position even if the funds deposited are trust property; the bank, though, would owe the duties of a trustee where it received the money in that capacity: *Space Investment Ltd v Canadian Imperial Bank of Commerce Trust Co (Bahamas) Ltd* [1986] 1 W.L.R. 1072.

(iv)   Fiduciary Relationship and Duty of Care

34-255 The general rule   Usually the relationship of banker and customer is not of a fiduciary nature.[787] Special circumstances, however, may constitute the banker a fiduciary agent, thus imposing on him a duty of full disclosure or a specific duty of care.[788] Three cases illustrate both the type of circumstances that may lead to the creation of a fiduciary relationship between banker and customer and the ambit of the doctrine. In the first case, *Woods v Martins Bank Ltd*,[789] the manager of a branch of the defendant bank was interested in obtaining the custom of the plaintiff, a young man without business experience, who had inherited a small legacy. The branch manager offered to advise the plaintiff on his investments and business affairs and eventually induced him to invest a substantial amount of money in shares of a private company. The manager failed to disclose to the plaintiff that that company was heavily indebted to the bank and that the head office was pressing for the reduction of its overdraft. The company went into liquidation and the shares turned out to be worthless. As a defence to the plaintiff's action in damages, the bank pleaded that the advice had been given to the plaintiff before he became a customer, to whom they might have owed a duty of care. Giving judgment for the plaintiff, Salmon J. held that, even if a relationship of banker and customer had not been established at the relevant time, the bank had nevertheless assumed fiduciary obligations towards the plaintiff when it agreed to become his financial adviser.[790]

---

[787] *Governor and Company of the Bank of Scotland v A Ltd* [2001] EWCA Civ 52, [2001] Lloyd's Rep. Bank. 73 at [25]; *JP Morgan Chase Bank v Springwell Navigation Corp* [2008] EWHC 1186 (Comm) at [573] (affirmed [2010] EWCA Civ 1221, [2010] 2 C.L.C. 705); *Forsta Ap-Fonden v Bank of New York Mellon SA* [2013] EWHC 3127 (Comm) at [173]; *Barclays Bank Plc v Svizera Holdings BV* [2014] EWHC 1020 (Comm) at [8]; *Bailey v Barclays Bank Plc* [2014] EWHC 2882 (QB) at [87]–[90]; *WW Property Investments Ltd v National Westminster Bank Plc* [2016] EWCA Civ 1142 at [57]; *Rehman v Santander UK Plc* [2018] EWHC 748 (QB) at [43]. The fact that the bank holds third party security to cover the customer's indebtedness does not convert the banker-customer relationship into a fiduciary one: *Kotonou v National Westminster Bank Plc* [2010] EWHC 1659 (Ch), [2011] 1 All E.R. (Comm) 1164 (held bank as lender owes no duty to borrower to call on third party security before it lapsed). Neither does a lender owe an equitable duty to act in good faith on a debt restructuring of its borrower merely because it holds security by way of mortgage when it does not exercise, or threaten to exercise, its powers under that security: *Standish v Royal Bank of Scotland Plc* [2018] EWHC 1829 (Ch) at [48]–[49]. But some activities of a multifunctional bank may give rise to fiduciary duties, e.g. acting as custodian of its customer's securities (*JP Morgan Chase Bank v Springwell Navigation Corp* [2008] EWHC 1186 (Comm) at [573] (affirmed [2010] EWCA Civ 1221, [2010] 2 C.L.C. 705); *Forsta Ap-Fonden v Bank of New York Mellon SA* [2013] EWHC 3127 (Comm) at [173]). Even then, the fact the bank is a fiduciary in some respects does not mean that it is a fiduciary in all respects (*Forsta Ap-Fonden v Bank of New York Mellon SA*, above, at [174]; *Saltri III v MD Mezzanine SA SICAR* [2012] EWHC 3025 (Comm), [2013] 1 All E.R. (Comm) 661 at [123]). For detailed coverage, see E.P. Ellinger, E. Lomnicka and C.V.M. Hare, *Ellinger's Modern Banking Law*, 5th edn (2011), Ch.5, s.4.

[788] See *Fahad Al Tamimi v Mohamad Khodari* [2009] EWCA Civ 1109, per Wilson L.J. at [42]: "The relationship between a lender and a borrower is not in principle a fiduciary relationship. The relationship between a bank manager and a customer may in certain circumstances acquire a fiduciary character".

[789] [1959] 1 Q.B. 55. See also *Standard Investments Ltd v Canadian Imperial Bank of Commerce*, 22 D.L.R. (4th) 410 (1985); *Hong Kong Bank of Canada v Phillips* [1998] Lloyd's Rep. Bank. 343; *United Pan-Europe Communications NV v Deutsche Bank AG* [2000] 2 B.C.L.C. 461, CA; *Diamantides v JP Morgan Chase Bank* [2005] EWCA Civ 1612. See also *Investors Compensation Scheme Ltd v West Bromwich Building Society* [1999] P.N.L.R. 496 at 509, Evans-Lombe J. (independent financial adviser).

[790] [1959] 1 Q.B. 55 at 72. Note that this case was decided before the principle of *Candler v Crane,*

Bundy's case   In the second case, *Lloyds Bank Ltd v Bundy*,[791] the Court of Appeal held that a bank owed a duty of "fiduciary care" to a customer from whom it had obtained a guarantee—covered by a charge over land—to secure an overdraft granted to another customer. Conceding that such a duty did not usually exist when a customer agreed to guarantee to his bank the obligations of a third party, Sir Eric Sachs emphasised that in the present case the guarantor—who was a customer of long standing—had relied on the bank's advice. As the bank had failed properly to advise the guarantor or to suggest that he obtain legal advice, the guarantee and charge were voidable on the ground of undue influence. The learned judge described the situations in which a fiduciary relationship could be created as follows:

> "... whilst disclaiming any intention of seeking to catalogue the elements of such a special relationship, it is perhaps of a little assistance to note some of those which have in the past frequently been found to exist where the court has been led to decide that this relationship existed as between adults of sound mind. Such cases tend to arise where someone relies on the guidance or advice of another, where the other is aware of that reliance and where the person upon whom reliance is placed obtains, or may obtain, a benefit from the transaction or has some other interest in it being concluded. In addition, there must, of course, be shown to exist a vital element ... referred to as confidentiality."[792]

34-256

Analysis of rule in Morgan's case   The principle in question has been clarified in *National Westminster Bank Plc v Morgan*.[793] The bank was asked to approve a refinancing arrangement for a customer whose improvident business ventures had led to his defaulting in payments under an existing mortgage, granted to a building society over the family home, owned jointly by the customer and his wife. As part of the proposed scheme, the object of which was to preclude the forced sale of the property by the building society, the bank demanded a charge over the same property. When the wife, who was also a customer of the bank, made it clear that she was unwilling to execute a charge covering the husband's business ventures, the branch manager advised her, erroneously but in good faith, that the charge was meant to cover only the amount advanced in respect of the refinancing arrangement aimed at salvaging the house. In reality, the bank's standard form of a charge was so phrased as to constitute the property a security for the chargors' total indebtedness to the bank. When the husband passed away, he was not indebted to the bank in respect of his business activities. The couple had, however, been in arrears of payments due under the refinancing arrangement and the bank proposed to sell the property to recover the amount due to it. Reversing the Court of Appeal's decision to set the mortgage aside, the House of Lords held that the bank had not committed a breach of a duty of care or a fiduciary duty owed to the wife. The relationship between the bank and the couple had remained one of banker and customer and, on the facts, there was no exercise of undue influence by the branch manager. Lord Scarman highlighted three points. First, the bank had not derived any hidden benefit from the transaction. The sole object of the refinancing scheme was

34-257

Christmas & Co [1951] 2 K.B. 164 was overruled by the House of Lords in *Hedley Byrne & Co Ltd v Heller & Partners Ltd* [1964] A.C. 465, so that liability could not be placed on negligence simpliciter.

[791] [1975] Q.B. 326.

[792] [1975] Q.B. 326 at 341. And see *Commonwealth Trading Bank of Australia v Smith* (1991) 102 Aust. L.R. 453; *Scaravelli v Bank of Montreal* (2004) 69 O.R. (3d) 295 at [37].

[793] [1985] A.C. 686.

to enable the couple to save their house from being sold by the building society. Secondly, the branch manager's statement was incorrect technically rather than in substance. Whilst the documents effectively secured the bank in respect of the husband's business debts, the bank had no intention of exercising any rights acquired by it under the charge in respect of such debts. Thirdly, the wife understood the general nature of the charge and of the transaction as a whole. In view of these facts, the mere inequality in the parties' bargaining power was immaterial. Emphasising the absence of a conflict of interests between the bank and the couple, his Lordship concluded that the bank had not been under a duty to advise the wife to seek independent legal advice.

34-258 **Limitations of general principle defined** It is clear from the cases considered in the foregoing paragraphs that banks are held to be subject to fiduciary duties or special duties of care only in exceptional cases. Basically, such a duty arises where the bank has assumed liability or has held itself out in a manner that justifies its imposition.[794] A duty of care is more readily invoked if the bank has derived some benefit, be it direct or indirect, from the transaction involved or if it placed itself in a situation which led to a conflict of interests between the customer and itself.[795] Cases of this sort are, of course, rare. In its ordinary dealings, the bank need not be unduly suspicious and cannot, for instance, be expected to initiate enquiries about the motive behind a payment instruction given to it by the customer's duly authorised agent unless there are some very clear indications that ought to alert the bank about the agent's fraudulent design.[796] Usually, all that is to be expected of a bank is the exercise of reasonable care in the discharge of its duties to customers. In determining whether a bank has acted negligently, regard must be had to all relevant circumstances as well as to standard banking practice. This principle emerges most clearly from an earlier authority, *Schioler v Westminster Bank Ltd*.[797] The plaintiff, a Danish national domiciled in Denmark but resident in the United Kingdom, maintained an account with the Guernsey branch of the defendant bank. Dividends due to the plaintiff from a Malaysian company were usually remitted by it for credit of this account in sterling, an arrangement under which the plaintiff was not liable to taxation in the United Kingdom. On one occasion, however, the dividend was remitted by a voucher expressed in foreign currency. In the absence of facilities in Guernsey for the negotiation of foreign currency drafts, the dividend voucher was forwarded by the Guernsey branch for collection to the bank's head office in England. The plaintiff, thereupon, became subject to payment of United Kingdom income tax, which was duly deducted by the bank. The plaintiff's action

---

[794] For such an exceptional case, see *Verity and Spindler v Lloyds Bank Plc* [1995] C.L.C. 1557 (bank manager assumed the role of borrowers' financial adviser); cf. *Murphy v HSBC Bank Plc* [2004] EWHC 467 (Ch) (bank assumed no responsibility to borrowers who had own solicitors and accountants to advise them).

[795] *Barclays Bank Plc v Quincecare Ltd* [1988] F.L.R. 166 at 185. Under the *Quincecare* duty, as it is known, a bank must refrain from executing an order to make a payment where it is "put on enquiry" that the order is an attempt to misappropriate funds.

[796] As in *Singularis Holdings Ltd (in liquidation) v Daiwa Capital Markets Europe Ltd* [2017] EWHC 257 (Ch), affirmed on other grounds [2018] EWCA Civ 84. There was no appeal on the judge's finding of the *Quincecare* duty of care (above), or breach of that duty, although Vos C. stressed (at [98]) that "it will be a rare situation for a bank to be put on inquiry; there is a high threshold" and that the instant case was "an unusual one, the circumstances of which are unlikely often to arise".

[797] [1970] 2 Q.B. 719.

in breach of contract was dismissed by Mocatta J., who held that the bank had not acted negligently in failing to ask for specific instructions when the dividend was received in foreign currency. As the bank had acted in accordance with established banking practice, it was not in breach of a duty of care.

Everyday transactions Another case in point is *Redmond v Allied British Banks* **34-259**
Plc.[798] The plaintiff paid to the credit of his account with the defendant bank a number of crossed cheques, bearing crossings accompanied by the words "not negotiable—account payee only", which bore on their backs the purported indorsements of the payees. These cheques were paid by the drawee bank when presented through the clearing system but as, in reality, the cheques had been circulated by persons who had no title to them, the defendant bank was sued in conversion by the true owners. The defendant bank settled these actions and then debited the plaintiff's account with the face value of the cheques. The plaintiff claimed that the bank ought to have warned him about the risk involved in the taking up of crossed cheques payable to a third party and bearing the words in question. Dismissing the action, Saville J. said that he could see no basis for a duty to advise or to warn a customer that there were risks attendant upon something which the customer proposed to do.[799] There was no need to imply such a duty in order to give business efficacy to the contract and there was no evidence to suggest that the circumstances of the transactions involved were such as to give rise to some duty of care in tort. His Lordship supported his view by a reference to the Privy Council's decision in *Tai Hing Cotton Mill Ltd v Liu Chong Hing Bank Ltd*.[800] It derives further support from cases[801] which show that the courts are unwilling to broaden the category of cases in which a duty of care in tort is imposed at law so as to enable a party to recover pure economic loss.[802]

---

[798] [1987] F.L.R. 307.

[799] See also *Winnetka Trading Corp v Julius Baer International Ltd* [2011] EWHC 2030 (Ch), [2012] 1 B.C.L.C. 588 at [90]–[97]. Similarly, an English bank acting as agent for collection of a cheque owes no duty of care to a foreign collecting bank, which is deemed to be its customer for these purposes, to advise on the effect of the Cheques Act 1992 on the meaning and significance of an "a/c payee only" crossing on the cheque: see *Honourable Society of the Middle Temple v Lloyds Bank Plc* [1999] 1 All E.R. (Comm) 193; *Linklaters (a firm) v HSBC Bank Plc* [2003] EWHC 1113 (Comm), [2003] 2 Lloyd's Rep. 545 (noted by Ellinger (2004) 120 L.Q.R. 226).

[800] [1986] A.C. 80, discussed below, para.34-345.

[801] *D & F Estates Ltd v Church Commissioners of England* [1989] A.C. 177; *Caparo Industries Plc v Dickman* [1990] 2 A.C. 605; *Murphy v Brentwood DC* [1991] 1 A.C. 398; see Vol.I, paras 18-024 et seq.

[802] As regards liability owed to third parties, arising in the context of an ordinary banking transaction, see: *TE Potterton Ltd v Northern Bank Ltd* [1993] 1 I.R. 413 (paying bank owes payee of cheque a duty to act carefully and honestly when advising payee of its reasons for dishonour of cheque); *Chapman v Barclays Bank Plc* [1997] Bank. L.R. 315, CA (bank owes no duty of care to third party who had financial interest in the borrower's affairs); *Wells v First National Commercial Bank* [1998] P.N.L.R. 552, CA (bank instructed to make funds transfer to named beneficiary owes no duty of care to that beneficiary and will not be liable to him if it fails to execute the instruction); *Abou-Rahmah v Abacha* [2005] EWHC 2662 (QB), [2006] 1 All E.R. (Comm) 247; affirmed. [2006] EWCA Civ 1492, [2007] 1 Lloyd's Rep. 115, but with no appeal on this issue (receiving bank does not owe a duty of care to the payer of funds, who is not its customer and to whom it has undertaken no special responsibility, to pay money received only to the beneficiary identified in the payer's instructions or, in the case of discrepancies, to clarify the identity of the beneficiary with the payer); *Customs and Excise Commissioners v Barclays Bank Plc* [2006] UKHL 28 [2007] 1 A.C. 181 (bank notified by a third party of freezing injunction granted to the third party against one of the bank's customers affecting an account held by the customer with the bank, owes no duty to the third party to take

34-260 **Effect of contractual documents on duty of care** Where a bank provides specialist banking services to financially sophisticated customers under the terms of contractual documentation drafted by specialist lawyers, the court will be slow to find a duty of care in tort going beyond the rights and obligations carefully set out in those documents.[803] There are a number of cases which illustrate that contractual terms, such as those which deny that advice has been given and/or relied upon, may prevent the coming into existence of any duty of care to advise.[804] The

---

reasonable care to comply with the terms of the injunction); *Riyad Bank v Ahli United Bank (UK) Plc* [2006] EWCA Civ 780, [2006] 2 Lloyd's Rep. 292 (where there is a contractual chain, the normal position is that the chain should not be bypassed by a claim in tort, but a duty of care may exist where discussions and representations are made directly to the party who suffers loss); *So v HSBC Bank Plc* [2009] EWCA Civ 296, [2009] 1 C.L.C. 503 (bank owes duty of care to third party when representing that it had accepted and intended to carry out its customer's instructions); *Chudley v Clydesdale Bank Plc (t/a Yorkshire Bank)* [2017] EWHC 2177 (Comm) at [248]–[250] (no sufficient proximity between bank and third party to establish duty of care on which to base claim that bank negligent in putting a "dangerous document" into circulation). Somewhat exceptionally, a bank arranging a capital market transaction was recently held liable for breach of a duty of care owed to third party bondholders: see *Golden Belt 1 Sukuk Company v BNP Paribas* [2017] EWHC 3182 (Comm) (bank arranging Sukuk—Islamic bond—issue owed tortious duty of care to bondholders to ensure promissory note that supported issuer's liability was properly executed).

803 *IFE Fund SA v Goldman Sachs International* [2006] EWHC 2887 (Comm), [2007] 1 Lloyd's Rep. 264 at [63], per Toulson J.; affirmed [2007] EWCA Civ 811, [2007] 2 Lloyd's Rep. 449 (syndicated loan); applied in *Maple Leaf Macro Volatility Master Fund v Rouvroy* [2009] EWHC 257 (Comm), [2009] 1 Lloyd's Rep. 475 at [369]. See also *Barclays Bank Plc v Svizera Holdings BV* [2014] EWHC 1020 (Comm) at [68]–[70] (applying the opinion of Lord Hodge in *Grant Estates Ltd v Royal Bank of Scotland Plc* [2012] CSOH 133 at [73] as to when a tortious duty of care to advise would arise in the case of a bank or other financial institution). But contrast *Sumitomo Bank Ltd v Banque Bruxelles Lambert SA* [1997] 1 Lloyd's Rep. 487, where Langley J. held that provisions as to the arranging bank's duties, rights and exonerations under the syndicated loan agreement did not prevent, and were not inconsistent with, a general duty of care being owed to syndicate members. See also *Golden Belt 1 Sukuk Company v BNP Paribas* [2017] EWHC 3182 (Comm), where standard disclaimers in Offering Circular did not prevent bank arranging Sukuk—Islamic bond—issue being held in breach of tortious duty of care to bondholders to ensure promissory note that supported issuer's liability was properly executed. The contractual documents may also regulate the existence and extent of a fiduciary relationship, especially where the parties are both substantial financial institutions dealing on an arm's length basis (*Forsta Ap-Fonden v Bank of New York Mellon SA* [2013] EWHC 3127 (Comm) at [177]–[178]; *Saltri III v MD Mezzanine SA SICAR* [2012] EWHC 3025 (Comm) at [123(f)]).

804 *Springwell Navigation Corp v JP Morgan Chase Bank* [2008] EWHC 1186 (Comm), affirmed [2010] EWCA Civ 1221, [2010] 2 C.L.C. 705; *IFE Fund SA v Goldman Sachs International* [2007] EWCA Civ 811, [2007] 2 Lloyd's Rep. 449; *Peekay Intermark v Australia & New Zealand Banking Group* [2006] EWCA Civ 386, [2006] 2 Lloyd's Rep. 511; *Valse Holdings v Merrill Lynch International Bank* [2004] EWHC 2471 (Comm); *Bankers Trust International Plc v PT Dharmala Sakti Sejahtera* [1996] C.L.C. 518; *Credit Suisse International v Stichting Vestia Groep* [2014] EWHC 3103 (Comm) at [113]–[114]. See also *Titan Steel Wheels Ltd v Royal Bank of Scotland Plc* [2010] EWHC 211 (Comm), [2010] 2 Lloyd's Rep. 92 (held contract terms gave rise to contractual estoppel or, alternatively, negatived the existence of a duty of care); *Raiffeisen Zentralbank Österreich AG v Royal Bank of Scotland Plc* [2010] EWHC 1392 (Comm), [2011] 1 Lloyd's Rep. 123 (held no representation/no responsibility provisions in Information Memorandum gave rise to contractual estoppel). The decision of the Court of Appeal in *Springwell Navigation Corp v JP Morgan Chase Bank* [2010] EWCA Civ 1221, [2010] 2 C.L.C. 705, is important because it upholds the doctrine of contractual estoppel, applying the approach taken by the Court of Appeal (possibly obiter) in *Peekay Intermark Ltd v ANZ Banking Group*, above. Followed in *Cassa di Risparmio della Repubblica di San Marino SpA v Barclays Bank Ltd* [2011] EWHC 484 (Comm), [2011] 1 C.L.C. 701 at [492]–[508]; *Standard Chartered Bank v Ceylon Petroleum Corp* [2011] EWHC 1785 (Comm) at [526]–[534], affirmed on different ground [2012] EWCA Civ 1049; *Barclays Bank Plc v Svizera Holdings BV* [2014] EWHC 1020 (Comm) at [58]–[63], [71]; *Crestsign Ltd v National Westminster Bank*

prevailing view has been that where these terms define the basis upon which the parties act, they do not constitute exclusion clauses falling within the ambit of the Unfair Contract Terms Act 1977 or s.3 of the Misrepresentation Act 1967,[805]

Plc [2014] EWHC 3043 (Ch) at [119]; *Credit Suisse International v Stichting Vestia Groep* [2014] EWHC 3103 (Comm) at [307]–[308] (contractual estoppel applied to agreement about a state of affairs in the future) and [309]–[310] (questioning whether contractual estoppel is really a form of estoppel at all); *Thornbridge Ltd v Barclays Bank Plc* [2015] EWHC 3430 (QB) at [111] (appeal dismissed, Unreported January 9, 2018); *Marz Ltd v Bank of Scotland Plc* [2017] EWHC 3618 (Ch) at [240]–[275]. But note that contract terms may not assist a bank when relied upon in a different context from the one in which they were intended to apply (*Camerata Property Inc v Credit Suisse Securities (Europe) Ltd* [2011] EWHC 479 (Comm), [2011] 2 B.C.L.C. 54 at [184]: for related proceedings, see [2012] EWHC 7 (Comm) and [2013] EWHC 29 (Comm)) or where the terms are limited in their scope (*UBS AG (London Branch) v Kommunale Wasserwerke Leipzig GmbH* [2014] EWHC 3615 (Comm) at [773]–[784]), and that a "disclaimer" cannot create a contractual estoppel when it is not part of the contract (*Taberna Europe CDO II Plc v Selskabet AF1.September 2008 (In Bankruptcy)* [2015] EWHC 871 (Comm) at [120]; reversed on appeal [2016] EWCA Civ 1262, where Court of Appeal held at [19]–[20] that a non-contractual "duty-negating" clause fell outside s.3 of the Misrepresentation Act 1967 because it was found in the very document that was said to contain the misrepresentation). For criticism of recent trend towards "documentary fundamentalism", see G. McMeel [2011] L.M.C.L.Q. 185. In the *Springwell* case [2008] EWHC 1186 (Comm) at [431]ff, Gloster J. held that an investment bank owed no general advisory duty to a sophisticated investor who was aware of the risks he was running. Her decision on this point was not challenged on appeal; however, the Court of Appeal (above, at [123]) accepted Gloster J.'s tentative conclusion (above, at [108]) that there might be a "low level duty of care" on the part of a salesman not to make any negligent misstatements and to use reasonable care not to recommend a highly risky investment without pointing out that it was such. However, the courts have tended to reject claims based on the existence of an advisory duty of care in the context of selling financial investments, e.g., most recently, *Property Alliance Group Ltd v Royal Bank of Scotland Plc* [2018] EWCA Civ 355; *London Executive Aviation Ltd v Royal Bank of Scotland Plc* [2018] EWHC 74 (Ch); *Marz Ltd v Bank of Scotland Plc* [2017] EWHC 3618 (Ch); *Finch v Lloyds TSB Bank Plc* [2016] EWHC 1236 (QB) at [52]–[58]; *Thornbridge Ltd v Barclays Bank Plc* [2015] EWHC 3430 (QB) at [96] (appeal dismissed, Unreported January 9, 2018); cf. *Rubenstein v HSBC Bank Plc* [2011] EWHC 2304 (QB), [2011] 2 C.L.C. 459 at [70], where there was a one-to-one enquiry about a specific investment transaction: reversed in part (on causation) [2012] EWCA Civ 1184, [2013] 1 All E.R. (Comm) 915. For brief discussion of statutory regulatory regime governing the sale of financial products by banks, see para.34-434 below.

[805] *IFE Fund SA v Goldman Sachs International* [2006] EWHC 2887 (Comm), [2007] 1 Lloyd's Rep. 264 at [70]–[71], per Toulson J., affirmed [2007] EWCA Civ 811, [2007] 2 Lloyd's Rep. 449 at [28]; *Springwell Navigation Corp v JP Morgan Chase Bank* [2008] EWHC 1186 (Comm) at [671], affirmed [2010] EWCA Civ 1221, [2010] 2 C.L.C. 705; *Titan Steel Wheels Ltd v Royal Bank of Scotland Plc* [2010] EWHC 211 (Comm), [2010] 2 Lloyd's Rep. 92 at [98]; *Raiffeisen Zentralbank Österreich AG v Royal Bank of Scotland Plc* [2010] EWHC 1392 (Comm), [2011] 1 Lloyd's Rep. 123 at [316]–[317]; *Marz Ltd v Bank of Scotland Plc* [2017] EWHC 3618 (Ch) at [240]–[275], distinguishing *First Tower Trustees Ltd v CDS (Superstores International) Ltd* [2017] 4 W.L.R. 73 at [31]–[32]. In *Springwell*, the Court of Appeal held (at [181]–[182]) that "no representation" and "non-reliance" provisions of the relevant contract were caught by s.3 of the Misrepresentation Act 1967 because they were "an attempt retrospectively to alter the character and effect of what had gone before and so in substance an attempt to exclude or restrict liability" (citing Christopher Clarke J. in *Raiffeisen*, above, at [315], who also said, at [314], that "the key question … is whether the clause attempts to rewrite history or parts company with reality"). Nevertheless, the Court of Appeal held that the terms were reasonable when taken in context and in the light of the fact that the principal behind Springwell was a sophisticated investor in emerging market investments who was conscious of the risks involved. cf. *Thornbridge Ltd v Barclays Bank Plc* [2015] EWHC 3430 (QB) at [105] (appeal dismissed, Unreported January 9, 2018), where H.H.J. Moulder, sitting as a judge of the High Court, said "the test is not whether the clause attempts to rewrite history or parts company with reality. The first step is to determine as a matter of construction whether the terms define the basis upon which the parties were transacting business or whether they were clauses inserted as a means of evading liability"; *Sears v Minco Plc* [2016] EWHC 433 (Ch) at [74]–[84] (see criticism of the

although such a term may constitute an unfair term when found in a "consumer contract" within the meaning of the Consumer Rights Act 2015.[806]

However, in *First Tower Trustees Ltd v CDS (Superstores International) Ltd*,[807] the Court of Appeal recently held that a non-reliance clause, binding on the representee through the doctrine of contractual estoppel, was caught by s.3 of the Misrepresentation Act 1967, and subject to the reasonableness test in the Unfair Contract Terms Act 1977, where the clause in substance excluded liability for misrepresentation which would otherwise have arisen. The reasoning of Leggatt L.J. appears to be of wide application[808]:

> "... whenever a contracting party relies on the principle of contractual estoppel to argue that, by reason of a contract term, the other party to the contract is prevented from asserting a fact which is necessary to establish liability for a pre-contractual misrepresentation, the term falls within s.3 of the Misrepresentation Act 1967."

34-261 **Money laundering** In *Shah v HSBC Private Bank (UK) Ltd*,[809] Hamblen J. considered what, if any, obligations a bank owed to its customer when it froze the customer's account having made an authorised disclosure under s.338 of the Proceeds of Crime Act 2002 (POCA). He held that the trigger for disclosure to the authorities under POCA was the bank's subjective suspicion that a requested transfer involved funds which were criminal property.[810] The suspicion had to be genuinely held but it did not matter whether or not there were reasonable grounds for the suspicion, nor did it have to be rational.[811] Thus far, the Court of Appeal

---

reasoning in these cases in *First Tower Trustees Ltd v CDS (Superstores International) Ltd* [2018] EWCA Civ 1396 at [66], [110]). For a non-exhaustive list of factors that may be taken into account when determining whether a "basis clause" or an "exclusion clause" for the purposes of the Unfair Contract Terms Act 1977 or s.3 of the Misrepresentation Act 1967, see *Carney v NM Rothschild & Sons Ltd* [2018] EWHC 958 (Comm) at [94] (at [97]–[100] the court also considered the effect of "basis clauses" in the context of the "unfair relationship" provisions in ss.140A and 140B of the Consumer Credit Act 1974). It should be noted that different, more stringent, rules apply in the case of fraud: see Vol.I, para.15-150.

[806] Consumer Rights Act 2015 (CRA 2015) Pt 2. Note also CRA 2015 s.50(1), which effectively makes anything that is said or written to a consumer about the bank, or the service provided by the bank, a term of any contract to supply the service as between bank and consumer if relied upon by the consumer: s.50(2) allows the bank to qualify any pre-contractual representations, but only if it does so on the "same occasion" or if it represents a "change to [what was said or written] that has been expressly agreed between the consumer and the trader". See further, para.38-572 below.

[807] [2018] EWCA Civ 1396 at [39]–[67], [89]. The particular non-reliance clause in issue was held to be unreasonable under the statutory test because it rendered a landlord's replies to its tenant's pre-contract enquiries worthless, but Lewison L.J. accepted, at [67], that such a clause may well be reasonable "in cases involving the sale of complex financial products to sophisticated investors".

[808] At [111]; e.g. Leggatt L.J.'s reasoning is arguably wide enough to catch a "no advice" clause (depending on the facts). But what of a clause which states that a bank gives no warranty of completeness of information provided and has no obligation to update such information? cf. *Parmar v Barclays Bank Plc* [2018] EWHC 1027 (Ch) at [133], where it was held that a bank cannot rely on a basis clause to exclude or restrict any duty where a claim is made by a private person under s.138D of the Financial Services and Markets Act 2000 for breach of statutory duty (see the FCA's Conduct of Business Sourcebook r.2.1.2).

[809] [2009] EWHC 79 (QB), [2009] 1 Lloyd's Rep. 328.

[810] At [45], applying *K Ltd v National Westminster Bank Plc* [2006] EWCA Civ 1039, [2007] 1 W.L.R. 311, where the Court of Appeal adopted the definition of suspicion given in *R. v Da Silva* [2007] 1 W.L.R. 303, stating that the bank only has to consider that there is a more than fanciful possibility that the relevant facts exist.

[811] At [45] and [47].

agreed with Hamblen J.[812] However, their Lordships considered that the judge had been wrong to say that the customer was left to rely only on an assertion of bad faith (which he had not made).[813] There was no reason why the customer could not require the bank to prove its case that it had the relevant suspicion and be entitled to pursue the case to trial so that the bank could make good its contention in this respect.[814] But their Lordships held that there was no reasonable prospect that a claim based on negligence would succeed.[815] Hamblen J. had accepted that a banker's duty of care was not completely excluded by POCA and that, in principle, delay in making a relevant disclosure might be a breach of that duty.[816] However, he had held that there was no evidence of such delay since all the disclosures had been made within two days of receiving the relevant payment instruction. Their Lordships agreed with the judge on this issue.[817]

(v) Banks and Undue Influence

Undue influence and suretyship transactions   Banks most commonly come up   34-262
against the doctrine of undue influence when they seek to enforce third party security.[818] In rare cases the bank may be accused of having exercised undue influence itself,[819] but it is more usual for a person who has given security to the bank to cover the indebtedness of the bank's customer to allege that they did so as a result of the undue influence, misrepresentation or other wrongdoing of that customer. The typical case is where the wife charges her interest in the matrimonial home to secure the borrowing of her husband. She may have done this as a result of his undue influence or misrepresentation. The wife may later seek to raise the husband's wrongdo-

---

[812] [2010] EWCA Civ 31, [2011] 1 All E.R. (Comm) 67 at [21]. Re-iterated by Supperstone J. when delivering judgment at the trial of the action: *Shah v HSBC Private Bank (UK) Ltd* [2012] EWHC 1283 (QB) at [67]–[69].

[813] At [22].

[814] Hence the Court of Appeal reversed Hamblen J.'s decision to give summary judgment to the bank on the customer's claim for damages for alleged loss suffered as a result of the bank's breach of duty in failing to carry out his payment instructions. Delivering judgment at the trial of the action (see [2012] EWHC 1283 (QB)), Supperstone J. dismissed the customer's claim, holding that (1) there was an implied term in the banking contract that permitted the bank, because it suspected money laundering, to delay the execution of the customer's payment instructions until it received consent under POCA (at [45], [236]); (2) there was no duty on the bank to provide the customer with information in relation to the delay and that, in any event, there was an implied term in the banking contract that permitted the bank to refuse to provide that information where doing so might contravene its duties under POCA (at [169], [171]–[172], [238]). For related proceedings, see [2011] EWCA Civ 1154 (on disclosure of the names of employees who had reported their suspicions); [2011] EWCA Civ 1669 (on amendment to allege bad faith on the part of bank employees).

[815] At [35]–[36].

[816] [2009] EWHC 79 (QB), [2009] 1 Lloyd's Rep. 328 at [58].

[817] [2010] EWCA Civ 31, [2011] 1 All E.R. (Comm) 67 at [35].

[818] See Vol.I, paras 8-058 et seq. for general discussion of the doctrine of undue influence.

[819] The normal bank–customer relationship does not give rise to a presumption of undue influence (*National Westminster Bank Plc v Morgan* [1985] A.C. 686, HL: see para.34-257 above), but see *Lloyds Bank Ltd v Bundy* [1975] Q.B. 326 (para.34-256 above) for an exceptional case. *Libyan Investment Authority v Goldman Sachs International* [2016] EWHC 2530 (Ch) illustrates just how hard it is for a claim based on undue influence (or unconscionable bargain) to succeed where commercial parties transact with each other and each side can be expected to negotiate their own terms without regard to the other side's interests. See also *Holyoake v Candy* [2017] EWHC 3397 (Ch) at [404]–[408] (court rejected allegation that loan agreement between seasoned businessmen induced by actual undue influence).

ing against the bank when it attempts to enforce the security against her. In *Barclays Bank Plc v O'Brien*,[820] the first of two seminal decisions of the House of Lords in this area, it was held that the wife's prospects of having the security set aside by the court turn on whether her husband acted as the bank's agent,[821] or whether the bank had actual or constructive notice of his undue influence or other wrongdoing.[822]

34-263 The burden is on the wife (or other surety) adequately to plead and prove that the bank had notice of the undue influence or wrongdoing.[823] In *Royal Bank of Scotland Plc v Etridge (No.2)*,[824] the second seminal case in this area, the House of Lords held that, where a wife offers to stand surety for her husband's debts, it is enough for her to show that the bank was aware of the husband/wife relationship. In other cases, the surety must establish that the bank knew that there was a non-commercial relationship between the surety and the debtor and that the transaction was on its face to the disadvantage of the surety. The burden of proof then shifts to the bank to show that it took all reasonable steps to bring home to the wife (or other surety) the risks involved in entering into the transaction.[825] The bank's failure to take all reasonable steps does not automatically mean that the security will be set aside. The wife (or other surety) must also establish either that the transaction was procured by undue influence (or other wrongdoing), or that the basic facts of the "evidential presumption" that it was so procured by undue influence exist and that presumption has not otherwise been rebutted.[826]

34-264 **O'Brien's case** In *Barclays Bank Plc v O'Brien*,[827] the husband, who was an accountant, persuaded his wife to execute a charge over the matrimonial home to back a guarantee given by him to secure the debts due to the bank from a company in which he had an interest. The relevant mortgage documents were executed by the wife at the bank's premises. She was not given the chance to read them and, in addition, the clerk who proffered the documents for her signature failed to draw her attention to a side-letter, in which the wife purported to acknowledge that she understood the nature of the transaction and that the bank had recommended that she take independent legal advice. The clerk further failed to carry out the branch manager's instruction to explain to her the nature of the transaction. Reversing the trial judge's decision, the Court of Appeal set the charge aside.[828] After a review of

---

[820] [1994] 1 A.C. 180.
[821] e.g. *Avon Finance Co Ltd v Bridger* [1985] 2 All E.R. 281; *Kingsnorth Trust Ltd v Bell* [1986] 1 W.L.R. 119. But in *O'Brien* (at 195), the House of Lords criticised the artificiality of the agency analysis in most surety transactions, and it is not likely to be applied unless the debtor acts as the bank's agent "in a real sense" (*CIBC Mortgages Plc v Pitt* [1994] 1 A.C. 200 at 211, HL).
[822] Note that the equitable concept of constructive notice is not used in a conventional manner in this context: see *Royal Bank of Scotland Plc v Etridge (No.2)* [2001] UKHL 44, [2002] 2 A.C. 773 at [39], [108] and [145].
[823] *Barclays Bank Plc v Boulter* [1999] 1 W.L.R. 1919, HL.
[824] [2001] UKHL 44, [2002] 2 A.C. 773 at [84].
[825] *Barclays Bank Plc v Boulter*, above.
[826] As to which, see Vol.I, paras 8-075—8-102. See, e.g. *Royal Bank of Scotland Plc v Chandra* [2011] EWCA Civ 192, [2011] N.P.C. 26 (held at [40] that no misrepresentation or undue influence); *Davies v AIB Group (UK) Plc* [2012] EWHC 2178 (Ch), [2012] 2 P. & C.R. 19 (held at [113]–[114] that no undue influence: husband made full disclosure of the entire transaction and all of the relevant documents so as to put wife's solicitor in the position to tender full and informed advice to her).
[827] [1994] 1 A.C. 180.
[828] [1993] Q.B. 109.

both the 19th-century decisions and the modern cases in point, Scott L.J. concluded that many of the relevant authorities treated a certain class of surety, encompassing married women and other persons such as aged relatives, as a "protected class". Scott L.J. concluded that—as a matter of policy—the existence of such a class of protected debtor should be recognised, although its existence was not postulated in all the authorities in point.

The House of Lords affirmed the Court of Appeal's decision, but on a different **34-265** reasoning. To start with, Lord Browne-Wilkinson emphasised that it was essential that a law designed to protect the vulnerable, such as wives and cohabitees, should not render the matrimonial home unacceptable as security to financial institutions. His Lordship then reviewed the authorities respecting undue influence and concluded that, although there was no presumption of undue influence as between husband and wife, it was open to the wife to prove that, in her particular case, she did leave decisions on financial affairs to her husband. By doing so she established that "she reposed confidence and trust in her husband in relation to financial affairs and therefore undue influence [was] to be presumed".[829]

Actual or constructive notice His Lordship then considered the situations in **34-266** which the undue influence exercised by the husband over the wife would induce a Court of Equity to set aside a charge or mortgage granted by the wife to a third party such as a bank. Naturally, such a charge would be set aside if the wrongdoing husband was acting as the bank's agent in obtaining the security from the wife. In such a case the bank would be fixed with the wrongdoing of its agent. His Lordship added:

"Apart from this, if the creditor bank has notice, actual or constructive, of undue influence exercised by the husband (and consequently of the wife's equity to set aside the transaction) the creditor will take subject to that equity and the wife can set aside the transaction against the creditor ... as well as against the husband."[830]

Lord Browne-Wilkinson concluded that, if the doctrine of notice was properly applied, there was no need to postulate a special equitable doctrine applicable to charges executed by a class of debtor comprising wives and other persons such as cohabitees and aged parents. The key to the problem was to identify the circumstance in which the bank or other creditor was to be taken to have had notice of the wife's (or other chargor's) equity to set aside the transaction. His Lordship emphasised that, generally, a person would have constructive notice of such an equity where he was in command of facts which put him on inquiry as to the possible existence of the defect. Applying this general principle, his Lordship said:

"... a creditor is put on inquiry when a wife offers to stand surety for her husband's debts by the combination of two factors: (a) the transaction is on its face not to the financial advantage of the wife; and (b) there is a substantial risk in transactions of that kind that,

---

[829] [1994] 1 A.C. at 190.
[830] [1994] 1 A.C. 190 at 191. For further consideration of what constitutes constructive notice, contrast the approach of Lord Brown-Wilkinson in *O'Brien*, at 195–196, with that of Millet J. in *MacMillan Inc v Bishopsgate Investment Trust Plc (No.3)* [1995] 1 W.L.R. 978, 1014; and for resolution of any inconsistency between the two approaches, see Lord Neuberger M.R. in *Sinclair Investments (UK) Ltd v Versailles Trade Finance Ltd* [2011] EWCA Civ 347, [2012] Ch. 435 at [109], as explained by Lord Clarke in *Crédit Agricole Corporation and Investment Bank v Papadimitriou* [2015] UKPC 13 at [12]–[21].

in procuring the wife to act as surety, the husband has committed a legal or equitable wrong that entitles the wife to set aside the transaction."[831]

34-267 Avoiding constructive notice His Lordship recognised that a bank could not be expected to conduct a detailed examination of the circumstances of each case in which a wife, a cohabitee or an aged parent offered to execute a charge over a piece of property. The bank could avoid being fixed with constructive notice by taking reasonable steps to satisfy itself that the wife's consent was freely given. It satisfies these requirements by insisting "that the wife attend a private meeting (in the absence of the husband) with a representative of the creditor at which she is told of the extent of her liability as surety, warned of the risk she is running and urged to take independent legal advice".[832]

34-268 O'Brien guidelines in practice The practice of banks, both before and after the House of Lords issued its guidance in *O'Brien*, has been, and remains, not to have a private meeting with the surety.[833] It appears that banks have preferred not to adopt this course, probably because of the risk that the surety could later assert that the bank had somehow misrepresented the position. Instead, banks have made it their standard practice to insist both that the surety obtains independent legal advice on the nature and effect of the documents that she is to sign, and that the legal adviser confirms to the bank in writing that such advice has been given.[834] In *Royal Bank of Scotland Plc v Etridge (No.2)*,[835] the House of Lords expressed general approval of this practice, subject to certain controls, and dropped the requirement that the bank must have a private meeting with the surety.

34-269 Etridge's case In 2001, the House of Lords revisited this "difficult corner of the law" in *Royal Bank of Scotland Plc v Etridge (No.2)*.[836] The House of Lords heard eight appeals together. In seven of the appeals, the appellant was a wife who had agreed to subject her property, usually her interest in the matrimonial home, to a charge in favour of the bank in order to provide security for the payment of her husband's debts, or the debts of a company by means of which her husband carried on business. In each case the bank had started proceedings for possession of

---

831 [1994] 1 A.C. 190 at 196. cf. *CIBC Mortgages Plc v Pitt* [1994] 1 A.C. 200, heard at the same time as *O'Brien*, where the loan appeared on its face to be a joint one for the benefit of both husband and wife.

832 [1994] 1 A.C. 190 at 196; but note that Lord Browne-Wilkinson added that, in circumstances in which a bank had knowledge of specific facts which rendered undue influence probable rather than a mere possibility, it ought to insist that (and not only to suggest) that independent advice be taken by the chargor.

833 *Royal Bank of Scotland Plc v Etridge (No.2)* [2001] UKHL 44, [2002] 2 A.C. 773 at [51].

834 *Royal Bank of Scotland Plc v Etridge (No.2)* [2001] UKHL 44, [2002] 2 A.C. 773 at [51]. This probably goes further than contemplated in *Barclays Bank Plc v O'Brien* [1994] 1 A.C. 180, since Lord Browne-Wilkinson considered (at 197) that it would only be the exceptional case in which the bank should not only advise the surety to obtain independent legal advice but should insist that she do so. See also the Standards of Lending Practice for Personal Customers (para.34-222 above) at p.7 (Account maintenance and servicing), point 8, and p.11 (Customer vulnerability), and the Standards of Lending Practice for Business Customers (para.34-223) at pp.6–7 (Product sale), points 13 and 14, pp.9–10 (Product execution), point 6; and pp.14–15 (Vulnerability).

835 [2001] UKHL 44, [2002] 2 A.C. 773 at [55].

836 [2001] UKHL 44, [2002] 2 A.C. 773. The quote is from Lord Hobhouse at [98]. The opinion of Lord Nicholls was said to command "the unqualified support of all members of the House": per Lord Bingham at [3].

the mortgaged property, but the wife had defended the action on the ground that her agreement to grant the charge was brought about by the undue influence or misrepresentation of her husband and that, in the circumstances, the bank should not be allowed to enforce the charge against her. In each case the issue was whether the bank had notice of the husband's impropriety or alleged impropriety. In each case the bank had some reason to believe that a solicitor had acted for the wife in the transaction in question. So the question for their Lordships to decide was the extent to which the solicitor's participation, or believed participation, had absolved the bank of the need to make further inquiries about the circumstances in which the wife was persuaded to agree to grant the charge, or to take any further steps to satisfy itself that her consent was a true and informed consent.[837]

Bank put on inquiry   In *Etridge*, the House of Lords recognised that Lord   **34-270** Browne-Wilkinson had not used the equitable concept of constructive notice in *O'Brien* in a conventional manner.[838] By contrast, in *Etridge* the House spoke in terms of the bank, or other creditor, being "put on inquiry".[839] Two factors combine to put the bank on inquiry: the non-commercial relationship between the surety and the debtor and the fact that the transaction is on its face to the disadvantage of the surety. This is a low threshold and Lord Nicholls held it to be crossed whenever a wife offers to stand surety for her husband's debts.[840]

Relationship between surety and debtor   A bank will be put on inquiry where   **34-271** a wife guarantees her husband's debts.[841] Similarly, the bank will be put on inquiry where a husband guarantees his wife's debts or there is a heterosexual or homosexual relationship between surety and debtor (cohabitation not being essential), provided the bank is aware of the relationship.[842] The same rule applies where the bank knows of a parent and child relationship between debtor and surety.[843] Similarly, the rule applies where the bank is aware that there is a relationship of trust and confidence as between surety and debtor even though that relationship is not sexual.[844] However, *Etridge* is a landmark decision because Lord Nicholls was prepared to go even further than this. His Lordship did not want to draw an arbitrary boundary between those relationships that would activate the *O'Brien* principle and those that would not. Lord Nicholls held that, in future, banks

---

[837] The eighth appeal before the House, *Kenyon-Brown v Desmond Banks & Co (a firm)*, was a case in which the wife had sued the solicitor who acted for her in this type of transaction alleging breaches of duty owed to her by the solicitor. This case raised an issue as to the extent of the duty lying on a solicitor who acts for a wife who is proposing to grant a charge over her property as security for her husband's, or his company's, debts.

[838] At [39], [108] and [145].

[839] At [44], where Lord Nicholls went on to accept that even this phrase is a misnomer as the bank is not required to make any inquiries.

[840] At [44].

[841] At [44], [46]. But that does not mean that the wife will easily be able to establish undue influence in the first place. Lord Nicholls (at [30]) did not think that, in the ordinary course, a wife's guarantee of her husband's business debts was to be regarded as a transaction which, failing proof to the contrary, was explicable only on the basis that it had been procured by the exercise of undue influence by the husband. See also Lord Scott at [162]. See above, Vol.I, paras 8-093—8-094.

[842] At [47].

[843] At [84].

[844] At [83], citing *Crédit Lyonnais Bank Nederland NV v Burch* [1997] 1 All E.R. 144.

should regulate their affairs on the basis that they are put on inquiry in every case where the relationship between the surety and the debtor is non-commercial.[845]

34-272 **Nature of the transaction** In *Etridge*, the House of Lords stressed that there would be other cases where a bank is not put on inquiry: e.g. where money is advanced to husband and wife jointly, unless the bank is aware that the loan is being made for the husband's purposes, as distinct from their joint purposes.[846] Cases where the wife stands surety for the debts of a company whose shares are held by her and her husband were declared to be less clear-cut.[847] However, Lord Nicholls considered that a bank is put on inquiry in such cases, even where the wife is a director or secretary of the company. He held that the shareholding interests, and the identity of the directors, was not a reliable guide to the identity of the person who actually had control of the conduct of the company's business.[848]

34-273 **Reasonable steps that a bank should take** Once put on inquiry, Lord Nicholls considered that a bank should not be expected to discover for itself whether a wife's consent had been procured by the exercise of undue influence, nor should it be expected to insist on confirmation from a solicitor that the solicitor has satisfied himself that the wife's consent has not been procured by undue influence.[849] Neither should the bank be compelled to hold a personal meeting with the surety.[850] According to Lord Nicholls[851]:

"The furthest a bank can be expected to go is to take reasonable steps to satisfy itself that the wife has had brought home to her, in a meaningful way, the practical implications of the proposed transaction. This does not wholly eliminate the risk of undue influence or misrepresentation. But it does mean that a wife enters into a transaction with her eyes open so far as the basic elements of the transaction are concerned."

---

[845] At [87]–[89]. See *Bank of Scotland Plc v Makris* Unreported May 15, 2009 (relationship between surety and debtor was held not to be non-commercial where debtor was joint venture company and surety was director and shareholder who took active interest in the company). See also *Trustees of Beardsley Theobalds Retirement Benefit Scheme v Yardley* [2011] EWHC 1380 (QB) at [47] (employee's guarantee of employer's obligations as tenant under lease). But the *O'Brien* principle only applies to suretyship transactions, i.e. tripartite transactions as described by Lord Nicholls in *Etridge* at [43]: *Chancery Client Partners Ltd v MRC 957 Ltd* [2016] EWHC 2142 (Ch) at [28]–[29]; *Deane v Coutts & Co* [2018] EWHC 1657 (Ch) at [125]–[127].

[846] *CIBC Mortgages Plc v Pitt* [1994] 1 A.C. 200, HL. See also *Mortgage Agency Services Number Two Ltd v Chater* [2003] EWCA Civ 490, [2004] 1 P. & C.R. 4 (joint loan to mother and son); *Bradley v Governor of the Bank of Ireland* [2016] NICH 11 (joint loan to mother and son). Similarly, a third party is unlikely to be put on constructive notice when the agreement will confer a joint tenancy on the wife: *Darjan Estate Co Plc v Hurley* [2012] EWHC 189 (Ch), [2012] 1 W.L.R. 1782 at [34], and above, Vol.I, para.8-119. But contrast *Davies v AIB Group (UK) Plc* [2012] EWHC 2178 (Ch), [2012] 2 P. & C.R. 19 at [117], obiter (bank aware that joint loan being made for purposes of husband's company, as distinct from their joint purposes).

[847] See, e.g. *Goode Durrant Administration v Biddulph* [1994] 2 F.L.R. 551 (a join loan case).

[848] At [49]. See *Mahon v FBN Bank (UK) Ltd* [2011] EWHC 1432 (Ch), [2011] B.P.I.R. 1029 (bank still put on inquiry despite wife being sole shareholder and company secretary); cf. *National Westminster Bank Plc v Alfano* [2012] EWHC 1020 (QB) at [54] (guarantors were directors or senior managers of debtor company). For loan made to family partnership, see *O'Neill v Ulster Bank Ltd* [2015] NICA 64, [2016] B.P.I.R. 126 at [17] (arguable that situation analogous to where wife stands surety for loan made to company in which she is a shareholder).

[849] At [53].

[850] At [53]. See also Lord Clyde at [94]–[95]; Lord Scott at [148].

[851] At [54].

Lord Nicholls stressed that, *in the ordinary case*, it would be reasonable for the bank to rely upon confirmation from a solicitor,[852] acting for the wife,[853] that he has advised the wife appropriately.[854] However, *in an extraordinary case*, where the bank knows that the solicitor has not duly advised the wife or if the bank knows facts from which it ought to have realised that the wife has not received the appropriate advice, it will proceed at its own risk.[855]

Future transactions Lord Nicholls also gave detailed guidance to banks as to how they should act in future when looking to the fact that the wife has been, or reasonably appears to have been, advised independently by a solicitor.[856] This guidance is not to be considered as optional.[857] It can be summarised as follows: **34-274**

(a) the bank should make direct contact with the wife and:
  (i) explain to her the reason why it requires written confirmation from a solicitor, acting for her, that he has fully explained the nature of the documents to her and the practical implications they will have for her; and
  (ii) ask her to nominate a solicitor to act for her and provide the necessary confirmation (she should be told that this may be the same solicitor that acts for her husband but that she may choose another solicitor if a solicitor is already acting for her and her husband). *The bank should not proceed with the transaction until it has received an appropriate response directly from the wife.*

(b) The bank must provide the wife's solicitor with such financial information as he needs for the purpose of explaining the nature of the documents and their practical implications to her. It should be routine practice for banks to send necessary financial information to the solicitor. What is required depends on the facts of the case but, ordinarily, it will include information on the purpose for which the proposed new facility has been requested, the current amount of the husband's indebtedness, the amount of his current

---

852 This includes the case where the certificate is given by a legal executive, provided that the advice was independent and was given with the authority of the legal executive's principal: *Barclays Bank Plc v Coleman* [2001] Q.B. 20 at [78], affirmed [2001] UKHL 44, [2002] 2 A.C. 773 at [292]. The mere fact that the wife has seen a solicitor is not enough without confirmation that he has given her independent advice: *Lloyds TSB Bank Plc v Holdgate* [2002] EWCA Civ 1543, [2003] H.L.R. 25; *First National Bank Plc v Achampong* [2003] EWCA Civ 487, [2004] 1 F.C.R. 18; cf. *Gov and Co of the Bank of Scotland v Hill* [2002] EWCA Civ 1081, [2002] 29 E.G.C.S. 152. See also *UCB Corporate Services Ltd v Williams* [2002] EWCA Civ 555, [2002] 3 F.C.R. 448 (bank did not even know wife had seen a solicitor).

853 In *National Westminster Bank Plc v Amin* [2002] UKHL 9, [2002] 1 F.L.R. 735, it was not clear that this requirement had been met.

854 At [56]. The steps that a solicitor should take when advising the wife or other surety are set out in Vol.I, para.8-122. See also *Padden v Bevan Ashford Solicitors* [2011] EWCA Civ 1616, [2012] P.N.L.R. 14 and [2013] EWCA Civ 824 (appeal following retrial).

855 At [56]–[57]; and also Lord Scott at [175]. See also *HSBC Bank Plc v Brown* [2015] EWHC 359 (Ch) (where despite certificate being signed by a solicitor, the bank ought to have realised that the surety had not received appropriate advice).

856 At [79]. See *Royal Bank of Scotland v Chandra* [2010] EWHC 105 (Ch), [2010] 1 Lloyd's Rep. 677, especially at [173]–[175], for a case where the court had to decide whether the transaction was "past" or "future" for the purposes of the *Etridge* guidance (no discussion of this issue on appeal: see [2011] EWCA Civ 192, [2011] N.P.C. 26).

857 Lord Hobhouse at [100], who thought that it should be applied equally to past as well as future transactions because it represented a reasonable response to being put on inquiry.

overdraft facility and the amount and terms of any new facility. A copy of any written application of the husband for a facility should also be sent to the solicitor. The bank will have to obtain the consent of the customer to the disclosure of confidential information, and the transaction should not be allowed to proceed without such consent (Lord Scott considered that a husband who proposes that his wife stands surety for his or his company's debts constitutes implied consent to disclosure,[858] but it is submitted that obtaining express consent to disclosure would be a much safer option from the bank's point of view, especially where the debtor is technically the husband's company[859]).

(c) In those exceptional cases where the bank believes or suspects that the wife has been misled by her husband or is not entering into the transaction of her own free will, the bank must inform the wife's solicitors of the facts giving rise to its belief or suspicion.

(d) The bank must in every case obtain from the wife's solicitor a written confirmation to the effect mentioned above.[860]

34-275 **Independent advice**   Should the solicitor acting for the wife act for her alone? Does it matter that the solicitor also acts for the husband and/or the bank in the transaction? In the *Etridge* case, Lord Nicholls considered this to be a much-vexed question: one, he stressed, which could not be answered by reference to decided cases.[861] Lord Nicholls balanced the factors that suggest that the solicitor should act for the wife alone against those factors that suggest that he may also act for the husband or the bank, provided he is satisfied that this is in the wife's best interests and is satisfied also that this will not give rise to any conflicts of duty or interest. In Lord Nicholls' opinion, the latter proved more weighty than the former.[862] At the heart of Lord Nicholls' reasoning was the understanding that when advising the wife the solicitor owes his duties, both legally and professionally, to her and her alone. He is concerned only with her interests.[863]

34-276 **No imputation of solicitor's knowledge to bank**[864]   Does the solicitor act as the bank's agent for these purposes so that the solicitor's knowledge that he has not

---

[858] At [190].

[859] See also the *Standards of Lending Practice for Personal Customers* (para.34-222 above) at p.7 (Account maintenance and servicing), point 8, and the *Standards of Lending Practice for Business Customers* (para.34-223 above) at pp.9–10 (Product execution), point 6.

[860] See also *Trustees of Beardsley Theobalds Retirement Benefit Scheme v Yardley* [2011] EWHC 1380 (QB) at [51]: guarantee of tenant's obligations under lease held unenforceable where landlord failed to obtain acknowledgement from solicitor that he had given appropriate advice to guarantor; *HSBC Bank Plc v Brown* [2015] EWHC 359 (Ch) (held bank proceeded at own risk where, despite certificate being signed by a solicitor, the bank ought to have realised that the surety had not received appropriate advice).

[861] At [69]–[70].

[862] At [74]. See also Lord Clyde at [96] and Lord Scott at [173].

[863] At [74]. See also *Kapoor v National Westminster Bank Plc* [2010] EWHC 2986 (Ch), where it was held that the wife had received independent legal advice, and the bank was entitled to rely on the solicitor's certificate that she had received that advice, despite the fact that the wife had ignored the bank's suggestion to consult a different solicitor than the one advising her husband.

[864] A separate question is whether knowledge of the surety's solicitor should be imputed to her. The general rule is that, subject to any statutory variation, a solicitor's knowledge is treated as that of his client (see *AIB v Martin and Gold* Unreported March 15, 1999, Jacob J.), but in *Davies v AIB Group (UK) Plc* [2012] EWHC 2178 (Ch), [2012] 2 P. & C.R. 19 at [116], without deciding the issue, Norris J. thought that some caution might be required in the context of undue influence

done his job properly, whatever he said on the certificate, can be imputed to the bank? Lord Nicholls answered this question in the negative.[865] The idea central to the arrangement is that in advising the wife the solicitor is acting for her and no one else. According to his Lordship, "[t]o impute to the bank knowledge of what passed between the solicitor and the wife would contradict this essential feature of the arrangement".[866] The mere fact that the bank, for its own purposes, asked the solicitor to advise the wife did not constitute the solicitor the bank's agent when giving that advice. Lord Nicholls concluded that, in the ordinary case, deficiencies in the advice given were a matter between the wife and the solicitor so that the bank was entitled to proceed on the assumption that a solicitor advising the wife has done his job properly. However, he held that the position would be different where the bank knew that the solicitor had not done his job properly, or if it knew facts from which it ought to have realised this. Similarly, Lord Scott thought that where the solicitor's only instructions came from the bank, and the bank was his only client, so that he never became the solicitor of the wife, his knowledge of what had or had not taken place regarding advice to the wife might well be imputed to the bank.[867]

Rescission Where a wife (or other surety) successfully raises an *O'Brien/* **34-277** *Etridge* defence, she is entitled to rescind the transaction with the bank.[868] The fact that the person who exercised the undue influence, or made the misrepresentation, is not himself a party to the transaction is basically irrelevant. If, for example, the bank has constructive notice to the effect that the wife has been subjected to undue influence by her husband, it would be irrelevant that the charge was executed by the wife alone and not jointly by the spouses.[869] Where the wife has received benefits under the transaction with the bank, she should be required, as a condition of rescission, to make counter-restitutio to the bank of the value of the benefit she has received.[870] However, the equitable remedy of rescission will not be made on terms where the wife obtained no benefit for herself from the transaction. In *TSB Bank Plc v Camfield*,[871] a wife was induced to stand surety by her husband's innocent misrepresentation that their maximum liability in respect of the loan for his business was £15,000, when in fact it was unlimited. The bank was held to have constructive notice of the misrepresentation and the issue turned on whether the security could be partially enforced up to £15,000. The Court of Appeal held that

---

arguments: "A principle of attributing the knowledge of an agent to the principal does not really assist in identifying how an intention to enter a transaction was produced—freely or under undue influence."

[865] At [77]–[78]. See also Lord Hobhouse at [122].

[866] At 77.

[867] At [180].

[868] Subject to the usual bars, including that restitutio in integrum is impossible (but it need not be precise); there has been affirmation or delay (*First National Bank Plc v Walker* [2001] 1 F.C.R. 21, CA); there has been intervention of a bona fide purchaser for value without notice (*CIBC Mortgages Plc v Pitt* [1994] 1 A.C. 200). See generally, Vol.I, para.8-103. If the property subject to the security is jointly owned by a husband and wife then, even though the security may not be enforceable against the wife, it may be against the husband, and so the court may still order the property to be sold, under the Trusts of Land and Appointment of Trustees Act 1996 s.14, in order to realise the husband's share: see *First National Bank Plc v Achampong* [2003] EWCA Civ 487, [2004] 1 F.C.R. 18 (noted by Thompson [2003] Conv. 314).

[869] *Royal Bank of Scotland Plc v Etridge (No.2)* [2001] UKHL 44, [2002] 2 A.C. 773 at [39], [144]–[146]; *Banco Exterior Internacional SA v Thomas* [1997] 1 W.L.R. 221.

[870] See *Dunbar Bank Plc v Nadeem* [1998] 3 All E.R. 876, CA; *Society of Lloyds v Khan* [1998] 3 F.C.R. 93. See also *National Commercial Bank (Jamaica) Ltd v Hew* [2003] UKPC 51 at [43].

[871] [1995] 1 W.L.R. 430.

the security was to be set aside in full. Nourse L.J. stated: "[t]he wife's right to have the transaction set aside *in toto* as against the husband is no less enforceable against the mortgagee".[872] The decision may be criticised on the ground that as the wife was prepared to guarantee payment of £15,000, it was appropriate to impose terms.[873] Of course, in a case of undue influence, where the surety's consent is totally vitiated, it is right that the security be set aside in full.[874] However, even in a case of undue influence it may occasionally be possible to sever tainted material from untainted material in an instrument, and to set aside only the former, so long as this does not amount to rewriting the contract.[875]

34-278 **Duty of care** In the normal course of events, a bank is under no duty of care to proffer explanations as to the nature and effect of a security document executed by a surety, or to advise the surety to take independent legal advice.[876] However, a duty of care may arise where there are special factors, e.g. where it is clear that the bank is being looked to for advice or is in some close relationship with the prospective surety of a kind which gives rise to a fiduciary relationship between them.[877] Whether a duty of care is owed depends upon all the circumstances of the case, including relevant evidence of banking practice.[878] Although it seems established that no duty of explanation or advice normally arises where the surety is not a customer of the bank, there is some uncertainty whether the same can be said where the surety is an existing customer of the bank. In *Cornish v Midland Bank Plc*,[879] where the Court of Appeal held that the bank had been negligent in the advice it

---

872 At 437.
873 But contrast C. Mitchell, P. Mitchell and S. Watterson (eds), Goff and Jones, *The Law of Unjust Enrichment*, 9th edn (2016), paras 40-14—40-15. For opposing arguments, see J. O'Sullivan "Undue Influence and Misrepresentation after O'Brien: Making Security Secure", Ch.3 of F.D. Rose (ed.), *Restitution and Banking Law* (1998), pp.64–69, and G. Virgo's reply, which appears in Ch.4 of the same book, pp.76–77. In *De Molestina v Ponton* [2002] 1 Lloyd's Rep. 271, Colman J. rejected partial rescission. In Australia rescission on terms is accepted (*Vadasz v Pioneer Concrete (SA) Pty Ltd* (1995) 184 C.L.R. 102, HC), as it is in New Zealand (*Scales Trading Ltd v Far Eastern Shipping Co Public Ltd* [1999] 3 N.Z.L.R. 26, CA; the Privy Council, having made a different factual finding, did not express an opinion on the issue, [2001] 1 N.Z.L.R. 513). See also J. Poole and A. Keyser, "Justifying Partial Rescission in English Law" (2005) 121 L.Q.R. 273.
874 But see *Castle Phillips Finance v Piddington* (1994) 70 P. & C.R. 59, an undue influence case, where the Court of Appeal was able to mitigate the effect of setting aside the charge in full by subrogating the creditor to an earlier, valid charge. Applied in *UCB Group Ltd v Hedworth* [2003] EWCA Civ 1717 (a case of sub-subrogation). By contrast, where an earlier charge is voidable for undue influence, a replacement charge, taken out as a condition of discharging the earlier charge, will also be voidable, even though the replacement charge was not itself procured by undue influence (*Yorkshire Bank Plc v Tinsley* [2004] EWCA Civ 816, [2004] 1 W.L.R. 2380, emphasising at [26], [32] and [39] that the two charges were "inseparably connected"). But this will only occur where the undue influence which procured the first charge remained "operative", in the sense that the grantor of the security was unaware that the first charge could have been set aside. The grantor will not be entitled to set aside the second charge where she was aware of her right to set aside the first charge before she entered into the second charge (*Wadlow v Samuel* [2007] EWCA Civ 155).
875 *Barclays Bank Plc v Caplan* [1998] 1 F.L.R. 532, Ch D.
876 *Chetwynd-Talbot v Midland Bank Ltd* (1982) 132 N.L.J. 901; *O'Hara v Allied Irish Banks Ltd* [1985] B.C.L.C. 52; *Westpac Banking Corp v McCreanor* [1990] 1 N.Z.L.R. 580; *Shivas v Bank of New Zealand* [1990] 2 N.Z.L.R. 327; *Barclays Bank Plc v Khaira* [1992] 1 W.L.R. 623; and *Union Bank of Finland v Lelakis* [1995] C.L.C. 27. cf. *Cornish v Midland Bank Plc* [1985] 3 All E.R. 513 at 522–523, per Kerr L.J.; *Shotter v Westpac Banking Corp* [1988] 2 N.Z.L.R. 316.
877 *Barclays Bank Plc v Khaira* [1992] 1 W.L.R. 623, 637, Morison Q.C., sitting as Deputy High Court judge.
878 *Union Bank of Finland v Lelakis* [1995] C.L.C. 27, 47, Clarke J.
879 [1985] 3 All E.R. 513, 522–523.

had given to its customer, the surety, Kerr L.J. went on to consider, obiter, whether the bank was under a duty of care to give an explanation of the security documents. Kerr L.J. came to the tentative conclusion that banks are under a duty to their own customers to proffer an adequate explanation of the nature and effect of the security documents they are about to sign. Kerr L.J.'s dictum has been considered in a number of subsequent cases and rejected in nearly all of them.[880] It is submitted that the better view is that customers should be treated in the same way as non-customers, and that there should normally be no duty of care to proffer an explanation or advice in either case. Imposition of a duty to proffer an explanation or advice would seem to undermine the arm's length nature of the banker-customer relationship.

Damages *O'Brien* and *Etridge* are not concerned with establishing liability for **34-279** damages or equitable compensation, but preventing a party from relying upon a transaction that is tainted by wrongdoing.[881] However, where a bank attempts to explain the nature and extent of the security documents to the surety, will it be liable in damages for negligent advice if it fails to do so properly? In *Midland Bank Plc v Perry*,[882] the trial judge held the bank liable for negligence in such circumstances. In *Cornish v Midland Bank Plc*,[883] it was conceded, with the approval of the Court of Appeal, that the bank owed the surety a duty of care to give a full and proper explanation of the security documents when it had undertaken the task of giving an explanation.[884] However, in *Barclays Bank Plc v O'Brien*,[885] Scott L.J. said that where equity required the bank to explain the nature of a security document to the surety, the bank was not to be placed under a duty of care. He distinguished between where the surety is a customer of the bank, or where the bank voluntarily assumes the role of adviser, when it may be under a duty to advise carefully, and where the bank explains the security documents and the transaction to the surety to avoid the security being set aside in equity, when a duty of care would not arise. Nevertheless, a bank which proffers an explanation or advice as to the security documents runs the risk of crossing the line and being held to have voluntarily assumed the role of an adviser.[886] It is no wonder, therefore, that banks have sought to avoid this risk by adopting the practice of requiring the surety to take independent legal advice.[887]

---

[880] *Westpac Banking Corp v McCreanor* [1990] 1 N.Z.L.R. 580; *Shivas v Bank of New Zealand* [1990] 2 N.Z.L.R. 327; *Barclays Bank Plc v Khaira* [1992] 1 W.L.R. 623; and *Union Bank of Finland v Lelakis* [1995] C.L.C. 27. cf. *Shotter v Westpac Banking Corp* [1988] 2 N.Z.L.R. 316. Kerr L.J.'s dictum was not considered by the Court of Appeal in *Barclays Bank Plc v O'Brien* [1993] Q.B. 109, where the issue appears to have been left open.

[881] *Deane v Coutts & Co* [2018] EWHC 1657 (Ch) at [126].

[882] [1987] F.L.R. 237 (no appeal on this point).

[883] [1985] 3 All E.R. 513.

[884] See also *Barclays Bank Plc v Khaira* [1992] 1 W.L.R. 623 at 634.

[885] [1993] Q.B. 109 at 140–141. See also Purchas L.J. at 156. The House of Lords did not deal with this issue.

[886] In *Midland Bank Plc v Kidwai* [1995] 4 Bank. L.R. 303, 307–308, Morritt L.J. emphasised that *O'Brien* principles do not require the bank to take on the duties of a solicitor or other independent adviser.

[887] *Royal Bank of Scotland Plc v Etridge (No.2)* [2001] UKHL 44, [2002] 2 A.C. 773 at [51]. See above, para.34-268.

(vi)   Banks as Constructive Trustees

34-280   Introduction   A bank's liability as constructive trustee is, conceptually, distinguishable from its liability for the breach of a fiduciary duty or of a special duty of care. Liability for the breach of such a duty is usually maintainable only in cases in which there is a proximate relationship between the bank and the person who seeks to hold it liable. Normally such a person would have to be a customer. By contrast, the bank's liability as a constructive trustee is incurred when another person, who is a trustee or otherwise subject to fiduciary duties, has committed a breach of trust or fiduciary duty and the bank has become involved in the matter in such a manner as to become answerable. The victim's claim is, thus, based on the bank's act or omission and not on his being able to establish proximity with it. It follows that although in many of the cases in which banks were sued as constructive trustees the claimant was a customer, the fate of his claim did not depend on this circumstance.

34-281   The nature of constructive trust claims   The starting point of any analysis of this area of law is the classic dictum of Lord Selborne L.C. in *Barnes v Addy*:

> "... strangers are not to be made constructive trustees merely because they act as the agents of trustees in transactions within their legal powers, transactions perhaps of which a Court of Equity may disapprove, unless (i) those agents receive and become chargeable with some part of the trust property, or (ii) unless they assist with knowledge in a dishonest and fraudulent design on the part of the trustees."[888]

Further, his Lordship continued, to ensure that "the transactions of mankind" can be conducted with safety, it is necessary that:

> "... persons dealing honestly as agents [be] at liberty to rely on the legal power of the trustees, and are not to have the character of trustees constructively imposed upon them".[889]

This qualification is relevant in respect of both branches of the doctrine.

34-282   The first type of liability is generally known as liability for "knowing receipt". The second type of liability was known as liability for "knowing assistance" until a change in the law in 1995 made it more appropriate to refer to it as liability for "dishonest assistance". In both cases liability is personal and not proprietary.[890] But there the similarity ends. The two types of liability are fundamentally different. As Lord Nicholls observed in *Royal Brunei Airlines v Tan*:

> "The first limb of Lord Selborne L.C.'s formulation is concerned with the liability of a person as a *recipient* of trust property or its traceable proceeds. The second limb is concerned with what, for want of a better compendious description, can be called the liability of an *accessory* to a trustee's breach of trust. Liability as an accessory is not dependent upon receipt of trust property. It arises even though no trust property has

---

[888] (1874) 9 Ch. App. 244 at 251.
[889] (1874) 9 Ch. App. 244 at 251.
[890] See *Re Montagu's ST* [1987] Ch. 264, 276, per Megarry V.C., dealing with knowing receipt; *Twinsectra Ltd v Yardley* [1999] Lloyd's Rep. Bank. 438, 467, per Potter L.J., dealing with dishonest assistance.

reached the hands of the accessory. It is a form of secondary liability in the sense that it only arises where there has been a breach of trust."[891]

Lord Nicholls went on to opine that whereas "recipient liability is restitution-based; accessory liability is not".[892]

The distinction between the two types of liability was again highlighted by the Court of Appeal in *Grupo Torras SA v Al-Sabah*:

34-283

"The basis of liability in a case of knowing receipt is quite different from that in a case of dishonest assistance. One is a receipt-based liability which may on examination prove to be either a vindication of persistent property rights or a personal restitutionary claim based on unjust enrichment by subtraction; the other is a fault-based liability as an accessory to a breach of fiduciary duty."[893]

It should be noted, however, that until the issue is authoritatively decided upon by the higher courts, the precise relationship between liability under the receipt category of constructive trusteeship and the law of restitution remains unclear and uncertain under English law.[894] By contrast, following the Privy Council's landmark decision in *Royal Brunei Airlines v Tan*, the requirements for accessory liability can now be stated with more certainty. Accessory liability is "fault-based"; the "touchstone of liability" is the accessory's dishonesty.[895]

Dishonest assistance   Liability for dishonest assistance will be imposed on anyone who has dishonestly been accessory to, or assisted in, a disposition of property in breach of trust or other fiduciary obligation. In such a case the accessory or assister is traditionally described as a "constructive trustee" and said to be "liable to account as a constructive trustee".[896] However, as the accessory or assister does not have to receive any trust property for this type of liability to arise, it seems misleading to describe him as a trustee at all.[897] In fact, the expressions "constructive trust" and "constructive trustee" are really "nothing more than a formula for equitable relief".[898] It would be more accurate, and less confusing, to regard dishonest participation in a breach of trust as a species of equitable wrong[899]: "the equitable counterpart of the economic torts",[900] or an "equitable tort".[901] These are cases of "ancillary liability" where the intervention of equity is "purely

34-284

---

[891] [1995] 2 A.C. 378 at 382.
[892] At 386.
[893] [2001] Lloyd's Rep. Bank. 36 at [122].
[894] See below, para.34-304.
[895] See below, para.34-290.
[896] See, e.g., *Westdeutsche Landesbank Girozentrale v Islington LBC* [1996] A.C. 669, 705, per Lord Browne-Wilkinson.
[897] *Agip (Africa) Ltd v Jackson* [1990] Ch. 265, 292, per Millett J.; *Paragon Finance Plc v DB Thakerar & Co (a firm)* [1999] 1 All E.R. 400, 409, per Millett L.J.; *Dubai Aluminium Co Ltd v Salaam* [2002] UKHL 48, [2003] 2 A.C. 366 at [141], per Lord Millett. See generally, W. Swadling, "The Fiction of the Constructive Trust" (2011) 64 C.L.P. 400, especially 414–416; contrast C. Mitchell and S. Watterson, "Remedies for Knowing Receipt" in C. Mitchell (ed.), *Constructive and Resulting Trusts* (2010), pp.115–158, especially 129.
[898] *Selangor United Rubber Ltd v Cradock (No.3)* [1968] 1 W.L.R. 155, 1582, per Ungoed-Thomas J.
[899] See *Grupo Torras SA v Al-Sabah* [2001] Lloyd's Rep. Bank. 36 at [123], CA; *Casio Computer Co Ltd v Sayo* [2001] EWCA Civ 661 at [14]. See also Lord Nicholls, "Knowing Receipt: The Need for a New Landmark" Ch.15 in Cornish et al (eds), *Restitution—Past, Present and Future* (Oxford: Hart Publishing, 1988), 244.
[900] *Twinsectra Ltd v Yardley* [2002] UKHL 12, [2002] 2 A.C. 164 at [127], per Lord Millett.
[901] *Abou-Rahmah v Abacha* [2006] EWCA Civ 1492, [2007] 1 Lloyd's Rep. 115 at [2], per Rix L.J.

remedial".[902] The remedy for the wrongdoing is compensation for the loss caused by the dishonest assistance.[903]

34-285 **Requirements for accessory liability** There are four requirements for accessory liability to be imposed:

(i) there must have been a trust or other fiduciary relationship;

(ii) there must have been a misfeasance or other breach of trust, though *Tan* establishes that such misfeasance or breach of trust need not itself be dishonest or fraudulent;

(iii) the person upon whom liability is to be imposed must, as a matter of fact, have been accessory to, or assisted in, the misfeasance or breach of trust, and

(iv) the accessory must have been dishonest.[904]

34-286 *(i) Trust or other fiduciary relationship* Although the *Barnes v Addy* doctrine started life as a response to the misapplication of trust funds by express trustees, its coverage has since been extended to include the breach of fiduciary duties by others. The doctrine is now commonly applied in the corporate context where directors and other senior officers of the company are deemed to owe fiduciary duties to the company.[905]

34-287 *(ii) Misfeasance or other breach of trust* In *Barnes v Addy*, Lord Selborne L.C. specifically referred to assistance "in a dishonest and fraudulent design on the part of the trustees".[906] An attempt by Ungoed-Thomas J., in *Selangor United Rubber Estates Ltd v Cradock (No.3)*,[907] to jettison the reference to dishonesty and fraud, was emphatically rejected by the Court of Appeal in *Belmont Finance Corp Ltd v*

---

[902] *Williams v Central Bank of Nigeria* [2014] UKSC 10, [2014] A.C. 1189 at [9], per Lord Sumption. The Supreme Court held (by a majority) that the words "trust" and "trustee" in s.21(1)(a) of the Limitation Act 1980 bear their orthodox meanings, and that "trustee" does not include those who are liable to account in equity because they have dishonestly assisted in a breach of trust or knowingly received trust property. It was also held (by an even narrower majority) that the words "party or privy" to a fraud or fraudulent breach of trust within s.21(1)(a) applies only to claims brought against trustees and not to claims brought against anyone else who is involved in the fraud or fraudulent breach of trust, and that, in consequence, the limitation period for claims against dishonest assisters and knowing recipients is six years (but note the effect of s.32 of the 1980 Act which, in certain cases, postpones the commencement of the six years). For useful notes, see S. Watterson [2014] C.L.J. 253 and P. Davies [2014] L.M.C.L.Q. 313.

[903] *Sinclair Investment Holdings SA v Versailles Trade Finance Ltd* [2007] EWHC 915 (Ch), [2007] 2 All E.R. (Comm) 993 at [120]–[125], where Rimer J. stressed that the remedy was personal and not proprietary. Sometimes an account of profits will be awarded against an accessory who profits from the assistance: see *Novoship (UK) Ltd v Mikhaylyuk* [2014] EWCA Civ 908, [2015] Q.B. 499, requiring a sufficiently direct causal connection between the accessory's gain and the dishonest assistance (noted by P. Davies (2015) 131 L.Q.R. 173; P. Devonshire [2015] C.L.J. 222); cf. *Akita Holdings Ltd v AG of Turks and Caicos Islands* [2017] UKPC 7, [2017] A.C. 590 and *Lifeplan Australia Friendly Society Ltd v Ancient Order of Foresters in Victoria Friendly Society Ltd* [2017] FCAFC 74, (2017) 250 F.C.R. 1 for approaches conflicting with *Novoship* (noted by P.G. Turner [2018] C.L.J. 255). For further discussion of the remedies available against a dishonest assister, see S.B. Elliott and C. Mitchell (2004) 67 M.L.R. 16; S. Baughen [2007] L.M.C.L.Q. 545, 556–558; P. Ridge (2008) 124 L.Q.R. 445.

[904] As summarised by Cresswell J. in *Bankgesellschaft Berlin AG v Makris* Unreported January 22, 1999.

[905] See, e.g. *Agip (Africa) Ltd v Jackson* [1990] Ch. 265; affirmed [1991] Ch. 547.

[906] (1874) 9 Ch. App. 244 at 252.

[907] [1968] 1 W.L.R. 1555.

Williams,[908] on the ground that to depart from it would introduce an undesirable degree of uncertainty over what degree of unethical conduct would suffice if dishonesty was not to be the criterion. It was not until 1995, when the Privy Council delivered its advice in *Royal Brunei Airlines v Tan*,[909] that the need to establish dishonesty or fraud on the part of the trustee or other fiduciary was finally abandoned as a prerequisite to accessory liability. This was the main point at issue in the case. Those earlier authorities holding that the breach of trust must be fraudulent may now be taken as overruled, although it should be noted that in most cases the breach of trust is likely to be a dishonest one.[910]

There remains uncertainty as to whether liability as a constructive trustee is **34-288** restricted to assistance in a breach of trust in relation to property or whether it also extend to a case of dishonest assistance in *any* breach of fiduciary duty. In *Tan*, Lord Nicholls stated that:

"… a liability in equity to make good resulting loss attaches to a person who dishonestly procures or assists in a breach of trust or fiduciary obligation".[911]

Lord Nicholls' formulation does not require the misapplication of trust property or its proceeds, but as the point was not in issue in that case, where trust property had certainly been misapplied, this cannot be taken as the last word on the subject. The issue was left open in a number of cases,[912] though in others the broader approach was rejected.[913] However, the Court of Appeal has recently held in *Novoship (UK) Ltd v Mikhaylyuk* that "the remedy of an account of profits is available against one who dishonestly assists a fiduciary to breach his fiduciary obligations, even if that breach does not involve a misappropriation of trust property".[914]

(iii) Accessory or assister   The person upon whom liability is to be imposed must **34-289** as a matter of fact have been accessory or assisted in the misfeasance or breach of trust. In many cases banks will not find it easy to avoid the charge that they were accessory to or assisted in a breach of trust, especially one that involves the fraudulent misapplication of trust funds. The provision of banking services to persons behaving in a fraudulent or improper manner often exposes a bank to potential liability under this head. The misapplied trust funds will usually be held in bank accounts and moved between bank accounts. The banks that hold those accounts, as well as any other bank involved as an intermediary in the funds transfer process, run the risk of being accused of providing assistance to the dishonest fiduciary. For example, payment by a bank on the instructions of fraudulent directors of a company of moneys of the company to another person may be such

---

908 [1979] Ch. 250.
909 [1995] 2 A.C. 378.
910 W. Blair (2000) 30 H.K.L.J. 74 at 88, n.44.
911 [1995] 2 A.C. 378 at 392.
912 *Brown v Bennett* [1999] 1 B.C.L.C. 649; *Fyffes Group Ltd v Templeman* [2000] 2 Lloyd's Rep. 643; *Goose v Wilson Sandiford & Co (No.2)* [2000] EWCA Civ 73, [2001] Lloyd's Rep. P.N. 189 at [88]; *Gencor ACP Ltd v Dalby* [2000] 2 B.C.L.C. 734, 757; *JD Wetherspoon Plc v Van de Berg & Co Ltd* [2009] EWHC 639 (Ch) at [518]; *Fiona Trust & Holding Corp v Privalov* [2010] EWHC 3199 (Comm) at [61].
913 *Satnam Investments Ltd v Dunlop Heywood & Co Ltd* [1999] 3 All E.R. 652, 651; *Petrotrade Inc v Smith* [2000] 1 Lloyd's Rep. 486, 491–492.
914 [2014] EWCA Civ 908, [2015] Q.B. 499 at [93]; per Longmore L.J. (delivering the judgment of the court). See also *Schenk v Cook* [2017] EWHC 144 (QB) at [85].

assistance.[915] More worrying still, at least from the bank's point of view, is that the mere provision of advisory services to the fiduciary can be deemed "assistance" where there is a sufficient causative link between that advice and the breach of trust,[916] even though the bank itself never comes into contact with the misapplied funds.[917] It is because the "assistance" net can be cast so widely that attention has focused so crucially on the level of mental intent required the person giving assistance for him to be held liable under this head of constructive trusteeship. Banks and other financial institutions involved in millions of money transmission activities on a daily basis, and so particularly vulnerable to the charge of "assistance", have always argued that the level of mental intent should be high.

34-290 *(iv) Dishonesty*   The accessory must have been dishonest. It is the presence of the necessary level of mental intent, which, following *Royal Brunei Airlines v Tan*,[918] is dishonesty, that is the fourth requirement for accessory liability to be imposed. *Tan* has finally settled an issue that has plagued the English courts for many years.[919] The decision is to be welcomed for bringing a greater degree of certainty to this notoriously difficult area.

34-291   In *Tan*, Lord Nicholls, speaking by way of obiter dicta, confirmed that "dishonesty is a necessary ingredient of accessory liability. It is also a sufficient ingredient".[920] Lord Nicholls also attempted to clarify the meaning of dishonesty in this context. The key passage from his judgment reads as follows:

> "Whatever may be the position in some criminal or other context (see, for instance, *R. v Ghosh* [1982] Q.B. 1053),[921] in the context of the accessory liability principle acting dishonestly, or with a lack of probity, which is synonymous, means simply not acting as an honest person would in the circumstances. This is an objective standard. At first sight this may seem surprising. Honesty has a connotation of subjectivity, as distinct from the objectivity of negligence. Honesty, indeed, does have a strong subjective element in that it is a description of a type of conduct assessed in the light of what a person actually knew at the time, as distinct from what a reasonable person would have known or appreciated. Further, honesty and its counterpart dishonesty are mostly concerned with advertent conduct, not inadvertent conduct. Carelessness is not dishonesty. Thus for the most part dishonesty is to be equated with a conscious impropriety. However, these subjective characteristics of honesty do not mean that individuals are free to set their own standards of honesty in particular circumstances. The standard of what constitutes honest conduct is not subjective. Honesty is not an optional scale, with higher or lower values according to the moral standards of each individual. If a person knowingly appropriates another's property, he will not escape a finding of dishonesty simply because he sees nothing wrong

---

[915] See, e.g. *Selangor United Rubber Estates Ltd v Cradock (No.3)* [1968] 1 W.L.R. 1555; *Karak v Rubber Co Ltd v Burden (No.2)* [1972] 1 W.L.R. 602.

[916] See *Brown v Bennett* [1999] 1 B.C.L.C. 649.

[917] In *Casio Computer Co Ltd v Sayo* [2001] EWCA Civ 661 at [15], the Court of Appeal held that loss caused by the breach of fiduciary duty is recoverable from the accessory without the need to show a *precise* causal link between the assistance and the loss.

[918] [1995] 2 A.C. 378.

[919] For a thorough review of the conflicting authorities, see E.P. Ellinger and E. Lomnicka, *Modern Banking Law*, 2nd edn (1994), pp.205–211.

[920] At 392.

[921] In *Ivey v Genting Casinos (UK) Ltd* [2017] UKSC 67, [2017] 3 W.L.R. 1212 the Supreme Court (obiter) has since adopted a unified test of dishonesty in both criminal and civil law which is essentially objective. Lord Hughes, delivering the judgment of the court, stated (at [74]) that the second (subjective) limb of the test propounded in *Ghosh* did not correctly represent the law. Noted by G. Virgo [2018] C.L.J. 18; M Dyson and P Jarvis (2018) 134 L.Q.R. 198.

in such behaviour. In most situations there is little difficulty in identifying how an honest person would behave. Honest people do not intentionally deceive others to their detriment. Honest people do not knowingly take others' property. Unless there is a very good and compelling reason, an honest person does not participate in a transaction if he knows it involves a misapplication of trust assets to the detriment of the beneficiaries. Nor does an honest person in such a case deliberately close his eyes and ears, or deliberately not ask questions, lest he learns something he would rather not know, and then proceed regardless."[922]

Lord Nicholls expressly referred to an "objective standard" of dishonesty. But he also spoke of honesty having "a strong subjective element" and that, for the most part, "dishonesty is to be equated with a conscious impropriety". This left room for doubt and uncertainty as to the precise test to be adopted when assessing whether or not an accessory has been dishonest.[923] However, the "now clearly established"[924] test of dishonesty was explained in *Barlow Clowes International Ltd v Eurotrust International Ltd* by Lord Hoffmann as follows[925]:

34-292

"Although a dishonest state of mind is a subjective mental state, the standard by which the law determines whether it is dishonest is objective. If by ordinary standards a defendant's mental state would be characterised as dishonest, it is irrelevant that the defendant judges by different standards. Their Lordships held this to be a correct state of the law and their Lordships agree."

In *Ivy v Genting Casinos (UK) Ltd*,[926] where the Supreme Court (obiter) adopted a unified test of dishonesty in both criminal and civil law, Lord Hughes acknowledged that the test of dishonesty was as set out by Lord Nicholls in *Royal Brunei Airlines Sdn Bhd v Tan*, and by Lord Hoffmann in Barlow Clowes, and continued:

"When dishonesty is in question the fact-finding tribunal must first ascertain (subjectively)

---

[922] At 389. Recklessness is not equivalent to dishonesty but it can be a sign of dishonesty: see Lord Nicholls at 389–391, as interpreted by Lewison L.J. in *Clydesdale Bank Plc v Workman* [2016] EWCA Civ 73, [2016] P.N.L.R. 18 at [48]–[53]. Lord Nicholls said that "[c]arelessness is not dishonesty" (above). See also *Ivey v Genting Casinos (UK) Ltd* [2017] UKSC 67, [2017] 3 W.L.R. 1212 at [62]; *Singularis Holdings Ltd (In Liquidation) v Daiwa Capital Markets Europe Ltd* [2017] EWHC 257 (Ch) at [147], affirmed on other grounds [2018] EWCA Civ 84.

[923] In *Twinsectra Ltd v Yardley* [2002] UKHL 12, [2002] 2 A.C. 164 a majority of the House of Lords held that a "combined test" of dishonesty was to be applied in a case of dishonest assistance; in other words, before there could be a finding of dishonesty it must be established that the defendant's conduct was dishonest by the ordinary standards of reasonable and honest people (the objective element) and that he himself realised that by those standards his conduct was dishonest (the subjective element).

[924] *Ivey v Genting Casinos (UK) Ltd* [2017] UKSC 67, [2017] 3 W.L.R. 1212 at [62], per Lord Hughes (obiter).

[925] [2005] UKPC 37, [2006] 1 W.L.R. 1476 at [10]. Lord Hoffmann was also a party to the *Twinsectra* decision (above). The objective test was also approved in *Abou-Rahman v Abacha* [2006] EWCA Civ 1492, [2007] 1 Lloyd's Rep. 115 at [59] (Arden L.J.); *Starglade Properties Ltd v Nash* [2010] EWCA Civ 1314 at [32] (Morritt C.). Note Gloster L.J.'s dissent in *UBS AG (London Branch) v Kommunale Wasserwrke Leipzig GmbH* [2017] EWCA Civ 1567 at [347] on ground that it was "impractical and unreal to introduce into commercial transactions the moral standards of the vicarage": Lord Briggs and Hamblen L.J. (the majority) held at [113] that "[w]here a party to an intended transaction deals with the other party's agent secretly and behind his back, and dishonestly assists that agent to abuse his fiduciary duties to the other party so as to bring that transaction about, then the first party's conscience may be affected not merely by the particular form of abuse by the agent of which it actually knew, but also by any other abuse [in this case, a bribe] which the agent chose to employ to bring about the transaction with the first party".

[926] [2017] UKSC 67, [2017] 3 W.L.R. 1212 at [74].

the actual state of the individual's knowledge or belief as to the facts. The reasonableness or otherwise of his belief is a matter of evidence (often in practice determinative) going to whether he held the belief, but it is not an additional requirement that his belief must be reasonable; the question is whether it is genuinely held. When once his actual state of mind as to knowledge or belief as to facts is established, the question whether his conduct was honest or dishonest is to be determined by the fact-finder by applying the (objective) standards of ordinary decent people. There is no requirement that the defendant must appreciate that what he has done is, by those standards, dishonest."

34-293 Knowing receipt   The liability of a recipient of property disposed of in breach of trust is generally known as liability for knowing receipt.[927] The liability is personal and is to restore the value of any property received in breach of trust.[928]

34-294 Requirements of recipient liability   There are three requirements, all of which must be met, for liability to arise under this category. They were summarised by Hoffmann L.J. in *El Ajou v Dollar Land Holdings*, when he stated that the claimant must show:

"... first, a disposal of his assets in breach of fiduciary duty; secondly, the beneficial receipt by the defendant of assets which are traceable as representing the assets of the [claimant]; and thirdly, knowledge on the part of the defendant that the assets he received are traceable to a breach of fiduciary duty."[929]

34-295 Types of knowing receipt   In *Agip (Africa) Ltd v Jackson*, Millett J. identified two main types of "knowing receipt" as follows:

"The first is concerned with that of the person who receives for his own benefit trust property transferred to him in breach of trust. He is liable as a constructive trustee if he receives with notice, actual or constructive, that it was trust property and that the transfer to him was a breach of trust; or if he received it without notice but subsequently discovered

---

[927] It has been said that, according to modern authority, the recipient "is now better simply described as a person who is accountable in equity on such grounds": *Relfo Ltd (In Liquidation) v Varsani* [2012] EWHC 2168 (Ch) at [71], per Sales J. (affirmed [2014] EWCA Civ 360), citing *Paragon Finance Plc v DB Thakerar & Co* [1999] 1 All E.R. 400, 409; *Dubai Aluminium Co Ltd v Salaam* [2002] UKHL 48, [2003] 2 A.C. 366 at [142]; *Sinclair Investments (UK) Ltd v Versailles Trade Finance Ltd (In Administrative Receivership)* [2011] EWCA Civ 347, [2011] 4 All E.R. 335 at [43]–[44]. Lord Sumption has described this form of liability as "ancillary" and equity's intervention as "purely remedial", see *Williams v Central Bank of Nigeria* [2014] UKSC 10, [2014] 2 W.L.R. 355 at [9] (and see also para.34-284 above).

[928] *Arthur v Att-Gen of the Turks and Caicos Islands* [2012] UKPC 30 at [37]. But for the purpose of claiming a contribution from another wrongdoer under the Civil Liability (Contribution) Act 1978, the remedy for knowing receipt is deemed to be "compensatory": see *Charter Plc v City Index Ltd* [2007] EWCA Civ 1382, [2008] 2 W.L.R. 950 at [32]. Whether the liabilities of knowing assistants and knowing recipients are distinct or whether knowing assistance and knowing receipt establish one overarching liability to account is uncertain: contrast *Novoship (UK) Ltd v Mikhaylyuk* [2014] EWCA Civ 908, [2015] Q.B. 499 with *Akita Holdings Ltd v AG of Turks and Caicos Islands* [2017] UKPC 7, [2017] A.C. 590 and *Lifeplan Australia Friendly Society Ltd v Ancient Order of Foresters in Victoria Friendly Society Ltd* [2017] FCAFC 74, (2017) 250 F.C.R. 1 (and see P.G. Turner [2018] C.L.J. 255).

[929] [1994] 2 All E.R. 685 at 700. On the requirement that the disposal of the assets must be in breach of duty, see M. Coglan and R. Nolan (2013) 129 L.Q.R. 359. On the question of tracing, the court may decide that funds held in the defendant's bank account were the traceable proceeds of funds originally held by the claimant, notwithstanding that the claimant cannot prove every stage in the process by which the funds were ultimately transferred to the defendant, see *Relfo Ltd (In Liquidation) v Varsani* [2014] EWCA Civ 360, especially at [56]–[68] (noted by S. Watterson [2014] C.L.J. 496).

the facts. In either case he is liable to account for the property, in the first case as from the time he received the property, and in the second as from the time he acquired notice.

The second and ... distinct class of case is that of a person, usually an agent of the trustees, who receives the property lawfully and not for his own benefit but who then either misappropriates it or otherwise deals with it in a manner inconsistent with the trust. He is liable to account as constructive trustee if he received the trust property knowing it to be such, though he will not necessarily be required in all circumstances to have known the exact terms of the trust."[930]

The second class is sometimes referred to as "liability for inconsistent dealing". But where the inconsistent dealing is not for the benefit of the agent, there seems to be a good case for saying that liability only arises if there has been dishonest assistance because beneficial receipt is the essence of the knowing receipt type constructive trust.[931]

Beneficial receipt   Liability depends on *beneficial* receipt of the property disposed   **34-296**
of in breach of trust or of its traceable product. Agents who receive trust money in a ministerial capacity, i.e. for the benefit of their principal and not for their own use and benefit, are not to be made liable for "knowing receipt".[932] In *Agip (Africa) Ltd v Jackson*,[933] Millett J. expressed the clear view (obiter) that paying and collecting banks could not normally be brought within the "knowing receipt" category since they do not generally receive money for their own benefit, acting only as their customer's agent, but that the position would be otherwise if the collecting bank uses the money to reduce or discharge the customer's overdraft, when it would be using the money for its own benefit.[934]

A bank account may fluctuate between credit and debit and so it may not be easy   **34-297**
to ascertain whether money received into the account was received beneficially or not. Writing extra-judicially, Lord Millett (as he now is) has emphasised that the mere continuation of a running account should not be sufficient to render the bank liable as a recipient: there must probably be some conscious appropriation of the sum paid into the account in reduction of the overdraft.[935] This provides an important gloss to his Lordship's dictum in *Agip*, although we await a court to adopt it.

Following Lord Millett's reasoning, if a bank receives trust property into an ac-   **34-298**
count in credit, knowing that it has been paid in breach of trust, the bank cannot be held liable under the "knowing receipt" category of constructive trust: it may, however, be held liable under the "dishonest assistance" category if the necessary elements of that head of liability are all present. Of course, a bank would be considered to have *beneficially* received trust property where it exercised a right of set-off against it once it was credited to the account, or debited its commission, fees or other charges against the trust property. Again, some conscious appropriation by the bank seems necessary.[936]

---

[930] [1990] 1 Ch. 265 at 291; affirmed [1991] Ch. 547.

[931] The point is made by William Blair Q.C. in (2000) 30 H.K.L.J. 74 at 82.

[932] *Uzinterimpex JSC v Standard Bank Plc* [2008] EWCA Civ 819, [2008] 2 Lloyd's Rep. 456 at [39].

[933] [1990] Ch. 265 at 292.

[934] Implicitly approved on appeal [1991] Ch. 547; and applied by the Supreme Court of Canada in *Citadel General Assurance Co v Lloyds Bank Canada*, 152 D.L.R. (4th) 411, 422–423 (1997).

[935] P.J. Millett (1991) 107 L.Q.R. 71, 83, n.46.

[936] It has been argued that a bank receives beneficially *all* money deposited, irrespective of the state of

34-299   In *Trustor AB v Smallbone (No.2)*,[937] Morritt V.C. held that a court was entitled to pierce the corporate veil and recognise receipt by a company as receipt by the individuals in control of the company if the company was used as a device or façade to conceal the true facts thereby avoiding or concealing any liability of those individuals.

34-300   **Level of knowledge required**   The third requirement, identified by Hoffmann L.J. in *El Ajou v Dollar Land Holdings*,[938] for receipt-based liability relates to the knowledge of the recipient. Liability depends on the recipient's knowledge of the breach of trust. For this purpose, reference is often made the five categories of "knowledge" set out by Peter Gibson J. in 1983 in *Baden v Société Générale pour Favoriser le Développement du Commerce et de l'Industrie en France SA*.[939] In that case the judge divided "knowledge" into the following five categories:

(1)   actual knowledge;

(2)   wilfully shutting one's eyes to the truth;

(3)   wilfully and recklessly failing to make such inquiries as a reasonable and honest man would make;

(4)   knowledge of circumstances which would indicate the facts to an honest and reasonable man; and

(5)   knowledge of circumstances which would put a reasonable man on inquiry.

Categories (1) to (3) represent "dishonesty"; categories (4) and (5) denote "negligence".

34-301   Some cases support the view that liability only arises if the recipient has knowledge falling within the first three *Baden* categories, i.e. only in cases of dishonesty or want of probity.[940] This approach has the superficial attraction of putting the level of knowledge necessary for the receipt category of liability on a par with the need for dishonesty under the assistance category. However, it ignores the fact that a recipient *beneficially* receives trust property, whereas the defendant may have assisted another's breach of trust without necessarily being personally enriched. This fact alone seems to argue in favour of some difference in measure between them. Other cases suggest that knowledge within the first three categories is required in commercial transactions, but that knowledge falling within any of the five categories (so as to include constructive notice) is enough in non-commercial

---

the account, as the bank is entitled to do as it pleases with money received to the credit of a customer provided it pays the customer an equivalent sum on demand: see Gleeson, "The Involuntary Launderer", Ch.5 in PBH Birks (ed.), *Laundering and Tracing* (1995), pp.126–127; Bryan, "Recovering Misdirected Money from Banks: Ministerial Receipt at Law and in Equity", Ch.10 in Rose, *Restitution and Banking Law* (1998), pp.180–187; cf. Mitchell, Ch.4 in Meredith Lectures 2002, *Dirty Money: Criminal and Civil Aspects* (2003), pp.199–226, citing the arguments of Moore, "*Restitution from Banks*", unpublished D.Phil dissertation, University of Oxford, 2000, that banks receive money beneficially when deposited by the account holder but only ministerially when deposited by someone else. Moore-Bick L.J., speaking obiter in *Uzinterimpex JSC v Standard Bank Plc* [2008] EWCA Civ 819, [2008] 2 Lloyd's Rep. 456 at [40], saw "a good deal of force in Dr Bryan's criticisms of the decision in *Agip v Jackson*".

[937] [2001] 1 W.L.R. 1177. But see *Law Society of England and Wales v Habitable Concepts Ltd* [2010] EWHC 1449 (Ch) for a case where the court refused to pierce the corporate veil.

[938] See above, para.34-294.

[939] [1993] 1 W.L.R. 509.

[940] See, e.g., *Nelson v Larholt* [1948] 1 K.B. 339; as interpreted in *Carl-Zeiss-Stiftung v Herbert Smith & Co (No.2)* [1969] 2 Ch. 276; *Re Montagu's Settlement Trusts* [1987] Ch. 264.

transactions.[941] A third line of cases support the view that liability arises whenever the recipient has knowledge falling within any of the five *Baden* categories, i.e. even negligence is enough to give rise to receipt-based liability.[942]

Unconscionability as the test of liability   In *BCCI v Akindele*[943] BCCI's liquida-   **34-302**
tors claimed that A, a Nigerian businessman, was liable to repay the proceeds of an investment agreement that had been executed by BCCI's directors in breach of trust. The liquidators claimed under both the "knowing receipt" and "dishonest assistance" heads of constructive trust. At first instance, both claims failed. There was no appeal on the assistance claim as the liquidators could not prove that A had been dishonest. The issue before the Court of Appeal turned on the level of knowledge required to impose liability under the receipt category. Nourse L.J. delivered the judgment of the Court, which can be summarised as follows. First, dishonesty is not a necessary ingredient of liability in knowing receipt. Secondly, just as there is a single test of dishonesty for knowing assistance (see *Tan*), there should be a single test of knowledge for knowing receipt. Thirdly, all that is necessary is that the recipient's state of knowledge must be such as to make it unconscionable for him to retain the benefit of the receipt. Fourthly, a test based on unconscionability, while it could not avoid difficulties of application, ought to avoid the difficulties of definition which have bedevilled other categorisations of the requisite degree of knowledge, such as the *Baden* five point scale.[944] Applying the test of unconscionability to the facts of the case, the Court of Appeal held that A's state of knowledge was not such as to have made him liable under the head of knowing receipt.

It is submitted that the rejection of dishonesty as the appropriate fault element   **34-303**
for knowing receipt is welcome. It is more appropriate to a cause of action founded on culpable acts, e.g. procuring or assisting a breach of trust, than it is to passive receipt.[945] However, the term "unconscionable" lacks objectivity and is open to subjective interpretation. This leads to uncertainty. In *Tan*, Lord Nicholls was particularly critical of the use of unconscionability as the test of liability for assistance:

---

[941] See *Eagle Trust Plc v SBC Securities Ltd* [1994] 1 B.C.L.C. 464, although Vinelott J. clouded the issue by relying on the concept of "inferred knowledge"; *Eagle Trust Plc v SBC Securities Ltd (No.2)* [1996] 1 B.C.L.C. 121; *Cowan de Groot Properties Ltd v Eagle Trust Plc* [1992] 4 All E.R. 700.

[942] See *Nelson v Larholt*, above, as interpreted in *Cowan de Groot Properties v Eagle Trust* [1992] 4 All E.R. 700; *Belmont Finance Corp Ltd v Williams Furniture Ltd (No.2)* [1980] 1 All E.R. 393; *International Sales and Agencies Ltd v Marcus* [1982] 3 All E.R. 551; *Houghton v Fayers* [2000] Lloyd's Rep. Bank. 145, CA; *Westpac Banking Corp v Savin* [1985] 2 N.Z.L.R. 41 NZCA; *Powell v Thompson* [1991] 1 N.Z.L.R. 597 at 607–610; *Citadel General Assurance Co v Lloyds Bank Canada*, 152 D.L.R. (4th) 411, 429 (1997), Can SC.

[943] [2001] Ch. 437; the *Akindele* test of "unconscionability" has been endorsed by the Court of Appeal in the following cases: *Criterion Properties Plc v Stratford UK Properties Ltd* [2002] EWCA Civ 1883, [2003] 1 W.L.R. 2108 at [20]–[39] (affirmed on different grounds: [2004] UKHL 28, [2004] 1 W.L.R. 1846); *Charter Plc v City Index Ltd* [2007] EWCA Civ 1382, [2008] Ch. 313 at [8]; *Uzinterimpex JSC v Standard Bank Plc* [2008] EWCA Civ 819, [2008] 2 Lloyd's Rep. 456 at [37]–[46]; and, following agreement of the parties, by the Privy Council in *Arthur v Att-Gen of the Turks and Caicos Islands* [2012] UKPC 30 at [33]–[36] (stressing the difference between proprietary and personal remedies).

[944] Nourse L.J. added (at 455), "I have grave doubts about its utility in cases of knowing receipt". See below, para.34-303.

[945] Nolan [2000] C.L.J. 447.

"... [i]f it means no more than dishonesty, then dishonesty is the preferable label. If it means something different, it must be said that it is not clear what that something different is. Either way, the term is best avoided in this context."[946]

There has already been speculation as to what the term "unconscionable" means in this context.[947] In *Criterion Properties Plc v Stratford UK Properties LLC*,[948] the Court of Appeal held that an assessment of unconscionability based merely on whether the recipient had actual knowledge of the circumstances which gave rise to the breach of duty "was too narrow and one-sided a view of the matter".[949] The court was to have regard to the recipient's actions and knowledge in the context of

---

[946] [1995] 2 A.C. 378 at 392.

[947] See, e.g. Barkehall Thomas (2001) 21 O.J.L.S. 239 at 253–264, who formulates guidelines so as to render the test economically efficient, and also Stevens [2001] R.L.R. 99, who considers Nourse L.J.'s analysis to be "flawed".

[948] [2002] EWCA Civ 1883, [2003] 1 W.L.R. 2108 at [38]; affirmed on different grounds: [2004] UKHL 28, [2004] 1 W.L.R. 1846.

[949] In *Papamichael v National Westminster Bank Plc* [2003] EWHC 164 (Comm), [2003] 1 Lloyd's Rep. 341 at [247], Judge Chambers Q.C. treated actual knowledge as a necessary condition for liability. In *Crown Dilmun v Sutton* [2004] EWHC 52 (Ch), [2004] 1 B.C.L.C. 468 at [200], Peter Smith J., reluctantly applying the Court of Appeal decision in *Criterion Properties*, held that "attribution of knowledge is not enough. It must be unconscionable for the ... defendant to retain the benefit". In *Starglade Properties Ltd v Nash* Unreported January 26, 2010, N. Strauss Q.C. (sitting as a deputy judge of the High Court) said, at [57], that unconscionability provides "a flexible test, which requires the court to consider what is right, taking into account the nature and extent of the defendant's knowledge and all the circumstances relating to the receipt. Actual knowledge which could put a reasonable man on enquiry, coupled with a failure to enquire, may suffice ...". (Although the Court of Appeal reversed the deputy judge's decision on the claim based on dishonest assistance (see para.34-296 above), there was no appeal against his decision on the knowing receipt claim: see [2010] EWCA Civ 1314 at [6].) In *Law Society of England and Wales v Habitable Concepts Ltd* [2010] EWHC 1449 (Ch), Norris J. held, at [16], that "[t]he unexplained nature of the bank credit and its sheer scale would call for enquiry to be made by anyone who wished to deal with the credit with a clear conscience". In *Armstrong DLW GmbH v Winnington Networks Ltd* [2012] EWHC 10 (Ch), S. Morris Q.C. (sitting as a deputy judge of the High Court) said, at [132], that, in a commercial context, *Baden* types (1) to (3) knowledge on the part of a defendant renders receipt of trust property unconscionable (adding that it is not necessary to show that the defendant realised that the transaction was "obviously" or "probably" in breach of trust or fraudulent; the possibility of impropriety or the claimant's interest is sufficient); and that *Baden* types (4) and (5) knowledge also renders receipt "unconscionable" but only if, on the facts actually known to the defendant, a reasonable person would either have appreciated that the transfer was probably in breach of trust or would have made inquiries or sought advice which would have revealed the probability of the breach of trust. In *Crédit Agricole Corporation and Investment Bank v Papadimitriou* [2015] UKPC 13 at [20], where the (different) issue was whether the appellant bank was a bona fide purchaser of assets without constructive notice of an existing proprietary interest in them, the Privy Council stated that "[t]he bank must make inquiries if there is a serious possibility of a third party having such a right or, put in another way, if the facts known to the bank would give a reasonable banker in the position of the particular banker serious cause to question the propriety of the transaction". Note Lord Sumption's (at [33]) statement that "[w]hether a person claims to be a bona fide purchaser of assets without notice of a prior interest in them, or disputes a claim to make him accountable as a constructive trustee on the footing of a knowing receipt, the question what constitutes constructive notice or knowledge is the same". See also *Thanakharn Kasikorn Thai Chamkat (Mahachon) v Akai Holdings Ltd* (2010) H.K.C.F.A.R. 479 at [135], where Lord Neuberger, delivering the judgment of the Hong Kong Court of Final Appeal, said that the test of "unconscionability" for knowing receipt was "effectively identical" to that of "irrationality" for determining whether a defaulting agent has apparent authority, and that "equity would follow the law" absent special circumstances (explained and criticised by R. Lee and L. Ho in (2012) 75 M.L.R. 91). In *Relfo Ltd (In Liquidation) v Varsani* [2012] EWHC 2168 (Ch) at [79]–[80] (affirmed [2014] EWCA Civ 360), Sales J. said "one needs to be a little careful in using this formulation" (i.e. unconscionability), and preferred to speak in terms of the "relevant knowledge" identified by Millett J. in *Agip (Africa) Ltd v Jackson* [1990] 1 Ch. 265,

the commercial relationship as a whole to determine whether the test of unconscionability was satisfied. In *Akindele*, Nourse L.J. was at pains to emphasise that the new test would enable the courts to give common sense decisions in the commercial context. This seems to mean that the courts will pay equal regard to the need for speed in commercial transactions, which limits the ability to investigate matters, while also recognising that there must be cases where there is no justification on the known facts for allowing a commercial man who has received funds paid in breach of trust to plead the shelter of the exigencies of commercial life.[950]

Strict liability   It was pointed out above that the English courts are increasingly   **34-304**
coming to regard "knowing receipt" as restitution-based. Certain distinguished judges and scholars argue in favour of a standard of strict liability subject only to the defences of bona fide purchaser without notice and change of position.[951] Nourse L.J. touched on the issue in *BCCI v Akindele*. His Lordship doubted whether strict liability coupled with a change of position defence would be preferable to fault-based liability in many commercial transactions.[952] Nourse L.J. thought it was commercially unworkable, and also contrary to the internal management rule of company law, that simply on proof of an internal misapplication of the company's funds, the burden should shift to the recipient to defend the receipt either by change of position or in some other way. There does seem good sense in this last observation. For the moment, the issue must await determination by the House of Lords.[953]

Duties of care: third parties   The relaxation of the test of knowledge in the *Royal*   **34-305**
Brunei case may have a bearing on yet another type of action that is occasionally brought against banks by persons other than customers, namely, an action in negligence based on the breach of a duty of care. Notably, in *Lipkin Gorman*,[954] the Court of Appeal indicated that, usually, such an action would succeed only in circumstances that might also give rise to an action in constructive trust. In a more recent case, *Chapman v Barclays Bank Plc*,[955] the Court of Appeal indicated, however, that such an action would lie only if a certain proximity between the bank

---

291F–G, when referring to the first of the two main types of knowing receipt (see para.34-295 above). In *Arthur v Att-Gen of the Turks and Caicos Islands* [2012] UKPC 30 at [40], Sir Terence Etherton, delivering the advice of the Privy Council, said "Knowing receipt in the *Akindele* sense is ... not merely absence of notice but unconscionable conduct amounting to equitable fraud. It is a classic example of lack of *bona fides*".

[950] See Butterworths *Corporate Law Update*, August 3, 2000.

[951] See Birks, "Receipt", in Birks & Pretto (eds), *Breach of Trust* (2002), 213; Lord Nicholls, writing extra-judicially, in Cornish et al (eds), *Restitution—Past, Present and Future* (1998), p.231; Lord Walker, "Dishonesty and Unconscionable Conduct in Commercial Life" (2005) 27 Sydney L.R. 187, 202.

[952] [2001] Ch. 437 at 456.

[953] Dicta from their Lordships' House favours strict liability: *Criterion Properties Plc v Stratford UK Properties LLC* [2004] UKHL 28, [2004] 1 W.L.R. 1846 at [4], per Lord Nicholls; *Twinsectra Ltd v Yardley* [2002] UKHL 12, [2002] 2 A.C. 164, 194, per Lord Millett; but contrast *Farah Constructions Pty Ltd v Say-Dee Pty Ltd* [2007] HCA 22 at [131] and [151]–[155], noted with approval by Conaglen and Nolan [2007] C.L.J. 515, 516, where the High Court of Australia (obiter) preferred fault-based liability over strict liability, applied in *Bell Group Ltd (In Liquidation) v Westpac Banking Corp* [2008] WASC 239, and see also D. Salmons [2017] C.L.J. 399.

[954] [1989] 1 W.L.R. 1340; reversed on different grounds [1991] 2 A.C. 548.

[955] [1997] 6 Bank. L.R. 315.

and the claimant could be established on the facts. It is believed that, generally, the chances of a third party are, accordingly, slim.[956]

34-306 Duty of secrecy   The relationship of banker and customer is of a confidential nature and, as a general rule, the banker is under a duty of secrecy. The leading English case is *Tournier v National Provincial Bank*, where Atkin L.J.[958] observed that this duty applies not only to information derived by the banker from the account, but extends also to information obtained from other sources, if the occasion upon which the information is obtained arises out of the banking relationship of the bank and its customer. It does not, however, preclude the bank from referring to or disclosing information which the enquirer can readily obtain from another source, such as a caution in bankruptcy proceedings and, presumably, a caveat.[959] Generally, though, the bank's duty of confidentiality does not terminate on the closing of the account and, presumably, survives the death of the customer. In *Tournier's* case the Court of Appeal indicated, further, that the banker may disclose such information in the following cases[960]:

(a)   when there is compulsion by law, e.g. when the banker is obliged to give evidence in legal proceedings[961];

---

[956]   See, e.g. *Jeremy D Stone Consultants Ltd v National Westminster Bank Plc* [2013] EWHC 208 (Ch) at [255]–[260].

[957]   Banks also have to take account of the EU's General Data Protection Regulation 2016/679 (GDPR), which applies as from May 25, 2018 and replaces the Data Protection Act 1998. In order to Brexit-proof the legislation, a new Data Protection Act 2018 effectively replicates the GDPR into UK law.

[958]   [1924] 1 K.B. 461, 485, and see Bankes L.J. at 474. In *Tournier* the bank's duty of confidentiality was held to be an implied term of the bank–customer contract; alternatively, it may arise from an express assurance of confidentiality by the bank (see, e.g. *Primary Group (UK) Ltd v Royal Bank of Scotland Plc* [2014] EWHC 1082 (Ch), where "negotiating damages" awarded, applying the now preferred nomenclature of *Morris-Garner v One Step (Support) Ltd* [2018] UKSC 20 at [3]), or out of an equitable obligation of confidence (see, e.g. *CF Partners (UK) LLP v Barclays Bank Plc* [2014] EWHC 3049 (Ch), where "negotiating damages" awarded). For case law relating to the prohibition of disclosure to other companies in the same group, see *Bank of Tokyo v Karoon* [1987] A.C. 45n, CA, 53–54; *Bhogal v Punjab National Bank* [1988] 2 All E.R. 296, 305, CA. See the *Standards of Lending Practice for Personal Customers* (para.34-222 above) at pp.7 (Account maintenance and servicing: "Firms will maintain the security of customers' data but may share information about the day-to-day running of a customer's account(s), including positive data, with credit reference agencies where the firm has agreed to follow the principles of reciprocity. [CONC 5]"), and for the same guidance with regard to business customers, see the *Standards of Lending Practice for Business Customers* (para.34-223 above) at pp.9–10 (Product execution), point 5. See also the *Lending Code*, revised 2nd edn (2014), para.[15] (customer's personal information to be treated as private and confidential).

[959]   *Christofi v Barclays Bank Plc* [1998] 1 W.L.R. 1245; affirmed [2000] 1 W.L.R. 937.

[960]   "Where the case is within one of the qualifications to the duty of confidence, the duty, *ex hypothesi*, does not exist": *El Jawhary v Bank of Credit and Commerce International SA* [1993] B.C.L.C. 396 at 400, per Nicholls V.-C. See also *Barclays Bank Plc v Taylor* [1989] 1 W.L.R. 1066 at 1074, per Lord Donaldson M.R.

[961]   Consider, e.g. the banker's duty of making payment to sequestrators and of disclosing to them the state of the customer's account: *Bucknell v Bucknell* [1969] 1 W.L.R. 1204; *Eckman v Midland Bank Ltd* [1973] Q.B. 519. For another instance of legal compulsion, see, e.g. the Income Tax Act 2007 s.771. See also the Bankers Books Evidence Act 1879 s.7, and the analysis in *Williams v Summerfield* [1972] 2 Q.B. 512; and in *R. v Marlborough St Metropolitan Stipendiary Magistrate Ex p. Simpson* [1980] Crim. L.R. 305; Police and Criminal Evidence Act 1984 s.9; the Companies Act 1985 ss.434(2), 452(1A); Insolvency Act 1986 ss.236, 366; Financial Services and Markets Act 2000

(b) when public interest calls for disclosure, e.g. when during war time the customer's activities disclose dealings with the enemy[962]; and

(c) when the disclosure is necessary in the banker's own interest, e.g. when, in order to claim repayment of an overdraft, he has to disclose that the customer's account is overdrawn.[963]

Pt XI. Note that disclosure of such information by way of a discovery will be ordered, as a matter of justice, in respect of proceedings in which the bank's customer is sued in fraud by a third party: *A v C* [1980] 2 All E.R. 347; *Bankers Trust Co v Shapira* [1980] 3 All E.R. 353; *C v S* [1999] Lloyd's Rep. Bank. 26 (giving important guidance to banks served with a disclosure order and also concerned with prosecution for "tipping off": two "tipping off" offences are now to be found in the Proceeds of Crime Act 2002 s.333A, with the separate offence of prejudicing an investigation in s.342; see also *Bank of Scotland v A Ltd* [2001] EWCA Civ 52, [2001] 1 W.L.R. 751; *Tayeb v HSBC Bank Plc* [2004] EWHC 1529 (QB), [2004] 4 All E.R. 1024). And note that where the bank is compelled to disclose, it is not under a duty to oppose the orders or to notify the customer: *Barclays Bank v Taylor* [1989] 1 W.L.R. 1066, CA. A bank is likewise not in breach of its duty of confidentiality where it produces documents as ordered in a subpoena duces tecum (now called a "witness summons" under the Civil Procedure Rules 1998): *Robertson v Canadian Imperial Bank of Commerce* [1994] 1 W.L.R. 824, PC.

Legislation to combat money laundering and the financing of terrorist activities is particularly draconian. A bank commits an offence if it fails to disclose to the National Crime Agency its knowledge or suspicion, or that it has reasonable grounds for knowledge or suspicion, that a customer is engaged in money laundering or terrorist offences (Proceeds of Crime Act 2002 s.330; Terrorism Act 2000 s.21A, as inserted by the Anti-terrorism, Crime and Security Act 2001 Sch.2 Pt 3). The threshold for suspicion is low: the bank only has to consider that there is a more than fanciful possibility that the relevant facts exist (*K Ltd v National Westminster Bank Plc* [2006] EWCA Civ 1039, [2007] 1 W.L.R. 311 at [16], applied in *Shah v HSBC Private Bank (UK) Ltd* [2009] EWHC 79 (QB), [2009] 1 Lloyd's Rep. 328 at [45], reversed [2010] EWCA Civ 31, [2011] 1 All E.R. (Comm) 67, but *K Ltd* applied at [21], and also applied by Supperstone J. at the trial of the action: [2012] EWHC 1283 (QB) at [67]–[69])). Subjectively, the bank may itself know or suspect the customer is engaged in money laundering or terrorist offences but, even if it does not, it may objectively have reasonable grounds for such knowledge or suspicion. Such disclosure is a "protected disclosure", i.e. it "is not to be taken to breach any restriction on the disclosure of information (however arising)" (Proceeds of Crime Act 2002 s.337(1); Terrorism Act 2000 s.21B(1), as inserted). In general terms, a customer who opens an account at a bank in the UK must be taken to have accepted and be entitled to assume that the bank will act in accordance with applicable anti-money laundering and terrorism legislation (*Tayeb v HSBC Bank Plc* [2004] EWHC 1529 (Comm), [2004] 4 All E.R. 1024 at [57], per Colman J.).

A bank (the paying bank) may be granted a *Norwich Pharmacal* order against another bank (the beneficiary's bank) compelling it to disclose information in relation to the identity of certain of its customers who were beneficiaries of electronic payments made as a result of the paying bank's own mistakes, e.g. making a duplicate payment, selection of an incorrect mandate or insertion of an incorrect account number, see *Santander UK Plc v National Westminster Bank Plc* [2014] EWHC 2626 (Ch); *Santander UK Plc v Royal Bank of Scotland Plc* [2015] EWHC 2560 (Ch) at [11]–[17], but with criticism of the ruling in *Santander UK Plc v National Westminster Bank Plc*, above, that a claim in unjust enrichment was a wrong capable of justifying a *Norwich Pharmacal* order (noted by M. Campbell [2016] L.M.C.L.Q. 42).

[962] For recent cases recognising the existence of an independent ground of disclosure under this qualification, see *Price Waterhouse v BCCI Holdings (Luxembourg) SA* [1992] B.C.L.C. 583; *Douglas v Pindling* [1996] A.C. 890, PC; *Pharaon v Bank of Credit and Commerce International SA (In Liquidation)* [1998] 4 All E.R. 455. For earlier tentative (and obiter) recognition, see *Libyan Arab Foreign Bank v Bankers Trust Co* [1989] Q.B. 728, 771, per Staughton J. See also *Rodaro v Royal Bank of Canada*, 59 O.R. (3d) 74 (2002), Ont CA, noted by Ogilvie (2004) 19 B.F.L.R. 103.

[963] See *Kaupthing Singer & Friedlander Ltd v Coomber* [2011] EWHC 3589 (Ch) at [52], [56]; *Deutsche Bank (Suisse) SA v Khan* [2013] EWHC 482 (Comm) at [384]–[393]. See also *Sunderland v Barclays Bank Ltd* (1938) 5 L.D.A.B. 163; *Nam Tai Electronics Inc v Price-waterhouseCoopers* [2008] 1 H.K.C. 427 at [49], [53], [54] HKCFA. See also *Primary Group (UK) Ltd v Royal Bank of Scotland Plc* [2014] EWHC 1082 (Ch) at [192], where disclosure was held not to be "reasonably

Finally, *Tournier's* case indicates that the banker is entitled to give information when expressly or impliedly authorised so to do by the customer.[964] There is an established trade practice that banks provide each other with credit references relating to their customers. In the past banks justified this practice on the ground that their customers gave their implied consent to it. However, in *Turner v Royal Bank of Scotland Plc*,[965] a case where the customer had a personal account with the bank, the Court of Appeal held that this practice was not sufficiently "notorious" (i.e. known to the bank's customers) to make it an implied term of the banker–customer contract.[966] The Court of Appeal ignored the fact that the customer also held a business account at the bank, and so it is unclear whether *Turner* applies to business customers.[967]

34-307 **Extraterritorial orders** Specific problems arise where courts in one country issue orders for the disclosure of information which are meant to have effect in another country.[968] In practice, this type of case arises principally where courts or grand juries in the United States issue orders addressed to overseas branches of

---

necessary" for the bank's own protection. The "interests of the bank exception" probably needs to be reassessed in the light of developments in the law of confidence, misuse of private information and data protection (as to which, see R. Spearman [2012] J.I.B.F.L. 78).

[964] It has been suggested that where such consent has been given not freely but under compulsion, for instance, by a foreign court, the bank ought to refuse to make disclosure: *Re ABC* [1985] F.L.R. 159 Cayman Islands. But see R. Cranston, E. Avgouleas, K. van Zwieten, C. Hare and T. van Sante, *Principles of Banking Law*, 3rd edn (2018), 266. For examples where legislation allows disclosure but only with customer consent, see the Small and Medium Sized Business (Credit Information) Regulations 2015 (SI 2015/1945) regs 3(2), 6(1)(b); the Small and Medium Sized Business (Finance Platforms) Regulations 2015 (SI 2015/1946) regs 3(4), 6(3)(b).

[965] [1992] 2 All E.R. (Comm) 664.

[966] *Turner* dealt with banking practice between 1986 and 1989, and therefore predates the 1994 revision of the *Banking Code* (for personal customers) which made banker's references subject to the express consent of the customer concerned. A similar requirement was contained in the *Business Banking Code* (for business customers) first published in 2002. Both Codes were replaced in November 2009 by a new Banking and Payment Services (BPS) conduct regime (see above, para.34-219). See now the Standards of Lending Practice for consumer customers and also for business customers (paras 34-222—34-223 above), although neither makes direct reference to the practice of giving banker's references. A bank has been held to owe a duty of care to its customer when providing information to credit reference agencies in relation to that customer, and to owe a duty of care to the customer's spouse where she was a joint holder of the same account and a co-director of the family business which largely depended on her husband's credit (but "almost certainly" not in the ordinary case): *Gatt v Barclays Bank Plc* [2013] EWHC 2 (QB) at [35], where held that bank was not liable to spouse in contract (she was also a customer of the bank), negligence or defamation where it sent computerised information about her husband to credit reference agencies stating that an account, which was a joint account with her, was "delinquent" because the overdraft exceeded the agreed limit. For the duty imposed on designated banks to provide information about their small and medium-sized business customers to designated credit reference agencies (CRAs), and the duty on designated CRAs to provide credit information about small and medium-sized businesses to finance providers, see the Small and Medium Sized Business (Credit Information) Regulations 2015 (SI 2015/1945).

[967] E.P. Ellinger, E. Lomnicka and C.V.M. Hare, *Ellinger's Modern Banking Law*, 5th edn (2011), pp.195–197.

[968] Where a requesting court located in another EU Member State (except Denmark) issues a letter of request to obtain evidence in the UK in relation to a "civil or commercial matter", the position is governed by Council Regulation (EC) 1206/2001 on the co-operation between Member States in the taking of evidence in civil or commercial matters. Where the requesting court is not located in another Member State, a letter of request is governed by the Hague Convention on the Taking of Evidence Abroad in Civil or Commercial Matters 1970, and, where the requested court is in the UK, the position is governed by the Evidence (Proceedings in Other Jurisdictions) Act 1975. See gener-

American banks or instruct a bank's American head office to acquire the information involved from its branches abroad. The customer of the respective overseas branch may, of course, object to the disclosure of the information and, where necessary, apply for an injunction to preclude his branch from complying with the American order. Predictably, English courts have shown no sympathy for the foreign courts' trespass into their jurisdiction. Thus, in *Re Westinghouse Uranium Contract*[969] the House of Lords held that a request for the disclosure of information made in a letter rogatory addressed by the United States District Court to the High Court ought to be denied if the information involved was subject to bank secrecy in the United Kingdom. Their Lordships placed considerable weight on an opinion submitted by the Attorney-General, who took the view that the wide investigatory procedures applicable under the United States' anti-trust law against foreign citizens constituted an infringement of the law of the United Kingdom.

In another case, *X A G v A Bank*,[970] Leggatt J. showed no hesitation in enjoining **34-308** an American bank from complying with an American Department of Justice's subpoena *duces tecum* which was supported by an order issued by the United States District Court, in which the bank's head office was instructed to produce in the United States records maintained with its London office. Holding that the proper law of the contract between the bank and the relevant customer was English law, his Lordship observed that if the order were carried out, it:

"... would take effect in London for the production of documents in breach of what might be termed a private interest in the sense that what is directly involved is a contract between banker and customer. But this indubitably is also a matter of public interest, because it raises issues of wider concern than those peculiar to the [instant] parties."[971]

Weighing all the circumstances of the case and taking into account the interests of both the bank and the customer, Leggatt J. enjoined disclosure.

English courts are, thus, strongly disinclined to uphold a foreign court's order **34-309** which is contrary to English law or which conflicts with what may be best termed the local public interest. A more recent instance of the same policy is to be seen in *Libyan Arab Foreign Bank v Bankers' Trust Co.*[972] In this case Staughton J. ordered an American bank to effect payment of an amount deposited with its London office, notwithstanding an order in which President Reagan sought to freeze balances maintained by Libyan Government bodies with all the branches of American banks. As a corollary to their firm stand against extraterritorial orders issued overseas, the English courts have shown an unwillingness to issue orders for the disclosure of evidence that would have to take effect outside the United Kingdom.[973]

---

ally, E.P. Ellinger, E. Lomnicka and C.V.M. Hare, *Ellinger's Modern Banking Law*, 5th edn (2011), pp.197–207.
[969] [1978] A.C. 547.
[970] [1983] 2 All E.R. 464.
[971] [1983] 2 All E.R. 464 at 477. But see *First American Corp v Sheikh Zayed Al-Nahyan* [1999] 1 W.L.R. 1154; *Pharaon v BCCI SA (In Liquidation)* [1998] 4 All E.R. 455: the public interest in making documents available in the foreign court in respect of international fraud usually outweighs concerns about bank confidentiality.
[972] [1988] 1 Lloyd's Rep. 259; and see *Libyan Arab Foreign Bank v Manufacturers Hanover Trust Co* [1988] 2 Lloyd's Rep. 494; and *Libyan Arab Foreign Bank v Manufacturers Hanover Trust (No.2)* [1989] 1 Lloyd's Rep. 608 (Hirst J.).
[973] *R. v Grossman* (1981) 73 Cr. App. R. 302; *MacKinnon v Donaldson, Lufkin & Jenrette Securities Corp* [1986] Ch. 482. See also *Société Eram Shipping Co Ltd v Compagnie Internationale de*

(viii) Termination of Relationship

34-310 Termination of relationship by consent The contract may fix the period the bank-customer relationship is to last, e.g. as with a fixed term deposit, so that there can be no early termination without the consent of both parties. By contrast, where an account is repayable on demand, as with a current account or easy access savings accounts, the customer may at common law terminate the relationship at any time by withdrawing the credit balance and closing the account.[974] For accounts that fall within the scope of the Payment Services Regulations 2017,[975] such as current accounts and easy access savings accounts, the contract may be terminated by the customer at any time, unless a period of notice (not exceeding one month) has been agreed.[976] The position is different where the bank wishes to terminate the relationship. At common law, as confirmed by Lord Hoffmann in *National Commercial Bank of Jamaica Ltd v Olint Corp Ltd*[977]:

> "... in the absence of express contrary agreement or statutory impediment, a contract by a bank to provide banking services to a customer is terminable upon reasonable notice."[978]

However, current accounts and easy access savings accounts will constitute "framework contracts" under the Payment Services Regulations 2017, so that a bank may only close an account opened for an indefinite period by giving at least two months' notice, if the contract so provides.[979]

Navigacion [2003] UKHL 30, [2003] 3 W.L.R. 21 at [22]–[23] and [67], HL (similar principles expressed when court refuses to grant third party debt order over credit balance in foreign bank account). cf. *Masri v Consolidated Contractors International Co SAL (No.2)* [2008] EWCA Civ 303, [32]–[35], per Lawrence Collins L.J., but see also *Masri v Consolidated Contractors International Co SAL (No.4)* [2008] EWCA Civ 876, [15]–[16], [80], [2009] UKHL 43, [19], [26]. Interestingly, in *Credit Suisse Trust Ltd v Intesa Sanpaolo SpA* [2014] EWHC 1447 (Ch), the English High Court granted *Norwich Pharmacal* relief to the victim of fraud by ordering the London branches of two Italian banks to provide information about a customer, despite the fact that the banking activity took place in Italy and all the information sought was held in Italy: the only link to the UK was that the banks had branches in London.

[974] But see *Bank of Baroda v Mahomed* [1999] Lloyd's Rep. Bank. 14, CA (limitation point arising because customer made separate demands for repayment).

[975] Payment Services Regulations 2017 (SI 2017/752) ("PSRs 2017"), as amended. See, previously, Payment Services Regulations 2009 (SI 2009/209), as amended ("PSRs 2009"). See above, paras.34-224 et seq., and below, paras 34-401 et seq.

[976] Termination of a "framework contract", such as one for a current account or easy access savings account, including the bank's right to charge for closing the account, is provided for in the PSRs 2017 reg.51 (see also PSRs 2009 reg.43). A framework contract is defined in reg.2(1) to mean "a contract for payment services which govern the future execution of individual and successive payment transactions and which may contain the obligation and conditions for setting up a payment account". The regulation does not affect the parties' rights to treat the framework contract, in accordance with the general law of contract, as unenforceable, void or discharged (PSRs 2017 reg.51(7); see also PSRs 2009 reg.43(7)). Where the framework contract is also a regulated agreement under the Consumer Credit Act 1974, PSRs 2017 reg.51 does not apply (PSRs 2017 reg.41(2); see also PSRs 2009 reg.34).

[977] [2009] UKPC 16 at [1].

[978] As to what constitutes a reasonable period of notice, see *Prosperity Ltd v Lloyds Bank Ltd* (1923) 39 T.L.R. 372 (refusing to grant a mandatory injunction ordering the bank to reopen the account). See also *National Commercial Bank of Jamaica Ltd v Olint Corp Ltd*, above, at [16]–[21], where application for injunction also refused on grounds that, where customer disputes closure of his account, damages will usually be an adequate remedy. cf. *N v S* [2015] EWHC 3248 (Comm) at [12]–[13], reversed [2017] EWCA Civ 253.

[979] PSRs 2017 reg.51(4) (see also PSRs 2009 reg.43(4)).

(c) The Current Account

(i) Rights and Duties of the Banker

Nature of relationship The relationship between the banker and a customer who   **34-311**
has opened a current account is that of debtor and creditor.[980] The debt is, however,
payable only on demand at the branch in which the account is kept.[981] Thus, it is
not the banker's duty to seek his creditor, the customer, and repay the debt. The
banker is under an obligation to honour cheques of the customer, provided an
adequate credit balance is available.[982] When drawing a cheque the customer, acting as principal, authorises his banker—his agent—to make payment.[983] A relationship of principal and agent is, accordingly, superimposed on the basic relationship
of creditor and debtor. In carrying out instructions given to the bank by its
customer—the principal—it must exercise reasonable care and skill.[984] Its main
duty, though, is to adhere strictly to the terms of its mandate.[985]

The mandate to pay: electronic means of payment In modern banking practice,   **34-312**
a bank usually agrees with its customer to honour payment instructions delivered
by electronic means, e.g. by use of a debit card, or by use of a password communicated to the bank over a telephone or internet link.[986] The bank is probably not
obliged to provide these services to its customer without special agreement whereas

---

[980] *Foley v Hill* (1848) 2 H.L. Cas. 28; *Joachimson v Swiss Bank Corp* [1921] 3 K.B. 110. A bank open-
ing a current account must satisfy certain "customer due diligence" requirements contained in the
Money Laundering, Terrorist Financing and Transfer of Funds (Information on the Payer) Regula-
tions 2017 (SI 2017/692) Pts 3–4, implementing the Fourth Money Laundering Directive 2015/849/
EU. It must also normally satisfy the requirements of the Banking Conduct of Business Sourcebook
(BCOBS) and the Payment Services Regulations 2017 (SI 2017/752), as amended. For details, see
E.P. Ellinger, E. Lomnicka and C.V.M. Hare, *Ellinger's Modern Banking Law*, 5th edn (2011), Ch.7,
s.2.

[981] *Joachimson v Swiss Bank Corp*, above; *Arab Bank Ltd v Barclays Bank DCO* [1954] A.C. 495. The
rule that repayment must be demanded at the branch of the bank that holds the account is ripe for
review in the light of modern technology and business practices when customers can now access
their accounts remotely, via cash machines and through debit cards, and where some banks operate
over the internet and through telephone banking services with no branches at all. The courts in one
overseas jurisdiction seem prepared to jettison the rule (*Damayanti Kantilal Doshi v Indian Bank*
[1999] 4 S.L.R. 1, 11, Sing CA).

[982] *Joachimson v Swiss Bank Corp*, above; *Bank of New South Wales v Laing* [1954] A.C. 135, 154;
Barclays Bank Ltd v WJ Simms Ltd [1980] 1 Q.B. 692, 699; *Sierra Leone Telecommunication Co
Ltd v Barclays Bank Plc* [1998] 2 All E.R. 821, 827; *Re Spectrum Plus Ltd* [2005] 2 A.C. 680 at [59].

[983] *London Joint Stock Bank v Macmillan* [1918] A.C. 777; *Westminster Bank v Hilton* (1926) 43 T.L.R.
124. This remains the case even where the account is overdrawn: *Coutts & Co v Stock* [2000] 1
W.L.R. 906 at 909, Lightman J., endorsed by the Court of Appeal (obiter) in *Hollicourt (Contracts)
Ltd v Bank of Ireland* [2001] 2 W.L.R. 290 at 296, 300.

[984] *Astro Amo Compania Naviera SA v Elf Union SA (The Zographia M)* [1976] 2 Lloyd's Rep. 382,
393; *Barclays Bank Plc v Quincecare Ltd* [1992] 4 All E.R. 363, 376.

[985] Conflict can exist between the bank's duty to honour the mandate and its duty to exercise reasonable care and skill in and about the execution of the mandate, e.g. where an agent authorised to draw
on his principal's bank account does so for his own benefit or for an unauthorised purpose: see *Lipkin
Gorman (a firm) v Karpnale Ltd* [1989] 1 W.L.R. 1340, CA, varied on another point: [1991] 2 A.C.
548; *Barclays Bank Plc v Quincecare Ltd* [1992] 4 All E.R. 363; *Verjee v CIBC Bank & Trust Co
(Channel Islands) Ltd* [2001] Lloyd's Rep. Bank. 279; *Singularis Holdings Ltd (In Liquidation) v
Daiwa Capital Markets Europe Ltd* [2017] EWHC 257 (Ch), affirmed [2018] EWCA Civ 84.

[986] The bank's standard terms and conditions often allow a customer to give, and the bank to act on,
oral instructions (see *Earles v Barclays Bank Plc* [2009] EWHC 2500 (QB) at [17]). On its true
construction, a "one signature" mandate expressed to authorise payment by cheques or other writ-

it is obliged to honour cheques drawn by its customer under the express or implied terms of the banker–customer contract which arises when an account is opened.[987] In fact, current accounts are now more commonly accessed by electronic means than by the customer drawing a cheque on the account. Banks have standard terms and conditions that govern the operation of a customer's current account and which provide for access to the account through electronic means. Such terms and conditions usually reflect the statutory rights and duties that apply through the provisions of the Payment Services Regulations 2017 (PSRs 2017),[988] and also the FCA's *Banking Conduct of Business Sourcebook*, which provide mandatory rules for those residual cases where the PSRs 2017 do not apply.[989] Regulation 82(5) of the PSRs 2017 provides that:

"... [w]here all the conditions of the payer's framework contract with the account servicing payment service provider have been satisfied, the account servicing payment service provider may not refuse to execute an authorised payment order irrespective of whether the payment order is initiated by the payer, through a payment initiation service provider, or by or through a payee, unless such execution is otherwise unlawful."[990]

Detailed consideration of the PSRs 2017 is found later in this chapter.[991] Cheques fall outside the PSRs 2017.[992]

34-313 **The mandate to pay: cheques** The customer's cheque is a mandate authorising the banker to honour the cheque when presented by the payee or a holder.[993] The mandate may be limited by the inclusion of a general or special crossing, as well as by including in the cheque words prohibiting transfer.[994]

34-314 **Limits on duty to honour cheque** There are several limitations to the banker's duty to honour a cheque drawn by the customer. First, the banker is under an obligation to honour a cheque only if the customer's account is either actually in credit, or, where it is in debit, if the customer has been granted an overdraft.[995] Thus, if the customer has made a deposit, but a cheque is presented before the banker has had reasonable time for crediting the amount deposited to the account, he is not liable

---

ten instructions and "for all other purposes" has been held to bind a partnership in respect of loan agreements signed by only one of the partners (*Kotak v Kotak* [2017] EWHC 1821 (Ch)).

[987] *Libyan Arab Foreign Bank v Bankers Trust Co* [1989] Q.B. 728, 749.

[988] SI 2017/752 ("PSRs 2017"), as amended. See, previously, Payment Services Regulations 2009 (SI 2009/209), as amended. For when the PSRs 2017 apply, see above, paras 34-224—34-225, and below, paras 34-401—34-404. The PSRs 2017 may be disapplied in favour of the Consumer Credit Act 1974 (PSRs 2017 regs 41, 64).

[989] BCOBS Ch.5, in particular BCOBS 5.1.11R (bank's liability for unauthorised payments) and 5.1.12R (banking customer's liability for unauthorised payments). BCOBS 5.1.11R–5.1.19R are similar to Pt 7of the PSRs 2017.

[990] For definition of a "framework contract", see reg.2(1) and para.34-310 above. But note the "force majeure" provision set out in reg.96.

[991] See below, paras 34-401 et seq.

[992] PSRs 2017 Sch.1 Pt 2(g), the exclusion under this paragraph also include travellers' cheques, bankers' drafts, paper-based vouchers and paper postal orders.

[993] At the time the account was opened, the customer will have identified those individuals who are authorised to sign cheques and draw on the account. But even a customer's irrevocable authority to a bank to accept the written demand of a particular person may later be overridden by the oral instructions of the customer himself: *Morrell v Workers Savings & Loan Bank* [2007] UKPC 3 at [10].

[994] As regards crossing cheques, see above, paras 34-158 et seq.; as regards words prohibiting transfer, see ss.8 and 81A of the Act, discussed in paras 34-026—34-028 and 34-165—34-168, above.

[995] See below, para.34-315.

if he dishonours the cheque.[996] Similarly, if the customer instructs his bankers to collect cheques and credit his account with the proceeds, he is not entitled to draw against these cheques until they have been cleared. However, once the account is credited the customer is, in the absence of stipulation to the contrary, entitled to draw the full amount, although some cheques paid in may not have been cleared.[997] Secondly, the cheque is a mandate requesting the banker to pay it at the branch at which the account is kept. The customer is not entitled to demand payment at another branch, and, if a cheque is, in point of fact, cashed for a holder at another branch of the bank, this branch is probably to be considered as discounting or collecting the cheque.[998] Thirdly, a cheque should be paid only if presented during ordinary business hours. However, if a banker pays a cheque shortly after business hours, he does not exceed his authority.[999] Finally, as a matter of practice, bankers do not honour cheques that have been outstanding for a long period, and one presented more than 6 months after the date of issue is unlikely to be paid.[1000] It is, likewise, the practice not to pay an undated cheque[1001]; but a banker would honour it, if the holder exercised his prima facie authority to complete the instrument within a reasonable time.

Overdrafts Where there are insufficient funds available to cover the full amount of the customer's cheque, the bank may refuse to honour it. In such circumstances the cheque stands as an offer by the customer to the bank to extend credit to him on the bank's usual terms as to interest and other charges, unless other terms have been agreed between them.[1002] The bank may either reject the offer or accept it by   **34-315**

---

996 *Marzetti v Williams* (1830) 1 B. & Ad. 415, 424.

997 *Capital and Counties Bank v Gordon* [1903] A.C. 240, 249.

998 *Woodland v Fear* (1857) 7 E. & B. 519. But see also above, para.34-311.

999 *Baines v National Provincial Bank* (1927) 32 Com. Cas. 216.

1000 In New Zealand it has been recognised that a cheque becomes stale after 6 months: *Commissioners of Inland Revenue v Thomas Cook (NZ) Ltd* [2003] 2 N.Z.L.R. 296 at [31]–[39], upheld on different grounds [2004] UKPC 53.

1001 *Griffiths v Dalton* [1940] 2 K.B. 264.

1002 *Emerald Meats (London) Ltd v AIB Group (UK) Ltd* [2002] EWCA Civ 460 at [12]; *Lloyds Bank Plc v Voller* [2000] 2 All E.R. (Comm) 978 at 982, CA; *Barclays Bank Ltd v W.J Simms, Son & Cooke (Southern) Ltd* [1980] Q.B. 677 at 699. The Supreme Court has held that bank charges levied on personal current account customers in respect of unauthorised overdrafts constitute part of the price or remuneration for the banking services provided and, in so far as the terms giving rise to the charges are in plain intelligible language, no assessment of the fairness of those terms, under the Unfair Terms in Consumer Contracts Regulations 1999, may relate to their adequacy as against the services provided: see *Office of Fair Trading v Abbey National Plc* [2009] UKSC 6, [2010] 1 A.C. 696 (but contrast European Court of Justice's strict interpretation of art.4(2) exception in underlying EC Directive 1993/13/EEC: *Kásler v OTP Jelzálogbank Zrt* (C-26/13) EU:C:2014:282; *Jean-Claude Van Hove v CNP Assurances SA* (C-96/14) EU:C:2015:262; *Andriciuc v Banca Românească SA* (C-186/16) EU:C:2017:703). Note that, in response to the Supreme Court's decision in *OFT v Abbey National Plc*, the Consumer Rights Act 2015 s.64(2), introduces an additional requirement for the application of the exclusion from the test of unfairness of terms relating to the main subject matter of the contract or the price/quality ratio: the term must be both transparent (expressed in plain and intelligible language and, in the case of a written term, legible: subs.(3)) and (which is new) prominent (brought to the consumer's attention in such a way that an average consumer would be aware of the term: subss. (4)–(5)), and not a term listed in Pt 1 of Sch.2 of the 2015 Act (subs.(6)) Pt 2 of the 2015 Act replaced the 1999 Regulations for contracts made on or after October 1, 2015 (see below, Ch.38)). Andrew Smith J. held at first instance in *Abbey National* that such bank charges could not be characterised as penalties because they were levied other than upon a breach of contract: [2008] EWHC 875 (Comm), [2008] 2 All E.R. (Comm) 625. When reviewing the penalty clause jurisdiction in *Cavendish Square Holding BV v Makdessi* [2015] UKSC 67, [2016] A.C. 1172, the

paying the cheque and, in doing so, allow the customer to overdraw.[1003] In the case of a joint account, all the account holders will be liable for the overdrawn balance where the bank advances funds at the request of only one of them, even though as between the account holders themselves this was unauthorised, so long as the bank acts within the terms of the original mandate agreed when the account was opened, e.g. where only one signature is required on the cheque.[1004]

34-316 **Combining accounts**   It has been held in *Garnett v M'Kewan*[1005] that if a customer has a current account which is in credit with one branch of the bank, and another account which is overdrawn with another branch, the banker is entitled to combine the two accounts,[1006] so as to set off the overdraft against the credit balance. The nature of this right and of its abrogation by contract are discussed in *National Westminster Bank Ltd v Halesowen Presswork and Assemblies Ltd.*[1007] The plaintiffs maintained an account with the defendant bank. In April 1968, when this account showed a substantial debit balance, an account No.2 was opened for the plaintiffs'

Supreme Court (at [40]–[43]) declined to follow the approach taken in Australia and retained the requirement that the penalty doctrine is only triggered by breach. The different approaches to the breach requirement in the two jurisdictions has been confirmed by the High Court of Australia in *Paciocco v ANZ Banking Group Ltd* [2016] HCA 28 at [7]–[10] and [119]–[127], and see also *Andrews v Australia and New Zealand Banking Group Ltd* [2012] HCA 30, (2012) 290 A.L.R. 595. For whether overdraft charges can be challenged as part of an "unfair credit relationship" under Consumer Credit Act 1974 ss.140A–D, see D. Cook, A. Ibrahim and A. Khan [2011] J.I.B.F.L. 212, and the expanding case law on these provisions, including *Plevin v Paragon Personal Finance Ltd* [2014] UKSC 61, [2014] 1 W.L.R. 4222; *Nelmes v Nram Plc* [2016] EWCA Civ 491; *McMullon v Secure the Bridge Ltd* [2015] EWCA Civ 884; *Barclays Bank Plc v McMillan* [2015] EWHC 1596 (Comm); *Deutsche Bank (Suisse) SA v Khan* [2013] EWHC 482 (Comm); *Carney v NM Rothschild & Sons Ltd* [2018] EWHC 958 (Comm).

[1003] *Barclays Bank Ltd v WJ Simms, Son & Cooke (Southern) Ltd* [1980] Q.B. 677. See also *Office of Fair Trading v Abbey National Plc* [2008] EWHC 875 (Comm), [2008] 2 All E.R. (Comm) 625 at [79] (bank must exercise its decision honestly and rationally). In *Verjee v CIBC Bank and Trust Co (Channel Islands) Ltd* [2001] Lloyd's Rep. Bank. 279, it was held that the mere fact that a cheque was drawn against an inadequate balance did not put the bank on inquiry and that, by honouring the cheque, the bank did not commit a breach of a duty of care to the customer.

[1004] *Royal Bank of Scotland Plc v Fielding* [2003] EWHC 986 (Ch) at [81], [85], per Hart J.; affirmed. [2004] EWCA Civ 64 (but Jonathan Parker J. suggesting (at [108]) (without deciding the point) that bank might breach its duty of care to one account holder if it continued to operate the account even though it "had some reason to suppose the mandate was being abused" by the other account holder, or (at [101]) had "notice that a fraud is bring committed").

[1005] (1872) L.R. 8 Ex. 10. See also *Barclays Bank Ltd v Okenarhe* [1966] 2 Lloyd's Rep. 87. For a detailed discussion see E.P. Ellinger, E. Lomnicka and C.V.M. Hare, *Ellinger's Modern Banking Law*, 5th edn (2011), pp.248–268, 884–891.

[1006] *Garnett v M'Kewan*, above, does not regard the right of combination as subject to notice; *National Westminster Bank Ltd v Halesowen Presswork and Assemblies Ltd* [1972] A.C. 785, 807, 810, 820 treats the question as still open but contains strong dicta suggesting that notice, even though with immediate effect, is required. For retail customers, the bank's right of set-off (or combination) is now regulated by the FCA's *Banking Conduct of Business Sourcebook* (BCOBS), which imposes certain information requirements pre-contract (BCOBS 4.1.4AG(2)(a)(i),(ii)), pre-use of set-off rights (BCOBS 4.1.4AG(2)(b)(i),(ii)) and post-use of set-off rights (BCOBS 4.1.4AG(2)(c)). BCOBS also imposes limits on the use of set-off rights against retail customers: see BCOBS 5.1.3AG(1),(2)(a) (customer must be left with a "subsistence balance"); BCOBS 5.1.3AG(2)(b)(i),(ii) (no set-off of personal debts against ring-fenced or earmarked funds) and BCOBS 5.1.3BG(1),(2) (refund is usual remedy unless not fair to do so). Neither the *Standards of Lending Practice for Personal Customers* nor the *Standards of Lending Practice for Business Customers* (paras 34-222—34-223 above) have detailed provisions about the use of the right of set off.

[1007] Above, reversing the decision of the Court of Appeal and restoring Roskill J.'s judgment: [1971] 1 Q.B. 1. See also Vol.I, paras 20-040 et seq.

trading operations. The bank agreed that, in the absence of a material change of circumstances, account No.1 would remain frozen for a period of four months. On June 12, 1968, the plaintiffs passed a resolution to wind up voluntarily. On June 19, the bank informed the liquidator that it had determined to set off the debit balance in account No.1 against the credit balance in account No.2. The majority of the House of Lords held that the bank was entitled to take this course. In the first place, the resolution to wind up involved a change in the circumstances under which the bank had agreed to keep the two accounts separate, whereupon the bank regained its right to combine the accounts. Secondly, the dealings between the plaintiffs and the bank were "mutual" within the meaning of s.31 of the Bankruptcy Act 1914.[1008] This provision, which has since been superseded by s.323 of the Insolvency Act 1986, conferred on the bank a statutory right of set off. Their Lordships pointed out that this right of set off, as well as the ordinary right to combine accounts, is to be distinguished from the banker's lien. Sums standing to the credit of the customer's account constitute a debt payable to him by the bank and the actual funds involved are the bank's property. The bank cannot have a lien over its own property.[1009]

Effect of agreement   *Halesowen's* case does not question the validity of an agreement abrogating the bank's right to combine accounts in situations in which s.31, or currently s.323, is inapplicable.[1010] An agreement to keep an account separate can be inferred where it is opened for a specific purpose, e.g. for the paying of an employee's wages,[1011] or when the customer indicates, when opening the account, that it may not be combined with other accounts and a note to this effect is entered in the ledger.[1012] Moreover, an account which the customer opens as trustee, or as agent or as nominee of another person, may not be combined with the customer's private account.[1013] Similarly, where an amount constituting a "retention fund" under a building contract is paid into a joint account in the names of the contractor and the landowner, the bank cannot combine the balance standing to the credit of this

34-317

[1008] Mutual dealings and set-off rules are now to be found in r.14.24 (administration) and r.14.25 (winding up) of the Insolvency (England and Wales) Rules 2016 (SI 2016/1024).

[1009] But note that it is now accepted that a bank can have a charge over funds deposited with it: *Re Bank of Credit and Commerce International SA* [1998] A.C. 214; overturning *Re Charge Card Services Ltd* [1987] Ch. 150; affirmed (on another point) [1989] Ch. 497; *Re Spectrum Plus Ltd* [2005] UKHL 41, [2005] 2 A.C. 680 at [60], per Lord Hope.

[1010] It appears that the right under s.323 cannot be abrogated by contract: *Halesowen's* case, above, at 805, 809, 824; *Fraser v Oystertec Plc* [2006] 1 B.C.L.C. 491 at [16].

[1011] *Re EJ Morel (1934) Ltd* [1962] 1 Ch. 21. cf. *Re James R Rutherford & Sons Ltd* [1964] 1 W.L.R. 1211. And see *Coca-Cola Financial Corp v Finsat International Ltd* [1998] Q.B. 43, CA. For a case involving a bank's refusal without notice to sanction further advances under a facility agreement, see: *Socomex Ltd v Banque Bruxelles Lambert SA* [1996] 1 Lloyd's Rep. 156 (Mance J.).

[1012] *Barclays Bank Ltd v Okenarhe* [1966] 2 Lloyd's Rep. 87. Usually the arrangement remains in effect only insofar as there is no substantial change in the circumstances: *British Guiana Bank v OR* (1911) 104 L.T. 754; *Halesowen's* case, above; cf. *Direct Acceptance Corp Ltd v Bank of New South Wales* (1968) 88 W.N. (N.S.W.) (Pt 1) 498. As regards the combination of a current account and a loan account, see *Bradford Old Bank Ltd v Sutcliffe* [1918] 2 K.B. 833, 847.

[1013] *Union Bank of Australia v Murray-Aynsley* [1898] A.C. 693; *Barclays Bank Ltd v Quistclose Investments Ltd* [1970] A.C. 567. But an account opened by a person as trustee may be subject to combination with that person's other accounts if the bank is not aware of the existence of a trust: *Thomson v Clydesdale Bank* [1893] A.C. 282; *Royal Bank of Scotland Plc v Wallace International Ltd* [2000] All E.R. (D) 78, CA. Section 85(b) of the Solicitors Act 1974 provides that "client accounts" of a solicitor may not be combined with his personal account.

account with the debit balance in the contractor's personal account.[1014] A question that has arisen in recent years is whether a bank is entitled to exercise an equitable set-off as against money standing to the credit of X's account, if the beneficial owner of the funds is Y, who is indebted to the bank. It has been held that such a right of set-off is exercisable only if X concedes, or the bank can clearly establish on the evidence, that the money is due to Y as equitable owner.[1015]

34-318 Customer's remedies for dishonour A cheque which is returned unpaid by a banker usually bears on its face a written answer. The practice of bankers to make such an answer is, however, compulsory only where the cheque is presented through a clearing house which so stipulates. Answers on unpaid cheques must be composed with some care. "Refer to drawer", is ordinarily met with in cases of want of funds, and may be libellous if used in other circumstances. Although the words seem merely to invite the presenter of the cheque to inquire of the drawer as to the reason of dishonour,[1016] they have acquired a certain notoriety.[1017] Where words are not plainly defamatory, the test is not what they would convey to a particular person, but what they would suggest to a person of average intelligence.[1018] In New Zealand "Present again" has been held to be libellous[1019] as of course are the words "Not sufficient".[1020]

34-319 Damages for breach of contract Apart from any rights that may arise in tort from the nature of the written answer, the wrongful dishonour of the cheque, in itself, entitles the customer to damages for breach of contract.[1021] For many years the amount of damages recoverable by the customer differed according to whether he was a trader or a non-trader. Where the customer was a trader or, probably a professional man, he could recover substantial damages for injury to his credit and reputation without proof of actual loss,[1022] but where he was a non-trader he could only recover nominal damages for breach of contract, unless he proved actual

---

[1014] *MPS Construction Pty Ltd (In Liquidation) v Rural Bank of NSW* [1980] A.C.L.R. 835, especially at 842–843 Aust.

[1015] *Punjab National Bank v Basna* [1988] F.L.R. 97. See also *Neste Oy v Lloyds Bank Plc* [1983] Com. L.R. 145, concerning the combination of an account maintained by the customer as an agent with his personal account. And see *Bhogal v Punjab National Bank* [1988] 2 All E.R. 296; followed in *Uttamchandani v Central Bank of India* (1989) 133 S.J. 262; and *Saudi Arabian Monetary Agency v Dresdner Bank AG* [2003] EWHC 3271 (Ch), [2004] 2 Lloyd's Rep. 19; affirmed. [2004] EWCA Civ 1074, [2005] 1 Lloyd's Rep. 12.

[1016] *Szek v Lloyds Bank* (1908), in *Legal Decisions Affecting Bankers*, Vol.II, p.159; *Flach v London and South Western Bank* (1915) 31 T.L.R. 334; *Plunkett v Barclays Bank* [1936] 2 K.B. 107; *Jayson v Midland Bank Ltd* [1968] 1 Lloyd's Rep. 409. cf. *Pyke v Hibernian Bank* [1950] Ir. Rep. 195.

[1017] See E.P. Ellinger, E. Lomnicka and C.V.M. Hare, *Ellinger's Modern Banking Law*, 5th edn (2011), pp.509–513. See also *Aktas v Westpac Banking Corp Ltd* [2010] HCA 25 (where the High Court of Australia, by a majority, rejected a defence of qualified privilege); criticised by Tobin & Hare [2012] L.M.C.L.Q. 1.

[1018] *Frost v London Joint Stock Bank* (1906) 22 T.L.R. 760.

[1019] *Baker v Australia and New Zealand Bank* [1958] N.Z.L.R. 907.

[1020] *Davidson v Barclays Bank* [1940] 1 All E.R. 316.

[1021] See also below, para.34-406, for the payer's rights against the payer's bank under the Payment Services Regulations 2017 (SI 2017/752), as amended, for non-execution or defective execution of an (electronic) payment transaction that falls within the scope of the Regulations; for the payee's rights against the payee's bank, see below, paras 34-409 et seq.

[1022] *Wilson v United Counties Bank Ltd* [1920] A.C. 102 at 112, per Lord Birkenhead.

loss.[1023] However, the distinction between traders and non-traders has now been swept away by the Court of Appeal in *Kpohraror v Woolwich Building Society*.[1024] Evans L.J. observed that in modern social conditions it is not only tradesmen for whom the dishonour of a cheque might be obviously injurious.[1025] The credit rating of individuals is as important for their personal transactions, including mortgages and hire-purchase and banking facilities, and it is notorious that central registers are kept containing information relevant to credit ratings. Accordingly, the Court of Appeal held that in every case (trader and non-trader alike) there is a presumption of fact that the customer suffers some injury to his credit and reputation when his cheque is wrongfully dishonoured.[1026] This development is to be welcomed for it acknowledges the important role of credit in modern consumer society.[1027]

Mandate and third parties A bank is entitled, and indeed bound, to refuse to honour its customer's cheque or other payment instruction where to do so would render it liable as an accessory to misfeasance or breach of trust.[1028] However, the bank must have positive evidence of misfeasance or breach of trust: mere suspicion is not enough to refuse its customer's instructions.[1029] The bank may face a dilemma in cases where it is aware that the customer is the subject of criminal investigation. On the one hand, if the bank allows the customer to operate the account and withdraw misappropriated funds, it could be held liable as a constructive trustee of the funds and made to account to the victim[1030]; on the other hand, if it raises the issue with the customer, it could commit a "tipping off" offence under the Proceeds of Crime Act 2002, where the disclosure is likely to prejudice an investigation.[1031] It was held by the Court of Appeal in *Governor & Company of the Bank of Scotland v A Ltd*,[1032] that in such a case the bank may ask the court for an interim declaration as to what information can be disclosed to the customer but once that information has been identified the bank had to take a commercial decision as to the course of action it then wishes to take, i.e. whether or not to contest proceedings brought by the customer for repayment of his deposit. Lord Woolf C.J. added that "it seems almost inconceivable that a bank which takes the initiative in seeking the court's guidance should subsequently be held to have acted dishonestly so as to incur accessory liability".[1033]

34-320

Proceeds of Crime Act 2002 A bank must freeze an account where it knows or

34-321

[1023] *Gibbons v Westminster Bank* [1939] 2 K.B. 882; *Rae v Yorkshire Bank Plc* [1988] F.L.R. 1, CA.
[1024] [1996] 4 All E.R. 119.
[1025] At 124.
[1026] For factors that may be relevant to an assessment of the quantum of general damages on wrongful dishonour of a cheque, see *Nicholson v Knox Ukiwa* [2007] EWHC 2430 (QB) at [83]–[118].
[1027] R. Hooley [1996] C.L.J. 189 at 191; cf. N. Enonchong (1997) 60 M.L.R. 412.
[1028] *Royal Brunei Airlines Sdn v Tan* [1995] 2 A.C. 378, PC. See above, paras 34-284—34-292.
[1029] *TTS International v Cantrade Private Bank* Unreported 1995, Royal Court of Jersey, but see (1995) 4 J. Int. Tr. 60.
[1030] See above, para.34-289.
[1031] s.333A ("tipping off" offences). See also s.342 (offence of prejudicing an investigation). The Terrorism Act 2000 s.39, as amended by the Anti-terrorism, Crime and Security Act 2001, also provides for a "tipping off" offence.
[1032] [2001] EWCA Civ 52, [2001] 1 W.L.R. 751.
[1033] At [47]. To similar effect, see *Tayab v HSBC Bank Plc* [2004] EWHC 1529, [2004] 4 All E.R. 1024 at [75]–[77].

suspects that the account contains the proceeds of crime.[1034] In practice, the bank cannot give an explanation to its customer for fear of committing a "tipping-off" offence,[1035] unless the relevant authorities (the National Crime Agency (NCA))[1036] consent or the court so directs.[1037] The bank does not act in breach of contract by refusing to honour its customer's payment instructions where it is suspicious that the money in the account is criminal property.[1038] The bank must report its knowledge or suspicion to NCA.[1039] If, after an initial period of seven days to investigate the matter, NCA refuses to give the bank consent to deal with the suspect account, it remains frozen for a further period of 31 days.[1040] At any stage the bank, or any other person affected by the freezing of the account, may ask NCA to look at the matter again.[1041] At the end of the 31 day moratorium, NCA must apply to the court for an order to prohibit further dealing with the funds in the account.[1042] Unless such an order has been made, the bank is now bound to act in accordance with its customer's instructions.

(ii) Termination of Duty to Pay

34-322 Countermand of payment Section 75(1) of the Bills of Exchange Act 1882 provides that the banker should not honour a cheque if the customer has

---

[1034] *Squirrell Ltd v National Westminster Bank Plc* [2005] EWHC 664 (Ch), [2006] 1 W.L.R. 637, considering s.328 of the Proceeds of Crime Act 2002 which creates an offence of facilitating the acquisition, retention, use or control of criminal property. The Money Laundering, Terrorist Financing and Transfer of Funds (Information on the Payer) Regulations 2017 (SI 2017/692), which replace the Money Laundering Regulations 2007 (SI 2007/ 2157), and the Transfer of Funds (Information on the Payer) Regulations 2007 (SI 2007/3298), do not change the principal offences under the POCA 2002, nor the regime for reporting money laundering suspicions.

[1035] s.333A ("tipping-off" offences). See also s.342 (offence of prejudicing an investigation).

[1036] The NCA replaced the Serious Organised Crime Agency in 2013.

[1037] *Bank of Scotland v A Ltd* [2001] EWCA Civ 52, [2001] 1 W.L.R. 751; *Amalgamated Metal Trading Ltd v City of London Police Financial Investigation Unit* [2003] EWHC 703 (Comm), [2003] 1 W.L.R. 2711. But see also *National Crime Agency v N* [2017] EWCA Civ 253 at [71], where Hamblen L.J. said that *Bank of Scotland v A*, a tipping-off case, had to be "considered with caution and cannot be regarded as providing general guidance" in the context of the statutory consent regime contained in POCA 2002.

[1038] *K Ltd v National Westminster Bank Plc* [2006] EWCA Civ 1039, [2007] 1 W.L.R. 311, where it was held that the bank does not have to adduce evidence to support any such suspicion or even show that there were reasonable grounds for the suspicion. But in *Shah v HSBC Private Bank (UK) Ltd* [2010] EWCA Civ 31, [2011] 1 All E.R. 67, the Court of Appeal held that where a customer brings non-summary proceedings against his bank claiming damages to compensate for loss caused to him because of the bank's failure to carry out his payment instructions, and the bank relies on its suspicion that the requested transfer involved funds which were criminal property, there was no reason why the bank should not be required at trial to prove that it had the relevant suspicion: at the trial the High Court held that HSBC did in fact have a genuine suspicion that the funds were criminal property, see [2012] EWHC 1283 (QB).

[1039] An "authorised disclosure" under s.338.

[1040] s.335. The court has recently been given power to extend the moratorium period up to 186 days through amendments to Pt 7 of the 2002 Act, introduced by the Criminal Finances Act 2017 s.10 (in force on October 31, 2017).

[1041] *R (on the application of UMBS Online Ltd) v Serious Organised Crime Agency* [2007] EWCA Civ 406. In *National Crime Agency v N* [2017] EWCA Civ 253 at [59]–[64], the Court of Appeal held that the court had jurisdiction to override the compulsory statutory consent procedure under POCA 2002 by granting interim relief, but stated that, as the balance of convenience is likely to lie in favour of the public interest in the prevention of money laundering in most cases, such intervention was likely to be exceptional.

[1042] s.41.

countermanded, or "stopped", it. If the banker pays a cheque after having received notice of countermand, he is not entitled to debit the customer's account. However, the notice given by the customer to the banker must be unambiguous and should identify the cheque: otherwise the banker is not at fault if he honours it.[1043] At the same time, if the notice is clear, it is effective, and the banker is not entitled to rely on a business practice prevailing in his firm in order to disregard it. In *Burnett v Westminster Bank Ltd*[1044] the plaintiff had one current account with the X branch of the defendant bank and another one with its Y branch. The payment of cheques drawn on the Y branch was done through a computer, which calculated whether there were sufficient funds in the account for meeting the cheque, and then forwarded it to the branch on which it was drawn, where the teller would check the signature. The computer identified the account and the branch on which the cheque was drawn by decoding numbers printed on each cheque with magnetic ink. Customers were, therefore, requested, in a clause printed on the folder of each cheque book, not to use cheque forms contained in it for drawing on any other account. Despite this clause, the plaintiff used a form contained in the cheque book supplied by the Y branch in order to draw a cheque on the X branch, changing the address in the form to that of the X branch. On the next day he gave notice of countermand to the X branch. The cheque was presented through the clearing house, and was forwarded by the computer to the Y branch and honoured. It was held on the facts that the clause demanding that forms contained in the cheque book be used for drawing cheques only on the Y branch, was not a term of the contract between the plaintiff and the defendant bank, and that notice of countermand given to the X branch, on which the cheque was drawn, was sufficient.

When effective   The notice of countermand becomes effective only when it   **34-323** reaches the teller or ledger clerk, and the mere fact that a letter countermanding payment has arrived at the banker's address at the time the cheque is honoured, does not render the banker liable. However, if the letter remains unopened for an unreasonable time, and as a result the teller is not notified of the countermand and the cheque is honoured, the banker may be liable in an action in negligence.[1045] Unless otherwise agreed, no particular form is required for an effective countermand. The countermand may be made orally, in person or by telephone, or by letter, telex, fax, email or other writing. However, in each case the bank must be able reasonably to satisfy itself that the countermand is that of its customer. The bank is not obliged to accept an unauthenticated message as countermand of its duty and authority to pay in accordance with its customer's mandate, although it may rely on the unauthenticated message to delay payment pending confirmation.[1046] Use of an agreed password may even authenticate a countermand given over the telephone or via the internet. Notice of countermand given at one branch is not an effective

---

[1043] *Westminster Bank v Hilton* (1926) 43 T.L.R. 124. See also *Giordano v Royal Bank of Canada* [1973] 3 O.R. 771 Canada.
[1044] [1966] 1 Q.B. 742.
[1045] *Curtice v London City and Midland Bank* [1908] 1 K.B. 293; *Reade v Royal Bank of Ireland* [1922] 2 Ir.R. 22.
[1046] *Curtice v London City and Midland Bank Ltd* [1908] 1 K.B. 293.

countermand at any other branch of the bank[1047]; but it is sufficient if the customer gives notice of countermand to the branch on which the cheque is drawn.[1048]

34-324   Payment Services Regulations 2017   The Payment Services Regulations 2017 ("PSRs 2017") reg.67(3) provide that the payer's consent to a payment transaction can be withdrawn at any time before the point at which the payment order can no longer be revoked under reg.83.[1049] Regulation 83(1) restricts the ability of a payment service user to revoke a payment order by providing that, subject to certain exceptions, the payment service user may not revoke a payment order after it has been received by the payer's payment service provider.[1050] In the case of a payment transaction initiated by a payment initiation service provider, by or through the payee, the payer may not revoke the payment order after giving consent to the payment initiation service provider to initiate the payment transaction or giving consent to execute the payment transaction to the payee.[1051] In the case of a direct debit, the payer may not revoke the payment order after the end of the business day preceding the day agreed for the debiting of funds.[1052]

34-325   Death of customer   Section 75(2) of the Act provides that *notice* of the customer's death terminates the banker's duty and authority to pay a cheque. This section seems to overcome, as regards payment of cheques, the principle that the authority of an agent is automatically determined by the principal's death and that the agent is liable for any act performed after it.[1053]

34-326   Mental disorder of customer   There is no authority regarding the effect of the insanity of the customer on the banker's duty to pay his cheques.[1054] It has been held in *Yonge v Toynbee*[1055] that the authority of an agent is determined by the principal's insanity. The relationship of customer and banker is not, however, solely that of principal and agent and it may, thus, be doubted whether the principle of *Yonge v Toynbee* applies. It is thought that *notice* of the customer's insanity terminates the banker's authority to pay cheques.[1056] Where an order is made under the Mental Capacity Act 2005 the position should be clearer.

34-327   Winding up   The bank has to exercise extreme caution where a customer, who is a body corporate, is being wound up. By s.127 of the Insolvency Act 1986, in a

---

[1047] *London Provincial and South Western Bank v Buszard* (1918) 35 T.L.R. 142.

[1048] *Burnett v Westminster Bank Ltd* [1966] 1 Q.B. 742; *Royal Bank of Canada v Boyce*, 57 D.L.R. (2d) 683 (1966).

[1049] Previously, Payment Services Regulations 2009 (SI 2009/209) ("PSRs 2009"), as amended, reg.55(3). See also PSRs 2017 reg.67(4) (PSRs 2009 reg.55(4)) for withdrawal of consent to the execution of a series of payment transactions. For application of the PSRs 2017 in general, see above, paras 34-224 et seq., and below, paras 34-402 et seq. The PSRs focus only on electronic means of payment, so that cheques fall outside their scope.

[1050] For the time of receipt of a payment order, see PSRs 2017 reg.81 (PSRs 2009 reg.65).

[1051] PSRs 2017 reg.83(2) (contrast differently worded PSRs 2009 reg.67(2)).

[1052] PSRs 2017 reg.83(3) (PSRs 2009 reg.67(3)). For further provisions relating to revocation, see PSRs 2017 reg.83(4)–(6) (PSRs 2009 reg.67(4)–(6)).

[1053] *Campanari v Woodburn* (1854) 15 C.B. 400. And see E.P. Ellinger, E. Lomnicka and C.V.M. Hare, *Ellinger's Modern Banking Law*, 5th edn (2011), pp.479–481.

[1054] But see *Drew v Nunn* (1879) 4 Q.B.D. 661; *Daily Telegraph Newspaper Co v McLaughlin* [1904] A.C. 776. See also Vol.I, paras 9-075 et seq.

[1055] [1910] 1 K.B. 215.

[1056] Hart, *Law of Banking*, 4th edn, p.302; F.H. Ryder, "Bankers and the Law relating to Lunacy" (1934) 55 J.I.B. 14; cf. Megrah, *The Banker's Customer*, 2nd edn, p.76.

winding-up of a company by the court, any disposition of the company's property made after the commencement of the winding-up is, unless the court orders otherwise, void. According to s.129 of the 1986 Act, the winding-up of a company by the court is deemed to commence at the time of the presentation of the petition for winding-up (or, if the company was already in voluntary liquidation, at the time when the resolution for voluntary winding-up was passed). Section 127 does not specify the appropriate remedy of the company's liquidator when the disposition is avoided but the Court of Appeal indicated in *Hollicourt (Contracts) Ltd v Bank of Ireland* that the right of recovery is restitutionary.[1057] Problems for the bank arise if, due to oversight or to its ignorance of the pending petition, the bank allows payments to be made into and out of the company's account. Until recently, all payments into and out of a company's bank account were considered to be dispositions of the company's property and void.[1058] That view has turned out to be too sweeping. Payments into an account in credit have been held not to constitute dispositions of the company's property as the amount standing to the credit of the customer's account is increased.[1059] Payments into an overdrawn account do constitute dispositions of the company's property and are void under s.127 unless validated by the court.[1060] Payments made out of a company's bank account, whether the account is in credit or overdrawn, have been held not to constitute a disposition of the company's property to the bank, which merely acts as the company's agent in making a disposition in favour of the third party.[1061] In any event, a bank is well advised to ask the company for a validation order under s.127 before allowing it to continue to operate the account as notice of the winding-up petition terminates the bank's authority to honour its customer's cheques.[1062] If a disposition is made in good faith in the ordinary course of business when the par-

---

[1057] [2001] Ch. 555, CA. A change of position defence may defeat the restitutionary claim, although this will depend on the circumstances of the particular case, and the issues raised by the application of that defence are different to those raised by a request for a validation order: see *Re Tain Construction Ltd* [2003] B.P.I.R. 1188.

[1058] *Re Gray's Inn Construction Ltd* [1980] 1 W.L.R. 711, CA.

[1059] *Re Barn Crown Ltd* [1994] 4 All E.R. 42, criticised in R.M. Goode, *Principles of Corporate Insolvency Law*, 4th edn (2011), para.13-131.

[1060] *Re Gray's Inn Construction Ltd*, above; *Re Tain Construction Ltd* [2003] B.P.I.R. 1188

[1061] *Hollicourt (Contracts) Ltd v Bank of Ireland*, above, CA, endorsing the ruling of Lightman J. in *Coutts & Co v Stock* [2000] 1 W.L.R. 906. But in *Officeserve Technologies Ltd (In Liquidation) v Anthony-Mike* [2017] EWHC 1920 (Ch), H.H.J. Paul Matthews, sitting as Judge of the High Court, stated obiter (at [88]) that whilst he agreed with Lightman J. that there is no disposition of the company's property to the bank on the facts of *Coutts & Co v Stock*, where the account was overdrawn, he considered that there is a disposition caught by s.127 where the account is in credit because the bank's liability to the company has been reduced. The judge (at [88]) preferred the reasoning of Blackburne J. at first instance in *Hollicourt (Contracts) Ltd v Bank of Ireland* [2000] 1 W.L.R. 895, although he did not refer to the Court of Appeal's reasoning when reversing Blackburne J. on appeal at [2001] Ch. 555, and (at [97]) relied on dicta of Lord Neuberger in *Akers v Samba Financial Group* [2017] UKSC 6, [2017] A.C. 424 at [74] to the effect that the giving up of contractual rights by a company would be a "disposition" within s.127.

[1062] *Pettit v Novakovic* [2007] B.P.I.R. 1643 at [7]. Presentation of the petition does not *automatically* terminate the bank's mandate: *Hollicourt (Contracts) Ltd v Bank of Ireland*, above. The principles that govern the validation of a disposition, either prospectively or retrospectively, are set out in *Re Gray's Inn Construction Ltd* [1980] 1 W.L.R. 711, CA; and in *Denney v John Hudson & Co Ltd* [1992] B.C.L.C. 901; see also *Wilson v 375 Live Ltd* [2015] EWHC 870 (Ch); *Re Gray's Inn Construction Ltd* was explained and amplified by the Court of Appeal in *Express Electrical Distributors Ltd v Beavis* [2016] EWCA Civ 765, [2016] 1 W.L.R. 4783, where Sales L.J. (at [56]) said validation would ordinarily only be granted "if there is some special circumstance which shows that the disposition in question ... has been ... for the benefit of the general body of unsecured creditors".

ties are unaware of the presentation of the petition, and it is completed before the winding-up order is made, the court is likely to validate it (unless it can be challenged as a preference).[1063]

34-328   **Bankruptcy**   The bankruptcy of an individual commences with the day on which the bankruptcy order is made.[1064] By s.284(1) of the 1986 Act any disposition of property made by the bankrupt between the presentation of the bankruptcy petition and the vesting of the bankrupt's estate in his trustee (i.e. the day he is appointed) is void, except to the extent that it is made with the consent of, or is ratified by, the court. The wording of s.284(1) is similar to that of s.127 of the 1986 Act, and so s.284(1) should apply to dispositions of the type caught by s.127.[1065] The discretion vested in the court under s.284(1) is also likely to be exercised in a way similar to the discretion vested under s.127. If the bank makes a payment which is caught by s.284(1), but does so unaware of the presentation of the petition, the court is likely to ratify the payment. The bank is given further protection by s.284(5) which allows it to maintain a debit if the bank pays against the bankrupt's payment instruction after the making of a bankruptcy order, unless the bank did so with notice of the bankruptcy or it is not reasonably practical to recover the amount from the payee. It would seem that the subsection only applies where the payment is made out of an overdrawn account, because only then has the bankrupt "incurred a debt to a banker" by reason of the making of the payment.[1066] A bank which receives a payment into the account before the bankruptcy order may be protected by s.284(4). By subs.(4), the amount paid into the account is irrecoverable if received before the commencement of the bankruptcy in good faith, for value and without notice of the presentation of the bankruptcy petition.

34-329   **Third party debt orders**   Service of a third party debt order (formerly called a "garnishee order") relieves the banker of his obligation to pay his customer's cheques or other payment instruction, until the order is discharged, regardless of the respective amounts of the balance and the judgment debt.[1067] In many interim third party debt orders, however, a named sum is now expressed as the limit attachable, in which case it is the practice of bankers to earmark such specified amount together with an additional sum to cover estimated costs and to allow the customer to operate on the remaining balance. An interim third party debt order citing a solicitor as

---

[1063] In *Re Tain Construction Ltd* [2003] B.P.I.R. 1188 it was held that this does not mean "prefer" in the technical sense of preference under the sections of the Insolvency Act 1986 avoiding transactions as preferences; rather, it means circumvention of the pari passu distribution of assets which is the policy of s.127 to achieve.

[1064] Insolvency Act 1986 s.278(a).

[1065] See above, para.34-327. But note that there are differences between the two regimes and differences between s.127 and s.284: *Pettit v Novakovic*, above. See also *Thomas v D'Eye* [2016] B.P.I.R. 883 at [49], per Baister R., who said of s.284, "we are not dealing with unjust enrichment generally but a particular statutory regime which gives rise to an account for money had and received to which there are limited defences".

[1066] *Paget's Law of Banking*, 14th edn (2014), para.14.48.

[1067] *Rogers v Whiteley* [1892] A.C. 118. See also *Edmunds v Edmunds* [1904] p.362. For a detailed analysis including the question of priorities, see E.P. Ellinger, E. Lomnicka and C.V.M. Hare, *Ellinger's Modern Banking Law*, 5th edn (2011), pp.459–470, and 477 for similarities and differences between a freezing injunction (which also relieves a bank of its duty to honour its customer's mandate) and an interim third party debt order.

a judgment debtor will attach the balance on the solicitor's "clients" account.[1068] A third party debt order attaches foreign currency balances maintained with a bank in the United Kingdom,[1069] but not with a foreign branch unless by the law applicable in that place an English order would be recognised as discharging the liability of the third party to the judgment debtor.[1070] The procedural rules relating to third party debt orders are to be found in Pt 72 of the Civil Procedure Rules 1998[1071] where reference is made to a third party debt order being made in respect of "any debt due or accruing due to the judgment debtor from a third party".[1072] The essential condition for the effectiveness of a third party debt order is that there should be a subsisting debt owed to the judgment debtor[1073]; execution cannot be levied against a debt if the judgment debtor has parted with his interest in it.[1074] Doubts as to whether money standing to the credit of a customer in a current account could be deemed "due or accruing" were resolved in *Joachimson v Swiss Bank Corp.*[1075] Ordinarily a demand is necessary before moneys so credited strictly fall due, but the Court of Appeal held that service of a garnishee summons operated as a demand.[1076] Compliance with a final third party debt order discharges the

---

[1068] *Plunkett v Barclays Bank* [1936] 2 K.B. 107, but the order is unlikely to be made final where the account is a trust account.

[1069] *Choice Investments Ltd v Jeromnimon (Midland Bank Garnishee)* [1981] Q.B. 149; *Camdex International Ltd v Bank of Zambia (No.3)* (1997) 6 Bank. L.R. 44, CA.

[1070] *Société Eram Shipping Co Ltd v Compagnie Internationale de Navigation* [2003] UKHL 30, [2004] 1 A.C. 260; *Kuwait Oil Tanker Co SAK v Qabazard* [2003] UKHL 31, [2004] 1 A.C. 300. The situs of the debt is vitally important. In *Taurus Petroleum Ltd v State Oil Marketing Company of the Ministry of Oil, Republic of Iraq* [2017] UKSC 64 at [31]–[32], [60], [72], [83], [124]–[125], the Supreme Court held (unanimously), overturning *Power Curber International Ltd v National Bank of Kuwait* [1981] 2 Lloyd's Rep. 394 on the point, that the general rule that the situs of a debt is the debtor's residence (i.e. the place where the debt is recoverable) applies to letters of credit: for a credit issued by the London branch of an overseas bank, when the credit incorporated UCP 600 (art.3 of which provides that "[b]ranches of a bank in different countries are to be considered as separate banks"), the situs of the debt due under the credit was London, thereby making the debt susceptible to a third party debt order made by an English court.

[1071] Pt 72 of the Civil Procedure Rules 1998 came into effect on March 25, 2002, replacing RSC Ord.49.

[1072] In *Alawiye v Mahamood* [2005] EWHC 277 (Ch), [2006] 3 All E.R. 668, Lindsay J. held that, in the absence of any contrary indication, the court could and should accept, as sufficient for the purposes of an interim third party debt order under CPR r.72.4, evidence in which the judgment creditor was able to say no more than that the judgment debtor had previously had an account with the third party bank and that it had previously been in credit. Lindsay J. also stated (obiter) that the fact that the account had previously been overdrawn did not of itself preclude there being a debt to the judgment debtor from the third party, at least where there is nothing to indicate that, overall, the bank is not a debtor to the judgment debtor.

[1073] An order can only be made when the debt is owed solely to the judgment debtor: *Taurus Petroleum Ltd v State Oil Marketing Company of the Ministry of Oil, Republic of Iraq* [2017] UKSC 64 at [24], citing Field J. at first instance [2013] EWHC 3494 (Comm), [2014] 1 Lloyd's Rep. 432 at [13].

[1074] *Taurus Petroleum Ltd v State Oil Marketing Company of the Ministry of Oil, Republic of Iraq* [2017] UKSC 64 at [68]. See also *Merchant International Co Ltd v Natsionalna Aktsionerna Kompaniia Naftogaz Ukrainy* [2014] EWCA Civ 1603; *Rekstin v Severo Sibirsko Gosudarstvennoe Aksionernoe Obschestvo Koseverputj and the Bank for Russian Trade Ltd* [1933] 1 K.B. 47; *Re General Horticultural Co* (1886) 32 Ch. D. 512, 515 (which, according to Lord Clarke in *Taurus*, above, at [45]–[46], does not establish any independent principle of "honest dealing", but merely reaffirms that a judgment creditor cannot by means of a third party debt order levy execution on property that does not belong to the judgment debtor).

[1075] [1921] 3 K.B. 110, 131.

[1076] As regards the right of the bank served with a third party debt order to deduct its expenses from the amount attached, see *Gerry Webb Transport v Brenner* [1985] C.L. 152.

bank's indebtedness to its own customer, but there is no discharge if the bank pays in reliance on only an interim order.[1077]

34-330 **Period of limitation** The amount credited to the customer's account is payable on demand.[1078] It follows that the six-year limitation period does not run against the customer in respect of his credit balance in a current account until a demand for payment has been made. It has been suggested that when the account is overdrawn the period of limitation runs against the bank from the date of the advance.[1079] However, if the banker grants the customer an overdraft, repayable on demand, the time begins to run from the time of the demand.[1080]

34-331 Where a customer (the payer) seeks redress against his own bank (the payer's bank) for an unauthorised or incorrectly executed (electronic) payment transaction under the Payment Services Regulations 2017,[1081] the payer must notify the payer's bank without delay, and in any event no later than 13 months after the debit date, on becoming aware of any unauthorised or incorrectly executed payment transactions.[1082]

34-332 **Effect of war** The effect of war on the banker's duty to pay his customer's cheques depends largely on legislation, e.g. the Trading with the Enemy Act 1939, which may prohibit the honouring of certain types of cheques, e.g. those of persons residing in territory occupied by the enemy. The outbreak of hostilities or of war may further suspend the banker's duty to pay if it becomes impossible to do so, e.g. if hostilities are carried on in his place of business. When the banking business can safely be resumed, the banker's duty to pay the customer's cheques is revived, and any credit balance becomes again payable on demand.[1083]

34-333 **Effect of extraterritorial orders** From time to time attempts are made by certain governments, such as the United States, to freeze or block accounts maintained by designated persons or bodies not only within the territory but even in places over which the government concerned has no sovereignty.[1084] An instance was President Reagan's Order of January 8, 1986 which sought to freeze all property and interests

---

[1077] *Crantrave Ltd v Lloyds TSB Bank Plc* [2000] Q.B. 917, CA. Where there is a prior equitable charge or flawed asset arrangement over the account, the court will not make a third party debt order final: *Fraser v Oystertec Plc* [2004] EWHC 1582 (Ch), [2005] B.P.I.R. 381.

[1078] *Joachimson v Swiss Bank Corp* [1921] 3 K.B. 110.

[1079] *Parr's Banking Co v Yates* [1898] 2 Q.B. 460.

[1080] *Lloyds Bank v Margolis* [1954] 1 W.L.R. 644. As regards a fresh demand and acknowledgment of the debt, see *Bank of Baroda v Mahomed* [1999] 1 Lloyd's Rep. Bank. 14, CA. See also Vol.I, paras 28-039—28-040.

[1081] SI 2017/752 ("PSRs 2017"), as amended. See previously, the Payment Services Regulations 2009 (SI 2009/209), as amended ("PSRs 2009"). See above, paras 34-224 et seq. (noting, in particular, the scope of the PSRs 2017), and below, paras 34-401 et seq.

[1082] PSRs 2017 reg.74(1) (PSRs 2009 reg.59(1)), makes the payment service user's reporting obligation a condition for redress under regs 76, 91, 92, 93 or 94 (PSRs 2009 regs 61, 75, 76 or 77). PSRs 2017 reg.74(2) (PSRs 2009 reg.59(2)) relieves the user of this obligation if the user's bank has failed to comply with the various information requirements set out in Pt 6 (PSRs 2009 Pt 5). The payee's rights to redress under these provisions are also subject to the same time-bar.

[1083] *Arab Bank Ltd v Barclays Bank DCO* [1954] A.C. 495. See also Vol.I, para.23-030.

[1084] Sanctions may also be imposed by the UN Security Council or the EU against states, governments, individuals and other entities in order to bring about a change in their policy or activity. For a recent example, where a bank was held to have been entitled to freeze the bank accounts of one of its customers, as it had reasonable cause to suspect, for the purposes of the Syria (European Union Financial Sanctions) Regulations 2012, that the funds in the account might be held by, controlled

of the Government of Libya and any entities controlled by it which were at that date, or came thereafter, into the possession or control of any "US persons including overseas branches of US persons". This Order created problems for Libyan banks, which maintained accounts with American banks. Whilst an attempt to challenge the Order in the United States would have been futile, attempts were, predictably, made to enforce payment of amounts deposited by Libyan bodies with American banks in other countries.

The Libyan Arab Bank cases   In the leading case, *Libyan Arab Foreign Bank v*   **34-334**
Bankers Trust Co,[1085] the L Bank, which was a Libyan government body, maintained a Eurodollars account with BT's office in London and another account, used predominantly for transfers and settlements, with BT's head office in the United States. After the making of the Order, the L Bank demanded payment in London of the US $140m deposited with the London office. BT refused, arguing that its contractual relationship with the L Bank was governed, in its entirety, by the law of the United States. It was, further, argued that even if the proper law of the deposit made in London was English law, payment should not be ordered as it would involve the performance of an act in the United States which was illegal under American law. To substantiate this second argument, BT called expert evidence to show that an amount of such magnitude could be cleared and settled only in the United States. Giving judgment for the L Bank, Staughton J. held that, although there was only one contract between the two banks, it was governed by two separate proper laws. American law governed the deposit made in the United States, whilst English law governed the deposit made in London.[1086] On this basis his Lordship concluded that President Reagan's Order did not affect the deposit made in London. He accepted, at the same time, that, in English law, it would be wrong to order BT to perform an act, such as the settlement of a debt or its payment through an American clearing system, if the process involved the performance in the United States of an act there illegal. Staughton J. held, however, that BT could pay the amount involved in cash in US dollars notes, as these could be imported without an infringement of American law from the United States. Alternatively, payment could be effected in pounds sterling of an amount equal to US $140m. His Lordship pointed out that the conversion of the currencies, namely the sale of the US

---

by or owned by her husband, who had been identified by the Council of the European Union as benefitting from or supporting the regime in Syria, see *Hmicho v Barclays Bank Plc* [2015] EWHC 1757 (QB). The UK has not opted into, and is not bound by, Regulation (EU) 655/2014 on the freezing of bank accounts, which enables a claimant to make a single application to the courts of one Member State to obtain a European Account Preservation Order, which freezes bank accounts held by a defendant in other Member States, without further intervention by the courts in those Member States.

[1085] [1989] Q.B. 728. See also *Libyan Arab Foreign Bank v Manufacturers Hanover Trust Co* [1988] 2 Lloyd's Rep. 494; and *Libyan Arab Foreign Bank v Manufacturers Hanover Trust (No.2)* [1989] 1 Lloyd's Rep. 608 (Hirst J.).

[1086] At common law, the bank-customer contract and the account contract are governed by the law of the place of the branch where the account is held. The same principle applied under the Contracts Applicable Law Act 1990, implementing the Rome Convention on the Law Applicable to Contractual Obligations (*Sierra Leone Telecommunications Co Ltd v Barclays Bank Plc* [1998] 2 All E.R. 820, 827) and continues to apply under EC Regulation 593/2008 on the Law Applicable to Contractual Obligations (in force December 17, 2009) arts 4(1)(b), 19(2), as the law applicable to banking operations is prima facie "the place where the branch … is located", although the applicable law may be that of the jurisdiction where the bank has its head office when two or more accounts are held in different jurisdictions (art.4(2)). See E.P Ellinger, E. Lomnicka and C.V.M. Hare, *Ellinger's Modern Banking Law*, 5th edn (2011), pp.380–381.

dollars and the purchase of the required pounds sterling, could be effected in London. It should be emphasised that in the instant case the contract between the banks did not include a jurisdiction or choice of law clause. The outcome may, possibly, have differed if the contract between the parties had been made subject to the law of New York. It is interesting to note that some banks seek to protect themselves against problems of the type here encountered by including in their standard terms and conditions respecting deposits in foreign currency a clause which makes payment subject to the "lawful and instant availability" of clearing facilities in the country in whose currency the account is denominated.

34-335 Closure of bank If the bank closes down or is being wound up, its duty to honour the customer's cheques is terminated. The balance standing to the customer's account becomes, in such cases, payable at once, and without the need of a demand.[1087]

(iii) Protection of Paying Banker in Cases of Unauthorised Payment

34-336 Payment Services Regulations 2009 and 2017 The law set out in this section of the chapter reflects the general common law and statutory position as it emerged before the enactment and coming into force of the Payment Services Regulations 2009 ("PSRs 2009").[1088] On January 13, 2018 the PSRs 2009 were revoked and replaced by the Payment Services Regulations 2017 ("PSRs 2017").[1089] The pre-2009 law remains applicable to cheques (as cheques fall outside the scope of the PSRs 2009 and PSRs 2017)[1090] and to other payment transactions that do not fall within the scope of the Regulations.[1091] In respect of payment transactions that fall within their scope, neither the PSRs 2009 nor the PSRs 2017 expressly preserve the common law position.[1092] We have already noted the restrictions on opting out of the PSRs 2009 and PSRs 2017 where the payment service user is a consumer, a micro-enterprise or a charity.[1093]

34-337 Discharge If the banker pays a cheque in compliance with the terms of his mandate, he is entitled to debit the customer's account. Likewise, he gives an effective discharge of the cheque by paying it in due course, and is entitled to debit the customer's account.[1094] Payment, it should be noted, is complete when the money is placed on the counter; if the cashier appreciates immediately thereafter

---

[1087] *Re Russian Commercial and Industrial Bank* [1955] Ch. 148. See also *Bank of Credit and Commerce International SA v Malik* [1996] B.C.C. 15.

[1088] SI 2009/209, as amended.

[1089] SI 2017/752, as amended. See generally, above, paras 34-224 et seq. and, below, paras 34-401 et seq.

[1090] PSRs 2017 Sch.1 Pt 2. The statutory protection relating to the payment and collection of cheques extends by virtue of the Cheques Act 1957 ss.1(2) and 4(2) to certain other instruments analogous to cheques. See below, paras 34-350 and 34-369.

[1091] For the scope of the PSRs 2017, see above, paras 34-225 et seq. and, below, paras 34-402 et seq. The contractual terms and conditions upon which the bank supplies its services would also require consideration in such cases.

[1092] But note, e.g., the express preservation of general common law rights in the context of the termination of a framework contract; see PSRs 2017 reg.51(7) (PSRs 2009 reg.43(7)), and see also above, para.34-310. See also below, para.34-404, and E.P. Ellinger, E. Lomnicka and C.V.M. Hare, *Ellinger's Modern Banking Law*, 5th edn (2011), pp.618–619.

[1093] PSRs 2017 regs 40(7), 63(5) (PSRs 2009 regs 33(4), 51(3), and see above, para.34-228.

[1094] s.59(1), discussed in para.34-123, above. (Note that a duty of care may be imposed on the banker where a fiduciary relationship between him and the customer comes into existence; above, paras 34-

that the customer's account is overdrawn, the money is not recoverable from the payee, even though, at the moment, he may be counting the money in the cashier's presence.[1095] If the banker does not pay the cheque in compliance with his mandate or in due course, he may nevertheless be able to rely on some special defences. Under the common law he is protected, if he is able to show either that the customer is precluded from asserting wrongful payment, or that such payment was caused by the customer's own fault or negligence. The Bills of Exchange Act 1882 and the Cheques Act 1957 provide special defences for bankers who pay cheques bearing forged or irregular indorsements. All these defences require a detailed discussion.

Estoppel The customer may, by his conduct, be precluded from asserting that the banker exceeded his mandate by paying a cheque. Thus, if the customer assured his banker, before payment of the cheque, that his signature was genuine, he would later on be precluded from asserting that it had been forged.[1096] In *Greenwood v Martins Bank*[1097] a husband was aware that his wife had forged and cashed his cheques, but did not disclose this fact to his bankers for a long period. In the meantime the wife forged further cheques and, when threatened by him with exposure, committed suicide. It was held that the husband was estopped from pleading the forgery of any of these cheques and that, as his silence had lulled his bankers into security, he could not recover from them the amount paid on any of these forgeries. It was further held that the detriment sustained by the bank was its inability, resulting from the customer's silence, to proceed against the wife. In a case like *Greenwood v Martins Bank Ltd*, the customer must have actual knowledge of the forgery, or have deliberately turned a blind eye, for an estoppel to be raised successfully against him. Constructive knowledge, in the sense that the customer had knowledge of circumstances which would cause a hypothetical reasonable customer to discover the fraud, is not enough.[1098]

34-338

The Liggett defence Where the banker is unable to establish an absolute defence based on an estoppel, he may nevertheless have a partial defence if it can be shown that the customer's loss is smaller than the amounts of the cheques wrongfully honoured. Thus, where cheques drawn by an employee without authority are wrongfully honoured by the banker but a portion of the proceeds is injected by the employee into the customer's business, the banker is obligated to re-credit the customer's account only with the amount misappropriated by the employee. This

34-339

---

255 et seq.)

[1095] *Chambers v Miller* (1862) 13 C.B.(N.S.) 125. cf. *Balmoral Supermarket Ltd v Bank of New Zealand* [1974] 2 N.Z.L.R. 155 (deposit held incomplete where bank robbery occurred while funds to be deposited were counted by teller). As to when payment is complete when effected through the clearing system or by giro, see below, paras 34-422—34-430.

[1096] *Brook v Hook* (1871) L.R. 6 Ex. 89, 99–100, and see above, para.34-051.

[1097] [1933] A.C. 51. See also *Bank of New Zealand v Auckland Information Bureau Inc* [1996] 1 N.Z.L.R. 420 NZCA (principle extended to unauthorised direct credit instructions). As to wider application of the principle, see *Geniki Investments International Ltd v Ellis Stickbrokers Ltd* [2008] 1 B.C.L.C. 662 at [44]–[46] (client/stockbroker relationship; where also held that duty arises on awareness of unauthorised transaction and that it is not necessary for customer to have knowledge of possible fraud behind transaction); cf. *Banque Nationale de Paris v Hew Keong Chan Gary* [2001] 1 S.L.R. 300 (High Court of Singapore).

[1098] *Price Meats Ltd v Barclays Bank Plc* [2000] 2 All E.R. (Comm) 346; *Patel v Standard Chartered Bank* [2001] Lloyd's Rep. Bank. 229. See also *Morison v London County and Westminster Bank Ltd* [1914] 3 K.B. 356; *Brown v Westminster Bank Ltd* [1964] 2 Lloyd's Rep. 187; *Tina Motors Pty Ltd v Australia and New Zealand Banking Group Ltd* [1977] V.R. 205.

rule is based on the equitable doctrine that a person who pays the debts of another without authority is allowed the benefit of such payment.[1099]

34-340 **Ratification** Where an agent exceeds his authority in drawing a given cheque, his act may be ratified by the principal. The ratification precludes the principal from seeking reimbursement from the drawee bank which has paid the cheque. Cases of this type arise where an agent draws on his principal's account a cheque for an amount exceeding his mandate or where a director, who is authorised to draw on the company's account jointly with another person, draws a cheque without obtaining that other person's signature. The latter type of case arose in *London Intercontinental Trust Ltd v Barclays Bank Ltd*.[1100] Here the cheques, which were honoured by the bank although they bore the signature of one director instead of the required two signatures, were drawn principally in order to transfer funds from one of the company's accounts to another. Initially, when the board of directors discovered the discrepancy, it resolved not to take any action. Subsequently, the company ran into financial difficulties and a new board was appointed. It was then resolved to bring an action against the bank, alleging that the cheques in question had been paid in breach of mandate. Slynn J. gave judgment for the bank on three grounds. First, he held that the director in question had the actual authority to transfer the relevant amounts so that he could have issued in his own name a written or oral instruction to this effect. The bank was, therefore, entitled to act on this specific instruction of the director although he gave it by means of cheques signed by himself only.

> "The bank as a result of its failure to observe the discrepancy took a risk in honouring the cheque that [the director] was not in fact authorised. In the case of both these cheques … he was so authorised."[1101]

Secondly, his Lordship concluded, on the facts, that the original meeting of the board had adopted the director's act with the full knowledge that the cheques had been improperly drawn. The company had therefore ratified the payment of these cheques by the bank. Thirdly, his Lordship noted that before the company brought its action against the bank it had pursued a claim in liquidation before the Stock Exchange on the basis that the transactions were valid. In this way the company made its election and was bound by it. An election, however, denotes ratification

---

[1099] *B Liggett (Liverpool) Ltd v Barclays Bank Ltd* [1928] 1 K.B. 48; *Lloyds Bank Ltd v Chartered Bank of India, Australia and China* [1929] 1 K.B. 40, 61; cf. *Re Cleadon Trust Ltd* [1939] Ch. 286, 302–303, 315; *Crantrave Ltd v Lloyds TSB Bank Plc* [2000] Q.B. 917, 924, 925; *Swotbooks.com Ltd v Royal Bank of Scotland Plc* [2011] EWHC 2025 (QB), [49]–[56]. See also *Associated Midlands Corp v Bank of New South Wales* [1983] 1 N.S.W.L.R. 533 Aust; *Limpgrange Ltd v BCCI SA* [1986] F.L.R. 36; *RCL Operators Ltd v National Bank of Canada* [1997] 6 Bank. L.R. 195, NB CA; *Majesty Restaurant Pty Ltd v Commonwealth Bank of Australia Ltd* (1999) 47 N.S.W.L.R. 593 Aust. For a detailed discussion, see Ellinger and Lee [1984] L.M.C.L.Q. 459; and see also E.P. Ellinger, E. Lomnicka and C.V.M. Hare, *Ellinger's Modern Banking Law*, 5th edn (2011), pp.500–501.

[1100] [1980] 1 Lloyd's Rep. 241; applied in *HJ Symons & Co v Barclays Bank Plc* [2003] EWHC 1249 (Comm). See also *Izodia v Royal Bank of Scotland International Ltd* Unreported August 1, 2006, Royal Court of Jersey: noted (2007) 3 J.I.B.F.L. 143.

[1101] [1980] 1 Lloyd's Rep. 241 at 249. Applied in *Senex Holdings Ltd (In Liquidation) v National Westminster Bank Plc* [2012] EWHC 131 (Comm), [2012] 1 All E.R. (Comm) 1130 at [18]–[20] (director had actual authority despite it being arguable that he was in breach of duty to company's creditors at the time he gave instructions to the bank).

only if it is final and unequivocal. In *Limpgrange Ltd v BCCI SA*[1102] Staughton J. held that an entry in the customer's books, which treated a debt as due from a third party rather than from the bank, did not in itself constitute a final election and hence did not amount to a ratification of the bank's unauthorised payment to the third party.

Pass books and periodic statement Credit entries in a periodic statement or pass   **34-341** book constitute prima facie evidence against the banker but may be rectified within a reasonable time to show the true facts.[1103] If in reliance on an erroneous credit entry the customer changes his position, the bank is estopped from asserting the mistake and, thus, is unable to recover the amount involved.[1104] But this principle applies only where the customer establishes that it would be inequitable to require him to effect reimbursement.[1105] The fact that the customer does not object to entries in his pass book or periodic statement does not preclude him from alleging, subsequently, that they have been wrongfully made. Modern English authorities indicate that in the absence of an express contractual undertaking, the customer is neither under any implied obligation to examine the debit entries in his pass book or periodic statement of account nor to check the validity of any cancelled cheques which the banker may forward him.[1106] It has been held that not even the return of a pass book to the banker by a customer, without comment and with the entries ticked, constitutes a settled account, and that the customer is not prevented from subsequently challenging the correctness of the entries.[1107] One possible solution is to incorporate a suitable clause in the bank's standard terms and conditions. Canadian cases indicate that if a customer signs an undertaking to examine a pass book or periodic statement and to inform the banker of any errors before a stated date, the banker will then be absolved by the customer's neglect, provided consideration for the undertaking is established.[1108] But the Privy Council's decision in *Tai Hing Cotton Mills Ltd v Liu Chong Hing Bank Ltd*[1109] suggests that to be effective, such a clause must impose on the customer a definite duty to peruse

---

[1102] [1986] F.L.R. 36; distinguished in *Swotbooks.com Ltd v Royal Bank of Scotland Plc* [2011] EWHC 2025 (QB) at [43]–[44], although held no ratification because account entries could not be considered in isolation (at [45]–[48]).

[1103] *Commercial Bank of Scotland v Rhind* (1860) 3 Macq. H.L. 643; *British and North European Bank v Zalzstein* [1927] 2 K.B. 92.

[1104] *Skyring v Greenwood* (1825) 4 B. & C. 281; *Holt v Markham* [1923] 1 K.B. 504; *Lloyds Bank v Brooks* (1951) 72 J.I.B. 114. See also *Holland v Manchester and Liverpool District Banking Co* (1909) 14 Com. Cas. 241.

[1105] *United Overseas Bank v Jiwani* [1976] 1 W.L.R. 964.

[1106] *Lewes Sanitary Steam Laundry Co Ltd v Barclay & Co Ltd* (1906) 95 L.T. 444; *Kepitigalla Rubber Estates Ltd v National Bank of India* [1909] 2 K.B. 1010; *Walker v Manchester and Liverpool District Banking Co* (1913) 108 L.T. 728; *Brewer v Westminster Bank* [1952] 2 All E.R. 650; *Wealden Woodlands (Kent) Ltd v National Westminster Bank Ltd* (1983) 133 New L.J. 719; *Royal Bank of Scotland Plc v Fielding* [2003] EWHC 986 (Ch); affirmed [2004] EWCA Civ 64. The principle is much criticised: Pollock (1910) 26 L.Q.R. 4; Holden (1954) 17 M.L.R. 41; Chorley, *Gilbart Lectures* (1954). For a detailed discussion, see E.P. Ellinger, E. Lomnicka and C.V.M. Hare, *Ellinger's Modern Banking Law*, 5th edn (2011), p.233.

[1107] *Chatterton v London and County Bank, The Times,* January 21, 1891.

[1108] *Mackenzie v Imperial Bank* [1938] 2 D.L.R. 764; *B & G Construction Co v Bank of Montreal* [1954] 2 D.L.R. 753; *Arrow Transfer Co v Royal Bank of Canada,* 19 D.L.R. (3d) 420 (1971); *Canadian Pacific Hotels Ltd v Bank of Montreal,* 40 D.L.R. (4th) 385 (1987); *Kelly Funeral Homes Ltd v Canadian Imperial Bank of Commerce,* 72 D.L.R. (4th) 276 (1990). See, generally, K.W. Perrett (1999) 14 B.F.L.R. 245.

[1109] [1986] A.C. 80. See also *Financial Institutions Services Ltd v Negril Negril Holdings Ltd* [2004]

his statement and, further, must convey to him that the entries made in the statement will be conclusively binding on him unless he queries them within the prescribed period.

34-342 **Customer's negligence in drawing cheque** If the customer has been so careless when drawing a cheque as to facilitate a fraud by a third party, he is precluded from asserting the forgery against the bank. In *London Joint Stock Bank v Macmillan*[1110] a clerk prepared a cheque for £2 payable to bearer. There was no sum in words then written on the cheque, but after it had been signed by his employers the clerk altered the figures to £120 and wrote the words "one hundred and twenty pounds" in the space provided. The clerk presented the cheque and, as the forgery was not readily apparent, received payment and absconded. The banker was held entitled to debit the customer's account. Lord Finlay L.C. said:

> "A cheque drawn by a customer is in point of law a mandate to the banker to pay the amount according to the tenor of the cheque. It is beyond dispute that the customer is bound to exercise reasonable care in drawing the cheque to prevent the banker being misled. If he draws a cheque in a manner which facilitates fraud, he is guilty of a breach of duty as between himself and the banker, and he will be responsible to the banker for any loss sustained by the banker as a natural and direct consequence of this breach of duty."[1111]

34-343 **Scope of principle** The principle in *Macmillan*'s case may well be extended so as to prejudice the right of recovery against the banker of a customer who has left in blank the amount payable on a promissory note made by him, or on a bill of exchange which he has accepted, provided that these instruments are expressed to be payable at a named bank.[1112] Where the note or bill is not expressed to be payable at a bank, however, it seems that no duty is owed to anyone to guard against fraud.[1113] Even in the case of cheques, a customer is not always considered negligent if he leaves a blank space. The question is, always, whether a reasonable man would leave such a blank space or not. In *Slingsby v District Bank*,[1114] the customer left a blank space between the name of the payee and the words "or order", and a fraudulent third party filled up this space by making the cheque payable to the payee "*per pro*" himself, and then negotiated the cheque by indorsing it in his own name. It was held that the customer was not negligent and that, although the alteration was not apparent, the banker could not debit the customer's account with the amount paid against the cheque.

34-344 **Carelessness not connected with the drawing of a cheque** Negligence of the customer which is not connected with the actual drawing of a cheque does not, usu-

---

UKPC 40 (conclusive evidence clause was not clear and unambiguous and so was construed narrowly against the bank). It may also be necessary to assess the clause in the light of the Consumer Rights Act 2015 Pt 2 (for "consumer contracts") or the Unfair Contract Terms Act 1977.

[1110] [1918] A.C. 777. The rule has been established for a long time: see *Young v Grote* (1827) 4 Bing. 253.

[1111] [1918] A.C. 777 at 789.

[1112] As to whether the customer may be entitled to plead contributory negligence on the bank's part, see below, para.34-370. As regards the bank's right to recover an amount paid under a mistake of fact from the payee, see above, paras 34-125 et seq.

[1113] *Scholfield v Londesborough* [1896] A.C. 514.

[1114] [1931] 2 K.B. 588 (affirmed [1932] 1 K.B. 544); cf. *Lumsden & Co v London Trustee Savings Bank* [1971] 1 Lloyd's Rep. 114, 121.

ally, afford a defence to a banker who has wrongfully honoured the cheque. Parke B. in *Bank of Ireland v Evans' Trustees*,[1115] which related to the negligent keeping of a seal, expressed to the House of Lords the unanimous opinion of the judges: "If there was negligence in the custody of the seal, it was very remotely connected with the act of transfer". The learned judge went on to explain that:

"If such negligence could disentitle the plaintiffs, to what extent is it to go? If a man should lose his cheque-book, or neglect to lock the desk in which it is kept, and a servant or stranger should take it up, it is impossible in our opinion to contend that a banker paying his forged cheque would be entitled to charge his customer with that payment. Would it be contended that if he kept his goods so negligently that a servant took them and sold them, he must be considered as having concurred in the sale, and so be disentitled to sue for their conversion on a demand and refusal?"

Tai Hing   Thus, while a customer must be careful not to facilitate fraud when   **34-345** drawing cheques, he is not under a duty to his banker to take reasonable care in organising his business so as to prevent opportunities for others to forge his cheques.[1116] Any doubts that could have existed on this point were settled by the Privy Council's decision in *Tai Hing Cotton Mill Ltd v Liu Chong Hing Bank Ltd*.[1117] A book-keeper perpetrated a series of frauds on his employers. In some cases he tricked them into signing blank or incomplete cheques which he converted and completed in a manner that suited his purposes. In other cases, he resorted to the cruder method of forging the required signatures. As the rogue, who had the custody of the firm's cheque books with its three banks, enjoyed his employers' utmost trust, there was no attempt to check his activities and his frauds went undetected for approximately six years. When he was eventually unmasked, the employers accepted responsibility for all cheques which carried genuine signatures, but demanded that the three banks recredit the firm's respective accounts with the amounts paid out against the forged cheques. The banks' defence was, principally, that the frauds were occasioned by the firm's negligence in the way it conducted its business, pleading that the firm should, accordingly, be estopped from disputing the validity of the payments made by the banks. Reversing the Hong Kong Court of Appeal's decision in favour of the banks, Lord Scarman emphasised that, on the facts, none of the contracts made between the firm and the banks included an express term imposing on the firm a duty to conduct its business in a manner aiming to combat the perpetration of a fraud. At common law, a customer's duty of care was confined to what could:

"... be seen to be plainly necessary incidents of the relationship. Offered such a [current account] service, a customer must obviously take care in the way he draws his cheque, and must obviously warn his bank as soon as he knows that a forger is operating his account."[1118]

His Lordship rejected the view that the customer's duty at common law went

---

[1115] (1855) 5 H.L. Cas. 389, 410–411. See also *Welch v Bank of England* [1955] Ch. 508.

[1116] *Lewes Sanitary Steam Laundry Co Ltd v Barclays & Co Ltd* (1906) 95 L.T. 444. See also *Kepitigalla Rubber Estates Ltd v National Bank of India* [1909] 2 K.B. 1010.

[1117] [1986] A.C. 80; applied in *Yorkshire Bank Plc v Lloyds Bank Plc* [1999] Lloyd's Rep. Bank. 191. For recent criticism, see C. Hare (2012) 23 J.P.F.L.P. 182.

[1118] [1986] A.C. 80 at 106. See also *Wealden (Woodlands) Kent Ltd v National Westminster Bank Ltd* (1983) 133 N.L.J. 719. For these purposes the customer must have actual knowledge of the forgery as opposed to constructive knowledge: *Price Meats Ltd v Barclays Bank Plc* [2000] 2 All E.R. (Comm) 346; *Patel v Standard Chartered Bank* [2001] Lloyd's Rep. Bank. 229.

further than this.[1119] As already pointed out, a wider duty could, however, be imposed on the customer by means of an express verification clause. A question which was not raised in *Tai Hing* is whether a bank may effectively recover losses resulting from the payment of forged cheques of the type here encountered by suing the rogue in deceit and by seeking to hold the employers vicariously liable.[1120]

34-346 **Forged indorsement** If an indorsement is forged on a cheque payable *to bearer*, and the banker pays it to a holder or his agent, he will—in the absence of special circumstances—be considered as having paid the cheque in due course. The holder, in such cases, obtains his title by the delivery to him of the cheque, and does not claim under the forged indorsement. If, however, a cheque payable *to order* bears a forged indorsement of the payee, a transferee is, it appears, not a holder,[1121] and payment to him does not constitute payment in due course. However, s.60 of the Bills of Exchange Act 1882 protects the banker in such cases. It provides that if a banker pays a cheque payable to order in good faith and in the ordinary course of business, he is deemed to have paid it in due course although it may bear a forged indorsement of the payee or of a subsequent holder.[1122] This section applies regardless of whether a cheque has been paid over the counter or through the clearing system.[1123] The phrase "in the ordinary course of business" probably means: the mode of transacting business which is adopted by the banking community at large.[1124] It has been held that if the banker pays a crossed cheque over the counter,[1125] or honours a cheque bearing an irregular indorsement,[1126] he does not pay it in the ordinary course of business. It is not certain whether a banker, who acts negligently, may nevertheless be considered as paying a cheque in the ordinary course of business. In *Carpenters' Co v British Mutual Banking Co*[1127] Greer L.J. expressed the view that, when a banker acts negligently, he cannot be regarded as

---

[1119] But note E.P. Ellinger, E. Lomnicka and C.V.M. Hare, *Ellinger's Modern Banking Law*, 5th edn (2011), p.496, n.330, which makes the point that whilst *Tai Hing* remains good law for cheques, "statutory developments have resulted in a potentially greater risk of liability for customers who pay by card or electronic funds transfer". See the Payment Services Regulations 2017 (SI 2017/752) as amended, regs 72(3), 77(3) (see, previously, the Payment Services Regulations 2009 (SI 2009/209), as amended regs 57(2), 62(2)(a).

[1120] The point was pleaded but not pursued in the *Tai Hing* case. It gains support from dicta of Richmond J. in *National Bank of New Zealand Ltd v Walpole and Patterson Ltd* [1975] 2 N.Z.L.R. 7, 14; and that of La Forest J. (dissenting) in *Boma Manufacturing Ltd v Canadian Imperial Bank of Commerce*, 140 D.L.R. (4th) 463, 499 (1996). It does not matter for these purposes that the employee (or agent) is acting in furtherance of his own interests and not those of his employer (or principal), so long as he is acting within the course of his employment (or within the scope of his actual or apparent authority): *Lloyd v Grace, Smith & Co* [1912] A.C. 716, HL; *Crédit Lyonnais Bank Nederland NV v Export Credit Guarantee Department* [2000] 1 A.C. 486, HL; as explained in *Dubai Aluminium Co Ltd v Salaam* [2002] UKHL 48, [2003] 2 A.C. 366 at [39], [114]. See also E.P. Ellinger, E. Lomnicka and C.V.M. Hare, *Ellinger's Modern Banking Law*, 5th edn (2011), pp.497–498, and C. Hare (2012) 23 J.B.F.L.P. 182 at 210–213.

[1121] See above, para.34-054, discussing s.24 of the Act.

[1122] s.60 applies only to cheques. As regards bills of exchange, see s.19 of the Stamp Act 1853, which gives a similar protection.

[1123] *Australian Mutual Provident Society v Derham* (1979) 39 F.L.R. 167, 173.

[1124] See also E.P. Ellinger, E. Lomnicka and C.V.M. Hare, *Ellinger's Modern Banking Law*, 5th edn (2011), pp.503–505.

[1125] *Smith v Union Bank* (1875) L.R. 10 Q.B. 291; affirmed (1875) 1 Q.B.D. 31, 35.

[1126] *Charles v Blackwell* (1877) 2 C.P.D. 151, 159–160; *Slingsby v District Bank* [1931] 2 K.B. 588; affirmed [1932] 1 K.B. 544. But note as regards protection in respect of cheques irregularly indorsed, below, para.34-348.

[1127] [1938] 1 K.B. 511.

paying a cheque in the ordinary course of business. Slesser L.J., who concurred with Greer L.J.'s judgment on other grounds, thought that a banker may be acting in the ordinary course of business despite his negligence, and his view was supported by Mackinnon L.J., who delivered a dissenting judgment.

Payment with negligence Section 60 appears wide enough to give adequate **34-347** protection to the banker both in the case of uncrossed as well as crossed cheques bearing a forged indorsement. But s.60 cannot apply to cheques crossed "account payee" or "account payee only" as such cheques are non-transferable (s.81A(1) of the Bills of Exchange Act 1882) and, therefore, cannot be payable to order as required by the section.[1128] Section 80, however, expressly provides a similar protection to a banker who pays a crossed cheque (a) in conformity with the tenor of the crossing; (b) in good faith and; (c) "without negligence". This last phrase thus replaces the words "in the ordinary course of business" of s.60. Section 80 appears to reproduce s.9 of the Crossed Cheques Act 1876 and the need to include it, in addition to s.60, in the 1882 Act has been questioned.[1129] However, there are points of difference between the two sections. Section 80 only covers crossed cheques, s.60 extends to crossed and uncrossed cheques. Section 60 only covers cheques payable to order, s.80 extends to cheques which under s.81A of the 1882 Act or otherwise are not transferable. A banker is not to be treated for the purposes of s.80 as having been negligent by reason only of his failure to concern himself with any purported indorsement of a cheque which under s.81A(1) of the 1882 Act or otherwise is not transferable.[1130] In other words, the paying banker can ignore any purported indorsement on the cheque, as it is the responsibility of the collecting banker to ensure that a non-transferable cheque is collected only for the account of the named payee. However, there may be additional circumstances, e.g. where the paying banker is reliably informed that the cheque has been stolen from the payee (assuming the drawer has not, as yet, countermanded payment), in which it might be negligent for a bank to pay a non-transferable cheque bearing a purported indorsement without first satisfying itself that it was in fact being paid to the person entitled to receive it.[1131]

Irregularity in or absence of indorsement Section 60 protects the paying banker **34-348** only in cases of a forged indorsement which is regular on its face. Section 1 of the Cheques Act 1957 protects a banker who, in good faith and in the ordinary course of business, pays a cheque which is not indorsed or is irregularly indorsed. It provides that a banker who pays such a cheque is deemed to have paid it in due course within the meaning of s.59 of the Bills of Exchange Act 1882.[1132] However, the Committee of London Clearing Bankers has taken the view that the public inter-

---

[1128] Since the Cheques Act 1992 introduced s.81A into the Bills of Exchange Act 1882, to the effect that crossed cheques marked "account payee" or "a/c payee", with or without the word "only", are not transferable, United Kingdom banks now almost invariably supply their customers with cheque forms which are crossed and pre-printed with the words "account payee", so that the cheque is valid only as between the parties to it.

[1129] Holden, *History of Negotiable Instruments in English Law*, p.229; *Chalmers and Guest on Bills of Exchange*, 18th edn (2017), para.14-027. A duty of care may be imposed on the banker where he owes his customer a fiduciary duty of care: above, paras 34-255 et seq.

[1130] Bills of Exchange Act 1882 s.81A(2).

[1131] *Chalmers and Guest on Bills of Exchange*, 18th edn (2017), para.14-028.

[1132] As regards such a cheque's effect as a receipt, see the Cheques Act 1957 s.3 as amended by art.5 of the Deregulation (Bills of Exchange) Order 1996 (SI 1996/2993).

est would best be served by retaining the need for indorsement in certain circumstances. These circumstances are set out in a circular of September 23, 1957,[1133] forwarded by that Committee to Clearing Bank Managers. The procedure laid down in this circular may, no doubt, be taken as establishing "the ordinary course of business" and if disregarded would deprive a banker of the protection of s.1. This is especially so because s.1 provides that the banker does not incur liability by "reason only of" the irregular indorsement. As from the date of the circular, the banker, when paying an irregularly indorsed cheque, not only pays despite this defect but also in disregard of standard banking practice. Insofar as that circular relates to the paying banker, it provides that indorsements will continue to be required where cheques or other instruments are cashed over the counter, but that otherwise the paying banker need not concern himself with indorsements unless the instruments are travellers' cheques, bills of exchange (other than cheques) and promissory notes.

34-349 **Where cheque avoided by forgery** Do the paying bank's statutory defences, under ss.60 and 80 of the Bills of Exchange Act 1882 and under s.1 of the Cheques Act 1957, apply where a cheque bears a forged signature of the drawer or if it has been materially altered by a fraudster? The paying bank's statutory defences do not apply where the drawer's signature is forged because the instrument is not a cheque at all. By s.24 of the Bills of Exchange Act 1882, a forged or unauthorised signature is "wholly inoperative" and so the instrument does not meet the statutory definition of a bill of exchange and, therefore, of a cheque.[1134] However, common law defences do remain open to the bank.[1135] In *Slingsby v District Bank*,[1136] Scrutton and Greer L.JJ. thought that a cheque, which, under s.64, was avoided by a material alteration, ceased to be a cheque and hence fell outside the ambit of these provisions. It is submitted that this remains good law. Indeed, in *Smith v Lloyds TSB Bank Plc*,[1137] where a claim was brought against a collecting bank in conversion, it was held by the Court of Appeal that:

> "… the effect of the presence of the word 'avoided' in s.64(1) of the 1882 Act is that the materially altered cheque or draft is, subject to the qualifications in the section, a worthless piece of paper."

Section 64(1) does go on to provide that, where the material alteration is not apparent, the instrument is enforceable in the hands of a holder in due course according to its original tenor. However, as most cheques drawn on United Kingdom banks are crossed and marked "account payee", so as to be non-transferable under s.81A(1) of the 1882 Act, this proviso is unlikely to apply much in practice.

34-350 **Extension of protection to other instruments** Section 1(2) of the Cheques Act 1957 gives a protection similar to that of subs.(1) to a banker who pays any such

---

[1133] Set out in *Chalmers and Guest on Bills of Exchange*, 18th edn (2017), para.17-003.

[1134] Bills of Exchange Act 1882 s.3(1). By s.73 of the 1882 Act, a cheque is defined as "a bill of exchange drawn on a banker payable on demand". See *Arrow Transfer Co Ltd v Royal Bank of Canada*, 27 D.L.R. (3d) 81, 104 (1972). See further, *Chalmers and Guest on Bills of Exchange*, 18th edn (2017), paras 2-013, 3-062, 17-063.

[1135] See above, paras 34-338 et seq.

[1136] [1932] 1 K.B. 544 at 559 (Scrutton L.J.), 562 (Greer L.J.). See also *Kulatilleke v Bank of India* (1958) 59 New L.R. (Ceylon) 190; *Kulatilleke v Bank of Ceylon* (1958) 59 New L.R. (Ceylon) 188; *Chalmers and Guest on Bills of Exchange*, 18th edn (2017), para.17-063.

[1137] [2000] 2 All E.R. (Comm) 693, 703.

count at a bank on the terms that cheques may be drawn on the account by either of them, then, in the absence of facts or circumstances which indicate that the account has been opened for some specific purpose, each party can draw upon it not only for the benefit of both parties, but also for his own benefit. Thus, in *Re Bishop deceased, National Provincial Bank Ltd v Bishop*[1150] a husband and wife opened a joint account and each of them was authorised to draw on it. The husband drew several cheques for the payment of shares purchased in his own name. It was held that these shares were the property of the husband, and were not held by him in trust for his wife and himself.

Survivorship As legal title to a chose in action cannot be held in common, a joint account must create joint legal co-ownership in the debt owed by the bank.[1151] Upon the death of a joint account holder, the legal title to the chose in action representing the joint account vests entirely in the remaining joint account holder(s) by virtue of a right of survivorship.[1152] The bank must meet the demands of that person and in doing so will thereby obtain a good discharge.[1153] Most modern standard-form joint account mandates contain a clause requiring the bank to honour payment instructions given by the surviving account holder(s).

34-355

Beneficial title to the chose in action representing the joint account determines whether the surviving account holder or the deceased account holder's estate is entitled to claim the deceased account holder's share of any balance standing to the credit of the joint account at the time of his death. In *Whitlock v Moree*,[1154] Lord Briggs, delivering the majority advice of the Privy Council, held that where documents relating to the opening of the joint account contained terms indicating on a true construction that the survivor was to be the sole owner,[1155] these terms applied to the legal and beneficial interest and no further investigation was neces-

34-356

Crantrave Ltd v Lloyds TSB Bank Plc [2000] Q.B. 917, CA. In *Crantrave v Lloyds TSB Bank Plc*, there was also support for the view that the bank might have a defence to a claim for breach of mandate where it could be established on the evidence that the customer had been "unjustly enriched" by the unauthorised payment ([2000] Q.B. 917 at 924, 925; see also *Majesty Restaurant Pty Ltd v Commonwealth Bank of Australia Ltd* (1999) 47 N.S.W.L.R. 593, for a case that might fall within this exceptional category). But no evidence of any "unjust factor" or "unconscionability" in *Swotbooks.com Ltd v Royal Bank of Scotland Plc* [2011] EWHC 2025 (QB), where S Phillips Q.C., sitting as a Deputy High Court judge, stated (at [54]) that "the fact that a bank wrongfully debited its customers' account by mistake and thereby paid a creditor of its customer without authority, does not of itself, in my judgment, make it unconscionable for the customer to recover the mistaken payment from the bank".

[1150] [1965] Ch. 450; followed in *Pettitt v Pettitt* [1970] A.C. 777, 815, HL. See also *Fielding v Royal Bank of Scotland Plc* [2004] EWCA Civ 64, where bank held entitled to follow express mandate and debit account on instructions of one of the joint account holders, but Jonathan Parker J. suggesting (at [108]) (without deciding the point) that bank might breach its duty of care to one account holder if it continued to operate the account even though it "had some reason to suppose the mandate was being abused" by the other account holder, or (at [101]) had "notice that a fraud is being committed".

[1151] See E.P. Ellinger, E. Lomnicka and C. Hare, *Ellinger's Modern Banking Law*, 5th edn (2011), pp.324 et seq., for detailed discussion of survivorship. See also D. Fox, *Property Rights in Money* (2008), para.7.52.

[1152] *McEvoy v Belfast Banking Co* [1935] A.C. 24, 43 (Lord Atkin). See also *Russell v Scott* (1936) 55 C.L.R. 440, 451 (Aust. HC); *Pecore v Pecore* [2007] S.C.C. 17, [2007] 1 S.C.R. 795 at [4], Can SC.

[1153] A. Malik and J. Odgers (eds), *Paget's Law of Banking*, 14th edn (2014), [5.21].

[1154] [2017] UKPC 44 at [29]–[32] (on appeal from the Bahamas): Lady Hale and Lord Sumption agreeing with Lord Briggs. But note the strong dissent of Lord Carnwath (with whom Lord Wilson agreed).

[1155] In this case, the account opening documents also contained an express assignment by each account holder to the two of them jointly of any money separately owned by that account holder. But Lord

sary, unless there were special circumstances such as evidence of fraud, duress, undue influence, misrepresentation and the like. In such circumstances, the account-opening documents are themselves dispositive of the beneficial interests in the chose in action and not merely incontrovertible proof of the transferor's intentions.[1156]

34-357 Where, on their true construction, the account-opening documents are silent as to the disposition of the beneficial interests in the joint account,[1157] a resulting trust may be presumed to arise in favour of the account holder who has contributed the money in the account, or a presumption of advancement applied where the relationship between the joint account holders are husband and wife or parent and child.[1158] However, the presumptions are frequently displaced. All the relevant facts and circumstances are considered in order to ascertain the intentions of the contributing account holder with a view to rebutting the presumption.[1159]

34-358 **Partnership accounts** Unless otherwise agreed, each partner is entitled to open an account in the firm's name or to draw upon any existing partnership account.[1160] Although in a sense it is a joint account, each partner is in fact acting as agent of the firm. Usually, however, the articles of a partnership specify the manner in which cheques should be drawn, and the signatures of two of the partners are commonly required.[1161] As it is common knowledge that most partnerships have articles, it stands to reason that a banker must take reasonable steps to inform himself of the provisions concerning the rights of the partners as regards the opening of accounts and the drawing of cheques.[1162] A partner is not entitled to open a partnership account in his own name.[1163]

Briggs stressed at [29] that this was not necessary for the application of the principle set out in the main text.

[1156] At [37], disagreeing with Lawrence Collins J. only on this particular issue in *Aroso v Coutts & Co* [2002] 1 All E.R. (Comm) 241 at [22].

[1157] In *Whitlock v Moree*, above, at [46]–[47], the Board agreed with the Bahamian Court of Appeal's interpretation of the account opening documents, and of the relevant clause in particular, as "a pellucidly clear declaration" that the survivor was to have the beneficial interest in the joint account. Absence of such a clear declaration might allow a court to distinguish the Privy Council's advice. Alternatively, an account opening document may expressly state that it only governs the relationship between the joint holder's right of disposal vis-à-vis the bank, and not the relationship as between the account holders themselves and their legal successors: see, e.g. *Sillett v Meek* [2007] EWHC 1169 (Ch).

[1158] *Aroso v Coutts & Co* [2002] 1 All E.R. (Comm) 241 at [22] (presumption of resulting trust). See *Niles v Lake* [1947] S.C.R. 294, Can SC; *Pecore v Pecore* [2007] S.C.C. 17, [2007] 1 S.C.R. 795, Can SC.

[1159] *Aroso v Coutts & Co*, above, at [22] (rebuttal of presumption of resulting trust); *Marshal v Crutwell* (1875) L.R. 20 Eq. 328 (rebuttal of presumption of advancement), cf. *Re Harrison* (1920) 90 L.J. Ch. 186 (no rebuttal of presumption of advancement). See also *Purvis v Purvis* [2018] EWHC 1458 (Ch) at [34] (no presumption of advancement).

[1160] Partnership Act 1890 ss.5, 6. As to whether a partner has authority to overdraw an account, see *Bank of Australasia v Breillat* (1847) 6 Moore P.C. 152, 193. See also *Kotak v Kotak* [2017] EWHC 1821 (Ch) at [118] et seq. (obiter) on whether a partner who signed a number of loan agreements had done "any act for carrying on in the usual way business of the kind carried on by the firm of which he is a member" within the second limb of s.5 of the 1890 Act. It was held in *Kotak v Kotak* that, on its true construction, a "one signature" mandate expressed to authorise payment by cheques or other written instructions and "for all other purposes" bound the partnership in respect of loan agreements signed by only one of the partners.

[1161] As regards the position where a cheque payable to a partnership is paid into a partner's personal account, see *Souhrada v Bank of NSW* [1976] 2 Lloyd's Rep. 444.

[1162] For an interesting case concerning an innocent partner's position where a dishonest partner has perpetrated irregularities respecting a trust account and, in consequence, caused loss to the bank, see

Trust accounts   A cheque drawn on a trust account should bear the signature of   **34-359**
all trustees, unless the trust instrument stipulates to the contrary.[1164] However, a
trustee may, by power of attorney, delegate for a period not exceeding 12 months
"all or any of the trusts, powers and discretions vested in him as trustee either alone
or jointly with any other person or persons".[1165] Delegation to a sole trustee is
permitted, but this cannot circumvent the rule requiring payment of capital money
to at least two trustees.[1166] The banker is not, generally, concerned with the propriety
of the acts of the trustees; he only has to satisfy himself that their acts are within
the apparent scope of their powers. Usually, in the absence of actual knowledge on
the part of the banker that a cheque is drawn by the trustee for improper purposes,
he is not liable. However, certain acts of the trustee should constitute a red flag.
Thus, a banker should be put on his guard if a trustee draws on trust funds and
directs the banker to credit the cheque to his overdrawn personal account. In *Foxton
v Manchester and Liverpool District Banking Co*,[1167] Fry, J. held that the burden of
proof in these circumstances is on the banker to show that the payment was
legitimate and proper, and if he fails to prove this he must reimburse the funds.
There is some authority[1168] for the view that before this principle may apply the
banker must have already struck a balance and known of the overdraft, or perhaps
even to have pressed for payment. The opinion of Fry J. has since, however, been
cited with approval by Farwell J.,[1169] and is the more likely to prevail.[1170]

Executors' accounts   An account opened by executors or administrators is to be   **34-360**
regarded as that of the estate. Each executor has the power to open an account, but
the other executors are entitled to countermand his actions and stop cheques drawn
by him.[1171] To avoid difficulties bankers usually insist on a mandate given by all the
executors or administrators before opening the account. While the executors have
no power to carry on the deceased's business or to borrow money for this purpose,
they are nevertheless authorised to wind up the estate and can, for that purpose,
pledge assets or give other securities over them.[1172] The banker can, thus, safely
grant an overdraft or advance money against such a security and, provided the
banker acts in good faith and without knowledge of a breach of trust on the part of
the executor, can enforce the security against the estate.[1173]

National Commercial Banking Corp of Australia Ltd v Batty (1986) 65 A.L.R. 385 Aust.
[1163] *Alliance Bank v Kearsley* (1871) L.R. 6 C.P. 433. For a detailed account, see E.P. Ellinger, E.
    Lomnicka and C.V.M. Hare, *Ellinger's Modern Banking Law*, 5th edn (2011), p.441.
[1164] For the nature of a trust account, see *Mann v Coutts & Co* [2003] EWHC 2138 (Comm), [2004] 1
    All E.R. (Comm) 1 at [154]–[165].
[1165] Trustee Act 1925, as amended by the Trustee Delegation Act 1999 s.5. Delegation may be to a trust
    corporation (Trustee Act 1925 s.25(3), as amended).
[1166] Trustee Delegation Act 1999 ss.7, 8. Previously delegation to a sole trustee was not permitted. See
    generally, *Hanbury and Martin's Modern Equity*, 20th edn (2015), para.21-019.
[1167] (1881) 44 L.T. 406, 408; and see *Space Investment Ltd v Canadian Imperial Bank of Commerce Trust
    Co (Bahamas) Ltd* [1986] 1 W.L.R. 1072.
[1168] *Gray v Johnston* (1868) L.R. 3 H.L. 1; *Coleman v Bucks and Oxon Union Bank* [1897] 2 Ch. 243.
[1169] *Att-Gen v De Winton* [1906] 2 Ch. 106, 116.
[1170] As regards the position when the banker's duties as trustee conflict with his being a banker, see *Re
    Pauling's Settlement Trusts* [1964] 1 Ch. 303, 339. See also above, paras 34-255 et seq.
[1171] *Gaunt v Taylor* (1843) 2 Hare 413; and see E.P. Ellinger, E. Lomnicka and C.V.M. Hare, *Ellinger's
    Modern Banking Law*, 5th edn (2011), pp.336–337.
[1172] This appears to follow from *Farhall v Farhall* (1871) L.R. 7 Ch. App. 123.
[1173] *Berry v Gibbons* (1873) L.R. 8 Ch. App. 747.

(d) Discount and Collection

34-361 Discount and collection compared In the vast majority of cases, cheques are not presented by the payee directly to the drawee bank but are remitted by him to his own banker, who arranges for their clearance. In such cases the payee's banker assumes either the role of a collecting banker or that of a discounting banker. When the banker presents the cheque to the drawee on behalf of his customer, he acts as a collecting banker and in the capacity of an agent. If the banker gives his customer value for the cheque before clearance, he presents it, in point of fact, in order to obtain payment for himself. He is in such a case a discounter and holder of the cheque. Whether a banker acts, in a specific case, as a collecting banker or as a discounting banker is a question of fact. The mere crediting of the customer's account before clearance, does not, in itself, constitute him a discounter; but if he agrees to grant the customer an overdraft against the cheque, or actually allows him to draw against it before clearance, he becomes a discounter.[1174] The two roles, however, are not exclusive of one another. A banker may at one and the same time be an agent for collection and a discounter or holder of that cheque for value. Thus, a banker who grants his customer an overdraft of £5 against an uncleared cheque for £100 has given value for it; but it cannot be said that—as a result—he ceases to be the customer's agent for collection.[1175]

34-362 Non-transferable cheques It is almost invariably the case today that where a cheque is delivered to a bank for collection the bank receives the cheque as agent for the customer for the purposes of collecting it on the customer's behalf and not as discounter.[1176] For these purposes, the collecting bank's customer may be another domestic or foreign bank using the collecting bank as its agent to gain access to the cheque clearing system.[1177] In theory, the collecting bank could give the customer value for the cheque and collect the cheque, to the extent of the value given, on its own behalf as a holder for value, but the fact that UK banks now almost invariably issue cheque forms to their customers which are crossed and pre-printed with the words "account payee", thereby making the cheque non-transferable,[1178] means

---

[1174] *Re Farrow's Bank* [1923] 1 Ch. 41; *AL Underwood Ltd v Barclays Bank* [1924] 1 K.B. 775; *Westminster Bank Ltd v Zang* [1966] A.C. 182; *Barclays Bank Ltd v Astley Industrial Trust* [1970] 2 Q.B. 527, 539. The same is true where the banker accepts a cheque in reduction of an overdraft: *McLean v Clydesdale Bank* (1883) 9 App. Cas. 95. For a detailed analysis, see *National Australia Bank Ltd v KDS Construction Services Pty Ltd* (1988) 76 A.L.R. 27 Aust. See also *Taylor v Australia and New Zealand Banking Group Ltd* Unreported May 26, 1988, Vic SC (both Australian authorities consider also whether the transaction constituted an undue preference). A Canadian authority suggests that the bank becomes a discounter even if the overdraft is granted by error: *Bank of Nova Scotia v Taylor* (1979) 60 A.P.R. 14.

[1175] *Barclays Bank Ltd v Astley Industrial Trust*, above, at 538.

[1176] But the proceeds are not held on trust for the customer; the bank merely incurs a commitment to credit the customer's account with an equivalent amount: *Emerald Meats (London) Ltd v AIB Group (UK) Ltd* [2002] EWCA Civ 460.

[1177] See *Importers Co Ltd v Westminster Bank Ltd* [1927] 2 K.B. 297; *Honourable Society of the Middle Temple v Lloyds Bank Plc* [1999] 1 All E.R. (Comm) 193; *Linklaters (a firm) v HSBC Bank Plc* [2003] EWHC 1113 (Comm), [2003] 2 Lloyd's Rep. 545 (Comm), noted by Ellinger (2004) 120 L.Q.R. 226.

[1178] Bills of Exchange Act 1882 s.81A(1).

that this is very rare indeed, for a collecting bank cannot become the holder of a non-transferable cheque.[1179]

Electronic presentation of cheques   The Small Business, Enterprise and Employ-   **34-363**
ment Act 2015 s.13, amends the Bills of Exchange Act 1882 to allow for the electronic presentation of cheques by the collecting bank to the drawee bank for payment.[1180] Under s.89E(1) of the 1882 Act, the Treasury was given power by regulations to make provision for the "responsible banker" to compensate any person for any loss of a kind specified by the regulations which that person incurs in connection with electronic presentation or purported electronic presentation of a cheque or other relevant instrument. The term "responsible banker" is defined in subs.(3) to mean (a) the banker who is authorised to collect payment of the instrument on a customer's behalf, or (b) if the holder of the instrument is a banker, that banker.

Made pursuant the Treasury's power contained in s.89E(1) of the 1882 Act, reg.5   **34-363A**
of the Electronic Presentment of Instruments (Evidence of Payment and Compensation for Loss) Regulations 2018[1181] ensures that if a customer of the bank which pays the cheque or the bank that pays the cheque ("the claimant") incurs a loss[1182] in connection with the electronic presentment, or purported electronic presentment, of a cheque (and that loss did not result from gross negligence or fraudulent activity on their part), and they have not already received compensation, they can obtain compensation from the bank which presented the cheque. The regulation sets out conditions to be met in order for compensation to be payable, including that the claimant has made a claim in accordance with reg.6, which sets out the procedure for such a claim. Importantly, a right to compensation can only arise where one of the following two criteria is met: (a) the electronic presentment or purported electronic presentment of the instrument was of a type described in s.89E(2)(c), (d) or (e) of the Bills of Exchange Act 1882[1183]; (b) the cheque was collected for or paid to a person other than its true owner.[1184] The claimant's right to compensation may also be affected by two additional factors. First, the claimant is not entitled to compensation if they are protected by s.80 of the Bills of Exchange Act 1882 (protection to banker and drawer where cheque is crossed).[1185] Secondly, the amount of compensation to be paid will be reduced where any act or omission of the claimant contributed to the loss.[1186]

Causes of action   If the collecting bank collects a cheque for anyone other than   **34-364**
the true owner, the bank may be liable to the true owner for conversion of the

---

[1179] See R. Hooley [1992] C.L.J. 432.

[1180] See above, paras 34-153—34-154A (especially for commencement dates).

[1181] SI 2018/832, made on July 10, 2018 and coming into force on the 21st day after that date (reg.1).

[1182] Meaning loss arising directly from the debiting of funds from the claimant's account and not further consequential loss (reg.5(4)).

[1183] s.89E(2)(c) covers "purported presentment for payment by any means involving provision of an electronic image of an instrument that may not be presented for payment in that way"; (d) covers "provision, in purported presentment for payment, of (i) an electronic image that purports to be, but is not, an image of a physical instrument (including an image that has been altered electronically), or (ii) an electronic image of an instrument which has no legal effect"; (e) covers "provision, in presentment or purported presentment for payment of an electronic image which has been stolen".

[1184] reg.5(1)(e), (2).

[1185] reg.7. For Bills of Exchange Act 1882 s.80, see below, para.34-347.

[1186] reg.8.

cheque.[1187] The value of the cheque is deemed to be its face value and the true owner can recover damages of that amount.[1188] However, where the cheque has been materially altered, the measure of damages is not the face value: the cheque is avoided under s.64(1) of the Bills of Exchange Act 1882 and becomes a worthless piece of paper.[1189] The true owner is the person with an immediate right to possession of the cheque.[1190] In cases of misappropriation, the identity of the true owner depends on whether the cheque has been delivered by the drawer to the payee. Problems sometimes arise where a cheque is stolen in the post. Where a cheque is sent by post by a debtor to pay his creditor, the issue turns on whether the creditor expressly or impliedly requested or authorised payment through the post: if he did then he is the true owner.[1191] If it is uncertain whether a cheque was misappropriated whilst in the hands of the drawer or the payee, by s.21(3) of the Bills of Exchange Act 1882 the payee will be deemed to have received a valid and unconditional delivery of the cheque, and hence be the true owner, until the contrary is proved.[1192] Alternatively, the amount received for the cheque may be recovered from the bank by the true owner as money had and received.[1193] In theory, the collecting bank may have a right of indemnity or recourse against its own customer who paid in the cheque for collection, but in practice this may prove worthless.[1194] As the collecting bank will have a defence to the restitutionary claim for money had and received if it has already paid the proceeds of the cheque over to its customer in good faith and in ignorance of the claim,[1195] the most common form of action brought by the true owner against the bank is an action in conversion.

34-365 **Protection of collecting banker** A defence available to a collecting banker against an action for the conversion of a cheque (or an action related thereto but

[1187] *Morison v London County and Westminster Bank Ltd* [1914] 3 K.B. 356; *AL Underwood Ltd v Barclays Bank* [1924] 1 K.B. 775; *Lloyds Bank Ltd v Savory & Co* [1933] A.C. 201; *Marquess of Bute v Barclays Bank* [1955] 1 Q.B. 202 (which shows that the claimant need not be the owner of the cheque, but may be a person entitled to immediate possession).
[1188] *Marquess of Bute v Barclays Bank* [1955] 1 Q.B. 202. For criticism of the face value rule, see E.P. Ellinger, E. Lomnicka and C.V.M. Hare, *Ellinger's Modern Banking Law*, 5th edn (2011), pp.683–685. The rule was described as a "legal fiction" by Lord Nicholls in *OBG Ltd v Allan* [2007] UKHL 21, [2007] 2 W.L.R. 920 at [227]–[228].
[1189] *Smith v Lloyds TSB Plc* [2000] 2 All E.R. (Comm) 693, CA. The proviso to s.64(1) cannot apply where the cheque is non-transferable: see above, para.34-349.
[1190] *Marquess of Bute v Barclays Bank Ltd* [1955] 1 Q.B. 202.
[1191] *Norman v Ricketts* (1886) 3 T.L.R. 182; and see also *Chalmers and Guest on Bills of Exchange*, 18th edn (2017), para.2-151.
[1192] *Surrey Asset Finance Ltd v National Westminster Bank Plc, The Times,* November 30, 2000; permission to appeal refused [2001] EWCA Civ 60.
[1193] *Bavins Jnr & Sims v London and South Western Bank* [1900] 1 Q.B. 270; *Morison v London County and Westminster Bank Ltd,* above; *United Australia Ltd v Barclays Bank Ltd* [1941] A.C. 1 (waiver of tort); cf. *John v Dodwell & Co* [1918] A.C. 563, 570. But this restitutionary claim may fail if the money is paid over to the principal. The collecting bank does not owe a duty of care to the drawee: *Yorkshire Bank Plc v Lloyd's Bank Plc* [1999] Lloyd's Rep. Bank. 191.
[1194] But see *Honourable Society of the Middle Temple v Lloyds Bank Plc,* above, where an English clearing bank was held entitled to claim a full indemnity from the overseas bank that had instructed it to act as the collecting agent of the overseas bank, applied in *Linklaters (a firm) v HSBC Bank Plc,* above, where Gross J. held that the fact the collecting agent was also the paying bank was of no significance to its claim for a complete indemnity and that there was no room for just and equitable apportionment between the two banks under the Civil Liability (Contribution) Act 1978 as this solution was inherently uncertain and carried with it a much increased risk of litigation. See also Ellinger (2004) 120 L.Q.R. 226.
[1195] See Vol.I, paras 29-186 et seq.

brought under the law of unjust enrichment) is provided in s.4 of the Cheques Act 1957, which has replaced and widened the scope of the protection previously afforded by s.82 of the Bills of Exchange Act 1882. Under s.4, a banker is not liable to the true owner of a cheque if he has received payment of it for a customer in good faith and without negligence despite any defects in the customer's title.[1196] To avail himself of this defence, the collecting banker must, thus, be able to prove, among other things, that he has acted without negligence. Where compliance with this standard is in issue, it is of primary importance to examine whether or not the banker has acted in conformity with prevailing banking practice. In *Lloyds Bank v Savory & Co*[1197] the required standard was described as based on:

"... the practice of *reasonable men* carrying on the business of bankers, and endeavouring to do so in such a manner as may be calculated to protect themselves and others against fraud".

Emphasis is to be placed on the words "reasonable men"; they imply that the courts will be reluctant to be guided by, or give effect to, a banking practice which is unreasonably lax or which may exonerate bankers from liability where they fail to exercise the degree of skill expected of conscientious businessmen.[1198] Some support for this submission is to be found in the fact that mere exigencies of business will not excuse negligence.[1199] However, the banker is not required to play the amateur detective and is not expected to be abnormally suspicious.[1200]

Instances of negligence   Negligence in the collection of cheques, within the   **34-366** meaning of s.4, may occur either at the time the account is opened or when the banker accepts a specific cheque for collection. In the past, the banker has been held to be negligent if he opens an account without taking up references of the customer,[1201] or without ascertaining the occupation of his prospective customer and, if he turns out to be an employee, to ascertain the name of his employer.[1202] It has also been held that the banker's failure to insist on an identification does not constitute negligence.[1203] There is, however, authority for the view that an immigrant, who wishes to open an account shortly after arriving from overseas and who is unable to provide a referee known to the banker or to one of his correspondents, should be asked to produce a passport or some other proof of

---

[1196] As regards the protection afforded by this section to a discounting banker, see para.34-371, below. As regards the meaning of the word "customer", see above, para.34-251. See generally, E.P. Ellinger, E. Lomnicka and C.V.M. Hare, *Ellinger's Modern Banking Law*, 5th edn (2011), Ch.15.

[1197] [1933] A.C. 201, 221; see Megrah (1956) 77 J.I.B. 256. In *Marfani & Co Ltd v Midland Bank Ltd* [1968] 1 W.L.R. 956, 957, Diplock L.J. observed that current banking practice provided a better guide for determining the absence or presence of negligence than cases decided 30 years earlier, when banking facilities were far less widespread.

[1198] See implied warning to this effect by Cairns J. in *Marfani & Co Ltd v Midland Bank Ltd*, above, at 981–982. And see *Thackwell v Barclays Bank Plc* [1986] 1 All E.R. 676, which also supports the view that a failure to make an enquiry is not excused by the fact that an answer would have allayed fears of fraud.

[1199] *Ross v London County and Westminster Bank* [1919] 1 K.B. 678.

[1200] *Penmount Estate Ltd v National Provincial Bank* (1945) 173 L.T. 344, 346. See also *Smith and Baldwin v Barclays Bank* (1944) 65 J.I.B. 171.

[1201] *Ladbroke v Todd* (1914) 30 T.L.R. 433; *Hampstead Guardians v Barclays Bank* (1923) 39 T.L.R. 229. cf. *Commissioners of Taxation v English, Scottish and Australian Bank* [1920] A.C. 683.

[1202] *Lloyds Bank v Savory & Co* [1933] A.C. 201.

[1203] *Marfani & Co Ltd v Midland Bank Ltd* [1968] 1 W.L.R. 956.

identity.[1204] Today, failure to check the identity of a customer is more likely to amount to negligence. This is because banks must ensure that they have proper procedures for identifying their customers so as to comply with the stringent requirements of the money laundering and terrorist financing legislation.[1205] Banks must also comply with the rules laid down by the Financial Services Authority to combat money laundering (one of the regulatory objectives of the Authority under the Financial Services and Markets Act 2000 is "the reduction of financial crime"). Banks are now less likely to require references when a new account is opened, which is not surprising as satisfactory references are relatively easy for a thief to fabricate.[1206]

34-367   Bankers have been held to have acted negligently in the actual collection of cheques in the following cases: where an employee, official or agent was allowed to place to his credit cheques payable to or, in some cases, drawn by his employer or principal[1207]; where a cheque was collected and credited to the private account of an agent although the cheque indicated that he obtained it in his representative capacity[1208]; where a banker collected a cheque crossed "a/c payee only" for a person other than the specified payee[1209]; and where a banker collected for his customer, without inquiry, cheques to an amount clearly out of proportion to the

---

[1204] *Lumsden & Co v London Trustee Savings Bank* [1971] 1 Lloyd's Rep. 114.

[1205] See the Money Laundering, Terrorist Financing and Transfer of Funds (Information on the Payer) Regulations 2017 (SI 2017/692), implementing the Fourth Money Laundering Directive 2015/849/EU. The Fifth Money Laundering Directive 2018/843/EU must be implemented in EU Member States by 10 January 2020. The Sanctions and Anti-Money Laundering Act 2018 comes into force on 29 March 2019 and, inter alia, enables the government to make regulations for the detection, investigation and prevention of money laundering or terrorist financing.

[1206] E.P. Ellinger, E. Lomnicka and C.V.M. Hare, *Ellinger's Modern Banking Law*, 5th edn (2011), pp.695–698.

[1207] *Morison v London County and Westminster Bank Ltd* [1914] 3 K.B. 356; *Ross v London County and Westminster Bank* [1919] 1 K.B. 678; *Souchette v London County and Westminster Bank* (1920) 36 T.L.R. 195; *AL Underwood Ltd v Bank of Liverpool* [1924] 1 K.B. 775; *Lloyds Bank v Savory & Co* [1933] A.C. 201. However, if business efficacy requires that certain cheques payable to a drawer be collected through the account of the agent and this procedure is adopted with the drawer's knowledge, he is estopped from suing the collector's banker: *Australia and New Zealand Bank Ltd v Ateliers de Constructions Electriques de Charleroi* [1967] 1 A.C. 86.

[1208] *Marquess of Bute v Barclays Bank* [1955] 1 Q.B. 202. cf. *Moser v Commercial Banking Co of Sydney Ltd* (1974) 22 F.L.R. 123 Aust: cheque payable jointly to husband and wife collected for husband's personal account; held to involve negligence.

[1209] *Bevan v National Bank* (1906) 23 T.L.R. 65; *House Property Co of London v London County and Westminster Bank* (1915) 31 T.L.R. 479; *Rhostar (Pvt) Ltd v Netherlands Bank of Rhodesia Ltd* [1972] 2 S.A.L.R. 703, especially 717; *National Commercial Banking Corp of Australia Ltd v Robert Bushby Ltd* (1984) 1 N.S.W.L.R. 559, affirmed sub. nom. *National Commercial Banking Corp of Australia Ltd v Batty* (1986) 65 A.L.R. 385. But note that if the payee authorises the collection of the cheque for the credit of an account other than his own, there is no conversion involved: *Souhrada v Bank of NSW* [1976] 2 Lloyd's Rep. 444, 452. Note further that there is no negligence in the collection for an account other than the ostensible payee's of a cheque crossed with the mere addition of the words "not negotiable": *Day v Bank of NSW* (1978) 19 A.L.R. 32 Aust. Following the passing of the Cheques Act 1992 (discussed above, para.34-165), in the absence of special circumstances, it would generally be negligent to collect payment of an "a/c payee" cheque for someone other than the named payee without further inquiry. But in each case the enquiry is fact sensitive and current banking practice is highly relevant to the issue of negligence (*Architects of Wine Ltd v Barclays Bank Plc* [2007] EWCA Civ 239, [2007] 2 All E.R. 285 at [12], per Rix L.J., who added that "[a] bank's evidence about its practice is, especially if unchallenged, relevant evidence of the current practice of bankers"). As regards the collection of an "a/c payee" cheque on the instructions of a non-clearing bank, see *Hon Society of the Middle Temple v Lloyds Bank* [1999] 1 All E.R. (Comm) 193; *Linklaters (a firm) v HSBC Bank Plc* [2003] EWHC 1113, [2003] 2 Lloyd's Rep. 545 (Comm), noted by Ellinger (2004) 120 L.Q.R. 226.

known position in life of the customer.[1210] A banker is, however, not considered negligent merely because he fails to compare the signature of the drawer with an indorsement, and consequently fails to discover that the customer is not only the payee but also the drawer of a company's cheque paid into his account.[1211]

Absent or irregular indorsement   Before 1957 a banker, who collected a cheque **34-368** bearing an irregular indorsement, was considered to have acted negligently and was therefore not protected by s.82 of the Bills of Exchange Act 1882.[1212] The law was changed by s.4(3) of the Cheques Act 1957, according to which a banker is not to be treated as having been negligent by reason only of his failure to concern himself with the absence of, or the irregularity in, indorsements. This provision must, however, be read in the light of the Circular of the Committee of London Clearing Bankers (namely the predecessors of the Committee of London and Scottish Banks) of September 23, 1957, which remains the basis of the prevailing banking practice in point. Just as this circular requires the paying banker to insist upon indorsements in certain circumstances, so also it gives detailed instructions for the guidance of the collecting banker. The effect of it is that as a matter of practice the collecting banker is expected to require indorsements of any cheque or other instrument:

(i)   which is tendered for an account other than that of the ostensible payee (in such a case the banker must look for the indorsement of the payee and of all subsequent indorsees other than that of the customer for whose account it is to be collected); or

(ii) on which the payee's name is misspelt, or the payee is incorrectly designated, and the surrounding circumstances are suspicious; or

(iii) which is payable to joint payees and tendered for an account to which not all are parties.

It follows that if a banker collects one of the instruments mentioned in the circular despite its being unindorsed or bearing an irregular indorsement, he may be considered as having acted negligently by ignoring a requirement of common banking practice.

Other documents   The statutory protection relates not only to the collection of **34-369** cheques, but under s.4(2) applies also to the collection of:

(a)   any document issued by a customer of a banker which, though not a bill of exchange, is intended to enable a person to obtain payment from that banker of the sum mentioned in the document[1213];

(b)   any document issued by a public officer which is intended to enable a person to obtain payment from the Paymaster-General or the Queen's and Lord Treasurer's Remembrancer of the sum mentioned in the document but is not a bill of exchange; and

---

[1210] *Lloyds Bank v Chartered Bank of India* [1929] 1 K.B. 40; *Motor Traders Guarantee Corp v Midland Bank* [1937] 4 All E.R. 90; *Nu-Stilo Footwear v Lloyds Bank* (1956) 77 J.I.B. 239; *Day v Bank of NSW* [1976] 2 Lloyd's Rep. 444, which also concerned the question of negligence arising from the bank's failure to inquire as regards the authority of an indorser who paid a cheque into his own account having indorsed it per pro the payee.

[1211] *Orbit Mining and Trading Co v Westminster Bank* [1963] 1 Q.B. 794.

[1212] *Bavins Jnr & Sims v London and South Western Bank Ltd* [1900] 1 Q.B. 270.

[1213] Such a document includes a cheque payable to "cash or order": *Orbit Mining and Trading Co v Westminster Bank* [1963] 1 Q.B. 794.

(c) any draft payable on demand drawn by a banker upon himself, whether payable at the head office or some other office of his bank.[1214]

It thus includes dividend and interest warrants, conditional orders and bankers' drafts. It does not include commercial bills of exchange or promissory notes.

34-370 **Contributory negligence** Can a plea of contributory negligence be raised as a partial defence to an action in conversion brought by the true owner of a cheque against a collecting banker? A positive answer to this question was given in *Lumsden & Co v London Trustee Savings Bank*.[1215] In that case a collecting banker failed to establish that he had acted without negligence in the collection of certain cheques and was therefore held not to be entitled to the protection of s.4 of the Cheques Act 1957. It was, however, held that the customer was guilty of contributory negligence to the extent of 10 per cent and the amount recoverable by him was reduced accordingly. Donaldson J.'s decision to allow this defence was based on the language of s.1 of the Law Reform (Contributory Negligence) Act 1945:

> "Where any person suffers damage as the result partly of his own fault and partly of the fault of any other person or persons ... the damages recoverable in respect thereof shall be reduced to such extent as the court thinks just and equitable ..."

The learned judge held that this provision does not confine the defence of contributory negligence to instances in which the claimant—against whom it is raised—owes a duty of care to the defendant. It is sufficient if the claimant's carelessness or fault has contributed to the occurrence of the loss. Whilst Australian authorities cast some doubts on the correctness of this decision,[1216] it has been affirmed in England by statute. Under s.47 of the Banking Act 1979 the defence of contributory negligence is available to a banker "in any circumstances in which proof of absence of negligence would be a defence in proceedings by reason of s.4 of the Cheques Act 1957".[1217]

34-371 **Protection of discounting banker** A discounting banker may, on occasions, be able to plead two defences against an action in conversion by the true owner of a cheque. First, s.4(1)(b) protects the banker not only if he collects the cheque for a customer but also when "having credited a customer's account with the amount of such an instrument, [he] receives payment thereof for himself". Thus, it is argu-

---

[1214] As regards the legal nature of such a draft, see *Commercial Banking Co of Sydney Ltd v Mann* [1961] A.C. 1, 7. See generally as regards bankers' drafts: *Chalmers and Guest on Bills of Exchange*, 18th edn (2017), paras 2-003, 2-012 and 2-040.

[1215] [1971] 1 Lloyd's Rep. 114; following *Helson v McKenzies (Cuba Street) Ltd* [1950] N.Z.L.R. 878.

[1216] *Wilton v Commonwealth Trading Bank* [1973] 2 N.S.W.R. 644; *Tina Motors Pty Ltd v ANZ Banking Group Ltd* [1977] V.R. 205, 208–209; *Day v Bank of NSW* (1978) 19 A.L.R. 32, 42 et seq.; *Grantham Homes Pty Ltd v Interstate Permanent Building Society Ltd* (1979) 37 F.L.R. 191; *Oxland Enterprises Pty Ltd v Gierke* (1980) 91 L.S.J.S. 276. See also dictum of Lord Wright in *Lloyds Bank v Savory & Co* [1933] A.C. 201, 229. cf. *Varker v Commercial Banking Co of Sydney Ltd* [1972] 2 N.S.W.R. 967.

[1217] The object of this provision was to ensure that the application to actions of this type of the plea of contributory negligence was not affected by s.11(1) of the Torts (Interference with Goods) Act 1977. Note that contributory negligence also constitutes a defence to an action for the breach of a contractual duty of care where the defendant is also liable in the tort of negligence for the same default: Vol.I, para.26-085. Note also that under reg.8 of the Electronic Presentment of Instruments (Evidence of Payment and Compensation for Loss) Regulations 2018 (SI 2018/832), compensation to be paid by a "responsible banker" under reg.5 is reduced if the claimant's behaviour contributed to the loss (see above, paras 34-153—34-154A).

able that a discounting banker may claim the defence of s.4 provided the cheque has been credited to the customer's account: he cannot rely on this section if the cheque has not gone through the customer's account, e.g. if the banker has paid cash against the cheque.[1218] The second defence which may, on occasions, be open to the discounting banker is to rely on his position as holder in due course of a cheque. If he can bring himself within the definition of a holder in due course, he is to be regarded as the owner of the instrument and an action in conversion against him will fail.[1219] However, in order to be considered a holder in due course, the banker must prove that he took the cheque in good faith and for value and that the cheque was, at that time, complete and regular on its face.[1220]

Regularity   The last requirement proved, on occasions, a pitfall, as a cheque is **34-372** considered regular on its face only insofar as, inter alia, it is regularly indorsed.[1221] However, it appears that this requirement has been mitigated by s.2 of the Cheques Act 1957, which confers on a banker who gives value for a cheque payable to order, which the holder delivers to him for collection without indorsing it, such rights as he would have had if it had been indorsed in blank. Two cases show that a discounting banker may rely on this section in order to establish that he is a holder in due course of an unindorsed cheque. In *Midland Bank Ltd v RV Harris Ltd*[1222] a customer of the plaintiffs paid into his account with them two cheques drawn by the defendant on Lloyds Bank and payable to the customer's firm. The cheques were dishonoured by Lloyds Bank and the plaintiffs brought an action claiming to be holders in due course of the cheques. It was proved that the customer was allowed to draw against the cheques before their clearance. Although the cheques did not bear an indorsement, it was held that, by s.2, the plaintiffs could be treated as holders in due course of the cheques despite the absence of an indorsement. In *Westminster Bank v Zang*[1223] a customer of the plaintiffs paid into the account of a company of which he was a director an unindorsed cheque, drawn by the defendant and payable to the customer's order. The defendant stopped the cheque and it was dishonoured by the drawee bank. The plaintiffs brought an action to enforce payment, claiming to be holders in due course. As it was proved that the plaintiffs did not give value for the cheque, it was held that they were not holders in due course or for value, and could not enforce payment. The House of Lords held, however, that if they had given value for the cheque, they would have been holders in due course despite the missing indorsement. It was further held that the fact that the cheque was not collected for the original payee was of no relevance.

Comparison with non-bank holder   *Zang's* case demonstrates that a banker may **34-373**

[1218] Under s.82 of the Bills of Exchange Act 1882 a banker was not protected if he credited the customer's account before clearance: *Capital and Counties Bank v Gordon* [1903] A.C. 240. This difficulty was removed by s.1 of the Bills of Exchange (Crossed Cheques) Act 1906, which provided that a banker collected a cheque within the meaning of s.82 notwithstanding that he credited his customer's account with the amount of the cheque before clearance. Under that section a discounting banker would not have been protected, as such a banker collects the cheque for himself and not for a customer. Section 4(1)(b), it should be noted, explicitly protects a banker who, having credited the customer's account, *receives payment for himself.*

[1219] See s.38(2) of the Act discussed in para.34-093, above.

[1220] See s.29 of the Act, discussed in para.34-072, above.

[1221] *Arab Bank Ltd v Ross* [1952] 2 Q.B. 216.

[1222] [1963] 1 W.L.R. 1021.

[1223] [1966] A.C. 182.

be considered a holder in due course in circumstances in which an ordinary member of the public—who is less familiar with negotiable instruments than a banker—would not be so considered. It should be noted that a person may be a holder in due course although he has acted with negligence.[1224] Accordingly, a discounting banker may find it useful to rely on his being a holder in due course of a cheque if he is not able to prove that he has acted without negligence. If he cannot show that he is a holder in due course, e.g. where he discounts an order cheque bearing a forged indorsement,[1225] he may still escape liability for conversion by relying on s.4, provided the cheque has been credited to the account of a customer.

34-374 **Non-transferable cheques** As UK banks now almost invariably issue their customers with cheque forms which are crossed and pre-printed with the words "account payee", thereby making the cheque non-transferable,[1226] the holder in due course defence will rarely be available to a collecting bank. The collecting bank cannot become a holder in due course, or indeed any other type of holder, of a non-transferable cheque when it is not the named payee.[1227] In consequence, the holder in due course defence need only be considered in those relatively rare cases where a cheque is uncrossed, or where the words "account payee" are absent or have been deleted by the drawer of the cheque.

34-375 **Protection in cases of forgery** It has been indicated that the true owner of a forged cheque, e.g. a company whose cheque has been forged by a director, may recover the face value of the cheque from the collecting banker, provided the latter cannot claim to be protected under s.4.[1228] Insofar as the action of the true owner against the collecting banker is one in conversion, it is submitted that the true owner should be allowed to recover only the true value of the instrument. Whilst the value of a genuine cheque or bill is the amount for which it is drawn, it should be observed that by alleging the forgery of the instrument, the owner, or claimant, claims that it is null and void.[1229] Why then should he be allowed to claim its face value? In *Mathew and Cousins v Sherwell*[1230] a person drew a cheque and delivered it, after his being declared a bankrupt, to the defendant. Sir James Mansfield dismissed an action by the assignee in bankruptcy for the conversion of the cheque, holding that even if the action succeeded the assignee could, at most, recover the value of the paper on which the cheque was written. The assignee was not allowed to claim that whilst the cheque was a nullity, it had the value of £300. This reasoning has been followed in modern cases decided in Australia and in Canada.[1231] Most recently, in

---

[1224] See above, para.34-075.

[1225] See above, para.34-053.

[1226] Bills of Exchange Act 1882 s.81A(1).

[1227] The requirements for holder in due course status are set out in s.29(1) of the Bills of Exchange Act 1882, and are considered in para.34-072 above.

[1228] *Orbit Mining and Trading Co v Westminster Bank* [1963] 1 Q.B. 794. See also *Stoney Stanton Supplies (Coventry) Ltd v Midland Bank Ltd* [1966] 2 Lloyd's Rep. 373, 385.

[1229] See ss.24 and 64 of the Act. And see above, para.34-349, considering the argument in respect of ss.60 and 80 of the Bills of Exchange Act 1882.

[1230] (1810) 2 Taunt. 439. cf. *Building and Civil Engineering Holidays Scheme Management Ltd v Post Office* [1964] 2 Q.B. 430, 444–447.

[1231] *Arrow Transfer Co Ltd v Royal Bank of Canada*, 19 D.L.R. (3rd) 420 (1971), affirmed 27 D.L.R. (3rd) 81 (1972) Can; *Number 10 Management Ltd v Royal Bank of Canada*, 69 D.L.R. (3d) 99, 105 (1977): *Koster's Premier Pottery Pty Ltd v Bank of Adelaide* (1981) 28 S.A.S.R. 355 Aust.

Smith v Lloyds TSB Group Plc,[1232] the English Court of Appeal has rejected the face value rule where a cheque had been "materially altered" by an unauthorised person so as to fall within s.64(1) of the Bills of Exchange Act 1882. The Court of Appeal held that such a cheque was a "worthless piece of paper".[1233] It may be that the true owner of the cheque could overcome such a result by relying on the law of unjust enrichment and suing the collecting banker for money had and received. Whilst there is authority indicating that the claimant, the true owner of the cheque, may do so,[1234] it is to be doubted if he would usually be able to succeed. It should be noted that the collecting banker receives the amount of the cheque as the agent of his customer, and it is doubtful whether an action for money had and received would succeed against such an agent once he has paid the amount of the collected cheque to his principal, the customer.[1235]

Duty to customer Quite regardless of whether the bank has accepted a cheque **34-376** for collection or on the basis of a discount arrangement, it owes its customer the duty to present the instrument for payment with ordinary diligence.[1236] Basically, the bank has a "reasonable time" to present the cheque for payment.[1237] In practice, the position is governed by the Clearing House Rules. Under the traditional banking procedure, cheques had to be presented for payment through the clearing house to the branch on which they were drawn.[1238] In 1996, the Bills of Exchange Act 1882 was amended to allow for cheque truncation.[1239] Under a fully truncated system only essential information about the cheque is sent electronically from the collecting bank to the drawee bank and not the cheque itself, which remains with the collecting bank. The declining use of cheques, coupled with high development costs, meant that a fully truncated cheque-clearing system was never developed in the UK. In fact those provisions introduced in 1996 to allow for cheque truncation (ss.74B and 74C of the Bills of Exchange Act 1882) have now been repealed by s.13 of the Small Business, Enterprise and Employment Act 2015, which introduces fresh amendments to the 1882 Act that allow for cheques to be cleared through presenta-

---

[1232] [2000] 2 All E.R. (Comm) 693.

[1233] At 703.

[1234] *Morison v London County and Westminster Bank Ltd* [1914] 3 K.B. 356, 365–366; *United Australia Ltd v Barclays Bank Ltd* [1941] A.C. 1, above, para.34-364.

[1235] *Morison v London County and Westminster Bank Ltd*, above, at 386; above, para.34-125; for the same reason he would lose on an action in money had and received based on the ratio in *Lipkin Gorman v Karpnale Ltd* [1991] 2 A.C. 548, above, para.34-131.

[1236] By contrast, where a collecting bank collects an instrument for a remitting bank, there is no privity of contract between the collecting bank and the customer of the remitting bank either at common law or under the Uniform Rules for Collections, 1995 revision (URC 522): *Grosvenor Casinos Ltd v National Bank of Abu Dhabi* [2008] EWHC 511 (Comm), [2008] 2 All E.R. (Comm) 112 at [157], Flaux J., distinguishing *Bastone & Firminger Ltd v Nasima Enterprises (Nigeria) Ltd* [1996] C.L.C. 1902 at 1908, Rix J., who thought the URC point arguable. See further, H. Bennett (2008) 124 L.Q.R. 532.

[1237] Note that as a collecting bank does not become a holder the position is not governed by s.45(2) of the Bills of Exchange Act 1882, although this provision furnishes a guideline. For a detailed discussion of the collecting bank's duties, see E.P. Ellinger, E. Lomnicka and C.V.M. Hare, *Ellinger's Modern Banking Law*, 5th edn (2011), pp.715 et seq.; the clearing house rules are discussed at pp.390 et seq.

[1238] *Barclays Bank v Bank of England* [1985] 1 All E.R. 385.

[1239] Bills of Exchange Act 1882 ss.74B–C, inserted by the Deregulation (Bills of Exchange) Order 1996 (SI 1996/2993). See *Chalmers and Guest on Bills of Exchange and Cheques*, 18th edn (2017), paras 13-021 et seq.; and, on cheque truncation generally, see also Vroegop [1990] L.M.C.L.Q. 244. See above, para.34-152.

tion of an electronic image of the cheque (known as "cheque imaging") in place of presentation of the cheque itself.[1240]

(e) The Giro System and Electronic Transfer of Funds[1241]

34-377 Introduction The word "giro", which is used to describe money transfer operations is derived from the Greek word for circle. Giro denotes the cyclic operation involved in the transfer of credit balances from one bank account into another.

34-378 Nature of a giro transfer The common thread that runs through all giro operations, paper-based or electronic, is that they involve the movement of a credit balance from one account to another brought about through adjustment of the balances of the payer's and the payee's accounts.[1242] The payer's account is debited and the payee's account is credited. This results in the debt owed to the payer by his bank being extinguished or reduced pro tanto (or, where his account is overdrawn, his liability to the bank increased) by the amount of the transfer to the payee, whilst the debt owed to the payee by his own bank is increased (or, where his account is overdrawn, his liability reduced) by the same amount.

34-379 Transfer of value A giro operation does not involve the transfer of property, simply the adjustment of separate property rights (i.e. choses in action) of the payer and the payee against their own banks.[1243] It is, therefore, something of a misnomer to speak of the "transfer" of funds as there is no actual transfer of coins and bank notes from the payer to the payee.[1244] Moreover, there is no assignment of any debt that may be owed to the payer by his own bank.[1245] As Staughton J. observed in *Libyan Arab Foreign Bank v Bankers Trust Co*[1246]:

> "'Transfer' may be a somewhat misleading word, since the original obligation is not assigned (notwithstanding dicta in one American case which speaks of assignment)[1247]; a new obligation by a new debtor is created."

[1240] See Pt 4A of the Bills of Exchange Act 1882 (as inserted by s.13). See above, paras 34-153—34-154A.

[1241] This section of the chapter draws heavily on Ch.13 of E.P. Ellinger, E. Lomnicka and C.V.M. Hare, *Ellinger's Modern Banking Law*, 5th edn (2011).

[1242] Usually the payer instructs his bank to debit his account with the amount of the transfer, but it is possible for a non-customer to instruct a bank to make a giro transfer simply by paying cash over the counter; much turns on the practice of individual banks as to whether they will accept giro transfer instructions from non-customers. Where the payee does not have a bank account, the funds are usually deposited into a general account at the receiving bank, and left at the payee's disposal.

[1243] *R. v Preddy* [1996] A.C. 815, 834, HL.

[1244] See *Foskett v McKeown* [2001] 1 A.C. 102, 128, per Lord Millett: "No money passes from paying bank to receiving bank or through the clearing system (where the money flows may be in the opposite direction) there is simply a series of credits and debits which are causally and transactionally linked". See also *Customs and Excise Commissioners v FDR Ltd* [2000] S.T.C. 672 at [37]; and *Dovey v Bank of New Zealand* [2000] 3 N.Z.L.R. 641, 648 NZCA; *European Bank Ltd v Citibank Ltd* [2004] NSWCA 76 at [57]–[62]; *Darkinjung Pty Ltd v Darkinjung Local Aboriginal Land Council* [2006] NSWSC 1217 at [13]; *Scottish Exhibition Centre Ltd v Commissioners for Revenue and Customs* [2008] S.T.C. 967 at [19], Ct of Sess. IH.

[1245] *R. v Preddy*, above (credit transfer); *Mercedes-Benz Finance Ltd v Clydesdale Bank Plc* [1997] C.L.C. 81, Ct of Sess. OH (debit transfer).

[1246] [1989] Q.B. 728, 750.

[1247] Presumably, Staughton J. was referring to *Delbrueck & Co v Manufacturers Hanover Trust Co*, 609 F. 2d. 1047 at 1051 (1979) (see below, para.34-426).

Transfer of *value*, rather than the transfer of funds, is probably a more accurate description of the giro process.

Credit and debit transfers   Giro operations can be classified as either credit   **34-380**
transfers or debit transfers according to the way the payment order is communicated to the payer's bank.

Credit transfers   A credit transfer represents a "push" of funds by the payer to   **34-381**
the payee. The payer instructs his bank to cause the account of the payee, at the
same or another bank, to be credited. The payer's payment order may be for an
individual credit transfer, e.g. by bank giro credit or CHAPS payment, or for a
recurring transfer of funds under a standing order (standing orders are instructions
given by a customer to his bank to make regular payments of a fixed amount to a
particular payee).[1248] On receipt of the payer's payment order, the payer's bank will
debit the payer's account, unless the payer has provided his bank with some other
means of reimbursement, and credit the payee's account where it is held at the same
bank, or, where the payee's account is held at another bank, forward a payment
order to the payee's bank, which will credit the payee's account.

Debit transfers   A debit transfer represents a "pull" of funds by the payee from   **34-382**
the payer. The payee conveys instructions to his bank to collect funds from the
payer. These instructions may be initiated by the payer and passed on to the payee,
e.g. as happens with the collection of cheques; alternatively, they may be initiated
by the payee himself pursuant to the payer's authority, as happens with direct debits
(where the payer signs a mandate authorising his bank to pay amounts demanded
by the payee).[1249] On receipt of instructions from the payee, the payee's bank usually provisionally credits the payee's account with the amount to be collected and
forwards instructions to the payer's bank, which will debit the payer's account. The
credit to the payee's account becomes final when the debit to the payer's account
becomes irreversible.

Clearing   Payment effected through a giro transfer system is initiated by a pay-   **34-383**
ment order given by the payer, or someone else acting with his authority, to his own
bank. In cases where the payment is not "in-house" (i.e. the payer and the payee
hold accounts at the same bank), the payer's payment order will lead to a further
payment order passing between the payer's bank and the payee's bank, sometimes
through the intermediation of other banks. The process of exchanging payment
orders between participating banks is known as clearing. Clearing may take place
through a series of bilateral exchanges of payment orders between banks, but in the
United Kingdom it is more common for clearing to take place multilaterally through
a centralised clearing house.

Paper-based and electronic system   Giro transfer systems are classified as either   **34-384**
paper-based or electronic depending on the medium used for inter-bank communication of payment instructions.[1250] In a paper-based funds transfer system the
paper embodying the payment instruction is physically transferred from one bank
to another, e.g. by direct courier or at a centralised clearing house. The credit clear-

---

[1248] See below, para.34-393.
[1249] See below, para.34-395.
[1250] B. Geva, *The Law of Electronic Funds Transfers* (1992–2002, looseleaf), s.1.03[4].

ing is a paper-based funds transfer system.[1251] By contrast, with an electronic funds transfer system the inter-bank communication of payment instructions is by electronic means, e.g. by magnetic tape, disc or, more usually, telecommunication link. The major inter-bank electronic funds transfer systems in the United Kingdom are the services operated by BACS Payment Schemes Ltd, called BACS, and the payment system run by the CHAPS Clearing Co Ltd, called CHAPS, and the Faster Payments Service, operated by the Faster Payments Scheme Ltd.[1252]

34-385   **Settlement**   Where the payer and the payee hold accounts at the same bank, the transfer of funds between the two accounts will usually involve a simple internal accounting exercise at the bank, known as an "in-house" transfer.[1253] The payer's account is debited and the payee's account is credited. The position will be different where the payer's account and the payee's account are held at different banks, known as an "inter-bank" transfer. In such cases an inter-bank payment order will pass from bank to bank, sometimes from the payer's bank directly to the payee's bank, otherwise via intermediary banks which each issue their own payment order to the next bank down the chain, until a payment order finally reaches the payee's bank. Each inter-bank payment order must be paid by the bank sending the instruction to the bank receiving it. It is this process whereby payment is made between the banks themselves of their obligations *inter se* which is known as settlement.

34-386   **Bilateral and multilateral settlement**   Settlement can occur on either a bilateral or multilateral basis. Bilateral settlement occurs where the bank sending the payment order and the bank receiving it are "correspondents", meaning that each holds an account with the other. Settlement is effected through an adjustment of those accounts. Multilateral settlement involves the settlement of accounts of the sending bank and the receiving bank held at a third bank. The third bank could be a common correspondent of the two banks, i.e. one where they both have accounts; alternatively, and more typically, the third bank could be a central bank.

34-387   **Gross and net settlement**   Settlement may be either gross or net. With gross settlement the sending and receiving banks settle each payment order separately without regard to any other payment obligations arising between them. This is usually done on a real-time basis, with settlement across the accounts of participating banks held at the central bank as each payment order is processed. With net settlement the mutual payment obligations of the parties are set off against each other and only the net balance is paid. This process occurs periodically with net balances being settled either at the end of the day ("same-day" funds) or on the following day ("next-day" funds). Net settlement may be either bilateral or multilateral.[1254] In a bilateral net settlement system, a participant's exposure is measured by reference to its net position with regard to each individual counterparty

---

[1251] As is the cheque clearing. But see above, paras 34-153—34-154A, for new Pt 4A of the Bills of Exchange Act 1882, as inserted by s.13 of the Small Business, Enterprise and Employment Act 2015, which allows for cheques and bank giro credits to be presented for payment by electronic means.

[1252] CHAPS is an electronic real-time sterling credit transfer system, normally used for high value transfers. The Faster Payments Service began operation in May 2008 and offers a near real-time facility for internet and telephone transfers between bank accounts, with standing orders being processed on a same day basis.

[1253] *Libyan Arab Foreign Bank v Bankers Trust Co* [1989] Q.B. 728, 750–751.

[1254] The text which follows is only concerned with payment netting and not with the netting of contractual commitments, e.g. as carried out in a variety of contracts such as foreign exchange

and not by reference to the system as a whole. In a multilateral net settlement system, a participant's position is measured by reference to its net position with regard to all other participants in the system as a whole. As a result, each participant will end up as a net net debtor or a net net creditor in relation to all other participants in the system. Multilateral netting may arise through direct determination of multilateral net positions, or indirectly by netting the net bilateral positions and thereby obtaining net net positions. In each case, settlement follows the multilateral netting process.

Clearing systems   The very nature of giro operations anticipates the existence of   **34-388**
a suitable clearing system. Geva has identified two senses in which the term "clearing system" can be used.[1255] First, in its narrow sense, the term refers to a mechanism for the calculation of mutual positions within a group of participants with a view to facilitating the settlement of their mutual obligations on a net basis. Secondly, in its broad sense, the term also extends to the settlement of those obligations.

Clearing house rules   The banks and building societies which are members of the   **34-389**
various clearing systems must have settlement accounts at the Bank of England.[1256] Other banks and building societies may gain access to these systems through agency agreements with those members. Members are bound by the rules of the clearing system through a multilateral contract.[1257] The rules must be interpreted against the background of the manner and operation of the particular clearing system. Any interpretation of the rules must also be in accordance with the nature of the rules themselves.[1258] A customer of a clearing bank may be bound by, and able to rely on, the clearing system rules against his own bank through an implied term of the banker–customer contract (it is always open for the clearing house rules to be expressly incorporated into a bank's contract with its customer but this is unlikely in practice). The customer is taken to have contracted with reference to the reasonable usage of bankers, including those clearing system rules which represent such reasonable usage.[1259] However, where clearing house rules derogate from the customer's existing rights, the usage codified in the rules will be deemed unreason-

---

contracts, repurchase agreements, securities trades and derivatives.

[1255] B. Geva (1991) 19 Can. B.L.J. 138.

[1256] Furthermore, Pt 5 of the Banking Act 2009 provides the statutory framework for oversight by the Bank of England of interbank payment systems that are systemically important (extended to service providers to such systems by the Banking Act 2009 (Service Providers to Payment Systems) Order 2017 (SI 2017/1167)). The Financial Services (Banking Reform) Act 2013 creates a new competition-focused, economic regulator of retail payment systems in the UK: the new Payment Systems Regulator became fully operational on April 1, 2015. For co-operative relationship between the main regulatory authorities in relation to payment systems in the UK, see the *Memorandum of Understanding between the Bank of England, the Financial Conduct Authority, the Payment Systems Regulator and the Prudential Regulation Authority* (July 2018). In 2015 the Payments Council was replaced by Payments UK, a trade association representing the UK payments industry. From July 1, 2017, Payments UK was integrated into a new finance and banking industry trade association called UK Finance (*https://www.ukfinance.org.uk*).

[1257] Probably on the same principle as applied in *Clarke v Dunraven (The Satanita)* [1897] A.C. 59.

[1258] R. Cranston, E. Avgouleas, K. van Zwieten, C. Hare and T. van Sante, *Principles of Banking Law*, 3rd edn (2018), p.353.

[1259] *Hare v Henty* (1861) 10 C.B.N.S. 65; *Re Farrow's Bank Ltd* [1923] 1 Ch. 41; *Parr's Bank Ltd v Thomas Ashby & Co* (1898) 14 T.L.R. 563; *Tayeb v HSBC Bank Plc* [2004] EWHC 1529 (Comm), [2004] 4 All E.R. 1024 at [57]. See also *Tidal Energy Ltd v Bank of Scotland Plc* [2014] EWCA Civ 1107, [2014] 2 Lloyd's Rep. 549, where the Court of Appeal, by a majority (Tomlinson L.J. at [48]–

able and will not bind the customer without his full knowledge and consent.[1260] In order to rely on the clearing house rules against a member bank other than his own bank, the customer would have to bring himself within the ambit of the Contracts (Rights of Third Parties) Act 1999, which may prove difficult, not least because the member banks may have "contracted out" of the Act.[1261] Agency arguments are likely to prove equally problematical.

34-390 **UK clearing systems** There are four major clearing systems for giro transfers in the United Kingdom.[1262] Each is run by an independent company.[1263] First, there is the credit clearing system, run by the Cheque and Credit Clearing Co Ltd, which is a paper-based credit transfer system used for the physical exchange of high-volume, low-value, credit collections such as bank giro credits. Secondly, there is BACS, operated by BACS Payment Schemes Ltd, which provides a high-volume, low-value, bulk electronic clearing service for credit and debit transfers, including standing orders, direct debits, wages and salaries, pensions and other government benefits. Thirdly, there is CHAPS, which is operated by the CHAPS Clearing Co Ltd. CHAPS is an electronic sterling credit transfer system, normally used for high value transfers.[1264] The fourth is operated by Faster Payments Scheme Ltd and called the "Faster Payments" system. It began operation in May 2008 and offers a near real-time facility for mobile, internet and telephone transfers between bank accounts, with standing orders being processed on a same day basis.[1265] Save for CHAPS, which is a real-time gross settlement system, the other clearing systems are multilateral net settlement systems with settlement of balances across the participants' accounts held at the Bank of England at the end of each day, or several times each day for the Faster Payments system.[1266] In 2015, BACS introduced pre-

---

[49] and Lord Dyson M.R. at [59], Floyd L.J. dissenting at [23]), held that banking practice could be relied on in order to construe a CHAPS transfer form (the judgments, even of the majority, are not easy to reconcile, but all three Lord Justices appear to agree that there can be reliance on banking practice for the purposes of interpretation where the practice is known or reasonably available to both the bank and its customer).

[1260] *Barclays Bank Plc v Bank of England* [1985] 1 All E.R. 385, 394; see also *Turner v Royal Bank of Scotland Plc* [1999] Lloyd's Rep. Bank. 231 CA.

[1261] See, e.g. CHAPS Reference Manual (version: January 5, 2018), p.19.

[1262] There is also the cheque clearing, but this is not classified as a giro system: see B. Geva (1991) 19 Can. B.L.J. 138, s.1.03[3].

[1263] See above.

[1264] CHAPS used to operate a euro credit transfer system but that system closed in May 2008. Euro payments can now be made over a system called TARGET2, which can be used to make domestic and cross-border payments in euro throughout the EU. The Bank of England decided not to participate in TARGET2; accordingly UK banks have made individual arrangements for cross-border euro payments, using TARGET2 via other Member States. UK banks also have a range of other euro payment mechanisms available to them. In order to promote a Single European Payment Area (SEPA), the European Payment Council has developed the SEPA Credit Transfer Scheme (SCT) and the SEPA Direct Debit Scheme (SDD). Since January 2008 (for the SCT) and May 2009 (for the SDD), it has been possible for UK banks to register to participate in these schemes. The SCT and SDD are harmonised payment instruments for making domestic and cross-border payments in Euros within the SEPA. See E.P. Ellinger, E. Lomnicka and C.V.M. Hare, *Ellinger's Modern Banking Law*, 5th edn (2011), pp.563–564.

[1265] It is now possible to send individual payments of up to £250,000 using the Faster Payments system, but individual banks and building societies set their own limits depending on how the payment is sent and the type of account their customer is sending from (*http://www.fasterpayments.org.uk*).

[1266] See E. Katz [2014] B.J.I.B.F.L. 462 on the elimination of settlement risk associated with net settlement in BACS and the Faster Payment Service.

funding to reduce the risk of settlement failure between participants.[1267] The Faster Payments system also has pre-funding requirements.[1268]

Individual money transfer forms (bank giro credit transfers)   The bank giro **34-391** credit, or the individual credit transfer form, is the basic facility used by the banks in money transfer operations. Prior to January 1, 1998, bank giro credit transfers were made using standard credit forms which left blank spaces for the payer to insert details concerning the transfer: the name of the payee's account and the other details concerning it; and the amount involved. However, many of these forms were completed inaccurately, which led to unacceptable delays in payment being made. Thus, since January 1998 inter-bank bank giro credits must be made using pre-printed credit forms, such as those found at the back of cheque books, or provided with utility bills. It is a matter for individual banks whether they will continue to accept blank credit forms completed in manuscript for intra-bank transfers.

The bank giro credit form sets out neither the payer's express request that the **34-392** bank execute the transfer nor his authorisation for the debiting of his account. The payer is, however, required to sign the form; his mandate to the bank as regards the remittance of the funds is based on his executing, in this manner, a standard bank giro credit. But the bank giro credit does not, even by implication, confer on the bank the authority to reimburse itself. The payer has to remit to the bank the required cash, a personal cheque, or cheques of third parties payable to himself.

Standing orders   Standing orders are used to arrange for periodic payments of **34-393** fixed amounts, such as monthly rents, instalments due under hire-purchase agreements, and annual subscriptions. The clearing banks have their own pro forma standing order forms with the payer supplying the same information as he used to provide on blank inter-bank credit forms before pre-printed credit forms became the norm. The form also enables the payer to provide the bank with a direction concerning the frequency and dates of payments. No specific funds are earmarked by the bank at the time it receives the instructions in order to enable it to reimburse itself. But the current form used by banks includes a clause, which authorises the bank to debit his account with the amount of each payment when it is made.[1269] The standing order is thus a self-contained instruction which need not be accompanied by the customer's cheque or by cash. Obviously, it can be used only by persons who maintain an account with the transferring bank.

In practice, organisations, such as charitable bodies, arrange for the printing of **34-394** standard forms which set out the details of their account. The payer completes this form by inserting the details concerning his account with the transferring bank. The order is transmitted to this bank by the payee. From a legal point of view, the practice does not lead to a departure from the principles to be discussed subsequently. The payee transmits the form as the payer's agent. In other cases, the creditor supplies the debtor with a pre-printed book of encoded bank giro credits,

---

[1267] R. Cranston, E. Avgouleas, K. van Zwieten, C. Hare and T. van Sante, *Principles of Banking Law*, 3rd edn (2018), p.351.

[1268] R. Cranston, E. Avgouleas, K. van Zwieten, C. Hare and T. van Sante, *Principles of Banking Law*, 3rd edn (2018), p.351.

[1269] But the bank is under no obligation to make the transfer if there are insufficient funds in the account to cover it, nor is it obliged to monitor the account subsequently to see whether sufficient funds have been credited to the account to cover the standing order: *Whitehead v National Westminster Bank Ltd, The Times,* June 9, 1982.

which the debtor uses to effect payments. Under this procedure, used by some local authorities and finance companies, a series of bank giro credits performs the function of a standing order.

34-395 **Direct debiting** The direct debiting scheme was introduced in 1967.[1270] It facilitates the prompt payment of amounts due under commercial and consumer contracts by enabling the supplier, dealer, or other creditor to obtain payment of amounts due to him by issuing a direct demand for payment to the debtor's bank. The procedure involves some extra paperwork at the initial stages but saves time thereafter. The creditor asks the debtor to sign a mandate executed on a standard form.[1271] The form is returned to the creditor, which either sends it to the debtor's bank or, where the Automated Direct Debit Instruction Service (AUDDIS) is used, kept by the creditor and details of the mandate are transmitted electronically to the debtor's bank.[1272] The form authorises the debtor's bank to pay amounts demanded by the creditor; there is no need to require on each occasion the confirmation of the indebtedness by the debtor. Although intimation of the sum payable is in the hands of the creditor, the mandate remains that of the debtor and the direct debit does not operate so as to vest in the creditor any rights of the debtor against its own bank.[1273]

34-396 All mandate forms used under the scheme must be variable in terms of amount, date and frequency; as such, neither the amount of the debit, its date or its frequency is specified on the form. However, the creditor must give the debtor at least 10 working days' notice (unless a shorter period of notice has been agreed) of the amount and date of the first direct debit and of any subsequent change to the amount and date of the direct debit. The creditor must then collect the direct debit payment on or within three working days after the specified due date as advised to the debtor; failure to do so results in the creditor having to give the debtor further notice of the new collection date. Conceptually direct debiting can be used for the settlement of any type of payment. In the majority of cases, however, direct debiting is used to arrange for the payment of varying amounts falling due at regular or irregular intervals, such as amounts payable in respect of electricity bills or for the supply of different quantities of a commodity ordered by a purchaser from a supplier from time to time as old stock is used up.

34-397 It is obvious that direct debiting is open to abuse. There are, however, control measures in operation which reduce this risk.[1274] First, a firm that wants to collect payment by direct debit must be sponsored by one of the banks and building societies which operate the scheme. Sponsorship is dependent on the sponsor being satisfied as to a number of factors, including the financial status and administrative

---

[1270] The system is currently administered by BACS and is governed by its own set of rules: *The Service User's Guide and Rules to the Direct Debit Scheme*.

[1271] There is also a Paperless Direct Debit service.

[1272] The creditor's failure properly to implement a correctly completed direct debit mandate might constitute a breach of an implied term of the underlying contract between them, or even a breach of a duty of care in tort owed by the creditor to the debtor: *Weldon v GRE Linked Life Assurance Ltd* [2000] 2 All E.R. (Comm) 914, Nelson J. With effect from January 1, 2008, the use of AUDDIS to submit direct debit instructions became mandatory for all new service users that submit direct to BACS (*The Service User's Guide and Rules to the Direct Debit Scheme*).

[1273] *Mercedes-Benz Finance Ltd v Clydesdale Bank Plc* [1997] C.L.C. 81, Ct of Sess. OH.

[1274] Payment Services Regulations 2017 (SI 2017/752) (as amended) reg.79 provides for refunds of payment transactions initiated by or through a payee, and reg.80 provides for requests for refunds for payment transactions initiated by or through a payee. See previously, the Payment Services Regulations 2009 (SI 2009/209), as amended, regs 63 and 64. For application of the PSRs 2009 and PSRs 2017, see paras 34-224—34-225 above, and para.34-402 below.

capability of the firm. Secondly, before being accepted into the scheme, the firm must provide all banks and building societies operating the scheme with an indemnity against any loss, including consequential loss, that may be caused to them, unless the loss was due to the bank or building society's own fault. Under the terms of the direct debit scheme, the debtor is guaranteed a full and immediate refund from his bank should there be an error in the direct debiting process by the creditor or the debtor's own bank, e.g. where a payment was made after the debtor cancelled his authority, where more than the notified sum was debited from the account, or the debit was made on the wrong date. Where the error is due to the fault of the creditor, the debtor's bank can claim a refund from the creditor under the terms of its indemnity.

Cancellation of a direct debit   Where the creditor and the debtor have agreed that   **34-398**
payment shall be by direct debit, subsequent cancellation of the direct debit mandate by the debtor gives the creditor a claim for breach of contract against him. In *Esso Petroleum Co Ltd v Milton*,[1275] the Court of Appeal treated such a claim as being similar to one that a creditor would have on a dishonoured cheque. In this case, the claimants owned two garages operated and managed by the defendant under licence. Under the terms of two licence agreements, one for each garage, the defendant was obliged to purchase all his petrol supplies from the claimants and pay for them on or before delivery by direct debit. The defendant was also forbidden from selling petrol at prices greater than those notified to him by the claimants. Towards the end of 1995, the claimants instructed the defendant to cut petrol prices in the face of stiff pricing competition and increased his site rentals. The defendant complained that this made his operations unprofitable and, in order to put pressure on the claimants, he cancelled his direct debit mandate when almost £170,000 was owing to the claimants for petrol supplied. The claimants applied for summary judgment against him. The defendant admitted the claim, but alleged that the increasingly stringent financial terms that the claimants had imposed amounted to a repudiatory breach of contract, and he counterclaimed damages which he sought to set off in equity in extinction of his debt to the claimants. The first instance judge dismissed the claimants' application for summary judgment, but the claimants successfully appealed on two grounds. The first was that the defendant's counterclaim, even if good, would not give rise to an equitable set-off. The second was that no set off or counterclaim is available where payment was made, or agreed to be made, by direct debit. On the second issue, the Court of Appeal held, by a majority, that the payment arrangements of the parties by direct debit were to be treated as assimilated to those of payment by cheque, and so applied the rule, well established in the case of cheques, that there can be no set-off or counterclaim arising from the underlying contract unless there is fraud or failure of consideration. This was, according to Thorpe L.J.,[1276] "a natural evolution" of the rule which applies to bills of exchange and cheques, and reflected, according to Sir John Balcombe,[1277] the modern commercial practice of treating a direct debit in the same way as a payment by cheque. By contrast, Simon Brown L.J., dissenting, held that there were insufficient similarities between cheques and direct debit arrangements to treat the two as equivalent.

[1275] [1997] 1 W.L.R. 938, applied in *Gibbs Mew Plc v Gemmell* [1999] 1 E.G.L.R. 43 CA; *Courage Ltd v Crehan* [1999] 2 E.G.L.R. 145 CA; *Esso Petroleum Co Ltd v Ilanchelian* Unreported March 19, 2001; *Geldof Metaalconstructie NV v Simon Carves Ltd* [2010] EWCA Civ 667 at [43].
[1276] *Esso Petroleum Co Ltd v Milton* [1997] 1 W.L.R. 938 at 606f.
[1277] *Esso Petroleum Co Ltd v Milton* [1997] 1 W.L.R. 938 at 607j.

34-399   It is respectfully submitted that Simon Brown L.J. was right, and the majority were wrong, on this issue.[1278] The analogy with a dishonoured cheque is flawed. Where a cheque is dishonoured, the payee obtains a cause of action through breach of the drawer's payment obligation embodied in the cheque itself.[1279] There is no similar promise embodied in a direct debit mandate, revocation of which does not of itself create a separate cause of action.[1280] Where a direct debit mandate is revoked, the creditor is left only with his claim for the debt due on the underlying contract. Why should the debtor lose his right of set-off when sued on the underlying contract? The mere fact that the payment was to be by direct debit should not of itself be enough to imply an exclusion clause into the contract. Such a term is neither obvious, nor necessary for business efficacy. If the debtor's right of set-off is to be excluded, this should be done through an express term of the underlying contract.[1281] The best explanation for applying the no set-off rule to bills of exchange and cheques is that it facilitates the free negotiation of such instruments for cash.[1282] However, direct debits are not transferable and do not require the same protection. It does not answer this point simply to assert, as the claimants did, that as most cheques are now non-transferable, being crossed "account payee only", no distinction should be drawn between such cheques and direct debits. Perhaps it would show greater consistency if non-transferable cheques were also kept outside the no set-off rule. There is, after all, a strong case to be made that "account payee only" cheques fall outside the Bills of Exchange Act 1882.[1283]

34-400   **Legal nature of the relationships between the parties**   The legal relationships between the parties to a giro transaction are governed by the law of contract in general and by the principles concerning agency in particular. Thus, for example, the instructions given to the paying banker in one of the bank giro forms constitutes a mandate reminiscent of the authority conferred on the drawee bank by a cheque.

34-401   **Statutory controls**   There is no comprehensive statutory regime within the United Kingdom governing all money transfer operations.[1284] Neither the law of negotiable instruments nor the principles of assignment are applicable. Limited statutory provision was made for "cross-border credit transfers" within the EEA through the Cross-

---

[1278] See criticisms of R. Hooley [1997] C.L.J. 500 and A. Tettenborn (1997) 113 L.Q.R. 374.

[1279] Bills of Exchange Act 1882 s.55(1)(a).

[1280] See, by analogy, *The Brimnes* [1975] 1 Q.B. 929, 949, 964–965, 969 CA.

[1281] In fact, the claimants in this case did attempt to rely on an express term of the licence agreements which purported to exclude any right of set-off, but the Court of Appeal held the term to be unreasonable under the Unfair Contract Terms Act 1977 (applying *Stewart Gill Ltd v Horatio Myer & Co Ltd* [1992] Q.B. 600, CA). In some cases there may be an issue as to whether the 1977 Act is engaged in the first place; see *African Export-Import Bank v Shebah Exploration and Production Co Ltd* [2017] EWCA Civ 845 (no set-off clause in facilities agreement based on industry standard form).

[1282] *Nova (Jersey) Knit Ltd v Kammgarn Spinnerei GmbH* [1977] 1 W.L.R. 713, 721, HL.

[1283] See J.K. MacLeod (1997) 113 L.Q.R. 133, 156.

[1284] But note that on November 25, 1992, by Resolution 47/34, the United Nations General Assembly approved the Report of the United Nations Commission on International Trade Law (UNCITRAL) and the Model Law on International Credit Transfers finalised at UNCITRAL's 25th Session of May 4–22, 1992; see *UN: General Assembly, Official Records, 4th Session*, Supp. No.17, A/47/17. The General Assembly recommended that all States enact legislation based on the Model Law. In the United States two statutory regimes are in force: the Electronic Fund Transfer Act 1978, applicable to consumer transactions, and art.4A of the Uniform Commercial Code, which applies to wholesale transfers.

Border Credit Transfer Regulations 1999,[1285] which implemented EC Directive 97/5. As from November 1, 2009, this regime was replaced by the Payment Services Regulations 2009 ("PSRs 2009"),[1286] implementing the EC Payment Services Directive.[1287] The PSRs 2009 introduced new conduct of business rules for payment services (incorporating both payment transactions and the operation of payment accounts) that fell within their scope.[1288] The conduct of business rules specified the information to be provided to the payment service user (Pt 5) and set out the rights and obligations of payment service users and providers (Pt 6). However, the PSRs 2009 focused only on electronic means of payment: paper-based payment transactions, such as cheques, were expressly excluded from the regime.[1289] The PSRs 2009 have since been revoked and replaced by the Payment Services Regulations 2017 ("PSRs 2017"),[1290] which implement in part the EU's Revised Payment Services Directive ("PSD2") in the UK.[1291] With certain exceptions as set out in reg.1, which include where the implementation period is linked to the coming into force of the secure communication and authentication requirements adopted under art.98 of PSD2, the PSRs 2017 came into force on January 13, 2018.[1292]

Payment Services Regulations 2017 The PSRs 2017 build on the PSRs 2009. **34-402** The main differences between them, which relate to matters considered in this section of *Chitty*, include the following.

(1) The PSRs 2017 are of wider scope than the PSRs 2009. Pts 5 and 6 of the PSRs 2009, with some exceptions, only applied if the service was provided from an establishment maintained by a payment service provider or its agent in the UK, the payment service providers of both the payer and the payee were within the EEA, and the transaction was in euros, sterling or another non-euro Member State currency.[1293] This changes with the PSRs 2017. So long as the payment services are provided from an establishment maintained by a service provider or its agent in the UK,[1294] Pts 6 (informational requirements) and 7 (rights and obligations) of the PSRs 2017 extend, with some exceptions, to (i) services relating to transactions in EEA currencies where the payment service providers of both the payer and the payee are located within the EEA, (ii) services relating to transactions in non-EEA currencies where the payment service providers of both the payer and the payee are located in EEA countries,[1295] and (iii) services relating to transactions where the payment service provider of either the payer or the payee, but not

---

[1285] SI 1999/1876.

[1286] SI 2009/209, as amended. For detailed analysis, see the 31st edition of *Chitty on Contracts*, Vol.II, Ch.34, Sect.2(e); E.P. Ellinger, E. Lomnicka and C.V.M. Hare, *Ellinger's Modern Banking Law*, 5th edn (2011), pp.601 et seq.

[1287] Directive 2007/64 of the European Parliament and of the Council on payment systems in the internal market ([2007] O.J. L319/1).

[1288] The PSRs 2009 also introduced an authorisation regime for providers of payment services which are neither credit institutions nor e-money institutions.

[1289] PSRs 2009 Sch.1 Pt 2(g).

[1290] SI 2017/752, as amended. See also, para.34-224 above.

[1291] Revised Payment Services Directive 2015/2366/EU.

[1292] PSRs 2017 reg.1(6).

[1293] PSRs 2009 regs 33(1), 51(1), (2): reg.73 (value date and availability of funds) applied whether or not the payment service providers of both the payer and the payee were located within the EEA.

[1294] PSRs 2017 regs 40(1)(a), 63(1)(a).

[1295] PSRs 2017 regs 40(1)(b)(ii), 63(1)(b)(ii).

both, is in the EEA.[1296] In the case of (ii) and (iii), Pts 6 and 7 apply only in respect of those parts of the transaction which are carried out in the EEA,[1297] and when they apply they do so in a more restricted manner than in the case of (i).[1298] Payment service providers are still able to opt out of all the informational requirements in Pt 6, and certain conduct requirements in Pt 7, when dealing with business customers, unless they are "micro-enterprises".[1299]

(2) The PSRs 2017 retain most of the exemptions contained in the PSRs 2009. For example, cheques and other paper-based transactions are outside the scope of the new regulations,[1300] as are payment transactions contained within a payment or a securities settlement system.[1301] A number of the exemptions have been clarified, such as where specific payment instruments can only be used in a limited way,[1302] and where providers of electronic communication networks provide additional services and those services are the purchase of digital content and voice-based services, or the purchase of tickets and donations to charities, within certain monetary limits.[1303]

(3) The PSRs 2017 extend to the activities of "payment initiation services" and "account information services",[1304] although in a much more limited way than with other payment services providers.[1305] A payment initiation service is an online service to initiate a payment order at the request of the payment service user with respect to a payment account held at another payment service provider.[1306] An account information service is an online service to provide consolidated information on one or more payment accounts held by a payment service user with another payment service provider or with more than one payment service provider, and includes such a service whether the information is provided (a) in its original form or after processing; and (b) only to the payment service user or to the payment service user and to another person in accordance with the payment service user's instructions.[1307] This would cover account aggregation services which provide customers with a consolidated view of their bank accounts and enable them to access their accounts online. The PSRs 2017 allow for access to payment accounts which are accessible online by payment initiation

---

[1296] PSRs 2017 regs 40(1)(b)(iii), 63(1)(b)(iii).

[1297] PSRs 2017 regs 40(2)(a),(3)(a), 63(2)(a), (3)(a).

[1298] PSRs 2017 regs 40(2)(b), (3)(b), 63(2)(b), (3)(b). Significantly, for a transfer in a non-EEA currency, regs 84 to 88 (amounts transferred and received and execution times) do not apply (reg.63(2)(b)).

[1299] PSRs 2017 regs 40(7), 63(5). There can be no contractual opt out if the payment service user is a consumer, a micro-enterprise or a charity as defined in reg.2.

[1300] PSRs 2017 Sch.1 Pt 2(g).

[1301] PSRs 2017 Sch.1 Pt 2(h).

[1302] PSRs 2017 Sch.1 Pt 2(k).

[1303] PSRs 2017 Sch.1 Pt 2(l).

[1304] PSRs 2017 Sch.1 Pt 1(g), (h).

[1305] PSRs 2017 regs 40(4), 63(4): Pts 6 and 7 do not apply to registered account information service providers or EEA registered account information service providers, except for, in the case of Pt 6 regs 59 and 60, and, in the case of Pt 7 regs 70, 71(7) to (10), 72(3) and 98 to 100.

[1306] PSRs 2017 reg.2.

[1307] PSRs 2017 reg.2.

service providers[1308] and by account information services,[1309] although access may be denied by an account servicing payment service provider (i.e. a payment service provider providing and maintaining a payment account for a payer) in certain circumstances (i.e. "reasonably justified and duly evidenced reasons relating to unauthorised or fraudulent access to the payment account").[1310]

(4)   The PSRs 2017 introduce changes to the way payment service providers authenticate payments. Save for exceptions permitted by the European Banking Authority (EBA), PSD2 requires all payment service providers to use "strong customer authentication" when a payer: (a) accesses a payment account online, (b) initiates an electronic payment transaction, and (c) carries out any action through a remote channel that may imply a risk of payment fraud or other abuses.[1311] In addition, where a payer initiates an electronic remote payment transaction, payment service providers must apply strong customer authentication that includes elements which dynamically link the transaction to a specific amount and a specific payee.[1312] Strong customer authentication means authentication based on two or more elements categorised as knowledge (i.e. something only the user knows, e.g. a password, code or PIN), possession (i.e. something only the user possesses, e.g. a token, smartcard or mobile phone) and inherence (i.e. something the user is, e.g. a biometric characteristic like a fingerprint or retina scan) that are independent in that breach of one does not compromise the reliability of the others.[1313] PSD2 mandates the EBA, in close cooperation with the European Central Bank, with development of regulatory technical standards, including those for strong customer authentication.[1314] This means that regs 68(3)(c), 69(2)(a) and (3)(d), 70(2)(a) and (3)(c) and 100 of PSRs 2017 (which deal with secure communication and authentication) only come into force 18 months after the date on which the EBA's regulatory technical standards, as adopted by the European Commission, come into force.[1315]

The PSRs 2017 contain similar (but not identical) conduct of business require-   **34-403**
ments to those found in Pts 5 and 6 of the PSRs 2009. Pt 6 of the PSRs 2017 sets out information requirements for payment services, and Pt 7 of the PSRs 2017 sets out rights and obligations in relation to payment services. Like reg.120(1) of the PSRs 2009, reg.148(1) of the PSRs 2017 makes any breach of the requirements of Pts 6 or 7 actionable by a "private person" who suffers loss as a result of the contravention, subject to defences and other incidents applying to actions for breach of statutory duty.[1316] However, and new to the PSRs 2017, it is provided, in

---

[1308] PSRs 2017 reg.69.
[1309] PSRs reg.70.
[1310] PSRs reg.71(7)—(10).
[1311] 2015/2366/EU ("PSD2") art.97(1))
[1312] PSD2 art.97(2).
[1313] PSD2 art.4(30); PSRs 2017 reg.2.
[1314] PSD2 art.98.
[1315] PSRs 2017 reg.1(6).
[1316] In PSR 2017 reg.148, a "private person" means (a) any individual, except where the individual suffers the loss in question in the course of providing payment services; and (b) any person who is not an individual, except where that person suffers the loss in question in the course of carrying on business of any kind (reg.148(3)). A fiduciary or representative may also, generally, bring the action on

reg.148(4), that where there is a contravention of a requirement under regs 76(5)(b), 77(6), 93(4) or 95 for a payment service provider to compensate another service provider, the payment service provider to which compensation is required to be paid is to be treated for the purposes of reg.148 as if it were a "private person".

34-404   The wide scope of the PSRs 2017 mean that they are likely to apply to most domestic electronic funds transfers within the UK, and to a large number of international funds transfers from the UK to other states, whether or not those states are within the EEA. In so far as a money transfer falls outside the scope of the PSRs 2017, it will be necessary to consider the position at common law. In respect of funds transfers falling within their scope, the PSRs 2017 do not expressly preserve the remedies that the parties might otherwise have had at common law.[1317] Whether this means that the PSRs 2017 establish an exclusive remedial regime when applicable must await determination by the courts.[1318]

34-405   **Position of payer's bank under the Payment Services Regulations 2017**[1319]   The payer's bank is placed under certain minimum requirements as to information which it must provide to its customer. These requirements differ according to whether the payment transaction takes place under a "single payment service contract" or a "framework contract".[1320] Part 7 of the PSRs 2017 governs the authorisation and execution of a payment instruction and creates a regime governing the rights and obligations of parties to a payment transaction. In this regard special provision is made for the use of a "payment instrument" in order to initiate a payment transaction. A payment instrument is any device, password or procedure used by the payer in order to initiate a payment transaction.[1321]

34-406   **Non-execution or defective execution**   An important difference from the posi-

---

behalf of a private person: reg.148(2). In the context of the similarly worded definition of "private person" in the FSMA 2000 (Rights of Action) Regulations 2001, "in the course of carrying on business of any kind" has been interpreted broadly by the courts so that a company carrying on business of any kind, irrespective of whether this related to financial services, falls outside the definition of "private person": for cases on the definition, see para.34-221 above.

[1317] But note, e.g., the express preservation of general common law rights in the context of termination of a framework contract, see PSRs 2017 reg.51(7), and see also above, para.34-310.

[1318] E.P. Ellinger, E. Lomnicka and C.V.M. Hare, *Ellinger's Modern Banking Law*, 5th edn (2011), pp.618–619. It seems to be arguable that the common law continues to apply in those cases where the payment service provider has exercised the "corporate opt-out" and contracted out of the PSRs 2017 conduct of business requirements (see above, para.34-402).

[1319] This paragraph, and those that follow, should be read in conjunction with para.34-402 (Payment Services Regulations 2017) above.

[1320] For a single payment service contract (defined in reg.2(1) of PSRs 2017 as, essentially, a one-off transaction) information requirements of payer's bank and payee's bank are to be found in PSRs 2017 regs 43–47 and Sch.4 (PSRs 2009 regs 36–39 and Sch.4). For "framework contracts" (defined in para.34-310 above) information requirements relating to both banks are contained in PSRs 2017 regs 48–54 and Sch.4 (PSRs 2009 regs 40–46 and Sch.4). For provisions common to both types of contract, see PSRs 2017 regs 55–59 (PSRs 2009 regs 47–50). For other information requirements, see PSRs 2017 regs 60 (information requirements for account information service providers), 61 (information on ATM withdrawal charges) and 62 (provision of information leaflet). Note also disapplications in relation to regulated contracts falling within the scope of the Consumer Credit Act 1974 (PSRs 2017 reg.41; PSRs 2009 reg.34), and for low-value payment instruments (PSRs 2017 reg.42; PSRs 2009 reg.35). Pt 6 of the PSRs 2017 does not apply to registered account information service providers or EEA registered account information service providers, except for regs 59 and 60 (PSRs 2017 reg.40(4)). The "corporate opt-out" (see above, para.34-402) to the information requirements of Pt 6 of the PSRs 2017 is found in reg.40(7) of those Regulations (PSRs 2009 reg.33(4)).

[1321] Key terms are defined in reg.2(1) of PSRs 2017: "'payment instrument' means any (a) personalised device; or (b) personalised set of procedures agreed between the payment service user and the pay-

tion at common law is that under the PSRs the payer's bank is subjected to a regime of strict liability for non-execution or defective execution of the payer's instructions, whereas the bank's liability at common law turns on its failure to exercise reasonable care and skill in and about the execution of the payer's payment instructions.[1322] In the case of a payment order initiated by the payer, as with a CHAPS transfer or a standing order, the payer's bank is liable to the payer for the correct execution of the payment transaction unless it can prove to the payer that the correct amount was received by the payee's bank on time.[1323] If the payer's bank is liable, it must refund the amount of the defective or non-executed transaction to the payer without undue delay, and, where applicable, restore the debited payment account to the state it would have been in had the transaction not occurred at all.[1324] Where the payment order is initiated by the payee, as with direct debits, the payer's bank will be liable to refund the payer the amount of the direct debit payment, and if necessary re-credit the payer's account, if the payee's bank has been able to prove that it carried out its end of the payment transaction properly, i.e. it has sent the payment instruction (in the correct amount and within the correct timescale), and the correct payee's details, to the payer's bank, so that failure to receive the correct amount of funds within the correct timescale lies with the payer's bank rather than with the payee's bank.[1325] The payer can also claim for any charges and any interest incurred as a result of the non-execution or defective execution of the payment

---

ment service provider, used by the payment service user in order to initiate a payment order"; "'payment order' means any instruction by a payer; or a payee to their respective payment service provider requesting the execution of a payment transaction"; "'payment transaction' means an act, initiated by the payer or payee, or on behalf of the payer, of placing, transferring or withdrawing funds, irrespective of any underlying obligations between the payer and payee".

[1322] See below, para.34-408.

[1323] PSRs 2017 reg.91(2) (PSRs 2009 reg.75(2)), but note that reg.91 only applies where a payment order is initiated *directly* by the payer (PSRs 2017 reg.91(1)): for non-execution or defective execution of a payment order initiated by the payer through a payment initiation service, see PSRs 2017 reg.93, which includes, in reg.93(2), (4), a requirement that a payment initiation service provider, on request, must immediately compensate an account servicing payment service provider for losses incurred or sums paid as a result of the refund to the payer. The general rule is that the payer's bank must ensure that the amount of the payment transaction is credited to the account of the payee's bank by the end of the business day following receipt of the payment order (PSRs 2017 reg.86(1); PSRs 2009 reg.70(1)); but subject to exceptions in the case of payment instructions initiated by way of a paper payment order, and certain payment transactions (e.g. not in euros or sterling) executed wholly within the EEA (PSRs 2017 reg.86(2), (3); PSRs 2009 reg.70(3), (4)). See also *Tidal Energy Ltd v Bank of Scotland Plc* [2013] EWHC 2780 (QB), [2013] 2 Lloyd's Rep. 605 at [22] (affirmed [2014] EWCA Civ 1107 without reference to this point), where H.H.J. Havelock-Allan Q.C. said (obiter) that if PSRs 2009 reg.75 had applied to the transfer (it did not because the PSRs had been expressly excluded by the bank's terms and conditions), the unique identifier given by the payer would have been incorrect because there was a mismatch between the payee's name, on the one hand, and the account number and sort code, on the other, in which case reg.74(2) would have applied. PSRs 2009 reg.74(2) provides: "Where the unique identifier provided by the payment service user is incorrect, the payment service provider is not liable under regulation 75 or 76 for non-execution or defective execution of the payment transaction, but the payment service provider—(a) must make reasonable efforts to recover the funds involved in the payment transaction; and (b) may, if agreed in the framework contract, charge the payment service user for any such recovery." For equivalent provision to PSRs 2009 reg.74(2), see PSRs 2017 reg.90(2).

[1324] PSRs 2017 reg.91(3) (PSRs 2009 reg.75(4)). Liability under reg.91 does not apply if reg.96 (force majeure) applies. The "corporate opt-out" (see above, para.34-402) applies to PSRs 2017 reg.91 (PSRs 2017 reg.63(5)(a)).

[1325] PSRs 2017 reg.92(6) (PSRs reg.76(5)). Liability under reg.92 does not apply if reg.96 (force majeure) applies. The "corporate opt-out" (see above, para.34-402) applies to PSRs 2017 reg.92 (PSRs 2017 reg.63(5)(a)).

transaction.[1326] However, in order to obtain the redress stated above, the payer must notify the payer's bank without delay, and in any event no later than 13 months after the debit date, on becoming aware of any unauthorised or incorrectly executed payment transactions.[1327] The payer's bank is given a right of recourse, which applies where the non-execution or defective execution of a payment transaction is "attributable" to the payee's bank or an intermediary bank.[1328]

34-407 **Unauthorised transactions**   For a payment transaction to be authorised, the payer must have given his consent to the execution of the payment transaction or to the execution of a series of payment transactions of which the payment transaction forms part.[1329] The payer may give his consent before or, if agreed, after the execution of the payment transaction, which must be in the form, and in accordance with the procedure, agreed between the payer and the payer's bank, and may be given via the payee or a payment initiation service provider.[1330] The payer's bank is liable to the payer for execution of an unauthorised payment transaction and it must refund the amount of the unauthorised payment to him.[1331] If the unauthorised payment has been debited from the payer's account, the payer's bank must restore the debit to that account.[1332] In order to claim a refund or restoration of his account following an unauthorised payment transaction, the payer must notify his bank without delay on becoming aware of the unauthorised nature of the transaction and, in any event, this must be done no later than 13 months after the debit date.[1333] In cases where the payer denies having authorised an executed payment transaction or claims that a payment transaction has not been correctly executed, it is for the payer's bank to prove that the payment transaction was authenticated, accurately recorded, entered in the bank's accounts and not affected by a technical breakdown or some other deficiency.[1334] For these purposes, "authenticated" means the use of any procedure which allows a payment service provider to verify the identity of a

---

[1326] PSRs 2017 reg.94 (PSRs 2009 reg.77). For "corporate opt-out", see PSRs 2017, reg.63(5)(a).

[1327] PSRs 2017 reg.74(1) (PSRs 2009 reg.59(1)), which makes the payment service user's reporting obligation a condition for redress under regs 76, 91, 92, 93 or 94 (PSRs 2009 regs 61, 75, 76 or 77). PSRs 2017 reg.74(2) (PSRs 2009 reg.59(2)) relieves the payment service user of this obligation if his bank has failed to comply with various information requirements in Pt 6 of the PSRs 2017.

[1328] PSRs 2017 reg.95 (PSRs 2009 reg.78). Arguably, this allows the payer's bank to short-circuit the contractual chain of banks and claim against a remote correspondent bank to whom the liability in question is attributable: see E.P. Ellinger, E. Lomnicka and C.V.M. Hare, *Ellinger's Modern Banking Law*, 5th edn (2011), pp.607 and 618.

[1329] PSRs 2017 reg.67(1); PSRs 2009 reg.55(1).

[1330] PSRs 2017 reg.67(2) (PSRs 2009 reg.55(2) did not include consent given via the payee or a payment initiation service provider). For withdrawal of consent, see PSRs 2017 reg.67(3)–(4) (PSRs reg.55(3)–(4)) (and above, para.34-328). A framework contract may give the payment service provider the right to stop the use of the payment instrument on reasonable grounds relating to (a) security of the payment instrument; (b) the suspected unauthorised or fraudulent use of the payment instrument or (c) in the case of a payment instrument with a credit line, a significantly increased risk that the payer may be unable to fulfil its liability to pay (PSRs 2017 reg.71(2); PSRs 2009 reg.56(2)).

[1331] PSRs 2017 reg.76(1)(a); PSRs 2009 reg.61(a).

[1332] PSRs 2017 reg.76(1)(b); PSRs 2009 reg.61(b).

[1333] PSRs 2017 reg.74(1) (PSRs 2009 reg.59(1)), which makes the payment service user's reporting obligation a condition for redress under regs 76, 91, 92, 93 or 94 (PSRs 2009 regs 61, 75, 76 or 77). PSRs 2017 reg.74(2) (PSRs reg.59(2)) relieves the payment service user of this obligation if his bank has failed to comply with various information requirements in Pt 6 of the PSRs 2017.

[1334] For PSRs 2017, see reg.75(1) (PSRs 2009 reg.60(1)), and also PSRs 2017 reg.75(2) which deals with the burden of proof where a transaction is initiated through a payment initiation service provider (if liable for an unauthorised transaction, the payment initiation service provider must compensate the

payment service user or the validity of the use of a specific payment instrument, including the use of the user's personalised security credentials.[1335] Use of a "payment instrument" recorded by the bank is not in itself necessarily sufficient to prove either that the payment transaction was authorised by the payer or that the payer acted fraudulently or failed with intent or gross negligence to comply with PSRs 2017 reg.72.[1336] The payer's obligations in relation to payment instruments and personalised security credentials are set out in PSRs 2017 reg.72: the payer must only use the instrument in accordance with its terms and conditions (so long as those terms and conditions are "objective, non-discriminatory and proportionate"), he must notify the payment service provider in the agreed manner and without undue delay on becoming aware of the loss, theft, misappropriation or unauthorised use of the payment instrument, and he must take all reasonable steps to keep safe personalised security credentials relating to the payment instrument or an account information service.[1337] If a payment service provider, including a payment initiation service provider, claims that a payer acted fraudulently or failed with intent or gross negligence to comply with reg.72, the payment service provider must provide supporting evidence to the payer.[1338] Under PSRs 2017 reg.77(3),[1339] the payer is liable for all losses incurred in respect of an unauthorised payment transaction where the payer has (a) acted fraudulently, or (b) has with intent or gross negligence failed to comply with reg.72, otherwise the payer's liability is restricted to £35 at most.[1340] However, in certain circumstances, a non-fraudulent payer will not be liable for any losses incurred in respect of an unauthorised payment transaction, namely where the losses arose after notification of the loss, theft, misappropriation or unauthorised use of the payment instrument to the payer's bank,[1341] where the bank failed to provide him with the appropriate means for notification,[1342] and where the payment instrument was used in connection with a "distance contract" (other than an excepted contract).[1343] The non-fraudulent payer will also not be liable for any losses where PSRs 2017 reg.100 requires the application of "strong customer authentication",[1344] but the payer's payment service provider did not require strong customer authentification.[1345] Where the payer's payment service provider had to make a refund to the payer/restore the debited payment account as the result of an

---

account servicing payment service provider that has had to refund the payer or restore his account: PSRs 2017 reg.76(5)).

[1335] PSRs 2017 reg.2(1). "Personalised security credentials" are defined in reg.2(1) to mean "personalised features provided by a payment service provider to a payment service user for the purposes of authentication".

[1336] PSRs 2017 reg.75(3) (PSRs 2009 reg.60(3), referring to payer's obligations in reg.57).

[1337] PSRs 2017 reg.73 (PSRs 2009 reg.58) sets out obligations of the payment service provider in relation to payment instruments.

[1338] PSRs 2017 reg.75(4).

[1339] PSRs 2009 reg.62(2).

[1340] PSRs 2017 reg.77(1) (PSRs 2009 reg.62(1): £50). However, under PSRs 2017 reg.77(2), the payer will not be liable for any losses if (a) the loss theft or misappropriation of the payment instrument was not detectable by the payer prior to the payment, unless the payer acted fraudulently, or (b) the loss was caused by acts or omissions of an employee, agent or branch of a payment service provider or of an entity which carried out activities on behalf of the payment service provider.

[1341] PSRs 2017 reg.77(4)(a) (PSRs 2009 reg.62(3)(a)).

[1342] PSRs 2017 reg.77(4)(b) (PSRs 2009 reg.62(3)(b)).

[1343] PSRs 2017 reg.77(4)(d) (PSRs reg.62(3)(c)).

[1344] See para.34-402 above.

[1345] PSRs 2017 reg.77(4)(c).

unauthorised payment transaction,[1346] the payer's payment service provider would be entitled to compensation from the payee or the payee's payment service provider (or both) where reg.100 required the application of strong customer authentication, but the payee or the payee's payment service provider did not accept strong customer authentication.[1347] The payer may also be entitled to a refund from the payer's bank where an authorised payment transaction is initiated by or through the payee, as with a direct debit. This will occur where the payer did not specify the exact amount of the payment when initially authorising the direct debit and the amount of the payment "exceeded the amount that the payer could reasonably have expected taking into account the payer's previous spending pattern, the conditions of the framework contract and the circumstances of the case".[1348]

34-408 **Position of the paying banker at common law** It is clear that the paying banker is under a duty to adhere to the terms of his authority. Presumably, he will be liable to compensate the customer for loss resulting from undue delay or from negligence in the execution of an order given in a giro form.[1349] He may, likewise, be precluded from debiting the customer's account with a wrongfully made payment.[1350] It is, at the same time, accepted that the contract between the customer and the paying banker is not governed by the doctrine of strict compliance encountered in documentary credit cases.[1351] In *Royal Products Ltd v Midland Bank Ltd*,[1352] which concerned the construction of a money transfer order given by a customer to his bank, Webster J. rejected the submission that in construing those instructions, the court should, as a matter of law or banking practice, give a legal implication to each detail of them, for it seemed to his Lordship that the doctrine which would lead to that result had little application to cases involving giro instructions.[1353] The main duty of the customer is to give unambiguous instructions and to exercise reasonable care in making out the giro forms. His liability is

---

[1346] PSRs 2017 reg.76(1).

[1347] PSRs 2017 reg.77(6).

[1348] PSRs 2017 reg.79(1), (2), but note restrictions in paras (5), (6) (PSRs 2009 reg.63(1), (2)). PSRs 2017 reg.79(3), sets out the payer's entitlement to an unconditional refund of the full amount of any direct debit transactions denominated in euro which comply with art.1 of Regulation (EU) 260/2012. The payer must make the request for a refund to his bank within eight weeks from the date on which the funds were debited (PSRs 2017 reg.80(1); PSRs 2009 reg.54(1)). The bank then has 10 business days in which to make the refund or justify its refusal to do so (PSRs 2017 reg.80(4); PSRs 2009 reg.54(5)).

[1349] But see *Dovey v Bank of New Zealand* [2000] 3 N.Z.L.R. 641, 651–652 (the Court of Appeal of New Zealand held that where the payer's bank had been instructed to make a transfer of funds by tested telex the bank was not in breach of contract by using an even faster method of transfer).

[1350] See *Tidal Energy Ltd v Bank of Scotland Plc* [2014] EWCA Civ 1107, [2014] 2 Lloyd's Rep. 549, where the Court of Appeal, by a majority, construing a CHAPS transfer order in accordance with banking practice, held that a CHAPS transfer was within mandate when the payment was made to an account matching the sort code and account number—but not the name of the payee/beneficiary customer—provided by the payer. For casenotes, see G. McMeel [2015] L.M.C.L.Q. 1; T.K.C. Ng (2015) 131 L.Q.R. 202; S. Booysen [2018] J.I.B.F.L. 405. An attempt by the bank to draft its terms and conditions of use of online facilities widely so as to impose liability on a consumer customer for unauthorised debits to his account, regardless of the circumstances, is likely to be held to be "unfair" under the Unfair Terms in Consumer Contracts Regulations 1999 or, for contracts made on or after October 1, 2015, Pt 2 of the Consumer Rights Act 2015 (which revokes and replaces the 1999 Regulations): see *Spreadex Ltd v Cochrane* [2012] EWHC 1290 (Comm) (consumer opened spread betting account via bookmaker's website).

[1351] See below, paras 34-523 et seq.

[1352] [1981] 2 Lloyd's Rep. 194, 199.

[1353] But the bank must, of course, exercise care and skill in its operation and is under a duty to adhere

in all probability similar to that of a customer who gives an ambiguous notice countermanding payment of a cheque or who facilitates a fraudulent alteration by negligently leaving blank spaces when the cheque is drawn.[1354]

Position of the payee's bank under the Payment Services Regulations 34-409 2017[1355]   Statutory duties are imposed on the payee's bank by the Payment Services Regulations 2017 ("PSRs 2017").[1356] Like the payer's bank, Pt 6 of the PSRs 2017 imposes information disclosure requirements on the payee's bank.[1357] Part 7 of the PSRs 2017 contains provisions relating to the rights and obligations of the payee's bank in the provision of payment services.[1358]

First, a number of provisions deal with the transmission of payment instruc-   **34-410** tions and the receipt of funds by the payee's bank. In the case of a direct debit, the payee's bank must transmit the payment order to the payer's bank within the time limits it has agreed with the payee.[1359] The payee's bank must then credit the amount of the payment to the payee's account following its receipt of the funds.[1360] The payee's bank must ensure that the amount of the payment is at the payee's disposal immediately after that amount has been credited to the payee bank's account.[1361] The transferred funds must start to earn interest by the end of the business day upon which the payee's bank received those funds.[1362]

Secondly, several provisions deal with the right to levy charges on the payee. The   **34-411** starting point is that the payee's bank must ensure that the full amount of the payment is transferred to the payee and that no charges are deducted from that amount.[1363] However, the payee and the payee's bank may agree to the deduction

---

to its instructions: see, e.g. the American case of *Mellon Bank v Securities Settlement Corp*, 710 F. Supp. 991 (N. J. 1989). In the normal course of events, the payer's bank will not owe the payee a duty of care in tort: *Wells v First National Commercial Bank* [1998] P.N.L.R. 552, CA; *National Westminster Bank Ltd v Barclays International Ltd* [1975] Q.B. 654; cf. *TE Potterton Ltd v Northern Bank Ltd* [1995] 4 Bank. L.R. 179 Irish HC. See also *Grosvenor Casinos Ltd v National Bank of Abu Dhabi* [2008] EWHC 511 (Comm), [2008] 2 All E.R. (Comm) 112 (held no privity of contract between drawee bank and payee of a bearer cheque when that bank was employed as collecting bank by payee's own bank—remitting bank—under Uniform Rules for Collections, 1995 revision, No.522); noted by H. Bennett (2008) 124 L.Q.R. 532.

[1354] See above, paras 34-322, 34-342. As regards the paying banker's right to reclaim an amount paid to the credit of the wrong account as money paid under a mistake of fact, see *Continental Caoutchouc and Gutta Percha Co v Kleinwort Sons & Co* (1904) 90 L.T. 474.

[1355] This paragraph, and those that follow, should be read in conjunction with para.34-402 (Payment Services Regulations 2017) above.

[1356] SI 2017/752, as amended. See, previously, Payment Services Regulations 2009 (SI 2009/209), as amended ("PSRs 2009"). See also above, paras 34-224 et seq. and 34-401.

[1357] Again a distinction is made between "framework contracts" and "single payment service contracts". See para.34-405 above. See also PSRs 2009 Pt 5.

[1358] See also PSRs 2009 Pt 6, and E.P. Ellinger, E. Lomnicka and C.V.M. Hare, *Ellinger's Modern Banking Law*, 5th edn (2011), pp.621 et seq. for detailed analysis of these provisions.

[1359] PSRs 2017 reg.86(5) (PSRs 2009 reg.70(6)).

[1360] PSRs 2017 reg.86(4), which is not restricted only to payment orders initiate by or through the payee (PSRs 2009 reg.70(5)).

[1361] PSRs 2017 reg.89(2), (3), which is not restricted only to payments received as a result of direct debits (PSRs 2009 reg.73(2)); and see also PSRs 2017 reg.87(2) (see also PSRs 2009 reg.71(2)), which applies where the payee has no account at the bank (PSRs 2017 reg.87(1); PSRs 2009 reg.71(1)).

[1362] PSRs 2017, reg.89(1) and, with specific reference to payment orders initiated by the payee, reg.92(4). See also PSRs 2017 reg.73(1).

[1363] PSRs 2017 reg.84(1); PSRs 2009 reg.68(1).

of the bank's charges before the funds are credited to the payee's account,[1364] so long as the payee is given information as to the full amount of the payment transaction and the amount of the charges.[1365] In the case of a direct debit, the payee's bank is liable to reimburse the payee for any unauthorised charges deducted from the amount transferred.[1366]

34-412   Thirdly, a number of provisions deal with the payee bank's liability for the non-execution or defective execution of a payment transaction. In the case of a payment order initiated by the payer, as with a CHAPS transfer or a standing order, the payer's bank is liable to the payer for the correct execution of the payment transaction unless it can prove that the funds were received by the payee's bank on time.[1367] However, if the payer's bank can prove that the funds were transferred to the payee's bank within the relevant time-limits, responsibility for the non-execution or defective execution of the payment transaction shifts to the payee's bank, which must then immediately make available to the payee a sum equivalent to the amount of the transfer and, were applicable, credit the corresponding amount to the payee's account.[1368] Where the payment transaction is initiated by the payee, as with direct debits, the payee's bank is liable to the payee for the correct transmission of the payment order to the payer's bank within the relevant time-limits.[1369] Where the payee's bank is so liable, it must immediately re-transmit the payment order to the payer's bank.[1370] The payee's bank must also ensure that the transaction is handled in accordance with PSRs 2017 reg.89, such that the amount of the transaction (a) is at the payee's disposal immediately after it is credited to the payee's bank, and (b) is value dated on the payee's payment account no later than the date the amount would have been value dated if the transaction had been executed properly.[1371] The payee's bank must, on request, make immediate efforts to trace the payment transaction and notify the payee of the outcome.[1372] It remains open to the payee's bank to prove that it correctly transmitted the payment order to the payer's bank in time, and in such a case liability for the non-execution or defective execution of the payment transaction shifts to the payer's bank, which must refund the amount of the payment to the payer and, where necessary, re-credit his account.[1373] The payee can also claim for any charges and any interest incurred as a result of the non-execution or

---

[1364] For controls on the level of charges, see PSRs 2017 reg.66 (PSRs 2009 reg.54).

[1365] PSRs 2017 reg.84(2); PSRs 2009 reg.68(2).

[1366] PSRs 2017 reg.84(3)(b); PSRs 2009 reg.68(3)(b). The payer's bank is responsible for reimbursing the payee for unauthorised deductions where the payer initiates the payment transaction (PSRs 2017 reg.84(3)(a); PSRs 2009 reg.68(3)(a)).

[1367] See also PSRs 2017 reg.91(2) (PSRs 2009 reg.75(2)); and for relevant time limits, see PSRs 2017 reg.86 (PSRs 2009 regs 70(1), (3), (4)) and above, para.34-406. PSRs 2017 reg.91 only applies where a payment order is initiated *directly* by the payer (reg.91(1)). For non-execution or defective execution of a payment order initiated by the payer through a payment initiation service, see reg.93.

[1368] See also PSRs 2017 reg.91(5), (6) and, for late execution, (7) (see also PSRs 2009 reg.75(5)). PSRs 2017 reg.91 only applies where a payment order is initiated *directly* by the payer (reg.91(1)). For non-execution or defective execution of a payment order initiated by the payer through a payment initiation service, see PSRs 2017 reg.93.

[1369] PSRs 2017 reg.92(2) (PSRs 2009 reg.76(2)). The payee's bank must transmit the relevant payment order within the time-limits agreed between the payee and his bank (PSRs 2017 reg.86(5); PSRs 2009 reg.70(6)). reg.76(2).

[1370] PSRs 2017 reg.92(3); PSRs 2009 reg.76(3).

[1371] PSRs 2017 reg.92(4).

[1372] PSRs 2017 reg.92(5), and note that the payee's payment service provider must act free of charge. See also PSRs 2009 reg.76(4), with no express reference to acting free of charge.

[1373] PSRs 2017 reg.92(6), (7), but if the payer's payment service provider proves that the payee's service provider has received the amount of the payment transaction, para.(6) does not apply and the payee's

defective execution of the payment transaction.[1374] However, in order to obtain the redress stated above, the payee must notify the payee's bank without delay, and in any event no later than 13 months after the debit date, on becoming aware of any incorrectly executed payment transactions.[1375] The payee's bank will not be liable for an incorrectly executed transfer where the unique identifier (e.g. the payer's account number, sort code or bank details) provided by the payee is incorrect, although the bank must make reasonable efforts to recover the funds involved in the transaction.[1376] The payee's bank can also avoid liability in cases of force majeure.[1377] It should also be noted that the payee's bank is given a right of recourse, which applies where the non-execution or defective execution of a payment transaction is "attributable" to the payer's bank or an intermediary bank.[1378]

Position of recipient (payee's) banker at common law   That the recipient   **34-413**
banker—like the paying banker—is engaged as an agent is indisputable; it is less certain who is to be regarded as his principal. Is the principal the person or bank that remits the amount or is it the customer for whose credit the amount is received? It will be convenient to discuss separately the position prevailing in the different types of giro operation.

Giro credit transfers   In an ordinary giro credit transfer the transferor issues his   **34-414**
instructions to the paying banker on the basis of the details concerning the payee's account, supplied in the payee's invoice or emerging from correspondence. When the payee furnishes these details to the transferor, he manifests his willingness to receive payment through giro channels. Thus, the payee's banker is to be treated as having the authority to receive on the payee's behalf any amount remitted for the credit of the designated account.[1379] It follows that the recipient banker is the payee's agent and that any amount remitted to him by a paying banker is tendered to him in that capacity.[1380] The same analysis would appear to be applicable also to standing orders and to traders' credits.

---

payment service provider must value date the amount on the payee's payment account no later than the date the amount would have been value dated if the transaction had been executed correctly (reg.92(8)). Compare PSRs 2009 reg.76(5).

[1374] PSRs 2017 reg.94 (PSRs 2009 reg.77), which includes charges and interest incurred as a result of late execution of the payment transaction.

[1375] PSRs 2017 reg.74(1) (PSRs 2009 reg.59(1)), which makes the payment service user's reporting obligation a condition for redress under regs 76, 91, 92, 93 or 94 (PSRs 2009 regs 61, 75, 76 or 77). PSRs 2017 reg.74(2) relieves the payment service user of this obligation if his bank has failed to comply with various information requirements in Pt 6 of the PSRs (see also PSRs 2009 reg.59(2), referring to Pt 5 of PSRs 2009).

[1376] PSRs 2017 reg.90(2); PSRs 2009 reg.74(2). See above, para.34-406.

[1377] PSRs 2017 reg.96; PSRs 2009 reg.79.

[1378] PSRs 2017 reg.95; PSRs 2009 reg.78. See also para.34-406 above.

[1379] See *Dovey v Bank of New Zealand* [2000] 3 N.Z.L.R. 641, 650 (the Court of Appeal of New Zealand held that by nominating the bank to which funds were to be transferred, the claimant gave that bank authority to accept funds on his behalf, even though the bank had yet to open an account for him). But a transfer of funds to a bank account of the creditor (or a release of funds to such an account), which is not the account stipulated in the underlying contract, is not payment, nor is it even a valid tender of payment (*PT Berlian Laju Tanker TBK v Nuse Shipping Ltd* [2008] EWHC 1330 (Comm), [2008] 1 C.L.C. 967 at [67]). Note that payment by a debtor into a third party's bank account identified in an email sent from the hacked email account of the creditor does not constitute payment to the creditor (*J Brazil Road Contractors v Belectric Solar Ltd* Unreported 22 January 2018, Canterbury CC).

[1380] But see *Customs and Excise Commissioners v National Westminster Bank Plc* [2002] EWHC 2204 (Ch), [2003] 1 All E.R. (Comm) 327 (held bank was not authorised to receive payment on its

34-415   Where a debtor makes a cash payment into a giro account, it is necessary to distinguish between a payment made directly to the bank at which the account is maintained and a payment to some other bank coupled with a request that the amount involved be remitted to the payee's bank. In the former case a single bank combines the roles of the paying banker and of the recipient banker; it seems clear that this bank receives payment from a stranger on behalf of its customer, the payee. In the latter case, just as in all other giro operations, the debtor effects payment by use of giro channels in reliance on the information supplied by the payee in an invoice or in correspondence. Presumably, the debtor makes payment to a bank other than the payee's for reasons of convenience. In such a case payment is accepted by that bank in compliance with its arrangement with other banks, as in the absence of such an agreement the bank would almost certainly refuse to act for a stranger. This reasoning suggests that a banker who receives a cash payment from a stranger for the credit of an account maintained with another bank, is to be regarded that other bank's agent. The bank which receives the cash payment does not enter into a contract with the debtor, or payer, and manifests no intention of acting on his behalf. Moreover, it is difficult to attribute to such a bank an intention to act on behalf of the payee, who—just like the payer—remains a stranger.[1381]

34-416   **In direct debits**   In direct debiting arrangements, the authority signed by the debtor is addressed to his own bank, i.e. the paying banker, who is, thus, engaged by the debtor. The fact that the document which contains the authority is delivered by the debtor to the payee, who delivers it to his own bankers (the recipient bankers), who in turn deliver or post it to the paying banker, has no bearing on the legal nature of the transaction. The ensuing presentation of direct debiting forms by the payee to the paying banker (usually through the recipient banker) is effected in reliance on the authority to pay, conferred by the debtor on the paying banker. In essence, the procedure involved in direct debiting resembles the presentation to the drawee bank of a cheque drawn by the payee to his own order on behalf of the owner of the cheque book. A cheque drawn by an agent on his principal's account for the payment of commission due to the agent and a cheque drawn by a firm's book-keeper on this firm's account for the payment of his own monthly wages, constitute illustrations in point. Moreover, when a direct debiting form is presented to the paying banker by a recipient banker engaged by the payee, the recipient banker acts on the payee's behalf in a manner resembling the presentation of a cheque by a collecting banker. However, a contractual relationship between the payee of the direct debiting form and the paying banker—who is acting on the debtor's behalf—is created by the indemnity furnished by the payee. It will be recollected that this indemnity is addressed to all bankers participating in the system.

34-417   **Relationship between transferor and recipient (payee's) banker**   The recipient (payee's) bank does not owe a duty of care to a non-customer transferor of a giro transfer to pay money received only to the recipient identified in the

---

customer's behalf simply because he had a current account with it).

[1381] That there is no privity of contract between the payee and an agent of his own bank: see *Calico Printers' Association Ltd v Barclays Bank Ltd* (1931) 36 Com. Cas. 71 (affirmed (1931) 36 Com. Cas. 197). That such a single transaction does not constitute the payer a "customer", see *Great Western Ry Co v London and County Banking Co* [1901] A.C. 414.

transferor's instructions, or to clarify any discrepancies in those instructions as to the recipient's identity with the transferor.[1382]

Position of correspondent (intermediary) bank under the Payment Services **34-418** **Regulations 2017**[1383]   Where a funds transfer falls within the scope of the Payment Services Regulations 2017 ("PSRs 2017"),[1384] the potential liability of the correspondent or intermediary bank differs from that at common law. In a case where there has been a failure to execute a payment order at all or on time, and this is "attributable" to the actions of a correspondent or intermediary bank, that bank must compensate the payer's bank (or payee's bank in the case of a direct debit) for any losses incurred as a result of the defective execution or non-execution of the payment order.[1385] Liability may be avoided where the payer originally provided an incorrect unique identifier (identifying the payee and his account),[1386] or in a case of force majeure.[1387] The position under the PSRs appears to differ from that at common law in two ways.[1388] First, whereas at common law the correspondent or intermediary bank's liability turns on its negligence, under the PSRs the bank's liability appears to be strict.[1389] Secondly, the common law appears to limit the payer's bank to recoupment of losses from the correspondent bank that it actually instructed, whereas the PSRs appear to offer the payer's bank a right of action against the correspondent bank responsible for the loss (or to which the loss is "attributable"), even though there is no direct contractual link between the two banks.

Position of correspondent (intermediary) bank at common law   Where there **34-419** is no correspondent banking relationship between the paying bank and the payee's bank, the paying bank effects the transfer by giving an appropriate instruction to an intermediary.[1390][1391] has been applied to international money transfers in *Royal*

[1382] *Abou-Rahman v Abacha* [2005] EWHC 2662 (QB), [2006] 1 All E.R. (Comm) 247, where Treacy J. refused to follow *Royal Bank of Canada v Stangl*, 32 A.C.W.S. (3d) 17 (1992), a Canadian decision to the opposite effect. The Court of Appeal affirmed Treacy J.'s decision but there was no appeal on this issue: [2006] EWCA Civ 1492, [2007] 1 Lloyd's Rep. 115.

[1383] This paragraph, and those that follow, should be read in conjunction with para.34-402 (Payment Services Regulations 2017) above.

[1384] SI 2017/752, as amended. See, previously, Payment Services Regulations 2009 (SI 2009/209), as amended ("PSRs 2009"). See also above, paras 34-224 et seq. and 34-401.

[1385] PSRs 2017 reg.95, and note that this also extends to non-execution or defective or late execution of payment transactions initiated through a payment initiation service. Compare PSRs 2009 reg.78.

[1386] PSRs 2017 reg.90; PSRs 2009 reg.74.

[1387] PSRs 2017 reg.96; PSRs 2009 reg.79.

[1388] *Ellinger's Modern Banking Law*, 5th edn (2011), pp.618–619, which also raises the question whether PSRs 2009 reg.78 is intended to be the only claim available to the payer's bank or whether it still allows the payer's bank to recoup its losses from the bank that it has instructed directly.

[1389] Subject to issues of causation.

[1390] Where an intermediary bank incurs liability as a result of carrying out the instructions of the payer's bank, it will usually be entitled to an indemnity or contribution from the payer's bank: *Hon Soc of the Middle Temple v Lloyds Bank Plc* [1999] 1 All E.R. (Comm) 193.

[1391] *Calico Printers' Association Ltd v Barclays Bank Ltd*, above. Note that the converse is true in other legal systems, such as in the United States: *Evra Corp v Swiss Bank Corp*, 522 F. Supp. 820 (1981) (reversed on another point 673 F. 2d 1982 (1982)): see also Uniform Commercial Code s.4A-305. A problem of conflict of laws arises therefore in certain cases involving international money transfers. And see Vroegop [1990] L.M.C.L.Q. 540, especially 550 et seq. Where a collecting bank collects an instrument for a remitting bank, there is no privity of contract between the collecting bank and the customer of the remitting bank either at common law or under the Uniform Rules for Collections, 1995 revision (URC 522): *Grosvenor Casinos Ltd v National Bank of Abu Dhabi* [2008]

Products Ltd v Midland Bank Ltd.[1392] The same authority further shows that the paying bank may be liable for its correspondent's negligence or default. In this case, a Maltese merchant, who maintained a current account with the defendant bank, instructed it to transfer an amount of £13,000 to the credit of his account with the B Bank in Malta. The N Bank in Malta, which was instructed by the defendant bank to effect the necessary transfer, executed it despite the fact that strong rumours about the B Bank's imminent collapse were circulating at the relevant time. The merchant claimed that the N Bank, with which he had his other account in Malta and with which he had accordingly a relationship of customer and banker, ought to have warned him about the position. He sought to hold the defendant bank responsible for the default and negligence alleged. Dismissing the action, Webster J. held that, on the facts, no negligence was attributable to the N Bank. But his Lordship observed that the paying bank owed its customer, the payer, a duty of care and skill in selecting its correspondent and added that, in the absence of a clause to the contrary, the paying bank could be vicariously liable for the negligence and default of its correspondent.[1393] It is, however, important to note that most modern banking forms include a clause under which a correspondent is engaged at the customer's risk and expense. As the paying bank is not in a position to exercise any control over its correspondent, such a clause appears reasonable.

34-420   **Revocation of payment order under the Payment Services Regulations 2017**[1394] Regulation 67(3) of the Payment Services Regulations 2017 ("PSRs 2017"),[1395] provides that the payer's consent to a payment transaction can be withdrawn at any time before the point at which the payment order can no longer be revoked under reg.83.[1396] PSRs 2017 reg.83(1) restricts the ability of a payment service user to revoke a payment order by providing that, subject to certain exceptions, the payment service user may not revoke a payment order after it has been received by the payer's payment service provider.[1397] In the case of a payment transaction initiated by a payment initiation service provider, or by or through the payee, the payer may not revoke the payment order after giving consent to the payment initiation service provider to initiate the payment transaction or giving consent to execute the payment transaction to the payee.[1398] In the case of a direct debit, the payer may not revoke the payment order after the end of the business day preceding the day agreed for the debiting of funds.[1399]

34-421   **Countermand of order at common law** In order to avoid uncertainty as to the

---

[1392] EWHC 511 (Comm), [2008] 2 All E.R. (Comm) 112 at [157], Flaux J., distinguishing *Bastone & Firminger Ltd v Nasima Enterprises (Nigeria) Ltd* [1996] C.L.C. 1902 at 1908, Rix J., who thought the URC point arguable. See further, H. Bennett (2008) 124 L.Q.R. 532.

[1392] [1981] 2 Lloyd's Rep. 194, 198.

[1393] This view derives support from the House of Lord's decision in *Equitable Trust Co of New York Ltd v Dawson Partners* (1927) 27 Ll.L. Rep. 49.

[1394] This paragraph, and those that follow, should be read in conjunction with para.34-402 (Payment Services Regulations 2017) above.

[1395] SI 2017/752, as amended. See, previously, Payment Services Regulations 2009 (SI 2009/209), as amended ("PSRs 2009") reg.55(3).

[1396] See also PSRs reg.67. For withdrawal of consent to the execution of a series of payment transactions, see PSRs 2017 reg.67(4) (PSRs 2009 reg.55(4)).

[1397] See also PSRs 2009 reg.67(1). For time of receipt of a payment order, see PSRs 2017 reg.81 (PSRs 2009 reg.65).

[1398] PSRs 2017 reg.83(2), and note the change in wording from PSRs 2009 reg.67(2).

[1399] PSRs 2017 reg.83(3); PSRs 2009 reg.67(3). For further provisions relating to revocation, see PSRs 2017 reg.83(4)–(6) (PSRs 2009 reg.67(4)–(6)).

payer's right of countermand, the payer's bank may include in its contract with the payer an express provision stipulating that the payer may not countermand his payment instruction after a certain point in the payment process. Alternatively, the payer may be bound by the express rules of the payment system used to make the transfer.[1400] Where there are no such express rules, the courts will apply the (less certain) principles of common law. Under those common law principles, as the payer is the paying banker's principal, he is entitled to countermand or revoke an instruction before it has been executed.[1401] The exact point of time at which the transfer is complete has to be discussed separately as regards two situations. The first is the "in house" payment, where a customer instructs his bank to credit the account of another customer who maintains his account with the same branch. The second type of case, involving "out house" payments, includes transfers made at the instruction of a customer for the credit of another customer's account with a different branch of the same bank. Such a transfer is effected by computer entries made by means of a process similar to the one used where the transferor and the transferee maintain their respective accounts with different banks.

In-house transfers   The question of when is payment complete in the case of an   **34-422**
in house transfer is covered by two conflicting authorities. In the first case—
Rekstin v Severo Sibirsko Gosudarstvennoe Akcinernoe[1402]—the facts were unusual.
A customer instructed his bank to transfer his total balance to the credit of another customer's account. After the bank had effected the transfer by making the necessary ledger entries but before notification was given to the payee, a judgment creditor served a garnishee order nisi (now called an "interim third party debt order") attaching the transferor's balance. It was held that at the time the order was served the amount transferred was still accruing to the transferor. It is important to emphasise that this conclusion was largely based on the fact that no debt was owed by the transferor to the transferee and that there was nothing to indicate that the transferee had anticipated payment. Thus, there was no evidence establishing the transferee's assent to the transfer of the amount involved. The bank, therefore, could not be regarded as having the authority to hold the amount transferred on the transferee's behalf.

Momm's case   A more flexible approach was adopted in *Momm v Barclays Bank*   **34-423**
International Ltd.[1403] On June 26, 1974 the defendant bank received an instruction from a customer, H, to credit the account of the plaintiff, another customer banking with the same branch, with an amount of £120,000. The payment instruction was given in execution of a currency exchange contract between H and the plaintiff. Although H's account did not have a sufficient credit balance, the assistant manager decided to credit the plaintiff's account. The necessary forms were prepared and processed forthwith by the defendant bank's computer. Later in the day, H suspended payment. On the next day the defendant bank reversed the credit entry which had appeared in the plaintiff's account. When the plaintiff, who was not notified of the credit entry and of its reversal, discovered the facts through a perusal of

---

[1400] *Tidal Energy Ltd v Bank of Scotland Plc* [2014] EWCA Civ 1107, [2014] 2 Lloyd's Rep. 549; *Tayeb v HSBC Bank Plc* [2004] EWHC 1529 (Comm), [2004] 4 All E.R. 1024.
[1401] On revocation of an agent's authority, see generally, above, paras 31-166 et seq.
[1402] [1933] 1 K.B. 47.
[1403] [1977] Q.B. 790, sub. nom. *Delbrueck & Co v Barclays Bank International Ltd* [1976] 2 Lloyd's Rep. 341.

H's books, he brought an action for a declaration that his account had been wrongfully debited on June 27. Giving judgment for the plaintiff, Kerr J. observed:

> "The issue is whether or not a completed payment had been made by the defendants to the plaintiffs on June 26. This is a question of law. If the answer is 'Yes,' it is not contested that the plaintiffs have a good cause of action. If there were no authorities on this point, I think that the reaction, both of a lawyer and a banker, would be to answer this question in the affirmative. I think that both would say two things. First, that in such circumstances a payment has been made if the payee's account is credited with the payment at the close of business on the value date, at any rate if it was credited intentionally and in good faith and not by error or fraud. Secondly, I think that they would say that if a payment requires to be made on a certain day by debiting a payor customer's account and crediting a payee customer's account, then the position at the end of that day in fact and in law must be that this has either happened or not happened, but that the position cannot be left in the air. In my view both these propositions are correct in law."[1404]

His Lordship distinguished *Rekstin's* case as having been decided on its special facts. Unlike the transferee in *Rekstin's* case, the plaintiff transferee in *Momm's* case was aware that a payment would be received at some point in execution of the currency exchange contract and had specified that it should be made into its account held at the defendant bank.

34-424 Out-house transfers The difficulty in determining the exact point of time at which an outhouse giro transfer is complete stems from the fact that the actual crediting of the payee's account can often precede the time at which his bank makes its actual decision to receive payment on his behalf. This is so because the crediting of the payee's account can be effected by the computer entry before the bank's officer makes his conscious decision to accept the money. It is clear that the payee's attitude to the problem may depend on the practical situation in which it arises. In cases in which the paying bank wishes to reverse the credit entry for its own purposes, e.g. because the transferor has countermanded payment or has become insolvent, the payee is likely to maintain that his consent to payment has been given in advance. On this basis, he would be able to argue that any countermand received after the execution of the credit entry in his account was ineffective. A reversal of entries would be ruled out altogether. The payee is likely to take a different stand where the amount involved is transferred under a contract which entitles him, in the event that an instalment due is not paid on time, to invoke an attractive forfeiture clause. If in such a case the computer credits the payee's account before the stipulated deadline but the voucher is presented thereafter, the payee has an interest in maintaining that payment has been completed only insofar as payment has been validly received on his behalf by the bank within the stipulated period.

34-425 Cases where payee claims payment is complete In *Royal Products Ltd v Midland Bank Ltd*[1405] Webster J. proceeded on the basis that a money transfer was complete and, accordingly, no longer subject to a countermand when the funds were made available to the payee's bank and accepted by it, intentionally, on the payee's behalf. This view derives further support from an observation made by Hirst J. in

---

[1404] [1977] Q.B. 790 at 799–800. cf. *Libyan Arab Foreign Bank v Bankers Trust Co* [1988] 1 Lloyd's Rep. 259, 273–274, where Staughton J. inclined to the view that an in-house payment was complete when the bank set the transferring procedure into motion. The point was, though, obiter.
[1405] [1981] 2 Lloyd's Rep. 194.

Libyan Arab Foreign Bank v Manufacturers Hanover Trust Co (No.2)[1406] in respect of a money transfer effected as between accounts maintained by two separate branches of a single bank. His Lordship concluded that the transfer was complete when the transferring branch debited the recipient branch's account with itself and the latter branch effected a matching "intentional bona fide" credit entry in the payee's account. Effectively, this meant that the transfer was complete, and hence irreversible, when the funds were made available to the payee. Similarly, in *Tayeb v HSBC Bank Plc*,[1407] where the payee's bank became suspicious of the origins of funds transferred into the payee's account using the CHAPS electronic transfer system and returned those funds to the payer's bank, Colman J. held that a CHAPS transfer was ordinarily irreversible once the payee's bank had authenticated the transfer, sent an acknowledgement message informing the payer's bank that the transfer had been received and credited the funds to the payee's account.[1408]

US authority A more detailed analysis is to be found in the decision of the United **34-426** States Second Circuit Court of Appeals in *Delbrueck & Co v Manufacturers Hanover Trust Co*,[1409] which involved another dispute arising out of the collapse of the Herstatt Bank on June 26, 1974. Here the plaintiff bank, which maintained an account with the defendant bank in New York, had entered into exchange contracts with Herstatt. On June 25, the plaintiff bank sent a telex to the defendant bank, instructing it to credit Herstatt's account with the C Bank with the amount due under these contracts. About one hour after Herstatt's closure (which under Eastern Standard Time took place at 10.30am on June 26) the defendant bank executed the transfer by means of the American automated clearing system known as CHIPS. Within the next 30 minutes the plaintiff bank countermanded payment by a telephone call and immediately thereafter confirmed this instruction by telex. However, as the CHIPS agreement precluded the countermand of a payment instruction after its release by the paying bank, the defendant bank did not order the C Bank to stop payment. Herstatt's account with the C Bank was actually credited with the amount involved at 9.00pm. Affirming the District Court's decision, Moore J. pointed out that a CHIPS message was received by the payee's bank almost as soon as it was released by the paying bank's computer terminal. Furthermore, it was common ground that funds transferred by means of CHIPS could be drawn upon by the payee as soon as the electronic message was received by the recipient bank. On this basis and taking into account the terms of the CHIPS agreement, Moore J. held that the payment became irrevocable and hence complete as soon as the mes-

---

[1406] [1989] 1 Lloyd's Rep. 608, 631–632.

[1407] [2004] EWHC 1529 (Comm), [2004] 4 All E.R. 1024 (noted by Ellinger (2005) 121 L.Q.R. 48).

[1408] At [60] and [85]. However, that judge stated (at [60]) that there was an appropriate analogy with the practice in relation to documentary credits where, at the time of presentation of documents, a bank with cogent evidence of fraud can decline to make payment (*United Trading Corp v Allied Arab Bank Ltd* [1985] 2 Lloyd's Rep. 554). He added (at [61]) that the same exception was likely in respect of illegal transactions (see *Mahonia Ltd v JP Morgan Chase Bank* [2003] 2 Lloyd's Rep. 911). See also *Tidal Energy Ltd v Bank of Scotland Plc* [2013] EWHC 2780 (QB), [2013] 2 Lloyd's Rep. 605 at [49] (affirmed [2014] EWCA Civ 1107, [2014] 2 Lloyd's Rep. 549), where held CHAPS payment complete where payee's bank, that is able to match account number and sort code to one of its accounts, credits that account with the money and sends an acknowledgement back to the payer's bank to indicate acceptance of the payment.

[1409] 609 F.2d 1047 (1979) (affirming 464 F. Supp. 989 (1979)). cf. *Mellon Bank v Securities Settlement Corp*, 710 F. Supp. 991 (1989), suggesting that where the clearing rules do not preclude countermand, payment is complete upon the crediting of the payee's account.

sage was received by the C Bank. The actual crediting of Herstatt's account by the C Bank was a mere matter of book-keeping and, accordingly, inconclusive.

34-427 **Cases in which payee refuses funds** Obviously, *Delbrueck's* case is of persuasive authority only. But it is significant that the Second Circuit effectively held that payment was complete at the time the funds became available to the drawee. This conclusion is in accord with the principles laid down in English authorities involving cases in which the payee asserted that an amount was "paid" out of the time specified in a charterparty or, in other words, argued that payment had not been completed when due. In the leading case of *Mardorf Peach Co Ltd v Attica Sea Carriers Corp of Liberia (The "Laconia")*[1410] the issue was whether an amount paid after the stipulated date was received by the bank in circumstances which indicated that the payee had waived the delay. It was established that the bank had commenced the steps required for the crediting of the payee's account but, on receiving his instruction to return the amount involved, remitted it back forthwith. One of the questions involved was whether the transfer of the funds to the payee had been executed before he issued his orders. Giving judgment for the payee, the shipowner, the House of Lords held inter alia that the transfer had not been executed before the amount was refunded as the bank had not made a conscious decision to accept payment. The steps taken by it for the processing of the telegraphic transfer order were purely provisional and procedural.[1411]

34-428 If this reasoning were applied to giro transfers, it would appear that the payee's bank must be given an opportunity to reject payment if ordered to do so by the payee within a reasonable time. At the same time, it seems unlikely that the payer has the right to countermand payment once the amount has been credited to the payee's account. *Momm's* case, discussed above, shows that notice to the payee is not required to effect transfer. It is arguable that the giro transfer should be regarded as executed as soon as the entries are made by the computer but that the recipient has the right to reject the payment made to him within a reasonable time.[1412]

34-429 **Availability as if cash** *The Laconia* was explained by the House of Lords in *The Chikuma*.[1413] In this case an amount due under a charterparty was credited by the payee's bank in Rome to the payee's account as of the due date, which was Thursday, January 22, 1976, but coupled with an indication that the "value date" was to be January 26, which fell on the Monday of the following week. Under Italian law, the funds were apparently available to the payee as from January 22 but interest on this deposit was to commence running on the 26th, namely the value date. Furthermore, if the payee had chosen to withdraw the funds on the 22nd, he

---

[1410] [1977] A.C. 850 (reversing [1976] Q.B. 835; questioning on this point *Astro Amo Compania Naviera SA v Elf Union SA (The Zographia M)* [1976] 2 Lloyd's Rep. 382; and overruling *Empresa Cubana de Fletes v Lagonisi Shipping Co Ltd (The Georgios C)* [1971] 1 Q.B. 488). See also *Tenax Steamship Co Ltd v The Brimnes (Owners) (The Brimnes)* [1975] Q.B. 929.

[1411] [1977] A.C., per Lord Wilberforce at 871–872. And see Lord Fraser of Tullybelton at 884.

[1412] But delay may not be fatal to the payee's right to reject where he was unaware of the payment being made to his account: *HMV Fields Properties Ltd v Bracken Self Selection Fabrics Ltd*, 1991 S.L.T. 31. Contrast *TSB Bank of Scotland Plc v Welwyn Hatfield DC and Council of the London Borough of Brent* [1993] 2 Bank. L.R. 267, where the payee was fully aware that funds had been transferred into the account.

[1413] *A/S Awilco of Oslo v Fulvia Spa di Navigazione of Cagliari (The Chikuma)* [1981] 1 W.L.R. 314. And see *Royal Products Ltd v Midland Bank Ltd* [1981] 2 Lloyd's Rep. 194, 209–210. See also *Tayeb v HSBC Bank Plc* [2004] EWHC 1529 (Comm), [2004] 4 All E.R. 1024 at [88].

would have incurred a liability to pay interest up to the 26th. Lord Bridge pointed out that, on this basis, the amount involved was not available to the payee on January 22 in the same way as cash. In reality, the arrangement was akin to an overdraft facility granted for the four days involved. To constitute payment, the amount involved would have had to be available for the payee's unconditional use on the due date.

This decision has been forcefully criticised[1414] on the basis that the position should have been regarded as governed by English law, under which the funds would have been treated as unequivocally available to the payee when the amount was credited to his account on January 22. It is believed that this criticism is questionable. Under prevailing English practice the amount involved would in all probability not have been credited to the payee's account before the due date although he might have been given preliminary notification of its receipt. Alternatively, if his account had been credited forthwith, the payee would have been specifically advised that the funds were not available for drawings until the 26th. It is clear that, in either case, payment would not have been complete on January 22.

34-430

(f)   The Deposit Account

Its nature   Sums paid by a customer into a deposit account may be payable on demand, but in most cases are payable either after notice or at a fixed date, e.g. three months after the date of deposit.[1415] The customer is not, as a rule, entitled to draw cheques on such an account.[1416] The advantage that the customer gains by opening a deposit account is that the banker pays interest—at a rate determined by him[1417]—on sums paid into such an account. If the customer is entitled to demand payment by giving notice, the rate of interest is usually rather low. If the amount is repayable at a fixed date, i.e. is a "fixed deposit", interest at a higher rate may be granted. In practice payment of amounts standing to the credit of deposit accounts will be granted on demand; but if the customer requests payment before the agreed date he stands to lose the interest.

34-431

Deposit receipts   Banks do not now issue deposit receipts or deposit books. It used to be the case that a deposit receipt or deposit book was given to the customer at the time of the deposit. These documents were not negotiable instruments.[1418] If the banker paid the amount standing to the credit of the deposit account to a third party, against the deposit receipt, he did so at his peril[1419] and was liable to pay again to the depositor. A delivery of the deposit receipt by the customer, with the intention

34-432

[1414] F.A. Mann (1981) 97 L.Q.R. 379.

[1415] The *Banking Conduct of Business Sourcebook* (BCOBS) and/or the Payment Services Regulations 2017 (SI 2017/752), as amended (previously, the Payment Services Regulations 2009 (SI 2009/209), as amended), place banks under various statutory requirements when opening certain types of savings accounts: see E.P. Ellinger, E. Lomnicka and C.V.M. Hare, *Ellinger's Modern Banking Law*, 5th edn (2011), Ch.9, s.1; and also para.34-311 above.

[1416] In *Hopkins v Abbott* (1875) L.R. 19 Eq. 222 Malins V.C. thought that cheques may be drawn on a deposit account stipulating for payment on demand. This view does not reflect modern practice: see E.P. Ellinger, E. Lomnicka and C.V.M. Hare, *Ellinger's Modern Banking Law*, 5th edn (2011), p.361.

[1417] The bank's right to fix its interest rate remains intact even if the bank is being wound up: *Bank of Credit and Commerce International v Malik* [1996] B.C.C. 15, reversed in part on another point: [1996] C.L. 677, CA.

[1418] *Pearce v Creswick* (1843) 2 Hare 286, 298; *Re Dillon, Duffin v Duffin* (1890) 44 Ch. D. 76.

[1419] *Evans v National Provincial Bank* (1897) 13 T.L.R. 429. The depositor's signature at the back of

of giving the transferee a right to the proceeds, amounted, however, to an equitable assignment.[1420] The transfer of a deposit receipt could also constitute a *donatio mortis causa*.[1421]

34-433 **Third party debt orders** Section 40 of the Senior Courts Act 1981, as amended by SI 2001/3649,[1422] makes the usual deposit account subject to attachment by way of third party debt order (formerly called "garnishee") proceedings: the sum in the deposit account is now to be deemed "due or accruing" notwithstanding that the withdrawal of money from the account is ordinarily subject to certain conditions.

(g) Giving Information on Financial Transactions

34-434 **Scope** Bankers give information concerning business transactions mainly in two types of cases: (a) where a customer asks the banker's advice as regards an investment[1423]; and (b) where a person, through his own bankers, requests another banker to give a reference on the standing of one of the customers of this other banker.

---

the note does not preclude him from pleading wrongful payment.

[1420] *Re Griffin* [1899] 1 Ch. 408.

[1421] *Re Dillon, Duffin v Duffin* (1890) 44 Ch. D. 76.

[1422] See, formerly, the Administration of Justice Act 1956 s.38.

[1423] The position at common law is considered in the paragraphs below. However, there is also a regulatory regime that controls the way a bank provides investment advice and sells investment products contained in the Financial Services and Markets Act 2000 and the Financial Conduct Authority's (FCA) Conduct of Business Sourcebook (COBS) (prior to April 1, 2013, the Financial Services Authority was the relevant regulatory body). Specific obligations on a bank turn on the type of customer with which it is dealing, and banks are required to categorise their clients as retail clients, professional clients and eligible counterparties. Breach of FCA conduct of business rules is actionable, as if it were an actionable breach of statutory duty, by a "private person" suffering loss (FSMA 2000 s.138D: prior to April 1, 2013, this was found in s.150 of the 2000 Act). For definition of a "private person", see para.34-221 above. For recent decisions on categorisation of clients, see *Maple Leaf Macro Volatility Master Fund v Rouvroy* [2009] EWHC 257 (Comm), [2009] 1 Lloyd's Rep. 475; *Wilson v MV Global UK Ltd* [2011] EWHC 138 (QB); *Bank Leumi (UK) Plc v Wachner* [2011] EWHC 656 (Comm); and see also J. Ahern [2011] J.I.B.F.L. 556. Recent decisions on what constitutes investment advice include *Rubenstein v HSBC Bank Plc* [2011] EWHC 2304 (QB), [2011] 2 C.L.C. 459, reversed in part [2012] EWCA Civ 1184, [2013] 1 All E.R. (Comm) 915; *Zaki v Credit Suisse (UK) Ltd* [2011] EWHC 2422 (Comm), [2011] 2 C.L.C. 523, affirmed [2013] EWCA Civ 14, [2013] 1 B.C.L.C. 640; *City Index Ltd v Balducci* [2011] EWHC 2562 (Ch), [2012] 1 B.C.L.C. 317; *Al Salaiman v Credit Suisse Securities (Europe) Ltd* [2013] EWHC 400 (Comm); *Thornbridge Ltd v Barclays Bank Plc* [2015] EWHC 3430 (QB); *Parmar v Barclays Bank Plc* [2018] EWHC 1027 (Ch). No claim for breach of statutory duty is available for breaches of FSMA 2000 which are not specifically defined in the Act as giving rise to a claim for breach of statutory duty (*Hall v Cable and Wireless Plc* [2009] EWHC 1793 (Comm), [2011] B.C.C. 543 at 548–549); there is no common law duty of care to comply with the FSMA 2000 regulatory regime (*Brown v InnovatorOne Plc* [2012] EWHC 1321 (Comm) at [1276]). In *Green & Rowley v Royal Bank of Scotland Plc* [2013] EWCA Civ 1197, [2013] 2 C.L.C. 634 the Court of Appeal held that the existence of a statutory means of enforcement of the (then current) conduct of business rules under FSMA 2000 s.150 (now under s.138D), meant that no separate co-extensive common law duty of care arose and there could be no claim for breach of those rules other than under s.150. The case was highly fact sensitive (which is something that the courts often stress: see, e.g. *London Executive Aviation Ltd v Royal Bank of Scotland Plc* [2018] EWHC 74 (Ch) at [160]). The bank had not undertaken an advisory duty. As Tomlinson L.J. said (at [23]): "*Absent that feature*, there is neither justification nor need for the imposition of a common law duty independent of but co-extensive with the remedy provided by statute" (emphasis added). *Green & Rowley* was distinguished in *Crestsign Ltd v National Westminster Bank Plc* [2014] EWHC 3043 (Ch) at [146]–[147], where the Deputy High Court Judge resisted "the fallacious reasoning that because common law duties and COBS duties

Advising on investments In general a bank is not under a legal obligation to **34-435**
provide advice, but if it gives advice then it must do so using reasonable care and
skill.[1424] In *Woods v Martins Bank*[1425] it was held that giving advice on financial matters to customers or potential customers is a banking business and that the banker
owes his customer a duty to act with reasonable care and skill in giving such advice.
The duty will be contractual where the claimant can prove a contract under which
the defendant bank has agreed to provide a service including the provision of
advice,[1426] otherwise the claimant must establish a tortious duty to advise, and such
a duty will arise only in exceptional circumstances.[1427] Its breach would, for
example, give rise to an action in damages where, in a transaction between the bank
and the customer, the customer has pursued to his detriment a course of action in
reliance on a negligent statement made by the bank.[1428] In view of the decision of
the House of Lords in *Hedley Byrne & Co v Heller & Partners*[1429] and the later deci-

---

are not co-terminous, and because [the claimant] is excluded from the class of persons able to sue
for breach of COBS duties, the banks can owe no common law duty which happens to overlap with
a COBS duty". In *CGL Group Ltd v Royal Bank of Scotland* [2017] EWCA Civ 1073 at [103], the
Court of Appeal held that banks do not owe a duty of care in tort to customers when carrying out a
regulatory review of potential swaps mis-selling cases which was required as a result of agreement
between the FCA and various banks. In *Elite Property Holdings Ltd v Barclays Bank Plc* [2018]
EWCA Civ 1688 at [59]–[65], the Court of Appeal held that a bank does not owe a contractual duty
to its customer as to its conduct of a FCA review, absent some clear expression of intention by the
bank to assume a contractual obligation. In *Flex-E-Vouchers Ltd v Royal Bank of Scotland* [2016]
EWHC 2604 (QB) at [53] and [67], it was held that there was no implied term in a swap sale contract
that the bank would comply with the requirements of the FSA/FCA's Handbook, including when it
conducted a regulatory review.

[1424] *Finch v Lloyds TSB Bank Plc* [2016] EWHC 1236 (QB) at [52].

[1425] [1959] 1 Q.B. 55, especially at 70–72, distinguishing *Banbury v Bank of Montreal* [1918] A.C. 626.
See also *Bank of Montreal v Young*, 60 D.L.R. (2d) 220 (1966). cf. *Mutual Life and Citizens' Assurance Co v Evatt* [1971] A.C. 793.

[1426] Supply of Goods and Services Act 1982 s.13; Consumer Rights Act 2015 s.49. cf. *Marz Ltd v Bank
of Scotland Plc* [2017] EWHC 3618 (Ch) (express contractual duties of advice specified in bank's
terms and conditions negated by express term of ISDA Master Agreement which prevailed as a
comprehensive and specifically applicable set of contractual terms relating to swap transaction);
Worthing v Lloyds Bank Plc [2015] EWHC 2836 (QB) (no strict contractual obligation to correct
original investment advice).

[1427] *Finch v Lloyds TSB Bank Plc* [2016] EWHC 1236 (QB) at [47]–[59] (borrower's claim that lender
owed a contractual or tortious duty to advise it about a potentially onerous clause in a loan agreement failed because there was no contract whereby the lender was to provide advice and there was
nothing exceptional about the relationship to justify the imposition of a tortious duty to advise,
especially where borrower represented by professional advisers and giving of advice might have been
contrary to lender's best interests). As to bank being under no duty in tort to disclose its internal risk
assessments and estimates of break costs of swaps contracts, see *Property Alliance Group Ltd v Royal
Bank of Scotland Plc* [2018] EWCA Civ 355 at [56]; *Marz Ltd v Bank of Scotland Plc* [2017] EWHC
3618 (Ch) at [332]; *London Executive Aviation Ltd v Royal Bank of Scotland Plc* [2018] EWHC 74
(Ch) at [244]–[254]; *Parmar v Barclays Bank Plc* [2018] EWHC 1027 (Ch) at [208]–[209], [215]–
[217]; and also *Deslauriers v Guardian Asset Management Ltd* [2017] UKPC 34 at [22] (lender
under no duty to advise borrower about internal policies or external influences, regulatory or
otherwise, which affect decision to reject application for additional loan). As regards the weight given
to a bank's promotional materials, see *James v Barclays Bank Plc* (1995) 4 Bank. L.R. 131; cf. *Finch
v Lloyds TSB Bank Plc*, above, at [58].

[1428] *Esso Petroleum Co Ltd v Mardon* [1976] Q.B. 801; *Box v Midland Bank Ltd* [1979] 2 Lloyd's Rep.
391, which shows also that a bank is liable for a branch manager's negligent statement; note that
judgment was reversed on the question of costs: [1981] 1 Lloyd's Rep. 434. See also *Verity and
Spindler v Lloyds Bank Plc* [1995] C.L.C. 1557.

[1429] [1964] A.C. 465. For a fuller account, see Vol.I, paras 7-091 et seq.

sion of the Privy Council in *Royal Bank Trust Co (Trinidad) Ltd v Pampellone*[1430] it is clear that a bank owes a similar duty of care where it agrees to advise a person who is neither an actual nor a potential customer. The latter authority, though, shows that the scope of the duty owed depends largely on the circumstances of the enquiry and, further, on the information the bank agrees to provide. In *Pampellone's* case the majority of the Judicial Committee held that, where the advice furnished by the bank to the enquirer was confined to his being supplied with a consultant's report on the subject of the enquiry, the bank could not be regarded as warranting or endorsing this advice and was not under a duty to suggest to the customer that reports of the type furnished could not be regarded as conclusive.[1431] An issue may arise as to whether advice was given or information merely provided.[1432] The *Hedley Byrne* duty to take care not to misstate is much narrower than the advisory duty where it was to be expected that relevant professional standards (e.g. FCA conduct of business rules) would form part of the assessment as to whether it had been broken.[1433] It has even been suggested there may be what has been described as a "mezzanine" duty or intermediate duty, occupying the middle ground between a full duty to advise on the one hand, and a limited duty not to mislead on the other, whereby the bank that chooses to explain the nature and effect of a proposed

---

[1430] [1987] 1 Lloyd's Rep. 218. See also *Federal Savings Credit Union Ltd v Hessian*, 98 D.L.R. (3d) 488 (1979).

[1431] When a person passes on information supplied by another, the question whether he is adopting that information as his own or making some representation about it is a question of interpretation depending on the facts (*Webster v Liddington* [2014] EWCA Civ 560, [2014] P.N.L.R. 26 at [36], and setting out a non-exhaustive list of possible scenarios at [46]). The test for determining which scenario applies is an objective one (*IFE Fund SA v Goldman Sachs International* [2006] EWHC 2887 (Comm), [2007] 1 Lloyd's Rep. 264 at [50], per Toulson J., affirmed [2007] EWCA Civ 811, [2007] 2 Lloyd's Rep. 449). Generally, bank does not make representation about accuracy or reliability of valuation or competence of third party valuer simply by passing on valuation report commissioned for bank's own internal purposes to intended borrower or guarantor (*Rehman v Santander UK Plc* [2018] EWHC 748 (Ch) at [37]). See above, Vol.I, para.7-012.

[1432] Although we have recently been reminded by Lord Sumption that the labels of advice and information are "neither distinct nor mutually exclusive categories": *Hughes-Holland v BPE Solicitors* [2017] UKSC 21, [2017] 2 W.L.R. 1029 at [39]. See also *Lloyds Bank Plc v McBains Cooper Consulting Ltd* [2018] EWCA Civ 452 at [33].

[1433] *Green & Rowley v Royal Bank of Scotland Plc* [2012] EWHC 3661 (QB) at [82], affirmed [2013] EWCA Civ 1197, [2013] 2 C.L.C. 634, and see, especially, [18] and [23], per Tomlinson L.J.; *Rubenstein v HSBC Bank Plc* [2011] EWHC 2304 (QB), [2011] 2 C.L.C. 459 at [87], reversed in part [2012] EWCA Civ 1184, [2013] 1 All E.R. (Comm) 915; *Shore v Sedgwick Financial Services Ltd* [2007] EWHC 2509 (Admin), [2008] P.N.L.R. 10 at [161]; *Seymour v Ockwell* [2005] P.N.L.R. 758 at 784; *Loosemore v Financial Concepts* [2001] Lloyd's Rep. P.N. 235 at 241; *Anderson v Openwork Ltd* [2015] EW Misc B14 (Slough County Court) at [13], [22]–[25]; *O'Hare v Coutts & Co* [2016] EWHC 2224 (QB) at [206]–[208], where Kerr J. adopted the test in *Montgomery v Lanarkshire Health Board* [2015] A.C. 1430, a medical negligence case, to define the standard of care to be applied in the explanation of risk as part of the provision of investment advice, and considered that compliance with COBS rules "is ordinarily enough to comply with a common law duty to inform, forming part of the duty to exercise reasonable skill and care; while breach of them will ordinarily also amount to a breach of that common law duty" (see also *Thomas v Triodos Bank NV* [2017] EWHC 314 (QB) at [89] for application of the test of materiality in the *Montgomery* case); *London Executive Aviation Ltd v Royal Bank of Scotland Plc* [2018] EWHC 74 (Ch) at [237]. See also *Grant Estates Ltd (In Liquidation) v Royal Bank of Scotland Plc* [2012] CSOH 133 at [79]. *Green & Rowley* was distinguished in *Crestsign Ltd v National Westminster Bank Plc* [2014] EWHC 3043 (Ch) at [147] on the ground that in *Green & Rowley* the court was concerned with whether a duty was owed at common law co-terminous with the (then current) COBS rules.

transaction owes a duty to do so fully, accurately and properly.[1434] However, in *Property Alliance Group Ltd v Royal Bank of Scotland Plc*,[1435] the Court of Appeal made clear that this was not the correct approach:

"The expression 'mezzanine' duty or intermediate duty, first coined in *Crestsign*, is best avoided. It appears to reflect the notion that there is a continuous spectrum of duty, stretching from not misleading, at one end, to full advice, at the other end. Rather, concentration should be on the responsibility assumed in the particular factual context as regards the particular transaction or relationship in issue."

High risk transaction   In modern trade banks advise their customers on high risk   **34-436** transactions, such as the trading in foreign exchange options. It is accepted that, in transactions of this type, the bank's duty of care is marginal because the risky nature of the markets involved is common knowledge.[1436] However, the bank is more likely to be held to a higher duty of care if it advises an unsophisticated customer to trade in a foreign currency in the course of a non-speculative transaction, for instance, encourages him to borrow in a foreign currency because the rate of interest charged on it is lower than applied to loans in the home currency.[1437] Whether or not a given customer is the type of investor capable of appreciating the risks involved in a market, to which he has access through the bank, is a question of fact. Thus, in *ANZ Banking Group Ltd v Cattan*[1438] the customer was given access to the Emerging Market Debt because the bank had assumed that his background and experience gave him the experience required for trading on this sector. Morison J. concluded that the bank's assessment of the customer's calibre was based on reasonable grounds. In the circumstances, the bank incurred no liability either by granting the customer access to the market or for failing to give him advice. In *JP Morgan Chase Bank v Springwell Navigation Corp*,[1439] Gloster J. held that a trader employed by an investment bank, who made recommendations and gave advice to a financially sophisticated investor as to the purchase of emerging market debt securities, did not assume responsibility to the investor so as to bring into play the full range of obligations of an investment advisor or asset manager. In *London Executive Aviation Ltd v Royal Bank of Scotland Plc*,[1440] Rose J. stated (obiter) that the authorities highlighted various factors that a court should take into account when considering

---

[1434] *Crestsign Ltd v National Westminster Bank Plc* [2014] EWHC 3043 (Ch) at [142]–[146], relying on *Bankers Trust International Plc v PT Dharmala Sakti Sejahtera* [1996] C.L.C. 518, 533D–E. See also *Wani LLP v Royal Bank of Scotland Plc* [2015] EWHC 1181 (Ch) at [34]–[36], [48]; *Thomas v Triodos Bank NV* [2017] EWHC 314 (QB) at [81]. But contrast the doubts as to the existence of such an intermediate duty expressed by the judge in *Thornbridge Ltd v Barclays Bank Plc* [2015] EWHC 3430 (QB) at [118]–[131] (appeal dismissed, Unreported January 9, 2018); and the restrictive interpretation of *Crestsign* adopted by Asplin J. in *Property Alliance Group Ltd v Royal Bank of Scotland Plc* [2016] EWHC 3342 (Ch) at [195]–[196] (on appeal, see main text below), which was endorsed in *Marz Ltd v Bank of Scotland Plc* [2017] EWHC 3618 (Ch) at [237] and in *London Executive Aviation Ltd v Royal Bank of Scotland Plc* [2018] EWHC 74 (Ch) at [236].

[1435] [2018] EWCA Civ 355 at [67].

[1436] *Stafford v Conti Commodity Services* [1981] 1 All E.R. 691 (concerning stockbrokers); *Lloyd v City Corp Australia* (1986) 1 N.S.W.L.R. 286 (forex trading); *McEvoy v ANZ Banking Group Ltd* [1988] Aust. Tort Rep. 80-151 (ditto).

[1437] *Foti v BNP* (1989) 54 S.A.S.R. 354, Sth Aust SC.

[1438] [2001] WL 852289.

[1439] [2008] EWHC 1186 (Comm) at [450]–[457], Gloster J. also held (at [475]–[491]) that disclaimers in the contractual documentation precluded the existence of a general advisory duty; affirmed [2010] EWCA Civ 1221, [2010] 2 C.L.C. 705 (no appeal on general advisory duty issue). See further, paras 34-260 and 34-434, above.

[1440] [2018] EWHC 74 (Ch) at [206]–[217]. Rose J. (at [159]–[205]) also provides a useful summary of

whether a duty of care had arisen between a bank and its customer: (i) the level of sophistication of the client; (ii) the absence of a written advisory agreement; (iii) the availability of advice from other sources; and (iv) the presence or absence of indicia of an advisory relationship.

34-437 **Banking references** The decision of the House of Lords in *Hedley Byrne & Co v Heller & Partners*[1441] indicates that if a banker agrees to give a reference concerning the financial position of one of his customers, he is likely to owe a duty of care not only to the banker who requests the information but also to the person for whom the information is, in fact, obtained. The latter can, thus, sue the reference-giving banker in negligence, if he sustains financial loss due to a carelessly given false reference.[1442] However, the prevailing view is that the reference-giving banker successfully excludes liability, by giving the information "without responsibility".[1443] In such cases, the reference-giving banker owes only a duty to act honestly.[1444] It has also been held that a bank that provides a reference by telephone on a given customer does not warrant to the enquirer that the person who made reference to the bank is the real customer rather than an imposter. The bank, in other words, does not assume a duty of care to the enquirer as to the true identity of the customer.[1445]

(h)   The Banker as Bailee

34-438 **Degree of care** One of the ancillary advantages of a banking account is that facilities are afforded for the safe custody of the customer's securities and other valuables. In some instances they are deposited loose, as in the case of marketable

---

the court's approach to claims for the negligent selling of financial products. See also *Property Alliance Group Ltd v Royal Bank of Scotland Plc* [2018] EWCA Civ 355, the first mis-selling case to be substantively determined by the Court of Appeal.

[1441] Above. On the question of proximity, see also *McInerny v Lloyds Bank Ltd* [1973] 2 Lloyd's Rep. 389, affirmed [1974] 1 Lloyd's Rep. 246.

[1442] For a summary of the three broad approaches to whether a duty of care exists, see *Customs & Excise Commissioners v Barclays Bank Plc* [2006] UKHL 28, [2007] 1 A.C. 181 at [82]–[83], although in *NRAM Ltd (formerly NRAM Plc) v Steel* [2018] UKSC 13, [2018] 1 W.L.R. 1190 at [24], assumption of responsibility was confirmed to be the "foundation of ... liability" for negligent misstatement. In the context of bankers' references, see *Playboy Club London Ltd v Banca Nazionale Del Lavoro SpA* [2018] UKSC 43 (defendant bank did not owe a duty of care to casino for negligent misstatement as to gambler's creditworthiness when request for reference came from associated company of casino acting as agent of casino which was its undisclosed principal: Supreme Court rejected argument that because casino was undisclosed principal of associated company the relationship between bank and casino was sufficiently proximate to found a duty of care as it was "equivalent to contract"). See also *Turner v Royal Bank of Scotland Plc* [2001] EWCA Civ 64, [2001] 1 All E.R. (Comm) 1057 (on causation and loss).

[1443] This is, indeed, the ratio in *Hedley Byrne*. And see *WB Anderson & Sons Ltd v Rhodes (Liverpool) Ltd* [1967] 2 All E.R. 850, 857. cf. dicta in *L Shaddock & Associates Pty Ltd v Paramatta City Council* (1981) 36 A.L.R. 385, 398 (Stephen J.). See also *Barclays Bank Plc v Grant Thornton UK LLP* [2015] EWHC 320 (Comm) (effectiveness of auditor's disclaimer of responsibility to third party bank).

[1444] That this duty is not excluded: see *Commercial Banking Co of Sydney Ltd v RH Brown & Co* [1972] 2 Lloyd's Rep. 360, HC of Aust. Note further that any exclusion of liability for negligence may perhaps be defeated under s.2(2) and/or s.3 of the Unfair Contract Terms Act 1977, and perhaps even by Pt 2 of the Consumer Rights Act 2015, where the enquirer can be classified as a "consumer". Sections 2 and 3 of the 1977 Act do not apply to "consumer contracts" and "consumer notices", but see the provision made about such contracts and notices in ss.62 and 65 of the 2015 Act. The Unfair Terms in Consumer Contract Regulations 1999 (SI 1999/2083) were revoked and replaced by Pt 2 of the 2015 Act (for commencement, see para.38-366 below).

[1445] *Gold Coin Jolliers SA v United Bank of Kuwait* [1997] 6 Bank. L.R. 60.

securities; in other cases they may be lodged in a locked box or sealed parcel.[1446] When the banker accepts documents for safe custody, he may not receive payment for this service. It is, however, doubtful whether the banker is in these cases to be regarded as a gratuitous bailee or a bailee for reward. In *Giblin v McMullen*[1447] the Privy Council held that, if a banker accepts without a reward the safe custody of documents, he is a gratuitous bailee. However, there is a relationship of contract between the banker and his customer and it may, therefore, be argued that although the banker does not receive a specific consideration for his services as bailee, he should be treated as a bailee for reward because of the consideration received by him under the general contract which he has with the customer. In any event, in *Houghland v RR Low (Luxury Coaches) Ltd*[1448] the view was expressed that it is unnecessary to put different types of bailment into watertight compartments, such as gratuitous bailments on the one hand and bailments for reward on the other. A bailee is under a duty to exercise, in each case, a degree of care warranted by the circumstances. As bankers, in order to attract customers, usually advertise that they offer facilities of safe custody, it is reasonable to presume that a high degree of care is required.[1449]

There is no English authority relating to the deposit of moneys by a customer in a night safe. It is thought that although the banker has no knowledge at the time of the actual deposit he is, nevertheless, a bailee for reward until the moneys are duly credited to the customer's account,[1450] whereupon the conventional debtor-creditor relationship is created.   **34-439**

Strict liability   There are some forms of loss for which the banker as bailee is liable even in the absence of negligence. Where he agrees for a reward to store items at a specified place and yet stores them elsewhere he is liable for any loss or damage at the later place, unless he can show that the loss or damage would have been inevitably occasioned had the terms of the contract been strictly observed.[1451] Similarly, and because misdelivery is tantamount to conversion,[1452] strict liability is imposed on a banker who surrenders the valuables to an unauthorised person. A banker is entitled to retain the valuables for a reasonable time in order to inquire into a suspected forgery or impersonation, but no amount of diligence will mitigate ultimate misdelivery whether the bailment is gratuitous or for reward. The satisfaction of a judgment for damages for conversion, however, transfers to the banker such title to the valuables as was vested in the bailor.[1453]   **34-440**

[1446] As regards the nature of the contract relating to the hire of a safe from a bank, see the decision of the High Court of Australia in *Commissioner of Taxation v Australia and New Zealand Banking Group Ltd* (1979) 53 A.L.J.R. 336, 339, which suggests that the retention by the bank of a spare key, enabling it to open the safe, gives it the "control" over the items there deposited.

[1447] (1869) L.R. 2 P.C. 317. See also *Kahler v Midland Bank* [1948] 1 All E.R. 811, 819–820 (affirmed [1950] A.C. 24).

[1448] [1962] 1 Q.B. 694, 698. See above, paras 33-008, 33-035, 33-056.

[1449] The causes of action against the bank may include breach of contract, tort, breach of duty as bailee and liability for conversion (as to which, see *Schwarzschild v Harrods Ltd* [2008] EWHC 521 (QB)).

[1450] So held in *Bernstein v Northwestern National Bank* (1945) 41 A. 2d 440. See also E.P. Ellinger, E. Lomnicka and C.V.M. Hare, *Ellinger's Modern Banking Law*, 5th edn (2011), pp.742–743.

[1451] cf. *Lilley v Doubleday* (1881) 7 Q.B.D. 510. See above, para.33-051.

[1452] *Stephenson v Hart* (1828) 4 Bing. 476, 482–483; *Hiort v London and North Western Ry* (1879) 4 Ex. D. 188, 194; *Glyn, Mills, Currie & Co v East and West India Dock Co* (1880) 6 Q.B.D. 475, 493 (affirmed (1882) 7 App. Cas. 591).

[1453] *USA v Dollfus Mieg et Cie SA* [1952] A.C. 582.

(i) Bankers' Commercial Credits[1454]

(i) The UCP

34-441 Purpose of credit The expansion of international trade in the last 150 years has necessitated the development of the bankers' commercial credit. Its purpose is to finance contracts of sale of goods where the delay between delivery on board and at destination is likely to be substantial.[1455] The inherent difficulties of overseas transactions are aggravated by the reluctance of both seller and buyer to tie up capital during shipment. Merchants have accordingly availed themselves of the accommodation facilities offered by bankers and in some cases by commercial houses which in return for an agreed commission furnish the credit that the merchants themselves are usually unable or unwilling to afford.[1456]

34-442 Modern practice Modern practice shows letters of credit being supplanted by open account as the means of settling trade transactions. Nevertheless, letters of credit remain extremely popular in regions such as Asia, where more than 60 per cent of all letters of credit are handled.[1457] The decline in use of letters of credit is likely to continue with the development of the Bank Payment Obligation (BPO), which is an irrevocable undertaking given by an obligor bank (usually the buyer's bank) to a recipient bank (which must be the seller's bank) to pay a specified sum under the condition of a successful electronic matching of data or acceptance of mismatches. In April 2013, the International Chamber of Commerce adopted the Uniform Rules for Bank Payment Obligations.[1458] The ICC suggests that the BPO is an alternative "electronic letter of credit". However, whilst the BPO has similarities with letters of credit, it is in many ways a very different type of payment process, e.g., unlike a letter of credit, there is no checking and transmission of physical documents by banks, with everything done electronically and automatically in the SWIFT Trade Services Utility; and, unlike the beneficiary of a letter of credit, the seller does not receive a payment undertaking directly from the obligor bank (the seller's claim is against the recipient bank, i.e. the seller's bank, according to the terms of any separate contractual agreement that the seller will usually have

---

[1454] See, in particular, *Benjamin's Sale of Goods*, 10th edn (2017), Ch.23; R. King, *Gutteridge and Megrah's Law of Banker's Commercial Credits*, 8th edn (2001); R. Jack, A. Malek and D. Quest, *Documentary Credits*, 4th edn (2009); P. Ellinger and D. Neo, *The Law and Practice of Documentary Letters of Credit* (2010); D. Horowitz, *Letters of Credit and Demand Guarantees: Defences to Payment* (2010).

[1455] The last 40 years have seen a substantial increase in the use of standby credits, which serve the same function as performance bonds. For a detailed discussion of standby credits and demand guarantees, see *Benjamin's Sale of Goods*, 10th edn (2017), Ch.24; R.K. Chhina, *Standby Letters of Credit in International Trade* (2013); R.F. Bertrams, *Bank Guarantees in International Trade*, 4th edn (2013). Note that the ICC has published revised Uniform Rules for Demand Guarantees (URDG 758) which came into effect on July 1, 2010; and see A. Affaki and R. Goode, *Guide to ICC Uniform Rules for Demand Guarantees URDG 758* (2011).

[1456] The object of the transaction is fully explained in *Guaranty Trust Co of New York v Hannay & Co* [1918] 2 K.B. 623, 652; *Pavia & Co SpA v Thurmann-Nielsen* [1952] 2 Q.B. 84, 88; *Trans Trust SPRL v Danubian Trading Co Ltd* [1952] 2 Q.B. 297, 304. For the use of irrevocable credits in transactions other than overseas sales, see *Barclays Bank DCO v Mercantile National Bank* [1973] 2 Lloyd's Rep. 541, US Cir Ct of App; *McInerny v Lloyds Bank Ltd* [1973] 2 Lloyd's Rep. 389, affirmed [1974] 1 Lloyd's Rep. 246 (acceptance credits).

[1457] A. Casterman (2014) 20(1) DCInsight 18.

[1458] ICC Publication No.750E. See also *The ICC Guide to the Uniform Rules for Bank Payment Obligations* (ICC Publication No.751E).

entered into with that bank, but this bilateral agreement is not part of the BPO itself).[1459] It remains to be seen whether the BPO will be widely adopted and eventually replace the letter of credit as a method of payment settlement in international trade transactions.

The parties to a commercial credit transaction   There are at least three parties   **34-443** in a commercial credit transaction. The buyer, having agreed in the contract of sale to furnish a commercial credit, approaches his own banker (the "issuing banker") and requests him to open a commercial credit in favour of the seller. The details of the credit to be opened are set out in an "application form", which is a form prepared by the banker, but filled up by the buyer and signed by him. The banker usually informs the buyer in writing of his willingness to open the commercial credit applied for. The application form will then constitute the basis of the contract between the buyer and his banker. In due course, the issuing banker sends to the seller the commercial credit, which specifies the conditions that the seller must perform in order to obtain payment under it. After receiving this credit, the seller ships the goods to the buyer and tenders the required documents (usually a bill of lading, an insurance policy and an invoice) to the issuing banker or his agent and obtains payment. As the issuing banker's business is, in most cases, carried on at the place of the buyer, the issuing banker frequently engages another banker, operating at the seller's place of business, and instructs him to notify the seller of the opening of the credit, and to make payment against the documents. This second banker is known as "intermediary" or "correspondent banker". It should be added that a commercial credit does not always promise payment of cash against the required documents. In most credits opened in the United Kingdom the issuing banker promises to accept a draft drawn under, and accompanied by the documents required in, the commercial credit. In most credits opened in South East Asia the issuing banker promises to negotiate (usually "without recourse")[1460] a draft, accompanied by the required documents, drawn by the seller on the buyer.[1461] On the Continent the issuing banker usually promises to pay cash against the documents. For most purposes these different modes of payment do not, however, lead to differences regarding the rights of the parties.

The Uniform Customs and Practice for Documentary Credits: their develop-   **34-444** **ment**   The wide use of commercial credits in international sales has led to a need for uniformity. The first attempt to provide a uniform system was undertaken by the International Chamber of Commerce (ICC) in 1933, when the first revision of the Uniform Customs and Practice for Documentary Credits, prepared by this institute was adopted by the bankers of several European countries. A second revision of the Code was promulgated by the ICC in 1951. Although this revision was adopted widely, it was rejected by the bankers in the United Kingdom and in most Commonwealth countries. However, the bankers in these countries adopted the next revi-

---

[1459] For analysis of the differences between the BPO and a letter of credit, see G. Wynne and H. Fearn, "The bank payment obligation: will it replace the traditional letter of credit—now, or ever?" [2014] B.J.I.B.F.L. 102. See also K. Vorpeil, "Bank payment obligations: alternative means of settlement in international trade" [2014] I.B.L.J. 41.

[1460] See the *Uniform Customs and Practice for Documentary Credits*, 2007 Revision (UCP 600) art.7(a) (no reference to negotiation by issuing bank "without recourse") and art.8(a)(ii) (express reference to negotiation by confirming bank "without recourse").

[1461] UCP 600 art.6(c), states that a credit must not be issued available by a draft drawn on the applicant.

sion, promulgated in 1962. This third revision settled many of the practical problems that plagued issuers of documentary credits. For this reason, it is not surprising that the third revision attained world-wide recognition. Nevertheless, the need for a further revision was felt by about the end of the decade. It was eventually undertaken by the ICC in collaboration with the United Nations Commission on International Trade Law (UNCITRAL). This revision, known as the 1974 Revision, was more comprehensive than the earlier versions. The 1974 Revision attained universal acceptance and was generally considered a satisfactory Code. But certain technological developments in communications and problems arising in respect of specific provisions of that Revision, especially as regards shipping documents, prompted a further review.[1462] The fourth Revision of the Uniform Customs and Practice for Documentary Credits which remained in effect for 10 years came into force on October 1, 1984. The 10 years following the promulgation of the 1983 Revision were marked by a rise in the volume of letters of credit issued all over the world and also by a substantial increase in disputes ensuing in litigation. Many of the inadequacies of the 1983 Revision surfaced in this process. Others became the subject of specific points of controversy referred to the ICC's banking commission. The 1993 Revision which came into effect on January 1, 1994,[1463] purported to cure these defects. There was also an attempt to improve the draftsmanship. All the same, the 1993 Revision was, basically, an updated and improved version of the 1983 Revision.

34-445 **The 2007 Revision** The latest revision of the *Uniform Customs and Practice for Documentary Credits* ("UCP 600") was approved unanimously at an International Chamber of Commerce Banking Commission meeting in October 2006. UCP 600 came into effect on July 1, 2007.[1464] A supplement to the UCP dealing with the electronic presentation of documents ("eUCP") has been reissued with UCP 600.[1465] To accompany this latest revision of the UCP, the ICC published a new version of *International Standard Banking Practice for Examination of Documentary Credits* ("ISBP"), which is a checklist of items that document examiners need to check for in their review of documents presented under the credit.[1466] A new version of ISBP was approved by the ICC Banking Commission in April 2013.[1467]

34-446 **Main changes in the 2007 revision** This is not the place for a detailed review of the changes introduced by UCP 600.[1468] Nevertheless, the main changes are summarised in this paragraph and those that follow. First, whereas the 1993 Revision of the UCP ("UCP 500") covered both revocable and irrevocable credits, UCP 600 only applies to irrevocable credits.[1469] Secondly, art.1 of UCP 600 states that UCP 600 is to apply "when the text of the credit expressly indicates that it is subject to

---

[1462] See, generally, problems considered by the ICC's Commission on Banking Techniques and Practice, ICC Brochures No.371, 399 and 434.
[1463] As ICC Brochure No.500.
[1464] ICC Publication No.600.
[1465] Discussed below in paras 34-457 et seq.
[1466] ICC Publication No.681.
[1467] ICC Publication No.745.
[1468] See E.P. Ellinger, "The Uniform Customs and Practice for Documentary Credits (UCP): their development and the current revisions" [2007] L.M.C.L.Q. 152; C. Debattista, "The New UCP 600—Changes to the Tender of the Seller's Shipping Documents under Letters of Credit" [2007] J.B.L. 329; J. Ulph, "The UCP 600: Documentary Credits in the Twenty-first Century" [2007] J.B.L. 355.
[1469] UCP 600 art.2 (see definition of "credit").

these rules".[1470] The wording constitutes a change from UCP 500, art.1, which says that the UCP applies "where they are incorporated into the text of the credit". Nevertheless, despite the wording of UCP 600 art.1, a court may well allow incorporation of the UCP based upon a previous course of dealing between the parties.[1471] Even in the absence of a previous course of dealing, it has also been suggested that English law would probably allow the incorporation of the UCP into the credit as a matter of business practice because it is so widely used by banks all over the world.[1472] Thirdly, UCP 600 contains a new definitions section (art.2) and interpretations section (art.3). Three definitions are particularly important. A "complying presentation" is defined to mean a presentation that is in accordance with the terms and conditions of the credit, the applicable provisions of the UCP rules and international standard banking practice. The concept of "honour" is also new to UCP 600 and is defined to mean (a) to pay at sight if the credit is available by sight payment; (b) to incur a deferred payment undertaking and pay at maturity if the credit is available by deferred payment[1473]; and (c) to accept a bill of exchange ("draft") drawn by the beneficiary and pay at maturity if the credit is available by acceptance. The concept of "negotiation" has caused problems in the past. Under UCP 500 art.10(b)(ii), "negotiation" was defined in terms of "the giving of value" for drafts and/or documents by the bank authorised to negotiate. There were issues as to what this meant and ICC Banking Commission Paper No.2 (September 1994) tried to deal with these issues. The new definition in UCP 600 refers to the "purchase" of drafts and/or documents "by advancing or agreeing to advance funds to the beneficiary on or before the banking day on which reimbursement is due to the nominated bank".

Some things have not changed. Most importantly, UCP 600 art.4, enshrines the autonomy principle into the UCP. UCP 600 art.5, states that "banks" deal with documents and not goods, services or performance to which the documents relate. The wording is slightly different from UCP 500 which in art.4 states that "all parties" concerned in documentary credit operations deal with documents and not with goods etc. The change in wording should be welcomed. Where the underlying contract is one of sale, the seller and the buyer clearly deal in goods even where the sale is on c.i.f. terms.[1474] Similarly, UCP 600 art.34, makes clear that in credit operations banks have no responsibility for anything other than conformity of the documents to the credit. **34-447**

Construction of the UCP English courts regard the provisions of the UCP as **34-448**

[1470] The UCP may be modified or excluded in specified respects by the terms of the credit (*Taurus Petroleum Ltd v State Oil Company of the Ministry of Oil, Republic of Iraq* [2017] UKSC 64 at [61]), although art.1 of UCP 600 provides that such modification or exclusion must be express.

[1471] *Benjamin's Sale of Goods*, 10th edn (2017), para.23-006.

[1472] E. McKendrick (ed.), *Goode on Commercial Law*, 5th edn (2016), 35.45, citing, by analogy, *Harlow and Jones Ltd v American Express Bank Ltd* [1990] 2 Lloyd's Rep. 343, 349, a case on the Uniform Rules for Collections. See also, R.K. Chhina, "The Uniform Customs and Practice for Documentary Credit (the USP): Are they merely a set of contractual terms?" (2016) 30 B.F.L.R. 245.

[1473] UCP 600 arts 7(c) and 8(c), establish a definite undertaking by issuing and confirming banks to reimburse on maturity whether or not the nominated bank prepaid or purchased its own acceptance or deferred payment undertaking before maturity. Art.12(b) provides that, by nominating a bank to accept or incur a deferred payment undertaking, an issuing bank gives the nominated bank authority to prepay or purchase a draft accepted or a deferred payment undertaking incurred by that bank. As to the effect of art.12(b) on the assignment of the beneficiary's rights under the credit to the nominated bank before maturity, see below, para.34-483.

[1474] *Arnold Karberg & Co v Blythe, Green, Jourdain & Co* [1916] 1 K.B. 495, per Bankes L.J.

standard contractual terms which must be incorporated into the credit and construed according to normal principles governing the construction of commercial contracts. The modern approach to the construction of commercial contracts is contextual,[1475] although the courts tend to take a more literal approach to the construction of standard form contracts that reflect market practice or upon which third parties are likely to rely.[1476] This is reflected in the way the Supreme Court recently approached the construction of letters of credit in *Taurus Petroleum Ltd v State Oil Company of the Ministry of Oil, Republic of Iraq*,[1477] where emphasis was placed upon the language of the credits, construed in their contractual context, and not upon extraneous circumstances. Nevertheless, when construing provisions of the UCP, the courts "seek to give effect to the international consequences underlying the UCP".[1478] In *Fortis Bank SA/NV v Indian Overseas Bank*, Thomas L.J. said that the UCP was to be construed:

"... in accordance with its underlying aims and purposes reflecting international practice and the expectations of international bankers and international traders so that it underpins the operation of letters of credit in international trade. A literal and national approach must be avoided."[1479]

The English courts have been willing to imply a term into the UCP,[1480] although Thomas L.J., without reaching a concluded view on the subject, has cautioned that, given its international status, "there would be real difficulties in using a rule of national law as to the implication of terms (if distinct from a method of construction) to write an obligation into the UCP".[1481]

34-449   Standard of examination of documents   UCP 600 art.14 is the key provision dealing with the standard of examination of the tendered documents. It draws together in one article, and makes some changes to, various provisions that were previously scattered across UCP 500. First, UCP 600 art.14(a), states that a bank must examine tendered documents to determine whether they appear on their face to constitute a complying presentation. Unlike UCP 500 art.13(a), UCP 600 does not expressly state that the bank must conduct its examination "with reasonable care".[1482] It was felt that the general reference to reasonable care was unnecessary as UCP 600, supplemented by ISBP, adopted a significantly more detailed ap-

---

[1475] See Vol.I, paras 13-041 et seq.

[1476] See Vol.I, para.13-051.

[1477] [2017] UKSC 64 at [8], [73]. The High Court of Australia adopted a similar approach to the construction of a performance bond in *Simic v New South Wales Land & Housing Corporation* [2016] HCA 47 at [8]–[11], [31], [77]–[101].

[1478] *Glencore International AG v Bank of China* [1996] 1 Lloyd's Rep. 135, 148, per Sir Thomas Bingham M.R.

[1479] [2011] EWCA Civ 58, [2011] 2 Lloyd's Rep. 33 at [29]. Opinions of the ICC Commission on Banking Technique and Practice and DOCDEX decisions provide evidence as to international banking practice: see *Benjamin's Sale of Goods*, 10th edn (2017), para.23-007.

[1480] *Seaconsar (Far East) Ltd v Bank Markazi Jomhouri Islami Iran* [1999] 1 Lloyd's Rep. 36, 39. See also *Bankers Trust Co v State Bank of India* [1991] 1 Lloyd's Rep. 587, 599, reversed on grounds of interpretation: [1991] 2 Lloyd's Rep. 443. In the context of performance bonds, the courts have consistently emphasised that it will be rare for a term to be implied into such a contract, see below, para.34-523.

[1481] *Fortis Bank SA/NV v Indian Overseas Bank* [2011] EWCA Civ 58, [2011] 2 Lloyd's Rep. 33 at [55]; cited with evident approval by Blair J. in *Deutsche Bank AG, London v CIMB Bank Berhad* [2017] EWHC 1264 (Comm) at [37].

[1482] In *Gian Singh & Co Ltd v Banque de l'Indochine* [1974] 2 All E.R. 754, 757–758, Lord Diplock

proach to compliance.[1483] A presentation either complies or it does not: if it does not, a bank that honours or negotiates is not entitled to reimbursement and cannot claim such entitlement on the basis that it exercised reasonable care in examining the presentation.[1484]

Secondly, under UCP 600 art.14(b), each bank has a maximum of five banking days following the day of presentation to determine if the presentation is complying. UCP 500 art.13(b), gave the bank a reasonable time, not to exceed seven banking days, to examine the documents and make the determination. UCP 600 brings greater certainty with the removal of the reference to a reasonable time and its replacement by a fixed period of five banking days following the date of presentation.

Other changes with regard to the standard of examination of documents can be listed as follows. First, UCP 500 art.43, provides that transport documents must be presented to banks not later than 21 days after the date of shipment (but in any event not later than the expiry date of the credit). UCP 600 art.14(c) restricts this rule by stating that a presentation including one or more *original* transport documents must be made by or on behalf of the beneficiary not later than 21 days after the date of shipment (but in any event not later than the expiry date of the credit). The rule does not apply to copies. Secondly, there are two key parts of UCP 600 art.14 that deal with data content. Article 14(d) provides that data in a document, when read in context with the credit, the document itself and international standard banking practice, need not be identical to, but must not conflict with, data in that document, any other stipulated document or the credit. The intention behind art.14(d) is clearly to move away from the mirror image approach to documentary compliance. Article 14(f) provides that if a credit requires presentation of a document other than a transport document, insurance document or commercial invoice, without stipulating by whom the document is to be issued or its data content, banks will accept the document as presented if its content appears to fulfil the function of the required document and otherwise complies with art.14(d). Article 14(f) seems to take data content out of the equation when there is no stipulation as to what it should be. Thirdly, UCP 600 art.14(g) states that a document presented but not required by the credit is to be disregarded and may be returned to the presenter. Fourthly, UCP 600 art.14(h) provides that non-documentary conditions are to be ignored. A non-documentary condition would be where the credit contains a reference to goods being of "US origin". This condition will be ignored unless the credit also calls for one of the tendered documents—most likely the certificate of origin—to indicate compliance with that condition. Fifthly, UCP 600 art.14(j), clarifies the position where the addresses and contact details (phone, fax, email, etc.) of the beneficiary and the applicant do not correspond.

34-450

Complying presentation   Under UCP 500 there was no precise statement as to when an issuing or nominated bank had to start the settlement process. By contrast, UCP 600 provides that the issuing bank must honour the credit when it determines

34-451

---

said that the UCP's express reference to reasonable care "does no more than restate the duty of the bank at common law".

[1483] G. Collyer, *Commentary on UCP 600* (2007, ICC Publication No.680), p.62.

[1484] *Benjamin's Sale of Goods*, 10th edn (2017), para.23-099, citing *Equitable Trust Co of New York v Dawson Partners Ltd* (1927) 27 Ll. L. Rep. 49, 52 (Lord Sumner); E.P. Ellinger [2007] L.M.C.L.Q. 166. cf. R. Cranston, E. Avgouleas, K. van Zwieten, C. Hare and T. van Sante, *Principles of Banking Law*, 3rd edn (2018), pp.521, 531.

that a presentation is complying.[1485] When a confirming bank determines that a presentation is complying, it must honour or negotiate and forward the documents to the issuing bank.[1486] When a nominated bank determines that a presentation is complying and honours or negotiates, it must forward the documents to the confirming bank or issuing bank.[1487]

34-452 **Discrepant documents, waiver and notice**   UCP 500 art.14(d)(ii) makes it clear that a rejection notice has to state "all" discrepancies in respect of which the bank refused the documents. UCP 600 art.16(c)(ii) retains the requirement, although it does so in slightly different language: the bank must give a "single notice" of rejection to the presenter and that notice must state "each discrepancy in respect of which the bank refuses to honour or negotiate". If the bank fails to comply with this requirement, or any other requirement of art.16, it is precluded from claiming that the documents do not constitute a complying presentation.[1488] This seems to mean that the bank may be precluded from raising a new objection when documents are retendered by the seller having cured the defect identified in the original notice of rejection. By contrast, in the normal course of events, the mere failure to raise a discrepancy when refusing an initial presentation does not estop a bank at common law from claiming that a subsequent presentation is non-compliant on the basis of that discrepancy.[1489]

34-453   Under UCP 500 art.14(d)(i) a bank which refuses documents must also state in its rejection notice whether it is holding the documents at the disposal of, or is returning them to, the presenter. The purpose of this provision is that, as soon as the documents have been rejected, they should be put back in circulation. However, problems have arisen where a bank serves a rejection notice and at the same time approaches the applicant for a waiver of the discrepancies, and if such waiver is received releases the documents without further notice. For example, in *Crédit Industriel et Commercial v China Merchants Bank*,[1490] the issuing bank's notice of rejection was held to be bad where it ended with the words:

"Should the disc[repancy] being accepted by the applicant, we shall release the documents to them without further notice to you unless yr instructions to the contrary received prior to our payment. Documents held at yr risk for yr disposal".

Steel J. considered that the conditional nature of the rejection was not saved by the potential for acceptance of contrary instructions prior to payment, particularly where no notice was to be given. The message constituted a continuing threat of conversion of the claimant's documents. UCP 600 art.16(c)(iii) contains additional options designed to avoid banks sitting on discrepant documents. The rejection notice must state that the bank (a) holds the documents pending further instructions from the presenter; (b) holds the documents until it receives a waiver from the applicant and agrees to accept it, and receives further instructions from the presenter prior to

---

[1485] UCP 600 art.15(a).
[1486] UCP 600 art.15(b).
[1487] UCP 600 art.15(c).
[1488] UCP 600 art.16(f) (but note that the preclusion does not apply to a non-confirming nominated bank). See *Fortis Bank SA/NV v Indian Overseas Bank* [2010] EWHC 84 (Comm), [2010] 2 Lloyd's Rep. 641, affirmed [2011] EWCA Civ 58, [2011] 2 Lloyd's Rep. 33.
[1489] *Kydon Compania Naviera v National Westminster Bank Ltd* [1981] 1 Lloyd's Rep. 68, 79. See also *Benjamin's Sale of Goods*, 10th edn (2017), para.23-222; *Paget's Law of Banking*, 14th edn (2014), para.36.19.
[1490] [2002] EWHC 973 (Comm), [2002] 2 All E.R. (Comm) 427.

agreeing to accept a waiver; (c) is returning the documents; or (d) is acting in accordance with instructions previously received from the presenter. The bank must act in accordance with the statement contained in the notice with reasonable promptness.[1491]

UCP 600 art.16(d) provides that the rejection notice must be given by telecom- **34-454** munication or, if that is not possible, by other expeditious means no later than the close of the fifth banking day following the day of presentation. This provision is more tightly worded than the equivalent provision in UCP 500. UCP 500 art.14(d)(i) requires notice to be given "*without delay* but no later than the close of the seventh banking day following the day of receipt of the documents". The net effect of UCP 600 arts 14(b) and 16(d) seems to be that a bank has a maximum of five banking days following presentation of the documents to determine if the presentation is compliant, but the longer it takes to make its determination, the less time it has available to it to give a notice of rejection to the applicant.

Original documents and copies   The basic rule is that original documents must **34-455** be tendered to the bank, unless the credit calls for copy documents. However, there has been uncertainty as to what constitutes an original document.[1492] Article 17 of UCP clears up that uncertainty. It states that at least one original of each stipulated document must be tendered,[1493] and provides that a bank must treat as original any document bearing an apparently original signature, mark, stamp or label of the issuer of the document, unless the document itself indicates that it is not original.[1494] Unless a document indicates otherwise, a bank is also to accept a document as original (i) if it appears to be written, typed, perforated or stamped by the document issuer's hand; or (ii) appears to be on the document issuer's original stationery; or (iii) states that it is an original, unless the statement appears not to apply to the document presented.[1495]

Commercial invoice   UCP 600 art.18 deals with the commercial invoice. Some **34-456** parts of the art.18 are the same as the equivalent provision (art.37) in UCP 500, e.g. the requirements in art.18(c) that the description of the goods in the commercial invoice should correspond with that in the credit (in all other documents, the goods may be described in general terms not inconsistent with the description of the goods in the credit). But some parts of art.18 are different. Article 18(a) states that in addition to the requirement that the invoice must be made out to the applicant and made by the beneficiary, it must be made out in the same currency as the credit. This is a useful clarification as it avoids any dispute as to whether the price is merely

---

[1491] *Fortis Bank SA/NV v Indian Overseas Bank* [2010] EWHC 84 (Comm), [2010] 2 Lloyd's Rep. 641, affirmed [2011] EWCA Civ 58, [2011] 2 Lloyd's Rep. 33 (where the issuing bank's failure to act in accordance with the disposal statements contained in its UCP 600 art.16(c)(iii) notices, was held, applying UCP 600 art.16(f), to precluded the bank from claiming that the documents did not constitute a complying presentation). In *Fortis Bank SA/NV v India Overseas Bank* [2011] EWHC 538 (Comm), [2011] 2 Lloyd's Rep. 190, J. Hirst Q.C., sitting as a Deputy Judge of the High Court, held (at [35]) that "in the absence of special extenuating circumstances, a bank which failed to despatch the documents within three banking days would have failed to act within reasonable promptness".

[1492] *Glencore International AC v Bank of China* [1996] 1 Lloyd's Rep. 135; *Kredietbank Antwerp v Midland Bank Plc* [1999] 1 All E.R. (Comm) 801; *Crédit Industriel et Commercial v China Merchants Bank* [2002] EWHC 973 (Comm), [2002] 2 All E.R. (Comm) 427.

[1493] UCP 600 art.17(a).

[1494] UCP 600 art.17(b).

[1495] UCP 600 art.17(c).

subject to conversion into the appropriate currency or whether a different stipulated currency makes the document non-compliant. Article 18(b) states that a bank may accept a commercial invoice in excess of the amount permitted in the credit provided the bank in question has not honoured or negotiated for an amount in excess of that permitted by the credit. The bank's decision to do so will be binding on all parties.

34-457 **The eUCP**   To facilitate the electronic transmission of documents tendered under letters of credit, the ICC has promulgated a new set of guidelines entitled the eUCP, which makes provision for the dematerialisation of documents for the purpose of their being transmitted and tendered electronically.[1496] According to art.e1(a), they accommodate the presentation of electronic records alone or in combination with paper documents.

34-458 **A supplement**   The eUCP do not replace the UCP but constitute a supplement. To avoid confusion, the letter "e" precedes the number of each article thereof. When the eUCP are incorporated in a letter of credit, it is not necessary also to incorporate the UCP because, under arts e1(b) and e2(a), the supplement incorporates the UCP in any facility subject to it. However, under art.e2(b), where the eUCP applies, its provisions prevail "to the extent that they would produce a result different from the application of the UCP". At the same time, the eUCP remains subordinate to the UCP if the letter of credit confers on the beneficiary the option of choosing between the presentation of paper documents and electronic records. If, in such a case, he:

> "… chooses to present only paper documents, the U.C.P. alone shall apply to that presentation. If only paper documents are permitted under an eUCP Credit, the U.C.P. alone shall apply."

34-459 **Seldom used**   To date, the eUCP are not in common use. In the case of letters of credit which call for the drawing of a bill of exchange, such letters of credit available by acceptance or by negotiation, banks and businessmen continue to opt for the presentation of paper documents because under the negotiable instruments laws prevailing in most countries a bill of exchange is issued, accepted and transferred by means of a "signature" in the traditional sense. The eUCP can be more readily used in the case of cash and deferred payment credits but even in these instances they are not popular. All the same, a brief discussion is required.

34-460 **Important definitions**   To blend the eUCP with the UCP where both apply to a letter of credit, art.e3(a) redefines certain terms for the purpose of applying the UCP to an electronic record presented under the eUCP. "Appears on their face"—used in art.14(a) of UCP 600—is applied to the examination of data content of an electronic record. The generic term "document" includes an "electronic record" and "place of presentation" of electronic records means an "electronic address". Of particular importance is that "'sign' and the like shall include an electronic signature". Where a letter of credit is subject to the eUCP, this definition would, accordingly, apply to "signature" of a document, for instance a marine bill of

---

[1496] ICC Brochure No.500/3; in force since 1 April 2002; and now see revision of eUCP (Version 1.1), in force since 1 July 2007.

lading.[1497] It would not, however, apply outside the ambit of the UCP, so that, under the provisions of the applicable local law[1498] a negotiable instrument, such as a bill of exchange, will still require a manual or facsimile signature.

Definitions of terms in eUCP   Further definitions, respecting the eUCP itself, are **34-461** spelt out in art.e3(b). An "electronic record" means data created, generated, sent, communicated or stored by electronic means, provided its sender and data source can be authenticated and provided further that it is capable of being examined for compliance with the terms and conditions of the eUCP credit. An "electronic signature" means a data process attached to or logically associated with an electronic record and executed to identify the person executing it and to signify his authentication of the electronic record. "Received" means the time when an electronic record enters the information system of the applicable recipient in a form capable of being accepted by that system. An acknowledgement of receipt does not imply an acceptance or refusal of the electronic record under an eUCP credit. A document in the traditional form is called a "paper document".

Format   Under art.e4, a credit must specify the formats in which electronic **34-462** records are to be presented. If no format is specified, any format would do. In art.e3(b)(iii), "format" is defined as the data organisation in which the electronic record is expressed. A word processing system, for instance, constitutes a "format".

Presentation   Article e5(a) requires that a place be stated for the presentation of **34-463** the electronic record and of paper documents. Under art.e5(b) electronic records may be presented separately and need not be presented at the same time. If the eUCP credit allows for the presentation of one or more electronic records, the beneficiary must give notice to signify that the presentation is complete. Such notice may be given as an electronic record or as a paper document and has to identify the credit to which it relates. Presentation is deemed not to have been made if the beneficiary's notice is not received. Article e5(d) restates this last provision as a general rule in respect of all presentations made under an eUCP credit. In effect, this means that the beneficiary has to ensure that his communications have been received by the bank. In addition, art.e5(f) provides that an electronic record that "cannot be authenticated" is deemed not to have been presented.

Bank's inability to receive   Article e5(e) deals with cases in which a bank is open **34-464** but its system is unable to receive a transmitted electronic record on the stipulated expiry date or on the designated last day of a designated period. In such a case, the bank is deemed to be closed on the relevant date, which is then postponed (or extended) to "the first following banking day on which such Bank is able to receive an electronic record". However, if the only electronic record remaining to be presented is the notice of completeness, it may be given by telecommunication or by a paper document and is deemed timely as long as it is sent before the bank is able to receive an electronic record.

Examination   Article e6 augments the provisions of art.14(a) of UCP 600. Under **34-465** art.e6(a), an electronic record at an external system or hyperlink to which reference is made constitutes the electronic record to be examined. The failure of a

---

[1497] UCP 600 art.20(a)(i). As regards "superimposed", "notation" and stamped, see art.e3(a)(v).
[1498] As to which see above, para.34-041.

stipulated system to provide the required access to the applicable electronic record constitutes a discrepancy. Under art.e6(b), the forwarding of electronic records by the nominated bank[1499] signifies that the bank has checked the apparent authenticity of the electronic record. Under art.e6(c), the inability of the issuing bank or of the confirming bank to examine an electronic record in a format required by the eUCP or, if no format is required, to examine it in the format presented is not a basis for the refusal of the documents.

34-466   **Time for examination of documents**   Under art.e7(a)(i), the time for the examination of the documents commences on the banking day following the banking day on which the beneficiary's notice of completeness was received. The maximum period of five banking days, prescribed in art.14(b) of UCP 600 is not—in itself—varied. Under art.e7(a)(ii), if the time for the presentation of documents or of the notice of completeness is extended, the time for the examination of the documents commences on the banking day following the day on which the bank to which presentation is to be made is able to receive the notice of completeness.

34-467   **Notice of refusal**   Article e7(b) does not modify the contents of the notice of refusal—spelt out in art.16(c) of UCP 600—which are to be served by a bank that decides to reject documents tendered to it. However, the clause provides that, if the rejected presentation includes electronic records and the bank that rejects the tender does not receive, within 30 days, instructions from the "presenter" [tenderor] as regards the disposition of the electronic records, "the Bank shall return any paper documents not previously returned to the presenter but may dispose of the electronic records in any manner deemed appropriate without any responsibility". Obviously, the electronic record may be shredded. Its return to the presenter would not serve any commercial purpose.

34-468   **Originals and copies**   Under art.e8, any requirement of the UCP or an eUCP for the presentation of one or more originals or copies of an electronic record is satisfied by the presentation of one electronic record. In respect of paper documents, the position remains governed by art.17 of UCP 600.[1500]

34-469   **Issuance**   According to art.e9, unless an electronic record contains a specific date of issuance, it is deemed to have been issued on the day on which it appears to have been sent by the issuer. The date of receipt is deemed to be the date on which it was sent if no other date is apparent.

34-470   **Transport**   If an electronic record evidencing transport does not specify a date of shipment or of dispatch, art.e10 provides that the date of the issuance of the record is to be treated as the relevant date. This presumption does not apply, however, if the record includes a notation setting out the date of shipment or of transport. Such a notation need not be separately signed or authenticated.

34-471   **Corruption of record**   Under art.e11(a), if upon its receipt an electronic record "appears to have been corrupted", the recipient—be it the issuing bank, the confirming or another nominated bank—may request the presenter that the record be re-

---

[1499] For the definition of "nominated bank" see below, para.34-475.
[1500] See above, para.34-455.

presented. Under sub-cl.(b)(ii) if the nominated bank, to which notice is given, is not the confirming bank, it must communicate the request to the issuing bank and any confirming bank. Under sub-cl.(b)(i), the time for examination is thereupon suspended and resumes when the electronic record is re-presented. Under sub-cl.(b)(iii)–(iv), if the electronic record is not presented again within thirty calendar days, the bank may treat the electronic record as not presented and "any deadlines are not extended".

Additional disclaimer The general disclaimer available to banks under the **34-472** articles of the UCP are discussed elsewhere in this chapter.[1501] Article 12 includes additional disclaimers available where documents are tendered electronically. It provides that by checking the apparent authenticity of an electronic record, banks assume no liability for the identity of the sender, the source of information or its complete and unaltered character other than that which is apparent in the electronic record received by the use of a commercially acceptable data process for the receipt, authentication and identification of electronic records. A bank is, accordingly, not entitled to ignore a red flag which is staring in its face in consequence of a patent irregularity in the electronic record received.

Assessment The eUCP were originally adopted by a majority vote of the Bank- **34-473** ing Commission.[1502] It remains to be seen whether the guidelines would eventually gain popularity. Two practical problems, that are not easily overcome, may continue to quench any enthusiasm for their use. One is that the electronic transmission of documents is bound to facilitate the recirculation of documents transmitted in this manner. Where a fraudster and his negotiating bank are in league, the eUCP is bound to play into their hands. The other problem, referred to earlier, arises where the documentary credit transaction involves the use of negotiable instruments drawn at a usance other than at sight. As negotiation and transfer require the indorsement of the instrument (by means of a physically executed signature) completed by its delivery, dematerialisation thereof is ruled out. As the remaining documents are, invariably, tendered together with the bill of exchange, their electronic transmission without the bill is of no practical benefit.

(ii) Types of Documentary Credits

Irrevocable credits Article 2 of UCP 600 defines a documentary credit ("credit") **34-474** as:

> "... any arrangement, however named or described, that is irrevocable and thereby constitutes a definite undertaking of the issuing bank to honour a complying presentation."

This marks an important change from UCP 500 which covered both revocable and irrevocable credits. But revocable credits are rare in practice and so the change is not unexpected. Article 2 also contains a definition of "honour", which means:

> "... to pay at sight if the credit is available by sight payment; to incur a deferred payment undertaking and pay at maturity if the credit is available by deferred payment; to accept a bill of exchange ('draft') drawn by the beneficiary and pay at maturity if the credit is available by acceptance".

[1501] See below, para.34-498.
[1502] By 63 to 3 votes: on November 7, 2001; see *Documentary Credit World*, Vol.6, issue 2, p.28—February 2002.

Article 2 defines a "complying presentation" of documents as one:

"... that is in accordance with the terms and conditions of the credit, the applicable provisions of [the UCP] and international standard banking practice."

34-475   UCP 600 art.7(a) sets out the issuing bank's payment undertaking in the following terms:

"Provided that the stipulated documents are presented to the nominated bank or to the issuing bank and that they constitute a complying presentation, the issuing bank must honour if the credit is available by:

i.   sight payment, deferred payment or acceptance with the issuing bank;
ii.   sight payment with the nominated bank and that nominated bank does not pay;
iii.   deferred payment with a nominated bank and that nominated bank does not incur its deferred payment undertaking or, having incurred its deferred payment undertaking, does not pay at maturity;
iv.   acceptance with a nominated bank and that nominated bank does not accept a draft drawn on it or, having accepted a draft drawn on it, does not pay at maturity;
v.   negotiation with a nominated bank and that nominated bank does not negotiate."

A "nominated bank" is defined in UCP 600 art.2 as "the bank with which the credit is available or any bank in the case of a credit available with any bank".

34-476   The opening of an irrevocable credit leads to a contract between the issuing bank and the seller.[1503] A documentary credit becomes irrevocable upon issue; that is, upon its release from the control of the issuing bank or confirming bank, irrespective of the time that it is delivered to or received by the beneficiary.[1504] However, for the purpose of determining whether the buyer has complied with its obligations under the contract of sale, the credit may be considered to be "opened" only when it is communicated to the beneficiary.[1505] In each case, it will be a question of construction of the contract concerned.[1506]

34-477   **Revocable credits**   Where the credit is revocable, the issuing bank is free to amend or cancel it at any time without notice to the beneficiary.[1507] Thus, the opening of a revocable credit does not lead to the creation of a contract between the issuing bank and the seller.[1508] All the issuing bank is required to do is reimburse any other bank for any payment, acceptance or negotiation made by such bank before

---

[1503] *Urquhart Lindsay & Co Ltd v Eastern Bank Ltd* [1922] 1 K.B. 318, 321–322; *Donald H Scott & Co Ltd v Barclays Bank Ltd* [1923] 2 K.B. 1, 13; *Trans Trust SPRL v Danubian Trading Co Ltd* [1952] 2 Q.B. 297, 304–305; *Midland Bank Ltd v Seymour* [1955] 2 Lloyd's Rep. 147, 166; *Hamzeh Malas & Sons v British Imex Industries Ltd* [1958] 2 Q.B. 127, 129; *McInerny v Lloyds Bank Ltd* [1973] 2 Lloyd's Rep. 389 (affirmed [1974] 1 Lloyd's Rep. 246). For the theoretical difficulties and their solution, see below, paras 34-500 et seq.

[1504] UCP 600 arts 7(b) and 8(b). cf. *Urquart Lindsay & Co Ltd v Eastern Bank Ltd* [1922] 1 K.B. 318, 321–322 (credit irrevocable once seller has acted on it); *Dexters Ltd v Schenker & Co* (1923) 14 Ll.L. Rep. 586, 588 (credit irrevocable from time it reaches hands of seller).

[1505] *Bunge Corp v Vegetable Vitamin Foods (Private) Ltd* [1985] 1 Lloyd's Rep. 613 at 617, Neill J.

[1506] R. King, *Gutteridge and Megrah's Law of Bankers' Commercial Credits*, 8th edn (2001), para.4-48, n.132.

[1507] UCP 500 art.8(a).

[1508] This was also the position in England before the adoption of the UCP: *Cape Asbestos Co Ltd v Lloyds Bank Ltd* [1921] W.N. 274.

receiving notice of amendments or cancellation.[1509] Revocable credits are rare and tend only to be found where the parties are not interested in security, e.g. they are members of the same group of companies, but where they are concerned to save costs. UCP 600 only applies to irrevocable credits; it does not apply to revocable credits.[1510] If the parties to the underlying contract want to use a revocable credit, they should make the credit subject to UCP 500, the 1993 revision of the UCP, which does extend to such credits. A credit that does not indicate whether it is revocable or irrevocable will be deemed to be irrevocable.[1511]

Confirmed and unconfirmed credits   Whether a commercial credit is confirmed   **34-478**
or unconfirmed depends on the role assumed by the correspondent banker. If the correspondent banker is merely instructed by the issuing banker to notify the seller about the opening of the commercial credit by the issuing banker and to accept, on behalf of the issuing banker, a tender of documents complying with the terms of the credit, the correspondent banker acts as an agent of the issuing banker. The correspondent banker assumes, in such cases, the role of an "advising banker", and the commercial credit is unconfirmed on the part of the correspondent banker, although it may contain an undertaking of the issuing banker and thus be irrevocable.[1512] If at the instruction of the issuing banker the correspondent banker confirms the credit, i.e. adds to the promise of the issuing banker an undertaking of his own to accept or negotiate a draft or to pay the amount of the credit to the seller against conforming documents, the correspondent banker becomes a confirming banker and the commercial credit is a confirmed credit.[1513] In practice the correspondent banker is asked to confirm a credit only if it is irrevocable.[1514] In an "irrevocable and confirmed credit" the seller obtains an undertaking of both the issuing and the correspondent banker.

Negotiation credits   The credit may be available by negotiation with a bank   **34-479**
nominated in the credit (or with any bank if the credit so provides).[1515] UCP 600 art.2 defines "negotiation" to mean the purchase by the nominated bank of bills of exchange ("drafts") drawn on a bank other than the nominated bank (e.g. drawn on the issuing bank), and/or documents under a complying presentation, by advancing or agreeing to advance funds to the beneficiary on or before the banking day

---

[1509] UCP 500 art.8(b).

[1510] See above, para.34-474.

[1511] UCP 600 art.3.

[1512] A bank asked to advise a credit by the issuing bank or the confirming bank must make sure it does not use language in its communications with the beneficiary that would lead a court to find that the bank had accepted direct liability for payment of the credit: see *Den Danske Bank A/S v Surinam Shipping Ltd* [2014] UKPC 10.

[1513] UCP 600 art.8(a). It was held in *Fortis Bank SA/NV v Indian Overseas Bank* [2009] EWHC 2303 (Comm), [2010] 1 Lloyd's Rep. 227, that an issuing bank that permitted the advising bank to confirm a letter of credit at the beneficiary's request and expense thereby authorised the bank to add its confirmation to the credit for the purposes of UCP 600 art.2, which provides that a "confirming bank" means "the bank that adds its confirmation to a credit upon the issuing bank's authorisation or request".

[1514] If the correspondent banker reserves to himself a right of recourse against the seller, his undertaking does not constitute a confirmation: *Wahbe Tamari & Sons Ltd v Colprogeca Sociedade Geral de Fibras, Cafes e Produtos Coloniais Lda* [1969] 2 Lloyd's Rep. 18.

[1515] As regards the construction of a credit in which it is not clear from the formula used whether it is a straight or negotiation credit, see *European Asian Bank AG v Punjab and Sind Bank (No.2)* [1983] 1 W.L.R. 642, especially 655.

on which reimbursement is due to the nominated bank. This enables the beneficiary to obtain funds without delay by selling the documents to the nominated bank (and so it is only of practical use to the beneficiary where payment under the credit is not immediate). A nominated bank that has honoured or negotiated a complying presentation and forwarded the documents to the issuing bank is entitled to reimbursement from the issuing bank under UCP 600 art.7(c).[1516] In *Société Générale SA v Saad Trading*,[1517] Teare J. held that (i) if the documents forwarded to the issuing bank are not compliant, the issuing bank is not obliged to reimburse the confirming bank under art.7(c) (and that the issuing bank is not bound by the view of the confirming bank that the documents are compliant)[1518]; and (ii) under art.7(c) the documents to be forwarded to the issuing bank must be the documents presented to the confirming bank under the credit (discretion on the part of the confirming bank as to which documents to forward would be contrary to the principle of strict compliance).[1519] In this case the confirming bank did not forward bills of exchange required to be presented under the letter of credit to the issuing bank, but as there was no dispute that the documents presented by the beneficiary to the confirming bank were compliant, the judge held that the issuing bank was not entitled to refuse to reimburse the confirming bank.[1520]

34-480 Branch as bank One important provision of UCP 600 which is relevant as regards both the confirmation of, and the negotiation of documents tendered under, a documentary credit, is to be found in art.2. It is provided that, for the purposes of the UCP, "branches of a bank in different countries are considered to be separate banks". It follows that there can be no doubt as regards the effect of the confirmation by the Standard Chartered Bank's office in Singapore of, for instance, a documentary credit issued by the same bank's office in London. Notably, the Singapore branch could also negotiate documents tendered by the beneficiary under a documentary credit opened by the London office.

34-481 Anticipatory credits In exceptional circumstances it may be stipulated both in the contract of sale and between the buyer and the issuing banker that credit facilities should in part be extended so as to assist the seller prior to shipment. The anticipatory (or packing) credit[1521] serves this purpose and in its so-called "red clause" authorises an early advance. Usually the advance is conditional upon the tender by the seller of such documents as the receipts of a warehouse or of a forwarding agent which may relate, as may be agreed, either to the goods

---

[1516] In the case of reimbursement of a nominated bank for having "honoured" a complying presentation, the issuing bank's obligation to reimburse arises only where the nominated bank has actually made the payment (*Deutsche Bank AG, London v CIMB Bank Berhad* [2017] EWHC 1264 (Comm) at [38]–[39]). UCP 600 art.7(c), adds that "[r]eimbursement for the amount of a complying presentation under a credit available by acceptance or deferred payment is due at maturity, whether or not the nominated bank prepaid or purchased before maturity". See UCP 600 art.8(c) for a similar undertaking of a confirming bank to reimburse another nominated bank that has honoured or negotiated a complying presentation and forwarded the documents to the confirming bank.

[1517] [2011] EWHC 2424 (Comm), [2011] 2 C.L.C. 629.

[1518] At [44].

[1519] At [45]–[46].

[1520] At [47].

[1521] e.g. *South African Reserve Bank v Samuel & Co* (1931) 40 Ll.L. Rep. 291. Anticipatory credits originated in the South African trade in hides.

themselves or even to the raw materials from which the goods are ultimately to be manufactured.

Standby credits   A substantial increase in the volume of standby credits has taken   **34-482**
place during the last few years. Whilst earlier on this facility was used predominantly in domestic transactions in the United States, it has now developed into an instrument of international trade. The standby credit serves the same function as a performance bond and a first demand guarantee. It is opened in order to protect the beneficiary against losses sustained from the non-performance or from the faulty performance of a contract made between himself and the applicant for the standby credit. Payment is usually due against the tender of a bill of exchange for the specified amount accompanied by a certificate in which the beneficiary attests the other party's default. Under art.1, UCP 600 is applicable to standby credits. The problems of this type of facility are discussed in detail elsewhere.[1522]

Transfer and assignment of credits[1523]   It is important to distinguish between the   **34-483**
assignment of a credit and its transfer. There is, it is submitted, nothing to prevent a seller from assigning to a third party his rights under any commercial credit. The seller has a contingent right to claim a liquidated amount and such a demand or claim can be assigned in equity and by way of a statutory assignment.[1524] That the UCP do not have the intention of precluding the assignment of this right is demonstrated by UCP 600 art.39, which reads:

"The fact that a credit is not stated to be transferable shall not affect the right of the beneficiary to assign any proceeds to which it may be or may become entitled under the credit, in accordance with the provisions of the applicable law."

This article relates only to the assignment of proceeds and not to the right to perform under the credit itself. Where such an assignment takes place, the seller continues to be the party who will tender the documents and the only effect of the assignment is that, when the seller tenders the required documents, payment will be made to the assignee.[1525] When a credit is *transferred*, a third party—known as second

---

[1522] *Benjamin's Sale of Goods*, 10th edn (2017), Ch.24, and see the *ICC's International Standby Practices*, ISP 98. For the use of such letters of credit instead of cash deposits, see *Ludgate Insurance Co Ltd v Citibank* [1996] 2 L.R.L.R. 247.

[1523] For a fuller account, see *Benjamin's Sale of Goods*, 10th edn (2017), paras 23-312 et seq. (discussing also the back-to-back credit).

[1524] See generally Vol.I, paras 19-043 et seq. (note that an undertaking to pay money is not a personal contract).

[1525] Note that in *Singer & Friedlander v Creditanstalt-Bankverein* [1981] Com. L.R. 69 the Commercial Court of Vienna held, accordingly, that the assignee was not entitled to tender in his own name a set of documents procured by the assignor. Whilst the assignee had the right to claim the proceeds from the bank, the documents had to be tendered by him on behalf of the assignor. As regards the priorities as between the rights of the assignee and the bank's claim of a set-off, see *Hongkong and Shanghai Banking Corp v Kloeckner & Co AG* [1990] 2 Q.B. 514; see also *Marathon Electrical Manufacturing Corp v Mashrebank* [1997] 2 B.C.L.C. 460, QB. And note that where a bank takes up documents tendered under a deferred payment credit by way of assignments, equities available against the beneficiary are also available against the bank: *Banco Santander SA v Banque Paribas* [1999] 2 All E.R. (Comm) 18; affirmed [2000] Lloyd's Rep. Bank. 165. But see now UCP 600 arts 7(c), 8(c) and 12(b) (see above, para.34-446). Art.12(b) was intended to shift the risk of fraud back to the issuing bank and reverse the outcome in *Santander*. But art.12(b) only refers to the nominated bank being authorised to "prepay or purchase" a deferred payment undertaking. This may have reversed the outcome in *Santander* so far as the authorisation issue was concerned,

beneficiary—is substituted both to the rights and obligations of the seller or part thereof.[1526]

34-484 **Article 38 of UCP 600** The transferability of documentary credits is governed by art.38 of the UCP 600 which reads:

"a. A bank is under no obligation to transfer a credit except to the extent and in the manner expressly consented to by that bank.

b. For the purpose of this article:

Transferable credit means a credit that specifically states it is 'transferable'. A transferable credit may be made available in whole or in part to another beneficiary ('second beneficiary') at the request of the beneficiary ('first beneficiary').

Transferring bank means a nominated bank that transfers the credit or, in a credit available with any bank, a bank that is specifically authorized by the issuing bank to transfer and that transfers the credit. An issuing bank may be a transferring bank.

Transferred credit means a credit that has been made available by the transferring bank to a second beneficiary.

c. Unless otherwise agreed at the time of transfer, all charges (such as commissions, fees, costs or expenses) incurred in respect of a transfer must be paid by the first beneficiary.

d. A credit may be transferred in part to more than one second beneficiary provided partial drawings or shipments are allowed. A transferred credit cannot be transferred at the request of a second beneficiary to any subsequent beneficiary. The first beneficiary is not considered to be a subsequent beneficiary.

e. Any request for transfer must indicate if and under what conditions amendments may be advised to the second beneficiary. The transferred credit must clearly indicate those conditions.

f. If a credit is transferred to more than one second beneficiary, rejection of an amendment by one or more second beneficiary does not invalidate the acceptance by any other second beneficiary, with respect to which the transferred credit will be amended accordingly. For any second beneficiary that rejected the amendment, the transferred credit will remain unamended.

g. The transferred credit must accurately reflect the terms and conditions of the credit, including confirmation, if any, with the exception of:
— the amount of the credit,
— any unit price stated therein,
— the expiry date,
— the period for presentation, or
— the latest shipment date or given period for shipment,
any or all of which may be reduced or curtailed.

The percentage for which insurance cover must be effected may be increased to provide the amount of cover stipulated in the credit or these articles.

The name of the first beneficiary may be substituted for that of the applicant in the credit.

---

but it is far from certain that it would have reversed the position of the nominated bank as assignee taking subject to equities (as to which see D. Horowitz [2008] J.B.L. 508).

[1526] The first beneficiary will usually want to keep information about his transaction with the second beneficiary away from the applicant for fear that the applicant will cut him out of the picture and deal directly with the second beneficiary. In *Jackson v Royal Bank of Scotland* [2005] UKHL 3, [2005] 1 W.L.R. 377 at [20]–[24], the House of Lords confirmed that an issuing bank owes the first beneficiary of a transferable letter of credit a duty of confidentiality with regard to this information (breach of duty of confidentiality when issuing bank reveals to applicant the extent of first beneficiary's "mark-up" on price charged).

If the name of the applicant is specifically required by the credit to appear in any document other than the invoice, such requirement must be reflected in the transferred credit.

h. The first beneficiary has the right to substitute its own invoice and draft, if any, for those of a second beneficiary for an amount not in excess of that stipulated in the credit, and upon such substitution the first beneficiary can draw under the credit for the difference, if any, between its invoice and the invoice of a second beneficiary.

i. If the first beneficiary is to present its own invoice and draft, if any, but fails to do so on first demand, or if the invoices presented by the first beneficiary create discrepancies that did not exist in the presentation made by the second beneficiary and the first beneficiary fails to correct them on first demand, the transferring bank has the right to present the documents as received from the second beneficiary to the issuing bank, without further responsibility to the first beneficiary.

j. The first beneficiary may, in its request for transfer, indicate that honour or negotiation is to be effected to a second beneficiary at the place to which the credit has been transferred, up to and including the expiry date of the credit. This is without prejudice to the right of the first beneficiary in accordance with sub-article 38(h).

k. Presentation of documents by or on behalf of a second beneficiary must be made to the transferring bank."

Bank's duty to transfer Article 38 of UCP 600 sets out the conditions to be   **34-485**
fulfilled for a credit to be transferable. The main requirements are that (a) the transferring bank must expressly consent to the extent and manner of the transfer; and (b) the credit must be specifically state that it is transferable. In *Bank Negara Indonesia 1946 v Lariza (Singapore) Pte Ltd*,[1527] the Privy Council held that, for the purposes of what is now art.38(a), the transferring bank's consent:

"... has to be an express consent made after the request [for transfer] and it has to cover both the extent and manner of the transfer request."[1528]

This means that a bank may issue a transferable credit and, if it is a credit where no other bank is involved, later refuse to allow the transfer at will. The decision has been rightly criticised for reducing the usefulness of the transferable credit for financing supply transactions.[1529]

(iii) The Contract between Seller and Buyer

The documentary credit clause The documentary credit transaction com-   **34-486**
mences when a buyer and a seller agree in their contract of sale that payment should be made through a commercial credit. The buyer is then under an obligation to furnish the seller with a commercial credit. This obligation of the buyer is a condition precedent to the seller's duty to ship the goods.[1530] The buyer must furnish the seller with the type of credit that has been agreed upon in the contract of sale. Thus,

---

[1527] [1988] A.C. 583.
[1528] At 599, per Lord Brandon.
[1529] C.M. Schmitthoff [1988] J.B.L. 49, 53.
[1530] *Dix v Grainger* (1922) 10 Ll.L. Rep. 496, 497; *Garcia v Page & Co Ltd* (1936) 55 Ll.L. Rep. 391, 392; *Trans Trust SPRL v Danubian Trading Co Ltd* [1952] 2 Q.B. 297, 304; *Lindsay & Co Ltd v Cook* [1953] 1 Lloyd's Rep. 328, 335; *Soproma SpA v Marine and Animal By-Products Corp* [1966] 1 Lloyd's Rep. 367. Provision of a letter of credit is a condition precedent to any obligation on the part of the seller to perform any aspect of the loading operation which is the seller's responsibility: *Kronos Worldwide Ltd v Sempra Oil Trading SARL* [2004] EWCA Civ 3, [2004] C.L.C. 136 at [19], per Mance L.J. In some cases the contract of sale may impose on the seller an obligation precedent

if the contract of sale provides for the opening of a confirmed credit, the furnishing of a revocable credit,[1531] or of an irrevocable but unconfirmed credit,[1532] is insufficient. Similarly, if the contract of sale calls for an irrevocable credit to be opened in London, the buyer does not perform his duty by furnishing an irrevocable credit available in another place.[1533] Difficulties arise if the contract of sale does not specify what type of commercial credit should be opened. As a revocable credit does not constitute good security, it may be presumed that the seller and buyer agree that an irrevocable credit should be furnished. In *Giddens v Anglo-African Produce Co Ltd*[1534] the contract of sale provided that a credit was to be "established" with a certain bank. The buyers furnished the sellers with a revocable credit of that bank, whereupon the sellers declined to ship the goods. An action by the buyers against the sellers was dismissed. Bailhache J. read the word "established" as describing the word "credit", and explained that the revocable credit furnished by the buyers could not be considered an "established credit". His Lordship thus appears to have treated the term "established credit" as synonymous with "irrevocable credit". The case indicates that if the contract of sale does not specify what type of credit should be opened, the courts tend to construe the contract as stipulating for an irrevocable credit. However, one authority indicates that if the parties fail to reach an agreement as to the nature of the credit to be furnished, or the documents against which payment is to be made, the contract of sale is incomplete.[1535]

34-487 **Time when credit is to be made available** If the contract of sale provides a date for the opening of the credit, the buyer must furnish it by that date.[1536] If the contract of sale requires that a credit be opened immediately, the buyer must have such time as is needed by a person of reasonable diligence to get such a credit established.[1537] A provision that a credit should be furnished within a few weeks, means within a reasonable time, and what constitutes reasonable time depends on the facts of each case.[1538] In most cases a contract of sale does not stipulate a time for the furnishing of the credit, but specifies a date or period for the shipment of the goods. When the contract of sale provides a period during which the goods are to be shipped, the

---

to the buyer's duty to furnish a credit: *Knotz v Fairclough, Dodd & Jones Ltd* [1952] 1 Lloyd's Rep. 226. And see *Transpetrol Ltd v Transol Olieprodukten Nederland BV* [1989] 1 Lloyd's Rep. 309, especially at 310–311 where Phillips J. treated a nonsensical condition precedent as irrelevant. A buyer who fails to open a credit may be able to defend the seller's claim for damages on the ground that it would have been illegal to have opened the credit: see *Soeximex SAS v Agrocorp International Pte Ltd* [2011] EWHC 2743 (Comm).

[1531] *Panoutsos v Raymond Hadley Corp* [1917] 2 K.B. 473.

[1532] *Soproma SpA v Marine and Animal By-Products Corp* [1966] 1 Lloyd's Rep. 367, 386. The credit must conform not only in form but also in substance to the type specified in the contract of sale. Thus, where a confirmed credit is required, the buyer does not discharge his duty by furnishing a credit in which the correspondent banker purports to give a confirmation but at the same time reserves a right of recourse: *Wahbe Tamari & Sons Ltd v Colprogeca Sociedade Geral de Fibras, Cafes e Produtos Coloniais Lda.* [1969] 2 Lloyd's Rep. 18, 21.

[1533] *Furst & Co v WE Fischer Ltd* [1960] 2 Lloyd's Rep. 340 and see *H & JM Bennett Europe Ltd v Angrexco Co Ltd* Unreported April 6, 1990, suggesting that the buyer is in breach of the contract of sale if he seeks to include onerous terms in the credit.

[1534] (1923) 14 Ll. L. Rep. 230.

[1535] *Schijveschuurder v Canon (Export) Ltd* [1952] 2 Lloyd's Rep. 196.

[1536] As regards the construction of an ambiguous clause, see *Schio Supply Co v Gatoil (USA) Inc* [1989] 1 Lloyd's Rep. 588, 591, CA.

[1537] *Garcia v Page & Co Ltd* (1936) 55 Ll.L. Rep. 391, 392.

[1538] *Etablissements Chainbaux SARL v Harbormaster Ltd* [1955] 1 Lloyd's Rep. 303.

buyer must furnish the commercial credit at the very beginning of this period, so that the seller may, if necessary, be able to ship the goods at its very first date. This rule applies both in the case of contracts c.i.f. and f.o.b.[1539] If the contract of sale specifies an actual date and not a period of shipment, the buyer must furnish the commercial credit within a reasonable time before that date.[1540] The reason for this is that the seller is entitled to have the credit before he actually prepares the goods for shipment. If the obligation of the buyer to open a credit is dependent upon the prior receipt of explicit instructions from the seller, the buyer is not obliged to obtain in the meantime from the banker a letter indicating that the credit will be established as soon as these instructions are received.[1541]

Defects in opening of credit   It is the duty of the buyer to ensure that the credit when opened satisfies the agreed specifications. In order to escape the danger of repudiation he must cure the credit of any initial defects before it is required; and if he does this the seller cannot afterwards complain.[1542] If the seller ships the goods despite the buyer's failure to open the credit either on the due date or in its appropriate form, the seller may be taken by his conduct to have waived his objections to the breach of contract. In *Panoutsos v Raymond Hadley Corp*[1543] payment had been agreed to be by a confirmed credit but the credit that was opened was in fact revocable. The seller, with notice of this defect, made certain shipments and applied to the buyer for an extension of time for the remaining shipments. Before that time had elapsed, the seller suddenly sought to cancel the contract on the ground that the credit was not in accordance with the original specifications. The Court of Appeal concluded that as the buyer had been led to suppose that the breach of the condition precedent had been waived, he was entitled to reasonable notice to enable him to comply with the condition and that the purported cancellation was unjustified.   **34-488**

Waiver or variation   A similar attitude was taken by the Court of Appeal in *Plasticmoda Societa Per Azioni v Davidsons (Manchester) Ltd*[1544] but a difference of opinion occurred in *WJ Alan & Co Ltd v El Nasr Export and Import Co.*[1545] The buyers undertook to furnish a confirmed credit covering the sale on f.o.b. terms of two shipments of coffee at a price of Kenyan shs. 262 per ton. The sellers did not raise any objection when the buyers furnished a confirmed credit expressed in sterling and, in point of fact, began to operate the credit and asked for an extension of the shipping time. After the second shipment but before the presentment of the documents, the pound sterling was devalued; the value of the Kenyan cur-   **34-489**

[1539] As regards contracts c.i.f., see *Pavia & Co SpA v Thurmann-Nielsen* [1952] 2 Q.B. 84, 88–89; but cf. *Sinason-Teicher Inter-American Grain Corp v Oilcakes and Oilseeds Trading Co Ltd* [1954] 1 W.L.R. 1394, 1400 which suggests that the credit should be opened at a reasonable time before the commencement of the shipping period. As regards contracts f.o.b., see *Ian Stach Ltd v Baker Bosley Ltd* [1958] 2 Q.B. 130; *Glencore Grain Rotterdam BV v Lebanese Organisation for International Commerce* [1997] 2 Lloyd's Rep. 386; *Kolmar Group AG v Traxpo Enterprises Pvt Ltd* [2010] EWHC 113 (Comm), [2010] 2 Lloyd's Rep. 653.

[1540] *Plasticmoda Societa per Azioni v Davidsons (Manchester) Ltd* [1952] 1 Lloyd's Rep. 527, 538.

[1541] *Nicolene Ltd v Simmonds* [1952] 2 Lloyd's Rep. 419; affirmed [1953] 1 Q.B. 543.

[1542] *Kronman & Co v Steinberger* (1922) 10 Ll.L. Rep. 39.

[1543] [1917] 2 K.B. 473. See also *Ian Stach Ltd v Baker Bosley Ltd* [1958] 2 Q.B. 130; *Furst & Co v WE Fischer Ltd* [1960] 2 Lloyd's Rep. 340; *Soproma SpA v Marine and Animal By-Products Corp* [1966] 1 Lloyd's Rep. 367.

[1544] [1952] 1 Lloyd's Rep. 527.

[1545] [1972] 2 Q.B. 189.

rency remained unaltered. The sellers obtained payment under the confirmed credit and then sued the buyers for the difference between the amount paid and the amount in Kenyan currency for which the credit ought to have been opened. The Court of Appeal held that the sellers were not entitled to recover. Lord Denning M.R. said:

> "... the sellers, by their conduct, waived the right to have payment by means of a letter of credit in Kenyan currency and accepted instead a letter of credit in sterling."[1546]

He emphasised that a person is entitled to rely on the waiver although no consideration has moved from him and although he has not sustained any detriment by acting on it. Megaw L.J. based his concurring judgment on a different ground. In his view the consequence of the acceptance of the sterling credit by the sellers was "that the original term of the contract of sale as to the money of account was varied from Kenyan currency to sterling".[1547] He conceded that if there were no variation of the contract, the buyers would still be entitled to succeed on the ground of waiver. But he thought that this principle would have a more suitable scope of application in cases involving a number of shipments. A similar view was expressed by Stephenson L.J., who doubted whether the waiver doctrine would apply in cases where the buyer had not altered his position to his detriment.

34-490 **Default by banker** As it is agreed in the contract of sale that payment should be made by the furnishing of a commercial credit, the seller has to claim payment from the bank in the first instance and only on the bank's default from the buyer.[1548] The buyer's obligation to pay the price of the goods is not absolutely discharged by the opening of the credit, and that upon the banker's default the seller can claim payment from the buyer.[1549] In *Saffron v Société Minière Cafrika*[1550] the High Court of Australia suggested that while this principle applies in the case of revocable and irrevocable but unconfirmed credits, the opposite is true in the case of a confirmed credit. It is, however, difficult to see why the furnishing of a confirmed credit should discharge the buyer. The only difference between a "confirmed" and an "irrevocable but unconfirmed" credit is that in the former the seller obtains a promise of both the issuing and the correspondent banker whilst in the latter he obtains only one promise, i.e. that of the issuing banker. It is submitted that the correct view is that the opening of a commercial credit (whether confirmed or unconfirmed) does not, in itself, discharge the buyer.[1551]

34-491 **Default after acceptance of draft** Authorities indicate, further, that even if the banker accepts a draft drawn under the commercial credit, the buyer is not

---

[1546] [1972] 2 Q.B. 189 at 214. A similar view was taken by Lord Denning in the *Plasticmoda* case, above, at 538. The principle had already a distinguished lineage. Denning L.J. traced it back through *Charles Rickards Ltd v Oppenhaim* [1950] 1 K.B. 616 to the decision of the House of Lords in *Hughes v Metropolitan Railway Company* (1877) 2 App. Cas. 439.

[1547] [1972] 2 Q.B. at 217. See also *Maran Road Saw Mill v Austin Taylor & Co Ltd* [1975] 1 Lloyd's Rep. 156.

[1548] *Soproma SpA v Marine and Animal By-Products Corp* [1966] 1 Lloyd's Rep. 367, 385–386.

[1549] *WJ Alan & Co v El Nasr Export and Import Co* [1972] 2 Q.B. 189 at 212. See also *Newman Industries Ltd v Indo-British Industries Ltd* [1956] 2 Lloyd's Rep. 219, 236, reversed on a different point: [1957] 1 Lloyd's Rep. 211; *Soproma SpA v Marine and Animal By-Products Corp*, above.

[1550] (1958) 100 C.L.R. 231, especially at 243–244.

[1551] So held by Lord Denning M.R. in *WJ Alan & Co Ltd v El Nasr Export and Import Co* [1972] 2 Q.B. 189, 212. Megaw and Stephenson L.JJ. did not express a view on this point: [1972] 2 Q.B. 189 at 218, 220.

discharged; if the banker subsequently dishonours the draft by non-payment, the seller is entitled to claim payment from the buyer.[1552] However, in order to save the buyer from having to pay twice, the courts will release him from any obligation assumed by him towards the defaulting issuing banker. In *Sale Continuation Ltd v Austin Taylor & Co Ltd*[1553] the defendants, as selling agents, contracted in London for the sale of timber by Malaysian principals to a Belgian buyer. The defendants, who for all practical purposes assumed the position of a buyer vis-à-vis the Malaysian sellers, instructed the plaintiffs, a firm of merchant bankers, to furnish the sellers with an irrevocable credit to be confirmed by a correspondent banker in Malaysia. In the application form the defendants promised to provide funds as soon as the plaintiffs should receive advice about the negotiation of the sellers' draft by the correspondent banker in Malaysia. A draft drawn by the sellers under the credit and accompanied by the required documents was, in due course, negotiated in Malaysia and accepted by the plaintiffs in London. Subsequently, but before payment of the draft, the documents were released by the plaintiffs to the defendants under a trust receipt, in which the defendants agreed to hold the documents and proceeds as trustees of the plaintiffs. Shortly afterwards the plaintiffs stopped payment and it was clear that they would dishonour the draft of the Malaysian sellers. The defendants thereupon refused to remit the price of the goods, paid to them by the Belgian buyer, to the plaintiffs, paying the amount due directly to the Malaysian sellers. An action brought by the receiver of the plaintiffs was dismissed. Paull J. held that the plaintiffs were under an obligation to honour the draft drawn by the Malaysian sellers under the commercial credit. By entering into a voluntary liquidation, the plaintiffs had evinced an intention not to fulfil this obligation and the defendants were, thereupon, discharged from their obligation to provide funds for meeting the plaintiffs' acceptance of the draft of the Malaysian sellers. When this draft was dishonoured by the plaintiffs, the defendants became entitled to be released from their obligations under the trust receipt and to pay the price directly to the Malaysian sellers.

Default after remittance of funds   It remains to be considered who should sustain **34-492** the loss if the buyer has paid the amount of the credit to the issuing banker, but the latter fails before making payment to the seller, e.g. after the acceptance of a draft drawn under the credit but before it is honoured. It has been held that in such a case the buyer is not entitled to claim that he has performed his entire bargain by furnishing the required letter of credit and by remitting to the banker the funds necessary for making payment. He is not discharged from his duty to pay the price to the seller, because the buyer promises "*to pay* by letter of credit not to provide by a letter of credit a source of payment which [*does*] *not pay*".[1554] Any damages that may be recoverable against the buyer in the event of the defalcation of the banker will

---

[1552] *Hindley v Tothill, Watson & Co* (1894) 13 N.Z.L.R. 13, 23, and the US cases of *Greenough v Munroe*, 53 F. 2d 362 (1931) at 364–365; *Bank of United States v Seltzer*, 251 N.Y.S. 637, 644 (1931); *Re Canal Bank and Trust Co's Liquidation* (1933) 152 So. 297, 300; and see Uniform Commercial Code s.5-117.

[1553] [1968] 2 Q.B. 849 following *Bank of United States v Seltzer*, above. As regards trust receipts, see below, paras 34-542 et seq.

[1554] *Maran Road Saw Mill v Austin Taylor Co & Ltd* [1975] 1 Lloyd's Rep. 156, 159 noted (1977) 40 M.L.R. 91. See also *ED & F Man Ltd v Nigerian Sweets and Confectionary Co Ltd* [1972] 2 Lloyd's Rep. 50, in which the seller was allowed to recover payment from the buyer although the issuing bank was nominated in the contract of sale. See *Benjamin's Sale of Goods*, 10th edn (2017), para.23-301.

be for non-payment of money. If, which has been doubted,[1555] the law rigidly limits those damages to the amount of the money due, together with such interest as may be due[1556] or as the court may award,[1557] the limitation will apply, provided that the credit has been opened. Damages for the failure of the buyer to open the credit are wider in extent, and embrace any loss to the seller that was at the time of the contract reasonably foreseeable by both parties as the probable consequence of the breach.[1558]

34-493 **Seller's rights where documents are faulty** What is the seller's position if the bank has lawfully rejected documents tendered under the documentary credit as it found them to contain discrepancies? It seems obvious that, if despite the bank's rejection of the documents, the buyer accepts the goods, he is bound to pay the price. The buyer cannot possibly retain the goods but claim that the bank's right to reject the documents discharges him from his duty to settle the price. The position is more difficult if the buyer uses the bank's rejection of the documents as a ground for the rejection of the goods. In *Shamsher Jute Mills v Sethia (London)*[1559] Bingham J. held that as the seller's inability to obtain the amount of the documentary credit was occasioned by his failure to tender a proper set of documents, he was unable to enforce the contract of sale. His Lordship, thus, treated the seller's failure to bring himself within the terms of the documentary credit as a breach of his duties under the contract of sale. But as the contract of sale and the documentary are deemed to be autonomous of, and unqualified by, each other, it is perhaps arguable that the seller's inability to recover under the documentary credit, due to a formality concerning the regularity of the documents, need not necessarily bar him from seeking a remedy under the contract of sale. The buyer's breach could, for instance, be seen in his refusal to instruct the bank to accept the documents despite the discrepancies. This argument, which would appear not to have been raised in the instant case, derives support from the fact that the opening of the documentary credit does not, in itself, constitute an unconditional discharge of the buyer's duty to pay the price.[1560] That the mutual rights of the seller and buyer are not abrogated by the opening of the credit is demonstrated by *Famouri v Dialcord Ltd*,[1561] in which it was held that the buyer would be entitled to sue the seller in deceit or in breach of contract where it turned out that documents were false or forged.

(iv) The Relationship of Issuing Banker and Buyer

34-494 **The application form** Pursuant to the contract of sale the buyer, in order to procure the issue of the credit, applies to a local banker setting out his requirements. This is usually made upon a standard "application form" provided by the banker and if accepted the details there recorded represent the limits of his authority. The buyer should specify how the credit is to be advised, e.g. by teletransmission, airmail or courier, the duration, extent and revocability or irrevocability of the

---

[1555] *Trans Trust SPRL v Danubian Trading Co Ltd* [1952] 2 Q.B. 297, 306, 307.
[1556] Late Payment of Commercial Debts (Interest) Act 1998; see above, Vol.I, paras 26-187 et seq., 26-277 et seq., 26-281 et seq.
[1557] In pursuance of Senior Courts Act 1981 s.35A.
[1558] On the basis of *Hadley v Baxendale* (1854) 9 Exch. 341; see *Trans Trust SPRL v Danubian Trading Co Ltd* [1952] 2 Q.B. 297; and *Ian Stach Ltd v Baker Bosley Ltd* [1958] 2 Q.B. 130.
[1559] [1987] 1 Lloyd's Rep. 388.
[1560] Above, para.34-490.
[1561] (1983) 13 New L.J. 153.

credit; details of the manner in which shipment and insurance is to be effected; an exact description of the goods; a list of the documents against which the banker is to make payment and the name of the person to whom or to whose order the bill of lading should be addressed. If the seller has nominated a correspondent banker, the issuing banker should be so instructed, for the credit may otherwise be issued directly to the seller or facilities be arranged through channels that may prove unacceptable. The standard form upon which application is made will ordinarily contain a clause entitling the issuing banker to retain the shipping documents as security pending reimbursement by the buyer, and sometimes an acknowledgment that if before reimbursement delivery is made to the buyer of either documents or goods in connection with which the credit is to be issued, the buyer will thereupon execute a trust receipt. Once the extent of the commission and the manner of reimbursement have been agreed the issuing banker will open the credit and thereby enter into separate relations with the seller.

The relations between the buyer and the issuing banker depend solely on the **34-495** terms of the contract between them and are not affected by rights or obligations which either of them has against or owes to other parties.[1562] Thus, if the banker, at the instruction of the buyer, issues an irrevocable credit, then despite any dispute that the buyer may thereafter have with the seller under the contract of sale, the buyer cannot of his own will compel the banker to cancel the credit.[1563] The application form, having been accepted by the banker, is not only final but must be rigidly observed. Whether the terms on which the banker is instructed to make payment may seem reasonable or unreasonable, and whether or not they stem from the contract of sale, the banker's right to reimbursement depends upon a strict and not a liberal interpretation.[1564] However, if the buyer's instructions are ambiguous, the issuing bank is entitled to reimbursement as long as he gives the instructions a reasonable interpretation and acts accordingly.[1565] This principle applies notwithstanding that the relationship between the buyer—the applicant for the credit—and the issuing bank is not purely one of principal and agent.[1566] Naturally, the bank cannot invoke this principle if the ambiguity resulted from a shortcoming in the drafting of a clause in the bank's standard form. Moreover, even where

---

[1562] See *Societe Generale SA v Saad Trading* [2011] EWHC 2424 (Comm), [2011] 2 C.L.C. 629 at [33], where Teare J. confirmed that the relationship between the applicant and the issuing bank was to be found in the facility agreement between them, and in the particular instructions, or mandate, which the former gave the latter to issue the credit, and held that the issuing bank was entitled to an indemnity from the applicant under the terms of the facility agreement. See also *Petrologic Capital SA v Banque Cantonale de Geneve* [2012] EWHC 453 (Comm) at [52]–[56], where S. Males Q.C., sitting as a deputy judge of the High Court, held that the applicant for a letter of credit could not rely on the Contracts (Right of Third Parties) Act 1999 so as to enforce an English law and exclusive jurisdiction clause contained in the letter of credit itself in an action to prevent the issuing bank from performing its obligations under the credit.

[1563] *Sovereign Bank of Canada v Belhouse, Dillon & Co* (1911) 23 Q.R. (K.B.) 413. See also *Kingdom of Sweden v New York Trust Co*, 96 N.Y.S. 2d 779, 791 (1949).

[1564] *Midland Bank Ltd v Seymour* [1955] 2 Lloyd's Rep. 147.

[1565] *Midland Bank Ltd v Seymour*, above, at 153, 168. cf. *European Asian Bank AG v Punjab and Sind Bank (No.2)* [1983] 1 W.L.R. 642, 656, where Goff L.J. suggested that where the ambiguity is patent, the bank ought to ask for a clarification; *Cooper v National Westminster Bank Plc* [2009] EWHC 3035 (QB), [2010] 1 Lloyd's Rep. 490 at [63].

[1566] *Credit Agricole Indosuez v Muslim Commercial Bank Ltd* [2000] 1 Lloyd's Rep. 275.

the bank—as agent—is entitled to invoke the principle under discussion, it must show that it has given the ambiguous instruction a reasonable construction.[1567]

34-496 **Strict adherence to mandate** If the buyer has stipulated the form of any document against which payment is to be made, the banker must at his peril insist upon complete compliance.

> "There is no room for documents which are almost the same, or which will do just as well. Business could not proceed securely on any other lines."[1568]

Applying this principle to the circumstances before the Court of Appeal in *Rayner & Co Ltd v Hambro's Bank Ltd*, Goddard L.J. remarked[1569]:

> "... if the bank wants to be reimbursed by the customer, it must show that it has performed its mandate. If I employ someone at a remuneration to pay money for me on getting a receipt in a particular form, and he pays the money without getting the receipt in that form, he has not carried out the duty which I imposed upon him. It would be no answer for him to say: 'But I got a receipt which in fact gives you all reasonable protection.' My answer to that would be: 'You are not concerned with the protection which you have given me. You are concerned to carry out the orders which I have given you.'"

However, if the buyer, after having come to know of the breach of authority of the issuing banker, adopts his act, he is considered to have ratified the act of the issuing banker and is obliged to reimburse him despite the breach.[1570]

34-497 **Deposit of security** The issuing banker may require funds or securities to be deposited by the buyer before any bills drawn under the credit should fall due. Provided there is sufficient evidence of appropriation,[1571] funds[1572] or securities[1573] so deposited will not go in satisfaction of general creditors of the banker in the event of failure prior to payment but are recoverable in full by the buyer.[1574] The issuing bank may be well advised to obtain security from the buyer (applicant) because the orthodox view is that, as the issuing bank's undertaking under a letter of credit involves a primary obligation and not a secondary one, it does not acquire a right of subrogation to the underlying commercial relationship between buyer and seller (beneficiary).[1575]

34-498 **Exemption clauses** Most application forms include clauses exempting the banker

---

[1567] *Patel v Standard Chartered Bank* [2001] Lloyd's Rep. Bank. 229.

[1568] *Equitable Trust Co of New York v Dawson Partners Ltd* (1927) 27 Ll.L. Rep. 49, 52; *South African Reserve Bank v Samuel & Co* (1931) 40 Ll.L. Rep. 291.

[1569] [1943] K.B. 37, 43. See also UCP 600 art.14.

[1570] *Midland Bank Ltd v Seymour* [1955] 2 Lloyd's Rep. 147. See also *Swotbooks.com Ltd v Royal Bank of Scotland Plc* [2011] EWHC 2025 (QB), [40]–[48] (held no ratification).

[1571] The burden of proof is not easily discharged: see *Re Barned's Banking Co Ltd, Massey's Case* (1870) 39 L.J. Ch. 635.

[1572] *Farley v Turner* (1857) 26 L.J. Ch. 710.

[1573] *Jombart v Woollett* (1837) 2 My. & C. 389.

[1574] See also S. Connelly, "Bank recovery and resolution: the case of contingent letters of credit under bail-in" [2016] J.I.B.F.L. 78.

[1575] See A. Ward and G. McCormack, "Subrogation and Bankers' Autonomous Undertakings" (2000) 116 L.Q.R. 121. The issue is touched upon, but without decision, by Vos J. in *Ibrahim v Barclays Bank Plc* [2011] EWHC 1897 (Ch), [2011] 2 C.L.C. 589 at [136]–[137]: there were no issues about subrogation on appeal, although Lewison L.J. stated (following citation of McCormack and Ward at 136) that it was "received wisdom that when an issuing bank honours a letter of credit its payment will discharge the obligation that gave rise to the need for the letter of credit" ([2012] EWCA

from responsibility for matters which are not in his control. In fact, even in the absence of an express exemption clause, an issuing banker is not responsible if it turns out that an apparently regular document, accepted by him from the seller, has been forged or obtained by fraud.[1576] At present, most exemption clauses are set out in UCP 600, which, as mentioned above, are incorporated in the contract between the buyer and the issuing banker. Article 14(a) specifies that bankers must examine documents tendered under a documentary credit to ascertain that they appear on their face to be in accordance with the terms of the credit; documents which appear on their face to be inconsistent with one another will be considered as non-complying.[1577] It is clear that the banker is not responsible if he fails to notice a defect that a prudent inspection would not disclose. Article 5 specifies that the banker is concerned solely with the documents and not with the goods. The issuing banker is, thus, not responsible if, despite the conformity of the documents, the goods are faulty. Article 34 provides that the banker does not assume any responsibility for the genuineness, sufficiency, accuracy and legal effect of any document. Article 35 provides that the banker assumes no responsibility for the consequences arising out of the delay or loss in transit of a message as well as for loss arising out of errors in the translation or decoding of messages. Under art.36 the banker is not responsible for any loss occurring due to the interruption of his business by strikes, riots, wars, acts of God and other causes beyond his control. Article 37 provides that if the issuing banker utilises the services of a correspondent banker, he does so at the risk of the buyer and assumes no liability, should the instructions transmitted to the correspondent banker not be carried out.[1578] Under art.37(d), the applicant for the credit—the buyer—is bound and liable to indemnify the banks against all obligations and responsibilities imposed by foreign laws and usages. It is to be doubted that the application of these articles is affected by the Unfair Contract Terms Act 1977 as the articles appear to satisfy the reasonableness tests laid down in s.11 of the Act.[1579]

(v)   The Relationship of Banker and Seller

Nature and form   In the case of a revocable credit the seller does not obtain a   **34-499**
binding promise of the issuing banker, and the credit may be revoked at any time prior to the acceptance of documents by the issuing banker. An irrevocable credit, on the other hand, creates a legally binding contract between the banker and the seller. If the credit is irrevocable but unconfirmed the contract is between the seller

---

Civ 640, [2012] 2 B.C.L.C. 1 at [59]).
[1576] *Woods v Thiedemann* (1862) 1 H. & C. 478; *Ulster Bank v Synnott* (1871) 5 Ir. R. Eq. 595; *Basse and Selve v Bank of Australasia* (1904) 90 L.T. 618; *Guaranty Trust Co of New York v Hannay & Co* [1918] 2 K.B. 623.
[1577] UCP 600 art.14(d). And see *National Bank of Egypt v Hannevig's Bank Ltd* (1919) 1 Ll.L. Rep. 69; *Legal Decisions Affecting Bankers*, Vol.III, pp.211, 213. See also *British Imex Industries Ltd v Midland Bank Ltd* [1958] 1 Q.B. 542, 552; *Singh & Co v Banque de L'Indochine* [1974] 1 Lloyd's Rep. 56, 60–61; affirmed [1974] 2 Lloyd's Rep. 1.
[1578] As regards the position where the UCP do not apply, see *Equitable Trust Co of New York v Dawson Partners Ltd* (1926) 27 Ll. L. Rep. 49. But art.37 does not preclude the buyer from disputing the regularity of documents taken up by the issuer's correspondent: *Credit Agricole Indosuez v Generale Bank (No.2)* [2000] 1 Lloyd's Rep. 123 (distinguished in *Societe Generale SA v Saad Trading* [2011] EWHC 2424 (Comm), [2011] 2 C.L.C. 629 at [49]–[53], on basis that documents when presented were compliant and not discrepant, so issuing bank could rely on reimbursement clause against applicant on basis that it had mistakenly indemnified confirming bank "in good faith").
[1579] See generally Vol.I, paras 15-062 et seq., especially para.15-096.

and the issuing banker. If the credit is both irrevocable and confirmed, the correspondent banker is jointly bound with the issuing banker towards the seller.[1580] A commercial credit, whether revocable or irrevocable, need not be in any specified form, but, in fact, most current forms follow a uniform pattern. It is at the outset both dated and numbered, and clearly sets out its duration and the amount of cover provided. It is addressed to the seller and states that, on the instructions of the buyer, the banker authorises the seller to draw bills of exchange up to the stated amount. There then follows the list of the documents which are to accompany the bill upon presentation and to be surrendered upon acceptance or payment. The letter of credit specifies the manner in which the documents are to be made out and the shipments to which they are to relate. The letter concludes with the undertaking to honour all bills of exchange drawn within the terms of the credit, provided that they bear on their face the number and date of the credit to enable identification.

34-500   Theoretical analysis   UCP 600 provides that the issuing bank becomes irrevocably bound to honour the credit as of the time it issues the credit,[1581] and that the confirming bank becomes irrevocably bound to honour or negotiate the credit as of the time it adds its confirmation to the credit.[1582] Each bank becomes contractually bound to the seller at these respective times. But it is far from clear as to what, if any, consideration is provided by the seller for these contractual promises. There have been a number of theories advanced to find the necessary consideration. It has been argued, for example, that consideration for the credit is the seller's agreement to present shipping documents to the bank or, alternatively, that the credit becomes binding as a result of the seller's reliance on it. However, none of these theories stand up to close scrutiny.[1583] There are flaws in the two theories highlighted above.[1584] First, the seller makes no promise to the bank to produce the shipping documents. Secondly, the idea that reliance by the seller makes the bank's promise binding is irreconcilable with the commercial understanding of the credit as irrevocable from the moment that it is issued. The enactment of the Contracts (Rights of Third Parties) Act 1999, which allows third parties (the beneficiary under the credit) to enforce rights conferred on them in other peoples' contracts (the contract between the applicant and the issuing bank), does not take the matter any further.[1585] Article 4(a) of UCP 600 provides that the beneficiary cannot avail himself of the contract between the banks, or between the applicant and the issuing bank, and this would effectively exclude the operation of the Act.[1586]

34-501   Mercantile usage   The best explanation of the legal nature of an irrevocable credit is based on regarding it as established by a mercantile usage recognised all over the

---

[1580] See above, para.34-478.

[1581] UCP 600 art.7(b).

[1582] UCP 600 art.8(b).

[1583] See R.M. Goode, "Abstract Payment Undertakings", Ch.9 of P. Cane and J. Stapleton (eds), *Essays for Patrick Atiyah* (1991), p.218.

[1584] Goode, as above, p.218.

[1585] M.A. Clarke, R.J.A. Hooley, R.J.C. Munday, L.S. Sealy, A.M. Tettenborn and P.G. Turner, *Commercial Law: Text, Cases and Materials*, 5th edn (2017), p.772.

[1586] M.A. Clarke, R.J.A. Hooley, R.J.C. Munday, L.S. Sealy, A.M. Tettenborn and P.G. Turner, *Commercial Law: Text, Cases and Materials*, 5th edn (2017), p.772; relying on the Contracts (Rights of Third Parties) Act 1999 s.1(2). See also *Petrologic Capital SA v Banque Cantonale de Geneve* [2012] EWHC 453 (Comm) at [52]–[56] (applicant for letter of credit held unable to rely on the Contracts (Right of Third Parties) Act 1999 to enforce English law and exclusive jurisdiction clause contained in the credit in an action to prevent the issuing bank from performing its obligations under the credit).

world. This explanation derives support from an observation of Jenkins L.J. in *Hamzeh Malas & Sons v British Imex Industries Ltd*[1587]:

> "[T]he opening of a confirmed letter of credit constitutes a bargain between the banker and the vendor of the goods, which imposes upon the banker an absolute obligation to pay ... An elaborate commercial system has been built up on the footing that bankers' confirmed credits are of that character, and, in my judgment, it would be wrong for this court in the present case to interfere with that established practice."[1588]

This decision further intimates that arguments assailing the validity of irrevocable credits will meet with little sympathy from the courts.[1589]

The autonomy of an irrevocable credit An irrevocable credit constitutes an independent contract between the issuing banker and the seller, and is not qualified by or subject to the terms of the contract of sale, made between the buyer and the seller,[1590] or the contract between the issuing banker and the buyer.[1591] It can be enforced by the seller even if the issuer is a foreign central bank. A plea of sovereignty on such an issuer's part is untenable.[1592] The autonomy of the issuing bank's undertaking is most clearly declared in art.4(a) of the UCP, but it has been well established in England for several decades.[1593] Thus, the buyer cannot enjoin the issuing bank from honouring a draft presented by the seller and accompanied

34-502

[1587] [1958] 2 Q.B. 127, 129. See also *International Banking Corp v Barclays Bank Ltd* (1925) 5 Legal Decisions Affecting Bankers 1, 4.

[1588] See also Kerr J. in *RD Harbottle Mercantile Ltd v National Westminster Bank Ltd* [1987] 1 Q.B. 146, 155–156; *Centi Force Engineering v Bank of Scotland*, *The Times*, December 23, 1992.

[1589] As, e.g., in *Taurus Petroleum Ltd v State Oil Company of the Ministry of Oil, Republic of Iraq* [2017] UKSC 64 at [25], [95], [100].

[1590] *Urquhart Lindsay & Co Ltd v Eastern Bank Ltd* [1922] 1 K.B. 318, 322–323.

[1591] The autonomy principle is not offended where the issuing bank exercises a right of set-off against the sum due to the beneficiary under the letter of credit: see, e.g. *Hong Kong and Shanghai Banking Corp v Kloekner & Co AG* [1990] 2 Q.B. 514; *Safa v Banque du Caire* [2000] 2 Lloyd's Rep. 600; *Lehman Brothers Commodity Services Inc v Credit Agricole Corporate and Investment Bank* [2011] EWHC 1390 (Comm), [2012] 1 All E.R. (Comm) 254 (issuing bank entitled to set-off sums owed to it under a separate, pre-existing ISDA Master Agreement, against sums owed by it to beneficiary under letter of credit).

[1592] *Trendtex Trading Corp v Central Bank of Nigeria* [1978] Q.B. 529, *Hispano Americana Mercantil SA v Central Bank of Nigeria* [1979] 2 Lloyd's Rep. 277, which also interprets the State Immunity Act 1978 s.3(3)(b). See also *Banca Carige SpA Casa di Risparmio di Genova e Imperio v Banco Nacional de Cuba* [2001] 1 W.L.R. 2039.

[1593] *Urquhart Lindsay & Co Ltd v Eastern Bank Ltd* [1922] 1 K.B. 318; *Hamzeh Malas & Sons v British Imex Industries Ltd* [1958] 2 Q.B. 127; *United City Merchants (Investments) Ltd v Royal Bank of Canada* [1983] A.C. 168; *Power Curber International Ltd v National Bank of Kuwait* [1981] 2 Lloyd's Rep. 394, 397. See also *RD Harbottle (Mercantile) Ltd v National Westminster Bank Ltd* [1978] 1 Q.B 146; *Edward Owen Engineering Ltd v Barclays Bank International Ltd* [1978] Q.B. 159; *Howe Richardson Scale Co Ltd v Polimex-Cekop* [1978] 1 Lloyd's Rep. 161; *Bolivinter Oil SA v Chase Manhattan Bank NA* [1984] 1 W.L.R. 392; *Turkiye Is Bankasi AS v Bank of China* [1998] 1 Lloyd's Rep. 250; *Petrologic Capital SA v Banque Cantonale de Geneve* [2012] EWHC 453 (Comm) at [56]; *National Infrastructure Development Co Ltd v BNP Paribas* [2016] EWHC 2508 (Comm) at [12]; *Petrosaudi Oil Services (Venezuela) Ltd v Novo Banco SA* [2017] EWCA Civ 9 at [55]; *Taurus Petroleum Ltd v State Oil Marketing Company of the Ministry of Oil, Republic of Iraq* [2017] UKSC 64 at [73], [84]. But the autonomy principle does not preclude looking at the terms of the credit to see what it is that the bank is paying: *Ibrahim v Barclays Bank Plc* [2012] EWCA Civ 640, [2012] 2 B.C.L.C. 1 at [61]. In the case of performance guarantees, the application of the autonomy doctrine depends on whether the document is a traditional or a first demand guarantee: see *Gold Coast Ltd v Caja de Ahorros del Mediterraneo* [2001] EWCA Civ 1806, [2002] 1 Lloyd's Rep. 617; *Marubeni Hong Kong & South China Ltd v The Government of Mongolia* [2005] EWCA

by the required documents merely because the seller has failed to perform his contract with the buyer, e.g. by supplying goods of an inferior quality.[1594] The autonomy of the bank's undertaking is considered to be of such importance that an English court will be prepared to uphold it, provided the credit is available in England, even if a foreign court has granted the buyer an injunction.[1595] There are only two exceptions to the autonomy doctrine.[1596]

Civ 395, [2005] 2 All E.R. (Comm) 289; *Uzinterimpex JSC v Standard Bank Plc* [2008] EWCA Civ 819, [2008] 2 Lloyd's Rep. 456; *Wuhan Guoyu Logistics Group Co v Emporiki Bank of Greece SA* [2012] EWCA Civ 1629, [2013] 1 All E.R. (Comm) 1191.

[1594] *Hamzeh Malas & Sons v British Imex Industries Ltd*, above. However, Andrew Smith J. has held in *Oliver v Dubai Bank Kenya Ltd* [2007] EWHC 2165 (Comm) that the autonomy principle was not infringed where a standby credit required presentation of a telex issued by the same bank that had issued the credit confirming that the beneficiary had fulfilled its commitments set out in the underlying contract, thereby giving that bank sole power to prevent the credit from becoming payable. He held (at [13]) that the requirement of the confirming telex did not offend the autonomy principle as the bank did not seek to rely upon any claims or defences which the applicant might have had.

[1595] *Power Curber International Ltd v National Bank of Kuwait* [1981] 2 Lloyd's Rep. 394; *National Infrastructure Development Co Ltd v Banco Santander SA* [2017] EWCA Civ 27 at [45]; *National Infrastructure Development Co Ltd v BNP Paribas* [2016] EWHC 2508 (Comm) at [17]. For detailed discussion of jurisdictional issues and the governing law of letters of credits, see M. Brindle and R. Cox (eds), *Law of Bank Payments*, 5th edn (2018), paras 8-123 et seq. In *Taurus Petroleum Ltd v State Oil Marketing Company of the Ministry of Oil, Republic of Iraq* [2017] UKSC 64 at [31]–[32], [60], [72], [83], [124]–[125], the Supreme Court held (unanimously), overturning *Power Curber* on the point, that the general rule that the situs of a debt is the debtor's residence (i.e. the place where the debt is recoverable) applies to letters of credit: for a credit issued by the London branch of an overseas bank, when the credit incorporated UCP 600 (art.3 of which provides that "[b]ranches of a bank in different countries are to be considered as separate banks"), the situs of the debt due under the credit was London, thereby making the debt susceptible to a third party debt order made by an English court.

[1596] For a possible further exception, see below, para.34-509. For the tendency to construe a bank's irrevocable undertaking, such a cumbersomely phrased performance bond, as autonomous, see *Siporex Trade SA v Banque Indosuez* [1986] 2 Lloyd's Rep. 146. In *Wuhan Guoyu Logistics Group Co v Emporiki Bank of Greece SA* [2012] EWCA Civ 1629, [2013] 1 All E.R. (Comm) 1191, Longmore L.J. (with the agreement of Rimer and Tomlinson L.JJ.) tried to find some consistency of approach when deciding whether a document was a suretyship guarantee or an autonomous "on demand" guarantee. He said (at [25]) that "while everything must in the end depend on the words actually used by the parties, there is nevertheless a presumption that, if certain elements are present in the document, the document will be construed in one way or the other". He cited and approved (at [26]) of the analysis in *Paget's Law of Banking*, 11th edn (1996), and now contained in almost identical words in the 14th edition (2014), para.34.8, which provides that: "where an instrument (i) relates to an underlying transaction between the parties in different jurisdictions, (ii) is issued by a bank, (iii) contains an undertaking to pay 'on demand' (with or without the words 'first' and/or 'written'); and (iv) does not contain clauses excluding or limiting the defences available to a guarantor, it will almost always be construed as a demand guarantee." It should be noted, however, that the Court of Appeal held that the instrument in this case was an "on demand" guarantee despite the fact that the fourth element of the presumption was absent. The same result followed in *Spliethoff's Bevrachtingskantoor BV v Bank of China Ltd* [2015] EWHC 999 (Comm) at [71] and [81], *Caterpillar Motoren GmbH and Co KG v Mutual Benefits Assurance Co* [2015] EWHC 2304 (Comm) at [21] and [27]; *South Lanarkshire Council v Aviva Insurance Ltd* [2016] CSOH 83 at [26] (Outer House of Court of Session) and *Bitumen Invest AS v Richmond Mercantile Ltd FZC* [2016] EWHC 2957 (Comm) at [31]. The presumption that an instrument gives rise to independent, primary liability seems to apply "[w]here ... the granter is a bank or other financial institution whose business includes the granting of financial instruments for a fee", e.g. an insurance company: *South Lanarkshire Council v Aviva Insurance Ltd*, above, at [25], per Lord Doherty, citing *Meritz Fire & Marine Insurance Co Ltd v Jan de Nul NV* [2010] EWHC 3362 (Comm), [2011] 1 All E.R. (Comm) 1049 at [65]–[66], per Beatson J.; *Caterpillar Motoren GmbH & Co KG v Mutual Benefits Assurance Co*, above, at [20], per Teare J.; *Spliethoff's Bevrachtingskantoor BV v Bank of China Ltd*, above, at [83], per Carr J.

Illegality The first arises in cases in which the transaction is tainted with illegality. **34-503**
Thus, if a letter of credit infringes the exchange control provisions of a country
which is a member of the International Monetary Fund Treaty, an English court
would refuse to enforce the credit in view of the Bretton-Woods Agreement Order
in Council 1946.[1597] But the respective contravention does not necessarily vitiate the
letter of credit *in toto*. The court will enforce payment of any part of the amount of
the credit which is unaffected by and hence lawfully due notwithstanding the
exchange control contravention.[1598] The illegality exception to the autonomy
doctrine is not confined to cases where payment of the credit infringes exchange
control provisions.[1599] In *Group Josi Re v Walbrook Insurance Co Ltd*,[1600] Staughton
L.J. expressed the view that a court would restrain a bank from paying under a letter of credit that was being used as a means of payment of an illegal arms sale, at
least where the illegality was clearly established and known to the bank. More
recently, in *Mahonia Ltd v JP Morgan Chase Bank*,[1601] Colman J. refused to strike
out an illegality defence to enforcement of a letter of credit where the underlying
contract was alleged to have been made for an illegal purpose, namely the
contravention of US Securities law.

The fraud rule The most important exception to the autonomy doctrine is where **34-504**
there is fraud on the part of the seller (the beneficiary of the credit), or his agent,

---

See also *Wuhan Guoyu Logistics Group Co Ltd v Emporiki Bank of Greece SA* [2013] EWCA Civ
1679, [2014] 1 Lloyd's Rep. 273, where it was held that money paid by bank to beneficiary under
the "on demand" guarantee was not held in trust for bank when, between beneficiary making demand
in good faith and payment being made to beneficiary, it had been conclusively determined by a final
arbitration award that the event which triggered demand had not in fact fallen due. In *Marubeni Hong
Kong & South China Ltd v The Government of Mongolia* [2005] EWCA Civ 395, [2005] 2 All E.R.
(Comm) 289 at [28], Carnwath L.J. said that cases where documents are issued by banks which are
"described as, or assumed to be, performance bonds ... provide no useful analogy for interpreting
a document which was not issued by a bank and which contains no overt indication of an intention
to create a performance bond or anything analogous to it". But the presumption that an instrument
issued by a non-bank party does not give rise to independent primary liability may be rebutted by
the clear language of the instrument itself, as in *IIG Capital LLC v Van Der Merwe* [2008] EWCA
Civ 542, [2008] 2 Lloyd's Rep. 187; *Meritz Fire & Marine Insurance Co Ltd v Jan de Nul NV*, above,
affirmed [2011] EWCA Civ 827, [2011] 2 Lloyd's Rep. 379; *ABM Amro Commercial Financed Plc
v McGinn* [2014] EWHC 1674 (Comm); *Caterpillar Motoren GmbH and Co KG v Mutual Benefits
Assurance Co*, above; *Bitumen Invest AS v Richmond Mercantile Ltd FZC*, above; *Ultrabulk AS v
Jagatramka* [2017] EWHC 2792 (Comm); *Multiplex Construction Europe Ltd v Dunne* [2017]
EWHC 3073 (TCC). For cases where the presumption was not rebutted, see *Vossloh Aktiengesells-
chaft v Alpha Trains (UK) Ltd* [2010] EWHC 2443 (Ch), [2011] 2 All E.R. (Comm) 307; *Carey Value
Added SL v Grupo Urvasco SA* [2010] EWHC 1905 (Comm), [2011] 2 All E.R. (Comm) 140; *North
Shore Ventures Ltd v Anstead Holdings Inc* [2011] EWCA Civ 230, [2011] 3 W.L.R. 628; *Autoridad
del Canal de Panama v Sacyr SA* [2017] EWHC 2228 (Comm).

[1597] Pt I art.8.

[1598] *United City Merchants (Investments) Ltd v Royal Bank of Canada* [1983] A.C. 168, affirming on this
point [1981] 1 Lloyd's Rep. 604, in which the Court of Appeal varied the conclusion of Mocatta J.
([1979] 2 Lloyd's Rep. 498), who thought the illegality in the underlying transaction vitiated the letter of credit in toto. As to effect of orders invalidating facilities in the place of issue, see *Shanning
International Ltd v Lloyds TSB Bank Plc* [2001] UKHL 31, [2001] 1 W.L.R. 1462.

[1599] See N. Enonchong, "The autonomy principle of letters of credit: an illegality exception?" [2006]
L.M.C.L.Q. 404. See generally, N. Enonchong, *The Independence Principle of Letters of Credit and
Demand Guarantees* (2011), Ch.8.

[1600] [1996] 1 W.L.R. 1152.

[1601] [2003] EWHC 1927 (Comm), [2003] 2 Lloyd's Rep. 911. It was later held at the trial of the action
that there was no illegality which affected the transaction: *Mahonia Ltd v JP Morgan Chase Bank*
[2004] EWHC 1938 (Comm).

in relation to the presentation of the documents.[1602] In *United City Merchants (Investments) Ltd v Royal Bank of Canada, (The American Accord)*, Lord Diplock said that the fraud exception arose[1603]:

"... where the seller, for the purposes of drawing on the credit, fraudulently presents to the confirming bank documents that contain, expressly or by implication, material representations of fact that to his knowledge are untrue."

However, if the fraud is that of an independent third party, as it was in the *United City Merchants* case, where the fraudulent ante-dating of a bill of lading was carried out by the loading brokers—who were the carrier's, and not the seller's, agents—then the seller can still enforce the credit, so long as he is unaware of the fraud at the time of presentation. Moreover, there is no separate exception to the autonomy doctrine that applies simply because the tendered document is a "nullity" in the sense that it is a forgery or executed without the authority of the person by whom it purports to be issued.[1604]

34-505 **Obtaining an injunction against a bank**   Even where the alleged fraud can be brought home to the seller, an injunction will be granted only if there is clear proof to support that it has taken place.[1605] A court will not readily intervene to stop payment under an irrevocable letter of credit because, as Kerr J. famously stated in *RD Harbottle (Mercantile) Ltd v National Westminster Bank Ltd*, irrevocable obliga-

---

[1602] See *Benjamin's Sale of Goods*, 10th edn (2017), paras 24-022 et seq.

[1603] [1983] 1 A.C. 168, 183. In *Sinocore International Co Ltd v RBRG Ltd* [2017] EWHC 251 (Comm) at [46], Phillips J. held that the authorities do not support a much wider proposition that a party who presents forged documents cannot obtain relief from the court in the transaction more generally, e.g. a claim for damages for a prior breach of the underlying contract.

[1604] *Montrod Ltd v Grundkotter Fleischvertriebs GmbH* [2001] All E.R. (Comm) 368; affirmed [2001] EWCA Civ 1954, [2002] 1 W.L.R. 1975. For a critique, see Hooley [2002] C.L.J. 279. The Singapore Court of Appeal has since recognised a separate "nullity" defence: *Beam Technology (Mfg) Pte Ltd v Standard Chartered Bank* [2003] 1 S.L.R. 597, noted by Chin and Wong [2004] L.M.C.L.Q. 14. See also K. Donnelly [2008] J.B.L. 316; P. Todd [2008] L.M.C.L.Q. 547; J. Ren [2015] J.B.L. 1.

[1605] Note that fraud in this context refers to common law fraud, namely deceit: *GKN Contractors Ltd v Lloyds Bank Plc* (1985) 30 Build. L.R. 48. See further on the meaning of fraud, as explained in the context of performance bonds, *Edward Owen Engineering Ltd v Barclays Bank International Ltd* [1978] 1 Lloyd's Rep. 166, 171, 172–173; *Bolivinter Oil SA v Chase Manhattan Bank NA* [1984] 1 W.L.R. 392; *Esal (Commodities) Ltd v Oriental Credit Ltd* [1985] 2 Lloyd's Rep. 546, 549; *Balfour Beatty Civil Engineering v Technical & General Guarantee Co Ltd* (1999) 68 Con. L.R. 180 at 190–191; *TTI Team Telecom International Ltd v Hutchison 3G UK Ltd* [2003] EWHC 762 (TCC), [2003] 1 All E.R. (Comm) 914. In *Enka Insaat Ve Sanayi AS v Banca Popolare dell'Alto Adige SpA* [2009] EWHC 2410 (Comm), [2009] C.I.L.L. 2777 at [24]–[25], the test applied by Teare J., when deciding whether to give summary judgment against a bank on a demand guarantee, was whether there was a real prospect that the bank would establish at trial that the only realistic inference was that the beneficiary did not honestly believe in the validity of its demand. In *National Infrastructure Development Co Ltd v Banco Santander SA* [2017] EWCA Civ 27 at [20]–[24], *Enka* was said to provide the correct approach where the beneficiary of a letter of credit seeks summary judgment against a bank, and that the position was different from those cases where the bank's own customer was seeking an interlocutory injunction against the bank (as in *Solo Industries UK Ltd v Canara Bank* [2001] 1 W.L.R. 1800 and *Alternative Power Solution Ltd v Central Electricity Board* [2014] UKPC 31, [2015] 1 W.L.R. 697: see main paragraph). See also N. Enonchong, "The problem of abusive calls on demand guarantees" [2007] L.M.C.L.Q. 83. Mere suspicions of a fraud do not justify the rejection of a regular set of documents: *Society of Lloyd's v Canadian Imperial Bank of Commerce* [1993] 2 Lloyd's Rep. 579.

tions assumed by banks are the life-blood of international commerce.[1606] An injunction should only be granted to restrain a bank from paying under a letter of credit where the fraud exception applies and the bank is aware of the fraud. Evidence must be clear, both as to the fact of fraud and as to the bank's knowledge.[1607] In *United Trading Corp v Allied Arab Bank Ltd*, Ackner L.J. stated that, in order to obtain an interlocutory injunction, the claimant had to establish that it is seriously arguable that, on the material available, "the only realistic inference is that the [beneficiary] could not honestly have believed in the validity of its demands on the performance bonds".[1608] This test sets a lower standard of proof at the pre-trial hearing than at the full trial, but it was later stressed by Rix J., in *Czarnikow-Rionda Sugar Trading Inc v Standard Bank London Ltd*, that this places on the court "an additional requirement to be careful in its discretion not to upset what is in effect a strong presumption in favour of the fulfilment of the independent banking commitments".[1609] The approach taken by Rix J. was later endorsed Mance L.J. in *Solo Industries UK Ltd v Canara Bank.*[1610] In *Alternative Power Solution Ltd v Central Electricity Board*, Lord Clarke, delivering the judgment of the Board of the Privy Council, agreed with the reasoning of Rix J. and Mance L.J., and continued[1611]:

> "It recognises that the test cannot be quite the same as at a trial and that the test at the interlocutory stage can properly be described as Ackner L.J. described it, namely whether it is seriously arguable that, on the material available, 'the only realistic inference is that [the beneficiary] could not honestly have believed in the validity of its demands on the performance bonds' and that the bank was aware of the fact. In the view of the Board the expression 'seriously arguable' is intended to be a significantly more stringent test than good arguable case, let alone serious issue to be tried. As Mance L.J. put it, a case of established fraud known to the bank, is, by its nature, one which, if it is good at all, must be capable of being established with clarity at the interlocutory stage. In summary, the Board concludes that it must be clearly established at the interlocutory stage that the only realistic inference is (a) that the beneficiary could not honestly have believed in the validity of its demands under the letter of credit and (b) that the bank was aware of the fraud."

The Board also accepted that[1612]:

> "… the reasons why reported cases of injunctions being granted (or continued) under the fraud exception are so rare are (a) because it is almost never possible to establish the test

---

[1606] [1978] Q.B. 146, 155; approved by Lord Denning M.R. in *Edward Owen Engineering Ltd v Barclays Bank international Ltd* [1978] Q.B. 159, 169.

[1607] *Bolivinter Oil SA v Chase Manhattan Bank NA* [1984] 1 W.L.R. 392, 393 (Sir John Donaldson M.R. was considering the position at the interlocutory stage).

[1608] [1985] 2 Lloyd's Rep. 554, 561.

[1609] [1999] 2 Lloyd's Rep. 187, 202.

[1610] [2001] 1 W.L.R. 1800 at [32].

[1611] [2014] UKPC 31, [2015] 1 W.L.R. 697 at [59] (Lord Mance was a member of the Board). The same standard of proof of fraud is required whether the injunction is sought against the bank or the beneficiary: see *Dong Jin Metal Co Ltd v Raymet Ltd* Unreported July 13, 1993, CA; *Deutsche Ruckversicherung AG v Walbrook Insurance Co Ltd* [1995] 1 W.L.R. 1017, 1030–1031; *Group Josi Re v Walbrook Insurance Co Ltd* [1996] 1 W.L.R. 1152, 1161–1162; *Czarnikow-Rionda Sugar Trading Inc v Standard Bank London Ltd* [1999] 2 Lloyd's Rep. 187, 190; *Solo Industries UK Ltd v Canara Bank* [2001] EWCA Civ 1059, [2001] 1 W.L.R. 1800 at [31]; *Simon Carves Ltd v Ensus UK Ltd* [2011] EWHC 657 (TCC), [2011] B.L.R. 340 at [29], [33(b)]; cf. *Themehelp Ltd v West* [1996] Q.B. 84. See generally, *Benjamin's Sale of Goods*, 10th edn (2017), para.24-034. See also below, paras 34-508 et seq.

[1612] At [79].

for fraud as opposed to a mere possibility of fraud, but also (b) because the balance of convenience will almost always militate against the grant of an injunction."

The Board stated[1613] that it agreed with Kerr J. in *RD Harbottle (Mercantile) Ltd v National Westminster Bank*, who said that the balance of convenience issue faced the applicant with an "insuperable difficulty",[1614] and also with Rix J. in the *Czarnikow-Rionda* case, who did not regard Kerr J. as necessarily saying that it could never be done, but added "that it would of necessity take extraordinary facts to surmount this difficulty".[1615]

34-506 **Tender by third party** A direct result of the multi-national character of the documentary credit transaction is that usually the forged documents are tendered to the issuing bank not by the seller, who is the beneficiary of the credit, but by an innocent third party such as a negotiating or discounting bank. In *Discount Records Ltd v Barclays Bank Ltd*[1616] Megarry J. held that the fraud principle could not be invoked against such a third party, as a holder in due course of the bill of exchange ought not to be enjoined from enforcing the credit by reason of the seller's fraud. The difficulty with this view is that a bill of exchange drawn under a documentary credit does not bear the issuing bank's acceptance at the time of its tender. For this reason it cannot confer any rights against the bank on the holder thereof. His being a holder in due course would therefore appear to be immaterial. It is true that, in the case of a negotiation credit,[1617] the holder of the bill may claim to be the promisee of the bank's undertaking in the letter of credit. He may therefore seek to enforce this promise rather than the bill of exchange.[1618] But, even so, it is to be doubted that the bank's undertaking involves a promise to accept documents which are forged or fraudulent and hence ineffective. In the case of a straight credit, in which the bank's promise is addressed to the beneficiary alone, it is even more strongly arguable that the third party should not be regarded as being in a better position than the beneficiary. Undoubtedly, both the beneficiary and a third party such as a negotiating bank are protected against a misuse of the fraud rule by its main limitation which is that, to invoke it, it is necessary to establish the occur-

---

[1613] At [81].

[1614] [1978] Q.B. 146, 155.

[1615] [1999] 2 Lloyd's Rep. 187, 202–204 (and, in particular, his conclusion at point (11)). See also *Tetronics (International) Ltd v HSBC Bank Plc* [2018] EWHC 201 (TCC) at [69] (balance of convenience means "such relief is extremely rare"). For an exceptional case where an injunction was granted, see *Kvaerner John Brown Ltd v Midland Bank Plc* [1998] C.L.C. 446, without consideration of the balance of convenience, thereby rendering the decision of doubtful authority.

[1616] [1975] 1 W.L.R. 315. See also *Hamzeh Malas & Sons v British Imex Industries Ltd* [1958] 2 Q.B. 127, at 130; and *European Asian Bank AG v Punjab and Sind Bank (No.2)* [1983] 1 W.L.R. 642, 645, suggesting that whether a third party is to be regarded an agent for collection or a holder depends on his position at the time of the tender. Contrast the position when it is alleged that a third party can enforce the credit as an undisclosed principal: see *Taurus Petroleum Ltd v State Oil Marketing Company of the Ministry of Oil, Republic of Iraq* [2013] EWHC 3494 (Comm), [2014] 1 Lloyd's Rep. 432 at [21], Field J. (obiter): the issue was not addressed by either the Court of Appeal [2015] EWCA Civ 835 or the Supreme Court [2017] UKSC 64.

[1617] As regards such credits, see above, para.34-479.

[1618] In *DCD Factors Plc v Ramada Trading Ltd* [2007] EWHC 2820 (QB), [2008] Bus. L.R. 654, Lloyd Jones J. held (at [32]) that it was artificial to inquire whether payment was sought under the bill of exchange or letter of credit when they formed different elements of one substantial transaction amounting to the negotiation of a negotiation credit.

rence of forgery or of fraud.[1619] It seems that this principle applies even if the injunction is sought only as against the beneficiary. In *Deutsche Rückversicherung AG v Walbrook Insurance Co Ltd*[1620] Phillips J. held that an injunction restraining the beneficiary from making a call under the credit would be granted only to the extent that it was also to be available as an order precluding the bank from making payment.

Banco Santander   The points just made are echoed in *Banco Santander SA v Bank Paribas*,[1621] which involved a deferred payment credit. A fraud respecting the documents came to light after the acceptance of the tender but before the date on which payment was due. The issuing bank refused to pay whereupon the negotiating bank instituted an action for the amount of the credit relying on its position as the beneficiary's assignee. The Court of Appeal held that the negotiating bank's right was subject to the equities available against the "assignor" and that, accordingly, that bank was not entitled to payment against the fraudulent documents.[1622] But their Lordship indicated that, if the negotiating bank had brought the action in its own rights—that is, as a negotiation bank—the fraud in the documents could not be asserted against it. Naturally, the bank would be entitled to sue in its own name only if the letter of credit sanctioned negotiation or—in other words—constituted a negotiation credit and provided that the "negotiation"[1623] of the documents could be established.

34-507

Restrictions on beneficiary's right to call for payment   In *Sirius International Insurance Corp (Publ) v FAI General Insurance Co Ltd*,[1624] the Court of Appeal held that the principle of autonomy did not mean that a beneficiary could draw on a letter of credit when he had expressly agreed not to do so unless certain conditions were satisfied and those conditions had not been met. In this case, the restrictions were contained in a separate agreement made between the beneficiary (Sirius) and the applicant (FAI). May L.J. stated that:

34-508

"... although those restrictions were not terms of the letter of credit, and although the bank would have been obliged and entitled to honour a request to pay which fulfilled its terms, that does not mean that, as between themselves and FAI, Sirius were entitled to draw on

---

[1619] *Discount Records Ltd v Barclays Bank Ltd* [1975] 1 W.L.R. 315.

[1620] [1996] 1 Lloyd's Rep. 345; but contrast as regards performance bonds *Themhelp Ltd v West* [1996] Q.B. 84. In *Armlea Plc v Gov & Co of the Bank of Scotland* Unreported June 4, 2004, where Lord Mackay (at [39]–[43]), sitting in the Outer House of the Court of Session, rejected a submission by a principal that it did not have to plead fraud when seeking an injunction against the bank to restrain payment under a demand guarantee (as opposed to where the bank wanted to avoid making payment, when fraud had to be pleaded). Lord Mackay (at [44]–[46]) also rejected a submission that the fraud exception only applied to demand guarantees involved in international commerce and not to those involved in domestic commerce.

[1621] [2000] Lloyd's Rep. Bank. 165; affirming [1999] 2 All E.R. (Comm) 18.

[1622] But see now UCP 600 arts 7(c), 8(c) and 12(b): and for discussion of whether art.12(b) would have had an effect on the assignment point in the *Santander* decision, see above, para.34-483.

[1623] As to which see above, para.34-479.

[1624] [2003] EWCA Civ 470, [2003] 1 All E.R. (Comm) 865, noted by Hare [2004] C.L.J. 288. For examples of Australian cases to similar effect, see *Selvas Pty Ltd v Hansen Yuncken (SA) Pty Ltd* (1987) 6 Australian Construction Law Rep. 36; *Boral Formwork v Action Motors* [2002] NSWSC 713.

the letter of credit if the express conditions of this underlying agreement were not fulfilled. They were not so entitled."[1625]

The Court of Appeal was also of the opinion that if draw-down was attempted in these circumstances, a court would be likely to grant an injunction restraining the beneficiary from drawing on the letter of credit in breach of express conditions contained in the underlying agreement. It should be noted that fraud was not alleged against Sirius and so the case did not fall within the fraud exception to the autonomy principle. The Court of Appeal held that an express condition of the separate agreement between the parties had not been met and that Sirius were not entitled to the proceeds of the credit. The House of Lords[1626] reversed that decision on the ground that the condition had been satisfied. Their Lordships found it unnecessary to examine arguments about the autonomy principle.

34-509   The *Sirius* case raises important questions about the extent of the autonomy principle. There must be some concern as to how far it undermines the principle and its consequential benefits of commercial certainty. However, the English courts have not shown themselves willing to embrace the wider principle of "unconscionable demand" which has gained judicial support in Singapore.[1627] It is not entirely clear what constitutes unconscionability, although it seems to be something more than unfairness and less than fraud, nor as to the standard of proof required to obtain injunctive relief on this ground.[1628] The uncertainty that this creates is obvious. Nevertheless, there have been dicta in recent English cases which suggests that the previous reluctance to apply a concept of "unconscionability" may not last forever.[1629] The concept might find acceptance in the area of independent guarantees, which merely perform a security function as opposed to being a mode of payment.[1630] In *Simon Carves Ltd v Ensus UK Ltd*,[1631] Akenhead J. granted an injunction restraining a beneficiary from seeking payment under an on-demand performance bond on the ground that the issuing bank had a strong case that, as between it and the beneficiary, the bond was null and void pursuant to the terms of the underlying contract. Akenhead J. said that:

[1625] At [27]. The right to drawdown must be clearly precluded by the express (as in *Sirius*) or implied terms of the underlying contract: *MW High Tech Projects UK Ltd v Biffa Waste Services Ltd* [2015] EWHC 949 (TCC) at [34] (where Stuart-Smith J. refused to imply term that prior call on parent company guarantee, which was a condition of a call on the on-demand retention bond, had to be "valid").

[1626] [2004] UKHL 54, [2004] 1 W.L.R. 3251.

[1627] See, e.g. *Samwoh Asphalt Premix Pte Ltd v Sum Cheong Piling Pte Ltd* [2002] B.L.R. 459; *McConnell Dowell Construction (Aust) Pty Ltd v Semcorp Engineering and Constructions Pte Ltd* [2002] B.L.R. 450; *BS Mount Sophia Pte Ltd v Join-Aim Pte Ltd* [2012] SGCA 28, [2012] 3 S.L.R. 352. See further, P. Ellinger and D. Neo, *The Law and Practice of Documentary Letters of Credit* (2010), pp.319 et seq. (the principle has emerged in Singapore with reference to independent guarantees as distinct from commercial letters of credit). See also Chhina [2016] L.M.C.L.Q. 412. In *National Infrastructure Development Co Ltd v Banco Santander SA* [2016] EWHC 2990 (Comm) (affirmed [2017] EWCA Civ 27), Knowles J. (at [26]–[27]) refused an invitation to develop the law to recognise a different approach to standby letters of credit used to settle performance obligations, as opposed to letters of credit used to settle primary payment obligations, and noted that the position under Singaporean law appeared to be different.

[1628] See Ganotaki [2004] L.M.C.L.Q. 148 at 152.

[1629] See, especially, the dicta of Potter L.J. in *Montrod Ltd v Grundkotter Fleischvertriebs* [2001] EWCA Civ 1954, [2002] 1 All E.R. (Comm) 257 at [59], and that of Judge Thornton Q.C., sitting as a deputy High Court judge, in *TTI Team Telecom International Ltd v Hutchison 3G UK Ltd* [2003] EWHC 762 (TCC), [2003] 1 All E.R. (Comm) 914 at [37].

[1630] See Ellinger and Neo, *The Law and Practice of Documentary Letters of Credit*, above, at p.319.

[1631] [2011] EWHC 657 (TCC), [2011] B.L.R. 340.

"... [i]n principle, if the underlying contract, in relation to which the bond has been provided by way of security, clearly and expressly prevents the beneficiary party to the contract from making a demand under the bond, it can be restrained by the Court from making a demand under the bond."[1632]

Akenhead J. was tentatively of the view, although not deciding the issue, that this constituted a second type of exception (the other being fraud) to the general principle that the court will not act to prevent a beneficiary calling on an on-demand bond.[1633]

Dealings in documents The principle that the commercial credit is not qualified **34-510** by the underlying contract of sale is linked with one further important rule. Article 5 of the UCP provides that in commercial credit transactions the parties deal in documents and not in goods. Thus, insofar as the seller tenders all the required documents, the banker is not entitled to reject them on the ground that the goods are not up to contract.[1634]

Examination of the documents Banks must examine all tendered documents to **34-511** determine, on the basis of the documents alone, whether or not the documents appear on their face to constitute a complying presentation, i.e. whether they constitute a presentation in accordance with the terms and conditions of the credit, the applicable provisions of the UCP and international standard banking practice.[1635] Under UCP 600 art.14(b), the issuing bank, the confirming bank and any other nominated bank acting on its nomination (including an advising bank) each has a maximum of five banking days following the day of presentation to determine if the presentation is complying. UCP 500 was differently worded. UCP 500 art.13(b), gave the bank a reasonable time, not to exceed seven banking days, to examine the documents and make the determination. What was a reasonable time could be a matter of some uncertainty, but it could certainly arise in less than seven banking days.[1636] Where the issuing bank, the confirming bank, or a nominated bank acting on its nomination, decides to refuse to honour or negotiate a credit, it must give a

---

[1632] At [33]. Applied by Edwards-Stuart J. in *Doosan Babcock Ltd v Comercializadora de Equipos y Materiales Mabe Limitada* [2013] EWHC 3201 (TCC), [2014] B.L.R. 33, who said at [36] that Akenhead J.'s judgment "has extended the law, but in my view it has done so adopting a principled and incremental approach that does not undermine the general principles applicable to making a call on a bond". It has been stressed that in order to obtain injunctive relief "it must be positively established that the beneficiary was not entitled to draw down under the underlying contract": *MW High Tech Projects UK Ltd v Biffa Waste Services Ltd* [2015] EWHC 949 (TCC) at [34], per Stuart-Smith J., citing *Permasteelisa Japan KK v Bouyguesstroi and Bank Intesa SpA* [2007] EWHC 3508 (QB), Ramsey J.).

[1633] At [34].

[1634] *Urquhart Lindsay & Co Ltd v Eastern Bank Ltd* [1922] 1 K.B. 318; *Hamzeh Malas & Sons v British Imex Industries Ltd* [1958] 2 Q.B. 127. But see also *Ibrahim v Barclays Bank Plc* [2011] EWHC 1897 (Ch), [2011] 2 C.L.C. 589 at [116] (UCP 600 art.5 did not prevent conditions attached to payment of letter credit providing indication of parties' intentions as to whether payment discharged a third party's debt in complex financial transaction), affirmed [2012] EWCA Civ 640, [2012] 2 B.C.L.C. 1 (Lewison L.J. at [61]: "the autonomy principle does not preclude looking at the terms of the letter of credit to see what it is that the bank is paying").

[1635] UCP 600 art.14(a).

[1636] As to the meaning of "reasonable time", see *Co-operative Centrale Raiffeisen-Borenleenbank BA v Sumitomo Bank Ltd* [1987] Fin. L.R. 275 varied [1988] Fin. L.R. 207; *Bankers Trust Co v State Bank of India* [1991] 2 Lloyd's Rep. 443; affirming [1991] 1 Lloyd's Rep. 587. *Seaconsar Far East Ltd v Bank Markazi Jomhouri Islami Iran* [1997] 2 Lloyd's Rep. 89; affirmed [1999] 1 Lloyd's Rep. 36, CA.

single notice to that effect to the presenter, i.e. the beneficiary, bank or other party that makes a presentation of documents under a credit.[1637] UCP 600 art.16(d), provides that the rejection notice must be given by telecommunication or, if that is not possible, by other expeditious means no later than the close of the fifth banking day following the day of presentation.[1638] The net effect of UCP 600 arts 14(b) and 16(d), seems to be that a bank has a maximum of five banking days following presentation of the documents to determine if the presentation is compliant, but that the longer it takes to make its determination, the less time it has available to it to give a notice of rejection to the applicant.[1639] If the bank fails to comply with the five (banking) day maximum period, it will not have served a proper notice which satisfies art.16(d) and, because of the effect of UCP 600 art.16(f),[1640] will be precluded from claiming that the documents do not comply with the credit.[1641] To avoid the problems resulting from the need of making a conclusive decision of whether to accept or reject the documents, UCP 500 gave the bank the option of paying "under reserve" or "against indemnity".[1642] The option is no longer available under UCP 600, which appears to be due to the bank now having the option to reject the tendered documents pending a waiver of discrepancies from the applicant.[1643]

34-512   **Rejection notice**   The notice of rejection must state the discrepancies in respect of which the document is being rejected. There has been some doubt as to whether a bank would be estopped from later raising further discrepancies not identified in the original rejection notice. The position at common law is that, absent special circumstances raising a true estoppel, the bank will not be prevented from relying upon discrepancies which were not listed in the original rejection notice.[1644] But the position was thought to be different under the UCP.[1645] The 1993 revision of the UCP clarified the issue by stating, for the first time, that the notice must specify *all* discrepancies in respect of which the bank refused the documents.[1646] UCP 600 art.16(c)(ii), retains the requirement, although it does so in slightly different language: the bank must give a "single notice" of rejection to the presenter and that notice must state "each discrepancy in respect of which the bank refuses to honour

---

[1637] UCP 600 art.16(c).

[1638] On what is meant by the word "given" in UCP 600 art.16(d), and whether or not it requires receipt of the notice by the presenter, see *Bulgrains & Co Ltd v Shinhan Bank* [2013] EWHC 2498 (QB) at [29]–[31]. UCP 600 art.16(d) is more tightly worded than the equivalent provision in UCP 500. UCP 500 art.14(d)(i) required notice to be given "without delay but no later than the close of the seventh banking day following the day of receipt of the documents". An issue could arise as to whether notice had been given "without delay": see, e.g. *Bayerische Vereinsbank Aktiengesellschaft v National Bank of Pakistan* [1997] 1 Lloyd's Rep. 59.

[1639] M.A. Clarke, R.J.A. Hooley, R.J.C. Munday, L.S. Sealy, A.M. Tettenborn and P.G. Turner, *Commercial Law: Text, Cases and Materials*, 5th edn (2017), p.827

[1640] See above, para.34-452.

[1641] J. Ulph, "The UCP 600: Documentary Credits in the Twenty-first Century" [2007] J.B.L. 355, 364.

[1642] As regards the position of the parties in such a case, see *Banque de l'Indochine et de Suez SA v JH Rayner (Mincing Lane) Ltd* [1983] Q.B. 711.

[1643] R. Cranston, E. Avgouleas, K. van Zwieten, C. Hare and T. van Sante, *Principles of Banking Law*, 3rd edn (2018), p.534.

[1644] *Kydon Compania Naviera SA v National Westminster Bank Ltd (The Lena)* [1981] 1 Lloyd's Rep. 68, 79. See also Benjamin's Sale of Goods, 10th edn (2017), para.23-222; Paget's Law of Banking, 14th edn (2014), para.36.19.

[1645] See *Hing Yip Hing Fat Co Ltd v Daiwa Bank Ltd* [1991] 2 H.K.L.R. 35, 45–51.

[1646] UCP 500 art.14(d)(ii).

or negotiate".[1647] If the bank fails to comply with this requirement, or any other requirement of art.16, it is precluded from claiming that the documents do not constitute a complying presentation.[1648] This seems to mean the bank may be precluded from raising a new objection when documents are retendered by the seller having cured the defects identified in the original notice of rejection.[1649]

Under UCP 500 art.14(d)(i), a bank which refused documents had also to state **34-513** in its rejection notice whether it was holding the documents at the disposal of, or was returning them to, the presenter. The purpose of this provision was that, as soon as the documents had been rejected, they should be put back in circulation. However, problems arose where a bank served a rejection notice and at the same time approached the applicant for a waiver of the discrepancies, and if such waiver was received released the documents without further notice.[1650] In *Crédit Industriel et Commercial v China Merchants Bank*,[1651] the issuing bank's notice of rejection was held to be bad where it ended with the words:

"Should the disc[repancy] being accepted by the applicant, we shall release the documents to them without further notice to you unless yr instructions to the contrary received prior to our payment. Documents held at yr risk for yr disposal."

Steel J. considered that the conditional nature of the rejection was not saved by the potential for acceptance of contrary instructions prior to payment, particularly where no notice was to be given.[1652] The message constituted a continuing threat of conversion of the claimant's documents. However, UCP 600 art.16, contains additional options designed to avoid banks sitting on discrepant documents. Under art.16(c)(iii) the rejection notice must state that the bank[1653]:

"(a) holds the documents pending further instructions from the presenter; or

---

[1647] Where the bank specifies discrepancies in the tendered documents, but fails to state that the bank is refusing to honour or negotiate as required by UCP 600 art.16(c)(i), and later serves another notice correcting the defect, it may be able to rely on the second notice as long as it serves that notice in time and adopts the same substantive reasons: *Bulgrains & Co Ltd v Shinhan Bank* [2013] EWHC 2498 (QB) at [32]–[33], distinguishing *United Bank Ltd v Banque Nationale de Paris* [1992] 2 S.L.R. 64, 76, as relied on by Benjamin's Sale of Goods, 10th edn (2017), para.23-211 (now also citing *Swiss Singapore Overseas Enterprises Pts Ltd v China CITIC Bank Corp Ltd (No.2)* [2014] 1 HKC 96 at [57]), arguing to the contrary. The bank's refusal statement may be explicit but it may also be implicit, either from use of a particular type of message format, as where a SWIFT standard-form MT734 message is transmitted from one bank to another, which will be universally understood by bankers as a refusal, or where there is a statement in a free form SWIFT message sent by one bank to another that it should be regarded as a MT734 message: *Bulgrains & Co Ltd v Shinhan Bank*, above, at [39] and [42].

[1648] UCP 600 art.16(f) (but note that the preclusion does not apply to a non-confirming nominated bank). See *Fortis Bank SA/NV v Indian Overseas Bank* [2010] EWHC 84 (Comm), [2010] 2 Lloyd's Rep. 641, affirmed [2011] EWCA Civ 58, [2011] 2 Lloyd's Rep. 33.

[1649] M.A. Clarke, R.J.A. Hooley, R.J.C. Munday, L.S. Sealy, A.M. Tettenborn and P.G. Turner, *Commercial Law: Text, Cases and Materials*, 5th edn (2017), p.827. See also above, para.34-452, and below, para.34-526.

[1650] UCP 600 art.16(b) allows the issuing bank "in its sole judgement" to approach the applicant for a waiver of discrepancies. The article expressly provides that this does not extend the maximum period of five banking days, allowed under art.14(b), for determination by the bank whether the presentation is complying.

[1651] [2002] EWHC 973 (Comm), [2002] 2 All E.R. (Comm) 427.

[1652] At [68].

[1653] But see *Bulgrains & Co Ltd v Shinhan Bank* [2013] EWHC 2498 (QB) at [50]–[51], where it was held that, in a communication between banks, it is enough that the rejection notice merely identifies the applicable provision, in that case "notify, as per UCP 600 article 16(c)(iii)(b)", without expressly stating what the issuing, confirming or nominated bank is proposing to do with the

(b)   holds the documents until it receives a waiver from the applicant and agrees to accept it, and receives further instructions from the presenter prior to agreeing to accept a waiver; or

(c)   is returning the documents; or

(d)   is acting in accordance with instructions previously received from the presenter."

The bank must act in accordance with the statement contained in the notice with reasonable promptness.[1654]

34-514   According to UCP 600 art.16(f), if the issuing bank or confirming bank fails to act in accordance with the provisions of art.16, it is precluded from claiming that the documents do not constitute a complying presentation. But the article makes no reference to the position of a nominated bank. However, if a nominated bank is employed by the issuing bank or confirming bank to take up and examine the documents on its behalf, the nominated bank's failure to comply with art.16 will bar the issuing bank or confirming bank from claiming that the documents are not conforming.[1655]

34-515   **The banker's recourse against the seller**   It is doubtful whether a banker, who accepts a faulty tender, has a right of recourse against the seller if the buyer rejects the documents tendered. The question must be considered both from the point of view of the law of negotiable instruments and the general principles of the law of contract. As regards the law of negotiable instruments, it should be borne in mind that the undertaking of the banker may assume one of three forms. First, he may promise to pay cash either when the documents are tendered or at a stipulated deferred date. Secondly, he may promise to accept and pay a bill of exchange drawn on himself by the beneficiary or, if the bill is to be drawn on a third party such as the confirming bank, promise that it would be duly honoured. Thirdly, the issuing banker may promise to negotiate a draft drawn by the seller on the buyer and accompanied by the documents. In the first case the law of negotiable instruments will, obviously, not apply. In the second case, where the banker is the acceptor of the draft and the seller the drawer, the law of negotiable instruments does not confer on the former a right of recourse against the latter. The third case, however, gives rise to problems. The seller here is the drawer and the banker an indorser or holder. Thus, if the draft is dishonoured by the drawee (the buyer), the issuing banker may claim to have a right of recourse against the seller under ss.43(2) or 47(2) of the

---

documents.

[1654] *Fortis Bank SA/NV v Indian Overseas Bank* [2010] EWHC 84 (Comm), [2010] 2 Lloyd's Rep. 641, affirmed [2011] EWCA Civ 58, [2011] 2 Lloyd's Rep. 33 (where the issuing bank's failure to act in accordance with the disposal statements contained in its UCP 600 art.16(c)(iii) notices, was held, applying UCP 600 art.16(f), to precluded the bank from claiming that the documents did not constitute a complying presentation). In *Fortis Bank SA/NV v India Overseas Bank* [2011] EWHC 538 (Comm), [2011] 2 Lloyd's Rep. 190, J. Hirst Q.C., sitting as a Deputy Judge of the High Court, held (at [35]) that "in the absence of special extenuating circumstances, a bank which failed to despatch the documents within three banking days would have failed to act within reasonable promptness". A bank which takes possession of a bill of lading for examination but then rejects it and holds it to the order of the person presenting it, refuses to accept delivery and thereby prevents the completion of the indorsement in its favour for the purposes of the Carriage of Goods by Sea Act 1992 s.5(2)(b), i.e. it does not become a holder of the bill of lading: see *Standard Chartered Bank v Dorchester LNG (2) Ltd, The Erin Schulte* [2014] EWCA Civ 1382, where held that s.5(2)(b) requires both an intention on the part of the indorser to transfer the document and an intention on the part of the indorsee to accept it (but note that the bank in this case was held to have become the holder of the bill of lading with the rights of suit under the contract of carriage for different reasons).

[1655] See E.P. Ellinger [1997] 3 (No.2) D.C.I. 9.

Bills of Exchange Act 1882. Moreover, the case of *M.A. Sassoon & Sons Ltd v International Banking Corp*[1656] lays down that the fact that a draft is stated to be drawn under a commercial credit does not necessarily exclude a right of recourse. However, this case did not concern the relationship of issuing banker and seller; it was a case in which a discounting banker sought to claim recourse against the seller, after the dishonour of a draft by the buyer.[1657] The issue is no longer a live one under UCP 600 as art.6(c) provides that a credit must not be issued available by a draft drawn on the applicant (the buyer).[1658]

Position at common law   In considering whether, in certain circumstances, the **34-516** general principles of the common law may confer on the banker a right of recourse against the seller, a distinction must be drawn between three types of case. First, the banker may wish to recover an amount paid to the seller, if the tender was affected with fraud. In this type of case the banker should be entitled to claim against the seller in deceit.[1659] Secondly, the banker may wish to reclaim payment from the seller if the buyer fails. It is, however, difficult to see on what principle he may establish such a claim, especially as a commercial credit constitutes a security given by the banker to the seller. Thirdly, the banker may wish to seek recourse to the seller if he has accepted, by mistake, a faulty set of documents tendered by the seller. It is, however, to be doubted whether the banker should be allowed to claim the amount back as money paid under a mistake of fact. In most cases the seller would change his position by parting with the documents against the banker's acceptance or payment and the banker should accordingly be precluded from claiming that the money was paid under a mistake of fact.[1660] UCP 600 art.16(f), supports this contention:

"... if an issuing bank or a confirming bank fails to act in accordance with the provisions of this article, it shall be precluded from claimant that the documents do not constitute a complying presentation."

Moreover, the issuing banker is under a duty to examine the documents tendered to him.[1661] The seller is, thus, entitled to presume that, if the banker accepts the documents tendered, the set is regular. In this situation the seller may perhaps be entitled to claim that the banker has waived inquiry and that he should, therefore, be precluded from claiming that he paid the amount of the credit under a mistake of fact.[1662]

The measure of damages   The modern cases support the proposition that if the **34-517** issuing or confirming bank fails to pay against presentation of conforming docu-

---

[1656] [1927] A.C. 711, 731.
[1657] cf. D. Sheehan, "Rights of Recourse in Documentary (and Other) Credit Transactions" [2005] J.B.L. 326.
[1658] Also UCP 600 art.8(a)(ii) provides that a confirming bank negotiates without recourse (provided there has been a complying presentation). See, further, Benjamin's Sale of Goods, 10th edn (2017), para.23-304 (distinction drawn between positions of issuing and confirming bank on the one hand, and non-confirming nominated banks on the other).
[1659] *KBC Bank v Industrial Steels (UK) Ltd* [2001] 1 All E.R. (Comm) 409; *Komercni Banka AS v Stone and Rolls Ltd* [2002] EWHC 2263 (Comm), [2003] 1 Lloyd's Rep. 383.
[1660] See on this point, Vol.I, paras 29-186 et seq. and above, paras 34-128 et seq.
[1661] Above, para.34-511.
[1662] Both in view of the seller's change of a position, as to which see above, para.34-133, and the principle considered in *Beevor v Marler* (1898) 14 T.L.R. 289.

ments under a letter of credit payable at sight, the beneficiary may sue in debt to recover the value of the credit, provided he is willing and able to transfer the documents to the bank against payment.[1663] If the beneficiary is willing and able to transfer the documents to the bank, he is entitled to recover the face value of the credit as a debt (subject to the right to recover any consequential losses as damages).[1664] If he is not willing or able to hand over the documents, the position is different; his claim is in damages for wrongful failure to honour the credit.[1665] In *Urquhart Lindsay & Co Ltd v Eastern Bank Ltd*[1666] the issuing banker opened an irrevocable credit covering several shipments of machinery. He wrongfully dishonoured one draft of the seller on the ground that, although the draft and documents complied with the terms of the commercial credit, the amount exceeded the sum agreed upon in the contract of sale. The seller treated the dishonour of the draft as a repudiation by the banker of the entire commercial credit. The seller was allowed to recover the difference between on the one hand the value of the materials left on his hands plus the cost of such as he would have further provided, and on the other hand what the seller would have been entitled to receive for the manufactured goods from the buyers. However, Rowlatt J. stressed that the damages could not exceed the amount of the credit.

34-518 **Damages for delay in payment**   It has been held that a bank is liable for loss directly resulting from a delay in the performance of its undertaking in the letter of credit. In *Ozalid Group Export Ltd v African Continental Bank Ltd*[1667] a letter of credit in favour of a British exporter was for an amount of US $125,939.22. Although the exporter tendered the required documents before the expiry of the credit, the bank made payment only after the lapse of two months. During this period the US dollar lost in parity vis-à-vis the pound sterling and, as a result, the exporter obtained £2987.17 less for the amount eventually paid in US dollars than he would have got if payment had been made promptly. Giving judgment for the exporter for this amount plus interest and disbursements, Donaldson J. observed that

---

[1663] *Standard Chartered Bank v Dorchester LNG (2) Ltd* [2014] EWCA Civ 1382 at [51], per Moore-Bick L.J., citing *Power Curber International Ltd v National Bank of Kuwait Ltd* [1981] 2 Lloyd's Rep. 394; *United City Merchants (Investments) Ltd v Royal Bank of Canada* [1983] A.C. 168; *Floating Dock v The Hong Kong and Shanghai Banking Corp* [1986] 1 Lloyd's Rep. 65; *Seaconsar Far East Ltd v Bank Markazi Jomhouri Islami Iran* [1999] 1 Lloyd's Rep. 36. In *Taurus Petroleum Ltd v State Oil Company of the Ministry of Oil, Republic of Iraq* [2017] UKSC 64, at [23], [64]–[65], [77]–[78], a majority of the Supreme Court construed an unusually worded letter of credit to give rise to two separate obligations: an obligation to pay the proceeds of the credit into the account of a third party in New York, which was owed to the beneficiary alone and which sounded in debt, and a separate collateral obligation to pay the proceeds into that account which was owed to the beneficiary and the third party jointly and which sounded in damages. For earlier authorities where the claim was held to sound in damages measured by reference to the face value of the credit, see *Belgian Grain and Produce Co Ltd v Cox & Co (France) Ltd* (1919) 1 Ll. L. Rep. 256; *Stein v Hambro's Bank of Northern Commerce* (1921) 9 Ll. L. Rep. 433, 507; reversed on a different point (1922) 10 Ll. L. Rep. 529; *Dexters Ltd v Schenker & Co* (1923) 14 Lloyd's Rep. 586. For the position on insolvency of the issuing bank or the confirming bank, see S. Connelly, "Bank recovery and resolution: the case of contingent letters of credit under bail-in" [2016] J.I.B.F.L. 78.

[1664] *Standard Chartered Bank v Dorchester LNG (2) Ltd* [2014] EWCA Civ 1382 at [51]–[52].

[1665] *Standard Chartered Bank v Dorchester LNG (2) Ltd* [2014] EWCA Civ 1382 at [51]; *Seaconsar Far East Ltd v Bank Markazi Jomhouri Islami Iran* [1999] 1 Lloyd's Rep. 36, 38 (col.1).

[1666] [1922] 1 K.B. 318, especially at 324. But establishing a causal link between breach of contract and loss remains essential, see *Fortis Bank SA/NV v India Overseas Bank* [2011] EWHC 538 (Comm), [2011] 2 Lloyd's Rep. 190 (where restitutionary claim also failed).

[1667] [1979] 2 Lloyd's Rep. 231.

the bank ought to have realised that the British exporter would have promptly converted any amount paid in US dollars into pounds sterling. His Lordship held that the exporter, the beneficiary of the credit, had the option of claiming payment in US dollars, or in pounds sterling.[1668]

"Notwithstanding that in the present case the price of the goods was agreed to be paid in US dollars, it is clear that the [exporter's] loss was incurred in sterling and that this was foreseeable by the [issuing bank]."[1669]

(vi) The Relationship of Issuing and Correspondent Bankers

Relationship of principals The status of the correspondent banker will vary with the role adopted. If the correspondent banker, situated in the country of the seller, has been designated in the contract of sale as the banker with whom the credit should be opened, the buyer need not be deterred from making arrangements through his own local banker. The local banker will instruct the correspondent banker to open a credit in favour of the seller. The correspondent is in those circumstances the real issuing banker[1670] for he has not merely passed on or added his support to the credit of the issuing banker, but has instead issued a credit under which he has taken upon himself sole liability to the seller. In that case it is difficult to resist the implication that between the two bankers the relationship is not that of principal and agent but rather that of two independent principals.

34-519

Principal and agent Where the correspondent does not assume sole liability but forwards to the seller with or without confirmation a letter of credit issued by the issuing banker, an agency relationship is more easily imputed. In such a case the correspondent banker acts as the agent of the issuing banker for the purpose of transmitting the credit of the issuing banker to the seller. At the same time, when the correspondent banker confirms the credit, he acts as principal, as he undertakes an obligation in his own name. The nature of the relationship between an issuing and confirming banker was of some significance in *Bank Melli Iran v Barclays Bank DCO*[1671] where inaction or silence of the issuing banker was held in the circumstances to provide sufficient evidence of ratification of those acts of the correspondent which were otherwise outside the scope of authority.[1672] The submission that the relationship between the issuing and the correspondent banker was not that of principal and agent but of customer and banker,[1673] where the principle of ratification would be inapplicable, was there rejected as contrary to the understanding of the House of Lords in *Equitable Trust Co of New York v Dawson Partners Ltd*.[1674] It is to be emphasised, as the House of Lords indicated, that the principal is the issuing banker and that the buyer is not a party to the relationship, and that there is no privity of contract between the buyer and the correspondent banker. UCP 600

34-520

[1668] His Lordship analysed in this context the principle of *Miliangos v George Frank (Textiles) Ltd* [1976] A.C. 443.

[1669] [1979] 2 Lloyd's Rep. 231 at 234.

[1670] *Skandinaviska Kreditaktiebolaget v Barclays Bank* (1925) 22 Ll.L. Rep. 523; *National Bank of Egypt v Hannevig's Bank Ltd* (1919) 1 Ll.L. Rep. 69.

[1671] [1951] 2 Lloyd's Rep. 367, [1951] 2 T.L.R. 1057. But see also *Credit Agricole Indosuez v Muslim Commercial Bank Ltd* [2000] 1 All E.R. (Comm) 172, 180, CA.

[1672] Following *Prince v Clark* (1823) 1 B. & C. 186.

[1673] For which some support may have been gathered from the analogy drawn in *Rayner & Co Ltd v Hambro's Bank Ltd* [1943] K.B. 37, 43.

[1674] (1927) 27 Ll. L. Rep. 49, 52, 53, 57.

art.2, provides that a "confirming bank" means "the bank that adds its confirmation to a credit upon the issuing bank's authorisation or request". It was held by Hamblen J., in *Fortis Bank SA/NV v Indian Overseas Bank*,[1675] that it amounts to a relevant authorisation for the purposes of UCP 600 where an issuing bank permits the advising bank to confirm a letter of credit at the beneficiary's request and expense.

34-521 Compliance with instructions   Just as the issuing banker must strictly comply with the instructions of the buyer so must the correspondent comply with those of the issuing banker. Any departure from the conditions laid down endangers his right to reimbursement and exposes him to an action for damages for breach of contract.[1676] The instructions to the correspondent may be merely to forward the credit,[1677] or more probably to pay or accept bills of exchange drawn on himself,[1678] or to pay, accept or negotiate[1679] bills drawn either on the issuing banker or on the buyer.

34-522 Effect of red signal   In some extraordinary cases a "red signal", or a clear indication of fraud, ought to put the negotiating bank on enquiry. In *Standard Bank London Ltd v Bank of Tokyo Ltd*[1680] one X asked the S Bank in London to finance certain transactions on the security of standby credits to be issued by the Kuala Lumpur office of BOT, a Japanese bank. Over a period of some 18 months, X delivered to the S Bank three letters of credit which, on their face, appeared to have been issued by BOT. In reality, all three documents were skilfully perpetrated forgeries. Any suspicions which the S Bank may have had were, however, allayed when it received in respect of each letter of credit a tested telex in which BOT confirmed the authenticity of the facility. But these tested telexes were also issued by the fraudsters, who got access to BOT's terminal and code. When called upon to pay, BOT denied liability. Its main argument was that the circumstances of each transaction were such as to put the S Bank on enquiry. The S Bank's failure to investigate, constituted a breach of a duty of care owed by it to BOT and, in consequence, the S Bank was not entitled to enforce the letters of credit. Waller J. gave judgment for the S Bank. Having cited the evidence of an expert witness, who described a "tested telex" as "the electronic signature of the bank sending the message", his Lordship emphasised that it was unchallenged that banks all over the world relied with complete confidence on tested telexes. "The tested telex system" he added "is meant to avoid arguments in relation to authority". Rejecting an argument to the effect that, in the instant case, the S Bank was put on enquiry, his Lordship said that:

[1675] [2009] EWHC 2303 (Comm), [2010] 1 Lloyd's Rep. 227 at [59]–[60].

[1676] But note that the issuer is liable where his instructions are ambiguous: *Midland Bank Ltd v Seymour* [1955] 2 Lloyd's Rep. 147. UCP 600 art.35, also provides a disclaimer on transmission and translation, but UCP 600 does not contain a provision equivalent to UCP 500 art.12 (incomplete or unclear instructions). See also *Habib Bank Ltd v Central Bank of Sudan* [2006] EWHC 1767 (Comm), [2006] 2 Lloyd's Rep. 412, on waiver of discrepancies by the issuing bank.

[1677] *Cape Asbestos Co Ltd v Lloyds Bank* [1921] W.N. 274.

[1678] *Donald H Scott & Co Ltd v Barclays Bank Ltd* [1923] 2 K.B. 1.

[1679] As to the position of a negotiating banker generally, see UCP 600 arts 7(c), 8(c) and 12. See also *Societe Generale SA v Saad Trading* [2011] EWHC 2424 (Comm), [2011] 2 C.L.C. 629 (see above, para.34-479). "Negotiation" is defined in UCP 600 art.2.

[1680] [1995] 2 Lloyd's Rep. 169. See also *Industrial & Commercial Bank Ltd v Banco Ambrosiano Veneto SpA* [2003] 1 S.L.R. 221.

"... the duty to inquire will depend on the circumstances of each and every case, and what should, or may, put someone on enquiry, will also depend on the circumstances of any individual case. Thus, the more usual the circumstances and the clearer a representation appears to be, the less the duty to inquire should be, and the less likely there will be circumstances which will put anyone on enquiry".

(vii) The Tender of Documents

Construction of terms of credit The insistence upon strict compliance is 34-523
continually reiterated. In *English, Scottish and Australian Bank v Bank of South Africa*, Bailhache J. remarked[1681]:

> "It is elementary to say that a person who ships in reliance on a letter of credit must do so in exact compliance with its terms. It is also elementary to say that a bank is not bound or indeed entitled to honour drafts presented to it under a letter of credit unless those drafts with the accompanying documents are in strict accord with the credit as opened."[1682]

This duty prevails in all the contracts which occur in a documentary credit transaction, i.e. the contract between the buyer and the banker, the contract of banker and seller and in the relationship of issuing and correspondent banker.[1683] The UCP lays down detailed rules concerning the requirements of the compliance of the documents, and there are also many authorities concerning this problem. The courts will imply additional terms into a banker's irrevocable credit only in rare and exceptional circumstances.[1684]

Modern review The doctrine of strict compliance has been fine tuned in 34-524

[1681] (1922) 13 Ll.L. Rep. 21, 24. But note that when the terms of the credit are construed, it is important to read it as a whole: *Elder Dempster Lines Ltd v Ionic Shipping Agency Inc* [1968] 1 Lloyd's Rep. 529, 535–536; see also *Kreditbank Antwerp v Midland Bank Plc* [1998] Lloyd's Rep. Bank. 173; affirmed [1999] Lloyd's Rep. Bank 219, where the trial judge said that where a credit was ambiguous any doubts should be resolved so as to give the transaction efficacy; but his words are not supported by the Court of Appeal. Whether the strict compliance rule applies to performance bonds and demand guarantees has been the subject of some uncertainty: but see *IE Contractors Ltd v Lloyds Bank Plc* [1990] 2 Lloyd's Rep. 496 at 500–501, per Staughton L.J. ("[i]t is a question of construction of the bond"), applied in *Sea-Cargo Skips AS v State Bank of India* [2013] EWHC 177 (Comm), [2013] 2 Lloyd's Rep. 477 at [30], *Lukoil Mid-East Ltd v Barclays Bank Plc* [2016] EWHC 166 (TCC) at [17]; *South Lanarkshire Council v Coface SA* [2016] CSIH 15 at [12]; *MUR Joint Ventures BV v Compagnie Monegasque de Banque* [2016] EWHC 3107 (Comm) at [26]–[28]. See also *Simic v New South Wales Land and Housing Corp* [2016] HCA 47 at [6], where French C.J., sitting in the High Court of Australia, stated: "Two complementary principles apply to letters of credit and performance bonds alike—the principle of strict compliance and the principle of autonomy or independence."

[1682] For a specific application of this maxim, see *Kydon Compania Naviera SA v National Westminster Bank Ltd (The Lena)* [1981] 1 Lloyd's Rep. 68, 74-75, where it was held that a tender of documents was bad because, inter alia, the bill of exchange was drawn on the issuing bank instead of on the applicant of the credit, who was designated as its drawee in the letter of credit. And see *Seaconsar Far East Ltd v Bank Mardazi Jamhouri Islami Iran* [1994] 1 Lloyd's Rep. 1, HL.

[1683] Contrast Dolan (1988) 105 Banking L.J. (U.S.) 380, who suggests that a less stringent standard is applicable in the relationship of issuing banker and buyer. See also Dolan, "A Principled Exception to the Strict Compliance Rule in Trilateral Letter of Credit Transactions" (2003) 18 B.F.L.R. 245.

[1684] *Cauxell Ltd v Lloyd's Bank, The Times,* December 26, 1995; *Uzinterimpex JSC v Standard Bank Plc* [2007] EWHC 1151 (Comm), [2007] 2 Lloyd's Rep. 187 at [157]–[158]; *South Lanarkshire Council v Aviva Insurance Ltd* [2016] CSOH 83 at [29], which cases, although dealing with performance bonds, ought to apply also to letters of credit. See also above, para.34-448.

Kreditbank Antwerp v Midland Bank Plc.[1685] One of the documents called for in a letter of credit was a "draft survey report issued by Griffith Inspectorate". The survey report tendered was executed on the letterhead of a firm describing itself as "Daniel C Griffith (Holland) BV" and signed for that company. However, a logo at the foot of the document stated "Inspectorate" and underneath it appeared the words: "Member of the Worldwide Inspectorate—dedicated to the elimination of risk". Holding that the document was regular, Evans L.J., in the Court of Appeal, noted that banks were concerned with the form of documents presented to them and not with the underlying facts. Accepting that mere trivialities or misprints had to be ignored,[1686] his Lordship observed:

"… the requirement of strict compliance is not equivalent to a test of exact literal compliance in all circumstances and as regards all documents. To some extent, therefore, the banker must exercise his own judgment whether the requirement is satisfied by the documents presented to him".[1687]

In respect of the certificate under consideration, his Lordship concluded[1688]:

"… the requirement of a Report … issued by 'Griffith Inspectorate' is amply met by the documents issued by the Dutch company named which declares itself a member of the Inspectorate Group. If there is a literal requirement that the name 'Griffith Inspectorate' shall appear in the documents, then it does so, assuming only that there is a world-wide Inspectorate group and that the company bearing the name Daniel Griffith (Holland) is a member of it. That is an assumption which, as the [trial] judge held, an experienced banker can be expected to assume".

34-525   **Summary**   *Kredietbank Antwerp*[1689] defeats any attempt to rely on a discrepancy based on asserting a "mirror image" test as the yardstick of strict compliance. At the same time, the Court of Appeal did not seek to modify the strict compliance

---

[1685] [1998] Lloyd's Rep. Bank 173; affirmed [1999] 1 All E.R. (Comm) 801.

[1686] The courts are willing to overlook a trivial defect in a tendered document where there is an *obvious* typographical error: see, e.g. *Bankers Trust Co v State Bank of India* [1991] 2 Lloyd's Rep. 443, where one of the tendered documents gave the buyer's telex number as 931310 instead of 981310. But where it is not obvious that the error is merely typographical, the bank is entitled to reject the tendered document as discrepant: see, e.g. *Bulgrains & Co Ltd v Shinhan Bank* [2013] EWHC 2498 (QB), where the claimant beneficiary was identified in the credit as "Bulgrains Co Ltd" but in the tendered commercial invoice as "Bulgrains & Co Ltd", and it was held (at [24]) "that there was a discrepancy as to name that was not clearly and demonstrably simply a typographical error and was material" (approving *United Bank Ltd v Banque Nationale de Paris* [1992] 2 S.L.R. 64, 73–74, Tin J.: "the name of the beneficiary is a very significant matter"): the judge added that even if there was no facility to insert an ampersand when (as here) using the SWIFT messaging system to transmit a credit to the beneficiary, the word "and" could and should have been used because it was properly part of the beneficiary's name (and see *Benjamin's Sale of Goods*, 10th edn (2017), para.23-127, questioning whether the issuing bank should have been prevented from raising the discrepancy because it was caused by an error in the terms of the credit attributable to the bank itself). See also *Beyene v Irving Trust Co Ltd* (1985) 762 Fed. Rep. 2d 4, US Second Circuit CA; cf. *Hing Yip Hing Fat Co Ltd v Daiwa Bank Ltd* [1991] 2 H.K.L.R. 35, Hong Kong SC. It must also be remembered that the wording of the credit remains of paramount importance. Even an apparently trivial discrepancy will justify rejection of the documents if the credit is specific as to that requirement: see, e.g. *Seaconsar Far East Ltd v Bank Markazi Jomhouri Islami Iran* [1993] 1 Lloyd's Rep. 236, CA (reversed on other grounds: [1994] 1 A.C. 438), where tendered documents did not bear the letter of credit number or buyer's name as required under the express terms of the credit.

[1687] [1999] 1 All E.R. (Comm) at 806.

[1688] [1999] 1 All E.R. (Comm) at 816.

[1689] [1998] 2 Lloyd's Rep. 173; affirmed [1999] 1 All E.R. (Comm) 801.

doctrine. This fundamental doctrine remains intact but is given a reasonable and not a literal, robotic, construction. Nevertheless, it remains the case that a bank has no discretion to accept a document issued by a party other than the issuer as designated and styled in the credit.[1690] In *Simic v New South Wales Land and Housing Corp*,[1691] where the beneficiary was incorrectly named in a performance bond as "New South Wales Land & Housing Department trading as Housing NSW ABN 45754121940" and correctly named in the demand for payment as "New South Wales Land and Housing Corporation ABN 24960729253", the High Court of Australia held the demand to be non-compliant, although the applicant's claim for rectification of the bond was upheld. French C.J. stated[1692]:

> "In the ordinary case, saving minor slips and misdescriptions, the designation of a person or entity as a beneficiary cannot simply, as a matter of construction, be transmuted into the designation of a different person or entity. Nor can a reference to a non-existent entity be construed as a reference to an existing entity with quite a different name."

Technical defences   If a tender of documents does not strictly comply with the requirements of the commercial credit, the banker is entitled to reject it. It does not matter whether the discrepancy is significant or minute. This is the position even after the Court of Appeal's decision in *Kredietbank Antwerp*, just discussed. The rule is that de minimis non curat lex does not apply in commercial credit transactions.[1693] Moreover, the person to whom the documents are tendered is entitled to raise any lawful objections against the documents, even if in fact his objection is purely technical and the true motive for his rejection of the documents is to be found in a falling market.[1694] English courts have held, consistently, that the fact that he does not, at the time of the rejection of the documents, raise all the defences available to him does not preclude him from setting up all of them at the trial.[1695] However, the law in point must now take account of UCP 600 arts 16(c)(ii) and 16(f), which appear to establish a preclusion.[1696]   **34-526**

UCP and technical defences   The latest revision of the UCP contains a number of provisions which are designed to ensure that tendered documents are not rejected for overly technical reasons. Three of these provisions merit special mention. First,   **34-527**

[1690] See *Benjamin's Sale of Goods*, 10th edn (2017), para.23-125—23-127.

[1691] [2016] HCA 47.

[1692] At [10].

[1693] *Moralice (London) Ltd v ED & F Man* [1954] 2 Lloyd's Rep. 526; *Soproma SpA v Marine and Animal By-Products Corp* [1966] 1 Lloyd's Rep. 367, 390; *Astro Exito Navegacion SA v Chase Manhattan Bank NA (The Messiniaki Tolmi)* [1986] 1 Lloyd's Rep. 455. But see *Bunge Corp v Vegetable Vitamin Foods (Pte) Ltd* [1985] 1 Lloyd's Rep. 613 (held de minimis rule did apply to underlying contract between applicant and beneficiary).

[1694] *Guaranty Trust Co of New York v Van Den Berghs* (1925) 22 Ll.L. Rep. 58, 112; affirmed 287, 477, 455. But see *Mannesman Handel AG v Kaunlaran Shipping Corp* [1993] 1 Lloyd's Rep. 89, in which Saville J., in a case governed by Swiss law, invoked a doctrine of good faith in the performance of contractual duties, to defeat an unconscionable reliance on a meaningless discrepancy.

[1695] *Skandinaviska Kreditaktiebolaget v Barclays Bank* (1925) 22 Ll.L. Rep. 523, 525; *Westminster Bank v Banca Nazionale Di Credito* (1928) 33 Ll.L. Rep. 306, 311; *Kydon Compania Naviera SA v National Westminster Bank Ltd (The Lena)* [1981] 1 Lloyd's Rep. 68, 78–80, which suggested that the position had not been changed by art.8 of the 1974 Revision of the UCP But it is probably too late to raise a new defence at the stage of an appeal: *Gian Singh & Co Ltd v Banque de L'Indochine* [1974] 2 Lloyd's Rep. 1, 12.

[1696] See above, paras 34-452 and 34-512. But see also *Benjamin's Sale of Goods*, 10th edn (2017), para.23-222 (as to the position of non-confirming nominated banks).

UCP 600 art.14(d) provides that data in a document, when read in context with the credit, the document itself and international standard banking practice, need not be identical to, but must not conflict with, data in that document, any other stipulated document or the credit. Documents need not be mirror images of each other, but they must not be inconsistent.[1697] Secondly, UCP 600 art.14(f) provides that if a credit requires presentation of a document other than a transport document, insurance document or commercial invoice, without stipulating by whom the document is to be issued or its data content, banks will accept the document as presented if its content appears to fulfil the function of the required document and otherwise complies with sub-art.14(d). Sub-article 14(f) seems to take data content out of the equation when there is no stipulation as to what it should be.[1698] For example, if the credit calls for an inspection certificate without more, the condition will be satisfied if an inspection certificate is presented even if it does not "pass" the goods. If the buyer wants tender of an inspection certificate which states that the goods have passed inspection, then he must specify this in his application to the issuing bank to open the credit and the credit must be issued in those terms.[1699] Thirdly, UCP 600 art.14(h), provides that non-documentary conditions are to be ignored. A non-documentary condition would be where the credit contains a reference to goods being of "US origin". Under the UCP this condition would be ignored unless the credit also called for one of the tendered documents—most likely the certificate of origin—to indicate compliance with that condition.[1700]

34-528 **Regularity of documents** In order to constitute a valid tender a document must, in the first place, be effective and, secondly, must be of the type current in the trade in question, i.e. a document on which questions cannot be raised.[1701] The set must also be regular as a whole. If the documents are inconsistent with each other the set is defective.[1702] Article 14(c) of UCP 600 settles the vexed problem of stale documents, i.e. documents presented before the expiry of the credit but after an unduly long time from the day of issue. UCP 600 art.14(c) provides that a presentation including one or more original transport documents must be made by or on behalf of the beneficiary not later than 21 days after the date of shipment (but in any event not later than the expiry date of the credit).

[1697] M.A. Clarke, R.J.A. Hooley, R.J.C. Munday, L.S. Sealy, A.M. Tettenborn and P.G. Turner, *Commercial Law: Text, Cases and Materials*, 5th edn (2017), p.783.
[1698] M.A. Clarke, R.J.A. Hooley, R.J.C. Munday, L.S. Sealy, A.M. Tettenborn and P.G. Turner, *Commercial Law: Text, Cases and Materials*, 5th edn (2017), p.783.
[1699] P. Downes, "UCP 600: not so strict compliance" [2007] B.J.I.F.L. 196, 197–198.
[1700] English courts have in the past construed non-documentary conditions in letters of credit as calling for production of a reasonable document evidencing its satisfaction: *Banque de l'Indochine et de Suez SA v JH Rayner (Mincing Lane) Ltd* [1983] Q.B. 711; *Floating Dock Ltd v Hong Kong and Shanghai Banking Corp* [1986] 1 Lloyd's Rep. 65; *Astro Exito Navegacion SA v Chase Manhattan Bank NA (The Messiniaki Tolmi)* [1986] 1 Lloyd's Rep. 455. Where the credit incorporates UCP 600, it is unclear whether an English court will continue to follow this approach on the ground that the terms of the credit should prevail as they reflect the intention of the parties. There is no direct authority on the point but *Credit Agricole Indosuez v Generale Bank (No.2)* [2000] 1 Lloyd's Rep. 123 suggests that the old approach will continue to be followed. See also *Kumagai-Zenecon Construction Co Ltd v Arab Bank Ltd* [1997] 3 S.L.R. 770; *Korea Exchange Bank v Standard Chartered Bank* [2006] 1 S.L.R. 565. See generally, E. Adodo, "Non-documentary Requirements in Letters of Credit Transactions: What is the Bank's Obligation Today?" [2008] J.B.L. 103.
[1701] *Skandinaviska Kreditakiebolaget v Barclays Bank*, above, at 525. See also *Karberg & Co v Blythe, Green, Jourdain & Co* [1916] 1 K.B. 495.
[1702] *Banque de l'Indochine et de Suez SA v J H Rayner (Mincing Lane) Ltd* [1983] Q.B. 711.

The ISBP   A novel source for the determination of the regularity of documents   **34-529**
tendered under letters of credit is the *International Standard Banking Practice for
the Examination of Documents under UCP 600* (the ISBP), originally issued by the
ICC in 2002.[1703] The current version of the ISBP was published in 2013.[1704] The
detailed provisions of the ISBP spell out the requirements of the document usually called for in documentary credit transactions and fill in many voids and
uncertainties left unanswered by the UCP. It remains to be seen how far these provisions will guide the courts in the determination of the regularity of documents
tendered under letters of credit. David Steele J.'s decision in *Credit Industriel et
Commercial v China Merchant Bank*[1705] indicates that, in general, the construction
of banking practice by the ICC is given weight in legal disputes respecting the law
of letters of credit. Once the ISBP become a regular tool of the banking world in
general, the courts would, undoubtedly, be guided by them. Nevertheless, the ISBP
merely represents one source of international standard banking practice: it is not the
exclusive source. Expert evidence can still be relied upon by the parties to a dispute
to establish a local or regional banking practice which may be at odds with that
found in the ISBP.[1706]

Originals and copies   An important innovation resulting from the use of electroni-   **34-530**
cally produced documents was reflected in art.20(b) of the UCP 500, under which
a document constitutes an original although it has been produced either by a
reprographic, automated or computerised system or as a carbon copy provided it
is marked as an original and, where necessary, appears to be signed. In *Glencore
International AG v Bank of China*,[1707] the Court of Appeal held that the two
requisites were cumulative. Accordingly, where it was sought to give the status of
an original to a document produced, or appearing to have been produced, by one
of the methods specified in art.20(b), it had to be marked as an original. Its being
signed by hand did not, in itself, convert it into an original. A very different conclusion was reached by the Court of Appeal in *Kreditbank Antwerp v Midland Bank
Plc*,[1708] which suggests that, where the appearance of a document establishes that
it is an original, a marking is superfluous. Both decisions were reviewed by Steel
J. in *Crédit Industriel et Commercial v China Merchants Bank*,[1709] who held that it
was appropriate to turn to the ICC's Policy Statement, published on July 12, 1999,
for guidance. In essence, the Policy Statement embodied the general principle
upheld in the *Kredietbank* case, namely that art.20(b) did not apply to a document
which appeared on its face to be an original. This is now the position under UCP
600 art.17, which addresses the issue as follows:

"a.   At least one original of each document stipulated in the credit must be presented.
b.   A bank shall treat as an original any document bearing an apparently original
signature, mark, stamp or label of the issuer of the document, unless the document
itself indicates that it is not an original.
c.   Unless a document indicates otherwise, a bank will also accept a document as an
original if it:

[1703] ICC Publication No.645.
[1704] ICC Publication No.745. An earlier version was published in 2007 to accompany the issue of UCP
600 (ICC Publication No.681).
[1705] [2002] EWHC 973 (Comm), [2002] 2 All E.R. (Comm) 427.
[1706] See Ellinger [2007] L.M.C.L.Q. 152, 159.
[1707] [1996] 1 Lloyd's Rep. 135.
[1708] [1998] Lloyd's Rep. Bank. 173; affirmed [1999] Lloyd's Rep. Bank. 219.
[1709] [2002] EWHC 973 (Comm), [2002] 2 All E.R. (Comm) 427.

> i. appears to be written, typed, perforated or stamped by the document issuer's hand; or
> ii appears to be on the document issuer's original stationery; or
> iii. states that it is original, unless the statement appears not to apply to the document presented."

Article 17 goes on to permit the presentation of either originals or copies if a credit requires presentation of copies of documents.[1710] In addition, if a credit requires presentation of multiple documents by using terms such as "in duplicate", "in two fold" or "in two copies", this can be satisfied by the presentation of at least one original and the remaining number in copies, except when the document itself indicates otherwise.[1711]

34-531 **Compliance with time** UCP 600 art.6(d)(i), provides that a credit must state an expiry date for presentation and that an expiry date stated for honour or negotiation will be deemed to be an expiry date for presentation. A presentation by or on behalf of the beneficiary must be made on or before the expiry date.[1712] Article 6(d)(ii) provides that the place of the bank with which the credit is available is the place for presentation (and that the place for presentation under a credit available with any bank is that of any bank). A place for presentation other than that of the issuing bank is in addition to the place of the issuing bank. The expiry date of the credit or the last day for presentation of documents may be extended by the operation of UCP 600 art.29, which applies where a time limit would otherwise expire on a day on which the bank to which presentation is to be made is closed.

34-532 **Compliance with amount** A draft in excess of the amount of the credit must be rejected by the banker as it does not comply with the terms of the credit.[1713] But where the sum demanded does not in itself exceed the amount of the credit, the bank has the discretion to make payment notwithstanding that the attached invoice is for an excessive figure.[1714]

34-533 **Quantity and weight** Article 30(b) of the UCP 600 permits, in the absence of stipulation to the contrary, a discrepancy of up to 5 per cent of the weight or quantity of the goods. The quantity must be stated in the documents either in the words of the commercial credit, or in such manner as to make it possible to calculate it.[1715]

34-534 **The description of the goods** At one time it was thought that each document should contain a full and accurate description of the goods in the words of the com-

---

1710 UCP 600 art.17(d).

1711 UCP 600 art.17(e).

1712 UCP 600 art.6(e).

1713 But note that a tolerance of 5 per cent less in the amount of the drawing is often permissible: art.30(c) of UCP 600. See also art.30(a) of UCP 600 construing "about" and "approximately". The tolerance provided for in subart.30(c) does not apply when the credit specifies a specific tolerance or uses the expressions referred to in subart.30(a).

1714 UCP 600 art.18(b). UCP 600 art.18(a)(iii) states that the invoice must be made out in the same currency as the credit.

1715 *London and Foreign Trading Corp v British and North European Bank* (1921) 9 Ll.L. Rep. 116. As regards the meaning of "about" or "approximately" see art.30(a) of UCP 600. And see *Kydon Compania Naviera SA v National Westminster Bank Ltd (The Lena)* [1981] 1 Lloyd's Rep. 68, 76, showing that this provision applies only to weight and quantity *strictu sensu*.

mercial credit.[1716] More recent authorities show that it is, in fact, sufficient if all the documents, when read together, give a full description of the goods.[1717] A similar solution is adopted by art.18(c) of the UCP 600 according to which the description of the goods in the commercial invoice must correspond with the description in the credit.[1718] In the remaining documents the goods may be described in general terms.[1719]

The bill of lading   The tender of a full set of bills of lading is required in most   **34-535**
commercial credits opened for the finance of c.i.f. and f.o.b. contracts.[1720] The bill of lading is, in fact, the banker's security for his advances to the seller.[1721] In most respects a bill of lading tendered under a commercial credit must fulfil all the requirements of a bill of lading tendered under a c.i.f. contract.[1722] The bill of lading must, of course, be of the type required in the commercial credit. A bill of lading dated after the last day specified for shipment is irregular.[1723]

UCP provisions   Several rules concerning the type of bill of lading to be tendered   **34-536**
in the absence of stipulation to the contrary are provided for by the UCP. Article 27 of UCP 600 defines a clean transport document as one which bears no superimposed clause or notation[1724] which expressly declares a defective condition of the goods or packing. The word "clean" need not appear on the transport document, even if the credit has a requirement for that transport document to be "clean on board".[1725] Articles 14(l) and 20 of UCP 600 entitle the banker to reject bills of lading issued by a forwarding agent who does not claim to be the carrier's agent, bills issued under and subject to the condition of a charterparty and bills of

---

[1716] See, e.g. *London and Foreign Trading Corp v British and North European Bank*, above; cf. *Rayner & Co Ltd v Hambro's Bank Ltd* [1943] K.B. 37.

[1717] *Midland Bank Ltd v Seymour* [1955] 2 Lloyd's Rep. 147; *Soproma SpA v Marine and Animal By-Products Corp* [1966] 1 Lloyd's Rep. 367; cf. *Bank Melli Iran v Barclays Bank DCO* [1951] 2 Lloyd's Rep. 367.

[1718] A discrepancy as to description of the goods in the invoice cannot be cured by the fact that a compliant description is given in another tendered document: *Bulgrains & Co Ltd v Shinhan Bank* [2013] EWHC 2498 (QB) at [25]. But even in the invoice the correspondence need not be literally identical: *Glencore International AG v Bank of China* [1996] 1 Lloyd's Rep. 135. And see *Kreditbank Antwerp v Midland Bank Plc*, above.

[1719] And see *Kydon Compania Naviera SA v National Westminster Bank Ltd (The "Lena")* [1981] 1 Lloyd's Rep. 68, 75–77; and note that in *Glencore International AG v Bank of China*, above, it was held that a packing list need not include a detailed description of the goods.

[1720] In such cases two bills out of a set of three are a bad tender: *Donald H Scott & Co Ltd v Barclays Bank Ltd* [1923] 2 K.B. 1. See now art.19(a)(iv) and ISBP para.70.

[1721] As regards the title conferred by the possession of the bill of lading on the consignee where there was no intention that title should pass to him, see *"The Future Express"* [1994] 2 Lloyd's Rep. 542, CA.

[1722] As to delivery of a mate's receipt and a mercantile usage establishing its negotiability in the trade between Sarawak and Singapore, see *Kum v Wah Tat Bank Ltd* [1971] 1 Lloyd's Rep. 439. And note that the transport documents must be dated, a requirement which remains intact notwithstanding the words "to be accepted as presented": *Credit Agricole Indosuez v Credit Swisse First Boston* [2001] 1 All E.R. (Comm) 1088.

[1723] *Credit Agricole Indosuez v Generale Bank* [2000] 1 Lloyd's Rep. 123.

[1724] A notation on a received for shipment bill of lading, certifying shipment on board is not a notation rendering the instrument unclean: *Westpac Banking Corp v South Carolina National Bank* [1986] 1 Lloyd's Rep. 311.

[1725] UCP 600 art.27. Note that under art.26(b) of UCP 600 a bill of lading is not rendered unclean by reason of clauses such as "shipper's load and count" or "said by shipper to contain".

lading covering shipment by sailing vessels.[1726] Article 20 of UCP 600 provides that bills of lading must show that the goods have been shipped on board a named vessel.[1727] Compliance with this requirement may be evidenced either by a bill of lading bearing words indicating loading or shipment on board a named vessel or by a notation on the bill to that effect.[1728] Article 20(c) of UCP 600 permits the tender of a bill of lading which includes a clause authorising transhipment.[1729] Under art.26(a) of UCP 600 a bill of lading which shows stowage on deck constitutes a bad tender. But a bill of lading that does not show that stowage on deck has taken place, may not be rejected merely because it includes a clause permitting such stowage.

34-537 **Other transport documents involving carriage of goods by sea** Article 21 of UCP 600 makes specific provisions respecting non-negotiable sea waybills. In most regards, the provisions applicable to such documents are similar to those governing marine bills of lading, except that the waybill need not be a negotiable document of title. Article 22 of UCP 600 governs charterparty bills of lading. Such a document may, of course, include a reference to its being subject to a charterparty. However, under art.22(b), "a bank will not examine such charter party contracts, even if they are required to be presented by the terms of the credit".

34-538 **Multimodal or combined transport documents** Multimodal or combined transport documents are covered in art.19 of UCP 600. Such a document must indicate the name of the carrier and has to be signed by the carrier, or his agent or by the master or an agent acting on his behalf. Another requirement is that the document indicate that the goods have been "dispatched, taken in charge or shipped on board at the place stated in the credit" (UCP 600 art.19(a)(ii)). The document must, further, indicate "the place of dispatch, taking in charge or shipment, and the place of final destination stated in the credit" (UCP 600 art.19(a)(iii)).

34-539 **Other transport documents** UCP 600 includes detailed provisions concerning transport documents used where carriage is by air or over land. Article 23 covers air transport documents, applying to them, basically, the main provisions applicable to bills of lading. Thus, the document has to indicate the name of the air carrier and be signed by the carrier or his agent and must show that the goods have been accepted for carriage (art.23(a)(i)(ii)). It must, further, indicate the airports of departure and of destination (art.23(a)(iv)). The principles respecting documents covering carriage by road, rail or inland waterways are regulated on similar lines in art.24. The provisions respecting courier and postal receipts are set out in art.25.

34-540 **Insurance documents** UCP 500 art.34 deals with "insurance documents" without further elaboration as to what the term covers. It certainly includes an insurance policy,[1730] and art.34(d) goes on to make it clear that certificates of insurance will

---

[1726] The tender of a combined transport bill of lading is, however, good.

[1727] But a received for shipment bill of lading is a good tender if the letter of credit does not provide for a bill of lading but a multimodal or combined transport document: art.19(a)(ii) of UCP 600.

[1728] UCP 600 art.20(a)(ii). cf. *Diamond Alkali Export Corp v Bourgeois* [1921] 3 K.B. 443, concerning the position at common law.

[1729] UCP 600 art.20(d), states that clauses in a bill of lading stating that the carrier reserves the right to tranship will be disregarded.

[1730] *Diamond Alkali Export Corp v Bourgeois* [1921] 3 K.B. 443; *Donald H Scott & Co Ltd v Barclays*

be accepted by banks unless the credit expressly stipulates otherwise. Cover notes issued by brokers will only be accepted if specifically authorised in the credit.[1731] UCP 600 art.28, makes it clear that that an insurance document includes an insurance policy, an insurance certificate or a declaration under an open cover, so long as these documents appear to be issued and signed by an insurance company, an underwriter or their agents or their proxies. But art.28(c) provides that cover notes will not be accepted. An insurance document may contain reference to any exclusion clause.[1732]

Invoices and certificates UCP 600 art.18(a) states that a commercial invoice (i) **34-541** must appear to have been issued by the beneficiary,[1733] (ii) must be made out in the name of the applicant,[1734] (iii) must be made out in the same currency as the credit, but (iv) need not be signed. Where the amount in which the invoice is made out exceeds the amount of the credit, the bank to which the invoice has been presented can accept it provided that the amount due for settlement does not exceed the value of the credit.[1735] UCP 600 art.18(c) provides that the description of the goods in the commercial invoice should correspond with that in the credit. Otherwise the data in the invoice need not be identical to, but must not conflict with, data in that or other documents, including the credit.[1736] In addition to the usual shipping documents, letters of credit not infrequently insist upon the tender of consular certificates or certificates of origin or of weight.[1737] Unless the credit stipulates by whom the certificate must be issued or the required data content, banks will accept the certificate as presented provided only that it appears to fulfil the function of the required certificate and that there is no conflict of data as prohibited by art.14(d).[1738]

(viii) The Nature and Effect of the Trust Receipt

Nature of trust receipt If the buyer is able to reimburse the issuing banker on **34-542** the arrival of the goods at their destination then the shipping documents are surrendered absolutely by the issuing banker to the buyer who is thus enabled to collect the goods from the ship and deal with them thereafter in the ordinary course of business. Frequently, however, the buyer looks to his dealings with the goods to provide him with the means of reimbursement and is anxious therefore to obtain the shipping documents before discharging his debt. A banker, willing to extend the

---

Bank Ltd [1923] 2 K.B. 1.
[1731] UCP 500 art.34(c).
[1732] UCP 600 art.28(i).
[1733] Except as provided for in UCP 600 art.38 (transferable credits).
[1734] Except as provided in subart.38(g).
[1735] UCP 600 art.18(b).
[1736] UCP, 600 art.14(d).
[1737] UCP 600 art.14(h), provides that non-documentary conditions are to be ignored. As regards the nature of a certificate of inspection, see *Commercial Banking Co of Sydney v Jalsard Pty Ltd* [1973] A.C. 279; note that the bank is not liable for the genuineness of a certificate: *Gian Singh & Co Ltd v Bank de L'Indochine* [1974] 1 Lloyd's Rep. 56; affirmed [1974] 2 Lloyd's Rep. 1. As regards the conformity of a certificate, see *Astro Exito Navegacion SA v Chase Manhattan Bank NA* [1986] 1 Lloyd's Rep. 455. As regards false certificates presented without the tenderor's knowledge of fraud, see *Montrod Ltd v Grundkotter Fleischvertriebs GmbH* [2001] All E.R. (Comm) 368; affirmed [2001] EWCA Civ 1954, [2002] 1 W.L.R. 1975.
[1738] UCP 600 art.14(f). On certificates generally, see *Benjamin's Sale of Goods*, 10th edn (2017), paras 23-193 et seq.

credit facilities beyond the period of shipment, obtains such protection as he can by requiring the buyer, in return for the shipping documents, to execute a trust receipt, variously described as a letter of trust or of lien. This is sometimes little more than an acknowledgment that the shipping documents and thence the goods and ultimately their proceeds will be held by the buyer on behalf of the banker; it usually, however, sets out various conditions as to insurance and storage of the goods pending disposal and in particular is likely to contain an undertaking to isolate the transaction in order to assist the earmarking of the proceeds of sub-sale. The buyer does not upon executing the receipt become a strict trustee, but he does thereby entitle the banker in the event of the buyer's insolvency to recover the goods or their proceeds in preference to ordinary creditors.[1739]

34-543 **Registration** The trust receipt steers a delicate course among the dangers of non-registration as either a bill of sale or a mortgage or charge under s.8 of the Bills of Sale Act 1882 or ss.859A–Q of the Companies Act 2006. Particular phraseology that has found favour with the courts was that before Astbury J. in *Re David Allester Ltd*[1740] where the trust receipt there considered had not been registered but was held to be nonetheless effective. It was emphasised that the rights of the banker over the goods had arisen originally under the pledge effected by the initial transfer to the banker of the bill of lading and the trust receipt was construed as but an authority stating the terms on which the pledgor was to realise the goods on the banker's behalf. The decision does much to safeguard a banker parting with a bill of lading initially received by way of security. Exceptionally, where some other document such as a delivery order is, instead of a bill of lading, initially received by the banker there is no pledge of the goods in the absence of attornment[1741] and the reasoning of Astbury J. is not then applicable. In those limited circumstances a trust receipt, contrary to the general rule, may perhaps wither without registration, but a banker is unlikely to extend credit facilities in the first place unless offered either the bill of lading, and accordingly the status of pledgee of the goods, or sufficient collateral security.

34-544 **Effect of the trust receipt** Whilst the trust receipt gives the banker priority over the ordinary creditors of the insolvent buyer, it does constitute the buyer a mercantile agent and thus enables him to pass a valid title under s.2(1) of the Factors Act 1889. In *Lloyds Bank v Bank of America National Trust and Savings Association*[1742] the plaintiffs had received from Strauss & Co Ltd bills of lading as securities for advances. Subsequently, upon Strauss & Co Ltd undertaking to sell the goods and hold the proceeds on trust, the bills of lading were released, but Strauss & Co Ltd then fraudulently pledged them with the defendants who took them in good faith and without notice of the plaintiffs' rights. Both Porter J. and the Court of Appeal rejected the plaintiffs' claim to recover the documents. Greene M.R. expressed the view of the court that Strauss & Co Ltd, for the purpose of the

---

[1739] *North Western Bank v Poynter* [1895] A.C. 56. See generally, E.P. Ellinger, "Trust Receipt Financing" [2003] J.I.B.L.R. 305.

[1740] [1922] 2 Ch. 211.

[1741] *Dublin City Distillery Ltd v Doherty* [1914] A.C. 823. See also Lord Wright's analysis of the common law of pledge in *Madras Official Assignee v Mercantile Bank of India Ltd* [1935] A.C. 53. In that case, railway receipts had been surrendered but the decision itself is not of wide application for their efficacy depended upon a local statute.

[1742] [1938] 2 K.B. 147.

Factors Act, had been not only mercantile agents but, together with the plaintiffs, the owners of the goods, and that there was no invalidity in their disposition to the defendants merely because of their dual capacity. The rights of the banker accordingly do not prevail in such circumstances against those of the bona fide third party purchaser for value.

(j) The Banker's Lien

Extent of lien By mercantile custom the banker has a general lien over all forms **34-545** of commercial paper deposited by or on behalf of a customer in the ordinary course of banking business. The custom does not extend to valuables lodged for the purpose of safe custody and may in any event be displaced by either an express contract or circumstances which show an implied agreement inconsistent with the lien.[1743] Thus in *Re Bowes*,[1744] where a policy of life assurance was deposited with a memorandum which expressed the deposit as security for all sums due up to a limit of £4,000, North J. held that a lien would not be implied so as to extend the effect of the security beyond the agreed overdraft. The most frequent example of circumstances inconsistent with the general lien is in the case of a deposit expressed to cover an advance for a specified purpose.[1745] However, once the original purpose has been fulfilled by repayment of the specified advance, if a customer knowingly permits the banker to retain the security, a general lien may ultimately be implied and its protection then claimed in respect of other advances.[1746]

The lien is applicable to negotiable instruments which are remitted to the banker **34-546** from the customer for the purpose of collection. When collection has been made the proceeds may be used by the banker in reduction of the customer's debit balance unless otherwise earmarked.[1747] It seems that where bonds are deposited and it is understood that the banker should cut off the coupons and collect the interest, then both bonds and coupons are subject to the lien.[1748] Prima facie neither would be so subject if the customer were to cut the coupons, for the arrangement would imply that the deposit related merely to safe custody. A similar implication would perhaps also exist with regard to share certificates where they are kept at a bank and the dividends are forwarded by the company to the banker on the instruction of the customer and are not dependent upon coupon cutting.

Third party interests A banker may not claim the protection of the lien in respect **34-547** of advances made after notice that the security belongs to or is subject to some interest of a stranger.[1749] Cozens-Hardy M.R. had made the wider suggestion that the lien

---

[1743] *Brandao v Barnett* (1846) 12 Cl. & F. 787.

[1744] (1886) 33 Ch. D. 586.

[1745] *Wilkinson v London and County Banking Co* (1884) 1 T.L.R. 63.

[1746] *Re London and Globe Finance Corp* [1902] 2 Ch. 416.

[1747] *Re Keever* [1967] Ch. 182. Note that the banker's right to combine the customer's accounts— discussed above, para.34-316—is distinguishable from the banker's lien. As the banker "owns" the money standing to the credit of the customer's account, he can have no lien over it: *National Westminster Bank Ltd v Halesowen Presswork and Assemblies Ltd* [1972] A.C. 785; *Re Charge Card Services Ltd* [1989] Ch. 497. Nevertheless, the credit balance on an account can be charged to the bank: *Re BCCI SA (No.8)* [1998] A.C. 214.

[1748] *Paget's Law of Banking*, 14th edn (2014), para.14.10 et seq.

[1749] *Jeffryes v Agra and Masterman's Bank* (1866) L.R. 2 Eq. 674; *Siebe Gorman & Co Ltd v Barclays Bank Ltd* [1979] 2 Lloyd's Rep. 142.

prevails over the property of the customer only,[1750] but, at least with regard to negotiable instruments, this may be doubted.[1751]

34-548 **Power of sale** Unlike other common law liens, that of the banker is not merely possessory in nature but is thought to carry with it a power of sale. Such a power over negotiable instruments is fortified by statute, for the banker is deemed to be a holder for value to the extent of the sum for which the lien exists.[1752]

[1750] *Cuthbert v Robarts, Lubbock & Co* [1909] 2 Ch. 226, 233.
[1751] *Brandao v Barnett* (1846) 12 Cl. & F. 787, 805–806.
[1752] Bills of Exchange Act 1882 s.27(3). See also Cheques Act 1957 s.2. But the banker cannot be the holder of a crossed cheque marked "account payee" or "account payee only" which is paid in for collection: see above, para.34-374.

CHAPTER 35

CARRIAGE BY AIR

David McClean

1.   INTRODUCTION[1]

Provisions governing carriage by air   The rules of the common law have   **35-001**
minimal importance in the law of carriage by air, virtually all of which is governed
by international conventions, or their provisions as applied to other instances of
carriage. In the case of passengers, EU legislation creates remedies for those who
suffer denied boarding, or cancellation of or long delay to their journey.[2] The common law rules apply only to carriage which is gratuitous and which is performed
neither by an air transport undertaking nor by the Crown. In the rare cases in which
the carrier's liability is to be determined by the common law rules as to negligence,
the maxim of res ipsa loquitur is available to assist the claimant.[3] There are now four
major conventions which have effect in English law: (a) the original Warsaw
Convention 1929 (and that convention as amended by Montreal Additional Protocol
No.1 of 1975 which substituted Special Drawing Rights (SDRs) for gold francs in
the provisions dealing with liability limits); (b) the Warsaw Convention 1929 as
amended by the Hague Protocol 1955, commonly known as "Warsaw-Hague" (and
that convention as amended by Montreal Additional Protocol No.2 of 1975 which
similarly substituted SDRs for gold francs); (c) Warsaw-Hague as further amended

---

[1]   See Shawcross and Beaumont, *Air Law*, Vol.1, Div.VII; Drion, *Limitation of Liabilities in
International Air Law* (1954); Miller, *Liability in International Air Transport* (1977); Mankiewicz,
The Liability Régime of the International Air Carrier (1981); Magdalénat, *Air Cargo* (1983).
[2]   European Parliament and Council Regulation 261/2004 of 11 February 2004 establishing common
rules on compensation and assistance to passengers in the event of denied boarding and of cancellation or of long delay in flights. See para.35-049.
[3]   *George v Eagle Air Services Ltd* [2009] UKPC 21, [2009] 1 W.L.R. 2133.

by Montreal Protocol No.4 of 1975, "the MP4 Convention"; and (d) the Montreal Convention 1999. European Union legislation has also been enacted which in some respects seeks to override the international legal regime in its application to Union air carriers.[4]

2. THE INTERNATIONAL CONVENTIONS

35-002 **The Warsaw Convention 1929** The Warsaw Convention of 1929 was drafted in order to remove inconsistencies between the national laws of the different countries[5] and to strike a fairer balance than might otherwise have been the case between carriers and passengers and owners of cargo in respect of their mutual rights and liabilities. The Convention sought to provide a set of uniform rules as to the carrier's liability and to settle jurisdictional questions and ensure a uniform limitation period. Under the Convention, the carrier was enabled to limit his liability. In return the passenger or owner of cargo did not have to prove negligence on the part of the carrier. Fault on the part of the carrier was presumed on proof of damage.[6] The Warsaw Convention was first given effect in the United Kingdom by the Carriage by Air Act 1932. The unamended Warsaw Convention continues to have effect as Sch.2 to the Carriage by Air Acts (Application of Provisions) Order 2004.[7] Schedule 3 to the same Order gives effect to Montreal Additional Protocol No.1 of 1975. The two Schedules differ only in respect of the currency units by reference to which liability limits are prescribed. The Warsaw Convention 1929 does not form part of the European Union legal order; but the Montreal Convention does.[8]

35-003 **The Hague Protocol 1955** The Warsaw Convention 1929 was amended by the Hague Protocol 1955, which attracted the support of most but not all of the parties to the original convention. The principal amendments effected by the Hague Protocol to the Warsaw Convention were as follows. First, the mandatory contents of the passenger ticket, baggage check and air waybill were much reduced, and the effect of failure to comply with them was rendered much less severe for the carrier.[9] Secondly, the maximum financial limit of liability for the death of or bodily injury to a passenger was doubled.[10] Thirdly, the troublesome phrase "wilful misconduct" which appeared in the English text of the Warsaw Convention was redefined as "intentional or reckless misconduct".[11] Fourthly, the carrier's employees and agents, as well as the carrier himself, could avail themselves of the limits of liability imposed by the Convention, provided that they were acting within the scope of their employment.[12] The Warsaw Convention as amended by The Hague Protocol of 1955 was given effect in the United Kingdom by the Carriage by Air Act 1961. The text of the Convention as set out in Sch.1 to the 1961 Act was amended by the Car-

---

4   See below, paras 35-018 et seq.
5   *Grein v Imperial Airways Ltd* [1937] 1 K.B. 50, 74–77.
6   See, generally, Lowenfeld and Mendelsohn (1967) 80 Harv.L.Rev. 497.
7   SI 2004/1899.
8   *Bogiatzi v Deutscher Luftpool* (C-301/08) EU:C:2009:649, [2009] E.C.R. I-10185; *Wallentin-Hermann v Alitalia-Linee Aeree Italiane SpA* (C-549/07) EU:C:2008:771, [2008] E.C.R. I-11061.
9   See below, paras 35-023, 35-025, 35-061, 35-065, 35-067.
10   See below, para.35-033.
11   See below, para.35-035.
12   See below, para.35-040. See, generally, Forrest (1961) 10 I.C.L.Q. 726.

riage by Air and Road Act 1979 so as to incorporate the amendments made by Montreal Additional Protocol No.2 of 1975.[13]

The Guadalajara Convention 1961 A Convention supplementary to the Warsaw **35-004**
Convention was signed at Guadalajara in 1961: it deals with the situation where the "contracting carrier" sub-contracts all or part of the contract of carriage to an "actual carrier".[14] This Convention was given statutory force by the Carriage by Air (Supplementary Provisions) Act 1962, which came into force on May 1, 1964.[15] The provisions of the amended Warsaw Convention are set out in the First Schedule to the Carriage by Air Act 1961, and the provisions of the Guadalajara Convention are set out in the Schedule to the Carriage by Air (Supplementary Provisions) Act 1962.[16] Both these Schedules are in two Parts, comprising an English and a French text; and under the Acts, the French text prevails if there is any inconsistency between them.[17]

The "MP4 Convention" The Guatemala City Conference 1971 modernised those **35-005**
provisions of the Warsaw Convention as amended at The Hague which governed the carriage of passengers and baggage, producing a Protocol which has never come into effect. The Montreal Conference 1975 carried out a similar task in respect of cargo, and the resulting Montreal Protocol No.4 contains the results of both exercises. The Protocol adopts the principle of the absolute liability of the carrier, subject only to contributory negligence. The defence available under art.20(1) of the Convention, that the carrier, his servants and agents have taken all necessary measures to avoid the damage, is removed in cases concerning cargo, except where liability is based on delay. The possibility existing under the earlier instruments of recovery beyond the prescribed maxima where the documentation was defective or on proof of intentional or reckless misconduct is removed in cases concerning cargo. There are changes in the rules governing cargo documentation, notably the possibility of using, instead of an air waybill, other means which would preserve a record of the carriage to be performed. The Protocol was given effect in English law by the Carriage by Air Acts (Implementation of Protocol No.4 of Montreal, 1975) Order 1999,[18] which added a new Sch.1A to the Carriage by Air Act 1961.

The Montreal Convention 1999 The Montreal Convention overhauls the whole **35-006**
"Warsaw system" covering the full range of issues dealt with in the earlier instruments, including liability for passengers, baggage, cargo and delay, and incorporates the effect of the Guadalajara Convention.[19] It clarifies the exclusivity of the Convention rules and provides that punitive, exemplary or other non-compensatory dam-

---

13 Carriage by Air and Road Act 1979 s.4(1).
14 See below, paras 35-045—35-047.
15 SI 1964/486.
16 The full text of the Hague Protocol is also published as Cmnd.3356 and that of the Guadalajara Convention as Cmnd.2354.
17 1961 Act s.1(2); 1962 Act s.1(2). In *Corocraft Ltd v Pan American Airways Inc* [1969] 1 Q.B. 616, a decision on the unamended Convention, the Court of Appeal preferred the French to the English text of that Convention, although there was no provision in the Act of 1932 corresponding to s.1(2) of the Acts of 1961 and 1962 (noted [1969] C.L.J. 40). Similarly, the United States courts give primacy to the French text of the unamended Convention: *Eastern Airlines Inc v Floyd*, 111 S.Ct. 1489 (1991).
18 SI 1999/1312.
19 For a pessimistic assessment of its treatment in national courts, see Tompkins (2014) 39 A.S.L. 203.

ages are not to be recoverable.[20] By July 31, 2018 it had 132 States Parties and so is the Convention most often applicable to international carriage by air. In its provisions as to jurisdiction, the Convention adds a "fifth jurisdiction" for passenger claims. It makes new and more modern provision as to passenger documentation. For damages not exceeding a prescribed amount for each passenger, the carrier is not able to exclude or limit its liability. The carrier is not liable for such damages to the extent that they exceed the prescribed amount if the carrier proves that (a) such damage was not due to the negligence or other wrongful act or omission of the carrier or its servants or agents; or (b) such damage was solely due to the negligence or other wrongful act or omission of a third party. The prescribed amount was 100,000 SDRs in the original text of the Convention; it was raised with effect from December 30, 2009 to 113,100 SDRs.[21] As to baggage, the Convention provides that the carrier must deliver to the passenger a baggage identification tag for each piece of checked baggage; the "baggage check" of the earlier instruments in the Warsaw system disappears. The cargo provisions are based, with minor improvements, upon those in Montreal Protocol No.4. Effect is given to the Convention in English law by the Carriage by Air Acts (Implementation of the Montreal Convention 1999) Order 2002.[22]

35-007 **Parties to the Conventions**   For the purposes of English law, the states which are parties to the various versions of the Warsaw Convention and the Montreal Convention 1999 are conclusively identified in the Order in Council made under the Carriage by Air Act 1961.[23]

3. SCOPE AND APPLICATION OF THE CONVENTIONS

35-008 **Scope of the Conventions**   Every version of the Warsaw Convention, and the Montreal Convention 1999, declares that it applies to all international carriage of persons, baggage or cargo performed by aircraft for reward.[24] The Conventions also apply to gratuitous carriage by aircraft performed by an air transport undertaking.[25] Carriage performed directly by the Crown, whether gratuitously or for reward, is

---

[20]   See *O'Carroll v Ryanair*, 2009 S.C.L.R. 125.

[21]   The decision to raise the amount was in the form of a decision of the ICAO Council under art.24 of the Convention, given effect in England by the Carriage by Air (Revision of Limits of Liability under the Montreal Convention) Order 2009 (SI 2009/3018).

[22]   SI 2002/263, which came into force on June 28, 2004.

[23]   s.2(1) as amended by SI 1999/1312 and SI 2002/263 (and see the Carriage by Air Acts (Application of Provisions) Order 2004 (SI 2004/1899) arts 5(2) and 6(2)). The power has been exercised in the Carriage by Air (Parties to Convention) Order 1999 (SI 1999/1313) and the Carriage by Air (Parties to Protocol No.4 of Montreal 1975) Order 2000 (SI 2000/3061), but not yet in relation to the Montreal Convention 1999.

[24]   Warsaw Convention 1929 art.1(1); Warsaw-Hague text art.1(1); MP4 Convention art.1(1); Montreal Convention 1999 art.1(1). "Aircraft" has been held to include a hot air balloon: *Laroche v Spirit of Adventure (UK) Ltd* [2009] EWCA Civ 12, [2009] Q.B. 778. "Reward" includes any form of consideration: see Civil Aviation Act 1982 s.105(1); *Corner v Clayton* [1976] 1 W.L.R. 800, 804–805 (no profit element required); *Herd v Clyde Helicopters Ltd*, 1996 S.L.T. 976 IH (lump sum payment for series of flights sufficed).

[25]   Warsaw Convention 1929 art.1(1); Warsaw-Hague text art.1(1); MP4 Convention art.1(1); Montreal Convention 1999 art.1(1). "Air transport undertaking" is not defined in the Conventions or in the United Kingdom implementing legislation; however, it is defined in s.95(5) of the Transport Act 2000, for the purposes of that Act, as meaning "an undertaking ... which includes the provision of services for the carriage by air of passengers or cargo for hire or reward".

also within the Conventions.[26] The Conventions themselves do not apply to the carriage of mail or postal packages: under English law such carriage is subject to Sch.1 to the Carriage by Air Acts (Application of Provisions) Order 2004, under art.2(2) of which the carrier is liable only to the relevant postal administration and in accordance with the rules applicable to the relationship between carriers and postal administrations.[27]

Carriage or other service   The Conventions apply to "carriage", and issues may   **35-009** present themselves as to whether the contract is one of carriage or for the provision of some other type of service. It has sometimes been argued that the notion of carriage implies that a flight is undertaken for the primary purpose of moving an individual or goods from Point A to Point B. This argument was not accepted by the House of Lords where it was held that in the absence of any relationship between the carrier and a person carried other than that of carrier and carried (for example, a relationship of employer and employee, or of instructor and student) the person carried was a passenger for the purposes of the Conventions.[28]

Applicable only to actions between carrier and passenger or goods owner   It   **35-010** must also be remembered that the Conventions only regulate the legal relations between the air carrier[29] and his passengers and owners of baggage and cargo. They do not embrace the legal relations between the carrier's customers and other persons or entities concerned with the carriage for whom the carrier is not in law responsible. Thus such liabilities in law as those of the manufacturers of the aircraft used for the carriage and those of the agencies (governmental or non-governmental) responsible for the airworthiness of the aircraft fall outside the Conventions. The liabilities of such entities are unlimited and are regulated by the normal principles of the law of tort.

Interpretation of the Convention   The Warsaw Convention 1929 is in a single   **35-011** text in the French language. The Hague Protocol of 1955 was drawn up in three authentic texts, in English, French and Spanish; it was, however, agreed that in case of any inconsistency the French text was to prevail.[30] In the case of the "MP4 Convention", there was a fourth authentic text in Russian, but the French text again prevails in case of inconsistency.[31] Both the English and the French texts of the Convention as amended by the Hague Protocol and of the MP4 Convention are given effect in England.[32] The Montreal Convention of 1999 is in six languages,

---

[26]   Carriage by Air Acts (Application of Provisions) Order 2004 (SI 2004/1899) art.8 (excluding, in art.8(2), cases where members of the Armed Forces are carried during a time of actual or imminent hostilities, severe international tension, or great national emergency).

[27]   Carriage by Air Acts (Application of Provisions) Order 2004 (SI 2004/1899) art.4.

[28]   *Herd v Clyde Helicopters Ltd* [1997] A.C. 534 (carriage of police personnel and equipment for operational purposes); *Laroche v Spirit of Adventure (UK) Ltd* [2009] EWCA Civ 12, [2009] Q.B. 778 (recreational flight in hot air balloon).

[29]   This expression can in certain circumstances embrace carriers other than the contracting carrier such as "successive carriers" and "actual carriers": see below, paras 35-045—35-047.

[30]   Hague Protocol, final clause; Carriage by Air Act 1961 s.1(8) as substituted by the Carriage by Acts (Implementation of the Montreal Convention 1999) Order 2002 (SI 2002/263) art.2(2).

[31]   Montreal Protocol No.4, final clause; Carriage by Air Act 1961 s.1(8) as substituted by the Carriage by Acts (Implementation of the Montreal Convention 1999) Order 2002 (SI 2002/263) art.2(2). For this convention, see above, para.35-005.

[32]   For the Warsaw-Hague text, see the Carriage by Air Act 1961 Sch.1. For the MP4 Convention text,

English, Arabic, Chinese, French, Russian and Spanish, all texts being equally authentic. However, the Carriage by Air Acts (Application of Provisions) Order 2004[33] gives effect in the United Kingdom only to the English versions of the unamended Warsaw Convention (despite that Convention having a single authentic text in French) and of that Convention as amended by Montreal Additional Protocol No.1; similarly, the Carriage by Air Acts (Implementation of the Montreal Convention 1999) Order 2002[34] gives effect only to the English text of the Montreal Convention. There have been relatively few reported cases in England on the interpretation of the Convention texts. The similarities between the various versions of the Warsaw Convention and of the Montreal Convention mean that a decision on one may well be applicable to some or all of the other texts. The paucity of decisions means that it is necessary to seek guidance from the decisions of courts in other Convention jurisdictions as to the operation of the detailed provisions of the Conventions.[35] The courts in the United States in particular have been prolific in their decisions, especially on the original Convention which was until 2003 the only version ratified by the United States. Many of these decisions display a great ingenuity in interpreting the Convention as far as possible in the passenger's favour in the event of claims for personal injuries.[36] The House of Lords has approved a liberal approach to the interpretation of English statutes giving effect to international Conventions generally[37] and has specifically held that ambiguities in, or doubts as to, the text of the Warsaw Convention may be resolved by cautious and infrequent reference to the *travaux préparatoires* of the international conferences which led up to the adoption of the Conventions. Their Lordships however stipulated that such reference should only be made when the material consulted is public and accessible and where it clearly and indisputably points to a definite legislative intention. The purpose of the Conventions is uniformity and the English courts should have recourse to the same aids to interpretation as would be used in other Convention jurisdictions.[38] However, while giving due weight to the need for uniformity of interpretation, an English court should approach the applicable Convention in an objective spirit in order to try to discover what its true intent is.[39] The starting-point for interpretation must always be the text of the Convention and not the

---

see the Carriage by Air Act 1961 Sch.1A as substituted by the Carriage by Air Acts (Implementation of Protocol No.4 of Montreal, 1975) Order 1999 (SI 1999/1312), a corrected French text being substituted by the Carriage by Acts (Implementation of the Montreal Convention 1999) Order 2002 (SI 2002/263) art.2(26).

[33] Carriage by Air Acts (Application of Provisions) Order 2004 (SI 2004/1899) arts 5(1) and 6(1).

[34] Carriage by Acts (Implementation of the Montreal Convention 1999) Order 2002 (SI 2002/263).

[35] For the weight to be given to decisions of foreign courts, see *Abnett v British Airways Plc* [1997] A.C. 430; *Morris v KLM Royal Dutch Airlines* [2002] 2 A.C. 628; *Gahan v Emirates* [2017] EWCA Civ 1530.

[36] See, e.g. *Lisi v Alitalia-Linee Aeree Italiane SpA* [1967] 1 Lloyd's Rep. 140, [1968] 1 Lloyd's Rep. 505 (but cf. the stricter approach commended in *Chan v Korean Air Lines Ltd*, 109 S.Ct. 1676 (1989)). For a comparative study of the approaches of United States and French courts to the interpretation of the Convention, see Miller, *Liability in Air Transport* (above, para.35-001 n.1).

[37] *James Buchanan and Co Ltd v Babco Forwarding and Shipping (UK) Ltd* [1978] A.C. 141, 152.

[38] *Fothergill v Monarch Airlines Ltd* [1981] A.C. 251, 278, 283, 287 and 294. cf. *Corocraft Ltd v Pan American Airways Inc* [1969] 1 Q.B. 616, 655; *Rustenburg Platinum Mines Ltd v South African Airways* [1977] 1 Lloyd's Rep. 564, 576–577; *Adatia v Air Canada* (1992) 2 S. & B. Av.R. VII/63, CA; *Tondriau (or Sauvage) v Air India*, 13 E.T.L. 126 (1978) Cour de Cassation, Brussels.

[39] *King v Bristow Helicopters Ltd* [2002] UKHL 7, [2002] 2 A.C. 628, especially, per Lord Hobhouse of Woodborough at [147]–[150]; *Swiss Bank Corp v Brink's-MAT Ltd* [1986] Q.B. 853; *Antwerp United Diamonds BVBA v Air Europe* [1996] Q.B. 317, CA.

language used, even by a court of the highest authority, in formulating a statement of its effect.[40] The terms of the carrier's conditions of contract or of carriage or of the documents of carriage (the passenger ticket or air waybill) cannot be relevant where the issue is one of interpretation of the Carriage by Air Act 1961 and the Convention to which it gives effect.[41]

Definition of international carriage   Each of the conventions contains a defini-   **35-012**
tion of "international carriage"; the differences between the various definitions are matters of drafting only. The definition as it appears in the Montreal Convention 1999[42] is:

"... any carriage in which, according to the agreement between the parties, the place of departure and the place of destination, whether or not there be a break in the carriage or a transhipment, are situated either within the territories of two States Parties, or within the territory of a single State Party if there is an agreed stopping place within the territory of another State, even if that State is not a State Party."[43]

Which of the various conventions, if any, applies to a particular case of carriage turns on the reference to the places of departure and destination in the definition of "international carriage" in each convention. It is crucial to identify the places of departure and destination, and to determine to which, if any, conventions the state in which each of those places is situated is a party. The most recent convention to which both states are parties will apply. In every case, what must be examined is the carriage of the particular passenger or cargo, not that of the aircraft effecting the carriage. Carriage between two points within the territory of a single high contracting party without an agreed stopping place within the territory of another state (for example between London and Belfast, or London and Gibraltar) is not international carriage.[44] For the purpose of determining whether or not the carriage is international, carriage to be performed by several successive air carriers will in some circumstances be deemed to be one undivided carriage: it must have been regarded by the parties as a single operation, whether it had been agreed upon under the form of a single contract or of a series of contracts.[45]

Conventions provide exclusive cause of action   The Conventions provide a   **35-013**
statutory cause of action which is not subject to the choice of law rules applying to claims in contract or tort.[46] Any action for damages, however founded, can only

---

[40] *Re Deep Vein Thrombosis and Air Travel Group Litigation* [2005] UKHL 72, [2006] 1 A.C. 495, commenting on over-reliance on the formulation in *Air France v Saks*, 470 U.S. 392 (1985).
[41] *Antwerp United Diamond BVBA v Air Europe* [1996] Q.B. 317, CA.
[42] Carriage by Air Act 1961 Sch.1B art.1(2).
[43] See *Grein v Imperial Airways Ltd* [1937] 1 K.B. 50; *Rotterdamsche Bank NV v BOAC* [1953] 1 W.L.R. 493.
[44] Carriage by Air Acts (Application of Provisions) Order 2004 (SI 2004/1899) Sch.2 art.1(2); Carriage by Air Act 1961 Sch.1 art.1(2), Sch.1A as inserted by SI 1999/1312 art.1(2); Sch.1B as inserted by SI 2002/263 art.1(2).
[45] Carriage by Air Acts (Application of Provisions) Order 2004 (SI 2004/1899) Sch.2 art.1(3); Carriage by Air Act 1961 Sch.1 art.1(3), Sch.1A as inserted by SI 1999/1312 art.1(3); Sch.1B as inserted by SI 2002/263 art.1(3).
[46] *Corocraft Ltd v Pan American Airways Inc* [1969] 1 Q.B. 616 (reversed on other grounds [1969] 1 Q.B. 616, CA); *Rothmans of Pall Mall (Overseas) Ltd v Saudi Arabian Airlines Corp* [1981] Q.B. 368, CA; *Holmes v Bangladesh Biman Corp* [1982] A.C. 1112, HL; *American Express Co v British Airways Board* [1983] 1 W.L.R. 701.

be brought subject to the conditions and limits of liability set out in the relevant convention.[47] The Convention does not purport to deal with all matters relating to contracts of international carriage by air; but in those areas with which it deals, such as the liability of the carrier, the code was intended to be uniform and to be exclusive also of any resort to the rules of domestic law. The words used in art.24 of the MP4 Convention and art.29 of the Montreal Convention 1999, "in the carriage of passengers, baggage and cargo ..." make very clear the exclusivity of the Convention rules across the whole field. That this is true of the earlier conventions has been established by judicial decisions of the highest courts in England, Ireland, South Africa and the United States.[48] The exclusivity principle was applied in the context of the Montreal Convention 1999 by the Supreme Court in *Hook v British Airways Plc; Stott v Thomas Cook Tour Operators*.[49] The Convention was intended to deal comprehensively with the carrier's liability for whatever might physically happen to passengers between embarkation and disembarkation. A claim for breach of duty under equality laws or alleging ill-treatment of a disabled passenger was precluded as within the substantive scope of the Convention.

35-014 **No contracting out** Article 23 of each version of the Warsaw Convention (and art.26 of the Montreal Convention 1999) provides that, with one exception,[50] any provision tending to relieve the carrier of liability or to fix a lower limit than that laid down in the applicable Convention is null and void, although without prejudice to the validity of the contract as a whole under the Convention.[51] Moreover art.32 of the various Warsaw texts provides that any clause contained in the contract by which the parties purport to infringe the rules laid down by the Convention, whether by deciding the law to be applied or by altering the rules as to jurisdiction, is also null and void (though arbitration clauses are allowed for the carriage of cargo, provided that the arbitration takes place in a Convention jurisdiction). However, art.33 (and art.27 of the Montreal Convention 1999) expressly permits the carrier to make regulations which do not conflict with the provisions of the Convention; and most carriers by air issue General Conditions of Carriage, one set for pas-

---

47 Carriage by Air Acts (Application of Provisions) Order 2004 (SI 2004/1899) Sch.2 art.24(1), (2); Carriage by Air Act 1961 Sch.1 art.24(1), (2); Sch.1A as inserted by SI 1999/1312 art.24(1), (2) (using different language); Sch.1B as inserted by SI 2002/263 art.29.

48 *Sidhu v British Airways Plc; Abnett v British Airways Plc* [1997] A.C. 430, HL; *Herd v Clyde Helicopters Ltd* [1997] A.C. 534, HL; *Deaville v Aeroflot Russian International Airlines* [1997] 2 Lloyd's Rep. 67; *R. v Secretary of State for the Environment, Transport and the Regions Ex p. IATA* [2000] 1 Lloyd's Rep. 242; *Morris v KLM Royal Dutch Airlines* [2001] EWCA Civ 790, [2001] 3 All E.R. 126; *King v Bristow Helicopters Ltd* [2002] UKHL 7, [2002] 2 A.C. 628; *Western Digital Corp v British Airways Plc* [2001] Q.B. 733, CA; *The Deep Vein Thrombosis and Air Travel Group Litigation* [2002] EWHC 2825; (affirmed [2003] EWCA Civ 1005, [2003] 3 W.L.R. 956) and [2005] UKHL 72, [2006] 1 A.C. 495; *Smyth & Co Ltd v Aer Turas Teoranta* Unreported February 3, 1997, SC (followed in *Nolan v Aer Lingus Group Ltd* Unreported November 9, 2009, Cir Ct, *McAuley v Aer Lingus Ltd* [2011] IEHC 89, and *Hennessey v Aer Lingus Ltd* [2012] IEHC 124); *Potgieter v British Airways Plc* (2005) 2 S.A. 133 (C); *El Al Israel Airlines Ltd v Tseng*, 119 S.Ct. 662 (1999).

49 [2014] UKSC 15, [2014] A.C. 1347. See para.35-048. The approach of the European Court in the context of Regulation 261/2004 is very different: see para.35-055. For a Canadian decision on the exclusivity of the Montreal Convention 1999, see *Thibodeau v Air Canada* 2014 SCC 67.

50 As to this, see 1961 Act Sch.1 art.23(2) (inherent defect, quality or vice & cargo); see, e.g. *Corocraft Ltd v Pan American Airways Inc* [1969] 1 Q.B. 616 (reversed on other grounds [1969] 1 Q.B. 616, CA).

51 For the rationale of this provision (to protect the passenger or other person dealing with the carrier against provisions of the kind which it describes), see *Abnett v British Airways Plc* [1997] A.C. 430.

sengers and baggage and another set for cargo. These conditions are commonly based on those recommended from time-to-time by the International Air Transport Association ("IATA"). Thus, contracts of carriage by air possess, as it were, a two-tier structure. The bottom tier of the contract is formed by the statute, and is mandatory. The upper tier of the contract is formed by the carrier's regulations which may fill gaps in the statutory provisions (or merely repeat such provisions), and may increase his statutory liabilities, but cannot reduce them. There is, therefore, practically no scope for the rules of the common law in carriage by air,[52] and in particular no scope for its distinction between common and private carriers.[53]

Jurisdiction   The English courts can assume jurisdiction in a claim for damages **35-015** under the conventions only in accordance with the jurisdictional rules they contain. In all versions of the Warsaw Convention, art.28 provides that an action for damages must be brought, at the option of the plaintiff, in the territory of one of the High Contracting Parties before one of the following[54]: (a) the court having jurisdiction where the carrier is ordinarily resident; or (b) the court having jurisdiction where the carrier has its principal place of business; or (c) the court having jurisdiction where the carrier has an establishment by which the contract has been made; or (d) the court having jurisdiction at the place of destination. The Montreal Convention 1999 retains these four grounds of jurisdiction (with changes of wording) and a fifth ground is added. Article 33 of that Convention provides that an action for damages must be brought, at the option of the plaintiff, in the territory of one of the States Parties, before one of the following: (a) the court of the domicile of the carrier; or (b) the court of the carrier's principal place of business; or (c) the court where the carrier has a place of business through which the contract had been made; or (d) the court at the place of destination; or (e) in respect of damage resulting from the death or injury of a passenger, before a court in the territory of a state party in which at the time of the accident the passenger had his or her principal and permanent residence and to or from which the carrier operates services for the carriage of passengers by air, either on its own aircraft, or on another carrier's aircraft pursuant to a commercial agreement, and in which that carrier conducts its business of carriage of passengers by air from premises leased or owned by the carrier itself or by another carrier with which it has a commercial agreement.[55]

The English court has held the four options in art.28(1) to be exhaustive[56]: it **35-016**

---

[52] The common law rules may still be of importance in connection with gratuitous carriage not performed by an air transport undertaking, which as we have seen (see above, para.35-001) is not within the scope of the Convention. See *Fosbroke-Hobbes v Airwork Ltd* [1937] 1 All E.R. 108; *Ludditt v Ginger Coote Airways* [1947] A.C. 233.

[53] As to whether a carrier by air can be a common carrier, see *Aslan v Imperial Airways Ltd* (1933) 45 Ll.L. Rep. 316, 322 (decided before the original Warsaw Convention came into operation); McNair pp.138–141; Shawcross and Beaumont, at Vol.1, para.VII[5]; Kahn-Freund pp.696–697. In *Aslan v Imperial Airways Ltd*, the flight documents expressly repudiated common carrier status. The matter appears to be of only academic interest now.

[54] Carriage by Air Acts (Application of Provisions) Order 2004 (SI 2004/1899) Sch.2 art.28(1); Carriage by Air Act 1961 Sch.1 art.28(1); Sch.1A as inserted by SI 1999/1312 art.28(1). See generally, Shawcross and Beaumont, at paras VII[416] et seq.; *Dicey, Morris and Collins on the Conflict of Laws*, 15th edn (2012), Vol.1, paras 15-008—15-019.

[55] Carriage by Air Act 1961 Sch.1B as inserted by SI 2002/263 art.33.

[56] Questions of procedure are governed by the *lex fori*, the law of the court seised of the case: Carriage by Air Acts (Application of Provisions) Order 2004 (SI 2004/1899) Sch.2 art.28(2); Carriage by Air Act 1961 Sch.1 art.28(2); Sch.1A as inserted by SI 1999/1312 art.28(2); Sch.1B as inserted

provides "a self-contained code".[57] If an action is begun in the English courts, which have jurisdiction under art.28(1), it is not open to the defendant to raise the plea of *forum non conveniens*[58]; if an action is commenced in a foreign court which appears not to have jurisdiction under art.28(1), an anti-suit injunction may be granted by the English court.[59] Article 28(1) is strictly applied, and its constraints cannot be avoided by the use of procedural rules for service of claim forms out of the jurisdiction.[60] Although there is little English judicial authority on art.28(1), it seems from cases in other jurisdictions that a corporate carrier is "ordinarily resident" in the jurisdiction where the central administration of the company is located: a branch office in England of a foreign carrier would not suffice for this purpose.[61] The place of central administration will, of course, also be the principal place of business of the carrier.[62] The "establishment by which the contract has been made" seemingly does not have to be owned by the carrier: it may be that of a general sales agent who carries on the carrier's business in the country in question.[63] A contract may be made by an establishment where the establishment has played a part in the meeting of minds of the parties.[64] Finally, the "place of destination" will be that identified in the particular passenger ticket or air waybill[65]: in the case of a round trip or return ticket, then, the place of destination will be the place of departure provided that the carriage was envisaged as a single operation.[66]

35-017   **Limitation of actions**   The right to damages in respect of the carrier's liability under arts 17 to 19 of the Convention is extinguished if an action is not brought within two years reckoned from the date of arrival at the destination, or from the date on which the aircraft ought to have arrived, or from the date on which the carriage stopped.[67] The "actions" referred to seemingly cover not only actions brought

---

by SI 2002/263 art.33(4). The English court would, therefore, determine whether a particular case falls under its jurisdiction, as opposed to that of a court in Scotland or Northern Ireland. See the Scottish decision to this effect: *Abnett v British Airways Plc*, 1995 S.C.L.R. 654.

57   *Rothmans of Pall Mall (Overseas) Ltd v Saudi Arabian Airlines Corp* [1981] Q.B. 368, per Roskill L.J. at 385; *Milor SRL v British Airways Plc* [1996] Q.B. 702, CA.

58   *Milor SRL v British Airways Plc* [1996] Q.B. 702, CA. United States courts are divided: in agreement with *Milor* is *Hosaka v United Airlines Inc*, 305 F. 3d 989 (2002), 9th Cir, cert. den. 537 US 1227 (2003); to the contrary is *Re Air Crash Disaster near New Orleans, Louisiana on July 9, 1982, Trivelloni-Lorenzi v Pan American World Airways Inc*, 821 F. 2d 1147 (1987), 5th Cir; both are cases on versions of the Warsaw Convention. A US Court of Appeals has held that *forum non conveniens* is available under the Montreal Convention 1999: *Re West Caribbean Airways SA* 305 F. 3d 989 (2002), 9th Cir, followed in *Pierre-Louis v Newvac Corp* 584 F. 3d 1052 (2009), 11th Cir. and *Galbert v West Caribbean Airways* 715 F. 3d 1290 (2013), 11th Cir.

59   *Deaville v Aeroflot Russian International Airlines* [1997] 2 Lloyd's Rep. 67 (injunction refused on facts).

60   *Rotterdamsche Bank NV v British Overseas Airways Corp* [1953] 1 W.L.R. 493.

61   *Rothmans of Pall Mall (Overseas) Ltd v Saudi Arabian Airlines Corp* [1981] Q.B. 368, per Roskill L.J. at 386; Shawcross and Beaumont, at Vol.1, para.VII[443]ff.

62   *Eck v United Arab Airlines Inc*, 360 F. 2d 804 (1966), US Ct of Appeals, 2nd Cir.

63   *Berner v United Airlines Inc*, 157 N.Y.S. 884 (1956); 170 N.Y.S. 2d 340 (1957), Bundesgerichtshof, March 23, 1976 (11 E.T.L. 873 (1976)).

64   *Orchestre Symphonique de Vienne v Trans World Airlines* (1971) I.A.T.A. A.C.L.R. No.418.

65   The place of destination will be the ultimate destination. This helps to determine whether or not carriage is "international carriage" within the meaning of the Convention: 1961 Act Sch.1 art.1(2); see above, para.35-012.

66   *Qureshi v KLM Royal Dutch Airlines*, 102 D.L.R. (3d) 205 (1979), Nova Scotia SC.

67   Carriage by Air Acts (Application of Provisions) Order 2004 (SI 2004/1899) Sch.2 art.29(1); Carriage by Air Act 1961 Sch.1 art.29(1); Sch.1A as inserted by SI 1999/1312 art.29(1); Sch.1B as

under the Carriage by Air Act 1961 but also those brought under the Fatal Accidents Act 1976 and the Law Reform (Miscellaneous Provisions) Act 1934. The right of action is seemingly completely destroyed and cannot be relied upon as a defence to an action brought by the carrier.[68] The two-year period cannot be suspended, interrupted or extended by reference to domestic law.[69] The expiry of the period of limitation extinguishes any cause of action under the Convention even when the carrier could not have limited his liability because of art.25.[70] The two-year period of limitation applies in lieu of any period specified under the Limitation Act 1980[71] or any other statute. It applies to actions against the carrier's employees or agents acting within the scope of their employment,[72] to actions against "actual carriers" under the Carriage by Air (Supplementary Provisions) Act 1962,[73] and also to arbitration proceedings,[74] but actions by the carrier to recover his fare, or for freight, however, are not subject to the two-year limitation period at all. The Convention makes no express provision concerning changes of party once the action has been commenced, but a change of party under CPR r.17.4 or 19.5 after the expiry of the two-year period cannot be allowed as this would conflict with the Convention.[75]

4. European Legislation: "the Montreal Regulation"

European Parliament and Council Regulation 889/2002 The European Union   **35-018** first legislated on carriage by air in Council Regulation 2027/97 of October 9, 1997 on air carrier liability in the event of accidents.[76] This was limited to passenger liability but anticipated a number of features of the Montreal Convention 1999. Regulation 2027/97 was radically amended, and in effect replaced, by European Parliament and Council Regulation 889/2002 of May 13, 2002[77] to align it fully with the Montreal Convention 1999 and to extend it to cover baggage liability.[78] The

---

inserted by SI 2002/263 art.35(1). English law will, as the *lex fori*, determine the method of calculating the period of limitation: Carriage by Air Acts (Application of Provisions) Order 2004 (SI 2004/1899) Sch.2 art.29(2); Carriage by Air Act 1961 Sch.1 art.29(2); Sch.1A as inserted by SI 1999/1312 art.29(2); Sch.1B as inserted by SI 2002/263 art.35(2).

[68] cf. *Aries Tanker Corp v Total Transport Ltd (The Aries)* [1977] 1 W.L.R. 185, HL, per Lord Wilberforce at 188; *Timeny v British Airways Plc* (1991) 102 A.L.R. 565 S. Australian SC.; *Mediterranean Freight Services Ltd v BP Oil International Ltd (The Fiona)* [1994] 2 Lloyd's Rep. 506, CA (obiter); *Agtrack (NT) Pty Ltd v Hatfield* [2005] HCA 38; *Air Link Pty Ltd v Paterson* [2005] HCA 39 and see *Bogiatzi v Deutscher Luftpool* (C-301/08) EU:C:2009:649, [2010] 1 All E.R. (Comm) 555.

[69] *Laroche v Spirit of Adventure (UK) Ltd* [2009] EWCA Civ 12, [2009] Q.B. 778.

[70] *Re Air Disaster at Lockerbie, Scotland on December 21, 1988*, 928 F. 2d 1267, 1286 (1991), US Ct of Appeals, 2nd Cir.

[71] Limitation Act 1980 s.33(2).

[72] Carriage by Air Act 1961 s.5(1).

[73] Carriage by Air (Supplementary Provisions) Act 1962 s.3(2).

[74] Carriage by Air Act 1961 s.5(3).

[75] *Hall v Heart of England Balloons Ltd* [2010] 1 Lloyd's Rep. 373, Birmingham Cty Ct, followed in *Jeffery v Thomas Cook Airlines Ltd* Unreported June 2, 2010, Macclesfield Cty Ct and *Foster v Thomas Cook Group Plc* Unreported March 31, 2011, Newcastle-upon-Tyne Cty Ct.

[76] For text see [1997] O.J. L285/1.

[77] For text see [2002] O.J. L140. See also the application of the amended Regulation by the Agreement on the European Economic Area 1992 as adjusted by the Brussels Protocol 1993 and the amendments made by Decisions of the EEA Joint Committee.

[78] The effect is that the Montreal Convention becomes part of the EU legal order: *Wallentin-Hermann v Alitalia-Linee Aeree Italiane SpA* (C-549/07) EU:C:2008:771, [2008] E.C.R. I-11061;

amending Regulation applied from June 28, 2004, the date on which the Montreal Convention entered into force for the European Union. The necessary changes to the law of the United Kingdom were made by the Air Carrier Liability Regulations 2004[79] and the Air Carrier Liability (No.2) Regulations 2004.[80] The Convention provisions which would otherwise be applicable do not apply to EU carriers to the extent that the amended Regulation has the force of law[81]; an EU carrier is one holding an air operating certificate issued by the authorities of a Member State. Pre-requisites for the issue of a licence include the carrier having a principal place of business in the Member State and that nationals of a Member State own or effectively control the carrier. The EU Regulation implements the relevant provisions of the Montreal Convention in respect of the carriage of passengers and their baggage and lays down certain supplementary provisions, and also extends the application of these provisions to carriage by air within a single Member State. The liability of an EU air carrier in respect of passengers and their baggage is declared to be governed by all provisions of the Montreal Convention relevant to such liability,[82] including its limitation provisions.[83] The Regulation obliges Member States to apply the Montreal Convention in cases where they are under a treaty obligation to apply some other instrument in the Warsaw system, and it may prove to be open to challenge in this respect. The Regulation also deals with the supplementary sum which, in accordance with art.22(2) of the Montreal Convention, may be demanded by a Union air carrier when a passenger makes a special declaration of interest in delivery of their baggage at destination. This sum is to be based on a tariff, to be made available to passengers on request, which is related to the additional costs involved in transporting and insuring the baggage concerned over and above those for baggage valued at or below the liability limit.[84]

35-019   **Advance payments**   Regulation 889/2002 makes provision in respect of advance or interim payments. The minimum advance in the event of death is the equivalent of 16,000 SDRs per passenger, and an advance payment is declared not to be returnable, except in the cases prescribed in art.20 of the Montreal Convention or where the person who received the advance payment was not the person entitled to compensation.[85]

35-020   **Conditions of carriage**   Regulation 889/2002 also deals with the provision of information to passengers.[86] All air carriers must, when selling carriage by air in the Union, ensure that a summary of the main provisions governing liability for pas-

---

Stott v Thomas Cook Tour Operators Ltd [2012] EWCA Civ 66 at [28]; *Air Baltic Corp AS v Lietuvos Respublikos specialiųjų tyrimų tarnyba* (C-429/14) EU:C:2016:88, [2016] 1 Lloyd's Rep. 407 at [23].

79   SI 2004/1418.
80   SI 2004/1974.
81   Carriage by Air Act 1961 s.1(2) as substituted by the Carriage by Acts (Implementation of the Montreal Convention 1999) Order 2002 (SI 2002/263) art.2(2); Carriage by Air Acts (Application of Provisions) Order 2004 (SI 2004/1899) art.3(2).
82   Regulation 2027/97 art.3(1) as substituted by Regulation 889/2002 art.1(4). For the effect of the Regulation on non-international carriage, see below, para.35-082.
83   *Bogiatzi v Deutscher Luftpool* (C-301/08) EU:C:2009:649, [2010] 1 All E.R. (Comm) 555 (a case under Regulation 2027/97 and the Warsaw Convention, but of wider application).
84   Regulation 2027/97 art.3a as inserted by Regulation 889/2002 art.1(5).
85   Regulation 2027/97 art.5 as substituted by Regulation 889/2002 art.1(7).
86   Regulation 2027/97 art.6 as substituted by Regulation 889/2002 art.1(8).

sengers and their baggage, including deadlines for filing an action for compensation and the possibility of making a special declaration for baggage, is made available to passengers at all points of sale including sale by telephone and via the internet. In order to comply with this requirement, Union air carriers (but not other air carriers) must use a notice set out in the Annex to the Regulation. In addition, all air carriers must in respect of carriage by air provided or purchased in the EU, provide each passenger with a written indication of the applicable limit for that flight on the carrier's liability in respect of death or injury, if such a limit exists; the applicable limit for that flight on the carrier's liability in respect of destruction, loss of or damage to baggage, and a warning that baggage greater in value than this figure should be brought to the airline's attention at check-in or fully insured by the passenger prior to travel; and the applicable limit for that flight on the carrier's liability for damage occasioned by delay. Failure to comply with the requirements of art.3a or art.6 of the amended Regulation is made an offence by the Air Carrier Liability Regulations 2004.[87]

Insurance requirements   Regulation 889/2002 requires a Union air carrier to be **35-021** insured up to a level that is adequate to ensure that all persons entitled to compensation receive the full amount to which they are entitled in accordance with the Regulation.[88] European Parliament and Council Regulation 785/2004 of April 21, 2004 on insurance requirements for air carriers and air operators,[89] which came into force on May 1, 2005, requires all air carriers and aircraft operators flying within, into, out of, or over the territory of a Member State to have specified levels of insurance cover in respect of their aviation-specific liability in respect of passengers (death and personal injury caused by accidents), for loss or destruction of or damage to baggage and cargo, and to third parties (death, personal injury and damage to property caused by accidents).[90] The insured risks must cover acts of war, terrorism, hijacking, acts of sabotage, unlawful seizure of aircraft and civil commotion. Insurance in respect of the carriage of mails is excluded.[91] In the United Kingdom, an air carrier or aircraft operator (other than a carrier or operator regulated by another Member State) who fails to comply with these requirements commits an offence.[92] The United Kingdom regulations require passenger liability insurance in the case of non-commercial operations by aircraft with a maximum take-off mass of 2,700 kg or less of at least 100,000 SDRs per passenger,[93] and designate the Civil Aviation Authority as the competent authority for the purposes of Regulation 785/ 2004.[94]

---

[87]   SI 2004/1418.
[88]   Regulation 2027/97 art.3(2) as substituted by Regulation 889/2002 art.1(4).
[89]   For text see [2004] O.J. L188.
[90]   Regulation 785/2004 art.4(1). The levels of cover were raised by Commission Regulation 285/ 2010 [2010] O.J. L87.
[91]   Regulation 785/2004 art.1(2). There are insurance requirements in this context: Council Regulation 2407/92 art.7.
[92]   Civil Aviation (Insurance) Regulations 2005 (SI 2005/1089) reg.5.
[93]   Civil Aviation (Insurance) Regulations 2005 reg.4; for penalties see reg.12.
[94]   Civil Aviation (Insurance) Regulations 2005 reg.3. The Secretary of State is exceptionally the competent authority in cases where a permit is required under arts 250 or 252 of the Air Navigation Order 2016 (SI 2016/765) in respect of certain aircraft registered outside the United Kingdom.

5. LIABILITY OF THE CARRIER

(a) Passengers: Death or Injury

35-022 **Who is a passenger?** In order to be a "passenger" a person need not personally have made a contract with the carrier.[95] It is sufficient if he is on board the aircraft with the carrier's consent, i.e. is not a stowaway. IATA Conditions thus define a passenger as "any person, except members of the crew, carried or to be carried in an aircraft pursuant to a ticket".[96] So a person whose ticket was bought by a parent, spouse, employer or friend would certainly be included, and so would the holder of a free pass.[97] The definition would make it appear that the carriage by the carrier of employees who are not members of the crew is carriage under the Conventions.[98] The mere fact that a flight is for recreational purposes and not for transport from point A to point B does not prevent the person being carried from being a passenger for the purposes of the Conventions.[99]

35-023 **Passenger ticket** The requirements as to passenger documentation vary depending on which convention is applicable. Where the Warsaw Convention 1929 applies, the carrier must deliver a passenger ticket which must contain the following particulars: (a) the place and date of issue; (b) the place of departure and of destination; (c) the agreed stopping places, provided that the carrier may reserve the right to alter the stopping places in case of necessity, and that if that right is exercised, the alteration shall not have the effect of depriving the carriage of its international character; (d) the name and address of the carrier or carriers; and (e) a statement that the carriage is subject to the rules relating to liability established by the Warsaw Convention.[100] Where the carriage is governed by the Warsaw-Hague text or the MP4 Convention, a ticket must be delivered (not necessarily by the carrier) containing: (a) an indication of the places of departure and destination; (b) if the places of departure and destination are within the territory of a single high contracting party, one or more agreed stopping places being within the territory of another state, an indication of at least one such stopping place; (c) a notice, generally referred to in practice as "The Hague notice", to the effect that, if the passenger's journey involves an ultimate destination or stop in a country other than the country of departure, the Warsaw Convention may be applicable and that the Convention governs and in most cases limits the liability of carriers for death or personal injury and in respect of loss of or damage to baggage.[101] The Montreal Convention 1999 provides that in respect of carriage of passengers an individual or collective document of carriage must be delivered. The document must: (a) give an indication of the places of departure and destination; (b) if the places of departure and destina-

---

[95] *Ross v Pan American Airways Inc*, 299 N.Y. 88 (1949); *Block v Compagnie Nationale Air France*, 386 F. 2d 323 (1967), US Ct of Appeals, 5th Cir.

[96] Passenger Conditions (PSC(24) 1724) art.1.

[97] *Western Digital Corp v British Airways Plc* [2001] Q.B. 733, CA.

[98] Drion, pp.58–62. cf. *Herd v Clyde Helicopters Ltd* [1997] A.C. 534; *Re Mexico City Aircrash of 31 October, 1979*, 708 F. 2d 400 (1983) US Court of Appeals, 9th Cir.

[99] *Laroche v Spirit of Adventure (UK) Ltd* [2009] EWCA Civ 12, [2009] Q.B. 778.

[100] Carriage by Air Acts (Application of Provisions) Order 2004 (SI 2004/1899) Sch.2 art.3(1).

[101] Carriage by Air Act 1961 Sch.1 art.3(1); Sch.1A as inserted by SI 1999/1312 art.3(1). See *Abnett v British Airways Plc* [1997] A.C. 430, HL; and the cargo case of *Fujitsu Computer Products Corp v Bax Global Inc* [2005] EWHC 2289 (Comm), [2006] 1 Lloyd's Rep. 231.

tion are within the territory of a single state party, one or more agreed stopping places being within the territory of another state, an indication of at least one such stopping place.[102] A ticket as such is not prescribed; any other (for example, electronic) means which preserve this information may be substituted.[103] The passenger must also be given written notice to the effect that where the Montreal Convention is applicable it governs and may limit the liability of carriers in respect of death or injury, and for destruction or loss of, or damage to baggage, and delay.[104]

Time of delivery of ticket Where a ticket is required by the terms of the applicable convention, it must be delivered before the start of the flight[105] if the passenger is to be bound by its terms. It was argued in a number of American cases that delivery had to be early enough to give the passenger a reasonable opportunity to take measures (such as buying insurance) to protect himself,[106] and that this consideration, taken with the need to give proper notice of the liability limitations, required the ticket to meet certain minimum requirements as to the size and legibility of its printed text.[107] Later United States decisions rejected these arguments, while recognising that a document could be so defectively printed as not to qualify as a "ticket" at all.[108]

35-024

Absence, irregularity or loss of passenger ticket The absence, irregularity, or loss of the ticket does not affect the existence or the validity of the contract of carriage which is, nonetheless, subject to the rules of the relevant convention. However, if in a case governed by the Warsaw Convention 1929, the carrier accepts a passenger without a passenger ticket having been delivered, the carrier is not entitled to avail himself of those provisions which exclude or limit liability.[109] The corresponding rule in cases under the Warsaw-Hague text or the MP4 Convention is that if, with the consent of the carrier, the passenger embarks without a passenger ticket having been delivered, or if the ticket does not include the prescribed notice as to the possible applicability of the Warsaw Convention,[110] the carrier is not

35-025

---

102 Carriage by Air Act 1961 Sch.1B as inserted by SI 2002/263 art.3(1).
103 Carriage by Air Act 1961 Sch.1B as inserted by SI 2002/263 art.3(2).
104 Carriage by Air Act 1961 Sch.1B as inserted by SI 2002/263 art.3(4).
105 *Fosbroke-Hobbes v Airwork Ltd* [1937] 1 All E.R. 108.
106 *Mertens v Flying Tiger Line Inc*, 341 F.2d. 851 (1965), US Ct of Appeals, 2nd Circuit; *Warren v Flying Tiger Line Inc*, 352 F.2d. 494 (1965), US Ct of Appeals, 9th Cir.
107 *Lisi v Alitalia-Linee Aeree Italiane SpA* [1967] 1 Lloyd's Rep. 140, US Ct of Appeals, 2nd Circuit; affirmed [1968] 1 Lloyd's Rep. 505, US SC. This decision also rested on an interpretation of the unamended Convention (as to the effect of omitting the required statement) which was later rejected by the US Supreme Court: *Chan v Korean Air Lines Ltd*, 109 S.Ct. 1676 (1989). In Canada, the legibility test in *Lisi v Alitalia-Linee Aeree Italiane SpA* was applied in respect of the "notice" required by the Warsaw-Hague text (*Montreal Trust Co v Canadian Pacific Airlines Ltd* [1977] 2 Lloyd's Rep. 80, SC of Canada), but not followed in the context in which it was decided, that of the "statement" in the unamended Convention, in *Ludecke v Canadian Pacific Airlines Ltd* [1979] 2 Lloyd's Rep. 260, SC of Canada.
108 *Chan v Korean Air Lines Ltd*, above.
109 Carriage by Air Acts (Application of Provisions) Order 2004 (SI 2004/1899) Sch.2 art.3(2). See *Preston v Hunting Air Transport Ltd* [1956] 1 Q.B. 454. The provisions excluding or limiting liability include art.20 (which enables the carrier to escape liability if he proves that he, his servants and agents have taken all necessary measures), art.21 (contributory negligence) and art.22 (limit to damages payable by the carrier).
110 See above, para.35-023.

entitled to avail himself of the provisions of art.22 limiting his liability.[111] Non-compliance with the provisions of the Montreal Convention 1999 as to passenger documentation does not affect the existence or the validity of the contract of carriage, which is, nonetheless, subject to the rules of the Convention including those relating to limitation of liability.[112] In cases under any of the Conventions, the provisions as to passenger documentation are excluded if the carriage is "in extraordinary circumstances outside the normal scope of an air carrier's business" (for example, a rescue flight to recover persons stranded by a natural disaster).[113]

35-026 **Information for passengers** An air carriage contractor (a carrier concluding a contract of carriage, a tour operator or ticket seller) must inform the passenger at the time of reservation of the identity of the operating air carrier or carriers, and notify the passenger if there is any change in the operating carrier.[114] There are further requirements as to the publication of air fares which must show separately any taxes, airport charges, and other charges, surcharges or fees such as those related to security or fuel that have been added to the basic fare. Optional price supplements must be communicated in a clear, transparent and unambiguous way at the start of any booking process and their acceptance by the customer must be on an "opt in" basis.[115]

35-027 **Right of refusal** Each convention makes it clear that its provisions do not prevent the carrier from refusing to enter into a contract of carriage.[116] The Passenger Conditions of Carriage recommended by IATA allow the carrier, in the reasonable exercise of its discretion to refuse to carry a passenger or his baggage on any flight after the date of a notice in writing to that effect; the passenger is entitled to a refund of any fare already paid. In addition, the Conditions reserve the right to refuse carriage if certain circumstances exist or in the carrier's reasonable belief may occur. These are (a) the need to comply with applicable laws; (b) the proposed carriage might endanger the safety, health or materially affect the comfort of other passengers or crew; (c) the passenger's mental or physical state presents a hazard or risk to the passenger concerned, other passengers, crew or property; (d) misconduct on a previous flight which may be repeated; (e) refusal to submit to a security check; (f)

---

[111] Carriage by Air Act 1961 Sch.1 art.3(2); Sch.1A as inserted by SI 1999/1312 art.3(2).

[112] Carriage by Air Act 1961 Sch.1B as inserted by SI 2002/263 art.3(5).

[113] Carriage by Air Act 1961 Sch.1 art.34; Sch.1A as inserted by SI 1999/1312 art.34; Sch.1B as inserted by SI 2002/263 art.51; Carriage by Air Acts (Application of Provisions) Order 2004 (SI 2004/1899) Sch.2 art.34.

[114] European Parliament and Council Regulation 211/2005 art.11. Failure to comply with is an offence by the Civil Aviation (Provision of Information to Passengers) Regulations 2006 (SI 2006/3303).

[115] European Parliament and Council Regulation 1008/2008 of 24 September 2008 on common rules for the operation of air services in the Community art.23(1); *Air Berlin Plc & Co Luftverkehrs KG v Bundesverband der Verbraucherzentralen und Verbraucherverbande—Verbraucherzentrale Bundesverband eV* (C-290/16) EU:C:2017:523. For enforcement in the UK, see Pt 2 of the Operation of Air Services in the Community (Pricing etc.) Regulations 2013 (SI 2013/486).

[116] Carriage by Air Acts (Application of Provisions) Order 2004 (SI 2004/1899) Sch.2 art.33; Carriage by Air Act 1961 Sch.1 art.33; Sch.1A as inserted by SI 1999/1312 art.33; Sch.1B as inserted by SI 2002/263 art.27. Note the possible relevance of Equality Act 2010 s.29 (discrimination in the provision of services). However in *Hook v British Airways Plc; Stott v Thomas Cook Tour Operators* [2014] UKSC 15, [2014] A.C. 1347 where the Act was not in issue, it was held that the Montreal Convention was intended to deal comprehensively with the carrier's liability so that a claim for breach of duty under equality laws or alleging ill-treatment of a disabled passenger was precluded.

failure to pay the applicable fare, taxes, fees or charges; (g) lack of necessary travel documents; (h) presentation of an unlawfully obtained or counterfeit ticket; (i) misuse of the ticket, as where coupons are used out of sequence to obtain a prohibited fare advantage; and (j) failure to observe the carrier's instructions with respect to safety or security.[117]

Liability for death and bodily injury Article 17 of the Warsaw Convention **35-028** 1929, which was not changed either by the Hague Protocol 1955 or by Montreal Protocol No.4 1975, provides that the carrier is liable for damage sustained in the event of death or wounding of a passenger or any other bodily injury suffered by a passenger if the accident which caused the damage so sustained took place on board the aircraft or in the course of any of the operations of embarking or disembarking.[118] The corresponding article in the Montreal Convention 1999 provides that the carrier is liable for damage sustained in case of death or bodily injury of a passenger upon condition only that the accident which caused the death or injury took place on board the aircraft or in the course of any of the operations of embarking or disembarking.[119] "Damage" in this context was held by the United States Supreme Court to mean "legally cognizable harm", art.17 leaving it to adjudicating courts to specify what harm is cognizable.[120] The European Court of Justice has held that the term "damage" must be given a uniform and autonomous interpretation, one identical throughout Ch.III of the Montreal Convention, notwithstanding the different meanings given to that concept in the domestic laws of the States Parties to the convention. As there was nothing in the Montreal Convention to indicate that the contracting States intended to attribute a special meaning to the concept of damage and to derogate from its ordinary meaning, the term "damage" was to be construed as including both material and non-material damage.[121]

In interpreting the phrase "in the course of any of the operations of embarking or disembarking" the court will enquire whether the passenger's movement through the airport procedures indicates that at the relevant time he was engaged upon the operation of embarking upon (or disembarking from) the particular flight in question.[122] This will involve looking at the location of the passenger at the relevant time, but also at other factors, which might include the activity in which the passenger was engaged, the degree of control exercised over the passenger by the carrier,[123] and the question whether the passenger was in the "zone of aviation-related risk".[124]

---

117 PSC(24)1724, art.7.1. For overbooked flights, see below, para.35-043.
118 Carriage by Air Acts (Application of Provisions) Order 2004 (SI 2004/1899) Sch.2 art.17.
119 Carriage by Air Act 1961 Sch.1B as inserted by SI 2002/263 art.17(1).
120 *Zicherman v Korean Air Lines Ltd*, 116 S.Ct. 629 (1996).
121 *Walz v Clickair SA* (C-63/09) EU:C:2010:251; [2010] E.C.R. I-4239.
122 *Adatia v Air Canada* (1992) 2 S. & B. Av. R. VII/63, CA; *Galvin v Aer Rianta* Unreported October 13, 1993, Irish High Ct; *Phillips v Air New Zealand* [2002] EWHC 800 (Comm), [2002] 1 All E.R. (Comm) 801; *Barraclough v Thomas Cook Airlines Ltd* Unreported April 23, 2010, Manchester Cty Ct (wheelchair incident 300 metres from departure gate; not "embarking").
123 See the tripartite test developed in the American cases of *Day v Trans World Airlines Inc*, 528 F. 2d. 31 (1975), US Ct of Appeals, 2nd Cir (cert. denied 429 US 890 (1976)); and *Evangelinos v Trans World Airlines Inc*, 550 F.2d. 152 (1976), US Ct of Appeals, 3rd Cir; and a test based on location in *MacDonald v Air Canada*, 439 F.2d. 1402 (1971), US Ct of Appeals, 1st Cir.
124 This approach is to be found in a number of cases in civil law jurisdictions: e.g. *Maché v Air France*, 20 R.F.D.A. 228 (1966) Cour de Cassation. See also *Hernandez v Air France*, 545 F. 2d. 279 (1976),

35-029 **"Accident"** The term "accident" is not defined for the purposes of the conventions. A statutory definition, for the purposes of accident investigation, defines "accident" as including "any fortuitous or unexpected event by which the safety of an aircraft or any person is threatened".[125] The United States Supreme Court has held that an "accident" must be an unexpected or unusual event or happening that is external to the passenger: it is not sufficient that the plaintiff suffers injury as a result of his or her own internal reaction to the usual, normal and expected operation of the aircraft.[126] It is clear that an aircraft crash, or a hijack, will constitute an accident, but so may less dramatic incidents such as extreme cases of turbulence, and incidents during flight such as the spillage of scalding hot drinks or the service of infected food. A United States decision held that sexual molestation by a fellow passenger was an "accident"[127]: the characteristics of air travel made the plaintiff vulnerable. The Court of Appeal followed that decision but questioned the need to establish that an accident had to be a characteristic of air travel[128]; that the assault was an accident was confirmed in the House of Lords.[129] It is not an accident when a passenger becomes ill during a normal flight; it has been held that the occurrence of deep vein thrombosis, and a failure to warn of the risk of its occurrence, cannot be an accident,[130] but where a passenger who later died had been refused a change of seat to avoid the cigarette smoke to which he was allergic, this was held to be an unusual event external to the passenger and so an "accident".[131] There is a range of judicial views on the question whether an omission may amount to an accident (and whether a distinction can properly be drawn between act and omission in this context).[132] Some United States courts have taken into account normal industry practice, seeing a departure from such practice as necessarily constituting an "unusual and unexpected event". The better view is that a court must always ask whether there was an "unexpected or unusual event"; some departures from an industry standard might be "accidents" in that sense but others not.[133]

1st Cir (cert. denied 97 S.Ct. 1592 (1977)), speaking of the need for a logical nexus between air travel per se and the accident. See Shawcross and Beaumont, at Vol.1, paras VII[721]–[723].

[125] Civil Aviation Act 1982 s.75(4).

[126] *Air France v Saks*, 105 S.Ct. 1338 (1985) cf. *Chaudhari v British Airways Plc, The Times,* May 7, 1997, CA (passenger with paralysis of the left side of his body could not claim that a fall on board the aircraft occurring as he tried to stand was an "accident"); *Barclay v British Airways Plc* [2008] EWCA Civ 1419, [2009] 1 All E.R. 871 (passenger's slip on standard feature of passenger cabin, a plastic strip covering the seat fix tracking, not an "accident"); *Buckley v Monarch Airlines Ltd* Unreported September 19, 2012, Manchester Cty Ct (spillage of hot drink held not an "accident": the spillage was unexplained, creating doubt as to the element of "externality"); *Ford v Malaysian Airline Systems Berhad* [2013] EWCA Civ 1163, [2014] 1 Lloyd's Rep. 301 (passenger unable to urinate during flight due to a medical condition, so "internal" to the passenger; diuretic administered by a doctor also on board; later tests suggested that treatment inappropriate; held not an "unusual" event for the purposes of art.17).

[127] *Wallace v Korean Air*, 214 F. 3d 293 (2000), 2nd Cir.

[128] *Morris v KLM Royal Dutch Airlines* [2001] EWCA Civ 790, [2001] 3 All E.R. 126.

[129] See *Morris v KLM Royal Dutch Airlines*, above; *King v Bristow Helicopters Ltd* [2002] UKHL 7, [2002] 2 A.C. 628.

[130] *Re Deep Vein Thrombosis and Air Travel Group Litigation* [2005] UKHL 72, [2006] 1 A.C. 495. For a full discussion, see Shawcross and Beaumont, at Vol.1, paras VII[691] et seq.

[131] *Olympic Airways v Husain*, 124 S.Ct. 1221 (2004).

[132] *Olympic Airways v Husain*, 124 S.Ct. 1221 (2004); *Povey v Qantas Airways Ltd* [2005] HCA 33, (2005) 216 A.L.R. 427; *Deep Vein Thrombosis and Air Travel Group Litigation* [2003] EWCA Civ 1005, [2004] Q.B. 234, per Lord Phillips of Worth Matravers M.R. and the same case on appeal, [2005] UKHL 72, [2006] 1 A.C. 495, per Lord Mance.

[133] The view taken in *Blansett v Continental Airlines Inc* 379 F 3d 177 (2004), 5th Cir.

Discussion of a departure from industry practice is appropriate for liability based on negligence, which is not relevant under the Montreal Convention.

"Bodily injury"   The term "bodily injury" is to be construed narrowly; mere   **35-030**
mental anxiety, unaccompanied by physical injury, will give rise to no liability under art.17. This conclusion was reached by the United States Supreme Court after many years in which American courts were divided as to the scope of "lésion corporelle" in the French text of the Convention,[134] and was later adopted by the House of Lords, resolving a difference of view between the English Court of Appeal and the Inner House of the Court of Session.[135] "Bodily injury" was held to mean a change in some part or parts of the body of the passenger which was sufficiently serious to be described as an injury; it does not include mere emotional upset such as fear, distress, grief or mental anguish. Post Traumatic Stress Disorder will not constitute "bodily injury" unless it has caused actual physical brain damage; there is no liability for mental injuries which are accompanied by, but not caused by physical injuries.[136]

Defences available to the carrier: "all necessary measures"   Under art.20 of the   **35-031**
Warsaw Convention 1929, the Warsaw-Hague text, and the MP4 Convention, the carrier is not liable if he proves that he and his employees or agents have taken all necessary measures to avoid the damage or that it was impossible for him or them to take such measures.[137] In the Montreal Convention 1999 the defence is available only in cases of liability for delay.[138] In that Convention, however, it is provided that in passenger cases to the extent that the damages exceed a prescribed amount,[139] the carrier is not liable if the carrier proves that (a) such damage was not due to the negligence or other wrongful act or omission of the carrier or its servants or agents; or (b) such damage was solely due to the negligence or other wrongful act or omission of a third party.[140] The English courts have rarely had to consider art.20 of the Convention. In *Chisholm v British European Airways*[141] a passenger was injured after she had left her seat when, because of turbulence, the passengers had been warned to fasten their seat belts and remain seated. The plaintiff disregarded the warnings given by illuminated signs, by the aircraft's public address system, and also by the cabin crew to each passenger. It was held that the carrier was not liable because his employees had taken all necessary measures to avoid the damage. The

---

[134]   *Eastern Airlines Inc v Floyd*, 111 S.Ct. 1489 (1991); *Kotsambasis v Singapore Airlines Ltd* (1997) 148 A.L.R. 498, NSWCA. The position stated in the text was accepted by counsel for both parties in *Sidhu v British Airways Plc* [1995] P.I.Q.R. P427, CA, but some doubt was expressed by Lord Hope on appeal in the same case: *Abnett v British Airways Plc* [1997] A.C. 430.

[135]   *Morris v KLM Royal Dutch Airlines*, above; *King v Bristow Helicopters Ltd* [2002] UKHL 7, [2002] 2 A.C. 628.

[136]   *Ehrlich v American Airlines Inc*, 360 F. 3d 366 (2004), 2nd Cir.

[137]   Carriage by Air Acts (Application of Provisions) Order 2004 (SI 2004/1899) Sch.2 art.20(1); Carriage by Air Act 1961 Sch.1 art.20; Sch.1A as inserted by SI 1999/1312 art.20.

[138]   Carriage by Air Act 1961 Sch.1B as inserted by SI 2002/263 art.19. For the application of the Montreal Convention 1999 to govern the liability of European Union air carriers, see above, para.35-018.

[139]   100,000 SDRs in the original text of the Convention, raised to 113,100 SDRs by a decision of the ICAO Council under art.24 of the Convention, given effect in England by the Carriage by Air (Revision of Limits of Liability under the Montreal Convention) Order 2009 (SI 2009/3018).

[140]   Carriage by Air Act 1961 Sch.1B as inserted by SI 2002/263 art.21(2).

[141]   [1963] 1 Lloyd's Rep. 626.

court considered that "all necessary measures" meant all *reasonable* measures or, as it was put more recently, "all measures necessary in the eyes of a reasonable man".[142] Thus, what looks like a strict liability under the Convention seems to have been relaxed, although the carrier must still prove more than that he was not negligent.[143] If the court had reached the opposite conclusion under art.20, the plaintiff's damages might perhaps have been reduced under art.21 by reason of her contributory negligence.[144] However, on somewhat similar facts to the *Chisholm* case but where the passengers had not been instructed to fasten their seat belts prior to the aircraft encountering forecast turbulence, the court held that the failure of the carrier's employees to warn the passengers was a breach of art.20. The fact that the plaintiff passenger had unfastened his seat belt at some time during a long flight did not constitute contributory negligence under art.21.[145]

35-032 **Contributory negligence** Under art.21 of the Warsaw Convention 1929,[146] which was unchanged by the Hague Protocol 1955,[147] if the carrier proves that the damage was caused by or contributed to by the negligence of the injured person, the court may, in accordance with the provisions of its own law, exonerate the carrier wholly or partly from its liability. This is retained, with a drafting change, in the MP4 Convention.[148] Under the Montreal Convention 1999, if the carrier proves that the damage was caused by or contributed to by the negligence or other wrongful act or omission of the person claiming compensation, or the person from whom his or her rights are derived, the carrier is wholly or partly exonerated from its liability to the claimant to the extent that such negligence or wrongful act or omission caused or contributed to the damage.[149]

35-033 **Upper financial limit of liability** In cases governed by the Warsaw Convention 1929, in the absence of a special contract, and unless the carrier loses the protection of art.22(1) of the Convention (by failing to deliver a passenger ticket, or on proof of wilful misconduct by the carrier, its servants or agents), its liability in the carriage of persons is limited to the sum of 125,000 francs for each passenger.[150] The figure of 8,300 SDRs was substituted for the amount in francs by Montreal Additional Protocol No.1 of 1975.[151] Under the Warsaw-Hague text and the MP4 Convention, and in the absence of a special contract, and unless the carrier loses the protection of art.22(1) of the Convention (by failing to deliver a passenger ticket,

---

[142] *Goldman v Thai Airways International Ltd* (1981) 125 S.J. 413 (reversed on other grounds [1983] 1 W.L.R. 1186, CA). A similar interpretation was arrived at in *United International Stables Ltd v Pacific Western Airlines Ltd* (1969) 5 D.L.R. 3d 67, SC of British Columbia; and *Manufacturers Hanover Trust Co v Alitalia*, 429 F.Supp. 964 (1977), US District Ct. The approach in this last decision was expressly approved in *Swiss Bank Corp v Brink's-MAT Ltd* [1986] Q.B. 853 at 96–97.
[143] *Swiss Bank Corporation v Brink's-MAT Ltd*, above, at 97.
[144] Kahn-Freund, p.727.
[145] *Goldman v Thai Airways International Ltd* (1981) 125 S.J. 413; reversed on another ground [1983] 1 W.L.R. 1186, CA: see below, para.35-037.
[146] Carriage by Air Acts (Application of Provisions) Order 2004 (SI 2004/1899) Sch.2 art.21.
[147] Carriage by Air Act 1961 Sch.1 art.21.
[148] Carriage by Air Act 1961 Sch.1A as inserted by SI 1999/1312 art.21(1).
[149] Carriage by Air Act 1961 Sch.1B as inserted by SI 2002/263 art.20. For the application of the Montreal Convention 1999 to govern the liability of European Union air carriers, see above, para.35-018.
[150] Carriage by Air Acts (Application of Provisions) Order 2004 (SI 2004/1899) Sch.2 art.22.
[151] Carriage by Air Act 1961 Sch.1 art.22.

or on it being shown that the damage resulted from the intentional or reckless misconduct of the carrier, its servants or agents), its liability in the carriage of persons is limited to the sum of 250,000 francs for each passenger.[152] In cases under the Montreal Convention 1999, there is no limit to the damages which may be payable once the liability of the carrier for the death of or injury to a passenger has been established. However, for damages not exceeding a prescribed amount[153] for each passenger, the carrier is not able to exclude or limit its liability. The carrier is not liable for such damages to the extent that they exceed the prescribed amount if the carrier proves that (a) such damage was not due to the negligence or other wrongful act or omission of the carrier or its servants or agents; or (b) such damage was solely due to the negligence or other wrongful act or omission of a third party.[154] The references to "special contract" mean in practice terms in the carrier's Conditions of Carriage.

A large number of airlines are now parties to agreements which have an effect similar to and supplement the provisions of the Montreal Convention 1999: the IATA Intercarrier Agreement on Passenger Liability of 1995 and its Intercarrier Implementation Agreement of 1996, and the ATA Implementing Agreement of 2005.[155]

Unfair terms   Under Pt 2 of the Consumer Rights Act 2015 various types of contractual term are classed as unfair and so not binding on the consumer. They include any term which has the object or effect of excluding or limiting the trade's liability in the event of the death of or personal injury to the consumer resulting from an act or omission of the trader. As already noted, in cases covered by the Montreal Convention 1999 any contractual provision tending to relieve the carrier of liability or to fix a lower limit than that laid down in the applicable Convention is null and void.[156] Part 2 of the Consumer Rights Act 2015 itself does not apply to a term of a contract, or to a notice, to the extent that it reflects (a) mandatory statutory or regulatory provisions, or (b) the provisions or principles of an international convention to which the United Kingdom or the EU is a party.[157] **35-034**

Misconduct   In cases governed by the Warsaw Convention 1929, the carrier is not entitled to avail itself of the provisions which limit or exclude its liability,[158] if the damage is caused by its wilful misconduct or by such default on its part as, in accordance with the law of the court seised of the case, is considered to be equivalent to wilful misconduct; or by the wilful misconduct or equivalent fault of any servant or agent of the carrier acting within the scope of his or her employment.[159] The **35-035**

---

152 Carriage by Air Act 1961 Sch.1A as inserted by SI 1999/1312 art.22.
153 100,000 SDRs in the original text of the Convention, raised to 113,100 SDRs by a decision of the ICAO Council under art.24 of the Convention, given effect in England by the Carriage by Air (Revision of Limits of Liability under the Montreal Convention) Order 2009 (SI 2009/3018).
154 Carriage by Air Act 1961 Sch.1B as inserted by SI 2002/263 art.21. For the application of the Montreal Convention 1999 to govern the liability of European Union air carriers, see above, para.35-018.
155 See generally, Shawcross and Beaumont, at Vol.1, paras VII[183] et seq.
156 See para.35-014.
157 Consumer Rights Act 2015 s.73. See generally Ch.38.
158 See above, para.35-025.
159 Carriage by Air Acts (Application of Provisions) Order 2004 (SI 2004/1899) Sch.2 art.25. See *Horabin v British Overseas Airways Corp* [1952] 2 All E.R. 1016; *Rustenburg Platinum Mines Ltd v South African Airways* [1977] 1 Lloyd's Rep. 564; *Thomas Cook Group Ltd v Air Malta Co Ltd*

test of "wilful misconduct" having proved unsatisfactory, a new formulation was adopted in the Hague Protocol of 1955. Under the Warsaw-Hague text and the MP4 Convention, the limits of the liability specified in art.22 do not apply if it is proved that the damage[160] resulted from an act or omission of the carrier, its servants or agents, done with intent to cause damage or recklessly and with knowledge that damage would probably result; provided that, in the case of such act or omission of a servant or agent, it is also proved that he or she was acting within the scope of his or her employment.[161] In the Montreal Convention 1999, intentional or reckless misconduct is relevant in passenger cases only in respect of liability for delay.[162]

35-036   This loss of the carrier's protection by virtue of misconduct has been much debated as far as the construction of the expressions "with intent to cause damage" and "recklessly and with knowledge that damage would probably result" is concerned. It seems clear that the probability of the result qualifies the nature of the act or omission of the carrier, i.e. if the nature of the act or omission necessarily makes damage—any damage—probable and not just possible, the requirements of the Convention provision will be met.[163] The probability does not have to be high or predominant[164]: one just anticipates damage from the act or omission. "Probably" just means that something is likely to happen.[165]

35-037   **A subjective test**   In construing the term "recklessly and with knowledge that damage would probably result" the courts have applied a subjective approach. It must be shown that the relevant actor himself had knowledge that damage would probably result. It is not enough to show that some other person had that knowledge, or that he would have had it if only he had applied his mind to the matter.[166] So in a case involving a failure by the commander of a passenger aircraft to give warnings of turbulence,[167] the Court of Appeal held that if the pilot did not know that damage would probably result from his omission, the court was not entitled to attribute to him knowledge which another pilot might have possessed or which he himself should have possessed. Similarly, it has been held that there can be no reliance on "background knowledge", facts within a pilot's knowledge but not present in his mind at the time of the relevant acts or omissions, even if, had he thought about them, they would have led to him appreciating the probability of damage, in this context.[168]

[1997] 2 Lloyd's Rep. 399; *Rolls Royce Plc v Heavylift-Volga DNEPR Ltd* [2000] 1 All E.R. (Comm) 796.

[160] See *Goldman v Thai Airways International Ltd* [1983] 1 W.L.R. 1186, CA, for the view that the damage anticipated must be of the same kind of damage as that suffered.

[161] Carriage by Air Act 1961 Sch.1 art.25; Sch.1A as inserted by SI 1999/1312 art.25.

[162] Carriage by Air Act 1961 Sch.1B as inserted by SI 2002/263 art.22(5). For the application of the Montreal Convention 1999 to govern the liability of European Union air carriers, see above, para.35-018.

[163] *Goldman v Thai Airways International Ltd* (1981) 125 S.J. 413. See, generally, Bin Cheng (1977) 2 *Annals of Air and Space Law* 55.

[164] *Goldman v Thai Airways International Ltd*, above.

[165] *Goldman v Thai Airways International Ltd* [1983] 1 W.L.R. 1186, CA, per Eveleigh L.J. at 1196; *Qantas Airways Ltd v SS Pharmaceutical Co Ltd* [1991] 1 Lloyd's Rep. 288, NSWCA.

[166] *SS Pharmaceutical Co Ltd v Qantas Airways Ltd* [1989] 1 Lloyd's Rep. 319, NSWSC.

[167] *Goldman v Thai Airways International Ltd* [1983] 1 W.L.R. 1186, CA. See also *Gurtner v Beaton* [1993] 2 Lloyd's Rep. 369, CA; *Connaught Laboratories Ltd v British Airways* (2002) 217 D.L.R. (4th) 717 Ont.

[168] *Nugent v Michael Goss Aviation Ltd* [2000] 2 Lloyd's Rep. 222, CA (but note the observations of

Taken to its logical conclusion, the subjective test would make it impossible for **35-038** a plaintiff to establish misconduct by the carrier other than in the exceptional case. It is submitted that a fairer balance has to be struck between the parties. That such a balance can be achieved was demonstrated by a Canadian decision in which it was held that where, on the evidence, goods must have been stolen by some employee of the carrier having access to them, and where it could be concluded that they had been stolen in the course of that employee's employment, it was not necessary specifically to identify the thief before concluding that in stealing them he had acted with intent to cause damage or recklessly and with knowledge that damage would probably result. A thief must be deemed to have knowledge that theft is damaging to the owner.[169]

Misconduct of course not only covers the acts or omissions of the carrier's **35-039** employees or agents but also embraces the acts or omissions of the carrier itself at corporate level. If therefore the carrier has a reckless system—say, with regard to the operation of procedures to ensure the safety of passengers—or if he has failed to modify his system in light of painful experience—this may lead to a finding of misconduct.

Liability of carrier's employees or agents   If the action is brought, not against **35-040** the carrier, but against his employees or agents, they are entitled to avail themselves of the limit of liability which the carrier himself could have invoked, provided they prove that they were acting within the scope of their employment. This is expressly provided in the Warsaw-Hague text,[170] the MP4 Convention,[171] and the Montreal Convention 1999,[172] and is generally taken to have been the case under the Warsaw Convention 1929.[173] It is further provided that, in that case, the aggregate amount recoverable from the carrier and his employees and agents is not to exceed that limit. If the damage resulted from an act or omission of the employee or agent done with intent to cause damage or recklessly and with knowledge that damage would probably result, that fact has the same effect on the liability of the carrier, his employees and agents as similar conduct by the carrier himself.

Fatal accidents   Section 3 of the Carriage by Air Act 1961 provides that refer- **35-041** ences in s.1 of the Fatal Accidents Act 1976 to a wrongful act, neglect or default shall include references to any occurrence which gives rise to liability under the applicable convention.[174] Hence, in the event of the death of a passenger, the Fatal Accidents Act 1976 will determine which dependants can recover damages for the loss of their breadwinner.[175] The damages are not limited to financial loss.[176]

Pill L.J. as to the possible relevance of the pilot's "fund of knowledge", the general knowledge his experience of flying brings him).
[169] *Swiss Bank Corp v Air Canada* (1981) 129 D.L.R. (3d) 85 at 95, 104, Federal Ct, Canada (affirmed (1987) 44 D.L.R. (4th) 680, Federal Ct of Appeal).
[170] Carriage by Air Act 1961 Sch.1 art.25A.
[171] Carriage by Air Act 1961 Sch.1A as inserted by SI 1999/1312 art.25A.
[172] Carriage by Air Act 1961 Sch.1B as inserted by SI 2002/263 art.30.
[173] *Reed v Wiser*, 555 F. 2d 1079 (1977), 2nd Cir.
[174] Carriage by Air Act 1961 s.3 as amended by SI 1999/1312 and SI 2002/263.
[175] *Kandalla v British European Airways* [1981] Q.B. 158.
[176] *Preston v Hunting Air Transport Ltd* [1956] 1 Q.B. 454.

35-042   **Several actions by one passenger**   The limitations on liability in art.22 of the Warsaw-Hague text, in the MP4 Convention, and in arts 21 and 22 of the Montreal Convention 1999 apply whatever the nature of the proceedings by which liability may be enforced. They apply to the aggregate liability of the carrier in all proceedings which may be brought against it under the law of any part of the United Kingdom, together with any proceedings brought against it outside the United Kingdom.[177] These provisions are also applied by the Carriage by Air Acts (Application of Provisions) Order 2004[178] to proceedings under the unamended Warsaw Convention and under that Convention as amended by Montreal Additional Protocol No.1; and by the Civil Liability (Contribution) Act 1978 to proceedings under that Act to recover contribution from any other person liable in respect of the same damage.[179] A court may, at any stage of the proceedings, make any such order as appears to the court to be just and equitable in view of the limits set in the Conventions and of any proceedings which have been, or are likely to be, commenced in the United Kingdom or elsewhere to enforce the liability in whole or in part.[180] The court is expressly given jurisdiction to award an amount less than it would have awarded if the limitation in the applicable Convention applied solely to the proceedings before the court, and can make any part of its award conditional on the result of any other proceedings.[181] Where there are claims under both the Fatal Accidents Act 1976 and the Law Reform (Miscellaneous Provisions) Act 1934 and the combined total damages would exceed the applicable Convention limit, the amounts recoverable under art.22(1) will be apportioned by the court in accordance with s.4(2) of the Carriage by Air Act 1961,[182] the court making such order as is just and equitable.

35-043   **Overbooking**   Whilst it is not unreasonable for a carrier to exclude liability for damage occasioned by delay in the event inter alia of facts beyond his control or facts not reasonably to be anticipated there seems no good reason for a carrier to escape liability when the likelihood of delay is in practical terms reasonably foreseeable. This could happen, for example, when a carrier overbooks the capacity of an aircraft on a particular flight as a matter of commercial policy, thus deliberately creating a risk that he will not be able to accommodate all the passengers who hold tickets and who turn up for the flight. The policy of overbooking was examined by the House of Lords in *British Airways Board v Taylor*,[183] a case on the applicability of s.14 of the Trade Descriptions Act 1968 to air carriers' reservations. Although at one stage, airlines sought to avoid liability through terms in their Conditions of Carriage, most have now adopted a "denied boarding compensation policy". It seems likely that liability for "overbooking" would arise outside art.19 which in all versions of the Warsaw Convention and in the Montreal Convention 1999 governs liability for delay. Decisions in other jurisdictions show a tendency to treat such cases as amounting to non-performance of the contract

---

[177] Carriage by Air Act 1961 s.4, as amended by SI 1999/1312 and SI 2002/263.
[178] SI 2004/1899 art.7.
[179] Civil Liability (Contribution) Act 1978 s.2(3).
[180] Carriage by Air Act 1961 s.4(2), as amended by SI 1999/1312 and SI 2002/263.
[181] Carriage by Air Act 1961 s.4(3), as amended by SI 1999/1312 and SI 2002/263.
[182] As amended by SI 2002/263.
[183] [1976] 1 W.L.R. 13.

rather than as creating delay in the carriage by air.[184] Denied boarding compensation under European Parliament and Council Regulation 261/2004[185] applies, inter alia, to denied boarding as a result of overbooking.

Successive carriers   A carriage to be performed by several successive carriers is **35-044** deemed to be one undivided carriage for the purposes of the Convention if it is regarded by the parties as a single operation, whether there is a single contract or a series of contracts, and it does not lose its international character merely because one contract or a series of contracts is to be performed entirely within the territory of the same state.[186] Each carrier who accepts passengers, baggage or cargo under such a carriage is subjected to the rules of the Convention, and is deemed to be one of the contracting parties to the contract of carriage insofar as the contract deals with that part of the carriage which is performed under his supervision.[187] In the case of carriage of this nature, however, the passenger or his representative can only sue the carrier who performed the carriage during which the accident or the delay occurred, except when by express agreement the first carrier assumed liability for the whole journey.[188] IATA Conditions negative any such agreement.[189] Hence, if part of the carriage not only is, but to the knowledge of the passenger is to be, performed by a carrier other than the one who made the contract, the liability of each carrier is limited to what happens during his part of the journey.

Contracting carriers and "actual" carriers   The situation is different, however, **35-045** if one carrier makes the contract with the passenger, and another carrier by virtue of authority from the first performs the whole or part of the carriage without becoming a "successive carrier" as above defined. This would happen if, for instance, the passenger was not told at the time when he made his contract that another carrier would perform the whole or part of the carriage. This situation is dealt with by the Guadalajara Convention 1961, which is supplementary to the Warsaw Convention and has the force of law in the United Kingdom by virtue of the Carriage by Air (Supplementary Provisions) Act 1962.[190] With minor drafting changes, the text of

---

[184] *Wolgel v Mexicana Airlines*, 821 F. 2d 442 (1987), US Ct of Appeals, 7th Circuit; Bundesgerichtshof, September 20, 1978, 1979 Z.L.W. 134.

[185] See para.35-049.

[186] Carriage by Air Acts (Application of Provisions) Order 2004 (SI 2004/1899) Sch.2 art.1(3); Carriage by Air Act 1961 Sch.1 art.1(3); Sch.1A as inserted by SI 1999/1312 art.1(2); Sch.1B as inserted by SI 2002/263 art.1(3). See *Rotterdamsche Bank NV v BOAC* [1953] 1 W.L.R. 493, see below, para.35-047. Both parties to the contract of carriage must regard the carriage as a single, individual operation: *Karfunkel v Compagnie Nationale Air France*, 427 F.Supp. 971 (1977), New York District Ct; *Bafana v Commercial Airways (Pty) Ltd* [1990] (1) S.A. 368, Witwatersrand Ct.

[187] Carriage by Air Acts (Application of Provisions) Order 2004 (SI 2004/1899) Sch.2 art.30(1); Carriage by Air Act 1961 Sch.1 art.30(1); Sch.1A as inserted by SI 1999/1312 art.30(1); Sch.1B as inserted by SI 2002/263 art.36(1). A carrier may be a successive carrier under art.30 even where the contract of carriage was incomplete to the extent that return flights were not agreed upon, provided that the completion of the contract and consequent amendment of the ticket were within the contemplation of the parties when the contract was made. The completion and amendment will relate back to the time of making of the contract, thus making the carrier in question a successive carrier: *Briscoe v Compagnie Nationale Air France*, 290 F.Supp. 863 (1968), New York District Ct.

[188] Carriage by Air Acts (Application of Provisions) Order 2004 (SI 2004/1899) Sch.2 art.30(2); Carriage by Air Act 1961 Sch.1 art.30(2); Sch.1A as inserted by SI 1999/1312 art.30(2); Sch.1B as inserted by SI 2002/263 art.36(2).

[189] PSC(24)1724 art.15.1.2(b).

[190] The 1962 Act was drafted so as to be supplementary to both the Warsaw Convention 1929 and the

the Guadalajara Convention is incorporated as Ch.V (arts 39 to 48) of the Montreal Convention 1999. The general effect is that in relation to the carriage performed by the actual carrier, an action for damages may be brought, at the option of the plaintiff, against that carrier or the contracting carrier, or against both together or separately. If the action is brought against only one of those carriers, that carrier will have the right to require the other carrier to be joined in the proceedings, the procedure and effects being governed by the law of the court seised of the case.[191] The rules of the applicable convention will govern all claims,[192] but the aggregate of the amounts recoverable from the actual carrier and the contracting carrier (and from their respective employees and agents acting within the scope of their employment) may not exceed the highest amount which could be awarded against either the contracting carrier under that Convention, or against the actual carrier under that Convention, as applied by the Guadalajara Convention.[193] Each carrier is, in general, benefitted by, and liable for, the other's acts and omissions and those of the other's employees or agents acting within the scope of their employment; but those of the actual carrier and of his employees or agents are of course only imputed to the contracting carrier in relation to that part of the carriage which the actual carrier performs, and vice versa.[194] Thus, if the actual carrier and his employees and agents took all necessary measures to avoid the damage, the contracting carrier can rely on this fact as a defence. On the other hand, no act or omission of the contracting carrier or his employees or agents will subject the actual carrier to liability exceeding the limits specified in art.22 of the Warsaw Convention[195]; nor can the actual carrier be adversely affected by any special contract between the passenger and the contracting carrier which has the effect of enlarging his liability, unless the actual carrier agreed to it.[196]

European legislation[197] requires the "air carriage contractor" to inform the passenger of the identity of the operating air carrier or carriers at the time of reservation, or on the identity of the relevant carrier becoming known, or at the latest at check-in (or on boarding if no check-in is required). It is an offence not to comply with this requirement.[198]

Warsaw-Hague text; it has been amended to perform the same function in respect of the MP4 Convention: Carriage by Air (Supplementary Provisions) Act 1962 s.2(1)(b), as amended by SI 1999/1312.

[191] Carriage by Air (Supplementary Provisions) Act 1962 Sch. art.VII; Carriage by Air Act 1961 Sch.1B as inserted by SI 2002/263 art.45.

[192] Carriage by Air (Supplementary Provisions) Act 1962 Sch. art.II; Carriage by Air Act 1961 Sch.1B as inserted by SI 2002/263 art.40.

[193] Carriage by Air (Supplementary Provisions) Act 1962 Sch. art.VI; Carriage by Air Act 1961 Sch.1B as inserted by SI 2002/263 art.44.

[194] Carriage by Air (Supplementary Provisions) Act 1962 Sch. art.III; Carriage by Air Act 1961 Sch.1B as inserted by SI 2002/263 art.41.

[195] Carriage by Air (Supplementary Provisions) Act 1962 Sch. art.III(2); Carriage by Air Act 1961 Sch.1B as inserted by SI 2002/263 art.41(2).

[196] Carriage by Air (Supplementary Provisions) Act 1962 Sch. art.III(2); Carriage by Air Act 1961 Sch.1B as inserted by SI 2002/263 art.41(2).

[197] European Parliament and Council Regulation 2111/2005 of December 14, 2005 on the establishment of a Community list of air carriers subject to an operating ban within the Community and on informing air transport passengers of the identity of the operating air carrier and repealing Article 9 of Directive 2004/36 arts 10–13.

[198] Civil Aviation (Provision of Information to Passengers) Regulations 2006 (SI 2006/3303).

Sub-contracted carriage   The Guadalajara Convention appears to assume that, **35-046**
as between the passenger and the contracting carrier, the contracting carrier is
entitled to sub-contract the contract of carriage to another carrier. Airlines' conditions of contract always reserve the right to substitute other carriers for the whole
or part of the journey in question.[199] In the absence of such a term, where for
example a passenger negotiated a contract with the owner of a light aircraft for a
flight to a family function on a basis akin to that of an air-taxi flight, it is not clear
whether the pilot could sub-contract the carriage to another. There is very little
English authority as to when a contract of carriage can be sub-contracted. Even if
an unauthorised sub-contracting amounted, on the facts of a particular case, to a
breach of contract, it is very doubtful whether this would disqualify the contracting carrier from relying on the defences and limitations of liability contained in the
Warsaw Convention.

It has been held sufficient to create a "successive carrier" situation where a   **35-047**
contractual carrier's timetable forms part of the contract of carriage and makes it
clear that part of the carriage is to be performed by another carrier.[200] This was in a
pre-Guadalajara Convention case. The provisions of the Guadalajara Convention
make it unnecessary, however, to contrive "successive carrier" relationships.

Disabled persons and persons with reduced mobility   European Parliament and   **35-048**
Council Regulation 1107/2006 concerning the rights of disabled persons and
persons with reduced mobility when travelling by air applies in respect of both
disabled persons and persons with reduced mobility, defined as: "any person whose
mobility when using transport is reduced due to any physical disability (sensory or
locomotor, permanent or temporary, intellectual disability or impairment, or any
other cause of disability, or age, and whose situation needs appropriate attention and
the adaptation to his or her particular needs of the service made available to all passengers)",[201] thus including the blind, the old and also those with a temporary
injury.[202] In the United Kingdom enforcement of Regulation 1107/2006 is by means
of a civil procedure which replaced the earlier criminal offences.[203] Regulation
1107/2006 applies to persons using or intending to use commercial passenger air
services departing from, transiting through or arriving at an airport in an EU
Member State; and departing from an airport in a third country to an airport in an
EU Member State, if the operating carrier is a Union air carrier (but only with regard
to the provisions on prevention of refusal of carriage and assistance by air
carriers).[204]

Air carriers, their agents and tour operators must not refuse, on grounds of disability or reduced mobility, to accept a flight reservation or embark a person
(provided the person has a valid ticket and reservation), and must not require that
the person can only travel if accompanied by another person who can give

---

[199] For code-shares, see IATA recommended conditions (PSC(24)1724) art.2.3.
[200] *Rotterdamsche Bank NV v British Overseas Airways Corp* [1953] 1 W.L.R. 493. The use of joint
designator codes, identifying two carriers in respect of the same journey, will have the same effect.
[201] Regulation 1107/2006 art.2(a).
[202] It applies with effect from July 26, 2007 with regard to the provisions on refusal of carriage, and
with effect from July 26, 2008 with regard to the other provisions: Regulation 1107/2006 art.18.
[203] Civil Aviation (Access to Air Travel for Disabled Persons and Persons with Reduced Mobility)
Regulations 2014 (SI 2014/2833), as amended by SI 2016/729 (which designates dispute resolution bodies).
[204] Regulation 1107/2006 art.1(2) and (3). See Viegas, (2013) 38 A.S.L. 47.

assistance.[205] If applicable safety requirements, the size of the aircraft or its doors, makes embarkation physically impossible, the air carrier (or its agent or tour operator) must make reasonable efforts to propose an acceptable alternative, and the person must be offered the right of reimbursement or re-routing, and must be given reasons.[206] Amongst other obligations, airlines, their agents and tour operators must provide specified types of assistance without charge to disabled persons.[207] This includes carriage of recognised assistance dogs in the cabin (subject to national regulations), transport of mobility equipment, making all reasonable efforts to arrange seating to meet the person's needs, assistance in moving to toilet facilities and all reasonable efforts to give an accompanying person a seat next to the disabled person.

In *Hook v British Airways Plc; Stott v Thomas Cook Tour Operators*[208] the claimant alleged a breach by the carrier of the obligation in art.10 to make reasonable efforts to meet his seating needs. It was held that although reg.9 of the Civil Aviation (Air Travel for Disabled Persons and Persons with Reduced Mobility) Regulations 2007[209] provides that a claim by a disabled person or a person with reduced mobility for an infringement of any of his rights under Regulation 1107/2006 may be made the subject of civil proceedings in the same way as any other claim in tort, this had to be interpreted so as to avoid conflict with the exclusivity provisions in art.29 of the Montreal Convention[210] which were binding on EU institutions. It followed that a claim for damages could not be made in respect of anything occurring during the time (when the passenger is on board the aircraft or in the course of any of the operations of embarking or disembarking)[211] in which the Convention is applicable.

(b)   Passengers: Denied Boarding, Cancellation and Long Delay

35-049   **Regulation 261/2004**   Under European Parliament and Council Regulation 261/2004,[212] compensation is payable and other assistance is to be provided to passengers denied boarding or subjected to cancellation of or long delay to their journey. This takes the form of standardised and immediate assistance in contrast to the individualised damage for delay under the Montreal Convention 1999.[213] It follows that Regulation 261/2004 does not operate to limit the liability of the carrier for delay under the Montreal (or Warsaw) Convention, and that the Montreal Convention does not preclude the payment of compensation under the

---

205   Regulation 1107/2006 art.3.
206   Regulation 1107/2006 art.4.
207   Regulation 1107/2006 art.10 and Annex 2.
208   [2014] UKSC 15, [2014] A.C. 1347. See Prassl, (2014) 130 LQR 538.
209   SI 2007/1895.
210   See para.35-013.
211   See para.35-028.
212   European Parliament and Council Regulation 261/2004 of February 11, 2004 establishing common rules on compensation and assistance to passengers in the event of denied boarding and of cancellation or of long delay in flights. Airlines must ensure that a clearly legible and visible notice containing prescribed wording as to the Regulation's provisions is displayed to passengers at check-in, and must provide passengers affected by denied boarding, cancellation or delay with a notice setting out the rules for compensation and assistance: art.14. For commentary on many aspects of the Regulation, see Bobek and Prassl (eds), *Air Passenger Rights: Ten Years On* (2016).
213   *R (on application of International Air Transport Association) v Department for Transport* (C-344/04) EU:C:2006:10, [2006] E.C.R. I-403.

Regulation.[214] Regulation 261/2004 applies to passengers departing from an airport in the EU, and to passengers departing from an airport in a third country on a flight operated by a Community carrier to an airport in an EU state, unless they received benefits or compensation and were given assistance in that third country.[215] Where connecting flights are concerned, the Regulation applies when the first leg is operated from an EU airport and this causes a connecting flight to be missed, even if the resulting denied boarding is on the second leg operated by a non-Community carrier and wholly outside the EU.[216]

The Regulation applies only to passengers who (a) have a confirmed reservation on the flight concerned and, except in the case of cancellation, present themselves for check-in as stipulated and at the time indicated in advance and in writing (including by electronic means) by the air carrier, the tour operator or an authorised travel agent (or, if no time is indicated, not later than 45 minutes before the published departure time); or (b) have been transferred by an air carrier or tour operator from the flight for which they held a reservation to another flight, irrespective of the reason.[217] Regulation 261/2004 does not apply to passengers travelling free of charge or at a reduced fare not available directly or indirectly to the public; but it does apply to passengers having tickets issued under a frequent flyer programme or other commercial programme by an air carrier or tour operator.[218] The Regulation only applies to passengers transported by motorised fixed wing aircraft.[219]

Jurisdiction Regulation 261/2004 does not contain any provisions regarding jurisdiction. It was confirmed by the European Court in *Rehder v Air Baltic Corp*[220] that the relevant jurisdictional rules are those in the Brussels I Regulation (recast).[221] For the purposes of art.7 of the Brussels I Regulation (recast) the place of departure and the place of destination may both be considered as places in which the services of an airline were to be supplied.[222] In the case of connecting flights, the place of performance of such a flight is the place of arrival of the second leg, as one of the main places of provision of services under a contract for carriage by air.[223] Liability under Regulation 261/2004 is always that of the operating carrier.[224] Where that carrier is not also the contracting carrier, the matter is nonetheless, despite the absence of a contract between the carrier and the operating carrier, "a matter relat-

35-050

---

[214] *Gahan v Emirates* [2017] EWCA Civ 1530 at [31]ff.

[215] Regulation 261/2004 art.3(1). See *Emirates Airlines Direktion für Deutschland v Schenkel* (C-173/07) EU:C:2008:400, [2008] E.C.R. I-5237.

[216] *Gahan v Emirates* [2017] EWCA Civ 1530 (effectively overruling *Sanghvi v Cathay Pacific Airways* [2011] EWHC 1684 (Ch), [2012] 1 Lloyd's Rep 46). A proposed revision of Regulation 261/2004 would secure the result reached in *Gahan*: see COM (2013) 130 final.

[217] Regulation 261/2004 art.3(2). See *Caldwell v easyJet Airline Co Ltd*, 2015 S.L.T. (Sh Ct) 223; *Kupeli v Kibris Turk Hava Yollari Sirketi* [2016] EWHC 930 (QB).

[218] Regulation 261/2004 art.3(3).

[219] Regulation 261/2004 art.3(4).

[220] (C-204/08) EU:C:2009:439, [2009] E.C.R. I-6073.

[221] European Parliament and Council Regulation 1215/2012 of December 12, 2012 on jurisdiction and the recognition and enforcement of judgments in civil and commercial matters (or its predecessor Regulation 44/2001).

[222] *Rehder v Air Baltic Corp* (C-204/08) EU:C:2009:439, [2009] E.C.R. I-6073.

[223] *flightright GmbH v Air Nostrum Líneas Aéreas del Mediterráneo SA* and *Barkan v Air Nostrum Lineas Aereas del Mediterraneo SA* (Joined Cases C-274/16 and C-448/16) EU:C:2018:160.

[224] This does not preclude claims for compensation or reimbursement by the operating carrier against third parties: Regulation 261/2004 art.13.

ing to a contract" for the purposes of art.7(1)(a) of the Brussels I Regulation (recast).[225]

35-051 **Limitation of actions** Regulation 261/2004 does not contain provisions concerning limitations of actions. In *Cuadrench Moré v Koninklijke Luchtvaart Maatschappij NV*[226] the European Court held that neither art.35 of the Montreal Convention nor art.29 of the Warsaw Convention was applicable (since compensation under Regulation 261/2004 falls outside the scope of those conventions); the matter was governed by the domestic legal system of each Member State, as long as those domestic systems safeguarded the rights of individuals derived from EU law. In England, the six-year limitation period under s.9 of the Limitation Act 1980 applies.[227]

35-052 **Denied boarding** "Denied boarding" is defined in Regulation 261/2004 as:

"... a refusal to carry passengers on a flight, although they have presented themselves for boarding under the conditions laid down in Article 3(2), except where there are reasonable grounds to deny them boarding, such as reasons of health, safety or security, or inadequate travel documentation."[228]

"Denied boarding" is not limited to overbooking cases.[229] When an operating air carrier reasonably expects to deny boarding on a flight, it must first call for volunteers to surrender their reservations in exchange for benefits under conditions to be agreed between the passenger concerned and the operating air carrier. Volunteers must be assisted in accordance with art.8 (in respect of reimbursement or re-routing), such assistance being additional to the agreed benefits.[230] If an insufficient number of volunteers comes forward to allow the remaining passengers with reservations to board the flight, the operating air carrier may then deny boarding to passengers against their will and immediately compensate them in accordance with art.7 and assist them in accordance with arts 8 and 9.[231]

35-053 **Cancellation** "Cancellation" is defined in Regulation 261/2004 as meaning "the non-operation of a flight which was previously planned and on which at least one place was reserved".[232] The Regulation distinguishes between cancellation and delayed departure, without defining "delay". The European Court has held that a flight is delayed for the purposes of art.6 of Regulation 261/2004, which is drafted in terms of delay in departure, if it is operated in accordance with the original planning and its actual arrival time is later than the scheduled arrival time; the flight can

---

[225] *flightright GmbH v Air Nostrum Líneas Aéreas del Mediterráneo SA* and *Barkan v Air Nostrum Lineas Aereas del Mediterraneo SA* (Joined Cases C-274/16 and C-448/16) EU:C:2018:160 (decided under the original Brussels I Regulation 44/2001).

[226] *Cuadrench Moré v Koninklijke Luchtvaart Maatschappij NV* (C-139/11) EU:C:2012:741, [2013] 2 All E.R. (Comm) 1152.

[227] *Dawson v Thomson Airways Ltd* [2014] EWCA Civ 845, [2015] 1 W.L.R. 883. For the relevance of provisions in the carrier's Conditions of Carriage, see *Vergara v Ryanair Ltd* 2014 S.L.T. (Sh Ct) 119.

[228] Regulation 261/2004 art.2(j).

[229] *Finnair Oyj v Timy Lassooy* (C-22/11) EU:C:2012:604, [2013] 1 C.M.L.R. 18.

[230] Regulation 261/2004 art.4(1).

[231] Regulation 261/2004 art.4(1). For the remedies under arts 8 and 9, see para.35-059.

[232] Regulation 261/2004 art.2(l).

be classified as cancelled only if the air carrier arranges for the passengers to be carried on another flight whose original planning is different from that of the flight for which the booking was made.[233] However, "cancellation" includes the situation in which the aircraft takes off but, for whatever reason, is subsequently forced to return to the airport of departure where the passengers are transferred on to another flight.[234] In the case of cancellation, the passengers concerned must (a) be offered assistance by the operating air carrier in accordance with art.8 (reimbursement or re-routing); and (b) be offered assistance by the operating air carrier in accordance with art.9(1)(a) (meals and refreshment) and 9(2) (messages), as well as, in event of re-routing when the reasonably expected time of departure of the new flight is at least the day after the departure as it was planned for the cancelled flight, the assistance specified in art.9(1)(b) and 9(1)(c) (hotel accommodation and associated transport); and (c) have the right to compensation by the operating air carrier in accordance with art.7.[235]

However, passengers are not entitled to compensation if (i) they are informed of the cancellation at least two weeks before the scheduled time of departure; or (ii) they are informed of the cancellation between two weeks and seven days before the scheduled time of departure and are offered re-routing, allowing them to depart no more than two hours before the scheduled time of departure and to reach their final destination less than four hours after the scheduled time of arrival; or (iii) they are informed of the cancellation less than seven days before the scheduled time of departure and are offered re-routing, allowing them to depart no more than one hour before the scheduled time of departure and to reach their final destination less than two hours after the scheduled time of arrival.[236] The operating carrier has the burden of proof concerning the questions as to whether and when the passenger has been informed of the cancellation.[237] An operating air carrier is also not obliged to pay compensation if it can prove that the cancellation is caused by extraordinary circumstances which could not have been avoided even if all reasonable measures had been taken.[238]

Delayed departure   The provisions as to delayed departure in Regulation 261/ **35-054** 2004 apply where a flight is expected to be delayed: (a) for two hours or more in the case of flights of 1,500 km or less; (b) for three hours or more in the case of intra-Community flights of more than 1,500 km and other flights between 1,500 and 3,500 km; or (c) for four hours or more in the case of other flights.[239] When an operating carrier reasonably expects a flight to be delayed beyond its scheduled time of departure for a period that attracts Regulation 261/2004, it must offer the af-

---

[233] *Sturgeon v Condor Flugdienst GmbH* (heard with *Böck v Air France SA* (Joined Cases C-402/04 and C-432/07) EU:C:2009:716, [2009] E.C.R. I-10923. In *Rose v easyJet Airline Co Ltd* Unreported 2015, Liverpool Cty Ct, the court held that a passenger who had been told, incorrectly, by the airline's representatives that the intended flight had been cancelled was entitled to the same remedies as if the cancellation had taken place. Sed quaere.

[234] *Sousa Rodríguez v Air France* (C-83/10) EU:C:2011:652, [2012] 1 C.M.L.R. 40.

[235] Regulation 261/2004 art.5(1). For the remedies under arts 8 and 9, see para.35-059.

[236] Regulation 261/2004 art.5(1)(c).

[237] Regulation 261/2004 art.5(4). When passengers are informed of the cancellation, an explanation must be given concerning possible alternative transport: art.5(2). The carrier is obliged to pay compensation where the airline informs the relevant travel agent in time, but the latter fails to inform the passenger: *Krijgsman v Surinaamse Luchtvaart Maatschappij NV* (C-302/16) EU:C:2017:359.

[238] Regulation 261/2004 art.5(3). For these extraordinary circumstances, see para.35-058.

[239] Regulation 261/2004 art.6(1).

fected passengers: (a) the assistance specified in art.9(1)(a) (meals and refreshment) and art.9(2) (free messages); and (b) when the reasonably expected time of departure is at least the day after the time of departure previously announced, the assistance specified in art.9(1)(b) and 9(1)(c) (hotel accommodation and associated transport); and (c) when the delay is at least five hours, the assistance specified in art.8(1)(a) (reimbursement or re-routing).[240] In any event, the assistance shall be offered within the time limits set out in art.6(1) with respect to each distance bracket.[241]

35-055 **Late arrival at destination** The remedies for delay in art.6 of Regulation 261/2004 define delay in terms of delayed departure. The text of the Regulation provides no remedy for late arrival at the destination. It was nonetheless held by the European Court in *Sturgeon v Condor Flugdienst GmbH*[242] that the Regulation gave a remedy for delayed arrival at destination, where the lateness was three hours or more (regardless of the length of the flight); and that the remedy was compensation, payable unless the carrier proves that the long delay was caused by extraordinary circumstances which could not have been avoided even if all reasonable measures had been taken, namely circumstances beyond the actual control of the air carrier. The decision was much criticised but was reaffirmed by the European Court in *Nelson v Deutsche Lufthansa GmbH*.[243] One question asked repeatedly was whether the compensation for loss of time caused by late arrival is compensatory or not and what the consequences of an affirmative answer would mean in the light of the Montreal Convention's embargo on non-compensatory damages. In *Nelson v Deutsche Lufthansa GmbH* the European Court held that as compensation for loss of time fell outside the definition of damage occasioned by delay in art.19 of the Montreal Convention, it also fell outside the scope of art.29 of the Montreal Convention, and thus the obligation under Regulation 261/2004 to compensate delayed passengers for their loss of time was compatible with art.29 of the Montreal Convention.[244] The approach of the Court to the interpretation of art.29 of the Montreal Convention is plainly at variance with that of the UK Supreme Court and the US Supreme Court in the landmark cases of *Hook v British Airways Plc*[245] and *El Al International Airlines Ltd v Tseng*,[246] according to which the Warsaw and Montreal Conventions are exclusive in the sense that if the damage arises out of international carriage to which the convention applies, no other basis for a claim is allowed, not only when the convention does provide in a basis for the claim, but also if it does not. There is liability under the *Sturgeon* rule whether or not there was also delay in the departure of the flight sufficient to attract art.6.[247]

---

[240] Regulation 261/2004 art.6(1).

[241] Regulation 261/2004 art.6(2). For the remedies under arts 8 and 9, see para.35-059.

[242] Heard with *Böck v Air France SA* (Joined Cases C-402/07 and C-432/07) EU:C:2009:716, [2009] E.C.R. I-10923.

[243] Heard with *R. (on the application of TUI Travel) v Civil Aviation Authority* (Joined Cases C-581/10 and C-629/10) EU:C:2012:657, [2013] 1 All E.R. (Comm) 385.

[244] Joined Cases C-581/10 and C-629/10, EU:C:2012:657 at [50]–[55].

[245] [2014] UKSC 15, [2014] A.C. 1347; see para.35-013.

[246] 119 S.Ct. 662 (1999).

[247] *Air France v Folkerts* (C-11/11) EU:C:2013:106, [2013] All E.R. (EC) 1133. See also *Guadrench More v Koninkijke Luchtvaart Maatschappij NV* (C-139/11) EU:C:2012:741, [2013] 2 All E.R. (Comm) 1152; *Coelho dos Santos v TAP Portugal* (C-365/11) and *Becker v Société Air France* (C-584/11) EU:C:2013:281; *Wegener v Royal Air Maroc SA* (C-537/17) EU:C:2018:361, [2018] Bus. L.R. 1366

Upgrading and downgrading If, as a result of over-booking or re-routing, an **35-056**
airline places a passenger in a higher class, it may not request any supplementary
payment, and if it places a passenger in a lower class it must reimburse the passenger (a) 30 per cent of the ticket price for flights of 1,500 km or less; (b) 50 per
cent of the ticket price for intra-EC flights of more than 1,500 km and other flights
between 1,500 and 3,500 kms; (c) 75 per cent of the ticket price for all other
flights.[248] In the case of journeys comprising several legs, downgrading occurring
on only one leg, the reimbursement is to be based on the price of the specific flight,
and not the overall ticket price. If the price of the individual leg is not specified on
the ticket, the basis should be the part of the overall ticket price that corresponds
to the quotient of the distance of the flight in question and the total distance that the
passenger is entitled to travel.[249] For this purpose, taxes and charges are excluded
from the concept of ticket price, as long as neither the requirement to pay those
taxes and charges, nor their amount, depends on the class for which that ticket has
been purchased.[250]

The remedies: compensation Where compensation is prescribed as a remedy **35-057**
under Regulation 261/2004, for denied boarding,[251] cancellation,[252] and under the
Sturgeon rule as to long delay in arrival at destination,[253] the level of compensation payable depends upon the length of the flight, namely (a) €250 for flights of
1,500 km or less; (b) €400 for intra-EC flights of more than 1,500 km and other
flights between 1,500 and 3,500 km; and (c) €600 for all other flights, the distance
being calculated to the last destination at which the denial of boarding or cancellation will delay the passenger's arrival.[254] "Distance" relates, in the case of air routes
with connecting flights, only to the distance calculated between the first point of
departure and the final destination on the basis of the "great circle" method, regardless of the distance actually flown.[255] The amount of mandatory compensation is
halved when the airline offers re-routing to final destination on a flight which arrives not later than two, three or four hours respectively later than the original
scheduled arrival time.[256] Article 12 of the Regulation provides that the compensation provided for by art.7 is "without prejudice to a passenger's rights to further
compensation", although the compensation granted under art.7 may be deducted
from such compensation. This allows a national court to award compensation for
damage, including non-material damage, under the Montreal Convention or under
the applicable domestic law of a Member State arising from breach of a contract
of carriage by air. It may not serve as a legal basis for a claim for compensation of
the expenses a passenger incurred because of the failure of that carrier to fulfil its
obligations to assist and provide care under art. 8 and art.9 of Regulation 261/
2004 in case of delay or cancellation of a flight.[257]

---

[248] Regulation 261/2004 art.10(2).
[249] *Mennens v Emirates Direktion fur Deutschland (C-255/15)* (C-255/15) EU:C:2016:472.
[250] *Mennens v Emirates Direktion für Deutschland* (C-255/15) EU:C:2016:472 at [38].
[251] Regulation 261/2004 art.4; see para.35-052.
[252] Regulation 261/2004 art.5(1); see para.35-053.
[253] See para.35-055.
[254] Regulation 261/2004 art.7(1).
[255] *Bossen v Brussels Airlines SA/NV* (C-559/16) EU:C:2017:644.
[256] Regulation 261/2004 art.7(2). See *Sanghvi v Cathay Pacific Airways* [2011] EWHC 1684 (Ch),
[2012] 1 Lloyd's Rep 46 at [27]–[28].
[257] *Sousa Rodríguez v Air France* (C-83/10) EU:C:2011:652, [2012] 1 C.M.L.R. 40; *McDonagh v*

35-058 **Compensation not payable in extraordinary circumstances** If the cancellation or delay of more than three hours in arrival at destination is caused by extraordinary circumstances, which could not have been avoided even if all reasonable measures had been taken, the carrier is not obliged to pay the standardised compensation provided for in art.7 of the Regulation; the burden of proof is on the carrier.[258] Two recitals address this issue: Recital (14) lists as situations that might constitute extraordinary circumstances:

"… cases of political instability, meteorological conditions incompatible with the operation of the flight concerned, security risks, unexpected flight safety shortcomings and strikes that affect the operation of an operating air carrier."

Recital (15) deals specifically with the impact of an air traffic management decision.[259] In *Wallentin-Hermann v Alitalia Linee Aeree Italiane SpA*,[260] the European Court noted that "extraordinary circumstances" was not defined in the text of the Regulation, and that as art.5(3) derogated from the principle of compensation it had to be interpreted strictly. The carrier must prove that the cancellation is caused by extraordinary circumstances which could not have been avoided even if all reasonable measures had been taken: the carrier must establish that, even if it had deployed all its resources in terms of staff or equipment and the financial means at its disposal, it would clearly not have been able—unless it had made intolerable sacrifices in the light of the capacities of its undertaking at the relevant time—to prevent the extraordinary circumstances with which it was confronted from leading to the cancellation of the flight.[261] The examples given in Recital (14) did not themselves constitute extraordinary circumstances, but they might produce such circumstances.

A technical problem caused by failure to maintain an aircraft is to be regarded as inherent in the normal exercise of an air carrier's activity, and not as amounting to "extraordinary circumstances".[262] The same is true even of unexpected problems, not attributable to poor maintenance, given the very complex operating systems of aircraft.[263] A collision with mobile boarding stairs has been held to be an event inherent in the normal exercise of the activity of the air carrier and consequently, cannot be considered as an extraordinary circumstance.[264] The same result has been reached in cases concerning bird strikes,[265] "wildcat" strike action by aircrew,[266] and

---

Ryanair (C-12/11) EU:C:2013:43 [2013] 2 C.M.L.R. 32; *Graham v Thomas Cook Group UK Ltd* [2012] EWCA Civ 1355.

[258] Regulation 261/2004 art.5(3). The National Enforcement Bodies under the Regulation produced in April 2013 a list of events they considered "extraordinary circumstances"; it has no legal force.

[259] See *British Airways Plc v Horstink & Snapper* Unreported February 16, 2015, Liverpool Cty Ct.

[260] C-549/07, EU:C:2008:771.

[261] *Wallentin-Hermann v Alitalia Linee Aeree Italiane SpA* (C-549/07) EU:C:2008:771; *Egltis v Latvijas Republikas Ekonomickas ministrija* (C-294/10) EU:C:2011:303, [2011] 3 C.M.L.R. 40. See *Dunbar v easyJet Airline Co Ltd*, 2015 GWD 36-570, Sh Ct (North Strathclyde, Paisley).

[262] *Wallentin-Hermann v Alitalia Linee Aeree Italiane SpA* (C-549/07) EU:C:2008:771; *Jet2.com Ltd v Huzar* [2014] EWCA Civ 791, [2014] 4 All E.R. 581.

[263] *Van der Lans v Koninklijke Luchtvaartmaatschappij NV* (C-257/14) EU:C:2015:618. cf. *Bland v Thomas Cook Airlines Ltd* Unreported January 21, 2016, Manchester Cty Ct (aircraft tyre damaged by foreign object on runway: extraordinary circumstance).

[264] *Siewert v Condor Flugdienst GmbH* (C-394/14) EU:C:2014:2377.

[265] *Pesková v Travel Service as* (C-315/15) EU:C:2017:342, [2017] Bus. L.R. 1134.

[266] *Krüsemann v TUIfly GmbH* (C-195/17; joined with many others) EU:C:2018:258, [2018] Bus. L.R. 1191.

lightning hitting the aircraft during take-off.[267] The spread of volcanic ash from an eruption of the Icelandic volcano Eyjafjallajökull in 2010 did amount to "extraordinary circumstances".[268] At least in certain circumstances, the sudden illness of the pilot may amount to "extraordinary circumstances".[269]

The remedies: reimbursement or re-routing, care The remedy of reimbursement or re-routing under art.8 of Regulation 261/2004 obliges the airline to offer the passenger the choice between (a) reimbursement of the full ticket cost for the part or parts of the journey not made, and for the part or parts already made if the flight is no longer serving any purpose in relation to the passenger's original travel plan, together with, when relevant, a return flight to the first point of departure at the earliest opportunity; and (b) re-routing under comparable transport conditions[270] to final destination at the earliest opportunity or, at the passenger's choice, at a later date.[271] In a number of cases the question has arisen whether a passenger whose flight has been seriously delayed at departure and who chooses the option to be reimbursed for the ticket price by the airline is still entitled to compensation of €250 under art.7 of the Regulation. Although the Regulation seems to be sufficiently clear in this matter concerning cancelations in art.5 (the answer would be affirmative), the Regulation lacks a clear provision on this matter for delays. Breach of art.8 does not give rise to a civil action for damages,[272] but is a matter for administrative enforcement, the Civil Aviation Authority being responsible for enforcement in the United Kingdom.[273]

35-059

The obligation under art.9 of Regulation 261/2004 on the airline to provide care entails the provision of (a) meals and refreshments in a reasonable relation to the waiting time[274]; (b) hotel and accommodation where necessary, and related transport; and (c) two telephone calls, telex or fax messages, or emails. The duty to provide care has been held to be ongoing and to last until (a) the passenger's arrival at the final destination or (b) the passenger's election to make his own way to the final destination.[275]

---

[267] *Monarch Airlines Ltd v Evans and Lee* Unreported January 14, 2016, Luton Cty Ct.

[268] *Marshall v Iberia Lineas Aereas de España SA* Unreported December 13, 2010, Mayor's and City of London Ct (reversed but not on this point, H.H.J. Birtles, 2011, Unreported); *Williams v KLM Royal Dutch Airlines* Unreported 2011, Taunton Cty Ct; *Rosen v EasyJet Airline Co Ltd* Unreported December 15, 2011, Croydon County Ct. However the volcanic eruption did not excuse the carrier from providing the remedies other than compensation: *McDonagh v Ryanair* (C-12/11) EU:C:2013:43, [2013] 2 C.M.L.R. 32.

[269] *Marchbank-Smith v Virgin Atlantic Airways Ltd* Unreported January 14, 2015, Manchester Cty Ct.

[270] See *Marshall v Iberia Lineas Aereas de España SA* Unreported 2011 (H.H.J. Birtles) (putting on a wait list not comparable to a confirmed flight).

[271] *Hendy v Iberian Lineas de España Ltd* Unreported March 21, 2011, Oxford County Ct; *Rozen v EasyJet Airline Co Ltd* Unreported December 15, 2011, Croydon County Ct.

[272] *Graham v Thomas Cook Group UK Ltd* [2012] EWCA Civ 1355.

[273] Civil Aviation (Denied Boarding, Compensation and Assistance) Regulations 2005 (SI 2005/975) reg.5(1). Dispute resolution bodies are specified in reg.5(2) as substituted by SI 2016/729.

[274] Regulation 261/2004 art.9.

[275] *Hendy v Iberian Lineas de España SA* Unreported March 21, 2011, Oxford County Ct; *Rozen v EasyJet Airline Co Ltd* Unreported December 15, 2011, Croydon County Ct.

(c) Baggage

35-060 Forms of baggage   In the law of carriage by air, baggage is of two kinds. There is hand baggage, i.e. "objects of which the passenger takes charge himself"[276] and keeps with him in the aircraft; and registered baggage, sometimes termed checked baggage, of which the carrier takes charge. This is carried in the hold of the aircraft in which the passenger travels, or of another aircraft. The IATA Conditions define baggage in general as "your personal property accompanying you in connection with your trip".[277] The terms "registered" or "registration" used in the Convention in relation to baggage are not defined, and the English court has been prepared to interpret the Convention's provisions in relation to the carrier's liability for baggage as if the terms "registered" or "registration" were not there.[278]

35-061 Baggage check   In cases falling under the Warsaw Convention 1929, for the carriage of registered baggage, the carrier must deliver a baggage check in practice combined with the passenger ticket. The baggage check must contain the following particulars: (a) the place and date of issue; (b) the place of departure and of destination; (c) the name and address of the carrier or carriers; (d) the number of the passenger ticket; (e) a statement that delivery of the baggage will be made to the bearer of the baggage check; (f) the number and weight of the packages; (g) the amount of any value at destination declared by the passenger; and (h) a statement that the carriage is subject to the rules relating to liability established by the Warsaw Convention.[279] The absence, irregularity or loss of the baggage check does not affect the existence or the validity of the contract of carriage, which is nonetheless subject to the rules in the Convention. Nevertheless, if the carrier accepts baggage without a baggage check having been delivered, or if the baggage check does not contain particulars (d), (f) and (h), then the carrier is not entitled to avail itself of those provisions[280] of the Convention which exclude or limit its liability.[281] In cases under the Warsaw-Hague text and the MP4 Convention, in respect of the carriage of registered baggage, a baggage check must be delivered which, unless combined with or incorporated in a passenger ticket which complies with the provisions of the Convention, must contain: (a) an indication of the places of departure and destination; (b) if the places of departure and destination are within the territory of a single high contracting party, one or more agreed stopping places being within the territory of another state, an indication of at least one such stopping place; and (c) a notice to the effect that, if the carriage involves an ultimate destination or stop in a country other than the country of departure, the Warsaw Convention may be ap-

---

276 Carriage by Air Acts (Application of Provisions) Order 2004 (SI 2004/1899) Sch.2 art.22(3); Carriage by Air Act 1961 Sch.1 art.22(3); Sch.1A as inserted by SI 1999/1312 art.1(3). The term "unchecked baggage" is used in the Montreal Convention 1999: Carriage by Air Act 1961 Sch.1B as inserted by SI 2002/263 art.17(4) where, however, it is provided that references to "baggage" include both "checked" and "unchecked" baggage. English courts have not examined the question of the proper categorisation of baggage originally taken on board by the passenger but subsequently handed to the aircraft crew for stowage in the hold.

277 PSC(24)1724 art.1.

278 *Collins v British Airways Board* [1982] Q.B. 734, CA, Kerr L.J. dissenting (at 182) considered that "registration" of baggage must require the completion of a document constituting a baggage check to the effect that the carrier had taken charge of registered baggage.

279 Carriage by Air Acts (Application of Provisions) Order 2004 (SI 2004/1899) Sch.2 art.4.

280 See above, para.35-025.

281 Carriage by Air Acts (Application of Provisions) Order 2004 (SI 2004/1899) Sch.2 art.4(4).

plicable and that the Convention governs and in most cases limits the liability of carriers in respect of loss of or damage to baggage.[282] The baggage check constitutes prima facie evidence of the registration of the baggage and of the conditions of the contract of carriage.[283] The absence, irregularity, or loss of the baggage check does not affect the existence or the validity of the contract of carriage, which is nonetheless subject to the rules of the Warsaw-Hague text. Nevertheless, if the carrier takes charge of the baggage without a baggage check having been delivered, or if the baggage check does not contain, and is not combined with or incorporated in a passenger ticket which contains, the prescribed notice as to the possible applicability of the Warsaw Convention, the carrier is not entitled to avail itself of the provisions of art.22(2) limiting its liability.[284] In cases under the Montreal Convention 1999, no baggage check is required but the carrier must deliver to the passenger a baggage identification tag for each piece of checked baggage.[285]

Liability for damage, destruction or loss   In all cases other than those under the **35-062** 1999 Convention, unless the carrier can establish one of the defences allowed by the applicable Convention (that is, either that it and its servants or agents had taken all necessary measures to avoid the damage or that it was impossible for it or for them to have taken such measures; or the defence of contributory negligence; or in cases under the 1929 Convention proof that the damage was occasioned by negligent pilotage or negligence in the handling of the aircraft or in navigation and that, in all other respects, the carrier and his servants and agents had taken all necessary measures to avoid the damage), it is liable for damage sustained in the event of the destruction, or loss of, or of damage to, any registered baggage, if the occurrence which caused the damage so sustained took place during the carriage by air.[286] For this purpose, "carriage by air" comprises the period during which the baggage is in the charge of the carrier, whether in an aerodrome or on board an aircraft or, in the case of a landing outside an aerodrome, in any place whatsoever.[287] Under the Montreal Convention 1999, the carrier is liable for damage sustained in case of destruction or loss of, or of damage to, checked baggage upon condition only that the event which caused the destruction, loss, or damage took place on board the aircraft or during any period within which the baggage was in the charge of the carrier. In the case of unchecked baggage, the carrier is liable if the damage resulted from its fault or that of its servants or agents. However, the carrier is not liable if and to the extent that the damage resulted from the inherent defect, quality, or vice of the baggage, checked or unchecked.[288] European Parliament and Council Regula-

---

282   Carriage by Air Act 1961 Sch.1 art.4(1); Sch.1A as inserted by SI 1999/1312 art.4(1). See *Collins v British Airways Board* [1982] Q.B. 734, CA.

283   Carriage by Air Act 1961 Sch.1 art.4(2); Sch.1A as inserted by SI 1999/1312 art.4(2).

284   Carriage by Air Act 1961 Sch.1 art.4(2); Sch.1A as inserted by SI 1999/1312 art.4(2).

285   Carriage by Air Act 1961 Sch.1B as inserted by SI 2002/263 art.3(3).

286   Carriage by Air Acts (Application of Provisions) Order 2004 (SI 2004/1899) Sch.2 art.18(1); Carriage by Air Act 1961 Sch.1 art.18(1); Sch.1A as inserted by SI 1999/1312 art.18(1). For the meaning of "damage", see *Walz v Clickair SA* (C-63/09) EU:C:2010:251, [2011] 1 All E.R. (Comm) 1037, and para.35-028, above.

287   Carriage by Air Acts (Application of Provisions) Order 2004 (SI 2004/1899) Sch.2 art.18(2); Carriage by Air Act 1961 Sch.1 art.18(2); Sch.1A as inserted by SI 1999/1312 art.18(2).

288   Carriage by Air Act 1961 Sch.1B as inserted by SI 2002/263 art.17(2), (4).

tion 889/2002 applies the Montreal Convention regime to govern the baggage liability of Union air carriers.[289]

35-063   In cases governed by the Warsaw Convention 1929, the liability of the carrier in respect of registered baggage is limited to a sum of 250 francs per kilogramme[290] of the lost or damaged package,[291] and liability in respect of objects of which the passenger takes charge himself is limited to 5,000 francs per passenger.[292] In cases governed by the Warsaw-Hague text, the limits remain as in the 1929 Convention.[293] Under the Warsaw-Hague text, however, when the loss, damage or delay of a part of the registered baggage, or of an object contained therein, affects the value of other packages covered by the same baggage check, the total weight of such package or packages must also be taken into consideration in determining the limit of liability.[294] The limits in the 1929 Convention and the Warsaw-Hague text as amended by Montreal Additional Protocols 1975 No.1 and No.2 respectively, and in cases under the MP4 Convention, are 17 SDRs per kilogramme for registered baggage, and 332 SDRs per passenger for unregistered baggage.[295] Under the Montreal Convention 1999 (and the rules of that Convention as applied to Union air carriers under EU law) the liability of the carrier in the case of destruction, loss, damage, or delay to checked or unchecked baggage was limited in the original text of the Convention to 1,000 SDRs for each passenger.[296] This limit was raised with effect from December 30, 2009 to 1,131 SDRs for each passenger.[297] The Convention limits apply per passenger; this means that it is not correct to apply the limit separately to claims in respect of material and non-material damage,[298] but that if a single piece of baggage contains property belonging to two or more passengers, each may recover the actual loss up to the convention maximum, and it is immaterial that there is only one baggage check.[299] In all cases, the carrier's liability in respect of registered or checked baggage may be increased if the passenger makes, at the time when the package was handed over to the carrier, a special declaration of the value at delivery and pays a supplementary sum if the case so requires. In that case, the carrier will be liable to pay a sum not exceeding the declared sum,

---

[289] See above, para.35-018.

[290] Carriage by Air Acts (Application of Provisions) Order 2004 (SI 2004/1899) Sch.2 art.22(2).

[291] cf. the cargo case of *Data Card Corp v Air Express International Corp* [1984] 1 W.L.R. 198.

[292] Carriage by Air Acts (Application of Provisions) Order 2004 (SI 2004/1899) Sch.2 art.22(3).

[293] Carriage by Air Act 1961 Sch.1 art.22(2) (3) (which, as amended by the Carriage by Air and Road Act 1979 s.4, actually contains the limits as amended by Montreal Additional Protocol No.2 of 1975); *Bland v British Airways Board* [1981] 1 Lloyd's Rep. 289, CA; *Collins v British Airways Board* [1982] Q.B. 734, CA.

[294] Carriage by Air Act 1961 Sch.1 art.22(2)(b). cf. the cargo case of *Allied Implants Technology Ltd v Lufthansa Cargo AG* [2000] 2 Lloyd's Rep. 46.

[295] Carriage by Air Acts (Application of Provisions) Order 2004 (SI 2004/1899) Sch.3 art.22(2), (3); Carriage by Air Act 1961 Sch.1 art.22(2), (3) (as amended by the Carriage by Air and Road Act 1979 s.4); Sch.1A as inserted by SI 1999/1312 art.22(2)(a), (3).

[296] Carriage by Air Act 1961 Sch.1B as inserted by SI 2002/263 art.22(2) (applied to European Union air carriers by Council Regulation 2027/97 art.3.1 as substituted by Parliament and Council Regulation 889/2002).

[297] By a decision of the ICAO Council under art.24 of the Convention, given effect in England by the Carriage by Air (Revision of Limits of Liability under the Montreal Convention) Order 2009 (SI 2009/3018).

[298] *Walz v Clickair SA* (C-63/09) EU:C:2010:251, [2011] 1 All E.R. (Comm) 1037.

[299] Bundesgerichtshof, March 15, 2011, XZR 99/10.

unless it proves that the sum is greater than the actual value to the passenger at delivery.[300]

Time for making claims   Where baggage is damaged, the person entitled to **35-064** delivery must complain to the carrier forthwith after the discovery of the damage, and, at the latest, within (a) under the Warsaw Convention 1929, three days from the date of receipt; and (b) under all the other conventions, seven days from the date of receipt. Where baggage is delayed, the complaint must be made at the latest within (a) under Warsaw Convention 1929, 14 days from the date on which the baggage has been placed at his or her disposal; and (b) under all the other conventions, 21 days from the date on which the baggage has been placed at his or her disposal.[301] "Days" means current days, not working days.[302] Every complaint must be made in writing and given or dispatched within the specified times[303]; an oral complaint recorded in the information system of the carrier, provided the record identifies the complainant, satisfies this requirement.[304] If no complaint is made within the prescribed time limits, no action lies against the carrier, save in the case of fraud on its part.[305] Notice of complaint is not required in the case of total loss or destruction.

(d)   Cargo

Air waybill   In cases governed by the Warsaw Convention 1929 or the Warsaw- **35-065** Hague text, every carrier of cargo has the right to require the consignor to make out and hand over to him a document called an air waybill.[306] Though the legal responsibility for making out the waybill and for ensuring the correctness of its contents is that of the consignor,[307] in practice the carrier can make out the waybill[308] and, if he does, is deemed to have done so on the consignor's behalf. When more than one package is consigned, the carrier has the right to require a separate waybill for each package.[309] Each air waybill is made out in a set of three: the consignor

[300] Carriage by Air Acts (Application of Provisions) Order 2004 (SI 2004/1899) Sch.2 art.22(2); Carriage by Air Act 1961 Sch.1 art.22(2)(a); Sch.1A as inserted by SI 1999/1312 art.22(2)(a); Sch.1B as inserted by SI 2002/263 art.22(2).

[301] Carriage by Air Acts (Application of Provisions) Order 2004 (SI 2004/1899) Sch.2 art.26(2); Carriage by Air Act 1961 Sch.1 art.26(2); Sch.1A as inserted by SI 1999/1312 art.26(2); Sch.1B as inserted by SI 2002/263 art.31(2).

[302] Carriage by Air Acts (Application of Provisions) Order 2004 (SI 2004/1899) Sch.2 art.35; Carriage by Air Act 1961 Sch.1 art.35; Sch.1A as inserted by SI 1999/1312 art.35; Sch.1B as inserted by SI 2002/263 art.52.

[303] Carriage by Air Acts (Application of Provisions) Order 2004 (SI 2004/1899) Sch.2 art.26(3); Carriage by Air Act 1961 Sch.1 art.26(3); Sch.1A as inserted by SI 1999/1312 art.26(3); Sch.1B as inserted by SI 2002/263 art.31(3).

[304] *Finnair Oyj v Keskinainen Vakuutusyhtio Fennia* (C-258/16) EU:C:2018:252.

[305] Carriage by Air Acts (Application of Provisions) Order 2004 (SI 2004/1899) Sch.2 art.26(4); Carriage by Air Act 1961 Sch.1 art.26(4); Sch.1A as inserted by SI 1999/1312 art.26(4); Sch.1B as inserted by SI 2002/263 art.31(4).

[306] Carriage by Air Acts (Application of Provisions) Order 2004 (SI 2004/1899) Sch.2 art.5(1); Carriage by Air Act 1961 Sch.1 art.5(1).

[307] Carriage by Air Acts (Application of Provisions) Order 2004 (SI 2004/1899) Sch.2 art.10(1); Carriage by Air Act 1961 Sch.1 art.10(1).

[308] Carriage by Air Acts (Application of Provisions) Order 2004 (SI 2004/1899) Sch.2 art.6(5); Carriage by Air Act 1961 Sch.1 art.6(5).

[309] Carriage by Air Acts (Application of Provisions) Order 2004 (SI 2004/1899) Sch.2 art.7; Carriage

and carrier retain one each, while the third copy is for the consignee and travels with the cargo.[310] In practice, sets of air waybills may include as many as 15 copies, with three "top copies". In practice, air waybills are not negotiable, though a provision introduced in the Hague Protocol 1955 makes it clear that negotiable air waybills are a possibility.[311]

35-066 **Statements in waybill** The statements in the waybill relating to the weight, dimensions and packing of the cargo, and to the number of packages, are prima facie evidence of the facts stated; but those relating to the quantity, volume and condition of the cargo do not constitute evidence against the carrier unless they both have been, and are stated in the waybill to have been, checked by him in the presence of the consignor, or relate to the apparent condition of the cargo.[312]

35-067 **Absence of waybill, etc** The absence, irregularity or loss of the document does not affect the existence or validity of the contract of carriage, which continues to be governed by the rules of the applicable convention. In a case governed by the Warsaw Convention 1929, the air waybill must contain many prescribed particulars, and if the carrier accepts cargo without an air waybill having been made out, or if the air waybill does not contain the prescribed particulars, the carrier is not entitled to avail itself of the provisions[313] which exclude or limit its liability.[314] In a case governed by the Warsaw-Hague text, the air waybill must contain the same notice as to the applicability of the Convention as is required for passenger tickets and baggage checks.[315] If, with the consent of the carrier, cargo is loaded on board the aircraft without an air waybill having been made out, or if the air waybill does not contain a notice to the effect that the Convention governs, the carrier cannot avail himself of the limitations on his liability contained in art.22.[316] This is subject to the same exception as in the case of passenger tickets and baggage checks.[317]

35-068 **Cargo documentation under recent conventions** The MP4 Convention and the Montreal Convention 1999 also provide that in respect of the carriage of cargo an air waybill must be delivered.[318] However, in cases governed by these conventions

---

by Air Act 1961 Sch.1 art.7.

[310] Carriage by Air Acts (Application of Provisions) Order 2004 (SI 2004/1899) Sch.2 art.6(1), (2); Carriage by Air Act 1961 Sch.1 art.6(1), (2).

[311] Carriage by Air 1961 Sch.1 art.15(3). See generally *Gatewhite Ltd v Iberia Lineas Aereas de España Soc* [1989] 1 Lloyd's Rep. 160.

[312] Carriage by Air Acts (Application of Provisions) Order 2004 (SI 2004/1899) Sch.2 art.11(2); Carriage by Air Act 1961 Sch.1 art.11(2).

[313] See above, para.35-025.

[314] Carriage by Air Acts (Application of Provisions) Order 2004 (SI 2004/1899) Sch.2 art.9; *Corocraft Ltd v Pan American Airways Inc* [1969] 1 Q.B. 616, CA.

[315] Carriage by Air Acts (Application of Provisions) Order 2004 (SI 2004/1899) Sch.2 art.8; see above, para.35-023. There must be an identifiable notice; it is not sufficient that there are conditions from which the applicability of the Convention may be discovered: *Fujitsu Computer Products Corp v Bax Global Inc* [2005] EWHC 2289 (Comm), [2006] 1 Lloyd's Rep. 231.

[316] Carriage by Air Acts (Application of Provisions) Order 2004 (SI 2004/1899) Sch.2 art.9; see below, para.35-071. An air waybill does not have to be signed under art.6(2) to be "made out" within the meaning of art.9 and the carrier can still limit his liability: *United International Stables Ltd v Pacific Western Airlines Ltd* (1969) 5 D.L.R. (3d) 67, SC of British Columbia.

[317] SI 2004/1899 art.34; see above, para.35-025.

[318] Carriage by Air Act 1961 Sch.1A as inserted by SI 1999/1312 art.5(1); Sch.1B as inserted by SI 2002/263 art.4(1).

any other means that would preserve a record of the carriage to be performed may, with the consent of the consignor, be substituted for the delivery of an air waybill. If such other means are used, the carrier must, if so requested by the consignor, deliver to the consignor a receipt for the cargo permitting identification of the consignment and access to the information contained in the record preserved by such other means.[319] Under the MP4 Convention, the impossibility of using, at points of transit and destination, the other means that would preserve the record of the carriage does not entitle the carrier to refuse to accept the cargo for carriage.[320]

Acceptability of goods for carriage   The IATA recommended Conditions of Carriage for Cargo entitle the carrier to examine the packaging and contents of all shipments,[321] to the extent permitted by law, to refuse carriage of cargo when circumstances so require.[322] The cargo must be packed in an appropriate way for air carriage so as to ensure that it can be carried safely with ordinary care in handling and so as not to injure or damage any persons, goods or property.[323] Where dangerous goods are to be carried, the consignor must furnish a dangerous goods transport document, describing and certifying the goods in accordance with the current Technical Instructions for the Safe Transport of Dangerous Goods by Air prepared by ICAO.[324]   **35-069**

Liability for damage, destruction or loss   In cases governed by the Warsaw   **35-070**
Convention 1929 or the Warsaw-Hague text, unless the carrier can establish one of the defences allowed by the applicable Convention (that is, either that it and its servants or agents had taken all necessary measures to avoid the damage or that it was impossible for them to have taken such measures; or in the case of the unamended Convention that the damage was occasioned by negligent pilotage or negligence in the handling of the aircraft and that in all other respects, the carrier and its servants and agents have taken all necessary measures to avoid the damage; or the defence of contributory negligence), it is liable for damage[325] sustained in the event of the destruction or loss of, or of damage to, any cargo if the occurrence[326] which caused the damage so sustained took place during the carriage by air.[327] For this purpose, "carriage by air" comprises the period during which the cargo is in the charge of the carrier, whether in an aerodrome or on board an aircraft, or in the case

---

[319] Carriage by Air Act 1961 Sch.1A as inserted by SI 1999/1312 art.26(4); Sch.1B as inserted by SI 2002/263 art.4(2).

[320] Carriage by Air Act 1961 Sch.1A as inserted by SI 1999/1312 art.5(3).

[321] CSC1601 art.3.6.

[322] CSC1601 art.3.1.1.2.

[323] CSC1601 art.3.3.1.

[324] Air Navigation (Dangerous Goods) Regulations 2002 (SI 2002/2786). These regulations are regularly amended, most recently by SI 2011/1454, to refer to the most recent edition of the Technical Instructions.

[325] For the meaning of "damage", see *Walz v Clickair SA* (C-63/09) EU:C:2010:251, [2011] 1 All E.R. (Comm) 1037, and para.35-028, above.

[326] *Winchester Fruit Ltd v American Airlines Inc* [2002] 2 Lloyd's Rep. 265.

[327] Carriage by Air Acts (Application of Provisions) Order 2004 (SI 2004/1899) Sch.2 art.18(1); Carriage by Air Act 1961 Sch.1 art.18(1). For the relationship between the Warsaw Convention and the CMR Convention see *Quantum Corp Inc v Plane Trucking Ltd* [2002] EWCA Civ 350, [2002] 2 Lloyd's Rep. 25; and *Schenker International (Australia) Pty Ltd v Siemens Ltd*, NSWCA, Appeal 40760 of 2001, 2002.

of a landing outside an aerodrome in any place whatsoever.[328] In cases governed by the MP4 Convention, the carrier is liable, subject to the question of contributory negligence for damage sustained in the event of the destruction or loss of, or damage to, cargo upon condition only that the occurrence which caused the damage so sustained took place during the carriage by air. However, the carrier is not liable if it proves that the destruction or loss of, or damage to, the cargo resulted solely from: (a) the inherent defect, quality or vice of the cargo; (b) defective packing of that cargo performed by a person other than the carrier or its servants or agents; (c) an act of war or an armed conflict; or (d) an act of public authority carried out in connection with the entry, exit or transit of the cargo.[329] Similar rules as to liability are to be found in the Montreal Convention 1999,[330] where there is a simplified definition of the period of carriage by air.[331]

35-071 Upper financial limit of liability In cases governed by the Warsaw Convention 1929, the liability of the carrier in respect of cargo is limited to a sum of 250 francs per kilogramme of the lost or damaged package.[332] In cases governed by the Warsaw-Hague text, the limits remain as in the 1929 Convention.[333] Under the Warsaw-Hague text, however, when the loss, damage or delay of a part of the cargo, or of an object contained therein, affects the value of other packages covered by the same air waybill, the total weight of such package or packages must also be taken into consideration in determining the limit of liability.[334] The limits in the 1929 Convention and the Warsaw-Hague text as amended by Montreal Additional Protocol 1975 No.1 and No.2 respectively, and in cases under the MP4 Convention are 17 SDRs per kilogramme.[335] The same limit was set in the original text of the Montreal Convention 1999 but the limit was raised with effect from December 30, 2009 to 19 SDRs per kilogramme.[336] In all cases, the carrier's liability may be increased if the consignor makes, at the time when the package was handed over to the carrier, a special declaration of the value at delivery and pays a supplementary sum if the case so requires. In that case, the carrier will be liable to pay a sum not exceeding the declared sum, unless it proves that the sum is greater than the actual value to the consignor at delivery.[337]

---

[328] Carriage by Air Acts (Application of Provisions) Order 2004 (SI 2004/1899) Sch.2 art.18(2); Carriage by Air Act 1961 Sch.1 art.18(2); *Swiss Bank Corp v Brink's-MAT Ltd* Unreported November 14, 1985, QBD; *Rolls Royce Plc v Heavylift-Volga DNEPR Ltd* [2000] 1 Lloyd's Rep. 653. cf. *Victoria Sales Corp v Emery Air Freight Inc*, 917 F. 2d 705 (1990), 2nd Cir; *United International Stables Ltd v Pacific Western Airlines Ltd* (1969) 5 D.L.R. (3d) 67, Brit Columbia SC.

[329] Carriage by Air Act 1961 Sch.1A as inserted by SI 1999/1312 art.18(3).

[330] Carriage by Air Act 1961 Sch.1B as inserted by SI 2002/263 art.18(1), (2).

[331] Carriage by Air Act 1961 Sch.1B as inserted by SI 2002/263 art.18(3), (4).

[332] Carriage by Air Acts (Application of Provisions) Order 2004 (SI 2004/1899) Sch.2 art.22(2); *Data Card Corp v Air Express International Corp* [1984] 1 W.L.R. 198.

[333] Carriage by Air Act 1961 Sch.1 art.22(2) (which, as amended by the Carriage by Air and Road Act 1979 s.4, actually contains the limits as amended by Montreal Additional Protocol No.2 of 1975).

[334] Carriage by Air Act 1961 Sch.1 art.22(2)(b); *Allied Implants Technology Ltd v Lufthansa Cargo AG* [2000] 2 Lloyd's Rep. 46.

[335] Carriage by Air Acts (Application of Provisions) Order 2004 (SI 2004/1899) Sch.3 art.22(2); Carriage by Air Act 1961 Sch.1 art.22(2), (3) (as amended by the Carriage by Air and Road Act 1979 s.4); Sch.1A as inserted by SI 1999/1312 art.22(2)(a); Sch.1B as inserted by SI 2002/263 art.22(2).

[336] By a decision of the ICAO Council under art.24 of the Convention, given effect in England by the Carriage by Air (Revision of Limits of Liability under the Montreal Convention) Order 2009 (SI 2009/3018).

[337] Carriage by Air Acts (Application of Provisions) Order 2004 (SI 2004/1899) Sch.2 art.22(2); Car-

Stoppage in transit   Under the Sale of Goods Act 1979, the consignor, if he is an   **35-072**
unpaid seller who has learnt of the insolvency of the buyer, has a right to instruct
the carrier to stop the goods while they are in transit.[338] The Convention gives the
consignor, as between himself and the carrier,[339] a much more extensive power of
withdrawing, stopping or deflecting cargo, which is not dependent on the insolvency
of the buyer or even on the existence of a contract of sale between the consignor
and consignee. Subject to his liability to carry out all his obligations under the
contract of carriage, and provided that the cargo has not arrived at the place of
destination[340] the consignor may withdraw the cargo at the aerodrome of departure
or destination, stop it in the course of the journey on any landing, direct that it shall
be delivered to a person other than the consignee named in the air waybill, or
require it to be returned to the aerodrome of departure. He must not exercise this
right of disposition in such a manner as to prejudice the carrier or other consignors
and he must repay any expenses occasioned by the exercise of the right.[341] The carrier may refuse to obey the consignor only if to obey is impossible.[342] The rights
which the consignee may have against the consignor as a result of the latter's action remain unaffected by the Convention. The consignor's right of disposal ceases
when that of the consignee begins, i.e. when the cargo arrives at the place of
destination.[343]

Delivery to the consignee   On arrival of the cargo, the carrier must give notice   **35-073**
of the fact to the named consignee, unless the contract provides to the contrary.[344]
The consignee is then entitled to require delivery of the air waybill and of the cargo
on payment of outstanding charges and compliance with any relevant conditions of
carriage set out in the waybill.[345] Under the IATA recommended Conditions of Car-

---

riage by Air Act 1961 Sch.1 art.22(2)(a); Sch.1A as inserted by SI 1999/1312 art.22(2)(a); Sch.1B
as inserted by SI 2002/263 art.22(2).

338   ss.44–46.
339   The Guadalajara Convention requires the orders of the consignor under art.12 of the Warsaw
Convention to be addressed to the contracting carrier rather than to an actual carrier: 1962 Act Sch.
art.IV.
340   Carriage by Air Acts (Application of Provisions) Order 2004 (SI 2004/1899) Sch.2 arts 12(4), 13(1);
Carriage by Air Act 1961 Sch.1 arts 12(4), 13(1); Sch.1A as inserted by SI 1999/1312 arts 12(4),
13(1); Sch.1B as inserted by SI 2002/263 arts 12(4), 13(1)
341   Carriage by Air Acts (Application of Provisions) Order 2004 (SI 2004/1899) Sch.2 art.12(1); Carriage by Air Act 1961 Sch.1 art.12(1); Sch.1A as inserted by SI 1999/1312 art.12(1); Sch.1B as
inserted by SI 2002/263 art.12(1). See generally *Morton-Norwich Products Inc v Intercen Ltd* [1978]
R.P.C. 501.
342   Carriage by Air Acts (Application of Provisions) Order 2004 (SI 2004/1899) Sch.2 art.12(2); Carriage by Air Act 1961 Sch.1 art.12(2); Sch.1A as inserted by SI 1999/1312 art.12(2); Sch.1B as
inserted by SI 2002/263 art.12(2). The IATA recommended Conditions of Carriage (CSC1601) use
the phrase "not reasonably practicable" where the convention texts have "impossible" (art.7.2.2);
this makes practical sense but the convention text awaits judicial interpretation on this point.
343   Carriage by Air Acts (Application of Provisions) Order 2004 (SI 2004/1899) Sch.2 arts 12(4), 13(1);
Carriage by Air Act 1961 Sch.1 arts 12(4), 13(1); Sch.1A as inserted by SI 1999/1312 arts 12(4),
13(1); Sch.1B as inserted by SI 2002/263 arts 12(4), 13(1).
344   Carriage by Air Acts (Application of Provisions) Order 2004 (SI 2004/1899) Sch.2 art.13(2); Carriage by Air Act 1961 Sch.1 art.13(2); Sch.1A as inserted by SI 1999/1312 art.13(2); Sch.1B as
inserted by SI 2002/263 art.13(2). See the IATA recommended Conditions of Carriage (CSC1601)
art.8.1.
345   Carriage by Air Acts (Application of Provisions) Order 2004 (SI 2004/1899) Sch.2 art.13(1); Carriage by Air Act 1961 Sch.1 art.13(1); Sch.1A as inserted by SI 1999/1312 art.13(1); Sch.1B as
inserted by SI 2002/263 art.13(1).

riage, the consignee must accept delivery of and collect the shipment at the airport of destination or a facility designated by the carrier, unless delivery service has been specified.[346] Delivery to the consignee is deemed to have been effected when the carrier has delivered to the consignee or its agent any authorisation required to obtain release of the shipment and the shipment has been delivered to customs or any other government authorities as required by applicable law or customs regulations.[347]

35-074   **Failure to take delivery**   If the consignee refuses or fails to take delivery of the cargo, the carrier's rights and powers are closely defined in the IATA recommended Conditions of Carriage. In the absence of previous instructions from the consignor given on the face of the air waybill in anticipation of this kind of emergency, or if such instructions cannot reasonably be complied with, the carrier will send notice of the failure to take delivery to the consignor, and may return the cargo to the airport of departure to await the instructions of the consignor, or may even, after 30 days, sell it.[348] In the case of perishable goods, delivery of which is refused, or which are unclaimed or for other reasons threatened with deterioration, the carrier may immediately take such steps as he sees fit for the protection of himself and other parties in interest, including storage, sale, abandonment and even destruction of the goods.[349] Expenses incurred in meeting the contingency of refusal to take delivery are charged to the consignor.[350]

35-075   **Time for making claims: damage or delay**   Where cargo is damaged, the person entitled to delivery must complain to the carrier forthwith after the discovery of the damage, and, at the latest, within (a) under the Warsaw Convention 1929, seven days from the date of receipt; and (b) under all the other conventions, 14 days from the date of receipt. Where cargo is delayed, the complaint must be made at the latest within (a) under Warsaw Convention 1929, 14 days from the date on which the baggage has been placed at his or her disposal; and (b) under all the other conventions, 21 days from the date on which the cargo has been placed at his or her disposal.[351] "Days" means current days, not working days.[352] Every complaint must be made in writing and given or dispatched within the specified times[353]; an oral complaint recorded in the information system of the carrier, provided the record

---

346   CSC1601 art.8.3.

347   CSC1601 art.8.2.

348   CSC1601 art.8.4. There will, of course, usually be in these circumstances a bailment giving the bailee ultimate powers of sale under the Torts (Interference with Goods) Act 1977 s.12.

349   CSC1601 art.8.5.

350   CSC1601 art.8.5.2.

351   Carriage by Air Acts (Application of Provisions) Order 2004 (SI 2004/1899) Sch.2 art.26(2); Carriage by Air Act 1961 Sch.1 art.26(2); Sch.1A as inserted by SI 1999/1312 art.26(2); Sch.1B as inserted by SI 2002/263 art.31(2). "Damage" includes the loss of part of the contents: *Fothergill v Monarch Airlines Ltd* [1981] A.C. 251; Carriage by Air Act 1961 s.4A as inserted by the Carriage by Air and Road Act 1979 s.4 and as amended by SI 2002/263. The test for the adequacy of the notice of complaint is an objective one: *Western Digital Corp v British Airways Plc* [2001] Q.B. 733, CA.

352   Carriage by Air Acts (Application of Provisions) Order 2004 (SI 2004/1899) Sch.2 art.35; Carriage by Air Act 1961 Sch.1 art.35; Sch.1A as inserted by SI 1999/1312 art.35; Sch.1B as inserted by SI 2002/263 art.52.

353   Carriage by Air Acts (Application of Provisions) Order 2004 (SI 2004/1899) Sch.2 art.26(3); Carriage by Air Act 1961 Sch.1 art.26(3); Sch.1A as inserted by SI 1999/1312 art.26(3); Sch.1B as inserted by SI 2002/263 art.31(3).

identifies the complainant, satisfies this requirement.[354] If no complaint is made within the prescribed time limits, no action lies against the carrier, save in the case of fraud on his part.[355] Notice of complaint is not required in the case of total loss or destruction.

Loss of cargo   In cases of loss, that is where there is no delivery, the conventions do not impose a time limit for complaint, but the IATA recommended Conditions of Carriage provide that complaint must be made in the case of non-delivery within 120 days of the date on which the goods ought to have arrived at the destination. In some jurisdictions such a contractual term has been approved on the ground that it does not conflict with anything in the Warsaw Convention rules, but the better view appears to be that such a notice requirement is void as tending to relieve the carrier of liability.[356] If the carrier admits the loss of the cargo, or if the cargo has not arrived at the expiration of seven days after the date on which it ought to have arrived, the consignee is entitled to put into force against the carrier the rights which flow from the contract of carriage.[357]   **35-076**

Who can sue the carrier?   If goods are lost or damaged during transit, the general rule of common law in the case of carriage by land is that the owner of the goods is the person entitled to sue the carrier.[358] If goods are being carried because they have been sold, the owner will usually be the consignee; and the consignor is deemed to contract with the carrier as agent for the consignee. These principles of the common law are in general, unaffected by the Convention, which, as we have just seen,[359] gives the right of action in the case of loss to the consignee,[360] and in the case of damage or delay requires the person entitled to delivery to complain in writing to the carrier before bringing his action.[361] The "person entitled to delivery" is normally the consignee, but may exceptionally be the consignor if he has exercised his extensive rights of stoppage *in transitu*.[362] A literal interpretation of the Convention text suggests that the consignor never has a right of action in the event of loss of goods. This appears to follow from the restriction of the right of action to the consignee in cases of loss and from the fact that all rights of action   **35-077**

---

354 *Finnair Oyj v Keskinainen Vakuutusyhtio Fennia* (C-258/16) EU:C:2018:252 (a baggage case).

355 Carriage by Air Acts (Application of Provisions) Order 2004 (SI 2004/1899) Sch.2 art.26(4); Carriage by Air Act 1961 Sch.1 art.26(4); Sch.1A as inserted by SI 1999/1312 art.26(4); Sch.1B as inserted by SI 2002/263 art.31(4).

356 Carriage by Air Acts (Application of Provisions) Order 2004 (SI 2004/1899) Sch.2 art.23; Carriage by Air Act 1961 Sch.1 art.23; Sch.1A as inserted by SI 1999/1312 art.23; Sch.1B as inserted by SI 2002/263 art.26. See Shawcross and Beaumont at Vol.1, para.VII[944]. Loss of part of the contents is treated as "damage": *Fothergill v Monarch Airlines Ltd* [1981] A.C. 251; Carriage by Air Act 1961 s.4A as inserted by the Carriage by Air and Road Act 1979 s.4 and as amended by SI 1999/1312 and SI 2000/263.

357 Carriage by Air Acts (Application of Provisions) Order 2004 (SI 2004/1899) Sch.2 art.13(3); Carriage by Air Act 1961 Sch.1 art.13(3); Sch.1A as inserted by SI 1999/1312 art.13(3); Sch.1B as inserted by SI 2002/263 art.13(3). See *Gatewhite Ltd v Iberia Lineas Aereas de España* [1989] 1 Lloyd's Rep. 160; and Shawcross and Beaumont at Vol.1, para.VII[933].

358 cf. below, paras 36-043—36-044.

359 See above, para.35-076.

360 Carriage by Air Act 1961 Sch.1 art.13(3).

361 Carriage by Air Act 1961 Sch.1 art.26(2).

362 See above, para.35-072.

must be brought subject to the conditions set out in the applicable Convention.[363] In practice actions are often brought in the name of consignors.[364]

35-078 At common law, in the case of carriage by land, a stranger to the contract of carriage, one who is neither the consignor nor the consignee, may be able to sue the carrier in tort or in bailment if he can show that the carrier owed him a duty of care, or if he can show the necessary proprietary interest on which to base an action for conversion. The question arises whether such a stranger can sue the carrier by air. It has been argued that he cannot, because the Convention text gives no rights of action to anyone except the consignor and consignee, and provides that any action for damages, however founded, can only be brought subject to the conditions and limitations set out in the applicable Convention[365]: with the significant exception that this is without prejudice to the question who can sue for the death of a passenger.[366] This is the conclusion which foreign courts have come to on this question, though by no means unanimously.[367] The English court has, however, followed a forceful Commonwealth decision[368] and held that there is nothing in the Convention to prevent the owner of goods from bringing an action in his own name against an air carrier if goods are lost or damaged: the Convention was silent when it could easily have excluded the rights of the real party in interest had that been the draftsman's intention. In the circumstances, the *lex fori* can fill the gaps and allow a right of action to those who, like the owner of the goods, could sue the carrier at common law.[369] It seems, then, that the Convention in granting rights of action to consignors and consignees which they would not have had at common law is not to be construed as having abrogated rights of action possessed by owners of goods at common law.[370]

35-079 **Who pays freight?** The Convention does not deal with the question of who is liable to the carrier for the payment of freight and other charges. This is dealt with by the IATA recommended Conditions of Carriage, of which three features are noteworthy here. First, the carrier is entitled to payment in full, whether or not the

---

363 Carriage by Air Acts (Application of Provisions) Order 1967 (SI 1967/480) Sch.2 arts 13(3) and 24(1); Carriage by Air Act 1961 Sch.1 arts 13(3) and 24(1); Sch.1A as inserted by SI 1999/1312 arts 13(3) and 24(1); Sch.1B as inserted by SI 2002/263 arts 13(3) and 29. cf. *Gatewhite Ltd v Iberia Lineas Aereas de España* [1989] 1 Lloyd's Rep. 160; *Western Digital Corp v British Airways Plc* [2001] Q.B. 733, CA.

364 See, e.g. *Samuel Montagu and Co Ltd v Swiss Air Transport Co Ltd* [1966] 2 Q.B. 306.

365 Carriage by Air Acts (Application of Provisions) Order 2004 (SI 2004/1899) Sch.2 art.24(1); Carriage by Air Act 1961 Sch.1 art.24(1); Sch.1A as inserted by SI 1999/1312 art.24(1); Sch.1B as inserted by SI 2002/263 art.29.

366 Carriage by Air Acts (Application of Provisions) Order 2004 (SI 2004/1899) Sch.2 art.24(2); Carriage by Air Act 1961 Sch.1 art.24(2); Sch.1A as inserted by SI 1999/1312 art.24(2); Sch.1B as inserted by SI 2002/263 art.29.

367 See Shawcross and Beaumont at Vol.1, paras VII[967] et seq.

368 *Tasman Pulp and Paper Co Ltd v Brambles JB O'Loghlen Ltd* [1981] 2 N.Z.L.R. 225.

369 *Gatewhite Ltd v Iberia Lineas Aereas de España Sociedad* [1990] 1 Q.B. 326; *Thomas Cook Group Ltd v Air Malta Co Ltd* [1997] 2 Lloyd's Rep. 399; *Western Digital Corp v British Airways Plc* [2001] Q.B. 733, CA. cf. dicta of Lord Hope of Craighead in *Abnett v British Airways Plc* [1997] A.C. 430; Lord Hope thought it more consistent with the purpose of the Convention to regard it as providing a uniform rule about who can sue for goods which are lost or damaged during carriage by air, with the result that the owner who is not a party to the contract has no right to sue in his own name; but the point was not fully argued.

370 *Tasman Pulp and Paper Co Ltd v Brambles JB O'Loghlen Ltd*, above, at 235.

cargo is lost or damaged or fails to arrive.[371] Secondly, the consignor guarantees payment of all the carrier's unpaid charges, advances, disbursements and any costs which the carrier may incur by reason of the carriage of cargo prohibited by law or incorrectly described. By taking delivery or exercising any other right under the contract of carriage, the consignee agrees to pay the charges, but not so as to discharge the consignor's guarantee.[372] Thirdly, the carrier has a lien on the cargo for all such charges; the lien is enforceable by sale after notice to the consignor or consignee.[373]

(e) Delay to Passengers, Baggage or Cargo

Liability for delay   Under the Conventions, the carrier is liable for damage occasioned by delay in the carriage by air of passengers, baggage or cargo.[374] The carrier may, however, rely on a number of defences: (a) proof that he and his servants or agents have taken all necessary measures to avoid the damage or that it was impossible to take them[375]; (b) in the case of the unamended Warsaw Convention 1929 that the damage was occasioned by negligent pilotage or negligence in the handling of the aircraft and that in all other respects, the carrier and its servants and agents have taken all necessary measures to avoid the damage[376]; and (c) contributory negligence.[377] In the carriage of baggage and cargo, the provisions as to timely notice of complaint apply.[378] Delay means failure to complete the carriage in a reasonable time.[379] The effect of the provisions in Conditions of Carriage that the carrier "does not guarantee flight times shown in timetables and they do not form part of your contract with us"[380] is merely to prevent the carrier being under a stricter liability than is imposed by the applicable Convention. Although "punitive, exemplary or non-compensatory" may not be awarded under the Montreal Convention 1999, damages may be awarded to compensate passengers for the stress, inconvenience, frustration and disruption to their holiday caused by the delay in the arrival of their baggage at their destination.[381] There can be liability to persons other than the delayed passenger. Article 19 of the Montreal Convention applies not only to the damage suffered by a passenger but also to the damage suffered by a person in its capacity as an employer who had concluded a contract of international carriage with an air carrier for the purpose of carriage of passengers who were its

35-080

---

[371] Conditions of Carriage art.5.4.2.

[372] Conditions of Carriage art.5.4.3.

[373] Conditions of Carriage art.5.4.3.

[374] Carriage by Air Acts (Application of Provisions) Order 2004 (SI 2004/1899) Sch.2 art.19; Carriage by Air Act 1961 Sch.1 art.19; Sch.1A as inserted by SI 1999/1312 art.19 (using different language); Sch.1B as inserted by SI 2002/263 art.19. For claims under EU Regulation 261/2004, see para.35-049.

[375] Carriage by Air Acts (Application of Provisions) Order 2004 (SI 2004/1899) Sch.2 art.20(1); Carriage by Air Act 1961 Sch.1 art.20; Sch.1A as inserted by SI 1999/1312 art.20; Sch.1B as inserted by SI 2002/263 art.19.

[376] Carriage by Air Acts (Application of Provisions) Order 2004 (SI 2004/1899) Sch.2 art.20(2).

[377] Carriage by Air Acts (Application of Provisions) Order 2004 (SI 2004/1899) Sch.2 art.21; Carriage by Air Act 1961 Sch.1 art.21; Sch.1A as inserted by SI 1999/1312 art.21; Sch.1B as inserted by SI 2002/263 art.20.

[378] See above, paras 35-053 and 35-075—35-076.

[379] *Panalpina International Transport Ltd v Densil Underwear Ltd* [1981] 1 Lloyd's Rep. 187. See also *Bart v British West Indian Airways Ltd* [1967] 1 Lloyd's Rep. 239, Guyana CA.

[380] See IATA Recommended Conditions (PSC(24)1724), art.9.1.1.

[381] *O'Carroll v Ryanair* 2009 S.C.L.R. 125.

employees.[382] Delay is to be distinguished from "non-performance", the latter falling outside the scope of the Montreal Convention.[383]

35-081 **Upper limit of liability** In cases governed by the Warsaw Convention 1929, the liability of the carrier for delay is limited to a sum of 125,000 francs per passenger; 250 francs per kilogramme in the case of registered baggage or cargo; and 5,000 francs per passenger in respect of objects of which the passenger takes charge.[384] In cases governed by the Warsaw-Hague text, the passenger limit is raised to 250,000 francs,[385] but the other limits are unchanged. The Warsaw-Hague figures are restated in Montreal Protocol No.2 of 1975 as 16,600 SDRs, 17 SDRs per kilogramme, and 332 SDRs per passenger,[386] and these limits were retained in the MP4 Convention.[387] The limit of the carrier's liability under the original text of the Montreal Convention 1999 was set in the carriage of passengers at 4,150 SDRs per passenger, in the carriage of baggage at 1,000 SDRs per passenger, and 17 SDRs per kilogramme of cargo[388]; the limits were raised 4,694 SDRs, 1,131 SDRs and 19 SDRs with effect from December 30, 2009.[389]

6. NON-INTERNATIONAL CARRIAGE

35-082 **Applicable rules** The Conventions treated above regulate only international carriage. Carriage which is not international carriage as defined in any of the Conventions falls outside the Convention system. The applicable law is to be found in two sources. Union air carriers engaged in the carriage of persons or baggage are subject to European Parliament and Council Regulation 889/2002,[390] which applies to national as well as international carriage. However, Regulation 889/2002 applies only to "air carriers" defined by art.2(1)(a) to mean air transport undertakings with valid operating licences, and to "Community air carriers" defined by art.2(1)(b) to mean air carriers with valid operating licences granted by a Member State; so, carriage within a single Member State to view a property from the air by a carrier not required to have a valid operating licence is not to be within the Regulation or (as it was not international carriage) the Montreal Convention.[391] The liability of other air carriers, and EU air carriers engaged in the carriage of cargo, is governed by Sch.1 to the Carriage by Air Acts (Application of Provisions) Order 2004,[392] which applies a modified version of the Montreal Convention 1999. Subject to the Regulation, the 2004 Order applies to all carriage by air other than carriage to which the Warsaw-Hague text, the MP4 Convention or the Montreal Conven-

---

[382] *Air Baltic Corp AS v Lietuvos Respublikos specialiųjų tyrimų tarnyba* (C-429/14) EU:C:2016:88, [2016] 1 Lloyd's Rep. 407.
[383] See Shawcross and Beaumont, on Air Law, para.VII1003.1 and the very full judgment in *Chaing v Air Canada* Unreported January 22, 2016, Kingston-upon-Thames Cty Ct.
[384] Carriage by Air Acts (Application of Provisions) Order 2004 (SI 2004/1899) Sch.2 art.22.
[385] Carriage by Air Act 1961 Sch.1 art.22 as originally enacted.
[386] Carriage by Air Act 1961 Sch.1 art.22 as amended by the Carriage by Air and Road Act 1979 s.4(1).
[387] Carriage by Air Act 1961 Sch.1A as inserted by SI 1999/1312 art.22.
[388] Carriage by Air Act 1961 Sch.1B as inserted by SI 2002/263 art.22.
[389] By a decision of the ICAO Council under art.24 of the Convention, given effect in England by the Carriage by Air (Revision of Limits of Liability under the Montreal Convention) Order 2009 (SI 2009/3018).
[390] See above, paras 35-018 et seq.
[391] *Prüller-Frey v Brodnig* (C-240/14) EU:C:2015:567, [2015] 1 W.L.R. 5031.
[392] SI 2004/1899. Note that art.2 is amended by SI 2004/1974.

tion 1999 applies, and Sch.1 applies to carriage which is not international carriage as defined in Schs 2 or 3 (applying the original Warsaw Convention and that Convention as amended by Montreal Additional Protocol No.1 of 1975).[393] To avoid giving too extensive a scope to the predecessor provisions, for it was arguable that the provisions of the United Kingdom Order applied to internal carriage in other countries, the House of Lords held that their application is limited to (a) carriage in which the places of departure and destination and any agreed stopping places are all within the United Kingdom or other British territory; and (b) non-convention carriage involving a place of departure or destination or an agreed stopping place in a foreign state and a place of departure or destination or an agreed stopping place in the United Kingdom or other British territory.[394]

The modified convention regime under Sch.1 to the 2004 Order   Only parts of   **35-083** the Montreal Convention 1999 are applied by the 2004 Order.[395] Chapter II (arts 3 to 16) dealing with documentation is omitted except for parts of art.3 requiring the carrier to deliver a baggage identification tag for each piece of checked baggage. Liability for death or injury is unlimited but if the carrier proves an absence of fault there is no liability beyond 100,000 SDRs. There are no provisions regulating the carriage of mail and postal packages save for a provision that in these cases the carrier is liable only to the relevant postal administration and in accordance with the rules applicable to the relationship between carriers and postal administrations.[396]

---

[393] Carriage by Air Acts (Application of Provisions) Order 2004 (SI 2004/1899) arts 3(1) and 4.
[394] *Holmes v Bangladesh Biman Corp* [1989] A.C. 1112.
[395] Carriage by Air Acts (Application of Provisions) Order 2004 (SI 2004/1899).
[396] 2004 Order Sch.1 art.2(2). See the Postal Services Act 2000 s.90; *American Express Co v British Airways Board* [1983] 1 W.L.R. 701; *Post Office v British World Airlines Ltd* [2000] 1 All E.R. (Comm) 532.

CHAPTER 36

CARRIAGE BY LAND

P. J. S. MacDonald Eggers

1. INTRODUCTION

(a) General

The law of carriage The law of carriage of goods[1] is a branch of the law of   **36-001**
bailment.[2] Like the law of bailment, it transcends the distinction between contract
and tort. The law of carriage of passengers[3] and their luggage[4] similarly transcends
this distinction. As the present work deals with the law of contract and not the law

---

[1] See below, paras 36-007 et seq.
[2] See above, Ch.2, and Palmer, *Bailment*, 3rd edn (2009). See also Holdsworth, *A History of English Law*, 2nd edn (1937), Vol.VIII, 259.
[3] See below, paras 36-054 et seq.
[4] See below, paras 36-068 et seq.

of tort, those aspects of the law of carriage which are part of the law of tort are discussed only briefly. The alternative remedies in tort open to a passenger or an owner of goods cannot, however, be ignored, as it is sometimes possible to bypass an exemption clause by bringing an action in tort against someone other than the contracting carrier.[5]

36-002 Internal carriage The law of carriage by land is of very ancient origin.[6] For centuries the common carrier occupied a special position in the law. Today, however, the common carrier is practically extinct.[7] The modern law of carriage is not so much enshrined in reported cases as exemplified by the contractual terms by which carriers define the conditions on which they are prepared to carry goods, passengers and luggage.[8] Any account of the modern law must necessarily take account of these contractual terms, many of which have become standard forms of contract. Some of these terms have, of course, themselves been the subject of judicial interpretation. As the rights and duties of carriers towards their customers differ from those of other intermediaries in the freight trade, it is important on occasion to distinguish between carriers by land and others concerned with the transport of goods, such as forwarding agents.[9]

36-003 International carriage In recent years, and particularly since 1952,[10] the international law of carriage by land has been developed by the adoption by the international community, especially in Europe, of multilateral treaties in this field. These treaties are designed to govern contracts of carriage by land between countries which have accepted the particular treaties. In particular they are intended to regulate the mutual rights and duties of carriers and their customers. The United Kingdom has accepted some of these treaties. In 1954, for example, the United Kingdom became a contracting party to two international conventions on carriage by rail.[11] In 1967, the United Kingdom became a party to an international conven-

---

5   See below, paras 36-044—36-046, 36-057, 36-078.
6   See *Southcote's Case* (1601) 4 Co. Rep. 83, 84.
7   See below, paras 36-009—36-010.
8   See Leslie, *Law of Transport by Railways*, 2nd edn (1928); Kahn-Freund, *The Law of Inland Transport*, 4th edn (1965), especially Pts 2 and 3; *Halsbury's Laws of England*, 5th edn (2008), Vol.7; Clarke, *International Carriage of Goods by Road: CMR*, 6th edn (2014); Clarke and Yates, *Contracts of Carriage by Land and Air*, 2nd edn (2008).
9   *Marston Excelsior Ltd v Arbuckle, Smith and Co Ltd* [1971] 2 Lloyd's Rep. 306; *Gillespie Bros and Co Ltd v Roy Bowles Transport Ltd* [1973] Q.B. 400; *Hair and Skin Trading Co Ltd v Norman Airfreight Carriers Ltd* [1974] 1 Lloyd's Rep. 443; *Chas Davis (Metal Brokers) Ltd v Gilyott and Scott Ltd* [1975] 2 Lloyd's Rep. 422. See, generally, Hill, *Freight Forwarders* (1972), pp.16–25; Hill [1975] L.M.C.L.Q. 139; see below, para.36-006.
10   This was when the first comprehensive Berne Rail Conventions CIM and CIV were signed. There had been earlier limited Berne Conventions on carriage by rail, the earliest being concluded in 1890. See, as to the history of the international conventions on carriage by rail, Kahn-Freund at pp.408–409. The United Kingdom ratified the Berne Conventions CIM and CIV of October 25, 1952, in 1954 and became a party to the revised CIM and CIV of February 25, 1961, on January 1, 1965 and to the further revised CIM and CIV of February 7, 1970, on January 1, 1975. Currently the United Kingdom is a party to COTIF, the revised and amalgamated convention concerning international carriage by rail of May 9, 1980. COTIF entered into force generally and for the United Kingdom on May 1, 1985, and was modified by the Protocol of June 3, 1999, which entered into force in the United Kingdom on July 1, 2006; see below, paras 36-079—36-081.
11   i.e. the Berne Conventions CIM and CIV of October 25, 1952.

tion on carriage of goods by road.[12] As a result of the United Kingdom government's acceptance of treaties such as these and their successors, the particular treaty régimes have become binding on the United Kingdom and as such can be said to form part of the English law of carriage by land insofar as their terms have been incorporated in Acts of Parliament either directly or by reference.[13]

The identification of a carrier   The common law has recognised a variety of car-   **36-004**
riers—those who accept custody of or responsibility for persons or goods for the purpose of transporting them to a destination agreed between the carrier and the customer. The classification of a carrier depends on how his business of carriage is conducted. There are common carriers, private carriers and other "special" carriers. The status of the last category is dependent on Parliament's intervention (by virtue of domestic legislation or the incorporation of international conventions) or unusual exceptions etched by the common law. Whilst these distinctions potentially have relevance in the realm of international carriage, more often they arise for consideration in connection with the internal carriage of goods and persons, and even then the distinctions have less importance than of old. For this reason, the categorisation of carriers will be discussed as part of the section on internal carriage. It should not, however, be forgotten that the distinction unexpectedly may be resuscitated when an international carriage falls for judicial consideration.

(b)   Definition of Carrier

Carrier   Before the law relating to carriers and carriage by land is considered in   **36-005**
depth below, a moment's thought should be dedicated to the issue whether in a given case a person should be described as a "carrier" at all. A "carrier" is a person who transports goods or passengers or both from any place to any place in the manner agreed with the passenger or the owner of the goods to be carried. The carrier need not be paid in any sense for this service. The test is whether the person said to be the carrier is in fact accepting the responsibility of the carriage.[14] Although a person's business involves, whether necessarily or by choice, the conveyance of goods, that does not necessarily mean that that person is a carrier. If a person undertakes to carry a passenger or goods only for reasons associated with his own personal or commercial expedience, then that person is not a carrier. The carriage is not the raison d'être of that person. If the carriage is wholly incidental to that person's business, then he will not be a carrier. For example, a warehouseman,[15] a stevedore[16] and a wharfinger[17] have all been held not to be carriers. The "carrier's"

---

[12]   i.e. CMR, signed at Geneva on May 19, 1956: see below, para.36-082.
[13]   See below, paras 36-079—36-081. As to the general rule regarding the municipal effect and interpretation of such treaty provisions, see *James Buchanan and Co Ltd v Babco Forwarding and Shipping (UK) Ltd* [1978] A.C. 141; and *Fothergill v Monarch Airlines Ltd* [1981] A.C. 251. The relationship between international law and national law is now clearly explained in art.8 of COTIF, as modified by the Protocol of June 3, 1999. For a survey of international carriage conventions and a search for a common substratum for all modes of carriage, see Clarke, "The transport of goods in Europe: patterns and problems of uniform law" [1999] L.M.C.L.Q. 36; Clarke and Yates, *Contracts of Carriage by Land and Air*, 2nd edn (2008).
[14]   *Aqualon (UK) Ltd v Vallana Shipping Corp* [1994] 1 Lloyd's Rep. 669, 676. cf. *M Bardiger Ltd v Halberg Spedition APS* Unreported October 26, 1990.
[15]   *Consolidated Tea and Lands Co v Oliver's Wharf* [1910] 2 K.B. 395; contra *Maving v Todd* (1815) 1 Stark 72; *Armour & Co Ltd v Tarbard Ltd* (1920) 37 T.L.R. 208.
[16]   *Scruttons Ltd v Midland Silicones Ltd* [1962] A.C. 446.

business should be examined to determine the purpose of the carriage.[18] Such questions generally are more difficult to answer in the case of goods, as opposed to passengers. In the case of passengers, whether a person is acting as an agent or a carrier generally is clear.

36-006   **Freight forwarder**   A forwarding agent, or freight forwarder, is a person who contracts with the owner of goods to arrange for the transportation of those goods, rather than to carry the goods himself.[19] A freight forwarder, therefore, usually is not classified as a carrier,[20] so long as he remains true to his calling. Unlike the warehouseman, the stevedore, and the wharfinger, the freight forwarder often never acquires possession (that is, custody) of the goods to be carried.[21] As the functions of a carrier and a freight forwarder are necessarily linked, uncertainty may arise as to whether a person describing himself as a freight forwarder is in fact a carrier.[22] A freight forwarder, or any goods-handler, may also contract or act as a carrier as an adjunct to their principal business.[23] It is a question of fact in every case whether a person is a carrier.[24]

---

[17]   *Chattock & Co v Bellamy & Co* (1895) 64 L.J. Q.B. 250.

[18]   *Lacey's Footwear (Wholesale) Ltd v Bowler International Freight Ltd* [1997] 2 Lloyd's Rep. 369 where the court examined the circumstances of the making of the contract of carriage.

[19]   As to the distinction between a forwarder (that is, a person who contracts with the carrier as a principal, so that the owner of the goods is not a party to the contract) and a forwarding agent (who contracts on behalf of the owner of the goods with the carrier), see *M Bardiger Ltd v Halberg Spedition APS* Unreported October 26, 1990; *Aqualon (UK) Ltd v Vallana Shipping Corp* [1994] 1 Lloyd's Rep. 669, 673. See also Clarke, *International Carriage of Goods by Road: CMR* 6th edn (2014), para.10a.

[20]   *Moto Vespa SA v MAT (Britannia Express) Ltd* [1979] 1 Lloyd's Rep. 175, 179; *Elektronska Industrija Oour TVA v Transped Oour Kintinentalna Spedicna* [1986] 1 Lloyd's Rep. 49, 52; cf. *Swiss Bank Corp v Brink's-MAT Ltd* [1986] 2 Lloyd's Rep. 79.

[21]   In *Kala Ltd v International Freight Services (UK) Ltd* Unreported June 7, 1988, the freight forwarder was held to have exercised legitimately a contractual lien and right of detention over goods, the right to the control of which the owners had given to the freight forwarder. The court distinguished the freight forwarder's right to possession of the goods from mere custody, which was held by the actual carrier.

[22]   The fact that a freight forwarder describes himself as such is not a decisive answer to the question, although assistance is gained from any written contract: *Lacey's Footwear (Wholesale) Ltd v Bowler International Freight Ltd* [1997] 2 Lloyd's Rep. 369; see also *Kala Ltd v International Freight Services (UK) Ltd* Unreported June 7, 1988; *M Bardiger Ltd v Halberg Spedition APS* Unreported October 26, 1990; and *Aqualon (UK) Ltd v Vallana Shipping Corp* [1994] 1 Lloyd's Rep. 669, 676. cf. *Texas Instruments Ltd v Nason (Europe) Ltd* [1991] 1 Lloyd's Rep. 146.

[23]   *Hellaby v Weaver* (1851) 17 L.T.O.S. 271; *Langley Beldon & Gaunt Ltd v Morley* [1965] 1 Lloyd's Rep. 297, 306; *Lee Cooper Ltd v CH Jeakins & Sons Ltd* [1967] 2 Q.B. 1; *Elektronska Industrija Oour TVA v Transped Oour Kintinentalna Spedicna* [1986] 1 Lloyd's Rep. 49, 52; *M Bardiger Ltd v Halberg Spedition Aps* Unreported October 26, 1990.

[24]   Taking into account matters such as how the carrier or forwarder describes himself, how he charges, how he arranges the carriage, and what documents he issues: *M Bardiger Ltd v Halberg Spedition Aps* Unreported October 26, 1990.

2. INTERNAL CARRIAGE

(a) Goods

(i) Common and Private Carriers

The common carrier   At common law, the rights and obligations of a carrier are   **36-007**
defined by contract and the status of the carrier. As regards status, the classification of the carrier as a common or private carrier[25] will identify certain of the carrier's duties and liabilities. A common carrier is a person who publicly professes,
orally or by conduct, to undertake for reward[26] to all such persons, indiscriminately,[27] who desire to employ him, the transportation of goods provided that he has
room.[28] It is a question of fact in each case whether a person is a common carrier.[29]
A common carrier does not lose his legal character because he limits the class of
goods he is prepared to carry[30] or the routes or areas over which he is ready to
operate.[31] He is entitled to fix these limitations, for to compel him to do otherwise
would be an intolerable and prohibitive imposition. Nor, again, does he relinquish
his status because one terminus is outside the jurisdiction,[32] or because he fails
altogether to fix his termini[33] or to specify the goods he is prepared to carry.[34]

---

[25] It has been mooted that there is another class of carrier, namely a carrier, whilst not a common carrier, who has assumed the responsibilities of a common carrier, by virtue of their public employment.
Such was the decision concerning lightermen in *Liver Alkali Co v Johnson* (1871-72) L.R. 7 Ex. 267;
(1873-74) L.R. 9 Ex. 338. However, this view has been rejected, at least so far as carriage by road
is concerned: *Nugent v Smith* (1876) 1 C.P.D. 423, 433; *Watkins v Cottell* [1916] 1 K.B. 10; *Belfast
Ropework Co Ltd v Bushell* [1918] 1 K.B. 210; cf. *Aslan v Imperial Airways Ltd* (1933) 149 L.T.
276, 278.

[26] That is, at a reasonable price: *Belfast Ropework Co Ltd v Bushell* [1918] 1 K.B. 210. If the carrier
gives an estimate and seeks to negotiate the price with his customer, thus reserving a discretion to
himself to refuse to carry the goods, he is not a common carrier: *Electric Supply Stores v Gaywood*
(1909) 100 L.T. 855. A gratuitous carrier is not a common carrier: *Tyly v Morrice* (1699) Carth. 485.

[27] In the provision of carriage services, discrimination against a person on the grounds of race, sex,
religion, belief or sexual orientation is prohibited under the Equality Act 2010 ss.4–13, 28–29.
Discrimination on the grounds of disability is also prohibited, but the prohibition does not apply in
certain circumstances: Equality Act 2010 s.31 and Sch.3 Pt 9.

[28] *Bennett v Peninsular & Oriental Steam-Boat Co* (1848) 6 C.B. 775, 787; *Watkins v Cottell* [1916]
1 K.B. 10, 14; *Belfast Ropework Co Ltd v Bushell* [1918] 1 K.B. 210, 212; *GN Ry v LEP Transport*
[1922] 2 K.B. 742, 765.

[29] *Tamvaco v Timothy* (1882) 1 Cab. El. 1; *Belfast Ropework Co Ltd v Bushell* [1918] 1 K.B. 210, 212;
Eastman Chemical International AG v NMT Trading Ltd [1972] 2 Lloyd's Rep. 25; *A Siohn & Co
Ltd v R H Hagland & Son (Transport) Ltd* [1976] 2 Lloyd's Rep. 428.

[30] *Johnson v Midland Railway Co* (1849) 4 Ex. 367, 373; *Date v Sheldon* (1921) 7 Ll.L. Rep. 53, 54.
Brind v Dale (1837) 8 Car. & P. 207 suggests that, if carriage is from place to place within the same
town, the carrier is not a common carrier. But the decision is an isolated one, without reasoning on
this point, and seems unsound in principle: see, Kahn-Freund at p.205; *Eastman Chemical
International AG v NMT Trading Ltd* [1972] 2 Lloyd's Rep. 25.

[31] cf. *Johnson v Midland Ry*, above, at 373.

[32] *Crouch v LNW Ry* (1854) 14 C.B. 255, 289; *Piancini v LSW Ry* (1856) 18 C.B. 226. cf. *Bennett v P
& O SS Co* (1848) 6 C.B. 775 at 787.

[33] *Date v Sheldon* (1921) 7 Ll.L. Rep. 53; also, *Belfast Ropework Co v Bushell* [1918] 1 K.B. 210 at
214. Leslie at p.25, suggests that the courts would read reasonable termini into the common law
contract of carriage.

[34] Here, too, Leslie at pp.8, 25, suggests that the courts would read in reasonable classes of goods, on
an analogy with the exclusion of dangerous goods and goods of an exceptional character from the
normal profession of common carrier.

36-008 **Abdication of status** The common carrier may voluntarily abdicate this status by giving notice that he will not accept custom from the public. Alternatively, the common carrier may shed this status as regards particular types of goods only.[35] A carrier therefore may choose to be a common carrier for such times, places, and goods as he considers it appropriate, provided that he offers carriage in accordance with the calling of the common carrier and is thereby prepared to accept the burden of that calling.

36-009 **The identification of a common carrier** How a carrier sees fit to describe himself is indecisive for the establishment of his status. The courts have regard solely to the substance of the matter.[36] But "express and detailed professions as a common carrier are rare. In most cases, the fact that a profession has been made, and its extent, have to be collected from the conduct of the carrier".[37] He is not a common carrier if he carries for particular persons only,[38] or if his practice is to pick and choose among offers which consignors make him,[39] or if, as a furniture-remover, his rule is not to accept whatever furniture is offered, but to inspect it to decide first whether he will take it, and at what rate.[40] A carrier will not be a common carrier if he reserves to himself the right of refusal of the goods which a customer asks him to carry.[41] The question is always one of fact to be determined objectively, not dependent entirely upon the subjective intention of the carrier,[42] nor his appearance to a particular customer. In answering this question, regard may be had to the carrier's stated or published conditions of carriage[43] and advertisements,[44] policies adopted by the carrier to his customers, the nature of the goods carried and the routes taken by the carrier. All aspects of the carrier's business may be considered in identifying the carrier's status.[45] The test whether a person is a common carrier generally will not turn upon whether passengers or goods are carried.[46] A common carrier may by special contract restrict his insurer's liability at common law[47] without losing his status as a common carrier.[48] To the extent that the

---

[35] *Johnson v Midland Railway Co* (1849) 4 Ex. 367; *Sutcliffe v Great Western Railway Co* [1910] 1 K.B. 478.

[36] *Belfast Ropework Co v Bushell* [1918] 1 K.B. 210 at 212; *Date v Sheldon* (1921) 7 Ll.L. Rep. 53 at 54; *Eastman Chemical International AG v NMT Trading Ltd* [1972] 2 Lloyd's Rep. 25; *A Siohn and Co Ltd v RH Hagland and Son (Transport) Ltd* [1976] 2 Lloyd's Rep. 428.

[37] Leslie at p.13.

[38] e.g. *Re Oxlade and NE Ry* (1864) 15 C.B.(N.S.) 680; *Consolidated Tea & Lands Co v Oliver's Wharf* [1910] 2 K.B. 395.

[39] e.g. *Belfast Ropework Co v Bushell* [1918] 1 K.B. 210.

[40] e.g. *Watkins v Cottell* [1916] 1 K.B. 10; *Scaife v Farrant* (1875) L.R. 10 Ex. 358, 364–365. See also *Electric Supply Stores v Gaywood* (1909) 100 L.T. 855.

[41] *Ingate v Christie* (1850) 3 Car. & K. 61; *Belfast Ropework Co Ltd v Bushell* [1918] 1 K.B. 210, 215; *A Siohn & Co Ltd v RH Hagland & Son (Transport) Ltd* [1976] 2 Lloyd's Rep. 428, 429–430, although in the last case, the court held that the carrier's decision not to carry goods for a particular customer who was unsatisfactory did not affect that carrier's status as a common carrier.

[42] *A Siohn & Co Ltd v RH Hagland & Son (Transport) Ltd* [1976] 2 Lloyd's Rep. 428.

[43] cf. *Lacey's Footwear (Wholesale) Ltd v Bowler International Freight Ltd* Unreported March 17, 1995; affirmed [1997] 2 Lloyd's Rep. 369.

[44] *A Siohn & Co Ltd v RH Hagland & Son (Transport) Ltd* [1976] 2 Lloyd's Rep. 428, 430.

[45] *Upston v Stark* (1827) 2 Car. & P. 598; *Chattock & Co v Bellamy & Co* (1895) 64 L.J. Q.B. 250.

[46] *Clarke v West Ham Corp* [1909] 2 K.B. 858, 879; *A Siohn & Co Ltd v RH Hagland & Son (Transport) Ltd* [1976] 2 Lloyd's Rep. 428.

[47] See below, para.36-018.

[48] *Baxendale v GE Ry* (1869) L.R. 4 Q.B. 244; *GN Ry v LEP Transport Co* [1922] 2 K.B. 742. cf.

provisions of the contract do not modify them, he is still subject to the liabilities and entitled to the rights of a common carrier at common law.

The near extinction of the common carrier Before 1963 the railway companies, **36-010** and their successor the British Transport Commission, were undoubtedly common carriers of most kinds of goods.[49] But now no person (including the franchised and privatised railway undertakings) shall be regarded as common carriers by railway.[50] Similarly, Transport for London[51] and the operators of the Channel Tunnel[52] have been declared by Parliament not to be common carriers by rail. Given the diversification in the railways industry,[53] it is perhaps not surprising that the common carrier by rail is now extinct. Moreover, during the last 100 years the courts have shown a tendency not to attach a common carrier's liability to carriers by road[54]; and today it seems that most carriers of goods by road are private carriers, except as regards passengers' luggage in public service vehicles.[55] Under the Road Haulage Association's Conditions of Carriage of 2009, the carrier stipulates that he is not a common carrier.[56] The point is of little practical importance, in view of the almost universal practice of all carriers, whether public or private, to contract out of their common law liability,[57] It should be noted that the provider of a "postal services" within the meaning of the Postal Services Act 2000 shall not be regarded as a common carrier.[58]

The private carrier Where for any of the reasons above stated, a carrier of goods **36-011** is not a common carrier, he will in virtually all cases[59] be a private carrier.[60] There is one additional reason why he might be a private carrier, namely, where he is merely a casual contractor for the transport of goods; for the common carrier is

---

    Crouch v LNW Ry (1854) 14 C.B. 255, 293; *Peek v N. Staffs Ry* (1863) 10 H.L. Cas. 473, 494 et seq.
49   *GN Ry v LEP Transport Co*, above, at 769.
50   Railways Act 1993 s.123; the Railways Regulations 1998 (SI 1998/1340) reg.23. The Transport Act 1962 s.43(6) provides that the British Waterways Board shall not be regarded as common carriers by inland waterway.
51   Greater London Authority Act 1999 s.156(8), Sch.11 para.31. See also London Regional Transport Act 1984 Sch.2 para.7(3); s.2(6).
52   Channel Tunnel Act 1987 s.19(2).
53   This diversification has been propelled by the EC Council Directive of July 29, 1991 (91/440) and the EU Council Directives of June 19, 1995 (95/18 and 95/19), which require the separation and allocation of the management of railway infrastructure and railway services. These Directives have been implemented by the Railways Regulations 1998 (SI 1998/1340). The United Kingdom has sought to achieve this by privatising the railway undertakings by a system of franchising pursuant to the Railways Act 1993 and the Railways Act 2005.
54   Kahn-Freund at pp.205–207, citing *Electric Supply Stores v Gaywood* (1909) 100 L.T. 855; *Watkins v Cottell* [1916] 1 K.B. 10; and *Belfast Ropework Co v Bushell* [1918] 1 K.B. 210.
55   See below, para.36-068.
56   For these Conditions, see below, para.36-032.
57   See McBain, "Time to abolish the common carrier" [2005] J.B.L. 545.
58   Postal Services Act 2000 s.99 (as amended by the Postal Services Act 2011 s.91 and Sch.12 para.30). *Lane v Cotton* (1701) 12 Mod. 472; *Whitfield v Le Despencer* (1778) 2 Cowp. 754, 764; *Triefus & Co Ltd v Above Office* [1957] 2 Q.B. 352.
59   See n.22, above.
60   The same carrier may, of course, operate some vehicles as a common carrier and some as a private carrier: *Date v Sheldon* (1921) 7 Ll.L. Rep. 53, 54.

required to engage in his business habitually.[61] The precise limits of "habitually" have not been judicially clarified.

36-012 **The consequences of the distinction between common and private carriers** The importance of the classification of a carrier as a common or private carrier lies in the liabilities of and remedies available to the carrier. Their importance is subject to the terms of the contract of carriage.[62] Subject to that contract, the key differences in the position of the two types of carrier are as follows. It is the duty of the common carrier to carry the goods entrusted to him by a customer, provided he can accommodate those goods on his conveyance.[63] A common carrier effectively undertakes, save in circumstances recognised by the common law as providing an exception, to indemnify the owner of the goods he carries for any loss or damage sustained by the goods[64]; whereas a private carrier is liable, as a consequence of the bailment of the goods to him, only if his conduct amounts to negligence.[65] The common carrier has the right to demand advance payment of freight[66] and has a common law right to exercise a particular lien over the goods in his charge for freight which is due.[67] The rights of limitation of the liability of the carrier differ depending upon status.[68] These rights and liabilities, and others, will be discussed below.

(ii)   Introduction to Carrier's Duties and Liabilities

36-013 **Introduction** The carrier's duties and liabilities are dependent on his designation as a common or private carrier. Once his status is determined, the liability of a common carrier is decided by reference to the obligations imposed on him by law. However, these responsibilities may be modified by the contract which he has concluded with the consignor, owner or forwarder of the goods. Additionally, there may be a liability in tort. The private carrier, on the other hand, will be liable simply under the contract he has concluded or in tort. The common or private carrier's liability may also rest in bailment, insofar as it is separate from liability in contract or tort.[69] The liability of the carrier in contract and tort may be concurrent.[70] We shall

---

61   See *Watkins v Cottell* [1916] 1 K.B. 10, 14; cf. too, *Brind v Dale* (1837) 8 Car. & P. 207; and *Belfast Ropework Co v Bushell* [1918] 1 K.B. 210.
62   Clarke, *International Carriage of Goods by Road: CMR*, 6th edn (2014), para.222.
63   *Jackson v Rogers* (1683) 2 Show. 327; *Boson v Sandford* (1685) 1 Show. 101, 104; *Lane v Cotton* (1701) 12 Mod. Rep. 472, 484; *Macklin v Waterhouse* (1828) 5 Bing 212; *Johnson v Midland Railway Co* (1849) 4 Ex. 367; *Carr v Lancashire and Yorkshire Railway Co* (1852) 7 Ex. 707; *Oxlade v North Eastern Railway Co* (1864) 15 C.B.N.S. 680; *Clarke v West Ham Corp* [1909] 2 K.B. 858, 877.
64   *Coggs v Bernard* (1703) 2 Ld. Raym. 909; *Dale v Hall* (1750) 1 Wils. K.B. 281; *Forward v Pittard* (1785) 1 Term Rep. 27; *Trent and Mersey Navigation v Wood* (1785) 3 Esp. 127; *Covington v Willan* (1819) Gow. 115; *Brooke v Pickwick* (1827) 4 Bing. 218; *Riley v Horne* (1828) 5 Bing. 217; *Brind v Dale* (1837) 8 Car. & P. 207. See below, para.36-018.
65   *Coggs v Bernard* (1703) 2 Ld. Raym. 909; *Hayman v Hewitt* (1798) Peake Add. Cas. 170; *Richardson v North Eastern Railway Co* (1872) L.R. 7 C.P. 75; *John Carter (Fine Worsteds) Ltd v Hanson Haulage (Leeds) Ltd* [1965] 2 Q.B. 495; *Morris v CW Martin & Sons Ltd* [1966] 1 Q.B. 716. See below, para.36-017.
66   *Batson v Donovan* (1820) 4 B. & Ald. 21; *Wyld v Pickford* (1841) 8 M. & W. 443. See below, para.36-050.
67   *Skinner v Upshaw* (1702) 2 Ld. Raym. 752, see below, para.36-052.
68   See below, paras 36-033—36-034.
69   See above, para.36-001.

consider below the nature of the carrier's liability in respect of the carriage of goods, from the perspective of both common and private carriers, as it may arise in each of the respects described above, for loss or damage, delay and misdelivery.

(iii)   Carrier's Liability imposed by Law

Common carrier   By reason of his public calling, the common carrier is subject, at common law, to three peculiar obligations: he must accept for transport goods tendered with the appropriate freight, provided he has space in his vehicles[71]; he must charge only a reasonable rate for their carriage[72]; and he is strictly responsible for all loss or damage which occurs in the course of transit. **36-014**

Wrongful refusal   If a common carrier refuses goods for which he has space, or demands an unreasonable rate, he commits, prima facie, the common carrier's tort of wrongful refusal of goods.[73] But the following grounds of justification for refusing to carry goods will be open to him, namely: **36-015**

(i)   that the goods are not of the class that he carries, either because they fall outside his specified categories, or because, none being specified, it is unreasonable to expect him to carry such goods[74];

(ii)   that the goods are dangerous,[75] or exceptional in character,[76] e.g. of exceptional size, or would, in the circumstances, expose the carrier to undue risk,[77] or have a value disproportionate to the security measures at his disposal[78];

(iii)   that the goods were tendered an unreasonable time before the carrier was ready for his journey[79];

(iv)   that the goods consigned were inadequately packed.[80]

The common carrier will not be liable if, in fact, there was no room for the particular consignment in the carrier's vehicle or vehicles,[81] or if the consignor refused to pay the freight in advance when so requested.[82]

Unreasonable charge   A common carrier must charge only a reasonable rate. If he demands and recovers an unreasonable charge, an action for money had and **36-016**

---

70   *Henderson v Merrett Syndicates Ltd* [1995] 2 A.C. 145; cf. *Tai Hing Cotton Mills Ltd v Liu Chong Hing Bank Ltd* [1986] A.C. 80.
71   e.g. *Jackson v Rogers* (1683) 2 Show. 327; *Lane v Cotton* (1701) 12 Mod. 472, 484; *Riley v Horne* (1828) 5 Bing. 217, 224.
72   e.g. *Pickford v Grand Junction Ry* (1841) 8 M. & W. 372, 377; *GW Ry v Sutton* (1869) L.R. 4 H.L. 226, 237. A rate is not unreasonable merely because it consists of a higher charge made for the greater risk attending the carriage of valuable goods: *Harris v Packwood* (1810) 3 Taunt. 264. cf. *Baxendale v Eastern Counties Ry* (1858) 4 C.B.(N.S.) 63.
73   *Jackson v Rogers* (1683) 2 Show. 327; *Crouch v LNW Ry* (1854) 14 C.B. 255.
74   See Leslie at p.8.
75   *Bamfield v Goole and Sheffield Transport Co Ltd* [1910] 2 K.B. 94, 115; Leslie at p.30.
76   *Date v Sheldon* (1921) 7 Ll.L. Rep. 53, 54.
77   *Edwards v Sherratt* (1801) 1 East 604.
78   *Batson v Donovan* (1820) 4 B. & Ald. 21, 32; Leslie at p.30.
79   *Lane v Cotton* (1701) 12 Mod. 472, 481.
80   *Munster v SE Ry* (1858) 4 C.B.(N.S.) 676, 701; *Sutcliffe v GW Ry* [1910] 1 K.B. 478, 503; *LNW Ry v Hudson* [1920] A.C. 324, especially at 340.
81   *Jackson v Rogers* (1683) 2 Show. 327; *Riley v Horne* (1828) 5 Bing. 217, 221.
82   *Wyld v Pickford* (1841) 8 M. & W. 443.

received will lie for the difference between the charge made and the charge that was reasonable.[83] But, though he cannot pick and choose among his customers, there is no rule at common law that he must treat all customers equally in the matter of charges.

"There was nothing in the common law to hinder a carrier from carrying for favoured individuals at an unreasonably low rate, or even gratis. All that the law required was, that he should not charge more than was reasonable."[84]

36-017 **Private carrier** The private carrier is under no obligation to accept any goods for carriage,[85] but once he has done so, usually for reward, his obligations are regulated by the contract which governs the carriage, or by the bailment to which his acceptance of the goods has subjected him.[86] The contract may stipulate expressly the time, route and charges of the carriage and set out the carrier's responsibilities as to the safety of the goods, which will be construed and enforced subject to the Unfair Contract Terms Act 1977 and Unfair Terms in Consumer Contracts Regulations 1999 or the Consumer Rights Act 2015 (which has replaced the 1999 Regulations for contracts made on or after October 1, 2015[87]). Where the contract is silent, the private carrier will bear the obligation of a bailee to exercise reasonable care of the goods and there will be implied into the contract, by virtue of the Supply of Goods and Services Act 1982, obligations to carry the goods to destination with reasonable care and skill,[88] within a reasonable time,[89] and at a reasonable price.[90] Similar rights are "treated as included" in respect of consumer service contracts under the Consumer Rights Act 2015.[91]

36-018 **Common carrier's liability for loss and damage** Liability for loss or damage merits fuller discussion. The private carrier's liability extends only to loss or damage caused by his own or his employees' negligence or want of reasonable care,[92] the burden of disproving which is on him[93] even if the carriage is gratuitous.[94] But the common carrier is, prima facie, strictly responsible for all loss or damage which occurs in the course of transit,[95] subject, at common law, to the plea of any of four "excepted perils", coupled with the disproof of negligence on the part of the carrier or his employees. Furthermore, a claim for loss of or damage to the goods carried cannot be enforced by a set-off against or a deduction from the freight which is due to the carrier.[96] Thus, the common carrier is, prima facie, liable where goods

---

83 *Baxendale v LSW Ry* (1866) L.R. 1 Ex. 137; *GW Ry v Sutton* (1869) L.R. 4 H.L. 226.
84 *GW Ry v Sutton*, above, at 237: advice of Blackburn J. to the House of Lords.
85 Subject to the Equality Act 2010 ss.4–13, 28–29, 31 and Sch.3 Pt 9.
86 *Hunt & Winterbotham (West of England) Ltd v BRS (Parcels) Ltd* [1962] 1 Q.B. 617; cf. Clarke, *International Carriage of Goods by Road: CMR*, 6th edn (2014), para.222.
87 See below, paras 38-389—38-426 et seq.
88 Supply of Goods and Services Act 1982 s.13.
89 1982 Act s.14.
90 1982 Act s.15.
91 Consumer Rights Act 2015 ss.49, 51, 52, 57. See below, paras 38-567—38-587.
92 *Coggs v Bernard* (1703) 2 Ld. Raym. 909; *Hayman v Hewitt* (1798) Peake Add. Cas. 170.
93 *Travers (Joseph) & Sons Ltd v Cooper* [1915] 1 K.B. 73.
94 *Houghland v RR Low (Luxury Coaches) Ltd* [1962] 1 Q.B. 694.
95 As to when transit begins and ends, see below, para.36-041.
96 *United Carriers Ltd v Heritage Food Group (UK) Ltd* [1995] 2 Lloyd's Rep. 269. Indeed, a judgment obtained by a carrier for freight should not be stayed pending the obtaining and execution of a judgment against the carrier for loss or damage (at 273). See below, para.36-050.

in his charge are lost or damaged through the wrongful acts of third parties,[97] including robbery[98] or riot,[99] or through an accidental fire[100] or other inevitable accident.[101] This liability is often described vividly, though strictly speaking inaccurately, as an "insurer's liability".[102] To escape his insurer's liability the common carrier must prove both (i) that the loss or damage was caused by an act of God, an act of the Queen's enemies, inherent vice in the goods or the consignor's own fault; and (ii) that no negligence or want of reasonable care on the part of the carrier or his employees contributed to the loss or damage.

Act of God   The archaic legal phrase "act of God" means an operation of natural   **36-019** forces (as opposed to an act of man[103]) which it was not reasonably possible to foresee and guard against, like lightning,[104] extraordinary weather conditions,[105] "some extraordinary natural event",[106] or a totally unexpected heart attack.[107]

Act of the Queen's enemies   Acts of the Queen's enemies probably do not include   **36-020** acts of rebels, and certainly not acts of rioters. This defence refers rather to the acts of the armed forces of a foreign power with which the country is at war.[108] It is open to question whether this exception would be construed to apply to all acts and incidents of war and hostilities.[109] However, as the liability of a common carrier is likely to continue to exist, if it exists at all, in respect of inland carriage only, the scope of the exception of acts of the Queen's enemies may be justified.

Inherent vice   "Inherent vice" in the goods consigned for carriage refers to the   **36-021** development of some latent characteristic or natural behaviour of the goods

---

[97] *Gosling v Higgins* (1808) 1 Camp. 451; *Evans v Hutton* (1842) 4 Man. & G. 954. This includes goods entrusted to a fraudulent sub-contractor with whom the carrier has contracted (as opposed to a person falsely holding himself out to the customer as the carrier): *John Rigby (Haulage) Ltd v Reliance Marine Insurance Co Ltd* [1956] 2 Q.B. 468; *Harrisons and Crossfield Ltd v London and North Western Railway Co* [1917] 2 K.B. 755. cf. the definition of "bogus sub-contractor" in a carriers' transit insurance policy in *London Tobacco Co (Overseas) Ltd v DFDS Transport Ltd* [1994] 1 Lloyd's Rep. 394.

[98] *Morse v Slue* (1671) 1 Vent. 190, 239 (ship); *Barclay v Cuculla* (1784) 3 Doug. K.B. 389 (ship); *Gibbon v Paynton* (1769) 4 Burr. 2298.

[99] *Forward v Pittard* (1785) 1 T.R. 27.

[100] *Forward v Pittard*, above; *Thorogood v Marsh* (1819) Gow. 105; *Hyde v Trent & Mersey Navigation Co* (1793) 5 Term Rep. 389.

[101] *Forward v Pittard*, above.

[102] *HIH Casualty and General Insurance Ltd v Chase Manhattan Bank* [2003] UKHL 6, [2003] 2 Lloyd's Rep. 61 at [66].

[103] *Forward v Pittard* (1785) 1 T.R. 27; and cf. *Oakley v Portsmouth and Ryde Steam Packet Co* (1856) 11 Ex. 618 (ship).

[104] *Forward v Pittard*, above.

[105] e.g. *Blyth v Birmingham Waterworks Co* (1856) 11 Exch. 781 (frost); *Briddon v GN Ry* (1858) 28 L.J. Ex. 51 (snow); *Nugent v Smith* (1876) 1 C.P.D. 423 (storm); *Makin v LNE Ry* [1943] K.B. 467 (flood).

[106] *Environment Agency v Empress Car Co (Abertillery) Ltd* [1999] 2 A.C. 22, 35.

[107] *Ryan v Youngs* [1938] 1 All E.R. 522.

[108] The restriction of the excepted peril to acts done by states with which the sovereign is at war is sound on historical grounds: see Holmes, *Common Law*, p.177. *Curtis v Mathews* [1918] 2 K.B. 825; and *HM Secretary of State for War v Midland & GW Ry* [1923] 2 Ir.R. 102, seem not to be true exceptions: the one case involved an act of the "Provisional Government" in Dublin during Easter Week, 1916, and in the other, the judgment was influenced by the fact that the Irish Bench, at the time of the "Troubles", considered a state of war to exist.

[109] See *Spinney's (1948) Ltd v Royal Insurance Co* [1980] 1 Lloyd's Rep. 406. Note the treatment in Clarke, *International Carriage of Goods by Road: CMR*, 6th edn (2014), para.236b–236f.

themselves (including their packaging and containers) which tends to their injury, deterioration or destruction, without the operation of any fortuitous, external cause.[110] In the context of the carriage of goods, "inherent vice" refers to the risk of deterioration of the goods as a result of their natural behaviour during the carriage or the inability of the goods to withstand the ordinary incidents of carriage without the involvement of an external fortuitous event.[111] For example, if an animal, for some reason like fright, injures or destroys itself in the course of transit in a way that it was not reasonable to foresee or guard against, its common carrier will normally escape liability.[112] Similarly, an inherent vice has been held to exist in the case of inadequate gin casks,[113] the explosion of fermented wine,[114] and defective vehicles that collapse while being transported.[115] For this purpose, any defect in the goods' packaging will be treated as an inherent vice.[116]

36-022 **Consignor's fault** If the loss, damage or destruction is due solely to the fault of the consignor (or his agent), the common carrier is free from liability. This defence may overlap with that of "inherent vice", as where fragile or perishable goods are consigned inadequately packed and without any indication to the carrier of the particular precautions which they demand. Examples of the defence in question are consignor's fraud,[117] defective packing,[118] misleading packing,[119] or insufficient or misleading addressing[120] by the consignor. It should be added that the carrier will probably be exonerated where, without negligence on his part, the loss or damage is due to the act of the consignee (or his agent).[121]

36-023 **Carrier's negligence** As already mentioned, the common carrier does not escape liability merely by proving that the loss or damage was due to an excepted peril.

---

[110] *Soya GmbH v White* [1983] 1 Lloyd's Rep. 122; *Global Process Systems Inc v Syarikat Takaful Malaysia Berhad* [2011] UKSC 5, [2011] 1 All E.R. 869. cf. *Blower v GW Ry* (1872) L.R. 7 C.P. 655, 662–663. The concept of "inherent vice" has been explored at length in the context of carriage of goods by sea and is included as a defence in the CMR Convention (art.17.2) and the CIM Convention (art.23.2). See below, paras 36-093, 36-127. See Rodière (1971) 6 E.T.L. 2, 16.

[111] *Soya GmbH v White* [1983] 1 Lloyd's Rep. 122, 126; *Noten BV v Harding* [1990] 2 Lloyd's Rep. 283; *Global Process Systems Inc v Syarikat Takaful Malaysia Berhad* [2011] UKSC 5, [2011] Lloyd's Rep. I.R. 302.

[112] *Blower v GW Ry*, above; *Kendall v LSW Ry* (1872) L.R. 7 Ex. 373. See also *Gill v Manchester Ry* (1873) L.R. 8 Q.B. 186; *Prior v LSW Ry* (1885) 2 T.L.R. 89. The carrier is required to comply with the regulations for the protection of animals laid down in the Welfare of Animals (Transport) (England) Order 2006 (SI 2006/3260) (Wales Order: SI 2007/1047), made pursuant to Animal Health Act 1981. Accordingly, the carrier may seek to require the consignor to warrant that the animals to be carried are in a fit state to be carried and properly packed and secured.

[113] *Hudson v Baxendale* (1857) 2 H. & N. 575.

[114] *Farrar v Adams* (1711) Buller N.P. 69 (c).

[115] *Johnson v NE Ry* (1888) 5 T.L.R. 68; *Lister v L & Y Ry* [1903] 1 K.B. 878.

[116] *Wilson, Holgate & Co Ltd v The Lancashire and Cheshire Insurance Corp Ltd* (1922) 13 Ll.L. Rep. 486, 487; *Mayban General Insurance BHD v Alstom Power Plants Ltd* [2004] EWHC 1038 (Comm), [2004] 2 Lloyd's Rep. 609 at [19]–[22] (overruled on other grounds in [2011] UKSC 5).

[117] *Tyly v Morrice* (1699) Carth. 485; *Gibbon v Paynton* (1769) 4 Burr. 2298.

[118] *Barbour v SE Ry* (1876) 34 L.T. 67; *Gould v SE & C Ry* [1920] 2 K.B. 186 (which shows that the defence is applicable even if the carrier is aware of the defective packing when he accepts the goods). cf. *Baldwin v LC & D Ry* (1882) 9 Q.B.D. 582; *LNW Ry v Hudson* [1920] A.C. 324; and see Kahn-Freund at pp.370–372.

[119] *Bradley v Waterhouse* (1828) 3 Car. & P. 318.

[120] cf. *Bradley v Dunipace* (1861) 7 Hurl. & N. 200 (ship); *Wise v GW Ry* (1856) 1 Hurl. & N. 63.

[121] *Nurrell v Larkin* (1831) 1 L.J. C.P.(N.S.) 2; *Butterworth v Brownlow* (1865) 19 C.B.(N.S.) 409. In these cases, the common carrier escaped being liable qua warehouseman, transit having been completed.

He must also show that no negligence on his part contributed thereto.[122] It may also be noted that though damage has been caused by an excepted peril, a common carrier will be liable in respect of subsequent aggravation of such damage by his negligence.[123]

Private carrier's liability for loss and damage   The private carrier's responsibility is to carry the goods entrusted to him with reasonable care, the degree of care depending on the nature and value of the goods, the nature of the agreed or anticipated conveyance and the standard of conduct reasonably expected of a competent carrier.[124] Unlike the common carrier, the private carrier's liability is not strict, although if the goods are lost or damaged, the burden will lie on the carrier to prove that he exercised the requisite degree of care or that the loss or damage was not caused by any failure to exercise such care.[125]   **36-024**

(iv)   Contractual Liability

Liability by the terms of the contract   The common carrier may modify the obligations which rest on him by virtue of his public status by means of the contract with the consignor or owner of the goods, in which case his liability will be determined by his "special contract". The private carrier will often[126] conduct the carriage of goods pursuant to a contract, which will regulate his liability. Indeed, the carrier may be subject to obligations implied by law.[127] The terms of the contract may be liable to be upset by the Unfair Contract Terms Act 1977,[128] insofar as they are exemption clauses, and the Unfair Terms in Consumer Contracts Regulations 1999, which renders as non-binding on a consumer any term which has not been "individually" negotiated and may be deemed "unfair".[129] Such terms will be controlled in respect of consumer contracts under the Consumer Rights Act 2015,   **36-025**

---

122 Act of God: *Blower v GW Ry* (1872) L.R. 7 C.P. 655, 663; *Talley v GW Ry* (1870) L.R. 6 C.P. 44, 51–52. Queen's enemies: *Blower v GW Ry*, above; *Talley v GW Ry*, above; cf. *Phillips v Clark* (1857) 2 C.B.(N.S.) 156, 164 (ship). Inherent vice: cf. *Blower v GW Ry*, above; cf. too, *Gill v Manchester Ry* (1873) L.R. 8 Q.B. 186. Consignor's fault: *Stuart v Crawley* (1818) 2 Stark. 323; contrast *Richardson v NE Ry* (1872) L.R. 7 C.P. 75.

123 *Notara v Henderson* (1872) L.R. 7 Q.B. 225 (ship). See, too, *Cox v LNW Ry* (1862) 3 F. & F. 77.

124 *A F Colverd & Co Ltd v Anglo-Overseas Transport Co Ltd* [1961] 2 Lloyd's Rep. 352; *James Buchanan & Co Ltd v Hay's Transport Services Ltd* [1972] 2 Lloyd's Rep. 535; *Johnson Matthey & Co Ltd v Constantine Terminals Ltd* [1976] 2 Lloyd's Rep. 215; *A Siohn & Co Ltd v RH Hagland & Son (Transport) Ltd* [1976] 2 Lloyd's Rep. 428; *Swiss Bank Corp v Brink's MAT Ltd* [1986] 2 Lloyd's Rep. 79; *Metaalhandel J A Magnus BV v Ardfields Transport Ltd* [1988] 1 Lloyd's Rep. 197.

125 *John Carter (Fine Worsteds) Ltd v Hanson Haulage (Leeds) Ltd* [1965] 2 Q.B. 495; *Morris v CW Martin & Sons Ltd* [1966] 1 Q.B. 716; *British Road Services Ltd v Arthur V Crutchley Co Ltd* [1968] 1 All E.R. 811. Any damages awarded against the private carrier may be reduced by reason of the claimant's contributory negligence pursuant to the Law Reform (Contributory Negligence) Act 1945, because the private carrier bears a duty of care both in contract and tort, as will be discussed below. See Vol.I, para.26-085.

126 This need not always be the case. For example, the private carrier may be a gratuitous or involuntary bailee.

127 For example, under the Supply of Goods and Services Act 1982.

128 *Frans Maas (UK) Ltd v Samsung Electronics (UK) Ltd* [2004] EWHC 1502 (Comm), [2004] 2 Lloyd's Rep. 251 at [154]–[161]; *Scheps v Fine Art Logistic Ltd* [2007] EWHC 541 (QB) at [30]–[32]. See below, Ch.38.

129 regs 4(1), 5(1), 8(1). See below, Ch.38. See also *Lacey's Footwear (Wholesale) Ltd v Bowler International Freight Ltd* [1997] 2 Lloyd's Rep. 369, 385. In *English Welsh & Scottish Railway Ltd v E On UK Plc* [2007] EWHC 599 (Comm), a contract for carriage of coal by rail was held to be void and unenforceable where it contained terms which the rail regulator determined to be an abuse

which replaces and revokes the 1999 Regulations for contracts made on or after October 1, 2015.[130]

36-026   **Special contracts**   In the modern law of carriage of goods by land the strict liability of the common carrier has almost completely disappeared, because carriers have for very many years entered into "special contracts" with their customers relieving them of the common carrier's heavy liability.[131] The common carrier's liability at common law as described in the preceding paragraphs is thus no longer part of the living law. Nonetheless, it has had a profound effect upon the contract practice of carriers by rail and road.

36-027   **Incorporation of terms**   The question whether exemption clauses form part of a contract of carriage of goods by land now depends almost entirely upon the common law. The rules of the common law on the incorporation of terms are fully discussed elsewhere.[132] Briefly, the consignor will be bound if he signed a consignment note which contains or refers to the exemption clauses[133]; and this, of course, is the most usual way in which such clauses are in practice incorporated in a contract for the carriage of goods. He will also be bound if he received without signing it a document such as a receipt or ticket[134] which contains or refers to exemption clauses, provided he knew that there was writing on the document and that this contained conditions, or provided the carrier did what was reasonably sufficient to give him notice of the conditions.[135] The more burdensome or unusual the clause restricting or excluding liability, the more closely notice of it must be made.[136] He may perhaps also be bound if the previous course of dealing between him and the carrier justifies the inference that he must have known not only that goods are always accepted for carriage upon conditions, but also what those conditions are.[137] He may well be bound by any such course of dealing or notice even if he never read

---

of a dominant market position.

[130] See below, paras 38-389—38-426 et seq.

[131] For an account of the evolution of "special contracts" in relation to the carriage of goods by land, see the 24th edn of this work, Vol.II, paras 2817–2818; Kahn-Freund at Ch.9. Note the sage suggestion of Lord Coke in *Southcote's Case* (1601) 4 Co. Rep. 83, 84.

[132] Vol.I, paras 13-008—13-018.

[133] *L'Estrange v F Graucob Ltd* [1934] 2 K.B. 394.

[134] See below, para.36-061.

[135] See, e.g. *Parker v SE Ry* (1877) 2 C.P.D. 416; *Watkins v Rymill* (1883) 10 Q.B.D. 178; *Thompson v LMS Ry* [1930] 1 K.B. 41; *Lacey's Footwear (Wholesale) Ltd v Bowler International Freight Ltd* [1997] 2 Lloyd's Rep. 369; *Cory Bros Shipping Ltd v Baldan Ltd* [1997] 2 Lloyd's Rep. 58, 61–62. cf. *T Comedy (UK) Ltd v Easy Managed Transport Ltd* [2007] EWHC 611 (Comm), [2007] 2 Lloyd's Rep. 397 at [28]–[31], where the Court held that such references would not override an already existing agreement between the parties.

[136] *Parker v South Eastern Railway* (1877) 2 C.P.D. 416, 428; *Thornton v Shoe Lane Parking Ltd* [1971] 2 Q.B. 163; *Interfoto Picture Library Ltd v Stiletto Visual Programmes Ltd* [1989] 1 Q.B. 433; see Vol.I, para.13-015.

[137] cf. *J Spurling Ltd v Bradshaw* [1956] 1 W.L.R. 461, 467; *Circle Freight International Ltd v Medeast Gulf Exports Ltd* [1988] 2 Lloyd's Rep. 427, CA; *Lacey's Footwear (Wholesale) Ltd v Bowler International Freight Ltd*, above, where it was held that a carrier's mailshots to a customer before their first contract did not amount to a prior course of dealing. In that case, the majority of the Court of Appeal concluded that a party's standard terms were incorporated because the other party was aware that carriers and forwarding agents tended to contract on the basis of limitation provisions, even though he had not turned his mind to the content of those provisions; whether the party who relied on such provisions had taken adequate steps to draw these provisions to the attention of the other was irrelevant. In such cases, it is legitimate to take into account the nature of the transaction and the position and character of the parties: see also *Poseidon Freight Forwarding Co Ltd v Davies*

the conditions and did not know what they were.[138] In any event, the carrier's capacity to impose terms purporting to exclude or restrict his liability for negligence in the case of loss or damage is now fettered in that any contractual term or notice to that effect has to satisfy the requirement of reasonableness under the Unfair Contract Terms Act 1977 and, where applicable, the requirement of fairness under the Unfair Terms in Consumer Contracts Regulations 1999.[139] Such provisions insofar as they affect consumers will be subject to the Consumer Rights Act 2015, which replaces and revokes the 1999 Regulations for contracts made on or after October 1, 2015.[140]

Construction of contracts A common carrier no less than a private carrier can 36-028 contract out of his liability for loss of or damage to the goods.[141] But he must do so in plain language: otherwise his common law liability remains and cannot be removed by "subtle implications or ambiguous words".[142] Such clauses of exemption or limitation will be construed strictly and narrowly[143] and, therefore, will operate to exclude liability for the negligence of the carrier if the clause expressly (or necessarily by implication) so provides.[144] Whilst the task at hand is to construe the exemption clause in order to understand the intention of the parties,[145] broadly if the clause makes no specific reference to negligence, liability for negligence will be excepted where the carrier's only realistic liability would lie in negligence[146]; but this is not necessarily so, as the question is one of construction and so it must be

---

Turner Southern Ltd [1996] 2 Lloyd's Rep. 388.

[138] *Hardwick Game Farm v Suffolk Agricultural Poultry Producers' Association* [1966] 1 W.L.R. 287, 308–309, 316–317, 339; affirmed [1969] 2 A.C. 31; *Lacey's Footwear (Wholesale) Ltd v Bowler International Freight Ltd* [1997] 2 Lloyd's Rep. 369, 378; cf. *McCutcheon v David MacBrayne Ltd* [1964] 1 W.L.R. 125 HL.

[139] Unfair Contract Terms Act 1977 ss.2(2) and 11. In *Granville Oil and Chemicals Ltd v Davies Turner and Co Ltd* [2003] EWCA Civ 570, [2003] 1 All E.R. (Comm) 819 at [31], the Court of Appeal upheld a nine-month time-bar in the British International Freight Association Standard Trading Conditions, having found that the road transport leg was sufficient to make the Act applicable to the contract (carriage by sea ordinarily being excluded from the operation of the Act), because the contract was between commercial parties and not consumers. In *Frans Maas (UK) Ltd v Samsung Electronics (UK) Ltd* [2004] EWHC 1502 (Comm), [2004] 2 Lloyd's Rep. 251, the court held that the limitation provision under the BIFA Conditions was reasonable. In *Rohlig (UK) Ltd v Rock Unique Ltd* [2011] EWCA Civ 18, [2011] 2 All E.R. (Comm) 1161 at [23], the Court of Appeal said, in upholding the time bar provision in the BIFA Conditions, that when considering the reasonableness of a standard condition the Court should not be astute to draw fine distinctions between cases which are broadly similar. In this case, at [24]–[25], the Court of Appeal compared the requirements of the 1977 Act and the 1999 Regulations. The party who relies on standard form conditions has to plead and bear the onus of proof that such terms are reasonable: *Sheffield v Pickfords Ltd* [1997] C.L.C. 648. The difficulties associated with the issue of incorporation of terms were highlighted in *Matrix Europe Ltd v Uniserve Northern Ltd* [2008] EWHC 11 (Comm), [2008] 1 Lloyd's Rep. Plus 27. See also below, Ch.38 as to the Unfair Terms in Consumer Contracts Regulations 1999 and the Consumer Rights Act 2015 which replaces and revokes the 1999 Regulations for contracts made on or after October 1, 2015.

[140] See below, paras 38-389—38-426.

[141] See above, para.36-008.

[142] *LNW Ry v Neilson* [1922] 2 A.C. 263, 266 (Lord Buckmaster).

[143] *Alexander v Railway Executive* [1951] 2 K.B. 882, 893.

[144] *Page v London Midland & Scottish Railway* [1943] 1 All E.R. 455; *Buckmaster v Great Eastern Railway Co* (1870) 23 L.T. 471.

[145] *Lamport & Holt Lines Ltd v Coubro Scrutton Ltd* [1982] 2 Lloyd's Rep. 42, 50.

[146] *Rutter v Palmer* [1922] 2 K.B. 87, 92; *Alderslade v Hendon Laundry Ltd* [1945] K.B. 189; *Shell Chemicals UK Ltd v P & O Roadtanks Ltd* [1995] 1 Lloyd's Rep. 297, 301.

clear that the parties intended to exclude liability for negligence.[147] There may be an important difference between the positions of common and private carriers in respect of exemption clauses which do not specifically refer to negligence. The potential liability of a common carrier includes and extends beyond negligence. Such a clause therefore would not protect the common carrier from his own negligence.[148] On the other hand, the private carrier may be liable in tort or contract if he fails to take reasonable care. It is probable that such a clause would protect the private carrier from liability for negligence,[149] but it is arguable that the clause would operate to except liability in contract, but not in tort.[150] Nevertheless, at common law a common carrier can contract out of liability for negligence,[151] or even for theft by his employees,[152] provided he uses clear enough words. Naturally the capacity of a carrier to contract out of his liability for negligence in the case of loss of or damage to goods has now been limited by the Unfair Contract Terms Act 1977 and any attempt so to do now has to satisfy the requirement of reasonableness under that Act.[153] As with exemption clauses, the reasonableness of provisions purporting to limit liability may fall to be assessed under the Unfair Contract Terms Act 1977, especially where the parties' bargaining strength is unequal, whether by reference to economic strength or to convenience or opportunity.[154] Similarly, where applicable, the relevant terms will have to satisfy the requirement of fairness under the Unfair Terms in Consumer Contracts Regulations 1999 or, for contracts made on or after October 1, 2015, the Consumer Rights Act 2015 (which replaces and revokes the 1999 Regulations).[155]

36-029 **Fundamental breach** The construction of exemption clauses is discussed elsewhere in this work, and various judicial techniques for confining them within narrow limits are there considered.[156] One of these techniques was formerly so important in the law of carriage of goods that it must be briefly mentioned. This was the so-called "doctrine" of fundamental breach (or breach of a fundamental term). If the carrier committed a fundamental breach of the contract of carriage, so that the other party had the right to terminate the contract, the carrier might be unable to rely on the exemption clauses in the contract at all, unless the other party, with full knowledge of the facts, elected to affirm and not to terminate the contract. The

---

[147] *Hollier v Rambler Motors (AMC) Ltd* [1972] 2 Q.B. 71; *Gillespie Bros & Co Ltd v Roy Bowles Transport Ltd* [1973] Q.B. 400, 415; *HIH Casualty and General Insurance Ltd v Chase Manhattan Bank* [2003] UKHL 6, [2003] 2 Lloyd's Rep. 61 at [11], [59]–[66], [95]. See above, Vol.I, paras 15-013—15-016.

[148] *Price & Co v Union Lighterage Co* [1903] 1 K.B. 750; affirmed [1904] 1 K.B. 412. See Kahn-Freund at pp.231–234. A similar analysis was considered by Lord Hoffmann in *HIH Casualty and General Insurance Ltd v Chase Manhattan Bank* [2003] UKHL 6, [2003] 2 Lloyd's Rep. 61 at [66]–[67] in the analogous case of the impact of an exemption clause on an assured's duty of disclosure, the negligent or non-negligent breach of which results in the voidability of the insurance contract.

[149] *Rutter v Palmer* [1922] 2 K.B. 87; *Turner v Civil Service Supply Association Ltd* [1926] 1 K.B. 50; *Fagan v Green and Edwards Ltd* [1926] 1 K.B. 102; *Bontex Knitting Works Ltd v St John's Garage* [1943] 2 All E.R. 690: affirmed [1944] 1 All E.R. 381n; *Harris Ltd v Continental Express Ltd* [1961] 1 Lloyd's Rep. 251; cf. *Alderslade v Hendon Laundry Ltd* [1945] K.B. 189.

[150] *White v John Warwick & Co Ltd* [1953] 2 All E.R. 1021.

[151] *Austin v MS & L Ry* (1852) 10 C.B. 454; *Carr v L & Y Ry* (1852) 7 Ex. 707; *Manchester, Sheffield & Lincs Ry v Brown* (1883) 8 App. Cas. 703.

[152] *Shaw v GW Ry* [1894] 1 Q.B. 373.

[153] Unfair Contract Terms Act 1977 s.2(2).

[154] *Overseas Medical Supplies v Orient Transport Services Ltd* [1999] 1 All E.R. (Comm) 981.

[155] See below, paras 38-385—38-426.

[156] See Vol.I, Ch.15.

carrier might be unable to do so if, for instance, he unjustifiably deviated from the agreed or customary route,[157] or sent perishable goods by goods train after contracting to send them by passenger train,[158] or left the goods even for a short time to their fate,[159] or unjustifiably delivered them to the wrong person,[160] or unjustifiably subcontracted the contract of carriage to another carrier of whom he must have known his customer would not approve.[161] The cases illustrating this doctrine in the law of carriage by land produced some fine distinctions and some anomalous results.[162] For instance, it is curious that if a lorry driver negligently left a loaded lorry unattended whilst he had a meal and the contents were stolen, his employer might have been guilty of fundamental breach[163]; but if he deliberately stole the contents himself, his employer was not so guilty.[164] Again, it is curious that if a thief tricked a carrier into employing him as a lorry driver by means of forged references, and then stole the goods, the carrier's negligence in not checking the references properly did not amount to fundamental breach[165]; but if a thief tricked a carrier into subcontracting the contract by posing as the representative of a non-existent haulage firm, the carrier's negligence in not checking his credentials properly might do so.[166] As regards the burden of proof, the Court of Appeal held that if the plaintiff pleads breach of contract or duty and nothing more, the burden of proving the absence of a fundamental breach by the carrier rests on the defendant.[167]

Rule of construction only   The House of Lords has, of course, emphasised that   **36-030** the "doctrine" of fundamental breach is not a rule of substantive law but a rule of construction to the effect that normally an exemption clause will be construed as

---

157 *Mallet v GE Ry* [1899] 1 Q.B. 309; *LNW Ry v Neilson* [1922] 2 A.C. 263.
158 *Gunyon v SE & C Ry* [1915] 2 K.B. 370; cf. *Sleat v Fagg* (1822) 5 B. & Ald. 342.
159 *Bontex Knitting Works Ltd v St John's Garage* [1943] 2 All E.R. 690; affirmed [1944] 1 All E.R. 381n. In *Suisse Atlantique Société d'Armement Maritime SA v NV Rotterdamsche Kolen Centrale* [1967] 1 A.C. 361, 435, Lord Wilberforce had doubts about the correctness of this decision, but was prepared to accept it as a case of deviation.
160 *Alexander v Railway Executive* [1951] 2 K.B. 882; contrast *Hollins v J Davy Ltd* [1963] 1 Q.B. 844.
161 *Garnham, Harris & Elton Ltd v Alfred W Ellis (Transport) Ltd* [1967] 1 W.L.R. 940, where the load (copper wire) was known to be particularly susceptible to theft.
162 For further anomalous results when goods are carried by rail at owner's risk, see below, para.36-031.
163 *Bontex Knitting Works Ltd v St John's Garage* [1943] 2 All E.R. 690. It should not be inferred from this case (where the circumstances were rather special) that every time a lorry driver left a loaded lorry unattended, this amounted to fundamental breach. The contrary has often been decided: see, e.g. *Harris Ltd v Continental Express Ltd* [1961] 1 Lloyd's Rep. 251, 260; *Colverd & Co Ltd v Anglo-Overseas Transport Co Ltd* [1961] 2 Lloyd's Rep. 352; *Mayfair Photographic Supplies (London) Ltd v Baxter, Hoare and Co Ltd* [1972] 1 Lloyd's Rep. 410.
164 *Carter (Fine Worsteds) Ltd v Hanson Haulage Ltd* [1965] 2 Q.B. 495. The decision of the majority of the Court of Appeal on this part of the case may need reconsideration—that it is clear that an employee who steals goods which have been bailed to his employer may be acting within the scope of his employment: *Morris v CW Martin Ltd* [1966] 1 Q.B. 716. In particular, the statement in [1965] 2 Q.B. 495 at 524–525 that fundamental breach must always be personal and not vicarious is questionable.
165 *Carter (Fine Worsteds) Ltd v Hanson Haulage Ltd*, above.
166 *Garnham, Harris & Elton Ltd v Alfred W Ellis (Transport) Ltd* [1967] 1 W.L.R. 940.
167 *Woolmer v Delmer Price Ltd* [1955] 1 Q.B. 291; *Levison v Patent Steam Carpet Cleaning Co Ltd* [1978] Q.B. 69. The latter decision of the Court of Appeal is at odds with the Court of Appeal's decision in *Hunt and Winterbotham (West of England) Ltd v BRS (Parcels) Ltd* [1962] 1 Q.B. 617; cf. *HC Smith Ltd v GW Ry* [1922] 1 A.C. 178. See *Euro Cellular (Distribution) Plc v Danzas Ltd* [2003] EWHC 3163 (Comm), [2004] 1 Lloyd's Rep. 521 at [60]–[64].

not applying to a situation created by fundamental breach.[168] As a result of this decision the scope of the "doctrine" is now somewhat uncertain.[169] The scope of an exemption clause in a particular contract of carriage will be a question of construction depending on the intention of the parties, and it will require very clear words for an exemption clause to be interpreted as wide enough to cover a fundamental breach of contract.[170] Obviously many of the decisions cited in this and the last paragraphs must now be read in light of the more recent expressions of view by the House of Lords, although it is fair to say that their Lordships did not expressly disapprove of any of these cases.[171] It has been assumed that the doctrine of fundamental breach as previously enunciated should continue to apply to deviations from the contractual carriage and the line of cases concerning deviation (generally involving carriage by sea) should continue to avoid the application of exemption clauses.[172] It is submitted that such cases, at least as they apply to carriage by land, should be tailored to the main line of authorities and the now evolved rule of construction, as an exemption clause may be so drafted to take account of deviations.[173]

36-031   **Exceptions to liability commonly found in special contracts**   Standard form contracts often distinguish between goods carried at the carrier's risk and goods carried at the owner's risk, the former attracting a higher freight.[174] Where the parties agree that the goods are carried at the carrier's risk, the carrier will be liable for loss, damage or delay but subject to a list of exceptions. The exceptions often relied on by carriers include the four common law excepted perils, namely, act of God, act of foreign enemy, inherent vice and consignor's fault,[175] and some others, e.g. any consequence of war, invasion, hostilities, civil war, insurrection,[176] requisition, destruction of or damage to property by or under any order of any government or public or local authority,[177] and seizure under legal process.[178] Additionally, the contract may provide that the carrier is liable for loss or damage caused by insuf-

---

[168] *Suisse Atlantique Société d'Armement Maritime SA v NV Rotterdamsche Kolen Centrale* [1967] 1 A.C. 361; *Photo Production Ltd v Securicor Transport Ltd* [1980] A.C. 827.

[169] See Vol.I, paras 15-023—15-027, where the question is fully discussed. See, generally, *Kenyon, Son and Craven Ltd v Baxter, Hoare and Co Ltd* [1971] 1 W.L.R. 519 (bailment); followed in *Gallaher Ltd v British Road Services Ltd* [1974] 2 Lloyd's Rep. 440 (carriage by road).

[170] *Photo Production Ltd v Securicor Transport Ltd*, above.

[171] With the possible exception of *Bontex Knitting Works Ltd v St John's Garage*: see above, n.163.

[172] *Photo Production Ltd v Securicor Transport Ltd* [1980] A.C. 827 at 845.

[173] *Kenya Railways v Antares Pte Ltd (The Antares) (Nos 1 and 2)* [1987] 1 Lloyd's Rep. 424, 430; *State Trading Corp of India Ltd v M Golodetz Ltd* [1989] 2 Lloyd's Rep. 277, 288–289. Such clauses when included in standard forms or used against consumers must always be reasonable: Unfair Contract Terms Act 1977 s.3(2)(b). See also Unfair Terms in Consumer Contracts Regulations 1999 Sch.2 para.1(b) and the Consumer Rights Act 2015 ss.62–65 and Sch.2 Pt 1 para.2. For contracts made on or after October 1, 2015 the 1999 Regulations are replaced and revoked by the 2015 Act (see below, paras 38-389—38-426).

[174] The distinction between exemption clauses and clauses allocating risk may be a fine one and may be controversial: see *HIH Casualty and General Insurance Ltd v Chase Manhattan Bank* [2001] EWCA Civ 1250, [2001] 2 Lloyd's Rep. 483 at [118]–[119]; reversed in part [2003] UKHL 6, [2003] 2 Lloyd's Rep. 61.

[175] See above, paras 36-018—36-022.

[176] There are numerous authorities concerning carriage and insurance contracts interpreting such "war risks" exceptions: see e.g. *Green v British India Steam Navigation Co Ltd* (1920) 4 Ll.L. Rep. 245; *Pesquerias y Secaderos e Bacalao de España SA v Beer* (1949) 82 Ll.L. Rep. 501; *Spinney's (1948) Ltd v Royal Insurance Co* [1980] 1 Lloyd's Rep. 406. As to "insurrection", *see National Oil Co of Zimbabwe (Private) Ltd v Sturge* [1991] 2 Lloyd's Rep. 281.

[177] *Sommer v Mathews* (1934) 49 Ll.L. Rep. 154.

ficient or improper packing, labelling or addressing[179] by riots, civil commotions,[180] strikes, lockouts, stoppage or restraint of labour[181] from whatever cause; or by the consignee not taking or accepting delivery within a reasonable time. Where goods are carried at the owner's risk, the carrier will generally only be liable for loss, damage or delay resulting from the carrier's "wilful misconduct". The contract will often provide that the onus of proving "wilful misconduct" lies on the owner of the goods. The meaning of "wilful misconduct"[182] means something a great deal more than negligence, even gross or culpable negligence, and the onus of proving it may be prove to be a heavy one,[183] because the House of Lords has held that the carrier is entitled to refuse to give any explanation as to how the loss or damage occurred.[184]

The Road Haulage Association's Conditions of Carriage   There are no standard **36-032** conditions of carriage applicable to the road haulage industry as a whole.[185] Consequently, some carriers seek to apply highly individual conditions, constrained only by the requirements of the Unfair Contract Terms Act 1977[186] and the Unfair Terms in Consumer Contracts Regulations 1999 (or the Consumer Rights Act 2015, which replaces and revokes the 1999 Regulations for contracts made on or after October 1, 2015).[187] There are, however, conditions of carriage issued by the Road Haulage Association Limited (RHA) which are used by most carriers by road. The most recent version of these conditions is that which became operative as from September 1, 2009.[188] It is common for individual variations of these conditions to be applied. However, even where a contract of carriage has not been expressly made subject to the Association's Conditions, a course of previous dealing may be held sufficient to bring the contract in question under the Conditions.[189] Under the RHA's Conditions, the carrier's liability incorporates a number of the exceptions referred to above[190] and there is a specific provision that the carrier is still liable, even in the case of an excepted peril, if he fails to use reasonable care to minimise the effect of that peril. The RHA's Conditions provide that the liability of the carrier in respect

---

[178]   cf. *Handelsbanken Norwegian Branch of Svenska Handelsbanken AB v Dandridge (The Aliza Glacial)* [2002] EWCA Civ 577, [2002] 2 Lloyd's Rep. 421.

[179]   *Gould v South Eastern and Chatham Railway Co* [1920] K.B. 186.

[180]   *Boggan v Motor Union Insurance Co Ltd* (1923) 16 Ll.L. Rep. 64.

[181]   The meaning of "stoppage or restraint of labour" was considered in *Young and Son Ltd v British Transport Commission* [1955] 2 Q.B. 177.

[182]   "Wilful misconduct" is a term which is used in the CMR Convention (see below, para.36-131) and in the Marine Insurance Act 1906 (see below, para.42-022). As a contractual term, the words may attract a different meaning through the process of contractual construction.

[183]   See, e.g. *Lewis v GW Ry* (1877) 3 Q.B.D. 195; *Graham v Belfast and Northern Counties Ry* [1901] 2 I.R. 13; *Forder v GW Ry* [1905] 2 K.B. 532; *Bastable v NB Ry*, 1912 S.C. 555; *Hartstoke Fruiterers Ltd v LMS Ry* [1942] 2 All E.R. 488; affirming on other grounds [1943] K.B. 362; *Horabin v BOAC* [1952] 2 All E.R. 1016; *Young & Son Ltd v BTC* [1955] 2 Q.B. 177; Kahn-Freund at pp.257–261.

[184]   *HC Smith Ltd v Great Western Railway* [1922] 1 A.C. 178.

[185]   See generally, Hill [1969] J.B.L. 100.

[186]   Unfair Contract Terms Act 1977 ss.2(2) and 11.

[187]   See below, paras 38-389—38-426.

[188]   The extent to which the conditions are applicable to contracts for the hire of vehicles by one carrier from another was discussed in *Gillespie Bros and Co Ltd v Roy Bowles Transport Ltd* [1973] Q.B. 400.

[189]   *Eastman Chemical International AG v NMT Trading Ltd* [1972] 2 Lloyd's Rep. 25. cf. *T Comedy (UK) Ltd v Easy Managed Transport Ltd* [2007] EWHC 611 (Comm), [2007] 2 Lloyd's Rep. 397, [28]–[31].

[190]   See above, para.36-031.

of physical loss, misdelivery of or damage to the consignment shall be limited to the lesser of the value of the goods, the cost of repair or £1,300 per tonne on the gross weight of the goods lost, misdelivered or damaged, and shall not be less than £10.[191] In relation to all other claims, the 1998 conditions limit the carrier's liability to the lesser of the carriage charges or the amount of the proved loss.[192] In either case, the customer may declare an increase in this limit, provided that additional carriage charges are agreed.[193]

36-033 **Upper financial limit of liability: the Carriers Act 1830** While imposing its very strict liability upon common carriers, the common law drew no distinction between different kinds of goods, nor did it give the carrier any general right to open and inspect the packages brought to him for transport, or to be informed of their contents.[194] Hence the stagecoach proprietors had a real grievance: they were required to carry articles potentially of great value without any means of knowing what they were carrying, and were strictly liable if the articles were stolen during transit. The Carriers Act 1830 was passed in order to remove this grievance.[195] It relieved the common carrier by land (and mail contractors and stagecoach proprietors) of liability for certain goods of a specially valuable or breakable nature and worth more than £10, unless a special declaration of value was made. The Act provides[196] that no common carrier by land for hire shall be liable for the "loss[197] of or injury to" a "parcel or package"[198] containing certain articles of a valuable or breakable nature enumerated in s.1 of the Act,[199] the total value of which exceeds £10, unless their value is declared on delivery to the carrier, and an increased charge paid (if demanded)[200] as compensation for the greater risk and care to be taken. The carrier must give notice that such an increased charge will be made by a notice fixed in legible characters in some public and conspicuous part of his premises[201] and must on request give a signed receipt for the parcel or package.[202] If no declaration of value is made by the consignor, or if he does not pay or promise to pay the increased charge, the carrier is under no liability for the loss of or injury to the

---

[191] RHA Conditions cl.11(1). This provision in the 1998 conditions was new and was inserted together with a new cl.8, as a result of the court's decision in *Spectra International Plc v Hayesoak Ltd* [1997] 1 Lloyd's Rep. 153, [1998] 1 Lloyd's Rep. 162. As to the meaning of consignment, see *Gillespie Bros and Co Ltd v Roy Bowles Transport Ltd* [1973] Q.B. 400; and *Acme Transport Ltd v Betts* [1981] 1 Lloyd's Rep. 131.

[192] RHA Conditions cl.11(2).

[193] RHA Conditions cll.11(1) and 11(2).

[194] *Walker v Jackson* (1842) 10 M. & W. 161; *Crouch v LNW Ry* (1854) 14 C.B. 255.

[195] The public had a grievance too: see 24th edition of this work, Vol.II, para.2817.

[196] s.1. See Kahn-Freund at pp.335–337, 345–354; Leslie at pp.182–216.

[197] For the meaning of "loss", see *Hearn v LSW Ry* (1855) 10 Ex. 793; *Piancini v LSW Ry* (1856) 18 C.B. 226; *Wallace v Dublin & Belfast Ry* (1874) I.R. 8 C.L. 341; *Millen v Brasch* (1882) 10 Q.B.D. 142. The Act provides no protection if the goods are lost or damaged by delay: *Hearn v London and South Western Ry Co* (1855) 10 Ex. 793; *Millen v Brasch* (1882) 10 Q.B.D. 142.

[198] See, e.g. *Whaite v L & Y Ry* (1874) L.R. 9 Ex. 67. cf. *Treadwin v GE Ry* (1868) L.R. 3 C.P. 308.

[199] See Leslie at pp.193–198; Kahn-Freund at pp.348–350. The list includes gold, silver, bank notes or coin, jewellery, precious stones, watches, clocks, stamps, maps, "writings", title deeds, paintings, glass, china, silk, furs, and lace. The Carriers Act Amendment Act 1865 excepted from this list "machine-made lace". The Statute Law (Repeals) Act 2004 repealed the 1865 Act (Sch.1 Pt 17, Group 11(4)), but re-introduced the exception into s.1 of the 1830 Act (Sch.2 para.1).

[200] *Behrens v GN Ry* (1861) 6 Hurl. & N. 366; affirmed (1862) 7 Hurl. & N. 950.

[201] Carriers Act 1830 s.2.

[202] s.3.

goods, unless it arose from any theft or forgery on the part of his employees.[203] If the carrier fails to post up the statutory notice, or to give the signed receipt on request, he is subject to the common carrier's liability for loss or damage.[204] If all the mandatory requirements of the Act are duly fulfilled, the owner may recover the value of the goods if they are lost or injured, and in addition the increased charge.[205] The carrier may still rely on the defence of the Carriers Act even though he has deviated from the route and so committed a fundamental breach of contract,[206] or has been guilty of "gross negligence".[207] One provision of the Act looks strange to modern eyes, namely that if no declaration of value is made, the carrier's liability is not merely limited to the now paltry sum of £10 but is excluded altogether.

Scope of application of the Carriers Act   The Carriers Act is still in force but **36-034** its practical importance today is very small. It applies to "mail contractors, stage coach proprietors, and other common carriers by land for hire". It does not apply to private carriers and therefore not to any carrier by rail[208] nor to the great majority of modern carriers by road, except in regard to passengers' luggage carried in public service vehicles (buses and coaches[209]), Though such luggage is carried "free of extra charge" and the Act only applies to "carriers for hire", the Act nevertheless applies to passengers' luggage when carried in such vehicles because the fare paid by the passenger is deemed to include freight for his luggage.[210] Indeed, this is probably the most important sphere of application of the Act today. The Act applies to "common carriers by land" and therefore not to carriers by sea, even though the ship belongs to a common carrier by land. Hence, in the case of a through journey by land and sea, the carrier is not protected by the Act[211] unless he can prove that the loss or injury occurred during the land part of the journey.[212]

---

[203] ss.1, 8. Section 8 originally referred to "the felonious acts" of servants. The words in the text were substituted by s.10 of and Sch.2 para.4, to the Criminal Law Act 1967 (as amended by the Theft Act 1968 s.33(3) and Sch.3 Pt III). As to who is a servant, see *Stephens v LSW Ry* (1886) 18 Q.B.D. 121. For the degree of proof necessary, see *Boyce v Chapman* (1835) 2 Bing. N.C. 222; *GW Ry v Rimell* (1856) 18 C.B. 575; *Metcalfe v LB & SC Ry* (1858) 4 C.B.(N.S.) 307; *Vaughton v LNW Ry* (1874) L.R. 9 Ex. 93; *Kirkstall Brewery Co v Furness Ry* (1874) L.R. 9 Q.B. 468; *M'Queen v GW Ry* (1875) L.R. 10 Q.B. 569. Some of these cases are difficult to reconcile.

[204] s.3.

[205] s.7. The carrier may, however, prove that the actual value is less than the declared value, in which case his liability is limited to the former: s.9. The value is the invoice price to the buyer, not the price paid by the seller: *Blankansee v LNW Ry* (1881) 45 L.T. 761.

[206] *Morritt v NE Ry* (1876) 1 Q.B.D. 302; *Millen v Brasch* (1882) 10 Q.B.D. 142. For fundamental breach, see above, paras 36-029—36-030.

[207] *Boys v Pink* (1838) 8 C. & P. 361; *Hinton v Dibbin* (1842) 2 Q.B. 646.

[208] Today, no person may be a common carrier by rail: Railways Act 1993 s.123; the Railways Regulations 1998 (SI 1998/1340) reg.23. See above, para.36-010.

[209] No conclusion to the contrary should, it is submitted, be drawn from *Houghland v RR Low (Luxury Coaches) Ltd* [1962] 1 Q.B. 694, where not only was it not argued that the defendant was a common carrier, but also the carriage was what is technically known as "contract carriage", i.e. where the coach is hired for a lump sum, and not "stage carriage" or "express carriage", where each passenger pays a separate fare.

[210] *Le Conteur v LSW Ry* (1865) L.R. 1 Q.B. 54; *Casswell v Cheshire Lines Committee* [1907] 2 K.B. 499.

[211] *LNW Ry v Ashton* [1920] A.C. 84.

[212] *Le Conteur v LSW Ry*, above.

36-035 **Dangerous and unusual goods** At common law even a common carrier was never obliged to carry dangerous goods.[213] The customer impliedly warrants that the goods to be carried are not dangerous, unless the carrier knew or had the means of knowing that the goods are dangerous.[214] The customer will be liable at law for all loss or damage caused by any breach of this warranty, whether he was aware of the dangerous nature of the goods or not.[215] The carriage of dangerous and radioactive goods in the United Kingdom is governed by regulations[216] made to implement European Parliament and Council Directive 2008/68/EC of September 24, 2008 on the approximation of the laws of the Members States concerning the inland transport of dangerous goods. These regulations implement the Annexes to the European Agreement concerning the International Carriage of Dangerous Goods by Road signed at Geneva on September 30, 1957, as amended ("ADR") and the Annex to the Regulation concerning the International Carriage of Dangerous Goods by Rail ("RID") which forms Appendix C to the Convention concerning International Carriage by Rail ("COTIF").[217]

36-036 **Deviation** At common law a carrier, whether common or private, must carry the goods entrusted to him by the agreed route or by his own usual route (though it may not be the shortest)[218] and he must not deviate unnecessarily from his usual or the agreed route.[219] What amounts to a justifiable deviation in carriage by land has not been settled with precision. Deviation is certainly necessary and justifiable to secure the safety of the goods,[220] and probably justifiable if, e.g. it is to avoid a peril to the goods that lies ahead on the route, or, possibly, to bypass a blockage of the route in order to obviate unreasonable delay. The effect of deviation as constituting a fundamental breach of contract and so disentitling the carrier from relying on his exemption clauses has already been considered.[221]

36-037 **Delay** At common law a carrier, whether common or private, must deliver the goods at the agreed time, or if no time has been agreed, within a reasonable time.[222] Unless the carrier's obligation to deliver the goods at destination at an agreed time

---

213 See above, para.36-015. See, generally, Hill [1978] L.M.C.L.Q. 74; *Effort Shipping Co Ltd v Linden Management SA; The Giannis NK* [1998] 1 All E.R. 495. The RHA Conditions by cl.1 define "dangerous goods" as meaning "goods named individually in the Approved Carriage List issued from time to time by the Health and Safety Commission, explosives, radioactive substances and any other substances presenting a similar hazard".

214 *Brass v Maitland* (1856) 6 El. & Bl. 470, 482; *Bamfield v Goole and Sheffield Transport Co Ltd* [1910] 2 K.B. 94.

215 *Farrant v Barnes* (1862) 1 C.B.N.S. 553; *Great Northern Railway Co v LEP Transport and Depository Ltd* [1922] 2 K.B. 742; *Bamfield v Goole and Sheffield Transport Co Ltd*, above; Girvin [1996] L.M.C.L.Q. 487.

216 See, for example, Carriage of Dangerous Goods by Rail Regulations 1996 (SI 1996/2089), Carriage of Explosives by Road Regulations 1996 (SI 1996/2093), Carriage of Dangerous Goods by Road Regulations 1996 (SI 1996/2095), Packaging Labelling and Carriage of Radioactive Material by Rail Regulations 2002 (SI 2002/2099), and Carriage of Dangerous Goods and Use of Transportable Pressure Equipment Regulations 2009 (SI 2009/1348, as amended by SI 2011/1885). See also European Commission Directives 96/86 and 96/87, implemented by Carriage of Dangerous Goods (Amendment) Regulations 1999 (SI 1999/303).

217 See below, paras 36-079—36-082.

218 *Hales v LNW Ry* (1863) 4 B. & S. 66, 71; *Myers v LSW Ry* (1869) L.R. 5 C.P. 1.

219 *Davis v Garrett* (1830) 6 Bing. 716 (barge); *Taylor v GN Ry* (1866) L.R. 1 C.P. 385, 388.

220 *Taylor v GN Ry*, above.

221 See above, paras 36-029—36-030.

222 See also Supply of Goods and Services Act 1982 s.14.

is construed strictly, he will be liable for delay only insofar as he has failed to exercise reasonable care to deliver the goods at the required time.[223] He is not liable for delay where it was due to any cause outside the range of reasonable foresight and his own control, like an act of God,[224] or the act of a third party,[225] imperfect addressing of the goods by the consignor,[226] a strike of the carrier's employees,[227] the need (which could not reasonably have been foreseen) to give priority to passenger traffic,[228] or an exceptional and not reasonably foreseeable press of traffic.[229] In the latter case, it is the carrier's duty to forward goods in the order in which he received them; failure to do this may amount to negligence.[230] If the carrier has failed to exercise the requisite degree of care so as to be liable for delay, the Carriers Act will afford him no protection.[231]

Detention Detention is only another form of delay; it means negligent failure to dispatch the goods in proper time from the station of dispatch or retention of the goods at the station of destination for more than a reasonable time.[232]   **36-038**

Measure of damages for delay At common law the carrier is liable for such damages resulting from delay as arise naturally, i.e. according to the usual course of things, from the breach of contract[233]; or, to put it differently, for such damages as were at the time of the contract reasonably foreseeable as likely to result from such breach.[234] He is not liable for loss of exceptional profit which the owner would have made[235] unless it is shown that he knew of the facts which would lead to such special loss if he was guilty of delay.[236] Several standard form contracts provide that in general the carrier will not be liable for indirect or consequential damages or for loss of a particular market, whether held daily or at intervals.[237]   **36-039**

Misdelivery If the carrier delivers the goods to the wrong person, he is liable for breach of contract and for conversion.[238] But the strict liability in the tort of conversion is modified in favour of carriers. Thus, provided the carrier delivers to the consignee named in the contract, in accordance with its terms, he is not guilty of   **36-040**

223 *Raphael v Pickford* (1843) 5 Man. G. 551; *Taylor v Great Northern Railway Co* (1866) L.R. 1 C.P. 385; *Panalpina International Transport Ltd v Densil Underwear Ltd* [1981] 1 Lloyd's Rep. 187.
224 e.g. *Briddon v GN Ry* (1858) 28 L.J. Ex. 51.
225 *Taylor v GN Ry* (1866) L.R. 1 C.P. 385.
226 *Caledonian Ry v William Hunter and Co* (1858) 20 D.(Ct. of Sess.) 1097.
227 *Sims v Midland Ry* [1913] 1 K.B. 103.
228 *Briddon v GN Ry* (1858) 28 L.J. Ex. 51; *Goddard v Midland Ry* (1899) 80 L.T. 624.
229 *Wallace v G & SW Ry* (1869) 17 W.R. 464.
230 *Page v GN Ry* (1868) I.R. 2 C.L. 228.
231 *Hearn v London and South Western Ry Co* (1855) 10 Ex. 793; *Millen v Brasch* (1882) 10 Q.B.D. 142.
232 See *Gordon v GW Ry* (1881) 8 Q.B.D. 44.
233 *Hadley v Baxendale* (1854) 9 Exch. 341, 354–355.
234 *Victoria Laundry (Windsor) Ltd v Newman Industries Ltd* [1949] 2 K.B. 528, 539–540; *Czarnikow Ltd v Koufos* [1969] 1 A.C. 350. See Vol.I, paras 26-052—26-072.
235 *Horne v Midland Ry* (1873) L.R. 8 C.P. 131.
236 *Simpson v LNW Ry* (1876) 1 Q.B.D. 274.
237 Such clauses essentially only purport to exclude damages which might be recoverable pursuant to the second limb of the rule in *Hadley v Baxendale* (1854) 9 Exch. 341, although each clause will have to be construed in its own context: *Croudace Construction Ltd v Cawoods Concrete Products Ltd* [1978] 2 Lloyd's Rep. 55; *British Sugar Plc v NEI Power Projects Ltd* (1998) 87 B.L.R. 42; *Deepak Fertilisers & Petrochemical Corp v ICI Chemicals & Polymers Ltd* [1999] 1 All E.R. (Comm) 69.
238 *Youl v Harbottle* (1791) Peake 68; *M'Kean v M'Ivor* (1870) L.R. 6 Ex. 36, 41.

breach of contract or conversion if the consignee is not otherwise entitled to the goods, e.g. because he is receiving stolen goods.[239] This privilege has been regarded as a just corollary to the common carrier's general duty to accept the goods of all[240]; but today it probably applies to all carriers, whether common or private. Again, if the carrier, in delivering, as he thinks, to the agreed consignee, is in fact tricked into delivering to the wrong person in circumstances which ought reasonably to have aroused suspicion in his mind that the person holding himself out as consignee was not lawfully entitled to the goods, the carrier will be liable for breach of contract, because of his fault, and for conversion.[241] But if he delivers the goods to the address to which they were consigned, and there are no suspicious circumstances to warn him that the person claiming delivery there is not in fact entitled to it, he will escape liability.[242] It is not necessarily misdelivery to deliver goods to a swindler who has induced the consignor to send him the goods. In some circumstances, delivery to the wrong person may amount to a fundamental breach of contract and so may prevent the carrier from relying on his exemption clauses,[243] but this will turn on the construction of the clause and the intentions of the parties.[244]

36-041 **Beginning and end of transit** It is important to determine when transit begins and ends, because the carrier's liability as a carrier only exists between these times: after the end of transit he is only subject to the (usually lesser) liability of a warehouseman.[245] Transit begins not when the vehicle begins to move[246] but when the goods are delivered to and accepted by the carrier or by one of his actually or ostensibly authorised employees or agents.[247] At common law transit ends when the goods are tendered to the consignee, whether he has accepted them or not. Where the goods are not to be delivered at the consignee's premises, transit ends a reasonable time after their arrival at the station or place of destination.[248]

36-042 **Stoppage in transit** Under the Sale of Goods Act 1979,[249] the consignor, if he is an unpaid seller who has learnt of the insolvency of the buyer, has a right to stop

---

[239] *M'Kean v M'Ivor*, above, at 41; *Fowler v Hollins* (1872) L.R. 7 Q.B. 616, 632; *British Traders Ltd v Ubique Transport Ltd* [1952] 2 Lloyd's Rep. 236. cf. Clarke at para.231.

[240] *Sheridan v New Quay Co* (1858) 4 C.B.(N.S.) 618; *Fowler v Hollins*, above, at 649–650.

[241] *Duff v Budd* (1822) 3 Brod. & Bing. 177; *Stephenson v Hart* (1828) 4 Bing. 476. Quaere: whether *Duff v Budd* and *Stephenson v Hart* are not in fact cases of involuntary bailment? *Stephenson v Hart* was so regarded in *Heugh v LNW Ry* (1870) L.R. 5 Ex. 51, 56–57, 58, but not in *M'Kean v M'Ivor* (1870) L.R. 6 Ex. 36 at 39. cf. the similar rule of reasonably careful delivery in the law of sale of goods: *Galbraith & Grant Ltd v Block* [1922] 2 K.B. 155; see below, para.44-245.

[242] *M'Kean v M'Ivor*, above; *Heugh v LNW Ry*, above; *British Traders Ltd v Ubique Transport Ltd* [1952] 2 Lloyd's Rep. 236. See also *Birkett v Willan* (1819) 2 B. & Ald. 356; Leslie at pp.92–96; Kahn-Freund at pp.298–301; Hughes (1931) 47 L.Q.R. 244 et seq.

[243] *Alexander v Railway Executive* [1951] 2 K.B. 882; contrast *Hollins v J Davy Ltd* [1963] 1 Q.B. 844; *Sze Hai Tong Bank Ltd v Rambler Cycle Co Ltd* [1959] A.C. 576; see above, paras 36-029—36-030.

[244] *Photo Production Ltd v Securicor Transport Ltd* [1980] A.C. 827.

[245] As to the liability of a warehouseman, see above, para.33-058. As to the distinction between the liability of carriers and that of other intermediaries in the freight trade see, generally, Hill, *Freight Forwarders* (1972), Chs 2 and 11. See above, para.36-006.

[246] *Sadler Brothers Co v Meredith* [1963] 2 Lloyd's Rep. 293, 307.

[247] *Soanes v LSW Ry* (1919) 88 L.J. K.B. 524; *Rigby (Haulage) Ltd v Reliance Marine Insurance Co Ltd* [1956] 2 Q.B. 468. Contrast *Slim v GN Ry* (1854) 14 C.B. 647; *Harrisons & Crossfield Ltd v LNW Ry* [1917] 2 K.B. 755; *Crows Transport Ltd v Phoenix Assurance Co Ltd* [1965] 1 W.L.R. 383. See also Leslie at pp.65–68; Kahn-Freund at pp.312–321.

[248] *Chapman v GW Ry* (1880) 5 Q.B.D. 278.

[249] ss.44–46; see below, paras 44-326—44-338. See Leslie at pp.74–84; Kahn-Freund at pp.304–306.

the goods while they are in transit, even though he is not the owner and even though he may not be a party to the contract of carriage. The meaning of "in transit" for the purposes of this rule is defined in the Act[250] and does not exactly coincide with its meaning for the purposes of holding the carrier liable as a carrier.[251] For instance, if the carrier wrongfully refuses to deliver the goods to the buyer, transit is at an end for the purposes of stoppage in transit[252] but not for the purposes of the carrier's liability. Conversely, if the goods are rejected by the buyer and the carrier continues in possession of them, transit continues for the purposes of stoppage in transit[253] but ends for the purposes of the carrier's liability. Failure to comply with a notice to stop the goods when the consignor is properly exercising his right exposes the carrier to an action in tort for conversion. Compliance with an invalid notice may make him similarly liable to the owner. Subject to the foregoing, the carrier is always bound (unless otherwise agreed) to follow the instructions of the owner of the goods, provided it is reasonably practicable to do so[254]; and he is entitled to assume that, in the absence of notice to the contrary, the owner is the consignee.[255]

Title to sue in contract   Where the owner has suffered loss or damage to his goods, and has contracted with the carrier, the owner may sue the carrier in an action on that contract. At common law, it is necessary that both the owner and the offending carrier are parties to that contract.[256] Difficulties of identifying the contracting parties arise, where the owner of the goods has sold or bought the goods during the transit, and where the contracting carrier has entrusted the carriage to a sub-carrier or has delivered the goods to a successive carrier.[257] In the case of a sale of the goods carried, an initial presumption is made that he who is the owner of the goods at the time of the breach has contracted with the carrier[258] and that that person is the consignee.[259] In that case, either the carrier has contracted directly with the consignee or the consignor of the goods has contracted with the carrier as the consignee's agent.[260] Insofar as the consignor is the consignee's agent, any representation made or variation agreed by the consignor, will bind the consignee,[261] provided it is made or agreed with the consignee's authority. Where the presumption is rebutted and it is established that the consignor, and not the consignee, is a party to the contract of carriage, the consignor will have title to sue the carrier. This

36-043

As to priority between the right of stoppage in transit and the carrier's lien, see below, para.36-052.
[250] s.45.
[251] See above, para.36-041.
[252] s.45(6).
[253] s.45(4).
[254] *Scothorn v S Staffs Ry* (1853) 8 Ex. 341.
[255] *Cork Distilleries Co v GS & W Ry* (1874) L.R. 7 H.L. 269.
[256] See Leslie at pp.51–63; Kahn-Freund at pp.209–212.
[257] See below, paras 36-046—36-047.
[258] *Dawes v Peck* (1799) 8 Term Rep. 330; *Fragano v Long* (1825) 4 B. & C. 219; *Dunlop v Lambert* (1839) 6 Cl. & F. 600, 627; *Coats v Chaplin* (1842) 3 Q.B. 483; *Coombs v Bristol and Exeter Ry* (1858) 3 Hurl. & N. 1, 510; *Murphy v Midland Great Western Ry* [1903] 2 I.R. 5.
[259] *Stephenson v Hart* (1828) 4 Bing. 476, 487; *Heugh v London and North Western Ry* (1870) L.R. 5 Ex. 51, 57–58; *Albacruz (Cargo Owners) v Albazero (Owners); The Albazero* [1977] A.C. 774.
[260] *Cork Distilleries Co v GS & W Ry* (1874) L.R. 7 H.L. 269, 277, 281; *Murphy v Midland Great Western Ry* [1903] 2 I.R. 5, 23, 30; *Albacruz (Cargo Owners) v Albazero (Owners) (The Albazero)* [1977] A.C. 774, 785–786, 842–848; *Texas Instruments Ltd v Nasan (Europe) Ltd* [1991] 1 Lloyd's Rep. 146, 148–149; Kahn-Freund at p.210.
[261] Clarke, *International Carriage of Goods by Road: CMR*, 6th edn (2014), para.216c. cf. *Leduc v Ward* (1888) 20 Q.B.D. 475.

may be to the detriment of the consignee, who may have no contractual rights, as the consignor might have no wish to sue the carrier for the benefit of the consignee, especially if the consignor has discharged his obligations to the consignee by delivering the goods to the carrier and has been paid by the consignee. However, there is a possibility of an implied contract coming into being when the consignee takes delivery of the goods from the carrier[262]; such implied contracts, however, raise numerous objections and are limited in their scope.[263] In cases where the consignor or consignee are not contracting parties, they may now be able to enforce a contractual term which was intended for their benefit pursuant to the Contracts (Rights of Third Parties) Act 1999.[264] Whether or not the owner of the goods is a party to the carriage contract, he may well have his rights in bailment and remedy in tort in respect of any loss of or damage to the goods.[265]

(v)   Liability in Tort

36-044   **Liability in tort**   A person whose goods are lost or damaged during transit has alternative remedies against the carrier either for breach of contract or for tort.[266] This has long been settled law.

"The declaration in an action against a carrier may be framed either upon the contract, charging the injury as a breach of contract; or upon the duty imposed by law, charging the injury as breach of duty or wrong."[267]

---

262 *Brandt v Liverpool Brazil & River Plate* [1924] 1 K.B. 575.

263 *The Aramis* [1989] 1 Lloyd's Rep. 213. The difficulties led to the passing of the Carriage of Goods by Sea Act 1992 in relation to sea carriage. Other devices which have been developed to circumvent the doctrine of privity include the so-called principle in *Dunlop v Lambert* (1839) 6 Cl. & F. 600; *Albacruz (Cargo Owners) v Albazero (Owners) (The Albazero)* [1977] A.C. 774, 847; *Alfred McAlpine Construction Ltd v Panatown Ltd* [2001] 1 A.C. 518) to the effect that the original contracting party has entered into the contract for the benefit for all his successors in title to the goods, and assignments (*Britain & Overseas Trading (Bristles) v Brooks Wharf & Bull Wharf* [1967] 2 Lloyd's Rep. 51, 60).

264 The 1999 Act does not apply to contracts for the carriage of goods by rail or road which are the subject of an international convention, save that provisions which provide for the exemption of a third party's liability may be enforced by that third party under s.1: s.6(5).

265 If the consignee engaged the carrier, they will have established a relationship of bailment at will: *Transcontainer Express Ltd v Custodian Security Ltd* [1988] 1 Lloyd's Rep. 128, 135. If the consignor contracted with the carrier and assigns the benefit of that contract to the consignee, the latter will succeed to the consignor's rights as bailor: *Sonicare International Ltd v East Anglia Freight Terminal Ltd* [1997] 2 Lloyd's Rep. 48, 53. cf. Clarke, *International Carriage of Goods by Road: CMR*, 6th edn (2014), para.216c. See above, paras 36-001, 36-013.

266 Although set-off against freight cannot be relied upon: *United Carriers Ltd v Heritage Food Group (UK) Ltd* [1995] 2 Lloyd's Rep. 269.

267 Bullen and Leake, *Precedents of Pleadings*, 3rd edn (1868), p.120; cf. 13th edn (1990), p.142. For modern cases, see *Harris Ltd v Continental Express Ltd* [1961] 1 Lloyd's Rep. 251; *Learoyd Bros Ltd and Huddersfield Fine Worsteds Ltd v Pope & Sons (Dock Carriers) Ltd* [1966] 2 Lloyd's Rep. 142; *Lee Cooper Ltd v CH Jeakins & Sons Ltd* [1967] 2 Q.B. 1; cf. *Morris v CW Martin Ltd* [1966] 1 Q.B. 716 (bailment); *Moukataff v BOAC* [1967] 1 Lloyd's Rep. 396 (carriage by air at common law); *Transmotors Ltd v Robertson, Buckley & Co Ltd* [1970] 1 Lloyd's Rep. 224 (bailment to subcontractor in carriage of goods); *James Buchanan v Hay's Transport Services* [1972] 2 Lloyd's Rep. 535 (gratuitous sub-bailment in carriage of goods); *Gillespie Bros & Co Ltd v Roy Bowles Transport Ltd* [1973] Q.B. 400. As to the scope of liability in tort where there is a contract between the tortfeasor and the claimant, see *Henderson v Merrett Syndicates Ltd* [1995] 2 A.C. 145; cf. *Tai Hing Cotton Mills Ltd v Liu Chong Hing Bank Ltd* [1986] A.C. 80. cf. Clarke, *International Carriage of Goods by Road: CMR*, 6th edn (2014), para.229a.

This does not mean that, if the contract contains exemption clauses, the claimant can disregard the contract and allege a wider liability in tort.[268] Exemption clauses may, indeed, be construed as being wide enough to indemnify a carrier against liability in tort, not only his own but also that of his employees,[269] although naturally such clauses as purport, in the case of loss or damage to goods, to exclude or limit liability for negligence must now satisfy the statutory test of reasonableness.[270] But the existence of the alternative remedy does mean that the claimant may be able to sue in tort if there is no privity of contract between him and the defendant, for example, where the consignor makes the carriage contract, but the consignee suffers loss at the carrier's hands. The remedy in tort will be of service to claimants where there is lack of privity in various situations.[271] First, for example, the claimant may be a stranger to the contract of carriage, as when his goods have been borrowed or stolen from him, or hired to a hirer under a hire-purchase contract, and are then handed to a carrier by the borrower, thief or hirer, for carriage to a consignee. Secondly, the defendant may be a stranger to the contract of carriage, as when the owner of goods contracts with a carrier, and then sues someone else whose act or omission caused the loss or damage, e.g. the carrier's employee, or another carrier to whom the contract of carriage was sub-contracted either in whole or in part.

Title to sue in tort A claimant claiming damages in tort for the loss of or damage to his goods will rely either on the tort of negligence or on the tort of conversion. If he relies on negligence, he will have to prove that the defendant owed him a duty of care and broke it,[272] and that he was the owner of the goods or entitled to possession of them at the time when the loss or damage occurred by reason of the negligent act.[273] If he relies on conversion, he will have to prove that he had an immediate right to possession,[274] unless he can show a permanent injury to his reversionary interest,[275] e.g. by reason of the destruction or loss of the goods.[276] However, if the relation between the claimant and defendant is that of head bailor

36-045

---

[268] *Hall v Brooklands Auto Racing Club* [1933] 1 K.B. 205, 213; contrast *White v John Warwick Ltd* [1953] 1 W.L.R. 1285.

[269] *Gillespie Bros & Co Ltd v Roy Bowles Transport Ltd* [1973] Q.B. 400; reversing [1971] 2 Lloyd's Rep. 521: this concerned the construction of cl.3(4) in the 1967 Conditions of the Road Haulage Association. The RHA amended and amplified this clause in light of the decision at first instance so as to cover a carrier in the event of his own negligence. The amendment proved unnecessary in light of the Court of Appeal's decision. See also *Hair and Skin Trading Co Ltd v Norman Airfreight Carriers Ltd* [1974] 1 Lloyd's Rep. 443 on the construction of the similar cl.20 under the RHA's 1961 Conditions. Clause 3(4) in the RHA Conditions 1967 was held only to regulate rights and duties arising strictly out of the carriage of goods and not, e.g. indemnities in respect of claims against a carrier by employees for breach of common law and statutory duties: *Boughen v Frederick Attwood Ltd* [1978] 1 Lloyd's Rep. 413. See *Cert Plc v George Hammond Plc* [1999] 2 All E.R. (Comm) 976 as to the scope of RHA Conditions 1991 cl.11. As to the employer's vicarious liability for the acts of his employees, see *Frans Maas (UK) Ltd v Samsung Electronics (UK) Ltd* [2004] EWHC 1502 (Comm), [2004] 2 Lloyd's Rep. 251.

[270] Unfair Contract Terms Act 1977 ss.2(2) and 11.

[271] The disabling effect of a lack of privity is now qualified by the Contracts (Rights of Third Parties) Act 1999.

[272] *Lee Cooper Ltd v CH Jeakins & Sons Ltd* [1967] 2 Q.B. 1.

[273] *Margarine GmbH v Cambay Prince Steamship Co Ltd* [1969] 1 Q.B. 219; *Leigh and Sillavan Ltd v Aliakmon Shipping Co Ltd* [1986] A.C. 785.

[274] *Kahler v Midland Bank Ltd* [1950] A.C. 24.

[275] *Mears v LSW Ry* (1862) 11 C.B.(N.S.) 850; *HSBC Rail (UK) Ltd v Network Rail Infrastructure Ltd* [2005] EWCA Civ 1437, [2006] 1 Lloyd's Rep. 358.

and sub-bailee, as it may be when the contract of carriage has been sub-contracted with the actual or ostensible authority of the owner, then the claimant may be in a more favourable position.[277] If he sues for negligence, he will not have to prove that the defendant owed him a duty of care, because this arises automatically from the relationship between the parties; and the onus of disproving negligence will be on the defendant.[278] If he sues for conversion, he will not have to prove that he has a better right to possession, because the defendant will probably be estopped from denying his head bailor's title.[279] A carrier who voluntarily takes into his possession the goods of some other person can only invoke the terms of the sub-bailment under which he received the goods from an intermediate bailee against the owner of the goods when the owner has actually, expressly or impliedly, or even ostensibly authorised the sub-bailment and thus consented to the terms of the sub-bailment.[280]

36-046 **Scope of exemption clauses: sub-contracting** An exemption clause contained in a contract can only operate contractually; and it is a fundamental principle of the common law that no one except a party to a contract can take any advantage from it.[281] Hence, even if an exemption clause purports to exonerate not only the carrier but also his employees or agents, they will not be entitled to the benefit of the clause if the claimant sues them in tort, because they are not parties to the contract of carriage.[282] Similarly, if the carrier sub-contracts the whole or part of the contract of carriage as principal, and not as agent, and the owner sues the sub-carrier in tort, the owner will not be bound by exemption clauses contained in the sub-contract, because he is not a party thereto.[283] However, it is different if the carrier contracted with the owner as agent for the sub-carrier, because in that case the sub-carrier is a party to the original contract[284]; or if he contracted with the sub-carrier as agent for

---

[276] *Moukataff v BOAC* [1967] 1 Lloyd's Rep. 396, 415.

[277] *KH Enterprise (Cargo Owners) v Pioneer Container (Owners) (The Pioneer Container)* [1994] 2 A.C. 324. A successor in title to the bailor's goods will be owed a duty in bailment by the bailee or sub-bailee if the original bailor assigns the benefit of the contract of carriage to the successor or if the bailee attorns to the successor: *Sonicare International Ltd v East Anglia Freight Terminal Ltd* [1997] 2 Lloyd's Rep. 48, 53; *East West Corp v DKBS* 1912 [2003] EWCA Civ 83, [2003] 1 Lloyd's Rep. 239 at [39]–[42]. See also *Spectra International Plc v Hayesoak Ltd* [1997] 1 Lloyd's Rep. 153, [1998] 1 Lloyd's Rep. 162.

[278] *Victoria Fur Traders Ltd v Roadline (UK) Ltd* [1981] 1 Lloyd's Rep. 570, 578.

[279] However, even if the claimant proves a sub-bailment, he may be caught by exceptions included in the terms on which the goods were received by the sub-bailee from the head bailee: *Johnson, Matthey & Co Ltd v Constantine Terminals Ltd* [1976] 2 Lloyd's Rep. 215; *Singer Co (UK) Ltd v Tees and Hartlepool Port Authority* [1988] 2 Lloyd's Rep. 164, 168. The claimant will, however, only be subject to the terms of the sub-bailment when he expressly or impliedly consented to them: *KH Enterprise (Cargo Owners) v Pioneer Container (Owners) (The Pioneer Container)*, above. See, generally, Palmer and McKendrick (eds), *Interests in Goods*, 2nd edn (1998), Ch.19 (Bell).

[280] *KH Enterprise (Cargo Owners) v Pioneer Container (Owners) (The Pioneer Container)* [1994] 2 A.C. 324 PC. See *Sandeman Coprimar SA v Transitos y Transportes Integrales SA* [2003] EWCA Civ 113, [2003] 2 W.L.R. 1496, [61]–[66], where it was held that the terms of the sub-bailment, which were based on the CMR Convention, applied as between the bailor and sub-bailee. See also *Cami Automotive Insurance v Westwood Shipping Lines Inc* 2009 FC 664, 2012 FCA 16 (Fed CA Canada).

[281] *Dunlop Pneumatic Tyre Co Ltd v Selfridge & Co Ltd* [1915] A.C. 847; Vol.I, Ch.18.

[282] *Scruttons Ltd v Midlands Silicones Ltd* [1962] A.C. 446.

[283] See the cases cited above, paras 36-044—36-045.

[284] *Hall v NE Ry* (1875) L.R. 10 Q.B. 437, 443; *Barratt v GN Ry* (1904) 20 T.L.R. 175; cf. *Gill v MS & L Ry* (1873) L.R. 8 Q.B. 186; *United States Steel Products Co v GW Ry* [1916] 1 A.C. 189, 205, 210,

the owner, because in that case the owner is a party to the sub-carrier's contract[285]; or if the owner consented to the sub-bailment on the terms of the exemption clause.[286] These common law principles are now subject to the Contracts (Rights of Third Parties) Act 1999, which might permit an employee, agent or sub-bailee to enforce the benefit of an exemption clause.[287]

Successive carriers If a carrier engages the services of another carrier to perform part of the contract of carriage, it is important to know whether he contracted to carry the goods to their ultimate destination, or only to the point where he hands them over to the second carrier.[288] In the former case the first carrier will be liable to the owner (subject, of course, to the conditions of carriage) for loss of or damage to the goods which happens at any stage of the journey. In the latter case the first carrier will only be liable for loss or damage which happens while the goods are in his hands. In both cases, of course, the second carrier may be liable to the owner in tort in accordance with the principles already discussed,[289] or for breach of contract, if the second carrier contracted directly with the owner or through the agency of the first carrier. **36-047**

(vi)   Claims against the Carrier

Time for making claims It may be important for a carrier to receive early warning of a claim for loss of or damage to goods which he has carried, so that he may investigate the claim, inform his insurers and decide whether the claim should be admitted or resisted.[290] The general law will allow the claimant to institute proceedings in respect of his claim at any time during the period sanctioned by the Limitation Act 1980. In order to shorten the time in which claims are notified to the carrier, several standard form contracts provide that claims for loss, damage, misdelivery or delay must be presented to the carrier within specified short time periods. The capacity of the carrier to prescribe time limits for the making of claims and the institution of legal proceedings is constrained by the Unfair Contract Terms Act 1977, which provides that where the Act prevents a contract term excluding or restricting liability, as unreasonable, it also prevents any term which purports to make that liability or its enforcement subject to restrictive or onerous conditions.[291] A term in a contract of carriage requiring notice of a claim for, say, loss of or damage to goods to be given within an exceptionally short period of time might conceivably be rendered ineffective by this section.[292] Where the carrier has contracted with a consumer, such terms imposing short time limits on the consumer's presentation **36-048**

213; *The Mahkutai* [1996] A.C. 650.

[285] *Hall v NE Ry*, above, at 442. For the difficulties involved in this agency device, see Vol.I, paras 15-050—15-052. cf. *Victoria Fur Traders Ltd v Roadline (UK) Ltd* [1981] 1 Lloyd's Rep. 570.

[286] See above, para.36-045.

[287] *Homburg Houtimport BV v Agrosin Ltd* [2003] UKHL 12, [2003] 2 W.L.R. 711 at [57]. Even though the 1999 Act does not apply to contracts for carriage by rail or road, which is subject to the rules of an international convention, the Act is expressed to apply even in such cases where the third party seeks to rely on an exemption clause: s.6(5).

[288] See Kahn-Freund at pp.325–334.

[289] See above, paras 36-044—36-045.

[290] See, generally, Clarke [1982] L.M.C.L.Q. 533.

[291] ss.2(2), 3, 11 and 13.

[292] *Granville Oil and Chemicals Ltd v Davies Turner and Co Ltd* [2003] EWCA Civ 570, [2003] 1 All E.R. (Comm) 819 at [31]. See *Rohlig (UK) Ltd v Rock Unique Ltd* [2011] EWCA Civ 18, [2011] 2 All E.R. (Comm) 1161.

of a claim may not be binding on the consumer if it has not been individually negotiated and it is unfair within the meaning of the Unfair Terms in Consumer Contracts Regulations 1999.[293] Such provisions will be subject to the Consumer Rights Act 2015, which replaces and revokes the 1999 Regulations for contracts made on or after October 1, 2015.[294]

(vii) Carrier's Rights

36-049 **Consignor's warranty of fitness** At common law the consignor impliedly warrants that the goods are fit and proper for carriage and are not dangerous.[295] This principle was originally developed as a corollary to the common carrier's duty to accept all consignments offered to him even if he was unable to inspect their contents; but now it probably extends to all carriers, whether or not they are under a duty to carry the goods, and whether or not the consignor knows of the danger.[296] The carrier may recover damages for breach of this warranty, whether in respect of personal injuries sustained by himself or his employees[297] or in respect of damage sustained by the carrier's own property or by the goods of other consignors[298]; and it is immaterial whether or not the carrier is himself liable to the other consignors.[299]

36-050 **Carrier's right to freight** As a compensation for the heavy burden of his profession the carrier is entitled to demand payment of his reasonable charges in advance.[300] But if the freight is not paid before the goods are consigned, the carrier may not sue for it until the goods are finally delivered,[301] unless the consignor exercises his right of stoppage in transit.[302] Several standard form contracts therefore provide that a claim or counterclaim shall not be made a reason for deferring or withholding payment of the carrier's charges. Even without such protection in the carriage contract, the carrier (whether common or private) is entitled to the payment of freight on the due date without any deduction or set-off being made to allow for any claim which the consignor may have under the contract of carriage.[303] This right to freight without set-off exists notwithstanding that the contract is for a series of carriages as opposed to one carriage and that the carrier may have obliga-

---

[293] 1999 Regulations regs 4(1), 5(1), 8(1) Sch.2 para.1(q).

[294] See below, paras 38-389—38-426.

[295] *Bamfield v Goole and Sheffield Transport Co* [1910] 2 K.B. 94; *GN Ry v LEP Transport Co Ltd* [1922] 2 K.B. 742.

[296] *Burley v Stepney Corp* [1947] 1 All E.R. 507, 510.

[297] *Farrant v Barnes* (1862) 11 C.B.(N.S.) 553; *Bamfield v Goole and Sheffield Transport Co*, above.

[298] *GN Ry v LEP Transport Co Ltd* [1922] 2 K.B. 742.

[299] *GN Ry v LEP Transport Co Ltd*, above, at 765; cf. *The Winkfield* [1902] P. 42.

[300] *Batson v Donovan* (1820) 4 B. & Ald. 21, 28; *Wyld v Pickford* (1841) 8 M. & W. 443. In an action for refusal to carry, actual tender of freight need not be shown, only that the consignor was ready and willing to pay: *Pickford v Grand Junction Ry* (1841) 8 M. & W. 372.

[301] *Barnes v Marshall* (1852) 18 Q.B. 785, 789.

[302] *Booth SS Co Ltd v Cargo Fleet Iron Co Ltd* [1916] 2 K.B. 570.

[303] *United Carriers Ltd v Heritage Food Group (UK) Ltd* [1995] 2 Lloyd's Rep. 269, 273; *A S Jones Ltd v Burton Gold Medal Biscuits* Unreported April 11, 1984. See also *Britannia Distribution Co Ltd v Factor Pace Ltd* [1998] 2 Lloyd's Rep. 420 (set off available against freight between freight forwarder and principal); cf. *Schenkers Ltd v Overland Shoes Ltd* [1998] 1 Lloyd's Rep. 498 (concerning the validity, under the Unfair Contract Terms Act 1977, of a "no set-off" clause in a freight forwarding contract, as opposed to a carriage contract). This "freight rule" is a rule of law originating in international commercial custom and so is not liable to be upset by the Unfair Contract Terms Act 1977 (cf. *Stewart Gill Ltd v Horatio Myer & Co Ltd* [1992] Q.B. 600). As to air freight, see *Schenker Ltd v Negocios Europa Ltd* [2017] EWHC 2921 (QB), [2018] 1 W.L.R. 718.

tions under the contract ancillary to that of carriage, although his claim must be for freight and not a charge unrelated to the carriage.[304]

Who pays freight? The person liable to pay the freight is the person with whom   **36-051**
the carrier contracts. Thus, if the consignor contracted as agent for the consignee, the consignee is obliged to pay[305]; but if the consignor contracted as principal, the carrier must recover from the consignor.[306] The consignor may, by express contract, exclude his liability for freight and leave the carrier with a remedy against the consignee alone: but the courts are very ready to imply an undertaking by the consignor to pay the freight if the consignee does not do so, even if the consignment note says in so many words that freight will be paid by the consignee.[307] Acceptance of the goods by the consignee is, in the absence of notice to the contrary, evidence of an implied contract to pay the carrier's charges: the consideration for this contract is the fact that the carrier parted with his lien.[308] The incidence of liability for freight must be distinguished from the right to sue the carrier for loss of or damage to the goods. This has already been considered.[309]

Carrier's lien At common law the common, but not the private,[310] carrier has a   **36-052**
particular lien upon the goods for the payment of his freight.[311] But, in the absence of a contract or of binding usage,[312] he has no general lien on the goods for debts owing by his customer in respect of previous transactions[313]; nor can he sell the goods in order to defray his expenses. Under several standard form contracts, however, the carrier has not only a particular lien but also a general lien against the owner of the goods.[314] The unpaid seller's right of stoppage in transit has priority over the carrier's general, but not particular, lien.[315] The carrier's contractual right to exercise a general lien under a standard form of contract may come into existence at the time at which the contract was made notwithstanding that it is not exercisable except upon the happening of a particular event, i.e. the carrying of the goods. The lien is conveniently described as a "possessory lien" because it is only if the carrier has possession that it can be exercised. This does not imply, however, that the lien does not come into existence until possession is assumed.[316] In practice, the lien cannot be exercised until the goods reach their destination or the unpaid seller stops them in transit. The carrier cannot, for instance, detain the goods at the

---

[304] *United Carriers Ltd v Heritage Food Group (UK) Ltd*, above.
[305] cf. *Dickenson v Lano* (1860) 2 F. & F. 188. See Kahn-Freund at pp.399–401.
[306] *GW Ry v Bagge* (1885) 15 Q.B.D. 625. As to the freight forwarder's liability for freight, see *Britannia Distribution Co Ltd v Factor Pace Ltd* [1998] 2 Lloyd's Rep. 420 at 423.
[307] See n.306, above.
[308] *World Transport Co v Tealing* [1936] 2 All E.R. 573.
[309] See above, para.36-043.
[310] *Electric Supply Stores v Gaywood* (1909) 100 L.T. 855.
[311] *Skinner v Upshaw* (1702) 2 Ld. Ray. 752.
[312] The courts require particularly strong evidence of such usage. See Leslie at pp.87–88.
[313] *Rushforth v Hadfield* (1806) 7 East 224, 228; *Aldred v Pearson* (1843) 1 L.T.(O.S.) 457.
[314] The "owner" is the consignee or other person entitled to delivery: *US Steel Products Co v GW Ry* [1916] 1 A.C. 189, 207–208, 211–212, 214. cf. *T Comedy (UK) Ltd v Easy Managed Transport Ltd* [2007] EWHC 611 (Comm), [2007] 2 Lloyd's Rep. 397.
[315] *US Steel Products Co v GW Ry*, above; *Booth SS Co Ltd v Cargo Fleet Iron Co Ltd* [1916] 2 K.B. 570.
[316] *George Barker (Transport) Ltd v Eynon* [1974] 1 W.L.R. 462.

beginning of the transit in purported exercise of a general lien.[317] On the other hand it may continue after the end of transit and while the carrier remains in possession of the goods as warehouseman. The common carrier's lien is exercisable against the true owner, though the consignor may have been a thief or other person having no right to deal with the goods.[318] Similarly, a private carrier's contractual lien is exercisable against the true owner.[319]

36-053 **Carrier's right to sell the goods** At common law, the carrier as agent of necessity[320] has a very restricted right to sell perishable goods (and perhaps livestock, which have to be tended, fed and watered[321]) and goods which are left on his hands or which he cannot deliver to their destination, e.g. because of a strike of his employees. But there must be a real business necessity for the sale; and he must first communicate with the owner, unless it is commercially impossible to do so; otherwise he will be liable in damages.[322] In a number of standard form contracts, the carrier reserves to himself the right to sell the goods in defined circumstances. The contractual right of sale is often exercised on the basis of the carrier's general or particular lien, if the lien is not satisfied within a reasonable time from the date when the carrier first gave notice of the exercise of the lien to the owner of the goods.[323]

(b) Passengers

36-054 **Carriage by rail** By Regulation (EC) 1371/2007 on rail passengers' rights and obligations, which entered into force on December 3, 2009, the European Parliament adopted certain provisions of Appendix A (CIV) to the International Convention on Carriage by Rail (COTIF) as applicable to the carriage of passengers and their luggage by rail by licensed railway undertakings, whether such railway journeys were carried out internationally (in more than one country) or domestically (in one country). The provisions of CIV are discussed in the context of international carriage later in this chapter and should now be read as also applicable to domestic carriage.[324] Obligations imposed by CIV on the railway undertakings cannot be limited or waived by a derogation or restrictive clause in the transport contract, although the railway undertakings may offer contract conditions more favourable for the passenger.[325] In addition, the Regulation provides for the provision of pre-journey information and information during the journey set out

---

317 *Wiltshire Iron Co v GW Ry* (1871) L.R. 6 Q.B. 776, 780.
318 *Exeter Carrier's Case*, cited in *Yorke v Grenhaugh* (1702) 2 Ld. Ray. 866, 867.
319 Leslie at pp.88–91; cf. *Singer Manufacturing Co Ltd v LSW Ry* [1894] 1 Q.B. 833. See also Clarke, *International Carriage of Goods by Road: CMR*, 6th edn (2014), para.251.
320 For agency of necessity, see above, para.31-035.
321 *Sachs v Miklos* [1948] 2 K.B. 23, 35; cf. *GN Ry v Swaffield* (1874) L.R. 9 Ex. 132. As to the entitlement to reimbursement of gratuitous bailees incurring reasonable expenses in safeguarding and preserving goods for the benefit of the owners thereof, see, generally, *China Pacific SA v The Food Corp of India (The Winson)* [1982] 1 Lloyd's Rep. 117 HL.
322 Compare *Sims v Midland Ry* [1913] 1 K.B. 103 with *Springer v GW Ry* [1921] 1 K.B. 257. See also Torts (Interference with Goods) Act 1977 s.12.
323 It has been suggested that such power of sale may be unreasonable within the meaning of the Unfair Contract Terms Act 1977: Yates (ed.), *Contracts for the Carriage of Goods* (1993), para.3.2.1.17.1 (Clarke).
324 See below, paras 36-079, 36-100—36-117.
325 art.6.

in Annex II,[326] and the taking out of adequate insurance by the railway undertaking in respect of its liability to passengers.[327] In the event of a claim or complaint by a passenger against the railway undertaking, the Regulation legislates for the provision of assistance and remedies (reimbursement and compensation) to the passenger.[328] Certain provisions of the Regulation are qualified or supplemented by the Rail Passengers' Rights and Obligations Regulations 2010, which entered into force on June 25, 2010.[329]

Common carriers   The common carrier of passengers is he who holds himself out **36-055** as willing to carry members of the public generally. This profession draws in its train the general duty to receive all persons as passengers who offer themselves in a fit state to be carried and ready to pay the proper and reasonable fare and prepared to conform to all reasonable requirements as to carriage, unless there is no longer any room in the conveyance for such persons.[330] As we have seen,[331] the privatised railway companies and Transport for London are not regarded as common carriers; whether common carrier or not, they are not obliged to carry any person who is in an unfit condition.[332] But the common carrier of passengers is not subject to the strict form of liability applicable to the common carrier of goods. Hence the distinction between common and private carriers has never been as important in the law of carriage of passengers as it has in the law of carriage of goods.

Liability for death or personal injuries   At common law the carrier's liability **36-056** for safety of his passengers is not strict but is based on fault. His duty is to see that reasonable care is taken for the safety of his passengers. The House of Lords has put it succinctly:

> "A carrier's obligation to his passengers, whether it be expressed in contract or in tort, is to provide a carriage that is as free from defects as the exercise of all reasonable care can make it."[333]

But he is not liable for harm suffered through a latent defect in his conveyance which could not reasonably be detected[334]; there is no implied warranty that the conveyance is fit for its purpose.[335] Nor is he liable for an accident to a very young child which would not have happened if the child had been properly looked after

---

[326] art.8.

[327] art.12.

[328] arts 14, 16, 17 and 18. Ch.V of the Regulation concerns the obligations of railway undertakings with respect to the carriage of disabled persons: see also Ch.3 of the Rail Passengers' Rights and Obligations Regulations 2010 (SI 2010/1504).

[329] SI 2010/1504.

[330] *Clarke v West Ham Corp* [1909] 2 K.B. 858, 876–877, 878, 879.

[331] Greater London Authority Act 1999 s.156(8), Sch.11 para.31; Railways Act 1993 s.123; the Railways Regulations 1998 (SI 1998/1340) reg.23. The privatised operators provide services for the carriage of passengers by railway pursuant to franchise agreements: Railways Act 1993 s.23. See above, para.36-010.

[332] *Garton v Bristol and Exeter Ry Co* (1861) 1 B. & S. 112 at 162. See also the *National Rail Conditions of Carriage* (published in May 2012) cl.59, which allows a railway company to refuse carriage to any person which it has reasonable grounds to believe is likely to act in a riotous, disorderly or offensive manner.

[333] *Barkway v South Wales Transport Co Ltd* [1950] 1 All E.R. 392, 403–404, per Lord Radcliffe. This is an obligation reinforced by the Supply of Goods and Services Act 1982 s.13.

[334] *Readhead v Midland Ry* (1869) L.R. 4 Q.B. 379; cf. *Hyman v Nye* (1881) 6 Q.B.D. 685, 687–688.

[335] *John Carter (Fine Worsteds) Ltd v Hanson Haulage (Leeds) Ltd* [1965] 2 Q.B. 495. The common

by the adult in whose care the child was travelling.[336]

36-057 **Liability in tort** A passenger who has paid for his ticket and is injured by the negligence of the carrier has the choice between suing for breach of contract or for the tort of negligence.[337] It follows that claims against a carrier for damages for personal injuries or death do not necessarily depend on the existence of a contract of carriage between the carrier and the injured or dead person. It is sufficient if he was in the train or vehicle with the carrier's permission, i.e. provided that he was not a trespasser or (perhaps) an unborn person.[338] He can recover damages for negligence whether he bought his ticket himself or whether it was bought for him by, e.g. a parent, spouse, employer or friend, or whether he was travelling on a free pass.[339] In the case of a trespasser, the carrier's only duty is one of a limited duty of care, perhaps being no more than to avoid the intentional or reckless infliction of harm.[340] But, apart from this exceptional case, the standard of care is the same for passengers who have paid for their tickets as it is for those who, for one reason or another, have made no contract with the carrier but are present in his conveyance with his express or implied permission. Another consequence of the passenger's alternative rights of action in contract or tort is that the injured passenger can sue not only the carrier, who is vicariously liable for the negligence of his employees acting in the scope of their employment, but also the employee who negligently caused the harm.[341] It is immaterial that the employee was not a party to the contract of carriage.

36-058 **Liability for negligence of independent contractors** At common law a carrier was liable for injury caused to a passenger in a contractual relation with the carrier, even when the injury was caused by the negligence of an independent contractor.[342] So, where a passenger held a ticket issued by the Great Western Railway and was injured in an accident caused by the negligence of the South Wales Railway, on whose lines the journey was partly run, it was held that the Great Western Railway were liable to the passenger.[343] This liability was based on an implied term in the contract that the Great Western Railway undertook that due care

---

law liability of the carrier probably is unchanged by the Occupiers' Liability Act 1957, whether the passenger has paid for the carriage or not.

[336] *O'Connor v BTC* [1958] 1 W.L.R. 346.

[337] *Foulkes v Metropolitan District Ry* (1880) 5 C.P.D. 157; *Kelly v Metropolitan Ry* [1895] 1 Q.B. 944, 946; *Taylor v MS & L Ry* [1895] 1 Q.B. 134.

[338] *Walker v GN Ry* (1891) 28 L.R.Ir. 69; contrast *Montreal Tramways v Leveille* (1933) 4 D.L.R. 337. Note, however, Congenital Disabilities (Civil Liability) Act 1976.

[339] *Marshall v York, Newcastle and Berwick Ry* (1851) 11 C.B. 655, 662; *Collett v LNW Ry* (1851) 16 Q.B. 984; *GN Ry v Harrison* (1854) 10 Ex. 376; *Austin v GW Ry* (1867) L.R. 2 Q.B. 442, 445–446; *Harris v Perry* [1903] 2 K.B. 219. In *Gray v Thames Trains Ltd* [2007] EWHC 1558 (QB) at [18], the carrier admitted negligence.

[340] *Clerk & Lindsell on Torts*, 21st edn (2014), paras 12-67—12-72; *Videan v BTC* [1963] 2 Q.B. 650; *Commissioner for Rys v Quinlan* [1964] A.C. 1054; *Herrington v British Railways Board* [1972] A.C. 877. cf. the liability of the carrier to a trespasser concerning the condition of his vehicle provided for by the Occupiers' Liability Act 1984 s.1. A passenger who holds a second-class ticket is not necessarily a trespasser if he travels in a first-class compartment: *Vosper v GW Ry* [1928] 1 K.B. 340, 349.

[341] *Cosgrove v Horsfall* (1945) 62 T.L.R. 140; *Adler v Dickson* [1955] 1 Q.B. 158; *Genys v Matthews* [1966] 1 W.L.R. 758; *Gore v Van der Lann* [1967] 2 Q.B. 31.

[342] *GW Ry v Blake* (1862) 7 Hurl. & N. 987; *John v Bacon* (1870) 39 L.J. C.P. 365; *Thomas v Rhymney Ry* (1871) L.R. 6 Q.B. 266.

[343] *GW Ry v Blake*, above.

would be used in carrying the passenger throughout the journey. This form of liability is unaffected by the Occupiers' Liability Act 1957, whether the injury is caused by the defective state of the vehicle in which the passenger is being carried,[344] or by any other form of negligence.[345] There does not appear to be any authority on the liability of a carrier for the negligence of an independent contractor to a passenger who is lawfully in the vehicle but who is not in a contractual relationship with the carrier, e.g. a person travelling on a free pass, or a person travelling on a ticket purchased for him by a third party (but not as his agent) such as a child travelling on a ticket purchased by his parent. As pointed out above,[346] such a person is (so far as the standard of care is concerned) normally in the same position as a passenger who has a contract with the carrier, and can sue in tort for breach of the ordinary duty of care; but it is not clear whether this tortious liability would involve liability for the negligence of an independent contractor. But where the injury is caused by the defective state of the vehicle (as opposed to other forms of negligence) the position may today be governed by the Occupiers' Liability Act 1957. Although this Act does not affect the obligations imposed on any person:

"by or by virtue of any *contract* ... for the carriage for reward of persons ..., in any vehicle, vessel, aircraft or other means of transport",[347]

it does affect the liability in *tort* of an occupier of any premises (including vehicles[348]). In particular a person is not vicariously liable for the negligence of an independent contractor under the Act[349]; and a passenger who has no contract with the carrier and is compelled to sue in tort may therefore be in a less favourable position in this particular respect than a passenger who can sue in contract.[350]

Res ipsa loquitur   The otherwise heavy burden of proof imposed on injured passengers (or their estates or dependants) is alleviated in one important respect. In many cases of accidents to passengers, especially passengers by rail, the long-established and frequently illustrated doctrine of res ipsa loquitur may apply, with the result that it is very often for the carrier to disprove negligence, and not for the passenger to prove it.[351]   **36-059**

Breach of statutory duty   Carriers are under numerous statutory duties relating to, e.g. the construction and equipment of vehicles, the qualifications of drivers, and the safety rules of rail and road.[352] In an action against a carrier for negligence, proof of the breach of a statutory duty of this kind may in certain circumstances amount   **36-060**

---

[344] See s.5(3).
[345] In this event the Act does not apply at all: s.1.
[346] See above, para.36-044.
[347] s.5(3).
[348] s.1(3).
[349] s.2(4)(b). See *Clerk & Lindsell on Torts*, 21st edn (2014), paras 12-56—12-58.
[350] But it is arguable that a passenger travelling on a ticket issued to a third party (e.g. a child) travels "by virtue of" a contract of carriage.
[351] See, e.g. *Skinner v LB & SC Ry* (1850) 5 Ex. 787; *Dawson v MS & L Ry* (1862) 5 L.T. 682; *Gee v Metropolitan Ry* (1873) L.R. 8 Q.B. 161; *Laurie v Raglan BS Ltd* [1942] 1 K.B. 152; *Radley v LPTB* [1942] 1 All E.R. 433; *Easson v LNE Ry* [1944] K.B. 421; *Brookes v LPTB* [1947] 1 All E.R. 506; *Hale v Hants and Dorset Motor Services Ltd* [1947] 2 All E.R. 628.
[352] See, e.g. the Railways Regulations 1998 (SI 1998/1340); Public Passenger Vehicles Act 1981 Pts II and III; Road Traffic Act 1988; and Orders and Regulations made thereunder.

to prima facie evidence of negligence.[353] But it is no more than that. Such breach of a statutory duty by a carrier does not found an independent action in tort in which negligence need not be proved.[354]

36-061   **Defences**   The defences open to the carrier (apart from special contract, considered immediately below) are those usual in actions for negligence in tort, including contributory negligence, volenti non fit injuria, and remoteness of damage. A discussion of these matters is outside the scope of this work.[355]

36-062   **Special contract**   At common law there was nothing to prevent a carrier from contracting out of his duty to take reasonable care for the safety of his passengers and out of other duties, e.g. the duty to carry them with reasonable speed. The technical procedure by which exemption clauses may be incorporated in standard form contracts of carriage through the issue of tickets has been established in the well-known line of "ticket cases", which are considered elsewhere.[356] Briefly, the passenger will be bound by the conditions if he knew that there was writing on the ticket and that this contained conditions, or if the carrier did what was reasonably sufficient to give the passenger notice of the conditions. A statement on the face of the ticket saying "For Conditions See Back" and a reference on the back to the railway timetables, bills and regulations is sufficient notice, even if the passenger cannot read.[357] The degree and specificity of notice will depend on the onerousness or unusual nature of the term said to be incorporated.[358] The terms and conditions alleged to be incorporated may not be binding on the consumer if they are unfair within the meaning of the Unfair Terms in Consumer Contracts Regulations 1999 or the Consumer Rights Act 2015, which replaces and revokes the 1999 Regulations for contracts made on or after October 1, 2015.[359] Most of the ticket cases were concerned with carriage by rail or carriage by sea, where the passenger does not normally board the train or the ship until after he has taken his ticket and made his contract. No doubt the principle of the cases is equally applicable to carriage by long-distance coach if the ticket is bought at a coach station or from a travel agency. But what is the position if the passenger enters the vehicle before taking a ticket, e.g. if he boards a bus, or arrives at a railway station too late to buy a ticket at the booking office, but is allowed to board the train and pay during the journey or on arrival at his destination?[360] In such cases it may be very important to establish when the contract was made, because an exemption clause will be of no effect un-

---

[353] *Blamires v L & Y Ry* (1873) L.R. 8 Ex. 283; *Croston v Vaughan* [1938] 1 K.B. 540, 551–552.
[354] *Phillips v Britannia Hygienic Laundry Co* [1923] 2 K.B. 832; *Stennett v Hancock* [1939] 2 All E.R. 578; *Clarke v Brims* [1947] 1 K.B. 497; *Barkway v South Wales Transport Co Ltd* [1950] 1 All E.R. 392, 400. See Kahn-Freund at pp.473–483. As to the effect of a breach of statutory duty on the level of the carrier's contribution to liability, see *Madden v Quirk* [1989] 1 W.L.R. 702.
[355] See *Clerk & Lindsell on Torts*, 21st edn (2014), Chs 2–3.
[356] See Vol.I, paras 13-008—13-018, and see above, para.36-027.
[357] *Thompson v LMS Ry* [1930] 1 K.B. 41; *Fosbroke-Hobbes v Airwork Ltd* [1937] 1 All E.R. 108. cf. *Parker v South Eastern Railway* (1877) 2 C.P.D. 416. The conditions alleged to be incorporated may not be binding on the consumer if they are unfair within the meaning of the Unfair Terms in Consumer Contracts Regulations 1999.
[358] *Thornton v Shoe Lane Parking Ltd* [1971] 2 Q.B. 163; *Interfoto Picture Library Ltd v Stiletto Visual Programmes Ltd* [1989] 1 Q.B. 433; see above, Vol.I, para.13-015.
[359] See below, paras 38-389—38-426.
[360] See *Hooper v Furness Ry* (1907) 23 T.L.R. 451.

less it is communicated to the passenger at or before that time.[361] There is some authority for saying that the contract of carriage is made when the passenger puts himself either on the platform of the bus or inside it.[362] The principle of the ticket cases still applies to exemption clauses excluding liabilities which the carrier can lawfully exclude, e.g. for delay. But they have ceased to have much significance in cases where personal safety is concerned, for reasons about to be discussed.

Limitations on carriers' contracting out of liability for death and personal **36-063**
injury   Section 2(1) of the Unfair Contract Terms Act 1977 renders ineffective the exclusion or restriction of the liability of any person for death or personal injury resulting from negligence by reference to any contractual term or to a notice given to persons generally or to particular persons. The general provision appears to supersede previous statutory prohibitions on the insertion of terms in contracts of carriage of passengers by land excluding or limiting such liability. Section 43(7) of the Transport Act 1962, which prohibited the Boards set up under that Act (including the British Railways Board and the London Transport Executive) from excluding or limiting their liability for death of, or personal injury to, passengers (other than those travelling on free passes) was, indeed, expressly repealed by the 1977 Act.[363] Section 29 of the Public Passenger Vehicles Act 1981 makes void any contract for the conveyance of a passenger in a public service vehicle[364] insofar as it purports to negative or restrict the liability of any person for the death of, or personal injury to, a passenger while being carried in, entering or alighting from the vehicle, or purports to impose any conditions with respect to the enforcement of any such liability. Section 149 of the Road Traffic Act 1988 renders of no effect any agreement between the user[365] of a vehicle on the road and a passenger whereby the liability of the user for death or personal injury is excluded or limited or whereby conditions are imposed on the enforcement of such liability. The various statutory provisions described above invalidate not only terms purporting to exclude or restrict liability but also terms purporting to impose any conditions with respect to the enforcement of any such liability. Thus the Unfair Contract Terms Act[366] prohibits the insertion of terms making the liability or its enforcement subject to restrictive or onerous conditions or excluding any right or remedy in respect of the liability where the Act prevents a contract term excluding or restricting liability, as unreasonable. Whilst the 1977 Act does not treat a contract term which requires disputes to be referred to arbitration as a term excluding or restricting liability,[367] the Unfair Terms in Consumer Contracts Regulations 1999 exposes such terms to

---

[361] cf. *Olley v Marlborough Court Ltd* [1949] 1 K.B. 532. See Vol.I, para.13-010.
[362] *Wilkie v LPTB* [1947] 1 All E.R. 258, 259.
[363] Unfair Contract Terms Act 1977 s.31(4) and Sch.4. See below, Ch.38.
[364] s.1 defines a "public service vehicle" as a motor vehicle used for carrying passengers for hire or reward. This definition does not require a plaintiff to demonstrate that there was a legally enforceable agreement or right to be carried or that payment had been made: *Rout v Swallow Hotels* [1993] R.T.R. 80 (where a hotel minibus provided for the benefit of hotel guests was held to be a public service vehicle); *DPP v Sikondar* [1993] R.T.R. 90 (where a vehicle used for the systematic carrying of girls to and from school, whose driver received the occasional contribution to the cost of petrol, was held to be a public service vehicle).
[365] That is, one who controls, manages or operates the vehicle: *Brown v Roberts* [1965] 1 Q.B. 1. See also *Stinton v Stinton* [1995] R.T.R. 157; *Hatton v Hall* [1997] R.T.R. 212.
[366] Unfair Contract Terms Act 1977 s.13(1).
[367] Unfair Contract Terms Act 1977 s.13(2).

emasculation as against a consumer if they are unfair within the meaning of those Regulations.[368]

36-064 **Exceptions to the general limitations on carriers' contracting out of liability**   It may happen that a carrier by land also provides within the United Kingdom or between the United Kingdom and the British Islands regular passenger shipping services complementary to his road or rail services. Prima facie such combined land-sea carriers would be prohibited under s.2(1) of the Unfair Contract Terms Act 1977 from excluding or restricting their contractual liability for the death of, and personal injury to, passengers on their ships. Parliament has, however, intervened and enabled carriers by sea to limit their liability in such cases as those listed in the previous paragraph. By a statutory instrument,[369] contracts for the domestic carriage of passengers and their luggage by sea have been, since April 30, 1987, subjected to a modified version of the Athens Convention relating to the Carriage of Passengers and their Luggage by Sea 1974 where, inter alia, under the contract the places of departure and destination are in the area consisting of the United Kingdom, the Channel Islands and the Isle of Man and there is no intermediate port of call outside that area.[370] The Athens Convention[371] (which embraces international carriage of passengers and their luggage by sea) makes a carrier liable for damage resulting from the death of, and personal injury to, a passenger during the course of carriage by sea due to the fault or neglect of the carrier.[372] Such fault is usually presumed in the case of death of, or personal injury to, a passenger.[373] The carrier is permitted to limit his liability for death and personal injury.[374]

36-065 **Standard forms of contract**   The carriage of passengers by rail in respect of domestic scheduled passenger train services on the railway network of Great Britain is subject to the *National Rail Conditions of Carriage* the most recent version of which applies from May 20, 2012. The train companies are obliged to contract on the basis of these terms or terms no less generous to the customer. There are no generally accepted conditions of carriage of passengers by road; the *National Rail*

---

[368] Such terms are automatically unfair in so far as they relate to a pecuniary claim of up to £5,000: Arbitration Act 1996 ss.89–91; Unfair Arbitration Agreements (Specified Amount) Order 1999 (SI 1999/2167).

[369] The Carriage of Passengers and their Luggage by Sea (Domestic Carriage) Order 1987 (SI 1987/670) made under the Merchant Shipping Act 1979 s.16. The 1979 Act has been repealed by the Merchant Shipping Act 1995. However, the 1987 Order continues to have force by virtue of the Interpretation Act 1978 s.17(2)(b), as if made under s.184 of the 1995 Act. Under s.184(5), the meaning of "contracts of carriage" exclude contracts which are not for reward. See also The Carriage of Passengers and their Luggage by Sea (United Kingdom Carriers) Order 1998 (SI 1998/2917) as regards United Kingdom carriers. See *South West Strategic Health Authority v Bay Island Voyages* [2015] EWCA Civ 708 at [2]–[5]. In this case, the Court of Appeal said that although the Convention applied to domestic carriage, its construction should take account of the fact that it is an international convention [28].

[370] Merchant Shipping Act 1995 art.2.

[371] The substantive provisions of the Convention are set out in the Merchant Shipping Act 1995 s.183, Sch.6 Pt I.

[372] Athens Convention art.3. As to the effect of the time limitation in art.16, see *Higham v Stena Sealink Ltd* [1996] 1 W.L.R. 1107; *South West Strategic Health Authority v Bay Island Voyages* [2015] EWCA Civ 708.

[373] Athens Convention art.3(3).

[374] Athens Convention art.7. See also the Merchant Shipping (Convention Relating to the Carriage of Passengers and their Luggage by Sea) Order 2014 (SI 2014/1361). See *R G Mayor v P&O Ferries Ltd (The Lion)* [1990] 2 Lloyd's Rep. 144.

Conditions of Carriage do, however, apply to the carriage of passengers in road vehicles owned or operated by the Train Company.[375]

Liability for delay   At common law the carrier owes a duty to take passengers to **36-066** their agreed destinations within a reasonable time and at a reasonable speed.[376] The customer will be entitled to recover damages for any breach of this duty.[377] But the damage must not be too remote: it does not cover the expense of ordering a special train in order that the traveller might arrive at a seaside resort in time for dinner.[378] At common law the mere fact that times of departure and arrival are published does not amount to a warranty that the times will be strictly adhered to.[379] The *National Rail Conditions of Carriage*, at cll.42 to 45, provide that the passenger is entitled to compensation for delay, cancellation or poor service within the control of the Train Company in accordance with the Passenger's Charter, published by the Train Company, subject to the minimum levels of compensation set out in the *National Rail Conditions of Carriage*, provided a claim is lodged within 28 days of the completion of the journey; the Train Company does not accept liability for loss (including consequential loss) caused by the delay or cancellation of any train. Minimum compensation takes the form of vouchers which entitle the passenger to discounts off the price of his next railway journey. The list of circumstances which are not within the Train Company's control include these wide ranging categories: acts or apprehended threats of vandalism or terrorism; suicides or accidents to trespassers; gas leaks or fires in lineside buildings not caused by the Train Companies or their employees or agents; line closures at the request of the police or emergency services; exceptionally severe weather conditions; industrial action, riot or civil commotion; fire or failure due to electrical failure or defects not caused by the Train Company, their employees or agents.

Carrier's right to receive the proper fare   If a passenger misuses his ticket by **36-067** breaking the conditions on which it was issued to him, he breaks his contract and may be liable to pay the fare or part of it over again. This principle may be illustrated by reference to the *National Rail Conditions of Carriage* and decided cases. Thus, a railway ticket is not transferable; it cannot be used by anyone except the person for whom it was bought.[380] Tickets are valid only for a limited period, namely the period of validity printed on the ticket or stated in the Train Company's publications, leaflets and notices relating to the ticket.[381] Tickets are only available for use between the stations shown on them and by the specified route.[382] Whilst most ticket types permit the passenger to stop his journey at a station short of that shown on his ticket, the Train Company may in some cases at certain times charge

---

375 *National Rail Conditions of Carriage* cl.60.
376 *Hurst v GW Ry* (1865) 19 C.B.(N.S.) 310. See also Supply of Goods and Services Act 1982 s.14.
377 *Hobbs v LSW Ry* (1875) L.R. 10 Q.B. 111. See, as to the damages claimed and awarded in this case, *M'Mahon v Field* (1881) 7 Q.B.D. 591, 594, 596–597; *Bailey v Bullock* [1950] 2 All E.R. 1167, 1170–1171.
378 *Le Blanche v LNW Ry* (1876) 1 C.P.D. 286.
379 *Lord v Midland Ry* (1867) L.R. 2 C.P. 339; *Lockyer v International Sleeping Car Co* (1892) 61 L.J. Q.B. 501. So far as *Denton v GN Ry* (1856) 5 El. & Bl. 860 and *Cooke v Midland Ry* (1892) 57 J.P. 388 held that advertised times do form terms in the contract of carriage, they would probably not be followed today, because the exhibition of a timetable would not be construed as an offer capable of acceptance by the passenger.
380 *National Rail Conditions of Carriage* cl.6.
381 *National Rail Conditions of Carriage* cl.11.
382 *National Rail Conditions of Carriage* cl.13.

a higher fare for the shorter journey. In those cases, the passenger must pay the appropriate fare for the journey actually made.[383] At common law a passenger has no right to break his journey at an intermediate station and resume it later.[384] Of course, the contract of carriage may provide otherwise.[385]

(c) Passengers' Luggage

36-068 Common carriers At common law, there appears to have been no obligation on a carrier to carry passengers' luggage free of extra charge or at all.[386] For evident commercial reasons, however, carriers habitually accepted their passengers' luggage, generally without extra charge; and, in the absence of special terms to the contrary, they incurred, in relation to the luggage, the liability of common carriers.[387] From the nature of their liability, they came to be regarded as common carriers of luggage by implication. No person, such as Transport for London or the franchised railway companies, shall be regarded as common carriers by rail.[388] It is likely, however, that Transport for London and the operators of public service vehicles (buses and coaches) outside London are common carriers of passengers' luggage by road, except in the case of "contract carriage" (where the vehicle is hired for a lump sum).[389] It should be noted, however, that the *National Rail Conditions of Carriage* purport to apply the conditions applicable to carriage of passengers' luggage by rail to luggage carried in road vehicles owned or operated by the Train Company or its agents.[390]

36-069 Permitted luggage All passengers by rail and road are entitled to take with them certain quantities of luggage. This right may be either statutory or contractual. As to the former, the traffic commissioners in granting road service licences under Pt III of the Public Passenger Vehicle Act 1981 can impose conditions as to the amount of luggage to be carried free of extra charge and can fix the charges for excess luggage. The *National Rail Conditions of Carriage* provide that the Train Company will accept small items of luggage (including animals) accompanying a passenger, subject to specified exceptions (such as large luggage), free of charge.[391] Although there is no precise limitation upon the size, quantity or weight of the luggage which accompanies the passenger, the Train Company may refuse to carry the luggage if there is no room for it. The Train Company may refuse to accept luggage additionally where the luggage might cause injury, inconvenience or property damage, its loading or unloading might cause delay or it is not carried or packed in a suitable manner, notwithstanding that such luggage has been accepted previously or is accepted normally.

36-070 Definition of passengers' luggage at common law At an early period it was

---

[383] *National Rail Conditions of Carriage* cl.16. See *GN Ry v Winder* [1892] 2 Q.B. 595; *GN Ry v Palmer* [1895] 1 Q.B. 862.
[384] *Ashton v L & Y Ry* [1904] 2 K.B. 313; *Bastaple v Metcalfe* [1906] 2 K.B. 288.
[385] See, for example, *National Rail Conditions of Carriage* cl.16.
[386] See Leslie at p.295.
[387] cf. *Lovett v Hobbs* (1680) 2 Show. 127 and the cases cited in Leslie at p.301.
[388] Greater London Authority Act 1999 s.156(8), Sch.11 para.31; Railways Act 1993 s.123; the Railways Regulations 1998 (SI 1998/1340) reg.23. See above, para.36-010.
[389] See Kahn-Freund at pp.598–599, 609; and see above, para.36-034 n.208.
[390] *National Rail Conditions of Carriage* cl.60.
[391] *National Rail Conditions of Carriage*, cll.47–49.

important to determine whether or not articles which a passenger took with him were "passengers' luggage" because not only did carriers undertake an insurer's liability towards such articles, but they also carried them without extra charge. Moreover, if articles which appear to be passengers' luggage, but in fact are not so, are lost or damaged, the carrier may avoid all liability on the ground that he never contracted to carry such articles. The classic definition of passengers' luggage at common law is that of Cockburn C.J. in *Macrow v Great Western Railway*.[392] According to this, passengers' luggage is ordinary, personal luggage, that is to say, luggage for personal use or convenience according to the habits or wants of the particular class to which the passenger belongs, with reference to either the immediate necessities or the ultimate purpose of his journey. The meaning of this definition will be elucidated in the paragraphs that follow.[393]

The requirement of personal use   From luggage carried for the passenger's personal use or convenience must be distinguished (a) articles taken by a passenger for the use of others, like sheets and blankets for a household[394] or a rocking-horse as a present for a child[395]; and (b) at common law articles taken by a passenger for the purposes of his profession, trade or business.[396] Under the *National Rail Conditions of Carriage*, however, passengers are permitted to take with them small items of luggage free of charge.[397] Thus, in carriage by rail, many of the cases on the carriage of luggage at common law might now be decided differently; and it would no longer be necessary to consider whether, e.g. the artist's sketches were done for his own amusement or for sale. It should be stressed that at common law it is not the ownership of the articles but their use that is of crucial importance. Thus, if the luggage is taken by the passenger for the use of someone else, the carrier is not liable[398]; conversely, if the luggage contains articles lent to the passenger by a friend, the carrier is liable.[399] Even an employee may recover for the loss of his employer's luggage, provided the luggage was required for the use of the employee,

36-071

---

[392] (1871) L.R. 6 Q.B. 612, 622.

[393] See Kahn-Freund at pp.600–608.

[394] *Macrow v GW Ry* (1871) L.R. 6 Q.B. 612.

[395] cf. *Hudston v Midland Ry* (1869) L.R. 4 Q.B. 366. In *Buckland v R* [1933] 1 K.B. 329, 340, McCardie J., in a useful and important survey of "passengers' luggage", said that "a smaller toy might well have been included in the phrase 'ordinary luggage' ". But the difficulty remains that the child was not a passenger.

[396] *Phelps v LNW Ry* (1865) 19 C.B.(N.S.) 321 (solicitor carrying client's title deeds for use in lawsuit); *Gilbey v GN Ry* (1920) 36 T.L.R. 562 (actor's theatrical clothing); *GW Ry v Evans* (1921) 38 T.L.R. 166 (professional musician's violoncello); *Mytton v Midland Ry* (1859) 28 L.J. Ex. 385 (professional artist's sketches); *Belfast & Ballymena Ry v Keys* (1861) 9 H.L. Cas. 556 (merchandise); *Hastie v GE Ry* (1911) 46 L.J.News. 507 (typewriter carried for business purposes). Distinguish *Jenkyns v Southampton Steam Packet Co* [1919] 2 K.B. 135 (army officer's revolver, ear-defenders, binoculars and flash-lamp), which is not strictly reconcilable with the above cases or the rule they illustrate, but is perhaps comprehensible when recalled as a case arising during the First World War.

[397] *National Rail Conditions of Carriage* cl.47. Many of the cases on passengers' luggage at common law arose on the construction of the expression "ordinary luggage" which occurred in the former railway companies' private Acts; but in no case was a distinction suggested between "ordinary luggage" and "passengers' luggage". The *National Rail Conditions of Carriage* no longer employ the term "ordinary luggage".

[398] *Becher v GE Ry* (1870) L.R. 5 Q.B. 241 (employee taking employer's luggage).

[399] *Jenkyns v Southampton Steam Packet Co* [1919] 2 K.B. 135.

e.g. a uniform.[400] The *National Rail Conditions of Carriage*, on the other hand, are concerned not with personal use but with the condition, size and weight of the luggage.

36-072   **Use in connection with journey**   At common law the articles must be for the passenger's use on the actual journey, or in connection with the journey. What the latter phrase means is, at present, uncertain. Articles for personal use during the passenger's stay in a hotel whilst away from home would certainly be articles for use in connection with the journey.[401]

36-073   **In the nature of a package**   At common law objects taken by the passenger must correspond with the image normally evoked by the word "luggage", i.e. something of a size and shape that can reasonably be carried as luggage.[402]

> "An article which is taken, as it were, loose … is subject to rather different considerations… . There is, in addition to the requirement that they are for some personal use, the requirement that they must be of the kind of goods that are usually denominated as luggage … it conveys the idea that they are carried about in a box or a bag or something of that kind."[403]

So bicycles,[404] invalid chairs[405] and radio sets[406] have not in the past been treated as passengers' luggage. Nor does the term include the articles carried by a passenger on his person.[407] Whether the phrase embraces, e.g. a passenger's coat, hat, umbrella, stick, handbag, book or toy that is placed on the luggage rack or on the seat remains open.[408] The Train Companies often will allow the carriage of such items under their conditions of carriage.

36-074   **Carriage of items not permitted by the contract**

> "If the carrier permits the passenger, either on payment or without payment of an extra charge, to take more than the regulated quantity of luggage, or knowingly permits him to take as personal luggage articles that would not come under that denomination, he will be liable for their loss, though not arising from his negligence."[409]

On the other hand:

> "If a passenger, who knows or ought to know that he is only entitled to have his ordinary personal luggage carried free of charge, chooses to carry with him merchandise, for which the company are entitled to make a charge, he cannot claim to be compensated in respect of any loss or injury by the company, to whom he has abstained from giving notice of the contents. In such a case he carries it at his own risk."[410]

Similarly, if a passenger puts luggage into a train or other vehicle, and the carrier

---

[400] *Meux v GE Ry* [1895] 2 Q.B. 387, 394.
[401] See *Britten v GN Ry* [1899] 1 Q.B. 243, 248.
[402] *Macrow v GW Ry* (1871) L.R. 6 Q.B. 612, 621; *Britten v GN Ry*, above, at 248–249.
[403] *Britten v GN Ry*, above, at 248 (Channell J.).
[404] *Britten v GN Ry*, above. See *National Rail Conditions of Carriage*, cl.48.
[405] *Cusack v LNW Ry* (1891) 7 T.L.R. 452.
[406] *Page v LMS Ry* [1943] 1 All E.R. 455, 457.
[407] cf. *Smitton v Orient Steam Navigation Co* (1907) 96 L.T. 848.
[408] But see *Le Conteur v LSW Ry* (1865) L.R. 1 Q.B. 54, 62. See also Kahn-Freund at p.610, n.79.
[409] *Macrow v GW Ry* (1871) L.R. 6 Q.B. 612, 619 (Cockburn C.J.). cf. *Page v LMS Ry* [1943] 1 All E.R. 455.
[410] *Cahill v LNW Ry* (1863) 13 C.B.(N.S.) 818, 819 (Cockburn C.J.). cf. *GN Ry v Shepherd* (1852) 8

discovers that it consists of merchandise or exceeds the permitted weight, the carrier can make the appropriate charge and retain the luggage until the charge is paid.[411]

Common carrier's liability for loss and damage The common carrier of passengers' luggage is strictly liable for loss or damage, subject to the four excepted perils,[412] unless he has limited his liability by special contract. The only one of the excepted perils which requires discussion here is the passenger's fault. In the case of luggage put in the luggage compartment of a coach, this defence could only be available where, e.g. the loss or damage occurs because the luggage is wrongly labelled or addressed or badly packed. But where the passenger takes the luggage into the coach with him, the application of the defence widens. The fact that the passenger retains possession of his luggage does not affect the nature of the carrier's liability; it only enhances the possibility of a successful defence. The carrier is still a common carrier, whether the luggage is placed in the luggage compartment or is taken inside by the passenger.[413] In the days when the railways were common carriers it was held that a passenger need not keep a watchful eye on his luggage throughout the journey.[414] But if the passenger is negligent in looking after his luggage, the carrier is not liable.[415] Thus if luggage disappears from the luggage compartment of a coach during transit, the carrier will very probably be liable.[416] He would also be liable if the luggage disappeared from inside the coach while it stopped for 10 minutes to allow the passengers to visit a toilet or to buy sandwiches.[417] But he might not be liable if the coach stopped for an hour in order that the driver and passengers might take a meal. Since the carriage of luggage is not gratuitous, even if it is carried "free of extra charge",[418] the defence of s.1 of the Carriers Act 1830 is also available.[419] A passenger's clothes, jewellery, watch and so on which he carries on his person or in his pockets are not passenger's luggage. For these, the carrier is under the same liability as he is towards the passenger himself: his liability is based on negligence.[420] 36-075

The carrier's contractual liability for loss and damage A common carrier, who has modified his status by a special contract, and a private carrier will be liable for loss and damage to the passenger's luggage in accordance with the terms of that contract.[421] Alternatively, the passenger may have remedies in tort.[422] Any contract terms which seek to exclude or restrict such liability in contract or for negligence 36-076

Ex. 30.

[411] *Rumsey v NE Ry* (1863) 14 C.B.(N.S.) 641.

[412] See above, paras 36-018—36-022.

[413] See *Le Conteur v LSW Ry* (1865) L.R. 1 Q.B. 54, 58–59; *GW Ry v Bunch* (1888) 13 App. Cas. 31, 42, 48, 53.

[414] *Ehinger v SE & C Ry* (1922) 38 T.L.R. 678; *Vosper v GW Ry* [1928] 1 K.B. 340; *Carr v LMS Ry* [1931] N.I. 94.

[415] *Talley v GW Ry* (1870) L.R. 6 C.P. 44. See also *National Rail Conditions of Carriage* cl.51.

[416] cf. *Houghland v RR Low (Luxury Coaches) Ltd* [1962] 1 Q.B. 694, where (as previously pointed out) the carriage was "contract carriage" and the carrier therefore not a common carrier.

[417] cf. *Carr v LMS Ry* [1931] N.I. 94.

[418] *Casswell v Cheshire Lines Committee* [1907] 2 K.B. 499.

[419] See above, paras 36-033—36-034.

[420] *Smitton v Orient Steam Navigation Co Ltd* (1907) 96 L.T. 848.

[421] Although such terms must not be unfair within the meaning of Unfair Terms in Consumer Contracts Regulations 1999, where applicable.

[422] *Meux v Great Eastern Ry Co* [1985] 2 Q.B. 387; *Houghland v RR Low (Luxury Coaches) Ltd* [1962]

must yield to the requirement of reasonableness under the Unfair Contract Terms Act 1977,[423] and fairness in respect of consumer contracts made on or after October 1, 2015, under the Consumer Rights Act 2015.[424] Under the *National Rail Conditions of Carriage*, the Train Companies are only liable for loss of or from, or for damage or delay to, luggage brought on to premises or taken into trains upon proof that such loss, damage or delay was caused by the fault of the Train Company. The Train Company's liability in respect of any item will not exceed the limit laid down in the EU Rail Passengers Rights and Obligations Regulation (1371/2007) or the item's value, whichever is lower. The Train Company will also take reasonable care of lost property. In any event, the Train Company's liability is limited to the lesser of the value of the item or a specified limit.[425] Under the *National Rail Conditions of Carriage*, the Train Company may remove or dispose of any property which might in their opinion cause damage or injury or inconvenience to persons or may sell or dispose of unclaimed property.[426]

36-077　**Beginning and end of transit**　As in the case of the carriage of goods,[427] it is important to determine in relation to the carriage of passengers' luggage when transit begins and ends, because it is only during this period that the carrier can be made liable as a carrier. The *National Rail Conditions of Carriage* no longer indicate when transit begins or ends. The decided cases are still of interest on the question when transit ends at common law, and decisive of the question when it begins; and no doubt the principles contained in the cases can be applied with caution to the somewhat different conditions of carriage by road. At common law, transit begins when the luggage is received for transport by the carrier or one of his actually or ostensibly authorised employees[428] a reasonable and proper time before the train is due to start. What is a reasonable and proper time is a question of fact depending on the circumstances of each case.[429] If luggage is handed to a railway porter at an earlier time than this, the carrier will not be liable if it is stolen, because it should have been placed in the left luggage office.[430]

36-078　**Liability in tort**　If there is no contract with the passenger, the carrier may still be liable in tort. Thus, an employee can recover for the loss of his personal luggage, though his employer paid for his ticket[431]; and the employer can recover for

---

1 Q.B. 694; *Sullivan v Ashway Coaches* [1981] C.L.Y. 302. See also below, para.36-077.

[423] 1977 Act ss.2(2), 3, 11.

[424] 2015 Act ss.62–65. The 2015 Act revokes the Unfair Terms in Consumer Contracts Regulations 1999: see below, paras 38-389—38-426.

[425] *National Rail Conditions of Carriage*, cl.50. As at May 6, 2014, the limit is £1,376.25.

[426] *National Rail Conditions of Carriage*, cll.52–57. See also Torts (Interference with Goods) Act 1977 s.12.

[427] See above, para.36-041.

[428] *Soanes v LSW Ry* (1919) 88 L.J. K.B. 524.

[429] *GW Ry v Bunch* (1888) 13 App. Cas. 31 (40 minutes at Paddington Station on Christmas Eve held reasonable); *Steers v Midland Ry* (1920) 36 T.L.R. 703 (luggage left, with station inspector's approval, for one hour in sleeping-car while passenger had a meal outside the station: held reasonable). See also *Lovell v LC & D Ry* (1876) 34 L.T. 127; *Leach v SE Ry* (1876) 34 L.T. 134; contrast *Welch v LNW Ry* (1886) 34 W.R. 166.

[430] *GW Ry v Bunch* (1888) 13 App. Cas. 31, 44, 53.

[431] *Marshall v York, Newcastle and Berwick Ry* (1851) 11 C.B. 655.

the loss of luggage owned by him but required for the use of the employee, e.g. a uniform, though the employer was not himself a passenger.[432]

3. INTERNATIONAL CARRIAGE

(a) Introduction

International Convention on Carriage by Rail The United Kingdom is a party **36-079** to an important multilateral treaty on international carriage by rail. This is the Convention concerning International Carriage by Rail known as COTIF, signed at Berne on May 9, 1980.[433] COTIF is both a revision and an amalgamation of three previous carriage by rail Conventions, respectively known as CIM, CIV and CAV, which had been in force in their most recent form since January 1, 1975.[434] The new Convention incorporates all three Conventions with certain amendments as sets of Uniform Rules forming two appendices to COTIF. Appendix A embraces the CIV Uniform Rules regarding the international carriage of passengers and their luggage by rail; Appendix B covers the CIM Uniform Rules regarding the international carriage of goods by rail. Whilst most of the basic provisions of CIM, CIV and CAV remain in force, many of the articles of the earlier Conventions have been re-numbered. The object of having such Uniform Rules as appendices to COTIF is to enable them to be amended much more readily and quickly than under the old Conventions. The new Convention also provides for an intergovernmental organisa-tion, known as OTIF, to monitor the performance of the Convention so far as international through traffic by rail between Member States is concerned, and to facilitate its development. The Central Office for International Carriage by Rail in Berne provides the OTIF Secretariat, and the Organisation's headquarters are in Berne. The CIM Uniform Rules have annexed to them four sets of regulations, concerning the international carriage by rail of dangerous goods ("RID"),[435] contain-ers ("RICO"),[436] express parcels ("RIEx")[437] and the international haulage by rail of private owners' wagons ("RIP").[438]

International Transport Conventions Act 1983 The United Kingdom govern- **36-080** ment has ratified COTIF. The Convention came into force generally, and for the United Kingdom, on May 1, 1985, the day agreed by Member States under art.24(1) of COTIF, once the necessary 15 states had ratified or acceded to the Convention. The entry into force of the Convention by virtue of art.24(2) of COTIF automati-cally abrogated the earlier Conventions CIM, CIV and CAV. United Kingdom legislation had previously been enacted to give COTIF the force of law in the United Kingdom in the shape of the International Transport Conventions Act 1983.[439] The provisions thus given the force of law were those set out in Com-mand Paper Cmnd.8535, which contains the English text of the Convention and the

---

[432] *Meux v GE Ry* [1895] 2 Q.B. 387.
[433] "COTIF" stands for "*Convention Relative aux Transports Internationaux Ferroviaires*". The European Union acceded to COTIF, with effect from July 1, 2011.
[434] An account of these Conventions and their effect in English law is given in paras 2877–2879 of the 25th edition of this work.
[435] CIM Annex I; CIM arts 4(D) and 5(1)(a). See above, para.36-035.
[436] CIM Annex III; CIM art.8(2).
[437] CIM Annex IV; CIM art.8(3).
[438] CIM Annex II; CIM art.8(1).
[439] International Transport Conventions Act 1983 s.1(1).

Uniform Rules.[440] References in the present text to the English text of COTIF and its Appendix A (CIV) and Appendix B (CIM) are drawn from the Command Paper Cmnd.8535, which is separate from the Act. The French text of COTIF is, however, the only authoritative text.[441] The 1983 Act provided for the entry into force of COTIF as far as the United Kingdom is concerned to be certified by an Order in Council under s.11(3) of the Act. The certification of May 1, 1985, as the date of entry into force was thus made.[442] Under s.11(3) of the 1983 Act, the Carriage by Railway Act 1972 was repealed in its entirety from that date: this was the Act which had incorporated into English law the Additional Convention (CAV) relating to the liability of railways for death of and personal injury to passengers. The International Transport Conventions Act 1983 empowers Her Majesty by Order in Council from time to time to certify which states are Member States for the purposes of COTIF.[443] A Protocol modifying COTIF was incorporated into English law and came into force on November 1, 1996.[444]

36-081   **Modification to COTIF: the Vilnius Protocol**   On June 3, 1999, a Protocol modifying COTIF was signed in Vilnius by a number of states, including the United Kingdom. In anticipation of the Protocol entering into force and the United Kingdom's ratification of the Protocol by Royal Prerogative, Parliament enacted s.103 of the Railways and Transport Safety Act 2003, which empowers the Secretary of State to make regulations for the purpose of giving effect to the modified Convention. By the Railways (Convention on International Carriage by Rail) Regulations 2005,[445] the Vilnius Protocol was implemented as part of the law of the United Kingdom. The modifications import a general revision to COTIF, reflecting major changes in railway management and operations particularly following EC Directive 91/440, 95/18 and 95/19[446] including the increasing separation of infrastructure management from the operation of train companies and the increase of competition on any one network. In place of the three existing annexures to COTIF, the Protocol introduces (a) entirely new CIV Uniform Rules (Appendix A), the modifications to which also ensure that minimum levels of compensation exist for certain incidents throughout all signatory states; (b) new CIM Uniform Rules (Appendix B); (c) a free-standing Appendix for the carriage of dangerous goods (RID) (Appendix C[447]); (d) new Uniform Rules for contracts for use of vehicles in international rail traffic (CUV), contracts for use of infrastructure in international rail traffic (CUI), the validation of technical standards and prescriptions applicable to railway material to be used in international traffic (APTU) and the technical admission of railway material used in international traffic (ATMF) (Appendices D to G). The 2005 Regulations, and therefore the Protocol (now referred

---

[440] International Transport Conventions Act 1983 s.1(3).

[441] COTIF art.28. Under art.45 of the modified COTIF (see below, para.36-081), the Convention shall be expressed in English, German and French, but in the case of divergence, the French text shall prevail.

[442] International Transport Conventions Act 1983 (Certification of Commencement of Convention) Order 1985 (SI 1985/612).

[443] International Transport Conventions Act 1983 s.2(1).

[444] SI 1994/1907. Note also the Supplementary Provisions agreed between Member States in 1993.

[445] SI 2005/2092.

[446] Implemented by the Railways Regulations 1998 (SI 1998/1340).

[447] The Carriage of Dangerous Goods and Use of Transportable Pressure Equipment Regulations 2009 (SI 2009/1348, as amended by SI 2011/1885) implement RID. A new Appendix C (RID) has been formulated to take the place of the 2011 RID, with effect from January 1, 2013, although there does not yet appear to be implementing legislation in the United Kingdom. See above para.36-035.

to as COTIF 1999), entered into force on July 1, 2006.[448] The United Kingdom has declared pursuant to art.42 of the Protocol that it will not apply the CUI, APTU and ATMF (Appendices E, F and G). In addition, pursuant to an agreement between the United Kingdom and France, the CIV Uniform Rules and the CIM Uniform Rules will not apply to carriage by means of rail shuttle services carrying road vehicles and their passengers performed exclusively between the Channel Tunnel terminals at Cheriton in Kent and Coquelles in the Pas-de-Calais.

International Conventions on Carriage by Road Two important multilateral treaties must be noted.[449] The United Kingdom is a party to the Convention on the Contract for the International Carriage of Goods by Road (CMR),[450] signed at Geneva on May 19, 1956.[451] This Convention entered into force for the United Kingdom on October 19, 1967. The English and French texts of this Convention are of equal authenticity. The Convention was implemented in English law by the Carriage of Goods by Road Act 1965, the English text of the Convention forming a Schedule to the Act. The Act came into force on June 5, 1967.[452] The United Kingdom has also ratified a Protocol to CMR.[453] The Protocol was implemented in English law by the Carriage by Air and Road Act 1979[454] and entered into force on December 28, 1980.[455]   **36-082**

Convention for Carriage of Passengers and Luggage by Road The United Kingdom may at some stage become a party to the Convention on the Contract for the International Carriage of Passengers and Luggage by Road (CVR),[456] signed at Geneva on March 1, 1973. The Convention entered into force on April 12, 1994. Although represented at the Diplomatic Conference which drew up the Convention, the United Kingdom government has not yet signed,[457] still less ratified, the Convention. Although implementing legislation in the shape of the Carriage of Passengers by Road Act 1974 was passed, the possibility of signature and ratification   **36-083**

---

[448] See *London Gazette* dated July 3, 2006; Railways (Convention on International Carriage by Rail) Regulations 2005 (SI 2005/2092) art.1.

[449] The United Kingdom has entered into bilateral treaties concerning international carriage of goods by road with several states: see, e.g. the Agreements with Yugoslavia of February 3, 1969 (Cmnd 4282; TS. No.18 (1970)) and with France of March 28, 1969 (Cmnd.4324; TS. No.27 (1970)). These treaties are, however, mere facilitation agreements, designed to provide for the terms of entry of vehicles and for permits and the like. They do not affect the contractual relation between carrier and customer in any way.

[450] Cmnd.3455; TS. No.90 (1967). See below, paras 36-117 et seq. "CMR" stands for *"Convention Relative au Contrat de Transport International des Marchandises par Route"*.

[451] There was also a European Agreement concerning the International Carriage of Dangerous Goods by Road signed at Geneva on September 30, 1957 ("ADR"). The Annexes to that Agreement, as amended, were incorporated into English law by the Carriage of Dangerous Goods and Use of Transportable Pressure Equipment Regulations 2007 (SI 2007/1573). See now SI 2009/1348 and SI 2011/1885. See above, para.36-035.

[452] Carriage of Goods by Road Act 1965 (Commencement) Order 1967 (SI 1967/819).

[453] Cmnd.8138; TS. No.6 (1981).

[454] See ss.3(3), 4(2) (4), 5 and 6(1)(b).

[455] Carriage by Air and Road Act 1979 (Commencement No.1) Order 1980 (SI 1980/1966).

[456] Cmnd.5622. See below, paras 36-149 et seq. "CVR" stands for *"Convention Relative au Contrat de Transport International des Voyageurs et des Bagages par Route"*.

[457] Only Luxembourg and the Federal Republic of Germany signed the Convention. The former states of Czechoslovakia and Yugoslavia acceded to it.

grows remote, given that the 1974 Act was repealed by the Statute Law (Repeals) Act 2004.[458]

36-084 **Multi-modal or combined transport** With the rise of containerised transport, it is becoming increasingly common for the contract of carriage of goods to contemplate the international transport of those goods by more than one mode of carriage, namely by road, rail, sea and/or air. Each mode of carriage presently is governed by its own international legal regime provided each mode involves international transport,[459] with few attempts to identify the scope of their application in cases of combined transport.[460] Difficulties may arise where there is an overlap between the scope of each of these regimes. It is not proposed to discuss this topic here at length. The International Convention on the Multimodal Transport of Goods 1980 is an attempt to legislate for such combined transport but has not yet entered into operation, having received significantly less ratifications than required.[461] By art.30(4), the Multimodal Convention will not apply to those states which are bound to apply the CMR or the CIM rules.

(b) Goods by Rail

36-085 **Scope of the Uniform Rules (CIM) under Appendix B to COTIF**[462] CIM regulates the form and conditions of the contract of carriage of goods by rail, the performance of the contract, its modification, the disposal of the goods being carried, liability for loss, damage and delay, compensation and enforcement of claims by action.[463]

36-086 **Application of CIM** CIM applies to every contract of carriage of goods by rail for reward when the place of taking over of the goods and the place designated for delivery are situated in two different Member States, irrespective of the place of business and the nationality of the parties to the contract of carriage.[464] It follows that CIM will apply even though the carriage is performed through the territory of a non-Member State[465] and that CIM will not apply if the place of taking over and the place of delivery are in the same state even though the carriage is performed

---

[458] s.1(1) and Sch.1 Pt 14. The 2004 Act also repealed those parts of the Carriage by Air and Road Act 1979 which provided for the implementation of the Protocol to the CVR which was agreed in 1979.

[459] CMR (road), CIM (rail), Warsaw Convention 1929, protocols and supplements (air—see above, Ch.35), and Hague Rules 1924 and Hague-Visby Rules 1968 (sea). Also note the Budapest Convention on Contracts for the Carriage of Goods by Inland Waterway (CMNI) signed on June 22, 2001. As to defining the modes of carriage, see Clarke, "The Shape of the Conventions on the Carriage of Goods" (2015) 50 E.T.L. 371, 375–376.

[460] CMR art.2; COTIF art.2(2) and 3(3); CIM art.48; Warsaw Convention arts 18(5) and 31; Hague-Visby Rules art.1.

[461] See also the *UNCTAD/ICC Rules for Multimodal Transport Documents* 1991. See generally de Wit, *Multimodal Transport* (1995). See Faghfouri, "International Regulation of Liability for Multimodal Transport—In Search of Uniformity" (2006) 5 *WMU Journal of International Affairs* 95. As an example of the difficulties in identifying the terms governing each leg of the combined transport of goods, see *Finagra (UK) Ltd v OT Africa Line Ltd* [1998] 2 Lloyd's Rep. 622.

[462] See above, para.36-079. As to the work being undertaken towards the harmonisation of CIM with the framework applied in Eastern Europe and Asia under the Agreement on International Goods Transport by Rail, administered by the Organisation for Cooperation between Railways, see Abel (2012) 12 S.T.L. 8.

[463] See Clarke and Yates, *Contracts of Carriage by Land and Air*, 2nd edn (2008).

[464] CIM art.1(1).

[465] *Azienda Autonoma Ferrovie dello Stato v La Pace* (1976) 11 E.T.L. 137, Corte di Cassazione Civile,

through the territory of another state. CIM will also apply to contracts of carriage of goods by rail where only one of the place of taking over or place of delivery are in a Member State provided the parties to the contract agree that CIM will apply.[466] CIM will further apply where the international carriage is the subject of a single contract which contract includes carriage by road or internal inland waterway as a supplement to the trans-frontier carriage by rail or carriage by sea or trans-frontier inland waterway if the latter services are listed in accordance with art.24 of COTIF.[467] However, CIM will not apply where the carriage is performed between stations situated on the territory of neighbouring states, when the infrastructure of the stations is managed by one or more infrastructure managers subject only to one of those states.[468] Any stipulation in the contract of carriage which, directly or indirectly, derogates from CIM shall be null and void, but such nullity shall not operate to nullify the other provisions of the contract.[469]

Interpretation of the Convention   Whilst there have been no English decisions   **36-087**
on the interpretation of CIM, some decisions of the courts of the Continental parties to the unmodified Convention have been reported. In view of the similarity of the provisions regarding the carrier's liability and the carrier's exemptions from liability between CIM and the Geneva Convention on the Contract for the International Carriage of Goods by Road (CMR),[470] the reported decisions on the interpretation of CMR are often of assistance in the interpretation of CIM.

The carrier's role   Under the contract of carriage, the carrier undertakes to carry   **36-088**
the goods consigned for reward to the place of destination and to deliver them at the destination to the consignee.[471] For this service, the carrier is entitled to the payment by the consignor of the carriage charge, customs duties and other costs.[472]

Consignment note   CIM requires the contract of carriage to be confirmed by a   **36-089**
consignment note which accords with a uniform model.[473] The uniform model is to be established by international associations of carriers in agreement with customers' associations and relevant customs authorities.[474] The consignment note is prima facie evidence of the conclusion and conditions of the contract and the taking over of the goods being carried.[475] CIM specifies a number of formal requirements for the consignment note, stipulating the particulars which the consignment note must contain (e.g. places of issue, taking over and delivery, names of consignor, carrier and consignee, and details of the goods to be carried), the responsibility for which largely falls on the consignor.[476] However, the absence, irregularity or loss of the consignment note shall not affect the existence or validity of the contract which the

---

Italy.
[466] CIM art.1(2).
[467] CIM art.1(3), (4). See *Anon.* (2013) 49 E.T.L. 228, BGH. As to rail-road traffic, see also CMR art.2(1) and para.36-119 below.
[468] CIM art.1(6).
[469] CIM art.5.
[470] Some of these decisions have been reported in such periodicals as *European Transport Law* (E.T.L.) and *Lloyds Maritime and Commercial Law Quarterly* (L.M.C.L.Q.).
[471] CIM art.6(1).
[472] CIM art.10(1).
[473] CIM art.6(2).
[474] CIM art.6(8).
[475] CIM art.12(1).
[476] CIM arts 7, 8.

Convention emphasises shall remain subject to CIM.[477] One consignment note shall be issued for each consignment and, unless the contracting parties agree otherwise, must not relate to more than one wagon load.[478] CIM contemplates that there will be two copies of the consignment note, the duplicate being given to the consignor.[479] CIM provides that the consignment note will not have effect as a bill of lading.[480]

36-090 **Loading, carriage and delivery** CIM contemplates two types of consignments which may be carried by rail, namely packages and full wagon loads. Unless the parties otherwise agree, the carrier is responsible for the loading and unloading of packages and the consignor is responsible for the loading of a wagon load and the consignee is responsible for the unloading of the wagon load.[481] The consignor is responsible for any defects in the packing of the goods unless the defects were apparent to the carrier on taking them over and the carrier made no reservations concerning the defects.[482] On arrival at the destination, the carrier must deliver the goods to the consignee and hand over the consignment note against the provision of a receipt and the payment of sums outstanding under the carriage contract.[483] Delivery also may be effected by the handing over of the goods to customs authorities, or the deposit of the goods for storage with the railway, with a forwarding agent or in a public warehouse, provided that such delivery is permitted by the provisions in force at the destination station.[484]

36-091 **Modification of the contract** The consignor shall be entitled to dispose of the goods and to modify the contract of carriage by giving "subsequent orders". Such orders may require the carrier to delay delivery of the goods or to deliver the goods to a consignee or to a destination other than the one identified in the consignment note.[485] The modification of the contract appears to be limited to these matters and must be effected by the consignor producing to the carrier the duplicate consignment note on which the modifications must be entered.[486] Such modifications must be "possible, lawful and reasonable", must not interfere with the normal working of the carrier's undertaking nor prejudice the consignors or consignees of other consignments and must not have the effect of splitting the consignment.[487] The consignee will acquire the right to modify the contract of carriage once the consignment note is drawn up, unless the consignor reserves the right to himself or herself

---

[477] CIM art.6(2). In *NMBS Holding/Belgische Naamloze Vennootschap voor transport door middel van het gecombineerd rail-weg-systeem TRW* (2007) 42 E.T.L. 656, the Hof van Cassatie van Belgie held that a claim for damages could be brought against the railway carrier, in absence of a railway bill, provided that the contractual relationship between the claimant and carrier could be established.

[478] CIM art.6(6).

[479] CIM art.6(4).

[480] CIM art.6(5).

[481] CIM art.13(1).

[482] CIM art.14.

[483] CIM art.17(1). In Antwerp, it has been held that the consignee named in the consignment note who acts as agent for the final consignee will become a party to the contract by acceptance of the goods or the consignment note: *Sobelgra NV v Nationale Maatschappij der Belgische Spoorwegen (NMBS)* (1997) 33 E.T.L. 714.

[484] CIM art.17(2).

[485] CIM art.18(1).

[486] CIM art.19(1). If the carrier accepts the consignor's orders to deliver the goods to some person other than the consignee named in the consignment note without requiring the duplicate consignment note to be produced, he will be liable for any loss or damage arising from that omission: art.19(7); *SA Nicolas Corman v SNCF* (1976) 11 E.T.L. 120, Court of Appeal, Paris.

[487] CIM art.19(3), (4).

on the consignment note.[488] The consignor will lose the right to modify the contract when the consignee has acquired the right of modification or has accepted from the carrier the consignment note or the goods or has demanded both.[489] Similarly, the consignee will lose the right of modification when he has requested or accepted the consignment note or the goods. Additionally, the consignee will lose the right when he has instructed the carrier to deliver the goods to another person, who requests the carrier to hand over the consignment note and deliver the goods; that person will not be entitled to modify the contract.[490] The consignor may have a right of stoppage in transit vis-à-vis the consignee pursuant to the Sale of Goods Act 1979 if English law governs the contract between them.[491]

Prevention of carriage or delivery   If the carriage of the goods has been **36-092** prevented by circumstances,[492] the carrier must decide whether it is preferable (presumably in the interests of the person entitled to dispose of the goods) to modify the route or to ask the person entitled for instructions.[493] If it is impossible to continue the carriage or to effect delivery, the person entitled shall be asked for his instructions. If the carrier is unable to obtain instructions, he shall take such steps which he considers to be in the best interests of the person entitled.[494] If circumstances exist which prevent delivery, the carrier must ask the consignor or (if the consignee has modified the contract) the consignee for instructions.[495] If the consignee refuses delivery, the consignor may give instructions, even if he is unable to produce the duplicate consignment note.[496] If circumstances alter permitting delivery before the receipt of instructions, the carrier shall deliver the goods to the consignee.[497] If the goods are of a perishable nature or if the carrier does not receive instructions, the carrier may sell the goods and, after deducting relevant costs, place the proceeds of sale at the disposal of the person entitled.[498]

Loss, damage and delay   The carrier is liable for loss (total or partial) of the **36-093** goods, damage and delay (i.e. for exceeding the transit periods[499]) unless he can prove an applicable exception to that liability.[500] The carrier is liable for his own employees and for any other persons, including the managers of the railway infrastructure on which the carriage is performed, whose services he uses in the

---

[488] CIM art.18(3).
[489] CIM art.18(2).
[490] CIM art.18(4), (5).
[491] See below, paras 44-326—44-338.
[492] The carrier will not be liable for any loss of or damage to the goods or delay caused by circumstances which are unavoidable by the carrier: art.23(2).
[493] CIM art.20(1).
[494] CIM art.20(2).
[495] CIM art.21(1), (4).
[496] CIM art.21(3).
[497] CIM art.21(2).
[498] CIM art.22(3), (4).
[499] The transit period is that which is agreed between the carrier and consignor or, in the absence of agreement, as specified in art.16.
[500] A failure to comply with the instructions of the person entitled to dispose of the goods during carriage may also render the carrier liable for loss or damage caused thereby: art.19(6). There is a facility by which the carrier may seek an exception to liability for losses arising by specified causes in respect of rail-sea traffic, provided that the relevant Member State made such provision in the listed services set out in art.24(1) of COTIF. As to the possibility of liability beyond that provided for under CIM where it is contractually incorporated, see *DSM Acrylonitrile BV e.a. v DB Schenker Rail Nederland* (2016) 51 E.T.L. 335, Rechtbank te Rotterdam.

performance of the carriage.[501] There are two kinds of exceptions. The first type arises where the relevant loss, damage or delay was caused by (1) the fault of the person entitled; (2) an order given by the person entitled other than as a result of the fault of the carrier; (3) inherent defect in the goods (decay, wastage, etc.)[502]; or (4) circumstances which the carrier could not avoid and the consequences of which he was not able to prevent.[503] The burden of proving any of these is on the carrier.[504] Thus far, the exceptions are very similar to those applicable to the common carrier at common law. But the second kind of exception comprises circumstances when loss or damage arises from the special risks inherent in one or more of the following circumstances: (a) carriage in open wagons when that has been agreed; (b) absence or inadequacy of packaging; (c) loading by the consignor or unloading by the consignee; (d) the nature of certain kinds of goods which particularly exposes them to loss or damage, especially through breakage, rust, interior and spontaneous decay, desiccation or wastage; (e) irregular, incorrect or incomplete description or numbering of packages; (f) the carriage of live animals; and (g) the carriage of consignments which, with the parties' agreement, must be accompanied by an attendant.[505] If the carrier establishes that loss or damage could be attributed to one or more of these exceptions, this is rebuttably presumed, unless in (a) above there is an abnormal shortage or a loss of a package.[506] If the goods are not delivered to the consignee or held at his disposal within 30 days after the expiry of the transit period, they are presumed to be lost.[507]

36-094 Ascertainment of loss or damage   Upon delivery, the person entitled may ask the carrier for an opportunity to examine the goods to determine the existence of any loss or damage. Any failure by the carrier to permit such an examination will entitle the person entitled to the goods to refuse to accept the goods, even when he has accepted the consignment note and/or paid the outstanding charges.[508] In the event of the discovery, presumption or allegation of partial loss of or damage to the goods, the carrier must, without delay prepare, if possible in the presence of the person entitled, a report concerning the condition of the goods and the nature, extent, cause and time of the loss or damage.[509] If the person entitled does not accept the report's findings, he can insist upon the circumstances surrounding the loss or damage to be investigated by an expert.[510]

36-095   Upper financial limits of liability   The carrier's liability for loss of the goods,

---

[501] CIM art.40.
[502] Where there is wastage in transit of goods which, by reason of their nature, is caused by the sole fact of carriage, the carrier will be liable only to the extent that the wastage exceeds specified allowances: art.31.
[503] CIM art.23(2).
[504] CIM art.25(1).
[505] CIM art.23(3). The unmodified Convention included an additional exception in respect of loss caused by a failure to comply with customs formalities. Such matters are now regulated by art.15. The carrier is under a general duty to maintain its rolling stock put at a customer's disposal in good condition: *NMBS v NV Fonciere Carner* (1976) 11 E.T.L. 780, Hof van Beroep, Brussels. See also art.24 which concerns railway vehicles consigned as goods.
[506] CIM art.25(2), (3).
[507] CIM art.29(1).
[508] CIM art.17(4).
[509] CIM art.42(1).
[510] CIM art.42(3).

whether total or partial, is limited to 17 units of account[511] per kilogramme of gross mass short,[512] unless the consignor and carrier agree that the consignor shall declare in the consignment note a value for the goods exceeding this limit or a special interest in delivery by entering an amount in figures on the consignment note, in which case compensation can be claimed up to the value or amount declared.[513] The compensation is calculated by reference to the commodity exchange quoted price or current market price or the usual value of the goods of the same kind and quality at the time and place at which the goods were taken over for the carriage.[514] The carrier must also refund the carriage charges, customs duties and other expenses paid in respect of the missing goods.[515] The carrier's liability for delay (i.e. for exceeding the transit periods) depends on whether actual loss or damage was thus caused. If actual loss or damage resulted from the delay, the compensation may not exceed four times the amount of the carriage charges, although the total compensation for the loss or damage caused by delay and otherwise may not exceed the compensation payable for a total loss.[516] The carrier's liability for damage is for the amount by which the goods have been diminished in value, but may not exceed the amount payable in respect of loss.[517] The maximum limits of compensation for loss, damage or delay are removed altogether if it was due to the carrier's wilful misconduct (namely, an act or omission which the carrier has committed either with intent to cause such loss or damage, or recklessly and with knowledge that such loss or damage would probably result).[518] The claimant may recover interest on the compensation payable at the rate of 5 per cent per annum from the time a claim, together with supporting documents, is submitted in accordance with the CIM

---

[511] However, the carrier is free to assume a greater liability: art.5. The unit of account is the Special Drawing Right ("SDR") defined by the International Monetary Fund ("IMF"): COTIF art.9(1). Its value is expressed in the national currency of a State Member of the IMF in accordance with IMF methods of valuation: art.9(2). States which are not Members of the IMF shall determine their own methods of calculating the value of the SDR: if their legislation does not permit this, the unit of account is deemed to be the equivalent of three gold francs, each gold franc weighing 1031 of a gramme and of millesimal fineness 900: art.9(3), (4). In any event the conversion of the gold franc must express in national currency a value approximating closely to the value calculated by reference to the IMF methods of valuation. In the case of judicial proceedings or arbitration in the United Kingdom, the SDR is converted into its sterling equivalent on the day of the judgment or award: Railways (Convention on International Carriage by Rail) Regulations 2005 (SI 2005/2092) reg.7.

[512] CIM art.30(2).

[513] CIM arts 34, 35.

[514] CIM art.30(1).

[515] CIM art.30(4). The charges do not include charges which would have been incurred in the event that the carriage was performed in accordance with the contract, would have contributed to the value of the goods at the destination, and which were not incurred as a result of the incident giving rise to the claim (*Anon.* (2004) 39 E.T.L. 93, Bundesgerichtshof). The claimant cannot recover any additional duty or VAT payable in respect of the goods which do not find themselves at their destination: *Anon.*, Cass. Paris, January 28, 1975; cf. *James Buchanan & Co Ltd v Babco Forwarding and Shipping (UK) Ltd* [1978] 1 Lloyd's Rep. 119; contra *Anon.* (1994) 29 E.T.L. 360, Supreme Court of Denmark (CMR). See below, para.36-130 n.727.

[516] CIM art.33(1), (2), (3).

[517] CIM art.32(1), (2). Under the unmodified Convention, in the event of damage by deterioration, the carrier's liability is calculated under the provisions concerning damage not delay: *Anon.* (1976) 11 E.T.L. 787, Bundesgerichtshof. Under art.33(4), in the case of damage to goods, not resulting from the transit period being exceeded, the compensation payable under art.33(1) shall, where appropriate, be payable in addition to that provided for in art.32.

[518] CIM art.36.

Uniform Rules,[519] or failing such a claim, from the time of the commencement of legal proceedings in respect of the claim.[520]

36-096 Successive and substitute carriers If carriage is governed by a single contract and is performed by several successive carriers, each carrier, by the very act of taking over the goods with the consignment note, shall become a party to the contract of carriage in accordance with the terms of the contract and shall assume the obligations arising therefrom. Each carrier shall be responsible in respect of carriage over the entire route up to delivery.[521] Where the carrier has entrusted all or part of the performance of the carriage to a substitute carrier, the carrier shall remain liable in respect of the entire carriage. The CIM provisions governing the liability of the carrier shall also apply to the liability of the substitute carrier for the carriage performed by him.[522] Actions based on the contract of carriage may be brought only against the first carrier, the last carrier or the carrier who performed that part of the carriage on which the event giving rise to the claim occurred.[523] A successive carrier may be sued if that carrier has been named, with his consent, in the consignment note as the carrier who must deliver the goods, even if that carrier has not received the goods or the consignment note.[524]

36-097 Claims Claims against the carrier relating to the contract of carriage must be made in writing only by those persons who have the right to claim.[525] The consignor may bring an action against the carrier until such time as the consignee has taken possession of the consignment note or accepted the goods or demanded that the consignment note be handed over and that the goods be delivered or asserted his right to modify the contract.[526] From that time, the consignee may bring an action against the carrier unless and until the person to whom the consignee has ordered the carrier to deliver the goods has accepted the consignment note or the goods or has demanded both.[527] Actions based on CIM may be brought in the Member States designated by the parties' agreement or where the defendant is domiciled or resident or where the goods were taken over by the carrier or where the place designated for delivery is situated.[528]

36-098 Extinction of claims Acceptance of the goods by the person entitled extinguishes all rights of action against the carrier arising from the contract of carriage in case

---

[519] CIM art.43. If no supporting documents are provided within a reasonable time so that the amount of the claim can be finally settled, no interest shall accrue between the expiry of the time allotted and the actual submission of such documents: art.37(3).

[520] CIM art.37(2).

[521] CIM art.26.

[522] CIM art.27(1), (2).

[523] CIM art.45(1).

[524] CIM art.45(2).

[525] CIM art.43(1), (2). The claim generally has to be supported by the consignment note: see art.43(3)–(6). In *NMBS Holding/Belgische Naamloze Vennootschap voor transport door middel van het gecombineerd rail-weg-systeem TRW* (2007) 42 E.T.L. 656, the Hof van Cassatie van Belgie held that a claim for damages could be brought against the railway carrier, in absence of a railway bill, provided that the contractual relationship between the claimant and carrier could be established.

[526] CIM art.44(1)(a).

[527] CIM arts 44(1)(b), 44(2). Hammerschmeidová, "Right of the consignee to bring an action" Bulletin of International Carriage by Rail 3/2010, 83. Where there is an inconsistency with EU rules on jurisdiction, see *Anon.*, Cour de Cassation de France, November 29, 2016, (2016) 51 E.T.L. 684.

[528] CIM art.46(1).

of partial loss, damage or delay,[529] subject to four exceptions. First, claims for partial loss or damage can be made if the damage was ascertained by the preparation of a report or if report was not prepared solely by reason of the carrier's fault.[530] Secondly, claims for loss or damage which is not apparent and not discovered until after acceptance can still be made, provided the person entitled to claim asks the carrier for a report within seven days of acceptance and proves that the loss or damage occurred between the time of taking over the goods for carriage and the time of delivery.[531] Thirdly, claims for delay in delivery can be made within 60 days of acceptance.[532] Fourthly, the claim is not extinguished if wilful misconduct can be proved.[533]

Limitation of actions   All actions arising from the contract of carriage are time-barred after one year, or two years in the case of, inter alia, wilful misconduct.[534] The period of limitation runs, in the case of partial loss, damage or delay in delivery, from the date of delivery; in the case of total loss, from the 30th day after the expiry of the transit period.[535] A written claim suspends the running of the period of limitation until such date as the carrier rejects the claim in writing.[536]   **36-099**

(c)   Passengers, Luggage and Vehicles by Rail

(i)   Application and Scope of the Convention

Scope of the Uniform Rules (CIV) under Appendix A to COTIF   The CIV Uniform Rules regulate the making and performance of the contract of carriage of passengers, luggage and vehicles by rail, the liability of the rail carrier for death of, and personal injury to, passengers, and for failure to keep to the timetable, the liability of the passenger and the relations between carriers.   **36-100**

Application of CIV   CIV provides a unified set of rules to be applied to every contract of carriage of passengers by rail for reward or free of charge, when the place of departure and the place of destination are situated in two different Member States, irrespective of the domicile or the place of business and the nationality of the parties to the contract.[537] CIV applies also to international carriage pursuant to a single contract which includes carriage by road or by internal inland waterway or, provided that the services are provided for in art.24(1) of COTIF, by sea or trans-frontier inland waterway.[538] CIV also applies, as far as the liability of the carrier in the case of death or personal injury is concerned, to persons accompanying a consignment whose carriage is effected in accordance with the CIM Uniform   **36-101**

---

529   CIM art.47(1).
530   CIM art.47(2)(a).
531   CIM art.47(2)(b). See Clarke, "Non-apparent damage to goods in transit" [1982] L.M.C.L.Q. 533.
532   CIM art.47(2)(c).
533   CIM art.47(2)(d).
534   CIM art.48(1). The limitation provision applies to claims based on the contract of carriage, whether brought by or against the rail carrier: *Anon.* (2005) 40 E.T.L. 395, Oberster Gerichtshof Österreich. Where CIM is contractually incorporated without limitation of the scope of its application, art.48 may not apply to all claims governed by the CIM: *Anon.*, Oberster Gerichtshof Österreich, April 6, 2016, (2016) 51 E.T.L. 443.
535   CIM art.48(2).
536   CIM art.48(3).
537   CIV art.1(1).
538   CIV art.1(2), (3).

Rules.[539] As with CIM, CIV will not apply where the carriage is performed between stations situated on the territory of neighbouring states, when the infrastructure of the stations is managed by one or more infrastructure managers subject only to one of those states.[540] By Regulation (EC) 1371/2007 of the European Parliament, since December 3, 2009, the provisions of CIV are now also applicable to domestic carriage (i.e. carriage within one State).[541] Any stipulation in the contract of carriage which, directly or indirectly, derogates from CIV shall be null and void, but such nullity shall not operate to nullify the other provisions of the contract.[542]

36-102 Rail-sea carriage As mentioned above, CIV applies to a single contract of international carriage by rail and sea provided that the carriage is performed on services listed pursuant to art.24(1) of COTIF.[543] It should be noted, however, that, whilst CIV may in certain circumstances cover aspects of rail-sea carriage, legislation in the United Kingdom has provided that as far as English law is concerned, the terms of the Athens Convention relating to the Carriage of Passengers and their Luggage by Sea 1974 are applied to any contract for international carriage by sea under which a place in the United Kingdom is the place of departure or destination.[544] The Athens Convention enables carriers by sea to limit their liability in respect of the death of, or personal injury to, a passenger. The terms of the Athens Convention have also been applied to carriage by sea by United Kingdom carriers and within the United Kingdom.[545]

36-103 The carrier's role Under the contract of carriage, the carrier is obliged to carry the passenger and, where appropriate, the passenger's luggage and vehicle to the place of destination and to deliver the luggage and vehicle at the place of destination.[546] Subject to the terms of the contract, the carrier is entitled to advance payment of the carriage charge.[547]

(ii) Passengers and Hand Luggage

36-104 The passenger's rights The passenger in possession of a valid ticket is entitled to be carried in accordance with the terms of the contract of carriage. The passenger is also entitled to take with him articles which can be handled easily (hand

---

[539] CIM art.1(4).
[540] CIV art.1(5).
[541] See above, para.36-054. See also the Rail Passengers' Rights and Obligations Regulations 2010 (SI 2010/1504), which entered into force on June 25, 2010; Rail Passengers' Rights and Obligations (Exemption) Regulations 2014 (SI 2014/2793). See also the Merchant Shipping (Convention Relating to the Carriage of Passengers and their Luggage by Sea) Order 2014 (SI 2014/1361).
[542] CIV art.5.
[543] CIV art.1(3).
[544] Merchant Shipping Act 1995 s.183. The Athens Convention came into force on April 30, 1987. See *South West Strategic Health Authority v Bay Island Voyages* [2015] EWCA Civ 708, the Court of Appeal held that the Convention did not apply to contribution claims between carriers (at [15]–[21]).
[545] The Carriage of Passengers and their Luggage by Sea (United Kingdom Carriers) Order 1998 (SI 1998/2917); Carriage of Passengers and their Luggage by Sea (Domestic Carriage) Order 1987 (SI 1987/670), which now takes effect as if made under the Merchant Shipping Act 1995 s.184. Under s.184(5), the term "contract of carriage" in the context of the Athens Convention excludes a contract which is not for reward.
[546] CIV art.6(1).
[547] CIV arts 8(1), 19, 25.

luggage), but it is the passenger's responsibility to supervise such hand luggage.[548] If a passenger is unable to produce a valid ticket, the carrier may require the passenger to pay a surcharge. If the passenger fails to pay the carriage charge or the surcharge, the carrier may require the passenger to discontinue the journey.[549] The carrier may also exclude a passenger from carriage or require a passenger to discontinue his journey, without refunding the carriage charge, if that passenger presents a danger for the safety and the good functioning of the operations of the rail operations or for the safety of the other passengers or if that passenger inconveniences other passengers in an intolerable manner.[550]

The ticket   The contract of carriage must be confirmed by one or more tickets is-   **36-105** sued to the passenger. However, the absence, irregularity, or loss of the ticket shall not affect the existence or validity of the contract, which remains subject to the application of the CIV Uniform Rules.[551] The ticket is prima facie evidence of the making and contents of the contract of carriage.[552] The terms and conditions of the contract are those which are legally in force in each Member State. Such conditions will determine the form and content of tickets.[553] The ticket may be established in the form of electronic data registration, which can be transformed into legible written symbols.[554] However, the ticket must identify the carrier and must state that the carriage is subject to the CIV Uniform Rules.[555] It is incumbent on the passenger to ensure that on receipt of the ticket that it has been made out in accordance with his instructions.[556] If the ticket is not made out in the passenger's name, the ticket is transferable, provided that the journey has not yet begun.[557]

Liability for death and personal injury   In general under CIV the carrier is li-   **36-106** able for damage resulting from the death of, or personal injury or any other physical or mental harm to, a passenger, when the damage is caused by an accident arising out of the operation of the railway and happening while the passenger is in, entering or alighting from, railway vehicles.[558] In the event of death, the carrier is liable for damages comprising the necessary costs following the death (including transport and funeral expenses) and is liable to the passenger's dependents, whom the passenger was legally obliged to maintain, for the loss of support.[559] In the case of personal injury (whether or not it leads to death), or other physical or mental harm, the carrier is liable for damage comprising any necessary costs (including

---

[548] CIV arts 12(1), 15.

[549] CIV art.9(1).

[550] CIV art.9(2).

[551] CIV art.6(2). This is subject to the carrier's right, as set out in art.9, to demand a surcharge in the event of the non-production of the ticket and to require the passenger to discontinue the journey if the carriage charge or surcharge is not paid. See *Nationale Maatschappij der Belgische Spoorwegen NV v Demey* (C-261/15) EU:C:2016:709, September 21, 2016 (preliminary ruling of ECJ as to passenger not in possession of a ticket).

[552] CIV art.6(3).

[553] CIV arts 3(c), 7(1).

[554] CIV art.7(5).

[555] CIV art.7(2).

[556] CIV art.7(3).

[557] CIV art.7(4).

[558] CIV art.26(1).

[559] CIV arts 27(1), 27(2). National law shall govern the rights of action of those whom the passenger was maintaining without a legal obligation so to do: art.27(2).

medical treatment and transport expenses) and compensation for financial loss due to incapacity to work or increased needs.[560]

36-107 Fatal accidents   Regulation 5 of the Railways (Convention on International Carriage by Rail) Regulations 2005[561] provides that where under the Convention a person has a right of action in respect of the death of a passenger by virtue of his being a person whom the passenger was under a legally enforceable duty to maintain, no action in respect of the passenger's death may be brought for the benefit of that person under the Fatal Accidents Act 1976, although actions under that Act may be brought for the benefit of any other person. The Regulations further provide that in actions brought under CIV the same benefit shall be excluded in the assessment of damages as would be excluded under s.4 of the Fatal Accidents Act 1976. Where separate proceedings can be brought under CIV and under the Fatal Accidents Act 1976, a court may, in assessing damages under the 1976 Act, take account of any damages awarded in proceedings under the Convention.

36-108 Carrier's exemptions from liability for death and personal injury   The carrier is relieved of liability for death or personal injury (a) if the accident was caused by circumstances not connected with the operation of the railway and which the carrier, despite the exercise of the care required in the circumstances, could not avoid and the consequences of which he could not prevent[562]; (b) to the extent that the accident was due to the passenger's fault[563]; and (c) if the accident was caused by the behaviour of a third party which the carrier, despite the exercise of the care required in the circumstances, could not avoid and the consequences of which it could not prevent.[564] If the accident is due to the behaviour of a third party and if the carrier is in any event not entirely relieved of liability, he shall be liable in full up to the limits imposed by CIV.[565]

36-109 Liability for delay   The carrier is liable to the passenger for loss or damage resulting from the fact that the journey cannot, or could not reasonably, be continued on the same day because of a cancellation, the late running of a train or a missed connection. The damages for which the carrier is liable comprises the reasonable costs of accommodation and the reasonable costs of notifying persons expecting the passenger.[566] The carrier will be exempt from such liability in similar circumstances exempting the carrier from liability for death and personal injury.[567]

36-110 Liability for hand luggage   In the event that the passenger dies or sustains a personal injury, the carrier shall also be liable for loss or damage resulting from the

---

[560] CIV art.28. National law shall govern the right to claim damages other than those set out in arts 27 and 28: art.29.

[561] SI 2005/2092. See also the Rail Passengers' Rights and Obligations Regulations 2010 (SI 1504/2010) reg.7.

[562] CIV art.26(2)(a).

[563] CIV art.26(2)(b).

[564] CIV art.26(2)(c). As to the relationship between Regulation (EC) 1371/2007 and art.32 CIV, see *ÖBB-Personenverkehr AG* (C-509/11) EU:C:2013:613, (2014) 49 E.T.L. 43. See also Pavliha and Hojnik (2014) 49 E.T.L. 5. Another undertaking using the same railway infrastructure shall not be considered as a third party for the purposes of this provision.

[565] CIV art.26(3).

[566] CIV art.32(1). National law shall govern the passenger's right to claim other heads of damage: art.32(3).

[567] CIV art.32(2). See above, para.36-108.

total or partial loss of, or damage to, hand luggage.[568] In other cases, the carrier shall not be liable for hand luggage the supervision of which is the responsibility of the passenger, unless the loss or damage was caused by the fault of the carrier.[569]

Upper financial limits of liability   The amount of damages to be awarded in cases **36-111** of death or personal injury under CIV are to be determined in accordance with national law. The limit of damages per passenger is fixed, for the purposes of the CIV Uniform Rules, at 175,000 units of account, where national law provides for an upper limit of less than that amount.[570] There is no specified financial limit of liability for delay. Where the carrier is liable for damage to, or loss of, hand luggage, the limit of compensation is 1,400 units of account per passenger.[571] The liability of the carrier is, however, not limited at all if the loss or damage results from an act or omission which the carrier has committed either with intent to cause such loss or damage or recklessly with the knowledge that such loss or damage probably will result.[572]

(iii)   Registered Luggage and Vehicles

Transport documents   A passenger may consign articles as registered luggage in **36-112** accordance with the application of general conditions of carriage.[573] The carrier's obligations concerning the forwarding of registered luggage must be established by a luggage registration voucher issued to the passenger. The absence, irregularity or loss of the voucher shall not affect the existence or validity of the contract of carriage, which remains subject to the application of the CIV Uniform Rules.[574] The voucher is prima facie evidence of the registration of the luggage and the contents of the contract of carriage.[575] The form and content of the voucher are determined in accordance with the general conditions of carriage.[576] The voucher must identify the carrier and must state that the carriage is subject to the CIV Uniform Rules.[577] It is incumbent on the passenger to ensure that on receipt of the voucher that it has been made out in accordance with his instructions.[578] Similar provisions exist in respect of vehicles, for which a carriage voucher must establish the carrier's contractual obligations.[579]

Loss, damage and delay   The carrier is liable for loss or damage resulting from **36-113** the total or partial loss of, or damage to, registered luggage or the vehicle carried between the time of taking over by the carrier and the time of delivery as well as from delay in delivery.[580] The carrier will be relieved from this liability to the extent that the loss, damage or delay was caused by a fault of the passenger, an order given

---

[568] CIV art.33(1).
[569] CIV art.33(2).
[570] CIV art.30(2). As to "units of account", see para.36-095.
[571] CIV art.34.
[572] CIV art.48.
[573] CIV art.12(2).
[574] CIV art.16(1), (2). As to the responsibility of successive and substitute carriers, see arts 38, 39.
[575] CIV art.16(3).
[576] CIV art.17(1).
[577] CIV art.17(2).
[578] CIV art.17(3).
[579] CIV arts 24, 25.
[580] CIV arts 36(1), 47. It is rebuttably presumed that when the carrier took over the registered luggage that it was apparently in good condition and that the number and mass of the items of luggage cor-

by the passenger other than as a result of the carrier's fault, an inherent defect or circumstances which the carrier could not avoid and the consequences of which he was unable to prevent.[581] Further, the carrier will be relieved of liability to the extent that the loss or damage arises from the special risks inherent in (a) the absence or inadequacy of packing; (b) the special nature of the luggage or vehicle; and/or (c) the consignment as luggage of articles not acceptable for carriage.[582] The person entitled to the luggage or vehicle may consider the luggage or vehicle lost, without adducing further proof, if has not been delivered within 14 days after a valid request for delivery has been made.[583]

36-114 **Upper financial limits of liability** The amount of the carrier's liability for loss of registered luggage, whether total or partial, depends on whether or not the passenger establishes the amount of loss or damage suffered. If the amount of loss is proved, the loss is limited to 80 units of account per kilogramme of gross mass short or 1200 units of account per item of luggage; if not, the carrier must pay liquidated damages of 20 units of account per kilogramme of gross mass short or 300 units of account per item of luggage.[584] The carrier must also refund the carriage charges.[585] Liability for damage is for the amount by which the luggage has been diminished in value, but may not exceed the amount payable in respect of loss.[586] As regards delay, if the passenger proves that he suffered loss or damage, the maximum amount payable as compensation is 0.80 units of account per kilogramme of gross mass of the luggage or 14 units of account per item of luggage delivered late; but if loss or damage is not proved, the measure of damages is liquidated at 0.14 units of account per kilogramme of gross mass of the luggage or 2.80 units of account per item of luggage delivered late.[587] The maximum limits of compensation for loss, damage or delay are removed altogether if it was due to the act or omission of the carrier which was done with the intent to cause loss or damage or recklessly with the knowledge that such loss or damage probably will result.[588] As regards vehicles, compensation for loss of or damage to the vehicle shall be calculated on the basis of the usual value of the vehicle subject to a limit of 8,000 units of account[589]; compensation for proven loss or damage resulting from delay is limited to the amount of the carriage charge.[590]

(iv) Claims

36-115 **Claims against carriers** A claim relating to liability for death or personal injury must be addressed in writing to the carrier against whom an action may be brought. Where successive carriers performed the carriage under a single contract, the claim

---

responded to the entries on the voucher: art.16(4). Delivery of the luggage or vehicle must be effected on surrender of the voucher: art.22(1). See *Anon.* (2013) 49 E.T.L. 470, BGH.
[581] CIV arts 36(2), 47. The carrier bears the relevant burden of proof: art.37(1).
[582] CIV arts 36(3), 47. The carrier bears the initial burden of proof, which thereafter falls upon the claimant: art.37(2). See *Anon.* (2013) 49 E.T.L. 470, BGH.
[583] CIV art.40(1).
[584] CIV art.41(1).
[585] CIV art.41(2).
[586] CIV art.42.
[587] CIV art.43(1).
[588] CIV art.48.
[589] CIV art.45.
[590] CIV art.44.

may also be made against the first or the last carrier as well as the carrier who has his principal place of business or whose agency concluded the contract in the state where the passenger is domiciled or resident.[591] An action in respect of death or personal injury may be brought only against the carrier (including substitute carriers) who was bound pursuant to the contract of carriage to provide the service of carriage in the course of which the accident happened.[592] Other claims based on the contract of carriage may be brought only against the first carrier, the last carrier or the carrier who performed that part of the carriage on which the event giving rise to the claim occurred.[593] A successive carrier may be sued if that carrier has been named, with his consent, in the voucher as the carrier who must deliver the luggage or vehicle, even if that carrier has not received them or the voucher.[594] Actions based on CIV may be brought before the courts or tribunals as agreed between the parties or in those Member States in which the defendant is domiciled or resident or has his principal place of business or agency which concluded the contract.[595]

Extinction of claims A claimant loses his right of action based on the carrier's liability for death or personal injury if he does not give notice of the accident to one of the carriers to which a claim may be presented within 12 months of his becoming aware of the loss or damage.[596] Nonetheless, the right of action is not lost if (a) notice has been given to one of the carriers against a claim brought within the relevant period; (b) the carrier who is liable has learned of the accident within the relevant period in some other way; (c) notice of the accident has not been given, or has been given late, as a result of circumstances for which the claimant is not responsible; or (d) the claimant proves that the accident was caused by fault of the carrier.[597] As regards other claims, acceptance of the luggage by the person entitled extinguishes all rights of action against the carrier arising from the contract of carriage in case of partial loss, damage or delay,[598] subject to four exceptions. First, claims for partial loss or damage can be made if the damage was ascertained in accordance with CIV.[599] Secondly, claims for loss or damage which is not apparent and not discovered until after acceptance can still be made, provided the person entitled to claim asks the carrier for ascertainment within three days of acceptance and proves that the loss or damage occurred between the time of taking over and the time of delivery.[600] Thirdly, claims for delay in delivery can be made within 21 days of acceptance.[601] Fourthly, the claim is not extinguished if the person entitled proves that the loss or damage was caused by fault on the part of the carrier.[602]

36-116

Limitation of actions Actions for damages brought under CIV based on the carrier's liability for death or personal injury are time-barred in the case of a pas-

36-117

---

591 CIV art.55(1).
592 CIV arts 26(5), 56(1).
593 CIV arts 55(2), 56(2).
594 CIV art.56(3).
595 CIV art.57(1).
596 CIV art.58(1).
597 CIV art.58(2).
598 CIV art.59(1). It is assumed that this provision applies alike to vehicles.
599 CIV arts 54, 59(2)(a).
600 CIV art.59(2)(b).
601 CIV art.59(2)(c).
602 CIV art.59(2)(d). cf. CIM art.47(2)(d).

senger who has sustained an accident, three years from the day after the accident. In the case of other claimants, actions are barred three years from the day after the death of the passenger or five years from the day after the accident, whichever is the earlier.[603] As regards all other claims, the period of limitation shall be one year (or two years in the case of wilful misconduct) (a) in the case of compensation for loss, from the 14th day after the person entitled calls for delivery; (b) in the case of compensation for partial loss, damage or delay in delivery, from the day when delivery took place; and (c) in all other cases involving the carriage of passengers, from the day of expiry of the validity of the ticket.[604] When a claim is made in writing to the carrier, the limitation period is suspended until the carrier against whom the claim has been made rejects it in writing.[605]

(d)   Goods by Road

36-118   **Application to the United Kingdom of the CMR Convention**   The Carriage of Goods by Road Act 1965 by s.1, enacts as part of the law of the United Kingdom the Geneva Convention on the Contract for the International Carriage of Goods by Road of 1956,[606] familiarly known as CMR, the substantive provisions of CMR being set out in the Schedule to the Act.[607] The Act came into force on June 5, 1967,[608] and has been extended to Gibraltar, the Isle of Man and Guernsey by Order in Council.[609] The 1965 Act was amended in certain respects by the Carriage by Air and Road Act 1979[610] in order to give effect as part of English law to a Protocol[611] adopted at Geneva in 1978–1979 which had amended the Convention.[612] Those parts of the 1979 Act which amended the 1965 Act came into force on December 28, 1980,[613] when the Protocol itself entered into force. Those parts of the 1979 Act have been extended to Gibraltar, the Isle of Man and Guernsey.[614] The 1965 Act, by s.2, gives power to Her Majesty by Order in Council conclusively to certify which states are parties to CMR: this power has been exercised.[615]

---

[603]   CIV art.60(1).

[604]   CIV art.60(2), (3).

[605]   CIV art.60(4).

[606]   Cmnd.3455; TS No.90 (1967). For the meaning of the abbreviation "CMR", see above, para.36-081.

[607]   See, generally, Hill [1968] J.B.L. 155; Fitzpatrick [1968] J.B.L. 311; Hill [1975] L.M.C.L.Q. 303; Donald [1975] L.M.C.L.Q. 420; Giles [1975] 24 I.C.L.Q. 379; Wijffels [1977] L.M.C.L.Q. 30; Hill [1977] L.M.C.L.Q. 212. For comprehensive accounts, see Donald, *The CMR* (1981); Clarke, *International Carriage of Goods by Road: CMR*, 6th edn (2014); Hill and Messent, *CMR: Contracts for the International Carriage of Goods by Road*, 3rd edn (2000); Clarke and Yates, *Contracts of Carriage by Land and Air*, 2nd edn (2008). For an appraisal of the problems of CMR as seen from particular national standpoints, see Loewe (1976) 11 E.T.L. 166, 311.

[608]   SI 1967/819.

[609]   SI 1967/820 (Gibraltar); SI 1969/1365 (Isle of Man); SI 1971/1743 (Guernsey). These Orders were made under s.9 of the Act. For the position of Jersey, see *Chloride Industrial Batteries Ltd v F &W Freight Ltd* [1989] 1 W.L.R. 823 CA.

[610]   1979 Act ss.3(3), 4(2) (4), 5 and 6(1)(b).

[611]   Cmnd.8138; TS No.6 (1981).

[612]   See below, para.36-130 (dealing with units of account).

[613]   SI 1980/1966.

[614]   SI 1981/604 (Gibraltar); SI 1981/1543 (Isle of Man); SI 1986/1882 (Guernsey).

[615]   Carriage of Goods by Road (Parties to Convention) Order 1967 (SI 1967/1683) as amended by SI 1969/385, SI 1973/596 and SI 1980/697.

The scope of CMR   CMR applies to every contract for the carriage[616] of goods[617]   **36-119**
by road in vehicles[618] for reward, when the place of taking over of the goods and
the place designated for delivery are situated in two different countries, at least one
of which is a party to the Convention.[619] CMR applies to any part of the agreed
international carriage even where the goods are carried on a vehicle which does not
leave its national territory.[620] The place of residence and the nationality of the parties are irrelevant,[621] as are their respective registered places of business.[622] The parties may have the same nationality.[623] Even if CMR does not apply to the carriage
contemplated by the contract, it is still open to the parties to agree to the application of CMR,[624] presumably in whole or in part. In that event, the fact that the carriage falls outside the scope of application of CMR set out in art.1 is of no
consequence. The Convention does not apply to carriage performed under the terms
of any international postal convention, to funeral consignments or to furniture
removal, nor does it apply to traffic between the United Kingdom and the Republic
of Ireland.[625] CMR does not cover every possible legal right or obligation arising

---

[616] In *Anon.* (2008) 43 E.T.L. 747, the Bundesgerichtshof held that a "contract of carriage" has an
autonomous meaning independent of national law. The Convention has been held to apply to an
umbrella agreement providing for multiple deliveries over a long period of time; there is no requirement that the Convention will apply only to those contracts where consignment notes may be issued contemporaneously with or soon after the contract is made: *Gefco (UK) Ltd v Mason* [1998] 2
Lloyd's Rep. 585. CMR will not apply to an existing relationship between the carrier and the
purchaser of goods, where the latter is not interested, directly or indirectly, in the contract of carriage:
Atlanta Companies, Judge & Dolph Ltd v Pvba Transport Leopold Laureys & Zonen (1996) 31
E.T.L. 843, Ghent.

[617] For the purposes of CMR, "goods" may include a trailer hauled by the carrier's vehicle if that is what
he contracted to carry: *NV Cobelfret v NV Transport Jaco* (1996) 31 E.T.L. 579, Antwerp.

[618] Defined in the Carriage of Goods by Road Act 1965 Sch. art.1(2). As to the limits of a contract of
carriage under CMR, see *Kruidenier Hzn CV v Vink CV* [1978] L.M.C.L.Q. 649, District Court,
Rotterdam. In *Anon.* (2006) 41 E.T.L. 228, Hof van Cassatie van België, it was held that where the
contract was silent on the mode of carriage and the circumstances were such that the parties did not
contemplate road transport, CMR was inapplicable. See also *NV DPD Belgium v Timmerman* (2011)
48 E.T.L. 82, where it was also held that courier services could fall within the scope of the
Convention.

[619] 1965 Act Sch. art.1(1). Jersey is not a "different country" from the United Kingdom for the purposes
of CMR: *Chloride Industrial Batteries Ltd v F & W Freight Ltd* [1989] 1 W.L.R. 823 CA. It is essential, for the Convention to apply, that the road carriage contemplated by the contract is
international. If the contract contemplated, for example, one road leg in one country and one sea leg
in another country, the Convention will not apply: *Princes Buitoni Ltd v Hapag-Lloyd Aktiengesellschaft* [1991] 2 Lloyd's Rep. 383.

[620] *NV Crowe and Co v Alliance Ass Cie Ltd* (1969) 4 E.T.L. 948, Hof van Beroep, Brussels.

[621] 1965 Act Sch. art.1(1).

[622] *Anon.* (1975) 10 E.T.L. 410, Oberlandesgericht, Celle.

[623] *Anon.* (1966) 1 E.T.L. 691, Landgericht, Bremen.

[624] *Princes Buitoni Ltd v Hapag-Lloyd Aktiengesellschaft* [1991] 2 Lloyd's Rep. 383, 385–386. Where
the CMR applies by agreement, rather than by the application of art.1, the parties are entitled to deviate from the terms of CMR (subject to any other restrictions applicable as a matter of national law):
Anon. (2013) 48 E.T.L. 619, BGH.

[625] 1965 Act Sch. art.1(4), (5) Protocol of Signature. As to the meaning of "furniture removal" in art.1(4),
see *Parr v Clark & Rose Ltd*, 2002 S.C.L.R. 222. In *Quantum Corp Inc v Plane Trucking Ltd* [2002]
EWCA Civ 350, [2002] 1 W.L.R. 2678 at [64], the Court of Appeal was dismissive of an argument
that the Protocol excluded the CMR Convention in respect of traffic between the UK and Ireland
even where the traffic took place in UK as part of an international carriage extending beyond the
UK and Ireland.

under a contract of carriage otherwise governed by the Convention; extraneous matters, such as liens, are governed by national law.[626]

36-120 Combined transport CMR applies where the vehicle is carried over part of the journey by sea, rail, inland waterways or air and the goods are not unloaded from the vehicle.[627] If, however, any loss, damage or delay in delivery occurs during the carriage by the other means of transport, and was not caused by an act or omission of the carrier by road, but by some event which could only have occurred in the course and by reason of that other means of transport, then, by art.2(1) of CMR, the road carrier's liability is not determined by the Convention, but by conditions prescribed by law for the carriage of goods by that means of transport.[628] In the absence of such conditions, the liability of the carrier by road is determined by CMR.[629] As CMR is intended to fit in with other Conventions governing carriage by other means of transport, reference may be had to those Conventions in cases covered by art.2(1) to establish the time at which carriage by road began or ended and carriage by the other means of transport was effective.[630]

36-121 Interpretation of the Convention CMR was somewhat loosely drafted. Consequently many provisions require judicial interpretation. The House of Lords has stated that the English text of the Convention, which is of equal authenticity to the French text, should be interpreted in a normal manner, unconstrained by technical rules of English law, or by English legal precedent, but adopting broad principles of general acceptation.[631] Assistance from the French text may be sought whether

---

[626] CMR occasionally, not always, specifies which municipal law applies. National legislation, however, should not be discriminatory against carriers from other EU Member States so as to offend art.76 of the EEC Treaty of Rome: *Anon.* (1993) 28 E.T.L. 592, Gerichtshof der Europäischen Gemeinschaften.

[627] 1965 Act Sch. art.2(1). In *Quantum Corp Inc v Plane Trucking Ltd* [2002] EWCA Civ 350, [2002] 1 W.L.R. 2678 at [15]–[18], [21], [62]–[63], the Court of Appeal, interpreting art.1, held that the CMR Convention applied to an international road leg which formed part of a larger contract where (a) the carrier promised unconditionally to carry by road and on a trailer; (b) the carrier reserved either a general or a limited option to elect to carry out some other means of carriage for all or part of the way; (c) the carrier left the means of transport open either entirely or as between a number of possibilities at least one of them being carriage by road; or (d) where the carrier undertook to carry by some other means but reserved either a general or limited option to carry by road. The concept of a contract for carriage by road embraced a contract providing for or permitting carriage of goods by road on one leg, when such carriage actually took place under such contract; the place of taking over and delivery under art.1(1) were to be read as referring to the start and end of the contractually provided or permitted road leg: at [39]. cf. *The OOCL Bravery* (1999) 35 E.T.L. 398, US District Ct SDNY. *Anon.*, Bundesgerichtshof (2009) 44 E.T.L. 196. See also *Anon.* (2013) 49 E.T.L. 228, BGH.

[628] *PVBA Transport Maes v NV Centraal Beheer Schadeverzekering* (1996) 31 E.T.L. 558, Netherlands. In *Anon.* (2011) 47 E.T.L. 87, the Oberlandesgerichtshof Düsseldorf held that a trailer in which the goods are carried, even without a tractor, is a vehicle for the purposes of art.2(1), that a fire on board a sea-going vessel is a typical risk for that means of transport under art.2(1), and that the Hague Rules are prescribed conditions within the sense of art.2(1).

[629] 1965 Act Sch. art.2(1). The Warsaw Convention may thus regulate aspects of a road carrier's liability in the case of road-air carriage. The Hague Rules have been applied to regulate the carrier's liability in road-sea carriage: *Thermo Engineers Ltd v Ferrymasters Ltd* [1981] 1 Lloyd's Rep. 200, 205. See, generally, Clarke, *International Carriage of Goods by Road: CMR*, 6th edn (2014), para.15.

[630] *Thermo Engineers Ltd v Ferrymasters Ltd*, above, at 204.

[631] *James Buchanan and Co Ltd v Babco Forwarding and Shipping (UK) Ltd* [1978] A.C. 141; *Hatzl v XL Insurance Co Ltd* [2009] EWCA Civ 223, [2010] 1 W.L.R. 470 at [33]–[34]. See, generally, Hardingham [1978] L.M.C.L.Q. 51; Clarke, para.3a. The House of Lords has approved a teleologi-

or not the English text is ambiguous.[632] Where the language used is capable of two interpretations, the court must seek to give effect to the intention of those who made the Convention.[633] There is comparatively little English authority on CMR.[634] Although there have been many reported decisions on the Convention in the courts of the Continental parties to CMR,[635] only limited guidance can be obtained from these as there has been no consistency of approach to matters of interpretation; on some provisions there are as many interpretations of CMR as there are contracting states.[636] Whilst the Court of Appeal has emphasised that English courts must nonetheless endeavour to interpret CMR as far as possible in the same way as in the courts of the Continental parties,[637] the House of Lords has warned of the dangers inherent in trying to assess a balance of foreign judicial opinion, especially where the decisions are not those of the highest courts.[638]

Consignment note Whilst the contract of carriage does not have to be written, **36-122** the contract must be confirmed by the making out of a consignment note[639] of which there must be three copies signed by the sender and the carrier, one copy being

---

cal approach to the interpretation of purely domestic statutes, unfettered by any rule requiring an exclusive reliance upon the occasionally inadequate words used in the statute itself: *Pepper (Inspector of Taxes) v Hart* [1993] A.C. 593. See Wijffels (2001) 36 E.T.L. 653.

632 *James Buchanan and Co Ltd v Babco Forwarding and Shipping (UK) Ltd*, above, at 152.

633 *James Buchanan and Co Ltd v Babco Forwarding and Shipping (UK) Ltd*, above, at 157; *Hatzl v XL Insurance Co Ltd* [2009] EWCA Civ 223, [2010] 1 W.L.R. 470 at [33]. cf. *Shell Chemicals UK Ltd v P & O Roadtanks Ltd* [1993] 1 Lloyd's Rep. 114, 115; affirmed on other grounds: [1995] 1 Lloyd's Rep. 297.

634 Most of the reported English decisions on CMR are referred to in the present text with the exception of *SCA (Freight) Ltd v Gibson* [1974] 2 Lloyd's Rep. 533; *Avandero (UK) Ltd v National Transit Insurance Co Ltd* [1984] 2 Lloyd's Rep. 613; and *London Tobacco Co (Overseas) Ltd v DFDS Transport Ltd* [1994] 1 Lloyd's Rep. 394, where the implications of a carrier's insurance cover against liability under CMR were discussed. The Court of Appeal has made significant contributions as far as the construction of the Convention is concerned: see, generally, *Ulster-Swift Ltd v Taunton Meat Haulage Ltd* [1975] 2 Lloyd's Rep. 502; affirmed [1977] 1 W.L.R. 625 CA; more fully reported at [1977] 1 Lloyd's Rep. 346; *James Buchanan and Co Ltd v Babco Forwarding and Shipping (UK) Ltd* [1977] Q.B. 208 CA; affirmed on different grounds [1978] A.C. 141; *Cummins Engine Co Ltd v Davis Freight Forwarding (Hull) Ltd* [1981] 2 Lloyd's Rep. 106; affirmed [1981] 1 W.L.R. 1363 CA.

635 Many decisions of the courts of the Continental parties to CMR on the interpretation of the Convention have been reported since 1966 in the periodical *European Transport Law*. The decisions are usually fully reported in the original language and have a headnote in English. Since 1974 some additional decisions of Continental courts have been reported in *Lloyd's Maritime and Commercial Law Quarterly*. Some of these Continental decisions are cited in the present text.

636 See, generally, Hill [1975] L.M.C.L.Q. 303; Hill (1976) 11 E.T.L. 182; Wijffels (1976) 11 E.T.L. 208; Loewe (1976) 11 E.T.L. 311: this last reference is to an authoritative commentary on CMR.

637 *James Buchanan and Co Ltd v Babco Forwarding and Shipping (UK) Ltd* [1977] Q.B. 208 at 213–214. See also *Ulster-Swift Ltd v Taunton Meat Haulage Ltd* [1977] 1 W.L.R. 625 at 631–632; *Fortis Corporate Insurance NV/Uni-Data Logistics BV/UPS SCS (Nederland) BV* (2009) 45 E.T.L. 101, Hoge Raad der Nederlanden. As to the influence (or lack of it) of Human Rights legislation, see *Re Deep Vein Thrombosis and Air Travel Group Litigation* [2002] EWHC 2825 (QB), [2003] 1 All E.R. (Comm) 418 at [180]–[182], [191]–[192], [229], [2003] EWCA Civ 1005, [2003] 3 W.L.R. 956.

638 *Fothergill v Monarch Airlines Ltd* [1981] A.C. 251 at 284. In *Morris v KLM Royal Dutch Airlines* [2002] UKHL 7, [2002] 2 A.C. 628 at [147], Lord Hobhouse said: "Whilst it is important to have regard to the international consensus upon the understanding of the provisions of international conventions and hence to what the courts in other jurisdictions have had to say about the provision in question, the relevant point for decision always remains: what do the actual words used mean?"

639 1965 Act Sch. art.4. The taking over of the goods is not a prerequisite to the formation of a contract of carriage: *Anon.* (1966) 1 E.T.L. 691, Landgericht, Bremen; or the application of CMR: *Gefco UK Ltd v Mason* [1998] 2 Lloyd's Rep. 585.

handed to the sender, one accompanying the goods, and one retained by the carrier.[640] The consignment note must contain a number of statements and particulars, including the names and addresses of the sender, the carrier and the consignee, the place and date of taking over the goods and the place of delivery, the description of the goods, the gross weight and the number of packages, and a statement that the carriage is subject to the provisions of the Convention.[641] The consignment note should also include a generally recognised description of the goods, if they are dangerous.[642] Other particulars which are pertinent to the contemplated carriage should be entered in the consignment note, such as carriage charges,[643] sender's charges, "cash on delivery" charges, insurance requirements, declarations of value,[644] and any other particulars which the parties deem useful.[645] The sender will be responsible for any losses, damages and expenses resulting from any deficiency or inadequacy in the particulars furnished in the consignment note.[646] On taking over the goods, the carrier is required to check the accuracy of such statements in the consignment note as to the number of packages, their marks and numbers and the apparent condition of the goods and packaging.[647] Where the carrier has no reasonable means of checking, he must enter his reservations, and the grounds for them, in the consignment note. He must also specify the grounds for any reservations with regard to the apparent condition of the goods and their packaging. These reservations do not bind the sender unless he has expressly agreed to be bound by them in the consignment note.[648] A carrier who does not make any reservations at the time at which the goods are handed over for carriage is presumed to have received them in good condition and has to prove that the damage established at the destination existed prior to the time at which he took them over.[649] When a carrier makes reservations concerning the apparent condition of the goods, they must be written on the consignment note when the goods are received. Reservations written on the sender's copy of the consignment note are inoperative

---

[640] Sch. art.5(1). Whether or not the consignment note is signed is a matter for national law determined by the rules of private international law: *Anon.* (2012) 48 E.T.L. 610, BGH. In the context of art.5(1), the "carrier" must be the original or contracting carrier. As to the difficulties which may arise when another consignment note is issued during the carriage, see *Harrison & Sons Ltd v R T Steward Transport Ltd* (1993) 28 E.T.L. 747, where the court placed more importance on the original consignment note in the context of art.34 (see below, para.36-135).

[641] Sch. art.6(1).

[642] Sch. arts 6(1)(f) and 22(1). See also the European Agreement concerning the *Carriage of Dangerous Goods by Road*, Cmnd.3769 (1968) and EU Council Directive 1994/55, November 21, 1994 on the approximation of laws within Member States concerning carriage of dangerous goods by road. As to the meaning of "dangerous", see *Anon.*, OLG Düsseldorf, January 23, 1992 (1992) Transp.R. 218; cf. *Effort Shipping Co Ltd v Linden Management SA (The Giannis NK)* [1998] 1 All E.R. 495.

[643] Sch. art.6(1)(i). See *T Comedy (UK) Ltd v Easy Managed Transport Ltd* [2007] EWHC 611 (Comm), [2007] 2 Lloyd's Rep. 397 at [60].

[644] Sch. art.6(2).

[645] Sch. art.6(3). See, for example, *Harrison & Sons Ltd v R T Steward Transport Ltd* (1993) 28 E.T.L. 747.

[646] Sch. arts 7(1) and 22(2).

[647] Sch. art.8(1). The carrier is not obliged to check the manner in which the goods were loaded (assuming that the carrier did not load the goods): *Generali Transports Assurances ea v Kuhne & Nagel ea* (2002) 37 E.T.L. 511.

[648] Sch. art.8(2).

[649] *SA De Zeven Provinciën v SPRL Ultra Rapid Wagner Freres* (1977) 12 E.T.L. 776, Commercial Court, Charleroi; *Anon.* (1993) 28 E.T.L. 745, Cass.

so long as the consignment note remains in the carrier's possession.[650] The sender may require the carrier to check the gross weight of the goods, their quality and the contents of the packages. The carrier may claim the cost of checking. The results of the checks must be entered in the consignment note.[651]

The consignment note as evidence of the contract The consignment note is **36-123** prima facie evidence[652] of the making of the contract of carriage,[653] the conditions of the contract and the receipt of the goods by the carrier[654]; and of the identity of the parties to the contract[655]; but the absence, irregularity or loss of the consignment note does not affect the existence or validity of the contract of carriage which remains subject to the provisions of the Convention.[656] However, if the consignment note does not contain the required statement that the carriage is subject to the provisions of the Convention, the carrier is liable for all expenses, loss and damage sustained through such omission by the person entitled to dispose of the goods,[657] i.e. he cannot rely on the limitations on his liability mentioned below.[658] This is a less drastic penalty than the similar one provided in the Warsaw Convention on Contracts of Carriage by Air,[659] because it does not apply automatically, but only if the claimant is prejudiced by the omission.

Sender's right of disposal The sender has the right to "dispose" of the goods, in **36-124** particular by asking the carrier to stop them in transit, to change the place of delivery or to substitute another consignee.[660] Article 12(5) of the Convention requires the right of disposal to be exercised by compliance with three conditions: first, the first (the sender's) copy of the consignment note must have the instruc-

---

[650] *NV Alptripan v NV Ruys and Co* (1976) 11 E.T.L. 271, Commercial Court, Antwerp.

[651] Sch. art.8(3).

[652] Whilst the signature on the consignment note may be printed or in the form of a stamp (art.5(1)), the absence of a signature will render the consignment note of neutral (or at best prima facie) evidential value: *City Vintages Ltd v SCAC Transport International* Unreported December 1, 1987. cf. *Anon.* (1998) 33 E.T.L. 427, BGH.

[653] The Convention does not state when and where the consignment note must be issued, save that art.5 requires one copy of the consignment note to accompany the goods, which might suggest that the note should be made out prior to the commencement of the carriage (cf. *M Bardiger Ltd v Halberg Spedition APS* Unreported October 26, 1990). Such matters, however, will affect the probative value of the consignment note as evidence of the contract of carriage: *Electronska Industrija Oour TVA v Transped Oour Kintinentalna* [1986] 1 Lloyd's Rep. 49, 51; *Texas Instruments Ltd v Nason (Europe) Ltd* [1991] 1 Lloyd's Rep. 146.

[654] Sch. art.9(1). Despite the issue of a CMR consignment note, the presumption of the existence of a contract was displaced in *Ulster-Swift Ltd v Taunton Meat Haulage Ltd* [1975] 2 Lloyd's Rep. 502; affirmed [1977] 1 Lloyd's Rep. 346, 358 CA.

[655] *Aqualon (UK) Ltd v Vallana Shipping Corp* [1994] 1 Lloyd's Rep. 669. See *Anon.* (2001) 36 E.T.L. 947, BGH.

[656] Sch. art.4. See *Gefco (UK) Ltd v Mason* [1998] 2 Lloyd's Rep. 585. Art.4 does not apply to the relations between successive carriers: *SGS-Ates Componenti Elettronici SpA v Grappo Ltd* [1978] 1 Lloyd's Rep. 281, 284. See below, para.36-135. See, generally, Clarke, *International Carriage of Goods by Road: CMR*, 6th edn (2014), Ch.2.

[657] Sch. art.7(3).

[658] This refers to para.36-130, below, and perhaps also to paras 36-127—36-128, below; but the matter is far from clear.

[659] See above, para.35-067.

[660] Sch. art.12(1). Dicta in one English case suggest that where goods are damaged in transit and the sender on hearing of the damage requires the goods to be returned to him, he is exercising his rights under art.12(1). When his instructions are carried out there may be a "delivery" for the purpose of calculating the CMR limitation period under art.32(1)(a) (see below, para.36-143): *Worldwide Carriers Ltd v Ardtran International Ltd* [1983] 1 Lloyd's Rep. 61, 65.

tions given pursuant to the right of disposal entered upon its face and must be given to the carrier[661]; secondly, the instructions must be possible to carry out and must not interfere with the carrier's undertaking or prejudice the senders and consignees of the other consignments carried by the carrier[662]; thirdly, the instructions must not result in a division of the consignment.[663] As in the Uniform Rules (CIM) under Appendix B to COTIF,[664] this right of stoppage in transit is much more extensive than in English law, because it does not depend on the consignee being an insolvent buyer or on the sender being an unpaid seller; but, as under CIM, it presumably applies only as between the sender and the carrier, and not as between the sender and the consignee. The sender's right of disposal ends when that of the consignee begins. This happens when the second copy of the consignment note is handed to the consignee[665] or when the goods arrive at the place designated for delivery and the consignee requires the carrier to deliver the goods and the second copy of the consignment notes[666] or, when the goods having failed to arrive at the contractual destination, the consignee seeks to enforce his rights under the contract of carriage.[667] When instructions are given to the carrier in accordance with the Convention, the carrier is obliged to obey them.[668] A failure to comply with valid instructions will render the carrier liable for all resulting loss or damage.[669] When the right of disposal is exercised, it is exercised without regard to the requirements of contracts other than the contract of carriage.[670] This right may be exercised in breach of the contract of sale,[671] although the right of disposal may be instrumental in passing property in the goods being carried.[672]

---

[661] Sch. art.12(5)(a). It seems that this condition is not essential: *Anon.* (1985) 20 E.T.L. 349, BGH. Indeed, under art.15(1), where the consignee refuses delivery of the goods, the sender may exercise the right of disposal without producing the first copy of the consignment note. Nevertheless, save for situations covered by art.15(1), the carrier will obey the instructions of the sender without the first copy of the consignment note at his risk: art.12(7).

[662] Sch. art.12(5)(b). The "interference" must be more than merely incidental: Hill & Messent, *CMR: Contracts for the International Carriage of Goods by Road*, 3rd edn (2000), para.5.5–5.7; Clarke, *International Carriage of Goods by Road: CMR*, 6th edn (2014), para.32a(f). If it is not possible to carry out the instructions, the carrier must notify the person entitled to dispose of the goods "immediately": art.12(6).

[663] Sch. art.12(5)(c). Whether "consignment" refers to the goods covered by the consignment note or all the goods carried by the carrier is unclear. The former construction is preferable, because the rights of those interested in the other consignments are protected by art.12(5)(b). Contra Hill & Messent, *CMR: Contracts for the International Carriage of Goods by Road*, 3rd edn (2000), paras 5.5–5.6.

[664] See above, para.36-091.

[665] Sch. art.12(2).

[666] Sch. art.13(1). The vesting of a right of action in the consignee under art.13(1) does not result in the sender losing his right of action: *NV VAPO v SPRL Frigo-Express-Adriaenssens and Zonen* (1976) 11 E.T.L. 295, Commercial Court, Antwerp.

[667] Sch. arts 12(2) and 13(1). If the consignee exercises the right of disposal by nominating another consignee, that new consignee cannot name yet another consignee (art.12(4)), unless it is the original consignee (*Anon.*, Arrond. Amsterdam 16.2.66 S. & S. No.69). The consignment note may provide that the consignee has the right of disposal from the time the consignment note is drawn up: art.12(3). It is only in this last circumstance that the consignee is obliged to produce a copy of the consignment note in exercising the right of disposal: art.12(5)(a).

[668] Sch. art.12(1) and (2). cf. *Anon.* (2002) 37 E.T.L. 817, BGH.

[669] Sch. art.12(7).

[670] cf. *Kala Ltd v International Freight Services (UK) Ltd* Unreported June 7, 1988.

[671] *Benjamin's Sale of Goods*, 8th edn (2010), paras 21-063—21-065.

[672] *Aqualon (UK) Ltd v Vallana Shipping Corp* [1994] 1 Lloyd's Rep. 669, 677. The right of disposal provided for in the CMR Convention must be distinguished from the right of disposal referred to in the Sale of Goods Act 1979 s.19.

Delivery The consignment note must specify the destination of the goods and the **36-125** name and address of the consignee.[673] With this information, it should be possible for the carrier to deliver the goods in accordance with the contract of carriage.[674] The consignee has the right to call for delivery of the goods. Under art.13(1), the consignee is entitled to take delivery of the goods and the second copy of the consignment note upon production by the consignee of a receipt.[675] Nothing more is required from the consignee.[676] There is therefore little safeguard for the carrier if faced with a demand for delivery by a plausible, but fraudulent, consignee.[677] The carrier must not knowingly or recklessly deliver the goods to the wrong person.[678] Further, if the carrier's suspicions about the credentials of the "consignee" are aroused, the carrier must explore whether these suspicions are justified.[679] The carrier must exercise a high degree of care that the person to whom he proposes to deliver the goods is the named consignee.[680] If the carriage or the delivery of the goods is rendered impossible, the carrier must seek instructions from the person entitled to dispose of the goods.[681] If the goods are still in transit, the carrier may perform the contract by taking such steps which seem to the carrier to be in the best interests of the person entitled to dispose of the goods.[682] If the carriage or delivery remains impossible, the carrier may avail himself of the rights of unloading, storage and sale referred to in art.16 [683]

Loss, damage and delay The carrier is liable for loss (total or partial), damage **36-126** and delay in delivery in substantially the same circumstances as he is under CIM.[684] The general assertion of a carrier's liability in art.17(1) of CMR thus broadly cor-

---

[673] Sch. art.6(1)(d) and (e).

[674] If the carrier does not have adequate information in this regard, he is obliged (at least as a matter of English law) to make reasonable enquiries and take reasonable steps to locate the place of delivery and the consignee.

[675] And payment of or security for charges outstanding and shown on the face of the consignment note: art.13(2). In *T Comedy (UK) Ltd v Easy Managed Transport Ltd* [2007] EWHC 611 (Comm), [2007] 2 Lloyd's Rep. 397 at [52]–[53], [60], the Court held that art.13(2) effectively created a particular lien, allowing the carrier to withhold delivery pending the payment of or the provision of security for the unpaid carriage charges; insofar as the contract of carriage created a general lien, allowing the carrier to retain the goods pending payment of other debts, or a wider particular lien, the relevant provision would be void pursuant to art.41 (see below, para.36-148).

[676] Contrast the use of bills of lading and warehouse warrants.

[677] Given the liability regime imposed by the Convention: see below, para.36-126.

[678] *Sze Hai Tong Bank Co v Rambler* [1959] A.C. 576; *Anon.* (1991) 26 E.T.L. 359, Court of Cassation, France. See also *Lacey's Footwear (Wholesale) Ltd v Bowler International Freight Ltd* [1997] 2 Lloyd's Rep. 369, where the driver delivered the goods to thieves notwithstanding being instructed otherwise; in this case, the carrier was held to be guilty of wilful misconduct because of the act of the driver by virtue of art.3. cf. *Vesta Forsikring A/S v JN Spedition A/S* (1998) 33 E.T.L. 70.

[679] cf. *Stephenson v Hart* (1828) 4 Bing. 476.

[680] cf. the common law position: *M'Kean v M'Ivor* (1870-71) L.R. 6 Ex. 30; Clarke, *International Carriage of Goods by Road: CMR*, 6th edn (2014), para.35.

[681] Sch. arts 14(1), 15(1) and 15(3). In *Anon.* (2003) 38 E.T.L. 512, Oberster Gerichtshof Österreich, it was held that delivery was not prevented if the carrier was able to carry the goods to the destination by alternative means. In *NV Gebroeders Van Arde/NV SBTC - Sotramari* (2007) 43 E.T.L. 99, the Hof van Beroep te Antwerpen held that a driver who noticed a defect in the cooling system of the refrigerated container being carried, which was followed by a slight explosion, but did not notify the principal or ask for instructions in accordance with art.14(1), but instead continued with the transport and delivered container to destination, was in breach of art.14(1).

[682] Sch. art.14(2).

[683] See below, para.36-142.

[684] Sch. art.17(1); see above, para.36-093. Art.17(1) does not in any event exhaust the carrier's liabilities: see also art.7(3) (above, para.36-123) and art.21 (failure of carrier to collect "cash on delivery"

responds to the position of a carrier in English law, quite apart from the Convention. Nonetheless art.17(1) does not exclude the carrier's liability for non-performance or for loss of or damage or delay to something other than the consigned goods, provided, of course, that this has not resulted from loss of or damage or delay to the consigned goods, in which case CMR does limit or exclude liability.[685] The loss or damage must occur between the time at which the carrier takes over the goods and the time of delivery.[686] The goods appear to be taken over by the carrier for the purposes of this provision when they pass from the control of the sender to that of the carrier, irrespective of when the carriage begins. "Delivery" similarly is marked by the goods leaving the carrier's control and passing into the control of the consignee.[687] The passing of control is a question of fact in the individual case. The terms "loss" and "damage" are used in an ordinary sense. Consequently even very serious damage to goods falls to be assessed for compensation purposes as damage under art.25 of the Convention rather than being regarded as "constructive total loss" embraced by art.23.[688] Delay occurs when the goods have not been delivered within the agreed time limit[689] or, if none has been agreed, within a reasonable time.[690] If goods have not been delivered within 30 days of the agreed time limit or, if none, within 60 days of the carrier taking over the goods, this is conclusive evidence of loss.[691] The effect of these provisions is to make the limitation period

---

charge from consignee). Other liabilities may arise under national law. See, generally, Clarke at Ch.5; *Anon.*, Rechtbank te Rotterdam, March 30, 2016, (2016) 52 E.T.L. 101.

[685] *Shell Chemicals UK Ltd v P & O Roadtanks Ltd* [1993] 1 Lloyd's Rep. 114, 116; affirmed on other grounds: [1995] 1 Lloyd's Rep. 297 (driver mistakenly collected a tank of detergent instead of contractual consignment of particular liquid chemical); *NV De Dijcker/NV Sonatra* (2007) 42 E.T.L. 427, Hof van Beroep te Antwerpen. See also *Anon.* (1993) 28 E.T.L. 917, where it was held that a claim based on inaccurate information provided by the carrier as to the location and expected arrival time of his vehicle was a claim under national law and not under the Convention. The Court of Appeal has confirmed that the CMR regime is inapplicable to personal injury suffered in the course of carriage: *Noble v RH Group Ltd* Unreported February 5, 1993. In *Tiense Suikerraffinaderij ea* (2014) 49 E.T.L. 337, the Hof van Cassatie van België held that other types of loss are governed by national law. See also *Dalesi v VC Europe BV* (2016) 52 E.T.L. 567, Gerechtshof Arnheim-Leeuwarden.

[686] As to the meaning of "taking over the goods", see *NV De Dijcker/NV Sonatra* (2007) 42 E.T.L. 427, Hof van Beroep te Antwerpen.

[687] Sch. art.15(1) provides that where circumstances prevent delivery of the goods after their arrival at the place designated for delivery, the carrier shall ask the sender for instructions. Where art.15(1) applies, there is no delivery within art.32(a) and consequently no limitation period begins to run: *Moto Vespa SA v MAT (Britannia Express) Ltd* [1979] 1 Lloyd's Rep. 175, 180. cf. *Castrol Industries Belgium nv v De Rijke Vloeistoffentransport bv* (1999) 35 E.T.L. 544, Antwerp. See Clarke, *International Carriage of Goods by Road: CMR*, 6th edn (2014), para.37.

[688] *William Tatton and Co Ltd v Ferrymasters Ltd* [1974] 1 Lloyd's Rep. 203, 206; *Worldwide Carriers Ltd v Ardtran International Ltd* [1983] 1 Lloyd's Rep. 61, 63–64. When a carrier has to return damaged goods for repairs, such return carriage is covered by the original contract which has not been executed by reason of the non-delivery of the goods at their destination: *SA Soffritti Milan v Usines Balteau* (1977) 12 E.T.L. 881, Court of Appeal, Brussels.

[689] This time limit will be binding, provided that it has been agreed, even if it has not been included in the consignment note: *Anon.* (1994) 29 E.T.L. 97, BGH; cf. art.6(2)(f). This is not surprising, given art.5.

[690] Sch. art.19. This article emphasises the need for diligence in the making up of complete loads when partial loads are taken. The provisions in the Convention regarding compensation for delay presuppose performance (albeit late) of the contract by the carrier. They do not apply when the carrier has not performed the contract of carriage at all: *Gondrand SA v Agrati* [1978] L.M.C.L.Q. 518, Court of Appeal, Milan.

[691] Sch. art.20(1). cf. *Anon.* (2001) 37 E.T.L. 353, BGH. See Clarke at paras 56, 58.

in art.32(1)(b)[692] (which applies in cases of total loss) apply in cases where goods are damaged but not delivered.[693]

The carrier's exemptions from liability: art.17(2)   The carrier's exemptions   **36-127**
from liability are almost identical to those listed in CIM.[694] The burden of proof is
also substantially the same.[695] Thus the carrier is exempted under art.17(2) from liability for loss, damage or delay in the event of (1) a wrongful act or neglect of the
claimant[696]; (2) instructions of the claimant given otherwise than as the result of a
wrongful act or neglect of the carrier[697]; (3) inherent vice of the goods[698]; and (4)
circumstances which the carrier could not avoid and the consequences of which he
was unable to prevent.[699] The burden of proving any of these exceptions is on the

---

[692] See below, para.36-143.
[693] *Worldwide Carriers Ltd v Ardtran International Ltd* [1983] 1 Lloyd's Rep. 61, 65; *ICI Plc v MAT Transport Ltd* [1987] 1 Lloyd's Rep. 354, 360. cf. *Royal Insurance Cie v Transport R Marcel* (1978) 13 E.T.L. 742, Tribunal de Commerce, Paris.
[694] Sch. art.17(2), (3) and (4): see generally, *Ulster-Swift Ltd v Taunton Meat Haulage Ltd* [1975] 2 Lloyd's Rep. 502: affirmed [1977] 1 Lloyd's Rep. 346 CA; Clarke at Ch.6. As to the relationship between art.17(2) and art.17(3), see *Wulck und Co v Chapman and Ball (International) Ltd* [1980] 2 Lloyd's Rep. 279, 282–283. See above, para.36-093.
[695] Sch. art.18. See Clarke at Ch.6.
[696] Whether the word "claimant" in this context refers to the person bringing the claim or those interested in the goods (that is, any person who might bring a claim under the contract) is unclear and subject to debate (Hill & Messent at para.6.16). Notwithstanding the unfortunate language used, the purpose of the Convention is to provide a defence to the carrier in circumstances where those interested in the goods or possessed of the right of disposal are responsible for the losses claimed. It is sug-gested that the latter construction is preferable (*Anon.* (1982) B.T. 73 App. Paris). Otherwise, absurd situations may arise, for example, where the carrier is faced with a claim by both the sender and the consignee. If the former construction were correct, the carrier could not avoid liability (if no other defence were available). If the sender or consignee is prejudiced by the latter construction, he might have a right of action against the other under the relevant contract between them. This broad interpretation is not so broad as to defeat claims against the carrier which clearly are not contemplated by the Convention. See, for example, *Noble v RH Group Ltd* Unreported, February 5, 1993. In *Datec Electronic Holdings Ltd v United Parcels Service Ltd* [2005] EWHC 221 (Comm), [2005] 1 Lloyd's Rep. 470 at [127]; reversed on other grounds [2005] EWCA Civ 1418, [2006] 1 Lloyd's Rep. 279 at [28]; cf. [2007] UKHL 23, [2007] 2 Lloyd's Rep. 114 at [29], the court held that the consignment of a package worth more than U$50,000, pursuant to a contract which provided that the value of a package may not exceed US$50,000, did not constitute a wrongful act for the purposes of art.17(2).
[697] *Anon.* (1998) 34 E.T.L. 371, BGH.
[698] Frozen meat carried on a refrigerated trailer has been held not to have any relevant inherent vice within the meaning of art.17(2): *Ulster-Swift Ltd v Taunton Meat Haulage Ltd* [1975] 2 Lloyd's Rep. 502, 505–506: affirmed [1977] 1 Lloyd's Rep. 346, 351–352 CA. cf. *Centrocoop Export-Import SA v Brit European Transport Ltd* [1984] 2 Lloyd's Rep. 618.
[699] There is little English authority on this exemption. Where a carrier proved that goods and the trailer on which they were carried were stolen by violent armed robbers, he was held to have established his defence under art.17(2): *G L Cicatiello SRL v Anglo-European Shipping Services Ltd* [1994] 1 Lloyd's Rep. 678. The Continental courts have construed the carrier's exemptions under this head narrowly. See, generally, Loewe (1976) 11 E.T.L. 311, 312–364. Sudden, violent braking of the vehicle has been held insufficient to absolve the carrier from liability: *PVBAKC v PVBA Roeckens* (1972) 7 E.T.L. 1058, Court of Conciliation, Antwerp; *SA Soffriti Milan v Usines Balteau* (1977) 12 E.T.L. 881, Court of Appeal, Brussels. Theft of the goods similarly does not exempt the carrier: *Anon.* (1969) 4 E.T.L. 888, Bundesgerichtshof; *Kuhne and Nagel v Transports Internationaux Van Mieghem* (1974) 9 E.T.L. 330, Court of Commerce, Brussels; *NV La Préservatrice v Well Transport* (1969) 14 E.T.L. 924, Hof van Beroep, Antwerp; *Føroya Sjovatrygging v PK Transport* (1998) 33 E.T.L. 52, Supreme Court, Denmark; *Anon.* (1998) 33 E.T.L. 60, BGH; cf. *m/v Nord Cloud* (2006) 41 E.T.L. 79, Hof van Beroep te Antwerpen. However, a "wildcat", unlawful strike has been held

carrier.[700] When the court has to decide whether or not a carrier could avoid circumstances and prevent consequences within the meaning of art.17(2), the carrier who raises art.17(2) as a defence must show that he could not have avoided the loss, if he is to escape the primary liability imposed on him by art.17(1). The carrier cannot escape liability by showing that he has complied with common practice if he could, by taking precautions, have prevented the loss. Whether or not he has shown due diligence or behaved reasonably by reference to the standards applied in the tort of negligence is not relevant.[701] Article 17(2) requires a carrier to attain a standard somewhere between taking every conceivable precaution, however extreme, and on the other hand doing no more than act reasonably in accordance with prudent carrier's practice. The words "could not avoid" are to be construed as having the rider "with the utmost care".[702] It is for the claimant to suggest (but not prove) what the carrier ought to have done and for the carrier then to rebut specific complaints thus put forward.[703] The exemptions under art.17(2) are not available to the carrier if the loss or damage arises by reason of the defective condition of his vehicle or the wrongful act or neglect of the person from whom he hired the

---

to relieve the carrier (*NV Westvlees v NV Saelens Intertransport Sitra* (1997) 32 E.T.L. 606). The carrier must particularise the unavoidable circumstances. If, e.g. the cause of a fire on a vehicle is unknown, the carrier's liability remains: *Transport van de Nederlanden v Zeilemaker's Transport-bedrijf* (1967) 2 E.T.L. 1013, Arrondissementsrechtbank, Alkmaar. The contributory negligence of other road users may not be a circumstance which the carrier could not avoid within the meaning of art.17(2): *Gebr H C en C J in'T Veen NV v Haluco BV* [1978] L.M.C.L.Q. 517, Court of Appeal, The Hague. A carrier has been exempted from liability under art.17(2) where goods were damaged or lost by reason of a traffic accident which the driver of the vehicle on which they were laden could not avoid under the circumstances even with the utmost care: *Anon.* (1975) 10 E.T.L. 516, Bundesgerichtshof. A tyre puncture has also been held to relieve a carrier of liability when the tyres were in good condition and had been checked both before and during the course of the journey: *NV Maatschappij van Assurantie v A J Koeneman* (1966) 1 E.T.L. 137, Arrondissementsrechtbank, Rotterdam. cf. *Anon.* (1993) 28 E.T.L. 293, Hof Antwerpen. However, in *'S-Hertogenbosch* (2014) 49 E.T.L. 701, the Gerechtshof held that a principal carrier was liable for the actions of a fraudster who pretended to be someone else and who was engaged by the principal carrier through a digital freight exchange system and that the carrier could not invoke this exemption, because it had chosen to use the exchange.

700 1965 Act Sch. art.18(1). This burden was discharged in *Centrocoop Export-Import SA v Brit European Transport Ltd* [1984] 2 Lloyd's Rep. 618. Under art.17(3) the carrier is not relieved of liability if the condition of the vehicle used by him to perform the carriage was defective. See *Walek & Co v Chapman Ball (International) Ltd* [1980] 2 Lloyd's Rep. 279. In addition, the carrier will not be able to avoid liability if the vehicle is unsuitable for the carriage of the particular goods in the carrier's charge: *Anon.* (1994) 29 E.T.L. 669, Cass.

701 *Michael Galley Footwear Ltd v Iaboni* [1982] 2 All E.R. 200, 206; *Thermo Engineers Ltd v Ferrymasters Ltd* [1981] 1 W.L.R. 1470, 1478–1479; *NV Valkeniersnatie v NV International Services and Freightforwarding* (2006) 41 E.T.L. 272, Hof van Beroep te Antwerpen. cf. *Sidney G Jones Ltd v Martin Bencher Ltd* [1986] 1 Lloyd's Rep. 54.

702 *JJ Silber Ltd v Islander Trucking Ltd* [1985] 2 Lloyd's Rep. 243, 247. Indeed, in The Netherlands, it has been held that where the carrier parked his lorry at night beside the gates of an illuminated industrial park and failed to drive for a further 50–60 km to a secure parking area, even though so to do would have breached—without any danger to road safety—the rules as to driving time, the carrier had not demonstrated that he acted carefully to avoid the loss: *Gebr Oegema BV v Amev Schadeverzekering NV* (1998) 34 E.T.L. 82. See also *Anon.* (1998) 34 E.T.L. 109, BGH; cf. *Anon.* (1997) 33 E.T.L. 829, BGH; *Anon.* (2013) 49 E.T.L. 334, Oberster Gerichtshof Österreich.

703 *JJ Silber Ltd v Islander Trucking Ltd* [1985] 2 Lloyd's Rep. 243, 247. In *GL Cicatiello SRL v Anglo European Shipping Services Ltd* [1994] 1 Lloyd's Rep. 678, the court rejected the claimants' suggestions that the carrier should have had installed a variety of security devices, had a second driver and sought a secure lorry park on the motorway from Rome to Naples, because the loss would have occurred in any event. cf. *M. Bardiger Ltd v Halberg Spedition APS* Unreported October 26, 1990; *National Semiconductors (UK) Ltd v UPS Ltd* [1996] 2 Lloyd's Rep. 212.

vehicle.[704] Where the relevant loss or damage is caused in part by the carrier's conduct for which he is liable and in part by one or more of the exempted causes, the carrier shall be liable only for that part of the loss or damage for which he is responsible, pursuant to art.17(5).[705]

The carrier's exemptions from liability: art.17(4)   The second type of excepted   **36-128** risks, embraced by art.17(4), covers loss or damage arising from the special risks inherent in one or more of the following circumstances: (a) carriage in open, unsheeted vehicles when their use has been expressly agreed and specified in the consignment note; (b) absence or inadequacy of packing of goods liable to wastage or damage if not properly packed[706]; (c) handling, loading, stowage or unloading of the goods by the sender, the consignee, or persons acting on their behalf[707]; (d) the nature of certain kinds of goods which particularly exposes them to total or partial loss or to damage, especially through breakage, rust, decay,[708] desiccation,

---

[704]   Sch. art.17(3). See *NW Ewals Cargo Care v Lear Corp Ltd* (2009) 45 E.T.L. 426, Hof van Beroep te Antwerpen. Given its subject matter and its location within the article, this provision does not apply to the defences under art.17(4): Clarke, *International Transport*, para.75f. See *Anon.* (2001) 38 E.T.L. 131, Oberster Gerichtshof Österreich; *Anon.* (2004) 39 E.T.L. 244, Oberster Gerichtshof Österreich; *NV De Dijcker/NV Sonatra* (2007) 42 E.T.L. 427, Hof van Beroep te Antwerpen.

[705]   *Anon.* (2007) 42 E.T.L. 766, Bundesgerichtshof.

[706]   This exemption was construed strictly in *Tetroc Ltd v Cross-Con (International) Ltd* [1981] 1 Lloyd's Rep. 192. cf. *Anon.*, App. Paris 19.10.93 (1993) B.T. 792. See also *Aquascutum Ltd v Europa Freight Corp* Unreported November 20, 1985; *Anon.*, Oberster Gerichtshof Österreich, April 27, 2016, (2016) 51 E.T.L. 560.

[707]   Whilst many decisions of Continental courts on the interpretation of art.17(4)(c) have been reported, these courts have differed widely in their approach. There has been a tendency to introduce legal concepts drawn from the particular municipal law. Some decisions suggest that the sender is always responsible for loading and stowage. Others make the carrier responsible and suggest that he has been guilty of a wrongful act and neglect if he has not checked loading and stowage, unless the parties agree contractually otherwise (*Anon.*, Oberster Gerichtshof Österreich, July 6, 2016, (2016) 51 E.T.L. 565), carried out by the sender. See, e.g. *Anon.*, Bundesgerichtshof, March 19, 2015, (2016) 51 E.T.L. 99. See Wijffels (1976) 11 E.T.L. 208, 211–229, for an analysis of Continental decisions interpreting art.17(4)(c) in 12 different ways. Whilst CMR does not expressly provide that unloading must be performed by the carrier, the carrier has been held responsible for unloading in the absence of stipulations to the contrary or exemptions resulting from the nature of the goods: *PVBA Wanman and Zorn v Transport Internationaux L'Essor Maritime Français* (1976) 11 E.T.L. 231, Hof van Beroep, Ghent. If the carrier notices during the carriage that the goods have been packed defectively within the meaning of art.17(4)(b) he must take all steps to avoid damage to the goods. Failure to do so will result in liability for any damage being apportioned between the carrier and the sender: *Anon.* (1976) 11 E.T.L. 261, Oberlandesgericht, Saarbrucken. A carrier who undertakes to unload goods is liable for the whole operation even if that carrier is a successive carrier: *Anon.* (1993) 28 E.T.L. 286, Hof Brussel. He should refuse to unload if in his view it is likely to prove dangerous. Alternatively, he should at least enter reservations: *SA Polysar France v Booy Clean Belgium* (1977) 12 E.T.L. 293, Commercial Court, Antwerp. Art.8 requires the carrier to check the condition of the goods and their packaging. Further, it has been held that art.17(4)(c) does not exonerate a carrier from checking the stowage of the goods performed by the sender. If the carrier performs the carriage, notwithstanding obvious inadequacies or defects in the stowage, the carrier will be liable for the resultant damage: *Anon.* (1993) 28 E.T.L. 618, Cass.; *GIE La Réunion Européene v SA Warin* (1995) 30 E.T.L. 688, Cass. However, it may be that the carrier is under no obligation to check the loading or stowage of the goods, if adequately performed by one who is accustomed to such operations (i.e. a specialist): *Anon.* (1993) 28 E.T.L. 768, Rechtbank van Koophandel te Antwerpen. See *Cigna Insurance Co of Europe v Intercargo NV* (1999) 34 E.T.L. 264. On the other hand, in *Anon.* (2007) 42 E.T.L. 766, Bundesgerichtshof, it was held that the carrier's liability would be reduced pursuant to art.17(5) where the carrier stowed the goods but subject to the sender's supervision.

[708]   The carrier was relieved of liability under this head in *Centrocoop Export-Import SA v Brit European Transport Ltd* [1984] 2 Lloyd's Rep. 618. As to the breadth of this defence, see *W Donald & Son*

leakage, normal wastage, or the action of moth or vermin; (e) insufficient or inadequate marks or numbers on packages; and (f) the carriage of livestock.[709] If the carrier establishes that the loss or damage could be attributed to one or more of these excepted risks, this is rebuttably presumed, provided that in (a) above there has not been an abnormal shortage or a loss of any package.[710] If a claimant rebuts, within the meaning of the second sentence of art.18(2), the presumption under the first sentence of that paragraph that loss or damage could be attributed to an excepted risk, the carrier is then liable for loss or damage under art.17(1). To disprove the presumption the standard of proof is that of the balance of probabilities.[711] The carrier under CMR art.18(4) is not entitled to the exemption granted by art.17(4)(d) above where he performs the carriage in a specially equipped vehicle, unless he proves that all steps incumbent on him in the circumstances with regard to the choice, maintenance and use of the equipment were taken.[712] Under art.18(5) the carrier, when carrying livestock, must show that he took all steps normally incumbent on him in the circumstances, despite the exemption in art.17(4)(f). There should be a reduction in the carrier's liability to the extent that the loss or damage was contributed to matters falling within one or more of the exemptions.[713]

36-129 **Sender's liability** The Convention identifies specified instances of liability which may attach to the sender under the contract of carriage. For example, the sender will be liable for loss, damage and expense caused by any inaccuracies in or inadequacies of the consignment note,[714] defective packing of the goods entrusted to the car-

---

(Wholesale Meat Contractors) Ltd v Continental Freeze Ltd, 1984 S.L.T. 182; *Anon.* (2013) 49 E.T.L. 213, Oberster Gerichtshof Österreich.

[709] See art.18(5) and *Hans Johan Kosta v Samson Transport Co A/S* (1997) 32 E.T.L. 230, Denmark.

[710] Sch. art.18(2), (3). Where a sender of dangerous goods has not informed the carrier of the nature of the danger and the necessary precautions and where this information has not been entered in the consignment note, the sender or the consignee has the burden of proving that the carrier knew the nature of the danger: art.22(1). The phrase *"could be attributed to"* means that the carrier need only prove that one or more of the excluded matters relied upon could plausibly have caused the damage, not that on a balance of probabilities the excluded matter did cause the damage: *Exportadora Valle de Colina SA v AP Moller-Maersk A/S* [2010] EWHC 3224 (Comm) at [24]–[26]. cf. *Hijka BV v Vermeulen* [1978] L.M.C.L.Q. 650 DC, Utrecht; *GIE Law Réunion Européene v SA Warin* (1995) 30 E.T.L. 688, Cass. See also *Hans Johan Kosta v Samson Transport Co A/S* (1997) 32 E.T.L. 230, Denmark. The carrier need not have entered reservations in the consignment note: *van Asten bvba v Mercator nv* (1999) 35 E.T.L. 386, Hof Cass., Belgium.

[711] *Ulster-Swift Ltd v Taunton Meat Haulage Ltd* [1977] 1 Lloyd's Rep. 346, 352; *Exportadora Valle de Colina SA v AP Moller-Maersk A/S* [2010] EWHC 3224 (Comm) at [24]–[26].

[712] When the court is considering whether or not a carrier has proved that he took all steps incumbent on him in the circumstances pursuant to art.18(4), the court can take into account not only the evidence adduced by the carrier as to the steps taken but also evidence as to the soundness or otherwise of the goods at the time of loading. Where the goods have admittedly deteriorated during the period of transport, the court is entitled to hold that the carrier has failed to discharge the burden of proof on him under art.18(4) if, on all the evidence, it was more likely than not that he had failed to take some unidentified step incumbent on him: *Ulster-Swift Ltd v Taunton Meat Haulage Ltd* [1977] 1 Lloyd's Rep. 346, 353. The court considered that this interpretation of art.18(4) was consistent with the view that in English law a claimant need not prove what was the precise, specific event by reason of which his goods were lost whilst in the custody of the carrier: cf. *Houghland v RR Low (Luxury Coaches) Ltd* [1962] 1 Q.B. 694. The court found that the carrier had discharged this burden of proof under art.18(4) in *Centrocoop Export-Import SA v Brit European Transport Ltd* [1984] 2 Lloyd's Rep. 618.

[713] Sch. art.17(5); *Anon.* (2007) 42 E.T.L. 766, Bundesgerichtshof.

[714] Sch. art.7(1).

rier,[715] the absence, irregularity or inadequacy of documents or information required to be given to the carrier for the purposes of customs or other formalities[716] and arising out of the carriage of dangerous goods, at least where the sender has failed to inform the carrier, and the carrier is not aware, of the dangerous nature of the goods.[717] Any other liability of the sender falls to be determined in accordance with the contract of carriage and national law.[718] The sender is also liable for freight (unless the contract provides otherwise). Such liability is not, however, one which can form the subject matter of a set-off against any liability owed by the carrier to the sender.[719] Unlike the liability of a carrier under the CMR regime,[720] compensation for the sender's liability is not subject to limitation.[721]

Upper financial limits of liability and measure of damages   Where a carrier is   **36-130** held liable for loss of the goods, the value of the goods is calculated for compensation purposes as being their value at the place and time at which they were accepted for carriage.[722] The value is fixed according to the commodity exchange price, or, failing that, the current market price, or, failing both, the normal value of goods of the same kind and quality.[723] The carrier's liability for loss of the goods is limited to 8.33 units of account per kilogramme of gross weight short,[724] unless

---

[715] Sch. art.10.

[716] Sch. art.11(2).

[717] Sch. art.22(2).

[718] cf. *Shell Chemicals UK Ltd v P & O Roadtanks Ltd* [1993] 1 Lloyd's Rep. 114; affirmed on other grounds [1995] 1 Lloyd's Rep. 297.

[719] *RII & D International Ltd v IAS Animal Air Services Ltd* [1984] 1 W.L.R. 573; *United Carriers Ltd v Heritage Food Group (UK) Ltd* [1995] 2 Lloyd's Rep. 269.

[720] Sch. arts 23–26.

[721] cf. *Shell Chemicals UK Ltd v P & O Roadtanks Ltd* [1993] 1 Lloyd's Rep. 114; affirmed on other grounds [1995] 1 Lloyd's Rep. 297. However, the time limitation provisions of the CMR Convention do apply to claims against the sender: art.32(1)(c); for example, see *Anon*, Arrond. Rotterdam June 5, 1992 (1993) S. & S. No.107; *AXA Assurances SA v Jan de Poorter bv* (2000) 35 E.T.L. 381, Hoge Raad der Netherlands; cf. *Van Vlierden L v Engelen V* (2000) 35 E.T.L. 671, Hof Cass., Belgium.

[722] Sch. art.23(1). See, generally, Clarke at Ch.8. CMR only provides compensation for loss of, or damage to, the goods carried. A claim for compensation for damage done, e.g. to the sender's or the consignee's tanks, cannot be brought within CMR: *English and American Insurance Co Ltd v Transport Nagels* (1977) 12 E.T.L. 420, Commercial Court, Antwerp. In *NV Valkeniersnatie v NV International Services and Freightforwarding* (2006) 41 E.T.L. 272, Hof van Beroep te Antwerpen, it was held that where a carrier was instructed to take out 100 per cent insurance, but failed so to do, he could not rely on the limits set out in art.23.

[723] Sch. art.23(2). Such exchange, market or normal value is a reference to the standard rate for the goods and ignores the peculiar situation of the goods in question: *Anon.* (1993) 28 E.T.L. 740, BGH. The current market price has been held not to include, e.g. any excise duty payable on the product sold in a home market: *James Buchanan and Co Ltd v Babco Forwarding and Shipping (UK) Ltd* [1977] Q.B. 208 CA; unanimously affirmed on this point: [1978] A.C. 141. Contra, *Anon.* (1994) 29 E.T.L. 360, Supreme Court of Denmark.

[724] Sch. art.23(3) as amended by the Carriage by Air and Road Act 1979 s.4(2). See *Topdanmark Forsikring A/S v DSV Road A/S* (2016) 51 E.T.L. 93, Supreme Court of Denmark. This section gave effect as part of English law, with effect from December 18, 1980, to a Protocol to CMR which entered into force on that date: see above, para.36-118. Prior to that time the unit used in the Convention was the gold franc: this franc had the same meaning as in the rail Conventions CIM, CIV and the Additional Convention CAV, which Conventions were abrogated when the new rail Convention COTIF entered into force on May 1, 1985: see above, paras 36-079—36-081. The Protocol which effected the changeover to units of account also added a new paragraph to CMR which became art.23(7) and which provided that the unit of account in the Convention was to be the Special Drawing Right (SDR) as defined by the International Monetary Fund ("IMF"). The amount speci-

the sender declared in the consignment note a higher value[725] or a special interest in delivery[726] against an agreed surcharge. The carrier must also refund the carriage charges, customs duties and other charges incurred in respect of the carriage.[727] The expression "the carriage" in this context is restricted to the carriage covered by the contract and does not embrace, for example, the return carriage charges and storage costs of goods damaged during the period of carriage covered by the contract.[728] The carriage charges, customs duties and other charges are refunded in full in the case of damage amounting to total destruction but only in proportion to the damage sustained in the event of damage not amounting to total destruction.[729] The carrier's liability for delay is limited to the carriage charges.[730] His liability for damage is the amount by which the goods have diminished in value, but may not

---

fied in art.23(3) is to be converted into the national currency of the State of the court seised of the case on the basis of the value of that currency on the date of the judgment or the date agreed upon by the parties. When, however, the amounts on which compensation under the Convention is based are not expressed in the currency of the country in which payment is claimed, conversion shall be at the rate of exchange applicable on the day and at the place of payment of compensation: 1965 Act Sch. art.27(2).

[725] Sch. art.24.

[726] Sch. art.26.

[727] Sch. art.23(4). The expression "other charges incurred in respect of the carriage" was construed by reference to the French text ("*les autres frais encourus a l'occasion du transport*") as meaning "any other expenses which the owner of the goods has to pay as a result of the carriage of the goods": *James Buchanan & Co Ltd v Babco Forwarding and Shipping (UK) Ltd* [1977] Q.B. 208 at 224, per Lawton L.J.: affirmed by the House of Lords [1978] A.C. 141. Lord Wilberforce (at 154) agreed that the English and French versions of art.23(4) are equally broad and loosely-drafted. They should, in his Lordship's opinion, be interpreted broadly so as to cover charges arising in the course of the removal from the failure of the carrier to carry in accordance with the contract of carriage. Viscount Dilhorne (at 158) construed the words "in respect of" as meaning "in consequence of" or "arising out of" in this context. See Clarke, *International Carriage of Goods by Road: CMR*, 6th edn (2014), para.98; *Anon.* (2004) 39 E.T.L. 93, Bundesgerichtshof. A survey fee incurred as part of the cost of realising the damaged value of goods falls within art.23(4): *ICI Plc v MAT Transport Ltd* [1987] 1 Lloyd's Rep. 354, 362; as do premiums for the insurance of the goods carried: *M Bardiger Ltd v Halberg Spedition Aps* Unreported, October 26, 1990. As to charges and duties due to the non-reconciliation of documents after the theft of goods during transport see, *Philip Morris Holland BV v Transportgroep Van der Graaf BV* (2006) 41 E.T.L. 804, Hoge Raad der Nederlanden. However, the cost of cleaning or destruction of the goods does not fall within art.23(4): *PB v O en A* (1999) 35 E.T.L. 566, Ghent. The plaintiff will be entitled to a refund under art.23(4) where the carrier is guilty of wilful misconduct, although the limitation "no further damages shall be payable" will not, in that event, apply: *Lacey's Footwear (Wholesale) Ltd v Bowler International Freight Ltd* [1997] 2 Lloyd's Rep. 369. See also *Transport Van Laer NV v Comexas Benelux NV* (2002) 37 E.T.L. 475; *Sandeman Coprimar SA v Transitos y Transportes Integrales SA* [2003] EWCA Civ 113, [2003] 2 W.L.R. 1496; *Philip Morris Products SA v Smidl SRO*, Unreported, November 17, 2017.

[728] *William Tatton Co Ltd v Ferrymasters Ltd* [1974] 1 Lloyd's Rep. 203. However in *James Buchanan & Co Ltd v Babco Forwarding and Shipping (UK) Ltd*, above, [1977] Q.B. 208 at 215, the Court of Appeal (per Lord Denning M.R.) expressed the opinion that, in light of their broader interpretation of the Convention, return carriage charges and storage costs should be allowed. See also *Thermo Engineers Ltd v Ferrymasters Ltd* [1981] 1 W.L.R. 1470, 1478.

[729] *William Tatton and Co Ltd v Ferrymasters Ltd* [1974] 1 Lloyd's Rep. 203.

[730] Sch. art.23(5). The compensation which may be awarded pursuant to this provision need not be the carriage charges themselves; the compensation is limited in quantum to the amount of those charges. The provision refers to "damage" resulting from delay. It is suggested that this is a reference to any financial deprivation suffered by the claimant, rather than to physical damage sustained by the goods: *Anon.* (1993) 28 E.T.L. 740, BGH. The claimant may recover both damages sustained directly or losses incurred as a result of his liability to another party: *Anon.* (1994) 29 E.T.L. 97, BGH. If goods are lost as a result of delay, it has been held that the limitation provisions under art.23(1)–(4) on the one hand and under art.23(5) on the other hand may be aggregated (*Deniz-Er v NV Soncotra* (2007) 42 E.T.L. 275, Hof van Beroep te Gent). This decision is to be doubted; see Clarke, *International*

exceed the amount payable in respect of loss.[731] The carrier is also liable to the sender for compensation for an amount representing the "cash on delivery" charge,[732] in the event that the carrier fails to collect that charge.[733] The court has power at any stage of the proceedings to make such order as appears to be just and equitable if the carrier's liability is limited, and may have regard to other proceedings which have been, or are likely to be, commenced in the United Kingdom or elsewhere.[734]

Wilful misconduct: an exception to limitation   Pursuant to art.29, the carrier **36-131** may not avail himself of the provisions excluding or limiting[735] his liability or shifting the burden of proof if the damage was caused by his wilful misconduct, or any default regarded by English law as equivalent to wilful misconduct. The burden of proof of wilful misconduct, of course, lies on the claimant.[736] Wilful misconduct appears to mean that the carrier or his agents or servants,[737] including the driver, has deliberately caused the loss or damage or was aware of the risk of loss or damage and ignoring that risk took no steps to avert it. For example, a driver who was well aware of the EEC Regulations governing the length of time for which it was permissible for a driver continuously to drive a vehicle, without rest, and who deliberately chose to ignore them, knowing that he was thus exposing himself, his load and other road users to a greater risk than if he complied with the Regulations, was held to

---

Carriage of Goods by Road: CMR, 6th edn (2014), para.59.

731 Sch. art.25. See generally, William Tatton and Co Ltd v Ferrymasters Ltd [1974] 1 Lloyd's Rep. 203.

732 Which should have been entered on the face of the consignment note (art 6(2)(c)). Given art.4, it is unlikely that the failure to enter the COD charge on the consignment note will deprive any contractual requirement that the charge be collected against delivery to the consignee of its force.

733 Sch. art.21. In Eastern Kayam Carpets Ltd v Eastern United Freight Ltd Unreported December 6, 1983, the court held that such a charge was not limited to freight and could extend to the price of the goods. The charge to be collected by the carrier could be in cash or in the form of a draft (Anon. (1970) 5 E.T.L. 670, Arrond. Breda). If the carrier is ordered to deliver the goods against receipt of a certified cheque, this order must be obeyed with all reasonable care to ensure that the carrier receives a certified cheque: Anon. (1994) 29 E.T.L. 464, Hof van Cassatie van België; cf. Eastern Kayam Carpets Ltd v Eastern United Freight Ltd, above; Anon. (1996) 31 E.T.L. 404, BGH. The COD charge would not include any document which did not represent payment of the charge (Eastern Kayam Carpets Ltd v Eastern United Freight Ltd, above). See also Coveretex v Dendertrans Int (1997) 32 E.T.L. 602.

734 s.3.

735 Sch. art.29(1); Although the carrier may still continue to rely on those provisions which "fix" his liability such as arts 23(1), (2) and 27(1), (2): Lacey's Footwear (Wholesale) Ltd v Bowler International Freight Ltd [1997] 2 Lloyd's Rep. 369; cf. art.28(1). Where art.29 applies to remove any limitation on liability, the plaintiff may recover loss of profits (Lacey's Footwear (Wholesale) Ltd v Bowler International Freight Ltd, above) or interest in excess of the 5 per cent limit provided for in art.27 (B. Paradise Ltd v Islander Trucking Ltd Unreported January 28, 1985). Such losses might be calculated in accordance with the applicable national law or arts 17–28: Anon. (2005) 40 E.T.L. 729, Bundesgerichtshof-Deutschland; Anon. (2010) 45 E.T.L. 625, Bundesgerichtshof. In Antwerp United Diamonds BVBA v Air Europe [1995] 2 Lloyd's Rep. 224, the Court of Appeal held, in the context of the Carriage By Air Act 1961, that the "misconduct" provision (similar to art.29) would permit compensation to be awarded in excess of the limit imposed by virtue of a special declaration of interest (which may be made under CMR pursuant to arts 24 and 26).

736 Sch. art.29(1). See Clarke at para.101; Datec Electronic Holdings Ltd v United Parcels Service Ltd [2005] EWCA Civ 1418, [2006] 1 Lloyd's Rep. 279, [2007] UKHL 23, [2007] 2 Lloyd's Rep. 114; Van Wijngen International BV v EFB European Freight Brokers VOF ea (2017) 52 E.T.L. 575, Rechtbank Rotterdam.

737 Sch. art.29(2).

be guilty of wilful misconduct within art.29(1).[738] On the other hand, it has been held by the Court of Appeal that there was no wilful misconduct merely because the driver was aware that he was sleepy and decided to continue to drive; if, however, the driver deliberately flouted the regulatory limits set for time and rest periods or was aware that he could not overcome his sleepiness (e.g. because his vehicle hit the side of the road), there would be wilful misconduct.[739] Where a carrier insisted that an employee should park a trailer carrying goods unattended in a public car park when he knew that there was a high risk of loss, he was held to have been guilty of wilful misconduct.[740]

36-132   **Scope of limitation provisions**   The CMR provisions relating to the limitation of compensation apply only in the event the carrier is liable for loss of, damage to or delay in the arrival of the goods placed in the carrier's charge.[741] The CMR provisions are relevant whether the carrier's liability arises under the contract or outside of the contract,[742] for example in tort or restitution. In respect of any other liability of the carrier[743] or any liability of any other party to the contract of carriage or at all, the CMR regime concerning compensation is inapplicable.

---

[738]   *Sidney G Jones Ltd v Martin Bencher Ltd* [1986] 1 Lloyd's Rep. 54, 58–60. The court applied the classic English authorities (such as *Lewis v Great Western Railway* (1877) 3 Q.B.D. 195; and *Forder v Great Western Railway* [1905] 2 K.B. 532) on "wilful misconduct" as a matter imposing liability on a railway where goods were carried at owner's risk. The court also relied on the well-known direction of Barry J. as to the meaning of the phrase "wilful misconduct" in the context of carriage by air under the original Warsaw Convention in *Horabin v British Overseas Airways Corp* [1952] 2 All E.R. 1016; see above, paras 35-035—35-039.

[739]   In *TNT Global SpA v Denfleet International Ltd* [2007] EWCA Civ 405, [2007] 2 Lloyd's Rep. 504. See also *Anon.* (2007) 43 E.T.L. 86, Bundesgerichtshof, where it was held that if the driver dozed off, that of itself was not wilful misconduct unless it was proved that the driver ignored clearly recognised symptoms of fatigue.

[740]   *Texas Instruments Ltd v Nason (Europe) Ltd* [1991] 1 Lloyd's Rep. 146. cf. *M Bardiger Ltd v Halberg Spedition APS* Unreported October 26, 1990; *Anon.* (1993) 28 E.T.L. 762, Rechtbank van Koophandel te Brussel. See also *National Semiconductors (UK) Ltd v UPS Ltd* [1996] 2 Lloyd's Rep. 212, 214–215; *Lacey's Footwear (Wholesale) Ltd v Bowler International Freight Ltd* [1997] 2 Lloyd's Rep. 369, where the carrier's employee's misconduct was not intentional, but "reckless carelessness"; *Alena Ltd v Harlequin Transport Services Ltd* (2002) 38 E.T.L. 218 at [29]–[31]. cf. *BVBA Transport Nys v NV Cigna Insurance Company of Europe EA* (1996) 31 E.T.L. 840, Brussels; *Nordland Transportkontor GmbH v Storebrand Skadeforsikring AS* (1996) 31 E.T.L. 563, Norway; *Anon.* (1996) 31 E.T.L. 703, BGH; *Micro Anvika Ltd v TNT Express Worldwide (Euro Hub) NV* [2006] EWHC 230 (Comm); *Anon.* (2006) 41 E.T.L. 668, BGH. See Wijffels (2001) 36 E.T.L. 653, where there is a brief survey of the differing interpretations given to "wilful misconduct" in the Contracting States. In Spain, Portugal, Belgium and The Netherlands, the carrier will not usually be deprived of his right of limitation if there has been no intention to deceive. In *Anon* (2012) 47 E.T.L. 556, the Hoge Raad der Nederlanden held that in order that the limitation should not apply, the carrier must have at least acted recklessly and with knowledge that damage would probably result. See also *Topdanmark Forsikring A/S v DSV Road A/S* (2016) 51 E.T.L. 93, Supreme Court of Denmark.

[741]   Sch. arts 23–26.

[742]   Sch. art.28(1).

[743]   For example, the failure by the carrier to perform the contract at all: *Anon.* (1994) B.T. 636 Comm. Carpentras; *Anon.* (1994) B.T. 736 App. Toulouse; cf. *Anon.* (1975) 10 E.T.L. 75, BGH. See also *Shell Chemicals UK Ltd v P & O Roadtanks Ltd* [1993] 1 Lloyd's Rep. 114; affirmed on other grounds [1995] 1 Lloyd's Rep. 297; *Anon.* (1993) 28 E.T.L. 917, BGH; *Noble v RH Group Ltd* Unreported February 5, 1993, where the Court of Appeal commented upon a late Respondents' Notice, holding that the Convention was not intended to regulate the carrier's liability for personal injury occurring during the carriage. See *Lacey's Footwear (Wholesale) Ltd v Bowler International Freight Ltd* [1997] 2 Lloyd's Rep. 369, as to the carrier's failure to comply with his obligation to insure the goods.

Interest   A claimant is entitled to claim interest on the compensation payable.   **36-133**
Article 27(1)[744] sets the interest recoverable at 5 per cent per annum and provides
that interest shall accrue from the date on which a claim in writing was sent to the
carrier, or in the absence of such a claim, from the date of the institution of legal
proceedings. The provision appears expressly to disallow interest accruing before
the written claim is made or legal proceedings are commenced.[745] Such a claim does
not have to be quantified; a general intimation of intention to hold the carrier liable is sufficient.[746] The date on which legal proceedings are commenced, so far as
English legal procedure is concerned, is the date on which the claim form is
issued.[747]

The parties to the contract   The Carriage of Goods by Road Act 1965 makes not   **36-134**
only the sender of the goods and the carrier parties to the contract, but also includes
as parties the consignee and any successive carrier and that carrier's employees and
agents.[748] This provision enables sub-contractors to obtain the benefit of exemption clauses in the principal contract of carriage. CMR in any event makes the carrier responsible for the acts and omissions of his employees and agents and of any
other persons of whose services he makes use for the performance of the carriage
when they are acting within the scope of their employment.[749] Such persons are
entitled to avail themselves of the provisions of the Convention which exclude or
limit the liability of the carrier.[750] The Convention does not itself list exhaustively
the parties to the contract. Whilst it does identify as parties the sender, the consignee

---

[744] This provision creates an entitlement to interest. The court has no discretion in the matter:
Elektronska Industrija Oour TVA v Transped Oour Kintinentalna Spedicna [1986] 1 Lloyd's Rep.
49, 53. See also *Frans Maas Groningen BV v Delta Lloyd Schadeverzekering NV* (1998) 34 E.T.L.
254, Netherlands; *Anon.* (2012) 48. E.T.L. 424, Oberster Gerichtshof Österreich. Art.27 also applies to claims under art.37: *Anon.* (2004) 39 E.T.L. 517, BGH.

[745] It seems also that interest at 5 per cent will run until payment is made (art.27(2)). Accordingly, it is
unlikely that interest at the Judgments Act 1838 rate will be allowed, although it appears that such
interest was awarded at first instance in *James Buchanan & Co Ltd v Babco Forwarding and Shipping (UK) Ltd* [1978] 1 Lloyd's Rep. 119 HL.

[746] *William Tatton and Co Ltd v Ferrymasters Ltd* [1974] 1 Lloyd's Rep. 203, 207; *Worldwide Carriers Ltd v Ardtran International Ltd* [1983] 1 Lloyd's Rep. 61, 66; *ICI Plc v MAT Transport Ltd*
[1987] 1 Lloyd's Rep. 354, 361.

[747] *Sidney G Jones Ltd v Martin Bencher Ltd* [1986] 1 Lloyd's Rep. 54. cf. *Dresser (UK) Ltd v
Falcongate Freight Management Ltd* [1991] 2 Lloyd's Rep. 557, where in the context of the Civil
Jurisdiction and Judgments Act 1982, service of the writ was held to be the operative date. Now see
Brussels I Regulation (Council Regulation 44/2001) art.30.

[748] s.14(2); see also Sch. arts 3, 28(2) and 34. See *M Bardiger Ltd v Halberg Spedition Aps* Unreported
October 26, 1990. CMR, however, will not apply to an existing relationship between the carrier and
a purchaser of the goods carried, where the latter is not interested in the contract of carriage: *Atlanta
Companies, Judge & Dolph Ltd v Pvba Transport Leopold Laureys & Zonen* (1996) 31 E.T.L. 843,
Ghent. In *Royal & Sun Alliance Insurance Plc v MK Digital Fze (Cyprus) Ltd* [2006] EWCA Civ
629, [2006] 2 Lloyd's Rep. 110 at [3], the Court of Appeal held that the contract was not one to which
the CMR Convention applied, because there was insufficient evidence that the claimant was a carrier, as opposed to a *commissionnaire de transport.*

[749] Sch. art.3. *Thermo Engineers Ltd v Ferrymasters Ltd* [1981] 1 Lloyd's Rep. 200, 206; *Noble v RH
Group Ltd* Unreported February 5, 1993; *Lacey's Footwear (Wholesale) Ltd v Bowler International
Freight Ltd* [1997] 2 Lloyd's Rep. 369. See also *Anon.* (1995) 30 E.T.L. 678, Tribunal Supremo
(Civil) de España. In *S-Hertogenbosch* (2014) 49 E.T.L. 701, the Gerechtshof held that a principal
carrier was liable for the actions of a fraudster who pretended to be someone else and who was
engaged by the principal carrier through a digital freight exchange system.

[750] Sch. art.28(2) which affords to such third parties the benefit of the CMR exclusion or limitation of
liability provisions in relation to extra-contractual liability. Although the Convention does not so
provide, it would be reasonable to assume that this protection of the exclusion and limitation provi-

and the carrier, it defines none of them.[751] Although the term "carrier" is not defined, the whole scheme of CMR supports the conclusion that "carrier" means someone who contracts to carry, irrespective of whether or not he in fact performs any part of the carriage in question. A person who has contracted to carry can perform the whole carriage by means of a sub-contractor whilst himself remaining liable under the Convention as a "carrier".[752] A freight forwarder is prima facie not a carrier under the Convention,[753] although he might be so regarded if he was himself to contract for the international carriage of goods by road, no matter what arrangements he made for sub-contracting. If the freight forwarder on the facts was the "sender" of the goods, as opposed to being merely the agent of the shipper or carrier, he might well be held to be subject to CMR under this head. All turns on what the freight forwarder contracted to perform on the facts of the particular case.[754]

36-135 **Title to sue** The Convention is also silent as to those who can invoke the carrier's liability. It seems clear that the person who concludes the contract of carriage with the carrier has a right of action, even if he has not himself suffered material damage. The sender will also have a right of action if he has suffered damage. Actions will normally be brought by the person entitled to dispose of the goods or

---

sions would extend to the third parties for whom the carrier is responsible under art.3.

[751] See, generally, Hill (1976) 11 E.T.L. 182, 192.

[752] *Ulster-Swift Ltd v Taunton Meat Haulage Ltd* [1977] 1 Lloyd's Rep. 346, 358–359, CA. cf. *Moto Vespa SA v MAT (Britannia Express) Ltd* [1979] 1 Lloyd's Rep. 175, 181; *Elektronska Industrija Oour TVA v Transped Oour Kintinentalna Spedicna* [1986] 1 Lloyd's Rep. 49.

[753] See *M Bardiger Ltd v Halberg Spedition Aps* Unreported October 26, 1990, where it was held that the CMR Convention does not apply to freight forwarders and any contract which they make, other than a contract of carriage.

[754] *Tetroc Ltd v Cross-Con (International) Ltd* [1981] 1 Lloyd's Rep. 192, 198 (freight forwarders held to be CMR carriers on the facts); *Kala Ltd v International Freight Services (UK) Ltd* Unreported June 7, 1988. See, generally, Clarke, *International Carriage of Goods by Road: CMR*, 6th edn (2014), para.10a. Where a CMR consignment note named a company as a carrier, the English court concluded that this was evidence of the identity of the carrier: *Aqualon (UK) Ltd v Vallana Shipping* [1994] 1 Lloyd's Rep. 669. There have been many divergent decisions of the courts of the Continental parties to CMR on the status of freight forwarders: see, e.g. *NV Koeltransport Rotterdam v Don Augustin Arxè* (1970) 5 E.T.L. 587, Gerechtshof, The Hague; *Anon.* (1971) 6 E.T.L. 273, Arrondissementsrechtbank, Rotterdam; *PVBA Mallentjer v NV Ruys & Co* (1975) 10 E.T.L. 235, Hof van Beroep, Brussels; *Schueremans v General Accident Fire and Life Ass Corp* (1972) 7 E.T.L. 865, Hof van Beroep, Brussels; *NV Marubeni-Lida v PVBA Kuhne and Nagel* (1974) 9 E.T.L. 608, Hof van Beroep, Brussels. A commission agent has been held not to be a carrier under the Convention: *Phoenix Assurance Ltd v NV Muller* (1969) 4 E.T.L. 1026, Tribunal de Commerce, Antwerp. As to the characteristics of a forwarding agency contract as opposed to a contract of carriage under the Convention, see *NV Hollandsche Assurantie v NV Gerlach Co* (1969) 4 E.T.L. 151, Gerechtshof, Amsterdam. A person to whom both international carriage of goods and the import and customs formalities are entrusted remains a CMR carrier even when he employs third parties to perform the actual carriage and personally only sees to the import and customs formalities: *Graphische Technik Bremen v NV Schenkers & Co* (1977) 12 E.T.L. 411, Commercial Court, Antwerp. The fact that a person describes himself as a forwarder and as offering "specialised trading services" and "full load and groupage services" does not imply that he is not prepared to make a contract of carriage as a principal. The method of invoicing may be of evidentiary significance: *Elektronska Industrija Oour TVA v Transped Oour Kintinentalna Spedicna*, above, at 52–53. Any party effecting carriage who draws up a freight invoice must by virtue of CMR art.1 be held to be a carrier rather than a forwarding agent, even if some other person carries out the actual operation of carriage: *SA Chemin de Fer Industriel Groups v Geszait* (1978) 13 E.T.L. 285, Commercial Court, Brussels. An organiser of a particular international carriage by road operation who was not instructed to perform the carriage personally but was told only to make arrangements for the carriage is an agent to whom CMR provisions are not applicable: *Soc Fratelli Gondrand v Lebole-Euroconf* (1978) 13 E.T.L. 407, Court of Appeal, Paris. See above, paras 36-005—36-006.

those claiming under him.[755] The consignee is given an express right of action against the carrier in the event of loss of the goods and (it seems) delay.[756]

Successive carriers   If carriage governed by a single contract under CMR is   **36-136** performed by successive road carriers, each of them is responsible for the performance of the whole operation, the second and each succeeding carrier becoming a party to the contract of carriage by his acceptance of the goods and the consignment note.[757] There is, then, joint and several responsibility.[758] A carrier can be a successive carrier under CMR even where he only carries out a national sector of the carriage.[759] The person with whom the sender, the consignee or another person interested in the goods makes a contract of carriage is the first or contracting carrier for the purpose of art.34 (and presumably, art.36) of CMR, whether or not he himself takes possession of the goods.[760] All subsequent carriers are likewise successive carriers within the meaning of the Convention, whether or not they in turn take possession of the goods.[761] Main contractors and sub-contractors may be successive carriers under CMR: the creation of this relationship will, however, depend on whether or not the sub-contractor becomes a party to the contract of carriage by accepting the goods and the consignment note.[762] The Convention appears, then, to create an artificial statutory contract between the person interested

---

[755] Sch. art.12(7). It is likely that the sender who has had the right of disposal would retain a title to sue, notwithstanding that the right of disposal has been acquired by the consignee. That is, both the sender and the consignee (and indeed any subrogated insurers) may claim damages on the basis of art.12: *Anon.* (1993) 28 E.T.L. 286, Hof Brussel. See the discussion in Hill & Messent, *CMR: Contracts for the International Carriage of Goods by Road*, 3rd edn (2000), para.5.8.

[756] Sch. art.13(1). *Texas Instruments Ltd v Nason (Europe) Ltd* [1991] 1 Lloyd's Rep. 146, 149. The English text of this article is somewhat ambiguous. The French text, however, confirms the view expressed in the text as to the consignee's right of action in the event of delay. See, generally, Clarke at para.40. After goods have been delivered to the consignee, he has a right of action in respect of damage to the goods without being required to prove that he has himself suffered loss: *Transport Internationaux Van Mieghen v Kuhne and Nagel* (1976) 11 E.T.L. 238, Court of Appeal, Brussels. The consignee also has a right of action where his identity may be deduced from a document attached to the consignment note: *Anon.* (1993) 28 E.T.L. 934, Hof Antwerpen. See also *GM De Rooy & Zonen International Transportbedriff Belgie v Philips Innovative Applications* (2007) 42 E.T.L. 390, Hof van Cassatie van Belgie.

[757] Sch. art.34. Carriers of goods in separate lots under separate consignment notes and governed by separate contracts are not successive carriers under a single contract within the meaning of art.34, even if employed by the same employer. Hence the presence within the jurisdiction of the English court of one carrier will not justify service on another carrier out of the jurisdiction in respect of that employer's claim to be indemnified for damaged goods in contribution proceedings under art.39(2) (see below, paras 36-140—36-141); *Arctic Electronics (UK) Ltd v McGregor Sea and Air Services* [1985] 2 Lloyd's Rep. 510. In England, it has been held that a sea carrier, who was sub-contracted by the road carrier who accepted the goods, could be a successive carrier under art.34, if the sea carrier became a party to the single contract for the whole of the carriage: *Dresser (UK) Ltd v Falcongate Freight Management Ltd* (1991) 26 E.T.L. 798; contra *NV Agfa Gevaert v NV Rhenus Belgium* (1989) 24 E.T.L. 574, App. Anvers. See also *Flegg Transport Ltd v Brinor International Shipping and Forwarding Ltd* [2009] EWHC 3047 (QB).

[758] *PVBA Transcom v Sasse Europa Auto Transport* (1975) 10 E.T.L. 419, Commercial Court, Brussels.

[759] *St Paul Fire and Marine Ins Co v SPRL Kuhne and Nagel* (1975) 10 E.T.L. 548, Commercial Court, Antwerp; *PVBA Wanman and Zorn v Transports Internationaux L'Essor Maritime Français* (1976) 11 E.T.L. 231, Hof van Beroep, Ghent.

[760] See *Anon.*, Hoge Raad der Nederlanden, September 11, 2015, (2016) 51 E.T.L. 109; Laurijssen (2016) 51 E.T.L. 121.

[761] Sch. arts 1(1) and 34; *Ulster-Swift Ltd v Taunton Meat Haulage Ltd* [1975] 2 Lloyd's Rep. 502, 508; affirmed [1977] 1 Lloyd's Rep. 346. cf. *NV Travaca v Roba Ltd* (1996) 31 E.T.L. 545, Belgium; *Anon.* (2002) 37 E.T.L. 809, Oberster Gerichtshof Österreich.

[762] *Muller Batavia Ltd v Laurent Transport Co Ltd* [1977] 1 Lloyd's Rep. 411, 415. *M Bardiger Ltd v*

in the goods and each successive or actual carrier.[763] The effect of art.34 is, therefore, to apply to each successive carrier the rights and obligations of "the carrier", as the term is used in arts 1 to 33 of CMR, save where the context makes it clear that only the first or contracting carrier is being referred to.

36-137 **Acceptance of consignment note** The term "acceptance of the ... consignment note" in art.34 should be given a natural and ordinary meaning.[764] Thus the consignment note, like the goods, is accepted when it is taken over by the carrier concerned with a view to carrying out the next part of the carriage pursuant to the terms of the consignment note. There can be an acceptance of the goods within the meaning of art.34 without a receipt being first given under art.35(1) by the accepting carrier, acceptance and the giving of a receipt being two distinct matters. Failure of the carrier to enter his name and address on the consignment note does not prevent acceptance of the consignment note under art.34.[765] It seems that a person cannot be a successive carrier under art.34 unless a consignment note is available for him to accept with the goods, and he accepts it.[766] Otherwise a carrier performing only a national sector of the carriage might assume that his obligations as a carrier were regulated

---

Halberg Spedition Aps Unreported October 26, 1990; *Union des Assurances de Paris v Planza Transports SA* (1995) 30 E.T.L. 675, Tribunal Federal Suisse; *Pauwels International nv v Alva Transport Salters nv* (1999) 35 E.T.L. 432, Mechelen. A successive carrier will be responsible for the acts of a sub-contractor (art.3). The sender has no right of action against a sub-contractor who is not also a successive carrier, under the contract of carriage between the sender and the carrier, at least under the CMR Convention and English law, although there may be a right of action under another national law (*NV Valkeniersnatie v NV International Services and Freightforwarding* (2006) 41 E.T.L. 272, Hof van Beroep te Antwerpen). The sender might have an extra-contractual claim against the sub-contractor, for example a claim arising out of the bailment of the goods to the sub-contractor, which bailment may be subject to the terms of the CMR contract of carriage (see, for example, *The Pioneer Container* [1994] 1 Lloyd's Rep. 593; *The Mahkutai* [1996] 2 Lloyd's Rep. 1); *Spectra International Plc v Hayesoak Ltd* [1997] 1 Lloyd's Rep. 153, [1998] 1 Lloyd's Rep. 162; *Sandeman Coprimar SA v Transitos y Transportes Integrales SA* [2003] EWCA Civ 113, [2003] 2 W.L.R. 1496. In the event of an extra-contractual claim against the sub-contractor, the latter can rely on the Convention's limitation and exclusion provisions (art.28(2)). If the sender has no right of action against the sub-contractor, he can sue the carrier, who is responsible for the sub-contractor's acts and omissions.

[763] *Ulster-Swift Ltd v Taunton Meat Haulage Ltd* [1975] 2 Lloyd's Rep. 502, 508; affirmed [1977] 1 Lloyd's Rep. 346, 358. *Aqualon (UK) Ltd v Vallana Shipping Corp* [1994] 1 Lloyd's Rep. 669, 673. It is possible that s.14(2)(d) of the 1965 Act extends the contract to persons for whom the carrier is responsible under art.3: *M Bardiger Ltd v Halberg Spedition Aps* Unreported October 26, 1990; contra, *Aqualon (UK) Ltd v Vallana Shipping Corp* [1994] 1 Lloyd's Rep. 669, 673. In *Harrison & Sons Ltd v RT Steward Transport Ltd* (1993) 28 E.T.L. 747, the court held, relying on the terms of s.14(2)(c) of the 1965 Act, that a "carrier" for the purposes of art.39 included a carrier who became a party to the contract of carriage whether by virtue of art.34 "or otherwise".

[764] In *Harrison & Sons Ltd v RT Steward Transport Ltd* (1993) 28 E.T.L. 747, the Court held that the "consignment note" referred to in art.34 was a reference to the original consignment note issued by the first carrier, and not a consignment note issued during an intermediate leg of the contractual journey. cf. *Dresser (UK) Ltd v Falcongate Freight Management Ltd* (1991) 26 E.T.L 798.

[765] *SGS-Ates Componenti Elettronici SpA v Grappo Ltd* [1978] 1 Lloyd's Rep. 281, 284. See, generally, Hardingham [1978] L.M.C.L.Q. 499.

[766] *Graphische Technik Bremen v NV Schenkers & Co* (1977) 12 E.T.L. 411, Commercial Court, Brussels; contra, *St Paul Fire and Marine Ins Co v SPRL Kuhne and Nagel* (1975) 10 E.T.L. 419, Commercial Court, Antwerp. *Harrison & Sons Ltd v RT Steward Transport Ltd* (1993) 28 E.T.L. 747; *Dresser (UK) Ltd v Falcongate Freight Management Ltd* (1991) 26 E.T.L. 798; *Parr v Clark & Rose Ltd*, 2002 SCLR 222. CMR art.4 dealing with the absence, irregularity or loss of the consignment note does not, seemingly, apply to the relationship between successive carriers.

only by municipal law or by his own trading conditions.[767] A successive carrier, however, can delegate to an agent or sub-contractor the task of accepting the consignment note for the purpose of art.34.[768]

Which carrier may be sued by those interested in the goods CMR envisages **36-138**
primary legal proceedings, seeking compensation under art.23(1) for breach of the contract of carriage, as being brought against a carrier by the sender or consignee of goods or by some person otherwise interested in the goods. Where there are successive carriers, such proceedings may be brought against the first or contracting carrier, the last carrier or the carrier who was performing that portion of the carriage during which the event causing the loss, damage or delay occurred, or any two or more of them.[769] A carrier can be a "last carrier" under art.36 even where he has not complied with art.35(1) in failing to enter his name and address on the consignment note accompanying the goods from a previous carrier.[770] A carrier may, furthermore, be a "last carrier" under this article even where he has issued a document covering the last stage of the carriage within the territory of a single contracting state.[771]

Proceedings against the carriers The effect of arts 31(1) and 34 is to enable a **36-139**
claimant to bring a single action against any or all of the carriers concerned. Such an action may only be instituted either (a) in a court of a contracting state agreed between the parties; or (b) in the court of a country where the defendant[772] is ordinarily resident, or has his principal place of business or the branch or agency through which the contract of carriage was made; or (c) in the courts of the place where the goods were taken over for carriage or the place where they were to be delivered.[773] Whilst art.36 limits the number of carriers against whom such primary proceedings may be instituted, art.34 seems to make a successive carrier potentially

---

[767] *SGS-Ates Componenti Elettronici SpA v Grappo Ltd*, above, at 284.
[768] *Coggins T/A PC Transport v LKW Walter International Transportorganisation AG* [1999] 1 Lloyd's Rep. 255.
[769] Sch. art.36. See, generally, *Cummins Engine Co Ltd v Davis Freight Forwarding (Hull) Ltd* [1981] 1 W.L.R. 1363, 1371 CA; *M Bardiger Ltd v Halberg Spedition Aps* Unreported October 26, 1990; *Sandeman Coprimar SA v Transitos y Transportes Integrales SA* [2003] EWCA Civ 113, [2003] 2 W.L.R. 1496; *Rosewood Trucking Ltd v Balaam* [2005] EWCA Civ 1461, [2006] 1 Lloyd's Rep. 429; Clarke at para.50. The restrictions of art.36 do not apply in the event of a counterclaim or the raising of a set-off in proceedings concerning the contract of carriage. As to the difficulties of raising a set-off against a claim for freight, see *United Carriers Ltd v Heritage Food Group (UK) Ltd* [1995] 2 Lloyd's Rep. 269.
[770] *SGS-Ates Componenti Elettronici SpA v Grappo Ltd* [1978] 1 Lloyd's Rep. 281, 284.
[771] *SA Precam v SPRL Independent Transport and Forwarding Agency* (1979) 14 E.T.L. 664, Tribunal de Commerce, Verviers. However, the carrier must accept the original consignment note in order to be treated as a successive carrier within the meaning of Ch.VI of the Convention: *Harrison & Sons Ltd v RT Steward Transport Ltd* (1993) 28 E.T.L. 747; *Dresser (UK) Ltd v Falcongate Freight Management Ltd* (1991) 26 E.T.L. 798. In France, it has been held that where a carrier has been instructed to perform the last leg of the carriage and that carrier does not participate in, but subcontracts, the actual performance of this last leg, that carrier will not be a last carrier for the purposes of art.36: *Skandia Insurance Company Ltd v Theo Adams Expeditie en Transport* (1995) 30 E.T.L. 685, Cass.
[772] In *Hatzl v XL Insurance Co Ltd* [2009] EWCA Civ 223, [2010] 1 W.L.R. 470, the Court of Appeal interpreted "*defendant*" as excluding insurers or assignees.
[773] Sch. art.31(1). See Clarke at para.50. In this respect, the allocation of jurisdiction pursuant to rules of the Civil Jurisdiction and Judgments Act 1982 is inappropriate, given the terms of art.71 of EC Regulation 44/2001: *Harrison & Sons Ltd v RT Steward Transport Ltd* (1993) 28 E.T.L. 747. cf. *Deaville v Aeroflot Russian International Airlines* [1997] 2 Lloyd's Rep. 67, 71 (Warsaw

liable in such proceedings for damage sustained during a portion of the carriage which he had not contracted to perform. It appears that the burden laid on a carrier by art.18(1) of proving that loss, damage or delay had occurred in such a way as to relieve him of liability under art.17(2) must be directly discharged by each successive carrier.[774]

36-140 **Carrier's rights of recovery from other carriers** A carrier who has paid compensation under art.23(1) of CMR may recover such compensation by way of contribution or indemnity, together with interest and costs, from other carriers under art.37.[775] This CMR contribution régime replaces that applicable under the Civil Liability (Contribution) Act 1978.[776] Provided that a carrier from whom contribution is claimed under art.37 has received due notice of the primary proceedings under CMR and has had an opportunity of entering an appearance therein, he cannot dispute the "validity of the payment made" to a claimant by the carrier seeking contribution from him if the amount of the compensation was determined by judicial authority.[777] The determination referred to in this context appears to be the determination of quantum. "Due notice" can, it seems, be given merely by letter.[778] Under the procedure of the English courts, a carrier receiving due notice of primary proceedings (assuming, of course, that he had not been made a defendant therein) could become a party to those proceedings if he wished to dispute the question of liability.[779] Whilst CMR is silent as to the extent to which a carrier receiving due notice of primary proceedings is bound by the determination therein of liability if he has not entered an appearance, he would seem to be estopped thereafter from denying liability in contribution proceedings.

36-141 **Contribution proceedings** Contribution proceedings are envisaged as being secondary to and consequential upon the main action. The procedure of the English courts, however, enables such proceedings to be brought by way of third-party proceedings in the main action, even if the carrier seeking contribution has not already paid the compensation.[780] The carrier must, however, pay the sender or

---

Convention). See below, para.36-146. However, it has been held that the Brussels Convention rules on *lis alibi pendens* (arts 21 and 22) (now arts 27 and 28 of EC Regulation 44/2001) continue to apply, because there are no provisions in CMR providing for parallel proceedings: *Frans Maas Logistics (UK) Ltd v CDR Trucking BV* [1999] 2 Lloyd's Rep. 179; *Royal & Sun Alliance Insurance Plc v MK Digital Fze (Cyprus) Ltd* [2005] EWHC 1408 (Comm), [2005] 2 Lloyd's Rep. 679 at [55]–[69]; reversed on other grounds [2006] EWCA Civ 629, [2006] 2 Lloyd's Rep. 110.

774 Subject, of course, to that carrier's right of recovery from other carriers concerned: Sch. art.37. See below, paras 36-140—36-141.

775 In *Rosewood Trucking Ltd v Balaam* [2005] EWCA Civ 1461, [2006] 1 Lloyd's Rep. 429, the Court of Appeal refused to allow a carrier who compensated the first carrier but who was not the first, last or responsible carrier within the meaning of art.36 to recover an indemnity from the responsible carrier.

776 s.5(1) as amended by Civil Liability (Contribution) Act 1978 s.9(1) and Sch.1; *ITT Schaub-Lorenz Vertriebsgesellschaft mbH v Birkart Johann Internationale Spedition GmbH & Co KG* [1988] 1 Lloyd's Rep. 487, 494.

777 Sch. art.39(1). See Clarke at paras 51–53.

778 *Cummins Engine Co Ltd v Davis Freight Forwarding (Hull) Ltd* [1981] 1 W.L.R. 1363 at 1374 CA.

779 e.g. under CPR r.19.2(2); see *Cummins Engine Co Ltd v Davis Freight Forwarding (Hull) Ltd*, above, at 1372.

780 *Cummins Engine Co Ltd v Davis Freight Forwarding (Hull) Ltd*, above, at 1372; *ITT Schaub-Lorenz Vertriebsgesellschaft mbH v Birkart Johann Internationale Spedition GmbH* [1988] 1 Lloyd's Rep. 487, 494 CA. See CPR Pt 20.

consignee before enforcing his right to recover against another carrier.[781] Article 37 provides that the carrier responsible for loss or damage should be solely liable for the compensation.[782] Where two or more carriers are responsible, each pays an amount in contribution proportionate to his share of liability. If no apportionment is possible, each responsible carrier is liable in proportion to his share of the payment for carriage.[783] If, however, it cannot be ascertained to which carrier liability is attributable, the amount of compensation is apportioned between all of them in proportion to their share of the payment for carriage.[784] In the absence of agreement to the contrary, separate contribution proceedings between carriers can only be brought before the courts of the country in which one of the carriers from whom recovery is sought is ordinarily resident or has his principal place of business or has the branch through which the contract of carriage was made.[785] These provisions apply only to recourse proceedings between carriers.[786] The jurisdictional provisions of art.31(1) do not apply to secondary contribution proceedings.[787]

Carrier's right to sell the goods　The carrier may sell the goods, without await- **36-142** ing instructions from the person entitled to dispose of them, (a) if the goods are perishable or their condition warrants such a course; (b) if the storage expenses would be out of proportion to the value of the goods; or (c) if after the expiry of a reasonable time he has not received from the person entitled to dispose of the goods instructions to the contrary which he may reasonably be required to carry out.[788] The proceeds of sale, after the deduction of the expenses chargeable against the goods, belong to the person entitled to dispose of the goods.[789]

Reservations at delivery and extinction of claims　If, upon taking delivery of **36-143** the goods, the consignee checks with the carrier the condition of the goods, the result of that check will be conclusive evidence of the condition of the goods at the time of delivery, unless any loss or damage sustained by the goods is not apparent and the consignee has sent to the carrier reservations in writing about the goods

---

[781] *ITT Schaub-Lorenz Vertriebsgesellschaft mbH v Birkart Johann Internationale Spedition GmbH*, above, at 494; *Frans Maas Logistics (UK) Ltd v CDR Trucking BV* [1999] 2 Lloyd's Rep. 179.

[782] "The carrier responsible" under art.37(a) must be a person who has made himself a party to the contract of international carriage: *ITT Schaub-Lorenz Vertriebsgesellschaft mbH v Birkart Johann Internationale Spedition GmbH*, above, at 493.

[783] See, generally, *Walek and Co v Chapman and Ball (International) Ltd* [1980] 2 Lloyd's Rep. 279.

[784] By Sch. art.38, a similar apportionment is provided in the event of the insolvency of one of the carriers.

[785] Sch. art.39(2): *Cummins Engine Co Ltd v Davis Freight Forwarding (Hull) Ltd* [1981] 1 W.L.R. 1363 at 1373, 1375. See, generally, Glass [1982] L.M.C.L.Q. 173. Art.39(2) of CMR does not provide for a compulsory and exclusive jurisdiction in disputes. See *British American Tobacco Switzerland SA v Exel Europe Ltd* [2015] UKSC 65, [2016] A.C. 262 at [36]–[37], [68]. It is presently open to question whether the jurisdiction provided for in art.39(2) is compulsory and exclusive: *Arctic Electronics (UK) Ltd v McGregor Sea and Air Services* [1985] 2 Lloyd's Rep. 510; contra, *Harrison & Sons Ltd v RT Steward Transport Ltd* (1993) 28 E.T.L. 747. Proceedings brought pursuant to art.39(2) would not require the leave of the court under CPR r.6.20: *Harrison & Sons Ltd v RT Steward Transport Ltd*, above. Whilst the carrier from whom a contribution is sought must be a party to the one contract of carriage (*Arctic Electronics (UK) Ltd v McGregor Sea and Air Services* [1985] 2 Lloyd's Rep. 510), it is not necessary that such a carrier is a successive carrier within the meaning of the Convention (*Harrison & Sons Ltd v RT Steward Transport Ltd*, above).

[786] *Anon.* (2007) 43 E.T.L. 94, Bundesgerichtshof.

[787] *Cummins Engine Co Ltd v Davis Freight Forwarding (Hull) Ltd*, above, at 1373.

[788] Sch. art.16(3).

[789] Sch. art.16(4).

within seven days of delivery.[790] Where the consignee takes delivery of the goods without checking their condition with the carrier and without providing reservations to the carrier, the fact that delivery has been accepted shall constitute prima facie evidence that the condition of the goods is that which is represented in the consignment note.[791] Such reservations must be sent to the carrier immediately (in the case of apparent loss or damage[792]) or in writing within seven days (in the case of loss or damage which is not apparent) and provide a general indication of the loss or damage sustained by the goods.[793] Such prima facie evidence may be controverted.[794] The acceptance of delivery in these circumstances does not mean that the consignee loses any right of action because of any failure to make a reservation.[795] Further, the taking of delivery will be evidence of the condition of the goods only so far as the interest of the consignee is concerned. No compensation is payable for delay unless a written reservation is sent to the carrier within 21 days from the time at which the goods were placed at the disposal of the consignee.[796] A failure to send such a reservation in the case of delay will result in the loss of a right of action.[797]

36-144   **Limitation of actions**   All actions arising from the contract of carriage are time-barred after one year, or three years in the case of wilful misconduct. As far as primary actions between owners of goods and carriers are concerned, art.32 provides that the period of limitation runs (a) in the case of partial loss, damage or delay in delivery, from the date of delivery; (b) in the case of total loss[798] from the thirtieth day after the expiry of the agreed time limit or, if none, from the sixtieth day from the date on which the goods were taken over by the carrier; and (c) in all other cases, on the expiry of three months after the making of the contract of carriage.[799] Article 32 is intended to be comprehensive and to cover all claims aris-

---

790   Sch. art.30(2).

791   Sch. art.39(1). The provision is inelegantly drafted by the use of the word "or", rather than "and": see *Transports Lesage et Compagnie SA v Transports Fromilhague* (1997) 34 E.T.L. 248, Cour de Cassation, France. Invisible damage, such as contamination of chemicals, can constitute inherent vice and can be the subject of reservations made within seven days of delivery of the goods. Provided that such reservations are made within that period, the absence of any protest in the consignment note at the time of delivery does not give rise to the presumption in the carrier's favour under art.30(1): *English and American Insurance Co Ltd v Transport Nagels* (1977) 12 E.T.L. 420, Commercial Court, Antwerp. See also Clarke [1982] L.M.C.L.Q. 533.

792   A verbal reservation is sufficient in the case of apparent damage: *Société Coop UTRAC v SPRL Legrand* (1970) 5 E.T.L. 716, Court of Appeal, Liège. Reservations are "sent" to the carrier within the meaning of art.30(1) if they are noted on the copy of the consignment note in the possession of and to be kept by the carrier: *Anon.* [1978] L.M.C.L.Q. 517, Court of Cassation, France.

793   *Anon.* (2004) 39 E.T.L. 400, Oberster Gerichtshof Österreich.

794   *Anon.* (1993) 28 E.T.L. 286, Hof Brussels; *Anon.* (1994) B.T. 623 App. Douai.

795   cf. *Anon.* (1993) 28 E.T.L. 265, BGH.

796   Sch. art.30(3).

797   *Anon.* (1993) 28 E.T.L. 265, BGH, where the court also held that the exceptions provided in art.29 were inapplicable to situations covered by art.30(3).

798   Total loss includes no more than what is called an actual total loss in s.57(1) of the Marine Insurance Act 1906. The concept of constructive total loss is not applicable to CMR: *ICI Plc v MAT Transport Ltd* [1987] 1 Lloyd's Rep. 354, 358.

799   Sch. art.32(1). See, generally, Clarke at paras 43–44. The limitation period applies equally to proceedings brought by and against the carrier: *Anon.* (1975) 10 E.T.L. 523, Bundesgerichtshof; *Anon.* (1976) 11 E.T.L. 266, Hof van Beroep, Amsterdam. As to claims in delict or tort, see *Anon.* (2005) 40 E.T.L. 878, Oberster Gerichtshof Österreich. CMR provides under art.15(1) that where circumstances prevent delivery of the goods after their arrival at the place designated for delivery,

ing under CMR.[800] When goods are damaged but not delivered (e.g. where, after receiving damage, they are returned to the sender), the period of limitation applied is that for total loss under art.32(1)(b), having regard to art.20(1).[801] Alternatively, if it is to be regarded as a claim for damage rather than loss, art.32(1)(c) applies in such a case, on the basis that it covers all cases where neither art.32(1)(a) nor art.32(1)(b) provides in the particular case a point from which the one-year CMR limitation period can run.[802] A written claim suspends the running of the period of limitation until such date as the carrier rejects the claim in writing.[803] In order to suspend the running of the limitation period, the claim holding the carrier liable must be notified to the carrier in an unambiguous manner by or on behalf of the person entitled to bring the claim and must be accompanied by such supporting documents so as to enable the carrier to define and pronounce his response to the claim, although it is not necessary that the claim describe precisely the level of

---

the carrier shall ask the sender for his instructions. Where art.15(1) applies, there is no "delivery" within the meaning of art.32(1)(a) and consequently no relevant period of limitation applies under the Convention: *Moto Vespa SA v MAT (Britannia Express) Ltd* [1979] 1 Lloyd's Rep. 175, 180 (see above, para.36-126). Combined road-sea transport is subject to CMR if the road transport is international within the meaning of the Convention. For the purposes of prescription, clauses in combined transport bills of lading are of no effect insofar as they conflict with CMR arts 31 and 32: *Atlas Assurance Co Ltd v Ocean Transport and Trading Ltd* (1976) 11 E.T.L. 279, Commercial Court, Antwerp; cf. *Agence Belgo-Danoise NV v Rederij HAPAG-Lloyd AG (The Hamburg Express)* (1976) 11 E.T.L. 691, Commercial Court, Antwerp; and *Atlas Assurance Co Ltd v Peninsular & Oriental Steam Navigation (The Osaka Bay)* (1977) 12 E.T.L. 843, Commercial Court, Antwerp.

[800] *Worldwide Carriers Ltd v Ardtran International Ltd* [1983] 1 Lloyd's Rep. 61, 65. See also *Frigo Express bvba v Frigo Traffic Company nv* (2004) 39 E.T.L. 521, Hof van Cassatie van België (claim by carrier against sub-carrier); *Transports Collomb Muret auto SA v Panini France SA* (2004) 39 E.T.L. 531, Cour de Cassation de France (claim by carrier against consignee); *NV Navex & Van Meerbeeck v BVBA Butti & Zonen* (2006) 41 E.T.L. 102, Rechtbank van Koophandel te Antwerpen (claim for customs debt); *Extra Logistics NV v Gebroeders Delhaize & Cie* (2014) 49 E.T.L. 341 (claim for storage charges after consignee refused to accept delivery). As to extra-contractual claims, see *NV Axa Belgium/NV Deceuninck Compound/NV AZO* (2008) 43 E.T.L. 379.

[801] *ICI Plc v MAT Transport Ltd* [1987] 1 Lloyd's Rep. 354, 360.

[802] *Worldwide Carriers Ltd v Ardtran International Ltd*, above, at 65. *Shell Chemicals UK Ltd v P & O Roadtanks Ltd* [1993] 1 Lloyd's Rep. 114, 116; affirmed [1995] 1 Lloyd's Rep. 297, 301. cf. *Royal Insurance Cie v Transport R. Marcel* (1978) 13 E.T.L. 742, Tribunal de Commerce, Paris. See, generally, Glass [1984] L.M.C.L.Q. 30.

[803] Sch. art.32(2). See Clarke at para.45. The term "claim" in art.32(2) refers to a claim for compensation when something has gone wrong in the course of the carriage. It does not refer to a request by one carrier against another, or against the consignor, for payment of the freight: *Muller Batavia Ltd v Laurent Transport Co Ltd* [1977] 1 Lloyd's Rep. 411, 416. A claim can be made within the meaning of art.32(2) by a damage assessor acting on behalf of parties interested in the goods: *SARL Prufer v Michel* (1977) 12 E.T.L. 300, Commercial Court, Mons; *Anon.* (1997) 32 E.T.L. 442, BGH (insurance broker). The burden of proof, inter alia, that a claim has been received rests upon the party relying on such an assertion: art.32(2). That burden was held to have been discharged in *Sidney G Jones Ltd v Martin Bencher Ltd* [1986] 1 Lloyd's Rep. 54, 64–65. A written claim does not require any particular formality: *Worldwide Carriers Ltd v Ardtran International Ltd*, above, at 66; *ICI Plc v MAT Transport Ltd*, above, at 361. For the purpose of art.32(2), a written claim may be sent to an agent of the carrier expressly or impliedly authorised to receive it, such as a carrier's liability insurer who is, on the facts, so authorised: *Poclain SA v SCAC SA* [1986] 1 Lloyd's Rep. 404, 406-407. A telex message holding the carrier liable is a written claim within the meaning of art.32(2): *NV Van Dijck v PVBA Welltransport* (1977) 12 E.T.L. 437, Commercial Court, Antwerp. See also *NV La Préservatrice v Well Transport* (1979) 14 E.T.L. 924, Hof van Beroep, Antwerp; *Anon.*, Cour d'Appel de Paris, December 14, 2011, Bulletin of International Carriage by Rail 1/2011, 6. A claim can be validly rejected in the carrier's name by a third party such as an insurance broker: *NV Rombouts Internationale Transporten v Vlatrex Continental BV* (1976) 11 E.T.L. 767, Gerechtshof, The Hague. A written claim which is not rejected suspends the limitation period as soon as it begins to run if it has not already begun to do so: *ICI Plc v MAT Transport Ltd*, above, at 361.

compensation claimed.[804] The owner of goods who wishes, when met by a plea of limitation, to set up suspension of the period of limitation, must show that the particular carrier relying on the time-bar has received a written claim from him or from someone acting on his behalf. A written claim made to the first carrier or to any one carrier does not suspend the running of the period of limitation against all carriers. A carrier obviously cannot reject a claim under art.32(2) unless it is made against him directly.[805] The rejection must be clear and unambiguous so that the claimant must understand that, time having been suspended since the claim was made, there has now come the time when the claimant must decide whether to start proceedings. The mere non-acceptance or non-admission of the claim is not sufficient. If the rejection is communicated in circumstances attracting privilege (for example, being marked "without prejudice"), the rejection will not restart the running of time within the meaning of art.32(2). In order to constitute a valid rejection for the purposes of art.32(2), the documents which were attached to the claim must be returned to the claimant; this requirement is not limited to such original documents as are provided by the claimant, but includes photocopies.[806] The period of limitation may also be extended in any of the ways applicable under the Limitation Act 1980.[807] A counterclaim served within the relevant limitation period stops time running under the Convention.[808] CMR however provides specifically that a right of action once time-barred cannot be exercised as a counterclaim or set-off.[809] Until a counterclaim has been served, a right of action by way of counterclaim is not exercised within the meaning of the Convention.[810]

36-145 Limitation of actions between carriers The limitation period applies to claims between carriers. The period begins to run either on the date of the final judicial decision fixing the amount of compensation payable under CMR, or, if there is no

---

[804] *Anon.* (1995) 30 E.T.L. 211, OGH; *Chatruco v Jura Belgie* (2010) 45 E.T.L. 623, Hof van Cassatie van Belgie. cf. *Sprl Transports Cremer v SA van de Casteele et Cie* (1996) 31 E.T.L. 833, Brussels. In *Delamode Plc v ECS European Containers* (2012) 48 E.T.L. 210, the Hof van Cassatie van België held that there was no requirement that the written claim state the amount of damage, provided that it contained sufficient information so as to allow the carrier to form an opinion as to the nature and quantum of damage so that the carrier can respond to the claim.

[805] *Worldwide Carriers Ltd v Ardtran International Ltd* [1983] 1 Lloyd's Rep. 61 at 66. Information imparted by one carrier to other carriers that a claim is being made against him by the owner of goods and that he intends to make a claim against those other carriers cannot constitute a "written claim" against those other carriers under art.32(2) in respect of a claim which the owners of goods are not making against those other carriers. See also *Sidney G Jones Ltd v Martin Bencher Ltd*, above, at 60–61.

[806] *Zerowatt SpA v International Express Company Ltd* Unreported October 6, 1989; *Microfine Minerals and Chemicals Ltd v Transferry Shipping Co Ltd* [1991] 2 Lloyd's Rep. 630. See also *NV Optitrade ea v NV Cat Benelux* (2004) 39 E.T.L. 407, Hof van Beroep te Antwerpen.

[807] Sch. art.32(3). See Vol.I, Ch.28.

[808] *Impex Transport Aktieselskabet v AG Thames Holdings Ltd* [1981] 1 W.L.R. 1547, 1552.

[809] Sch. art.32(4). The fact that CMR by arts 32(4) and 36 contemplates the possibility of a set-off or counterclaim does not exclude the operation of the general rule that a claim against a carrier in respect of loss of, or damage to, cargo or in respect of delay, cannot be asserted by way of a deduction from freight. The rule enunciated by the House of Lords in *Aries Tanker Corp v Total Transport Ltd* [1977] 1 W.L.R. 185 applies to contracts subject to CMR: *RH and D International Ltd v IAS Animal Air Services Ltd* [1984] 1 W.L.R. 573. See also *United Carriers Ltd v Heritage Food Group (UK) Ltd* [1995] 2 Lloyd's Rep. 269. As to air freight, see *Schenker Ltd v Negocios Europa Ltd* [2017] EWHC 2921 (QB), [2018] 1 W.L.R. 718.

[810] *Impex Transport Aktieselskabet v AG Thames Holdings Ltd*, above, at 1557–1558. See CPR Pt 20. See, generally, Rose [1982] L.M.C.L.Q. 33 and [1984] L.M.C.L.Q. 199.

such judicial decision, from the actual date of payment.[811] In the context of claims between carriers the term "carrier" means any person who contracts to carry. It is not restricted to claims between successive carriers within the meaning of art.34.[812] The courts have, however, emphasised that the term "claims" in art.39(4) embraces claims by one successive carrier against another in respect of that other's responsibility for something which has gone wrong in the course of the carriage where breach by that other of his obligations either to the consignor or to his predecessor as carrier has resulted in damage and a claim for compensation at the end of the line. The term "claims" has no application to claims between successive carriers in respect of moneys due not for breach of the contract of carriage (i.e. compensation for something which has gone wrong) but as payment for services duly performed. Articles 34 to 40 of the Convention are solely concerned with resolving the rights *inter se* of successive carriers where something has gone wrong en route.[813]

Jurisdiction   Article 31(1) prescribes those states in which legal proceedings may be brought in connection with any contract of carriage to which the CMR Convention applies, in addition to the state agreed between the parties,[814] namely the state of the residence of the defendant, the state where the goods are taken over by the carrier, the place designated for delivery of the goods or the state which has been agreed by the parties.[815] This is intended to provide a self-contained code for the allocation of jurisdiction,[816] so that Regulation (EU) 1215/2012 is inapplicable

36-146

---

[811] Sch. art.39(4).
[812] See above, para.36-135; *Ulster-Swift Ltd v Taunton Meat Haulage Ltd* [1977] 1 Lloyd's Rep. 346, 358–360; *Harrison & Sons Ltd v RT Steward Transport Ltd* (1993) 28 E.T.L. 747. cf. *NV Travaca v Roba Ltd* (1996) 31 E.T.L. 545, Belgium.
[813] *Muller Batavia Ltd v Laurent Transport Co Ltd* [1977] 1 Lloyd's Rep. 411 at 415.
[814] *Catlin Insurance Co (UK) v Gusia* (2013) 49 E.T.L. 222, Rechtbank van Koophandel te Antwerpen.
[815] A carrier who did not agree to a particular jurisdiction, and had no notice of a particular jurisdiction agreement, would not be bound by that agreement: *British American Tobacco Switzerland SA v Exel Europe Ltd* [2012] EWHC 694 (Comm), [2012] 2 Lloyd's Rep. 1 at [46]–[51], [2015] UKSC 65, [2016] A.C. 262 at [26]. Accordingly, a successive carrier cannot be sued in proceedings brought against the primary carrier pursuant to a jurisdiction agreement between the claimant and the primary carrier, if the successive carrier did not agree to that clause and if the jurisdiction agreement is not in the consignment note, subject to the other heads of jurisdiction in CMR: *British American Tobacco Switzerland SA v Exel Europe Ltd* [2015] UKSC 65, [2016] A.C. 262. In *Anon.* (2002) 37 E.T.L. 80, BGH, it was held that art.31 extends to extra-contractual claims. See also *Anon.*, Oberster Gerichtshof Österreich, February 25, 2015, (2015) 50 E.T.L. 700. Art.31(1) does not lay down any formal requirements for any jurisdiction agreement between the parties (cf. art.23 of EC Regulation 44/2001). Whether the factual requirement of an "agreement" on jurisdiction will be construed in the manner adopted by the European Court of Justice in the context of art.23 of EC Regulation 44/2001 is unclear. In *LSG-RA Leutner GmbH v BVBA Ideal Transport* (2006) 41 E.T.L. 570, the Hof van Beroep te Gent held that the parties are free to choose a jurisdiction without stating it in the waybill and that the agreement was to be adjudged by reference to national law; see, however, (2007) 42 E.T.L. 401, Hof van Cassatie van Belgie. There is much to be said in favour of a consistent approach, given the difficulties posed by multi-modal transport involving carriage by road (which in isolation would be governed by CMR) and by sea (which in isolation would require jurisdiction agreements to comply with art.23 of the Brussels I Regulation).
[816] *Arctic Electronics (UK) Ltd v McGregor Sea and Air Services* [1985] 2 Lloyd's Rep. 510, 514. Art.31 gives the plaintiff the option to choose the forum, so that the forum should not be able to exercise any otherwise available power to decline jurisdiction: cf. *Milor Srl v British Airways Plc* [1996] 3 All E.R. 537; *Deaville v Aeroflot Russian International Airlines* [1997] 2 Lloyd's Rep. 67, 72 (Warsaw Convention art.28). In *Ideal Transport v LSG-RA Leutner GmbH* (2007) 42 E.T.L. 401, the Hof van Cassatie van Belgie held that the choice offered by art.31 was cumulative and a contractual

insofar as the same rule is provided for in both conventions,[817] provided that the applicable rule in CMR is highly predictable, facilitates the sound administration of justice, enables the risk of concurrent proceedings to be minimised, and is construed harmoniously with the objectives of the Regulation, ensuring the free movement of judgments in the European Union.[818] In the event of more than one set of proceedings being commenced in more than one state, art.31(2) provides that the later action will not be entertained if it concerns the same parties and is brought on the same grounds.[819] The claimant may bring proceedings against the first carrier, the last carrier or the carrier who was performing that part of the carriage where the relevant loss, damage or delay has occurred.[820] When the defendant carrier seeks recourse against other carriers concerned in the carriage, such action is governed by art.39(2), which is more restrictive than art.31(1). Such recourse must (not may, as suggested by the provision itself) be brought in the state of residence of one of those carriers.[821] Article 39(2) is concerned only with actions among carriers and

---

choice of forum did not necessarily prevail.

[817] Council Regulation 1215/2012 art.71. This Regulation applies to proceedings instituted on or after January 10, 2015: Civil Jurisdiction and Judgments (Amended) Regulations 2014 (SI 2014/2947) reg.1. See *Harrison & Son Ltd v RT Steward Transport Ltd* (1993) 28 E.T.L. 747; *British American Tobacco Switzerland SA v Exel Europe Ltd* [2015] UKSC 65, [2016] A.C. 262; *Nickel & Goeldner Spedition GmbH v "Kintra" UAB* (C-157/13) EU:C:2014:2145, [2015] Q.B. 96 (CJEU). However, note the ECJ's decision in *Réunion Européenne SA v Spliethoffs Bevrachtingskantoor BV* [1999] C.L.C. 282, which concerned multi-modal carriage by sea, then land, and the application of the Brussels Convention. See *Anon.*, Oberster Gerichtshof Österreich (2003) 38 E.T.L. 656, 658, 661; *DFDS Transport A/S v Dieter Mehrholz Internationale Transporte* (2004) 39 E.T.L. 74, Supreme Court of Denmark; *Royal & Sun Alliance Insurance Plc v MK Digital Fze (Cyprus) Ltd* [2005] EWHC 1408 (Comm), [2005] 2 Lloyd's Rep. 679 at [55]–[69]; reversed on other grounds [2006] EWCA Civ 629, [2006] 2 Lloyd's Rep. 110.

[818] *TNT Express Nederland BV v AXA Versicherung AG* (C-533/08) EU:C:2010:243, [2011] R.T.R. 11. In the same case, the ECJ held that it did not have jurisdiction to interpret art.31 of CMR. See *British American Tobacco Switzerland SA v Exel Europe Ltd* [2015] UKSC 65, [2016] A.C. 262 at [48]–[58]. See also *Nipponkoa Insurance Co (Europe) Ltd v Inter-Zuid Transport BV* (C-452/12) EU:C:2013:858, (2013) 49 E.T.L. 165, ECJ, where it was held that art.31 must be interpreted in a manner which ensures conditions which are no less favourable than the objectives under the Regulation.

[819] *Andrea Merzario Ltd v Internationale Spedition Leitner Gesellschaft mbH* [2001] EWCA Civ 61, [2001] 1 Lloyd's Rep. 490. cf. the French text of the CMR Convention: *"pour la même cause"*. Arts 21 and 22 of the Brussels Convention have been held to remain applicable, because CMR does not regulate the matters of *lis alibi pendens*: *Frans Maas Logistics (UK) Ltd v CDR Trucking BV* [1999] 2 Lloyd's Rep. 179; *Royal & Sun Alliance Insurance Plc v MK Digital Fze (Cyprus) Ltd* [2005] EWHC 1408 (Comm), [2005] 2 Lloyd's Rep. 679 at [55]–[69]; reversed on other grounds [2006] EWCA Civ 629, [2006] 2 Lloyd's Rep. 110. This question was identified but not resolved in *Harrison & Son Ltd v RT Steward Transport Ltd* (1993) 28 E.T.L. 747. cf. *Deaville v Aeroflot Russian International Airlines* [1997] 2 Lloyd's Rep. 67, 71 (Warsaw Convention). See Council Regulation 44/2001 arts 27 and 28. In *Anon.* (2006) 41 E.T.L. 561, the Oberster Gerichtshof Österreich held that lis pendens must be assumed under art.31 where the respective claims are for negative declaratory relief and affirmative relief (contra *Anon.* (2004) E.T.L. 255, BGH; *Anon.* (2004) E.T.L. 264, BGH.

[820] Sch. art.36. However, art.36 is not a provision stipulating in which jurisdiction proceedings by cargo claimants may be brought; that is a matter for art.31. See *British American Tobacco Switzerland SA v Exel Europe Ltd* [2015] UKSC 65, [2016] A.C. 262 at [19]–[20], [34]–[47], [67], [69].

[821] See above, paras 36-140—36-141. *Harrison & Son Ltd v RT Steward Transport Ltd* (1993) 28 E.T.L. 747; *Cummins Engine Co Ltd v Davis Freight Forwarding (Hull) Ltd* [1981] 2 Lloyd's Rep. 402, 408–409; contra, *Arctic Electronics (UK) Ltd v McGregor Sea and Air Services* [1985] 2 Lloyd's Rep. 510, adopting the view of Eveleigh L.J. in *Cummins Engine Co Ltd v Davis Freight Forwarding (Hull) Ltd* [1981] 2 Lloyd's Rep. 402, 409. In *Blue Water Shipping A/S v Melship Eesti OÜ* (2000) 35 E.T.L. 772, the Supreme Court of Denmark held that art.39 referred to the residence of

not claims by cargo interests (whose claims are governed by art.31).[822] It appears not to be open to the carriers to agree an alternative forum for the determination of the carrier's recourse claim, except possibly arbitration.[823]

Arbitration   The contract of carriage may contain an arbitration clause if the clause provides that the arbitration tribunal shall apply the Convention.[824] There must be an express provision to this effect.[825] If there is a valid arbitration clause, the English courts will stay proceedings and refer the matter to the arbitration tribunal in question.[826]   **36-147**

No contracting out   Any stipulation which would directly or indirectly derogate from the provisions of the Convention is null and void,[827] but only to the extent of the derogation.[828] Successive carriers can agree among themselves as to their liability to contribution and the effect thereon of the insolvency of one of them.[829] Compensation under CMR must be assessed solely in accordance with the terms of the Convention itself, and the principles applicable to the assessment of damages at common law are irrelevant.[830]   **36-148**

---

the defendant successive carrier and not the claimant successive carrier. cf. art.40.

[822] *British American Tobacco Switzerland SA v Exel Europe Ltd* [2015] UKSC 65, [2016] A.C. 262 at [36]–[37], [62], [68].

[823] Sch. art.33, which gives force to an arbitration clause in the contract of carriage, will bind the parties to the contract of carriage. Such parties are identified in s.14(2)(c) of the 1965 Act.

[824] Sch. art.33. By s.7(2) of the 1965 Act as amended, the time at which an arbitration is commenced is determined by the Arbitration Act 1996 s.14(3)–(5).

[825] *AB Bofors-UVA v AB Skandia Transport* [1982] 1 Lloyd's Rep. 410, 413; *Inco Europe Ltd v First Choice Distribution* [1999] 1 All E.R. 820, 831 (a clause which required the arbitrators to observe "the applicable imperative legal stipulations including the provisions of international transport treaties" was held to be valid). However, see *Anon.* (2010) 45 E.T.L. 637, Oberster Gerichtshof Österreich. See, generally, Glass [1984] L.M.C.L.Q. 30.

[826] Arbitration Act 1996 s.9; *AB Bofors-UVA v AB Skandia Transport*, above, at 413.

[827] Sch. art.41(1). A carrier's general conditions of contract can never relieve him of his liability if such conditions derogate from CMR: *SA Chemin de Fer Industriel Groups v Geszait* (1978) 13 E.T.L. 285, Commercial Court, Brussels; *Datec Electronic Holdings Ltd v United Parcels Service Ltd* [2005] EWCA Civ 1418, [2006] 1 Lloyd's Rep. 279 at [24].

[828] *Datec Electronic Holdings Ltd v United Parcels Service Ltd* [2005] EWCA Civ 1418, [2006] 1 Lloyd's Rep. 279 at [24], [2007] UKHL 23, [2007] 2 Lloyd's Rep. 114 at [30]; *T Comedy (UK) Ltd v Easy Managed Transport Ltd* [2007] EWHC 611 (Comm), [2007] All E.R. (D) 469 at [52]–[53]; *Anon.*, Oberster Gerichtshof (2008) 44 E.T.L. 311. See also *Noble v RH Group Ltd* Unreported February 5, 1993, where it was held that liability of the carrier for accidents occurring during the unloading of the goods, as opposed to their carriage, and for personal injury was not intended to be regulated by the Convention and therefore any provisions dealing with such liability were not affected by art.41. Quaere whether unloading of goods may be equated with delivery so as to engage art.17; it would depend on whether the carrier is responsible for the unloading of the goods. In *Anon.* (2009) 45 E.T.L. 110, the Bundesgerichtshof held that a clause in the contract regulating the kind of goods which the carrier was not willing to carry was not in conflict with art.41.

[829] Sch. art.40. This permits carriers engaged in secondary contribution proceedings (see above, paras 36-140—36-141) to derogate from arts 37 and 38. Contractual provisions purporting to give exemptions from liability have been held valid as regards the mutual relationship between successive carriers: *Anon.* (1976) 11 E.T.L. 290, Landgericht, Duisburg.

[830] *William Tatton and Co Ltd v Ferrymasters Ltd* [1974] 1 Lloyd's Rep. 203, 206; *James Buchanan and Co Ltd v Babco Forwarding and Shipping (UK) Ltd* [1977] Q.B. 208, 219 CA: affirmed [1978] A.C. 141.

(e) Passengers and Luggage by Road

36-149 **Application and scope of the CVR Convention** The Carriage of Passengers by Road Act 1974 by s.1(1) was passed to enact, as part of the law of the United Kingdom, the Geneva Convention on the Contract for the International Carriage of Passengers and Luggage by Road (CVR) of 1973,[831] the main provisions of the Convention being set out in the Schedule to the Act. The Convention entered into force on April 12, 1994. The United Kingdom has not yet become a party to the Convention. In 2004, the 1974 Act was repealed by the Statute Law (Repeals) Act 2004.[832] The Convention applies to every contract for the carriage of passengers and their luggage in vehicles by road for reward when the carriage takes place in the territory of more than one state and the place of departure or the place of destination, or both, are situated in the territory a contracting state, irrespective of the place of residence and nationality of the parties to the contract.[833] The Convention applies where carriage by road is interrupted by another mode of transport, at least so far as the portions of carriage performed by road are concerned, even if such portions are not international.[834] It also applies to loss or damage caused by an incident connected with the carriage by the vehicle where the vehicle itself is carried over part of the journey by another mode of transport, provided that the loss or damage occurred either while the passenger was inside the vehicle or entering or alighting therefrom.[835]

36-150 **Transport documents** Where passengers are carried, the carrier must issue an individual or collective ticket showing the name and address of the carrier and containing a statement to the effect that the contract is subject to CVR.[836] The ticket is prima facie evidence of the particulars shown on it[837] but the absence, irregularity or loss of the ticket shall not affect the existence or validity of the contract of carriage, which remains subject to the provisions of the Convention.[838] The carrier is liable for any damage caused to the passengers by a breach of his obligations in relation to the ticket.[839] The ticket is, in general, transferable at any time before the journey begins.[840] The carrier may, and at the request of the passenger shall, issue a luggage registration voucher giving the number and nature of the pieces of luggage handed to him.[841] The voucher has to contain an express statement as to the applicability of the Convention.[842] Its issue is prima facie evidence that the luggage appeared to be in good order when handed over.[843] A carrier acting in good faith makes a valid delivery of the luggage if he delivers it to the holder of the

---

831 See above, para.36-082. See, generally, Hodgin [1976] L.M.C.L.Q. 1.
832 s.1(1) and Sch.1 Pt 14. The 2004 Act also repealed those parts of the Carriage by Air and Road Act 1979 which provided for the implementation of the Protocol to the CVR which was agreed in 1979.
833 CVR art.1(1).
834 CVR art.2.
835 CVR art.3.
836 CVR art.5(1) and (2).
837 CVR art.6.
838 CVR art.5(1).
839 CVR art.5(3).
840 CVR art.7.
841 CVR art.8(1).
842 CVR art.8(2).
843 CVR art.9.

voucher.[844] He may require any person claiming the luggage but not producing the voucher to prove his right to the luggage and to produce adequate security for the luggage if the proof appears insufficient.[845]

Personal injuries The CVR carrier is liable for loss or damage resulting from the death or wounding of, or from any other bodily or mental injury caused to, a passenger as a result of an accident connected with the carriage and occurring while the passenger is inside the vehicle or is entering or alighting from it.[846] If the accident was caused by circumstances which the carrier could not have avoided even by using the diligence required by the facts of the case, he will be relieved of liability.[847] The carrier will not, however, be relieved of liability if the accident resulted from any physical or mental failing of the driver or from any defect in or malfunctioning of the vehicle or from any wrongful act or neglect of any person from whom the carrier hired the vehicle.[848] The national law of the country where the court seised of the case is located determines not only the extent of an injury giving rise to compensation but also the persons who are entitled to compensation for such injury.[849]

36-151

Loss of, or damage to, luggage The carrier is liable for loss or damage resulting from the total or partial loss of luggage and for damage thereto.[850] This liability for luggage handed to the carrier extends over the whole period from the time when he takes charge of the luggage until he delivers it or deposits it in a safe and convenient place,[851] if it is not claimed on the arrival of the vehicle.[852] The carrier is in general responsible for other luggage (which term includes personal effects carried or worn by the passenger) while it is in the vehicle but is only held responsible for luggage which is stolen or cannot be found if it has been placed in his care. The only exception to this is in the event of an accident.[853] The carrier is relieved of liability if the loss or damage results from an inherent defect in the luggage or from a special risk inherent in its perishable or dangerous nature or from circumstances which the carrier could not have avoided even if he had used the diligence required by the facts of the case.[854] As in the case of personal injuries, the carrier is responsible for the failings of the driver, the defects in the vehicle and the wrongful acts of any person from whom he has hired the vehicle.[855] Luggage not delivered within 14 days from the date on which the passenger claims it is deemed to have been lost.[856]

36-152

---

844 CVR art.10(1).
845 CVR art.10(2).
846 CVR art.11(1).
847 CVR art.11(2).
848 CVR art.11(3).
849 CVR art.12.
850 CVR art.14(1).
851 CVR art.10(3).
852 CVR art.14(1).
853 CVR art.14(1).
854 CVR art.14(2).
855 CVR art.14(3).
856 CVR art.15.

36-153 **Upper financial limits of liability**   The CVR carrier's liability and that of his employees and agents[857] in the event of death of or personal injury to passengers is limited to 83,333 units of account[858] for each victim in respect of the same occurrence.[859] This amount is exclusive of both legal or other costs incurred by the parties and of interest.[860] A higher limit may be agreed between the parties to the contract of carriage.[861] It is, however, competent for any contracting state to set a higher limit of liability or to set no limit at all. When a carrier has his principal establishment in such a state (or in a non-contracting state which has a higher limit, or no limit at all) the law of that state prevails in relation to the determination of the total amount of damages.[862] The carrier's liability and that of his employees and agents in the event of total or partial loss of, or damage to, luggage for which he is responsible cannot exceed 166.67 units of account for each piece of luggage or 666.67 units of account for each passenger. Compensation in respect of personal effects carried or worn by the passenger is limited to 333.33 units of account for each passenger.[863] These amounts, once again, are exclusive of legal or other costs and of interest.[864] If, however, loss or damage results from wilful misconduct or gross negligence by the carrier or by a person for whom he is responsible (i.e. his employees and agents and all other persons whose services he uses to perform his obligations under the Convention),[865] the carrier cannot rely on those provisions of CVR which exclude his liability in whole or in part or which limit the compensation payable.[866]

36-154 **Carrier's exemptions from liability**   The carrier's exemptions under arts 11(2) and 14(2) have already been described.[867] The carrier may also be exonerated wholly or in part if any loss or damage resulted from the wrongful act or neglect of the passenger or from conduct by the passenger not conforming to the normal conduct of a passenger.[868] The carrier is not liable for loss or damage caused by a nuclear incident if by the law of a particular contracting state the operator of a nuclear installation is liable instead for such loss or damage.[869]

36-155 **Extinction of claims and limitations of actions**   The period of limitation for actions arising out of death or personal injury to passengers is three years from the date on which the person suffering loss or damage in this respect had or should have had knowledge of it. This period of limitation cannot, however, exceed five years from the date of the accident.[870] The period of limitation for all other actions arising out of carriage under the Convention is one year from the date on which the vehicle arrived at the place of destination of the passenger or (in the case of non-

---

857 CVR arts 4 and 18(1).
858 CVR art.19, inserted by the Protocol to the CVR 1979 (Cmnd.7481). The unit of account is the Special Drawing Right (SDR).
859 CVR art.13(1).
860 CVR art.13(2).
861 CVR art.13(3).
862 CVR art.13(1).
863 CVR art.16(1).
864 CVR art.16(2).
865 CVR art.4.
866 CVR art.18(2).
867 See above, paras 36-150—36-151.
868 CVR art.17(1).
869 CVR art.17(3).
870 CVR art.22(1).

arrival) from the date on which the vehicle ought to have arrived at that place of destination.[871] The receipt of luggage by a passenger without complaint on his part is prima facie evidence that it was delivered complete and in good condition. Any complaint must be made to the carrier orally or in writing within seven days of actual receipt of the luggage by the complainant passenger.[872] The passenger is, however, relieved of this obligation if the loss or condition of the luggage has been duly checked by the passenger and the carrier.[873]

Jurisdiction   A claimant instituting proceedings arising out of carriage under the Convention may bring an action in any court or tribunal of a contracting state designated by agreement between the parties. He may also institute proceedings in the courts or tribunals of the state within whose territory either (a) the loss or damage occurred; or (b) the place of departure or destination of the carriage was located; or (c) the defendant had his principal place of business or was habitually resident or had the place of business through which the contract of carriage was made.[874]   **36-156**

No contracting out   Any stipulation which would directly or indirectly derogate from the provisions of the Convention is null and void.[875] In particular any clause assigning to the carrier the benefit of any insurance made in favour of the passenger or any similar clause, or any clause shifting the burden of proof, is null and void.[876] Any proceedings to enforce a liability imposed on the carrier under CVR are subject to the terms and limits laid down in the Convention.[877]   **36-157**

---

[871] CVR art.22(2).
[872] CVR art.20(1).
[873] CVR art.20(2).
[874] CVR art.21(1).
[875] CVR art.23(1).
[876] CVR art.23(2).
[877] CVR art.18(1).

CHAPTER 37

CONSTRUCTION CONTRACTS

Vincent Moran Q.C. and William Webb

1. The Nature of Construction Contracts

(a) Definitions

37-001   **Construction**   The term "construction" comprehends any form of building or assembling, but is usually confined to the creation of, or the carrying out of work to or in connection with, immovable property. Construction embraces the carrying out of both building and engineering works. The same principles, with some adaptation, apply to construction in relation to other property such as ships, aircraft, plant and machinery, as well as computer hardware and software.

37-002   **Construction contract**   English law, with some exceptions, contains no rules or principles which would regulate the performance of construction work, and hence construction contracts subject to English or other similar legal systems[1] generally employ relatively elaborate forms of contract setting out the rights and duties of the parties, which have been said to resemble a "legislative code".[2] The term "construction contract" includes both "building contract" and "engineering contract", which will have particular characteristics depending upon the technical subject matter of the contract under consideration. Building usually indicates a structure intended for occupation whereas engineering will embrace any form of construction, which need

---

[1]   This covers all common law jurisdictions including the United States; and even where Code law exists defining rights and duties in relation to construction activities, there is an increasing tendency to use standard forms similar to the English models.

[2]   *Amalgamated Building Contractors v Waltham Holy Cross UDC* [1952] 2 All E.R. 452, per Lord Denning at 453.

not be static. The former tends to employ the JCT[3] Standard Form of Building Contract and the latter the ICC[4] form in the case of civil engineering works or other specialist forms. The JCT and ICC forms are referred to in this chapter to illustrate the many legal points which can arise and the way in which the standard forms deal with them. Many construction contracts are now let on individually drafted contract forms, but on analysis their terms will usually be found to be based on one or more of the standard forms dealt with in this chapter.

Work, materials and design   Construction contracts involve the provision of **37-003** work (also referred to as labour and, more recently, services) and materials (including goods, plant or equipment). In addition, construction contracts usually involve an element of "design", a ubiquitous and imprecise term which is often a source of dispute. At its lowest level, design involves the choice of appropriate materials and working methods, where not specified in the contract. At another level, design includes determination of the detailed physical characteristics of the building or works to comply with stated requirements or performance criteria. Such a contract is usually termed "design and build" but there are many intermediate stages. Similarly, "management" is comprehended to some degree in all construction contracts. Where this is the primary contribution of the contractor, who is intended otherwise to sub-let all physical work, the arrangement is usually called a "management contract".[5]

Building contract   A building contract has been judicially described as: **37-004**

"… an entire contract for the sale of goods and work and labour for a lump sum price payable by instalments as the goods are delivered and the work is done …"[6]

although the payment for work by instalments is not a necessary feature of all construction contracts[7]; and nor are all building contracts for a lump sum. The subject matter of construction contracts will often require complex and specialist provisions and contractual machinery not often found in other commercial contracts, such as provisions in relation to the grant of an extension of time for completion of the contract works. However, consistent with the above definition, the law relating to construction contracts is the application in a particular context of the general principles of the law of contract, and no more.[8]

---

3   Joint Contracts Tribunal.
4   Until 2011 this form was sponsored by and bore the name of the Institution of Civil Engineers (ICE). The ICE in 2011 withdrew its sponsorship and the (substantially unamended) form is now issued by its other sponsors, the Civil Engineering Contractors Association (CECA) and the Association of Consulting Engineers (ACE) under the new name of the Infrastructure Conditions of Contract (ICC).
5   See below, para.37-015.
6   Lord Diplock in *Modern Engineering (Bristol) Ltd v Gilbert-Ash (Northern) Ltd* [1974] A.C. 689 at 717B and 722G. This is referred to in *Beaufort Developments (NI) Ltd v Gilbert-Ash (NI) Ltd* [1999] 1 A.C. 266, 290.
7   A construction contract falling within the definition provided by ss.104 and 105 of the Housing Grants, Construction and Regeneration Act 1996 must now contain provision for payment by instalments unless it is specified in the contract that the duration of the work is to be less than 45 days (s.109).
8   Lord Reid in *Modern Engineering (Bristol) Ltd v Gilbert-Ash (Northern) Ltd* [1974] A.C. 689, 699H: "… When parties enter into a detailed building contract there are, however, no overriding rules or principles covering their contractual relationship beyond those which generally apply to the construc-

37-005 **Statutory definition** The above description of construction contracts[9] now needs to take account of the Housing Grants, Construction and Regeneration Act 1996 which, in ss.104 and 105, provides an extensive, but by no means comprehensive, statutory definition of "construction contract". Thus, by s.104(2) of the Housing Grants, Construction and Regeneration Act 1996, a construction contract will include an agreement to do architectural, design or surveying work,[10] or an agreement to provide advice on building, engineering, interior or exterior decoration or on the laying-out of landscape,[11] in relation to construction operations. However, drilling for oil or gas, tunnelling generally, plant or steel work for nuclear processing, power generation, water or effluent treatment or chemical, oil, gas, steel or food and drink production and the supply (excluding installation) of components, materials, plant and machinery generally are all excluded from the definition and therefore the provisions of the Housing Grants, Construction and Regeneration Act 1996.[12] In addition, by statutory instrument[13] Private Finance Initiative (PFI) contracts and highway and sewerage works for adoption are excluded from the definition of "construction contract". These exclusions together cover a major portion of what is generally regarded as construction work. Furthermore, the structure of s.105 in terms of "inclusions" and "exclusions" leads to the position that a contract between a contractor and an owner of a crane for the hire of a crane plus a driver was held to be a contract for construction operations which formed an integral part of, or were preparatory to, or were for rendering complete, construction operations within s.105(1)(a).[14]

37-006 **Application of Housing Grants, Construction and Regeneration Act 1996** The Housing Grants, Construction and Regeneration Act 1996 is to apply whether or not the contract is subject to English law, provided the construction operations are within the jurisdiction.[15] Furthermore, the Housing Grants, Construction and Regeneration Act 1996 provides that

"... where an agreement relates to construction operations and other matters, this part applies to it only so far as relates to construction operations."[16]

---

tion of contracts ...". See also, Lord Lloyd of Berwick in *Beaufort Developments (NI) Ltd v Gilbert-Ash Ltd* [1999] 1 A.C. 266, 290: "... Standard forms of building contract have often been criticised by the courts for being unnecessarily obscure and verbose. But in fairness one should add that it is sometimes the courts themselves who have added to the difficulty by treating building contracts as if they were subject to special rules of their own ...".

9 For a table of the dates on which the relevant provisions of the Housing Grants, Construction and Regeneration Act 1996 came into force, see Housing Grants, Construction and Regeneration Act 1996 (Commencement No.3) Order 1997 (SI 1997/2846).
10 s.104(2)(a).
11 s.104(2)(b).
12 The statutory definition has been further considered in *Nottingham Community Housing Association Ltd v Powerminster Ltd* [2000] B.L.R. 309; *Shepherd Construction Ltd v Mecright Ltd* [2000] B.L.R. 489; and *ABB Zantingh Ltd v Zedal Building Services Ltd* [2001] B.L.R. 66. It is also to be noted that a party can become estopped from contending, at the stage of enforcement of the Adjudicator's Decision, that the Housing Grants, Construction and Regeneration Act 1996 and the Scheme do not apply; see *Maymac Environmental Services Ltd v Faraday Building Services Ltd* (2000) 75 Con. L.R. 101.
13 See s.105(3).
14 *Baldwins Industrial Services Plc v Barr Ltd* [2003] B.L.R. 176.
15 s.104(6), (7).
16 s.104(5). For a consideration of the principles that apply to such "hybrid" contracts, see *Equitix Ltd*

The notional division of contracts in relation to payment obligations may be workable but the resolution of disputes by adjudication[17] in relation to part only of a contract, or the operation of a right of suspension[18] in relation to part of the work, may require further consideration.[19]

(b) Types of Construction Contract—Payment

Range of subject matter   From the descriptions of construction contracts above, it follows that there is a very broad range of subject matter which will fall under this heading, ranging from the refurbishment of a domestic dwelling to the construction of a power station or a motorway. In view of this diversity of technical subject matter, and the vastly different requirements and anticipated roles of the parties to the contracts, construction contracts can be usefully considered as falling into one of several broad categories, depending upon how the obligations of the parties are defined and arranged.   **37-007**

Lump sum contract   In a lump sum contract, the contractor is required to carry out and complete the entirety of the identified contract works for a fixed sum agreed in advance, or, as is more usual, if there are changes in the scope of the named contract works, for "… such other sum as shall become payable under this contract".[20] In the case of lump sum contracts, the proposed contract works will be of a known extent (that is, not at the development/design stage) and described in detail in a specification, bill of quantities or in drawings or in a combination of these. Where the specification or bill of quantities forms part of the contract,[21] provided the work is sufficiently described, the contractor will be taken to have included for that work in his fixed price.[22] Where work is not sufficiently described, and its existence is not reasonably to be inferred from the language of the contract,[23] the contractor will be entitled to recover payment in addition to the fixed price.[24] A lump sum contract may include responsibility for design and management.   **37-008**

Degree of completion required   An important question in the context of lump sum contracts is the extent to which completion of the entire contract must be achieved before the lump sum price is payable, assuming the absence of any right of the contractor to payment by instalments. The general position is that where, on a true construction, a contract is an entire contract, then the contractor is entitled to recover nothing on the contract before the work is completed.[25] However, this does not mean that the employer will be able to avoid payment of the fixed price by reference to defects or omissions since: **37-009**

---

v *Bester Generation UK Ltd* [2018] EWHC 177 (TCC) per Coulson J. at [19]–[23].
[17] s.108 and see below, paras 37-262 et seq.
[18] s.112.
[19] The Housing Grants, Construction and Regeneration Act 1996 has been amended by the Local Democracy, Economic Development and Construction Act 2009 but ss.104 and 105 are unchanged.
[20] art.2 of the Articles of Agreement, JCT Standard Building Contract (2011 edn).
[21] *Patman & Fotheringham v Pilditch* (1904) 2 H.B.C., 4th edn, 368.
[22] *A-Jac Demolition (London) Ltd v Urlin Rent-A-Car Inc* (1990) 74 O.R. 2nd 474 DC.
[23] *Williams v Fitzmaurice* (1858) 3 H. & N. 844.
[24] *C Bryant & Son Ltd v Birmingham Hospital Saturday Fund* [1938] 1 All E.R. 503.
[25] *Hoenig v Isaacs* [1952] 2 All E.R. 176, 178H, per Somervell L.J.; and see *Sumpter v Hedges* [1898] 1 Q.B. 673.

"It is not every breach of that term which absolves the employer from his promise to pay the price, but only a breach which goes to the root of the contract, such as an abandonment of the work when it is only half done. Unless the breach does go to the root of the matter, the employer cannot resist payment of the price. He must pay it and bring a cross-claim for the defects-and omissions, or, alternatively, set them up in diminution of the price ...[26]"

37-010 **Remeasurement contract** Work carried out under a remeasurement contract is measured and valued as the work proceeds, so that there is no pre-agreed lump sum. There is typically a bill of quantities in which the quantities are estimated, the rates inserted being intended to form the basis for the remeasurement of work[27] carried out, in the case of the ICC Form of Contract, by the engineer, although the task of preparing interim statements and a final account for submission to the engineer is an obligation upon the contractor.[28] Equally, under cl.56(2) of ICC (2011 edn), a mechanism exists whereby the engineer can vary the agreed rates where the quantities differ sufficiently from those described in the bills of quantities as to change the nature of the work undertaken,[29] since the contractor is entitled to price on the quantities in the bill.[30]

37-011 **Prime cost contracts** In this type of contract (used most often in connection with works requiring substantial design development during the course of the work) the contractor is paid the actual or prime cost of carrying out the works or (in the case of management contracts) of procuring the contract works, plus a fee or other element for profit (which may or may not depend upon the final value of the works). The JCT Management Contract is a Prime Cost contract, the definition and detailed machinery for the ascertainment of the prime cost being set out in a contract schedule. Any definition of Prime Cost will exclude certain costs which the contractor is required to bear. Thus, there will usually be express exclusions of cost resulting from any negligence by the contractor in performing his obligations under the contract.

A prime cost contract may contain an express term that the contractor will incur cost with reasonable efficiency and care. However, in the absence of an express term the question whether such a term is to be implied will depend on the circumstances surrounding the making of the contract.

37-012 **Hybrid contracts** Since construction contracts cover such a wide range of activities, contracts will be found which combine the above methods of payment and which contain or include others. Many contracts contain payment mechanisms related to performance, especially for work which includes maintenance; and in others, the sum payable depends on the contractor's success in meeting an agreed cost-limit or "target".

---

[26] *Hoenig v Isaacs* [1952] 2 All E.R. 176, 181A, per Denning L.J. The question of what is required for substantial completion is discussed in *Keating on Construction Contracts*, 10th edn (2016), para.4-019.

[27] See, for example, cl.56(1) of the ICC (2011), formerly the *ICE Form*, 7th edn (1999).

[28] ICC Form cl.60.

[29] See *Keating on Construction Contracts*, 9th edn (2012), p.1180 (commentary on cl.56(2) of the 2011 ICC Form); Abrahamson, *Engineering Law and the ICE Contracts*, 4th edn (1979, reprinted 1996), p.210.

[30] The question of re-rate under the ICE 5th edn is considered in Construction Award No.6 (1992) in [1995] Con. L. Yb. 57. See also *Kelly Pipelines Ltd v British Gas Plc* (1989) 48 B.L.R. 126.

(c)   Types of Construction Contract—Procurement

Standard procurement   The JCT and ICC forms of contract represent a type of   **37-013**
procurement which has become traditional during most of the 20th century. Such
contracts are based on a full description of the works to be executed being provided
by or on behalf of the employer, to be produced respectively by the architect or
engineer, who is intended then to become the contract administrator under the
construction contract. Prospective contractors are invited to bid in competition for
the work described, the contract usually being awarded to the lowest tenderer.[31] The
general principle is that the employer, through his agents, provides the design and
the contractor builds to it. But even in this form of contract contractors may, to a
greater or lesser extent, accept some form of design responsibility. Other methods
of procurement have existed in the past and many alternatives presently exist for
the commissioning of construction works, and are considered below. While the JCT
and ICC Forms of Contract are no longer dominant in the construction industry,
they remain well-known and are frequently used as the basis of ad hoc forms. They
are used in this chapter to illustrate many of the issues under consideration.

Design and build contracts   This type of contract may be regarded as a "pack-   **37-014**
age deal" whereby the employer obtains all or substantially all of the design work
and construction through the main contractor, although the construction work may
be performed by sub-contractors and the design by a sub-contracted professional
team. The JCT Standard Form of Building Contract with Contractor's Design 1981
Edition (now 2011) and the ICC Design and Construct Version[32] are examples of
such contracts. These forms each incorporate within the contract documents
"Employer's Requirements", in which the works to be produced are described in
terms of performance and any other requirements the employer wishes to lay down.
The tenderer is required to produce "Contractor's Proposals", which set out in detail
the way in which the employer's requirements are to be fulfilled, such proposals
also being incorporated into the contract. Design and build contracts are usually
based on prime cost, but may also contain lump sum elements where the detailed
design work precedes the contract. Expressions such as "design and build" (or
"turnkey" or "package deal" contracts) can often obscure[33] the precise nature of the
rights and obligations of the parties to a particular contract. In *Viking Grain Storage v TH White Installations*[34] the court considered whether the contractor (White)
had assumed a responsibility for the design of a grain drying and storage
installation. After considering the evidence in relation to the formation of the
contract, the Official Referee said[35]:

---

[31]   The dangers of encouraging low bidding have been much discussed. Tendering for public works and
        services is now subject to European Directives, implemented by the Public Contracts Regulations
        2006 or the Public Contracts (Scotland) Regulations 2006 under which (inter alia) a contracting
        authority may award a contract on the basis of the most economically advantageous tender
        ("MEAT"), a principle which may also be applied outside the range of the Regulations. See also
        Bowsher and Moser, "Damages for breach of the EC Public Procurement Rules in the United
        Kingdom" (2005) 15 P.P.L.R. 195.
[32]   (2011) edition.
[33]   See I. N. Duncan Wallace, "Contracts for Industrial Plant Projects" (1984) 1 I.C.L.R. 322.
[34]   (1985) 33 B.L.R. 103.
[35]   (1985) 33 B.L.R. 103 at 110–111.

"Those documents and the conduct of the parties as borne out by the correspondence before me, from 29 January 1980, point unequivocally, in my view, to the assumption by White of responsibility for all aspects of the project, including its design from start to finish ... The lump sum price was to include the services which were to be laid on. The specifications and drawings for the civil works were prepared by White; as were those for drainage and other services, for the buildings and for the functional parts of the installation ..."

Where the contractor takes on design work, and there is reliance on his skill and judgment,[36] then, save where the implication of a term is displaced by the express terms of the contract, there will be an implied term as to the fitness of those works for their intended purpose.[37] This is a valuable implied term to an employer because it will be no defence for the contractor to show that he has taken reasonable skill and care in the preparation of the relevant aspect of design. Most standard forms, however, seek to limit the contractor's responsibility to one of reasonable skill and care. Contractors may engage a professional firm to carry out the design element of a design and build contract as a sub-contractor. In such circumstances the relevant standard of care owed to the contractor will be at least a duty to take reasonable care, although it is possible for a strict obligation (analogous to that ordinarily owed by a contractor to his client in respect of construction issues) to be owed.[38] Similarly, the employer may engage professionals to safeguard his own interests and to inspect the contractor's design and work.

37-015 **Management contracts** This expression refers to a variety of different types of contract under which the principal role of the contractor is the management of the construction operation as opposed to the physical performance of the work, which is usually substantially or wholly sub-contracted. Although the physical work is subcontracted, the management contractor will often undertake primary responsibility for carrying out the work in accordance with the time limits and quality requirements specified in the contract. However, the forms of contract usually limit the liability of the management contractor, often by reference to sums recovered from the sub-contractor who may be in default.[39] Management contracts generally require the whole of the physical work to be sub-let and treated as prime cost, with the main contractor receiving remuneration in the form of a management fee, rather than pay-

---

[36] *Young & Marten v McManus Childs* [1969] 1 A.C. 454, 472; *Norta Wallpapers v John Sisk & Sons* (1976) 14 B.L.R. 49 (a decision of the Irish Supreme Court); *IBA v EMI and BICC* (1980) 14 B.L.R. 1, 44–46; *University of Warwick v Sir Robert McAlpine* (1988) 42 B.L.R. 1 at 10–16 (in which Garland J. considered all of the decisions referred to above).

[37] *Samuels v Davies* [1943] 1 K.B. 526; *Greaves & Co (Contractors) Ltd v Baynham Meikle & Partners* [1975] 1 W.L.R. 1095; *Independent Broadcasting Authority v EMI Electronics Ltd and BICC Construction Ltd* (1980) 14 B.L.R. 1; *Viking Grain Storage Ltd v TH White Installations Ltd* (1985) 33 B.L.R. 103. In *John Lelliott (Contracts) Ltd v Byrne Bros (Formwork) Ltd* (1992) 31 Con. L.R. 89 at 92 His Honour Judge Newey Q.C. said: "I think that the effect of the cases is that when a party to a contract agrees to supply a structure for a particular purpose knowing that his knowledge and skill will be relied upon by the other party the courts will readily imply a term requiring that it will be fit for that purpose, but that express terms of the contract, particular facts or general background may result in this not being so ...". See also *Rotherham MBC v Frank Haslam Milan* (1996) 78 B.L.R. 1, CA.

[38] See *Greaves and Co Ltd v Baynham Meikle* [1975] 1W.L.R. 1095, CA; and *George Hawkins v Chrysler UK Ltd* (1986) 38 B.L.R. 36.

[39] See *Copthorne v Arup Associates* (1997) 85 B.L.R. 22 (a case on the JCT Form of Management Contract, 1987 edn).

ment based on value of the work executed. Standard forms of management contract are issued by both the JCT and ICC and these also provide the basis for further ad hoc forms devised by parties, often with specific projects in mind.

Term contracts Such arrangements are commonly used for the carrying out of large numbers of small repetitive items such as excavation and backfilling to carry out work to statutory undertakers' equipment in highways (holes in the road). The relevant authority may let a contract to carry out such work as may be instructed within a given period, at rates which are specified or ascertainable. Part of the consideration may be in the form of a periodic "retainer" to cover overheads and there may be provisions covering substantial changes to the anticipated quantity of work. It is a matter of construction in each case, whether the arrangement consists of one continuing contract or a series of contracts created when orders are placed.[40]   **37-016**

Joint ventures Contracts are frequently undertaken by two or more contractors operating as a "joint venture". This has no effect on the position of the employer other than through the advantage of having two or more contractors who are usually required to accept joint and several liability. The structure of the joint venture may take any legal form. If a partnership is used, each partner will undertake direct liability to the employer; or if a company structure is used, the companies forming the joint venture will be required to enter into direct collateral agreements with the employer. As between the joint venturers *inter se* there will be a management structure which will define inter alia the sharing of cost and profit, the provision of capital, the management of the project and the settlement of any disputes between the joint venturers. The rights of joint venturers *inter se* will be determined by the general law of partnership or companies. Joint ventures may be formed to bid for a single project or for a number of projects; or for a continuing business. Provision will need to be made for the costs of tendering for unsuccessful projects, particularly where it is intended to form the joint venture only upon the tender being accepted.   **37-017**

Private Finance Initiative ("PFI") This represents the most far-reaching change to the UK (and worldwide) construction industry since the early 1990s. The PFI provides an alternative means of financing major public projects through the use of private equity finance. The PFI "contractor" enters into a contract with the intended user of the project or facilities, under which the user covenants to pay fees or charges over the period of the PFI contract, which is usually 25 years. The necessary land will usually be transferred to the PFI contract for the period so that the arrangement operates in a manner similar to a mortgage of the property, which is usually to be returned to the original owner at the end of the period. While the PFI contract will be governed by particular and special conditions (further dealt with below[41]) the design and construction of the facilities or works will be carried out under a series of contracts and sub-contracts similar to and governed by the same principles as conventional construction contracts.   **37-018**

---

[40]   See *Brogden v Metropolitan Railway* (1877) 2 App. Cas. 666. For an indication of the way in which the courts approach term (or "maintenance") contracts, see *Bonnells Electrical Contractors v London Underground* (1995) C.I.L.L. 1110.
[41]   See paras 37-023, 37-039.

(d) Standard Forms of Contract

37-019 Use of standard forms   Construction contracts are often characterised by, and have also been criticised for,[42] the use of lengthy and elaborate standard forms.[43] Given the frequent long-term nature of construction contracts, detailed machinery is required which permits adjustment of the relationship between the parties in changed circumstances (for example, by the use of variation and price escalation clauses).[44] Although standard forms have been thought of as resembling legislative codes of the parties,[45] their effect is no different to any other written form of contract.[46] There are now many clauses in the most frequently used standard forms which are the subject of decisions of the courts and the broad approach of the courts to such decided cases is that reasonable businessmen are entitled to assume that the authoritative construction of particular words will be followed.[47] Where bespoke forms are encountered it is almost invariably found that the bulk of the provisions are nevertheless based on one or more of the standard forms, with amendments as required by the particular client. However, it is also commonplace for standard forms to be substantially amended.[48] In these circumstances it is important to remember that[49] "Comparison of one contract with another can seldom be a useful aid to construction and may be ... positively misleading ...".

37-020 The contract administrator   A common feature of practically all standard forms of contract (as well as most bespoke forms) is the widespread use of a third party, variously given the title engineer, architect, supervising officer, or project manager, who is given an important administrative role involving both action as the employer's agent and decisions taken on the basis of an impartial professional opinion.[50] Such persons are compendiously referred to in this chapter as the contract administrator.

37-021 Institutional standard forms   Standard forms issued by public and local authori-

---

[42] *Peak Construction v McKinney Foundations* (1970) 1 B.L.R. 111, 114.
[43] There have been some deliberate attempts to simplify construction and engineering contracts, and perhaps the most important example is the New Engineering and Construction Contract ("NECC").
[44] For a discussion of adjustments to long-term contracts, see Ewan McKendrick, "The Regulation of Long-term Contracts in English Law" in Beatson and Friedmann (eds), *Good Faith and Fault in Contract Law* (1995).
[45] *Amalgamated Building Contractors Ltd v Waltham Holy Cross UDC* [1952] 2 All E.R. 452.
[46] Save that a printed form may constitute "written standard terms" of one party for the purposes of the Unfair Contract Terms Act 1977 s.3(1). Despite the terms of the DoE Consultation Paper, "*Fair Construction Contracts*", issued in May 1995 following the Latham Report, the Housing Grants, Construction and Regeneration Act 1996 Pt II draws no distinction between standard and non-standard or "bespoke" (see May 1995 Consultation Paper) forms contract. Accordingly, the provisions of the Housing Grants, Construction and Regeneration Act 1996 apply in the same way to both types of construction contract.
[47] *British Sugar v NEI Power Projects* (1997) 87 B.L.R. 42 at 501, per Waller L.J. (a case on the meaning of "consequential loss").
[48] For a discussion on the use of bespoke and amended standard forms in the construction industry see DoE Consultation Paper, "*Fair Construction Contracts*", May 1995.
[49] *Mitsui Construction Company Ltd v The Att-Gen of Hong Kong* (1986) 33 B.L.R. 1, 18, PC.
[50] *Sutcliffe v Thackrah* [1974] A.C. 727; *Ashville Investments Ltd v Elmes Contractors Ltd* [1989] 1 Q.B. 488 at 506; but see *Beaufort Developments (NI) Ltd v Gilbert-Ash Ltd* [1999] 1 A.C. 266, 290. See also *Scheldebouw BV v St James Homes (Grosvenor Dock) Ltd* [2006] EWHC 89 (TCC), [2006] B.L.R. 113, where Jackson J. described how, when undertaking a decision-making function, a contract administrator had a duty to act in a manner that was independent, impartial, fair and honest.

ties for both building and civil engineering work were well known in the nineteenth century.[51] Forms officially sanctioned by the construction institutions emerged only during the twentieth century. Best known are the JCT Standard Form of Building Contract (until 1977 known as the RIBA Form) and the ICC Conditions of Contract (until 2011 known as the ICE Conditions). The JCT Form is published in three versions: with quantities, without quantities, and with approximate quantities. The ICE 7th Edition of 1999 and the ICC Form are described as "Measurement Version" but are also available as a "Term Version". References in this chapter are to the Measurement Version. Both the JCT and ICC Forms are available as versions for design and build and there are also standard sub-contract documents. Many standard forms of sub-contract have been issued by the institutions which have produced main contract standard forms,[52] but some are issued by sectional bodies such as contractors' organisations.[53] Particular types of construction activity have generated distinct standard forms, such as that issued by the Institutions of Mechanical Engineers and of Engineering and Technology (formerly the Institution of Electrical Engineers) known as MF/1 (Rev 4, 2000). This form is suitable for the construction of process plant and equipment where the contractor's obligation is to include the attainment of specified performance criteria or output levels at the end of the construction period. Other standard forms are issued by the same Institutions and also by the Institution of Chemical Engineers for process plant contracts. For international engineering and construction work a suite of standard form exists, known as the FIDIC Forms.[54]

Other standard forms   Since the 1970s increasing numbers of variants of these forms have been issued including forms for design and build contracts, for management contracts and for minor and intermediate works.[55] A standard form used by many government departments was issued by the former Property Services Agency and known as GC/Works/1. A new suite of such forms, known as GC/Works/1 to 10, was produced in 1998 and 1999. There have been various attempts to produce a "common" standard form of construction contract of a kind to be found in some European countries.[56] Such a form was recommended by the Banwell Committee (1964), but without result. During the 1980s an initiative was launched by the British Property Federation, again without lasting effect. In 1991, however, the ICE published the New Engineering Contract (now called the Engineering and Construction Contract), which aimed at providing, in a unified format, a complete range of

37-022

---

[51]   See I. Duncan Wallace, *Construction Contracts: Principles and Policies in Tort and Contract* (1986), paras 27-09—27-14.

[52]   Such as the JCT Domestic Sub-Contract 1981 ("DOM/1") recommended for use where the JCT 80 has been used in the main contract. In practice, the use of DOM/1 is more widespread than this: its popularity seems to be based upon the focus upon interim payment and "cashflow" in its terms. The equivalent in the JCT 2011 Form is the Standard Building Sub-Contract (SBCSub/A).

[53]   Notably the CECA "Blue Form" of sub-contract which is used where the ICE Conditions are part of the main contract.

[54]   *Federation Internationale des Ingenieurs Conseils.* While successive versions up to the 4th edn of 1987 were based closely on the format, including clause numbering of the ICE conditions, in 1998 FIDIC departed from tradition by producing a new suite of forms, covering a wide range of construction activities, in a new format which may be regarded a sui generis, although much of the detailed drafting owes its origin to earlier standard forms.

[55]   The *JCT Intermediate Form of Building Contract* 2011 edn and the *JCT Agreement for Minor Building Works* 2011 are particularly widespread standard forms.

[56]   Notably Denmark, Holland and Sweden.

contract documents covering all types of procurement and construction through the use of "core clauses" with optional additions. This form of contract was specifically recommended in the Latham Report[57] as being conducive to best practice contracting. Its use of present tense language has been controversial[58] but the form is now used in a wide variety of projects. The NEC is now in its 3rd edition (2005) and has been used for a number of high profile contracts, including the London 2012 Olympic projects. There are also sets of standard forms for the engagement of architects and engineers for use in different circumstances, some of which are issued by the relevant professional bodies such as the Royal Institute of British Architects or the Association of Consulting Engineers.

37-023 **PFI contract forms** Since the advent of PFI contracting different forms of contract have emerged, initially drafted by private law firms. As projects have grown and expanded into new areas the task of achieving some form of standardisation has been undertaken not by the traditional construction industry institutions, but by HM Treasury which, since July 1999, has published and periodically revised a document entitled Standardisation of PFI Contracts ("SoPC"). An edition, known as Version 4, was issued in March 2007 and may be downloaded free from the Treasury website.[59] SoPC provides very detailed guidance, including draft contract provisions, for the preparation of PFI contracts. The contents of such contracts are further reviewed below. As already noted contracts for the performance of the design and construction work involved in the PFI project are based on conventional contracts and governed by the same principles save where PFI-specific legislation applies.

(e) Content of Standard Forms

37-024 **Typical features** Whilst differing greatly both in their precise provisions and in their attempt to accommodate particular kinds or levels of construction activity, standard forms often have typical features of content and structure. Some of these are considered below by reference to the following popular standard forms of contract: the Joint Contracts Tribunal Standard forms (JCT 98 and JCT SBC 2005), Intermediate JCT form (IFC 98 and IC 2005), JCT Minor Works form (MW 98 and 2005) and the *Infrastructure Conditions of Contract*, 2011 (formerly the ICE Conditions 7th edn). The JCT in 2005 published a new suite of standard form contracts. The contract forms within the 2005 suite have been significantly reorganised in terms of structure and clause numbering, although the JCT SBC 2005 contains most of the material contained in the JCT 98 form. JCT 98 was itself largely a consolidation of the JCT 1980 form. The form was again re-issued in 2011, substantially to incorporate new payment provisions following amendment of the Housing Grants, Construction and Regeneration Act 1996. Despite appearances, JCT 2005 and 2011 forms represent in substance the latest in a policy of continuity. The major changes from that which went before are as follows[60]:

---

57   See para.5.1.9.
58   See Valentine (1996) 12 Const. L.J. 305.
59   *http://www.hm-treasury.gov.uk.*
60   See generally *Keating on Construction Contracts*, 10th edn (2016), at para.20-008—20-020.

(1)   the integration in the main body of the JCT SBC 2005 form of certain provisions previously contained in a JCT supplement;
(2)   some amendments to the wording of important provisions;
(3)   some omissions from the JCT 98 form (such as nominated sub- contractors provisions);
(4)   abandonment of the long-used title "Standard Form of Building Contract" in favour of "Standard Building Contract" ("SBC").

Contractor's general obligations   The overriding obligations upon the contrac-   **37-025**
tor are often set out at the beginning of the standard form. Clause 2.1 of JCT 2011 provides a general description of the contractor's obligations and provides that the work shall be carried out and completed in a proper and workmanlike manner. Clause 2.3 also provides further general obligations in respect of the quality of materials, goods and workmanship. In contracts involving some element of contractor's design, there will also ordinarily be general design obligations. Under the ICC Form, the contractor's general responsibilities are set out in cl.8,[61] whilst the duties and authority of the engineer are set out in cl.2.[62]

Priority of contract documents   Standard forms will typically identify which of   **37-026**
the contract documents will have priority in the case of conflict, and then go on to provide for the adjustment of discrepancies in such documents. Clause 1.3 of the JCT 2011 Form provides that:

"The Agreement and these Conditions are to be read as a whole but nothing contained in the Contract Bills or the CDP Documents shall override or modify the Agreement or these Conditions."

The Contract Bills will have been specifically agreed by the parties for the purposes of a particular contract, whereas the Contract Conditions will be the printed standard form. The clear words of cl.1.3 and the other similar provisions of other standard form contracts displace the general rule of construction[63] that the written words specifically agreed by the parties will prevail over printed words in this way: if there is a direct conflict, then the conditions will prevail, but otherwise the bills may supplement what is stated in the conditions.[64] Clause 5 of the ICC Form adopts a different approach to the priority of contract documents in two principal ways: (i) the clause provides that the several documents forming the contract are to be taken as mutually explanatory of one another; and (ii) ambiguities or discrepancies are to be explained and adjusted by the engineer, who is then to issue an appropriate instruction in writing (under cl.13).

Extras and changes   Variations will often be required in construction contracts   **37-027**

---

[61]   This clause is substantially the same as cl.8 in the ICE 5th edn, save that by cl.8(2) of the ICE 7th edn, on which the ICC Conditions are based, the contractor is stated not to be responsible for the design or specification of the Permanent Works except as may be expressly provided in the contract, and the contractor is required to exercise all reasonable skill, care and diligence in designing any part of the Permanent Works for which he is responsible. For a discussion of the interrelationship between cl.8(2) and cl.12 of the ICE 5th edn, see *Humber Oil Terminals Trustee Ltd v Harbour and General Works (Stevin) Ltd* (1991) 59 B.L.R. 1, CA.
[62]   On the general position of the engineer, see: *Sutcliffe v Thackrah* [1974] A.C. 727, HL; *Pacific Associates v Baxter* [1990] 1 Q.B. 993, CA.
[63]   See *Keating on Construction Contracts*, 10th edn (2016), para.3-041; Lewison, *The Interpretation of Contracts*, 6th edn (2015) para.7.04.
[64]   *English Industrial Estates v Wimpey* [1973] 1 Lloyd's Rep. 118, CA.

as a result of changes to the employer's requirements or alterations to the design not apparent at tender. Clause 5.1 of JCT 2011 provides a definition of "Variation" for the purposes of those conditions and cll.5.2 to 5.10 deal with valuation. Equivalent provisions appear in other JCT contracts. In the ICC Form (2011 edn), the procedure for ordered variations is set out in cl.51, and the basis for valuation in cl.52. An important point of contrast here is that the ICC Form (2011 edn) contains no equivalent of the JCT provisions for separate recovery of loss and expense caused by matters materially affecting regular progress of the works, so that, under the ICC Form, any cost incurred in connection with a variation must be recovered through cl.52.[65]

37-028   **Instructions**   Standard forms will provide a machinery for the contract administrator to give instructions to the contractor to secure the construction of the works in conformity with the contract.[66] Instructions will be necessary where drawings and specifications produced for pricing and tender purposes are found to be insufficiently comprehensive to build the finished product. Whilst the precise scope of the authority of the contract administrator will depend upon the construction of the contract,[67] he will not have power to modify the express terms of the contract, and there will usually be an implied term that instructions are to be given at a time which is reasonable in all the circumstances of the particular contract.[68] Clauses 3.10 to 3.21 of the JCT 2011 Form deal with the architect's instructions. Clause 3.10 requires the contractor to comply with all instructions issued to him by the architect insofar as the architect is expressly empowered by the contract to issue such instructions and cll.3.14 to 3.21 set out those instructions which the architect is empowered to issue. Clause 3.10.1 of JCT 2011 provides that where an instruction is one requiring a variation the contractor need not comply to the extent that he makes a reasonable objection. Otherwise, if the contractor fails to comply with an instruction within seven days, cl.3.11 permits the employer to employ others to execute the relevant work and pass on all additional costs to the contractor. Clause 2(6) of the ICC Form deals with the method by which instructions can be given by the engineer; cl.7(1) deals with the situation where further drawings, specifications and instructions are "... necessary for the purpose of the proper and adequate construc-

---

65   See *Keating on Construction Contracts*, 9th edn (2012), pp.1169–1174. On cl.52 ICE 5th edn, see the commentary in Abrahamson, *Engineering Law and the ICE Contracts*, 4th edn (1996), pp.178 et seq. and also the decision in *Henry Boot Construction Ltd v Alston Combined Cycles Ltd* [1999] B.L.R. 123.

66   In *AMF International Ltd v Magnet Bowling Ltd* [1968] 1 W.L.R. 1028, 1046 Mocatta J. said: "It is the function and right of the builder to carry out his own building operations as he thinks fit. The architect, on the other hand, is engaged as the agent of the owner for whom the building is being erected, and his function is, inter alia, to make sure that in the end, when the work has been completed, the owner will have a building properly constructed in accordance with the contract and any supplementary instructions which the architect may have given ...".

67   For example, the power to omit work and give it to another contractor, on which see *Commissioner for Main Roads v Reed & Stuart* (1974) 12 B.L.R. 55 (a decision of the High Court of Australia).

68   *Neodox Ltd v Borough of Swinton and Pendlebury* (1958) 5 B.L.R. 34 (a decision on the ICE Conditions), where Diplock J. went on to say (at 46–47): "I think that in general clauses 10 and 18 give to the engineer the power to determine the method by which works are to be executed, such as the excavation of trenches where there are alternative methods possible; and I think, too, that clause 6 of the specification, on its true construction, entitles the engineer to decide when and where timbering or other forms of sheeting are to be used. His decision as to whether one method or another is satisfactory to him must, of course, be a honest one, but it does not seem to me that the Corporation warrant his competency or skill, or warrant that his decision will be reasonable ...".

tion and completion of the works ..." and cl.7(4) deals with the question of late instructions.

Certificates   In most construction contracts, the entitlement of the contractor to   **37-029**
payment or extensions of time depends on the certificate or decision of the architect, engineer or other professional identified in the contract.[69] For example, the elaborate provisions of cl.4 of JCT 2011 deal with certificates (interim and final) and payment of the contractor. Clauses 4.9 to 4.13 of JCT 2011 deal with certification of interim payment and cl.4.15 provides for issue of the final certificate. Clause 60 of the ICC Form deals with certificates and payment. It is to be noted that many of the most prevalent standard forms use words such as "opinion", and so call for an assessment by the contract administrator, based upon his skill and judgment.

Time for completion   The parties will usually make express provision for a   **37-030**
completion date or at least a completion period, and many construction contracts have optional additional requirements for sectional or phased handover of parts of the works.[70] Clause 14 of the ICC Form provides for the submission by the contractor to the engineer for his acceptance of a programme "... showing the order in which he proposes to carry out the Works having regard to the provisions of clause 42(1)" (possession of the site and access). The status and effect of the stipulations as to time in a building contract are matters of construction in the particular case: sectional handover of work may be required; time may be fixed by reference to specified start and finish dates; programmes submitted by the contractor may, but need not, create enforceable obligations; or time may be expressly stated to be of the essence, thereby allowing the innocent party to treat breach as putting the contract at an end.[71] The courts have shown a distinct reluctance to accept the proposition that building contracts are easily undermined by events which impact upon the time for completion.[72] Where the express term governing time for completion is lost, then time is sometimes described as being rendered "at large" (so that completion will be required in a reasonable time). The courts have not always been content with this solution to the problem of time, as in *Bruno Zornow v Beechcroft Developments*[73] where the Court considered that it made commercial sense to imply a date for completion into an agreement which varied works covered by an agreement which did contain a completion date.[74] In the absence of an enforceable express stipulation as to time, the court will normally imply a term into a contract that completion is to be within a reasonable time.[75] In the absence of express words governing the rate of progress to be achieved by the contractor within the period

---

[69]   Generally, see *Ashville Investments Ltd v Elmer Contractors Ltd* [1989] Q.B. 488, 507; (1987) 37 B.L.R. 60 at 79.
[70]   Many of the JCT Forms have Sectional Completion Supplements; although under the reformulated JCT 2011 suite these provisions are incorporated into the main body of the standard form.
[71]   The general position is that time is not of the essence in building contracts; see the discussion in *Keating on Construction Contracts*, 10th edn (2016), paras 8-005—8-011.
[72]   *McAlpine Humberoak v McDermott International Inc* (1992) 58 B.L.R. 1, CA.
[73]   (1989) 51 B.L.R. 16 (a case where the contract incorporated the 1963 edn of the JCT, 1977 revision, with quantities, substantially amended).
[74]   Whilst the decision of the Judge is open to question, the case is illustrative of the way in which the courts will often strive to retain at least some enforceable stipulation as to time, to reflect commercial realities.
[75]   *Hick v Raymond & Reid* [1893] A.C. 22, 32; Supply of Goods and Services Act 1982 s.14.

for completion[76] it seems that, depending upon the circumstances of the particular case, there may be room for the implication of a term that the contractor will proceed with reasonable diligence, or it may be that the sole obligation upon the contractor is that of completing within the period for completion.[77]

37-031 **Extensions of time and liquidated damages**   Standard forms will often contain detailed provisions identifying the circumstances in which, and the precise means by which, the time for completion may be extended (so that such other provisions of the contract as, say, those permitting the levy of liquidated damages for delay, will not apply). Clause 2.32 of JCT 2011 deals with the entitlement to deduct liquidated damages for non-completion and cll.2.26 to 2.29 deal with extensions of time. In the ICC Form, extensions of time are dealt with by cl.44, and liquidated damages by cl.47.[78]

37-032 **Valuation and payment**   The provisions in any given standard form relating to interim and final valuation and payment will be central to the contractor's cash flow. For any "construction contract" within the meaning of s.104 of Housing Grants, Construction and Regeneration Act 1996, ss.109–113 will have an important impact upon provisions relating to payment. Equally, from the point of view of cash flow, in circumstances where rights of set-off otherwise existing at common law can be restricted or curtailed by the use of clear words,[79] standard forms of sub-contract may, in particular, contain detailed notice provisions governing the entitlement of the main contractor to set-off sums in respect of defects or delays to the works.[80] These provisions will need to be adhered to in detail to avoid loss of the right to set-off.[81]

37-033 **Insurance of the works**   Given the expense and risk of damage involved in construction projects, standard forms will typically make extensive provision for the insurance of the works.[82] Clauses 6.4 to 6.9 of JCT 2011 require the contractor to take out and maintain insurance in respect of claims for injury to persons or property and also deal with the insurance of the works. Clauses 23 and 21 respectively of the ICC Form contains similar requirements.

37-034 **Correction of defects**   Standard forms will often make specific provision for the correction of defects during the course of the works. Clauses 3.17 to 3.20 of JCT 2011 deal with the power of the architect to issue instructions to ensure that the

---

[76]   See *West Faulkner Associates v London Borough of Newnham* (1994) 71 B.L.R. 1, CA on cl.25(1)(b) of the *JCT Local Authorities Form with Quantities*, 1963 edn (1977 revision) and the meaning of "... to proceed regularly and diligently with the Works ...".

[77]   *Greater London Council v Cleveland Bridge and Engineering Company Ltd* (1986) 34 B.L.R. 50 (Staughton J. at first instance), cf. 72, 78, per Parker L.J.

[78]   For extension of time and recovery of liquidated damages generally see below, paras 37-115—37-123.

[79]   Lord Diplock in *Modern Engineering v Gilbert-Ash* [1974] A.C. 689, 717. However: (i) a provision restricting a right of set-off contained in written standard terms of business may fall within Unfair Contract Terms Act 1977 s.13(1)(b) so that it will be subject to a requirement of reasonableness; and (ii) there can be no restriction on the right of set-off in insolvency: *Stein v Blake* [1996] A.C. 243, HL.

[80]   As cl.23 of DOM/1.

[81]   *Mellowes Archital v Bell Projects* (1997) 87 B.L.R. 26, CA; *Rupert Morgan Building Services (LLC) Ltd v Jervis* [2003] EWCA Civ 1563, [2004] 1 W.L.R. 1867, [2004] B.L.R. 18.

[82]   See below, para.37-132.

works meet the standards described in the contract. In the ICC Form, the removal, substitution and re-execution of unsatisfactory work and materials (by instruction in writing from the engineer to the contractor) during the progress of the works is dealt with by cl.39.

Termination Construction contracts will typically provide machinery identify-   **37-035**
ing the circumstances in which defaults of either party will entitle the innocent party to terminate the contractor's employment under the contract. These often complex procedures will need to be operated with considerable care since a party purport-ing to terminate a contract without an entitlement to do so will generally be found to have repudiated the contract. The relevant provision of JCT 2011 (cl.8) is organised around the occurrence of defined specified defaults. Clause 8.3.1 makes clear that the provisions of the contract do not affect the rights and remedies avail-able at common law. Thus, in the case of repudiatory breach by the contractor, cl.8.4 would not preclude the employer from treating the contract as at an end, as in *Sutcliffe v Chippendale & Edmondson.*[83] The employer has an option either to ac-cept the repudiation and treat the contract as at an end, or to comply with the contractual termination provisions. Under the ICC Form, termination of the contractor's employment is dealt with by cl.65.

Disputes Standard forms of building contract will typically contain provisions for   **37-036**
the resolution of disputes or differences, whether by litigation, arbitration, expert determination or adjudication.[84] The JCT suite of contracts provide for the parties to elect between litigation and arbitration as their ultimate form of dispute resolu-tion with litigation being the default position if the parties fail to specify. This is to be contrasted with the position that applied up to and including the 1998 versions of the JCT Form, which provided for arbitration to the default form of dispute resolution. Where there is an arbitration agreement, s.9(4) of the Arbitration Act 1996 entitles either party to a stay of legal proceedings save where the narrow circumstances identified in s.9 of the 1996 Act apply.[85] All forms of JCT contract also include provision for the temporary resolution of disputes by adjudication. This is required in all domestic construction contracts by virtue of s.108 of the Housing Grants, Construction and Regeneration Act 1996 but by making express provision for adjudication the parties to the contract will be permitted to adjudicate even if

---

[83]   (1971) 18 B.L.R. 149 at 160–162, a decision on the 1963 edn of the *Standard Form of Building Contract or RIBA Form.*
[84]   For the statutory right of a party to a "construction contract" to refer a dispute arising under the contract for adjudication, see Housing Grants, Construction and Regeneration Act 1996 s.108.
[85]   See *Halki Shipping Corp v Sopex Oils Ltd* [1997] 1 W.L.R. 1268, decision of Clarke J., affirmed by the Court of Appeal at [1998] 1 W.L.R. 726; *Beaufort Developments (NI) Ltd v Gilbert-Ash NI Ltd* [1999] 1 A.C. 266, 281; *Birse Construction Ltd v St David Ltd* [1999] B.L.R. 194; *Jitendra Bhailbhai v Dilesh R Patel* [2000] Q.B. 551, CA. Furthermore, a party dealing as a "consumer" within the meaning of the Unfair Terms in Consumer Contracts Regulations 1994 may be able to avoid a mandatory stay by arguing that the arbitration clause is unfair: *Zealander v Laing Homes Ltd* (2000) 2 T.C.L.R. 724. In *Ahmad Al-Naimi v Islamic Press Agency Inc* [2000] 1 Lloyd's Rep. 522, [2000] B.L.R. 150, the Court of Appeal said that, in a case where the issue is whether the underlying dispute is subject to an agreement to arbitrate at all, the court has a choice whether to decide that issue itself, or to stay proceedings whilst that issue is referred to arbitration. Significantly, both parties in *Al-Naimi* had asked the judge at first instance and the Court of Appeal to resolve the question of jurisdiction on the affidavit evidence. Chadwick L.J. went on (at 156) to say that the correct approach was that set out by Judge Humphrey Lloyd Q.C. in *Birse Construction Ltd v St David Ltd* [1999] B.L.R. 194.

they would otherwise have fallen outside the scope of the Act, for example because one of the parties is a residential occupier with the meaning of s.106 of the Act.

(f) PFI Contracts

37-037 **Private Finance Initiative** Historically, major construction projects have been financed either publicly, through local authorities and government departments, or privately through the raising of equity and loans.[86] With increasing pressure on public finances in the last two decades, many different schemes have been evolved for the raising of private project finance. For example, many inner city redevelopment schemes have been financed through sale and lease-back arrangements coupled with planning agreements promoted by local authorities. During the 1980s some local authorities raised finance for their own projects by deferred loan agreements under which the financier became the project employer, thereby giving rise to issues as to the recoverability of loss.[87] In 1992 the government announced its support for a new policy known as the Private Finance Initiative ("PFI"). This involved relaxation of previous finance policy, encouragement of public-private joint ventures and promotion of opportunities for private sector financing. There is no definition of PFI, which has now extended well beyond construction projects, into the provision of services formerly provided through public finance in many different fields. An early and substantial example of PFI is the cross-channel rail link. PFI is now regarded as falling under the broader description of Private-Public Partnerships ("PPP") in which construction may play a varying role. PPP contracts may involve PFI arrangements coupled with privatisation of former publicly operated facilities. PFI may be based on differing methods of financing. The most usual, which is dealt with here, is referred to as the Project Finance model. The capital value of PFI projects entered into up to 2006 is estimated at around £50bn.[88] While the value of projects is increasing, a number currently being in excess of £1bn, PFI still represents only a small proportion of the total annual capital value of the UK construction market at around £60bn.

37-038 **Operation of PFI schemes** A scheme based on project finance PFI usually involves the creation of a special purpose vehicle ("SPV") company which is intended to undertake the primary contractual obligation (for example, to construct or refurbish a hospital and to operate certain services within it), financed through equity and loans in whatever proportions the promoters may decide. The involvement of government or public authorities is usually limited to the provision of land, with operating agreements under which the project is usually to revert back to public ownership (as in the case of the channel tunnel) but may involve outright sale. PFI is currently utilised for the provision of schools, roads, prisons, hospitals and other capital projects and services. The essence of PFI projects is that they involve long-term operation agreements (which are outside the ambit of this section), coupled with construction contracts in which the terms are modified to fit the

---

[86] Historically, canals and railways in the UK were privately financed, while roads, harbours and military works were financed by the public purse. See, for example, Hawke and Reed (1969) 2 *Economic History Review* 269–286 and the discussion of railways in Atiyah, *The Rise and Fall of Freedom of Contract* (1979).

[87] See *Darlington BC v Wiltshier Northern* [1995] 1 W.L.R. 68; (1994) 69 B.L.R. 1; *Linden Gardens Trust v Lanesta Sludge Disposal* [1994] 1 A.C. 85; (1993) 63 B.L.R. 1; *Alfred McAlpine Construction v Panatown* [2001] 1 A.C. 518.

[88] http://www.amaresearch.co.uk.

wider roles being undertaken by the parties. For example, contractors are likely to have a financial interest in the project, and to undertake substantially enhanced risks under the construction contract. The design will also play an important role in the overall viability of the project, and its provision is likely to be integrated with the arrangements for financing and constructing the capital works.[89] PFI projects have given rise to a number of legal difficulties, including issues of authority and vires.[90] There are a number of statutory provisions designed to support PFI in various sectors.[91] Certain construction contracts entered into under the PFI are excluded from the operation of the Housing Grants, Construction and Regeneration Act 1996[92] and are thus not required to conform to the payment provisions under the Act, nor to include the right to adjudication.[93]

Typical provisions of PFI contracts   PFI contracts contain many provisions   **37-039**
similar to those of conventional construction contracts and with the same objective of securing the satisfactory construction of capital works comprising or forming part of the services to be provided to the user (in the contract referred to as "the authority") over the duration of the contract. The major difference is that there are no provisions for payment by the authority in respect of the capital costs, which is to be paid for out of the "unitary charge" payable once the services become available. The exception is so called "compensation events" which are intended to cater for matters arising before the "service commencement date" which are at the authority's risk and which result in delay or increased costs to the contractor (equivalent to claims under more conventional construction contracts). Matters giving rise to such compensation include breach by the authority, authority changes[94] and discriminatory or specific changes in law as defined.[95] For the construction of the facility or works, the PFI contract is intended to operate as a design and build contract with the authority's requirements being set out in an output specification. The contractor's proposals for realisation of the authority's requirements are set out in the initial tender and developed in detail after award of the contract. Compliance with the output specification is intended to be secured through provisions for submission of information to the authority as the design is developed, by quality management systems and provisions for inspection and tests at completion.[96] The construction phase (which concludes with "service commencement") may be subject to delays in the same way as conventional construction projects and in the event that the authority anticipates incurring loss as a result of late service commencement, there may be a provision for liquidated damages to be payable on a conventional basis. The PFI contractor will be expected to transfer all conventional construction risks, including delay, to the contractor carrying out the works, who will usually enter into a conventional design and build contract with the PFI contractor.

Other features of PFI contracts   There are many other features usually found in   **37-040**

---

[89] See generally Haley (1999) 15 Const. L.J. 220.
[90] See *Crèdit Suisse v Waltham Forest LBC* [1997] Q.B. 362; *Crèdit Suisse v Allerdale BC* [1997] Q.B. 306.
[91] Residual Liabilities (National Health Service) Act 1996, National Health Service (Private Finance) Act 1997, Local Authorities (Capital Finance) Regulations 1997 (SI 1997/319).
[92] The Construction Contracts (England and Wales) Exclusion Order 1998 (SI 1998/648).
[93] s.108.
[94] SoPC s.13.
[95] SoPC s.14.6.
[96] SoPC ss.3.4, 3.5 and 3.6.

PFI contracts which are designed to regulate the relations between the parties over the 25-year (or other) span of the contract. Thus, depending on the nature of the service there will be detailed provision for monitoring performance by the PFI contractor (through sub-contractors) and for payment of the unitary charge and appropriate adjustments thereto. There will be provisions for early termination for authority default or contractor default and for termination on other grounds including voluntary termination, in each case involving complex accounting procedures to accommodate many levels of financial interest in the project including particularly that of the project's financiers (lenders). As an alternative to termination, PFI contracts usually provide for the authority to have a right of "step-in" on the ground of serious but short-term default by the contractor which the authority is in a position to resolve, the intention being that the authority will subsequently "step-out" and allow the contract to continue. A related device is usually provided under a direct agreement between the authority and the senior lenders under which, in the event of termination or threatened termination for contractor default, the lenders may step-in to protect their investment (which is otherwise inadequately secured) with similar provisions for step-out. Different standard models exist for such provisions and there is no standardised recommendation. While there have been a limited number of PFI "failures" many projects have proved financially successful to the promoters such that SoPC now contains recommendations for "refinancing" provisions aimed at securing a partial return for the authority in the event that a PFI contractor decides to "sell" the project at a profit, reflecting the secured long-term income under the contract. The current recommendation is for a 50% sharing of the refinancing gains.[97] Thus, it can be seen that a PFI project involves a large number of complex and interrelated contracts between the authority, the PFI contractor, financiers, principal and sub-contractors, designers and other professionals, usually accompanied by many cross-warranties or collateral contracts between those not in primary contractual relationships. Bidding and negotiating all the necessary contracts is costly and time-consuming, such that there is usually a staged bidding arrangement, with the final stage of negotiation being conducted only with one preferred bidder whose bid is considered the most favourable.

37-041 **Example of PFI project** A decision of the Technology and Construction Court[98] dealt with a range of complex issues in contract (and tort) which illustrate the practical operation of a PFI project. The claimant (BL) entered into a PFI contract with a local authority (LCC) for the collection, recycling and disposal of domestic waste. The contract required construction of a recycling plant which was the subject of the dispute. An essential feature of the plant was a large drum known as the ball mill in which waste was broken down into its constituent parts for different forms of treatment and disposal. BL entered into a back-to-back contract with an associated company (BW) which undertook to discharge BL's obligations as to construction of the plant. BW engaged MEH under a contract to design and build the plant, MEH entering into a direct performance warranty with BL. MEH sub-contracted the work to HU who in turn entered into a contract for the design and construction of the ball mill with OT. After practical completion of the ball mill further works were required during the commissioning process, including welding and grinding. The additional works were carried out by P. During a tea-break a fire broke out

---

[97] SoPC s.34.
[98] *Biffa Waste Services v Maschinenfabrik Ernst Hese GmbH* [2008] EWHC 6 (TCC), [2008] B.L.R. 155; see also *Amey Birmingham Highways Ltd v Birmingham City Council* [2018] EWCA Civ 264.

caused by the negligence of HU and P. A substantial delay ensued which was partly mitigated by running the ball mill with a temporary liner at additional cost. BL and BW claimed liquidated damages and the additional cost incurred against MEH under the design and build contract and the direct agreement. Ramsey J. held that MEH were liable to BW for liquidated damages, but such damages were an exhaustive remedy and there was no liability for the additional cost of mitigation measures. MEH had no remaining liability to BL whose action was therefore stayed. The case illustrates the complexity of PFI contractual arrangements and the application of conventional legal analysis to those arrangements.[99]

Foreign projects The means of financing the project has a major influence on the method of procurement. In the developing world much construction work has been financed by the World Bank or the European Bank for Reconstruction and Redevelopment, each of which has favoured standard procurement methods using the FIDIC forms of contract. PFI has also become widely used in a variety of forms depending on the particular project. The procurement methods employed are variously known as Build Operate Transfer ("BOT"), Build Own Operate Transfer ("BOOT") and latterly, Design Build Finance Operate ("DBFO"). Projects vary greatly in their financial and administrative detail, but all involve the provision of capital works financed through external private sources. The promoters are granted leases or licenses to provide and operate the capital works, with the objective of recouping their investment and profit, the works ultimately being transferred to the government or other promoter of the scheme. Such projects have included power stations, hydro-electric schemes and all forms of building and construction throughout the developing world. Contracts usually involve multi-national parties and may be subject to any national law chosen by the parties as the governing or proper law, which may occasionally be English law. Disputes, particularly under the FIDIC form of contract, involve multi-stage processes, usually with the final stage being arbitration under the ICC Rules with an agreed neutral seat.

37-042

2. FORMATION OF CONTRACT

(a) General Principles

General principles The law relating to the formation of construction contracts is no more than the application of general principles of contract[100] in a particular context. Given that the process of construction contract procurement is often long, complex and costly, and the pressures at tender stage are often very considerable, disputes linked to contract formation are amongst the most frequent to come before the courts.[101] In construction contracts, as with other kinds of contract, the parties are bound by what they have agreed. However, in order to distinguish between binding promises which the courts will enforce and the whole range of tender docu-

37-043

---

[99] Although the decision in first instance in *Biffa Waste* as to the vicarious liability of OT for the negligence of P has now been reversed by the Court of Appeal, see [2008] EWCA Civ 1257, [2009] 3 W.L.R. 324, [2009] B.L.R. 1.

[100] See Vol.I, Ch.1.

[101] *VHE Construction v Alfred McAlpine Construction Ltd* (April, 1997), reported in attenuated form in (1997) C.I.L.L. 1253. See *Ove Arup & Partners International Ltd v Mirant Asia-Pacific Construction (Hong Kong) Ltd* [2003] EWCA Civ 1729, [2004] B.L.R. 49.

ments, offers, negotiations and counter-offers which will typically precede the formation of a contract, the law imposes certain essential requirements.

37-044   Offer and acceptance   The link between an offer and acceptance of that offer[102] is almost invariably essential to the formation of a contract. In most situations it will be clear by the canons of offer and acceptance that the parties must be taken to have reached an agreement and that it covered all the matters which they thought necessary, so that there is a contract in law.[103] Occasionally, where it proves impossible to discern a clear offer or a clear acceptance then, when judged objectively, a contract may still be found to have been made since the canons of offer and acceptance are not the last word and may be incapable of precise application.[104] In particular, in cases where work has commenced in anticipation of agreement being reached, the courts will look for clear words (such as "subject to contract") to establish that the parties did not intend to, and did not enter into, a binding legal relationship.[105] However, an analysis in terms of offer and acceptance will generally be the only way of ensuring that the parties have given a clear outward expression of agreement, which also promotes certainty.[106] For construction cases in which an analysis of offer and acceptance was applied in the context of work which had commenced, see *Peter Lind v Mersey Docks and Harbour Board*[107] (no coincidence of offer and acceptance) and the decision in *Hall & Tawse South Ltd v Ivory Gate Ltd*[108] (coincidence of offer and acceptance).

37-045   Consideration[109]   In order for a promise to be enforceable it must be supported by "something of value in the eye of the law"[110] which is given in exchange, unless the promise was made by deed. Typically, in the context of construction contracts, the consideration provided by the employer is the promise to pay the contract price, and the consideration provided by the contractor is the promise to carry out the works. The separate promise of performance of an existing contractual obligation can also constitute valuable consideration.[111]

---

102   See Vol.I, Ch.2.
103   This requires an objective assessment of the effect of what was said and done, and is not concerned with the subjective, undisclosed intentions of the parties. See *Hussey v Horne-Payne* (1879) 4 App. Cas. 311, 323; *Storer v Manchester City Council* [1974] 1 W.L.R. 1403, 1408H; *Harmony Shipping v Saudi-Europe Line (The Good Helmsman)* [1981] 1 Lloyd's Rep. 377 at 414; *Pagnan v Feed Products* [1987] 2 Lloyd's Rep. 601, 610. See also, Howarth (1984) 100 L.Q.R. 265.
104   *Percy Trentham v Architral Luxfer* [1993] 1 Lloyd's Rep. 25, 27; (1992) 63 B.L.R. 44, 52–55.
105   *Percy Trentham v Architral Luxfer*, above; *Sykes (Wessex) Ltd v Fine Fare Ltd* [1967] 1 Lloyd's Rep. 53 at 57; and see *Birse Construction Ltd v St David Ltd* [1999] B.L.R. 194 *Adonis Construction v O'Keefe Soil Remediation* [2009] EWHC 2047 (TCC).
106   *Brogden v Metropolitan Railway* (1877) 2 App. Cas. 666, 693; *Gibson v Manchester City Council* [1979] 1 W.L.R. 294, 297.
107   [1972] 2 Lloyd's Rep. 234.
108   (1998) 62 Con. L.R. 117.
109   See Vol.I, Ch.4. For a discussion of the doctrine of consideration in the context of third party rights, see Law Commission Report No.242 (1996) 68–73.
110   *Thomas v Thomas* (1842) 2 Q.B. 851, 859.
111   *North Ocean Shipping v Hyundai Construction* [1979] Q.B. 705; *Pao On v Lau Yiu Long* [1980] A.C. 614, PC; *Comyn Ching v Oriental Tube* (1979) 17 B.L.R. 47, CA; *Williams v Roffey Bros* [1991] 1 Q.B. 1, CA.

Intention to create legal relations   The parties must intend that their agreement   **37-046**
was to give rise to legal consequences.[112] In commercial or business agreements the
intention to create legal relations is presumed and must be clearly rebutted by the
party seeking to deny it.[113] The parties to the contract must have the capacity to
make the contract.[114]

Certainty   "The parties are to be regarded as masters of their contractual fate. It   **37-047**
is their intentions which matter and to which the Court must strive to give effect".[115]
The parties must express themselves such that their meaning can be determined by
others with a reasonable degree of certainty.[116] The courts do not recognise a
contract to negotiate, or an "agreement to agree", since this would be too
uncertain.[117] A "lock out" agreement will be recognised by the courts if it is sufficiently certain. As Lord Ackner said in *Walford v Miles*[118]:

> "There is clearly no reason in the English contract law why A, for good consideration,
> should not achieve an enforceable agreement whereby B agrees, for a specified period of
> time, not to negotiate with anyone except A in relation to the sale of his property ..."

It is to be noted that in *Lambert v HTV Cymru (Wales) Ltd*[119] the Court of Appeal
(distinguishing *Walford v Miles*), held that a clause requiring a party to "... use all
reasonable endeavours to obtain a right of first negotiation from any assignee of the
purchaser for the author to write 'conceptual' children's books in connection with
the film to be negotiated in good faith" was sufficiently certain to found an enforceable obligation.

Essential terms   It is for the parties to decide the terms of the contract between   **37-048**
them,[120] and these must include all the terms which are essential to allow the
contract "to be workable as a matter of commercial common sense".[121] Typically
in construction contracts, matters such as the scope of work, the time for completion and the price will need to be finalised in order to make the contract workable,
but there is no prescriptive definition of what will be an essential term in every case.
It is for the parties to decide what is essential or important to their reaching agreement,[122] where the parties have indeed failed to agree a term which is essential to

---

112 See Vol.I, Ch.4.
113 *Edwards v Skyways* [1964] 1 W.L.R. 349, [1964] 1 All E.R. 494.
114 See Vol.I, Ch.9.
115 *Pagnan v Feed Products* [1987] 2 Lloyd's Rep. 601, 611.
116 *Scammel v Ouston* [1941] A.C. 251, 255; *Teekay Tankers Ltd v STX Offshore & Shipbuilding Co Ltd*
[2017] EWHC 253 (Comm), [2018] 1 All E.R. (Comm) 279.
117 *Courtney & Fairbarn v Tolaini Brothers* [1975] 1 W.L.R. 297, 301–302; *Mallozzi v Carapelli* [1976]
1 Lloyd's Rep. 407; *Albio Sugar v Williams Tankers* [1977] 2 Lloyd's Rep. 457; *Scandinavian Trading Tanker Trees v Cripps* (1983) 267 E.G. 596; *Walford v Miles* [1992] 2 A.C. 128, 136C to 137H.
118 [1992] 2 A.C. 128, 139D.
119 [1998] EWCA Civ 387, [1998] F.S.R. 874.
120 *Pagnan v Feed Products* [1987] 2 Lloyd's Rep. 601, 611.
121 *Trollope and Colls v Atomic Power Constructions* [1963] 1 W.L.R. 333, 337. See also *Nicolene v
Simmonds* [1953] 1 Q.B. 543, 552 (and the reference to "essential terms"); *Hillas v Arcos* (1932)
38 Com. Cas. 23, 43; *Rossiter v Miller* (1878) 3 App. Cas. 1124, 1151. Applied in *J Murphy & Sons
Ltd v Johnston Precast Ltd* [2008] EWHC 3024 (TCC), where it was held that a contractor and sub-
contractor had concluded a binding contract when the contractor had faxed an order for the sub-
contractor to make and supply a pipe.
122 *Pagnan v Feed Products* [1987] 2 Lloyd's Rep. 601, 619.

the working of their agreement, the court cannot fill the gap.[123] This situation is to be distinguished from the position where the court is able to imply a term which gives effect to the plain intention of the parties, as in *Trollope & Colls v Atomic Power Constructions*[124] where, in relation to the implication of a term, Megaw J. said[125]:

> "I do not think that a term such as this can be implied simply for the purpose of upholding the existence of a contract, unless it can clearly be seen that it conforms with what the parties truly intended and with what they both would have accepted as a matter of course had the question been raised in the course of the negotiations or at the moment of making the supposed contract ..."[126]

In practice, the question will often arise whether *price* is an essential requirement of a particular construction contract. In each case, it will be necessary to look at what was said and done by the parties and determine what the parties intended would be essential for an agreement, as emphasised by Goff J. in *British Steel Corp v Cleveland Bridge*.[127] In this case it was decided that price was indeed an essential term on which (among other essential terms) no final agreement was ever reached, so that there was no contract between the parties.

(b)   Contract/No Contract

37-049   **Concluded agreement**   Construction contracts are often the product of lengthy negotiation over a range of issues such as scope of work, price, time for completion, specification and performance criteria. It will be a question of importance and often one of some complexity to decide at what point (if at all) in the negotiations the parties reached a concluded agreement. Some important guidelines are set out in *Trollope & Colls v Atomic Power Constructions*[128] and *Pagnan v Feed Products*[129] which can be summarised in the following propositions[130]:

---

[123] *Mmecen v Inter Ro-Ro and Gulf Ro-Ro Services (The Samah and Lina V)* [1981] 1 Lloyd's Rep. 40, 43, referred to in the construction case, *Mitsui Babcock Energy v John Brown Engineering* (1996) 51 Con. L.R. 129, 183.

[124] [1963] 1 W.L.R. 333.

[125] at 341.

[126] See also, *Arbiter Investments Ltd v Wiltshier London* (1991) 7 Const. L.J. 49; *Mitsui Babcock Energy v John Brown Engineering* (1996) 51 Con. L.R. 129, 183.

[127] [1984] 1 All E.R. 504, 511g–j.

[128] [1963] 1 W.L.R. 333.

[129] [1987] 2 Lloyd's Rep. 601, 619, per Lloyd L.J. The principles set out by Lloyd L.J. were expressly referred to in *Mitsui Babcock Energy v John Brown Engineering* (1996) 51 Con. L.R. 129, 166–167. See also *Birse Construction Ltd v St David Ltd* [1999] B.L.R. 194.

[130] See *RTS Flexible Systems Ltd v Molkeri Alois Muller GmbH & Co* [2010] UKSC 14, [2010] 1 W.L.R. 753 at [48]–[49] where the Supreme Court held that these same principles applied whether one was considering a contract concluded in correspondence or by oral communications and conduct. See also *Iliffe & Iliffe v Feltham Construction Ltd* [2014] EWHC 2125 (TCC), per Stuart-Smith J. at [79]–[82] for a summary of the relevant principles in a construction context. In *Hamid v Francis Bradshaw Partnership* [2013] EWCA Civ 470, [2013] B.L.R. 447, the Court of Appeal found that where an issue arises as to the identity of a party referred to in a written contract extrinsic evidence is admissible to assist in the resolution of that issue and that, if an objective analysis shows that a party has been misdescribed in the document, the court may correct that error as a matter of construction, not rectification; however, in *Liberty Mercian Ltd v Cuddy Civil Engineering Ltd* [2013] EWHC 2688 (TCC), [2014] B.L.R. 179, it was held that in order to identify the true parties to a written contract the principle of misnomer may only apply to replace the identified contracting party with

(i) in order to determine whether a contract has been concluded in the course of negotiations, one must look to the negotiations as a whole[131];

(ii) there must be an intention by both parties, continuing up to the date of the supposed contract, to make a contract;

(iii) at the date of the supposed contract, the parties must have been of one mind on all the terms which they then regarded as being required in order that a contract should come into existence;

(iv) the terms on which the parties were of one mind must not omit any term which, even though the parties did not realise it, was in fact essential to be agreed if the contract was to be commercially workable;

(v) in relation to the agreement of further terms the parties must intend that agreement would become binding forthwith, even though there were terms still to be agreed;

(vi) there must be some manifestation which indicated with sufficient clarity the acceptance by the offeree of the offer as then made to him, such acceptance complying with any stipulation in the offer itself as to the manner of acceptance.

Subject to contract clauses   Where the negotiations of the parties are expressed to be "subject to contract" (or similar words are used to refer to a more formal document being executed at a future time) then there will generally be no concluded contract.[132] Although the factual matrix in which the words are used may be considered, the prima facie effect of the words *"subject to contract"* will only be taken away by the most compelling of circumstances. The words "subject to contract" have therefore acquired a clear legal meaning and once introduced they only cease to have effect if the parties expressly or by necessary implication so agree.[133] Agreement expressed to be subject to a more formal document being executed in the future creates a rather lower hurdle to be overcome in establishing that the agreement is nevertheless binding.[134]   **37-050**

Effect of standard forms[135]   The existence of standard forms generated by the parties as "standard terms of business" creates additional complexities in issues of contract formation, especially where each party seeks to impose its terms on the   **37-051**

---

another entity in circumstances there was a clear mistake on the face of the instrument when it is read by reference to its relevant background or context and where it is clear what correction should be made.

131 See also, *Hussey v Horne-Payne* (1879) L.R. 4 App. Cas. 311; *Port Sudan Cotton v Chettiar* [1977] 2 Lloyd's Rep. 5, 10; *Bushwall Properties v Vortex* [1976] 1 W.L.R. 591, 603; *British Steel Corp v Cleveland Bridge* [1984] 1 All E.R. 504, 509; *Pagnan v Granaria* [1986] 2 Lloyd's Rep. 547, 548; *VHE Construction v Alfred McAlpine Construction* (1997) C.I.L.L. 1253, 1254; *Global Asset Capital Inc v Aabar Block SARL* [2017] EWCA Civ 37, [2017] 4 W.L.R. 163.

132 *Winn v Bull* (1877) 7 Ch. D. 29, 31–32; *Von Hatzfeldt-Wildenburg v Alexander* [1912] 1 Ch. 284, 288–289; *CH Rugg & Co Ltd v Street* [1962] 1 Lloyd's Rep. 364, 369; *Fraser Williams v Prudential Holborn* (1993) 64 B.L.R. 1, 9; *Lexair Ltd (in administrative receivership) v Edgar W Taylor* (1993) 65 B.L.R. 87, 98; *Manchester Cabins Ltd v The Metropolitan Borough of Bury* Unreported 1997.

133 As in *Alpenstow v Regalian* [1985] 1 W.L.R. 721. See also *Confetti Records v Warner Music* [2003] EWHC 1274 (Ch), [2003] All E.R. (D) 61 (Jun), Ch D.

134 *Harvey Shopfitters Ltd v ADI Ltd* [2003] EWCA Civ 1757, [2004] 2 All E.R. 982.

135 Generally, see Furmston, Norisada and Poole, *Contract Formation and Letters of Intent* (1997), Ch. 4; Rawlings (1979) 42 M.L.R. 715; Adams [1983] J.B.L. 297; Jacobs (1985) 34 I.C.L.Q. 297.

other. The expression "battle of forms"[136] refers to the situation where there is an offer, followed by a series of counter-offers, all seeking to introduce the respective parties' written standard terms of business. The conflict between competing written terms may often be resolved in favour of the party who puts forward the latest terms and conditions; and if they are not objected to by the other party, then he may be taken to have agreed to them.[137] While it has been said that "In many of these cases our traditional analysis of offer, counter-offer, rejection and acceptance and so forth is out-of-date ..."[138] an analysis based upon simple standards (not rigid rules) of offer and acceptance is almost invariably the correct and practical approach for ascertaining the actual or presumed intentions of the parties to see if they were *ad idem*.[139]

37-052 **Decisions on contract/no contract** Some of the more significant court decisions are here summarised. In *British Steel Corp v Cleveland Bridge*[140] the plaintiffs (steel fabricators) were approached by the defendants to supply steel-cast nodes for incorporation into a building. The plaintiff prepared an estimate for the works based on incomplete information. In February 1979 the defendant gave a letter of intent which (i) stated the defendant's intention to place a contract with the plaintiff based on prices quoted; (ii) proposed that the contract incorporate the defendant's standard form of sub-contract (which provided for unlimited liability on the part of the plaintiff for consequential loss arising out of late delivery); and (iii) required the plaintiff "to proceed immediately with the works pending the preparation and issuing to you of the official form of sub-contract". The plaintiff did not reply to the letter of intent; the defendant then indicated that it required delivery of the nodes in a particular sequence; and there followed further discussions after which the specification was substantially changed. The plaintiff proceeded to manufacture and deliver the nodes, although the parties were unable to agree on progress payments and liability for loss for late delivery. By December 1979, all but one of the nodes had been delivered. The defendant refused to make any interim payment for the nodes delivered, and instead sent a claim to the plaintiff for damages for late delivery. The plaintiff issued proceedings, contending that no contract had been made between the parties, and claiming the value of the nodes. Robert Goff J. held that there was no contract, and said[141]:

"In the present case, an unresolved dispute broke out between the parties on the question of whether CBE's or BSC's standard terms were to apply, the former providing no limit to the seller's liability for delay and the latter excluding such liability altogether. Accordingly, when, in a case such as the present, the parties are still in a state of negotiation, it is impossible to predicate what liability (if any) will be assumed by the seller for, e.g. defective goods or late delivery, if a formal contract should be entered into. In these circumstances, if the buyer asks the seller to commence work 'pending' the parties entering into a formal contract, it is difficult to infer from the buyer acting on that request that he is assuming any responsibility for his performance, except such responsibility as will

---

[136] *Butler Machine Tool Co Ltd v Ex-Cell-O Corp (England) Ltd* [1979] 1 W.L.R. 401, 404, [1979] 1 All E.R. 965, 968f.
[137] *Butler Machine Tool Co Ltd v Ex-Cell-O Corp (England) Ltd*, above, at 404.
[138] *Butler Machine Tool Co Ltd v Ex-Cell-O Corp (England) Ltd*, above, at 404.
[139] See *Chichester Joinery v John Mowlem* (1987) 42 B.L.R. 100 for a case in which an analysis of offer and acceptance is applied to competing standard terms of business.
[140] [1984] 1 All E.R. 504.
[141] At 510j to 511a.

rest on him under the terms of the contract which both parties confidently anticipate they will shortly enter into."

In *Drake and Scull v Higgs and Hill (Northern)*[142] the defendants were main contractors for certain works to a Liverpool hospital, and they invited the plaintiffs to tender for the supply and installation of mechanical and electrical installations. There was extensive correspondence between the parties in relation to design obligations, the plaintiffs' daywork rates, and whether formal contract documentation would be entered into. The Official Referee found that all matters of dispute were resolved by May 1991, save for the fixing of the plaintiffs' daywork rates, which both parties regarded as essential. No further relevant correspondence passed until May 1993. The plaintiffs commenced work in April 1992 and completed in July 1993. The Official Referee, finding a contract between the parties, said: **37-053**

"I am satisfied that, by May 11, all the terms save one necessary for a binding sub-contract to come into being were 'agreed'. That is to say, inter alia, price, commencement date of the contract, duration of the contract and obligations under the contract. The fact that D&S had no design obligations save for the extremely limited development of design requirements was only reached on May 11, but it was resolved on that date. The only matter which was not agreed at that time were the daywork rates. It is clear that up to May 12, both parties were regarding agreement on daywork rates as an essential matter. The potential importance of reaching agreement may be gauged from the fact that in the absence of agreement D&S have as yet been unable to recover any payment for the daywork that they have done. But I have reached the conclusion on the basis of the arguments advanced by Mr. Collins Q.C. that if the failure to agree daywork rates was the only matter which might have prevented the coming into being of a contract, that lacuna would be made good by the implication of a term that D&S should be paid a reasonable sum."

In *Mitsui Babcock Energy v John Brown Engineering*,[143] the defendants were the main contractors for the construction of a 600 MW combined cycle power station. They engaged the plaintiffs to design, manufacture and install two generators. In May 1992 the defendants issued a letter of intent to the plaintiffs, followed by negotiation over performance tests which were provided for in cl.35 of the standard form MFI. The defendants pressed for strict compliance with the design requirements and for payment of substantial sums as liquidated damages if the generators failed to pass the performance tests. In the result, cl.35 was struck out and a marginal annotation "to be discussed and agreed" was inserted. The contract documents were signed on behalf of both parties in June 1993. In September 1995, the defendants sent a letter to the plaintiffs alleging that there was no contract. The Official Referee holding that there was a contract, said[144] that "... the parties made a coherent and workable contract ..." which was not invalidated by the failure to arrive at an agreement on cl.35. The Official Referee also observed that the parties operated the contract provisions up to September 1995. **37-054**

In *ERDC Group Ltd v Brunel University*,[145] the Court found that, for a period prior to September 1, 2002, the series of letters of intent[146] issued by Brunel, and worked to by ERDC, were sufficient to create a binding contract. However, on the **37-055**

---

[142] (1995) 11 Const. L.J. 214.
[143] (1996) 51 Con. L.R. 129.
[144] At 184.
[145] [2006] EWHC 687 (TCC), [2006] B.L.R. 255.
[146] For a review of cases on letters of intent, see Whittaker, "What are your intentions?" *New Law Journal* (July 28, 2006) p.1200.

unusual facts of the case, the court concluded that, in the period after September 1, 2002, there was no contract and, furthermore, the move to the non-contractual basis did not justify a departure from contract rates and prices in favour of remuneration based on ERDC's costs.

(c) Tenders

37-056 **Tendering procedure** The employer will typically send out an invitation to tender to a list of pre-selected contractors or even to a single contractor, and the contractors will submit offers to carry out the work in the form of a tender. For larger construction projects, the tender procedure will often be complex, protracted and costly for the prospective contractors. The submission of a tender is an offer by the contractor to carry out work, so that a tenderer is always at risk of having his tender rejected. This is generally to be regarded as an occupational hazard of the contractor's business.[147] Any claim to recover the costs of tendering will fail if it is made clear that no contract will be entered into unless a certain condition is satisfied, and the condition is not satisfied, or if negotiations are conducted on the assumption that either party is free to withdraw from them and the defendant does withdraw before a contract is concluded.[148]

37-057 **Qualifications to general rule** The contractor may be able to recover payment of a reasonable sum where the tenderer carries out work which (i) goes beyond or is distinct from the work ordinarily carried out by a tenderer free of charge; and (ii) is carried out at the prospective employer's request[149] and for the prospective employer's benefit. However, the basis upon which negotiations are carried on between the parties may mean that the tenderer will not be able to bring himself within the requirements of what is a restitutionary remedy.[150] Alternatively, where the ground for rejection of a tender conflicts with some binding undertaking or representation relating to how the submitted tender will be treated, then the tenderer will be able to recover damages for breach of the contract which will be implied into the tender arrangements. In *Blackpool Aero Club v Blackpool BC*[151] the Court of Appeal held that, in all the circumstances, the Council's rules for the submission of tenders gave rise to a contractual right (not a mere expectation) on the part of the tenderer that his tender, submitted in accordance with the rules, would be considered.[152] In *MJB Enterprises Ltd v Defence Construction (1951) Ltd*,[153] the Supreme Court of Canada decided that, although on a true construction of the contract there was no obligation upon the putative employer to award a contract to the lowest tenderer, there was a term to be implied into the contract (to give effect to the presumed intentions of the parties) which obliged the putative employer only

---

147 *William Lacey (Hounslow) Ltd v Davis* [1957] 1 W.L.R. 932, 934; *Fairclough Building v Borough Council of Port Talbot* (1992) 62 B.L.R. 82, 94.135a.
148 See *Rackline Ltd v The National Library of Wales* (1997) C.I.L.L. 1268 for consideration of whether, on the construction of a contract for work in stages, the contractor was entitled to work on all stages.
149 *William Davis (Hounslow) Ltd v Lacey* [1957] 1 W.L.R. 932; *Craven-Ellis v Canons Ltd* [1936] 2 K.B. 403.
150 Goff and Jones, *The Law of Unjust Enrichment*, 8th edn (2011), Ch.26. *Regalian Properties v London Docklands Development Corp* (1995) 11 Const. L.J. 127; *Blackpool Aero Club v Blackpool BC* [1990] 1 W.L.R. 1195, CA.
151 [1990] 1 W.L.R. 1195, CA.
152 At 1202.
153 (2000) T.C.L.R. 235.

to accept a compliant tender. The tender process must also now be considered in the light of relevant EU legislation and relate domestic regulatory provisions.[154]

Good faith and partnering   English law does not recognise a more general duty   **37-058**
of good faith which might prevent the employer rejecting tender offers at any stage, or ending negotiations at any time.[155] Given the general antipathy of English law towards a broader understanding of pre-contractual duties and obligations of good faith, professionals in the construction industry have sought to develop new approaches to the problems of financial risk experienced by tenderers, as well as the risk, cost and uncertainty to which the employer is exposed. The phenomenon of "partnering" in the construction industry (an expression covering a loose amalgam of different strategies for cooperation and collaboration between contracting parties) can be considered in this light. Partnering arrangements may be based on the long-term relationship between contractor and employer or may be project-specific. Partnering charters set out the broad aims of the parties, such as cooperation in a spirit of openness and team work. Partnering agreements may provide for more concrete collaboration between the parties, such as shared use of information and resources. The essence of partnering is that it is intended not to create enforceable contractual rights, and is therefore beyond the scope of this chapter.

Estoppel   Given the substantial amount of preparation and negotiation which will   **37-059**
typically accompany building projects, it is relevant to consider whether such matters as estoppel by representation or proprietary estoppel are capable of giving rise to new rights of the parties, or whether an estoppel operates exclusively as a rule of evidence.[156] The balance of authority,[157] is in favour of estoppel by representation being an evidential matter, rather than something which can create new substantive rights. However, once A is estopped from denying against B certain

---

[154] In *Harmon CFEM Facades (UK) Ltd v The Corporate Officer of the House of Commons* (1999) 67 Con. L.R. 1, Judge Humphrey Lloyd Q.C. held that the House of Commons had failed in a number of different ways to conduct a tendering process in accordance with Public Works Regulations, and also in accordance with the principles of fairness and equality which were held to derive from a contract to be implied from the procurement regime required by the European Directives, as interpreted by the European Court (see at 168–169). Note also that the decision in *R. v Tower Hamlets LBC Ex p. Gary Luck (trading as G Luck Arboricultural and Horticultural Services)* (1999) 15 Const. L.J. 235, where a council refused to include the applicants in their list of tenderers, the applicants' remedy under the Public Services Contract Regulations 1993 was damages and a judicial review was inappropriate.

[155] *Walford v Miles* [1992] 2 A.C. 128 at 140C. On good faith, see: Nili Cohen, "Pre-Contractual Duties: Two Freedoms and the Contract to Negotiate" in Beatson and Friedmann, *Good Faith and Fault in Contract Law* (1995); Furmston, Norisada and Poole, *Contract Formation and Letters of Intent* (1997) Ch.10; and also the Australian decision in *Hughes Aircraft Systems International v Airservices Australia* (1997) 146 A.L.R. 1, noted by Furmston in (1998) 114 L.Q.R. 362. By way of comparison, see the Privy Council treatment of fairness and good faith in an appeal from the New Zealand Court of Appeal in *Pratt Contractors Ltd v Transit New Zealand* [2004] B.L.R. 143. For a case where the court (in this case the Court of Appeal in the SAR of Hong Kong) decided that the terms of a settlement agreement were no more than an agreement to agree, applying *Walford v Miles*, see *Hyundai Engineering & Construction Co Ltd v Vigour Ltd* [2005] B.L.R. 416. See also *Monde Petroleum SA v WesternZagros Ltd* [2016] EWHC 1472 (Comm), [2017] 1 All E.R. (Comm) 1009.

[156] See Wilken and Ghaly, *Waiver Variation and Estoppel*, 3rd edn (2012), paras 9.04–9.12; Halliwell, *Equity and Good Conscience in a Contemporary Context* (1997), Ch.2. For a discussion of good faith in the context of construction contracts and the building industry, see "Good Faith in Construction Contracts—The Hidden Agenda" (1999) 15 Const. L.J. 288.

[157] *Bell v Marsh* [1903] 1 Ch. 528 at 540; *London Joint Stock Bank Ltd v Macmillan* [1918] A.C. 777, 818; *Evans v Bartlam* [1937] A.C. 473 at 484; *Hopgood v Brown* [1955] 1 W.L.R. 213, 223.

facts, this is a step on the way[158] to establishing a cause of action, since certain legal consequences will flow from the facts which A is now unable to deny.[159] Estoppel may therefore play an important role in the *evidence* considered by the court on the issue whether there was a concluded and binding agreement. In *Mitsui Babcock Energy Ltd v John Brown Engineering Ltd*,[160] for example, the Official Referee decided there was a contract, but also indicated that he would, if necessary, be prepared to rely upon evidence of conduct amounting to an estoppel in reaching the same conclusion. That estoppel in contract formation is likely to be confined to an evidential role is further supported by the rejection, in the construction context, of the contention that an estoppel can found a contract.[161]

(d) Letters of Intent

37-060 **Purpose** In construction contracts, there will typically be a wide range of contractual and commercial issues to be resolved between the parties to the intended contract, prior to its finalisation. Pressures to commence the intended works will often also be considerable. The use of a letter of intent, or letter of comfort, is intended to give some measure of security to the party commencing work, pending the conclusion of the contract. Although always a matter of construction in all the circumstances of the particular case,[162] a letter of intent will typically involve the expression of an intention by A to enter into a contract with B at some point in the future, coupled with an indication from A to B that B should commence work.[163]

37-061 **Effect of letter of intent** This will be partly a matter of construction of the particular document[164] and partly a question of legal analysis. In many cases, the terms of the letter of intent will mean that it cannot have the effect of creating enforceable promises in the form of a contract; indeed, this will often be its main objective.[165] In *British Steel v Cleveland Bridge*,[166] Cleveland Bridge requested BSC

---

[158] *Low v Bouverie* [1891] 3 Ch. 82, 105.

[159] *Low v Bouverie* [1891] 3 Ch. 82, 112. See also *Haden Young Ltd v Laing O'Rourke Midlands Ltd* [2008] EWHC 1016 (TCC), [2008] All E.R. (D) 49 (Jun), where Ramsey J. held that a party was not estopped from contending that no contract had been concluded. An estoppel could not be used to create a legal relationship where there was no such relationship at the outset. It was prohibited to use an alleged estoppel to assert an obligation equivalent to a cause of action and the Court should not bridge the lacuna in "no contract" cases by reference to estoppel.

[160] (1996) 51 Con. L.R. 129, 186.

[161] *J Murphy & Sons Ltd v ABB Daimler-Benz Transportation (Signal) Ltd* [1998] All E.R. (D) 718 (Dec).

[162] *Wilson Smithett v Bangladesh Sugar* [1986] 1 Lloyd's Rep. 378, 379. In this case, a letter of intent was construed as constituting acceptance of an offer which was then binding on both parties.

[163] *British Steel Corp v Cleveland Bridge and Engineering Co Ltd* [1984] 1 All E.R. 504; *Monk Construction Ltd v Norwich Union Life Assurance Society* (1992) 62 B.L.R. 107; *Turriff Construction Ltd v Regalia Knitting Mills Ltd* (1971) 9 B.L.R. 20; *Kleinwort Benson Ltd v Malasia Mining Corp* [1989] 1 W.L.R. 379, [1989] 1 All E.R. 785; *Wilson Smithett v Bangladesh Sugar* [1986] 1 Lloyd's Rep. 378; *Hall & Tawse South Ltd v Ivory Gate Ltd* (1998) C.I.L.L. 1376; *Jarvis Interiors Ltd v Galliard Homes Ltd* [2000] B.L.R. 33; Furmston, Norisada and Poole, *Contract Formation and Letters of Intent* (1998), Ch.5.

[164] *Wilson Smithett v Bangladesh Sugar* [1986] 1 Lloyd's Rep. 378, 379, per Leggatt L.J.: "The fact that it has the particular label that it has does not brand it at the outset as a contractual document or as a non-contractual document".

[165] See, for example, the decision of the Court of Appeal in *RTS Flexible Systems Ltd v Molkerei Alois Muller GmbH & Co* [2009] EWCA Civ 26, [2009] B.L.R. 181. However, see now the decision of the Supreme Court at [2010] UKSC 14, [2010] 1 W.L.R. 753, where this decision was reversed. The

to proceed immediately with the work pending the preparation and issuing of the official form of sub-contract. Robert Goff J. said[167]:

"In these circumstances, if the buyer asks the seller to commence work 'pending' the parties entering into a formal contract, it is difficult to infer from the buyer acting on that request that he is assuming any responsibility for his performance, except such responsibility as will rest on him under the terms of the contract which both parties confidently anticipate they will shortly enter into ..."

Exceptional situations A letter of intent may result in a binding contract. In *Turriff Construction v Regalia*[168] the judge found on the facts that, although the letter of intent stated that the proposed contract was "subject to agreement on an acceptable contract", those words referred only to the full contract and not to the preliminary contract by which the plaintiffs were to be indemnified for the cost of the work properly undertaken by them pending the conclusion of the full contract.[169] In *Wilson Smithett v Bangladesh Sugar*[170] the judge considered that the letter of intent was the acceptance of an offer leading to a binding contract, despite the requirement for the submission of a security deposit/performance bond. Where, as in *Turriff v Regalia*, there is a preliminary contract between A and B, then B's entitlement to be paid is based upon the implied term of that preliminary contract that A will pay B a reasonable sum for the work done. Where, as in *BSC v Cleveland Bridge*, there is no contract, then the legal basis for recovery by B of a quantum meruit or reasonable sum is *not* by the implication of a promise or assurance of payment, but by the application of the law of unjust enrichment[171]: the law imposes an obligation on the party making the request to pay a reasonable sum for the work done in pursuance of the request.

37-062

3. CONTRACT TERMS

Introduction The range of obligations contained in a given construction contract will, in common with other kinds of contract, be derived from a number of different sources, and the general principles relating to express and implied terms, and the principles applicable to their construction, are not considered in detail here.[172] However, a number of issues of particular relevance in the context of construction contracts are considered briefly below.

37-063

(a) General Principles Apply

Contract material The period of pre-contract preparation and negotiation will often be complicated and lengthy; there may be preliminary investigations (for

37-064

---

case is discussed in detail in Vol.I, para.2-126.
166 [1984] 1 All E.R. 504.
167 At 510j to 511a.
168 (1971) 9 B.L.R. 20.
169 See also *Bryen & Langley Ltd v Boston* [2005] B.L.R. 508, where it was held that the fact that one of the parties had stated in a letter that their agreement should be contained in a formal JCT Standard Form of Contract 1998 to be drawn up and signed in due course did not prevent the parties from being taken to have already concluded a contract on the terms of the JCT form prior to its formal execution.
170 [1986] 1 Lloyd's Rep. 378.
171 *BSC v Cleveland Bridge* [1984] 1 All E.R. 504, 511.
172 See Vol.I, Ch.13 on express terms and Ch.14 on implied terms.

example, site investigations, viability studies, negotiations with landlords and sub-contractors) which take months or years to complete. There will often be discussions, formal meetings (recorded or unrecorded), correspondence, memoranda and "heads of agreement" before the parties arrive at a contract. The question will often arise whether, and to what extent, prior negotiations and other kinds of extrinsic evidence, can be relied upon to construe the contract.[173] The object of the construction of a written agreement is to discover the intentions of the parties to the agreement.[174]

37-065   **Application of principles**   The use of standard forms may pose particular problems, as do other practices common in the drawing up of construction contracts. Where there are conflicts between contractual documents or provisions, the court must construe the intentions of the parties from the documents taken as a whole, reading the documents together unless there are manifest contradictions.[175] Standard forms will often identify the priority to be accorded to the different contract documents, for example, by stating that nothing contained in the specification or the bills of quantities shall override or modify the application or interpretation of the Articles and Conditions of the standard form.[176] While words should be given their natural and ordinary meaning, the court must strive to give meaning to the words chosen by the parties. The court will not easily reach the conclusion that formal contract documents contain mistakes of language. However:

"... if detailed semantic and syntactical analysis of words in a commercial contract is going to lead to a conclusion that flouts business commonsense, it must be made to yield to business commonsense."[177]

In *Somerfield Stores Ltd v Skanska Rashleigh Weatherfield Ltd*,[178] the Court of Appeal held that while the terms of a commercial contract must be construed in the light of the relevant factual matrix and commercial common sense, that did not permit the court to rewrite the parties' agreement merely because the terms appeared unexpected or unwise.[179] Although the "matrix of fact" is broad,[180] evidence of previous negotiations,[181] declarations of subjective intent,[182] and of conduct oc-

---

[173] Although evidence of prior negotiations would normally not be admissible as part of the factual matrix to assist in construing contracts (see *Chartbrook Ltd v Persimmon Homes Ltd* [2009] UKHL 38, [2009] 1 A.C. 1101), in *Maggs (t/a BM Builders) v Marsh* [2006] EWCA Civ 1058, [2006] B.L.R. 395, the Court of Appeal found that the subsequent conduct of the parties was admissible evidence in connection with the construction of a partly written and partly oral contract.

[174] *Marquis of Cholmondley v Clinton* (1820) 2 Jac. & W. 1, 91.

[175] *Pagnan v Tradax Ocean Transportation* [1987] 2 Lloyd's Rep. 342, 348, 350, [1987] 3 All E.R. 565, 571, 574.

[176] IFC 98 Form cl.1.3.

[177] *Antaios Compania Naviera SA v Salen Rederierna AB* [1985] A.C. 191, 201; *Investors Compensation Scheme Ltd v West Bromwich Building Society* [1998] 1 W.L.R. 896, 913. In the context of a badly drafted building contract, see *Mitsui Construction Company Ltd v Att-Gen of Hong-Kong* (1986) 33 B.L.R. 1, 14, PC.

[178] [2006] EWCA Civ 1732.

[179] Although if there are two possible meanings the more commercial construction is likely to be preferred, see *Rainy Sky SA v Kookmin Bank* [2011] UKSC 50, [2011] 1 W.L.R. 2900.

[180] See the decision in *Investors Compensation Scheme Ltd v West Bromwich Building Society* [1998] 1 W.L.R. 896, HL.

[181] See also *Chartbrook Ltd v Persimmon Homes Ltd* [2009] UKHL 38, [2009] 1 A.C. 1101 where it was confirmed by the House of Lords that evidence of prior negotiations would normally not be

curring after conclusion of a contract will not be admissible.[183] Following the broad approach taken by the House of Lords in the *ICS v West Bromwich* case, it is to be noted that a more restrictive and conventional approach has subsequently been taken by the Court of Appeal[184] on pragmatic grounds of time and cost, as well as authority. When construing a construction contract, even one entirely contained in writing, it is therefore permissible to have regard to the factual background known to each parties at or before the date of the conclusion of the contract,[185] although a proper balance should be struck between a consideration of the factual background and the words used by the parties, especially if the latter yield a fairly clear conclusion.[186] A more difficult question arises where parties make deletions to a printed document. There is authority both in support of and against the proposition that the court can have regard to the deletions in the interpretation of the concluded contract.[187] From a practical point of view, deletions will only become significant where there is obvious ambiguity in the retained words, and consideration of the deleted words in these circumstances is permissible.[188]

(b) Contract Documents

Formal contract   Many different documents will be brought into existence for a construction project. Some of these will be incorporated into the formal contract, often bound together with a form setting out "general" conditions. Whether the form is standard or bespoke, certain formal details will need to be incorporated such as the price, the contract period or completion date and a description of the work. In addition the engineer or architect (and under the JCT Form, the quantity surveyor) will be identified. These, and other specific details may be included in an appendix, or in separate articles of agreement, which are also convenient if the contract is to be under seal. In addition to a set of general conditions there may be "special" or "particular" conditions which may give rise to issues of priority. The fundamental distinction to be drawn is between documents which are incorporated into and become part of the formal contract and those which are not. It is partly a question of fact and one of construction whether particular documents should be considered as contract documents.   **37-066**

Description of work   Documents setting out details of the work to be undertaken will usually be prepared specifically for the contract. These may include a set of "contract drawings", specifications and bills of quantities. Other specific docu-   **37-067**

---

admissible as part of the factual matrix to assist in construing contracts.
[182] *Investors Compensation Scheme Ltd v West Bromwich Building Society* [1998] 1 W.L.R. 896, 913b.
[183] *Whitworth Street Estates (Manchester) Ltd v James Miller & Partners* [1970] A.C. 583, 603; *Wates Ltd v Greater London Council* (1983) 25 B.L.R. 1, 29.
[184] *National Bank of Sharjah v Dellborg* [1997] EWCA Civ 2070, CA; *Scottish Power Plc v Britoil (Exploration) Ltd* [1997] EWCA Civ 2752. See also *William Hare v Shepherd Construction* [2010] EWCA Civ 283, [2010] B.L.R. 358 at [18], where the Court of Appeal held that when construing an exclusion clause, any ambiguity in the meaning or effect of the clause is a matter counted against the party seeking to rely upon the clause.
[185] See *Volta Developments Ltd v Waltham Forest Friendly Society Ltd* [2008] All E.R. (D) 306 (Mar) and *Prenn v Simmonds* [1971] 1 W.L.R. 1381 at 1384.
[186] See *Wayne Martin v David Wilson Homes Ltd* [2004] 3 E.G.L.R. 77 and now *Wood v Capita Insurance Services Ltd* [2017] UKSC 24, [2017] A.C. 1173 at [9]–[14].
[187] See *Keating on Construction Contracts*, 10th edn (2016) para.3-010 and 3-012 for a discussion of the authorities.
[188] *Louis Dreyfus et Cie v Parnaso Cia Naviera SA* [1959] 1 Q.B. 498, 515, CA.

ments may be drawn up for incorporation into the contract, such as a method statement[189] schedules of "daywork" charges and correspondence intended to have contractual effect. Various provisions may be found within the conditions of contract regulating the effect of such incorporated documents. They may, for example, all be given equal status and the contract administrator may be empowered to "explain and adjust" the terms where any discrepancy appears.[190] Alternatively, there may be a stated order of precedence. There may also be a reference within the contract to other documents not forming part of the substantive obligations but having a secondary effect, such as a standard method of measurement.

37-068 **Status of bill**   Misunderstanding can arise as to the status of a bill of quantities. The document usually comprises a brief description of each item of work by reference to a standard catalogue of descriptions usually termed a standard method of measurement. To each such item the person compiling the bill adds the appropriate quantity which has been "taken off" the tender drawings, so that the contractor may insert his rate and thereby gross up the contract price. The status and use of bills of quantities (and in particular the abbreviated descriptions of the work and any other provisions that may be included) vary significantly between the Standard Forms. Where the bill of quantities is a full contract document (as under the ICC Form) any other provisions incorporated into the bill will similarly have full contractual effect. Under the JCT 98 Form and JCT SBC 2005 and 2011, however, the bill is limited in its status to defining the quality and quantity of the work and may not override or modify the conditions.[191] Consequently, any provision purporting to modify the conditions which is contained within the bill, such as a provision for sectional completion, may be of no effect even though the apparent intention of the parties is to the contrary.[192] The effect of the bill is also dependent upon whether the contract provides for remeasurement of the work and whether the conditions provide for "correcting" the bill in the event of departure from the standard method of measurement.[193]

37-069 **Incorporated documents**   Most construction contracts will incorporate other material by reference, with either full or qualified contractual effect. Thus, in many public works contracts "standard" specifications are incorporated by reference, the contract documents containing merely lists of amendments and substituted clauses. Quality may be defined by reference to identified British standards or other public documents, although the mere incorporation of "appropriate British standards" may lead to uncertainty. Standard pricing documents such as schedules of daywork charges may similarly be incorporated and then amended by reference only by the parties.

37-070 **Sub-contract conditions**   These commonly incorporate, by reference, relevant provisions of the main contract, in order to create a "back-to-back" obligation. This may be achieved by deeming the sub-contractor to have notice of the main contract and requiring that the sub-contractor perform the obligations of the main contrac-

[189] See *Yorkshire Water Authority v McAlpine* (1985) 32 B.L.R. 114.
[190] See ICC Form of Contract cl.5.
[191] JCT 98 cll.14.1, 2.2.1; JCT SBC 2005 cll.1.3, 2.3.
[192] *Gleeson v London Borough of Hillingdon* (1994) Con. L. Yb. 111; *English Industrial Estates v Wimpey* [1973] 1 Lloyd's Rep. 118.
[193] See below, para.37-143.

tor in relation to the sub-contract works and indemnify the contractor against liability incurred by reason of any breach.[194] Such a device will not avail the employer where the sub-contractor's obligation is more extensive than that of the main contractor, e.g. where a nominated sub-contractor is employed to carry out design work which does not form part of the main contract.

Non-contractual documents Depending upon a true construction of the contract   **37-071** as a whole, certain documents may be intended not to bind the parties to their literal terms, but to have more limited effect. Thus, a programme setting out the contractor's intended sequence of work, even though the contract may require its provision, will generally not constitute a contract document. Were it to bind the parties literally, the inevitable failure of one or both parties to comply in every respect would render one or both parties in breach. Where programmes are to be referred to in the contract documents, the obligation will generally be to produce and review a sequence of working, but not to comply with each detail. Where important stages of the work are to be completed by particular dates, sectional completion may be provided for. There will be other documents which are supplied to the contractor by the employer (or a member of the professional team) which form part of the background information available to the contractor at tender and which may be of critical importance in relation to particular types of claims that may be made by the contractor. For example, in civil engineering contracts the contractor will usually be supplied with site investigation data upon which the initial design of the works will have been based. The content of the site investigation report will become significant in relation to any claim made by the contractor asserting additional cost or delay caused by unforeseen ground conditions.[195]

(c) Implied Terms

General principles Where problems or conflicts occur which are not clearly ad-   **37-072** dressed by the express terms of the construction contract, then parties will frequently seek to imply a term into their contract which will enable them to achieve their objective such as, for example, access to the site or to particular working areas of the site, or timely provision of drawings and information.[196] The general rules governing the implication of terms by the courts apply to construction contracts in the same way as to contracts generally, and they are considered in detail elsewhere.[197] The basic principles are that[198]:

---

[194] CECA Form of Sub-contract cl.3. See the approach of the Court of Appeal in *Acqua Design Ltd v Kier Regional Ltd* [2002] EWCA Civ 797, [2003] B.L.R. 111 to the question of whether certain provisions of the Standard DOM/1 Form of Sub-Contract were incorporated into a negotiated sub-contract.

[195] See cl.12 of the ICC Form.

[196] For a discussion of the basic principles, see Peden (2001) 117 L.Q.R. 459. Note also that in the decision in *Bloor Construction (UK) Ltd v Bowmer & Kirkland (London) Ltd* [2000] B.L.R. 314, it was decided that the power of an adjudicator under the Housing Grants, Construction and Regeneration Act 1996 to correct an error arising from an accidental error or omission in his decision arose by way of an implied term.

[197] See above, Vol.I, Ch.14.

[198] For a clear statement of the principles involved, see *BP Refinery (Westernport) Pty Ltd v Shire of Hastings* (1978) 52 A.L.J.R. 20, 26; *Phillips Electronique v British Sky Broadcasting Ltd* [1995] E.M.L.R. 472, CA. See the decision of the Court of Appeal in *Ultraframe (UK) Ltd v Tailored Roofing Systems Ltd* [2004] 2 All E.R. (Comm) 692, [2004] B.L.R. 341. In *Marks & Spencer Plc v BNP*

(i)   the term must be reasonable and equitable[199];
(ii)   the term must be necessary to give business efficacy to the contract, so that no term will be implied if the contract is effective without it[200];
(iii)   the term must be so obvious that "it goes without saying"[201];
(iv)   the term must be capable of clear expression[202];
(v)   the term must not contradict any express term of the contract.[203]

37-073 **Necessary terms** The courts will imply terms into a construction contract where necessary to achieve the intentions of both[204] of the parties to a contract,[205] and where necessary to make the contract work as a matter of business efficacy.[206] It follows from the requirement of necessity that the courts will not imply terms which, in effect, improve the contract made by the parties,[207] or which is but one of many routes by which a problem may be addressed.[208] A term will be implied only where there is an obvious gap in the contract which requires filling.[209] A term may be implied into a contract notwithstanding the existence of an entire agreement clause.[210]

37-074 **Non-prevention** One of the most important implied terms in the context of construction is that the employer[211] will not hinder or prevent the contractor from carrying out its obligations in accordance with the terms of the contract and from executing the works in a regular and orderly manner.[212] Where the express terms of the contract are silent as to obstructions and access, then it will be important to

---

Paribas Securities Services Trust Co (Jersey) Ltd [2015] UKSC 72, the Supreme Court reaffirmed the applicability of these five principles and provided further guidance as to their usage.

[199] *Young and Marten Ltd v McManus Childs Ltd* [1969] 1 A.C. 454, 465, HL; *Liverpool City Council v Irwin* [1977] A.C. 239, 262, HL.

[200] *The Moorcock* (1889) 14 P.D. 64, 68, CA; *Reigate v Union Manufacturing Co* [1918] 1 K.B. 592, 605, CA. In *Clin v Walter Lilly & Co Ltd v Clin* [2018] EWCA Civ 490 it was held that in order to make a Design Portion JCT Contract work effectively there was an implied term to the effect that the employer, who had the responsibility for obtaining planning permission, should take due diligence to obtain the same, and that this obligation included a requirement to provide in good time to the local authority the information that its planning officers require and are lawfully entitled to expect in order to grant the necessary consents.

[201] *Shirlaw v Southern Foundries (1926) Ltd* [1939] 2 K.B. 206, 227, CA.

[202] *Shell UK Ltd v Lostock Garage Ltd* [1976] 1 W.L.R. 1187, 1196.

[203] *Tamplin (FA) Steamship Co Ltd v Anglo-Mexican Petroleum Products Co Ltd* [1916] 2 A.C. 397, 422; *Lynch v Thorne* [1956] 1 W.L.R. 303, 311.

[204] *Duke of Westminster v Guild* [1985] Q.B. 688, 699; *Barratt Southampton v Fairclough Building Ltd* (1988) 27 Con. L.R. 62, 70.

[205] *Liverpool City Council v Irwin* [1977] A.C. 239, 253, HL.

[206] *Trollope & Colls Ltd v North West Metropolitan Regional Hospital Board* [1973] 1 W.L.R. 601, 609, HL.

[207] *The Moorcock* (1889) 14 P.D. 64, 68, CA.

[208] *Trollope & Colls Ltd v North West Metropolitan Regional Hospital Board* [1973] 1 W.L.R. 601, 610, HL.

[209] *Adams Holden & Pearson v Trent Regional Health Authority* (1989) 47 B.L.R. 34, 49; *Barratt Southampton Ltd v Fairclough Building Ltd* (1988) 27 Con. L.R. 62, 70; *GLC v Cleveland Bridge and Engineering Co* (1984) 34 B.L.R. 50, 78.

[210] See *Harrison v Shepherd Homes Ltd* [2011] EWHC 1811 (TCC), 27 Const. L.J. 709, per Ramsey J. at [54]–[66].

[211] The employer will be responsible for acts of prevention by the contract administrator: *London Borough of Merton v Leach* (1985) 32 B.L.R. 51.

[212] *London Borough of Merton v Stanley Hugh Leach Ltd* (1985) 32 B.L.R. 51, 79 where Vinelott J. applied dicta of Vaughan Williams L.J. in *Barque Quilpue v Bryant* [1904] 2 K.B. 264, 274 to the JCT Standard Form, 1963 edn, 1971 Revision. For a decision in which the principle was applied in a

establish an implied term that the contractor is to be given access to the site where work is to be carried out.[213] In *Milburn Services Ltd v United Trading Group*,[214] the court implied a term that the sub-contractor was to have access to the works notwithstanding that the main contract contained an "entire agreement clause". However, where non-prevention and access are concerned, the courts will only imply obligations which are strictly necessary to the performance of contractual obligations, so that exclusive access to the site, or a complete absence of debris prior to commencement, are unlikely to be the subject of implied terms.[215] In *Bernhard's Rugby Landscapes Ltd v Stockley Park Consortium Ltd*[216] the court was not prepared to imply a term of cooperation to enable a party to carry out its contract works in accordance with its own method statement and/or programme where the manner of execution of these activities was entirely a matter for the party seeking to imply the term. The degree of co-operation to be implied depends in each case on the obligations undertaken, rather than on what is reasonable.[217] Claims for damages arising out of delay to the works will often be based on breach of an implied term as to non-prevention. There will generally be an implied term as to the timely delivery of information, instructions and drawings, since although the employer will be entitled to issue information as the works proceed,[218] he is not entitled to issue information in such a way as prevents or impedes performance by the contractor.[219] Such matters are, however, frequently covered by express terms, which will preclude further implication. Also, it should be noted that in *Leander Construction Ltd v Mulalley & Co Ltd*[220] it was held that ordinarily there will be no implied term in a building contract that the contractor should proceed regularly and diligently with the works prior to the contract completion date.

Co-operation   Construction contracts will often require a high degree of col-   **37-075** laboration between the contractor and the employer (or his representative under the contract), and between the main contractor and his specialist sub-contractors. The implication of a term as to cooperation between contracting parties is well-established[221] and arises as a matter of law since otherwise A might frustrate the performance of an obligation by B which was dependent on action being taken or not taken by A. The precise scope of A's implied obligation to cooperate in his contract with B will depend upon the nature of the obligations under the contract, but it is thought that, in most cases, A's obligation to cooperate is more in the nature of an obligation to maintain the state of affairs between A and B, rather than an obligation upon A positively to facilitate the performance of obligations which B

---

construction contract, see *Allridge (Builders) Ltd v Grandactual Ltd* (1997) C.I.L.L. 1225.
[213] *Roberts v Bury Commissioners* (1870) L.R. 5 C.P. 310, 320, 325.
[214] (1995) 52 Con. L.R. 130.
[215] *Allridge (Builders) Ltd v Grandactual Ltd* (1997) C.I.L.L. 1225.
[216] (1997) 82 B.L.R. 39.
[217] *Mackay v Dick* (1881) 6 App. Cas. 251, 263. See also: *Nala Engineering Ltd v Roselec Ltd* (1999) C.I.L.L. 1534; and *Scottish Power Plc v Kvaerner Construction (Regions) Ltd* (1999) S.L.T. 721 Outer House.
[218] *Neodox Ltd v Swinton & Pendlebury Borough Council* (1958) 5 B.L.R. 78.
[219] *London Borough of Merton v Stanley Hugh Leach* (1985) 32 B.L.R. 51; *J & J Fee Ltd v The Express Lift Co Ltd* (1993) 34 Con. L.R. 147; *Royal Brompton Hospital NHS Trust v Hammond (No.4)* (1999) 69 Con. L.R. 170.
[220] [2011] EWHC 3449 (TCC), [2012] B.L.R. 152.
[221] *Mackay v Dick* (1881) 6 App. Cas. 251, 263; *Luxor (Eastbourne) Ltd v Cooper* [1941] A.C. 108, 118; *Mona Equipment Ltd v Rhodesia Railways Ltd* [1949] 2 All E.R. 1014, 1018.

has undertaken to carry out.[222] Thus, the appointment or re-appointment of a contract administrator and, where the contract administrator is an employee, securing compliance with his terms of employment, will fall within the obligation to co-operate.[223] So, too, will the provision of access by a contractor to a sub-contractor where certain dates for completion are contractual obligations.[224] The implication of an obligation that the employer should positively assist the contractor in the execution of his works will depend upon the circumstances of the particular case, but is likely to be rare, given the basic principles governing the implication of terms generally.

37-076 **Standard of workmanship** The contractor must carry out his works using all proper skill and care, and the standard required in the particular case is to be gathered from all the circumstances of the contract.[225] Where a contractor is required to obtain materials (where specified by the employer), the implied term as to workmanship requires the contractor to make a proper inspection of the materials before using them, and the contractor will be responsible for defects in the materials obtained by him if such defects would have been apparent upon reasonable inspection.[226] There is authority to suggest that the implied obligation upon the contractor as to workmanship is more onerous than the requirement to identify reasonably apparent defects in materials, and will, in appropriate circumstances, become a duty to warn.[227] Depending upon all the relevant circumstances, the implied term may require the contractor to inform their employer's architect of defects in the design of which he is aware,[228] or it may extend to defects which the contractor believes to exist in the works.[229] In *Edward Lindenberg v Joe Canning*[230] the judge, having heard expert evidence, concluded that the fact that such an obviously important structural feature as the chimney breast being indicated on plans as non-load-bearing should "by itself" have led the defendant contractor to have had grave doubts about the plan which he ought, in turn, to have raised with the surveyor overseeing the works.[231]

37-077 **Duty to warn** A duty to warn will arise where there is an obvious danger. In *Plant Construction Plc v Clive Adams Associates*,[232] certain temporary works were, to the knowledge of the defendant, obviously dangerous, so that the obligation to carry

---

[222] *Mona Oil Equipment & Supply Co Ltd v Rhodesia Railway Ltd* [1949] 2 All E.R. 1014.

[223] *Perini Corp v Commonwealth of Australia* [1969] 2 N.S.W.L.R. 530; (1969) 12 B.L.R. 82, 104.

[224] *Jardine Engineering v Shimizu* (1992) 63 B.L.R. 96.

[225] *Young & Marten Ltd v McManus Childs Ltd* [1969] 1 A.C. 454, 465, per Lord Reid; *Greaves & Co (Contractors) Ltd v Baynham Meikle & Partners* [1975] 1 W.L.R. 1095, 1098, per Lord Denning M.R.

[226] *Young & Marten Ltd v McManus Childs Ltd* [1969] 1 A.C. 454, 466, 470 and 479.

[227] For a critical consideration of cases on the duty to warn, see: Wilson and Rutherford (1994) 10 Const. L.J. 90.

[228] *Equitable Debenture Assets Corp Ltd v William Moss* (1983) 2 Con. L.R. 1.

[229] *Victoria University of Manchester v Hugh Wilson* (1984) 2 Const. L.R. 43. And see in the context of an engineer's duty to warn about dangerous temporary works, *Hart Investments Ltd v Fidler and Larchpack Ltd* [2007] B.L.R. 526.

[230] (1992) 62 B.L.R. 147.

[231] See also *Harrison v Shepherd Homes Ltd* [2011] EWHC 1811 (TCC), 27 Const. L.J. 709, per Ramsey J. at [39]–[52], where it was held, albeit as a matter of construction of the relevant express term, that where a contractor carries out both design and construction of the works, the obligation to carry out the work in a proper and workmanlike manner extends to any design work as well as to the construction work undertaken.

[232] [2001] B.L.R. 137.

out the works with the skill and care of an ordinary competent contractor carried with this an obligation to warn of the danger perceived.[233]

Fitness of materials Where the contractor is responsible for the supply of materials for the building works, there will be an implied warranty that the materials (i) will be reasonably fit for their purpose; and (ii) will be of good quality.[234] In each case, the warranties can be excluded or negated by reference to the express agreement of the parties, or by reference to evidence of the intentions of the parties.[235] In order for the implication to arise there must be reliance on the skill of the contractor.[236] The provision of materials must also conform to the requirements of the Supply of Goods and Services Act 1982. **37-078**

Fitness of works There will be a further implied warranty that the work carried out by the contractor will, on completion, be reasonably fit for its particular purpose where: (i) the employer makes known to the contractor the particular purpose for which the building is required; (ii) the work is of a kind which the contractor holds himself out as performing; and (iii) the employer relies on the contractor's skill and judgment.[237] The scope for the implication of a warranty as to fitness for intended purpose will vary considerably depending upon the nature of the express obligations of the contractor. Where the express obligations of the contractor are broadly in the nature of "design and build" obligations, then there will be far greater room for the implication of the warranty as to fitness for intended purpose.[238] Where, however, the contractor is required to carry out work in accordance with detailed plans or a specification provided by another, then there is little room for the implication of the warranty.[239] In *MT Hojgaard A/S v E.ON Climate and Renewables UK*[240] it was held at first instance that the contractor was in breach of an express fitness for purpose term requiring a certain design life for transition pieces in a windfarm structure, notwithstanding the design's compliance with the other DNV standard design specifications in the contract. The Supreme Court[241] upheld that finding, stating that where a contract requires an item to be produced in accordance with prescribed criteria and in accordance with a prescribed design which will inevitably **37-079**

---

233 See also *Aurum Investments Ltd v Avonforce Ltd (In Liquidation)* [2001] 2 All E.R. 385.

234 *Young & Marten v McManus Childs Ltd* [1969] 1 A.C. 454, HL; *Gloucestershire CC v Richardson* [1969] 1 A.C. 480, HL; *Rotherham MBC v Frank Haslam Milan & Co Ltd and MJ Gleeson (Northern) Ltd* (1996) 78 B.L.R. 1, CA. The implied warranties form a parallel to the warranties contained in s.14 of the Sale of Goods Act 1979. In respect of contracts for the supply of computer software, see *St Albans City & District Council v ICL* [1996] 4 All E.R. 481, CA.

235 *Young & Marten Ltd v McManus Childs Ltd* [1969] 1 A.C. 454, 474, per Lord Upjohn, referring to *G H Myers & Co v Brent Cross Service Co* [1934] 1 K.B. 46, 55, per du Parcq J.

236 *IBA v EMI & BICC* (1980) 14 B.L.R. 1, 47, HL.

237 *Greaves v Baynham Meikle* [1975] 1 W.L.R. 1095, 1098G, per Lord Denning M.R.

238 *IBA v EMI and BICC* (1980) 14 B.L.R. 1, 47 where Lord Scarman said (obiter) that: "... in the absence of a clear, contractual indication to the contrary, I see no reason why one who in the course of business contracts to design, supply and erect a television aerial mast is not under an obligation to ensure that it is reasonably fit for the purpose for which he knows it is intended to be used ...". See also *Viking Grain v TH White* (1985) 33 B.L.R. 103.

239 *Lynch v Thorne* [1956] 1 W.L.R. 303, 311, CA; *Norta Wallpapers (Ireland) Ltd v John Sisk & Sons (Dublin) Ltd* (1976) 14 B.L.R. 49, where the Irish Supreme Court held (at 63–64) that there was no room for the implication that the contractor warranted that a factory roof would be reasonably fit for its intended purpose in circumstances where the roof had been chosen by a specialist sub-contractor.

240 [2014] EWHC 1088 (TCC), [2014] B.L.R. 450.

241 [2017] UKSC 59, [2017] B.L.R. 477.

result in the product falling short of that criteria, the contractor will often be obliged to improve upon the aspects of the prescribed design contained in the contract. Whether this is true in any given case is likely to turn upon the nature of the inconsistency in the contract and the relative expertise of the contractor and the employer, or its designing architect.

37-080 **Construction and sale of a dwelling** When a purchaser buys a house from a builder who contracts to build it, there will be implied warranties: (i) that the builder will do the work in a good and workmanlike manner; (ii) supplying good and proper materials for the work; and (iii) that the house will be reasonably fit for human habitation.[242] However, the "threefold implication" will not arise if the contractor simply sells a house which he has previously constructed.[243]

(d)   Statutes Relevant to Construction

37-081 **Introduction** Statute plays an increasingly important part in determining the obligations which arise in construction contracts independent of the agreement of the parties. Some of the more important legislation is considered here.[244]

37-082 **Statutory implied terms** The Supply of Goods and Services Act 1982 (Pt II) ("SOGSA 1982") is applicable to contracts[245] for the supply of a service, and this includes construction contracts, e.g. through supply of building materials and work.[246] Subject to the possibility of exclusion or restriction in accordance with s.16, a supplier of a service acting in the course of business is obliged to carry out the service with reasonable skill and care[247]; there will be an implied term that the supplier will carry out the service within a reasonable time[248]; and there will be an implied term that the party contracting with the supplier will pay a reasonable charge.[249] The obligations created by SOGSA 1982 may be negatived or varied by express agreement, by the course of dealing between the parties, or by such usage as binds both parties to the contract; but a term implied by SOGSA 1982 is not negatived by an express term of the contract between the parties unless it is inconsistent with it.[250]

37-083 **Defective Premises Act 1972** Section 1(1) provides:

"(1)   A person taking on work for or in connection with the provision of a dwelling

---

[242] *Hancock v BW Brazier (Anerley) Ltd* [1966] 1 W.L.R. 1317, 1332F; *Greaves v Baynham Meikle* [1975] 1 W.L.R. 1095, 1098G. See *Harrison v Shepherd Homes Ltd* [2011] EWHC 1811 (TCC), 27 Const. L.J. 709 for a consideration of when such obligations will survive a conveyance of the property.

[243] *Minster Trust Ltd v Traps Tractors Ltd* [1954] 1 W.L.R. 963, 975.

[244] For the Housing Grants, Construction and Regeneration Act 1996 (as now amended), see below, paras 37-145 et seq.

[245] Made on or after July 4, 1983.

[246] For a case where SOGSA 1982 is considered in the context of a construction contract, see *Charlotte Thirty Ltd and Bison Ltd v Croker Ltd* (1990) 24 Con. L.R. 46. Contracts for the supply of materials are normally governed by the Sale of Goods Act 1979 (see below, Ch.44); see *Jewsons Ltd v Boykan* [2004] 1 Lloyd's Rep. 505, [2004] B.L.R. 31 on fitness for purpose under s.14(3) in the building context.

[247] s.13.

[248] s.14.

[249] s.15. By s.2 what is a reasonable charge is a question of fact.

[250] s.16.

(whether the dwelling is provided by the erection or by the conversion or enlargement of a building) owes a duty—

(a)   if the dwelling is provided to the order of any person, to that person; and

(b)   without prejudice to paragraph (a) above, to every person who acquires an interest (whether legal or equitable) in the dwelling;

to see that the work which he takes on is done in a workmanlike or, as the case may be, professional manner, with proper materials and so that as regards that work the dwelling will be fit for habitation when completed."

The following points in relation to s.1(1) may be noted:

(i)   although the word "dwelling" is nowhere defined in the statute, it "... implies a building used or capable of being used as a residence for one or more families, and provided with all necessary parts and appliances, such as floors, windows, staircases, etc. ..."[251];

(ii)   s.1(1) is directed at the creation of new dwellings, either by construction or by adaptation, and is not concerned with works of rectification to an existing dwelling[252];

(iii) fitness for habitation is a measure of the standard required to be achieved in the performance of the obligations imposed by s.1(1), so that it is a necessary ingredient to a cause of action that the plaintiff can show that the dwelling is not fit for habitation[253];

(iv)   the question of whether a dwelling is fit for habitation is one of fact and degree and can extend to defects of quality which render the dwelling unsuitable for its purpose as well as to dangerous defects[254];

(v)   to be fit for habitation, a dwelling must be capable of occupation for a reasonable time without risk to the health or safety of the occupants and without undue inconvenience or discomfort for the occupants[255];

(vi)   if, when a dwelling is complete, it lacks some essential attribute, then, notwithstanding that the defect is latent rather than patent, the dwelling will be unfit for habitation and come within the scope of s.1(1).[256]

Unfair Contract Terms Act 1977[257]   This Act applies for the most part to contract   **37-084** terms that seek to exclude or restrict liability, whether that liability arises in contract

---

[251]   *Halsbury's Laws* (Vol.31, 4th re-issue), p.246.

[252]   *Jacobs v Moreton & Partners* (1994) 72 B.L.R. 92, 105.

[253]   *Thompson v Clive Alexander & Partners* (1992) 59 B.L.R. 77, 87; *Alexander v Mercouris* [1979] 1 W.L.R. 1270, 1274B, per Buckley L.J.: "The duty is one to be performed during the carrying on of the work. The reference to the dwelling being fit for habitation indicates the intended consequence of the proper performance of the duty and provides a measure of the standard of the requisite work and materials ...". These decisions were followed in *Murray v Jack Lunn (Construction) Ltd* Unreported 1996. See also *Harrison v Shepherd Homes Ltd* [2011] EWHC 1811 (TCC), 27 Const. L.J. 709, where the Court held that it was bound by *Alexander v Mercouris* to find that "fitness for habitation" provided a measure of the required "work and materials" obligation, although Ramsey J. stated obiter that absent this authority he would have found that the duty created by s.1(1) was a threefold duty analogous to that at common law under *Hancock v Brazier* and not a single duty (see at [124]–[153]).

[254]   See *Bole v Huntsbuild* [2009] EWCA Civ 1146, 127 Con. L.R. 154, per Dyson L.J. at [29] and also *Harrison v Shepherd Homes Ltd* [2011] EWHC 1811 (TCC), 27 Const. L.J. 709, per Ramsey J. at [154]–[165].

[255]   *Rendlesham Estates Plc v Barr Ltd* [2014] EWHC 3968 (TCC).

[256]   *Andrews v Schooling* [1991] 1 W.L.R. 783, 790.

[257]   See generally Vol.I, Ch.15.

or in tort. Where a consumer makes a contract with the seller or supplier of goods, then the contract will also fall within the Unfair Terms in Consumer Contracts Regulations 1999 or the Consumer Rights Act 2015 as applicable.[258] It should be noted, however, that for contracts entered into after October 1, 2015, in respect of business to consumer contracts only, the provisions of UCTA 1977 and the Unfair Terms in Consumer Contracts Regulations 1999 no longer apply. When applicable the two regimes, which exist in parallel, play an important part in the regulation of contractual terms in the context of construction. The Act affects contractual terms which arise in the course of business[259] in three different (though frequently overlapping) ways: (i) control over contractual terms which purport to exclude or restrict liability in negligence[260]; (ii) control over contractual terms which purport to exclude or restrict liability in relation to implied terms in contracts of sale or hire purchase; (iii) a more general power of review of contract clauses, by s.3, exercisable in the particular circumstances described in the section. The section applies between contracting parties where one of them deals as a consumer or on the other's written standard terms of business. It is not necessary for a party's terms and conditions to be incorporated in their entirety to trigger the application of this section and a single incorporated clause taken from a party's standard terms and conditions may, on the right facts, be sufficient.[261] In these circumstances, contract terms which purport to exclude or restrict liability for breach of contract or which purport to entitle one party to render a contractual performance substantially different from that reasonably expected of him at the time the contract was made, may to that extent be ineffective.[262]

37-085 **Exclusion depends on reasonableness** In each situation identified above, the exclusion or restriction of liability will be ineffective except insofar as the contract term satisfies the requirement of "reasonableness", a concept which is explained in s.11 and elaborated in guidelines in Sch.2 which are frequently regarded as being of general application.[263] The burden of proof in relation to reasonableness is on the party seeking to uphold the disputed clause,[264] and it is also for the party who relies on standard form conditions to plead the facts and matters on which it relies if it seeks to contend that its conditions are reasonable.[265]

---

258 See Vol.I, para.15-168.
259 That is, liability for breach of obligations or duties arising from things done or to be done by a person in the course of a business: s.1(3).
260 See, for example, *Phillips Products Ltd v Hyland* [1987] 1 W.L.R. 659; *Smith v Eric S Bush* [1990] A.C. 831.
261 See *Commercial Management (Investments) Ltd v Mitchell Design & Construct Ltd* [2016] EWHC 76 (TCC).
262 See *Langstane Housing Association Ltd v First Riverside Construction Ltd* [2009] CSOH 52, 124 Con. L.R., where the Outer House of the Court of Session held that a net contribution clause in the retainer of an engineer did not fall within the scope of cl.16 or 17 of the Act (as it applies in Scotland), but that had it done so it would have satisfied the fair and reasonable test and have been effective.
263 For judicial reference to Sch.2 in the construction context, see: *Rees Hough Ltd v Redland Reinforced Plastics* (1984) 27 B.L.R. 136; *Barnard Pipeline Technology Ltd v Marston Construction Co Ltd* (1992) C.I.L.L. 743; *Edmund Murray Ltd v BSP International Foundations Ltd* (1992) 33 Con. L.R. 1, CA. See also: *Pegler Ltd v Wang (UK) Ltd* [2000] B.L.R. 218; *Casson v Ostley* [2003] B.L.R. 147; *Stent Foundations Ltd v MJ Gleeson Group Plc* [2001] B.L.R. 134; and *Watford Electronics Ltd v Sanderson CFL Ltd* [2001] 1 All E.R. (Comm) 696, [2001] B.L.R. 143.
264 Unfair Contract Terms Act 1977 s.11(5).
265 *Sheffield v Pickfords Ltd* [1997] EWCA Civ 984; *Lacey's Footwear Ltd v Bowler* [1997] 2 Lloyd's

Reasonableness in construction   The test of "reasonableness" has been of wide   **37-086**
application in construction contracts, indicating that the courts will consider a wide
range of circumstances in determining whether the test has been met. In *Rees Hough
v Redland Reinforced Plastics*[266] a clause purporting to limit the liability of the
designer and supplier of defective pipes to defects notified within three months of
supply was held to be unreasonable. In *Smith v Eric Bush* the disclaimer contained
in a building society valuation for a modest dwelling was held to be unreasonable[267] since the valuer assumes a responsibility to both mortgagee and purchaser
by agreeing to carry out a valuation for mortgage purposes knowing that the valuation will probably be relied upon by the purchaser in order to decide whether or
not to enter into a contract to purchase the house.[268] In *The Chester Grosvenor Hotel
Company Ltd v Alfred McAlpine Management Ltd*,[269] a management contract
provided that the client could not recover from the project manager sums for delay
in excess of monies received by the project manager from the works contractors.
The clause was held to be reasonable in circumstances where the parties were
substantial concerns dealing at arm's length; the parties had choice open to them
in relation to contracting party and terms. In *Stewart Gill Ltd v Horatio Myer Ltd*[270]
a clause in a contract for the supply and installation of an overhead conveyor system
which purported to exclude rights of set-off was held to be unreasonable. In *Barnard
Pipeline Technology Ltd v Marston Construction Company Ltd*[271] a clause which
provided that the liability of the supplier of pipes for defects was to be limited to
the cost of replacement or repair of the goods supplied was held to be reasonable,
in circumstances where there was equality of bargaining power and the parties had
had previous dealings. In *St Albans City & DC v ICL*[272] a clause limiting the liability of the supplier of computer software to the price or £100,000, and excluding liability for specific types of loss, was held to be unreasonable, the trial judge
observing, inter alia, that the defendant had called no evidence to show that it was
fair and reasonable to limit their liability to £100,000 or to any other sum. In *James
Moore v Yakeley Associates*[273] it was held that a clause limiting the liability of an
architect to £250,000 was reasonable.

Unfair Contract Terms in Consumer Contracts Regulations   The regime of the   **37-087**
Act exists in parallel with that imposed by the Unfair Terms in Consumer Contracts
Regulations 1999 which replace the Unfair Terms in Consumer Contracts Regulations 1994, which implemented a European Council Directive[274] on Unfair Terms
in Consumer Contracts.[275] The Regulations apply to contracts concluded after July
1, 1995[276] between a "consumer" and a seller or supplier—although it should be
noted that they no longer apply to contracts entered into after October 1, 2015.

Rep. 369.
[266] (1984) 27 B.L.R. 136, 153.
[267] [1990] 1 A.C. 831, 847D, 859A.
[268] at 847D.
[269] (1991) 56 B.L.R. 115, 133–135.
[270] [1992] Q.B. 600, 606, 609, [1992] 2 All E.R. 257, 261a, 263a–e.
[271] (1991) C.I.L.L. 743.
[272] [1996] 4 All E.R. 481.
[273] (1998) 62 Con. L.R. 76.
[274] 93/13 of April 5, 1993.
[275] [1993] O.J. L95/29. For a discussion of the directive, see: Beale, "Legislative Control of Fairness:
      The Directive on Unfair Terms on Consumer Contracts" in Beatson and Friedmann, *Good Faith and
      Fault in Contract Law* (1995).
[276] reg.1 of the 1994 Regulations states that they "… shall come into force on 1st July 1995 …"; reg.1

Schedule 2 to the Regulations contains an indicative, rather than exhaustive, list of the terms which are regarded as causing a significant imbalance which operates to the detriment of the consumer, and may therefore be considered to be unfair under the Regulations. The 1999 Regulations confer upon the Office of Fair Trading a power to go to the court to prevent the continued use of unfair terms brought to his attention.[277] For contracts made on or after October 1, 2015, the Consumer Rights Act 2015 revokes and replaces the 1999 Regulations.[278]

37-088   **The Building Regulations**[279]   The power to make building regulations as part of the system of building control in England and Wales is vested in the Secretary of State by operation of s.1 of the Building Act 1984.[280] The regulations currently in force are the Building Regulations 2010,[281] as amended by successive Amending Regulations issued from 2011 and continuing.[282] The Building Regulations themselves are a concise document, with the applicable technical detail being found in a series of approved documents. An important aspect of the scheme for building regulation is that there is a dual system in operation: there is building control carried out by local authorities, and then there is control by way of certificates issued by approved inspectors operating under the Building (Approved Inspectors, etc.) Regulations, the latest version of which is the 2010 Regulations.[283] Up to 2005 the only Approved Inspector was NHBC Building Control Services Ltd, a subsidiary of the NHBC,[284] but a list of individual approved inspectors is now maintained by the Construction Industry Council.

37-089   **Civil liability in relation to the Building Regulations**   Given the status of s.38 of the Building Act 1984 (not brought into force), the civil liability of the building contractor for breaches of the building regulations will depend upon the terms of the contract between him and the employer. Where the building contract contains no express provision requiring compliance with statutory requirements,[285] liability for breach of the building regulations may arise through breach of express or implied terms as to materials or workmanship and it is also thought that there may generally be an implied term in building contracts that the works will be carried out and completed in accordance with the building regulations.[286] The fact that the works have been inspected and approved by a local authority building inspector as being compliant with the Building Regulations is no defence to a civil claim against

---

of the 1999 Regulations "… on 1st October 1999".

[277] reg.8. A "Bulletin" is produced by the Office of Fair Trading containing, inter alia, "Case Studies" where the Regulations have been applied to standard terms in consumer transactions.

[278] See above, para.15-168.

[279] See *Keating on Building Contracts*, 10th edn (2016), para.16-046; Powell-Smith and Billington, *The Building Regulations—Explained and Illustrated*, 10th edn (1995, 1998 reprint).

[280] The Act came into force on December 1, 1984 when the relevant powers were to be exercised by the Department for the Environment. Since 2007 the relevant powers are transferred to the Department for Communities and Local Government.

[281] SI 2010/2214.

[282] There are other specialist regulations also derived from the 1984 Act: the Building (Approved Inspectors, etc.) Regulations 2010 (SI 2010/2215), the Building (Inner London) Regulations 1987 (SI 1987/748), the Building (Disabled People) Regulations 1987 (SI 1987/1445), the Building (Prescribed Fees) Regulations 1994 (SI 1994/2020), each of which are also regularly amended by further SIs.

[283] SI 2010/2215.

[284] National House Building Council.

[285] *Townsend (Builders) v Cinema News* (1958) 20 B.L.R. 118, CA; *Equitable Debenture Assets Corp v William Moss* (1984) 2 Con. L.R. 1.

[286] See *Keating on Construction Contracts*, 10th edn (2016), para.4-060.

the builder if there has, in fact, been a breach of the Building Regulations[287] although where there is a factual dispute as to what was built it may be of evidential relevance.

Since the decision of the House of Lords in *Murphy v Brentwood DC*[288] a local **37-090** authority, exercising its functions in relation to the building regulations (such as the approval of plans, the supervision of work and the issue of relevant notices), is not generally liable either to an original or a subsequent owner for the cost of repairing a building which is, in breach of the building regulations, in a defective state.[289] Equally, an expert instructed by a local authority to advise the authority about the ground conditions and adequacy of foundations for dwellings built on an old mining area, owed no duty of care to a first purchaser or the then owner/occupier to prevent or avoid the occurrence of pure economic loss.[290]

Approved inspectors The duty of the approved inspector is to supervise build- **37-091** ing works to ensure that they comply with the requirements of the building regulations. The position of the approved inspector has[291] been contrasted with that of the local authority in that whereas the local authority has a discretion whether to inspect, the approved inspector must inspect at the stages set out in the building regulations.

(e) Tort in Construction

Overview Although the law applicable to the modern construction industry is **37-092** often perceived as being solely concerned with the operation of standard forms contracts, a broad range of statutory and common law obligations are also encountered in the construction context. The tort of negligence has in recent times played a particularly important role which has, however, now been significantly reduced and redefined.

Modern role of negligence The departure from *Anns v Merton LBC*[292] in *Murphy* **37-093** *v Brentwood DC*[293] had a fundamental impact upon the duties and liabilities which arise in the construction industry,[294] bringing with it the distinction between physical damage to person or other property[295] (recoverable on the basis of *Donoghue v*

---

[287] *Hunt v Optima Cambridge Ltd* [2013] EWHC 681 (TCC), 148 Con. L.R. 27.

[288] [1991] 1 A.C. 398.

[289] Ending 14 years of such claims, which commenced with *Anns v Merton LBC* [1978] A.C. 728.

[290] *Preston v Torfaen BC* (1993) 36 Con. L.R. 48, CA.

[291] See Powell-Smith and Billington, *The Building Regulations—Explained and Illustrated*, 11th edn (1999).

[292] [1978] A.C. 728, HL.

[293] *Murphy v Brentwood DC* [1991] 1 A.C. 398, HL.

[294] For discussion, see Cane, *Tort Law and Economic Interests*, 2nd edn (1996), pp.208–214; and Baatz, "The language of duty" in *Construction Law—Themes and Practice* (1998).

[295] *Jacobs v Moreton & Partners* (1994) 72 B.L.R. 92; *Tunnel Refineries Ltd v Bryan Donkin Co Ltd* (1998) C.I.L.L. 1392. But see *Bellefield Computer Services Ltd v E Turner & Sons Ltd* [2000] B.L.R. 97 for a rejection of an attempt to circumvent the effect of *Murphy* by the suggestion of a distinction to be drawn in negligence claims between the damage to the negligently constructed building itself and items which are within but not part of the building. See also the decisions in *Linklaters Business Services v Sir Robert McAlpine Ltd* [2010] EWHC 1145 (TCC), [2010] B.L.R. 537 (at the interlocutory stage) and at [2010] EWHC 2931 (TCC), 133 Con. L.R. 211 (after trial) and *Broster v Galliard Docklands Ltd* [2011] EWHC 1722 (TCC), [2011] B.L.R. 569 which all followed *Bellefield* and discuss of the law of negligence as it applies to duties of care owed by contractors in

Stevenson)[296] and economic loss (irrecoverable save where there is some factor beyond the mere occurrence of the loss and the fact that its occurrence could be foreseen[297]). This distinction is reflected in a number of decisions on building projects,[298] although it is to be observed that there has been a divergence of view between the English courts and other common law jurisdictions on this controversial subject.[299]

37-094 **Tort and contract** Following the decision in *Henderson v Merrett Syndicates*[300] there has been further clarification of the underlying principles of tortious liability, which were traced back to *Hedley Byrne v Heller & Partners*[301] with its frequent references to one party having assumed or undertaken a responsibility to another in respect of the application of a particular skill, then relied on by the other party. In the light of the assumption of responsibility principle developed in *Henderson v Merrett*,[302] the specialist building contractor is by no means immune from claims for pure economic loss in tort, although the situations where such liability may still arise will be narrow.[303] Accordingly, the Court of Appeal has held that a specialist contractor carrying out maintenance work (in this case the removal of asbestos) assumed a responsibility to the owner of the building which invited reliance no less than the work carried out by any other professional adviser, so that pure economic loss was recoverable.[304] This is to be contrasted with the Court of Appeal's decision in *Robinson v PE Jones (Contractors) Ltd*,[305] where it was held that a builder did not owe a home owner a duty of care in tort (concurrent with the obligations owed under the building contract between the same parties) in respect of economic losses associated with the quality of the building works to be undertaken pursuant to the building contract. It was decided that ordinarily the position of a builder in this respect is to be distinguished from that of a professional, who generally would be found to owe a concurrent duty of care in respect of such economic losses in parallel to any contractual obligations created by its retainer with the client. Adopting the same approach in the case of building contracts would

---

the context of alleged complex structures.
[296] [1932] A.C. 562, HL.
[297] *Murphy v Brentwood DC* [1991] 1 A.C. 398, 487.
[298] *Hydrocarbons Great Britain Ltd v Cammell Laird Shipbuilders Ltd* (1991) 58 B.L.R. 123; *Lancashire and Cheshire Association of Baptist Churches Inc v Howard & Seddon Partnership* (1991) 65 B.L.R. 21, [1993] 3 All E.R. 467; *Morse v Barrett (Leeds) Ltd* (1993) 9 Const. L.J. 158; *Londonwaste Ltd v AMEC Civil Engineering Ltd* (1997) 83 B.L.R. 136.
[299] *Bryan (Allan) v Judith Maloney* (1995) (Australia) reported at 74 B.L.R. 35; *Winnepeg Condominium Corp No.36 v Bird Construction Co Ltd and Smith Carter Partners* (1995) (Canada) reported at 74 B.L.R. 1 and 11 Const. L.J. 306; *Invercargill City Council v Noel Gordon Hamlin* (1996) (New Zealand) reported at 78 B.L.R. 78; affirming 72 B.L.R. 39 and 11 Const. L.J. 285.
[300] [1995] 2 A.C. 145, HL.
[301] [1964] A.C. 465, HL.
[302] See also *White v Jones* [1995] 2 A.C. 207, HL.
[303] See Cartwright (1997) 13 Const. L.J. 157 and the decision of Ramsey J. in *Biffa Waste Services v Maschinenfabrik Ernst Hese* [2008] B.L.R. 155. The decision in first instance in *Biffa Waste* as to the vicarious liability of a contractor for the negligence of a third party has now been reversed by the Court of Appeal, see [2008] EWCA Civ 1257, [2009] 3 W.L.R. 324, [2009] B.L.R. 1.
[304] *Barclays Bank v Fairclough* (1995) 76 B.L.R. 1, CA. See also *BSkyB Ltd v HP Enterprise Services UK Ltd* [2010] EWHC 86 (TCC), [2010] B.L.R. 267 at [341]–[358], where it was held that when considering whether a duty of care existed in respect of an alleged negligent misstatement, the impact of the contractual regime must be considered and a duty of care should not be permitted to circumvent or escape a contractual exclusion or limitation of liability clause.
[305] [2011] EWCA Civ 9, [2011] 3 W.L.R. 815, [2011] B.L.R. 206.

involve the wholesale subordination of the law of tort into the law of contract and the parties had to be taken to have agreed that the rights and obligations between them were to be derived from the building contract alone. Following the Court of Appeal decision in *Wellesley Partners LLP v Withers LLP*[306] the contractual rules on remoteness, and possibly also causation, would continue to apply even where there are concurrent duties of care in contract and tort.

Liability of professionals A further aspect of liability in tort which is of substantial importance in construction is the liability of professionals within the industry, such as engineers, architects, project managers and quantity surveyors.[307] Although such professionals will typically have contracts of retainer with the employer (such retainer being often more formal than in other professions), the parallel liability in tort (based on the principles enunciated in *Hedley Byrne v Heller*,[308] *Henderson v Merrett Syndicates*[309] and *White v Jones*[310]) may be important in particular circumstances, such as where the claim in contract is time-barred.[311] The duties assumed by the architect or the engineer will depend upon terms of their assumption of responsibility, but there will typically be a duty to design the works[312] and then to supervise the contractor, limited to ensuring that the work is completed in accordance with the contract, so that detailed method of working will be a matter for the builder. Accordingly, cl.3.22 of the RIBA terms provide that the client "… shall hold the contractor, and not the Architect, responsible for the contractor's management and operational methods and for the proper carrying out and completion of the Works and for health and safety provisions on the site …".[313] However, where the contract specifies a particular method of working as an important feature

37-095

---

[306] [2015] EWCA Civ 1146.

[307] See Hodgin (ed.), *Professional Liability: Law and Insurance* (Lloyd's 1996) Ch.3; note also the potential for liability to arise in the tort of negligence in respect of economic loss even absent the existence of a contractual relationship, as with the architect in *Burgess v Lejonvarn* [2017] EWCA Civ 254.

[308] [1964] A.C. 465, HL.

[309] [1994] 2 A.C. 145, HL.

[310] [1995] 2 A.C. 207, HL.

[311] Note that in *Samuel Payne v John Setchell Ltd* [2002] B.L.R. 489 H.H.J. Humphrey Lloyd Q.C. found that ordinarily there would be no concurrent duty of care owed in tort by a construction professional in respect of pure economic losses caused to his client as a result of the incompetent performance of his services. It was concluded that *both* a contractor and an engineer should ordinarily only be taken to owe a tortious duty to take reasonable care against causing their contractual client personal injury or damage to property other than to the building or construction work that is itself the subject of their work/services. It is thought, however, that the judgment gave insufficient weight to the decision in *Henderson v Merrett* and it is notable that the approach taken has not been followed in subsequent construction professional cases. Thus in *Mirant Asia Pacific v Ove Arup* [2005] P.N.L.R. 10 H.H.J. Toulmin Q.C. declined to follow the Court's reasoning in *Payne v Setchell*, holding instead that *Henderson* principles applied in the case of an engineer's concurrent duty of care to his client in respect of economic losses referable to design errors. It should also be noted that the approach taken in *Payne v Setchell* to this issue was not followed by H.H.J. Seymour Q.C. in *Tesco v Costain* (2003) C.I.L.L. 2062. Reference should also be made to *Bellefield Computer Services Ltd v E Turner & Sons Ltd* [2000] B.L.R. 97 where Schieman L.J. observed that in his view the builder in that case did owe a duty of care to the original owner of a property in respect of damage caused to the building itself.

[312] In the absence of an express provision to the contrary, an architect is under a duty to review his design as necessary until the works are complete: *Brickfield Properties v Newton* [1971] 1 W.L.R. 862, CA; and for the position after completion, see *Eckersley v Binnie & Partners* (1988) 18 Con. L.R. 1, per Bingham L.J. But see now *New Islington and Hackney HA v Pollard Thomas and Edwards Ltd* [2001] B.L.R. 74.

[313] See also *Clayton v Woodman & Sons (Builders) Ltd* [1962] 2 Q.B. 533, CA.

of the design, then there is clearly a duty upon the architect to supervise that work. The architect may also have an obligation in relation to general on-site supervision, and both the ACE and the RIBA conditions of appointment contemplate this as a possibility where necessary. Such an obligation will not be discharged by reference to, for example, a clerk of works installed by the architect or by the employer, since the architect will retain overall control.[314] The extent of the supervision which the architect should supply will depend upon the project concerned, but should be sufficient to carry out the job successfully.[315] The professional named in the building contract also has a duty of care towards his client in respect of the certificates which he issues,[316] whether interim or final.[317] However, the right of the building contractor to pursue a claim in negligence against the certifier is limited in the light of *Pacific Associates v Baxter*[318] where the Court of Appeal struck out a claim by contractors under a FIDIC form of engineering contract against the engineers under the contract. It should be noted that a professional may limit its potential liability by way of a net contribution clause. In *West v Ian Finlay & Associates*,[319] it was held by the Court of Appeal that such a clause contained in an architect's retainer should be construed in accordance with the normal meaning of the unambiguous words used in it, that as a result it should apply to a main contractor as well as specialist sub-contractors and that it did not fall foul of the Unfair Terms in Consumer Contracts Regulations 1999[320] as an unfair term nor fail the test of reasonableness under the Unfair Contract Terms Act 1977.

4. PARTICULAR FEATURES

(a) Variations

37-096 **Introduction** It is commonplace that construction works, as finally built, will vary from what was contemplated at the date when the contract was priced by the contractor and executed between the parties. Without express authority there is no power to order the contractor to carry out extra work,[321] and an unauthorised change to the works, if not corrected, may become a breach of contract. Under the law applying in the USA, both State and Federal, there is a principle which limits the power to order variations to those which fall within the general scope of the work. Variations outside this limit are termed "Cardinal Changes", and entitle the contrac-

---

[314] *Leicester Gardens v Trollope* (1911) 75 J.P. 197.
[315] *Alexander Corfield v David Grant* (1992) 59 B.L.R. 102. The liability of construction professionals in negligence has been considered in *J D Williams & Co Ltd v Michael Hyde & Associates Ltd* [2001] B.L.R. 99 (the application of the *Bolam* test); and *Baxall Securities Ltd and Norbain SDC v Sheard Walshaw Partnership* [2002] B.L.R. 100, CA (consideration of the duties of the architect in a particular case of flooding and latent defects). It must of course be remembered that the test for negligence is a particular one (*Bolam v Friern Hospital Management Committee* [1957] 1 W.L.R. 582). For notable examples, see: *Department of National Heritage v Steensen Varming Mulcahy* (1998) 60 Con. L.R. 33; and *London Underground Ltd v Kenchington Ford Plc* (1998) 63 Con. L.R. 1.
[316] *Sutcliffe v Thackrah* [1974] A.C. 727, 737, HL. See also *John Barker Construction Ltd v London Portman Hotel Ltd* (1996) 83 B.L.R. 31.
[317] *London Borough of Merton v Lowe* (1981) 18 B.L.R. 130, CA.
[318] [1990] 1 Q.B. 993; (1988) 44 B.L.R. 33, CA; and see also *Leon Engineering & Construction Co Ltd v Ka Duk Investment Co Ltd* (1989) 47 B.L.R. 139 Hong Kong.
[319] [2014] EWCA Civ 316, [2014] B.L.R. 324.
[320] SI 1999/2083.
[321] *Dodd v Churton* [1897] 1 Q.B. 562.

tor to damages.[322] No such doctrine exists under English law, although there is high authority suggesting that there may be an implied limit on changes that may be ordered.[323] There may be a limit, prescribed by the contract, on variations which may be ordered. This may be in the form of a stated proportion of the value of the works which may not be exceeded without consent[324]; or there may be a provision entitling the contractor to additional payment if net additions or deductions exceed a stated limit.[325] There may be a limit arising by implication in particular circumstances.[326] Otherwise, there will ordinarily be no limit, provided the changes fall within the express terms of the contract.[327]

What constitutes a variation   Modern construction contracts generally contain   **37-097** complex variation clauses which empower the contract administrator to order a wide range of changes under the power to give a variation. Such clauses usually comprise a series of examples rather than a definition.[328] The effect of such clauses will be to designate particular actions of the contract administrator as variations under the contract, e.g. an instruction which restricts access to the site[329]; or an instruction to change the specified sequence of construction.[330] A departure from the contract requirements not instructed by the contract administrator will not constitute a variation, although the contract administrator may be given authority to sanction such a departure as a variation.[331] Even where there is no additional work, there may be a variation where an instruction has the effect of depriving the contractor of choice. Thus in *English Industrial Estates v Kier Construction*[332] the contractor had a choice whether to crush demolition waste on site or to import fill. An instruction of the engineer to crush all hard arisings was held to constitute a variation order by limiting the contractor's choice. In *Strachan & Henshaw Ltd v Stein Industrie (UK) Ltd*[333] the Court of Appeal considered whether the instruction given to the plaintiff sub-contractor to remove its cabins from next to the workface to a distance of half a mile away (involving an alleged increase in "walking time") was an "alteration to the Works" and a variation within the meaning of cl.27 of the MF/1 Conditions of Contract (as amended). It was held that the instruction given by the defendant contractor in relation to the location of the cabins did not alter the *"work to be done by the Contractor under the Contract"* which was the phrase used in cl.1.1 to define *"the Works"* and so there was no variation under cl.27. Variations under a contract are to be distinguished from variations *of* the contract itself. The wording of the particular contract may be relevant to whether a variation under or of the contract is recognised. However, in *MWB Business Exchange Centres Ltd v Rock Advertis-*

---

[322]   See *Construction Claims and Liability*: Simon, sect.11.2, Wiley.
[323]   *Thorn v London Corp* (1876) 1 App. Cas. 120.
[324]   Model Form MF/1 cl.27.2.
[325]   *FIDIC Conditions* 4th edn cl.52.3: additional payment in excess of 15 per cent. The 1998 edition contains a more conventional provision for the adjustment of rates where quantities are varied by more than 10 per cent: cl.12.3(a).
[326]   *Parkinson v Commissioner of Works* [1949] 2 K.B. 632.
[327]   *McAlpine Humberoak v McDermott* (1992) 58 B.L.R. 1.
[328]   See ICC Form cl.51(1).
[329]   JCT cl.5.1.2.1.
[330]   ICC Form cl.51(1).
[331]   JCT SBC 2011 cl.3.14.4.
[332]   (1991) 56 B.L.R. 93.
[333]   (1997) 87 B.L.R. 52, CA.

ing Ltd[334] it was held by the Supreme Court that where a contract contained an anti-oral variation clause and one party alleged a variation to the same was agreed orally, the anti-oral variation clause precluded an informal variation of the contract being effective unless some words or conduct unequivocally representing that the variation was valid notwithstanding its informality gave rise to an estoppel. Something more would be required for that purpose than the informal promise itself.[335]

37-098 **Work not constituting a variation** The carrying out of "additional" work not mentioned in the contract will not constitute a variation if the work is included within the contractor's overall obligation to complete.[336] An instruction of the contract administrator to carry out particular work, where the contractor would otherwise have been obliged to carry out the same or similar work, has been held to be a variation.[337] But the better view, it is thought, is that there is no variation unless the contractor is required to carry out work additional to that necessarily included in the contract. In practice the question whether work which the contractor has not priced is a variation for which extra payment is due constitutes a dispute under the contract, to be determined by an adjudicator or arbitrator.[338] Note that under cl.51(3) of the ICC Form the contractor is not to be paid for any variation necessitated by the contractor's default. While an ordered variation may consist of additional quantities of work, the mere carrying out of work in quantities additional to those stated does not, without more, constitute a variation. Additional quantities or reduced quantities may entitle the contractor to claim compensation where the change in quantities impacts upon the underlying nature of the work and the contractor's tender assumptions or tender prices.[339]

37-099 **Payment for variations** The valuation of variations will either be carried out by reference to a mechanism contained within the contract, or on the broader basis of a reasonable valuation of the work. The contract mechanism may provide for a reasonable valuation in default of applicable rates.

37-100 **Valuation under the contract** The Standard Forms of Contract make elaborate provision for the valuation of variations, which usually involve valuations of the work at rates and prices contained in (or to be ascertained from) the contract documents. Where additional work differs from the contract work, either by its nature or the conditions which it is executed, the additional work may be valued using the contract rates as a basis, or the contract may provide that reasonable rates are to be ascertained.[340] Work which cannot be measured may be ordered to be

---

[334] [2018] UKSC 24.

[335] [2018] UKSC 24 at [16].

[336] *Sharpe v San Paulo Railway* (1873) L.R. 8 Ch. App. 597; *Williams v Fitzmaurice* (1858) 3 H. & N. 844; *Bottoms v Mayor of York* (1892) II Hudson's Building Contracts (4th edn) 208.

[337] *Simplex Concrete Piles v St Pancras BC* (1958) 14 B.L.R. 80.

[338] See *Howard de Walden v Costain* (1991) 55 B.L.R. 124; *Kirk & Kirk v Croydon Corp* (1956) J.P.L. 585; and *English Industrial Estates* (1991) 56 B.L.R. 93; and see generally *"The inclusive price principle—A tribute to Ian Duncan Wallace QC"* by HH Judge Anthony Thornton Q.C. July 2007, published by the Society of Construction Law at *http://www.scl.org.uk.*

[339] See ICC Form cl.56(2)—rates or prices rendered unreasonable; and FIDIC (1993 edn) cl.12.3(a). For a case where a claim for extra payment for hard work conditions encountered on excavation was rejected, see: *Worksop Tarmacadam Company Ltd v Hanneby* (1995) 55 Con. L.R. 105.

[340] See JCT 98 cl.13.5, JCT SBC 2005 cl.5.10, ICC Form cl.52(1), FIDIC (1998 edn) cl.12.3(b). Clause 52 of the ICE 6th edn, was considered by the Court of Appeal in *Henry Boot Construction Ltd v*

executed at daywork rates,[341] and the contract may provide a schedule of daywork rates to be used in these circumstances. More modern forms of contract seek to quantify both the value and the time impact of variations in advance of their being instructed.[342] In the absence of agreement, however, the variation and its effect must be valued subsequent to its order and carrying out. Standard Forms of Contract usually provide for additional compensation arising from the issue of variation instructions, typically in terms of general "loss and expense" incurred in addition to payment due in respect of the variation itself[343] or by way of adjustment of other contract rates which have been rendered "unreasonable or inapplicable" by the variation.[344] Where the contract does not contain a bill of quantities, provision is usually made for the contractor to submit a Schedule of Rates to be utilised in the valuation of variations. In *Henry Boot Construction Ltd v Alstom Combined Cycles Ltd*[345] it was held that mistakes in the contractor's rates and prices were to be disregarded for the purposes of arriving at a new rate pursuant to cl.52(1) of the ICE 6th edition even though the practical effect of such an approach was to give the contractor a windfall.[346]

Reasonable valuation   Where there are no rates or prices in the contract documents covering the variation in question and the contract does not provide for a reasonable rate to be determined, the contractor will be entitled to a reasonable sum on the basis of an implied term as to payment.[347] What is a reasonable sum will be a question requiring consideration of all the factors in the case, and there are no rigid rules which will apply in such cases. Although "cost plus a percentage for profit" is often associated with reasonable remuneration[348] there are situations where the contractor may recover on a more generous basis to take account of such matters as the value of the contractor's work to the employer.[349] On the question of what is a reasonable sum, the shipping case of *Greenmast Shipping v Jean Lion et Cie*[350] is instructive and has been referred to in a number of decisions on building contracts.[351] In that case, owners were entitled to payment in a situation where there was held to be an implied contract to pay for a vessel laying off Aqaba for nine days whilst the charterers resolved certain problems in relation to the sale of the vessel's cargo. Saville J. approached the question of remuneration "... by asking simply   **37-101**

Alstom Combined Cycles Ltd [2000] B.L.R. 247; and the entitlement to an uplift for overheads and profit as part of a fair valuation under the "third limb" of cl.52 was considered in *Weldon Plant Ltd v The Commission for New Towns* [2000] B.L.R. 496.

341   See above, para.37-067.
342   See ICC Design and Construct Version cl.52(1) and New Engineering and Construction Contracts cl.62.
343   See JCT 98 cl.26.1 and JCT SBC 2005 cll.4.23 to 4.26.
344   ICC Form cl.52(4).
345   (2000) 69 Con. L.R. 27, CA.
346   For observations on the decision at first instance, see: I. Duncan Wallace (2000) 16 Const. L.J. 40.
347   *Thorn v London Corp* (1876) 1 App. Cas. 120; *Parkinson v Commissioner of Works* [1949] 2 K.B. 632, CA; *Pilgrim Shipping Co Ltd v The State Trading Co of India Ltd (The Hadjitsakos)* [1975] 1 Lloyd's Rep. 356, 369; *Costain Civil Engineering Ltd v Zanen Dredging and Contracting Co Ltd* (1996) 85 B.L.R. 77, 94.
348   *Sanjay Lachhani v Destination Canada (UK) Ltd* (1997) 13 Const. L.J. 279.
349   *Costain v Zanen* (1996) 85 B.L.R. 77.
350   [1986] 2 Lloyd's Rep. 277.
351   *Laserbore Ltd v Morrison Biggs Wall Ltd* (1993) C.I.L.L. 896; *Costain Civil Engineering v Zanen Dredging and Contracting Co Ltd* (1996) 85 B.L.R. 77.

what would be a fair commercial rate for the services provided outside the charter-party …".[352]

(b)   Instructions, Certificates and Approval

37-102   Introduction   These are three types of "event" typically provided for under the terms of a construction contract as part of the machinery of performance: the giving of instructions, the issue of certificates and the grant of approval. The effect of each will depend on the terms of the individual contract but there are some general principles which can be formulated from the cases. Each such event involves a decision in writing, or confirmed in writing, of the contract administrator. With limited exceptions, all such decisions are subject to review by adjudication or by arbitration or litigation, subject to any other dispute resolution process that may be incorporated into the contract.

37-103   Instructions   A construction contract will usually provide expressly for the issue of instructions, which allow for the ongoing direction and supervision of the works and of the contractor. The ICC Form cl.13(1), provides that the contractor "shall comply with and adhere strictly to the Engineer's instructions on any matter …". Clause 13(3) then provides "if such instructions require any variation to any part of the Works the same shall be deemed to have been given pursuant to Clause 51". These common provisions express the general principle that an "instruction" may or may not constitute a variation: if it does so, it will not be prevented from taking effect as such by being called an instruction; an instruction not amounting to a variation will take effect in accordance with the terms of the contract.[353] Examples of other types of instruction (not amounting to variations) are an instruction to commence the works,[354] an instruction to suspend the progress of the works (often referred to as an Order),[355] an instruction to carry out tests on materials or workmanship,[356] an instruction nominating a sub-contractor,[357] an instruction (referred to as a request) to furnish vouchers to prove the quality of materials[358] and an instruction to remove from the site work materials or goods[359] or any person employed thereon.[360] Every construction contract requires large numbers of instructions of the foregoing, and of many other, types for their practical operation. The power to give instructions may need to be implied as a matter of necessity, where not expressly stated in the contract documents.[361]

37-104   Certificates   Most construction contracts expressly require the issue of docu-

---

[352] [1986] 2 Lloyd's Rep. 277, 279.
[353] cl.13(3) of the ICC Form also provides for the possibility of additional payment where instructions disrupt the contractor's arrangements.
[354] ICC Form cl.41(1)(b), where the contractor is to be "notified".
[355] ICC Form cl.40(1).
[356] ICC Form cl.36(1).
[357] JCT 98 cl.35.1. Note that no equivalent provisions remains in JCT SBC 2005.
[358] JCT 98 cl.8.2.1.
[359] JCT 98 cl.8.4.1 and JCT SBC 2011 cl.3.18.1.
[360] JCT 98 cl.8.6 and JCT SBC 2011 cl.3.21.
[361] Where work is carried out in the absence of a formal instruction, then it will often be necessary for the contractor to rely upon estoppel arguments in order to recover payment for additional work carried out in the absence of an instruction or confirmation of verbal instruction, but nevertheless accepted by the employer. For a consideration of these issues, see *Ministry of Defence v Scott Wilson Kirkpatrick* [2000] B.L.R. 20, CA. See also the decision of the Court of Appeal of New South Wales in *Trimis v Mina* [2000] T.C.L.R. 346.

ments called "certificates" by the Contract Administrator. There is no definition of the term, but a certificate is usually taken to embody a decision requiring the exercise of professional skill and judgment on issues which will often require subjective assessments.[362] The subject matter of certificates and of instructions may overlap, but the latter normally embodies no more than an administrative decision, while the former may involve the initial resolution of a dispute. In *Kaye v Hosier and Dickinson* it was said that the architect:

"... has to issue certificates showing how much money is owing. Incidentally, his certificates and instructions may resolve some controversial points, and he has to act fairly, but he is not primarily or characteristically adjudicating on disputes."[363]

Certificates may be categorised into interim (or payment) certificates, final certificates and certificates of record. They will be issued throughout the contract, as required by progress of the works. Completion will involve certificates of all three types. Although it is rare for a construction contract to specify the precise form for a certificate, to be effective the document should clearly and unambiguously represent the physical expression of the certifying process.[364] Further, a certificate is subject to the general rules of construction.[365]

Interim certificates These are the means whereby instalment payments are ef-   **37-105**
fected, the most usual arrangement being for monthly valuations to be made on the basis of an approximate measure of work carried out.[366] This will be appropriate whether the contract is for a lump sum or subject to remeasure. In the latter case, however, work will need to be accurately measured as each section is completed, for the purpose of the final account.[367] It was held by the House of Lords in *Gilbert-Ash v Modern Engineering*[368] that an interim certificate created a debt which could, subject to any contractual term to the contrary, be reduced or extinguished by set-off, reversing decisions of the Court of Appeal to the contrary.[369] An alternative form of interim payment not involving measurement is referred to as "milestone" payments, whereby the contract sum is divided into predetermined amounts to be released at dates or stages (milestones) of the work. Such payments may, depending on the terms of the contract, require a form of certificate, e.g. as to completion of the requisite work stages. Milestone payments may also be made subject to the achievement of stipulated rates of progress. Milestone payments have been recommended eventually to replace interim payments based on monthly measurement.[370] Although the value stated in interim certificates may be corrected in subsequent certificates,[371] the contract administrator will be required to give more than a merely

---

[362] See, for example, JCT 2011 cl.2.28 ("If, in the opinion of the Architect, ... the Architect shall ... give an extension of time ... as he then estimates to be fair and reasonable ...").
[363] [1972] 1 W.L.R. 146.
[364] See *BR and EP Cantrell v Wright & Fuller Ltd* [2003] B.L.R. 412 at 413.
[365] [2003] B.L.R. 412 at 430–431.
[366] See *Secretary of State for Transport v Birse Farr Joint Venture* [1993] 62 B.L.R. 36 at 53.
[367] See ICC Form cll.55–57.
[368] [1974] A.C. 689.
[369] *Dawnays v Minter* [1971] 1 W.L.R. 1205; *Frederick Mark v Schield* [1972] 1 Lloyd's Rep. 9; *GKN Foundations v Wandsworth LBC* [1972] 1 Lloyd's Rep. 528; *John Thompson v Wellingborough Steel* (1972) 1 B.L.R. 69; *Token Construction v Naviewland Properties* (1973) 1 B.L.R. 48.
[370] "Latham" *Report—Constructing the Team*, HMSO 1994.
[371] See *Rupert Morgan Building Services Ltd v Jervis* [2003] EWCA Civ 1563, [2004] 1 W.L.R. 1867,

superficial glance at the works prior to the issue of a certificate.[372] Furthermore, where the contract provides for interim payments to be made in respect of "... the total value of the sub-contract work on site properly executed by the sub-contractor ..."[373] or similar terms,[374] then defective work should not be included in a valuation, and should be included only when rectified at a later stage.

37-106 **Final certificate** This is provided for under most construction contracts, although the terminology and the effect of such a certificate will vary between different forms of contract. A final certificate may take effect only as a statement of account[375] but in most cases it also certifies the work as being finally complete.[376] The certificate may also be made conditionally final and binding on the parties as to the opinion of the contract administrator on quality of the work.[377] A claim to have a sum included in a final certificate constitutes a separate and different cause of action to a claim to have a sum, even if the same, included in an interim certificate.[378]

37-107 **Certificates of record** The third type of certificate (not always so called) signifies events such as completion of the works[379] and making good of defects.[380] Other examples are a certificate that the contractor has failed to complete the works by the completion date[381] and a certificate of the contractor's default prior to termination of employment.[382] Examples which are not called certificates, but operate as such, are extensions of time[383] and the valuation of a contractual claim or variation, which will subsequently be incorporated into the next interim payment certificate.

37-108 **Recovery without a certificate** It is a matter of construction of the underlying contract whether a certificate is a condition precedent to recovery of the sum of money to be certified. In *Lubenham v South Pembroke DC*[384] the Court of Appeal held that a certificate issued under the JCT Standard Form of Building Contract, 1963 edition, where there was a patently incorrect deduction, was nevertheless bind-

---

CA at 1870. In *Urang Commercial Ltd v Century Investments Ltd* [2011] EWHC 1561 (TCC), 138 Con. L.R. 233 it was held, following the decision in *Rupert Morgan*, that the effect of the interim payment provisions under a JCT form of contract was that when a sum was certified as a "sum due" the employer had to pay the relevant amount on the date specified unless an appropriate withholding notice was issued within time (although there was no requirement to serve such a notice in respect of other claims made by the contractor).

[372] *Sutcliffe v Chippendale & Edmondson* (1971) 18 B.L.R. 149; *Townsend v Stone Toms & Partners* (1984) 27 B.L.R. 26, CA.

[373] DOM/1 Conditions cl.21.4. These words were considered (in the context of alleged defects) in *Barrett Steel Building Ltd v Amec Construction Ltd* Unreported March 3, 1997 (see 15-CLD–10-07).

[374] See IFC 98 cl.4.2.1(a) and JCT IC 2005 cll.4.6 and 4.7, and JCT MW 2005 cl.4.3.

[375] See ICC Form cl.60(4).

[376] See JCT 98 cll.30.8, 30.9 and JCT SBC 2011 cl.4.15.

[377] JCT 2011 cl.1.10. In certain circumstances, the protection afforded by a Final Certificate may arise on the basis of an estoppel; see *Tameside MBC v Barlows Securities Group Services Ltd* (1999) C.I.L.L. 1559. See *Cantrell v Wright and Fuller Ltd* [2003] EWHC 1545 (TCC), [2003] B.L.R. 412.

[378] See *Henry Boot Construction Ltd v Alstom Combined Cycles Ltd* [2005] EWCA Civ 814, [2005] 1 W.L.R. 3850 at 3870 3873, CA.

[379] JCT 98 cl.17.1, and JCT SBC 2011 cl.2.30, ICC Form cl.48(2).

[380] JCT 98 cl.17.4, and JCT SBC 2011 cl.2.39, ICC Form cl.61(1).

[381] JCT 98 cl.24.1 and JCT SBC 2011 cl.2.31.

[382] ICC Form cl.65(1).

[383] JCT 98 cl.25, and JCT SBC 2011 cll.2.26 to 2.29, ICC Form cl.44.

[384] (1986) 33 B.L.R. 39.

ing, so that the contractor could not assert entitlement to a further sum. May L.J., giving the judgment of the court, held:

"Whatever the cause of the undervaluation, the proper remedy available to the contractor is, in our opinion, to request the Architect to make the appropriate adjustment in another certificate, or if he declines to do so, to take the dispute to arbitration under clause 35. In default of arbitration or a new certificate the conditions themselves give the contractor no right to sue for the higher sum. In other words we think that under this form of contract the issue of a certificate is always a condition precedent to the right of the contractor to be paid."

Where the certificate is a condition precedent to recovery of payment, a sum otherwise due may be recovered without a certificate in the following circumstances: (i) where the condition precedent has been waived by the other parties to the contract; (ii) where the certifier has been disqualified by improper conduct[385]; (iii) where there has been prevention by or on behalf of the employer[386]; and (iv) where the certifier becomes incapacitated without being replaced.[387] In practice, however, it will usually be more convenient to rely on the powers of an arbitrator to review and revise any certificate, which will ordinarily include the power to grant a certificate which has been refused by the certifier.[388] Where the dispute is litigated, the same powers will be available to the court.[389] In *Henry Boot Ltd v Alstom Combined Cycles Ltd*[390] it was explained by the Court of Appeal that the absence of a certificate is not a bar to the right to payment even where it is expressed to be a condition precedent (at least where the contract administrator's decision is not expressed to be binding) because a court or arbitrator can find that a party was entitled to payment in a larger sum than certified.

Liability of the certifier   It was held in *Sutcliffe v Thackrah*[391] that the immunity **37-109** assumed to attach to an arbitrator[392] did not apply to a certifier, reversing earlier authority to the contrary.[393] The decision applied both to the issue of an interim or final certificate. The House recognised, however, the possibility that the function of a certifier might involve a "sufficient judicial element to require an arbitrator's immunity to attach".[394] Examples of "certification" which could attract immunity are the engineer's decision under cl.66 of earlier versions of the ICE Conditions, or the decision of an adjudicator under the terms of a contract.[395]

Approvals   Most construction contracts require a variety of approvals to be given **37-110** by the contract administrator. These may be expressed in positive terms requiring "approval" to be expressed, or they may require the "satisfaction" of the engineer

---

385 *Panamena Europea Navigacion v Frederick Leyland* [1947] A.C. 428; *Hickman v Roberts* [1913] A.C. 229.
386 *Roberts v Bury Commissioners* (1870) L.R. 5 C.P. 310; *Croudace v London Borough of Lambeth* (1986) 33 B.L.R. 20.
387 *Perini Pacific v Commonwealth of Australia* (1969) 12 B.L.R. 82; *Croudace v Lambeth* (1986) 33 B.L.R. 20.
388 See JCT 98 cl.41.4, JCT SBC 2011 cl.9.5 and ICC Form cl.66(8).
389 *Beaufort Developments v Gilbert-Ash NI* [1999] 1 A.C. 266.
390 [2005] EWCA Civ 814, [2005] 1 W.L.R. 3850 at 3861.
391 [1974] A.C. 727.
392 See now Arbitration Act 1996 s.29.
393 *Chambers v Goldthorpe* [1901] 1 Q.B. 624.
394 per Lord Reid.
395 See below.

or architect. The Standard Form of Building Contract 1963 edition required the works generally to be to the architect's satisfaction, but this is modified in the 1998 edition, such satisfaction now being applicable "where and to the extent that approval of the quality of materials or of the standards of workmanship is a matter for the opinion of the Architect"; and in such a case the work is to be to his "reasonable satisfaction".[396] In the JCT SBC 2005 and 2011, cl.1.10 is to similar effect. The ICC Form, however, requires the whole of the works to be "to the satisfaction of the Engineer".[397] Other examples of an express approval are in relation to the "mode, manner and speed of construction of the works" which are to be "acceptable to the Engineer" under the ICC Form[398]; and in relation to the contractor's programme which is required to be accepted by the engineer.[399] The effect of the giving or withholding of such approvals is dependent on the terms of the contract. In general, however, action which is within the discretion of the contract administrator will not afford the contractor any ground of claim, while action outside the area of contractual discretion will give rise to a right to compensation, as a variation or as a breach.[400] Non-approval within the discretion of the contract administrator may give rise to express rights under the terms of the contract.[401]

(c) Completion, Maintenance and Performance

37-111 **Scope of obligations** Construction contracts can be divided into an initial construction period followed by a post-completion period during which different types of contract impose different requirements. In the simplest case the contract may contain provisions which apply post-completion, for correction of latent defects which appear during a stipulated period. Alternatively, the contract may require works to be maintained for a stipulated period. Where the subject matter of the contract is plant or machinery, there is usually an obligation to operate and demonstrate performance, as part of the substantive obligations. In the case of process plant, performance is likely to include both consumption of resources and output in terms of product quality and rate. Various questions arise where fully conforming performance is not achieved, which are considered further below.

37-112 **Completion** Standard form contracts will usually be found to stipulate the degree of completion required to bring the construction period to an end. This may be referred to as "*practical*" completion[402] or "*substantial*" completion which may also be subject to passing any final testing or commissioning prescribed by the contract.[403] There may also be provisions entitling the contractor to achieve completion notwithstanding outstanding work.[404] In the absence of qualifying provisions, the work must be sensibly finished even though subject to defects or uncompleted

---

396 1998 edn cl.2.1.
397 ICC Form cl.13(1).
398 ICC Form cl.13(2).
399 ICC Form cl.14(2).
400 But see above as to effect of actions of the supervisor on the employer.
401 See ICC Form cl.13(3) where the contractor is entitled to compensation if an instruction of the engineer gives rise to costs which could not have been foreseen.
402 JCT 2011, cl.2.30.
403 ICC Form cl.48(1).
404 ICC Form cl.49(1).

details for which allowance is made.[405] The achievement of completion is unaffected by the subsequent manifestation of defects that were latent at the date of completion,[406] although such defects will entitle the owner to an abatement of, or set-off against, the contract price or any instalment payable upon completion.[407]

Maintenance and defects correction   These terms are sometimes used **37-113** interchangeably. Editions of the ICE Conditions of Contract up to the 5th (1973) referred to "maintenance" as meaning the correction of defects. The position is clarified under the 7th edition of the ICE Conditions and under the same provision of the ICC Form.[408] Maintenance, properly so called, refers to maintaining the works, by repair or renewal, during a specified period. Such an obligation will require express words, as opposed to the correction of defects for which the contractor will in any event be liable (see below) by way of damages for breach. The JCT Standard Form of Building Contract has traditionally referred to the period during which the contractor corrects "defects, shrinkages or other faults" as the defects liability period. While the contract could provide for the contractor's liability for latent defects to be limited to such a period, it is clear that this is not the effect of the JCT Form of Contract. The effect of the "defects liability" provisions is not to render the contractor liable to correct defects (such liability existing in any event) but to afford the contractor a right to receive notice of defects in the stipulated period and to have the opportunity of correcting them at his own expense, as opposed to what may be the greater expense of bringing in other contractors. Once completion is achieved, any latent defect appearing in the work renders the contractor in breach and liable in damages which will not be capped by any provision for liquidated damages in respect of loss of use of the works. Conversely, defects appearing before the achievement of completion may be regarded as a "temporary disconformity" not ordinarily sounding in separate damages.[409] In *Oksana Mul v Hutton Construction Ltd*[410] Akenhead J. held that cl.2.30 of the JCT Intermediate Form of Contract, which created a right for the employer to deduct sums from the contract sum in respect of unremedied defects in certain circumstances, did not exclude the employer's parallel right to claim damages for defects present in the works as at practical completion.

Performance obligations   Contracts for the provision of process plant and **37-114** machinery are usually divided into an initial construction period, followed by a post-completion period during which the plant must be operated and performance demonstrated.[411] The provisions as to testing are usually accompanied by a detailed protocol involving stages, such as an initial period of operation followed by performance tests over a prescribed period. The contract may provide prescribed penalties or deductions as compensation in respect of failure to meet required

---

[405] *Hoenig v Isaacs* [1952] 2 All E.R. 176; *Bolton v Mahadeva* [1972] 1 W.L.R. 1009.
[406] *Jarvis v Westminster CC* [1970] 1 W.L.R. 637.
[407] *Gilbert-Ash v Modern Engineering* [1974] A.C. 689, HL.
[408] cl.49 of ICE 7th edn and ICC Form.
[409] This passage is based on the (dissenting) judgment of Lord Diplock in *P & M Kaye v Hosier & Dickenson* [1972] 1 W.L.R. 146, but see further *Lintest v Roberts* (1980) 13 B.L.R. 38, where defects prior to completion were held to give rise to a vested right of correction.
[410] [2014] EWHC 1797 (TCC), [2014] B.L.R. 529.
[411] For an example of a project with substantial performance testing, see *Mitsui Babcock Energy Ltd v John Brown Engineering Ltd* (1996) 51 Con. L.R. 129 where it was unsuccessfully argued that a failure of the parties to agree on performance testing meant that there was no contract at all.

performance levels. The detailed performance requirements will be specific to each item of plant or machinery, but standard forms exist which prescribe the basic contract structure.[412] In addition to performance of obligations, the contract may require other services, such as training of operating personnel, the provision of spares for the plant, as-built drawing of the works and detailed operating manuals and instructions.

(d)   Extension of Time and Liquidated Damages

37-115   Date for completion   Construction contracts almost invariably stipulate a period or date for commencement and/or completion. The contractor must be afforded the opportunity to carry out the work within the stipulated period.[413] Any act of prevention, such as the ordering of variations or late access to working areas, will release the contractor from the fixed period unless the contract provides machinery for adjustment of the time period.[414] The major consequence of time becoming "at large" is that by operation of the so-called "prevention principle" the employer thereby loses its ability to rely upon any liquidated and ascertained damages clause in the contract. The prevention principle is based on the notion that a promisee cannot insist upon the performance of an obligation which he has prevented the promisor from performing. In a building contract, acts of prevention (such as variation instructions) do not have to amount to breaches of contract in order to trigger the application of the prevention principle. However, for the act relied upon to amount to an act of prevention, it must actually prevent the contractor from carrying out the works within the contract period. Thus, in *Adyard Abu Dhabi v SD Marine Services*[415] it was held that where there were concurrent causes of delay (one the contractor's responsibility and the other the employer's) the prevention principle does not operate because the delay would have occurred anyway absent the employer's delay event happening.

37-116   Extension of time   Clauses relating to the grant of extensions of time for completion are to be regarded as being inserted for the benefit of the employer, to permit re-fixing of the completion period where delay is occasioned by the employer. It follows that an extension of time clause is to be construed contra proferentem, against the employer, and that general words such as "other unavoidable circumstances" will not be construed so as to apply to specific delay occasioned by the employer.[416] Extension of time clauses under standard forms of contract usually contain elaborate machinery providing for the giving of notice by the contractor and for decisions by the contract administrator, which may be given in stages.[417] There is generally no objection to an extension of time being given retrospectively.[418] The contractor's notice may be made a condition precedent to the

---

[412] See for mechanical & electrical plant, Form MF/1 and for chemical plant the I. Chem. E. Conditions.

[413] *Wells v Army & Navy Co-op* (1902) 86 L.T. 764, HBC (4th edn), Vol.2, p.346.

[414] *Dodd v Churton* [1897] 1 Q.B. 562.

[415] [2011] EWHC 848 (Comm), [2011] B.L.R. 384.

[416] *Peak v McKinney* (1969) 1 B.L.R. 111.

[417] ICC Form cl.44, JCT SBC 2011 cl.2.27. In *Walter Lilly & Co Ltd v DMW Developments Ltd* [2012] EWHC 1773 (TCC), [2012] B.L.R. 503 it was held (at [362]–[365]) that cl.25.3.3 of the JCT Standard Form of Building Contract required a consideration of what events critically delayed the works as they went along, as opposed to a purely retrospective exercise.

[418] *Amalgamated Building Contractors v Waltham Holy Cross UDC* [1952] 2 All E.R. 452.

right to extension,[419] but it is more usual to permit the grant of an extension in the absence of notice, in order to avoid time becoming "at large". Alternatively, on a proper construction of the contract the procedural requirements may only be "directory", in which case a failure to comply with the same will only be capable of sounding in damages as opposed to preventing the contractor obtaining an extension of time. Where there is ambiguity as to whether or not notification is a condition precedent to an extension of time, it is to be construed not to be.[420]

Relevant delay   The right to extension will be conditional on proof of the relevant events and may also require proof that "completion of the Works is likely to be delayed thereby".[421] It has been held that under the JCT form of building contract, in order to establish an entitlement to an extension of time, it is necessary to show that the relevant event relied upon was likely to or did in fact cause actual delay to the progress of the works and thereby to the completion date for the works as a whole.[422] In *Balfour Beatty v Chestermount Properties* it was therefore held that delay to the completion date must be assessed by reference to the progress of the works in relation to the then-projected completion date.[423] Following this approach, in *Adyard Abu Dhabi v SD Marine Services* it was held that merely establishing delay caused to a particular work activity which does not impact on the completion date of the works as a whole, or theoretical delay, will not suffice.[424] In *Adyard* the Court rejected the claimant shipbuilder's submission that an employer's risk event need only be measured against the contractual completion date and that this did not require any factual analysis of competing causes of delay to the actual progress of the works that the claimant might be responsible for.

    Alternatively, the right to extension may be conditioned on showing that "delay ... has been suffered by the contractor as a result of" the relevant event.[425] In the latter case, the contractor may be entitled to an extension even though the work has not been shown to be delayed beyond the completion date. Such an extension may have the effect of allowing the contractor to mitigate the effect of his own delay or to claim compensation for delay caused by some other event for which the employer is liable.

    Any extension of time awarded will invariably be added by reference to the period immediately following the contractual completion date, even if the delaying event in fact occurred at some other point in time, such as substantially after

37-117

---

419 See *Bremer Handelsgeseuschaft mbH v Vander Avenne Izegem PVBA* [1978] 2 Lloyd's Rep. 109, HL for the general approach to the construction of a notice clause as a condition precedent, requiring the time for service and resultant loss of rights from a failure to comply to be expressed. But note the less stringent approach taken in *Steria Ltd v Sigma Wireless Communications Ltd* [2008] B.L.R. 79.

420 *Steria Ltd v Sigma Wireless Communications Ltd* [2008] B.L.R. 79 TCC at [88] and [89]. See also *WW Gear Construction Ltd v McGee Group Ltd* [2010] EWHC 1460 (TCC) where it was indicated that in deciding whether a clause was or was not a condition precedent to recovery, the ordinary rules of contractual construction should apply (see at [11]–[13]).

421 JCT 98 cl.25.3.1.2 and JCT SBC 2011 cl.2.28.1 and see generally *Henry Boot v Central Lancashire NTDC* (1980) 15 B.L.R. 1.

422 See *Balfour Beatty v Chestermount Properties Ltd* (1993) 62 B.L.R. 1 at 27; *Henry Boot Construction (UK) Ltd v Malmaison Hotel (Manchester) Ltd* (1999) 70 Con. L.R. 32; and *City Inn Ltd v Shepherd Construction Ltd* [2010] B.L.R. 473 (per Lord Osborne at [42]).

423 (1993) 62 B.L.R. 1, per Colman J. at [25] and [29]–[32].

424 [2011] EWHC 848 (Comm), [2011] B.L.R. 384, per Hamblen J. at [257]–[292].

425 ICC Form cl.44(2).

the original completion date.[426] This could produce incongruous results in terms of liability for damages arising from late completion or claims for loss and expense, but it is submitted that such problems can be reduced or eliminated entirely by correctly applying the causation requirements of such subsequent claims rather than focussing too strictly on the period in respect of which an extension of time has been granted.

37-118 **Assessment of entitlement** The assessment of any extension of time entitlement involves an exercise of judgment by the contract administrator which must be fair and rational. In *John Barker Construction Ltd v London Portman Hotel Ltd*[427] it was held that an architect, when considering what a "fair and reasonable" extension of time would consist of under cl.25 of the JCT Standard Form of Building Contract With Quantities (1980 edition), must (i) apply any relevant provisions of the building contract, (ii) make a logical and methodical analysis of the effect any relevant events had or were likely to have on the programme, and (iii) conduct a calculation of the relevant critical delay, rather than simply make an impressionistic general assessment of the same. Although the need for a logical and methodical analysis to underpin any award of an extension of time has been doubted.[428] It is submitted that Arbitrators and Courts are likely to require contract administrators to discharge this function in a way that contains some form of logical and methodical assessment.

37-119 **Time at large** Where the work is delayed by the employer and an appropriate extension of time is not granted, time is said to be "at large", i.e. the contractual date is no longer binding. The contractual obligation is then replaced by an obligation to complete within a reasonable time.[429] Time will be "at large" where delay is caused by the employer and no machinery exists under the contract allowing the completion date to be re-fixed.[430] The same applies where the contract administrator fails to extend time.[431] In *McAlpine Humberoak v McDermott International*,[432] the contract provided for an extension of time but contained no machinery whereby it was to be granted. The Court of Appeal held that this did not prevent time being re-fixed, if necessary by the court, so as to permit the recovery of general (not liquidated) damages by the employer. Where the contract contains an arbitration

---

[426] *Carillion Construction Ltd v Emcor Engineering Services Ltd* [2017] EWCA Civ 65 where this was described as an extension being awarded on a "contiguous" basis.

[427] (1996) 83 B.L.R. 31.

[428] See the dicta of H.H.J. Seymour Q.C. in *Royal Brompton Hospital NHS Trust v Hammond (No.7)* 76 Con. L.R. 148 at 176, which appeared to approve the adoption of an impressionistic approach.

[429] *Pentland Hick v Raymond and Reid* [1893] A.C. 22; *British Steel v Cleveland Bridge* (1981) 24 B.L.R. 94. In *Shawton Engineering Ltd v DGP International Ltd (t/a Design Group Partnership)* [2005] EWCA Civ 1359, [2006] B.L.R. 1, the Court of Appeal held that when time was at large the determination of a reasonable time for completion was a composite question that had to be judged objectively as at the time when the question arose and in the light of all relevant circumstances— and not simply, e.g. by a consideration of the time required to complete any work associated with the instruction of a variation.

[430] *Stanmor Floors Ltd v Piper Construction Midlands Ltd* Unreported May 4, 2000; *Multiplex Construction (UK) Ltd v Honeywell Control Systems (No.2)* [2007] EWHC 447 (TCC), [2007] B.L.R. 195. See also the general observations of Fraser J. on the time at large principle in *North Midland Building Ltd v Cyden Homes Ltd* [2017] EWHC 2414 (TCC), upheld on appeal, [2018] EWCA Civ 1744.

[431] *Peak v McKinney* (1969) 1 B.L.R. 111.

[432] (1992) 58 B.L.R. 1.

clause, time may similarly be re-fixed by the arbitrator's award, provided that the contract allows for an extension on the appropriate grounds.

Concurrent delay Concurrent delay can be defined as a period of project over-run which results from two or more effective causes of delay which are of approximately equal causative potency.[433] Under the JCT and similar forms of construction contracts, as long as it is established that the relevant event relied upon as the basis of an extension of time claim is at least a concurrent cause of actual delay to the completion date of the works, the contractor will be entitled to an extension of time.[434] The approach of the Scottish Courts in this situation, to permit an apportionment of the relevant period of delay between the parties so as to permit a partial award of an extension of time to the contractor,[435] probably does not reflect the law of England.[436]

37-120

Liquidated damages Most construction contracts make provision for recovery of pre-fixed or "liquidated" damages for delay in completion by the contractor. While such damages may be regarded as limiting the contractor's liability,[437] all the modern authorities treat such damages potentially as a penalty, recoverable only where it is shown to be a "genuine pre-estimate of loss".[438] There are very few instances in which the stipulated damages have been successfully challenged on the ground they were not a genuine pre-estimate. In *Alfred McAlpine Capital Projects Ltd v Tilebox Ltd*,[439] the court provided a useful summary of the law relating to liquidated damages and penalty clauses in the construction field: the pre-estimate of liquidated and ascertained damages did not have to be correct to be enforceable; the test for whether a clause was an unenforceable penalty was an objective one; for a pre-estimate to be unreasonable there had to be a substantial difference between the estimated and actual damage sustained; and the court would normally be predisposed to uphold the terms of the parties' agreement in this respect when made in a commercial context between parties with comparable bargaining power.

37-121

---

[433] See John Marrin Q.C., "Concurrent Delay" (2002) 18 Const. L.J. 6 at 436, as approved in *Adyard Abu Dhabi v SD Marine Services* [2011] EWHC 848 (Comm), per Hamblen J. at 277.

[434] See *Henry Boot Construction (UK) Ltd v Malmaison Hotel (Manchester) Ltd* (1999) 70 Con. L.R. 32. The *Malmaison* approach was apparently approved in *Motherwell Bridge Construction Ltd v Micafil Vakuumtechnik* (2002) 81 Con. L.R. 44, per H.H.J. Toulmin, CBE, Q.C., at 559–564; see also *Walter Lilly & Co Ltd v Mackay & DMW Developments Ltd* [2012] EWHC 1773 (TCC) where it was held that concurrent delay was sufficient to establish an entitlement to an extension of time under the JCT form, per Akenhead J. at 362–370; and *Saga Cruises BDF Ltd v Fincantieri SpA* [2016] EWHC 1875 (Comm) at [249]–[251].

[435] See *John Doyle Construction Ltd v Laing Management (Scotland) Ltd* [2004] B.L.R. 295; and *City Inn v Shepherd Construction Ltd* [2010] B.L.R. 437. See also the obiter dicta in support of this approach in the decision of the High Court of Hong Kong in *W. Hing Construction Co Ltd v Boost Investments Ltd* [2009] B.L.R. 338 at [61]–[62].

[436] See the discussion of this issue by Ramsey J. in the papers entitled "Claims for Delay & Disruption: the impact of *City Inn*", presented at the annual TECBAR conference in January 2011 and in the TECBAR Review for Spring 2011. See also *Walter Lilly & Co Ltd v DMW Developments Ltd* [2012] EWHC 1773 (TCC), [2012] B.L.R. 503, where it was held that, under the JCT extension of time clause wording and similar forms of construction contracts, as long as it is established that the relevant event relied upon as the basis of an extension of time claim by a contractor is at least a concurrent cause of actual delay to the completion date of the works, the contractor will be entitled to an extension of time (see at [362]–[370]).

[437] See *Suisse Atlantique v Rotterdamsche Kolen Centrale* [1967] 1 A.C. 361.

[438] *Dunlop v New Garage* [1915] A.C. 79.

[439] [2005] EWHC 281 (TCC), [2005] B.L.R. 271.

The fact that damages may be difficult or even impossible to estimate does not lead to the conclusion they must be a penalty.[440] There are, conversely, many cases in which the deduction of liquidated damages has been challenged on the ground of improper operation of the contract machinery,[441] or inability to fix the damages with precision,[442] or failure to establish the applicable completion date.[443] The leading case is *Peak v McKinney*,[444] where delay occurred on a local authority housing contract as a result of the discovery of defective work. Additional delay, not of the contractor's making, was caused by the employers' inaction. Liquidated damages were deducted but the Court of Appeal held that the words of the extension of time clause "or other unavoidable circumstances" should be construed *contra proferentem*, and therefore did not permit the architect to grant an extension on account of the employer's delay. Consequently, time was at large and no liquidated damages could be recovered. The court further held that in such a case the employer was "left to his ordinary remedies; that is to say, to recover such damages as he can prove flow from the contractor's breach".[445]

37-122 Revised rule on penalty clauses In *Cavendish Square Holding BV v Makdessi* the Supreme Court held that the true test for a penalty is whether the impugned provision is a secondary obligation which imposes a detriment on the contract-breaker out of all proportion to any legitimate interest of the innocent party in the enforcement of the primary obligation.[446] This test is likely to be more permissive of liquidated damages clauses and any cases pre-dating this decision must be treated with care.

An interesting question which arises is whether, upon the liquidated damages provisions in the contract becoming unenforceable, the amount of liquidated damages nevertheless takes effect as a limit on the unliquidated damages which can be recovered. A number of charterparty cases suggest that damages can be recovered in excess of the cap.[447] There is no direct authority dealing with the question in the case of construction contracts, although there is some support for the view that the unenforceable liquidated damages clause should indeed operate as a limit on the damages which can be recovered.[448]

37-123 Recovery of damages Contracts will often require the employer to take certain procedural steps in relation to the contractor before he will become entitled to deduct liquidated damages. In *JF Finnegan v Community Housing Association Ltd*[449] it was held that JCT 80 cl.24.2.1 makes the requirement of notice in writing from the employer a condition precedent to the deduction of liquidated damages for the employer. Furthermore, the notice (which, it was conceded, could accompany

---

[440] *Clydebank Engineering v Don Jÿse y Z Quierdo* [1905] A.C. 6.
[441] *Ramac v Lesser* [1975] 2 Lloyd's Rep. 430.
[442] *Brammell & Ogden v Sheffield CC* (1983) 29 B.L.R. 73.
[443] *Miller v LCC* (1934) 50 T.L.R. 479.
[444] *Miller v LCC* (1934) 50 T.L.R. 479.
[445] per Salmon L.J. at 121.
[446] [2015] UKSC 67 at [32], [255] and [291]. See above, paras 26-190 et seq.
[447] *Wall v Rederialktiebolaget Luggade* [1915] 3 K.B. 66; *Watts v Mitsui* [1917] A.C. 227.
[448] See *Hudson on Building Contracts*, para.10-022 referring to the decision of the Supreme Court of Canada in *Elsley v Collins Insurance* (1978) 83 D.L.R. (3d) 1. Despite opportunities to do so, the English Court of Appeal has declined to deal with the point: see *Rapid Building v Ealing Family Housing* (1984) 29 B.L.R. 5, 16.
[449] (1995) 77 B.L.R. 22, CA, approving *A Bell & Son (Paddington) Ltd v CBF Residential Care and Housing Association* (1989) 46 B.L.R. 102.

the deduction and need not precede it) needed to specify: (i) whether the employer is making any deduction of liquidated damages; and (ii) what sum is being deducted, the whole or only part of the liquidated damages.

(e)   Bonds and Guarantees[450]

The nature of suretyship[451]   Suretyship is a general term which describes a situation where A (the surety) agrees to take responsibility for an existing (or future) liability of B (the principal) to a third party C (the beneficiary) such that the liability of A to C is additional to the liability of B to C. Within the general category of contracts of suretyship, there are contracts of guarantee and contracts of indemnity. In a contract of guarantee, the guarantor (A) promises to be responsible—with the principal (B)—for the performance of the principal's obligations to the beneficiary (C) so that the guarantor will be personally liable if the principal fails to perform his obligations to the beneficiary (C) to the same extent as the principal (B).[452] A contract of indemnity is not predicated upon the failure in performance of the principal (B). Although it will often, in practice, be understood as between the surety (A) and the principal (B) that the principal is to be primarily liable to the beneficiary (C), under a contract of indemnity, the surety has a liability to make good the loss suffered by the beneficiary (C) which is not dependent in any way on the continuing liability of the principal (B).[453] Whether a contract is one of guarantee or indemnity will be a matter of construction of all the words used in the document,[454] although the contract will be one of indemnity, and not guarantee, if there are circumstances in which the liability of the surety is separate or different from that of the principal.[455]

37-124

Suretyship in the construction context   In the construction industry there are a variety of situations in which some form of security will be sought by an employer or contractor in relation to particular features of, or all of, a given project. A retention bond may be given by a contractor in return for early release of retention, or for payment in full without deduction, so as to provide him with the cash to complete the project without recourse to separate borrowing. Where a contract provides for payment to be made by the employer to the contractor in advance of work being carried out, then typically the employer will require a bond as security from the contractor. In *Wardens and Commonality of the Mystery of Mercers of the City of London v New Hampshire Insurance Company*[456] the Court of Appeal construed a document as a guarantee of liability for sums which had not been earned under the terms of the building contract but had been paid in advance in order to

37-125

---

[450] See generally, Andrews and Millett, *Law of Guarantees*, 3rd edn (2008); Phillips, *The Modern Contract of Guarantee*, 3rd edn (1996); Moss and Marks, *Rowlatt on Principal and Surety*, 5th edn (1999).

[451] See, generally, Ch.45.

[452] *Moschi v Lep Air Services Ltd* [1973] A.C. 331, 348, HL.

[453] *Yeoman Credit Ltd v Latter* [1961] 1 W.L.R. 828, 830; *Davys v Buswell* [1913] 2 K.B. 47, 53.

[454] *Moschi v Lep Air Services Ltd* [1973] A.C. 331, 349; *Alfred McAlpine Construction Ltd v Unex Corp Ltd* (1994) 38 Con. L.R. 63, CA.

[455] *Yeoman Credit Ltd v Latter* [1961] 1 W.L.R. 828, 832; *Argo Caribbean Group v Lewis* [1976] 2 Lloyd's Rep. 289, 296. See also Phillips, *The Modern Contract of Guarantee*, 3rd edn (1996), pp.25–31.

[456] [1992] 1 W.L.R. 792, [1992] 2 Lloyd's Rep. 365, CA.

avoid liability for VAT which would have become payable on the works at a future date.

37-126 Performance bonds[457]   The type of suretyship most frequently encountered in the construction context is the performance bond (or performance guarantee). Some of the issues encountered in relation to this type of security are considered here. The underlying commercial purpose of the performance bond will depend upon the nature of the particular project and the particular terms of the bond. However, the purpose of a performance bond in a construction contract will often be quite different from that of a bond provided in connection with other commercial contracts such as a contract of international trade. In many commercial contracts, the bond is regarded as an easily realisable source of capital which can be used to maintain the transaction upon the occurrence of a default. In construction contracts, rapid availability of funds is less important than the existence of such funds where, for example, the contractor becomes insolvent. This divergence between the purpose of performance bonds in construction contracts and their use in other commercial fields, is one explanation for the difference in views between the Court of Appeal[458] and the House of Lords[459] in the *Trafalgar House* case (below).

37-127 Categories of bond   Performance bonds may be considered as falling into one of two categories. Conditional performance bonds exist where the guarantor only becomes liable to the party entitled to claim the bonded sum (the beneficiary), on proof of breach of the terms of the underlying building contract, or on proof of both breach and loss as a result of the breach.[460] Unconditional or (more usually) "on demand" bonds exist where, on a true construction of the words used in the bond, the guarantor is liable to pay the beneficiary the bonded sum when the demand is made in the manner provided for in the bond, without the need for the beneficiary to prove breach of the underlying building contract or damage (or both). It is a question of construction in each case whether a bond, taken as a whole, is conditional or "on demand" and, in the former case, the nature of the conditions attaching to the bond will also be a matter of the construction of the often complex and archaic[461] language still used in such documents. In *IE Contractors Ltd v Lloyds Bank Plc and Rafidain Bank*[462] Staughton L.J. said:

> "The question is 'What was the promise which the bank made to the beneficiary under the credit, and did the beneficiary avail himself of that promise?' The degree of compliance required by a performance bond may be strict, or not so strict. It is a question of the construction of the bond ..."

Accordingly, although the words "on demand" may appear in the bond, they are not

---

[457] See generally Ch.45.

[458] (1994) 66 B.L.R. 42.

[459] [1996] A.C. 199.

[460] See *OTV Birwelco Ltd v Technical and General Guarantee Co Ltd* [2002] 4 All E.R. 668; (2002) 84 Con. L.R. 117.

[461] *Trade Indemnity Co Ltd v Workington Harbour and Dock Board* [1937] A.C. 1, 17; *Tins' Industrial Co Ltd v Kono Insurance Ltd* [1987] 3 H.K.C. 71, 77; *Trafalgar House Construction (Regions) Ltd v General Surety and Guarantee Co Ltd* [1996] A.C. 199; *Paddington Churches Housing Association v Technical and General Guarantee* [1999] B.L.R. 244.

[462] [1990] 2 Lloyd's Rep. 496, 500.

a term of art and so are not determinative[463] of the question of whether the bonded sum is payable on a conditional or on an "on demand" basis, since the bond must be construed as a whole. The courts have indicated the importance of construing bonds in the light of their overall presumed commercial purpose.[464] However, the basis and precise nature of the liability of the bondsman is ultimately a question of construction.

Conditional bonds Conditional bonds are based upon breach of the underlying building contract by the contractor, and because they are based on a failure by the principal to perform, conditional bonds are in the nature of contracts of guarantee.[465] In *Trafalgar House Construction (Regions) Ltd v General Surety & Guarantee Co Ltd*[466] the House of Lords considered the effect of the following words in a performance bond: **37-128**

> "... or if on default by the Subcontractors the Surety shall satisfy and discharge the damages sustained by the Main Contractor hereby up to the amount of the above-written Bond ..."

Dealing with the first part of the clause (default), Lord Jauncey (with whom Lord Lloyd and Lord Steyn agreed) said,[467] after having considered the authorities,[468] that he had no hesitation in concluding that the performance bond amounted to a guarantee so that all questions of sums due and cross-claims could be raised in answer to the demand made. It was held that the words in the bond "... damages sustained by the main contractor ..." were not sufficient[469] to exclude the normal legal incidents of suretyship, with the result that the extent of the remaining obligation under the bond could only be determined after taking account of any unpaid sums and set-offs.

Termination of the underlying contract In the case of a conditional performance bond which exists for the benefit of the employer in circumstances of default by the contractor (such as a failure to complete the contract works), the employer must be careful to ensure that it acts in such a way towards the contractor that its right to claim damages from the contractor, and its entitlement to call the bond, are preserved. In *Perar BV v General Surety and Guarantee Co Ltd*[470] there was a main contract substantially based on JCT 81 with contractor's design and cl.27.2 providing for the automatic termination of the contractor's employment in the event of administrative receivership. Prior to completion of the works, the contractor went into administrative receivership and was said to have abandoned the works. The plaintiff (as assignee of the rights of the employer under the bond) sought to recover **37-129**

---

[463] cf. *Tins' Industrial Co Ltd v Kono Insurance Ltd* [1987] 3 H.K.C. 71, 76G where the Court of Appeal of Hong Kong appear to have been impressed with absence of the words "on demand" in reaching the conclusion that this was a conditional bond.

[464] For a careful analysis of a guarantee in a construction context, see: *Try Build Ltd v Blue Star Garages* (1998) 66 Con. L.R. 90.

[465] See Andrews and Millett, *Law of Guarantees*, 2nd edn (1995), para.1.4.

[466] [1996] 1 A.C. 199, HL.

[467] [1996] 1 A.C. 199, 207D and G.

[468] In particular, *Trade Indemnity Co Ltd v Workington Harbour and Dock Board* [1937] A.C. 1, HL ("the *Workington* case").

[469] By contrast with the words used in *Hyundai Shipbuilding & Heavy Industries Co Ltd v Pournaras* [1978] 2 Lloyd's Rep. 502, CA.

[470] (1994) 66 B.L.R. 72, CA.

the sum under the bond from the defendant surety. The claim was rejected at first instance. On appeal the Court of Appeal held that if, following automatic termination, the contractor had no right to continue with the contract work then he could have no duty to do so, and therefore was not in breach in failing to continue the works. For the same reasons, there had been no "default" of the contractor within the meaning of the bond in circumstances where the building contract provided specific machinery following on from the automatic termination. In *Laing Management Ltd v Aegon Insurance Co (UK) Ltd*[471] it was held that although the appointment of an administrative receiver was not itself repudiatory conduct, the acceptance of other acts as repudiatory breaches in the statement of claim, meant that a claim in damages for the costs of completion could be recovered under the bond. In *Aviva Insurance UK Ltd v Hackney Empire Ltd*,[472] it was held that a side agreement made between an employer and a contractor arising out a dispute relating to delay to a project did not have the effect of discharging a bond provided by the claimant in favour of the defendant employer. In *CIMC Raffles Offshore (Singapore) Ltd v Schahin Holding SA*[473] the Court of Appeal indicated that it would be difficult to disapply by the wording of a guarantee the doctrine[474] whereby a material variation to the contract guaranteed, without the guarantor's consent, may lead to the discharge of the guarantee.

37-130 **"On demand" bonds**   Where a performance bond is, on its true construction, unconditional (or "on demand") then the obligation of the surety will arise merely upon a demand being made (in the manner prescribed in the bond) by the beneficiary.[475] In *Bache & Co (London) Ltd v Banque Vernes et Commerciale de Paris SA*[476] a commercial guarantee provided for payment by the surety forthwith of the amount stated in the demand, such notice of default being conclusive evidence that the liability of the surety had accrued in that amount. The Court of Appeal upheld the claim of the beneficiary to sums under the bond. In *Esal (Commodities) Ltd v Oriental Credit Ltd*[477] it was held that, on a construction of the material words in the bond, the beneficiary did not have to demonstrate breach since it was thought that this would be wholly inconsistent with the entire object of the transaction.[478]

37-131 **Final accounting**   Where a beneficiary makes a claim on an unconditional bond, then he is entitled without more to the whole sum stated in the bond from the surety. However, in the absence of clear words to the contrary (which may, in any event, be construed as a penalty[479]) there will be an accounting exercise between the parties at some stage after the bond has been called. If the amount of the bond is not sufficient to satisfy the beneficiary's claim for damages then he can bring proceedings for his loss, giving credit for the amount received under the bond. However,

---

[471] (1997) 55 Con. L.R. 1.
[472] [2012] EWCA Civ 1716, [2013] B.L.R. 57.
[473] [2013] EWCA Civ 644, [2013] B.L.R. 458.
[474] *Holme v Brunskill* (1877) 3 Q.B.D. 495; see generally below, para.45-104.
[475] In these circumstances, the principal remaining defence to a summary call on the bond will be that the call involves fraud, on which see the decision in *Balfour Beatty Civil Engineering Ltd v Technical & General Guarantee Co Ltd* (1999) 66 Con. L.R. 90.
[476] [1973] 2 Lloyd's Rep. 437, CA.
[477] [1985] 2 Lloyd's Rep. 546, CA.
[478] [1985] 2 Lloyd's Rep. 546, 549 (col.2).
[479] *Cargill International SA v Bangladesh Sugar and Food Industries Corp* [1998] 1 W.L.R. 461.

if, following the accounting exercise, the amount received by the beneficiary under the bond exceeds the loss sustained, then the surety is entitled to recover the overpayment.[480]

(f) Insurance

Introduction On most construction projects, there will be a number of levels of insurance[481] cover against different kinds of loss, the relevant policies being held by different participants. On major projects, a compendious arrangement is sometimes encountered known as "Project Insurance", which is intended to supersede (or duplicate) all the levels of cover as discussed below. The majority of projects, however, involve many individual policies which frequently overlap in practice. There is no general statutory requirement to provide insurance under construction projects. Individual parties may, however, be under statutory duties to insure, e.g. employers in respect of their employees.

37-132

Insurance of the works In the absence of other cover, e.g. through project insurance, the construction contract will usually require the contractor to effect insurance of the works. This will usually include goods and materials awaiting incorporation and may cover the contractor's plant and equipment. The insurance cover required may be in respect of loss from any cause (all risks) save for specified excepted risks.[482] Alternatively, some forms of contract require insurance only against specified perils. Where the work is to be carried out to, or to form part of, existing works or buildings, the contract must specify whether cover is required in respect of the existing works. Some contracts require insurance of the works to be in joint names,[483] which will enable either party to recover in the event of loss. In *London Borough of Barking & Dagenham v Stamford Asphalt Co Ltd*,[484] a case concerning conditions 6.2 and 6.3B of the JCT Agreement for Minor Building Works, it was held that, on the assumption that the sub-contractor's negligence had caused certain fire damage to the employer's property, then the failure of the employer to obtain condition 6.3B insurance did not affect the employer's right of

37-133

---

[480] *Cargill International SA v Bangladesh Sugar and Food Industries Corp* [1998] 1 W.L.R. 461, 465 See also: *ENS Ltd v Derwent Cogeneration Ltd* (1998) 62 Con. L.R. 141, 182.

[481] See Wright, *Construction Insurance* (1997). Following the Latham Report Working Group 10 of the Construction Industry Board has produced *Liability law and latent defects insurance* (1997, Thomas Telford).

[482] See ICC Form cl.20 and JCT 80 cl.22, JCT SBC 2011 cl.6.8.

[483] e.g. ICC Form cl.21(1). For consideration by the House of Lords of the JCT 1998 contractual machinery providing for Joint Names insurance, see *CRS v Taylor Young Partnership* [2002] UKHL 17, [2002] 1 W.L.R. 1419 where it was held that the effect of the contractual joint names insurance scheme was to exclude the normal rules for compensation for negligence and breach of contract and see also *Bovis Construction Ltd v Commercial Union Assurance Co* [2001] 1 Lloyd's Rep. 416. But note that the approach taken in *CRS v Taylor Young Partnership* was held not to be a rule of law and was distinguished on the facts in *Tyco Fire & Integrated Solutions Ltd v Rolls Royce Motor Cars Ltd* [2008] EWCA Civ 286, [2008] B.L.R. 285 where the joint names insurance provision under the particular building contract under consideration found not to exclude the contractor's potential liability for negligence causing damage to existing structures as provided for in other clauses of the contract. In *TFW Printers Ltd v Interserve Project Services Ltd* [2006] EWCA Civ 875, [2006] B.L.R. 299, the Court of Appeal held, in a case concerning a modified version of the JCT Agreement for Minor Building Works, that the employer's obligation under cl.6.3B to provide joint names' insurance cover against specified perils expired on practical completion of the works.

[484] (1997) 82 B.L.R. 25, CA, approving the reasoning of Otton J. in *National Trust v Haden Young Ltd* (1993) 66 B.L.R. 88 (upheld by the Court of Appeal at (1994) 72 B.L.R. 1).

recovery against the contractor under condition 6.2, since neither condition referred to or qualified the other.[485] However, the position in this respect under the JCT Minor Works Building Contract 2011 has probably been materially altered by the express exclusion from the terms of the cl.5.2 indemnity of loss and damage to any property required to be insured under cl.5.4B by a specified peril. Thus the employer may, in this case, bear the sole risk of damage to the existing structures caused by specified perils, even if due to the contractor's negligence.

37-134 Third party liability insurance Construction contracts must also make provision for liability to third parties arising out of the works. The usual scheme is to render the contractor responsible for any such loss, and to require liability insurance in respect of it.[486] While insurance of the works will usually be effected by a bespoke policy, liability insurance will often be covered by a contractors all risks ("CAR") policy which will contain a variety of cover, usually including some cover in respect of materials, workmanship and design.

37-135 Professional indemnity Insurance will usually be held by the professional team (architect, engineer and quantity surveyor) termed professional indemnity ("PI") insurance. Such policies will provide cover in respect of loss arising from design fault, which will usually be an excepted risk under the contractor's works insurance. The cover will, however, usually be limited to negligent acts or omissions. A potential lacuna therefore exists where loss arises from a design fault which is non-negligent.[487] PI insurance may also provide cover in respect of defective work where negligent supervision is established.

(g) Retention

37-136 Definition Monies held on account of retention form part of the sums certified by the contract administrator and earned by the contractor but which are not payable to the contractor until the final stages of the contract works. Typically, once practical completion is reached the next certificate will include one half of the retention monies; and the second half will be stated to be due upon the certificate issued after the certificate of making good defects. The amount of retention as a percentage deducted from successive interim certificates can vary and will depend upon the provisions of the construction contract. In some cases retention can be a substantial percentage of the certified value,[488] but in modern contracts based on the standard forms, retention is typically between 3 to 5 per cent of the value certified.

37-137 Purpose and operation Under the JCT 2011 Standard Form, the status of retention, and the rights and obligations of the parties in relation to sums retained, is defined in cl.4.18.1 in the following way:

"... the Employer's interest in the Retention is fiduciary as trustee for the Contractor (but without obligation to invest) ..."

The operation of the retention fund can be viewed from the perspective of the

---

[485] (1997) 82 B.L.R. 25 at 36B, per Auld L.J.
[486] JCT 98 cl.21, JCT SBC 2005 cl.6.1 to 6.4, ICC Form cl.23.
[487] See *Queensland Railways v Manufacturers Insurance* [1969] 1 Lloyd's Rep. 214.
[488] In *Rayack Construction Ltd v Lampeter Meat Co Ltd* (1979) 12 B.L.R. 30, the retention was 50 per cent and this was to be retained during the whole of the five year defects liability period.

(main) contractor, the employer and a nominated sub-contractor.

Position of contractor The words impose a trustee type obligation upon the   **37-138**
employer with the result that (i) the employer will be in breach of trust if he seeks
to use the retention monies for his own purposes[489]; and (ii) as long as the employer
is not in liquidation or administrative receivership,[490] the court will enforce these
obligations by requiring the employer (on application by the contractor) to set aside
the retention fund[491] without the need for the contractor to show that the employer
is financially at risk.[492] The contractor can require the employer to set up a retention trust account at any time during the life of the contract[493] (provided the application is not too late),[494] and the insolvency of the contractor or the termination of his
employment under the contract is not a bar to such remedy.[495]

Position of employer The stages at which retention typically becomes payable—   **37-139**
practical completion and the issue of the certificate of making good defects—
provide a clear indication that the practical purpose of retention is to ensure satisfactory completion by the contractor and by nominated sub-contractors. However,
insofar as the employer has rights of deduction under the contract against the
contractor, then he will (i) have a valid excuse for not having set up the retention
fund in the first place; and (ii) have a right to withdraw sums from it. In *Henry Boot
Building v Croydon Hotel*[496] the plaintiff contractor under a JCT Form of Contract
was refused a mandatory injunction to set aside retention of £355,179 in
circumstances where certificates had been issued by the architect under cl.22
entitling the defendant employer to liquidated damages in excess of the retained
sums. There are also dicta in *Rayack Construction* (see above) which suggest that
the employer may be entitled to have recourse to retention on the strength of a claim
for damages for breach of the contract (and not just in relation to claims under the
contract).[497]

5. PAYMENT

(a) Measure and Value

Payment generally Payment under construction contracts typically involves the   **37-140**
initial identification in the contract of a sum of money, variously called the "contract
sum"[498] or "tender total".[499] The contractor is entitled to this sum, or such other sum
as may become payable in accordance with the contract conditions. In practice, the

---

[489] *Wates Construction v Franthom Property* (1991) 53 B.L.R. 23, 37, CA.
[490] *Re Jartay Developments Ltd* (1982) 22 B.L.R. 134; *Mac-Jordan Construction v Brookmount Erostin* (1991) 56 B.L.R. 1, CA.
[491] *Rayack v Lampeter* (1979) 12 B.L.R. 30: *Concorde Construction Co Ltd v Colgan Co Ltd* (1984) 29 B.L.R. 125; *Henry Boot Building v Croydon Hotel* (1985) 36 B.L.R. 41, CA; *Wates Construc-tion v Franthom Property* (1991) 53 B.L.R. 23, CA; *Mac-Jordan Construction v Brookmount Erostin* (1991) 56 B.L.R. 1, CA.
[492] *Rayack v Lampeter Meat* (1979) 12 B.L.R. 30, 38.
[493] *Finnegan v Ford Sellars Morris Developments* (1991) 53 B.L.R. 38.
[494] *GPT Realisations v Panatown* (1992) 61 B.L.R. 88.
[495] *Re Arthur Sanders Ltd* (1981) 17 B.L.R. 125.
[496] (1985) 36 B.L.R. 41, CA.
[497] *Rayack Construction v Lampeter Meat* (1979) 12 B.L.R. 30, 38.
[498] JCT Form art.2.
[499] ICC Form cl.(1)(1)(i).

contractor is most unlikely to be paid the exact sum identified in the contract, given that every contract may be subject to variations,[500] claims,[501] fluctuation payments[502] or other factors by which the figure will require adjustment. Although the resolution of issues of payment will be a matter of the construction of the contract documents in the particular case, certain general principles can be identified and are discussed below.

37-141 **Lump sum** Where the effect of the agreement, in accordance with the contract conditions, is to carry out the work for a stated amount, it is referred to as "lump sum", a technical expression so understood by valuers.[503] The simplest form of lump sum contract is that in which the technical description of the works is contained in a specification and/or drawings, the terms of the contract requiring expressly, or as a matter of construction, that the contractor is to perform the whole of the work so described for the stated figure. This was the case in *Sharpe v Sao Paulo Railway*[504] where, although the contractor was involved in substantially more work than he could have anticipated, his promise to complete a railway from terminus to terminus meant that the increased work was not extra work under the contract. This represents the usual mode of contracting in the USA and many other parts of the world. In the majority of UK contracts, however, a bill of quantities[505] is also incorporated into the contract, primarily for the calculation of interim payments, but also having other effects.

37-142 **Effect of bill of quantities** A bill of quantities does not prevent the contract operating as lump sum. The JCT Form of Contract, with quantities, operates in this way, providing expressly that the employer will pay the contractor "the contract sum or such other sum as shall become payable hereunder".[506] The effect of a lump sum contract containing bills of quantities is that the contractor takes the risk that the given quantities will over—or under—state the true quantities. Only if it is shown that the bills have been prepared erroneously from the drawings will the contractor be entitled to seek an adjustment of the contract price.[507]

37-143 **Remeasurement** A contract containing quantities in which the sum finally due to the contractor is to be ascertained by recalculating each stated quantity from the actual amount of work performed, is referred to as a "remeasurement" contract. Various editions of the ICE Conditions and the ICC Form are to this effect, typically providing that the engineer shall "determine by admeasurement the value in accordance with the contract of the work done"[508] and providing further that the quantities set out in the bill "are not to be taken as the actual and correct quantities of the works".[509] Remeasurement contracts are practically limited to civil engineering projects, where substantial changes can occur, particularly in relation to earthworks and foundations. The contract sum is to be recalculated using the actual

---

[500] See para.37-096.
[501] See para.37-238.
[502] See para.37-168.
[503] See *Keating on Construction Contracts*, 10th edn (2016), paras 4-001—4-026.
[504] (1873) L.R. 8 Ch. App. 597.
[505] See para.37-068.
[506] JCT Form art.2.
[507] See below, para.37-143.
[508] ICC Form cl.56(1).
[509] ICC Form cl.55(1).

quantities and the quoted rates; but the ICC Form also provides that the rate may be adjusted where an increase or decrease of the quantities stated in the bill "of itself shall so warrant".[510]

Error or omission   Where a bill of quantities is used, questions may arise as to **37-144** the precise work included in each item. If the effect of the contract conditions is that the drawings or other contract description are to prevail over the bill, the risk of any error or omission in the bill will be that of the contractor. However, it is now a common and almost invariable practice to provide that the bills are "deemed to have been prepared" in accordance with a stated method of measurement.[511] There are a range of standard methods of measurement ("SMMs") available for building, civil engineering, highways and other works, each of which sets out details of "deemed" item coverage. The contract conditions may then provide for the consequences of any departure from the SMM. Both the JCT Form[512] and the ICC Form[513] require any error in description or omissions, by reference to the relevant SMM, to be corrected and treated as equivalent to a variation.

(b)   Interim Payment Under the Housing Grants, Construction and Regeneration Act 1996

Payment under the Housing Grants, Construction and Regeneration Act **37-145** **1996**   The Housing Grants, Construction and Regeneration Act 1996 ("the 1996 Act") applies to all construction contracts in England and Wales with limited exceptions.[514] One of the major features of the 1996 Act is detailed rules regarding the availability and procedure for interim payments during construction projects which limit the parties' freedom to contract in important respects. As a result, the interim payment requirements of the Housing Grants Act are now relatively standard across the industry, being found in many standard forms. The particular requirements of the Act are:

(i)   a party to a construction contract is entitled to interim payments provided the duration of the work is expected to be 45 days or greater[515];

(ii)   the construction contract must provide an adequate mechanism for determining what payments become due under the contract and when[516];

(iii)   the construction contract must provide a final date for payment in relation to any sum which becomes due[517];

(iv)   the construction contract must require one of the parties, or a specified person such as an architect or contract administrator, to give a notice specifying the sum due not later than five days after the payment due date.[518] This is referred to as a payment notice;

(v)   if the payer intends to pay less than the amount stated in the payment

---

[510] ICC Form cl.56(2).
[511] ICC Form cl.57.
[512] JCT SBC 2011 c.2.14.
[513] ICC Form cl.55(2).
[514] s.105 of the 1996 Act sets out certain excluded areas of construction operations, and s.106 provides that contracts with residential occupiers are excluded from the 1996 Act.
[515] 1996 Act s.109(1).
[516] 1996 Act s.110(1)(a).
[517] 1996 Act s.110(1)(b).
[518] 1996 Act s.110A(1).

notice, it must issue a further notice prior to the final date for payment.[519] This is referred to as a pay less notice.

37-146 Right to interim payments Whilst the Act requires that a contract make provision for interim payments and specifies a particular procedure to be followed in each instance, the parties are afforded considerable latitude as to the frequency and amount of the payments. Many construction contracts provide for interim payments to be made on a monthly basis or pursuant to progress milestones with a similar degree of regularity and commonly the value of each interim payment is broadly in line with the value of the work carried out to date, subject to a retention being kept by the employer. However, the Act does not mandate such approaches and it is permissible for the total amount of interim payments to fall far short of the value of the work carried out. The only limit imposed by the Act appears to be that the parties must incorporate the statutory requirement in good faith.[520] Whilst it has been judicially suggested that a cynical regime prescribing one interim payment of an insignificant amount would probably not satisfy the Act, it has been held that interim payments which in fact stopped many months prior to completion satisfied the requirements of the Act.[521]

37-147 Due dates and final dates Rather than a single deadline for payment, the 1996 Act introduces two relevant dates—the due date for payment and the final date for payment.[522] Despite its name, it is not expected that payments will be made on or before the due date. Instead, it is the final date for payment which represents the last occasion upon which a payment can be made without giving rise to a breach of contract and a right to recover interest. The due date serves little purpose other than to mark the start of a window within which the payment and pay less notices referred to in the Act must be served. The parties are free to determine when the due date is, when the final date for payment is and when, between the two dates, pay less notices must be served.

37-148 Payment notices The Act envisages that a payment notice may be given by one of three parties referred to as the payer, the payee or a specified person; designations which in practice refer to the employer, the contractor and the construction professional such as an architect or engineer. The parties are expected to specify in the contract who is to provide the notice and the deadline for the notice, which may not be more than five days after the due date.[523] As discussed below, in large construction contracts it is most common to choose an architect or an engineer to issue valuation certificates for the purposes of interim payments and provided they are valid such certificates will ordinarily constitute the relevant payment notice. In order to be valid, s.110A provides that the notice must set out the sum considered to be due and the basis upon which that sum has been calculated. Any notice served

---

[519] 1996 Act s.111.

[520] *Balfour Beatty Regional Construction Ltd v Grove Developments Ltd* [2016] EWCA Civ 990, [2017] 1 W.L.R. 1893 at [57].

[521] *Balfour Beatty Regional Construction Ltd v Grove Developments Ltd* [2016] EWCA Civ 990, [2017] 1 W.L.R. 1893 at [57]–[58].

[522] Introduced by s.110(1)(a) and 110(1)(b) respectively.

[523] If the parties fail to specify the date, then the Scheme for Construction Contract implies a deadline of five days after the due date.

must be in a form which would be recognised by a reasonable recipient as a payment notice with contractual effect.[524]

Payment notices in default   Section 110B of the 1996 Act provides that the payee   **37-149** may issue its own payment notice if the payer or a specified person who is due to issue the payment notice misses the contractual deadline. This is to prevent the employer, or professionals engaged by the employer, from unilaterally delaying or avoiding interim payments by refusing to issue payment notices. If pursuant to the contract the payee has previously issued an application for payment complying with the requirements of a payment notice then this notice will automatically be treated as the payment notice in default and no further notice need be issued.[525] It has been held that any document relied upon by the payee must be in "substance, form and intent" the payment notice or application for payment required by the contract or the 1996 Act,[526] but a more recent formulation has been to ask whether the reasonable recipient of the document in question would have realised that it was an application or payment notice with contractual force and with all the consequences that may entail.[527] To the extent that there is a difference between these two formulations, the latter is to be preferred. Whether a given document complies with the contractual requirements is a question of objectively interpreting the contractual requirements and the document served. Provided a reasonable recipient would have understood the status of the document, there is no reason for imposing additional requirements of specific substance, form or intent. If the payment notice in default is served later than the contractual deadline for the original payment notice, the final payment date will be extended.[528]

Pay less notices   Section 111 of the 1996 Act provides that a party wishing to pay   **37-150** less than the sum stated in the applicable payment notice must issue a pay less notice by the relevant deadline. Whilst the Act is written in such a manner that this provision takes direct effect, such that there is no need for the contract to expressly set out the entitlement to serve a pay less notice, most standard form contracts do so. It is, however, expected that the contract will set out the deadline for service of the pay less notice[529] and if this does not occur the Scheme for Construction Contracts implies a deadline of seven days prior to the final date for payment.[530] The content of the document is effectively the same as a payment notice. It must set out the sum the payer considers to be due on the date the notice is served and the basis on which that sum is calculated.[531] In addition, the document must be such that the reasonable recipient of the document would realise that it was a pay less notice.[532] Nevertheless, it is not fatal if the document does not describe itself as a pay less notice or is otherwise misleading as to its purpose. A document which was stated to be a final certificate but which was served in the appropriate window for a pay

---

[524] *Grove Developments Ltd v S&T (UK) Ltd* [2018] EWHC 123 (TCC), [2018] B.L.R. 173 at [29].
[525] 1996 Act s.110B(4)
[526] *Jawaby Property Investment Ltd v The Interiors Group Ltd* [2016] EWHC 557 (TCC), [2016] B.L.R. 328 at [59].
[527] *Grove Developments Ltd v S&T (UK) Ltd* [2018] EWHC 123 (TCC), [2018] B.L.R. 173 at [26]–[27].
[528] 1996 Act s.110B(3).
[529] 1996 Act s.111(7)(a).
[530] Scheme for Construction Contracts para.10.
[531] 1996 Act s.111(4).
[532] *Grove Developments Ltd v S&T (UK) Ltd* [2018] EWHC 123 (TCC), [2018] B.L.R. 173 at [29].

less notice was upheld as a valid pay less notice on the basis that a reasonable recipient would have realised that the sender was confused about the true legal position and would therefore have recognised that the document should be treated as a pay les notice.[533]

37-151 **Effect of failure to serve a pay less notice**   If the employer fails to serve a pay less notice, then the payee is entitled to recover the full sum stated in the payment notice without deduction, set-off or abatement.[534] This is frequently pursued by way of adjudication, a statutory form of dispute resolution also introduced by the 1996 Act, but can also be pursued directly in litigation.[535] It has been held that this aspect of the 1996 Act only works in favour of the party carrying out the work (the contractor or sub-contractor) and cannot be relied on by the employer to recover sums due in its direction, such as liquidated damages.[536]

The amount which the employer has to pay as a result of having failed to serve the requisite notices may well exceed the true value of the works as calculated pursuant to the contractual valuation mechanism. This is an inevitable risk of the statutory regime and does not provide any defence to the employer, although it may subsequently recover any overpayment. The cases are mixed as to the time and method by which this can occur. Some cases suggest that the employer must wait until the final payment to recover any overpaid sums,[537] whilst other cases have found that the employer can immediately seek a determination of the true value of the works and, once confirmed, recover any overpayment.[538] Pending clarification from the Court of Appeal, it is thought that the latter is the better view and that, by analogy with the position following an erroneous adjudicator's decision,[539] there is an implied term that any overpayment can be recovered which can be relied upon at any time after the overpayment has been made.[540]

37-152 **Circumstances where the payer can avoid paying the notified sum**   On the exceptional facts of *Melville Dundas Ltd v George Wimpey UK Ltd*[541] the terms of the contract were found to avoid the need to serve a withholding notice, so that no payment needed to be made even though no withholding notice had been served by the required deadline. In that case, the contractor had applied for an interim payment, but by the final date for payment the employer had neither made a payment nor served a withholding notice. The contractor then became insolvent and the

---

533   *Surrey and Sussex Healthcare NHS Trust v Logan Construction (South East) Ltd* [2017] EWHC 17 (TCC), [2017] 1 All E.R. (Comm) 586.
534   *Rupert Morgan Building Services (LLC) Ltd v Jervis* [2003] EWCA Civ 1563, [2004] 1 WLR 1867.
535   As happened in *Rupert Morgan Building Services (LLC) Ltd v Jervis* [2003] EWCA Civ 1563, [2004] 1 W.L.R. 1867.
536   *Balfour Beatty Construction Northern Ltd v Modus Corovest (Blackpool) Ltd* [2008] EWHC 3029 (TCC), [2009] C.I.L.L. 2660. However, it is difficult to find such a limit in the wording of the Act and the point has not been tested at Court of Appeal level or above.
537   *ISG Construction Ltd v Seevic College* [2014] EWHC 4007 (TCC), [2015] 2 All E.R. (Comm) 545; *Harding v Paice* [2014] EWHC 3824 (TCC), 157 Con. L.R. 98, affirmed at [2015] EWCA Civ 1231, [2016] 1 W.L.R. 4068.
538   *Grove Developments Ltd v S&T (UK) Ltd* [2018] EWHC 123 (TCC), [2018] B.L.R. 173 at [103].
539   *Aspect Contracts (Asbestos) Ltd v Higgins Construction Plc* [2015] UKSC 38, [2015] 1 W.L.R. 2961.
540   This view also appears to be supported at Court of Appeal level by the decision in *Rupert Morgan Building Services (LLC) Ltd v Jervis* [2003] EWCA Civ 1563, [2004] 1 W.L.R. 1867 and can possibly be inferred from obiter comments in the Court of Appeal decision in *Harding v Paice* [2015] EWCA Civ 1231, [2016] 1 W.L.R. 4068.
541   [2007] UKHL 18, [2007] UKHL 18, [2007] B.L.R. 257.

employer on this ground terminated the contract. It was held that the words of cl.27.5.5.1 of the JCT Standard Form of Building Contract (With Design 1998 edition) were clear and that the contractor ceased to become entitled to any further payment whatever once the contract had been terminated, that there was no conflict between this clause and s.111(1) of the 1996 Act and therefore that the failure to serve a withholding notice in respect of the interim payment did not affect the parties' rights. Potentially this decision creates a problem for contractors or suppliers seeking to obtain payment, at least in a termination situation.[542] An amendment to the Housing Grants, Construction and Regeneration Act 1996 appears to confirm the effect of *Melville Dundas* in providing that the obligation to pay the notified sum does not apply where the contract provides for payment to be suspended upon insolvency.[543]

Right to suspend work   The Act further reinforces the right to prompt payment **37-153** by providing a statutory right to suspend performance, subject first to giving seven days' notice.[544] The period during which performance is so suspended is to be disregarded in computing the time taken to complete any work affected by exercise of the right.

Pay-when-paid and pay-when-certified clauses   Section 113 of the 1996 Act **37-154** (prohibition of conditional payment provisions) prevents reliance upon what are often termed "pay-when-paid" clauses except in the case of the insolvency of the employer (or any other person, payment by whom is a precondition to payment of the third party under the contract). While s.113 will prevent some of the potentially harsh effects of "pay-when-paid" clauses seen in other jurisdictions,[545] the insolvency exception will mean that in certain cases the sub-contractor will, in practice, be accepting substantial risks in relation to the outcome of a construction project. In these circumstances, the effect of a particular "pay-when-paid" clause will be a matter of construction, requiring clear and unambiguous words, and requiring careful consideration of whether, on a true construction, the clause affects the right to payment or only the time for payment.[546]

The amendments made to the Act in 2011 introduced at s.110(1A) further limitations by prohibiting terms which make payment conditional upon the performance of obligations under another contract or the decisions of any other person as to whether obligations under another contract have been performed. This amendment prevents "pay-when-certified" clauses whereby a sub-contractor's payment is conditional upon money being certified for payment under the main contract, a com-

---

[542] The decision in *Melville Dundas* was applied in *Pierce Design International Ltd v Mark Johnston* [2007] EWHC 1691 (TCC), [2007] B.L.R. 381.

[543] s.111(10) as inserted by the Local Democracy, Economic Development and Construction Act 2009; 1996 Act s.111(10).

[544] 1996 Act s.112.

[545] Hong Kong: *Hong Kong Teakwood Works v Shui On Construction Ltd* [1984] H.K.L.R. 235; *Schindler Lifts (Hong Kong) Ltd v Shui On Construction Ltd* [1985] H.K.L.R. 118; (1985) 29 B.L.R. 95, Singapore; *Brightside Mechanical and Electrical Services Group Ltd v Hyundai Engineering and Construction Co Ltd* (1988) 41 B.L.R. 110.

[546] *Iezzi Construction Pty v Curumbin Crest Development Pty* (1995) 2 Qd. R. 350 Australia; *Smith and Smith Glass Ltd v Winstone Cladding Systems Ltd* [1992] 2 N.Z.L.R. 473 New Zealand. See "Back to Back Payment Clauses—'If and When'" at (1995) C.I.L.L. 1029.

mon way by which main contractors sought to circumvent the prohibition on pay-when-paid clauses described above.

(c) Interim Payment Generally

37-155 **Right to interim payment** As set out above, in most construction contracts in England and Wales the Housing Grants, Construction and Regeneration Act 1996 requires an interim payment regime to be included, failing which one will be implied from the Scheme for Construction Contracts. In contracts to which the 1996 Act does not apply, it is nevertheless common for parties to make express provision for interim payments due to the financing demands of large-scale construction projects.

37-156 **Interim measurement** Where there is a bill of quantities, the contract conditions usually provide for approximate monthly measurement to be taken, based on the quantities and rates set out in the bill. In the case of a lump sum contract, the quantity surveyor will estimate the proportions of the total stated quantities which have been performed. In the case of a remeasurement contract, the work may need to be physically measured. This is particularly important where work is to be covered up by succeeding work.[547] Standard forms of contract frequently provide for interim payments to be made in respect of goods and materials on site but not yet incorporated, and even goods and materials manufactured but not yet delivered.[548] The bill of quantities may also contain items other than measured work, such as preliminaries (i.e. fixed charges covering items such as insurance or the provision of site facilities) and method related charges.[549] All such items will be paid proportionally through periodic interim measurement, subject to retention and to any other adjustment permitted under the contract.

37-157 **Milestone payments** As an alternative to the somewhat cumbersome process of monthly measurement, a lump sum contract may provide for periodic payments in the form of a series of separate lump sums payable at stated intervals or by reference to stages of the work. Such payments are referred to as "milestones" and have been given the *imprimatur* of Sir Michael Latham in his report.[550] The payments need not be equal and may be graduated to create an incentive to achieve completion. Their release may be made conditional upon performance to quality and/or programme requirements.

37-158 **Interim certificates** Interim payments may become payable directly in accordance with the contract conditions; or they may be payable only upon the certificate of the contract administrator. In the latter case the certificate is usually a condition precedent to the right to claim payment.[551] Where a certificate has been withheld by the contract administrator an arbitration clause may empower the arbitrator to award what is due, despite the absence of a certificate[552]; and where proceedings are brought, the court may exercise the same power to open up, review and revise

---

[547] See ICC Form cl.56(3).
[548] See, generally, JCT 80 cl.30, JCT SBC 2011 cl.4.17, and ICC Form cl.60(1)(b), (c).
[549] See *Civil Engineering Standard Method of Measurement*, 2nd edn (1985).
[550] *Constructing the Team*, HMSO 1994.
[551] See generally *Keating on Construction Contracts*, 10th edn (2016), Ch.5.
[552] Both the JCT Form and the ICC Form contain such arbitration clauses.

any certificate or decision given under the contract.[553] At common law, it has been held that a certificate creates a debt which is susceptible to right of set-off, unless the contract otherwise provides.[554] This position is, however, substantially altered by s.111 of the Housing Grants, Construction and Regeneration Act 1996 which requires a notice to be served in a tight timeframe if the employer does not intend to pay the full sum stated in a certificate.[555]

Requirement for completion   If there is no statutory or express contractual right **37-159** to interim payment, a construction contract normally operates as an entire contract[556] so that payment is conditional upon the achievement of substantial completion.[557] The same rule will apply to instalments in respect of defined sections of the work. In addition, it is not uncommon for payments to be made in advance of carrying out the work. For example, in major international projects, advance payment in foreign currency may be provided for to finance the establishment of the site or importation of plant. Such payments are likely to be conditional upon the provision of a repayment bond. Where advance payments are made, there is likely to be a reduction in subsequent periodic payments proportional to the value of the work performed.

Set-off   The right of the employer (under a main contract) or the contractor (under **37-160** a sub-contract) to make deductions from sums which might otherwise be due under the terms of the contract, but for the existence of, for example, defects and delays to the works, is an important aspect of modern construction industry practice which often leads to formal disputes. From the point of view of the contractor or sub-contractor, regular income from work as it progresses is vital for cash flow. However, the employer will not wish to pay interim valuations in circumstances where there are existing problems with the works. The general law on set-off applies equally to construction contracts, but it is important to note that in most cases the employer will need to serve a pay less notice by the contractual deadline if it wishes to rely on a set-off. Otherwise, the employer will be required to pay the sum stated as due in the preceding payment notice without deduction by reference to such set-off.

Abatement   The principle of abatement,[558] settled in *Mondel v Steel*,[559] applies to **37-161** contracts for the sale of goods or for work or labour, and was described in *Gilbert-Ash (Northern) Ltd v Modern Engineering (Bristol) Ltd*[560] when Lord Morris said:

"... it has long been an established principle of law that if one man does work for another, the latter, when sued, may defend himself by showing that the work was badly done and that the claim made in respect of it should be diminished ..."

There are a number of points on the principle of abatement which are of significance in the construction context. First, provisions of a building contract which exclude

---

[553] *Beaufort Developments v Gilbert-Ash NI* [1999] 1 A.C. 266, HL.
[554] *Gilbert-Ash v Modern Engineering* [1974] A.C. 689; *Mondel v Steel* (1841) 8 M. & W. 858; *Hanak v Green* [1958] 2 Q.B. 9.
[555] See below, para.37-150.
[556] *Gilbert-Ash v Modern Engineering* [1974] A.C. 689, HL, per Lord Diplock.
[557] See above, para.37-009.
[558] Derham, *Set-off*, 2nd edn (1996), pp.124–130.
[559] (1841) 8 M. & W. 858.
[560] [1974] A.C. 689, HL.

equitable set-off may not be sufficiently clear to exclude the common law defence of abatement. Where, for example, notices of set-off have not been complied with, then contractual and equitable set-off may not be open, but there will be an independent right to abate.[561] Secondly, the rule of abatement applies only to matters that go to reduce the value of the work performed or of the goods sold and it does not apply to claims based on delay.[562] Where there is an abatement by reference to defective work, the question becomes one of how to value an abatement. The measure of an abatement is how much less the subject matter of the action is worth by reason of the breach; but in *Duquemin v Slater*[563] it was decided, by reference to the case of sale of goods, that the cost of repair could not be taken into account. It is thought that in many cases of abatement by reference to defects, the cost of remedial works will, in practical terms, be an important factor in deciding the extent of a right to abate.[564] As with set-off, unless the abatement is already taken into account in the preceding payment notice, an employer will generally need to have served a pay less notice in order to withhold payment on the basis of an abatement.

(d) Cost-based Payment

37-162 **Introduction** Where construction work is the subject of competitive tendering payment, both for the original contract work and for any varied work, is usually to be calculated on the basis of the tendered figures. Various devices exist for deriving rates to be used for the payment of variations where these are to be based on the original tendered figures. An alternative method of payment is one based on "cost". This requires appropriate definition since it is doubtful whether the term could have any absolute meaning. This section discusses a number of situations in which cost-based payments arise and the way in which such claims are to be valued.

37-163 **Claims based on cost** The standard forms of contract frequently contain provisions for particular payments to be based on cost rather than quoted rates. Under the ICC Form, a substantial number of provisions entitling the contractor to additional payment state that the payment is to be cost-based. For example, for delay in the provision of necessary instructions, the contractor is to be paid "the amount of such costs (incurred) as may be reasonable"[565]; in respect of encountering conditions which could not reasonably have been foreseen, the contractor is entitled to be paid "the amount of any costs which may reasonably have been incurred by the contractor together with a reasonable percentage addition thereto in respect of profit" by reason of such conditions or obstructions[566]; and in respect of general instructions issued by the Engineer the contractor is entitled to be paid any "cost beyond that reasonably to have been foreseen by an experienced contractor at the time of tender ... as may be reasonable except to the extent that such ... extra costs

---

[561] *Acsim (Southern) Ltd v Danish Contracting and Development Co Ltd* (1989) 47 B.L.R. 59, CA; *Mellowes Archital v Bell Projects* (1997) 87 B.L.R. 26, CA.

[562] *Mellowes Archital v Bell Projects* (1997) 87 B.L.R. 26, 40, CA.

[563] (1993) 65 B.L.R. 124.

[564] See *Barrett Steel Building Ltd v Amec Construction Ltd* Unreported March 3, 1997 and the reference to *Linden Gardens v Lenesta Sludge Disposals Ltd* [1994] 1 A.C. 85, 111.

[565] ICC Form cl.7(4)(a).

[566] ICC Form cl.12(6).

result from the contractors' default".[567] The form also includes a definition of "cost" as "all expenditure properly incurred or to be incurred whether on or off the site including overhead finance and other charges properly allocatable thereto but does not include any allowance for profit".[568] These provisions are typical of those found in many Standard Forms of Contract. The JCT Standard Form of Building Contract, on the contrary, contains uniform procedures and definitions applying to all such claims, by which the contractor is entitled to recover:

"... direct loss and/or expense ... for which he would not be reimbursed by a payment under any other provision of this contract."

This is thought to be equivalent to cost. The contract itself does not contain a definition, but the words have been interpreted by the courts as being equivalent to damages,[569] and such as to include interest or finance costs.[570]

Prime cost There is no fixed definition of this term which generally refers to work **37-164** which is intended to be valued in accordance with a definition contained in the contract. This may be in the form of a lengthy schedule of sums which are to be allowable (and those which are not) so as to arrive at a definite computation of the sum payable. Various forms of prime cost contract have been issued containing elaborate definitions of sums recoverable in respect of labour, materials, plant and sub-contracted work. In all such cases, express provision needs to be made for the cost of supervision and of other forms of overhead, and all other matters which may give rise to dispute.

Prime cost sums Another distinct use of the term "prime cost" occurs in rela- **37-165** tion to intended sub-contracts.[571] In such cases, it is customary to include a prime cost or PC sum chosen by the employer within the tender, with provision within the conditions of contract for the work in question to be executed by a sub-contractor, the actual cost of the sub-contracted work being substituted for the PC sum.[572] The sum to be paid constitutes actual cost to the contractor but not prime cost as may be defined. The usual procedure is for the employer (or the contract administrator) to obtain a lump sum tender from the prospective nominated sub-contractor whose payment will then be determined in accordance with the terms of the sub-contract, the final total replacing the PC sum for the purpose of the main contractor's account.

Dayworks This is a form of prime cost payment usually provided for under **37-166** conditions of contract where the supervisor is empowered to order particular work

---

[567] ICC Form cl.13(3).
[568] ICC Form cl.1(5).
[569] *Wraight v PH & T (Holdings)* (1968) 13 B.L.R. 26.
[570] *Minter v WHTSO* (1980) 13 B.L.R. 1; *Rees & Kirby v Swansea CC* (1985) 30 B.L.R. 1. Note that in *Sempra Metals Ltd v Inland Revenue* [2007] UKHL 34, [2007] 3 W.L.R. 354, the House of Lords has radically reassessed the circumstances in which a claimant may be entitled to claim compound interest. It was held that (i) the Court could award compound interest where a claimant was seeking restitution of money paid under a mistake; and (ii) the Court had a common law jurisdiction to award interest, simple or compound, as damages on claims for non-payment of debts as well as other claims for breach of contract and tort. It is therefore now open to claimants to plead and prove their actual interest losses as a result of a late payment of a debt, and this may include compound interest.
[571] See below, para.37-179.
[572] See *NWM Hospital Board v Bickerton* [1970] 1 W.L.R. 607 for the House of Lords' interpretation of the process of nomination and accounting.

to be executed on dayworks, usually on the basis that the work in question cannot properly be valued by measurement.[573] The term refers to lists of rates for labour, plant and materials together with appropriate mark-ups in respect of all additional charges. The rates in question may be included as an annex to the contract or reference may be made to published schedules.[574]

37-167 **Provisional sums** This term appears in most forms of contract and refers to a sum of money (specified) which is to be "provided" in the contractor's price, to be expended as directed (usually by the contract administrator). It is therefore in the nature of a contingency item, where the contractor will be paid according to the instructions which may be given.

(e) Price Fluctuations

37-168 **Meaning** Where the contract provides for the contractor to be compensated in respect of price increases, the additional payments are referred to as "fluctuation". Such payments may be provided for whether the underlying contract is lump sum or subject to remeasure. Variations which are priced on the basis of rates contained in the contract may be subject to fluctuation payments, but not claims based on cost, which will be assumed to be current unless the contrary is stated. Contracts which provide for payment of such increases are commonly known as "fluctuation contracts" while those which are not so subject are usually termed "fixed price" (although the price is fixed only in this limited sense).

37-169 **Net fluctuation clauses** Such provisions allow the contractor to recover the net increase in various costs on which the tender is deemed to be based by computing the actual price increase in respect of elements of the work actually carried out on a monthly basis. The JCT Forms of Contract print a separate clause applying to "rates of contribution levy and tax" payable by an employer, which is intended to apply in all cases.[575] A more extensive clause covers net increases in labour and materials costs, in addition to employer's contribution, levy and tax.[576] In respect of materials, goods, electricity and fuel, the clause is intended to operate from a list of "basic prices" provided by the contractor from which increases or decreases may be determined. Variants of this type of clause are found in many other standard construction contracts. Such clauses are important and may give rise to disputes in times of financial instability where the price, e.g. of hydrocarbon products to be used in the works may be subject to rapid and substantial change. The clauses also operate in reverse, at least in theory, where prices decrease. The objective of these clauses is for the contractor to recover the actual price increase in respect of the stipulated components. The price of any element not listed in the clause will be deemed to be fixed.

37-170 **Formula adjustment** An alternative and somewhat simpler means of assessing price fluctuation is by use of a set of formulae for different components of the work.

---

[573] See JCT 2011 cl.5.7 and ICC Form cll.52(5), 56(4).
[574] See definition of Prime Cost of Daywork carried out under a building contract issued by the RICS, and the BEC and Schedule of Dayworks carried out incidental to contract work issued by the FCEC (now CECA).
[575] JCT SBC 2011 cll.4.21 and 4.22, and Sch.7.
[576] JCT SBC 2011 cll.4.21 and 4.22.

Such clauses are found both in the ICC Form[577] and in the JCT Forms.[578] The ICC model represents the simplest form of calculation, whereby a predetermined apportionment of the constituents of the work is made, which is then applied to published cost index figures to calculate the fluctuation payment each month. The clause thus operates irrespective of actual constituents of the work which has been carried out. An alternative version of the standard clause exists for fabricated structural steelwork whereby the apportionment can itself be adjusted. These clauses operate on the basis of "Baxter" indices, named after their originator. The JCT formula clause operates in a similar manner, but is based on Formula Rules issued by the Joint Contracts Tribunal. The clause applies to all work carried out save for items based on actual cost or current prices, including dayworks.

(f) Quantum Meruit

Where available Payment based upon quantum meruit (literally "what he **37-171** deserves") is an important and surprisingly frequent feature of the construction industry and is most likely to arise in one of two particular situations which it is important to distinguish. First, where there is no contract,[579] a builder who carries out work at the request of, and for the benefit of, the employer, will be entitled to a quantum meruit by way of reasonable sum, for the work carried out. It is now clear that the underlying basis for such a claim is the law of unjust enrichment.[580] In *British Steel Corp v Cleveland Bridge and Engineering Co Ltd*[581] Robert Goff J. found that no contract had been concluded since the parties had not agreed the price or other essential terms, but held that the plaintiffs could recover on a quantum meruit for the work they had done, stating that:

"... if, contrary to their expectation, no contract was entered into, then the performance of the work is not referable to any contract the terms of which can be ascertained, and the law simply imposes an obligation on the party who made the request to pay a reasonable sum for such work as has been done pursuant to that request, such an obligation sounding in quasi contract or, as we now say, in restitution ..."

Secondly, where the contract contains no express provision relating to payment, both generally or in respect of specific matters such as a particular variation, the contractor will be entitled to a reasonable sum for the work carried out[582] on the basis of an implied term to that effect. The distinction between the contract and no-contract scenarios is important because it affects the basis upon which the valuation of a reasonable sum is carried out.[583]

Quantum meruit on repudiation It has been suggested that a contractor, whose **37-172**

---

[577] The clause is published as a separate insert.
[578] JCT SBC 2011 cll.4.21 and 4.22 and Sch.7.
[579] See Goff and Jones, *The Law of Unjust Enrichment*, 8th edn (2011), Mannolini (1996) M.L.R. 111; Ball (1983) L.Q.R. 572.
[580] See above, Vol.I, Ch.29. In *Costello v MacDonald* [2011] EWCA Civ 930 it was held by the Court of Appeal that there was no basis for a restitutionary claim for payment based upon unjust enrichment by the claimant building contractor against the owners of land on which a property was built because there was in existence a building contract for the works between the claimant and a company owned by the defendants that for tax reasons had been used as the employer for the project.
[581] [1984] 1 All E.R. 504.
[582] See *Turriff Construction v Regalia Knitting Mills* (1971) 9 B.L.R. 20. See also the decision of the Court of Appeal in *Furmans Electrical Contractors v Elecref Ltd* [2009] EWCA Civ 170.
[583] *Benedetti v Sawaris* [2013] UKSC 50 at [9].

contract is brought to an end by the repudiation of the employer, which is accepted by the contractor, may claim quantum meruit in respect of the whole of the contract works, as an alternative to claiming the value of work done together with loss of profit.[584] However, the better view is that older authorities supporting such a right cannot stand in the face of modern House of Lords authority; and that a contractor may not benefit from his own poor performance and obtain payment on a more favourable basis.[585] Thus, the contractor cannot put the contract to one side and recover the whole value of work done on the basis of a quantum meruit since in any event the contract, on repudiation, is determined only insofar as it is executory.[586]

37-173 **Assessment of a reasonable sum** The courts have laid down no rigid guidelines to be applied in the assessment of a reasonable sum although it is clear that the contractor should be paid a fair commercial rate for the work done in all the relevant circumstances.[587] The basis for any such assessment of a reasonable sum can be a source of controversy, since the employer may wish to confine recovery to the contractor's actual or tender costs,[588] whereas the contractor may want the reasonable sum to reflect the value which his work ultimately represented to the employer.[589] Although in some instances a reasonable sum will be calculated on the basis of actual cost plus an uplift for profit and overheads, it will be a matter of importance in the particular case whether, for example, the contractor who has obtained his resources at an especially low cost will be obliged to share that benefit with the employer, or whether a more objective view of "fair commercial rate" should be adopted. The correct answer will depend upon the legal basis of the quantum meruit claim.[590] If the claim is in unjust enrichment, then the focus should be on the enrichment received by the employer whereas if the claim is on the basis of an implied term, then the intention of the parties will be used but it is likely that market rates will be applied.

6. SUB-CONTRACTS

(a) Sub-Contractors

37-174 **Use of sub-contractors** In the majority of the more substantial construction projects, the main contractor will engage specialist sub-contractors to carry out particular parts of the overall works identified in the main contract. So, in the context of a large commercial development, the main contractor will typically engage a specialist mechanical and electrical ("M&E") sub-contractor to carry out relevant works and there will be other "works packages" which will similarly be let under the direction of the main contractor or the professional team. In addition,

---

584 *Planchè v Colburn* (1831) 8 Bing 14; *Appelby v Myers* (1867) L.R. 2 C.P. 651 at 659; *Lodder v Slavey* [1904] A.C. 442 at 453, PC.

585 *Keating on Construction Contracts*, 10th edn (2016), paras 9-060—9-062.

586 *Bank of Boston v European Grain* [1989] A.C. 1056, 1098, HL; *Photo Production v Securicor* [1980] A.C. 827, 849.

587 *Greenmast Shipping v Jean Lion (The Saronikos)* [1986] 2 Lloyd's Rep. 277; *Laserbore Ltd v Morrison Biggs Wall Ltd* (1993) C.I.L.L. 896.

588 An approach discussed in *Sanjay Lachhani v Destination Canada (UK) Ltd* (1997) 13 Const. L.J. 279, 284.

589 Discussed in *Costain Civil Engineering v Zanen Dredging* (1996) 85 B.L.R. 77.

590 *Benedetti v Sawaris* [2013] UKSC 50 at [9].

sub-contracting often includes the more basic "building" elements of the work, such as foundation work, bricklaying, carpentry and the like. There are a number of standard forms of sub-contract which are used extensively within different parts of the construction industry in conjunction with particular standard forms of main contract. Sub-contractors are often liable for losses up the contractual chain pursuant to indemnity clauses. In *Greenwich Millennium Village Ltd v Essex Services Group*,[591] the Court of Appeal found that an indemnity clause in a contract between a sub-contractor and its labour only sub-sub-contractor operated to indemnify the sub-contractor in respect of a loss partly caused by its own negligence in failing to spot defects in works. This was because it was held as a matter of commercial common sense that is how the wording of the clause should be construed, notwithstanding the absence of clear words indicating such an intention.

Standard forms—civil engineering In the civil engineering context, the CECA **37-175** (originally FCEC) form of sub-contract (also known as the "blue form") was designed for use in conjunction with the ICE Conditions of Contract, up to the 7th edition, and has been widely used.[592] The form will continue to be used in conjunction with the ICC Form. In a number of decisions the courts have considered ways in which the CECA form allows the sub-contractor to have the benefit (in a broad sense) of matters which are commercially relevant to the sub-contractor but occur between the employer and the main contractor. In *Mooney v Boot*[593] the plaintiff carried out certain drainage works under the blue form for the defendant main contractor. The main contractor was subsequently paid a lump sum settlement by the employer in respect of claims which included a claim for delay and disruption to drainage works. The Court of Appeal decided that the words "such contractual benefits ... as may be claimable" in cl.10(2)[594] of the sub-contract meant that the sub-contractors could attach to such contractual benefits as may be claimed by the main contractor in good faith, and were not confined to such benefits as become due under the main contract, so that they included any unapportioned settlement windfall. In *Redland Aggregates v Shepherd Hill Engineering* [595] the Court of Appeal considered the interrelation between the arbitration clause under the FCEC sub-contract (cl.18) and the ICE main contract (cl.66). The practical effect of that decision is that all three parties may join in a single arbitration, but where the main contractor is unwilling or unable to proceed with a joint arbitration in the manner contemplated by cl.18(2) FCEC, then the main contractor will not be able to prevent the sub-contractor from proceeding with its own arbitration under cl.18(1).

Standard forms—building In the context of building contracts, there are a **37-176** number of standard forms of sub-contract available. The particular form selected will also depend upon whether the sub-contractor is domestic and selected by the contractor, or nominated on behalf of the employer. As with engineering sub-contracts, standard forms of building contract raise issues as to the extent to which

---

[591] [2014] EWCA Civ 960.

[592] The edition of July 1998 was intended for use with the sixth edition of the ICE Conditions but has been reprinted with amendments (April 2001) for use with the seventh edition. A similar form (also reprinted April 2001) is intended for sub-contracts under the ICE Design and Construct Conditions.

[593] (1996) 80 B.L.R. 66, CA.

[594] "On receiving any such contractual benefits from the Employer (including any extension of time) the Contractor shall in turn pass on to the Sub-Contractor such proportion if any thereof as may in all the circumstances be fair and reasonable."

[595] [1999] B.L.R. 252, CA; affirmed by the House of Lords, [2000] 1 W.L.R. 1621, [2000] B.L.R. 385.

the sub-contractor can rely on events under the main contract. In *Birse Construction v Co-operative Wholesale Society*[596] the Court of Appeal considered the relationship between the JCT Standard Form 1963 (Private with Quantities) main contract and a sub-contract substantially in the form of the NFBTE/FASS/BEC Form of Sub-Contract 1963 in the context of "name borrowing". It was held that it was implicit in the JCT scheme of main contract and sub-contract that where, in an arbitration under the main contract, the arbitrator made an award of a sum which should have been certified as due under the sub-contract, that sum was to be treated under the sub-contract as duly certified, so that the award became binding in the arbitration under the sub-contract.

37-177 **No right to direct payment** In the absence of any provisions in the main contract to the contrary, the rules in relation to privity of contract will mean that the contractual relationship between the employer and the main contractor and between the main contractor and the sub-contractor will be quite distinct and separate.[597] It follows that, in the absence of a valid assignment from the contractor, the sub-contractor will not be able to sue the employer for goods supplied or work done under his sub-contract with the main contractor. Accordingly, in *Hampton v Glamorgan CC*[598] a builder contracted with a council to build a school in accordance with the specification and other documents contained in the contract. Part of the contract works comprised the provision of low pressure heating apparatus, and a specialist sub-contractor was asked to provide a scheme for this part of the works. During the course of the works, the builder paid the sub-contract on account, but was eventually unable to pay the balance so that sub-contractor sued the council. It was held that on a true construction of the building contract there was no privity between the sub-contractor and the council, so the sub-contractor's claim failed.[599] If the employer (following the demise or failure of the main contractor) gives an verbal assurance to the sub-contractor that he will be paid if he completes his work, then it is possible that such action could be construed as an enforceable promise to pay,[600] as opposed to a guarantee which may be unenforceable.[601] Equally, a direct instruction by the employer to the sub-contractor may be construed as a promise to pay the sub-contractor.[602] In each case, it is a question of construction of the contract as to what rights and obligations have been conferred, or imposed, on the parties.[603]

37-178 **Direct liability for default** The employer will generally have no right of recourse against the sub-contractor for defects in that sub-contractor's work. However, a direct right of recourse may be created by use of a collateral warranty. These devices are widespread in the construction industry and their use is by no means limited to sub-contractors. Their subject matter may extend to compliance with design and programme requirements, as well as quality (see further section (b) below). The

[596] (1997) 84 B.L.R. 58, CA.
[597] *Scobie & McIntosh Ltd v Clayton Bowmore Ltd* (1990) 49 B.L.R. 119, 129–130.
[598] [1917] A.C. 13, HL.
[599] [1917] A.C. 13, 21.
[600] *Smith v Rudhall* (1862) 3 F. & F. 143; *Conrad v Kaplan* (1914) 18 D.L.R. 37.
[601] *Poucher v Treahey* (1875) 37 U.C.R. 367.
[602] *Dixon v Hatfield* (1825) 2 Bing. 439.
[603] *Actionstrength Ltd v International Glass Engineering IN.GL.EN SpA* [2003] UKHL 17, [2003] 2 A.C. 541; and *Brican Fabrications Ltd v Merchant City Developments Ltd* [2003] B.L.R. 512 Court of Session.

possibility of direct recourse is further subject to the effect of the Contracts (Rights of Third Parties) Act 1999.[604]

(b) Nomination

Meaning This refers to a practice which has evolved over many years, initially **37-179** in the building industry, whereby a sub-contractor is selected or "nominated" by or on behalf of the employer to carry out designated work, usually of specialist nature. The objective is to ensure that particular items of work are executed by specialists to known standards. Nomination has traditionally been applied to elements such as lifts and mechanical services within buildings. Appropriate contractual devices have evolved whereby the work in question, usually designated as a Prime Cost or PC sum in the bill of quantities, is required to be executed by a sub-contractor to be selected and notified to the main contractor. The sub-contract price will be negotiated by or on behalf of the employer. The main contractor will be presented with a "nomination" instruction in which all the major terms of the sub-contract are specified. For the protection of the main contractor, the standard forms have traditionally provided for certain terms to be included in the nominated sub-contract. The prospective sub-contractor must also undertake to carry out the work within a period conformable with the requirements of the main contract. Upon acceptance of a nomination by the main contractor, the employer drops out of the picture, leaving the prospective sub-contract parties free to negotiate any outstanding terms. The main contractor subsequently receives payment due in accordance with the nomination, in place of the PC sum. The main contractor is usually entitled additionally to a stipulated level of profit and/or discount on the sums paid. Nomination under JCT forms of contract progressively lost its advantages as a result of limitations on the liability of the main contractor and, as a result, was removed from JCT forms in 2005. It remains in other standard forms which have not so qualified the main contractor's liability; and it may be found that the principles developed in the cases apply to other ad hoc contracts where the employer retains the right to select or approve sub-contractors, even though not called nomination.

Effect on privity rule It is an important feature of nomination that there is no **37-180** transgression of the privity rule. Neither the employer nor the architect assumes any responsibility towards the nominated sub-contractor, as to payment or otherwise, nor does the nominated sub-contractor undertake, via the nomination system, any obligation towards the employer (but see below). This is so even though, as is commonly the position, the prospective nominated sub-contractor has performed and is intended to perform design work. Where such design work is carried out prior to and as part of the tendering process for the Prime Cost work, the product of the successful design will be incorporated into the nomination, and will take effect as an instruction of the architect. Where subsequent design work, including the provision of necessary construction details, is carried out by the nominated sub-

---

[604] The case of *Junior Books v Veitchi* [1983] 1 A.C. 520 also remains as an unlikely but possible route to liability, in the tort of negligence, but on its own facts. In that case, the House of Lords refused to strike out a claim for economic loss brought by an employer against a nominated sub-contractor, in respect of defects in the flooring resulting from negligence of the sub-contractor. While the dissenting judgment of Lord Brandon received specific approval in *D & F Estates v Church Commissioners* [1989] A.C. 177, the case has not been disapproved and is now to be regarded, it appears, as based on the existence of a special relationship, equivalent to contract: see *Murphy v Brentwood DC* [1991] 1 A.C. 398, 466, 481. See above, Vol.I, para.1-217.

contractor after the sub-contract has been entered into, the status of the design information so produced is uncertain. Where the main contract includes design responsibility, such information may be regarded as being provided pursuant to such responsibility. Where this is not the case, the status of design information remains uncertain. The question requires to be addressed in order to determine responsibility for such information being provided late and causing delay. The standard forms contain a number of express provisions relevant to these issues.

37-181 **Direct warranties** These difficulties have been regulated, to some extent, by the development of a variety of direct or "collateral" warranties for use between the employer and the nominated sub-contractor. These may consist simply of undertakings by the sub-contractor in relation to design services; or there may be parallel obligations undertaken by the employer to operate the direct payment provisions under the main contract in favour of the nominated sub-contractor, if not paid. The origin of warranties may be traced to the case of *Shanklin Pier v Detel Products*.[605] During the 1970s and 1980s[606] the use of warranties was somewhat eclipsed by the apparent availability of remedies in tort. The law having now been clarified,[607] warranties remain the prime source of establishing direct liability between parties otherwise displaced in the contractual chain, typically employer and sub-contractor.[608] As regards design, such warranties typically undertake a direct obligation to the employer to carry out such design services as are required. The warranty will usually cover past and future design work, and may include an obligation timeously to provide such details as may be required by the main contractor. In most cases the warranty is expressed, not in absolute terms, but as an undertaking to exercise (and to have exercised) reasonable skill and care, commensurate with the ordinary duty undertaken by the architect. Such a warranty, therefore, fills a lacuna in the network of obligations undertaken in relation to design and construction, but creates a theoretical gap in respect of non-negligent design error or delay.

37-182 **Advantage of nomination** The nomination system can be seen as providing for the employer both the advantage of specialist and selected materials and components, while preserving the overall responsibility of the main contractor. Additionally, the employer has the advantage of specialised design services with a direct right of action against the designer being created by warranty. Under the JCT (and former RIBA) Standard Forms of Building Contract (prior to the 2005 suite), separate provision was made for nominated sub-contractors and nominated suppliers.[609] The 1998 edition of the forms continued this distinction, nominated sub-contractors being the subject of a lengthy and detailed code.[610] In traditional forms of building contract it has not been uncommon to find the value of nominated work amounting to one third or more of the total building cost. Nominated sub-contracting has been used in civil engineering, although to a lesser extent. The 5th edition of the ICE Conditions included, for the first time, fully detailed provisions

---

605 [1951] 2 K.B. 854.

606 See *Dutton v Bognor Regis UDC* [1972] 1 Q.B. 373; and *D & F Estates v Church Commissioners* [1989] A.C. 177.

607 *Murphy v Brentwood DC* [1991] 1 A.C. 398.

608 The possible use of the Contracts (Rights of Third Parties) Act 1999 to fill gaps in the contractual chain has been eschewed generally by the construction industry in favour of continued use of warranties.

609 See 1939 edition, cll.22, 23 and 1963 edn, cll.27, 28.

610 JCT 98 cl.35 and see also cl.36.

governing nomination,[611] which is continued with some modification into the 6th and 7th editions and the ICC Form.[612] As a result of various decisions of the court and of the drafting bodies, nomination has become less utilised in favour of "listed" sub-contractors (see below).[613] The JCT SBC 2005 and 2011 forms do not provide for nominated sub-contractors at all; but now provides instead for the "three person" procedure.[614]

Re-nomination   A number of questions concerning liability for performance of **37-183** a nominated sub-contractor or supplier remained uncertain under the Standard Forms until resolved by decisions of the courts. Notably, the House of Lords decided in *NW Metropolitan Hospital Board v Bickerton*[615] that where a nominated sub-contractor repudiated by failing to complete or failing to perform, the architect was obliged to re-nominate so that the employer would bear the increased cost of carrying out the work. The decision was given in relation to the JCT 1963 edition but subsequently given contractual effect both in later editions of the JCT Form[616] and in the ICE Conditions.[617] It was further held by the Court of Appeal in *Fairclough v Rhuddlan BC*[618] that, where a nominated sub-contractor repudiated, the main contractor was not responsible for defects in the nominated work discovered after repudiation. The re-nomination had, therefore, to include for the remedial work, necessarily at the employer's cost.

Delay   As part of the bargain by which the employer acquired the right to **37-184** nominate, successive editions of the Standard Form of Building Contract have exonerated the main contractor from responsibility for delay caused by a nominated sub-contractor.[619] The effect of this was not merely to relieve the main contractor but, in effect, to leave the sub-contractor without liability for its own delay, save for any loss suffered by the main contractor through such delay. The employer's loss may be covered by a direct warranty (see above) but recovery will be subject to proof by the employer of fault, rather than the onus falling on the sub-contractor to prove entitlement to extension of time. In practice, the effect of exonerating the main contractor from liability for delay by a nominated sub-contractor has usually meant that such loss could not be recovered. However, where delay resulted from the need to re-nominate a replacement sub-contractor, it was held by the House of Lords in *Percy Bilton v GLC*,[620] that such delay was not the responsibility of the employer, not being caused by his fault nor covered by any of the express provisions of the contract. Furthermore, once a nominated sub-contractor has achieved apparent completion, the subsequent discovery of latent defects does not constitute

611 See cll.58, 59 A, B, C.
612 See cll.58, 59.
613 The continuing utility of nomination has, however, been recognised by the inclusion of such provisions in more modern forms such as GC/Works/1 (1998) and FIDIC (1998), generally without relieving the main contractor of overall responsibility, as provided by earlier forms.
614 See below, para.37-185.
615 [1970] 1 W.L.R. 607.
616 JCT 98 cl.35.
617 ICE 5th edn cl.59B.
618 (1985) 30 B.L.R. 26.
619 See above, para.37-179. See JCT 1963 edn cl.23(g) and JCT 98 cl.25.4.7.
620 [1982] 1 W.L.R. 794.

delay on the part of a nominated sub-contractor.[621] These decisions apply only to the JCT Form of Contract prior to the 2005 suite. Other major Standard Forms do not provide a direct right of extension in respect of delay by a nominated sub-contractor. In the absence of such a provision, the general rule is that the main contractor remains liable and must pass on any such liability to the sub-contractor.

37-185 **Listed sub-contractors** The difficulties surrounding nomination, as outlined above, led to employers seeking alternative means of selection, not involving any reduction in the liability of the main contractor. The JCT suite of contracts have since 2005 omitted the previous formal procedures associated with nominated sub-contractors as well as provisions for "listed" or "specified" sub-contractors which were also found in earlier form of the contract. The 2016 forms provide, in their place, a "three-person procedure". Thus, under cl.3.8 of JCT Standard Form of Contract 2016 the contract bills may list not fewer than three persons from whom the contractor may select at his sole discretion a sub-contractor to carry out the work described in the bills.[622]

7. THE CONTRACT ADMINISTRATOR

(a) Engineers, Architects and Quantity Surveyors

37-186 **Introduction** This section deals with professionals who are appointed under the terms of a construction contract, not as a party to the contract, but to perform designated functions. Engineers, architects, surveyors and other professionals are appointed under standard forms, and other bespoke contracts, to exercise the powers and duties assigned to a third party, variously designated as the supervising officer, project manager, contract administrator, employer's agent or, more traditionally, the engineer or architect. The appointment may be of an individual or, more usually, a professional partnership. There may also be a corporate or ex-officio appointment, e.g. a borough surveyor. In the case of a partnership or company, the contract may require identification of the individual who is to act. Otherwise, the question of how a partnership or corporation is to form a professional opinion appears not to have been the subject of any judicial consideration. A common abuse of the standard forms is for the corporate employer to be appointed also as the contract administrator, including the role of giving a professional opinion on matters of difference. Such procedure, while open to criticism, has been upheld by the courts on the basis of a concession, accepted by the court, that "in all its judgments, decisions and certificates the employer was obliged to act honestly, fairly and reasonably".[623] Later authority, however, has cast doubt on whether such an appointment can be effective.[624] The ICE Conditions of Contract for Minor Works required the employer to appoint "a named individual to act as Engineer" and the

---

[621] *Jarvis v Westminster Corp* [1970] 1 W.L.R. 637.

[622] See generally *Keating on Construction Contracts*, 10th edn (2016) at paras 20-229—20-231.

[623] *Balfour Beatty v DLR* (1996) 78 B.L.R. 42. The basis of the case was the decision in *Northern Regional Health Authority v Crouch* [1984] Q.B. 644, now reversed by *Beaufort Developments Ltd v Gilbert-Ash NI Ltd* [1999] 1 A.C. 266, HL.

[624] *Scheldebouw BV v St James Homes (Grosvenor Dock) Ltd* [2006] EWHC 89 (TCC), [2006] B.L.R. 113.

same wording is adopted in the ICC Form.[625] The roles of the most prominent professionals likely to be encountered under standard forms of contract are described below.

Architect   An architect, in order to practise under the title, must be registered by   **37-187**
the Architect's Registration Council pursuant to s.20 of the Architects Act 1997.[626]
In addition to having an ongoing responsibility for the design[627] and often for obtaining all necessary planning and other permissions for the works,[628] the architect, under many standard forms of building contract, will be responsible for the supervision and monitoring of the works, and this will often include the issuing of instructions, variations and certificates. In relation to the grant of certificates, the assessments which the architect will be required to make call for the formation of an opinion[629] which will often be subjective and open to interpretation. However, the architect will owe a duty to his client, the building owner, to use reasonable care in issuing his certificates.[630]

Engineer   This term is used generically in that different types of construction   **37-188**
contract will contemplate people with qualifications from different specialist bodies (e.g. the Institution of Mechanical Engineers or the Institution of Civil Engineers). Typically, the engineer will carry out a similar range of functions under engineering contracts as is performed by the architect in the context of building contracts.

Quantity surveyor   A quantity surveyor may have different functions at differ-   **37-189**
ent stages in a construction contract, but will generally be concerned with the quantity (measure) and value of work. Before commencement of the works, the quantity surveyor will typically be involved in drawing up the bills of quantities (for the employer) or pricing the bills of quantities (for the contractor). During the contract works, a quantity surveyor will be engaged in the preparation and submission of interim applications (for the contractor), or in measuring and valuing work (either as a professional named in the contract,[631] or informally for the employer).[632]

---

625   ICE Conditions cl.2.1 The ICC Form cl.2(2)(a) requires, where the engineer is not an individual, that a chartered engineer be named to act on behalf of the engineer.

626   See ss.118–125 of the Housing Grants, Construction and Regeneration Act 1996 in relation to the regulation of architects. For a discussion of the architect and his role, see: *Munckenbeck and Marshall v Kensington Hotel* (1999) 15 Const. L.J. 231.

627   *Brickfield Properties Ltd v Newton* [1971] 1 W.L.R. 862, CA; *University of Glasgow v William Whitfield* (1988) 42 B.L.R. 66; *New Islington and Hackney Housing Association Ltd v Pollard Thomas and Edwards Ltd* [2001] B.L.R. 74.

628   In some cases an architect may be under a duty to take some steps to ascertain the financial viability of tenderers, as in *Partridge v Morris* (1995) C.I.L.L. 1095.

629   See JCT SBC 2011 cl.4.9.

630   *Arenson v Arenson* [1977] A.C. 405, HL; *Michael Salliss & Co v Calil and William F Newman* (1987) 13 Con. L.R. 68; see also *Pacific Associates v Baxter* (1988) 44 B.L.R. 33, [1990] 1 Q.B. 993, CA and *Galliford Try Infrastructure Ltd v Matt McDonald Ltd* [2008] EWHC 1570 (TCC).

631   As provided for by art.4 of the Articles of Agreement used in conjunction with JCT.

632   In *Dhamija v Sunningdale Joineries Ltd* [2010] EWHC 2396 (TCC), [2011] P.N.L.R. 9, it was held that ordinarily there would be no implied term of a quantity surveyor's retainer to the effect that there was a positive obligation to ensure that only properly executed work was valued or to inspect work being valued to consider whether the same were properly executed or not; but there would be an implied obligation, where the quantity surveyor was aware of the related terms of the building contract, to take reasonable care to value only properly executed work (per Coulson J. at [18]–

37-190 **Project manager**   A project manager will often be used by the employer in complex construction projects to organise and coordinate the activities of the contractor and the professional team (i.e. architect, quantity surveyor, specialist engineers, etc.). However, the scope of the project management function will be shaped by the particular character of the project involved, so that any general definition of the role is unlikely to assist on the question what, on a true construction of the terms of a particular contract, are the rights and obligations of the parties.[633] It has been held that a project manager had a duty to his client to ensure that contractor's liability insurance was in place.[634]

(b) Role Under Contracts

37-191 **Dual role**   The role of professionals who may be identified in construction contracts will depend upon a true construction of the terms contained in the particular contract.[635] Generally, the role will be divided between actions taken as the employer's agent, where the contract administrator must act in the employer's best interest, and those involving a professional opinion. In the latter case, the role of the architect has been described in the following terms:

> "The building owner and the contractor make their contract on the understanding that in all such matters the Architect will act in a fair and unbiased manner and it must therefore be implicit in the owner's contract with the Architect that he shall not only exercise due care and skill but also reach such decisions fairly, holding the balance between his client and the contractor."[636]

Such duty is sometimes said to be "independent", but the term is unnecessary and potentially misleading given that the contract administrator is invariably employed by, and can therefore be dismissed by, the employer.[637] The proper analysis, it is submitted, is that the employer undertakes that a person will be appointed (or reappointed as necessary) who is capable of performing the actions required by the contract. However, the employer does not promise that the actions will be performed.[638]

37-192 **Action as agent**   When giving instructions for a variation, the contract administrator acts as the employer's agent, and requires appropriate authority. Likewise, certain instructions involving consequences akin to variation of the works involve acting as agent, e.g. an instruction given under cl.13 of the ICC Form (see above, s.3(b)). An instruction nominating a sub-contractor will be given as the employer's agent. In matters of approval of the work for compliance with the contract require-

---

[26]).

[633] *Pozzolanic Lytag Ltd v Bryan Hobson Associates* [1999] B.L.R. 267; and *Costain Ltd v Bechtel Ltd* [2005] EWHC 1018 (TCC).

[634] *Pozzolanic Lytag Ltd v Bryan Hobson Associates* [1999] B.L.R. 267.

[635] For a consideration of the duties of members of a large professional team in a particular context, see *Chesham Properties Ltd v Bucknall Austin Project Management Services Ltd* (1996) 53 Con. L.R. 22.

[636] *Sutcliffe v Thackrah* [1974] A.C. 727, 737.

[637] See the description of the architect in *Beaufort Developments Ltd v Gilbert Ash Ltd* [1999] 1 A.C. 266, 276, per Lord Hoffmann ("...He is a professional man but can hardly be called independent"). See also: *John Holland Construction and Engineering Ltd v Majorca Products* (Supreme Court of Victoria, July 26, 1996) reported in (2000) 16 Const. L.J. 114.

[638] See *Perini Corp v Commonwealth of Australia* (1969) 12 B.L.R. 82, SC NSW.

ments, the contract administrator also acts as the employer's agent, being under a duty to ensure that the employer does not suffer loss through certification of defective work or materials. In cases where approval, or "satisfaction" are a matter of professional judgment, the contract administrator's role is likely to be that of reaching a decision "fairly, holding the balance between his client and the contractor" (see above).

Authority Where the contract terms empower the contract administrator to take 37-193 particular actions, his unqualified appointment by the employer necessarily involves authority, by holding out, to exercise all such power. In addition, the contract administrator will have an implied authority to do other things reasonably necessary and ancillary to those matters for which express authority is given.[639] It follows that any limitation of authority to exercise the powers set out in the contract must be notified to the contractor, if the employer is to avoid being bound. In practice, there may be a limitation on the authority of the Contract Administrator to perform functions which are necessary to the operation of the contract, such as granting extensions of time. For this reason, many standard forms expressly require any limitation upon the authority of the Contract Administrator to be stated.[640]

Acting impartially Actions of the contract administrator which are to be taken 37-194 having regard to the interests of both parties, involving the giving of a professional opinion, are sometimes termed "impartial" decisions. Actions falling within this category include valuing the works for the purpose of issuing interim and final payment certificates, granting extensions of time, accepting the contractor's programme,[641] giving a certificate of default as part of the termination procedure[642] and many other specific instances. Even though acting impartially, the contract administrator acts pursuant to his duty to the employer, under the contract of employment. The employer, in turn, has an obligation under the construction contract to appoint a contract administrator who can carry out the duties required under the contract (see above).[643]

Challenging the contract administrator Under a traditional standard form 37-195 construction contract, the decision of the Contract Administrator is binding, subject to challenge by arbitration or litigation, which, in some cases could not be brought until completion of the works. The position is also now radically altered by the Housing Grants, Construction and Regeneration Act 1996 which provides, in respect of construction contracts within the Act, for a right of adjudication at any time.[644] The effect is that either party now[645] may immediately challenge any decision of the contract administrator. The adjudicator's decision is to be binding until

---

[639] See the decision of the Court of Appeal in *Naylor & Naylor v JL Builders & Son* [2009] EWCA Civ 1621 where it was held that the contractual functions of an agent were not to extend beyond what he was expressly instructed to do or what was reasonably incidental thereto.
[640] See FIDIC (1998 edn) cl.3.1 and ICC Form cl.2(1)(b).
[641] ICC Form cl.14(2).
[642] ICC Form cl.65(1), JCT 2011 cl.8.4.
[643] For an analysis of the duties of a "Construction Manager", where those duties involve the issue of certificates, see the judgment of Jackson J. in *Scheldebouw BV v St James Homes (Grosvenor Dock) Ltd* [2006] EWHC 89 (TCC), [2006] B.L.R. 113.
[644] s.108.
[645] Provided the contract was entered into on or after May 1, 1998.

the dispute is finally determined by legal proceedings or arbitration.[646] Under the ICE Conditions provision was made, after the decision of the contract administrator, for a "second stage" decision on matters of dispute or difference, which were required to be referred to the engineer for his decision before a further challenge by arbitration[647]; and under the *FIDIC Conditions* (1998 edition), disputes are to be referred, after an initial decision, to a Dispute Adjudication Board.[648] Where the contract in question is subject to the Act, the existence of a dispute gives rise to an immediate right to refer the matter for adjudication, followed by arbitration or litigation, thus rendering the engineer's decision otiose. The ICE Conditions were initially amended in an attempt to avoid any "dispute" arising until after the matter had been referred to the engineer, so as to postpone the right to refer a dispute for adjudication. This was palpably contrary to s.108(2)(a) of the Act, by which the contract must enable the parties to give notice "at any time of his intention to refer a dispute to adjudication". The amendment was subsequently withdrawn and the ICE Conditions and now the ICC Form thus contain no provision for a further decision of the engineer, and provide for adjudication at any time.

Decisions of the contract administrator under the main contract are frequently referred to in forms of sub-contract, where the sub-contractor may be bound to comply with instructions given under the main contract. Other provisions may link the rights of the sub-contractor to payment, extensions of time and other matters to decisions given by the contract administrator under the main contract. The question arises whether the sub-contractor has the right to challenge such decisions under the main contract and if so in what manner.[649] In the light of *Beaufort Developments v Gilbert-Ash NI*[650] it is thought that there would be no difficulty in challenging such decisions under a sub-contract, in the absence of clear words giving the decisions binding effect. Any such challenge would also be subject to the right of adjudication at any time. Difficulties may nevertheless arise where the decision is also challenged under the head contract, unless the proceedings can be joined.

37-196 **Project manager and employer's agent**   These terms are met in particular types of contract, e.g. the new Engineering and Construction Contract. The particular role created is entirely dependent upon the conditions of contract. Usually, such appointment indicates a person or body appointed to act solely on behalf of the employer. In the case of the project manager, there may be additional management functions allowing greater control and direction of the works than normally exercised by a contract administrator.

(c)   Liability of Contract Administrator

37-197 **Basis of liability**   The contract administrator owes duties under his contract of appointment to the employer. He will be liable for the negligent exercise of those du-

---

646 s.108(3). For discussion of the status of the adjudicator's decision, see *Macob Civil Engineering Ltd v Morrison Construction Ltd* [1999] 3 B.L.R. 93; and *Outwing Construction Ltd v H Randell and Son Ltd* [1999] B.L.R. 156.

647 ICE 7th edn cl.66.

648 FIDIC (1998 edn) cl.20.2.

649 See *Modern Engineering v Miskin* [1981] 1 Lloyd's Rep. 135; (1980) 15 B.L.R. 82 where the point was decided by an arbitrator, who was then removed for misconduct.

650 [1999] 1 A.C. 266.

ties, whether involving acts as the employer's agent or acts performed impartially.[651] Earlier authority suggested that the contract administrator might have immunity from suit on the basis that acting impartially involved a "judicial" element.[652] It is clear that no such immunity attaches to the ordinary process of certifying but the possibility remains of actions under particular contracts being regarded as of a "judicial" nature. The contract administrator will be additionally liable for breach of authority for actions done without appropriate authority where the employer is bound by virtue of the terms of the main contract.

Standard of duty   The contract administrator owes a duty in contract, implied if **37-198** not express, to act with reasonable skill and care.[653] The duty of a professional man in a construction context (albeit involving a claim in tort) was considered in *Eckersley v Binnie & Partners*[654] where Bingham L.J. (dealing with the liability of engineers who had failed to provide against the possibility of methane migration into a water transfer pipe and dissenting in the result from the majority of the Court of Appeal) said that a professional man:

"... must bring to any professional task he undertakes no less expertise, skill and care than other ordinary competent members would bring but need bring no more. The standard is that of the reasonable average. The law does not require of a professional man that he be a paragon combining the qualities of polymath and prophet."

In *Greaves v Baynham Meikle & Partners*[655] an engineer was held liable on the basis that work under his design was not fit for purpose, despite there being no findings of negligence. The particular circumstances of the case were that the engineer was employed by a design and build contractor who was himself assumed to be liable on a fitness for purpose basis. The decision has not been followed in similar circumstances,[656] and may be regarded as limited to its own facts. Most design and build contracts now limit the contractor's design responsibility to that which would be assumed by a separately engaged design professional.[657] In the absence of such limitation, however, there is likely to be an implied term of fitness for purpose which could render the design and build contractor similarly liable.[658] It is also to be noted that where design work is carried out by the contractor under the *FIDIC Conditions* the works are expressly required to be "fit for the purposes for which the works are intended".[659]

Liability in particular circumstances   In circumstances where construction **37-199** projects have become far more complex in recent years, there are many profession-

651 *Sutcliffe v Thackrah* [1974] A.C. 727.
652 See *Chambers v Goldthorpe* [1901] 1 K.B. 624, overruled by *Sutcliffe v Thackrah* [1974] A.C. 727. But an express contractual term requiring a "first class" service has been held to be more onerous than a duty to exercise reasonable skill and care: *Conoco Phillips Petroleum Co Ltd v Snamprogetti Ltd* [2003] All E.R. (D) 134.
653 *Bolam v Friern Hospital Management Committee* [1957] 1 W.L.R. 582; and see *Holland Hannen & Cubitts v WHTSO* (1985) 35 B.L.R. 1.
654 (1988) 18 Con. L.R. 1.
655 [1975] 1 W.L.R. 1095.
656 *George Hawkins v Chrysler* (1986) 38 B.L.R. 36.
657 ICE Design and Construction Conditions cl.8(2).
658 *IBA v EMI & BICC* (1980) 14 B.L.R. 1 and 11 B.L.R. 29, CA; *Viking Grain Storage v TH White Installations* (1985) 3 Con. L.R. 52.
659 *FIDIC Plant and Design-Build Conditions (Yellow Book)*, cl.4.1; *FIDIC Construction Conditions (Red Book)* cl.4.1(c).

als in addition to the traditional architect/engineer to take responsibility for particular features of a project. Again, the liability of such professionals will depend upon their terms of engagement and the responsibilities assumed by them in fact. In *Pozzolanic Lytag Ltd v Bryan Hobson Associates*[660] it was held that a project manager had a duty to his client to ensure that all adequate insurance arrangements for the liability of a building contractor were in place, as required by the contract for the proposed project. In the same way, decisions in relation to the liability of architects have indicated the increasing range of functions performed by architects, such as decisions to proceed with a given development[661] and advice given on the acceptability of tenderers.[662] However, the scope of an architect's obligations will always depend upon his brief and all the circumstances of the project, so that in *Tesco Stores Ltd v The Norman Hitchcox Partnership Ltd*[663] the court decided that the architect did not owe any duty towards the employer to inspect the supermarket shell works during or at the end of their construction merely as a consequence of the architect's retainer to design those works.

37-200 **Liability to third parties** Engineers, architects and surveyors may incur liability to third parties under the general law of tort[664] and under the special circumstances envisaged by the law relating to negligent misstatement.[665] The important distinction between these heads of liability is that the former is generally limited to a liability in respect of physical damage, including personal injury,[666] while the latter may include purely economic loss, as now understood.[667] Of particular interest is the possible liability of the contract administrator to the building contractor.[668] In *Pacific Associates v Baxter*,[669] the plaintiff contractor sought to recover damages against the defendant engineer, who had rejected the contractor's claim under the contract. In subsequent arbitration proceedings, the claim succeeded but was settled for a small proportion of the contractor's loss. The contractor sought to recover the balance from the engineer on the basis of negligent administration of contract. The claim was struck out as disclosing no reasonable cause of action, on the basis that the defendant had entered into a contractual relationship with the employer, against whom the contractor had separate rights to bring arbitration proceedings. There had been no voluntary assumption of responsibility to the plaintiff and no duty upon the engineer had been established. The main contract, additionally, contained a disclaimer by which the defendant declined to accept any responsibility for the plaintiff, but the conclusions of the Court of Appeal may be seen as standing independent of such disclaimer.[670]

---

660 [1999] B.L.R. 267.
661 *Gable House Estates Ltd v The Halpern Partnership and Bovis Construction Ltd* (1995) 48 Con. L.R. 1.
662 *Partridge v Morris* (1995) C.I.L.L. 1095.
663 (1997) 56 Con. L.R. 42.
664 *D & F Estates v Church Commissioners* [1989] A.C. 177; *DoE v Thomas Bates* [1991] 1 A.C. 499; and *Murphy v Brentwood DC* [1991] 1 A.C. 398.
665 *Hedley Byrne v Heller* [1964] A.C. 465.
666 See *Clay v Crump* [1964] 1 Q.B. 533; and *Spartan Steel v Martin* [1973] Q.B. 27.
667 *Sutherland Shire Council v Heyman* (1985) 60 A.L.R. 1, HC Australia.
668 See *Old School v Gleeson* (1976) 4 B.L.R. 103.
669 [1990] 1 Q.B. 993.
670 See also *South Nation River v Auto Concrete Curb* (1993) 11 Con. L.J. 155 Canada SC but see *John Mowlem v Eagle Star Insurance (No.1)* (1992) 62 B.L.R. 126. Also, in *Leon Engineering Construction v Ka Duk Investments* (1989) 47 B.L.R. 139, the Supreme Court of Canada held that it was argu-

(d) Contract with Employer

Standard terms   Contracts for professional services require no formality. The **37-201** professional bodies, however, issue standard forms of engagement which make detailed provisions as to duties, work stages and payment. Provision may be made for a "scale fee", which is dependent upon the valuation of the works at various stages. Architects and engineers, at least, are now frequently required to submit lump sum design "tenders", with the resulting fee being paid in stages to be agreed. Standard conditions of engagement invariably provide for an express duty of reasonable skill and care together with certain exclusions or limitations such as:

> "The client shall hold the contractor and not the Architect responsible for the contractor's management and operational methods and for the proper carrying out and completion of the works and for health and safety provisions on site."[671]

Delegation   A professional may not delegate design duties without express **37-202** authority. In *Moresk Cleaners v Hicks*[672] an architect delegated the design of reinforced concrete work to a sub-contractor. It was held that the architect had the option of arranging for the client to employ the specialist designer or of employing the specialist himself, while retaining responsibility for the design. An architect may, however, properly delegate a specialist design process details of which would not be revealed by the supplier. Thus in *Merton LBC v Lowe*[673] an architect was held to be entitled to delegate the design of a specialist ceiling finish. Waller L.J. stated:

> "Pyroc were nominated sub-contractors employed for a specialist task of making a ceiling with their own proprietary material. It was the defendant's duty to use reasonable care as Architects. In view of successful work done elsewhere, they decided that to employ Pyroc was reasonable. No witness called suggested that it was not at the beginning."

The architects were, however, held liable under their general design responsibility for failing to take adequate steps to remedy defects which subsequently became apparent.

Continuing duty   A continuing duty to review a design was upheld by the Court **37-203** of Appeal in *Brickfield Properties v Newton*[674] where Sachs L.J. said:

> "The Architect is under a continuing duty to check that his design will work in practice and to correct any errors which may emerge. It savours the ridiculous for the Architect to be able to say 'true my design was faulty, but of course I saw to it that the contractors followed it faithfully'."

Although there is authority that duties last until completion of the works,[675] it is probably right that duties endure beyond completion. The extent of a continuing

---

able that engineers would be liable for negligent misstatement in respect of errors in tender documents.

[671] RIBA Standard Form of Appointment (SFA/92), published as an Appendix in *Keating on Building Contracts*, 6th edn (1995). A similar wording is contained in SFA198 (see App.C to the 7th edition of *Keating on Construction Contracts*).

[672] [1966] 2 Lloyd's Rep. 338.

[673] (1982) 18 B.L.R. 130.

[674] [1971] 1 W.L.R. 862, 873.

[675] *Chelmsford DC v Evers* (1985) 25 B.L.R. 99, 106; *Equitable Debenture Assets Corp v William Moss* (1984) 2 Con. L.R. 1, 24.

post-completion design duty gives rise to serious potential difficulties. In *Eckersley v Binnie*,[676] where an explosion attributed to methane occurred some years after completion of a project, Bingham L.J. considered the nature of a duty continuing into the future. He said[677]:

> "What is plain is that if any such duty at all is to be imposed, the nature, scope and limits of such a duty require to be very carefully and cautiously defined. The development of the law on this point, if it ever occurs, will be gradual and analogical."

However, the "continuing" duty to review the design only arises after the initial breach associated with a defective design, when a "trigger event" occurs to put the architect on notice that a review is or may be required.[678]

The extent to which the courts will impose continuing obligations to warn or advise will, in practice, be determined by the manner and extent to which the parties provide for this in their contract.

8. BREACH AND NON-PERFORMANCE

(a) General Principles

37-204   **The basis for a claim for breach**   In construction contracts, as with contracts generally, it is fundamental to distinguish[679] between claims made under the contract and claims for breach of the contract which are the subject of this section. A breach of contract by party A which has not been excused will give party B a right to claim at least nominal damages simply on the basis that there has been "an infraction of a legal right".[680] Where B can go further and show that A's breach of contract is causative of a type of loss which the law will allow, and where the loss claimed is not too remote,[681] then B will be entitled to claim substantial damages.[682] Although an award of damages is a question of fact in the particular case,[683] the broad principle behind any award of damages for breach of contract remains "where a party sustains a loss by reason of a breach of contract he is, so far as money can do it, to be placed in the same situation with respect to damages as if the contract had been performed".[684] A further principle is that before considering any question of causation or remoteness of damage it is necessary to consider whether the

---

[676] (1988) 18 Con. L.R. 1.

[677] The judgment of Bingham L.J. was a dissenting opinion on the question of liability of the engineers, but his observations on the continuing nature of the design obligation, while obiter, are of great significance.

[678] See *New Islington and Hackney Housing Association Ltd v Pollard Thomas and Edwards Ltd* [2001] B.L.R. 74 at 80.

[679] In complex building cases, the distinction can sometimes be in danger of being overlooked: see *McAlpine Humberoak v McDermott International (No.1)* (1992) 58 B.L.R. 1, 22, CA.

[680] *The Mediana* [1900] A.C. 113, 116.

[681] See the discussion of the rule in *Hadley v Baxendale* (1854) 9 Ex. 341 in *McGregor on Damages*, 19th edn (2014), paras 8-157 et seq.; and in *Keating on Construction Contracts*, 10th edn (2016) at paras 9-007—9-016; and also *Balfour Beatty Construction (Scotland) Ltd v Scottish Power Plc*, 1994 S.C. (H.L.) 20; (1994) 71 B.L.R. 20, HL.

[682] See also the discussion of the general principles when considering an award of damages in relation to defective premises in *Harrison v Shepherd Homes Ltd* [2011] EWHC 1811 (TCC), 27 Const. L.J. 709, per Ramsey J. at [234]–[264].

[683] *British Westinghouse Electric & Manufacturing Co Ltd v Underground Electric Railways Co Ltd* [1912] A.C. 673, 688.

[684] *Robinson v Harman* (1848) 1 Ex. 850, 855. For other clear expressions of the principle see *Wertheim*

type or kind of loss in respect of which damages are claimed was within the contractual scope of the obligation that has been breached.[685]

Mitigation of loss   A plaintiff must take all reasonable steps to minimise the loss   **37-205**
to him as a result of breach, but the plaintiff is under no obligation to take any step which a reasonable and prudent man would not ordinarily take in the course of his business.[686] The plaintiff need not, for example, take steps which would involve him in complicated litigation[687] or steps which he cannot financially afford.[688] In the context of construction contracts, a failure by the employer (or by the contract administrator on his behalf) to permit the contractor to return to the site to correct minor defects (often referred to as "snagging") may amount to a failure to mitigate.[689] Likewise, where more substantial defects appear post-completion the employer should consider whether it is reasonable to permit or invite the contractor to carry out repairs. The decision will be a complex matter where the repairs proposed by the contractor are less extensive than those advised by the employer's expert advisers.[690]

Betterment   If, following defective work by the builder in breach of contract, the   **37-206**
plaintiff takes the step of rebuilding to a higher standard than necessary, or to a standard higher than the building contract, properly performed, would have produced, then the plaintiff must give credit for the element of betterment.[691] However, betterment will not apply where the plaintiff obtains a building which,

---

v Chicoutimi Pulp Co [1911] A.C. 301, 307; Monarch SS Co Ltd v Karlhamns Oljefabriker [1949] A.C. 196 at 220; Radford v De Froberville [1977] 1 W.L.R. 1262, 1268; DO Ferguson v M Sohl (1992) 62 B.L.R. 95, 103; Ruxley Electronics Ltd v Forsyth [1996] 1 A.C. 344, 365. See also Fuller and Perdue (1936-37) 46 Yale L.J. 52, 373.

685   See South Australia Asset Management Ltd v York Montague Ltd [1997] A.C. 191; and Transfield Shipping Inc v Mercator Shipping Inc [2009] 1 A.C. 61 (on which see further above, Vol.I, paras 26-137 et seq.). For an application of these principles in a construction contract context, see HOK Sport Ltd v Aintree Racecourse Co Ltd [2003] B.L.R. 155; Earl Terrace Properties v Nilsson Design [2004] B.L.R. 273 and Hancock v Tucker [1999] Lloyd's P.N. 814. See also John Grimes Partnership Ltd v Gubbins [2013] EWCA Civ 37, [2013] B.L.R. 126 where the Court of Appeal held that if the type or kind of loss was, at the time of contract, reasonably foreseeable by the defendant as not unlikely to result from his breach (had a breach been contemplated at that time) then such a type or kind of loss was not too remote (see at [17]–[19]).

686   British Westinghouse Electric v Underground Electric Railways [1912] A.C. 673, 689.

687   Pilkington v Wood [1953] Ch. 770, 777.

688   Clippens Oil Co Ltd v Edinburgh and District Water Trustees [1907] A.C. 291; Perry v Sidney Phillips & Son [1982] 1 W.L.R. 1297, [1982] 1 All E.R. 1005, 1013; Trans Trust SPRL v Danubian Trading Co Ltd [1952] 2 Q.B. 297, 306.

689   City Axis Ltd v Daniel P Jackson (1998) 64 Con. L.R. 84.

690   See Great Ormond Street Hospital v McLaughlin & Harvey (1987) 19 Con. L.R. 25; and Kaye v Hosier & Dickinson [1972] 1 W.L.R. 146.

691   British Westinghouse Electric and Manufacturing v Underground Electric Railways [1912] A.C. 673, 691; Richard Roberts v Douglas Smith Stimson (1988) 46 B.L.R. 50; Skandia Property (UK) v Thames Water (1998) C.I.L.L. 1326. An appeal against this decision was dismissed; see [1999] B.L.R. 338. See Linklaters Business Services v Sir Robert McAlpine Ltd [2010] EWHC 2931 (TCC), 133 Con. L.R. 211, per Akenhead J. at [145]–[146], where Skandia was distinguished and a claimant was permitted to recover damages based upon the cost of replacing damaged pipework instead of remedying defects to insulation and corrosion to pipework locally because, in all the circumstances, this was a reasonable decision to have made (not least because bona fide experienced experts advised that replacement was required and there was no suggestion that this advice was negligent or that further experts should have been called in to provide advice as well).

whilst necessarily newer and better than the defective building, is a reasonable choice of replacement in all the circumstances.[692]

37-207 **Causation** For a plaintiff to succeed in his claim for substantial damages, he must show an effective[693] causal connection between breach and loss, and causation will be a matter of fact in each case to be determined by the application of common sense.[694] In practical terms, causation is at the core of most construction disputes, since the connection, or possible competing connections, between breach and loss will not be clear-cut, and will be a matter of impression or inference from the primary facts.[695] In *Lamb v Jarvis*[696] the court considered that the defective jointing of pipework by the plaintiff, taken with the defendant's defective groundworks, had jointly caused leaks which were the damage forming the subject matter of the remedial scheme for which the plaintiff sought payment from the defendant. Faced with the problems of causation and apportionment, it was held[697] that the court was entitled to arrive at an apportionment between the parties, rather than being bound to arrive at a conclusion on an "all or nothing" basis.[698]

(b) Breach by Employer

37-208 **Introduction** Although the contractor, in practice, may follow a less systematic pattern, claims for damages by the contractor against the employer are based upon the assumption that the contractor, in tendering for given works, has: (i) analysed the scope of the work by reference to documentation and/or inspection of the works; (ii) identified his basic costs (labour and materials) of carrying out the work; (iii) included in his tender prices a margin for overheads (vehicles, head office costs) and for profit; and (iv) foregone other profitable work in tendering for the given works. Since claims for damages are based upon the compensation of loss incurred, the assumptions identified above will need (along with many other factors) to be

---

692 *Harbutts Plasticine v Wayne Tank & Pump Co* [1970] 1 Q.B. 447. See also *Voaden v Champion* [2002] 1 Lloyd's Rep. 623 at [85]–[89] where the test of reasonableness in this sense is set out.

693 *Monarch Steamship Co v Karlshamns Oljefabriker* [1949] A.C. 196, 226.

694 *Galoo Ltd v Bright Grahame Murray* [1994] 1 W.L.R. 1360, 1369–1375, CA. See also *Nulty v Milton Keynes BC* [2013] EWCA Civ 15, [2013] B.L.R. 134, where the Court of Appeal held that the civil balance of probability test meant no less and no more than the court having to be satisfied on rational and objective grounds that the case for believing that the suggested means of causation occurred was stronger than the case for not believing it (at [35]). But also note the unusual approach taken to the burden of proof in relation to the application of the "but for" test in *West v Ian Finlay & Associates* [2013] EWHC 868 (TCC) (reversed on other grounds, [2014] EWCA Civ 316, [2014] B.L.R. 324). In this case the defendant architect was found to have been negligent in failing to notice the poor quality of the M&E services installations in the renovation of the claimants' property, but argued that there was no loss because the work under this contract would never have been properly carried out and completed by the M&E contractor irrespective of how competently it had acted. It was held that given the nature of its breaches of duty, the onus was on the defendant to show that even if it had acted with reasonable care the damage would probably still have occurred, applying the approach adopted by the Court of Appeal in the context of a road traffic personal injury claim in *Phethean-Hubble v Coles* [2012] EWCA Civ 349, [2012] R.T.R. 31.

695 For building cases in which causation is directly discussed, see *Pratt v George J Hill Associates* (1987) 38 B.L.R. 25, CA; *Gable House Estates v The Halpern Partnership* (1995) 48 Con. L.R. 1; *Skandia Property (UK) Ltd and Vala Properties BV v Thames Water* (1997) 57 Con. L.R. 65.

696 (1998) 60 Con. L.R. 1.

697 Following the decision in *Tennant Radiant Heat Ltd v Warrington Development Corp* [1988] 1 E.G.L.R. 41, CA.

698 See also the discussion of approaches to causation in *Keating on Construction Contracts*, 10th edn (2016), paras 8-025—8-028.

revisited on the facts of each case, to ascertain the true extent of the contractor's recoverable loss. Some of the principal areas of liability of the employer to pay damages to the building contractor are considered below.

Payment for work done   The contractor's entitlement to be paid (both in timing   **37-209** and amount) will be derived from the terms of the construction contract, and failure to pay will amount to a breach. Although non-payment by the employer is not generally a breach which will entitle the contractor to treat the contract as at an end,[699] the failure of the employer to pay under a "construction contract" falling within the Housing Grants, Construction and Regeneration Act 1996[700] will confer upon the contractor a right to suspend work. If there is no express provision relating to time for payment, then payment is to be made within a reasonable time in all the circumstances.[701] Where the employer wrongfully terminates the contract prior to completion by the contractor, then the contractor is entitled to be paid (either under the contract or as damages)[702] for work done, and the rate of payment will be by reference to the rates and prices in the contract, and not on the basis of a reasonable sum. Additionally, in respect of that portion of the work which the contractor was prevented from completing, the contractor may claim either the expenditure which he has wasted following the employer's breach, or alternatively loss of profit on the work.[703]

Withdrawal of work   Although the general rule may be altered or displaced by   **37-210** the terms of the contract, the contractor has a legitimate expectation and contractual right to carry out the work contained in the contract. The employer cannot generally remove work from a contractor in order to have that work carried out by a third party.[704] The contractor will be entitled to recover by way of damages for breach the loss of profit element on the work withdrawn, by reason of the reduced amount of turnover. In assessing such a claim for loss of profit, the court will have to consider whether the work was indeed profitable, as well as assessing how far (if at all) the loss of profit on the particular item of work reduced the overall profit of the contractor's business.

Delay and disruption   Where the employer, in breach of the express or implied   **37-211** terms of the contract, interrupts or otherwise interferes with the work of the contractor[705] then the contractor may incur costs which are additional to the extra direct cost of carrying out the work. The different heads of recovery for delay and disruption

---

[699] *D R Bradley (Cable Jointing) Ltd v Jefco Mechanical Services Ltd* Unreported 1988 (see 6-CLD-07-21).

[700] See s.112 of the Housing Grants, Construction and Regeneration Act 1996, as amended by the Local Democracy, Economic Development and Construction Act 2009.

[701] Here again the applicability of the Housing Grants, Construction and Regeneration Act 1996 must be considered.

[702] *Canterbury Pipe Lines v Christchurch Drainage* (1979) 16 B.L.R. 76 Court of Appeal of New Zealand.

[703] *Felton v Wharrie* (1906) H.B.C. (4th edn) Vol.2, 398, CA. See also the discussion in *Keating on Construction Contracts*, 10th edn (2016), paras 9-058—9-063.

[704] *Gallagher v Hirsch* [1899] N.Y. 454 App. Div. 467; *Carr v JA Berriman Pty Ltd* (1953) 27 A.J.L.R. 273; *Commissioners of Main Roads v Reed and Stuart* (1974) 12 B.L.R. 55; *Abbey Developments Ltd v PP Brickwork Ltd* [2003] C.I.L.L. 2033 (TCC).

[705] Common examples will be delayed, reduced and interrupted access to the works, or late procurement of planning or building permissions (on which see *Ellis-Don v Parking Authority of Toronto* (1978) 28 B.L.R. 98, 110).

(increased preliminaries, overheads, loss of profit, loss of productivity, increased costs as a result of inflation, interest for non-payment of money) are considered in detail in the specialist textbooks.[706] Disruption claims are difficult to establish. The contractor must prove that there was disruption to its activities, that this was caused by a breach of contract or a matter that the employer is contractually responsible for and that the sum/loss claimed flowed from the same. In *Walter Lilly & Co Ltd v DMW Developments Ltd*[707] Akenhead J. stated that there is no set way to prove these elements and that it is open to contractors to prove them with whatever evidence will satisfy the tribunal to the requisite standard of proof. However, it is to be noted that the calculation of loss of overheads and profit in construction contracts will often be evaluated together by reference to the "Hudson formula" which takes a percentage for head office cost or profit and multiplies this by the contract sum. This is multiplied by the period of delay (in weeks), divided by the contract period. The formula has been the subject of consideration by the courts,[708] but it is thought that it must be used with some regard being paid to some factors which the formula may ignore, such as the effect of re-deployment of resources during the period of delay and the likelihood that the profit multiplier will not take account of the element for profit already contained within the contract sum. It appears also that claims for overhead and profit have to be established in principle, i.e. the contractor must show that there was other work available that, but for the employer's breach, would have been undertaken in the relevant period.[709] In *Cleveland Bridge UK Ltd v Severfield-Rowen Structures Ltd*[710] it was held that where the Court is satisfied that some (more than de minimis) disruption must have occurred as a result of the contractor's breaches, it should make a reasoned assessment, albeit one based on the minimum loss or expense probably attributable to the same.

(c) Breach by the Contractor

37-212 **Introduction** Claims for damages by the employer following breach by the contractor are considered in this section by reference to: (i) failure to build; (ii) defective work; (iii) delay; (iv) consequential loss; and (v) claims for non-pecuniary loss. In considering the types of claims typically made by the employer in construction contracts, the application of general principles relating to the duty to mitigate and the requirement to account for betterment[711] should be borne in mind.

---

[706] See for example *Keating on Construction Contracts*, 10th edn (2016), paras 9-048—9-054.

[707] [2012] EWHC 1773 (TCC), [2012] B.L.R. 503 at [486c].

[708] *Ellis-Don v Parking Authority of Toronto* (1978) 28 B.L.R. 98 Supreme Court of Ontario; *Finnegan v Sheffield City Council* (1988) 43 B.L.R. 124; see also *Walter Lilly & Co Ltd v Mackay & DMW Developments Ltd* [2012] EWHC 1773 (TCC) where it was held that the use of a formula, supported by relevant factual evidence of opportunities foregone, was a legitimate and helpful way of establishing this head of loss, per Akenhead J. at 540–543.

[709] See generally *Keating on Construction Contracts*, 10th edn (2016), paras 9-049—9-059. In *Walter Lilly & Co Ltd v DMW Developments Ltd* [2012] EWHC 1773 (TCC), [2012] B.L.R. 503 it was held that the use of a formula, supported by relevant factual evidence of opportunities foregone, was a legitimate way of establishing this head of loss; but that in order to prove a claim for loss of profit and head office overheads caused by delay it had to be shown on the balance of probabilities that, but for the delay, the claimant would have secured other work which would have contributed to such overheads and/or generated profit and the loss would not have been sustained (see at [540]–[543]).

[710] [2012] EWHC 3652.

[711] See section (a) above.

Failure to build   Where the contractor fails to build at all or in part, then the   **37-213**
normal measure of damages is the cost to the employer of completing the building
works in a reasonable manner less the contract price. The leading authority on the
point is still *Mertens v Home Freeholds*.[712] The employer may also recover in
respect of increased costs arising through delay in completion following the
contractor's failure to build.[713]

Defective work   Where, after completion, there are defects in the works, the   **37-214**
employer will normally be entitled to damages equal to the costs of making good
the defects (this is sometimes referred to as the costs of reinstatement).[714] However,
whilst such an award of damages puts the plaintiff (employer) into the position he
would be in if the contract had been properly performed in the first place, it is still
for the plaintiff to show that reinstatement is a reasonable response to the damage
in question.[715] In *Ruxley Electronics & Constructions Ltd v Forsyth*[716] the plaintiff
contractor was engaged to build a swimming pool for Mr Forsyth which was to have
a diving area 7ft 6ins deep, whereas the pool which was built had a diving area with
a depth of 6ft. The pool was suitable for diving and the failure to follow the requirement as to depth was found to have had no effect on the value of Mr Forsyth's
property. Mr Forsyth counterclaimed the cost of re-building the pool to the depth
specified in the contract with the plaintiff contractor, which was estimated at
£21,560. The House of Lords (reversing the decision of the Court of Appeal)
awarded Mr Forsyth modest damages for loss of amenity, and not the costs of
reinstatement.[717] The judgments in *Ruxley*, both in the Court of Appeal and House
of Lords dealt with the question of the intention of the innocent party to carry out
re-instatement. The position appears to be that the court normally has no concern
with the use to which an award of damages will be put and an undertaking to reinstate would be irrelevant. However, intention may be relevant to the reasonableness of re-instatement.[718]

Delay   Where a contractor, without excuse, fails to complete in accordance with   **37-215**

---

[712] [1921] 2 K.B. 526, 535, CA. There are no other authorities on this point, although in *DO Ferguson v M Sohl* (1992) 62 B.L.R. 95, 104, the relevant passage from the judgment of Lord Sterndale M.R. in *Mertens* was referred to by Hirst L.J. without adverse comment.

[713] See also *Dodd Properties v Canterbury CC* [1980] 1 W.L.R. 433.

[714] *East Ham Corp v Bernard Sunley & Sons Ltd* [1966] A.C. 406, HL. See *Brit Inns Ltd v BDW Trading Ltd* [2012] EWHC 2143 (TCC), 145 Con. L.R. 181 for an example of the approach to the measure and proof of damages in claims for defective work and loss of profits.

[715] See *Atkins v Scott* (1990) 7 Const. L.J. 215, CA.

[716] [1996] 1 A.C. 344, HL.

[717] Note in particular the passage in the speech of Lord Mustill at 360. See on this, McInnes, "The Yellow Brick Road: Ruxley revisited" (1998) 14 Const. L.J. 33. See also *Bovis Lend Lease v RD Fire Protection* (2003) 89 Con. L.R. 169, where the cost of reinstatement was also refused. See also *Harrison v Shepherd Homes Ltd* [2011] EWHC 1811 (TCC), 27 Const. L.J. 709, per Ramsey J. at [263]–[264], for a summary of the general principles to apply when considering an award of damages for defective premises and, in particular, the circumstances in which damages based on the cost of reinstatement, diminution in value and loss of amenity and inconvenience will be appropriate.

[718] See [1996] A.C. 344, per Lord Jauncey at 359 and Lord Lloyd at 372–373 and [1994] 1 W.L.R. 650, per Staughton L.J. at 658; and see *Radford v DeFroberville* [1977] 1 W.L.R. 1262. For a decision in which a claimant had no intention of conducting the postulated repair work and where this was found to be relevant to the reasonableness of adopting reinstatement costs as the basis for the measure of damages, see *London Fire and Emergency Planning Authority v Halcrow Gilbert Associates Ltd* [2007] EWHC 2546 (TCC).

the timescale provided for within the contract,[719] then the employer will either be entitled to levy "liquidated and ascertained damages" at the contractual rate[720] or he will be entitled to claim general (unliquidated) damages referable to the loss incurred by reason of the delay. Furthermore, where the form of contract provides for the contractor to proceed with the works regularly and diligently,[721] then a failure to do so may entitle the employer to dismiss the contractor from the site[722] if the breach is to be regarded as repudiatory (see below). This is to be distinguished from termination under the terms of the contract. Where (which will be rare in construction contracts) time is stated to be of the essence, then failure by the contractor will mean that the employer is entitled to treat the contract as at an end and dismiss the contractor from the site.[723]

37-216 Consequential loss   In construction projects, defects in the works will often have a wider impact upon the employer's existing operations and production process. Such losses will rarely be said to arise naturally according to the usual course of things and, accordingly, consequential losses will usually fall under the second limb of *Hadley v Baxendale*[724]: that is, damage which, in the reasonable contemplation of both parties at the time of making the contract would, had they thought about it, have had a very substantial degree of probability.[725] Construction contracts will often have clauses limiting or excluding liability for "consequential loss", and the effect of such clauses will be a matter of construction,[726] although it may also be important to consider whether such exclusion is reasonable for the purposes of the Unfair Contract Terms Act 1977.[727]

37-217 Non-pecuniary loss   Where building works are to the plaintiff's main dwelling, he will be able to recover modest damages for anxiety and distress associated with the defective work of the building contractor.[728] However, this head of loss will not be recoverable as between commercial parties, or where the plaintiff's property is substantially for investment purposes.[729]

---

[719] Or within a reasonable time: *Hick v Raymond & Reid* [1893] A.C. 22, 32.

[720] See above, para.37-031.

[721] In *Leander Construction Ltd v Mulalley & Co Ltd* [2011] EWHC 3449 (TCC) it was held that ordinarily there will be no implied term in a building contract that the contractor should proceed regularly and diligently with the works prior to the contract completion date.

[722] *West Faulkner Associates v London Borough of Newham* (1994) 71 B.L.R. 1, CA. See also *Sabic UK Petrochemicals Ltd v Punj Lloyd Ltd* [2013] EWHC 2916 (TCC), [2014] B.L.R. 43, where it was held in relation to an express term requiring a contractor to carry out and complete the works with due diligence that a consideration of what was required to satisfy this obligation was linked to the parties' other contractual obligations and, in particular, on the facts of the case to the contractor's obligation to meet a milestone date for the commencement of commissioning.

[723] *Rickards v Oppenheim* [1950] 1 K.B. 616, 628, CA.

[724] (1854) 9 Ex. 341. This is the broad effect of *British Sugar Plc v NEI Power Projects Ltd* (1997) 87 B.L.R. 42, CA.

[725] *Balfour Beatty Construction (Scotland) Ltd v Scottish Power Plc*, 1994 S.C. (H.L.) 20; (1994) 71 B.L.R. 20, HL.

[726] *British Sugar Plc v NEI Power Projects Ltd* (1997) 87 B.L.R. 42, CA; *Hotel Services Ltd v Hilton International Hotels (UK) Ltd* [2000] 1 All E.R. (Comm) 750, [2000] B.L.R. 235.

[727] See above, para.37-084.

[728] *Rawlings v Rentokil Laboratories* [1972] E.G.D. 744; *Perry v Sidney Phillips* [1982] 1 W.L.R. 1292; *Ruxley Electronics v Forsyth* [1996] A.C. 344, 360–361, HL. See also, Franklin, "Mere Heartache" (1992) 7 Const. L.J. 318; Humphries, "Contractual Damages for Mental Distress" (1996) S.J. 182.

[729] *Hutchinson v Harris* (1978) 10 B.L.R. 19, 37.

(d) Repudiation and Discharge

Repudiatory breach   Where one party so acts or expresses himself as to show that   **37-218**
he does not mean to accept the obligations of the contract any further, then this may,
depending on the circumstances, amount to a repudiatory breach of contract.[730]
Generally, a breach of contract will only give rise to a claim for damages, and the
innocent party will be obliged to continue its outstanding performance of the
contract notwithstanding the breach.[731] However, where there is a breach of a condition which amounts to a refusal to perform going to the root of the contract, then
there will be a repudiatory breach[732] entitling the innocent party, on acceptance of
the repudiation, to treat the contract as at an end.[733] The act of repudiation may
consist of a clear unqualified refusal, but will more probably involve some other
breach which goes to the root of the contract, or may be such as to indicate an intention no longer to be bound by the contract.[734] In considering where there has been
a repudiation, it is necessary to look at the conduct and the circumstances of the parties as a whole.[735]

Acceptance   The innocent party faced with a repudiatory breach can do one of two   **37-219**
things: (i) affirm the contract in a clear way; or (ii) accept the repudiation by making it plain that by reason of the repudiatory act of the defaulting party, he considers that the contract is at an end.[736]

What will amount to repudiation?   What will amount to a repudiation of the   **37-220**
contract will depend upon the terms which the parties have agreed and the relative
importance which they have placed on them. In relation to acts or defaults of the
contractor, a refusal to carry out work is likely to evince the appropriate intention
no longer to be bound. Poor workmanship, however, will generally not be sufficient to constitute repudiation,[737] unless there is a manifest inability to comply with
the requirements of the contract indicative of a basic inability, or basic lack of
competence and intention, to perform the contract. Unless time is of the essence,
delay may amount to a repudiation only where the delay gives rise to the inference that the defaulting party does not intend to be bound by the terms of the
contract. In relation to acts or defaults of the employer, an act of prevention such
as a refusal to grant the contractor access to the site, or dismissal of the contractor
from the site, is likely to amount to a repudiation. A failure by the employer to pay

---

[730] *Heyman v Darwins* [1942] A.C. 356, 378, HL.
[731] *Channel Tunnel Group v Balfour Beatty* [1992] Q.B. 656, 666, CA.
[732] *Woodar Investment Development v Wimpey Construction UK* [1980] 1 W.L.R. 277, 283. See also
Eminence Property Developments Ltd v Heaney [2010] EWCA Civ 1168, [2011] 2 All E.R. (Comm)
223, where the Court of Appeal held, following *Woodar*, that the legal test for repudiatory conduct
was whether, looking at all the circumstances of the case objectively, from the perspective of a
reasonable person in the innocent party's position, the contract breaker had clearly shown an intention to abandon and altogether refuse to perform the contract (per Etherton L.J. at [33]–[61]).
[733] *Photo Productions Ltd v Securicor Transport Ltd* [1980] A.C. 827, 849; see also *Scobie & McIntosh
v Clayton Bowmore* (1990) 49 B.L.R. 119.
[734] *General Billposting Co Ltd v Atkinson* [1909] AC 118, 122; *Sutcliffe v Chippendale and Edmondson*
(1971) 18 B.L.R. 149, 157, 161 (Sir William Stabb Q.C.); *Woodar Ltd v Wimpey Ltd* [1980] 1 W.L.R.
277, 282–283, HL. See also *Price v Great Yarmouth BC* (2003) T.C.L.R. 1, CA at 9.
[735] *Woodar Ltd v Wimpey Ltd* [1980] 1 W.L.R. 277, 281, HL.
[736] *Fercometal v Mediterranean Shipping* [1989] A.C. 788, 805, HL. On acceptance of repudiatory
breach, see also *Laing Management Ltd v Aegon Insurance Co (UK) Ltd* (1997) 55 Con. L.R. 1.
[737] There were not sufficient in *Sheffield v Conrad* (1987) 22 Con. L.R. 108, CA.

the contractor could amount to a repudiation, depending on the terms as to payment, and the circumstances of the refusal,[738] but generally there is no right to suspend work where payment is withheld from the contractor.[739] It is to be noted that s.112 of the Housing Grants, Construction and Regeneration Act 1996 gives rise to a right to suspend in specified circumstances of default.

37-221 **Repudiation and contractual termination** Save where the contract provides that the machinery of contractual termination[740] is an exclusive remedy of the parties, then such machinery will not exclude the remedies available at common law following an act of repudiation.[741] However, the often complex machinery for termination of employment under a given contract will have to be operated with care and precision. In particular, standard form contracts will often identify particular defaults the occurrence of which will entitle the other party to terminate. The contract will also often identify periods of time during which the innocent party must give proper notice of default to the party in breach[742] so that the specified default can be made good. A party who operates the machinery of contractual termination without justification under the contract is likely to be regarded as having repudiated the contract, since operation of the machinery will typically be accompanied by a refusal to perform obligations under the contract.[743]

(e) Frustration and Force Majeure

37-222 **Frustration** This is a principle which addresses those situations where the underlying objectives of the parties in entering into a contract are defeated, without fault of either party, through changes in circumstances which are unforeseen, or on

---

[738] In *Alan Auld Associates Ltd v Rick Pollard Associates* [2008] EWCA Civ 655, [2008] B.L.R. 419, it was held by the Court of Appeal that in a contract for the provision of engineering services, which was analogous to an employment contract, a party's persistent and cynical failure to pay invoices in spite of repeated complaints from the party providing the services amounted to a repudiatory breach of contract. Also, note that in *Mayhaven Healthcare Ltd v Bothma & Bothma* [2009] EWHC 2634 (TCC), [2010] B.L.R. 154 it was held that the question of whether a contractor's wrongful suspension of works amounts to a repudiatory breach of contract was not capable of a simple answer, as it would depend upon the terms of the contract, the nature of the breach and all the facts and circumstances of the case.

[739] *Supamarl v Federated Homes Ltd* (1981) 9 Con. L.R. 25; *Channel Tunnel Group v Balfour Beatty* [1992] Q.B. 656, 666, CA. See also *Multiplex Constructions (UK) Ltd v Cleveland Bridge UK Ltd* [2006] EWHC (TCC) 1341, (2006) 107 Con. L.R. 1, where it was held that a contractor's failure to make payments to its sub-contractor in accordance with a supplementary agreement did not amount to a repudiatory breach of contract in all the circumstances, especially having regard to the fact that the contractor had referred the relevant payment dispute to adjudication.

[740] See paras 37-244—37-246 below.

[741] *Architectural Installation v James Gibbons* (1989) 46 B.L.R. 91. However, *Lockland Builders v John Kim Rickwood* (1995) 77 B.L.R. 38, CA indicates that it may be easier to exclude common law rights following repudiatory breach than was previously thought. Note that in *Golden Straight Corp v Nippon Kisen Kubishika Kaisha* [2007] UKHL 12, [2007] 2 W.L.R. 891 the House of Lords held that the assessment of damages for wrongful repudiation could take into account events which took place after the date of the acceptance of the repudiatory breach.

[742] See cll.8.4 and 8.9, JCT 2011.

[743] *Architectural Installation Services v James Gibbons* (1989) 46 B.L.R. 91. See also *Stocznia Gdynia SA v Gearbulk Holdings Ltd* [2009] EWCA Civ 75, [2009] 3 W.L.R. 677, [2009] B.L.R. 196, where it was held by the Court of Appeal that a party did not lose its right to treat a contract as repudiated and to recover damages for repudiation simply because it exercised its contractual termination rights; and that on the facts there was no inconsistency between recovering instalments of the price, pursuant to the termination provisions, and claiming damages at common law for loss of bargain.

the occurrence of particular types of supervening events. The general rule is that contractual obligations are binding and absolute, so that a party is not absolved from performance merely because this has become more expensive, more difficult or even proves to be impossible.[744] Prior to the decision in *Taylor v Caldwell*,[745] parties were regarded as capable of making provision for the occurrence of supervening events in their contracts, so that a very strict view prevailed. In its modern form, the doctrine of frustration, as seen in the case of construction contracts as well as other kinds of contract, involves the identification of situations where it would be unjust and unreasonable to hold parties to their contracts.[746] However, the authorities indicate that a plea of frustration ought not to be lightly invoked, since the operation of the doctrine has been kept within very narrow limits. In particular, to see if the doctrine applies "you have first to construe the contract and see whether the parties have themselves provided for the situation which has arisen. If they have provided for it, the contract must govern".[747]

Frustration of construction contract   In construction contracts, frustration arising out of delay will be kept within very narrow confines, such as occurred in *Metropolitan Water Board v Dick Kerr & Co*.[748] Here, indefinite delay was imposed by a government order to stop work under the Defence of the Realm Acts which was held not to fall under the extension of time provision in the contract. Frustration will almost invariably have no application to a case of ground conditions which render construction impossible, since the onus is upon the contractor to ascertain at tender stage whether there are difficulties which may affect the site. Unexpected adverse weather conditions will only excuse non-performance by the contractor to the extent provided by the contract terms.[749] Since the courts will not generally release parties from the consequences of poor bargains, unforeseen increases in costs and price in the course of a construction contract will not give rise to frustration save where increases make the obligations radically different from those contemplated.[750]

37-223

Force majeure   Parties to commercial contracts will often make provision for situations where circumstances beyond the control of the parties render performance impossible by one of the contracting parties.[751] Most of the standard forms of contract include clauses dealing with force majeure covering such matters as war, strikes, fire, weather and government action, but each clause must be construed carefully to ascertain its true scope and effect.

37-224

---

[744] *Paradine v Jane* (1646) Al. 26; 82 E.R. 897, where it was held that the tenant was not released from the obligation to pay rent in circumstances where the lease had become dispossessed by Royalists during the English Civil War; *The Company of Proprietors of the Brecknock and Abergavenny Canal Navigation Co v Pritchard* (1796) 6 Term Rep. 750 (the defendant builders were not released from a liability to maintain a bridge which was washed away by flood); see also *Davis Contractors Ltd v Fareham UDC* [1956] A.C. 696, 729, HL (serious shortages of labour caused work to take 22 months rather than the anticipated 8 months).

[745] (1863) 3 B. & S. 826.

[746] *J Lauritzen AS v Wijsmuller BV (The Super Servant Two)* [1990] 1 Lloyd's Rep. 1, CA.

[747] *The Eugenia* [1964] 2 Q.B. 226, 239, CA; *Bank Line Ltd v Capel* [1919] A.C. 435, 456, HL.

[748] [1918] A.C. 119, HL, also considered by the Privy Council in *Wong Lai Yong v Chinachem* (1979) 13 B.L.R. 81.

[749] (1888) 52 J.P. 392.

[750] *Wates Ltd v Greater London Council* (1983) 25 B.L.R. 1, 35, CA.

[751] For one judicial definition of force majeure see *Lebeaupin v Crispin* [1920] 2 K.B. 714, 718.

(f) The Privity Rule and its Exceptions

37-225 **The privity rule** The general rule of the common law is that no-one but the parties to a contract can be entitled under it, or bound by it.[752] The privity rule is best seen as distinct from the rule that consideration must move from the promisee,[753] since privity is concerned with who can enforce a contract, whereas the doctrine of consideration regulates the kinds of promises which the parties can enforce.[754]

37-226 **Criticism of the privity rule** The privity rule has been the subject of trenchant criticism, both from the judiciary and from academic lawyers.[755] Some of the most important decisions on the contemporary scope of the privity rule have been cases on construction contracts, reflecting the complex array of parties affected by construction work. For example, in complex projects, the owner of the land and the party employing the builder will rarely go on to occupy the building on completion, since rights of ownership or occupation will be the subject of a lease, sale, assignment or other transfer.[756] Accordingly, it will frequently occur that the party who suffers the loss and damage caused by defects in the building will be different from the party with which the builder has a direct contractual relationship.

37-227 **Exceptions to the privity rule** The response of the courts to the problems created by the rule has been to couple the suggestion for systematic[757] reform by the legislature,[758] with a process of developing exceptions to the privity rule on a case-by-case basis. Although the precise scope of the exceptions to the privity rule is unclear, it is nevertheless apparent that in allowing exceptions the underlying rationale, at least in part, is this: what was in the contemplation of the parties at the time when the building contract was entered into? The starting-point for the development of what has now been described as a "contract-based"[759] approach to the privity rule is the proposition that consignor in a contract for the carriage of goods by sea under a bill of lading is entitled to substantial damages from the car-

---

[752] *Tweddle v Atkinson* (1861) 1 B. & S. 393 (but see the comments in *Darlington BC v Wiltshier Northern Ltd* [1995] 1 W.L.R. 68, 76G, per Steyn L.J.); *Dunlop Pneumatic Tyre Co Ltd v Selfridge & Co Ltd* [1915] A.C. 847 at 853 ("Our law knows nothing of a *jus quaesitum tertio* arising by way of contract"); *Beswick v Beswick* [1968] A.C. 58 at 72, 78, 83 and 92, HL; and see generally Law. Com. No.242 *Privity of Contract: Contracts for the Benefit of Third Parties* (1996).

[753] *Dunlop Pneumatic Tyre Co Ltd v Selfridge & Co Ltd* [1915] A.C. 847, 853.

[754] See the Contracts (Right of Third Parties) Act 1999. In *Themis Avraamides v Mark Colwill and Stephen Martin (t/a Bathroom Trading Company)* [2006] EWCA Civ 1533, [2007] B.L.R. 76, a building case concerning the installation of defective bathroom equipment, it was held that s.1(3) of the Contracts (Rights of Third Parties) Act 1999 required the third-party beneficiary to be expressly identified in order for the subsection to be relied upon.

[755] Some of the most important sources of criticism are reviewed in *Darlington BC v Wiltshier Northern* [1995] 1 W.L.R. 68, 73, and 77.

[756] In *Technotrade Ltd v Larkstore Ltd* [2006] EWCA Civ 1079, [2006] 1 W.L.R. 2926, [2006] B.L.R. 345, the Court of Appeal held that the rights and benefits under a ground investigation report prepared for the original owner of some development land could be assigned to and relied upon by a purchaser of the land in a claim for breach of contract by the purchaser against the party that produced the report in respect of damage that had occurred between the date of sale of the land and the assignment. But a claimant cannot pursue claims in relation to a contract as an assignee where the terms of the relevant contract preclude the assignment, see *Ruttle Plant Hire v Secretary of State for the Environment, Food and Rural Affairs* [2007] EWHC 2870 (TCC).

[757] See *Darlington BC v Wiltshier Northern Ltd* [1995] 1 W.L.R. 68, 76E.

[758] Contracts (Rights of Third Parties) Act 1999: see generally Ch.18.

[759] *Alfred McAlpine Construction Ltd v Panatown Ltd* [2001] 1 A.C. 518.

rier, although property in the goods had passed to a third party when the damage occurred.[760]

Decisions on privity   A number of important cases in the construction field have **37-228** raised privity issues. In *St Martin's Property Corp v Sir Robert McAlpine*[761] the contract between the employer and the contractor contained a prohibition on assignment save where the contractor gave his consent in writing. The employer subsequently assigned ownership in the site to a third party, but that assignment was ineffective to transfer to the third party the benefit of the building contract. The House of Lords held that the employer was entitled to recover damages for defects where the loss was suffered by the third party.[762] Having referred to *Dunlop v Lambert* Lord Browne-Wilkinson said:

> "In my judgment the present case falls within the rationale of the exceptions to the general rule that a plaintiff can only recover damages for his own loss. The contract was for a large development of property which, to the knowledge of both the Corporation and McAlpine, was going to be occupied, and possibly purchased, by third parties and not by the Corporation itself. Therefore it could be foreseen that damage caused by a breach would cause loss to a later owner and not merely to the original contracting party, Corporation."

In *Darlington BC v Wiltshier Northern Ltd*[763] the Council employer entered into **37-229** an arrangement to procure the construction of a recreational centre which would not be affected by restrictions on its powers of borrowing. There was a contract between the building contractor and a bank and a second contract between the bank and the Council, whereby the bank contracted to procure the construction of the centre for the Council and to assign all benefits to the Council. The Court of Appeal held that since the building contracts, to the knowledge of both parties, were entered into for the benefit of the Council, then it was foreseeable that the Council, as assignee of the bank's rights, would claim substantial damages, even though (in contrast to the *McAlpine* case) the bank never acquired or transmitted to the Council any proprietary interest in the centre.[764] In *Alfred McAlpine v Panatown*,[765] for reasons of VAT liability, the building contract was concluded between the builder (McAlpine) and a company (Panatown) within the same group as the owner of the site which wished to develop the site (Unex), although there was also a Duty of Care Deed between McAlpine and Unex. Panatown proceeded against McAlpine for damages for breach of contract. The Court of Appeal[766] held that Panatown was entitled to recover substantial damages from McAlpine, on the basis that it was "intended or contemplated" that Panatown should have such a right. However, the House of Lords allowed the appeal of *McAlpine* on the basis that the *Linden Gardens* exception to the general rule that a party could only claim substantial dam-

---

[760] *Dunlop v Lambert* (1839) 6 Cl. & F. 600 as explained in *The Albazero* [1977] A.C. 774, 847.

[761] This appeal was heard with *Linden Gardens Trust Ltd v Lenesta Sludge Disposals Ltd* [1994] 1 A.C. 85, HL.

[762] Note the broader principle on which Lord Griffiths was prepared to decide the matter (at 96–97) and with which Steyn L.J. agreed in *Darlington BC v Wiltshier Northern Ltd* [1995] 1 W.L.R. 68, 80, although not adopted in *Alfred McAlpine v Panatown* [2001] 1 A.C. 518.

[763] [1995] 1 W.L.R. 68, CA.

[764] [1995] 1 W.L.R. 68, 75.

[765] [2000] 1 A.C. 518.

[766] (1998) 88 B.L.R. 67.

ages in respect of its own loss, did not apply on the facts of this case as *Unex* and *McAlpine* had their own direct contractual relationship under the duty of care deed.

(g) Non-performance Not Amounting to Substantial Breach

37-230 Introduction Construction contracts often create obligations whose non-fulfilment does not or may not amount to breach sounding in substantial damages at the suit of the party adversely affected. This is usually because, on analysis, there is no "breach" at the time in question, the right of the injured party being transferred into some secondary obligation under the terms of the contract. Alternatively, where non-fulfilment or default occurs on the part of the engineer/architect, who is not a party to the primary contract, no direct or immediate remedy may be available against the employer.[767]

37-231 Complaint by employer Non-performance not amounting to breach occurs in the case of (i) failure to comply with quality obligations,[768] where the employer's right before completion will be limited to nominal damages, contractual rights of rectification and other rights available in the case of serious default[769]; and (ii) failure to comply with a programme issued under the terms of the contract, which will usually give rise to a secondary obligation to prepare a revised programme or to take steps to expedite progress if so instructed.[770] An obligation to achieve sectional completion will be enforceable provided it is clear that separate damages are intended to be recovered. If liquidated damages are provided for failure to achieve overall completion, the failure to achieve completion of a section within the specified time will sound in damages whether or not separate liquidated damages are provided for the section.[771] Where the employer is concerned about the quality of the works prior to their completion, then as discussed above, the employer will rarely be justified in ejecting the contractor from the site.[772] The employer will need to exercise considerable caution before preventing his contractor from returning to complete and carry out snagging to the works, since any such acts of prevention may amount to a failure to mitigate loss. In *City Axis v Daniel P Jackson*[773] it was held that the defendant employer had acted unreasonably in refusing the plaintiff access to complete certain building works, and that the failure to permit snagging constituted a failure to mitigate loss.

37-232 Complaint by the contractor Where the contractor is aggrieved by failure of the

---

[767] The alternative analysis is that the employer has a right to nominal damages for breach of contract, which, in the rare cases where substantial loss will result if the error is not immediately dealt with, becomes a right to substantial damages or other remedy. On this analysis, the contractor is protected by the fact that if the error is remediable, he will always have the right to attempt to remedy it first.

[768] See *Kay v Hosier & Dickinson* [1972] 1 W.L.R. 146 at 165D-H where such non-fulfilment is characterised as a "temporary disconformity" in a dissenting speech by Lord Diplock. Lord Diplock's dictum has, however, never been enthusiastically adopted; see: *Lintest Building v Roberts* (1980) 13 B.L.R. 38 at 44; *Nene Housing Society Ltd v National Westminster Bank Ltd* (1980) 16 B.L.R. 22 at 32; *Surrey Heath BC v Lovell Construction Ltd and Haden Young Ltd* (1988) 42 B.L.R. 25; *Guinness Plc v CMD Property Developments Ltd* (1995) 76 B.L.R. 40 at 57–58; *Pearce and High Ltd v Baxter* Pt 3 [1999] B.L.R. 101, CA.

[769] Principally termination of employment.

[770] ICC Form cl.46.

[771] *Turner v Mathind* (1992) 23 Con. L.R. 16 at 27, CA.

[772] See *Sutcliffe v Chippendale & Edmondson* (1971) 18 B.L.R. 157, 165; and the references to *Yeoman Credit Ltd v Apps* [1962] 2 Q.B. 508, CA.

[773] 64 Con. L.R. 84.

contract administrator to carry out specified duties under the contract, e.g. to certify appropriately, or to grant extensions of time, such failure will not generally be actionable against the employer[774]; nor generally, will the failure be actionable against the contract administrator.[775] Complex questions can arise where non-fulfilment of the duties of the contract administrator impede or prevent proper operation of the contract machinery vis-à-vis the contract parties. In such a situation, the courts have proceeded on the basis that the actions of the contract administrator, even if patently flawed, should continue to bind the parties until revised by arbitration or other agreed procedure.[776]

9. REMEDIES BY ENFORCEMENT

(a) Control by Contract Administrator

Introduction Commercial contracts may contain both primary obligations (e.g. description of subject matter, delivery dates, etc.) and secondary obligations[777] which take effect upon breach or non-performance of the former (e.g. an obligation to pay liquidated damages). In construction contracts such extensive use is made of secondary obligations that it may be said that the principal and often exclusive remedies for non-performance are to be found within the contract terms, through direct enforcement. The principal agency through which this is achieved (by whichever party enforcement is sought) will usually be the contract administrator. Thus, while claims for breach of contract will usually be available, they are often in practical terms limited, in the case of the employer to those arising from latent defects which are manifested after completion and, in the case of the contractor, to claims similar to or even duplicating those available under the contract terms.   **37-233**

Alternative to breach The Standard Forms of Contract empower the contract administrator to give decisions whose effect is to correct potential breaches, so as to bring the work back into conformity, where there is a departure from the requirements of the contract. Under JCT SBC 2011, for example, the architect may issue instructions for the removal from site of any work or materials not in accordance with the contract.[778] Similar powers exist under ICC Form, which also contains elaborate provisions for testing to ascertain compliance with the contract.[779] Where the work is brought back into conformity as a result of Contract Administrator instructions, there will be no further contractual consequence save that the contractor remains liable to the employer for any delay and must himself bear any expense which results from the need for the instruction in the first place. However, where the basis of the instruction is disputed, both the cost and delay consequences may form the subject of a claim by the contractor.   **37-234**

Delay by contractor Intervention by the contract administrator where the   **37-235**

---

[774] *London Borough of Merton v Leach* (1985) 32 B.L.R. 51, 78; and see *Perini v Commonwealth of Australia* (1969) 12 B.L.R. 82.

[775] *Pacific Associates v Baxter* (1988) 44 B.L.R. 33.

[776] *Lubenham Fidelities v South Pembrokeshire DC* (1988) 33 B.L.R. 39; and see *Channel Tunnel Group v Balfour Beatty* [1993] A.C. 334; (1993) 61 B.L.R. 1, HL.

[777] See *Photoproductions v Securicor Transport* [1980] A.C. 827; *Lombard North v Butterworth* [1987] Q.B. 527.

[778] JCT SBC 2011 cl.3.18.1.

[779] See cll.36, 38 and 39.

contractor's default consists of delay (as opposed to defects in quality) involves more difficult concepts, since delay will usually be measured by a programme which is not itself an express obligation of the contractor. No breach, therefore occurs until the completion date is reached, save for the possibility of establishing a failure to proceed with due expedition[780] or regularly and diligently. In *West Faulkner Associates v London Borough of Newham*[781] it was held that cl.25(1)(b) of the JCT form for use by Local Authorities (1963 edn 1977 rev.) required the contractor to proceed both regularly and diligently, and that the contractor could be dismissed from the site if he failed to do either. Some contracts empower the contract administrator to give instructions which are intended to result in more expeditious progress.[782] The exercise of such powers, however, frequently lead to disputes where the contractor claims to be entitled to extension of time. In such a case, the instruction may be contended to be an instruction to accelerate.[783]

37-236 **Operation of the contract**   Many of the powers of the contract administrator are essential to operation of the procedures of the contract. Thus, payment provisions depend on the proper operation of the procedure for interim and final certificates of payment, including detailed provisions for measurement and valuation. These powers include decisions on whether work and materials conform to the requirements of the contract, as well as decisions on "claims" made by the contractor. Where delay occurs, the contract requires decisions on whether or not extension of time is merited, where rejection will almost invariably lead, when the completion date is passed, to a claim by the employer for delay damages. The contract administrator must exercise his power to consider the grant of extensions of time as much for the benefit of the employer as for the benefit of the contractor. This is because the courts will not allow a claim for liquidated damages by an employer who has effectively prevented completion.[784]

37-237 **Powers of control generally**   Standard forms of construction contract, particularly those of a more traditional kind, tend to vest the contract administrator with wide and seemingly arbitrary powers of control which appear to place the appointed person in full charge of the works. Thus, under ICC Form, cl.13(1) provides that the contractor shall "complete the Works in strict accordance with the contract to the satisfaction of the Engineer and shall comply with and adhere strictly to the Engineer's instructions on any matter connected therewith (whether mentioned in the contract or not". Such clauses do not, however, in practice lead to the engineer taking control of the works, since by doing so the engineer would risk incurring liability on behalf of the employer for any variation to the works that might be ordered.[785] The standard forms generally provide other means of claiming compensation in addition, where the contractor's ability to carry out the works as he may choose is interfered with.[786] Engineers and architects will therefore generally be reluctant to exercise powers vested in them, save where this is clearly neces-

---

[780] See ICC Form cl.41(2).

[781] (1994) 71 B.L.R. 1, CA.

[782] See, e.g. ICC Form cl.46.

[783] In the absence of direct English authority, see *Norair Engineering v US* (1981) 666 F. 546; and *Morrison Knudsen v BC Hydro* (1978) 85 D.L.R. 3d 186; (1978) 7 Const. L.J. 227.

[784] *Percy Bilton Ltd v GLC* [1982] 1 W.L.R. 794; (1982) 20 B.L.R. 1, HL.

[785] The term "variation" tends to be given a wide definition under most standard construction contracts: see, e.g. ICC Form cl.51, JCT 98 cl.13 and JCT SBC 2005 cl.5.1.

[786] See ICC Form cl.13(3), JCT 98 cl.26 and JCT SBC 2005 cll.4.23 to 4.26.

sary or (in the case of a variation) authorised by the client, who must bear the financial consequence. Other powers typically available to the contract administrator, and which will in practice be utilised with caution, include powers to suspend or postpone work[787] and to terminate the contractor's employment under the contract (see below).

(b) Claims

Claims by contractor The term "claim" is often applied to any application **37-238** involving payment beyond the stated contract sum (in the case of a lump sum contract) or beyond the sum of the remeasured quantities applied to the contract rates (in the case of a remeasurement contract). Claims typically include payment for disputed extras and payment under the provisions of the contract which allow for additional recovery in specified circumstances. A claim brought pursuant to the terms of a contract is for enforcement of its terms, subject to proof of the facts asserted where these are disputed, and so is a claim under the contract, rather than being a claim for breach. In addition, the term "claim" is often applied to a claim for damages for breach.[788] Such claims often overlap with or form an alternative to a contractual claim, the facts relied on and the financial consequences asserted being common. Where this is so, consideration needs to be given to whether the effect of the contract is to render the contractual claim an exclusive remedy. Generally, the reverse is the case The effect of bringing an alternative claim for breach may be to avoid the effect of a notice provision which would bar the claim under the contract terms.

Claims by employer—delay Claims under the terms of the contract brought by **37-239** the employer are usually limited to claims for delay damages, which are frequently expressed as liquidated (i.e. predetermined) damages involving no requirement of proof. Whether a delay claim is for liquidated or actual damages, it is rarely necessary for the employer to launch proceedings since, under most systems of procurement, the employer is the debtor and may simply set-off the sum claimed. The claim will then require proof as a counterclaim to any proceedings for non-payment which may be brought by the contractor.[789]

Claims by employer—quality Claims by the employer relating to the quality of **37-240** the work arising during the period of performance are generally intended to be settled by the contract administrator by decisions given under express powers, i.e. to reject non-conforming work. The work should, therefore, comply fully with the contract at the date of the completion certificate.[790] Latent defects appearing during the "defects liability period"[791] or "rectification period"[792] amount to a breach of contract, which the contractor, by virtue of these provisions, is entitled to be

---

[787] ICC Form cl.40, JCT 2011 cl.3.15.

[788] For an analysis of the problems of quantifying claims for time and money, see: *Ascon Contracting Ltd v Alfred McAlpine Construction (Isle of Man) Ltd* (1999) 66 Con. L.R. 119.

[789] For contracts subject to the Housing Grants, Construction and Regeneration Act 1996 a counterclaim also requires appropriate notice, pursuant to s.111 of intention to pay less than the sum otherwise due to the contractor.

[790] With the exception of particular powers whereby the Contract Administrator may accept completion subject to minor or outstanding work see, e.g. ICC Form cll.48, 49.

[791] See JCT 98 cl.17.

[792] See JCT SBC 2005 cll.2.34 and 2.39.

given the opportunity to correct.[793] Where the contractor fails to carry out such correction or there is a dispute, the employer remains the debtor through the retention fund, to which recourse may be had to satisfy any loss. It is therefore similarly unlikely that the employer will need to bring proceedings. With the possible exception of a claim for termination or repudiation, claims by the employer (other than claims by set-off) are in practice limited to those arising from latent defects in the work. Such claims are not usually subject to any action by the contract administrator, who will be functus officio. Such a claim will be for breach of contract[794] and will be subject to the effect of any final certificate as well as limitation.

37-241 **Particular provisions for claims**   Each form of contract has its own characteristic types of claim, based on risks typically encountered by a particular industry. Thus, in civil engineering work, unexpected sub-surface conditions are a frequent cause of difficulty. The ICE Conditions and subsequently the ICC Form has, from its inception, made provision for dividing this risk between the parties such that the contractor undertakes the risk of ground conditions which could reasonably be foreseen by an experienced contractor and the employer takes the risk where such conditions could not reasonably be so foreseen.[795] Where such a claim is established the conditions of contract entitle the contractor to be paid for the additional cost incurred, including delay. Building contracts are typically silent as regards ground conditions which will therefore be at the contractor's risk unless conditions exist which should have been measured in accordance with the relevant standard method of measurement[796] or unless the circumstances can be brought within any other provision of the contract. Adverse ground conditions are typical of claims in which the risk may be placed upon the employer (as under the ICC Form), but where the contract is silent, the risk will fall upon the contractor (as under the JCT Form). Another example is cost inflation (fluctuations) where the risk will fall upon the contractor unless transferred to the employer by the terms of the contract.

37-242 **Claims for loss and expense**   The JCT Form of Contract contains a well-known claim provision entitling the contractor to payment of "direct loss and/or expense" arising from a variety of matters including late provision of instructions, failure to give access and architect's instructions requiring a variation.[797] Such a claim is conditional upon timely notice[798] and upon the loss or expense being such that it would "not be reimbursed by payment under any other provision in this contract". In the case of a variation, therefore, the contractor is entitled to recover payment for the work itself pursuant to the valuation provisions included in the contract,

---

[793]   See *Kaye v Hosier & Dickinson* [1972] 1 W.L.R. 146, HL.

[794]   In *McGlinn v Waltham Contractors Ltd* [2007] EWHC 149 (TCC), [2007] 111 Con. L.R. 1 it was held that a claimant who had demolished and rebuilt his property due to building defects was only entitled to damages based upon the cost of repairing the defects, rather than the higher cost of demolishing and rebuilding the property, because the defects complained of were aesthetic rather than structural and he had not acted reasonably in demolishing the building.

[795]   ICC Form cl.12.

[796]   Such as rock or running sand.

[797]   JCT SBC 2016 cll.4.20 and 4.21.

[798]   See *WW Gear Construction Ltd v McGee Group Ltd* [2010] EWHC 1460 (TCC), 131 Con. L.R. 63, where the JCT Standard Trade Contract (TC/C) Conditions 2002 (as amended) were construed to make a timely request in writing a pre-condition for an entitlement to recover loss and expense under the contract, and where it was indicated that in deciding whether a clause was or was not a condition precedent to recovery, the ordinary rules of contractual construction should apply (at [11]–[13]).

together with any additional loss and/or expense incurred.[799] Normally a contractor will be unable to recover loss and expense in relation to delay where it would have suffered the exact same loss and expense anyway, even absent the relevant matters alleged to be the employer's responsibility, as a result of causes within the contractor's control or for which it is contractually responsible.[800] The ICC Form contains no similar provision, but allow a claim based on variations where it is established that the effect is to render "any rate or price contained in the contract ... unreasonable or inapplicable".[801] The engineer is then empowered to increase the rate in question so as to compensate the contractor. Claims for late instructions or failure to give access are dealt with under other specific clauses. In contrast to the last paragraph, claims for loss and/or expense or rate adjustment are matters which may, absent provisions under the contract, still be regarded as employer's risks since they arise from interference through the issuing of variations. Such claims may otherwise be expressed, in the alternative, as claims for breach.

Extensions of time and claims   Where a ground of claim also gives rise to an   **37-243** extension of time, part of the quantification of the claim will be the time-dependent element of the loss or additional cost. Not all grounds of claim give rise to delay, nor do all entitlements to extension of time carry a right to payment. For example, exceptionally adverse weather is usually recognised (but subject to the precise wording of the contract) as qualifying for an extension but any additional cost is at the contractor's risk. Under the JCT 2016, cl.2.29 lists those relevant events which entitle the contractor to an extension of time[802] and cl.4.24 lists those relevant matters which entitle the contractor to recover loss and expense including time related costs. A comparison of those two clauses reveals those issues which entitle the contractor to additional time but not additional money. Under the ICC Form grounds of claim carrying an entitlement to reimbursement are contained within individual clauses.[803] Extensions of time are dealt with by a general clause as well as in a number of individual clauses.[804]

(c)   Termination of Employment

Meaning   This refers to termination of the employment of the contractor under the   **37-244** contract, as opposed to bringing the contract itself to an end. Other terms, including "forfeiture", appear in different forms of the contract but the effect is the same.

---

[799] Loss and/or expense has been equated to common law damages: *Wraight v PT & H (Holdings)* (1968) 13 B.L.R. 26.

[800] See *De Beers v Atos Origin IT Services* [2011] B.L.R. 274, per Edwards-Stuart J. at [177]–[178]. The distinction between the test of causation that applies to extension of time and loss and expense provisions using the JCT wording was confirmed in *Walter Lilly & Co Ltd v DMW Developments Ltd* [2012] EWHC 1773 (TCC), [2012] B.L.R. 503, per Akenhead J. at [362]–[370] and [540]–[543].

[801] ICC Form cl.52(4).

[802] Relevant Events are discussed in *Henry Boot Construction (UK) Ltd v Malmaison Hotel (Manchester) Ltd* (1999) 70 Con. L.R. 32. A contractor may be entitled to an extension of time not only if the matter relied upon is the dominant cause of delay, but also if it has only "equal causative potency", see *Henry Boot Construction v Malmaison*; *Steria Ltd v Sigma Wireless Comm Ltd* [2008] B.L.R. 79 and *Keating on Construction*, 10th edn (2016) at para.8-025 to 8-028.

[803] For example, cl.7: late instructions; cl.12: adverse ground conditions; cl.13: engineer's instructions.

[804] See cll.7, 12, 13 above and cl.44. For a consideration of the different approach to causation in the context of a claim for damages compared to an extension of time claim, see *Costain Ltd v Charles Haswell & Partners Ltd* [2009] EWHC 3140 (TCC), 128 Con. L.R. 154.

Both parties remain bound by terms of the contract which are to apply upon termination coming into effect. These will include provisions for the drawing up of accounts, including those relating to completion of the work by others. The consequences of termination for default are broadly equivalent to the effect of acceptance of a repudiatory breach of contract as terminating the contract. In the case of termination of the contractor's employment pursuant to the terms of the contract, however, the contract makes express provision for the consequences. Termination is brought about by service of appropriate notices, whose effect may be subject to subsequent proof of the matters asserted.

37-245 **Termination by employer** A provision entitling the employer to terminate on the ground of various defaults is found in practically every form of construction contract. The grounds upon which such termination is available, however, differ. Generally, termination of the contractor's employment will be at the employer's option and will not occur until the service of a notice to that effect. It is not uncommon for contract to require a notice of default to be served prior to the termination, giving the contractor a chance to remedy any breach. For example, under cl.8.4 of the JCT 2011 contract, the employer must give 14 days' notice of various defaults such as a failure to proceed regularly and diligently with the works before he is entitled to terminate. By contrast, in the event of contractor insolvency under cl.8.5, the right to terminate arises immediately and even before it is exercised certain interim measures take automatic effect.

37-246 **Termination by contractor** Some, but not all, forms of contract provide for termination by the contractor. The JCT Form allows termination by the contractor on various grounds, notably non-payment on a certificate after notice, and suspension of the works.[805] The *ICE Form* introduced, in the 7th edition, a right of termination available to the contractor following events equivalent to insolvency of the employer, or where the employer attempts to assign without prior consent, and this continues in the ICC Form.[806] Where the grounds of termination under the contract are equivalent to repudiation, termination may be effected both under the contract and, in the alternative, in common law. It is possible that the two remedies may be seen as involving mutual inconsistency. There is authority, however, to the effect that both remedies may be exercised in the alternative.[807] The remedy provided, following a valid termination for default,[808] whether by employer or contractor, is usually equivalent to common law damages following termination at law, but with added contractual remedies. Thus, there is usually a provision that upon termination by the employer the contractor must assign the benefit of sub-contracts.[809] Under the 6th edition of the ICE Conditions, property in plant and materials was deemed to vest in the employer when on the site and could subsequently be used

---

[805] See JCT SBC 2011 cl.8.9.
[806] This latter provision is surprising given that any such purported assignment will be of no effect: *Linden Gardens Trust Ltd v Lenesta Sludge Disposals Ltd* [1994] 1 A.C. 85; *Hendry v Chartsearch* [1998] EWCA Civ 1276.
[807] *Supamarl v Federated Homes* [1981] 9 Con. L.R. 25; *Architectural Installation Services v James Gibbon* (1989) 46 B.L.R. 91; but see also *Lockland Builders v John Kim Rickwood* (1995) 77 B.L.R. 38, CA and para.37-218, above.
[808] See *Laing Management Ltd v Aegon Insurance Company (UK) Ltd* (1997) 55 Con. L.R. 1 where it was decided that the exercise of a contractual right to terminate was not to be treated as acceptance of a repudiatory breach so as to discharge both parties from future performance.
[809] See, e.g. JCT 98 cl.27.4 and JCT SBC 2011 cl.8.7.2.3.

by the employer after any termination.[810] These provisions were removed from the 7th edition and do not appear in the ICC Form.

Termination of employment and fundamental breach compared It is 37-247 important to note that in the case of termination by either the employer or the contractor, the grounds provided under the contract may fall far short of what could be regarded as fundamental breach, leading to a right to terminate the contract in law.

Termination at will Many forms of contract provide for termination, solely by 37-248 the employer, without ground of default, providing a remedy broadly equivalent to that generally available under civil law in respect of an administrative contract.[811] Such provisions exist in Form GC Works/1, formerly issued for use by UK government departments. In such cases, the contractor will usually be entitled to full compensation, including loss of profit. The JCT Form of Contract provides for termination without fault where the works are suspended for specified reasons, including force majeure.[812] Such termination may be effected by either party.

Disputed termination To be effective, the act of termination by one party must 37-249 be followed by withdrawal from the site. In the case of termination by the employer it is possible that the contractor may seek to resist physical removal from the site pending final resolution of the question whether the employer was entitled to take such action. In *Hounslow v Twickenham Gardens*[813] the contractor refused to leave the site after service of notice of termination under a JCT Form of Contract. The employer sought an injunction which was refused by Megarry J. on the ground that the employer was under an implied obligation not to revoke the contractor's licence to occupy the site except in accordance with the contract. It was held that the employer had not, for the purpose of the injunction proceedings, conclusively established the validity of its termination notices. It was stated:

"I fully accept the importance to the Borough on social grounds as well as others of securing the due completion of the contract, and the unsatisfactory nature of damages as an alternative. But the contract was made, and the Contractors are not to be stripped of their rights under it, however desirable that may be for the Borough. A contract remains a contract even if (or perhaps especially if) it turns out badly."

This decision has been much criticised and has not been followed in a number of cases including *Chermar v Pretest*[814] and *Tara Civil Engineering v Moorfield Developments*.[815] In the latter case, where a contractor disputed notice of termination served under the ICE Conditions, the Court rejected the contractor's claim to be entitled to remain on the site in the interim, holding that the issues raised by the parties were to be decided by arbitration. Pending ultimate resolution, the balance of convenience was strongly in favour of the court supporting the engineer's

---

[810] ICE 6th edn cll.53, 63(2).
[811] See further N. Brown and J.S. Bell, *French Administrative Law*, 5th edn (1998).
[812] See JCT SBC 2011 cl.8.11.
[813] [1971] Ch. 233.
[814] 8 Const. L.J. 44.
[815] (1989) 46 B.L.R. 72.

decision.[816] It would appear unlikely that the courts will now support a challenge to an apparently bona fide exercise of a contractual right of termination by granting an injunction.

37-250 **Mutual termination** In some cases both parties have sought, virtually simultaneously, to exercise rights of termination. This was the case in *Att-Gen of Hong Kong v Ko Hon Mau*,[817] where the contractor gave notice of termination under the HK Public Works Highways Maintenance Conditions. Ten days later, the Government gave cross-notice of termination and physically re-entered the site taking possession of the contractor's plant. The contractor sought to enforce his right to take possession of the plant, which was resisted by the Government. The Hong Kong Court of Appeal upheld the contractor's right on the basis that his notice was first in time, both notices being accepted as bona fide. The court observed that both notices were provisional in the sense that they would only take final effect at the conclusion of the arbitration proceedings.

(d) Final Certificates

37-251 **Binding effect** The issue of the final certificate (for which provision is made in most standard forms of contract) will occur in the final stages of the work of the contract administrator. This may have a profound effect on the ability of either party subsequently to enforce the terms of the contract. In JCT 2011, cl.1.10 provides for the issue of a Final Certificate, which may be disputed within 28 days after issue, but will become binding both as to matters of quality and payment to the extent that it is not specifically challenged. The significance and effect of the issue of a final certificate which is not challenged within the specified period, will be a matter of construction.[818] In *Crown Estates Commissioners v John Mowlem*[819] the Court of Appeal held that the final certificate issued under JCT 80 was conclusive in respect of all works under the contract, since on a true construction of cl.30.9.1.1 all matters of standards and quality of work and materials were for the reasonable opinion of the architect and so were concluded (in the absence of arbitration) by the issue of a final certificate. A similar decision had previously been reached in relation to the IFC 84 Form in *Colbart v Kumar*.[820] The consequence of these decisions is that, under these forms of contract, no evidence may be called to contradict or qualify the architect's decision as expressed in the final certificate, so that it is effectively binding on the parties on all relevant questions of fact. However, although the final certificate operates as an evidential bar, it does not constitute a cessation of liability for the purposes, for example, of the Civil Liability (Contribution) Act 1978.[821]

37-252 **Decisions criticised** The decision in *Crown Estates* was the subject of trenchant criticism[822] and it is also to be observed that the JCT changed the wording of the clause to overcome the perceived difficulties created by *Crown Estates*. The cur-

---

[816] Following *American Cyanamid v Ethicon* [1975] A.C. 396.
[817] (1988) 44 B.L.R. 144.
[818] See generally as to the effect of final certificates *Kaye v Hosier and Dickinson* [1972] 1 W.L.R. 146, HL; and *East Ham Corp v Bernard Sunley & Sons Ltd* [1966] A.C. 406, HL.
[819] (1994) 70 B.L.R. 1, CA.
[820] (1992) 59 B.L.R. 89.
[821] *Oxford University Fixed Assets Ltd v Architects Design Partnership* (1999) 64 Con. L.R. 12.
[822] Duncan Wallace (1995) 11 Const. L.J. 184.

rent version of the clause gives the final certificate conclusive effect in respect of the quality of work or materials only if the contract documents make it clear that the parties have agreed to abide by the decision of the architect in issuing the final certificate for the relevant parts or requirements of the works. However, decisions on final certificates in other standard forms indicate that a broad construction of the relevant contract terms is still preferred. In *Matthew Hall Ordtech v Tarmac Roadstone*[823] it was held that on a true construction of cl.38.5 of the *Institution of Chemical Engineers Model Form of Conditions of Contract for Process Plants* (1981 rev.) the final certificate is conclusive evidence that all work has been completed in accordance with the requirements of the contract. However, it is to be observed that the Scottish Court of Session has given a more restrictive view to the effect of a Final Certificate issued under JCT 63 (July 1977 revision) Form of Contract.[824]

10. DISPUTES

(a) Nature of Disputes

Disputes under construction contracts In contrast to a contract for sale of goods, where disputes may relate to the quality of the goods as delivered or to the date of delivery, disputes under construction contracts can arise from every aspect of the production of the works required by the contract, including the speed of production. Moreover, as regards quality, as a consequence of the proper application of the contract terms, the works as finally delivered may be expected to accord to the requirements of the contract and to give rise to subsequent disputes only in respect of latent defects. Disputes concerning pre-delivery performance of the work are likely to involve, in addition to the original contract requirements, consideration of instructions, variations and approvals, both in terms of their timing and overall effect. Where delay occurs, there may be detailed disputes as to the causes, including scrutiny of programmes and progress reports. In all such cases, decisions may have been made by the contract administrator which may (with limited exceptions) subsequently be challenged by way of adjudication, arbitration or litigation. Disputes may thus encompass all aspects of quality, timing and payment. The question of whether a "dispute" or "difference" has in fact arisen may be important in the context of dispute resolution procedures, particularly in the case of adjudication or arbitration, where a dispute or difference must have arisen before those procedures are operated, in order to vest the adjudicator or arbitrator with jurisdiction. The most authoritative discussion of this topic, in the context of arbitration but equally applicable to adjudication, is in *Amec Civil Engineering Ltd v Secretary of State for Transport*,[825] and in *Collins (Contractors) Ltd v Baltic Quay Management (1994) Ltd*,[826] where Clarke L.J. accepted as "broadly correct" the test set out in the form of the seven propositions by Jackson J. in the first instance decision in *Amec*.

37-253

---

[823] (1997) 87 B.L.R. 96.
[824] *Belcher Food Products Ltd v Miller & Black*, 1999 S.L.T. 142 (opinion of Lord Gill).
[825] [2005] EWCA Civ 291, [2005] 1 W.L.R. 2339.
[826] [2004] EWCA Civ 1757, [2005] B.L.R. 63.

(b)   Conditions Precedent

37-254   **Multi-stage disputes**   While disputes are a widespread feature of construction contracts, their incidence is usually controlled by the terms of the contract. Generally, more elaborate contracts will provide for a series of stages through which a dispute may or must proceed before arbitration or litigation become available to the parties. Where a particular stage, on the true construction of the contract, is mandatory, it will operate as a condition precedent to the right to pursue the claim to the next stage.[827] Subject to any question of waiver, the failure to comply with such a condition precedent may afford the other party a defence to the claim.[828] Such conditions precedent may arise through necessary implication from the express requirements of the contract. An example is the requirement for a claim or contention to be referred to the engineer under earlier versions of the ICE Conditions of Contract.[829] The 1998 edition of FIDIC similarly requires disputes which have not been settled through reference to the engineer to be referred to a Dispute Adjudication Board. The effect of these provisions (subject to the effect of the Housing Grants, Construction and Regeneration Act 1996 where applicable) is that the matter in question must have been so referred, and other provisions of the contract (such as the service of timely notice) also complied with, as a condition precedent to an arbitrator subsequently appointed having jurisdiction. Complex issues of fact and construction can arise under such clauses, for example where the engineer has failed to give a clear response under the contract.[830] Care must also be exercised in complying with the requirements for the commencement of arbitration proceedings within agreed time periods since the courts will make use of the power under s.12 of the Arbitration Act 1996 (to extend time for reference to arbitration) sparingly, and not to overcome the carelessness or ignorance of one of the parties.[831]

37-255   **Enforcement of conditions precedent**   The modern attitude of the courts to such provisions was expressed by Lord Mustill in *Channel Tunnel Group v Balfour Beatty Construction*[832] as follows:

> "Having made this choice I believe that it is in accordance not only with the presumption exemplified in the English cases cited above that those who make arrangements for the resolution of disputes must show good reasons for departing from them, but also with the interests of the orderly regulation of international commerce, that having promised to take their complaints to the experts and if necessary to the arbitrators, that is where the

---

[827]   See *Channel Tunnel Group v Balfour Beatty* [1993] A.C. 334, per Lord Mustill at 353.

[828]   A party who concurs in arbitration proceedings without raising any alleged condition precedent may found a waiver or estoppel or even give rise to an ad hoc submission: see *Jones v Balfour Beatty* (1992) 42 Con. L.R. 1; and see also Arbitration Act 1996 s.73 as to the timely raising of questions of jurisdiction.

[829]   cl.66, as to which see *Monmouthshire CC v Costelloe & Kemple* [1965] 5 B.L.R. 83 at 91; *Anglian Water v RDL Contracting* (1988) 43 B.L.R. 98; *Wigan Metropolitan BC v Sharkey Bros* (1988) 43 B.L.R. 115; *ECC Quarries v Merriman* (1988) 45 B.L.R. 90; *Mid Glamorgan CC v The Land Authority for Wales* (1990) 49 B.L.R. 61; *Havant BC v South Coast Shipping Company* (1998) 14 Const. L.J. 420; *Edmund Nuttall v RG Carter* [2002] B.L.R. 312. The ICE Conditions were substantially amended in the light of the Housing Grants, Construction and Regeneration Act and the ICC Form now contains no requirement for an engineer's decision.

[830]   See I.N.D. Wallace Q.C., *Construction Contracts: Principles and Policies in Tort and Contract*, Ch.18—The Timebar in FIDIC cl.67.

[831]   *Harbour and General Works v Environmental Agency* [1999] 1 All E.R. (Comm) 953, [1999] B.L.R. 143.

[832]   [1993] A.C. 334.

appellants should go. The fact that the appellants now find their chosen method too slow to suit their purpose, is to my way of thinking quite beside the point."

The case concerned the enforcement by the court, pursuant to its inherent jurisdiction, of a dispute resolution procedure involving reference to a panel of experts, to be followed by arbitration, where one party had sought an injunction from the court in respect of an issue which was to be so referred. Where litigation has been commenced without the parties having fully complied with mandatory steps in the dispute resolution procedure, the Courts will ordinarily enforce the agreed procedure by granting a stay of the proceedings until such time as the preceding steps in the procedure have been complied with, although there is a residual discretion not to grant a stay.[833]

(c) Arbitration

Alternative fora Most standard form construction contracts,[834] and particularly **37-256** those in use internationally, provide for arbitration as the final means of resolution of disputes between the parties to the contract.[835] In the case of an arbitration agreement contained in a domestic construction contract (being one in which both parties and the seat of the arbitration are located in England and Wales), arbitration and litigation effectively provide alternative fora for the resolution of disputes. Either party is, however, entitled to enforce an arbitration agreement[836] irrespective of the wish of the other party to bring concurrent court proceedings against other parties which may not be available in arbitration,[837] or of any other considerations which might render litigation more appropriate. The discretion formerly available to the court is no longer available under the Arbitration Act 1996.[838]

Jurisdiction of court In *Northern RHA v Derek Crouch Construction*[839] the Court **37-257** of Appeal held that, where an arbitration clause empowered the arbitrator to "open up review and revise" a certificate of the architect, the court did not possess such a

---

[833] See *DGT Steel and Cladding Ltd v Cubitt Building and Interiors Ltd* [2007] EWHC 1584 (TCC) at paras 5–13 and cases cited therein.

[834] It should be noted that the default position in respect of dispute resolution under the JCT 2005 suite of contracts is now litigation, not arbitration. This represents a change from previous editions of the JCT Standard Form suite of contracts, although the parties are of course free to make arbitration the final means of dispute resolution by way of an appropriate amendment or by ad hoc agreement to refer.

[835] Arbitration clauses are to be construed in the same way as any other contractual clause. However, whilst arbitration clauses, like any other clause, can be unenforceable for ambiguity, the court will generally lean heavily towards a construction of the words used by the parties which gives a sensible and effective interpretation to the arbitration clause. See *Star Shipping AS v China National Foreign Trade Transportation Corp (The Star Texas)* [1993] 2 Lloyd's Rep. 445, CA; *Lobb Partnership Ltd v Aintree Racecourse Co Ltd* [2000] B.L.R. 65.

[836] See Arbitration Act 1996 s.9.

[837] See *Taunton Collins v Cromie* [1964] 1 W.L.R. 633, a case under the Arbitration Act 1950, which gave the court discretion to refuse a stay where litigation was considered more appropriate.

[838] The statutory provisions which created a discretion were s.4(1) of the Arbitration Act 1950 and s.86 of the Arbitration Act 1996 (not brought into effect). For decisions on the mandatory stay provided by s.9(4) of the Arbitration Act 1996, see: *Halki Shipping v Sopex Oils* [1998] 1 W.L.R. 726, CA; *Birse Construction Ltd v St David Ltd* [2000] B.L.R. 57, CA; *Ahmad Al-Naimi (trading as Buildmaster Construction Services) v Islamic Press Agency Inc* [2000] B.L.R. 150, CA. The requirements for a "step" within the meaning of s.9(3) of the Arbitration Act 1996 were considered in *Bhailbhai Patel v Dilesh R Patel* [2000] Q.B. 551, [1999] B.L.R. 227, CA.

[839] [1984] Q.B. 644.

power but was limited to enforcing the terms of the contract. The effect was that any dispute which involved challenging decisions given by an architect, engineer or other contract administrator had to be brought by arbitration. This was followed in a number of subsequent cases.[840] The decision has, however, now been conclusively reversed by the House of Lords in *Beaufort Developments v Gilbert-Ash*,[841] with the effect that words expressly empowering an arbitrator to grant particular remedies will not be construed as limiting those remedies to arbitration proceedings. While the contract may provide for certificates to bind the court:

"... in all other respects, where a party comes to the court in the search for an ordinary remedy under the contract or for a remedy in respect of an alleged breach of it, the court is entitled to examine the facts and to form its own opinion upon them in the light of the evidence. The fact that the Architect has formed an opinion on the matter will be part of the evidence. But, as it will not be conclusive evidence, the Court can disregard his opinion if it does not agree with it."[842]

(d) Litigation

37-258 Technology and Construction Court In cases where the parties do not enter into, or do not seek to enforce, an arbitration agreement, either party is free to litigate any issue arising under a construction contract, subject to the effect of any certificate[843] or decision rendered binding under the terms of the contract.[844] The existence of an arbitration clause, if not enforced, is immaterial.[845] Proceedings may be brought in the Technology and Construction Court (TCC) list of the Business and Property Courts, where cases are heard by specialist judges experienced in construction matters.

37-259 Particular features of the TCC For the purposes of Pt 49 of the Civil Procedure Rules, the TCC is considered as specialist proceedings. Every claim allocated to the TCC will be allocated to the multi-track and the rules relating to track allocation will not apply.[846] "TCC business" includes any claim which involves issues or questions which are technically complex or for which trial by a judge of the TCC is for any other reason desirable. TCC business may be dealt with either in the High Court or in the county court. Under their former name as Official Referees' Courts, original procedures were introduced, many of which have been adopted generally

---

840 Including the decisions of the Court of Appeal in: *Rapid Building v Ealing Family Housing Association* (1984) 29 B.L.R. 5; *Turner & Goudy v McConnell* [1985] 1 W.L.R. 898; *CM Pillings v Kent Instruments* (1985) 30 B.L.R. 80; *Youll v Arthur White (Contractors) Ltd* Unreported March 5, 1987; *Benstrete Construction v Hill* (1987) 38 B.L.R. 115; *Ashville Investments v Elmer Contractors* [1989] Q.B. 488; *North West Reg Thames RHA v Shephard Robson* (1995) 50 Con. L.R. 79; *Balfour Beatty Civil Engineering v Docklands Light Railway* (1996) 78 B.L.R. 42.
841 [1999] 1 A.C. 266.
842 per Lord Hope at 291–292.
843 The question of final certificates was further considered in *London Borough of Barking & Dagenham v Terrapin Construction Ltd* [2000] B.L.R. 479, CA (in the context of JCT 1981 with Contractor's Design); and in *Tameside MBC v Barlow Securities Group Services Ltd* [2001] B.L.R. 113, CA.
844 See above.
845 See *Beaufort Development v Gilbert-Ash* [1998] 2 W.L.R. 860.
846 TCC Practice Direction (March 11, 1999). For changes, consult the website of the Lord Chancellor's Department. See also Pt 60 of the CPR (which came into force on March 25, 2002), the Supplementary Practice Direction and the *TCC Guide* (2nd edn) with effect from October 3, 2007.

throughout the courts. These include the exchange of expert evidence,[847] exchange of witness statements[848] and meetings between experts without prejudice.[849] Procedures not commonly adopted in other divisions include preparation of pleadings and particulars in the form of schedules. A schedule which sets out, in columns, the items in dispute with a note of the contention of each party and the sums contended for is popularly known as a "Scott Schedule".[850]

Presentation of claims   The nature and often complicated factual basis for many   **37-260** claims made in construction litigation will mean that special difficulties arise in the way they are presented and pleaded in court. Where an alleged loss may be attributed to a series of possible competing technical causes, there is a question as to the degree of particulars and detailed analysis of nexus which must be set out in the written presentation of the case. In a "global claim" or "total cost claim"[851] the claimant will identify alleged breaches, events alleged to permit recovery and alleged loss suffered, but the loss will be given as a global sum without specific linkages to particular alleged causative events. The practical difficulties and necessary limitation in pleading an accurate apportionment of loss between competing causes was accepted in *Crosby v Portland UDC*[852]; but in other cases, a far more demanding approach to the requirements of pleading has been adopted.[853] The modern approach is to permit global claims to be brought and to proceed to trial but to recognise that a party seeking to prove a claim on a global or total costs basis carries a greater burden than a party seeking to prove the same claim on a particularised or itemised basis.[854]

Alternative dispute resolution (ADR)   Where a commercial agreement between   **37-261** parties requires ADR to be undertaken, the strong tendency of the courts, especially in the specialist divisions, is to refuse to permit a party to pursue proceedings without having first instituted ADR proceedings.[855] There is a separate jurisdiction to stay proceedings in accordance with the principles set out in the CPR, and in *Shirayama Shokusan Company Ltd v Danovo Ltd*[856] Blackburne J. concluded that the court had jurisdiction to order the parties to mediate even where one party was opposed to any mediation, and although the prospects for success of such a process

---

847 Originally RSC Ord.38 rr.35–37, now CPR r.35.5.
848 Originally RSC Ord.38 r.2A, now CPR r.32.4.
849 Originally RSC Ord.38 r.38, now CPR r.35.12.
850 After a former Official Referee, George Alexander Scott (1920–1933). See now *Civil Procedure 2008* (*The White Book*), para.2C-71.
851 See *Mid-Glamorgan CC v J Devonald Williams* (1991) 29 Con. L.R. 129. See the review of the decided cases on "global" claims by Lord Macfayden in *John Doyle Construction Ltd v Laing Management (Scotland) Ltd* [2002] B.L.R. 393 Court of Session. Subsequent to the opinion of the Lord Ordinary, see the opinions of Lords MacLean, Johnston and Drummond Young in the Extra Division of the Inner House of the Court of Session (following a reclaiming motion by the management contractor) in *Laing Management (Scotland) Ltd v John Doyle Construction Ltd* [2004] B.L.R. 295.
852 (1967) 5 B.L.R. 121.
853 *Wharf Properties Ltd v Eric Cumine Associates (No.2)* (1991) 52 B.L.R. 1, PC.
854 *Walter Lilly & Co Ltd v Mackay* [2012] EWHC 1773 (TCC) per Akenhead J. at [486]; *John Sisk & Son Ltd v Carmel Building Services Ltd* [2016] EWHC 806 (TCC) per Carr J. at [55]–[56].
855 *Cable & Wireless Plc v IBM UK Ltd* [2002] EWHC 2059 (Comm), [2003] B.L.R. 89.
856 [2003] EWHC 3306 (Ch), [2004] B.L.R. 207.

was limited. A refusal by one party to mediate will often, though not necessarily, have adverse costs consequences, but each case will depend on its own facts.[857]

(e) Adjudication

37-262 **Adjudication by statute** The Housing Grants, Construction and Regeneration Act 1996 imposes a requirement that all construction contracts covered by the Act include adjudication as a form of dispute resolution. The Act applies to all construction contracts in England and Wales save for certain excluded operations[858] and contracts with residential occupiers.[859]

37-263 **Statutory requirements** The 1996 Act lays down a series of requirements for an adjudication procedure in any construction contract as defined. Section 108 requires that the contract shall:

(a) enable a party to give notice at any time of his intentions to refer a dispute to adjudication;

(b) provide a timetable with the object of securing the appointment of the adjudicator and referral of the dispute to him within seven days of such notice;

(c) require the adjudicator to reach a decision within 28 days of referral or such longer period as is agreed by the parties after the dispute has been referred;

(d) allow the adjudicator to extend the period of 28 days by up to 14 days, with the consent of the party by whom the dispute was referred;

(e) impose a duty on the adjudicator to act impartially; and

(f) enable the adjudicator to take the initiative in ascertaining the facts and the law.

Section 108 of the Housing Grants, Construction and Regeneration Act 1996 further provides that a party to a construction contract has the right to refer a dispute for adjudication, that the contract is to provide that the decision of the adjudicator is binding until finally determined by arbitration or other means, and that the contract provides for immunity of the adjudicator.

37-264 **The statutory scheme** If the contract does not comply with the requirements of s.108 of the Housing Grants, Construction and Regeneration Act, the Scheme for Construction Contracts[860] ("the Scheme") applies.[861] The Scheme sets out, inter alia, the powers and responsibilities of the adjudicator together with a strict timetable for the conduct of the adjudication proceedings. However, the Housing Grants, Construction and Regeneration Act 1996 makes no provision for the enforcement of an adjudicator's award. Accordingly, one of the early questions raised by the Housing Grants, Construction and Regeneration Act 1996 was the attitude which the court would take to enforcement.

---

[857] *The Wethered Estate Ltd v Michael Davis* [2006] B.L.R. 86, Ch D.

[858] 1996 Act s.105(2).

[859] 1996 Act s.106.

[860] The Scheme for Construction Contracts (England and Wales) Regulations 1998 (SI 1998/649).

[861] The Scheme applied in *Macob Civil Engineering Ltd v Morrison Construction Ltd* [1999] B.L.R. 93; and in *Outwing Construction Ltd v H Randall & Son Ltd* [1999] B.L.R. 156.

In *Macob Civil Engineering Ltd v Morrison Construction Ltd*,[862] MCL, the unsuccessful party in an adjudication, argued that, given that the adjudicator's determination was challenged,[863] it was not a "decision" within para.23 of the Scheme. Dyson J. rejected this argument pointing out that, if it were correct, it would substantially undermine the effectiveness of the Scheme, which was intended by Parliament "... to introduce a speedy mechanism for settling disputes in construction contracts on a provisional interim basis ...".[864] MCL also sought a mandatory stay to arbitration under s.9 of the Arbitration Act 1996, but this was rejected on the facts of the case.[865] Finally, Dyson J. indicated that the usual remedy for failure to pay in accordance with an adjudicator's decision will be for the successful party to issue proceedings claiming the sum due, followed by an application for summary judgment.[866] In *Ringway Infrastructure Services Ltd v Vauxhall Motors Ltd*[867] Akenhead J. held that the cause of action to enforce an adjudicator's award was contractual and that for the purposes of an award of interest under s.35A of the Senior Courts Act 1981, it accrued when the defendant failed to honour the decision.

The enforcement of adjudicator's awards Following *Macob*, the courts have **37-265** taken a robust approach to the enforcement of adjudicator's awards, although in the light of the decision of the Court of Appeal in *Halki Shipping v Sopex Oils*[868] it is not altogether easy to see why the question of enforcement ought not to be a matter to be referred to arbitration. However, the effect of the decisions on the enforcement of adjudicator's awards may be summarised as follows[869]:

(1) A decision of an adjudicator whose validity is challenged as to its factual or legal conclusions or as to procedural error remains a decision that is both enforceable and should be enforced.[870]

(2) A decision that is erroneous, even if the error is disclosed by the reasons, will still not ordinarily be capable of being challenged and should, ordinarily, still be enforced.[871]

(3) A decision may be challenged on the ground that the adjudicator was not empowered by the Housing Grants, Construction and Regeneration Act to make the decision because there was no underlying construction contract

---

[862] [1999] B.L.R. 93.

[863] In this case, both on the merits and on the basis of certain breaches of natural justice.

[864] [1998] B.L.R. 93 at 97.

[865] To this extent, the interrelationship between s.9 of the Arbitration Act 1996 (as considered in *Halki* [1998] W.L.R. 726, CA) and the Scheme may benefit from further consideration by the courts.

[866] The decision in *Outwing Construction Ltd v H Randall & Son Ltd* [1999] B.L.R. 156 further emphasises the robust approach taken by the courts in implementing the presumed intention of the legislature where enforcement of the Scheme is concerned.

[867] (2007) 115 Con. L.R. 149.

[868] [1998] 1 W.L.R. 726, CA.

[869] See *Sherwood & Casson Ltd v Mackenzie Engineering Ltd* (2000) 2 T.C.L.R. 418.

[870] *Macob v Morrison* [1999] B.L.R. 93; *C&B Scene Concept Design Ltd v Isobars Ltd* [2002] B.L.R. 93, CA.

[871] *Bouygues (UK) Ltd v Dahl-Jensen (UK) Ltd* [2000] B.L.R. 49. The adjudicator is permitted to take the initiative in ascertaining the facts and the law, but the proper ambit of the dispute will be determined by the notice of adjudication, properly construed, and the adjudicator will ordinarily have no jurisdiction to decide what is the real dispute between the parties: *McAlpine PPS Pipeline Systems Joint Venture v Transco Plc* [2004] EWHC 2030 (TCC), [2004] B.L.R. 352.

between the parties[872] or because the adjudicator has gone outside his terms of reference[873] or because there has been a breach of the rules of natural justice,[874] although in the case of the latter it has been emphasised that enforcement will only be refused in the clearest cases.[875]

(4) Adjudication is intended to be a speedy process in which mistakes will inevitably occur. Accordingly, the court should guard against characterising a mistaken answer to an issue, which is within the adjudicator's jurisdiction, as being an excess of jurisdiction. Furthermore, the court should give a fair, natural and sensible interpretation to the decision in the light of the disputes that are the subject of the reference.[876]

(5) An issue as to whether a construction contract ever came into existence, which is an issue challenging the jurisdiction of the adjudicator, so long as it is reasonably and clearly raised, must be determined by the court on the balance of probabilities with, if necessary, oral and documentary evidence.[877]

(6) Generally the courts will view an alleged set off against an adjudicator's

---

[872] *The Project Consultancy Group v The Trustees of the Gray Trust* [1999] B.L.R. 377. *Redworth Construction Ltd v Brookdale Healthcare Ltd* [2006] EWHC 1994 (TCC), [2006] B.L.R. 366. In *Treasure & Son Ltd v Martin Dawes* [2008] B.L.R. 24 Akenhead J. held that there was jurisdiction for the adjudicator to make the decision under consideration notwithstanding the fact that there had been an oral variation of the original written contract that contained the adjudication clause. But see *Lead Technical Services Ltd v CMS Medical Ltd* [2007] EWCA Civ 316, [2007] B.L.R. 251 where the Court of Appeal held that there was an arguable case that an adjudicator had no jurisdiction because the relevant contract was partly oral. See also *Pegram Shopfitters Ltd v Tally Wiejl (UK) Ltd* [2003] EWCA Civ 1750, [2004] 1 W.L.R. 2082 in which the Court of Appeal held that it had been wrong to enter summary judgment on an adjudicator's decision where it had been contended that there was no contract at all between the parties. As to the need for all of the material terms to be contained in writing, see *RJT Consulting Engineers Ltd v DM Engineering (NI) Ltd* [2002] B.L.R. 217.

[873] *Bouygues (UK) Ltd v Dahl-Jensen (UK) Ltd* [2000] B.L.R. 49.

[874] *Quietfield Ltd v Vascroft Construction Ltd* [2006] EWCA Civ 1737, [2007] B.L.R. 67, on appeal from [2006] EWHC 174 (TCC), (2006) 109 Con. L.R. 29. For an example of a breach of natural justice being found by the Court, see *CJP Builders Ltd v William Verry Ltd* [2008] EWHC 2025 (TCC), [2008] B.L.R. 545. See also *Vision Homes Ltd v Lancsville Construction Ltd* [2009] EWHC 2042 (TCC), [2009] B.L.R. 525, where it was held that no breach of natural justice occurred; and *PC Harrington Contractors Ltd v Tyroddy Construction Ltd* [2011] EWHC 813 (TCC), where it was held that an adjudicator had acted in breach of natural justice by not dealing with a specific defence raised by a party and by not giving either party an opportunity to deal with a jurisdictional issue that arose and which was decided in the adjudication.

[875] *Carillion Construction Ltd v Devonport Royal Dockyard Ltd* [2005] EWCA Civ 1358, [2006] B.L.R. 15. Note that in *Speymill Contracts Ltd v Baskind* [2010] EWCA Civ 120, [2010] B.L.R. 257 the Court of Appeal confirmed that fraud or deceit could be raised as a defence in adjudication enforcement proceedings provided that it was a real defence to the claims being made and was supported by clear and unambiguous evidence.

[876] *Carillion Construction Ltd v Devonport* [2005] EWCA Civ 1358, [2006] B.L.R. 15.

[877] *The Project Consultancy Group v The Trustees of the Gray Trust* [1999] B.L.R. 377. See also *Adonis Construction v O'Keefe Soil Remediation* [2009] EWHC 2047 (TCC), where it was held that there was no written contract for the purposes of the Housing Grants, Construction and Regeneration Act 1996 in circumstances where the sub-contractor had never signed the order for works and where the draft order did not amount to an offer capable of acceptance to form a contract. See *Naylor Construction Services Ltd v Acoustafoam Ltd* [2010] B.L.R. 183 (TCC), where it was held that all material terms were sufficiently set out in the relevant documents. Also in *Durham CC v Kendall* [2011] EWHC 780 (TCC), [2011] B.L.R. 425, it was held, following *RJT Consulting*, that an agreed minute of a meeting was capable of being a written record for these purposes if it recorded the agreement in writing of a material term.

decision as an attempt to frustrate the operation of the 1996 Act which will ordinarily not be permitted, especially where the subject matter of the set off has been implicitly dealt with in the adjudicator's decision.[878]

Some procedural aspects of adjudication   The decisions of the courts on **37-266** adjudication have also clarified a number of procedural issues which may be summarised as follows:

(1)   A party to a "construction contract" to which the provisions of the Housing Grants, Construction and Regeneration Act 1996 apply, can refer a matter to adjudication at any time and even in the course of ongoing court proceedings.[879] Section 107 of the original Act required the contract to be "in writing", which was held to require that the whole of the contract should be evidenced in writing.[880] The section is repealed by the Local Democracy, Economic Development and Construction Act 2009 with respect to contracts entered into on or after October 1, 2011.

(2)   A party responding to an adjudication notice can raise any matter by way of response to the claim (including set-off and counterclaim) provided that all of those matters are raised in the responding party's notice of intention to withhold payment or, in a case subject to the amendments introduced by the Local Democracy, Economic Development and Construction Act 2009, that those matters are raised in the notice of intention to pay less than the notified sum.[881]

(3)   Neither the Housing Grants, Construction and Regeneration Act 1996 nor the Scheme confers on an adjudicator the power to award costs in adjudication proceedings and the parties' freedom to agree otherwise is the contract is severely limited by s.108A of the Act. Further, s.5A(2A) of the Late Payment of Commercial Debts (Interest) Act 1998 cannot be relied upon as a basis for recovering costs.[882]

(4)   Although much will depend upon the terms of the particular contract, the mere fact that the responding party to an adjudication has failed to serve a proper notice of intention not to pay sums otherwise due will not relieve the referring party from the obligation to demonstrate entitlement and prove its case.[883] This is an issue which, however, the Court of Appeal declined to consider in *C&B Scene Concept Design v Isobars*.[884]

---

[878]   *Ferson Contractors Ltd v Levolux AT Ltd* [2003] B.L.R. 118.
[879]   *Herschel Engineering Ltd v Breen Property Ltd* [2000] B.L.R. 272. See also *Connex South Eastern Ltd v MJ Building Services Group Plc* [2005] EWCA Civ 193, [2005] 1 W.L.R. 3323, [2005] B.L.R. 201, where the Court of Appeal held that the words "at any time" were to be given their literal and ordinary meaning and that therefore a dispute could be referred to adjudication (subject to the possibility that the right to adjudicate has been waived or was the subject of an estoppel) even after the expiry of a relevant limitation period—although, of course, the responding party would be able to take the limitation point as part of its defence in this event.
[880]   *RJT Consulting Engineers Ltd v D M Engineering (NI)* [2002] B.L.R. 217.
[881]   *VHE Construction Plc v RBSTB Trust Ltd* [2000] B.L.R. 187; *Northern Developments (Cumbria) Ltd v J & J Nichol* [2000] B.L.R. 158; and see s.111(3) of the Housing Grants, Construction and Regeneration Act 1996 as inserted by the Local Democracy, Economic Development and Construction Act 2009.
[882]   *Enviroflow Management Ltd v Redhill Works (Nottingham) Ltd* [2017] EWHC 2159 (TCC).
[883]   *Woods Hardwick Ltd v Chiltern Air Conditioning Ltd* [2001] B.L.R. 23; *SL Timber Systems v Carillion Construction Ltd* [2001] B.L.R. 516 (Lord Macfayden, Outer House).
[884]   [2002] B.L.R. 93.

(5) Mere procedural breaches of little consequence are not to be taken as vitiating the decision reached by an adjudicator[885] but the adjudicator does have an obligation to follow the Scheme and "… to conduct the proceedings in accordance with the rules of natural justice or as fairly as the limitations imposed by Parliament permit …".[886]

(6) The general law in relation to actual or apparent bias will apply to the conduct of adjudicators, but the courts have indicated that a robust approach will be taken, so that a telephone conversation with one side may not amount to apparent bias[887]; and where the adjudicator receives privileged material, he may properly continue if he concludes that there can be no legitimate fear that he might not have been impartial.[888] However, where an adjudicator is very critical of a party for not producing a witness who was never asked to attend, this may amount to bias,[889] as may a large number of former appointments by one of the parties, particularly if combined with certain conduct during the conduct of the adjudication.[890]

(7) Although the possibility has been raised that some disputes may be so complex that it is impossible for them to be dealt with fairly within the timescales available in the adjudication process,[891] such concerns have subsequently not found favour with the courts, particularly in cases where substantial extensions of time have been agreed between the parties.[892]

(8) Where a contract has been entered into under duress, then that contract is voidable; and so, if it has in fact been avoided by the innocent party, then the agreement to adjudicate is unenforceable and the adjudicator will have no jurisdiction.[893]

37-267 **Contractual adjudication schemes** In most cases, Standard Forms of Contract have now been amended to take account of the Housing Grants, Construction and Regeneration Act 1996 by the addition of conforming adjudication procedures which apply in place of the Scheme. A party who signs up to such a contract without amending the dispute resolution provisions will be bound by the adjudication clause even if he would not ordinarily fall within the Act, for example because one of the parties is a residential occupier.[894] The solution generally adopted for enforcement of an adjudication decision is to provide that the arbitration clause does not apply to an adjudication decision, leaving the parties free to enforce through the courts.

37-268 **Effect of an adjudicator's decision** Unless the contract provides otherwise, the decision of an adjudicator, at least in the statutory context, is taken to be temporar-

---

[885] See *Discain Project Services Ltd v Opecprime Development Ltd (No.1)* [2000] B.L.R. 402; and *Balfour Beatty Construction Ltd v Lambeth LBC* [2002] EWHC 597 (TCC), [2002] B.L.R. 288.

[886] *Glencot Developments v Ben Barrett* [2001] B.L.R. 207; and *Discain Project Services Ltd v Opecprime Ltd (No.1)* [2000] B.L.R. 402.

[887] *Amec Capital Projects Ltd v Whitefriars City Estates Ltd* [2004] EWCA Civ 1418, [2005] B.L.R. 1.

[888] See *Specialist Ceiling Services Ltd v ZVI Construction (UK) Ltd* [2004] B.L.R. 403; cf. *Paice v Harding (t/a MJ Harding Contractors)* [2015] EWHC 661 (TCC).

[889] As in *A&S Enterprises Ltd v Kema Holdings Ltd* [2005] EWHC 3365 (QB), [2005] B.L.R. 76.

[890] As in *Cofely Ltd v Bingham* [2016] EWHC 240 (Comm).

[891] *AWG v Rockingham Motorway Speedway Ltd* (2004) T.C.L.R. 6.

[892] *CIB Properties Ltd v Birse Construction Ltd* [2005] 1 W.L.R. 2252.

[893] *Capital Structures Plc v Time & Tide Construction Ltd* [2006] B.L.R. 226.

[894] *Treasure & Son Ltd v Dawes* [2007] EWHC 2420 (TCC).

ily binding, meaning that it must be complied with, but can be overturned by a subsequent Court decision showing it to be wrong. There is a difficult issue as to the legal basis on which an unsuccessful party to adjudication may seek to obtain repayment of sums paid over to a referring party as a result of an adjudicator's decision. In *Aspect Contracts (Asbestos) Ltd v Higgins Construction Plc*[895] it was held by the Supreme Court that there was an implied term in the contract under consideration (as a result of para.23(2) of the Scheme) to the effect that the losing party had a right to refer the dispute to court and, if successful, have any money paid out returned to it.[896]

(f) International Disputes

Forum, jurisdiction and choice of law Many construction projects involve contracts or sub-contracts of an international character. In such cases problems of forum, jurisdiction and choice of law may arise. Such questions are to be determined in accordance with the applicable rules of conflict of laws. As regards litigation, where issues arise between parties from European states, questions of forum and jurisdiction will be governed by the Brussels Convention[897] and the Judgments Regulations[898] and matters of choice of law by the Rome Convention.[899] Where the matters are before the court in England and Wales, the relevant enacting legislation in relation to forum is the Civil Jurisdiction and Judgments Act 1982[900] and, in the case of choice of law, the Contracts (Applicable Law) Act 1990. **37-269**

Arbitration Prima facie, neither Convention applies to arbitration, which is overwhelmingly the most frequently used form of dispute resolution in international construction matters. In the case of an international arbitration[901] whether the seat is in England and Wales or abroad, the procedural law will, prima facie, be that of the seat of the arbitration[902] together with such rules as may be stated in or incorporated by the arbitration agreement. Many such contracts incorporate either the ICC[903] or the LCIA[904] Rules, each of which provide for the arbitration to be administered. **37-270**

The proper law or governing law, in the absence of express choice, will be determined by the applicable rules of conflict of laws, but is almost invariably specified in the terms of the contract.[905] Where there is no choice of applicable law but the arbitration is subject to Institutional Rules, these may empower the Tribunal to

---

[895] [2015] UKSC 38.

[896] cf. above, para.28-056.

[897] Convention on Jurisdiction and the Enforcement of Judgments in Civil and Commercial Matters 1968, as amended.

[898] Which came into force on March 1, 2002; with the necessary changes to the Civil Jurisdiction and Judgments Act 1982 being made by the Civil Jurisdiction and Judgments Order 2001 (SI 2001/ 3929).

[899] Convention on the Law Applicable to Contractual Obligations 1980.

[900] As extended by the Civil Jurisdiction and Judgments Act 1991 and to the Civil Jurisdiction and Judgments Order 2001 (SI 2001/3929).

[901] There is no universal definition, but art.1(3) of the UNCITRAL Model Law on International Commercial Arbitration, provides that an arbitration is international, inter alia, if the parties have their places of business in different states.

[902] *Miller v Whitworth Street Estates* [1970] A.C. 583; and see also Arbitration Act 1996 s.2.

[903] International Chamber of Commerce, Paris.

[904] London Court of International Arbitration.

[905] See, for example, FIDIC (1998 edn) cl.1.4.

apply rules of law to the merits of the dispute which are not necessarily the same as the proper or governing law which would be applied by a court.[906]

37-271   Where the seat of an international arbitration is in London (or technically England and Wales) Pt I of the Arbitration Act 1996 applies[907] including the right to seek leave to appeal against an award on a point of law.[908] The parties may by agreement exclude any right of appeal[909] and both the ICC and LCIA Arbitration Rules contain such an exclusion agreement. Where appeal is not excluded the question of law must be a question of English law.[910] In *Reliance Industries Ltd v Enron Oil and Gas India Ltd*[911] the applicant sought to argue that there was a question of English law arising out of the award of an arbitral tribunal within the meaning of s.69 of the Arbitration Act 1996 on the basis that, although the substantive law was Indian law, the arbitrators had in practice applied English law. The arbitrators had in fact applied Indian law, which happened to be the same as English law on the point in question, but it was held by the Commercial Court that there was no basis for an appeal under the Arbitration Act. In *Braes of Doune Wind Farm v Alfred McAlpine*[912] the arbitration clause provided that the seat of the arbitration was Glasgow but the arbitration was to be subject to the English Arbitration Act 1996. On an application to the TCC in London for leave to appeal it was held that, on the construction of the arbitration agreement, the venue of the hearing was to be Glasgow but seat of the arbitration was England so that the court had jurisdiction to entertain the application.

37-272 **New York Convention 1958**   The successor of the Geneva Convention 1927,[913] the New York Convention on the Recognition and Enforcement of Foreign Arbitral Awards 1958 is probably the most important international instrument relating to international commercial arbitration, providing for the recognition and enforcement of arbitration agreements and of foreign arbitral awards. In particular in relation to international arbitration agreements, the Convention requires the national courts of contracting states to refuse to allow a dispute which is the subject of an arbitration agreement to be litigated if an objection is raised by any party to the arbitration agreement.[914] This is given effect to by s.9 of the English Arbitration Act 1996, which applies whether or not the seat is in England and Wales.[915] Enforcement of awards under the New York Convention is provided for under English law by Pt III ss.100–104 of the Arbitration Act 1996.

---

[906] See ICC Rules of Arbitration 1998 art.17.1 and LCIA Arbitration Rules 1998 art.22.3.
[907] By s.2(1) of the Act.
[908] Under s.69.
[909] Arbitration Act 1996 s.69(1).
[910] Arbitration Act 1996 s.82(1)(a).
[911] [2002] 1 All E.R. (Comm) 59, [2002] B.L.R. 36.
[912] [2008] EWHC 426 (TCC), [2008] B.L.R. 321.
[913] Which remains in force in England by virtue of Pt II of the Arbitration Act 1950, and s.99 of the Arbitration Act 1996.
[914] See further, Redfern and Hunter, *Law and Practice of International Commercial Arbitration*, 4th edn (2004); Dicey, Morris and Collins, *The Conflict of Laws*, 14th edn (2007), Ch.16. See also Collins, *Essays in International Litigation and the Conflict of Laws* (1994), Ch.5 on arbitration.
[915] Arbitration Act 1996 s.2(2).

CHAPTER 38

CONSUMER CONTRACTS

Simon Whittaker

1. Introduction

Development of the law The English common law of contract has rarely been **38-001**
developed by the courts in a way which regulates directly and specifically contracts
between traders and consumers, although many developments of the law more
generally have had the incidental effect of providing protection for consumer parties to such contracts. So, for example, the general requirement that standard terms
can be incorporated into a contract only on reasonable notice, while not restricted
to the case where the person to be bound by the term is a consumer, has had an
significant role in protecting consumers from unfair contract terms.[1] Similarly,

---

[1] An early example may be found in *Parker v South Eastern Ry* (1877) 2 C.P.D. 416, 421, 423 and
see Vol.I, paras 13-014—13-017. There remain the important exceptions to this general requirement of reasonable notice where the other party has signed a document containing, or incorporating by reference, the terms in question (*L'Estrange v F Graucob* [1934] 2 K.B. 394) or where

implied terms in contracts of sale of goods where the seller contracts in the course of business protected consumer buyers as well as buyers contracting in the course of business,[2] a breadth of application which continued when these terms were given legislative expression in the Sale of Goods Act 1893.[3] And a consumer party to a contract can exercise a right to rescission of a contract concluded as a result of a misrepresentation made by the other party as can a misrepresentee who is not a consumer.[4] A rare example of the restriction of a development of the common law for the benefit of consumers, or at least of non-traders, can be seen in *Barclays Bank Plc v O'Brien*,[5] *Royal Bank of Scotland v Etridge (No.2)*[6] and the case-law following these leading decisions.[7] In these cases, the courts recognised that a surety may defeat a claim under the contract of suretyship by a bank which has extended credit to that surety's spouse or partner on the ground of misrepresentation or undue influence by that spouse or partner, but they have restricted this protection to the situation where the relationship between the surety and the spouse/debtor is non-commercial.[8]

38-002 **Legislative protection for consumer contractors** The beginnings of modern protection for consumers in relation to the contracts which they conclude can be seen in the 1970s. So, first, in 1973 the Supply of Goods (Implied Terms) Act controlled the exclusion by a seller of his liability arising from breach of the statutory implied terms in respect of title, description and quality and fitness for purpose set out in the Sale of Goods Act 1893.[9] Under the 1973 Act, while any exemption clauses in respect of the implied warranty of title were rendered void,[10] as regards the other liabilities a distinction was drawn between "consumer sales" (where an exemption clause was rendered void) and other cases (where the term was "not enforceable to the extent that it is shown that it would not be fair and reasonable to show reliance on the term").[11] The 1973 Act defined "consumer sale" for the purposes of this rule, in terms of a sale of goods concluded by a

"... seller in the course of business where the goods—

    (a)   are of a type ordinarily bought for private use or consumption; and

    (b)   are sold to a person who does not buy or hold himself out as buying them in the course of a business."[12]

However, when this tentative control of exemption clauses was extended by the Unfair Contract Terms Act 1977, the protection for consumers was rearranged and the reference to "consumer sales" was not replaced by reference to "consumer

---

standard terms form part of a course of dealing and see Vol.I, paras 13-002, 13-011.
2   *Jones v Bright* (1829) 5 Bing. 533; *Jones v Just* (1868) L.R. III Q.B. 197.
3   Sale of Goods Act 1893 ss.12–15, which were repealed and replaced by the Sale of Goods Act 1979 ss.12–15.
4   See Vol.I, paras 7-112 et seq.
5   [1994] 1 A.C. 180.
6   [2001] UKHL 44, [2002] 1 A.C. 773.
7   [2001] UKHL 44, [2002] 1 A.C. 773 at [87] and [89] and see Vol.I, paras 8-110 et seq.
8   Vol.I, para.8-118.
9   Sale of Goods Act 1893 ss.12–15.
10 1973 Act s.4 creating new Sale of Goods Act 1893 s.55(3).
11 1973 Act s.4 creating new Sale of Goods Act 1893 s.55(4).
12 1973 Act s.4 creating new Sale of Goods Act 1893 s.55(7).

contracts", but instead by the notion of a person "dealing as consumer".[13] As the courts made clear, this definition could apply so as to protect not merely consumers in the sense defined by the 1973 Act, but also to businesses (even if incorporated) where the contract is neither an integral part of their business nor, if incidental to their business, of a type which they regularly enter.[14] Further important legislation for the protection of consumers was enacted by the Consumer Credit Act 1974, where the protection extended (and still extends) to a range of individuals including sole traders, small partnerships and unincorporated associations.[15] Moreover, in 1994 the well-known provisions in the Sale of Goods Act 1979 (which replaced the 1893 Act) implying terms as to the quality and fitness for purpose of the goods sold were amended so as to make them more appropriate for consumers, in particular, the reference to "merchantable quality" being replaced by one to "satisfactory quality".[16]

The importance of European law   However, from the late 1980s EEC (later EC   **38-003** and now EU) law has become increasingly important as a source of legislative protection for consumer contractors, typically by way of directive and therefore requiring implementation by the UK into national law, whether by statute or, as has been more usual, by secondary legislation under the European Communities Act 1972.[17] Some of these legislative instruments have required national rules governing consumer contracts which are concluded in particular ways (as in the case of "doorstep selling"[18] and "distance contracts"[19]); some have required rules governing aspects of particular types of contracts (as in the case of contracts for the sale of goods,[20] timeshare contracts,[21] package travel contracts,[22] consumer credit[23] and

---

[13]   Unfair Contract Terms Act 1977 s.12 (definition). Reference to a person "dealing as consumer" was then made relevant to the controls in s.3(1) (contractual liability generally), s.4 (indemnity clauses), s.6(2) (statutory implied terms in sale of goods) and s.7(2) (statutory implied terms in miscellaneous contracts under which goods pass).

[14]   *R. B. Customs Brokers Co Ltd v United Dominions Trust Ltd* [1988] 1 W.L.R. 321 and see Vol.I, para.15-074.

[15]   See below, para.39-005.

[16]   Sale and Supply of Goods Act 1994 s.1. This change was recommended by Law Commission, *Sale and Supply of Goods*, Law Com. No.160 § 3.27.

[17]   European Communities Act 1972 s.2(2).

[18]   Directive 85/577/EEC to protect the consumer in respect of contracts negotiated away from business premises [1985] O.J. L372/31 implemented in UK law by the Consumer Protection (Cancellation of Contracts Concluded Away from Business Premises) Regulations 1987 (SI 1987/2117), which were replaced by the Cancellation of Contracts made in a Consumer's Home or Place of Work, etc. Regulations 2008 (SI 2008/1816). The current law is contained in the Consumer Contracts (Information, Cancellation and Additional Charges) Regulations 2013 (SI 2013/3134) ("2013 Regulations") on which see below, paras 37-059 et seq.

[19]   Directive 97/7/EC on the protection of consumers in respect of distance contracts [1997] O.J. L144/19 implemented in UK law by the Consumer Protection (Distance Selling) Regulations 2000 (SI 2000/2334) (the current law is contained in the 2013 Regulations, on which see below paras 38-061 et seq.); Directive 2002/65/EC concerning the distance marketing of consumer financial services [2002] O.J. L271/16 art.3(2) implemented principally by the Financial Services (Distance Marketing) Regulations 2004 (SI 2004/2095) on which see below, para.38-136.

[20]   Directive 99/44/EC on certain aspects of the sale of consumer goods and associated guarantees [1999] O.J. L171/7 ("Consumer Sales Directive", "1999 Directive") and see below, para.38-433.

[21]   Directive 94/47/EC on the protection of purchasers in respect of certain aspects of contracts relating to the purchase of the right to use immovable properties on a timeshare basis [1994] O.J. L280/83 and see for the current legislation below, paras 38-148—38-154.

[22]   Directive 90/314/EEC on package travel, package holidays and package tours [1990] O.J. L158/

passenger transport[24]); and perhaps the most prominent example, the Unfair Terms in Consumer Contracts Directive 1993, subjected most contract terms which had not been "individually negotiated" in *all* consumer contracts to a test of unfairness.[25] At this earlier stage in its development, EU contract law generally required only "minimum harmonisation", that is to say, the European legislation required only minimum rights or protections for the consumer, thereby allowing Member States to enact national laws which are more protective of consumers than the EU law required.[26] However, at the beginning of the present century, the European Commission started a wide-ranging review of EC/EU legislation in the area of contract law, with particular reference to consumer law,[27] and this had a number of consequences for EU (and therefore UK) consumer contract law. First, the Commission has sought (and to an extent achieved) the reform and consolidation of existing directives so as to provide greater consistency between them, this being noticeable particularly in the Consumer Rights Directive 2011,[28] which, inter alia, consolidated the information duties required by the directives concerning "doorstep selling" (later "off-premises contracting")[29] and "distance contracts",[30] though it did not consolidate the requirements contained in directives on guarantees in contracts for the sale of goods[31] nor on unfair contract terms[32] as had earlier been proposed.[33] Other earlier consumer contract directives have also been subject to reform and consolidation, for example, on timeshare contracts[34] and package travel contracts.[35]

59; [1994] O.J. L280/83, repealed and replaced by Directive (EU) 2015/2302 on package travel and linked travel arrangements [2015] O.J. L326/1. See below, paras 38-137—38-147.

23 Directive 87/102/EEC on consumer credit [1987] O.J. L42/48 repealed and replaced by Directive 2008/48/EC on credit agreements for consumers [2008] O.J. L133/66.

24 e.g. Regulation (EC) 261/2004 establishing common rules on compensation and assistance to passengers in the event of denied boarding and of cancellation or long delay of flights [2004] O.J. L46/1.

25 Directive 93/13/EEC [1993] O.J. L95/29 ("1993 Directive"), below, para.38-218.

26 See, notably, Directive 93/13/EEC of April 5, 1993 on unfair terms in consumer contracts, art.8 and see below, para.38-022.

27 See Communication from the Commission to the Council and the European Parliament on European Contract Law COM(2001) 398 final; Communication from the Commission to the European Parliament and the Council, *A more coherent European Contract Law, An Action Plan* COM(2003) 68 final; European Contract Law and the revision of the acquis: the way forward COM(2004) 651 final; EU Commission, *Green Paper from the Commission on policy option for progress towards a European Contract Law for consumers and businesses* COM(2010) 348 final.

28 Directive 2011/83/EU on consumer rights [2011] O.J. L304/64 ("Consumer Rights Directive" or "2011 Directive"), below, para.38-060.

29 Directive 85/577/EEC to protect the consumer in respect of contracts negotiated away from business premises [1985] O.J. L372/31.

30 Directive 97/7/EC on the protection of consumers in respect of distance contracts [1997] O.J. L144/19. The Consumer Rights Directive did not, however, include elements from the Directive 2002/65/EC concerning the distance marketing of consumer financial services [2002] O.J. L271/16.

31 Directive 99/44/EC on certain aspects of the sale of consumer goods and associated guarantees [1999] O.J. L171/7 (the "Consumer Sales Directive").

32 Directive 93/13/EEC of April 5, 1993 on unfair terms in consumer contracts [1993] O.J. L95/29 ("Unfair Terms in Consumer Contracts Directive" or "1993 Directive").

33 Proposal for a Directive of the European Parliament and of the Council on Consumer Rights of 8 October 2008 COM(2008) 614/3 final, Chs IV and V.

34 Directive 2008/122/EC on the protection of consumers in respect of certain aspects of timeshare, long-term holiday product, resale and exchange contracts [2009] O.J. L33/30 repealing and replacing Directive 94/47/EC on the protection of purchasers in respect of certain aspects of contracts relating to the purchase of the right to use immovable properties on a timeshare basis [1994] O.J. L280/83; Directive 2008/48/EC on credit agreements for consumers [2008] O.J. L133/66.

35 Directive (EU) 2015/2302 on package travel and linked travel arrangements [2015] O.J. L326/1

Secondly, the Commission has sought to move directives in the area of consumer protection from requiring "minimum harmonisation" to requiring "full harmonisation", that is to say, the European legislation sets rights or protections for the consumer for which Member States must provide but which they must not exceed in the interests of greater protection for the consumer.[36] Thirdly, and related to this, by the Unfair Commercial Practices Directive 2005 the European legislator enacted an important general and "fully harmonised" framework for the regulation of unfair commercial practices business-to-consumer.[37] While the 2005 Directive is expressly stated as being "without prejudice to contract law and, in particular, to the rules on the validity, formation or effect of a contract"[38] and the UK's first implementation reflected this scope,[39] in 2014 the UK legislator nonetheless chose to give some "contract law" effects to certain aspects of the 2005 Directive's requirements, thereby creating new rights to redress for consumers against their trader contracting partners.[40] Fourthly, the EU legislator brought earlier European Conventions on jurisdiction and the recognition and enforcement of judgments (the "Brussels Convention")[41] and on the law applicable to contractual obligations (the "Rome Convention")[42] directly within the fold of EU law by enacting regulations to replace them.[43] These regulations set uniform rules of private international law governing

---

revoking and replacing Directive 90/314/EEC on package travel, package holidays and package tours.

[36] e.g. Directive 2011/83/EU on consumer rights art.4; Directive 2008/48/EC on credit agreements for consumers recital 9, though as the following recitals explain, the directive leaves a good deal of competence in Member States as regards matters outside its carefully delineated scope; Directive (EU) 2015/2302 on package travel and linked travel arrangements [2015] O.J. L326/1 art.4 (full harmonisation with exceptions). See also the Proposal for a Directive of the European Parliament and of the Council on certain aspects concerning contracts for the supply of digital content COM(2015) 634 final art.4 and the Amended Proposal for a Directive of the European Parliament and of the Council on certain aspects concerning contracts for the online and other distance sales of goods COM(2017) 637 final art.3.

[37] Directive 2005/29/EC concerning unfair business-to-consumer commercial practices [2005] O.J. L149/22 ("Unfair Commercial Practices Directive" or "2005 Directive") especially art.4. The Directive excludes certain areas from "full harmonisation", notably, art.3(9) (financial services) and see generally below, paras 38-159 et seq.

[38] Directive 2005/29/EC art.3(2), on which see Whittaker in Weatherill and Bernitz (eds), *The Regulation of Unfair Commercial Practices under EC Directive 2005/29, New Rules and New Techniques* (2007), Ch.8.

[39] The Consumer Protection from Unfair Trading Regulations 2008 (SI 2008/1277) ("2008 Regulations") reg.29 (as enacted) provided explicitly that "an agreement shall not be void or unenforceable by reason only of a breach of these regulations" but said no more as to the wider lack of effect of the Regulations on the "law of contract", apparently on the basis that they set out the consequences of the new controls and did not need to set out other non-consequences.

[40] Consumer Protection (Amendment) Regulations 2014 (SI 2014/870) inserting, notably, new Pt 4A Consumers' Rights to Redress in Consumer Protection from Unfair Trading Regulations 2008 (SI 2008/1277). See further, below paras 38-172 et seq.

[41] Convention on Jurisdiction and the Enforcement of Judgments in Civil and Commercial Matters 1968.

[42] Rome Convention on the Law Applicable to Contractual Obligations 1980.

[43] Regulation (EC) 593/2008 on the law applicable to contractual obligations ("Rome I") [2008] O.J. L177/6; Regulation (EC) 864/2007 applicable to non-contractual obligations ("Rome II Regulation") [2007] O.J. L199/40 (some of whose provisions bear an important relationship with contract, notably art.12 *"culpa in contrahendo"*); Council Regulation 44/2001 on jurisdiction and the recognition and enforcement of judgments in civil and commercial matters [2001] O.J. L12/1 ("Brussels I Regulation") first replaced the Brussels Convention and then was itself replaced as from January 10, 2015 by Regulation (EU) 1215/2012 of 12 December 2012 on jurisdiction and the recognition and enforcement of judgments in civil and commercial matters (recast) ("the Brussels Ibis Regulation").

applicable law for "contractual obligations" and jurisdiction, recognition and the enforcement of judgments in "matters relating to a contract"[44] as well as special rules for, for example, consumers in these contexts.[45] The present significance of these private international law rules governing consumer contracts is that the European Court of Justice has interpreted the concepts which they use (notably, "consumer"), and this case-law may be helpful in the interpretation of the same or similar concepts in the EU substantive law legislation governing consumer contracts.[46]

38-004 **Impact of "Brexit" on UK consumer contract law** On March 29, 2017 the Prime Minister, the Right Hon. Mrs Theresa May MP, set in motion the process of the departure of the United Kingdom from the European Union ("Brexit") under art.50 of the Treaty of the European Union (TEU).[47] The likely significance of this on English contract law is noted generally in Vol.I, Ch.1 of the present work.[48] While much still remains unclear, a number of issues arising from this fundamental change were settled by the European Union (Withdrawal) Act 2018 (notably, the status of past and future decisions of the Court of Justice of the EU for the interpretation of EU legislation implemented in UK law[49]); moreover, the 2018 Act would in principle preserve existing consumer protection legislation derived from EU law on "exit day" (provisionally set as March 29, 2019 at 11.00pm).[50] Until "exit day," the UK remains fully a member of the EU and the status of EU law and the decisions of the Court of Justice of the EU remain the same.

38-005 **Earlier approaches to UK implementation of European directives** For a long time UK implementation of the various European directives governing consumer contracts was often effected in a piecemeal way. Indeed, in many instances, directives were implemented by standalone statutory instrument, thereby creating new and distinct bodies of legislative controls; this can be seen in the context of package travel, package tours and package holidays,[51] doorstep selling[52] and distance contracts.[53] In the case of the Unfair Terms in Consumer
Contracts Directive 1993, the resulting standalone statutory instrument created a set of legislative rules which overlapped considerably with, but formally were

---

[44] Brussels Ibis Regulation art.7(1); Rome I Regulation generally.
[45] Brussels Ibis Regulation arts 17–19; Rome I Regulation art.6.
[46] See below para.38-016.
[47] The Prime Minister's authority to do so was given by the European Union (Notification of Withdrawal) Act 2017 s.1.
[48] Vol.I, paras 1-014—1-018.
[49] Vol.I, para.1-017.
[50] Vol.I, para.1-016.
[51] Package Travel and Linked Travel Arrangements Regulations 2018 (SI 2018/634) revoking and replacing Package Travel, Package Holidays and Package Tours Regulations 1992 (SI 1992/3288) on which see below, paras 38-137—38-147.
[52] Consumer Protection (Cancellation of Contracts Concluded Away from Business Premises) Regulations 1987 (SI 1987/2117) later replaced by the Cancellation of Contracts made in a Consumer's Home or Place of Work, etc. Regulations 2008 (SI 2008/1816). As will be explained, the latter have been revoked and replaced by the Consumer Contracts (Information, Cancellation and Additional Charges) Regulations 2013 (SI 2013/3134): below, paras 38-061 et seq.
[53] Consumer Protection (Distance Selling) Regulations 2000 (SI 2000/2334) which have been revoked and replaced by the Consumer Contracts (Information, Cancellation and Additional Charges) Regulations 2013 (SI 2013/3134) (below, paras 37-061 et seq.); Financial Services (Distance Marketing) Regulations 2004 (SI 2004/2095) (below, para.38-136).

entirely separate from, the existing domestic legislation in the area, the Unfair Contract Terms Act 1977. In the context of unfair contract terms, the resulting complexity attracted a good deal of criticism, and, in turn, a recommendation from the Law Commissions that the legislation should be recast into a single enactment.[54] In the case of other directives, the UK legislature sought to integrate their requirements within existing legislative frameworks. In the case of timeshare contracts, this was easily achieved as these had already been the subject of regulation by UK statute.[55] However, in other cases, the process was more difficult, a particularly striking example being found in the legislative implementation of the Consumer Sales Directive of 1999, which was effected in English law principally by the insertion of a new Pt 5A into the Sale of Goods Act 1979.[56] This amendment created a series of dedicated rights for consumer buyers in respect of the "contractual non-conformity" of the goods in addition to (and in an awkward relationship with) the classic rights of rejection of the goods, restitution of the price and damages for breach of the implied statutory conditions governing satisfactory quality and fitness for purpose also foreseen by the Sale of Goods Act.[57] Here, therefore, implementation of the European directive lead to very considerable substantive complexity and, to an extent, overlap, even though it was effected by change to existing wider legislation.

Major reforms to UK consumer contract legislation: (i) the Consumer Rights Act 2015[58]   Recent legislation has sought to remedy some of the problems caused by this piecemeal and overly complex approach to legislative implementation of EU consumer law, prompted to an extent by the requirement to implement the Consumer Rights Directive of 2011 (which sought to bring more consistency into the underlying EU framework as regards pre-contractual information duties imposed on sellers and suppliers to consumers), but even more by a view in government that UK legislative implementation should be consistent, easier to find and easier to understand.[59] The principal result of this view is the Consumer Rights Act 2015, whose provisions re-implement earlier EU directives requiring consumer rights in respect of contractual non-conformity of goods sold to consumers and the control of unfair contract terms, but do so in a way which seeks to integrate their requirements into a wider framework, in part drawn from other domestic UK legislation (notably, the Unfair Contract Terms Act 1977,[60] the Sale of Goods Act

38-006

---

[54] Law Commission, Scottish Law Commission, *Unfair Terms in Contracts* (Law Com. No.292, Scot Law Com. No.199, 2005).

[55] Timeshare Act 1992, which preceded the Directive 94/47/EC on the protection of purchasers in respect of certain aspects of contracts relating to the purchase of the right to use immovable properties on a timeshare basis. The 1994 Directive was implemented by amendment of the Timeshare Act 1992 by regulation: Timeshare Regulations 1997 (SI 1997/1081). Subsequently, the UK's treatment of timeshare and related contracts has been made by the Timeshare, Holiday Products, Resale and Exchange Contracts Regulations 2010 (SI 2010/2960) on which see below, paras 38-148—38-154.

[56] On this implementation, see below, paras 38-439 et seq.

[57] s.14.

[58] On general differences between the law applicable to consumer contracts and the general law after these legislative changes see Whittaker (2017) 133 L.Q.R. 47.

[59] BIS, *Enhancing consumer confidence by clarifying consumer law* (July 2012); BIS, *Enhancing consumer confidence through effective enforcement, consultation on consolidating and modernising consumer law enforcement powers* (March 2012).

[60] e.g. Consumer Rights Act 2015 s.65 reflecting Unfair Contract Terms Act 1977 s.2 (1), below,

1979,[61] and the Supply of Goods and Services Act 1982[62]) and in part developed specially for the purpose (as in the case of the new rules governing contracts for the supply of "digital content"[63]). In this way, the 2015 Act reflects a broad strategy of separating the most prominent special rules governing contracts between traders and consumer from the legislative schemes applicable to contracts between other categories of contractor. So, notably, the Unfair Contract Terms Act 1977 (as amended by the 2015 Act) no longer contains any rules restricted to the situation where one party "deals as consumer".[64]

38-007 **(ii) Consumer Contracts (Information, Cancellation and Additional Charges) Regulations 2013**[65] However, the UK legislature did not seek to place all relevant consumer contract law in the Consumer Rights Act 2015. So, rather confusingly, the UK implemented the Consumer Rights Directive 2011 principally by enactment of standalone regulations, the Consumer Contracts (Information, Cancellation and Additional Charges) Regulations 2013 ("2013 Regulations"), rather than in the Consumer Rights Act.[66] The 2013 Regulations are principally concerned with rules governing a trader's information duties and the consumer's rights of cancellation in off-premises contracts and distance contracts other than relating to financial services, though they also create other particular consumer protection rules, notably, in relation to inertia selling and additional charges.[67]

38-008 **(iii) Creating rights to redress in respect of certain unfair commercial practices** As earlier noted, in 2014 the UK legislator chose to give some "contract law" effects to certain aspects of the Unfair Commercial Practices Directive 2005's prohibitions by inserting new provisions into the Consumer Protection from Unfair Trading Regulations 2008 ("the 2008 Regulations") which had earlier implemented the directive, thereby creating new rights to redress for consumers against their trader contracting partners.[68] As a result, a consumer to whom a misleading statement has been made by a trader or who has been subject to an aggressive com-

---

para.38-409.

[61] Consumer Rights Act 2015 ss.9–11, 13 reflecting Sale of Goods Act 1979 ss.13–15: below, paras 38-497—38-499, 38-501.

[62] Consumer Rights Act 2015 ss.9–11, 13 reflecting Supply of Goods and Services Act 1982 ss.3–5 (on which see below, paras 38-497—38-499, 38-501); Consumer Rights Act 2015 ss.49, 51–53 reflecting Supply of Goods and Services Act 1982 ss.13–16: below paras 38-571, 38-577—38-578.

[63] Consumer Rights Act 2015 ss.33–47: below, paras 38-540 et seq.

[64] Consumer Rights Act 2015 s.75, Sch.4 paras 5–11 on which see Vol.I, Ch.15 where it is explained that certain persons who "deal as consumer" do not count as "consumer" and are therefore no longer protected under either the 1977 or the 2015 Act: see especially paras 15-073—15-079.

[65] SI 2013/3134 ("2013 Regulations").

[66] An exception is found in the Consumer Rights Act 2015 ss.28 (delivery of goods) and 29 (passing of risk), which implement the Consumer Rights Directive 2011 arts 18 and 20 (which were formerly implemented by the 2013 Regulations regs 42 and 43): below paras 38-526—38-527. A further exception is that the 2015 Act gives contractual force to information supplied by a trader as required by the 2011 Directive art.6(5): 2015 Act s.11(4)–(5), 12 (goods contracts); s.36(3)–(4), 37 (digital content contracts); and s.50(3) and (4) (services contracts), on which see below, paras 38-499—38-500, 38-548—38-549 and 38-575 respectively.

[67] SI 2013/3134 Pt 4 see below, paras 38-061 et seq.

[68] Consumer Protection (Amendment) Regulations 2014 (SI 2014/870) inserting, notably, new Pt 4A Consumers' Rights to Redress in Consumer Protection from Unfair Trading Regulations 2008 (SI 2008/1277). Rights are also created for consumers in respect of payments which they have made: for the details see below paras 38-172 et seq.

mercial practice may enjoy a short-lived "right to unwind in respect of a business to consumer contract", a "right to a discount" and/or a right to damages.[69] These new consumer rights are related to the wider provisions governing unfair commercial practices from which they spring in the Consumer Protection from Unfair Trading Regulations 2008, but they are separate from the broader framework of consumer rights against traders established by the 2015 Act. Moreover, the rights to redress under the amended 2008 Regulations bear a complex relationship with traditional rights for contracting parties established by the common law[70] and by the Misrepresentation Act 1967.[71] These complexities, which will be explained below, are hardly welcome, even if the new provisions create rights for consumers which they would not otherwise enjoy.[72]

(iv) Special rules governing consumer contracts of insurance In parallel to these developments specifically relating to consumer protection and principally concerned with legislation implementing EU directives, the English and Scottish Law Commissions undertook a series of studies into the law governing misrepresentation and non-disclosure in contracts of insurance.[73] The first tranche of legislation resulting from their recommendations was the Consumer Insurance (Disclosure and Representations) Act 2012, which made new provision governing a consumer assured's duty of utmost good faith and the insurer's remedies for breach. The second tranche of legislation is the Insurance Act 2015, which, inter alia, abolishes the rule permitting a party to a contract of insurance to avoid the contract on the ground that the utmost good faith has not been observed by the other party,[74] sets out new rules governing non-consumer insurance contracts and supplements the 2012 Act's provisions governing consumer insurance contracts. These new provisions are discussed in Ch.42 (Insurance) of the present work.[75]

38-009

The relationship between "contract law" and prohibitions or preventive measures This chapter will follow the general approach of this work in focussing on "contract law" in the sense of the law which sets out the circumstances in which consumer contracts are concluded, the grounds of their invalidity and/or of the invalidity of their terms, the relative rights and obligations which they create for their parties, and the remedies which arise on their breach ("contract law" in the narrow and usual sense), rather than on the wider laws which regulate the behaviour of contracting parties, whether through structures such as the regulation of financial services, administrative powers of control and review or the criminal law.[76] However, in the case of consumer law, this contrast is blurred in a number of important ways, since modern consumer protection legislation has often combined rules governing contract law in the narrow sense (for example, providing a

38-010

---

[69] Consumer Protection from Unfair Trading Regulations 2008 Pt 4A.

[70] e.g. the relationship between the right to rescind a contract for misrepresentation and the "right to unwind" the contract for a misleading statement under the 2008 Regulations (as amended).

[71] e.g. the relationship between the rights to/possibility of award of damages for misrepresentation under the Misrepresentation Act 1967 s.2(1) and 2(2) and the right to damages in respect of a misleading statement under the 2008 Regulations (as amended).

[72] Below, paras 38-172 et seq.

[73] See below, para.42-045.

[74] Insurance Act 2015 s.13.

[75] See below, paras 42-030—42-032, 42-046—42-050.

[76] See Vol.I, para.1-001.

consumer with a right of cancellation of the contract, rendering unfair terms not binding on consumers, or creating special rights in respect of breach of contract) with preventive measures of the behaviour of traders with which these contract law rules are concerned.[77] Many of these preventive measures have been required by European directives which also set out the "contract law" consumer protection measures, and this combination has been relied on by the European Court of Justice as a reason for national courts having a duty to raise the issue of the consumer's protection of their own motion.[78] At the same time, the Unfair Commercial Practices Directive 2005, which requires a fully harmonised framework of the control of unfair commercial practices business-to-consumer distinguishes expressly between its own concern with the prohibition of unfair commercial practices and "contract law and, in particular, … the rules on the validity, formation or effect of a contract", this being the case whether those rules are EU or national,[79] though, as earlier indicated, UK law has recently chosen to enact legislation which provides rights to redress for consumers in respect of certain unfair commercial practices by traders.[80]

38-011 **The structure and scope of this chapter** This chapter will consider the law governing consumer contracts under the following headings: the relationship of EU and UK consumer contract law; definitions of consumer contract; information requirements and consumers' rights of cancellation; unfair commercial practices and the consumer's rights to redress; the control of unfair contract terms; and contracts for the supply of goods, digital content or services. This chapter will not discuss the law governing consumer credit agreements, which is discussed in Ch.39, nor, as already noted, rules governing consumer insurance contracts, which are discussed in Ch.42. Chapters 35 Carriage by Air and 36 Carriage by Land discuss the law governing these contracts including for the protection of passengers.[81] Moreover, the present chapter will not discuss the legislative and regulatory frameworks governing the provision of financial services put in place by the Financial Services and Markets Act 2000 and the Financial Services Act 2012.

38-012 **Changes in the law** The preceding paragraphs make clear that there has been very considerable change in the legislation governing consumer contracts in the course of the present decade. In general, this chapter will set out the law as it is in force at the time of writing,[82] with some reference to the earlier law where this is helpful to understand its development. However, in the case of the regulation of unfair contract terms and the special rules and remedies applicable to contracts for the sale of goods and related contracts, hire and contracts for the supply of services and (where the earlier law remains applicable to contracts entered into before October 1, 2015, when the relevant provisions in the Consumer Rights Act 2015

---

[77] See below, paras 38-132—38-134 (in relation to "off-premises contracts" and "distance contracts"); paras 38-353—38-364, 38-419—38-426 (unfair contract terms) and para.38-534 (remedies for non-conformity in the context of sale of goods, etc.).

[78] See below, para.38-019.

[79] Directive 2005/29 art.3(2), recital 9. cf. Consumer Rights Directive 2011 art.3(5) below, paras 38-063—38-065.

[80] Consumer Protection from Unfair Trading Regulations 2008 (SI 2008/1277) Pt 4A (as inserted by Consumer Protection (Amendment) Regulations 2014 (SI 2014/870) and see below, paras 38-172 et seq.

[81] See above, paras 35-071—35-073.

[82] i.e. July 31, 2018.

came into force)[83] this chapter will discuss first the old law (together with the important interpretation given to it both by the European Court of Justice and by English courts) and then the new law, highlighting similarities and differences with the earlier position.[84]

2. The Relationship of EU and UK Consumer Contract Law

(a) The Continuing Interpretative Significance of EU Directives

EU regulations and directives[85]   The vast majority of EU legislative instru-   **38-013**
ments governing the substantive law of consumer contracts has been in the form of directives rather than regulations,[86] unlike EU private international law which has been enacted by EU regulation.[87] As the European treaties have made clear, a regulation has "general application" and is "binding in its entirety and directly applicable in all Member States".[88] By contrast, a directive is "binding, as to the result to be achieved, upon each Member State to which it is addressed, but shall leave to the national authorities the choice of form and methods",[89] Use of directives by the EU legislator therefore allows a Member State a degree of leeway in terms of the juristic or procedural mechanisms by which it is to be implemented. This degree of choice in the "form and methods" of implementation of a directive must be distinguished from the question of whether it allows a Member State to go further than the directive requires, which, in the context of consumer protection, turns on the distinction between "minimum" and "full harmonisation" and on the scope of the particular instrument.[90] While the UK legislator's earlier approach to the implementation of EEC consumer protection law sought to take full advantage of the degree of leeway allowed by directives (as can be seen in the "domestication" of the Product Liability Directive's requirements by the Consumer Protection Act 1987),[91] from the 1990s the UK legislator generally preferred to take a more cau-

---

83   The Consumer Rights Act 2015 (Commencement No.3, Transitional Provisions, Savings and Consequential Amendments) Order 2015 (SI 2015/1630) art.3(a)–(c) (with the exceptions and qualifications made by arts 4 and 6 as amended by SI 2016/484 art.2(3)); see further below, paras 38-216, 38-366 and 38-437).

84   See below, paras 38-220—38-364, 38-365—38-426 and 38-432 et seq. respectively.

85   On the effects of the UK leaving the EU see above, para.38-005 and Vol.I, paras 1-014—1-018.

86   An example of an EU regulation creating rights for consumers (though not formally limited to consumers) is Regulation (EC) 261/2004 establishing common rules on compensation and assistance to passengers in the event of denied boarding and of cancellation or long delay of flights [2004] O.J. L46/1 (the "Denied Boarding Regulation"), on which see above, paras 35-045 et seq.

87   Notably, Regulation (EC) 593/2008 on the law applicable to contractual obligations ("Rome I") [2008] O.J. L177/6; Council Regulation 44/2001 on jurisdiction and the recognition and enforcement of judgments in civil and commercial matters [2001] O.J. L012/1 ("Brussels I Regulation") which was itself replaced by Regulation (EU) 1215/2012 of 12 December 2012 on jurisdiction and the recognition and enforcement of judgments in civil and commercial matters (recast) ("the Brussels I Ibis Regulation"); Regulation (EC) 864/2007 applicable to non-contractual obligations ("Rome II Regulation") [2007] O.J. L199/40 (some of whose provisions bear an important relationship with contract, notably art.12 "culpa in contrahendo").

88   art.288 TFEU (formerly art.249 EC).

89   art.288 TFEU (formerly art.249 EC).

90   Below, paras 38-022—38-028.

91   Directive 1985/374/EEC concerning liability for defective products. HL Deb. Vol.483 col. 851 (Lord Lucas) (government's purpose was "to make clear those of [1985 Directive's] provisions which are unfamiliar to our law or might otherwise give rise to debate").

tious route, sometimes following almost word for word the text of a directive, an approach sometimes known as "copy-out", of which the Unfair Terms in Consumer Contracts Regulations provide a well-known example.[92] An important exception to this general pattern (though not one which affects the rights of individual consumers) can be seen in relation to the measures put in place by the UK legislature for the enforcement of European consumer protection rules. Here, the various directives require Member States to put in place "adequate and effective means" for the prevention of the practices controlled by them (for example, the use by traders of unfair contract terms) and this has given Member States very considerable discretion as to the mechanisms by which they do so.[93] The Consumer Rights Act 2015 followed a similar route as regards the preventive and enforcement measures which it consolidated and reformed, but its provisions which set out the consumer's substantive rights against traders did not follow the earlier pattern of UK implementation and instead sought to integrate, at least to an extent, the European rules within earlier domestic legislative rules, while at the same time "improving" and adding to them so as to conform to UK consumer protection policy.[94]

38-014 **Significance of EU source of English consumer contract law for its interpretation** EU directives remain important even after their implementation into English law by statute or statutory instrument. This importance stems from the fact that as a matter of EU legal principle and of English judicial practice UK implementing legislation must "as far as possible" be interpreted by English courts so as to give effect not merely to the terms but also the purposes of a directive, this principle of conforming interpretation sometimes being said to lead to the "indirect effect" of directives.[95] Thus, where the terms of a directive (on their proper, i.e. EU, interpretation) have one significance, this must wherever possible prevail over any significance which is apparently intended by the words of the United Kingdom's implementing legislation.[96] The Court of Justice of the EU has recognised, however, that:

---

[92] Unfair Terms in Consumer Contracts Regulations 1994 (SI 1994/3159), which were revoked and replaced by the Unfair Terms in Consumer Contracts Regulations 1999 (SI 1999/2083) ("1999 Regulations"). For criticisms of "copy-out" in this context see Bright and Bright (1995) 111 L.Q.R. 655; Reynolds (1994) 111 L.Q.R. 1.

[93] e.g. Directive 93/13/EEC art.7; *Nemzeti Fogyasztóvédelmi Hatóság v Invitel Távközlési Zrt* (C-472/10) EU:C:2012:242, April 26, 2012 at para.38 and see below, paras 38-353—38-364.

[94] Below, paras 38-370—38-375.

[95] For the main European decisions see *Von Colson and Kammann v Land Nordrhein-Westfalen* (C-14/83) EU:C:1984:153 [1984] E.C.R. 1891, *Marleasing SA v La Comercial Internacionale de Alimentacion SA* (C-106/89) EU:C:1990:395, [1990] E.C.R. I-4135, *Pfeiffer v Deutsches Rotes Kreuz, Kreisverband Waldshut eV* (C-397–403/01) EU:C:2004:584, [2004] E.C.R. I-8835, *Schulte v Deutsche Bausparkasse Badenia AG* (C-350/03) EU:C:2005:637, [2005] E.C.R. I-9215 at para.71 and see Prechal, *Directives in EC Law*, 2nd edn (2005), Ch.8; Craig and De Búrca, *EU Law*, 6th edn (2015), pp.209 et seq. For the UK see in particular *Robertson v Swift* [2014] UKSC 50, [2014] 1 W.L.R. 3438 at [20]–[23] approving the summary of the impact of this principle by Sir Andrew Morritt, C. at *Vodafone 2 v Commissioners for Her Majesty's Revenue and Customers* [2010] Ch. 77 at [37]; *United States of America v Nolan* [2015] UKSC 63, [2016] A.C. 463 where Lord Mance (with whom Lord Neuberger of Abbotsbury, Baroness Hale of Richmond and Lord Reed agreed) at [14] described the principle of conforming interpretation as "a cardinal principle of European Union and domestic law".

[96] *Robertson v Swift* [2014] UKSC 50, [2014] 1 W.L.R. 3438 at [30]–[33] provides a good example of this in the context of the Cancellation of Contracts made in a Consumer's Home or Place of Work, etc. Regulations 2008 (SI 2008/1816) implementing the Doorstep Selling Directive 1985.

"... the obligation for a national court to refer to the content of a directive when interpreting and applying the relevant rules of domestic law is limited by general principles of law and cannot serve as the basis for an interpretation of national law *contra legem* [i.e. contrary to the clear words of the legislation]."[97]

Moreover, the Court of Justice has consistently held that "even a clear, precise and unconditional provision of a directive seeking to confer rights or impose obligations on individuals cannot of itself apply in proceedings exclusively between private parties".[98] So, in the usual case of a dispute arising from consumer contract law (which seeks to confer rights on consumers against traders), where an English court considers itself unable to interpret national implementing legislation so as to conform to the requirements of the underlying EU directive, then it must apply the national legislation even though this would lead to the UK being in breach of its Treaty obligations: in principle, directives do not have "horizontal effects".[99] Finally, where UK law does implement a EU directive, and the Court of Justice of the EU[100] has ruled on the meaning of or laid down principles in relation to that directive, UK courts must follow that ruling or those principles.[101]

"Autonomous" and national interpretations   In interpreting the terms of a direc-   **38-015**
tive, an important distinction is to be drawn according to whether the Court of Justice has treated or is likely to treat a particular issue as one on which a European view should be taken (giving rise to an "autonomous" or "independent" interpretation) or as one which should be left to the national laws of the Member States. For this purpose, the Court of Justice has stated that:

"According to settled case-law, the need for a uniform application of European Union law and the principle of equality require that the terms of a provision of European Union law which makes no express reference to the law of the Member States for the purpose of determining its meaning and scope must normally be given an independent and uniform interpretation throughout the European Union."[102]

For those issues where a particular legal concept is itself defined (at least in part) by a directive or regulation, it is clear that an "autonomous" interpretation is at least to this extent to be taken.[103] So, for example, in *Kásler* the Court of Justice held that

---

97   *Kásler v OTP Jelzálogbank Zrt* (C-26/13) EU:C:2014:282, April 30, 2014 para.65 (in the context of Directive 93/13 on unfair terms in consumer contracts).
98   *Faccini Dori v Recreb Srl* (C-91/92) EU:C:1994:292, [1994] E.C.R. I-03325 paras 22–25 (in the context of the consumer's right of cancellation under the Doorstep Selling Directive 85/577/EEC); *Association de médiation sociale v Union locale des syndicats CGT* (C-176/12) EU:C:2014:2, January 15, 2014, para.36.
99   *Marshall v Southampton and South-West Hampshire Area Health Authority* (152/84) EU:C:1986:84, [1986] E.C.R. 723 para.48; Craig and De Búrca, *EU Law*, 6th edn (2015) pp.200–209.
100 Formerly the European Court of Justice.
101 European Communities Act 1972 s.3(1).
102 *Ekro BV Vee- en Vleeshandel v Produktschap voor Vee en Vlees* (C-327/82) EU:C:1984:11; [1984] E.C.R. 00107 para.11; *UsedSoft GmbH v Oracle International Corp* (C-128/11) EU:C:2012:407 para.39 and see similarly *Infopaq International* (C-5/08) EU:C:2009:465, [2009] E.C.R. I-6569 para.27; *Stichting ter Exploitatie van Naburige Rechten (SENA) v Nederlandse Omroep Stichting (NOS)* (C-245/00) EU:C:2003:68, [2003] E.C.R. I-1251 para.23; *BKK Mobil Oil Körperschaft des öffentlichen Rechts v Zentrale zur Bekämpfung unlauteren Wettbewerbs eV* (C-59/12) EU:C:2013:634, October 3, 2013 para.25.
103 Other examples of the ECJ/CJEU taking autonomous interpretations of concepts in EU consumer directives may be found in *easyCar (UK) Ltd v Office of Fair Trading* (C-336/03) EU:C:2005:150;

the terms used by art.4(2) of the Directive on unfair terms in consumer contracts (which create an exclusion from its general test of unfairness) must be given an autonomous interpretation, and the Court then set out "the criteria that the national court may or must apply when examining a contractual term" for this purpose.[104] In some contexts in constructing such an autonomous interpretation, the Court of Justice may rely on academic instruments setting out "European contract law"[105] on the basis that these reflect principles common to the laws of Member States.[106] However, as the passage from the Court of Justice recognises, the Court's development of autonomous interpretations of concepts used by EU legislation finds an exception in the case of provisions which expressly refer to the law of the Member States for the purpose of determining its meaning and scope. An important example of this may be found in context of consumer contracts in the Consumer Rights Directive 2011 art.3(5) of which states that:

"This Directive shall not affect national general contract law such as the rules on the validity, formation or effect of a contract, in so far as general contract law aspects are not regulated in this Directive."

As will be explained, this rather opaque provision is intended to allocate the interpretation of *some* of the "contract law" concepts used by the Directive to national law, even though the Directive requires the enactment of contract law rules.[107] Moreover, even in the absence of a provision such as art.3(5) of the 2011 Directive, the Court of Justice may depart from its normal approach requiring an autonomous interpretation as regards some concepts used by a directive, principally

---

[2005] E.C.R. I-1947 paras 20–24 ("contract for the provision of transport services" under Directive 97/7/EC on the protection of consumers in respect of distance contracts art.3(2)); *Leitner v TUI Deutschland GmbH & Co KG* (C-168/00) EU:C:2002:163, [2002] E.C.R. I-02631 ("damage" for the purposes of Directive 90/314/EEC of 13 June 1990 on package travel, package holidays and package tours art.5); *Wallentin-Hermann v Alitalia-Linee Aeree Italiane SpA* (C-549/07) EU:C:2008:771, [2008] E.C.R. I-11061 ("extraordinary circumstances" for the purposes of the Denied Boarding Regulation).

104 *Kásler v OTP Jelzálogbank Zrt* (C-26/13) EU:C:2014:282, April 30, 2014 at paras 38, 45–51 and see below, paras 38-250—38-251.

105 Notably, Lando and Beale (eds) *Principles of European Contract Law* Pts I and II (1999), Lando, Clive, Prüm and Zimmermann, *Principles of European Contract Law* Pt III (2003); *Principles, Definitions and Model Rules of European Private Law, Draft Common Frame of Reference* (DCFR) prepared by the Study Group on a European Civil Code and the Research Group on EC Private Law (Acquis Group), 2010, six volumes. Although subsequently withdrawn by the EU Commission, the CJEU could nevertheless take into account the Proposal for a Regulation on a Common European Sales Law COM(2011) 635 final, whose Annex I setting out a Common European Sales Law ("CESL") contains provisions on many issues applicable to contracts generally. On the CESL and its possible remaining significance see Vol.I, para.1-013.

106 See, e.g. *Masdar (UK) Ltd v EC Commission* (T-333/03) [2007] 2 All E.R. (Comm) 261 where the Court of First Instance accepted reference to the work of the *Study Group on a European Civil Code* in order to develop a EU law of restitution for unjustified enrichment under art.288 (formerly 215) EC; *Hamilton v Volksbank Filder eG* (C-412/06) EU:C:2008:215 (A.G. Poires Maturo at para.24 referring to time limits for the exercise of a right as being a "principle common to the laws of the Member States" and citing the possible future DCFR); A.G. Trstenjak's reference to art.167(3) CESL in the context of the 1993 Directive in *Banco Español de Crédito SA v Calderón Camino* (C-618/10) EU:C:2012:349, para.42.

107 See below, paras 38-063—38-065. Identical provision to art.3(5) of the 2011 Directive is found in Directive (EU) 2015/2302 on package travel and linked travel arrangements [2015] O.J. L326/1 art.2(3) (this Directive repeals and replaces Directive 90/314/EEC on package travel, package holidays and package tours [1990] O.J. L158/59). On this see below, paras 38-142—38-147.

on the ground of the difficulty of construction of an autonomous interpretation (as may be the case for the definition of "contract" itself).[108] Where this is the case, the Court may allow national legislation or national courts to take their own view of the meaning of a concept, subject in particular to the principle of the effectiveness of the protection for consumers.[109]

Interpretative approach of Court of Justice   As is well known, the Court of   **38-016**
Justice of the EU takes a less literal and more teleological approach to the interpretation of legislation than is traditional in English law, this meaning that the purposes of a directive, especially as set out in its recitals, must be kept in mind in resolving any question of interpretation of its provisions.[110] Furthermore, the recitals to directives often seek to explain provisions in their main text and the Court of Justice takes these explanations into account in its interpretation of the text, although it will not allow the recitals to contradict that text.[111] So, for example, the text of the Consumer Rights Directive of 2011 follows earlier European legislative practice in providing that:

"... 'consumer' means any natural person who, in contracts covered by this Directive, is acting for purposes which are outside his trade, business, craft or profession."[112]

However, recital 17 of the Directive glosses this definition by adding that:

"... in the case of dual purpose contracts, where the contract is concluded for purposes partly within and partly outside the person's trade and the trade purpose is so limited as not to be predominant in the overall context of the contract, that person should also be considered as a consumer."

Given the interpretative significance given by the Court of Justice to a directive's recitals, the definition in the text of the 2011 Directive must therefore be read subject to this gloss.[113] The Court may also take into account the *travaux préparatoires* of a regulation or directive in interpreting its provisions.[114] Moreover, the different language versions of regulations and directives are equally authoritative and so recourse may need to be had at times to language versions other than

---

[108] See below, paras 38-229—38-230.
[109] cf. e.g. *Veedfald v Århus Amtskommune* (C-203/99) EU:C:2001:258, [2001] E.C.R. I-03569 at para.27 (in the context of Directive 85/374/EEC concerning liability for defective products [1985] O.J. L210/29 art.9).
[110] See, e.g. in the context of the Denied Boarding Regulation *Sturgeon v Condor Flugdienst GmbH* (C-402/07 and C-432/07) EU:C:2009:716, [2009] E.C.R. I-10923 paras 40–42.
[111] *Société d'Importation Edouard Leclerc-Siplec v TF1 Publicité SA* (412/93) EU:C:1995:26, [1995] E.C.R. I-00179 at paras 45–47.
[112] Directive 2011/83/EU on consumer rights, art.2(1). See similarly Directive 93/13/EEC on unfair terms in consumer contracts art.2(b) (in the same terms, except without reference to "craft").
[113] This is the case in the context of the UK's implementation of the Consumer Rights Directive 2011 which defines "consumer" explicitly in this way: 2013 Regulations reg.4; Consumer Rights Act 2015 s.2(3) and see below, para.38-041. It remains a more controversial question whether this gloss on the standard definition of "consumer" should and would be read over to *other* EU secondary legislation: below, para.38-036.
[114] Schönberg and Frick (2003) 28 *European Law Review* 149. For a recent example in the consumer law context see *Faber v Autobedrijf Hazet Ochten BV* (C-497/13) EU:C:2015:357, June 4, 2015 at paras 54, 61 and 72 (referring to the European Commission's explanatory memorandum to the proposal for the Consumer Sales Directive 1999, COM(95) 520 final).

English.[115] The Court of Justice also takes in account wider EU legal principle (such as the principles of legal certainty, effectiveness or the "principle of the procedural autonomy" of national laws[116]); and more recently, it has also taken into account relevant provisions of the Charter of Fundamental Rights of the European Union.[117] Finally, as part of its seeking to interpret every provision of EU law in the light of EU law as a whole,[118] the Court of Justice sometimes takes into account its case-law interpreting a concept in one context in deciding the interpretation of the same or a similar concept in another. This quest for consistency of interpretation can be seen in relation to some of its decisions in the area of EU consumer contract law.[119]

38-017   Interpretation, application and "guidance" by the Court of Justice   While in principle the Court of Justice holds that the interpretation of EU law is ultimately for itself, it recognises that the application of EU law is for national courts, a division of function reflected in the preliminary ruling procedure by which a national court may or, where a question of interpretation is raised in a case before a national court "against whose decisions there is no judicial remedy under national law", must ask the Luxembourg court for its interpretative view.[120] However, the line between interpretation and application can be blurred, especially in the case of evaluative concepts such as the "unfairness of a contract term" (as set out in the Unfair Terms in Consumer Contracts Directive 1993). In this particular context, the approach of the Court of Justice was for long quite restrained, holding that while it:

"... may interpret general criteria used by the Community legislation in order to define the concept of unfair terms ... it should not rule on the application of these general criteria to a particular term, which must be considered in the light of the particular circumstances of the case in question."[121]

However, while still formally adhering to this position, since 2011 the Court has chosen to explain in some detail the considerations that a national court should take into account in applying the test of unfairness, by way of "guidance".[122] The Court

---

[115] *Srl CILFIT and Lanificio di Gavardo SpA v Ministry of Health* (C-283/81) EU:C:1982:335, [1982] E.C.R. 03415 at para.18; *Kyocera Electronics Europe GmbH v Hauptzollamt Krefeld* (C-152/01) EU:C:2003:623, [2003] E.C.R. I-13821 at paras 32–33 and see below, para.38-051 ("trader").

[116] e.g. *Asturcom Telecommunicaciones SL v Rodríquez Nogueira* (C-40/08) EU:C:2009:615, [2009] E.C.R. I-9579, below para.38-333.

[117] e.g. *Asociación de Consumidores Independientes de Castilla y León v Anuntis Segundamano España SL* (C-413/12) EU:C:2013:800.

[118] *Srl CILFIT and Lanificio di Gavardo SpA v Ministry of Health* (C-283/81) EU:C:1982:335, [1982] E.C.R. 03415 at para.20.

[119] e.g. *BKK Mobil Oil Körperschaft des öffentlichen Rechts v Zentrale zur Bekämpfung unlauteren Wettbewerbs eV* (C-59/12) EU:C:2013:634, October 3, 2013 at [33]–[35] where the CJEU analogised between definitions of "consumer" for the purposes of Directive 2005/29/EC concerning unfair business-to-consumer commercial practices [2005] O.J. L149/22 art.2(b) and the Brussels Convention on Jurisdiction and the Enforcement of Foreign Judgments in Civil and Commercial Matters of September 27, 1968 art.13 (jurisdiction on consumer contracts).

[120] art.267 TFEU (formerly art.177 EC). The most important qualification on the duty to refer is found in the doctrine of *acte clair*, where "the correct application of Community law [is] so obvious as to leave no scope for any reasonable doubt as to the manner in which the question raised is to be resolved": *Srl CILFIT and Lanificio di Gavardo SpA v Ministry of Health* (283/81) EU:C:1982:335, [1982] E.C.R. 03415 at para.16; Craig and De Búrca, *EU Law*, 6th edn (2015) 500–501.

[121] *Freiburger Kommunalbauten GmbH Baugesellschaft & Co KG v Hofstetter* (C-237/02) EU:C:2004:209, [2004] 2 C.M.L.R. 13 at para.22.

[122] *Pereničová v SPS finance spol. sro* (C-453/10) EU:C:2012:144, para.44; *Nemzeti Fogyasztóvédelmi*

has taken a similar view of other provisions within the Unfair Terms in Consumer Contracts Directive, so in *Matei v SC Volksbank România SA* the Court ruled, in relation to the exclusion from the test of unfairness of terms which reflect the main subject matter of the contract and in relation to the price/quality ratio in art.4(2),[123] that:

"... although it is for the national court alone to rule on the classification of [the relevant terms] in accordance with the particular circumstances of the case, the fact remains that the Court has jurisdiction to elicit from the provisions of Directive 93/13, in this case the provisions of Article 4(2), the criteria that the national court may or must apply when examining a contractual term."[124]

Approach of English courts English courts have sought to follow the interpreta- **38-018** tive practice of the Court of Justice and, where necessary or helpful, look at the recitals to a directive as an aid to its interpretation,[125] consider other language versions of its text,[126] and, of course, apply the interpretations and guidance of the Court of Justice in their own decision-making.[127] In the following discussion, therefore, while primary reference will be made to the UK legislation implementing an EU directive in English law on the general assumption that it reflects that directive, where necessary reference will be made to this wider body of authoritative material.

The duty of national courts to intervene of their own motion to protect EU **38-019** **consumer rights** In a series of cases starting with *Océano Grupo Editorial*, the European Court of Justice has held that national courts have both a power and a duty to raise of their own motion the question of the unfairness of a term in a consumer contract falling within the Unfair Terms in Consumer Contracts Directive,[128] as long as the national court "has available to it the legal and factual elements necessary

---

Hatóság v Invitel Távközlési Zrt (C-472/10) EU:C:2012:242 at para.22; *RWE Vertrieb AG v Verbraucherzentrale Nordrhein-Westfalen eV* (C-92/11) EU:C:2013:180, para.48; *Aziz v Caixa d'Estalvis de Catalunya, Tarragona i Manresa* (C-415/11) EU:C:2013:164 at para.66; *Constructora Principado SA v Menéndez Álvarez* (C-226/12) EU:C:2014:10, January 16, 2014 at para.20; *Sebestyén v Kővári* (C-342/13) EU:C:2014:1857, April 3, 2014, para.25. See further below, paras 38 270—38-271, 38-278 and 38-314.

[123] Below, paras 38-245 et seq.
[124] *Matei v SC Volksbank România SA* (C-143/13) EU:C:2015:127, February 26, 2015, para.53, referring to *Kásler v OTP Jelzálogbank Zrt* (C-26/13) EU:C:2014:282, April 30, 2014 para.45.
[125] *Freiburger Kommunalbauten GmbH Baugesellschaft & Co KG v Hofstetter* (C-237/02) EU:C:2004:209, [2004] 2 C.M.L.R. 13 at para.22 (unfair contract terms). For examples in the English courts see: *Director General of Fair Trading v First National Bank Plc* [2001] UKHL 52, [2002] 1 A.C. 481 (Unfair Terms in Consumer Contracts Directive 1993); *Sean Titshall v Qwerty Travel Ltd* [2011] EWCA Civ 1569, [2011] C.T.L.C. 219 at [5] (Package Travel Directive 1990)
[126] e.g. Lord Rodger of Earlsferry's discussion of the German and French texts of art.4(2) of Directive 93/13/EEC in *Director General of Fair Trading v First National Bank Plc* [2001] UKHL 52 at [64].
[127] e.g. *Robertson v Swift* [2014] UKSC 50, [2014] 1 W.L.R. 3238 at [23]–[24], [27]–[28]; *ParkingEye Ltd v Beavis* [2015] UKSC 67, [2015] 3 W.L.R. 1373 at [105]–[106], [208] and [308] (although the learned Justices of the SC differed as to the proper application of the CJEU's case-law): see below, paras 38-275—38-277.
[128] *Océano Grupo Editorial SA v Murciano Quintero* (C-240/98 to C-244/98) EU:C:2000:346, [2000] E.C.R. I-4941; *Mostaza Claro v Centro Móvil Milenium SL* (C-168/05) EU:C:2006:675, [2006] E.C.R. I-10421. On this case-law see below, paras 38-331—38-335. For a general discussion of these questions see Whittaker in Leczykiewicz and Weatherill (eds) *The Involvement of EU Law in Private Relationships* (2013) Ch.6.

for that task".[129] This position is justified by the Court by the need to ensure that the consumer enjoys effective protection in view of the real risk that he is unaware of his rights or encounters difficulties in enforcing them.[130] This line of cases appeared at first to be distinct from the Court's general case-law governing the question whether a national court must raise an issue of EU law of its own motion under *Van Schijndel*,[131] according to which national procedural rules on this question must not be less favourable than those governing similar domestic actions nor render virtually impossible or excessively difficult the exercise of rights conferred by EU law.[132] Moreover, in *Rampion*[133] the Court of Justice extended this special judicial protection for consumers, holding that a national court must have the power to raise the rights of the consumer under the Consumer Credit Directive 1986[134] of its own motion, given that that directive's purpose was to ensure the creation of a common consumer credit market and the protection of consumers.[135] On the other hand, in *Martín Martín* the Court held that a national court of appeal may, of its own motion, declare void a contract which infringes the Doorstep Selling Directive's provisions on consumer protection,[136] even though the issue had not been raised at first instance,[137] but in doing so it preferred to follow its approach in *Van Schijndel*, seeing this limitation on the power of national courts as "justified by the principle that, in a civil suit, it is for the parties to take the initiative, and that, as a result, the court is able to act of its own motion only in exceptional cases where the public interest requires intervention".[138] According to the Court, the Doorstep Selling Directive 1985 seeks to redress the imbalance and, therefore, disadvantage with which consumers, as "weaker parties" are faced with in the circumstances of doorstep selling by providing them with a right of cancellation, notice of which the business must give to them.[139] This notice of the consumer's rights "plays a central role in the overall scheme of the directive ... for the exercise of that right and, therefore,

---

[129] *Pannon GSM Zrt v Erzsébet Sustikné Győrfi* (C-243/08) EU:C:2009:350, [2009] E.C.R. I-4713 at para.32; *Bucura v SC Bancpost SA* (C-348/14) EU:C:2015:447, July 9, 201 para.44. On the possibility that a Member State may incur liability for a court's failure to protect a consumer's EU law rights see *Tomášová v Republic of Slovenská* (C-168/15) EU:C:2016:602 July 28 2016, below, para.38-331.

[130] *Océano Grupo Editorial SA v Murciano Quintero* (C-240/98 to C-244/98) EU:C:2000:346 at para.26.

[131] *Van Schijndel v Stichting Pensioenfonds voor Fysiotherapeuten* (C-430/93 and C-431/93) EU:C:1995:441, [1995] E.C.R. I-4705 ("*Van Schijndel* (C-430/93 and C-431/93)"); *Peterbroeck, Van Campenhout & Cie SCS v Belgium* (C-312/93) EU:C:1995:437; [1995] E.C.R. I-4599; *Heemskerk BV and Firma Schaap v Productschap Vee en Vlees* (C-455/06) EU:C:2008:650, [2008] E.C.R. I-08763.

[132] *Van Schijndel* (C-430/93 and C-431/93) at para.17.

[133] *Rampion v Franfinance SA* (C-429/05) EU:C:2007:575, [2007] E.C.R. I-8017 ("*Rampion* (C-429/05)").

[134] Directive 87/102/EEC [1987] O.J. L42/48.

[135] *Rampion* (C-429/05) at para.59; *Radlinger v Finway a.s.* (C-377/14) EU:C:2016:283, April 21, 2016 at paras 62–74 (information duties) and see below, para.38-068.

[136] Directive 85/577/EEC. The Directive itself requires only that the consumer be given a right of cancellation of the contract, but the Court held that a national court was entitled to declare a contract void in these circumstances: first, because the Directive allows national authorities a discretion in determining the consequences which follow the infringement in question; and second, because the Directive puts in place only a minimum level of harmonisation: *Martín Martín v EDP Editores SL* (C-227/08) EU:C:2009:792, [2009] E.C.R. I-11939, paras 32–33. On this directive generally and its replacement by the Consumer Rights Directive 2011 see below, paras 38-059—38-060.

[137] *Martín Martín v EDP Editores SL* (C-227/08) EU:C:2009:792, [2009] E.C.R. I-11939, para.18.

[138] C-227/08 para.20.

[139] C-227/08 paras 21–26.

for the effectiveness of consumer protection sought by the Community legislature"[140]: positive intervention allows the national court to "compensate for the imbalance between the consumer and the trader" in the context.[141] More recently, this approach has been adopted by the Court in the context of the Unfair Contract Terms Directive itself[142] as well as to the availability of different rights for the consumer in respect of non-conformity of goods bought under the Consumer Sales Directive 1999.[143]

A wider duty to request information from parties? In *Faber v Autobedrijf* **38-020**
Hazet Ochten BV[144] the Court of Justice of the EU considered whether a national court has a duty to consider of its own motion whether a party to a contract subject to a dispute was a "consumer", so as to attract the application of national legislation implementing that directive. In doing so, the Court followed its own general approach under *Van Schijndel*, so as to subject any national procedural rules to the principles of equivalence and effectiveness.[145] According to the Court:

> "In that regard, it is, in principle, for the national court, for the purpose of identifying the legal rules applicable to a dispute which has been brought before it, to assign a legal classification to the facts and acts on which the parties rely in support of their claims. That legal classification is a prerequisite in a case in which, like that in the main proceedings, the guarantee or warranty in respect of the goods sold, on which the applicant is relying, may be governed by different rules depending on the purchaser's status. Such a classification does not, in itself, imply that the court is, of its own motion, exercising a discretion, but merely that it is establishing and ascertaining whether there is a statutory condition which determines the applicable legal rule."[146]

This view reflects a general approach in many continental national procedural laws according to which it is the role of a civil court to classify the facts and transactions ("acts"[147]) on which parties base their claims following the principle *iura novit curia* ("the court knows the law"), but it contrasts sharply with the approach of the common law generally (and English law in particular) where in principle it is for the parties to characterise in legal terms the basis of their claims.[148] Following *Van*

---

[140] C-227/08 para.27.
[141] C-227/08 para.28.
[142] *Banif Plus Bank Zrt v Csipai* (C-472/11) EU:C:2013:88; [2013] W.L.R. (D) 76 at para.27; *Asturcom Telecommunicaciones SL v Rodriquez Nogueira* (C-40/08) EU:C:2009:615, [2009] E.C.R. I-9579, below, para.38-333. See also *Margarit Panicello v Hernández Martínez* (C-503/15) EU:C:2017:126, A.G. Opinion of September 15, 2016 at [127]–[128] (the CJEU judgment of February 16, 2017 did not comment on these issues).
[143] Directive 1999/44/EEC; *Duarte Hueros v Autociba SSA and Automóviles Citroen España SA* (C-32/12) EU:C:2013:637, [2014] 1 C.M.L.R. 53 especially at paras 31–43 (in the context of a national rule denying a court the power recognise the consumer's right to reduction of the price on the ground of non-conformity where the consumer had claimed unsuccessfully rescission of the contract). cf. *Radlinger v Finway a.s.* (C-377/14) EU:C:2016:283, April 21, 2016 at paras 62–74 where the CJEU recognised an obligation on the national court to consider whether the information duties of the trader under the Consumer Credit Directive 2008 had been complied with simply by reference to the need to ensure the protection of the consumer and to its earlier case-law.
[144] C-497/13 EU:C:2015:357, June 4, 2015 ("*Faber* (C-497/13)").
[145] *Van Schijndel v Stichting Pensioenfonds voor Fysiotherapeuten* (C-430/93 and C-431/93) EU:C:1995:441, [1995] E.C.R. I-4705 above, para.38-019.
[146] *Faber* (C-497/13) at para.38.
[147] cf. the French version of para.38, which refers to "*faits et actes*".
[148] See generally Whittaker in Leczykiewicz and Weatherill (eds), *The Involvement of EU Law in*

Schijndel, the Court of Justice did not treat the court's duty here to be one governed merely by national law to be applied in the EU law context by way of application of the principle of equivalence,[149] but rather one which may need to reflect the principle of effectiveness:

"... the principle of effectiveness requires a national court before which a dispute relating to a contract which may be covered by that directive has been brought to determine whether the purchaser may be classified as a consumer, even if the purchaser has not expressly claimed to have that status, as soon as that court has at its disposal the matters of law and of fact that are necessary for that purpose *or may have them at its disposal simply by making a request for clarification*."[150]

To decide otherwise would be "tantamount to making the consumer subject to the obligation to carry out a full classification of his situation himself, failing which he would lose the rights which the EU legislature intended to confer on him" by the 1999 Directive.[151] As will be seen, from the point of view of English law the radical element here is the requirement that, where a national court cannot on the facts as otherwise available to it determine whether a case before it falls within the scope of national legislation implementing an EU consumer protection directive, it may be required as a matter of EU law to request a party to clarify the factual position so as to be able to do so.[152]

38-021 **Significance for English law** In the context of the regulation of unfair contract terms, the significance of the case-law following *Océano Grupo Editorial*[153] has long been recognised and this has now been given legislative expression in the UK by the Consumer Rights Act 2015 which provides that, in proceedings before a court which relate to a term of a consumer contract[154]:

"The court must consider whether the term is fair even if none of the parties to the proceedings has raised that issue or indicated that it intends to raise it"[155]

provided that:

"... the court considers that it has before it sufficient legal and factual material to enable it to consider the fairness of the term."[156]

Private Relationships (2013) Ch.6.
[149] *Faber* (C-497/13) at para.39.
[150] *Faber* (C-497/13) at para.46 (emphasis added).
[151] *Faber* (C-497/13) at para.44. For this purpose, the Court held that it is irrelevant whether or not a consumer is assisted by a lawyer: *Faber* (C-497/13) at para.47.
[152] cf. the more cautious approach of A.G. Sharpston, advising that the national court should not have a duty to go beyond the ambit of the dispute as defined by the parties and not, therefore, where the legal and factual elements are neither already part of the file or are obtainable in accordance with *national* procedural law: Opinion in *Faber* (C-497/13) of November 27, 2014, especially at paras 70–73.
[153] *Océano Grupo Editorial SA v Murciano Quintero* (C-240/98 to C-244/98) EU:C:2000:346, [2000] E.C.R. I-4941.
[154] Consumer Rights Act 2015 s.71(1) and see below, para.38-392 in particular on the question whether restricting the court's duty to the situation where "proceedings before a court *relate to* a term of a consumer contract" is compatible with the case-law of the CJEU.
[155] Consumer Rights Act 2015 s.71(2).
[156] Consumer Rights Act 2015 s.71(3).

Outside this context, the UK legislation (primary and secondary) which implements EU consumer contract directives does not refer to any power or duty in courts to raise the issue of any rights which the consumer may have under EU law of their own motion. However, given the case-law in *Rampion*,[157] *Martín Martín*,[158] and *Faber v Autobedrijf Hazet Ochten BV*,[159] it is clear that a court in England and Wales may have a duty to raise of its own motion the issue of whether a party to proceedings is a "consumer" and, if so, what rights he or she may enjoy under the legislation implementing EU consumer contract law subject principally to the condition that the right is important for the effectiveness of the particular consumer protection which is foreseen by the EU directive; and a court may even be required to request a party to clarify the facts to do so.

(b) The Intensity of Harmonisation Required by EU Legislation

"Minimum harmonisation" As earlier noted, earlier European directives seeking to harmonise consumer contract law did so in a way which explicitly required only "minimum harmonisation". The typical example[160] may be found in the case of the Unfair Terms in Consumer Contracts Directive 1993, art.8 of which allows Member States to

38-022

> "... adopt or retain the most stringent provisions compatible with the Treaty in the area covered by this Directive, to ensure a maximum degree of protection for the consumer."

Provision to this effect has consequences for the lawfulness of any national extension of protections as a matter of EU. For example, in *Caja de Madrid*[161] the Court of Justice held that Spanish legislation implementing the 1993 Directive in a way which does not include the exclusion from the requirement of fairness of terms provided by art.4(2) of the 1993 Directive is compatible with that Directive and with EU law more generally, as the exclusion falls within the "material scope" of the Directive and therefore within art.8's minimum harmonisation clause.[162] As regards the condition in art.8 of the Directive that any such extension of the protection of consumers must be "compatible with the Treaty", the Court of Justice ruled that the

---

[157] *Rampion v Franfinance SA* (C-429/05) EU:C:2007:575, [2007] E.C.R. I-8017.

[158] Directive 85/577/EEC; *Martín Martín v EDP Editores SL* (C-227/08) EU:C:2009:792, [2009] E.C.R. I-11939 paras 32–33.

[159] C-497/13 EU:C:2015:357, above, para.38-020.

[160] This was seen as the typical example by the ECJ in *Commission v France* (C-52/00) EU:C:2002:252, [2002] E.C.R. I-3827, April 25, 2002 at para.18 (where Directive 85/374/EEC on liability for defective products was held to require "complete harmonisation").

[161] *Caja de Ahorros y Monte de Piedad de Madrid v Asociación de Usuarios de Servicios Bancarios (Ausbanc)* (C-484/08) EU:C:2010:309, [2010] E.C.R. I-04785 ("*Caja de Madrid* (C-484/08)"). The CJEU has also accepted that national legislation which prohibits the terms listed in the annex to the 1993 Directive (a "black list") rather than constituting an "indicative list" (a "grey list") is also compatible with EU law given the minimum harmonisation foreseen by that Directive: *Matei v SC Volksbank România SA* (C-143/13) EU:C:2015:127, February 26, 2015, paras 60–61.

[162] *Caja de Madrid* (C-484/08) at paras 30–35. For an example in the UK context see *Robertson v Swift* [2014] UKSC 50, [2014] 1 W.L.R. 3438 at [18] approving in this respect the decision of the CA sub. nom. *Swift v Robinson* [2013] EWCA Civ 1794, [2013] Bus. L.R. 479 at [48]–[54] (holding intra vires the extension by UK regulations made under the European Communities Act 1972 s.2(2) so as to include contracts made when a trader visits the consumer's house at the latter's request which was not required by the Doorstep Selling Directive 85/577/EEC (the SC reversed the CA's decision on other grounds).

Treaty provisions cited for this purpose by one of the parties to the national litigation as precluding the omission of art.4(2) of the Directive from its national implementing legislation did not give rise to clear and unconditional obligations on Member States and therefore could not have this effect.[163] As a result, in principle, art.8 allows Member States to extend the scheme of control required by the 1993 Directive where these fall within the "material scope" of the Directive, that is to say, "the laws, regulations and administrative provisions of the Member States relating to unfair terms in contracts concluded between a seller or supplier and a consumer"[164] with the exception of "contractual terms which reflect mandatory statutory or regulatory provisions and the provisions or principles of international conventions to which the Member States or the Community are party".[165] However, the power of national legislatures to extend the protection set out by minimum harmonisation directives does not mean that issues not expressly covered by a directive remain within in the competence of national legislatures and, therefore, national law, at least if the issue is implicitly covered by the Directive as correctly interpreted. So, for example, in *Leitner* the European Court of Justice rejected the argument that the lack of the inclusion of "non-material damage" (notably, loss of enjoyment) as a damage for which a package tour operator is responsible under the Package Travel Directive 1990 in cases where it has failed to perform its contract with the consumer does not mean that the issue of the recoverability of "non-material damage" was within the competence of national legislatures, holding instead that "damage" must be interpreted as including "non-material damage" in this context.[166]

38-023   **"Minimum harmonisation" and national legislation beyond the scope of the instrument**   The power recognised by a "minimum harmonisation" clause in a EU directive to maintain or introduce stricter provisions to extend the protection for consumers is restricted to the scope of that directive.[167] However, after the enactment of a directive, in principle Member States remain competent to enact laws outside its scope, subject to any other EU law obligation to the contrary. To give a very clear example, the enactment of the (minimum harmonisation) Unfair Terms in Consumer Contracts Directive did not (and does not) prevent Member States from enacting rules to govern unfair terms in contracts falling outside its scope, notably, commercial contracts or contracts between two private individuals neither of whom are acting in the course of business, as is the case in English law in the Unfair Contract Terms Act 1977. Moreover, there is no reason why a Member State should not for this purpose adopt the regulatory framework used by a directive.[168]

---

[163] *Caja de Madrid* (C-484/08) at paras 45–49 in relation to arts 2, 3(1)(g), 4(1) EC. See also *Buet v Ministère public* (C-382/87) EU:C:1989:198, [1989] E.C.R. 1235; *Gysbrechts and Santurel Inter BVBA* (C-205/07) EU:C:2008:730, [2008] E.C.R. I-09947. cf. *Alemo-Herron v Parkwood Leisure Ltd* (C-426/11) EU:C:2013:521 especially at para.32 qualifying the impact of a "minimum harmonisation" clause in Directive 2001/23 relating to the safeguarding of employees' rights in the event of transfers of undertakings, businesses or parts of undertakings or businesses [2001] O.J. L82/16 arts 3(1) and (8) by reference to art.16 of the EU Charter of Fundamental Right which "covers, inter alia, freedom of contract", on which see Vol.I para.1-034.

[164] 1993 Directive art.1(1).

[165] 1993 Directive art.1(2), on which see below, paras 38-233—38-240.

[166] *Leitner v TUI Deutschland GmbH & Co KG* (C-168/00) EU:C:2002:163, [2002] E.C.R. I-02631 paras 16, 23 and 24.

[167] *Caja de Madrid* (C-484/08) paras 29–35.

[168] e.g. *Di Pinto* (C-361/89) EU:C:1991:118, [1991] E.C.R. I-01189 at para.22 (national extension of

Examples of "minimum harmonisation" directives   Apart from the 1993 Direc-   **38-024**
tive, a number of EU legislative instruments in the area of consumer contract law
still require only "minimum harmonisation", notably, the Consumer Sales Directive 1999,[169] and the Denied Boarding Regulation.[170]

"Full harmonisation"   In the later 1990s the European Commission became dis-   **38-025**
satisfied with the effect of "minimum harmonisation" as a tool for the development of the internal market, seeing the extensions of protection for consumers (and
others) by national laws which this allows as creating "legal fragmentation"
between those laws and, therefore, distortions in competition and inhibitions to the
development of the internal market.[171] The Commission has therefore sought to
move from minimum harmonisation to "full harmonisation" both as regards areas
already covered by EU legislation and in new areas of EU legislative intervention.
In the context of consumer law, "full harmonisation" requires Member States to put
in place the rights which the relevant instrument requires for their protection, but
it prohibits Member States from going further than these requirements and putting
in place stricter consumer protection. This means that a directive held to require
"full harmonisation" will not merely prohibit Member States from enacting
implementing legislation which goes beyond the instrument's requirements, but will
also require them to cut down any existing national rules for the protection of
consumers which do so. Here, therefore, the "material scope" of the EU legislative instrument becomes of crucial importance, for any "full harmonisation"
required by it applies only within the scope of the instrument and not beyond it. For
example, in 2002 the Court of Justice held that the Product Liability Directive
1985[172] required "complete harmonisation" of national laws within its scope.[173] In
its implementing legislation France had imposed liability on producers in respect
of damage to property caused by their defective products without the restrictions
contained in the Directive which set a lower threshold of 500 ECU and which
concern only an item of property which "is of a type ordinarily intended for private
use or consumption" which "was used by the injured person mainly for his own
private use or consumption" (which will be termed here "consumer property").[174]
The Court of Justice held first that the omission of the lower threshold was
incompatible with the Directive's requirement of "complete harmonisation",[175] but
in a later case, it held that French implementing legislation's imposition of liability on producers in respect of *any* damage to property caused by a defective

---

protection of Directive on "doorstep selling" for the benefit of businesses not precluded by Directive as this extension falls outside its scope).
[169] Directive 99/44/EC art.8(2). This position would change if the Amended Proposal for a Directive
of the European Parliament and of the Council on certain aspects concerning contracts for the online
and other distance sales of goods COM(2017) 637 final, were enacted, as art.3 of the proposal
provides for full harmonisation.
[170] Regulation (EC) 261/2004 establishing common rules on compensation and assistance to passengers in the event of denied boarding and of cancellation or long delay of flights, art.1(1) referring to "minimum rights for passengers".
[171] This is clearly set out in the Consumer Rights Directive 2011 (as enacted) recitals 6 and 7.
[172] Council Directive 1985/374/EEC concerning liability for defective products, [1985] O.J. L210/29.
[173] *Commission v France* (C-52/00) EU:C:2002:252, April 25, 200; [2002] E.C.R. I-3827; *Commission v Greece* (C-154/00) EU:C:2002:254 April 25 2002; *González Sánchez v Medicina Asturiana
SA* (C-183/00) EU:C:2002:255 April 25 2002.
[174] Directive 85/374/EEC art.9(b).
[175] *Commission v France* (C-52/00) EU:C:2002:25, paras 26–34.

product including property intended for business use and employed for that purpose (and therefore without the restrictions in the Directive) did not fall foul of the "complete harmonisation" required by the Directive: the Directive does not seek exhaustively to harmonise the field of liability for defective products beyond the matters regulated by it and the definition of "damage" in the Directive is restricted to consumer property.[176] Moreover, even if an issue is not regulated by a provision in a directive which requires full harmonisation, but the issue is nevertheless held to fall within its scope, then Member States are in principle precluded from regulating that issue as the directive has to this extent a "pre-emptive" effect.[177]

38-026 **Examples of "full harmonisation" and "partial full harmonisation": Unfair Commercial Practices Directive 2005**[178] Perhaps the most important example of "full harmonisation" in EU consumer protection law is found in the Unfair Commercial Practices Directive 2005, which contains a so-called "internal market clause" according to which:

> "Member States shall neither restrict the freedom to provide services nor restrict the free movement of goods for reasons falling within the field approximated by this Directive."[179]

The Court of Justice has held that this provision means that the 2005 Directive requires "full harmonisation" of "the laws, regulations and administrative provisions of the Member States on unfair commercial practices harming consumers' economic interests" within its scope, except where the 2005 Directive itself recognises exceptions to, or qualifications on, this position.[180] Crucially, therefore, in principle, Member States *must not* prohibit business-to-consumer commercial practices within the scope of the 2005 Directive *unless* they are prohibited under the controls set out by the 2005 Directive itself.[181] However, the 2005 Directive is stated as being "without prejudice to contract law and, in particular, to the rules on the validity, formation or effect of a contract", this being the case whether those rules are EU or national.[182] As a result, the 2005 Directive neither requires any changes to "contract law" nor, equally importantly, prohibits any changes to "contract law" even if they would otherwise appear to fall within its scope. This means, inter alia, that Member States remain competent to use the framework of

---

[176] *Moteurs Leroy Somer v Dalkia France* (C-285/08) EU:C:2009:351, [2009] E.C.R. I-4733 paras 25–32.

[177] See Weatherill, *EU Consumer Law and Policy*, 2nd edn (2013), 84–85 on "pre-emptive effect". For the impact of full harmonisation on issues within a EU legislative instrument but not overtly regulated by it see Whittaker (2009) *European Review of Contract Law* 2.

[178] See also Directive (EU) 2015/2302 on package travel and linked travel arrangements [2015] O.J. L326/1: art.4 sets a general principle of full harmonisation, with certain exceptions which the Directive itself sets out.

[179] Directive 2005/29/EC concerning unfair business-to-consumer commercial practices [2005] O.J. L149/22 ("2005 Directive") art.4.

[180] Directive 2005/29/EC art.1. On the scope of the 2005 Directive see recitals 6–9 and art.3.

[181] *VTB-VAB NV Total Belgium NV* (C-261/07 and C-299/07) EU:C:2009:244, [2009] E.C.R. I-2949 at para.63; *Mediaprint Zeitungs- und Zeitschriftenverlag GmbH & Co KG v "Österreich"-Zeitungsverlag GmbH* (C-540/08) EU:C:2010:660, [2010] E.C.R. I-10909 at para.27, *Zentrale sur Bekämpfung unlauteren Weebewerbs eV v Plus Warenhandelsgessellschaft mbH* (C-304/08) EU:C:2010:12, [2010] E.C.R. I-00217 at para.41, *Wamo BVBA v JBC NV* (C-288/10) EU:C:2011:443, [2011] E.C.R. I-5835 at para.33. There is an important exception to "full harmonisation" in relation to "financial services": 2005 Directive art.3(9).

[182] 2005 Directive art.3(2), recital 9.

control of the 2005 Directive (or just one or more of its controls) as the basis of "contract law" remedies in national legislation despite the Directive's generally required "full harmonisation". While the UK did not do so in its original implementation of the 2005 Directive,[183] in 2014 its implementing legislation was amended so as to create a series of "rights to redress" for consumers against traders in respect of *some* unfair commercial practices, thereby taking advantage of this remaining competence.[184] Moreover, as will be seen, the relationship between the 2005 Directive's requirement of full harmonisation and national laws which implement directives in the area of contract law (such as the Directive on unfair terms in consumer contracts) and which take advantage of their "minimum harmonisation" is not straightforward.[185]

Financial Services Distance Contracts Directive 2002 This Directive[186] sets full **38-027** harmonisation as its general rule, but then exempts from this rule its central provisions imposing information requirements, thereby imposing there only minimum harmonisation.[187]

Consumer Rights Directive 2011 As originally proposed in 2008 the Consumer **38-028** Rights Directive would have moved four existing directives from minimum to full harmonisation (including the Consumer Sales Directive and the Unfair Terms in Consumer Contracts Directive),[188] but the Consumer Rights Directive 2011[189] as enacted has a more restricted ambit, reworking earlier provisions concerning "off-premises contracts" and "distance contracts"[190] (though not in the area of financial services[191]), adding new provisions governing pre-contractual information requirements for consumer contracts more generally,[192] and making other particular changes.[193] Article 4 declares that:

"Member States shall not maintain or introduce, in their national law, provisions diverging from those laid down in this Directive, including more or less stringent provisions to ensure a different level of consumer protection, unless otherwise provided for in this Directive."

---

[183] Consumer Protection from Unfair Trading Regulations 2008 (SI 2008/1277) (as originally enacted).
[184] Consumer Protection (Amendment) Regulations 2014 (SI 2014/870) inserting, notably, new Pt 4A Consumers' Rights to Redress in the 2008 Regulations (SI 2008/1277). See further below, paras 38-172 et seq. cf. art.L.132-10 of the French *Code de la consommation*, which renders contracts made as a result of an aggressive commercial practice a nullity, although the Code does not provide expressly for a similar effect in the case of misleading commercial practices.
[185] See below, paras 38-421—38-426 in relation to the Consumer Rights Act 2015.
[186] Directive 2002/65/EC concerning the distance marketing of consumer financial services, art.4(2) (relating to the Directive's information requirements). The Directive is implemented in UK law by the Financial Services (Distance Marketing) Regulations 2004 (SI 2004/2095) see below, para.38-136.
[187] 2002 Directive recital 13, arts 3 and 4.
[188] Proposal for a Directive of the European Parliament and of the Council on Consumer Rights of 8 October 2008 COM(2008) 614/3 final.
[189] Directive 2011/83/EU on consumer rights [2011] O.J. L304/64 and see below, para.38-060.
[190] Directive 2011/83/EU on consumer rights arts 6–16.
[191] Directive 2011/83/EU art.3(3)(d). Directive 2002/65/EC concerning the distance marketing of consumer financial services remains in force and, as earlier noted, its information provisions require only minimum harmonisation: art.4(2).
[192] Directive 2011/83/EU art.5.
[193] Directive 2011/83/EU Ch.IV ("Other consumer rights").

It will be seen, therefore, that the Consumer Rights Directive sets a general rule of "full harmonisation" but then notes that the Directive itself provides for some exceptions to this effect, for example, in relation to information requirements applicable to contracts other than "off-premises contracts" or distance contracts.[194] Moreover, the Consumer Rights Directive defines its scope elaborately, stating generally that it applies to "any contract concluded between a trader and a consumer" but then setting out a series of qualifications and restrictions.[195]

3. DEFINITIONS OF CONSUMER CONTRACT

(a) Introduction

38-029 **Definition by reference to contracting parties** As will be seen, each UK statute or statutory instrument governing consumer contracts defines the ambit of the protections which it provides specially for its own purposes. In terms of their subject matter, some protections apply to particular types of contracts, such as "contracts to supply goods to a consumer"[196] or "holiday accommodation contracts",[197] while others apply in principle to *all* types of contract in this sense, notably protections against unfair terms,[198] and in respect of "on-premises contracts", "off-premises contracts" or "distance contracts".[199] However, whatever the subject matter of the contracts which they govern, the contracts affected by these statutes and statutory instruments are also restricted by reference to the categories of contracting party: broadly speaking, consumers on the one hand, and traders (or persons acting in the course of a business) on the other. While there remain significant differences in the ways in which these two categories of party are described in the legislation, the modern UK law (following to an extent EU law in this respect) has become increasingly consistent. The following paragraphs will therefore explain the background (UK and EU) to the definitions of the parties to consumer contracts in UK legislation, leaving any particular points of qualification or refinement to later paragraphs dealing with the particular statutes or statutory instruments to which they relate.

(b) "Consumer"

38-030 **Background** Although until recently the approach of English law to the definition of the person to be protected by its consumer protection legislation was particular and contextual, three broad approaches could be identified.[200] First, the Consumer Credit Act 1974 applied (and still applies) its principal controls to "consumer credit agreements", defined as agreements between an individual (the "debtor") and any other person (the "creditor") by which the creditor provides the

---

[194] Directive 2011/83/EU art.5(4).
[195] Directive 2011/83/EU art.3.
[196] Consumer Rights Act 2015 Pt 1 Ch.2.
[197] Timeshare, Holiday Products, Resale and Exchange Contracts Regulations 2010 (SI 2010/2960) regs 3 and 4, below, para.38-149.
[198] Consumer Rights Act 2015 Pt 2; formerly the Unfair Terms in Consumer Contracts Regulations 1999: below, paras 38-222, 38-386.
[199] Consumer Contracts (Information, Cancellation and Additional Charges) Regulations 2013 (SI 2013/3134) reg.7(1), with the exclusions set out in the remainder of reg.7. The categories of contract are themselves are defined by reg.5: below paras 38-069 et seq.
[200] cf. above, para.38-002.

debtor with credit of any amount.[201] Secondly, the Unfair Contract Terms Act 1977 protected persons "dealing as consumer" against exemption clauses and indemnity clauses.[202] Thirdly, a number of particular statutes and statutory instruments implementing EU directives protected "consumers" defined in a near-standard form of words derived from their parent directives, as in the case of the Doorstep Selling Regulations 1987[203] and the Unfair Terms in Consumer Contracts Regulations 1999.[204] Of these three approaches, the Consumer Credit Act's definition of the ambit of its controls by reference to the person provided with credit remains distinct and special for its purposes, the established domestic approach being subject to a further layer of complexity by the restricted scope of new controls required by the Consumer Credit Directive 2008.[205] This law is discussed in Ch.39 of the present work.[206] By contrast, since 2012 UK legislation has sought to bring a considerable degree of consistency to the definition of the "protected party" (the consumer) in its consumer contract protection law, these changes being inspired in part by the concern to provide a consistent approach to the interpretative gloss given to "consumer" at the EU level by the Consumer Rights Directive 2011.[207]

The following paragraphs will therefore discuss earlier case law of the European Court of Justice on the standard definition of "consumer" in EU legislation and English case-law on UK implementing legislation; they will then explain the significance of the reformulation given to the definition in the UK legislation, itself reflecting the model set by the Consumer Rights Directive. **38-031**

"Consumer" in EU law   While the precise (English) form of words defining "consumer" in the text of the directives of the consumer *acquis* varies, the definition found in the Doorstep Selling Directive of 1985 set a pattern which was much used. It provided that: **38-032**

> "'Consumer' means a natural person who, in transactions covered by this Directive, is acting for purposes which can be regarded as outside his trade or profession."[208]

Given the extent of its use, this will be termed here the EU standard definition.[209]

---

[201] Consumer Credit Act 1974 s.8(1) (as amended) and see below, para.39-016.

[202] On this law (now abrogated by the Consumer Rights Act 2015) see Vol.I, Ch.15 and especially paras 15-073—15-079.

[203] Consumer Protection (Cancellation of Contracts Concluded Away from Business Premises) Regulations 1987 (SI 1987/2117) reg.2(1) ("Doorstep Selling Regulations 1987") ("'consumer' means a person, other than a body corporate, who, in making a contract to which these Regulations apply, is acting for purposes which can be regarded as outside his business") and cf. Directive 85/577/EEC art.2 ("'consumer' means a natural person who, in transactions covered by this Directive, is acting for purposes which can be regarded as outside his trade or profession").

[204] SI 1999/2083 reg.3(1) ("'consumer' means any natural person who, in contracts covered by these Regulations, is acting for purposes which are outside his trade, business or profession") and cf. Directive 93/13/EEC art.2(b) ("'consumer' means any natural person who, in contracts covered by this Directive, is acting for purposes which are outside his trade, business or profession").

[205] Directive 2008/48/EC concerning credit agreements for consumers [2008] O.J. L133/66, replacing Directive 87/102/EEC concerning consumer credit O.J. L42/48.

[206] See below, para.39-011.

[207] Consumer Rights Directive 2011 recital 17; art.2(1) and see below, paras 38-036, 38-041.

[208] Directive 85/577/EEC art.2 (repealed and replaced by Directive 2011/83/EU on consumer rights, Ch.III and art.31).

[209] The following directives followed this definition, with very minor variations: Directive 93/13/EC on unfair terms in consumer contracts art.2(b); Directive 97/7/EC on the protection of consumers in respect of distance contracts art.2(2) (directive repealed and replaced by Directive 2011/83/EU

38-033 **"Natural persons"** This standard definition restricts consumers to "natural persons"[210] and therefore, unlike a person "dealing as consumer" under the Unfair Contract Terms Act as enacted, a company cannot rely on UK regulations implementing a directive containing this definition, even if it acts "for purposes which are outside [its] business",[211] unless the implementing legislation (or other UK legislation) extends the scope of its controls to persons contracting in this way.[212] It is more controversial as a matter of EU law whether a body of natural persons, such as an unincorporated association like a sports club, can be a "consumer" for the purposes of this type of definition.[213]

38-034 **European case-law** The Court of Justice of the EU has made clear that it will take an autonomous definition of the concept of "consumer" for the purposes of the EU secondary legislative instruments which use this term.[214] In this respect, the Court of Justice is likely to take into account the purpose of this body of legislation, which it sees as being protective of consumers, while still acknowledging that the need for harmonisation is justified by the requirements of the internal market.[215] So, for

---

on consumer rights, Ch.III and art.31); Directive 98/6/EEC on consumer protection in the indica-tion of the prices of products offered to consumers [1998] O.J. L80/27 art.2(e); Directive 99/44/EC on certain aspects of the sale of consumer goods and associated guarantees art.1(2)(a); Directive 87/102/EEC concerning consumer credit, art.1(2)(a) (repealed and replaced by Directive 2008/48/EC concerning credit agreements for consumers art.3(a)); Directive 2000/31/EC "Directive on electronic commerce" [2000] O.J. L178/1 art.2(e); Directive 2002/65/EC concerning the distance marketing of consumer financial services art.2(d). More complex versions of the same approach to definition of "consumer" can be seen in Directive 94/47/EEC art.2 (first Timeshare Directive). Directive 90/314/EEC on package travel, package holidays and package tours, art.2(4) adopted a much more elaborate definition specific to its context (*Cape Snc v Idealservice Srl* (C-541/99) EU:C:2001:625, [2001] E.C.R. I-09049), but the 1990 Directive was repealed (as of January 1, 2018) by Directive (EU) 2015/2302 on package travel and linked travel arrangements [2015] O.J. L326/1 and the 2015 Directive substitutes for "consumer" the new category of "traveller" which "means any person who is seeking to conclude a contract, or is entitled to travel on the basis of a contract concluded, within the scope of [the] Directive": art.3(6). As recital 7 explains, the majority of travellers buying pack-ages or linked travel arrangements are "consumers within the meaning of Union consumer law", but the Directive's protections should extend to "business travellers including members of liberal profes-sions, or self-employed or other natural persons where they do not make travel arrangements on the basis of a general agreement". See below, para.38-342.

[210] *Cape Snc v Idealservice Srl* (C-541/99 and C-542/99) EU:C:2001:625, [2001] E.C.R. I-09049.

[211] *Cape Snc v Idealservice Srl* (C-541/99 and C-542/99) EU:C:2001:625; 1999 Regulations reg.3(1). On "dealing as consumer" under the 1977 Act (before it was amended by the Consumer Rights Act 2015) see Vol.I, paras 15-073—15-079.

[212] For English law, the 1999 Regulations were extended to consumer arbitration agreements defining "consumer" for this purpose as legal as well as natural persons: Arbitration Act 1996 s.90; *Heifer International Inc v Christiansen* [2007] EWHC 3015 (TCC), [2008] All E.R. (D) 120 (Jan) and see below, para.38-225. This extension remains in place under the Consumer Rights Act 2015, below, para.38-412.

[213] cf. the decision of the French First Chamber of the *Cour de cassation* of June 4, 2014, [2014] Bull. civ.1 no.102, [2014] E.C.C. 30 which held that a co-ownership association (a *syndicat de copropriétaires*) which is treated as having legal personality by French law could not count as "consumer" for the purposes of French legislation implementing Directive 93/13/EEC art.7 both on the ground of its possessing legal personality and on the ground that such an association (even though formed by private individuals) has as its object an economic activity in the upkeep and manage-ment of the property and therefore was not "*non-professionnel*" (non-business).

[214] e.g. *Cape Snc v Idealservice Srl* (C-541/99) EU:C:2001:625, [2001] E.C.R. I-09049 paras 16–17 (Unfair Terms in Consumer Contracts Directive); *France v Di Pinto* (361/89) EU:C:1991:118, [1991] E.C.R. I-1189 (Doorstep Selling Directive).

[215] This is typically required by the competence on which the directives have been made, this being

example, the Court has explained in relation to the Unfair Terms in Consumer Contracts Directive that:

"... the system of protection established by Directive 93/13 is based on the idea that the consumer is in a weak position vis-à-vis the trader as regards both his bargaining power and his level of knowledge, which leads to the consumer agreeing to terms drawn up in advance by the trader without being able to influence the content of those terms."[216]

However, the Court has taken a fairly restrictive view of "consumer" for these purposes,[217] particularly when contrasted with the expansive view taken by English law for the purposes of the Unfair Contract Terms Act, where it has been held that a business which makes a contract of a kind which does not form a regular part of its business may "deal as consumer".[218] So, for example, in *Di Pinto*[219] the question arose whether a trader could ever be a "consumer" for the purposes of the Doorstep Selling Directive, which used the standard defining language for "consumer" earlier noted.[220] The European Court held that:

"... the criterion for the application of protection lies in the connection between the transactions which are the subject of the canvassing and the professional activity of the trader: the latter may claim that the directive is applicable only if the transaction in respect of which he is canvassed lies outside his trade or profession. Article 2, which is drafted in general terms, does not make it possible, with regard to acts performed in the context of such a trade or profession, to draw a distinction between normal acts and those which are exceptional in nature."[221]

The Court added that:

"Acts which are preparatory to the sale of a business, such as the conclusion of a contract for the publication of an advertisement in a periodical, are connected with the professional activity of the trader although such acts may bring the running of the business to an end, they are managerial acts performed for the purpose of satisfying requirements *other than the family or personal requirements of the trader*."[222]

The last italicised phrase could be seen as suggesting that a person does not act as a consumer unless contracting for their "family or personal needs". In *Benincasa v Dentalkit*[223] the European Court considered the concept of consumer for the

---

art.114 TFEU (formerly art.95 EC).

[216] *Pereničová v SOS finance, spol. sro* (C-453/10) EU:C:2012:144, [2012] 2 C.M.L.R. 28 para.27 repeating similar formulations in earlier judgments from *Mostaza Claro v Centro Móvil Milenium SL* (C-168/05) EU:C:2006:675, [2006] E.C.R. I-10421 (which used "seller or supplier" rather than "trader"). See similarly *BKK Mobil Oil Körperschaft des öffentlichen Rechts v Zentrale zur Bekämpfung unlauteren Wettbewerbs eV* (C-59/12) EU:C:2013:634, October 3, 2013 para.35 in the context of the Unfair Commercial Practices Directive 2005.

[217] Reich (1995) 4 *European Review of Private Law* 285, 292–293.

[218] Unfair Contract Terms Act 1977 s.12; *R. & B. Customs Brokers Co Ltd v United Dominions Trust Ltd* [1988] 1 W.L.R. 321: on which see Vol.I, para.15-074.

[219] *France v Di Pinto* (361/89) EU:C:1991:118, [1991] E.C.R. I-1189.

[220] Directive 85/577 to protect the consumer in respect of contracts negotiated away from business premises [1985] O.J. L372/31 art.2 (repealed and replaced by Directive 2011/83/EU on consumer rights [2011] O.J. L304/64).

[221] EU:C:1991:118, [1991] E.C.R. I-1189 at [15].

[222] EU:C:1991:118, [1991] E.C.R. I-1189 at [16] (emphasis added).

[223] C-269/95 EU:C:1997:337, [1997] E.C.R. I-3767.

purposes of art.13 of the Brussels Convention,[224] upholding its previous view that this referred to "private final consumer" in this context[225]:

> "Consequently, only contracts concluded for the purpose of satisfying an individual's own needs in terms of private consumption come under the provisions designed to protect the consumer as the party deemed to be the weaker party economically."[226]

The Court of Justice has held that, in order to determine whether a person was acting as a consumer for the purposes of the Directive on unfair terms in consumer contracts, a national court should take into account:

> "… all the circumstances of the case, particularly the nature of the goods or service covered by the contract in question, capable of showing the purpose for which those goods or that service is being acquired."[227]

This was seen as a "functional criterion".[228] However, the concept of "consumer" is:

> "… objective in nature and is distinct from the concrete knowledge the person in question may have, or from the information that person actually has."[229]

As a result, while lawyers may constitute "traders" in their contracts with their own clients,[230] they may, even if they are technically knowledgeable, nonetheless act as consumers in other transactions as they may be weaker parties compared to the traders with whom they deal.[231] For example, in *Bachman* a transport company (of which A was director) concluded a contract of loan with a finance company, B, the loan being guaranteed by A's mother, C, and secured on her home. When the company was faced with insolvency, D (A's brother) concluded a contract of novation of the original loan contract with B under which he undertook to pay back the loan over a period at interest.[232] Subsequently, D sought to establish that he had entered this contract of novation as a consumer and was therefore entitled to challenge some of its terms as unfair under national legislation implementing the 1993 Directive. The Court of Justice of the EU held that a physical person in D's position could be a consumer if the national court found that he acted for private purposes (notably, to save his mother from the imminent enforcement of the

---

224 Brussels Convention on Jurisdiction and the Enforcement of Foreign Judgments in Civil and Commercial Matters of September 27, 1968 replaced by Council Regulation 44/2001 on jurisdiction and the recognition and enforcement of judgments in civil and commercial matters [2001] O.J. L12/1, which was itself replaced as from January 10, 2015 by Regulation (EU) 1215/2012 of 12 December 2012 on jurisdiction and the recognition and enforcement of judgments in civil and commercial matters (recast) ("the Brussels Ibis Regulation").

225 EU:C:1997:337, [1997] E.C.R. I-3767 at para.15; *Shearson Lehman Hutton* (C-89/91) EU:C:1993:15, [1993] E.C.R. I-139 at paras 20 and 22.

226 EU:C:1997:337, [1997] E.C.R. I-3767 at [17].

227 *Costea v SC Volksbank România SA* (C-110/14) EU:C:2015:538, April 23, 2015 at para.23.

228 *Tarčau v Banca Comercială Intesa Sanpaolo România SA* (C-74/15) EU:C:2015:772, Order of CJEU November 19, 2015 at para.27.

229 *Costea v SC Volksbank România SA* (C-110/14) EU:C:2015:538, April 23, 2015 at para.21. See similarly, *Tarčau v Banca Comercială Intesa Sanpaolo România SA* (C-74/15) EU:C:2015:772, Order of CJEU November 19, 2015 para.27 on which see below, paras 38-226 and 45-156.

230 *Šiba v Devėnas* (C-537/13) EU:C:2015:14, January 15, 2015 [2015] Bus. L.R. 291 paras 23 and 24.

231 *Costea v SC Volksbank România SA* (C-110/14) EU:C:2015:538, April 23, 2015 at paras 20–27.

232 *Bachman v FAER IFN SA* (C-535/16) EU:C:2017:321 (Order of the Court of April 27, 2017, available in French).

guarantee of the original loan) rather than for business or professional purposes or in "manifest connection" with a role in the (insolvent) transport company.[233]

Contracts with mixed purposes   In *Gruber v Bay Wa AG*[234] the European Court   **38-035**
of Justice held that, for the purposes of the special consumer jurisdiction under art.13 of the Brussels Convention, a person who concludes a contract for goods intended for purposes which are in part within and in part outside of his trade or profession (in the case itself, a farmer who bought tiles to roof a building used both for agricultural and for domestic purposes) may not rely on the special rules in the Convention provided for consumer contracts:

> "... unless the trade or professional purpose is so limited as to be negligible in the overall context of the supply, the fact that the private element is predominant being irrelevant in that respect."[235]

The Court further held that a national court must assess whether this is the case by reference to all the evidence, but it:

> "... must not take account of facts or circumstances of which the other party to the contract [the business supplier] may have been aware when the contract was concluded, unless the person who claims the capacity of consumer behaved in such a way as to give the other party to the contract the legitimate impression that he was acting for the purposes of his business."[236]

While this observation was made in the context of a person (the alleged "consumer") acting partly for business and partly for non-business purposes, it suggests more generally that a person who in fact contracts as a consumer but gives the trader the impression that he acts in the course of a business cannot rely on his status as consumer.[237]

The Consumer Rights Directive and its possible wider influence   On the other   **38-036**
hand, while the Consumer Rights Directive of 2011 (which principally repealed and replaced the earlier Doorstep Selling Directive and Distance Contracts Directive[238]) uses an almost identical form of words to define consumer as is used by the EU standard definition as earlier identified,[239] recital 17 states that:

---

[233] See similarly *Dumitraş v BRD Groupe Société Générale* (C-534/15) EU:C:2016:700, Order of the CJEU of September 14, 2016 at paras 38-29 (absence of "functional links" between guarantor and company debtor (such as being a director or holding non-negligible shares) could justify national court in finding that the guarantor was a consumer).

[234] C-464/01 EU:C:2005:32, [2005] E.C.R. I-439.

[235] EU:C:2005:32, [2005] E.C.R. I-439 at [54]. This approach was followed at first instance by *Turner & Co (GB) Ltd v Abi* [2010] EWHC 2078 (QB), [2011] 1 C.M.L.R. 17 at [32]–[41]. In *Ali v Spirit Motor Transport Ltd* Unreported January 24, 2014 (Leeds County Court) it was held a purchase for dual purposes was not a consumer contract with the meaning of the Cancellation of Contracts made in a Consumer's Home or Place of Work, etc. Regulations 2008 (SI 2008/1816) unless the trade purpose was negligible, 75 per cent not being negligible for these purposes.

[236] EU:C:2005:32, [2005] E.C.R. I-439 at [54].

[237] cf. Unfair Contract Terms Act 1977 s.12(1)(a) which provided that a person "deals as consumer" if "he neither makes the contract in the course of a business nor holds himself out as doing so", on which see Vol.I, para.15-074.

[238] Below, para.38-060.

[239] "'Consumer' means any natural person who, in contracts covered by this Directive, is acting for purposes which are outside his trade, business, craft or profession". The main difference is the ad-

"... in the case of dual purpose contracts, where the contract is concluded for purposes partly within and partly outside the person's trade and the trade purpose is so limited as not to be predominant in the overall context of the contract, that person should also be considered as a consumer."

While rather awkwardly phrased, this recital therefore includes a person as a "consumer" where they act mainly for non-trade purposes and it therefore reflects a more extensive view of the understanding of "consumer" by the EU legislature than was taken by the Court of Justice in the context of the Brussels Convention in *Gruber v Bay Wa AG*,[240] where any business purpose other than one which is "so limited as to be negligible" deprives a person of their status as consumer.[241] The Consumer Rights Directive seeks to achieve this by indicating the proper interpretation to be taken to the standard form of words defining consumer and, owing to the significance of the recitals to a directive for the interpretation of its text,[242] this gloss on "consumer" therefore clearly governs the definition in the Consumer Rights Directive itself; and this directive did make an insertion into the 1993 Directive, though not one of substantive significance.[243] Moreover, this gloss may well have a wider significance as it could encourage the Court of Justice to hold that "consumer" can include persons *mainly* acting outside their trade or profession for the purposes of other substantive law directives in the consumer *acquis*, distinguishing its more restrictive approach in *Gruber* on the basis that it concerned the special (and therefore exceptional) provisions in the Brussels Convention governing international jurisdiction.[244] This way of thinking was, indeed, adopted by Advocate General Crux Villalón in *Costea v SC Volksbank România SA*.[245]

38-037   Most recently in *Schrems v Facebook Ireland Ltd* the Court of Justice again considered the issue of a contract with mixed purposes for the purposes of the special international jurisdiction for consumers provided by arts 15 and 16 of the Brussels Regulation, though in a very different context from its earlier decision in *Gruber*.[246] In *Schrems*, the applicant for various declarations had been a user of the social network Facebook for some years, initially for his own personal purposes (such as exchanging photographs and chatting), but he later opened a "Facebook

---

ditional reference to "craft": cf. above, para.38-032.

[240] C-464/01 EU:C:2005:32, [2005] E.C.R. I-439 ("*Gruber* (C-464/01)").

[241] Above, para.38-035.

[242] Above, para.38-016.

[243] The 2011 Directive art.32 inserts a new art.8a in the 1993 Directive which requires Member States to inform the EU Commission of any exercises of their power to extend the protection for consumers by way of art.8. See also Directive 2013/11/EU of May 21, 2013 on ADR for consumer disputes [2013] O.J. L165/63 art.4(1)(a) of which defines "consumer" in the standard way, but its recital 18 then glosses this definition in an almost identical way as 2011 Directive recital 17. A similar pattern is found in Directive 2014/17/EU of February 4, 2014 on credit agreements for consumers relating to immovable property [2014] O.J. L60/34 (the "Mortgage Credit Directive") recital 12 and art.4(1), referring to the definition of "consumer" in Directive 2008/48/EC of April 23, 2008 on credit agreements for consumers [2008] O.J. L133/66 art.3(1). This supports the view that the Court of Justice should hold that this gloss is to be applied more generally to definitions of "consumer" in the EU consumer protection *acquis*, unless the context otherwise requires. cf. however, the Amended Proposal for a Directive of the European Parliament and of the Council on certain aspects concerning contracts for the online and other distance sales of goods COM(2017) 637 final whose recitals do not contain a gloss of this kind in respect of its standard definition of "consumer" in art.2(b).

[244] Above, para.38-035.

[245] (C-110/14) EU:C:2015:538, April 23, 2015 especially at paras 35–47. The CJEU in its judgment of September 3, 2015 did not address this issue.

[246] C-498/16 EU:C:2018:37, January 25, 2018 ("*Schrems* (C-498/16)").

page" so as to report to internet users on his legal proceedings against Facebook Ireland, his lectures, media appearances, etc. and to publicise his books in relation to alleged infringements of data protection. He founded an association which seeks to uphold the fundamental right to data protection and had assigned to him, by more than 25,000 people worldwide, claims to be brought in the proceedings from which a reference was made to the Court of Justice. In terms of its interpretation of "consumer" for these purposes, the Court of Justice in *Schrems* recognised that, while the concepts in the Brussels Regulation had to be interpreted:

"... independently, by reference principally to the general scheme and objectives of that regulation ... account must, in order to ensure compliance with the objectives pursued by the legislature of the European Union in the sphere of consumer contracts, and the consistency of EU law, also be taken of the definition of 'consumer' in other rules of EU law."[247]

One issue before the Court of Justice was the proper approach to a case where an individual acted partly outside his trade or profession and party within it.[248] In this respect, the Court expressly followed its earlier decision in *Gruber* to the effect that the link between an individual and his trader or profession must be:

"... so slight as to be marginal and, therefore, had only a negligible role in the context of the supply in respect of which the contract was concluded, considered in its entirety.[249]"

As regards the particular case before it, the Court considered that where digital social network services are used over a long time, changes in their use are relevant to the user's status as (or as not) "consumer". The Court added that:

"... [t]his interpretation implies, in particular that a user of such services may, in bringing an action, rely on his status as a consumer only if the predominantly[250] non-professional use of those services, for which the applicant initially concluded a contract, has not subsequently become predominantly professional."[251]

With respect, use of a criterion of "predominance" of one purpose over another differs significantly from the approach in *Gruber* where any non-negligible business or professional purpose rules out a person's being a consumer; instead this approach is that adopted by the Consumer Rights Directive as earlier explained.[252] The Court of Justice's position on the understanding of "consumer" in relation to mixed purpose contracts therefore remains uncertain, although its judgment in *Schrems* appears to be moving towards including as a "consumer" a person who acts predominantly for non-business purposes. In the particular circumstances of *Schrems* itself, the Court considered that neither the actual expertise of the ap-

---

[247] *Schrems* (C-498/16) at para.28 referring to its observations in *Vapenik v Thurner* (C-508/12) EU:C:2013:790, December 5, 2013 which concerned Regulation (EC) No.805/2004 of the European Parliament and of the Council of 21 April 2004 creating a European Enforcement Order for uncontested claims [2004] O.J. L143/15.

[248] The CJEU also held that where consumers assign their claims to another individual, the latter cannot rely on the special provisions in the Brussels Regulation provided for "consumers" as regards those assigned claims, as art.16(1) assumes that the action being brought is by the consumer against the other party to the contract: *Schrems* (C-498/16) at paras 42–49.

[249] *Schrems* (C-498/16) at para.32, citing *Gruber* (C-464/01) at para.39.

[250] The original here and later in the paragraph states "predominately".

[251] *Schrems* (C-498/16) at para.38.

[252] Above, para.38-036.

plicant which he might have acquired in the field covered by Facebook's services[253] nor his various activities (publishing, lecturing, etc.) undertaken for the purposes of representing the rights and interests of service users (including as to personal data) could deprive him of the status of "consumer", not least as the contrary interpretation would disregard the objective set out in art.169(1) TFEU of promoting the right of consumers to organise themselves in order to safeguard their interests.[254] Here, therefore, wider EU law principle was used to guide the application of the concept of "consumer".

38-038 **Earlier UK standard definition of "consumer" and its interpretation by English courts**   As earlier noted, until recently, the UK legislature implemented the standard EU definition of "consumer" faithfully, in general not seeking to extend it to cover non-human persons nor those acting partly in the course of business.[255] So, for example, the Unfair Terms in Consumer Contracts Regulations 1999 provided that:

> "... 'consumer' means any natural person who, in contracts covered by these Regulations, is acting for purposes which are outside his trade, business or profession."[256]

Later versions of this standard definition in other instruments have replaced "natural person" with "individual", but this was clearly not intended to make any substantive difference.[257]

38-039 **United Kingdom case-law on earlier definition**   In *Standard Bank London Ltd v Apostolakis*[258] the proper understanding of the standard definition of "consumer" in the Unfair Terms in Consumer Contracts Regulations 1999 arose in unusual circumstances. The defendants were wealthy individuals (a civil engineer and a lawyer) who had used their personal funds for dealings in foreign exchange under an "umbrella contract" with a bank in Athens, where they resided. The question arose as to the validity of an exclusive jurisdiction clause of the English courts in this contract, either under art.13 of the Brussels Convention or the 1999 Regulations. It was held first that this was a "consumer contract" for the purposes of art.13.[259] According to Longmore J.:

---

[253] Citing *Costea v SC Volksbank România SA* (C-110/14) EU:C:2015:538, above, paras 38-034 and 38-252.

[254] *Schrems* (C-498/16) at paras 39–40.

[255] This was not the universal practice. For example, when the Consumer Sales Directive 1999 was implemented by inserting a new Pt 5A Additional rights of buyer in consumer cases, it applied where "the buyer deals as consumer" rather than merely to a "consumer" buyer, thereby applying to the wider category of person identified by the Unfair Contract Terms Act 1977: Sale of Goods Act 1979 s.61(5A) referring to the construction of "dealing as consumer" under the Unfair Contract Terms Act 1977 Pt 1: see below, para.38-444 (before s.61(5A)'s repeal by the Consumer Rights Act 2015 s.60 and Sch.1 para.35(3)).

[256] SI 1999/2083 reg.3(1) "consumer". See similarly Consumer Protection (Distance Selling) Regulations (SI 2000/2334) reg.3(1) "consumer"; Cancellation of Contracts made in a Consumer's Home or Place of Work, etc. Regulations 2008 (SI 2008/1816) reg.2(1) "consumer".

[257] Financial Services (Distance Marketing) Regulations 2004 (SI 2004/2095) reg.2(1).

[258] *Standard Bank London Ltd v Apostolakis (No.1)* [2000] I.L. Pr. 766 (Longmore J.); *Standard Bank London Ltd v Apostolakis (No.2)* [2001] Lloyd's Rep. Bank. 240 (Steel J.).

[259] [2000] I.L. Pr. 766.

"It is certainly not part of a person's trade as a civil engineer or a lawyer ... to enter into foreign exchange contracts. They were using the money in a way which they hoped would be profitable but merely to use money in a way which they hoped would be profitable is not enough ... to be engaging in trade."[260]

Even if the wording used by the European Court in *Benincasa*[261] were applied literally, the foreign exchange contracts:

"... were for the purpose of satisfying the needs of [the defendants], defined as an appropriate use of their income, and that that need was a need in terms of private consumption. Consumption cannot be taken as literally consumed so as to be destroyed but rather consumer in the sense that a consumer consumes, viz. he uses or enjoys the relevant product."[262]

It was later assumed that the defendants were also "consumers" for the purposes of the Unfair Terms in Consumer Contracts Directive 1993 and held that, apart from this decision under the Convention, the choice of jurisdiction clause was "unfair" within the meaning of the 1999 Regulations.[263]

However, in *Maple Leaf Macro Volatility Master Fund v Rouvroy*[264] Andrew **38-040** Smith J. questioned the conclusion of Longmore J. as regards the status as consumer of the defendants in the *Apostolakis* case, which he saw as concerning the question whether the dealing of the defendants there was of a nature that they were to be regarded as carrying on a trade. Andrew Smith J. distinguished the case before him, which instead concerned the question whether an agreement made by directors of (and major shareholders in) a company for funding of a securities transaction to regain control of that company was so connected with their business activities as not to be regarded as outside their trade. He held that it was not to be so regarded, so that the directors did not qualify as "consumers" either for the purposes of art.15 of the Brussels I Regulation or of the Unfair Terms in Consumer Contracts Regulations 1999.[265] In *Prostar Management Ltd v Twaddle*,[266] a professional

---

260 [2000] I.L. Pr. 766, 771, per Longmore J.
261 *Benincasa v Dentalkit* (C-269/95) EU:C:1997:337, [1997] E.C.R. I-3767, above, para.38-034.
262 [2000] I.L. Pr. 766, 773.
263 *Standard Bank London Ltd v Apostolakis (No.2)* [2001] Lloyd's Rep. Bank. 240.
264 [2009] EWHC 257 (Comm), [2009] 1 Lloyd's Rep. 475.
265 [2009] EWHC 257 (Comm) at [209] and [270]. The Brussels Convention on jurisdiction and the enforcement of judgements in civil and commercial matters 1968 art.13 was replaced by Regulation (EU) 1215/2012 of 12 December 2012 on jurisdiction and the recognition and enforcement of judgments in civil and commercial matters (recast) ("the Brussels Ibis Regulation") art.17. In commenting on the contrast between the *Apostolakis* and *Rouvroy* decisions, the HC in *AMT Futures Ltd v Mazillier, Dr Meier & Dr Guntner Rechtsanwaltsgesellschaft mbH* [2014] EWHC 1085 (Comm), [2015] 2 W.L.R. 187 at [58] considered that the dividing line between investors who count as "consumers" and those who do not "is likely to be heavily dependent on the circumstances of each individual and the nature and pattern of investment". (This point was not discussed on appeal to the CA or the SC: [2015] EWCA Civ 143, [2015] Q.B. 699; [2017] UKSC 13, [2017] 2 W.L.R. 853.) See also *Barclays Bank Plc v Kufner* [2008] EWHC 2319 at [31], [2009] 1 All E.R. (Comm) 1 (person entering guarantee contract to acquire (through an offshore company) the component parts of a ship chartering business not a "consumer"); *Heifer International Inc v Christiansen* [2007] EWHC 3015 (TCC), [2008] All E.R. (D) 120 (Jan) at [243]–[250] (offshore company set up to purchase a residential property for its beneficial owners acted "for purposes outside [its] trade, business, or profession" when it entered contracts for the purchase and renovation of the property in question); *Wilson v MF Global UK Ltd* [2011] EWHC 138 (QB) at [129]–[131] (claimant trading through defendant in volatile financial market apparently held not a "consumer"); *Turner & Co (GB) Ltd v Abi* [2010] EWHC 2078 (QB), [2011] 1 C.M.L.R. 17 at [42] (shareholder director of a business com-

footballer claimed that he acted as "consumer" for the purposes of the 1999 Regulations in relation to his receipt of services under a management agreement for the promotion of his career, profile and sponsorship. The Glasgow and Strathkelvin Sheriff Court had regard to the decisions of the European Court in *Di Pinto*[267] and *Benincasa*[268] and rejected this claim, holding that being a footballer was the defender's "trade or profession" and that the contract in question could not be regarded as being outside it.[269] In *Overy v Paypal (Europe) Ltd*[270] the High Court, having reviewed the European case-law on the proper understanding of "consumer" including the Court of Justice's decision in *Gruber*,[271] held that the claimant, a professional photographer who opened a "business account" with an online provider of electronic payment services and who used it partly for the purposes of his photography business and partly to sell his house by means of an online competition, did not count as a "consumer" so as to be protected by the 1999 Regulations: first, while the competition was "not an adventure in the nature of trade", he also intended to use it for his photography business and "that purpose could not reasonably be regarded as one which was insignificant or negligible"[272]; and, secondly, by the nature of the application which he made online and the information which the claimant provided in so doing, "he clearly conducted himself in such a way as to lead to the obvious conclusion that he was acting in his trade or professional capacity".[273] Finally, in *Ashfaq v International Insurance Co of Hannover Plc* the Court of Appeal applied the approach of the High Court in *Overy v Paypal (Europe) Ltd* to the context of an individual who had concluded a contract of insurance on a house which he let to tenants as part of a letting business.[274] In these circumstances, the individual did not contract as a "consumer" within the meaning of the 1999

missioning an agent to sell the business not acting as a "consumer" but for the purposes of that business); *The Office of Fair Trading v Foxtons Ltd* [2009] EWHC 1681 (Ch), [2009] 29 E.G. 98 (C.S.) at [28] (owners of property seeking to lease it acted as "consumers" in entering a letting agency contract with an estate agent, although other "professional" or "commercial" landlords would not); *RTA (Business Consultants) Ltd v Bracewell* [2015] EWHC 630 (QB), [2015] Bus. L.R. 800 at [51]–[60] (person contracting with estate agent for the sale of his business not a "consumer" for the purposes of the Cancellation of Contracts made in a Consumer's Home or Place of Work, etc. Regulations 2008 (SI 2008/1816)); *R. (on the application of Bluefin Insurance Services Ltd) v Financial Ombudsman Service Ltd* [2014] EWHC 3413, [2015] Bus. L.R. 656 at [121]–[128] (director of company taking out a Directors and Officers Insurance Policy was not a "consumer" for the purposes of the Financial Ombudsman Service's jurisdiction (which was defined by reference, inter alia, to the definition of "consumer" in the 1993 Directive) as the insurance concerned his liability for acts in the course of his trade, business, or profession); *Kinloch v Coral Racing Ltd* [2017] CSOH 43, 2017 S.L.R. 856 at [158]–[159] (claimant held to be a professional gambler and therefore not a "consumer" for the purpose of the 1999 Regulations). cf. *Evans v Cherry Tree Finance Ltd* Unreported April 13, 2007, Ch D (concession that if any purposes for which the claimant contracted were outside his trade or business, then he was a consumer as defined by the regulations).
266 [2003] S.L.T. (Sh. Ct.) 11.
267 *France v Di Pinto* EU:C:1991:118, [1991] E.C.R. I-1189.
268 C-269/95 EU:C:1997:337, [1997] E.C.R. I-3767.
269 [2003] S.L.T. (Sh. Ct.) 11 at [12]–[14].
270 [2012] EWHC 2659 (QB), [2013] Bus. L.R. Digest D1.
271 C-464/01 EU:C:2005:32, above, paras 38-034—38-035.
272 [2012] EWHC 2659 (QB) at [174]–[175] per Judge Hegarty Q.C. and cf. *Gruber v Bay Wa AG* (C-464/01) EU:C:2005:32, [2005] E.C.R. I-439 at para.54 discussed above, para.38-035.
273 [2012] EWHC 2659 (QB) at [176] per Judge Hegarty Q.C. and cf. *Gruber v Bay Wa AG* (C-464/01) EU:C:2005:32, [2005] E.C.R. I-439 at para.54 discussed above, para.38-035.
274 [2017] EWCA Civ 357, [2017] H.L.R. 29.

Regulations, not least as the contract was in the form of a business insurance.[275] These decisions, it should be noted, were all made before the Court of Justice had given judgment in *Schrems v Facebook Ireland Ltd.*[276]

The new UK standard legislative definition of "consumer"   In 2012 the Law   **38-041** Commissions recommended that any new Acts on consumer law should specify that an individual who uses a product *wholly or mainly* for non-business use should be protected, considering the approach of the European Court of Justice in *Gruber v Bay Wa AG*[277] to be too narrow and noting that this approach had already been adopted by the Consumer Insurance (Disclosure and Representations) Bill then before Parliament.[278] As enacted, the Consumer Insurance (Disclosure and Representations) Act 2012 defines the consumer party to a contract of insurance as being:

> "… an individual who enters into the contract wholly or mainly for purposes unrelated to the individual's trade, business or profession."[279]

The same, more extensive approach was adopted by the Consumer Rights (Payment Surcharges) Regulations 2012[280] and the Consumer Contracts (Information, Cancellation and Additional Charges) Regulations 2013 on their implementing the Consumer Rights Directive.[281] The 2013 Regulations provide that:

> "'Consumer' means an individual acting for purposes that are wholly or mainly outside the individual's trade, business, craft or profession."[282]

The Consumer Rights Act 2015 adopted an identical definition[283] and, furthermore, abolished the special protection for those "dealing as consumer" contained in the Unfair Contract Terms Act 1977 and the Sale of Goods Act 1979, instead placing the substance of these protections within the framework of its own protection of "consumers".[284] In this way, the UK legislator has adopted the definition of consumer in the Consumer Rights Directive 2011 even though that directive does not impose any requirements as regards unfair contract terms or consumer guarantees in contracts of sale of goods.[285]

The key change here from the earlier standard UK definition is the addition of   **38-042** the words "wholly or mainly", allowing to this extent an individual who contracts

---

275 [2017] EWCA Civ 357 at [45]–[57]. cf. *Chesterton Global Ltd v Finney* Unreported April 30, 2010, Lambeth County Ct where an individual who leased a "buy-to-let" property was held to have done so as a "consumer".

276 Above, para.38-037.

277 C-464/01 EU:C:2005:32, [2005] E.C.R. I-439.

278 Law Commission and Scottish Law Commission, *Consumer Redress for Misleading and Aggressive Practices* Law Com. No.332, Scot. Law Com. No.226 (2012), paras 6.11–6.13.

279 Consumer Insurance (Disclosure and Representations) Act 2012 s.1 and see below, para.42-031.

280 SI 2012/3110 reg.2 "consumer".

281 SI 2013/3134 reg.4: see below, para.38-069.

282 SI 2013/3134 reg.4 "consumer" (which refers to "craft" as foreseen by the 2011 Directive).

283 Consumer Rights Act 2015 s.2(3). In the case of "sales contracts" the 2015 Act s.2(5) and (6) qualify this definition in some situations: see below, para.38-487.

284 Below, paras 38-372, 38-384.

285 Consumer Rights Act 2015 s.76(2) referring to s.2(3). See also the Alternative Dispute Resolution for Consumer Disputes (Competent Authorities and Information) Regulations 2015 (SI 2015/542) reg.3 "consumer" on which see below, para.38-155.

partly for business purposes to be protected. The new definition of "consumer" in the Consumer Rights Act 2015 applies to its provisions on the rights of consumer buyers and other transferees of goods earlier provided by the Sale of Goods Act 1979 and the Supply of Goods and Services Act 1982,[286] and to the new rights of consumers under "digital content contracts".[287] This adoption by the 2015 Act of the definition of consumer drawn from the Consumer Rights Directive 2011 therefore allows a consistent definition between the 2015 Act and the UK secondary legislation implementing the Consumer Rights Directive itself, viz the Consumer Rights (Payment Surcharges) Regulations 2012[288] and the Consumer Contracts (Information, Cancellation and Additional Charges) Regulations 2013.[289] Finally, when in 2014 the UK legislator created "rights to redress" for consumers in respect of certain unfair commercial practices, it changed the definition of "consumer" both for these particular purposes and for the wider purposes of the regulation of unfair commercial practices.[290] As a result, the definition of "consumer" in the UK legislation implementing the Unfair Commercial Practices Directive 2005 (which establishes "full harmonisation" within its scope) defines "consumer" for this purpose following the approach of the Consumer Rights Directive 2011 rather than the 2005 Directive itself.

38-043 **Compatibility with EU law**   It has earlier been suggested that the interpretative gloss of the EU legislation's standard definition of "consumer" provided by the Consumer Rights Directive 2011 may persuade the Court of Justice of the EU to extend the protection of other consumer protection directives in the area of contract law to persons acting wholly or mainly for purposes which are outside that person's business or profession[291] and it has been seen that the Court of Justice in *Schrems* appears to have moved in this direction.[292] If this were the case, then clearly the new standard UK definitions would merely reflect the true EU position. However, if this were *not* the case, it is submitted that the UK extension of the scope of its implementing legislation would in principle be compatible with EU law, as it would extend the scheme of the relevant directives to persons outside their scope. As earlier explained, such an extension is permissible in EU law, whether a directive requires "full harmonisation" or merely "minimum harmonisation".[293]

38-044 **The "average consumer"**   EU legislation and case-law has been seen as reflecting "standards" by which consumers' behaviour or understanding should be viewed: "confident" or sophisticated consumers; "average" consumers; and "vulnerable"

---

[286] Consumer Rights Act 2015 ss.2(3), 3–32; 48–57 ("goods contracts").

[287] Consumer Rights Act 2015 ss.2(3), 33–47.

[288] SI 2012/3110 reg.2 "consumer": and see generally below, para.38-427—38-428.

[289] SI 2013/3134. See *Christopher Linnett Ltd v Harding (t/a MJ Harding Contractors)* [2017] EWHC 1781 (TCC) at [84] (sole trader not a "consumer" for the purposes of the 2013 Regulations when contracting with an adjudicator for services as acting "wholly (or at least mainly) inside [his] trade or business").

[290] Consumer Protection from Unfair Trading Regulations 2008 (SI 2008/1277) reg.2(1) (as amended by Consumer Protection (Amendment) Regulations 2014 (SI 2014/870) reg.2(3) below, para.38-168.

[291] Above, paras 38-036—38-037.

[292] Above, para.38-037.

[293] Above, paras 38-023 and 38-025. This was the view taken by the Law Commissions Law Com. No.332, Scot. Law Com. No.226 (2012), para.6.13.

consumers.[294] However, of these approaches, the dominant one in the Court of Justice is the standard of the "average consumer" who is "reasonably well informed and reasonably observant and circumspect", a standard well established by it in the context of legislation on misleading advertising and the marketing of particular products.[295] This standard is not, however, a uniform one and this was reflected in the way in which the concept of "average consumer" was described and used by the Unfair Commercial Practices Directive 2005.[296] As earlier noted, the 2005 Directive creates a fully harmonised "general framework" for preventive measures of consumer protection though it is "without prejudice to contract law".[297] For this purpose, the 2005 Directive distinguishes between: (i) the average consumer; (ii) the average member of the group where a commercial practice is directed to a particular group of consumers; and (iii) the average member of a clearly identifiable group of consumers who are particularly vulnerable to the practice or the underlying product because of their mental or physical infirmity, age or credulity in a way which the trader could reasonably be expected to foresee.[298] Given this background, the "average consumer" is therefore a necessary element in the UK's legislation on unfair commercial practices, which, as earlier noted, has recently been extended to create certain rights to redress for consumers against traders.[299]

The wider significance of "average consumer" in EU and UK consumer protection law   As earlier noted, the 2005 Directive's treatment of the standard of average consumer reflects the Court of Justice's established case-law and the Court has recently seen it as relevant to other EU consumer protection legislation.[300] A key example may be found in relation to the Unfair Terms in Consumer Contracts Directive 1993, where the standard by which the consumer (and particular the consumer's understanding) is to be assessed has been held by the Court of Justice of the EU to be relevant to the requirement of fairness and of "plain, intelligible language".[301]   **38-045**

294 See further Weatherill in Weatherill and Bernitz (eds), *The Regulation of Unfair Commercial Practices under EC Directive 2005/29* (2007), Ch.7.
295 The ECJ case-law in question can be seen in *Pippig Augenoptik GmbH & Co KG v Hartlauer Handelsgesellschaft mbH* (C-44/01) EU:C:2003:205, [2003] E.C.R. I-3095 at [55]; *De Landtsheer Emmanuel SA v Comite Interprofessionnel du Vin du Champagne* (381/05) [2007] Bus. L.R. 1484; *Lidl Belgium GmbH & Co KG v Etablissementen Franz Colruyt NV* (356/04) [2007] Bus. L.R. 492 at [78] (misleading advertising); *Gut Springenheide GmbH and Rudolf Trusky v Oberkreisdrektor des Kreises Steinfurt-Amft fur Lebensmitteluberwachung* (C-210/96) EU:C:1998:369, [1998] E.C.R. I-4657 (marketing standards for eggs); *Estée Lauder Cosmetics GmbH & Co OHG v Lancaster Group GmbH* (C-220/98) EU:C:2000:8, [2000] E.C.R. I-0117 (marketing of cosmetics); *Mundipharma v Office for Harmonisation in the Internal Market (Trade Marks and Designs)–Altana Pharma (RESPICUR)* (T-256/04) EU:T:2007:46, [2007] E.C.R. II-449 (trademarks); *Tifosi Optics Inc v Office for Harmonisation in the Internal Market (Trade Marks and Designs) (OHIM)* (T-531/12) EU:T:2014:855 (trade marks). See also the recent discussion of "average consumer" in *OFT v Purely Creative* [2011] EWHC 106 (Ch), [2011] E.C.C. 20 at [73]–[74]; *Secretary of State for Business, Innovation and Skills v PLT Antimarketing Ltd* [2015] EWCA Civ 76, [2015] C.T.L.C.8 at [30]–[31] for the purposes of the 2008 Regulations.
296 Directive 2005/29/EC concerning unfair business-to-consumer commercial practices [2005] O.J. L149/22, recitals 18 and 19; arts 5(2)(b) and (3), 6(1) and (2), 7(1) and (2), and 8. This directive is implemented in UK law by the Consumer Protection from Unfair Trading Regulations 2008 (SI 2008/1277), on which see below, paras 38-157 et seq.
297 Directive 2005/29 art.3(2), below, para.38-157 but cf. paras 38-172 et seq.
298 These distinctions are drawn from 2005 Directive art.5(2) and 5(3), below, para.38-169.
299 Above, para.38-003 and see below, paras 38-172 et seq.
300 cf. Whittaker in Weatherill and Bernitz at Ch.8.
301 Directive 93/13/EEC arts 3 and 5 respectively.

So, in *Banco Español de Crédito, SA v Calderón Camino* Advocate General Trstenjak referred to the Court's general case-law on average consumer in the context of the procedural position of a consumer in relation to the assessment of the fairness of terms under the 1993 Directive.[302] And in *Kásler* the Court of Justice of the EU adopted the standard of "the average consumer, who is reasonably well informed and reasonably observant and circumspect" for the purposes of the application of the requirements of plain, intelligible language in arts 4(2) and 5 of the 1993 Directive.[303] The "transparency" of terms is also relevant to their fairness under art.3 of that Directive.[304] This interpretative approach of the Court of Justice was adopted explicitly by the Consumer Rights Act 2015, which uses the standard of the "average consumer", meaning "a consumer who is reasonably well-informed, observant and circumspect" for the purpose of determining the "prominence" of a term, "prominence" being a new condition for the "core exclusion" of terms from the test of fairness of terms which specify the main subject matter of the contract, etc.[305]

38-046 **Other legislative contexts** The "average consumer" may be a useful benchmark for assessing the demands of requirements in other EU consumer protection directives. So, for example, the Consumer Rights Directive 2011 (implemented in UK law mainly by the Consumer Contracts (Information, Cancellation and Additional Charges) Regulations 2013) imposes a general information requirement on traders in relation to consumer contracts that they provide the consumer with various information "in a clear and comprehensible manner".[306] On the other hand, where UK legislation neither implements nor is based on a scheme provided by EU legislation, then the idea of the "average consumer" has no direct relevance, stemming, as it does, from European case-law and thinking. So, for example, the UK legislation governing consumer insurance (which does not reflect EU law) itself defines those things which a consumer/insured ought to know for the purposes of their duty of fair representation,[307] rather than appealing to a general standard such as the "average consumer assured".

38-047 **Consumers as the supplier of goods or services?** Typically, a "consumer" is a person who receives goods or services from a trader,[308] but the standard definition of consumer (both in EU law and in recent UK legislation[309]) is not explicitly

---

[302] *Banco Español de Crédito, SA v Calderón Camino* (C-618/10) EU:C:2012:349, Opinion of February 14, 2012 para.73.

[303] *Kásler v OTP Jelzálogbank Zrt* (C-26/13) EU:C:2014:282, April 30, 2014 at para.74. On the other hand, the CJEU did not adopt the perspective of the "average consumer" for the purposes of *identification* of the clauses to which art.4(2) of the 1993 Directive applied: see below, paras 38-254 and 38-261, 38-262.

[304] Below, paras 38-285—38-286.

[305] Consumer Rights Act 2015 s.64(4) and (5) on which see below, paras 38-398—38-399.

[306] Consumer Rights Directive 2011 art.5(1), 6(1) and 7(1) ("plain, intelligible language"); Consumer Contracts (Information, Cancellation and Additional Charges) Regulations 2013 (SI 2013/3134) regs 9(1), 10(1) and 13(1).

[307] Insurance Act 2015 ss.3 and 4 and see below, paras 42-046—42-047.

[308] cf. "dealing as consumer" under the Unfair Contract Terms Act 1977 before this concept was abolished by the Consumer Rights Act 2015. Under the 1977 Act, a person might "deal as consumer" in supplying goods or services to a person contracting in the course of business: Peel (ed.), *Treitel on The Law of Contract*, 14th edn (2015), para.7-054; Vol.I, para.15-074.

[309] Above, paras 38-036, 38-041.

restricted in this way, since an individual who acts for purposes that are (wholly or mainly[310]) outside his or her trade, business, craft or profession may equally *supply* goods or services to a trader, for example, in the case of a person who sells their second-hand car to a dealer or a person who guarantees a relative's debts to a bank. Moreover, in the case of consumer contract law derived from EU law, its declared purpose of the protection of consumers as the weaker or less informed party[311] may apply equally to an individual who *supplies* goods or services to a trader as to one who receives them. It is submitted, however, that the question whether such an individual is included within the various legislative schemes of protection in EU or UK law cannot be given a general answer, but must instead be considered in the context of each scheme, for while some legislation is clear on the question, other legislation is more open to argument. For example, the Unfair Commercial Practices Directive 2005 states that it applies to "unfair *business-to-consumer* commercial practices",[312] defined as:

"... act, omission, course of conduct or representation, commercial communication including advertising and marketing, by a trader, directly connected with the promotion, sale or supply of a product to consumers."[313]

The general test of an unfair commercial practice also suggests that it applies only to commercial practices in relation to "products" supplied *to* a consumer[314] and the European Commission's view is that the 2005 Directive does not apply to "consumer-to-business relations".[315] On the other hand, the main examples of unfair commercial practices in the 2005 Directive (misleading statements, misleading omissions and aggressive behaviour) are not worded in a way which suggests such a restriction.[316] Moreover, the 2005 Directive is concerned with commercial *practices* business-to-consumer, both from the point of view of fairness of competition between traders and of the protection of "consumers",[317] and unfair commercial practices can take place where an individual supplies goods or services to a trader on the basis of, for example, a misleading statement, omission or aggressive practice. But if the Commission's view is correct, then the Consumer Protection from Unfair Trading Regulations 2008 go further than the 2005 Directive requires, as they define "commercial practice" as any act, etc. "by a trader, which is directly connected with the promotion, sale or supply of a product *to or from* consumers".[318] This extension also applies to the rights to redress for consumers

---

310 On this point, see above, para.38-036.
311 See above, para.38-034.
312 Directive 2005/29/EC concerning unfair business-to-consumer commercial practices [2005] O.J. L149/22 art.1.
313 Directive 2005/29/EC art.2(d).
314 Directive 2005/29/EC art.5, especially 5(2)(b).
315 First Report from the Commission to the European Parliament, the Council and the European Economic and Social Committee on the application of Directive 2005/29/EC, etc. accompanying Communication Com (2013) 138 final, p.10.
316 Directive 2005/29/EC arts 6–8.
317 Directive 2005/29/EC recitals 1–5.
318 SI 2008/1277 reg.2(1). It is submitted that this extension of the scheme of the 2005 Directive is compatible with its general requirement of "full harmonisation" as, on the narrower view taken by the Commission, consumer-to-business commercial practices fall outside the 2005 Directive's scope and therefore beyond the force of this requirement: cf. above, para.38-025.

against traders created by amendment in 2014 of the 2008 Regulations.[319] By contrast, the Consumer Rights Act 2015 Pt 1 states explicitly that its provisions governing "goods contracts" apply only to "contracts for a trader to supply goods *to a consumer*"[320]: this restriction makes sense, of course, given that these provisions create rights for *buyers*.[321] And while the wording of the Unfair Terms in Consumer Contracts Directive 1993 (formerly implemented in UK law by the Unfair Terms in Consumer Contracts Regulations 1999 and now by the Consumer Rights Act 2015)[322] is not completely clear, the Court of Justice has recently held that there is no requirement that the "consumer" be the recipient of goods or services and so the Directive may apply to a contract under which a natural person acting other than in the course of business guarantees a loan made by a creditor to a commercial company.[323]

38-048 **Burden of proof as to "consumer"** Before its amendment by the Consumer Rights Act 2015, the Unfair Contract Terms Act 1977 provided expressly that "it is for those claiming that a party does not deal as consumer to show that he does not" and this burden of proof applied both to the 1977 Act's provisions controlling exemption clauses and indemnity clauses, and to the provisions in the Sale of Goods Act 1979 creating rights for buyers "dealing as consumer".[324] By contrast, earlier UK legislation implementing other EU directives governing consumer contracts did not set express burdens of proof as to whether a person was a "consumer" so as to benefit from their provisions, following in this respect the directives themselves.[325] It is not entirely clear how EU law would treat the issue of burden of proof on this issue for the purposes, for example, of the Unfair Terms in Consumer Contracts Directive 1993[326] or the Consumer Rights Directive 2011.[327] It may be that the Court of Justice of the EU would hold that, given the absence of any provision in the European legislation on this issue especially where this is in contrast to other issues,[328] the issue of burden of proof lies with national laws as part of the law of procedure and following the general principle of the autonomy of national laws in

---

[319] SI 2008/1277 reg.27A(2)(b) referring to "consumer to business contract" (though restricted to sale of goods) and see below, para.38-177.

[320] Consumer Rights Act 2015 s.3(1). See similarly s.33(1) ("contract for a trader to supply digital content to a consumer") and s.48(1) ("contract for a trader to supply a service to a consumer"): below, paras 38-465 et seq.

[321] The main exception to this is 2015 Act s.51's provision regarding the imposition of a reasonable price on the consumer under "services contracts": below, para.38-578.

[322] See below, paras 38-211 et seq.

[323] *Tarčau v Banca Comercială Intesa Sanpaolo România SA* (C-74/15) Order of CJEU November 19, 2015, on which see below, para.38-226 and para.45-156. In *Harvey v Dunbar Assets Plc* [2017] EWCA Civ 60, [2017] Bus. L.R. 784 at [69]–[70] the CA was prepared to assume from this decision (without deciding) that an individual who guarantees a company debt *can* be a consumer, provided that he is not connected to the company and has been acting outside his business, trader or profession, though it held that the individual before them was held not to satisfy those conditions.

[324] Sale of Goods Act 1979 Pt 5A s.61(5A) which expressly applies the same burden of proof. Similar provision was made for provisions applying to those "dealing as consumer" under the Supply of Goods and Services Act 1982 s.18(4). These provisions were repealed and replaced by the Consumer Rights Act 2015, on which see below, paras 38-049, 38-385.

[325] e.g. Unfair Terms in Consumer Contracts Regulations 1999 on which see below, para.38-225.

[326] Directive 93/13/EEC.

[327] Directive 2011/83/EU.

[328] cf. e.g. the position as to the "individual negotiation" of a term under Directive 93/13/EEC art.3(2).

this area.[329] On the other hand, the Court could hold that the issue requires an autonomous European view and therefore place the burden of proof as to the issue on the consumer following the general principle common to national laws that it is in general for a person alleging something to prove it (*actori incumbit probatio*).[330] However, recent case-law of the Court of Justice in the context of the Consumer Sales Directive imposes a duty on national courts to consider whether a party to litigation is a "consumer" as part of its role in the classification of facts in legal terms and in order to give proper effect to the directive's policy of consumer protection, and this case-law strongly suggests that while in principle it is for the parties to adduce and establish the *facts* on which such a classification is founded (supplemented as needs be by the court requesting clarification), the classification of a party as "consumer" itself is for the court by way of neutral assessment rather than being appropriate to the allocation of a burden of proof.[331]

Recent UK legislation Recent UK consumer protection legislation differs in relation to the issue of burden of proof as to "consumer". For example, the new legislation governing consumer insurance contracts sets no express burden of proof on this issue.[332] This is also the case as regards the Consumer Contracts (Information, Cancellation and Additional Charges) Regulations 2013, which, inter alia, imposes duties of information on traders and provides consumers with rights of cancellation in certain circumstances,[333] and the Consumer Protection from Unfair Trading Regulations 2008, both as regards its provisions prohibiting unfair commercial practices and its new provisions creating rights to redress for consumer in respect of certain such practices.[334] The reason for this lack of express provision as to burden of proof in these sets of regulations is that they implement EU directives which require "full harmonisation" and such a rule could be seen as extending the protection for consumers within their respective scopes.[335] In contrast, the Consumer Rights Act 2015 provides that:

38-049

> "A trader claiming that an individual was not acting for purposes wholly or mainly outside the individual's trade, business, craft or profession must prove it."[336]

This burden of proof applies for the purposes of Pt 1 of the Act (which provides rules governing contracts between a trader and a consumer for the trader to supply

---

[329] cf. below, para.38-335—38-336.

[330] See, e.g. *Systran SA and Systran Luxembourg SA v Commission* (T-19/07) of December 16, 2010, para.206 (where the General Court stated in the context of the Commission's non-contractual liability that "[a]s a general rule, as the Commission claims, where there is a dispute over the existence of a right, it is for the person claiming that the right does or does not exist to substantiate that claim (actori incumbit probatio)").

[331] *Faber v Autobedrijf Hazet Ochten BV* (C-497/13) EU:C:2015:357, June 4, 2015, above, para.38-020. cf. below, para.38-337.

[332] Consumer Insurance (Disclosure and Representations) Act 2012 s.1 defining "consumer insurance contract" and adopted by Insurance Act 2015 s.1.

[333] Consumer Contracts (Information, Cancellation and Additional Charges) Regulations 2013 (SI 2013/3134) reg.4 "consumer".

[334] Consumer Protection from Unfair Trading Regulations 2008 (SI 2008/1277) reg.2(1) "consumer" as amended by Consumer Protection (Amendment) Regulations 2014 (SI 2014/870).

[335] The 2008 Regulations (SI 2008/1277) implement the Unfair Commercial Practices Directive 2005 on whose "full harmonisation" see below, para.38-159; the 2013 Regulations (SI 2013/3134) implement the Consumer Rights Directive 2011 on whose "full harmonisation" see below, para.38-062.

[336] Consumer Rights Act 2015 s.2(4).

goods, digital content or services) and of Pt 2 of the Act (which provides rules governing unfair contract terms). Some of these rules are new and original (not being drawn from EU law),[337] but the majority are drawn either from earlier domestic UK legislation[338] or from EU directives requiring only minimum harmonisation.[339] The main exception to this pattern is found in the 2015 Act's provisions governing the delivery of and passing of risk in goods in contracts to supply goods[340] which implement provisions in the Consumer Rights Directive 2011 which requires (generally and in these cases) "full harmonisation".[341] In these situations, it is therefore possible that the 2015 Act fails properly to implement this Directive in that, to this extent, it goes beyond its requirements within its scope.

(c)   The Other Party to Consumer Contracts—"Traders"

38-050   Background   The fact that one of the parties to a contract has concluded it in the course of a business has long been significant in English contract law, the best-known example being the restriction of the statutory implication of terms as to quality and fitness for purpose of goods sold to sellers so acting.[342] Whether a person does or does not contract "in the course of a business" is also relevant under the Unfair Contract Terms Act 1977, many of whose controls are restricted to exemption clauses governing "business liability",[343] and some of whose controls were for the benefit of persons "dealing as consumer", an element of whose definition contained a requirement that the other party does have to make the contract in the course of a business.[344] While the Consumer Rights Act 2015 abolishes the category of persons "dealing as consumer"[345] and repeals and reforms some of the "business liabilities" contained in the Sale of Goods Act 1979, the notion of a party contracting "in the course of a business" remains significant in some non-consumer contracts, as discussed elsewhere in the present work.[346] For present purposes, modern legislation governing consumer contracts (both EU and UK) defines the non-consumer party to a consumer contract by reference, broadly speaking, to that person's acting in the course of a business, but the precise wording used has differed considerably depending on the context.

---

[337]   e.g. Consumer Rights Act 2015 ss.33–47 (contracts to supply digital content).

[338]   Unfair Contract Terms Act 1977; Sale of Goods Act 1979; Supply of Goods and Services Act 1982.

[339]   Directive 93/13/EEC art.8; Directive 99/44/EEC art.8, above, paras 38-022—38-024.

[340]   2015 Act s.28–29.

[341]   Consumer Rights Directive 2011/83/EEC arts 18 and 20. As will be explained, the 2015 Act also implements the Directive 2011 art.6(5) to the extent to which it gives contractual force to the information required of and given by traders to consumers under those Regulations: 2015 Act ss.11(4)–(6), 12; 36(3)–(4); and 50(3), below, paras 38-499—38-500, 38-548—38-549 and 38-575 respectively.

[342]   Sale of Goods Act 1893 s.14(2) (which required that the goods are of a description which it is in the courses of the seller's business to supply); Sale of Goods Act 1979 s.14(2) and (3) (sale of goods in the course of a business).

[343]   Unfair Contract Terms Act 1977 s.1(3) (as amended).

[344]   Unfair Contract Terms Act 1977 s.12(1)(b). As earlier noted, the Consumer Rights Act 2015 s.75, Sch.4 para.11 deletes the notion of "dealing as consumer" from the 1977 Act: see below, paras 38-372 and see Vol.I, paras 15-073—15-079.

[345]   Consumer Rights Act 2015 s.75, Sch.4 para.11 and see below, paras 38-372.

[346]   e.g. Sale of Goods Act 1979 s.14 (amended by the 2015 Act s.60, Sch.1 para.13); Supply of Goods and Services Act 1982 s.4 (as amended by the 2015 Act s.60, Sch.1 para.40), s.13. See below, para.44-096.

EU legislation   Unlike the relatively consistent approach to the definition of   **38-051**
"consumer" in EU consumer protection legislation,[347] EU directives have used a
wide variety of terms and definitions to describe the party to a consumer contract
other than the consumer depending on the particular subject matter of that
legislation. So, for example, the Unfair Terms in Consumer Contracts Directive
refers to the "seller or supplier" of goods and services, meaning:

"... any natural or legal person who, in contracts covered by this Directive, is acting for
purposes relating to his trade, business or profession, whether publicly owned or privately
owned."[348]

The term "seller or supplier" is not, however, reflected in some other language versions of the 1993 Directive, which instead refer to a "professional" or "tradesman", defined in a similar manner.[349] Other directives refer to the trader party to a
consumer contract by reference to the type of contract in question, as in the case
of a "seller" under the Consumer Sales Directive 1999 which principally concerns
contracts for the sale of goods, and who is then defined in a similar way to the 1993
Directive except that it omits the reference to public or private ownership.[350] The
UK's implementation of these directives reflected this diversity of terminology and
of definition.[351] However, the Unfair Commercial Practices Directive 2005 may be
seen as marking the beginning of a more consistent approach in this respect, providing that:

"... 'trader' means any natural or legal person who, in commercial practices covered by
this Directive, is acting for purposes relating to his trade, business, craft or profession and
anyone acting in the name of or on behalf of a trader."[352]

This general form of words was taken up by the Consumer Rights Directive 2011,
which provides that:

"... 'trader' means any natural or legal person, *irrespective of whether privately or publicly
owned*, who is acting, including through any other person acting in his name or on his

---

[347]   Above, para.38-032.
[348]   Directive 93/13/EEC art.2(c).
[349]   The non-consumer party to the contract is termed *professionnel* in the French and *Gewerbetreibender*
in the German versions of Directive 93/13/EEC art.2(c).
[350]   Directive 99/44/EEC art.1(2)(c). The French version of this provision refers to "business activity,
whether public or private" (*"activité professionnelle, qu'elle soit publique or privée"*). See similarly,
Timeshare Directive 94/47 art.2 ("vendor") and Package Travel Directive 90/314/EEC art.2(2) and
(3) ("organizer" and "retailer"), though this approach was amended by Directive (EU) 2015/2302
on package travel and linked travel arrangements [2015] O.J. L326/1, which revokes and replaces
the 1990 Directive. Art.3 of the 2015 Directive defines "organiser" and "retailer" as categories of
"trader", which is itself defined and which extends to persons facilitating a "linked travel
arrangement": see below, paras 38-142 et seq. The directives differ also as to whether they mention
that the business party acts through an agent: cf. the Doorstep Selling Directive 85/577/EEC art.2
("anyone acting in the name or on behalf of a trader") and the Unfair Terms in Consumer Contracts
Directive 93/13/EEC art.2(c) which makes no such reference.
[351]   The 1999 Directive was first implemented in English law by amendment of the Supply of Goods
(Implied Terms) Act 1973, the Sale of Goods Act 1979 and the Supply of Goods and Services Act
1982 (as explained below, paras 38-439 et seq.), all of which define the trader party to the contract
as "seller", "bailor" or "supplier" as the case may be.
[352]   Directive 2005/29/EC art.2(b).

behalf, for purposes relating to his trade, business, craft or profession in relation to contracts covered by this Directive."[353]

It will be seen, though, that while "trader" is used in both cases, there remains no textual consistency in relation to the question whether the trader is public or private (in activity or ownership) and whether the trader acts personally or through an agent.

38-052 **European case-law** However, the Court of Justice has taken a very broad approach to the expression acting "in the course of business" and "trader" in the context of EU consumer protection legislation. In *Veedfald v Århus Amtskommune*[354] the Court of Justice considered the meaning of a defence to liability in a producer in art.7(c) of the Product Liability Directive 1985 where the producer can prove that "the product was neither manufactured by him for sale or any form of distribution for economic purpose nor manufactured or distributed by him in the course of his business".[355] In *Veedfald* a public hospital argued that, as it had produced and used the product in question in the course of providing publicly funded health care for which its patient did not pay, it therefore did not do so for an economic purpose or in the course of [its] business within the meaning of art.7(c).[356] However, the European Court disagreed, holding that the fact that products are manufactured for a service for which the patient has not paid and which is financed from public funds:

> "... cannot detract from the economic and business character of that manufacture. The activity in question is not a charitable one which could therefore be covered by the exemption from liability provided for in Article 7(c) of the Directive. Besides, the [defendant hospital] itself admitted at the hearing that, in similar circumstances, a private hospital would undoubtedly be liable for the defectiveness of the product pursuant to the provisions of the Directive."[357]

This last point was clearly addressed to the argument put to the Court that the application of the 1985 Directive's scheme of liability to public hospitals would have harmful consequences for public health care and place them at a disadvantage in relation to private health schemes.[358] While this decision concerned a provision in a defence to liability and the European Court interprets such defences narrowly (especially where they reduce the protection of consumers[359]), it suggests that the Court is likely to interpret "course of business" in other consumer protection directives so as to further their purposes of the facilitation of the internal market by reducing distortions of competition and the furtherance of the protection of consumers.[360]

38-053 **BKK Mobil Oil and Šiba v Devėnas** This broad approach is confirmed by *BKK Mobil Oil* where the Court of Justice of the EU considered the proper approach to

---

[353] Directive 2011/83/EU art.2(2) (emphasis added) and see also recital 16.
[354] *Veedfald v Århus Amtskommune* (C-203/99) EU:C:2001:258, [2001] E.C.R. I-3569.
[355] Directive 1985/374/EEC art.7(c).
[356] EU:C:2001:258, [2001] E.C.R. I-3569 at [20].
[357] EU:C:2001:258, [2001] E.C.R. I-3569 at [21].
[358] EU:C:2001:258, [2001] E.C.R. I-3569 at [20].
[359] EU:C:2001:258, [2001] E.C.R. I-3569 at [15].
[360] See, e.g. 1993 Directive recitals 1–2.

be taken to the definition of "trader" and "business" for the purposes of the Unfair Commercial Practices Directive,[361] in the context of the question whether a health insurance fund established as a public law body in German law is subject to the controls in that Directive. As earlier noted, the Directive provides:

"... 'trader' means any natural or legal person who, in commercial practices covered by this Directive, is acting for purposes relating to his trade, business, craft or profession and anyone acting in the name of or on behalf of a trader."[362]

First, the Court held that an "autonomous and uniform" European interpretation must be given to this definition, and, as a result, "the classification, legal status and specific characteristics of the body at issue under national law are irrelevant".[363] The Court further held that the definition of "trader" is "particularly broad" not excluding "either bodies pursuing a task of public interest or those which are governed by public law" and must be determined "in relation to the related but diametrically opposed concept of 'consumer', which refers to any individual not engaged in commercial or trade activities".[364] In the Court's view, given that the health insurance fund's members were manifestly consumers, the fund must be treated as a "trader" and "whether the body at issue or the specific task it pursues are public or private is irrelevant".[365] In this respect, the Court of Justice did not follow the advice of Advocate General Bott, who saw "the common thread" running through a number of EU consumer protection directives, including the Unfair Terms in Consumer Contracts Directive 1993 and the Consumer Rights Directive 2011, as being:

"... that a trader may be a natural person or a public-law or private-law body who, in his relations with consumers, is acting for purposes relating to his trade or profession, *which presupposes that he acts within the framework of a regular profit-making activity*."[366]

Moreover, in *Šiba v Devėnas* the Court of Justice applied its approach to "trader" in the 2005 Directive to "seller or supplier" under the 1993 Directive, holding therefore that the public or private nature of the specific task which forms the subject matter of the contract cannot determine the Directive's application.[367] This

---

361 *BKK Mobil Oil Körperschaft des öffentlichen Rechts v Zentrale zur Bekämpfung unlauteren Wettbewerbs eV* (C-59/12) EU:C:2013:634, October 3, 2013 (*"BKK Mobil Oil* (C-59/12)").

362 Directive 2005/29/EC art.2(b).

363 *BKK Mobil Oil* (C-59/12) at paras 25–26.

364 *BKK Mobil Oil* (C-59/12) at paras 32–33 citing by analogy *Shearson Lehman Hutton v TVB Treuhandgesellschaft für Vermögensverwaltung und Beteiligungen mbH* (C-89/91) EU:C:1993:15, [1993] E.C.R. I-00139 at para.22 on art.13 of the Brussels Convention on jurisdiction and the enforcement of judgments in civil and commercial matters.

365 *BKK Mobil Oil* (C-59/12) at paras 36–38.

366 *BKK Mobil Oil* (C-59/12) A.G. Opinion February 12, 2014 at para.42 (emphasis added). cf. Vol.I, para.15-072 where it is said that "business" for the purposes of s.1(3) of the Unfair Contract Terms Act 1977 does not require acting with the view to profit relying principally on *Town Investments Ltd v Department of Environment* [1978] A.C. 359 (government department could conclude a "business tenancy").

367 C-537/13 EU:C:2015:14, January 15, 2015 [2015] Bus. L.R. 291, para.28. See similarly *Karel de Grote-Hogeschool Katholieke Hogeschool Antwerpen VZW v Kuijpers* (C-147/16) EU:C:2018:320, May 17, 2018 at paras 44–60 (not-for-profit independent educational institution subsidised mostly by public funds can be a "seller or supplier" in relation to a contract by which the student agrees to repay sums due in respect of registration fees and a study trip, though the CJEU apparently distinguished such a contract from the provision of the education itself on the basis that it is not a "service" within the meaning of art.57 TFEU). A.G. Sharpston in her opinion of November 30, 2017

case-law strongly suggests that the Court of Justice would take a similarly very broad interpretation of the definition of the trader party to a consumer contract for the purposes of other directives in the consumer *acquis*, without the need for any explicit reference to a business being "publicly owned or privately owned".[368]

38-054 **A regular part of his business?** For the purposes of domestic legislation, English courts have come to contrasting views on the question whether, in order to act "in the course" of a business, a person must contract in a way which forms part of the regular course of dealing of that business. On the one hand, in *R. & B. Customs Brokers Co Ltd v United Dominions Trust Ltd* the Court of Appeal held that a person may "deal as consumer" within the meaning of the Unfair Contract Terms Act 1977, even though contracting as part of its business if the contract was neither integral to its business or forms a regular part of it.[369] On the other hand, in *Stevenson v Rogers* the Court of Appeal held that a person who contracts as part of his business does so "in the course of" that business for the purposes of the implication of the term as to quality of goods sold in the Sale of Goods Act 1979,[370] this decision being influenced by the change in wording from the 1893 Act which required that the "goods [were] bought by description from a seller who deals in goods of that description".[371] While apparently inconsistent, these two decisions have in common that they extended the ambit of the legislative controls in question, whether in terms of the imposition of liability for failures in quality of goods sold or the control of exemption clauses. As regards consumer contracts, the legislative contexts of these earlier decisions have changed, since the Consumer Rights Act 2015 now provides for the statutory terms to be included in consumer contracts for the supply of goods, digital content and services and the rules governing unfair contract terms, using a single definition of "trader" for both these purposes.[372] In doing so, the 2015 Act thereby implements EU directives affecting sales of goods and unfair contract terms.[373]

38-055 **EU law** This then raises the question as to the likely view of the Court of Justice as to the need for regularity in contracting for a trader to act in the course of a business for the purposes of EU consumer protection legislation. This may, of course, be influenced by the particular wording or context of the directive in question, but the Court of Justice of the EU would resolve the question by reference to its purposes in the light of general EU principle. In this respect, EU legislation in this context is intended to create protection for consumers as "weaker" and less well-informed parties throughout the European Union and by this means increase consumer confidence and thus the facilitation of the establishment of the internal

---

the same case at para.50 considered, however, that the definition of "seller or supplier" in the 1993 Directive is (at least textually) wider than the terms used in other consumer instruments.

[368] cf. *Karel de Grote-Hogeschool Katholieke Hogeschool Antwerpen VZW v Kuijpers* (C-147/16) EU:C:2018:320, Opinion of A.G. Sharpston, November 30, 2017 at para.50.

[369] [1988] 1 W.L.R. 321.

[370] [1999] Q.B. 1028; *Feldarol Foundry Plc v Hermes Leasing (London) Ltd* [2004] EWCA Civ 747, (2004) 101 (24) L.S.G. 32.

[371] Sale of Goods Act 1893 s.14(2); [1999] Q.B. 1028, 1035–1040.

[372] Consumer Rights Act 2015 ss.2(2) and (7) (Pt 1); s.76(2) (applying the Pt 1 definitions for Pt 2), below, paras 38-365 et seq. and especially 38-383; 38-465 et seq. and especially 38-482.

[373] i.e. Unfair Terms in Consumer Contracts Directive 1993; Consumer Sales Directive 1999.

market.[374] In this respect, a consumer will not usually be aware or able to become aware of the nature of the business of a supplier of goods or services and, therefore, whether or not the contract which he intends to conclude does or does not form a regular part of its business. In terms of authority, as has been seen, the Court of Justice in *BKK Mobil Oil* did not require a trader's act to fall "within the framework of a regular profit-making activity" as had its Advocate General.[375] As a result, it is submitted that, in principle, the consumer should not be deprived of the protections required by a directive merely because the contract in question is unusual for the supplier. Finally, the question has arisen as to the circumstances in which a person who offers to sell goods through an internet platform does so as a "trader" for the purposes of the Unfair Commercial Practices Directive or the Consumer Rights Directive.[376] According to Advocate General Szpunar in *Kamenova*, an individual who on one occasion offers to sell eight different goods (some new, some second-hand) does not do so, but he emphasised that in deciding this question national courts should take into account whether the platform was organised and set up for profit; how many sales were made and for how long; whether the seller possessed a legal status which allowed it to make "commercial transactions"[377]; whether he was subject to VAT; whether he acted for a trader, or for an agent of a trader, and received some remuneration (as in the case of "influencers"); whether he bought things for resale so as to render his activity regular, frequent or simultaneous to a business (as where he sells goods from home as well as online); whether the level of profit generated by sales confirms that the transaction forms part of a business activity; and/or whether the products for sale are of the same type or value, in particular, if the offer is restricted to a limited number of products.[378] These various elements were seen by Advocate General Szpunar as allowing national courts to decide whether a person exercises a commercial activity which thereby places him in a position of superiority in relation to a consumer and, therefore, whether there is a situation of imbalance between trader and consumer.[379]

Trader as "intermediary" of non-trader   In *Wathelet v Garage Bietheres & Fils SPRL*[380] a consumer had bought a second-hand car from a garage, the car in fact being owned by a private individual on behalf of whom the garage sold the car. Although the issue was disputed, the national court held that there was "strong, specific and circumstantial evidence indicating that [the private individual] was not informed that it was a private sale".[381] The question arose as to whether a trader who acts as intermediary on behalf of a non-professional seller counts as a "seller" within the meaning of the Consumer Sales Directive 1999 so as to bear the liabilities which   **38-056**

---

[374] e.g. 1993 Directive recitals 5, 6 and 10. On the role of EU consumer law as protecting the consumer as weaker party and less well-informed party see further *Pereničová v SOS finance, spol. sro* (C-453/10) EU:C:2012:144, [2012] 2 C.M.L.R. 28 para.27.

[375] *BKK Mobil Oil* (C-59/12) and cf. A.G. Bott's Opinion at para.42 quoted more fully above, para.38-053.

[376] *Komisiaza zashtita na potrebeitelite v Kamenova* (C-105/17) EU:C:2018:378 Opinion of A.G. Szpunar of May 31, 2018 (available in French) ("*Kamenova* (C-105/17) Opinion of A.G. Szpunar").

[377] In some national laws, "commercial transactions" ("*actes de commerce*") are defined by law and may be restricted to persons enjoying the status to do so.

[378] *Kamenova* (C-105/17) Opinion of A.G. Szpunar at paras 49–52

[379] *Kamenova* (C-105/17) Opinion of A.G. Szpunar at para.53.

[380] C-149/15 EU:C:2016:840, [2017] 1 W.L.R. 865 ("*Wathelet* (C-149/150)").

[381] *Wathelet* (C-149/15) at para.22.

that directive imposes on "sellers", whether or not the trader is remunerated and whether or not the trader informed the prospective buyer that the seller is a private individual.[382] The Court of Justice of the EU held in this respect that the sale was a "private sale" as the owner of the vehicle was a private individual, the garage acting as a trader and as authorised intermediary.[383] The concept of "seller" must be given an autonomous interpretation for the purposes of the 1999 Directive and, while the definition in the Directive does not cover intermediaries, it should be interpreted as covering:

"… a trader acting as intermediary on behalf of a private individual who has not duly informed the consumer of the fact that the owner of the goods sold is a private individual",

which is for the national court to decide on the facts,[384] taking into account the degree of participation and the amount of effort employed by the intermediary in the sale, the circumstances in which the goods were presented to the consumer, and the latter's behaviour.[385] This interpretation of the Directive was explicitly said not to depend on whether the intermediary is remunerated for so acting.[386] This result was justified by the Court of Justice by the need to ensure the high level of consumer protection required by the 1999 Directive which would be put at risk if the consumer's ignorance concerning the capacity in which the trader acts were allowed to deprive him of the rights provided by the Directive.[387] In English law, it would seem that in these circumstances the trader would be considered to be the agent of an undisclosed principal,[388] and so could be sued on the contract of sale as "seller" on this basis.[389]

38-057 **Recent UK legislation: a standard approach to "trader"** The Consumer Rights (Payment Surcharges) Regulations 2012,[390] the Consumer Contracts (Information, Cancellation and Additional Payments) Regulations 2013 and the Consumer Rights Act 2015 all refer to the non-consumer party to the contracts to which they apply as a "trader" and state that:

---

[382] *Wathelet* (C-149/15) at para.23. According to the 1999 Directive art.1(1)(c) "*seller*: shall mean any natural or legal person who, under a contract, sells consumer goods in the course of his trade, business or profession". On the significance of the 1999 Directive and its implementation in English law see below, paras 38-433 et seq.

[383] *Wathelet* (C-149/15) at paras 24–26.

[384] *Wathelet* (C-149/15) at paras 28–30 and 45.

[385] *Wathelet* (C-149/15) at para.44.

[386] *Wathelet* (C-149/15) at para.45. Remuneration was seen as part of the contractual relationship between the individual owner of the goods and the intermediary and therefore outside the scope of the Directive: *Wathelet* (C-149/15) at para.43.

[387] *Wathelet* (C-149/15) at paras 36–42.

[388] There is a degree of uncertainty here as the A.G.'s Opinion refers to an intermediary acting *in the name of* as well as on behalf of the individual and the former suggests that the agency is disclosed, whereas the CJEU states the facts as being that the consumer was told that her apparent seller acted as an intermediary only after the contract had been concluded: *Wathelet* (C-149/15) at para.14.

[389] See Vol.I, para.31-063. The general law of agency applies to contracts for the sale of goods: Sale of Goods Act 1979 s.62(2); *Benjamin's Sale of Goods* 10th edn (2017), para.3-002.

[390] SI 2012/3110 reg.2 "trader" (as amended by SI 2013/3134 Sch.4 para.15(2)) and see generally below, para.38-428.

"... 'trader' means a person acting for purposes relating to that person's trade, business, craft or profession, whether acting personally or through another person acting in the trader's name or on the trader's behalf."[391]

"Business" includes the activities of any government department or local or public authority.[392] While the form of the definitions of "trader" and "business" in the Consumer Protection from Unfair Trading Regulations 2008 (as amended in 2014) differ slightly from this form of words, the substance of all the new statutory definitions is identical except that a "trader" is stated as including "a person acting in the name of or on behalf of a trader"[393] except for the purposes of the consumer's new rights to redress against "traders".[394]

EU and UK legislative interpretation All the recent UK consumer contract **38-058** legislation where these definitions of "trader" are encountered reflect EU directives which use and define the "trader".[395] In this respect, as earlier noted, the Court of Justice of the EU has adopted a broad approach to the definition of "trader" for the purposes of two of these directives[396] and is likely to take the same approach to the other relevant consumer protection directives.[397] In particular, the Court has

---

[391] Consumer Contracts (Information, Cancellation and Additional Charges) Regulations 2013 (SI 2013/3134) reg.4 "trader"; Consumer Rights Act 2015 s.2(2).

[392] The Consumer Rights (Payment Surcharges) Regulations 2012 (SI 2012/3110) reg.3 "business" (as inserted by SI 2013/3134 Sch.4 para.15(3)(a)); Consumer Contracts (Information, Cancellation and Additional Charges) Regulations 2013 (SI 2013/3134) reg.5 "business"; Consumer Rights Act 2015 s.2(7).

[393] Consumer Protection from Unfair Trading Regulations 2008 (SI 2008/1277) reg.2(1) "business" and "trader" (as amended by SI 2014/870). The effect of this inclusion is to subject a trader's agent to a possible personal responsibility in respect of the commission of an unfair commercial practice, as foreseen by reg.8 (offences relating to unfair commercial practices).

[394] Consumer Protection from Unfair Trading Regulations 2008 (SI 2008/1277) reg.2(1) "trader" (b) (as amended by SI 2014/870). The definition of the non-consumer party to "consumer insurance contracts" under the Consumer Insurance (Disclosure and Representations) Act 2012 and Insurance Act 2015 (neither of which implement EU legislation) differs, designating that party as "a person who carries on the business of insurance and who becomes a party to the contract by way of that business (whether or not in accordance with permission for the purposes of the Financial Services and Markets Act 2000)" (2012 Act s.1(b) "consumer insurance contract"); Insurance Act 2015 s.1: and see below, para.42-031.

[395] In the case of the Consumer Rights (Payment Surcharges) Regulations 2012, the Consumer Contracts (Information, Cancellation and Additional Payments) Regulations 2013 and the Consumer Rights Act 2015 the UK legislation implements the relevant directive; in the case of the Consumer Protection from Unfair Trading Regulations 2008 (as amended in 2014), the regulations as a whole implement a directive (the Unfair Commercial Practices Directive 2005), even though the consumer's rights to redress are not required by that directive: below, paras 38-157 et seq.

[396] *BKK Mobil Oil Körperschaft des öffentlichen Rechts v Zentrale zur Bekämpfung unlauteren Wettbewerbs eV* (C-59/12) EU:C:2013:634, October 3, 2013 (Unfair Commercial Practices Directive 2005); *Šiba v Devėnas* (C-537/13) EU:C:2015:14 (Unfair Terms in Consumer Contracts Directive 1993) above, paras 38-052—38-053.

[397] i.e. the Consumer Sales Directive 1999 and the Consumer Rights Directive 2011. If this were not the case and these directives were interpreted by the CJEU as having a narrower understanding of "trader", it is submitted that the broader UK statutory definitions would be compatible with EU law, as their references to a trader acting through an agent and to a trader undertaking activities of a public character would then represent extensions of the protective schemes of the directives to persons otherwise outside their scope of application and so such an extension would not fall foul even of those directives which require "full harmonisation": cf. the Unfair Commercial Practices Directive 2005 and the Consumer Rights Directive 2011 (both of which in principle require "full harmonisation") and the Unfair Terms in Consumer Contracts Directive 1993 and the Consumer Sales Direc-

recognised that public authorities can be "traders" and that there is, therefore, no requirement that a trader acts with a view to profit.[398] Moreover, if the arguments earlier set out hold good, this would also mean that the definition of "trader" would not require any contract made with a consumer to form an integral part of the trader's business or be concluded with any degree of regularity by him.[399]

4. Information Requirements and Consumers' Rights of Cancellation

(a) Introduction

38-059 **Rationale** In the context of the protection of the economic interests of consumers, the European legislator has long seen the use of duties of information in traders towards consumers before the conclusion of a contract as an important regulatory technique.[400] As Weatherill observes:

"These techniques do not address directly the content of the bargain between trader and consumer. Contractual terms remain to be fixed by private negotiation.[401] The assumption underlying [this] type of regulatory technique ... is that an imbalance of economic power can be sufficiently corrected by adjusting the environment within which the bargain is struck by giving the consumer extra information in advance and extra time to consider the implications."[402]

Rather than a single regime, the EU legislator enacted a series of distinct regimes dealing with contracts made in particular circumstances or with particular categories of contract. As a result, duties of information were imposed on traders in relation to contracts made in particular circumstances (notably, contracts made away from business premises ("doorstep selling")[403] and contracts made at a distance[404]) or contracts where the consumer is seen as particularly at risk of abuse, as in the case of timeshare contracts[405] and package holidays.[406] Other information requirements were imposed on the providers of "information society services" (such as selling goods online) which apply for the benefit of all their recipients, but in the case of

tive (both of which require merely "minimum harmonisation"): see above, paras 38-022, 38-024 and 38-026 and 38-028.
[398] Above, para.38-053.
[399] Above, para.38-055 for the arguments in support of this view.
[400] Weatherill, *EU Consumer Law and Policy*, 2nd edn (2013), Ch.4.
[401] cf. though, the important controls on unfair contract terms put in place by Directive 93/13/EEC on unfair terms in consumer contracts, below, para.38-212.
[402] Weatherill, *EU Consumer Law and Policy*, 2nd edn (2013), p.92, who also considers criticisms of this technique.
[403] Directive 85/577/EEC to protect the consumer in respect of contracts negotiated away from business premises [1985] O.J. L372/31 ("Doorstep Selling Directive 1985").
[404] Directive 97/7/EC on the protection of consumers in respect of distance contracts [1997] O.J. L144/19; Directive 2002/65/EC concerning the distance marketing of consumer financial services [2002] O.J. L271/16.
[405] Directive 94/47/EC on the protection of purchasers in respect of certain aspects of contracts relating to the purchase of the right to use immovable properties on a timeshare basis, revoked and replaced by the Timeshare Directive 2008/122/EC ("Timeshare Directive 2009"), below, paras 38-148 et seq.
[406] Directive 90/314/EEC on package travel, package holidays and package tours repealed and replaced by Directive (EU) 2015/2302 on package travel and linked travel arrangements [2015] O.J. L326/1 and see below, paras 38-137 et seq. esp. at paras 38-139 and 38-144.

consumers cannot be excluded by agreement.[407] Often the imposition of information duties on the trader before the conclusion of a contract has been combined with the provision of a cooling-off period within which consumers are entitled to cancel[408] the contract.[409] The justifications for these rights of cancellation have differed according to context: in timeshare contracts, the right is provided so as to give consumers the "opportunity of fully understanding their rights and obligations under the contract"[410]; in distance contracts, it is justified on the ground that the consumer is not able to see the goods before concluding the contract,[411] and in off-premises contracts because of the risk of surprise and the frequent inability of consumers to compare the offer made with other offers.[412] Following the then general pattern, these directives required merely "minimum harmonisation".[413]

The Consumer Rights Directive 2011 The main provisions of the 2011 directive are concerned with the reformulation of the information requirements and rights of cancellation for door-step selling (renamed "off-premises contracting") and distance contracts generally (but not distance contracts related to financial services[414]), but the directive also introduces new information requirements in traders to consumers in contracts which are neither off-premises contracts nor distance contracts, and requires certain other measures for the protection of consumers in relation to contracts (for example, in relation to the imposition of "additional payments").[415] After implementation of the 2011 Directive in UK law by the

38-060

---

[407] Directive 2000/31/EC on certain legal aspects of information society services, in particular electronic commerce, in the Internal Market ("Directive on electronic commerce") [2000] O.J. L178/1 art.10. This requirement is implemented in UK law by the Electronic Commerce (EC Directive) Regulations 2002 (SI 2002/2013), below, para.38-156.

[408] The EU directives refer here to "withdrawal" rather than "cancellation" of a contract, but recent UK secondary legislation refers to "cancellation" when the directives refer to "withdrawal" and instead use "withdrawal" to describe a consumer's right to revoke his *offer*: Consumer Contracts (Information, Cancellation and Additional Charges) Regulations 2013 (SI 2013/3134) ("2013 Regulations") regs 29(3), 32(1), 33, 34 and 38 and see below, para.38-113. This chapter will follow the usage in these UK regulations.

[409] Weatherill, *EU Consumer Law and Policy*, 2nd edn (2013), p.92.

[410] Timeshare Directive 2009 recital 11.

[411] Directive 97/7/EC recital 14 and see similarly Consumer Rights Directive 2011 recital 37.

[412] Directive 85/577/EEC recital 3 and see similarly Consumer Rights Directive 2011 recital 37 which refers also to the risk of psychological pressure. See also *Martín Martín v EDP Editores SL* (C-227/08) EU:C:2009:792, [2009] E.C.R. I-11939 para.22 where the ECJ stated that the Doorstep Selling Directive was "designed to protect consumers against the risks inherent in the conclusion of contracts away from business premises ... as the special feature of those contracts is that as a rule it is the trader who initiates the contract negotiations, and the consumer has not prepared for such door-to-door selling by, inter alia, comparing the price and quality of the different offers available", a passage relied on by the SC in *Roberton v Swift* [2014] UKSC 50, [2014] 1 W.L.R. 3438 at [9]. The ECJ has held that where a consumer was in one of the situations of "doorstep selling" as set out by the Doorstep Selling Directive 1985, then he enjoyed a right of renunciation of the contract even though "specific conduct or an intention to manipulate on the part of the trader" are not established: *Travel Vac SL v Antelm Sanchis* (C-423/97) EU:C:1999:197, [1999] E.C.R. I-2195 at para.43.

[413] Directive 85/577/EEC art.8; Directive 97/7/EC art.14; Directive 94/47/EC art.11. On the significance of "minimum harmonisation" generally see above, paras 38-022—38-023.

[414] These remain governed by Directive 2002/65/EC.

[415] Consumer Rights Directive 2011 Ch.IV "Other Consumer Rights". On the 2011 Directive generally see European Commission, *DG Justice Guidance Document concerning Directive 2011/83/EU*, etc. (June 2014) ("DG Justice Guidance Document on 2011 Directive") available at *http://ec.europa.eu/justice/consumer-marketing/files/crd_guidance_en.pdf*. See also European Commission, *Report from the Commission to the European Parliament and the Council on the application of Direc-*

Consumer Contracts (Information, Cancellation and Additional Charges) Regulations 2013 (the "2013 Regulations"),[416] these regulations contain the general and most important information and cancellation provisions governing consumer contracts. However, there are other, special provisions governing particular categories of contract: "distance contracts" for the supply of financial services,[417] timeshare,[418] package travel[419] and contracts concluded by electronic means.[420] There are also information requirements imposed on traders in relation to alternative dispute resolution (ADR).[421] This section will focus on the 2013 Regulations, but its final paragraphs will outline the legislation governing these special categories.[422]

38-061 **Consumer Contracts (Information, Cancellation and Additional Charges) Regulations 2013** The UK implemented most (though not all) of the requirements of the Consumer Rights Directive by the Consumer Contracts (Information, Cancellation and Additional Charges) Regulations 2013 (the "2013 Regulations").[423] The 2013 Regulations therefore revoked and replaced earlier UK regulations implementing the directives which the 2011 Directive itself replaced, the Cancellation of Contracts made in a Consumer's Home or Place of Work, etc. Regulations 2008[424] and the Consumer Protection (Distance Selling) Regulations 2000.[425]

---

tive 2011/83/EU, COM(2017) 259 final (with accompanying Commission Staff Working Document SWD (2017) 169 final).

[416] SI 2013/3134.

[417] Financial Services (Distance Marketing) Regulations 2004 (SI 2004/2095) below, para.38-136.

[418] Timeshare, Holiday Products, Resale and Exchange Contracts Regulations 2010 (SI 2010/2960) below, paras 38-148—38-154

[419] The Package Travel and Linked Travel Arrangements Regulations 2018 (SI 2018/634) revoking and replacing the Package Travel, Package Holidays and Package Tours Regulations 1992 (SI 1992/3288); see below, paras 38-137—38-147.

[420] Electronic Commerce (EC Directive) Regulations 2002 (SI 2002/2013) reg.9, below, para.38-156. There are two further situations foreseen by the Consumer Rights Act 2015 in which traders must provide information to consumers and others. First, ss.83–88 impose a duty on letting agents to publicise their fees, though the enforcement measures provided by s.87 of the Act do not affect the validity of any contract made. Secondly, ss.90–95 (as amended by the Digital Economy Act 2017 s.105 as from April 6, 2018) impose on persons who resell tickets for a recreational, sporting or cultural event in the UK through a secondary ticketing facility a number of information duties (e.g. as to the ticket, the venue, etc.), prohibit the original seller from cancelling resold tickets or blacklisting persons reselling (in both cases subject to conditions), but again the enforcement measures provided by s.93 do not affect the validity of any contract made.

[421] Directive 2013/11/EU of May 31, 2013 on alternative dispute resolution for consumer disputes [2013] O.J. L165/63, below, para.38-155.

[422] See below, paras 38-135 et seq.

[423] SI 2013/3134 (in force June 13, 2014). The Consumer Rights Act 2015 ss.11(4) and (5), 12 (goods contracts), s.36(3) and (4), 37 (digital content contracts) and s.50 (services contracts) give effect to the Consumer Rights Directive 2011 art.6(5)'s requirement that information provided by traders as required by the 2011 Directive (in relation to off-premises and distance contracts) forms part of the contract: see below, paras 38-105, 38-499—38-500, 38-548—38-549 and 38-575. The Consumer Rights (Payment Surcharges) Regulations 2012 (SI 2012/3110) (as amended by the Payment Services Regulations 2017 (SI 2017/752)) give effect to the Consumer Rights Directive 2011 art.19 on which see below, para.38-428.

[424] SI 2008/1816, itself replacing Consumer Protection (Cancellation of Contracts Concluded away from Business Premises) Regulations 1987 (SI 1987/2117) implementing the Directive 85/577/EEC. The 2008 Regulations (SI 2008/1816) therefore do not apply to contracts entered into on or after June 13, 2014, being the date of coming into force of the 2013 Regulations: 2013 Regulations reg.2(b).

[425] SI 2000/2334 implementing Directive 97/7/EC. The 2000 Regulations (SI 2000/2334) therefore do

This section will principally explain the provisions of the 2013 Regulations governing information and cancellation,[426] and will note the special rules governing, for example, timeshare contracts,[427] but will leave until later in this chapter the UK's legislation implementing the Consumer Rights Directive's requirements other than those relating to information and cancellation.[428] As yet there is no case-law on either the 2011 Directive or the 2013 Regulations, but, where still relevant, reference will be made to European and English case-law on the directives and regulations which they respectively replaced.

"Full harmonisation" with qualifications   The Consumer Rights Directive **38-062** makes clear that, in principle, it requires "full harmonisation" of the matters within its scope, but adds "unless otherwise provided for in this Directive".[429] There are a number of matters which remain required only as a matter of "minimum harmonisation", notably, the information requirements imposed on traders where the contracts which they conclude with consumers are neither off-premises contracts nor distance contracts[430] (termed "on-premises contracts" by the 2013 Regulations[431]) and the 2011 Directive also provides expressly for options for Member States in relation to some of its provisions. For example, while in the case of the effect of cancellation by a consumer on "ancillary contracts" the Directive provides the general rule that cancellation shall automatically terminate such ancillary contracts "without any costs for the consumer", it adds that "Member States shall lay down detailed rules on the termination of such contracts".[432] The following discussion will explain how the 2013 Regulations relate to the underlying provisions in the 2011 Directive only where this is relevant to their interpretation or application.

Autonomous interpretations and "national general contract law"   Article 3(5) **38-063** of the Consumer Rights Directive states that:

"This Directive shall not affect national general contract law such as the rules on the validity, formation or effect of a contract, in so far as general contract law aspects are not regulated in this Directive."

---

not apply to contracts entered into on or after June 13, 2014, being the date of coming into force of the 2013 Regulations: 2013 Regulations reg.2(a).
[426] They also note the earlier provisions governing information and cancellation in the Financial Services (Distance Marketing) Regulations 2004 (SI 2004/2095) which implemented the Distance Contracts for Financial Services Directive 2002 [2002] O.J. L271/16. On these regulations see below, para.38-136.
[427] See below, paras 38-148 et seq.
[428] The Consumer Rights Directive's provisions (arts 18 and 20) on delivery of goods and the passing of risk in "sales contracts" were implemented in UK law first by the 2013 Regulations regs 42 and 43, but were reimplemented by the Consumer Rights Act 2015 ss.28 and 29. The Consumer Rights Directive's provisions on fees for the use of means of payment (art.19) were implemented by the Consumer Rights (Payment Surcharges) Regulations 2012 (SI 2012/3110) (on which see below, para.38-428) and its provision on "communication by telephone", "additional payments" and inertia selling (arts 21, 22 and 27 respectively) were implemented by the 2013 Regulations regs 41, 40 and 39 respectively (on which see below, paras 38-430—38-431).
[429] Consumer Rights Directive 2011 art.4.
[430] Consumer Rights Directive 2011 art.5(4).
[431] 2013 Regulations reg.5 "on-premises contract".
[432] Consumer Rights Directive 2011 art.15. Further examples may be found in art.6(7) (language requirements) and art.7(4) (off-premises contracts concerning certain works of repairs or maintenance where payment does not exceed €200).

This provision is contained within an article entitled "scope" and, at first sight, resembles closely art.3(2) of the Unfair Commercial Practices Directive 2005 which states that it is "without prejudice to contract law and, in particular, to the rules on the validity, formation or effect of a contract".[433] It is true that art.3(5) of the Consumer Rights Directive and art.3(2) of the Unfair Commercial Practices Directive rest on a distinction between "(general) contract law" and other aspects of their respective requirements (and notably the compliance measures for the enforcement of the duties and prohibitions imposed on traders[434]), but the functions of the two provisions differ significantly. For while art.3(2) of the Unfair Commercial Practices Directive excludes "contract law" entirely from its scope and, therefore, from the impact of the full harmonisation which the 2005 Directive generally imposes in respect of its prohibitions on unfair commercial practices business-to-consumer,[435] art.3(5) of the 2011 Directive implicitly acknowledges that *some* of its provisions *do* regulate "(general) contract law". As Recital 14 to the 2011 Directive explains:

"This Directive should not affect national law in the area of contract law for contract law aspects that are not regulated by this Directive. Therefore, this Directive should be without prejudice to national law regulating for instance the conclusion or the validity of a contract (for instance in the case of lack of consent). Similarly, this Directive should not affect national law in relation to the general contractual legal remedies, the rules on public economic order, for instance rules on excessive or extortionate prices, and the rules on unethical legal transactions."

So, art.3(5) of the 2011 Directive does not put aside "contract law" from its scope, but rather specifies that "contract law" issues raised by its own provisions (and therefore within its scope) but *not regulated* by it, are to be regulated by "national general contract law". The 2011 Directive therefore expressly allocates this category of unregulated contractual issues to national law with the result that, under its own case-law, the Court of Justice of the EU should not seek to construct "autonomous" European views as to these issues.[436] In this way, the 2011 Directive's allocation of "unregulated" contractual issues to national contract law has a direct impact on the

---

[433] Directive 2005/29/EC art.3(2), on which see Whittaker in Weatherill and Bernitz (eds), *The Regulation of Unfair Commercial Practices under EC Directive 2005/29, New Rules and New Techniques* (2007), Ch.8 and below, para.38-160. The guidance provided by the European Commission on art.3(5)'s application is limited, as it provides merely two particular examples ("if national contract law makes it possible for rights and obligations under an existing contract to be transferred from one consumer to another, no new contract would be concluded to which the Directive would apply" and "how a trader may enforce a consumer's liability for the diminished value of the goods under art.14(2)": DG Justice Guidance Document on 2011 Directive, paras 2.7 and 6.4.4. respectively.

[434] Consumer Rights Directive 2011, especially arts 23–24. The central example of the duties on traders to be so enforced are found in relation to duties of information under arts 5 and 6.

[435] Unfair Commercial Practices Directive 2005 arts 4, 5 and 11 and see above, para.38-026 and below 38-424—38-427 on the significance of this for aspects of the Consumer Rights Act 2015. Article 3(2) of the 2005 Directive does not prevent Member States from giving "contract law" significance to its provisions, as the UK has recently done by amendment in 2014 of the Consumer Protection from Unfair Trading Regulations 2008 (SI 2008/1277) by the Consumer Protection (Amendment) Regulations 2014 (SI 2014/870) inserting, notably, new Pt 4A Consumers' Rights to Redress, on which see below, paras 38-172 et seq.

[436] cf. above, para.38-015. Presumably, however, this allocation of contract issues left unregulated by the 2011 Directive to national contract law would be subject to the general principles of EU law, notably, the principle of the effectiveness. cf. for this purpose, the approach of the CJEU to the principle of the autonomy of national procedural law, above, paras 38-019—38-020.

way in which the 2013 Regulations are to be interpreted and applied.

Contract law issues regulated by the 2011 Directive   Three examples may be **38-064** provided of issues of contract law regulated by the 2011 Directive. A first example may be found in the provision stating that information given by traders to consumers before the consumer is bound by an off-premises or distance contract in performance of the duties which the Directive imposes "shall form an integral part" of the contract in question "and shall not be altered unless the contracting parties expressly agree otherwise".[437] A second set of examples may be found in the Directive's provisions that exercise by a consumer of a right of cancellation "shall terminate the obligations of the parties ... to perform the distance or off-premises contract"[438] with consequential obligations for both the trader and the consumer.[439] A third example may be found in relation to inertia selling, which had earlier been prohibited when practiced business-to-consumer by the Unfair Commercial Practices Directive 2005.[440] However, the 2005 Directive did not create any contractual remedy in respect of this practice and so the 2011 Directive requires "the contractual remedy of exempting the consumer from the obligation to provide any consideration for such unsolicited supply or provision".[441]

Contract law issues within the 2011 Directive but not regulated by it   Recital **38-065** 14 of the 2011 Directive quoted above refers to the conclusion or validity of a contract on the ground of lack of consent as examples of contract law aspects not regulated by its provisions which are therefore left to national contract law.[442] This is relevant to the Directive's central provisions which require traders to provide consumers with information "[b]efore the consumer is bound by a contract ... or any corresponding offer",[443] as the issues whether and, if so, when the consumer is so bound are not regulated by the Directive itself; these issues therefore fall to be determined by the common law rules governing the conclusion of a contract.[444] In this respect, while the 2011 Directive refers to the possibility of a consumer being bound by an *offer* (as is recognised in some European national laws[445]), the 2013

---

[437]   Consumer Rights Directive 2011 art.6(5). On this see below, para.38-105.

[438]   Consumer Rights Directive 2011 art.12(a) (referring to "withdrawal" rather than "cancellation", on which see below, para.38-065).

[439]   Consumer Rights Directive 2011 arts 13 and 14.

[440]   Consumer Rights Directive 2011 art.27; Unfair Commercial Practices Directive 2005 2005/29/EC art.5(5), Annex point 29, implemented in UK law by the Consumer Protection from Unfair Trading Regulations 2008 (SI 2008/1277) reg.3(4)(d), Sch.1 para.29.

[441]   Consumer Rights Directive 2011 recital 60; art.27. This change was effected in UK law by amendment of the Consumer Protection from Unfair Trading Regulations 2008 (SI 2008/1277) by the 2013 Regulations reg.39 (as itself amended by SI 2014/870).

[442]   Above, para.38-063.

[443]   Consumer Rights Directive 2011 arts 5(1) and 6(1) and see the 2013 Regulations regs 9(1), (10(1) and 12(1).

[444]   See Vol.I, Ch.2. Recent examples in relation to the earlier Cancellation of Contracts made in a Consumer's Home or Place of Work, etc. Regulations 2008 (SI 2008/1816) may be found in *Cox v Woodlands Manor Care Home Ltd* [2015] EWCA Civ 415, [2015] 3 Costs L.O. 327, where the Court of Appeal held that a conditional fee agreement had been made at a consumer's home where it was signed, even though it was subject to a condition depending on the possibility of funding from legal expenses insurance and *Howes Percival Ltd v Page* [2013] EWHC 4104 (Ch) at [237] unreported where it was held to be "little more than happenstance" that one of the meetings between parties took place at the consumers' home, neither the contract nor an offer being made there.

[445]   e.g. French law where the *Code civil* now so provides: arts 1114–1116 C. civ. (as created by *Ordon-*

Regulations reflect the general English common law position that a person is not bound by an offer until it is accepted, thereby concluding a contract.[446]

38-066 **Mandatory nature of 2013 Regulations** While the 2013 Regulations do not themselves provide that the information requirements which they impose are mandatory, the Consumer Rights Directive does so, providing that where the law applicable to the contract is the law of a Member State, "consumers may not waive the rights conferred on them by the national measures transposing" the Directive.[447] The Directive further provides that any contract terms "which directly or indirectly waive or restrict the rights resulting" from it "shall not be binding on the consumer".[448] As a result, and following the principle of the conforming interpretation of national measures implementing a directive,[449] any contract term seeking to exclude or restrict the trader's duties of information or any of the legal consequences set out by the 2013 Regulations for the provision of or failure to provide information which they require would not be binding on a consumer.[450] Similarly, any waiver by the consumers of their rights under the Regulations would not be binding on the consumer, whether this waiver took place before or after any resulting contract was concluded.[451]

38-067 **Express consent or agreement of consumer** On the other hand, a number of provisions in the Regulations set out the legal position which would apply to a situation generally, but then provide for a different position if the consumer expressly agrees with the trader, or requests or consents otherwise. This is the case, for example, as regards any change to the information supplied by the trader before concluding a contract which must be "expressly agreed between the consumer and

---

nance No.2016/131 of February 10, 2016).

[446] See Vol.I, para.2-094. Following its earlier pattern in arts 5(1) and 6(1), the 2011 Directive later provides for the effects of consumer withdrawal from the contract in cases of concluded contracts and "in cases where an offer was made by the consumer": art.12. In implementing these provisions, the UK Regulations distinguish between a consumer's right of *cancellation of his contract* (following here the 2011 Directive's provisions to this effect) and the possibility of a consumer *withdrawing his offer*. In the case of the latter, the circumstances in which a consumer can withdraw his offer will be set by the common law, but the 2013 Regulations (following the 2011 Directive) set some of the effects of the consumer's exercise of such a power of withdrawal, notably, as to recovery of any sums paid in advance: below, para.38-123.

[447] 2011 Directive art.25, first sentence. The Department of Business Innovation & Skills, *Directive 2011/83/EU on consumer rights, Draft Transposition Note* (August 2013) p.14 states that "no specific implementation" is required for 2011 Directive art.25 as the provisions of the Regulations are mandatory. cf. the express provisions on "no contracting-out" in the Consumer Protection (Distance Selling) Regulations 2000 (SI 2000/2334) reg.25 and the Cancellation of Contracts made in a Consumer's Home or Place of Work, etc. Regulations 2008 (SI 2008/1816) reg.15. The 2011 Directive makes no explicit anti-avoidance provision as regards choice of applicable law (unlike, e.g. the Unfair Terms in Consumer Contracts Directive 1993 art.6(2), below, para.38-352) with the result that the controls on choice of law are those generally applicable under the Rome I Regulation arts 3(4) and 6: Dicey, Morris and Collins, *The Conflict of Laws*, 15th edn (2012), Vol.II, para.33-179.

[448] 2011 Directive art.25, second sentence.

[449] Above, para.38-014.

[450] cf. the position as regards information actually supplied by the trader which, under the Consumer Rights Act 2015, is treated as included as a term of the contract, liability for breach is subjected to stringent controls by the same Act: 2015 Act ss.11(3), 12, and 31(1)(c) and (d) (goods contracts) below, para.38-531; s.36(3), 37 and 47(1)(c) and (d) (digital content contracts), below, para.38-539; and s.50(3) and 57(2) (services contracts), below, paras 38-585—38-586.

[451] See below, para.38-120.

the trader",[452] an express choice of a more expensive kind of delivery of goods,[453] and an express request by the consumer for services to be supplied before the end of the cancellation period,[454] and an express consent by the consumer for digital content to be supplied before the end of the cancellation period.[455] These examples are all expressly foreseen by the 2011 Directive and therefore form qualifications on the mandatory nature of its provisions.

Duty of court in relation to compliance with information duties   The Court of   **38-068** Justice of the EU has held that the purpose of consumer protection pursued by a number of directives requires national courts to raise of their own motion issues relating to possible rights for the consumer under national laws implementing those directives.[456] In *Radlinger v Finway a.s.*[457] the Court of Justice applied this case-law to the context of the information requirements imposed on traders to consumers by the Consumer Credit Directive 2008. The particular justification for such a duty as regards information requirements was that the consumer is in

> "… a weak position vis-à-vis the seller or supplier, as regards both his bargaining power and his level of knowledge, which leads to the consumer agreeing to terms drawn up in advance by the seller or supplier without being able to influence the content of those terms."[458]

The Court of Justice continued:

> "In that regard, information, before and at the time of concluding a contract, on the terms of the contract and the consequences of concluding it is of fundamental importance for a consumer. It is, in particular, on the basis of that information that the consumer decides whether he wishes to be bound by the conditions drafted in advance by the seller or supplier."[459]

There is a real risk, moreover, that the consumer may not rely on a legal rule protecting him owing to lack of awareness.[460] Effective consumer protection therefore requires national courts to consider whether the information duties in the 2008 Directive have been complied with and, if that have not, they must draw all the consequences provided by national law, in the context, as regards penalties imposed as required by that directive.[461] It is submitted that this reasoning applies by analogy to other information requirements imposed on traders by EU directives for the benefit of consumers and, therefore, that the Court of Justice would

---

[452] 2013 Regulations reg.9(4) (on-premises contracts); reg.10(6) (off-premises contracts) and 13(7) (distance contracts), below, para.38-105.

[453] 2013 Regulations reg.34(2), below, para.38-124.

[454] Regulations reg.36(1).

[455] 2013 Regulations reg.37(1). Other examples are found in reg.11(2) (consumer expressly agrees for information to be on another durable medium rather on paper in the case of off-premises contracts in connection with repair or maintenance); and reg.34(7) (express agreement of consumer to different means of payment for reimbursement of payments made).

[456] Above, paras 38-019—38-021.

[457] C-377/14 April 21, 2016 ("*Radlinger* (C-377/14)").

[458] *Radlinger* (C-377/14) at para.63, referring to *ERSTE Bank Hungary Zrt v Sugár* (C-32/14) EU:C:2015:637, October 1, 2015 at para.39 (which concerned the 1993 Directive).

[459] *Radlinger* (C-377/14) at para.64, referring to *Constructora Principado SA v Menéndez Álvarez* (C-226/12) EU:C:2014:10, January 16, 2014 at para.25 (which concerned the 1993 Directive).

[460] *Radlinger* (C-377/14) at paras 65, 70 and 74 (an obligation and not merely a power).

[461] *Radlinger* (C-377/14) at para.73.

equally require national courts to raise the question whether these other information requirements have been fulfilled and, if not, with what effect. This special role of national courts in relation to information duties must be borne in mind when considering the range of legal consequences of non-compliance with the information requirements under the 2013 Regulations.[462]

(b)   Contracts Covered by the 2013 Regulations

38-069   **All consumer contracts**   Article 3(1) of the 2011 Directive states that:

> "This Directive shall apply, under the conditions and to the extent set out in its provisions, to any contract concluded between a trader and a consumer. It shall also apply to contracts for the supply of water, gas, electricity or district heating, including by public providers, to the extent that these commodities are provided on a contractual basis."

As a result, and although it is nowhere stated explicitly, the 2013 Regulations also apply in principle to *all types of consumer contract*, defined by reference to their parties, although some provisions have a more restricted ambit.[463] For this purpose, the 2013 Regulations use the standard definition of "trader" and of "consumer" adopted by recent UK consumer law:

> "… 'consumer' means an individual acting for purposes that are wholly or mainly outside the individual's trade, business, craft or profession."[464]

> "… 'trader' means a person acting for purposes relating to that person's trade, business, craft or profession, whether acting personally or through another person acting in the trader's name or on the trader's behalf."[465]

> "… 'business' includes the activities of any government department or local or public authority."[466]

The background to these definitions and their likely significance have already been discussed.[467]

38-070   **"A contractual basis"**   As just noted, art.3(1) of the 2011 Directive specifically includes within its scope:

> "… contracts for the supply of water, gas, electricity or district heating, including by public providers, to the extent that these commodities are provided on a contractual basis."

This statement reinforces the definition of "trader", which includes a "legal person, irrespective of whether privately or publicly owned",[468] but it also makes a further point, that is, that these commodities must be supplied under a *contract*, as distinct

---

[462]   See below, paras 38-104 et seq.

[463]   cf. below para.38-079 on the question whether the 2011 Directive (and therefore the 2013 Regulations) apply (at least sometimes) to contracts consumer-to-business as well as business-to-consumer.

[464]   2013 Regulations reg.4 "consumer".

[465]   2013 Regulations reg.4 "trader".

[466]   2013 Regulations reg.5 "business".

[467]   Above, paras 38-030—38-049, 38-050—38-058 respectively.

[468]   2011 Directive art.2(2), reflected in substance by the definition of "trader" and "business" in the 2013 Regulations regs 4 and 5 respectively.

from, in particular, a public law or statutory basis. Given that the Directive does not explain for these purposes what "contractual basis" means, it could be argued that art.3(5)'s allocation of contract law issues raised (but not regulated) by the Directive to national contract law would include the issue whether these commodities are supplied under a "contract", rather than determining this issue on the basis of an autonomous view of "contract".[469] So, for example, in English law where these commodities are supplied under a statutory duty to do so, the courts have held this supply to be non-contractual.[470] As a result, these supplies would not be subject to the requirements which the 2011 Directive (and therefore the 2013 Regulations) would otherwise impose. On the other hand, the Court of Justice of the EU could instead hold—despite art.3(5)—that it should take an autonomous view of "contractual basis" for the purposes of the 2011 Directive given that this condition is fundamentally important to the directive's scope and, therefore, to the achievement of the directive's purposes.[471]

Distinctions according to the circumstances in which the contracts are made Within the broad category of consumer contracts, the most prominent distinction in the 2013 Regulations is between "off-premises contracts", "distance contracts" and "on-premises contracts", all three of which are defined by reference to the circumstances in which they are concluded, as well as by the status of their parties. The detailed definitions of each of these categories will be set out later, but at this stage it is helpful to note that "on-premises contracts" is a residual category, defined simply as "a contract between a trader and a consumer which is neither a distance contract nor an off-premises contract".[472] **38-071**

Distinctions according to the subject matter of the contract The 2011 Directive which the 2013 Regulations implement distinguishes *four* categories of contract according to their subject matter: (i) sales contracts, (ii) services contracts, (iii) contracts for the supply of digital content not on a tangible medium,[473] and (iv) contracts for the supply of water, gas or electricity where they are not put up for sale in a limited volume or set quantity, or district heating.[474] However, this fourfold classification is not followed entirely by the 2013 Regulations, which instead include within "service contracts" the contracts falling within the Directive's category (iv).[475] As a result, the 2013 Regulations distinguish between three distinct **38-072**

---

469 Above, para.38-065.
470 *Read v Croydon Corp* [1938] 4 All E.R. 631; *Norweb Plc v Dixon* [1995] 1 W.L.R. 637 and see Vol.I, para.1-037.
471 cf. the discussion of the possible construction of an autonomous view of "contract" for the purposes of Directive 93/13/EEC on unfair terms in consumer contracts, below, paras 38-229—38-230.
472 2013 Regulations reg.5 "on-premises contracts".
473 As the 2011 Directive recital 19 states: "[i]f digital content is supplied on a tangible medium, such as a CD or a DVD, it should be considered as goods within the meaning of this Directive". cf. *Software Incubator Ltd v Computer Associates UK Ltd* [2018] EWCA Civ 518 (contract for the supply of software does not constitute a "sale of goods" for the purposes of the Commercial Agents (Council Directive) Regulations 1993 (SI 1993/3053)).
474 This is made clear by recital 19, which states that the latter two types of contract "should be classified, for the purpose of this Directive, neither as sales contracts nor as service contracts". This is then followed through by its definitions of "goods", "sales contract" and "service contract" in art.2(3), (5) and (6) respectively.
475 2013 Regulations reg.5 "service". This treatment in the 2013 Regulations is compatible with the 2011 Directive's requirements as it applies the same rules to supplies of water, gas or electricity where

categories of consumer contract defined according to their subject matter and, at times, regulate them specially: "sales contracts", "service contracts" and "contracts for the supply of digital content not on a tangible medium".[476] While it is nowhere clearly stated by the Regulations, it would seem clear from the requirements of the 2011 Directive, that the provisions in the Regulations which impose requirements on traders in respect of information apply to all these three types of contract, even though some of the elements of their definitions appear to be restricted to sales and services contracts.[477] As will be seen, though, some of the rules governing consumer contracts apply only to sales contracts, service contracts,[478] or contracts for the supply of digital content not on a tangible medium,[479] and this three-fold distinction is particularly clear in the rules governing the commencement of the "normal period" for cancellation in off-premises and distance contracts,[480] and in the way in which some particular information requirements are described.[481] As will be seen, this three-fold distinction according to the subject matter of consumer contracts is also reflected in the Consumer Rights Act 2015, though it is treated there differently.[482]

38-073   **"Sales contract" and "service contract"**   The 2013 Regulations define "sales contract" as:

"... a contract under which a trader transfers or agrees to transfer the ownership of goods to a consumer and the consumer pays or agrees to pay the price, including any contract that has both goods and services as its object."[483]

"Goods" for these purposes are defined as:

"... any tangible moveable items, but that includes water, gas and electricity if and only if they are put up for sale in a limited volume or set quantity".[484]

---

they are not put up for sale in a limited volume, etc. as to services: arts 5(2), 7(3), 8(8), 9(2)(a) and (c), 14(4)(a) and 17(2).

476   "Tangible medium" is not explicitly defined by the Directive nor by the Regulations, but reg.5 defines "goods" as "any tangible moveable items, but that includes water, gas and electricity if and only if they are put up for sale in a limited volume or a set quantity".

477   See notably, element (d) of the definition of "off-premises contract" in reg.5 which refers to the trader's intended "selling goods or services to the consumer"; and the requirement in the definition of "distance contract" also in reg.5 that the contract should be concluded under "an organised distance sales or service-provision scheme": for these, see below, paras 38-081—38-085, 38-086—38-089.

478   For "sales contract" see reg.12(4)(a); reg.28(3) (below, para.38-112); reg.30(3)–(6) (below, para.38-117); reg.34(5) and (9) (below, para.38-114) and reg.35(1) (below, para.38-128); for "service contract" see reg.30(2)(a) (below, para.38-073) and reg.36(2) (below, para.38-074).

479   2013 Regulations reg.12(5), 16(3), 30(2)(b) and 37.

480   2013 Regulations reg.30 (below, para.38-117).

481   2013 Regulations Sch.1 paras (a), (c), (e); Sch.2 paras (a), (f), (j), the references to "digital content" being added by SI 2014/870 reg.9(3) and (4).

482   Consumer Rights Act 2015 Pt 1 Ch.2 (goods contracts); Ch.3 (digital content contracts, though the exclusion from this category of digital content contracts supplied on a tangible medium is inherent in the definition of "goods contracts" and these contracts require a price, below, para.38-541) and Ch.4 ("services contracts"). In particular, the 2015 Act does not distinguish sharply as regards the different types of contract under which digital content is supplied, but rather allows its categories of contract (and therefore their regulation) to overlap (either with "goods contracts" or "services contracts") as its subject matter requires. See below, paras 38-484, 38-504 and 38-543.

483   2013 Regulations reg.5 "sales contract" reflecting closely 2011 Directive art.2(5). cf. Consumer Rights Act 2015 s.5, below, para.38-486—38-488.

484   2013 Regulations reg.5 "goods"; 2011 Directive art.2(3).

"Service contract" is defined as:

"... a contract, other than a sales contract, under which a trader supplies or agrees to supply a service to a consumer and the consumer pays or agrees to pay the price."[485]

And "service" is stated as including:

"(a)   the supply of water, gas or electricity if they are not put up for sale in a limited volume or a set quantity, and
(b)   the supply of district heating."[486]

Contracts for the supply of goods and services   It will be seen from the definition of "sales contract" set out above, that this category includes "any contract that has both goods and services as its object". This appears to mean that the rules governing "sales contracts" rather than the rules governing "service contracts" apply to these mixed contracts.[487] At first sight, this does not follow recital 50 of the 2011 Directive, according to which: **38-074**

"For contracts having as their object both goods and services, the rules provided for in this Directive on the return of goods should apply to the goods aspects and the compensation regime for services should apply to the services aspects."

However, on turning to the relevant provisions in the 2013 Regulations, it will be seen that while reg.35 governing the return of goods in the event of cancellation is restricted to "sales contracts", the provisions in reg.36 which set out the "compensation regime for services" supplied are not restricted to "service contracts" but rather to the situation where "a service has been supplied in the cancellation period".[488] This allows the nuanced approach required by the 2011 Directive to be applied under the 2013 Regulations.

Contracts for the supply of digital content   "Digital content" is defined by the 2013 Regulations as "data which are produced and supplied in digital form".[489]As recital 19 to the 2011 Directive explains: **38-075**

---

[485]   2013 Regulations reg.5 "service contract"; 2011 Directive art.2(6). cf. Consumer Rights Act 2015 s.48, below, para.38-568.

[486]   2013 Regulations reg.5 "service", picking up the explanation in 2011 Directive recital 25 of its own use of "service" in the definition of "service contract" in art.2(6). Recital 25 continues by noting that "district heating refers to the supply of heat, inter alia, in the form of steam or hot water, from a central source of production through a transmission and distribution system to multiple buildings, for the purpose of heating". From the point of view of legislative drafting, the inclusion of these types of contract within "service contract" allows the Regulations to state the relevant cancellation period in a single provision (2013 Regulations reg.30(2)(a), on which see below, para.38-117) whereas the 2011 Directive makes specific provision for them which is identical to service contracts as more generally understood: Directive 2011/83/EU arts 9(2)(a) and (c). cf. the different treatment of "services contracts" under the Consumer Rights Act 2015 s.48, below, para.38-568.

[487]   See above, para.38-073. cf. DG Justice Guidance Document on 2011 Directive, para.2.2 which argues that contracts which contain elements of both goods and services should be classified either as "sales contracts" or "services contracts" depending on which element reflects their main purpose, relying in particular on case-law of the CJEU governing the Treaty provisions on free movement of goods and the freedom to provide services: *Burmanjer* (C-20/03) EU:C:2005:307 [2005] E.C.R. I-4133 at paras 34–35.

[488]   2013 Regulations reg.36(3)–(6) (on which see below, para.38-128). cf. reg.36(2) which concerns the loss of the consumer's right to cancel a "service contract".

[489]   2013 Regulations reg.5 "digital content"; 2011 Directive art.2(11). This definition is adopted by the Consumer Rights Act 2015 s.2(9), below, para.38-540.

"Digital content means data which are produced and supplied in digital form, such as computer programs, applications, games, music, videos or texts, irrespective of whether they are accessed through downloading or streaming, from a tangible medium or through any other means."[490]

However, neither the 2013 Regulations nor the 2011 Directive define contracts for the supply of digital content even though they regulate them specially,[491] but recital 19 explains that:

"If digital content is supplied on a tangible medium, such as a CD or a DVD, it should be considered as goods within the meaning of this Directive."

This fits with the definitions of "sales contracts" in both the Directive and the Regulations as the tangible medium would constitute "goods" ("tangible moveable item") and the digital content would form an element of those goods.[492] On the other hand, "contracts for digital content which is not supplied on a tangible medium" would not fall within the definition of sales contracts nor are they specifically included within service contracts, unlike contracts for the supply of water, gas or electricity where they are not put up for sale in a limited volume or set quantity, or district heating.[493] Reflecting this view, the 2013 Regulations make special provision governing this category of contract as regards the consumer's loss of the right to cancel if he or she has consented to the beginning of performance.[494] Moreover, in the view of the European Commission, the distinction drawn by recital 19 of the 2011 Directive between digital content supplied under a sales contract or services contract and digital content supplied in non-tangible digital form means that contracts for online digital content are subject to the Directive even if they do not involve the payment of a price by the consumer, as there is no requirement as to contracts for the supply of digital content in digital form equivalent to the requirement of payment of a price as regards sales and service contracts.[495] As the Commission acknowledges, this view leads not merely to a considerable expansion of the scope of the application of the Directive, but it also leads to the drawing of difficult lines as to the application of the Directive in relation to the free supply of digital content (i.e. without payment of a price), but the Commission argues that the Directive should not apply to online digital content provided by means of broadcasting of information on the internet "without the express conclusion of a contract" nor "in itself" to access to a website or a download from a website. In this respect, it may be that the Court of Justice would consider it necessary to find an autonomous definition of contract for this purpose, but it could hold that the definition of a "contract" should instead fall under art.3(5)'s general allocation of issues

---

[490] 2011 Directive recital 19, first sentence.
[491] 2013 Regulations reg.12(5) (below, para.38-101); reg.16(3) (below, para.38-101); reg.30(2) and 30(6) (below, para.38-117); reg.37 (below, para.38-128). cf. Consumer Rights Act 2015 s.33 which defines "contract to supply digital content" for the purpose of Ch.3 of the Act specially for its purposes: below, para.38-541.
[492] On which see above, para.38-073.
[493] See above, para.38-073.
[494] 2013 Regulations reg.37; 2011 Directive art.14(4)(b).
[495] *DG Justice Guidance Document on 2011 Directive*, para.12.1. See also EU Commission, *Report from the Commission to the European Parliament and the Council on the application of Directive 2011/83/EU* (etc.) COM(2017) 259 final, para.5 noting that "some interested parties consider that the application of the [2011 Directive] to 'free' digital content is not absolutely clear". This is reflected in the treatment of "digital content contracts other than for a price paid by the consumer" in 2013 Regulations regs 9(3), 10(5) and 13(6), below, para.38-105.

not governed by the Directive to "national general contract law" as earlier explained.[496] Moreover, there remains a difficult line between the supply of free digital content online (which, according to the Commission, is covered by the Directive) and free online services, such as cloud storage or webmail, where the main contractual obligation of the trader is not to provide digital content but rather a service allowing the creation, processing, storing or sharing of data that is produced by a consumer.[497] Such free online services are clearly not covered by the 2011 Directive (nor by the 2013 Regulations) since "service contracts" are defined contracts for the supply of a service to the consumer in return for a price.[498] In this respect, the position under the Consumer Rights Act 2015 differs. The 2015 Act identifies a distinct legislative category of "a contract for the supply of digital content" for the purposes of its own provisions in Ch.3 of Pt 1, being "a contract for a trader to supply digital content to a consumer" where "it is supplied for a price paid by the consumer" or where:

"… it is supplied free with goods or services or other digital content for which the consumer pays a price, and … it is not generally available to consumers unless they have paid a price for it or for goods or services or other digital content,"[499]

where "price" is specially defined so as to include "the consumer using, by way of payment, any facility for which money has been paid".[500] This leaves contracts for the supply of digital content for some consideration other than for a price as so understood outside the provisions of Ch.3, but they may well fall within the scope of Ch.4's provisions on "services contracts" which (unlike the 2013 Regulations) are *not* defined so as to require the payment of a *price* by the consumer.[501] And of course, where the digital content is supplied on a tangible medium (such as on a CD) which can count as "an item that includes digital content", then Ch.1's provisions on "goods contracts" may apply.[502]

Exclusions from the scope of the 2013 Regulations   The 2013 Regulations   **38-076** exclude from their general scope a number of types of contracts and of contracts concluded in certain ways,[503] as well as excluding certain types of contracts from their provisions requiring traders to give consumers information,[504] and from their provisions governing the consumer's right of cancellation.[505] In terms of exclusions from their general scope, reg.6 provides that the 2013 Regulations do not apply to gambling contracts[506]; contracts for services of a banking, credit, insurance,

---

[496] Above, paras 38-063—38-067 and 38-070.
[497] EU Commission, *Report from the Commission to the European Parliament and the Council on the application of Directive 2011/83/EU* (etc.) COM(2017) 259 final, para.5 (arguing that the 2011 Directive should be amended so as to include such free online digital services).
[498] 2011 Directive art.2(6); 2013 Regulations reg.5, above, para.38-073.
[499] 2015 Act s.33(1) and (2), and see below, paras 38-541—38-542.
[500] 2015 Act s.33(3), below, para.38-541.
[501] 2015 Act s.48, below, para.38-568; cf. 2013 Regulations reg.5 "service contract", above, para.38-073.
[502] See below, para.38-487 and esp. in relation to 2015 Act s.16, below, para.38-504.
[503] 2013 Regulations reg.6.
[504] 2013 Regulations reg.7(2)–(4), below, para.38-077. The information requirements for off-premises contracts are also excluded as regards repair or maintenance contracts" as defined: 2013 Regulations reg.11.
[505] 2013 Regulations regs 27(2)–(3), 28 on which see below, paras 38-112.
[506] 2013 Regulations reg.6(1)(a) which explains this category.

personal pension, investment or payment nature[507]; contracts for the creation of immovable property or of rights in immovable property[508]; contracts for rental of accommodation for residential purposes[509]; contracts for the construction of new buildings or the construction of substantially new buildings by the conversion of existing buildings[510]; contracts for the supply of foodstuffs, beverages or other goods intended for current consumption in the household and which are supplied by a trader on frequent and regular rounds to the consumer's home, residence or workplace[511]; package travel within the scope of the Package Travel Directive 2015[512]; and timeshare and related contracts within the scope of the Timeshare Directive.[513] Moreover, the 2013 Regulations do not apply to contracts concluded

---

[507] 2013 Regulations reg.6(1)(b); 2011 Directive arts 2(12) and 3(3)(d). There are two exceptions for the case of the effect of cancellation or withdrawal on "ancillary contracts" (reg.38(4)) and "additional payments" (reg.40(3), discussed below, para.38-430): 2013 Regulations reg.6(3). In the case of off-premises contracts, this exclusion marks a significant difference from the 2008 Regulations (SI 2008/1816) which applied to contracts of consumer credit with certain exclusions: regs 5 and 6. In the case of "distance contracts" (but not off-premises contracts), duties of information and rights of cancellation are provided by the Financial Services (Distance Marketing) Regulations 2004 (SI 2004/2095) reg.2(1) of which defines "financial service" identically to the excluded contracts in reg.6(1)(b) of the 2013 Regulations: SI 2004/2095 implementing Directive 2002/65/EC concerning the distance marketing of consumer financial services, on which see below, para.38-136.

[508] 2013 Regulations reg.6(1)(c), implementing 2011 Directive art.3(3)(e). In *Travel Vac SL v Antelm Sanchis* (C-423/97) EU:C:1999:197, [1999] E.C.R. I-2195 at para.25 the ECJ held that the Doorstep Selling Directive 1985 could apply to a contract of timeshare despite an exclusion of contracts relating to immovable property (art.3(2)(a)) identical to the one provided by the 2011 Directive art.3(3)(e) as long as the contract "concerns the provision of separate services of a value higher than that of the right to use the property". However, in *Schulte v Deutsche Bausparkasse Badenia AG* (C-350/03) EU:C:2005:637, [2005] E.C.R. I-9215 paras 77–80 the ECJ held that this did not mean that the 1985 Directive could apply to a separate contract of sale of immovable property even though it formed part of a single economic unit in which service elements predominated. This point is now resolved in its specific context by 2011 Directive art.3(3)(h) (implemented in UK law by 2013 Regulations reg.6(1)(h)) which excludes from its scope contracts falling under the Timeshare Directive 2008/122/EC. Similarly, in *Friz GmbH v von der Heyden* (C-215/08) EU:C:2010:186, [2010] E.C.R. I-02947 the ECJ held that Directive 85/577 could apply to a contract under which the consumer entered a "real property fund by means of the acquisition of holdings in a partnership in exchange for a capital investment" despite its exclusion of contracts concerning rights to immovable property, but such a contract is likely to fall within the exclusion of "contracts for services of a banking, credit, insurance, personal pension, investment or payment nature" in the 2011 Directive art.3(3)(d) as explained by art.2(12) (implemented by the 2013 Regulations reg.6(1)(b)).

[509] 2013 Regulations reg.6(1)(d).

[510] 2013 Regulations reg.6(1)(e).

[511] 2013 Regulations reg.6(1)(f).

[512] 2013 Regulations reg.6(1)(g) referring to "package travel contracts" within the scope of Directive (EU) 2015/2302 on package travel and linked travel arrangements [2015] O.J. L326/1, which repealed and replaced Directive 90/314/EEC on package travel, package holidays and package tours. This exclusion does not therefore apply to "linked travel arrangements" which are not therefore excluded from the scope of the 2011 Directive: 2015 Directive art.3(2), (3) and (5) and art.27(2) (amending the 2011 Directive art.3(3)). See below, paras 38-137—38-141. While art.12(5) of the 2015 Directive provides that, as regards off-premises contracts, Member States may provide in their national laws that the traveller has the right to withdraw from a package travel contract within a period of 14 days *without giving any reason*, unlike the general position provided for termination by travellers under the 2015 Directive, the UK government decided not to make provision to this effect in the Package Travel and Linked Travel Arrangements Regulations 2018: see Department of Business, Energy & Industrial Strategy, *Updating Consumer Protection in the Package Travel Sector, Government Response* (April 2018), paras 79 and 84.

[513] Directive 2008/122/EC on the protection of consumers in respect of certain aspects of timeshare, long-term holiday product, resale and exchange contracts ("Timeshare Directive 2009"); 2013

by means of automatic vending machines or automated commercial premises[514]; contracts concluded with a telecommunications operator through a public telephone for the use of the telephone[515]; contracts concluded for the use of one single connection, by telephone, internet or fax, established by a consumer[516]; or to contracts under which goods are sold by way of execution or otherwise by authority of law.[517]

Contracts not excluded (or not excluded entirely) by the 2013 Regulations though excluded from the 2011 Directive Contracts for social services, including social housing, childcare and support for families and persons permanently or temporarily in need, including long-term care are excluded from the 2011 Directive,[518] but not from the 2013 Regulations.[519] The 2011 Directive also excludes generally contracts for healthcare,[520] but the 2013 Regulations exclude only contracts for the supply of a medicinal product by administration by a prescriber, or under a prescription or directions given by a prescriber or for the supply of a product by a health care professional in certain circumstances from the effect of its provisions governing information requirements and the consumer's right of cancellation.[521]   **38-077**

Contracts for passenger transport services While not excluded from the scope of the 2013 Regulations as a whole,[522] "contracts to the extent that they are for passenger transport services" are excluded from the provisions governing the consumer's rights of cancellation[523] and are excluded from their provisions governing information requirements, with the exception of requirements applicable to distance contracts concluded by electronic means.[524] For this purpose, "contracts for the provision of transport services" in the predecessor to this exclusion in the   **38-078**

Regulations reg.6(1)(h): on the Timeshare Directive 2009 see below, paras 38-148—38-154.

514 2013 Regulations reg.6(2)(a).
515 2013 Regulations reg.6(2)(b).
516 2013 Regulations reg.6(2)(c).
517 2013 Regulations reg.6(2)(d).
518 2011 Directive art.3(3)(a).
519 On the lawfulness of this extension as a matter of EU law, see above, para.38-025.
520 2011 Directive art.3(3)(b) "healthcare" being defined by reference to Directive 2011/24/EU on the application of patients' rights in cross-border healthcare [2011] O.J. L88/45 art.3(a), which provides that: "'healthcare' means health services provided by health professionals to patients to assess, maintain or restore their state of health, including the prescription, dispensation and provision of medicinal products and medical devices."
521 2013 Regulations reg.7(2) and reg.27(2) and (4) (with definitions provided by reg.7(5)).
522 The 2011 Directive art.3(3)(k) excludes generally contracts for passenger transport services from its scope with the exceptions of art.8(2) (information requirements for distance contracts concluded by electronic means), art.19 (fees for the use of means of payment) and art.22 (additional payments). As a result, the provisions in the 2013 Regulations governing information requirements for distance contracts concluded by electronic means (reg.14(1)–(5)), additional payments (reg.40) and helpline charges over basic rate (reg.41) apply to contracts for passenger transport services. The 2011 Directive art.19's provisions (fees for the use of means of payment) are implemented by the Consumer Rights (Payment Surcharges) Regulations 2012 (SI 2012/3110) reg.5 of which does not exclude payments made for the purposes of contracts for the passenger transport services: on which see below, para.38-428.
523 2013 Regulations reg.27(2)(c).
524 2013 Regulations reg.7(3); reg.14(1)–14(5) (both as set out by 2011 Directive arts 3(3)(k) and 8(2)). The 2011 Directive recital 27 justifies this exclusion on the basis that these contracts are already subject to EU legislation or to regulation at a national level.

Distance Contracts Directive[525] was interpreted very broadly by the European Court of Justice as referring to all contracts governing services in the field of transport and not merely to contracts of carriage, and as a result included a contract for hire of a car.[526] However, recital 27 to the 2011 Directive explains that while passenger transport is generally excluded from the scope of the Directive,[527] "in relation to transport of goods *and car rental which are services,* consumers should benefit" from the Directive's protection, with the important exception of the right of cancellation.[528]

38-079   Consumer-to-business contracts?   As noted above, the Consumer Rights Directive 2011 (which the 2013 Regulations implement) states that it "shall apply, under the conditions and to the extent set out in its provisions, to any contract concluded between a trader and a consumer",[529] thereby expressing itself in a way which is neutral as to whether it is the trader or the consumer who supplies goods or services under a contract.[530] The definitions of "trader" and "consumer" used by the 2011 Directive (and also the 2013 Regulations) are equally neutral on this point.[531] However, as has been seen, the definitions of "sales contract" and "service contract" are cast in terms under which the trader supplies the goods or services to the consumer and on this ground the European Commission has tentatively argued that the 2011 Directive does not apply to contracts under which the consumer transfers goods to a trader.[532] On the other hand, the definitions of "off-premises contract", "distance contract", and "on-premises contract" differ as to whether they are expressed in a way which suggests that contracts under which a consumer supplies goods or services to a trader are included or excluded from their scope. The issue will therefore be addressed in the context of each category of contract in turn.[533]

38-080   The temporal application of the 2013 Regulations   The 2013 Regulations apply generally in relation to contracts entered into on or after June 13, 2014.[534] Given what has earlier been said in relation to the Consumer Rights Directive's

---

[525] Directive 97/7/EC art.3(2).

[526] *easyCar (UK) Ltd v Office of Fair Trading* (C-336/03) EU:C:2005:150; [2005] E.C.R. I-1947 especially at paras 22–27.

[527] The exceptions are noted above in this paragraph.

[528] (emphasis added). This particular exclusion is effected by art.16(l) referring explicitly to "car rental services", implemented in UK law by 2013 Regulations reg.28(1)(h): see below, para.38-112.

[529] 2011 Directive art.3(1), first sentence, on which see above, para.38-069.

[530] The English version of recital 7 to the 2011 Directive refers to its regulating "certain aspects of business-to-consumer contracts across the Union" which suggests that it applies only to contracts under which the trader supplies goods or services *to* the consumer, but this terminology is not reflected in all the language versions. For example, the French version of recital 7 refers merely to its governing *"certains aspects des contrats entre les entreprises et les consommateurs au sein de l'Union"*, the Italian version to *"taluni aspetti dei contratti tra imprese e consumatori nell'Unione"* and the German version to *"bestimmte Aspekte von Verträgen zwischen Unternehmen und Verbrauchern unionsweit"* (all of which can be translated as "certain aspects of contracts between businesses and consumers across the Union"). It is submitted, therefore, that no significance should be attached to the use of the convenient English jargon expression "business-to-consumer" in this recital or in recitals 5 and 9.

[531] Above, para.38-069.

[532] Above, para.38-073; 2011 Directive art.2(4) and (6) (2013 Regulations reg.5); *DG Justice Guidance Document on 2011 Directive*, para.2.1.

[533] Below, paras 38-083 and 38-088.

[534] 2013 Regulations reg.1(2).

acknowledgement of the role of national contract law for contract law issues not regulated by the Directive,[535] it is submitted that the question when a contract was "entered into" for the purposes of this regulation must be determined by reference to the general English law of contract, rather than on the basis of an autonomous European rule or rules.[536] As noted above, earlier UK regulations may apply to off-premises contracts and distance contracts (but not to on-premises contracts which were not included in earlier EU or UK legislative schemes) made on or before June 12, 2014, though the scope of the contracts to which these regulations apply and the content of their requirements differ.[537]

(i) "Off-Premises Contracts"

"Off-premises contracts" The 2013 Regulations reg.5 provides that: **38-081**

"... 'off-premises contract' means a contract between a trader and a consumer which is any of these—
- (a) a contract concluded in the simultaneous physical presence of the trader and the consumer, in a place which is not the business premises of the trader;
- (b) a contract for which an offer was made by the consumer in the simultaneous physical presence of the trader and the consumer, in a place which is not the business premises of the trader;
- (c) a contract concluded on the business premises of the trader or through any means of distance communication immediately after the consumer was person-ally and individually addressed in a place which is not the business premises of the trader in the simultaneous physical presence of the trader and the consumer;
- (d) a contract concluded during an excursion organised by the trader with the aim or effect of promoting and selling goods or services to the consumer."

Regulation 5 further explains that:

"... business premises[538] in relation to a trader means—
- (a) any immovable retail premises where the activity of the trader is carried out on a permanent basis, or
- (b) any movable retail premises where the activity of the trader is carried out on a usual basis."

These definitions reflect very closely the Consumer Rights Directive 2011, which the 2013 Regulations implement.[539] Taken together, they mean that "off-premises contract" is a wider category than the contracts covered by the earlier UK Cancellation of Contracts made in a Consumer's Home or Place of Work, etc. Regulations 2008, and these Regulations were themselves of broader application than the

---

[535] 2011 Directive art.3(5), above, paras 38-063—38-065.
[536] For which see, in particular, Vol.I, Ch.2 of the present work.
[537] Cancellation of Contracts made in a Consumer's Home or Place of Work, etc. Regulations 2008 (SI 2008/1816) replacing Consumer Protection (Cancellation of Contracts Concluded Away from Business Premises) Regulations 1987 (SI 1987/2117); Consumer Protection (Distance Selling) Regulations 2000 (SI 2000/2334).
[538] Consumer Rights Directive 2011 recital 22 explains that "[b]usiness premises should include premises in whatever form (such as shops, stalls or lorries) which service as a permanent or usual place of business for the trader". It then provides a series of illustrations of this broad approach.
[539] Consumer Rights Directive 2011 art.2(8) and (9) respectively.

Doorstep Selling Directive 1985 which the Consumer Rights Directive 2011 replaced.[540] In this respect, the 2013 Regulations define the contracts negatively, so as to cover all contracts which are *not* concluded on the trader's premises, rather than seeking to set out (as did the 2008 Regulations) the situations in which contracts are not so made (notably, those made "during a visit by the trader to the consumer's home or place of work, or to the home of another individual"[541]). The exception to this approach is that the 2013 Regulations specifically include contracts concluded "during an excursion organised by the trader with the aim or effect of promoting and selling goods or services to the consumer" (as, for example, where a trader organises an apparently recreational coach or boat trip and then seeks to sell goods or services on the coach or boat).[542] Clearly, though, the main example of the application of this definition is the case where the trader visits the consumer at the latter's home or place of work.[543] While aspect (d) of the definition of "off-premises contracts" looks as though it is restricted to sales contracts or service contracts, it is submitted that it also includes contracts for the supply of digital content not on a tangible medium[544] as these attract special regulation regarding their confirmation.[545]

38-082   Moreover, the definition of "off-premises contracts" in the 2013 Regulations specifically seeks to prevent the trader being able to make technical points as to where (according to national contract law[546]) a contract was concluded, by including contracts "for which an *offer* was made by the consumer in the simultaneous physical presence of the trader and the consumer, in a place which is not the business premises of the trader"[547] and contracts concluded "immediately after the consumer was personally and individually addressed in a place which is not the business premises of the trader in the simultaneous physical presence of the trader and the consumer" even though the contract was itself "*concluded on* the business premises of the trader or through any means of distance communication".[548] For these purposes, it makes no difference that the trader was or was not invited to the home or workplace of the consumer (the non-business premises).[549] As recital 21

---

540 Cancellation of Contracts made in a Consumer's Home or Place of Work, etc. Regulations 2008 (SI 2008/1816) reg.5 (defining the scope of the contracts to which the Regulations apply); Doorstep Selling Directive 1985 art.1(1).

541 SI 2008/1816 reg.5(a).

542 2013 Regulations reg.5 "off-premises contract" (d); cf. SI 2008/1816 reg.5(b). In *Travel Vac SL v Antelm Sanchis* (C-423/97) EU:C:1999:197, [1999] E.C.R. I-2195 at para.38 the ECJ held (in relation to the equivalent provision in Directive 85/577/EEC (art.1(1)) that a contract "concluded in a situation in which a trader has invited a consumer to go in person to a specified place at a certain distance from the place where the consumer lives, and which is different from the premises where the trader usually carries on his business and is not clearly identified as premises for sales to the public, in order to present to him the products and services he is offering, must be considered to have been concluded during an excursion organised by the trader away from his business premises within the meaning of Directive 85/577".

543 Consumer Rights Directive 2011 recital 21.

544 Above, para.38-075.

545 2013 Regulations reg.12(5).

546 See above, paras 38-063—38-065 on the role of national contract law here.

547 2013 Regulations reg.5 "off-premises contract" (b) (emphasis added); cf. SI 2008/1816 reg.5(c).

548 2013 Regulations reg.5 "off-premises contract" (c) (emphasis added), e.g. where a trader's representative approaches a particular consumer in the street with an offer for a subscription magazine and the contract is immediately signed on the trader's nearby business premises: *DG Justice Guidance Document on 2011 Directive*, para.3.3.

549 Consumer Rights Directive 2011 recital 21. The earlier UK Regulations (SI 2008/1816) implemented

explains:

> "In an off-premises context, the consumer may be under potential psychological pressure or may be confronted with an element of surprise, irrespective of whether or not the consumer has solicited the visit."[550]

It is submitted that, for these purposes, the Supreme Court's view in *Robertson v Swift* that earlier UK regulations implementing the Doorstep Selling Directive 1985 were not restricted to contracts which were negotiated and concluded during a *single* visit to the consumer's home[551] remains valid, as there is no requirement either in the 2011 Directive or in the 2013 Regulations that an off-premises contract is concluded during a single visit on non-business premises.[552] On the other hand, recital 22 of the 2011 Directive also explains that:

> "The definition of an off-premises contract should not cover situations in which the trader first comes to the consumer's home strictly with a view to taking measurements or giving an estimate without any commitment of the consumer and where the contract is then concluded only at a later point in time on the business premises of the trader or via means of distance communication on the basis of the trader's estimate. In those cases, the contract is not to be considered as having been concluded immediately after the trader has addressed the consumer if the consumer has had time to reflect upon the estimate of the trader before concluding the contract."[553]

Consumer-to-business contracts? The definition of "off-premises" contract is **38-083** ambivalent as to whether contracts under which a consumer supplies goods or services to a trader are included. For while the first three of the situations falling within an "off-premises contract" are neutral on this point, the fourth is expressly concerned with contracts:

> "... concluded during an excursion organised by the trader with the aim or effect of promoting and selling goods or services to the consumer."[554]

This means, therefore, that *this* example of an "off-premises contract" appears to be restricted to contracts business-to-consumer, but, at a purely textual level, this example could either support an argument that this reflects the general position for off-premises contracts or that the other examples provided by the definition are not so restricted. In any event, much of the information required of traders and the consequences of the exercise of the consumer's right to cancel is appropriate only

---

Directive 85/577/EEC (art.1(1) of which provided that it did not apply to contracts concluded during a visit made at the consumer's express request) "so as to embrace visits a trader made to the consumer's home at the request of the consumer" and this extension was held lawful both as a matter of EU law (as the 1985 Directive art.8 allowed "more favourable provision" to protect consumers) and under s.2(2) of the European Communities Act 1972: *Swift v Robertson* [2013] EWCA Civ 1794, [2013] Bus. L.R. 479 at [48]–[54] approved (though no longer in issue) by the SC sub. nom. *Robertson v Swift* [2014] UKSC 50, [2014] 1 W.L.R. 3438 at [18].

[550] 2011 Directive recital 21, second sentence.

[551] *Robinson v Swift* [2014] UKSC 50, [2014] 1 W.L.R. 3438 at [17], describing as "plainly right" the decision of the Court of Appeal below sub. nom. *Swift v Robinson* [2013] EWCA Civ 1794, [2013] Bus. L.R. 479 at [40]–[43], [67] and [68], though the point was no longer in issue before the SC.

[552] 2013 Regulations reg.5 "off-premises contract".

[553] 2011 Directive recital 22, fourth and fifth sentences.

[554] 2011 Directive art.2(8)(d); 2013 Regulations reg.5 "off-premises contract" (d). Above, para.38-081 and see generally above, para.38-079.

to the provision of goods or services by traders to consumers.[555]

38-084 Dietzinger For this purpose the European Court of Justice's decision in *Dietzinger* may be significant, as there it held that the earlier Doorstep Selling Directive 1985 (which the 2011 Directive's provisions on off-premises contracts replaced) applied to a contract of guarantee concluded by a person other than in the course of his trade or profession which guaranteed a contract supplying goods or services by a person in the course of his trade, etc. to a person who was *not* acting in the course of his trade, etc. despite the fact that the 1985 Directive was expressed as applying to "contracts under which a trader supplies goods or services to a consumer",[556] the Court observing that "nothing in the wording of the directive requires that the person concluding the contract under which goods or services are to be supplied be the person to whom they are supplied",[557] as long as the "consumer assumes obligations towards the trader with a view to obtaining goods or services from him".[558] The reason for this inclusive approach by the Court of Justice was the purpose of the 1985 Directive, which was "to protect consumers by enabling them to withdraw from a contract concluded on the initiative of the trader rather than of the customer, where the customer may be unable to see all on the implications of his act."[559] Given that the 2011 Directive's provisions governing off-premises contracts share this purpose with the 1985 Directive, it could be argued that these provisions (and therefore the 2013 Regulations) should also apply to off-premises contracts under which a consumer agrees to provide goods or services to a trader, as well to contracts under which a trader agrees to provide goods or services to a consumer. Moreover, given the changed and generally more neutral wording used to describe the contracts to which the 2011 Directive generally applies, it is submitted that this may be the case even if the consumer does not also conclude a contract for the provision of goods or services from the trader as required by the Court in *Dietzinger*.

38-085 Examples If the 2011 Directive applies in principle to contracts under which a consumer supplies goods or services to a trader as well as to one under which a consumer receives goods or services from a trader, then the information and cancellation provisions in the 2013 Regulations would apply, for example, to a contract under which a consumer sells goods to an antique dealer who has visited him at home. However, the position of contracts of guarantee made by a consumer to a trader who provides credit to a third party (whether or not that third party was also a consumer) is less certain. For even if in principle such a contract qualifies as a "consumer contract" for the purposes of the 2011 Directive and the 2013 Regulations, it may fall within the exclusion from their scope of "contracts for financial services", that is, "contracts for services of a banking, credit, insurance, personal pension, investment or payment nature".[560] On the other hand, it could be argued that a contract of guarantee undertaken by a "consumer" does not count as a

---

[555] Below, paras 38-091 et seq.
[556] Directive 85/577 art.1(1); *Bayerische Hypotheken- und Wechselbank AG v Dietzinger* (C-45/96) EU:C:1998:111, [1998] E.C.R. I-1199.
[557] C-45/96 EU:C:1998:111, [1998] E.C.R. I-1199 at para.19.
[558] C-45/96 EU:C:1998:111, [1998] E.C.R. I-1199 at para.22.
[559] C-45/96 EU:C:1998:111, [1998] E.C.R. I-1199 at para.19.
[560] 2013 Regulations reg.6(1)(b); 2011 Directive art.3(3)(d), "financial service" being defined by art.2(12).

"contract for services of a banking ... nature" and therefore falls outside this exclusion, particularly given that exclusions to schemes of consumer protection in EU legislation are to be interpreted strictly.[561]

(ii) Distance Contracts

Definition   The 2013 Regulations provide that: **38-086**

"... 'distance' contract means a contract concluded between a trader and a consumer under an organised distance sales or service-provision scheme without the simultaneous physical presence of the trader and the consumer, with the exclusive use of one or more means of distance communication up to and including the time at which the contract is concluded."[562]

This definition reflects word-for-word the definition found in the 2011 Directive.[563] It contains a number of elements.

"A contract concluded ... under an organised distance sales or service-   **38-087**
provision scheme"   Neither the 2013 Regulations nor the text of the 2011 Directive defines these notions, but recital 20 of the Directive explains that:

"The notion of an organised distance sales or service-provision scheme should include those schemes offered by a third party other than the trader but used by the trader, such as an online platform. It should not, however, cover cases where websites merely offer information on the trader, his goods and/or services and his contact details."

A clear example of a "distance contract" would be where the consumer views goods offered for sale on a seller's website and is able to buy those goods online, paying through secure pages, but it would not apply where the consumer views goods on a seller's website, yet cannot buy them online. However, as recital 20 to the Directive explains, it also includes cases where a:

"... consumer visits the business premises merely for the purpose of gathering information about the goods or services and subsequently negotiates and concludes the contract at a distance."[564]

On the other hand, according to recital 20, "distance contract" does not include contracts negotiated at the business premises of the trader and finally concluded by distance communication, contracts initiated by means of a distance communication but finally concluded at the business premises of the trader, and contracts where a consumer makes a reservation by means of a distance communication to request the provision of a service, giving as an example a consumer telephoning to request an appointment with a hairdresser. These cases would, therefore, fall outside both "distance contracts" and "off-premises contracts" and therefore, under the 2013

---

[561] *Veedfald v Århus Amtskommune* (C-203/99) EU:C:2001:258, [2001] E.C.R. I-3569 at para.15; *easyCar (UK) Ltd v Office of Fair Trading* (C-336/03) EU:C:2005:150; [2005] E.C.R. I-1947 at para.21; *Kásler v OTP Jelzálogbank Zrt* (C-26/13) EU:C:2014:282, April 30, 2014 at para.42; *Kušionová v SMART Capital a.s.* (C-34/13) EU:C:2014:2189, September 10, 2014 at para.77.
[562] 2013 Regulations reg.5 "distance contract".
[563] 2011 Directive art.2(7).
[564] 2011 Directive recital 20.

Regulations, into the residual category of "on-premises contracts".[565] Finally, the contract must be concluded under an "organised distance sales or service-provision scheme" and the requirement of an organised scheme means that:

"... if a trader only exceptionally concludes a contract with a consumer by e-mail or telephone, after being contacted by the consumer, such a contract should not be considered a distance contract under the Directive."[566]

It has been held that a scheme whereby, for a fee, the Royal Institute of Chartered Surveyors nominates adjudicators as part of its statutory function as an adjudicator nomination body is not an "organised distance sales scheme" so that a contract concluded with the adjudicator does not count as a "distance contract" for the purposes of the 2013 Regulations.[567] While the form of words used in this aspect of the definition of "distance contract" suggests that it is restricted to sales contracts and services contracts, it is submitted that it should be seen as extending to schemes under which contracts for the supply of digital content not on a tangible medium (which are neither sales contracts nor services contracts[568]) are provided, since they attract a special rule governing confirmation.[569]

38-088 **Contracts consumer-to-business?** While the definition of distance contract makes clear the breadth of the contracts covered by the provisions in the 2013 Regulations on distance contracts, it is expressed in a way which indicates that the contracts involve the provision of goods or services by a trader *to a consumer*.[570] At a purely textual level, therefore, this suggests these provisions do not apply to contracts under which a consumer supplies goods or services to a trader.

38-089 **"Means of distance communication"** Unlike the earlier legislation on distance contracts,[571] the 2013 Regulations (following the text of the 2011 Directive) do not define or illustrate what is meant by "means of distance communication", but recital 20 of the Directive explains that:

"The definition of distance contract should cover all cases where a contract is concluded between the trader and the consumer under an organised distance sales or service-provision scheme, with the exclusive use of one or more means of distance communication (such as mail order, Internet, telephone or fax) up to and including the time at which the contract is concluded."

(iii) *"On-Premises Contract"*

38-090 **A residual category** The 2013 Regulations provide that:

---

[565] Above, paras 38-071 and below, para.38-090.
[566] *DG Justice Guidance Document on 2011 Directive*, para.5.1.
[567] *Christopher Linnett Ltd v Harding (t/a MJ Harding Contractors)* [2017] EWHC 1781 (TCC), [2018] Bus. L.R. 179 at [86].
[568] Above, para.38-075.
[569] 2013 Regulations reg.16(3).
[570] cf. above, para.38-079.
[571] Directive 97/7/EC art.2 (4) "means of distance communication" referring to an "indicative list" in Annex I, implemented by SI 2000/2334 reg.3(1) "means of distance communication"; Sch.1.

"... 'on-premises contract' means a contract between a trader and a consumer which is neither a distance contract nor an off-premises contract."[572]

The 2011 Directive does not refer to "on-premises contracts", but instead imposes information requirements on traders in respect of contracts other than distance or off-premises contracts.[573] The use by the 2013 Regulations of the notion of "on-premises contracts" as they define it achieves the same result, but given the breadth and relative complexity of the definitions of "off-premises contract" and "distance contract", the term "on-premises contract" risks causing confusion. For example, as has been seen, the 2013 Regulations include within an "off-premises contract":

"... a contract *concluded on the business premises* of the trader ... immediately after the consumer was personally and individually addressed in a place which is not the business premises of the trader in the simultaneous physical presence of the trader and the consumer."[574]

Therefore, some contracts concluded on the business premises of the trader will *not* count as "on-premises contracts" for the purposes of the 2013 Regulations. Moreover, some contracts concluded entirely by means of distance communication[575] (such as email or telephone) will not constitute a "distance contract" as they are not made "under an organised distance sales or service-provision scheme".[576] Confusingly, such a contract would count as an "on-premises contract" within the meaning of the 2013 Regulations.

(c)   Information Requirements

(i)   General

"Giving information", "providing it" and "making it available"   The 2011 **38-091** Directive requires some information to be given, some provided and some made available by the trader to the consumer.[577] The differences between the provision and giving of information and merely making it available was considered by the Court of Justice of the EU in *Content Services Ltd*[578] in the context of the earlier Distance Contracts Directive, which required the trader to give the consumer written confirmation of information which he should receive.[579] The Court held that for this purpose the words "given" and "receive" should be given their usual meaning in everyday language, taking into account their context and, therefore, "refer to a process of transmission".[580] As a result, and taking into account the directive's purpose of consumer protection, a trader who merely provides a hyperlink on a

---

[572] 2013 Regulations reg.5 "on-premises contract".
[573] 2011 Directive art.5.
[574] 2013 Regulations reg.5 "off-premises contract" (c) (emphasis added), above, para.38-081.
[575] On which see above, para.38-089.
[576] 2013 Regulations reg.5, above, para.38-087.
[577] 2011 Directive arts 5(1), 6(1), 7(2), 7(4)(a) ("the trader shall provide"); arts 7(1) and 8(1) ("the trader shall give"); and art.8(1) ("the trader shall ... make that information available"): see further below, para.38-092.
[578] *Content Services Ltd v Bundesarbeitskammer* (C-49/11) of July 5, 2012 ("*Content Services Ltd* (C-49/11)").
[579] Directive 97/7/EC art.5(1).
[580] *Content Services Ltd* (C-49/11) paras 32–33.

website or within an email which allows the consumer to access the relevant information does not give that information, nor does the consumer receive it, as the consumer: "must act in order to acquaint himself with the information in question and he must, in any event, click on that link."[581] In so holding, the Court contrasted this position with the Directive's requirements as to pre-contractual information, with which the consumer was to be "provided" by the trader, considering that this was a "more neutral formulation" in the vast majority of its linguistic versions.[582]

38-092   The terminology in the Consumer Rights Directive   In turning to the Consumer Rights Directive 2011, the terminology has changed. As regards all three types of contract (off-premises contracts, distance contracts and other contracts) the trader is generally required to *provide* the consumer with the listed information before the consumer is bound[583]; but for off-premises contracts the Directive then requires the information to be *given*, though their confirmation is to be *provided*.[584] By contrast, in the case of distance contracts, the trader must *give* the necessary information before the consumer is bound "or make that information available to the consumer in a way appropriate to the means of distance communication",[585] although there is no similar alternative as regards the confirmation which the trader must provide after the distance contract is concluded.[586] As recital 36 explains:

> "In the case of distance contracts, the information requirements should be adapted to take into account the technical constraints of certain media, such as the restrictions on the number of characters on certain mobile telephone screens or the time constraint on television sales spots. In such cases the trader should comply with a minimum set of information requirements and refer the consumer to another source of information, for instance by providing a toll free telephone number or a hypertext link to a webpage of the trader where the relevant information is directly available and easily accessible."[587]

38-093   The terminology in the 2013 Regulations   This special treatment of distance contracts is reflected in the 2013 Regulations' rules governing pre-contractual information requirements, explaining that, for these purposes "something is made available to a consumer only if the consumer can reasonably be expected to know how to access it".[588] However, the 2013 Regulations then add that the confirmation to be given to the consumer "is treated as provided as soon as the trader has sent it or done what is necessary to make it available to the consumer"[589] and they also allow information governing "on-premises contracts"[590] and information in connection with repair or maintenance contracts concluded off-premises[591] to be made available instead of being given. It will be seen, therefore, that while the "making available" of information as an alternative to its provision is foreseen by

---

581   *Content Services Ltd* (C-49/11) paras 33 and 37.
582   *Content Services Ltd* (C-49/11) para.35, referring to Directive 97/7/EC art.4(1).
583   2011 Directive arts 5(1) and 6(1).
584   2011 Directive art.7(1) and 7(2).
585   2011 Directive art.8(1).
586   2011 Directive art.8(7).
587   2011 Directive recital 36.
588   2013 Regulations reg.13(1) and reg.8.
589   2013 Regulations reg.16(5).
590   2013 Regulations reg.9(1).
591   2013 Regulations reg.11(2).

the 2011 Directive as regards pre-contractual information for distance contracts,[592] the other examples of use of this phrase in the 2013 Regulations find no counterpart in the 2011 Directive, and therefore must be vulnerable to the argument that to this extent they fail properly to implement the minimum requirements of the 2011 Directive.

Vulnerable consumers　While neither the 2013 Regulations nor the text of the   **38-094** 2011 Directive refer to the type of consumer the trader must have in mind in providing information which they require, recital 34 of the Directive states:

"In providing that information, the trader should take into account the specific needs of consumers who are particularly vulnerable because of their mental, physical or psychological infirmity, age or credulity in a way which the trader could reasonably be expected to foresee. However, taking into account such specific needs should not lead to different levels of consumer protection."

A trader must therefore bear in mind the particular needs of vulnerable consumers, in particular in the manner in which information is provided.[593] This echoes the treatment of the "average consumer" by the Unfair Commercial Practices Directive 2005, which similarly requires traders to take into account in their business-to-consumer practices the particular vulnerability of consumers which the trader can reasonably be expected to foresee.[594]

Burden of proof　In case of dispute about a trader's compliance with the provi-   **38-095** sions in Pt 2 of the 2013 Regulations imposing information and confirmation requirements in relation to off-premises and distance contracts, it is for the trader to show that the provision in question was complied with, though this rule does not apply to proceedings relating to an offence relating to a trader's failure to give notice of the right to cancel nor to proceedings relating to compliance with an injunction to secure compliance with the Regulations.[595]

(ii)　Off-Premises Contracts and Distance Contracts

Application of the requirements　Part 2 of the 2013 Regulations imposes a series   **38-096** of requirements on traders[596] to give or (in the case of distance contracts) to make available[597] to consumers[598] information before they are bound by an off-premises contract[599] or distance contract[600] and to provide consumers with a copy or confirma-

---

[592]　2011 Directive art.8(1), though art.8(7) does not so refer as regards confirmation of the contract.
[593]　The 2011 Directive art.6(7) (relating to off-premises and distance contracts) also provides that Member States may maintain or introduce in their national laws language requirements regarding contractual information, so as to ensure that such information is easily understood by the consumer.
[594]　Unfair Commercial Practices Directive 2005/29/EC art.5(3), recital 18 glossing the notion of "average consumer": see above, para.38-044.
[595]　2013 Regulations reg.17; 2011 Directive art.6(9). There is no equivalent provision in the 2013 Regulations setting a burden of proof as to the information requirements in relation to "on-premises contracts", following the 2011 Directive.
[596]　On the meaning of "trader" see above, paras 38-069, 38-050—38-058.
[597]　On the significance of "make available to" see above, paras 38-091—38-092.
[598]　On the meaning of "consumer" see above, paras 38-069, 38-030 et seq.
[599]　On the definition of "off-premises contract" see above, paras 38-081—38-085.
[600]　On the definition of "distance contract" see above, paras 38-086—38-089.

tion of any resulting contract.[601] In principle, these requirements apply to all types of "consumer contract" with the exceptions already noted,[602] but in addition Pt 2 excludes from its scope certain contracts for the supply of medicinal or other health care products[603] and off-premises contracts under which the payment to be made by the consumer is not more than £42.[604]

38-097 **Information requirements** The 2013 Regulations provide that, before the consumer is bound by an off-premises contract, the trader must give the consumer in a clear and comprehensible manner a list of required information.[605] In the case of distance contracts, the trader must give or make available[606] the information in a clear and comprehensible manner and in a way appropriate to the means of distance communication used.[607] In all these requirements, it is submitted that the requirement that the information be provided or made available in a clear and comprehensible manner should be assessed from the point of view of the "average consumer", taking into account any particular vulnerability of consumers in the context which the trader can reasonably be expected to foresee.[608]

38-098 **The information required** Schedule 2 to the 2013 Regulations[609] lists the information so required:

"(a) the main characteristics of the goods, services or digital content,[610] to the extent appropriate to the medium of communication and to the goods, services or digital content[611];

(b) the identity of the trader (such as the trader's trading name);

(c) the geographical address at which the trader is established and, where available, the trader's telephone number, fax number and e-mail address, to enable the consumer to contact the trader quickly and communicate efficiently;

(d) where the trader is acting on behalf of another trader, the geographical address and identity of that other trader;

(e) if different from the address provided in accordance with paragraph (c), the geographical address of the place of business of the trader, and, where the trader acts on behalf of another trader, the geographical address of the place of business of that other trader, where the consumer can address any complaints;

(f) the total price of the goods, services or digital content inclusive of taxes, or where the nature of the goods, services or digital content is such that the price cannot reasonably be calculated in advance, the manner in which the price is to be calculated;

(g) where applicable, all additional delivery charges and any other costs or, where those

---

[601] 2013 Regulations reg.12 (off-premises contracts); reg.16 (distance contracts): below, para.38-101.

[602] For the contracts to which Pt 2 applies, see reg.7(1) and above, paras 38-069—38-079, which notes the contracts excluded from the scope of the Regulations as a whole.

[603] 2013 Regulations reg.7(2).

[604] 2013 Regulations reg.7(4) reflecting an option for Member States provided by the 2011 Directive art.3(4) and explained by recital 28 on the basis that to this extent it would relieve traders from an administrative burden.

[605] 2013 Regulations reg.10(1) (off-premises contracts).

[606] See above, paras 38-091—38-092 on the significance of "make available".

[607] 2013 Regulations reg.13(1), on which see above, para.38-089.

[608] See above, para.38-094.

[609] As amended by SI 2014/870.

[610] "Digital content" means "data which are produced and supplied in digital form": 2013 Regulations reg.5 "digital content".

[611] On the special significance of this requirement under the Consumer Rights Act 2015 s.11(4) (goods contracts) and s.36(3) (digital content contracts), see below, paras 38-499 and 38-548 respectively.

charges cannot reasonably be calculated in advance, the fact that such additional charges may be payable;

(h)   in the case of a contract of indeterminate duration or a contract containing a subscription, the total costs per billing period or (where such contracts are charged at a fixed rate) the total monthly costs;

(i)   the cost of using the means of distance communication for the conclusion of the contract where that cost is calculated other than at the basic rate;

(j)   the arrangements for payment, delivery, performance, and the time by which the trader undertakes to deliver the goods, to perform the services or to supply the digital content;

(k)   where applicable, the trader's complaint handling policy;

(l)   where a right to cancel exists, the conditions, time limit and procedures for exercising that right in accordance with regulations 27 to 38;

(m)   where applicable, that the consumer will have to bear the cost of returning the goods in case of cancellation and, for distance contracts, if the goods, by their nature, cannot normally be returned by post, the cost of returning the goods;

(n)   that, if the consumer exercises the right to cancel after having made a request in accordance with regulation 36(1), the consumer is to be liable to pay costs in accordance with regulation 36(4);

(o)   where under regulation 28, 36 or 37 there is no right to cancel or the right to cancel may be lost, the information that the consumer will not benefit from a right to cancel, or the circumstances under which the consumer loses the right to cancel;

(p)   in the case of a sales contract, a reminder that the trader is under a legal duty to supply goods that are in conformity with the contract;

(q)   where applicable, the existence and the conditions of after-sale customer assistance, after-sales services and commercial guarantees;

(r)   the existence of relevant codes of conduct, as defined in regulation 5(3)(b) of the Consumer Protection from Unfair Trading Regulations 2008, and how copies of them can be obtained, where applicable;

(s)   the duration of the contract, where applicable, or, if the contract is of indeterminate duration or is to be extended automatically, the conditions for terminating the contract;

(t)   where applicable, the minimum duration of the consumer's obligations under the contract;

(u)   where applicable, the existence and the conditions of deposits or other financial guarantees to be paid or provided by the consumer at the request of the trader;

(v)   where applicable, the functionality,[612] including applicable technical protection measures, of digital content[613];

(w)   where applicable, any relevant compatibility of digital content with hardware and software that the trader is aware of or can reasonably be expected to have been aware of[614];

(x)   where applicable, the possibility of having recourse to an out-of-court complaint and redress mechanism, to which the trader is subject, and the methods for having access to it".[615]"

---

[612] 2013 Regulations reg.5 provides that "'functionality' in relation to digital content includes region coding, restrictions incorporated for the purposes of digital rights management, and other technical restrictions".

[613] On the particular significance of this category of information under the Consumer Rights Act 2015 s.36(3), see below, para.38-548.

[614] On the particular significance of this category of information under the Consumer Rights Act 2015 s.36(3), see below, para.38-548.

[615] 2013 Regulations Sch.2, which notes that in the case of a public auction (as defined by reg.5 "public auction" and explained by the 2011 Directive recital 24) the information listed in paras (b) to (e) may be replaced with the equivalent details for the auctioneer.

The information relating to the consumer's cancellation right in paras (l), (m) and (n) above may be provided by means of the "model instructions on cancellation" set out by the Regulations, and if the trader uses this model correctly filled in, this is to be treated as compliance with those requirements.[616] The Regulations also provide that, if a right to cancel exists, the trader must give (or, in the case of distance contracts, make available to) the consumer a cancellation form which they set out.[617] In the case of off-premises contracts, the information and any cancellation form must be given on paper or, if the consumer agrees, on another durable medium and must be legible[618]; for distance contracts, it must be legible in so far as the information is provided on a durable medium.[619] In the case of distance contracts, the 2013 Regulations qualify the general rules as to the provision of information where they are concluded through a means of distance communication which allows limited space or time to display the information.[620]

38-099   **Distance contracts concluded by electronic means**   There are special information requirements for distance contracts concluded by electronic means.[621] Moreover, where the contract places the consumer under an obligation to pay, the trader must ensure that "the consumer, when placing the order, explicitly acknowledges that the order implies an obligation to pay", failing which the consumer is not bound by the contract or order.[622]

38-100   **Telephone calls to conclude a distance contract**   If a trader makes a telephone call to the consumer with a view to concluding a distance contract, the trader must, at the beginning of the conversation with the consumer, disclose the trader's identity, where applicable, the identity of the person on whose behalf the trader makes the call, and the commercial purpose of the call.[623]

38-101   **Provision of copy or confirmation of contract**   In the case of off-premises contracts, the trader must give the consumer a copy of the signed contract or confirmation of the contract on paper or, if the consumer agrees, on another durable

---

[616] 2013 Regulations reg.10(3) (off-premises contracts); reg.13(3) (distance contracts), referring to the "Model instructions for cancellation" in Sch.3 Pt A.

[617] 2013 Regulations reg.10(1)(b) (off-premises contracts); reg.13(1)(b) (distance contracts); Sch.3 Pt B.

[618] 2013 Regulations reg.10(2). Regulations 10 (3), (4), and (6) makes further incidental provision as to these requirements. Regulation 11 makes special provision for the provision of information in connection with repair or maintenance contracts. "Durable medium" is defined by reg.5 as: "paper or email, or any other medium that—(a) allows information to be addressed personally to the recipient, (b) enables the recipient to store the information in a way accessible for future reference for a period that is long enough for the purposes of the information, and (c) allows the unchanged reproduction of the information stored". On "durable medium" see *Content Services Ltd v Bundesarbeitskammer* (C-49/11) July 5, 2012 paras 39–50 in the context of the Distance Contracts Directive 1997: "a durable medium must ensure that the consumer, in a similar way to paper form, is in possession of the [relevant] information ... to enable him to exercise his rights where necessary": (C-49/11) at para.42.

[619] 2013 Regulations reg.13(2).

[620] 2013 Regulations reg.13(4).

[621] 2013 Regulations reg.14.

[622] 2013 Regulations reg.14(3)–(5).

[623] 2013 Regulations reg.15 implementing Consumer Rights Directive 2011 art.8(5). On the sanctions for a trader failing to do so, see 2013 Regulations regs 44 et seq., below, paras 38-132 et seq.

medium[624]; in the case of distance contracts, the trader must give or make available[625] to the consumer confirmation of the contract on a durable medium.[626] In either case, the trader must act within a reasonable time after the conclusion of the contract and, in any event, not later than the time of delivery of any goods or beginning of the performance of any service supplied under the contract,[627] and any confirmation must include all the information which should have been provided before the contract was concluded, unless already so provided in a durable medium.[628]

(iii) On-Premises Contracts

In principle, the information requirements imposed on traders in respect of on-premises contracts apply to all types of "consumer contracts" with the exceptions already noted.[629] In this respect, the trader must give or make available[630] the information to the consumer in a clear and comprehensible manner[631] if that information is not already apparent from the context.[632] However, the information requirements do:

38-102

"... not apply to a contract which involves a day-to-day transaction and is performed immediately at the time when the contract is entered into."[633]

As the Departmental Implementing Guidance explained:

"The principle behind the exemption for day-to-day transactions sold on premises is that the consumer will be very familiar with the goods or services and their cost, so that the level of information required by the Regulations would be superfluous. Thus buying a cup of coffee, the daily paper, weekly groceries, a tube of toothpaste, etc. would all constitute day-to-day transactions. By their nature, such transactions are likely to be low cost items."[634]

Presumably, the question whether a contract is an example of a "day-to-day transac-

---

[624] 2013 Regulations reg.12(1) and (3). On the definition of "durable medium" in reg.5, see above, para.38-098. In the case of off-premises contracts for the supply of digital content not on a tangible medium and the consumer has given the consent and acknowledgment in respect of its supply during the cancellation period, then the copy or confirmation must include confirmation of the consent and acknowledgment: 2013 Regulations reg.12(5) and see below, para.38-115.

[625] See above, paras 38-091—38-092 on the significance of "make available to".

[626] 2013 Regulations reg.16(1) and (5). On the definition of "durable medium" in reg.5, see above, para.38-098. In the case of distance contracts for the supply of digital content not on a tangible medium where the consumer has given the consent and acknowledgment in respect of its supply during the cancellation period, then the copy or confirmation must include confirmation of the consent and acknowledgment: 2013 Regulations reg.16(3) and see below, para.38-115.

[627] 2013 Regulations reg.12(4) (off-premises contracts); reg.16(4) (distance contracts).

[628] 2013 Regulations reg.12(2) (off-premises contracts) and reg.16(2) (distance contracts) referring to Sch.2. The relevant information is detailed at para.38-098 above.

[629] For the contracts to which Pt 2 of the 2013 Regulations applies, see above, paras 38-069, 38-072—38-079, which note the contracts excluded from the scope of the Regulations as a whole.

[630] See above, paras 38-091—38-092 on the significance of "make available".

[631] See above, para.38-097.

[632] 2013 Regulations reg.9(1).

[633] 2013 Regulations reg.9(2).

[634] Department for Business Innovation & Skills, *Consumer Contracts (Information, Cancellation and Additional Charges) Regulations, Implementing Guidance* (December 2013) C, para.6. The inclusion of this exemption reflects the exercise of an option for Member States under the Consumer Rights Directive 2011 art.5(3).

tion" is to be judged by its frequency in the practice of the average consumer. Although this exclusion may be justified (as does the Department's Guidance) on the basis of the likely familiarity of the consumer with the subject matter of such a transaction, it may also reflect a concern for the practical inconvenience and administrative cost of the imposition of information requirements on traders in relation to such transactions.

38-103 **The information required** Schedule 1 to the 2013 Regulations[635] lists the information required:

> "(a)   the main characteristics of the goods, services or digital content, to the extent appropriate to the medium of communication and to the goods, services or digital content[636];
>
> (b)   the identity of the trader (such as the trader's trading name), the geographical address at which the trader is established and the trader's telephone number;
>
> (c)   the total price of the goods, services or digital content inclusive of taxes, or where the nature of the goods, services or digital content is such that the price cannot reasonably be calculated in advance, the manner in which the price is to be calculated;
>
> (d)   where applicable, all additional delivery charges or, where those charges cannot reasonably be calculated in advance, the fact that such additional charges may be payable;
>
> (e)   where applicable, the arrangements for payment, delivery, performance, and the time by which the trader undertakes to deliver the goods, to perform the service or to supply the digital content;
>
> (f)   where applicable, the trader's complaint handling policy;
>
> (g)   in the case of a sales contract, a reminder that the trader is under a legal duty to supply goods that are in conformity with the contract;
>
> (h)   where applicable, the existence and the conditions of after-sales services and commercial guarantees;
>
> (i)   the duration of the contract, where applicable, or, if the contract is of indeterminate duration or is to be extended automatically, the conditions for terminating the contract;
>
> (j)   where applicable, the functionality,[637] including applicable technical protection measures, of digital content[638];
>
> (k)   where applicable, any relevant compatibility of digital content with hardware and software that the trader is aware of or can reasonably be expected to have been aware of.[639]"

(iv)   The Effects of the Information Requirements

38-104 **General** The information requirements imposed on traders as outlined above may have a number of different consequences: the provision of inaccurate information and the failure to provide information are both made to constitute breach of

---

[635] As amended by SI 2014/870.

[636] On the special significance of this requirement under the Consumer Rights Act 2015 s.11(4) (goods contracts) and s.36(3)(digital content contracts), see below, paras 38-499 and 38-548 respectively.

[637] 2013 Regulations reg.5 provides that "'functionality' in relation to digital content includes region coding, restrictions incorporated for the purposes of digital rights management, and other technical restrictions".

[638] On the particular significance of this category of information under the Consumer Rights Act 2015 s.36(3), see below, para.38-548.

[639] On the particular significance of this category of information under the Consumer Rights Act 2015 s.36(3), see below, para.38-548.

contract[640]; in the context of off-premises contracts and distance contracts, a trader's failure to provide information on the consumer's right to cancel affects the period within which the consumer may cancel[641]; and, in the context of off-premises contracts, this failure may constitute a criminal offence.[642] In addition, the various requirements imposed on traders may be enforced by injunction on the application of a weights and measures authority.[643] Finally, the provision of inaccurate information or the failure to provide information may constitute an unfair commercial practice within the meaning of the Consumer Protection from Unfair Trading Regulations 2008.[644] As earlier noted, in *Radlinger v Finway a.s.* the Court of Justice held that the effectiveness of the protection provided by information requirements for consumers in the Consumer Credit Directive 2008 means that a national court must raise of its own motion the issue whether these requirements have been fulfilled and, if they have not, must "draw all the consequences provided for under national law".[645] This strongly suggests that the Court would equally hold that a national court must also raise the issue whether a trader has fulfilled the information requirements under the Consumer Rights Directive and, therefore, in the UK context, the 2013 Regulations.

The contractual significance of information supplied   For all three types of   **38-105**
contracts (off-premises contracts, distance contracts and on-premises contracts), the 2013 Regulations as made provided that any information which is given by a trader to a consumer as they require "is to be treated as included as a term of the contract"[646] and that:

"... a change to any of that information, made before entering into the contract or later, is not effective unless expressly agreed between the consumer and the trader."[647]

In general English law, the effect of making the information given a term of the

---

[640] Below, paras 38-105—38-106.
[641] 2013 Regulations reg.31, below, para.38-118.
[642] Below, para.38-107.
[643] Below, paras 38-108, 38-132.
[644] Below, paras 38-109—38-111.
[645] *Radlinger v Finway a.s.* (C-377/14) April 21, 2016 at paras 62–74 and see above, para.38-068.
[646] 2013 Regulations reg.9(3) (on-premises contract); reg.10(5) (off-premises contract); and reg.13(6) (distance contract).
[647] 2013 Regulations reg.9(4) (on-premises contract); reg.10(4) (off-premises contract); and reg.13(7) (distance contract). While the Consumer Rights Directive 2011 art.6(5) requires these provisions for off-premises and distance contracts, art.5 concerning contracts other than off-premises and distance contracts does not do so. It is submitted, though, that, art.3(5) of the Directive leaves this issue to national contract law, here reflected in the 2013 Regulations reg.9(4): on the significance of art.3(5) of the 2011 Directive see above, paras 38-063—38-065. The 2013 Regulations refer to changes to "information, made before entering into the contract *or later*", whereas art.6(5) of the 2011 Directive states that information forming a part of the contract "shall not be altered unless the contracting parties expressly agree otherwise". A simple example may be found in the case of the parties agreeing by exchange of emails to a different time of delivery of the goods. It may be thought that the wording of the Regulations is broad enough to forbid changes by the trader to information provided even where these are made under an express variation clause in the contract. However, according to the European Commission, while a provision in a trader's standard terms stating that it may derogate from the information provided would not satisfy art.6(5)'s requirement for the express agreement of the parties, art.6(5) would not prevent changes made to the *terms* of a contract after it has been concluded (apparently) under an express variation clause, though the latter would be subject to control under the Unfair Terms in Consumer Contracts Directive 1993: *DG Justice Guidance Document on 2011 Directive*, para.4.2.5 and see below on the control of variation clauses under the 1999 Regulations (paras 38-312—38-315) or the Consumer Rights Act 2015 Pt 2 (paras 38-389 et

contract would in principle be that the trader is held to have promised that the information is accurate, with the result that any inaccuracy would constitute a breach of contract by the trader, with the normal set of remedies for breach at common law. However, as regards those goods contracts and digital content contracts to which it applies,[648] the Consumer Rights Act 2015 expressly made provision for this purpose by stating that information concerning the main characteristics of the goods or digital content provided by the trader as required by the 2013 Regulations[649] is to be included as a term of the contract under its provisions on sale or supply by description,[650] with the result that breach of these terms gives rise to the rights for consumers which the Act then sets out[651]; and the 2015 Act further provided that other information required by the 2013 Regulations for these contracts and for services contracts, is to be treated as a term of these contracts[652] with the result that breach gives rise to rights for the consumer which vary according to the category of contract in question.[653] After the enactment of these provisions in the 2015 Act, the 2013 Regulations were amended so that their own broad provisions governing the contractual significance of information were replaced with a residual provision to similar effect but applicable only to contracts for the supply of digital content *other than* for a price paid by the consumer.[654]

38-106 **Effect on the contract of failure to provide information** Under the earlier Cancellation of Contracts made in a Consumer's Home or Place of Work, etc.

---

seq.) (which implement the 1993 Directive). If the Commission's view holds good, if possible, the terms of the 2013 Regulations must be read so as to conform to this reading of the 2011 Directive, as here it requires "full harmonisation": 2011 Directive art.4 and above, para.38-062.

[648] The 2013 Regulations apply to contracts entered into on or after June 13, 2014: reg.1(2). The relevant provisions of the Consumer Rights Act 2015 Pt 1 came into force on October 1, 2015: below, paras 38-366 and 38-437.

[649] 2013 Regulations Sch.1 para.(a) or Sch.2 para.(a) (goods contracts); Sch.1 paras (a), (j) and (k) or Sch.2 paras (a), (v) or (w) (digital contents contracts), which make clear that the categories of information are wider as regards digital content contracts.

[650] Consumer Rights Act 2015 s.11(4)–(6) (goods contracts); s.36(3)–(5) (digital content contracts).

[651] Consumer Rights Act 2015 ss.11(7) and 19 (goods contracts); ss.36(5), 42 (digital content contracts): see below, paras 38-493, 38-499 and 38-512 et seq.; 38-544, 38-548 and 38-557 et seq.

[652] 2015 Act s.12 (goods contracts) on which see below, para.38-500; s.37 (digital content contracts) on which see below, para.38-549; and s.50 (services contracts) on which see below, para.38-572—38-576.

[653] 2015 Act s.19(5) (goods contracts) on which see below, paras 38-493, 38-512 et seq.; s.42(4) (digital content contracts) on which see below, paras 38-544, 38-557 et seq.; and s.54 (services contracts) on which see below, paras 38-570, 38-580 et seq.

[654] Consumer Contracts (Amendment) Regulations 2015 (SI 2015/1629) regs 4–6 (replacing 2013 Regulations reg.9(3) (on-premises contracts), reg.10(5) (off-premises contracts) and reg.13(6) (distance contracts)). (These amendments to the 2013 Regulations apply to contracts entered into on or after October 1, 2015: SI 2015/1629 reg.1.) The intention was that the 2013 Regulations should still apply to contracts under which digital content is supplied which do not fall within the definition of "digital content contracts" in the 2015 Act: Explanatory Note to SI 2015/1629, which states that the amendments are "in consequence of the Act and revoke provisions of the 2013 Regulations to the extent they are replicated in the Act". The retention of the residual category of contracts for the supply of digital content in the 2013 Regulations as amended is required by their broad scope following in this respect the Consumer Rights Directive 2011: see above, para.38-075. Under the 2015 Act Pt 1 Ch.3, "a contract for a trader to supply digital content to a consumer" is of two types: where digital content "is supplied for a price paid by the consumer" (s.33(1)) and where "(a) it is supplied free with goods or services or other digital content for which the consumer pays a price, and (b) it is not generally available to consumers unless they have paid a price for it or for goods or services or other digital content" (s.33(2)): below, paras 38-541—38-542.

Regulations 2008,[655] a trader's failure to provide the information to the consumer as they required rendered a contract unenforceable against the consumer.[656] There is no equivalent provision in the 2013 Regulations, but they do provide that every contract to which Pt 2 applies[657] is to be treated as including a term that the trader has complied with the information requirements which it sets out, with the exception of those required of traders by telephone with a view to concluding a distance contract.[658] This provision has no equivalent in the 2011 Directive, but can be seen as part of the UK's provision of "adequate and effective means" to ensure compliance with the Directive,[659] and/or as setting out "general contract law" effects of the Directive's provisions which the latter does not itself regulate.[660] The use by the Regulations of the technique of deemed contract term means that any failure to provide information as required by the Regulations would constitute a breach of contract, with the consequences set out by the general common law.[661] In addition to these effects on the contract, as regards off-premises contracts and distance contracts, failure in a trader to provide information on the consumer's right to cancel results in an extension of the period of cancellation from 14 days to a year, unless in the meanwhile the trader provides the consumer with the requisite information.[662]

Criminal law: off-premises contracts   In the case of off-premises contracts (but **38-107** not distance contracts or on-premises contracts), the 2013 Regulations create an offence for a trader who enters into an off-premises contract but fails to give the consumer the required information on the consumer's right of cancellation.[663] A person guilty of such an offence is liable on summary conviction to an unlimited fine.[664] The Regulations make further and incidental provision on the creation of this offence, including a defence of due diligence for the trader.[665] In England and Wales, this offence is to be enforced and prosecuted by weights and measures authorities, often known as the local trading standards service.[666]

---

655 There was no equivalent provision in the Consumer Protection (Distance Selling) Regulations 2000 (SI 2000/2334).
656 SI 2008/1816 reg.7(6); *W v Veolia Environmental Services (UK Plc)* [2011] EWHC 2020 (QB), [2012] 1 All E.R. (Comm) 667; *Allproperty Claims Ltd v Tang* [2015] EWHC 2198 (QB) at [45] and cf. *Kell v Department of Energy and Climate Change* Unreported July 23, 2015, Newcastle upon Tyne County Ct.
657 i.e. off-premises contracts, distance contracts and on-premises contracts: 2013 Regulations reg.7 and see paras 38-069—38-079.
658 2013 Regulations reg.18 referring specifically to the information requirements in regs 9–14 and 16.
659 2011 Directive art.23(1).
660 As permitted by 2011 Directive art.3(5) as explained above, paras 38-063—38-065.
661 See Vol.I, Chs 24, 26 and 27. In particular, this could lead to termination for breach of contract subject to the normal requirement that breach by the trader substantially deprived the consumer of the benefit of the contract and/or damages: Vol.I, para.24-041.
662 2013 Regulations reg.31, on which see below, para.38-118.
663 2013 Regulations reg.19, referring to the information listed in paras (l), (m) or (n) of Sch.2 (on which see above, para.38-098).
664 Until March 12, 2015 the maximum fine available on summary conviction was £5,000 (level 5 on the standard scale), but on that date this was changed to an unlimited fine by the Legal Aid, Sentencing and Punishment of Offenders Act 2012 s.85.
665 2013 Regulations regs 20–23. Regulations 24–26 (powers of investigation, obstruction of authorised officers, and freedom from self-incrimination, respectively) were revoked by the Consumer Rights Act 2015 (Consequential Amendments) Order 2015 (SI 2015/1726) art.2, Sch. Pt 2 para.7; the 2015 Act was amended so as to include the 2013 Regulations in the list of legislation to which the investigatory powers in that Act (Sch.5) apply: SI 2015/1726 art.2, Sch. Pt 1 para.6.
666 2013 Regulations reg.23.

38-108   Enforcement of information requirements   The information requirements set out by the 2013 Regulations attract the general enforcement measures available to weights and measures authorities for the enforcement of the Regulations generally, as noted later in this section.[667]

38-109   Relationship between information requirements and law governing unfair commercial practices   In principle, a trader's failure to provide the information required by the 2013 Regulations or, as the case may be, a failure to provide such information accurately, may constitute (respectively) a "misleading omission" or "misleading action" within the meaning of the Consumer Protection from Unfair Trading Regulations 2008 ("2008 Regulations"), subject in particular to the condition that doing so caused, or was likely to cause, the average consumer to take a transactional decision he would not have taken otherwise and to the other conditions which those 2008 Regulations set out.[668] Where this is the case, then the consequences of such failures would give rise to the enforcement measures and (in the case of misleading actions but not misleading omissions) to the rights to redress for consumers which those Regulations provide in addition to the consequences and enforcement measures already noted in relation to the 2013 Regulations themselves.[669]

38-110   Misleading omissions   In this respect, the position as regards misleading omissions is clear, as reg.6(1) of the 2008 Regulations provides that:

> "(1)   A commercial practice is a misleading omission if, in its factual context, taking account of the matters in paragraph (2)—
>
> (a)   the commercial practice omits material information,
>
> (b)   the commercial practice hides material information,
>
> (c)   the commercial practice provides material information in a manner which is unclear, unintelligible, ambiguous or untimely, or
>
> (d)   the commercial practice fails to identify its commercial intent, unless this is already apparent from the context,
>
> and as a result it causes or is likely to cause the average consumer to take a transactional decision he would not have taken otherwise."

And for this purpose, reg.6(3) provides that "material information" means:

> "(a)   the information which the average consumer needs, according to the context, to take an informed transactional decision; and
>
> (b)   any information requirement which applies in relation to a commercial communication as a result of an EU obligation."

As a result, for example, a trader's failure to provide the information required by the 2013 Regulations (which implement the Consumer Rights Directive 2011) falls within reg.6(3)(b) so as to satisfy the "material information" element of the 2008 Regulations' definition of a "misleading omission".[670] This means that such a failure could give rise to the enforcement measures available under the 2008 Regula-

---

667   2013 Regulations Pt 6, below, para.38-132—38-134.
668   SI 2008/1277 reg.5 and especially 5(2)(b) (misleading actions) and reg.6 especially 6(1) (misleading omissions), below, paras 38-165 et seq.
669   2008 Regulations (as amended by SI 2014/870), Pt 4 Enforcement; Pt 4A Consumers' Rights to Redress: on the latter, see below, paras 38-172 et seq.
670   This reflects accurately the Unfair Commercial Practices Directive 2005 art.7(5), which refers to a "non-exhaustive list" in its Annex II, and the latter includes Directive 97/7/EC on distance contracts,

tions,[671] though not to any right to redress for consumers under these Regulations as these do not extend to "misleading omissions".[672]

Misleading actions   Similarly where a trader provides a consumer with false   **38-111** information of the types required by the 2013 Regulations, this could in principle constitute a "misleading action" within the meaning of the 2008 Regulations, subject to the other conditions for the incidence of this particular form of unfair commercial practice.[673] As will be seen, the definition of a "misleading action" under the 2008 Regulations is quite complex, but its central element concerns a commercial practice where "it contains false information and is therefore untruthful" in relation to a series of matters which it then specifies,[674] these matters being drawn directly from the 2005 Directive on which the 2008 Regulations are based.[675] In this respect, it is submitted that this possibility is not prevented by art.3(4) of the Unfair Commercial Practices Directive 2005 (which the 2008 Regulations implement), according to which:

"In the case of conflict between the provisions of this Directive and other Community rules regulating specific aspects of unfair commercial practices, the latter shall prevail and apply to those specific aspects."

As recital 10 of the 2005 Directive explains, art.3(4) seeks to ensure that the Directive's relationship with existing Community law is coherent, and so

"... applies only in so far as there are no specific Community law provisions regulating specific aspects of unfair commercial practices, such as information requirements and rules on the way the information is presented to the consumer."

In the result,[676] art.3(4) therefore resolves:

---

arts 4 and 5 of which were the predecessor provisions to the information requirements now contained in the Consumer Rights Directive 2011 arts 6 and 7 which are implemented in UK law by the 2013 Regulations regs 13 and 14. For the "complementary nature" of information obligations under specific EU legislation and the provision in art.7(5) of the 2005 Directive (implemented by reg.6(3)(b) of the 2008 Regulations), see *Abcur AB v Apoteket Farmaci, Apoteket AB and Apoteket Farmaci AB* (C-544/13 and C-545/13) July 16 2015 at paras 78–82 (medicinal products for human use). For discussion of the significance of "misleading omission" under reg.6(3)(a) of the 2008 Regulations see *Secretary of State for Business, Innovation and Skills v PLT Antimarketing Ltd* [2015] EWCA Civ 76, [2015] C.T.L.C.8 at [30]–[31] where the Court of Appeal identified the "critical question" as being "whether the average consumer can be said to need to obtain that information from the trader in question, rather than obtain it (for example) by shopping around, and finding out for himself whether something better, or cheaper, is on offer": *Secretary of State for Business, Innovation and Skills v PLT Antimarketing Ltd* at [31] per Briggs L.J. (with whom Ryder and Richards L.JJ. agreed) later referring to this as "the "needs" test": *Secretary of State for Business, Innovation and Skills v PLT Antimarketing Ltd* at [40]. cf. the approach of the CJEU to art.6 of the 2005 Directive's requirements as regards "misleading actions" in *Nemzeti Fogyasztóvédelmi Hatóság v UPC Magyarország Kft* (C-388/13) of April 18, 2015 at paras 53–54 (where a trader provides erroneous information to the consumer, the fact that the consumer could himself have obtained the correct information is irrelevant).

[671] On which see below, paras 38-170—38-171.
[672] Below, para.38-185.
[673] 2008 Regulations reg.5 and see below, paras 38-179—38-183.
[674] 2008 Regulations reg.5(2)(a) and 5(4).
[675] Unfair Commercial Practices Directive 2005 art.6(2). On the 2005 Directive, see below, para.38-159 et seq.
[676] See also below, para.38-422.

"... irreconcilable conflict between substantive norms, i.e. situations where the same business-to-consumer commercial practice would qualify as 'unfair' under one provision and 'non-unfair' ... under another provision. In such cases, the EU special provision shall 'prevail'."[677]

While the information requirements in the 2011 Directive must "prevail" over the more general information requirements set out by the 2005 Directive, a failure accurately to provide this information *may* constitute a "misleading action" under the 2005 Directive (subject to its other conditions, notably, that the information "deceives or is likely to deceive the average consumer" and "causes or is likely to cause the average consumer to take a transactional decision he would not have taken otherwise"[678]). In the result, in the UK context the provision of false or misleading information of the types required by the 2013 Regulations[679] may constitute a "misleading action" and so give rise to the enforcement measures set out by the 2008 Regulations and they may also give rise to a right to redress for individual consumers, as these rights can arise in respect of the commission of a misleading action.[680] Where this is the case, the consumer's rights to civil redress in respect of a misleading action and the consumer's rights for breach of contract in respect of information provided by a trader under the 2013 Regulations (and treated as a term of the contract under the Consumer Rights Act 2015)[681] may in principle co-exist, though it is submitted that the courts would so interpret the two regimes that the consumer could not in these circumstances obtain double recovery.

---

[677] Orlando (2011) *European Review of Contract Law* 25 at 50–51 (emphases omitted), and see below, para.38-161.

[678] 2008 Regulations reg.5(2)(a) and (b). In *Abcur AB v Apoteket Farmaci, Apoteket AB and Apoteket Farmaci AB* (C-544/13 and C-545/13) July 16 2015 the CJEU held that art.3(4) of the 2005 Directive "applies only in so far as there are no specific EU law provisions regulating specific aspects of unfair commercial practices, such as information requirements and rules on the way the information is presented to the consumer" in relation to medical products for human use (at para.79) and that, where the specific provisions conflict with the provisions in the 2005 Directive, the former "take precedence and apply to those specific aspects of unfair commercial practices" (at para.81), but in the result, this allowed advertising practices relating to such medical products to fall within the scope of the 2005 Directive "provided that the conditions for the application of that directive are satisfied" (at para.83). Moreover, it is submitted that the line of argument in the text is not contradicted by *Citroën Commerce GmbH v Zentralvereinigung des Kraftfahrzeuggewerbes zur Aufrechterhaltung lauteren Wettbewerbs eV (ZLW)* (C-476/14) July 7, 2016 at paras 44–46 where the CJEU held that the provision in the 2005 Directive regarding the materiality of certain information in invitations to purchase for the purposes of misleading omissions (which included "the price inclusive of taxes" (art.7(4)(c))) could not apply to the case before them "as the aspect relating to the selling price referred to in an advertisement", as that issue was governed by Directive 98/6/EC on consumer protection in the indication of the prices of products offered to customers [1998] O.J. L80/27 art.3(1)'s provision on "selling price": the 1998 Directive governed this "specific aspect" within the meaning of art.3(4) of the 2005 Directive, which therefore "cannot apply as regards that aspect" (C-476/14 judgment at para.45). This case therefore provides an example of where the "special provision" must prevail, as explained in the text.

[679] See above, paras 38-098 (off-premises and distance contracts) and 38-103 (on-premises contracts).

[680] 2008 Regulations regs 27A(4)(a), 27B(1)(a) below, paras 38-172 et seq. especially at 38-178.

[681] Above, para.38-105.

(d)　The Consumer's Right of Cancellation or Withdrawal

(i)　The Situations in Which the Right Arises and its Duration

The contracts affected　Part 3 of the 2013 Regulations creates rights of cancel-　**38-112**
lation for consumers, and regulates the effect of their exercise and of the withdrawal
of an offer by a consumer, in respect of off-premises and distance contracts but not
on-premises contracts.[682] Part 3 excludes the same types of contracts from the application of these provisions as they exclude from Pt 2's information requirements,[683] in addition to those types of contracts or contracts made in particular
circumstances which are excluded entirely from the scope of the 2013
Regulations.[684] Part 3 also excludes from its scope contracts for the supply of goods
or services of certain types or supplied in certain circumstances, for example, for
the supply of goods made to the consumer's specifications,[685] wine bought *en
primeur*,[686] newspapers, periodicals or magazines supplied other than under a
subscription,[687] contracts for the supply of accommodation, transport of goods,
vehicle rental services, catering or services relating to leisure activities, if the
contract provides for a specific date or period of performance[688] and contracts
concluded at a public auction.[689] Moreover, the rights conferred by Pt 3 cease to be
available to the consumer in the case of contracts for the supply of sealed goods
which are not suitable for return due to health protection or hygiene reasons, if they
become unsealed after delivery; contracts for the supply of sealed audio or sealed
video recordings or sealed computer software, if the goods become unsealed after
delivery; and any sales contract, if the goods become mixed inseparably (according to their nature) with other items after delivery.[690]

The right to cancel the contract and the right to withdraw an offer　The 2013　**38-113**
Regulations distinguish between the consumer's right to cancel the off-premises
contract or distance contract after it has been concluded and the consumer's right
to withdraw an offer which he or she has made.[691] The right to cancel itself is cre-

---

[682]　2013 Regulations reg.27(1) (referring to Pt 3). For the definition of these contracts see above, paras
38-081 (off-premises contract); 38-086 (distance contract) and 38-090 (on-premises contract).

[683]　2013 Regulation reg.27(2)–(4) and cf. reg.7(2)–(5) whose contents are noted above, para.38-077.
The only qualification on this position is that contracts for passenger transport services are wholly
excluded from Pt 3 of the 2013 Regulations, whereas their exclusion from Pt 2 finds an exception
in the case of distance contracts concluded by electronic means: see above, para.38-078.

[684]　Above, para.38-076.

[685]　2013 Regulations reg.28(1)(b).

[686]　2013 Regulations reg.28(1)(d) as explained by 2011 Directive recital 49.

[687]　2013 Regulations reg.28(1)(f).

[688]　2013 Regulations reg.28(1)(h).

[689]　2013 Regulations reg.28(1)(g); "public auction" is defined by reg.5 "public auction". The full list
is contained in 2013 Regulations reg.28.

[690]　2013 Regulations reg.28(3).

[691]　The terminology adopted by the Regulations for this purpose differs from the terminology used by
the 2011 Directive, which refers to what appears in the Regulations as the right to cancel as a right
to withdraw. As earlier noted at para.38-065, the Directive also provides for the case (as recognised
by some national laws) of a consumer being bound by *an offer* (art.5(1), art.6(1)) and therefore appears to extend the consumer's right to withdraw to the situation where he would otherwise be bound
by his offer to *conclude* a distance or off-premises contract: art.12(b) describing the effects of
withdrawal, even though arts 9 to 11 which describe the right of withdrawal itself and its exercise
do not refer to this.

ated and delineated by the Regulations in terms of when it starts, how long it exists and the effects of its exercise. As reg.29(1) provides, "[t]he consumer may cancel a distance or off-premises contract at any time in the cancellation period without giving any reason, and without incurring any liability" except in the circumstances which the Regulations themselves set out.[692] By contrast, reg.29(3) provides that:

> "(3)   Paragraph (1) does not affect the consumer's right to withdraw an offer made by the consumer to enter into a distance or off-premises contract, at any time before the contract is entered into, without giving any reason and without incurring any liability."

This provision does not create any right in a consumer to withdraw an offer, but rather implicitly recognises that such a right exists (as it does in English law at common law[693]) and that this right is not affected by the recognition of the right to cancel the contract created by the Regulations. As explained in Vol.I of the present work, at common law a person (the offeror) has a general right to withdraw his or her offer before it has been accepted by the offeree; and this right of withdrawal is subject to a requirement of communication of the withdrawal to the offeree, though this may be satisfied by communication other than from the offeror and is subject to exceptions.[694] By contrast, the Regulations require the consumer to inform the trader of the decision to withdraw any offer made to a trader in respect of the contracts covered by Pt 3, and provides that, where a consumer does so, the trader must in principle reimburse payments received from the consumer (subject to exceptions and qualifications), and that any "ancillary contract" made by the consumer is automatically terminated.[695] As a result, while the circumstances in which a consumer may withdraw an offer to contract in respect of an off-premises or distance contract are determined by the common law, the Regulations set both a legal requirement of informing the trader that is distinct from the requirement of communication of a withdrawal or revocation of offer at common law and two distinct legal consequences of its exercise. In both respects, the 2013 Regulations therefore seek to harmonise the circumstances in which a consumer can withdraw an offer and can cancel any concluded contract. This is clearly sensible in terms of legislative policy, as otherwise a trader could argue that the Regulations' provisions on the reimbursement of payments made by a consumer and on ancillary contracts do not apply to offers made but not accepted by the trader, since no contract was concluded and, therefore, no right of cancellation of *the contract* was generated. This is all the more the case as a trader could seek to rely either on the general common law position or on its own standard terms of business to claim that its own communications constitute mere invitations to treat and a communication to it from a consumer constitutes an offer accepted only on further communication by the trader.[696] On the other hand, the Regulations make no provision in respect of any possible right in a consumer to revoke an acceptance which he or she

---

[692]   2013 Regulations reg.29(1) referring to regs 34(3) and (9), 35(5) and 36(4), on which see below, paras 38-124, 38-125, 38-127 and 38-129.

[693]   Vol.I, para.2-094. Withdrawal of an offer is often described as its revocation.

[694]   Vol.I, paras 2-095—2-097.

[695]   2013 Regulations regs 32(1), 34 and 38.

[696]   On the general rules at common law, see Vol.I, paras 2-011—2-014 (offer and invitation to treat); paras 2-026 et seq. (acceptance).

has posted,[697] except by way of its own right of cancellation.

The right to cancel: general As earlier noted, the 2013 Regulations provide that: **38-114**

"... [t]he consumer may cancel a distance or off-premises contract at any time in the cancellation period without giving any reason, and without incurring any liability",[698]

though they then provide four circumstances in which the consumer may incur some liability as a result of the exercise of the right to cancel.[699] While the Consumer Rights Directive 2011 justifies the right to cancel in distance contracts on the basis that, as the consumer has not seen the goods, he or she "should be allowed to test and inspect the goods he has bought to the extent necessary to establish the nature, characteristics and the functioning of the goods" and the right to cancel in off-premises contracts "because of the potential surprise element and/or psychological pressure" in this situation, the Directive (and in turn the Regulations) do not attempt to restrict the right to cancel to cases where these grounds are relevant, but instead allow the consumer to cancel "without giving any reason".[700]

Supply of services or digital content in cancellation period The 2013 Regula- **38-115** tions provide that the trader must not begin the supply of a service before the end of the cancellation period[701] unless the consumer has made an express request to this effect and, in the case of an off-premises contract, this was made on a durable medium.[702] Where the trader begins performance of the service at such a request by the consumer, the latter ceases to have the right to cancel the contract once the service has been fully performed, provided that he or she acknowledged that this would be the case when performance of the service began.[703] Similarly, a trader must not begin to supply digital content not on a tangible medium[704] unless the consumer has given express consent and has acknowledged that the right to cancel will be lost.[705] Where these conditions are satisfied, however, the consumer ceases to have a right to cancel the contract.[706]

The cancellation period The earlier directives on doorstep selling and distance **38-116** contracts set a period of seven days within which the consumer could cancel these

---

[697] Vol.I, paras 2-060—2-061.

[698] 2013 Regulations reg.29(1).

[699] 2013 Regulations reg.29(1), referring to reg.34(3), 34(9), 34(5) and 36(4) on which see below, paras 38-124, 38-125, 38-127 and 38-129.

[700] 2011 Directive recital 37.

[701] On which, see below, paras 38-116—38-117.

[702] 2013 Regulations reg.36(1). On the definition of "durable medium" in reg.5, see above, para.38-098.

[703] 2013 Regulations reg.36(2). This restriction on the availability of the right of cancellation does not apply to contracts for the supply of water, gas, electricity or district heating (on which see above, para.38-073). For the consequences of a consumer's exercise of a right to cancel falling outside this restriction where services are supplied during the cancellation period; see 2013 Regulations reg.36(3)–(6), below, paras 38-128—38-130.

[704] For "digital content" see 2013 Regulations reg.5, above, para.38-075. On "tangible medium" see above, para.38-075.

[705] 2013 Regulations reg.37(1).

[706] 2013 Regulations reg.37(2). For the consequences of a consumer's exercise of a right to cancel falling outside this restriction, see reg.37(3)–(4).

types of contract,[707] but their requirement of only "minimum harmonisation"[708] led to differing cancellation periods in the laws of Member States.[709] The Consumer Rights Directive 2011 saw these differences as causing legal uncertainty and compliance costs for traders, and so requires instead a uniform period of 14 days,[710] this being faithfully reflected in the 2013 Regulations.[711] Under the Directive, this period refers to 14 days after the relevant day ("days" referring to calendar days),[712] and this is given effect by the 2013 Regulations by referring to each cancellation period as ending, for example, "at the end of 14 days *after the day on which* the contract is entered into".[713] However, this apparent simplicity is then marred by the considerable complexity of the provisions governing the commencement of this period and its extension by up to a year for the situation where the trader has not notified the consumer of the existence of the right.[714] This scheme is set by the 2013 Regulations by means of provision in reg.30 governing the "normal cancellation period" and in reg.31 governing the extended cancellation period where the information requirement is breached.

38-117 **Normal cancellation period**   The 2013 Regulations set the day relevant to the start of the 14-day cancellation period differently according to the particular type of contract in question. So, in the case of service contracts[715] and contracts for the supply of digital content which is not supplied on a tangible medium, the cancellation period starts on the day after the contract is entered into,[716] the latter to be determined by the application of the normal rules at common law governing the formation of contract.[717] In the case of "sales contracts",[718] the Regulations set a basic rule according to which the cancellation period ends at the end of 14 days after the day on which the goods come into the physical possession of either the consumer or of a person, other than the carrier, identified by the consumer to take possession of them.[719] This rule is then nuanced for the cases where the sales contract concerns multiple goods ordered in one order but delivered on different days (the day on which the last of the goods comes into the possession of the consumer, etc.); multiple lots of goods or pieces of something delivered on different days (the day on which the last of the lots or pieces come into the possession of the consumer, etc.); and for the regular delivery of goods during a defined period of more than one day (the day on which the first of the goods comes into the possession of the consumer, etc.).[720] For these purposes, it is submitted that the notion

---

707   Directive 85/577/EEC art.5(1); Directive 97/7/EC art.6(1).
708   On which see above, para.38-022.
709   Directive 2011/83/EU recital 40.
710   Directive 2011/83/EU art.9.
711   2013 Regulations regs 30 and 31.
712   Directive 2011/83/EU recital 41 referring to Council Regulation (EEC, Euratom) 1182/71, [1971] O.J. L124/1.
713   2013 Regulations reg.30(2) (emphasis added). A similar formulation is used in regs 30(3), (4), (5) and (6) and 31(2) and (3).
714   Directive 2011/83/EU arts 9 and 10.
715   For the definition of "service contract" see above, para.38-073.
716   "Digital content" means "data which are produced and supplied in digital form": 2013 Regulations reg.5 "digital content".
717   This results from Directive 2011/83/EU reg.3(5) as explained by paras 38-063—38-065, above.
718   For the definition of "sales contract" see above, para.38-073.
719   2013 Regulations reg.30(3).
720   2013 Regulations reg.30(4)–(6).

of goods "coming into the physical possession of the consumer" would attract an autonomous European significance, since the 2011 Directive (which the Regulations implement) uses this notion in relation to sales contracts in the context of the consumer's right of cancellation[721] and in relation to its provisions governing the delivery of goods and the passing of risk.[722] In this respect, in the case of the passing of risk, recital 55 of the Directive explains that "a consumer should be considered to have acquired the physical possession of the goods when he has received them".[723] In order to achieve a coherent interpretation of the Directive, this explanation should also be used as regards "coming into physical possession of the consumer" for the purposes of the consumer's right of cancellation. On this basis, the question whether goods have come into the physical possession of a consumer would become whether he has received them, but the precise significance of this in a particular case would remain for national courts as a matter of the application of the law to the facts as they find them.[724]

Cancellation period extended for breach of information requirement Where **38-118** a trader did not provide the consumer before the conclusion of the contract with information on the right to cancel as the Regulations require,[725] the cancellation period ends at the end of 12 months after the day on which it would otherwise have ended under the normal cancellation periods (for example, for service contracts the day of the conclusion of the contract),[726] unless in the meanwhile the trader provides the consumer with that information, when the cancellation period ends 14 days after the consumer receives that information.[727] These rules mark a significant change from the unsatisfactory position under the earlier directives, under which the period for exercise of the right of cancellation in doorstep selling contracts started only on receipt by the consumer of notice of that right[728] and was therefore held to be inconsistent with any temporal limitation in national law[729]; and in distance contracts where a trader's failure to inform led to the right lasting for three months or until seven days after the information had been supplied.[730] The 2011 Directive

---

[721] Directive 2011/83/EU art.9(2)(b).
[722] Directive 2011/83/EU arts 18 and 20, which were first implemented by 2013 Regulations regs 42 and 43, but were then re-implemented by the Consumer Rights Act 2015 ss.28 and 29: see below, paras 38-526—38-527. These provisions all refer to goods coming into the possession of the consumer or a person identified by the consumer to take the possession of the goods.
[723] The explanation in this recital supports the view that the Directive requires an autonomous view of the notion of "goods coming into the physical possession" of the consumer and this means that art.3(5)'s saving of *unregulated* contract law issues for national law would not apply, even if this notion were seen as belonging to "contract law": on the significance of art.3(5), see above, paras 38-063—38-065.
[724] Above, para.38-017.
[725] 2013 Regulations regs 10(1) (off-premises contracts); 13(1) (distance contracts). The information requirement is contained in Sch.2 para.(l). In *Hamilton v Volksbank Filder eG* (C-412/06) EU:C:2008:215, [2008] E.C.R. I-02383 at paras 34–36 the ECJ held that the supply of incorrect information on the consumer's right of cancellation is equivalent to no information and this was confirmed by the form of words used by Directive 2011/83/EU art.10, 2013 Regulations reg.31(1).
[726] 2013 Regulations reg.31(1) and see above, para.38-117 for the normal cancellation periods applicable to other types of contract.
[727] 2013 Regulations reg.31(2).
[728] Directive 85/577/EEC art.5.
[729] *Heininger v Bayerische Hypo- und Vereinsbank AG* (C-481/99) EU:C:2001:684, [2001] E.C.R. I-09945 at paras 44–48.
[730] Directive 97/7/EC art.6.

instead requires a uniform period of 12 months throughout the EU in the interests of legal certainty.[731]

38-119 **Exercise of the right to cancel** The 2013 Regulations provide generally that "to cancel a contract ... the consumer must inform the trader of the decision to cancel it",[732] either by using a "form following the model cancellation form" which the Regulations themselves provide[733] or by making "any other clear statement setting out the decision to cancel the contract".[734] Where a trader gives consumers the option of using such a form or other statement on the trader's website, the Regulations provide that the consumers need not use it, but if they do, the trader must communicate to them an acknowledgement of receipt of the cancellation on a durable medium[735] without delay.[736] Where a consumer cancels by making "any other clear statement setting out the decision to cancel the contract", the Regulations provide that:

"... the consumer is to be treated as having cancelled the contract in the cancellation period if the communication is sent before the end of that period."[737]

It is for a consumer to show that the contract was cancelled in the cancellation period which the Regulations set out.[738]

38-120 **No effective waiver of right by consumer** As earlier noted, under the 2013 Regulations, where the right to cancel exists, the consumer may choose to cancel without giving any reason. In other situations where English law recognises a right in a party to a contract to set that contract aside (whether rescission for misrepresentation or termination for breach of contract), such a party may instead choose to affirm the contract and so lose the right to set it aside.[739] While the 2013 Regulations do not so provide, the 2011 Directive (which they implement) states expressly that, where the law applicable to the contract is the law of a Member State, "consumers may not waive the rights conferred on them by the national measures transposing this Directive".[740] Given the duty of national courts to interpret the Regulations so as to conform to the UK's obligation faithfully to implement the Directive,[741] it is submitted that a consumer would not lose any right of

---

731 Directive 2011/83/EU recital 43. The uniform nature of this period stems from the Directive's general requirement of "full harmonisation" in art.4, see above, para.38-062.

732 2013 Regulations reg.32(2), referring to cancellation under reg.29(1). cf. above, para.38-113 on the position as regards the consumer's right to withdraw an offer.

733 2013 Regulations reg.32(3)(a); Sch.3 Pt B.

734 2013 Regulations reg.32(3)(b).

735 On "durable medium" see 2013 Regulations reg.5 as noted above, para.38-098.

736 2013 Regulations reg.32(4).

737 2013 Regulations reg.32(5).

738 2013 Regulations reg.32(6).

739 See Vol.I, paras 7-133—7-134 (misrepresentation) and 24-003 (breach of contract).

740 Directive 2011/83/EU art.25, first sentence. Article 25 distinguishes this from the exclusion of cancellation by agreement by its second sentence providing that "any contractual terms which directly or indirectly waive or restrict the rights resulting from the Directive shall not be binding on the consumer". cf. *Salat v Barutis* [2013] EWCA Civ 1499, [2014] E.C.C. 2 at [22] (CA "inclined to agree" that under the Cancellation of Contracts made in a Consumer's Home or Place of Work, etc. Regulations 2008 (SI 2008/1816) (which were replaced by the 2013 Regulations) a consumer cannot affirm a contract that would otherwise be unenforceable against him).

741 Above, para.38-014.

cancellation under the Regulations by any purported affirmation of the contract or waiver of the right to do so. On the other hand, this position is unlikely to be of great practical significance given the short-lived nature of the right of cancellation, except in the case where the trader has not informed the consumer of the right of cancellation, but in that case it is unlikely that the consumer would know of it and therefore be found in possession of the knowledge of the right requisite for affirmation or waiver.[742]

Contract unenforceable where right of cancellation exists Under the earlier Cancellation of Contracts made in a Consumer's Home or Place of Work, etc. Regulations 2008, a trader's failure to provide the information to the consumer rendered a contract unenforceable against the consumer and, as a result, it was held that a company which hired a car to a consumer could not recover the hire costs from an insurer liable for damage caused to the consumer's car which the hired car replaced.[743] While the 2013 Regulations do not make express provision as to the unenforceability of an off-premises contract or distance contract in these circumstances,[744] it is submitted that, where a right of cancellation in a consumer exists, then the contract is unenforceable against the consumer, with the potential for similar effects on the liability of a third party. **38-121**

(ii)   The Effects of Cancellation or Withdrawal

General effect of cancellation The 2013 Regulations provide that where a consumer exercises the right of cancellation which they create, "cancellation ends the obligations of the parties to perform the contract".[745] This form of words, which follows closely the 2011 Directive,[746] is restricted to the parties' obligations to *perform* the contract, but it is submitted that the notion of "performance" for these purposes should not be interpreted narrowly so as to include only the main obligations of the parties to supply goods or services (on the one hand) or to pay (on the other), but should be seen as extending at least to certain types of incidental obligations, such as an obligation in a consumer to take a dispute to arbitration (to the extent to which a contract term creating such an obligation were otherwise to be binding on the consumer[747]) as well, of course, to any secondary obligation to pay damages for non-performance which might otherwise have arisen. On the other hand, the 2013 Regulations assume that cancellation by the consumer does not terminate *all* the obligations arising from the contract itself, as they provide that the trader must bear the direct cost of returning the goods where he has agreed to do so[748] and the "contract is to be treated as including a term that the trader must bear the direct cost of the consumer returning the goods" where the trader failed to **38-122**

---

[742] See Vol.I, paras 7-134 and 24-003.

[743] SI 2008/1816 reg.7(6); *W v Veolia Environmental Services (UK Plc)* [2011] EWHC 2020 (QB), [2012] 1 All E.R. (Comm) 667 at [49] and [54] applying to this context *Dimond v Lovell* [2000] UKHL 27, [2002] 1 A.C. 384.

[744] Above, para.38-106.

[745] 2013 Regulations reg.33(1)(a).

[746] Directive 2011/83/EU art.12(a).

[747] In English law, such an arbitration clause would not be binding on a consumer where a claim refers to a "modest amount", currently £5,000, under the Arbitration Act 1996 ss.89, 90 on which see below, para.38-302 (unfair contract terms).

[748] 2013 Regulations reg.35(5)(a).

provide the consumer with the information about the consumer bearing those costs as the Regulations elsewhere provide.[749] These provisions therefore assume that the intended effect of these contract terms survives cancellation. Moreover, the 2013 Regulations provide that cancellation by the consumer gives rise to obligations in the trader to reimburse payments received from the consumer and obligations in the consumer to return goods received and to pay an amount in respect of any diminution in the value of the goods as a result of their handling beyond what is necessary to establish their nature, characteristics and functioning, in both cases subject to a series of provisos and qualifications[750] or, in the case of some services, to pay to the trader a proportionate amount for the supply of the service during the cancellation period,[751] though it is earlier provided that, apart from these specified situations, the consumer may cancel "without any liability".[752] Overall, in this way the 2013 Regulations seek to set out the principal consequences of cancellation for both the parties and to preclude any other "liabilities" in the consumer, this reflecting the 2011 Directive's concern to address these issues at a European level in contrast to the earlier directives whose provisions gave rise to uncertainty as to whether they were to be settled by the Court of Justice by the development of autonomous interpretations or by national laws.[753] On the other hand, where cancellation of the contract gives rise to issues between the parties other than those regulated by the 2011 Directive (as implemented by the 2013 Regulations), then art.3(5) of the Directive allocates them to national contract law for resolution.[754]

38-123 **Reimbursement by the trader of payments received from the consumer**   As regards *all* the types of contract (sales contracts, service contracts and contracts for the supply of digital content not on a tangible medium) which may give rise to a right of cancellation,[755] on cancellation or withdrawal of an offer by the consumer, the trader must reimburse "all payments, other than payments for delivery,[756] received from the consumer", subject only to the possibility of some allowance being made in respect of the diminution in value of the goods as a result of their handling by the consumer.[757] This general right of restitution of monies paid is clearly not dependent on the normal rules of English common law in similar circumstances, notably the requirement of total failure of consideration.[758] Under the Regulations, reimbursement must be made without delay, and in any event not later than the following specified days: in the case of sales contracts, if the trader has not offered to collect the goods, the end of 14 days after the day on which the

---

[749] 2013 Regulations reg.35(5)(b), 35(6); the information requirement is contained in Sch.2 para.(m).
[750] 2013 Regulations regs 34 and 35 on which see below, paras 38-123 et seq.
[751] 2013 Regulations reg.36(3)–(6), below, para.38-129.
[752] 2013 Regulations reg.29(1).
[753] For the earlier case-law on these issues see: *Travel Vac SL v Antelm Sanchis* (C-423/97) EU:C:1999:197, [1999] E.C.R. I-2195 at paras 53–60, *Schulte v Deutsche Bausparkasse Badenia AG* (C-350/03) EU:C:2005:637, [2005] E.C.R. I-9215 at paras 67–69, 82–93, *Hamilton v Volksbank Filder eG* (C-412/06) EU:C:2008:215, [2008] E.C.R. I-02383 at paras 37–49 (all doorstep selling), *Messner v Firma Stefan Krüger* (C-489/07) EU:C:2009:502, [2009] E.C.R. I-07315, *Handelsgesellschaft Heinrich Heine GmbH v Verbraucherzentrale Nordrhein-Westfalen eV* (C-511/08) EU:C:2010:189; [2010] E.C.R. I-03047 (both distance contracts).
[754] Above, paras 38-063—38-065.
[755] Above, para.38-112.
[756] On which see below, para.38-124.
[757] 2013 Regulations reg.34(1) referring to reg.34(10).
[758] On which see Vol.I, paras 29-057 et seq.

trader receives the goods back or, if earlier, the day on which the consumer supplies evidence of having sent the goods back; otherwise, the end of 14 days after the day on which the trader is informed of the consumer's decision to withdraw the offer or cancel the contract.[759] The trader must make the reimbursement using the same means of payment as the consumer used for the initial transaction, unless the consumer has expressly agreed otherwise; and the trader must not impose any fee on the consumer in respect of the reimbursement.[760]

Payments for delivery The trader must reimburse any payment for delivery[761] **38-124** received from the consumer, unless the consumer expressly chose a kind of delivery costing more than the "least expensive common and generally acceptable kind of delivery offered by the trader", in which case the trader must reimburse any payment for delivery received from the consumer up to the amount the consumer would have paid if the consumer had chosen that kind of delivery.[762]

Allowance for diminution in value as a result of handling In the case of sales **38-125** contracts, if the value of the goods is diminished:

> "… by any amount as a result of handling of the goods by the consumer beyond what is necessary to establish the nature, characteristics and functioning of the goods, the trader may recover that amount from the consumer, up to the contract price."[763]

For these purposes, the Regulations explain that handling of this kind takes place in particular if "it goes beyond the sort of handling that might reasonably be allowed in a shop".[764] While not so restricted by the Regulations, a trader's right of recovery on this ground will normally apply only to cases of cancellation of the contract, as it assumes that the trader has already supplied the goods to the consumer and such a supply will normally take place only after a contract is concluded (and therefore after the consumer's right to withdraw his or her offer has ceased[765]). This "recovery" by the trader may take the form either of a deduction from any payment to be reimbursed from the consumer or by a payment to be made by the consumer to the trader.[766] A trader who has failed to provide the consumer with information on the right to cancel as required by the Regulations has no right to recovery on this ground.[767]

Return of goods by the consumer in the event of cancellation In general, where **38-126** a contract is cancelled by the consumer, the latter must send back the goods to the trader or hand them over to the trader or to a person authorised by him to receive them[768] without undue delay and in any event not later than 14 days after the day

---

[759] 2013 Regulations reg.34(4)–(6) (as amended by SI 2015/1629 reg.7).

[760] 2013 Regulations reg.34(7) and (8).

[761] "Delivery" means "voluntary transfer of possession from one person to another": 2013 Regulations reg.5. And see above, para.38-117.

[762] 2013 Regulations reg.34(2) and (3).

[763] 2013 Regulations reg.34(9).

[764] 2013 Regulations reg.34(12); 2011 Directive recital 47.

[765] Above, para.38-113.

[766] 2013 Regulations reg.34(10).

[767] 2013 Regulations reg.34(11). On this information requirement see above, para.38-118.

[768] 2013 Regulations reg.35(2). Regulation 35(3) explains that the consumer must send them back to any address specified by the trader for this purpose or for the consumer to contact him and, failing

on which the consumer informs the trader that he or she is cancelling the contract.[769] The consumer must bear the cost of doing so (but no other cost),[770] unless the trader has agreed to bear them or unless the trader has failed to provide the consumer with the information about the consumer bearing those costs as the Regulations require.[771] The exceptions to this position are found in the cases where the trader has offered to collect the goods or where in the case of an off-premises contract, the goods were delivered to the consumer's home when the contract was entered into and could not, by their nature, normally be returned by post.[772] In these cases, it is the trader's responsibility to collect the goods and the consumer is not required to bear any cost of returning them unless the trader offered to collect the goods and the consumer has agreed to bear the cost of his or her doing so.[773]

38-127 **Trader's duties have contractual force**   The 2013 Regulations provide that in the case of cancellation of a contract, the contracts are "to be treated as including a term" that the trader must reimburse payments (including, where applicable, delivery payments) according to the rules earlier noted[774] and to bear the direct cost of the consumer returning the goods where he or she has agreed to do so.[775] There is no equivalent provision in the Consumer Rights Directive, but the Directive permits Member States to give contractual force to the duties which it requires for traders, either as a matter of their general duty to put in place adequate and effective means to ensure compliance with the Directive or as a matter of their residual competence as regards "contract law" issues raised by the Directive but not regulated by it since the latter means that the remedial consequences of giving the trader's duties contractual force rests with general English law on this subject.[776] For this purpose, it is not clear whether breach of a trader's duty of reimbursement and to bear the cost would be remedied by the action for the agreed sum or damages, the difference being that the latter would extend to losses caused by the breach rather than simply the sum in question, subject to the restrictions generally applicable for this purpose.[777] It should be noted that the Regulations do not include any parallel provision setting the *consumer's* duties (viz to send back the goods[778] at his or her own cost) as a term of the contract.[779]

38-128 **Supply of services or digital content in cancellation period**   As earlier explained, where services or digital content not on a tangible medium are supplied during the cancellation period at the request of the consumer, the consumer may lose the right to cancel the contract which would normally be available.[780]

---

this, any place of business of the trader.
769 2013 Regulations reg.35(4).
770 2013 Regulations reg.35(5)(a) and (7).
771 2013 Regulations reg.35(5). The information requirement is set out by Sch.2 para.(m), above, para.38-098.
772 2013 Regulations reg.35(1).
773 2013 Regulations reg.35(1) and (8) (as amended by SI 2013/3134 reg.9(2)).
774 2013 Regulations reg.34(1), (2) (on which see above, paras 38-123—38-124); reg.34(13).
775 2013 Regulations reg.35(2) and (5)(a) (on which see above, para.38-126); reg.35(6).
776 2011 Directive art.3(5), above, paras 38-063—38-065.
777 See Vol.I, paras 21-041, 26-009.
778 2013 Regulations reg.35(2)(a).
779 2013 Regulations reg.35(5).
780 2013 Regulations regs 36(1)–(2), 37(1)–(2), above, para.38-115 (which set out the further conditions for the application of this restriction).

In the case of services supplied during the cancellation period where the **38-129** consumer does not lose the right to cancel in this way and the consumer chooses to exercise this right, the 2013 Regulations distinguish two situations. On the one hand, where the service is supplied in response to an express request (made, in the case of an off-premises contract, on a durable medium), in principle the consumer must pay the trader an amount for the supply of the service for the period for which it is supplied, ending with the time when the trader is informed of the consumer's decision to cancel, in proportion to what has been supplied in comparison with the full coverage of the contract.[781] This amount is to be calculated on the basis of the total contract price or, if this is excessive,[782] on the basis of the market value of the service that has been supplied at the time of the conclusion of the contract calculated by comparing prices for equivalent services supplied by other traders.[783] On the other hand, where the service is not supplied in response to a request by the consumer as outlined above or where the trader has failed to provide the consumer with information on his or her right to cancel or on his or her liability to pay the reasonable cost[784] of any services requested, then "[t]he consumer bears no cost for the supply of the service, in full or in part, in the cancellation period".[785]

Special provision is made for contracts under which digital content is supplied **38-130** not on a tangible medium. In this case, where the digital content is supplied during the cancellation period in circumstances in which the consumer does not lose the right to cancel by reason of his express request that it should be so supplied,[786] and the consumer chooses to exercise this right, the 2013 Regulations provide that the consumer bears no cost for the supply (whether in full or in part) of the digital content in the cancellation period[787] as long as the consumer did not give "prior express consent to the beginning of the performance of the digital content before the end of the 14 day cancellation period" (as explained earlier[788]), the consumer gave that consent but did not acknowledge when giving it that the right to cancel would be lost, *or* the trader failed to provide confirmation of the consumer's consent or acknowledgment.[789] Where none of these situations apply, then under 2011 Directive the consumer is liable to pay a reasonable cost in respect of receipt of the digital content,[790] but the provision in the Regulations governing liability in the consumer to pay a reasonable cost is worded in a way which is restricted to contracts for the supply of a service,[791] which are generally distinguished in the Regulations from

---

[781] 2013 Regulations reg.36(4).
[782] Directive 2011/83/EU recital 50 suggests that the burden of proof as to the excessive character of the price lies on the consumer.
[783] 2013 Regulations reg.36(5) implementing Directive 2011/83/EU art.14(3). The reference to the time of the conclusion of the contract reflects the gloss contained in recital 50 of the Directive.
[784] This description is not used by 2013 Regulations reg.36(4) but is used by Sch.2 para.(n).
[785] 2013 Regulations reg.36(6). In this form of words "in full or in part" could refer either to the supply or the cost, whereas Directive 2011/83/EU art.14(4)(a) makes clear that it refers to the supply. The categories of information referred to in the text are required to be supplied by the trader under regs 10(1)(a) and 13(1)(a) as set out in Sch.2 paras (l) and (n), on which see above, para.38-093.
[786] On which see 2013 Regulations reg.37(1) and (2), above, para.38-115.
[787] 2013 Regulations reg.37(4) which refers confusingly to "no cost for supply of the digital content, in full or in part" in which "in full or in part" could refer either to the supply or the cost, whereas Directive 2011/83/EU art.14(4)(b) makes clear that it refers to the supply.
[788] Above, para.38-115 referring to 2013 Regulations reg.30.
[789] 2013 Regulations reg.37(4) referring to regs 12(5) and 16(3).
[790] 2011 Directive art.14(3).
[791] 2013 Regulations reg.36(4) and (5), above, para.38-129.

contracts for the supply of digital content not on a tangible medium.[792] It may be thought, however, that the fact that the Regulations provide that the consumer bears no cost for the supply of digital content in the cancellation period if one of the three situations apply suggests that the consumer *must* bear the cost of supply where they do not. There is, though, no provision in the relevant regulation to this effect.[793]

38-131 **Effect of withdrawal or cancellation on ancillary contracts** Regulation 38 makes special provision for the effect of withdrawal of an offer or cancellation of a consumer contract on "ancillary contracts". For this purpose:

> "An "ancillary contract", in relation to a distance or off-premises contract (the 'main contract'), means a contract by which the consumer acquires goods or services related to the main contract, where those goods or services are provided—
> (a) by the trader, or
> (b) by a third party on the basis of an arrangement between the third party and the trader."[794]

Regulation 38 makes clear that such an ancillary contract may include the provision of a financial service.[795] Examples of such an "ancillary contract" include an extended warranty, insurance (for example, for a purchase of jewellery) or a credit agreement to finance goods or services,[796] but not all contracts of this type concluded at the same time as the purchase of goods or services from a trader are "ancillary contracts" for the purposes of reg.38 as the latter requires that the ancillary contract is provided either by that trader or by a "third party on the basis of an arrangement between the third party and the trader". Where these conditions are satisfied, reg.38 provides that where a consumer withdraws an offer or cancels the main contract, then "any ancillary contracts are automatically terminated, without any costs for the consumer" other than the costs foreseen by the provisions governing the consumer's liability for "costs" on cancellation of that main contract.[797] When a trader is informed by a consumer of a decision to withdraw an offer or cancel a contract, the trader must inform any other trader with whom the consumer has an ancillary contract that it is terminated.[798] In terms of payments, the Departmental Implementing Guidance explains that "responsibility for refund should follow the original flow of funds", so that if the money for the ancillary contract was paid directly to the trader they should reimburse the consumer and recover from the third party; but if the money was paid directly by the consumer to the third party, the third party should refund the money to the consumer.[799]

---

[792] Above, paras 38-073 and 38-075.
[793] cf. reg.36(4) and (5) (supply of service in cancellation period) and reg.37(4) (supply of digital content in cancellation period).
[794] 2013 Regulations reg.38(3).
[795] 2013 Regulations reg.38(4) (technically putting aside the general exclusion of financial services contracts from the scope of the Regulations in reg.6(1)(b)).
[796] Department for Business Innovation & Skills, *Consumer Contracts (Information, Cancellation and Additional Charges) Regulations, Implementing Guidance* (December 2013) A, para.5.
[797] 2013 Regulations reg.38(1), referring to reg.34(3) (on which see para.38-124); reg.34(9) (on which see para.38-125); reg.35(5) (on which see para.38-126); and reg.36(4) (on which see para.38-129).
[798] 2013 Regulations reg.38(2).
[799] Department for Business Innovation & Skills, *Consumer Contracts (Information, Cancellation and Additional Charges) Regulations, Implementing Guidance* (December 2013) G, para.20.

(e) Enforcement

The scheme in the 2013 Regulations The 2013 Regulations provide their own **38-132** dedicated regime for the enforcement of the requirements which they set out. Under this regime, local weights and measures authorities are designated as "enforcement authorities"[800] and it is provided that it is their duty to consider any complaint made to them about contravention of the Regulations unless it appears to be frivolous or vexatious or another enforcement authority has notified the Competition and Markets Authority (CMA)[801] that it agrees to consider the complaint, in which case that other authority comes under a duty to do so.[802] An enforcement authority may apply for an injunction against any person who appears to it to be responsible for a contravention of the Regulations and a court hearing such an application may grant an injunction "on such terms as it thinks fit to secure compliance with these Regulations".[803] However, the Regulations envisage that an enforcement authority may instead seek an undertaking from a person in respect of its contravention and/or future compliance with the Regulations as they provide that an enforcement authority must notify the CMA of "any undertaking given to it by or on behalf of any person who appears to it to be responsible for a contravention of these Regulations".[804] An enforcement authority must also notify the CMA of the outcome of any application to a court for an injunction and of the terms of any undertaking given to the court or order made by it, or the outcome of any application made by such an authority to enforce a previous court order.[805] For all these purposes, clearly the main concern is with the enforcement of the various requirements made of traders by the Regulations,[806] but the Regulations enforcement regime is not restricted to this context and could in principle extend to the enforcement of the duties which they impose *on consumers*, notably, the duty to return goods after cancellation of a distance or off-premises contract.[807] This is specifically foreseen by the 2011 Directive's preamble, which provides that:

> "In situations where the trader *or the consumer* does not fulfil the obligations relating to the exercise of the right of withdrawal, penalties provided for by national legislation in accordance with this Directive should apply as well as contract law provisions."[808]

However, it will surely be very rare for an enforcement authority to seek to exercise its enforcement powers under the 2013 Regulations against a consumer.

"Enforcement orders" under the Enterprise Act 2002 Under Pt 8 of the **38-133**

---

[800] This is true of Great Britain; in Northern Ireland, the enforcement authority is the Department of Enterprise, Trade and Investment in Northern Ireland: 2013 Regulations reg.44(3).

[801] As from April 1, 2014, the Office of Fair Trading was abolished and its functions taken over by the Competition and Markets Authority (CMA).

[802] 2013 Regulations reg.44(1) and (2).

[803] 2013 Regulations reg.45(1) and (2).

[804] 2013 Regulations reg.46(a).

[805] 2013 Regulations reg.46(b) and (c).

[806] Notably, the information requirements (above, paras 38-091 et seq.) and the trader's responsibilities to reimburse payments made by the consumer following the latter's cancellation of a contract (above, para.38-123).

[807] 2013 Regulation reg.35, above, para.38-126.

[808] 2011 Directive recital 48, second sentence (emphasis added). The Directive expresses the consequences of withdrawal by the consumer in terms of obligations on the trader and the consumer (arts 13 and 14); its provisions on enforcement and penalties are found in arts 23 and 24.

Enterprise Act 2002, the CMA (replacing the OFT)[809] and other persons or bodies termed "enforcers", may apply to the court for an "enforcement order" against a person to stop breaking legislation enacted for the benefit of consumers.[810] The 2002 Act distinguishes for this purpose between "domestic infringements"[811] (which are concerned with enforcement of national protections by UK-based enforcers) and "Community infringements" (for which cross-border enforcement was created and which also covers domestic action by UK enforcers in respect of breaches of specified UK laws implementing the Directives specified by the Consumer Injunctions Directive).[812] A number of the directives and their UK implementing legislation which are the subject of this chapter are included for the purposes of "Community infringements" and these include, for present purposes, the Consumer Rights Directive 2011[813] and the 2013 Regulations.[814] "Enforcers" are divided into "general enforcers",[815] which include the CMA and local weights and measures authorities in Great Britain; "designated enforcers", which are any public or private body in

---

[809] As from April 1, 2014, the OFT was abolished and its functions under the 1999 Regulations taken over by the Competition and Markets Authority ("CMA"): Enterprise and Regulatory Reform Act 2013 (Competition) (Consequential, Transitional and Saving Provisions) (No.2) Order 2014 (SI 2014/549) Sch.1 para.26; Public Bodies (The Office of Fair Trading Transfer of Consumer Advice Scheme Function and Modification of Enforcement Functions) Order 2013 (SI 2013/783) art.10.

[810] The Enterprise Act 2002 Pt 8 came into force on June 20, 2003: The Enterprise Act 2002 (Commencement No.3, Transitional and Transitory Provisions and Savings) Order 2003 (SI 2003/1397) art.2. It replaced the Fair Trading Act 1973 Pt III and the Stop Now Orders (EC Directive) Regulations 2001 (SI 2001/1422). Its provisions concerning "Community infringements" implement into UK law Directive 2009/22/EC on injunctions for the protection of consumers' interests [2009] O.J. L110/30. It has been held that the conduct of a person taking place *before* the coming into force of Pt 8 of the Enterprise Act 2002 can form the basis of granting an order under it: *Office of Fair Trading v MB Designs (Scotland) Ltd* [2005] S.L.T. 691 at [23], OH of the Ct of Sess., where Pt 8 is discussed more generally. The powers contained in the Enterprise Act 2002 were extended (in particular) by the Enterprise Act 2002 (Amendment) Regulations 2006 (SI 2006/3363) implementing arts 4(6) and 13(4) of the Regulation 2006/2004 on co-operation between national authorities responsible for the enforcement of consumer protection laws (the Regulation on consumer protection co-operation), as amended by Directive 2005/29/EC. The Consumer Rights Act 2015 s.79 Sch.7 changed the powers contained in Pt 8 of the 2002 Act, as noted in the present and following paragraphs, in relation to conduct which occurs, or which is likely to occur, after its commencement: 2015 Act s.79(2). This section (together with the other provisions in Pts 1 and 2 of the Act) came into force on October 1, 2015: see below, para.38-366.

[811] Enterprise Act 2002 s.211 (which was amended on the coming into force of s.75 and Sch.7 of the 2015 Act).

[812] Enterprise Act 2002 s.212; OFT, *Enforcement of consumer protection legislation, Guidance on Pt 8 of the Enterprise Act* (2003), para.3.15. The first consumer injunctions directive (98/27/EC) of 1998 was revoked and replaced by the Directive 2009/22/EC on injunctions for the protection of consumers' interests (2009) O.J. L 110/1 whose list in Annex I of relevant directives is much amended.

[813] Enterprise Act 2002 ss.210 and 212, Sch.13 Pt 1 para.9F. The list in Sch.13 also includes the Package Travel Directive 2015 ("Directive (EU) 2015/2302") (Sch.13 Pt 1 para.4; see below, para.38-137—38-138); the Unfair Terms in Consumer Contracts Directive 93/13 (Sch.13 Pt 1 para.5; see below, para.38-218); the Consumer Sales Directive 1999/44/EC (Sch.13 Pt 1 para.8; see below, para.38-433) and the Unfair Commercial Practices Directive 2005/29/EC (Sch.13 Pt 1 para.9C; see below, para.38-159); and art.62 of Directive 2015/2366/EU of the European Parliament and of the Council of November 25, 2015 on payment services in the internal market (Sch.13 Pt 1 para.16: see below, para.38-428).The powers of a court in relation to "enforcement orders" are contained in s.217 of the 2002 Act and with the coming into force of the Consumer Rights Act 2015 are extended so as to allow a court to require a person against whom an order is made to take "enhanced consumer measures": see below, para.38-134.

[814] Enterprise Act 2002 (Part 8 EU Infringements) Order 2014 (2014/2908) art.4, Sch.

[815] Enterprise Act 2002 s.213(1).

the United Kingdom which the Secretary of State designates as a person or body one of whose purposes is the protection of the collective interests of consumers and which include the Civil Aviation Authority, the Information Commissioner and the Rail Regulator[816]; "Community enforcers", which are qualified entities listed for this purpose by the EU, the list including a number of public and private bodies (notably, consumers' associations)[817]; and "CPC enforcers", which are bodies or persons designated by the Secretary of State under the EU Regulation on consumer protection co-operation,[818] these including the CMA, local weights and measures authorities and certain other public bodies and persons.[819] The inclusion of "Community enforcers" within the class of those entitled to apply for enforcement orders reflects the policy of the EU to promote cross-border policing under its own consumer protection legislation.[820] The designation of "CPC enforcers" seeks to give effect to a policy of encouraging and facilitating co-operation between European national authorities in the enforcement of consumer protection.[821] Where a domestic or a Community infringement (including therefore an infringement of the requirements of the 2013 Regulations) harms the collective interest of consumers,[822] an "enforcer" can apply to the court for an enforcement order, but only after engaging in appropriate consultation with the person against whom the order would be made and, if the enforcer is not the CMA, after the enforcer has given notice to the CMA of the enforcer's intention to apply for the enforcement order, and the appropriate minimum period has elapsed.[823] Where a court finds that an infringement has been committed or is likely to be committed by the defendant to proceedings brought under these provisions, it may make an enforcement order, notably, to prevent the defendant from continuing the relevant conduct.[824]

"Enhanced consumer measures" The Consumer Rights Act 2015[825] amends the **38-134** Enterprise Act 2002 Pt 8 so as to extend a court's power to make an "enforcement

---

[816] Enterprise Act 2002 s.213(2)–(4); the Enterprise Act 2002 (Part 8 Designated Enforcers: Criteria for Designation, Designation of Public Bodies as Designated and Transitional Provisions) Order 2003 (SI 2003/1399) art.5, Sch.1.

[817] Enterprise Act 2002 s.213(5); Directive 2009/22/EC on injunctions for the protection of consumers' interests. The list of qualified bodies is listed by the EU Commission and published in the Official Journal.

[818] Regulation (EC) 2006/2004 on cooperation between national authorities responsible for the enforcement of the consumer protection law [2004] O.J. L364/1. Regulation (EC) 2006/2004 is repealed and replaced with effect from January 17, 2020 by Regulation (EU) 2017/2394 of the European Parliament and of the Council of December 12, 2017 on cooperation between national authorities responsible for the enforcement of consumer protection laws and repealing Regulation (EC) No.2006/2004 O.J. L 345/1.

[819] Enterprise Act 2002 s.213(5A).

[820] Directive 2009/22/EC recitals 4–8.

[821] Regulation 2006/2004 recitals.

[822] Enterprise Act 2002 ss.211(1)(c), 212(1). On the requirement of "harming the collective interest of consumers" see *Office of Fair Trading v MB Designs (Scotland) Ltd* [2005] S.L.T. 691 at [23], [1], [13]–[16].

[823] Enterprise Act 2002 s.214(1) as replaced by Public Bodies (the Office of Fair Trading Transfer of Consumer Advice Scheme Function and Modification of Enforcement Functions) Order 2013 (SI 2013/783) art.9(2) and amended by Enterprise and Regulatory Reform Act 2013 (Competition) (Consequential, Transitional and Saving Provisions) Order 2014 (SI 2014/892) Sch.1 para.7.

[824] 2002 Act ss.217–218 (as amended). Section 219 of the 2002 Act provides a power in enforcers to accept an undertaking from a person who has engaged, is engaging or who is likely to engage in conduct constituting an infringement in specified circumstances.

[825] The Consumer Rights Act 2015 s.79 (which made these amendments) was brought into force on

order" under that Act to require a person against whom the order is made to take "enhanced consumer measures".[826] There are three categories of enhanced consumer measures: the "redress category", the "compliance category", and the "choice category".[827] Each of these categories of measure are defined by the legislation,[828] but for present purposes of most interest is the "redress category", which includes:

"(a)   measures offering compensation or other redress to consumers who have suffered loss as a result of the conduct which has given rise to the enforcement order or undertaking,

(b)   where the conduct referred to in paragraph (a) relates to a contract, measures offering such consumers the option to terminate (but not vary) that contract,

(c)   where such consumers cannot be identified, or cannot be identified without disproportionate cost to the subject of the enforcement order or undertaking, measures intended to be in the collective interests of consumers."[829]

It will be seen that this was an innovative new power, allowing a court to order a trader to offer compensation to consumers who have suffered loss as a result of an infringement of a legislative provision for their protection or the option of terminating any contract to which that infringement relates. However, this power is subject both to the conditions of the availability of an enforcement order under Pt 8 generally (and in particular that an infringement harms the *collective* interests of consumers[830]) and to a general requirement that such enhanced consumer measures may be ordered only as the court considers to be just and reasonable[831] and to a series of particular conditions set by the Act for this purpose.[832]

(f)   Special Rules for Financial Services Contracts, Timeshare Contracts, Package Travel Contracts, Contracts Concluded by Electronic Means and ADR

(i)   Introduction

38-135   Special rules governing particular contracts in EU law   As outlined above,[833] the general framework for the information requirements imposed on traders and rights of cancellation for consumers required by the Consumer Rights Directive 2011 and implemented by the Consumer Contracts (Information, Cancellation and Additional Charges) Regulations 2013 is supplemented by a series of other special

---

October 1, 2015: the Consumer Rights Act 2015 (Commencement No.3, Transitional Provisions, Savings and Consequential Amendments) Order 2015 (SI 2015/1630) art.3(d) and (i). Section 79(2) of the Act provides that these amendments "have effect only in relation to conduct which occurs, or which is likely to occur, after the commencement of [s.79]".

[826]   2002 Act s.217(10A) as inserted by 2015 Act s.79, Sch.7 para.7. The 2015 Act also extended the court's power in relation to taking undertakings: 2002 Act s.217(10B). See Department for Business, Innovation and Skills, *Enhanced Consumer Measures, Guidance for Enforcers of Consumer Law* (May 2015).

[827]   See 2002 Act s.219A(2)–(5) as inserted by 2015 Act s.79, Sch.7 para.8.

[828]   2002 Act s.219A(1) as inserted by 2015 Act s.79, Sch.7 para.8.

[829]   2002 Act s.219A(2) as inserted by 2015 Act s.79, Sch.7 para.8.

[830]   2002 Act ss.211(1) and 212(2), above, para.38-133.

[831]   2002 Act s.219B(1) as inserted by 2015 Act s.79, Sch.7 para.8.

[832]   2002 Act s.219B and 219C as inserted by 2015 Act s.79, Sch.7 para.8. Similar conditions are imposed on the taking of undertakings by an enforcer: 2002 Act ss.219(5ZA) and (5ZB), 219A and 219B as inserted by 2015 Act s.79, Sch.7 paras 7 and 8.

[833]   Above, paras 38-060 et seq.

rules required by EU legislation governing particular categories of contract or governing particular situations. This is the case as regards the rules governing "distance contracts" for the supply of financial services, which are excluded from the scope of the 2011 Directive and also the 2013 Regulations, and remain subject to the dedicated regime provided by the Financial Services (Distance Marketing) Regulations 2004[834] which implemented the Financial Services Distance Marketing Directive 2002.[835] Moreover, EU directives on timeshare[836] and package travel[837] impose special information requirements and rights of cancellation implemented in UK law by regulation and in the case of both of these types of contracts, the directives added other special rules governing these contracts which it will be convenient to discuss here.[838] EU legislation has required Member States to ensure that ADR is available for consumer disputes[839] and, in doing so, has required them to impose on trader's information as to the availability of ADR.[840] Finally, the Electronic Commerce (EC Directive) Regulations 2002 (implementing the relevant provisions of the Electronic Commerce Directive 2000) impose pre-contractual information requirements in respect of contracts made by electronic means by persons providing an information service to all whether or not their recipient is a consumer, but disallow their exclusion where the recipient is a consumer.[841]

(ii)   The Distance Marketing of Financial Services

Summary   As earlier noted, contracts for the provision of financial services are   **38-136** excluded from the scope of the 2013 Regulations,[842] but the earlier Financial Services (Distance Marketing) Regulations 2004[843] make very broadly similar

---

[834]   SI 2004/2095.

[835]   Directive 2002/65/EC concerning the distance marketing of consumer financial services [2002] O.J. L271/16 below, para.38-136.

[836]   The UK first imposed legislation in this context by the Timeshare Act 1992, which preceded Directive 94/47/EC on the protection of purchasers in respect of certain aspects of contracts relating to the purchase of the right to use immovable properties on a timeshare basis. The 1994 Directive was implemented by amendment of the Timeshare Act 1992 by regulation: Timeshare Regulations 1997 (SI 1997/1081). Subsequently, the UK's regulation of timeshare and related contracts has been made by the Timeshare, Holiday Products, Resale and Exchange Contracts Regulations 2010 (SI 2010/2960) which implements the later Directive 2008/122/EC on the protection of consumers in respect of certain aspects of timeshare, long-term holiday product, resale and exchange contracts [2009] O.J. L33/30 (which itself replaced the 1994 Directive). See below, paras 38-148—38-154.

[837]   The Package Travel and Linked Travel Arrangements Regulations 2018 (SI 2018/634) implementing Directive (EU) 2015/2302 on package travel and linked travel arrangements [2015] O.J. L326/1 and replacing the Package Travel, Package Holidays and Package Tours Regulations 1992 (SI 1992/3288) implementing Directive 90/314/EEC of 13 June 1990 on package travel, package holidays and package tours [1990] O.J. L158/59; [1994] O.J. L280/83. See below, paras 38-137—38-147.

[838]   The international conventions and UK and EU laws providing for the protection of passengers are discussed in Ch.35, Carriage by Air and Ch.36 Carriage by Land, paras 36-079 et seq.

[839]   Directive 2013/11/EU of 21 May 2013 on alternative dispute resolution for consumer disputes [2013] O.J. L165/63; Regulation (EU) 524/2013 of 21 May 2013 on online dispute resolution for consumer disputes (Regulation on consumer ODR) [2013] O.J. L165/1.

[840]   Directive 2013/11/EU art.13 implemented in UK law by the Alternative Dispute Resolution for Consumer Disputes (Competent Authorities and Information) Regulations 2015 (SI 2015/542) reg.19 below, para.38-155.

[841]   SI 2002/2013 reg.9, below, para.38-156.

[842]   2013 Regulations reg.6(1)(b), above, para.38-076.

[843]   SI 2004/2095, implementing Directive 2002/65/EC concerning the distance marketing of consumer financial services [2002] O.J. L271/16, cf. above, para.38-027.

provision for distance contracts for the provision of financial services[844] as the 2013 Regulations make in relation to other contracts. So, a "distance contract" under the 2004 Regulations is defined as:

"... any contract concerning one or more financial services concluded between a supplier and a consumer under an organised distance sales or service-provision scheme run by the supplier or by an intermediary, who, for the purpose of that contract, makes exclusive use of one or more means of distance communication up to and including the time at which the contract is concluded."[845]

The 2004 Regulations impose information requirements on the supplier of the service which are similar to those under the 2013 Regulations though tailored to suit the subject matter of the contracts, and this information is to be provided "in a clear and comprehensible manner appropriate to the means of distance communication used".[846] However, certain categories of financial service contracts are excluded from these pre-contractual requirements[847] and the 2004 Regulations also exclude more generally from their principal provisions governing information duties and the consumer's right to cancel some contracts for and supplies of financial services where equivalent provision is made by other regimes, notably, contracts and supplies made by a supplier who is an "authorised person, the making or performance of which constitutes or is part of a regulated activity carried on by him" within the meaning of the Financial Services and Markets Act 2000[848] and those made by suppliers established in another State within the EEA where the law of that State regulates the contract or supply in accordance with the 2002 Directive.[849] The 2002 Regulations' provisions on cancellation by the consumer are also similar to those under the 2013 Regulations (though they make a series of detailed exceptions to the availability of the consumer's right to cancel[850]) and so provide that the consumer may cancel within a period of 14 days from the conclusion of the contract, unless the supplier has failed to provide information as they require, in which case the

---

[844] "Financial service" means any service of a banking, credit, insurance, personal pension, investment or payment nature: 2004 Regulations reg.2(1).

[845] 2004 Regulations reg.2(1) "distance contract".

[846] 2004 Regulations reg.7 especially reg.7(2) and Sch.1. A restricted range of information is required where a financial services distance contract is also a contract for payment services to which the Payment Services Regulations 2017 apply: reg.7(1A) and reg.8(1A) as amended by the Payment Services Regulations 2017 (SI 2017/752) (in force generally January 13, 2018).

[847] 2004 Regulations reg.7(6) and (7) (consumer credit agreements and authorised non-business overdraft agreements).

[848] 2004 Regulations reg.4(2) referring to regs 7–11, 15 (with the qualifications made by reg.4(5)). Regulation 4(3) disapplies the 2004 Regulations regs 7 and 8 (i.e. the main information requirements) as regards contracts made by a supplier who is an "appointed representative" within the meaning of s.39(2) of the Financial Services Markets Act 2000, where the making or performance of that contract constitutes or is part of a regulated activity within the meaning of s.22 of the 2000 Act (apart from an "exempt regulated activity" within the meaning of s.325(2) of that Act) carried on by the supplier, with similar exclusions as regards supplies by such persons as regards reg.15 (which concerns unsolicited services). Regulation 4(4) makes the same exclusions as regards contracts or supplies where the supplier is bound, etc. by "rules of a designated professional body which are equivalent to those regulations" and the making or performance of that contract or the supply constitutes or is part of an exempt regulated activity carried on by the supplier. Regulation 6(3) and (4) make certain saving provisions in respect of these exclusions.

[849] 2004 Regulations reg.4(1) referring to regs 7–14, 15. See further reg.4 more generally.

[850] 2004 Regulations reg.11, e.g. contract where the price of that service depends on fluctuations of the money market outside the supplier's control.

period is 14 days after the day of supply of that information.[851] The effect of an exercise of the right to cancel is that the notice of cancellation terminates the contract at the time when it is given,[852] with a consequential refund of monies paid by the consumer subject to a charge made by the supplier in respect of a "service actually provided by the supplier in accordance with the contract".[853] Equally, the consumer must refund any sums or return any property transferred to him or her under the contract.[854] The 2004 Regulations specify that any contract term which is inconsistent with their application is void[855] and that they will apply notwithstanding any choice of applicable law of a State which is not an EEA State if the contract or supply has a close connection with the territory of an EEA State.[856] The 2004 Regulations entrust their enforcement to the Financial Conduct Authority,[857] the Competition and Markets Authority and local weights and measure authorities, depending on the nature of the alleged breach,[858] and this enforcement may include an application for an injunction.[859]

(ii)   Package Travel, Package Holidays, Package Tours and Linked Travel Arrangements

Introduction   The Package Travel Directive 1990[860] (the "1990 Directive") made   **38-137** a series of "minimum harmonisation" requirements for the protection of consumers[861] and was implemented into UK law by the Package Travel, Package Holidays and Package Tours Regulations 1992[862] ("1992 Regulations"). However, the 1990 Directive was repealed and replaced by Directive (EU) 2015/2302 on package travel and linked travel arrangements,[863] and its new requirements are made on the general basis of "full harmonisation" of the laws of Member States.[864] In the case of the UK, the Package Travel and Linked Travel Arrangements Regulations 2018 were issued by the government (the "2018 Regulations") on May 24, 2018[865] and came into force generally on July 1, 2018 as required by the Directive.[866] The following paragraphs therefore continue to discuss the 1992 Regulations (implementing the 1990 Directive) but will then outline the provisions of the new 2018 Regulations.

---

851   2004 Regulations regs 9 and 10.
852   2004 Regulations reg.9(2).
853   2004 Regulations reg.13, especially reg.13(3) and (6).
854   2004 Regulations reg.13(11) and (12).
855   2004 Regulations reg.16(1) reflecting 2002 Directive art.12(1).
856   2004 Regulations reg.16(3) reflecting 2002 Directive art.12(2). To this extent, the general rules in the Rome I Regulation are therefore qualified: Regulation (EC) 593/2008 on the law applicable to contractual obligations ("Rome I Regulation") on which see Vol.I, paras 30-018 et seq.
857   2004 Regulations reg.17.
858   2004 Regulations reg.17.
859   2004 Regulations reg.19. Further enforcement provisions are set out in regs 20–23.
860   Directive 90/314/EEC of 13 June 1990 on package travel, package holidays and package tours: [1990] O.J. L158/59.
861   1990 Directive art.8. On the nature of "minimum harmonisation" see above, para.38-022.
862   SI 1992/3288.
863   [2015] O.J. L326/1 ("2015 Directive"). Repeal of the 1990 Directive is with effect from July 1, 2018: 2015 Directive art.29.
864   2015 Directive art.4.
865   The Package Travel and Linked Travel Arrangements Regulations 2018 (SI 2018/634).
866   2018 Regulations reg.1. See also the documents available at *https://www.gov.uk/government/consultations/updating-consumer-protection-in-the-package-travel-sector*, including Department of Business, Energy & Industrial Strategy, *Updating Consumer Protection in the Package Travel Sector, Government Response* (April 2018).

(aa)   Package Travel, Package Holidays and Package Tours Regulations 1992

38-138   **Scope of the 1992 Regulations**[867]   The 1992 Regulations apply to "packages" defined as the "pre-arranged combination"[868] of at least two of three components (transport, accommodation or other tourist services not ancillary to either) and "accounting for a significant proportion of the package", when sold or offered for sale at an inclusive price[869] and the service covers a period of more than 24 hours or includes overnight accommodation.[870] The "organiser" refers to the person who "otherwise than occasionally, organises packages and sells or offers them for sale, whether directly or through a retailer"; the "retailer" refers to "the person who sells or offers for sale the package put together by the organiser"; and the "consumer" generally refers to "the person who takes or agrees to take the package".[871] In addition to the rules outlined below, the Regulations protect the consumer in the event of the insolvency of the organiser or retailer.[872]

38-139   **Information, withdrawal and cancellation**   The 1992 Regulations prohibit the organiser and the retailer from supplying to the consumer any "descriptive matter concerning a package, the price of a package or any other conditions applying to the contract" which contains any misleading information.[873] The Regulations require organisers of package travel, etc. to provide brochures which set out information about the price and other matters which they set out in a Schedule,[874] and in principle any particulars supplied in such a brochure are contractually binding on the organiser and may give rise to a claim for damages.[875] The Regulations also impose on the organiser and/or the retailer a duty to provide specified travel information (such as visa requirements, health formalities or security for money paid over) before the contract is concluded and further practical travel information before the start of the journey: breach of these duties constitutes a criminal offence.[876] The Regulations impose requirements as to the contents and form of the contracts to which they apply,[877] to allow consumers to transfer their bookings, governing price revision and notice to the consumer of any significant alterations

---

[867]   As noted above, para.38-137, on the coming into force of the 2018 Regulations implementing the Package Travel Directive 2015, the 1992 Regulations (and their amending regulations) were revoked, but they will continue to apply to contracts concluded before the commencement date of the new regulation, i.e. July 1, 2018: 2018 Regulations reg.37.

[868]   On which see *Club-Tour, Viagens et Turismo SA v Gonçalves Garrido* (C-400/00) EU:C:2002:272, [2002] E.C.R. I-4051.

[869]   On which see *Sean Titshall v Qwerty Travel Ltd* [2011] EWCA Civ 1569, [2011] C.T.L.C. 219.

[870]   1992 Regulations reg.2(1) "package", with further refinements.

[871]   1992 Regulations reg.2(1) "organiser" and "retailer" and (2) (specifying other uses of "consumer").

[872]   1992 Regulations regs 16–22.

[873]   1992 Regulations reg.4(1). Breach of this duty may give rise to liability to compensate the consumer for any resulting loss: reg.4(2).

[874]   1992 Regulations reg.5.

[875]   1992 Regulations reg.6(1), with exceptions set out in reg.6(2) and (3). The consumer's claim is limited to damages by the stipulation that the particulars take effect as contractual warranties: reg.6(1).

[876]   1992 Regulations regs 7 and 8. For incidental provision as to these and the other offences created by the Regulations see regs 24–27.

[877]   1992 Regulations reg.9.

to essential terms.[878] In this respect, the Regulations insert into the contract an implied term to the effect that where the organiser is constrained before departure to alter significantly an essential term of the contract, such as the price (to the extent to which the Regulations allow him to do so under their price revision rules), the organiser will notify the consumer to enable him to decide what to do and, in particular, to "withdraw from the contract without penalty or to accept a rider to the contract specifying the alterations made and their impact on the price".[879] Where the consumer withdraws from a contract under this provision or where the organiser cancels the package for any reason other than the fault of the consumer, the consumer is entitled to take a substitute package (either of equivalent or superior quality or, if lower quality, with a reduction in price) or to repay him all monies paid as soon as possible,[880] together with compensation.[881] Other terms are implied into the contract to provide for cases where, after departure, a significant proportion of the services contracted for are not provided or the organiser realises that this will be the case; here, the organiser must make suitable alternative arrangements with compensation as appropriate.[882]

Liability for proper performance of the contract   The 1992 Regulations also **38-140** make the organiser and retailer of a package:

"... liable to the consumer for the proper performance of the obligations under the contract, irrespective of whether such obligations are to be performed by that other party or by other suppliers of services."[883]

The organiser and retailer are liable for "any damage caused" to the consumer as a result of the improper performance of the contract,[884] unless it is due neither to their

---

878   1992 Regulations regs 10–12.
879   1992 Regulations reg.12(a). It will be noted that the 1992 Regulations refer to a right to *withdraw* in the consumer, rather than a right to *cancel* in the consumer (unlike the 2013 Regulations which distinguish between a right to cancel a contract and a right to withdraw an offer, above, para.38-113). The 1992 Regulations instead use cancellation to refer to the organiser's act of cancellation of the package as set out in regs 13(1)–(2).
880   1992 Regulations reg.13(1)–(2).
881   1992 Regulations reg.13(3)–(4). Compensation is not available where the package is cancelled owing to the package not reaching a minimum number of persons where this was indicated to the consumer in its description or where it is cancelled by reason of "unusual and unforeseeable circumstances beyond the control of the party by which could not have been avoided even if all due care had been exercised", but the latter does not include overbooking.
882   1992 Regulations reg.14.
883   1992 Regulations reg.15(1). The contract must oblige the consumer to communicate to the supplier of the services concerned or to the organiser or retailer any failure in the services at the place where they are supplied: 1992 Regulations reg.15(9).
884   "Improper performance" depends on the terms of the contract and in the absence of an assumption of an absolute obligation on the part of the supplier of the service, reasonable care will be required: *Hone v Going Places Ltd* [2001] EWCA Civ 947 at [15]–[16]; applied in *Evans v Kosmar Villa Holidays Plc* [2007] EWCA Civ 1003, [2008] 1 W.L.R. 297 at [21] and *Committeri v Club Mediterranee SA* [2016] EWHC 1510 (QB) at [29], where it was also held (at [49]–[53]) that liability arising from national law implementing the 1990 Directive and therefore arising in respect of "the proper performance of the obligations arising from the contract" is contractual rather than non-contractual for the purposes of the EU private law instruments on applicable law, i.e. Regulation 593/2008 on the law applicable to contractual obligations ("Rome I") [2008] O.J. L177/6 (on which see Vol.I, paras 30-019 et seq.) and Regulation 864/2007 of the European Parliament and of the Council law applicable to non-contractual obligations ("Rome II Regulation") [2007] O.J. L199/40. See also *X v Kuoni Travel Ltd* [2018] EWCA Civ 938, [2018] 1 W.L.R. 3777 at [33]–[37] (express term ac-

own fault or to that of another supplier of services[885] because it is attributable to the consumer, or to other specified circumstances.[886] For this purpose, damages in respect of "damage" suffered by the consumer may include compensation for personal injuries and, following the position established at common law, physical discomfort and mental distress, including for disappointment and loss of enjoyment.[887] The Regulations provide that liability on this basis cannot be excluded in respect of personal injury or death, but liability for a term of the contract may limit the amount of compensation in respect of other damage unless the limitation is unreasonable.[888]

38-141 **Enforcement** The 1992 Regulations made no dedicated provision for enforcement of their requirements by injunction, but the Enterprise Act 2002 included the 1990 Directive in the list of instruments which might give rise to a "Community infringement" and so applied Pt 8 of the 2002 Act for their purposes[889]; and the 1992 Regulations were specified as the UK law which gave effect to this Directive for this purpose.[890] However, this position changed on the revocation of the 1992 Regulations by the 2018 Regulations, where the latter were substituted for the 1992 Regulations for these purposes as noted below.[891]

(bb) Package Travel and Linked Travel Arrangements Regulations 2018

38-142 **Package Travel Directive 2015 and the 2018 Regulations** As earlier noted, the 1990 Directive was repealed and replaced by Directive (EU) 2015/2302 on package travel and linked travel arrangements.[892] A principal aim of this new directive was to adapt the protection for consumers in relation to package travel earlier required by the 1990 Directive in the light of major changes in the market, notably, as a result of the increasing importance of the internet as a medium through which

---

cepting responsibility if "holiday arrangement" "is not of a reasonable standard", but act of electrician employee in guiding consumer through hotel grounds and sexually assaulting her was not part of the "holiday arrangements").

[885] It has been held that the reasonable care of the service supplier must be judged by the standards of the place where the service is provided: *Lougheed v On the Beach Ltd* [2014] EWCA Civ 1538 at [16] applying *Wilson v Best Travel Ltd* [1993] 1 All E.R. 353 (which was decided at common law). In *X v Kuoni Travel Ltd* [2018] EWCA Civ 938 at [38], [40]–[48] a majority of the CA held that an electrician employee of a hotel (which *was* a supplier of the service to the consumer) did not himself supply a service within the meaning of reg.15(2) of the 1992 Regulations so as to allow the possible application of the defences to liability there contained.

[886] 1992 Regulations reg.15(2).

[887] See *Milner v Carnival Plc* [2010] EWCA Civ 389, [2010] P.I.Q.R. Q3. For the common law position see *Jarvis v Swann Tours Ltd* [1973] Q.B.233; *Jackson v Horizon Holidays* [1975] 1 W.L.R. 1468 and see Vol.I, para.26-155. In *Leitner v Tui Deustchland GmbH & Co KG* (C-168/00) EU:C:2002:163, [2002] E.C.R. I-2631 the ECJ held that "damage" under the Package Travel Directive 1990 includes loss of enjoyment and therefore national laws must allow recovery for this type of loss in their national legislation implementing the Directive.

[888] 1992 Regulations reg.15(4)–(5). The contract may also provide for compensation to be limited in accordance with international conventions which govern the relevant services forming part of the package: reg.15(3).

[889] Enterprise Act 2002 ss.210(6)(b) and (7), 212; Sch.13 Pt 1 para.4 (before July 1, 2018); Enterprise Act 2002 (Part 8 Community Infringements Specified UK Laws) Order 2003 (SI 2003/1374) Sch.1 para.3.

[890] Enterprise Act 2002 (Part 8 Community Infringements Specified UK Laws) Order 2003/1374 Sch.1.

[891] Below, para.38-147.

[892] [2015] O.J. L326/1 ("2015 Directive"). Repeal of the 1990 Directive is with effect from July 1, 2018: 2015 Directive art.29.

travel services are made available.[893] As earlier noted, the UK government has issued regulations for the implementation of the 2015 Directive in UK law, the Package Travel and Linked Travel Arrangements Regulations 2018 (the "2018 Regulations") which revoked the 1992 Regulations and which came into force generally on July 1, 2018,[894] applying to contracts made on or after that date.[895] The following paragraphs will outline the most significant of their features for the purposes of contract law.

Scope of the Regulations   The 2018 Regulations govern "packages offered for   **38-143** sale or sold by traders to travellers" and to "linked travel arrangements" facilitated by traders for travellers.[896] "Trader" is defined generally for this purpose, and refers to the organiser or retailer of package travel, the facilitator of a linked travel arrangement, or a travel service provider.[897] The protection of "travellers" (rather than "consumers" as under the 1992 Regulations, though this was specially defined[898]) means that individuals who are business travellers are included except where their travel arrangements are made on the basis of a general agreement.[899] The key notion of a "package" is redefined extensively when compared to the 1992 Regulations, requiring a combination of two different elements of "travel services" for the purpose of the same trip or holiday, subject to a series of particular conditions.[900]

"'Travel service' means

(a)   the carriage of passengers;
(b)   accommodation which is not intrinsically part of the carriage of passengers and is not for residential purposes;
(c)   rental of
  (i)   cars;
  (ii)   other motor vehicles [as defined by reference];
  (iii)   or motorcycles [as defined by reference];
(d)   any other tourist service not intrinsically part of a travel service within the meaning of paragraph (a), (b) or (c)."[901]

According to recital 18 of the Directive, "any other tourist service" would include, for example:

"... admission to concerts, sport events, excursions or event parks, guided tours, ski passes and rental of sports equipment such as skiing equipment, or spa treatments."

---

[893]   2015 Directive recital 2.

[894]   2018 Regulations reg.1(2) (with the exception there noted).

[895]   2018 Regulations reg.1(2); reg.37(2) (preserving the 1992 Regulations in relation to contracts concluded under them before July 1, 2018).

[896]   2018 Regulations reg.3(1) (with the exceptions set by reg.3(2)); cf. 2015 Directive art.2(1) (with the exceptions set by art.2(2)).

[897]   2018 Regulations reg.2(1) "trader".

[898]   Above, para.38-138.

[899]   This is the combined effect of the definition of "traveller" in reg.2(1) and the exclusion from the scope of the Regulations in reg.3(2)(c) of "packages and linked travel arrangements purchased on the basis of a general agreement", defined (reg.3(3)) as an: "agreement which is concluded between a trader and another person acting for a trade, business, craft or profession, for the purpose of booking travel arrangements in connection with that trade, business, craft or profession." cf. 2015 Directive arts 2(2)(c), 3(6) and recital 7.

[900]   2018 Regulations reg.2(5) and (6); cf. 2015 Directive art.3(2) ("package") and recitals 10 and 11, 17 to 19.

[901]   2018 Regulations reg.2(1) "travel service"; cf. 2015 Directive art.3(1).

The 2018 Regulations introduce the notion of a "linked travel arrangement", defined as:

> "… at least two different types of travel service purchased for the purpose of the same trip or holiday, not constituting a package, resulting in the conclusion of separate contracts with the individual travel service providers, if a trader facilitates—
>
> (a) on the occasion of a single visit to, or contact with, a trader's point of sale, the separate selection and separate payment of each travel service by travellers; or
>
> (b) in a targeted manner, the procurement of at least one additional travel service from another trader where a contract with such other trader is concluded at the latest 24 hours after the confirmation of the booking of the first travel service."[902]

Recital 9 of the 2015 Directive explains that this is:

> "… where online or high street traders facilitate the procurement of travel services by travellers leading the traveller to conclude contracts with different travel services providers, including through linked booking processes, which do not contain the features of a package and in relation to which it would not be appropriate to apply all of the obligations applicable to packages."[903]

As regards both the definition of "package" and "linked travel arrangement", where not more than one type of travel service of the kind listed in the first three paragraphs of its definition ((a) to (c)) is combined with one or more "other tourist service" as referred to in para.(d) of the definition of "travel service", then the arrangement will not count as a "package" or, as the case may be, a "linked travel arrangement" if those services do not account for a significant proportion of the value of the combination (or combined value of the services) and are not advertised as, and do not otherwise represent, an essential feature of package combined, or the combination, trip or holiday and, moreover, in the case of packages, subject to a further condition that the "other tourist service" or services are not selected or purchased after the performance of a travel service of the kind listed in paras (a), (b) or (c) of the definition of "travel service" has started.[904] According to recital 9 of the 2015 Directive, linked travel arrangements take place:

> "… where online or high street traders facilitate the procurement of travel services by travellers leading the traveller to conclude contracts with different travel services providers, including through linked booking processes, which do not contain the features of a package."

In terms of the first example, it may thought to be unusual in practice for the "separate selection and separate payment of each travel service" to take place "on the occasion of a single visit, or contact with, a trader's point of sale". More generally, many respondents to the government's consultation on the implementation of the 2015 Directive expressed concerned as to the lack of clarity of what constitutes

---

[902] 2018 Regulations reg.2(3); cf. 2015 Directive art.3(5).

[903] See further explanations of "linked travel arrangement" and how it differs from other arrangements see the 2015 Directive, recitals 12 to 17.

[904] 2018 Regulations reg.2(4) (in relation to "linked travel arrangement") and reg.2(6) (b) (in relation to "package"); cf. 2015 Directive art.3(2)(b) ("package"); 3(5) ("linked travel arrangement"). Recital 18 of the 2015 Directive explains that "[i]f other tourist services account for 25% or more of the value of the combination, those services should be considered as representing a significant proportion of the value of the package or linked travel arrangement."

a "linked travel arrangement".[905] However, very few of the requirements of the Directive or the 2018 Regulations apply to "linked travel arrangements", the most significant examples being that a traveller will benefit from requirements concerning the protection of travellers from the insolvency of the facilitator of the arrangement,[906] and that a trader has a duty to inform the traveller that he will not benefit from any of the rights applying exclusively to *packages* under the Regulations and that each service provider will be solely responsible for the proper contractual performance of the service, though he will benefit from insolvency protection.[907]

Information requirements for package travel contracts The 2018 Regulations set out a detailed list of information to be provided to the traveller by the organiser or, where applicable, retailer[908] by means of standard forms before the traveller is bound by a package travel contract, including as to the main characteristics of the travel service (as set out), details about the trader, the total price of the package together with arrangements for payment and a number of other matters.[909] The information must be provided "in a clear, comprehensible and prominent manner" and, if in writing, in legible form.[910] The most important of this information (notably as to the main characteristics of the travel service and the price) "forms an integral part of the package travel contract" and "must not be altered unless the traveller expressly agrees otherwise" with the organiser or, as the case may be, retailer.[911] The 2018 Regulations also provide that the organiser or retailer must provide the traveller with a copy or confirmation of the contract, setting out the "full content of the package", including the information which should have been (or was) supplied in advance of the contract and further information about the travel service (e.g. special requirements of the traveller accepted by the organiser) and practical matters (such as the name, etc. of the organiser's local representative or equivalent, and of the traveller's right (created by the Regulations and subject to conditions) to transfer the contract on reasonable notice to another traveller before the start of the package.[912] The Regulations set out a series of strict controls on the circumstances in which the price of a package travel contract may be increased or other terms of the contract changed.[913]

38-144

---

[905] Department of Business, Energy & Industrial Strategy, *Updating Consumer Protection in the Package Travel Sector*, Government Response (April 2018), paras 50–51 and 54.

[906] 2018 Regulations reg.26(1)–(6). cf. 2015 Directive art.19, recitals 16, 43 and 44. See also 2018 Regulations reg.28 (liability for booking errors).

[907] 2018 Regulations reg.26(7) and (8); the 2018 Regulations set out the required form of words for this information in different circumstances in Schs 6 to 10.

[908] Where a package is sold through a retailer, 2018 Regulations reg.4 determines the responsibility for the provision of the information as between its organiser and the retailer by reference to the notion of a "relevant person", which is then used by the subsequent provisions (regs 5 to 7).

[909] 2018 Regulations regs 4 and 5 referring to Schs 1 to 4; cf. 2015 Directive art.5(1) and (2).

[910] 2018 Regulations reg.5(4): cf. 2015 Directive art.5(3).

[911] 2018 Regulations reg.6(1). Regulation 6(4) provides that it is an implied condition that the organiser or retailer complies with reg.6's provisions and this means that a failure to do so would constitute a breach of contract in the organiser or retailer entitling the traveller to terminate the contract. Art.6(1) of the 2015 Directive requires contractual force to be given to pre-contractual information in a similar way to the general scheme contained in the Consumer Rights Directive 2011 art.6(5) on which see above, para.38-105.

[912] 2018 Regulations reg.7; Schs 1 and 5; cf. 2015 Directive art.7. For the right to transfer itself see 2018 Regulations reg.9.

[913] 2018 Regulations regs 10 and 11; cf. 2015 Directive arts 10 and 11.

38-145 **Termination of the contract** The 2018 Regulations provide that in general a traveller "may terminate the package travel contract at any time before the start of the package" though he may be required to pay "an appropriate and justifiable termination fee to the organiser" (concerning which further details are specified)[914] and may also terminate the contract without paying any termination fee:

> "… in the event of unavoidable and extraordinary circumstances occurring at the place of destination or its immediate vicinity and which significantly affect—
>
> (a) the performance of the package, or
> (b) the carriage of passengers to the destination." [915]

In these circumstances, the traveller can obtain a full refund of any payments made for the package but no additional compensation.[916] Conversely, the organiser is also empowered to terminate the contract where he:

> "… is prevented from performing the contract because of unavoidable and extraordinary circumstances and notifies the traveller of the termination of the contract without undue delay before the start of the package."[917]

Where this is the case, the organiser must refund any payments made by the traveller for the package, but is not liable for any additional compensation.[918]

38-146 **Responsibility for the performance of the package** The 2018 Regulations set a general principle that the organiser[919] is liable for the performance of the travel services included in the package travel contract "irrespective of whether those services are to be performed by the organiser or by other travel service providers"[920] and imposes on him a duty to remedy any lack of conformity of the service with the contract within a reasonable period set by the traveller, unless this is impossible or entails "disproportionate costs, taking into account the extent of the lack of conformity and the value of the travel services affected".[921] The Regulations make further detailed provision as to the traveller's remedies for non-conformity of the travel service with the contract, including a power in the traveller to remedy it himself where the organiser refuses to remedy the lack of conformity or where

---

914 2018 Regulations reg.12(2)–(6). The provisions of reg.12 are implied as a term in every package travel contract: reg.12(1). cf. 2015 Directive art.12(1).

915 2018 Regulations reg.12(7).

916 2018 Regulations reg.12(8).

917 2018 Regulations reg.13(2)(b) and (3) and see reg.14 on refunds in the event of termination; cf. 2015 Directive art.12(3)(b). The organiser may also terminate the contract where the package was stated as being for a minimum number of persons and that number is not enrolled at various times before its start depending on the duration of the package: reg.13(2)(a) and (3).

918 2018 Regulations reg.13(3) and see reg.14 on refunds in the event of termination; cf. 2015 Directive art.12(3).

919 The UK government decided not to extend responsibility for performance of package contracts to their retailers as well as their organisers: Department of Business, Energy & Industrial Strategy, *Updating Consumer Protection in the Package Travel Sector, Government Response* (April 2018), paras 88–91.

920 2018 Regulations reg.15(2); cf. 2015 Directive art.13(1).

921 2018 Regulations reg.15(4). Where the exceptions apply, the traveller enjoys the possibility of a price reduction or compensation: reg.15(5) referring to reg.16. cf. 2015 Directive art.13 and specifically art.13(3).

immediate remedy is required[922]; a duty in the organiser to make suitable alternative arrangements if a significant proportion of the travel service cannot be provided as agreed[923]; a power in the traveller to terminate the contract without paying a termination fee where "a lack of conformity substantially affects the performance of the package" and "the organiser fails to remedy the lack of conformity within the reasonable period" set by the traveller;[924] a general right to:

"... an appropriate price reduction for any period during which there is a lack of conformity, unless the organiser proves that the lack of conformity is attributable to the traveller",[925]

and a right to "appropriate compensation for any damage which the traveller sustains as a result of any lack of conformity", unless the latter was attributable to the traveller, to a third party unconnected with the provision of the travel services included in the package travel contract and is unforeseeable or unavoidable, or was due to unavoidable and extraordinary circumstances.[926]

Effectiveness of traveller's protection and enforcement   Part 5 of the 2018 **38-147** Regulations makes provision for the effectiveness of the protection of travellers from the insolvency of the organisers of package travel and linked travel arrangements.[927] The Regulations make it an offence in an organiser or retailer of a package, or a facilitator of a linked travel arrangement, to fail in their respective duties of information and, in the case of the former, in respect of the content of the package travel contract, and in respect of certain failures as regards the traveller's insolvency protection.[928] The Regulations specify that local weights and measures authorities and the Civil Aviation Authority are the enforcement authorities for these purposes.[929] In addition, the Regulations substitute the 2015 Directive for the 1990 Directive in the list of instruments which may give rise to a "Community infringement" and so apply Pt 8 of the Enterprise Act 2002 for their purposes; and they substitute the 2018 Regulations as the regulations specified as the UK law giving effect to the 2015 Directive for these purposes.[930] Finally, the Regulations render

---

[922] 2018 Regulations reg.15(6), which entitles the traveller to a reimbursement of the expenses necessary to do so; see also reg.15(7) (no requirement in these circumstances for the traveller to set a period nor to wait the expiry of any reasonable period in fact set).

[923] 2018 Regulations reg.15(8)–(10) and (12).

[924] 2018 Regulations reg.15(11); cf. 2015 Directive art.13(6). Further detailed provision is made where in certain circumstances the traveller requires repatriation or is unable to return as agreed in the contract owing to unavoidable and extraordinary circumstances: reg.15(12)–(16).

[925] 2018 Regulations reg.16(2); cf. 2015 Directive art.14(1).

[926] 2018 Regulations reg.16(3) and (4); cf. 2015 Directive art.14(3) and above, para.38-340 under the 1992 Regulations.

[927] cf. 2015 Directive arts 17 to 18, and 19(1).

[928] As regards package travel, see 2018 Regulations regs 5(5) (information); reg.7(12) (failure in respect of the content of the contract, etc.), and regs 19(9) and 25 (insolvency requirements); as regards linked travel arrangements, see reg.26(10) (information and insolvency requirements). See further regs 32–34 (due diligence defence, liability of persons other than the principal offender, and prosecution time limit).

[929] 2018 Regulations reg.31 (in Northern Ireland, the enforcement authority is the Department for the Economy in Northern Ireland).

[930] 2018 Regulations reg.38(3) referring to 2002 Act Sch.13 Pt 1 para.4; reg.38(7) amending the Enterprise Act 2002 (Part 8 Community Infringements Specified UK Laws) Order 2003 (SI 2003/1374) Sch.1.

any waiver or contractual arrangement purporting to restrict the application of the Regulations not binding on the traveller.[931]

(iii) Timeshare and Related Contracts

38-148 **Timeshare and related contracts** The Timeshare, Holiday Products, Resale and Exchange Contracts Regulations 2010 (the "Timeshare Regulations" or "2010 Regulations")[932] implement in the UK the EU Timeshare Directive 2009, revoking and replacing earlier legislation.[933] The Timeshare Directive 2009 provides generally for "full harmonisation", and the 2010 Regulations follow its substantive requirements closely, though with considerable reordering and rephrasing.[934] Very broadly, the 2010 Regulations impose on the trader a range of pre-contractual information duties, make specific and demanding formal and language requirements for the contracts affected, and, in addition, provide the consumer with a 14-day right of withdrawal which is extended where the trader fails to provide the consumer with a withdrawal form and/or "key information".[935]

38-149 **The contracts affected** The 2010 Regulations govern two types of contract ("timeshare contracts" and "long-term holiday product contracts"),[936] together with two further types of contract which are related to them: "resale contracts" and "exchange contracts".[937] A timeshare contract is defined as

"… a contract between a trader and a consumer—

(a) under which the consumer, for consideration, acquires the right to use overnight accommodation for more than one period of occupation, and

(b) which has a duration of more than one year, or contains provision allowing for the contract to be renewed or extended so that it has a duration of more than one year." [938]

For this purpose, "accommodation" includes a reference to "accommodation within a pool of accommodation".[939] A "long-term holiday product contract" is defined as

"… a contract between a trader and a consumer—

---

[931] 2018 Regulations reg.30(2) and (3).

[932] SI 2010/2960.

[933] Directive 2008/122/EC on the protection of consumers in respect of certain aspects of timeshare, long-term holiday product, resale and exchange contracts ("Timeshare Directive 2009"). The earlier UK legislation was the Timeshare Act 1992 and the Timeshare Regulations 1997 (SI 1997/1081) (as amended in 2003), which were revoked by the 2010 Regulations reg.36.

[934] Timeshare Directive 2009 recital 3. On full harmonisation, see above, para.38-025. The text of the Directive allows exceptions to the general requirement of full harmonisation, so, e.g. art.5(1)(a)–(b) allow Member States in which the consumer is resident to make further requirements as to the language in which the contract is provided to the consumer than are required by art.5(1), first sentence of the Directive itself. This option has been exercised by the UK in the 2010 Regulations reg.18.

[935] 2010 Regulations regs 12–15 (information requirements), regs 15–18; regs 20–24 (right of withdrawal for consumer, below, paras 38-150—38-152).

[936] 2010 Regulations regs 3 and 4–6. On the related contracts, see below.

[937] 2010 Regulations, defined in regs 9 and 10. The 2010 Regulations came into force on February 23, 2011: 2010 Regulations reg.1(2).

[938] 2010 Regulations reg.7(1).

[939] 2010 Regulations reg.7(2).

(a)   the main effect of which is that the consumer, for consideration, acquires the right to obtain discounts or other benefits in respect of accommodation, and

(b)   which has a duration of more than one year, or contains provision allowing for the contract to be renewed or extended so that it has a duration of more than one year,

irrespective of whether the contract makes provision for the consumer to acquire other services."[940]

The two related contracts which are also affected by the 2010 Regulations are resale contracts defined as:

"... a contract between a trader and a consumer under which the trader, for consideration, assists the consumer in buying or selling rights under a timeshare contract or under a long-term holiday product contract"[941]

and exchange contracts defined as:

"... a contract between ... a consumer who is also party to a timeshare contract, and ... a trader, under which the consumer, for consideration, joins a timeshare exchange system."[942]

Timeshare contracts and long-term holiday product contracts and these two related contracts are together termed "holiday accommodation contracts" by the Regulations and, if they satisfy a series of conditions and do not fall within a series of exclusions, then qualify as "regulated contracts".[943] For the purposes of the four contracts described above, the definitions of "trader" and "consumer" follow closely the definitions of the 1990 Directive, without any extension to the consumer acting "wholly or mainly" for non-business purposes.[944] In addition to these four

---

940   2010 Regulations reg.8.

941   2010 Regulations reg.9.

942   2010 Regulations reg.10(1). Regulation 10(2) explains that "[a] "timeshare exchange system" is a system which allows a consumer access to overnight accommodation or other services in exchange for giving other persons temporary access to the benefits deriving from the consumer's timeshare contract.

943   The structure of the UK legislation is quite complex. Technically, the four types of contract (timeshare, long-term holiday product contract, resale contract and exchange contract) are all "holiday accommodation contracts": reg.4. Regulation 5 then determines to which holiday accommodation contracts the Regulations apply, the relevant rules in fact determining the Regulations' application as a matter of private international law: this is discussed below, para.38-153. A "regulated contract" refers to "a holiday accommodation contract" to which the Regulations apply in this technical sense, as long as it is not an "excluded arrangement" within the meaning of reg.6. The provisions on "excluded arrangements" reflect recitals 6 and 7 of the Timeshare Directive 2009 which explain that timeshare contracts for its purposes do not cover the arrangements excluded by reg.6(1)–(4): these consist of multiple reservations of accommodation to the extent that they do not imply rights and obligations beyond those arising from the separate reservations; lease agreements which provide for a single continuous period of occupation and hotel loyalty schemes (which it defines). Regulation 6(5) also excludes contracts of insurance where the effecting or the carrying out of the contract constitutes a regulated activity for the purposes of the Financial Services and Markets Act 2000 (which do not appear to fall within the scope of the 2009 Directive).

944   2010 Regulations reg.11(1): "... 'consumer' means an individual who is not acting for the purposes of a trade, business, craft or profession" and: "... 'trader' means (a) a person acting for purposes relating to that person's trade, business, craft or profession, or (b) anyone acting in the name of, or on behalf of, a person falling within paragraph (a)". Regulation 11(2) adds that this applies where either of these is either the party or a would-be party to the "regulated contract". The definitions in the 2009 Directive are found in art.2(1)(e) and (f). For discussion of the treatment of "consumer"

"regulated contracts", "ancillary contracts" and "related credit agreements" are automatically terminated if the consumer withdraws from a regulated contract under the Regulations.[945]

38-150 **Information requirements** The 2010 Regulations impose a number of requirements on traders to give[946] "key information in relation to the contract" to the consumer in good time before entering a "regulated contract".[947] The "key information" is defined by reference to "standard information forms" which the 2010 Regulations themselves provide, the four forms (for timeshare contracts, long-term holiday product contract, resale contracts and exchange contracts respectively[948]) consisting of a series of headings under which the trader is required to fill in the relevant particular information, so, for example, in relation to timeshare contracts this includes a short description of the immovable property, the exact nature and content of the consumer's rights under the contract, and summaries of the services and facilities which the consumer will enjoy, and the consumer's right of withdrawal.[949] The information must be provided by the trader using the relevant form,[950] must be "clear, comprehensible and accurate" and "sufficient to enable the consumer to make an informed decision about whether or not to enter into the contract",[951] and must be provided in an official language of an EEA State in which the consumer is resident or is a national.[952] A trader's failure in any of these requirements constitutes a criminal offence.[953] The Regulations make further requirements as to the advertising and marketing of a "regulated contract", again buttressed by criminal penalties.[954]

38-151 **Formalities** The 2010 Regulations require that a regulated contract[955] must be in writing and include the identity, place of residence and signature of the parties, the date and place of conclusion of the contract, must include the "key information" in relation to the contract[956] as "terms of the contract, and with no changes, other than permitted changes",[957] and must include the standard withdrawal form which

---

and "trader" in EU law, see above, paras 38-034—38-036 and 38-051—38-055.
[945] 2010 Regulations regs 22(2)(b) and (6)–(7) (ancillary contracts) and 23 (related credit agreements), below, para.38-152.
[946] The information must be provided in writing, free of charge, and "in a manner which is easily accessible to the consumer": 2010 Regulations reg.12(5)(b)–(c). cf. the discussion above, para.38-091 between a trading "providing" (or giving) and "making available" information. The 2009 Directive art.4 requires the trader to "provide the consumer" with the information in question.
[947] For the significance of "regulated contract" see 2010 Regulations regs 3–4 as explained by para.38-149.
[948] 2010 Regulations reg.13(2). The forms are set out in 2010 Regulations Schs 1–4 (for timeshare contracts, long-term holiday product contract, re-sale contracts and exchange contracts respectively). Regulation 13(1) imposes further rules as to the completion of these forms.
[949] 2010 Regulations reg.12, referring to Sch.1 Pts 1–3.
[950] 2010 Regulations reg.12(5)(a).
[951] 2010 Regulations reg.12(4).
[952] 2010 Regulations reg.12(6)–(7).
[953] 2010 Regulations reg.12(5) and (8). Further provision for these offences is made by regs 27–32.
[954] 2010 Regulations reg.14. Further provision for these offences is made by regs 27–32.
[955] On which, see above, para.38-149.
[956] As defined by 2010 Regulations reg.12, above, para.38-150.
[957] 2010 Regulations reg.15(4). "Permitted changes" are defined as: "changes to the key information which were communicated to the consumer in writing before the conclusion of the contract and which (a) were expressly agreed between the trader and the consumer, or (b) resulted from unusual

they set out.[958] The trader must draw the consumer's attention to three important matters (the consumer's right of withdrawal and its length, and the prohibition on "advanced consideration"[959]) and obtain the consumer's signature in relation to *each* section of the contract dealing with them, and the trader must provide the consumer with a copy of the contract.[960] Any failure by the trader in any of these respects constitutes a criminal offence and the contract is rendered unenforceable against the consumer.[961] The Regulations make provision for the language in which the contract must be drawn up[962] and, in the case of timeshare contracts whose subject is a "single item of specific immovable property situated in a EEA State" a certified translation of the contract into an official language of that State.[963]

Consumer's right to withdraw   The 2010 Regulations provide that a consumer   **38-152** may withdraw[964] from a "regulated contract"[965] by written notice[966] without giving any reason and may use the standard withdrawal form which should have been included in the contract to do so.[967] The basic withdrawal period is 14 days beginning with the date of conclusion of the contract or the date on which the consumer receives a copy of the contract, whichever is later,[968] but if no standard withdrawal form is included in the contract the period is extended until the form is provided to the consumer plus 14 days up to a limit of a year and 14 days[969]; and if the "key information"[970] is not provided by the trader, the period is extended until that information is provided plus 14 days up to a limit of three months and 14 days.[971] The exercise of this right of withdrawal by a consumer terminates the parties' obligations under the relevant "regulated contract"[972]; and where this is a timeshare contract or long-term holiday accommodation contract, it terminates their obligations under any "ancillary contract" by which the consumer acquires services which

---

and unforeseeable circumstances beyond the trader's control, the consequences of which could not have been avoided even if all due care had been exercised". "Permitted changes" must be expressly mentioned in the contract: reg.15(6). cf. the similar provisions affecting the information provided under the requirements in the Consumer Contracts (Information, Cancellation and Additional Charges) Regulations 2013, above para.38-105.

958   2010 Regulations reg.15(7); Sch.5.
959   On this prohibition see 2010 Regulations reg.25, below, para.38-152.
960   2010 Regulations reg.16(1)–(3).
961   2010 Regulations reg.15(8) (referring to the reg.15 requirements) and reg.16(4) (referring to the reg.16 requirements). Further provision for these criminal offences is made by regs 27–32.
962   2010 Regulations reg.17.
963   2010 Regulations reg.18.
964   Notice that, unlike the 2013 Regulations which distinguish between a right to cancel a contract and a right to withdraw an offer (above, para.38-113), the 2010 Regulations refer to the right of the consumer to withdraw from a contract (reg.20(1)) and to a right to terminate long-term holiday product contracts (reg.24).
965   On which see 2010 Regulations regs 3–6 and above, para.38-149.
966   Written notice is deemed as given at the time it is sent by the consumer: 2010 Regulations reg.20(2).
967   2010 Regulations reg.20. The requirement of inclusion of the form is made by reg.15(7).
968   2010 Regulations reg.21(1)–(2).
969   2010 Regulations reg.21(3)–(4).
970   On which see 2010 Regulations reg.12 and above, para.38-150.
971   2010 Regulations reg.21(5) and (6). Regulation 21(7) provides that where the trader has failed in both requirements the withdrawal period ends with the later of the two dates set. Where an exchange contract is related to a timeshare contract and offered to the consumer at the same time, the withdrawal period for both contracts is the one applicable to the timeshare contract: reg.21(8)–(10).
972   As defined by 2010 Regulations regs 3–6 and see above, para.38-149.

are related to the main contract either provided by the trader or by a third party under an arrangement between the latter and the trader[973]; withdrawal by the consumer from a timeshare contract also terminates the parties' obligations under any exchange contract which is related to it.[974] On withdrawal, the consumer is not liable for any costs or charges in respect of the regulated contract or any ancillary contract affected, including any costs or charges corresponding to services provided before withdrawal,[975] and any related credit agreement is automatically terminated at no cost to the consumer.[976] As regards timeshare contracts, long-term holiday product contracts and exchange contracts, it is an offence for a person to accept any consideration (and notably, any payment[977]) before the end of the period for withdrawal allowed for the consumer and, in the case of resale contracts, to accept any consideration before the sale of those rights takes place or the contract in question is otherwise terminated.[978] In addition to a right of withdrawal, in the case of a long-term holiday product contract which is a "regulated contract", the consumer may terminate the contract without penalty by giving notice of termination no later than 14 days after any day on which the consumer receives a request for payment of an instalment (other than the first instalment) as set out by the payment schedule which the Regulations require for this category of contract.[979]

38-153 **Exclusion by agreement or choice of law**   The 2010 Regulations provide that a term of a "regulated contract"[980] is void to the extent that it purports to allow the consumer to waive the rights conferred on them by these Regulations.[981] Article 12 of the 2009 Directive makes overt provision for its application "in international cases", but in the scheme of the 2010 Regulations these special controls on choice of applicable law are given effect by reg.5's provisions specifying the "holiday accommodation contracts" to which the Regulations apply.[982] The background to this special provision is that under the Rome I Regulation, the contracts falling within the scope of the 2009 Directive[983] may fall under art.3's general provisions allowing choice of law and art.6's special provisions governing consumer contracts[984] or,

---

[973] 2010 Regulations reg.22(2)(b) and (6). In the case of long term holiday product contracts, withdrawal terminates an obligation to pay any penalty or further instalments of the payment schedule as required by reg.26: reg.22(3).

[974] 2010 Regulations reg.22(7) referring to reg.21(10) and deeming such a contract to be "ancillary" for the purposes of reg.22(6).

[975] 2010 Regulations reg.22(4) and (5).

[976] 2010 Regulations reg.23(1) and (2). Regulation 23(4) defines such a related credit agreement as being one "under which credit which fully or partly covers any payment under the regulated contract is granted to the consumer by (a) the trader, or (b) a third party on the basis of an arrangement between the third party and the trader".

[977] "Consideration" includes payments, guarantees, reservations of money on account, and acknowledgements of debt: 2010 Regulations reg.25(6).

[978] 2010 Regulations reg.25.

[979] 2010 Regulations reg.24. The requirements for a payment schedule are set out by reg.26.

[980] Above, para.38-149.

[981] 2010 Regulations reg.19.

[982] 2010 Regulations reg.5; "holiday accommodation contracts" are defined by reg.4. These two elements, together with the provisions in reg.6 excluding certain arrangements, are then put together for the definition of "regulated contract" by reg.3, as explained above, para.38-149.

[983] Regulation (EC) 593/2008 on the law applicable to contractual obligations ("Rome I Regulation") reg.6(4)(b) refers to the repealed Timeshare Directive 1994, but the 2009 Directive art.18 requires this reference to be construed as referring to the 2009 Directive.

[984] Rome I Regulation art.6(4)(b).

where they do not, art.4's default provisions governing contracts even where (as in the case of timeshare contracts) they concern rights in rem in immovable property and tenancies.[985] In very broad terms, the 2009 Directive[986] (and so also the 2010 Regulations) seek to give consumers additional protection to that provided by the Rome I Regulation[987] so as to prevent the avoidance of their controls by choice of applicable law, in a similar way to the anti-avoidance provisions in the Unfair Terms in Consumer Contracts Directive 1993[988] and the Consumer Sales Directive 1999.[989] As a result, reg.5 provides that the 2010 Regulations apply to a "holiday accommodation contract"[990] in any one of three circumstances. First, where the contract is to any extent governed by the law of the United Kingdom, or of a part of the United Kingdom.[991] Secondly, where the contract is to any extent governed by the law of a country other than an EEA State, but the relevant accommodation[992] is in immovable property situated in an EEA State, and "the parties to the contract are to any extent subject to the jurisdiction of a court in the United Kingdom in relation to the contract".[993] And thirdly, where the contract is to any extent governed by the law of a country other than an EEA State, is not directly related to immovable property, and the trader carries on commercial or professional activities in the United Kingdom or by any means directs such activities to the United Kingdom and the contract falls within the scope of those activities.[994] Finally, it would appear that an express choice of law clause in a contract falling within the scope of the 2010 Regulations may be assessed for its fairness under the general controls on unfair contract terms implementing the Unfair Terms in Consumer Contracts Directive 1993, i.e. the Consumer Rights Act 2015 Pt 2 (and formerly the Unfair Terms in Consumer Contracts Regulations 1999).[995]

Enforcement   The 2010 Regulations provide that the offences which they create are to be punished by fines,[996] and makes further incidental provision relating to these offences[997]; their enforcement is entrusted to local weights and measures authorities.[998] Obligations owed by traders to consumers under the Regulations in relation to the key information requirements and to the form, formalities, language and translation of the contract are "duties owed" by them and are actionable accordingly and any civil liability arising as a result cannot be excluded by any

38-154

---

985   Rome I Regulation art.4(1)(c) and (d) on which see Dicey, Morris and Collins, *The Conflict of Laws*, 15th edn (2012), Vol.II, paras 33-044, 33-047—33-048. On these provisions of the Rome I Regulation generally see Vol.I, para.30-103.
986   2009 Directive art.12(2).
987   2009 Directive recital 17.
988   1993 Directive art.6(2) below, paras 38-352 and 38-418.
989   1999 Directive art.7(2) below, para.38-533.
990   Defined by 2010 Regulations regs 4 and 7–10, above, para.38-149.
991   2010 Regulations reg.5(1) and (2).
992   Defined as "(i) the accommodation which is the subject of the contract, or (ii) in a case where a pool of accommodation is the subject of the contract, some or all of the accommodation in that pool": 2010 Regulations reg.5(5)(a).
993   2010 Regulations reg.5(1), (3) and (5)(b).
994   2010 Regulations reg.5(1), (4) and (5)(b).
995   cf. *Verein für Konsumenteninformation v Amazon EU Sàrl* (C-191/15) July 28, 2016, see below, para.38-321.
996   2010 Regulations reg.27.
997   2010 Regulations regs 28–32.
998   2010 Regulations reg.32 (in Northern Ireland, the Department of Enterprise Trade and Investment in Northern Ireland).

contract term, notice or other provision.[999] While the 2010 Regulations make no dedicated provision for enforcement of their requirements by injunction, the Enterprise Act 2002 includes the Timeshare Directive 2009 in the list of directives and regulations which may give rise to a "Community infringement" and so apply Pt 8 of the 2002 Act for their purposes[1000]; and the 2010 Regulations are specified as the UK law which gives effect to the 2009 Directive.[1001] As a result, where an infringement by a trader of any of the requirements for consumers in the 2010 Regulations harms the collective interest of consumers,[1002] an "enforcer" may apply to the court for an enforcement order, subject to the conditions set out earlier.[1003]

(iv) Trader's Information Duties in Relation to ADR

38-155   **EU law and ADR**   EU legislation has provided for the establishment of a European online dispute resolution (ODR) platform[1004] and has required Member States to ensure that ADR is available for consumer disputes by the "ADR Directive",[1005] although the legislation does not make ADR mandatory.[1006] The European ODR platform was established by the EU Commission and is available to allow consumers and traders in the EU and the EFTA states to resolve disputes relating to the online purchase of goods and services without going to court.[1007] As part of the wider scheme, the ADR Directive requires Member States to impose on traders a duty to inform consumers as to the availability of ADR.[1008] Following the scope of the Directive as a whole, this requirement applies to domestic and cross-border disputes[1009] relating to contractual obligations stemming from sales contracts or service contracts[1010] between traders and consumers, where the consumer claims against the trader.[1011] Implementing this requirement in the UK, the Alternative Dispute Resolution for Consumer Disputes (Competent Authorities and Information) Regulations 2015 (the "2015 Regulations") distinguish between two

---

999   2010 Regulations reg.35 (1)–(2), (4)–(5).

1000 Enterprise Act 2002 ss.210(6)(b) and (7), 212; Sch.13 Pt 1 para.9E, 212(1).

1001 Enterprise Act 2002 (Part 8 Community Infringements Specified UK Laws) Order 2003 (SI 2003/1374) Sch.1 para.1.

1002 Enterprise Act 2002 s.212.

1003 Enterprise Act 2002 s.214(1). See above, paras 38-133—38-134.

1004 Regulation (EU) 524/2013 of 21 May 2013 on online dispute resolution for consumer disputes (Regulation on consumer ODR) [2013] O.J. L165/1.

1005 Directive 2013/11/EU of 21 May 2013 on alternative dispute resolution for consumer disputes [2013] O.J. L165/63.

1006 ADR Directive art.1 referring to the availability of ADR procedures to consumers "on a voluntary basis", though adding that the Directive is without prejudice to national legislation making participation in such procedures mandatory provided that such legislation does not prevent the parties from exercising their right of access to the judicial system: see further *Menini and Rampanelli v Banco Populare Societa Cooperativa* (C-75/16) of June 14, 2017 at paras 45 et seq.

1007 See *https://ec.europa.eu/consumers/odr/main/?event=main.home.show*.

1008 ADR Directive art.13.

1009 ADR Directive art.2(1). The Directive is implemented in UK law by the Alternative Dispute Resolution for Consumer Disputes (Competent Authorities and Information) Regulations 2015 (SI 2015/542) (the "2015 Regulations"), as amended by the Alternative Dispute Resolution for Consumer Disputes (Amendment) Regulations 2015 (SI 2015/1392).

1010 "Sales contracts" and "services contracts" are defined by the ADR Directive art.4(1)(c) and (d) (as implemented by the 2015 Regulations reg.5). Recital 16 explains that this means that the Directive applies to disputes between traders and consumers "in all economic sectors, other than the exempted sectors" and includes "disputes arising from the sale or provision of digital content for remuneration".

1011 ADR Directive recital 16; art.2 (with exclusions there made), especially art.2(2)(g).

situations.[1012] First, where a trader is obliged to use ADR services provided by an ADR entity or EU listed body[1013] under an enactment, the rules of a trade association to which the trader belongs, or a term of a contract, the trader must provide the name and website address of the ADR entity or EU listed body on its website, if it has one and in the "general terms and conditions of sales or service contracts between the trader and a consumer where they exist".[1014] Secondly, where a trader has exhausted its internal complaint handling procedure when considering a complaint from a consumer relating to a sales contract or a service contract:

"... the trader must inform the consumer, on a durable medium:

(a)   that the trader cannot settle the complaint with the consumer;
(b)   of the name and website address of an ADR entity or EU listed body which would be competent to deal with the complaint, should the consumer wish to use alternative dispute resolution; and
(c)   whether the trader is obliged, or prepared, to submit to an alternative dispute resolution procedure operated by that ADR entity or EU listed body." [1015]

These requirements apply in addition to any information requirements applicable to traders regarding out-of-court redress procedures contained in any other enactment [1016] The 2015 Regulations make similar provision as to the provision of information by online traders and online marketplaces to consumers regarding the ODR platform.[1017] In addition to these information requirements, the ADR Directive makes other requirements in relation to consumer contracts which are implemented by the 2015 Regulations, including that Member States must ensure that an agreement between a consumer and a trader to submit complaints to an ADR entity is not binding on the consumer if it was concluded before the dispute has materialised and if it has the effect of depriving the consumer of his right to bring an action before the courts for the settlement of the dispute.[1018]

(v)   Contracts Concluded by Electronic Means

Summary   The Electronic Commerce (EC Directive) Regulations 2002 (the   **38-156** "Electronic Commerce Regulations 2002") reg.9 (implementing art.10 of the Electronic Commerce Directive 2000[1019]) imposes a duty on providers of informa-

---

[1012] Alternative Dispute Resolution for Consumer Disputes (Competent Authorities and Information) Regulations 2015 (SI 2015/542) reg.19 (as amended by SI 2015/1392) (the amendment came into force on July 9, 2015 but could not take effect until the commencement of SI 2015/542 reg.19 on October 1, 2015).
[1013] 2015 Regulations (as amended by SI 2015/1392) reg.4 provides that an "ADR entity" means a person whose name appears on a list maintained by the Secretary of State or other person specified by the Regulations (reg.5 referring to Sch.1 Pt 1 col.1; Pt 2) as satisfying a list of requirements: reg.9(4), 10 and Sch.3. An "EU listed body" means a person, other than an ADR entity, whose name appears on a list referred to in the ADR Directive art.20(2): 2015 Regulations reg.5.
[1014] 2015 Regulations reg.19(1).
[1015] 2015 Regulations reg.19(2).
[1016] 2015 Regulations reg.19(3).
[1017] 2015 Regulations reg.19A (as amended by SI 2015/1392) (in force January 9, 2016). For the European ODR platform, see above in this paragraph.
[1018] ADR Directive art.10(1); 2015 Regulations reg.14B (inserted by SI 2015/1392 reg.2(8)) (in force on July 9, 2015).
[1019] Directive 2000/31/EC on certain legal aspects of information society services, in particular electronic

tion society services, such as selling goods online,[1020] to provide information on specified matters before the conclusion of contract to be concluded by electronic means.[1021] The matters on which information must be provided "in a clear, comprehensible and unambiguous manner" relate to the different technical steps to follow to conclude the contract, whether or not the concluded contract will be filed by the service provider and whether it will be accessible, the technical means for identifying and correcting input errors prior to the placing of an order, and the languages offered for the conclusion of the contract[1022]; the provider must make available[1023] any terms and conditions applicable to the contract to recipients in a way which allows them to store and reproduce them[1024]; and it must also indicate any relevant code of conduct to which it subscribes and how they may be accessed.[1025] The provider must acknowledge receipt of any order without undue delay and by electronic means and must make available[1026] the technical means which allow the identification and correction of input errors.[1027] With the exception of the duty to make terms and conditions available, these duties do not apply to "contracts concluded exclusively by exchange of electronic mail or by equivalent individual communications".[1028] Moreover, while the duties apply for the benefit of all "recipients" of the service, they may be excluded by agreement only where the parties are not consumers.[1029] The Electronic Commerce Regulations 2002 provide that the duties which they impose on service provides in this respect[1030] shall be enforceable by the recipient of the service in the tort of breach of statutory duty[1031]

---

commerce, in the Internal Market ("Directive on electronic commerce") [2000] O.J. L178/17.

[1020] The Electronic Commerce Regulations 2002 (SI 2002/2013) reg.2(1) defines "service provider" as "any person providing an information society service" and explains "information society service" by reference to the 2000 Directive art.2(a) (which itself refers to Directive 98/34/EC laying down a procedure for the provision of technical standards and regulations [1998] O.J. L204/37 art.1(2)) and recital 17's explanation that it covers "any service normally provided for remuneration, at a distance, by means of electronic equipment for the processing (including digital compression) and storage of data, and at the individual request of a recipient of a service", though recital 18 further explains, inter alia, that "[i]nformation society services span a wide range of economic activities which take place on-line" and "are not solely restricted to services giving rise to on-line contracting but also, in so far as they represent an economic activity, extend to services which are not remunerated by those who receive them, such as those offering on-line information or commercial communications, or those providing tools allowing for search, access and retrieval of data" and see *Criminal Proceedings against Vanderborght* (C-339/15) of May 4, 2017 at paras 37 to 50 (advertising relating to dentistry services by means of a website created by a member of a regulated profession constitutes a commercial communication which is part of an information society service or which constitutes such a service for the purposes of art.8 of the 2000 Directive).

[1021] SI 2002/2013 reg.9. Regulations 6–8 impose other requirements on society service providers: to make available general information (such as the name of the provider, geographical address, etc.) in a form which is "easily, directly and permanently accessible"; to ensure the clarity of commercial communications provided; and to ensure that unsolicited commercial communications sent by electronic mail are clearly and unambiguously identifiable as such as soon as it is received.

[1022] Electronic Commerce Regulations 2002 reg.9(1).

[1023] On this concept cf. above, para.38-091.

[1024] Electronic Commerce Regulations 2002 reg.9(3). This requirement may be enforced by court order: reg.14.

[1025] Electronic Commerce Regulations 2002 reg.9(2).

[1026] On this concept cf. above, para.38-091.

[1027] Electronic Commerce Regulations 2002 reg.11(1) and (2).

[1028] Electronic Commerce Regulations 2002 reg.9(4) and 11(3).

[1029] Electronic Commerce Regulations 2002 reg.9(1) and (2), and 11(1).

[1030] i.e. under Electronic Commerce Regulations 2002 regs 6–8, 9(1) and 11(1)(a).

[1031] Electronic Commerce Regulations 2002 reg.13.

and that, in the case of a failure in the service provider to make available means of allowing a person to identify and correct input elements, a person may rescind any contract made, unless a court orders otherwise on the former's application.[1032] Apart from the last provision, the service provider's failures to perform these duties are not stated as affecting the validity of any contract made, but as a "Community infringement" they may attract enforcement measures under Pt 8 of the Enterprise Act 2002.[1033]

5. UNFAIR COMMERCIAL PRACTICES AND THE CONSUMER'S RIGHTS TO REDRESS

(a) Introduction

Legislative history In 2008 the UK government enacted the Consumer Protection from Unfair Trading Regulations (the "2008 Regulations"),[1034] repealing a good deal of the Trade Descriptions Act 1968 and implementing a new scheme for the control of "unfair commercial practices" business-to-consumer as required by the Unfair Commercial Practices Directive 2005 (the "2005 Directive"). When is sued, the 2008 Regulations had no impact on "contract law" in the sense that the commission of an unfair commercial practice by a trader which led to a contract with a consumer was not on this ground invalid[1035]; nor did they create any "private rights" of redress for the consumer in respect of such an unfair commercial practice, such as by way of a claim for damages for any loss caused to the consumer as a result. However, in 2014 the UK government issued a further set of regulations to create a new set of "rights to redress" for consumers in respect of *certain* unfair commercial practices by traders by the insertion of a new Pt 4A into the 2008 Regulations.[1036] These rights to redress consist of a "right to unwind" a concluded contract or a payment made by a consumer to a trader,[1037] a right to a discount[1038] and a right to damages.[1039] As will be explained, the relationship between these new rights to redress and existing rights at common law, in equity and, in particular, under s.2 of the Misrepresentation Act 1967 is not straightforward.[1040]

38-157

The structure of this section This section will look briefly at the Unfair Commercial Practices Directive, at the general scheme of the 2008 Regulations prohibiting unfair commercial practices and then at the rights to redress for consumers.

38-158

[1032] Electronic Commerce Regulations 2002 reg.15 referring to the duty in reg.11(1)(b).

[1033] Enterprise Act 2002 s.210(6) and 212; Sch.13 Pt 1 para.9; Enterprise Act 2002 (Part 8 Community Infringements Specified UK Laws) Order 2003 (SI 2003/1374) Sch.1 para.1 (2002 Regulations regs 6, 7, 8, 9 and 11 as "specified UK laws"). On these enforcement powers see above, paras 38-133—38-134.

[1034] SI 2008/1277. In the following the "2008 Regulations" refers to SI 2008/1277 as amended principally by SI 2014/870 in contrast to the "2008 Regulations (as issued)", which refers to the 2008 Regulations before their amendment in 2014.

[1035] 2008 Regulations reg.29 (as issued).

[1036] Consumer Protection (Amendment) Regulations 2014 (SI 2014/870). These Regulations also made certain other amendments to the 2008 Regulations, notably, in respect of their definitions: SI 2014/870 reg.2.

[1037] 2008 Regulations regs 27E–27H.

[1038] 2008 Regulations reg.27I.

[1039] 2008 Regulations reg.27J.

[1040] Below, paras 38-172 et seq.

(b)   The Unfair Commercial Practices Directive 2005

38-159   General   The Unfair Commercial Practices Directive 2005 requires Member States to put in place a very general framework of control prohibiting unfair business-to-consumer commercial practices.[1041] Its purposes in doing so combine concerns with the protection of the economic interests of consumers and the prevention of unfair competition in the interests of competitors, with an internal market concern that *national* unfair competition laws should not be allowed to act as a barrier to cross-border trade.[1042] To achieve the last of these purposes, the 2005 Directive generally requires "full harmonisation", with the result that, within its scope, Member States *must not prohibit* business-to-consumer commercial practices *unless* they are prohibited as unfair under the controls set out by the 2005 Directive itself.[1043] On the other hand, within its scope, the purpose of the Directive is to protect consumers and, according to the Court of Justice of the EU, its provisions are "essentially designed with the consumer as the target and victim of unfair commercial practices in mind" and on the assumption that the consumer is "in a weaker position, particularly with regard to the level of information, in that the consumer must be considered to be economically weaker and less experienced in legal matters" than the trader.[1044]

38-160   Scope of the 2005 Directive   For present purposes, there are two important aspects of the scope of the Directive. First, it applies to "unfair business-to-consumer commercial practices … before, during and after a commercial transaction in relation to a product".[1045] As noted by the Court of Justice of the EU, the Directive gives a "particularly wide definition"[1046] to "business-to-consumer commercial practices" for this purpose, as this refers to:

"… any act, omission, course of conduct or representation, commercial communication including advertising and marketing, by a trader directly connected with the promotion, sale or supply of a product to consumers."[1047]

[1041] See in particular the essays in Collins (ed.) *The Forthcoming EC Directive on Unfair Commercial Practices, Contract, Consumer and Competition Law Implications* (2004) and in Weatherill and Bernitz (eds), *The Regulation of Unfair Commercial Practices under EC Directive 2005/29, New Rules and New Techniques* (2007).

[1042] Bernitz in Weatherill and Bernitz (eds), *The Regulation of Unfair Commercial Practices under EC Directive 2005/29, New Rules and New Techniques* (2007), Ch.3 at p.37; Stuyck in Bernitz and Weatherill, Ch.9 at pp.171–172.

[1043] 2005 Directive art.4; *VTB-VAB NV Total Belgium NV* (C-261/07 and C-299/07) EU:C:2009:244, [2009] E.C.R. I-2949 at [63]; *Mediaprint Zeitungs- und Zeitschriftenverlag GmbH & Co KG v "Österreich"-Zeitungsverlag GmbH* (C-540/08) EU:C:2010:660, [2010] E.C.R. I-10909 at [27], *Zentral sur Bekämpfung unlauteren Weebewerbs eV v Plus Warenhandelsgessellschaft mbH* (C-304/08) EU:C:2010:12, [2010] E.C.R. I-00217 at [41], *Wamo BVBA v JBC NV* (C-288/10) EU:C:2011:443, [2011] E.C.R. I-5835 at [33]; *Europamur Alimentación SA v Direccion General de Commercio y Protección del Consumidor de la Comunidad Autónoma de la Región de Murcia* (C-295/16) October 19, 2017 at paras 34–35, and 43. There is also an important exception to "full harmonisation" in relation to "financial services": 2005 Directive art.3(9). cf. above, paras 38-025—38-026.

[1044] *Nemzeti Fogyasztóvédelmi Hatóság v UPC Magyarország Kft* (C-388/13) of April 18, 2015 at paras 52–53 referring to *BKK Mobil Oil Körperschaft des öffentlichen Rechts v Zentrale zur Bekämpfung unlauteren Wettbewerbs eV* (C-59/12) EU:C:2013:634, October 3, 2013 para.36.

[1045] 2005 Directive art.3(1).

[1046] *Total Belgium & Galatea* (C-261/07 and C-299/07) EU:C:2009:244 at [49].

[1047] 2005 Directive art.2(d). A "commercial practice" therefore covers "any measure taken in relation

A "product" is also understood very broadly, as it means "any goods or service including immovable property, rights and obligations".[1048] Overall, therefore, a good deal of what traders do in relation to the conclusion and performance of contracts with consumers falls within the scope of the 2005 Directive. On the other hand, secondly, the 2005 Directive provides that it is "without prejudice to contract law and, in particular, to the rules on the validity, formation or effect of a contract".[1049] As a result, the national, as well as EU,[1050] legal rules of "contract law" are not affected by the 2005 Directive and this means, in particular, that national contract laws are protected from the potential impact of the Directive's full harmonisation. For this purpose, the reference "in particular" to the rules on the validity, formation or effect of a contract strongly suggest that "contract law" refers to rules governing the relative rights and obligations of parties to a contract.[1051] On the other hand, this also means that Member States are free in principle to give "contract law" significance to some or all of the prohibitions of unfair commercial practices as the Directive understands them.

Relationship with other EU legislation The 2005 Directive was intended as a **38-161** "framework directive" with the result that more particular EU provisions on unfair business-to-consumer commercial practices (such as those required by the Unfair Contract Terms Directive[1052] or the Consumer Rights Directive[1053]) retain their force within this wider framework: the special rules derogate from the general.[1054] According to art.3(4) of the 2005 Directive:

[note] not only to the conclusion of a contract but also to its performance, and in particular the measures taken in order to obtain payment for the product": *UAB "Gelvora" v Valstybinė vartotojų teisių apsaugos tarnyba* (C-357/16) of July 20, 2017 at para.21. The CJEU further held that where the claims assigned to a debt collection agency originated in the supply of a service (the provision of credit at interest), its debt recovery activities may be regarded as a "product" within the meaning of art.2(c) of the 2005 Directive and may constitute an unfair "commercial practice" as the measures which it adopts are liable to influence the consumer's decision in respect of payment of the product: C-357/16 at paras 21–25. For this purpose, the fact that the existence of the debt was confirmed by a court decision and that that decision was passed for enforcement to a bailiff is without consequence: C-357/16 at para.31.

[1048] 2005 Directive art.2(c). On the CJEU's interpretation of "product" to include practices in which a debt collection agency engages to recover the debt, see *UAB "Gelvora" v Valstybinė vartotojų teisių apsaugos tarnyba* (C-357/16) of July 20, 2017 noted in the previous note.

[1049] Directive 2005/29/EC art.3(2), on which see Whittaker in Weatherill and Bernitz (eds), *The Regulation of Unfair Commercial Practices under EC Directive 2005/29, New Rules and New Techniques* (2007), Ch.8. Art.3(3), (7)–(10) of the 2005 Directive contains further matters in respect of which the Directive is "without prejudice", for example, "any conditions of establishment or of authorisation regimes, or to the deontological codes of conduct or other specific rules governing regulated professions in order to uphold high standards of integrity on the part of the professional", on which see *Criminal Proceedings against Vanderborght* (C-339/15) of May 4, 2017 at paras 26–30.

[1050] 2005 Directive recital 9.

[1051] Whittaker, in Weatherill and Bernitz (eds), *The Regulation of Unfair Commercial Practices under EC Directive 2005/29, New Rules and New Techniques* (2007) and cf. above, para.38-063 for a similar understanding of "contract law" for the purposes of the Consumer Rights Directive 2011 art.3(5).

[1052] Directive 93/13/EEC, on which see below, paras 38-218.

[1053] Above, paras 38-060.

[1054] EC Commission, Green Paper on European Union Consumer Protection COM(2001) 531 final, para.3.4 and see Bernitz in Weatherill and Bernitz, *The Regulation of Unfair Commercial Practices under EC Directive 2005/29* (2007) 33 at 44. See also Opinion of A.G. Bot in *Vueling Airlines SA v Instituto Galego de Consumo de la Xunta de Galicia* (C-487/12) of January 23 2014 para.61 referring to provisions on the pricing of air carriage in Regulation (EC) 1008/2008 on common rules for

"In the case of conflict between the provisions of this Directive and other Community rules regulating specific aspects of unfair commercial practices, the latter shall prevail and apply to those specific aspects."

As earlier noted, this provision resolves:

"... irreconcilable conflict between substantive norms, i.e. situations where the same business-to-consumer commercial practice would qualify as 'unfair' under one provision and 'non-unfair' ... under another provision. In such cases, the EU special provision shall 'prevail'."[1055]

So, UK legislative provisions implementing other EU directives and thereby creating "rules regulating specific aspects of unfair commercial practices" prevail over the national rules implementing the 2005 Directive (that is, the 2008 Regulations), but only where those UK legislative provisions follow the *requirements* of that other EU directive itself.

38-162 A transitional period for "minimum harmonisation" legislation On the other hand, art.3(5) of the 2005 Directive protected from the force of its "full harmonisation" national legal prohibitions of business-to-consumer commercial practices which were "more restrictive or prescriptive" than the 2005 Directive and which implemented the requirements of EU "minimum harmonisation" legislation, but only where this was already provided by national law for the protection of consumers at the time of the coming into force of the 2005 Directive and only for a transitional period of six years, ending on June 11, 2013.[1056] This means, therefore, that, after this date, national legal provisions which prohibit the use or recommendation for use of unfair terms *beyond* the requirements of minimum harmonisation directives *without* an evaluation of the fairness of that "commercial practice" within the meaning of the 2005 Directive are inconsistent with the 2005 Directive; in particular, national law is not entitled to add to the list of commercial practices provided by Annex 1 of the 2005 Directive which "shall in all circumstances be regarded as unfair".[1057] As will be seen in relation to the regulation of unfair contract terms under the Consumer Rights Act 2015, the relationship which the 2005 Directive envisages between its own fully harmonised requirements and other more particular, minimum harmonisation directives can cause problems for national

---

the operation of air services in the Community [2008] O.J. L293/3 art.23 as "*lex specialis*" in relation to the general rules in the Directive 2005/29/EC and Directive 2011/83/EU. (This point was not referred to by the CJEU in its decision of September 18, 2014.) See also above, para.38-111, discussing *Citroën Commerce GmbH v Zentralvereinigung des Kraffahrzeuggewerbes zur Aufrechterhaltung lauteren Wettbewerbs eV (ZLW)* (C-476/14) July 7, 2016 at paras 44–46.

[1055] Orlando (2011) *European Review of Contract Law* 25 at 50–51 (emphases omitted), above, para.38-111.

[1056] 2005 Directive art.3(5); *European Commission v Belgium* (C-421/12) of July 10, 2014 at [73]. This permission was subject to a condition that the measures were "essential to ensure that consumers are adequately protected against unfair commercial practices and must be proportionate to the attainment of this objective". This transitional period was not extended as was foreseen as possible by the 2005 Directive art.3(5), third sentence: EU Commission, First Report on the application of Directive 2005/29/EC of the European Parliament and of the Council of 11 May 2005 concerning unfair business-to-consumer commercial practices in the internal market, etc. COM(2013) 139 final, para.2.4 (stating that no such extension should be made).

[1057] 2005 Directive art.5(5), recital 17; *Zentral sur Bekämpfung unlauteren Weebewerbs eV v Plus Warenhandelsgessellschaft mbH* (C-304/08) EU:C:2010:12, [2010] E.C.R. I-00217 at [45]; *Wamo BVBA v JBC NV* (C-288/10) EU:C:2011:443, [2011] E.C.R. I-5835 at [37].

implementing measures which go beyond the controls which these directives require.[1058]

Scheme of control of the 2005 Directive   Under the 2005 Directive, there are   **38-163**
three main ways in which a commercial practice is to be held unfair. First, there is
a general test of an unfair commercial practice where:

"(a)   it is contrary to the requirements of professional diligence, and
(b)   it materially distorts or is likely to materially distort the economic behaviour with
regard to the product of the average consumer whom it reaches or to whom it is addressed, or of the average member of the group when a commercial practice is
directed to a particular group of consumers."[1059]

The Directive then defines or explains most of the elements of this general evaluative test.[1060] Secondly, the 2005 Directive identifies two commercial practices
which "in particular ... shall be unfair": misleading commercial practices (whether
constituted by action or omission) and aggressive commercial practices.[1061] Thirdly,
the 2005 Directive sets out a list of "those commercial practices which shall in all
circumstances be regarded as unfair",[1062] without, that is, any "case-by-case" evaluation of the practice under the earlier tests,[1063] though the list itself divides these
examples between "misleading commercial practices"[1064] and "aggressive commercial practices".[1065]

Enforcement   Following its broad declaration that "unfair commercial practices   **38-164**
shall be prohibited",[1066] the 2005 Directive requires Member States to put in place
"adequate and effective means" to enforce compliance with its provisions and to
lay down penalties for the infringement of national provisions implementing its
requirements.[1067] Moreover, the 2005 Directive adds itself to the list of legislation
which attract the cross-border injunctive relief under the Consumer Injunctions
Directive and the Regulation on Consumer Protection Co-operation.[1068]

[1058] Below, paras 38-421—38-426.
[1059] 2005 Directive art.5(2)(a) and (b).
[1060] 2005 Directive art.2 (definitions); art.5(3) (explaining the material distortion of the economic
behaviour of the average consumer).
[1061] 2005 Directive arts 5(4), 6–8.
[1062] 2005 Directive art.5(5); Annex I.
[1063] 2005 Directive recital 17; *Zentrale sur Bekämpfung unlauteren Weebewerbs eV v Plus Warenhandelsgessellschaft mbH* (C-304/08) EU:C:2010:12, [2010] E.C.R. I-00217 at para.45.
[1064] 2005 Directive Annex I points 1–23.
[1065] 2005 Directive Annex I points 24–31.
[1066] 2005 Directive art.5(1).
[1067] 2005 Directive arts 11 and 13.
[1068] 2005 Directive art.16; Directive 98/27 on injunctions for the protection of consumers' interests
[1998] O.J. L166/51 (itself repealed and replaced by Directive 2009/22/EC on injunctions for the
protection of consumers' interests [2009] O.J. L110/30); Regulation (EC) 2006/2004 on cooperation between national authorities responsible for the enforcement of the consumer protection law
[2004] O.J. L364/1. Regulation (EC) 2006/2004 is repealed and replaced with effect from January
17, 2020 by Regulation (EU) 2017/2394 of the European Parliament and of the Council of 12
December 2017 on cooperation between national authorities responsible for the enforcement of
consumer protection laws and repealing Regulation (EC) No 2006/2004 O.J. L 345/1. The
significance of this addition is explained below, para.38-171.

(c)   The General Scheme of the 2008 Regulations

38-165   **Faithful implementation of the 2005 Directive**   When enacted in 2008, the Consumer Protection from Unfair Trading Regulations followed very faithfully the scope and pattern of the controls of unfair commercial practices required by the 2005 Directive[1069] and repealed or amended a number of primary and secondary UK legislative provisions so as to conform to the Directive's general standard of full harmonisation.[1070] This faithful implementation was continued when the Regulations were amended in 2014 so as to create the consumer's new rights to redress, although some amendments were also made to the definitions applicable both to the existing regime and to the new provisions.[1071] So, reg.3 provides that "unfair commercial practices are prohibited"[1072] and provides a general test according to which:

> "A commercial practice is unfair if—
>
> (a)   it contravenes the requirements of professional diligence; and
> (b)   it materially distorts or is likely to materially distort the economic behaviour of the average consumer with regard to the product."[1073]

Regulation 3 also provides that:

> "A commercial practice is unfair if—
> (a)   it is a misleading action under the provisions of regulation 5;
> (b)   it is a misleading omission under the provisions of regulation 6;
> (c)   it is aggressive under the provisions of regulation 7; or
> (d)   it is listed in Schedule 1."

In this way, the Regulations reflect exactly the ways in which a commercial practice is to be held unfair under the 2005 Directive.[1074]

38-166   **"Commercial practice"**   Under the 2008 Regulations:

> "'... commercial practice" means any act, omission, course of conduct, representation or commercial communication (including advertising and marketing) by a trader, which is directly connected with the promotion, sale or supply of a product to or from consumers,

---

[1069] 2008 Regulations regs 3–7. The main definitional provisions are contained in reg.2.

[1070] 2008 Regulations reg.30(1); Schs 2 and 4.

[1071] See below, para.38-168. The most important amendment was the redefinition of "consumer" so as to extend the protection of the 2008 Regulations to "individuals acting for purposes that are wholly *or mainly* outside that individual's business": 2008 Regulations reg.2(1) "consumer". cf. above, paras 38-036—38-038.

[1072] 2008 Regulations reg.3(1).

[1073] 2008 Regulations reg.3(3). On this general test see *Deroo-Blanquart v Sony Europe Ltd* (C-310/15) of September 7, 2016, referring to art.5 of the 2005 Directive.

[1074] 2005 Directive art.5. The 2005 Directive art.5(4)(a) treats misleading actions and misleading omissions as examples of a single category of misleading commercial practices. Sch.1 of the 2008 Regulations lists 31 "commercial practices which are in all circumstances considered unfair". For the interpretation of one example of these prohibited practices by the CJEU see *"4finance" UAB v Valstybinė vartotojų teisių* (C-515/12) of April 3, 2014; *Loterie Nationale-National Loterij NV van publiek recht v Adriaensen, De Kesel and The Right Frequency VZW* (C-667/15) of December 15, 2016 (concerning 2005 Directive Annex I point 14 implemented by 2008 Regulations Sch.1 para.14 (pyramid promotional schemes)).

whether occurring before, during or after a commercial transaction (if any) in relation to a product.'[1075]

This definition follows closely the 2005 Directive[1076] with the qualification that it concerns behaviour "by a trader, which is directly connected with the promotion, sale or supply of a product *to or from* consumers".[1077] If or to the extent to which the 2005 Directive does not itself cover commercial practices consumer *to* a trader,[1078] to this extent the 2008 Regulations extend their prohibitions beyond the scope of the Directive.[1079] In the case of the consumer's rights to redress, the 2008 Regulations proscribe the circumstances in which this extension applies.[1080]

"Commercial practice" and isolated events   Can a commercial practice consist **38-167** of an isolated event, for example, a single false statement inducing a contract or must it form part of a wider scheme? The definition of "commercial practice" could be read as concerned with the nature of the act or omission and not with whether it needs to be repeated, or part of a scheme, in order to amount to a practice and, as has been noted, the Court of Justice of the EU has held that the definition of "commercial practice" in the 2005 Directive is "particularly wide",[1081] a width that is linked to the main purposes of the Directive in creating a fully-harmonised system of fair competition as well as consumer protection throughout the EU.[1082] In terms of English authority, while the Crown Court earlier held that a misrepresentation that relates to only one consumer and one contract will not amount to a "practice" within the meaning of the 2008 Regulations,[1083] the Court of Appeal held in *R. v X Ltd* the Crown Court's reasoning in the case to be unpersuasive[1084]: a commercial practice can be derived from a single incident, this finding textual support in the reference in the definition to *"any act ... by a trader which is directly connected with the* promotion, sale or *supply of a product"*[1085] and in the Court of Justice's view

---

[1075] 2008 Regulations reg.2(1) "commercial practice" and cf. above, para.38-160 on the CJEU's interpretation of this notion.

[1076] The definition of "commercial practice" in reg.2(1) combines the definition of "business-to-consumer commercial practices" in art.2(d) of the 2005 Directive, with art.3(1)'s definition of the scope of the Directive, with the clarification that there is no need for a commercial transaction to have been made.

[1077] 2008 Regulations reg.2(1) (emphasis added).

[1078] On which see above, para.38-047.

[1079] It is submitted that this extension of the scheme of the 2005 Directive is therefore compatible with its general requirement of "full harmonisation" as, on the narrower view of the scope of the 2005 Directive taken by the European Commission, consumer-to-business commercial practices fall outside the 2005 Directive's scope and therefore beyond the force of this requirement: cf. above, para.38-023. On such an extension beyond the scope of a "full harmonisation" directive, see above, para.38-025.

[1080] 2008 Regulations reg.27A(2)(b), below, para.38-177.

[1081] *VTB-VAB NV Total Belgium NV* (C-261/07 and C-299/07) EU:C:2009:244, [2009] E.C.R. I-2949 at para.49; *Mediaprint Zeitungs- und Zeitschriftenverlag GmbH & Co KG v "Österreich"-Zeitungsverlag GmbH* (C-540/08) EU:C:2010:660, [2010] E.C.R. I-10909 at para.17; *Zentrale sur Bekämpfung unlauteren Weebewerbs eV v Plus Warenhandelsgessellschaft mbH* (C-304/08) EU:C:2010:12, [2010] E.C.R. I-00217 at para.36; *Wamo BVBA v JBC NV* (C-288/10) EU:C:2011:443, [2011] E.C.R. I-5835 at para.33; *Pereničovà v SOS finance, spol. sro* (C-453/10) EU:C:2012:144, at para.38.

[1082] Above, para.38-159.

[1083] *R. (on the application of Tower Hamlets LBC) v Steele* [2012] C.T.L.C. 109.

[1084] *R. v X Ltd* [2013] EWCA Crim 818, [2014] 1 W.L.R. 591 at [24].

[1085] [2013] EWCA Crim 818 at [22] (emphasis added by Court of Appeal).

that the definition of "commercial practice" in the Directive is wide.[1086] On the other hand, the Court of Appeal considered that the question whether a single incident can constitute, or perhaps better, can reflect a commercial practice will depend on the circumstances: "the concept is concerned with systems"[1087] and, while "a single failing (or perhaps more than one failing) to one customer may not be sufficient", on the facts the jury was entitled to find that there was a failure in the process.[1088] However, this English case-law has been overtaken by the decision of the Court of Justice of the EU in *UPC Magyarország*.[1089] In that case, a provider of cable television services (the trader) had informed a customer (the consumer) that the service for which he had paid finished on a particular date, but by reason of "a simple clerical error" gave the consumer the wrong date. As a result, the consumer terminated the contract after the end of the period already paid for and was charged an amount for the remaining period, even though he had contracted for the provision of a cable service from another provider. The Hungarian National Consumer Protection Authority brought proceedings against the trader on the basis that its provision of erroneous information was a "misleading commercial practice", but the trader argued that an "isolated administrative error relating to a single client" could not constitute a "commercial practice" within the meaning of the 2005 Directive. In this respect, the Court of Justice referred to its earlier case-law on the "particularly wide" character of the Directive's definition of "commercial practice",[1090] and noted that:

"… the sole criterion referred to in [art.2(d) of the Directive] is that the trader's practice must be directly connected with the promotion, sale or supply of a product or service to consumers."[1091]

Having held that the provision of misleading information by a trader as part of an after-sales service to a consumer satisfies all the elements of a "misleading action" under the Directive,[1092] the Court of Justice observed that:

"In this regard, it should be stated that the fact that the action of the professional concerned took place on only one occasion and affected only one single consumer is immaterial in this context.

Neither the definitions set out in Articles 2(c) and (d), 3(1) and 6(1) of the Unfair Commercial Practices Directive nor the latter, considered as a whole, contain any indication that the act or omission on the part of the professional must be recurrent or must concern more than one consumer."

In the light of the need to protect consumers which underlies that directive, those

---

[1086] [2013] EWCA Crim 818 at [26] referring to *Zentrale sur Bekämpfung unlauteren Weebewerbs eV v Plus Warenhandelsgessellschaft mbH* (C-304/08) EU:C:2010:12, [2010] E.C.R. I-00217 at para.36.

[1087] [2013] EWCA Crim 818 at [23].

[1088] [2013] EWCA Crim 818 at [33].

[1089] *Nemzeti Fogyasztóvédelmi Hatóság v UPC Magyarország* (C-388/13) of April 16, 2015 ("*UPC Magyarország* (C-388/13)"). cf. *Pereničovà v SOS finance, spol. sro* (C-453/10) EU:C:2012:144 at para.41, where the CJEU held that "commercial practice" included the indication in an individual credit agreement of an APR lower than the real rate which therefore constitutes false information as to the total cost of the credit and hence the price", without requiring explicitly that this false indication formed part of a wider practice on the part of the creditor.

[1090] *UPC Magyarország* (C-388/13) para.34.

[1091] *UPC Magyarország* (C-388/13) para.35.

[1092] 2005 Directive art.2(c), 3(1) and 6(1); recital 13; *UPC Magyarország* (C-388/13) paras 36–40.

provisions cannot be interpreted as imposing conditions of that kind where they do not even set out such conditions explicitly.[1093] Moreover, according to the Court of Justice, the contrary view would have "serious disadvantages".[1094] First, a requirement of frequency of acts or number of consumers affected without any threshold to determine whether an act or omission would come within the scope of the Directive would threaten its compatibility with the principle of legal certainty; and, secondly, it would be extremely difficult for the consumer to establish that other individuals had been harmed by that same trader.[1095] On the other hand, the frequency of the unfair commercial practice complained would be relevant to any sanction attached to that practice by national law in fulfilment of its duty to impose penalties which are "effective, proportionate and dissuasive".[1096] In conclusion, it is submitted, therefore, that the decision of the Court of Justice in *UPC Magyarország* makes clear that an isolated act or omission by a trader may constitute an unfair commercial practice within the meaning of the 2005 Directive and this view should be followed by English courts rather than the approach of the Court of Appeal in *R. v X Ltd.*[1097]

Other definitions The 2008 Regulations follow the 2005 Directive in defining a   **38-168**
number of the important elements of their controls.[1098] So, *"product"* refers to goods, a service, digital content, immoveable property, and rights or obligations".[1099] And:

> "… 'professional diligence' means the standard of special skill and care which a trader may reasonably be expected to exercise towards consumers which is commensurate with either—
>
> (a)   honest market practice in the trader's field of activity, or
> (b)   the general principle of good faith in the trader's field of activity." [1100]

[1093] *UPC Magyarország* (C-388/13) paras 41–43 citing, as regards the final point, *CHS Tour Services GmbH v Team4 Travel GmbH* (C-435/11) of September 19, 2013.

[1094] *UPC Magyarország* (C-388/13) para.44.

[1095] *UPC Magyarország* (C-388/13) paras 45 and 46. The reference to the *consumer* establishing that other individuals have been harmed looks inappropriate in the context of the 2005 Directive, which does not seek to establish any *rights* for consumers against the trader, but is concerned rather to prohibit certain categories of actions and omissions of traders: see above, para.38-157. This is confirmed by the nature of the national proceedings in *UPC Magyarország* (C-388/13), which were brought by the Hungarian National Authority for Consumer Protection at the request of the individual consumer affected by the trader's "practice" and resulted in the imposition of a fine on the trader. Indeed, this aspect of the 2005 Directive was later emphasised in the CJEU's judgment (at para.56).

[1096] 2005 Directive arts 11 and 13; *UPC Magyarország* (C-388/13) at para.57; *Köck v Schutzverband gegen unlauteren Wettbewerb* (C-206/11) of January 17, 2013 para.44. The CJEU also held that the unintentional nature of the trader's actions, whether or not it has caused the consumer any harm and whether the consumer could have obtained correct information elsewhere, are not relevant to the question whether the trader has committed a misleading commercial practice, though the first two of these would be relevant to the question of an appropriate penalty: *UPC Magyarország* (C-388/13) at paras 47–54, 58.

[1097] [2013] EWCA Crim 818, above.

[1098] The definitions are contained in 2005 Directive art.2.

[1099] 2008 Regulations reg.2(1) "product", which also makes special provision for this purpose for cases where a trader demands payment from a consumer in full or partial settlement of C's liabilities, where the "product" is to be treated as that full or partial settlement: 2008 Regulations reg.2(1A) and (1B). As will be explained, there are restrictions on the definition of "product" for the purposes of the consumer's rights to civil redress: 2008 Regulations regs 27C and 27D, below, para.38-176. The definition of "product" in the 2005 Directive is found in art.2(b).

[1100] 2008 Regulations reg.2(1) "professional diligence"; 2005 Directive art.2(h).

However, as earlier noted, the definitions of "consumer" and "trader" were refined on the amendment of the 2008 Regulations in 2014, so that:

"... 'consumer' means an individual acting for purposes that are wholly or mainly outside that individual's business."

"... 'trader' means a person acting for purposes relating to that person's business, whether acting personally or through another person acting in the trader's name or on the trader's behalf."[1101]

And trader "includes a person acting in the name of or on behalf of a trader" except for the purposes of Pt 4A's rights of civil redress.[1102] Finally, the 2008 Regulations define "transactional decision" for their *general* purposes as:

"... any decision taken by a consumer, whether it is to act or to refrain from acting, concerning—
   (a) whether, how and on what terms to purchase, make payment in whole or in part for, retain or dispose of a product; or
   (b) whether, how and on what terms to exercise a contractual right in relation to a product." [1103]

As will be seen, however, this definition does not apply for the purposes of the consumers' rights to redress.[1104]

38-169 **"Average consumer"** As noted above,[1105] the idea of the "average consumer" is drawn by the 2005 Directive from the case-law of the European Court of Justice and explained quite elaborately in its text and recitals.[1106] The 2008 Regulations follow the Directive and thereby adopt a variable objective approach. The starting point is that:

"In determining the effect of a commercial practice on the average consumer where the practice reaches or is addressed to a consumer or consumers account shall be taken of the material characteristics of such an average consumer including his being reasonably well informed, reasonably observant and circumspect."[1107]

However, where a commercial practice is "directed to a particular group of consumers, a reference to the average consumer shall be read as referring to the average member of that group"[1108] and:

"In determining the effect of a commercial practice on the average consumer—
   (a) where a clearly identifiable group of consumers is particularly vulnerable to the practice or the underlying product because of their mental or physical infirmity,

---

[1101] 2008 Regulations reg.2(1) "consumer" and "trader" and see above, paras 38-032 et seq. and 38-050 et seq.
[1102] 2008 Regulations reg.2(1) "trader".
[1103] 2008 Regulations reg.2(1) "transactional decision"; 2005 Directive art.2(k).
[1104] 2008 Regulations reg.27B(2), below, para.38-183.
[1105] Above, paras 38-044—38-045.
[1106] 2005 Directive recitals 18 and 19; art.5(2)(b), 5(3).
[1107] 2008 Regulations reg.2(2).
[1108] 2008 Regulations reg.2(4).

age or credulity in a way which the trader could reasonably be expected to foresee, and

(b) where the practice is likely to materially distort the economic behaviour only of that group,

a reference to the average consumer shall be read as referring to the average member of that group."[1109]

This final provision is stated as being without prejudice to "the common and legitimate advertising practice of making exaggerated statements which are not meant to be taken literally".[1110] Although this is not set out in the 2008 Regulations, recital 18 of the 2005 Directive explains that it:

"... takes as a benchmark the average consumer, who is reasonably well-informed and reasonably observant and circumspect, *taking into account social, cultural and linguistic factors*",[1111]

adding that:

"... [t]he average consumer test is not a statistical test. National courts and authorities will have to exercise their own faculty of judgement, having regard to the case-law of the Court of Justice, to determine the typical reaction of the average consumer in a given case.[1112]"

Criminal offences   Part 3 of the 2008 Regulations creates a series of criminal of-   **38-170**
fences in traders where they knowingly or recklessly engage in a commercial practice which fails the general test of unfairness,[1113] where the practice constitutes a misleading action,[1114] a misleading omission[1115] or an aggressive commercial practice,[1116] or where it consists of a commercial practice prohibited in all circumstances.[1117] These crimes may, on summary conviction, lead to a fine not exceeding the statutory maximum, or, on conviction on indictment, to a fine or imprisonment for a term not exceeding two years or both.[1118] In principle, a person convicted of an offence under the Regulations may be ordered to pay compensation to the victim (the consumer),[1119] but this power has been interpreted as requiring evidence of loss and has in general been little used.[1120] The 2008 Regulations

---

[1109] 2008 Regulations reg.2(5).

[1110] 2008 Regulations reg.2(6).

[1111] Emphasis added. See also *Konsumentombudsmannen v Ving Sverige AB* (C-122/10) of May 12, 2011 paras 21–22; *Criminal Proceedings against Canal Digital Denmark A/S* (C-611/14) of October 26, 2016 at para.39.

[1112] And see *Criminal Proceedings against Canal Digital Denmark A/S* (C-611/14) at para.39.

[1113] 2008 Regulations reg.8 (subject to the conditions there specified).

[1114] 2008 Regulations reg.9 referring to reg.5, but excluding the case foreseen by reg.5(3)(b).

[1115] 2008 Regulations reg.10 referring to reg.6.

[1116] 2008 Regulations reg.11 referring to reg.7.

[1117] 2008 Regulations reg.12 referring to Sch.1, but excluding for these purposes the commercial practices foreseen by Sch.1 paras 11 ("advertorial") and 28 (including in an advertisement a direct exhortation to children to buy advertised products or persuade their parents or other adults to buy advertised products for them).

[1118] 2008 Regulations reg.13. Until March 12, 2015 the maximum fine available on summary conviction was £5,000 (level 5 on the standard scale), but on that date this was changed to an unlimited fine by the Legal Aid, Sentencing and Punishment of Offenders Act 2012 s.85.

[1119] Powers of Criminal Courts (Sentencing) Act 2000 s.130(4).

[1120] Law Commission, Scottish Law Commission, *Consumer Redress for Misleading and Aggressive Practices* (2012) Law Com No.332; Scot Law Com No.226, Cm 8323 para.2.44, 2.46.

make further provision incidental to the creation of these offences,[1121] including for a defence of due diligence.[1122]

38-171 **Enforcement by authorities** Apart from these criminal offences, the 2008 Regulations are buttressed by two systems of enforcement of their prohibition of unfair commercial practices. First, Pt 4 of the Regulations sets out a special scheme of enforcement, under which every weights and measures authority has a duty to enforce the regulations, and the CMA has a power to do so,[1123] in both cases taking into account the desirability of encouraging control of unfair commercial practices by such established means as it considers appropriate in all the circumstances.[1124] These enforcement authorities have the power to make test purchases and powers of entry and investigation.[1125] Secondly, the 2008 Regulations amended the Enterprise Act 2002 so as to include the 2005 Directive in the list of directives and regulations which give rise to a "Community infringement" and also to designate the 2008 Regulations as the specified UK law so as to apply Pt 8 of the 2002 Act for their purposes.[1126] As a result, where an infringement of the prohibition against unfair commercial practices by a trader harms the collective interest of consumers,[1127] an "enforcer" can apply to the court for an enforcement order, subject to the conditions set out earlier.[1128] The 2008 Regulations also provide that, where an enforcer has brought an application for an enforcement order under Pt 8 of the 2002 Act against a trader in respect of a contravention of the requirements of the 2005 Directive, the court has a power to require that trader to provide evidence as to the accuracy of any factual claim made as part of a commercial practice by that trader.[1129] Where the trader fails to do so or fails to do so adequately, "the court may consider that the factual claim is inaccurate".[1130]

[1121] 2008 Regulations reg.14 (time limit for prosecution); reg.15 (offences committed by bodies of persons); reg.16 (offence due to the default of another person); reg.17 (due diligence defence); reg.18 (innocent publication of advertisement defence).

[1122] 2008 Regulations reg.17.

[1123] 2008 Regulations reg.19(1) and (1A). In Northern Ireland, this duty is owed by Department of Enterprise, Trade and Investment in Northern Ireland. The duty to enforce does not extend to the consumer's rights to redress in Pt 4A of the Regulations: reg.19(1).

[1124] 2008 Regulations reg.19(4).

[1125] There powers were earlier contained in the 2008 Regulations regs 20–25, but as from October 1, 2015 (SI 2015/1630 art.3(h)) these provisions were revoked and replaced by more general provision in the Consumer Rights Act 2015 s.77, Sch.5 (para.10 of which refers to the enforcement of the 2008 Regulations reg.19(1) and (1A). (Commencement No.3, Transitional Provisions, Savings and Consequential Amendments) Order 2015 (SI 2015/1630) art.5, Sch.2 para.115 subject to transitional provisions set out in art.8.)

[1126] 2008 Regulations reg.26; Enterprise Act 2002 Sch.13 9C; Enterprise Act 2002 (Part 8 Community Infringements Specified UK Laws) Order 2003 (SI 2003/1374) Sch.1 para.1 as inserted by 2008 Regulations Sch.2 Pt 2 para.100.

[1127] Enterprise Act 2002 ss.211(1)(c), 212(1). See above, para.38-133.

[1128] Enterprise Act 2002 ss.214–218 (as amended) and see above, paras 38-133—38-134.

[1129] Enterprise Act 2002 s.218A(1) and (2) as inserted by 2008 Regulations reg.27.

[1130] Enterprise Act 2002 s.218A(3) as inserted by 2008 Regulations reg.27.

(d)   The Rights to Civil Redress for Consumers

(i)   Introduction

The Law Commissions' recommendations   The rights to redress for consum-   **38-172**
ers introduced by amendment of the 2008 Regulations by the 2014 Regulations
resulted from recommendations of the Law Commissions in their report *Consumer
Redress for Misleading and Aggressive Practices* (the "Law Commissions'
Report").[1131] The Law Commissions considered that there were considerable social
problems not being addressed properly by existing law, expressing a particular
concern with the extent to which vulnerable persons, such as the elderly or the
disabled, were being targeted by "scams" or pressured into buying goods or
services.[1132] The Law Commissions identified two main deficiencies in the existing law. First, in the case of misleading actions by traders, the law governing
remedies for misrepresentation is "fragmented, complex and unclear",[1133] with
particular uncertainty as to the relationship between rescission and damages[1134] and
difficulties for consumers in the valuation of their loss.[1135] Secondly, in the case of
aggressive commercial practices, the law governing remedies for duress, undue
influence and (especially) unconscionable conduct is unclear and restrictive, being "not readily accessible to non-lawyers"[1136] and leaving important gaps in protection for the victim of "scams", there being in particular no clear right to damages
to victims of duress.[1137] The Law Commissions' purpose in making their recommendations was therefore to "simplify the consumer remedies against misleading
practices and to improve protection against aggressive practices".[1138] However,
contrary to the views of consumer groups and the Office of Fair Trading,[1139] the Law
Commissions recommended that the new rights be "targeted" in the sense that they
should not arise in respect of all unfair commercial practices prohibited by the 2008
Regulations. In particular, the new rights should apply only in the case of misleading actions and aggressive practices: as a result, a misleading *omission* and a commercial practice found unfair under the general test in the 2008 Regulations should
not give rise to the new rights to redress[1140]; and a commercial practice listed as
unfair in all circumstances would not do so unless it would be likely to cause the
average consumer to enter into a contract or make a payment which they would not
otherwise have done.[1141] As this further indicates, the new rights should not arise

---

[1131] Law Com No.332; Scot Law Com No.226 (2012); Cm 8323. See also Department for Business In-
novation & Skills, Misleading and Aggressive Practices—A New Private Right for Consumers,
Government response to consultation on the draft regulations (April 2014) p.3 noting that the
Government had in their draft regulations accepted almost all the Commissions' recommendations.

[1132] Law Commissions' Report (2012) SS.3 and 21, paras 1.13, 1.15, 3.50, 3.55, 4.22 and 8.58. An
example of such a case is *R. v X Ltd* [2013] EWCA Crim 818, [2014] 1 W.L.R. 591.

[1133] Law Commissions' Report (2012) S.12, p.x.

[1134] In particular, under Misrepresentation Act 1967 s.2(2), on which see Vol.I, paras 7-105—7-111.

[1135] Law Commissions' Report (2012), para.4.15.

[1136] Law Commissions' Report (2012) S.16, p.x.

[1137] Law Commissions' Report (2012), paras 3.49 et seq. On this law see Vol.I, Ch.8 and especially
para.8-057.

[1138] Law Commissions' Report (2012), para.1.4.

[1139] Law Commissions' Report (2012), para.1.37.

[1140] The general test was seen as "so uncertain as to be intrinsically unsuited to form the basis of private
law rights": Law Commissions' Report (2012), para.2.15.

[1141] Law Commissions' Report (2012), paras 4.46 and 5.5.

merely as a result of a misleading or aggressive practice, as they should be subject to a condition that they contributed to the conclusion of a contract or the making of a payment.[1142] These restrictions were seen by the Law Commissions as needed as wider availability could generate "unpredictable" costs on traders".[1143] In terms of the new remedies for consumers arising from misleading or aggressive practices, the Law Commissions recommended a two-tiered approach: the first tier would provide the consumer with a short-lived right to unwind the contract or payment, with full refund of any payments made; and, where the goods or services have been fully consumed, where there has been delay or where the consumer chooses to keep the contract, a right to a discount based on "pre-set bands" of percentages of the price of the contract; the second tier would provide a right to damages recoverable only on proof of loss or harm by the consumer.[1144]

38-173 **The structure of the new law** Rather than introducing primary legislation, as foreseen by the Law Commissions,[1145] the new rights for consumers were introduced by amendment of the 2008 Regulations by the 2014 Regulations.[1146] Despite a principal purpose of the new law being to introduce a new simple regime for consumers, the new law is itself complex and bears a complex relationship with the general law of misrepresentation, duress and undue influence. Nevertheless, the fundamental distinction made by the 2008 Regulations (as so amended) is between general conditions for the availability of the new rights to redress[1147] and particular conditions, attributes and consequences of the three different rights to redress: the right to unwind; the right to a discount; and the right to damages.[1148] In order to enjoy a right to redress, a consumer must establish that both sets of conditions are satisfied.[1149] The 2008 Regulations (as so amended) then make consequential provision for the procedural expression of the new rights to redress and on the relationship of the new rights to existing law.[1150] This section will follow this broad structure.

38-174 **No duty on court to raise issue of consumer's rights to redress** The Court of Justice of the EU has recognised that national courts may have a duty to raise of their own motion the existence of a right for consumers in national law which reflects EU legislation for the protection of consumers.[1151] While the rights to redress in Pt 4A of the 2008 Regulations are tied to the commission by a trader of certain unfair commercial practices whose prohibition reflects the Unfair Commercial Practices Directive 2005 (whose purpose was, inter alia, to protect consumers), that Directive does not provide for any rights for consumers such as are contained in Pt 4A.[1152] As a result, the Pt 4A rights to redress are not rights in EU law and do not,

---

[1142] Law Commissions' Report (2012), para.5.6.
[1143] Law Commissions' Report (2012), para.4.42 and see paras 4.57–4.63.
[1144] Law Commissions' Report (2012), paras 8.24 et seq.
[1145] Law Commissions' Report (2012), para.5.16.
[1146] Consumer Protection (Amendment) Regulations 2014 (SI 2014/870). On the consumer's rights to redress under the 2008 Regulations, see Bant and Paterson (2018) 80 M.L.R. 895.
[1147] 2008 Regulations regs 27A–27D.
[1148] 2008 Regulations regs 27E–27J.
[1149] 2008 Regulations reg.27A(1).
[1150] 2008 Regulations regs 27K–27L.
[1151] Above, paras 38-019—38-021.
[1152] Above, paras 38-159—38-160.

therefore, attract the case-law of the Court of Justice which may impose duties in national courts to raise the rights of consumers of their own motion.

Temporal application of the new law The provisions of the 2014 Regulations   **38-175** amending the 2008 Regulations and creating the new rights to redress came into force on October 1, 2014 "and apply in relation to contracts entered into, or payments made, on or after that date".[1153]

(ii) General Conditions for the Availability of the Rights to Redress

Introduction In very broad terms, Pt 4A of the 2008 Regulations requires that the   **38-176** consumer must establish that a misleading action or aggressive commercial practice by a trader was a significant factor in the consumer's decision to enter a contract or make a payment to the trader in respect of a product supplied. This broad picture is expressed by subjecting the general availability of the consumer's rights to redress to three conditions: (i) the existence of a contract between the trader and the consumer or a payment made by the consumer to the trader; (ii) the commission of a misleading action or aggressive practice by the trader or by a "producer" of goods or digital content[1154]; and (iii) that the prohibited practice is a significant factor in the consumer's decision to enter the contract or make the payment.[1155] As will be seen, the first two of these conditions are the subject of considerable nuance.[1156] Moreover, following the recommendations of the Law Commissions,[1157] the 2008 Regulations qualify the general definition of "product"[1158] for the purposes of the Pt 4A rights by excluding from it immoveable property apart from an assured tenancy or a contract of lease for the supply of holiday accommodation[1159] and

---

[1153] SI 2014/870 reg.1(3). The 2014 Regulations reg.9's provisions making minor amendments to the Consumer Contracts (Information, Cancellation and Additional Charges) Regulations 2013 (SI 2013/ 3134) came into force on June 13, 2014 immediately before the latter Regulations themselves: 2014 Regulations reg.1(2). For the 2013 Regulations generally, see above, paras 38-061 et seq.

[1154] Defined as "data which are produced or supplied in digital form": 2008 Regulations reg.2(1) "digital content".

[1155] 2008 Regulations reg.27A(2), (4) and (6).

[1156] Below, paras 38-177—38-189.

[1157] Law Commissions Report (2012), paras 6.93–6.118. Their main reasons were that land transactions apart from residential leases are subject to a well-established and understood law of conveyancing, and consumers have access to redress schemes; in the case of financial services, there are already sophisticated mechanisms in place to protect consumers and the remedies they recommend may be unsuited to the considerable amounts of money which these services may involve. On the other hand, consumer credit agreements and debt collection should be included within the new scheme as they are often inextricably linked to the supply of goods and services and cause many problems.

[1158] The general definition is found in 2008 Regulations reg.2(1) "product", above, para.38-168.

[1159] 2008 Regulations reg.27C provides that "product" does not include "immoveable property other than a relevant lease", defining the latter in relation to England and Wales as an assured tenancy within the meaning of Pt I of the Housing Act 1988 or a lease under which accommodation is let as holiday accommodation, but then excluding leases granted by a private registered provider of social housing as defined by s.80(3)(a) of the Housing and Regeneration Act 2008 or by a registered social landlord as understood by Pt I of the Housing Act 1996, leases of a dwelling-house or part of a dwelling-house granted on payment of a premium calculated by reference to a percentage of the value of the dwelling-house or part of or the cost of providing it or under which the lessee (or the lessee's representatives) will or may be entitled to a sum calculated by reference, directly or indirectly, to the value of the dwelling-house or part and leases granted to a person as a result of the exercise by a local housing authority within the meaning of the Housing Act 1996 of its functions under Pt VII (homelessness) of that Act: 2008 Regulations reg.27D(1)–(3).

services provided in the course of carrying on a "regulated activity" within the meaning of the Financial Services and Markets Act 2000 other than where the service consists of the provision of credit for a transaction between the borrower and the lender or for a transaction between the borrower and a person other than the lender.[1160]

38-177 **First condition: contract or payment** As has been seen, the prohibition of unfair commercial practices in the 2008 Regulations applies where these practices materially distort or are likely materially to distort the economic behaviour of the average consumer with regard to the "product", understood very broadly.[1161] There is no requirement that the trader concludes a contract with a consumer or otherwise actually causes the consumer to take some other "transactional decision" with or for the benefit of the trader. This very broad approach reflects the general concern of the 2008 Regulations (reflecting the 2005 Directive) with the prevention of unfair commercial practices, rather than with "contract law". However, following the recommendations of the Law Commissions, the 2008 Regulations take here a much more restrictive approach, requiring that one of three types of transaction must have taken place between the trader and the consumer for a right to redress to be available. First, where:

"(a)   the consumer enters into a contract with a trader for the sale or supply of a product by the trader (a 'business to consumer contract')."[1162]

This is the broadest category of situation, applying to all contracts for the sale or supply by a trader to a consumer of a *product*, defined very broadly as "goods, a service, digital content, immoveable property, and rights or obligations",[1163] though with the restrictions on immoveable property and the exclusion of financial services as earlier explained.[1164]

[1160] 2008 Regulations reg.27D(1) excludes generally from the definition of "product" a service provided in the course of carrying on a "regulated activity" within the meaning of s.22 of the Financial Services and Markets Act 2000 (as illustrated by the list in Sch.2 of that Act), but then reg.27D(2) specifically saves from this exclusion "restricted-use credit agreements" as defined by the Financial Services and Markets Act 2000 (Regulated Activities) Order 2001 (Order 2001/544) art.60L(1) "restricted-use credit agreements" para.(a) or (b) (but *not* (c)), i.e. a credit agreement "to finance a transaction between the borrower and the lender, whether forming part of that agreement or not" or "to finance a transaction between the borrower and a person ('the supplier') other than the lender": cf. below, paras 39-027—39-028 on these two categories of "restricted-use credit agreement" and their significance under the Consumer Credit Act 1974 s.11(1). This saving provision is itself subject to an exception in the cases of agreements under which the obligation of the borrower to repay is secured by a legal or equitable mortgage on land (other than timeshare accommodation), "mortgage" including a charge for these purposes and "timeshare accommodation" meaning overnight accommodation which is the subject of a timeshare contract within the meaning of the Timeshare, Holiday Products, Resale and Exchange Contracts Regulations 2010 (SI 2010/2960) reg.7: 2008 Regulations reg.27D(3) and (4). Finally, it is expressly provided that Pt 4A of the 2008 Regulations (and therefore the consumer's rights to redress) may apply to the supply of a product even though that supply may constitute an activity within art.39F (debt-collecting) of the Financial Services and Markets Act 2000 (Regulated Activities) Order 2001: 2008 Regulations reg.27D(5).

[1161] Above, para.38-168.

[1162] 2008 Regulations reg.27A(2)(a).

[1163] 2008 Regulations reg.2(6), above, para.38-168.

[1164] 2008 Regulations regs 27D and 27E, above, para.38-176.

"(b)   the consumer enters into a contract with a trader for the sale of goods to the trader (a 'consumer to business contract')."[1165]

This situation applies to the converse situation of a "consumer to business contract", but its ambit is much more restricted than the first situation, as it concerns only sales of goods to the trader (such as the sale by a consumer of a second-hand car or jewellery) and, furthermore, is subject to a further restriction in that it does not apply where the trader supplies or agrees to supply a *product* to the consumer as well as agreeing to pay the consumer.[1166] Where a consumer enters a contract of part-exchange with a trader, for example, of a second-hand car, it is submitted that such a contract would fall within (a) as "a contract with a trader for the sale or supply of a product by the trader", even though it also involves the supply of goods by the consumer.

"(c)   the consumer makes a payment to a trader for the supply of a product (a 'consumer payment')."[1167]

The Law Commissions identified a real social problem in the extent to which unscrupulous traders and others harass consumers into paying debts, whether these are real or invented.[1168] In their view, debt collection following a consumer contract clearly falls within the scope of the 2008 Regulations' prohibitions, but the position as regards other circumstances (such as wheel-clamping charges, demands in respect of parking charges, requests for compensation for alleged copyright infringements and "civil recovery" against shoplifters) is less clear.[1169] The third situation described at (c) is restricted to payments to a trader for the supply of a product[1170] and therefore restricts the application of the rights to redress for consumers (notably, "unwinding the payment" and damages for any deception ("misleading statement") or harassment ("aggressive practice") to this situation.[1171]

Second condition: "prohibited practice"   Here, the 2008 Regulations require   **38-178** either that the "trader engages in a prohibited practice in relation to the product" or that, in the case of contracts of sale of goods or the supply of digital content, the "producer" does so in certain circumstances.[1172] For both purposes, the Regulations restrict "prohibited practice" to "misleading actions" under reg.5 and "aggressive commercial practices" under reg.7 and, following the Law Commissions' recommendations, therefore do not extend the availability of consumer rights to redress to commercial practices qualifying as unfair under the general test.[1173] In the case of commercial practices designated by the Regulations in general as unfair in all circumstances,[1174] the rights to redress are available only if the commercial practice in question satisfies the test for misleading action or aggressive practice.

[1165] 2008 Regulations reg.27A(2)(b).
[1166] 2008 Regulations reg.27A(3).
[1167] 2008 Regulations reg.27A(2)(c).
[1168] Law Commissions' Report (2012), para.4.34.
[1169] Law Commissions' Report (2012), para.4.35.
[1170] On the definition of "product" for these purposes, see above, para.38-176.
[1171] Below, paras 38-195 and 38-185.
[1172] 2008 Regulations reg.27A(4), and see below, paras 38 188—38-189.
[1173] 2008 Regulations reg.27B. See above, para.38-165 (on the general test) and para.38-172 (for the Law Commissions' views).
[1174] 2008 Regulations reg.3(4)(d); Sch.1, above, para.38-172 and cf. 38-163.

This means in particular that they must cause or be likely to cause the average consumer to take a transactional decision he would not have taken otherwise.[1175]

38-179 **Misleading actions** Under reg.5, a commercial practice may constitute a "misleading action" either under a very general test of its containing false or deceptive information[1176] or in relation to two special cases.[1177]

38-180 **False or deceptive information** This is the most important category. Regulation 5(2) provides that a commercial practice constitutes a "misleading action"

> "(a) if it contains false information and is therefore untruthful in relation to any of the matters in paragraph (4) or if it or its overall presentation in any way deceives or is likely to deceive the average consumer in relation to any of the matters in that paragraph, even if the information is factually correct; and
>
> (b) it causes or is likely to cause the average consumer to take a transactional decision he would not have taken otherwise."

The lists of matters referred to in reg.5(4) are:

> "(a) the existence or nature of the product;
> (b) the main characteristics of the product (as defined in paragraph 5);
> (c) the extent of the trader's commitments;
> (d) the motives for the commercial practice;
> (e) the nature of the sales process;
> (f) any statement or symbol relating to direct or indirect sponsorship or approval of the trader or the product;
> (g) the price or the manner in which the price is calculated;
> (h) the existence of a specific price advantage;
> (i) the need for a service, part, replacement or repair;
> (j) the nature, attributes and rights of the trader (as defined in paragraph 6);
> (k) the consumer's rights or the risks he may face."

The Regulations then provide details as to what is included in the "main characteristics of the product",[1178] and what are the "nature, attributes and rights" as far as concern the trader,[1179] and the "consumer's rights" for these purposes.[1180]

38-181 In *Canal Digital Denmark A/S*[1181] the Court of Justice of the EU considered whether art.6(1) of the 2005 Directive governing misleading actions (implemented in UK law by reg.5(2) of the 2008 Regulations) applies to a case where a trader provides television packages by subscription either on a monthly or on a six-monthly charge, but has particularly highlighted the monthly charge in its marketing, while the six-monthly charge is omitted entirely or presented only in a less conspicuous way.[1182] Having noted the significance of the "average consumer" to

---

[1175] 2008 Regulations regs 5(2)(b), 5(3) and 7(1)(b). Moreover, "transactional decision" is defined specially for these purposes: reg.27B(2), below, para.38-183.
[1176] 2008 Regulations reg.5(2) and see below, para.38-180.
[1177] 2008 Regulations reg.5(3) and see below, para.38-182.
[1178] 2008 Regulations reg.5(5).
[1179] 2008 Regulations reg.5(6).
[1180] 2008 Regulations reg.5(7).
[1181] *Criminal Proceedings against Canal Digital Denmark A/S* (C-611/14) October 26, 2016 ("*Canal Digital Denmark A/S* (C-611/14)").
[1182] *Canal Digital Denmark A/S* (C-611/14) at para.36.

whom the practice is addressed,[1183] the Court of Justice held that in determining whether commercial practices of this sort "deceive or are likely to deceive the average consumer in relation to the price" the national court must:

"... determine, having regard to all the relevant circumstances, whether the commercial communication concerned has the effect of suggesting to the average consumer an attractive price which, ultimately, is proven to be misleading."[1184]

For this purpose:

"... consideration may be given, where relevant, to the fact that offers for TV channels are characterised by a wide variety of proposals and combinations that are generally highly structured, both in terms of cost and content, resulting in a significant asymmetry of information that is likely to confuse consumers."[1185]

On the other hand, the Court of Justice noted that, unlike art.7's provisions governing misleading *omissions*, art.6(1) "contains no reference to limitations of space or time related to the communication medium used", so that:

"... time constraints that may apply to certain communication media, such as television commercials, cannot be taken into account when assessing whether a commercial practice is misleading under art.6(1)."[1186]

However, where the price of a "product" is divided into several components, one of which is emphasised in the marketing, while the other is omitted or presented less prominently, the average consumer may be led to a mistaken perception of the overall offer, particularly in that he is being offered a particularly advantageous price.[1187] This guidance on the proper approach to the interpretation and application of art.6(1) of the 2005 Directive makes clear that the *omission* of some information regarding an aspect of the "product" (there, its price) may form part of a misleading action rather than constituting only a misleading omission, thereby taking a broad interpretation of "misleading action" for this purpose, a position of particular significance for the purposes of the consumer's rights to redress in UK law, as these are available for misleading actions but not misleading omissions.[1188] The Court of Justice also identified an important difference between the two categories of misleading commercial practices (actions and omissions) as a matter of EU law, in that, where:

"... the medium used to communicate the commercial practice imposes limitations of space or time, these limitations and any measures taken by the trader to make the informa-

---

[1183] See above, paras 38-180 and 38-169.
[1184] *Canal Digital Denmark A/S* (C-611/14) at para.40.
[1185] *Canal Digital Denmark A/S* (C-611/14) at para.41.
[1186] *Canal Digital Denmark A/S* (C-611/14) at para.42.
[1187] *Canal Digital Denmark A/S* (C-611/14) at paras 43–44. The CJEU also explained that "the price is, in principle, a determining factor in the mind of the average consumer, when he has to make a transactional decision" (para.46), this being relevant to the requirement in art.6(1) that the relevant commercial practice must cause or be likely to cause the average consumer "to take a transactional decision that he would not have taken otherwise" (and see 2008 Regulations reg.5(2)(b), though note that in the Regulations "transactional decision" is defined specially for the purposes of the consumers rights to redress under Pt 4A: 2008 Regulations reg.27B(2) and see below, para.38-183).
[1188] Above, para.38-178.

tion available to consumers by other means shall be taken into account in deciding whether information has been omitted"

whereas no such allowance for the medium used is to be made as regards a misleading action.[1189] On the other hand, art.7(4) of the Directive makes special provision regarding certain categories of information (including as to price) in "invitations to purchase" whose omission "shall be regarded as material", whereas art.6 makes no similar provision regarding invitations to purchase for the purposes of misleading actions.[1190] Overall, therefore, the Court of Justice accepted that a particular commercial practice may constitute at the same time a misleading action *and* a misleading omission, subject to the particular conditions and taking account of the particular considerations set out by arts 6 and 7 of the 2005 Directive respectively.

38-182   The special cases   Reflecting the 2005 Directive,[1191] reg.5(3) identifies two special cases of a commercial practice constituting a "misleading action", viz where:

"(a)   it concerns any marketing of a product (including comparative advertising) which creates confusion with any products, trade marks, trade names or other distinguishing marks of a competitor; or

(b)   it concerns any failure by a trader to comply with a commitment contained in a code of conduct[1192] which the trader has undertaken to comply with, if—

(i)   the trader indicates in a commercial practice that he is bound by that code of conduct, and

(ii)   the commitment is firm and capable of being verified and is not aspirational, and it causes or is likely to cause the average consumer to take a transactional decision he would not have taken otherwise, taking account of its factual context and of all its features and circumstances."[1193]

38-183   Definitions: "transactional decision"   Both as regards the general test and the special cases, the general definitions of the Regulations apply (including as to "consumer"[1194] and "average consumer"[1195]), with the exception of "transactional decision" which is defined specially for the purposes of the availability of the rights to redress as:

"... any decision taken by a consumer to enter into a contract with a trader for the sale or supply of a product by the trader, or for the sale of goods to the trader, or to make a payment to a trader for the supply of a product."[1196]

This redefinition for the purposes of the rights to redress is necessary in order to link the definitions of misleading actions and aggressive practices to the circumstances governed by the first condition of the availability of these rights[1197]; the definition of "transactional decision" provided generally for the prohibition of

---

[1189] *Canal Digital Denmark A/S* (C-611/14) at paras 42 and 58–63.

[1190] *Canal Digital Denmark A/S* (C-611/14) at paras 52–58.

[1191] 2005 Directive art.6(2).

[1192] A "code of conduct" is defined by the 2008 Regulations reg.2 as: "an agreement or set of rules (which is not imposed by legal or administrative requirements), which defines the behaviour of traders who undertake to be bound by it in relation to one or more commercial practices or business sectors".

[1193] 2008 Regulations reg.5(3).

[1194] Above, para.38-168.

[1195] Above, para.38-169.

[1196] 2008 Regulations reg.27B(2).

[1197] 2008 Regulations reg.27A(2) and (3), above, para.38-177.

unfair commercial practices by the Regulations (following the Directive[1198]) is much wider[1199] and reflects their application to practices "before, during and after a commercial transaction (if any) in relation to a product".[1200]

Comparison with the law of misrepresentation   Overall, the types of behaviour **38-184** covered by "misleading action" as defined by reg.5 cover very many, though not all, the behaviour which may be the subject of a claim for misrepresentation under the general law. Under the general law, an actionable misrepresentation requires a false statement of fact or law and, in principle, this excludes false statements of opinion or future fact.[1201] This means that some pre-contractual statements by a trader may count as a misrepresentation even though they do not constitute a "misleading action" within the meaning of the 2008 Regulations (as not falling within the matters enumerated by reg.5(4) or the special cases).[1202] Conversely, some statements of intention may count as a misleading action under the 2008 Regulations, for example, a "failure by a trader to comply with a commitment contained in a code of conduct which the trader has undertaken to comply with"[1203] though they would not count as an actionable misrepresentation under the general law if at the time the contract was made the trader intended to comply with the code of conduct. Finally, if (contrary to the position adopted above) an isolated misrepresentation by a trader or its employee that was not part of a scheme or within the employee's actual authority[1204] does not constitute a "commercial practice",[1205] it would not fall within "prohibited practice" and could not give rise to the new rights to redress. This result would be the unforeseen consequence[1206] of using a legislative scheme designed for the prohibition of trader behaviour enforceable through administrative measures, court orders or penalties,[1207] not requiring the conclusion of any transaction,[1208] and specifically inapplicable to "contract law"[1209] as the basis of civil redress for individual consumers in respect of the particular contracts which they make with traders. Certainly, if "commercial practice" cannot extend (or cannot extend in the circumstances) to an isolated case of misrepresentation, then even in consumer cases the general law of misrepresentation will remain of importance.[1210]

Misleading omissions   Regulation 6 of the 2008 Regulations specifically includes **38-185** an "misleading omission" as an example of the unfair commercial practices which they prohibit, explaining that this includes situations where:

[1198] 2005 Directive art.2(k).
[1199] 2008 Regulations reg.2(1) "transactional decision".
[1200] 2008 Regulations reg.2(1) "commercial practice" above, para.38-166.
[1201] Vol.I, paras 7-007 et seq.
[1202] Above, paras 38-179—38-182.
[1203] 2008 Regulations reg.5(3)(b).
[1204] i.e. the employee did not have express, implied or "usual" authority: see above, paras 31-043 et seq.
[1205] cf. the discussion above, paras 38-167—38-168 as to the question whether a "commercial practice" may be found in relation to an isolated transaction.
[1206] The Law Commissions' Report appears to assume that "commercial practice" can apply to an isolated transaction: paras 2.10 and 2.11.
[1207] 2005 Directive arts 5(1); 11–13.
[1208] The definition of "commercial practice" refers to "before, during or after a commercial transaction (if any)": *R. v X Ltd* [2013] EWCA Crim 818 at [23]; 2005 Directive recital 13.
[1209] 2005 Directive art.3(2), above para.38-160.
[1210] This law will not be excluded: see below, para.38-208.

"(a)   the commercial practice omits material information,
(b)   the commercial practice hides material information,
(c)   the commercial practice provides material information in a manner which is unclear, unintelligible, ambiguous or untimely, or
(d)   the commercial practice fails to identify its commercial intent, unless this is already apparent from the context,

and as a result it causes or is likely to cause the average consumer to take a transactional decision he would not have taken otherwise."[1211]

"Material information" is defined as referring to:

"(a)   the information which the average consumer needs, according to the context, to take an informed transactional decision; and
(b)   any information requirement which applies in relation to a commercial communication as a result of an EU obligation."[1212]

So, in the case of the second category, a trader's failure to provide the information required of traders in respect of distance contracts, off-premises contracts, on-premises contracts or timeshare contracts,[1213] would constitute a misleading omission, subject to it having the designated effect or likely effect on the average consumer's decision-making.[1214] However, following the recommendation of the Law Commissions, the 2014 amendments to the 2008 Regulations do not include "misleading omissions" as defined by reg.6 as a "prohibited practice" for the purposes of the consumer's right to redress.[1215] The effect of this is clear in relation to a "pure omission", so that, notably, a failure in a trader to provide the pre-contractual information required by UK legislation implementing EU law will not in itself give rise to rights to redress in consumers,[1216] nor will a failure to provide information "which the average consumer needs, according to the context, to take an informed transactional decision".[1217] However, the position is less clear in the case of a trader providing information in either of these categories, but doing so inaccurately or incompletely. At first sight, such commercial behaviour by a trader could fall within reg.6(1)(c)'s reference to the provision of "material information in a manner which is unclear, unintelligible, ambiguous or untimely" and therefore

---

[1211] 2008 Regulations reg.6(1).
[1212] 2008 Regulations reg.6(3) and see *Carrefour Hypermarchés SAS v ITM Alimentaire International SASU* (C-562/15) of February 8, 2017. Further provision is made for information to be supplied where a commercial practice is an invitation to purchase: 2008 Regulations reg.6(4). On "invitation to purchase" see 2005 Directive art.2(i) and *Konsumentombudsmannen v Ving Sverige AB* (C-122/10) of May 12 2011 paras 27–33 and esp. at para.28 ("an invitation to purchase is a specific form of advertising to which is attached a stricter obligation to provide information"), where it was held that the list of information deemed material by art.7(4) (implemented by reg.6(4) of the 2008 Regulations) is an exhaustive one: C-122/10 at paras 68–72.
[1213] On which see above, paras 38-098, 38-103 and 38-150.
[1214] On the significance of reg.6's requirements as to misleading omissions generally see *OFT v Purely Creative* [2011] EWHC 106 (Ch), [2011] E.C.C. 20 at [73]–[74]; *Secretary of State for Business, Innovation and Skills v PLT Antimarketing Ltd* [2015] EWCA Civ 76, [2015] C.T.L.C.8 at [30]–[31]; *Deroo-Blanquart v Sony Europe Ltd* (C-310/15) of September 7, 2016 especially at paras 48–49 ("material information" refers to "key items of information which the consumer needs to make an informed transactional decision", assessed in all the circumstances).
[1215] Above, para.38-172.
[1216] A failure to supply information required by EU legislation in itself constitutes "material information" whose omission falls within reg.6: reg.6(3)(b).
[1217] 2008 Regulations reg.6(3)(a).

outside the scope of availability of the rights to redress. On the other hand, the definition of "misleading action" in reg.5 is very broad, in that it includes both false information and information whose "overall presentation in any way deceives or is likely to deceive the average consumer".[1218] It is submitted that "half-truths" and other statements which, while true, are misleading would be caught by reg.5 and therefore attract the possibility of rights to redress for consumers[1219] and is, therefore, broadly similar to the position under the general law of misrepresentation where such true but misleading statements can be actionable.[1220] Such a broad approach to misleading action was taken by the Law Commissions,[1221] which gave as examples a case where a consumer buys a lawnmower, which works satisfactorily but the consumer is not aware that the mower requires an unusual and hard-to-obtain fuel, and the case where a travel agent sells a package holiday in an exotic foreign destination to a consumer, but fails to tell the consumer that there has recently been an outbreak of cholera at the destination.[1222] In the case of the first example, if a trader sold the mower as petrol-driven or a "motor-mower", it seems correct that the overall presentation is misleading, but in the second example, to include a failure to provide information as to the cholera as a "misleading action" would obliterate the distinction between positive statements and non-disclosure. On the other hand, after the Law Commission's recommendations and the resulting amendments to the 2008 Regulations were made in 2014, the Court of Justice of the EU in *Canal Digital Denmark A/S*[1223] provided guidance on the interpretation and application of arts 6 and 7 of the 2005 Directive on misleading actions and misleading omissions respectively, making clear, first, that the provision of incomplete information may constitute a misleading action, and that, secondly, the same commercial practice may constitute both a misleading action and a misleading omission, subject in either case to its satisfying the particular conditions and taking into account the particular factors which are required by the 2005 Directive. As a result, merely because a commercial practice appears to fall within one of the examples of a misleading omission (in the earlier example, "material information in a manner which is unclear, unintelligible, ambiguous or untimely") does not prevent it from also counting as a misleading action (notably, as information whose "overall presentation in any way deceives or is likely to deceive the average consumer").

Aggressive practice   Regulation 7(1) provides: **38-186**

"(1)   A commercial practice is aggressive if, in its factual context, taking account of all of its features and circumstances—

(a)   it significantly impairs or is likely significantly to impair the average consumer's freedom of choice or conduct in relation to the product concerned through the use of harassment, coercion or undue influence; and

---

[1218] 2008 Regulations reg.5(2)(a), above, para.38-180.
[1219] 2008 Regulations reg.27B(1)(a), above, para.38-178.
[1220] See Vol.I, para.7-021.
[1221] Report paras 7.22–7.23 arguing that "deceives" in reg.5(2)(a) should be understand in the context to mean "mislead" rather than deliberately mislead.
[1222] Report paras 7.26–7.28. The examples had been provided by H. Collins, *A Private Right of Redress for Unfair Commercial Practices: A Report for Consumer Focus* (April 2009) who referred to them as examples of misleading omissions.
[1223] *Criminal Proceedings against Canal Digital Denmark A/S* (C-611/14) of October 26, 2016 and see above, para.38-181.

(b)   it thereby causes or is likely to cause him to take a transactional decision he would not have taken otherwise."

"Consumer", "average consumer", "product" and "transactional decision" are defined in the same way as they are for the purposes of the rights to redress for consumers in respect of misleading actions.[1224] Regulation 7(2) then explains that:

"(2)   In determining whether a commercial practice uses harassment, coercion or undue influence account shall be taken of—
(a)   its timing, location, nature or persistence;
(b)   the use of threatening or abusive language or behaviour;
(c)   the exploitation by the trader of any specific misfortune or circumstance of such gravity as to impair the consumer's judgment, of which the trader is aware, to influence the consumer's decision with regard to the product;
(d)   any onerous or disproportionate non-contractual barrier imposed by the trader where a consumer wishes to exercise rights under the contract, including rights to terminate a contract or to switch to another product or another trader; and
(e)   any threat to take any action which cannot legally be taken."

For these purposes, "coercion" includes the use of physical force[1225] and "undue influence" means:

"... exploiting a position of power in relation to the consumer so as to apply pressure, even without using or threatening to use physical force, in a way which significantly limits the consumer's ability to make an informed decision."[1226]

There is no definition of "harassment".

38-187   Examples; comparison with general law   As the Law Commissions pointed out, the list of practices unfair in all circumstances illustrates the sort of practices which could fall within the category of aggressive practices: creating the impression that the consumer cannot leave the premises until a contract is formed, conducting personal visits to the consumer's home and ignoring the consumer's legitimate request to leave or not to return, and making persistent and unwanted solicitations by telephone, fax, email or other remote media except in circumstances and to the extent justified to enforce a contractual obligation.[1227] The Law Commissions recommended that the definition of an aggressive practice for the purposes of the consumer's rights to redress should track the definition in reg.7 with some modifications so as, in particular, to avoid reference to "undue influence" which would cause confusion with the doctrine of undue influence under the general law, to define "harassment" as "unreasonable behaviour which is likely to cause alarm, distress or serious annoyance and inconvenience" and to make clear that no "course of

---

[1224] 2008 Regulations reg.2(1) "consumer"; reg.2(2)–(6) "average consumer"; reg.27B(2) "transactional decision": see above, paras 38-168, 38-169 and 38-183 respectively. Regulation 2(1) defines "product" generally (see above, para.38-168), but this definition is then qualified by regs 27C–27D for the purposes of the rights to redress provided by Pt 4A as explained below, para.38-176.
[1225] 2008 Regulations reg.7(3)(a).
[1226] 2008 Regulations reg.7(3)(b).
[1227] 2008 Regulations Sch.1 paras 24, 25 and 26. For examples of "aggressive commercial practices" see *R. v Waters* [2016] EWCA Crim 1112, [2017] E.C.C. 5 (high-pressured sale of furniture to elderly person); *R v Jackson* [2017] EWCA Crim 78 (pressurising elderly and vulnerable person to agree to pay for work trader said he had carried out).

conduct" is required for there to be harassment for this purpose.[1228] These recommendations are not, however, reflected in the law as made, which simply adopts the definition of "aggressive commercial practice" in the Regulations generally without change as the basis of the consumer's new rights, except in relation to the definition of "transactional decision".[1229] This has the advantage of relative simplicity, but it does allow the confusion which the Law Commissions foresaw between "undue influence" for the purposes of the new rights for consumers and "undue influence" under the general law, the main difference being that the latter typically involves the abuse of a special relationship of trust between the parties,[1230] which is unlikely to be the case in the context of consumer contracts. Moreover, the idea of "undue influence" in the Regulations (following the 2005 Directive) is much broader and less technical than undue influence under the general law, though the significance of vulnerable groups of consumers (notably, by reason of "age, physical or mental infirmity or credulity"[1231]) for the purposes of "average consumer" may sometimes have a similar resonance to some of the traditional concerns of the general law of undue influence or, indeed, equitable relief against unconscionable bargains.[1232] Indeed, the Regulations' reference to "the exploitation of a position of power"[1233] without limiting it to a relationship of trust and confidence suggests that the exploitation of a consumer's urgent need for the product may amount to an aggressive practice. The contrast between the definition of "aggressive practices" and the facts which would attract the common law doctrine of duress is also marked, as the latter typically involves an illegitimate threat to the person, goods or economic interests of the party to the contract.[1234] On the other hand, if (contrary to the view adopted above) "aggressive practice" requires a course of conduct in a trader and cannot apply merely to an isolated example of pressure being exerted on an individual consumer, then the general law of duress, undue influence and unconscionable bargains would retain their significance even in the context of consumer contracts and some cases seen by the Law Commissions as requiring a remedy would be left without one.[1235]

Prohibited practice by a "producer"   In the preceding discussion of the second **38-188** condition for the availability of the consumer's rights to redress, the prohibited practice has been engaged in by the trader with whom the consumer has made a contract or to whom the trader has made a payment. However, reg.27A(4)(b) provides that the second condition for the availability of their rights may equally be satisfied in certain cases where it is the producer of goods or digital content which so engages, being:

"(b)   in a case where a consumer enters into a business to consumer contract for goods
         or digital content—
    (i)   a producer engages in a prohibited practice in relation to the goods or digital
           content, and

[1228] Law Commissions' Report (2012), paras 7.67–7.82.
[1229] 2008 Regulations reg.27B(1)(b), (2) above, para.38-183.
[1230] Law Commissions' Report (2012), para.7.66 and see Vol.I, paras 8-058 et seq. where the complexities of the general law are explained.
[1231] 2008 Regulations reg.2(5)(a), above, para.38-169.
[1232] Vol.I, paras 8-132 et seq.
[1233] 2008 Regulations reg.7(3)(b).
[1234] Vol.I, Ch.8 especially paras 8-010—8-011.
[1235] Above, paras 38-166—38-167.

(ii)   when the contract is entered into, the trader is aware of the commercial practice that constitutes the prohibited practice or could reasonably be expected to be aware of it."

The Regulations then define "producer" to include a manufacturer, EEA importer or a person who presents themselves as a producer.[1236]

38-189   The 2008 Regulations generally do not distinguish between different categories of trader which engage in unfair commercial practices: retailers, wholesalers, producers or agents may all fall under their prohibitions and, therefore, the preventive measures or criminal offences which they set out.[1237] By contrast, the rights to civil redress under Pt 4A of the Regulations require that the trader has made a contract with the consumer, or that the consumer has made a payment to the trader, thereby focussing the consumer's civil rights against the retailer of goods or services and reflecting the importance of the consumer's right to unwind the transaction so made.[1238] This focus was supported by the Law Commissions, which recommended against allowing consumers to claim directly against producers and perpetrators of unfair practices other than retailers.[1239] The 2014 Regulations as enacted retain this focus but go further and provide that the trader who supplies goods or digital content may be liable to the consumer's rights to redress where it is their producer, rather than the trader/supplier itself, who has engaged in a prohibited practice (i.e. misleading action or aggressive practice), subject to the condition that, at the time of the contract, "the trader is aware of the commercial practice that constitutes the prohibited practice or could reasonably be expected to be aware of it".[1240] This liability in a retailer of goods or digital content for these types of unfair commercial practices in the producer therefore parallels closely the retailer's contractual liability for lack of satisfactory quality of the goods or digital content supplied even in circumstances where this failure is caused by their own supplier or their manufacturer. For under the Consumer Rights Act 2015 the question whether goods or digital content supplied under a contract are of satisfactory quality may take into account any public statement made in advertising or labelling about the specific characteristics of the goods or digital content by the producer or trader (or their representatives), but this will not be the case, inter alia, where the trader shows that he was not aware, and could not reasonably have been aware, of the statement.[1241] In this way, the new law governing the consumer's rights to redress for misleading statements reflects closely the new law governing the consumer's rights in respect of the satisfactory quality of the goods under the contract.

38-190   **Third condition: "A significant factor in the consumer's decision"**   The third condition for the availability of the consumer's rights to redress is that "the

---

[1236] 2008 Regulations reg.27A(5). This definition is modelled on the one provided by Directive 1999/44/EC on certain aspects of the sale of consumer goods and associated guarantees [1999] O.J. L171/12 art.2(d), implemented in UK law by Sale of Goods Act 1979 s.14(2D)–(2F), 61(1) "producer" and Consumer Rights Act 2015 ss.9(5), 59(1) "producer", below, paras 38-440 and 38-497 respectively.

[1237] Law Commissions' Report (2012), para.6.64.

[1238] Above, para.38-172. Law Commissions' Report (2012), para.6.65.

[1239] Law Commissions' Report (2012), paras 6.73–6.75.

[1240] 2008 Regulations reg.27A(4)(b)(ii).

[1241] Consumer Rights Act 2015 s.9(5), (6) and 7(a) (goods); s.34(5), (6) and (7)(a) (digital content): see below, paras 38-497 and 38-546 respectively.

prohibited practice is a significant factor in the consumer's decision to enter into the contract or make the payment".[1242] As earlier explained, the Regulations' definition of "prohibited practice" for the purposes of the consumer's rights to redress requires that the misleading action or aggressive practice causes or is likely to cause the average consumer to enter into a contract with a trader or to make a payment to a trader for the supply of a product.[1243] However, in addition, the third condition of the availability of the consumer's rights to redress is that the prohibited practice in question is a significant factor in that consumer's decision to enter the contract or make the payment. The Law Commissions rejected the adoption of a test of "but for" causation between the prohibited practice and the consumer's decision, on the basis that it would be unrealistic to expect consumers to prove that without the commercial practice they would not have entered the contract at all: "often there will be no way of telling why a consumer acted in that particular way following an aggressive or misleading practice".[1244] On the other hand, "putting no weight on causation would be inconsistent with the compensatory aim of private rights".[1245] The "significant factor" test was seen as a compromise position.[1246] The Law Commissions concluded that:

> "In practice, this means that consumers will need to provide some evidence that they saw or heard the misleading statement, or experienced the aggressive practice before making the decision to buy or pay and that they were influenced by it. Thereafter, it will be enough if the misleading or aggressive practice is sufficiently serious to cause a reasonably well informed, observant and circumspect consumer to enter into the contract or to make a payment."[1247]

Comparison with the general law of misrepresentation, duress and undue **38-191**
influence   Although the Law Commissions thought otherwise,[1248] the "significant factor" test to determine the causal connection required between the consumer's decision to enter the contract differs from the rules governing misrepresentation, duress and undue influence under the general law. In the case of misrepresentation, the test of "inducement" is that it is sufficient for the claimant to show that the misrepresentation was *one* of the inducing causes of the misrepresentee's decision to enter the contract[1249]: what is required is that the misrepresentee would not have entered the contract or would not have entered the contract *on the same terms* but for the misrepresentation.[1250] However, an exception to this general pattern is found

---

[1242] 2008 Regulations reg.27A(6). See also Bant and Paterson (2017) 80 M.L.R. 895 at 902 et seq.
[1243] 2008 Regulations reg.27B and see above, paras 38-180—38-183 and 38-186. The *Law Commissions Report* 2014 para.7.85 referred to this element as an objective test, seeing it as similar to the "materiality" test of the general law of misrepresentation, on which see Vol.I, para.7-041.
[1244] *Law Commissions Report* 2014 paras 7.107–7.108.
[1245] *Law Commissions Report* 2014 para.7.108.
[1246] *Law Commissions Report* 2014 para.7.114.
[1247] *Law Commissions Report* 2014 para.7.115.
[1248] *Law Commissions Report* 2014 para.7.109 stating that the "significant factor" test "is in line with existing law, particularly in Scotland", but referring to a discussion in their earlier Joint Consultation Paper *Consumer Redress for Misleading and Aggressive Practices* (2011) Consultation Paper No.199, Discussion Paper No.149 paras 8.7–8.8 which describes incompletely the position in English law (describing the "but for" test as requiring the entering of a contract and not also including the entering of a contract on different terms), and which observes that "[i]n Scotland there has been little discussion of misrepresentation and causation".
[1249] Vol.I, para.7-038.
[1250] Vol.I, paras 7-038—7-039.

in the rules governing rescission for fraud, where it is sufficient if there is evidence to show that the misrepresentee was materially influenced by the misrepresentation merely in the sense that it had some impact on his thinking: it is no defence for the misrepresentor to show that the misrepresentee would still have made the contract.[1251] The courts have applied this special rule for fraud to cases of duress to the person and to cases of actual undue influence,[1252] but the better view is that the causal requirement for duress of goods and economic duress is that the victim must show that the duress was a "significant cause" of the victim's entering the contract, in the sense that, but for the threat, he would not have entered the contract or would not have entered it on the same terms.[1253] Given that the Law Commissions foresaw that the "significant factor" test retains *some* causal role for the prohibited practice in the consumer's decision to enter the contract or to make the payment, it is submitted that the courts are likely to seek to apply their general approach in their interpretation of "significant factor" for the purposes of the consumer's rights to redress under the Regulations with the result that the third condition would be satisfied where the consumer could establish that, but for the prohibited practice, he or she would not have entered the contract or made the payment, or would not have done so on the same terms. However, if the courts wished instead to take a more generous view, they could treat the prohibited practices as more akin to fraud, duress of the person and actual undue influence, with the result that, the trader could not escape liability under the rights to redress merely by establishing that the consumer would anyway have entered the contract or made the payment or would have done so on the same terms. This more generous view may be appropriate as a matter of policy as regards aggressive practices which involve intentional behaviour on the part of the trader ("harassment, coercion or undue influence"[1254]), but may well be less so for misleading actions, which may be committed by a trader purely innocently.[1255]

(iii)   The Three Rights to Redress

38-192   **Overview of the consumer's rights**   A consumer who enters a contract with, or makes a relevant payment to, a trader as the result of a "prohibited practice"[1256] may have a "right to redress"[1257] in the form of one or more remedies (termed "rights" by the 2008 Regulations): to "unwind" the contract or payment[1258] or, in the case of business to consumer contracts, to obtain a discount,[1259] and in either case to claim damages.[1260] According to the Law Commissions, the overall strategy of the

---

[1251] Vol.I, para.7-040 relying on *Edgington v Fitzmaurice* (1885) 29 Ch. D. 459, 483.

[1252] Vol.I, para.7-040, 8-026, *Barton v Armstrong* [1976] A.C. 104 (duress to the person); para.8-074, *UCB Corporate Services Ltd v Williams* [2002] EWCA Civ 555, [2003] 1 P. & C.R. 12 at [86] (actual undue influence). Cases of presumed undue influence are treated differently, as where it is presumed that one party had influence over the other and that a transaction between them was one "not readily explicable by the relationship" between them, it will be presumed (or inferred) that the transaction was the result of an abuse of an influence unless the presumption is rebutted: Vol.I, para.8-075.

[1253] Vol.I paras 8-027—8-028.

[1254] 2008 Regulations reg.7(1)(a).

[1255] 2008 Regulations reg.5(2) and (3).

[1256] Above, paras 38-178—38-191.

[1257] 2008 Regulations reg.27A(1).

[1258] 2008 Regulations regs 27E–27H; below, paras 38-193—38-195.

[1259] 2008 Regulations reg.27I; below, paras 38-196—38-197.

[1260] 2008 Regulations reg.27J; below, paras 38-198—38-203.

new rights was "to approximate the outcomes under the current law, but in a simplified way".[1261] The consumer may enforce a right to redress by a claim in civil proceedings.[1262] The claim will be subject to the Limitation Act 1980 as if it were an action founded on a simple contract.[1263]

The right to unwind the contract: business to consumer contracts If a   **38-193**
consumer has entered a "business to consumer" contract[1264] and the three conditions of the general availability of the consumer's rights to redress[1265] are fulfilled, the consumer will have a right to "unwind" the contract provided that (i) the consumer indicates to the trader that he or she rejects the product within a limited period,[1266] (ii) that the "product" remains "capable of rejection"[1267] and (iii) the consumer has not already exercised the right to discount for the same contract and prohibited practice.[1268] The period is 90 days from the later of the day on which the contract was made or, in effect, on which the consumer first received delivery or performance.[1269] The product is incapable of rejection only if (as the case may be) the goods have been fully consumed, services have been fully performed,[1270] digital content was available to the consumer for a fixed period that has expired,[1271] the

---

[1261] Law Commissions Report (2012), para.8.19.

[1262] 2008 Regulations reg.27K.

[1263] 2008 Regulations reg.27K(5).

[1264] i.e. one under which the trader is to supply a product to the consumer: see above, para.38-177.

[1265] See above, paras 38-177—38-191.

[1266] 2008 Regulations reg.27E(1)(a). The drafting of the 2008 Regulations is curious: rather than conferring a right to unwind that the consumer may exercise and that will expire if the consumer does not exercise it within a limited period, the consumer will have a right only if he or she exercises it within the period. If the consumer has the right and exercises it, the contract comes to an end: 2008 Regulations reg.27E(1)(a) and 27F(1).

[1267] 2008 Regulations reg.27E(1)(b).

[1268] 2008 Regulations reg.27E(10).

[1269] See 2008 Regulations reg.27E(3)–(7). cf. the 30 day period for the consumer's "short-term right to reject" goods under the Consumer Rights Act 2015 s.20 and 22, below, para.38-516.

[1270] Law Commissions Report (2012), para.8.77 considered that a consumer who abandons services midperformance (e.g. a consumer who is misled about a theatre performance and who leaves before the final curtain call) should have a right to a full refund. However, the reason for excluding the right to unwind (with consequential refund) under the Regulations where services have been fully performed is far from clear, given that the prohibited practice may have resulted in the consumer contracting for services that were of no value to him or her even though fully completed, while in other cases a consumer may derive a considerable benefit from services that have only been performed in part yet be entitled to a refund of the whole price. Note, however, that in some circumstances the consumer may obtain a 100 per cent discount of the price (below, para.38-196) as foreseen by Law Commissions Report (2012), para.8.78.

[1271] Note that the 2008 Regulations clearly contemplate the consumer being entitled to reject digital content, whereas under the Consumer Rights Act 2015 Ch.3, a consumer who has been supplied digital content that does not conform to the statutory requirements has no right to reject, the drafters having taken the view that there cannot be a right to reject when there is nothing to give back: see Consumer Rights Act 2015 ss.42 especially at 42(7), below, para.38-561. It is not clear how digital content that is supplied on a tangible medium is to be treated under the 2008 Regulations, as goods or as digital content. It seems better to view them as goods, so that the consumer must make the tangible medium available for collection by the trader, but if the digital content was to be available to the consumer for only a limited period to regard the goods as "fully consumed" when that period expires, so that the consumer will lose the right to unwind just as with other types of digital content. This distinction would accord with the treatment of digital content under the Consumer Contracts (Information, Cancellation and Additional Charges) Regulations 2013 (SI 2013/3134) (above, paras 38-061 et seq.). The 2013 Regulations provide that a consumer who has concluded an off-premises or distance contract for the supply of digital content not on a tangible medium with

lease has expired or the right conferred on the consumer has been fully exercised.[1272] If the consumer has a right to unwind (which, as stated above, requires that the consumer has notified the trader that he or she rejects the product), the contract comes to an end and the consumer and the trader are released from their obligations under it[1273]; the trader must give the consumer a refund[1274]; and, if the contract was for the sale or supply of goods, the consumer must make the goods available for the trader to collect.[1275] Where the consumer has paid money under the contract, in principle the amount paid must be refunded without any deduction for use,[1276] though this is qualified by detailed provisions governing cases in which the consumer has transferred something other than money[1277] and also where the contract was for the sale or supply of goods on a regular basis.[1278] This general position is to be compared with the effects of cancellation by a consumer of an off-premises or distance contract, as cancellation also brings to an end the obligations of the parties to the contract, but generates an obligation in the trader to reimburse all payments received from the consumer other than payments for delivery (subject to a possible qualification for diminution in value through their handling) and in principle also an obligation in the consumer to return any goods supplied.[1279]

38-194 **The right to unwind the contract: consumer to business contracts** If the consumer has entered a contract under which the consumer is to sell goods to the trader,[1280] the consumer has the right to treat the contract as at an end,[1281] so that the

---

a right of cancellation, but then qualify this where the trader begins performance with the express consent of the consumer and with an acknowledgement that the right to cancel will be lost: 2013 Regulations reg.36(1) and (2), above, para.38-115.

[1272] 2008 Regulations reg.27E(8)–(9).

[1273] 2008 Regulations reg.27F(1)(a). It is not clear whether this would affect obligations that are normally intended to survive termination or avoidance of the contract, such as obligations of confidentiality.

[1274] 2008 Regulations reg.27F(1)(b); see further below.

[1275] 2008 Regulations reg.27F(1)(c). Under other legislation the term "contract for the supply of goods" includes contracts for work and materials, which will result in the goods being incorporated into other goods (as when parts are used to repair a car) or land (as in a building contract) (e.g. under the Supply of Goods and Services Act 1982 s.1); under the Consumer Rights Act 2015, the contract will be regarded as a mixed contract, partly for the supply of goods and partly for services, see ss.1(3)–(5) below, paras 38-484 and 38-488. The 2008 Regulations also refer to a "mixed contract", i.e. "a contract relating to a product which consists of any two or more of goods, a service, digital content, immoveable property or rights", but only for the purposes of setting the "relevant day" for the start of the 90-day period for the right to unwind: reg.27E(5) and (6). If the goods cannot readily be detached (cf. *Borden (UK) Ltd v Scottish Timber Products Ltd* [1979] 3 W.L.R. 672, CA; *Hendy Lennox (Industrial Engines) Ltd v Grahame Puttick* [1984] 2 All E.R. 152 (QBD)), it can be said that they will have ceased to have an independent existence and therefore should be treated as "fully consumed" within reg.27E(8)(a), with the result that the consumer has no right to redress.

[1276] 2008 Regulations reg.27F(3). Law Commissions Report (2012), paras 8.83–8.96 rejecting an analogy with the then applicable position under Sale of Goods Act 1979 s.48C(3). This provision is reflected in the "final right to reject" in the Consumer Rights Act 2015 s.24(8)–24(10), below, para.38-519.

[1277] 2008 Regulations reg.27F(4)–(6).

[1278] 2008 Regulations reg.27F(7)–(10).

[1279] Consumer Contracts (Information, Cancellation and Additional Charges) Regulations 2013 (SI 2013/3134) regs 33–38 above, paras 38-123—38-126.

[1280] 2008 Regulations reg.27A(3) has the effect that contracts under which "the trader supplies or agrees to supply a product to the consumer as well as paying or agreeing to pay the consumer" (such as part-exchange contracts) are not "consumer to business" contracts; they may instead count as "business to consumer" contracts: above, para.38-177. There are special provisions for "unwinding" contracts under which the consumer has transferred something other than money: see 2008 Regula-

parties are released from their obligations under it. There is no time limit, except as applies under the general limitation period.[1282] If the consumer exercises the right to unwind, he or she will have a right to the return of the goods transferred if they can be returned in the condition they were in when sold by the consumer, and must refund any payment made by the trader. If the goods cannot be returned in the same condition, the consumer has the right to be paid the amount (if any) by which the market price of the goods when the trader paid for them exceeds what the trader paid for them.[1283]

Unwinding payments   Where the three general conditions for the availability of   **38-195**
a right to redress are satisfied,[1284] a consumer who has made a payment in full or partial settlement of the consumer's liabilities or purported liabilities to the trader for a product as a result of a prohibited practice, may recover that payment to the extent that the consumer was not required (i.e. legally liable) to make it.[1285] In other words, the right to unwind a payment applies only if the payment made was not due: the consumer cannot, for example, recover a payment that was due on the ground that the consumer would not have made the payment at that time but for a misleading action or aggressive practice on the part of the trader.[1286]

The right to a discount   In the case of a business to consumer contract, if the   **38-196**
consumer has not exercised the right to unwind the contract,[1287] the consumer has

---

tions reg.27F(4)–(5).

[1281] The phrase "treat the contract as at an end" seems to be used here in a different sense from its use in the Consumer Rights Act 2015. Under the Act, it is assumed that a consumer may enjoy "a right to treat the contract as at an end" for breach of an express term and for this purpose "treating a contract as at an end means treating it as repudiated": Consumer Rights Act 2015 s.19(11)(e) and 19(13) (goods contracts); s.54(7)(f) (services contracts), that is, what is often called termination for breach of contract, which is coupled with a right to damages for breach of contract. The 2015 s.20(4) Act also sees its special consumer rights to reject goods as involving the treating of the contract as at an end and may be accompanied with damages: 2015 Act ss.19(3), (4), (10) and (11)(a): see below, paras 38-513—38-523 and (on the general law) Vol.I, paras 24-001 et seq. It cannot be intended that a consumer who unwinds a consumer to business contract entered into as the result of a prohibited practice by a trader should recover damages for breach of contract; the consumer's right to damages is governed by reg.27J, see below, paras 38-198—38-203.

[1282] 2008 Regulations 27K(5), applying the general six-year period applicable to actions founded on simple contract under s.6 of the Limitation Act 1980. It seems unlikely that the consumer will lose this right by inaction unless it is possible to infer an agreement (for good consideration) to abandon the right, or possibly a promissory estoppel which prevents the consumer from enforcing the right (see above, paras 4-086 et seq.), but see below, para.38-210 on the question whether these general exclusions of a claim by a consumer apply in the context of Pt 4A rights.

[1283] 2008 Regulations reg.27G(6).

[1284] Above, paras 38-177—38-191.

[1285] 2008 Regulations reg.27H. The Law Commissions Report (2012), para.8.102 acknowledged that a payment made as a result of misleading actions or threats could be recovered under the general law of unjust enrichment, but this law was seen by consumer groups as "complex and difficult" and so the new law should make this recovery "more accessible". On the general law see Vol.I, paras 29-033 et seq. (mistake) and 29-094 et seq. (compulsion).

[1286] Nor is there any right to a discount in relation to consumer payments, below, para.38-196. On the other hand, this restriction limits the right to unwind the payment rather than the consumer's right to redress more generally, so that the consumer who pays a sum that is due may have a right to damages under reg.27J: see below, para.38-198.

[1287] The drafting in reg.27I(1)(b) seems inconsistent with earlier provisions. In the case of a business to consumer contract, the consumer does not have a right to unwind at all unless the consumer notifies the trader within the stated period, etc. If the consumer has this right, unwinding then seems to

a right to a discount.[1288] If the consumer has made one or more payments to the trader, the consumer may recover a relevant percentage; if payments are still to be made, they may be reduced accordingly. For these purposes, for most contracts, the 2008 Regulations provide "pre-set bands"[1289] the relevant percentages are as follows:

"(a) if the prohibited practice is more than minor, it is 25%,
(b) if the prohibited practice is significant, it is 50%,
(c) if the prohibited practice is serious, it is 75%, and
(d) if the prohibited practice is very serious, it is 100%."[1290]

It is clear, therefore, that where the prohibited practice is minor or less than minor, no discount is available.[1291] The seriousness of the prohibited practice is to be assessed by reference to:

"(a) the behaviour of the person who engaged in the practice,
(b) the impact of the practice on the consumer, and
(c) the time that has elapsed since the prohibited practice took place."[1292]

The Law Commissions accepted that pre-set bands for discounts could operate unfairly in purchases where there is clear evidence of the difference between what the product was worth and what the consumer paid for it, for example, in a £10,000 purchase where the trader can show that the loss was 10 per cent, the court may be faced with a harsh choice if it were only able to give 25 per cent or nothing.[1293] The 2008 Regulations reflect this concern by providing an exception to their application for cases where the amount payable under the contract is more than £5,000 and there is clear evidence that the market price of the product is lower than the contract price: here, the relevant percentage is "the percentage difference between the market price of the product and the amount payable for it under the contract" rather than one of the pre-set bands.[1294] The wording of this provision is ambiguous, but it is submitted that it refers to the percentage by which the contract price exceeds the market price (which on the facts of the example given above would be 11.11 per cent), rather than the percentage by which the market price is lower than the contract price (which on the same facts would be 10 per cent), since if the second percentage were intended, the amount of the discount would be the difference between the contract price and the market price, and it would have been simpler to say so. This replacement of the pre-set bands by this special test means that where traders sell or supply high-value products their behaviour (and therefore any penal element)

---

follow automatically. (See above, para.38-193.) But the intention behind the words "if the consumer has not exercised the right to unwind" seems clear enough.

[1288] 2008 Regulations reg.27I(1). The fact that the consumer has not exercised the right to unwind in respect of the contract assumes that the consumer had such a right but did not exercise it. This means that a consumer who has made a payment which was *due* cannot enjoy a right of discount under reg.27I as he or she does not enjoy a right to unwind the contract under reg.27H in these circumstances: above, para.38-195.

[1289] Law Commissions Report (2012), paras 8.125–8.135.

[1290] 2008 Regulations reg.27I(4).

[1291] cf. Law Commissions Report (2012), para.8.137 setting a lowest band of "0 per cent if [the prohibited practice is] negligible".

[1292] 2008 Regulations reg.27I(5).

[1293] Law Commissions Report (2012), para.8.133.

[1294] 2008 Regulations reg.27I(6) and (7).

cannot be taken into account[1295]; nor can the time that has elapsed since the prohibited practice took place or the "impact of the practice on the consumer" to the extent to which this is not already reflected in the special percentage discount applicable.

Nature of the right to a discount   The most obvious purpose of the discount is   **38-197**
to provide a simple mechanism to compensate the consumer who has been misled or pressured into buying a product that is worth less than the consumer had agreed to pay, but who cannot (or chooses not to) unwind the contract.[1296] However, it is clear that these discounts are not just a form of price reduction,[1297] since (except where the price is over £5,000) there is no reference to the actual value of the product. Although the Law Commissions' original intention was that "the consumer would receive compensation in the form of a discount on the price ... the new [legislation] should use broad bands of *detriment*",[1298] the Regulations refer to "the seriousness of the prohibited *practice*" (emphases supplied), not the seriousness of the loss to the consumer. The "impact on the consumer" is just a factor to be taken into account together with the behaviour of the person (trader or producer[1299]) and the time that has elapsed since the prohibited practice took place, and is not the measure to be used, while the nature of the trader's behaviour would not normally be relevant to calculation of damages. Nor is the discount a form of "aggravated" damages (seeking to compensate the consumer for the additional hurt caused by the trader's practices[1300]), as this is a head under which the consumer may recover damages.[1301] The right to a discount seems therefore to be partly aimed at compensation for loss of value and partly a form of civil penalty.[1302] If this is so, then its practical implication could be that its award would not affect any further amount that a consumer may be able to recover on some other basis, such as damages for fraud or for breach of contract, as Pt 4A prevents double recovery only of "compensation".[1303]

The right to damages   The 2008 Regulations provide the consumer who has   **38-198**
entered a contract as the result of a prohibited practice by the trader with a right to damages, whether or not the consumer unwinds the contract or claims a discount.[1304] Where the prohibited practice is a misleading action, this new right to damages has

---

[1295] See below, para.38-197.
[1296] Note that damages recoverable under the 2008 Regulations reg.27J may not include "the difference between the market price of a product and the amount payable for it under a contract": reg.27J(3), see below, para.38-199.
[1297] See below, paras 38-518, 38-559 and 38-582 for price reduction in the context of failures in conformity of goods, digital content and services under the Consumer Rights Act 2015.
[1298] *Consumer Redress for Misrepresentation and Aggressive Practices: a Joint Consultation Paper* (LCCP 199/SLCDP 149, 2011), paras 14.49–14.50. The Report does not explicitly depart from the emphasis on detriment, though it states that the level of discount should depend on: "(1) the impact of the commercial practice on the value of the product; (2) the trader's behaviour; and (3) the amount of time that has passed..." (para.8.136). The same factors are listed in reg.27I(5), but the behaviour of the person who engaged in the practice is now listed first.
[1299] Above, para.38-188.
[1300] See Vol.I, para.26-049. Law Commission Report, *Aggravated, Exemplary and Restitutionary Damages* Law Com. No.247 (1997), Pt II.
[1301] See below, para.38-198.
[1302] cf. Law Commission Report, *Aggravated, Exemplary and Restitutionary Damages* Law Com. No.247 (1997), para.5.25.
[1303] 2008 Regulations reg.27L(2)(b) and see below, para.38-204.
[1304] 2008 Regulations reg.27A(1); reg.27J.

a particularly uncomfortable relationship with the existing bases of recovery under the law of misrepresentation, both at common law and under the Misrepresentation Act 1967.[1305] By contrast, where the prohibited practice consists of an aggressive commercial practice, as the Law Commissions intended, the Regulations create a right to damages which does not clearly otherwise exist under the general law.[1306]

38-199 **Measure of recovery for financial loss** A consumer who has entered a contract as the result of a prohibited practice by the trader may recover damages for financial loss incurred which he would not have incurred if the prohibited practice had not taken place.[1307] In this respect, the Regulations specify that this right to damages:

"... does not include the right to be paid damages in respect of the difference between the market price of a product and the amount payable for it under a contract."[1308]

This formula imposes an ambiguous restriction. It could mean that the consumer cannot recover damages representing a good bargain, i.e. representing the difference between the price paid for goods or services and their *higher* market value (oddly referred to as "market price") (the first hypothesis), as was apparently intended by the Law Commissions.[1309] Such a restriction would accord with the established position as regards the measure of damages for fraud, negligent misstatement at common law, and under s.2(1) of the Misrepresentation Act 1967, often expressed in terms of allowing a misrepresentee to recover a "tort measure" rather than a "contract measure".[1310] On the other hand, the formula could equally mean that the consumer cannot recover damages to compensate him for a bad bargain, i.e. representing the difference between the price paid for goods or services and their *lower* market value (the second hypothesis). Or, of course, it could be thought to refer equally to both hypotheses. In the case of the second hypothesis, it may be unusual for a consumer to need to rely on a claim for damages in order to recover for loss caused by a bad bargain in this way. Where he can exercise the right to unwind the contract under the Regulations or the right to rescind at common law (which remains available in principle in parallel to the rights to redress[1311]), then he will be able to recover any price paid and so throw the bad bargain back onto the

---

[1305] Below, paras 38-199 and 38-201.

[1306] Law Commissions' Report (2012), paras 3.49 et seq., above, para.38-172. On this law see Vol.I, Ch.8 and especially para.8-057.

[1307] 2008 Regulations, reg.27J(1)(a). The form of words "which he would not have incurred if the prohibited practice had not taken place" suggests a "but/for" test of causation applicable to claims for damages, even though the causal test applicable to the availability of the rights to redress in general is the test of "significant factor" (see 2008 Regulations reg.27A(6), above, para.38-190). Bant and Paterson (2018) 80 M.L.R. 895 at 920–921 argue that the requirement in reg.27J(1) should be interpreted as reflecting a concern that the consumer claimant is left "no better off" by reason of the award that he would have been had the prohibited practice not taken place.

[1308] 2008 Regulations reg.27J(1)(a) and (3).

[1309] The Law Commissions described the loss recoverable as "consequential economic loss", giving the example of a consumer "who is sold a new bed in an aggressive way and then throws away the old bed to make room for it": Report (2012), para.8.145. The relevant measure of damages under Pt 4A therefore follows the "reliance measures" rather than the "expectation measure" of damages: Report (2012), para.8.3–8.15.

[1310] See *Doyle v Olby (Ironmongers) Ltd* [1969] 2 Q.B.158; *Royscot Trust Ltd v Rogerson* [1991] 2 Q.B. 297 and Vol.I, paras 7-056, 7-079, 7-099.

[1311] Below, para.38-205.

trader (even though the consumer also has to return any goods transferred).[1312] And if the right to unwind or right to rescind is not, or is no longer, available to the consumer, then he may still have a right to a discount under the Regulations,[1313] although, except where the price payable was more than £5,000, the amount of such a discount is not determined by reference to the difference between the market value (again, referred to as the "price") and the amount payable under the contract, but rather to the "seriousness" of the prohibited practice, as earlier explained.[1314] Nevertheless, there could be cases in which a consumer could not recover in respect of his bad bargain, either by way of recovery of the price or a discount. This would not matter were it not for the fact that where a consumer has a right to redress under the Regulations, he does not have a right to damages under s.2(1) of the 1967 Act, as will later be explained.[1315] This unattractive result could be avoided if the restricting formula in the Regulations were interpreted to refer only to the first hypothesis so as to preclude recovery in respect of loss of any good bargain, on the basis that this is the likely intention of the legislator given that it accords with the position under the general law of misrepresentation to which this legislative right to damages is clearly related. In drawing these parallels with the general law of misrepresentation, it is well to remember, however, that the right to damages under the Regulations applies not merely to contracts (or payments) resulting from misleading actions, but also from aggressive commercial practices.

Non-financial losses   The Regulations provide that the consumer may also claim damages for "alarm, distress or physical inconvenience or discomfort"[1316] that would not have occurred if the prohibited practice had not taken place.[1317] This provision seems particularly likely to be relevant to cases where the prohibited practice was an aggressive commercial practice, but applies equally where it was a misleading action.   **38-200**

Reasonably foreseeable losses   In the case both of financial and non-financial losses, the Regulations restrict the damages recoverable by a consumer to the "loss that was reasonably foreseeable at the time of the prohibited practice".[1318] In this respect, the criterion of reasonable foreseeability reflects the position under the general law of remoteness in the tort of negligence and for breach of contract,[1319] rather than the special rule of directness applicable to damages in the tort of deceit and applied by the Court of Appeal to liability under s.2(1) of the Misrepresentation Act 1967 (though this has been the object of criticism).[1320] On the other hand, the Regulations require that it is the *loss* that was reasonably foreseeable, rather than (as under the general law governing the tort of negligence and breach of contract) the *type* or *kind* of loss. The form of words in the Regulations is therefore appar-   **38-201**

[1312] Above, para.38-193.

[1313] Above, para.38-196.

[1314] Above, para.38-196.

[1315] Misrepresentation Act 1967 s.2(4), below, para.38-208.

[1316] reg.27J(1)(b).

[1317] See reg.27J(1)(a) and (b).

[1318] reg.27J(4).

[1319] *Overseas Tankship (UK) Ltd v Morts Dock & Engineering Co (The Wagon Mound No.1)* [1961] A.C. 388, see Vol.I, paras 1-203 and 7-099 (tort of negligence). On the rules of remoteness for breach of contract see Vol.I, paras 26-117 et seq.

[1320] *Doyle v Olby (Ironmongers) Ltd* [1969] 2 Q.B.158; *Royscot Trust Ltd v Rogerson* [1991] 2 Q.B. 297 and Vol.I, paras 7-056 et seq., and 7-078.

ently more restrictive than the general law, as a type of loss may be reasonably foreseeable even where the particular loss suffered by the consumer was not so foreseeable at the time of the prohibited practice.

38-202 **Defence of due diligence** The trader's liability to damages under the Regulations is subject to what amounts to a defence of due diligence on the part of the trader and which was intended to reflect the position under s.2(1) of the Misrepresentation Act 1967, though using the language of the criminal law defence in the Regulations.[1321] Thus under reg.27J:

> "(5) A consumer does not have the right to damages if the trader proves that—
>   (a) the occurrence of the prohibited practice in question was due to—
>   (i) a mistake,
>   (ii) reliance on information supplied to the trader by another person,
>   (iii) the act or default of a person other than the trader,
>   (iv) an accident, or
>   (v) another cause beyond the trader's control, and
>   (b) the trader took all reasonable precautions and exercised all due diligence to avoid the occurrence of the prohibited practice."

Again, though, it should be borne in mind that damages are available under the Regulations not merely in respect of misleading actions (which may well be innocent in the sense of both honest and careful so as to attract this defence) and in respect of "aggressive commercial practices". Although the definition of "aggressive commercial practice" is broad enough to apply to non-intentional or even non-negligent conduct on the part of the trader, most cases of "harassment or coercion" as opposed to "undue influence" may well be thought as unlikely to attract the application of this due diligence defence.

38-203 **Damages in respect of payments made as a result of prohibited practices** The right to damages is not confined to consumers who have entered a contract with a trader as the result of a prohibited practice: it extends to consumers who have made a payment to the trader in respect of a product as the result of a prohibited practice. This includes not only payments that were not in fact due but also payment of sums that were due.[1322] There will seldom be a viable claim for financial loss in such cases,[1323] but it is not hard to imagine cases in which the consumer should be compensated for distress caused by an aggressive practice, which consists of "harassment, coercion or undue influence".[1324]

[1321] Law Commissions Report (2012) 8.165–8.173; 2008 Regulations reg.17(1), above, para.38-170.
[1322] See above, para.38-177. There is no right to unwind nor to a discount if the payment was in fact due: above, para.38-195.
[1323] In the case of a debt paid, the amount was already due, so there is unlikely to be financial loss, unless, possibly, where in order to pay the trader the consumer resorts to an (even more) expensive form of credit such a pay-day loan. In the case of a payment of a sum that was not due, the normal remedy would be to unwind the settlement agreement. In addition, the exclusion of damages for the difference between the market price of a product and the amount payable for it under a contract (reg.27J(3)), read with the definition of "product" in cases of payment (reg.2(1)), seems to preclude an award under reg.27J for loss caused by paying sums that were not due.
[1324] 2008 Regulations reg.7, above, para.38-186.

General relationship of "rights to redress" and claims under the wider law Regulation 27L provides that: **38-204**

"(1) Nothing in [Part 4A] affects the ability of a consumer to make a claim under a rule of law or equity, or under an enactment, in respect of conduct constituting a prohibited practice."

The only limitation in reg.27L is that the consumer may not recover compensation under both the Regulations and another rule or enactment.[1325] There is no definition of "compensation" for this purpose, and the question is whether it is wider than merely money awards solely aimed at the indemnisation of the loss or harm caused to the consumer. It is submitted that "compensation" is wider than "damages" (which are normally based on loss[1326]) and, in particular, should be interpreted so as to cover "compensation orders" made by criminal courts, even though the courts take into account factors other than the harm caused to the victim.[1327] This interpretation would fit with the intention of the Law Commissions, which foresaw that the consumer's right to a discount could form part of such a compensation order, though the Regulations do not so provide.[1328] Moreover, if this wider interpretation were taken, it would mean that any award of a discount under the Regulations (despite their possibly penal aspect) would also count as "compensation" for the purposes of any award of damages, whether under the Regulations themselves or under the general law.

Rescission for misrepresentation, duress or undue influence Regulation 27L **38-205**
therefore means that, subject to their own conditions, a consumer may have a right to rescind the contract for misrepresentation,[1329] duress, undue influence or unconscionability,[1330] whether or not he also has a right to redress under the Regulations. There may be occasions when the consumer will want to rely on this remedy, rather than on the right to unwind the contract under the 2008 Regulations.[1331]

Damages for fraud Regulation 27L also means that, subject to its own condi- **38-206**
tions, a consumer may have a right to damages in the tort of deceit for fraud, whether or not he also has a right to redress under the Regulations. Where a

---

[1325] reg.27L(2).

[1326] A possible exception could be punitive damages, but these are not awarded in claims for breach of contract, though they may exceptionally be awarded for claims in tort: Vol.I, para.26-048.

[1327] Powers of Criminal Courts (Sentencing) Act 2000 s.130(4). While the making of an order "is not part of the sentence of the court strictly speaking", there is an "important relationship between the sentence of the court and the desirability or otherwise of making one": *R. v Brogan* [1975] 1 All E.R. 879, 881, 880 per Scarman J.

[1328] Law Commissions Report (2012), para.5.19 which refers to the consumer's right to unwind as well as the right to a discount. The power of a criminal court under the Powers of Criminal Courts (Sentencing) Act 2000 s.130(4) extends to the award of "such amount as the court considers appropriate, having regard to any evidence and to any representations that are made by or on behalf of the accused or the prosecutor" but, as the *Law Commissions Report*, para.2.43 noted, this has been interpreted restrictively by the courts so as to preclude an award where there was neither agreement nor sufficient proof of the amount of damage: *R. v Vivian* [1979] 1 W.L.R. 291, 293; *R. v Horsham Justices, Ex p. Richards* [1985] 1 W.L.R. 986.

[1329] On the right to rescission generally see Vol.I, paras 7-112 et seq.

[1330] On which see Vol.I, paras 8-054 et seq., 8-103.

[1331] Above, para.38-187—38-191.

consumer can establish fraud, the remedy at common law may have advantages over the damages remedy provided by the Regulations in respect of misleading actions, in particular as the test of remoteness in the tort of deceit is one of directness, whereas the test of remoteness under the Regulations is foreseeability of the consumer's loss.[1332]

38-207 **Remedies for breach of contract**   In the case of a misleading action, if it can be shown that the trader's statement amounted to an element of the description of the product,[1333] or (because it was information that the trader was required to give under the Consumer Contracts (Information, Cancellation and Additional Charges) Regulations 2013[1334]) it was "included as a term of the contract",[1335] or if it amounted to an express term of the contract,[1336] and that the statement was false, the consumer may have the right to terminate the contract and will have a right to damages, though the damages must not include compensation awarded under Pt 4A of the 2008 Regulations.[1337] It may be difficult to determine whether, or to what extent, a consumer who has been awarded a discount has been compensated in respect of the difference between the value the product would have had if it had complied with the contract and its actual value.[1338]

38-208 **Misrepresentation Act 1967 s.2 disapplied**   However, on the creation of the consumer's rights to redress in 2014, the Misrepresentation Act 1967 was amended so that a consumer who has a right to redress under Pt 4A of the 2008 Regulations in respect of the conduct constituting misrepresentation no longer has a right to damages under s.2 of the Act.[1339] Section 2(4) of the 1967 Act therefore provides that s.2:

"... does not entitle a person to be paid damages in respect of a misrepresentation if the person has a right to redress under Part 4A of the [2008 Regulations] in respect of the conduct constituting the misrepresentation."

The thinking behind this disapplication was that leaving two possible grounds for consumer claims would lead to greater complexity in litigation.[1340] Nevertheless, s.2(4) is a very strange provision. In the case of the right to damages under s.2(1) of the 1967 Act, s.2(4)'s effect is not merely to prevent consumers from claiming damages under s.2 of the 1967 Act where they have a right to *damages* under the 2008 Regulations, but where they have a right to *redress*, that is, including a right to unwind the contract or to a discount. This would not matter if it were not for the

---

[1332] *Doyle v Olby (Ironmongers) Ltd* [1969] 2 Q.B.158 and see Vol.I, para.7-057; 2008 Regulations reg.27J(4), above, para.38-201.

[1333] e.g. Consumer Rights Act 2015 s.11 (formerly Sale of Goods Act 1979 s.13).

[1334] SI 2013/3134.

[1335] SI 2013/3134 regs 9(3), 10(5) and 13(6); Consumer Rights Act 2015 s.11(4) and 12(2) (goods contracts); ss.36(3) and 37(2) (digital content contracts) and 50(3) (services contracts): see above, para.38-105 and below, paras 38-499—38-500, 38-548—38-549 and 38-575 respectively.

[1336] See Vol.I, para.13-003.

[1337] reg.27L(2)(a).

[1338] See above, para.38-197.

[1339] SI 2014/870 reg.5 inserting new Misrepresentation Act 1967 s.2(4). It is provided that this disapplication does not affect claims under Consumer Credit Act 1974 s.75(1) against a creditor under a debtor-creditor-supplier agreement: 1967 Act s.2(5) (as inserted). See below, para.39-030.

[1340] Law Commissions Report (2012), paras 7.133–7.134.

fact that a consumer could have a right to unwind the contract or to a discount but no practical right to damages under the 2008 Regulations, notably, where his loss was not foreseeable by the trader at the time of engaging in the prohibited practice.[1341] In this situation, the consumer would almost certainly have a right to a discount[1342] (the right to unwind may have expired[1343]) and therefore could not rely on s.2(1) in order to recover damages under the more generous (if criticised) rule of remoteness there applicable.[1344] Moreover, apart from different rules of remoteness of damage, other differences between claims under s.2(1) and claims for damages under the 2008 Regulations may make them more or less attractive to a consumer depending on context. So, while the right to damages under the Regulations may compensate the consumer's "alarm, distress or physical inconvenience or discomfort", these heads of loss are less clearly recoverable under s.2(1)[1345]; on the other hand, while the limitation periods for rights to redress and claims under s.2(1) are both six years, the time of accrual may differ.[1346] And while contributory negligence may be a defence to a claim under s.2(1),[1347] it is less clear that such a defence would apply to a claim for damages under Pt 4A.[1348] Certainly, the drawing of an exclusive line between claims under s.2 and the consumer's right to redress under the 2008 Regulations places considerable stress on the scope of availability of the new rights, which, as has been seen, is complex. In particular, where the contract does not concern a "product" as redefined for the purposes of Pt 4A,[1349] the consumer may claim only under s.2 and not under the 2008 Regulations.

The consumer's rights to redress and s.2(2) of the 1967 Act   Moreover, the   **38-209**
relationship between a consumer's right to redress and the application of s.2(2) of the 1967 Act which provides a power in a court to award damages in lieu of rescission is not clear.[1350] Section 2(4) of the 1967 Act provides that:

"… this *section* does not entitle a person to be paid damages in respect of a misrepresentation if the person has a right to redress … in respect of the conduct constituting the misrepresentation" (emphasis added).

[1341] 2008 Regulations reg.27J(4), above, para 38-201.

[1342] The exception would be where the prohibited practice is not sufficiently serious to qualify as "minor" in the first band of reg.27I(4)(a), above, para.38-196.

[1343] Above, para.38-193.

[1344] On this rule see Vol.I, para.7-080.

[1345] They are recoverable in the tort of deceit (Vol.I, para.7-070) and the fiction of fraud in the Misrepresentation Act 1967 s.2(1) (Vol.I, para.7-080) suggests that they should therefore equally be recoverable in this context.

[1346] 2008 Regulations reg.27K(5) provides that the period is "as if it were an action founded on simple contract", thereby attracting a six-year period from the time of accrual of the cause of action, which is normally the breach of contract: Vol.I, para.28-032. Accrual of the cause of action in tort for the purposes of s.2 Misrepresentation Act is often the date when the contract is entered into, but may be a later date: Vol.I, para.28-034.

[1347] *Gran Gelato Ltd v Richcliff (Group) Ltd* [1992] Ch. 560, Vol.I, para.7-084.

[1348] The question would turn on whether the trader's liability to damages under the Regulations qualifies as "fault" as being an "act or omission which gives rise to a liability in tort" within the meaning of s.1(1) and s.4 of the Law Reform (Contributory Negligence) Act 1945. At no point do the 2008 Regulations classify the trader's liability under reg.27J as tortious, and the limitation period designated is the period applicable to claims under a simple contract (reg.27K(5)); on the other hand the consumer's rights to damages under reg.27J arises from the commission of a "prohibited practice" rather than from any breach of contract.

[1349] Above, para.38-176.

[1350] Vol.I, paras 7-105 et seq.

This could be thought to rule out the possibility of an award of damages under s.2(2) as well as damages under s.2(1), but it is submitted that s.2(4) should not be so interpreted, as its unattractive consequence would be that where a consumer has a right to redress under the Regulations, then the court would lose its power to refuse rescission (for example, in respect of an insignificant and purely innocent misrepresentation), as the court would not be in a position to "declare the contract subsisting *and award damages* in lieu of rescission" as provided by s.2(2).[1351] This consequence would be avoided if s.2(2) were interpreted as not "entitling" the misrepresentee/consumer to damages given that the award of damages is subject to the discretion of the court, as this would then mean that the disapplication in s.2(4) would not affect s.2(2) at all.

38-210   **Waiver or contractual exclusion of rights to redress**   Can the consumer's rights to redress be lost by "waiver" (including, for example, affirmation of the contract so as to lose the right to unwind) or by contractual agreement, whether in the original consumer contract between the parties or subsequently? Under the general law of misrepresentation contract terms which exclude liability for misrepresentation are subject to a test of reasonableness,[1352] and in the case of consumer contracts, are subject to the general test of unfairness in the Consumer Rights Act 2015,[1353] but the 2008 Regulations are silent on the issue whether a trader can exclude liability under the rights to redress, as is the 2005 Directive—in the latter case, unsurprisingly given that the Directive puts aside "contract law" from its scope.[1354] However, the 2008 Regulations provide that:

> "Except as provided by Part 4A, an agreement shall not be void or unenforceable by reason only of a breach of these Regulations."[1355]

This provision reflects the earlier (and still residual) position that the 2008 Regulations (following the 2005 Directive) do not affect "contract law", while excepting the situations where Pt 4A does affect contracts, notably, by the grant of rights to unwind the contract, a discount and damages.[1356] What this means is that the commission of an unfair commercial practice within the meaning of the 2008 Regulations does not itself affect the enforceability of any agreement made between a consumer or a trader except as provided by Pt 4A: it leaves open, therefore, the unenforceability of a contract term or contractual agreement which seeks to exclude or modify the effect of the rights to redress under Pt 4A. In the absence of express provision in the 2008 Regulations, it is submitted that such a *contract term* in the original consumer contract would fall under the general test of unfairness of terms in consumer contracts.[1357] On the other hand, where a consumer concluded a

---

[1351] Emphasis added.

[1352] Misrepresentation Act 1967 s.3 on which see Vol.I, paras 7-145—7-157.

[1353] This is noted by the Misrepresentation Act 1967 s.3(2) (as inserted by the 2015 Act) in disapplying s.3(1)'s own controls from the terms of consumer contracts. On the controls in Pt 2 of the 2015 Act, see below, paras 38-372 and 38-389 et seq.

[1354] 2005 Directive art.3(2), above, para.38-160. cf. Consumer Rights Directive 2011 art.25 which provides that "consumers may not waive the rights conferred on them by the national measures transposing" the Directive, above, para.38-166.

[1355] 2008 Regulations reg.29.

[1356] Above, para.38-204.

[1357] Consumer Rights Act 2015 s.62(4) and (5), below, paras 38-389 et seq. And see, formerly, Unfair Terms in Consumer Contracts Regulations 1999 (SI 1999/2083) reg.5, below paras 38-241 et seq.

contract with a trader whose "main subject matter" was to settle or otherwise exclude the consumer's right to redress under the 2008 Regulations, this contract would not fall to be tested for its fairness as it would fall within the special exclusion for terms that specify the main subject matter of the contract.[1358] Such an agreement (if contractual) or a payment could themselves give rise to a right to redress under Pt 4A, subject to the general conditions for their availability and any particular conditions applicable to the particular right to redress in question.[1359] More generally, however, the legislative controls on unfair terms in consumer contracts would not affect any non-contractual waiver under the general law by the consumer of his or her rights under Pt 4A of the Regulations, but the absence of provision in Pt 4A for waiver or affirmation as an exception to the availability of these rights argues against their applying and this position would further the purpose of the new consumer rights which are designed to be simpler and clearer than the general law.[1360] In particular, in the case of the consumer's right to unwind, the Regulations provide that the consumer enjoys this right only for a very short period (90 days) and further provides that, if the consumer has exercised the right to a discount, the consumer no longer enjoys the right to unwind. This structure argues that, within the 90-day period and unless the consumer has opted for a discount, he should not lose his right to unwind by action which would constitute affirmation under the general law.

6. THE CONTROL OF UNFAIR CONTRACT TERMS

(a) Introduction

The general position English law has long taken the view that the principles of freedom of contract and the binding force of contracts in general rule out review of the fairness of either the contract as a whole or of particular terms of the contract.[1361] As regards the fairness of particular contract terms, this general position at common law can be seen most explicitly in its approach to the validity of exemption clauses: for once agreed by the parties to a contract, they are effective to exclude liability both in contract and in tort,[1362] even extending to liability for causing death and personal injuries by negligence.[1363] The courts have tempered this position by the development of demanding tests for the incorporation of terms, especially exemption clauses,[1364] restrictive approaches to the interpretation of standard terms *contra proferentem*,[1365] and the recognition of exceptions (for

38-211

[1358] SI 1999/2083 reg.6(2)(a), below, paras 38-245 et seq.; Consumer Rights Act 2015 s.64, below, paras 38-394 et seq.

[1359] So, for example, a right to unwind a payment made would not exist in the case of payments which were owed under such a settlement contract, but a right to damages could do so: above, paras 38-195 and 38-203.

[1360] Above, para.38-172.

[1361] See Vol.I, paras 1-031 et seq. See notably, the rule that consideration need not be adequate: Vol.I, para.4-014.

[1362] *Nicholson v Willan* (1804) 5 East 507.

[1363] This is clear a fortiori from the effectiveness of non-contractual notices to this effect: e.g. *White v Blackmore* [1972] 3 All E.R. 158.

[1364] Vol.I, paras 13-008 et seq. and see especially *Interfoto Picture Library Ltd v Stiletto Visual Programmes Ltd* [1989] 1 Q.B. 433.

[1365] Vol.I, paras 15-007 et seq.

example, as regards the exclusion of remedies for personal fraud[1366] and penalty clauses[1367]), but these rules remain relatively restrained exceptions to the general position.

38-212 **Legislative control of the fairness of contract terms** By contrast, the impact of legislation on the fairness of contract terms has been very considerable and particularly so in the case of consumer contracts. Sometimes this control has been effected by the creation of rights or obligations on the parties to particular types of contracts which are not susceptible of contrary exclusion by agreement, notably as regards contracts of consumer credit,[1368] tenancy[1369] and employment.[1370] Other than this regulation of particular types of contract, before 1995 the most important restriction on the effectiveness of contract terms was the Unfair Contract Terms Act 1977, which subjected exemption and limitation clauses (and certain related clauses) both as regards persons "dealing as consumer"[1371] and commercial parties to considerable restrictions.[1372] While this Act also imposed a requirement of reasonableness on the effectiveness of indemnity clauses in consumer contracts,[1373] until the UK was required to implement the Unfair Terms in Consumer Contracts Directive 1993 (the "1993 Directive"),[1374] English law contained no system of control on the basis of fairness applicable to all or most other types of contract term. The 1993 Directive requires Member States to put in place two types of control. First, very broadly, it requires that terms in all types of consumer contracts that have not been "individually negotiated" are binding on consumers only if they are "fair",[1375] with the important exception of terms which define the main subject matter of the contract and as regards the price/quality ratio, provided that they are plain and intelligible (the "core exclusion")[1376]; it also requires more generally that written terms be plain and intelligible.[1377] Secondly, the 1993 Directive requires Member States to put in place adequate and effective means to prevent the continued use of unfair terms in consumer contracts.[1378] The 1993 Directive requires only "minimum harmonisation" and so in principle allows Member States to retain or adopt more protective measures for consumers in national laws within its scope.[1379]

[1366] Vol.I, para.7-145.

[1367] Vol.I, paras 26-190 et seq.

[1368] See Consumer Credit Act 1974, and para.39-100.

[1369] e.g. Landlord and Tenant Act 1985 s.8 (terms as to fitness for human habitation to be "implied, notwithstanding any stipulation to the contrary").

[1370] See paras 40-219 et seq.

[1371] The protections were provided for persons "dealing as consumer": Unfair Contract Terms Act 1977 ss.3–7, 12, Vol.I paras 15-073—15-079.

[1372] See above, Vol.I, para.15-062.

[1373] Unfair Contract Terms Act 1977 s.4 and see above, Vol.I, paras 15-088—15-090.

[1374] Directive 93/13/EEC on unfair terms in consumer contracts [1993] O.J. L95/21 ("1993 Directive") and see below, paras 38-218—38-319.

[1375] 1993 Directive arts 3, 4(1) and 6, below, paras 38-241 et seq.

[1376] 1993 Directive art.4(2), on which see below, paras 38-245 et seq.; 38-394 et seq. Terms which reflect legislation or the common law are also excluded from the scope of the Directive as a whole: 1993 Directive art.1(2), below, paras 38-233—38-240 and 38-388.

[1377] 1993 Directive art.5 and see below, paras 38-347 et seq. and 38-414—38-417.

[1378] 1993 Directive art.7.

[1379] 1993 Directive art.8. On "minimum harmonisation" and its significance see above, paras 38-022—38-023. For the difficulties caused by the relationship of the 1993 Directive and the Unfair Commercial Practices Directive 2005, see below, paras 38-421—38-426.

UK legislation implementing the 1993 Directive   The 1993 Directive was first   **38-213**
implemented into UK law by the Unfair Terms in Consumer Contracts Regulations 1994,[1380] but these regulations were revoked and replaced by the Unfair Terms
in Consumer Contracts Regulations 1999 ("the 1999 Regulations").[1381] The main
differences between the two sets of regulations were that the 1999 Regulations followed even more closely the terms of the Directive's provisions[1382] and they made
provision to enable a number of "qualifying bodies" to apply to the courts for
injunctive relief against the use or recommendation for use of unfair terms, whereas
under the 1994 Regulations this could be done only by the Director General of Fair
Trading.[1383] Implementation of the 1993 Directive in this way left unaffected the
controls on contract terms in the Unfair Contract Terms Act 1977, some of whose
provisions governed consumer contracts as understood by the Regulations.[1384]

Reform proposals   The existence of two overlapping legislative regimes govern-   **38-214**
ing unfair contract terms attracted considerable criticism and in 2005 the English
and Scottish Law Commissions published a joint report recommending major
legislative reform.[1385] Their proposals included the creation of a unified legislative
regime for the control of unfair terms in consumer contracts, putting together the
controls provided by the Unfair Contract Terms Act 1977 and the Unfair Terms in
Consumer Contracts Regulations 1999; preserving the protection given by the
Unfair Contract Terms Act 1977 in business contracts; and extending existing
protection against unfair contract terms for consumers to small businesses.
Meanwhile at the European level, the European Commission proposed changes to
the 1993 Directive, placing it in a wider proposal for a Consumer Rights Directive
which would have seen the provisions on unfair terms in consumer contracts in the
1993 Directive (with amendments) change from requiring minimum harmonisation to the "full harmonisation" of national laws.[1386] However, the Consumer Rights
Directive as enacted in 2011 required no change to the substance of the existing
regime of control under the 1993 Directive,[1387] although one of its provisions may

---

[1380] SI 1994/3159. The 1994 Regulations came into force on July 1, 1995 but were revoked and replaced
by the Unfair Terms in Consumer Contracts Regulations 1999 (SI 1999/2083). The 1994 Regulations applied to contracts made on or after July 1, 1995 (though the 1993 Directive art.10(1) required
national implementing measures to govern contracts concluded after December 31, 1994) and the
1999 Regulations apply to contracts made on or after October 1, 1999, and before the coming into
force of the provisions governing unfair contract terms in the Consumer Rights Act 2015 on October
1, 2015, as explained below, para.38-215.

[1381] SI 1999/2083. The 1999 Regulations were subject to minor amendments noted at the relevant
paragraphs of this section.

[1382] This may be seen in certain definitional provisions of the 1999 Regulations, in their implementation of art.1(2) of the Directive and in their lack of an exclusion of certain types of contract which
appears in the preamble to the Directive, but not in its text see 31st edn (2012) of the present work,
Vol.I, paras 15-017, 15-023 and 15-038.

[1383] See below, para.38-353.

[1384] This is most obviously the case as regards contracts where one party "deals as consumer" (Unfair
Contract Terms Act 1977 ss.3–7, 12) but is also the case as regards the controls on liability for
negligence under the 1977 Act s.2: on which see Vol.I, paras 15-073—15-078 and 15-081 et seq.

[1385] Law Commission, Scottish Law Commission, *Unfair Terms in Contracts* (Law Com. No.292, Scot
Law Com. No.199, 2005).

[1386] Proposal for a Directive on Consumer Rights of October 8, 2008 COM(2008) 614/3 final whose arts
30–39 concerned unfair contract terms; the principle of "full harmonisation" was set by art.4. On
the significance of "full harmonisation" see above, paras 38-025—38-026.

[1387] Directive 2011/83/EU on consumer rights [2011] O.J. L304/64. Its main requirements concern

be useful in interpreting aspects of the 1993 Directive.[1388] This left the way open for the UK legislator to reform the national controls on unfair terms without waiting for new legislation at the EU level.

38-215 **Consumer Rights Act 2015** The Consumer Rights Act 2015[1389] ("the 2015 Act" or "the Act") reflects the view of the Law Commissions and the UK government that UK consumer law (and especially consumer contract law) was unnecessarily complex, at times inconsistent (especially in relation to the two sets of legislative provisions governing unfair contract terms[1390]) and scattered in an unhelpful way across a series of legislative enactments, some primary legislation and some secondary, some implementing EU legislation and some purely domestic.[1391] However, the 2015 Act did not follow the Law Commissions' earlier strategy of placing the controls on unfair contract terms in a single Act and, to a considerable extent, a single framework,[1392] but instead divided the control of unfair terms sharply between terms found in consumer contracts (regulated by the 2015 Act, principally in Pt 2) and terms (principally exemption clauses[1393]) in other contracts (regulated by the Unfair Contract Terms Act 1977). Moreover, the 2015 Act was also concerned to provide new, dedicated rules for consumer rights in respect of goods, digital content and services (Pt 1 of the Act), and as a result deleted provisions specifically governing consumer contracts from other more general legislation, notably, the Sale of Goods Act 1979, and disapplied many other of the provisions of those Acts as regards "consumer contracts".[1394] The 2015 Act also introduced significant reforms to the law governing the enforcement of consumer protection laws, domestic and EU, with amendments, inter alia, of Pt 8 of the Enterprise Act 2002 so as to create a new possibility for courts to order "enhanced consumer measures" to individuals affected by breach of a consumer protection measure.[1395] These changes af-

---

information and cancellation rights in off-premises and distance contracts (on which see above, para.38-060), implemented in UK law by the Consumer Contracts (Information, Cancellation and Additional Charges) Regulations 2013 (SI 2013/3134), on which see above, paras 38-061 et seq. Other provisions in the 2011 Directive are implemented by the Consumer Rights Act 2015 ss.28 and 29 (on which see below, paras 38-526 and 38-484) and the Consumer Rights (Payment Surcharges) Regulations 2012 (SI 2012/3110): below, para.38-527. The provisions on unfair contract terms in consumer contracts in the Proposal for a Directive on Consumer Rights appeared in a somewhat modified form in the Commission's Proposal for a Regulation on a Common European Sales Law COM(2011) 635 final, Annex, arts 79–85 CESL, but this proposal was withdrawn by the EU Commission in December 2014: Vol.I, para.1-013.

[1388] See above, para.38-036.

[1389] The Consumer Rights Act 2015 was accompanied by a set of *Explanatory Notes* prepared by the Department for Business, Innovation and Skills ("*Explanatory Notes* 2015"). See also Conway, *Consumer Rights Act, Briefing Paper* (House of Commons Library, SN 6588, October 1, 2015).

[1390] Unfair Contract Terms Act 1977; Unfair Terms in Consumer Contracts Regulations 1999.

[1391] *Explanatory Notes* 2015, paras 5–9. Law Commission, Scottish Law Commission, Unfair Terms in Consumer Contracts (2005) Law Com No.292, Scot Law Com No.199 ("Law Com. Unfair Terms (2005)"); Law Commission, Scottish Law Commission, *Unfair Terms in Consumer Contracts: Advice to the Department for Business, Innovation and Skills* (March 2013) ("Law Com. Advice (2013)"); BIS, *Enhancing Consumer Confidence by Clarifying Consumer Law* (July 2012) ("BIS, Clarifying Consumer Law"). See also BIS, *Enhancing Consumer Confidence through Effective Enforcement, Consultation on consolidating and modernising consumer law enforcement powers* (March 2012).

[1392] Above, para.38-214.

[1393] The Unfair Contract Terms Act 1977 as amended by the 2015 Act applies only to exemption clauses and other clauses falling within s.3(2)(b) of the 1977 Act: see Vol.I, paras 15-080 et seq.

[1394] See generally below, paras 38-465 et seq.

[1395] Consumer Rights Act 2015 s.79; Sch.7 above, para.38-134.

fected the powers of regulators in respect of the prevention of unfair contract terms. In summary, the 2015 Act's strategy in relation to unfair contract terms had four aspects[1396]: first, it re-implemented the Directive on unfair terms in consumer contracts, following closely the Directive's general approach, but modifying some of its rules in a way more protective of consumers; secondly, it amended the Unfair Contract Terms Act 1977 so as no longer to apply to terms in "consumer contracts" or "consumer notices" as defined by the new Act; thirdly, it provided that the trader's liability arising from breach of new statutory terms in "goods contracts", "digital content contracts" and "services contracts" governing the quality, fitness for purpose, etc. of their subject matter do not bind the consumer[1397]; and, fourthly, the 2015 Act extended the enforcement measures (injunctions against, and undertakings, by traders[1398]) which it put in place for the control of unfair terms reflecting the Directive to contract terms rendered not binding on consumers under its provisions more generally, as well as to "consumer notices" also rendered not binding on consumers under the Act.[1399]

Temporal application of the 2015 Act's provisions on unfair terms   The Act   **38-216**
received Royal Assent on March 26, 2015; its substantive provisions governing unfair contract terms contained in Pts 1 and 2 were brought into force on October 1, 2015.[1400] The Act provides that the Secretary of State may make "transitional, transitory or saving provision in connection with the coming into force of any provision of this Act" by order made by statutory instrument.[1401] Parts 1 and 2 of the Act were brought into force generally so as to apply to contracts made on or after October 1, 2015.[1402] Thus contracts made before October 1, 2015, and notices that

---

[1396] See below, paras 38-370—38-374.

[1397] Below, paras 38-465 et seq. (with the qualifications there noted).

[1398] These are detailed in 2015 Act Sch.4, on which see below, para.38-420.

[1399] 2015 Act ss.31(7), 47(5), 57(7), 70 and Sch.3, on which see below, para.38-374. In addition, the provisions in Pt 2 of the 2015 Act which implemented the 1993 Directive were designated as a specified UK law for the purposes of s.212 of the Enterprise Act 2002 ("Community infringements"), and acts or omissions in respect of any provision in Pt 2 of the 2015 Act are specified as possible "domestic infringements" for the purposes of s.211 of the Enterprise Act 2002. For the details and more general discussion of these powers see below, paras 38-420—38-426.

[1400] The Consumer Rights Act 2015 (Commencement No.3, Transitional Provisions, Savings and Consequential Amendments) Order 2015 (SI 2015/1630) art.3(a)–(c). (There is an exception as regards Pt 1 Ch.4's provisions governing services contracts which did not apply to "consumer transport services" (as defined by the Order) until October 1, 2016: 2015 Order arts 4 and 6(2) as amended by the Consumer Rights Act 2015 (Commencement No.3, Transitional Provisions, Savings and Consequential Amendments) (Amendment) Order 2016 (SI 2016/484) art.2.) But see further below, para.38-437. Section 100(1) and (2) provides that ss.96–98 ("this chapter") which created powers in the Secretary of State to make consequential provisions, to make transitional, transitory and saving provisions, for financial provision come into force on the day on which the Act is passed, i.e. March 26, 2015 (Royal Assent). See also below, para.38-366.

[1401] 2015 Act s.88.

[1402] The Consumer Rights Act 2015 (Commencement No.3, Transitional Provisions, Savings and Consequential Amendments) Order 2015 (SI 2015/1630) art.6(1) provide that the provisions of Pts 1 and 2 brought into force on October 1, 2015 do *not* apply to any contract entered into before October 1, 2015 which would, apart from its provisions, be covered by Pts 1 or 2 nor to any notice provided or communicated before October 1, 2015 which would constitute a "consumer notice" and so be covered by Pt 2 of the Act. Article 6(3) of the 2015 Order therefore preserves the effect of the amendments to the law required by the Sale and Supply of Goods to Consumers Regulations 2002 (on which see below, paras 38-439 et seq.) in relation to any contract entered before October 1, 2015 despite the revocation of those Regulations by the Act; and art.6(4) preserves the effect of the Unfair

might apply to events that occurred before that date, continue to be governed by the pre-Act law, i.e. the Unfair Terms in Consumer Contract Regulations 1999 and, so far as it affects consumers, the Unfair Contract Terms Act 1977.

38-217 **The structure of this section** This section will consider first the 1993 Directive itself, which remains central to an understanding of the provisions in both the 1999 Regulations and the 2015 Act which have implemented it in English law; secondly, it will discuss the 1999 Regulations (the "old law"), together with English case-law interpreting them and case-law of the European Court of Justice interpreting the Directive. Thirdly, it will set out the new general scheme for the control of unfair terms in Pt 2 of the 2015 Act (the "new law"). This section of the chapter refers to the *Explanatory Notes* accompanying the Consumer Rights Act 2015.[1403] The 2015 Act's provisions preventing the exclusion of the consumer's rights arising under contracts for the supply of goods, digital content and services will be considered later in the context of the provisions setting out the rights themselves.[1404] Fourthly, a final part of this section will consider three particular cases of control required by the Consumer Rights Directive 2011 in relation to the imposition by traders of monetary charges on consumers, whether or not any contract term provides for these charges: payment charges, "additional payments" and helpline charges.[1405]

(b) The Directive on Unfair Terms in Consumer Contracts

38-218 **Introduction** On April 5, 1993 the EC Council enacted a directive on Unfair Terms in Consumer Contracts ("the Directive").[1406] It was made under art.95 of the EC Treaty (now art.114 TFEU), which empowered the European legislator to issue directives for the approximation of provisions laid down by laws, regulations or administrative action which have as their object the establishment and functioning of the common market, making particular mention of proposals in the field of

---

Terms in Consumer Contracts Regulations 1999 (on which see above, paras 38-220 et seq.) in relation to "any contract or notice relating to any contract" entered into before October 1, 2015 which is provided or communicated before October 1, 2015 and which would otherwise be covered by Pts 1 or 2 of the Act, despite the revocation of those Regulations by the 2015 Act. Similarly, those provisions brought into force on October 1, 2016 in Pt 1 of the 2015 Act in relation to any "contract to supply a consumer transport service" do not apply to contracts entered before that date and the provisions in the Unfair Contract Terms Act 1977 therefore still apply to those contracts until that date: SI 2015/1630 arts 4 and 6(2) (as amended by SI 2016/484 art.2(3)). On the temporal application of the enforcement provisions of the 2015 Act, see below, para.38-366.

[1403] These were prepared by the Department of Business, Innovation and Skills ("*Explanatory Notes* 2015").

[1404] Below, paras 38-531—38-532,38-564 and 38-586.

[1405] Below, paras 38-427—38-431.

[1406] Directive 93/13 on unfair terms in consumer contracts [1993] O.J. L95/21 ("1993 Directive"). For discussion of the Directive or the Unfair Terms in Consumer Contracts Regulations, see Dean (1993) 56 M.L.R. 581; Collins (1994) 14 O.J.L.S. 229; Macdonald (1994) J.B.L. 441; Hondius (1994) 7 *Journal of Contract Law* 34; Willett (1994) Con. L.J. 114; Beale in Beatson and Friedmann (eds), *Good Faith and Fault in Contract Law* (1995), Ch.9; Bright and Bright (1995) 111 L.Q.R. 655; Weatherill (1995) 3 *European Review of Private Law* 307, especially 316 et seq. cf. Joerges at 175; Collins at 353; de Moor at 257; Weatherill, *E.C. Consumer Law and Policy* (2005), pp.115 et seq.; Howells and Wilhelmsson, *E.C. Consumer Law* (1997), pp.88 et seq.; Beatson, *Anson's Law of Contract*, 28th edn (2002), pp.200–203, 300 et seq.; Macdonald [1999] C.L.J. 413; Whittaker (2000) 116 L.Q.R. 95; Bright (2000) 20 L.S. 331; Whittaker (2004) *ZEuP* 75; Whittaker (2010) 73 M.L.R. 106.

consumer protection which must "take as a base a high level of protection".[1407] The preamble to the Directive makes clear that its purposes are: (i) to reduce distortions in competition between sellers of goods[1408] and suppliers of services caused by differences in rules governing terms in consumer contracts; (ii) to create effective uniform legal protection for consumers from the imposition of unfair contract terms,[1409] especially (but not exclusively) where this concerns transactions with suppliers in Member States other than their own[1410]; and (iii) to enhance the awareness of consumers as to the rules of law which govern consumer contracts in Member States other than their own, for otherwise they may be deterred from entering direct transactions with suppliers in other Member States.[1411] The Directive requires only minimum requirements for the control of fairness and transparency of terms in consumer contracts, it being expressly acknowledged that Member States are free to retain or to introduce systems of control which are more protective of consumers.[1412] This means, inter alia, that decisions of courts of other Member States concerning the interpretation of their legislation implementing the Directive have to be treated with considerable care, as their interpretation may be of national legislation which (lawfully) goes further than the Directive requires.[1413]

Significance of the Directive for English law   As earlier explained, the Directive remains important even after its implementation into UK law by the 1999 Regulations or the 2015 Act, as English courts must wherever possible give effect not merely to the terms but also the purposes of the Directive, and to decisions of the Court of Justice interpreting its provisions.[1414] In the following discussion, therefore, while reference will be made to the terms of the Regulations and the 2015 Act, where necessary reference will be made to the Directive itself. For this purpose, the Court of Justice will normally take "autonomous" interpretations of its concepts, and has done so in respect of some of the key concepts.[1415] More generally, the Court of Justice has developed two important areas of case-law governing the

38-219

[1407] EC Treaty art.95(3) (now art.114(3) TFEU).
[1408] But see discussion, below, paras 38-222 et seq.
[1409] Directive 1993 recital 9.
[1410] This is clear from recital 2's use of the phrase "*notably*, when [sellers or suppliers] sell or supply in other Member States" (emphasis added) and in recital 7 ("both at home and throughout the internal market"). See also *Sziber v ERSTE Bank Hungary Zrt* (C-483/16) EU:C:2018:367 paras 56–59.
[1411] Directive 1993 recital 5.
[1412] Directive 1993 art.8 and see *Caja de Ahorros y Monte de Piedad de Madrid v Asociación de Usuarios de Servicios Bancarios (Ausbanc)* (C-484/08) EU:C:2010:309, [2010] 3 C.M.L.R. 43 (in relation to art.4(2) of the Directive, on which see above, para.38-022), *Pereničová v SOS finance, spol. sro* (C-453/10) EU:C:2012:144, [2012] 2 C.M.L.R. 28 paras 34–36 (in relation to art.6(1) in fine of the Directive). The Proposal for a Directive on Consumer Rights of October 8, 2008 COM(2008) 614/3 final art.4 (full harmonisation) sought to change this position as regards the 1993 Directive, but the relevant provisions (arts 30–39 of the Proposal) were not present in the Directive as enacted: Directive 2011/83/EU on consumer rights [2011] O.J. L304/64.
[1413] e.g. the decision of the French Cour de Cassation in Civ.(1) March 15, 2005, Bulletin civil I No.135 which held that the French legislation protecting *consommateurs ou non-professionnels* against unfair contract terms could apply for the protection of a corporation as included within the term *non-professionnel* as long as it acted outside its business, even though both the Directive itself and the ECJ make clear that "consumer" refers only to human persons: 1993 Directive art.2(b) and above, para.38-032.
[1414] Above, paras 38-014 et seq. but cf. as to the likely effects of the UK's leaving of the EU, above, para.38-004 and Vol.I, paras 1-014—1-018.
[1415] See, notably, in respect of the concepts used in art.4(2) of the 1993 Directive: below, paras 38-250—38-253.

Directive, recognising a duty in national courts to address the issue of the fairness of a term falling within the Directive's controls of their own motion[1416] and providing national courts with considerable and increasingly elaborate "guidance" as to the proper application of the notion of "fairness" itself and of the related requirement that a term be plain and intelligible.[1417] The significance of this case-law for the UK's implementation of the Directive will be found in the exposition of the provisions of the 1999 Regulations and in the commentary made on the provisions of the 2015 Act.

(c) The Old Law: the Unfair Terms in Consumer Contracts Regulations 1999

38-220 **Temporal application of the 1999 Regulations** The 1999 Regulations apply to contracts made on or after October 1, 1999 and before October 1, 2015, when the provisions governing unfair contract terms in the Consumer Rights Act 2015 were brought into force so as to apply to contracts made on or after that date.[1418]

38-221 **Summary of impact of the 1999 Regulations** The 1999 Regulations subject a very wide range of types of terms in consumer contracts to two requirements: (i) that the terms should be "fair"; and (ii) that when in writing they should be written in "plain, intelligible language" (the latter being sometimes referred to as a requirement of "transparency"). There are two levels of effect in respect of any failure to fulfil these requirements. At the level of the relationship between the parties to a contract, a term which fails the requirement of fairness is not binding on the consumer, while a term which fails the requirement of transparency is to be interpreted *contra proferentem* and may be subjected to the test of fairness even if it relates to the contract's price or main subject matter.[1419] At a more general level, the 1999 Regulations empowered the Competition and Markets Authority (CMA) (formerly the Office of Fair Trading (OFT)[1420]) and a number of other bodies to bring proceedings for an injunction to prevent a person using a term which they consider is unfair or unclear.[1421] The OFT published guidance on its approach to its powers under the Regulations and on why it considered that certain kinds of standard terms used in contracts with consumers have the potential for unfairness under the Regulations, some of which is general and some of which specific to certain market sectors.[1422] These publications provide useful guidance as to the

---

[1416] Below, paras 38-331—38-333.

[1417] Below, paras 38-269—38-271.

[1418] Above, para.38-216.

[1419] Below, paras 38-339—38-346, 38-261, 38-262 and 38-351.

[1420] As from April 1, 2014, the OFT was abolished and its functions under the 1999 Regulations taken over by the CMA: Enterprise and Regulatory Reform Act 2013 (Competition) (Consequential, Transitional and Saving Provisions) (No.2) Order 2014 (SI 2014/549) Sch.1 para.26; Public Bodies (The Office of Fair Trading Transfer of Consumer Advice Scheme Function and Modification of Enforcement Functions) Order 2013 (SI 2013/783) art.10. See further below, paras 38-353 et seq.

[1421] 1994 Regulations reg.8; 1999 Regulations reg.12 (as amended), and see below, paras 38-353 et seq.

[1422] See notably, OFT, *Unfair contract terms guidance* (2008) OFT311 available at *http://www.oft.gov.uk/about-the-oft/legal-powers/legal/unfair-terms/guidance*. These guidance notes replaced regular "unfair contract terms bulletins", to which reference is on occasion still made as they provided more context for the examples which they set out. The OFT's guidance remains available on the CMA's website: *https://www.gov.uk/government/collections/cma-consumer-enforcement-guidance*. The CMA has published guidance setting out its understanding of the Consumer Rights Act 2015: *Unfair contract*

likely application of the test of unfairness, but the OFT's views have not always been followed by the courts.[1423]

(i) The Types of Contracts Governed by the 1999 Regulations

All types of consumer contracts The 1999 Regulations (following the English **38-222** version of the 1993 Directive) provide that they apply in relation to "unfair terms in contracts concluded between a seller or supplier and a consumer",[1424] but they define "seller or supplier" without reference to the types of contracts involved.[1425] Moreover, the terminology of sale and supply is not used at the same points in the Directive in a number of its other language versions, which instead use words translatable as "trader" (such as the French, *professionnel*) instead of "seller and supplier" and recital 10 of the Directive explains that its rules "should apply to *all* contracts concluded between sellers or suppliers and consumers".[1426] The general view of commentators has long been that the 1993 Directive applies to all types of consumer contracts defined by reference only to the status of their parties: the "seller and supplier" and the "consumer"[1427] and this was put beyond doubt by the Court of Justice in *Brusse v Jahani BV*,[1428] *Šiba v Devėnas*,[1429] and *Tarčau*.[1430] In *Brusse v Jahani BV* the Court of Justice considered a question on the proper interpretation of the definition of "seller or supplier" in the context of Dutch law, given that, like the English version, the Dutch version of the Directive uses "seller" to describe the business party to the contract.[1431] Having reviewed the various language versions of the Directive, the Court noted that, whatever the terminology used in the

---

terms guidance, *Guidance on the unfair contract terms provisions in the Consumer Rights Act*, (July, 2015) available at *https://www.gov.uk/government/uploads/system/uploads/attachment_data/file/450440/Unfair_Terms_Main_Guidance.pdf*. See also CMA, *Consumer law compliance review: cloud storage, Findings report* (May 27, 2016), esp. Ch.5, available at *https://www.gov.uk/government/uploads/system/uploads/attachment_data/file/526447/cloud-storage-findings-report.pdf*.

[1423] *Director General of Fair Trading v First National Bank Plc* [2001] UKHL 52, [2002] 1 A.C. 481 and see below, para.38-246 and see also *OFT v Abbey National Plc* [2009] UKSC 6, [2010] 1 A.C. 696 below, paras 38 247—38-248 and cf. *Office of Fair Trading v Ashbourne Management Services Ltd* [2011] EWHC 1237 (Ch), [2011] E.C.C. 32.

[1424] 1999 Regulations reg.4(1); 1993 Directive art.1. The 1994 Regulations reg.3(1) and Sch.1 paras (a)–(d) were expressed as not applying to contracts relating to employment, contracts relating to succession rights, any contract relating to rights under family law and any contract relating to the incorporation and organisation of companies or partnerships. This reflected 1993 Directive recital 10, as noted below in this paragraph.

[1425] 1999 Regulations reg.3(1), "seller or supplier".

[1426] (Emphasis added): *"que ces règles doivent s'appliquer à tout contrat conclu entre un professionnel et un consommateur"*. Similar formulations are found in the Italian, Spanish and German versions of the Directive; 1993 Directive art.2.

[1427] On the 1993 Directive see Tenreiro (1993) 7 *Contrats-Concurrence-Consommation* 1; Trochu (1993) D.S. Chron 315, 317; Weatherill, *EU Consumer Law and Policy* (2005) p.117; Calais-Auloy and Steinmetz, *Droit de la consommation*, 7th edn (2006), para.179 (although referring to the French legislation implementing the Directive). The arguments in favour of this position have been rehearsed in successive editions of the present work, Vol.I, Ch.15 since its 27th edition.

[1428] C-488/11 EU:C:2013:341, May 30, 2013.

[1429] C-537/13 EU:C:2015:14, January 15, 2015 [2015] Bus. L.R. 81 (*"Šiba v Devėnas (C-537/13)"*). See also *Karel de Grote–Hogeschool Katholieke Hogeschool Antwerpen VZW v Kuijpers* (C-147/16) of May 17, 2018 at paras 53–54.

[1430] *Tarčau v Banca Comercială Intesa Sanpaolo România SA* (C-74/15) Order of CJEU November 19, 2015 (*"Tarčau (C-74/15)"*).

[1431] C-488/11 EU:C:2013:341, paras 25–27 (*"verkoper"*).

different versions, they all defined the business party in the same way (as reflected in the definition in the 1999 Regulations reg.3(1)) and that therefore:

"... beyond the term used to designate the other party to the contract with the consumer, the legislature's intention was not to restrict the scope of the directive solely to contracts concluded between a seller and a consumer."[1432]

Noting the reference in recital 10 to "all contracts" concluded between sellers and suppliers and consumers,[1433] the Court concluded that:

"... it is therefore by reference to the capacity of the contracting parties, according to whether or not they are acting for purposes relating to their trade, business or profession that the directive defines the contracts to which it applies."[1434]

This view of the scope of the Directive reflects the purpose of the Directive in the protection of consumers as "weaker parties" as regards both their bargaining power and their level of knowledge.[1435] As a result, the Court held that a contract of residential tenancy concluded between a landlord acting for purposes relating to his trade, business or profession and a tenant acting for purposes which do not relate to his trade, business or profession fell within the scope of the Directive.[1436] In *Šiba v Devėnas*,[1437] the Court of Justice followed its earlier view in *Brusse* and therefore held that contracts for the supply of legal services fell within the scope of the Directive, even though the lawyer supplying those services exercised a "liberal profession" (which is distinguished from a business in the laws of some Member States).[1438] And in *Tarčau v Banca Comercială Intesa Sanpaolo România SA*, the Court of Justice followed this earlier case-law and therefore held that the 1993 Directive could apply to a contract of guarantee undertaken by a natural person act-

---

[1432] *Brusse v Jahani BV* (C-488/11) EU:C:2013:341 ("*Brusse* (C-488/11)"), para.28. On the definition in the Regulations see below, para.38-224.

[1433] 1993 Directive recital 10 notes that, "as a result" of its application to "all contracts concluded between sellers or suppliers and consumers", it does *not* apply to "contracts relating to employment, contracts relating to succession rights, contracts relating to rights under family law and contracts relating to the incorporation and organization of companies and partnership agreements". Generally, these exclusions (which were reflected in the text of the 1994 Regulations reg.3(1), Sch.1) are straightforward given that the parties to these types of contract would not qualify as "seller or supplier" and "consumer" within the meaning of the 1993 Directive, but there is a particular difficulty with this interpretation as regards contracts of employment. While normally these will not count as "consumer contracts" as neither the "supplier of the service" (the employee) *nor* the would-be recipient of the service (the employer) act for purposes outside their "trade, business or profession", there may be circumstances in which the employer could appear to count as a "consumer", e.g. in the case of a private individual employing a nanny for his or her children (perhaps using for this purpose the standard terms of the nanny's professional association), where it could be argued that the individual does so as a consumer of the professional services of the nanny. In theory, there could here be both a "consumer contract" and a contract of employment, but it may be that the CJEU could read recital 10 as reflecting an understanding that the existence of a contract of employment is incompatible with there being a "consumer contract" within the meaning of the 1993 Directive. In this respect, there is a preliminary reference pending before the CJEU asking whether an employer which grants loans to an employee for the purchase of a home are acting as "seller or supplier" and "consumer" respectively for the purposes of the 1993 Directive: *Pouvin v Electricité de France* (C-590/17).

[1434] *Brusse* (C-488/11) para.30.

[1435] *Brusse* (C-488/11) para.31.

[1436] *Brusse* (C-488/11) para.34.

[1437] *Šiba v Devėnas* (C-537/13) January 15, 2015.

[1438] *Šiba v Devėnas* (C-537/13) at paras 17, 20–24.

ing other than in the course of business under which he or she guaranteed the obligations of a debtor company to a commercial lender.[1439] According to the Court of Justice:

"... [t]he purpose of the contract is ... subject to the exceptions listed in the recital 10 of the Directive ... , irrelevant in determining the scope of the directive."[1440]

As a result, the Directive (and therefore the 1999 Regulations) do not restrict the categories of contract to which they apply in the sense of the types of subject matter with which they are concerned; the contracts to which they apply are defined exclusively by reference to the status of the two parties: "seller and supplier" and "consumer".[1441] On the other hand, in *Šiba v Devėnas* the Court held that the nature of the subject matter of the contract would be relevant to the assessment of the fairness of its terms.[1442]

Further examples The Directive's Annex setting out an indicative list of terms   **38-223**
which may be unfair (appearing in Sch.2 to the 1999 Regulations) assumes that it applies to non-physical property, including transactions in transferable securities, financial instruments and to the purchase or sale of foreign currency, traveller's cheques or international money orders denominated in foreign currency.[1443] This being so, contracts of assignment or of the licensing of contractual rights (for example, a right to use computer software) are also included within the ambit of the Regulations; and English courts have held or assumed that the Regulations apply to a wide variety of types of consumer contract, notably, contracts of residential tenancy[1444]; contracts for the supply of a newly-built house,[1445] contracts for the provision of

---

[1439] *Tarčau v Banca Comercială Intesa Sanpaolo România SA* C 74/15 Order of CJEU November 19, 2015 ("*Tarčau* (C-74/15)") (an "order" is made by the CJEU where it considers that the question for a preliminary ruling admits of no reasonable doubt). See similarly *Bucura v SC Bancpost SA* (C-348/14) EU:C:2015:447, July 9, 201 (available in French) paras 35–38 (1993 Directive may apply where the alleged "consumer" contracted as "co-debtor" to a person concluding a contract of consumer credit); *Dumitraş v BRD Groupe Société Générale* (C-534/15) Order of the CJEU of September 14, 2016 (contract of guarantee by individual in context of group of companies); *Bachman v FAER IFN SA* (C-535/16) (Order of the Court of April 27, 2017, available in French) (contract of novation under which individual undertook obligations arising under earlier commercial contract of loan). See also *Air Berlin Plc & Co Luftverkehrs KG v Bundesverband der Verbraucherzentralen und Verbraucherverbande-Verbracherzentrale Bundesverband eV* (C-290/16) of July 6, 2017 at para.44, holding that the 1993 Directive is a "general directive for consumer protection, intended to apply to all sectors of economic activity" and therefore national legislation implementing the 1993 Directive could apply to the contracts of air transport falling within the scope of Regulation (EC) 1008/2008 of the European Parliament and of the Council on common rules for the operation of air services in the Community in the absence of express provision in that Regulation to the contrary (which there is not).

[1440] *Tarčau* (C-74/15) at para.22. On the status of these "exceptions" see below, para.38-222, in relation to the 1993 Directive recital 10.

[1441] See below, paras 38-224—38-227 on the definitions of these terms.

[1442] 1993 Directive art.4(1); C-537/13 at paras 33–35, below, para.38-284.

[1443] 1999 Regulations Sch.2 para.2(c). On the role of this Schedule more generally, see below, paras 38-299 et seq.

[1444] *London Borough of Newham v Khatun* [2004] EWCA Civ 55, [2005] Q.B. 37 and see *Peabody Trust Governors v Reeve* [2008] EWHC 1432 (Ch) at [30], [2009] L. & T.R. 6; *Shaftsbury House (Developments) Ltd v Lee* [2010] EWHC 1484 (Ch) at [54], *Rochdale BC v Dixon* [2011] EWCA Civ 1173, [2012] H.L.R. 6.

[1445] *Zealander v Laing Homes Ltd* (2000) 2 T.C.L.R. 724. The CJEU has assumed that the 1993 Directive applies to contracts for the purchase of immovable property by a consumer from a builder:

financial services,[1446] contracts of membership of a gymnasium,[1447] and the contract under which a person enjoys free parking for a limited period.[1448]

38-224 **"Sellers or suppliers"** Regulation 3(1) of the 1999 Regulations provides that:

> "... 'seller or supplier' means any natural or legal person who, in contracts covered by these Regulations, is acting for purposes relating to his trade, business or profession, whether publicly owned or privately owned."[1449]

Restricting consumer protection to situations where the other party is acting "in the course of a business" is familiar to English lawyers from the Unfair Contract Terms Act 1977, many of whose controls are restricted to exemption clauses governing "business liability",[1450] but the proper interpretation for the purposes of the Directive (and therefore the Regulations) may differ. As explained earlier in relation to the proper EU approach to the definition of the non-consumer party to consumer contracts generally,[1451] in *BKK Mobil Oil*[1452] the Court of Justice held that the concept of "trader" and "business" (which are identical) for the purposes of the Unfair Commercial Practices Directive 2005 are broadly defined and must include public bodies even if they conclude contracts in the course of pursuing a task in the public interest[1453]; the significance of these terms:

> "... must be determined in relation to the related but diametrically opposed concept of 'consumer', which refers to any individual not engaged in commercial or trade activities."[1454]

And in *Šiba v Devėnas* the Court of Justice followed this case-law in relation to "seller or supplier" under the 1993 Directive, holding therefore that the public or private nature of the specific task which forms the subject matter of the contract cannot determine that Directive's application.[1455] This view also precludes any requirement that the "seller or supplier" acts with a view to profit as public bodies providing services to citizens/consumers will often not do so.[1456] Finally, it is submitted that, once the parties to the contract satisfy the definitions of "seller or supplier" and

---

Constructora Principado SA v Menéndez Álvarez (C-226/12) EU:C:2014:10, January 16, 2014.

[1446] *Director General of Fair Trading v First National Bank* [2001] UKHL 52, [2002] 1 A.C. 481 (below, para.38-246); *Abbey National Plc v Office of Fair Trading* [2009] UKSC 6, [2010] 1 A.C. 696 (the "Bank Charges" case) (below, paras 38-247—38-248). The 1993 Directive recital 19 assumes that contracts of insurance may fall within its scope. As will be seen, contracts of loan to a consumer secured by mortgage on property have recently formed a significant part of the CJEU's case-law: below, para.38-270.

[1447] *Office of Fair Trading v Ashbourne Management Services Ltd* [2011] EWHC 1237 (Ch), [2011] E.C.C. 31.

[1448] *ParkingEye Ltd v Beavis* [2015] UKSC 67, [2016] A.C. 1172, below, paras 38-275—38-277.

[1449] cf. 1994 Regulations reg.2 "sellers", "suppliers" and "business".

[1450] Unfair Contract Terms Act 1977 ss.1(3) (as amended) and 14.

[1451] Above, paras 38-050—38-058.

[1452] *BKK Mobil Oil Körperschaft des öffentlichen Rechts v Zentrale zur Bekämpfung unlauteren Wettbewerbs eV* (C-59/12) EU:C:2013:634, October 3, 2013 ("*BKK Mobil Oil* (C-59/12)"), above para.38-053.

[1453] *BKK Mobil Oil* (C-59/12) at paras 32–33, above para.38-053.

[1454] *BKK Mobil Oil* (C-59/12) para.33.

[1455] *Šiba v Devėnas* (C-537/13) para.28.

[1456] *Karel de Grote–Hogeschool Katholieke Hogeschool Antwerpen VZW v Kuijpers* (C-147/16) of May 17, 2018 at para.51.

"consumer" under the 1993 Directive (and therefore the 1999 Regulations), there is no need to establish that the particular contract concluded between them formed a regular part of the seller or supplier's business activity.[1457]

"Consumer"   Regulation 3(1) of the 1999 Regulations provides that: **38-225**

> "… 'consumer' means any natural person who, in contracts covered by these Regulations, is acting for purposes which are outside his trade, business or profession."[1458]

Unlike the definition in the Consumer Rights Act 2015 which refers to acting for purposes which are "wholly or partly" outside his trade, etc.,[1459] this follows exactly the definition in the 1993 Directive.[1460] As earlier explained, it therefore restricts consumers to "natural persons" and rules out the possibility of a company relying on the provisions of the Regulations even if it acts "for purposes which are outside [its] business".[1461] The possibly wider significance of "consumer" in the Directive (and therefore the 1999 Regulations) has been discussed earlier,[1462] as has the English case-law on the Regulations themselves[1463] and the possible relevance of the concept of the "average consumer" for these purposes.[1464]

"Consumers" as "suppliers"   The general question whether a person who supplies, other than in the course of his business, goods or services to a business (as, for example, in the case of a consumer selling a used car or jewellery to a trader) can count as a "consumer" for the purposes of EU consumer protection law has been raised earlier, but the question must be addressed specifically in relation the 1993 Directive.[1465] In this respect, the English version of arts 1 and 2 of the Directive, which describe the business party to the contract as the "seller or supplier" may be thought to support an understanding of a consumer as "recipient". Also in favour of this view is the concern of the Directive with enhancing the fairness of competition of the supply of property and services, which may be thought to make sense only where the latter are indeed competing, i.e. where their *provision* is by "businesses".[1466] And in general, as has been seen, the European Court has taken a   **38-226**

[1457] Above, para.38-054.

[1458] cf. 1994 Regulations reg.2, "consumer". No burden of proof as to being a "consumer" is set by the 1999 Regulations, following the 1993 Directive art.2(b).

[1459] Consumer Rights Act 2015 s.2(3), above paras 38-041—38-042 and below, para.38-384.

[1460] 1993 Directive art.2(b).

[1461] *Cape Snc v Idealservice Srl* (C-541/99 and C-542/99) EU:C:2001:625, [2001] E.C.R. I-09049. For English law, the 1999 Regulations are extended to consumer arbitration agreements including as "consumer" for this purpose legal as well as natural persons: Arbitration Act 1996 s.90; *Heifer International Inc v Christiansen* [2007] EWHC 3015 (TCC), [2008] All E.R. (D) 120 (Jan) and see below, para.38-302.

[1462] Above, paras 38-035—38-036. Neither the 1993 Directive nor the 1999 Regulations set a burden of proof as to "consumer".

[1463] Above, paras 38-038—38-040.

[1464] Above, paras 38-044—38-045. As explained below, the "average consumer" has been made relevant by the CJEU to the requirement of plain, intelligible language in 1993 Directive arts 4(2) and 5 (below, paras 38-261, 38-262 and 38-350).

[1465] Above, para.38-047. cf. the position under the Unfair Contract Terms Act 1977 in relation to which it has been stated that "a person can "deal as consumer" in disposing of goods, no less than in acquiring goods or services": Peel (ed.), *Treitel on The Law of Contract*, 14th edn (2015), para.7-054.

[1466] cf. the change of phrasing used in defining consumer contracts under the Rome Convention of June 19, 1980 on the law applicable to contractual obligations and its successor in Rome I Regulation (Regulation (EC) 593/2008 on the law applicable to contractual obligations). Under art.5(1) Rome

restrictive interpretation of the notion of "consumer" even in the context of consumer protection legislation.[1467] On the other hand, other language versions of arts 1 and 2 of the 1993 Directive do not assume a sale or supply *by the business*, instead using terms to describe the non-consumer party to the contract such as *professionnel* in the French and *Gewerbetreibender* in the German.[1468] Moreover, as earlier noted,[1469] the justification for the protection of consumers against unfair terms accepted by the Court of Justice of the EU is that "consumers" are weaker than traders in their bargaining power and level of knowledge and that this leads to their agreeing to terms whose content they cannot influence and this justification applies with equal force to "consumers" who supply as to those who receive. The view taken by successive editions of the present work has been that the 1993 Directive can apply to contracts under which "consumers" supply persons acting in the course of business and this view was recently confirmed explicitly by the Court of Justice of the EU in its decision in *Tarčau v Banca Comercială Intesa Sanpaolo România SA*.[1470] In that case, the national court had considered that the 1993 Directive applied only to contracts for the supply of goods or services to consumers, but the Court of Justice held the Directive applies to "all contracts" between consumers and sellers or suppliers.[1471] Given that the directive defines the scope of the contracts to which it applies by reference to the capacity of its contracting parties, that is, "according to whether or not they are acting for purposes relating to their trade, business or profession,"[1472] a contract under which a natural person agrees to secure the contractual obligations owed by a commercial company to a banking institution under a credit agreement will fall within the scope of the directive, if the national court finds that that natural person (as "consumer") "acted for private purposes" rather than that he:

"... acted for purposes relating to his trade, business or profession or because of functional links he has with that company, such as a directorship or non-negligible shareholding."[1473]

Referring to the decision in *Tarčau*, the English Court of Appeal has been prepared to assume, without deciding, that the 1993 Directive (and therefore the 1999

Convention a consumer contract is defined as "[a] contract the object of which is the *supply of goods or services to a person ('the consumer')* for a purpose which can be regarded as being outside his trade or profession, or a contract for the provision of credit for that object", whereas under art.6(1) Rome I the special provisions governing consumer contracts apply to "a contract concluded by a natural person for a purpose which can be regarded as being outside his trade or profession (the consumer) with another person acting in the exercise of his trade or profession (the professional)".

[1467] Above, para.38-034.
[1468] cf. above, para.38-222.
[1469] Above, para.38-034.
[1470] C-74/15 Order of CJEU November 19, 2015 ("*Tarčau* (C-74/15)").
[1471] *Tarčau* (C-74/15) at para.22 and see above, para.38-222.
[1472] *Tarčau* (C-74/15) at para.23.
[1473] *Tarčau* (C-74/15) at para.29. For the earlier English decisions on this point see *Barclays Bank Plc v Kufner* [2008] EWHC 2319 (Comm), [2009] 1 All E.R. (Comm) 1 at [28]–[29] Field J. (guarantor acting for purposes of trade or business); *Royal Bank of Scotland v Chandra* [2010] EWHC 105 (Ch), [2010] 1 Lloyd's Rep. 677 at [102] (affirmed [2011] EWCA Civ 192, [2011] Bus. L.R. D149 on other grounds) (principal debtor not consumer); *United Trust Bank Ltd v Dohil* [2011] EWHC 3302 (QB) at [73] (guarantor acting for purposes of trade or business) not following *The Governor and Co of the Bank of Scotland v Singh* Unreported June 17, 2005, QBD Mercantile Ct, Manchester, at [85]–[90]; *Manches LLP v Freer* [2006] EWHC 991 (QB); *Williamson v Governor of the Bank of Scotland* [2006] EWHC 1289 (Ch) at [42]–[46]. On this see below, paras 45-156—45-158.

Regulations) applied to a case where an individual guarantees the debt of a company, as long as that individual is not connected with the company and has been acting outside his business, trade or profession.[1474]

"Consumers" as agents for non-consumers Where an individual (A) contracts **38-227** for goods or services acting outside his trade, business or profession from a person (B) who does act within the course of the latter's business but A acts in doing so as agent for a third person (C) who acts in the course of his business, then the contract thereby formed between B (the supplier) and C (the principal)[1475] does not count as a consumer contract and so falls outside the controls of the 1999 Regulations. However, where in such circumstances A also undertakes personal liabilities under the contract which he makes on behalf of the principal,[1476] then the contract may qualify as a consumer contract and so fall within the Regulations for this purpose. So, it has been held that where after a fire an owner of a house (A) entered a contract for its reinstatement with a builder (B) as agent for his insurer (C) (which had exercised its contractual right to repair the property rather than pay an indemnity) but under which he (A) also undertook personal liabilities in respect of payment for the building work, then the terms of the contract could be assessed for fairness under the Regulations.[1477]

Third parties and consumers Under the Contracts (Rights for Third Parties) Act **38-228** 1999 the parties to a contract may create a right of enforcement in a third party, subject to a series of conditions.[1478] Where such a contract is a "consumer contract" within the meaning of the 1999 Regulations, then in principle its terms would be subject to their controls in the normal way and therefore could extend to the assessment of fairness of a term which, for example, sought to exclude or limit the extent to which the consumer could invoke the liability of a third party (such as a manufacturer) or otherwise sue a third party. On the other hand, where parties to a contract (whether or not it is a consumer contract) seek to create a right in a third party (a "consumer" in the sense that he or she is not acting in a course of business), but also sought to limit that right (for example, by a limitation clause) it would appear that that third party could *not* invoke the controls of the 1999 Regulations. This follows from the fact that the 1999 Regulations (following the 1993 Directive) apply only for the protection of consumers who are party to the contract with the trader, as reflected in the definition of "consumer" itself as "any natural person who, *in contracts covered by these Regulations*, is acting for purposes which are outside his trade [etc.]".[1479]

[1474] *Harvey v Dunbar Assets Plc* [2017] EWCA Civ. 60, [2017] Bus. L.R. 784 at [68]–[72] On the facts it was very difficult for the individual guarantor to maintain that he had no connection with the company nor was acting in the course of business in making the guarantee, and so the CA refused permission to amend the grounds of appeal so as to include the challenge to the guarantee under the 1999 Regulations.

[1475] See para.31-054.

[1476] See para.31-084.

[1477] *Domsalla v Dyason* [2007] EWHC 1174 (TCC) at [92], [2007] B.L.R. 348.

[1478] For the details see Vol.I paras 18-090 et seq.

[1479] 1999 Regulations reg.3(1); 1993 Directive art.2(b). This was the view of the Law Commission: *Privity of Contract: Contracts for the Benefit of Third Parties* Law Com. No.242 (1996) Cm 3329 para.13.10. cf. the position under the Consumer Rights Act 2015 s.72, below, paras 38-402—38-404. For the position of a third party assignee of the consumer's rights in relation to contract terms "not binding" on the consumer as unfair, see below, para.38-345.

38-229 **An autonomous view of "contract"?**   So far in this discussion it has been assumed that the transaction which falls (arguably) within the ambit of the 1999 Regulations qualifies as a "contract" within the meaning of this notion in English law. However, the question arises whether the Court of Justice of the EU would indeed rely on the classifications of the domestic laws of the Member States for this purpose, or would instead adopt an autonomous view of this concept.[1480] The Court of Justice would decide between these two positions on the basis of which of them is likely to be most effective in enabling the Directive to achieve its purposes[1481] and on the difficulty of constructing a European conception of contract for the purposes of the Directive.[1482] As regards the latter, it is to be noted that the Court has already embarked on such an undertaking for the purposes of European instruments on international jurisdiction.[1483] As regards the purposes of the Directive, both reduction in distortions in competition and the protection of consumers would be enhanced by the Court's taking an autonomous view of "contract" for the purposes of the Directive, for such a view would clearly enhance the harmonising purpose of the Directive and thereby make more effective its policy of consumer protection within the EU.

38-230   If the Court of Justice were to take such an autonomous view of contract, it is likely that it would do so on the basis of an agreement between the parties or an agreement intended to have legal effects.[1484] If the Court of Justice were to do so, this would sometimes require an English court to classify as contractual for the purposes of the Directive a transaction which in English law is considered non-

---

[1480] On "autonomous" interpretations generally, above, para.38-015. For this issue in relation to the 1993 Directive and development of the consequences noted in the following discussion, see Whittaker (2000) 116 L.Q.R. 95. cf. the position under the Consumer Rights Directive 2011 art.3(5) which would apparently allocate the question of what constitutes a "contract" for its purposes to national general contract laws: above, paras 38-063—38-065, 38-070.

[1481] cf. the approach of A.G. Sir Gordon Slynn in *Arcado SPRL v Haviland SA* EU:C:1988:127, (9/87) [1988] E.C.R. 1539 at 1548.

[1482] *Industrie Tessili Italiana Como v Dunlop AG* (12/76) EU:C:1976:133, [1976] E.C.R. 1473.

[1483] Brussels Convention on jurisdiction and the enforcement of judgements in civil and commercial matters 1968 art.5(1), whose equivalent provision is provided by Regulation (EU) 1215/2012 of 12 December 2012 on jurisdiction and the recognition and enforcement of judgments in civil and commercial matters (recast) ("the Brussels Ibis Regulation"): *Martin Peters Bauunternehmung GmbH v Zuid Nederlandse Aannemers Vereniging* (34/82) EU:C:1983:87, [1983] E.C.R. 987 and *Jakob Handt & Co GmbH v Traitements Mécano-chimiques des Surfaces SA* (26/91) EU:C:1992:268, [1992] E.C.R. I-3967. However, care is needed in using this case-law by analogy, since the ECJ adopted a very wide approach to "matters relating to contract" for these purposes see, e.g. *Engler v Janus Versand GmbH* (C-27/02) EU:C:2005:33, [2005] E.C.R. I-00481 at para.51 (the sending of a prize notification by a trader which was not followed by the ordering of any goods by the consumer to whom it was addressed fell within art.5(1) as a "matter relating to contract" as based on a "legal obligation freely consented to by one person towards the other and on which the claimant's action is based", even though no contract had been concluded for the purposes of art.13 of the Convention).

[1484] Whittaker (2000) 116 L.Q.R. 95. See, notably, the definition of "contract" for the purposes of the Amended proposal for a Directive of the European Parliament and of the Council on certain aspects concerning contracts for the online and other distance sales of goods COM(2017) 637 final art.2(g) to the effect that "'contract' means an agreement intended to give rise to obligations or other legal effects", thereby adopting the definition in the proposed Common European Sales Law art.2 in Proposal for a Regulation on a Common European Sales Law COM(2011) 635 final (proposal withdrawn by the Commission in December 2014), on which see above, Vol.I paras 1-013 and 1-025. In this respect, recital 17 to the Amended Proposal claims that its definition reflects "the common traditions of all Member States".

contractual.[1485] Three examples may be given. First, the laws of most of the Member States contain no requirement conceptually equivalent to English law's doctrine of consideration.[1486] This raises the possibility of including within the ambit of the Directive the terms on which professional services are provided gratuitously. Secondly, the relationship between the beneficiary of a trust and the trustee may sometimes be considered "contractual" for the purposes of the Directive (and therefore the Regulations), even though it is not in the general English law.[1487] Thirdly, some provisions of public services, such as water and electricity, may be held to be "contractual" for the purposes of the Regulations even though they are non-contractual under general English law.[1488] In this respect, the European Commission has drawn attention to its statement in the Council's minutes in connection with the adoption of the common position concerning art.2 of the Directive on the notion of the contract which "points out that the notion of contract also includes transactions involving supplies of goods or services in a regulatory framework".[1489] Moreover, in *Schulz & Egbringhoff*,[1490] in the context of the exclusion from the 1993 Directive of contract terms required by legislation,[1491] Advocate General Wahl distinguished between contracts under which electricity or gas was supplied under contracts by suppliers under a legal "universal service obligation" some of whose terms were set by legislation, which he referred to as "contracts, which are governed by national legislation, [which] do not fall within the sphere of freedom of contract"[1492] and those made in the absence of such an obligation under "special contracts" which are "concluded on the basis of freedom of contract".[1493] This ap-

---

[1485] On the other hand, some legal relationships which involve elements of agreement in one or both parties may nevertheless be properly characterised as "non-contractual" in English law owing to the nature or extent of their regulation: e.g. the relationship between a student on the Bar Professional Training Course and the Bar Council: *R. (on the application of Prescott) v General Council of the Bar* [2015] EWHC 1919 (Admin) at [79].

[1486] There was no more than a superficial conceptual similarity between the former French law doctrine of *la cause* and the doctrine of consideration and there is no similarity in terms of their respective overall functions: see Whittaker, in Bell, Boyron and Whittaker, *Principles of French Law*, 2nd edn (2008), pp.321–322; H. Kötz and A. Flessner, *European Contract Law* (trans. Weir, 1997), Vol.I, pp.54 et seq. In 2016, the notion of *la cause* was deleted from the French *Code civil* on the wider reform of French contract law by *Ordonnance* No.2016/131 of February 10, 2016.

[1487] cf. *Gray v Taylor* [1998] 1 W.L.R. 1093 in which the Court of Appeal held that a person occupying an almshouse under a charitable trust was not a tenant.

[1488] For the non-contractual nature of the supply of electricity and water to domestic consumers (even though they pay), see the Electricity Act 1989 ss.16, 22 and *Norweb v Dixon* [1995] 1 W.L.R. 636 and the Water Industry Act 1991 ss.53–56 and *Read v Croydon Corp* [1938] 4 All E.R. 631. cf. the position in relation to gas under the Gas Act 1995 ss.7 and 8 amending Gas Act 1986 ss.7 and 8.

[1489] European Commission, *Report on Directive 93/13/EEC on unfair terms in consumer contracts*, COM(2000) final, p.15.

[1490] A.G. Opinion, *Schulz v Technische Werke Schussental GmbH und Co KG, Egbringhoff v Stadwerke Ahaus GmbH* (C-359 and C-400/11) of May 8, 2014. The CJEU's decision of October 23, 2014 did not reflect on the differences between the two categories of contract.

[1491] 1993 Directive art.1(2), below, paras 38-233—38-240.

[1492] A.G. Opinion, C-359 and C-400/11 at para.34.

[1493] A.G. Opinion, C-359 and C-400/11 at para.38 (as in the earlier decision of the CJEU in *RWE Vertrieb AG v Verbraucherzentrale Nordrhein-Westfalen eV* (C-92/11) EU:C:2013:180, March 21, 2013, below, para.38-234. cf. *Roundlistic Ltd v Jones* [2016] UKUT 325 (LC) at [100] (appeal pending), where it was held that a lease of residential premises granted by a landlord to its tenant was a contract concluded between those parties, despite the fact that it was concluded within the context of the obligation on the landlord to grant a new lease pursuant to the Leasehold Reform, Housing and Urban Development Act 1993, though it was further held that these terms of the new lease were excluded from the scope of the 1999 Regulations on the basis that they reflected "mandatory statutory provi-

proach therefore distinguishes between two categories of *contract*, those which are closely regulated by law (both as regards an obligation to conclude the contract in the supply and some of its terms) and those not so regulated, and thereby assumes that the fact of such regulation does not preclude the transaction from being classed as a contract for the purposes of the 1993 Directive.[1494] On the other hand, where terms of a consumer contract are required by law in this way they fall within the exclusion from the scope of the 1993 Directive as being terms which reflect "mandatory statutory or regulatory provisions".[1495]

38-231 **Differences from the ambit of the Unfair Contract Terms Act 1977** It will be apparent that the types of contracts governed by the 1999 Regulations differ significantly from those governed by the provisions of the Unfair Contract Terms Act 1977 *before* their amendment by the Consumer Rights Act 2015.[1496] First, while the ambit of the Regulations is restricted to consumer contracts, a significant number of provisions of the 1977 Act apply to non-consumer contracts, notably, as regards any exclusion of liability for negligence,[1497] of contractual liability in general where it arises from breach of a written standard term[1498] and as regards the implied terms as to title, quality, etc. in sale of goods.[1499] Secondly, on the other hand, as regards consumer contracts, the net of the Regulations is rather wider than the 1977 Act, notably in their inclusion of contracts of insurance,[1500] sale at auction of second-hand goods,[1501] contracts which relate to the creation or transfer of a right or interest in intellectual property,[1502] and contracts for the sale, etc. of land.[1503] Thirdly, the 1977 Act may apply to non-contractual notices,[1504] whereas the Regulations apply only to contract terms, though it has been noted that "contract" may be given for this purpose a meaning different from its general significance in English law.[1505]

(ii) Contract Terms Excluded from the 1999 Regulations

38-232 **General** Unlike the Unfair Contract Terms Act 1977 (whose controls principally affect exemption clauses)[1506] the types of contract terms caught by the Regulations are very varied; indeed, the starting point of the Regulations (following the Direc-

---

sions" within the meaning of reg.4(2), on which see below, para.38-238.

[1494] For the A.G., therefore, the terms of the contracts before the Court (which did not reflect freedom of contract) fell within the special provisions on the transparency of contract terms in the relevant Energy Directives and not the 1993 Directive: C-359 and C-400/11 at para.47.

[1495] 1993 Directive art.1(2) and see below, paras 38-233—38-240.

[1496] In particular, after its amendment in 2015, the 1977 Act no longer applies to the terms of "consumer contracts" as defined by s.61 of the 2015 Act. See generally on these amendments Vol.I, paras 15-062 et seq.

[1497] Unfair Contract Terms Act 1977 s.2 and see Vol.I, paras 15-081—15-083.

[1498] s.3, and see Vol.I, paras 15-084—15-087.

[1499] s.6, above, Vol.I, para.15-093.

[1500] These are excluded from ss.2–4 of the 1977 Act by s.1(2) and Sch.1 para.1(a).

[1501] This is by virtue of the more restricted definition of consumer in this respect in s.12 of the 1977 Act, see Vol.I, para.15-076.

[1502] This type of contract is excluded from ss.2–4 of the 1977 Act by s.1(2), Sch.1 para.1(c) and see Vol.I, para.15-117.

[1503] These are excluded from ss.2–4 of the 1977 Act by s.1(2) Sch.1 para.1(b), see Vol.I, para.15-117.

[1504] ss.2 and 14, and see Vol.I, para.15-081.

[1505] See above, para.38-229 and below, para.38-388.

[1506] See Vol.I, para.15-062.

tive) is that their controls apply to *all* types of terms, the legislation referring simply to "unfair terms in contracts concluded between a seller or a supplier and a consumer".[1507] From this starting point, there are two sets of derogations. First, the Regulations exclude altogether from their controls contract terms which reflect "mandatory statutory or regulatory provisions" and those which reflect "the provisions of international conventions".[1508] These exclusions (and the question as to whether the Regulations apply to implied terms) will be considered in the following paragraphs. Secondly, the two requirements created by the Regulations differ somewhat in the range of terms which they govern. So, the requirement that terms be in "plain, intelligible language" applies to *any written term* of the contract,[1509] whereas the requirement of fairness applies to any term (whether written or oral)[1510] "which has not been individually negotiated", unless that term defines the main subject matter of the contract in a "plain, intelligible" way, etc. under the "core exclusion".[1511] These qualifications on the general starting point will be considered with the treatment of the requirements themselves.[1512]

Terms which reflect "mandatory statutory or regulatory provisions" of English law   Regulation 4(2)(a) of the 1999 Regulations,[1513] following closely art.1(2) of the 1993 Directive, excludes from their scope: **38-233**

"... contractual terms which reflect ... mandatory statutory or regulatory provisions (including such provisions under the law of any Member State or in EU legislation having effect in the United Kingdom without further enactment)."[1514]

For this purpose recitals 13 and 14 of the Directive explain that:

"Whereas the statutory or regulatory provisions of the Member States which directly or indirectly determine the terms of consumer contracts are presumed not to contain unfair terms; whereas, therefore, it does not appear to be necessary to subject the terms which reflect mandatory statutory or regulatory provisions ... ; whereas in that respect the wording 'mandatory statutory or regulatory provisions' in Article 1(2) also covers rules which, according to the law, shall apply between the contracting parties provided that no other arrangements have been established;

Whereas Member States must however ensure that unfair terms are not included, particularly because this Directive also applies to trades, businesses or professions of a public nature."

Recital 13 therefore makes clear that the adjective "mandatory" does not restrict the category of legal rules which impose terms on the parties to a contract to those whose effect is incapable of exclusion by agreement, rules which are, therefore,

---

[1507] 1999 Regulations reg.4(1); 1993 Directive arts 2(a), 3(1).

[1508] 1999 Regulations reg.4(2)(a).

[1509] 1999 Regulations reg.7; 1993 Directive art.5 and recital 11.

[1510] It is perhaps unusual for an oral term to be other than "not individually negotiated", but it is conceivable, particularly given the rule as to the burden of proof as to this issue (on which see below, para.38-243), for example, where a trader simply stipulates orally that a particular non-refundable deposit must be paid for goods or where a trader's standard terms are read by its agents to the consumer over the telephone.

[1511] 1999 Regulations regs 5(1), 6(2) and see below, paras 38-245 et seq.

[1512] Below, paras 38-241 et seq. respectively.

[1513] The Consumer Rights Act 2015 s.73 retains this exclusion from the controls on unfair terms in Pt 2 of the Act, below, para.38-388.

[1514] cf. 1994 Regulations reg.3(1), Sch.1 para.(e)(i) which omitted "mandatory".

"mandatory" in the normal sense, i.e. belonging to *ius cogens*.[1515] Instead, "mandatory" also includes rules which simply apply by law in the absence of any express contractual provision, but which *may* be the subject of contrary contractual exclusion, i.e. rules belonging to *ius dispositivum*.[1516] This is therefore a potentially wide category of exclusion of terms from the ambit of the controls of the Regulations, and one of particular importance in the provision of public services, where some or even many of the terms are set by legislation. This is certainly the context of the application of the exclusion found in art.1(2) of the Directive in other European national laws where the practice is more widespread of the setting of standard terms for certain services by administrative decree.[1517]

38-234   Case-law of the CJEU   In *RWE Vertrieb AG v Verbraucherzentrale Nordrhein-Westfalen eV*,[1518] the Court of Justice of the EU clarified the interpretation of the exclusion of terms provided by art.1(2) of the 1993 Directive.[1519] In that case, the German law governing the supply of natural gas to consumers distinguished between supplies by gas suppliers under "standard tariff contracts", where the supplier was under a legal obligation to conclude contracts with consumers, and "special contracts", where they were not. German legislation set the general terms and conditions of supply of the standard tariff contracts, but did not do so for the special contracts. However, the wording of the standard conditions of the *special* contracts concluded by the supplier in the main proceedings corresponded to those required for the tariff contracts by the legislation, and in this sense, they "reflected" those legal provisions. The issue before the Court was whether the contract terms in the special contracts of supply of natural gas to consumers fell under the controls of unfairness in the German legislation implementing the 1993 Directive or whether they fell instead within the exclusion in that legislation foreseen by art.1(2) of that Directive. Referring to recital 13 of the Directive, the Court of Justice considered that this exclusion is justified by the fact that "it may legitimately be supposed that the national legislature struck a balance between all the rights and obligations of the parties to certain contracts",[1520] and held that this reasoning does not apply to the situation where a consumer contract merely reproduces a rule of national law applicable to *another* category of contracts to which the national legislation in question does not apply:

[1515] This also rules out any association with the meaning found in private international law: see, e.g. Regulation (EC) 593/2008 on the law applicable to contractual obligations ("Rome I") [2008] O.J. L177/6 art.9.

[1516] This is made clear by French jurists for whom the distinction between *ius cogens* (*loi impérative*) and *ius dispositivum* (*loi supplétive*) is traditional: see notably Ghestin and Marchessaux-Van Melle J.C.P. 1995 I.3854 at No.6. As will be seen, however, art.1(2) has been held *not* to apply to terms which reflect the wording of legislation but where the legislation does not apply to the category of contract in question: *RWE Vertrieb AG v Verbraucherzentrale Nordrhein-Westfalen eV* (C-92/11) EU:C:2013:180, below, para.38-234.

[1517] e.g. the standard terms on which passengers travel by train on the French national carrier, *SNCF*, on which see Whittaker in Freedland and Auby (eds), *The Public Law/Private Law Divide* (2006), pp.243, 249 et seq.

[1518] *RWE Vertrieb AG v Verbraucherzentrale Nordrhein-Westfalen eV* (C-92/11) EU:C:2013:180, March 31, 2013 ("*RWE Vertrieb AG (C-92/11)*").

[1519] *RWE Vertrieb AG (C-92/11)*.

[1520] *RWE Vertrieb AG (C-92/11)* at para.29.

"... [a]n intention of the parties to extend the application of those rules to a different contract cannot be equated to the establishment by the national legislature of a balance between all the rights and obligations of the parties to the contract."[1521]

The Court of Justice concluded, therefore, that the Directive applies to terms such as those in the "special contracts" of supply of gas to consumers before it.[1522] The Court therefore held that art.1(2) does not apply to contract terms in a legislative scheme where the scheme does not apply to the contract in question,[1523] but it assumed that the exclusion found in art.1(2) *does* apply to terms in a contract which copy out legislative or other legal rules which would otherwise apply to that contract, even where those legislative rules do not themselves *require* to be so expressed in the contract, as art.1(2)

"... extends to terms which reflect provisions of national law that apply between the parties to the contract independently of their choice or those that apply by default in the absence of other arrangements established by the parties."[1524]

In *Kušionová*[1525] the Court of Justice followed its earlier approach to art.1(2) in *RWE Vertrieb AG*, noting that this exclusion should be interpreted strictly[1526] and that it is for the national court to determine whether a particular contract term falls within this test. On the other hand, the Court of Justice in *RWE Vertrieb AG* did not consider directly the question whether art.1(2)'s exclusion applies to contract terms which are not directly determined by national legislation but which are approved or otherwise regulated under a legislative scheme or to contract terms which are varied under a lawful exercise of a statutory power in the seller or supplier.[1527] A significant example of the former would be where the terms of supply of a public service are drawn up by the (commercial) supplier of that service, but then subjected either to a requirement of approval by an administrative body or to a structure of review by a "watchdog" institution. If this approval or review were undertaken under "legislative or regulatory provisions" the latter could be said to "determine indirectly" the content of the contracts, as foreseen by recital 13 of the Directive. On the other hand, the Court of Justice could instead distinguish between those provisions which *determine* and those which *provide for approval* of the terms on which services are provided, only the former being within the terms of art.1(2). This distinction could be supported by the clearly restrictive approach of the Court of Justice to the exclusion in art.1(2) in *RWE Vertrieb AG*, following its general approach to exclusions from schemes for the protection of consumers.[1528]

[1521] *RWE Vertrieb AG* (C-92/11) at para.29.

[1522] *RWE Vertrieb AG* (C-92/11) at para.38.

[1523] cf. *Peabody Trust Governors v Reeve* [2008] EWHC 1432 (Ch), [2009] L. & T.R. 6 at [40]–[62], where it was said that a variation clause which successfully incorporated the power of variation provided by s.103 in a tenancy contract to which that provision did *not* apply would be unfair within the meaning of the 1999 Regulations.

[1524] *RWE Vertrieb AG* (C-92/11) para.26; *Kušionová v SMART Capital a.s.* (C-34/13) of September 10, 2014 para.79; *Andriciuc v Banca Românească* (C-186/16) of September 20, 2017 at paras 27–31.

[1525] *Kušionová v SMART Capital a.s.* (C-34/13) of September 10, 2014.

[1526] *Kušionová v SMART Capital a.s.* (C-34/13) para.77.

[1527] cf. Unfair Contract Terms Act 1977 s.29(2) (contract term to be taken as satisfying the requirement of reasonableness "if it is incorporated or approved by, or incorporated pursuant to a decision or ruling of, a competent authority acting in the exercise of any statutory jurisdiction or function and is not a term in a contract to which the competent authority is itself a party": Vol.I, para.15-124.

[1528] C-92/11 EU:C:2013:180.

38-235 **Optional terms and mandatory content** However, in *Engilbertsson* the EFTA Court took a more extensive view of the exclusion in art.1(2) of the 1993 Directive despite its formal recognition "that derogations from EEA consumer protection law must be interpreted strictly".[1529] In that case, which considered a reference from an Icelandic court, a consumer contract for a mortgage loan contained an indexation clause to govern repayments by the consumer. Under national law such a clause was not mandatory, but, if used, the parties were "bound to a substantial extent by the scheme set out in regulatory and statutory provisions of national law".[1530] In these circumstances, the EFTA Court held that the exclusion in art.1(2) of the 1993 Directive applies to a term in a consumer contract "whose inclusion in the category of contract is optional but whose substance is mandatory", as the inequality of bargaining power between the parties does not influence the content of the terms to the detriment of the consumer.[1531] As a result, the national court must assess "whether and to what extent the regulatory scheme is exhaustive and that the seller or supplier therefore has no right to unilaterally set out certain aspects in terms and conditions at a contractual level".[1532] However, the EFTA Court recognised that, where a national court found that certain aspects of the subject-matter of a term were set by national legal provisions and so excluded from the scope of the Directive, the trader must nevertheless make the consumer aware of the content of those provisions so that the consumer can "foresee, on the basis of clear, intelligible criteria, the alterations that may occur to the principal of the loan".[1533]

38-236 **"Legislative provisions" and common law rules** Article 1(2) of the 1993 Directive refers to "contractual terms which reflect mandatory *statutory or regulatory* provisions" and this suggests that it is not concerned with contract terms which reflect the position *at common law*.[1534] As has been seen, however, the Court of Justice has assumed that art.1(2) applies to terms in a contract which copy out legislative rules which would otherwise apply to that contract, even where those legislative rules do not themselves *require* to be so expressed in the contract.[1535] If this is indeed the case, then it is submitted that art.1(2) should equally apply so as to exclude contract terms which mirror the otherwise applicable legal rule whether its source is found in statute or the common law, for art.1(2)'s reference to "legisla-

---

[1529] *Engilbertsson v Íslandsbanki hf* (E-25/13) of August 28, 2014 ("*Engilbertsson* (E-25/13)") at para.77. The EFTA Court decided under the Agreement between the EFTA States on the Establishment of a Surveillance Authority and a Court of Justice art.34. Under art.3(2) of the same Agreement, the EFTA Court "shall pay due account to the principles laid down by the relevant rulings by the Court of Justice of the European Communities given after the date of signature of the EEA Agreement and which concern the interpretation of that Agreement or of such rules of the Treaty establishing the European Economic Community ... in so far as they are identical in substance to the provisions of the EEA Agreement or to the provisions of Protocols 1 to 4 and the provisions of the acts corresponding to those listed in Annexes I and II to the present Agreement".

[1530] *Engilbertsson* (E-25/13) at para.74.

[1531] *Engilbertsson* (E-25/13) at para.75.

[1532] *Engilbertsson* (E-25/13) at para.78.

[1533] *Engilbertsson* (E-25/13) at paras 78, 142–143, citing the CJEU's case-law on variation clauses under the 1993 Directive in *Nemzeti Fogyasztóvédelmi Hatóság v Invitel Távközlési Zrt* (C-472/10) EU:C:2012:242, April 26, 2012 paras 24, 26, 28–29 on which see below, para.38-314.

[1534] Emphasis added. This question does not arise if art.1(2) of the 1993 Directive is restricted to terms which are determined by the law, as the common law does not require any *express terms* to be included in consumer contracts. For the position as regards *implied terms*, see below, para.38-240.

[1535] Above, para.38-234.

tive" as opposed to "legal" provisions[1536] (the latter of which could equally refer to the common law as to legislation) can be explained by the fact that the vast majority of the national laws of Member States at the time of the enactment of the directive set out their legal rules governing contracts in legislation rather than by way of common law. Moreover, the reason for the exclusion as set out in recital 13 and noted in *RWE Vertrieb AG* that "it may legitimately be supposed that the national legislature struck a balance between all the rights and obligations of the parties to certain contracts",[1537] applies equally to regulation by the common law.

Statutory power in party to vary term   The question also arises whether art.1(2)   **38-237**
of the Directive (and therefore reg.4(2)(a) of the 1999 Regulations) applies to a term inserted into a contract by exercise of a power enjoyed by a party to the contract under statute, or to a term in a contract varied by a party in the same circumstances. In *Rochdale BC v Dixon* the Court of Appeal considered whether a term in a public sector secure periodic tenancy which had been varied by the lawful exercise of the public authority's statutory power under ss.102 and 103 of the Housing Act 1985 was unfair within the meaning of the 1999 Regulations.[1538] If valid, the term in question as so varied enabled the local authority landlord to collect the tenant's water charges for the water company and, therefore, to subject the tenant to the risk of eviction on non-payment of these charges. The Court of Appeal held that such a term was not unfair for a number of reasons, including that any exercise of the statutory power was taken by the democratically elected councillors of the local authority and possessed its own consultation procedure.[1539] While the point was not before the Court of Appeal, it could be argued that a term varied under a lawful exercise of a statutory power should be seen as falling within the exclusion in art.1(2) of the Directive as a term which reflects a legislative provision, but it is submitted that the Court of Justice of the EU would be unlikely to agree: art.1(2) is to be strictly construed[1540] and such a variation by the "seller or supplier" would not fall squarely within the justification for the exclusion, that is, that:

> "… it may legitimately be supposed that the national legislature struck a balance between all the rights and obligations of the parties to certain contracts."[1541]

Statutory obligation to grant contract on same terms   In *Roundlistic Ltd v*   **38-238**
Jones,[1542] a new lease had been granted to a tenant by her landlord under its obligation imposed by the Leasehold Reform, Housing and Urban Development Act 1993.[1543] The Upper Tribunal (Lands Chamber) noted that the terms upon which the landlord was obliged to grant the new lease were provided by the Act and that, while there was scope for some alternations in the terms, the Act's starting-point was that the new lease was to be on the same terms as the existing lease subject to certain

---

[1536] For this purpose, no reliance can be made on the reference in recital 13 to "rules which, according to the law" as other language versions make clear that here "the law" translates legislation rather than "law" (for example, it appears in French as *la loi* rather than *le droit*).

[1537] *RWE Vertrieb AG* (C-92/11) at para.29.

[1538] [2011] EWCA Civ 1173, [2012] H.L.R. 6.

[1539] [2011] EWCA Civ 1173 at [68] (Rix L.J. with whom Rimer and Elias L.JJ. agreed).

[1540] *Kušionová v SMART Capital a.s.* (C-34/13) of September 10, 2014 para.77.

[1541] *RWE Vertrieb AG* (C-92/11) at para.29, above, para.38-234.

[1542] [2016] UKUT 325 (LC) (appeal pending).

[1543] i.e. ss.43, 56 and 57.

limited modifications.[1544] In these circumstances, the Upper Tribunal concluded that the 1999 Regulations did not apply to the terms of the new lease on the basis that they fell within the exclusion in reg.4(2) as "mandatory statutory provisions".[1545] It is submitted, however, that this decision extends the scope of application of reg.4(2) beyond the likely interpretation by the Court of Justice of the EU of art.1(2) of the 1993 Directive which reg.4(2) implements[1546]: art.1(2) is to be strictly construed[1547] and there is a difference between contract terms required by legislation itself (where "it may legitimately be supposed that the national legislature struck a balance between all the rights and obligations of the parties to certain contracts"[1548]) and contract terms which reflect an earlier contract between the parties whose content has not been the object of any legislative consideration or imposition.

38-239 **Terms which reflect "the provisions of international conventions"** The Regulations also provide that their requirements do not apply to:

"… contractual terms which reflect … the provisions or principles of international conventions to which the Member States or the European Union are party."[1549]

As the 1993 Directive makes clear, this exclusion is particularly concerned to exclude terms in conventions "in the transport area",[1550] notably the Warsaw Convention on international carriage by air.[1551] It should be noted that the exception applies to terms which reflect national legislation which uses the *principles* of international conventions to which the Member States or the Community are party, such as in the area of domestic carriage of goods.[1552]

38-240 **No application to implied terms** In *Baybut v Eccle Riggs Country Park Ltd* the High Court noted that the Regulations are not expressly limited to express contract terms,[1553] but nevertheless considered that they do not apply to implied terms of any type: not to terms implied by statute, as these fall within the exclusion of terms which reflect "mandatory statutory or regulatory provisions" or the "provisions of international conventions"[1554]; nor to terms implied at common law, whether in law

---

[1544] [2016] UKUT 325 (LC) at [101].

[1545] [2016] UKUT 325 (LC) at [101]. It had been held that the new lease was a "contract" for the purposes of the 1999 Regulations despite its compulsory elements: see above, para.38-230.

[1546] See notably *RWE Vertrieb AG* (C-92/11), above, para.38-234.

[1547] *Kušionová v SMART Capital a.s.* (C-34/13) of September 10, 2014 para.77

[1548] *RWE Vertrieb AG* (C-92/11) at para.29. See also the explanation of the exclusion in art.1(2) in recital 13 of the 1993 Directive that "the statutory or regulatory provisions of the Member States which directly or indirectly determine the terms of consumer contracts are presumed not to contain unfair terms".

[1549] 1999 Regulations reg.4(2)(b).

[1550] 1993 Directive art.1(2).

[1551] See above, paras 35-002 et seq.

[1552] On the other hand, a term of a contract which is governed by an international convention but which does not reflect the provisions of that convention remains subject to the controls in the 1993 Directive: cf. *Air Berlin Plc & Co Luftverkehrs KG v Bundesverband der Verbraucherzentralen und Verbraucherverbande-Verbracherzentrale Bundesverband eV* (C-290/16) of July 6, 2017 at paras 44–45 (emphasising the applicability of the 1993 Directive to international contracts of carriage of passengers by air, though not addressing this point).

[1553] Unreported November 2, 2006, Ch D at [20], referring to 1999 Regulations regs 4, 5 and 6(2).

[1554] Unreported November 2, 2006, Ch D at [22] and see above, para.38-233.

or "to make contracts work by filling a technical lacuna in the contract" on the basis that it is difficult to see how these terms (which are implied only where they are reasonable[1555]) could ever be found unfair within the meaning of the Regulations.[1556] The court also noted that all the examples given in the "indicative list" of terms which may be regarded as unfair in the Schedule to the 1999 Regulations are express terms,[1557] to which it may be added that the exclusion from the requirement of fairness of individually negotiated terms makes little sense except in the context of express terms.[1558] Finally, while the English version of the 1993 Directive is no more explicit on the question of implied term than the UK Regulations, some of its other language versions use words which are more appropriate to describe what an English lawyer would see as an express term: so the French version of art.1(1) of the Directive refers to its application to "*clauses abusives*"; the German version to "*mißbräuchliche Klauseln*". Overall, the better view is indeed that the Regulations have no application to implied terms as understood by English law.[1559]

(iii) The Requirement of Fairness

Introduction It has been noted that the Regulations make two requirements of contract terms, that they be fair and that they be expressed in plain, intelligible language and that the range of terms to which these two requirements apply differs to a degree.[1560] In this section, the first of these requirements will be examined.   **38-241**

(aa) The Exclusion of Terms Which Have Been "Individually Negotiated"

In general In addition to the exclusion from the scope of the 1999 Regulations as a whole of contract terms required by legislation or international convention,[1561] the 1999 Regulations—unlike the new law under the Consumer Rights Act 2015—exclude from the test of unfairness contract terms which have been "individually negotiated".[1562] This exclusion reflects a view strongly urged at the time that the inclusion within the scope of the proposed directive on unfair contract terms of "individually negotiated terms" would represent "a drastic restriction of the autonomy of the individual".[1563] Clearly, there is considerable practical similar-   **38-242**

[1555] See Vol.I, para.14-012.

[1556] Unreported November 2, 2006, Ch D at [22].

[1557] Unreported November 2, 2006, Ch D at [23] and see below paras 38-299 et seq. It is submitted that this would apply also to the statutory terms which Pt 1 of the Consumer Rights Act 2015 "treats as included" in the contracts to which it applies: see, e.g. in relation to "goods contracts" below, paras 38-492 et seq.

[1558] Unreported November 2, 2006, Ch D at [23].

[1559] This view was endorsed by Andrew Smith J. in *OFT v Abbey National Plc* [2008] EWHC 875 (Comm), [2008] 2 All E.R. (Comm) 625 at [102] (decision upheld by Court of Appeal, which itself was overturned by SC on other grounds in [2009] UKSC 6, [2010] 1 A.C. 696, below, paras 38-247—38-248).

[1560] See above, para.38-232.

[1561] Above, paras 38-233—38-241.

[1562] 1999 Regulations reg.5(1); 1993 Directive art.3; *Engilbertsson v Íslandsbanki hf* (E-25/13) (EFTA Court) of August 28, 2014 at paras 125–126. On the Consumer Rights Act 2015 see below, para.38-389.

[1563] Brandner and Ulmer (1991) 29 C.M.L.R. 647 at 652; Howells and Wilhelmsson, *EC Consumer Law*

ity between this exclusion and the restriction of the requirement of reasonableness to "written standard terms of business" found in s.3 of the Unfair Contract Terms Act 1977,[1564] but there are also some technical differences. First, the test in the Regulations includes within the requirement of fairness a *non-standard* term as long as it was drafted in advance and presented or imposed on the consumer; and secondly, there is no requirement equivalent to s.3's restriction to "terms *of business*", a restriction which has led the courts to exclude from the test of reasonableness under the 1977 Act a standard term of employment of a bank on the basis that its relevant business for this purpose was banking.[1565] A third possible difference appears to be more formal than substantive. Under the Regulations the exclusion of "individually negotiated terms" leaves within the control of fairness standard terms other than those belonging to the seller or supplier, for example, terms proposed or promoted by a trade association or third party intermediary; but while in s.3 of the 1977 Act the "written standard terms" are stated as being "the other's" (i.e. those of the person acting in the course of a business and relying on a contract term falling within the section's controls), it is likely that this expression would include the standard terms of a third party habitually used by that business.[1566]

38-243 **"Individual negotiation"** Moreover, reg.5(2) of the 1999 Regulations weight the issue of individual negotiation firmly in favour of the consumer, providing that:

> "... a term shall always be regarded as not having been individually negotiated where it has been drafted in advance and the consumer has therefore not been able to influence the substance of the term."

The Regulations place the burden of proof as to the issue of individual negotiation on the person who claims that a term has been so negotiated.[1567] In *UK Housing Alliance Ltd v Francis*[1568] the Court of Appeal held that the mere fact that a consumer had instructed solicitors in relation to the conclusion of the contract and that these had the opportunity of considering and therefore of influencing the allegedly unfair terms did not mean that any individual term had been individually negotiated: the supplier must prove that the relevant term was individually negotiated and reg.5(2) "imposes an absolute prohibition on a finding of individual negotiation if there has not been an ability to influence the substance of a term", and "it does not follow from the existence of the ability to influence the substance of a term that the term has, in fact, been individually negotiated".[1569] Finally, the Regulations also provide

---

(1997), p.91.

[1564] On which cf. Vol.I, para.15-084. This requirement in s.3(1) of the 1977 Act was originally an alternative to the case where the party "deals as consumer", but the 2015 Act has deleted this alternative condition: Vol.I, paras 15-084 and 15-079.

[1565] *Keen v Commerzbank AG* [2006] EWCA Civ 1536, [2007] I.C.R. 623 at [103]–[104].

[1566] *African Export-Import Bank v Shebah Exploration and Production Co Ltd* [2017] EWCA Civ 845, [2018] 1 W.L.R. 487 at [20] expressly approving the example of use of the RIBA form of engagement in *British Fermentation Products Ltd v Compare Reavell Ltd* [1999] 2 All E.R. (Comm) 389 at [46] (H.H.J. Bowsher Q.C.) and see Vol.I, para.15-084.

[1567] 1999 Regulations reg.5(4).

[1568] [2010] EWCA Civ 117, [2010] Bus. L.R. 1034. cf. *Khurana v Webster Construction Ltd* [2015] EWHC 758 (TCC) at [52] (a term presented by a party in a letter as an offer for consideration and possible acceptance by the other where there is no evidence that it had been drafted prior to the production of the letter in question was not "drafted in advance").

[1569] [2010] EWCA Civ 117 at [19], per Longmore L.J. (applied by *Harrison v Shepherd Homes Ltd* [2011] EWHC 1811 (TCC), [103]–[105]).

that:

> "Notwithstanding that a specific term or certain aspects of it in a contract has been individually negotiated, these Regulations shall apply to the rest of a contract if an overall assessment of it indicates that it is a pre-formulated standard contract."[1570]

Thus, the presence of an individually negotiated term in a consumer contract does not necessarily exclude the application of the Regulations to the rest of the contract. This means that, for example, the general terms of a standard form contract of consumer sale whose delivery date for the goods, price or other particular aspect of the contract has been "individually negotiated" will not escape the requirement of fairness altogether.

Standard terms put forward by the consumer   In *Bryen & Langley Ltd v Boston* **38-244** the question arose as to how, if at all, the 1999 Regulations affected standard terms (here, terms of one of the JCT standard building contracts) put forward by a consumer (or rather by his professional advisers) and incorporated into a consumer contract.[1571] In the Court of Appeal Rimer J. noted that the consumer before him had had:

> "... the opportunity to influence the terms on which the contractors were being invited to tender, even though he may not have taken it up; and [that] there is therefore at least an argument"

that the terms were not therefore "not individually negotiated"; but he expressed no view on this point which had not been argued, it being held instead that in these circumstances any term of the standard contract would not fail the requirement of fairness as it would not cause a significant imbalance in the rights and obligations of the parties to the detriment of the consumer *contrary to the requirement of good faith*.[1572] It is submitted with respect that the latter indicates the correct approach. There is nothing in the provisions of the 1999 Regulations or the 1993 Directive to support the proposition that standard terms put forward by a consumer fall for that reason within their exclusion of individually negotiated terms, particularly bearing in mind that this exclusion is to be interpreted strictly following the general approach of the Court of Justice of the EU to exceptions to European legislative schemes of consumer protection.[1573] For while a consumer who proposes a set of standard terms may sometimes have "been able to influence the substance of the term" (by amending or deleting the standard terms which he himself proposes), this will not always be the case. Moreover, the exclusion from the requirement of fairness affects contract terms which have been the object of "individual negotiation", whereas a term in a set of standard terms proposed by the consumer remains standard (and often unknown to, or not understood by, the consumer and possibly even his professional advisers) and not therefore (at least normally) "*individually negotiated*". For these reasons, the putting forward of standard terms by a consumer

---

[1570] 1999 Regulations reg.5(3).
[1571] [2005] EWCA Civ 973, [2005] All E.R. (D) 507 (Jul) on appeal from [2004] EWHC 2450 (TCC), 98 Con. L.R. 82.
[1572] [2005] EWCA Civ 973 at [46] and cf. [2004] EWHC 2450 (TCC) at [43] (Judge Richard Seymour Q.C.).
[1573] 1993 Directive art.3(1) and (2); 1999 Regulations reg.5(1)–(4). On the strict interpretation of exceptions to EU schemes of consumer protection see above, para.38-234 and below, para.38-250.

should be dealt with in terms of the requirement of good faith, rather than in terms of their "individual negotiation".[1574]

(bb) The "Core Exclusion"

38-245 The "core exclusion" in the 1999 Regulations Regulation 6(2) of the 1999 Regulations (reflecting very closely art.4(2) of the Directive) provides that:

"In so far as it is in plain intelligible language, the assessment of fairness of a term shall not relate—

(a) to the definition of the main subject matter of the contract, or
(b) to the adequacy of the price or remuneration, as against the goods or services supplied in exchange." [1575]

This is an important provision, reflecting the focus of concern of the Directive on unfair *terms*, rather than on unfair *contracts* and so ruling out (in principle) from its ambit any review of contracts on the basis that they represent a bad bargain for the consumer: to this extent, the exclusion contained in art.4(2) reflects the general principle of freedom of contract.[1576] However, both its interpretation and its application have caused considerable difficulty, this stemming in part from the awkwardness of the drafting of the Directive, which does not make clear whether it seeks to exclude a category of terms from the test of fairness or whether instead it seeks to exclude certain types of issue from the evaluation of the fairness of terms.[1577] The Directive itself recognises the potential difficulty in applying the exclusion found in art.4(2) and attempts to explain how it may apply in the context of one particular example, contracts of insurance.[1578] While the exclusion in reg.6(2) of the Regula-

---

[1574] See below, para.38-293.

[1575] And cf. 1994 Regulations reg.3(2).

[1576] This view was pressed strongly at the time of the *travaux préparatoires* of the Directive in relation to the EC Commission's Proposal for a Council Directive on unfair terms in consumer contracts COM(90) 322 final, which did not restrict the control of unfair contract terms in this way: see notably, Brandner and Ulmer (1991) 28 C.M.L.R. 645 especially at 655–657; Niglia, *The Transformation of Contract in Europe* (2003) pp.119–145.

[1577] The *position* of art.4(2) of the Directive suggests that it excludes certain types of issue from the evaluation of the fairness of terms, as does the first part of its text ("*assessment* of the unfair nature of the terms *shall relate neither* to the definition of the subject matter") and it may be thought unusual for a particular term itself to "relate … to the adequacy of the price or remuneration, *as against* the goods or services supplied in exchange". On the other hand, the last phrase of art.4(2) suggests the exclusion of a category of term ("in so far as *these terms* are in plain intelligible language") and this is supported by recital 19, according to which "assessment shall not be made of *terms which describe* the main subject matter of the contract nor the quality/price ratio of the goods or services supplied" continuing that "the main subject matter of the contract and the price/quality ratio may nevertheless be taken into account in assessing the fairness of *other* terms". As will be seen, the CJEU has held that the way in which the exclusion in art.4(2) applies differs according to its two limbs, see below, paras 38-250—38-252.

[1578] 1993 Directive recital 19 states that "… it follows [from the exclusion in art.4(2)] inter alia, that in insurance contracts, the terms which clearly define or circumscribe the insured risk and the insurer's liability shall not be subject to such assessment since these restrictions are taken into account in calculating the premium paid by the consumer". There is no equivalent explanatory provision in either the 1994 or the 1999 Regulations. cf. *Bankers Insurance Co Ltd v South* [2003] EWHC 380, [2003] P.I.Q.R. P28 at [21] (exclusion in travel insurance agreed as defining "main subject matter of the contract") and see below, para.38-259 discussing *Van Hove v CNP Assurances SA* (C-96/14) EU:C:2015:262, April 23, 2015.

tions has been considered and applied by the House of Lords in *DGFT v First National Bank Plc*[1579] and the Supreme Court in *Abbey National Plc v The Office of Fair Trading*,[1580] later decisions of the Court of Justice of the EU, notably in *Kásler*[1581] and *Matei*,[1582] have clarified the proper interpretation of art.4(2) of the Directive and have provided guidance to national courts on the application of national legislation which implements it in a way which departs considerably from the Supreme Court's views in *Abbey National Plc*. English courts are bound to follow this case-law of the Court of Justice in their decisions on reg.6(2) of the Regulations as it implements art.4(2) of the Directive without amendment.[1583]

The First National Bank Plc decision   In *Director General of Fair Trading v First National Bank Plc*[1584] the House of Lords took a restrictive approach to the interpretation of the exclusion from the test of fairness now found in reg.6(2) of the 1999 Regulations. There, a contract of consumer credit contained a term by which: **38-246**

> ... interest on the amount which becomes payable [on default] shall be charged in accordance [with rates stipulated by the contract] ... until payment after as well as before any judgment (such obligation to be independent of and not to merge with the judgment)."

The effect of this agreement (if valid) would be that where the bank obtains judgment against a borrower, interest would be payable at the contractual rate on the outstanding principal plus accrued interest unpaid at the date of judgment until the judgment is discharged by payment. It would prevent the independent obligation to pay interest to merge in the judgment, the provision for interest at the contractual rate continuing to apply after judgment. The bank argued that this contract term did not fall to be assessed for fairness under the Regulations because it concerned the adequacy of the bank's remuneration as against the services supplied, namely the loan of money.[1585] The House of Lords disagreed. In the view of Lord Bingham of Cornhill:

> "The object of the Regulations and the Directive is to protect consumers against the inclusion of unfair and prejudicial terms in standard-form contracts into which they enter, and that object would plainly be frustrated if reg.3(2)(b) were so broadly interpreted as to cover any terms other than those falling squarely within it. In my opinion the term, as part of a provision prescribing the consequences of default, plainly does not fall within it. It does not concern the adequacy of the interest earned by the bank as its remuneration but is designed to ensure that the bank's entitlement to interest does not come to an end on the entry of judgment."[1586]

[1579] [2001] UKHL 52, [2002] 1 A.C. 481, below, para.38-246.
[1580] [2008] EWHC 875 (Comm), [2009] EWCA Civ 116, [2009] 2 W.L.R. 1286, [2009] UKSC 6, [2010] 1 A.C. 696; Whittaker (2010) 73 M.L.R. 106 and see below, paras 38-247—38-248.
[1581] *Kásler v OTP Jelzálogbank Zrt* (C-26/13) EU:C:2014:282, April 30, 2014, paras 38-249 et seq.
[1582] *Matei v SC Volksbank România SA* (C-143/13) EU:C:2015:127, February 26, 2015.
[1583] European Communities Act 1972 s.3(1), but see *Casehub Ltd v Wolf Cola Ltd* [2017] EWHC 1169 (Ch), [2017] 5 Costs L.R. 835, noted below, para.38-264. Under the "minimum harmonisation" clause in the 1993 Directive art.8 UK law is entitled to narrow the core exclusion which it provides in the interests of more extensive consumer protection and this has apparently been effected by the Consumer Rights Act 2015 s.64, below, paras 38-394—38-403.
[1584] [2001] UKHL 52, [2002] 1 A.C. 481 and see Whittaker (2004) *ZEuP* 75.
[1585] [2001] UKHL 52 at [10].
[1586] [2001] UKHL 52 at [12] See similarly [2001] UKHL 52 at [34] (Lord Steyn). References to reg.3(2)(b) refer to the earlier Unfair Terms in Consumer Contracts Regulations 1994 (SI 1994/

In this respect, the fact that the contract term before them was a "default provision" clearly weighed with the House.[1587] Having said this, though, in applying the test of fairness to this contract term, for the House of Lords the fact that it related to the payment of interest which was part of the "essential bargain" between the parties argued in favour of its fairness.[1588] In the result, the House of Lords held that the term in question did *not* fall within the exclusion found in art.4(2) of the Directive, but nevertheless "carries into effect what the parties themselves would regard as the essence of the transaction" and was held valid.[1589]

38-247 **OFT v Abbey National Plc** In *OFT v Abbey National Plc*,[1590] the question arose as to whether the OFT was entitled to consider the unfairness of certain terms of contracts between banks and their current account consumer customers under which the banks imposed charges when the customer requested or instructed the bank to make a payment for which they did not hold the necessary funds in the account and which was not covered by an arranged facility (the "relevant terms"). As regards the nature of the exclusion, at first instance, Andrew Smith J. expressed the view that reg.6(2)(b) excludes an assessment relating to the adequacy of the price from a term to which it applies[1591]; and, on appeal, the banks adopted this position with the result that the question to be determined by the Supreme Court was whether, in assessing the fairness of the terms, the OFT was entitled to take into account "the adequacy of the price or remuneration, as against the goods or services supplied in exchange", on the ground that "[a]ny assessment based on matters *not* relating to the appropriateness in amount of the price or remuneration is *not* excluded by regulation 6(2)(b)".[1592] The Supreme Court therefore considered whether the relevant terms provided for the "price or remuneration in exchange for the services" supplied by the bank so as to fall within this exclusion. For this purpose, it held, first, that the banks provided a "package of services" to their customers, which:

> "... include the collection and payment of cheques, other money transmission services, facilities for cash distribution ... and the provision of statements in printed or electronic form."[1593]

Secondly, the Supreme Court held that the payments for which the terms provided constituted part of the "price or remuneration" in exchange for this package of services so as to attract the application of the exclusion, rejecting the Court of Appeal's view that in deciding whether a term provided for the "price or remuneration" a court should adopt the point of view of the typical consumer and consider whether the relevant terms provided for the "essential bargain" between the

---

3159).

[1587] [2001] UKHL 52 at [11]–[12], [34], [43].

[1588] [2001] UKHL 52 at [20] and see below, para.38-272.

[1589] [2001] UKHL 52 at [56], per Lord Millett and see below, para.38-272.

[1590] [2008] EWHC 875 (Comm), [2009] EWCA Civ 116, [2009] 2 W.L.R. 1286, [2009] UKSC 6, [2010] 1 A.C. 696; Whittaker (2011) 74 M.L.R. 106.

[1591] [2008] EWHC 875 at [423]–[424]. cf. above, para.38-245.

[1592] [2009] UKSC 6 at [95], per Lord Mance; similarly, at [57]–[60], per Lord Phillips While Lord Walker of Gestingthorpe was "inclined to agree" that for the purposes of the appeal the dispute as to the nature of the exclusion was a distraction, he also saw that "in the long run it may become an issue of great practical importance": [2009] UKSC 6 at [29] and see at [61] (Lord Phillips).

[1593] [2009] UKSC 6 at [40], per Lord Walker and cf. at [80] and [81] (where this view is apparently taken by Lord Phillips), and at [98] (Lord Mance).

parties.[1594] According to the Supreme Court, the Court of Appeal's reference to the view of the typical consumer was not supported by the *travaux préparatoires* of the Directive, whose concern with the protection of the parties' consent was amply reflected in its distinct exclusion from review of terms which are "individually negotiated" and by the proviso to the exclusion found in art.4(2) that the terms in question be in plain and intelligible language.[1595] Instead, "the identification of the price or remuneration ... is a matter of objective interpretation by the court".[1596]

Applying this view of reg.6(2)(b), the Supreme Court agreed that the bank **38-248** charges in issue before it constituted part of the price or remuneration for the package of services provided by the banks. According to Lord Walker (with whom Baroness Hale and Lord Neuberger agreed):

"... [t]hey are an important part of the banks' charging structure, amounting to over 30 per cent of their revenue stream from all personal current account customers. The facts that the charges are contingent, and that the majority of customers do not incur them, are irrelevant".[1597]

With respect, this comes close to saying that the fact that the banks made a good deal of money out of the charges generated by the relevant terms means that they provided for part of the price or remuneration for the package of services, so adopting the position of the supplier of the goods or services, rather than an objective view. Lord Mance (with whom Baroness Hale and Lord Neuberger M.R. also agreed) took a somewhat different approach:

"... viewing the matter at the level of the banking contracts, the comparison is between, on the one hand, the package of services offered by the banks (some or all of which may or may not be used by any particular customer) and, on the other, the customer's commitment to pay *such charges as may arise from whatever facilities he does use*. At this level, the banks' case is that price or remuneration is or includes the customer's potential liability for charges, rather than the payments which he or she has actually to make if and when such charges are incurred."[1598]

Lord Mance therefore viewed the OFT's challenge to the proportionality of the relevant charges to the cost of providing particular services (as opposed to the overall package of services) as beside the point[1599]:

"... [i]f the agreement to incur the relevant charges is part of an overall package contract, its vulnerability to challenge and, if permissible, any assessment of its fairness under the Directive and the Regulations must ... depend upon an analysis of such agreement as part of the package contract."[1600]

He held, in conclusion, that "the concepts of 'price or remuneration' must ... be capable in principle of covering, under a banking contract, an agreement to make

---

[1594] [2009] EWCA Civ 116 at [91]–[92].

[1595] [2009] UKSC 6 at [45] (Lord Walker); similarly at [78] (Lord Phillips), [108], [112] and [115] (Lord Mance). In relation to this particular issue, *OFT v Foxtons Ltd* [2009] EWHC 1681 (Ch), [2009] 29 E.G. 98 (C.S.) (which was decided on the basis of the CA's decision in *OFT v Abbey National Plc*) was overtaken by the decision of the SC in the latter case.

[1596] [2009] UKSC 6 at [113] per Lord Mance.

[1597] [2009] UKSC 6 at [47] and see at [88] (Lord Phillips).

[1598] [2009] UKSC 6 at [98] (emphasis added).

[1599] [2009] UKSC 6 at [99].

[1600] [2009] UKSC 6 at [100].

a payment in a particular event".[1601] So, while Lord Mance accepted that some terms providing for the payment of money did not fall within reg.6(2)(b) even though they could not be said to be "default terms",[1602] the relevant charges clearly did so fall. The Supreme Court further held that, even if the Court of Appeal had been right in requiring reg.6(2)(b) to be applied from the point of view of the typical consumer so as to focus on what was or was not "ancillary" to the main bargain, the relevant terms would still fall within its exclusion. For this purpose, Lord Walker could not see how "charges amounting to 30 per cent of the revenue stream were 'not part of the core or essential bargain'".[1603] Lord Mance agreed:

"... [t]he uneconomic nature of the relevant charges from the customers' viewpoint constitutes the importance of the charges from the banks' viewpoint, and the plain intelligible language of the banking contracts made evident that there must be a considerable element of cross-subsidy in respect of customers where they remained in credit".[1604]

This view enabled the Supreme Court to hold that, quite apart from the doctrine of *acte clair* (on which the Supreme Court was divided[1605]) it did not need to refer the question of the proper interpretation of art.4(2) of the Directive to the Court of Justice of the EU since the *application* of reg.6(2) was a matter for itself as a national court.[1606]

38-249   European case-law   Since the decision of the Supreme Court in *OFT v Abbey National Plc*, the Court of Justice of the EU has considered the exclusion contained in art.4(2) of the 1993 Directive on eight occasions.[1607] This European case-law takes a very different view of the interpretation of art.4(2) from that adopted by the Supreme Court in *OFT v Abbey National Plc* and provides significant guidance on its application which must be used by English courts.[1608] Of these cases, the most important are *Kásler, Matei, Van Hove* and *Andriciuc*.[1609]

[1601] [2009] UKSC 6 at [104].

[1602] [2009] UKSC 6 at [101].

[1603] [2009] UKSC 6 at [47].

[1604] [2009] UKSC 6 at [117].

[1605] Lord Walker ([2009] UKSC 6 at [49]), Lord Mance ([2009] UKSC 6 at 115) and Baroness Hale ([2009] UKSC 6 at [91]) considered that the doctrine of *acte clair* would have applied; Lord Phillips ([2009] UKSC 6 at [91]) and Lord Neuberger ([2009] UKSC 6 at [120]) would have held that it did not. On the general division of function between national courts and the CJEU see above, para.38-017.

[1606] [2009] UKSC 6 at [50] (Lord Walker), [117] (Lord Mance) and at [120] (Lord Neuberger).

[1607] *Caja de Ahorros y Monte de Piedad de Madrid v Asociación de Usuarios de Servicios Bancarios (Ausbanc)* (C-484/08) EU:C:2010:309, June 3, 2010 [2010] 3 C.M.L.R. 43; *Pohotovosť s.r.o. v Korčkovska* (C-76/10) of November 16, 2010 (available only in French); *Nemzeti Fogyasztóvédelmi Hatóság v Invitel Távközlési Zrt* (C-472/10) EU:C:2012:242, April 26, 2012 ("*Invitel* (C-472/10)"); *Kásler v OTP Jelzálogbank Zrt* (C-26/13) EU:C:2014:282, April 30, 2014 ("*Kásler* (C-26/13)"); and *Matei v SC Volksbank România SA* (C-143/13) EU:C:2015:127, February 26, 2015 ("*Matei* (C-143/13)"); *Van Hove v CNP Assurances SA* (C-96/14) EU:C:2015:262, April 26, 2015 ("*Van Hove* (C-96/14)"); *Bucura v SC Bancpost SA* (C-348/14) EU:C:2015:447, July 9, 2015; and *Andriciuc v Banca Românească* (C-186/16) of September 20, 2017 ("*Andriciuc* (C-186/16)").

[1608] For this reason, it is submitted that the reasoning of English courts which have applied the interpretation of art.4(2) of the 1993 Directive by the SC in *OFT v Abbey National Plc* or otherwise without reference to the recent case-law of the CJEU as described in the text should not be relied on or should be relied on only in the light of the case-law of the CJEU: for these earlier decisions see *Office of Fair Trading v Ashbourne Management Services Ltd* [2011] EWHC 1237 (Ch), [2011] E.C.C. 31 (terms which set a minimum duration for gym membership of one year with either no or only a very

Kásler and Matei   These cases both concerned terms of contracts of consumer   **38-250**
credit, the details of which will be noted later,[1610] its ruling in *Kásler* being followed closely by *Matei*. The Court of Justice held that the exclusion in art.4(2) of
the Directive must be strictly interpreted as it provides an exception to the test of
unfairness[1611] and that its terms require an "autonomous and uniform interpretation throughout the European Union" taking into account its context and the purpose
of the legislation.[1612] Moreover, while it is for national courts alone to rule on the
classification of a term in a contract (as falling within or outside these terms), the
Court of Justice can "elicit [from art.4(2)] the criteria that the national court may
or must apply when examining a contractual term".[1613] The Court further held that
art.4(2) distinguished clearly between two categories of contract term, which are
concerned respectively with terms that concern the main subject matter of the
contract and terms relating to the "adequacy of the price and remuneration on [the]
one hand, as against the services or goods supplied, on the other".[1614]

First, where a term concerns the "main subject matter of the contract" the Court   **38 251**
of Justice considered that it should not be examined as to its unfairness at all. According to the Court:

> "… contractual terms falling within the notion of the 'main subject-matter of the contract'
> … must be understood as being those that lay down the essential obligations of the
> contract and, as such, characterise it. By contrast, terms ancillary to those that define the
> very essence of the contractual relationship cannot fall within the notion of the 'main
> subject-matter of the contract' within the meaning of Article 4(2)."[1615]

For this purpose, the fact that a term has been individually negotiated cannot
constitute a relevant criterion given that, if the term was so negotiated, it would fall
outside the scope of the Directive.[1616] The Court in *Kásler* then explained that in
identifying the terms covered by the first limb of art.4(2) national courts should have

---

limited possibility of cancellation without liability fell within the main subject matter of the contract
but remained reviewable for fairness on other grounds); *Foxtons Ltd v O'Reardon* [2011] EWHC
2946 (QB) (term in exclusive estate agency contract for sale of property provided that agent's fee
was payable on exchange of contracts fell within reg.6(2)(a) as it defined the main subject matter
of the contract). cf. *Financial Services Authority v Asset L.I. Inc (t/a Asset Land Investment Inc)*
[2013] EWHC 178 (Ch) at [132] (terms in contracts for the sale of land under a collective investment scheme which described services undertaken by the seller held not to relate to the *main* subject
matter of the contract, which was the sale and purchase of land). On appeal, the Court of Appeal
considered that the issue of the unfairness of the terms was unnecessary for the issues before the
court, but it would have agreed with the court below: [2014] EWCA Civ 435, [2015] 1 All E.R. 1
at [96]–[99]. cf. the view of the HC in *Casehub Ltd v Wolf Cola Ltd* [2017] EWHC 1169 (Ch), [2017]
5 Costs L.R. 835 noted below, para.38-264, that it was bound to follow the decision of the SC in
Abbey National Plc rather than the guidance of the CJEU.
[1609] Below, paras 38-250 et seq.
[1610] Below, paras 38-254—38-257.
[1611] *Kásler* (C-26/13) at para.42; *Matei* (C-143/13) para.49.
[1612] *Kásler* (C-26/13) at paras 37–38; *Matei* (C-143/13) para.50.
[1613] *Kásler* (C-26/13) at para.45; *Matei* (C-143/13) para.53.
[1614] *Kásler* (C-26/13) at paras 43–51 and 52–58 respectively; *Matei* (C-143/13) paras 54–55.
[1615] *Kásler* (C-26/13) at [49]–[50]; similarly *Matei* (C-143/13) para.54. Subsequent editions of the present
work have explained art.4(2) on the basis that it draws a distinction between the term or terms which
express the substance of the bargain and "incidental" (if important) terms which surround them, a
formulation quoted with apparent approval by Lord Bingham of Cornhill in *Director General of Fair
Trading v First National Bank Plc* [2001] UKHL 52 at [12]: see 31st edn, Vol.I, para.15-060.
[1616] *Kásler* (C-26/13) at [47]–[48], referring to 1993 Directive art.3(1).

regard to a wide range of circumstances (in the context, "the nature, general scheme and the stipulations of the loan agreement, and its legal and factual context"), but in doing so it did not echo the language used by Advocate General Wahl, who had advised that "the [national] court must decide in each individual case the essential obligation(s) which must *objectively* be regarded as essential in the general scheme of the contract", asking itself whether a term "contributes objectively, in one way or another, to the *legal or commercial definition of the essential characteristics of the contract*".[1617] In this way, the Court of Justice required courts to take a broad contextual approach to the identification of the main subject matter of the contract, rather than the more abstract approach based on the legal definition of the contract which its Advocate General advocated.

38-252   Secondly, the second limb of art.4(2) of the Directive covers terms relating to "the adequacy of the price and remuneration on [the] one hand, as against the services or goods supplied, on the other"[1618] and so the starting point for the application of this exclusion is also the identification of a contract term which has this characteristic. However, in the view of the Court of Justice:

> "… it is clear from the wording of Article 4(2) of Directive 93/13 that the second category of terms that cannot be examined as regards unfairness is limited in scope, for that exclusion concerns only the adequacy of the price or remuneration as against the services or goods supplied in exchange."[1619]

The explanation for this exclusion is that "no legal scale or criterion exists that can provide a framework for, and guide, such a review".[1620] So, where a term describes "the quality/price ratio of the goods or services supplied" then it is excluded from the review of unfairness only as regards this issue. As a result of this restricted significance of the second limb of the exclusion:

> "Terms relating to the consideration[1621] due by the consumer to the lender or having an impact on the actual price to be paid to the latter by the consumer thus do not, in principle, fall within the second category of terms, except as regards the question whether the amount of consideration or the price as stipulated in the contract are adequate as compared with the service provided in exchange by the lender."[1622]

38-253   Thirdly, a term falling within one of the examples in the "indicative list" of terms in the Annex to the Directive will not fall within the exclusion contained in art.4(2) of the Directive, since, given the purpose of this list is to "serve as a 'grey list' of terms which may be regarded as unfair", such an inclusion would "to a large extent be deprived of its effectiveness if they were excluded from the outset from an assessment of their unfairness pursuant to Article 4(2)".[1623]

[1617] *Kásler* (C-26/13) A.G. Wahl, Opinion of February 12, 2014 at [49] (original emphasis) and [53] (emphasis added).

[1618] *Kásler* (C-26/13) at para.52; *Matei* (C-143/13) para.55.

[1619] *Kásler* (C-26/13) at para.54 and 55; *Matei* (C-143/13) para.55.

[1620] *Kásler* (C-26/13) at para.54.

[1621] In the French version of this judgment, "consideration" appears as "*la contrepartie*" and in the German as "*Gegenleistung*", that is in both cases, something in return.

[1622] *Matei* (C-143/13) para.56.

[1623] *Matei* (C-143/13) para.60. Under the Consumer Rights Act 2015 s.64(6), this position is made explicit as this provides that the section providing for the "core exclusion" "does not apply to a term of a contract listed in Part 1 of Schedule 2", i.e. the indicative list of terms foreseen by the Annex to the 1993 Directive: see below, para.38-398.

Guidance on the application of the exclusion In *Kásler* a contract of consumer   **38-254**
credit denominated in a foreign currency set the exchange rate for repayment of the
loan by the consumer at the creditor bank's "selling rate" by one term, whereas
another term set the exchange rate for payment of the original sums lent by the bank
to the consumer at the bank's "buying rate". The loan was denominated in the
foreign currency (there, Swiss francs) to ensure stability of the repayment advanced
and did not make available any foreign currency to the consumer borrower. In these
circumstances, and applying its interpretation of art.4(2) of the Directive,[1624] the
Court of Justice held that it was for the national referring court:

> "... to determine, having regard to the nature, general scheme and the stipulations of the
> loan agreement, and its legal and factual context, whether the term setting the exchange
> rate for the monthly repayment instalments constitutes an essential element of the debtor's
> obligations, consisting in the repayment of the amount made available by the lender."[1625]

However, the Court of Justice held that the second limb of the exclusion in art.4(2)
could not apply to the term before the national referring court:

> "... such a term, in so far as it contains a pecuniary obligation for the consumer to pay,
> in repayment instalments of the loan, the difference between the selling rate of exchange
> and the buying rate of exchange of the foreign currency, *cannot be considered as
> 'remuneration'*, the adequacy of which as consideration for a service supplied by the
> lender cannot be subject of an examination as regards unfairness under Article 4(2)."[1626]

This was the case on the basis that this difference could not constitute something
in return ("consideration") for any foreign exchange service supplied by the lender
in this respect.[1627]

These views of the Court of Justice therefore differ from those expressed by the   **38-255**
Supreme Court in *OFT v Abbey National Plc*[1628] in two ways. First, the Court of
Justice considered that contract terms relating to the calculation of moneys payable by the consumer should be considered in relation to each limb of the exclusion in art.4(2) (so, for example, a price term *may* define the very essence of the
contractual relationship so as to fall within the "main subject matter of the
contract"), whereas the Supreme Court in *OFT v Abbey National Plc* assumed that
the relevant terms setting bank charges would fall only under the second limb of
the exclusion.[1629] It may be added that it would be difficult to argue that the relevant
terms in *OFT v Abbey National Plc* constituted an "essential element" of the bank
customer's contract as understood by the Court of Justice, especially given that their
contingent nature meant that they would not apply to all customers. Secondly, the
Supreme Court in *OFT v Abbey National Plc* considered whether the sums arising
under the relevant terms constituted part of the price or remuneration for "the package of services provided by the banks",[1630] whereas the Court of Justice in *Kásler*
held that the difference between the selling rate of exchange and the buying rate of

---

[1624] Above, paras 38-250—38-251.
[1625] *Kásler* (C-26/13) at para.54.
[1626] *Kásler* (C-26/13) at para.59 (emphasis added).
[1627] *Kásler* (C-26/13) at para.58.
[1628] [2009] UKSC 6, above, paras 38-247—38-248.
[1629] i.e. 1999 Regulations reg.6(2)(b).
[1630] [2009] UKSC 6 at [40], per Lord Walker and cf. at [80] and [81] (where this view is apparently taken
by Lord Phillips), and at [98] (Lord Mance), above, para.38-247.

exchange of the foreign currency, could not be considered as "remuneration" as there was nothing done by the creditor in exchange *for this difference*, thereby rejecting an approach which would have instead looked at the difference as forming part of the remuneration for the package of financial services provided by the creditor. So, for the Court of Justice, the exclusion in the second limb of art.4(2) applies only where there is something specifically in return for the "price or remuneration" provided by the term in question.

38-256   **Matei**   In *Matei* the Court of Justice offered guidance to a Romanian court on the application of legislation implementing art.4(2) of the Directive to two terms in a contract of consumer credit: a term under which the consumer debtor could be required to pay the creditor a "risk charge" calculated on the basis of the balance of the loan and payable monthly throughout its duration, and a term authorising the creditor to alter the rate of interest "in the event of significant changes on the financial markets" (the variation clause).[1631] As regards the variation clause, the Court of Justice saw four reasons why such a clause should fall outside the scope of the exclusion in art.4(2): first, the Court so held in the earlier case of *Invitel* in relation to a similar term[1632]; secondly, such a clause is included in the first paragraph of the Annex to the Directive as a term which may be considered unfair unless it satisfies certain conditions set by its second paragraph and this inclusion would be deprived of its effectiveness if it were excluded from the outset from the test of unfairness by way of art.4(2)[1633]; thirdly, the term looks "ancillary" as it contains an adjustment mechanism for the interest rate which is set by a term which is likely to be part of the main subject matter of the contract[1634]; and, fourthly, the second limb of the exclusion did not appear to be in issue before the national court, as the latter was concerned rather with

> "... the conditions and criteria enabling the lender to make that alteration, in particular on the ground of alleging 'significant changes in the money market' and so was not concerned with the limited issue of any alleged inadequacy of the level of the altered interest rate as against any consideration that may have been supplied in exchange for the alteration."[1635]

So, the view of the Court of Justice was very clearly that the interest variation term fell outside the scope of art.4(2), though it was careful to add that this view was "subject to verification by the referring court".[1636]

38-257   In the case of the terms providing for a "risk charge" to be applied by the lender, according to the Court of Justice "several elements suggest that they do not fall within the exclusion laid down by Article 4(2)".[1637] As regards the first limb of the exclusion, in deciding whether the terms defined the "very essence of the contractual relationship" or are instead "ancillary", the national court must take into account:

[1631] *Matei* (C-143/13) paras 26–27.
[1632] *Nemzeti Fogyasztóvédelmi Hatóság v Invitel Távközlési Zrt* (C-472/10) EU:C:2012:242, April 26, 2012 at para.23; *Matei* (C-143/13) para.58 and see below, para.38-314.
[1633] *Matei* (C-143/13) paras 59–61 referring to 1993 Directive Annex paras 1(j) and 2(b).
[1634] *Matei* (C-143/13) para.62.
[1635] *Matei* (C-143/13) para.63.
[1636] *Matei* (C-143/13) para.63.
[1637] *Matei* (C-143/13) para.64.

"... the essential aim pursued by the 'risk charge' which consists in ensuring repayment of the loan. That clearly constitutes an essential obligation on the part of the consumer in exchange for making available the amount of the loan."[1638]

For this purpose, the Court considered that:

"... taking account of the objective of protecting consumers which must guide the interpretation of the provisions of [the 1993 Directive] ... the mere fact that the 'risk charge' may be regarded as representing a relatively important part of the APR and, therefore, the income received by the lender from the credit agreements concerned is in principle irrelevant for the purposes of determining whether the terms providing for that charge define the 'main subject-matter' of the contract."[1639]

In deciding whether the term providing for the "risk charge" fell within the second limb of the exclusion, in the view of the Court of Justice "certain information in the documents submitted to the Court seems rather to indicate that this is not the case", though it remained for the referring court to decide whether the term does fall within the exclusion.[1640] The information in question suggests that the dispute below

"... does not concern the adequacy of the amount of the risk charge as compared with a service provided by the lender (of whatever kind) since it is submitted that the lender does not provide any actual service which could constitute consideration for that charge, so that the question of the adequacy of that charge does not arise."[1641]

Instead,

"... the dispute ... essentially covers the grounds justifying the terms in question, and in particular, whether, in so far as they require the consumer to pay commission of a substantial amount which aims to ensure the repayment of the loan, even though it is argued that that risk is already guaranteed by a mortgage and that, in exchange for that charge, the bank does not provide a real service to the consumer solely in the consumer's interests, those terms must be regarded as unfair, within the meaning of Article 3 of [the 1993 Directive]."[1642]

So, if the national court were to hold that this was the case, the exclusion in the second limb of art.4(2) would not be in issue as the challenge to the term would not concern the adequacy of the remuneration in relation to a service supplied in return by the creditor.

Of these elements of guidance in the application of art.4(2), two contrast clearly **38-258** with the approach taken by the Supreme Court in *OFT v Abbey National Plc*: the first, is that in common with its approach in *Kásler*,[1643] for the application of the second limb of the exclusion the Court requires a distinct service to be identified in exchange for which the "price or remuneration" is to be paid[1644]; the second is that for the application of the first limb, the Court of Justice specifically ruled it to be "in principle irrelevant" that the "risk charge" generated a relatively important

---

[1638] *Matei* (C-143/13) para.67.

[1639] *Matei* (C-143/13) para.68.

[1640] *Matei* (C-143/13) para.69.

[1641] *Matei* (C-143/13) para.70 referring by analogy to *Kásler* (C-26/13) at para.58, above, para.38-254.

[1642] *Matei* (C-143/13) para.71.

[1643] *Kásler* (C-26/13) at para.59, above, para.38-255.

[1644] cf. [2009] UKSC 6 at [40], per Lord Walker and cf. at [80] and [81] (where this view is apparently taken by Lord Phillips) and at [98] (Lord Mance), above, para.38-247.

part of the income received by the creditor from their contracts with consumers, whereas three members of the Supreme Court in *OFT v Abbey National Plc* saw the fact that the relevant terms imposing bank charges generated an important part of the banks' revenue stream as relevant to the question whether the charges amounted to part of the "price or remuneration" for the package of services under the second limb.[1645]

38-259   **Van Hove**   In the case of contracts of insurance, recital 19 of the 1993 Directive sought to explain the exclusion in art.4(2) by stating that:

> "… it follows [from the exclusion in art.4(2)] inter alia, that in insurance contracts, the terms which clearly define or circumscribe the insured risk and the insurer's liability shall not be subject to such assessment since these restrictions are taken into account in calculating the premium paid by the consumer."

In *Van Hove v CNP Assurances SA*[1646] the Court of Justice considered the significance of this in a reference from a French court concerning the application of the core exclusion in relation to a consumer contract of insurance. There the consumer had concluded two contracts of loan with a lender and at the same time had concluded with an insurer a contract of insurance which guaranteed cover of all the loan repayments "due from the borrowers to the contracting party in the event of death, permanent and absolute invalidity or 75% of such loan repayments in the event of total incapacity for work". A further term stated that the insured "shall be regarded as being in a state of total incapacity for work if, after 90 consecutive days' interruption of activity following an accident or illness ('the waiting period'), he finds himself unable to take up any activity, paid or otherwise".[1647] After suffering a work-related accident, the consumer was assessed by the national social security authorities as having a permanent partial incapacity at 72 per cent, but the insurer's doctor advised it that the consumer's state of health allowed him to carry on appropriate employment on a part-time basis and the insurer therefore refused to cover his loan repayments as he was no longer "unable to take up any activity, paid or otherwise" within the meaning of the contract. The consumer claimed that these terms were unfair, and the French court therefore asked the Court of Justice whether art.4(2) should be interpreted as covering such terms in a contract of insurance. The Court of Justice, following faithfully its early approach to art.4(2) in *Kásler* and *Matei*, held that in deciding whether a term falls within the "main subject-matter of the contract" a national court should consider whether it lays down "the essential obligations of the contract" which "characterise it" or whether it is an ancillary term.[1648] For this purpose, the Court felt able to drawn on its own case-law which held for the purposes of EU provisions on VAT, that:

> "… the essentials of an insurance transaction are that the insurer undertakes, in return for prior payment of a premium, to provide the insured, in the event of materialisation of the risk covered, with the service agreed when the contract was concluded."[1649]

[1645] [2009] UKSC 6 at [47] (Lord Walker, with whom Baroness Hale and Lord Neuberger agreed), above, para.38-248.

[1646] C-96/14 EU:C:2015:262, April 23, 2015 ("*Van Hove* (C-96/14)").

[1647] *Van Hove* (C-96/14) paras 11–12.

[1648] *Van Hove* (C-96/14) paras 31, 33 referring to *Kásler* (C-26/13) para.50; *Matei* (C-143/13) para.54 above, para.38-251.

[1649] *Van Hove* (C-96/14) para.34 referring to *Card Protection Plan (CCP) Ltd v Commissioners of*

Having cited recital 19 of the Directive, the Court held that the contract term in issue which defines the concept of "total incapacity for work" and other conditions which the consumer must meet to receive cover for the loan may circumscribe the insurer's risk and "lay down the essential obligations of the insurance contract at issue", but whether or not it did was for the national court to decide, taking into account the "nature, general scheme and the stipulations of the contract and its legal and factual context".[1650] However, the Court of Justice then considered the significance of the condition for the application of the exclusion in art.4(2) that the term be in "plain, intelligible language" as discussed more generally in the following paragraph.

Andriciuc The recent decision of the Court of Justice in *Andriciuc v Banca* **38-260**
Românească (C-186/16) provides a good example of a case where it clearly considered that the contract term in question fell *within* the exclusion provided by art.4(2).[1651] In that case, the consumers, resident in Romania and with incomes in Romanian currency, had contracted loans from a bank under which they had to make monthly repayments in the same foreign currency (Swiss francs) as that in which the contracts had been concluded, with the consequence that the risk in fluctuations as between the Romanian currency and the Swiss franc was borne entirely by the consumers. The consumers sought to challenge the fairness of the terms providing for the loan to be repaid in the same currency in which it was made, but the question arose whether those terms fell within the exclusion in Romanian legislation implementing art.4(2) of the Directive. Having referred to its own case-law in *Kásler*, *Matei* and *Van Hove*,[1652] the Court of Justice concluded that "a number of elements in the documents before the Court" indicate that the relevant terms are covered by the notion of "main subject matter of the contract" within the meaning of the first limb of art.4(2).[1653] The Court observed:

> "In that connection, it must be observed that, under a loan agreement, the lender undertakes, in particular, to make available to the borrower a certain sum of money and the latter undertakes, in particular, to repay that sum, usually with interest, on the scheduled payment dates. Therefore, the essential obligations of such a contract relate to a sum of money which must be determined by the stipulated currency in which it is paid and repaid. Thus, as the Advocate General observed…, the fact that a loan must be repaid in a certain currency relates, in principle, not to an ancillary repayment arrangement, but to very nature of the debtor's obligation, thereby constituting an essential element of a loan agreement."[1654]

In this respect, the Court of Justice distinguished the situation before it from *Kásler* on the basis that, although the loans there were denominated in foreign currency, they had to be repaid in the national currency according to the selling rate of the exchange applied by the bank, whereas in *Andriciuc* the loans had to be repaid in

---

Customs & Excise (C-349/96) EU:C:1999:93, [1999] E.C.R. I-973 para.17; *Skandia* (C-240/99) EU:C:2001:140, [2001] E.C.R. I-01951 para.37; and *Commission v Greece* (C-13/06) EU:C:2006:765, [2006] E.C.R. I-11563 para.10.

[1650] *Van Hove* (C-96/14) paras 36–37, following *Kásler* at paras 50 and 51, above, para.38-251.
[1651] *Andriciuc v Banca Românească* (C-186/16) of September 20, 2017 ("*Andriciuc* (C-186/16)").
[1652] Above, paras 38-250—38-259.
[1653] *Andriciuc* (C-186/16) at paras 27–31.
[1654] *Andriciuc* (C-186/16) para.38 referring to the Opinion of A.G. Wahl, para.46 et seq.

the same foreign currency as that in which they were issued.[1655] As a result, the Court of Justice was clear that the term setting the repayment in Swiss francs fell within the exclusion of art.4(2), subject to the proviso that it was drafted in plain intelligible language.[1656]

38-261 **The condition that the "terms are in plain intelligible language"[1657]** The exclusions from the assessment of unfairness contained in art.4(2) of the Directive and reflected in reg.6(2) of the 1999 Regulations are subject to the condition that the relevant terms are expressed in plain and intelligible language: where they are not the terms are for this reason subject to the test of unfairness.[1658] The Court of Justice has made clear both the importance and the demanding character of this condition. First, in *Pohotovost' sro v Korckovskà*[1659] the Court of Justice held that the omission of the APR (which, together with other "essential terms of the contract"[1660] was required by the Consumer Credit Directive of 1987[1661]) from a term of a contract of consumer credit which concerned the cost of the loan could be seen by a national court as having a decisive impact on the question whether that term was "in plain intelligible language", and, if it was so held, the term failed the condition for the application of art.4(2) and fell to be assessed for its fairness under art.3 of the Directive.[1662] This decision has considerable implications given the breadth of scope of application and the extent of information requirements imposed by the law (and EU law in particular) in relation to consumer contracts.[1663] Secondly, in *Kásler* the Court of Justice explained more generally the significance of the condition that the "terms are in plain intelligible language", holding that it has the same scope as the requirement of plain intelligible writing in art.5 of the 1993 Directive,[1664] and that the latter includes a requirement that the consumer should actually be given an op-

---

[1655] *Andriciuc* (C-186/16) at para.40.

[1656] *Andriciuc* (C-186/16) at para.41. On its decision on the proviso, see below, para.38-262.

[1657] Under the Consumer Rights Act 2015 s.64, this condition has apparently been extended so as to impose a condition that a term is both "transparent and prominent": see below, paras 38-398—38-399.

[1658] For examples in the English courts see *Bankers Insurance Co Ltd v South* [2003] P.I.Q.R. P.28 at [24] (exclusion in travel insurance held "plain and intelligible"); *Financial Services Authority v Asset L.I. Inc (t/a Asset Land Investment Inc)* [2013] EWHC 178 (Ch), [2013] 2 B.C.L.C. 480 at [132] (terms in contracts for the sale of land under a collective investment scheme which described services undertaken by seller held not to be in "plain, intelligible" language and so reviewable for unfairness even if they otherwise fell within the exclusion of reg.6(2) of the 1999 Regulations). On appeal, the Court of Appeal considered that the issue of the unfairness of the terms was unnecessary for the issues before the court, but it would have agreed with the court below: [2014] EWCA Civ 435, [2015] 1 All E.R. 1 at [96]–[99].

[1659] C-76/10 of November 16, 2010 (available only in French). The decision was an "order" (*ordonnance*) made under art.104(3) of the Rules of Procedure of the Court of Justice, according to which a "question referred to the Court for a preliminary ruling is identical to a question on which the Court has already ruled, or where the answer to such a question may be clearly deduced from existing case-law, the Court may, after hearing the Advocate General, at any time give its decision by reasoned order in which reference is made to its previous judgment or to the relevant case-law".

[1660] Directive 87/102 on consumer credit [1987] O.J. L42/48 art.4(3).

[1661] Directive 87/102 on consumer credit [1987] O.J. L42/48 art.4(2)(a).

[1662] C-76/10 para.72, citing *Caja de Madrid* (C-484/08) para.32. The CJEU also held that the national court could find that the term was unfair as a result of the omission of the APR: C-76/10 para.73.

[1663] See above, paras 38-059 et seq., especially in respect of "on-premises contracts", off-premises contracts and distance contracts.

[1664] *Kásler* (C-26/13) at para.69. On art.5 see below paras 38-347 et seq. (1999 Regulations reg.7) and paras 38-414—38-417 (Consumer Rights Act 2015 s.68).

portunity of examining all the terms of the contract.[1665] The Court then noted that it had previously held in the context of art.5 that pre-contractual information on the terms of the contract and the consequences of concluding it is of "fundamental importance for a consumer" as it provides the basis on which "he decides whether he wishes to be bound by the terms previously drawn up by the seller or supplier".[1666] For this reason, "the requirement of transparency" of contract terms in the 1993 Directive (including in art.4(2)) cannot be "reduced merely to their being formally and grammatically intelligible", but must be understood in a broad sense given that the Directive is based on the idea that the consumer is in a position of weakness compared to the trader "in particular as regards his level of knowledge".[1667] As a result, the requirement of transparency requires that the "consumer is in a position to evaluate, on the basis of clear, intelligible criteria, the economic consequences for him which derive from" the term in question; the reasons for the trader using the term and its relationship with other contractual terms should be clear and intelligible.[1668] In the context of the terms before it, which concerned the application of different exchange rates to different aspects of the contract of consumer credit,[1669] the national referring court must therefore:

"... determine whether, having regard to all the relevant information, including the promotional material and information provided by the lender in the negotiation of the loan agreement, the *average consumer, who is reasonably well informed and reasonably observant and circumspect*, would not only be aware of the difference, generally observed on the securities market, between the selling rate of exchange and the buying rate of exchange of a foreign currency, but also be able to assess the potentially significant economic consequences for him resulting from the application of the selling rate of exchange for the calculation of the repayments for which he would ultimately be liable and, therefore, the total cost of the sum borrowed."[1670]

It will be seen therefore, that the Court of Justice requires national courts to consider as a condition for the application of the exclusion in art.4(2) not merely whether a term is formally or grammatically clear but also whether (in its context) it allows the average consumer to understand its practical significance for himself.[1671]

For this purpose, *Van Hove* provides an example of how very demanding the requirement of transparency can be. There, a contract of insurance contained a term which restricted cover for the consumer to the situation where he suffered from "total incapacity for work" where "after 90 consecutive days' interruption of activity following an accident or illness ... he finds himself unable to take up any activity, paid or otherwise".[1672] The French court had considered that while "plain and precise", this term is capable of being understood in various ways, including that it does not rule out payment other than where the consumer is not fit to carry on any activity whatsoever[1673] so that it cannot be ruled out that, even though gram-

38-262

[1665] *Kásler* (C-26/13) at para.67 referring to 1993 Directive recital 12.
[1666] *Kásler* (C-26/13) at para.70 referring to *RWE Vertrieb AG v Verbraucherzentrale Nordrhein-Westfalen eV* (C-92/11) EU:C:2013:180, March 21, 2013 at para.44, below, para.38-350.
[1667] *Kásler* (C-26/13) at paras 71–72.
[1668] *Kásler* (C-26/13) at para.75.
[1669] Above, para.38-254.
[1670] *Kásler* (C-26/13) at para.74 (emphasis added).
[1671] On the wider significance of the "average consumer" in EU law see above, paras 38-044—38-046.
[1672] *Van Hove v CNP Assurances SA* (C-96/14) of April 23, 2015, on which see above, para.38-259.
[1673] *Van Hove* (C-96/14) para.42.

matically intelligible, "the scope of that term was not understood by the consumer".[1674] The notion of "activity, paid or otherwise" is, in the view of the Court of Justice, "extremely broad and vague"; moreover, the consumer may not necessarily have been aware of the difference between the concept of "total incapacity for work" under the contract and "partial permanent incapacity" within the meaning of French social security law.[1675] It was, therefore, for the national court to assess all the information available to the consumer as well as the contract itself, in deciding whether an average consumer would have understood this difference and its potentially significant economic consequences.[1676] Moreover, the fact that the insurance contract was related to loan contracts could also be relevant as:

> "... [t]he consumer cannot be required ... to have the same vigilance regarding the extent of the risks covered by that insurance contract as he would if he had concluded that contract and the loan contracts separately."[1677]

It will be seen that, in this way, the understanding of the average consumer of the significance of a contract term is crucial to the application of the exclusion in art.4(2), though it is relevant to the condition of transparency rather than to the identification of the terms subject to the exclusion.[1678] A similarly demanding approach was taken in *Andriciuc*, which concerned a term requiring repayment of a loan in a foreign currency where the loan was itself issued in that same currency.[1679] The Court of Justice noted that, in deciding whether the contract:

> "... puts the consumer in a position to evaluate, on the basis of clear, intelligible criteria, the economic consequences for him which derive from [the contract]",[1680]

a national court should refer to all relevant facts, "including the promotional material and information provided by the lender in the negotiation of the loan agreement" with the view to ascertaining whether:

> "... all the information likely to have a bearing on the extent of his commitment have [sic] been communicated to the consumer, enabling him to estimate in particular the total cost of his loan."[1681]

In this respect, the Court of Justice noted the Recommendation of the European Systematic Risk Board on lending in foreign currencies to the effect that financial

---

[1674] *Van Hove* (C-96/14) para.43.

[1675] *Van Hove* (C-96/14) paras 45–46.

[1676] *Van Hove* (C-96/14) para.47.

[1677] *Van Hove* (C-96/14) para.48. As will be seen, the Consumer Rights Act 2015 follows this approach in its provision implementing art.4(2) of the Directive by expressly referring to the "average consumer" for the purpose of its condition that the term be prominent as well as transparent: see 2015 Act s.64(2)–(5) below, paras 38-395—38-401.

[1678] cf. the approach of the Court of Appeal in *OFT v Abbey National Plc* (reversed by the SC in the same case) which adopted the viewpoint of an average consumer to distinguish between those contract terms which set the "price or remuneration" and other terms, as suggested by earlier editions of the present Work: [2009] EWCA Civ 116, [2009] 2 W.L.R. 1286 at [72] referring to the present work (30th edn, 2008) Vol.I para.15-058, reversed [2009] UKSC 6, [2010] 1 A.C. 696 at [113]. On the decision of the SC, see above, paras 38-247—38-248.

[1679] *Andriciuc v Banca Românească* (C-186/16) of September 20, 2017 ("*Andriciuc* (C-186/16)") above, para.38-260

[1680] *Andriciuc* (C-186/16) at para.45.

[1681] *Andriciuc* (C-186/16) at paras 46–47.

institutions:

> "... must provide borrowers with adequate information to enable them to take well-informed and prudent decisions and should at least encompass the impact on instalments of a severe depreciation of the legal tender of the Member State in which a borrower is domiciled and of an increase of the foreign interest rate."[1682]

As a result, in the case of such a contract, the consumer/borrower must be clearly informed that he is being exposed to a certain foreign exchange risk which may become difficult to bear if there is a fall in value of the currency in which he receives his income and the lender must set out the possible variations in exchange rate and the risks in taking out a loan in a foreign currency.[1683] In this respect, of particular interest is the Court of Justice's use of a European recommendation to help determine the content of the information to be supplied by a trader if it is to satisfy the requirement that a term is in plain, intelligible writing.

A variable objective test It has been seen from its treatment by the Unfair Com- **38-263**
mercial Practices Directive, that the test of the "average consumer" is not necessarily uniform, but can instead be a test which (while objective) varies according to context.[1684] It is submitted that similar distinctions could helpfully be drawn in the context of the transparency of contract terms especially as regards the extent to which a consumer could be expected to read, understand and appreciate the practical significance for his own position of the terms of the contract, for while a national court would generally be justified in assessing these questions bearing in mind an "average consumer" (neither very sophisticated and careful nor, conversely, of under average intelligence or careless), where a trader has targeted its goods or services (and therefore its contract terms) towards a particular group of consumers, then this standard should be varied so as to take this into account. It is submitted, moreover, that in the context of contract terms, this standard could be varied in either direction. So, if a business targets particularly vulnerable consumers (for example, offering loans to low-income or poor-credit would-be borrowers), then the "average consumer" should be to an extent lowered; but if a business targets its sophisticated financial products towards high-income individuals (who may be independently advised), then the "average consumer" should be to this extent raised. And, as the General Court has observed in the context of EU legislation on trade marks, "the average consumer's level of attention is likely to vary according to the category of goods or services in question".[1685] In this way, the "average consumer" is an objective standard variable according to its context.

OFT v Abbey National Plc viewed in the light of the European case-law In **38-264**
earlier paragraphs, it has been explained that the approaches to the interpretation and proper application of the exclusion in art.4(2) of the Directive (reg.6(2) of the

---

[1682] *Andriciuc* (C-186/16) at para.49 referring to Recommendation ESRB/2011/1 of September 21, 2011 on lending in foreign currencies, [2011] O.J. C342/1, Recommendation A—Risk awareness of borrowers, para.1 [2011] O.J. C342/1.

[1683] *Andriciuc* (C-186/16) at para.50.

[1684] Above, paras 38-044 and 38-169.

[1685] *Tifosi Optics Inc v Office for Harmonisation in the Internal Market (Trade Marks and Designs) (OHIM)* (T-531/12) EU:T:2014:855 para.36; *Mundipharma v Office for Harmonisation in the Internal Market (Trade Marks and Designs) OHIM-Altana Pharma (RESPICUR)* (T-256/04) EU:T:2007:46, [2007] E.C.R.II-449 at para.42.

Regulations) taken by the Supreme Court in *OFT v Abbey National Plc* and by the Court of Justice of the EU in its later case-law differ significantly.[1686] Under the approach of the Court of Justice, there are three questions for a court considering the possible application of reg.6(2) to terms such as those considered by the Supreme Court in *OFT v Abbey National Plc* (i.e. terms in a contract for a current account which imposed charges on consumer customers when they requested or instructed the bank to make a payment without sufficient funds or credit).[1687] First, under the first limb of the exclusion in reg.6(2), the court should consider whether the terms could be said to "lay down the essential obligations of the contract and, as such, characterise it".[1688] It is submitted that it would be most unlikely that a court would so decide, particularly given the contingent nature of the terms in question.[1689] Secondly, under the second limb of the exclusion, the court should consider whether any payments to be made under the terms constitute the "remuneration" in exchange for a specific service provided by the bank (rather than as part of the remuneration for a wider package of services). Here, it could be argued that the banks provided a "specific service" to customers when or before the charge was levied by processing their instruction to pay and then paying,[1690] but it is submitted that Andrew Smith J.'s view on this question in *OFT v Abbey National Plc* is correct, that is, that the such charges are not payments *in exchange* for those services, but charges levied because the services are supplied in particular circumstances.[1691] If this view is correct, then the exclusion in reg.6(2) would not apply to terms imposing such bank charges, without reference to the third question. Thirdly, even if in principle the terms imposing bank charges were to fall within the exclusion in reg.6(2), they would do so only if they passed the requirement of transparency. For this purpose, the Court of Justice requires not merely that the terms are grammatically intelligible, but that the average consumer would be able to evaluate the economic consequences of the term for his or her own position. The answer to this question would depend not merely on the clarity or even prominence of the drafting of the terms in question but on how any particular term would be viewed by the average consumer given the wider context in which the contract in question was made.[1692] However, in *Casehub Ltd v Wolf Cola Ltd* the High Court rejected the invitation of the claimant consumer that it should not follow the Supreme Court's decision in *Abbey National Plc* in relation to the exclusion in art.4(2) as implemented by s.64 of the Consumer Rights Act 2015 on the basis that Supreme Court's decision was inconsistent with the later decisions of the CJEU in *Kásler* and *Matei*, on the

---

[1686] See above, paras 38-255 and 38-258.

[1687] See above, paras 38-250—38-253.

[1688] *Kásler* (C-26/13) at para.49 and see above, para.38-251.

[1689] cf. above, para.38-247.

[1690] cf. the Court of Appeal in *OFT v Abbey National Plc* [2009] EWCA Civ 116, [2009] 2 W.L.R. 1286 at [17] referring to the discussion of Andrew Smith J. [2008] EWHC 875 (Comm), [2008] 2 All E.R. (Comm) 625 at [373] et seq. and especially at [402]–[413]. The Court of Appeal did not require to decide this issue: at [113].

[1691] *OFT v Abbey National Plc* [2008] EWHC 875 (Comm), [2008] 2 All E.R. (Comm) 625 at [406]. It is true that Andrew Smith J. referred to the understanding of the typical consumer for this purpose (and this does not form part of the approach of the CJEU at this stage of its analysis), but Andrew Smith J. considered that it rested equally on the substance and reality of the matter. The Supreme Court did not take a view on this issue as it held that payments made under the terms formed part of the remuneration for a package of services: [2009] UKSC 6, [2010] 1 A.C. 696 especially at [42], [47], [81], [89], [100]–[104], and [104], above, para.38-247.

[1692] cf. above, paras 38-261—38-263.

grounds that it was bound by the Supreme Court's decision as a matter of precedent and that it was "far from clear that the CJEU cases ... have the effect for which [the claimant] contends".[1693] It will later be argued, however, that, with respect, this approach was not justified as a matter of authority.[1694]

(cc) The Composite Test of Unfairness

The test in the Regulations Regulation 5(1) of the 1999 Regulations provides that: **38-265**

"A contractual term which has not been individually negotiated shall be regarded as unfair if, contrary to the requirement of good faith, it causes a significant imbalance in the parties' rights and obligations arising under the contract, to the detriment of the consumer."[1695]

Regulation 6(1) further provides that:

"Without prejudice to regulation 12,[1696] the unfairness of a contractual term shall be assessed, taking into account the nature of the goods[1697] or services for which the contract was concluded and by referring, at the time of the contract,[1698] to all the circumstances attending the conclusion of the contract and to all the other terms of the contract or another contract on which it is dependent."[1699]

These provisions reflect accurate the test of fairness in the 1993 Directive[1700] and provide the framework for a sophisticated and composite test of unfairness, its combination of different ideas and considerations being clearly aimed at reducing the degree of uncertainty and discretion which is given to a court in requiring it to judge the fairness of a term. This test can be broken down into two principal elements: the basic test of unfairness (including the significance of the requirement of good faith and the range of considerations relevant to its application); and the significance and contents of the "indicative" or "grey list" of terms found in Sch.2 of the 1999 Regulations,[1701] to which may be added other illustrations of potentially unfair terms, which will be discussed in the following paragraphs.

The basic test The basic test of unfairness of a term is that: **38-266**

"... contrary to the requirement of good faith it causes a significant imbalance in the parties' rights and obligations under the contract, to the detriment of the consumer."

The significance of this test gave rise to considerable comment,[1702] and for some its use of the notion of good faith introduced into English law a new and somewhat

---

[1693] [2017] EWHC 1169 (Ch), [2017] 5 Costs L.R. 835 at [53]–[54] and see further below, para.38-400.
[1694] Below, para.38-400.
[1695] cf. Consumer Rights Act 2015 s.62(4), below, para.38-390.
[1696] See below, paras 38-353 et seq.
[1697] On the appropriateness of this limitation to goods, see above, para.38-222.
[1698] On which see below, paras 38-324—38-238.
[1699] cf. Consumer Rights Act 2015 s.62(5), below, para.38-390.
[1700] 1993 Directive arts 3 and 4(1).
[1701] See below, paras 38-299 et seq. cf. Consumer Rights Act 2015 s.63 and Sch.2, below, para.38-391.
[1702] Collins at 229; Beale, Ch.9 pp.242 et seq.; Weatherill (1995) 3 *European Review of Private Law* 307; Howells and Willhemson at p.88, pp.96 et seq.; Beatson pp.200–203, 300 et seq., pp.291 et seq.; Bright in Burrows and Peel, *Contract Terms* (2007), Ch.9.

alien concept. In this respect, it is helpful to bear in mind the origins of the reference to good faith, this flowing from its use in the German legislation which significantly influenced the Directive.[1703] In turn, this German legislation can be seen as the legislative recognition of existing judicial controls on unfair contract terms, this law-making being justified by the Civil Code's general provision requiring good faith of parties to contracts[1704]: "good faith" in this context can be seen as little more than a convenient legal pigeon-hole in which to have placed within the structure of the Civil Code judicial developments which took into account a range of considerations deemed appropriate to the control in hand.[1705] For this reason, it could be thought that the reference to "good faith" in the Directive is no more than a bow in the direction of these origins. Indeed, such a very limited significance to the phrase "contrary to the requirement of good faith" has been adopted by some French writers[1706] and this was reflected in its omission from France's implementing legislation.[1707] For a French lawyer it is unnecessary for two reasons: first, because the French Civil Code already makes a general requirement of the performance of contracts in good faith[1708] (an argument of no significance for English law), but, secondly, because a business supplier could not be considered to remain in good faith if he were to seek to enjoy the disproportionate advantages set out in the contract concluded with the consumer.[1709] From this perspective, the requirement that the term "causes a significant imbalance in the parties' rights and obligations under the contract to the detriment of the consumer" is sufficient in itself.

38-267 **"Significant imbalance" and the role of good faith** However, this French view of good faith misunderstands the particular function of the requirement of good faith in the scheme of the Directive. According to this scheme, the first and basic element of the requirement of fairness is that the term "causes a significant imbalance in the parties' rights and obligations arising under the contract, to the detriment of the consumer". However, not all contract terms which cause such a

---

[1703] i.e. *Gesetz zur Regelung des Rechts der Allgemeinen Geschäftsbedingungen* ("Standard Contract Terms Act") of 1976, translated in part by Dannemann in Markesinis, Lorenz and Dannemann, at pp.908 et seq. (The German Standard Contracts Act 1976 itself was abrogated and replaced by a revised BGB para.307(1).) The first draft of the Directive was much closer to the German legislation, applying to commercial as well as to consumer contracts. Apart from the German law, the laws of some other Member States law had used the notion of good faith in their control of unfair contract terms, for example, Spanish law: Paisant, *Recueil Dalloz Sirey*, 1995 Chronique p.99, p.100.

[1704] BGB para.242 and see Zimmermann, *The New German Law of Obligations* (2005), pp.173–178.

[1705] Zimmermann and Whittaker, *Good Faith in European Contract Law* (2000), Ch.1. It is noteworthy that the German Standard Terms Act of 1976 did not attempt to explain the requirement of good faith by reference to the already elaborate case-law based on para.242 BGB, but instead listed the clauses which are either necessarily void or are void if they fail a test of "reasonableness": see Standard Contract Terms Act 1976 paras 9–11.

[1706] See Larroumet, *Droit Civil, Les obligations Le contrat*, 5th edn (2003), Tome 3, p.422; Paisant, at p.100.

[1707] *Loi* 95/96 of February 1, 1995, now art.L.132-1 al. 1 Code de la consommation (as amended) Again, this reflects French legislative and judicial tradition which preferred to use the notion of the abuse of rights (hence, "*clauses abusives*") rather than the (admittedly closely related) notion of good faith.

[1708] In the case of the Code civil as first enacted in 1804, good faith was expressed only as applying to the performance of contracts (art.1134 al. 3 C.civ.), but after reform to French contract law in 2016, art.1104 requires that "negotiated, formed and performed in good faith".

[1709] Paisant at p.100.

significant imbalance are to be held unfair. Recital 16 of the Directive explains, therefore, the special role of the requirement of good faith.

"Whereas the assessment, according to the general criteria chosen, of the unfair character of the terms, in particular in sale or supply activities of a public nature providing collective services which take account of solidarity among users, must be *supplemented by a means of making an overall evaluation of the different interests involved; whereas this constitutes the requirement of good faith*; whereas, in making an assessment of good faith, particular regard shall be had to the strength of the bargaining positions of the parties, whether the consumer had an inducement to agree to the term and whether the goods or services were sold or supplied to the special order of the consumer; whereas the requirement of good faith may be satisfied by the seller or supplier where he deals fairly and equitably with the other party whose legitimate interests he has to take into account."[1710]

So, according to recital 16, the role of the requirement as to good faith is to ensure that the test of "significant imbalance" ("the general criteria chosen") is not applied in any sense mechanically, but rather the court should in making its assessment of a contract term look to "an overall evaluation of the interests involved". It is interesting, for this purpose, that while some of the factors which the recital mentions as being significant to this evaluation are familiar to English lawyers from the assessment of "reasonableness" under the Unfair Contract Terms Act 1977[1711] and may indeed be thought to represent an attempt to interpret good faith particularly for the benefit of common lawyers, the recital gives as a first and particular context for this supplementary requirement of good faith as "sale or supply activities of a public nature providing collective services which take account of solidarity among users".[1712] This inclusion shows that the function of the requirement of good faith is to ensure that *all* possible relevant considerations may be taken into account in making the overall assessment of the fairness of a term, even where these considerations relate to the public interest and therefore not necessarily to the position of either of the parties to the contract.[1713] Furthermore, two of the other circumstances

38-268

[1710] Emphasis added.

[1711] Unfair Contract Terms Act 1977 s.11(1) and Sch.2. The elements specified by recital 16 were included in Sch.2 of the 1994 Regulations, expressly to be taken account of in the assessment of good faith. However, their omission from the text of the 1999 Regulations made no substantive change as their presence in the preamble to the Directive requires them to be taken into account in the interpretation of its text and, therefore, the text of the 1999 Regulations.

[1712] This reference to taking account of "solidarity among users" has little resonance for English lawyers, but it may allude to the idea found, for example, in French administrative law which requires that those who use a public service must have equal access to it and be equally treated by it: Bell, Boyron and Whittaker, *Principles of French Law*, 2nd edn (2008), pp.170–171. This degree of inclusiveness in the evaluation of the fairness of contract terms would also allow a court to take into account their effect on the "Convention rights" of third parties as well as of the parties themselves under the Human Rights Act (cf. Vol.I, para.1-097; Whittaker (2001) 21 O.J.L.S. 193, 213. This suggestion finds some support from reference to "fundamental rights" and, more recently, the Charter of Fundamental Rights of the EU in the context of the 1993 Directive: see Opinion A.G. Tizziano in *Mostaza Claro v Centro Móvil Milenium SL* (C-168/05) EU:C:2006:675, [2007] 1 C.M.L.R. 222 at [59] quoting *Krombach v Bamberski* (C-7/98) EU:C:2000:164, [2000] E.C.R. I-0193 (relevance of "fundamental rights" to fairness of arbitration clause); *Sánchez Morcillo v Banco Bilbao Vizcaya Argentaria SA* (C-169/14) EU:C:2014:2099, July 17, 2014 especially at para.50 (relevance of Charter of Rights art.47 to national procedural law on the consumer's right of appeal and the effectiveness of the consumer's protection under 1993 Directive art.7).

[1713] The words "the function of the requirement of good faith ... fairness of a term" in the text were quoted with approval by the Court of Appeal in *West v Ian Finlay & Associates* [2014] EWCA Civ 316, [2014] B.L.R. 324 at [45].

mentioned by the recital as possible elements in this "overall evaluation" illustrate circumstances in which a "significant imbalance in the parties' rights and obligations arising under the contract to the detriment of the consumer" may be justified and therefore fair, where:

"... the consumer had an inducement to agree to the term [or] ... the goods or services were sold or supplied to the special order of the consumer."

Another element draws attention to the significance of the relative bargaining power of the parties (which will normally rest with the seller or supplier but which may exceptionally rest with the consumer). The final circumstance re-emphasises the inclusive nature of the requirement of good faith, stating that this may be satisfied:

"... by the seller or supplier where he deals fairly and equitably with the other party whose legitimate interests he has to take into account."

This is clearly related to the requirement in art.4(1) of the Directive that in assessing the fairness of a term, a court should consider "all the circumstances attending the conclusion of the contract".

38-269   What all this means, therefore, is that the Directive does require an autonomous interpretation of the concept of good faith, but not one drawn from the significances or uses to which the concept (or related concepts) have been put in the laws of the Member States generally.[1714] The concept of good faith is autonomous in the sense that it is specifically European (rather than to be left to the interpretation of national law or national courts), but it is also autonomous in the sense that it is particular to the context of the control of unfair contract terms. This can be seen in recent case-law in the Court of Justice in *Aziz*[1715] and *Menéndez Álvarez*.[1716]

38-270   **Aziz and Menéndez Álvarez**   In *Aziz* the Court of Justice explained the test of "significant imbalance" and the proper approach to the condition that this imbalance must arise "contrary to the requirement of good faith" in a reference from a Spanish court asking for guidance as to whether three terms in a contract of loan secured by a mortgage of residential property to be repaid over 33 years were unfair within the meaning of the Directive.[1717] First, as the Court had previously explained, "the system of protection introduced by the directive is based on the idea that the consumer is in a weaker position vis-à-vis the seller or supplier, as regards both his bargaining power and his level of knowledge" and the Directive's provision that unfair terms are not binding on the consumer "aims to replace the formal balance which the contract establishes between the rights and obligations of the parties with

---

[1714] On the difficulties of identifying a practical meaning of "good faith" and its linguistic equivalents see Zimmermann and Whittaker, *Good Faith in European Contract Law* (2000), p.690 and see above, Vol.I, paras 1-047—1-048.

[1715] *Aziz v Caixa d'Estalvis de Catalunya, Tarragona i Manresa* EU:C:2013:164, March 14, 2013 ("*Aziz* (C-415/11)"). On the question of the compatibility of Spanish procedural law and the effectiveness of the Directive's protection of consumers, see below, para.38-333.

[1716] *Constructora Principado SA v Menéndez Álvarez* (C-226/12) EU:C:2014:10, January 16, 2014 ("*Menéndez Álvarez* (C-226/12)").

[1717] *Aziz* (C-415/11).

an effective balance which re-establishes equality between them".[1718] The Court then held that:

> "... in order to ascertain whether a term causes a 'significant imbalance' in the parties' rights and obligations arising under the contract, to the detriment of the consumer, it must in particular be considered what rules of national law would apply in the absence of an agreement by the parties in that regard. Such a comparative analysis will enable the national court to evaluate whether and, as the case may be, to what extent, the contract places the consumer in a legal situation less favourable than that provided for by the national law in force. To that end, an assessment should also be carried out of the legal situation of that consumer having regard to the means at his disposal, under national legislation, to prevent continued use of unfair terms."[1719]

The Court continued:

> "With regard to the question of the circumstances in which such an imbalance arises 'contrary to the requirement of good faith', having regard to the sixteenth recital in the preamble to the directive ... the national court must assess for those purposes whether the seller or supplier, dealing fairly and equitably with the consumer, could reasonably assume that the consumer would have agreed to such a term in individual contract negotiations."[1720]

The Court of Justice therefore requires national courts to make a hypothetical judgment as to what the *seller or supplier* could *reasonably assume* as to the agreement of the consumer, an approach which links the judicial control of the fairness of contract terms to the condition that the terms in question were not "individually negotiated",[1721] seeing the court's control as a substitute for the consumer's own decision-making. For this purpose, Advocate General Kokott, to whose Opinion the Court had referred with approval, added that:

> "In this connection, it is important inter alia whether such contractual terms are common, that is to say they are used regularly in legal relations in similar contracts, or are surprising, whether there is an objective reason for the term and whether, despite the shift in the contractual balance in favour of the user of the term in relation to the substance of the term in question, the consumer is not left without protection."[1722]

The Court of Justice, by way of "guidance" to the national court, then explained the proper question for it to consider in relation to an acceleration clause in a contract of loan under which the lender would have been entitled to call in the totality of the loan on expiry of the 33 years where the consumer borrower failed to pay any of the principal or the interest on the loan.[1723] Where a borrower under a long-term loan defaulted over a "limited specific period", the national court should:

> "... assess in particular ... whether the right of the [lender] to call in the totality of the loan is conditional upon the non-compliance by the consumer with an obligation which

---

[1718] *Aziz* (C-415/11) at paras 44–45, referring to *Banco Español de Crédito, SA v Calderón Camino* (C-618/10) EU:C:2012:349, June 14, 2012 at paras 39–40.

[1719] *Aziz* (C-415/11) at para.68.

[1720] *Aziz* (C-415/11) at para.69. The approach in *Aziz* was followed closely in the order of the CJEU in *Sebestyén v Kővári* (C-342/13) EU:C:2014:1857, April 3, 2014 at paras 27–28.

[1721] 1993 Directive art.3, especially 3(2), above, paras 38-242—38-244.

[1722] *Aziz* (C-415/11) Opinion of A.G. Kokott, at para.75.

[1723] See also below, para.38-307 (default interest clause).

is of essential importance in the context of the contractual relationship in question, whether that right is provided for in cases in which such non-compliance is sufficiently serious in the light of the term and amount of the loan, whether that right derogates from the relevant applicable rules and whether national law provides for adequate and effective means enabling the consumer subject to such a term to remedy the effects of the loan being called in."[1724]

So, while the Court did indeed refer to the position under the national law applicable in the absence of the relevant term, it first took a view as to the proper position in respect of the operation of such a clause, that is, that the obligation is "of essential importance" and/or the consumer's non-compliance "is sufficiently serious". Here, therefore, the Court of Justice requires the national court to compare the position under the contract term and the position which *should* be the case given what it considers to be these proper considerations. The Court of Justice, following its Advocate General's advice, also found the "indicative list" in the Annex to the Directive (and found in the 1999 Regulations Sch.2) particularly helpful in setting out the considerations the national court should take into account.[1725]

38-271   Similarly, in *Menéndez Álvarez*[1726] the Court of Justice held that in general the notion of "significant imbalance" in the test of unfairness of contract terms in the 1993 Directive "cannot be limited to a quantitative economic evaluation based on a comparison between the total value of the transaction which is the subject of the contract and the costs charted to the consumer" under the term which is challenged, and instead must extend to consideration of a comparison between the parties' rights and obligations under that term and under the national law rules which would apply in the absence of any such agreement.[1727] According to the Court:

"... a significant imbalance can result solely from a sufficiently serious impairment of the legal situation in which the consumer, as a party to the contract in question, is placed by reason of the relevant national provisions, whether this be in the form of a restriction of the rights which, in accordance with those provisions, he enjoys under the contract, or a constraint on the exercise of those rights, or the imposition on him of an additional obligation not envisaged by the national rules."[1728]

As a result, the national court should assess the fairness of a contract term which imposed on a consumer purchaser of residential property from a builder the liability to pay national capital gains tax which would otherwise lie on the builder as vendor of the property which had benefited from the increase in the value of the property, taking account, in particular, the information which the consumer purchaser had received about this before the contract was made.[1729] For these purposes, the Court of Justice further held that the fact that the contract term in question stated that "the consumer's assumption of responsibility for payment of the capital gains tax [had] been taken into account in determining the sale price does not itself constitute proof of consideration [i.e. something in return] which the

---

[1724] *Aziz* (C-415/11) at para.73.

[1725] *Aziz* (C-415/11) at para.74 and see below, paras 38-299 et seq.

[1726] *Constructora Principado SA v Menéndez Álvarez* (C-226/12) EU:C:2014:10, January 16, 2014.

[1727] *Menéndez Álvarez* (C-226/12) at paras 21–22.

[1728] *Menéndez Álvarez* (C-226/12) at para.23.

[1729] *Menéndez Álvarez* (C-226/12) at paras 26–27.

consumer would have benefited from", although it assumed that proof of an *actual* reduction in price would be relevant to the fairness of the term.[1730]

Fairness and good faith in First National Bank Plc In *Director General of Fair Trading v First National Bank Plc*[1731] decided some 10 years before the judgments of the Court of Justice in *Aziz*[1732] and *Menéndez Álvarez*,[1733] the House of Lords discussed the requirement of good faith and the test of unfairness more generally for the purposes of the Directive as implemented by the 2004 Regulations.[1734] As to good faith, Lord Bingham of Cornhill observed: **38-272**

> "The requirement of good faith in this context is one of fair and open dealing. Openness requires that the terms should be expressed fully, clearly and legibly, containing no concealed pitfalls or traps. Appropriate prominence should be given to terms which might operate disadvantageously to the customer. Fair dealing requires that a supplier should not, whether deliberately or unconsciously, take advantage of the consumer's necessity, indigence, lack of experience, unfamiliarity with the subject matter of the contract, weak bargaining position or any other factor listed in or analogous to those listed in Schedule 2 to the [1994] Regulations.[1735] Good faith in this context is not an artificial or technical concept; nor, since Lord Mansfield[1736] was its champion, is it a concept wholly unfamiliar to British lawyers. It looks to good standards of commercial morality and practice. Regulation 4(1) lays down a composite test, covering both the making and the substance of the contract, and must be applied bearing clearly in mind the objective which the Regulations are designed to promote."[1737]

Clearly, then, Lord Bingham saw good faith as an extremely inclusive concept, potentially comprising elements of both procedural and substantive fairness.[1738] However, with the greatest respect, the idea of a business "taking advantage" of the consumer (even if unconsciously) is potentially restrictive, having overtones of bad faith which is clearly unnecessary[1739] and is not reflected in the later case-law of the Court of Justice in *Aziz*[1740] and *Menéndez Álvarez*.[1741]

West v Ian Finlay & Associates In *West v Ian Finlay & Associates*,[1742] the Court of Appeal took a rather different approach to the requirement of "significant imbal-   **38-273**

[1730] *Menéndez Álvarez* (C-226/12) at para.29.

[1731] [2001] UKHL 52, [2002] 1 A.C. 481; Macdonald (2002) 65 M.L.R. 763; Dean (2002) 65 M.L.R. 773; Whittaker (2004) *ZEuP* 75.

[1732] *Aziz v Caixa d'Estalvis de Catalunya, Tarragona i Manresa* (C-415/11) EU:C:2013:164, March 14, 2013 ("*Aziz* (C-415/11)"), above, para.38-270.

[1733] *Menéndez Álvarez* (C-226/12), above, para.38-271.

[1734] Unfair Terms in Consumer Contracts Regulations 1994 (SI 1994/3159) revoked and replaced by the 1999 Regulations as noted, above, para.38-213.

[1735] The 1994 Regulations Sch.2 listed the elements found in recital 16 of the 1993 Directive.

[1736] See *Carter v Boehm* (1766) 3 Burr. 1905, 1910, quoted Vol.I, para.1-044.

[1737] [2001] UKHL 52 at [17], with whom Lord Steyn (at [39]), Hope of Craighead (at [40]), Millett (at [53]) and Rodger of Earlsferry (at [62]) agreed.

[1738] Beale in Beatson and Friedman (eds), *Good Faith and Fault in Contract Law* (1995), Ch.9, p.245.

[1739] cf. Macdonald (2002) 65 M.L.R. 763 at p.769.

[1740] *Aziz v Caixa d'Estalvis de Catalunya, Tarragona i Manresa* (C-415/11) EU:C:2013:164, March 14, 2013 ("*Aziz* (C-415/11)").

[1741] *Constructora Principado SA v Menéndez Álvarez* (C-226/12) EU:C:2014:10, January 16, 2014 ("*Menéndez Álvarez* (C-226/12)").

[1742] [2014] EWCA Civ 316, [2014] B.L.R. 324. Vos L.J. delivered a judgment to which all members of the Court of Appeal contributed.

ance in the parties' rights and obligations arising under the contract" than the Court of Justice in *Aziz* and *Menéndez Álvarez*, neither of which were discussed even though they preceded the Court of Appeal's decision.[1743] *West* concerned, inter alia, the fairness of a "net contribution clause" in a contract of appointment between a house-owner and the defendant architectural firm for the alteration and renovation of their house. The Court of Appeal held that, as a matter of construction, the effect of the clause was to limit the defendant's loss or damage to the amount that it was reasonable for it to pay having regard to "the contractual responsibilities of other consultants, contractors and specialists appointed by [the claimants]".[1744] Its practical effect was to place on the claimants the risk of the insolvency of the contractors engaged to undertake the work done on the houses, a risk which had transpired; the clause also meant that the claimant would have to bring proceedings against any defaulting contractor who may be jointly and severally liable with the defendant, and to await the outcome of any contribution proceedings before obtaining full satisfaction.[1745] Having set out the test of the unfairness of contract terms in the 1999 Regulations and having referred to examples of exclusions of liability in the "indicative list" in Sch.2, the Court of Appeal relied on passages from the speeches in the House of Lords in the *First National Bank* case on the test of unfairness,[1746] and concluded that "in evaluating the application of regulation 5(1) of the UTCC Regulations, it is necessary to consider significant imbalance and good faith separately as well as together in making the ultimate overall assessment".[1747] The Court of Appeal then noted a range of considerations which it thought relevant on the facts to this assessment, including the fact that the clause would make the claimants bear the insolvency risk of contractors which they had chosen, that the clause is "by no means unusual" in the context, that other terms of the contract stipulated that the defendant did not warrant the solvency of others, and that the claimants should hold the contractors which they appointed responsible for the performance of their services.[1748] The Court of Appeal then turned to the requirement of good faith which it saw, following dicta in the *First National Bank* case, as requiring that the defendants should not take advantage of the claimants nor set any "a concealed trap or pitfall".[1749] Nor were the claimants in a weak bargaining position, given their financial experience.[1750] On the other hand, although the clause was presented in an open way, it did not draw the reader's attention to the fact that it was shifting the insolvency risk of the other contractors from the defendant to the claimants, and nor did the defendant itself, despite RIBA guidelines to this effect.[1751] Overall, balancing out all these elements, the Court concluded, therefore, that the

---

[1743] *Aziz* (C-415/11); *Menéndez Álvarez* (C-226/12), on which see above paras 38-270—38-271. *West v Ian Finlay & Associates* was heard on appeal on February 25, 2014 and judgment was handed down by the Court of Appeal on March 27, 2014.

[1744] [2014] EWCA Civ 316 at [30]. There was, therefore, no room for the application of the required interpretation of *ambiguous* contract terms in favour of the consumer set out in 1999 Regulations reg.7(2): [2014] EWCA Civ 316 at [32] and see below, para.38-347.

[1745] [2014] EWCA Civ 316 at [49].

[1746] *Director General of Fair Trading v First National Bank Plc* [2001] UKHL 52, [2002] 1 A.C. 481 especially at [17], [24], [54] and [56], on which see above, para.38-272.

[1747] [2014] EWCA Civ 316 at [46].

[1748] [2014] EWCA Civ 316 at [51], [52] and [53] respectively.

[1749] [2014] EWCA Civ 316 at [55] and [57].

[1750] [2014] EWCA Civ 316 at [56] and [59].

[1751] [2014] EWCA Civ 316 at [57]–[58].

requirement of good faith had been satisfied on the facts.[1752] Moreover, while the clause plainly caused an imbalance in the parties' rights and obligations, the Court of Appeal did not consider this "so weighted" in favour of the defendants as to cause a *significant* imbalance given:

"(a) The prevalence of the usage of the [clause] in standard RIBA forms, (b) the fact that the clause would be regarded as not unusual in a commercial contract, and (c) the fact that it was the [claimants] who in this case would be taking the final decision on the future choice of main contractor, very likely being alive (bearing in mind [one of the claimant's] banking background) to the fact that that contractor's financial stability was a matter of importance."[1753]

The Court of Appeal therefore held the clause was not unfair under the 1999 Regulations, principally on the ground that there was no failure to fulfil the requirement of good faith, though secondarily on the ground that it did not cause a significant imbalance in the parties' rights and obligations to the detriment of the consumer.

Many of the elements which the Court of Appeal took into account in coming to its overall evaluation of the term were properly relevant given the guidance given both by the Directive itself and by the Court of Justice *Aziz* and *Menéndez Álvarez*, although, with respect, the fact that the net contribution clause is not unusual in a *commercial* contract should not have been considered relevant.[1754] Moreover, the Court of Appeal's emphasis on the need to evaluate the *significance* of the imbalance in the rights and obligations of the parties is consistent with the guidance in *Menéndez Álvarez*, as the Court of Justice there accepted that "[a] significant imbalance can result solely from a *sufficiently serious* impairment of the legal situation in which the consumer, as a party to the contract in question, is placed by reason of the relevant national provisions".[1755] On the other hand, while the Court of Appeal accepted that the requirement of good faith required the evaluation of "all possible relevant considerations ... in making the overall assessment of the fairness of a term",[1756] it did not "assess for those purposes whether the seller or supplier, dealing fairly and equitably with the consumer, could reasonably assume that the consumer would have agreed to such a term in individual contract negotiations" as required by the Court of Justice in *Aziz*, although its reference to the common usage of the clause could be thought of as a relevant to such a hypothetical assessment.[1757]

38-274

[1752] [2014] EWCA Civ 316 at [58] and [59].

[1753] [2014] EWCA Civ 316 at [59].

[1754] On this guidance, see above, paras 38-270—38-271. It is surprising that the Court of Appeal found this relevant as it had earlier noted that, while a commercial party commissioning building work would protect its interests by insurance or the taking of a performance bond from the main contract, in the consumer context "it is common practice for the architect to protect his position by insurance, but uncommon for a consumer client to obtain insolvency insurance protection or a performance bond from a contractor": [2014] EWCA Civ 316 at [52].

[1755] *Menéndez Álvarez* (C-226/12) at [23] (emphasis added).

[1756] [2014] EWCA Civ 316 at [45] quoting the 31st edition of this work, Vol.I, para.15-074; and [57]–[58].

[1757] C-415/11 at [69] and see above, para.38-270.

38-275 ParkingEye Ltd v Beavis[1758] In *ParkingEye Ltd*, the Supreme Court considered the guidance of the Court of Justice on the test of unfairness in the 1993 Directive in *Aziz*[1759] in deciding how the test of unfairness in the 1999 Regulations would apply to a term in a contract under which a consumer could park for free in a car park for up to two hours, but would incur a charge of £85 for overstaying this permitted period or for breaking other rules set by the management company of the car park, such as parking only within marked bays.[1760] A notice to this effect in "large, prominent and legible" print was displayed on signs at the entrance of the car park and around it.[1761] A user of the car park (the "consumer") overstayed the two-hour limit by nearly an hour and the management company sought to recover the charge from him. The Supreme Court considered that the contract was a licence to park cars on the terms posted at its entrance, that the charge was not a charge for the right to park or even to overstay at the car park, but arose only on certain breaches of the contract by the user.[1762] The car park was operated in this way as its owner was concerned to ensure that motorists should park for free to attract customers for the retailers to which it had leased other parts of its site, but that these customers should not overstay their parking period so as to increase the potential number of customers. The purposes of the charge were therefore to manage the efficient use of parking spaces in the interests of the owner, the retailers and other would-be customers and to provide an income stream for the car park's managers to meet its costs and make a profit.[1763] In considering the fairness of the term imposing the charge under the 1999 Regulations, the Supreme Court followed the guidance of the Court of Justice of the EU in *Aziz*,[1764] which it saw as the "leading case on the topic" provided by that court.[1765] It noted Advocate General Kokott's advice in *Aziz*, which was followed by the Court of Justice, that the requirement that the "significant imbalance" in the contracting parties' rights and obligations to the detri-

---

[1758] [2015] UKSC 67, [2015] 3 W.L.R. 1373. Subsequent to the decision of the SC (but without reference to it) it has been said that a term of a new lease granted pursuant to the landlord's obligation under the Leasehold Reform, Housing and Urban Development Act 1993 and therefore replicating a term in an earlier lease in subject to the 1999 Regulations, was not "contrary to the requirement of good faith", though it had earlier been held that that the 1999 Regulations did not apply to the term as it fell within the exclusion in reg.4(2): *Roundlistic Ltd v Jones* [2016] UKUT 325 (LC) at [101] and [104]; see above, para.38-238.

[1759] *Aziz v Caixa d'Estalvis de Catalunya, Tarragona i Manresa* (C-415/11) March 14, 2013 discussed above, para.38-270.

[1760] [2015] UKSC 67 at [90] and [123].

[1761] [2015] UKSC 67 at [91].

[1762] [2015] UKSC 67 at [94].

[1763] [2015] UKSC 67 at [97]–[98].

[1764] *Aziz v Caixa d'Estalvis de Catalunya, Tarragona i Manresa* (C-415/11).

[1765] [2015] UKSC 67 at [105] (Lord Neuberger of Abbotsbury, Lord Sumption and Lord Carnwath) (with whom Lord Hodge (at [289]) and Lord Clarke of Stone-cum-Ebony (at [291]) agreed on these points); [204] and [208] (Lord Mance); Lord Toulson agreed on the importance of the *Aziz* decision (at [306]–[308]), but dissented on its significance on the facts of *ParkingEye Ltd*: see below. The SC also held that the term imposing the charge was not a penalty clause at common law as the management company had a legitimate interest in imposing these charges which could not be satisfied by damages even though the amount did not represent any loss caused to them by the breaches by the user and, secondly, the sum was *not* out of all proportion to its interest or the owner's interests: [2015] UKSC 67 at [99]–[101] (Lord Neuberger, Lord Sumption and Lord Carnwath); [197]–[199] (Lord Mance); Lord Toulson did not express a decided view on this issue: at [316]. *ParkingEye Ltd v Beavis* was joined with *Cavendish Square Holding BV v Makdessi* which concerned the common law regarding contractual penalty clauses in a commercial context, on which see Vol.I, paras 26-190 et seq.

ment of the consumer should be contrary to good faith allows account to be taken of the legitimate interests of the parties to organise their own legal relationship even in a way which derogates from national legal rules otherwise applicable.[1766] In this respect, the Supreme Court noted the formula used by the Court of Justice to assess good faith by reference to the hypothetical test of whether the seller or supplier "could reasonably assume that the consumer would have agreed to such a term in individual negotiations" and the views of Advocate General Kokott on the relevant circumstances for this purpose, such as whether or not the term would be surprising.[1767]

38-276 A majority of the Supreme Court held that the contract term on which the £85 charge was based was fair within the meaning of the Regulations. While the term did create an imbalance in the parties' rights and obligations to the detriment of the consumer, both the management company and the owners of the car park had a legitimate interest in imposing a liability on consumers in excess of any damages recoverable in inducing them to observe the two-hour time limit: indeed "charging overstayers £85 underpinned the business model which enabled members of the public to park free of charge for two hours" and was:

"... fundamental to the contractual relationship created by [consumers'] acceptance of the terms of the notice, whose whole object was the efficient management of the car park."[1768]

In the view of the majority, the hypothetical test in *Aziz* was objective:

"... the question is not whether [the defendant consumer] himself would in fact have agreed to the term imposing the £85 charge in a negotiation, but whether a reasonable motorist in his position would have done so. In [its] view, a reasonable motorist would have agreed."[1769]

Motorists generally and the defendant in particular *did* accept the term and while this would not usually have much weight as regards standard terms, the term in question "could not have been briefer, simpler or more prominently proclaimed".[1770] Moreover, objectively, they had every reason to accept the terms, as they were allowed to park free for two hours in return for the risk of the £85 charge if they overstayed.[1771] The terms were beneficial to motorists themselves as they freed up parking spaces, as well as being beneficial to the management company, the site owner and the retailers and the level of the charge was not exorbitant: the terms were therefore "objectively reasonable".[1772] In this respect, Lord Mance's view was more nuanced, considering that the Court of Justice of the EU in *Aziz* could not be

---

[1766] [2015] UKSC 67 at [106], referring to A.G. Kokott's Opinion at paras 73 and 87. Recital 16 of the 1993 Directive itself explains the requirement of good faith as allowing "an overall evaluation of the different interests involved" as noted above, para.38-267.

[1767] [2015] UKSC 67 at [106]; A.G. Kokott's Opinion in *Aziz* (C-415/11) at para.75 quoted above, para.38-270.

[1768] [2015] UKSC 67 at [106] (Lord Neuberger, Lord Sumption and Lord Carnwath, with whom Lord Hodge (at [289]) and Lord Clarke (at [291]) agreed on this point).

[1769] [2015] UKSC 67 at [108] (referring for this purpose to A.G. Kokott's Opinion in *Aziz* at para.75, though her reference was to "an objective reason for the term" rather than specifically an objective approach to the hypothetical test).

[1770] [2015] UKSC 67 at [108].

[1771] [2015] UKSC 67 at [109].

[1772] [2015] UKSC 67 at [109]. See also at [111]–[113] rejecting further arguments as to the unfairness of the term.

taken to have identified the hypothetical test as conclusive, but rather as relevant to the assessment of fairness of a term, given that the Directive requires a court to take into account all circumstances for this purpose.[1773] Lord Mance found the argument that the management company could not reasonably have assumed that customers in the defendant's position would have agreed to the scheme in individual contractual negotiation "less easy to address", as such a customer, if asked, would have been satisfied with the proposal of two hours of free parking, but would probably have asked for "some form of gradated payment in the event of overstaying".[1774] Nevertheless, Lord Mance concluded that the term was not unfair within the meaning of the Regulations, as a term of this sort is simple and familiar and clear notice was given; there is no significant imbalance in the parties' rights and obligations given that the consumer is given a valuable privilege (the free parking) in return for a promise to pay a sum in the event of overstaying; and, finally, the charge is not disproportionately high.[1775] By contrast, Lord Toulson dissented on this issue. In his view, the term on which the charge was based did create a significant imbalance in the parties' rights and obligations to the detriment of the consumer as the charge far exceeded any amount which was otherwise likely to be recoverable as damages.[1776] Moreover, he considered that the hypothetical test which *Aziz* used to explain the requirement of good faith is "significantly more favourable to the consumer" than is the general common law governing penalty clauses, as its starting point is the special protection of consumers rather than that parties should be kept to their bargains.[1777] In his view, no assumption can fairly be made that a consumer would have agreed to the term in individual negotiations and the burden of proof is on the trader to establish that he would have done as it makes no allowance for circumstances, allows period of grace and provides no room for adjustment.[1778] He therefore concluded that the term was unfair.[1779]

38-277 **Comments** The Supreme Court in *ParkingEye Ltd* took care to follow and apply the guidance of the Court of Justice of the EU on the interpretation and application of the test of unfairness in the 1993 Directive. In this respect, however, while the hypothetical test used by the Court of Justice in *Aziz* to explain the significance of the requirement of good faith was expressed in general terms, it is submitted that it should not be taken as the touchstone of that requirement. Instead, Lord Mance's interpretation of the hypothetical test as *relevant* to the assessment of good faith but not conclusive of it is to be preferred, not least as recital 16 of the Directive itself explains the significance of good faith by reference to a series of other matters and without reference to the hypothetical test.[1780] Moreover, the hypothetical test is itself open to criticism. First, on the basis that it requires a court to take a view as to the assumptions of a reasonable trader in the position of the actual trader (what he would have assumed) and of a reasonable consumer in the position of the actual consumer (what he would have decided). Such fictitious tests tend to shift the focus

---

[1773] [2015] UKSC 67 at [208], having noted (at [202]–[203]), the 1999 Regulations reg.6(1) and the 1993 Directive recital 16 to this effect.
[1774] [2015] UKSC 67 at [209].
[1775] [2015] UKSC 67 at [212], adopting the conclusions of Judge Maloney Q.C. at trial.
[1776] [2015] UKSC 67 at [307].
[1777] [2015] UKSC 67 at [308].
[1778] [2015] UKSC 67 at [309]–[310].
[1779] [2015] UKSC 67 at [314].
[1780] Above, para.38-267.

of the court away from the level of the substantive imbalance caused to the consumer by the term in issue and the wider interests of the parties and others with which the test of unfairness should be concerned. Secondly, on the basis that the hypothetical test assumes that the fundamental problem with the terms of consumer contracts is that they are not individually negotiated and that on this ground the consumer's freedom of contract is undermined, rather than that consumers are to be protected because they are "weaker parties" as regards both their bargaining power and their level of knowledge.[1781] Moreover, Lord Mance's interpretation of the Court of Justice's guidance also avoids the difficulty otherwise found in relation to the new law under the Consumer Rights Act 2015 whose controls on unfair contract terms are not restricted to terms which are not individually negotiated, as it would make little sense to apply the hypothetical test to a term which had in fact been individually negotiated.[1782] In terms of the application of the hypothetical test on the facts of *ParkingEye Ltd*, with respect, the view of the majority of the Supreme Court that the terms in *ParkingEye Ltd* were not unfair as a matter of consumer law coupled with its reformulation of the common law governing penalty clauses[1783] is likely to give rise to concern that traders can effectively impose on consumers the payment of sums for breaches of contract even where the level of the sums is unrelated to any loss actually suffered by those traders.

"Unfairness" under the 1993 Directive and "unfair commercial practices"   In   **38-278** *Pereničová* the Court of Justice of the EU considered the relationship between a finding of an "unfair commercial practice" within the meaning of the Unfair Commercial Practices Directive 2005[1784] and a finding of the unfairness of a contract term within the meaning of the 1993 Directive.[1785] The particular significance of this relationship before the Court was that, under the 2005 Directive, a finding of an "unfair commercial practice" has no impact on the validity of any contract or contract term to which the unfair practice relates,[1786] whereas under the 1993 Directive, an unfair contract term is not binding on the consumer and may invalidate the contract as a whole.[1787] The Court noted that the definition of an "unfair commercial practice" is "particularly wide"[1788] and "applies to unfair business-to-consumer commercial practices, before, during or after a commercial transaction relating to goods or service".[1789] The 2005 Directive provides a general test for the

---

[1781] See above, para.38-270.

[1782] See below, para.38-389.

[1783] See Vol.I, paras 26-190 et seq.

[1784] Directive 2005/29 concerning unfair business-to-consumer commercial practices in the internal market [2005] O.J. L149/22 ("2005 Directive"), implemented in UK law by the Consumer Protection from Unfair Trading Regulations 2008 (SI 2008/1277). On the 2005 Directive and these implementing regulations, see above, paras 38-157—38-210.

[1785] *Pereničová v SOS finance, spol. sro* (C-453/10) EU:C:2012:144, [2012] 2 C.M.L.R. 28.

[1786] Directive 2005/29 art.3(2). This was also the position in UK law when the 2005 Directive was first implemented in UK law by the Consumer Protection from Unfair Trading Regulations 2008 (SI 2008/1277), but changed by the Consumer Protection (Amendment) Regulations 2014 (SI 2014/870) inserting, notably, new Pt 4A Consumers' Rights to Redress in the 2008 Regulations. On these amendments see above, paras 38-172—38-210.

[1787] 1993 Directive art.6(1) on which see below, paras 38-339 et seq.

[1788] *Plus Warenhandelsgeselschaft* (C-304/08) EU:C:2010:12, [2010] E.C.R. I-217 at para.36; *Mediaprint Zeitungs- und Zeitschriftenverlag* (C-540/08) EU:C:2010:660, [2011] 1 C.M.L.R. 48 at para.17.

[1789] *Pereničová v SOS finance, spol. sro* (C-453/10) EU:C:2012:144 ("*Pereničová* (C-453/10)") para.39.

unfairness of a commercial practice,[1790] which is supplemented by three particular examples of unfair commercial practices,[1791] including "misleading actions",[1792] and a blacklist of practices which "shall in all circumstances be regarded as unfair".[1793] In *Perenicová* a consumer credit agreement had misstated the APR, as the lender had not included within its calculation some charges relating to the loan.[1794] In the view of the Court of Justice this would constitute a "misleading commercial practice" within the meaning of the 2005 Directive if the national court were to find that it "causes or is likely to cause the average consumer to take a transaction decision that he would not have taken otherwise",[1795] but the referring court wished to know whether such a finding would mean that the APR term in question would also be unfair under the 1993 Directive. For this purpose, the Court of Justice observed that art.4(1) of the 1993 Directive:

"… gives a particularly wide definition of the criteria for making such an assessment, by expressly including 'all the circumstances' attending the conclusion of the contract in question … In those circumstances, … a finding that a commercial practice is unfair is one element among others on which the competent court may base its assessment of the unfairness of contractual terms under Article 4(1) of Directive 93/13. That element, however, is not such as to establish, automatically and on its own, that the contested terms are unfair. It is for the referring court to decide on the application of the general criteria set out in Articles 3 and 4 of Directive 93/13 to a specific term, which must be considered in the circumstances of the particular case."[1796]

In the result, "a finding that a commercial practice is unfair has no direct effect on whether the contract is valid" under the 1993 Directive.[1797]

38-279 **Particular elements within the test of unfairness** It has been seen that the basic test on which courts must review the terms of consumer contracts comprises a number of elements. The overall requirement is that a term is judged unfair and for this purpose the starting point is the criterion of "significant imbalance", this then being qualified by the need to ensure the evaluation of all interests involved (under the requirement of good faith). The Directive (and the Regulations) then go further and specify a number of factors to be taken into account in determining the issue of fairness (the nature of the goods or services, all the circumstances attending the conclusion of the contract and all the other terms of the contract or of another contract on which it is dependent) and finally provide a list of illustrative terms

---

[1790] 2005 Directive art.5(1).

[1791] 2005 Directive art.5(4).

[1792] 2005 Directive art.6.

[1793] 2005 Directive art.5(5), Annex I.

[1794] *Perenicová* (C-453/10) para.22.

[1795] *Perenicová* (C-453/10) para.41, following art.5(2)(b) as explained by art.2(b) and 2(k) of the 2005 Directive.

[1796] *Perenicová* (C-453/10) paras 42–44.

[1797] *Perenicová* (C-453/10) para.46. A.G. Kokott has argued that, where relevant to the fairness of a term of a consumer contract under the Unfair Terms in Consumer Contracts Directive 1993, a national court has an obligation to raise the unfairness of any relevant *commercial practice* within the meaning of the Unfair Commercial Practices Directive 2005: *Margarit Panicello v Hernández Martínez* (C-503/15) A.G. Opinion of September 15, 2016 at [127]–[128]. The CJEU (judgment of February 16, 2017) did not comment on these issues as it ruled that it had no jurisdiction to hear the request for a preliminary ruling.

which *may* be unfair.[1798] The following paragraphs will look at these elements in turn. In doing so, reference will sometimes be made to the views of the former Office of Fair Trading (OFT), as expressed in its published guidance and bulletins.[1799] While a court was "in no sense bound by the guidance provided by the Office of Fair Trading", it can provide "helpful commonsense indications of what is likely to be considered to be fair".[1800] As from March 31, 2014 the OFT was abolished and from April 1, 2014 its role under the 1999 Regulations transferred to the Competition and Markets Authority (CMA). The CMA has continued to make available the guidance on the 1999 Regulations issued by the OFT,[1801] and has issued some new guidance of its own.[1802]

"A significant imbalance in the parties' rights and obligations arising under the contract, to the detriment of the consumer" As earlier noted, this phrase encapsulates the key idea of the notion of unfairness for the purposes of both sets of Regulations, requiring that the *term* creates an imbalance in the parties' legal rights and obligations and that this imbalance pass a threshold of significance. Two aspects of this definition have become clear either by case-law or as a result of the OFT's work in policing terms in consumer contracts. **38-280**

Potential for unfairness The Court of Justice has held that the assessment of the fairness of a contract term must be made by reference to the time of the conclusion of the contract,[1803] but in doing so it added that the court should take into account all the circumstances which could have been known at that time and which could affect the future performance of the contract: **38-281**

> "… since a contractual term may give rise to an imbalance between the parties which only manifests itself during the performance of the contract."[1804]

This temporal focus of the assessment also makes clear that a contract term will be judged according to its *potential* unfairness: if a term could give rise to a "significant imbalance in the parties' rights", etc. (given the particular and concrete factors to be outlined below), then it is no answer for a seller or supplier wishing to rely on it to say that on the facts it does not do so nor that it was never intended to be relied

---

[1798] See below, paras 38-299 et seq.

[1799] Notably, OFT, *Unfair contract terms* (2008) OFT311 available at *https://www.gov.uk/government/publications/unfair-contract-terms-guidance-2*. Further guidance is available as regards particular market sectors. It is to be noted that the way in which the test of unfairness will apply in disputes between the parties to a contract will differ in certain respects from the way in which it is to be applied in preventative proceedings (on which, see below, para.38-357), but these are not significant for present purposes.

[1800] *Peabody Trust Governors v Reeve* [2008] EWHC 1432 (Ch), [2009] L. & T.R. 6 at [54], per G. Moss Q.C., referring to OFT, *Guidance on Unfair Terms in Tenancy Agreements* (November 2001).

[1801] The CMA has also published guidance on the provisions in the Consumer Rights Act 2015 governing unfair contract terms: CMA, *Unfair contract terms guidance, Guidance on the unfair terms provisions in the Consumer Rights Act* (July 2015).

[1802] e.g. CMA, *Guidance for lettings professionals on consumer protection law; Helping you comply with your obligations* (June 13, 2014, CMA31).

[1803] 1993 Directive art.4(1) (implemented by 1999 Regulations reg.6(1)) refers to an assessment "at the time of the conclusion of the contract" and see further below, paras 38-325—38-326.

[1804] *Andriciuc v Banca Românească* (C-186/16) of September 20, 2017 para.54 referring to *Bucura v SC Bancpost SA* (C-348/14) EU:C:2015:447, July 9, 2015 para.48.

on so as to do so.[1805] So, for example, if a price variation clause gives a supplier an unlimited discretion to vary the price (a term which can for this purpose be assumed to be potentially unfair given its lack of limitation or justification[1806]), then it would not be binding on the consumer with the result that even a moderate variation of the price (itself not in the context apparently unfair) would not be effective against the consumer: the unfairness of the term makes it "not binding" on the consumer.[1807] As Advocate General Szpunar has observed, "reasonable conduct in a context where a contractual term is unfair does not render the term fair."[1808]

38-282 **The significance of imbalance** Secondly, the OFT attached very considerable significance to the notion of balance, so that a term which may look, prima facie, severely prejudicial to the rights of a consumer may yet be considered fair if it is counterbalanced by a corresponding term which could act to the consumer's advantage. Various examples of this thinking are given in the OFT's reports, such as a seller's right to increase prices being coupled with a realistic right in the consumer to get out of the contract without penalty.[1809] In the context of cancellation rights, for example, in the view of the OFT:

> "… [f]airness and balance require that consumers and suppliers should be on an equal footing as regards rights to end or withdraw from the contract. The supplier's rights should not be excessive, nor should the consumer's be over-restricted. This does not, however, mean a merely formal equivalence in rights to cancel, but rather that both parties should enjoy rights of equal extent and value."[1810]

An example of the importance of imbalance for the determination of the fairness of a term may be found in *Spreadex Ltd v Cochrane*.[1811] There a consumer had agreed to use a trader's online platform for the making of spread bets with the trader, a spread betting bookmaker. On the premise (which the court rejected) that this

---

[1805] See the explicit reference to the potential unfairness of a term by the CJEU in *Banco Primus SA v Gutiérrez García* (C-421/14) of January 26, 2017 at para.67. See also the views expressed in OFT, *Unfair Contract Terms*, Bulletin No.1 (May 1996), paras 1.2, p.5; *Bulletin No.3* (March 1997), p.7; *Financial Services Authority v Asset L.I. Inc (t/a Asset Land Investment Inc)* [2013] EWHC 178 (Ch), [2013] 2 B.C.L.C. 480 at [135]; [2014] EWCA Civ 435, [2015] 1 All E.R. 1 at [99]; cf. *Stewart Gill Ltd v Horatio Myer & Co Ltd* [1992] Q.B. 600 (in relation to the reasonableness test under the Unfair Contract Terms Act 1977 s.11).

[1806] And see 1999 Regulations Sch.2 para.1(l), below, paras 38-312—38-315.

[1807] In *Banco Bilbao Vizcaya Argentaria SA v Quintano Ujeta* (C-602/13) Order of June 11, 2015 paras 47–50 (available only in French) an acceleration clause in a contract of consumer credit secured on the consumer's residence created a right in the lender to call in the principal and interest immediately on non-payment of interest even though the default position in national law subjected this right to three months of lateness. The national court held the acceleration clause unfair on this ground and the CJEU held that the fact that the trader had chosen to wait for three months to call in the principal and interest did not affect the fact that the effect of unfairness is to render the clause "not binding" on the consumer. (On the inability of the trader to rely on the default position in national law in these circumstances, see below, para.38-342). See also *Radlinger v Finway a.s.* (C-377/14) April 21, 2016 at para.95 (potential cumulative effect of all penalty clauses on consumer the basis for assessment of fairness).

[1808] *Banco Primus SA v Gutiérrez García* (C-421/14) A.G. Opinion February 2, 2016 para.85. (The judgment of the CJEU of January 26, 2017 did not refer to this issue.)

[1809] OFT, *Unfair Contract Terms*, Bulletin No.1 (May 1996), para.1.5, p.6.

[1810] OFT, *Unfair Contract Terms* (2008) OFT311, para.6.1.1.

[1811] [2012] EWHC 1290 (Comm), [2012] Info. T.L.R. 1.

agreement was in principle contractually binding,[1812] a term of the contract under which the consumers were deemed to have authorised all trading under their account number was held unfair within the meaning of the Regulations: under the agreement for use of the online platform, the bookmaker assumed no obligations and the customer was granted no rights, whereas under this term, the consumer would be liable for any trade on the account not made or authorised by him. "The result is ... and most clearly, a significant imbalance in the parties' rights and obligations".[1813]

Factors in fairness While in principle the 1999 Regulations are concerned with the unfairness of contract terms, rather than with the fairness of the parties' behaviour more generally, certain aspects of their mutual behaviour may be relevant in the assessment of fairness. For, as has been seen,[1814] the Regulations require that in assessing the fairness of a term account shall be taken of the nature of the goods or services, all the circumstances attending the conclusion of the contract and all other terms of the contract or of a contract on which it is dependent.[1815] While formally this provision requires certain factors to be taken into account (raising the possibility of arguing that only these should be), it is submitted that, quite apart from the inherent openness of the concept of fairness itself, other considerations may be taken into account in assessing fairness by way of application of the requirement of good faith which forms an element within the assessment of fairness.[1816]   **38-283**

"The nature of the goods or services" In certain types of case, the nature of the goods or services could argue for the fairness of a term which in other contexts would clearly be unfair. So, for example, in *Bryen & Langley Ltd v Boston*[1817] it was considered material to the issue of fairness of a term that the transaction before the court was not of a "normal 'consumer' type, like buying a television set", but, for the individual or individuals concerned, a major project such as the costly construction of a building which would be undertaken only with the benefit of appropriate professional advice. A second example may be found in the context of clauses allowing the forfeiture of a purchaser's deposit in contracts of sale of land. Here, at first sight the loss of ten per cent of the purchase price if the purchaser withdraws from the contract suggests that such a clause is unfair, but it may not be given the   **38-284**

[1812] [2012] EWHC 1290 (Comm) at [14]–[16] (absence of consideration) and see below, para.38-304 (note). cf. *Roundlistic Ltd v Jones* [2016] UKUT 325 (LC) at [103] where it was held that the fact that the terms of a new long lease (subject to the 1999 Regulations) granted on the same terms as a lease for which it was substituted (which had 80 years remaining and which was not subject to the 1999 Regulations) meant that a term of the new lease could not be said to "cause" a significant imbalance in the rights and obligations of the contracting parties: "[i]f there was a significant imbalance it already existed". See also *Abbott v RCI Europe* [2016] EWHC 2602 (Ch) at [45]–[47] (term of a contract under which consumers "deposited" their own timeshare rights with a company so as to enable them to exchange those rights for access to other properties held fair as creating no significant imbalance given the fetters imposed by law on the company's exercise of its discretion under the term and the power in the consumers to cancel the contract without penalty).

[1813] [2012] EWHC 1290 (Comm) at [17], per David Donaldson Q.C. referring also to other factors to the same end, notably the inadequate manner in which the potential customer's agreement was sought: at [21].

[1814] See above, para.38-265.

[1815] 1999 Regulations reg.6(1).

[1816] See above, paras 38-267—38-270.

[1817] [2004] EWHC 2450 (TCC), 98 Con. L.R. 82 at [45]; [2005] EWCA Civ 973, [2005] All E.R. (D) 507 (Jul) (appeal allowed on other grounds).

need of the seller to cover transaction costs and also to be indemnified for likely loss of profit on the transaction. Indeed, a term allowing a person (the alleged consumer) who had agreed to participate in a world voyage by clipper to cancel the contract at a charge of 75 per cent of the price was held to be fair as not disproportionate in the context since that person's commitment to the venture was important.[1818] It may be under this heading that a court could properly consider the impact of (good) industry practice in relation to the type of contract in question in assessing a term's fairness.

38-285 **"All the circumstances attending the conclusion of the contract"** This is clearly a very inclusive formulation.[1819] Here, two possible factors will be mentioned, both of which can be thought of as circumstances relating to the conclusion of the contract. First, the fact that a seller or supplier has put pressure on a consumer to conclude the contract or to do so in haste and without time to think about its significance would point strongly against the fairness of any term which prejudices the consumer, even if this pressure did not amount to either duress or undue influence within the meaning of the general law[1820] or an unfair commercial practice within the meaning of the 2008 Regulations.[1821] Secondly, the degree of genuine opportunity for the consumer to read, understand, consider and decide upon the terms of a contract is also an important factor in their overall fairness. This may be supported by reference to recital 20's statement that "the consumer should actually be given an opportunity to examine all the terms"[1822] and the Schedules' inclusion in the "indicative list" of a term which has the object or effect of "irrevocably binding the consumer to terms with which he had no real opportunity of becoming acquainted before the conclusion of the contract".[1823] Now, a term which irrevocably binds a consumer to the contract is typically to be found in any contract which does not provide for a consumer to withdraw from the contract and so, absent such a provision, the terms of any contract which the consumer did not have a real opportunity of being acquainted are vulnerable to a charge of unfairness. Positively, therefore, a seller or supplier whose explanatory pre-contractual brochure[1824] makes

---

[1818] *Boyde v Clipper Ventures Plc* 2013 S.C.L.R. 313, 2013 G.W.D. 12-243.

[1819] *Pereničovà* (C-453/10) para.42, above, para.38-278. The CJEU has therefore held that national legislation cannot apply a restricted legal standard for the assessment of a contract term, such as a restriction on the rate of default interest to three times the interest otherwise owed under the contract: *Ibercaja Banco SAU v Cortés González* (C-613/15) March 17, 2016 at para.33. And see *Financial Services Authority v Asset L.I. Inc (t/a Asset Land Investment Inc)* [2013] EWHC 178 (Ch) at [134]–[137] (terms seeking to restrict the seller's liability in contracts for the sale of land under a collective investment scheme held unfair given, inter alia, the "telesales pitch" by the sellers). On appeal, the Court of Appeal considered that the issue of the unfairness of the terms was unnecessary for the issues before the court, but it would have agreed with the court below: [2014] EWCA Civ 435, [2015] 1 All E.R. 1 at [96]–[99].

[1820] See above, Vol.I, Ch.8.

[1821] cf. above, paras 38-159 et seq.

[1822] See *Nemzeti Fogyasztóvédelmi Hatóság v Invitel Távközlési Zrt* (C-472/10) EU:C:2012:242, April 26, 2012 at para.27, referring to the requirement of "plain, intelligible writing" in art.5 of the Directive, on which see below, paras 38-347 et seq.

[1823] 1999 Regulations Sch.2 para.1(i). See further *RWE Vertrieb AG v Verbraucherzentrale Nordrhein-Westfalen eV* (C-92/11) EU:C:2013:180, March 21, 2013 paras 43–44 referring to 1993 Directive art.5 and recital 20, and emphasising the importance of the provision of pre-contractual information for the fairness of a variation clause, below, para.38-315.

[1824] OFT, *Unfair Contract Terms*, Bulletin No.2 (September 1996), para.2.22, p.12 (though considering this to be particularly a matter for the good faith of the trader). cf. the reference in *Andriciuc v Banca*

clear the otherwise surprising terms on which he deals or whose staff follow a practice of advising their customers of the terms in a clear and intelligible manner may be more likely to succeed in arguing that the terms in question are fair. This links in with the common law's traditional concern with notice of terms,[1825] but it goes further in that a "real opportunity" is referred to and it may be thought that the more theoretical the opportunity, the more likely a term is to be held to be unfair.[1826]

This approach to fairness is related to the Regulations' requirement that the contract terms themselves be expressed in plain and intelligible language[1827] and it is therefore submitted that a lack of plainness or intelligibility is *relevant* to the assessment of a term under the Regulations' requirement of fairness. So, for example, a term which provided that:

"Should any other disagreement arise in connection with or out of this contract the matters in dispute shall be referred in accordance with the Arbitration Act 1950 or any statutory modification or re-enactment therefore for the time being in force",

has been held insufficient to set out clearly its intended nature and effect as an arbitration clause in the circumstances, this being a factor in the court's holding the clause unfair within the meaning of the Regulations.[1828] And the Court of Justice has emphasised the importance of the quality of pre-contractual information relating to contract terms for the assessment of their fairness, relating this to the requirement of plain intelligible language in art.5 of the 1993 Directive (implemented by reg.7 of the 1999 Regulations).[1829] So, where, for example, the fact that the amount of a tax imposed by law on a vendor of property was made payable by a consumer purchaser of residential property by a term of the contract of sale was unknown at the date on which the contract was concluded and was "to be determined only ex post by the relevant [tax] authority", would argue for the unfairness of that term, for "if that is the case, this could lead to uncertainty on the part of the consumer as to the extent of the commitment undertaken".[1830] On the other hand, the fact that a term is plain and intelligible does not rule out a finding that it is unfair.[1831] For this purpose, it is submitted that while generally the Court of Justice will adopt the variable objective standard of the "average consumer",[1832] where a business knows (or, possibly, can reasonably foresee) that a *particular* consumer with whom it deals has a lesser likely understanding of its contract terms, then this should be relevant to

---

Românească (C-186/16) of September 20, 2017 at paras 46–47 to an the trader's "promotional material" for the purposes of the requirement of plain intelligible language, above, para.38-262.

[1825] See Vol.I, paras 13-008 et seq.

[1826] The common law approach appears, by contrast, to distinguish between the general law of notice, where the unusual or onerous nature of a contract term is relevant to the degree of notice required (*Interfoto Picture Library Ltd v Stiletto Visual Programmes Ltd* [1989] Q.B. 433) and the rule governing signed documents, where it is not: *L'Estrange v F Graucob* [1934] 2 K.B. 394. See Peel (ed.), *Treitel on The Law of Contract*, 14th edn (2015), paras 7-004—7-010.

[1827] See below, paras 38-347—38-351.

[1828] *Mylcrist Builders Ltd v Buck* [2008] EWHC 2172 (TCC), [2009] 2 All E.R. (Comm) 259 at [56].

[1829] *Nemzeti Fogyasztóvédelmi Hatóság v Invitel Távközlési Zrt.* (C-472/10) EU:C:2012:242, [26]–[28], below, para.38-314; *RWE Vertrieb AG v Verbraucherzentrale Nordrhein-Westfalen eV* (C-92/11) EU:C:2013:180, March 21, 2013 at [44], below, para.38-315; *Constructora Principado SA v Menéndez Álvarez* (C-226/12) EU:C:2014:10, January 16, 2014 at para.26.

[1830] *Menéndez Álvarez* (C-226/12) at para.27.

[1831] *Sebestyén v Kovári* (C-342/13) EU:C:2014:1857, April 3, 2014 at para.34.

[1832] Above, paras 38-044 and 38-261, 38-262 and below, para.38-350.

the assessment of the fairness of the terms, notably, as a result of the requirement of good faith.[1833]

38-286 Lack of plainness or intelligibility sufficient?   What is more open to contention is whether a lack of plainness or intelligibility (often referred to as transparency) can render a term unfair within the meaning of the Regulations without more.[1834] The key hurdle to allowing it to do so is the first element of the composite test of unfairness, viz that the term must cause "a significant imbalance in the parties' rights and obligations arising under the contract, to the detriment of the consumer".[1835] Clearly, a case can be imagined where a term (while not plain and intelligible) does not attempt to create such an imbalance (notably, where any imbalance is to the *benefit* of the consumer) and so would not be rendered unfair by the Regulations; but in this situation it is difficult to see why the consumer would wish to argue that such a term was "not binding" on him (though a body entrusted with a policing role in relation to unfair contract terms may nevertheless wish to intervene).[1836] However, where a contract term either seeks to bind a consumer to a particular duty or seeks to create rights which do not benefit him (notably, as compared to his existing rights or the rights of the seller or supplier under the contract more widely), a court could find that such an "imbalance" in the rights and obligations of the parties was "significant" merely on the ground that the consumer was not able to appreciate its extent: as the Director General of Fair Trading observed:

"... it would clearly be difficult to maintain that unintelligible or ambiguous terms were *not* unfair if they had some potential for detriment to the consumer."[1837]

The final step in this direction (noted without comment by the European Commission) is that courts in some Member States have held that a failure in the requirement of transparency itself constitutes "unfairness" within the meaning of the Directive.[1838] However, this equating of the two requirements contained in the Directive does not accord with the way in which they are set out in the Directive as distinct both in their content and even more in their effects.[1839] Indeed, if a mere failure in transparency would lead without more to a failure in fairness this would render the distinctive treatment of the requirement of transparency entirely otiose. For this reason, the Law Commissions' view that "non-transparent terms" are not automatically unfair, though the lack of transparency is an important factor in the

---

[1833] Below, paras 38-267 et seq.

[1834] cf. Study Group on a European Civil Code and Research Group on EC Private Law (Acquis Group), *Principles, Definitions and Model Rules of European Private Law*, Interim Outline edn (2008), *Draft Common Frame of Reference* art.II.-9:402(2) which provides that "[i]n a contract between a business and a consumer a term which has been supplied by the business in breach of the duty of transparency ... may on that ground alone be considered unfair". No similar provision was contained in the Proposal for a Regulation for a Common European Sales Law COM(2011) 635 final, Annex I, arts 79–83 CESL.

[1835] 1999 Regulations reg.5(1), above, para.38-266 and see Bright in Burrows and Peel, *Contract Terms* (2007), p.172 at 184–186.

[1836] On this see below, paras 38-353 et seq.

[1837] OFT, *Unfair Contract Terms*, Bulletin No.2 (September 1996), p.8.

[1838] EC Commission, Report on the Implementation of Directive 93/13/EEC on unfair terms in consumer contracts COM(2000) 248 final, p.18.

[1839] Below, paras 38-339—38-351.

evaluation of their fairness[1840] is to be supported.[1841]

"All the other terms of the contract"   The Regulations require courts to take into   **38-287**
account the other terms of the contract before them in assessing the unfairness of
a term. It is to be noticed that *all* the terms should be looked at, including terms
which may fall within the "core exclusion" as relating to the contract's main subject
matter or price/quality ratio.[1842] In the view of the Director General of Fair Trading, an example of "another term" of a contract which may argue for the fairness
of a term which by itself looks unfair may be found in a term which provides the
consumer with a cooling-off period during which he may decide to cancel the
contract without penalty.[1843]

"The ... terms ... of another contract on which it is dependent"   It would seem   **38-288**
from the general formulation of this phrase that there is no requirement that the
other contract on which the consumer contract is dependent must itself be a
consumer contract within the meaning of the Regulations (though in the vast majority of situations it will be) nor even that the other contract be between the same parties as the one whose term is to be assessed.[1844] A situation in the consumer context
in which two contracts are related may be found in the context of the financing of
a consumer sale. Here, it would seem that whatever controls already exist on the
fairness of the terms of either the sale or the financing contract,[1845] the terms of the
one may go to the fairness of the terms of the other. For example, the fairness of
the terms of purchase of a house could be assessed taking into account the terms
of a loan contract secured on the house taken out by a consumer purchaser/
mortgagor. However, this example shows the difficulties that would arise in this
respect, where the mortgagee is not also the seller, for it may be thought unfair for
a mortgagee to be prejudiced by the terms of the sale of which it may know nothing and have even less control. This may lead a court to imply into the phrase
"another contract" a requirement that this contract be between the parties to the
consumer contract whose terms are to be assessed.

The test of unfairness applied in the First National Bank Plc case   In *Direc-*   **38-289**
tor General of Fair Trading v First National Bank Plc[1846] the Director General of
Fair Trading challenged the fairness of a term in a contract of consumer credit the
effect of which (if valid) would be that where the bank obtains judgment against a
borrower, interest would be payable at the contractual rate on the outstanding
principal plus accrued interest unpaid at the date of judgment until the judgment is

---

[1840] Law Com., Scottish Law Com., *Unfair Terms in Consumer Contracts: Advice to the Department for Business, Innovation and Skills* (March 2013), para.S.34; para.6.60.
[1841] cf. *Verein für Konsumenteninformation v Amazon EU Sàrl* (C-191/15) July 28, 2016 at para.68 where, as will be seen below, para.38-321, the CJEU came close to saying that an express choice of law clause in a consumer contract *will* be unfair if the trader does not explain that its effect is limited by the restrictions imposed by art.6(2) of the Rome I Regulation on the law applicable to contractual obligations, on the basis that this means that the term fails the requirement of plain intel- ligible language.
[1842] 1993 Directive recital 19. On the "core exclusion" see above, paras 38-245—38-264.
[1843] OFT, *Unfair Contract Terms*, Bulletin No.2 (September 1996), p.12.
[1844] cf. *Domsalla v Dyason* [2007] EWHC 1174 (TCC) at [77] (wide range of contracts related to the consumer contract in question considered as part of "all the circumstances").
[1845] Notably, under the Consumer Credit Act 1974 on which see below, Ch.39.
[1846] [2001] UKHL 52, [2002] 1 A.C. 481; Whittaker (2004) *ZEuP* 75.

discharged by payment. The Court of Appeal held that the term was unfair as the borrower's attention is not specifically drawn to the point of payment of interest at the contractual rate beyond judgment in instalments by the bank at or before the conclusion of the contract—nor indeed at any later stage.[1847] In its view, the existence of the court's powers by statute to order payment by instalments and to modify the contractual rate of interest as a result does not prevent the term from operating unfairly "in a majority of cases where instalment orders are made without the consideration by the courts of those provisions".[1848] The bank has the stronger bargaining position and the clause comes as an "unfair surprise". However, the House of Lords unanimously reversed this decision and held that the term was fair within the meaning of the Regulations. So, for Lord Bingham of Cornhill:

> "The essential bargain is that the bank will make funds available to the borrower which the borrower will repay, over a period, with interest. Neither party could suppose that the bank would willingly forgo any part of its principal or interest. If the bank thought that outcome at all likely, it would not lend. If there were any room for doubt about the borrower's obligation to repay the principal in full with interest, that obligation is very clearly and unambiguously expressed in the conditions of contract. There is nothing unbalanced or detrimental to the consumer in that obligation; the absence of such a term would unbalance the contract to the detriment of the lender."[1849]

The unfairness of the situation in which consumer borrowers relied on the terms of judgments made against them for payment of their debt to lenders and were later surprised by a demand for payment of *contractual* interest under a term such as the one in issue was caused by the absence of procedural safeguards provided for a consumer on default by the applicable primary and secondary legislation rather than by the contract term itself.[1850]

38-290   Other factors in the assessment of good faith or fairness   Other factors have been suggested as relevant to determining whether the requirement of good faith is satisfied, though most could equally well be thought of simply as going to the issue of fairness in general.

38-291   Price/quality ratio   A notable example is found in the preamble to the Directive which allows the "price/quality" ratio of the contract to be taken into account in assessing a term *other than* one which itself describes the main subject matter of the contract or the quality/price ratio of the goods or services supplied.[1851] The relevance of the price/quality ratio to the fairness of incidental terms may be seen to be reflected in recital 16's reference to the consumer's receipt of an inducement as an element within the application of the requirement of good faith.

38-292   EU recommendations   It has been suggested that EU recommendations in the field of consumer protection may be referred to by a court in assessing the fairness of a term.[1852] This suggestion has recently been given support by the Court of

---

[1847] [2000] Q.B. 672, 688.
[1848] [2000] Q.B. 672, per Peter Gibson L.J. The powers are contained in Consumer Credit Act 1974 ss.129, 136.
[1849] [2001] UKHL 52 at [20]. Lords Steyn, Hope of Craighead, Millett and Rodger of Earlsferry agreed.
[1850] [2001] UKHL 52 at [23], [61], [66].
[1851] 1993 Directive recital 19.
[1852] Howells and Wilhelmsson *E.C. Consumer Law* (1997) at p.103.

Justice's reference to an EU recommendation for the purposes of determining whether a contract term has satisfied the requirement of plain intelligible language.[1853]

Consumer benefiting from advice, well-informed or experienced Where a **38-293** consumer's professional agent put forward a standard set of terms which were held to have been incorporated into the contract, and thereby "imposed these terms" on the supplier of a service, the Court of Appeal regarded:

> "... the suggestion that there was any lack of good faith or fair dealing by [the supplier] with regard to the ultimate incorporation of these terms into the contract as repugnant to common sense ... It was not for [the suppliers] to take the matter up with [the consumer] and ensure that he knew what he was doing; they knew that he had the benefit of the services of a professional ... to advise him on the effects of the terms "[1854]

In this way, even if a particular term of the standard contract (here, an arbitration clause) were found to cause a "significant imbalance in the parties' rights and obligations under the contract, to the detriment of the consumer" as envisaged by reg.5(1) of the 1999 Regulations, this would not be "contrary to the requirement of good faith", with the result that the contract term would not be unfair within the meaning of the Regulations. Similarly, where it is shown that the consumers were independently wealthy, experienced in business and legally advised, that the negotiation of the contract was conducted aggressively on their behalf, that significant changes were procured to the seller or supplier's usual terms and that the terms challenged were expressed fully, clearly and legibly, and given appropriate prominence "with no concealed pitfalls", a court may conclude that the requirement of good faith is satisfied and so the terms are not unfair under the 1999 Regulations.[1855] Even in the absence of legal advice, the financial experience of the consumer may be relevant to the application of the test of unfairness in the circumstances, as it makes it more likely that he or she will understand the significance of the term.[1856] But the mere fact that a consumer benefits from legal advice in relation to a term does not necessarily tip the balance in favour of their fairness. So, for example, in *Harrison v Shepherd Homes Ltd*[1857] consumer purchasers, concluding a standard contract of purchase with builders, were legally advised, but while this "opportunity for them to be advised [had] to be weighed in the overall assessment of good faith", in fact they were "not alerted to any problems with the terms" and so this did not detract sufficiently from other circumstances so as to

---

[1853] *Andriciuc v Banca Românească* (C-186/16) of September 20, 2017 para.49, above, para.38-260.

[1854] *Bryen & Langley Ltd v Boston* [2005] EWCA Civ 973, [2005] All E.R. (D) 507 (Jul) at [46], per Rimer J. (with whom Clarke ([56]) and Pill L.JJ. [56] agreed). This decision has been treated as holding generally that the arbitration provisions in the JCT Minor Works Contract "even if proffered by the contractor in circumstances which would make it procedurally unfair for the contractor to rely on them vis-à-vis a consumer, do not cause a significant imbalance in the parties' rights and obligations": *Domsalla v Dyason* [2007] EWHC 1174 (TCC) at [92], per H.H.J. Thornton Q.C. On the issue whether terms in these circumstances remain not "individually negotiated" see above, para.38-244.

[1855] *Deutsche Bank (Suisse) SA v Khan* [2013] EWHC 482 (Comm) at [372]–[380].

[1856] *West v Ian Finlay & Associates* [2014] EWCA Civ 316, [2014] B.L.R. 324 at [60] and see above para.38-273.

[1857] [2011] EWHC 1811 (TCC), (2011) 27 Const. L.J. 709.

establish the "fair and open dealing" which the Regulations require.[1858]

38-294 Particularly vulnerable consumers It has been seen that the Court of Justice has developed the notion of the "average consumer" for a number of legal purposes and that the Unfair Commercial Practices Directive 2005 gave it a prominent role for the purposes of its general scheme of regulatory control of commercial practices business-to-consumer, so to ensure, inter alia, the protection of consumers who are vulnerable "because of their mental or physical infirmity, age or credulity in a way which the trader could reasonably be expected to foresee".[1859] And while not mentioned in the 1993 Directive, the Court of Justice has used the standard of the "average consumer" as the proper standpoint for the assessment of the requirement of plain intelligible language under that Directive.[1860] It is submitted that the taking advantage by a business of the vulnerability of a consumer understood in the sense earlier noted would clearly be relevant to the issue of the business's failing to have "dealt fairly and equitably with the consumer" and therefore the requirement of good faith,[1861] even though the consumer possessed the requisite legal capacity to conclude the contract in question under the law governing minors' contracts or the law governing lack of mental capacity.[1862]

38-295 The language type of the contract In general, a domestic consumer contract governed by English law is normally to be expressed in the English language and where reference is made to the "intelligibility" of the language used this normally refers to the style of language rather than to its type. However, it should not be universally assumed that English should be the only language in which such a contract should be expressed: for if a seller or supplier contracts with consumers whose first language is known or can reasonably be foreseen by it to be other than English, then it may be "contrary to the requirement of good faith" for the business to rely entirely on terms set out in English.[1863] And where, for example, a contract for the provision of financial services was made with consumers who were Greek and non-resident in the UK, the court considered that the term under consideration "called for *translation* and careful explanation".[1864] A similar approach could also be taken in the case of a cross-border contract concluded via the internet and on terms set out on the seller or supplier's website.[1865]

[1858] [2011] EWHC 1811 (TCC), at [113], per Ramsey J. (and similarly at [116] and [119]).

[1859] Directive 2005/29/EC concerning unfair business-to-consumer commercial practices art.5(3) and see above, para.38-169.

[1860] 1993 Directive arts 4(2), 5; *Kásler v OTP Jelzálogbank Zrt* (C-26/13) EU:C:2014:282, April 30, 2014 para.74, above, paras 38-261, 38-262 and below, para.38-350.

[1861] Above, paras 38-267 et seq.

[1862] See Vol.I, paras 9-005 et seq. and 9-075 et seq. respectively.

[1863] See further Whittaker, *Cambridge Yearbook of European Studies* (2006), Vol.8, Ch.10; Loos (2017) EuCML 54. Legislation sometimes makes requirements as to the language of pre-contractual information and the contract itself, as in the case of timeshare and related contracts where the required information and the contract must be provided in an official language of the EEA State in which the consumer is resident or is a national: Timeshare, Holiday Products, Resale and Exchange Contracts Regulations 2010 (SI 2010/2960) regs 12(4)–(7) and 17, above, paras 38-150—38-151. cf. Consumer Rights Act 2015 s.30(4) (guarantees to consumers in relation to goods offered within UK must be in English), below, para.38-528.

[1864] *Standard Bank London Ltd v Apostolakis (No.2)* [2001] Lloyd's Rep. Bank 240, 250 (emphasis added).

[1865] On which see Whittaker, *Cambridge Yearbook of European Studies* (2006), Vol.8, Ch.10, passim.

Terms deemed to be unfair within the meaning of the Regulations While **38-296**
generally the question whether a contract term is "unfair" within the meaning of the
Regulations is a matter for the composite test described in the preceding paragraphs,
on occasion legislation has deemed a particular type of term in consumer contracts
to be unfair within the meaning of the Regulations. This is true of arbitration clauses
where they relate to claims for a "modest amount"[1866] and also of contract terms:

> "... providing that a consumer bears the burden of proof in respect of showing whether a
> distance supplier or an intermediary complied with any or all of the obligations placed
> upon him resulting from the Directive"

of 2002[1867] concerning the distance marketing of consumer financial services.[1868]

"Fairness" under the Regulations and "reasonableness" under the Unfair **38-297**
Contract Terms Act 1977[1869] It has been noted that some of the considerations
to be taken into account by a court in assessing the fairness of a term for the
purposes of the Regulations (in particular in relation to the requirement of good
faith) are the same or very similar to those to be taken into account in assessing the
"reasonableness" of a term under the Unfair Contract Terms Act 1977.[1870] Moreover,
while the specific factors which are to be taken into account may differ somewhat,
the "definitions" of the two concepts are both very inclusive, allowing a court to
take into account whatever factors it thinks right in judging whether a term should
be enforced, as long as these relate to the term (as opposed to post-contractual dealings between the parties).[1871] There is, therefore, a profound similarity in the two
tests in that they both require a court to decide whether a particular contract term
should be enforceable according to a range of considerations, some of which relate
to the contract itself and some of which relate to the relative positions of the parties to the contract or the circumstances in which the contract was made. All this
does not mean, however, that the two tests have the same significance, but their differences do not stem from use of the language, on the one hand, of "reasonableness" and, on the other, of "fairness" and "good faith". Instead, they flow from the
differences in ambit of the two pieces of legislation, in particular as regards the
types of term to be tested. For while the Unfair Contract Terms Act 1977 deals
almost exclusively with exemption clauses, the requirement of fairness in the
Regulations affects any type of contract term as long as it is "ancillary"[1872] and has
not been "individually negotiated".[1873] Clearly, the considerations which are ap-

---

[1866] Arbitration Act 1996 ss.89, 90; Unfair Arbitration Agreements (Specified Amount) Order 1999 (SI
1999/2167). This law was amended on the revoking of the 1999 Regulations and their replacement
by the Consumer Rights Act 2015: see further below, para.38-302 and 38-412.

[1867] Directive 2002/65 concerning distance marketing of consumer financial services [2002] O.J. L271/
16.

[1868] The Financial Services (Distance Marketing) Regulations 2004 (SI 2004/2095) reg.24, amending
1999 Regulations regs 3(1) and 5(5). On these Regulations see above, para.38-136.

[1869] See above, para.38-212 and Vol.I, paras 15-062 et seq. on the effect of the Consumer Rights Act 2015
on the Unfair Contract Terms Act 1977.

[1870] See above, para.38-268 and Vol.I, paras 15-096 et seq.

[1871] This is made clear by the phrase in 1999 Regulations reg.6(1) directing the court to refer "*at the time
of the conclusion of the contract*, to all the circumstances attending the conclusion of the contract":
and see above, paras 38-265 and 38-285.

[1872] i.e. not falling within the first limb of the "core exclusion" in 1999 Regulations reg.6(2)(a): see above,
paras 38-245 et seq. especially at 38-251.

[1873] See above, paras 38-242—38-244

propriate in judging the "fairness" of terms other than exemption clauses are likely to differ considerably from those which are appropriate to that context. There are indeed existing parallels for this in wider English law: so, for example, the factors which are to be taken into account by a court in judging the "reasonableness" of a term of a contract which is in restraint of trade are not the same as those in judging the "reasonableness" of an exemption clause: the terminology of reasonableness is shared but the impact of this requirement differs according to the type of term in question, and the factors in determining reasonableness differ according to the reasons for which the term is viewed with suspicion (whether excluding a person's claim which would otherwise exist or unduly fettering a person's freedom).[1874] In a similar way, the application of the requirement of fairness for the purposes of the 1999 Regulations differs according to its context. In the result, therefore, while the application of the test of "fairness" for the purposes of the Regulations to exemption clauses is unlikely to differ from the application of the test of "reasonableness" under the 1977 Act, its application to other clauses will differ appropriately to the context of both the type of term and the type of contract in question.[1875]

38-298 **Procedural issues**[1876] In *Tew v Bank of Scotland*[1877] a number of claimants sought to establish the unfairness of terms in a particular category of mortgage ("shared appreciation mortgages") made with them by certain lenders, including the defendants to the proceedings. The question before Mann J. was whether the court should make a Group Litigation Order (GLO) in relation to these claims. Under Pt 19.10 to 19.15 CPR such an order is available so as "to provide for the case management of claims which give rise to common or related issues of fact or law". Mann J. held that while some issues arising from claims by a number of consumers that the terms of their contracts of a particular type were unfair within the meaning of the 1999 Regulations could be the object of a GLO (such as whether or not the relevant terms fell within the exclusion in reg.6(2)[1878]), the determination of the fairness of the terms could not.

> "On the face of the legislation, the facts of individual cases are capable of affecting the assessment of fairness, and they cannot be disregarded as such."[1879]

The learned judge added that:

> "This is not a case where one of necessity has to hypothesise a typical consumer, as one does in a regulatory challenge.[1880] There are real consumers, with real transactions, who are complaining that the transactions are unfair to them. It is in their particular contexts that the unfairness falls to be assessed, and it is not a sensible exercise to divide that exercise up in the way suggested",[1881]

[1874] cf. Vol.I, para.15-096 and paras 16-123 et seq.

[1875] cf. though, the differences in relation to the burden of proof discussed below, paras 38-335 et seq.

[1876] See also below, para.38-334 in relation to *Sales Sinués v Caixabank SA, Drame Ba v Catalunja Caixa SA* (Joined Cases C-381/14 and C-385/14) April 14, 2016 concerning stays of individual claims by consumers.

[1877] [2010] EWHC 203 (Ch).

[1878] [2010] EWHC 203 (Ch) at [36]–[37].

[1879] [2010] EWHC 203 (Ch) at [25], per Mann J.

[1880] See 1999 Regulations regs 12–14 and below, paras 38-353 et seq.

[1881] [2010] EWHC 203 (Ch) at [27], per Mann J.

so as to construct "common issues". In the particular context of the case before him, Mann J. instead gave directions for the trial of lead cases in order to get the fairness issue decided.[1882]

(dd)   The "Indicative List" of Terms

Introduction   Following the list in the Annex to the 1993 Directive exactly, Sch.2 **38-299** of the 1999 Regulations contains an identical "indicative and non-exhaustive list of the terms which may be regarded as unfair".[1883] This list has been termed a "grey list",[1884] for the terms which it contains are not necessarily to be held unfair (a "black list"), but this terminology may be misleading as inclusion within the list does not formally give rise to any presumption that a term will be unfair.[1885] On the other hand, the Court of Justice has emphasised the list's importance, observing that:

> "If the content of the annex [to the Directive] does not suffice in itself to establish automatically the unfair nature of a contested term, it is nevertheless an essential element on which the competent court may base its assessment as to the unfair nature of that term."[1886]

Given its merely illustrative nature, it may appear odd that the second part of Sch.2 purports to restrict the scope of particular examples of terms found in the first part, but this reinforces the importance which was attached by the drafters of the Directive to the illustrative list.[1887] Even so, it needs to be emphasised that a type of term included on the list may be held by a court to be fair in the circumstances before it. Moreover, as earlier explained, the appearance of a contract term on the list has a second significance, for where it does so it will be held to fall outside the "core exclusion" set by art.4(2) of the Directive and provided by reg.6(2) of the 1999 Regulations.[1888]

The list in para.1 of Sch.2 of the 1999 Regulations includes a wide variety of **38-300** terms and these not merely illustrate the application of the requirement of fairness, but also the range of types of terms which are subject to the Regulations' controls (in particular in contrast to the limited ambit of the Unfair Contract Terms

---

[1882] [2010] EWHC 203 (Ch) at [37].

[1883] 1999 Regulations reg.5(5), Sch.2 para.1; 1993 Directive, Annex. For the role of the list of terms under the Consumer Rights Act 2015 see below, para.38-391.

[1884] *Matei v SC Volksbank România SA* (C-143/13) EU:C:2015:127, February 26, 2015 para.60.

[1885] cf. the position under the Proposal for a Regulation on a Common European Sales Law COM(2011) 635 final, Annex I art.84 CESL (a list of "contract terms which are always unfair") and art.85 CESL (a list of "contract terms which are presumed to be unfair"). On the proposal, see Vol.I, para.1-013.

[1886] *Nemzeti Fogyasztóvédelmi Hatóság v Invitel Távközlési Zrt* (C-472/10) EU:C:2012:242, April 26, 2012 para.26, and see below para.38-314; *Sebestyén v Kővári* (C-342/13) EU:C:2014:1857, April 3, 2014 at para.32.

[1887] 1999 Regulations Sch.2 para.2. The ECJ has held that national legislation implementing the 1993 Directive need not itself include the list in the Directive's Annex. However: "Inasmuch as [it] is of indicative and illustrative value, it constitutes a source of information both for the national authorities responsible for applying the implementing measures and for individuals affected by those measures", and so its "form and method of implementation [must] offer a sufficient guarantee that the public can obtain knowledge of it". The Court held that the European Commission had failed to show that this requirement was not satisfied where (in Sweden) the Annex had been included in the *travaux préparatoires* of the implementing legislation and where these constitute an important aid to legislative interpretation: *Commission v Sweden* (C-478/99) EU:C:2002:281, [2002] E.C.R. I-04147.

[1888] Above, para.38-253.

Act 1977). In the following paragraphs, these terms will be noted and briefly discussed, the examples retaining the letter which they bear in para.1 of the Schedule.

38-301 Exclusion or limitation clauses   Terms which have the object or effect of:

"(a) excluding or limiting the legal liability of a seller or supplier in the event of the death of a consumer or personal injury to the latter resulting from an act or omission of that seller or supplier;

(b) inappropriately excluding or limiting the legal rights of the consumer vis-à-vis the seller or supplier or another party in the event of total or partial non-performance or inadequate performance by the seller or supplier of any of the contractual obligations, including the option of offsetting a debt owed to the seller or supplier against any claim which the consumer may have against him;

...

(q) excluding or hindering the consumer's right to take legal action or exercise any other legal remedy, particularly by requiring the consumer to take disputes exclusively to arbitration not covered by legal provisions, unduly restricting the evidence available to him or imposing on him a burden of proof which, according to the applicable law, should lie with another party to the contract."

Many of the terms within these examples would be classed as exemption clauses within the meaning of the Unfair Contract Terms Act 1977,[1889] or would come within the broader category of contract term falling within s.3(2) of that Act,[1890] but, as earlier noted, the ambit of the controls in the 1977 Act is sometimes narrower than the ambit of the Regulations.[1891] So, for example, a clause in a contract for the purchase of new homes by which the builders/sellers alleged that they were not liable for any failure to carry out the design of the works with proper skill and care was held unfair within the meaning of the 1999 Regulations, even though the purchasers were legally advised.[1892] Moreover, the Regulations are not restrained by any such limiting definitions as are found in the 1977 Act, and, as the OFT has put it:

"If a term achieves the same effect as an unfair exemption clause, it will be unfair whatever its form or mechanism. This applies, for instance, to terms which 'deem' things to be the case, or get consumers to declare that they are—whether they really are or not—with the aim of ensuring no liability arises in the first place."[1893]

An example of a term which requires a declaration may be found in the case of a contract for the provision of medical services under which the consumer/patient declares that he knows medical facts which could only be known with any certainty by experts.[1894] The High Court has found (in circumstances described as unusual) a "withholding notice clause" in the JCT Minor Works standard contract by which the consumer/employer's right of set off can be exercised only if the appropriate

---

[1889] s.13 and see above, Vol.I, para.15-069.
[1890] See above, Vol.I, paras 15-070, 15-084—15-086
[1891] Above, para.38-231.
[1892] *Harrison v Shepherd Ltd* [2011] EWHC 1811 (TCC) at [111]–[113]; affirmed on other grounds [2012] EWCA Civ 904.
[1893] OFT, Unfair Contract Terms Guidance OFT311 (2008), para.1.5. See also CMA, *Consumer law compliance review: cloud storage, Findings report* (May 27, 2016), above, para.38-221 (note), paras 5.59–5.66 (on exclusions or limitations of liability in contract for the provision of "cloud computing" services).
[1894] OFT, Unfair Contract Terms Guidance OFT311, Annex A, p.8.

notice has been served in time to the building contractor to be unfair within the meaning of the Regulations.[1895] Moreover, the OFT interpreted the impact of clauses which limit the consumer's right to offset a debt broadly. So, in its view:

"There is no objection to terms which state the consumer's normal legal obligation to pay promptly and in full what is properly owing—that is, the full price, on satisfactory completion of the contract. But suspicion falls on terms which say, or clearly imply, that the consumer must in all cases complete his payment of the whole contract price, without any deduction, as soon as the supplier chooses to regard his side of the bargain as finished. They are likely to be seen as excluding the right of set-off even if they do not actually mention that right."[1896]

And in *Aziz*[1897] the Court of Justice of the EU saw para.1(q) of the Annex to the Directive[1898] as relevant to the fairness of a term under which a lender under a long-term contract of loan secured by a mortgage of residential premises was able unilaterally to determine the amount of debt unpaid, this having considerable procedural advantages under the national procedural law applicable. In these circumstances, the national court

"... must in particular assess whether and, if appropriate, to what extent, the term in question derogates from the rules applicable in the absence of agreement between the parties, so as to make it more difficult for the consumer, given the procedural means at his disposal, to take legal action and exercise rights of the defence."[1899]

Arbitration and adjudication clauses   Paragraph 1(q) quoted above,[1900] refers to   **38-302**
a term which requires a "consumer to take disputes exclusively to arbitration not covered by legal provisions".[1901] This may refer to arbitration or adjudication clauses which give no option to the consumer. Here, it has been specifically provided that an arbitration clause in a "consumer contract"[1902] is deemed necessarily unfair where it relates to a claim for a "modest amount" set at the time of writing at £5,000.[1903] However, even where a claim for more than this amount is subject under a

---

[1895] *Domsalla v Dyason* [2007] EWHC 1174 (TCC), at [94]–[97]. cf. *West v Ian Finlay and Associates* [2014] EWCA Civ 316, [2014] B.L.R. 324 ("net contribution clause" whose effect was to limit the liability of an architect to its own reasonable responsibility for the loss or damage suffered by its employer not unfair in the circumstances): see above, para.38-273.

[1896] *Unfair Contract Terms Guidance* OFT311 (2008), para.2.5.3.

[1897] *Aziz v Caixa d'Estalvis de Catalunya, Tarragona i Manresa* (C-415/11) of March 14, 2013.

[1898] Implemented in UK law by the 1999 Regulations Sch.2 para.1(q).

[1899] *Aziz* (C-415/11) at para.75.

[1900] See above, para.38-301.

[1901] On the timing of challenge to the validity of an arbitration clause on the grounds of its unfairness, see *Mostaza Claro v Centro Móvil Milenium SL* (C-168/05) EU:C:2006:675, [2006] E.C.R. I-10421; *Asturcom Telecommunicaciones SL v Rodriquez Nogueira* (C-40/08) EU:C:2009:615, [2009] E.C.R. I-9579 below, paras 38-331 and 38-333.

[1902] The definition of "consumer contract" is somewhat wider for this purpose than for the purposes of the Regulations in general as it is provided that the consumer may be a legal person as well as a natural one: Arbitration Act 1996 s.90.

[1903] Arbitration Act 1996 ss.89, 90; Unfair Arbitration Agreements (Specified Amount) Order 1999 (SI 1999/2167) (in force January 1, 2000). These provisions are amended by the Consumer Rights Act 2015, which revoked and replaced the 1999 Regulations: below, para.38-412. Under Directive 2013/11/EU on alternative dispute resolution for consumer disputes [2013] O.J. L165/63 (the "ADR Directive") art.10 Member States must ensure that an agreement between a consumer and a trader to submit complaints to an ADR entity (as defined by art.4(1)(h)) is not binding on the consumer if it was concluded before the dispute has materialised and if it has the effect of depriving the consumer of his right to bring an action before the courts for the settlement of the dispute and that in ADR

consumer contract to arbitration or adjudication the relevant term may be held unfair.[1904] So, for example, in *Zealander v Laing Homes Ltd*[1905] the claimant had contracted to buy a new house and certain other items from the defendant, this house being covered in part by the National House Builders Council "Build Mark" Agreement, which contained a compulsory arbitration clause. The Technology and Construction Court refused to stay his claim for damages in respect of defects in the house, holding that the clause was unfair within the meaning of the Regulations in that it created a "significant imbalance" between the parties since the claimant, who had been in a position of disparity with the defendant builder, would have to take separate proceedings for the matters covered by the "Build Mark" Agreement and those falling outside it, which would put the claimant at a financial disadvantage. Similarly, in *Picardi v Cuniberti*,[1906] the same court held unfair a clause in a contract between two consumers and their architect under which either party could refer any dispute or difference to adjudication, the adjudicator to be appointed by the parties or, absent their agreement, nominated by the architect's own professional body. Applying the approach of Lord Bingham of Cornhill in *Director General of Fair Trading v First National Bank Plc*,[1907] the court held that:

"... a procedure which the consumer is required to follow, and which will cause irrecoverable expenditure in either prosecuting or defending it, is something which may hinder the consumer's right to take legal action. The fact that the consumer was deliberately excluded by Parliament from the statutory regime of the [Housing Grants Construction Regeneration Act 1996] reinforces this view."[1908]

On the other hand, in *Westminster Building Co Ltd v Beckingham*[1909] a private individual (the "consumer") who had commissioned a firm of builders to renovate

---

procedures which aim at resolving the dispute by imposing a solution the solution imposed may be binding on the parties only if they were informed of its binding nature in advance and specifically accepted this. This requirement is implemented in UK law by the Alternative Dispute Resolution for Consumer Disputes (Competent Authorities and Information) Regulations 2015 (SI 2015/542) reg.14B (as inserted by SI 2015/1392 reg.2(8)) (in force on July 9, 2015) and see further above, para.38-155.

[1904] cf. *Mostaza Claro v Centro Móvil Milenium SL* (C-168/05) EU:C:2006:675, [2006] E.C.R. I-10421 where a Spanish court considered unfair an arbitration clause in a consumer mobile telephone contract which referred all disputes to arbitration and gave the consumer a period of 10 days in which to refuse arbitration or, if she did not, to file submissions and present evidence in her defence. While the ECJ reaffirmed that the question whether a term is unfair within the meaning of the Directive is for national courts (below, para.38-329), A.G. Tizziano noted (at paras [32]–[37] and [49] of his Opinion) that this clause "severely limited" the consumer's fundamental right to a fair hearing.

[1905] (2003) 19 Const. L.J. 350. See also *Mylcrist Builders Ltd v Buck* [2008] EWHC 2172 (TCC), [2009] 2 All E.R. (Comm) 259 at [54]–[60], the court taking into account, inter alia, the low level of the sums involved relative to the costs of arbitration, the clause's lack of transparency as to its effect, and the lack of involvement of the consumer's professional advisers in drafting the contract.

[1906] [2002] EWHC 2923. This decision was strictly obiter given that the court held that the term was not incorporated into the contract at common law.

[1907] [2001] UKHL 52, [2002] 1 A.C. 481, above, para.38-272.

[1908] [2002] EWHC 2923 at [131]. The court also noted that the guidance of the RIBA whose standard form the architect had used, clearly required its members individually to negotiate such an adjudication clause.

[1909] [2004] EWHC 138 (TCC) at [31]. See similarly *Lovell Projects Ltd v Legg* (TCC) [2003] B.L.R. 452. cf. *Bryen & Langley Ltd v Boston* [2005] EWCA Civ 973, [2005] All E.R. (D) 507 (Jul) (arbitration clause in JCT standard contract held binding where the *consumer* imposed it on the supplier); *Heifer International Inc v Christiansen* [2007] EWHC 3015 (TCC), [2008] All E.R. (D) 120 (Jan) (Danish arbitration clause fair as inserted by consumer's own lawyers: the Regulations were "not intended to protect clients from their own legal advisers": at [299], per H.H.J. Toulmin Q.C.); and

his property under a contract falling outside the Housing Grants, Regeneration and Construction Act 1996 was held bound by an adjudication clause which it contained since this clause was not unfair in the circumstances: its terms were couched in plain and intelligible language and had been decided upon by the consumer's professional agents, chartered surveyors, who could have given him competent and objective advice as to its existence and effect.[1910] Moreover, in *Du Plessis v Fontgary Leisure Parks Ltd*[1911] the Court of Appeal held that a term of a contract between the owner of a holiday caravan park and the owner of a caravan in respect of use of a designated pitch for 10 years under which any dispute about an increase in pitch fee under a term of the contract could be referred to arbitration only with the support of 51 per cent or more of the park's caravan owners was not unfair under the Regulations, the Court seeing the

> "... good sense of permitting arbitration only if it was requested by a substantial body of caravan owners. Pitch fees had to be set consistently for the whole park. It would not be practicable to administer the leisure park if pitch fees were negotiated or determined on an individual basis."[1912]

Choice of jurisdiction clauses[1913]   In *Océano Grupo Editorial SA v Murciano Quintero* the European Court of Justice held that a choice of local jurisdiction clause in a consumer contract which purported to give jurisdiction to the court where the business supplier was established even though the consumers were domiciled in another part of Spain was unfair within the meaning of art.3 of the Unfair Terms in Consumer Contracts Directive 1993, the European Court seeing this type of term as falling within the category set out in subpara.(q) of para.1 of the Annex to that Directive.[1914] While this aspect of the European Court's decision has no direct significance for English law, in *Standard Bank London Ltd v Apostolakis (No.2)* its impact was extended by analogy to a choice of *national* jurisdiction clause.[1915] In that case, the defendants were two wealthy individuals resident in Greece who had entered foreign exchange contracts with a bank in Athens and who had commenced proceedings on the contracts in Athens. The claimant bank failed in its proceedings in England for an injunction to restrain the defendants from continuing their proceedings in Greece. Steel J. expressed the view that, whether or not the case fell within art.13 of the Brussels Convention so as to give the Greek courts exclusive jurisdiction,[1916] the term which gave exclusive jurisdiction to the English courts was unfair within the meaning of the Regulations given the cost and inconvenience of requiring the defendants to defend an action in England, the contrast with this requirement and the claimant's reservation to itself of a right to sue the defendants in England or in any country where they had assets or were

38-303

---

see above, para.38-244.
[1910] See similarly *Khurana v Webster Construction Ltd* [2015] EWHC 758 (TCC) at [53].
[1911] [2012] EWCA Civ 409 and see also below, para.38-313.
[1912] [2012] EWCA Civ 409 at [57], per Jackson L.J. (with whom Lloyd and Ward L.JJ. agreed).
[1913] cf. the position as regards choice of law clauses discussed below, para.38-321.
[1914] *Océano Grupo Editorial SA v Murciano Quintero* (C-240/98 to C-244/98) EU:C:2000:346, [2000] E.C.R. I-4941, especially at [22] and see below, para.38-331.
[1915] [2001] Lloyd's Rep. Bank 240.
[1916] This was the main ground of the decision: *Apostolakis (No.2)* [2001] Lloyd's Rep. Bank 240 at [40]. The equivalent provision of art.13 of the Brussels Convention is now found in Regulation (EU) 1215/2012 of December 12, 2012 on jurisdiction and the recognition and enforcement of judgments in civil and commercial matters (recast) ("the Brussels Ibis Regulation") and see especially arts 17–19.

amenable to suit and the fact that the defendants had been faced with "potentially confusing sets of jurisdiction clauses calling for translation and careful explanation", neither of which had taken place.[1917] However, the decision in *Apostolakis (No.2)* was distinguished in *Chopra v Bank of Singapore Ltd* on the basis that the clause in the latter case conferred only non-exclusive jurisdiction, the contract was in a language (English) known to the consumers and was "fairly simple and straightforward"; there was, moreover, no evidence that if they had known about the clause they would not have entered the contract.[1918]

38-304   "Potestative conditions"   Terms which have the object or effect of:

"(c)   ... making an agreement binding on the consumer whereas provision of services by the seller or supplier is subject to a condition whose realisation depends on his own will alone."

It may be thought that in English law such a term may render the contract as a whole void for uncertainty or lack of consideration, in that it appears to give the seller or supplier an effective choice whether or not to do anything under the contract,[1919] a term which in the Romanist terminology is known as a "potestative condition".[1920] This term's presence in the list may be explained by the fact that this result is not uniformly shared throughout the Member States.[1921]

38-305   Unbalanced forfeiture clauses   Terms which have the object or effect of:

"(d)   ... permitting the seller or supplier to retain sums paid by the consumer where the latter decides not to conclude or perform the contract, without providing for the consumer to receive compensation of an equivalent amount from the seller or supplier where the latter is the party cancelling the contract."

The type of terms described in this paragraph include terms under which either a part-payment or deposit paid by a consumer may be forfeited and proved to be a significant object of the OFT's work. In this respect, important factors in the fairness of such a term are the proportion between the sum to be forfeited and any loss to be suffered by the seller or supplier by the consumer's cancellation[1922] and, as para.(d) mentions, the existence of any counter-balancing provision in the contract for the benefit of the consumer.

38-306   Penalty clauses   Terms which have the object or effect of:

[1917] [2001] Lloyd's Rep. Bank 240, 250. It had previously been held that these contracts were "consumer contracts" for the purposes of the 1999 Regulations: *Standard Bank London Ltd v Apostolakis (No.1)* [2000] I.L. Pr. 766 and see above, para.38-039.

[1918] [2015] EWHC 1549 (Ch) at [139]–[140].

[1919] de Moor (1995) 3 *European Review of Private Law* 257, 269 and cf. below, para.38-308. cf. *Spreadex Ltd v Cochrane* [2012] EWHC 1290 (Comm), [2012] Info. T.L.R. 1 at [14]–[16] where it was held that an agreement under which a consumer had access to an online interactive platform for the making of "spread bets" in commodities was not contractually binding for lack of consideration since on its terms the spread betting bookmaker made no commitment as to the provision of the online service, the holding of the consumer's account or the acceptance of any bet made.

[1920] Thomas, *Textbook of Roman Law* (1976), p.237.

[1921] For example, while such a term may lead to the annulment of a contract in French law (being termed a *condition potestative*, see art.1174 C. civ. (as enacted) and Nicholas, *The French Law of Contract*, 2nd edn (1991), pp.159 et seq.), it would not necessarily do so in German law (cf. German Standard Contract Terms Act 1976 para.10(3), replaced from 2000 by BGB para.308(3)).

[1922] OFT, *Unfair contract terms guidance* (2008) OFT311 (above, para.38-221 (note)), para.6.2.

"(e)   requiring any consumer who fails to fulfil his obligation to pay a disproportionately high sum in compensation".

The type of term described in this paragraph bears a considerable similarity to the common law understanding of a "penalty clause", since the disproportionately high nature of a sum to be paid on breach argues in favour of it being a penalty.[1923] Clearly, though, clauses which are penal in their potential effect may be subjected to the test of fairness under the Regulations, whether or not they count as penalties in the common law sense.[1924] So, for example, it has been held that a clause which requires a consumer to pay interest at 8 per cent over the Bank of England current base rate on sums due to the business under the contract 30 days after the issue of an account is unfair within the meaning of the 1999 Regulations, even though it constituted a genuine pre-estimate of damage likely to be suffered by the claimant in the event of non-payment and therefore not a penalty clause under the then accepted approach at common law,[1925] this decision on the unfairness of the term resting principally on the grounds that the term was unusual and not balanced by a similar term governing unpaid monies such as damages which may fall due *to* the consumer.[1926] In *Office of Fair Trading v Ashbourne Management Services Ltd*,[1927] one standard form consumer contract for gym club membership of a year's duration with monthly payments by the consumer contained an express term allowing the business to terminate on the ground of the consumer's breach where the term was not a technical condition and the breach did not require to be repudiatory. Where the term further provided that the consumer was liable for all sums which *would have fallen due* if the contract had not been terminated early on the ground of breach, it was held to be both a penalty at common law and unfair.[1928] By contrast, in another standard form contract for gym membership before the court, a plain and intelligible term allowed termination only for repudiatory breach, and its requirement for accelerated payment of sums which would have fallen due (subject to a discount for this acceleration) was held to be neither a penalty at common law nor unfair within the meaning of the Regulations.[1929]

The question whether the sum to be paid by the consumer is disproportionate **38-307** depends on the nature of the contract and the context more generally. So, a term allowing a person (the alleged consumer) who had agreed to participate in a world voyage by clipper to cancel the contract at a charge of 75 per cent of the price was

---

[1923] See *Cavendish Square Holding BV v Makdessi, ParkingEye Ltd v Beavis* [2015] UKSC 67, [2015] 3 W.L.R. 1373, discussed Vol.I, paras 26-190 et seq. The decision of the SC in *ParkingEye Ltd* in relation to the 1999 Regulations is noted above, para.38-307 and also above, paras 38-275—38-277.

[1924] cf. Vol.I, paras 26-190 et seq. In *Kindlance v Murphy* Unreported December 12, 1997, NI Ch D an "interest acceleration clause" in a contract of mortgage was held unfair within the meaning of the 1994 Regulations. For an example of the upholding as fair of a clause requiring a consumer to pay a sum on his own termination of the contract, see *Gosling v Burrard-Lucas* [1999] 1 C.L. 197. For a further decision on allegedly penalty-like terms in financial services contracts see *Evans v Cherry Tree Finance Ltd* Unreported April 13, 2007, Ch D (early redemption clause with six-month deferment unfair in the circumstances).

[1925] *Munkenbeck & Marshall v Harold* [2005] EWHC 356 (TCC), [2005] All E.R. (D) 227. The common law position was recast by the SC in *Cavendish Square Holding BV v Makdessi, ParkingEye Ltd v Beavis* [2015] UKSC 67, [2015] 3 W.L.R. 1373, discussed Vol.I, paras 26-190 et seq.

[1926] [2005] EWHC 356 (TCC) at [12] and [15].

[1927] [2011] EWHC 1237 (Ch), [2011] E.C.C. 32.

[1928] [2011] EWHC 1237 (Ch) at [188]–[190] referring to *Financings Ltd v Baldock* [1963] 2 Q.B. 104.

[1929] [2011] EWHC 1237 (Ch) at [207] referring to *Lombard North Central Plc v Butterworth* [1987] Q.B. 527.

held to be fair as not disproportionate in the context since that person's commitment to the venture was important.[1930] In *Aziz*[1931] the Court of Justice of the EU considered the proper approach to a term in a long-term contract of loan secured by a mortgage of residential premises which set an annual default interest of 18.75 per cent automatically to sums not paid when due without the need for notice to the debtor. In these circumstances, the European Court advised that the national court must assess the national legal rules which would otherwise apply and compare the rate of default interest (if any) set by law and set by the contract term "in order to determine whether [the latter] is appropriate for securing the attainment of the objectives pursued by it in the Member State concerned and does not go beyond what is necessary to achieve them".[1932] Finally, it should be recalled that the example in paragraph (e) merely sets out a term which "*may* be regarded as unfair".[1933] For example, as earlier noted, in *ParkingEye Ltd v Beavis*[1934] the Supreme Court held that a term in a contract under which a consumer parked for free in a car park for up to two hours, but who incurred a charge of £85 for overstaying this permitted period was not unfair even though this amount did not reflect the potential loss caused by its breach to the managers of the car park,[1935] as the amount was not disproportionate to the legitimate interest of the managers of the car park, its owners and its other users in the efficient management of the car park.[1936]

38-308 **Cancellation clauses**   Terms which have the object or effect of:

"(f)   … authorising the seller or supplier to dissolve the contract on a discretionary basis where the same facility is not granted to the consumer, or permitting the seller or supplier to retain the sums paid for services not yet supplied by him where it is the seller or supplier himself who dissolves the contract."

It could be argued that an executory contract which contains a term permitting either party to "dissolve" it without any prejudicial consequence (such as the payment of expenses or the loss of a deposit) is itself void for lack of consideration, for consideration is illusory where it is alleged to consist of a promise the terms of which leave performance entirely to the discretion of the promisor (unless something else of value in the eyes of the law is required instead).[1937] However, this is clearly not the assumption of the Regulations (nor indeed of the Unfair Contract Terms Act 1977[1938]), which is that such clauses are, in principle, valid. Moreover, from the point of view of consumer protection, it does not help a consumer to say that a clause which allows a seller or supplier to cancel without prejudicial consequence renders the contract as a whole void, for this releases the seller or sup-

---

[1930] *Boyde v Clipper Ventures Plc* 2013 S.C.L.R. 313; 2013 G.W.D. 12-243. The CJEU has held that where more than one term in a consumer contract requires the consumer to pay sums in compensation for failure to perform his obligation, the national court should assess the cumulative effect of all such terms in assessing their disproportionate effect, whether or not the trader actually insists on their enforcement: *Radlinger v Finway a.s.* (C-377/14) April 21, 2016 at paras 92–95.

[1931] *Aziz v Caixa d'Estalvis de Catalunya, Tarragona i Manresa* (C-415/11) March 14, 2013.

[1932] *Aziz* (C-415/11) at para.74. Where such a term is held unfair and not binding on the consumer, the court must not instead apply the national rules otherwise applicable: below, para.38-342 discussing *Banco Bilbao Vizcaya Argentaria SA v Quintano Ujeta* (C-602/13) Order of June 11, 2015.

[1933] 1999 Regulations reg.5(5) (emphasis added); Sch.2 para.1(e).

[1934] [2015] UKSC 67, [2015] 3 W.L.R. 1373 on which see above, para.38-275—38-277.

[1935] [2015] UKSC 67, [2015] 3 W.L.R. 1373 at [97] (concession by the car park's managers).

[1936] See above, para.38-276.

[1937] See above, para.38-304.

[1938] s.3(2)(b)(ii).

plier just the same, whereas a holding that the clause is unfair means merely that the *clause* does not bind the consumer, thereby leaving the *contract* binding for both. Conversely, however, a term which allows a seller or supplier to retain a deposit when the consumer cancels the contract may well be held fair. So, for example, a clause requiring the parents of a pupil accepted at an independent school to give a term's written notice when cancelling their acceptance of a place, failing which a term's fees would be payable has been held fair within the meaning of the Regulations.[1939]

Terms relating to notice in contracts of indeterminate duration Terms which have the object or effect of:

    "(g) ... enabling the seller or supplier to terminate a contract of indeterminate duration without reasonable notice except where there are serious grounds for doing so."

38-309

Terms in a contract of indefinite duration which allow one or other party to terminate it are, in principle, valid in English law, as may be seen from the law governing contracts of employment and partnerships.[1940] Paragraph 1(g) describes a term which seeks to provide for the termination of a contract of indefinite duration without reasonable notice (a concept familiar to the common law) unless there are serious grounds for doing so. The OFT applied this example to a contract for the provision of estate agency services which allowed the agency to cancel the contract at any time, preferring its replacement with a term which allowed termination only on 14 days' notice.[1941] It is to be noted, though, that para.2 of Sch.2 of the 1999 Regulations excludes from the scope of para.1(g) a range of terms in contracts for the supply of financial services, transactions in transferable securities, etc.[1942]

"Automatic extension clauses" Terms which have the object or effect of:

38-310

    "(h) ... automatically extending a contract of fixed duration where the consumer does not indicate otherwise, when the deadline fixed for the consumer to express this desire not to extend the contract is unreasonably early."

Thus, for example, a term in a contract for the provision of a vehicle declamping service which stipulated that the annual contract was to be renewed unless the consumer gave notice not less than four weeks before its expiry was considered potentially unfair by the OFT (it being coupled with a clause requiring the payment of a very high percentage of the annual fee if the period for notice was not

---

[1939] *Broadwater Manor School v Davis* [1999] C.L.Y. 1801 Worthing County Court. See also OFT, *Unfair contract terms guidance* (2008) OFT311 above, para.38-221 (note), paras 6.1–6.2.

[1940] See below, paras 40-162 et seq. as regards employment and the Partnership Act 1890 s.26(1) as regards partnerships.

[1941] OFT, *Unfair contract terms guidance* (2008) OFT311 above, para.38-221 (note), para.7 and Annex I, p.71.

[1942] 1999 Regulations Sch.2 para.2(a) states that: "Paragraph 1(g) is without hindrance to terms by which a supplier of financial services reserves the right to terminate unilaterally a contract of indeterminate duration without notice where there is a valid reason, provided that the supplier is required to inform the other contracting party or parties thereof immediately". Para.2(c) provides that para.1(g) does not apply to: "[T]ransactions in transferable securities, financial instruments and other products or services where the price is linked to fluctuations in a stock exchange quotation or index or a financial market rate that the seller or supplier does not control; and contracts for the purchase or sale of foreign currency, traveller's cheques or international money orders denominated in foreign currency".

observed).[1943]

38-311   Binding terms and the relevance of notice   Terms which have the object or effect of:

> "(i)   irrevocably binding the consumer to terms with which he had no real opportunity of becoming acquainted before the conclusion of the contract."

As has already been noted, this example of a possible unfair term has very important implications.[1944] For the vast majority of consumer contracts written standard terms contain a term which binds the consumer irrevocably to the contract, although some rely simply on a requirement of a consumer's signature. Where a contract does contain such a term, then para.1(i) suggests that *this term* may be unfair in the absence of a real opportunity of knowing about *other terms* of the contract and if it is, *this term* (and therefore the contract as a whole) will not be binding on the consumer.[1945] In this way, the Regulations allow a court to make more onerous requirements of notice than has been the case at common law.[1946]

38-312   Variation clauses[1947]   Terms which have the object or effect of:

> "(j)   ... enabling the seller or supplier to alter the terms of the contract unilaterally without a valid reason which is specified in the contract;
> (k)   enabling the seller or supplier to alter unilaterally without a valid reason any characteristics of the product or service to be provided;
> (l)   providing for the price of goods to be determined at the time of delivery or allowing a seller of goods or supplier of services to increase their price without in both cases giving the consumer the corresponding right to cancel the contract if the final price is too high in relation to the price agreed when the contract was concluded."

These three examples of possibly unfair terms are clearly related, each allowing a seller or supplier to vary an aspect of the contract (whether its terms, its subject matter or its price) to the possible prejudice of the consumer.[1948] First, para.2(b) of Sch.2 to the 1999 Regulations provides that para.1(j) is:

[1943] OFT, *Unfair Contract Terms*, No.2 (September 1996), p.18 and see OFT, *Unfair contract terms guidance* (2008) OFT311, above, para.38-221, n.1270, para.8. See also CMA, *Consumer law compliance review: cloud storage, Findings report* (May 27, 2016), paras 5.50–5.58 (on terms which automatically renew fixed-term contract for the provision of "cloud computing" services), available at *https://www.gov.uk/government/uploads/system/uploads/attachment_data/file/526447/cloud-storage-findings-report.pdf*.

[1944] See above, para.38-285.

[1945] See below, para.38-340.

[1946] See above, Vol.I, paras 13-008 et seq.

[1947] cf. the position under the Consumer Rights Act 2015 (in force October 1, 2015), which provides that certain categories of information provided by the trader about goods or digital content are to be treated as included as a term of the relevant contract and that "any change to any of that information, made before entering into the contract or later, is not effective unless expressly agreed between the consumer and the trader" (2015 Act ss.11(4)–(5) and 12(2)–(3) (goods contracts); ss.36(3)–(4) and 37(2)–(3) (digital content contracts)) and which makes similar provision in respect of information provided by the trader in respect of a services contract (2015 Act s.50(2) and (3)). On these provisions see below, paras 38-105, 38-499 and 38-548 respectively.

[1948] The CMA has expressed concern as to the fairness of contract terms under which the provider of "cloud computer" services reserves to itself broad powers of unilateral variation of the terms of the contract or the characteristics of the services: see CMA, *Consumer law compliance review: cloud storage, Findings report* (May 27, 2016), above, para.38-221 (note), paras 5.24–5.38. In addition to the general controls on variation clauses put in place by the 1999 Regulations and discussed in the text, the Package Travel and Linked Travel Arrangements Regulations 2018 (SI 2018/634) reg.6

"... without hindrance to terms under which a seller or supplier reserved the right to alter unilaterally the conditions of a contract of indeterminate duration, provided that he is required to inform the consumer with reasonable notice and that the consumer is free to dissolve the contract."

So, it would seem that a term which allows variations of contract terms under these conditions is likely to be considered to be fair, but this will depend on the circumstances. So, in *Peabody Trust Governors v Reeve*,[1949] a term in a standard contract of tenancy used by a registered social landlord which purported to reserve to itself:

"... almost *carte blanche* in the field of variations, apart from the areas of rent and statutory protection, so as to provide in effect that the terms of the tenancy agreement will be whatever the [landlord] says they are to be from time to time"

was held unfair: the tenant's right to walk away from the contract in such a context is illusory as he or she has no real choice.[1950] More generally, the OFT considered that:

"... [a] right in a party to alter the terms of the contract after it has been agreed, regardless of the consent of the other party, is under strong suspicion of unfairness ... If a term could be used to force the consumer to accept increased costs or penalties, new requirements, or reduced benefits it is likely to be considered unfair whether or not it is meant to be used in that way."[1951]

On the other hand, a term is more likely to be found fair if it has a narrow effect, for example, allowing variations to reflect changes in the law or where it can be exercised only for clear reasons which are stated in the contract.[1952] Finally, it is to be noted that paras 1(j) and 1(l) are stated as being limited in their scope in various ways regarding certain terms in contracts for the provision of financial services, transactions in transferable securities, etc.[1953]

---

above, para.38-144 (replacing the Package Travel, Package Tours and Package Tours Regulations 1992 (SI 1992/3288) regs 12 and 13, above, para.38-139) makes special provision for the variation of the package travel contracts to which they apply.

[1949] [2008] EWHC 1432 (Ch), [2009] L. & T.R. 6.

[1950] [2008] EWHC 1432 (Ch) at [56]–[57], per Mr G. Moss Q.C.

[1951] OFT, *Unfair contract terms guidance* (2008) OFT311, above, para.38-221 (note), paras 10.1–10.2.

[1952] OFT, *Unfair contract terms guidance* (2008) OFT311, above, para.38-221 (note), para.10.3.

[1953] 1999 Regulations Sch.2 para.2 states that: "(b) Paragraph 1(j) is without hindrance to terms under which a supplier of financial services reserves the right to alter the rate of interest payable by the consumer or due to the latter, or the amount of other charges for financial services without notice where there is a valid reason, provided that the supplier is required to inform the other contracting party or parties thereof at the earliest opportunity and that the latter are free to dissolve the contract immediately; ... (c) Paragraphs 1(g), (j) and (l) do not apply to: transactions in transferable securities, financial instruments and other products or services where the price is linked to fluctuations in a stock exchange quotation or index or a financial market rate that the seller or supplier does not control; contracts for the purchase or sale of foreign currency, traveller's cheques or international money orders denominated in foreign currency; (d) Paragraph 1(l) is without hindrance to price indexation clauses, where lawful, provided that the method by which prices vary is explicitly described." For an example of guidance on the application of the Directive to a price indexation clause see *Engilbertsson v Íslandsbanki hf* (E-25/13) of August 28, 2014 (EFTA Court) at paras 97–98, 141–146 (emphasising the importance of the clarity and quality of information provided to the consumer about such a clause).

38-313   Du Plessis v Fontgary Leisure Parks Ltd[1954]   In *Du Plessis v Fontgary Leisure Parks Ltd* the Court of Appeal considered the fairness under the 1999 Regulations of a term in a licence agreement between the owner of a holiday caravan and the owner of a holiday caravan park (from which the caravan was purchased) in respect of use of a designated pitch for 10 years for a period of just over 10 months each year. Under the contract, the caravan owner paid a pitch fee reviewable every year under a procedure complying with an industry-wide code of practice, this procedure including a possibility of referring the proposed fee increase to a special arbitrator if 51 per cent or more of the caravan owners on the site objected to it. Under the relevant term, any review of the pitch fee by the park owner was to be made having regard to five specified criteria (including changes to the costs of living and sums spent on the facilities) or to "any other relevant factor". A year after the conclusion of the contract, the park owner sought to introduce a grading of pitches so as to charge different fees according to their size and location and it notified all caravan owners (including the claimant) of this intention. The increases were not sent to arbitration as the claimant did not have the support of more than 51 per cent of the caravan owners to do so. After grading, the claimant's pitch fell into the highest grade and her fee chargeable increased from £1,895 to £2,160 and, on her refusal to pay the increase, her contract was terminated and she sold her caravan at a loss. Before the Court of Appeal, the claimant argued that the term of the contract under which the park owner had purported to increase her pitch fee did not as a matter of construction allow increases on the ground of site grading and that, if it did, it was unfair and not binding on her under the 1999 Regulations. The Court held, first, that the increases caused by the introduction of grading fell within the words "any other relevant factor" in the relevant term as a matter of construction, there being no room for application of reg.7(2)'s *contra proferentem* rule as this phrase was not ambiguous.[1955] Secondly, the Court held that this aspect of the relevant term was not unfair under the Regulations as it did not create an imbalance in the parties' rights and obligations to the detriment of the claimant consumer: it formed part of a carefully balanced review procedure, any increase could be challenged by the courts even in the absence of arbitration, and the relevant term did not fall within the paragraphs in the Schedule to the Regulations on which the claimant relied,[1956] noting in particular that:

> "... the method by which the pitch fee would be varied was 'explicitly described', as required by paragraph 2(d) of Schedule 2 to the 1999 Regulations."[1957]

38-314   Invitel case   Subsequently, in *Invitel*[1958] the Court of Justice of the EU set out the criteria to be taken into account by a national court in considering a term in a contract for the supply of telephone services which imposed a fee in respect of payment of invoices by "money order" (or postal order) without specifying the method of the calculation of these fees. The Court of Justice treated such a term as being one which allowed the service provider to amend the fees charged for the service, as it meant that "the consumer pay[s] fees which had not initially been agreed

---

[1954] [2012] EWCA Civ 409 (April 2, 2012).

[1955] [2012] EWCA Civ 409 at [37]–[42] and cf. below, paras 38-347—38-351.

[1956] i.e. 1999 Regulations Sch.2 paras 1(i), (j), (k) and (l).

[1957] [2012] EWCA Civ 409 at [51], per Jackson L.J. (with whom Lloyd and Ward L.JJ. agreed). See further the comment, below, para.38-314.

[1958] *Nemzeti Fogyasztóvédelmi Hatóság v Invitel Távközlési Zrt* (C-472/10) EU:C:2012:242, April 26, 2012 ("*Invitel* (C-472/10)").

between the parties".[1959] Having considered the examples in the "indicative list" of terms in the Annex to the Directive, paras 1(j), 1(l) and 2(b) and (d), the Court held that:

"... in assessing the unfair nature of a term such as that at issue in the main proceedings, the question whether the reasons for, or the method of, the variation of the fees connected with the service provided were specified and whether the consumer had the right to terminate the contract is particularly relevant."[1960]

The actual opportunity of the consumer to examine the terms and their consequences and the service provider's obligation under art.5 of the Directive to draft the terms in plain intelligible language were also relevant.[1961] Overall,

"... the possibility for the consumer to foresee, on the basis of clear, intelligible criteria, the amendments, by a seller or supplier, of the [general business conditions] with regard to the fees connected to the service to be provided is of fundamental importance."[1962]

Where certain aspects of the method of amendment of fees are required by "mandatory statutory or regulatory provisions" within the meaning of art.1(2) of the Directive,[1963] or where those provisions provide a right for the consumer to terminate the contract, then the consumer must be informed of these provisions.[1964] Although the Court of Justice's guidance in *Invitel* was given in the context of a different type of consumer contract and a different type of variation clause,[1965] it is submitted that, had the Court of Appeal in *Du Plessis v Fontgary Leisure Parks Ltd*[1966] had the benefit of the guidance given by the Court of Justice in *Invitel*,[1967] it might have reached a different conclusion on the fairness of the tariff review clause before it in that case. For, while the circumstances taken into account by the Court of Appeal would still have argued in favour of the fairness of the term,[1968] it could have been argued that the term which provided for an increase in the fee payable by the caravan owner (the consumer) having regard to "any other relevant factor" (even though it described the method of variation explicitly) did not allow the caravan owner "*to foresee*, on the basis of clear, intelligible criteria, the amendments" of the fees, a possibility which the Court of Justice in *Invitel* considered to be of "fundamental importance".[1969]

RWE Vertrieb AG   In *RWE Vertrieb AG*[1970] the Court of Justice followed its   **38-315**

[1959] *Invitel* (C-472/10) at para.17.

[1960] *Invitel* (C-472/10) at para.26.

[1961] *Invitel* (C-472/10) at para.27.

[1962] *Invitel* (C-472/10) at para.28.

[1963] Above, para.38-233.

[1964] *Invitel* (C-472/10) at para.28. See also *Engilbertsson v Íslandsbanki hf* (E-25/13) of August 28, 2014 at paras 77, 142–143 and above, para.38-235.

[1965] In *Du Plessis* [2012] EWCA Civ 409 (April 2, 2012), above, para.38-313, the relevant term allowed the trader to vary the fee payable on various grounds according to a prescribed process; in *Invitel* (C-472/10), the relevant term allowed the trader to impose a fee in respect of payments made by money order without specifying the method of calculation of the fee or its amount.

[1966] [2012] EWCA Civ 409 (April 2, 2012), above, para.38-313.

[1967] *Invitel* (C-472/10).

[1968] [2012] EWCA Civ 409 at [47]–[52], above, para.38-313.

[1969] *Invitel* (C-472/10) para.28 (emphasis added).

[1970] *RWE Vertrieb AG v Verbraucherzentrale Nordrhein-Westfalen eV* (C-92/11) EU:C:2013:180, March 21, 2013 ("*RWE Vertrieb AG* (C-92/11)").

earlier approach in *Invitel*[1971] in the context of a standard term in a contract for the supply of gas to consumers which allowed the supplier unilaterally to vary the gas supply price without indicating the grounds, conditions or scope of such a variation.[1972] While accepting that the decision as to the fairness of such a term is for the national court to decide, the Court of Justice emphasised the importance for this purpose of the information provided to the consumer *before* the contract was made, for

"... [i]t is on the basis of that information in particular that he decides whether he wishes to be bound by the terms previously drawn up by the seller or supplier."[1973]"

In the context of assessing a price variation clause, the national court must consider whether the seller or supplier set out in a transparent fashion the reason for and method of the variation of the charges for the service to be provided, so that the consumer can foresee the alterations that may be made and, secondly, whether the consumer has the right to terminate the contract if the charges are in fact altered.[1974] While the Annex to the Directive at several points acknowledges that in contracts of indeterminate length the supplier has a legitimate interest in being able to alter the charge for the service,[1975] a lack of information for the consumer before contract:

"... cannot, in principle, be compensated for by the mere fact that consumers will, during the performance of the contract, be informed in good time of a variation of the charges and of their right to terminate the contract if they do not wish to accept the variation."[1976]

In this way, the strict requirements as to the provision of information for consumers and the acceptance of the possibility of a right in the seller unilaterally to vary the terms of the contract "correspond to a balancing of the interests of the two parties".[1977] Finally, it is also "of fundamental importance ... that the right of termination given to the consumer is not purely formal but can actually be exercised" and, for this purpose, various circumstances should be taken into account, including whether or not the market concerned is competitive.[1978]

38-316 **"Supplier's discretion" clauses** Terms which have the object or effect of:

"(m) ... giving the seller or supplier the right to determine whether the goods or services supplied are in conformity with the contract, or giving him the exclusive right to interpret any term of the contract."

For example, according to the OFT, a term which allows a supplier of goods to

---

[1971] *Invitel* (C-472/10), above, para.38-314.

[1972] For the CJEU's decision on the possible application of art.1(2) of the 1993 Directive to the term in question, see above, para.38-234.

[1973] *RWE Vertrieb AG* (C-92/11) at para.44. This importance was emphasised as regards the particular category of contract by the legislative duties with respect to transparency regarding contract terms and conditions imposed on the suppliers of gas by Directive 2003/55 of June 26, 2003 concerning common rules for the internal market in natural gas and repealing Directive 98/30/EC [2003] O.J. L176/57 art.3(3). The CJEU referred to the "requirements of good faith, balance and transparency" laid down by the 1993 and 2003 directives: *RWE Vertrieb AG* (C-92/11) at para.47.

[1974] *RWE Vertrieb AG* (C-92/11) at paras 48–49, citing *Invitel* (C-472/10) at paras 24, 26 and 28.

[1975] *RWE Vertrieb AG* (C-92/11) at para.40 referring to the 1993 Directive Annex, point 1(j), point 2(b) and also Directive 98/30/EC (above) art.3(3), Annex A, points (a) and (b).

[1976] *RWE Vertrieb AG* (C-92/11) at para.51.

[1977] *RWE Vertrieb AG* (C-92/11) at para.53.

[1978] *RWE Vertrieb AG* (C-92/11) at para.43.

undertake his own test or inspection to determine whether they are faulty would be likely to be unfair, though a term which provides for an independent test or inspection would be more likely to be fair, provided that its cost is not borne by the consumer if a complaint is well-founded.[1979]

"Entire agreement clauses"   Terms which have the object or effect of: **38-317**

"(n)   ... limiting the seller's or supplier's obligation to respect commitments undertaken by his agents or making his commitments subject to compliance with a particular formality."

The first part of this paragraph describes an important group of contract terms, often termed "entire agreement clauses".[1980] These clauses are of various kinds, but in general their aim is to ensure that a court concludes that it was the intention of the parties that a written document contains all the terms of the contract, for in the absence of such a finding a court can look at the oral as well as the written agreement of the parties.[1981] Here, the OFT took a strong view against the fairness of such terms:

"Good faith demands that each party to a contract is bound by his or her promises and by any other statements which help secure the other party's agreement. If a standard-form contract excludes liability for words that do not appear in it, there is scope for consumers to be misled with impunity."[1982]

For example, the OFT considered unfair the following term:

"All the terms of the Contract between the Company and the Customer are contained in the Contract and in these conditions and no oral or written arrangements between the Customer and any agent or representative of the company not contained in the Contract shall be in any way binding upon the Company."[1983]

As will be seen in this illustration, sometimes an entire agreement clause will   **38-318** seek to avoid liability in a seller or supplier by unreasonably restricting or purporting to restrict the authority of its agent.[1984] So, it has been held that where in the context of a particular type of contract (such as for the supply of replacement doors and windows) there is a very clear risk of statements being made by agents which do not conform to the contract's written terms, this risk is:

"... sufficiently great to make it unfair and contrary to the requirement of good faith for a supplier of such products to make use of a term which restricts liability for such statements",

e.g. by requiring any representation or promise made before or at the time of conclu-

---

[1979] OFT, *Unfair contract terms guidance* (2008) OFT311, above, para.38-221 (note), paras 13.2–13.3.
[1980] OFT, *Unfair contract terms guidance* (2008) OFT311, above, para.38-221 (note), para.14.
[1981] See Vol.I, para.13-117 in relation to the "parol evidence rule".
[1982] OFT, *Unfair contract terms guidance* (2008) OFT311, above, para.38-221 (note), para.14.1.1.
[1983] OFT, *Unfair contract terms guidance* (2008) OFT311, above, para.38-221 (note), Annex I, p.96 which notes the substitute term which was considered fair, which allowed the company to state, inter alia, that it "intends to rely upon the written terms set out here and on the other side of this document. If you require any changes, please make sure you ask for these to be put in writing".
[1984] OFT, *Unfair contract terms guidance* (2008) OFT311, above, para.38-221 (note), para.14.1.2. Such a clause attempts to denude the agents of their apparent or ostensible authority: cf. above, paras 31-057 et seq.

sion of the contract to be added to the contract and signed by both parties.[1985] On the other hand, in *Shaftsbury House (Developments) Ltd v Lee*[1986] an entire agreement clause excluding liability for any representations or statements not included in the written agreement in a contract of sale by a developer of an apartment "off plan" was held not unfair within the meaning of the Regulations, although on the facts this decision was hypothetical given that the court had found no actionable misrepresentations in the circumstances. By contrast, in *Djurberg (t/a Hampton Riviera) v Small*, the High Court held an entire agreement clause in a contract for the sale of a luxury house-boat was unfair given the bargaining position of the contracting parties and their dealings.[1987]

38-319 **"Unequal opt out clauses"**   Terms which have the object or effect of:

"(o)   obliging the consumer to fulfil all his obligations where the seller or supplier does not perform his".

An example of such a term may be found in a contract for the provision of airtime by a mobile telephone service which allowed its provider "from time to time without notice to suspend the Network service", but further provided that:

"Notwithstanding any suspension of the Network service ... the Customer shall remain liable for all charges due throughout the period of suspension unless [the supplier] at its sole discretion determines otherwise."[1988]

Not surprisingly, given its width, the OFT considered that this particular example of an "unequal opt out clause" was potentially unfair, and negotiated its replacement with a clause which advised the consumer to arrange insurance to cover any monthly charges and provided for a refund by the provider of the service if the consumer is unable to use the services in certain circumstances for a continuous period of three days.[1989]

38-320 **Assignment clauses**   Terms which have the object or effect of:

"(p)   ... giving the seller or supplier the possibility of transferring his rights and obligations under the contract, where this may serve to reduce the guarantees for the consumer, without the latter's agreement."

According to the OFT:

"If a supplier sells ('assigns') his business, consumers will find themselves dealing with someone else if the contract is a continuing one (like an insurance contract) or, when it is for a single transaction, if any problem arises with the goods or services supplied to them.

[1985] *Office of Fair Trading v MB Designs (Scotland) Ltd* [2005] S.L.T. 691 at [46], per Lord Drummond Young (OH of the Ct of Sess., in the context of granting an interim order under Pt 8 of the Enterprise Act 2002, on which see para.38-361).

[1986] [2010] EWHC 1484 (Ch) at [64]. See similarly *Harrison v Shepherd Ltd* [2011] EWHC 1811 (TCC) at [118]–[120]; affirmed on other grounds [2012] EWCA Civ 904.

[1987] Unreported September 1, 2017, Ch D at [124] discussing together unfairness under the 1999 Regulations and unreasonableness under s.3 of the Misrepresentation Act 1967 and s.11 of the Unfair Contract Terms Act 1977.

[1988] OFT, *Unfair Contract Terms*, Bulletin No.3 (March 1997), p.77 and see generally OFT, *Unfair contract terms guidance* (2008) OFT311 (above, para.38-221 (note)), para.15.

[1989] OFT, *Unfair Contracts Terms*, Bulletin No.3, p.77. See also CMA, *Consumer law compliance review: cloud storage, Findings report* (May 27, 2016) (above, para.38-221 (note)), paras 5.39–5.49.

Their legal position should be unaffected by the 'assignment'. A term is unlikely to be fair if it allows the supplier to sell on to someone else who offers a poorer service."[1990]

One possible solution is for the consumer to be consulted and the assignment to be permitted only if he or she consents or for the supplier's assignment clause to be without prejudice to the consumer's rights.[1991] While para.1(p) does not concern assignment of rights by the consumer, a supplier's assignment clause is particularly likely to be unfair if the contract prevents the consumer from transferring his own rights under the contract, given the reference in the general test of unfairness to the need for rights to be balanced.[1992] And the OFT intervened so as to prevent certain consumer contracts from preventing the assignment by the consumer of his rights under the contract more generally, this being most common as regards express guarantees of goods. In its view:

"Guarantees, while they remain current, can add substantial value to the main subject matter of the contract. If consumers cannot sell something still under guarantee with the benefit of that guarantee, they are effectively deprived of part of what they have paid for."[1993]

On the other hand, the OFT accepted that suppliers have a legitimate interest in ensuring that they are not subject to baseless claims under guarantees and so there is no objection to terms which require the purchaser (or "assignee") of goods, if he or she wishes to rely on the guarantee, to establish that it was properly assigned or that the transfer is subject to the reasonable consent of the supplier.[1994] In a different context, "non-transferable ticketing" in air-travel contracts was the subject of criticism by the OFT.[1995]

Choice of law clauses In *Verein fur Konsumenteninformation v Amazon EU Sarl*, **38-321** the Court of Justice considered the relationship between the fairness under the 1993 Directive of a standard choice of law clause in a consumer contract and the rules governing choice of applicable law in the Rome I Regulation[1996] in the context of term of an online trader's standard contract which designated the law of Luxembourg (which was the place of the trader's "seat") as "applicable to the exclusion of the United Nations Convention on the international sale of goods".[1997] The Court noted that arts 3(1) and 6(1) of the Rome I Regulation recognise that in principle the parties to a consumer contract may choose the law applicable to it, but that art.6(2) adds that, subject to certain conditions, any such choice of law does not "have the result of depriving the consumer of the protection afforded to him by provisions that cannot be derogated from by agreement" under the law of his

---

[1990] OFT, *Unfair contract terms guidance* (2008) OFT311 (above, para.38-221 (note)), para.16.1.
[1991] OFT, *Unfair contract terms guidance* (2008) OFT311 (above, para.38-221 (note)), para.16.2.
[1992] See above, paras 38-265—38-271.
[1993] OFT, *Unfair contract terms guidance* (2008) OFT311 (above, para.38-221 (note)), para.18.4.2. On the enforceability of guarantees under the Sale and Supply of Goods to Consumers Regulations 2002 reg.15, revoked and replaced (as from October 1, 2015) by the Consumer Rights Act 2015 s.30; see below, paras 38-462 and 38-528.
[1994] OFT, *Unfair contract terms guidance* (2008) OFT311 (above, para.38-221 (note)), para.18.4.3.
[1995] OFT, *Unfair Contract Terms*, Bulletin (July 1999), para.1.8.
[1996] C-191/15 July 28, 2016 ("*Amazon EU Sàrl (C-191/15)*"), on which see Ruhl (2018) 55 CML Rev. 201.
[1997] C-191/15 July 28, 2016 ("*Amazon EU Sàrl (C-191/15)*").

habitual residence[1998] and this may include national law rules implementing the 1993 Directive even where they ensure a higher level of protection for the consumer than the Directive requires.[1999] The Court of Justice of the EU therefore considered the proper approach to a national court's consideration of the fairness of such a express choice of law under the 1993 Directive, whose starting point should be the position under the Rome I Regulation, and that therefore:

"... a pre-formulated term on the choice of the applicable law designating the law of the Member State in which the seller or supplier is established is unfair only in so far as it displays certain specific characteristics inherent in its wording or context which cause a significant imbalance in the rights and obligations of the parties."[2000]

For this purpose, the unfairness of a such a term may result from its failure to conform to the requirement of plain and intelligible language by the trader in failing to inform the consumer that the effects of such a term are qualified by the mandatory statutory provisions of the consumer's place of residence provided for his protection.[2001] If the national court finds that the trader has failed to do so and "so leads the consumer into error by giving him the impression that only the law of [the Member State chosen] applies to the contract", then the choice of law clause would itself be an unfair term.[2002]

38-322 **Other potentially unfair terms** The guidance of the OFT (adopted by the CMA[2003]) contains a number of types of terms found in consumer contracts which it considers are likely to be considered to be unfair within the meaning of the Regulations.[2004] These include terms which allow the supplier to impose unfair financial burdens, such as a right to demand payment of unspecified amounts by way of security deposit,[2005] put on the consumer the onus to judge technical matters in which the supplier is expert but in which the consumer is not (for example, placing on a consumer the determination whether a driveway was ready for resurfacing with tarmacadam)[2006]; terms where the apparent supplier of the service states in small print that he acts only as agent for another person (for example, in the provision of a holiday cottage)[2007]; and "unfair enforcement clauses", for example, a term which grants to a seller of goods a right to enter the consumer's home and repossess the goods in certain circumstances without recourse to the court.[2008]

38-323 Apart from these examples, an important type of term which may be thought of as vulnerable under the Regulations is one which allows the seller or supplier to

---

[1998] Regulation (EC) 593/2008 on the law applicable to contractual obligations ("Rome I") [2008] O.J. L177/6.

[1999] *Amazon EU Sàrl* (C-191/15) at para.59 (noting art.8 of the Directive).

[2000] *Amazon EU Sàrl* (C-191/15) at para.67.

[2001] *Amazon EU Sàrl* (C-191/15) at paras 69–70.

[2002] *Amazon EU Sàrl* (C-191/15) at para.71.

[2003] Above, para.38-221, n.1270.

[2004] OFT, *Unfair contract terms guidance* (2008) OFT311 para.18.

[2005] OFT, *Unfair contract terms guidance* (2008) OFT311 para.18.1.2.

[2006] OFT, *Unfair Contract Terms*, Bulletin No.3 (March 1997), p.24.

[2007] OFT, *Unfair Contract Terms*, Bulletin No.3, p.28.

[2008] OFT, *Unfair contract terms guidance* (2008) OFT311 para.18.3.3. As has been seen, a person travelling under a package travel contract may transfer the benefit of that contract, subject to a certain conditions: see the Package Travel and Linked Travel Arrangements Regulations 2018 reg.9 replacing the Package Travel, Package Holidays and Package Tours Regulations 1992 reg.10 (transfer of bookings), above, paras 38-144 and 38-139 respectively.

terminate the contract on a minor breach by the consumer, whether this stems from a very slight breach of a significant term or the breach of a very minor term of the contract (notably, where the contract classes the terms in question as "conditions" as opposed to warranties).[2009] Other types of clauses which may be thought to be potentially unfair are those which restrict a consumer's legal or equitable rights, such as in relation to discharge of a guarantee on variation of the contract or negligence in relation to the security[2010]; a term which permits the supplier to pass on information about the consumer more freely or widely than would otherwise be allowed under the Data Protection Act.[2011] Moreover, it has been held that a contract term which provides that the consumer must indemnify the business in respect of its legal or other costs in any action or proceedings and pay it a reasonable sum in respect of time spent in connection with such an action or proceedings was unfair within the meaning of the 1999 Regulations, even though the court saw the force of the argument that such a term could protect the business against unfair treatment by the customer who could use the business's unrecoverable costs to negotiate a discount on the unpaid contract price: the term remained unbalanced by any similar provision for the benefit of the consumer.[2012] Terms under which an estate agent charged commission on the renewal of a lease by the tenant and on the sale of the property to the tenant have been held unfair, although the court was careful to state that its decision did not mean that all renewal commission clauses were unfair since the clauses in question were capable of operating onerously and not enough had been done to draw them to the attention of the consumer.[2013] On the other hand, it has been held that a term in a sale and leaseback contract under which the tenant/consumer loses the right to the final part of the purchase price (constituting a third of the total figure) on termination of the lease by the landlord under the tenancy agreement (where this final part would otherwise have been be payable on expiry of ten years or the giving up of the tenancy by the tenant) was not unfair within the meaning of the Regulations on the ground that the term did not create a significant imbalance in the rights and obligation of the parties to the detriment of the consumer and was not contrary to the requirement of good faith.[2014] According to Longmore L.J., while it is possible to conceive of circumstances where such a term might create such an imbalance:

"... especially if the original contract price was below the market price and the rental market (or perhaps the sale market) was buoyant at the time of the possession ... the matter has to be judged at the time when the contract is made and it would be equally pos-

---

[2009] See Vol.I, paras 13-019 et seq. and Whittaker in Burrows and Peel, *Contract Terms* (2007), 255, 262–263.

[2010] This example depends on the wider interpretation being given to "consumer contract" as explained above, para.38-226. (Such a term would not come within Sch.2 para.1(b) of the 1999 Regulations as it would not relate to a right in respect of the other party's inadequate *performance*.)

[2011] OFT, *Unfair contract terms guidance* (2008) OFT311 Annex I, p.122.

[2012] *Munkenbeck & Marshall v Harold* [2005] EWHC 356 (TCC), [2005] All E.R. (D) 227 at [12]–[15].

[2013] *The Office of Fair Trading v Foxtons Ltd* [2009] EWHC 1681 (Ch), [2009] 29 E.G. 98 (C.S.) at [91]–[95], [101], [103]–[106]. The decision on unfairness of the renewal commission clauses was taken after the court had held that they did not fall within the exclusion of reg.6(2) on the ground that they were not "plain and intelligible" (at [70], [74]), even if they formed part of the "core bargain".

[2014] *UK Housing Alliance (North West) Ltd v Francis* [2010] EWCA Civ 117, [2010] Bus. L.R. 1034, especially at [27]–[29]. cf. *Solitaire Property Management Co Ltd v Holden* [2012] UKUT 86 (LC) at [34] (term under which landlord holds funds supplied by tenant in case of "temporary deficiency" in moneys available to meet service charge expenses found fair).

sible to envisage a stagnant market in which the landlord would find it difficult to re-let the property or even re-sell it. In those circumstances the retention of what is less than one third of the price does not cause any imbalance let alone a significant one".[2015]

And it has been held that a term in a loan agreement under which the lender was entitled to recover the legal and other costs of enforcing its terms and recovering the money did not cause any significant imbalance in the parties' rights and obligations to the detriment of the consumer and was not unfair.[2016]

(ee)   The Timeframe for Assessment of the Fairness of a Term

38-324   **General**   While it was common ground in the *First National Bank* case that:

> "... fairness must be judged as at the date the contract is made, although account may properly be taken of the likely effect of any term that is then agreed and said to be unfair ..."[2017]

on examination the issue of the relevant time for the assessment of fairness is not without difficulty and a distinction needs to be drawn between the assessment of a term as between the parties to a consumer contract (termed an "assessment *in concreto*" by the European Court) and assessment of a term in the context of preventive measures (termed an "assessment *in abstracto*" by the European Court).[2018]

38-325   **Assessment as between the parties: the timeframe**   As between the parties to a consumer contract, the court assesses the fairness of the terms included in the contract before it and, as earlier explained, the basic test of unfairness focuses on the (purported) effect of the term on the relative rights and obligations of the parties to the contract.[2019] In doing so, the assessment is "concrete" in the sense that it can take into account the particular circumstances of the making of the individual contract: were any terms not easily comprehensible actually explained to the consumer? Did the business bring any pressure to bear on the consumer? More broadly, did the business "deal fairly and equitably with the other party"?[2020] The facts relevant to these questions would *precede* the point at which the contract itself is concluded. In this respect, it is perhaps surprising that reg.6(1) of the 1999 Regulations provides that:

> "... the unfairness of a contractual term shall be assessed taking into account the nature of the goods or services for which the contract was concluded and by referring, *at the time of conclusion of the contract*, to all the circumstances attending the conclusion of the contract,"

[2015] [2010] EWCA Civ 117 at [27].

[2016] *Shaw v Nine Regions Ltd* [2009] EWHC 3553 (QB).

[2017] *Director General of Fair Trading Plc v First National Bank Plc* [2001] UKHL 52, [2002] 1 A.C. 481 at [13], per Lord Bingham, quoted by Andrew Smith J. in *OFT v Abbey National Plc (Bank Charges)* [2008] EWHC 875 (Comm), [2008] 2 All E.R. (Comm) 625 at [442]. See similarly [2009] EWCA Civ 116, [2009] 2 W.L.R. 1286 at [106] (though the CA's decision was reversed on other grounds [2009] UKSC 6, [2010] 1 A.C. 696, above, paras 38-247—38-248). Lord Bingham's proviso accords with the relevance of a term's potential for unfair results in determining its unfair nature: above, para.38-281.

[2018] *Commission v Spain* (C-70/03) EU:C:2004:505, [2004] E.C.R. I-0799 at para.16.

[2019] Above, para.38-266.

[2020] Above, paras 38-266 et seq.

following here exactly the wording of the Directive.[2021] It is submitted, however, that the purpose of setting "the time of conclusion of the contract" as the relevant point of reference is not to exclude prior circumstances but rather to exclude circumstances or facts which occur *after* the conclusion of the contract: in principle the Directive is concerned with the fairness of contract terms not with the fairness of the behaviour of business parties in the course of performance or non-performance of the contract.[2022] In this respect, the timeframe for assessment of fairness of a term was recently explained by the Court of Justice in *Andriciuc*.[2023] In that case consumer/borrowers brought proceedings against the bank/lender in which they challenged the fairness of a term requiring repayment of the loans in a foreign currency where the loans were issued in that same currency on the ground that the term put all the risk of devaluation of the currency of their income on them as consumers without so informing them.[2024] One issue before the Court was whether the significant imbalance in the parties' rights and obligations under the contract has to be evaluated "strictly by reference to the time when the contract was concluded" or whether:

"... that imbalance [may] also extend to the case where, during the performance of the contract, ... performance by the consumer has become excessively burdensome in comparison with the time when the contract was concluded because of significant variations in the exchange rate."[2025]

In this respect, it held that the assessment must be made by reference to the time of the conclusion of the contract[2026]:

"... taking into account of all the circumstances which could have been known to the seller or supplier at that time, and which were of such a nature that they could affect the future performance of the contract, since a contractual term may give rise to an imbalance between the parties which only manifests itself during the performance of the contract."[2027]

In this way, while the assessment must be made as at the time of the conclusion of the contract, the test of unfairness does have a forward-looking aspect, for, as earlier explained, a contract term must be assessed according to its potential for unfairness in the future.[2028]

Assessment as between the parties: "the conclusion of the contract" Given **38-326** what has just been said, the question arises as to when a contract is to be held concluded for this purpose. As was noted by the High Court in *OFT v Abbey*

[2021] 1993 Directive art.4(1) (emphasis added).

[2022] cf. Directive 2005/29 concerning unfair business-to-consumer commercial practices in the internal market [2005] O.J. L149/22 which "applies to unfair business-to-consumer commercial practices, before, during or after a commercial transaction relating to goods or service": see above, para.38-166 and *Pereničovà v SOS finance, spol. sro* (C-453/10) EU:C:2012:144, para.39, above, para.38-278.

[2023] *Andriciuc v Banca Românească* (C-186/16) of September 20, 2017 ("*Andriciuc* (C-186/16)")

[2024] Above, para.38-281.

[2025] *Andriciuc* (C-186/16) at para.17.

[2026] *Andriciuc* (C-186/16) at para.54 referring to 1993 Directive art.4(1) and *Bucura v SC Bancpost SA* (C-348/14) EU:C:2015:447, July 9, 2015 para.48 and cf. above, para.38-281.

[2027] *Andriciuc* (C-186/16) para.54.

[2028] Above, para.38-281.

National Plc,[2029] the meaning or application of the expression "the conclusion of the contract" may give rise to particular difficulty where "new" terms are introduced into the relationship between parties to a contract concluded earlier. It is submitted that the Court of Justice of the EU could wish to take an autonomous view of this issue and could for this purpose draw on European contract law instruments, such as the *Principles of European Contract Law*.[2030] However, it may instead consider that this issue should fall to be determined by national contract laws, taking a lead from the provision with this effect in the Consumer Rights Directive 2011.[2031]

38-327 **Assessment in preventive proceedings: the timeframe** However, the timeframe for the assessment of terms in proceedings brought by the CMA or by "qualifying bodies" under the 1999 Regulations may well differ from the timeframe set for assessment *in concreto*.[2032] For the purpose of preventive measures taken under reg.12 of the 1999 Regulations, the 1993 Directive provides that:

> "Member States shall ensure that, in the interests of consumers and of competitors, adequate and effective means exist to prevent the continued use of unfair terms in contracts concluded with consumers by sellers or suppliers."[2033]

It adds that this shall include action before courts or administrative bodies:

> "... for a decision as to whether contractual terms drawn up for general use are unfair, so that they can apply appropriate and effective means to prevent the continued use of such terms"[2034]

and it makes clear that action can be taken against trade associations to the same end. The European Court described the assessment of contract terms in this way as "*in abstracto*"[2035] and this refers to the characteristic of these proceedings that they do not concern the terms of an individual contract, but rather the terms applicable to contracts of a particular type or types made by a particular business, several businesses or merely recommended for use by a trade association. This "abstract" character means that *individual* circumstances of the conclusion of a contract cannot be taken into account by a court in its assessment of fairness as they will differ from case to case. On the other hand, a court should take into account the general and likely circumstances surrounding the making of contracts in the area concerned

---

[2029] *OFT v Abbey National Plc (Bank Charges)* [2008] EWHC 875 (Comm) at [442]. While upheld by the Court of Appeal, the latter's decision was reversed by the SC on other grounds: [2009] UKSC 6, [2010] 1 A.C. 696, above, paras 38-247—38-248.

[2030] Lando and Beale (eds) *Principles of European Contract Law* Pts I and II (1999), Lando, Clive, Prüm and Zimmermann, *Principles of European Contract Law* Pt III (2003) arts 2:101–2:211; *Principles, Definitions and Model Rules of European Private Law, Draft Common Frame of Reference* (DCFR) prepared by the Study Group for a European Civil Code and the Research Group on EC Private Law (Acquis Group) (OUP, 2010, 6 vols), Vol.I, arts II.-4:101—II.-4:211. cf. above, para.38-229 on the question whether the CJEU would adopt an autonomous view of the concept of "contract" itself.

[2031] art.3(5), above, para.38-063 where other EU legislative provisions to similar effect are noted.

[2032] 1999 Regulations regs 10–13, below, paras 38-353 et seq. The timeframe in respect of the assessment of the fairness or the "plain, intelligible" character of terms in the context of proceedings by "enforcers" under the Enterprise Act 2002 appears to be clear as these proceedings are aimed at orders against persons to stop breaking legislation enacted for consumers where it harms their collective interest: see below, para.38-361.

[2033] 1993 Directive art.7(1).

[2034] 1993 Directive art.7(2).

[2035] *Commission v Spain* (C-70/03) EU:C:2004:505, [2004] E.C.R. I-0799 at para.16.

and this suggests that the timeframe for the assessment of the terms of contracts in preventive proceedings is a present and future one, the court looking at the fairness of the terms of the contract (under the basic test) as at the date of the proceedings taking into account the *likely future* circumstances of the actual conclusion of contracts under the terms in question.[2036]

"Continued use"   The Regulations refer to the prevention of the "continued use" of unfair terms: does this refer to the continued use of terms in contracts already concluded between consumers and businesses or only to the continued use of terms for the making of future contracts? It may be thought that the wording of art.7 of the Directive (on which these preventive measures rest) suggests the latter, as does the way in which the European Court has described these measures (although in a case not addressed to this issue).[2037] However, in *The Office of Fair Trading v Foxtons Ltd* the Court of Appeal held that the preventive measures foreseen by art.7 of the 1993 Directive were intended to cover existing as well as future contracts, so that an injunction could be granted under reg.12 of the 1999 Regulations so as to prevent a business from relying on a term found unfair for their purposes in contracts already existing between that business and consumers.[2038]   **38-328**

(ff)   The Relative Roles of the Court of Justice of the EU, National Courts and the Parties

The relative roles of the Court of Justice of the EU and national courts in relation to the issue of fairness   In *Océano Grupo Editorial SA v Murciano Quintero* the European Court itself ruled that a domestic jurisdiction clause in a consumer contract was unfair within the meaning of the 1993 Directive with the result that the Spanish court applying for a preliminary ruling and seized of a claim by the business against the consumer was entitled to deny jurisdiction on the ground of the unfairness of this term.[2039] However, when in *Freiburger Kommunalbauten GmbH Baugesellschaft & Co KG v Hofstetter*[2040] the Court of Justice was asked directly by a national court to decide whether a clause in the consumer contract before it was unfair within the meaning of the 1993 Directive, it refused to do so, noting that: **38-329**

> "… in referring to concepts of good faith and significant imbalance between the rights and obligations of the parties, Art.3 of the [1993] Directive merely defines in a general way the factors that render unfair a contractual term that has not been individually negotiated."[2041]

Given the range of factors which the Directive requires to be taken into account in assessing the fairness of a contract term:

[2036] And see below, para.38-357.

[2037] *Commission v Spain* (C-70/03) EU:C:2004:505, [2004] E.C.R. I-0799 at para.16 (referring to the task of courts under art.7 "to assess *in abstracto* the unfair character of a term which may be incorporated into contracts which have not yet been concluded").

[2038] [2009] EWCA Civ 288, [2010] 1 W.L.R. 663 and see below, para.38-358.

[2039] C-240/98 to C-244/98 EU:C:2000:346, [2000] E.C.R. I-4941 and see below, para.38-331.

[2040] C-237/02 EU:C:2004:209, [2004] 2 C.M.L.R. 13.

[2041] [2004] 2 C.M.L.R. 13 at [19]–[21].

"... the consequences of the term under the law applicable to the contract must also be taken into account. This requires that consideration be given to the national law."[2042]

So, while the Court of Justice:

"... may interpret general criteria used by the Community legislation in order to define the concept of unfair terms ... it should not rule on the application of these general criteria to a particular term, which must be considered in the light of the particular circumstances of the case in question."[2043]

As a result, following the general principle that it is for national courts to apply EU law to the facts before them,[2044] it is generally for a national court to decide whether a contract term satisfies the requirements for it to be regarded as unfair within the meaning of art.3(1) of the Directive.[2045] This starting point has been reaffirmed by the Court of Justice in subsequent cases, but, starting with *Invitel*,[2046] the Court has proved very willing to give guidance to the national court of referral as to the "indications which [that court] may or must apply when examining a contractual term" under the test of fairness in the Directive[2047] and, in doing so, has sometimes drawn factors from the illustrative list of terms which may be unfair in the Annex to the Directive.[2048] The Court of Justice has also explained the significance of the reference to good faith.[2049]

38-330 **Judicial discretion and domestic appeals** In the context of the Unfair Contract Terms Act 1977, it has been said that while a decision on the reasonableness of a contract term is not merely an exercise of judicial discretion (and so in practice all but immune to appeal)[2050] there "will sometimes be room for a legitimate differ-

---

[2042] [2004] 2 C.M.L.R. 13 at [21]; e.g. *Director General of Fair Trading Plc v First National Bank Plc* [2001] UKHL 52, [2002] 1 A.C. 481, above, para.38-272.

[2043] [2004] 2 C.M.L.R. 13 at [22] distinguishing (at [23]) its earlier decision in *Océano Grupo Editorial SA v Murciano Quintero* EU:C:2000:346, [2000] E.C.R. I-4941 on the basis that the clause there satisfied all the criteria necessary for it to be judged unfair without consideration of all the circumstances in which the contract was concluded or the advantages and disadvantages which the term would have under the applicable national law. On the general division of functions between the CJEU and national courts, see above, para.38-017.

[2044] Above, para.38-017.

[2045] [2004] 2 C.M.L.R. 13 at [25]. See also *Mostaza Claro v Centro Móvil Milenium SL* (C-168/05) EU:C:2006:675, [2006] E.C.R. I-10421 at [22]–[23].

[2046] *Nemzeti Fogyasztóvédelmi Hatóság v Invitel Távközlési Zrt* (C-472/10) EU:C:2012:242, April 26, 2012 paras 21–22, above, para.38-314; *Aziz v Caixa d'Estalvis de Catalunya, Tarragona i Manresa* (C-415/11) of March 14, 2013 at paras 66–67, above, para.38-270; *RWE Vertrieb AG v Verbraucherzentrale Nordrhein-Westfalen eV* (C-92/11) EU:C:2013:180, March 21, 2013 at paras 48–54, above, para.38-315; *Constructora Principado SA v Menéndez Álvarez* (C-226/12) EU:C:2014:10, January 16, 2014 at paras 20–25, above, para.38-271; *Sebestyén v Kővári* (C-342/13) EU:C:2014:1857, April 3, 2014 at paras 25–35; *Verein für Konsumenteninformation v Amazon EU Sàrl* (C-191/15) July 28, 2016 at paras 65–71, above, para.38-321; *Românească* (C-186/16) of September 20, 2017 at para.58, above, para.38-325.

[2047] *Constructora Principado SA v Menéndez Álvarez* (C-226/12) EU:C:2014:10, January 16, 2014 at para.20.

[2048] C-472/10 EU:C:2012:242, April 26, 2012 at paras 24–28 and see above, para.38-314.

[2049] *Aziz v Caixa d'Estalvis de Catalunya, Tarragona i Manresa* (C-415/11) of March 14, 2013; *Constructora Principado SA v Menéndez Álvarez* (C-226/12) EU:C:2014:10, January 16, 2014, above, paras 38-270—38-271.

[2050] See, e.g. the approach of the courts to the exercise of judicial discretion in relation to the award of a "just sum" under the Law Reform (Frustrated Contracts) Act 1943 s.1(3): Vol.I, para.23-090.

ence of judicial opinion",[2051] this indicating a judicial desire to discourage appeals on the issue of reasonableness.[2052] While the test of unfairness for the purposes of the Regulations has a number of features in common with the test of reasonableness under the 1977 Act,[2053] the composite character of the former requires courts to take into account a number of elements, each of which may require "interpretation" and not merely application. And English appellate courts have not appeared unwilling to reverse first instance decisions on the fairness of a term where they disagreed with their application of the test.[2054]

The power and duty of national courts to intervene of their own initiative In **38-331**
Océano Grupo Editorial SA v Murciano Quintero,[2055] which concerned proceedings brought by suppliers against consumers, the European Court of Justice held that, at least where a term in a consumer contract was clearly unfair within the meaning of the Directive, the national court is entitled to raise the issue of fairness of its own initiative, this being necessary to ensure that the consumer enjoys effective protection in view of the real risk that he is unaware of his rights or encounters difficulties in enforcing them.[2056] In the particular circumstances of the case, the term in question was a choice of local jurisdiction within Spain which chose the court of the place of establishment of the seller or supplier: here, the Spanish court was entitled to refuse jurisdiction on the basis that the clause was unfair within the meaning of the Directive. While in *Océano Grupo Editorial SA*[2057] the Court of Justice was careful to express its view in terms of a *power* in national courts to intervene of their own initiative,[2058] in *Mostaza Claro v Centro Móvil Milenium SL*[2059] the Court of Justice went further, holding that national courts have a duty to intervene of their own initiative in order to ensure that the protection promised by the Directive is effectively ensured for consumers. In that case, the Court ruled that a national court faced with a claim by a consumer for annulment of an arbitral award against her must annul the award if it considers that the arbitration clause on the basis of which the arbitration took place was invalid as an unfair term in a consumer contract within the meaning of the Directive, even though the consumer had not raised the issue of invalidity in the course of the arbitral proceedings and would normally be prevented from raising the issue by a subsequent action for annulment of the award as a matter of national procedural law. According to the Court:

> "The nature and importance of the public interest underlying the protection which the Directive confers on consumers justify ... the national court *being required to assess of its own motion* whether a contractual term is unfair, compensating in this way for the imbalance which exists between the consumer and the seller or supplier."[2060]

[2051] *George Mitchell (Chesterhall) Ltd v Finney Lock Seeds Ltd* [1983] 2 A.C. 803, 816, per Lord Bridge.
[2052] Peel (ed.), *Treitel on The Law of Contract*, 14th edn (2015), para.7-082 and see Vol.I, para.15-101.
[2053] Above, para.38-297.
[2054] e.g. *Director General of Fair Trading v First National Bank Plc* [2001] UKHL 52, [2002] 1 A.C. 481 reversing the Court of Appeal [2000] Q.B. 672 which itself had reversed the HC; *Bryen & Langley Ltd v Boston* [2005] EWCA Civ 973, [2005] All E.R. (D) 507 (Jul).
[2055] C-240/98 to C-244/98 EU:C:2000:346, [2000] E.C.R. I-4941.
[2056] EU:C:2000:346, [2000] E.C.R. I-4941 at [26].
[2057] See also *Cofidis SA v Fredout* (C-473/00) EU:C:2002:705, [2002] E.C.R. I-10875.
[2058] Whittaker (2001) 117 L.Q.R. 215, 217–218 (arguing for recognition of such a duty).
[2059] C-168/05 EU:C:2006:675, [2006] E.C.R. I-10421.
[2060] C-168/05 EU:C:2006:675, at [38] (emphasis added).

In *Pannon GSM Zrt v Erzsébet Sustikné Györfi*[2061] the Court of Justice confirmed that a national court bears an *obligation* to examine of its own motion the issue of the possible fairness of a contract term within the meaning of the Directive, but it restricted this obligation to the situation "where it has available to it the legal and factual elements necessary for that task".[2062] This qualification, whose language echoes the formulation used by the Court in *Freiburger Kommunalbautern*[2063] to describe the role of national courts in assessing the fairness of terms under art.3 of the Directive, recognises that in some situations a national court will not be in a position to come to a view as to the fairness of a term in the circumstances, possibly in part owing to the absence of consumer's own representations or evidence adduced for this purpose. Moreover, the Court of Justice added that:

"In carrying out that obligation, the national court is not ... required under the Directive to exclude the possibility that the term in question may be applicable, if the consumer, after having been informed of it by that court, does not intend to assert its unfair or non-binding status."[2064]

So, a national court's obligation to assess the fairness of a contract term does not mean that it should refuse to apply the term where the consumer itself wishes it, a position which fits entirely with art.6(1)'s provision that an unfair term will "not be binding on the consumer".[2065] Indeed, where a national court, having raised the issue of its own motion, considers that a term in a consumer contract in proceedings before it is unfair within the meaning of the Directive, it must as a general rule inform the parties to the dispute of that fact and invite them to set out their views on the matter by way of application of the principle of *audi alteram partem* found in art.47 of the Charter of Fundamental Rights of the European Union.[2066] As will be seen, under the new law governing the control of unfair terms in consumer contracts under the Consumer Rights Act 2015, legislative provision is made to give explicit effect to this case-law of the Court of Justice.[2067]

38-332 **"National procedural autonomy" and its limits** In *VB Pénzügyi Lizing Zrt v Schneider* the Court of Justice of the EU was asked whether a national court's duty to address the fairness of a term in a consumer contract meant that it is obliged to undertake, of its own motion, an examination with a view to establishing the factual and legal elements necessary for this purpose.[2068] In the view of A.G. Trstenjak, EU law does not require:

[2061] C-243/08 EU:C:2009:350, [2009] E.C.R. I-4713.

[2062] C-243/08 at [32] and see *Bucura v SC Bancpost SA* (C-348/14) EU:C:2015:447, July 9, 201 para.44. In *Tomášová v Republic of Slovenská* (C-168/15) EU:C:2016:602 July 28 2016 at paras 33–34 (available only in French), the CJEU held that only on its decision in *Pannon* had it made clear that national courts have an *obligation* to consider the fairness of terms in consumer contracts and that therefore before the date of this decision a national court could not be said to have committed a sufficiently serious breach of EU law by its failure to do so for the purpose of state liability under the *Francovich* principle (on which see Craig and de Búrca, *EU Law*, 6th edn (2015) pp.251 et seq.).

[2063] *Kommunalbauten GmbH Baugesellschaft & Co KG v Hofstetter* (C-237/02) EU:C:2004:209, [2004] 2 C.M.L.R. 13 at [21] and [22] and see above, para.38-329.

[2064] C-243/08 EU:C:2009:350, at [33] and see similarly at [35].

[2065] 1993 Directive art.6(1), below, para.38-339.

[2066] *Banif Plus Bank Zrt v Csipai* (C-472/11) EU:C:2013:88; [2013] W.L.R. (D) 76 at [29]; *Brusse v Jahani BV* (C-488/11) EU:C:2013:341, May 30, 2013 at para.52.

[2067] See 2015 Act s.71 and below, para.38-392.

[2068] C-137/08 EU:C:2010:659 at [45] (although the national court's question had earlier (para.[25]) been expressed in permissive rather than mandatory terms).

"… the national court to undertake an investigation of its own motion for the purpose of obtaining the legal and factual elements necessary to assess the unfairness of a contractual term where it does not have such elements available to it. The powers of the national court are determined rather by national procedural law … [I]n the laws of the Member States, civil law is characterised by the principle that it is for the parties to take the initiative, under which the parties are responsible for submitting all relevant facts on which the court must then base its decision."[2069]

The Court of Justice acknowledged its earlier case-law under which the guarantee of protection intended by the Directive may require positive action by the court unconnected with the actual parties to the contract, but it then identified a two-stage process. So:

"In the exercise of the functions incumbent upon it under the provisions of the Directive, the national court must ascertain whether a contractual term which is the subject of the dispute before it falls within the scope of that Directive. If it does, that court must assess that term, if necessary, of its own motion, in the light of the requirements of consumer protection laid down by that Directive."[2070]

Given that the Directive:

"… applies to any term conferring exclusive territorial jurisdiction which was not individually negotiated appearing in a contract concluded between a seller or supplier and a consumer"

Then:

"… the national court must … in all cases and whatever the rules of its domestic law, determine whether or not the contested term was individually negotiated."[2071]

For this purpose, the force of the burden of proof as to individual negotiation being on the business would appear to mean that a national court would be entitled to assume that a term was not individually negotiated unless the business established otherwise.[2072] The Court of Justice continued that:

"As regards the second stage of that examination, it must be found that the contractual term which is the subject of the dispute in the main proceedings provides, as the referring court states, for the exclusive territorial jurisdiction of a court which is not the court in whose jurisdiction the defendant lives or the one with jurisdiction for the place where the applicant has its registered office but the one which is situated close to the registered office of the appellant both geographically and in terms of transport links."[2073]

Since it had determined in *Océano Grupo Editorial* that a national jurisdiction clause "*must* be regarded as unfair within the meaning of the Article 3 of the Direc-

---

[2069] A.G. Trstenjak's *Opinion* paras 107–116, especially at para.110 (original emphasis) and 115.
[2070] C-137/08 EU:C:2010:659 at para.49. See similarly *Karel de Grote-Hogeschool Katholieke Hogeschool Antwerpen VZW v Kuijpers* (C-147/16) of May 17, 2018 at para.30. It is for a national court to ascertain whether the terms which are the subject of the dispute pending before it fall within the exclusion of "terms which reflect mandatory statutory or regulatory provisions" so as to fall outside the scope of the Directive: *Brusse v Jahani BV* (C-488/11) EU:C:2013:341, May 30, 2013, at para.33 referring to 1993 Directive art.1(2) and see above, paras 38-233—38-240.
[2071] C-137/08 EU:C:2010:659 at [51].
[2072] See above, para.38-243.
[2073] C-137/08 EU:C:2010:659 at [52].

tive",[2074] the Court of Justice did not consider it necessary to address the wider implications of the question addressed to it and, in particular, whether a national court has a power or a duty to examine facts *not* available to it on the face of the documents put before it by the business.[2075]

38-333   Behind this case-law of the Court of Justice is an implicit recognition of the principle that national courts "know the law" (this principle being known widely under the Latin tag *"iura novit curia"*) and specifically that they therefore are on notice as to the ambit of the protection required by the Directive so as to enable them—and indeed to require them—to intervene of their own initiative.[2076] On the other hand, the laws of civil procedure differ very considerably between Member States in terms of the relative roles of the courts and the parties to litigation in the identification of the facts on the basis of which they claim and their characterisation in legal terms, and this realisation forms one reason for the Court's acceptance of the "principle of the procedural autonomy of the Member States".[2077] However, while this principle provides the starting point for the Court of Justice, it then subjects national rules in question to the double test of the principle of effectiveness and the principle of equivalence.[2078] So, for example, in *Asturcom Telecommunicaciones SL v Rodriquez Nogueira*[2079] the Court of Justice of the EU considered whether a national court seized with a claim to enforce an arbitral award

---

[2074] C-137/08 EU:C:2010:659 at [53] (emphasis added) and [54].

[2075] cf. A.G. Trstenjak's interpretation of *Pénzügyi* in *Banco Español de Crédito, SA v Calderón Camino* (C-618/10) EU:C:2012:349 (Opinion of February 14, 2012) para.32, considering that the Court there "imposed on the national court an obligation under EU law to investigate in order to establish the necessary facts and law ... In the absence of precise indications from the Court, it could be assumed that regard should be had to the procedural law of each individual Member State" in determining how precisely this was to be done. For the decision of the CJEU, see below in this paragraph.

[2076] Whittaker (2001) 117 L.Q.R. 215; Whittaker in Leczykiewicz and Weatherill (eds), *The Involvement of EU Law in Private Relationships* (2013) Ch.6. See also above, para.38-020 discussing *Faber v Autobedrijf Hazet Ochten BV* (C-497/13) EU:C:2015:357, June 4, 2015.

[2077] *Cofidis SA v Fredout* (C-473/00) EU:C:2002:705 at para.28; *Asturcom Telecommunicaiones SL v Rodriguez Nogueira* (C-40/08) EU:C:2009:615, [2009] E.C.R. I-9579 at para.38.

[2078] See generally Craig and de Búrca, *EU Law, Text, Cases and Materials*, 6th edn (2015), pp.239 et seq.

[2079] C-40/08 EU:C:2009:615, [2009] E.C.R. I-9579. See also *Banco Español de Crédito, SA v Calderón Camino* (C-618/10) EU:C:2012:349, June 14, 2012. This case concerned, inter alia, the question whether, under a national order for payment procedure a national court must consider the fairness of the terms of a consumer contract on which the basis of which payment is claimed, the term in question being a term fixing the interest rate for late payment. The CJEU distinguished *Pannon* (C-243/08) EU:C:2009:350, above para.38-331 and *Pénzügyi* (C-137/08) EU:C:2010:659, above, para.38-332 on the basis that the case before it concerned the national court's responsibilities in the context of an order for payment procedure before the consumer lodged an objection, holding that the national procedure before it breached the principle of effectiveness as it completely prevented the national court from assessing the fairness of a term relating to late payments in a contract of consumer credit: C-618/10 EU:C:2012:349, at paras 45, 49–57; see similarly *Finanmadrid EFC SA v Albán Zambrano* (C-49/14) EU:C:2016:98, February 18, 2016. See also *Aziz v Caixa d'Estalvis de Catalunya, Tarragona i Manresa* (C-415/11) EU:C:2013:164, March 14, 2013 at paras 50, 59–64; *Sánchez Morcillo v Banco Bilbao Vizcaya Argentaria SA* (C-169/14) EU:C:2014:2099, July 17, 2014; *Banco Santander SA v Sánchez López* (C-598/15) EU:C:2017:945, December 7, 2017 (all three concerning Spanish procedures for the enforcement of mortgages); *Jőrös v Aegon Magyarország Hitel Zrt* (C-397/11) EU:C:2013:340, May 30, 201 at paras 29–38 and *Brusse v Jahani BV* (C-488/11) EU:C:2013:341, May 30, 2013 paras 42–46 (both concerning national rules and the role of *appellate* courts in circumstances where the unfairness of term had not been raised at first instance); *Baczó v Raiffeisen Bank Zrt* (C-567/13) EU:C:2015:88, February 12, 2015 (national rules governing competent national court to hear consumer claims); *ERSTE Bank Hungary Zrt v Sugár* (C-32/14) EU:C:2015:637, October 1, 2015 (effectiveness of the protection of consumers in context of national law governing notaries); *BBVA SA v Peñalva López* (C-8/14) EU:C:2015:731, October 29,

against a consumer where the arbitrators acted under an arbitration clause in a consumer contract can and/or must consider the unfairness of that arbitration clause within the meaning of the 1993 Directive, even where the consumer was neither present in the arbitration proceedings nor applied to the appropriate court for the annulment of the arbitrators' decision (as she was entitled under the applicable national law). The Court of Justice took as its starting point "the principle of res judicata":

"... [i]n the absence of Community legislation in this area, the rules implementing the principle of res judicata are a matter for the national legal order, in accordance with the principle of the procedural autonomy of the Member States. However, those rules must not be less favourable than those governing similar domestic actions (principle of equivalence); nor may they be framed in such a way as to make it in practice impossible or excessively difficult to exercise the rights conferred by Community law (principle of effectiveness)."[2080]

Applying this to the particular circumstances:

"... the need to comply with the principle of effectiveness cannot be stretched so far as to mean that, in circumstances such as those in the main proceedings, a national court is required not only to compensate for a procedural omission on the part of a consumer who is unaware of his rights, as in the case which gave rise to the judgment in *Mostaza Claro*,;[[2081];] but also to make up fully for the total inertia on the part of the consumer concerned who, like the defendant in the main proceedings, neither participated in the main proceeding nor brought an action for annulment of the arbitration award, which therefore became final."[2082]

As regards the principle of equivalence, the Court of Justice held that:

"... the conditions imposed by domestic law under which the courts and tribunals may apply a rule of Community law of their own motion must not be less favourable than those governing the application by those bodies of their own motion of rules of domestic law of the same ranking."[2083]

Given that art.6(1) of the 1993 Directive (which holds unfair terms "not binding on the consumer") is a mandatory rule, where a national court seized with an action for enforcement of a final arbitral award would, under domestic rules of procedure, assess of its own motion whether an arbitration clause was in conflict with domestic rules of this character, then it would be obliged to do so for the purposes of the 1993 Directive, as long as it has available the legal and factual elements necessary for this task.[2084] In this way, the Court of Justice sought to balance the policy of protection of the consumer pursued by the 1993 Directive and the policy of promoting

---

2015 (time-limit for relying on unfairness of terms specified by transitional legislation); *Radlinger v Finway a.s.* (C-377/14) EU:C:2016:283, April 21, 2016 at paras 51–59 (court's duty applies to insolvency proceedings).

[2080] C-40/08 EU:C:2009:615 at para.38.

[2081] C-168/05 EU:C:2006:675, [2006] E.C.R. I-10421.

[2082] C-40/08 EU:C:2009:615 at para.47.

[2083] C-40/08 EU:C:2009:615 at para.49.

[2084] C-40/08 EU:C:2009:615, paras 50–55. In English law under the Arbitration Act 1996 a person subject to an arbitral award may bring proceedings challenging the substantive jurisdiction of that award, whether or not he participated in the arbitral proceedings, but he must normally do so within certain time-limits and subject to certain restrictions: see above, paras 32-157—32-161. Where a person alleged to be a party to arbitral proceedings took no part in them, that person may challenge

the finality of decision-making (even of private arbitral decisions), and, at a more general level, to balance the demands of EU legal principle (or principles) and the so-called principle of the "autonomy" (and therefore integrity of approach) of national procedural laws. By doing so, in this context to an extent the Court has drawn back from its apparently greater willingness to intervene in (and override) national approaches to the relative roles of national courts and the parties to civil litigation previously revealed in *Océano Grupo Editoriale*[2085] and *Mostaza Claro*.[2086] On the other hand, more recently in *Faber* in the context of the Consumer Sales Directive 1999, the Court of Justice showed a greater willingness to use the principle of effectiveness to override national procedural law, notably so as to require a national court to request parties to clarify the facts which they put forward so as to enable it to determine whether or not national law implementing EU consumer protection legislation is applicable.[2087]

38-334 **Collective actions and stays of proceedings** Under the Civil Procedure Rules, the courts possess a power to stay the whole or part of any proceedings or judgment either generally or until a specified date or event.[2088] This power was used to stay the many thousands of proceedings relating to "bank charges" which had been brought by consumers against their banks until the general legal issues relating to the contract terms on the basis of which these charges were imposed were resolved by the courts in proceedings between the OFT against eight major banks for a declaration as to the ambit of the "core exclusion" allowed by art.4(2) of the 1993 Directive.[2089] However, in *Sales Sinués and Drame Ba*[2090] the Court of Justice of the EU considered the lawfulness of the staying of individual actions brought by

---

the arbitral award on the ground that there was no valid arbitral agreement by bringing court proceedings for a declaration or injunction or other appropriate relief, or he may challenge the award on the ground of the arbitral tribunal's lack of substantive jurisdiction: Arbitration Act 1996 ss.72(1)(a) and 67(1)(a) respectively. And where the other party seeks to enforce any such arbitral award by permission of the court, this permission will not be granted where the person against whom it is sought to be enforced shows that the tribunal lacked substantive jurisdiction to make the award, though any such an objection to jurisdiction must be made timeously: Arbitration Act s.73(2), below para.32-186. It is submitted that this national system of challenges to the jurisdiction of an arbitral award (including one grounded on the "non-binding" nature of an arbitration clause unfair within the meaning of the 1993 Directive) would satisfy the principle of effectiveness as explained by the European Court in the *Asturcom Telecommunicaciones SL* case. Moreover, for the purposes of this system of challenges, no distinction is to be made by an English court (whether in proceedings challenging the award or in considering defences to an application to enforce an award) as between a challenge on the ground of the non-binding nature of the arbitration agreement under the 1993 Directive and on any other legal ground which challenges the validity of the arbitration agreement and, in this way, the principle of equivalence is also satisfied.

[2085] C-240/98 to C-244/98 EU:C:2000:346, [2000] E.C.R. I-4941.

[2086] C-168/05 EU:C:2006:675, [2006] E.C.R. I-10421.

[2087] *Faber v Autobedrijf Hazet Ochten BV* (C-497/13) EU:C:2015:357, June 4, 2015 on which see above, para.38-020. cf. A.G. Kokott's view that, where relevant to the fairness of a term of a consumer contract under the Unfair Terms in Consumer Contracts Directive 1993, a national court has an obligation to raise the unfairness of any *commercial practice* within the meaning of the Unfair Commercial Practices Directive 2005: *Margarit Panicello v Hernández Martínez* (C-503/15) EU:C:2017:126, A.G. Opinion of September 15, 2016 at [127]–[128]. The CJEU (judgment of February 16, 2017) did not comment on these issues.

[2088] CPR r.3.1(f).

[2089] *Office of Fair Trading v Abbey National Plc* [2009] UKSC 6, [2010] 1 A.C. 696 at [17] and [61]. For general discussion of this case, see above, paras 38-247—38-248 and 38-264.

[2090] *Sales Sinués v Caixabank SA, Drame Ba v Catalunja Caixa SA* (Joined Cases C-381/14 and C-385/14) EU:C:2016:909, April 14, 2016 ("*Sales Sinués* (Joined Cases C-381/14 and C-385/14)").

consumers pending the outcome of "collective proceedings" on a preliminary reference from a Spanish court. There, individual proceedings had been brought by consumers for the annulment of a particular category of allegedly unfair terms ("interest rate floor clauses") in their contracts of consumer credit with banks, and the latter had asked the courts seized of these proceedings to stay them under a national provision allowing the staying of proceedings with the same subject matter pending the outcome of "collective proceedings" brought by a consumers' association under national legislation implementing art.7 of the 1993 Directive. Under Spanish law, the individual consumers could join the collective proceedings, but only subject to various constraints not imposed in respect of the individual proceedings. The Court of Justice explained the different purposes and legal effects of individual actions by consumers and collective actions under art.7, and that the principle of procedural autonomy allows national laws to establish the rules applicable to those collective actions subject to the principles of equivalence and effectiveness.[2091] As regards the latter, the Court held that it was clear from the national court's reference that the national legal provision under which the consumers' individual actions may be stayed would lead to those consumers no longer being able individually to assert the rights which the 1993 Directive recognises other than by joining the collective proceedings.[2092] This:

> "... is liable to undermine the effectiveness of the protection intended by that directive, in view of the differences in the purpose and nature of the consumer-protection mechanisms given specific expression by those actions."[2093]

For if the consumer joins the collective proceedings, national civil procedure rules would prevent the court which heard them from considering the circumstances relating to the individual consumer contract, the individual consumer would be dependent on the period set for the collective proceedings without consideration of his particular circumstances and he would be subject to further procedural constraints: these rules therefore do not constitute an adequate or effective means of bringing the continued use of unfair terms to an end contrary to art.7[2094]; and as regards the consumer's individual proceedings which would be stayed:

> "... the need to ensure consistency between judicial decisions cannot justify such a lack of effectiveness since ... the difference in nature between judicial control exercised in the context of a collective action and that exercised in the context of an individual action should, in principle, prevent the risk of incompatible judicial decisions."[2095]

Moreover, the "need to avoid overburdening the courts" cannot justify the effective exercise of a consumer's own individual ("subjective") rights.[2096] While the decision in *Sales Sinués and Drame Ba* has no direct application in the English

---

[2091] *Sales Sinués* (Joined Cases C-381/14 and C-385/14) at paras 30–32.
[2092] *Sales Sinués* (Joined Cases C-381/14 and C-385/14) at para.35.
[2093] *Sales Sinués* (Joined Cases C-381/14 and C-385/14) para.36.
[2094] *Sales Sinués* (Joined Cases C-381/14 and C-385/14) at paras 37–39.
[2095] *Sales Sinués* (Joined Cases C-381/14 and C-385/14) at para.41.
[2096] *Sales Sinués* (Joined Cases C-381/14 and C-385/14) at para.42. The judgment of the Court of Justice is expressed in terms of the precluding of a national provision which *requires* the national court *automatically* to suspend the consumer's individual action without considering its effect on the protection of the consumer and without that consumer being able to dissociate himself from the collective proceedings, even though (as A.G. Szpunar made clear at paras 29, 45 and 74) the national provision itself appears to provide a discretion rather than to impose a duty. This is apparently explained by the existence of uncertainty at the national level as to the proper force of the provi-

context, it does emphasise that any power under the English Civil Procedure Rules to stay consumers' individual proceedings must not be exercised in a way which undermines the practical exercise of their own individual rights under the UK legislation implementing the 1993 Directive.

38-335 **The burden of proof as to fairness**   In English law, the decision of an issue such as the reasonableness of a contract term is a matter requiring the allocation of a burden of proof.[2097] So, s.11(5) of the Unfair Contract Terms Act 1977 provides that "[i]t is for those claiming that a contract term or notice satisfies the requirement of reasonableness to show that it does". This provision reverses the normal burden of proof in civil cases at common law according to which burdens of proof rest on a person claiming something to establish it.[2098] By contrast with the 1977 Act, neither the 1999 Regulations nor the 1993 Directive provide a rule for the burden of proof as to the issue of the fairness of a term,[2099] in contrast to the position as to the "individual negotiation" of a term where the burden is placed on the seller or supplier to show that a term is individually negotiated.[2100] In theory, there are three possible approaches which the Court of Justice of the EU could take if the question as to the proper burden of proof as to the fairness of a term were to be submitted to its decision: (i) that the issue of burden of proof as to fairness is a matter for national law; (ii) that an autonomous European view must be taken as to the issue of burden of proof; and (iii) that the assessment of the fairness of a contract term for the purposes of the 1993 Directive is not itself a matter for the imposition of *any* burden of proof.

38-336 **A national or an autonomous rule of burden of proof?**   It is submitted that the case-law of the Court of Justice already noted which holds that it is the duty of national courts to address the question of the fairness of a term in a consumer contract of their own initiative[2101] is incompatible with a simple imposition of the burden of proof on consumers as to the issue of fairness in the normal common law sense, since it assumes that there is no need for the consumer to allege, let alone to establish, its unfairness. Moreover, the European Court's view that the role of national courts in this respect is a matter for EU law (rather than for national law by way of the principle of subsidiarity or under the principle of the procedural autonomy of Member States) suggests that the Court would also see the issue of burden of proof as to unfairness as one on which an autonomous view should be taken, subject to any extension of the protection for consumers which the 1993 Directive allows to Member States.[2102] In this respect, the general rule in the national

---

sion in question.

[2097] At common law, the reasonableness of a covenant in restraint of trade is considered an issue attracting a burden of proof, it being for the person seeking to rely on it to show its reasonableness: above, Vol.I, para.16-126. Some of the laws of other Member States treat issues such as the fairness of a contract term as one for burden of proof. So, e.g. the French legislation implementing the 1993 Directive expressly places the burden of proof on the issue of fairness on the consumer: art.L.132-1, al. 3 *Code de la consommation*.

[2098] See above, Vol.I, para.15-100.

[2099] This remains the case under general rules governing unfair terms in the Consumer Rights Act 2015, below, para.38-393.

[2100] 1993 Directive art.3(2) para.3 and see above, para.38-243.

[2101] See above, paras 38-331 et seq.

[2102] 1993 Directive art.8 and see above, para.38-218.

laws of Member States is that it is for a person to establish what he alleges,[2103] but to this it could be countered that the effectiveness of the protection of consumers requires that the burden of proof should lie on the seller or supplier, as it does in the Unfair Contract Terms Act 1977[2104] and as it does under the 1993 Directive as to the "individual negotiation" of terms.[2105]

"Neutral" assessment of fairness However, it is submitted that the Court of **38-337**
Justice is more likely to hold that the issue of the fairness of a contract term is not itself an issue proper for the imposition of a burden of proof on either party to the contract, but rather for a neutral judicial assessment.[2106] This is the position of the European Commission, which has expressed the view that:

> "... strictly speaking there is no problem concerning the burden of proof, because the unfair nature of a clause is not a matter of facts to be substantiated by the parties concerned, but a matter of law which the court must independently decide upon accord-ing to the rules of law (*jura novit curia*),[2107] Unfairness is therefore very much a matter of law, but potentially may depend on elements of fact which the court may not know and this becomes for burden of proof for one or the other side which may want the clause to be declared unfair or not unfair as the case may be."[2108]

This position may be supported at a textual level by noting the contrast between the Directive's provision of a rule governing the burden of proof as to the "individual negotiation" of a term[2109] (a predominantly factual issue) and the issue of unfair-ness (an issue for judicial assessment). If this way of thinking were followed by the Court of Justice, then a national court would have to decide the issue of the fair-ness of a contract term (whether this issue were raised by the consumer or of its own initiative) on the basis of the facts brought to its attention by the parties. These facts themselves (for example, as to the circumstances in which the contract was concluded[2110]) would remain subject to burdens of proof following the normal rules of the national laws of the Member States (and thereby preserving to this extent the general principle of the procedural autonomy of Member States).[2111] Against this position, however, is the fact that in two recent EU legislative *proposals*, the treat-ment of the control of unfair terms has distinguished between three categories of

---

[2103] "*Actori incumbit probatio*". See, for example, French law: Ghestin and Goubeaux, *Droit civil, Introduction générale*, 3rd edn (1990), p.536; and German law: Stadler in Ebke and Finkin (eds), *Introduction to German Law* (1996), Ch.13, pp.357, 367.

[2104] s.11(5).

[2105] 1993 Directive art.3(2); 1999 Regulations reg.5(4), above, para.38-243.

[2106] cf. the approach of English law to the issue of reasonableness in unfair dismissal. For while an employer bears the burden of proof of showing that dismissal took place for reasons which were "potentially fair", once this has been shown, the tribunal assesses whether or not the employer "acted reasonably or unreasonably" as a "neutral issue", although the parties may adduce facts or argu-ments in support of their positions: *Boys and Girls Welfare Society v McDonald* [1996] I.R.L.R. 129, 132.

[2107] i.e. "The court knows the law" and sometimes found as *curia novit legem*. The idea behind this maxim is that while in civil cases it is for the parties to bring the facts to the court, it is for the courts to apply the law to those facts, even in the absence of any legal submissions by the parties.

[2108] Proceedings of the Conference, "*The Unfair Terms Directive: 5 years On*" (July 1999), *The Implementation of Directive 93/13 into the National Legal Systems*, Final Report to Workshop 3, "*The definition of 'unfairness'*", pp.141–142, available at *http://ec.europa.eu/consumers/archive/cons_int/safe_shop/unf_cont_terms/event29_en.htm*.

[2109] 1993 Directive art.3(2), para.3.

[2110] See above, para.38-285.

[2111] On this principle and its qualifications see above, paras 38-332—38-333.

situation: first, terms (as listed) which are always unfair; secondly, terms (as listed) which are *presumed* to be unfair (where it would be for the trader to establish that a term is *fair*); and, thirdly, other terms (under a general provision) which are unfair if they cause "a significant imbalance in the parties' rights and obligations arising under the contract, to the detriment of the consumer, contrary to good faith and fair dealing".[2112] This tri-partite scheme suggests that, as regards terms falling within the general test of unfairness, it is for the consumer to establish that a term is unfair.

38-338   Finally, it is submitted that the view that the issue of the fairness of a contract term under the Regulations is in principle a matter for a neutral assessment by the court, rather than being itself the object of a burden of proof is equally suitable to proceedings brought by the CMA or by one of the "qualifying bodies" for an injunction in their preventive roles.[2113] One practical difference between the two types of way in which the issue of unfairness arises is that as between contracting parties there is likely to be more discussion as to the facts surrounding the making of the contract (which remain subject to burden of proof), whereas proceedings brought to prevent the continued use or recommendation for use of unfair terms are relatively more "abstract"[2114] and by their nature less likely to require the consideration of facts which need to be established.[2115]

(gg)   The Effects of a Finding That a Term is Unfair

38-339   "Not binding on the consumer"   Article 6(1) of the Directive provides that:

> "Member States shall lay down that unfair terms used in a contract concluded with a consumer by a seller or supplier shall, as provided for under their national law, not be binding on the consumer and that the contract shall continue to bind the parties upon those terms if it is capable of continuing in existence without the unfair terms."

The wording of reg.8 of the 1999 Regulations follows this formulation closely, except that understandably it omits reference to national law.[2116] The idea of an unfair contract term being "not binding" on a consumer was deliberately adopted by the European legislator as a "neutral" way of expressing the effect of a finding of "unfairness", making clear the practical effect which it sought to achieve without adopting any one of the various terminologies or techniques used by national laws in similar circumstances (such as holding the term invalid, a nullity, void or

---

[2112] This was the position under the Proposal for a Regulation on a Common European Sales Law COM(2011) 635 final, Annex I, arts 83–85 CESL (withdrawn by the Commission in December 2014), itself following the scheme of the earlier Directive on Consumer Rights of October 8, 2008 COM(2008) 614/3 final whose principal provisions on unfair terms (arts 30–39) did not appear in the Directive as enacted in 2011: Directive 2011/83/EU on consumer rights [2011] O.J. L304/64.

[2113] See below, paras 38-353 et seq.; cf. *Director General of Fair Trading v First National Bank Plc* [2000] 1 W.L.R. 98, 112 where it is noted that counsel for the DGFT conceded that it was for him to show that the term used by the defendant bank was unfair.

[2114] In *Commission v Spain* (C-70/03) EU:C:2004:505, [2004] E.C.R. I-0799 at para.16 the ECJ distinguished between proceedings between parties to a consumer contract ("assessment in concreto") and "actions for cessation which involve persons or organisations representative of the collective interest of consumers" (under art.7 of the 1993 Directive) ("assessment in abstracto").

[2115] Even here, however, facts may be relevant: e.g. a particular contract term may be more intelligible (and therefore more likely to be fair) if the business which uses it explains its significance either by a brochure or the practice of its agents.

[2116] See similarly Consumer Rights Act 2015 ss.62(1) and (3), 67, below, para.38-401.

"deemed not to have been written").[2117] Moreover, art.6(1)'s reference to an unfair term being "not binding on the consumer" means that a consumer may choose that the term in question *should* apply.[2118] So, for example, the European Court has held that where a national court holds unfair a term which determines internal territorial jurisdiction, it may nevertheless apply that term and take jurisdiction "if the consumer opposes [its] non-application".[2119] Apart from this situation, where a national court has found a term to be unfair of its own motion, it must not apply it.[2120] As a result, a court must be able to establish all the consequences of the finding of the unfairness of a term without waiting for the consumer, who has been fully informed of his rights, to submit a statement requesting that the term be declared invalid.[2121]

Examples of the "non-bindingness" of unfair terms   In the vast majority of cases which concern the unfairness of "incidental terms" the effect of a finding of unfairness is straightforward and unproblematic. So, for example, a consumer is not affected by any purported exercise of any power granted by the term (such as a variation of the price or subject matter of the contract by the seller or supplier); not prejudiced by any allocation of risk indicated by the term (such as contained in an exemption clause); nor is the consumer obliged to conform to a procedure stipulated by the term (such as in the case of an arbitration clause or choice of jurisdiction clause). By contrast, in principle, the seller or supplier remains bound by the term, even if it is unlikely that a consumer would wish to hold him to it (given that ex hypothesi the term purports to cause a significant imbalance in his rights or obligations to his detriment). However, in some cases the "non-bindingness" of a contract term may sometimes lead to the failure of the contract itself[2122] and, in other cases, the effect of "non-bindingness" of a term must be complemented by the non-application of any national law rules which would (in the absence of that term) otherwise apply.[2123]

38-340

"The contract shall continue to bind the parties upon those terms if it is capable of continuing in existence without the unfair terms"   The Court of Justice of the EU has held that the purpose of the 1993 Directive:

38-341

> "... consists in restoring the balance between the parties while in principle preserving the validity of the contract as a whole, not in abolishing all contracts containing unfair terms ... As regards the criteria for assessing whether a contract can, indeed continue to exist without the unfair terms, it must be noted that both the wording of article 6(1) ... and the requirements concerning the legal certainty of economic activities plead in favour of an objective approach in interpreting that provision, so that ... the situation of one of the parties to the contract, in this case the consumer, cannot be regarded as the decisive criterion determining the fate of the contract."[2124]

As a result, under the Directive itself, a national court cannot base its decision on

---

[2117] Tenreiro (1995) *European Review of Private Law* 273, 280 et seq.

[2118] This is explicitly stated by the Consumer Rights Act 2015 s.62(3), below, para.38-401.

[2119] *Pannon GSM Zrt v Erzsébet Sustikné Györfi* (C-243/08) EU:C:2009:350, [2009] E.C.R. I-4713 at [35].

[2120] *Pannon GSM* (C-243/08) EU:C:2009:350, [2009] E.C.R. I-4713 at para.35; *Jőrös v Aegon Magyarország Hitel Zrt* (C-397/11) EU:C:2013:340, May 30, 201 at para.41.

[2121] *Jőrös v Aegon Magyarország Hitel Zrt* (C-397/11) EU:C:2013:340, May 30, 201 at para.42.

[2122] Below, para.38-341.

[2123] Below, para.38-342.

[2124] *Pereničová v SOS finance, spol. sro* (C-453/10) EU:C:2012:144, [2012] 2 C.M.L.R. 28 ("*Pereničová*

the continuance of the contract solely on a possible advantage for the consumer of its annulment,[2125] although it may do so if national law so provides owing to the minimum nature of the harmonisation required by art.8 of the Directive.[2126] By contrast, the Court of Justice has held that a national provision which empowers a national court to *replace* unfair terms with a modified (and fair) term is not compatible with art.6(1) of the Directive.[2127] However, a national court is not precluded "in accordance with the principles of the law of contract, from deleting an unfair term and substituting for it a supplementary provision of national law" (i.e. a national legal rule applicable to the issue governed by the term in the absence of other or contrary agreement[2128]) where this would enable "real balance between the rights and obligations of the parties to be restored" and where otherwise the invalidity of the unfair term would require the court to annul the contract in its entirety with disadvantageous consequences to the consumer.[2129] A key example could be found in the case of a term relating to the main subject matter of the contract which fails the condition set by art.4(2) that it must be "plain and intelligible" and which is found to be unfair and so not binding on the consumer[2130]; if a supplementary rule allows a court to govern the issue of the main subject matter, then reliance on it could rescue the contract from overall invalidity.[2131] A possible example in English law may be found in the position as regards the price in a contract for the sale of goods. If a term setting the price of the goods falls outside the exclusion in reg.6(2) of the 1999 Regulations and is found to be unfair and not binding on the consumer, it could be argued that the court could substitute a "reasonable price" for the price fixed under that contract term by way of s.8 of the Sale of Goods Act 1979, for in this situation the price could be said not to have been "fixed by the contract", left by the contract to be fixed in a manner agreed by the contract or have been determined by the course of dealing between the parties as foreseen by that section.[2132] On the other hand, it could be countered that, where a contract term fixing the price has been found unfair and "not binding" on the consumer, it nevertheless cannot be said that there is no price "fixed by the contract" so as to allow the

---

(C-453/10)") paras 31–32; *Jőrös v Aegon Magyarország Hitel Zrt* (C-397/11) EU:C:2013:340, May 30, 201 at paras 44–48.

[2125] *Pereničovà* (C-453/10) para.33.

[2126] *Pereničovà* (C-453/10) at paras 34–35.

[2127] *Banco Español de Crédito, SA v Calderón Camino* (C-618/10) EU:C:2012:349, June 14, 2012, paras 69–73. See also *Brusse v Jahani BV* (C-488/11) EU:C:2013:341, May 30, 2013 at paras 54–60; *Kásler v OTP Jelzálogbank Zrt* (C-26/13) EU:C:2014:282, April 30, 2014 ("*Kásler* (C-26/13)") at paras 76–79; *Unicaja Banco, SA v Hidalgo Rueda* (C-482/13, C-484/13, C-485/12 and C-487/13) EU:C:2015:21, January 21, 2015 at paras 28–32. See also Opinion of A.G. Wahl, *Banco Santander v Demba* (C-96/16) EU:C:2018:643 at paras 82–92 advising that where a term in a contract of consumer credit fixing default interest has been held not binding, the court may nevertheless impose interest under another term of the contract imposing "ordinary interest" itself not held unfair and so not binding.

[2128] In English law, in principle such a supplementary rule may be fixed by statute (as in the case of rules governing contracts of sale of goods under the Sale of Goods Act 1979) or at common law, whether expressed in terms of a general legal position (such as the law governing termination for repudiatory breach) or by way of implied term.

[2129] *Kásler* (C-26/13) at paras 82–84; *Unicaja Banco, SA v Hidalgo Rueda* (C-482/13, C-484/13, C-485/12 and C-487/13) EU:C:2015:21, January 21, 2015 at para.33.

[2130] See above, para.38-261, 38-262.

[2131] *Kásler* (C-26/13) at paras 81–83.

[2132] Sale of Goods Act 1979 s.8(1) and (2) and see below, paras 44-051—44-052.

application of s.8(3).[2133]

No application of national "supplementary rules" more generally   As has been   **38-342**
noted above, the Court of Justice of the EU allows a national court to apply a
national supplementary rule (that is, one applicable in the absence of other or
contrary agreement[2134]) to govern an issue regulated by a contract term found unfair
and therefore not binding on the consumer, where otherwise the contract would fail
to the prejudice of the consumer, subject to the condition that such an application
would enable a "real balance between the rights and obligations of the parties to be
restored".[2135] However, the Court of Justice has emphasised that this acceptance of
the application of national rules in substitution for a contract term held unfair is
limited to these particular circumstances.[2136] In *Banco Bilbao Vizcaya Argentaria
SA* the strictness of this position for the trader was confirmed by the Court in
considering whether a Spanish court could apply its general rules governing interest on late payments of debts provided by the Spanish Civil Code for the situation
where no contract term setting a rate of interest has been fixed instead of an express
term in a consumer contract of loan setting default interest found unfair under
national legislation implementing the 1993 Directive.[2137] In its Order,[2138] the Court
held that the effect of art.6(1) of the Directive is that:

> "... national courts are bound solely to exclude the application of the unfair contract term
> so that it produces no binding effects on the consumer, without their being empowered
> to revise its content. Indeed, the contract must in principle subsist without any modifica-
> tion other than the suppression of the unfair contract terms to the extent to which such a
> survival of the contract is legally possible under the rules of national law."[2139]

As a result, where a court declares a penalty clause in a consumer contract to be
unfair, art.6(1) "cannot be interpreted as allowing the national court ... to reduce
the amount of the penalty imposed on the consumer instead of excluding entirely

---

[2133] Peel (ed.), *Treitel on The Law of Contract*, 14th edn (2015), para.7-120. cf. Bridge, *The Sale of Goods*, 3rd edn (2014), para.9.44 who notes (without referring to s.8(3) of the 1979 Act) that in these circumstances the absence of a power in the court to rewrite the contract means that the contract can-not continue and so must be unwound. Similar issues would arise in relation to price terms found unfair and not binding in contracts for the provision of services in relation to the Supply of Goods and Services Act 1982 s.15.

[2134] The French expression used is *"une disposition de droit national à caractère supplétif"*. This invokes the classic civil law distinction between legal provisions applying subject to other or contrary agree-ment (*les lois supplétives de volonté* or *ius dispositivum*) and legal provisions applying irrespective of the parties' agreement (*les lois impératives* or *ius cogens*).

[2135] *Kásler v OTP Jelzálogbank Zrt* (C-26/13) EU:C:2014:282, April 30, 2014 at paras 82–84; *Unicaja Banco SA v Hidalgo Rueda* (C-482/13, C-484/13, C-485/12 and C-487/13) EU:C:2015:21, January 21, 2015 ("*Unicaja Banco, SA* (C-482/13, etc.)") at para.33.

[2136] *Unicaja Banco SA* (C-482/13, etc.) at para.33.

[2137] *Banco Bilbao Vizcaya Argentaria SA v Quintano Ujeta* (C-602/13) EU:C:2015:397, Order of June 11, 2015 (available only in French) ("*Bilbao Vizcaya Argentaria SA* (C-602/13)"). The CJEU fol-lowed this ruling closely in very similar circumstances in *Banco Grupo Cajatres SA v Manjón Pinilla* (C-90/14) EU:C:2015:465, July 8, 2015 at paras 33–38.

[2138] The fact that the CJEU decided in the form of an Order rather than a judgment reflects its view that its response to the national court's question could clearly be deduced from its existing case-law: *Bilbao Vizcaya Argentaria SA* (C-602/13), para.29 referring to art.99 of the Court's own rules of procedure.

[2139] *Bilbao Vizcaya Argentaria SA* (C-602/13) at para.33. The translations from the French text of the CJEU's Order here and in the remainder of this paragraph are the editor's.

the application of the clause"[2140]; such a power of revision would "contribute to the elimination of the deterrent effect exercised on traders by the pure and simple non-application of such unfair contract terms as regards consumers", to the extent to which traders would be tempted to use them knowing that, if they were later invalidated, they could still look to the court to protect the interest with which the term was concerned.[2141] Moreover, in the case of a penalty clause such as the default interest clause before it, its annulment would not have any negative consequences for the consumer as the amounts which he or she would have to pay would necessarily be less.[2142] This decision has some potentially radical consequences in the context of English law. First, in the particular context of *Banco Bilbao Vizcaya Argentaria SA*, where a term in a consumer contract imposing a contractual rate interest for late payment of any sum owed by the consumer is held unfair and not binding on the consumer under the 1999 Regulations, a court could not award the trader actual interest losses caused by this late payment even if pleaded and proved as is generally possible at common law,[2143] nor, apparently, could a court exercise a statutory discretion to impose interest in respect of any such late payment.[2144] Secondly, the approach of the Court of Justice to "supplementary provisions of national law" is not restricted to the context of late payments of sums of money. For example, where a term in a consumer contract imposes on the consumer liability to pay a sum of money on breach of contract is held unfair and not binding on the consumer under the 1999 Regulations,[2145] the trader would *not* be entitled to recover damages for any loss actually caused by the consumer's breach under the general common law, as here the common law rules on damages must be viewed as "supplementary rules" which would substitute for the (unfair) term in the consumer contract. Such an effect of a finding of unfairness of a contract term under the 1999 Regulations contrasts strikingly with the effect of a finding that a term is a penalty clause at common law, as such a finding does not prevent the injured party from recovering damages at common law against the party in breach in respect of proven and legally recoverable losses.[2146] It is difficult to foresee, however, how far the approach of the Court of Justice in *Bilbao Vizcaya Argentaria SA* should be taken. For example, if a term in a consumer contract providing a power of termination in the trader for breach of contract by the consumer in certain circumstances were found unfair under the 1999 Regulations, it could be argued that such a finding prevents the trader from relying on the general common law of repudiatory breach so as to terminate the contract in respect of the circumstances foreseen by the term in question. Certainly, such a result would have a strong deterrent effect on traders including unfair termination clauses, and thus contribute to the effectiveness of the protection of consumers. However, even if this were the case, it is submitted that such a result should not prevent the trader from terminating the contract on the

---

[2140] *Bilbao Vizcaya Argentaria SA* (C-602/13) at para.34.

[2141] *Bilbao Vizcaya Argentaria SA* (C-602/13) at para.36.

[2142] *Bilbao Vizcaya Argentaria SA* (C-602/13) at para.39. The CJEU accepted that this lack of negative effect would be "subject to verification by the referring court".

[2143] cf. Vol.I paras 26-273—26-275 explaining the general common law position.

[2144] See Vol.I, paras 26-281—26-286, referring notably to the Senior Courts Act 1981 s.35A.

[2145] Such a contract term is foreseen as one which "may be regarded as unfair" by the 1999 Regulations reg.5(5); Sch.2 para.1(e), see above, paras 38-306—38-307. An example may be found in *Munkenbeck & Marshall v Harold* [2005] EWHC 356 (TCC), [2005] All E.R. (D) 227, above, para.38-306.

[2146] *McGregor on Damages*, 20th edn (2017), paras 15-026—15-027; and see *Cavendish Square Holding BV v Makdessi, ParkingEye Ltd v Beavis* [2015] UKSC 67, [2015] 3 W.L.R. 1373 at [9].

grounds of breach by the consumer on grounds not foreseen by the unfair contract term, whether under a fair (and therefore binding) express term or at common law.

Restitution of money paid by the consumer Neither the 1993 Directive nor the **38-343** 1999 Regulations make express provision regarding any possible restitutionary consequences of a finding that a term is "not binding" on the consumer on the ground of its unfairness. In this respect, art.6(1) of the Directive refers to an unfair term not binding the consumer "as provided for under their national law" and this neutrality as between the conceptual mechanisms of "non-bindingness" (such as invalidity or nullity) could suggest that other possible consequential effects of "non-bindingness" (notably, as to the availability of restitution and its incidents) are similarly a matter for national law. However, in *Gutiérrez Naranjo* the Court of Justice of the EU made clear that the restitutionary consequences of non-bindingness are, in principle, a matter for EU law.[2147] The background to this judgment was that in 2013 the Spanish Supreme Court had held terms in consumer loan contracts providing that the variable interest rate would not go below a certain threshold ("floor clauses") were not transparent and were unfair under Spanish legislation implementing the 1993 Directive, but the same court later held that while the effect of this unfairness was to render the terms invalid, this did not affect claims for restitution in respect of which a judgment with the force of res judicata had been given nor claims in respect of monies paid under the clauses *after* the date of its judgment on unfairness, the latter on the basis of "considerations of legal certainty, good faith and risk of serious economic difficulties".[2148] Advocate General Mengozzi had advised the Court of Justice that this limitation on the temporal effect of its judgment was a matter for Spanish law subject to the principles of equivalence and effectiveness, the latter of which was not infringed as the national court was entitled (exceptionally) to balance the purposes of the 1993 Directive (including its deterrent effect) and "the macroeconomic challenges to the already weakened banking system of a Member State".[2149] However, the Court of Justice disagreed. Taking into account, in particular, that art.6(1) of the 1993 Directive is a:

"… mandatory provision that is intended to replace the formal balance established by the contract between the rights and obligations of the parties with an effective balance that re-establishes equality between them",[2150]

art.6(1):

"… must be interpreted as meaning that a contractual term held to be unfair must be regarded, in principle, as never having existed, so that it cannot have any effect on the consumer. Therefore, the determination by a court that such a term is unfair must, in principle, have the consequence of restoring the consumer to the legal and factual situation that he would have been in if that term had not existed.
It follows that the obligation for the national court to exclude an unfair contract term

---

[2147] *Gutiérrez Naranjo v Cajasur Banco SAU, Palacios Martinez v Banco Bilbao Vizcaya Argentaria SA (BBVA), Banco Popular Español, SA v Irles López* (Joined Cases C-154/15, C-307/15 and C-308/15) EU:C:2016:980, December 21, 2016 ("*Gutiérrez Naranjo* (Joined Cases C-154/15, C-307/15 and C-308/15)").

[2148] Opinion of A.G. Mengozzi, *Gutiérrez Naranjo* (Joined Cases C-154/15, C-307/15 and C-308/15) at para.21 and see also the decision of CJEU in *Gutiérrez Naranjo* at paras 18–26.

[2149] Opinion, *Gutiérrez Naranjo* (Joined Cases C-154/15, C-307/15 and C-308/15) at para.72.

[2150] *Gutiérrez Naranjo* (Joined Cases C-154/15, C-307/15 and C-308/15) at para.55.

imposing the payment of amounts that prove not to be due entails, in principle, a corresponding restitutory [sic] effect in respect of those same amounts."[2151]

The Court of Justice therefore considered that while the reference to national law in art.6(1) means that Member States may define:

"... the detailed rules under which the unfairness of a contractual clause is established and the actual legal effects of that finding are produced",

the consumer must be allowed "a right of restitution of advantages wrongly obtained".[2152] While exceptions to this position may be made in respect of claims subject to res judicata and while reasonable time-limits may be imposed for the bringing of proceedings, only the Court of Justice of the EU itself is entitled to decide upon temporal limitations to be placed on its own interpretations of a rule of EU law.[2153] By contrast, the Spanish Supreme Court's restriction of claims by consumers to payments made before its own decision on the unfairness of the relevant terms was tantamount to depriving the consumers affected of their rights to obtain repayment in full of the amounts overpaid.[2154] The national court therefore had failed to provide the adequate and effective means of preventing the continued use of the relevant unfair terms as required by art.7(1) of the 1993 Directive.[2155]

38-344 The particular issues presented to the Court of Justice in *Gutiérrez Naranjo* are not directly relevant to the interpretation and application of the 1999 Regulations (nor indeed their successor provisions in the Consumer Rights Act Pt 2[2156]) by English courts. However, *Gutiérrez Naranjo* makes clear that EU law requires in principle that a consumer who has paid money under a contract term found unfair has a right to recovery of that money, as in the case of penalty clause, an unfair price variation clause or an unintelligible[2157] and unfair clause setting the price itself. However, the exact legal nature of this recovery and its incidents (for example, as regards any limitation period applicable or even any defence of change of position by the seller or supplier or contributory fault in the consumer) could still be thought to be a matter for national (and therefore English) law, as being "detailed rules" governing the effect of the non-bindingness of the term in question, subject to the qualification that the practical effect of the nature and incidents of the recovery must not prejudice the effectiveness of the consumer's protection.[2158] In terms of the classification of such a claim as a matter of the English law of restitution, it could be thought that recovery of money paid by a consumer could be placed on the ground

---

[2151] *Gutiérrez Naranjo* (Joined Cases C-154/15, C-307/15 and C-308/15) at paras 61–62.
[2152] *Gutiérrez Naranjo* (Joined Cases C-154/15, C-307/15 and C-308/15) at paras 64–66.
[2153] *Gutiérrez Naranjo* (Joined Cases C-154/15, C-307/15 and C-308/15) at paras 67–71.
[2154] *Gutiérrez Naranjo* (Joined Cases C-154/15, C-307/15 and C-308/15) at para.72.
[2155] *Gutiérrez Naranjo* (Joined Cases C-154/15, C-307/15 and C-308/15) at para.73.
[2156] Below, paras 38-365 et seq.
[2157] This further requirement stems from the proviso to the "core exclusion" from the test of unfairness: see above, para.38-261, 38-262.
[2158] *Gutiérrez Naranjo* (Joined Cases C-154/15, C-307/15 and C-308/15) at paras 66 and 69. On limitation of actions cf. *Cofidis CA v Fredout* (C-473/00) EU:C:2002:705, [2002] E.C.R. I-10875 (national limitation period held unable to prevent court intervening as regards the fairness of a contract term) and *Hamilton v Volksbank Filder eG* (C-412/06) EU:C:2008:215, [2008] E.C.R. I-2383 especially A.G. Maduro's Opinion at para.24 ("The existence of a general principle of limitation should therefore be recognised, while leaving the Member States the necessary discretion to implement it in their respective legal systems").

of the failure of basis on which it had been paid (traditionally called failure of consideration)[2159] or possibly on the ground of a mistake of law.[2160]

Terms "not binding" on consumer and third parties Where a contract term **38-345**
does not bind a consumer by reason of the 1999 Regulations, this may in certain circumstances have legal consequences for third parties to the contract. For example, if a term in a consumer contract which stipulates that the rights under it may not be transferred (e.g. a non-transferable air ticket[2161]) is found unfair within the meaning of the Regulations, then if these rights would otherwise be transferable[2162] the consumer would be entitled to assign them to a third party and the third party would receive valid assigned rights under the contract; and if the third party had incited the consumer to assign his rights under the contract knowing of the non-assignment clause, then that third party would nonetheless not be guilty of the tort of inducing breach of contract as the contract would not have been broken.[2163] In the very different context of contingency fee agreements, if a litigant (the consumer) were not bound by a term of a contingency fee agreement setting his advocate's success fee (on the basis that the term was both not "plain and intelligible" and unfair[2164]), then no costs order could be made by a court against a losing defendant (third party to the agreement) in respect of this fee since the court's statutory power to do so is restricted to "fees *payable* under a conditional fee agreement (including one which provides for a success fee)": if the term is not binding against the consumer, then the success fee would not by payable under the agreement.[2165] On the other hand, in principle the protection of the 1999 Regulations extends only to the consumer party of a consumer contract. For example, in *Mayhook v National Car Parks*[2166] a term in a contract of car parking under which the person who contracted was deemed to do so on behalf of the legal owner of the vehicle as well as of himself was held unfair under the 1999 Regulations in that it caused a significant imbalance in the relationship of the car park with the *owner* of the vehicle with the result that the car park was liable to that owner in damages for the wrongful detention of the vehicle for unpaid parking charges. With respect, however, the 1999 Regulations do not protect persons other than the consumer party to a consumer contract, whereas in the above situation the vehicle owner (who may or may not be a "consumer") is not party to the contract of parking and cannot be

---

[2159] See Vol.I, paras 29-057 et seq.

[2160] *Chesterton Global Ltd v Finney* Unreported April 30, 2010, Lambeth County Ct; *Re Welcome Financial Services Ltd* [2015] EWHC 815 (Ch) at [106] and see generally on this ground of recovery Vol.I, paras 29-033—29-058.

[2161] cf. above, para.38-320. cf. also the treatment of contract terms in contracts of sale of tickets for recreational, sporting and cultural events in the UK which provide for the cancellation of the ticket or blacklisting of the buyer on resale of the ticket by the "secondary ticketing" provisions in the Consumer Rights Act 2015 s.91(2), (3), (7) and (8) (in force on May 26, 2015: 2015 Act s.100(4) and see the Consumer Rights Act 2015 (Consequential Amendments) Order 2015 (SI 2015/1726) arts 2–4; Sch. paras 2–5).

[2162] So, for example, the rights in question are not too personal for this purpose: see Vol.I, paras 19-055—19-056.

[2163] On the need for breach of contract (and not mere interference with contract) for this tort see *OGB Ltd v Allan, Douglas v Hello! Ltd, Mainstream Properties Ltd v Young* [2007] UKHL 21, [2008] 1 A.C. 1 at [34] et seq. where the tort was described as being an "accessory" liability to breach of contract.

[2164] See above, para.38-261, 38-262, but cf. above, para.38-341.

[2165] Courts and Legal Services Act 1990 s.58A(6) (emphasis added) and see CPR Pt 44.3A, Practice Direction about Costs supplementing Pts 43–47 CPR para.9.1.

[2166] *Cambridge CC* Unreported November 29, 2012.

made so by a term of the contract to which he or she is not in privity under the general law of privity of contract and agency. The position would be different if the vehicle owner had given its driver actual or ostensible authority to conclude the contract of parking (this not being the case in *Mayhook*), as this would allow the formation of a consumer contract between the car park and the vehicle owner to which the 1999 Regulations could then apply. Finally, more difficult is the position of a person who, while not party to the original contract, enjoys rights under the contract by way of assignment or grant. For example, a landlord (the "trader") may grant a long lease to a tenant (the "consumer"), the contract of tenancy constituting a "consumer contract" for the purposes of the 1999 Regulations.[2167] If the tenant sells the lease to a third party, the question could arise as to whether that third party can claim the benefit of the controls of the 1999 Regulations on the fairness of its terms, even though not party to the original contract and, in some situations, even though not himself a "consumer".[2168] It could be argued that the protections which the 1993 Directive (and therefore the 1999 Regulations) provide are personal to the consumer party to the contract with the trader and therefore cannot be enjoyed by a third party. However, it is submitted that in principle where under the contract of transfer the third party enjoys the *contractual* rights of the consumer, then he should also be able to claim the benefit of the protections of the 1999 Regulations which his own transferor would have enjoyed: the purpose of the requirement of fairness under the 1999 Regulations is to "re-balance" the parties' rights and obligations under the consumer contract and it is these "rebalanced" rights which the third party acquires.[2169]

38-346 Other consequences Apart from the above consequences as between the parties to a consumer contract, the use or recommendation for use by a seller or supplier of an unfair term in a consumer contract may attract preventive measures in the CMA and a number of other "qualifying bodies" under dedicated provisions in the 1999 Regulations.[2170]

(iv) The Requirement of Plain and Intelligible Language

38-347 Regulation 7 of the 1999 Regulations provides that:

"(1) A seller or supplier shall ensure that any written term of a contract is expressed in plain, intelligible language.
(2) If there is any doubt about the meaning of a written term, the interpretation which is most favourable to the consumer shall prevail except in proceedings brought under regulation 12."[2171]

[2167] *London Borough of Newham v Khatun* [2004] EWCA Civ 55, [2005] Q.B. 37 and see above, paras 38-222—38-223.

[2168] cf. the position in *Roundlistic Ltd v Jones* [2016] UKUT 325 (LC) where, however, these points were not raised: on this case, see above, para.38-230. See also *Casehub Ltd v Wolf Cola Ltd* [2017] EWHC 1169 (Ch), [2017] 5 Costs L.R. 835 at [25]–[31] (assignment by consumers of their restitutionary claims under the 1999 Regulations to claimant company held valid) and see further below, para.38-400.

[2169] On the idea that the purpose of the requirement of fairness is to re-balance the parties' rights, see *Aziz v Caixa d'Estalvis de Catalunya, Tarragona i Manresa* (C-415/11) EU:C:2013:164, March 14, 2013 at paras 44–45, on which see, para.38-270.

[2170] See below, paras 38-353 et seq.

[2171] On proceedings brought under reg.12, see below, paras 38-353 et seq.

There are two aspects of this requirement, which is often termed the requirement of transparency: first, relating to its content and, secondly, relating to its effects.

The place of the requirement in the Regulations   It was earlier seen that the   **38-348**
transparency of the terms of consumer contracts (whether written or otherwise) is relevant to their assessment under the test of fairness, even though the more likely position is that a mere failure in "plainness" or "intelligibility" does not without more render a contract term unfair.[2172] However, the requirement in reg.7 of the 1999 Regulations is clearly distinct from the wider test of unfairness and at first sight it appears to focus on the form of drafting of the terms, rather than either their intended legal effect or their accessibility. The requirement has two limbs: terms must be both plain and intelligible. These are distinct as:

"A term might be obscure and difficult to understand at all, but bear only one meaning for anyone who manages to fathom it."[2173]

The OFT indicated what it viewed as the virtues towards which the drafter of a consumer contract should strive and which its own work was aimed at promoting.[2174] Its starting point was that the contracts should normally be comprehensible by the consumer without recourse to legal advice.[2175] As a result, the contract should avoid legal jargon (such as, for example, "representation", "warranty", "consequential damages", "force majeure") and references to a consumer's "statutory rights"; it should express itself in direct and ordinary language, notably by using the first and second person rather than by naming and defining the parties to the contract; and it should minimise the number of cross-references. Headings in the contract may be helpful, and the size of the print should be large enough to be legible without difficulty.[2176]

English courts have accepted that the "plain and intelligible" character of a   **38-349**
contract term is to be assessed from the standpoint of the typical (or average) consumer.[2177] So, for example, it has been held that a term which uses a vague word may not be "plain and intelligible" even though it is not so vague as to render the term void for legal uncertainty.[2178] In this respect:

"Any lawyer worth his salt can usually contrive possible alternative meanings of contractual words, and the fact that this can be done does not of itself make any given language insufficiently plain and intelligible. For that to result the alternative wording, or

---

[2172] Above, paras 38-285—38-286.

[2173] *OFT v Abbey National Plc (Bank Charges)* [2008] EWHC 875 (Comm) at [87], per Andrew Smith J.

[2174] OFT, *Unfair contract terms guidance* (2008) OFT311, above, para.38-221 (note), paras 19.1 et seq. As from April 1, 2014, the OFT was abolished and its functions under the 1999 Regulations taken over by the Competition and Markets Authority ("CMA"), on which see below, paras 38-353 et seq.

[2175] OFT, *Unfair contract terms guidance* (2008) OFT311, above, para.38-221 (note), para.19.3.

[2176] OFT, *Unfair contract terms guidance* (2008) OFT311, above, para.38-221 (note), para.19.4–19.8. It is submitted that the requirement of "plain, intelligible writing" does not affect the language type in which it is to be drawn up, but that this type may be relevant to the test of unfairness: see Whittaker, *Cambridge Yearbook of European Studies* (2006), Vol.8, Ch.10, above para.38-295.

[2177] See above, para.38-044.

[2178] *Office of Fair Trading v Foxtons Ltd* [2009] EWHC 1681 (Ch), [2009] 29 E.G. 98 (C.S.), (2009) 106(30) L.S.G. 14 [60]–[75] especially at [62]; *Office of Fair Trading v Ashbourne Management Services Ltd* [2011] EWHC 1237 (Ch), [2011] E.C.C. 31 at [155]; *Allproperty Claims Ltd v Tang* [2015] EWHC 2198 (QB) at [45].

uncertain effect, must be one of substance or significance, and not merely of legal contrivance."[2179]

It has also been accepted that reg.7(2)'s rule governing "doubt about the meaning of a written term" extends to the case where two sub-clauses in a contract term are entirely contradictory, with the result that the sub-clause which is most favourable to the consumer must prevail as reflecting "the interpretation most favourable to the consumer".[2180] On the other hand, the mere fact that a term may arguably be implied into a written contract does not mean that there is doubt as to the meaning of the written terms themselves.[2181]

38-350 **Broad approach to the requirement of transparency in the CJEU** However, the Court of Justice of the EU has held that the requirement that contract terms are in plain, intelligible language in art.5 of the Directive (which has the same scope as the condition for the "core exclusion" in art.4(2)[2182]) "cannot be ... reduced merely to their being formally and grammatically intelligible".[2183] First, in *RWE Vertrieb AG*[2184] the Court linked the requirement of plain, intelligible language in art.5 of the Directive to recital 20's explanation that "the consumer must actually be given an opportunity to examine all the terms of the contract".[2185] It then added that:

"Information, before concluding a contract, on the terms of the contract and the consequences of concluding it is of fundamental importance for a consumer. It is on the basis of that information in particular that he decides whether he wishes to be bound by the terms previously drawn up by the seller or supplier."[2186]

Later, in *Kásler* the Court held that the requirement meant that a court must determine whether, having regard to all the information provided by the business, including any promotional material or information provided in advance of the conclusion of the contract, "the average consumer, who is reasonably well informed and reasonably observant and circumspect"[2187] would understand not merely the grammatical sense of the words used by the contract term in question but also its

---

[2179] *Office of Fair Trading v Foxtons Ltd* [2009] EWHC 1681 (Ch) at [73], per Mann J. (in the context of the proviso concerning "plain intelligible language" in reg.6(2) of the 1999 Regulations).

[2180] *Peabody Trust Governors v Reeve* [2008] EWHC 1432 (Ch), [1009] L. & T.R. 6 at [30] and [33]; cf. *West v Ian Finlay and Associates* [2014] EWCA Civ 316, [2014] B.L.R. 324 at [30]–[32] where it was held that the relevant term was not ambiguous as the "normal meaning of the words [was] crystal clear". As a result, the interpretative presumption in reg.7(2) of the 1999 Regulations did not apply.

[2181] *The County Homesearch Co (Thames & Chilterns) Ltd v Cowham* [2008] EWCA Civ 26, [2008] 1 W.L.R. 909 at [21]. Regulation 7(2) of the 1999 Regulations has no application where the term is not ambiguous: *Du Plessis v Fontgary Leisure Parks Ltd* [2012] EWCA Civ 409 at [40], above, para.38-313.

[2182] *Kásler v OTP Jelzálogbank Zrt* (C-26/13) EU:C:2014:282, April 30, 2014 ("*Kásler* (C-26/13)") at para.69.

[2183] *Kásler* (C-26/13) at para.71.

[2184] *RWE Vertrieb AG v Verbraucherzentrale Nordrhein-Westfalen eV* (C-92/11) EU:C:2013:180, March 21, 2013 ("*RWE Vertrieb AG* (C-92/11)") above para.38-315; *Verein für Konsumenteninformation v Amazon EU Sàrl* (C-191/15) EU:C:2016:612, July 28, 2016 at paras 67–71 and above, para.38-321.

[2185] *RWE Vertrieb AG* (C-92/11) at para.43.

[2186] *RWE Vertrieb AG* (C-92/11) at para.44.

[2187] On the significance of the "average consumer" see above, para.38-044.

practical consequences for him in his or her own context.[2188] This very demanding and substantive (as opposed to merely formal) approach to the requirement of plain intelligible language clearly has very close links with the Court of Justice's approach to the requirement of *fairness* for the purposes of art.3 of the Directive as seen, notably, in *Invitel*.[2189]

The effects of failure to comply with the requirement of transparency Regulation 7 of the 1999 Regulations refers only to one of the effects of a failure in a term to fulfil the requirement of use of plain and intelligible language: that where there is as a result doubt as to its meaning it must be interpreted in a way most favourable to the consumer.[2190] At first sight this effect does not seem to add much to the traditional general position at common law which has long recognised a rule of construction that an ambiguous written instrument shall be construed against the person who made it (*contra proferentem*), but recent cases indicate that, under the general law, construction *contra proferentem* will be used by courts only where recourse to the context of the contract (its "matrix of fact") has been exhausted,[2191] whereas the requirement in the 1993 Directive (and the 1999 Regulations) is expressed as a legal rule applicable to cases where a term in a consumer contract is ambiguous. Apart from this effect, any failure to fulfil the requirement of plain and intelligible language will attract preventive measures under Pt 8 of the Enterprise Act 2002 and may also attract preventive measures under the 1999 Regulations themselves.[2192] Moreover, as has been noted, a contract term which fails the requirement of transparency will not fall within the "core exclusion" in respect of the test of unfairness.[2193]

(v) Prevention of Avoidance by Choice of Law

Choice of law of non-Member State It is to be noted that, in keeping with the Unfair Contract Terms Act 1977 though subtly differently,[2194] the 1999 Regulations contain a provision aimed at preventing the avoidance of their provisions by an express choice of law. Regulation 9 of the 1999 Regulations provides that:

> "These Regulations shall apply notwithstanding any contract term which applies or purports to apply the law of a non-Member State, if the contract has a close connection with the territory of the Member States."[2195]

While this provision clearly disallows an express choice of law to avoid the application of the Regulations where the law chosen belongs to a non-Member State, it allows the choice of the law of a Member State, relying in this respect on the effect of the Directive to ensure a minimum protection for consumers throughout the

38-351

38-352

[2188] *Kásler* (C-26/13) at paras 71–75 especially at 74 and see para.38-261, 38-262 et seq. on the interpretation and application of the proviso of transparency of the terms otherwise falling within the exclusion in reg.6(2) of the 1999 Regulations (reflecting art.4(2) of the 1993 Directive).

[2189] *Nemzeti Fogyasztóvédelmi Hatóság v Invitel Távközlési Zrt* (C-472/10) EU:C:2012:242, April 26, 2012 and see above, para.38-314.

[2190] *AJ Building and Plastering Ltd v Turner* [2013] EWHC 484 (QB), [2013] Lloyd's Rep. IR at [53]; *Khurana v Webster Construction Ltd* [2015] EWHC 758 (TCC) at [56].

[2191] cf. Vol.I, para.15-012.

[2192] Below, paras 38-355 and 38-361.

[2193] 1999 Regulations reg.6(2), above, para.38-261, 38-262.

[2194] s.27 and see Vol.I, para.30-009.

[2195] cf. Consumer Rights Act 2015 s.74, below, para.38-418.

European Union.[2196] The European Court of Justice has noted that art.6(2) of the 1993 Directive (implemented in English law by reg.9 of the 1999 Regulations) "merely states that the contract is to have a close connection with the territory of the Member States" in order to attract the application of the 1993 Directive's provisions.[2197] This "deliberately vague", "general expression seeks to make it possible to take account of various ties depending on the circumstances of the case" and so while the legislature of a Member State may properly seek to give it concrete effect by the use of presumptions, it cannot circumscribe it by:

> "… a combination of predetermined criteria for ties such as the cumulative conditions as to residence and conclusion of the contract referred to in Art.5 of the Rome Convention."[2198]

Moreover, in addition to this special control of clauses choosing the law of a non-Member State, an express choice of law clause in a consumer contract may be assessed as unfair under the national law implementing the 1993 Directive applicable to its assessment under the Rome I Regulation, as explained earlier.[2199]

(vi)   The Prevention of Unfair Terms

38-353   Introduction   Article 7 of Directive of 1993 requires Member States to:

> "… ensure that, in the interests of consumers and of competitors, adequate and effective means exist to prevent the continued use of unfair terms in contracts concluded with consumers by sellers or suppliers."

And it further provides that these:

> "… means … shall include provisions whereby persons or organizations, having a legitimate interest under national law in protecting consumers, may take action according to the national law concerned before the courts or before the competent administrative bodies for a decision as to whether contractual terms drawn up for general use are unfair, so that they can apply appropriate and effective means to prevent the continued use of such terms."

These requirements were first implemented into English law by imposing duties and granting powers in relation to the policing of unfair terms to the Director General of Fair Trading,[2200] but, while retaining this role for the Director General of Fair Trading, the 1999 Regulations also created similar duties and powers in a number of other bodies ("qualifying bodies"), entrusted with "watch-dog" roles for particular commercial sectors, but one of which—the Consumers' Association—is a private body with a very general concern with the protection of the interests of consumers. Subsequently, there have been a number of adjustments to

---

[2196] cf. the provisions governing choice of law in consumer contracts in EC Regulation 593/2008 on the law applicable to contractual obligations ("Rome I") [2008] O.J. L177/6 arts 3 and 6 see below, Vol.I, paras 30-066 et seq., 30-148 et seq.

[2197] *Commission v Spain* (C-70/03) EU:C:2004:505, [2004] E.C.R. I-0799 at [32]. Article 5 of the Rome Convention was replaced by Regulation (EC) 593/2008 (above, previous note) art.6, which introduced new conditions for the protection of consumers against loss of the protection of rules of the law of their habitual residence by choice of applicable law: below, Vol.I, paras 30-148 et seq.

[2198] EU:C:2004:505, [2004] E.C.R. I-0799 at [32] and [33].

[2199] Above, para.38-321.

[2200] 1994 Regulations reg.8.

the measures available to prevent the use of unfair contract terms. First, the office of the Director General of Fair Trading was replaced with a body corporate, the OFT,[2201] but in 2014 the OFT was itself abolished and its powers under the 1999 Regulations transferred to the Competition and Markets Authority (CMA).[2202] As a result, as amended, the 1999 Regulations provide the CMA and a number of "qualifying bodies" with important powers to police the fairness of contract terms, including powers to receive and consider complaints and powers to apply to a court for an injunction to stop any person caught by the Regulations requirements from using or recommending for us, an unfair contract term drawn up for general use in contracts concluded with consumers.[2203] Secondly, Pt 8 of the Enterprise Act 2002 put in place a further layer of support for the protection of consumers by giving a number of "enforcers" strengthened powers to obtain courts orders (known as "enforcement orders") against businesses which do not comply with their legal obligations to consumers and it included failures by businesses to fulfil the requirements of fairness and of transparency under 1999 Regulations for this purpose.[2204] One effect of these changes was to create the possibility of the cross-border policing of unfair contract terms, as "Community enforcers" recognised by other Member States and published at the European level are empowered to bring proceedings before UK courts.[2205] Finally, the enactment of the Consumer Protection from Unfair Trading Regulations 2008[2206] raises the possibility of preventive measures or criminal offences under these Regulations being used to sanction the use of unfair contract terms.[2207]

Temporal application of enforcement powers provided by the 1999 Regulations **38-354** As earlier noted, the Consumer Rights Act 2015 revoked the 1999 Regulations and replaced its provisions governing unfair terms and their enforcement with its own new provisions,[2208] and the relevant provisions of the 2015 Act were brought into force by an Order in 2015 (the "2015 Order") on October 1, 2015.[2209] However, the 2015 Order provides that the new provisions so brought into force[2210] do not apply to "any contract entered into before 1st October 2015 which would, apart from these provisions, be covered by Parts 1 or 2 of the Act" and provides instead that:

"... the Unfair Terms in Consumer Contracts Regulations 1999 continue to have effect

---

[2201] Enterprise Act 2002 ss.1, 2. This change came into effect on April 1, 2003: Enterprise Act 2002 (Commencement No.2, Transitional and Transitory Provisions) Order 2003 (SI 2003/766) art.2.

[2202] Below, para.38-356. As will later be explained, on the bringing into force of Pt 2 of the Consumer Rights Act 2015 on October 1, 2015, the 1999 Regulations were revoked and the CMA and other bodies (termed "regulators") have enjoyed a new set of powers of enforcement of the new law governing unfair terms in consumer contracts which the 2015 Act contains: below, paras 38-419 et seq. For discussion of the temporal application of these new powers see below, paras 38-354 and 38-366.

[2203] 1999 Regulations regs 10–15.

[2204] See further below, para.38-361.

[2205] Below paras 38-361 and above 38-133—38-134.

[2206] SI 2008/1277.

[2207] See below, paras 38-362—38-364.

[2208] Above, para.38-353.

[2209] The Consumer Rights Act 2015 (Commencement No.3, Transitional Provisions, Savings and Consequential Amendments) Order 2015 (SI 2015/1630) art.3(c), (g) and (h) referring in particular to the provisions in Pt 2 and Schs 3 (enforcement of the law of unfair contract terms and notices) and 5 (investigatory powers, etc.) and Sch.4 para.34 of which revokes the 1999 Regulations.

[2210] The 2015 Order art.6(1) provides that this applies only to the provisions in paras (a) to (c) and (g) of art.3 and therefore not to the 2015 Act's provisions on investigatory powers in art.3(h) of the 2015 Order.

in relation to any contract or notice relating to any such a contract despite the revocation of those Regulations by the Act."[2211]

This means that the preventive powers contained in the 1999 Regulations, rather than those in the 2015 Act, still apply to contracts made before October 1, 2015 despite the general revocation. In practice, this will concern the use by a trader of a contract made with a consumer or consumers before that date. This is likely to be of continuing significance in the case of contracts of continuing significance or duration, including many financial services contracts such as life insurance, or a loan by a building society or bank to finance the purchase of a house.[2212]

38-355 **Preventive measures and written contract terms which fail the requirement of "plain and intelligible writing"**   While both art.7 of the 1993 Directive and the 1999 Regulations themselves[2213] on their terms restrict the availability of their preventive measures to *unfair* contract terms, the Director General of Fair Trading interpreted the policing role imposed on him by the Regulations as including a concern with their formal as well as their substantive fairness.[2214] Often, such a role can be justified on the basis that any failure in plainness or intelligibility of contract terms forms an element within their wider unfairness.[2215] However, the Director General took the view that these policing measures extend to written contract terms which fail the requirement of "plain and intelligible writing" in and of itself. The main argument in favour of this position rests on the following reasoning. Article 5(2) of the Directive provides that:

> "... the rule on interpretation [*contra proferentem* which applies where a term is not plain and intelligible] shall not apply in the context of the procedures laid down in Article 7(2),"

and art.7(2) imposes on Member States the duty to provide for action to be taken by "persons or organisations, having a legitimate interest under national law in protecting consumers" to prevent the continued use of "unfair terms"; so, although art.7 refers expressly only to "unfair terms", art.5(2)'s exclusion of one aspect of its application under art.7 assumes that it will otherwise figure in the role accorded to persons by Member States under art.7. The main difficulty with this line of argument is that it appears to run contrary to the approach of the European Court of Justice in *Commission v Spain*, where it held that the reason why the rule of interpretation *contra proferentem* of ambiguous terms found in art.5 should not apply in proceedings under art.7 lies in the need to enhance the effectiveness of preventive proceedings against *unfair* terms[2216] since otherwise a potentially unfair term could be rescued by interpretation. This reasoning appears to assume, therefore, that proceedings under art.7 cannot be founded *merely* on a failure of term to be plain and intelligible and this position has apparently been accepted at first instance.[2217] Whatever the proper view as to the question of the availability of policing measures under art.7 of the 1993 Directive, the various "enforcers" acting under

---

[2211] The Consumer Rights Act 2015 (Commencement No.3, Transitional Provisions, Savings and Consequential Amendments) Order 2015 (SI 2015/1630) arts 3 and 6(1)(a) and 6(4).

[2212] See further the explanation by the FCA in this respect at *https://www.fca.org.uk/firms/unfair-contract-terms*.

[2213] 1999 Regulations regs 12–14.

[2214] OFT, *Unfair Contract Terms*, Bulletin No.2 (September, 1996), p.9.

[2215] Above, paras 38-285—38-286

[2216] *Commission v Spain* (C-70/03) EU:C:2004:505, [2004] E.C.R. I-0799 at paras 16 and 17.

[2217] *OFT v Abbey National Plc* [2008] EWHC 875 (Comm), [2008] 2 All E.R. (Comm) 625 at [86].

Pt 8 of the Enterprise Act 2002 enjoy certain powers to intervene under that Act on the basis of a failure to fulfil the requirement of plain and intelligible writing in the 1993 Directive since the Consumer Injunctions Directive[2218] (which Pt 8 implemented) required the introduction of injunctions aimed at the protection of the collective interests of consumers where there is "any act contrary" to the directives listed in its annex, and this annex includes the 1993 Directive in toto.[2219]

The role of the Competition and Markets Authority (CMA) and "qualifying bodies" Until March 28, 2013 the 1999 Regulations imposed on the OFT a duty to consider any complaint made to it that any contract term drawn up for general use is unfair, unless the complaint appeared to it to be frivolous or vexatious or unless a "qualifying body" had notified it that it would consider the complaint.[2220] However, as from that date a new regime has applied to preventive measures taken under the 1999 Regulations and, from April 1, 2014, the OFT was abolished and the lead role in respect of the regulatory control of unfair terms in consumer contracts placed in the hands of the newly-formed Competition and Markets Authority (CMA).[2221] Under this regime, the CMA or a "qualifying body" *may* consider complaints that any contract term drawn up for general use is unfair.[2222] Where the CMA agrees to consider a complaint, it comes under a duty to do so; similarly, where a qualifying body agrees to consider a complaint, it comes under a duty to do so, but it must also notify the CMA of its agreement to do so.[2223] The Regulations empower the CMA or, subject to certain conditions, a qualifying body to apply to a court for an injunction against any person appearing to them to be using, or recommending for use, an unfair term drawn up for general use in contracts concluded with consumers.[2224] They specify that the decision by either the CMA or a qualifying body whether or not to apply for an injunction under reg.12 is subject to a requirement of giving reasons where it has resulted from a complaint which it was under a duty to consider.[2225] In deciding whether or not to apply for an injunction, they may, if they consider it appropriate to do so, have regard to any undertaking given to them by or on behalf of any person as to the continued use of such a term in contracts concluded with consumers.[2226] The 1999 Regulations empower a court to which the CMA or a qualifying body has applied to grant an injunction on

38-356

While upheld by the Court of Appeal, the latter's decision was reversed by the SC on other grounds [2009] EWCA Civ 116, [2009] 2 W.L.R. 1286; [2009] UKSC 6, [2010] 1 A.C. 696 (above, paras 38-247—38-248). The point referred to in this paragraph was not in issue before either the Court of Appeal or the Supreme Court: [2009] EWCA Civ 116 at [38].

[2218] Directive 98/27 on injunctions for the protection of consumers' interests [1998] O.J. L166/51, which was repealed and replaced by codified Directive 2009/22/EC on injunctions for the protection of consumers' interests, O.J. L110/30 (in force December 29, 2009).

[2219] Directive 98/27 art.1(2); Annex, No.9; Directive 2009/22/EC art1(2), Annex 1, No.5.

[2220] 1999 Regulations reg.10(1) as in force before March 28, 2013. On the earlier work of the OFT, see Bright (2000) 20 L.S. 331.

[2221] Enterprise and Regulatory Reform Act 2013 (Competition) (Consequential, Transitional and Saving Provisions) (No.2) Order 2014 (SI 2014/549) ("Order 2014/549") Sch.1 para.26; Public Bodies (The Office of Fair Trading Transfer of Consumer Advice Scheme Function and Modification of Enforcement Functions) Order 2013 (SI 2013/783) ("Order 2013/783") art.10.

[2222] 1999 Regulations reg.10(1) and 10(2) (as amended by Order 2013/783 art.10; Order 2014/549 Sch.1 para.26). Order 2013/783 art.10(4) revoked 1999 Regulations reg.11 (which had governed the consideration of complaints by qualifying bodies).

[2223] 1999 Regulations reg.10(3) (as amended by Order 2013/783 art.10; Order 2014/549 Sch.1 para.26).

[2224] 1999 Regulations reg.12(1) and (2) (as amended by Order 2014/549 Sch.1 para.26).

[2225] 1999 Regulations reg.10(4) (as amended by Order 2013/783 art.10; Order 2014/549 Sch.1 para.26).

[2226] 1999 Regulations reg.10(5) (as amended by Order 2013/783 art.10; Order 2014/549 Sch.1 para.26).

such terms as it thinks fit, and this may relate not only to use of a particular contract term drawn up for general use but to any similar term or term having like effect used or recommended for use by *any person*.[2227] The CMA and qualifying bodies (except the Consumers' Association) also enjoy investigatory powers for these purposes.[2228] Finally, the Regulations require the CMA to publish details of any undertakings made to it or to a court, or order or other outcome of any application made by a court and empowers it to arrange for the dissemination of information and advice concerning the operation of the Regulations.[2229]

38-357 **Application of the fairness test in preventive proceedings**   Article 5 of the Directive provides that:

> "In the case of contracts where all or certain terms offered to the consumer are in writing, these terms must always be drafted in plain, intelligible language. Where there is doubt about the meaning of a term, the interpretation most favourable to the consumer shall prevail. This rule on interpretation shall not apply in the context of the procedures laid down in Article 7(2)."[2230]

In *Commission v Spain*[2231] the European Court held that:

> "The distinction made in Article 5 of the directive concerning the applicable rule of interpretation, as between actions involving an individual consumer and actions for cessation which involve persons or organisations representative of the collective interest of consumers may be accounted for by the different aims pursued by those actions. In the former case, the courts or competent bodies are required to make an assessment in concreto of the unfair character of a term contained in a contract which has already been concluded, while in the latter case it is their task to assess in abstracto the unfair character of a term which may be incorporated into contracts which have not yet been concluded. In the former case, an interpretation favourable to the individual consumer concerned benefits him or her immediately. By contrast, in the latter case, in order to obtain, by way of prevention, the most favourable result for consumers as a whole, it is not necessary, where there is doubt, to interpret the term in a manner favourable to them. Accordingly, an objective interpretation makes it possible to prohibit more frequently the use of an unintelligible or ambiguous term, which results in wider consumer protection."[2232]

As a result, before the revocation of the 1999 Regulations on October 1, 2015, the CMA or qualifying body (and, ultimately, the court) in considering preventive proceedings taken under them would often have had to assess in the abstract the unfair character of a term which might be incorporated into contracts which had not yet been concluded. However, as has earlier been explained,[2233] after October 1, 2015 the enforcement powers in the 1999 Regulations apply only in relation to

---

[2227] 1999 Regulations reg.12(3) and (4).

[2228] These powers are contained in the 1999 Regulations reg.13 on whose temporal application, see above, para.38-354.

[2229] 1999 Regulations reg.15 (as amended by Order 2014/549 Sch.1 para.26). A qualifying body must notify the CMA of any undertakings given to it by a person as to the continued use of a term which it considers unfair in contracts concluded with consumers, the outcome of any application made by it to a court under reg.12 and of the terms of any undertaking given to, or order made by, the court and of the outcome of any application made by it to enforce a previous order of the court: 1999 Regulations reg.14 (as amended by Order 2014/549 Sch.1 para.26).

[2230] 1993 Directive art.5.

[2231] *Commission v Spain* (C-70/03) EU:C:2004:505, [2004] E.C.R. I-0799.

[2232] C-70/03 EU:C:2004:505, at [16].

[2233] Above, para.38-354.

contracts made before that date and, as a result, the subject matter of preventive proceedings under the Regulations will relate to the use of unfair terms in contracts already so made and not to future contracts. It remains the case, however, that in this type of proceedings it is not possible to have regard to all the actual circumstances attending the conclusion of any particular contract, nor to have regard to other terms of any particular contract (or contract to which it is related), and so the court should take "into account the effects of contemplated or typical relationships between the contracting parties".[2234] For this purpose, it is submitted that the standard of the "average consumer" is an appropriate viewpoint from which to assess the potential for unfairness as well as the plain and intelligible character of the terms.[2235]

Nature of relief: injunctions and declarations In *Office of Fair Trading v Foxtons Ltd*[2236] the Court of Appeal considered the ambit, nature and appropriate content of relief to be granted by a court on the success of proceedings brought by the OFT (and, therefore, other "qualifying bodies").[2237] It held, first, that the preventive measures foreseen by art.7 of the 1993 Directive and provided for by reg.12 of the 1999 Regulations were intended to cover existing as well as future contracts.[2238] Secondly, it held that the decision whether or not to grant an injunction will depend on the circumstances of the case.[2239] In this respect, Waller L.J. observed that: **38-358**

"... in a situation where on a general challenge a court has found a term or terms in a set of standard conditions in use in current contracts unfair, it must be a proper exercise of its power to grant an injunction to prevent enforcement of that term or terms in existing contracts."[2240]

Arden L.J. took a rather more qualified approach, noting that the granting of an injunction in this context must accord with the general principles of Community law and so be both effective and proportionate (so that the interference with the rights of the business by the grant of the injunction is justified by the need to protect the consumer interests).[2241] Thirdly:

"... [t]he terms of the injunction (or declaration) can only ultimately be worked out against the background of precisely what the court has found to be unfair."[2242]

Fourthly, a court's decision in relation to preventive proceedings does not bind a subsequent court by way of res judicata in deciding an individual challenge to the fairness of a term by a consumer,[2243] so that a term not found unfair generally in preventive proceedings may be held unfair in the particular circumstances of the

---

[2234] *Director General of Fair Trading v First National Bank Plc* [2001] UKHL 52, [2002] 1 A.C. 481 at [33], per Lord Steyn.

[2235] Above, paras 38-044 and 38-350.

[2236] [2009] EWCA Civ 288, [2010] 1 W.L.R. 663.

[2237] Below, para.38-360 and cf. above, para.38-356.

[2238] [2009] EWCA Civ 288 at [43]–[44], [63]–[70] (Waller and Arden L.JJ. respectively). cf. [2009] EWCA Civ 288 at [86] (Moore-Bick L.J.). On the replacement of the OFT by the CMA for these purposes, see above, para.38-356. On the position of "qualifying bodies" see below, para.38-360.

[2239] [2009] EWCA Civ 288 at [73] (Arden L.J.) and [49] (Waller L.J.).

[2240] [2009] EWCA Civ 288 at [48].

[2241] [2009] EWCA Civ 288 at [73] (Arden L.J.) and see [99] (Moore-Bick L.J.).

[2242] [2009] EWCA Civ 288 at [51] (Waller L.J.) and similarly at [73] (Arden L.J.).

[2243] [2009] EWCA Civ 288 at [71] (Arden L.J.).

case in relation to an individual consumer.[2244] On the other hand:

> "... if there is an injunction which extends to existing contracts, the ability of the supplier to initiate or participate in [individual] proceedings will be governed by the terms of that injunction."[2245]

Finally, a finding in preventive proceedings that a term or terms in standard consumer contracts is or are unfair may appropriately be the subject of a declaration by the court, even though this may necessarily have an effect on non-parties to those proceedings.[2246] It is submitted that the approach of the Court of Appeal is consistent with the later decision of the Court of Justice of the EU in *Invitel*.[2247] There the Court of Justice held that effective implementation of the "deterrent nature and dissuasive purpose" of the preventive measures under art.7 of the Directive requires that a term in a set of standard terms used by a seller or supplier with a number of consumers which is declared unfair in an action for an injunction brought against that seller or supplier should:

> "... not [be] binding on either the consumers who are parties to the actions for an injunction or on those who have concluded with that seller or supplier a contract to which the same [standard terms] apply."[2248]

It is submitted that this result can be effected by an English court in exercising its discretion under reg.12(3) and (4).

38-359 Burden of proof in proceedings It has earlier been argued that the better view is that, as between the parties to a consumer contract, there is no burden of proof as to the issue of the fairness of a contract term as normally understood, but rather that the court should make a neutral assessment of this issue on the basis of those facts adduced by the parties to the proceedings.[2249] It is submitted that this should also be the case as regards an application brought by the CMA or one of the

---

[2244] [2009] EWCA Civ 288 at [46] (Waller L.J.).

[2245] [2009] EWCA Civ 288 at [71], per Arden L.J. cf. [2009] EWCA Civ 288 at [86] and [96] Moore-Bick L.J.

[2246] [2009] EWCA Civ 288 at [71], per Arden L.J. cf. [2009] EWCA Civ 288 at [86] and [96], per Moore-Bick L.J. Subsequently, Mann J. held that certain categories of terms in the contracts concluded by the defendant in these earlier proceedings (Foxtons Ltd, an estate agent supplying management services under "letting only service contracts" to non-business ("consumer") landlords) were unfair within the meaning of the Regulations: [2009] EWHC 1681 (Ch), [2009] 29 E.G. 98 (C.S.). The final order made by Mann J. identified these categories of terms, declared them unfair and not binding on the consumers with whom they had already been made and forbad the defendant from using or recommending them for use, save with the prior permission of the OFT and from relying on these same categories of terms appearing in existing contracts with their consumer customers: *http://webarchive.nationalarchives.gov.uk/20140402142426/http://www.oft.gov.uk/shared_oft/reports/Foxtons/Sealed_order*.

[2247] *Nemzeti Fogyasztóvédelmi Hatóság v Invitel Távközlési Zrt* (C-472/10) EU:C:2012:242, April 26, 2012 and cf. above, para.38-314. cf. *Biuro podróży "Partner" Sp. z o.o, Sp. komandytowa w Dąbrowie Górniczej v Prezes Urzędu Ochrony Konkurencji i Konsumentów* (C-119/15) EU:C:2016:987, December 25, 2016 at para.40 (trader fined for use of terms *equivalent to* a standard condition of business declared unlawful in other proceedings and placed on a national register must have a right to challenge the assessment of unfairness and the penalty as a result of the right to an effective judicial remedy under art.47 of the Charter of Fundamental Rights of the European Union).

[2248] C-472/10 EU:C:2012:242, April 26, 2012 at paras 37–38.

[2249] See above, paras 38-335—38-338.

"qualifying bodies" for the grant of an injunction.[2250] Indeed, this is a context where a neutral assessment is even more appropriate given that the assessment is made "in the abstract" (for the generality of circumstances in which the allegedly unfair term is used) than is the case as between the parties to the consumer contract, where the particular circumstances of the conclusion of the contract in question may be relevant.[2251] On the other hand, it is submitted that a court will not grant an injunction against a business on such an application unless it is satisfied that the term in question is unfair, whether or not this is expressed in terms of placing a burden of proof on the applicant body.

"Qualifying bodies" The 1999 Regulations extend the power to police unfair   **38-360**
terms in consumer contracts to a range of bodies other than the CMA, these being termed "qualifying bodies". Rather than providing a general definition or set of criteria by which a body may qualify for the purpose of bringing proceedings for an injunction under the 1999 Regulations, the latter simply list in Sch.1 those bodies or classes of body which in law do so.[2252] Apart from the Consumers' Association, the list includes regulators of former public utilities, such as the Gas and Electricity Markets Authority but also, at a local level, every weights and measures authority (known as "Trading Standard Service").[2253] Where a qualifying body agrees to consider a complaint, it comes under a duty to consider that complaint and must notify the CMA of its agreement to consider that complaint.[2254] A qualifying body is empowered to bring proceedings for an injunction against any person appearing to that body to be using, or recommending for use, an unfair term drawn up for general use in contracts with consumers, subject to a condition of prior notification of 14 days to the CMA unless the CMA consents to a shorter period of notification.[2255] In deciding whether or not to apply for an injunction, a qualifying body may take into account any undertaking given to it as to the continued use of the term and bears a duty to give reasons for its decision.[2256] As in the case of the CMA, qualifying bodies (except the Consumers' Association) possess investigatory powers[2257] and the courts' power to grant injunctions or declarations is the same as for proceedings brought by the CMA.[2258]

"Enforcement orders" under the Enterprise Act 2002 In addition to the pow-   **38-361**

[2250] cf. *Director General of Fair Trading v First National Bank Plc* [2001] 1 W.L.R. 98, 112 where counsel for the DGFT conceded that it was for him to show that the term used by the defendant bank was unfair.

[2251] Above, para.38-337.

[2252] 1999 Regulations reg.1 "qualifying body".

[2253] The full list is as follows: the Information Commissioner; the Gas and Electricity Markets Authority; the Northern Ireland Authority for Utility Regulation (which took over the functions of the Director General of Electricity Supply for Northern Ireland and the Director General of Gas for Northern Ireland); the Water Services Regulation Authority; the Office of Rail Regulation; every weights and measures authority in Great Britain; the Department of Enterprise, Trade and Investment in Northern Ireland; the Financial Conduct Authority (FCA, which took over the powers and role of the Financial Services Authority; the functions of the FCA under the 1999 Regulations are to be treated as functions of the FCA under the Financial Services and Markets Act 2000: 1999 Regulations reg.16 (as amended)); the Consumers' Association: 1999 Regulations Sch.1 as amended.

[2254] 1999 Regulations reg.10(3) (as amended by Order 2013/783 art.10; Order 2014/549 Sch.1 para.26).

[2255] 1999 Regulations reg.12(2) (as amended by Order 2014/549 Sch.1 para.26).

[2256] 1999 Regulations regs 10(4) and (5) (as amended by Order 2013/783 art.10; Order 2014/549 Sch.1 para.26).

[2257] See above, para.38-354 (note).

[2258] 1999 Regulations reg.12(3).

ers provided by the 1999 Regulations, the CMA and other persons or bodies may enjoy powers of enforcement under the Enterprise Act 2002. Under Pt 8 of that Act a number of bodies, termed "enforcers", may apply to the court for an "enforcement order" against a person to stop breaking legislation enacted for the benefit of consumers.[2259] These powers have been noted earlier.[2260]

38-362 **Consumer Protection from Unfair Trading Regulations 2008**   As has been seen, these Regulations implement in UK law the Unfair Commercial Practices Directive 2005.[2261] They set a very broad standard of commercial behaviour for traders in relation to consumers in a general provision which prohibits practices which contrary to "professional diligence" "materially distort or are likely to materially distort the economic behaviour of the average consumer with regard to the product",[2262] ("product" here being defined very broadly to include goods or services, digital content, immoveable property and rights or obligations[2263]). This standard is fleshed out by the setting of two main examples of unfair commercial practices (misleading actions and misleading omissions and aggressive practices[2264]) and is supplemented by a black list of particular commercial practices which "are in all circumstances considered unfair".[2265] "Unfair commercial practices" are prohibited and the 2008 Regulations create a series of offences relating to unfair commercial practices and a number of enforcement powers in public bodies.[2266] In the result, where, for example, a trader

> "... knowingly or recklessly engages in a commercial practice which contravenes the requirements of professional diligence ... and the practice materially distorts or is likely to materially distort the economic behaviour of the average consumer with regard to the product","

then the trader is guilty of a criminal offence and for this purpose

> "... a trader who engages in a commercial practice without regard to whether the practice contravenes the requirements of professional diligence shall be deemed recklessly to engage in the practice, whether or not the trader has reason for believing that the practice might contravene those requirements."[2267]

In 2014 the Consumer Protection from Unfair Trading Regulations 2008 were

---

[2259] 2002 Act Pt 8 came into force on June 20, 2003: The Enterprise Act 2002 (Commencement No.3, Transitional and Transitory Provisions and Savings) Order 2003 (SI 2003/1397) art.2. Pt 8 has been subject to considerable amendment, most recently by the extension of the powers of the court to order "enhanced consumer measures" enacted by the Consumer Rights Act 2015 s.79(1) and Sch.7 of the 2015 Act. These amendments to the 2002 Act were brought into force on October 1, 2015 by the 2015 Order art.3(e)) and s.79(2) of the Act provides expressly that they "have effect only in relation to conduct which occurs, or which is likely to occur, after the commencement of [s.79]".

[2260] Above, paras 38-133—38-134.

[2261] Directive 2005/29/EC concerning unfair business-to-consumer commercial practices [2005] O.J. L149/22 and see above, paras 38-159 et seq.

[2262] Consumer Protection from Unfair Trading Regulations 2008 (SI 2008/1277) reg.3(1)–(3). The Regulations came into force on May 26, 2008 and were significantly amended by SI 2014/870).

[2263] SI 2008/1277 reg.2(1) "product" (as amended).

[2264] SI 2008/1277 regs 3(2), 3(4)(a)–(d) and 5–7.

[2265] SI 2008/1277 reg.3(4)(d); Sch.1.

[2266] SI 2008/1277 Pts 3 and 4 respectively.

[2267] SI 2008/1277 reg.8. Regulation 13 sets the penalties for these offences as being "on summary conviction, to a fine not exceeding the statutory maximum and, on conviction on indictment, to a fine or imprisonment for a term not exceeding two years or both".

amended, inter alia, so as to create rights to (civil) redress in consumers in respect of certain categories of unfair commercial practices, i.e. "misleading actions" and "aggressive commercial practice".[2268] The consumer's right of redress may include a "right to unwind" the contract after rejection of goods or services (where the consumer has a general right to refund), a right to a discount and a right to damages.[2269]

Use or recommendation for use of contract terms as a "commercial prac- **38-363**
tice" The Court of Justice has noted that "commercial practice" is given a "particularly wide definition" by the 2005 Directive[2270] and the 2005 Directive makes clear that such a commercial practice may take place "before, during and after a commercial transaction in relation to a product".[2271] This strongly suggests that the use or recommendation for use by a trader of contract terms with consumers may constitute a business-to-consumer "commercial practice" for the purposes of the Unfair Commercial Practices Directive 2005,[2272] and this has been assumed by the Court of Justice in *Pereničová*[2273] and decided by the UK High Court.[2274] In the case of contracts entered into before October 1, 2015, this gives rise to the possibility of the use in such a contract of standard terms which are unfair (in part) because they are not in plain and intelligible language may be held to constitute a misleading action within the meaning of the 2008 Regulations.[2275]

If the use of unfair terms by a business in their dealings with consumers is held **38-364** to constitute an unfair commercial practice, then the preventive measures and, subject to their own conditions, criminal offences provided for the policing of unfair commercial practices would apply[2276] in addition to the particular consequences foreseen by the 1999 Regulations themselves. This is compatible with the "full harmonisation" required by the 2005 Directive[2277] since the requirements of the 1999 Regulations reflect exactly and do not go beyond the substantive requirements of the 1993 Directive and therefore fall within the rule in the 2005 Direc-

---

[2268] See generally above, para.38-172. These amendments came into force on October 1, 2014: SI 2014/870 reg.1(3).

[2269] SI 2014/870 reg.2 inserting regs 27E–27K into the 2008 Regulations.

[2270] *Total Belgium & Galatea* (C-261/07 and C-299/07) EU:C:2009:244 at para.49.

[2271] 2005 Directive art.3(1).

[2272] It would appear that the question whether such a "commercial practice" may consist of an isolated event would not or would only rarely arise in the context of use or recommendation for use of unfair contract terms which have not been individually negotiated, as such a use would normally rest on a continuing practice of the business using standard terms in their dealings with consumers on more than one isolated occasion: cf. above, para.38-167.

[2273] *Pereničová v SOS finance, spol. sro* (C-453/10) EU:C:2012:144, paras 37–41 (although the issue before the CJEU was whether the finding of an unfair commercial practice under the 2005 Directive would in itself render a term unfair and so not binding on the consumer under the 1993 Directive, on above, para.38-278). A.G. Trstenjak in her opinion in *Pereničová* of November 29, 2011 at para.90 in the course of a wider discussion of the 1993 and 2005 directives observed that "it is conceivable that the unfairness of a commercial practice consists in the very use in consumer contracts of unfair terms within the meaning of Directive 93/13. [citation] The trader's use of such terms is likely to be seen as a misleading act, since false information is provided or the consumer is unclear as to the actual scale of the contractual rights and obligations, especially with regard to rights and obligations arising from the clauses which are unfair and so invalid for the consumer".

[2274] *OFT v Ashbourne Management Services Ltd* [2011] EWHC 1237 (Ch), [2011] E.C.C. 31 especially at [227] and [240].

[2275] On "misleading actions" see above, paras 38-179—38-182; on the significance of the requirement of transparency, see above, paras 38-347 et seq.

[2276] Above, para.38-170.

[2277] Above, para.38-159.

tive which allows special EU rules to derogate from the general rules in 2005 "framework" Directive.[2278] However, as has been noted, since their amendment in 2014, the commission of a misleading action may also attract "rights to redress" in consumers, these including, inter alia, a right to unwind a contract where the trader with which he has made it has engaged in an unfair commercial practice in relation to the goods or services, etc. provided under the contract.[2279] This possible consequence of the use by a trader of unfair standard terms is compatible with the 2005 Directive as the latter does not affect national contract law.[2280] Where such a right to redress exists, a consumer who has concluded a contract containing an unfair contract term may be able to escape the binding force of the contract as a whole by exercising the right to unwind the contract, and not merely the binding force of the particular term in question (which is the normal consequence of a finding that a term is unfair).[2281] For this purpose, however, it must be recalled that both the scope of protection for consumers and the tests of unfairness of commercial practices and of contract terms are distinct under the two sets of Regulations (following the Directives which they implement) so that, in particular, the mere finding of an unfair commercial practice will not render any related contract term unfair.[2282]

(d)   The New Law: The Consumer Rights Act 2015

(i)   Introduction and Overview

38-365   Background   As earlier explained, the Consumer Rights Act 2015[2283] ("the 2015 Act" or "the Act") revoked and replaced the 1999 Regulations as well as removing from the Unfair Contract Terms Act 1977 provisions applicable to persons "dealing as consumer" and disapplying the remaining provisions from "consumer contracts" as understood by the 2015 Act.[2284] The Act was also concerned to introduce significant reforms to the law governing the enforcement of consumer protection laws, domestic and European, with amendments, inter alia, of Pt 8 of the Enterprise Act 2002 so as to create a new possibility for courts to order "enhanced consumer measures" to individuals affected by breach of a consumer protection measure.[2285] These changes affect the powers of regulators in respect of the prevention of unfair contract terms.

38-366   Temporal application of the 2015 Act's provisions on unfair terms   The Act

---

[2278] Unfair Commercial Practices Directive 2005 art.3(4), above, para.38-161 where it is explained that this applies only to national rules implementing the requirements of a EU directive without exercise of the power to extend the protection for consumers under a "minimum harmonisation" clause, as where the latter applies there is a six-year transitional rule in the 2005 Directive art.3(5). cf. the position under the Consumer Rights Act 2015 which (to an extent) extends the protection foreseen by the 1993 Directive: see below, paras 38-420—38-426.

[2279] See above, paras 38-172 et seq.

[2280] Directive 2005/29 art.3(2), recital 9, above, para.38-160.

[2281] 1999 Regulations reg.8(1) and (2), above, paras 38-339 et seq. which explains that where a term is held unfair and not binding under the 1999 Regulations the contract as a whole continues to bind the parties as long as it is capable of continuing in existence without the unfair term.

[2282] *Pereničovà v SOS finance, spol. sro* (C-453/10) EU:C:2012:144, para.41, above para.38-278.

[2283] The Act is accompanied by a set of Explanatory Notes prepared by the Department for Business, Innovation and Skills ("*Explanatory Notes* 2015").

[2284] Above, para.38-215.

[2285] Consumer Rights Act 2015 s.79; Sch.7 and see above, para.38-134 and below, para.38-420.

received Royal Assent on March 26, 2015; its substantive provisions governing unfair contract terms were brought into force on October 1, 2015.[2286] Parts 1 and 2 of the Act were brought into force generally so as to apply to contracts made on or after October 1, 2015.[2287] As has been seen, contracts made before October 1, 2015 remain governed by the 1999 Regulations.[2288]

Overview of the 2015 Act In order to give effect to the policies pursued by the Act, Pt 1 first defines a new, consistent terminology to be used to describe the "consumer" and the "trader"[2289] and then sets out the principal substantive rights to be enjoyed by consumers under each of a series of types of contract: "contracts to supply goods" or "goods contracts" (which are "sales contracts", contracts for the hire of goods, hire-purchase agreements and "contracts for the transfer of goods") (Ch.2)[2290]; "contracts to supply digital content" or "digital content contracts" (Ch.3)[2291]; and "contracts to supply a service" or "services contracts" (Ch.4).[2292] So, for example, Ch.2 governing contracts to supply goods provides for the inclusion of terms in these contracts that the goods are of satisfactory quality, fit for any particular purpose made known to the trader by the consumer, and are as described, these terms being modelled closely on the well-known statutory implied terms found, inter alia, in the Sale of Goods Act 1979 and the Supply of Goods and Services Act 1982.[2293] Chapters 2 to 4 of the Act are discussed in detail later in this chapter.[2294] The following paragraphs refer to the *Explanatory Notes* accompanying the Consumer Rights Act 2015.[2295]

Part 2 of the Act contains provisions which seek to re-implement the Unfair

38-367

38-368

[2286] The Consumer Rights Act 2015 (Commencement No.3, Transitional Provisions, Savings and Consequential Amendments) Order 2015 (SI 2015/1630) art.3(a)–(c). The exception to this general position is found in relation to "consumer transport services" where the relevant provisions in the Act apply only from October 1, 2016: 2015 Order arts 4 and 6(2) as amended by the Consumer Rights Act 2015 (Commencement No.3, Transitional Provisions, Savings and Consequential Amendments) (Amendment) Order 2016 (SI 2016/484) art.2; and see above, para.38-216. The Act's provisions in Pt 3 Ch.3 imposing a duty on letting agents to publicise fees were brought into force from May 27, 2015: Consumer Rights Act 2015 (Commencement) (England) Order 2015 (SI 2015/965). See also the Consumer Rights Act 2015 (Commencement No.1) Order 2015 (SI 2015/1333) (bringing into force on May 27, 2015 ss.77 and Sch.5 insofar as they relate to Ch.5 of Pt 3 (investigatory powers in relation to secondary ticketing) to the extent that they are not already in force and 82 (appointment of judges to Competition Appeal Tribunal)); Consumer Rights Act 2015 (Commencement No.2) Order 2015 (SI 2015/1584) (bringing into force certain empowering provisions in relation to s.81 (private actions in competition law) on August 3, 2015); the Consumer Rights Act 2015 (Commencement No.2 and Transitional Provision) (England) Order 2015 (SI 2015/1575) (bringing into force Ch.4 of Pt 3 of the Act (higher education and student complaints) on September 1, 2015 with transitional provisions).
[2287] The Consumer Rights Act 2015 (Commencement No.3, Transitional Provisions, Savings and Consequential Amendments) Order 2015 (SI 2015/1630) (the "2015 Order") arts 3(a)–(c), 6(1), (3) and (4).
[2288] Above, paras 38-220 et seq.
[2289] 2015 Act s.2(2)–(7) "trader" and "consumer", on which see below, paras 38-383 and 38-384—38-385 respectively. The 2015 Act s.2(1) restricts these definitions to Pt 1, but s.76(2) adopts them for the purposes of interpretation in Pt 2.
[2290] 2015 Act s.3. While the Act's provisions refer throughout Ch.2 to contracts to supply goods, the following paragraphs will use the shorter (equivalent) terminology used by the Act of "goods contracts".
[2291] 2015 Act s.33.
[2292] 2015 Act s.48, which does not, however, define "service contract".
[2293] 2015 Act ss.9–11 and see Sale of Goods Act 1979 ss.13–14; Supply of Goods and Services Act 1982 ss.3, 4, 8 and 9.
[2294] See below, paras 38-432, 38-435 and 38-465 et seq.
[2295] These were prepared by the Department of Business, Innovation and Skills ("*Explanatory Notes*

Terms in Consumer Contracts Directive 1993 ("the 1993 Directive") in the UK, replacing (and revoking) the Unfair Terms in Consumer Contracts Regulations 1999 ("1999 Regulations")[2296] and, in doing so, making limited but significant changes to the ambit of the controls on unfair terms in consumer contracts.

38-369   Part 3 of the Act makes "miscellaneous and general" provision on various matters, of which its clauses governing enforcement powers of regulatory authorities are most significant for present purposes, their details being contained in Sch.5 (investigatory powers) and Sch.7 (which provides, inter alia, for "enhanced consumer measures" under Pt 8 of the Enterprise Act 2002).[2297] Both these changes affect the law governing the control on unfair terms in consumer contracts, as will appear in the following paragraphs.

38-370   **The strategies of the 2015 Act in relation to contract terms**   There are four principal strategies adopted by the Act in relation to the control of unfair terms in consumer contracts.[2298]

38-371   First, as earlier noted, implementation of the Directive on unfair terms in consumer contracts of 1993, earlier effected by the Unfair Terms in Consumer Contracts Regulations 1999, is effected by the Act, principally by Pt 2. In general, and following the pattern set by the 1999 Regulations, these provisions follow closely the language of the 1993 Directive, but the Act extends its protection, notably as regards the category of persons protected by the requirements of fairness and plain, intelligible language by broadening the definition of "consumer",[2299] by including individually negotiated terms under the test of unfairness,[2300] and by imposing an additional requirement for the application of the exclusion from the test of unfairness of terms relating to the main subject matter of the contract or the price/quality ratio allowed by art.4(2) of the 1993 Directive in response to its interpretation by the Supreme Court in *Abbey National Plc v The Office of Fair Trading*.[2301] Moreover three further examples are included in the "indicative list" of terms which may be unfair,[2302] and all these terms are thereby specifically prevented from falling under the exclusion of terms relating to the main subject matter, etc. provided by s.64 of the Act.[2303]

38-372   Secondly, the Unfair Contract Terms Act 1977 was amended so as no longer to apply to terms in "consumer contracts" or "consumer notices" as defined by the 2015 Act: instead the 1977 Act applies only to other notices and to terms in other contracts, i.e. those between traders and those between individuals who are neither

---

2015").

[2296] 2015 Act s.75; Sch.4 para.34. On the 1999 Regulations, see above, paras 38-220 et seq.

[2297] See above, para.38-134 and below, para.38-420. 2015 Act Pt 3 also sets out various new rules, including for private actions in competition law (s.81); a new duty of letting agents to publicise fees (ss.83–88); and concerning "secondary ticketing" (ss.90–95).

[2298] The CMA has published guidance on the unfair contract terms provisions in the 2015 Act: *Unfair contract terms guidance, Guidance on the unfair terms provisions in the Consumer Rights Act 2015* (CMA37, July 2015).

[2299] 2015 Act s.2(3) and (4) as applied to Pt 2 by s.76(2), below, para.38-384.

[2300] 2015 Act s.62 below, para.38-389.

[2301] [2009] UKSC 6, [2010] 1 A.C. 696 on which see above, paras 38-247—38-248 and see below, paras 38-394—38-400.

[2302] 2015 Act Sch.2 Pt 1 paras 5, 12 and 14 and see below, para.38-391 and cf. above, paras 38-299 et seq.

[2303] 2015 Act s.64(6) and see below, para.38-398.

[1142]

traders nor consumers.[2304] The provisions so amended were of two types. First, there were provisions expressly governing contracts between a person seeking to exclude or limit their "business liability" as against a person "dealing as consumer", where the provisions governing, and references to, contracts within this category were deleted, as was the definition of "dealing as consumer" for this purpose.[2305] Secondly, there were provisions governing contracts between a person seeking to exclude or limit their "business liability" for negligence as against any person, whether in respect of death or personal injury or other loss or damage.[2306] Moreover, s.2 of the Unfair Contract Terms Act 1977 was amended so as not to apply to a "consumer notice",[2307] i.e.:

"... a notice to the extent that it relates to rights or obligations as between a trader and a consumer, or purports to exclude or restrict a trader's liability to a consumer."[2308]

Similarly, s.3 of the Misrepresentation Act 1967 was amended so as not to apply to "a term in a consumer contract within the meaning of Pt 2 of the Consumer Rights Act 2015".[2309] The details of these amendments are discussed in Vol.I, Ch.15 "Exemption Clauses"[2310] and Ch.7 "Misrepresentation" respectively.[2311] Here, though, it should be noted that, while this strategy had the effect of placing most (though not all) of the law governing the validity of terms in consumer contracts within the Consumer Rights Act,[2312] it also had the effect of making the application of the legislation (the Unfair Contract Terms Act 1977 or the Misrepresentation Act 1967 s.3 on the one hand, the Consumer Rights Act on the other) turn on the distinction between a person who contracts as a "consumer" with a "trader" within the meanings of the 2015 Act and where that person contracts other than as "consumer". As will be seen, the definition of "consumer" provided by the Act is

---

[2304] Law Com. Advice (2013) S. 44 (noting that the 1977 Act may also apply to "employment contracts").
[2305] 2015 Act s.75; Sch.4 para.5 (amending 1977 Act s.3 "liability arising in contract"); para.6 (deleting 1977 Act s.4 "unreasonable indemnity clauses"); para.7 (deleting 1977 Act s.5 "'guarantees' of consumer goods"); para.8 (amending 1977 Act s.6 "sale and hire purchase"); para.9 (amending 1977 Act s.7 "Miscellaneous contracts under which goods pass"); para.10 (deleting 1977 Act s.9 "effect of breach") and para.11 (deleting 1977 Act s.12 "dealing as consumer"). As regards "consumers", under the 2015 Act these terms are either governed by particular provisions (e.g. liability of seller to consumer in goods contracts by s.31, on which see below paras 38-531) or are subject to the general test of unfairness provided by s.62, on which see below, paras 38-389 et seq.
[2306] 2015 Act s.75; Sch.4 para.4 (amending 1977 Act s.2 "negligence liability"). These terms are subject to control under ss.62 and 65 of the 2015 Act: see below, paras 38-390 and 38-409.
[2307] 2015 Act s.75; Sch.4 para.4 (amending 1977 Act s.2 "negligence liability"). "Consumer notices" are controlled by ss.62(2), (6)–(7) and 65 of the 2015 Act, on which see below, paras 38-406—38-407, 38-409.
[2308] 2015 Act s.61(4) and see below, para.38-387.
[2309] 2015 Act s.75; Sch.4 para.1. These terms are controlled under the 2015 Act by the general test of unfairness provided by s.62, on which see below, paras 38-389 et seq.
[2310] See Vol.I, paras 15-062 et seq.
[2311] See Vol.I, para.7-149.
[2312] It does not include all the law, either at common law (such as the rule rendering ineffective an attempted exclusion of liability for personal fraud: see Vol.I, para.7-145) or in legislation creating rules governing consumer contracts whose effect cannot be excluded or restricted (or only subject to conditions) (e.g. the Package Travel and Linked Travel Arrangements Regulations 2018 (SI 2018/634) reg.30 (benefiting "travelers") on which see above, para.38-143 or the Timeshare, Holiday Products, Resale and Exchange Contracts Regulations 2010 (SI 2010/2960) reg.19: see above, paras 38-134 and 38-141 respectively). Moreover, provisions in other UK legislation make the rules (or some of the rules) which they set out incapable of exclusion by contract: e.g. Consumer Protection Act 1987 s.7 (no exclusion of product liability imposed by Pt 1 of that Act).

fact-sensitive and, therefore, in some cases the legislation applicable will be difficult to determine.[2313]

38-373 Thirdly, Pt 1 of the Act provides very widely that a term in the types of contract to which it applies (i.e. "contracts to supply goods", "contracts to supply digital content", and "contracts to supply a service")[2314] is not binding on the consumer to the extent that it would exclude or restrict the trader's liability arising under a number of the substantive provisions which it sets out[2315] (such as in respect of breach of the terms as to description, quality or fitness for purpose, etc. of goods inserted into contracts to supply goods[2316] or under rules on delivery of goods or the passing of risk[2317]). These provisions will be discussed in the context of the new provisions to which they relate.[2318]

38-374 Fourthly, the Act extended the enforcement measures (injunctions against and undertakings by traders) which it puts in place for the control of unfair terms in Pt 2 of the Act (and detailed in Sch.3) to contract terms rendered not binding on consumers under Pt 1 of the Act, as well as to "consumer notices" also rendered not binding on consumers under Pt 2 of the Act.[2319]

38-375 It will be seen, therefore, that the Consumer Rights Act 2015 sought to extend the framework governing the terms of consumer contracts well known from the 1999 Regulations (and reflecting closely the 1993 Directive) so as to cover "consumer notices" and the framework of the enforcement measures provided for unfair terms in consumer contracts by the 1999 Regulations so as to cover a range of invalid exclusions of liability in traders to consumers. By contrast, the 2015 Act subsumed the control of the exclusion of liability for misrepresentation (formerly specially governed by the Misrepresentation Act 1967 s.3) in traders to consumers under the general scheme of control of unfair terms and unfair notices which it provides. The following paragraphs discuss the treatment by the 2015 Act of unfair contract terms under the following headings: the relationship of the Act's provisions on unfair terms to EU law[2320]; the scope of the controls on contract terms and notices in Pt 2 of the Act[2321]; contract terms and notices not binding on the consumer

---

[2313] See below, para.38-384.
[2314] 2015 Act Chs 2, 3 and 4.
[2315] 2015 Act s.31 (contracts to supply goods); s.47 (contracts to supply digital content); s.57 (contracts to supply services).
[2316] 2015 Act ss.9–17.
[2317] 2015 Act ss.28–29.
[2318] Below, paras 38-465 et seq. For discussion of the controls of exemption clauses contained in Pt 1 of the 2015 Act, see below paras 38-531, 38-564, and 38-586. As there set out, there are qualifications on this broad picture in the case of contracts for the hire of goods (s.31(5)–(6), below, para.38-531) and contracts for services (s.57 of the Act, below, para.38-586).
[2319] 2015 Act s.70; Sch.3. In addition, the relevant provisions of the 2015 Act are specified as the UK law which gives effect to the 1993 Directive for the purposes of Pt 8 of the Enterprise Act 2002: Enterprise Act 2002 (Part 8 Community Infringements Specified UK Laws) Order 2003/1374 Sch.1 (referring to the 2015 Act ss.2, 61–64, 67–70, 72 to 74; Schs 2 and 3 and Sch.5 Pt 3) as amended by the Enterprise Act 2002 (Part 8 Community Infringements and Specified Laws) (Amendment) Order 2015 (SI 2015/1628) art.2. Moreover, acts or omissions in respect of any provision in Pts 1 and 2 of the 2015 Act are specified as possible "domestic infringements" for the purposes of s.212 of the Enterprise Act 2002: Enterprise Act 2002 (Part 8 Domestic Infringements) Order 2015 (SI 2015/1727) art.2. On the compatibility of the latter with EU law, see below, paras 38-421—38-426.
[2320] Below, paras 38-376 et seq.
[2321] Below, paras 38-382 et seq.

where assessed as unfair[2322]; contract terms and notices not binding on the consumer in all circumstances[2323]; the requirement for transparency[2324]; prevention of avoidance by choice of law[2325]; and the enforcement of rules governing unfair contract terms and notices.[2326]

(ii) The Relationship of the Consumer Rights Act to EU Law

Interpretation of provisions in the 2015 Act implementing the 1993 Directive   As earlier explained,[2327] the Court of Justice has held that the concepts and expressions used by the provisions of the 1993 Directive must normally be given an "autonomous" European interpretation[2328] and this means that, following the principle of the "indirect effect" of directives (sometimes known as the principle of conforming interpretation of national legislation implementing EU directives), English courts are under a duty to interpret the provisions of the 2015 Act seeking to implement the 1993 Directive "as far as possible" in a way so as to give proper effect to the UK's obligations under the Directive.[2329] As a result, the decisions of the Court of Justice on the 1993 Directive which have explained its own interpretative role relative to the roles of national courts,[2330] which have ruled on the proper interpretation of concepts used by the 1993 Directive or have provided guidance on their application by national courts,[2331] have explained the duty of national courts to raise the issue of the unfairness of a term in a consumer contract of their own motion,[2332] and the relationship between the test of unfairness of contract terms under the 1993 Directive and the unfairness of commercial practices under the Unfair Commercial Practices Directive 2005[2333] are relevant equally to the UK's reimplementation of that Directive by the 2015 Act as they are under the 1999 Regulations. This continuing relevance also holds good as regards case-law of the Court of Justice on other European legislative instruments on which it may draw in any future interpretation of the Directive's concepts, as in its case-law on the concept of "consumer".[2334] However, this last example raises a different issue, as the 2015 Act defines "consumer" in a way which may be broader in one respect than the interpretation of the Court of Justice to "consumer"[2335]; and this raises the question whether UK law is entitled as a matter of EU law to extend its legislative

38-376

[2322] Below, paras 38-389 et seq.

[2323] Below, paras 38-408 et seq.

[2324] Below, paras 38-414 et seq.

[2325] Below, paras 38-418 et seq.

[2326] Below, paras 38-419 et seq.

[2327] See above, para.38-015.

[2328] Kásler v OTP Jelzálogbank Zrt (C-26/13) EU:C:2014:282, April 30, 2014 at [37].

[2329] Above, para.38-017.

[2330] Above, para.38-329.

[2331] See above, paras 38-250—38-262, 38-270—38-271 and 38-314—38-315.

[2332] See, notably, Océano Grupo Editorial SA v Murciano Quintero (C-240/98 to C-244/98) EU:C:2000:346, [2000] E.C.R. I-4941; Mostaza Claro v Centro Móvil Milenium SL (C-168/05) EU:C:2006:675, [2006] E.C.R. I-10421 on which above, paras 38-331—38-332. The 2015 Act seeks to give legislative recognition to this case-law in s.71 "Duty of court to consider fairness of term" on which see below, para.38-392.

[2333] Directive 2005/29 concerning unfair business-to-consumer commercial practices in the internal market [2005] O.J. L149/22 ("2005 Directive") and see above, para.38-278 and, notably, Pereničová v SOS finance, spol. sro (C-453/10) EU:C:2012:144.

[2334] Above, paras 38-034—38-035.

[2335] 2015 Act s.2(3) (applicable to Pt 1, and applied to Pt 2 by s.76(2)) and see below para.38-384.

controls on unfair terms drawn from the 1993 Directive beyond those required by that Directive.

38-377 **"Minimum harmonisation" and "full harmonisation" in the EU law governing unfair contract terms** The question whether EU law permits national legislation controlling unfair contract terms beyond the requirements of the 1993 Directive is a complex one, turning on the relationship between three EU legislative instruments: the 1993 Directive itself, the Unfair Commercial Practices Directive 2005, and the Consumer Injunctions Directive 2009.[2336] In summary, the 1993 Directive requires Member States to put in place national measures to ensure that unfair contract terms are "not binding" on consumers and also to prevent the use of unfair terms in consumer contracts,[2337] but requires only "minimum harmonisation" and therefore in principle allows Member States to retain or enact measures within the scope of the Directive which are more protective of consumers.[2338] Secondly, the Unfair Commercial Practices Directive 2005 requires Member States to prohibit "unfair business-to-consumer commercial practices" within its scope, but requires "full harmonisation" and so forbids Member States from maintaining or putting in place measures within its scope which are *more* protective of consumers.[2339] In principle, as has been explained, the use or recommendation for use of an unfair term in a consumer contract may constitute an "unfair commercial practice" so as to fall within the scope of the 2005 Directive, but the 2005 Directive states that it is "without prejudice to contract law, and in particular the rules on the validity, formation or effect of a contract", whether this law is EU or national.[2340] Thirdly, the 2009 Directive requires Member States to allow national "qualified entities" (whether designated public bodies or consumers' associations) to bring proceedings for an injunction aimed at the protection of the collective interests of consumers in support of a list of European legislative instruments, including, inter alia, the 1993 Directive and the 2005 Directive and these injunctions are available in respect both of national infringements (that is, where all elements of the infringement take place within one Member State) and cross-border ("intra-Community") infringements, where an infringement in one Member State affects the collective interests of consumers in another.[2341] This Directive appears to assume that these injunctions can and should be available to prevent the use of terms which are unfair in national law even where the latter has extended the protection of the 1993 Directive under its "minimum harmonisation" clause.[2342] For present purposes, it will be seen that a broad distinction can be drawn between national provisions which affect the relative rights of contracting parties (and notably the binding character of the contract terms in question) which belong to

---

[2336] Directive 2009/22/EC on injunctions for the protection of consumers' interests, [2009] O.J. L110/30 ("2009 Directive"). These questions were not fully addressed by the Law Commissions, which relied on the "minimum harmonisation" character of the 1993 Directive to allow the UK to provide more protection to consumers than is required by that directive, without considering the possible impact of the 2005 Directive on preventive measures: Law Com., Scottish Law Com., *Unfair Terms in Consumer Contracts: Advice to the Department for Business, Innovation and Skills* (March 2013), para.S5.

[2337] 1993 Directive arts 6 and 7.

[2338] 1993 Directive art.8, above, para.38-022.

[2339] 2005 Directive arts 4 (full harmonisation); arts 5–9 and see above, paras 38-159—38-160.

[2340] Above, para.38-363; 2005 Directive art.3(2), recital 9, above, para.38-160.

[2341] 2009 Directive arts 1–2, 4, recitals 3, 7.

[2342] 2009 Directive recital 4 and see below, para.38-425.

"contract law" as understood by (and as excluded from the scope of) the 2005 Directive and enforcement measures (and notably injunctions) to prevent the use or recommendation for use of unfair terms at the request of the CMA and other regulators.

English law before the Consumer Rights Act 2015 Under the law as it stood **38-378** before the coming into force of the 2015 Act, the implementation in UK law of the 1993 Directive by the 1999 Regulations did not seek to go beyond the requirements of that Directive: the general approach was to "copy-out" the European provisions.[2343] The 1999 Regulations provided both that unfair terms are not binding on consumers and for preventive measures to be taken by the CMA and other qualifying bodies.[2344] By contrast, while English law more widely controlled unfair terms beyond the requirements imposed by the 1993 Directive (notably, by the Unfair Contract Terms Act 1977[2345]), it did not provide any dedicated provision for preventive measures in respect of the use or recommendation for use of contract terms so controlled, though it did specify the whole of the 1977 Act for the purposes of "domestic infringements" under Pt 8 of the Enterprise Act 2002.[2346] The 2005 Directive was (and is) implemented in UK law by the Consumer Protection from Unfair Trading Regulations 2008, which, inter alia, created a series of criminal offences relating to unfair commercial practices.[2347] And the 2009 Directive is implemented in UK law by Pt 8 of the Enterprise Act 2002, which provides for "enforcement orders" in respect, inter alia, of "Community infringements", and the 1999 Regulations (which implemented the 1993 Directive) and the 2008 Regulations (which implemented and still implement) the 2005 Directive were specified for this purpose.[2348] All this meant that the use by a trader of unfair terms in its dealings with consumers might attract the preventive measures provided by the 1999 Regulations, an "enforcement order" under Pt 8 of the Enterprise Act 2002 and/or a criminal sanction in respect of an "unfair commercial practice" (where the latter's conditions are satisfied).[2349]

Extension of controls on unfair contract terms under the Consumer Rights **38-379**
Act While the main purpose of the 2015 Act in relation to unfair contract terms was the placing of the law in a single legislative instrument (rather than being found in part in the Unfair Contract Terms Act 1977 and in part in the 1999 Regulations),[2350] the Act also extended the law governing unfair terms beyond UK law's previous position in a number of ways. The question whether EU law permits the law of a Member State to extend its law governing unfair contract terms in this way depends on whether this law concerns the relative rights of contracting parties under the contract ("contract law", so as to escape the 2005 Directive's "full harmonisation") or whether it prohibits practices by traders in relation to the use or recommendation for use of contract terms (whether this prohibition is effected by injunc-

---

[2343] Above, paras 38-221 et seq.
[2344] 1999 Regulations reg.8; regs 10, 12–15 respectively.
[2345] In particular, Unfair Contract Terms Act 1977 ("1977 Act") ss.2, 6(3) and 7(2).
[2346] The Enterprise Act 2002 (Part 8 and Domestic Infringements) Order 2003 (2003/1593) art.2 and Sch. Pt 1 referring to s.211 of the 2002 Act, on which see above, para.38-133.
[2347] Above, paras 38-165 et seq.
[2348] Enterprise Act 2002 s.212 (as amended) and see above, para.38-361.
[2349] See, e.g. *OFT v Ashbourne Management Services Ltd* [2011] EWHC 1237 (Ch), [2011] E.C.C. 31 and above, paras 38-353—38-364.
[2350] Above, para.38-212.

tion, criminal sanction or other enforcement measures) so as possibly to fall foul of the 2005 Directive's "full harmonisation". At this stage, the position regarding the first of these will be noted, leaving the latter for discussion in the context of the 2015's Act treatment of enforcement measures more generally.[2351]

38-380 **More extensive controls of unfair contract terms by national law than required by the 1993 Directive** The general position (which certainly applies to "contract law"[2352]) is that the laws of Member States may in principle provide for the control of unfair contract terms beyond those required by the 1993 Directive, either (within its scope) under its "own minimum harmonisation clause" or (outside its scope) under the Member States' general competence in this area.

38-381 **Extension of controls on the validity of contract terms beyond the 1993 Directive** The 2015 Act made a number of extensions to the protections required by the 1993 Directive but within its material scope. First, in general the Act renders terms which seek to exclude or limit liability in a trader for breach of the terms inserted in contracts to supply goods, digital content or services not binding on consumers, whether or not they were individually negotiated and without any assessment of their fairness under the general test provided by the 1993 Directive.[2353] Secondly, the general scheme for the control of unfair terms in Pt 2 of the Act goes beyond the protection for consumers required by the 1993 Directive by including "individually negotiated" terms under the test of unfairness,[2354] by imposing a second condition for the application of the exemption that they be "prominent" as well as transparent (that is, expressed in plain and intelligible language, which is required explicitly by the 1993 Directive),[2355] by adding three examples to the "indicative list" of terms,[2356] and by extending the protection for consumers against the choice of law applicable to the contract other than the law of an EEA State.[2357] Moreover, the 2015 Act also appears to extend the controls on unfair contract terms beyond the scope of the 1993 Directive, for example, by defining "consumer" as an individual "acting for purposes that are wholly *or mainly* outside that individual's trade", etc.[2358]

[2351] See below, paras 38-421 et seq.

[2352] Above, para.38-377. cf. below paras 38-421—38-426 on controls which do not belong to "contract law".

[2353] 2015 Act s.31 referring to ss.9–17, 28–29 (contracts to supply goods); s.47 (referring to ss.34–36, 41 and 46 (contracts to supply digital content); s.57, referring to ss.49–52 (contracts to supply services). For the most part, this position reflects the present position in English law: Unfair Contract Terms Act 1977 s.6(2) and 7(2). Some, but not all, of the cases so regulated reflect particular rules in EU law which have the same effect: see below, paras 38-531, 38-564 and 38-586.

[2354] 2015 Act s.62 thereby not following 1993 Directive art.3(1) and 3(2) and see below, para.38-389.

[2355] 2015 Act s.64, on which see below, paras 38-394—38-400 and cf. 1993 Directive art.4(2) *in fine*.

[2356] 2015 Act Sch.2 Pt 1 paras 5, 12 and 14 on which see below, para.38-391.

[2357] 2015 Act s.74 on which see below, para.38-418.

[2358] 2015 Act s.2(3) and 76(2) and see below, para.38-384. This is an apparent extension as the position of the CJEU on the definition of "consumer" for the purposes of the 1993 Directive is not certain: above, paras 38-035—38-037. A further example of an extension beyond the requirements of the 1993 Directive may be found in the Act's treatment of "secondary contracts": s.72, below, paras 38-402—38-405.

(iii) Scope of Controls on Contract Terms and Notices in Pt 2 of the Consumer Rights Act

"Terms in consumer contracts" and "consumer notices"   Part 2 of the   **38-382**
Consumer Rights Act 2015 applies to the terms of consumer contracts (implementing the 1993 Directive and replacing the 1999 Regulations and making certain other
provision in consequence of the deletion of protections for consumers from the
Unfair Contract Terms Act 1977).[2359] Secondly, Pt 2 extends its controls to certain
terms of "secondary contracts", whether or not the latter count as "consumer
contracts".[2360] And, thirdly, Pt 2 applies to "consumer notices" (in general, replacing s.2 of the Unfair Contract Terms Act 1977 in relation to a trader's liability to
consumers).[2361] The Act defines "trader" and "consumer" for these purposes.

"Trader"   Under Pt 2 of the Act "trader" means: **38-383**

> "... a person acting for purposes relating to that person's trade, business, craft or profes-
> sion, whether acting personally or through another person acting in the trader's name or
> on the trader's behalf."[2362]

"Business" is then defined to include "the activities of any government department or local or public authority".[2363] Taken together these definitions follow the
definition of "trader" in the Consumer Rights Directive 2011[2364] but also reflect the
definition of "seller or supplier" in the 1993 Directive.[2365] One consequential
advantage of using "trader" is that it avoids the implication that contracts by which
consumers supply goods or services *to* traders are necessarily excluded from the
controls on unfair contract terms.[2366] As has been earlier explained,[2367] the Court of
Justice of the EU has held that the very similar definition of "trader" for the
purposes of the Unfair Commercial Practices Directive 2005[2368] is "particularly
broad", not excluding "either bodies pursuing a task of public interest or those
which are governed by public law" and must be determined "in relation to the
related but diametrically opposed concept of 'consumer', which refers to any
individual not engaged in commercial or trade activities".[2369] Moreover, in *Šiba v*

[2359] See below, paras 38-389 et seq.

[2360] See below, paras 38-402—38-405.

[2361] Above, para.38-406.

[2362] 2015 Act s.2(2) applied to Pt 2 by s.76(2).

[2363] 2015 Act s.2(7) applied to Pt 2 by s.76(2).

[2364] Directive 2011/83/EU on consumer rights [2011] O.J. L304/64 art.2(2); *Explanatory Notes* 2015, para.34.

[2365] 1993 Directive art.2(c) and see above, para.38-224. One difference between the two definitions is that the Act refers expressly to a trader acting either "personally or through another person acting in the trader's name or on the trader's behalf", but it is submitted that such a situation should also be read into the definition in 1993 Directive art.2(c). A "person" is sufficiently broad to include both a "natural" and "legal" person as specified by art.2(c).

[2366] cf. above, para.38-226.

[2367] See generally, above, paras 38-050 et seq.

[2368] 2005 Directive art.2(b).

[2369] *BKK Mobil Oil Körperschaft des öffentlichen Rechts v Zentrale zur Bekämpfung unlauteren Wet-tbewerbs eV* (C-59/12) EU:C:2013:634, October 3, 2013 at [32]–[33] citing by analogy *Shearson Lehman Hutton* (C-89/91) EU:C:1993:15, [1993] E.C.R. I-139 para.22 on art.13 of the Brussels Convention on jurisdiction and the enforcement of judgments in civil and commercial matters: see above, para.38-050.

Devênas[2370] the Court of Justice applied this earlier approach to the definition of "trader" for the purposes of the 1993 Directive. As a result, "trader" is wide enough to include not-for-profit organisations, such as charities, mutual and cooperatives, where they carry on a business.[2371]

38-384 **"Consumer"** Under Pt 2 of the Act "consumer" means "an individual acting for purposes that are wholly or mainly outside that individual's trade, business, craft or profession".[2372] This definition reflects accurately the wording of the definitions of "consumer" in the 1993 Directive, and, therefore, the 1999 Regulations, with the significant exception of the reference to the individual's purposes being *mainly* outside that individual's trade, etc.[2373] As a matter of policy, this refinement was recommended by the Law Commissions in response "to a concern that many consumers occasionally use products such as mobile phones or home computers for work purposes".[2374] As earlier explained, the new wording follows the UK's implementation of the Consumer Rights Directive 2011,[2375] and reflects a wider UK legislative strategy in defining "consumer" for contract law purposes.[2376] To the extent to which the redefinition extends the scope of protection of the 1993 Directive,[2377] it is compatible with EU law.[2378] On the other hand, the protections provided for persons "dealing as consumer" contained in the Unfair Contract Terms Act 1977 were repealed by the Act,[2379] and this means principally that persons who would have fallen within this category but outside the new definition of "consumer", such as a company concluding a contract which is neither an integral part of its business nor, if only incidental to it, of a type which it regularly concludes,[2380] are no longer protected on this basis.[2381] Unlike the 1977 Act's definition of "dealing as consumer", the definition of "consumer" in the 2015 Act does not exclude a person in fact acting wholly or mainly outside his trade but holding himself out as acting in the course of a trade,[2382] but it is submitted that the likely view of the Court of Justice in this situation is that such a person should not be allowed to take advantage of the protection provided for consumers as the trader would legitimately consider

---

[2370] C-537/13 EU:C:2015:14, January 15, 2015, above, para.38-053. See also *Karel de Grote– Hogeschool Katholieke Hogeschool Antwerpen VZW v Kuijpers* (C-147/16) EU:C:2018:320, May 17, 2018, paras 49–60.

[2371] *Explanatory Notes* 2015, para.35.

[2372] 2015 Act s.2(3) as applied to Pt 2 by s.76(2).

[2373] 1993 Directive art.2(b).

[2374] Law Com. Advice (2013), para.7.100; cf. BIS, *Clarifying Consumer Law*, paras 4.25–4.31.

[2375] Directive 2011/83/EU on consumer rights [2011] O.J. L304/64 art.2(1), recital 17.

[2376] See above, paras 38-041—38-042.

[2377] This depends on the interpretation to be given to "consumer" by the CJEU, on which see above, paras 38-036—38-037.

[2378] Above, para.38-381.

[2379] 2015 Act s.75, Sch.4 paras 5–11.

[2380] *R. & B. Customs Brokers Co Ltd v United Dominions Trust Ltd* [1988] 1 W.L.R. 321, on which see Vol.I, para.15-074.

[2381] Such a person may still be protected on other grounds, notably, on the ground that it is acting on the other party's "written standard terms of business" under the Unfair Contract Terms Act 1977 s.3 (exemption clauses and related clauses), on which see Vol.I, paras 15-084—15-087. The Law Commissions considered that this change "carries with it only a negligible loss of protection" and would avoid "a very complicated piece of legislation carrying little benefit for businesses": Law Com. Advice (2013), para.7.115.

[2382] Unfair Contract Terms Act 1977 s.12(1)(a); 2015 Act s.2(3).

that he was acting for business purposes.[2383] The 2015 Act did not take a position on the question whether a person acting other than in the course of a business who *supplies* goods or services may count as a "consumer" for the purposes of Pt 2's provisions and so the answer to this question must follow the proper interpretation of the 1993 Directive in this respect.[2384]

Burden of proof as to "consumer"   Following the pattern set by the Unfair   **38-385**
Contract Terms Act 1977 (rather than the position under the 1999 Regulations), the 2015 Act provides that a trader claiming that an individual was *not* acting for purposes wholly or mainly outside the individual's trade, etc. must prove it.[2385]

"Consumer contract"   A "consumer contract" is defined as a "contract between   **38-386**
a trader and a consumer",[2386] and it is specifically provided that this does not include a contract of employment or apprenticeship.[2387] In the case of Pt 2's controls on unfair contract terms, this reflects the likely exclusion from the scope of the 1993 Directive of contracts relating to employment".[2388] "Consumer contract" should otherwise be interpreted as including all types of contracts concluded between "traders" and "consumers", including, for example, contracts for the sale, etc. of an interest in land or contracts of guarantee by the "consumer", following the proper interpretation of the 1993 Directive.[2389] This does not mean, however, that all the provisions in Pt 2 of the 2015 Act apply to terms in all types of consumer contracts, for certain types of contract are excluded or certain types of liability are excluded from its provisions barring the exclusion or restriction of liability for death or personal injury resulting from negligence, following the position earlier set out by the Unfair Contract Terms Act 1977.[2390]

"Consumer notice"   Unlike the 1999 Regulations, Pt 2 of the 2015 Act subjects   **38-387**
"consumer notices" to a test of fairness and a requirement of transparency modelled on the similar tests set out by the 1999 Regulations (following the 1993 Directive) for contract terms.[2391] In part, this reflects the need to protect consumers under the 2015 Act as much as they were protected under s.2 of the Unfair Contract Terms

---

[2383] cf. above, para.38-035; *Gruber v Bay Wa AG* (C-464/01) EU:C:2005:32, [2005] E.C.R. I-439 at para.54.

[2384] On which see above, para.38-226. The controls on contract terms in Pt 1 of the 2015 Act are restricted to the protection of consumers who *receive* goods, digital content or services as the contracts to which that Part relates are all expressed in terms of the supply of goods, digital content or services by traders to consumers: 2015 Act s.1(3).

[2385] 2015 Act s.2(4) as applied to Pt 2 by s.76(3). The position as regards persons "dealing as consumer" is found in Unfair Contract Terms Act 1977 s.12(3) (which, together with the rest of s.12) is deleted by the 2015 Act (s.75; Sch.4 para.11). No burden of proof as to "consumer" is set by the 1999 Regulations reg.3(1), following in this respect the 1993 Directive art.2(b): above, paras 38-048—38-059, 38-225.

[2386] 2015 Act ss.61(1), (3) and 76(1).

[2387] 2015 Act s.61(2).

[2388] 1993 Directive recital 10; art.1 and see above, para.38-222 (note). Employees remain protected from the exclusion of liability for negligence by their employers under the Unfair Contract Terms Act 1977 s.2 and from the effect of exemption clauses and certain related clauses contained in their employers' "written standard terms of business" under s.3 of the same Act, as foreseen by Law Com. Advice (2013), para.7.120: Vol.I, paras 15-081—15-087.

[2389] Above, paras 38-222—38-223.

[2390] Consumer Rights Act ss.65 and 66; Unfair Contract Terms Act 1977 ss.1(3) and 2(1) and see below, para.38-409.

[2391] On the position under the 1999 Regulations, see above, paras 38-241 et seq.

Act (which applies to the exclusion of liability for negligence by "notice" as well as by contract term), but the new provisions go further in several respects.[2392] Thus, s.61(4) of the Act provides that Pt 2 of the Act applies to a notice (a "consumer notice"[2393]) to the extent that it:

"(a) relates to rights or obligations as between a trader and a consumer, or

(b) purports to exclude or restrict a trader's liability to a consumer."

For this purpose, it does not matter:

"... whether the notice is expressed to apply to a consumer, as long as it is reasonable to assume it is intended to be seen or heard by a consumer."[2394]

For these purposes, "notice" is defined to include "an announcement, whether or not in writing, and any other communication or purported communication".[2395] On the other hand, in keeping with the Act's definition of "consumer contract", the Act excludes from the definition of "consumer notice" "a notice relating to rights, obligations or liabilities as between an employer and an employee."[2396]

38-388 Terms or notices reflecting "mandatory statutory or regulatory provisions" or international conventions The Consumer Rights Act 2015 adopts the exclusion from the scope of the controls set out by art.1(2) of the 1993 Directive and included in the 1999 Regulations[2397] by excluding from Pt 2 terms which reflect "mandatory statutory or regulatory provisions" or the provisions or principles of an international convention to which the UK or the EU is a party,[2398] but it extends this exclusion to "consumer notices". So, s.73 of the Act provides that Pt 2 governing unfair contract terms and notices:

"... does not apply to a term of a contract, or to a notice, to the extent that it reflects—

(a) mandatory statutory or regulatory provisions, or

[2392] It was earlier argued that the concept of "contract" in the 1993 Directive is likely to require an autonomous European interpretation and that, if one were taken by the CJEU, it would be based on the agreement of the parties without any requirement such as the English law doctrine of consideration: above, paras 38-229—38-230. The effect of non-contractual notices to exclude liability of an occupier of premises if sufficiently drawn to the claimant's (licensee's) attention is well established at common law, and based on the acceptance of the risk by entering the premises subject to this condition: *Ashdown v Samuel William & Sons Ltd* [1957] 1 Q.B. 409. This legal position was confirmed by the Occupiers' Liability Act 1957 s.2, though then controlled by the Unfair Contract Terms Act 1977 s.2 (as originally enacted and as still applicable outside the context of "consumer notices"). While the exclusion of liability by notice is not to be equated with the defence of volenti non fit injuria, it could nonetheless be said to rest on an implied non-contractual agreement between the visitor and the occupier of the premises who seeks to rely on the exclusion notice. Following this line of reasoning, notices disclaiming liability (which are seen as non-contractual by English law) could be seen as "contractual terms" under a European concept of contract as agreement. This would in turn mean that the 2015 Act's provisions which subject "consumer notices" to the controls set out by the 1993 Directive would not in principle go beyond that Directive's requirements.
[2393] 2015 Act s.61(7).
[2394] 2015 Act s.61(6).
[2395] 2015 Act s.61(8).
[2396] 2015 Act s.61(5) and cf. 2015 Act s.61(2), above, para.38-386.
[2397] 1999 Regulations reg.4(2).
[2398] See above, paras 38-233—38-240.

(b)   the provisions or principles of an international convention to which the United Kingdom or the EU is a party." [2399]

The Act explains that for this purpose "'mandatory statutory or regulatory provisions' includes rules which, according to law, apply between the parties on the basis that no other arrangements have been established".[2400] The interpretation of the exclusion in art.1(2) of the 1993 Directive which is reflected in s.73 of the Act has been set out by the Court of Justice in case-law earlier discussed.[2401]

(iv)   Contract Terms and Notices Not Binding on the Consumer Where Assessed as Unfair

(aa)   Terms of Consumer Contracts

Contract terms subject to the test of unfairness; "individually negotiated **38-389** **terms" included**   Apart from the exclusion of terms which reflect mandatory statutory provisions or the provisions of international conventions as explained above,[2402] under the Consumer Rights Act 2015 there is only one exclusion from the test of unfairness of terms in consumer contracts, i.e. the "core exclusion" allowed by art.4(2) of the 1993 Directive.[2403] In particular, the Act does not subject the application of the test of unfairness to a condition that the term be "individually negotiated" as foreseen by the 1993 Directive and as enacted by the 1999 Regulations.[2404] The inclusion of terms in consumer contracts which have been "individually negotiated" under the test of unfairness reflects the position under the Unfair Contract Terms Act, and the Law Commissions considered it desirable in the interest of simplicity that all the controls on unfair terms should have the same scope.[2405] Moreover, the Law Commissions considered that this inclusion would have little practical effect, as it is rare for consumers to negotiate about any term except the price or main subject matter (which are subject to special treatment under the Act) and a term which has been genuinely individually negotiated is very likely to be fair.[2406]

General test of unfairness   The formulation of the general test of unfairness of   **38-390** terms in consumer contracts in the Act is all but identical to the test required by the 1993 Directive and enacted by the 1999 Regulations, providing that:

> "A term is unfair if, contrary to the requirement of good faith, it causes a significant imbalance in the parties' rights and obligations under the contract to the detriment of the consumer."[2407]

[2399] 2015 Act s.73(1).
[2400] 2015 Act s.73(2); 1993 Directive recital 13.
[2401] See above, para.38-234.
[2402] Above, para.38-388.
[2403] 2015 Act s.64 and see below, paras 38-394—38-400.
[2404] 1993 Directive art.3(1) and 3(2); 1999 Regulations reg.5(1)–(4), on which see above, paras 38-242—38-244.
[2405] Law Com. Advice (2013), paras 7.64–7.65.
[2406] Law Com. Advice (2013), paras 7.64–7.65.
[2407] 2015 Act s.62(4); 1993 Directive art.3(1); 1999 Regulations reg.5(1).

Also following the earlier legislative pattern, though rewritten in more elegant English, the Act provides that:

"Whether a term is fair is to be determined—

(a) taking into account the nature of the subject matter of the contract, and

(b) by reference to all the circumstances existing when the term was agreed and to all of the other terms of the contract or of any other contract on which it depends."[2408]

The only change of wording of any significance here is the reference to "the subject matter of the contract" rather than the "nature of the goods or services for which the contract was concluded" (as in the 1993 Directive and the 1999 Regulations[2409]), but it is submitted that even this change makes no substantive difference.[2410] As a result, the discussion of the general test of unfairness of contract terms found in relation to the 1993 Directive and the 1999 Regulations earlier discussed is equally relevant to the test of unfairness found in the Consumer Rights Act,[2411] with the following qualification. As explained earlier in relation to the test of unfairness in the 1999 Regulations, the Court of Justice of the EU in *Aziz* advised that, under the requirement of good faith, the national court must assess whether the trader:

"... dealing fairly and equitably with the consumer, could reasonably assume that the consumer would have agreed to such a term in individual contract negotiations."[2412]

There is a particular difficulty in applying this approach to the test of unfairness in the Consumer Rights Act 2015, as the latter can apply to terms which *have been* individually negotiated as well as to terms which have not.[2413] Where it does, explaining the requirement of good faith by reference to a hypothetical test of what the trader could objectively have assumed the (reasonable) consumer would have agreed in individual negotiations would make little sense, given that, ex hypothesi, the consumer had in fact agreed to the term in question.[2414] It is submitted that this difficulty disappears if the hypothetical test is treated as *relevant* to the assessment of good faith rather than being conclusive of it,[2415] as this allows a court to be able to interpret the requirement of good faith in the context of an individually negotiated term on other and broader grounds, as is indeed suggested by recital 16 of the 1993 Directive itself.[2416] This is apparently the view taken by the CMA, which has observed that the "requirement of good faith ... allows for proper account to be

---

[2408] 2015 Act s.62(5).

[2409] 1993 Directive art.4(1); 1999 Regulations reg.6(1).

[2410] cf. the French version of the 1993 Directive art.3(1) which refers to "*la nature des biens ou services qui font l'objet du contrat*", which translates as "the nature of the goods or services which form the subject matter of the contract".

[2411] See above, paras 38-265 et seq.

[2412] *Aziz v Caixa d'Estalvis de Catalunya, Tarragona i Manresa* (C-415/11) EU:C:2013:164, March 14, 2013 at para.69, and see above, para.38-270.

[2413] 2015 Act s.62(1), (4) and (5), above, para.38-389.

[2414] cf. the discussion of the hypothetical test in *Aziz* in *ParkingEye Ltd v Beavis* [2015] UKSC 67, [2015] 3 W.L.R. 1373 above, paras 38-275—38-277.

[2415] This view was taken by Lord Mance in *ParkingEye Ltd v Beavis* [2015] UKSC 67 at [208], above, para.38-276.

[2416] Above, paras 38-267—38-268.

taken of the significance of any real negotiation that has actually taken place", but considers that

"... any contention that a particular consumer has actually influenced the substance of a term has to be tested against a detailed consideration of the circumstances existing at the time the contract was concluded. In [the CMA's] view, individual consumers rarely in practice have the required knowledge and bargaining power to ensure that contractual negotiations involving them are effectively conducted on equal terms."[2417]

The "indicative list of terms" Again following the 1993 Directive and the 1999 **38-391** Regulations,[2418] the 2015 Act includes a list of terms in consumer contracts that "may be regarded as unfair" for the purposes of the controls in Pt 2, the scope of these examples being qualified in a similar way as is found in the 1999 Regulations.[2419] The significance of the examples in the list therefore remains the same as the examples in the list in the 1999 Regulations.[2420] The vast majority of the 20 examples included in the list in the Act are substantively identical to the 17 found in this earlier instrument, differing only in minor points of drafting and in the replacement of "seller or supplier" with "trader",[2421] but there are three new examples.[2422] The Act makes provision for amendment of the "indicative list" (and

---

[2417] CMA, *Unfair contract terms guidance, Guidance on the unfair terms provisions in the Consumer Rights Act 2015* (CMA37, July 2015), para.2.30.

[2418] 1993 Directive art.3(3) and Annex; 1999 Regulations reg.5(5) and Sch.2 and see above, para.38-299 et seq.

[2419] s.63(1); Sch.2 Pts 1 and 2 respectively. Section 63(2) of the Act clarifies that a term listed in Sch.2 Pt 2 (which is thereby excluded from the scope of the examples in the indicative list in Sch.2 Pt 1) may nevertheless be assessed for fairness unless it is excluded from the scope of the test of fairness either as a term reflecting "mandatory statutory or regulatory provisions", etc. under s.73 or as a term specifying the main subject matter of the contract, etc. under the "core exclusion" in s.64.

[2420] See above, para.38-299. The 2015 Act s.64(6) provides expressly that terms listed in the Act Sch.2 Pt 1 cannot fall within the exclusion provided by s.64 on which see below, paras 38-394—38-400. While the list of terms in Sch.2 applies to "contract terms" rather than to "consumer notices", the CMA's view is that its "indicative list" also serves to illustrate the forms that unfairness can take in non-contractual notices: CMA, *Unfair contract terms guidance, Guidance on the unfair terms provisions in the Consumer Rights Act 2015* (CMA37, July 2015), para.1.25 and Pt 5 (which considers the practical significance of the examples in the list more generally).

[2421] 2015 Act Sch.2 Pt 1; 1999 Regulations Sch.2.

[2422] 2015 Act Sch.2 Pt 1 para.5: "[a] term which has the object or effect of requiring that, where the consumer decides not to conclude or perform the contract, the consumer must pay the trader a disproportionately high sum in compensation or for services which have not been supplied". This term is related to other examples found in the 1999 Regulations Sch.2 para.1(e) and (f) (included in the Act in Sch.2 Pt 1 paras 6 and 7) but has original elements, notably in its application to the case where "the consumer decides not to conclude or perform the contract". Sch.2 para.12 "[a] term which has the object or effect of permitting the trader to *determine* the characteristics of the subject matter of the contract after the consumer has become bound by it" (though this is subject to a qualification in Sch.2 para.23 as regards contracts which last indefinitely), which is clearly related to the example in para.13 (reflecting 1999 Regulations Sch.2 para.1(k)) which concerns terms enabling the trader "to *alter unilaterally* without a valid reason any characteristics of the goods, digital content or services to be provided". Sch.2 para.1(14): "A term which has the object or effect of giving the trader the discretion *to decide the price* payable under the contract after the consumer has become bound by it, where no price or method of determining the price is agreed when the consumer becomes bound" (though this example is also qualified by Sch.2 paras 23, 24 and 25), which builds on the first part of the example provided in the 1999 Regulations Sch.2 para.1 (l) (a term "providing for the price of goods to be determined at the time of delivery"), except that it extends to terms allowing the trader discretion to decide the price at any time. On possible changes to the "indicative list" as set out by the 1993 Directive (and partially reflected in the 2015 Act) see

its qualifications) by the Secretary of State by order made by statutory instrument.[2423]

38-392 **Duty of court in relation to the issue of fairness** The 2015 Act seeks to give explicit effect to the case-law of the Court of Justice of the EU as regards the duty of national courts to consider the fairness of a term in a consumer contract within the scope of the controls set out by the 1993 Directive.[2424] This follows the recommendation of the Law Commissions, which considered that such a statement would be helpful to bring this obligation to the attention of the courts and, especially, the lower courts.[2425] Section 71 of the Act therefore provides that:

> "(1)   Subsection (2) applies to proceedings before a court which relate to a term of a consumer contract.
> (2)   The court must consider whether the term is fair even if none of the parties to the proceedings has raised that issue or indicated that it intends to raise it.
> (3)   But subsection (2) does not apply unless the court considers that it has before it sufficient legal and factual material to enable it to consider the fairness of the term."

The qualification on the ambit of the duty made by s.71(3) reflects closely the qualification put on the national court's duty by the Court of Justice of the EU in *Pannon*[2426] but this should be read subject to later case-law in the Court of Justice in the context of the Consumer Sales Directive 1999 that appears to require a national court to request clarification from a party before it to enable it to determine whether one of the parties is a consumer and, therefore, falls within national legislation implementing EU consumer protection law.[2427] The Act also restricts the court's duty to the situation where "proceedings before a court *relate to* a term of a consumer contract"[2428] and this, together with the wording of s.71(2), suggests that the duty to consider the fairness of a contract term arises only where the proceedings before the court *relate to the term which is to be so considered for its fairness*.[2429] While similar wording has sometimes been used by the Court of Justice of the EU,[2430] it is submitted that such an interpretation of s.71 would risk imposing on English courts a more limited duty than is foreseen by the case-law of the Court of Justice to which s.71 ostensibly seeks to give effect. For, under that case-

---

Law Com. Advice (2013), paras 5-47 et seq. For discussion of these new examples of terms in the list see CMA, *Unfair contract terms guidance, Guidance on the unfair terms provisions in the Consumer Rights Act 2015* (CMA37, July 2015), paras 5.15.1–5.15.7, 5.22.11–5.22.12 and 5.23.1–5.23.7.

[2423] 2015 Act s.63(3)–(5).

[2424] See, notably, *Mostaza Claro v Centro Móvil Milenium SL* (C-168/05) EU:C:2006:675, [2006] E.C.R. I-10421; *Pannon GSM Zrt v Erzsébet Sustikné Györfi* (C-243/08) EU:C:2009:350, [2009] E.C.R. I-4713 and on this case-law and its progeny, above, paras 38-019—38-021, 38-331—38-335.

[2425] Law Com. Advice (2013), para.7.90.

[2426] *Pannon GSM Zrt v Erzsébet Sustikné Györfi* (C-243/08) EU:C:2009:350, [2009] E.C.R. I-4713 at [32], above, para.38-331.

[2427] *Faber v Autobedrijf Hazet Ochten BV* (C-497/13) EU:C:2015:357, June 4, 2015 on which see above, para.38-020.

[2428] 2015 Act s.71(1) (emphasis added).

[2429] cf. the observation in the *Explanatory Notes* 2015 para.341 in relation to s.71 that "the courts would only have to look at the term or terms in question, not the entire contract; this reflects the principle in Case C-137/08 *VB Pénzügyi v Schneider* in 2010".

[2430] Notably, *VB Pénzügyi Lizing Zrt v Schneider* (C-137/08) EU:C:2010:659, [2010] E.C.R. I-847 at para.49 referring to the duty of the court to decide whether "a contractual term *which is the subject of the dispute* before it falls within the scope of the Directive" (emphasis added).

law, a national court before which proceedings are brought relating to a consumer contract is under a duty to assess of its motion terms on which the trader *relies*, even though the terms are not ones to which the proceedings can be said to *relate*. So, for example, the Court of Justice has held that a national court must of its own motion raise the fairness of a national jurisdiction clause relied on by a trader to provide that court with jurisdiction to hear its claim against a consumer for payment under a consumer contract[2431]: such proceedings would not naturally be said to *relate* to the jurisdiction clause, but rather to the term or terms of the contract imposing on the consumer his or her duty to pay. The effect of this possible difference between the formulation of the Act and requirements of the case-law of the Court of Justice can be avoided if the phrase "proceedings before a court which relate to a term of a consumer contract" is interpreted as requiring only that the proceedings concern in a general sense the term to be considered for its fairness, if need be, by way of the conforming interpretation required of national courts by EU law.[2432] What this discussion suggests, however, is that it may be unwise for national legislation to seek to give effect to case-law of the Court of Justice which is both complex and, to an extent, still developing.[2433]

Burden of proof as to fairness of a contract term Unlike the position under the   **38-393**
Unfair Contract Terms Act 1977 as regards the reasonableness of contract terms,[2434] neither the 1993 Directive nor the 1999 Regulations set an express burden of proof as to the fairness or unfairness of terms. As earlier explained,[2435] while the position is not clear, the Court of Justice is most likely to take the view that the issue of fairness of terms under the 1993 Directive is not itself one appropriate to the allocation of a burden of proof, but instead for a "neutral assessment" of the term, although any facts on which the trader or consumer relies for this purpose would be subject to the normal rules of burden of proof established by national law.[2436] As a result, the Law Commissions considered that no provision should be made as to the burden of proof as to fairness of a term the new legislation, beyond the statement as to the duty of courts to raise the issue of fairness of their own motion,[2437] since "[t]o put the burden of proof on the consumer, even if it was just to prove a prima facie case, may not fit with the requirements of the EU law".[2438] Following this view, the Consumer Rights Act 2015 does not provide for the allocation of a burden of proof as to the fairness of terms, except to the extent to which it imposes a duty in courts to consider the issue of fairness of their own motion.[2439] This therefore leaves the issue of burden of proof as to fairness in the same state as under the 1999 Regulations.

The "core exclusion" from the assessment of fairness The proper interpreta-   **38-394**
tion of the exclusion to the test of unfairness of contract terms provided by art.4(2)

[2431] *Pannon GSM Zrt v Erzsébet Sustikné Györfi* (C-243/08) EU:C:2009:350, at para.35; *VB Pénzügyi Lizing Zrt v Schneider* (C-137/08) EU:C:2010:659 at para.56.
[2432] Above, para.38-014.
[2433] See above, para.38-020.
[2434] s.11(5) (reasonableness).
[2435] See paras 38-335—38-337.
[2436] See para.38-337.
[2437] Above, para.38-392.
[2438] Law Com. Advice (2013), para.7.91.
[2439] 2015 Act s.71, above, para.38-392.

of the 1993 Directive (and implemented faithfully by reg.6(2) of the 1999 Regulations) has caused considerably difficulty.[2440] This exclusion was the subject of the decision of the UK Supreme Court in *Abbey National Plc v The Office of Fair Trading*,[2441] where it ruled that terms under which banks imposed charges when their consumer customers requested or instructed the banks to make a payment for which they did not hold the necessary funds and which were not covered by an arranged facility fell within the exclusion from the test of unfairness provided by reg.6(2) so as to preclude the OFT from taking into account "the adequacy of the price or remuneration, as against the goods or services supplied in exchange" in their assessment of the fairness of the terms.[2442] The Supreme Court's view of the exclusion was criticised as too broad and insufficiently protective of the consumers[2443] and led the Department for Business, Innovation and Skills (BIS) to ask the Law Commissions to advise it on the exclusion in reg.6(2) of the 1999 Regulations as part of a wider updated advice on the creation of a single harmonised regime to replace the Unfair Contract Terms Act and the 1999 Regulations.[2444] The Law Commissions' advice to BIS had the advantage of guidance by the Court of Justice on the significance of art.4(2) of the 1993 Directive, notably in *Caja de Madrid* and *Pohotovosť*,[2445] but not in the important later decisions in *Kásler*, *Matei* and *Van Hove*.[2446]

38-395   The Law Commissions' Advice   The Law Commissions advised that the UK's implementation of the exclusion in art.4(2) should be reformed as the "current law is unacceptably uncertain. It requires significant legal expertise to navigate, and even then the outcome is unpredictable. Both consumers and traders may suffer from this uncertainty".[2447] The Law Commissions considered that the first limb of the exclusion in art.4(2) (concerning the main subject matter of the contract) excludes from the test of unfairness a category of contract terms, whereas the second part (referring to "the adequacy of the price and remuneration, on the one hand, as against the services or goods supplied in exchange, on the other") instead excludes the amount of the price as against the services or goods supplied in exchange from the assessment of the fairness of a term.[2448] As regards the second limb, they interpreted the Supreme Court's decision in *Abbey National Plc v The Office of Fair Trading*[2449] as rejecting a distinction between the main price and ancillary price or charges for the purposes of identifying "price and remuneration" under art.4(2),[2450] and stated that "[p]rice is therefore intended to be a broad concept which

---

[2440] See above, paras 38-245—38-264.
[2441] [2009] UKSC 6, [2010] 1 A.C. 696.
[2442] See above, paras 38-247—38-248.
[2443] e.g. Whittaker (2010) 73 M.L.R. 106.
[2444] Law Com. Advice (2013).
[2445] *Caja de Ahorros y Monte de Piedad de Madrid v Asociación de Usuarios de Servicios Bancarios (Ausbanc)* (C-484/08) EU:C:2010:309, [2010] E.C.R. I-04785; *Pohotovosť s.r.o. v Korčkovska* (C-76/10) EU:C:2010:685.
[2446] *Kásler v OTP Jelzálogbank Zrt* (C-26/13) EU:C:2014:282, April 30, 2014 ("*Kásler* (C-26/13)"); and *Matei v SC Volksbank România SA* (C-143/13) EU:C:2015:127, February 26, 2015 ("*Matei* (C-143/13)"); *Van Hove v CNP Assurances SA* (C-96/14) EU:C:2015:262, April 23, 2015 ("*Van Hove* (C-96/14)"), above, paras 38-250—38-263.
[2447] Law Com. Advice (2013) S. 14.
[2448] Law Com. Advice (2013), para.3.100–3.102.
[2449] [2009] UKSC 6, [2010] 1 A.C. 696 especially at [41], [78] and [113].
[2450] Law Com. Advice (2013), paras 3.13 and 4.61. It is submitted, though, that while the SC rejected

includes ancillary and contingent charges".[2451] They considered that the "price" should be understood as "money consideration" following the definition in the Sale of Goods Act 1979.[2452] While they considered that the reference to "remuneration" in art.4(2) of the Directive was unlikely to refer to consideration furnished other than in money (such as terms requiring consumers to grant traders intellectual property rights), if it did, as a matter of policy they recommended that the exclusion should not cover this situation.[2453]

The purpose of the Law Commissions' recommendations was to clarify the exclusion allowed by art.4(2) and to discourage traders from using "hidden price terms" which undermine the competitiveness of the market by offering low headline prices and then adding hidden extras, which both "causes detriment to consumers and disadvantages honest traders who are upfront about their charges".[2454] Rather than proposing that the exclusion should not apply to payments which are "incidental or ancillary to the main purpose of the contract" as they had previously suggested, the Law Commissions therefore recommended that:

38-396

> "... price or main subject matter terms should be exempt from review only if they are transparent and prominent. Both approaches distinguish between the terms which consumers take into account in their decision to buy the product and those which become lost in small print. The emphasis on prominence, however, offers a practical way of distinguishing between a headline price and other charges. It also emphasises that whether a term is exempt is within the control of the trader."[2455]

For this purpose, the Law Commissions recommended that future legislation should make clear that a requirement of transparency of terms required that they should be "plain and intelligible", legible and readily available to the consumer,[2456] considering that this did not "gold-plate" the Directive (i.e. did not go beyond its requirements).[2457] Moreover, the Law Commissions recommended that the legislation should add a new condition that a term must also be "prominent" to fall within the exclusion,[2458] meaning by this that:

38-397

> "... it is presented during the sales process in such a way that a reasonable consumer would be aware of the term even if they did not read the full contractual document."[2459]

---

the approach of the Court of Appeal below, its own approach is more complex than the Law Commissions' interpretation allows, as some of its members acknowledged that *some* charges fell outside the scope of art.4(2), notably, those charges which fall within examples of terms within the "indicative list": see [2009] UKSC 6 at [43], [101] referring to 1999 Regulations Sch.2 paras 1(d), (e), (f) and (l).

[2451] Law Com. Advice (2013), para.4.61.

[2452] Law Com. Advice (2013), para.4.63 referring to Sale of Goods Act 1979 s.2(1). The Law Commissions considered that terms providing for "early termination charges" should attract distinct treatment and therefore recommended that they should be added to the new legislation's "indicative list of terms" (foreseen by the 1993 Directive art.3(3)), whose members would be excluded explicitly from the benefit of the exclusion: Law Com. Advice (2013), paras 4.61 and 5.82. For implementation of this recommendation see 2015 Act Sch.2 Pt 1 para.5.

[2453] Law Com. Advice (2013), paras 4.63–4.64.

[2454] Law Com. Advice (2013), para.2.39.

[2455] Law Com. Advice (2013) S. 18 and see further Pts 2 and 3 of the Advice.

[2456] Law Com. Advice (2013), paras 4.25–4.26.

[2457] Law Com. Advice (2013), para.4.17 referring in particular to the significance of recital 20 which explains that "the consumer should actually be given an opportunity to examine all the terms".

[2458] Law Com. Advice (2013), paras 4.27–4.48.

[2459] Law Com. Advice (2013), para.4.27.

For this purpose, the EU standard of the "average consumer" (that is, "a reasonably well informed, observant and circumspect" consumer) should be adopted.[2460] The Law Commissions considered that there is "considerable overlap between the concepts of transparency and prominence", but that while transparent terms will not always be prominent, prominent terms will usually be available and legible, but may not necessarily be in plain and intelligible language.[2461] Moreover, the additional requirement of "prominence" would apply only as a condition for the application of the exclusion drawn from art.4(2) and would not affect the general requirement of transparency of terms.[2462] While not saying so explicitly, the Law Commissions apparently saw the imposition of this condition additional to the one required by art.4(2) of the 1993 Directive as permissible given the "minimum harmonisation" which it requires.[2463]

38-398   Consumer Rights Act 2015 s.64   Section 64(1) of the Act provides:

> "A term of a consumer contract may not be assessed for fairness … to the extent that—
>   (a)   it specifies the main subject matter of the contract, or
>   (b)   the assessment is of the appropriateness of the price payable under the contract by comparison with the goods, digital content or services supplied under it".[2464]

Section 64 further provides that this excludes a term from an assessment only if it is "transparent and prominent".[2465] For this purpose:

> "(3)   A term is transparent … if it is expressed in plain and intelligible language and (in the case of a written term) is legible.[2466]
>   (4)   A term is prominent … if it is brought to the consumer's attention in such a way that an average consumer would be aware of the term.
>   (5)   In subsection (4) "average consumer" means a consumer who is reasonably well-informed, observant and circumspect."

The exclusion which s.64 provides is specified as not applying to a term in the list of "indicative terms" provided by Pt 1 of Sch.2.[2467]

[2460] Law Com. Advice (2013), paras 4.41–4.45.

[2461] Law Com. Advice (2013), para.4.47.

[2462] Law Com. Advice (2013), para.4.48.

[2463] Law Com. Advice (2013), para.3.99. This position is implicit given the Law Commissions' contrasting treatment of the requirement of transparency, which they saw as implementing art.4(2) as properly understood: Law Com. Advice (2013), para.4.17.

[2464] 2015 Act s.64(1). The reference to "goods, digital content or services" may look restrictive (not applying, e.g. to contracts for the sale of land or insurance contracts), but it is submitted that the exclusion may apply to any type of "consumer contract" to which Pt 2 of the 2015 Act (following the 1993 Directive) applies: cf. above, paras 38-222—38-223 and 38-386.

[2465] 2015 Act s.64(2).

[2466] This definition of "transparency" is expressed as applying for the purposes of Pt 2 of the Act and therefore applies equally to the general requirement of transparency of terms in consumer contracts in s.68(1), below, para.38-414.

[2467] s.64(6); Sch.2 Pt 1, above, para.38-391. This is uncontroversial as regards the examples of terms also contained in the Annex to the 1993 Directive, as these terms are specified by the Directive art.3(3) as ones "which may be regarded as unfair" and therefore have been held by the CJEU to fall outside art.4(2): *Matei* (C-143/13) at paras 59–61, above, para.38-253. However, this exclusion from s.64 may well go further than the requirements of the Directive as regards terms added by the Act to this list: on which see above, para.38-391. On the compatibility of such an extension with EU law see above, paras 38-377—38-381; 38-421—38-426.

Comments; relationship to recent case-law of the CJEU It will be seen, **38-399**
therefore, that s.64 follows a number of the recommendations of the Law
Commissions. First, it adopts the view that the nature of the two limbs of art.4(2)
of the 1993 Directive differs: the first limb excludes from assessment for its fairness "a term ... to the extent that it specifies the main subject matter of the
contract"; whereas the second limb excludes a term from assessment for its fairness:

> "... to the extent that the assessment is of the appropriateness of the price payable under
> the contract by comparison with the goods, digital content or services supplied under it."

This view finds clear support in the more recent judgments of the Court of Justice
in *Kásler* and *Matei*.[2468] Secondly, s.64(3) explains the condition of transparency of
a term as concerning both its expression in plain and intelligible language and, in
the case of written terms, legibility, but, contrary to the recommendation of the Law
Commissions, s.64 does not also require that the term be "readily available".[2469] It
is submitted, however, that this omission makes no substantive difference, as the
Court of Justice in *Kásler* held that arts 4(2) and 5 of the 1993 Directive reflect the
same requirement of plain and intelligible language and that, for these purposes,
recital 20 states that "the consumer should actually be given an opportunity of
examining all the terms of the contract".[2470] As a result, an English court would have
to give effect to this aspect of the condition of the transparency of terms under
art.4(2) in its interpretation of s.64(3). Indeed, the Court of Justice in *Kásler* went
much further, holding that the requirement of transparency does not merely require
that the term is "formally and grammatically intelligible",[2471] but also that the
"consumer is in a position to evaluate, on the basis of clear, intelligible criteria, the
economic consequences for him which derive from" the term in question: the
trader's reasons for using the term and its relationship with other contractual terms
should be clear and intelligible.[2472] For this purpose, the Court of Justice set as the
standard for evaluation "the average consumer, who is reasonably well informed
and reasonably observant and circumspect".[2473] Thirdly, s.64(4) explains the new
condition of "prominence" as recommended by the Law Commissions in terms of
it being "brought to the consumer's attention in such a way that an average
consumer would be aware of the term". The *Explanatory Notes* to the Act provide
as an example of this condition that terms governing the price or subject matter are
"in the small print".[2474] The Law Commissions apparently assumed that this additional condition would go beyond the condition of "plain intelligible language"

[2468] *Kásler* (C-26/13) at paras 43, 49–51 and 52–55; *Matei* (C-143/13) at para.70 and see above, paras
38-251—38-252.

[2469] cf. above, para.38-397.

[2470] *Kásler* (C-26/13) at paras 66–68 and above, paras 38-261, 38-262 which discusses the later case-
law of the CJEU in *Matei* and *Van Hove* which confirms its earlier approach in *Kásler*. In the view
of A.G. Wahl, the requirement of plain intelligible language "implies that *the consumer acquires
actual knowledge* of all the terms": *Andriciuc v Banca Românească* (C-186/16) EU:C:2017:703
("*Andriciuc* (C-186/16)"), A.G. Opinion of April 26, 2016 at para.62. This point was not specifically addressed in the judgment of the CJEU of September 20, 2017.

[2471] *Kásler* (C-26/13) at para.71.

[2472] *Kásler* (C-26/13) at para.75 and see also *Andriciuc* (C-186/16) at paras 45–50, above, para.38-262.

[2473] *Kásler* (C-26/13) at para.74; *Andriciuc* (C-186/16) at para.47.

[2474] *Explanatory Notes* 2014 paras 307–308. See also the guidance in CMA, *Unfair contract terms guidance, Guidance on the unfair terms provisions in the Consumer Rights Act 2015* (CMA37, July
2015), paras 3.20–3.32.

set by art.4(2) of the Directive,[2475] but this assumption is open to doubt given the very broad interpretation of this condition in *Kásler*, *Matei*, *Van Hove* and *Andriciuc*, for in those cases, as earlier noted, the Court of Justice required the national court to consider not merely whether a relevant term had been "brought to the consumer's attention in such a way that an average consumer would be aware of the term",[2476] but that the average consumer "is in a position to evaluate, on the basis of clear, intelligible criteria, the economic consequences for him which derive from that term".[2477] In sum, the additional condition of "prominence" set by the 2015 Act may not go far enough to give proper effect to the interpretation of the Court of Justice without the aid of the principle of conforming interpretation by national courts of legislation implementing EU law.[2478] On the other hand, if and to the extent to which the Act's condition of "prominence" does indeed go further than the 1993 Directive (as interpreted) in the interests of providing greater protection for consumers than it requires, then the Act's compatibility with EU law is covered by the Directive's "minimum harmonisation" clause as regards its "contract law effects", though it may not be so covered as to its provision of enforcement measures.[2479] Fourthly, the strategy of the 2015 Act in dealing with the problem of "hidden price terms" by requiring that they must be "prominent" rests on the Law Commission's very broad interpretation of the expression "price and remuneration" found in art.4(2) of the Directive[2480] so as to cover all terms which impose money obligations on consumers.[2481] This view is reflected directly in s.64(1)(b) of the 2015 Act which excludes from the assessment of the term "the appropriateness of the price payable under the contract by comparison with the goods, digital content or services supplied" under the contract. It is submitted that this reformulation of the second limb of the exclusion in art.4(2) of the Directive may be broader in its effect than the interpretation given to that limb by the Court of Justice. In *Kásler*, the Court considered whether a term in a contract of consumer credit denominated in a foreign currency which set the exchange rate for repayment by the consumer of the loan at the creditor bank's "selling rate" could be assessed for its unfairness, where another term set the exchange rate for repayment of the original sums lent by the bank to the consumer at the bank's "buying rate".[2482] It held that the second limb of the exclusion in art.4(2) *could not apply* to the repay-

---

[2475] Above, para.38-397.

[2476] 2015 Act s.64(4).

[2477] *Kásler* (C-26/13) at para.75; *Matei* (C-143/13) at para.74; *Van Hove* (C-96/14) at para.41; *Andriciuc* (C-186/16) at para.45.

[2478] On which, see above, para.38-014. In both respects, it is striking that the Package Travel Directive 2015 (Directive (EU) 2015/2302 on package travel and linked travel arrangements (on which see above, para.38-242) requires a set of information, changes to information provided and the alteration of terms of the contract to be communicated to the traveller in a "prominent" as well as a "clear and comprehensible" manner: arts 5(3), 6(1), 7(4) and 19(2). However, rather than suggesting that "prominence" is a distinct requirement, it is submitted that this coupling of an explicit requirement of prominence with the long-established requirement that information, etc. be "clear and intelligible" is likely to encourage the CJEU to see prominence as already inherent in the "clear and intelligible" requirement made in other EU consumer protection directives, including the 1993 Directive.

[2479] See above, paras 38-377—38-381 and below, paras 38-421—38-426. This would also apply to the three added examples of terms which may be unfair of terms in the "indicative list" as membership of this list excludes the application of the exclusion in s.64 of the Act: s.64(6).

[2480] The Law Commissions saw their view as reflecting the position of the SC in *OFT v Abbey National Plc*, see above, para.38-395 (which criticises this interpretation).

[2481] Law Com. Advice (2013), para.4.61, above, para.38-395.

[2482] See above, note to paras 38-250—38-254.

ment term, as such a term:

> "… in so far as it contains a pecuniary obligation for the consumer to pay, in repayment instalments of the loan, the difference between the selling rate of exchange and the buying rate of exchange of the foreign currency, *cannot be considered as 'remuneration'*, the adequacy of which as consideration for a service supplied by the lender cannot be subject of an examination as regards unfairness under Article 4(2)",

of the Directive,[2483] apparently on the basis that this difference did not constitute something in return ("consideration") for any foreign exchange service supplied by the lender.[2484] As earlier explained, the Court of Justice therefore saw the second limb of the exclusion in art.4(2) as ruling out comparison of the sum payable under a contract term (there, the repayment term) as against any services provided *for such a sum*, thereby implicitly rejecting the Supreme Court's approach which looked globally at the sums payable (or contingently payable) under the term as against the package of services provided by the trader in respect (in part) of those sums.[2485] Moreover, this contrast between the approach of the Court of Justice and the Supreme Court in *OFT v Abbey National Plc* was made clearer by the Court of Justice's judgment in *Matei*, where it again required the identification of a distinct service in exchange for which the "price or remuneration" is to be paid.[2486] It is submitted that in these circumstances English courts should seek to give effect to the interpretation and guidance of the Court of Justice of the EU in their application of s.64(1)(b) of the 2015 Act following the principle of the conforming interpretation of UK legislation implementing EU directives, though the difficulty in doing so would be whether the English court would consider this "possible" given the wording of s.64(1)(b), its background in the Law Commissions' earlier *Advice* and the decision of the Supreme Court in *OFT v Abbey National Plc*.[2487]

In this respect, in *Casehub Ltd v Wolf Cola Ltd* the High Court rejected the invitation of the claimant (to whom consumers had assigned their claims[2488]) that it should not follow the Supreme Court's decision in *Abbey National Plc* in relation to the exclusion in s.64 of the 2015 Act on the basis that it was inconsistent with the later decisions of the CJEU in *Kásler* and *Matei*, on the grounds that it was bound by the Supreme Court's decision and that it was "far from clear that the CJEU cases … have the effect for which [the claimant] contends".[2489] In *Casehub*, the consumers (and other customers) had contracted with the defendant for the internet storage of data by way of "cloud computing". Under their contracts, the defendant charged its customers a £20 monthly subscription fee for a fixed term of 12 months; if a customer terminated its agreement within the minimum term, a cancellation fee was payable calculated as a lump sum equivalent to the total remaining monthly charges less a 10 per cent discount said to reflect the fact that the customer was paying early. Due to system problems, a number of the defendant's customers did not receive their log-in information to access the service and they therefore terminated

38-400

[2483] *Kásler* (C-26/13) at para.59 (emphasis added).

[2484] *Kásler* (C-26/13) at para.58.

[2485] Above, paras 38-247—38-248, 38-255.

[2486] *Matei* (C-143/13) at para.70 and see, above, para.38-257.

[2487] On the principle of "conforming interpretation" and its limits, see above, para.38-014.

[2488] The HC held that these assignments of the consumers' restitutionary claims against the defendant were valid and not unenforceable on the ground of maintenance and champerty: [2017] EWHC 1169 (Ch), [2017] 5 Costs L.R. 835 at [25]–[31].

[2489] [2017] EWHC 1169 (Ch), [2017] 5 Costs L.R. 835 at [53]–[54]

their contracts within the first month, being then charged a £196 cancellation fee. The claimant contended that the cancellation fee provisions in the consumer contracts were unlawful as unfair under s.62 of the 2015 Act and that therefore the consumers were not liable to pay the fees and could recover fees already paid. However, the High Court rejected this claim, holding that the cancellation fees provisions in the contracts came within the exclusion provided by s.64 of the Act. The assessment of the fairness of these terms would involve "the assessment ... of the appropriateness of the price payable under the contract" under s.64(1)(b), since, while the cancellation fee does not comprise the price payable under the contract, it was a monetary obligation on the customer which formed part of that price in accordance with the approach of the Supreme Court in *Abbey National Plc* to contracts providing for a package of ways of charging for a package of services.[2490] With respect, however, it is doubtful whether the High Court's approach to the authority of the Supreme Court's decision is correct given the requirement in s.3(1) of the European Communities Act 1972 that questions of the meaning of EU law (here, art.4(2) of the 1993 Directive) must be determined in accordance with "the principles laid down by and any relevant decision of the European Court" and given that the High Court did not explain how the European case-law did not have the effect contended for in relation to the Supreme Court's decision. Moreover, the inclusion within the exclusion in s.64(1)(b) of a term under which a fee is charged on "cancellation" of the contract by the consumer did not take into account the presence in Sch.2 Pt 1 of the 2015 Act (which lists terms which may be regarded as unfair) of:

"... [a] term which has the object or effect of requiring that, where the consumer decides not to conclude or perform the contract, the consumer must pay the trader a disproportionately high sum in compensation or for services which have not been supplied."

It is more than arguable that the cancellation fee term in the cloud computing contract in *Casehub* fell within this example of a term in that it required the consumers to pay "a disproportionately high sum in compensation or for services which [were] not supplied"; and under s.64(6) of the Act (following case-law of the Court of Justice), s.64 "does not apply to a term of a contract listed in Part 1 of Schedule 2".[2491]

38-401   **Effects of a finding of unfairness of a contract term**   The effects of a finding by a court that a term of a consumer contract is unfair under the Consumer Rights Act follow closely the position under the 1999 Regulations and the 1993 Directive.[2492] As a result, "[a]n unfair term of a consumer contract is not binding on the consumer",[2493] it being clarified that "[t]his does not prevent the consumer from relying on the term or notice if the consumer chooses to do so".[2494] On the other hand:

[2490] [2017] EWHC 1169 (Ch) at [49]–[56] referring in particular to [2009] UKSC 6 at [42] (Lord Walker) and [78] (Lord Phillips), on which see above, paras 38-247—38-248.

[2491] Above, para.38-398.

[2492] See above, paras 38-339—38-346.

[2493] 2015 Act s.62(1). See similarly 1993 Directive art.6(1) and 1999 Regulations reg.8(1). For discussion of the effect of a finding of unfairness in a "secondary contract" under s.72 of the Act see below, paras 38-402—38-405.

[2494] 2015 Act s.62(2). This also follows the CJEU's ruling that where a court raises the issue of fairness

"Where a term of a consumer contract is not binding on the consumer as a result of [Part 2 of the Act], the contract continues, so far as practicable, to have effect in every other respect."[2495]

And, thirdly, use by a trader of an unfair term in a consumer contract may attract the special enforcement measures of the law of unfair terms provided by Sch.3 of the Act[2496] or the making of an "enforcement order" under Pt 8 of the Enterprise Act 2002 where it harms the collective interests of consumers, and it *may* constitute an "unfair commercial practice" so as to attract the criminal sanctions provided by the Consumer Protection from Unfair Trading Regulations 2008.[2497]

(bb)   Certain Types of Term of "Secondary Contracts"

Extending the controls of Pt 2 to certain types of term in "secondary contracts"   Section 72 of the Consumer Rights Act 2015 Act applies the rules of Pt 2 to "a term of a contract ('the secondary contract')" that "reduces the rights or remedies or increases the obligations of a person under another contract ('the main contract')",[2498] "that would apply to the term if it were in the main contract".[2499] For these purposes, it does not matter "whether the parties to the secondary contract are the same as the parties to the main contract" or "whether the secondary contract is a consumer contract".[2500] On the other hand, these rules do not apply "if the secondary contract is a settlement of a claim arising under the main contract".[2501] This provision has no counterpart in the 1999 Regulations (or the 1993 Directive), but is related to s.10 of the Unfair Contract Terms Act 1977, which provides that: **38-402**

> "A person is not bound by any contract term prejudicing or taking away rights of his which arise under, or in connection with the performance of, another contract, so far as those rights extend to the enforcement of another's liability which [Part I of the Act] prevents that other from excluding or restricting."

The purpose of this anti-avoidance provision has been said to prevent a person (a) from enforcing against another person (B) a clause in a contract between them (the "secondary contract") which provides that B is not to sue a third person (C) under a contract between B and C and which would have been ineffective under the 1977 Act if it had been contained in the contract between B and C (the "main contract").[2502] It therefore applies, for example, to the case where a term in a direct contract between a manufacturer of goods and a person purports to affect the rights of that person as buyer under the Sale of Goods Act 1979 against the retailer from

---

of a term of its own motion and finds it unfair, then it must not apply it unless "the consumer, after having been informed of it, does not intend to assert its unfair or non-binding status": *Pannon GSM Zrt v Erzsébet Sustikné Györfi* (C-243/08) EU:C:2009:350, para.33.

[2495] 2015 Act s.67. See similarly 1993 Directive art.6(1) and 1999 Regulations reg.8(2).

[2496] 2015 Act s.70, which refers also to the provision of investigatory powers available to the CMA and other regulators for these purpose which are set out in Sch.5.

[2497] See below, paras 38-419—38-420.

[2498] 2015 Act s.72(1).

[2499] 2015 Act s.72(2).

[2500] 2015 Act s.72(3).

[2501] 2015 Act s.72(4).

[2502] Peel (ed.), *Treitel on The Law of Contract*, 14th edn (2015), para.7-084. This lack of enforceability could result either directly from a provision of the Act (e.g. s.2(1), s.6(2)) or from a finding of "unreasonableness" of such a term (e.g. s.2(2) or s.6(3) as assessed under s.11).

whom he or she purchases the goods[2503] or to the case where a supplier (B) contracts to supply a customer (C) with a product under a contract (the main contract) containing no exemption clause, but the customer (C) also enters a servicing contract with A (the secondary contract) under which C is precluded from exercising his rights against B under the main contract.[2504] While the scope of s.10 has been described as "enigmatic",[2505] it has been held not to apply to the compromise or waiver of an existing contractual claim such as the release by a person of rights which have accrued to him as the result of the breach of another contract to which he is party[2506] nor to the case where the parties to the main contract and the secondary contract are the same.[2507]

38-403   It will be seen that s.72 of the 2015 Act has considerable similarities with s.10 of the 1977 Act, but also significant differences.[2508] First, as will be seen, s.72 would apply to the situation where a person (a), *whether or not a trader* for these purposes, concludes a contract (the "secondary contract", A/B) with another person, B, *whether or not B is a "consumer"* for these purposes, which includes a term which reduces B's rights or remedies or increases his or her obligations towards a third person (C) where C is a "trader" and B is a "consumer" within the meaning of the Act so that this main contract (B/C) qualifies as a "consumer contract". In this situation, the term of the secondary contract is subject to the rules of Pt 2 of the Act governing fairness and transparency as they would apply if it were in the main contract.[2509] Secondly, unlike the 1977 Act as it has been interpreted, s.72 of the 2015 Act would also apply to the situation where a person, A (a "trader" for these purposes), and B (a "consumer" for these purposes), conclude a "consumer contract" (the "main contract") and also conclude a further contract (the "secondary contract") which contains a term that reduces B's rights or remedies against or increases his or her obligations towards A under the main contract, whether or not A qualifies as "trader" or B as "consumer" for the purposes of this secondary contract and whether or not that contract otherwise fails to qualify as a "consumer contract".[2510] In this situation, equally, the terms of the secondary contract is subject to the rules of Pt 2 of the Act governing its fairness and transparency. While the

---

[2503] See Vol.I, para.15-128.

[2504] *Tudor Grange Holdings Ltd v Citibank N.A.* [1992] Ch. 53 at [66].

[2505] Vol.I, para.15-128.

[2506] *Tudor Grange Holdings Ltd v Citibank N.A.* [1992] Ch. 53; Vol.I, para.15-128.

[2507] *Tudor Grange Holdings Ltd v Citibank N.A.* [1992] Ch. 53 at [66]; Peel (ed.), *Treitel on The Law of Contract*, 14th edn (2015), para.7-084.

[2508] The Law Commissions had earlier recommended that its proposed unified legislation on unfair terms should contain provision, applicable to all the types of contract governed by it, subjecting terms in secondary contracts to the same controls as if they appeared in the main contract, but that genuine agreements to settle existing disputes should be exempted: Law Commissions, *Unfair Terms* (2005), paras 3.141–3.142.

[2509] Unlike the controls on the terms of secondary contracts imposed by the Unfair Contract Terms Act 1977 s.10 (which apply to the "prejudicing or taking away" of rights which Pt 1 of that Act prevents) the controls imposed by s.72 of the 2015 Act on the terms of the secondary contract are those provided by Pt 2 of the Act (i.e. principally the test of unfairness, the requirement of transparency and the special controls on liability for negligence in s.65) and they do not, therefore, extend to the controls imposed by Pt 1 of the Act on contract terms which seek to exclude or limit liabilities or rules provided for consumer contracts and provided by s.31 (exclusion of liability: goods contracts), s.47 (exclusion of liability: digital content contracts), and s.57 (exclusion of liability: services contracts).

[2510] Notably, if the secondary contract is a contract of employment which is excluded from the definition of "consumer contract" by the 2015 Act s.61(2), above, para.38-386.

examples of exclusion or limitation clauses in the "indicative list" provided by Sch.2 of the 2015 Act would not apply directly for this purpose (given that they are concerned with the exclusion or limitation of liability in a trader to a consumer under a consumer contract),[2511] they could nevertheless provide useful guidance mutatis mutandis. Thirdly, as has been noted, following the interpretation taken of the scope of s.10 of the 1977 Act, s.72(4) expressly provides that it shall not apply to a settlement of a claim arising under the main contract.[2512]

The effect of unfairness on terms in "secondary contracts"   Unlike the position under s.10 of the Unfair Contract Terms Act 1977 (which provides that a person is not bound by a term falling under it[2513]), the controls imposed by s.72 of the 2015 Act on the terms of secondary contracts are those provided by Pt 2 of that Act (i.e. the test of unfairness and the requirement of transparency) and this means that, in general, a term in a secondary contract falling under s.72 may or may not bind according to whether or not it is assessed as unfair under the general test provided by s.62.[2514] Following the general rule, where a term in a secondary contract is found unfair by way of application of s.72, it is apparently not binding on the person whose rights or remedies are reduced or obligations increased, even though there is no provision in the 2015 Act which has this explicit effect.[2515]

38-404

While, as earlier noted, the provisions governing "secondary contracts" find no direct counterpart in the 1993 Directive, to the extent to which they govern terms in "consumer contracts" they clearly come within its scope, but to the extent to which they govern terms other than in "consumer contracts" within the meaning of the 1993 Directive they fall outside its scope and therefore in principle within the general competence of national law.[2516] In either situation, any extension beyond the 1993 Directive having effect on the contract term (being part of "contract law") itself is compatible with EU law.[2517] On the other hand, the controls on the terms of secondary contracts in s.72 may form the object of enforcement measures provided by Sch.3 of the Act.[2518] To the extent to which the availability of these

38-405

[2511] 2015 Act Sch.2 Pt 1 paras 1 and 2.

[2512] *Tudor Grange Holdings Ltd v Citibank N.A.* [1992] Ch. 53 at 66–67.

[2513] Above, para.38-402.

[2514] 2015 Act s.62(4) and (5), above, paras 38-389 et seq. The exception is found where ss.65 and 66 impose bars on the effectiveness of certain types of term (notably terms which exclude or limit a trader's liability for death or personal injury resulting from negligence) on which see below, para.38-409.

[2515] 2015 Act s.72(2) provides merely that "the term is subject to the provisions of this Part that would apply to the term if it were in the main contract". In the case of a term in a main contract (which must be a "consumer contract") the primary effect of a finding of unfairness is that the term is "not binding on the consumer": s.62(1). However, if this provision were applied as it stands to the case of a term in a secondary contract then it would appear to restrict the effect of the finding of unfairness in that secondary contract to the situation where the person affected is a "consumer" for the purposes of *that* contract, which appears inconsistent with s.72(3)(b) which provides that "it does not matter for the purposes [of s.72] ... whether the secondary contract is a consumer contract". It is clearly (if implicitly) the intention of s.72 that a person who acts as a "consumer" in the main contract should not lose the benefit of the rights which he or she enjoys under that contract by agreement with a third party, even if he acts *other than* as a consumer for the purposes of that secondary contract.

[2516] cf. above, paras 38-022—38-023, 38-377.

[2517] Above, para.38-380.

[2518] 2015 Act s.70(1) refers to Sch.3 providing functions for regulators "in relation to the enforcement of this Part" i.e. Pt 2.

enforcement powers go beyond the 1993 Directive and also fall within the scope of the Unfair Commercial Practices Directive 2005, they may fall foul of the "full harmonisation" which the latter Directive requires.[2519]

(cc) Consumer Notices

38-406   **The test of unfairness**   The Consumer Rights Act 2015 provides that:

> "A [consumer] notice is unfair if, contrary to the requirement of good faith, it causes a significant imbalance in the parties' rights and obligations to the detriment of the consumer."[2520]

This assessment must be made taking into account "the nature of the subject matter of the notice" and "by reference to all the circumstances existing when the rights or obligations to which it relates arose and to the terms of any contract on which it depends".[2521] It will readily be seen that this test of unfairness is modelled closely on the test applied to contract terms set out by the Act and reflecting the 1993 Directive.[2522] The substantive control of "notices" is not (at least explicitly) required by the 1993 Directive (which governs contract terms),[2523] but reflects rather the well-known provisions in the Unfair Contract Terms Act 1977 governing, notably, the exclusion of business liability for death and personal injury, and for "other loss or damage" caused by negligence.[2524] The approach of the Act here is two-fold: first, as will be seen, it bars the exclusion or restriction of liability for death or personal injuries resulting from negligence by notice, subject to certain exclusions.[2525] Secondly, the Act subjects the exclusion by notice of *all other liabilities* in traders to consumers to the new test of unfairness which has just been set out: this therefore applies to exclusions of liability for personal injuries or death caused by negligence in the cases excluded from the special bar[2526] and to exclusions of liability for other loss or damage. So, as regards the latter, for example, a notice of disclaimer of liability by a surveyor engaged by a building society purporting to exclude his or her liability to the (consumer) purchaser of the residence bought by the consumer with the help of a loan by the building society as seen in *Smith v Eric S. Bush*[2527] would

---

[2519] See below, paras 38-421—38-426.

[2520] 2015 Act s.62(6). On the definition of "consumer notice" see 2015 Act ss.61(4), 76(1) and above, para.38-387.

[2521] 2015 Act s.62(7).

[2522] 2015 Act s.62(4) and (5); 1993 Directive arts 3(1) and 4(1).

[2523] But see the argument at para.38-387 (note) that the control of non-contractual notices as understood at common law may be required as a matter of the autonomous interpretation of "contract" for the purposes of the 1993 Directive.

[2524] Unfair Contract Terms Act 1977 s.2. The 1977 Act s.5 "consumer guarantees" also applied to "notices", but s.5 was deleted by the Consumer Rights Act s.75; Sch.4 para.7 following the recommendation of the Law Commissions which saw it as unnecessary: *Unfair Terms in Contracts* (2005), para.3.48.

[2525] 2015 Act ss.65 and 66 on which see below, para.38-409.

[2526] 2015 Act s.66(4) excludes from the bar in s.65 terms or notices excluding or limiting the liability of an occupier of premises to a person who obtains access for recreational purposes, subject to certain conditions. However, this exclusion does not apply to the controls of the fairness of contract terms and consumer notices in s.62 of the 2015 Act (on which see above, para.38-390 and in this paragraph) as noted by *Clerk and Lindsell on Torts*, 22nd edn (2017), paras 12-52—12-53.

[2527] Joined with the decision in *Harris v Wyre Forest DC* [1990] 1 A.C. 831.

now fall to be assessed for its fairness under the 2015 Act[2528] rather than under s.2(2) of the 1977 Act. However, the 2015 Act goes further than the 1977 Act, as it subjects "consumer notices" in general to the test of fairness and this therefore includes non-contractual exclusions or limitation of liability by a trader for loss or damage other than caused by negligence.[2529] This would therefore allow the control of "end user licence agreements" (which commonly accompany contracts for software and other digital products and which not only include terms about how far the consumer may copy the information, but also restrictions of a range of liabilities including for defamation or breach of privacy)[2530] and "browse wrap licences" (which many internet sites use and which state that by downloading material the consumer will be taken to have agreed to the owner's terms and conditions, even where there is no box or icon to tick).[2531]

Effect of a finding of unfairness of a "consumer notice" The Consumer Rights   **38 407** Act 2015 provides that "an unfair consumer notice is not binding on the consumer".[2532] Moreover, the Act extends its scheme of enforcement measures required for the prevention of unfair contract terms by the 1993 Directive to "consumer notices".[2533] As will be seen, to the extent to which these measures constitute the prohibition of a "business-to-consumer commercial practice" within the meaning of the Unfair Commercial Practices Directive 2005, they may fall foul of its "full harmonisation".[2534]

(v)   Contract Terms and Notices Not Binding on the Consumer in All Circumstances

Four special categories   Under the Consumer Rights Act 2015, there are four   **38-408** categories of situation where terms in consumer contracts or "consumer notices" are made not binding on the consumer without any evaluation of their fairness as is provided for contract terms and consumer notices generally.

(i) Terms or notices excluding or restricting liability for death or personal injury   **38-409** *resulting from negligence*   Section 65(1) of the 2015 Act provides that:

> "... [a] trader cannot by a term of a consumer contract or by a consumer notice exclude or restrict liability for death or personal injury resulting from negligence."

This provision therefore reproduces for the consumer context s.2(1) of the Unfair Contract Terms Act 1977.[2535] For this purpose, s.65 reproduces the definitions of

---

[2528] 2015 Act s.62(6) and (7).

[2529] This follows the recommendation of Law Com. Advice (2013), para.7.26.

[2530] Law Com. Advice (2013), paras 7.18–7.19, 7.26.

[2531] Law Com. Advice (2013), paras 7.20–7.21.

[2532] 2015 Act s.62(2)

[2533] The heading of the 2015 Act s.70 confusingly refers only to the "enforcement of the law of unfair contract terms", but s.70(1) itself refers to the conferral of functions on the CMA and other regulators in relation to the enforcement of Pt 2 and, therefore, the law governing "consumer notices" as well as governing terms in consumer contracts. This is confirmed explicitly by Sch.3 (entitled "Enforcement of the law on unfair contract terms and notices" and which sets out the enforcement powers), para.1(d) of which provides that the Schedule applies to "a consumer notice".

[2534] Below, paras 38-421—38-426.

[2535] On which see Vol.I, paras 15-081—15-083.

"personal injury" and, with minor changes, "negligence" provided by the 1977 Act.[2536] Again following the 1977 Act, the 2015 Act excludes from the scope of these special controls any contract in so far as it is a contract of insurance, including a contract to pay an annuity on human life and any contract so far as it relates to the creation or transfer of an interest in land[2537]; and it provides that s.65 does not affect the validity of any discharge of indemnity given by a person in consideration of the receipt by that person of compensation in settlement of any claim the person has[2538] and does not apply to the liability of an occupier of premises to a person who obtains access to the premises for recreational purposes if the person suffers loss or damage because of the state of premises and allowing the person access for those purposes is not within the purposes of the occupier's trade, business, craft or profession.[2539] It is to be noted that these exclusions from the effect of s.65 leave applicable the general controls on terms or notices on the basis of their fairness and transparency.[2540]

38-410 *(ii) Contract terms seeking to exclude Pt 1 liabilities*   The Consumer Rights Act 2015 Pt 1 imposes on traders a series of liabilities in the three categories of contracts to which it applies: contracts to supply goods; contracts to supply digital content; and contracts to supply services.[2541] Part 1 of the Act also provides in general that the liabilities arising under its provisions in this way cannot be excluded or restricted by a term of the relevant contract.[2542] So, for example, a term of a consumer contract of sale of goods cannot exclude liability arising from breach of the term that the quality of the goods is satisfactory or that the goods are reasonably fit for any purpose made known by the consumer to the trader before the contract is made,[2543] thereby reflecting and, as regards consumer contracts, replacing the well-known controls in s.6 of the 1977 Act.[2544] Also following the 1977 Act, this control on the exclusion of liability extends to a series of terms of similar function.[2545] The rendering of contract terms ineffective in this way by Pt 1 of that Act generally takes effect without the need for any judicial assessment of their fairness under the general test of unfairness under Pt 2 of the Act.[2546] None of these controls in Pt 1 of the Act are required by the 1993 Directive, although some are required by the Consumer Sales Directive 1999, and, to a much lesser extent, the

---

[2536] 2015 Act s.65(3) and (4) respectively; Unfair Contract Terms Act 1977 s.1(1) ("negligence"); s.14 ("personal injury"). 2015 Act ss.65(2) (on relationship to voluntary acceptance of risk) and 65(5) (immaterial whether breach inadvertent or intentional or liability direct or vicarious) make similar provision as is found in the 1977 Act, ss.2(3) and 1(4) respectively.

[2537] 2015 Act ss.65(6) and 66(1) and cf. Unfair Contract Terms Act 1977 s.1(2); Sch.1 para.1(a) and (b).

[2538] 2015 Act ss.65(6) and 66(2) and cf. Unfair Contract Terms Act 1977 s.1(2); Sch.1 para.5 (which is restricted to cases of compensation for pneumoconiosis).

[2539] 2015 Act ss.65(6) and 66(4) and cf. Unfair Contract Terms Act 1977 s.1(3)(b) (which refers to "recreational or *educational* purposes").

[2540] 2015 Act ss.62, 68 and 69.

[2541] 2015 Act Pt 1, Chs 2, 3 and 4 respectively and see below, paras 38-465 et seq.

[2542] 2015 Act s.31 (contracts to supply goods), s.47 (contracts to supply digital content) and s.57 (contracts to supply services) and see below, paras 38-531, 38-564 and 38-586 (which note the qualifications on this general position).

[2543] 2015 Act ss.9 and 10; s.31(1)(a) and (b).

[2544] Unfair Contract Terms Act 1977 s.6(2) (which the 2015 Act s.75, Sch.4 para.8(3) deleted).

[2545] e.g. 2015 Act s.31(2) reflecting the definition in the Unfair Contract Terms Act 1977 s.13.

[2546] For the details see 2015 Act ss.31, 47 and 57 below, paras 38-531, 38-564 and 38-586 respectively (which explain the qualifications on this general position).

Consumer Rights Directive 2011.[2547] To the extent to which these controls on contract terms are not so required, their effect on the binding nature of the term between the contracting parties is clearly permitted by EU law under the "minimum harmonisation" clause in the 1993 Directive, but the position is more difficult as regards the availability of enforcement measures linked to these controls as a result of the "full harmonisation" required by the Unfair Commercial Practices Directive 2005.[2548]

(iii) Contract terms and burden of proof under the Distance Marketing of **38-411**
Financial Services Directive The Consumer Rights Act 2015 provides specially so as to deem unfair a term of a consumer contract which

"... has the effect that the consumer bears the burden of proof with respect to compliance by a distance supplier or an intermediary with an obligation under any enactment or rule implementing"

the Distance Marketing of Financial Services Directive 2002.[2549] The consequences of such deemed unfairness follow the consequences of a term assessed as unfair as earlier explained.[2550]

(iv) Consumer arbitration The Consumer Rights Act 2015 retained the special **38-412**
rule in the Arbitration Act 1996 according to which a term in a consumer contract which constitutes an arbitration agreement is deemed unfair so far as it relates to a pecuniary claim in a modest amount (£5,000 at the time of writing).[2551] Arbitration agreements in consumer contracts which relate to claims for larger sums may be assessed for their fairness under the general rule in s.62 of the Act.[2552]

In each of these four categories of case, the contract term or (as the case may be) **38-413**
notice is not binding on the consumer, but the wider consequences of the non-bindingness of a term as between the contracting parties differ as between them. As regards the two cases where a contract term is deemed unfair (arbitration agreements and terms governing burden of proof in distance contracts for the supply of financial services), the provisions of Pt 2 which govern the effects of the non-bindingness of a term apply so that the consumer is able to rely on the clause and

---

[2547] Directive 99/44/EC on certain aspects of the sale of consumer goods and associated guarantees [1999] O.J. L171/7 art.7(1). The Consumer Rights Directive 2011 (whose provisions are "imperative" under art.25) is relevant to the trader's liability under s.11(4) and s.12 (below, paras 38-499—38-500); s.36(3) and s.37 (below, paras 38-548—38-549) and s.50(3) (below, para.38-573). The 2011 Directive is also relevant to ss.28 and 29 of the Act: below, paras 38-526—38-527.

[2548] See below, paras 38-421—38-426.

[2549] 2015 Act s.63(6) and (7); Directive 2002/65/EC concerning the distance marketing of consumer financial services [2002] O.J. L271/16; 2015 Act s.63(6) and (7) (which provides definitions for this purpose). This provision reflects the 1999 Regulations reg.5(6) and (7) as inserted by the Financial Services (Distance Marketing) Regulations 2004 (SI 2004/2095) reg.24(3). On the latter generally, see above, para.38-136.

[2550] Above, para.38-401.

[2551] Arbitration Act 1996 ss.89–91 as amended by 2015 Act s.75, Sch.4 paras 30–32, referring to Pt 2 of the Act for these purposes. The special rule in the Arbitration Act 1996 s.90 extending the definition of a "consumer" so as to include a legal person is also retained. The amount is specified by the Unfair Arbitration Agreements (Specified Amount) Order 1999 (SI 1999/2167). cf. above, para.38-302.

[2552] Above, para.38-390. For this latter purpose, the definition of "consumer" follows the general scheme as provided by the 2015 Act s.2(2) and s.76(2) on which see above, para.38-384.

as regards its possible effect on the wider contract.[2553] In the case of the exclusion of liability for negligence, the 2015 Act provides simply that "[a] trader *cannot* by a term of a consumer contract ... exclude or restrict liability for death or personal injury resulting from negligence",[2554] not thereby deeming a contract term seeking to do so "unfair" and so "not binding" within the meaning of Pt 2 so as to attract its wider effects. It is submitted, though, that this is unlikely to cause any practical problems as a consumer has no reason to *rely* on such a clause and the ineffectiveness of such an exemption clause would not have the effect of rendering the continuation of the wider contract impracticable.[2555] Similarly, while Pt 1 makes no special provision for any wider effects of the non-bindingness of contract terms seeking to exclude Pt 1 liabilities, such an effect is most unlikely to have any effect on the wider contract.[2556] On the other hand, the 2015 Act applies the special enforcement regime for unfair terms which it provides in Sch.3 to all four of these categories of ineffective contract term.[2557]

(vi) The Requirement for Transparency

38-414 **Application to contract terms and consumer notices** Section 68(1) of the Consumer Rights Act 2015 headed "Requirement for transparency" provides that:

"A trader must ensure that a written term of a consumer contract, or a consumer notice in writing, is transparent."

As regards contract terms, it is provided that:

"... [a] term is transparent ... if it is expressed in plain and intelligible language and (in the case of a written term) is legible."[2558]

Section 68(2) provides specially that "[a] consumer notice is transparent ... if it is expressed in plain and intelligible language and it is legible".

38-415 **Contract terms** In the case of contract terms, the 2015 Act's intention is to implement art.5 of the 1993 Directive without extending the protection which it requires for consumers, since the additional requirement of "legibility" is seen as implicit in the Directive's requirement of plain, intelligible writing, a view which accords with the wide interpretation given to it by the Court of Justice of the EU.[2559] Un-

---

[2553] 2015 Act s.62(1) (as applied by Arbitration Act 1996 s.91(1) as amended) (arbitration agreements); s.62(1) (as applied by s.63(6) (distance contracts). For these consequences see ss.62(3) and 67 of the Act, above, para.38-401.

[2554] 2015 Act s.65(1) (emphasis added).

[2555] cf. 2015 Act ss.62(3) and 67. There is an argument that s.67 could apply to terms ineffective under s.65 as the text of the former refers to terms "not binding on the consumer" which *does* properly describe the effect of s.65 even though it does not use this terminology.

[2556] 2015 Act ss.31, 47 and 57 (Pt 1 liabilities); s.67.

[2557] 2015 Act ss.31(7), 47(5) and 57(7) (Pt 1 liabilities); s.70(1) (terms deemed unfair under ss.63(6) and by the Arbitration Act 1996 s.91). While the heading of s.70 refers to the "enforcement of the law on *unfair* contract terms" (emphasis added), the text of s.70 refers "to the enforcement of this Part" and this clearly includes the enforcement of the rule contained in s.65: and cf. *Explanatory Notes* 2015, paras 333–334. On this enforcement regime more generally see below, paras 38-419 et seq.

[2558] 2015 Act s.64(3) (made in the context of the exclusion of terms specifying the subject matter, etc. but applying for the purposes of Pt 2 generally).

[2559] See this above, paras 38-350 and 38-397.

like the Act's implementation of the similar condition for the exclusion in art.4(2) of the 1993 Directive, the Act does not generally further require that written contract terms be "prominent",[2560] but it has earlier been argued that this further requirement may be included with the requirement of plain intelligible language as this has been interpreted by the Court of Justice of the EU.[2561]

"Consumer notices in writing"   On the other hand, the 2015 Act extends the   **38-416**
requirement for transparency to "consumer notices in writing", which is not apparently required by the 1993 Directive.[2562]

Effects of failure to fulfil requirement for transparency   First, s.69(1) of the   **38-417**
2015 Act provides:

"If a term in a consumer contract, or a consumer notice, could have different meanings, the meaning that is most favourable to the consumer is to prevail."

This seeks to implement the requirement in art.5 of the 1993 Directive (earlier implemented in reg.7(2) of the 1999 Regulations), with the difference that this rule of interpretation is not restricted to the interpretation of *written* terms (as is reg.7(2)[2563]) and that it extends to "consumer notices". This rule reflects the traditional approach at common law under construction *contra proferentem*.[2564] Secondly, the 2015 Act provides that the enforcement measures provided for regulators for the enforcement of the law of unfair terms applies to the enforcement of the requirement of transparency of terms and notices as it does to the requirement of fairness,[2565] a position which was not stated in the 1999 Regulations.[2566] Following the 1993 Directive (and the 1999 Regulations), the 2015 Act provides that the special rule of construction does not apply for the purposes of proceedings for an injunction under this enforcement regime.[2567]

(vii)   Prevention of Avoidance by Choice of Law

Special rule governing choice of law of non-Member State   As required by the   **38-418**
1993 Directive for contracts within its scope[2568] (and following the 1999 Regulations, though using a different wording),[2569] s.74 of the Consumer Rights Act 2015

[2560] cf. s.64(2) and (4) and above, para.38-398.

[2561] Above, para.38-399.

[2562] cf. above, para.38-387 (note) on the possibility that "consumer notices" do fall within the 1993 Directive's autonomous definition of contract terms. On the definition of "consumer notice" see above, para.38-387.

[2563] The position under the 1993 Directive in this respect is not entirely clear. The first sentence of art.5 (which requires plain, intelligible writing), is restricted expressly to "contracts where all or certain terms offered to the consumer are in writing"; while the second sentence ("[w]here there is doubt about the meaning of a term, the interpretation most favourable to the consumer shall prevail") is not so restricted, it could be thought that its scope remains restricted by what has been stated in the first sentence.

[2564] See Vol.I, para.15-012.

[2565] 2015 Act s.70(1) referring to "the enforcement of this Part", i.e. Pt 2.

[2566] For argument that these measures did extend to the requirement of transparency, see above, para.38-355; Law Com. Advice (2013), paras 6.60–6.63.

[2567] 2015 Act s.69(2); 1993 Directive art.5; 1999 Regulations reg.7(2).

[2568] 1993 Directive art.6(2).

[2569] 1999 Regulations reg.9 on which see above, para.38-352.

provides that, where a consumer contract has a close connection with the UK, a choice of law of a country or territory other than an EEA State[2570] as the contract's applicable law does not affect the application of Pt 2's provisions governing unfair contract terms.[2571] This special rule required by the 1993 Directive[2572] differs from the general position provided by the Rome I Regulation,[2573] to which the Act helpfully cross-refers to indicate to the reader the rules applicable in the absence of a choice of the law of a country or territory other than an EEA.[2574] Article 6(1) of the Rome I Regulation provides the law of the consumer's habitual residence as the applicable law governing consumer contracts in the absence of agreement otherwise:

"... provided that the professional:

(a) pursues his commercial or professional activities in the country where the consumer has his habitual residence, or

(b) by any means, directs such activities to that country or to several countries including that country,

and the contract falls within the scope of such activities."

Furthermore, where these same conditions are satisfied, art.6(2) of the Rome I Regulation provides that any agreement in the consumer contract on applicable law may not:

"... have the result of depriving the consumer of the protection afforded to him by provisions that cannot be derogated from by agreement by virtue of the law which, in the absence of choice, would have been applicable on the basis of paragraph 1."

If these conditions are *not* satisfied, then the rules governing the law applicable to the consumer contract fall under the general scheme governing contracts in the Rome I Regulation.[2575] It seems clear that the special provision governing agreements on applicable law in the 1993 Directive takes precedence over the general scheme set out in the Rome I Regulation (which makes uniform provision governing the law applicable to contractual obligations) and is best seen as constituting a special "overriding mandatory provision" in the sense of art.9 of that Regulation.[2576] It is to be noted that, to the extent to which the Act extends the definition of

---

[2570] The EEA States comprise the EU Member States plus Iceland, Liechtenstein and Norway. The 1993 Directive forms part of the EU law which these latter States have agreed to apply: Agreement on the European Economic Area (updated version to April 12, 2014) art.72; Annex XIX para.7(a).

[2571] It is to be noted that the restriction of s.74's special rule to the application of Pt 2, means that it does not apply so as specially to protect the rules rendering terms not binding on consumers under Pt 1 of the Act, i.e. those rules governing the exclusion or restriction of liability arising from Pt 1 provisions by 2015 Act ss.31, 47 and 57. cf. similar provision in 2015 Act s.32 in respect of "contracts to supply goods" under Pt 1 Ch.2 of the Act, reflecting the Consumer Sales Directive 1999 art.7(2), below, para.38-533.

[2572] 1993 Directive art.6(2).

[2573] Regulation (EC) 593/2008 of the European Parliament and of the Council of 17 June 2008 on the law applicable to contractual obligations ("Rome I") [2008] O.J. L177/6 on which generally see Vol.I, paras 30-019 et seq.; Dicey, Morris and Collins, *The Conflict of Laws*, 15th edn (2012), Vol.II, paras 33-126 et seq. and, in relation to the 1993 Directive art.6(2), paras 33-168—33-173.

[2574] 2015 Act s.74(2).

[2575] Rome I Regulation, notably, arts 3 and 4 on which see Vol.I, paras 30-066—30-125.

[2576] Rome I Regulation arts 9 and 23 (on which generally see Vol.I, paras 30-024 and 30-211 et seq.); Plender and Wilderspin, *The European Private International Law of Obligations*, 3rd edn (2009), paras 9-092—9-093.

"consumer contract" beyond the definition taken by the Court of Justice for the purposes of the 1993 Directive,[2577] the 2015 Act also extends the application of this special rule governing choice of law.[2578] Such an extension of the applicable law rule may be reconciled with the uniform character of the rules set out for contractual obligations generally by the Rome I Regulation,[2579] but only to the extent to which it gives effect to "overriding mandatory rules" of the UK as part of the law of the forum or of the law of place of performance of the contract's obligations.[2580] The 2015 Act makes no provision equivalent to the exclusion of "international supply contracts" nor the rules governing *English* choice of law clauses as are found in the Unfair Contract Terms Act.[2581] It should be noted, however, that the Court of Justice of the EU has held that where a consumer contract contains a choice of law clause which designates the law of another Member State, that term may itself be an unfair term within the meaning of the 1993 Directive.[2582]

(viii)   Enforcement

Summary of position before enactment of the Consumer Rights Act   38-419
2015   Before the bringing into force of Pts 1 and 2 of the Consumer Rights Act 2015 on October 1, 2015, there were three sets of enforcement mechanisms which might be available to prevent the use or recommendation for use of unfair contract terms.[2583] The 1999 Regulations provided for applications for injunctions to be made by the Competition and Markets Authority (CMA) and other qualifying bodies against the use, recommendation for use or drawing up for general use of terms in consumer contracts that are unfair within the meaning of those Regulations.[2584] These powers did not extend to controls in English law of unfair contract terms which are not required by the 1993 Directive and implemented by the Regulations (notably, those found in the Unfair Contract Terms Act 1977[2585]). Secondly, Pt 8 of

---

[2577] See above, paras 38-035—38-036 (especially in relation to the definition of "consumer" in 2015 Act s.2(3) as an individual acting "wholly *or mainly* outside that individual's trade", etc.).

[2578] s.74(1) *in fine* provides that "this *Part* [i.e. Pt 2] applies despite that choice".

[2579] See especially Rome I Regulation Ch.2 "Uniform Rules".

[2580] Rome I art.9. In the absence of such a specially extended applicable law rule, the substantive controls in the 2015 Act on unfair contract terms which are *not* required by the 1993 Directive could be given effect despite a choice of law other than of UK law as legal provisions which cannot be derogated from by agreement under (and subject to the conditions of) Rome I Regulation arts 3(3) and 6(2), on which see Vol.I, paras 30-082 and 30-148 et seq.

[2581] Unfair Contract Terms Act ss.26 and 27 on which see Vol.I paras 15-122 and 15-125 respectively. As regards ss.26 and 27(1), this reflects the earlier recommendations of the Law Commissions for consumer contracts (made in relation to the Rome Convention on the law applicable to contractual obligations 1980, which preceded the Rome I Regulation): Law Commission and Scottish Law Commission *Unfair Terms in Contracts* (2005) Pt 7, especially paras 7.6 and 7.9; their recommendations as regards s.27(2) were more nuanced, but are not reflected directly in the 2015 Act, except to the extent to which s.74 applies its rule on choice of law so as to protect the controls on unfair contract terms in Pt 2 of the Act other than those required by the 1993 Directive.

[2582] *Verein für Konsumenteninformation v Amazon EU Sàrl* (C-191/15) EU:C:2016:612, July 28, 2016, above, para.38-321.

[2583] Above, paras 38-353—38-364. On the temporal application of the enforcement powers in Sch.3 of the 2015 Act (as described below, para.38-420) see above, para.38-366.

[2584] 1999 Regulations reg.12.

[2585] In particular, the Unfair Contract Terms Act 1977 ss.2, 6(3) and 7(2). They did not apply directly either to contract terms which are invalid at common law, such as terms seeking to exclude liability for personal fraud (on which see Vol.I, para.7-145) or penalty clauses (on which see Vol.I, paras 26-190 et seq.) though in both cases terms in consumer contracts that are invalid at common law are

the Enterprise Act 2002 provides for "enforcement orders" in respect, inter alia, of "Community infringements", and the latter include infringements of the UK's legislative measures implementing the 1993 Directive and the Unfair Commercial Practices Directive 2005.[2586] Thirdly, use or recommendation for use of unfair terms in consumer contracts may constitute an "unfair commercial practice" within the meaning of the Consumer Protection from Unfair Trading Regulations 2008 which set out the prohibitions required by the Unfair Commercial Practices Directive 2005.[2587] The 2008 Regulations provide, inter alia, for a series of criminal offences relating to unfair commercial practices as well as for enforcement measures under Pt 8 of the Enterprise Act 2002.[2588] This means, for example, that the use by a trader of unfair terms in its dealings with consumers could attract the preventive measures provided by the 1999 Regulations, an "enforcement order" under Pt 8 of the Enterprise Act 2002 and/or a criminal sanction as an "unfair commercial practice" (where the latter's special conditions are satisfied).[2589]

38-420   **Enforcement measures under the Consumer Rights Act 2015**   The approach of the 2015 Act to the enforcement of the controls which it requires for unfair terms and notices reflects this earlier law, but extends the special scheme (earlier set out by the 1999 Regulations and now set out by Sch.3 of the Act) to the Act's controls on terms generally[2590] as well as providing that the investigatory powers needed for these purposes are the same as for the enforcement of consumer protection legislation more widely.[2591] Under Sch.3 of the Act, the CMA and other "regulators"[2592] (who are the same as the "qualifying bodies" foreseen by the 1999 Regulations[2593]) possess a power to apply for an injunction against a person if it thinks that the person is "using, or proposing or recommending the use of, a term or notice" in the following circumstances[2594]: where a term or notice purports to exclude or restrict liability imposed by Pt 1 (for example, in respect of the satisfactory quality of goods supplied) or business liability for death or personal injury resulting

---

likely to be "unfair" within the meaning of the 1999 Regulations.

[2586] Enterprise Act 2002 s.212 (as amended) implementing the Consumer Injunctions Directive 2009 and see above, paras 38-133—38-134 and below, para.38-420. cf. the position as regards "domestic infringements" under Pt 8 of the 2002 Act, which extend, inter alia, to the Unfair Contract Terms Act 1977: Enterprise Act 2002 (Part 8 Domestic Infringements) Order 2003 (SI 2003/1593) art.2 and Sch. Pt 1.

[2587] 2008 Regulations reg.26 and see above, paras 38-362—38-364; *OFT v Ashbourne Management Services Ltd* [2011] EWHC 1237 (Ch), [2011] E.C.C. 31.

[2588] 2008 Regulations reg.26 and see above, para.38-170—38-171.

[2589] See, e.g. *OFT v Ashbourne Management Services Ltd* [2011] EWHC 1237 (Ch), [2011] E.C.C. 31 and see above, para.38-362.

[2590] 2015 Act ss.31(7), 47(5), 57(7) and 70(1).

[2591] 2015 Act s.70(2), applying the investigatory powers in Sch.5 (which replace the special provisions on investigatory powers in the 1999 Regulations reg.13): see especially s.77 and Sch.5 paras 2(d), 6 ("unfair contract terms enforcer"), and 13(7) and (8). On the temporal application of these powers, see above, para.38-366 (note), where the qualifications on this general position are noted.

[2592] The 2015 Act replaces the expression "qualifying body" used by the 1999 Regulations and instead refers to all those empowered to enforce its provisions governing unfair contract terms (including the CMA) as "regulators": 2015 Act Sch.3 para.8(1).

[2593] See above, para.38-360; 2015 Act Sch.3 para.8(1), though para.8(2) allows the Secretary of State to amend this list (the Director General of Electrical Supply of Northern Ireland and the Director General of Gas for Northern Ireland were replaced by the Northern Ireland Authority for Utility Regulation).

[2594] 2015 Act Sch.3 para.3(1).

from negligence[2595]; where a term or notice is unfair within the meaning of Pt 2 "to any extent"[2596]; and where a term or notice fails the requirement of transparency.[2597] Schedule 3 also provides regulators with powers to consider complaints about a term or notice in the same circumstances,[2598] and to accept an undertaking from a person against whom it has applied, or thinks it is entitled to apply for an injunction.[2599] Courts may grant an injunction on such conditions, and against such respondents to the proceedings, as it thinks appropriate.[2600] The powers in regulators are therefore wider in their scope of application than those contained in the 1999 Regulations in three principal ways: first, they apply to those provisions in the 2015 Act which reflect provisions in the 1977 Act and which render terms not binding on consumers without any assessment of their fairness[2601]; secondly, they apply to terms assessed as unfair under the general test even where (owing to the extended character of the scope of this test) they would not fall to be assessed under the 1999 Regulations (or the 1993 Directive)[2602]; and, thirdly, they apply to "consumer notices" in the same way as they apply to contract terms.[2603] In addition, the 2015 Act does not affect the possibility of enforcement measures being taken under Pt 8 of the Enterprise Act 2002 in respect of "Community infringements" which harm the collective interests of consumers and these include acts or omissions which contravene the 1993 Directive[2604] or which contravene laws of an EEA State (including the UK) which give effect to that Directive and which "provide additional permitted protections" beyond its minimum requirements, if "such additional protection is permitted by that Directive".[2605] For this purpose, the relevant provisions in Pt 2 of the 2015 Act which implement the 1993 Directive have been designated as a specified UK law for the purposes of s.212 of the 2002 Act[2606] and in addition, acts or omissions in respect of any provision in Pt 2 of the

---

[2595] 2015 Act Sch.3 para.3(2) referring to ss.31, 47, 57 and 65(1) of the Act and see above, para.38-409 and below, paras 38-531, 38-564 and 38-586.

[2596] 2015 Act Sch.3 para.3(3). This includes both terms or notices assessed as unfair under s.62 and terms deemed to be unfair under s.63(6) or the Arbitration Act 1996 s.91, on which see above, paras 38-389 et seq. and 38-412.

[2597] 2015 Act Sch.3 para.3(5) and see s.68, above, paras 38-414—38-416. The application of the enforcement measures to this requirement is therefore made explicit by the Act, though it was not under the 1999 Regulations and see above, para.38-355.

[2598] 2015 Act Sch.3 para.2 (reflecting 1999 Regulations reg.10).

[2599] 2015 Act Sch.3 para.6(1).

[2600] 2015 Act Sch.3 para.5(1). This broadly reflects 1999 Regulations reg.12(3) and (4).

[2601] 2015 Act Sch.3 para.3(2), above, paras 38-409—38-410, 38-412.

[2602] The scope of the test of unfairness is widened in the following ways: the definition of "consumer" is extended by s.2(3) and 76(2), above, para.38-384; the subjection of terms which have been individually negotiated to the test of unfairness by s.62, above, para.38-389; the exclusion from the assessment of fairness of terms which specify the main subject matter of the contract, etc. in s.64 is subjected to an additional condition of "prominence", above, paras 38-398—38-400. The 2015 Act does not expressly apply the Sch.3 enforcement regime to its controls on the effectiveness of certain terms on choice of applicable law as set out in s.74, as the latter is not expressed as rendering such terms unfair or otherwise not binding on consumers so as to fall within one of the categories in Sch.3 para.(2), (3) or (5) as required by para.3(1)(b), but art.6(2) of the 1993 Directive requires Member States to "take the necessary measures to ensure that the consumer does not lose the protection granted" by it and so such an effect could possibly be achieved by way of "conforming interpretation" as explained above, para.38-418.

[2603] 2015 Act ss.62(2), (6) and (7), 65 and 68; Sch.3 para.3(3) and (5).

[2604] Enterprise Act 2002 s.212(1)(a).

[2605] Enterprise Act 2002 s.212(1)(b) and (2).

[2606] Enterprise Act 2002 s.212(3); Enterprise Act 2002 (Part 8 Community Infringements Specified UK

2015 Act are specified as possible "domestic infringements" for the purposes of s.211 of the Enterprise Act 2002.[2607] Furthermore, the 2015 Act enhanced the consumer measures which are available under Pt 8 of the Enterprise Act so as to include, for example, measures offering compensation or other redress to consumers who have suffered loss as a result of the conduct which has given rise to the enforcement order.[2608] Thirdly, although not mentioned by the 2015 Act, in principle the use or recommendation for use of an unfair term or notice by a trader in its commercial practices with consumers can constitute an "unfair commercial practice" within the meaning of the Consumer Protection from Unfair Trading Regulations 2008.[2609]

38-421 **Compatibility of extensions of preventive measures with EU law?** The question arises, however, whether the extension of the enforcement measures required by art.7 of the 1993 Directive as foreseen by the 2015 Act are compatible with EU law. At first sight, such extensions are so compatible either to the extent to which they fall within the scope of that Directive and, therefore, within its permissive "minimum harmonisation" clause or outside the scope of the 1993 Directive and therefore within the general competence of the UK.[2610] However, as earlier noted, the difficulty arises from the impact of the "full harmonisation" generally required by the Unfair Commercial Practices Directive on national measures (apart from "contract law") which prohibit business-to-consumer commercial practices within the scope of the 2005 Directive.

38-422 **The impact of "full harmonisation" under the Unfair Commercial Practices Directive 2005** Where it applies, the impact of full harmonisation under the 2005 Directive is that Member States must not prohibit a "business-to-consumer commercial practice" falling within its scope unless it is prohibited under the controls of the Directive itself.[2611] As earlier noted, the use or recommendation for use of an unfair contract term or terms by a trader with a consumer or consumers may constitute a commercial practice in that trader within the meaning of the Unfair Commercial Practices Directive 2005[2612] and so may be held unfair under the Consumer Protection from Unfair Trading Regulations 2008.[2613] It has also been seen that the 2005 Directive provides for three qualifications on its scope (and therefore also on the full harmonisation which it requires). First, its prohibitions on unfair commercial practices are "without prejudice" to EU or national contract law[2614]; secondly, it provides that specific national rules governing commercial

---

Laws) Order 2003 art.3, Sch., as amended by the Enterprise Act 2002 (Part 8 Community Infringements and Specified UK Laws) (Amendment) Order 2015 (SI 2015/1628) art.2(2)(a), listing 2015 Act ss.2, 61–64, 67–70, 72–74, Schs 2 and 3 and Sch.5 Pt 3.

[2607] Enterprise Act 2002 s.211(2); Enterprise Act 2002 (Part 8 Domestic Infringements) Order 2015 (SI 2015/1727) art.2.

[2608] Consumer Rights Act 2015 s.79, Sch.7 inserting new s.219A in the Enterprise Act 2002. The example is found in s.219A(2)(a): see above, para.38-134.

[2609] Below, paras 38-362—38-363.

[2610] cf. above, paras 38-022—38-023, 38-377—38-381.

[2611] Above, para.38-159.

[2612] Above, paras 38-157 et seq. (which, at para.38-167, include discussion of the question whether an isolated event, such as a single use of an unfair term may count as a "commercial practice" for these purposes).

[2613] SI 2008/1277 on which see above, para.38-165.

[2614] 2005 Directive art.3(2), above, para.38-160.

practices business-to-consumer which implement specific EU rules (for example, in relation package travel[2615]) "prevail and apply" rather than the general scheme of controls foreseen by the 2005 Directive.[2616] And, thirdly, rules governing commercial practices which are more protective of consumers in national legislation implementing minimum harmonisation directives are protected from the 2005 Directive's "full harmonisation", but only for a transitional period which ended on June 11, 2013.[2617] This means that, after the expiry of this transitional period, in principle national legislation which prohibits business-to-consumer commercial practices as understood by the 2005 Directive other than under the Directive's own scheme is compatible with its requirement of full harmonisation only if its rules are *required* by other EU legislation or if they belong to "contract law". This impact of "full harmonisation" is made particularly clear by the existence of the (now expired) transitional position for national legislation implementing minimum harmonisation directives more strictly than they require.

"Contract law" for these purposes   It has earlier been suggested that "contract law" for the purposes of the "without prejudice" provision in the 2005 directive refers to the law which governs the relative rights and obligations of the parties to a contract.[2618] The natural contrast to this "contract law" is, it is submitted, regulatory or preventive measures of the practices of traders. This contrast is confirmed by recital 15 of the 2005 Directive in the context of explaining the significance of national information requirements and the condition of "materiality" of "misleading omissions".[2619]   **38-423**

> "Where Member States have introduced information requirements over and above what is specified in Community law, on the basis of minimum clauses, the omission of that extra information will not constitute a misleading omission under this Directive. By contrast Member States will be able, when allowed by the minimum clauses in Community law, to maintain or introduce more stringent provisions in conformity with Community law so as to ensure a higher level of protection of consumers' individual contractual rights."

Putting this contrast into the context of the Unfair Terms in Consumer Contracts Directive, the 2005 Directive does not prevent Member States from implementing its "contract law" provisions so as to be more protective of consumers, the "contract law" effects referring here principally to its requirement that unfair terms are not binding on consumers and that terms which fail the requirement of transparency are interpreted in favour of consumers.[2620] On the other hand, the measures required by the Directive of Member States to prevent the use or recommendation for use of

---

[2615] At the time, Directive 90/314/EEC of 13 June 1990 on package travel, package holidays and package tours, notably, art.3. The 1990 Directive is repealed and replaced by Directive (EU) 2015/2302 on package travel and linked travel arrangements [2015] O.J. L326/1, art.4 of which requires (generally) "full harmonisation": see above, paras 38-137 et seq.

[2616] 2005 Directive art.3(4), above, para.38-161 and see *Citroën Commerce GmbH v Zentralvereinigung des Kraftfahrzeuggewerbes zur Aufrechterhaltung lauteren Wettbewerbs eV (ZLW)* (C-476/14) EU:C:2016:527, July 7, 2016 at paras 44–46, noted above, para.38-111 (note).

[2617] 2005 Directive art.3(5), above, para.38-162.

[2618] 2005 Directive art.3(2) and see above, para.38-160. cf. similarly Consumer Rights Directive 2011 art.5(3), above, para.38-063.

[2619] 2005 Directive art.7, above, para.38-185.

[2620] 1993 Directive arts 5 and 6(1).

unfair terms in consumers contracts[2621] do not in this sense belong to "contract law".

38-424 **Significance for the Consumer Rights Act 2015**   This is significant for the 2015 Act to the extent to which it extends the *enforcement* measures put in place to prohibit contract terms to situations which the 1993 Directive does not require[2622] and yet which fall within the scope of the 2005 Directive.[2623] First, these measures are available to prevent the use or recommendation for use by a third party of contract terms which seek to exclude the trader's liability for breach of certain terms inserted by Pt 1 of the Act into contracts with consumers (such as to the satisfactory quality of goods supplied or the trader's right to supply goods[2624]) without any evaluation of the fairness of the terms (under the 1993 Directive) or of the fairness of this commercial practice (under the 2005 Directive).[2625] Secondly, these enforcement measures are available under the 2015 Act to prevent the use or recommendation for use of contract terms which seek to exclude the trader's business liability for death or personal injury resulting from negligence, similarly without regard to any evaluation of their fairness.[2626] Thirdly, as earlier noted, the 2015 Act extends the ambit of the test of unfairness by imposing a condition that terms relating to the subject matter of the contract, etc. are exempted from this test under the "core exclusion" only if prominent as well as transparent and these apparent extensions apply for the purposes of the Act's enforcement measures as well as for the "contract law" effects.[2627] Finally, the Act extends the scope of enforcement measures to "notices" as well as to "contract terms", an extension not expressly foreseen by the 1993 Directive.[2628] All these extensions of enforcement measures concerning the "com-

---

[2621] 1993 Directive art.7, above, paras 38-353 and 38-421.

[2622] If the 1993 Directive *does* require these measures, then they fall within 2005 Directive art.3(4), above, para.38-161.

[2623] On the other hand, extensions of controls on unfair terms which do not fall within the scope of the 2005 Directive (such as those which protect persons other than "consumers", on which see above, para.38-384) are not affected by its requirement of "full harmonisation".

[2624] 2015 Act ss.9, 17, 31(1) (a) and (i).

[2625] For the details of when the 2015 Act does hold a term not binding on the consumer without any evaluation of its fairness, see 2015 Act ss.31, 47 and 57 and below, paras 38-531, 38-564 and 38-586 respectively. The application of the Sch.3 powers is provided for by the 2015 Act ss.31(7); 47(5); 57(7). Sch.3, para.3(2)(a)–(c) then specifically provide that a "regulator" (such as the CMA) may apply for an injunction against a person if it thinks that the person is using, or proposing or recommending the use of, terms purporting to exclude or restrict liability in these situations. The position of terms seeking to exclude or limit the trader's liability in respect of the quality or fitness for purposes of goods in contracts of sale of goods differs from the general picture described in the text, as here EU law provides that such terms are not binding on consumers without any evaluation of their fairness: Directive 1999/44/EC on certain aspects of the sale of consumer goods and associated guarantees [1999] O.J. L171/12 art.7(1). While the 1999 Directive does not provide for measures to be put in place by Member States to ensure the effectiveness of this consumer protection (in contrast to the position under the 1993 Directive art.7), the 1999 Directive is included in the list of those whose national implementing measures must be supported by injunctions under the Consumer Injunctions Directive 2009, on which see below, para.38-425. As a result, it may be argued that injunctive relief in respect of such clauses is protected from the effect of "full harmonisation" under the 2005 Directive as it stems from a Community rule "regulating specific aspects of unfair commercial practices" within the meaning of 2005 Directive art.3(4), as explained above, para.38-161.

[2626] 2015 Act ss.65 and 70(1); Sch.3 para.3(2)(d). As regards the ineffectiveness to exclude liability in this situation, this is clearly modelled on the Unfair Contract Terms Act 1977 s.2(1), but that Act made no provision for "preventive measures".

[2627] 2015 Act ss.64(4), 70(1) and Sch.3 and see above, paras 38-394—38-399.

[2628] 2015 Act s.61(1), 70(1), Sch.3, especially para.1(d). cf. though, above para.38-387 (note), where it is argued that the treatment of "consumer notices" by the Act could be seen as reflecting a European

mercial practices" of the use or recommendation for use of consumer terms or notices without the need for an evaluation under the 2005 Directive appear to be precluded by that Directive as a result of its full harmonisation.

The Consumer Injunctions Directive 2009 However, there is a possibility that **38-425** these extensions (or some of these extensions) could shelter behind the special EU rules for "consumer injunctions" first enacted in a directive of 1998 and now found in the consolidating Consumer Injunctions Directive of 2009.[2629] As earlier noted the 2009 Directive requires Member States to permit national "qualified entities" to bring proceedings for an injunction aimed at the protection of the collective interests of consumers" as foreseen by a list of European legislative instruments, including the 1993 Directive and the 2005 Directive, and these injunctions must be available in respect both of national infringements (where all elements of the infringement take place within one Member State) and cross-border ("intra-Community") infringements.[2630] The purpose of the Consumer Injunctions Directive is to ensure that mechanisms are available in all Member States to require compliance with the European consumer *acquis*, and so allow "infringements harmful to the collective interests of consumers to be terminated in good time".[2631] Recital 4 of the 2009 Directive states:

> "As far as the purpose of bringing about the cessation of practices that are unlawful under the national provisions applicable is concerned, the effectiveness of national measures transposing the Directives in question, *including protective measures that go beyond the level required by those Directives*, provided that they are compatible with the Treaty and allowed by those Directives, may be thwarted where those practices produce effects in a Member State other than that in which they originate."[2632]

This recital is not explicitly reflected in the text of the 2009 Directive, art.1(2) of which defines "infringement" as "any act contrary to the Directives listed in Annex I as transposed into the internal legal order of the Member States which harms the collective interests referred to in paragraph 1", and which therefore suggests that it refers only to infringements of national laws where the latter reflect requirements of these directives, an interpretation which may be supported by reference to the 2009 Directive's main purpose, which is with procedural mechanisms rather than with substantive rights. Moreover, the argument that, owing to recital 4, the 2009 Directive allows Member States to provide for injunctions in respect of national laws implementing minimum harmonisation directives beyond the level

---

interpretation of "contract term" so as to fall within the requirements of the 1993 Directive.

[2629] Directive 98/27 on injunctions for the protection of consumers' interests [1998] O.J. L166/51, which was repealed and replaced by codified Directive 2009/22/EC on injunctions for the protection of consumers' interests, [2009] O.J. L110/30 ("2009 Directive").

[2630] 2009 Directive arts 1–2, 4; recitals 3, 7. On the application of the 2009 Directive, see European Commission, *Report from the Commission to the European Parliament and the Council concerning the application of Directive 2009/22/EC of the European Parliament and of the Council on injunctions for the protection of consumers' interest* COM(2012) 635 final.

[2631] 2009 Directive recital 3.

[2632] Emphasis added. The 2009 Directive art.7 allows Member States "to adopt or maintain in force provisions designed to grant qualified entities and any other person concerned more extensive rights to bring action at national level" but this "minimum harmonisation" clause appears to be concerned with the nature of the "rights to bring action" (beyond the injunctions required by the Directive) rather than with the substantive circumstances of the infringements to which the injunctions or other relief relate.

required by those directives, faces the difficulty that this would appear to conflict with the position set out by the text of the 2005 Directive, which (after the expiry of the six-year transitional period) permits the prohibition of business-to-consumer commercial practices by national law outside its own framework only where this prohibition reflects the requirements of EU legislation itself.[2633] Certainly the Consumer Injunctions Directive does not purport to allow Member States to implement minimum harmonisation directives in such a way as to prohibit business-to-consumer commercial practices beyond those directives' requirements in a way which does not conform to the (earlier) Unfair Commercial Practices Directive.

38-426 **Conclusion** If the line of argument in the above paragraphs holds good, then enforcement measures against the "commercial practices" of the use or recommendation for use of contract terms beyond the situations required by the 1993 Directive are in principle precluded unless they are first subjected to an evaluation of their fairness under the 2005 Directive. Given the absence of any reference to the need for such an assessment in the text of the 2015 Act, either generally or specifically in relation to the extensions of the scope of enforcement measures in relation to unfair terms which it contains, this therefore casts doubt on the compatibility with EU law of the relevant provisions of the Consumer Rights Act to the extent to which they foresee such an extension.[2634] The effects of such an incompatibility would be complex and cannot be fully explored here. In some instances, an English court may fell able to "read down" the provisions of the 2015 Act so as to ensure compatibility with the 2005 Directive, by way of the principle of "conforming interpretation".[2635] An example may be found in relation to the requirement of "prominence" for the application of the exclusion of terms which reflect the main subject matter of contracts, as this requirement could be interpreted by an English court as giving effect to the broad interpretation of the Court of Justice to the requirement of "plainness and intelligibility" even though the Act (following the Law Commissions) treats it as an additional, distinct requirement.[2636] On the other hand, some extensions of the enforcement controls on contract terms contained in the Act (notably, those in respect of the exclusion of liability for death or personal injuries caused by negligence[2637] or the exclusion of Pt 1 liabilities[2638]) would be much more difficult to read down so as to be compatible with the 2005 Directive. This would then raise the possibility of infringement proceedings by the European Commission against the UK under art.258 TFEU,[2639] and/or the possibility of liability in damages under the well-known *Francovich* and *Brasserie du Pêcheur* case-law of the Court of Justice.[2640]

[2633] 2005 Directive art.3(4) and (5), above, paras 38-161—38-162.

[2634] Above, para.38-420.

[2635] See above, para.38-014.

[2636] cf. above, paras 38-395—38-399.

[2637] 2015 Act ss.65 and 66, above, paras 38-409 and 38-424.

[2638] 2015 Act ss.31(7), 47(5) and 57(7), above, para.38-373, with the qualification as regards the exclusion of terms excluding the liability of a seller of goods as explained in para.38-424 (note).

[2639] On which see Craig and de Búrca, *EU Law, Texts, Cases, and Materials*, 6th edn (2015), Ch.12.

[2640] *Francovich v Italy* (C-6/90 and C-9/90) EU:C:1991:428, [1999] E.C.R. I-5357; *Brasserie du Pêcheur SA v Germany, R. v Secretary of State for Transport, Ex p. Factortame Ltd* (C-46/93 and C-48/93) EU:C:1996:79, [1996] E.C.R. I-1029 and see Craig and de Búrca, *EU Law, Texts, Cases, and Materials*, 6th edn (2015), pp.251 et seq.

(e) Special Rules Governing Consumer Payments

The Consumer Rights Directive 2011   In addition to information requirements   **38-427**
and rights of cancellation,[2641] the Consumer Rights Directive 2011 provides for
"other consumer rights" and these include special rules governing "fees for the use
of means of payment", "communication by telephone" and "additional
payments".[2642] These provisions are implemented in the UK by regulations as the
following paragraphs explain. The focus of these rules is to control the imposition
of disguised, unforeseen or otherwise unfair payments on consumers incidental to
the payment for the goods and services under the contract. To the extent to which
these payments are imposed under terms of a contract between the trader and the
consumer, they constitute controls of such terms, as any payment imposed other
than in accordance with the rules which they set out are required to be ineffective
under the 2011 Directive.[2643] However, as will be seen, their impact on contracts is
more direct than this suggests as they seek to control the *level* of the charges to be
imposed by a trader in certain circumstances. Moreover, in the case of payment
surcharges, UK implementation of the Second Payment Services Directive 2015[2644]
has led to the abolition of any charge for use of certain payment instruments except
where these are "commercial".[2645]

Payment surcharges: the controls   The Consumer Rights (Payment Surcharges)   **38-428**
Regulations 2012 as made[2646] implemented art.19 of the Consumer Rights Directive and reg.4 therefore provides that a trader must not charge consumers in respect
of the use of a given means of payment fees that exceed the cost borne by the trader
for the use of that means (such as an administration, booking or handling fee),[2647]
where the payment is made for the purposes of a sales contract, a service contract
or a contract for the supply of water, gas, electricity, district heating or digital
content.[2648] Regulation 4's prohibition does not refer to any particular method of

---

[2641] These are implemented in UK law by the Consumer Contracts (Information, Cancellation and Additional Charges) Regulations 2013 (SI 2013/3134) ("2013 Regulations"). For these aspects of the
2013 Regulations requirements, see above, paras 38-060 et seq.

[2642] Consumer Rights Directive 2011 arts 19, 21 and 22. The scope of these provisions in terms of the
contracts to which they apply is set by art.17. On the 2011 Directive generally, see above, paras 38-
060 and 38-062—38-067.

[2643] 2011 Directive art.25 "imperative nature of the Directive", second sentence: see above, para.38-
066.

[2644] Directive (EU) 2015/2366 of the European Parliament and of the Council of 25 November 2015 on
payment services in the internal market [2015] O.J. L337/35, art.62(3)–(4).

[2645] Below, para.38-428.

[2646] SI 2012/3110 ("2012 Regulations") (and as amended by the 2013 Regulations (SI 2013/3134)).

[2647] 2012 Regulations reg.4. "Trader" and "consumer" are defined by reg.2 in the new standard UK
definitions described above, paras 38-050—38-058 (especially at 38-057) and 38-030—38-049
(especially at 38-041) respectively. For explanation of what can properly be charged by a trader as
the "cost" for use see *DG Justice Guidance Document on 2011 Directive*, para.9.3.

[2648] 2012 Regulations reg.5(1). The definitions of these various categories of contract provided by reg.3
of the 2012 Regulations is mirrored by those found in the 2013 Regulations reg.5, on which see
above, paras 38-073—38-075. Regulation 5(1) and (2) of the 2012 Regulations exclude from the rule
against excessive charges a series of "excluded contracts" as allowed by the 2011 Directive, notably
including contracts for financial services contracts, this list following the exclusions in 2013 Regulations reg.6, with the addition of contracts for social services and health services (as explained by
reg.5(2)(a) and (b)). Regulation 6 of the 2012 Regulations provides a temporary exemption from the
prohibition in reg.4 where the trader's business is an existing micro-business or a new business as
explained in their Schedule.

payment (such as a credit or debit card) and therefore applies to any means of payment that a trader decides to accept, including cash, cheques, prepaid cards, charge cards, etc. and this means that any new methods of paying will also be subject to this prohibition as the technology relating to payments develops.[2649] This law applies to contracts entered into on or after April 6, 2013.[2650] However, this protection for consumers was supplemented by a wide prohibition on payment surcharges[2651] on the amendment of the Consumer Rights (Payment Surcharges) Regulations 2012 by the Payment Services Regulations 2017,[2652] implementing a requirement imposed by the Second Payment Services Directive 2015.[2653] Under the 2015 Directive, a payee, such as a retailer, "shall not request charges for the use of payment instruments" where their interchange fees are capped under the Interchange Fees Regulation 2015,[2654] and this includes the majority of consumer debit and credit cards.[2655] However, the UK's implementation of this aspect of the 2015 Directive went further than this requirement, as the Directive permits where a Member State considers that this is needed to encourage competition and promote the use of efficient payment instruments.[2656] As a result, under reg.6A(1) of the 2012 Regulations (as inserted by the 2017 Regulations), "a payee[2657] must not charge a payer[2658] any fee in respect of payment by means of a payment instrument" as long as it is not a commercial card or other payment instrument,[2659] whether or not it is a card-based payment instrument within the meaning of the Interchange Fees Regulation 2015; nor must a payee charge in respect of a payment service (such as a direct debit) in euro.[2660] As a result (and subject to territorial limitations[2661]),

---

[2649] Department of Business, Energy & Industrial Strategy, *The Consumer Rights (Payment Surcharges) Regulations 2012, Guidance* (June 2018), para.8.5.

[2650] 2012 Regulations reg.1(1) and (2). Reg.6 provides for a temporary exemption from the requirements of reg.4 for micro-businesses and new business as defined by the Sch. to the Regulations.

[2651] 2012 Regulations reg.6A. The new rules contained in reg.6A apply to charges made on or after January 13, 2018, except for charges under contracts entered into before July 18, 2017 (the date on which the 2017 Regulations were made): 2012 Regulations reg.1(3) as inserted by the 2017 Regulations Sch.8 (as regards the temporal effect on contracts of reg.6A); 2017 Regulations reg.1(6) (in relation to the prohibition on charging in reg.6A).

[2652] SI 2017/752 ("2017 Regulations") reg.156; Sch.8 Pt 3 para.12.

[2653] Directive (EU) 2015/2366 of the European Parliament and of the Council of 25 November 2015 on payment services in the internal market [2015] O.J. L337/35 ("2015 Directive"), art.62(3)–(4).

[2654] Regulation (EU) 2015/251 of the European Parliament and of the Council of 29 April 2015 on interchange fees for card-based payment transactions [2015] O.J. L123/1 ("Interchange Fees Regulation 2015").

[2655] Explanatory Memorandum to the 2017 Regulations, para.7.16.

[2656] 2015 Directive art.62(5).

[2657] A "payee" for the purposes of reg.6A is defined in reg.3 of the 2012 Regulations (as inserted) by reference to reg.2(1) of the 2017 Regulations as "a person who is the intended recipient of funds which have been the subject of a payment transaction". Unlike reg.4, therefore, reg.6A is not restricted to payments made to traders.

[2658] Under reg.3 of the 2012 Regulations (as inserted and referring to reg.2(1) of the 2017 Regulations) "… 'payer' means—(a) a person who holds a payment account and initiates, or consents to the initiation of, a payment order from that payment account; or (b) where there is no payment account, a person who gives a payment order".

[2659] 2012 Regulations reg.6A(1)(a)(ii) and (b)(ii). "Commercial card" is defined by art.2(6) of the Interchange Fees Regulation 2015 as "any card-based payment instrument issued to undertakings or public sector entities or self-employed natural persons which is limited in use for business expenses where the payments made with such cards are charged directly to the account of the undertaking or public sector entity or self-employed natural person".

[2660] "Payment service" is defined by reference to Regulation (EU) 260/2012 of the European Parliament and of the Council of March 14, 2012 establishing technical and business requirements for

reg.6A(1) imposes a ban on surcharging applicable to all non-commercial retail payment instruments.[2662] According to the Explanatory Memorandum to the 2017 Regulations,

> "... this is intended to level the playing field across all non-commercial retail payment instruments and create a clearer picture for consumers in which they know the full price of the product/service they are purchasing upfront and are confident that there will be no additional charges when they come to pay using a particular payment instrument."[2663]

Where reg.6A(1) does not apply owing in particular to the method of payment used (and subject to its own conditions), reg.4 still prohibits traders from charging consumers more than the direct cost borne by them for use of the relevant means of payment.[2664] Finally, reg.6A(2) imposes the latter type of control in respect of most payments between businesses made with commercial payment instruments.[2665]

Payment surcharges: enforcement   The 2012 Regulations provide for the **38-429** enforcement of reg.4 (the prohibition of excessive charges) and reg.6A (prohibition of any charge in respect of certain payment instruments) by local weights and measures authorities, who may take undertakings or apply to the court for an injunction for these purposes.[2666] Any contract term which requires the payment of a fee charged in contravention of reg.4 or reg.6A is unenforceable to the extent of that contravention and the contract for the purposes of which the payment is made is to be treated as providing for the fee to be repaid to the extent that the charging of the fee contravenes reg.4 or reg.6A.[2667] In addition, the relevant provisions of the 2012 Regulations have been designated as the "specified UK law" for the purposes of "Community infringements" under s.212 of the Enterprise Act 2002[2668] and this means that the various powers provided by Pt 8 of the 2002 Act are available for their enforcement.[2669]

Additional payments   Regulation 40 of the Consumer Contracts (Information, **38-430** Cancellation and Additional Charges) Regulations 2013 ("2013 Regulations")[2670] implements art.22 of the Consumer Rights Directive and provides that:

---

credit transfers and direct debits in euros [2012] O.J. L95/22.

[2661] These are contained in the 2012 Regulations reg.6B.

[2662] Explanatory Memorandum to the 2017 Regulations para.7.16.

[2663] Explanatory Memorandum to the 2017 Regulations para.7.16.

[2664] See above, in this paragraph.

[2665] This is the effect of reg.6A(2)'s use of the very general terms "payer" and "payee" as earlier noted.

[2666] 2012 Regulations regs 8-9 (amended by the 2017 Regulations only to the extent to reflect the substantive changes inserted by means of reg.6A of the 2012 Regulations). In Northern Ireland the enforcement authority is the Department of Enterprise, Trade and Investment in Northern Ireland.

[2667] 2012 Regulations reg.10.

[2668] Enterprise Act 2002 (Part 8 EU Infringements) Order 2014 (SI 2014/2908) art.3 and Sch. The Consumer Rights Directive 2011 and art.62(3) (second sentence), (4) and (5) of the Payment Services Directive 2015 are listed in the 2002 Act Sch.13 paras 9F and 16 respectively.

[2669] See above, paras 38-059 et seq.

[2670] For the contracts included and generally excluded from the scope of the 2013 Regulations see reg.6 above, paras 38-069, 38-076—38-078. However, despite the general exclusion of contracts for the provision of financial services under reg.6(1)(b), the 2013 Regulations specifically apply reg.40's controls where an additional payment is for financial services, unless the trader's main obligation is to supply financial services: reg.6(3) and 40(3).

"(1) Under a contract between a trader and a consumer, no payment is payable in addition to the remuneration agreed for the trader's main obligation unless, before the consumer became bound by the contract, the trader obtained the consumer's express consent.

(2) There is no express consent (if there would otherwise be) for the purposes of this paragraph if consent is inferred from the consumer not changing a default option (such as a pre-ticked box on a website)."[2671]

As suggested by reg.40(2)'s example, the principal target of this provision is the use of "pre-ticked" boxes to generate payments for additional services, for example, on websites selling passenger air-transport in relation to charges for bags or insurance. This provision appeared in the Consumer Rights Directive Proposal of 2008 as an element in the "transparency requirements" for contract terms, forming part of the proviso to its treatment of the questions at present governed by art.4(2) of the 1993 Directive.[2672] While art.22 of the Consumer Rights Directive as enacted stands alone, it rests on a similar distinction between contractual payments to be made by consumers which concern the main subject matter of the contract (which in principle fall within the exclusion from the test of fairness in art.4(2) of the 1993 Directive) and payments "in addition to the remuneration agreed" which, under art.22, require the consumer's express consent.[2673] Where a trader receives an additional payment which is not payable under a contract under reg.40, the contract is to be treated as providing for the trader to reimburse the payment to the consumer.[2674] More generally, the enforcement measures available in respect of this prohibition in reg.40 follow those available more generally under the 2013 Regulations.[2675]

38-431 Helpline charges over basic rate Regulation 41 of the 2013 Regulations,[2676] implementing art.21 of the Consumer Rights Directive 2011, provides that, where a trader operates a telephone line for the purpose of consumers contacting the trader by telephone in relation to contracts entered into with the trader, a consumer contacting the trader must not be bound to pay more than the basic rate. Although "basic rate" is not defined by the Directive nor the Regulations for this purpose, the Court of Justice of the EU has held that it refers to "an ordinary rate for a telephone call at no additional cost for the consumer" i.e. the cost of a call to a standard geographic landline or mobile telephone line and that this means that traders are not allowed to charge consumers premium rates even where they do not make a profit in doing so.[2677] Any amount paid by the consumer in excess of such a rate is recoverable by them.[2678] Again, the enforcement measures available in respect of the

---

[2671] SI 2013/3134. The definitions of "trader" and "consumer" are provided by the 2013 Regulations reg.4 and follow the new standard UK definitions: above, 38-050—38-058 (especially at 38-057) and 38-030—38-049 (especially at 38-041) respectively.
[2672] The Proposal for a Directive on Consumer Rights of October 8, 2008, COM(2008) 614/3 final art.32(2).
[2673] cf. above, paras 38-245 et seq.
[2674] 2013 Regulations reg.40(4).
[2675] 2013 Regulations regs 44–46 and see above, paras 38-132 et seq.
[2676] SI 2013/3134.
[2677] *Zentrale zur Bekämpfung unlauteren Wettbewerbs Frankfurt am Main eV v comtech GmbH* (C-568/15) EU:C:2017:154, March 2, 2017 at paras 27–32.
[2678] 2013 Regulations reg.41(2).

prohibition in reg.41 follow those available more generally under the 2013 Regulations.[2679]

7. CONTRACTS FOR THE SUPPLY OF GOODS, DIGITAL CONTENT OR SERVICES

(a) Introduction

Legislative background   Between the enactment of the Sale of Goods Act 1893   **38-432** and the amendment in 2002 of its successor, the Sale of Goods Act 1979[2680] the legislative frameworks governing contracts for the sale of goods did not themselves apply special rules to govern consumer contracts, that is, broadly speaking, contracts between sellers acting in the course of business and buyers *not* acting in the course of business, though they distinguished between sellers acting or not acting in the course of business.[2681] On the other hand, from 1973 legislation controlling the validity of contract terms seeking to exclude or to limit the seller's liability under the statutory implied terms in ss.13 to 15 of the Sale of Goods Act 1979 did distinguish according to the position of the buyer, first by reference to "consumer sales"[2682] and then, under the Unfair Contract Terms Act 1977, by reference to a buyer "dealing as consumer".[2683] This pattern was also followed in the case of contracts of hire-purchase[2684] and "miscellaneous contracts under which goods pass",[2685] such as contracts of hire of goods[2686] or for work and materials.[2687]

[2679] 2013 Regulations regs 44–46 and see above, paras 38-132 et seq.

[2680] These amendments were effected by the Sale and Supply of Goods to Consumers Regulations 2002 (SI 2002/3045) implementing Directive 1999/44/EEC ("the Consumer Sales Directive 1999").

[2681] As regards the latter, s.12 of the Sale of Goods Act 1979 does not require the seller to be contracting in the course of business, whereas s.14(2) and (3) of the same Act does so require. This does not mean that the legislature was not concerned with the implications of consumer sales for the drafting of the legislation and the amendments to the wording of the terms as to the quality of goods in s.14 of the 1979 Act were made in part so as to ensure that it was appropriate to consumer sales as much as to commercial sales: in particular, "merchantable quality" became "satisfactory quality", which was then explained by reference to a series of "aspects of the quality of the goods": see Law Commission Report *Sale and Supply of Goods*, Law Com. No.160 (1987) especially § 2.10; Sale and Supply of Goods Act 1994 s.1.

[2682] Supply of Goods (Implied Terms) Act 1973 s.4 creating new Sale of Goods Act 1893 s.55(4) and (7) (repealed by Unfair Contract Terms Act 1977).

[2683] Unfair Contract Terms Act 1977 s.6(2)(a) (in relation to the terms implied by the Sale of Goods Act 1979 ss.13–15).

[2684] Unfair Contract Terms Act 1977 s.6(2)(b) (in relation to the terms implied by the Supply of Goods (Implied Terms) Act 1973 ss.9–11).

[2685] Unfair Contract Terms Act 1977 s.7(2) (in relation to terms implied "from the nature of the contract"). For example, in most contracts for the transfer of goods (other than sale of goods or hire-purchase), such as a contract for the supply of work and materials, terms are implied by the Supply of Goods and Services Act 1982 ss.2–5.

[2686] Unfair Contract Terms Act 1977 s.7(2); Supply of Goods and Services Act 1982 ss.7–10.

[2687] Supply of Goods and Services Act 1982 ss.2–5 ("contracts for the transfer of goods" not being contracts for the sale of goods or hire-purchase agreements). In the case of contracts for the supply of services, a supplier in the course of business owes a duty to take reasonable care in the supply of the service by a term implied by the Supply of Goods and Services Act 1982 s.13 and any purported exemption of liability for breach of this term is ineffective in respect of claims for death or personal injury and, in respect of other loss or damage, is subject to the test of reasonableness under the Unfair Contract Terms Act 1977 s.2 (negligence liability): neither statutes distinguished for this purpose according to whether the recipient of the services was "dealing as consumer".

38-433 **Consumer Sales Directive 1999**   However, this established pattern of treatment was changed on implementation of the Consumer Sales Directive of 1999.[2688] The main purpose of this directive is to require uniform rules governing certain aspects of contracts of sale of goods by sellers acting in the course of a business to consumer buyers[2689] on the basis of "minimum harmonisation",[2690] but its scope extends also to "contracts for the supply of goods to be manufactured and produced".[2691] The Directive has three main requirements to be given effect in national laws. First, it requires that "the seller must deliver goods to the consumer which are in conformity with the contract of sale", defining "conformity" in terms familiar to the English lawyer from the statutory implied terms of ss.13 to 15 of the Sale of Goods Act 1979 that the goods comply with their description, are fit for any purpose made known by the consumer to the seller and accepted by him, are "fit for the purposes for which goods of the same type are normally used" and "show the quality and performance which are normal in goods of the same type and which the consumer can reasonably expect",[2692] as well as generally being in "conformity with the contract of sale", i.e. any express contract terms.[2693] However, some aspects of the 1999 Directive's requirement of conformity were new to English law at the time, notably, the specified relevance to the quality which a consumer can reasonably expect of goods of "public statements on the specific characteristics of the goods made about them by the seller, the producer or his representative".[2694] Secondly, the Directive requires a series of rights for consumer buyers in respect of the "contractual non-conformity" of the goods: at a first level, a right to repair or replacement of the goods[2695]; and, if these remedies are unavailable or fail,[2696] a right to "an appropriate reduction in the price"[2697] and a right to "rescission" of the contract as long as the non-conformity of the goods is not minor.[2698] The Directive also makes incidental provision for these rights of conformity, notably as regards proof of non-conformity[2699] and the limitation period for the rights which it requires for consumers.[2700] Thirdly, the Directive requires that "guarantees" by sellers or producers to consumers[2701] shall be binding.[2702]

[2688] Directive 1999/44/EC on certain aspects of the sale of consumer goods and associated guarantees [1999] O.J. L171/12 ("Consumer Sales Directive" or "1999 Directive").

[2689] 1999 Directive art.1(2)(a) "consumer"; (b) "consumer goods"; and (c) "seller".

[2690] 1999 Directive art.8.

[2691] 1999 Directive art.1(4) deeming these to be "contracts of sale" for the purposes of the Directive.

[2692] 1999 Directive art.2(1), 2(2)(c) and (d). The formulations of these requirements are elaborated further in the Directive.

[2693] 1999 Directive art.2(1), recital 7.

[2694] 1999 Directive art.2(2)(d) and (4).

[2695] 1999 Directive art.3(3).

[2696] On the specific requirements in this respect as implemented in UK law, see below, paras 38-451—38-517 and 38-518.

[2697] 1999 Directive art.3(5).

[2698] 1999 Directive art.3(5) and (6).

[2699] 1999 Directive art.5(3).

[2700] 1999 Directive art.5(1) and (2).

[2701] Defined in 1999 Directive art.1(2)(e).

[2702] 1999 Directive art.6.

First implementation of 1999 Directive: amendment of existing legisla- 38-434
tion   The 1999 Directive was first implemented in the UK by the Sale and Supply of Goods to Consumers Regulations 2002 ("the 2002 Regulations")[2703] and took effect principally by the amendment of existing UK legislation: the Sale of Goods Act 1979,[2704] the Supply of Goods and Services Act 1982,[2705] the Supply of Goods (Implied Terms) Act 1973,[2706] and the Unfair Contract Terms Act 1977.[2707] In particular, the 2002 Regulations inserted a new Pt 5A into the 1979 Act (a new Pt 1B into the 1982 Act) providing a new scheme of remedies based on the Directive for those dealing as consumer.[2708] The 2002 Regulations also made provision for "consumer guarantees" as required by the 1999 Directive, which was not inserted into any existing primary legislation.[2709] In implementing the Directive in this way, the new English law provisions were extended so as to benefit persons "dealing as consumer" within the meaning of the Unfair Contract Terms Act 1977 and not merely "consumers" as understood by the 1999 Directive.[2710] This law still applies to contracts made before October 1, 2015, when the relevant provisions of the Consumer Rights Act 2015 came into force, and will be discussed later as "the old law".[2711]

Second implementation of the 1999 Directive   However, the Consumer Rights 38-435
Act 2015 took a radically different approach to implementation of the Consumer Sales Directive 1999 and introduced wider reform to the substantive rights of consumers against traders in respect of the conformity of goods, digital content or services with the contract. Part 1 of the 2015 Act identifies three broad categories of consumer contract: "contracts for a trader to supply goods to a consumer" or "goods contracts" (Ch.2)[2712]; "contracts for a trader to supply digital content to a consumer" or "digital content contracts" (Ch.3)[2713]; and "contracts for a trader to supply a service to a consumer" or "services contracts" (Ch.4)[2714]; providing for each category a series of terms which are "treated as included" in the contract, these being broadly equivalent to the traditional implied terms of earlier legislation, as

---

[2703] SI 2002/3045.
[2704] 2002 Regulations regs 3–6, amending Sale of Goods Act 1979 ss.14, 20, 32 and 61(1) and inserting new Pt 5A.
[2705] 2002 Regulations regs 7–12, amending Supply of Goods and Services Act 1982 ss.4, 9, 11D, 11J and 18 and inserting new Pt 1B.
[2706] 2002 Regulations regs 13 amending Supply of Goods (Implied Terms) Act 1973 ss.10 and 15.
[2707] 2002 Regulations reg.14 amending Unfair Contract Terms Act 1977 s.12 (for English law).
[2708] Below, paras 38-439 et seq.
[2709] 2002 Regulations reg.15. The definitions in reg.2 apply only to this provision as the remainder of the substantive provisions of the 2002 Regulations provide for amendments of other legislation (as explained in the text) whose terms fall to be interpreted, therefore, by the legislation which these amendments concern.
[2710] This legislative decision took effect by amendment of the existing legislation whose provisions applied for the benefit of those "dealing as consumer" by reference to the 1977 Act: e.g. Sale of Goods Act 1979 s.48A(1)(a); s.61(5A). As explained in the previous note, the definition of "consumer" provided by 2002 Regulations reg.2 (which followed the definition in the 1999 Directive art.1(2)(a)) did not apply to these amendments. On the general approach to the definition of "consumer" in the EU consumer protection directives see above, paras 38-032 et seq.
[2711] Below, paras 38-439 et seq.
[2712] Consumer Rights Act 2015 s.3(1).
[2713] 2015 Act s.33(1).
[2714] 2015 Act s.48(1).

amended and supplemented.[2715] Secondly, in respect of each category of contract, the 2015 Act provides a series of "rights to enforce terms" about their subject matter (goods, digital content or services).[2716] Part 1 of the 2015 Act also gives effect to certain aspects of the Consumer Rights Directive 2011, notably its requirement that information provided by the trader about the goods or services as set out by the Directive is to form part of the contract[2717] and its rules governing delivery of goods and the passing of risk in goods in sales contracts.[2718] Thirdly, the 2015 Act provides very widely that a term in a contract to which it applies cannot exclude or restrict the trader's liability arising under its substantive provisions.[2719] In this way, the 2015 Act sought to set out in a single enactment the rules governing the issues arising between the parties to consumer contracts. As will be explained in more detail below, as a result, the 2015 Act therefore disapplied earlier legislation affecting these categories of contracts so as no longer to apply to them or to apply to them only with qualifications.[2720] On the other hand, in the case of "goods contracts"/ contracts of sale of goods, the 2015 Act did not seek to regulate all the issues governed by the 1979 Act and these other provisions remain applicable even though the buyer is a consumer.[2721] Moreover, other consumer protection legislation may apply to the parties to a contract falling within Pt 1 of the 2015 Act, as may the common law itself.[2722]

38-436   **Proposed EU directives on distance contracts for the sale of goods and on contracts for the supply of digital content**   The EU Commission has published two proposals for directives which would, if enacted and implemented in UK law, require the amendment of the 2015 Act's provisions governing contracts of sale of goods and contracts for the supply of digital content. The first is a proposal for a directive on aspects of the law governing sales of goods, which, when first proposed, was restricted to "distance contracts"[2723] but which was amended in 2017 so as no longer to do so.[2724] If enacted, the amended version of the directive would revoke the Consumer Sales Directive 1999[2725] and would require the UK to amend Ch.2 of Pt 1 of the 2015 Act according to its new requirements. The second is a proposal for a directive on aspects of the law governing the distance supply of digital content,[2726] which, if enacted, would require the amendment of Ch.3 of Pt 1

[2715] i.e. the Supply of Goods (Implied Terms Act) 1973, the Sale of Goods Act 1979 and the Supply of Goods and Services Act 1982.

[2716] 2015 Act s.19 (goods contracts); s.42 (digital content contracts); and s.54 (services contracts) and see below, paras 38-493, 38-557—38-580 respectively.

[2717] 2011 Directive art.6(5), above, para.38-105; 2015 Act ss.11(4)–(6), 12 (goods contracts); s.36(3)– (4) and 37 (digital content contracts); and ss.50(3)–(4) (services contracts) and see below, paras 38-499—38-500, 38-548—38-549 and 38-575 respectively.

[2718] 2011 Directive arts 18 and 20; 2015 Act ss.28–29, below, paras 38-526 and 38-527.

[2719] 2015 Act s.31 (goods contracts), s.47 (digital content contracts) and s.57 (services contracts) and see below, paras 38-531, 38-564 and 38-586 respectively (where the qualifications on this are explained).

[2720] 2015 Act s.60 and Sch.1 and see below, para.38-473.

[2721] Below, para.38-473.

[2722] Below, paras 38-475—38-476.

[2723] Proposal for a Directive of the European Parliament and of the Council on certain aspects concerning contracts for the online and other distance sales of goods COM(2015) 635 final.

[2724] Amended proposal for a Directive of the European Parliament and of the Council on certain aspects concerning contracts for the sales of goods, etc. COM(2017) 637 final ("Amended Sales of Goods Proposal 2017").

[2725] Amended Sales of Goods Proposal 2017 art.21.

[2726] Proposal for a Directive of the European Parliament and of the Council on certain aspects concern-

of the 2015 Act.[2727] Both proposed directives would require "full harmonization"[2728] and this would make their implementation in English law particularly difficult.

Temporal application of Pt 1 of the 2015 Act   As earlier noted, subject to one   **38-437** qualification, the relevant provisions of the 2015 Act were brought into force so as to apply to contracts made on or after October 1, 2015.[2729]

Structure of this section   The following paragraphs will therefore treat in turn the   **38-438** "old law" governing contracts made before October 1, 2015 Act and the "new law" under the Consumer Rights Act 2015 governing contracts made on or after that day.

(b)   The Old Law: Special Rules for Buyers and Hirers in Consumer Cases

Introduction   The following paragraphs apply to contracts made on or after   **38-439** March 31, 2003, this being the date of the coming into force of the Sale and Supply of Goods to Consumers Regulations 2002[2730] and before October 1, 2015, being the date of the coming into force of the relevant provisions of the Consumer Rights Act 2015.[2731] As earlier noted, these amendments took effect by way of amendment of the Sale of Goods Act 1979 (for contracts for the sale of goods),[2732] the Supply of Goods (Implied Terms) Act 1973 (for hire-purchase agreements),[2733] the Supply of Goods and Services Act 1982 (for contracts for the transfer of goods

---

ing contracts for the supply of digital content COM(2015) 634 final ("Digital content directive proposal 2015").

[2727] On this law, see below, paras 38-535—38-566.

[2728] Amended sales of goods proposal 2017 art.3; Digital content directive proposal 2015 art.4.

[2729] The Consumer Rights Act 2015 (Commencement No.3, Transitional Provisions, Savings and Consequential Amendments) Order 2015 (SI 2015/1630) (the "2015 Order") arts 3(a)–(c). The exception is found in relation Pt 1 Ch.4 whose provisions governing services contracts did not apply to certain "consumer transport services" (certain rail passenger services, carriage by air, and sea and inland waterway transport, all as specially defined by the 2015 Order art.2) until October 1, 2016: 2015 Order arts 4 and 6(2) as amended by the Consumer Rights Act 2015 (Commencement No.3, Transitional Provisions, Savings and Consequential Amendments) (Amendment) Order 2016 (SI 2016/484) art.2. The main reason for this delay in the bringing into force of the 2015 Act in this area was a concern that the Act's provisions (especially s.57's controls on the exclusion or restriction of liability in the carrier) would risk complexity and duplication with sectoral transport schemes: Department of Transport, *Applying the Consumer Rights Act 2015 to the rail, aviation and maritime sectors, Response to Consultation, Moving Britain Ahead* (July 2016). Although the Department of Transport (para.2.4) had earlier announced that the exemption from the application of s.57(3) of the 2015 Act (governing *restrictions* on liability) would continue to apply to passenger services operated by EU licensed rail passenger operators until October 1, 2017 (see *draft* Consumer Rights (Rail Passenger Service Exemption, Enforcement and Amendments) Order 2016 (laid before Parliament, July 7, 2016)). On September 6, 2016 it was announced that the 2015 Act would apply in full to all passenger transport services, including mainline rail passenger services as from October 1, 2016: *https://www.gov.uk/government/publications/consumer-rights-act-application-to-transport-services*. See above, para.38-366.

[2730] SI 2002/3045.

[2731] See above, para.38-437. SI 2015/1630 art.6(3) preserves the effect of the amendments to the law made by the 2002 Regulations in relation to contracts entered into before October 1, 2015.

[2732] 2002 Regulations regs 3–6, amending Sale of Goods Act 1979 ss.14, 20, 32 and 61(1) and inserting new Pt 5A.

[2733] 2002 Regulations regs 13 amending Supply of Goods (Implied Terms) Act 1973 ss.10 and 15.

other than sale of goods or hire-purchase agreement),[2734] and the Unfair Contract Terms Act 1977 (as regards the control of exclusions of liability arising under these provisions).[2735] The following paragraphs will set out the particular provisions applying only to consumer contracts for the sale of goods, referring in the course of doing so to parallel provisions governing hire-purchase agreements and other contracts for the transfer of goods.

(i) Amendment to the Statutory Implied Term as to Quality of Goods

38-440 **Amendment to Sale of Goods Act 1979 s.14** The Sale and Supply of Goods to Consumers Regulations 2002[2736] inserted subss.(2D) to (2F) into s.14 of the 1979 Act so as to read:

"(2)   Where the seller sells goods in the course of a business, there is an implied term that the goods supplied under the contract are of satisfactory quality.

(2A)   For the purposes of this Act, goods are of satisfactory quality if they meet the standard that a reasonable person would regard as satisfactory, taking account of any description of the goods, the price (if relevant) and all the other relevant circumstances.

(2B)   For the purposes of this Act, the quality of goods includes their state and condition and the following (among others) are in appropriate cases aspects of the quality of the goods—

(a)   fitness for all the purposes for which goods of the kind in question are commonly supplied,

(b)   appearance and finish,

(c)   freedom from minor defects,

(d)   safety, and

(e)   durability.

(2C)   The term implied by subsection (2) above does not extend to any matter making the quality of goods unsatisfactory—

(a)   which is specifically drawn to the buyer's attention before the contract is made,

(b)   where the buyer examines the goods before the contract is made, which that examination ought to reveal, or

(c)   in the case of a contract for sale by sample, which would have been apparent on a reasonable examination of the sample.

(2D)   If the buyer deals as consumer or, in Scotland, if a contract of sale is a consumer contract, the relevant circumstances mentioned in subsection (2A) above include any public statements on the specific characteristics of the goods made about them by the seller, the producer or his representative, particularly in advertising or on labelling.

(2E)   A public statement is not by virtue of subsection (2D) above a relevant circumstance for the purposes of subsection (2A) above in the case of a contract of sale, if the seller shows that—

(a)   at the time the contract was made, he was not, and could not reasonably have been, aware of the statement,

(b)   before the contract was made, the statement had been withdrawn in public or, to the extent that it contained anything which was incorrect or misleading, it had been corrected in public, or

(c)   the decision to buy the goods could not have been influenced by the statement.

[2734] 2002 Regulations regs 7–12, amending Supply of Goods and Services Act 1982 ss.4, 9, 11D, 11J and 18 and inserting new Pt 1B.

[2735] 2002 Regulations reg.14 amending Unfair Contract Terms Act 1977 s.12 (for English law).

[2736] SI 2002/3045 reg.3(2).

(2F)   Subsections (2D) and (2E) above do not prevent any public statement from being a relevant circumstance for the purposes of subsection (2A) above (whether or not the buyer deals as consumer ... if the statement would have been such a circumstance apart from those subsections."

Similar provisions were inserted into the Supply of Goods (Implied Terms) Act 1973 (for hire-purchase agreements)[2737] and the Supply of Goods and Services Act 1982 (for contracts for the transfer of goods other than sale of goods or hire-purchase agreement[2738] and for contracts of hire[2739]). These amendments therefore introduced new matters under the heading of "relevant circumstances" for the assessment of the goods "satisfactory quality".[2740] These are public statements concerning the goods made by the seller, the producer[2741] or his representative, particularly in advertising or labelling. These could previously be taken into account in determining the quality of the goods: but this change specifically makes them "relevant circumstances" for that purpose, though only where the buyer deals as consumer.[2742] As will be seen, the amendments provide exceptions for statements of which the seller could not have known, which have been withdrawn or which could not have influenced the decision to buy.

(ii)   Passing of Risk

Risk passes only on delivery   The 2002 Regulations amended s.20 of the Sale of **38-441** Goods Act 1979 so as to provide that where the buyer "deals as consumer",[2743] the normal rules which it provides for the passing of risk "must be ignored and the goods remain at the seller's risk until they are delivered to the consumer".[2744] Although this may accord better with the intention of the parties in a consumer transaction, it must be borne in mind that under the 1979 Act delivery may be effected without necessarily handing over physical possession of the goods: delivery may be actual or constructive.[2745] It is, though, more difficult to see why the seller should be required to bear the risk even with respect to loss caused by the buyer's fault, at least where this is caused by the goods' deterioration.[2746]

[2737] 2002 Regulations reg.13 inserting Supply of Goods (Implied Terms) Act 1973 s.10(2D)–(2F) and amending s.15(1).

[2738] 2002 Regulations reg.7 inserting Supply of Goods and Services Act 1982 s.4(2B)–(2D) and reg.12 amending s.18(1).

[2739] 2002 Regulations reg.10 inserting Supply of Goods and Services Act 1982 ss.9(2B)–(2D) and 10 and reg.12 amending s.18(1).

[2740] 2002 Regulations reg.3, implementing 1999 Directive art.2(2)(d) and (4).

[2741] 2002 Regulations reg.6(1), amending Sale of Goods Act 1979 s.61(1), to mean "the manufacturer of goods, the importer of goods into the European Economic Area or any person purporting to be a producer by placing his name, trade mark or other distinctive sign on the goods".

[2742] Sale of Goods Act 1979 s.61(5A) referring to "dealing as consumer" within the meaning of the Unfair Contract Terms Act 1977 Pt 1 (and especially s.12) and see Vol.I, paras 15-073—15-078.

[2743] As defined by reference to Unfair Contract Terms Act 1977 s.12: 1979 Act s.61(5A) and see Vol.I, paras 15-073—15-078.

[2744] Inserted by reg.4 of the Sale and Supply of Goods to Consumers Regulations 2002 (SI 2002/3045).

[2745] See below, para.44-241.

[2746] Sale of Goods Act 1979 s.20(2) which is also to be ignored: see *Benjamin's Sale of Goods* 9th edn (2014), para.6-026. Ignoring s.20(3) (which provides that nothing in s.20 "affects the duties or liabilities of either seller or buyer as bailee or custodier of the goods of the other party") appears to make no change in the law.

(iii)   Special Remedies for Buyers Dealing as Consumers

38-442   Introduction   The most important changes introduced by the Sale and Supply of Goods to Consumers Regulations 2002[2747] were the insertion of a new Pt 5A into the Sale of Goods Act 1979 so as to create special remedies in respect of the goods which are not in conformity with the contract of sale for the benefit of buyers "dealing as consumer",[2748] with similar insertions introduced into the Supply of Goods and Services Act 1982 (for contracts for the transfer of goods other than sale of goods or hire-purchase agreements).[2749] These changes became effective on March 31, 2003 and it may be assumed that the Regulations as a whole only apply to contracts entered into on or after that date,[2750] not (since they do not entirely deal with remedies) to contracts in respect of which remedies are sought to be exercised after that date.[2751] As earlier noted, the purpose of the new provisions was to comply as regards remedies with the requirements of Consumer Sales Directive's provisions requiring rights for consumers in respect of the non-conformity of goods.[2752] The remedies added by Pt 5A were in large part new to the common law: a right in certain circumstances to demand repair or replacement of the goods, a right to a reduction in the price, and a specific right to rescission more limited than the general right already existing at common law. All three notions are of recognisably civil law origin.[2753] To an extent, these remedies extended the rights of the consumer in England and Wales, but the wider law continues and is often more advantageous to consumers than the special provisions.[2754] Moreover, the interaction of the special remedies with the wider remedies under the Sale of Goods Act and the general law is complex. The new remedies do not apply to defects in title, late delivery or non-delivery, which are governed by the general law.[2755]

38-443   General section   The remedies are introduced by a general section which refers to all the remedies referred to above:

> "**48A.**—(1)   This section applies if—
>
>   (a)   the buyer deals as consumer … and
>
>   (b)   the goods do not conform to the contract of sale at the time of delivery.
>
>   (2)   If this section applies, the buyer has the right—

[2747] SI 2002/3045. The 2002 Regulations were revoked on the coming into force of the Consumer Rights Act 2015: 2015 Act s.60, Sch.1 para.53 above, para.38-437 and below, paras 38-465 et seq.

[2748] SI 2002/3045 regs 7–11 amend the Supply of Goods and Services Act 1982. A more detailed discussion of the changes effected by the Regulations appears in the 9th edn of *Benjamin's Sale of Goods* (2014), paras 12-073 et seq.

[2749] 2002 Regulations regs 7–12, inserting Supply of Goods and Services Act 1982 Pt 1B (ss.11M–11S).

[2750] And before October 1, 2015: see above, para.38-437.

[2751] These provisions are repealed and replaced by the Consumer Rights Act 2015 as regards contracts concluded on or after October 1, 2015: see below, paras 38-437 et seq.

[2752] 1999 Directive art.3.

[2753] See generally Whittaker, *Liability for Products: English Law, French Law and European Harmonisation* (2005) Ch.19 especially at pp.570–571.

[2754] Below, paras 38-456—38-457. The 1999 Directive art.8(1) provides that the rights which it foresees "shall be exercised without prejudice to other rights which the consumer may invoke under the national rules governing contractual or non-contractual liability" and art.8(2) permits Member States to retain rules which are stricter than those which the Directive requires by way of "minimum harmonisation", on which see above, para.38-022.

[2755] See below, paras 44-080 et seq. and 44-236 et seq.

    (a)   under and in accordance with section 48B below, to require the seller to repair or replace the goods, or

    (b)   under and in accordance with section 48C below—

        (i)   to require the seller to reduce the purchase price of the goods to the buyer by an appropriate amount, or

        (ii) to rescind the contract with regard to the goods in question.

   (3)   For the purposes of subsection (1)(b) above goods which do not conform to the contract of sale at any time within the period of six months starting with the date on which the goods were delivered to the buyer must be taken not to have so conformed at that date.

   (4)   Subsection (3) above does not apply if—

    (a)   it is established that the goods did so conform at that date;

    (b)   its application is incompatible with the nature of the goods or the nature of the lack of conformity."

A similar introductory provision was inserted into the Supply of Goods and Services Act 1982 for contracts for the transfer of goods other than sale of goods or hire-purchase agreement, referring to rights in the transferee against the transferor.[2756]

Dealing as consumer   As will appear below, Pt 5A is by virtue of its opening provision, s.48A, directed at situations where the buyer deals as consumer. Although the word "consumer" is defined in reg.2 of the 2002 Regulations, this definition is not relevant here[2757] because the sections discussed here were inserted into the Sale of Goods Act 1979, and the 1979 Act provides that "dealing as consumer" is to be construed by reference to Pt I of the Unfair Contract Terms Act 1977,[2758] the relevant definition appearing in s.12 (which was itself amended by the 2002 Regulations[2759]). The understanding of "dealing as consumer" is discussed in relation to the Unfair Contract Terms Act 1977 in Vol.I, Ch.15 of the present work[2760]: the main significance of the change here is that for the purposes of the special remedies, where the buyer is an individual (a "natural person") there is no requirement that the goods sold also be consumer goods.[2761]   **38-444**

Conformity with the contract of sale   The special additional rights for consumers arise where the goods do not conform to the contract and the notion of "contractual non-conformity" is therefore central to their availability. The Sale of Goods Act 1979 as amended by the 2002 Regulations provides that for the purposes of Pt 5A "goods do not conform to a contract of sale if there is, in relation to the goods, a breach of an express term of the contract or a term implied by ss.13, 14 or 15" of the same Act.[2762]   **38-445**

[2756] 2002 Regulations reg.9; Supply of Goods and Services Act 1982 s.11M.

[2757] It is only relevant to reg.15 to "consumer guarantees" on which see below, para.38-462.

[2758] Sale of Goods Act 1979 s.61(5A). Similarly as regards the rights of transferees of goods, the 2002 Regulations inserted them into the Supply of Goods and Services Act 1982 ss.11M–11S; s.18(4) of the 1982 Act provides that "dealing as consumer" is to be construed in accordance with Pt 1 of the Unfair Contract Terms Act 1977.

[2759] 2002 Regulations reg.14(1)–(3).

[2760] See Vol.I, paras 15-073—15-078.

[2761] 1977 Act s.12(1A) (inserted by 2002 Regulations reg.14). Also, the exception for sale by competitive tender no longer operates in such a case, and that for sales by auction is much reduced: s.12(2) (as amended by 2002 Regulations reg.14).

[2762] 1979 Act s.48F. As earlier noted, the 2002 Regulations made a small change to s.14 so as to reflect the definition of "conformity" in art.2 of the 1999 Directive: see above, para.38-440. For wider

38-446 **Presumption of non-conformity on delivery** Section 48A(3) of the 1979 Act provides that:

"… goods which do not conform to the contract of sale at any time within the period of six months starting with the date on which the goods were delivered to the buyer must be taken not to have so conformed at that date."

This provision is of considerable practical importance to consumers, as doubt as to when the unsatisfactory quality or defect in goods arose may be difficult to establish. There is an exception for cases where such a presumption would be "incompatible with the nature of the goods or the nature of the lack of conformity",[2763] for example, where the goods would deteriorate naturally over six months. It is uncertain whether the period starts again after redelivery of repaired or replaced goods, but in principle it seems that it should. This subsection creates a rebuttable presumption[2764] which applies only for the purposes of the Pt 5A remedies as opposed to the common law rights.[2765]

38-447 **First level of remedies: repair or replacement of the goods** At a first level, the consumer has the right to require repair or replacement of the goods. According to s.48B of the 1979 Act[2766]:

"(1)   If section 48A above applies, the buyer may require the seller—
 (a)   to repair the goods, or
 (b)   to replace the goods.
(2)   If the buyer requires the seller to repair or replace the goods, the seller must—
 (a)   repair or, as the case may be, replace the goods within a reasonable time but without causing significant inconvenience to the buyer;
 (b)   bear any necessary costs incurred in doing so (including in particular the cost of any labour, materials or postage).
(3)   The buyer must not require the seller to repair or, as the case may be, replace the goods if that remedy is—
 (a)   impossible, or
 (b)   disproportionate in comparison to the other of those remedies, or
 (c)   disproportionate in comparison to an appropriate reduction in the purchase price under paragraph (a), or rescission under paragraph (b), of section 48C(1) below.[2767]
(4)   One remedy is disproportionate in comparison to the other if the one imposes costs on the seller which, in comparison to those imposed on him by the other, are unreasonable, taking into account—
 (a)   the value which the goods would have if they conformed to the contract of sale,

---

discussion of the statutory implied terms see below, paras 44-086 et seq. Similar provision was made by the Supply of Goods and Services Act 1982 s.11S for contracts for the transfer of goods as understood by that Act.

[2763] 1979 Act s.48A(4)(b).

[2764] 1979 Act s.48A(4)(a); 1999 Directive recital 8, art.5(3), on which see *Faber v Autobedrijf Hazet Ochten BV* (C-497/13) EU:C:2015:357, June 4, 2015, below, paras 38-495, 38-496.

[2765] Similar provision is made by the Supply of Goods and Services Act 1982 s.11M(3) and (4) for contracts for the transfer of goods as understood by that Act.

[2766] Similar provision is made by the Supply of Goods and Services Act 1982 s.11N for contracts for the transfer of goods as understood by that Act.

[2767] subpara.(c) does not appear in the 1999 Directive, which leaves the transition between the major remedies there rather vague.

(b)   the significance of the lack of conformity, and

(c)   whether the other remedy could be effected without significant inconvenience to the buyer.

(5)   Any question as to what is a reasonable time or significant inconvenience is to be determined by reference to—

(a)   the nature of the goods, and

(b)   the purpose for which the goods were acquired."

Right is that of buyer   It should be noted that the right is that of the buyer: the seller has no right to demand to effect repair or replacement.[2768] However, the buyer's choice is limited by requirements of possibility and proportionality and the overall power of the court to decide that another Pt 5A remedy is more appropriate.[2769] Repair[2770] is obviously more appropriate to large artefacts, particularly if they are installed, as in the case of a boiler.[2771] In the case of many mass-produced, especially electronic, goods, replacement may well be cheaper and more efficient than repair. Section 48B(2)(b) places the expense of achieving either of these on the seller,[2772] though it seems that the buyer would be bound to cooperate in the execution of these procedures.[2773] The question of risk during such procedures is not addressed, but by the same reasoning it would seem that it should be on the seller.

38-448

Limits on the right   The limits on the right to demand repair or replacement stated in the section are not difficult to understand, though their application in practice may be more difficult. Considerable use is made of the notion that one remedy should not be disproportionate to others (whether repair as opposed to replacement, or (in

38-449

[2768] Compare Vienna Convention on the International Sale of Goods (see below, para.44-014) art.48.

[2769] 1979 Act s.48E below, para.38-455.

[2770] This word is defined in s.61(1) of the 1979 Act, as amended by reg.6: "repair" means, in cases where there is a lack of conformity of the goods, to bring the goods into conformity with the contract". It has been held under the common law that a repairing seller may owe a duty to state what was wrong with the goods: see below, para.44-285. The wording of the regulation does not make such reasoning easy here, unless failing to do so could be regarded as causing inconvenience to the buyer under s.48C(2)(b), below, para.38-451.

[2771] art.2(5) of the 1999 Directive requires that the remedies of repair or replacement apply to situations where goods are defectively installed by the seller. This is effected under the 2002 Regulations by treating the contract as one for work and materials: see s.11S(1)(b) of the Supply of Goods and Services Act 1982, inserted by reg.9. This, however, brings in s.13 of the 1982 Act, which deals with supply of services, and under which the duty is one of reasonable care only, whereas the Sale of Goods Act duties are strict. It is not clear that this result is compatible with art.2(5) of the Directive which provides that "any lack of conformity resulting from incorrect installation of the consumer goods shall be deemed to be equivalent to lack of conformity of the goods if installation forms part of the contract of sale of the goods and the goods were installed by the seller or under his responsibility" and thereby assimilates defective installation with defect in the goods themselves.

[2772] In *Gebr Weber GmbH v Wittmer* (C-65/09 and C-87/09) EU:C:2011:396, [2011] E.C.R. I-05257 at para.55, the CJEU held that, under the 1999 Directive, a seller must pay for the replacement of defective goods correctly installed. However, the CJEU appeared to suggest that considerations of proportionality could lead to the reduction of the sum payable, which might in turn lead to availability of the remedies of reduction of price and rescission. It is not easy to see any warrant for such a progression in the Regulations. The ECJ earlier held that national legislation permitting the seller to invoice the buyer for use of the goods, where they are replaced after a period, is contrary to the requirement that repair or replacement are "free of charge" (words not appearing in the UK Regulations): *Quelle AG v Verbraucherzentralen und Verbraucherverbande* (C-404/06) EU:C:2008:231, [2008] E.C.R. I-2685.

[2773] See *Benjamin's Sale of Goods*, 9th edn (2014), para.12-085.

the Regulations but not the Directive) one of these as compared with reduction of the price or rescission). In some cases repair or replacement would be completely inappropriate or indeed impossible, e.g. where specific goods are bought, or where all goods such as those ordered would be unsuitable for their purpose. Section 48B(4) makes clear that the test of disproportionality is one based on cost and does not specifically allow in the balancing process reference to the buyer's loss of confidence in the supplier or his interest in intangible satisfaction. Although the buyer may presumably at common law obtain damages for loss of use when the goods are being repaired or replaced[2774] it is unlikely that they can be obtained for annoyance, disappointment or frustration.

38-450 **Enforcement** The presence of these rules no doubt encourage the seller to repair or replace, but s.48E, which deals with "Powers of the Court", gives the court the power actually to order specific performance of the seller's duties.[2775] For English law, this power was new. It is limited by the considerations of proportionality specified in s.48B above, and also by the discretion of the court, which may take into account whether or not other remedies under Pt 5A (reduction of the price and rescission) are more appropriate. However, it only operates within Pt 5A and there appears to be no power to consider (as a court from which an order of specific performance is sought at present would do) whether an award of damages at common law (or indeed rejection at common law) would be more appropriate.[2776]

38-451 **Second level of remedies: reduction of purchase price or rescission of contract** These remedies derive ultimately from the Roman *actio quanti minoris* and *actio redhibitoria*. Section 48C reads:

"(1)   If s.48A above applies, the buyer may—
   (a)   require the seller to reduce the purchase price of the goods in question to the buyer by an appropriate amount, or
   (b)   rescind the contract with regard to those goods,
if the condition in subs.(2) below is satisfied.
   (2)   The condition is that—
   (a)   by virtue of s.48B(3) above the buyer may require neither repair nor replacement of the goods; or
   (b)   the buyer has required the seller to repair or replace the goods, but the seller is in breach of the requirement of s.48B(2)(a) above to do so within a reasonable time and without significant inconvenience to the buyer.
   (3)   For the purposes of this Part, if the buyer rescinds the contract, any reimbursement to the buyer may be reduced to take account of the use he has had of the goods since they were delivered to him."[2777]

[2774] See below, para.44-456.

[2775] This relevant provision reads as follows: "48E (1) In any proceedings in which a remedy is sought by virtue of this Part the court, in addition to any other power it has, may act under this section. (2) On the application of the buyer the court may make an order requiring specific performance or, in Scotland, specific implement by the seller of any obligation imposed on him by virtue of section 48B above".

[2776] See Harris (2003) 119 L.Q.R. 541; *Benjamin's Sale of Goods*, 9th edn (2014), para.12-116 and below, paras 38-521—38-522 in relation to the law under the Consumer Rights Act 2015.

[2777] Similar provision is made by the Supply of Goods and Services Act 1982 s.11P for contracts for the transfer of goods as understood by that Act.

Reduction of price   This remedy as such was new to English law, though s.53(1)   **38-452**
of the Sale of Goods Act[2778] would often give similar results. The effect of subs.(2)
is that, together with the remedy of rescission, it operates only when there is no
scope for repair or replacement or where the seller has failed to effect repair or
replacement within a reasonable time or without significant inconvenience to the
buyer: it is in this sense that these remedies arise at a second level. The assumption behind the remedy of reduction in price is that the buyer keeps the goods and
affirms the contract, but the price is adjusted to a level appropriate to the goods
retained taking into account the failure in conformity. It will certainly not be appropriate unless the goods as delivered are suitable to the purpose for which they
were acquired. It would seem that the price itself is a ceiling from which a percentage reduction is to be made; but the actual value of the goods from which the
reduced value is taken as a percentage should be assessed at the time of delivery.[2779]
If, therefore, the value of the goods has fallen between sale and delivery, the
percentage calculation for reduction of the price would still be taken on the basis
of the agreed price, and this calculation might sometimes yield more than the damages which would be recoverable.[2780] The use of the price reduction as opposed to
that of rescission is at the buyer's choice (subject to the discretion of the court as
to what is appropriate as later explained).[2781] In most cases, a common law award
of damages (which would be available instead or in addition) would prove a
superior remedy, especially as consequential loss can be included. It is unlikely
therefore that the reduction of the price remedy will be of much value in England
and Wales, except in the situation where the value of the goods falls (a situation less
relevant to consumer than to commercial contracts), or if the buyer has difficulty
in proving loss, as where he bought the goods for a gift to another.

Rescission[2782]   This is available as an alternative to reduction of the price, and is   **38-453**
again only available if there is no scope for repair or replacement. Subject to the
court's discretion if the consumer brings proceedings, it appears that the choice
between this remedy and reduction of the price lies with the buyer. A powerful right
to reject exists in any case under the general law[2783] and the right to rescind under
the special provisions is unlikely to be particularly useful.[2784] The 1999 Directive
in fact provides that the consumer is not entitled to have the contract rescinded if
the defect is "minor", a limitation which does not appear in the amendments to the
1979 Act effected by the 2002 Regulations, reflecting a wider UK policy that rejection by consumers should be possible for minor defects.[2785] The nature and effect
of rescission is left unexplained by s.48C, and while the operative word in the

---

[2778] Diminution or extinction of price: see below, para.44-411.
[2779] Some guidance may be drawn from art.50 of the Vienna Convention (see above, para.44-014), which
provides that the buyer may reduce the price "in the same proportion as the value that the goods actually delivered had at the time of delivery bears to the value that conforming goods would have had
at that time".
[2780] Some useful examples are given by Nicholas (1989) 115 L.Q.R. 211, 225–226. See also *Benjamin's
Sale of Goods*, 9th edn (2014), para.12-093.
[2781] See 1979 Act s.48E(3) and (4), below para.38-455.
[2782] See Hogg 2003 S.L.T. 27.
[2783] See below, paras 44-066 et seq.
[2784] It should also be borne in mind that a consumer buyer may have a right of cancellation within a brief
specified period without giving reasons, under regulations governing contracts concluded off-
premises and distance sales: above, paras 38-112 et seq.
[2785] See Law Com No.160 Scots Law Com No.104, *Sale and Supply of Goods* (1987) at 4.13–4.14.

French version of the Directive is *"résolution"*, which suggested termination ab initio with restitution, counter-restitution and damages,[2786] recital 15 appears to allocate these sorts of detail to national law as it provides that "the detailed arrangements whereby rescission of the contract is effected may be laid down in national law".[2787] In English law, it would be more in keeping with the general approach to termination for breach of contract for the effect of "rescission" under s.48C to be prospective rather than retrospective; and it may also be thought that this would be more substantively appropriate. In the present context rescission would therefore mean the rejection of non-conforming goods, termination of the contract for breach and recovery of the price if paid.[2788] Even where a consumer exercises the right to rescind under s.48C, the common law right to damages for breach persists. There could, however, be more problems in a consumer instalment contract.[2789]

38-454 **Allowance for use** Where the buyer justifiably returns goods, he is at common law normally entitled to the whole of the price back without allowance for any use of the goods which he may have had in the interim.[2790] Section 48C(3), however, requires a reduction of the price to take account of such use,[2791] but it only applies to a buyer who rescinds under Pt 5A and not to one who rescinds at common law. This is another reason why the common law remedy may be preferable for a buyer.

38-455 **Discretion as to appropriate remedy** Where the consumer brings proceedings seeking a remedy under Pt 5A of the Act the court has a discretion under s.48E of the 1979 Act as to the appropriate remedy for the consumer.[2792] Section 48E provides that, if the buyer requires the seller to give effect to a remedy under s.48B (i.e. repair or replacement) or s.48C (reduction of purchase price) or "has claims to rescind the contract" under s.48C, but the court decides that another remedy under either s.48B or s.48C is appropriate,[2793] the court may proceed:

"(a)   as if the buyer had required the seller to give effect to the other remedy, or if the other remedy is rescission under section 48C

(b)   as if the buyer had claimed to rescind the contract under that section."[2794]

It is further provided that, if the buyer has claimed to rescind the contract, the court may order that any reimbursement to the buyer is reduced to take account of the use he has had of the goods since they were delivered to him.[2795] In exercising these powers, a court may make an order "unconditionally or on such terms and condi-

---

[2786] arts 1183 and 1184 French Civil Code (as enacted).

[2787] cf. above, para.38-016 on the relevance of recitals to a directive for the interpretation of its provisions.

[2788] *Benjamin's Sale of Goods*, 9th edn (2014), para.12-097.

[2789] *Benjamin's Sale of Goods*, 9th edn (2014), para.12-101. There is no indication as to whether the goods can be returned when damaged without the buyer's fault, a point uncertain at common law also: see below, para.44-290; *Benjamin's Sale of Goods*, 9th edn (2014), para.12-100.

[2790] Below, para.44-066; *Benjamin's Sale of Goods*, 9th edn (2014), paras 12-069—12-070.

[2791] It is not clear how such valuation is to be determined: see Law Com Consultation Paper No.188, *Consumer Remedies for Faulty Goods* (2008), paras 7.36–7.38.

[2792] Similar provision is made by the Supply of Goods and Services Act 1982 s.11R(3)–(4) for contracts for the transfer of goods as understood by that Act.

[2793] 1979 Act s.48E(3).

[2794] 1979 Act s.48E(4).

[2795] 1979 Act s.48E(5); similarly, 1982 Act s.11R(5).

tions as to damages, payment of the price and otherwise as it thinks just".[2796]

Relation to common law remedies[2797]   The point has been made that in many or   **38-456**
most situations, the common law remedies of rejection and/or damages are superior
for a buyer, and advisers may find it prudent to take care not to fall by accident into
some of the procedures of Pt 5A. Their most distinctive feature was the introduction of the new procedures for repair or replacement. It may be an advantage to a
consumer to demand one of these, to which there is a legal right rather than a mere
possibility of a practical solution by this means. There is, however, a concomitant
drawback: if the consumer does not make this demand in circumstances where it
would be appropriate (a matter likely only to be settled by a court at a later stage),
he loses the right to proceed to the other Pt 5A remedies of reduction of the price
and rescission; and even if he does so proceed, the court is entitled under s.48E to
decide that another remedy (under the new provisions) is appropriate. The common law remedies of rejection and/or damages remain. But there is a danger here
that the right to reject could be lost by acceptance of the goods (especially by lapse
of time) under s.35 of the Sale of Goods Act,[2798] which does not apply to a person
who proceeds under Pt 5A. Part 5A contains, however, one specific reference to the
common law, which is as follows:

> "**48D.**—(1)   If the buyer requires the seller to repair or replace the goods the buyer
> must not act under subs.(2) until he has given the seller a reasonable time in which to
> repair or replace (as the case may be) the goods.
>   (2)   The buyer acts under this subsection if—
>   (a)   in England and Wales or Northern Ireland he rejects the goods and terminates
>   the contract for breach of condition[2799];
>   (b)   ...
>   (c)   he requires the goods to be replaced or repaired (as the case may be).[2800]"

In the result therefore, although a consumer buyer is under no obligation to   **38-457**
demand repair or replacement, if he does so he cannot revert to what may be called
the "common law route" without giving the seller a reasonable time to effect what
was demanded: he is locked into the system of special consumer remedies. There
may then be dangers of loss of the right to reject by retention of the goods for a
reasonable time under s.35, though s.35(6)(a)[2801] should ameliorate this. All in all
it is theoretically (though doubtless often not practically) desirable for a buyer to
indicate which route he is taking, the statutory or the common law.[2802]

Partial rejection and quantitative shortages   These are the subject of special   **38-458**

[2796] 1979 Act s.48E(6); similarly, 1982 Act s.11R(6).
[2797] See *Benjamin's Sale of Goods*, 9th edn (2014), paras 12-105, 12-106, 12-112 and especially para.12-
    120. The question whether a buyer who has lost the right to reject can still rescind under s.48C(1)
    was left open in *Douglas v Genvarigill Co Ltd* [2010] CSOH 14 at [37]. But in *Lowe v W Machell
    Joinery Ltd* [2011] EWCA Civ 794, [2012] 1 All E.R. (Comm) 153, it was assumed that the com-
    mon law remedy of rejection remains open to a person who does not choose to pursue the special
    statutory remedies: see at [51]–[52].
[2798] See below, paras 44-278 et seq.
[2799] The possibility of other forms of repudiatory breach is not alluded to.
[2800] Similar provision is made by the Supply of Goods and Services Act 1982 s.11Q for contracts for the
    transfer of goods as understood by that Act.
[2801] See below, paras 44-283—44-284.
[2802] See *Benjamin's Sale of Goods*, 9th edn (2014), para.12-097.

provisions in the Sale of Goods Act,[2803] but Pt 5A gives no guidance[2804] as regards the new procedures. A consumer who is party to a dispute involving such problems would do best therefore to seek to remain within the common law regime.

38-459 **Fixed time limits** The Consumer Sales Directive 1999 envisaged that national laws would set fixed limits for the exercise of the remedies for the consumer which it required, such special "delays" being common in civil law systems.[2805] Since such limits (other than the general limitation of actions) are not used in common law they do not appear in Pt 5A. The result is that the procedures of Pt 5A are subject only to the normal English limitation period of six years,[2806] and even this is applicable only to those who need to seek the aid of judicial procedures. It may well be that the various criteria of proportionality and appropriateness, together with the increasing difficulty of proof as time goes on, make this a theoretical point, but there is no doubt that the procedures of Pt 5A as enacted, including rescission, are not subject to any special time limits.

38-460 **Affirmation and waiver** Conversely, the common law rules are subject to general principles of waiver of breach and affirmation of contract (election), and in particular to s.35 of the Sale of Goods Act, under which the right to reject is lost after (inter alia) the lapse of a reasonable time.[2807] Whether or not the existence of any principle such as that of waiver is envisaged as operating under Pt 5A is not clear, though some of the numerous references to disproportionality, inconvenience and so forth would solve many problems.[2808] Since the principle of waiver is a general one of common law (even if its actual operation is controversial),[2809] based on justice and equity, it is difficult to see a reason for excluding its operation in the context of Pt 5A.[2810] However, there are certainly no rules as to lapse of time in Pt 5A, and if the new regime is intended as exclusive for the person operating it, this

---

[2803] 1979 Act ss.30, 35A: see below, paras 44-257 et seq., paras 44-286 et seq.

[2804] Other than a reference to rescinding the contract "with regard to those goods": 1979 Act s.48C(1)(b).

[2805] e.g. art.1648 French Civil Code (which was amended in 2005 so as to provide a two-year delay for claims under the guarantee against latent defects applicable to contracts of sale generally). The 1999 Directive art.5(1) provides that "the seller shall be held liable under Article 3 where the lack of conformity becomes apparent within two years as from delivery of the goods. If, under national legislation, the rights laid down in Article 3(2) are subject to a limitation period, that period shall not expire within a period of two years from the time of delivery". On the distinction between time-limits on liability in the seller and on the period during which the consumer can exercise the rights arising in respect of that liability see *Ferenschild v JPC Motor SA* (C-133/16) EU:C:2017:541, July 13, 2017.

[2806] Limitation Act 1980: see Vol.I, Ch.28. This is also true of the consumer remedies arising under the Supply of Goods and Services Act 1982 Pt 1B.

[2807] See below, paras 44-278 et seq.

[2808] It is submitted that the 1999 Directive's provision in art.8(1) that "any contractual terms or agreements concluded with the seller before the lack of conformity is brought to the seller's attention which directly or indirectly waive or restrict the rights resulting from this Directive shall, as provided for by national law, not be binding on the consumer" refers to agreements or waiver in the contract and, in any event, before the consumer's right to non-conformity has arisen and therefore has no bearing on the question whether any subsequent waiver by the consumer buyer should affect his rights in respect of non-conformity. Moreover, as earlier noted, recital 15 of the Directive provides that "the detailed arrangements whereby rescission of the contract is effected may be laid down in national law" and the question whether a consumer may effectively waive his right to rescission would fall naturally within such "detailed arrangements".

[2809] See Vol.I, paras 22-040 et seq.

[2810] See *Benjamin's Sale of Goods*, 9th edn (2014), para.12-110.

may mean that the right to reject (rescind) can be exercised at a later time than would be permissible under the general law.

Exclusion by contract   Since the regulations make provision for the remedies of a buyer in respect of the quality requirements in consumer sales, they come within s.6(2) of the Unfair Contract Terms Act 1977 (read with ss.12 and 13(1))[2811] and so cannot be excluded.[2812] The 1977 Act does not, however, apply to international supply transactions at all,[2813] and hence the new provisions can be excluded, as can other terms which might normally be regarded as unfair, for international consumer sales coming within the definition of international supply transactions.[2814] It is submitted that, in the case of buyers who are "consumers" within the meaning of the 1999 Directive (and not merely persons "dealing as consumer" within the wider meaning of the 1977 Act[2815]) the exclusion of control of exemption clauses for international sales is incompatible with the 1999 Directive's requirement that·   **38-461**

> "… any contractual terms or agreements concluded with the seller before the lack of conformity is brought to the seller's attention which directly or indirectly waive or restrict the rights resulting from this Directive shall, as provided for by national law, not be binding on the consumer."[2816]

It would be difficult to see, however, how an English court could interpret the 1977 Act so as not to apply this exclusion to consumer purchases even with the aid of the principle of conforming interpretation of legislation seeking to implement EU law.[2817]

(iv)   Consumer Guarantees and Warranties

Consumer guarantees   The Sale and Supply of Goods to Consumers Regulations 2002[2818] contain provisions relating to "consumer guarantees", for example, of the type frequently given to customers by manufacturers of motor vehicles and electrical equipment.[2819] The regulations do not require such a guarantee to be given. But, if goods are sold or otherwise supplied to a consumer[2820] which are offered with   **38-462**

[2811] s.12 ("dealing as consumer" as amended by the 2002 Regulations) and as applied to the 1979 Act by s.61(5A) of that Act; s.13 defining "exemption clause": see Vol.I, paras 15-073—15-078, 15-069 respectively.

[2812] This is also the case as regards the remedies arising under the Supply of Goods and Services Act 1982 Pt 1B, since the control on the exclusions of liability arising under the 1982 are also effected by the 1977 Act: see notably, s.2 and 7.

[2813] See below, para.44-125.

[2814] Unfair Contract Terms Act 1977 s.26. But (before the coming into force of the Consumer Rights Act 2015) the Unfair Terms in Consumer Contracts Regulations may apply. There are further problems regarding the conflict of laws aspects of the Act: see below, para.44-125.

[2815] See above, para.38-384.

[2816] Consumer Rights Directive 1999 art.7(1).

[2817] cf. above, para.38-014.

[2818] SI 2002/3045 reg.15, amended by SI 2008/1277 Sch.2 para.97. This provision was deleted on the coming into force of the Consumer Rights Act 2015 on October 1, 2015: s.75, Sch.3 para.7: below, para.38-528.

[2819] reg.15 implements the Consumer Sales Directive 1999 art.6.

[2820] Defined in 2002 Regulations reg.2. Regulation 15 thereby goes beyond what is required by the Consumer Sales Directive 1999 art.6 whose scope is restricted to the contracts of sale and work and materials to which the Directive applies: art.2(e) "guarantee".

a consumer guarantee,[2821] the guarantee takes effect at the time the goods are delivered as a contractual obligation owed by the guarantor[2822] under the conditions set out in the guarantee statement and the associated advertising. The guarantee must be in plain intelligible language; where the goods are offered within the UK, it must be in English; and it must contain certain essential particulars.[2823] The guarantor must also ensure that the guarantee contains a statement that the consumer has statutory rights in relation to the goods which are sold or supplied and that those rights are not affected by the guarantee.[2824] The guarantee must be made available, on request, to the consumer in writing or in another durable medium which is available and accessible to him.[2825]

38-463   Terms in a consumer guarantee which purport to exclude or restrict liability for loss or damage resulting from the negligence of a manufacturer or distributor of goods may be rendered ineffective by s.5 of the Unfair Contract Terms Act 1977[2826] and terms that are unfair by the Unfair Terms in Consumer Contracts Regulations 1999.[2827]

38-464   **Extended warranties**   The Supply of Extended Warranties on Domestic Electrical Goods Order 2005[2828] imposes an obligation on suppliers of domestic electrical goods,[2829] who also supply or offer to supply extended warranties for those goods, to provide certain information to consumers before the sale of an extended warranty and gives consumers cancellation and termination rights in relation to such warranties.[2830]

(c)   The New Law: Consumer Rights in Respect of Goods Contracts, Digital Content Contracts and Services Contracts

38-465   **The law recast by the 2015 Act: "goods contracts", "digital content contracts" and "services contracts"**   As noted earlier, Pt 1 of the 2015 Act identifies three broad categories of consumer contract: "contracts for a trader to supply goods to a consumer" or "goods contracts" (Ch.2)[2831]; "contracts for a trader to supply digital

---

[2821] Defined in reg.2.

[2822] "Guarantor" is defined by reg.2 of the 2002 Regulations as "a person who offers a consumer guarantee to a consumer" and is therefore wider that the 1999 Directive art.2(e) and 6 which restrict the application of the provisions in the latter to sellers or producers as defined by art.2(c) and (d) and supplemented by art.2(4).

[2823] For a commentary on these provisions, see *Benjamin's Sale of Goods*, 9th edn (2014), para.14-079. On the requirement of plain intelligible language, cf. above, paras 38-347 et seq. As 2002 Regulations reg.15 implements art.6 of the 1999 Directive, the interpretation of this requirement should follow the approach taken by the CJEU for the purposes of the Unfair Terms in Consumer Contracts Directive 1993 arts 4(2) and 5, as there explained.

[2824] SI 2002/3045 reg.15(2A), inserted by SI 2008/1277 reg.30(1), Sch.2 para.97.

[2825] SI 2002/3045 reg.15(3).

[2826] See Vol.I, para.15-091.

[2827] See above, paras 38-220 et seq.

[2828] SI 2005/37, amended by SI 2006/355 art.4(3). This order is not affected by the Consumer Rights Act 2015.

[2829] Defined in art.1(3).

[2830] *Benjamin's Sale of Goods*, 10th edn (2017), para.14-185.

[2831] Consumer Rights Act 2015 s.3(1).

content to a consumer" or "digital content contracts" (Ch.3)[2832]; and "contracts for a trader to supply a service to a consumer" or "services contracts" (Ch.4).[2833]

Terms "treated as included" First, for each broad category, the 2015 Act **38-466** provides a series of terms which are "treated as included" in the contract, these being broadly equivalent to the traditional implied terms of earlier legislation, as amended and supplemented.[2834] In this respect, in the case of "goods contracts", the Act sought to implement the Law Commissions' recommendations in its report *Consumer Remedies for Faulty Goods*.[2835] Within "goods contracts", further distinctions between different contracts are made, for example, for the purposes of the term that the trader has the right to supply the goods where a distinction is drawn between contracts for the hire of goods and other goods contracts.[2836]

"Rights to enforce terms" Secondly, in respect of each category of contract, the **38-467** 2015 Act provides a series of "rights to enforce terms" about their subject matter (goods, digital content or services).[2837] In the case of "goods contracts" and "digital content contracts", these rights are modelled broadly on the rights in respect of contractual non-conformity of goods provided by the 1999 Directive and earlier implemented by Pt 5A in the Sale of Goods Act 1979,[2838] but there are a series of adjustments and differences.[2839]

Other aims Thirdly, Pt 1 of the 2015 Act also gives effect to certain aspects of **38-468** the Consumer Rights Directive 2011, notably its requirement that information provided by the trader about the goods or services as set out by the Directive is to form part of the contract[2840] and its rules governing delivery of goods and the passing of risk in goods in sales contracts.[2841] Moreover, as will be seen, the provisions of the 2015 Act governing "digital content contracts" are original in the sense that they find no direct equivalent in EU legislation nor earlier UK legislation, though some of the provisions themselves have echoes of both. The 2015 Act's provisions on "services contracts"[2842] are based principally on earlier provisions in the Supply of Goods and Services Act 1982, supplemented by the creation of new rights to "repeat performance" and to price reduction.[2843]

Trader liabilities not subject to exclusion Fourthly, in general Pt 1 of the 2015 **38-469** Act provides that a term in a contract to which it applies cannot exclude or restrict

---

[2832] 2015 Act s.33(1).

[2833] 2015 Act s.48(1).

[2834] i.e. the Supply of Goods (Implied Terms Act) 1973, the Sale of Goods Act 1979 and the Supply of Goods and Services Act 1982.

[2835] Law Com No.317, Scot Law Com No.216, Cm 7725 (2008).

[2836] 2015 Act s.17 below, paras 38-507—38-509.

[2837] 2015 Act s.19 (goods contracts); s.42 (digital content contracts); and s.54 (services contracts) and see below, paras 38-493, 38-544 and 38-570 respectively.

[2838] 1982 Act Pt 1B.

[2839] See below, paras 38-512 et seq. and 38-557 et seq. for the details.

[2840] 2011 Directive art.6(5), above, para.38-105; 2015 Act ss.11(4)–(6), 12 (goods contracts); s.36(3)–(4) and 37 (digital content contracts); and ss.50(3)–(4) (services contracts): see below, paras 38-499—38-500, 38-548—38-549 and 38-575 respectively.

[2841] 2011 Directive arts 18 and 20; 2015 Act ss.28–29, below paras 38-526—38-527.

[2842] 2015 Act Pt 1 Ch.4.

[2843] 2015 Act ss.54–56, below, paras 38-580 et seq.

the trader's liability arising under its substantive provisions, though this strict position is qualified in the case of contracts of hire and in relation to contracts for services.[2844]

38-470 **Disapplication of general legislation** Fifthly, the corollary of the 2015 Act's enactment of special and separate provision for consumer contracts in certain respects is that it amended other, earlier legislation affecting these categories of contracts so as no longer to apply to them or to apply to them only with qualifications.[2845]

38-471 **Law outside the 2015 Act still applicable** On the other hand, this does *not* mean that all the law governing consumer contracts for the supply of goods, digital content or services is found in the 2015 Act, as the following paragraphs will explain.

38-472 **Issues regulated by the 2015 Act and no longer regulated by the Sale of Goods Act** As will be seen, special provision is made in the 2015 Act[2846] for the issues formerly (and still generally) governed by the 1979 Act's provisions on statutory implied terms as to title, sale by description, quality or fitness for purpose and sale by sample[2847] and, as a result, the 2015 Act disapplied these provisions in the 1979 Act so as no longer apply to "goods contracts" within the meaning of Pt 1 of the 2015 Act.[2848] So, for example, s.14 of the Sale of Goods Act 1979 was amended so as to remove earlier insertions governing buyers "dealing as consumer"[2849] and to provide that:

> "This section does not apply to a contract to which Chapter 2 of Part 1 of the Consumer Rights Act 2015 applies (but see the provision made about such contracts in sections 9, 10 and 18 of that Act)."[2850]

Similarly, the 2015 Act makes special provision for "goods contracts" regarding delivery of goods generally,[2851] delivery of the wrong quantity,[2852] instalment deliveries,[2853] and the passing of risk[2854] and, as a result, it disapplied the relevant provisions governing the delivery applicable to contracts of sale of goods generally.[2855] The 2015 Act provides a new scheme of remedies for the consumer under "goods contracts" and therefore, apart from deleting Pt 5A of the 1979 Act,[2856]

[2844] 2015 Act s.31 (goods contracts), s.47 (digital content contracts) and s.57 (services contracts) and see below, paras 38-531, 38-564 and 38-586 respectively.

[2845] 2015 Act s.60 and Sch.1.

[2846] 2015 Act ss.9–18, below, paras 38-492 et seq.

[2847] 1979 Act ss.11–15.

[2848] 2015 Act s.60; Sch.1, paras 8, 10–14.

[2849] 2015 Act s.60 and Sch.1 para.13(2) deleting s.14(2D) to (2F) of the 1979 Act.

[2850] 2015 Act s.60 and Sch.1 para.13(3).

[2851] 2015 Act s.28, below, para.38-526.

[2852] 2015 Act s.25, below, para.38-524.

[2853] 2015 Act s.26, below, para.38-525.

[2854] 2015 Act s.29, below, para.38-527.

[2855] 1979 Act ss.20, 29(3), 30–33; 35–36; 2015 Act s.60, Sch.1 paras 17–22. The 2015 Act s.60, Sch.1 para.23 provides that s.34 of the 1979 Act's provisions on the buyer's right of examining the goods do not affect the operation of s.22 of the 2015 Act (time limit for short-term right to reject), on which see below, para.38-516.

[2856] On which see above, paras 38-442 et seq.

it disapplied other provisions in the 1979 Act which are otherwise inconsistent with this new scheme.[2857]

Issues still regulated by the Sale of Goods Act 1979 This means, however, that the 2015 Act left unaffected a number of provisions of the 1979 Act, which are therefore potentially applicable to the contracts to which the 1979 applies.[2858] This applies to provisions in the 1979 Act governing capacity to buy and sell,[2859] how contracts of sale of goods are made,[2860] existing or future goods,[2861] perished goods,[2862] goods perishing before sale but after agreement to sell,[2863] ascertainment of price,[2864] agreement to sell at a valuation,[2865] stipulations about time,[2866] when property passes (though the 2015 Act refers instead to "ownership" rather than "property"),[2867] sales by a person other than the owner,[2868] duties of sellers and buyers in general,[2869] payment and delivery as concurrent conditions,[2870] delivery (other than about the timing for delivery[2871]), the buyer's liability for not taking delivery of goods,[2872] the unpaid seller's lien,[2873] the seller's action for the price,[2874] damages for non-acceptance against the buyer[2875] and auction sales.[2876] While this is quite a catalogue, it will be seen that many of the issues still governed by the 1979 Act are unlikely to arise between the parties to a consumer contract, the main exception being the seller/trader's rights in respect of the price and in respect of the consumer buyer's non-acceptance.

38-473

Supply of Goods (Implied Terms) Act 1973 and the Supply of Goods and Services Act 1982 The effect of the 2015 Act is that a consumer contract falling under Pt 1 of the 2015 Act is no longer governed by the provisions of the Supply of Goods (Implied Terms) Act 1973 (hire-purchase agreements) or of the Supply of Goods and Services Act 1982 (contracts for the transfer of property in goods,

38-474

[2857] 2015 Act s.60, Sch.1 paras 24–30 and 32 disapplying 1979 Act s.35 (acceptance), s.35A (right of partial rejection), and s.36 (buyer not bound to return rejected goods), s.51 (damages for non-delivery), s.52 (specific performance), s.53 (remedy for breach of warranty), s.54 (interest) and referring the reader to the relevant provisions of the 2015 Act. The 2015 Act s.60, Sch.1 also makes other minor amendments to the 1979 Act consequential on its enactment of Pt 1.

[2858] For these purposes, it must first be noted that while Ch.2 of Pt 1 of the 2015 Act applies to "goods contracts" as it defines them (2015 Act ss.3 and 5, below, paras 38-486—38-488), the 1979 Act applies to "contracts of sale of goods" as it defines them: 1979 Act ss.1–2.

[2859] 1979 Act s.3, on which see Vol.I, paras 9-013—9-015 and below para.44-033.

[2860] 1979 Act s.4, though parallel provision is made for all the contracts to which Pt 1 of the 2015 Act applies: 2015 Act s.1(2).

[2861] 1979 Act s.5 on which see below, para.44-038.

[2862] 1979 Act s.6 on which see below, para.44-046.

[2863] 1979 Act s.7 on which see below, paras 44-047—44-048.

[2864] 1979 Act s.8 on which see below, paras 44-051—44-052.

[2865] 1979 Act s.9 on which see below, para.44-053.

[2866] 1979 Act s.10 on which see below, para.44-128.

[2867] 2015 Act s.4; 1979 Act ss.16–19, 20A–20B, below, paras 44-130—44-188.

[2868] 1979 Act ss.21–26, below, paras 44-193—44-235.

[2869] 1979 Act s.27 on which see below, para.44-236.

[2870] 1979 Act s.28 on which see below, para.44-237.

[2871] 1979 Act s.29. The 2015 Act disapplied s.29(3) as regards Pt 1 consumer contracts.

[2872] 1979 Act s.37 on which see below, para.44-291.

[2873] 1979 Act ss.41–48 on which see below, paras 44-315 et seq.

[2874] 1979 Act s.49 on which see below, paras 44-359 et seq.

[2875] 1979 Act s.50 on which see below, paras 44-367 et seq.

[2876] 1979 Act s.57.

contracts for the hire of goods and contracts for services).[2877] Unlike the Sale of Goods Act 1979, there are no provisions in the 1973 or 1982 Act which still apply both to consumer contracts and to contracts generally, reflecting the generally narrower scope of the regulation of the categories of contract to which they apply.

38-475 **Common law and equity** Part 1 of the 2015 Act itself recognises that its rights to enforce the terms of the contracts may be supplemented by "other remedies" at common law or in equity, which, depending on the category of contract in question, may include specific performance, damages, "relying on the breach against a claim by the trader for the price", "treating the contract as an end" or recover of money paid on the basis of a failure of consideration.[2878] Moreover, even though not flagged up by the Act in this way, the common law may apply so as to provide other rights for the consumer. This is the case, for example, as regards the law of misrepresentation (to the extent to which it is not disapplied by the Consumer Protection from Unfair Trading Regulations 2008 as amended in 2014[2879]), the law of undue influence or duress.[2880]

38-476 **Other legislation** Apart from the rules in Pt 2 of the 2015 Act governing unfair terms in consumer contracts generally,[2881] other consumer protection legislation may also apply to the three broad categories of contract governed by Pt 1 of the 2015 Act, notably, the Consumer Contracts (Information, Cancellation and Additional Charges) Regulations 2013[2882] and the Consumer Protection from Unfair Trading Regulations 2008.[2883]

38-477 **Interpretation of 2015 Act Pt 1** Many concepts used by the 2015 Act are defined by it.[2884] For example, the 2015 Act provides that contracts to supply goods are treated as including a term that "the trader must have the right to sell or transfer the goods at the time when ownership of the goods is to be transferred",[2885] and defines "ownership" for this purpose,[2886] though it then refers its reader to the 1979 Act "for the time when ownership of goods is transferred" in relation to contracts of sale.[2887]

[2877] In the case of the 1973 Act, the disapplication of the provisions applicable to hire-purchase agreements was effected by 2015 Act s.60, Sch.1 paras 1–7 (which do so by substituting "relevant hire-purchase agreement" for "hire-purchase agreement" in the 1973 Act and then defining a relevant hire-purchase agreement as one which "is not a contract to which Chapter 2 of Part 1 of the Consumer Rights Act 2015 applies", as well as making consequential amendments to the 1973 Act. In the case of the 1982 Act, some provisions formerly applicable only to consumers were deleted (notably, Pt 1B), the scope set out in ss.1, 6 and 12 was amended so as not to apply to contracts to which Ch.2 of Pt 1 of the 2015 Act applies, these not being "relevant" contracts of the types governed by the Act; other consequential amendments were also made: 2015 Act s.60, Sch.1, paras 37–44, 50–52.

[2878] 2015 Act s.19(9)–(13) below, para.38-523; s.42(6)–(7) (digital content) below, para.38-562; and s.54(6)–(7) (services contracts) below, para.38-584.

[2879] SI 2008/1277 (as amended): see above, para.38-208 and Vol.I, Ch.7.

[2880] See Vol.I, Ch.8.

[2881] Above, paras 38-365 et seq.

[2882] SI 2013/3134: see above, paras 38-060 et seq.

[2883] SI 2008/1277 (as amended): see above, paras 38-157 et seq.

[2884] See notably, 2015 Act ss.2, 3–8, 33, 48 and 59.

[2885] 2015 Act s.17 provides exceptions for contracts for the hire of goods (s.17(1)(a)) and where circumstances show or imply that the trader intended to transfer only a more limited title (s.17(1) and (4)–(7)).

[2886] 2015 Act s.4(1) "the general property in goods, not merely a special property".

[2887] 2015 Act s.4(2) referring to 1979 Act ss.16–20B.

Other concepts used by the 2015 Act are left undefined by it. It is submitted that the proper interpretation of these concepts depends on whether the provision in which they appear reflects EU legislation. Where it does (even in cases where the Act goes beyond what that legislation requires), then its interpretation may require an autonomous European interpretation.[2888] Where, on the other hand, the concept does not reflect EU legislation or has not received and would not receive such an autonomous interpretation, then its interpretation would be subject to the normal rules governing the interpretation of UK statutes. In the case of concepts known to the common law or previously (or more generally) used by domestic statutes, in principle reference should be made to their interpretation under this wider English law. However, where a particular concept is used in provisions which reflect EU law and in other provisions which do not (but reflect domestic legislation) difficulty may arise. So, for example, "possession" is used by the Act in its definition of "hire of goods" (which does not reflect EU law),[2889] but it is also used in the Act's provisions governing the passing of risk[2890] and, by reference, on the delivery of goods,[2891] both of which reflect provisions in the Consumer Rights Directive 2011.[2892]

New terminology used by the Act   The declared purpose of the Act was to make   **38-478**
the law governing consumer rights more accessible to consumers, or at least to their advisers.[2893] As a result, some of the familiar terminology of the common law and of earlier legislation was abandoned and replaced by new terminology which was intended to be more easily comprehended. The most prominent example of this is the replacement of the terminology of "implied term" familiar both from the common law and from statute since the Sale of Goods Act 1893 with provisions that provide that a contract "is to be treated as including a term", for example, that the quality of goods is satisfactory.[2894] It is not clear that such a statutory deeming provision is any more accessible to non-lawyers than the traditional terminology, but in the following paragraphs these terms will be referred to as "statutory terms". On the other hand, use of "condition" by the 2015 Act is more complex. The 2015 Act abandons the technical sense (used both by the 1979 Act and the common law) of a condition as a type of term the slightest breach of which will in principle give rise in the injured party to a right to terminate the contract ("treat the contract as repudiated"),[2895] but it recognises that a contract to supply goods may be conditional as well as absolute,[2896] and then refers specially to a "conditional sales contract" as one where the trader retains ownership in the goods until certain conditions are met (typically payment).[2897] Moreover, the terminology used by the Act to describe the

---

[2888] Above, para.38-015.
[2889] 2015 Act s.6.
[2890] 2015 Act s.29 referring to "physical possession".
[2891] 2015 Act s.28; "delivery" is defined by s.59(1) as the "voluntary transfer of possession from one person to another".
[2892] 2011 Directive arts 18 and 20 (both referring to "physical possession"). See further, below, paras 38-526 and 38-527.
[2893] BIS, *Enhancing Consumer Confidence by Clarifying Consumer Law* (July 2012), paras 2.1–2.3.
[2894] 2015 Act s.9(1).
[2895] On this usage, see 1979 Act s.11(3) and more generally Vol.I, paras 13-019 et seq. The 2015 Act instead provides its own remedies which bring the contract to an end: e.g. below, paras 38-513 and 38-518 ("goods contracts").
[2896] 2015 Act s.3(5)(c).
[2897] 2015 Act s.5(3).

effects, for example, of failures of conformity in goods, is not uniform. The 2015 Act places the new statutory terms under a heading "What statutory *rights* are there under a goods contract?"[2898] and under a later heading asks "What *remedies* are there if statutory rights under a goods contract are not met?"[2899] However, s.19 (which follows this second heading and sets out the general framework for the consumer's rights) refers to the consumer's "*rights* to enforce terms about goods",[2900] for example, the "right to reject",[2901] except when referring to "other remedies" available to the consumer, such as damages, specific performance, which arise under the general law.[2902] On the other hand, later provisions setting out the details of the consumers "rights to enforce" do sometimes refer instead to the consumer's "remedy".[2903] This apparent inconsistency is not helpful. Moreover, at times the terminology adopted by the 2015 Act to define a technical distinction (with normative significance) may not be readily apparent without a close familiarity with its provisions. This is the case notably as regards the distinction between a "contract to supply goods" and "contracts for the transfer of goods" (the former being used to describe the broad category of contracts to which Ch.2 applies and which consists of "sales contracts", contracts for the hire of goods, hire purchase agreements and contracts for the transfer of goods[2904] and the latter being a residual category of contract under which the trader transfers or agrees to transfer ownership of goods to the consumer, which is neither a sales contract nor a hire-purchase agreement).[2905]

38-479 **Legislative style of the 2015 Act**   The general legislative style is to expound the law in relatively short sentences and to make frequent cross-reference within the text of the provisions to other sections of the Act itself or, on occasion, to other legislation. A prominent example is that each section of the Act which inserts a statutory term ends with a provision referring the reader to the relevant provision within the Act which provides for the consumer's rights against the trader in respect of breach of the term.[2906] Conversely, s.31's provision rendering a contract term which seeks to exclude the trader's liability arising under the provisions of Pt 1, lists the relevant sections for this purpose.[2907]

(i)   General Definitions

38-480 **Scope of application of Pt 1 of the 2015 Act**   Part 1 of the 2015 Act applies only to three broad categories of consumer contract: "contracts for a trader to supply goods to a consumer" or "goods contracts" (Ch.2)[2908]; "contracts for a trader to supply digital content to a consumer" or "digital content contracts" (Ch.3)[2909]; and

---

[2898] Heading prefacing s.9 of the 2015 Act (emphasis added).
[2899] Heading prefacing s.19 of the 2015 Act (emphasis added).
[2900] 2015 Act s.19 title.
[2901] 2015 Act s.20.
[2902] 2015 Act s.19(9)–(11).
[2903] 2015 Act s.23(4) and (5).
[2904] 2015 Act s.3(1) and (2).
[2905] 2015 Act s.8.
[2906] e.g., as regards "goods contracts", ss.9(9), 10(6), 12(5), 13(3), 14(3), 15(2) referring to s.19.
[2907] 2015 Act s.31(1) and see below, para.38-531.
[2908] Consumer Rights Act 2015 s.3(1).
[2909] 2015 Act s.33(1).

"contracts for a trader to supply a service to a consumer" or "services contracts" (Ch.4).[2910] The particular elements of these contracts will be explained in turn below,[2911] but certain "key definitions" are of more general application.

"Consumer"   For the purposes of Pt 1 of the 2015 Act: **38-481**

> "'Consumer' means an individual acting for purposes that are wholly or mainly outside that individual's trade, business, craft or profession."[2912]

This reflects the new standard UK definition of "consumer" and reflects the EU definition of "consumer", with the gloss that it includes as "consumer" a person who acts *mainly* outside his trade, etc.[2913] Following similar provision in the Unfair Contract Terms Act 1977, the 2015 Act provides that:

> "A trader claiming that an individual was not acting for purposes wholly or mainly outside the individual's trade, business, craft or profession must prove it."[2914]

"Trader"   The 2015 Act provides that: **38-482**

> "'Trader' means a person acting for purposes relating to that person's trade, business, craft or profession, whether acting personally or through another person acting in the trader's name or on the trader's behalf."[2915]

And "… 'business' includes the activities of any government department or local or public authority".[2916] This definition of the other party to a consumer contract has become standard in modern UK legislation governing consumer contracts and follows closely the position in EU law, as explained earlier.[2917]

Contracts business-to-consumer   It has earlier been seen that EU legislation (and   **38-483** therefore UK legislation which reflects it exactly without extension) may not make clear whether it applies so as to protect persons dealing other than in a course of business where they *supply* goods or services as opposed to where they *receive* goods or services.[2918] However, Pt 1 of the 2015 Act makes clear that its provisions apply only to contracts under which a trader supplies goods, digital content or services *to* consumers.[2919] This makes substantive sense as it seeks to create rights in buyers or customers (the consumer) and it also reflects the position under the EU legislation which some of the Act's provisions implement.[2920]

[2910] 2015 Act s.48(1).

[2911] Below, paras 38-485 et seq., 38-535 et seq. and 38-567 et seq. respectively.

[2912] 2015 Act s.2(3).

[2913] For discussion of the significance of "consumer" see above, paras 38-032 et seq. The 2015 Act s.2(5) and (6) makes a specific exclusion from this definition of "consumer" in relation to "sales contracts" as explained below, para.38-487.

[2914] 2015 Act s.2(4) cf. Unfair Contract Terms Act 1977 s.12(3) in relation to a person "dealing as consumer", itself deleted by the 2015 Act.

[2915] 2015 Act s.2(2).

[2916] 2015 Act s.2(7).

[2917] Above, paras 38-050 et seq.

[2918] Above, para.38-047.

[2919] 2015 Act ss.1(1), 3(1), 33(1) and 48(1).

[2920] i.e. 1999 Directive especially art.2(c) defining the business party as "seller", arts 2 and 3 imposing duties on the seller and rights in the consumer against the seller; Consumer Rights Directive 2011 arts 18 and 20 (which both make clear that they apply where the trader sells goods to the consumer).

38-484 **Mixed contracts** Chapters 2 to 4 of Pt 1 of the 2015 Act make provision for "goods contracts", "digital content contracts" and "services contracts" respectively, but it is specifically provided that each chapter applies even if the contract also covers something covered by another chapter, so that a "mixed contract" may be governed by two or all three of the chapters.[2921] Special provision is also made for particular mixed contracts.[2922] On the other hand, as will be seen, within the broad category of "goods contracts", sharp distinctions are drawn between contracts for the hire of goods and hire-purchase agreements,[2923] hire-purchase agreements and conditional sales agreements,[2924] and a "contract for transfer of goods" is defined as a residual category of contracts for the transfer of ownership of goods which is not a sales contract or a hire-purchase agreement.[2925]

(ii) "Goods Contracts"

(aa) The Four Types of "Goods Contracts"

38-485 **Introduction** The 2015 Act provides that there are four types of "goods contracts" to which Ch.2 of Pt 1 applies: a "sales contract", a "contract for the hire of goods", a "hire-purchase agreement" and a "contract for transfer of goods".[2926] These may include contracts entered into between one part owner and another, contracts for the transfer of an undivided share in goods and contracts that are absolute and contracts that are conditional.[2927] These contracts are referred to by the Act either as contracts to supply goods or "goods contracts".[2928]

38-486 **"Sales contracts"** The 2015 Act provides that:

"A contract is a sales contract if under it—
    (a)   the trader transfers or agrees to transfer ownership of goods to the consumer, and
    (b)   the consumer pays or agrees to pay the price."[2929]

Apart from the substitution of "ownership of goods" for "the property in goods", this definition follows closely the definition of "contract of sale of goods" in the 1979 Act,[2930] and this substitution makes no substantive difference given that the

---

[2921] 2015 Act s.1(4)–(5); s.3(7).

[2922] 2015 Act s.1(6) referring to ss.15 and 16, below, paras 38-503—38-504.

[2923] 2015 Act s.6(2), below, para.38-489.

[2924] 2015 Act s.7(4), below, para.38-490.

[2925] 2015 Act s.8, below, para.38-491.

[2926] 2015 Act s.3(2). Ch.2 does not apply to a contract for a trader to supply coins or notes to a consumer for use as currency; a contract for goods to be sold by way of execution or otherwise by authority of law; a contract intended to operate as a mortgage, pledge, charge or other security; or a contract made by deed and for which the only consideration is the presumed consideration imported by the deed: s.3(3). Particular provisions of the Act may apply or may apply differently according to the different types of "goods contracts" which *are* included: s.3(6) and, e.g. s.17 (trader to have right to supply the goods, etc.) on which see below, paras 38-507—38-510.

[2927] 2015 Act s.3(5). cf. 1979 Act s.2(2)–(3), below, para.38-478.

[2928] 2015 Act s.3(4); heading preceding s.3.

[2929] 2015 Act s.5(1). cf. *Software Incubator Ltd v Computer Associates UK Ltd* [2018] EWCA Civ 518 where it was held that a contract for the supply of software does not constitute a "sale of goods" for the purposes of the Commercial Agents (Council Directive) Regulations 1993 (SI 1993/3053).

[2930] 1979 Act s.2(1) below, paras 44-020 et seq.

2015 Act defines "ownership" as "the general property in goods, not merely a special property".[2931]

"Goods"   "Goods" are defined by the 2015 Act as: **38-487**

"... any tangible moveable items, but that includes water, gas and electricity if and only if they are put up for supply in a limited volume or set quantity."[2932]

This reflects the wording of the definition of "consumer goods" in the 1999 Directive, rather than "goods" in the 1979 Act.[2933] Moreover, reflecting an option for Member States under the 1999 Directive,[2934] the 2015 Act generally excludes from the application of Ch.2's provisions *sales* contracts where the goods are "second hand goods sold at public auction, and ... individuals have the opportunity of attending the sale in person", though it does so by deeming the buyer not to be a "consumer" in these circumstances,[2935] but the 2015 Act does not make this exclusion in relation to those of its provisions which implement the Consumer Rights Directive 2011, as that Directive does not allow for such an exclusion.[2936]

Contract for work and materials as "sales contract"   The 2015 Act also   **38-488**
includes within "sales contracts" certain contracts which might be treated by English law as being contracts for work and materials,[2937] thereby implementing the 1999 Directive.[2938] Section 5(2) of the 2015 Act provides that:

[2931] 2015 Act s.4(1) and cf. 1979 Act s.61(1) defining "property" as "general property in goods, and not merely a special property", on which see below, para.44-015. In the *PST Energy 7 Shipping LLC v OW Bunker Malta (The Res Cogitans)* [2016] UKSC 23, [2016] 2 W.L.R.1193 the SC held (in a commercial context) that a contract providing for possession of goods to be given, coupled with a legal entitlement to sue or consumer them before the property in them is transferred upon payment is not a contract of sale of goods within the meaning of the Sale of Goods Act 1979 (see below, para.44-020). On the significance of this decision for the definition of "sales contract" for the purposes of the 2015 Act, see *Benjamin's Sale of Goods*, 10th edn (2017), paras 14-062—14-065.

[2932] 2015 Act s.2(8). cf. the definition of "goods" under the 1979 Act s.61(1) as "all personal chattels other than things in action and money" with further explanations, on which see below, para.44-015.

[2933] 1999 Directive art.1(2)(b), though this provision also excludes from its definition of "consumer goods" "goods sold by way of execution or otherwise by authority of law". cf. above, para.38-056, which discusses *Wathelet v Garage Bietheres & Fils SPRL* (C-149/15) EU:C:2016:840, [2017] 1 W.L.R. 865 on when a trader who acts on behalf of a private individual is to be treated as a "seller" of goods under the Consumer Sales Directive 1999.

[2934] 1999 Directive art.1(3).

[2935] 2015 Act s.2(5). This restriction does not apply to the other types of "goods contracts" governed by Ch.2, but these other types of contract would not normally be the subject of public auction.

[2936] See 2015 Act s.2(6) referring to s.11(4) and (5) and 12 (both of which concern the information requirements under the 2011 Directive), s.28 (delivery) and s.29 (passing of risk) and "the other provisions of Chapter 2 as they apply in relation to those sections". The 2011 Directive makes special requirements as regards the information to be provided by the trader (art.6(3)) at "public auctions" (which it defines by art.2(13)), and excludes contracts so made from the rights of cancellation which a consumer may otherwise enjoy under the Directive: art.16(k). On these rights of cancellation see above, paras 38-112 et seq. See further on auction sales and the 2015 Act *Benjamin's Sale of Goods*, 10th edn (2017), para.14-056.

[2937] cf. below, para.44-026 on the position under the Sale of Goods Act 1979.

[2938] 1999 Directive art.1(4) on which see *Schottelius v Seifert* (C 247/16) EU:C:2017:638 where the CJEU confirmed that the 1999 Directive does not apply to contracts for the provision of work and materials other than the two types of such contract which it specifically includes. Thus art.1(4) deems "contracts for the supply of consumer goods to be manufactured or produced" to be "contracts of sale" and art.2(5) provides that "[a]ny lack of conformity resulting from incorrect installation of the

"A contract is a sales contract (whether or not it would be one under subsection (1)) if under the contract—

(a) goods are to be manufactured or produced and the trader agrees to supply them to the consumer,

(b) on being supplied, the goods will be owned by the consumer, and

(c) the consumer pays or agrees to pay the price."

So, for example, a contract under which a tailor produces a made-to-measure suit for a consumer is a sales contract.[2939] Similarly, the 2015 Act specifically provides that for the purposes of Pt 1: a "conditional sales contract" means:

"... a sales contract under which—

(a) the price for the goods or part of it is payable by instalments, and

(b) the trader retains ownership of the goods until the conditions specified in the contract (for the payment of instalments or otherwise) are met; and it makes no difference whether or not the consumer possesses the goods."[2940]

In keeping with the position under the general law,[2941] the 2015 Act provides that a contract cannot be a hire-purchase agreement if it is a conditional sales contract,[2942] but the 2015 Act also contains provisions which apply specifically to conditional sales contracts for the purposes of the consumer's "right to reject".[2943]

38-489 **"Contracts for the hire of goods"** Section 6(1) of the 2015 Act provides that:

"A contract is for the hire of goods[2944] if under it the trader gives or agrees to give the consumer possession of the goods with the right to use them, subject to the terms of the contract, for a period determined in accordance with the contract."

This definition rewrites the definition provided for contracts generally by the Supply of Goods and Services Act 1982, replacing its reference to a person bailing or agreeing to bail goods to another by way of hire,[2945] with the phrase giving "the consumer possession of the goods with the right to use them". As earlier noted, a contract for the hire of goods is not a hire-purchase agreement.[2946].

38-490 **"Hire-purchase agreements"** The 2015 Act provides that a contract is a hire-purchase agreement if "under the contract goods are hired[2947] by the trader in return for periodical payments by the consumer" and if under the contract "ownership of the goods[2948] will transfer to the consumer if the terms of the contract are complied with and:

---

consumer goods shall be deemed to be equivalent to lack of conformity of the goods if installation forms part of the contract of sale of the goods and the goods were installed by the seller or under his responsibility". On the latter, see below, para.38-503 concerning s.15 of the 2015 Act.

[2939] *Explanatory Notes* 2015 para.58.

[2940] 2015 Act s.5(3).

[2941] Below, para.44-028.

[2942] 2015 Act s.7(4).

[2943] 2015 Act ss.20(14), 22 (3)(a) and 24(11) on which see below, paras 38-514 and 38-516.

[2944] See 2015 s.2(8) and above, para.38-487 for the definition of "goods".

[2945] 1982 Act s.6(1).

[2946] 2015 Act s.6(2)

[2947] "Hired" is to be read in accordance with s.6(1): 2015 Act s.7(2).

[2948] On "ownership of the goods" see 2015 Act s.4(1) and above, para.38-477.

"(a)   the consumer exercises an option to buy the goods,

(b)   any party to the contract does an act specified in it, or

(c)   an event specified in the contract occurs."[2949]

It is provided that a contract is not a hire-purchase agreement if it is a conditional sales contract.[2950] These provisions substantively follow the definition in the Supply of Goods (Implied Terms) Act 1973, with the substitution of "ownership" for "property" and "hired" for "bailed".[2951]

"Contracts for transfer of goods"   The 2015 Act provides that: **38-491**

"A contract to supply goods is a contract for transfer of goods[2952] if under it the trader transfers or agrees to transfer ownership[2953] of the goods to the consumer and—

(a)   the consumer provides or agrees to provide consideration otherwise than by paying a price, or

(b)   the contract is, for any other reason, not a sales contract or a hire-purchase agreement.[2954]"

As earlier explained, "contracts for transfer of goods" is therefore the residual category of "goods contracts".[2955] An example can be found where a trader supplies goods to a consumer in return for the supply by the consumer of other goods and money (as in the part-exchange of a second-hand car).[2956] Another example may be found in a contract under which a trader agrees to repair the consumer's property using materials or spare parts which the trader supplies.[2957]

(bb)   The Statutory Terms and "Goods Conforming to a Contract"

Introduction   The following paragraphs will set out the terms which the 2015 Act   **38-492** provides are to be treated as included in the contracts to which Ch.2 of Pt 1 applies (the "statutory terms"),[2958] as well its provisions governing "conformity of the goods",[2959] but before doing so it is helpful to note that breach of the statutory terms which these provisions insert into contracts and the non-conformity of the goods

---

[2949] 2015 Act s.7(1)–(3).

[2950] 2015 Act s.7(4) and see s.5(3) for "conditional sales contract", above, para.38-488.

[2951] Supply of Goods (Implied Terms) Act 1973 s.15(1) "hire-purchase agreement". See also the definition of "hire-purchase agreement" under the Consumer Credit Act 1974 s.189(1), above, paras 39-306 et seq. and especially paras 39-310 and 39-356 (effect of the Consumer Credit Act 1974).

[2952] On the definition of "goods" see 2015 Act s.2(8) and above para.38-487.

[2953] On the definition of "ownership" see 2015 Act s.4(1) and above para.38-477.

[2954] 2015 Act s.8.

[2955] Above, para.38-478.

[2956] *Explanatory Notes* 2015 para.58.

[2957] In *Wood v TUI Travel PLC (t/a First Choice)* [2017] EWCA Civ 11, [2017] 1 Lloyd's Rep. 322 esp. at [27] it was held that where a contract for a holiday for consumers under which a hotel is to provide food and drink, in the absence of express agreement to the contrary, the property in the meal transfers to them when it is served, whether or not that meal is accompanied with a service. As a result, such a contract is a "contract for the transfer of property in goods" under s.4 of the Supply of Goods of Services Act 1982. (The decision related to a contract made before the coming into force of the 2015 Act on October 1, 2015.)

[2958] 2015 Act ss.9–14, 17–18.

[2959] 2015 Act ss.15 and 16, below, paras 38-503—38-504.

to the contract do not relate to the Act's scheme of rights to enforce terms about contracts in an entirely straightforward way.[2960]

38-493 **The relationship between the statutory terms, non-conformity of the goods and the consumer's remedies** At common law and under the Supply of Goods (Implied Terms) Act 1973, the Sale of Goods Act 1979 and the Supply of Goods and Services Act 1982 (before the latter two were amended by the Sale and Supply of Goods to Consumers Regulations 2002[2961]), the customer's remedies in respect of the goods or services rests on his or her establishing breach of that contract, whether that breach relates to an express or to an implied term, though for the purposes of the availability of rejection of goods and "treating the contract as repudiated" the 1979 Act uses the distinction between conditions (where rejection is available) and warranties (where it is not).[2962] To this relatively simple framework, the 2002 Regulations added a supplementary set of rights for those dealing as consumer, which, following the 1999 Directive, rested on establishing that the goods do not conform to the contract,[2963] conformity being defined as referring to the situation where there was breach of an express term of the contract or to one of the statutory implied terms as to the goods' description, quality or fitness for purpose[2964]: in effect, therefore, the consumer's remedies still required proof of breach of contract. However, the position under the 2015 Act is more complicated, though it does not adopt the apparently opaque, traditional distinction between conditions and warranties. The position under the 2015 Act is best understood by starting with s.19's overview of the consumer's rights to enforce terms about contracts. Section 19 begins by defining what is meant by reference to "goods conforming to a contract" for its own purposes and for the purposes of later provisions governing particular consumer remedies,[2965] being references to:

"(a)   the goods conforming to the terms described in sections 9, 10, 11, 13 and 14,
(b)   the goods not failing to conform to the contract under section 15 or 16, and
(c)   the goods conforming to requirements that are stated in the contract."[2966]

At first sight, this looks very inclusive, but there are two omissions from this catalogue: first, breach of the term inserted by s.12 of the Act, which gives contractual force to information required to be and actually supplied by the trader to the consumer under the Consumer Contracts (Information, Cancellation and Additional Charges) Regulations 2013 other than information concerning the main characteristics of the goods[2967]; and secondly, breach of the terms inserted by s.17

[2960] See below, paras 38-512 et seq.
[2961] SI 2002/3045 above, paras 38-442 et seq.
[2962] 1979 Act s.11 see below, para.44-056.
[2963] e.g. 1979 Act s.48A(1)(b); 1999 Directive art.2 above, paras 38-433 et seq. The person dealing as consumer had the benefit of a presumption of non-conformity as explained above, para.38-446.
[2964] e.g. 1979 Act s.48F, above, para.38-445. This special scheme therefore did not apply in respect of breach by the seller, etc. of the implied condition as to title or right to possession in the 1973 Act s.8, the 1979 s.12 or the 1982 Act ss.2 and 7.
[2965] 2015 Act s.19(1) referring to ss.22–24 of the same Act.
[2966] 2015 Act s.19(1) (a)–(c).
[2967] On which see above, paras 38-060 et seq. and especially at 38-105 and below, para.38-500. The special remedial consequence of breach of this statutory term is set by s.19(5) of the 2015 Act. Information provided by the trader concerning the main characteristics of the goods as required by the 2013 Regulations is inserted as a term of the contract under s.11 of the 2015 Act, which is included within the general scheme of s.19(1): below, para.38-499.

of the Act, which concern the trader's right to supply the goods, etc.[2968]; each of these omitted cases are provided with their own special remedial consequences.[2969] Section 19(3) then provides more generally that goods that do not conform to the contract because of the breach of the statutory terms earlier listed[2970] or under s.16 (goods not conforming to contract if digital content does not conform) give rise to the short-term right to reject, the right to repair or replacement and the right to a price reduction or the final right to reject,[2971] but s.19(3) does not apply to non-conformity under s.15 (installation as part of conformity of the goods) nor to breach of requirements stated in the contract, both of which are stated as giving rise to the right to repair or replacement and the right to a price reduction or the final right to reject, but not, therefore, to the short-term right to reject.[2972] Moreover, this position has three further nuances. First, the pattern of remedies for breach of the statutory terms or non-conformity just set out[2973] is subject to s.25's provisions on delivery by the trader of the wrong quantity of goods.[2974] Secondly, the consumer's short-term right to reject and the consumer's right to reject in respect of breach of a term as to the trader's right to supply are subject to s.26's provisions on instalment deliveries.[2975] And, thirdly, as s.19(8) explains, s.28 makes special provision about remedies for the consumer for breach of a term about the time for delivery of goods in sales contracts; these remedies do not rest on "non-conformity" of the goods to the contract and fall outside the remedial scheme foreseen by s.19.[2976]

To a considerable extent this pattern results from substantive differences between the statutory terms which the Act inserts and from the resulting appropriateness of some but not all the remedies which the Act foresees for consumers, but the complexity of the statutory provisions is unattractive in legislation aimed at simplification in the interests of accessibility of the law to consumers and their advisers. The following paragraphs will, therefore, refer to the relevant remedies arising for breach of the particular statutory terms or non-conformity of the goods with the contract individually, leaving until later detailed discussion of the remedies themselves and their relationship with "other remedies".[2977]

38-494

[2968] The special remedial consequence of breach of this term is set by s.19(6) of the 2015 Act: below, paras 38-507—38-511. Confusingly, while s.19(1) does not include goods conforming to the terms in s.17 as "conforming goods" for its own purposes or for the purposes of ss.22–24, s.21(12) specifically includes goods conforming to the terms in s.17 as goods conforming to the contract for the purposes of s.21 which concerns the partial rejection of goods by the consumer. Moreover, s.19(2) provides that for the purposes of ss.19, and 22 to 24, a failure to conform as defined by subs.(1)(a) to (c) is not a failure to conform to the contract if it has its origin in materials supplied by the consumer. Finally, it is not entirely clear whether s.19's reference to "the goods conforming to requirements that are stated in the contract" refers merely to a subset of express terms as ordinarily understood by English law, especially given that s.18(1) refers to the possibility of such an express term using this traditional expression: on which see below, para.38-505.

[2969] The special remedial consequence of breach of these statutory terms are set by the 2015 Act by s.19(5) and 19(6) respectively: below, paras 38-500 and 38-511.

[2970] i.e. inserted by 2015 Act ss.9, 10, 11, 13 and 14 (again omitting reference to s.12).

[2971] 2015 Act s.19(3), referring to ss.20, 22–24 of the same Act.

[2972] 2015 Act s.19(4) referring to ss.20, 23–24 of the same Act.

[2973] i.e. under s.19(3)–(6) of the 2015 Act.

[2974] 2015 Act s.19(7) referring to s.19(3) to (6): below, para.38-524.

[2975] 2015 Act s.19(7) referring to s.19(3)(a) and (6) respectively: below, para.38-525.

[2976] Below, para.38-526.

[2977] Below, paras 38-512 et seq.

38-495 **Presumption of non-conformity on delivery** Following the requirement of art.5(3) of the 1999 Directive as regards the contracts of sale (including sale and installation) to which it applies,[2978] s.19(14) provides that:

> "... goods which do not conform to the contract at any time within the period of six months beginning with the day on which the goods were delivered to the consumer must be taken not to have conformed to it on that day."

This rule does not apply if it is established that the goods did conform to the contract on that day or if its application is incompatible with the nature of the goods or with how they fail to conform to the contract.[2979] According to the Court of Justice of the EU in *Faber v Autobedrijf Hazet Ochten BV*,[2980] in order to benefit from the presumption, a consumer must first establish that a "lack of conformity" exists (though he or she need not establish its cause or that its origin is attributable to the seller[2981]) and, secondly, that this lack of conformity became "physically apparent" within six months of delivery of the goods.[2982] Having done so, the consumer need not establish that the lack of conformity existed at the time of delivery, the short period of six months allowing an assumption that it already existed "in embryonic form" on delivery.[2983] On the other hand, the seller may provide evidence that the lack of conformity did not exist on delivery, by establishing that its "cause or origin ... is to be found in an act or omission which took place after that delivery".[2984] But if the seller fails to do so, the consumer buyer can rely on the rights derived from the 1999 Directive.[2985]

38-496 The 2015 Act extends the benefit of this rebuttable presumption of non-conformity to all "goods contracts",[2986] and not merely to contracts of sale of goods and for the supply of goods to be manufactured or produced ("sales contracts" under the 2015 Act s.5[2987]) as required by the 1999 Directive.[2988] However, the presumption of non-conformity in s.19 of the 2015 Act applies only for the purposes of the consumer's right to repair or replacement and right to a price reduction or final right to reject and not, therefore, for the purposes of the consumer's short-term right to reject.[2989] Moreover, the presumption applies only in respect of breaches of the statutory terms governing the quality, fitness for particular purpose and description of goods, goods matching a sample or model,[2990] for non-conformity arising from

---

[2978] 1999 Directive art.5(3), formerly implemented by the 2002 Regulations as noted above, para.38-446.

[2979] 2015 Act s.19(15).

[2980] C-497/13 EU:C:2015:357, June 4, 2015 ("*Faber* (C-497/13)").

[2981] *Faber* (C-497/13) at para.70.

[2982] *Faber* (C-497/13) at para.71.

[2983] *Faber* (C-497/13) at para.72 quoting European Commission, Explanatory Memorandum to the proposal for a European Parliament and Council Directive on the sale of consumer goods and associated guarantees, COM(95) 520 final, p.12.

[2984] *Faber* (C-497/13) at para.73.

[2985] *Faber* (C-497/13) at para.74.

[2986] As defined by s.3(1), above, paras 38-485—38-491, following the general scheme of Ch.2 of Pt 1 as reflected in s.19.

[2987] 2015 Act s.5 on which see above, paras 38-486—38-487.

[2988] 1999 Directive art.1(1) and (4).

[2989] 2015 Act s.19(14) referring to s.19(3)(b) and (c) and (4) (and so not including s.19(3)(a)'s provision on the short-term right to reject.

[2990] 2015 Act s.19(14) referring to s.3(b) and (c) and (4), which themselves refer to ss.9, 10, 11, 13, and 14.

inadequate installation of the goods,[2991] arising from digital content that does not conform,[2992] or because of a breach of requirements that are stated in the contract.[2993] The presumption does not, therefore, apply to breach of the terms relating to the trader's right to supply.[2994]

Goods to be of satisfactory quality The 2015 Act divides the famous provision **38-497** in s.14 of the Sale of Goods Act 1979 and equivalent provisions in the Supply of Goods (Implied Terms) Act 1973 and Supply of Goods and Services Act 1982,[2995] into two parts: s.9(1) inserts into all "goods contracts"[2996] a statutory term that the goods are of satisfactory quality, whereas s.10 inserts a statutory term that the goods are fit for any particular purpose made known to the trader.[2997] The content of s.9 follows closely the wording of s.14(2) of the 1979 Act as amended by the 2002 Regulations, s.9(2)–(7) providing that:

"(2) The quality of goods is satisfactory if they meet the standard that a reasonable person would consider satisfactory, taking account of—
  (a) any description of the goods,
  (b) the price or other consideration for the goods (if relevant), and
  (c) all the other relevant circumstances (see subsection (5)).
(3) The quality of goods includes their state and condition; and the following aspects (among others) are in appropriate cases aspects of the quality of goods—
  (a) fitness for all the purposes for which goods of that kind are usually supplied;
  (b) appearance and finish;
  (c) freedom from minor defects;
  (d) safety;
  (e) durability.
(4) The term mentioned in subsection (1) does not cover anything which makes the quality of the goods unsatisfactory—
  (a) which is specifically drawn to the consumer's attention before the contract is made,
  (b) where the consumer examines the goods before the contract is made, which that examination ought to reveal, or
  (c) in the case of a contract to supply goods by sample, which would have been apparent on a reasonable examination of the sample.
(5) The relevant circumstances mentioned in subsection (2)(c) include any public statement about the specific characteristics of the goods made by the trader, the producer or any representative of the trader or the producer.[2998]
(6) That includes, in particular, any public statement made in advertising or labelling.

[2991] 2015 Act s.19(14) referring to 19(4) which itself refers to s.15.

[2992] 2015 Act s.19(14) referring to 19(3) which itself refers to s.16.

[2993] 2015 Act s.19(14) referring to s.19(4) which itself refers to breach of requirements that are stated in the contract.

[2994] 2015 Act s.19(14) refers to s.19(3)(b) and (c) and (4), none of which relate to breach of the terms in s.17. Breaches of the terms included by s.12 are also omitted, but they do not give rise to the rights mentioned by s.19(3) and (4): s.19(5).

[2995] i.e. 1973 Act s.10 and the 1982 Act s.4 and 9.

[2996] On which see above, paras 38-485 et seq.

[2997] Below, para.38-498.

[2998] 2015 Act s.59(1) defines "producer in relation to goods or digital content" as the manufacturer, the importer into the European Economic Area, or any person who purports to be a producer by placing the person's name, trade mark or other distinctive sign on the goods or using it in connection with the digital content", a definition deriving from the 1999 Directive art.1(2)(d).

(7)   But a public statement is not a relevant circumstance for the purposes of subsection (2)(c) if the trader shows that—

    (a)   when the contract was made, the trader was not, and could not reasonably have been, aware of the statement,

    (b)   before the contract was made, the statement had been publicly withdrawn or, to the extent that it contained anything which was incorrect or misleading, it had been publicly corrected, or

    (c)   the consumer's decision to contract for the goods could not have been influenced by the statement."

Section 9 further provides that a term about the quality of the goods may be treated as included in a goods contract as a matter of custom.[2999] It is submitted that earlier case-law on the significance of the implied term in s.14(2) of the 1979 Act will remain helpful for the interpretation of s.9 of the 2015 Act,[3000] though the latter's consumer context will need to be borne in mind. Under s.19 of the Act, goods which do not conform to the term described in s.9 are not "conforming goods" and may attract (subject to their own conditions) the short-term right to reject, the right to repair or replacement and the right to a price reduction or the final right to reject,[3001] as well as any "other remedies" available under the general law.[3002] The 2015 Act provides that contract terms which seek to exclude or restrict liability in the trader arising under s.9 are not binding on the consumer.[3003]

38-498   **Goods to be fit for particular purpose**   Section 10 of the 2015 Act inserts a statutory term into all "goods contracts"[3004] based on s.14(3) of the 1979 Act and equivalent provisions in the 1973 and 1982 Acts,[3005]

"... if before the contract is made the consumer makes known to the trader (expressly or by implication) any particular purpose for which the consumer is contracting for the goods"[3006]

"The contract is to be treated as including a term that the goods are reasonably fit for that purpose, whether or not that is a purpose for which goods of that kind are usually supplied."[3007]

[2999] 2015 Act s.9(8). cf. below, para.44-094.

[3000] On which see below, paras 44-095 et seq.

[3001] 2015 Act s.19(1)(a) and s.19(3) referring to ss.20 and 22 (short-term right to reject, on which see below, paras 38-513—38-516); s.23 (right to repair or replacement, on which see below, para.38-517) and s.24 (the right to a price reduction or the final right to reject, on which see below, paras 38-518—38-519).

[3002] 2015 Act s.19(9), as explained and restricted by s.19(10)–(13), below, para.38-523.

[3003] 2015 Act s.31(1)(a) and see below, para.38-531.

[3004] On which see above, paras 38-485 et seq.

[3005] i.e. 1973 Act s.10 and the 1982 Act s.4 and 9.

[3006] 2015 Act s.10(1). Section 10(2) (qualified by s.10(4)) provides that the statutory term also applies to a contract to supply goods if "(a) the goods were previously sold by a credit-broker to the trader, (b) in the case of a sales contract or contract for transfer of goods, the consideration or part of it is a sum payable by instalments, and (c) before the contract is made, the consumer makes known to the credit-broker (expressly or by implication) any particular purpose for which the consumer is contracting for the goods" and see the definitions of "credit-broker" and "credit-brokerage" in s.59(1) of the 2015 Act. As explained below in relation to the equivalent provision in the 1979 Act s.14, thus intends to include instalment credit transactions where the supplier of the goods, e.g. a retailer, sells the goods to a finance company which then sells them to the buyer on credit terms, the effect of the provision being to make the actual seller subject to the statutory term: see below, para.44-106.

[3007] 2015 Act s.10(3).

However, this term is not to be "treated as included" if "the circumstances show that the consumer does not rely, or it is unreasonable for the consumer to rely, on the skill or judgment of the trader".[3008] Section 10 further provides that a term about the fitness of the goods for a particular purpose may be treated as included in a goods contract as a matter of custom.[3009] Under s.19 of the Act, goods which do not conform to the term described in s.10 are not "conforming goods" and may attract (subject to their own conditions) the short-term right to reject, the right to repair or replacement and the right to a price reduction or the final right to reject,[3010] as well as any "other remedies" available under the general law.[3011] The 2015 Act provides that contract terms which seek to exclude or restrict liability in the trader arising under s.10 are not binding on the consumer.[3012]

Goods to be as described   Section 11(1)–(3) of the 2015 Act follow closely the   **38-499**
earlier legislative provision for implied term in the 1979 Act for sale by description (and the equivalent provisions in the 1973 Act and the 1982 Act),[3013] providing that contracts to supply goods[3014] by description[3015] "are to be treated as including a term that the goods will match the description".[3016] However, the 2015 Act made important new provision for this purpose by way of implementation of the Consumer Rights Directive 2011 and all but replacing its earlier implementation by the Consumer Contracts (Information, Cancellation and Additional Charges) Regulations 2013 (the "2013 Regulations")[3017] to the effect that:

3008 2015 Act s.10(4).

3009 2015 Act s.10(5). cf. below, para.44-094.

3010 2015 Act s.19(1)(a) and s.19(3) referring to ss.20 and 21 (short-term right to reject, on which see below, paras 38-513—38-516); s.23 (right to repair or replacement, on which see below, para.38-517) and s.24 (the right to a price reduction or the final right to reject, on which see below, paras 38-518—38-519).

3011 2015 Act s.19(9), as explained and restricted by s.19(10)–(13), below, para.38-523.

3012 2015 Act s.31(1)(b) and see below, para.38-531.

3013 1973 Act s.9; 1979 Act s.13; 1982 Act s.3 and 8.

3014 i.e. all "goods contracts", on which see above, paras 38-485 et seq.

3015 s.11 retains the technical expression the supply of goods "by description" for the purposes of the statutory term which it treats as included in goods contracts. As explained below in relation to s.13 of the 1979 Act, sale by description may be used in relation to two situations: where the buyer contracts in reliance on the description of the goods in contracts without having seen them and, secondly, where the buyer has seen the goods, but the stated characteristics of the goods are still intended to form part of the description by which they are sold: below, paras 44-086—44-087. This means that not all descriptions used by a seller in relation to goods will be relevant to "sale by description" under s.13 of the 1979 Act and, given the use of "by description" in s.11(1)–(3), it is submitted that the interpretation given to s.13 of the 1979 Act will be equally applicable to s.11 of the 2015 Act. cf. s.36 of the 2015 Act which sets out a statutory term that digital content will match any description without using the terminology of contracting "by description": below, para.38-548.

3016 2015 Act s.11(1). Section 11(2)–(3) provide that "if the supply is by sample as well as by description, it is not sufficient that the bulk of the goods matches the sample if the goods do not also match the description" and "a supply of goods is not prevented from being a supply by description just because (a) the goods are exposed for supply, and (b) they are selected by the consumer": for discussion of the equivalent provisions in the 1979 Act s.13 see below, paras 44-088—44-092.

3017 SI 2013/3134. The 2011 Directive art.6(1)(a) and (5) (as regards off-premises and distance contracts). The 2011 Directive does not require that information provided by the trader in respect of other contracts (governed by art.4 and termed "on-premises contracts" by the 2013 Regulations) should "form an integral part" of the contract, but the 2013 Regulations reg.9(3) (and see above, para.38-105) and the 2015 Act (as is explained in the text) do so require. After their amendment, the relevant provisions of the 2013 Regulations apply only to contracts for the supply of digital content *other than* for a price paid by the consumer, i.e. those digital content contracts not falling within the defini-

"(4) Any information that is provided by the trader about the goods and is information mentioned in paragraph (a) of Schedule 1 or 2 to [the 2013 Regulations] (main characteristics of goods) is to be treated as included as a term of the contract.

(5) A change to any of that information, made before entering into the contract or later, is not effective unless expressly agreed between the consumer and the trader."[3018]

The inclusion of this information in s.11 of the 2015 Act has the effect of attracting a broader range of remedies under the Act than is provided for breach of the terms derived from information supplied by the trader inserted by s.12 of the 2015 Act, which will be considered in the following paragraph, since breach of the statutory terms inserted by s.11 leads to the goods not "conforming" within the meaning of s.19(1) of the Act and thereby makes available (subject to their own conditions) the short-term right to reject, the right to repair or replacement and the right to a price reduction or the final right to reject,[3019] as well as any "other remedies" available under the general law.[3020] This is not the case as regards "other information" within the meaning of s.12 of the 2015 Act. The 2015 Act provides that contract terms which seek to exclude or restrict liability in the trader arising under s.11 are not binding on the consumer.[3021]

38-500 **Other pre-contract information included in contract** Section 12 of the 2015 Act applies to all goods contracts[3022] and provides that where a trader was required to provide information under the Consumer Contracts (Information, Cancellation and Additional Charges) Regulations 2013,[3023] any of that information that was provided by the trader other than the information concerning the main characteristics of the contract[3024] "is to be treated as included as a term of the contract".[3025] Section 12(3) provides that a change to any of that information, made before entering into the contract or later, is not effective unless expressly agreed between the consumer and the trader.[3026] As will be seen, the 2015 Act therefore distinguishes between information concerning the main characteristics of the contract (which

---

tion of the contracts governed by the 2015 Act Pt 1 Ch.3: see below, paras 38-530—38-542. It is to be noted, though that the scope of the 2013 Regulations is restricted in a number of important ways: see above, paras 38-076—38-077, 38-096.

[3018] 2015 Act s.11(4)–(5). In contrast to the general position, for the purposes of s.11(4)–(5), goods contracts include contracts where the goods are second-hand goods and are sold at public auction: 2015 Act s.11(6) referring to s.2(5) and (6) on which see above, para.38-487.

[3019] 2015 Act s.19(3) and see below, paras 38-513—38-516, 38-517 and 38-518—38-519.

[3020] 2015 Act s.19(9), as explained and restricted by s.19(10)–(13), below, para.38-523.

[3021] 2015 Act s.31(1)(c) and see below, para.38-531.

[3022] On which see above, para.38-485.

[3023] SI 2013/3134 reg.9 (on-premises contracts), reg.10 (off-premises contracts) and reg.13 (distance contracts). As earlier noted, while the 2011 Directive art.6(1)(a) and (5) requires information provided before the conclusion of off-premises and distance contracts to form part of the contract, it does not make the same requirement as regards information provided by the trader in respect of other contracts (governed by art.5 and termed "on-premises contracts" by the 2013 Regulations) but the 2013 Regulations reg.9 (and see above, para.38-105) and the 2015 Act (as is explained in the text) do so require.

[3024] Any information which concerns the main characteristics of the goods is to be treated as a term of the contract under 2015 Act s.11(4), as noted above, para.38-499.

[3025] 2015 Act s.12(1) and (2). See the similar provision in relation to contracts "for the supply of digital content other than for a price paid by the consumer" in 2013 Regulations reg.9(3) (on-premises contracts), reg.10(5) (off-premises contracts), and reg.13(6) (distance contracts) (as regards the latter two reflecting the 2011 Directive art.6(5)).

[3026] See the similar provision in relation to contracts "for the supply of digital content other than for a price paid by the consumer" in 2013 Regulations reg.9(3) (on-premises contracts), reg.10(5) (off-

becomes a statutory term under s.11) and other information (which becomes a statutory term under s.12). The significance of this treatment lies in the differences in remedies available for breach of the terms in the two sections. As has been seen, breach of a statutory term inserted by s.11 makes available (subject to their own conditions) the short-term right to reject, the right to repair or replacement and the right to a price reduction or the final right to reject,[3027] as well as any "other remedies" available under the general law.[3028] However, breach of any statutory term inserted by s.12 does not render the goods "non-conforming" within the meaning of s.19.[3029] Instead, s.19(5) provides that:

"If the trader is in breach of a term that section 12 requires to be treated as included in the contract, the consumer has the right to recover from the trader the amount of any costs incurred by the consumer as a result of the breach, up to the amount of the price paid or the value of other consideration given for the goods."

This is clearly a very much more restricted remedy than the set of remedies available in respect of breach of the terms treated as included more generally[3030] as it is restricted to "the amount of any costs incurred by the consumer as a result of the breach". The *Explanatory Notes* to the 2015 Act state that this remedy could be supplemented by a claim for damages under the general law where the consumer has incurred costs or losses above this amount,[3031] but if this is right, it is difficult to see what practical role the restriction in s.19(5) is intended to play.[3032] The 2015 Act provides that contract terms which seek to exclude or restrict liability in the trader arising under s.12 are not binding on the consumer.[3033]

Goods to match sample Section 13 of the 2015 Act applies to a "contract to supply goods by reference to a sample of the goods that is seen or examined by the consumer before the contract is made",[3034] and provides that such a contract is to be treated as including a term that:

38-501

"(a) the goods will match the sample except to the extent that any differences between

---

premises contracts) and reg.13(6) (distance contracts) (all as amended by SI 2015/1629 regs 4–6 on the bringing into force of the 2015 Act) and, as regards the latter two, reflecting the 2011 Directive art.6(5)).

[3027] 2015 Act s.19(3).

[3028] 2015 Act s.19(9), as explained and restricted by s.19(10)–(13), below, para.38-523.

[3029] This follows from the terms of s.19(1)(a) and s.19(3) which do not include s.12 in their lists of relevant terms.

[3030] i.e. under 2015 Act ss.9–11, 13 and 14 and in respect of non-conformity under s.16.

[3031] 2015 Act s.19(9)(a), (10) and 11(a); *Explanatory Notes* 2015 para.89. A consumer could not, however, rely on the general law so as to terminate the contract for breach of any terms inserted by s.12: 2015 Act s.19(12)–(13). The *Explanatory Notes* 2015 para.89 explain in relation to the recovery of costs that where there is other consideration given instead of a price, the cap on the recoverable costs would be the value of that consideration.

[3032] On the other hand, if the *Explanatory Notes* are wrong and the consumer's claim for compensation for breach (including by way of damages) is restricted as s.19(5) suggests, there would be a question whether the Act properly implements the Consumer Rights Directive 2011 art.6(5), on which see above, para.38-105.

[3033] 2015 Act s.31(1)(d) and see below, para.38-531.

[3034] 2015 Act s.13(1). On "contracts to supply goods" generally, see above, para.38-485. The formulation of the type of contract to which s.13 applies follows the wording of the 1973 Act s.11 and the 1982 Act ss.5 and 10 (contracting "by reference to a sample") rather than the 1979 Act s.15 ("where there is an express or implied term" to the effect the contract for sale is by sample, on which see below, para.44-113), but it is submitted that there is no substantive difference in this respect.

the sample and the goods are brought to the consumer's attention before the contract is made, and

(b)   the goods will be free from any defect that makes their quality unsatisfactory and that would not be apparent on a reasonable examination of the sample.[3035]"

This statutory term differs from the term implied by s.15 of the 1979 Act (and the equivalent provisions in the 1973 and 1982 Acts[3036]), in that, instead of referring to "the bulk" corresponding with the sample in quality,[3037] it instead provides more simply (and more appropriately for the consumer context) that the goods will match the sample except to the extent that any differences between the sample and the goods are brought to the consumer's attention before the contract was made.[3038] Under s.19 of the Act, goods which do not conform to the term described in s.13 are not "conforming goods" and may attract (subject to their own conditions) the short-term right to reject, the right to repair or replacement and the right to a price reduction or the final right to reject,[3039] as well as any "other remedies" available under the general law.[3040] The 2015 Act provides that contract terms which seek to exclude or restrict liability in the trader arising under s.13 are not binding on the consumer.[3041]

38-502   **Goods to match a model seen or examined**   Section 14 of the 2015 Act makes new provision governing contracts to supply goods[3042] "by reference to a model of the goods that is seen or examined by the consumer before entering into the contract",[3043] providing that such a contract is to be treated as including:

> "... a term that the goods will match the model except to the extent that any differences between the model and the goods are brought to the consumer's attention before the consumer enters into the contract."[3044]

No definition is given by the Act of "model" for this purpose, but the accompanying *Explanatory Notes* give as an example a case of a consumer viewing a television on the floor of a shop but receiving a boxed television from the stockroom; if the television received does not match the model seen, its seller would be liable for breach of the statutory term in s.14.[3045] Under s.19 of the Act, goods which do not conform to the term described in s.14 are not "conforming goods" and may attract (subject to their own conditions) the short-term right to reject, the right to repair or replacement and the right to a price reduction or the final right to reject,[3046] as well

---

[3035] 2015 Act s.13(2).

[3036] 1973 Act s.11; 1982 Act ss.5 and 10.

[3037] 1979 Act s.15(2)(a) and see below, para.44-114. See similarly 1973 Act s.11(1)(a) and(b); 1982 Act ss.5(2)(a) and (b) and 10(a) and (b).

[3038] 2015 Act s.13(2)(a).

[3039] 2015 Act s.19(1)(a) and s.19(3) referring to ss.20 and 22 (short-term right to reject, on which see below, paras 38-513—38-516); s.23 (right to repair or replacement, on which see below, para.38-517) and s.24 (the right to a price reduction or the final right to reject, on which see below, paras 38-518—38-519).

[3040] 2015 Act s.19(9), as explained and restricted by s.19(10)–(13), below, para.38-523.

[3041] 2015 Act s.31(1)(e) and see below, para.38-531.

[3042] On which see above, para.38-485.

[3043] 2015 Act s.14(1).

[3044] 2015 Act s.14(2).

[3045] *Explanatory Notes* 2015 para.77.

[3046] 2015 Act s.19(1)(a) and s.19(3) referring to ss.20 and 22 (short-term right to reject, on which see

as any "other remedies" available under the general law.[3047] The 2015 Act provides that contract terms which seek to exclude or restrict liability in the trader arising under s.14 are not binding on the consumer.[3048]

Installation as part of conformity of the goods   Section 15 of the 2015 Act **38-503** makes special provision for this purpose, stating that:

"... goods do not conform to a contract to supply goods if—
    (a)   installation of the goods forms part of the contract,
    (b)   the goods are installed by the trader or under the trader's responsibility, and
    (c)   the goods are installed incorrectly."[3049]

This reflects a requirement to the same effect in the 1999 Directive.[3050] If the installation is carried out in the circumstances foreseen by s.15, the trader must see that the goods are installed correctly: a strict obligation, rather than an obligation to take reasonable care and skill.[3051] Under s.19 of the Act, goods which do not conform to the contract under s.15 are not "conforming goods" within the meaning of that section,[3052] but attract their own set of remedies (subject to their own conditions): the right to repair or replacement and the right to a price reduction or the final right to reject,[3053] as well as any "other remedies" available under the general law.[3054] This means that where goods do not conform to the contract owing to their incorrect installation, the consumer does not have the short-term right to reject.[3055] The 2015 Act provides that contract terms which seek to exclude or restrict liability in the trader arising under s.15 are not binding on the consumer.[3056]

Goods not conforming to contract if digital content does not conform   Part 1 **38-504** of the 2015 Act defines "digital content" as "data which are produced and supplied in digital form"[3057] and distinguishes generally between "contracts for a trader to supply digital content to a consumer" (which are regulated specially by Pt 1

---

below, paras 38-513—38-516); s.23 (right to repair or replacement, on which see below, para.38-517) and s.24 (the right to a price reduction or the final right to reject, on which see below, paras 38-518—38-519).

[3047] 2015 Act s.19(9), as explained and restricted by s.19(10)–(13), below, para.38-523.

[3048] 2015 Act s.31(1)(f) and see below, para.38-531.

[3049] 2015 Act s.15(1)

[3050] 1999 Directive art.2(5), earlier implemented in UK law by the 1982 Act s.11S(1). Article 2(5) of the Directive also provides that any lack of conformity from incorrect installation is to be deemed equivalent to lack of conformity of the goods where the product is intended to be installed by the consumer, is installed by the consumer and the incorrect installation is due to a shortcoming in the installation instructions. Under the 2015 Act, this result follows from the application of ss.9–11 as the goods accompanied by inadequate installation instructions would not themselves be of satisfactory quality, etc. (on which see above, paras 38-498—38-499) rather than requiring any dedicated provision.

[3051] cf. 1982 Act s.13 and 2015 Act s.49 on which see below, para.38-571.

[3052] 2015 Act s.19(1)(b).

[3053] 2015 Act s.19(4) referring to s.23 (right to repair or replacement, on which see below, para.38-517) and ss.20 and 24 (the right to a price reduction or the final right to reject, on which see below, paras 38-518—38-519).

[3054] 2015 Act s.19(9)(b), as explained and restricted by s.19(10)–(13), below, para.38-523.

[3055] This right is explained by 2015 Act s.22. This restricted range of remedies in respect of incorrect installation is compatible with the 1999 Directive, which does not require a remedy such as the short-term right to reject.

[3056] 2015 Act s.31(1)(g) and see below, para.38-531.

[3057] 2015 Act s.2(9).

Ch.3[3058]) and contracts where the digital content is included within goods, which may be regulated by Pt 1 Ch.2 of the Act.[3059] This appears from s.16(1) of the Act which provides that:

"Goods (whether or not they conform otherwise to a contract to supply goods) do not conform to it if—

    (a)   the goods are an item that includes digital content, and

    (b)   the digital content does not conform to the contract to supply that content (for which see section 42(1))."

As a result, where digital content is included within goods (for example, a disk) and the digital content does not conform to the contract,[3060] then the goods themselves will not conform to the contract. Under s.19 of the Act, this means that the consumer may enjoy (subject to their own conditions) the short-term right to reject, the right to repair or replacement and the right to a price reduction or the final right to reject,[3061] as well as any "other remedies" available under the general law.[3062] This range of remedies includes the short-term and final right to reject which are not are available under Ch.3 in respect of digital content supplied other than where included in goods.[3063] The 2015 Act provides that contract terms which seek to exclude or restrict liability in the trader arising under s.16 are not binding on the consumer.[3064]

38-505   **No other terms about quality or fitness except express terms**   As earlier noted, the 2015 Act abandoned the traditional terminology of implied term in favour of a statutory formula according to which a relevant term is "treated as included" in the contract. However, the Act still finds it necessary to state that the statutory terms so included are not to be supplemented by other terms about quality or fitness, mirroring the earlier statutory formula as to implied terms.[3065] The result is s.18(1) according to which:

"Except as provided by sections 9, 10, 13 and 16, a contract to supply goods is not to be treated as including any term about the quality of the goods or their fitness for any particular purpose, unless the term is expressly included in the contract."[3066]

There are two points to be noted here. First, s.18(1) refers to only *some* of the statutory terms contained in Pt 1 Ch.2 of the Act: it refers to the terms concerning

---

[3058] Below, paras 38-535 et seq. The 2015 Act s.33(4) further specifies that "[a] trader does not supply digital content to a consumer for the purposes of this Part merely because the trader supplies a service by which digital content reaches the consumer".

[3059] cf. s.42(3) which refers to s.16 as applying "if an item including digital content is supplied".

[3060] For this purpose s.42(1) of the 2015 Act provides that digital content does not conform to the contract where it does not conform to the statutory terms imposed by s.34 (satisfactory quality), s.35 (fitness for particular purpose) and s.36 (description), on which see below, paras 38-546, 38-547 and 38-548 respectively.

[3061] 2015 Act s.19(1)(b) and s.19(3) referring to ss.20 and 22 (short-term right to reject, on which see below, paras 38-513—38-516); s.23 (right to repair or replacement, on which see below, para.38-517) and s.24 (the right to a price reduction or the final right to reject, on which see below, paras 38-518—38-519).

[3062] 2015 Act s.19(9)(b), as explained and restricted by s.19(10)–(13), below, para.38-523.

[3063] On which see 2015 Act s.42(2).

[3064] 2015 Act s.31(1)(h) and see below, para.38-531.

[3065] e.g. 1979 Act s.14(1).

[3066] 2015 Act s.18(2) notes that s.18(1) is subject to provision made by any enactment (whenever passed or made); "enactment" is defined by s.59(1).

satisfactory quality, fitness for purpose, goods matching a sample, and goods not conforming to contract if digital content does not conform to the contract,[3067] but it does not refer to the statutory term as to goods being as described, relating to pre-contractual information other than relating to the main characteristics of the goods, to goods matching a model seen or examined, nor to the trader's right to supply the goods, etc.[3068] As regards the terms which appear in the general legislation (such as the 1979 Act) as implied terms, this follows the earlier legislative pattern[3069] and the exclusions more generally continue to make substantive sense. Secondly, however, s.18(1) refers to a term that is "expressly included in the contract" as to the quality or fitness for any particular purpose of the goods. Again, it must be right for the new statutory terms to be capable of being supplemented by express terms, but it is unfortunate that the key provision in s.19 governing the consumer's rights to enforce terms about goods does not refer to express terms about the goods, their quality or fitness for purpose, but instead refers to "the goods conforming to requirements that are stated in the contract".[3070] It is submitted, however, that the latter expression is wide enough to include express terms as to the quality or fitness for any particular purpose of the goods within the meaning of s.18(1), as well as to any other stipulation ("requirement") as to the goods (such as their place of manufacture or their colour). The significance of this is that breach of a "requirement stated in the contract" gives rise only to a limited set of remedies, notably *not* including the short-term right to reject, as noted in the following paragraph.

Rights for consumer in respect of goods failing to conform to requirements stated in the contract   Section 19(4) of the 2015 Act provides that where there is a breach of a requirement stated in the contract,[3071] the consumer has the right to repair or replacement and the right to a price reduction or the final right to reject,[3072] but not therefore the short-lived right to reject.[3073] The consumer may also enjoy the "other remedies" available under the general law[3074] and, exceptionally, in the case of a breach of an express term[3075] these "other remedies" include the right to treat the contract as at an end (i.e. to terminate the contract).[3076] Under the general law, the consumer will have a right to terminate if the breach of the express term has the effect of depriving the consumer of the substance of what the consumer was contracting for or if the express term "goes to the root of the contract" and thus amounts to a condition.[3077]   **38-506**

Trader to have right to supply the goods, etc.   Section 17 provides statutory terms governing the trader's right to supply the goods, reflecting here the diversity of types of contract included under the broad category of "goods contracts". So, s.17   **38-507**

[3067] Above, paras 38-497, 38-498, 38-501 and 38-504 respectively.

[3068] 2015 Act ss.11, 12, 14 and 17 respectively.

[3069] e.g. 1979 Act s.12 (implied terms about title, etc.) and s.13 (sale by description)

[3070] 2015 Act s.19(1)(c) defining "goods conforming to a contract" for the purposes of ss.19, 22 to 24; s.19(4).

[3071] On which see above, para.38-505.

[3072] 2015 Act ss.20, 23 and 24 on which see below, paras 38-513—38-516 and 38-517—38-519.

[3073] 2015 Act s.22 below, para.38-516.

[3074] 2015 Act s.19(9)(c).

[3075] See above, para.38-505.

[3076] 2015 Act s.19(10)–(13) and esp. (11)(e) and see below, para.38-523.

[3077] See Vol.I, paras 24-035 et seq.

distinguishes between a "contract for the hire of goods" and other goods contracts, i.e. sales contracts, hire-purchase contracts and contracts for the transfer of goods,[3078] and then provides for cases where the parties to the contract intend that it should transfer a more limited title.[3079]

38-508 **Contracts for the hire of goods**   Section 17(1) of the 2015 Act provides that a contract for the hire of goods is to be treated as including a term that:

> "... at the beginning of the period of hire the trader must have the right to transfer possession of the goods by way of hire for that period."[3080]

Section 17(3) provides a further statutory term:

> "... that the consumer will enjoy quiet possession of the goods for the period of the hire except so far as the possession may be disturbed by the owner or other person entitled to the benefit of any charge or encumbrance disclosed or known to the consumer before entering into the contract."

These terms reflect closely the position under the 1982 Act, except that they do not use the language of bailment.[3081] Again following the 1982 Act s.17 provides that it does not affect the right of the trader to repossess the goods where the contract provides or is to be treated as providing for this.[3082] The 2015 Act makes special provision governing contract terms which seek to exclude or restrict liability in the trader arising under s.17 in respect of contracts for the hire of goods.[3083]

38-509 **Other "goods contracts"**   In the case of other goods contracts, i.e. sales contracts, hire-purchase contracts and contracts for the transfer of goods,[3084] s.17(1) provides that the contract is to be treated as including a term:

> "... that the trader must have the right to sell or transfer the goods at the time when ownership of the goods is to be transferred."[3085]

Section 17(2) provides for a further term to be treated as included that:

> "(a) the goods are free from any charge or encumbrance not disclosed or known to the consumer before entering into the contract,
>
> (b) the goods will remain free from any such charge or encumbrance until ownership of them is to be transferred, and
>
> (b) the consumer will enjoy quiet possession of the goods except so far as it may be disturbed by the owner or other person entitled to the benefit of any charge or encumbrance so disclosed or known."

These statutory terms follow closely the terms implied generally by the 1979 Act (and equivalent terms implied by the 1973 and 1982 Acts).[3086] The 2015 Act

---

[3078] On these categories, see above, paras 38-486—38-491.

[3079] 2015 Act s.17(4)–(7).

[3080] 2015 Act s.17(1)(a).

[3081] 1982 Act s.7(1) and (2).

[3082] 2015 Act s.17(8) reflecting the 1982 Act s.7(3).

[3083] 2015 Act s.31(5) and (6) and see below, para.38-531.

[3084] On these categories, see above, paras 38-486—38-488, 38-490—38-491.

[3085] 2015 Act s.17(1)(b). "Ownership" is defined by s.4(1), as noted at para.38-477 (note).

[3086] 1979 Act s.12(1) and (2); 1973 Act s.8(1); 1982 Act s.2(1) and (2). For discussion of s.12 of the 1979 Act see below, paras 44-075 et seq.

provides that terms in these goods contracts which seek to exclude or restrict liability in the trader arising under s.17 are not binding on the consumer.[3087]

Contracts where the parties intend that a more limited title should be transferred   As regards all types of "goods contracts",[3088] s.17 provides special treatment: **38-510**

> "... if the contract shows, or the circumstances when they enter into the contract imply, that the trader and the consumer intend the trader to transfer only—
> (a)   whatever title the trader has, even if it is limited, or
> (b)   whatever title a third person has, even if it is limited.[3089]

Where this is the case, the contract is to be treated as including a term that all charges or encumbrances known to the trader and not known to the consumer were disclosed to the consumer before entering into the contract and a term that the consumer's quiet possession of the goods will not be disturbed by the trader, and will not be disturbed by a person claiming through or under the trader, unless that person is claiming under a charge or encumbrance that was disclosed or known to the consumer before entering into the contract.[3090] Where the parties intend that the trader should transfer only whatever title a third person has, even if it is limited, then the contract is also to be treated as including a term that the consumer's quiet possession of the goods will not be disturbed by the third person, and will not be disturbed by a person claiming through or under the third person, unless the claim is under a charge or encumbrance that was disclosed or known to the consumer before entering into the contract.[3091] These provisions mirror (with some rewording) earlier provisions in the 1979 Act and the equivalent provisions in the 1973 and 1982 Acts.[3092]

Rights arising from breach of terms in s.17   As earlier noted, s.19 of the 2015 Act does not deem goods supplied in breach of the terms included by s.17 to render the goods "non-conforming" for its purposes.[3093] Instead, s.19(6) provides that breach of the term included by s.17(1) on the trader's right to supply gives rise to a right in the consumer to reject the goods,[3094] which may include a right of partial   **38-511**

[3087] 2015 Act s.31(1)(i) and see below, para.38-531. The position as regards hire of goods is governed by s.31(5) and (6) as explained below, para.38-531.

[3088] On which see 2015 Act s.3(2), above, para.38-485.

[3089] 2015 Act s.17(4).

[3090] 2015 Act s.17(5) and (6).

[3091] 2015 Act s.17(7) referring to s.17(4)(b).

[3092] 1979 Act s.12(3)–(5); 1973 Act s.8(2) and 1982 Act s.2(3)–(5). For discussion of these aspects of the 1979 Act see below, para.44-084. Section 17 of the 2015 Act does not affect the protection for private purchasers of motor vehicles under the Hire-Purchase Act 1964 s.27 (which concerns purchases from a seller who has vehicle under hire-purchase agreement or conditional sale agreement and does not yet own the vehicle) and the private purchaser in good faith and without notice of those agreements and deems the transfer of the vehicle to take effect as if the seller's title had been vested: *Explanatory Notes* 2015 para.83.

[3093] This follows from the terms of s.19(1): see above, para.38-493. There is an exception as regards the partial rejection of non-conforming goods under s.21: 2015 Act s.21(12). This is also the case as regards the application of the broad scheme of consumer remedies in s.19(3) of the 2015 Act.

[3094] 2015 Act s.19(6), referring to s.20. Section 20(3) provides that the right to reject under s.19(6) is not limited by ss.22 and 24 which has the effects in particular that the right to reject on this ground is not constrained by the time-limits set by s.22 nor is any refund affected by any deduction for use

rejection.[3095] Breach of such a term or of the terms treated as included by the remainder of s.17[3096] may give rise to "other remedies" under the general law (notably, damages), though these remedies do not include a right to reject the goods and terminate the contract.[3097] The 2015 Act provides in principle that contract terms which seek to exclude or restrict liability in the trader arising under s.17 are not binding on the consumer, but makes special provision in respect of contracts of hire.[3098]

(cc)   The Scheme of Remedies for the Consumer

38-512   **Introduction**   As earlier noted, the 2015 Act makes elaborate provision as regards the different circumstances which give rise to the remedies (often termed "rights" by the Act) which the Act provides for the consumer. This availability has been noted in respect of each of the statutory terms, special provisions as to the non-conformity of the goods and breach of requirements stated in the contract.[3099] The following paragraphs will therefore consider the new remedies themselves, termed "rights to enforce terms about goods". These include the short-term right to reject; the right to repair or replacement, and the right to a price reduction or the final right to reject. The relationship between these special rights and other remedies under the general law will be explained.[3100]

38-513   **The right to reject: general provisions**   Section 20 of the 2015 Act makes general provision concerning the two rights to reject, which is then supplemented by more particular treatment of the circumstances in which a consumer may reject some but not all of the goods,[3101] and special provisions governing the time limit for the short-term right to reject and the final right to reject.[3102] Each of the short-term right to reject and the final right to reject entitles the consumer to "reject the goods and treat the contract as at an end", subject to special rules governing severable contracts.[3103] The right to reject is exercised "if the consumer indicates to the trader that the consumer is rejecting the goods and treating the contract as at an end" whether by way of something said or done as long as it is in a way which is clear

---

under s.24.

[3095] 2015 Act s.21, s.12 of which specifically includes within goods conforming to the terms in s.17 to goods conforming to the contract for its own purposes. On s.20 and 22 generally, see below, paras 38-513—38-515.

[3096] i.e. 2015 Act s.17(2) (above, para.38-509), s.17(3) (above, para.38-508) and s.17(5)–(7) (above, para.38-510).

[3097] 2015 Act s.19(9)(a) (which refers generally to breach of a term that Ch.2 requires to be treated as included in the contract), (10)–(13). On these general remedies, see below, para.38-523.

[3098] 2015 Act s.31(1)(i), (5) and (6) and see below, para.38-531.

[3099] The key provisions are in s.19 of the 2015 Act. For the particular terms, etc. and their relationship to the remedies provided see above, paras 38-497—38-511.

[3100] Below, para.38-523.

[3101] 2015 Act s.21.

[3102] 2015 Act ss.20(1) and (2), 22 and 24.

[3103] 2015 Act s.20(4) referring to ss.(20) and (21). In summary, s.20(20) provides that where the contract is a severable contract and the contract is a goods contract other than sale, the provisions concerning defective delivery in instalments in s.26(3) do not apply to the final right to reject; s.20(21) adds that, depending on the terms of the contract and the circumstances of the case, the consumer is entitled to reject the goods to which a severable obligation relates or exercise a right to reject in respect of the whole contract. cf. 1979 Act s.11(4), below, para.44-069.

enough to be understood by the trader.[3104] This formulation adopts a terminology of the consumer *treating* the contract as at an end, rather than, for example, terminating or rescinding the contract[3105] and it assimilates this to rejection of the goods.[3106] Of more practical significance are the general provisions governing the effects of rejection. Here, the 2015 Act provides that in principle the trader has a duty to give the consumer a refund and the consumer has a duty to return or make the goods available for collection by the trader or (if there is an agreement for the consumer to return rejected goods) to return them as agreed.[3107]

Trader's duty to refund On rejection of the goods by the consumer, the trader **38-514** has a duty to refund any money paid under the contract.[3108] In the case of a contract for the hire of goods, the consumer's entitlement to a refund extends only to anything paid for a period of hire that the consumer does not get because the contract is treated as at an end[3109] and a similar rule applies to hire-purchase agreements and conditional sales contracts, even though the payments so made may exceed the value of having the goods.[3110] The trader must give any refund without undue delay, and in any event within 14 days beginning with the day on which the trader agrees that the consumer is entitled to a refund and using the same means of payment as the consumer used, unless the consumer expressly agrees otherwise[3111]; the trader must not impose any fee on the consumer in respect of the refund.[3112] Where a consumer is not entitled to receive a refund (whether as a result of not having paid any money or otherwise[3113]), he or she may be entitled to claim damages.[3114]

[3104] 2015 Act s.20(5) and (6).

[3105] cf. Vol.I, para.24-035 (the injured party treating the contract as discharged on the ground of total or partial failure to perform) and Peel (ed.), *Treitel on The Law of Contract*, 14th edn (2015), para.18-001 referring to "termination for breach" and discussing the varied terminology used for this purpose by the common law.

[3106] cf. below, para.44-066.

[3107] 2015 Act s.20(7). Whether or not the consumer has a duty to return the rejected goods, the trader must bear any reasonable costs of returning them, other than any costs incurred by the consumer in returning the goods in person to the place where the consumer took physical possession of them: 2015 Act s.20(8).

[3108] 2015 Act s.20(10) and (18). Special provision is made where the consumer transferred something other than money under the contract, where the consumer is entitled to receive back the same amount of that thing, unless no substitute can be provided, in which case the consumer is entitled to receive back the thing transferred in its original state: s.20(11)–(12). If the thing cannot be given back in its original state, then the consumer is not entitled to receive a refund, but may be entitled to claim damages: 2015 Act s.20(18)(b) and (19).

[3109] 2015 Act s.20(13). This rule applies also to things transferred by the consumer other than money. The 2015 Act s.20(18)(c) provides that to the extent that anything the consumer transferred cannot be divided so as to give back only the amount, or part of the amount, then the consumer has no entitlement to receive a refund. In this situation, the consumer may be entitled to claim damages: 2015 Act s.20(19).

[3110] 2015 Act s.20(14) referring to the return only of the part of the price paid. On the definition of these contracts see 2015 Act s.7 and 5(3) respectively, above, paras 38-490 and 38-478 respectively.

[3111] 2015 Act s.20(15) and (16). cf. similar provisions applicable to the consumer's right of reimbursement under the 2013 Regulations reg.34(4)–(6), above, para.38-123.

[3112] 2015 Act s.20(17). cf. similar provisions applicable to the consumer's right of reimbursement under the 2013 Regulations reg.34(7), above, para.38-123.

[3113] 2015 Act s.20(18) especially (b) and (c) noted above in this paragraph.

[3114] 2015 Act s.20(19), below, para.38-523.

38-515 **Partial rejection of goods** The 2015 Act makes detailed provision modelled on the general pattern in s.20 outlined above so as to allow a consumer to reject some but not all of the goods, where the goods so rejected do not conform to the contract.[3115]

38-516 **Time limit for short-term right to reject** The consumer's right to repair or replacement and right to a price reduction or final right to reject reflect closely the scheme of rights for consumers required by the 1999 Directive (and first brought into English law by the 2002 Regulations[3116]), but these rights are not always more attractive to consumers than the classic right to reject goods for breach of condition under the 1979 Act, though this classic right may be lost by "acceptance" of the goods, which may take place by lapse of time.[3117] It was for this reason that implementation of the 1999 Directive by the 2002 Regulations did not in principle preclude consumers from relying on this classic right unless they had required the trader to repair or replace the goods.[3118] The strategy of the 2015 Act was instead to provide a special "short-term right to reject" for consumers instead of the classic right[3119] but in addition to the Directive's four-fold scheme of rights. The circumstances in which this right to reject arises and the manner and consequences of its exercise are determined under the general provisions contained in s.20 of the Act,[3120] but s.22 makes particular provision as to its short-lived character. Section 22(1) provides that:

> "A consumer who has the short-term right to reject loses it if the time limit for exercising it passes without the consumer exercising it, unless the trader and the consumer agree that it may be exercised later."[3121]

In principle, the time-limit for exercising the short-term right to reject is the end of 30 days beginning with the first day after ownership or (in the case of a contract for the hire of goods, a hire-purchase agreement or a conditional sales contract[3122]) possession of the goods has been transferred to the consumer and the goods have been delivered.[3123] However, where the consumer requests or agrees to the repair or replacement of goods, the period set by the time limit stops running from the date of that request or agreement until the date that the consumer receives the goods in

---

[3115] 2015 Act s.21. For this purpose "non-conformity" includes goods which do not conform to the statutory term in s.17 of the Act as to the trader's right to supply, etc.: 2015 Act s.21(12).

[3116] Above, paras 38-442 et seq.

[3117] 1979 Act s.35 on which see below, paras 44-304—44-315.

[3118] 1979 Act s.48D, above, para.38-456. Under the general law, a buyer is not deemed to have accepted the goods merely because he or she requests their repair: Sale of Goods Act 1979 s.35(6) and below, para.44-237.

[3119] This is made clear by s.19(12) and (13)'s provisions governing termination for breach: see below, para.38-523 ("other remedies" for the consumer).

[3120] The short-term right to reject may also arise in respect of partial rejection of goods under s.21 of the Act.

[3121] 2015 Act s.22(2) provides that an agreement under which the short-term right to reject would be lost before the time limit passes is not binding on the consumer.

[3122] On these contracts see above, paras 38-489, 38-490 and 38-478 respectively.

[3123] 2015 Act s.22(3), which adds the further condition for the case where the contract requires the trader to install the goods or take other action to enable the consumer to use them, that the trader has notified the consumer that the action has been taken. Section 22(4) further provides that where any of the goods are of a kind that can reasonably be expected to perish after a shorter period, the time limit for exercise of the right in respect of those goods is the end of that shorter period.

response to them.[3124] And where goods supplied by the trader in response to such a request or agreement do not conform to the contract, the consumer has a further seven days after receipt of those goods or, if longer, any unexpired time set under the original time limit extended by the time between his request or agreement and receipt of those goods.[3125]

Right to repair or replacement   These rights reflect the first level of remedies   **38-517** required by the 1999 Directive and formerly implemented in UK law by the 2002 Regulations.[3126] They reflect the idea, widespread in modern civil law, that a creditor of an obligation should be able to obtain the cure of a defective performance from the debtor; they are rights to *corrective* performance by the trader, rather than rights simply to performance of the trader's original (primary) obligation arising under the contract.[3127] Section 23 provides that where the consumer requires the trader to repair or replace the goods,[3128] the trader must do so "within a reasonable time and without significant inconvenience to the consumer" and must bear any necessary costs incurred in doing so (including in particular the cost of any labour, materials or postage).[3129] However, s.23(3) and (4) provide that:

"(3)   The consumer cannot require the trader to repair or replace the goods if that remedy (the repair or the replacement)—
    (a)   is impossible, or
    (b)   is disproportionate compared to the other of those remedies.
(4)   Either of those remedies is disproportionate compared to the other if it imposes costs on the trader which, compared to those imposed by the other, are unreasonable, taking into account—
    (a)   the value which the goods would have if they conformed to the contract,
    (b)   the significance of the lack of conformity, and
    (c)   whether the other remedy could be effected without significant inconvenience to the consumer."

For this purpose, a reasonable time or significant inconvenience is to be determined taking account of the nature of the goods and the purpose for which the goods were acquired.[3130] This generally follows the position under the 2002 Regulations, except that under s.23 of the Act the seller cannot refuse to repair or replace the goods on the ground that this would be disproportionate in comparison with an appropriate price reduction or rescission.[3131] Also in keeping with the position adopted by the UK legislature under the 2002 Regulations (though not foreseen by the 1999 Directive)[3132] a consumer who requires or agrees to the repair of goods or, as the case may be, the replacement of the goods cannot require the trader to provide the other of those two remedies nor exercise the short-term right to reject, without giving the

---

[3124] 2015 Act s.22(6) and (8) effecting this by setting and defining a "waiting period".
[3125] 2015 Act s.22(7) and (8).
[3126] 1999 Directive art.3(3)–(4). On implementation by the 2002 Regulations see above, paras 38-447—38-449.
[3127] Whittaker (2017) 133 L.Q.R. 47 at 61–63.
[3128] 2015 Act s.23(1) refers back to s.19(3) and (4) as to the circumstances in which the consumer has the right to repair or replacement, as set out above, para.38-493.
[3129] 2015 Act s.23(2).
[3130] 2015 Act s.23(5).
[3131] cf. 1979 Act s.48B(3)(c) (as inserted by 2002 Regulations) above, para.38-447.
[3132] 1999 Directive art.3(2) and (3) and see above, para.38-433.

trader a reasonable time to repair or, as the case may be, replace them, unless giving the trader that time would cause significant inconvenience to the consumer.[3133] For this purpose, the Act clarifies that "… 'repair' in relation to goods that do not conform to a contract, means making them conform".[3134]

38-518 Right to price reduction or final right to reject These rights reflect the second level of remedies required by the 1999 Directive and formerly implemented in UK law by the 2002 Regulations.[3135] Under the right to a price reduction, the consumer may require the trader to reduce or extinguish[3136] the price[3137] which the consumer is required to pay under the contract, and/or to receive a refund from the trader for anything already paid by the consumer above the reduced amount.[3138] In this respect, neither the 1999 Directive nor the Act explain the precise purpose of a price reduction (beyond referring to reduction by an "appropriate amount"[3139]), but it would seem that (following its origins in the civil law[3140]) in general the reduction should reflect the difference in value between what was received by the consumer compared to what he should have received if the goods had conformed to the contract.[3141] Section 24(5) of the Act further provides, however, that:

> "A consumer who has the right to a price reduction and the final right to reject may only exercise one (not both), and may only do so in one of these situations—
> (a) after one repair or one replacement, the goods do not conform to the contract;
> (b) because of section 23(3) the consumer can require neither repair nor replacement of the goods; or
> (c) the consumer has required the trader to repair or replace the goods, but the trader is in breach of the requirement of section 23(2)(a) to do so within a reasonable time and without significant inconvenience to the consumer."[3142]

[3133] 2015 Act s.23(6) and (7),

[3134] 2015 Act s.23(8).

[3135] 1999 Directive art.3(5)–(6). On implementation by the 2002 Regulations see above, paras 38-451—38-454.

[3136] This is the effect of s.24(2)'s provision that: "[t]he amount of the reduction may, where appropriate, be the full amount of the price or whatever the consumer is required to transfer". From the fact that the Act does not allow a right of rejection in respect of digital content (see below, para.38-561), it would appear that the drafters of the Act took the view that there can be no right to reject where the consumer has nothing physical to hand back. Where the consumer is in this position as regards a "goods contract", a consumer could recover a 100 per cent reduction in price.

[3137] "Price reduction" may also apply to anything else the consumer is required to transfer under the contract: s.24(1) and (2). However, where this is the case, the right to a price reduction does not apply where what the consumer is (before the reduction) required to transfer under the contract (whether or not already transferred) cannot be divided up so as to enable the trader to receive or retain only the reduced amount, or if anything transferred which cannot be the subject of substitution cannot be given back in its original state: s.24(4) referring to s.20(12) in this respect.

[3138] 2015 Act s.24(1). Section 24(3) provides that s.20(10)–(17) applies to the consumer's right to receive a refund as outlined above, para.38-514.

[3139] 1999 Directive art.3(2) and (5) ("appropriate reduction"); 2015 Act s.24(1)(a) (reduction by an "appropriate amount").

[3140] In Roman law, the *actio quanti minoris* in sale reflected, e.g., in art.1644 of the French Code civil. cf. the "right to a discount" under the 2008 Regulations, above, paras 38-196—38-197.

[3141] cf. *Principles, Definitions and Model Rules of European Private Law, Draft Common Frame of Reference* (DCFR) prepared by the Study Group for a European Civil Code and the Research Group on EC Private Law (Acquis Group) (2010) art.III.-3:601 Right to reduce price. See also below, para.38-582 in relation to 2015 Act s.56 (price reduction in relation to services contracts).

[3142] On these requirements see above, para.38-517.

For the purposes of subs.(5)(a) there has been a repair or replacement if the consumer has requested or agreed to repair or replacement of the goods (whether in relation to one fault or more than one), and the trader has delivered goods to the consumer, or made goods available[3143] to the consumer, in response to the request or agreement.[3144]

Final right to reject and deduction for use   Unlike the short-lived right to reject **38-519** (where no deduction for use can be made by the trader), if the consumer exercises the final right to reject, in principle any refund to the consumer may be reduced by a deduction for use, taking into account of the use the consumer has had of the goods in the period since they were delivered.[3145] However, the trader may make no deduction to take account of use in any period when the consumer had the goods only because the trader failed to collect them at an agreed time or if the final right to reject is exercised in the first six months after the goods were delivered and ownership or (depending on the nature of the contract) possession was transferred to the consumer.[3146]

Time-limits in the scheme of the Directive and limitation of actions   Article **38-520** 5(1) of the Consumer Sales Directive 1999 provides that:

> "The seller shall be held liable under Article 3 where the lack of conformity becomes apparent within two years as from delivery of the goods. If, under national legislation, the rights laid down in Article 3(2) are subject to a limitation period, that period shall not expire within a period of two years from the time of delivery."

In *Ferenschild*[3147] the Court of Justice of the EU held that art.5(1) distinguishes between two types of time-limits: the first governing the period of *liability* of the seller where non-conformity of the goods becomes apparent and which is set in principle as two years from the time of delivery of the goods[3148]; the second governing the:

> "... period of time during which the consumer can actually exercise the rights that arose in the period of liability of the seller, with regard to the latter."[3149]

Under the Directive, Member States may choose whether or not to impose a time-limit of the second type[3150] and the UK in its implementation of the 1999 Directive (whether under the 2002 Regulations or the 2015 Act) has not chosen to do so.

[3143] For these purposes goods that the trader arranges to repair at the consumer's premises are made available when the trader indicates that the repairs are finished: 2015 Act s.24(7).

[3144] 2015 Act s.24(6).

[3145] 2015 Act s.24(8). For the general provisions governing the right to reject see 2015 Act s.20, above, paras 38-513—38-515.

[3146] 2015 Act s.24(9) and (10) and (11), (c) of which adds a further condition in respect of goods where the contract required the trader to install the goods or take other action to enable the consumer to use them, that the trader has notified the consumer that the action has been taken. The 2015 Act s.24(10) makes an exception to the rule preventing any deduction being made where the consumer exercised the final right to reject within six months for the case of motor vehicles or goods of a description to be specified by order of the Secretary of State as set out by s.24(10), (12)–(15).

[3147] *Ferenschild v JPC Motor SA* (C-133/16) EU:C:2017:541, July 13, 2017 ("*Ferenschild* (C-133/16)").

[3148] *Ferenschild* (C-133/16) at paras 33–34.

[3149] *Ferenschild* (C-133/16) at para.35.

[3150] *Ferenschild* (C-133/16) at para.36.

As regards the period of liability of the seller, following the position under the 1979 Act,[3151] the 2015 Act did not retain the relatively short period for liability in the seller foreseen by art.5 of the Directive and therefore instead generally allows consumers to bring their claims under the 2015 Act within the general limitation period of six years provided by the Limitation Act 1980.[3152] While an exception to this pattern is found in the case of the "short-term right to reject" which has a time-limit of 30 days,[3153] this is compatible with the 1999 Directive as the short-term right to reject is not required by the Directive but is additional to (and therefore more protective than) the Directive's own scheme of consumer rights, as permitted by its minimum harmonisation character.[3154]

38-521 **Discretion as to appropriate remedy** The 2015 Act s.58 provides that in any proceedings in which one of the special remedies provided for consumers by Ch.2[3155] is sought, the court enjoys additional two powers.[3156] First, on the application of the consumer, the court may make an order requiring specific performance by the trader of any obligation imposed on the trader in respect of repair or replacement of the goods.[3157] For this purpose, an order of specific performance would not seek to enforce the primary obligations of the contract, whether based on an express, implied or statutory term; instead, specific performance would seek to enforce the trader's secondary obligation (arising on breach of the obligations arising on breach of the relevant statutory term) to repair or replace the goods, and thereby protect the consumer's right to *corrective* performance.[3158] Secondly, where a consumer claims the right to repair or replacement or the right to a price reduction or the final right to reject (termed the "relevant remedies" by s.58), but the court decides that the provisions governing these rights "have the effect that exercise of another of

---

[3151] Above, para.38-459.

[3152] Limitation Act 1980 s.5 (six years from accrual of the cause of action). The general rule in contract is that the cause of action accrues when the breach takes place rather than when any damage may have been suffered: see Vol.I, paras 28-032 et seq. While art.5(1) of the 1999 Directive requires liability in the seller for two years from the date of delivery, it is submitted that breach will not precede delivery in this context. The UK equally chose not to exercise the option provided by art.7(2) of the 1999 Directive which allows Member States to provide that in the case of second-hand goods, the seller and the consumer buyer may agree contract terms which have a time period of liability shorter than the two years set by art.5(1) first sentence as long as it is not less than one year.

[3153] 2015 Act s.22 and above, para.38-516 (which explain the starting-points for this period).

[3154] 1999 Directive arts 3 and 8(2) and cf. *Ferenschild* (C-133/16) at para.48.

[3155] 2015 Act s.58(1), referring to s.19(3) and (4) and therefore to the legal grounds of the consumer's rights in respect of the statutory terms as to quality, fitness for purpose, etc. under the special rules governing conformity of the goods or for breach of requirements that are stated in the contract as there provided: above, para.38-493. The powers of the court in s.58 therefore do not extend to proceedings brought in respect of the costs incurred by the consumer under s.19(5) in relation to breach of the statutory terms under s.12, nor to the right of rejection foreseen by s.19(6) as regards breach of the statutory term as to the trader's right to supply under s.17. Moreover, while the remedies for consumers foreseen by s.19(3) and (4) are the short-term right to reject, the right to repair or replacement and the right to a price reduction or the final right to reject, s.58's provisions affect only the latter 4 of these remedies. Section 58 makes similar provision in respect of the special rights which Chs 3 and 4 of Pt 1 of the Act create in respect of digital contents contracts and services contracts, on which see below, paras 38-560 and 38-583 respectively.

[3156] As explained above, para.38-455, these powers in the court were earlier provided by the Sale and Supply of Goods to Consumers Regulations 2002 (SI 2002/3045) on the first implementation of the Consumer Sales Directive 1999, even though they were not foreseen by that Directive.

[3157] 2015 Act s.58(2) referring to s.23 of the Act, above, para.38-517.

[3158] Whittaker (2017) 133 L.Q.R. 47 at 61–63 and see above, para.38-517.

these rights is appropriate", "the court may proceed as if the consumer had exercised that other right".[3159] The court may make an order under s.58 unconditionally or on such terms and conditions as to damages, payment of the price and otherwise as it thinks just.[3160] Finally, on their terms, the court's powers under s.58 do not extend to the "other remedies" for consumers as this is understood by the Act and as explained below.[3161]

The court's discretions in relation to sales contracts In the case of contracts for **38-522** the *sale* of goods ("sales contracts"), the consumer's right to repair or replacement of goods in the 2015 Act reflects requirements of the Consumer Sales Directive 1999 and therefore the provisions of the Act relating to them must be interpreted with this in mind and in the light of the principle of effectiveness, here, of the consumer's protection.[3162] For this purpose, in *Weber and Putz* the Court of Justice of the EU assumed that the consumer's specific rights (i.e. repair or replacement) under the Directive were enforceable in kind against the seller, holding that national law must not allow replacement to be refused by a trader on the ground of disproportionality with regard to the value of the goods as conforming and the significance of the non-conformity, even though in the circumstances this meant that the trader had to bear the costs of the removal of goods installed by the consumer and the reinstallation of the replacement goods.[3163] This suggests that an English court should not refuse specific performance in support of the consumer's right to repair or replacement of goods sold on the ground that damages would be an adequate remedy, as this would to this extent replace the consumer's "European rights" with damages and so render them ineffective; it also suggests that the court should not take into account other traditional elements governing the availability of specific performance stemming from its equitable nature on the basis that the Directive itself provides only two circumstances (impossibility and disproportionality compared to the other specific remedy) where the trader is entitled to refuse to repair or replace.[3164] Finally, following the decision in *Weber and Putz* itself, in the case of "sales contracts", the court's powers to substitute another "appropriate right" under s.58 is incompatible with the 1999 Directive in that it allows a court to refuse a right to repair or replacement in circumstances other than those which are foreseen by art.3 of the Directive.

Other remedies for the consumer The 2015 Act acknowledges that, in principle, **38-523** its provision of special rights for consumers under Ch.2 does not prevent them seeking other remedies in respect of breach of the terms that it treats as included in the contract, on the special grounds on which goods do not conform to the contract

---

[3159] 2015 Act s.58(4) and (5). The "relevant remedies" are defined by s.58(8)(a), referring to ss.23 and 24. For this purpose, if the consumer has claimed to exercise the final right to reject, the court may order that any reimbursement to the consumer is reduced by a deduction for use, to take account of the use the consumer has had of the goods in the period since they were delivered to the extent provided by s.24(9) and (10): 2015 Act s.58(5) and (6).

[3160] 2015 Act s.58(7).

[3161] Below, para.38-323.

[3162] See Whittaker (2017) 133 L.Q.R. 47 at 63–66. On the Consumer Sales Directive 1999 generally, see above, para.38-433. On "sales contracts" see above, paras 38-486—38-488.

[3163] *Gebr Weber GmbH v Wittmer, Putz v Medianess Electronics GmbH* (C-65/09 and C-87/09) EU:C:2011:396, [2011] 3 C.M.L.R. 27 at paras 63–78.

[3164] 1999 Directive art.3(3), reflected in 2015 Act s.23(3)–(4) and see above, para.38-517.

under ss.15 and 16, or for breach of a requirement stated in the contract.[3165] In respect of all three of these sets of cases, and depending on the circumstances, these other remedies may include damages, seeking specific performance or relying on the breach against a claim by the trader for the price[3166]; the conditions and characteristics of these remedies are found in the law applicable to contracts generally.[3167] A consumer may exercise a right to treat the contract as at an end (which the Act explains as meaning "treating it as repudiated"[3168] and which is often termed rescission or termination for breach of contract) under the general law only for breach of an express term[3169]; a consumer may treat the contract as at end on the ground of breach of Ch.2's statutory terms or on the special grounds of the conformity of the goods in ss.15 and 16 only under the rights to reject which the Act itself creates.[3170] The Act provides that a consumer may exercise a remedy other than the remedies which itself creates (though not so as to recover twice for the same loss), instead of such a special remedy, or where no such special remedy is provided.[3171] Moreover, the 2015 Act does not prevent a consumer from claiming a remedy on grounds other than breach of the statutory terms or special grounds of non-conformity. So, for example, a consumer who has suffered personal injury or damage to property caused by a defect in a product (the goods) may be able to recover damages in tort under the statutory product liability provisions contained in Pt 1 of the Consumer Protection Act 1987.[3172]

38-524   **Delivery of wrong quantity**   The 2015 Act s.25 makes provision for the case where the trader delivers under a "goods contract"[3173] a quantity of goods to the consumer less than or more than the trader contracted to supply, in a way which is very closely based on the law provided for contracts of sale of goods under s.30 of the 1979 Act.[3174] Section 25 provides that where the trader delivers to the consumer a quantity of goods less than the trader contracted to supply, the consumer may reject them, but if the consumer accepts them, the consumer must pay for them at the contract rate.[3175] Conversely, where the trader delivers to the consumer a quantity of goods larger than the trader contracted to supply, the consumer may accept the goods included in the contract and reject the rest, or may reject all of the goods; but

---

[3165] 2015 Act s.19(9).

[3166] 2015 Act s.19(11) (a), (b) and (d) respectively.

[3167] See in relation to damages and specific performance Vol.I, Chs 26 and 27 respectively. Note that the 2015 Act disapplies the 1979 Act ss.51 (damages for non-delivery), 52 (specific performance), 53 (remedy for breach of warranty) and 54 (interest) from contracts to which Ch.2 of Pt 1 applies: 2015 Act s.60, Sch.1 paras 28–30 and 32 as noted above, para.38-472 (note). On the other hand, as regards contracts of sale of goods, the question whether a consumer buyer may rely on the trader's breach in resisting the seller's claim for the price remains governed by the 1979 Act ss.27, 28 and 49 (none of which the 2015 Act amends): on which see below, paras 44-236—44-237 and 44-359 et seq.

[3168] 2015 Act s.19(13).

[3169] 2015 Act s.19(11)(e). cf. above, paras 38-505—38-506 on the relationship between breach of an express term and breach of a requirement stated in the contract.

[3170] 2015 Act s.19(12) referring to s.19(3), (4) and (6), on these rights see above, paras 38-513—38-516 and 38-518—38-519.

[3171] 2015 Act s.19(10).

[3172] This 1987 Act implements Directive 1985/374/EEC concerning liability for defective products, [1985] O.J. L210/29. For discussion of the requirements of the 1987 Act see below, paras 44-449 et seq. and *Clerk and Lindsell on Torts*, 22nd edn (2017), paras 11-45 et seq.

[3173] 2015 Act s.3(1) and (2), above, para.38-485.

[3174] On which see below, paras 44-257—44-261.

[3175] 2015 Act s.25(1). There is no EU legislative background to this provision.

if the consumer accepts all of the goods delivered, the consumer must pay for them at the contract rate.[3176] Where a consumer is entitled to reject goods under s.25, then any further entitlement to treat the contract as at an end depends on the terms of the contract and the circumstances of the case.[3177] Section 25 of the 2015 Act does not restrict the consumer's right of rejection where the shortfall or the excess is so slight that it would be unreasonable to do so, as did s.30 of the 1979 Act where the buyer did not deal as consumer before its amendment by the 2015 Act.[3178] While at common law the right to reject is subject to the principle *de minimis non curat lex* so that a trifling departure from the exact quantity stipulated does not entitle the buyer to reject the goods,[3179] it is submitted that this restriction should not be read into s.25 of the 2015 Act as to do so could (if marginally) undermine the clarity of approach desirable in the context of consumer contracts. On the other hand, following s.30 of the 1979 Act,[3180] s.25 of the 2015 Act provides that it is subject to any usage of trade, special agreement, or course of dealing between the parties.[3181] While s.25 is not protected from exclusion or restriction by s.31 of the 2015 Act,[3182] it is submitted that a contract term which seeks to vary or exclude the rules in s.25 would fall under the requirements for transparency and fairness in Pt 2 of the 2015 Act and, subject to the conditions which that Part sets out, may not be binding on the consumer on the ground of its unfairness.[3183]

Instalment deliveries   The 2015 Act s.26 provides for instalment deliveries under **38-525** "goods contracts"[3184] in very similar terms as s.31 of the 1979 Act, with modifications so as to fit these rules into the framework which the 2015 Act provides for consumers.[3185] As a result, s.26 provides that, under a goods contract, the consumer is not bound to accept delivery of the goods by instalments, unless that has been agreed between the consumer and the trader.[3186] Where, however, the contract provides for the goods to be delivered by stated instalments, which are to be separately paid for[3187]:

[3176] 2015 Act s.25(2) and (3).

[3177] 2015 Act s.25(4). Section 25(5) and (6) provide for the manner of rejection in a similar manner to s.20(5) and (6) above, para.38-513, with the distinction that the consumer may not necessarily also indicate that the contract is at an end. Section 25(8) provides that it is subject to any usage of trade, special agreement, or course of dealing between the parties. A consumer may also claim damages in respect of delivery of the wrong quantity: s.25(7).

[3178] 1979 Act s.30(2A)–(2D) below, para.44-260. The 2015 Act s.60, Sch.1 para.19 deletes the restriction in s.30(2A) to buyers other than dealing as consumer and disapplies s.30 where Ch.2 of Pt 1 of the 2015 Act applies.

[3179] Below, para.44-260 with authorities there cited.

[3180] 1979 Act s.30(5).

[3181] 2015 Act s.25(8).

[3182] On which see below, para.38-531.

[3183] See especially 2015 Act ss.62 and 68 and above, paras 38-389 et seq. and 38-414 et seq. It is to be noted that, unlike the Unfair Terms in Consumer Contracts Regulations 1999 (SI 1999/2083) (on which see above, paras 38-242—38-244) the controls on fairness in Pt 2 of the 2015 Act extend to terms that have been individually negotiated: above, para.38-389.

[3184] On which see 2015 Act s.3(1) and (2), above, para.38-485.

[3185] On the 1979 Act s.31 see below, paras 44-262—44-268. The 2015 Act s.60, Sch.1 para.20 disapplies s.31 where Ch.2 of Pt 1 of the 2015 Act applies.

[3186] 2015 Act s.26(1).

[3187] 2015 Act s.26(2).

"If the trader makes defective deliveries[3188] in respect of one or more instalments, the consumer, apart from any entitlement to claim damages, may be (but is not necessarily) entitled—

(a) to exercise the short-term right to reject or the right to reject under section 19(6)[3189] (as applicable) in respect of the whole contract, or

(b) to reject the goods in an instalment."[3190]

The consumer's entitlement to exercise the rights in (a) or (b) depend on the terms of the contract and the circumstances of the case.[3191] While s.26 of the 2015 Act is not itself protected from contrary exclusion or restriction by s.31 of the Act, the trader's liabilities which give rise to the consumer's short-term right to reject[3192] or to the right to reject provided by s.19(6)[3193] to which s.31 refers are so protected.[3194] Finally, s.26(6) provides that:

"If the consumer neglects or refuses to take delivery of or pay for one or more instalments, the trader may—

(a) be entitled to treat the whole contract as at an end, or

(b) if it is a severable breach, have a claim for damages but not a right to treat the whole contract as at an end."

The trader's entitlement to exercise the rights in (a) or (b) depends on the terms of the contract and the circumstances of the case.[3195]

(dd)   Other Rules About Goods Contracts

38-526 **Delivery of goods in sales contracts** Section 28 of the 2015 Act makes special provision concerning the delivery of goods in "sales contracts",[3196] thereby implementing the Consumer Rights Directive 2011 art.18[3197] and replacing its earlier implementation by the Consumer Contracts (Information, Cancellation and Additional Charges) Regulations 2013.[3198] Section 28 provides that:

"… unless the trader and the consumer have agreed otherwise, the contract is to be treated as including a term that the trader must deliver[[3199]] the goods to the consumer."[3200]

[3188] For this purpose, "making defective deliveries" does not include failing to make a delivery in accordance with s.28: 2015 Act s.26(5). On s.28 see below, para.38-526.

[3189] On which see above, para.38-493 (setting out the situations in which this right is available) and paras 38-513—38-516 and 38-518—38-519 (setting out the nature and effects of exercise of these rights).

[3190] 2015 Act s.26(3).

[3191] 2015 Act s.26(4).

[3192] This is provided by s.19(3) of the Act.

[3193] Above, para.38-511 (trader's right to supply, etc.).

[3194] 2015 Act s.31(1) below, para.38-531.

[3195] 2015 Act s.26(7).

[3196] For the definition of this category of contract for this purpose, see 2015 Act s.5, above, paras 38-486—38-488. However, the 2015 Act's general exclusion of sales of second-hand goods sold at public auction does not apply for the purposes of s.28, following the definition of "goods" in art.2(3) of the Consumer Rights Directive: 2015 Act s.2(5) and (6)(a); s.28(14).

[3197] 2011 Directive art.18. On the 2011 Directive more generally, see above, paras 38-060 et seq.

[3198] SI 2013/3134 reg.42 (revoked by SI 2015/1629 reg.8).

[3199] "Delivery" means "voluntary transfer of possession from one person to another": 2015 Act s.59(1). This is the same definition as is contained in s.61(1) of the 1979 Act. While the significance of "delivery" varies under the general law in the 1979 Act, it is normally sufficient for the seller to make the goods available to the buyer and it may take place by constructive means and without any transfer

Moreover,

"... unless there is an agreed time or period [for the delivery of the goods[3201]], the contract is to be treated as including a term that the trader must deliver the goods—

    (a)   without undue delay, and

    (b)   in any event, not more than 30 days after the day on which the contract is entered into." [3202]

Where the trader has an obligation to deliver the goods at the time the contract is entered into, that time counts as the "agreed" time for these purposes.[3203] Where the trader does not deliver the goods in accordance with these rules, s.28 provides that the consumer may treat the contract as at an end if:

"(a)   the trader has refused to deliver the goods,[3204]

 (b)   delivery of the goods at the agreed time or within the agreed period is essential taking into account all the relevant circumstances at the time the contract was entered into, or

 (c)   the consumer told the trader before the contract was entered into that delivery in accordance with subsection (3), or at the agreed time or within the agreed period, was essential."[3205]

The Act's *Explanatory Notes* expect that in most cases where a consumer purchases goods expecting to receive them immediately, that immediate delivery will be essential in all the circumstances,[3206] and adds that examples of goods for which delivery within the initial period might be taken to be essential would include a wedding dress or a birthday cake.[3207] Where the trader does not deliver the goods in accordance with the above rules in any other circumstances, the consumer may specify a period that is appropriate in the circumstances and require the trader to deliver the goods before the end of that period[3208] and if the trader fails to do so, may treat the contract as at an end.[3209] Where the consumer exercises a right to treat

---

of the actual physical custody of the goods: below, para.44-241; *Benjamin's Sale of Goods*, 10th edn (2017), para.8-002. It is submitted, however, that the meaning of "delivery" in s.28 of the 2015 Act should follow its meaning in art.18 of the Consumer Rights Directive which it implements, and the latter requires that the trader "shall deliver the goods by transferring the physical possession or control of the goods", which suggests more than merely making the goods available for collection by the buyer. This is confirmed by the explanation in recital 55 of "delivery" in art.20 of the Directive in relation to the passing of risk that "a consumer should be considered to have acquired the physical possession of the goods when he has received them". Article 20 of the 2011 Directive is implemented by s.29 of the 2015 Act, on which see below, para.38-527.

[3200] 2015 Act s.28(2).

[3201] 2015 Act s.28(4)(a).

[3202] 2015 Act s.28(3). Although s.28 implements art.18 of the 2011 Directive, the time of the conclusion of the contract must be determined in accordance with the general rules of English contract law as set out by Vol.I Ch.2: 2011 Directive art.3(5) as explained above, paras 38-063—38-065.

[3203] 2015 Act s.28(4)(b).

[3204] s.28(6)(a) (following the 2011 Directive art.18(2) (second paragraph) does not distinguish between the trader's refusal to deliver the goods before or after the due time for performance and, therefore, could apply in circumstances which the common law would see as anticipatory breach consisting of renunciation of the contract (on which see Vol.I, paras 24-018, 24-024).

[3205] 2015 Act s.28(5) and (6).

[3206] *Explanatory Notes* 2015 para.152.

[3207] *Explanatory Notes* 2015 para.153.

[3208] 2015 Act s.28(7).

[3209] 2015 Act s.28(5) and (7)–(8).

the contract as at an end under s.28, the trader must without undue delay reimburse all payments made under the contract.[3210] On the other hand, where the consumer has such a right but does not exercise it, s.28 provides that the consumer may cancel the order for any of the goods or reject goods that have been delivered, whereupon "the trader must without undue delay reimburse all payments made under the contract in respect of any goods for which the consumer cancels the order or which the consumer rejects".[3211] Apart from making special provision in this respect where any of the goods form a commercial unit,[3212] s.28 does not explain what is meant by "cancellation" for this purpose, a term which is not otherwise used by Pt 1 of the 2015 Act.[3213] The "right to reject the goods" may refer to the special short-term right to reject or final right to reject (as the case may be) as foreseen by the 2015 Act itself.[3214] If this is the case, then the effect of these provisions appears to be that it allows the consumer not to pay (or to recover payments made) for goods rejected, which amounts to a form of partial termination. This remedy is not foreseen by art.18 of the 2011 Directive, which, apart from termination of the contract for which it provides, could be thought to allow national law only to provide additional *remedies*,[3215] rather than providing additional circumstances in which termination of a different kind may be effected; if this were so, then this aspect of s.28 would be problematic since art.18 of the 2011 Directive requires "full harmonisation".[3216] Certainly, s.28 of the 2015 Act (following explicitly art.18 of the Directive) adds that it does not prevent the consumer seeking other remedies where it is open to the consumer to do so.[3217] Finally, the rules on delivery in s.29 of the 1979 Act apply to delivery under "sales contracts" where they count as contracts for the sale of goods within the meaning of the 1979 Act,[3218] except as regards s.29(3)'s provision that where under the contract of sale the seller is bound to send the goods to the buyer, but no time for sending them is fixed, the seller is bound to send them within a reasonable time.[3219] For this purpose, however, it should be noted that delivery under s.29 of the 1979 Act includes (where appropriate) making the goods available for the buyer to collect,[3220] whereas under s.28 of the 2015 Act delivery seems to refer to the trader actually handing over the goods

---

[3210] 2015 Act s.28(9) referring to subss.(6) and (8).

[3211] 2015 Act s.28(10).

[3212] If any of the goods form a commercial unit, the consumer cannot reject or cancel the order for some of those goods without also rejecting or cancelling the order for the rest of them. A unit is a "commercial unit" if division of the unit would materially impair the value of the goods or the character of the unit: 2015 Act s.28(11) and (12).

[3213] "Cancellation" is referred to in relation to secondary ticketing in s.91 of the 2015 Act; and is included in some of the examples of contract terms which may be unfair for the purposes of Pt 2 of the Act: s.63, Sch.2 Pt 1 paras 4 and 15.

[3214] Above, paras 38-513—38-516, 38-518—38-519.

[3215] 2011 Directive art.18(4).

[3216] 2011 Directive art.4, above, para.38-062. A possible way out of this problem would be to hold that "cancelling the order" refers to a right to cancel an off-premises contract or distance contract under the 2013 Regulations (in which the content of s.28 was earlier contained), but the context of the provision in s.28 does not suggest that this is so: see SI 2013/3134 reg.42(10)–(11) and above, paras 38-112 et seq.

[3217] 2015 Act s.28(13). Such a remedy could include a claim for damages for breach of contract under the general law: 2011 Directive recital 53.

[3218] On the differences between these two categories see above, paras 38-486—38-488. For discussion of s.29 of the 1979 Act see below, paras 44-241 et seq.

[3219] s.29(3) is disapplied to contracts to which Ch.2 of Pt 1 of the 2015 Act applies: 2015 Act s.60, Sch.1 para.18, inserting new subs.(3A) in s.29 of the 1979 Act.

[3220] Below, para.44-244.

to the consumer.[3221] The 2015 Act provides that contract terms which seek to exclude or restrict liability in the trader arising under s.28 are not binding on the consumer.[3222]

Passing of risk   Section 29 of the 2015 Act makes special provision for the pass-   **38-527**
ing of risk in goods under "sales contracts" and the Act therefore disapplies the general provisions governing the passing of risk in s.20 of the 1979 Act as regards contracts to which s.29 of the 2015 Act applies.[3223] Under s.29, a sales contract is to be treated as including a term to the effect that the goods[3224] remain at the trader's risk until they come into the physical possession of the consumer or a person identi-fied by the consumer to take possession of the goods, unless the goods are delivered to a carrier who is commissioned by the consumer to deliver the goods other than a carrier the trader named as an option for the consumer: in the second situation, the goods are at the consumer's risk on and after delivery to the carrier.[3225] The main difference between this set of rules and the general rules retained for s.20 of the 1979 Act is that in the latter there is a presumption that the risk passes with the pass-ing of property in the goods, rather than on their delivery.[3226] The 2015 Act provides that contract terms which seek to exclude or restrict liability in the trader arising under s.29 are not binding on the consumer.[3227]

Goods under guarantee   Section 30 of the 2015 Act implements art.6 of the   **38-528**
Consumer Sales Directive 1999, thereby replacing its earlier implementation by the Sale and Supply of Goods to Consumers Regulations 2002[3228] and while the draft-ing differs between the two, the substance remains the same. Accordingly, s.30 ap-plies where there is a contract to supply goods,[3229] and there is a guarantee in rela-tion to the goods. A "guarantee" for these purposes is:

"... an undertaking to the consumer given without extra charge by a person acting in the course of the person's business (the "guarantor"[3230]) that, if the goods do not meet the specifications set out in the guarantee statement or in any associated advertising—

(a)   the consumer will be reimbursed for the price paid for the goods, or

---

[3221] See, in particular, s.28(2) of the 2015 Act and see above, para.38-526 (note).

[3222] 2015 Act s.31(1)(j) and see below, para.38-531.

[3223] 2015 Act s.60; Sch.1 para.17 (thereby replacing s.20(4) which applied to buyers dealing as consumer). The 2015 Act s.29 implements the Consumer Rights Directive 2011 art.20 and replaced its earlier implementation by the 2013 Regulations reg.43 (which was itself revoked by the Consumer Contracts (Amendment) Regulations 2015 (SI 2015/1629) reg.8 as regards contracts entered into on or after October 1, 2015).

[3224] The 2015 Act's general exclusion of sales of second-hand goods sold at public auction does not ap-ply for the purposes of s.29, following the definition of "goods" in art.2(3) of the Consumer Rights Directive: 2015 Act s.2(5) and (6)(a); s.29(6).

[3225] 2015 Act s.29(1)–(4). Section 29(5) notes that this final rule does not affect any liability of the car-rier to the consumer in respect of the goods. On "delivery" see above, para.38-526 (note).

[3226] See 1979 Act s.20(1) and below, paras 44-189 et seq.

[3227] 2015 Act s.31(1)(k) and see below, para.38-531.

[3228] SI 2002/3045 reg.15, above, para.38-462.

[3229] 2015 Act s.30(1) and see 2015 Act s.3(1) and (2), above, para.38-485.

[3230] There is no definition of "guarantor" in the 2015 Act except the designation in s.30(2), with the result that any person who gives a guarantee as is described there (whether the trader party to the goods contract, the producer of the goods or any other person) can be a "guarantor" subject to the condi-tion that they act in the course of their business. On the definition of "business" for this purpose see 2015 Act s.2(7) and above, para.38-482 as explained by paras 38-052—38-055.

(b)   the goods will be repaired, replaced or handled in any way." [3231]

The Act provides that the guarantee "takes effect, at the time the goods are delivered, as a contractual obligation owed by the guarantor" under the conditions set out in the guarantee statement and in any associated advertising.[3232] The guarantor must ensure that the guarantee sets out in plain and intelligible language[3233] the contents of the guarantee and the essential particulars for making claims under the guarantee and that it states that the consumer has statutory rights in relation to the goods and that those rights are not affected by the guarantee.[3234] Section 30 makes further detailed provision as to the contents and availability to the consumer of the guarantee.[3235]

38-529   **Exclusion or limitation of liability by a "guarantee"**   As earlier noted, s.30(3) provides that a "guarantee" "takes effect as a contractual obligation owed by the guarantor under the conditions set out in the guarantee statement and in any associated advertising" and s.30(4) adds that the guarantor must ensure that the guarantee "states that the consumer has statutory rights in relation to the goods and that those rights are not affected by the guarantee". This reflects the Act's perception of the legitimate function of guarantees as being undertakings by traders as to consumer rights to reimbursement of the price, or repair or replacement of the goods not available (or not necessarily available) otherwise to the consumer.[3236] Clearly, any attempted exclusion of the liabilities imposed on a guarantor in his capacity as the trader who sells or supplies goods to the consumer by Ch.2 of Pt 1 of the Act would fall foul of the controls which the Act provides as regards those liabilities.[3237] On the other hand, where the guarantee of goods is made by a trader other than such a seller or supplier (for example, their manufacturer) but seeks to exclude or limit the liability of the seller/supplier of the goods (also a trader), it is submitted that s.72 of the Act could come into play so as to control these attempted restrictions in the guarantee, a "secondary contract" for this purpose.[3238] In this respect, as has been seen, s.72 provides that a term in such a secondary contract which attempts to reduce the rights of the consumer buyer in the main contract (of sale or supply) would be subject to the general test of fairness in Pt 2 of the 2015 Act, rather than

---

[3231] 2015 Act s.30(2).

[3232] 2015 Act s.30(3). This would mean that any failure in respect of the undertakings in the guarantee would give rise to the normal remedies for breach of contract (and notably damages) provided under the general law: on damages see Vol.I, Ch.26.

[3233] As the 2015 Act s.30 implements art.6 of the 1999 Directive, it is submitted that the interpretation of this requirement should follow the approach taken by the CJEU for the purposes of the Unfair Terms in Consumer Contracts Directive 1993 arts 4(2) and 5, as explained above, paras 38-261, 38-262 and 38-350.

[3234] 2015 Act s.30(4). Where the goods are offered within the territory of the United Kingdom, the guarantee must be written in English: 2015 Act s.30(4).

[3235] These contents must include the name and address of the guarantor and the duration and territorial scope of the guarantee. The guarantor and any other person who offers to supply to consumers the goods which are the subject of the guarantee must, on request by the consumer, make the guarantee available to the consumer within a reasonable time, in writing and in a form accessible to the consumer: 2015 Act s.30(5)–(7).

[3236] See also 1999 Directive recital 21 ("[w]hereas, for certain categories of goods, it is current practice for sellers and producers to offer guarantees on goods against any defect which becomes apparent within a certain period; whereas this practice can stimulate competition").

[3237] 2015 Act s.31 and see below, para.38-531.

[3238] See below, paras 38-402—38-403.

subject to the controls on the liabilities imposed on the trader/supplier provided by Pt 1 of the 2015 Act.[3239] The position of limitations of liability in respect of the "contractual obligations" imposed by the Act in respect of the undertakings given by a trader in the guarantee which do *not* purport to affect the seller/supplier's liabilities in Pt 1 Ch.2 of the Act is more difficult, as, for example, an undertaking by the seller or the manufacturer to repair the goods without the restrictions on that "right to repair" set out by the 2015 Act,[3240] but subject to a limitation on the cost of such a replacement. The reference in s.30 to the guarantee taking effect "under the conditions set out in the guarantee" suggests that such a restriction should be given effect without any assessment of its fairness, but it could be argued that such a restriction is a term of the "guarantee contract" recognised by s.30 and is, therefore, subject to the general controls on the fairness of terms in Pt 2 of the 2015 Act.

Enforcement of the duties on guarantors and other traders by s.30   The du-   **38-530**
ties on guarantors and other traders imposed by s.30 may be enforced by injunction on the application of the CMA or a local weights and measures authority.[3241] Moreover, as s.30 implements the 1999 Directive, it attracts the enforcement measures put in place for "Community infringements" which harm the collective interests of consumers under Pt 8 of the Enterprise Act 2002 as explained earlier.[3242]

(ee)   Exclusion of Liability and Choice of Law

Exclusion of liability arising under Pt 1 Ch.2 of the 2015 Act   As earlier   **38-531**
explained, the 2015 Act repealed or disapplied provisions in the Unfair Contract Terms Act 1977 governing the contracts to which Ch.2 applies, and instead makes its own provision controlling the exclusion of liabilities arising under its provisions,[3243] though this follows the pattern of the relevant provisions in the 1977 Act to a considerable extent. As a result, s.31 of the 2015 Act provides generally that a term of a goods contract[3244] is not binding on the consumer to the extent that it would exclude or restrict the trader's liability under the statutory terms which it treats as included,[3245] in respect of its special provisions governing non-conformity of the goods,[3246] and governing delivery of goods and the passing of risk.[3247] Sec-

---

[3239] 2015 Act s.72(2).

[3240] 2015 Act s.23 and see above, para.38-517.

[3241] 2015 Act s.30(8)–(10).

[3242] Enterprise Act 2002 s.212; Sch.13 Pt 1 para.8; s.30 of the 2015 Act is designated as a "specified law" for the purposes of s.212 (Enterprise Act 2002 (Part 8 EU Infringements) Order 2014 (SI 2014/2908) art.4 and Sch.) and may be the basis of a "domestic infringement" under s.211 of the 2002 Act (Enterprise Act 2002 (Part 8 Domestic Infringements) Order 2015 (SI 2015/1727) art.2) and see above paras 38-133—38-134.

[3243] See above, para.38-372. On the general strategy of the 2015 Act in relation to the control of unfair contract terms, see above, paras 38-370—38-375.

[3244] 2015 Act s.3(1) and (2), above, para.38-485.

[3245] i.e. 2015 Act s.9 (goods to be of satisfactory quality), s.10 (goods to be fit for particular purpose), s.11 (goods to be as described), s.12 (other pre-contract information included in contract); s.13 (goods to match a sample); s.14 (goods to match a model seen or examined) and s.17 (trader to have right to supply the goods, etc.): 2015 Act s.31(1)(a)–(f), (i). On these provisions see above, paras 38-497—38-502 and 38-507—38-511.

[3246] i.e. 2015 Act s.15 (installation as part of conformity of the goods with the contract) and s.16 (goods not conforming to contract if digital content does not conform): 2015 Act s.31(1)(g) and (h). On these

tion 31 then explains what is meant by the exclusion or limitation of liability in terms which closely follow s.13 of the Unfair Contract Terms Act 1977, providing that the exclusion or restriction of liability:

"... also means that a term of a contract to supply goods is not binding on the consumer to the extent that it would—

    (a)   exclude or restrict a right or remedy in respect of a liability ... ,

    (b)   make such a right or remedy or its enforcement subject to a restrictive or onerous condition,

    (c)   allow a trader to put a person at a disadvantage as a result of pursuing such a right or remedy, or

    (d)   exclude or restrict rules of evidence or procedure.

    (3)   The reference in subsection (1) to excluding or restricting a liability also includes preventing an obligation or duty arising or limiting its extent." [3248]

Section 31 makes special provision in respect of the control of express terms in contracts for the hire of goods which seek to exclude or restrict liability in the trader in respect of the statutory term governing the trader's right to supply the goods, subjecting such a term to the test of unfairness under Pt 2 of the 2015 Act.[3249] On the other hand, s.31 does not control the effectiveness of contract terms seeking to exclude or restrict the trader's liabilities arising under s.25 (delivery of wrong quantity) or s.26 (instalment deliveries), both of which refer (for different purposes) to the agreement of the parties in relation to the application of their own provisions.[3250] In this respect, it is submitted that for these purposes exclusion or limitation clauses could fall within the general controls on terms in consumer contracts provided by Pt 2 of the 2015 Act, notably, by reference to the requirement of fairness and the requirement for transparency.[3251]

38-532   **Enforcement of provisions on exclusion of trader's liabilities**   As earlier explained in relation to the 2015 Act's treatment of unfair contract terms more generally, the Act applies the enforcement measures provided for the control of unfair contract terms under Pt 2 (and derived from the 1993 Directive[3252]) to its

---

provisions see above, paras 38-503—38-504 respectively.

[3247] 2015 Act ss.28 and 29 respectively: 2015 Act s.31(j) and (k), on which see above, paras 38-526 and 38-527 respectively.

[3248] 2015 Act s.31(2) and (3). Section 31(4) (following the 1977 Act s.13(2)) provides that an agreement in writing to submit present or future differences to arbitration is not to be regarded as excluding or restricting any liability for its purposes, but it should be noted that an arbitration clause in a consumer contract may be "unfair" and therefore not binding on a consumer under s.62 of the Act, and that the Arbitration Act 1996 provides that a term which constitutes an arbitration agreement is deemed to be unfair if the claim is for less than an amount currently £5,000: see above, para.38-412. For discussion of s.13 of the 1977 Act, see Vol.I, para.15-069, much of which is relevant to the interpretation of these provisions.

[3249] 2015 Act s.31(5)–(6) referring to liability under s.17 (on which see above, para.38-508). For the test of unfairness under Pt 2 of the Act see s.62 and above, paras 38-389 et seq. It is not clear what particular effect is intended by this reference to Pt 2 of the Act which would in any event apply to a term seeking to exclude liability under s.17, whether or not that term was individually negotiated.

[3250] 2015 Act s.25(4) and (8) (above, para.38-524); s.26(2) and (4) and (7) above, para.38-525.

[3251] 2015 Act ss.62 and 68 above, paras 38-389 et seq. and 38-414—38-417 respectively.

[3252] 1993 Directive art.7.

controls of exclusion clauses in Pt 1 of the Act as here reflected in s.31.[3253] These enforcement measures have been discussed earlier,[3254] as have the technical difficulties of compatibility of their extension in this way as a matter of EU law.[3255]

Special rule governing choice of law   As required by the Consumer Sales Directive 1999 as regards those contracts of sale of goods falling within its scope,[3256] s.32 makes special provision for choice of law for "sales contracts".[3257] Accordingly, s.32 provides that where the law of a country or territory other than an EEA State is chosen by the parties to be applicable to a sales contract, but the sales contract has a close connection with the United Kingdom, Ch.2 applies despite that choice.[3258] In this way, s.32 makes very similar provision to s.74 of the 2015 Act for the purposes of Pt 2's controls on unfair terms, in this case following the Unfair Terms in Consumer Contract Directive's own special provision on choice of law.[3259] However, reflecting the fact that some of the provisions in Ch.2 reflect the Consumer Rights Directive 2011 rather than the Consumer Sales Directive 1999, and that the 2011 Directive makes no special provision for choice of law, s.32 excludes from its special provision those sections of Ch.2 which reflect the 2011 Directive.[3260] For the cases where these exclusions apply, the Rome I Regulation on the law applicable to contractual obligations applies instead.[3261]

38-533

Enforcement of Pt 1 more generally   As earlier explained, enforcement authorities enjoy considerable powers under Pt 8 of the Enterprise Act 2002 to enforce

38-534

[3253] 2015 Act s.31(7) referring to Sch.3.

[3254] Above, paras 38-419 et seq.

[3255] The difficulty arises from the fact that the controls on exclusion clauses governing liability under s.31 of the 2015 Act go beyond the scope of the controls required by the Consumer Sales Directive 1999 (whose controls on the exclusion of liability in art.7(1) apply only to contracts for the sale of goods within its definition in art.1) and, where this is the case, beyond the intensity of the controls required by Unfair Terms in Consumer Contracts Directive 1993 (in that they invalidate such clauses in all circumstances rather than subjecting them to the test of unfairness) and that enforcement measures in respect of the "commercial practice" of use of such exemption clauses would therefore fall foul of the "full harmonisation" of the Unfair Commercial Practices Directive 2005. For an explanation of this difficulty see above, paras 38-421—38-426. The difficulty does not exist as regards the controls on the exclusion of liability under ss.11(4) and (5), 12, 28 and 29 of the 2015 Act which are required by the Consumer Rights Directive 2011 art.25.

[3256] 1999 Directive art.7(2). The relevant provisions of the 1999 Directive apply to contracts for the sale of goods and deem contracts for the supply of consumer goods to be manufactured and produced to be included in this category for this purpose: art.1(2)(b) "consumer goods", (c) "seller" and art.1(4)) above, paras 38-486—38-488.

[3257] Defined by s.5.

[3258] 2015 Act s.32(1).

[3259] 1993 Directive art.6(2). For discussion of s.74 of the Act, art.6(2) of the 1993 Directive and their relationship to the general provisions governing applicable law in Regulation (EC) 593/2008 on the law applicable to contractual obligations ("Rome I Regulation") see above, para.38-418.

[3260] 2015 Act s.32(2). The relevant provisions are 2015 Act ss.11(4) and (5) and 12 (implementing the 2011 Directive's provisions governing information requirements, on which see above, paras 38-105, 38-499—38-500); s.28 (delivery, on which see above, para.38-526); s.29 (passing of risk, on which see above, para.38-527) and s.31(1)(d), (j) and (k) ((which concern the exclusion of liability under ss.12, 28 and 29, on which see above, para.38-531).

[3261] 2015 Act s.32(3) referring to Regulation (EC) 593/2008 on the law applicable to contractual obligations ("Rome I Regulation") on which generally see Vol.I, paras 30-019 et seq. The application of these rules may lead to the application of English law under the Act even though the contract is governed generally by the law of another EU Member State, as in the case where art.6 of the Rome I Regulation applies.

designated UK legislation and EU legislation.[3262] As has been seen, many (though not all) of the provisions of Ch.2 of the 2015 Act reflect requirements of the Consumer Sales Directive 1999 or the Consumer Rights Directive 2011, and any breach of these requirements would constitute "Community infringements" within the meaning of Pt 8 of the 2002 Act.[3263] The relevant provisions in Ch.2 of the 2015 Act which implement the 1999 Directive or the 2011 Directive or which "provide additional permitted protections" have therefore been designated as specified UK laws for the purposes of s.212 of the 2002 Act.[3264] In addition, acts or omissions in respect of any provision in Pt 1 of the 2015 Act are specified as possible "domestic infringements" for the purposes of s.211 of the Enterprise Act 2002.[3265]

(iv) Digital Content Contracts

38-535 **Introduction** Chapter 3 of Pt 1 of the 2015 Act makes original provision governing important aspects of "digital content contracts", which it defines for these purposes.[3266] Under earlier law, it was by no means clear whether a person who "buys" digital content does so under a contract of sale of goods, a contract for services or something else.[3267] As a result, consumers who purchase digital content were unclear as to what rights they might have, how they should seek to enforce those rights against the trader and whether these rights were subject to exclusion by agreement. The 2015 Act sought therefore to create a "new category of digital content in consumer law with a bespoke set of rights and remedies appropriate to the unique nature of digital content".[3268] In doing so, however, the 2015 Act drew on earlier legislation in a number of important ways, adapting earlier provisions to suit the new context as well as supplementing them so as to provide for the distinctive features of the modern supply of digital content to consumers.

38-536   First, the 2015 Act adopts the definition of "digital content" used by the Consumer Contracts (Information, Cancellation and Additional Charges) Regulations 2013, that is "data which are produced and supplied in digital form",[3269] which was itself drawn from the Consumer Rights Directive 2011.[3270] As has been seen,

---

[3262] Above, paras 38-133—38-134.

[3263] Enterprise Act 2002 s.212; Sch.13 Pt 1 paras 8 and 9F lists these directives for this purpose.

[3264] Enterprise Act 2002 s.212(3); Enterprise Act 2002 (Part 8 Community Infringements Specified UK Laws) Order 2003 (SI 2003/1374) art.3; Sch., as amended by the Enterprise Act 2002 (Part 8 Community Infringements and Specified UK Laws) (Amendment) Order 2015 (SI 2015/1628) art.2(2)(b) listing 2015 Act ss.2, 3, 9–11, 13–15, 19, 23, 24, 30–32, 58 and 59 (1999 Directive); art.3(2) listing 2015 Act ss.5, 11(4)–(6), 12, 19, 28, 29, 36(3)–(4), 37, 38, 42, 50 and 54 (2011 Directive).

[3265] Enterprise Act 2002 s.211(2); Enterprise Act 2002 (Part 8 Domestic Infringements) Order 2015 (SI 2015/1727) art.2.

[3266] cf. the Proposal for a Directive of the European Parliament and of the Council on certain aspects concerning contracts for the supply of digital content COM(2015) 634 final; see above, para.38-436.

[3267] *Explanatory Notes* 2015 para.169 referring to Bradgate, "*Consumer rights in digital products: A research report prepared for the UK Department for Business, Innovation and Skills*", Institute for Commercial Law Studies, Sheffield and BIS, available at: *http://www.bis.gov.uk/assets/biscore/ consumer-issues/docs/c/10-1125-consumer-rights-in-digital-products*. cf. *Software Incubator Ltd v Computer Associates UK Ltd* [2018] EWCA Civ 518 where it was held that a contract for the supply of software does not constitute a "sale of goods" for the purposes of the Commercial Agents (Council Directive) Regulations 1993 (SI 1993/3053).

[3268] *Explanatory Notes* 2015, para.172.

[3269] SI 2013/3134 reg.5 "digital content"; 2015 Act s.2(9).

[3270] Consumer Rights Directive 2011 art.2(11).

the 2013 Regulations impose important information requirements on traders in relation to the consumer contracts to which they apply and these include contracts under which digital content is supplied, also creating rights of cancellation in respect of "off-premises contracts" and distance contracts.[3271] On the other hand, the legislative treatment of contracts under which digital content is supplied under the 2013 Regulations and the 2015 Act differs, as will be explained[3272] and the 2015 Act defines specially the *types* of contract for the supply of digital content to which it applies.[3273]

Secondly, the 2015 Act adopts the scheme of statutory terms governing satisfactory quality, fitness for purpose, description and pre-contract information which it uses for "goods contracts" and familiar from earlier legislation in order to create rights for consumers in respect of these matters in relation to digital content contracts.[3274] In doing so, the Act makes only those changes which are necessary given the change in subject matter of the contracts between the two contexts.[3275] On the other hand, the Act's provisions on the trader's right to supply the digital content to the consumer differ significantly from its provisions governing "goods contracts".[3276] Moreover, the Act makes original provision to regulate the situation where a consumer has concluded a contract to supply digital content and the consumer's access to the content on a device requires transmission to the device, or where, after the trader has supplied the digital content, the consumer is to have access to a "processing facility" under arrangements made by the trader.[3277] The Act also provides specially for the case where digital content is supplied under a contract subject to the right of the trader or a third party to modify that content.[3278]

38-537

Thirdly, the 2015 Act adopts three of the special remedies for consumers provided by Pt 1 Ch.2 of the Act in respect of "goods contracts" for use by consumers in respect of digital content contracts: the right to repair or replacement and price reduction.[3279] On the other hand, while the Act makes clear that a consumer may claim a refund in respect of breaches by the trader of the statutory terms, and that this refund may be in full,[3280] the Act does not provide for any right in the consumer to reject the digital content or to treat the digital content contract as at an end, similar to the right to reject provided by Pt 1 Ch.2 of the Act for consumers in relation to goods.[3281] The Act provides the consumer with new remedies of repair or compensa-

38-538

[3271] Above, paras 38-060 et seq.

[3272] Below, para.38-543.

[3273] 2015 Act s.33, below, paras 38-540—38-542.

[3274] 2015 Act ss.34–38 (digital content contracts) reflecting ss.9–12 of the Act (goods contracts), on which see above, paras 38-497—38-500.

[3275] Below, paras 38-544 et seq.

[3276] 2015 Act s.41 (digital content contracts), on which see below, paras 38-555—38-556 and cf. s.17 discussed above, paras 38-507—38-511.

[3277] 2015 Act s.39 below, paras 38-551—38-553.

[3278] 2015 Act s.40, below, para.38-554.

[3279] 2015 Act ss.42–44, below, paras 38-557 et seq.

[3280] 2015 Act s.44(1) and (2) (which treats the refund as a consequence of the application of price reduction). Section 45 provides a direct right to a refund of (in principle) "all money paid by the consumer for the digital content" where the trader is in breach of the statutory term as to the right to supply in s.41(1): 2015 Act ss.42(5) and 45.

[3281] On the new remedies and how they relate to "other remedies" available under the general law, see below, paras 38-557 et seq. On the remedies under goods contracts, see above, paras 38-512 et seq.

tion in respect of digital content which causes damage to a device or to other digital content.[3282]

38-539   Finally, the 2015 Act makes similar provision as is made in Pt 1 Ch.2 so as to render terms which seek to exclude or restrict the trader's liability for breach of the statutory terms not binding on the consumer.[3283] It also applies the enforcement regime provided by Pt 2 of the Act for the control of unfair terms generally to the particular context of its controls on exclusion and limitation clauses.[3284]

(aa)   "Digital Content Contracts"

38-540   **"Digital content"**   As earlier noted, the 2015 Act defines "digital content" as "data which are produced and supplied in digital form".[3285] The *Explanatory Notes* to the Act explain that this includes software, music, computer games and applications (or "apps")[3286] and that:

> "… [i]n the case of digital content which is supplied under contract from a trader to a consumer, and largely or wholly stored and processed remotely, such as software supplied via cloud computing, some digital content will always be transmitted to the consumer's device so that they can interact with the digital content product that they have contracted for."[3287]

Digital content so transmitted may fall within the scope of Ch.3 as long as it is supplied pursuant to a contract to which it applies, as set out below.

38-541   **The contracts covered by Pt 1 Ch.3 of the 2015 Act**   Chapter 3 provides that its provisions apply to contracts under which digital content is supplied of two distinct types.[3288] First, s.33(1) provides that it applies to:

> "… a contract for a trader to supply digital content to a consumer, if it is supplied or to be supplied for a price paid by the consumer."[3289]

And secondly, according to s.33(2) Ch.3 also applies to:

> "… a contract for a trader to supply digital content to a consumer, if—
>
> (a)   it is supplied free with goods or services or other digital content for which the consumer pays a price, and
>
> (b)   it is not generally available to consumers unless they have paid a price for it or for goods or services or other digital content."

[3282] 2015 Act s.46 below, para.38-563.

[3283] 2015 Act s.47, below, para.38-564.

[3284] 2015 Act s.47(5), below, para.38-566.

[3285] 2015 Act s.2(9).

[3286] *Explanatory Notes* 2015 para.166. cf. the illustrations of "digital content" provided by the Consumer Rights Directive 2011 recital 19, quoted above, para.38-075.

[3287] *Explanatory Notes* 2015 para.166.

[3288] s.33(8) of the 2015 Act provides, however, that s.33 does not limit the application of s.46's provisions providing a remedy for damage to a device or to other digital content caused by digital content, except as regards its limitation in s.33(4), on which see below, para.38-552 (note). The 2015 Act s.33(5)–(6), (9)–(10) provides the Secretary of State with powers by order to apply to other contracts for a trader to supply digital content to a consumer subject to certain conditions.

[3289] 2015 Act s.33(1).

This second example is the less obvious, but reflects the fact that digital content is frequently supplied as part of a wider arrangement, for example, when software is given away with a paid-for magazine in circumstances where it is not generally available to consumers for free.[3290] For this purpose, s.33(3) explains that the references in these earlier definitions to:

"... the consumer paying a price include references to the consumer using, by way of payment, any facility for which money has been paid."[3291]

The idea of something being paid for with "a facility for which money has been paid" is new and the Act's *Explanatory Notes* provide as examples

"... a token, virtual currency, or gift voucher, that was originally purchased with money (e.g. a magic sword bought within a computer game that was paid for within the game using "jewels" but those jewels were originally purchased with money)."[3292]

As a result, any contract which falls within one or other of the definitions in s.33(1) or s.33(2) will be governed by Ch.3 and both are equally termed a "contract to supply digital content" by the Act[3293] or simply "digital content contract", the latter of which will be the term used in the following paragraphs.

On the other hand, Ch.3 of the 2015 Act does not apply to contracts for the supply of digital content other than for a price paid by the consumer, such as where the consumer provides information to the trader in return for the supply of digital content. This is reflected in the amendments made to the 2013 Regulations in consequence of the enactment of the 2015 Act. Formerly, the 2013 Regulations had themselves implemented the requirement in the Consumer Rights Directive 2011[3294] that information provided by the trader to the consumer as required by the Regulations was treated as a term of the contract and cannot be changed effectively unless this has been expressly agreed between them: these provisions applied to all the contracts covered by the Regulations, i.e. for the supply of goods, digital content or services.[3295] However, after the 2015 Act, as in the case of goods and services,[3296] pre-contract information provided by a trader in relation to a digital content contract is made a term of the contract by the Act itself,[3297] but only in relation to those "digital content contracts" to which Ch.3 applies. As a result, the provisions in the 2013 Regulations providing for the contractual status of pre-contract information supplied, etc. were amended so as to apply only to those contracts omitted from the scope of Ch.3, i.e. contracts "for the supply of digital content other than for a price paid by the consumer".[3298] However, while this means that information supplied in respect of digital content contracts other than for a price paid by the consumer are made terms of the contract, the 2013 Regulations do not specify the remedial

38-542

[3290] *Explanatory Notes* 2015 para.174.

[3291] 2015 Act s.33(3).

[3292] *Explanatory Notes* 2015 para.174.

[3293] 2015 Act s.33(7).

[3294] Art.6(5) (although this effect is not required by the 2011 Directive as regards "on-premises contracts") and see above, paras 38-075 and 38-105.

[3295] 2013 Regulations regs 9(3) and (4); 10(5) and (6); and 13(6) and (7) (until their amendment in 2015) (although this effect is not required by the 2011 Directive as regards "on-premises contracts".

[3296] 2015 Act ss.11(4) and (5) (goods); 50(3) and (4) (services).

[3297] 2015 Act ss.36(3) and (4); s.37, below, paras 38-548—38-549.

[3298] 2013 Regulations regs 9(3), 10(5) and 13(6) as inserted by the Consumer Contracts (Amendment) Regulations 2015 (SI 2015/1629) reg.4.

consequences of breach of those terms, unlike the 2015 Act which distinguishes for this purpose between certain important categories of information (such as its main characteristics) and other types of pre-contractual information.[3299]

38-543 **"Digital content contracts" and other contracts in Pt 1 of the Act** The treatment of digital content contracts by s.33 of the Act has two main consequences. First, as suggested by the 2015 Act's general provisions governing "mixed contracts",[3300] a digital content contract within the meaning of Ch.3 may also be a "goods contract" within the meaning of Ch.2, that is, where both goods and digital content are supplied under the contract or where goods are supplied under the contract and digital content is supplied for free under the particular circumstances set out in s.33(2). Indeed, as earlier explained, s.16 of the Act makes particular provision for the case where goods do not conform to the contract if the goods consist of an item that includes digital content and the digital content does not conform to the contract.[3301] This regulatory overlap differs from the pattern under the Consumer Contracts (Information, Cancellation and Additional Charges) Regulations 2013, which distinguish between sales contracts (which are defined as relating to tangible moveable items, which may include digital content, as in the case of a CD) and "contracts for the supply of digital content not on a tangible medium" (which do not require payment of a "price" by the consumer) and then regulates them distinctly.[3302] Secondly, a contract for a trader to supply a service to a consumer or "services contract" governed by Pt 1 Ch.4 of the 2015 Act may also constitute a "digital content contract" and so fall within Pt 1 Ch.3, but s.33(4) provides that:

"... [a] trader does not supply digital content to a consumer for the purposes of this Part merely because the trader supplies a service by which digital content reaches the consumer."

This clarification of the significance of the Act's definition of "digital content contract" reflects the view of the EU Commission taken for the purposes of the Consumer Rights Directive 2011 that where a trader's main obligation is not to provide digital content but rather to provide a service (for example, allowing the creation, processing, sorting or sharing of data that is produced by a consumer) the contract is not for the supply of digital content even though some digital content reaches the consumer, though it may be a contract for the supply of a service.[3303] A particular significance of this provision is discussed below.[3304]

[3299] 2015 Act s.36(3) and 37, below, paras 38-548—38-549.

[3300] 2015 Act s.1(4)–(6), above, para.38-484.

[3301] Above, para.38-504. This overlap is also noted by the 2015 Act s.42(3) for the case where "an item including the digital content is supplied".

[3302] 2013 Regulations reg.5 "sales contract" and "goods", above, para.38-075.

[3303] EU Commission, *Report from the Commission to the European Parliament and the Council on the application of Directive 2011/83/EU* (etc.) COM(2017) 259 final, para.5 and see above, para.38-075.

[3304] Below, para.38-552 (note).

(bb)   The Statutory Terms

The relationship between the statutory terms, non-conformity of the digital   **38-544**
content and the consumer's remedies   Following in very broad terms the pattern set by Ch.2 for "goods contracts",[3305] s.42 of the 2015 Act sets out the relationship between the statutory terms "treated as included" in digital content contracts, the consumer's rights to enforce terms about digital content and any "other remedies" which the consumer may enjoy. In doing so, it draws a three-fold distinction. First, s.42 provides that for these purposes[3306] "digital content conforming to a contract" refers to the content's conforming to the statutory terms governing its quality, fitness for a particular purpose and description[3307] and where it does not conform to the contract in this sense, the consumer has a right to repair or replacement and the right to a price reduction.[3308] Secondly, s.42 provides that where pre-contractual information other than as to the digital content's main characteristics, functionality or compatibility forms the basis of a statutory term of the contract,[3309] breach of this term creates a right in the consumer to recover from the trader the amount of any costs incurred as a result of the breach, up to the amount of the price paid for the digital content or for any facility used by the consumer.[3310] This reflects a similarly limited remedy created for information provided by the trader under goods contracts other than where it relates to the main characteristics of the goods.[3311] Thirdly, s.42 provides that where the trader is in breach of the statutory term relating to the trader's right to supply the digital content, the consumer has a special right to a refund which in principle extends to all money paid.[3312] It is to be noted that this three-fold scheme does not provide for the case of "requirements that are stated in the contract" as Ch.2 does in the case of "goods contracts"[3313] nor for the case where the contract contains an express term about the quality or its fitness for any particular purpose even though such an express term is specifically foreseen by the Act.[3314] As regards the latter, it is submitted that the remedial and other consequences of breach of such an express term would be governed by the general law and this could lead to a claim for damages and, subject to its general conditions, a claim by the consumer to treat the contract as at an end under the law of termination for breach of contract.[3315] In this respect, while the Act provides expressly for the relationship between the special remedies for the consumer which s.42 recognises and other remedies which the consumer may enjoy

---

[3305] 2015 Act s.19, above, para.38-493.

[3306] Technically, s.42(1) makes this definition both for the purposes of s.42 and of s.43 (which concerns the right to repair or replacement): below, para.38-558.

[3307] 2015 Act s.42(1) referring to ss.34, 35 and 36 of the Act, below, paras 38-546, 38-547 and 38-548 respectively.

[3308] 2015 Act s.42(2) referring to ss.43 and 44 on which see below, paras 38-558 and 38-559 respectively.

[3309] Under 2015 Act s.37, below, para.38-549. Where information is provided in relation to the digital content's main characteristics, functionality or compatibility, it becomes a term of the contract under s.36 whose breach renders the content non-conforming within the meaning of s.42(1), with the remedial consequences provided by s.42(2): below, para.38-548.

[3310] 2015 Act s.42(4) which provides that "facility" is to be understood in the sense in which it is used by s.33(3) (on which see above, para.38-541).

[3311] 2015 Act ss.12 and 19(5), above, para.38-500.

[3312] 2015 Act ss.41, 42(5) and 45 on which see below, paras 38-555—38-556.

[3313] 2015 Act s.19(1)(c) and 19(4), above, paras 38-493 and 38-506.

[3314] 2015 Act s.38(1).

[3315] On which see Vol.I, Ch.24 (discharge by breach) and Ch.26 (damages).

under the general law (and excludes from these other remedies the consumer's treating the contract as at an end[3316]), the latter concerns only other remedies which the consumer may enjoy as a result of breach of the statutory terms in the Act[3317] and not, therefore, any express term.

38-545 Presumption of non-conformity The 2015 Act s.42 adopts the presumption of non-conformity on delivery which the Act earlier uses in relation to "goods contracts" and which is drawn from the Consumer Sales Directive 1999[3318] and so provides that:

> "… digital content which does not conform to the contract at any time within the period of six months beginning with the day on which it was supplied must be taken not to have conformed to the contract when it was supplied,"[3319]

This does not apply if it is established that the digital content did conform to the contract when it was supplied or if its application is incompatible with the nature of the digital content or with how it fails to conform to the contract.[3320]

38-546 Digital content to be of satisfactory quality The 2015 Act s.34 makes almost identical provision as to the satisfactory quality of digital content supplied under a "digital content contract"[3321] as s.9 of the Act makes in relation to the satisfactory quality of goods supplied under a "goods contract",[3322] itself being familiar from earlier statutory provisions, notably governing sale of goods.[3323] Section 34 provides that:

> "(1) Every contract to supply digital content is to be treated as including a term that the quality of the digital content is satisfactory.
>
> (2) The quality of digital content is satisfactory if it meets the standard that a reasonable person would consider satisfactory, taking account of—
>
> (a) any description of the digital content,
>
> (b) the price mentioned in section 33(1) or (2)(b) (if relevant), and
>
> (c) all the other relevant circumstances (see subsection (5)).
>
> (3) The quality of digital content includes its state and condition; and the following aspects (among others) are in appropriate cases aspects of the quality of digital content—
>
> (a) fitness for all the purposes for which digital content of that kind is usually supplied;
>
> (b) freedom from minor defects;
>
> (c) safety;
>
> (d) durability.
>
> (4) The term mentioned in subsection (1) does not cover anything which makes the quality of the digital content unsatisfactory—

[3316] 2015 Act s.42(8).

[3317] 2015 Act s.42(6) and (8) referring to breach of terms to which s.42(2), (4) or (5) apply.

[3318] 2015 Act s.19(14) and (15) above, paras 38-495, 38-496; Consumer Sales Directive 1999 art.5(3).

[3319] 2015 Act s.42(9), which specifies that its provision is for the purposes of s.42(2). As earlier noted, s.42(1) defines non-conformity of the digital content for this purpose as referring to where it is supplied other than in conformity with the statutory terms as to quality, fitness for particular purpose and description set by ss.34, 35 and 36 of the Act: above, para.38-544.

[3320] 2015 Act s.42(10).

[3321] On this category see 2015 Act s.33(1), (2) and (7) and above, paras 38-540—38-541. On the 1979 Act s.14, see below, paras 44-095 et seq.

[3322] 2015 Act s.9, above, para.38-497.

[3323] 1979 Act s.14(2).

> (a)   which is specifically drawn to the consumer's attention before the contract is made,
>
> (b)   where the consumer examines the digital content before the contract is made, which that examination ought to reveal, or
>
> (c)   where the consumer examines a trial version before the contract is made, which would have been apparent on a reasonable examination of the trial version.
>
> (5)   The relevant circumstances mentioned in subsection (2)(c) include any public statement about the specific characteristics of the digital content made by the trader, the producer or any representative of the trader or the producer.
>
> (6)   That includes, in particular, any public statement made in advertising or labelling.
>
> (7)   But a public statement is not a relevant circumstance for the purposes of subsection (2)(c) if the trader shows that—
>
> (a)   when the contract was made, the trader was not, and could not reasonably have been, aware of the statement,
>
> (b)   before the contract was made, the statement had been publicly withdrawn or, to the extent that it contained anything which was incorrect or misleading, it had been publicly corrected, or
>
> (c)   the consumer's decision to contract for the digital content could not have been influenced by the statement.
>
> (8)   In a contract to supply digital content a term about the quality of the digital content may be treated as included as a matter of custom."

Apart from replacement of the references to "goods" with references to "digital content", s.34 omits s.9's reference to "appearance and finish"[3324] as a possible aspect of the quality of digital content (for obvious reasons). Secondly, s.34(4)(c) replaces s.9's provision for the case of a contract to supply goods by sample (to the effect that the statutory term does not cover anything which would have been apparent on a reasonable examination of the sample[3325]), with provision for the case where the consumer examines a "trial version" before the contract is made, to the effect that the statutory term does not cover anything which would have been apparent on a reasonable examination of the trial version. It is to be noted that s.34(5)–(7) also makes public statements relevant to the standard that a reasonable person would consider satisfactory in s.9(5)–(7) which reflects a requirement of the Consumer Sales Directive, even though the Directive itself does not apply to digital content contracts.[3326] In order to achieve a harmonious interpretation between these provisions of the Act in s.9 and s.34, a court would need therefore to follow whatever interpretation were taken by the Court of Justice to the Directive's provisions underlying s.9. In terms of the significance of "satisfactory quality" in the context of digital content contracts, according to the Act's *Explanatory Notes*:

> "… a reasonable person's expectations as to quality are likely to vary according to the nature of the content and some aspects of quality set out in subsection (3) may not be relevant in particular cases. So for example a reasonable person might expect a simple music file to be free from minor defects so that a track which failed to play to the end would not be of satisfactory quality. However, it is the norm to encounter some bugs in a complex game or piece of software on release so a reasonable person might not expect that type of digital content to be free from minor defects. Consequently the application

---

[3324] 2015 Act s.9(3)(b).

[3325] 2015 Act s.9(4)(c).

[3326] 1999 Directive art.1(2)(b) "consumer goods". The provision governing public statements is found in art.2(2)(d) and (4). On these provisions see above, para.38-497.

of the quality aspect 'freedom from minor defects' to digital content will depend on reasonable expectations as to quality."[3327]

Under s.42 of the Act breach of the statutory term in s.34 gives rise in the consumer to the right to repair or replacement and the right to a price reduction, and may also give rise to other remedies under the general law.[3328]

38-547 Digital content to be fit for particular purpose   Section 35 of the 2015 Act makes identical provision for digital content contracts[3329] as s.10 makes for goods contracts,[3330] subject only to the replacement of the latter's references to "goods" with "digital content". As a result, where the consumer makes known to the trader (expressly or by implication) any particular purpose for which the consumer is contracting for the digital content,[3331]

"... the contract is to be treated as including a term that the digital content is reasonably fit for that purpose, whether or not that is a purpose for which digital content of that kind is usually supplied."[3332]

It is provided that this term is not to be included if the circumstances show that the consumer does not rely, or it is unreasonable for the consumer to rely, on the skill or judgment of the trader.[3333] A contract to supply digital content may be treated as making provision about the fitness of the digital content for a particular purpose as a matter of custom.[3334] Under s.42 of the Act breach of a statutory term inserted by s.35 will give rise in the consumer to the right to repair or replacement and the right to a price reduction, and may also give rise to other remedies under the general law.[3335]

38-548 Digital content to be as described   Section 36 of the 2015 Act provides that:

"(1)   Every contract to supply digital content is to be treated as including a term that the digital content will match any description of it given by the trader to the consumer.
(2)   Where the consumer examines a trial version before the contract is made, it is not sufficient that the digital content matches (or is better than) the trial version if the digital content does not also match any description of it given by the trader to the consumer."

It will be noted that s.36 does not use the technical expression of contracting "*by description*" used by s.11's provision governing the statutory term as to the description of goods, which itself reflects the general position under the 1979 Act.[3336] Instead, s.36 stipulates that "any description" of the digital content will form the

---

[3327] *Explanatory Notes* 2015 para.179.
[3328] 2015 Act s.42(1) and (2) on the operation of which, see above, para.38-544. On the consumer's rights and remedies see below, paras 38-557 et seq.
[3329] See the special definition of this category by s.33, above, paras 38-540—38-542.
[3330] See above, para.38-498. cf. Sale of Goods Act 1979 s.14(3), below, paras 44-105 et seq.
[3331] 2015 Act s.35(1).
[3332] 2015 Act s.35(3). Section 35(2) and (4) provide for the application of subs.(3) in the case of sale by a credit-broker to a trader and the consumer makes the particular purpose known to the credit-broker. "Credit-broker" and "credit-brokerage" are defined by s.59(1) of the Act.
[3333] 2015 Act s.35(4).
[3334] 2015 Act s.35(5).
[3335] 2015 Act s.42(1) and (2) on the operation of which, see above, para.38-544. On the consumer's rights and remedies see below, paras 38-557 et seq.
[3336] 2015 Act s.11 (above, para.38-499). On the 1979 Act s.13, see below, paras 44-086—44-087.

basis of the statutory term which it inserts in the contract. Moreover, s.36(2) adapts the parallel provision in s.11(2) of the 2015 Act so as to fit the more inclusive general approach to descriptions taken by s.11(1) and also to replace references to "sample" with references to "trial version", following the precedent set by the Act in relation to the statutory term as to satisfactory quality in s.34.[3337] Section 36 follows the approach earlier set by the Act in relation to goods contracts, by providing that information within some of the categories required to be provided by the trader under the Consumer Contracts (Information, Cancellation and Additional Charges) Regulations 2013[3338] and actually supplied by the trader to the consumer is to be included as a term of the contract.[3339] The categories in question are: "the main characteristics of the ... digital content, to the extent appropriate to the medium of communication and to the ... digital content"; "where applicable, the functionality,[3340] including applicable technical protection measures, of digital content"; and "where applicable, any relevant compatibility of digital content with hardware and software that the trader is aware of or can reasonably be expected to have been aware of".[3341] This reflects the Consumer Rights Directive's requirement that information supplied by the trader as it requires should form an integral part of the consumer contract[3342]; equally, a change to any of that information, made before entering into the contract or later, is not effective unless expressly agreed between the consumer and the trader.[3343] More generally, according to the Act's *Explanatory Notes*:

> "The policy intention is that matching the description should mean that the digital content should at least do what it is described as doing. It is not intended that "matches the description" should mean that the digital content must be exactly the same in every aspect. This section would not, for example prevent the digital content going beyond the description, as long as it also continues to match the description. This is particularly relevant for updates that may enhance features or add new features. As clarified in section 40, as long as the digital content continued to match the original product description and conform to the pre-contractual information provided by the trader, improved or additional features would not breach this right."[3344]

Under s.42 of the Act breach of a statutory term inserted by s.36 gives rise in the consumer to the right to repair or replacement and the right to a price reduction, and

---

[3337] 2015 Act s.34(4)(c), above, para.38-546.

[3338] SI 2013/3134 especially regs 9, 10 and 13 referring to Schs 1 and 2 of the Regulations: see above, paras 38-060 et seq. and especially para.38-105.

[3339] 2015 Act s.36(3)–(4). As earlier noted, similar provision is made for contracts for the supply of digital content other than for a price paid by the consumer (which fall outside the definition of "digital content contract" in s.33, above, paras 38-541—38-544) in the 2013 Regulations themselves: reg.9(3), 10(5) and 13(6).

[3340] 2013 Regulations reg.5 provides that "'functionality' in relation to digital content includes region coding, restrictions incorporated for the purposes of digital rights management, and other technical restrictions".

[3341] 2013 Regulations Sch.1 paras (a), (j) and (k) (on-premises contracts); Sch.2 paras (a), (v) and (w) (off-premises contracts and distance contracts): for the full lists of information in these Schedules see above, paras 38-103 and 38-098 respectively.

[3342] 2011 Directive art.6(5) (though applicable only to off-premises contracts and distance contracts): above, para.38-105.

[3343] 2015 Act s.36(4); 2011 Directive art.6(5) (as regards off-premises contracts and distance contracts): above, para.38-105.

[3344] *Explanatory Notes* 2015 para.185. On 2015 Act s.40, see below, para.38-554.

may also give rise to other remedies under the general law.[3345]

38-549 **Other pre-contract information included in contract** Section 37 of the 2015 Act makes similar provision for digital content contracts as does s.12 for goods contracts,[3346] and provides that where the Consumer Contracts (Information, Cancellation and Additional Charges) Regulations 2013[3347] required the trader to provide to the consumer before the contract became binding information other than about the main characteristics, functionality or compatibility of the digital content (which are dealt with by s.36[3348]), any information that was provided by the trader is to be treated as included as a term of the digital content contract.[3349] The categories of information to which s.37 therefore applies are set out above in relation to the 2013 Regulations themselves.[3350] Section 37 provides that a change to any of that information, made before entering into the contract or later, is not effective unless expressly agreed between the consumer and the trader.[3351] However, breach of the statutory terms foreseen by s.37 of the Act does not give rise to the three rights more widely provided by Ch.3 for consumers, as s.42(4) instead provides that in these circumstances the consumer has the right to recover from the trader:

> "… the amount of any costs incurred by the consumer as a result of the breach, up to the amount of the price paid for the digital content or for any facility[3352] … used by the consumer."[3353]

A consumer may, however, enjoy other remedies (notably, damages) in respect of breach of the statutory term in s.37, with the exception of a right to treat the contract as at an end.[3354]

38-550 **No other requirement to treat term about quality or fitness as included** Section 38(1) provides that a contract to supply digital content is not to be treated as including any term about the quality of the digital content or its fitness for any particular purpose except as the Act itself provides,[3355] unless the term is expressly included in the contract.[3356] Where such an express term is concluded, its breach

---

[3345] 2015 Act s.42(1) and (2) on the operation of which, see above, para.38-544. On the consumer's rights and remedies see below, paras 38-557 et seq.

[3346] Above, para.38-500.

[3347] SI 2013/3134 regs 9, 10 and 13 on which see above, paras 38-061 et seq. and especially 38-096— 38-103. It is to be noted, though, that the scope of the 2013 Regulations is restricted in a number of important respects: see above, paras 38-076—38-078, 38-096.

[3348] Above, para.38-548. The information relevant to s.37 is set out by 2013 Regulations Sch.1 paras (b)– (i) (on-premises contracts); Sch.2 paras (b)–(u) and (x) (off-premises contracts and distance contracts): for the full lists of information in these Schedules see above, paras 38-103 and 38-098 respectively. As earlier noted, similar provision is made for contracts for the supply of digital content other than for a price paid by the consumer (which fall outside the definition of "digital content contract" in s.33, above, para.38-105) in the 2013 Regulations themselves: reg.9(3), 10(5) and 13(6).

[3349] 2015 Act s.37(1)–(3) and cf. above, para.38-105.

[3350] 2013 Regulations Schs 1 and 2, above, paras 38-103 and 38-098.

[3351] 2015 Act s.37(3).

[3352] "Facility" is not defined by the 2015 Act but it is used by s.33(3), on which see above, para.38-541.

[3353] cf. 2015 Act s.19(5) making similar provision as regards "goods contracts", above, para.38-500. For the general scheme of the 2015 Act in relation to the availability of consumer remedies in respect of digital content, see above, para.38-544.

[3354] 2015 Act s.42(6)–(8), below, para.38-562.

[3355] i.e. under 2015 Act ss.34 and 35, above, paras 38-546 and 38-547 respectively.

[3356] 2015 Act s.38(2) provides that the rule in s.38(1) is subject to provision made by any other enact-

may give rise to remedies for breach provided by the general law, apparently even as regards a right to treat the contract as at an end for major breach of contract.[3357] This marks an apparent contrast with the general position under the 2015 Act, which does not allow a consumer to treat a digital content contract as at an end by reason of breach of the statutory terms which it treats as included in the contract.[3358]

Supply by transmission and facilities for continued transmission   Section 39   **38-551** of the 2015 Act makes original provision relating to supply by transmission of the digital content under a digital content contract,[3359] creating, inter alia, a special statutory term regarding a processing facility to which the consumer is granted access.

Time of supply by transmission   First, s.39 provides a special rule as to the time   **38-552** of supply of digital content where it takes place by transmission rather than by supply on a tangible medium, such as a disk. Transmission of this kind could take place, for example, where digital content is bought or used via the internet or through a satellite transmission under an arrangement with an internet service provider or mobile network operator,[3360] and where digital content is supplied in this way, it will usually travel through one or more intermediaries before it reaches the consumer's device.[3361] According to the Act's *Explanatory Notes*:

> "Some of these intermediaries, for example an Internet Service Provider ("ISP"), have been chosen by and are within the contractual control of the consumer. Other intermediaries, however, will be within the contractual control of the trader, or under arrangements initiated by the trader. For example, a supplier of streamed movies (the trader) may contract with a content delivery network who will deliver the data from the trader's server to the ISPs who will then deliver the content to the consumer."[3362]

For these purposes, s.39 provides that where the consumer's access to the content on a device requires its transmission to the device under arrangements initiated by the trader,[3363] the digital content is taken as supplied either when the content reaches the device (for example, directly to a consumer's satellite dish[3364]), or, if earlier, when the content reaches another trader chosen by the consumer to supply (such as an internet service provider[3365]) under a contract with the consumer, a service by which digital content reaches the device.[3366] The result of these intricate provi-

---

ment, whenever passed or made. cf. 2015 Act s.18 above, para.38-505 for the equivalent provision in relation to goods contracts.

[3357] For this right under the general law see Vol.I, Ch.24.

[3358] This follows from the fact that 2015 Act s.42(6)–(8) (which provides for and restricts "other remedies" for the consumer) does not apply to breaches of express terms, but is instead restricted to breaches of the statutory terms foreseen by ss.34, 35, 36, 37 and 41(1) of the Act.

[3359] On the definition of this category of contracts see 2015 Act s.33, above, paras 38-540—38-544.

[3360] *Explanatory Notes* 2015 para.191.

[3361] *Explanatory Notes* 2015 para.192.

[3362] *Explanatory Notes* 2015 para.192.

[3363] While this is specially provided for the purposes of Ch.3, this definitional provision applies only in the circumstances set out by s.39(1) of the 2015 Act: s.39(2).

[3364] *Explanatory Notes* 2015 para.193.

[3365] *Explanatory Notes* 2015 para.193.

[3366] 2015 Act s.39(2). A trader which is in the contractual control of the consumer and which only provides a service by which the digital content reaches the consumer is not providing digital content for the purposes of Ch.3: 2015 Act s.33(4), though may be subject to provision in Ch.4 governing the provision of services: *Explanatory Notes* 2015 para.193.

sions is that where the digital content fails to meet the quality standards set by the statutory terms because of a problem for which the trader (T) or an intermediary in the contractual control of the trader is responsible, then the trader will be liable.[3367] On the other hand, where the digital content fails to meet these quality standards because of a problem with the consumer's device or with the delivery service supplied by an independent trader with whom the consumer has contracted (such as an ISP or mobile network provider), the trader (T) would not be liable "since that trader (T) cannot be at fault in any way for the problem and has no way of rectifying it".[3368]

38-553 Facilities for continued transmission   Secondly, where there is a contract to supply digital content and "after the trader (T) has supplied the digital content, the consumer is to have access under the contract to a processing facility under arrangements made by T",[3369] under s.39(5) of the Act:

> "… [t]he contract is to be treated as including a term that the processing facility (with any feature that the facility is to include under the contract) must be available to the consumer for a reasonable time, unless a time is specified in the contract."[3370]

For these purposes:

> "A processing facility is a facility by which T or another trader will receive digital content from the consumer and transmit digital content to the consumer (whether or not other features are to be included under the contract)."[3371]

As a result, according to the Act's *Explanatory Notes*, these provisions:

> "… apply to digital content where use of the content in line with the contract requires some digital content to be transferred via the internet between the consumer's device and a server (processing facility) operated by or within the contractual control of T. Examples of this type of digital content would be massively multiplayer online games ("MMOs") and software accessed on the Cloud such as a music streaming facility."[3372]

In these circumstances, s.39(5)'s statutory term means that the consumer should be able to use their digital content in the way described for a reasonable time, unless an express term provides a different time.[3373] Finally, the sections of the Act which insert statutory terms in the contract governing the quality, fitness for a particular purpose and description of digital content are applied to all digital content transmitted to the consumer on each occasion under the facility, while it is provided under the contract, as they apply to the digital content first supplied.[3374] Breach of these statutory terms as well as the special statutory term as to access for the consumer to a processing facility foreseen by s.39(5) may give rise to the right to repair or replacement or the right to a price reduction, or other remedies under the general

---

[3367] *Explanatory Notes* 2015 para.194.
[3368] *Explanatory Notes* 2015 para.194 and see further Krebs (2017) J.B.L. 376.
[3369] 2015 Act s.39(3).
[3370] 2015 Act s.39(5).
[3371] 2015 Act s.39(4).
[3372] *Explanatory Notes* para.195.
[3373] *Explanatory Notes* para.195.
[3374] 2015 Act s.39(6) referring to ss.34, 35 and 36, on which see above, paras 38-546, 38-547 and 38-548 respectively.

law, except a right to treat the contract as at an end.[3375]

Quality, fitness and description of content supplied subject to modifica- **38-554**
tion According to the Act's *Explanatory Notes*, s.40 of the 2015 Act:

> "... reflects a unique issue for digital content in that manufacturers and traders are techni-
> cally able to change or update digital content after the initial provision of the digital
> content. This may be set out in the terms and conditions of the licence. In the majority of
> cases, this is to the benefit of consumers and often includes important updates to the digital
> content. Requiring consent for every update would create problems for business, both due
> to the logistics of contacting every consumer and getting their consent and the problems
> that would arise when some consumers do not accept updates, thus resulting in many dif-
> ferent versions of software in circulation and unnecessary disputes with consumers when
> digital content stops working due to lack of updates."[3376]

Section 40 therefore allows a contract to provide that a trader or a third party (such
as the digital content manufacturer) may update digital content, as long as the
contract stated that such updates would be supplied and as long as the term by which
it does so is not unfair within the meaning of Pt 2 of the 2015 Act.[3377] Accordingly,
s.40(1) first provides that, where under a contract a trader supplies digital content
to a consumer subject to the right of the trader or a third party to modify the digital
content, the Act's provisions inserting statutory terms as to satisfactory quality, fitness for a particular purpose and description of the digital content "apply in relation to the digital content as modified as they apply in relation to the digital content
as supplied under the contract".[3378] However, as regards any description of the
digital content, this

> "... does not prevent the trader from improving the features of, or adding new features
> to, the digital content, as long as—
>
> (a) the digital content continues to match the description of it given by the trader to
> the consumer, and
> (b) the digital content continues to conform to the information provided by the trader
> as mentioned in subsection (3) of section 36, subject to any change to that
> information that has been agreed in accordance with subsection (4) of that
> section." [3379]

The references to s.36(3) and (4) here concern the information as to the main
characteristics, functionality and compatibility of the digital content which is
required to be provided and is in fact provided by the trader under the Consumer
Contracts (Information, Cancellation and Additional Charges) Regulations 2013.[3380]
For these purposes, the presumption of non-conformity applicable to the rights arising from breach of the statutory terms governing the quality, fitness for particular
purpose and description of digital content generally does not apply to cases

---

[3375] 2015 Act s.39(7) and s.42(1), (6)–(8) and see below, paras 38-557 et seq.
[3376] *Explanatory Notes* 2015 para.196.
[3377] i.e. 2015 Act s.62 on which see above, paras 38-389 et seq.
[3378] 2015 Act s.40(1) referring to ss.34, 35 and 36 on which see above, paras 38-546, 38-547 and 38-
548 respectively.
[3379] 2015 Act s.40(2).
[3380] SI 2013/3134 regs 9, 10 and 13 and see above, paras 38-060 et seq., especially 38-096—38-103 (for
the information requirements) and above, para.38-548 (on s.36 of the 2015 Act).

governed by s.40 and so as regards these cases the consumer must establish the failures of the digital content as provided for by s.40.[3381] Finally, a claim on the grounds that digital content does not conform to a statutory term concerning satisfactory quality, fitness for particular purpose or description as applied by s.40(1) to digital content which has later been modified "is to be treated as arising at the time when the digital content was supplied under the contract and not the time when it is modified".[3382] This therefore means that any claim for breach must be brought within six years of the date when the digital content was first supplied, rather than at the date when the modification took place.[3383]

38-555 **Trader's right to supply digital content** Section 41 of the 2015 Act provides for a new statutory term to be included in contracts to supply digital content that the trader has the right to supply the digital content, mirroring the terms provided for goods contracts, but reflecting the fact that under many digital content contracts the trader does not agree to transfer to the consumer any property rights (such as intellectual property rights to the digital content).[3384] Section 41(1) therefore provides that:

> "Every contract to supply digital content is to be treated as including a term—
>
> (a) in relation to any digital content which is supplied under the contract and which the consumer has paid for, that the trader has the right to supply that content to the consumer;
>
> (b) in relation to any digital content which the trader agrees to supply under the contract and which the consumer has paid for, that the trader will have the right to supply it to the consumer at the time when it is to be supplied."[3385]

While, as has been explained, in Ch.3 generally "contract to supply digital content" includes not merely contracts where the content is supplied for a price paid by the consumer, but also where it is supplied free with goods, services or other digital content for which the consumer does pay a price and where it is not generally available without payment of a price,[3386] s.41(1) subjects the insertion of the statutory terms as to the trader's right to supply to the condition that the digital content was paid for by the consumer. Where s.41(1) applies, the statutory term as to the trader's right to supply concerns both digital content supplied under the contract itself and to digital content which the trader *agrees* to supply under the contract, for example, by way of later modification.

38-556 **Special refund remedy for breach** As earlier noted, breach of the statutory term that the trader has the right to supply digital content provided by s.41(1) of the 2015

[3381] This follows from the restricted terms of s.42's provisions governing the presumption of non-conformity. So, s.42(9) applies the presumption only for the purposes of s.42(2), which refers to the consumer's rights arising from "non-conformity" as defined by s.42(2), i.e. where the digital content does not conform to the statutory terms in ss.34, 35 and 36. On the presumption of non-conformity, see above, para.38-545.

[3382] 2015 Act s.40(3).

[3383] This follows from s.5 of the Limitation Act 1980's provision that the action under a simple contract "shall not be brought after the expiration of six years from the date on which the cause of action accrued", on which see Vol.I, para.28-002 and paras 28-031 et seq.

[3384] *Explanatory Notes* 2015 paras 199–200.

[3385] 2015 Act s.41(1).

[3386] For the definition of this category see 2015 Act s.33, above, paras 38-540—38-542.

Act gives rise to a special right in the consumer to a refund provided by s.45.[3387] This right reflects the idea that digital content cannot be returned and, therefore, the consumer must not have a right of rejection.[3388] Under s.45, this special right "gives the consumer the right to receive a refund from the trader of all money paid by the consumer for the digital content",[3389] unless "the breach giving the consumer the right to a refund affects only some of the digital content supplied under the contract" in which case, "the right to a refund does not extend to any part of the price attributable to digital content that is not affected by the breach".[3390] In keeping with other provisions in the 2015 Act governing refunds,[3391] s.45 provides that a refund must be given without undue delay, and in any event within 14 days beginning with the day on which the trader agrees that the consumer is entitled to a refund; it must be given using the same means of payment as the consumer used to pay for the digital content, unless the consumer expressly agrees otherwise; and the trader must not impose any fee on the consumer in respect of the refund.[3392]

(cc)   The Scheme of Remedies for the Consumer

Special rights for the consumer   It has been seen that the Act provides the   **38-557**
consumer with a special right to a refund by s.45 of the 2015 Act for breach of the statutory term as to the trader's right to supply the digital content[3393] and a very limited right to recover the amount of any costs incurred in respect of breach of the statutory term as to information contained in s.37 of the Act.[3394] More generally, s.42 provides that, where the trader has committed a breach of a statutory term as to the satisfactory quality, fitness for a particular purpose or description of the digital content as provided by ss.33, 34 and 36 of the Act, the consumer has a right of repair or replacement (under s.43) and a right to a price reduction (under s.44).[3395] The Act acknowledges that the consumer may also enjoy a remedy for breach of one of these statutory terms under the general law.[3396]

First level of remedies: right to repair or replacement   Much of s.43's provi-   **38-558**
sion for the right to repair or replacement of digital content under digital content contracts follows word for word s.23's provision for the right to repair or replacement of goods under goods contracts,[3397] with the exception that "digital content" is substituted for "goods".[3398] Under goods contracts, these rights to corrective performance in the consumer[3399] implement in UK law the Consumer Sales Direc-

---

[3387] 2015 Act s.42(5). cf. below, para.38-559 for the more general situation where a consumer may be able to obtain a partial or even full refund by way of price reduction under s.44 of the Act.
[3388] See below, para.38-561.
[3389] 2015 Act s.45(1).
[3390] 2015 Act s.45(2).
[3391] Notably, s.20(15)–(17) (refund under goods contracts), above, para.38-514. Similarly, s.44(4)–(6) (refund as a result of price reduction in relation to digital content contract), below, para.38-559.
[3392] 2015 Act s.45(3)–(5).
[3393] Above, para.38-556.
[3394] Above, para.38-549.
[3395] 2015 Act s.42(1)–(2), above, para.38-544. On these rights see below, paras 38-558 and 38-559 respectively.
[3396] 2015 Act s.42(6)–(8), below, para.38-562.
[3397] On which see above, para.38-517.
[3398] This is true of s.43(1)–(4).
[3399] Above, para.38-517; Whittaker (2017) 133 L.Q.R. 47 at 61–63.

tive 1999,[3400] and while the Directive's requirements do not extend to contracts for the supply of digital content other than where supplied as part of a "tangible movable item",[3401] an English court is likely to interpret the provisions of s.43 which use the same words as s.23 in a harmonious way, and the latter must "wherever possible" be interpreted so as to conform the Directive's requirements.[3402] Section 43(2)–(4) of the 2015 Act provide that:

"(2)   If the consumer requires the trader to repair[3403] or replace the digital content, the trader must—

    (a)   do so within a reasonable time and without significant inconvenience to the consumer; and

    (b)   bear any necessary costs incurred in doing so (including in particular the cost of any labour, materials or postage).

(3)   The consumer cannot require the trader to repair or replace the digital content if that remedy (the repair or the replacement)—

    (a)   is impossible, or

    (b)   is disproportionate compared to the other of those remedies.

(4)   Either of those remedies is disproportionate compared to the other if it imposes costs on the trader which, compared to those imposed by the other, are unreasonable, taking into account—

    (a)   the value which the digital content would have if it conformed to the contract,

    (b)   the significance of the lack of conformity, and

    (c)   whether the other remedy could be effected without significant inconvenience to the consumer."

However, in certain respects s.43 amends the scheme foreshadowed by s.23, and the differences in the contexts of s.23 and s.43 may also require differences in interpretation. So, s.43(5) provides that:

"(5)   Any question as to what is a reasonable time or significant inconvenience is to be determined taking account of—

    (a)   the nature of the digital content, and

    (b)   the purpose for which the digital content was obtained or accessed."

This differs from the parallel provision governing goods contracts,[3404] in that it refers to the purpose for which the digital contained was "obtained or accessed" rather than, under s.23(5) "for which the goods were acquired". This reflects the fact that Ch.3's statutory terms governing the quality, etc. of digital content may apply not merely to digital content acquired under the contract to supply digital content, but also to digital content which is later supplied or accessed.[3405] Moreover, s.43's provisions require the consumer to give the trader time to perform repairs or, as the case may be, to replace the digital content (unless giving the trader that time would cause significant inconvenience to the consumer) and so relate only to these two rights,

---

[3400] 1999 Directive art.3(2) and (3), above, para.38-433.

[3401] 1999 Directive art.1(2)(b) "consumer goods".

[3402] Above, para.38-014.

[3403] 2015 Act s.43(8) provides that in Ch.3 "'repair' in relation to digital content that does not conform to a contract, means making it conform". It is therefore distinct from an update of digital content to which s.40 of the Act applies: on s.40 see above, para.38-554.

[3404] Above, para.38-517.

[3405] See above, para.38-553 in relation to s.39 of the 2015 Act.

unlike s.23's equivalent provisions which relate also to the consumer's short-term right to reject the goods: this follows from the absence of any provision for the consumer to reject digital content, either under a short-term or a final right of rejection.[3406] However, unlike the position applicable to "goods contracts", where the consumer has the right to a reduction in price if the goods do not conform to the contract after one repair or replacement by the trader,[3407] the consumer will not necessarily have the right to a reduction of price after requiring repair or replacement of digital content under s.43 even though the digital content still does not conform to the contract, but will do so only if the consumer has required the trader to repair or replace the digital content and the trader has not done so within a reasonable time and without significant inconvenience to the consumer.[3408] This difference reflects the fact that it is the nature of some forms of digital content (such as games) that they may contain a few "bugs" on release, which may require multiple fixing by the trader.[3409]

Second level of remedy: right to price reduction   Section 44 of the 2015 Act   **38-559** provides for a right to price reduction for a consumer in respect of digital content which has failed to conform to the statutory terms as to quality, etc. which the Act itself provides.[3410] While to an extent this remedy reflects the pattern established by the Act for consumers in relation to "goods contracts" which implements the Consumer Sales Directive 1999,[3411] s.44 does not couple the right to price reduction with any right to reject the digital content or to rescind or otherwise terminate the contract. Under s.44(1)–(3):

> "(1)   The right to a price reduction is the right to require the trader to reduce the price to the consumer by an appropriate amount (including the right to receive a refund for anything already paid above the reduced amount).
> (2)   The amount of the reduction may, where appropriate, be the full amount of the price.
> (3)   A consumer who has that right may only exercise it in one of these situations—
>> (a)   because of section 43(3)(a) the consumer can require neither repair nor replacement of the digital content, or
>> (b)   the consumer has required the trader to repair or replace the digital content, but the trader is in breach of the requirement of section 43(2)(a) to do so within a reasonable time and without significant inconvenience to the consumer."

Thus, in common with the position as regards the consumer's right to a price reduction or final right to reject in respect of goods,[3412] the consumer's right to a price reduction in respect of digital content applies only at a second level, where the first level remedies of repair or replacement are either not available or the trader has failed to perform them within a reasonable time and without significant inconvenience to the consumer, though the details of the circumstances differ.[3413] On the other

---

[3406] 2015 Act s.43(6) and (7), below, para.38-561.
[3407] 2015 Act s.24(5)(a), above, para.38-518.
[3408] 2015 Act s.44(3)(b), below, para.38-559.
[3409] *Explanatory Notes* 2015 para.204.
[3410] 2015 Act s.42(1) and (2).
[3411] 2015 Act s.24; 1999 Directive art.3(5), above, paras 38-433, 38-518—38-519.
[3412] 2015 Act s.24(5), above, para.38-518.
[3413] The legislative expression here is odd, as s.44(3) does not say that the consumer has a right to a price reduction in these circumstances, but rather that the consumer may only exercise such a right in these

hand, where a consumer has a right to a price reduction, is entitled to exercise it and does exercise it, in common with other provisions in the Act, any refund must be given without undue delay, and in any event within 14 days beginning with the day on which the trader agrees that the consumer is entitled to a refund, using the same means of payment as the consumer used to pay for the digital content, unless the consumer expressly agrees otherwise, and the trader must not impose any fee on the consumer in respect of the refund.[3414]

38-560 Discretion as to appropriate remedy Section 58 of the 2015 Act provides that in any proceedings in which one of the three special remedies provided for consumers by Ch.3[3415] is sought, the court enjoys two additional powers. First, on the application of the consumer, the court may make an order requiring specific performance by the trader of any obligation imposed on the trader in respect of repair or replacement of the digital content.[3416] Secondly, where a consumer claims the right to repair or replacement or the right to a price reduction (termed the "relevant remedies" by s.58), but the court decides that the provisions governing these rights "have the effect that exercise of another of these rights is appropriate", "the court may proceed as if the consumer had exercised that other right".[3417] The court may make an order under s.58 unconditionally or on such terms and conditions as to damages, payment of the price and otherwise as it thinks just.[3418] These powers do not extend to the "other remedies" for consumers as this is understood by the Act and as explained in a later paragraph.[3419]

38-561 No right to reject digital content for breach of the statutory terms Before publication of the Consumer Rights Bill, the Government consulted on the question whether future legislation should include within the new rights for consumers in respect of failures of quality, etc. in digital content a right to reject the digital content (with full refund) modelled on what became the short-term right to reject goods.[3420] The Government considered that the "unique nature of digital content means that this is not a straightforward decision", as

> "… the concept of returning goods does not easily transfer to digital content since copies could be retained and any attempt to return the digital content to the trader could in fact result in another copy of digital content."[3421]

As enacted, the 2015 Act makes no provision for a right to reject digital content with a full refund, though, as has been seen, its provisions governing price reduction may in an appropriate case lead to a full refund.[3422] On the other hand, as earlier noted, in principle the 2015 Act does not prevent a consumer from treating the contract

---

circumstances.

[3414] 2015 Act s.44(4)–(6).

[3415] 2015 Act s.58(1), referring to s.42(2): the right to repair or replacement (under s.43) and the right to a price reduction (under s.44) (which are the "relevant remedies" under s.58(8)(b)).

[3416] 2015 Act s.58(2) referring to s.43 of the Act, above, para.38-558.

[3417] 2015 Act s.58(3) and (4).

[3418] 2015 Act s.58(7).

[3419] Below, para.38-562.

[3420] BIS, *Enhancing Consumer Confidence by Clarifying Consumer Law* (July 2012) ("BIS, Clarifying Consumer Law"), paras 7.137 et seq. which summarise the arguments for and against.

[3421] BIS, Clarifying Consumer Law, para.7.138.

[3422] 2015 Act s.44(2), above, para.38-559.

as at an end under the general law on the ground of breach of an *express* term as to the quality, etc. of the goods, and while this would lead to a refund of money paid by the consumer only if the consumer established a total failure of consideration, the consumer would be entitled to damages for non-performance of the contract as a whole, any value the consumer has retained being deducted.[3423] Of more practical importance, perhaps, may be the consumer's admittedly very short-lived right to cancel a contract under which digital content is supplied under the Consumer Contracts (Information, Cancellation and Additional Charges) Regulations 2013, not least because this right is not subject to establishing that the digital content was in any sense faulty.[3424]

Other remedies in respect of breach of the statutory terms The 2015 Act   **38-562**
acknowledges that, in principle, its provision of special rights for consumers under Pt 1 Ch.3 does not prevent them seeking other remedies in respect of breach of the statutory terms as to satisfactory quality, fitness for particular purpose, description, information supplied and the trader's right to supply.[3425] In this respect, and depending on the circumstances, these other remedies may include damages, seeking to recover money paid where the consideration for payment of the money has failed, and seeking specific performance or relying on the breach against a claim by the trader for the price[3426]; the conditions and characteristics of these remedies are found in the law applicable to contracts generally.[3427] However, the Act does not allow a consumer faced with breach of one of the statutory terms to treat the contract as at an end even if the general law would otherwise so allow,[3428] following its general refusal to provide a right of rejection of digital content to which such a right to treat the contract as at an end would be connected.[3429]

(dd)   Compensation for Damage to Device

Consumer Rights Act 2015 s.46   Under s.46 of the 2015 Act, where a trader sup-   **38-563**
plies digital content to a consumer under a contract and the digital content causes damage to a device or to other digital content which belongs to the consumer and "the damage is of a kind that would not have occurred if the trader had exercised reasonable care and skill", the consumer may require the trader either to repair the damage or compensate the consumer for the damage with an appropriate

---

[3423] See Vol.I, Ch.24 and especially para.24-052 and see also paras 29-057—29-067 (referring to "failure of basis"). The *possibility* of such a right of termination of the contract is allowed by the fact that the provisions in s.42(6)–(8) governing "other remedies" and preventing the consumer from treating the contract as at an end are restricted to breach of the statutory terms in ss.34–37 and 41(1) of the 2015 Act.

[3424] SI 2013/3134 and see above, paras 38-061 et seq. and 38-112 et seq.

[3425] 2015 Act s.42(6) referring to s.42(2), (4) and (5).

[3426] 2015 Act s.42(7)(a), (b), (c) and (e) respectively.

[3427] See Vol.I, Ch.26 (damages), Ch.27 (specific performance and injunction) and paras 21-028—21-039 on the question whether a party to a contract may rely on the other party's breach in resisting the latter's claim for the price. In the case of recover of money paid, the general condition at common law is that the injured party (the consumer) has to establish a total failure of consideration (or basis) and this would apparently always be impossible in the context of the supply of digital content since it requires that the contract is discharged, which s.42(8) forbids: for discussion of the requirement generally see Vol.I, paras 29-057 et seq.

[3428] 2015 Act s.42(8).

[3429] See above, para.38-561.

payment.[3430] For this purpose, any repair by the trader must be done within a reasonable time and without significant inconvenience to the consumer, and at the trader's cost.[3431] The consumer may bring civil proceedings to enforce any right under s.46 and such a claim is treated as an action founded on simple contract for the purposes of limitation of actions.[3432] According to the Act's *Explanatory Notes* the intention behind s.46 is "to engage the principles behind a negligence claim but limit the type of loss that can be claimed",[3433] so as to create a remedy for the case, for example, where a consumer downloads software that contains a virus which causes loss or damage to the consumer's device or to other digital content.[3434] For this purpose, however, it is by no means clear that a claim in the tort of negligence would exist, for no duty of care has been recognised by the courts in this context and in the case of damage to other digital content, it would be a nice question whether this would constitute damage to property or pure economic loss.[3435] This supplements any remedy which the consumer may enjoy where a consumer can establish that a breach of a statutory term (either in a goods contract in which digital content is supplied or in a digital content contract) has caused the damage.[3436] Section 46 is an innovatory provision in a number of ways. First, while the consumer's remedies require proof of a causal link between the digital content supplied by a trader under a contract and damage to the consumer's "property" (whether this is a device or digital content), they do not require proof that this damage was caused by the negligence of the trader supplying it; instead, the consumer's remedies arise where "the damage is of a kind that would not have occurred if the trader had exercised reasonable care and skill", which appears to be at most a statutory expression of res ipsa loquitur as to the trader's negligence. Secondly, the consumer's remedies pick up the Act's more general recourse to a right of repair, though here the trader may be required to repair something (whether a device or digital content) which it did not itself supply under the contract. However, the trader is permitted to opt to pay compensation instead of repairing. Thirdly, while the *Explanatory Notes* to s.46 compare the position under a "negligence claim", the consumer's remedies under s.46 arise only where digital content is supplied by a trader to a consumer under a

---

[3430] 2015 Act s.46(1)–(2). The compensation payment must be made without undue delay, and in any event within 14 days beginning with the day on which the trader agrees that the consumer is entitled to the payment; and the trader must not impose any fee on the consumer in respect of the payment: s.46(5) and (6).

[3431] 2015 Act s.46(3), subs.(b) of which specifies that these necessary costs include in particular the cost of any labour, materials or postage. Section 46(4) provides that: "any question as to what is a reasonable time or significant inconvenience is to be determined taking account of (a) the nature of the device or digital content that is damaged, and (b) the purpose for which it is used by the consumer".

[3432] 2015 Act s.46(8) and see especially Limitation Act 1980 s.5 and Vol.I, paras 28-031 et seq.

[3433] *Explanatory Notes* 2015 para.219.

[3434] *Explanatory Notes* 2015 para.219.

[3435] On the case-law surrounding recovery of pure economic loss in the tort of negligence see *Clerk and Lindsell on Torts*, 22nd edn (2017), paras 1-44 and 9-97 et seq. There would also be difficulties facing a consumer claiming that "digital content" supplied would itself constitute a "defective product" for the purposes of the statutory product liability in Pt 1 of the Consumer Protection Act 1987 as it is by no means clear that a "product" for this purpose includes non-physical property apart from electricity: see 1987 Act s.1(1), *Clerk and Lindsell on Torts*, paras 11-49—11-51 and Whittaker (1989) 105 L.Q.R. 125.

[3436] The relevant provisions of the 2015 Act are found in ss.9–11, 16 (goods contracts) and ss.34–36 (digital content contracts). Liability in damages under the general law for breach of the statutory terms inserted by these provisions is foreseen by s.19(9)–(10), and (11)(a) (goods contracts) and s.42(6) and (7)(a) (digital content contracts).

contract, and the consumer's claim is subjected to the general *contractual* period of limitation.

(ee) Exclusion of Liability and Enforcement

Exclusion of liability   Section 47 provides an almost identical pattern of control   **38-564**
of any attempted exclusion or restriction of liability as the Act earlier makes as regards the exclusion of the trader's liabilities under goods contracts, rendering such terms "not binding on the consumer to the extent that [the term] would exclude or restrict the trader's liability" arising under the provisions which insert statutory terms relating to the satisfactory quality, fitness for particular purpose, description, other pre-contractual information and trader's right to supply.[3437] Section 47 makes identical provision for this purpose as the Act earlier makes as regards goods contracts in relation to the meaning of excluding or restricting liability which is modelled on s.13 of the Unfair Contract Terms Act 1977.[3438] The exception to this pattern is that a trader's liabilities arising under s.46 in relation to damage to a device or other digital content caused by digital content may be excluded or restricted to the extent that it would satisfy the controls on unfair terms in consumer contracts generally in Pt 2 of the 2015 Act.[3439]

Choice of law   Unlike the position in relation to "goods contracts" in Pt 1 Ch.2[3440]   **38-565**
and the controls on unfair terms in Pt 2 of the 2015 Act,[3441] Ch.3 of the Act makes no special provision as regards the effect of choice of law on the protections for consumers which it sets out. This reflects the fact that, unlike these earlier provisions,[3442] Ch.3's provisions are not required by EU legislation which itself sets out a special rule on the effect of choice of law. This means that the effect of any choice of law falls to be governed under the general private international law rules applicable and, in particular, the Rome I Regulation on the law applicable to contractual obligations.[3443]

Enforcement   Section 47(5) of the 2015 Act provides that a regulator may enforce   **38-566**
s.47's provisions rendering terms seeking to exclude the trader's liability not binding on a consumer under the scheme of enforcement which the Act provides generally for the control of unfair contract terms.[3444] This scheme has been described

---

[3437] 2015 Act s.47(1) referring to ss.34–37 and 41 of the Act. In one respect, the controls differ, as s.47 renders terms seeking to exclude the trader's liability in respect of breach of s.41 (trader's right to supply digital content) not binding on the consumer in all circumstances, whereas the controls in s.31 on the exclusion of the trader's liability in respect of breach of s.17 (trader's right to supply the goods, etc.) under a contract of hire is subject to a test of fairness: 2015 Act s.31(5)–(6). On the controls on the exclusion of the trader's liabilities under "goods contracts" see 2015 Act s.31 and above, para.38-531.

[3438] 2015 Act s.47(2)–(4). cf. 2015 Act s.31(2)–(4) as explained above, para.38-531.

[3439] 2015 Act s.47(6) and see 2015 Act s.62 and above, paras 38-389 et seq.

[3440] 2015 Act s.32 (implementing Consumer Sales Directive 1999 art.7(2)), above, para.38-533.

[3441] 2015 Act s.74 (implementing Unfair Terms in Consumer Contracts Directive 1993 art.6(2)) above, para.38-418.

[3442] See above, para.38-533 (notes).

[3443] Regulation (EC) 593/2008 of the European Parliament and of the Council of 17 June 2008 on the law applicable to contractual obligations ("Rome I") [2008] O.J. L177/6 on which generally see Vol.I, paras 30-019 et seq.

[3444] 2015 Act Sch.3.

earlier, as have the difficulties of its use in relation to commercial practices which consist of the use or recommendation for use of terms in ways which do not reflect EU legislative requirements.[3445] In the case of digital content contracts, as has earlier been noted, Ch.3 of the 2015 Act does not implement any EU legislation (though some of its provisions are modelled on the Consumer Sales Directive beyond the latter's scope[3446]), with the exception of certain provisions implementing the Consumer Rights Directive 2011.[3447] As a result, the relevant provisions in Ch.3 of Pt 1 of the 2015 Act which implement the 2011 Directive or which "provide additional permitted protections"[3448] have been designated as specified UK laws for the purposes of s.212 of the 2002 Act.[3449] In addition, acts or omissions in respect of any provision in Pt 1 of the 2015 Act are specified as possible "domestic infringements" for the purposes of s.211 of the Enterprise Act 2002.[3450]

(v) Services Contracts

(aa) Introduction

38-567 **Background** The general motivations for the inclusion of provisions in Pt 1 of the Consumer Rights Act 2015 governing "services contracts"[3451] reflects long-standing concerns in the Law Commission and in government that English law's treatment of these contracts in the context of consumer-contracting was piecemeal and incomplete. The main provisions applicable were those governing "contracts for the supply of a service" put in place by the Supply of Goods and Services Act 1982 (the "1982 Act") applicable irrespective of the status of the contracting parties. To a considerable extent, the new provisions in Pt 1 Ch.4 of the 2015 Act which apply to contracts "for a trader to supply a service to a consumer" or "services contracts", reflect the earlier provisions in the 1982 Act (with some change of wording), but Ch.4 makes new provision for the contractual status of information supplied by the trader to the consumer (whether or not it was required to be supplied under the Consumer Contracts (Information, Cancellation and Additional Charges) Regulations 2013 ("2013 Regulations"),[3452] for new special remedies for the consumer if the trader breaches the statutory terms which it creates (being the "right

---

[3445] See above, paras 38-419 et seq.

[3446] Above, paras 38-546 (statutory term as to satisfactory quality) and paras 38-558—38-559 (special remedies for consumer).

[3447] 2011 Directive art.6(5) in relation to s.36(3)–(4) and s.37, as explained above, paras 38-548 and 38-549. As earlier noted in para.38-410 (note), the 2011 Directive art.25 renders all its provisions "imperative" and so incapable of exclusion by agreement in all circumstances.

[3448] Enterprise Act 2002 s.212(1)(b).

[3449] Enterprise Act 2002 s.212(3); Enterprise Act 2002 (Part 8 EU Infringements) Order 2014 (SI 2014/2908) art.4; Sch. (as amended by the Enterprise Act 2002 (Part 8 Community Infringements and Specified UK Laws) (Amendment) Order 2015 (SI 2015/1628) art.3(2)) listing, inter alia, 2015 Act ss.36(3)–(4), 37, 38 and 42.

[3450] Enterprise Act 2002 s.211(2); Enterprise Act 2002 (Part 8 Domestic Infringements) Order 2015 (SI 2015/1727) art.2.

[3451] The 2015 Act's substantive provisions on "services contracts" generally came into force on October 1, 2015, but an exception was made as regards certain categories of "consumer transport service" which came into force on October 1, 2016 as noted above, para.38-437 and below para.38-568 (note).

[3452] 2015 Act s.50. On the 2013 Regulations generally, see above, paras 38-061 et seq.

to repeat performance" and the right to a price reduction)[3453] and dedicated and original controls on the exclusion by agreement of liability in the trader.[3454]

No statutory definition of "services contracts"   Ch.4 of the 2015 Act applies to **38-568** "a contract for a trader to supply a service to a consumer" which it terms a "contract to supply a service"[3455] or (in its headings) "services contracts", the last name being used in the following paragraphs. Apart from the fact that this makes clear that Ch.4 does not apply to contracts for services to be supplied by a consumer to a trader,[3456] the only further clarification given is that the Act states that this "does not include a contract of employment or apprenticeship".[3457] In these respects, Ch.4 follows the precedent set by the 1982 Act,[3458] and, as a result, the understanding of the contracts to be governed by Ch.4's provisions will fall to be decided, at least in part, by reference to the traditional distinction between contracts for services and contracts of employment (sometimes called contract of service).[3459] This leaves a very wide range of contracts within the scope of Ch.4's provisions.[3460] In particular, the government clearly assumed that "contracts for services" included contracts of transport, as it delayed the coming into force of Ch.4 in relation to certain categories of "consumer transport services".[3461] Moreover, it must be recalled that the 2015 Act specifically provides that each of Chs 2 to 4 can apply even if the contract covers something covered by another chapter of Pt 1.[3462] The 2015 Act amended the 1982 Act so that the contracts to which Ch.4 applies are no longer governed by the relevant provisions of the 1982 Act.[3463]

Limited EU legislative background   In general, the provisions of Ch.4 of Pt 1 **38-569** of the 2015 Act do not implement EU legislation, but an exception to this position is found in relation to s.50, which provides that information required to be supplied by the trader to the consumer under the 2013 Regulations is to be treated as a term of the contract: this implements a particular aspect of the Consumer Rights Directive 2011.[3464]

[3453] 2015 Act s.54–56.
[3454] 2015 Act s.57.
[3455] 2015 Act s.48(4).
[3456] The definitions of "consumer" and "trader" in s.2(2)–(7) of the 2015 Act apply. On these see above, paras 38-384 and 38-383 respectively.
[3457] 2015 Act s.48(2).
[3458] 1982 Act s.12(1) and (2).
[3459] See below, paras 40-002, 40-005, 40-010 et seq.
[3460] In common with the 1982 Act s.12(4)–(5), s.48(5)–(8) of the 2015 Act empowers the Secretary of State to provide by Order that a provision within Ch.4 does not apply in relation to a service of a description specified in the order.
[3461] The Consumer Rights Act 2015 (Commencement No.3, Transitional Provisions, Savings and Consequential Amendments) Order 2015 (SI 2015/1630) arts 4 and 6(2) as amended by the Consumer Rights Act 2015 (Commencement No.3, Transitional Provisions, Savings and Consequential Amendments) (Amendment) Order 2016 (SI 2016/484) art.2, and see above, para.38-437.
[3462] 2015 Act s.1(4)–(5) referring to these as "mixed contracts": above, para.38-484. The 2015 Act therefore omits provision similar to s.12(3) of the 1982 Act which includes within the definition of contract for the supply of a service a contract whether or not goods are also to be transferred or bailed by way of hire under the contract.
[3463] 2015 Act s.60, Sch.1 paras 37–38 and 51 amending, notably, s.12 of the 1982 Act.
[3464] 2011 Directive art.6(5) on which see above para.38-105 and on s.50 of the 2015 Act see below, para.38-575.

(bb)   The Statutory Terms

38-570   **The relationship between the statutory terms, non-conformity of the service to the contract and the consumer's remedies**   Following the legislative pattern set by Pt 1's provision governing goods and digital content,[3465] the 2015 Act makes special provision as to how breach of the statutory terms which it inserts into contracts for a trader to supply services to a consumer relates to the scheme of remedies for the consumer which it sets out. For this purpose, s.54(2) of the Act defines "a service conforming to a contract"[3466] as a reference to:

> "(a)   the service being performed in accordance with section 49, or
> (b)   the service conforming to a term that section 50 requires to be treated as included in the contract and that relates to the performance of the service.[3467]"

As will be seen, s.49 inserts into the contract a statutory term that the service is to be performed with reasonable care and skill,[3468] and s.50 makes original provision according to which "anything that is said or written to the consumer" by the trader "about the trader or about the service" may (subject to the conditions there specified) become a term of the contract and any information provided by the trader as required by the 2013 Regulations will become a term of the contract.[3469] In this respect, s.54(2)(b)'s definition of "a service conforming to a contract" is therefore restricted: it does not include breaches of all the terms treated as included by s.50, but is limited to those where the term (and therefore the information) "relates to the performance of the service". Where the service does not conform to the contract in the special sense just outlined, the consumer has a "right to require repeat performance" and the right to a price reduction, subject to the conditions and qualifications on the availability on these rights which are later set out.[3470] On the other hand, where the trader is in breach of a statutory term required by s.50 which does *not* relate to the service or is in breach of the statutory term requiring the trader to perform within a reasonable time inserted by s.52, then, the consumer has a special right only to a price reduction.[3471] In keeping with its approach to the remedies available to the consumer under Chs 2 and 3 in relation to goods contracts and digital content contracts,[3472] s.54 of the Act also provides that it does not prevent a consumer seeking "other remedies" under the general law for a breach of the statutory terms imposing duties on the trader under Ch.4, though, unlike the earlier provisions, it includes within these other remedies a right to treat the contract as at an end.[3473]

[3465] 2015 Act s.19 (goods contracts) and s.42 (digital content contracts), above, paras 38-493 and 38-544 respectively.

[3466] This definition is stated as being for the purposes of the relevant provisions, i.e. ss.54 and 55 of the Act.

[3467] 2015 Act s.54(2).

[3468] Below, para.38-571.

[3469] 2015 Act s.50(1)–(3), below, paras 38-572—38-576.

[3470] 2015 Act ss.54(3), 55 and 56 and see below, paras 38-580—38-583.

[3471] 2015 Act ss.54(4) and (5), 56 and see below, para.38-582.

[3472] 2015 Act s.19(9)–(13) and s.42(6)–(8) on which see above, paras 38-523 and 38-562 respectively.

[3473] 2015 Act s.54(6)–(7). The restriction to statutory terms imposing duties on the trader follows from the restriction in s.54(6) to breach of terms to which subs.(3)–(5) apply and these provisions do not apply to s.51's statutory term as to reasonable price to be paid by the consumer: on s.51 see below, para.38-578.

Service to be performed with reasonable care and skill   Reflecting both the   **38-571**
common law of implied term and s.13 of the 1982 Act, s.49(1) provides that:

> "Every contract to supply a service is to be treated as including a term that the trader must
> perform the service with reasonable care and skill."

Given that no special explanation is provided for what is meant by "reasonable
care" for these purposes, recourse should be made to earlier case-law on this notion in the context of the 1982 Act and more generally at common law.[3474] Similarly,
the consumer bears the burden of proof of establishing that the trader failed to
exercise reasonable care in the performance of the service. Breach of this statutory term may give rise to a right in the consumer to repeat performance or a price
reduction,[3475] as well as the possibility of a remedy for breach of contract under the
general law.[3476]

Information about the trader or service to be binding   Section 50 of the 2015   **38-572**
Act makes new, significant and quite complex provision rendering "anything that
is said or written to the consumer" and certain categories of information supplied
by the trader to the consumer binding on the trader by the creation of new statutory terms of the contract. For this purpose, s.50 distinguishes two situations.

Things "said or written" by the trader irrespective of a duty to do so   First,   **38-573**
s.50(1) provides that:

> "Every contract to supply a service is to be treated as including as a term of the contract
> anything that is said or written to the consumer, by or on behalf of the trader, about the
> trader or the service, if—
> (a)   it is taken into account by the consumer when deciding to enter into the
>   contract, or
> (b)   it is taken into account by the consumer when making any decision about the
>   service after entering into the contract."

So, "anything that is said or written to the consumer, by or on behalf of the trader,
about the trader or the service" will constitute a term of the contract, subject to the
two conditions set by (a) or (b) and a qualification set by s.50(2).[3477] Section 50(1)
is therefore restricted to things "said or written" "about the trader or the service";
the second of these is obvious, but an example of the first may be found in a commitment made by a trader to paying its workers a "living wage".[3478] When compared
to the general position under the law of misrepresentation, "anything that is said or
written" is very inclusive as it is not restricted to information (which may imply
something factual) and could, therefore, include what the common law would treat
as a representation of opinion or future fact[3479]; on the other hand, at common law
a misrepresentation of fact can take place by conduct,[3480] whereas conduct could not
be said to constitute "anything that is *said or written*". As regards the two condi-

---

[3474] cf. Vol.I, para.14-044.
[3475] 2015 Ac s.54(2)–(3) as explained above, para.38-570. The remedies of repeat performance and price
   reduction are explained below, paras 38-581—38-583.
[3476] 2015 Act s.54(6) and (7), below, para.38-584.
[3477] Below, para.38-574.
[3478] *Explanatory Notes* 2015 para.249.
[3479] cf. Vol.I, paras 7-007 et seq.
[3480] See Vol.I, paras 7-019—7-020.

tions, the condition in (a) is straightforward as it provides a particular form of causal link between "what is said or written" by the trader and the consumer's decision to enter into the contract. This is familiar from the law of misrepresentation, where an actionable misrepresentation must induce the contract.[3481] However, the alternative condition in (b) is new and allows anything said or written which relates to the trader or the service if it is to be taken into account by the consumer "when making any decision about the service *after* entering into the contract".[3482] The latter condition could be satisfied where what is said or written to the consumer relates to the choices which he or she will enjoy in the course of performance of the contract.

38-574   As noted earlier, the impact of s.50(1) is qualified and this is effected by s.50(2), according to which:

> "Anything taken into account by the consumer as mentioned in subsection (1)(a) or (b) is subject to—
>
> (a) anything that qualified it and was said or written to the consumer by the trader on the same occasion, and
>
> (b) any change to it that has been expressly agreed between the consumer and the trader (before entering into the contract or later)."

So, the impact of s.50(1) may be qualified either by what the trader says or writes at the time or by any change agreed between the consumer, whether before entering the contract or at some later date.[3483] Despite these qualifications, it will be seen that the 2015 Act gives contractual force to pre-contractual statements in a range of situations where it would not be clearly the case under the general law of "warranty".[3484]

38-575 Information supplied as required by 2013 Regulations   The second situation foreseen by s.50 is provided by s.50(3), which provides that, without prejudice to s.50(1),[3485] information which the trader was required to provide to the consumer under the Consumer Contracts (Information Cancellation and Additional Charges) Regulations 2013 is to be treated as a term of the contract.[3486] Following the pattern set by statutory terms which the 2015 Act provides for "goods contracts" and "digital content contracts",[3487] s.50(4) requires that change to any of the information mentioned in s.54(3), "made before entering into the contract or later, is not effective unless expressly agreed between the consumer and the trader".

38-576 Remedies for breach   Where a trader breaches a statutory term treated as included

---

[3481] See Vol.I, para.7-036.

[3482] 2015 Act s.50(1)(b) (emphasis added).

[3483] In principle, such a term in a consumer contract which effected such a change could itself be an unfair term and so not binding on the consumer under s.62 of the 2015 Act, on which see above, paras 38-389 et seq.

[3484] See Vol.I paras 7-004, 13-003—13-005.

[3485] Above, para.38-573.

[3486] 2015 Act s.54(3); 2013 Regulations regs 9, 10 and 13 on which see generally above, paras 38-061 et seq. and (for the information requirements themselves), paras 38-098 and 38-103, implementing (in particular) the 2011 Directive art.6(5) (as explained above, para.38-105). It is to be noted, though, that the scope of the 2013 Regulations is restricted in a number of important respects: see above, paras 38-076—38-078, 38-096.

[3487] 2015 Act s.11(5) and 12(3) (goods contracts), above, paras 38-499 and 38-500; ss.36(4) and 37(3) (digital content contracts), above, paras 38-548 and 38-549.

in the contract under s.50(1) or (3), the consumer's special remedies differ according to whether the term (and therefore what was said or written or the information
provided) related to the service (in which case they may consist of the right to repeat
performance or price reduction)[3488] or to the trader, when it may consist only of price
reduction,[3489] though in both cases the consumer may equally enjoy a remedy for
breach of contract under the general law.[3490]

Service to be performed within a reasonable time   Section 52 of the 2015 Act   **38-577**
makes very similar provision as does s.14 of the 1982 Act for contracts for services
more generally, setting a statutory term "that the trader must perform the service
in a reasonable time",[3491] where

"(a)   the contract does not expressly fix the time for the service to be performed, and does
        not say how it is to be fixed, and
(b)   information that is to be treated under section 50 as included in the contract does
        not fix the time either."[3492]

This condition differs substantively from s.14 only in that it refers for this purpose
to information which has been incorporated into the contract under s.50. As earlier
noted, breach by the trader of a statutory term inserted by s.52 gives rise to a right
to a price reduction and may give rise to other remedies for breach of contract under
the general law.[3493]

Reasonable price to be paid for a service   Section 51 of the 2015 Act provides   **38-578**
that, where the consumer has not paid a price or other consideration for the service,
and where the contract does not expressly fix a price or other consideration, and
does not say how it is to be fixed, and "anything that is to be treated under section
50 as included in the contract does not fix a price or other consideration either", then
"the contract is to be treated as including a term that the consumer must pay a
reasonable price for the service, and no more".[3494]

While s.51 reflects closely s.15 of the 1982 Act, it is unusual in the 2015 Act in
that it may lead to the imposition of an obligation on the consumer to the trader,
but it is required so as to allow the neat separation of the 2015 Act (applicable to
consumer contracts) and the 1982 Act (applicable to other contracts); and the final
three words "and no more" allow s.51 to make some claim as being useful for the
protection of consumers. The 2015 Act makes no provision for breach by the
consumer of any term inserted into the contract by s.51 and this is therefore left to
the general law, notably the trader's action for the price.[3495]

Express terms; relation of statutory terms to other law on contract terms   The   **38-579**
2015 Act provides that the special remedies which it provides for the consumer "do

---

[3488] 2015 Act s.54(2)–(3) above, para.38-570.
[3489] 2015 Act s.54(4) above, para.38-570.
[3490] 2015 Act s.54(6)–(7), below, para.38-584.
[3491] 2015 Act s.50(2). "What is reasonable time is a question of fact": 2015 Act 52(3).
[3492] 2015 Act s.52(1).
[3493] 2015 Act s.54(5)–(6), above, para.38-570. On the right to a price reduction, see below, para.38-
       582.
[3494] 2015 Act s.51(1) and (2). "What is a reasonable price is a question of fact": 2015 Act s.51(3).
[3495] See Vol.I, para.26-009 (though ex hypothesi, the trader's claim for enforcement of the statutory term
       inserted by s.51 would not be for an *agreed* sum).

not affect any rights that the contract provides for, if those are not inconsistent".[3496] So, for example, a clause in a contract may provide the consumer with a power of termination of the contract, whether for breach by the trader or on some other ground. At common law, such an express clause takes effect on its terms as properly construed and, given that the Act makes no provision of this sort in its scheme of rights for the consumer, a right in the consumer under such an express clause would not be inconsistent with the consumer's special remedies. As will be seen, the Act makes further provision as to the possible exclusion or limitation of the special rights which it creates for consumers in relation to services.[3497] Secondly, the 2015 Act provides that nothing in Ch.4 "affects any enactment or rule of law that imposes a stricter duty on the trader"[3498] and is also:

"... subject to any other enactment which defines or restricts the rights, duties or liabilities arising in connection with a service of any description."[3499]

These provisions all follow closely similar provisions in the 1982 Act.[3500]

(cc)   The Scheme of Remedies for the Consumer

38-580   **Introduction**   In the case of services contracts, the range of special remedies is reduced to two: a right to repeat performance and a right to price reduction. Where the consumer has *both* these rights in the sense that the breach of the statutory term in question gives rise to them both under s.54(3),[3501] then the Act places them at two levels: the right to repeat performance first, the right to price reduction second. However, in cases where the consumer has only the special remedy of price reduction (i.e. where the trader is in breach of a s.50 term that does not relate to the service or in breach of the term to perform within a reasonable time[3502]), then, of course, there is no hierarchy of remedies: the consumer is restricted to, but also can immediately rely on, the right to price reduction.

38-581   **A right to repeat performance**   This is an original and, at first sight, a rather startling remedy. It clearly reflects in very broad terms the right to repair or replacement provided by the 2015 Act for consumers under goods contracts and digital content contracts[3503] in that it seeks to ensure that consumers receive the

---

[3496] 2015 Act s.54(1).

[3497] 2015 Act s.57, below, para.38-586.

[3498] e.g. *Greaves & Co (Contractors) Ltd v Baynham Meikle & Partners* [1975] 1 W.L.R. 1095, above, para.37-198.

[3499] 2015 Act s.53. An example may be found in the case of contracts for services governed by the carriage of air conventions (notably, the Warsaw Convention and the Montreal Convention, on which see above, paras 35-002 et seq.) which, in the view of the UK government, remain the exclusive basis of liability on the routes to which they apply even after the 2015 Act applies to them: Department of Transport, *Applying the Consumer Rights Act 2015 to the rail, aviation and maritime sectors, Response to Consultation, Moving Britain Ahead* (July 2016), para.2.8.

[3500] 1982 Act s.16(2)–(4).

[3501] As earlier seen, under s.54(3), the consumer has a right both to require repeat performance and the right to a price reduction where the service does not conform to the contract in the special sense set by s.54(2) (which refers to breach of the term relating to reasonable care in s.49 and breach of a term in s.50 and the term relates to the performance of the service): see above, para.38-570.

[3502] 2015 Act s.54(4) and (5), above, para.38-570.

[3503] Above, paras 38-517 and 38-558.

performance which they pay for reflecting their right to corrective performance.[3504] Accordingly, s.55(1)–(4) provides that:

"(1)   The right to require repeat performance is a right to require the trader to perform the service again, to the extent necessary to complete its performance in conformity with the contract.

(2)   If the consumer requires such repeat performance, the trader—
   (a)   must provide it within a reasonable time and without significant inconvenience to the consumer; and
   (b)   must bear any necessary costs incurred in doing so (including in particular the cost of any labour or materials).

(3)   The consumer cannot require repeat performance if completing performance of the service in conformity with the contract is impossible.

(4)   Any question as to what is a reasonable time or significant inconvenience is to be determined taking account of—
   (a)   the nature of the service, and
   (b)   the purpose for which the service was to be performed."

Where a consumer has this right,[3505] the only restriction on its availability is therefore that "the consumer cannot require repeat performance if completing performance of the service in conformity with the contract is *impossible*".[3506] For this purpose, impossibility could relate not merely to physical impossibility but also to impossibility in the sense that a *repeat* performance would be impossible, as in the case where performance of the services is time specific.[3507] Nevertheless, this is a very different position from the general law governing the availability of specific performance of a contract for the provision of services,[3508] though as will be explained, the consumer's right to require repeat performance will not necessarily lead to an order of specific performance of the service by the trader.[3509] As earlier noted, the right to repeat performance is placed at a first level of the consumer's special remedies in the sense that, where a consumer "has" both remedies, the right to a price reduction arises only where the right to repeat performance is unavailable or has failed in two specified senses.[3510] The new right to repeat performance may be illustrated by reference to the facts of the well-known decision of the House of Lords in *Ruxley Electronics and Construction Ltd v Forsyth*, where a landowner (apparently qualifying as a "consumer" within the meaning of the 2015 Act) commissioned the building of a swimming pool of a stipulated depth, and when it failed to conform to the stipulation, claimed the cost of reinstatement by way of damages for breach of contract.[3511] This claim failed, on the basis that this cost was disproportionate to the advantage to be gained by the landowner from reinstatement. However, such a contract would qualify as a contract for services within the meaning of Ch.4 of the 2015 Act; the contractual stipulation as to the depth of the pool would count as something "said or written" to the consumer under s.50(1) and, given that it would relate to performance of the service so as to fall within s.54(2)(b)

[3504] Above, para.38-517; Whittaker (2017) 133 L.Q.R. 47 at 61–63.
[3505] In the sense that it is in principle available under 2015 Act s.54(2)–(3).
[3506] 2015 Act s.55(3) (emphasis added).
[3507] *Explanatory Notes* 2015 para.263.
[3508] See Vol.I, Ch.27.
[3509] 2015 Act s.58(1)–(3), below, para.38-583.
[3510] See below, para.38-582.
[3511] [1996] A.C. 344 on which see Vol.I, para.26-040.

would therefore give rise to the right to repeat performance under s.54(3)(a). What is much less clear is whether a court would wish to order specific performance in support of the consumer's claim to repeat performance in circumstances such as these.[3512]

38-582   A right to price reduction   According to s.56(1) of the Act:

> "(1)   The right to a price reduction is the right to require the trader to reduce the price to the consumer by an appropriate amount (including the right to receive a refund for anything already paid above the reduced amount).
>
> (2)   The amount of the reduction may, where appropriate, be the full amount of the price."

For these purposes, s.56 makes similar provision as to the payment of any refund without undue delay, by the same means of payment, and without the imposition of a fee as Pt 1 provides more widely for refunds.[3513] The *Explanatory Notes* to the Act suggest that a reduction in the price by an appropriate amount will normally mean that the price is reduced by the difference in value between the service the consumer paid for and the value of the service as provided and that this will take into account the benefit which the consumer has derived from the service.[3514] However, they acknowledge that there may be some cases where the trader's breach has not reduced the value of the service to the consumer:

> "This could occur, for example, where the trader has not complied with information they gave about themselves.[3515] For example, if the trader tells the consumer that they will pay their workers the living wage and this is important to the consumer and a reason why they decided to go with this particular trader, arguably this does not affect the value of the service but the consumer would still have the right to request a reduction of an "appropriate amount" to account for the breach."[3516]

As earlier explained, the right to a price reduction is either available by itself (as in the cases where the trader has broken a term inserted by s.50 which does not relate to performance of the service or the statutory term to perform within a reasonable time[3517]) or coupled with a right to repeat performance. Where it is available by itself, the consumer can exercise it freely as foreseen by s.56(1) and (2). However, where the consumer "has" both the remedies in the sense of s.54(2)–(3) of the Act (which makes these two remedies available to a consumer where the trader breaches the statutory term of reasonable care or a term that s.50 treats as included which relates to performance of the service), then the Act sets the right to repeat performance at a first level and allows the right to price reduction only at a second level.[3518] This is effected by s.56(3) of the 2015 Act, according to which:

[3512] See 2015 Act s.58(2), below, para.38-583; Whittaker (2017) 133 L.Q.R. 47 at 65–66.

[3513] 2015 Act s.56(4)–(6). cf. 2015 Act s.20(15)–(17) (goods contracts), above, para.38-514.

[3514] *Explanatory Notes* 2015 para.266. cf. above, para.38-518 in relation to price reduction in respect of "goods contracts".

[3515] This would fall under s.50(1) of the 2015 Act.

[3516] *Explanatory Notes* 2015 para.267.

[3517] 2015 Act s.54(4)–(5) referring to s.50 and s.52 respectively, above, para.38-570.

[3518] cf. the position as regards "goods contracts" under ss.23 and 24 of the Act, above, paras 38-517— 38-518.

"A consumer who has [the right to a price reduction] and the right to require repeat performance[3519] is only entitled to a price reduction in one of these situations—

(a)   because of section 55(3) the consumer cannot require repeat performance; or

(b)   the consumer has required repeat performance, but the trader is in breach of the requirement of section 55(2)(a) to do it within a reasonable time and without significant inconvenience to the consumer."

This is drafted in an odd way, as it provides that where a consumer *has* a right to a price reduction, he or she "is only entitled" to it in one of these two situations. Be that as it may, the effect of this provision is that in the circumstances where the Act provides the consumer with *both* these rights, he or she must in principle require the right to repeat performance first and proceed to price reduction only if the first right is impossible or if the trader has failed to repeat performance within a reasonable time and without significant inconvenience to the consumer. This means, in effect, that, in principle, under the special scheme of remedies, the consumer must first require the trader to re-perform the service and thereby give the trader another chance to perform in conformity with the contract and another chance to earn (or keep) the price. There may, however, be a way by which a consumer who wishes to require price reduction could do so without first requiring repeat performance, notably, where the consumer had lost confidence in the trader. If "impossibility of performance" by the trader, were held to include the situation where the trader cannot perform without co-operation by the consumer,[3520] then, on a literal reading of s.55(3), the consumer could not require repeat performance and this in turn could then be said to trigger the availability of the right to price reduction.[3521] However, such a reading is unnatural, as it would be odd to hold that the consumer does not have a *right* to repeat performance (and so can enjoy a right to price reduction) owing to a decision which the consumer has himself or herself made (the decision not to co-operate with the trader's further performance). Either way, the special scheme of rights for the consumer in s.54 to 56 of the Act does not affect the availability of a remedy for breach of contract under the general law and, particularly in the case of a serious breach where the consumer has lost confidence in the trader, any right in the consumer to terminate the contract for breach and/or claim damages may seem more attractive.

Discretion as to appropriate remedy   Section 58 of the 2015 Act provides that **38-583** in any proceedings in which one of the two special remedies provided for consumers by Ch.4[3522] is sought, the court enjoys two additional powers. First, on the application of the consumer, the court may make an order requiring specific performance by the trader of any obligation imposed on the trader in respect of

---

[3519] The circumstances in which these rights are "had" by a consumer are set by s.54(2)–(3), above, para.38-570.

[3520] cf. by analogy, the rules governing an injured party's right to affirm a contract, perform and sue for the price under the general law: this right is subject to a condition that performance by the injured party does not require co-operation by the party in breach: see Vol.I, paras 26-114—26-116.

[3521] 2015 Act s.56(3)((a).

[3522] 2015 Act s.58(1), referring to s.54(3): the right to repeat performance (under s.55) and the right to a price reduction (under s.56) (which are the "relevant remedies" under s.58(8)(c)). These powers do not extend to the "other remedies" for consumers as this is understood by the Act and as explained below, para.38-584.

repeat performance.[3523] Secondly, where a consumer claims the right to repeat performance or the right to a price reduction (termed the "relevant remedies" by s.58), but the court decides that the provisions governing these rights "have the effect that exercise of another of these rights is appropriate", "the court may proceed as if the consumer had exercised that other right".[3524] The court may make an order under s.58 unconditionally or on such terms and conditions as to damages, payment of the price and otherwise as it thinks just.[3525] Neither the right to repeat performance nor the right to price reduction in relation to services contracts implement any requirement of EU law,[3526] and so there is no problem of compatibility with EU law in relation to the potentially restrictive effect of a court's exercise of its discretions in s.58 in relation to Ch.4.[3527] However, if a court were simply to apply the approach of the general law as to the availability of specific performance in relation to the right to repeat performance (albeit in relation to the performance of primary obligations rather than obligations to correct a non-conforming performance), this could well undermine the policy of consumer protection envisaged by the Act. On the other hand, to return to the example suggested by *Ruxley Electronics Construction Ltd v Forsyth*,[3528] a court may well be reluctant to order a builder to rebuild a swimming pool in conformity with the contract under threat of contempt of court, particularly where s.58 allows it instead to order a price reduction. A possible way of reconciling the need to maintain the genuine character of the consumer's right to repeat performance and the proper concerns of a court in this sort of case with awarding specific performance, may be found in the court's power to award damages in lieu of specific performance provided by s.50 of the Senior Courts Act 1981 (which reflects earlier provision in s.2 of the Chancery Amendment Act 1858, commonly known as Lord Cairns' Act).[3529] For if a court were to refuse to award specific performance in support of a consumer's claim for repeat performance under the 2015 Act, it could instead award damages in lieu of specific performance of the trader's *obligation to repeat performance* and so allow the consumer to obtain the cost of reinstatement of the swimming pool. As the Supreme Court has recently explained in relation to damages in lieu of an injunction, damages awarded under Lord Cairns' Act may not necessarily be measured in the same way as damages recoverable at common law[3530]: damages in substitution for specific performance "are a monetary substitute for what is lost by the withholding of the relief".[3531] As a result, the measure of damages in lieu of specific performance of a trader's obligation to repeat performance should reflect the particular nature of the obligation whose enforcement has been sought, i.e. the trader's secondary obligation to *repeat* performance, rather than the trader's primary

---

[3523] 2015 Act s.58(2) referring to s.55 of the Act, above, para.38-581.

[3524] 2015 Act s.58(3) and (4).

[3525] 2015 Act s.58(7).

[3526] Above, para.38-569.

[3527] cf. above, para.38-522 in relation to the right to repair or replacement in "sales contracts".

[3528] [1996] A.C. 344 on which see Vol.I, para.26-040.

[3529] 2015 Act s.58(1) specifically preserves "any other power [the court] has" as well as the powers which s.58 provides. For this suggestion see Whittaker (2017) 133 L.Q.R. 47 at 66.

[3530] *Morris-Garner v One Step (Support) Ltd* [2018] UKSC 20, [2018] 2 W.L.R. 1353 at [47] explaining that the remark of Lord Wilberforce in *Johnson v Agnew* [1980] A.C. 367, 400, [1979] 1 All E.R. 883 which appears to suggest the contrary should be treated with care. And see Vol.I, para.27-097.

[3531] *Morris-Garner v One Step (Support) Ltd* [2018] UKSC 20 at [95] per Lord Reed (with whom Lady Hale, Lord Wilson and Lord Carnwath agreed).

obligation to build a (conforming) swimming pool. This would allow a consumer to gain damages to cover the cost of reinstatement even though under the general law an injured party could not do so on the ground that this would be disproportionate.

"Other remedies"   The 2015 Act does not prevent the consumer seeking other   **38-584**
remedies for a breach of a statutory term imposing a duty on the trader as earlier set out, "in addition to one of the special remedies which it provides for the consumer "but not so as to recover twice for the same loss".[3532] These remedies include a consumer claiming damages, seeking to recover money paid where the consideration for payment of the money has failed; seeking specific performance; relying on the breach against a claim by the trader under the contract; and exercising a right to treat the contract as at an end.[3533]

(dd)   Exclusion of Liability

Introduction: before the 2015 Act   At common law, in principle a person who   **38-585**
contracts to perform a service for another person may limit or exclude their liability in respect of any defective performance, following the general principle of freedom of contract.[3534] By contrast, under the statutory scheme in the Unfair Contract Terms Act 1977 before its amendment by the 2015 Act, where a person acting in the course of a business seeks by contract to exclude or limit their liability for negligence, such an exemption clause is ineffective as regards the trader's liability for death and personal injury and effective as regards other losses only to the extent that the clause satisfies the "reasonableness test".[3535] These controls therefore apply where a trader seeks to exclude its liability for breach of the implied term in the 1982 Act that it must perform a service with reasonable care and skill.[3536] Beyond this case, any exemption of liability by a trader providing a service might fall foul of the controls put in place for contractual liability generally by the 1977 Act,[3537] or under the Unfair Terms in Consumer Contracts Regulations 1999.[3538]

Exclusion of liability for breach of the statutory terms   However, s.57 of the   **38-586**
2015 Act makes special provision to control the exclusion or limitation of the trader's liabilities to the consumer in respect of breach of the statutory terms which it provides for the consumer in respect of services and, for this purpose, makes a series of distinctions between the grounds on which the consumer's remedies arise and also as between the exclusion and the limitation of the trader's liability. So, first, s.57(1) provides:

[3532] 2015 Act s.54(6).
[3533] 2015 Act s.54(7) and see Vol.I, paras 21-028—21-039 (whether a party to a contract may rely on the other party's breach in resisting the latter's claim for the price); Ch.24 (right to treat the contract as at an end on the ground of breach); Ch.26 (damages), Ch.27 (specific performance and injunction); and paras 39-057 et seq. (recovery of money of paid on a total failure of consideration (or basis)).
[3534] See Vol.I, paras 1-031 et seq., but see also Ch.15, paras 15-001—15-022.
[3535] 1977 Act s.1(3) (defining "business liability"); s.2 (controlling the exclusion of liability for negligence); s.11 (the reasonableness test): see Vol.I, paras 15-081—15-082.
[3536] Supply of Goods and Services Act 1982 s.13.
[3537] 1977 Act s.3: see Vol.I, paras 15-084—15-086.
[3538] See above, paras 38-220 et seq. especially at paras 38-265 et seq.

"A term of a contract to supply services is not binding on the consumer to the extent that it would exclude the trader's liability arising under section 49 (service to be performed with reasonable care and skill)."[3539]

Here, it will be seen, an *exclusion* of liability (whether arising under the special remedies provided by the Act or the general law) is rendered totally ineffective. Secondly, and similarly, according to s.57(2) "a term of a contract to supply services is not binding on the consumer to the extent that it would exclude the trader's liability arising under section 50 (information about trader or service to be binding)", though this is subject to s.50(2)'s own provision allowing the trader to qualify what it says or writes to the consumer or change it where expressly agreed with the consumer.[3540] Again, this control applies only to *exclusions* of liability (whether arising under the special remedies which the Act provides in this case or under the general law[3541]). Thirdly, however, s.57(3) makes more general provision as regards a contract term under which the trader purports to *restrict* its liability arising from breach of the statutory terms as to performance with reasonable care, information supplied by the trader, and performance within a reasonable time[3542]: these are not binding on the consumer if the term "would prevent the consumer in an appropriate case from recovering the price paid or the value of any other consideration".[3543] The effect of this rather convoluted provision is therefore to render ineffective as regards these liabilities a clause which *restricts* the trader's liability (a limitation clause) unless the limitation is set at a level above the contract price. However, as s.57(3) itself acknowledges, this does not necessarily mean that a limitation clause which does allow the consumer to recover against the trader up to the level of the contract price will be effective, as it may still be not binding on the consumer under the general controls on unfair contract terms in Pt 2 of the 2015 Act.[3544]

(ee) Enforcement

38-587 **Enforcement of provisions on exclusion of trader's liabilities**   As earlier explained in relation to the 2015 Act's treatment of unfair contract terms more generally, the Act applies the enforcement measures provided for the control of unfair contract terms under Pt 2 (and derived from the 1993 Directive[3545]) to its controls of contract terms in Pt 1 of the Act.[3546] Secondly, the provisions in Ch.4

[3539] On this statutory term, see above, para.38-571.

[3540] Above, paras 38-573—38-574.

[3541] Above, paras 38-581—38-584.

[3542] s.57(3) refers to the restriction of liability arising under ss.49 and 50 and, where they apply, ss.51 and 52. The inclusion of s.51 is odd as this provides for the setting of a reasonable price to be paid *by the consumer* and therefore it cannot give rise to any liability in the trader.

[3543] 2015 Act s.57(3).

[3544] 2015 Act s.57(3) and on these general controls see especially 2015 Act s.62 and above, paras 38-220 et seq. especially at paras 38-223 et seq. There is a particular difficulty in the case of a term limiting liability at a level *above* the price paid by the consumer in respect of a term included in the contract under s.50(3) of the Act as regards information supplied as required by the 2013 Regulations (above, para.38-575), as the controls contained in s.57 of the Act appear to permit such a term subject only to assessment of its fairness under the general test in Pt 2 of the Act, whereas s.50(3) implements art.6(5) of the Consumer Rights Directive 2011, art.25 of which generally requires its provisions to be "imperative", so that such a term should not be binding on the consumer without such an assessment: see above, paras 38-066 and 38-105.

[3545] 1993 Directive art.7.

[3546] 2015 Act s.57(7) referring to Sch.3. See above, paras 38-419 et seq.

of the 2015 Act which implement the Consumer Rights Directive 2011 or which "provide additional permitted protections"[3547] (notably, the provisions in s.50 giving contractual effect to certain categories of information provided by the trader to the consumer) have been designated as specified UK laws for the purposes of s.212 of the Enterprise Act 2002 Act so as to attract enforcement orders in relation to "Community infringements".[3548] And, thirdly, acts or omissions in respect of any provision in Pt 1 of the 2015 Act are specified as possible "domestic infringements" for the purposes of s.211 of the Enterprise Act 2002.[3155]

[3547] Enterprise Act 2002 s.212(1)(b).

[3548] Enterprise Act 2002 s.212(3); Enterprise Act 2002 (Part 8 Community Infringements Specified UK Laws) Order 2003 art.3. The Consumer Rights Directive 2011 is also listed for this purpose in the 2002 Act Sch.13 para.9F.

Chapter 39

CREDIT AND SECURITY

Eva Lomnicka

1.   THE REGULATION OF CONSUMER CREDIT[1]

39-001   **In general**   Laws regulating the lending of money have been in operation in England for a considerable period of time. But, historically, the statutory control of money-lending ("lender credit") was treated quite distinctly from the control applied to the extension of credit to a purchaser of goods who was allowed to pay for them by instalments ("vendor credit"). As a result, the statutory regulation of credit transactions was at one time determined solely by the legal form in which the transaction was cast, irrespective of its economic function. And certain types of credit transaction, which could not easily be allocated to either of these self-contained categories, escaped any form of control. The Consumer Credit Act 1974 broke down these barriers in order to ensure that, wherever protection is required for the consumer, that protection is in principle available whatever the form of credit transaction adopted.[2]

39-002   **Changes since 1974**   As will be noted below, the Consumer Credit Act 1974 has been amended significantly since coming into force.[3] The most far-reaching amendments were those in the Financial Services Act 2012 (and orders made thereunder), which overhauled the regulatory architecture for financial services regulation by extensively amending the Financial Services and Markets Act 2000 (FSMA 2000) so as to create, inter alia, a new financial market regulator: the Financial Conduct Authority (FCA), in part replacing the Financial Services Authority. In anticipation of the abolition of the existing consumer credit regulator, the Office of Fair Trading (OFT), on April 1, 2014,[4] the Financial Services Act 2012 also enabled the Treasury by Order[5] to transfer consumer credit regulation to the FCA. This was achieved by enabling any activity requiring a consumer credit licence under the 1974 Act to become a "regulated activity" under the FSMA 2000.[6] Hence, essentially, since April 1, 2014 regulatory powers over consumer credit (and hire) activity, in particular authorisation (in place of licensing), supervision and enforcement, are exercised by the FCA under the FSMA 2000. Moreover, consumer credit advertisements (and quotations) are regulated under the FSMA 2000 "financial promotion" regime.[7] In addition, some provisions of the 1974 Act that imposed

---

[1]   See Guest and Lloyd, *Encyclopedia of Consumer Credit Law* (1975, looseleaf); Goode, *Consumer Credit: Law and Practice* (looseleaf); Goode, *Consumer Credit Law* (1989); Harding, *Consumer Credit and Consumer Hire* (1995); Philpott et al, *The Law of Consumer Credit and Hire* (2009).

[2]   See the wide definition of "credit" for the purposes of the regime, considered below, para.39-019.

[3]   Most of the Act came into force on May 19, 1985; see SI 1983/1551 and SI 1989/1128.

[4]   By the Enterprise and Regulatory Reform Act 2013 s.26(3).

[5]   The two main Orders were: (i) the Financial Services and Markets Act 2000 (Regulated Activities) (Amendment) (No.2) Order 2013 (SI 2013/1881) and (ii) the Financial Services Act 2012 (Consumer Credit) Order 2013 (SI 2013/1882).

[6]   See FSMA 2000 s.22 and the previous footnote. SI 2013/1881 made considerable amendments to the Financial Services and Markets Act 2000 (Regulated Activities) Order 2001 (SI 2001/544), the so-called "RAO" (made under the FSMA 2000 s.22), which now contains the definitions of (a) those "credit-related" regulated activities that are now regulated under the FSMA 2000 and (b) exempt agreements (see below, paras 39-038 et seq.).

[7]   See especially the FSMA 2000 s.21 and the Financial Promotion Order 2005 (SI 2005/1529), as amended, esp. by SI 2013/1881.

obligations on credit and hire providers[8] have been repealed and replaced by "rules" in a new "Module" of the *FCA Handbook*: "CONC". However, much of the 1974 Act still remains in force (with the FCA replacing the OFT as the main regulator and the Treasury replacing the Secretary of State). In particular, the formality and information requirements (both at the time of contracting and thereafter) are still imposed by the 1974 Act (and the regulations already made thereunder), although they are now enforced by the FCA using the (more extensive) powers conferred by the FSMA 2000.

The Mortgage Credit Directive   Until the Mortgage Credit Directive (MCD)[9] was implemented, there were two statutory regimes for the regulation of land mortgages, both eventually administered by the Financial Conduct Authority[10]: one under the Consumer Credit Act 1974 (for, essentially, certain second charge mortgages) and one under FSMA 2000 (for, essentially, first legal charge residential mortgages). The need to implement the MCD provided the opportunity for aligning the two regimes. Hence, essentially, all residential mortgages are now within the FSMA 2000 regime and hence are exempted from the Consumer Credit Act 1974 regime.[11] Moreover, there is a separate "lighter-touch" regulatory regime for certain consumer "buy-to-let" mortgages.[12]   **39-003**

The future of consumer credit regulation   By 2019, a five-year review of consumer credit regulation is expected to have been undertaken[13] and it may be that the dual FSMA 2000 and 1974 Act regime will be replaced by a single FSMA 2000 regime (although it may be that those parts of the 1974 Act that cannot be replicated in an FCA rulebook (for example, the unfair relationship[14] and the connected lender liability[15] provisions) will remain in the 1974 Act).   **39-004**

Scope of Consumer Credit Act 1974   The Consumer Credit Act 1974 gave effect to the recommendations of the *Crowther Committee on Consumer Credit*[16] for the regulation of the supply to individuals (including sole traders, small partnerships and unincorporated associations) of credit throughout the United Kingdom.[17]   **39-005**

---

8   e.g. CCA 1974 ss.51, 51A–51B, 55A, 55B, 74A–74B, 81, 82A, 160A.
9   Directive 2014/17/EU implemented on March 21, 2016. See *Implementation of the EU Mortgage Credit Directive* (HMT September 5, 2014); *Implementing the Mortgage Credit Directive and the new regime for second charge mortgages* (FCA CP14/20); *Implementation of the EU Mortgage Credit Directive: summary of Proposals* (HMT January 26, 2015) and *Implementing the Mortgage Credit Directive and the new regime for second charge mortgages: feedback to CP14/20 and final rules* (FCA PS15/9).
10   Since the transfer of consumer credit regulation from the OFT to the FCA: see above, para.39-002.
11   Credit agreements within the MCD art.3(1)(b)—for the acquisition or retention of interests in land or buildings—are also taken out of the CCA 1974 regime: see SI 2015/910 art.3 and Sch.1 para.2(2), amending CCA 1974 s.8(3).
12   See below, para.39-531.
13   The FCA has begun the review process: see *Call for Input: Review of retained provisions of the Consumer Credit Act*, February 2016. See now, *The Interim Report*, August 2018.
14   CCA 1974 ss.140A–140C; see below, paras 39-212 et seq.
15   CCA 1974 ss.75 and 75A; see below, paras 39-303—39-305.
16   Cmnd.4596 (1971).
17   Initially, the Act only regulated credit below £5,000. The limit was raised from £5,000 to £15,000 from May 20, 1985, by SI 1983/1878 and to £25,000 from May 1, 1998, by SI 1998/996. As noted below, para.39-010, the Consumer Credit Act 2006 abolished that limit except for the purposes of the exemption of agreements made for the debtor's business purpose (previously CCA 1974 s.16B,

It provided for the licensing of those who carried on the business of granting consumer credit[18] and of ancillary credit activities.[19] The Act repealed[20] the previous statutes that regulated the supply of credit or the advertisement of credit such as the Pawnbrokers Acts 1872 to 1960,[21] the Moneylenders Acts 1900 to 1927,[22] the Hire-Purchase Act 1965,[23] and the Advertisements (Hire-Purchase) Act 1967.[24] It replaced these enactments with a single statute, far more uniform in its application, although with necessary concessions to differing forms of credit business.

Many types of credit business that were previously subject to no control became regulated by the Act.[25] Further, the licensing system established by the Act extended, not merely to those engaged in the granting of consumer credit, but also to those engaged in businesses ancillary thereto.[26]

39-006 Consumer hire agreements   The 1974 Act also regulates consumer hire agreements if the hirer is an individual (including a sole trader, small partnership or unincorporated association).[27] A licence was required for a consumer hire business[28] and various businesses ancillary thereto.[29]

39-007 Extension of the 1974 Act   Certain provisions of the 1974 Act, in particular those that deal with unfair relationships,[30] apply to all credit agreements where the debtor is an individual even if the agreement is otherwise "exempt".[31]

---

see now RAO art.60C(3)–(7), below, para.39-046). However, agreements providing for credit in excess of £60,260 are outside the scope of the Consumer Credit Directive (see below, para.39-011) and hence are not covered by many provisions implementing that Directive (especially: CCA 1974 ss.55C, 66A, 75A and 77B); they may also fall within the "high net worth" exemption (previously in CCA 1974 s.16A, see now RAO art.60H, below, para.39-045), which is not available to agreements within the scope of the Directive.

[18] See below, para.39-061. Licensing under the CCA 1974 has been replaced by authorisation under the FSMA 2000: see below, paras 39-061 et seq.
[19] See below, paras 39-230 et seq.
[20] CCA 1974 s.192(3)(b), (4) Sch.5; SI 1977/325 (c.11); SI 1977/802 (c.30); SI 1979/1685 (c.42); SI 1980/50 (c.3); SI 1981/280 (c.6); SI 1983/1551.
[21] The progressive repeal of these Acts was effected by SI 1977/325 (c.11); SI 1980/50 (c.3); SI 1983/1551.
[22] See *Meston on Moneylenders*, 5th edn. The progressive repeal of these Acts was effected by SI 1977/325 (c.11); SI 1977/802 (c.30); SI 1979/1685 (c.42); SI 1980/50 (c.3); SI 1981/280; and SI 1983/1551.
[23] SI 1983/1551. See *Chitty on Contracts*, 23rd edn, Ch.7; Goode, *Hire-Purchase Law and Practice*, 2nd edn; Guest, *The Law of Hire-Purchase* (1966).
[24] The repeal of the whole of this Act was effected by SI 1980/50 (c.3).
[25] e.g. bank lending, credit cards, check trading, some land mortgages, mail order business.
[26] See below, paras 39-230 et seq.
[27] See below, paras 39-035 et seq. As was the case with credit agreements (see above, para.39-005), initially the Act only regulated *hire* agreements below £5,000. The limit was raised from £5,000 to £15,000 from May 20, 1985, by SI 1983/1878 and to £25,000 from May 1, 1998, by SI 1998/996. As also noted below, para.39-010, the Consumer Credit Act 2006 abolished that limit except for the purposes of the exemption for agreements made for the hirer's business purpose (previously CCA 1974 s.16B, see now RAO art.60O, below, para.39-046). The Consumer Credit Directive (see below, para.39-011) and hence the provisions enacted to implement it do not apply to hire agreements.
[28] See below, para.39-061. Licensing under the CCA 1974 has been replaced by authorisation under the FSMA 2000: see below, para.39-063.
[29] See below, para.39-230.
[30] CCA 1974 ss.140A–140C, see below, paras 39-212 et seq.
[31] Unless it is exempt under RAO art.60C(2) (previously CCA 1974 s.16(6C)) (see s.140A(5)). For exempt agreements, see below, paras 39-038 et seq.

Regulations, orders, etc The 1974 Act was merely a blueprint for the system of regulation that it established. It was supplemented by a considerable amount of subordinate legislation[32] made by the Secretary of State,[33] which was (and in so far as still in force, is) both detailed and complex. **39-008**

Contracting-out Contracting-out of the protections conferred by the 1974 Act is prohibited.[34] **39-009**

Consumer Credit Act 2006 Since the enactment of the Consumer Credit Act 1974, the consumer credit market changed dramatically both in relation to the increased amount of credit provided and in relation to the range of credit facilities offered to consumers. After a review of the Act,[35] its regime was amended in two stages. First, a number of Regulations (in particular, the Advertisements,[36] the Agreements[37] and the Early Settlement[38] Regulations) were replaced or amended extensively. Secondly, the Consumer Credit Act 2006 introduced a number of changes to the 1974 Act itself. In particular, the scope of the 1974 Act was widened[39] by removing the financial limit in general, although the financial limit of £25,000 was retained if the agreement was for the debtor's or hirer's purely *business* purposes.[40] Changes were made to the licensing system and the powers of the OFT were increased to enable it to impose "requirements" and "civil penalties" on licensees.[41] The provisions allowing the court to reopen "extortionate credit bargains" were replaced by the wider "unfair relationship" provisions.[42] Moreover, the provisions rendering agreements that breached certain formal requirements "irredeemably unenforceable"[43] were repealed. **39-010**

---

[32] See SI 1975/2123, 2124; SIs 1976/191, 837, 1002; SIs 1977/325, 328, 329, 330, 331, 802, 2163; SIs 1979/661, 667, 1685; SIs 1980/51, 59; SIs 1981/280, 614; SIs 1983/1551, 1552, 1553, 1554, 1555, 1556, 1557, 1558, 1559, 1560, 1561, 1562, 1564, 1565, 1566, 1567, 1568, 1569, 1570, 1571, 1878; SIs 1984/435, 436, 1046, 1107, 1108, 1109, 1600; SIs 1985/621, 666, 705, 1192; SI 1988/2047; SIs 1989/591, 596, 869, 1125, 1126, 1128, 1841, 2237; SIs 1991/817, 1393, 1949, 2844; SIs 1993/346, 2922; SI 1994/2420; SIs 1995/1250, 2914; SIs 1996/1445, 3081; SI 1997/211; SIs 1998/996, 997, 998, 1203, 1944; SIs 1999/1956, 2725, 3177; SIs 2000/290, 291, 1797; SIs 2004/1481, 1482, 1483, 1484, 2619, 3236, 3237; SI 2006/1273; SIs 2007/827, 1167, 1168; SIs 2008/645, 668, 1751; SIs 2010/139, 1011, 1012 (revoked), 1013, 1014, 1970; SI 2011/11; SI 2012/1745; SI 2012/2798.

[33] Since the transfer of consumer credit regulation to the FCA (see above, para.39-002), the Treasury has become the responsible government department for making subordinate legislation under the CCA 1974.

[34] CCA 1974 s.173(1), (2). But see s.173(3) (later consent). See also *Wilson v Robertsons (London) Ltd (No.2)* [2006] EWCA Civ 1088, [2007] C.C.L.R. 1.

[35] See the White Paper *Fair, Clear and Competitive: The Consumer Credit Market in the 21st Century*, 2003, Cm.6040. For a comment on the proposals, see Lomnicka [2004] J.B.L. 64.

[36] See below, para.39-067.

[37] See below, paras 39-080 et seq.

[38] See below, paras 39-158 et seq.

[39] But the definition of "individual" in s.189(1) was narrowed so as only to include partnerships of two or three (non-corporate) persons. Hence (see below, para.39-016) agreements with larger partnerships were taken out of regulation.

[40] See the exemption in RAO art.60C(3)–(7) (credit) and RAO art.60O (hire) (previously CCA 1974 s.16B), below, para.39-046, for "business" agreements above that amount.

[41] These provisions were eventually replaced by those in FSMA 2000; see below, para.39-063.

[42] CCA 1974 ss.140A–140C, see below, paras 39-212 et seq.

[43] viz CCA 1974 s.127(3)–(5). The term "irredeemably unenforceable" was coined by Lord Hoffmann in *Dimond v Lovell* [2002] A.C. 384. See below, paras 39-093 and 39-200.

39-011 Consumer Credit Directive The implementation of the Consumer Credit Directive 2008,[44] resulted in yet more significant changes to the 1974 Act and the regulations made thereunder.[45] To a large extent those changes were not extended to agreements outside the scope of the Directive, namely: (a) hire agreements, (b) agreements secured on land,[46] (c) pawn agreements, (d) credit agreements for business purposes, and (e) agreements providing for credit in excess of the Directive's financial ceiling (£60,260).[47] Hence there are now two regulatory regimes in some circumstances: the old regime applying to such "non-Directive" regulated agreements and a new "Directive" regime applying to regulated credit agreements within the scope of the Directive. However, some of the "Directive" protections have been extended to "non-Directive" agreements either in order to maintain a coherent regime (so they apply to hire-purchase as well as to conditional sale agreements, and to a large extent to pawn agreements) or because they are regarded as appropriate protections in any event.[48] Moreover, when it comes to the formal requirements for regulated credit agreements,[49] creditors who would otherwise be outside the new "Directive" regime may generally "opt into" it.

39-012 Banks and investment firms authorised in other EEA states The implementation of the EU's Banking Directive[50] and Markets in Financial Instruments Directive[51] was affected by legislative provisions contained in or made under the

---

44 Directive 2008/48/EC, [2008] O.J. L133/66, replacing Consumer Credit Directive (87/102). See also Directive 2011/90/EU of November 14, 2011 amending the APR assumptions in Pt II of Annex I to the 2008 Directive, implemented on January 1, 2013 by the Consumer Credit (Total Charge for Credit) (Amendment) Regulations 2012 (SI 2012/1745): see below, para.39-059.

45 The Directive was implemented by a series of statutory instruments: (a) Consumer Credit (EU) Regulations 2010 (SI 2010/1010, as amended by SI 2010/1969 and SI 2010/1011) (the main implementing regulations, amending, inter alia, the 1974 Act); (b) Consumer Credit (Total Charge for Credit) Regulations 2010 (SI 2010/1011, as amended by SI 2011/11 and since revoked by SI 2013/1881 art.21(gg)) (see below, para.39-059); (c) Consumer Credit (Advertisements) Regulations 2010 (SI 2010/1012 replaced by SI 2010/1970 and since revoked by SI 2013/1881 art.21(hh)) (see below, para.39-067); (d) Consumer Credit (Disclosure of Information) Regulations 2010 (SI 2010/1013, as amended by SI 2010/1969 and SI 2011/11) (see below, para.39-076); (e) Consumer Credit (Agreements) Regulations 2010 (SI 2010/1014, as amended by SI 2010/1969) (see below, paras 39-080 and 39-082).

46 But see now the Mortgage Credit Directive (above, para.39-003) which required the imposition of regulation on (essentially) all residential mortgages.

47 But when the Mortgage Credit Directive (see above, para.39-003) was implemented on March 21, 2016, the Consumer Credit Directive was extended to apply to unsecured loans above this financial limit to renovate residential property and hence the Consumer Credit Act 1974 was amended accordingly in relation to so-called "residential renovation agreements" (as defined in CCA 1974 s.189(1) to refer to the Directive definition): see amendments to the 1974 Act made by SI 2015/910 art.3 and Sch.1 para.2(3)–(9).

48 e.g. the *FCA Handbook* CONC 4.2 and 4.3 (previously CCA 1974 s.55A), CONC 5 and 6.2 (previously CCA 1974 s.55B) and CCA 1974 s.66A are applicable to regulated "business" credit agreements; *FCA Handbook* CONC 5 and 6.2 (previously CCA 1974 s.55B) and the financial promotion restrictions in CONC 3 are applicable to credit above £60,260 (see below, para.39-067).

49 See below, paras 39-080 et seq.

50 Directive 2013/36/EU (and related texts), so-called "CRR/CRD IV", replacing Directive 2006/48, replacing Directive 2000/12, which in turn replaced the Second Banking Coordination Directive 89/646.

51 "MiFID" (Directive 2004/39), replacing the Investment Services Directive (ISD), Directive 93/22, was itself replaced by "MiFID II" (Directive 2014/65/EU) and "MiFIR" (Regulation EU No.600/2014) in January 2017.

Financial Services and Markets Act 2000.[52] The philosophy underlying the Directives is that of "home state control", i.e. the authorisation and regulation of the institutions concerned are matters for the home state, with the host state having only a limited regulatory role. As a result of these provisions the control exercisable by virtue of the Consumer Credit Act 1974 and the Financial Services and Markets Act 2000 is presently reduced in the case of (broadly) an institution established in an EEA state ("home state") other than the United Kingdom that is authorised to carry on the relevant activity by its home state regulator.[53] Such a firm is presently entitled to establish a branch or provide services in another EEA state (the entitlement is sometimes referred to as "the single market passport") in accordance with the EU Treaty as applied in the EEA and subject to the conditions of the relevant single market directive.[54] If it seeks to exercise its passport rights in the United Kingdom it will presently qualify for authorisation by satisfying certain formal conditions such as informing the Financial Conduct Authority (FCA) of its intentions and being informed of the rules that apply to the conduct of its activities in the United Kingdom.[55] In particular, such a firm that qualifies for authorisation is presently ordinarily exempted from the need to apply for FCA authorisation.[56] The expected impact of "Brexit" on the operation of the "single market passport" is presently uncertain.

The Standards of Lending Practice These "Standards",[57] which set the benchmark of good lending practices, are issued by the Lending Standards Board and replace the old "Lending Code" (which itself replaced, in part, the provisions of the old Banking Code[58]). Like the Code, they are voluntary "soft law" in the sense that lending institutions agree to be bound by them in their dealings with both personal and (small) business customers but the Standards do not, as such, give rise to legal rights or obligations.[59] The scope and content of the Standards differ from that of the consumer credit regulatory regime but there is a considerable degree of overlap. In some respects the protection is more extensive than that of the statutory regime and in other respects it is less extensive. But nothing in the Code can detract from the statutory regulatory system or diminish the protection afforded to debtors and hirers, or their sureties, contained in that regime.[60]

39-013

Other EU Directives Other EU Directives have had an impact on the statutory regulatory regime, in particular, the Electronic Commerce Directive 2000,[61] the Distance Marketing of Consumer Financial Services Directive 2002,[62] the Unfair

39-014

---

52 FSMA 2000 ss.31(1)(b), 37 and Sch.3, as amended.
53 FSMA 2000 Sch.3 Pt I para.5.
54 FSMA 2000 Sch.3 Pt I para.7.
55 FSMA 2000 Sch.3 Pt I paras 12–15.
56 FSMA 2000 Sch.3 Pt I para.15(3).
57 They can be downloaded from *https://www.lendingstandardsboard.org.uk/the-slp*.
58 The other parts of the old Banking Code are replaced by the BCOBS Module of the *FCA Handbook*.
59 But the Banking Code is relevant to the extent of the common law duty owed by a bank subscribing to the Code; see *Thomas v Triodos Bank NV* [2017] EWHC 314 (QB).
60 See CCA 1974 s.173, above, para.39-009
61 Directive 2003/31, implemented, as far as consumer credit is concerned, primarily by the Consumer Credit Act 1974 (Electronic Communications) Order 2004 (SI 2004/3236) made under the Electronic Communications Act 2000.
62 Directive 2002/65, implemented by the Financial Services (Distance Marketing) Regulations 2004 (SI 2004/2095), see below, para.39-126.

Commercial Practices Directive 2005,[63] the Revised Payment Services Directive 2015 ("PSD2")[64] and the Consumer Rights Directive 2011.[65] The Mortgage Credit Directive 2014[66] resulted in further significant changes to the statutory regime, in particular the transfer of second charge residential mortgage regulation to the Financial Services and Markets Act 2000 regime. English law, as altered by the implementation of these directives, is not expected to be amended as a result of Brexit, at least in the near future.[67]

(a) Terminology

39-015 **New concepts** The draftsman of the Consumer Credit Act 1974 found it impossible to set up a system of wide-ranging control without devising new concepts, and consequently introduced, in Pt II of the Act (ss.8 to 20) and elsewhere, an entirely new and complex terminology. An understanding of this terminology is essential to an understanding of the regulatory regime. Examples illustrating the use of this terminology are provided in Pt II of Sch.2 to the 1974 Act.[68] On the transfer of consumer credit regulation to the FCA,[69] that terminology has been adopted (with minor changes[70]) in legislative provisions made under the FSMA 2000, in particular the RAO.[71]

39-016 **"[Consumer] credit agreement"** The 1974 Act defines a "consumer credit agreement" as an agreement[72] between an individual ("the debtor") and any other person ("the creditor") by which the creditor provides[73] the debtor with credit[74] of any

---

[63] Directive 2005/29, implemented by the Consumer Protection from Unfair Trading Regulations 2008 (SI 2008/1277), as amended by the Consumer Protection (Amendment) Regulations 2014 (SI 2014/870) in relation to contracts entered into on or after October 1, 2014. See, generally, above, paras 38-157 et seq.

[64] Replacing the old Payment Services Directive 2007, Directive 2007/64/EC. PSD2 has been implemented, as far as consumer credit is concerned, primarily by the Payment Services Regulations 2017 (SI 2017/752). Overlap with the 1974 Act is, to some extent, avoided: see, in particular regs 41 and 64. See further, paras 34-224 and 39-510 et seq.

[65] Directive 2011/83/EU. The Government implemented that part of the Directive that amended previous Directives conferring cancellation rights in certain sales on consumers, by the Consumer Contracts (Information, Cancellation and Additional Charges) Regulations 2013 (SI 2013/3134), an order under the European Communities Act 1972. See further below, para.39-125. See now the Consumer Rights Act 2015 (for contracts made on or after October 1, 2015) which updates and clarifies the law on goods and services and unfair contract terms, considered further above in paras 38-365 et seq.

[66] See above, para.39-003.

[67] See above, Vol.I, paras 1-016 et seq.

[68] But see s.188(2), (3). Note *Southern Pacific Mortgage Ltd v Heath* [2009] EWCA Civ 1135: Example 16 regarded as erroneous by Lloyd L.J.

[69] See above, para.39-002.

[70] For example the terms "lender" and "borrower" are used (in line with the terminology already used by the *FCA Handbook* in relation to the regulation of mortgages) rather than "creditor" and "debtor".

[71] The Financial Services and Markets Act 2000 (Regulated Activities) Order 2001 (SI 2001/544), as amended. See especially RAO arts 60B(3) and 60L.

[72] For the Act to apply there must be an "agreement", and not merely, e.g. an offer or letter of intent or proposal (see Vol.I, Ch.2). There may, however, be difficulty in ascertaining whether there is an agreement for a line of credit or whether the actual credit agreement is made in pursuance of the line of credit or both.

[73] i.e. agrees to provide: see CCA 1974 Sch.2 Example 21 and *National Westminster Bank Plc v Story* [1999] C.C.L.R. 70, CA.

[74] See below, para.39-019.

amount.[75] The expression "individual" is stated to include a partnership consisting of two or three persons not all of whom are bodies corporate and any other unincorporated body not consisting entirely of bodies corporate.[76] Hence an agreement for the provision of credit where the debtor is a body corporate will not be a "consumer credit agreement".[77] But if the debtor is an unincorporated body, such as a society or club, or is a sole trader or partnership of three or fewer persons, there can be a "consumer credit agreement" notwithstanding that the debtor carries on a business and that the credit is advanced for business purposes.[78] The definition of "credit agreement" in the RAO is almost identical, with the use of the terms "borrower" and "lender" instead of "debtor" and "creditor".[79] Therefore the application of the regulatory regime is generally determined by the status of the debtor/borrower and not by the purpose of the advance, subject to two qualifications in relation to "business" credit.[80] First, as noted below,[81] "business" agreements for over £25,000 are exempt from regulation. Second, as a result of the implementation of the Consumer Credit Directive[82] (which does not apply to "business" credit) the regulatory regime is less onerous in a number of respects in relation to regulated "business" credit agreements, although creditors may choose to opt into the "Directive" formal requirements for regulated credit agreements.[83]

"Regulated" consumer credit agreement   Since the transfer of consumer credit **39-017** regulation to the FCA,[84] the definition of "regulated" credit agreement is now in the Financial Services and Markets Act 2000 (Regulated Activities) Order 2001,[85] the so-called "RAO". A consumer credit agreement is a regulated agreement within the meaning of the 1974 Act[86] and for the purposes of RAO[87] if it is not an "exempt

---

75   CCA 1974 s.8(1). Section 8 was amended (i) (from April 6, 2008) by the Consumer Credit Act 2006 ss.2(1) and 5; (ii) (from October 31, 2008) by SI 2008/2826; (iii) (from April 1, 2014) by SI 2013/1881 and (iv) (from February 28, 2014) by SI 2014/436 (s.8(1) does not apply to a "green deal plan", because CCA 1974 s.189B applies instead (see below, para.39-257)). See the almost identical definition in RAO art.60LB(3). As noted above (para.39-005), originally the Act imposed a financial limit.
76   CCA 1974 s.189(1), as amended (from April 6, 2007) by the Consumer Credit Act 2006 s.1. See CCA 1974 Sch.2 Pt II Examples 19, 24. See the almost identical definition of "relevant recipient of credit" in RAO art.60L.
77   Except under CCA 1974 s.185(5), as amended by the Consumer Credit Act 2006 s.5(8), where such a body corporate contracts jointly with an individual. See *Bank of Ireland (UK) Plc v McLaughlin* [2014] NIQB 104 (corporate debtor not within CCA 1974).
78   See CCA 1974 Sch.2 Pt II Examples 7, 15, 19.
79   RAO art.60B(3) (for the definition of "relevant recipient of credit", see RAO art.60L).
80   Moreover, the application of the financial promotion provisions in CONC 3 do not apply to prospective *business* debtors: CONC 3.1.6R(1) (as was the case with the now repealed 2004 Advertising Regulations), see below, para.39-067.
81   RAO art.60C(3)–(7) (previously CCA 1974 s.16B), below para.39-046.
82   See above, para.39-011.
83   See below, para.39-080.
84   See above, para.39-002.
85   SI 2001/544, made under the FSMA 2000 s.22 (as amended in this regard by SI 2013/1881). See RAO art.60B(3) and the next footnote.
86   s.8(3), cross-referring to the definition in the RAO Ch.14A. But (as a result of the implementation of the Mortgage Credit Directive (see above, para.39-003) on March 21, 2016) there is the further qualification that, for the agreement to be a "regulated credit agreement" for the purposes of the CCA 1974, the agreement must *not* be for the acquisition or retention of property rights in land or a building (see amendment to s.8(3) in SI 2015/910 art.3 and Sch.1 para.2(2)).
87   RAO art.60B(3), and note the transitional provisions (for agreements made before April 1, 2014).

agreement", as also defined in the RAO.[88] An agreement that would not otherwise be a "regulated" agreement but is stated to be "regulated" and is documented as such, is not treated as a "regulated" agreement for the purposes of the regulatory regime.[89]

39-018 **"Debtor"/"borrower" and "creditor"/"lender"** The expressions "debtor" and "creditor" are used in the 1974 Act to refer respectively to the individual receiving credit and the person providing credit under a consumer credit agreement, or the person[90] to whom his rights and duties under the agreement have passed by assignment[91] or operation of law, and in relation to a prospective consumer credit agreement includes the prospective debtor or creditor.[92] The definitions of "borrower" and "lender" in the RAO are almost identical.[93] There is no requirement that the creditor/lender carries on a consumer credit, or any, business.[94]

39-019 **"Credit"** The expression "credit" is not defined in the 1974 Act or the RAO,[95] but is stated in both instruments to include "a cash loan, and any form of financial accommodation".[96] These words embrace all types of loan (e.g. moneylenders' loans, bank and building society loans, overdrafts, pawnbrokers' loans, advances on mortgage, etc.), the sale of goods on instalment credit terms (e.g. credit sales, conditional sales, budget accounts, option accounts, subscription accounts, etc.), the supply of services on credit, check trading, credit cards and charge cards[97] and debit cards.[98] In fact, any agreement for, say, the supply of goods or services where "credit" is extended (in the sense of the grant of a contractual right to defer the payment of a debt, whether the payment is to be made in one amount or by instal-

---

[88] In RAO arts 60C–60HA, see below, paras 39-038 et seq.

[89] *NRAM Plc v McAdam & Hartley* [2015] EWCA Civ 751, reversing [2014] EWHC 4174 (Comm).

[90] The assignment by an individual debtor of his rights under a consumer credit agreement to a company does not alter the status of the agreement.

[91] See the *FCA Handbook*, CONC 6.5 (previously CCA 1974 s.82A (added in implementation of the Consumer Credit Directive, see above, para.39-011)): in the case of an assignment of a regulated agreement other than one secured on land, the assignee must "arrange for" notice to be given to the debtor if arrangements for servicing the credit change from the debtor's perspective.

[92] s.189(1). See *Jones v Link Financial Ltd* [2012] EWHC 2402 (QB), [2012] C.C.L.R. 3 (extent of application of CCA 1974 to legal assignee of creditor).

[93] RAO art.60L(1).

[94] But see "non-commercial agreements", below para.39-049. A lender who enters into a regulated credit agreement by way of business requires FCA authorisation, see below para.39-062.

[95] The essence of credit is the contractual right to defer payment of an existing debt, or to incur a debt and defer its payment: *R. v Mitchell* [1955] 1 W.L.R. 1125; *R. v Garlick* (1958) 42 Cr. App. R. 141; *Grant v Watton (Inspector of Taxes)* [1999] S.T.C. 330, 345; *Dimond v Lovell* [2000] 1 Q.B. 261; affirmed [2002] 1 A.C. 384. For the problems which arise, see Guest and Lloyd *Encyclopedia of Consumer Credit Law* (1975, looseleaf) at para.2-010; and Goode, *Consumer Credit: Law and Practice*, Pt C, Ch.24. See also *Santander UK Plc v Harrison* [2013] EWHC 199 (QB), [2013] C.C.L.R. 4: the capitalisation of arrears (by adding them to the outstanding capital balance and increasing the monthly repayments correspondingly) whilst being the provision of "credit" was not the provision of a "cash loan" (for the purposes of SI 2008/831 art.4(1) which uses the term "cash loan", see below, para.39-148).

[96] CCA 1974 s.9(1); RAO art.60L (and see art.61(3)(c) in relation to mortgages). See CCA 1974 Sch.2 Pt II Examples 16, 19, 21. This wide definition of "credit" is also adopted in numerous other statutory provisions, e.g. the Consumer Protection (Distance Selling) Regulations 2000 (SI 2000/2334) reg.3(1); the Financial Services (Distance Marketing) Regulations 2004 (SI 2004/2095) reg.2(1).

[97] See CCA 1974 Sch.2 Pt II Example 16.

[98] But see below, para.39-488.

ments)[99] will be a consumer credit agreement if the debtor is an individual. In many commercial agreements, payment is to be made in arrear; such agreements can therefore be consumer credit agreements (if the debtor is not a body corporate or large partnership), although they may be "exempt agreements"[100] and hence will not necessarily be regulated agreements.

Hire agreements   The words "any other form of financial accommodation" do not **39-020** cover hire agreements (e.g. rental or leasing agreements) as hire agreements are contained within a separate category for which special statutory provision is made.[101] But, the hiring of goods to an individual under a hire-purchase agreement is deemed to be the provision of fixed-sum credit.[102]

"Credit exceeding £25,000"   Although the Consumer Credit Act 2006 removed **39-021** the financial limit so that agreements providing credit of any amount may now be regulated agreements,[103] the limit has been retained for the purposes of the exemption for credit advanced for purely *business* purposes.[104] Hence, in that context, it is still necessary to decide if "credit exceeding £25,000"[105] is provided. These words are relatively easy to apply where the agreement is one for the provision of fixed-sum credit[106]: the amount of the credit will be the amount agreed to be lent (whether

---

[99] See *Storlink UK v Thomas* [1996] C.L.Y. 1225, Cty Ct; *Dimond v Lovell* [2000] 1 Q.B. 261, affirmed [2002] 1 A.C. 384. Contrast *Legal and General Assurance Soc v Cooper* [1994] C.L.Y. 2656, Cty Ct (advance of monies against future commission did not constitute the provision of "credit"); *Tilby v Perfect Pizza Ltd* (2002) N.L.J. 397, [2003] C.C.L.R. 9 (ATE insurance premium payable only when risk arose did not involve "credit"); *Nejad v City Index Ltd* [2000] C.C.L.R. 7 (so-called "credit allocation" in betting context not "credit" as indebtedness would not necessarily arise); *McMillan Williams v Range* [2004] EWCA 294, [2004] 1 W.L.R. 1858 (no "credit" where unclear at the outset if indebtedness would arise); *Maple Leaf Macro Volatility Master Fund v Rouvroy* [2009] EWHC 257, [2009] C.C.L.R. 9 (no "credit" in funding agreement where no certainty that obligations to pay under the agreement would arise); *OFT v Ashbourne Management Services Ltd* [2011] EWHC 1237 (Ch) (monthly payment for gym membership did not give rise to "credit"); *Burrell v Helical (Bramshott Place) Ltd* [2015] EWHC 3727 (Ch) (no deferment of any obligation to pay hence no "credit").

[100] By virtue of the RAO art.60F (previously CCA 1974 s.16(5)) and the Exempt Agreements Order (SI 1989/869) art.3, made thereunder the following (inter alia) are "exempt agreements" (see below, paras 39-038 et seq.): (i) certain "borrower-lender-supplier" agreements (see below, para.39-030) for fixed-sum credit (see below, para.39-026) where the number of payments to be made by the borrower does not exceed 12 (previously four) if those payments are required to be made within a period of 12 months (or less) beginning with the date of the agreement and (ii) certain "borrower-lender-supplier" agreements (see below, para.39-030) for running-account credit (see below, para.39-024) where the number of payments to be made by the borrower in repayment of the whole credit per period of not more than three months does not exceed one. In both cases (as a result of the Consumer Credit Directive (see above, para.39-011)) there must be no charge for the credit. Further, by virtue of the RAO art.60G, certain "borrower-lender" agreements (see below, para.39-033) at low rates of charge are exempt.

[101] CCA 1974 s.15 and RAO arts 60N–60R, see below, para.39-035 and above, paras 33-085 et seq.; *Moorgate Mercantile Leasing Ltd v Isobel Gell and Ugolini Dispensers (UK) Ltd* [1986] 2 C.L. 39, Cty Ct. But see *Dimond v Lovell* [2000] Q.B. 216; *Burdis v Livsey* [2002] EWCA Civ 510, [2003] Q.B. 36 ("credit hire" agreements where hire payments were deferred were also credit agreements); and Guest and Lloyd *Encyclopedia of Consumer Credit Law* (1975, looseleaf) at para.2-016.

[102] CCA 1974 s.9(3) and RAO art.60L(8). See below, para.39-357.

[103] See above, para.39-010.

[104] RAO art.60C(3)–(7) (previously CCA 1974 s.16B), below para.39-046.

[105] For credit otherwise than in sterling, see CCA 1974 s.9(1) and RAO art.60L(9).

[106] Defined in CCA 1974 s.10(1)(b) and RAO art.60L; below, para.39-026.

this is to be drawn down in a lump sum or by instalments). In the case of a credit sale or conditional sale agreement, or a hire-purchase agreement,[107] relating to goods, the amount of the credit will be the balance financed, i.e. the cash price less the deposit (if any). But in the case of running-account credit,[108] the application of the £25,000 limit is by no means simple.[109]

39-022 **The Consumer Credit Directive: "credit exceeding £60,260"**   The Consumer Credit Directive[110] does not generally apply to agreements providing credit in excess of €100,000 and hence, in general, agreements providing credit in excess of that amount (which has been converted to £60,260 for the purposes of implementing the Directive in the United Kingdom) are not affected by the provisions that are derived from the Directive.[111] However, the duty to assess creditworthiness[112] as well as credit promotion regulation[113] apply regardless of the credit amount. Moreover, although creditors offering credit in excess of £60,260[114] prima facie remain subject to the "old" regime as regards formal agreement requirements,[115] they may "opt into" the new "Directive" regime.[116]

39-023 **"Charge for credit"**   For the purposes of the 1974 Act, an item entering into the total charge for credit[117] (e.g. interest, credit charges or other time/price differential charges, and certain other fees or charges) is not to be treated as credit even though time is allowed for its payment.[118]

---

107 Which is an agreement for "fixed-sum credit", see CCA 1974 s.9(3) and RAO art.60L(8); see also below, para.39-357.
108 Defined in CCA 1974 s.10(1)(a) and RAO art.60L; below, para.39-024.
109 See below, para.39-025.
110 See above, para.39-011.
111 Viz: CCA 1974 ss.55C, 60(5)(c), 61, 66A, 75A, 77B and *FCA Handbook*, CONC 4.2 and 4.3 (previously CCA 1974 s.55A). Moreover, the "high net worth" exemption in RAO art.60H (previously CCA 1974 s.16A) below, para.39-045, remains applicable to such agreements. But when the Mortgage Credit Directive (see above, para.39-003) was implemented on March 21, 2016, that financial threshold ceased to apply to "residential renovation agreements" (as defined in CCA 1974 s.189(1) to mean, essentially, unsecured loans to renovate residential property): see amendments made to the 1974 Act in SI 2015/910 art.3 and Sch.1 paras 2(3)–(9).
112 In the *FCA Handbook*, CONC 5 and 6.2 (previously CCA 1974 s.55B) considered further below, para.39-078.
113 In the *FCA Handbook*, CONC 3 (previously SI 2010/1970) considered further below, para.39-067.
114 When the Mortgage Credit Directive (see above, para.39-003) was implemented on March 21, 2016, so-called "residential renovation agreements" (as defined in CCA 1974 s.189(1) to mean, essentially, unsecured loans to renovate residential property) above this threshold became subject to the "new" (consumer credit) directive regime: see amendments made by SI 2015/910 art.3 and Sch.1 paras 3, 11, 13, 14.
115 See below, paras 39-080 et seq.
116 See below, para.39-080.
117 Defined in CCA 1974 ss.20(1), 189(1); below, para.39-059.
118 s.9(4) (see the equivalent provision in the RAO art.60L(11); added by SI 2015/853 art.3(5)). See CCA 1974 Sch.2 Pt II Examples 5, 19; and *Huntpast Ltd v Leadbeater* [1993] C.C.L.R. 15; *Humberclyde Finance Ltd v Thompson* [1997] C.C.L.R. 23; *Wilson v First County Trust Ltd* [2001] Q.B. 407; *Wilson v Robertsons (London) Ltd* [2005] EWHC 1425; *Griffiths v Welcome Financial Services Ltd* [2007] C.C.L.R. 3. In respect of a loan of money advanced in part to discharge prior mortgage arrears, see the apparently conflicting decisions (as to whether these arrears were a "charge for credit") of the Court of Appeal in *Watchtower Investments Ltd v Payne* [2001] EWCA Civ 1159 (followed in *London North Securities Ltd v Meadows* [2005] EWCA Civ 956); and *McGinn v Grangewood Securities Ltd* [2002] EWCA Civ 522. *London North Securities Ltd v Meadows* was distinguished in *Black Horse Ltd v Hanson & Ant* [2009] EWCA Civ 73, [2009] C.C.L.R. 6, where

"Running-account credit" This expression is defined, for the purposes of the **39-024** 1974 Act and the RAO, as "a facility under a [consumer] credit agreement[119] whereby the debtor/borrower or another "is enabled to receive from time to time" from the creditor/lender or a third party "cash, goods or services to an amount or value such that, taking into account payments made by or to the credit of the debtor/ borrower, the credit limit (if any) is not at any time exceeded".[120] Examples of running-account credit are bank overdrafts, shop budget accounts, credit cards and charge cards, debit cards, and option accounts.[121]

"Credit limit" In relation to running-account credit, "credit limit" is defined to **39-025** mean, as respects any period, the maximum debit balance which, under the credit agreement, is allowed to stand on the account during that period.[122] But any term of the agreement allowing that maximum to be exceeded merely temporarily is to be disregarded.[123]

For the purpose of deciding whether or not running-account credit gives rise to an exempt "business" credit agreement,[124] the transaction will be within the £25,000 limit (and hence not exempt) if the credit limit does not exceed £25,000.[125] However, there is an anti-avoidance provision in s.10(3)(b) of the 1974 Act and in the RAO which sets out three situations where running-account credit is deemed not to exceed £25,000, whether or not there is a credit limit, and if there is, notwithstanding that it exceeds £25,000. The first situation is where the debtor is not enabled to draw at any one time an amount that, so far as it represents credit, exceeds £25,000.[126] The second situation is where the agreement provides that, if the debit balance rises above a given amount (not exceeding £25,000), the rate of the total charge for credit increases or any other condition favouring the creditor or his associate comes into operation.[127] The third situation is where, at the time the

a dealer erroneously added VAT to the price and hence included it when he stated the "amount of the credit" in the agreement. It was held that this VAT amount, although erroneously charged, did form part of the "credit" and was not part of the total charge for credit. See also *Southern Pacific Securities 05–2 Plc v Walker* [2010] UKSC 32 (deferred broker's administration fee and interest thereon within s.9(4) and hence not part of "credit").

119 The CCA 1974 uses the expression "consumer credit agreement" (defined in s.8(1)) and the RAO uses the expression "credit agreement" (defined in RAO art.60B) but both have an almost identical meaning, see above, para.39-016.

120 CCA 1974 s.10(1)(a) (as amended (from April 6, 2008) by the Consumer Credit Act 2006 s.5(2)(a)) and RAO art.60L. See also CCA 1974 ss.18, 78, 82, 108, 118, 120 and 185.

121 See CCA 1974 Sch.2 Pt II Examples 15, 16, 18 and 23. It is a moot point whether traders' running accounts or milk, newspaper, etc. accounts are for "running-account credit" or "fixed-sum credit". The distinction is important, inter alia, in respect of the RAO art.60F (previously the Consumer Credit (Exempt Agreements) Order 1989 (SI 1989/869) art.3(1)(a)). See also *Goshawk Dedicated (No.2) Ltd v Bank of Scotland* [2005] EWHC 2906 (Ch), [2006] C.C.L.R. 1.

122 CCA 1974 s.10(2) and RAO art.60L(7). See also CCA 1974 Sch.2 Pt II Examples 6, 7, 19, 22, 23.

123 CCA 1974 s.10(2) and RAO art.60L(7). This is to permit, for example, a bank to honour cheques drawn on it in (temporary) excess of an agreed overdraft. See also CCA 1974 ss.18(5), 82(4), Sch.2 Pt II Examples 22, 23.

124 Within RAO art.60C(3)–(7) (previously CCA 1974 s.16B), see below, para.39-046.

125 CCA 1974 s.10(3)(a), as amended (from April 6, 2008) by the Consumer Credit Act 2006 s.5(2)(b).

126 CCA 1974 s.10(3)(b)(i). See the corresponding provision in RAO art.60L(10)(b)(i), added by SI 2015/853 art.3(6). Thus if a bank grants business overdraft facilities to an individual of £60,000 (or even without limit), but stipulates that, say, he shall only be entitled to draw £10,000 in any one month, there will be a regulated credit agreement.

127 CCA 1974 s.10(3)(b)(ii). See the corresponding provision in RAO art.60L(10)(b)(ii), added by SI 2015/853 art.3(6). An example would be where the agreement provides for an increase in interest

agreement is made it is probable, having regard to the terms of the agreement and any other relevant considerations, that the debit balance will not at any time rise above £25,000.[128] A creditor cannot therefore avoid the operation of the regulatory regime in relation to business credit, for example, by agreeing to provide running-account credit up to £30,000, when it is probable from the outset that the debtor will not require more than £25,000.[129]

39-026 **"Fixed-sum credit"** This is any facility, other than running-account credit, under a [consumer] credit agreement[130] whereby the debtor/borrower is enabled to receive credit (whether in one amount or by instalments).[131] That which is not running-account credit is therefore fixed-sum credit. Examples of fixed-sum credit are moneylenders' loans, bank and building society loans, pawnbrokers' loans, hire-purchase,[132] credit sale and conditional sale agreements, and check trading.[133]

39-027 **"Restricted-use credit"** A restricted-use credit agreement is defined both in the 1974 Act[134] and the RAO.[135] There are three categories of restricted-use credit agreement. The first (category (a)) is a credit agreement[136] to finance a transaction between the debtor/borrower and the creditor/lender, whether forming part of that agreement or not.[137] Examples of this category of agreement are hire-purchase,[138] credit sale and conditional sale agreements (whether the credit is provided by the supplier himself, or by a financier under the "direct collection" method of busi-

---

128 rate, or for provision of security by the debtor, if the debit balance exceeds £10,000.

128 CCA 1974 s.10(3)(b)(iii). See the corresponding provision in RAO art.60L(10)(b)(iii), added by SI 2015/853 art.3(6). See also CCA 1974 Sch.2 Pt II Example 7.

129 The considerable uncertainty created by this anti-avoidance provision is to some extent mitigated, but by no means wholly removed, by s.171(1) (agreement by the parties that, in their opinion, s.10(3)(b)(iii) does not apply to the agreement).

130 The CCA 1974 uses the expression "consumer credit agreement" (defined in s.8(1)) and the RAO uses the expression "credit agreement" (defined in RAO art.60B) but both have an almost identical meaning, see above, para.39-016.

131 CCA 1974 s.10(1)(b) (as amended (from April 6, 2008) by the Consumer Credit Act 2006 s.5(2)(a)) and RAO art.60. See also CCA 1974 ss.18, 77, 107, 118, 120, 139. See CCA 1974 s.189C(1)(a): a "green deal consumer credit agreement" (as defined in CCA 1974 s.189B(8) to mean a green deal plan (as defined in CCA 1974 s.189(1)) that is to be treated as a consumer credit agreement for the purpose of the 1974 Act by virtue of CCA 1974 s.189B(1)) is to be treated as an agreement for fixed-sum credit within s.10(1)(b). For "green deal plans" see below, para.39-257.

132 CCA 1974 s.9(3) and RAO art, 60L(8); see below, para.39-357.

133 See also CCA 1974 Sch.2 Pt II Examples 9, 10, 17, 23 and note the controversy over traders', etc. "running accounts" noted above, para.39-025.

134 CCA 1974 s.11(1), which also provides that the expression "restricted-use credit" is to be construed in the Act accordingly. See also ss.12, 13, 19(1)(c), 58(2), 69, 71, 72, 74(2).

135 RAO art.60L(1), (2).

136 The CCA 1974 s.11(1) uses the term "regulated consumer credit agreement" but it is suggested that the RAO definition (in referring to "credit agreement") is the more logical as whether an agreement is regulated or not will depend on whether it is for restricted use (and hence a borrower-supplier or borrower-lender-supplier agreement: see below, para.39-030).

137 CCA 1974 s.11(1)(a) and RAO art.60L(1). See *National Westminster Bank Plc v Story* [1999] C.C.L.R. 70, Cty Ct (there must be a contractual commitment "to finance" rather than a mere common purpose, see below, para.39-028). See also *Consolidated Finance Ltd v McCluskey* [2012] EWCA Civ 1325 (CCA 1974 s.11(1) inapplicable due to absence of either an express or implied term as to the provision of finance), followed in *Consolidated Finance Ltd v Collins* [2013] EWCA Civ 475.

138 CCA 1974 s.9(3) and RAO art.60L(8); below, para.39-357. See also CCA 1974 Sch.2 Pt II Example 10.

ness where the goods are sold by the supplier to the financier and then let or sold by the financier to the debtor), and mail order credit and shop budget and option accounts. The second (category (b)) is a credit agreement[139] to finance a transaction between the debtor/borrower and a person (the "supplier") other than the creditor/lender.[140] Examples of this category of agreement are loans for the purchase of land, loans where the loan is paid directly to a dealer (other than the creditor) who supplies goods or services to the debtor/borrower, check trading agreements, and credit card agreements (insofar as the card is used to obtain goods or services and not money).[141] The third (category (c)) is a credit agreement[142] to refinance any existing indebtedness of the debtor's/borrower's whether to the creditor/lender or another person.[143]

An agreement is not a restricted-use credit agreement if the credit is in fact **39-028** provided in such a way as to leave the debtor/borrower free to use it as he chooses, even though certain uses would contravene that or any other agreement.[144] Thus, for example, if a moneylenders' or bank loan is advanced to a debtor for a particular purpose which is stipulated in the agreement,[145] but in fact is paid over to the debtor so that he could (albeit in breach of the agreement) use it in whatever manner he wished, the agreement is not a restricted-use credit agreement.[146] Nor is an agreement a restricted-use credit agreement unless it contains an express or implied term

---

[139] CCA 1974 s.11(1) uses the term "regulated consumer credit agreement" but it is suggested that the RAO definition (in referring to "credit agreement") is the more logical as whether an agreement is regulated or not will depend on whether it is for restricted use (and hence a borrower-supplier or borrower-lender-supplier agreement: see below, para.39-030).

[140] CCA 1974 s.11(1)(b) and RAO art.60L(1). This category applies even if the identity of the supplier is unknown at the time the agreement is made: CCA 1974 s.11(4) and RAO art.60L(2)(b). See *OFT v Lloyds TSB Bank Plc* [2006] EWCA Civ 268: despite "very extensive" number of outlets where debtor could use card, agreement still "restricted-use".

[141] See also CCA 1974 Sch.2 Pt II Examples 12, 14, 16. The word "transaction" is not defined in the Act or RAO and will extend to a transaction in land, accommodation, facilities or choses in action (such as shares) as well as goods or services. See *Sutherland Professional Funding Ltd v Bakewells (A Firm)* [2013] EWHC 2685 (QB): the "supplier" in relation to loan made to finance litigation was the solicitor who paid various disbursements to others, not the individual recipients of the disbursements. See CCA 1974 s.189C(2): where a "green deal consumer credit agreement" (as defined in CCA 1974 s.189B(8) to mean a green deal plan (as defined in CCA 1974 s.189(1)) that is to be treated as a consumer credit agreement for the purpose of this Act by virtue of CCA 1974 s.189B(1)) is a regulated agreement, it is to be treated as a restricted-use agreement within s.11(1)(a). For "green deal plans" see below, para.39-257.

[142] CCA 1974 s.11(1) uses the term "regulated consumer credit agreement" but it is suggested that the RAO definition (in referring to "credit agreement") is the more logical as whether an agreement is regulated or not will depend on whether it is for restricted use (and hence a borrower-supplier or borrower-lender-supplier agreement: see below, para.39-030).

[143] CCA 1974 s.11(1)(c) and RAO art.60L(1). See also CCA 1974 Sch.2 Pt II Example 13. See *Consolidated Finance Ltd v Collins* [2013] EWCA Civ 475 (on facts, a CCA 1974 s.11(1)(c) not a CCA 1974 s.11(1)(b) case).

[144] CCA 1974 s.11(3) and RAO art.60L(2)(a). *National Home Loans Corp Plc v Hannah* [1997] C.C.L.R. 7, Cty Ct; *Citibank International v Schlieder, The Times,* March 26, 1999. It has been confirmed that the fact that credit is, in fact, provided in such a way that the debtor is not free to use it as he chooses does not, without more, render it "restricted use" as credit is only "restricted use" if it falls within one of the categories in s.11(1): see *National Westminster Bank Plc v Story* [1999] C.C.L.R. 70, CA.

[145] If it is a term of a regulated agreement, it must be so stipulated: see CCA 1974 s.61(1)(b), below, para.39-083.

[146] cf. CCA 1974 Sch.2 Pt II Example 12.

that the credit is to be used for a particular purpose[147] even though there are mechanisms in place to ensure that he will not receive the credit unless it is so used.[148]

39-029 **"Unrestricted-use credit"** An unrestricted-use credit agreement is a credit agreement[149] that is not a restricted-use credit agreement.[150] Hence, in order to discover if an agreement is for "unrestricted-use" credit, it is necessary first to consider if it is for "restricted-use" credit.[151] If it is not, then the agreement is necessarily an "unrestricted-use" credit agreement. Examples of unrestricted-use credit agreements are pawnbrokers' loans, bank overdrafts, bank cash cards, and (usually) bank and building society personal loans, and credit cards (insofar as the card is used to obtain money and not goods or services).[152]

39-030 **"Debtor-creditor-supplier agreement"/"borrower-lender-supplier agreement"** One of the most important types of agreement classified in the 1974 Act and RAO is a "debtor-creditor-supplier agreement" (for the purposes of the 1974 Act) and "borrower-lender-supplier agreement" (for the purposes of the RAO).[153] The definitions of these two terms in the 1974 Act and RAO are almost identical, the different wording (debtor/borrower, creditor/lender) reflecting the different terminology in the two regulatory regimes. Such an agreement is defined as a credit agreement falling into one of three categories:

The first category is a category 12(a) restricted-use credit agreement, that is, one to finance a transaction between the debtor/borrower and the creditor/lender, whether forming part of that agreement or not.[154] It is important to realise that, despite the fact that the expression "debtor-creditor-supplier agreement"/"borrower-lender-supplier agreement" might suggest three parties (as in the usual tripartite arrangement between debtor, financier and dealer), within this category also fall agreements where only two parties are involved, as where a dealer carries his own instalment credit or a shop or mail order house allows the debtor/borrower credit for the purchase of the creditor/lender's own goods or services.[155]

39-031 The second category is a category 12(b) restricted-use credit agreement, that is, one to finance a transaction[156] between the debtor/borrower and a person (the "sup-

---

[147] *National Westminster Bank Plc v Story* [1999] C.C.L.R. 70, CA. See para.39-027, above.

[148] *National Home Loans Corp Plc v Hannah* [1997] C.C.L.R. 7, Cty Ct.

[149] CCA 1974 s.11(1) uses the term "regulated consumer credit agreement" but it is suggested that the RAO definition (in referring to "credit agreement") is the more logical as whether an agreement is regulated or not will depend on whether it is for restricted use (and hence a borrower-supplier or borrower-lender-supplier agreement: see below, para.39-030).

[150] CCA 1974 s.11(2) and RAO art.60L(1). CCA 1974 s.11(2) (but not the RAO provision) adds that the expression "unrestricted-use credit" is to be construed in the Act accordingly.

[151] See above, para.39-027 and note *OFT v Lloyds TSB Bank Plc* [2006] EWCA Civ 268 (affirmed as regards another issue: [2007] UKHL 48).

[152] See also CCA 1974 Sch.2 Pt II Examples 12, 16, 18, 21.

[153] See, in particular, CCA 1974 ss.19(1), 56, 69–75. Of these provisions, ss.70(3) and 75 are of particular importance and exemption under the RAO arts 60C–60G (see below, paras 39-038 et seq.), especially arts 60F and 60G, may depend on whether the agreement is "borrower-lender-supplier" or "borrower-lender".

[154] CCA 1974 s.12(a) and RAO art.60L. See above, para.39-027.

[155] See *Dimond v Lovell* [2002] 1 A.C. 384 (hire agreement where credit given for hire charges is a CCA 1974 s.12(a) agreement as regards the credit element).

[156] See above, para.39-027.

plier") other than the creditor/lender,[157] provided that it is made by the creditor/lender under pre-existing arrangements, or in contemplation of future arrangements, between himself and the supplier.[158] The definitions of "pre-existing arrangements" and "future arrangements"[159] are complex.[160] But typical examples of pre-existing arrangements between a creditor/lender and the supplier are those that exist between a financier and its dealers by whom loan business is channelled to the financier, between a credit card issuer and recognised suppliers (of goods or services) who have agreed to accept the card[161] and between a check trading company and the suppliers who have agreed to honour its checks.[162] The expression "in contemplation of future arrangements" is more difficult to construe and reference must be made to its precise wording.[163] But the mere fact that the credit agreement is entered into in the knowledge or subject to a term that the creditor/lender will pay the amount of the loan direct to the supplier does not necessarily involve a debtor-creditor-supplier or borrower-lender-supplier agreement if the creditor/lender holds himself out as willing to make, in specified circumstances, payments of that kind to suppliers generally.[164]

The third category is a category 12(c) unrestricted-use credit agreement, that is, **39-032** one made by the creditor/lender under pre-existing arrangements between himself and a person (the "supplier") other than the debtor/borrower in the knowledge that the credit is to be used to finance a transaction between the debtor/borrower and the supplier.[165] If, for example, as the result of an arrangement previously made between a financier and a dealer, a customer is directed by the dealer to the financier and obtains a loan, then, notwithstanding that the loan is at the free disposition of the debtor/borrower,[166] there will be a debtor-creditor-supplier or borrower-lender-supplier agreement if the financier knows that the loan will be used to purchase goods or services from the dealer.[167]

"Debtor-creditor agreement"/"borrower-lender agreement" Important **39-033** incidents are also attached to the classification of a credit agreement as a "debtor-

---

[157] See above, para.39-027.
[158] CCA 1974 s.12(b) and RAO art.60L.
[159] CCA 1974 s.187 (as amended by Banking Act 1987 s.89, which added a new subs.(3A) excluding arrangements for the electronic transfer of funds from a current account at a bank, e.g. EFTPOS transactions) and RAO art.60L(3)–(5). See below, para.39-488.
[160] See Guest and Lloyd, *Encyclopedia of Consumer Credit Law* (1975, looseleaf) at para.2-188.
[161] See *OFT v Lloyds TSB Bank Plc* [2006] EWCA Civ 268 (affirmed as regards another issue: [2007] UKHL 48) holding that "arrangements" exist in "four-party" credit card situations (see below, para.39-486) between card issuers and suppliers (even suppliers abroad) through network schemes such as VISA and Mastercard. See also *Bank of Scotland v Truman* [2005] EWHC 583, [2005] C.C.L.R. 3.
[162] CCA 1974 s.187(1) and RAO art.60L(3). See also CCA 1974 Sch.2 Pt II Example 16, and s.187(4), (5).
[163] See s.187(2), (4) and RAO art.60L(4), (5).
[164] CCA 1974 s.187(3) and RAO art.60L(5)(a). See also CCA 1974 Sch.2 Pt II Example 21.
[165] CCA 1974 s.12(c) and RAO art.60L.
[166] This is so whether any other use than a transaction between the customer and the dealer would be a breach of the credit agreement (see CCA 1974 s.11(3) and RAO art.60L(2)(a), above, para.39-028, and CCA 1974 Sch.2 Pt II Example 8) or whether the loan is, under the agreement, technically at the free disposition of the borrower.
[167] But certain similar transactions may be excluded by CCA 1974 s.187(3) and RAO art.60L(5)(a). See CCA 1974 Sch.2 Pt II Example 21 (cheque guarantee cards)—but since June 2011, no longer in use.

creditor" or "borrower-lender" agreement.[168] Again[169] the former term is used in the 1974 Act and the latter in the RAO but the definitions of these two terms in both instruments are almost identical. It is the intention of the two regimes that any credit agreement that is not a debtor-creditor-supplier/borrower-lender-supplier agreement, is a debtor-creditor/borrower-lender agreement. The three categories of this type of agreement are:

(i)   a category 12(b) restricted-use credit agreement[170] which is *not* made by the creditor/lender under pre-existing arrangements, or in contemplation of future arrangements, between himself and the supplier[171]; or

(ii)   a category 12(c) restricted-use credit agreement,[172] that is, to re-finance any existing indebtedness of the debtor's/borrower's, whether to the creditor/lender or another person[173]; or

(iii)   an unrestricted-use credit agreement that is not made by the creditor/lender under pre-existing arrangements between himself and a person (the "supplier") other than the debtor/borrower in the knowledge that the credit is to be used to finance a transaction between the debtor/borrower and the supplier.[174]

Examples of debtor-creditor/borrower-lender agreements are moneylending agreements and bank loans (where the money is at the free disposition of the borrower), overdrafts, pawnbrokers' loans, credit cards (insofar as the card is used to obtain money and not goods or services), and many cash card agreements.[175]

39-034   **"Credit-token agreement"**   A credit-token agreement is a regulated agreement for the provision of credit[176] in connection with the use of a credit-token.[177] Section 14(1) of the 1974 Act[178] defines a credit-token to mean a card, check, voucher, coupon, stamp, form, booklet or other document or thing given to an individual[179] by a person carrying on a consumer credit business,[180] who undertakes—(a) that on the production of it (whether or not some other action is also required) he will supply cash, goods and services (or any of them) on credit; or (b) that where, on production of it to a third party (whether or not any other action is also required),

---

[168]   See ss.49(1), 74(1). And exemption may depend on whether the agreement is borrower-lender or borrower-lender-supplier, see above para.39-030.

[169]   Compare the case of "debtor-creditor-supplier agreements" and "borrower-lender-supplier agreements", see above, para.39-030.

[170]   See above, para.39-027.

[171]   CCA 1974 s.13(a) and RAO art.60L(1). This excludes agreements within CCA 1974 s.12(b) (and the corresponding agreements within the definition of "borrower-lender-supplier agreement" within art.60L); above, para.39-031.

[172]   See above, para.39-027.

[173]   CCA 1974 s.13(b) and RAO art.60L(1).

[174]   CCA 1974 s.13(c) and RAO art.60L(1). This excludes agreements within CCA 1974 s.12(c) (and the corresponding agreements within the definition of "borrower-lender-supplier agreement" within art.60L); above, para.39-032.

[175]   See also CCA 1974 Sch.2 Pt II Examples 8, 16, 17, 18, 21.

[176]   See CCA 1974 s.9(1) (para.39-019, above) and s.14(3) (considered below).

[177]   CCA 1974 s.14(2). See also CCA 1974 ss.63(4), 64(2), 66, 70(5), 84, 85, 171(4), 170, SI 1983/1553 Sch.2 Pt I para.17 (Sch.2 was replaced by SI 2004/1482); SI 1983/1555, as amended, below, paras 39-494 et seq.

[178]   The definition in the *FCA Handbook* Glossary is similar.

[179]   Defined in s.189(1), see above, para.39-016.

[180]   Defined in CCA 1974 s.189(1) to mean any business in so far as it comprises or relates to providing credit (or otherwise being a creditor) under regulated consumer credit agreements.

the third party supplies cash, goods and services (or any of them), he will pay the third party for them (whether or not deducting any discount or commission), in return for payment to him by the individual.[181] Examples of credit-tokens are two-party and three-party (or four-party[182]) credit cards,[183] checks issued by check trading companies by which the holder is enabled to purchase goods from approved suppliers,[184] certain debit cards,[185] and (in certain instances)[186] cash cards by which cash can be obtained from an automatic machine.[187] Less obvious documents may also be included, for example "preferred customer" letters issued by a creditor to a debtor upon the successful conclusion of a credit agreement which entitles the debtor, on production of it, to obtain further credit. And in *Elliot v Director General of Fair Trading*[188] a Divisional Court held that the need, inter alia, to enter into a credit agreement before the credit was extended was "some other action" (within section 14(1)(a)) and did not prevent the document—a card with the size, shape and appearance of an ordinary credit card—from being a credit-token.[189] But a document is not a credit-token if it does not have to be produced in order to obtain cash, goods or services. It is further submitted that cheque forms issued by a bank, and cheques and drafts drawn on a bank, are not credit-tokens in that the undertaking of the bank (vis-à-vis its customer) is not to "supply cash", but to pay the instrument. Moreover, it seems clear that electronic purses insofar as they merely store "e-cash" are not "credit-tokens".[190]

"Consumer hire agreement"[191]   A "consumer hire agreement" is defined in the **39-035** 1974 Act[192] and the RAO[193] to mean an agreement made by a person ("the owner") with an individual[194] (the "hirer") for the bailment[195] of goods to the hirer, being an

---

181 Where CCA 1974 s.14(1)(b) applies, it is arguable that a deemed provision of credit arises under s.14(3): see below, para.39-488. See also CCA 1974 Sch.2 Pt II Examples 2, 14, 16, 21, 22. Alternatively (a preferable view), s.14(3) may merely determine *when* and *by whom* credit is provided.

182 *OFT v Lloyds TSB Bank Plc* [2006] EWCA Civ 268 (affirmed as regards another issue: [2007] UKHL 48).

183 See below, para.39-472.

184 See below, para.39-481.

185 See below, para.39-477 and Guest and Lloyd, *Encyclopedia of Consumer Credit Law* (1975, looseleaf) at para.2-015: probably only where issued under an agreement for the provision of credit.

186 See Guest and Lloyd, *Encyclopedia of Consumer Credit Law* (1975, looseleaf) at para.2-015.

187 CCA 1974 s.14(4).

188 [1980] 1 W.L.R. 977.

189 It therefore seems that a document that, in law, is an invitation to treat may be a credit-token. The Divisional Court held that "undertakes" in s.14(1) does not require a contractual agreement or the possibility of a contractual agreement.

190 See below, para.39-480 and Guest and Lloyd, *Encyclopedia of Consumer Credit Law* (1975, looseleaf) at para.2-015.

191 Provisions of the CCA 1974 and RAO applicable both to consumer credit and consumer hire agreements are dealt with in the present chapter. For provisions applicable solely to consumer hire agreements, see above, paras 33-085 et seq.

192 CCA 1974 s.15(1).

193 RAO art.60N(3) and note the use of the phrase "individual or relevant recipient of credit [sic]", which means the same as "individual" in the CCA 1974 s.189(1).

194 Defined in s.189(1) (and see previous note), see above, para.39-016.

195 Or in Scotland, "the hiring". It was held in *TRM Copy Centre (UK) Ltd v Lanwell Services Ltd* [2009] UKHL 35 that "bailment" must be construed as confined to an agreement for hire (i.e. an agreement by which the bailor transfers or agrees to transfer to the bailee possession of and the right to use the goods in exchange for payment in cash or kind). Any wider construction would create

agreement which—(a) is not a hire-purchase agreement[196]; and (b) is capable of subsisting for more than three months.[197] The original version of the definition in the 1974 Act imposed a financial limit[198] but this has been removed except in relation to "business" hire.[199] The 1974 Act and RAO thus embrace, not only domestic rental agreements, but also, by reason of the fact that the word "individual"[200] includes sole traders and small partnerships, and any unincorporated body of persons,[201] equipment leases and contract-hire agreements even though made for the business purposes of the hirer.[202] However, as noted below,[203] "business" hire for over £25,000 is exempt from regulation. The application of the 1974 Act and RAO is therefore (apart from this "business" exemption) determined by the status of the hirer and not by the purpose of the advance. As the Consumer Credit Directive[204] does not apply to hire agreements, such agreements are not affected by those provisions of the 1974 Act introduced in implementation of that Directive. Nor is there any possibility of owners "opting into" the "Directive" regime.

39-036 **"Regulated" consumer hire agreement** Since the transfer of consumer credit (and hire) regulation to the FCA,[205] the definition of "regulated" consumer hire agreement is now in the RAO.[206] A consumer hire agreement is a regulated

---

anomalies (see Palmer and Yates [1979] C.L.J. 180). And see *Eurocopy (Scotland) Plc v Lothian Health Board* 1995 S.L.T. 1356 (photocopier held to be provided under a contract of "hire" in circumstances where there was no charge, provided minimum amount of paper was purchased).

[196] For the definition of "hire-purchase agreement", see CCA 1974 s.189(1) and below, para.39-356. Hire-purchase is characterised as fixed-sum *credit* for the purposes of the CCA 1974 and RAO see below, para.39-357.

[197] This will exclude, e.g. agreements for hire of plant for a *fixed* term of one month, but not an agreement from month to month of indefinite duration. It was confirmed in *Burdis v Livsey* [2002] EWCA Civ 510, [2003] Q.B. 36, CA that the period referred in CCA 1974 s.15(1)(b) is the period of hire and not the payment (or any other) period.

[198] CCA 1974 s.15(1)(c), repealed by the Consumer Credit Act 2006 s.2(2). The limit was raised from £5,000 to £15,000 from May 20, 1985, by SI 1983/1878 and to £25,000 from May 1, 1998, by SI 1998/996.

[199] See RAO art.60O (previously CCA 1974 s.16B), below, para.39-046, which exempts "business" hire agreements where the hirer has to make payments exceeding £25,000.

[200] Or in the case of the RAO the term "relevant recipient of credit [sic]", above.

[201] See above, para.39-016. cf. CCA 1974 s.185(5).

[202] See CCA 1974 Sch.2 Pt II Examples 20, 24.

[203] RAO art.60O (previously CCA 1974 s.16B, below), para.39-046. If the agreement provides, for example, for an automatic adjustment of hire rentals in the event of corporation tax or other changes, it is submitted that the amount that the hirer is required to pay, calculated as at the outset of the agreement, is the relevant figure. cf. CCA 1974 Sch.2 Pt II Example 24. Further, VAT should be included in calculating the £25,000 limit as it is a payment required to be made by the hirer by the agreement (being a tax charged on the supply of the goods and thus part of the consideration for the hiring): *Apollo Leasing Ltd v Scott*, 1984 S.L.T. 90; Value Added Tax Act 1994 ss.1, 89. More difficult problems are posed by agreements that, upon the expiration of the hiring, provide for a rebate of rentals based on (for example) the price fetched by the goods on resale, so that in effect the hirer pays less than £25,000. It is submitted that the rebate provision will not render the agreement a consumer hire agreement if the rebate is paid after the hirer has made payments in excess of £25,000. But if the rebate is to be *set-off* against the final (usually large) rental, the possibility that the hirer will not be required to make payments in excess of £25,000 would appear to constitute the agreement a regulated hire agreement.

[204] See above, para.39-011.

[205] See above, para.39-002.

[206] SI 2001/544, made under the FSMA 2000 s.22 (as amended in this regard by SI 2013/1881). See RAO art.60N(3) and the next footnote.

consumer hire agreement within the meaning of the 1974 Act[207] and for the purposes of RAO[208] if it is not an "exempt agreement" as also defined in the RAO.[209]

"Owner" and "hirer"   The expressions "owner" and "hirer" are used in the 1974   **39-037**
Act to refer respectively to a person who bails goods and the individual to whom goods are bailed under a consumer hire agreement, or the person[210] to whom his rights and duties under the agreement have passed by assignment or by operation of law, and in relation to a prospective consumer hire agreement includes the prospective bailor or hirer.[211] The definition of "owner" in the RAO is almost identical.[212] There is no requirement that the owner carries on a consumer hire, or any, business.[213]

"Exempt agreements": general   Certain credit and consumer hire agreements are   **39-038**
designated "exempt agreements" by the RAO.[214] As such they are excluded from being "regulated agreements".[215] With two exceptions,[216] the fact that a credit agreement is an exempt agreement does not prevent the application to it of the "unfair relationship" provisions in ss.140A to 140C.[217] Exempt agreements fall into a number of categories, which will now be considered.

Exempt land mortgages   There are essentially three main types of exempt agree-   **39-039**
ments where the credit is secured on land.[218] The first[219] is a credit agreement that is a "regulated mortgage contract" (or "regulated home purchase plan"), both as

---

[207] s.15(2), cross-referring to the definition in the RAO.

[208] RAO art.60N(3).

[209] In RAO arts 60O–60Q, see below, paras 39-044 et seq.

[210] The assignment by an individual hirer of his rights under a consumer hire agreement to a company does not alter the status of the agreement.

[211] CCA 1974 s.189(1). In the case of a hire-purchase agreement, the parties are respectively the "creditor"/"lender" and "debtor"/"borrower" as hire-purchase is characterised as fixed-sum credit, not hire: see below, para.39-357.

[212] RAO art.60N(3). Curiously, "hirer" is not defined in the RAO except (see the definition of "consumer hire agreement" (see para.39-035, above)), as being the counterparty to the owner.

[213] But see "non-commercial" agreements, below, para.39-049. An owner who enters into regulated consumer hire agreements by way of business requires FCA authorisation, see below, para.39-062).

[214] The Financial Services and Markets Act 2000 (Regulated Activities) Order 2001 (SI 2001/544) arts 60C–60H (credit) and arts 60O–60Q (hire), inserted by the Financial Services and Markets Act 2000 (Regulated Activities) (Amendment) (No.2) Order 2013 (SI 2013/1881) art.6. These new provisions replace the old CCA 1974 ss.16–16C. The "credit" exemptions were amended significantly when the Mortgage Credit Directive (see above, para.39-003) was implemented on March 21, 2016: see amendments in SI 2015/910 art.3 and Sch.1 para.4. See also below, para.39-531.

[215] See above, paras 39-017, 39-036. For further discussion, see Guest and Lloyd, *Encyclopedia of Consumer Credit Law* (1975, looseleaf), para.2-017; and Goode, *Consumer Credit: Law and Practice* (looseleaf), Pt C, Ch.26.

[216] Land mortgages and home purchase plans that are "exempt agreements" under RAO art.60C(2), see below, para.39-039.

[217] CCA 1974 s.140A(5). On ss.140A–140C, see below, paras 39-212 et seq. These provisions do not apply to *hire* agreements, but see CCA 1974 s.132 (above, para.33-090).

[218] See also (i) below, para.39-040 and (ii) the exemption for "borrower-lender-supplier" agreements secured on land and financing the purchase of land where the number of payments is 12 (previously four) or less in RAO art.60F(4), referred to below in para.39-041.

[219] RAO art.60C(2). When the Mortgage Credit Directive (see above, para.39-003) was implemented on March 21, 2016 this exemption was extended to all (not just first charge) residential mortgages: see amendment to art.60C(2) in SI 2015/910 art.3 and Sch.1 para.4(13) and the amendment to the definition of "regulated mortgage contract" in art.61 by SI 2015/910 art.3 and Sch.1 para.4(21).

defined in the RAO.[220] The effect of this exemption is to remove from the control of the 1974 Act[221] the majority of land mortgages (as well as "regulated home purchase plans") where the borrower is an individual, the loan is secured by a mortgage on land in the EEA and at least 40 per cent of that land is used as a dwelling house by the borrower or his family. The reason for this exemption from the Consumer Credit Act 1974 regime is that such agreements are regulated under the Financial Services and Markets Act 2000. Secondly,[222] certain types of credit agreements[223] secured by a land mortgage[224] where the lender is either a local authority or a lender specified by the FCA in its rules and falling within various categories,[225] also constitute exempt agreements. The list of institutions that may be so "specified" (and hence whose land mortgages of a specified description may be "exempt agreements") includes banks, building societies, insurers, friendly societies, organisations of employers or workers, charities and land improvement companies.[226] The third main type of exempt land mortgage[227] is a consumer credit agreement secured by a land mortgage of a dwelling where the lender is a housing authority.[228]

39-040 **"Investment mortgages" exemption** The removal of the financial limit[229] in the Consumer Credit Act 1974 potentially brought those land mortgages above that

---

[220] RAO arts 61(3) (as amended by SI 2015/910 art.3 and Sch.1 para.4(21)) and 63F (added by the Financial Services and Markets Act 2000 (Regulated Activities) (Amendment No.2) Order 2006 (SI 2006/2383)), respectively. This exemption was previously in CCA 1974 s.16(6C)–(6E), added on October 31, 2004 by the Financial Services and Markets Act 2000 (Regulated Activities) Order 2001 (SI 2001/544) art.90(2) and amended (to add the reference to "regulated home purchase plan") on April 6, 2007 by the Financial Services and Markets Act 2000 (Regulated Activities) (Amendment No.2) Order 2006 (SI 2006/2383) art.25(2). This category now (since the implementation on March 21, 2016 of the Mortgage Credit Directive (see above, para.39-003): see below, para.39-531) covers most residential mortgages.

[221] As noted above, para.39-038, whilst the "unfair relationship" provisions in CCA 1974 ss.140A–140C generally apply to "exempt agreements", those provisions do not apply to these two categories of exempt agreements (see s.140A(5)). However CCA 1974 s.126 (as substituted by 2013/1881 art.20(38), as amended by SI 2014/506) applies to preclude enforcement of a land mortgage securing a "regulated mortgage contract" (but not a "home purchase plan") without a court order: s.126(1)(b).

[222] RAO art.60E(1)–(4). This exemption was previously in CCA 1974 s.16(1), (2), as amended. Note that since March 21, 2016 this exemption does not apply in so far as it is not permitted by the Mortgage Credit Directive (see above, para.39-003): see new RAO art.60HA, added by SI 2015/910 art.3 and Sch.1 para.4(19).

[223] A "relevant credit agreement relating to the purchase of land" as precisely defined in RAO art.60E(7) (and see art.60E(8)–(10)).

[224] "legal or equitable mortgage secured on land" as defined in RAO art.60L(1).

[225] Those specified in RAO art.60E(3). Under the old CCA 1974 provisions, the institutions (and the relevant agreements) were specified by the Exempt Agreements Order 1989 (SI 1989/869) (as extensively amended).

[226] The list also includes bodies corporate "named or specifically referred to in any public general Act" and bodies corporate "named or specifically referred to in an order" made under "a relevant housing provision" (as defined in RAO art.60E(7)).

[227] RAO art.60E(5). Note that since March 21, 2016 this exemption does not apply in so far as it is not permitted by the Mortgage Credit Directive (see above, para.39-003): see new RAO art.60HA added by SI 2015/910 art.3 and Sch.1 para.4(19).

[228] "Housing authority" is defined in RAO art.60E(7). This exemption was previously in CCA 1974 s.16(6A), (6B) inserted by the Housing and Planning Act 1986 s.22.

[229] See above, para.39-005.

limit (that were not otherwise exempt[230]) within regulation. This unintended consequence in relation to certain "investment" (especially "buy-to-let") mortgages was obviated by the introduction of an exemption[231] for credit agreements secured by a land mortgage where less than 40 per cent of the land is used, or intended to be used, as the borrower's[232] dwelling.[233] However, lending for consumer "buy-to-let" agreements is regulated under a special regime.[234]

Exempt credit agreements: number of payments Certain "borrower-lender-supplier"[235] agreements may gain exemption if the number of payments[236] to be made by the borrower does not exceed a certain number.[237] The most important exemptions are such agreements (i) for "fixed-sum credit"[238] where the number of payments does not exceed 12 if those payments are required to be made within a period not exceeding 12 months beginning with the date of the agreement[239] and (ii) for "running-account credit"[240] where the whole amount outstanding is payable in one instalment per period. As a result of the implementation of the Consumer Credit Directive,[241] further conditions were added. For both the fixed-sum and the running-account exemption, there is now the further condition that the credit must either be

39-041

---

[230] See above, especially para.39-039 for the many exemptions available for land mortgages but note the changes to these exemptions on March 21, 2016 when the Mortgage Credit Directive (see above, para.39-003) was implemented.

[231] RAO art.60D (previously CCA 1974 s.16C, added on October 1, 2008 by the Legislative Reform (Consumer Credit) Order 2008 (SI 2008/2826); see the transitional provisions (ensuring that the financial limit was not removed for these agreements until the exemption came into force) in SI 2008/831 art.3(1) and Sch.2). As is the case in all other exempted land mortgages (except for those exempted by RAO art.60C(2)), the "unfair relationship" provisions in ss.140A–140C (see below, paras 39-212 et seq.) apply. And CCA 1974 s.126 also applies to art.60D mortgages: CCA 1974 s.126(2).

[232] Or "related person of the borrower" (as defined in art.60D(3)(b)). For the position of credit provided to trustees, see art.60D(2)(b).

[233] There is no requirement that the debtor actually rent out the land. When the Mortgage Credit Directive (see above, para.39-003) was implemented on March 21, 2016, this exemption ceased to apply to credit agreements within art.3(1)(b) of that Directive i.e. those for the acquisition or retention of interests in land or buildings: see amendment to art.60D in SI 2015/910 art.3 and Sch.1 para.4(14). But such mortgages are in any event not within the CCA 1974 regime: see CCA 1974 s.8(3) as amended by SI 2015/910 art.3 and Sch.1 para.2(2).

[234] See above, para.39-003 and below, para.39-531.

[235] See above, para.39-030, not "borrower-lender" agreements, see above, para.39-033. But this exemption does not apply to (a) agreements financing the purchase of land (but note the special exemption for certain such agreements in art.60F(4), noted below); (b) conditional sale or hire-purchase agreements or (c) agreements secured by a pledge: RAO art.60F(2)(e), (3)(e) referring to (7).

[236] "Payment" is defined in RAO art.60F(8) (as amended by SI 2015/853 art.3(5)) as a payment comprising or including either the repayment of capital or the payment of interest or any other charge which forms part of the total charge for credit (as to which, see above, para.39-059).

[237] RAO art.60F (as amended by SI 2015/352 and 2015/853). It essentially re-enacts, *but with some changes*, (the now revoked) Consumer Credit (Exempt Agreements) Order 1989 (SI 1989/869) art.3, made under (the now repealed) CCA 1974 s.16(5)(a). Art.3 was substantially amended as a result of the implementation of the Consumer Credit Directive (see above, para.39-011).

[238] See above, para.39-026.

[239] See (on the old provision, where the number of payments had to be four or less, see above) *Zoan v Rouamba* [2001] 1 W.L.R. 1509; *Ketley v Gilbert* [2001] 1 W.L.R. 986; *O'Hagan v Wright* [2001] NICA 26, [2003] C.C.L.R. 6; *Clarke v Tull* [2002] EWCA Civ 510, [2002] C.C.L.R. 4; *Thew v Cole* [2003] EWCA Civ 1828, [2004] R.T.R. 410; *Stevenson v Dudley Social Services* [2006] C.L.Y. 704, Cty Ct; *Barons Finance Ltd & Reddy Corp Ltd v Makanju* [2013] EWHC 153 (QB), [2013] C.C.L.R. 3; *Consolidated Finance Ltd v Collins* [2013] EWCA Civ 475.

[240] See above, para.39-024.

[241] See above, para.39-011.

secured on land or be provided without interest or any other charge (or in the case of running-account credit, with "no or insignificant charges").[242] Moreover, the running-account exemption only applies if the period does not exceed three months. There is a special exemption for borrower-lender-supplier agreements financing the purchase of land if the number of payments is not more than four (irrespective of the period over which they are payable) and the credit is either secured on land or provided without interest or other charges.[243]

39-042 **Exempt credit agreements: low-cost of credit** Certain "borrower-lender" agreements[244] may gain exemption if the total charge for credit is below certain thresholds.[245] Essentially there are three categories of such "low cost credit" agreements. The first category applies to credit union loans[246] and the other two categories apply to credit agreements offered to a particular class and not offered to the public generally.[247]

39-043 **Exempt credit agreements: other categories** There are two further categories of exempt credit agreements. The first is credit agreements made in connection with trade in goods or services with a connection with a country outside the United Kingdom.[248] The second is credit agreements by banks or investment firms for the purpose of allowing the borrower to carry out a transaction relating to financial instruments (for example, in the context of settlement mismatches or margin-trading).[249]

---

[242] RAO art.60F(2)(d); art.60F(3)(d). And see the exemption in RAO art.60F(4) noted below.

[243] RAO art.60F(4). Note that since March 21, 2016 this exemption does not apply in so far as it is not permitted by the Mortgage Credit Directive (see above, para.39-003): see new RAO art.60HA, added by SI 2015/910 art.3 and Sch.1 para.4(19). There are also special exemptions for the financing of insurance premium exemptions in RAO art.60F(5) and (6).

[244] See above, para.39-033, not "borrower-lender-supplier" agreements, see above para.39-030.

[245] RAO art.60G. It essentially re-enacts, *but with some changes*, (the now revoked) Consumer Credit (Exempt Agreements) Order 1989 (SI 1989/869) art.4, made under (the now repealed) CCA 1974 s.16(5)(b). Art.4 was substantially amended as a result of the implementation of the Consumer Credit Directive (above, para.39-011). Note the amendments made to art.60G when the Mortgage Credit Directive (see above, para.39-003) was implemented on March 21, 2016 (to render it compatible with the Directive) by SI 2015/910 art.3 and Sch.1 para.4(17).

[246] RAO art.60G(2). The rate of total charge for credit must not exceed 42.6 per cent. Note the new art.60G(2)(c) added when the Mortgage Credit Directive (see above, para.39-003) was implemented on March 21, 2016 (to render it compatible with the Directive) by SI 2015/910 art.3 and Sch.1 para.4(17)(a)(ii).

[247] See (i) RAO art.60G(3) (if interest is the only charge and the interest may not *at any time* be more than the sum of 1 per cent and the highest of the base rates published by the banks listed in art.60G(7) on the date 28 days before the date on which the interest is charged) and (ii) RAO art.60G(4) (if the rate or amount of any item entering into the total charge for credit cannot be *increased* after the date of the agreement and that rate must not exceed 1 per cent above the highest bank rate of the banks listed in art.60G(7) as it stood 28 days before the date of the agreement). Note the amendments to art.60G(3) and (4) made (referring to (8)) when the Mortgage Credit Directive (see above, para.39-003) was implemented on March 21, 2016 (the render them compatible with the Directive) by SI 2015/910 art.3 and Sch.1 para.4(17).

[248] RAO art.60C(8). It essentially re-enacts, *but with some changes*, (the now revoked) Consumer Credit (Exempt Agreements) Order 1989 (SI 1989/869) art.5, made under (the now repealed) CCA 1974 s.16(5)(c). Some ordinary foreign trade transactions would otherwise be caught.

[249] RAO art.60E(6). It essentially re-enacts, *but with some changes*, (the now revoked) Consumer Credit (Exempt Agreements) Order 1989 (SI 1989/869) art.5A, added in implementation of the Consumer Credit Directive (see above, para.39-011) art.2(2)(h), by SI 2010/1010 reg.67A (inserted by SI 2010/1969).

Exempt consumer hire agreements   There is one special[250] category of exempt **39-044** consumer hire agreement: where the owner is a body corporate authorised by or under any enactment to supply electricity, gas or water and the subject of the agreement is a meter or metering equipment.[251]

High net worth (HNW) "opt-out" exemption   There is an exemption for certain **39-045** credit and consumer hire agreements made with "high net worth" (HNW) borrowers or hirers.[252] Four conditions need to be satisfied: (a) the borrower or hirer must be an "individual"[253]; (b) the agreement itself must include a prescribed signed "declaration"[254] that the borrower or hirer agrees to forgo the "protection and remedies" applicable to regulated agreements[255]; (c) a "statement of high net worth",[256] must have been made[257] in relation to the borrower or hirer; and (d) this statement of high net worth must have been made during the year ending with the date of the agreement. However, as this exemption is incompatible with the Consumer Credit Directive,[258] it is only available for agreements outside the scope of the Directive: credit agreements secured on land,[259] agreements where credit in excess of £60,260 is provided[260] and hire agreements.

---

[250] See also the exemptions (also available for credit agreements) considered below in para.39-045 (HNW exemption) and para.39-046 (business purpose exemption).

[251] RAO art.60P. It essentially re-enacts, *but with some changes*, (the now revoked) Consumer Credit (Exempt Agreements) Order 1989 (SI 1989/869) art.6, made under (the now repealed) CCA 1974 s.16(6).

[252] RAO art.60H (credit) and art.60Q (hire) (previously CCA 1974 s.16A, added by the Consumer Credit Act 2006 s.3). The exemption mirrors the one for "certified sophisticated investors" in relation to financial promotion under the Financial Services and Markets Act 2000 (Financial Promotion) Order 2005 (SI 2005/1529) art.50.

[253] i.e. a natural person and not a partnership or unincorporated association (or corporation, although these cannot make regulated agreements anyway). See above, para.39-016.

[254] Complying with the relevant FCA rules (see the *FCA Handbook*, CONC App 1.4.6) (previously the (now repealed) Consumer Credit (Exempt Agreements) Order 2007 (SI 2007/1168) art.3 and Sch.1).

[255] Although (see above, para.39-038) the "unfair relationship" provisions in ss.140A–140C (below, paras 39-212 et seq.) apply and the declaration must say so.

[256] Again complying with the relevant FCA rules (see *FCA Handbook*, CONC App 1.4.6) (previously the (now repealed) Consumer Credit (Exempt Agreements) Order 2007 (SI 2007/1168) art.5 and Sch.2).

[257] It must be made by a person of a description "specified" by the FCA rules (and hence not by the borrower or hirer themselves) and must state that, in that person's opinion, the borrower or hirer either has an income or has net assets above a certain (specified by the rules) amount (presently net annual income after tax of above £150,000) or net assets (which are defined to exclude the primary residence and pension rights) of at least £500,000. A copy of this statement must be provided to the lender or owner before the agreement is made.

[258] See above, para.39-011.

[259] To render it compatible with the Mortgage Credit Directive (see above, para.39-003) art.60H was amended when that Directive was implemented on March 21, 2016: see (i) new RAO art.60HA, added by SI 2015/910 art.3 and Sch.1 para.4(19) and (ii) amendment made by SI 2015/910 art.3 and Sch.1 para.4(18).

[260] See RAO art.60H(b) (and above, para.3-022). But when the Mortgage Credit Directive (see above, para.39-003) was implemented on March 21, 2016, the credit exceeding £60,260 could not be for the purpose of (a) the renovation of residential property or (b) acquiring or retaining property rights in land or buildings: see amendments to art.60H in SI 2015/910 art.3 and Sch.1 para.4(18). But agreements within (b) are in any event outside the 1974 regime: see amendment to s.8(3) in SI 2015/910 art.3 and Sch.1 para.2(2)).

39-046 **"Business purpose" exemption** Although the Consumer Credit Act 2006 generally removed the financial limit (of £25,000 at the time the 2006 Act was passed),[261] that limit has been retained for "business purpose" credit or hire agreements.[262] Hence those credit and consumer hire agreements entered into "wholly or predominantly" for the borrower's or hirer's "business purposes" where the credit provided or hire payments to be made exceed £25,000[263] are exempt agreements.[264] As it may not always be obvious whether the agreement is entered into "wholly or predominantly" for "business" purposes, there is a rebuttable presumption that arises where the agreement includes a declaration by the borrower or hirer to that effect.[265] However, the presumption does not apply if, at the time the agreement was made, the lender or owner[266] "knows or has reasonable cause to suspect" that the declaration is not true.[267] If the presumption does not apply, the question of whether the agreement is "wholly or predominantly" for "business" purposes will need to be established in the usual way and, as it will be the lender or owner who will be seeking to invoke the exemption, the onus will then be on them to establish the business purpose on the part of the borrower or hirer.

39-047 **"Business purpose": Consumer Credit Directive** The Consumer Credit Directive[268] does not apply to "business" lending. Nevertheless, a number of provisions resulting from the implementation of the Directive have been extended to regulated "business" credit agreements, in particular, the duty to provide pre-contractual explanations,[269] the duty to assess creditworthiness[270] and the 14-day right of withdrawal in s.66A of the 1974 Act.[271] Moreover, although creditors providing regulated business credit prima facie remain subject to the "old" regime as regards

---

[261] See above, para.39-005.
[262] RAO art.60C(3)–(7) (credit) and RAO art.60O (hire) (previously CCA 1974 s.16B, added by the Consumer Credit Act 2006 s.4). As noted above, paras 39-016 and 39-035, in general, "business" credit and hire is within the scope of the regulatory regime. The old CCA 1974 provision was unsuccessfully invoked in *Bassano v Alfred Toft, Peter Biddulph, Peter Biddulph Ltd, Borro Loan Ltd, Borro Loan 2 Ltd* [2014] EWHC 377 (QB), [2014] C.C.L.R. 8. See also, on RAO art.60C(3)–(7), *Newmafruit Farms Ltd v Pither* [2016] EWHC 2205 (QB), [2017] C.C.L.R. 8.
[263] For a discussion of how this limit is calculated, see para.39-021 (credit) and 39-035 (hire).
[264] See *Woolsey v Payne* [2015] EWHC 968 (Ch) (meaning of "business purposes" in old s.16B). The exemption also applies to "green deal plans" (see RAO art.60C(4) and for "green deal plans" see below, para.39-257) but they must be entered "wholly" (not "wholly or predominantly") for business purposes.
[265] RAO art.60C(5) and art.60O(2). The declaration must comply with FCA rules (see *FCA Handbook*, CONC App.1.4.8). Although this is not made explicit (cf. the presumptions in CCA 1974 s.171(1), (2)), it seems clear that this presumption can be rebutted by evidence to the contrary adduced by the borrower or hirer.
[266] Or any person who has acted on his behalf in connection with the entering into of the agreement, for example a broker.
[267] RAO art.60C(6) and art.60O(3). If there is more than one lender or owner, then it is enough for this to be the case in relation to only one. It seems clear that (if the agreement contains the declaration) the onus is on the borrower or hirer to establish this. See *Wood v Capital Bridging Finance Ltd* [2015] EWCA Civ 451 (presumption rebutted).
[268] See above, para.39-011.
[269] In the *FCA Handbook*, CONC 4.2 and 4.3 (previously CCA 1974 s.55A): see below, para.39-077.
[270] In the *FCA Handbook*, CONC 5 and 6.2 (previously CCA 1974 s.55B): see below, para.39-078.
[271] See below, para.39-101.

formal agreement requirements,[272] they may instead opt into the new "Directive" regime.[273]

"Small agreement"   Section 17 of the 1974 Act defines "small agreements". **39-048** These are subject to "lighter" regulation.[274] A small agreement is (a) a regulated consumer credit agreement for credit not exceeding £50,[275] other than a hire-purchase[276] or conditional sale[277] agreement; or (b) a regulated consumer hire agreement which does not require the hirer to make payments exceeding £50, provided that (in either case) the agreement is an agreement which is either unsecured[278] or secured[279] by a guarantee or indemnity only (whether or not the guarantee is itself secured). In the case of running-account credit,[280] the credit limit must not exceed £50.[281] Section 17 also contains provisions designed to prevent the splitting up of agreements into two or more agreements below the £50 limit.[282] Although the Consumer Credit Directive[283] allows Member States to apply a threshold of £160 and to exclude agreements under that amount, on the implementation of the Directive it was decided not to apply that threshold but to maintain the less onerous regulatory regime only for agreements below £50.[284]

"Non-commercial agreement"   The application of the regulatory regime is, in **39-049** principle, not limited to situations where creditor/lender or owner carries on the *business* of granting credit or letting goods on hire, although FCA authorisation is only required by those acting "by way of business".[285] A loan by one individual to another will, for example, be a regulated credit agreement as long as it is not

---

[272] See below, paras 39-076 et seq.

[273] See below, para.39-080.

[274] In so far as the *FCA Handbook* uses the term "small borrower-lender-supplier agreement" (see CONC 2.9.2(2)R), this is defined by the Glossary by reference to CCA 1974 s.17. Pt V of the CCA 1974 (except ss.55, 56 and 66A), which relates to the form and content of regulated agreements, does not apply to "small" debtor-creditor-supplier agreements for restricted use: CCA 1974 s.74(1)(d) and see subss.(2) and (4). The older 2004 Disclosure Regulations made under s.55 apply (unless the creditor has opted into the "Directive" regime): SI 2004/1481 reg.2, as amended by SI 2010/1010 reg.75 and SI 2010/1969 reg.24, see below, para.39-076. The following sections do not apply to any "small" agreements: CCA 1974 ss.77A and 78(7) (periodic statements), s.85(3) (issue of new credit-tokens), ss.86B and 86C (notice of sums in arrears), s.86E (notice of default sums) and s.130A (interest on judgment debts). Moreover, *FCA Handbook*, CONC 2.9 (previously CCA 1974 s.51) prohibiting unsolicited credit-tokens does not apply to "small borrower-lender-supplier agreements". But CCA 1974 ss.77B (statement of account on request) and 78A (notification of variation of interest), added in consequence of the implementation of the Consumer Credit Directive (see above, para.39-011), do apply.

[275] The limit may be raised under CCA 1974 s.181 and was raised from £30 to £50 by SI 1983/1878. See CCA 1974 Sch.2 Pt II Examples 16, 17, 21, 22.

[276] Defined in CCA 1974 s.189(1); below, para.39-356.

[277] Defined in CCA 1974 s.189(1); below, para.39-442.

[278] See the definition of "security" in CCA 1974 s.189(1); below, para.39-180.

[279] CCA 1974 s.189(1).

[280] Defined in CCA 1974 ss.10, 189(1); above, para.39-024.

[281] CCA 1974 s.17(2) (as amended by the Consumer Credit Act 2006 s.5(3)) and note ss.10(2) and 10(3)(a). See also CCA 1974 Sch.2 Pt II Examples 16, 21, 22.

[282] s.17(3), (4).

[283] See above, para.39-011.

[284] See *Consultation on Proposals for Implementing the Consumer Credit Directive*, BERR, April 2009, para.1.11.

[285] See below, para.39-062.

exempt.[286] Dispensation is, however, granted from certain provisions[287] of the 1974 Act to "non-commercial agreements", defined to mean a consumer credit agreement or a consumer hire agreement not made by the creditor or owner in the course of a business[288] carried on by him.[289]

39-050 **"Multiple agreement"**   Section 18 of the 1974 Act, which is an anti-avoidance provision,[290] defines the expression "multiple agreement". Of all the sections in the Act it is this section which has given rise in practice to the greatest difficulty of interpretation.[291] Subsections (1), (2) and (3) appear to envisage four situations. First, where the terms of the agreement are such as to place a *part* of it within one category of agreement mentioned in the Act and another *part* of it within a category not so mentioned (for example, a "save and loan" agreement where the loan part is a consumer credit agreement and the savings part falls outside the Act).[292] Secondly, where the terms of the agreement are such as to place a *part* of it within one category of agreement mentioned in the Act, and another *part* of it within a different category of agreement so mentioned.[293] Thirdly, where the terms of the agreement are such as to place a *part* of it within two or more categories of agreement mentioned in the Act, the other part or parts falling outside the Act, or within one

---

[286] See above, paras 39-038 et seq.

[287] Pt V of the Act (except s.56), which relates to the form and content of regulated agreements, and withdrawal from and cancellation of regulated agreements, does not apply to "non-commercial" agreements: s.74(1)(a). The following sections also do not apply to non-commercial agreements: CCA 1974 ss.75(1), 77–79, 80(1), 82, 83, 86B, 86C, 86E 103(1), 107–109, 110(1), 112, 114–122, 123 and 130A.

[288] i.e. *any* business, as defined in CCA 1974 s.189(1), (2); see also below, para.39-062. There is an identical definition of "non-commercial agreement" in the *FCA Handbook* Glossary.

[289] CCA 1974 s.189(1). The CCA 1974 does not make provision in s.171 as to the onus of proof, but it would seem that the burden lies on the person alleging the agreement to be a non-commercial agreement. In *Khodari v Tamimi* [2009] EWCA Civ 1109, [2010] C.C.L.R. 3 a series of large loans over six years in a private context by a banker "to foster the relationship with an important client" at gambling clubs were held not to have been made "in the course of business" and hence to be "non-commercial" loans. For another example of a non-commercial agreement, see *Bassano v Alfred Toft, Peter Biddulph, Peter Biddulph Ltd, Borro Loan Ltd, Borro Loan 2 Ltd* [2014] EWHC 377 (QB), [2014] C.C.L.R. 8. See also *Woolsey v Payne* [2015] EWHC 968 (Ch).

[290] See Auld L.J. in *National Westminster Bank Plc v Story* [1999] C.C.L.R. 70, CA.

[291] See Guest and Lloyd, *Encyclopedia of Consumer Credit Law* (1975, looseleaf) at para.2-019; Goode, *Consumer Credit: Law and Practice* (looseleaf), Pt C, paras 25.101 et seq. The reform of s.18 was considered in the review that lead to the Consumer Credit Act 2006 (see the DTI Consultation Document, *Tackling loan sharks—and more!* (July 2002)) but as the impact of s.18 was diminished both by the repeal of s.127(3)–(4) and the removal of the financial limit, no proposals for reform were forthcoming. The Home Credit Market Investigation Order 2007 (made by the Competition Commission under the Enterprise Act 2002 ss.161 and 164 and amended in 2011) art.9 is in almost identical terms to s.18. For appellate case-law see *National Westminster Bank Plc v Story* [1999] C.C.L.R. 70 and *Southern Pacific Mortgage Ltd v Heath* [2010] EWCA Civ 1135, [2010] C.C.L.R. 4. See also: *National Home Loans Corp Plc v Hannah* [1997] C.C.L.R. 7, Cty Ct; *Wilson v First County Trust Ltd (No.1)* [2003] C.C.L.R. 1; *Ocwen v Coxall* [2004] C.C.L.R. 7; *London North Securities Ltd v Meadows* [2005] EWCA Civ 956, [2005] C.C.L.R. 7. For cases where s.18 was held inapplicable, see *Dimond v Lovell* [2002] 1 A.C. 384; Burdis v Livsey [2002] EWCA Civ 510, [2003] Q.B. 36; *Goshawk Dedicated (No.2) Ltd v Bank of Scotland* [2005] EWHC 2908 (Ch), [2006] C.C.L.R. 1.

[292] CCA 1974 s.18(1)(a) and Sch.2 Example 18. But see s.18(6) (exemption for furnished lettings). cf. *National Home Loans Corp Plc v Hannah* [1997] C.C.L.R. 7, Cty Ct.

[293] CCA 1974 s.18(1)(a) and Sch.2 Example 16 (but Example 16, in suggesting that an agreement could fall within both s.18(1)(a) and 18(1)(b), was regarded as erroneous by Lloyd L.J. in *Southern Pacific Mortgage Ltd v Heath* [2009] EWCA Civ 1135).

category, or likewise within two or more categories.[294] Fourthly, where the agreement is a "single" or *unitary* agreement, not in parts, and the terms of the agreement are such as to place it within two or more categories of agreement mentioned in the Act.[295] In all four situations, there is a "multiple agreement". But where *part* of an agreement falls within the first three situations mentioned above, that part is to be treated for the purposes of the Act as a *separate agreement*, and the Act applies to it accordingly.[296] However, in the fourth situation, the agreement is to be treated as an agreement in each of the categories in question, and the Act applies to it accordingly,[297] but it is not split into separate agreements.[298]

"Category of agreement"   The expression "category of agreement" is not defined   **39-051**
in the 1974 Act. However, it would appear to mean a type of agreement that the Act makes special provision for and hence is not limited to the broad categories of agreement created by Pt II[299] of the Act.[300] It also seems that the words "two or more categories"[301] must mean disparate categories.[302]

"Part" of an agreement   The greatest difficulty that has arisen relates to the   **39-052**
interpretation and application of the word "part".[303] The problem initially surfaced with respect to credit agreements where the debtor elects to take out payment protection insurance, the amount of the premium being financed by the creditor under the principal credit agreement.[304] Suppose, for example, that the principal credit agreement is a hire-purchase or conditional sale agreement,[305] or a debtor-creditor loan.[306] Does the inclusion in the agreement of payment protection insurance give rise to "parts", requiring each part to be treated for the purposes of the Act as a separate agreement? Or is the agreement (though multiple) a unitary agreement, not in parts, so that such separate treatment is not required?[307] Suppose that an agreement contains two elements, each of which falls within a different category

---

[294] CCA 1974 s.18(1)(b).

[295] CCA 1974 s.18(1)(b). For an example, see *Southern Pacific Mortgage Ltd v Heath* [2010] EWCA Civ 1135, [2010] C.C.L.R. 4: (obiter) credit card agreements and (ratio) the loan agreement in that case, were "single" (or unitary) agreement within s.18(1)(b).

[296] CCA 1974 s.18(2). Where part of an agreement falls within the third situation, the agreement (i.e. the separate agreement constituted by subs.(2)) is also to be treated as an agreement in each of the categories in question, and the Act applies to it accordingly (s.18(3)). See also s.18(4) (construction and apportionment).

[297] CCA 1974 s.18(3).

[298] The opening words of subs.(2) make it clear that the subsection is applicable only where *part* of an agreement falls within subs.(1) and see *Southern Pacific Mortgage Ltd v Heath* [2010] EWCA Civ 1135, [2010] C.C.L.R. 4.

[299] CCA 1974 ss.10–19.

[300] And so would include, e.g. "hire purchase", "conditional sale" and "credit sale" agreements: see CCA 1974 s.189(1). But see *National Westminster Bank Plc v Story* [1999] C.C.L.R. 70.

[301] CCA 1974 s.18(1)(b).

[302] *Southern Pacific Mortgage Ltd v Heath* [2010] EWCA Civ 1135, [2010] C.C.L.R. 4; *National Home Loans Corp Plc v Hannah* [1997] C.C.L.R. 7, Cty Ct.

[303] See Guest and Lloyd, *Encyclopedia of Consumer Credit Law* (1975, looseleaf) at para.2-019.

[304] Giving rise to a debtor-creditor-supplier agreement (within CCA 1974 s.12(b), see above, para.39-029) for restricted-use (see above, para.39-027) fixed-sum credit (see above, para.39-026).

[305] Additional difficulties arise in this case because of the wording of CCA 1974 ss.90, 100: see Guest and Lloyd, *Encyclopedia of Consumer Credit Law* (1975, looseleaf) at paras 2-019, 2-091, 2-101.

[306] See above, para.39-033.

[307] The Agreement Regulations (see below, paras 39-080 et seq.) in fact resolved this particular dilemma by making special provision for such a case: see SI 1983/1553 reg.2(8) and (9) and SI 2010/1014 reg.3(6) and (7).

of agreement mentioned in the Act. To determine whether this gives rise to "separate agreements",[308] it is necessary to decide whether these elements constitute "parts"[309] or whether the agreement remains a unitary agreement, not in parts.[310] It is generally agreed that the answer does not depend on whether the parties have literally divided the agreement into parts.[311] But there is a wide spectrum of opinion on the test to be applied.[312] On one view s.18 is essentially an anti-avoidance provision and an agreement will be a unitary multi-category agreements, not in parts, if it is an integrated package which could not be split up without affecting the character of the transaction.[313] On another, more cautious, view, however, the first question to be asked is whether the terms of the agreement treat the two elements differently, e.g. different rates of interest, different terms of repayment, different security. If they do, then the two elements may constitute "parts". Secondly, even if the elements are not differently so treated, is there a substantial degree of disparity between them, having regard to their subject-matter, their legal nature and the operation of the Act? If so, it would be prudent to assume that the two elements constitute parts. So, for example, a hire-purchase agreement coupled with a loan to finance single premium payment protection insurance would give rise to "parts", as each element differs in legal nature[314] and for the purposes of the Act.[315] Further problems which have emerged (but to which the same tests might be applied) relate to loans where one element of the loan is unrestricted-use credit, that is at the free disposition of the borrower, and another element is restricted-use credit, re-financing the borrower's indebtedness to another creditor or creditors[316]; to exempt agreements,[317] where one element of the loan is advanced for an exempt purpose and another for a purpose which is non-exempt; and to credit card agreements where the card may be used to obtain goods or services (a debtor-creditor-supplier agreement) or cash (usually a debtor-creditor agreement).[318]

39-053   Consequences if part is a separate agreement   One of the most important

---

[308] CCA 1974 s.18(2).

[309] The second situation mentioned above, para.39-050.

[310] CCA 1974 s.18(1)(b). The fourth situation mentioned above, para.39-050.

[311] CCA 1974 s.18(5) and Sch.2 Examples 16 and 18.

[312] See, e.g. Goode, *Consumer Credit Law and Practice* (looseleaf); Guest and Lloyd, *Encyclopedia of Consumer Credit Law* (1975, looseleaf) at para.2-019.

[313] Goode, above. In *Southern Pacific Mortgage Ltd v Heath* [2010] EWCA Civ 1135, [2010] C.C.L.R. 4 the Court of Appeal essentially approved the "Goode" view, holding that a loan in excess of the (then) financial limit similar to that in *National Home Loans Corp Plc v Hannah* [1997] C.C.L.R. 7, Cty Ct, fell within s.18(1)(b) in that although aspects fell within two categories of agreement, it was not in "parts" and hence was not notionally "split" by virtue of s.18(2). cf. *National Westminster Bank Plc v Story* [1999] C.C.L.R. 70.

[314] The hire-purchase element is a contract of hire of goods whereas the loan for the insurance is a contract of loan.

[315] The hire-purchase element is a debtor-creditor-supplier agreement within CCA 1974 s.12(a), whereas the loan for the insurance is a debtor-creditor-supplier agreement within CCA 1974 s.12(b), to which the Act attributes very different incidents, see, e.g. s.75 (below, para.39-303).

[316] In this case, however, unless there are differing terms, it is submitted that the agreement is a unitary agreement, not in parts, since each element is a contract of loan, and the Act attributes no very different incidents to restricted-use/unrestricted-use credit. But see *National Westminster Bank Plc v Story* [1999] C.C.L.R. 70.

[317] See above, paras 39-038 et seq.

[318] See CCA 1974 Sch.2 Example 16. See now *Southern Pacific Mortgage Ltd v Heath* [2010] EWCA Civ 1135, [2010] C.C.L.R. 4: (obiter) credit card agreements (and (ratio)) the loan agreements in that case were a "single" (or unitary) agreement within s.18(1)(b)) and Example 16 was regarded as erroneous in suggesting that an agreement could fall within both s.18(1)(a) and 18(1)(b).

consequences[319] of each part being required to be treated as a separate agreement is that the formal requirements of the Consumer Credit (Agreements) Regulations 1983,[320] the Consumer Credit (Agreements) Regulations 2010[321] and of the Consumer Credit (Cancellation Notices and Copies of Documents) Regulations 1983,[322] will, unless otherwise provided, apply distinctly to each part.[323] The resulting complexity of documents is likely to confuse, rather than to assist, the debtor or hirer. Few creditors and owners, however, have thought it necessary, for example, to serve separate enforcement,[324] default[325] or termination[326] notices in respect of each part which falls to be treated as a separate agreement.

Running-account credit   In the case of an agreement for running-account **39-054** credit,[327] a term of the agreement allowing the credit limit to be exceeded merely temporarily is not to be treated as a separate agreement or as providing fixed-sum credit in respect of the excess.[328]

"Linked transaction"[329]   The effect of the regulatory regime is not confined to the **39-055** regulation of consumer credit or consumer hire agreements alone. It extends to "linked transactions", or transactions ancillary to the consumer credit or consumer hire agreement.[330] The definition of a linked transaction is contained in s.19(1) and (2) of the 1974 Act,[331] and the word "transaction" is, of course, wider than

---

319 When the CCA 1974 imposed a general financial limit, a further important consequence was that the separate agreements might have been below the limit (and hence regulated) whereas the "whole" agreement was above it (and hence not regulated). This issue might still arises in relation to a "business" agreement above the limit in the exemption provided for in RAO art.60C(3)–(7) (credit) and RAO art.60O (hire); see above, para.39-046.

320 SI 1983/1553, as amended, see below, para.39-081.

321 SI 2010/1014, as amended by SI 2010/1969 regs 41–45, see below, para.39-082.

322 SI 1983/1557, as amended; see below, para.39-086.

323 But see reg.2(8) and (9) (previously reg.2(7A) inserted by SI 1984/1600) of the Consumer Credit (Agreements) Regulations 1983, as amended by SI 2004/1482 reg.4 (alleviation in the case of certain types of payment protection insurance). And see the identical provision in reg.3(6) and (7) of the Consumer Credit (Agreements) Regulations 2010 (SI 2010/1014).

324 CCA 1974 s.76; see below, para.39-64.

325 CCA 1974 s.87; see below, para.39-166.

326 CCA 1974 s.98; see below, para.39-172.

327 Defined in CCA 1974 ss.10, 189(1); above, para.39-024.

328 CCA 1974 s.18(5). See also CCA 1974 ss.10(2), 82(4). This covers a bank honouring cheques drawn on it in (temporary) excess of an agreed overdraft. See CCA 1974 Sch.2 Pt II Examples 22, 23.

329 See Guest and Lloyd, *Encyclopedia of Consumer Credit Law* (1975, looseleaf), para.2-020; and Goode, *Consumer Credit: Law and Practice* (looseleaf), Pt C, Ch.43.

330 See CCA 1974 ss.57(1), 67, 69(1), 70, 72, 95(2), 96, 113(8)–141(1), 142(2), 173, 179. See also CCA 1974 s.140C(4)(b) and note s.140C(5) and (6)(b) (a "linked transaction" is a "related agreement" for the purpose of ss.140A and 140B (the "unfair relationship" provisions, see below, paras 39-212 et seq.)). In *Townson v FCE Bank Plc (t/a Ford Credit)* Unreported June 23, 2016, Birmingham Cty Ct a PPI policy that was a "linked transaction" (within s.19(1)(c), see below, para.39-057) was held to be a "related transaction" in the context of the "unfair relationship" provisions. "Linked transactions" are not to be confused with the Consumer Credit Directive concept of "linked credit agreements" to which s.75A (see below, para.39-305) applies.

331 See also CCA 1974 Sch.2 Pt II Example 11. The definition of "attached contract" in the Financial Services (Distance Marketing) Regulations 2004 (SI 2004/2095) reg.12(2) is similar to s.19(1)(a), (1)(b) and (1)(c)(i). The term "linked transaction" is also used in RAO art.60E(7)(c) (definition of "relevant credit agreement relating to the purchase of land") and is defined (in RAO art.60E(8)) in an almost identical fashion.

"contract" or "agreement".[332] A transaction entered into by the debtor[333] or hirer, or a relative[334] of his, with any other person ("the other party"), *except one for the provision of security*[335] is a linked transaction in relation to an actual or prospective regulated agreement (the "principal agreement") of which it does not form part if it falls within one of the categories (a), (b) or (c) in s.19(1).

The first category[336] of transaction (in s.19(1)(a)) is one that is entered into by the debtor or hirer, or a relative of his, in compliance with a term of the principal agreement.[337] Therefore if, for example, a regulated hire-purchase or conditional sale agreement relating to a motor vehicle requires the debtor to insure the vehicle during the continuance of the agreement, or if a regulated consumer hire agreement requires the hirer to enter into a contract for the maintenance of the goods during the continuance of the agreement, the contract of insurance and the contract for maintenance (respectively) are "linked transactions", notwithstanding that the other party to the contract is in no way connected with the creditor and notwithstanding that the debtor is left completely free to choose the source of insurance or maintenance.

39-056   The second category of transaction (in s.19(1)(b)) is one where the principal agreement is a debtor-creditor-supplier agreement[338] and the transaction is financed, or to be financed, by the principal agreement. Therefore if, for example, a debtor obtains a loan from a financier to enable him to obtain goods from a dealer, and the loan is advanced by the financier under pre-existing arrangements or in contemplation of future arrangements with the dealer, the contract between the debtor and the dealer for the purchase of the goods is a linked transaction. Similarly, where the debtor uses a credit card, debit card or check, in order to obtain goods or services from a supplier, the contract for the supply of the goods or services is a linked transaction.

39-057   The third category (in s.19(1)(c)) is subdivided into three sub-categories and is so complex that reference should be made to the precise wording of the Act.[339] Essentially, this category covers a number of situations where a person (not necessarily the creditor or owner himself) initiates the transaction by suggesting it to the debtor or hirer, or his relative.[340] Thus, for example, if a creditor or broker informs the debtor that a valuation or survey must be carried out as a pre-condition for the grant of credit, or suggests to the debtor that it would be advisable to take out a pay-

---

[332] cf. *Greenberg v IRC* [1972] A.C. 109 (on s.43(4)(i) of the Finance Act 1960).
[333] See CCA 1974 s.189B(3), Sch.2A: in CCA 1974 s.19, references to "debtor" in relation to "green deal plans" (as defined in s.189(1), see below, para.39-257) are to be read as references to the "improver", as defined in CCA 1974 s.189B(6).
[334] Defined in CCA 1974 ss.184(1), 189(1).
[335] See below, para.39-180 (including a contract of guarantee or indemnity), and CCA 1974 Sch.2 Pt II Example 11. An insurance policy that is assigned to the creditor may be a linked transaction since it is the contract of assignment (and not the policy contract itself) that constitutes the "provision of security".
[336] See also CCA 1974 Sch.2 Pt II Example 11.
[337] The wording contemplates that the transaction must be made *after* the principal agreement (in that it can only then be made "in compliance with a term" of that agreement). But see CCA 1974 s.19(1)(c), below.
[338] Above, para.39-030. See *Citibank International v Schneider, The Times,* March 26, 1999 (where this condition was not satisfied and hence s.19(1)(b) held not to apply) and *Goshawk Dedicated (No.2) Ltd v The Governor and Company of the Bank of Scotland* [2005] EWHC 2906 (Ch) (solicitors' disbursements were linked transactions within s.19(1)(b) in being financed by a debtor-creditor-supplier agreement).
[339] See also CCA 1974 s.19(2). See also CCA 1974 Sch.2 Pt II Example 11.
[340] Defined in CCA 1974 ss.184(1), 189(1).

ment protection policy,[341] the contract of valuation, survey or insurance will be a linked transaction if the other party to it knew, at the time the transaction was initiated, that the credit agreement had been made or contemplated that it might be made.[342]

Linked transaction of no effect until principal agreement made   One of the particular incidents of a transaction being a "linked transaction", if entered into before the making of the principal agreement, is that it has no effect until such time (if any) as the principal agreement is made.[343] But regulations have excluded certain linked transactions, namely, contracts of insurance, guarantees of goods and agreements for deposit and current accounts, from the operation of this provision.[344]

39-058

"Total charge for credit" and "APR"   Before the transfer of consumer credit regulation to the FCA,[345] s.20(1) of the 1974 Act required the Secretary of State to make regulations containing such provisions as appeared to him appropriate for determining the "true" cost to the debtor of the credit provided or to be provided under an actual or prospective consumer credit agreement (the "total charge for credit" and "annual percentage rate" (APR)).[346] In consequence of the subsequent implementation of the Consumer Credit Directive[347] there were two sets of regulations: the original Consumer Credit (Total Charge for Credit) Regulations 1980[348] and (in implementation of the Directive) the Consumer Credit (Total Charge for Credit) Regulations 2010.[349] The 1980 Regulations only applied to agreements secured on land (as these were outside the scope of the Directive) unless the creditor had opted into the "Directive" regime.[350] They prescribed what items were to be treated as entering into the total charge for credit, how their amount was to be ascertained, and the method of calculating the APR[351] of the total charge for credit. These regulations provided for the inclusion in the total charge for credit not only of the interest on the credit but also certain other charges. In principle, all charges

39-059

---

[341]   See *Townson v FCE Bank Plc (t/a Ford Credit)* Unreported June 23, 2016, Birmingham Cty Ct: PPI policy within s.19(1)(c).

[342]   CCA 1974 ss.19(1)(c)(i), (ii), 19(2)(a), (b), (c). It is to be presumed in any proceedings, unless the contrary is proved, that when a person initiated a transaction (as mentioned above) he knew the principal agreement had been made, or contemplated that it might be made: CCA 1974 s.171(2).

[343]   CCA 1974 s.19(3). See also CCA 1974 s.57 (effect of withdrawal, below, para.39-098), CCA 1974 s.69(1)(i) (effect of cancellation below, para.39-106), CCA 1974 s.96 (effect of early repayment, below, para.39-163), CCA 1974 s.140C(4)(b) ("related agreement" in "unfair relationship" provisions, below, paras 39-212 et seq.).

[344]   CCA 1974 s.19(4); SI 1983/1560 (also applicable in relation to ss.69 and 96—see previous note). The regulations were made by the Secretary of State but since the transfer of consumer credit regulation to the FCA (see above, para.39-002) the Treasury is now the responsible government department.

[345]   See above, para.39-002.

[346]   See also CCA 1974 ss.9(4), 69, 70, 93, 95, 155 and Sch.2 Pt II Examples 5, 10; SI 1983/1553 and SI 2010/1014.

[347]   See above, para.39-011.

[348]   SI 1980/51 (revoking SI 1977/327), as amended by SIs 1985/1192, 1989/596, 1999/3177 and SI 2010/1010. The Financial Services Authority adopted much of the Regulations in the "MCOB" part of its Handbook, applicable to those land mortgages it regulated (and the FCA now regulates).

[349]   SI 2010/1011, as amended by SI 2011/11.

[350]   See below, para.39-080.

[351]   The original method of calculating the APR was completely changed by the amendment of the 1980 Regulations by SI 1999/3177 in order to implement the first Consumer Credit Directive, Council Directive 87/102 ([1987] O.J. L42/48). A computer program is usually necessary to calculate the APR.

payable under the transaction[352] by the debtor or a relative[353] of his whether to the creditor or any other person (and thus whether the creditor derived any benefit from them or not) were included,[354] although various charges were specifically excluded.[355] Further, the regulations contained the formula for the calculation of the APR[356] and for the making of assumptions in calculating the total charge for credit and the APR where certain relevant factors could not be ascertained.[357] The 2010 "Directive" Regulations contained similar provisions prescribing what items were to be treated as entering into the total charge for credit, how their amount was to be ascertained, and the method of calculating APR. These regulations also provided for the inclusion in the total charge for credit not only of the interest on the credit but also certain other specified "costs".[358] Further, they also contained the formula for the calculation of the APR[359] and for the making of assumptions in calculating the total charge for credit and the APR where certain relevant factors could not be ascertained.[360] On the transfer of consumer credit regulation to the FCA, the FCA was given the power to make rules defining the "total change for credit".[361] Hence both sets of the Total Charge for Credit Regulations have been repealed and replicated by two sets of FCA rules.[362]

39-060 **Significance of "total charge for credit" and "APR"** The "true" cost of credit is significant in two main respects. First, one of the most important recommenda-

---

352 Defined widely to include not only the credit agreement but also (i) any other transaction entered into in compliance with the credit agreement (i.e. a linked transaction with CCA 1974 s.19(1)(a), see above, para.39-055); (ii) any contract for the provision of security relating to the credit agreement; (iii) any credit brokerage contract relating to the agreement; and (iv) any contract required to be made or maintained as a condition of making the credit agreement.
353 Defined in CCA 1974 ss.184(1), 189(1).
354 SI 1980/51 reg.4 as amended by SIs 1989/596 and 1999/3177. So, in principle, finance charges, commitment fees, brokerage fees (see the amendment made by SI 1989/596), documentation fees (see *Wilson v First County Trust Ltd (No.1)* [2001] Q.B. 407; *Wilson v Robertsons (London) Ltd* [2005] EWHC 1425 (Ch)), membership fees, surveyors' fees, legal fees and similar charges (see *Griffiths v Welcome Financial Services Ltd* [2007] C.C.L.R. 3 (mortgage indemnity fee)) could be included. On the meaning of "charge" where part of the loan must pay off arrears under a previous loan, see *Watchtower Investment Ltd v Payne* [2001] EWCA Civ 1159, which was followed in *London North Securities Ltd v Meadows* [2005] EWCA Civ 956; but distinguished in *McGinn v Grangewood Securities Ltd* [2002] EWCA Civ 522. And see *Ocwen v Hughes* [2004] C.C.L.R. 4, Cty Ct (optional credit insurance premiums).
355 SI 1980/51 reg.5 as amended by SIs 1985/1192, 1989/596 and 1999/3177. For example, insurance premiums (other than premiums under insurance contracts within reg.4(c) and see *London North Securities Ltd v Meadows* [2005] EWCA Civ 956), certain maintenance charges, membership fees, default charges, and charges for money transmission services. See *Huntpast Ltd v Leadbeater* [1993] C.C.L.R. 15 (insurance premium and legal costs); *Humberclyde Finance Ltd v Thompson* [1997] C.C.L.R. 23 (payment waiver premium).
356 SI 1980/51 Pt III (as amended by SI 1999/3177).
357 SI 1980/51 Pt IV.
358 SI 2010/1011 reg.4 (in different terms to SI 1980/51 regs 4 and 5, noted above).
359 SI 2010/1011 reg.5 and Sch.
360 SI 2010/1011 reg.6—again in different terms to SI 1980/51 Pt IV. Reg.6 was amended (from January 1, 2013) by SI 2012/1745, implementing Directive 2011/90/EU which amended Pt II of Annex I to Directive 2008/48/EC.
361 RAO art.60M. See the definition of "total charge for credit" in CCA 1974 s.20 and RAO art.60L, referring to rules made under RAO art.60M.
362 In the CONC Module of the *FCA Handbook*. See CONC App 1.1 (Total charge for credit rules for certain agreements secured on land replicating the "old" 1980 regulations) and CONC App 1.2 (Total charge for credit rules for other agreements, replicating the "Directive" 2010 regulations).

tions of the Crowther Committee on Consumer Credit[363] was that creditors should be compelled to disclose the "true" cost of credit to persons obtaining or wishing to obtain credit. This approach is also reflected in the Consumer Credit Directive. Accordingly the total charge for credit and the APR must be disclosed when credit is promoted[364] and in documents comprising regulated credit agreements.[365] Second, as noted above, certain low-cost "borrower-lender" agreements may gain exemption if the total charge for credit is below certain thresholds.[366]

(b)   Authorisation of Credit and Hire Businesses[367]

Activities requiring FCA authorisation   From April 1, 2014, the 1974 Act licensing regime (as reformed by the Consumer Credit Act 2006) was replaced by the authorisation regime under the Financial Services and Markets Act 2000 (FSMA 2000), operated by the Financial Conduct Authority (FCA). The FSMA 2000 imposes a "general prohibition" on anyone undertaking a "regulated activity" in the United Kingdom[368] unless they are either an "authorised" or an "exempt" person.[369] The two activities of (i) entering into a "regulated credit agreement"[370] as lender and (ii) exercising or having the right to exercise a lender's rights and duties under a regulated credit agreement, are "specified" under the Financial Services and Markets Act 2000 (Regulated Activities) Order 2001 ("RAO").[371] This means that if undertaken "by way of business",[372] they are "regulated activities"[373] and hence can only be carried on in the United Kingdom by an authorised or exempt person. Similarly, the two activities of (i) entering into a "regulated consumer hire agreement"[374] as owner and (ii) exercising or having the right to exercise an owner's rights and duties under a regulated consumer hire agreement, are also "specified" under the RAO.[375] Hence again, if undertaken "by way of business"[376] they are "regulated activities"[377] and can only be carried on in the United Kingdom by an authorised or exempt person. Authorisation is therefore not required by businesses (a) that provide credit or hire only to companies or partnerships of over three persons[378]; and/or (b) that provide credit or hire only under exempt agreements.[379] But authorisation is required, for, e.g. bank lending, moneylending, hire-

39-061

---

[363]   Cmnd.4596 (1971) paras 6.5.15–21.

[364]   *FCA Handbook*, CONC 3; below, para.39-067.

[365]   s.60; below, paras 39-080 et seq.

[366]   RAO art.60G, see above, para.39-042.

[367]   See Guest and Lloyd, *Encyclopedia of Consumer Credit Law* (1975, looseleaf), paras 2-022—2-042; and Goode, *Consumer Credit: Law and Practice* (looseleaf), Pt C, Ch.27.

[368]   See FSMA 2000 s.418.

[369]   FSMA 2000 s.19. See below, para.39-064: trading whilst unauthorised. For "exempt persons" see FSMA 2000 s.38 (Exemption by Treasury Order) and s.39 ("appointed representatives").

[370]   See above, para.39-017.

[371]   SI 2001/544 art.60B, as inserted by the Financial Services and Markets Act 2000 (Regulated Activities) (Amendment) (No.2) Order 2013 (SI 2013/1881) art.6.

[372]   See below, para.39-062.

[373]   FSMA 2000 s.22.

[374]   See above, para.39-036.

[375]   SI 2001/544 art.60N, as inserted by the Financial Services and Markets Act 2000 (Regulated Activities) (Amendment) (No.2) Order 2013 (SI 2013/1881) art.6.

[376]   See below, para.39-062.

[377]   FSMA 2000 s.22.

[378]   As such persons cannot enter into consumer credit and consumer hire agreements (see above, paras 39-016 and 39-035, respectively) and hence "regulated agreements" (see above, paras 39-017 and 39-036, respectively).

purchase,[380] conditional and credit sale, credit card, check trading, pawnbroking, mortgage lending,[381] leasing and rental businesses. Shops and stores providing budget or option accounts or other credit facilities require authorisation, as do mail order businesses. Other business activities in relation to credit and hire (most of which are termed "ancillary credit businesses" under the 1974 Act) also require authorisation and are considered further below.[382]

39-062 **"Business"**   Only "specified activities" undertaken "by way of business" are "regulated activities" requiring authorisation.[383] Whilst sometimes a special meaning is given to the expression "by way of business" in relation to certain regulated activities,[384] for credit and hire businesses the expression is left undefined in the FSMA 2000,[385] although the FCA has provided some guidance in its Handbook, which has been found helpful in the case-law.[386]

39-063 **Authorisation and regulatory control**   Authorisation under the FSMA 2000 brings with it all the regulatory control that the FCA may exercise under that Act over "authorised persons". Hence, as well as having to satisfy the conditions for obtaining and then maintaining "authorisation",[387] authorised persons are subject to the *FCA Handbook*, which has a special "Module" of rules[388] and guidance devoted to consumer credit: the CONC Module.[389] Moreover, the FCA has power to ban products[390] and control high cost lending.[391] The FCA has extensive powers of monitoring "authorised persons"[392] and a wide variety of disciplinary powers ranging from varying, suspending or withdrawing authorisation[393] to the imposition of

---

[379] For exempt agreements, see above, paras 39-038 et seq.

[380] See RAO art.60L(8) above, para.39-024; below, para.39-357.

[381] But note the exemptions for land mortgages, see above, para.39-038; below, para.39-529. Residential mortgages within RAO art.61 (so-called "regulated mortgage contracts") are not "regulated agreements" (see RAO art.60C(2)) and hence not "regulated agreements" for the purpose of the CCA 1974 regime; but they are regulated (as "regulated mortgage contracts" under the parallel FSMA 2000 regime. See below, para.39-529.

[382] See below, paras 39-230 et seq.

[383] FSMA 2000 s.22.

[384] See the Financial Services and Markets Act 2000 (Carrying on Regulated Activities by Way of Business) Order 2001 (SI 2001/1177), as amended, made under FSMA 2000 s.419.

[385] The CCA 1974 definitions of "business" in s.189 (see s.189(1) (the expression "business" in the Act includes profession or trade) and s.189(2) (occasional transactions to be ignored)) have not been repealed and (as confirmed in *Newmafruit Farms Ltd v Pither* [2016] EWHC 2205 (QB), [2017] C.C.L.R. 8) are technically not relevant to the meaning of the terms in FSMA 2000 s.22. See, on the CCA 1974 definition, *Bassano v Alfred Toft, Peter Biddulph, Peter Biddulph Ltd, Borro Loan Ltd, Borro Loan 2 Ltd* [2014] EWHC 377 (QB), [2014] C.C.L.R. 8 (one-off loan).

[386] See *FCA Handbook*, PERG 2 (referred to in the mortgage case *Helden v Strathmore Ltd* [2010] EWHC 2012 (Ch), approved in [2011] EWCA Civ 542).

[387] See FSMA 2000 Pt 4A. Note especially s.55B ("threshold conditions") and also the "control of business transfers" powers in FSMA 2000 Pt VII.

[388] Breach is generally actionable by "private persons" (as defined) suffering loss: FSMA 2000 s.138D, as noted below.

[389] For the FCA's rule-making powers, see FSMA 2000 Pt 9A.

[390] FSMA 2000 s.137D.

[391] FSMA 2000 s.137C. See further below, para.39-292.

[392] See its far-reaching powers to obtain information in FSMA 2000 Pt XI.

[393] See FSMA 2000 ss.55J (variation or cancellation) and s.206A (suspension). Note also its power to impose requirements under ss.55L, 55N, 55O and prohibitions and restrictions under FSMA 2000 s.55P.

penalties[394] and requiring remedial action.[395] The FCA's disciplinary powers are subject to an appeal to the Upper Tribunal.[396] However, an authorised person that breaches the FCA rulebook is not subject to any criminal penalty[397] and their agreements are generally not impeachable on that ground alone,[398] although such a breach is generally actionable by "private persons" (as defined) suffering loss.[399] Finally, the Financial Ombudsman Scheme[400] applies to disputes between authorised persons and their customers.

Trading whilst unauthorised   Undertaking regulated activities in the consumer   **39-064**
credit context whilst not an authorised or exempt person and thus breaching the "general prohibition"[401] is a criminal offence[402] and special provision was made for the specific funding of teams detecting illegal money lenders (so-called "loan sharks") in the Bank of England and Financial Services Act 2016.[403] Moreover, agreements made by a person in contravention of the general prohibition are unenforceable and voidable by the counterparty, although the FCA has power to order otherwise if satisfied that this is "just and equitable".[404] The undertaking of credit or hire activities by an authorised person otherwise than in accordance with their authorisation (for example, if their authorisation does not extend to undertaking credit or hire activities) is similarly a criminal offence[405] and agreements are similarly unenforceable and voidable, subject to the FCA determining otherwise.[406]

Trading "through" unauthorised persons   Agreements made by an authorised   **39-065**
person "through" someone acting in breach of the general prohibition or outside their authorisation are also unenforceable and voidable, subject to the FCA determining otherwise.[407]

FCA determinations to enforce agreements   If the FCA dismisses the applica-   **39-066**

---

[394] See FSMA 2000 s.206. The FCA may also publicly censure: FSMA 2000 s.205.
[395] See FSMA 2000 s.384. The FCA may also apply to court for injunctions (s.380) or restitution orders (s.382).
[396] See FSMA 2000 s.55Z4 (for powers under Pt 4A) and ss.208(4), 384(6) (for other sanctions).
[397] See FSMA 2000 s.138E(1).
[398] See FSMA 2000 s.138E(2)—but there is an exception (s.138E(3)) for the special high cost credit rules under s.137C and the product intervention rules under s.137D.
[399] FSMA 2000 s.138D
[400] See FSMA 2000 Pt XVI.
[401] See above, para.39-061.
[402] FSMA 2000 s.23(1). Unlicensed trading was also a criminal offence under (the now repealed) CCA 1974 ss.39(1), 167 and Sch.1. See *R. v Linegar* [2009] EWCA Crim 648 (sentencing appeal).
[403] See the new Pt XXB added to FSMA 2000, in force July 16, 2016.
[404] FSMA 2000 ss.26, 28A. The position was similar under the CCA 1974 (see the now repealed s.40) but with the OFT having the power to "validate" agreements made by unlicensed traders (see *Smerdon v Ellis* [1997] C.L.Y. 960, Cty Ct; *Rendle v Hicks* [1998] C.L.Y. 2504, Cty Ct; *Barons Finance Ltd & Reddy Corp Ltd v Makanju* [2013] EWHC 153 (QB), [2013] C.C.L.R. 3). In other, non "credit-related activities", an application needs to be made to *the court* to uphold the agreements: FSMA 2000 s.28.
[405] FSMA 2000 s.23(1A)–(1G). To preserve the position under the CCA 1974 (see above), this is only the position in relation to "credit-related activities" (i.e. those activities that were previously subject to the CCA licensing regime). An authorised person who acts outside their authorisation in relation to other regulated activities only faces disciplinary action.
[406] FSMA 2000 ss.26A, 28A.
[407] FSMA 2000 ss.27, 28A. This introduces a degree of "self-policing" into the authorisation regime. In other, non "credit-related activities", an application needs to be made to the *court* to uphold the agreements: s.28.

tion to enforce an agreement ("except on technical grounds only") any security provided in relation to the agreement is avoided.[408] There is an appeal to the Upper Tribunal in respect of these FCA determinations.[409]

(c) Seeking Business[410]

39-067 **Advertising and quotations** Originally, Pt IV of the 1974 Act dealt with advertising and quotations, but since April 1, 2014, following the transfer of consumer credit regulation from the OFT to the FCA,[411] those activities are now regulated under the FSMA 2000 "financial promotion" regime.[412] In consequence of the implementation of the Consumer Credit Directive[413] there were two sets of regulations made under the (now repealed) provisions of the 1974 Act,[414] concerning the form and content of credit[415] advertisements: the Consumer Credit (Advertisements) Regulations 2004[416] and (in implementation of the Directive) the Consumer Credit (Advertisements) Regulations 2010.[417] The FCA rules (in the *FCA Handbook*, CONC 3) largely replicate the detailed and prescriptive provisions of these two sets of old Advertising Regulations.[418] Infringement of these provisions is no longer a criminal offence[419] but (as well as giving rise to the usual consequences for breach of FCA rules[420]) may also breach the Consumer Protection from Unfair Trading Regulations 2008.[421] Regulations under the 1974 Act[422]

---

[408] CCA 1974 ss.113(3)(c), 106.

[409] FSMA 2000 s.28B.

[410] See Guest and Lloyd, *Encyclopedia of Consumer Credit Law* (1975, looseleaf), paras 2-044—2-055; and Goode, *Consumer Credit: Law and Practice* (looseleaf), Pt C, Ch.28.

[411] See above, para.39-002.

[412] See especially FSMA 2000 s.21 and the Financial Services and Markets Act 2000 (Financial Promotion) Order 2005 (SI 2005/1529) (the "FPO")). See the amendments to the FPO made by the Financial Services and Markets Act 2000 (Regulated Activities) (Amendment) (No.2) Order 2013 (SI 2013/1881) art.17. Hence CCA 1974 ss.43–45, 47, 52 and 53 have been repealed.

[413] See above, para.39-011.

[414] For a case on the breach of the old CCA 1974 Advertising Regulations in the context of internet advertising, see *Motor Depot Ltd, Philip Wilkinson v Kingston Upon Hull City Council* [2012] EWHC 3257 (Admin).

[415] The Advertisements Regulations 2004 originally also applied to *hire* advertisements, but hire was removed from the scope of the Regulations by the Consumer Protection from Unfair Trading Regulations 2008 (SI 2008/1277) reg.30(1) and Sch.2 para.108. However, hire is now subject to the FCA promotion rules.

[416] SI 2004/1484 amended by SIs 2004/2619, 2007/827, 2008/1277 (removing hire agreements from regulation), 2010/1010, 2010/1969. These regulations constituted the third major revision of the CCA 1974 advertisements regime (the previous two being contained in SI 1980/54, as amended and SI 1989/1125, as amended).

[417] SI 2010/1970 (replacing SI 2010/1012).

[418] The (now repealed) CCA 1974 s.45, which prohibited advertisements where goods, etc. were not sold for cash, is replicated as a "rule" in CONC 3.5.2R and 3.6.3R.

[419] As it was under the CCA 1974 s.167 and Sch.1 (relevant provision repealed by the Financial Services and Markets Act 2000 (Regulated Activities) (Amendment) (No.2) Order 2013 (SI 2013/1881) art.20(64)).

[420] See above, para.39-063.

[421] SI 2008/1277, and hence give rise to a criminal offence or, for contracts made on or after October 1, 2014, civil redress. CCA 1974 s.46 (which also made it an offence to publish "false or misleading" advertisements) was repealed (from May 26, 2008) by SI 2008/1277 reg.30(1) and Sch.2 para.18. For case-law on s.46 (which may still be of persuasive relevance to offences under the 2008 Regulations), see *Home Insulation Ltd v Wadsley* [1988] 10 C.L. 48; *Metsoja v H Norman Pitt & Co Ltd* [1989] Crim. L.R. 560; *Rover Group Ltd and Rover Finance Ltd v Sumner* [1995] C.C.L.R.

also prescribed the content of quotations in certain cases[423] and their provisions have also been largely replicated as "rules" in the *FCA Handbook*.[424]

Canvassing It is an offence[425] to canvass[426] debtor-creditor[427] agreements off trade premises,[428] except in response to a request in writing made on a previous occasion and signed by or on behalf of the person making it.[429] **39-068**

Circulars to minors It is also an offence[430] for a person, with a view to financial gain, to send to a minor a document inviting him to borrow money, obtain goods on credit or hire, obtain services on credit, or apply for information or advice on borrowing money or otherwise obtaining credit, or hiring goods.[431] **39-069**

Infringement Failure to comply with those provisions of Pt IV that remain in force[432] do not affect the validity or enforceability of any agreement.[433] **39-070**

(d) Antecedent Negotiations[434]

"Antecedent negotiations" These are defined[435] by s.56(1) of the 1974 Act to mean any negotiations with the debtor[436] or hirer of the following alternative descriptions: first, negotiations conducted by the creditor or owner in relation to any regulated agreement; second, negotiations conducted by a credit-broker[437] in relation to goods sold or proposed to be sold by the credit-broker to the creditor before **39-071**

1; *Dudley MBC v Colorvision Plc* [1997] C.C.L.R. 19.

[422] Under CCA 1974 s.52, as amended (on October 1, 2004) by RAO art.90(4). See SI 1999/2725 as amended by SI 2000/1797 and SI 2001/544. The first quotations regulations (SI 1980/55, as amended) were replaced by SI 1989/1126, as amended, and were much wider in scope and were revoked by SI 1997/211.

[423] In connection with a prospective credit agreement (a) that would or could be secured by a mortgage or charge on the debtor's home, or (b) under which repayments of credit would be made in a currency other than sterling.

[424] See CONC 4.1.

[425] CCA 1974 s.167 and Sch.1.

[426] CCA 1974 ss.48, 189(1).

[427] See above, para.39-033.

[428] CCA 1974 s.48.

[429] CCA 1974 s.49. A Determination has been made by the Director General of Fair Trading under s.49(3) (the FCA now being the responsible authority), with respect to the exclusion of current accounts from s.49(1), (2). See Guest and Lloyd, *Encyclopedia of Consumer Credit Law* (1975, looseleaf) at para.4-4800. See also ss.153, 154 (below, para.39-252). For additional obligations imposed on such lenders, see the Home Credit Market Investigation Order 2007, as amended in 2011, made by the Competition Commission under the Enterprise Act 2002 ss.161, 164.

[430] CCA 1974 s.167 and Sch.1.

[431] CCA 1974 s.50. cf. *Alliance and Leicester Building Society v Leicestershire CC, The Times,* March 15, 1993. For a (now repealed) exemption with respect to student loans, see the Education (Student Loans) Act 1990 Sch.2 para.3(A) (as amended).

[432] Sections 48–49 (see above, para.39-068) and s.50 (see above, para.39-069).

[433] CCA 1974 s.170(1). For criminal penalties, see CCA 1974 ss.49, 50, 167(1), (2) and Sch.1 (as amended).

[434] See Guest and Lloyd, *Encyclopedia of Consumer Credit Law* (1975, looseleaf) at para.2-057.

[435] See also CCA 1974 Sch.2 Pt II Examples 1, 2, 3, 4.

[436] But not with a guarantor of the debtor: *Lombard North Central Plc v Gate* [1998] C.C.L.R. 51, Cty Ct. See CCA 1974 s.189B(3), Sch.2A: in s.56, references to "debtor" in relation to "green deal plans" (as defined in CCA 1974 s.189(1), below, para.39-257) are to be read as references to the "improver"/ "first bill payer", as defined in CCA 1974 s.189B(6).

[437] Defined in CCA 1974 s.189(1); below, para.39-231.

forming the subject of a debtor-creditor-supplier agreement falling within s.12(a)[438]; third, negotiations conducted by the supplier[439] in relation to a transaction financed or proposed to be financed by a debtor-creditor-supplier agreement falling within s.12(b) or (c).[440] It is to be noted that negotiations conducted by a third party other than the creditor or owner (either himself or by his employees or common law agents) in respect of a debtor-creditor[441] or hire[442] agreement do not fall within s.56(1).

39-072 The first category of antecedent negotiations mentioned above is self-explanatory, and it is clear that it will embrace negotiations conducted by an employee or an agent of the creditor or owner. The second category covers negotiations conducted by, for example, a dealer in relation to goods to be sold by the dealer[443] to a financier and which are to be the subject of a hire-purchase, conditional sale or credit sale agreement between the financier and the debtor (the usual "tripartite" transaction). It is to be noted that this category relates only to negotiations in relation to *goods* and to the goods sold or proposed to be sold by the dealer to the financier.[444] The third category refers, for instance, to negotiations conducted by a supplier of goods or services who supplies them for money advanced by a financier to the debtor as a restricted-use loan[445] under pre-existing arrangements between the financier and the supplier.

39-073 The person by whom negotiations are so conducted with the debtor or hirer is referred to as the "negotiator".[446]

39-074 For the purposes of the Act, antecedent negotiations are to be taken to begin when the negotiator and the debtor or hirer first enter into communication (including com-

---

[438] See above, para.39-030.

[439] Defined in CCA 1974 s.189(1).

[440] See above, paras 39-031, 39-032.

[441] See above, para.39-033.

[442] See above, para.39-035, and *Moorgate Mercantile Leasing Ltd v Isobel Gell and Ugolini Dispensers (UK) Ltd* [1986] 2 C.L. 39, Cty Ct; *Mynshul Asset Finance v Clarke* [1992] C.L.Y 487, Cty Ct; *Williams (JD) & Co v McCauley, Parson and Jones* [1994] C.C.L.R. 78; *Woodchester Leasing Equipment v British Association of Canned and Preserved Foods Importers and Distributors Ltd* [1995] C.C.L.R. 51, CA; *PB Leasing Ltd v Patel and Patel (t/a Plankhouse Stores)* [1995] C.C.L.R. 82, Cty Ct; *Powell v Lloyd's Bowmakers* [1996] S.L.T. 117, [1996] C.C.L.R. 50 Sh Ct. But contrast the following cases where the supplier was found to be, on the facts, the common law agent of the owner: *Woodchester Leasing Equipment v Clayton* [1994] C.C.L.R. 87; and *Lease Management Services Ltd v Purnell Secretarial Services Ltd* [1994] C.C.L.R. 127.

[443] See *Black Horse Ltd v Langford* [2007] EWHC 907, [2007] C.C.L.R. 5: s.56(1)(b) did not apply to a dealer who (although having the status of a "credit broker") sold the goods to an intermediary who then sold to the creditor in that the dealer was not the "credit broker" who sold the goods to the creditor. But note the Law Commissions' Joint Report: *Consumer Redress for Misleading and Aggressive Practices* (March 2012), Cm.8323, Recommendation 51, recommending that s.56 should be "clarified" to cover dealers acting through intermediaries.

[444] But see *UDT v Whitfield and First National Securities* [1987] C.C.L.R. 60, Cty Ct; and *Forthright Finance Ltd v Ingate* [1997] 4 All E.R. 99, CA (finance house held liable for dealer's failure to fulfil his undertaking to the debtor to discharge the outstanding balance on a vehicle traded-in by the debtor as part of a transaction to take a new vehicle on hire-purchase). Contrast *Powell v Lloyd's Bowmaker Ltd*, 1996 S.L.T. (Sh Ct) 117.

[445] See above, para.39-027; below, para.39-302. See *Scotland v British Credit Trust Ltd* [2014] EWCA Civ 790 (main loan, but not loan for PPI, was "restricted-use") (and see below).

[446] CCA 1974 s.56(1). See also CCA 1974 Sch.2 Pt II Examples 1, 2, 3, 4.

munication by advertisement[447]), and to include any representations[448] made by the
negotiator to the debtor or hirer and any other dealings between them.[449]

Negotiator as agent   Once antecedent negotiations have been shown to exist, the   **39-075**
negotiator, though not in fact the common law agent of the creditor, is deemed to
have conducted the negotiations in the capacity of agent of the creditor as well as
in his actual capacity.[450] Thus the creditor will be liable for express misrepresentations by his deemed agent,[451] and for any contractual undertakings given by the
deemed agent.[452] This deemed agency and liability for the acts or omissions of the
deemed agent cannot be excluded by agreement.[453]

(e)   The Agreement[454]

Pre-contract disclosure[455]   Regulations may be made under s.55 of the 1974   **39-076**
Act,[456] requiring specified information to be disclosed in the prescribed manner to
the debtor or hirer before a regulated agreement is made.[457] Failure to comply with
the regulations made under s.55 renders the agreement enforceable against the
debtor or hirer on an order of the court only.[458] In consequence of the implementation of the Consumer Credit Directive[459] there are now two sets of "Disclosure"

---

[447]   Defined in CCA 1974 s.189(1).

[448]   Defined in CCA 1974 s.189(1). See *Scotland v British Credit Trust Ltd* [2014] EWCA Civ 790
(representations that PPI (not financed by a "restricted-use" agreement) was a condition of the main
loan (a restricted-use agreement) were held to have been made in relation to the main loan and hence
within s.56(1)(c)) (and see above).

[449]   CCA 1974 s.56(4).

[450]   CCA 1974 s.56(2). See also below, para.39-302. Unlike CCA 1974 s.75(2), below, para.39-303, no
express right of indemnity is conferred on the creditor against the negotiator but a right to contribution would arise under Civil Liability (Contribution) Act 1978 (confirmed obiter in *Scotland v British Credit Trust Ltd* [2014] EWCA Civ 790). For the relevance of s.56 in attributing activities of others to the creditor in the context of the "unfair relationship" provisions (below, para.39-222) see
Plevin v Paragon Personal Finance Ltd [2013] EWCA Civ 1658 (point not considered on appeal
[2014] UKSC 61) and *Scotland v British Credit Trust Ltd* [2014] EWCA Civ 790 (s.56(2) rendered
activities of "negotiator" relevant).

[451]   See Vol.I, Ch.7, and below, para.39-302.

[452]   These may in consequence become terms of the regulated agreement: see CCA 1974 s.61(1)(b);
below, para.39-083. It is a moot point whether collateral warranties would be so incorporated.

[453]   CCA 1974 s.56(3) (and see, more generally, CCA 1974 s.170(1)).

[454]   See Guest and Lloyd, *Encyclopedia of Consumer Credit Law* (1975, looseleaf), paras 2-056, 2-061—
2-066; and Goode, *Consumer Credit: Law and Practice* (looseleaf), Pt C, Ch.30.

[455]   The Payment Services Regulations 2017 (SI 2027/752) regs 43 and 48 impose additional information requirements prior to the making of "payment services contracts" (or certain payments
thereunder), a term that covers *certain* credit agreements (see generally, above, paras 34-224 et seq.),
but note the modification for agreements that are CCA 1974-regulated agreements in reg.41(3).

[456]   s.55 does not apply to the types of agreement listed in CCA 1974 s.74(1)(a) (non-commercial agreement, see above, para.39-049), in s.74(1)(b) ("authorised business overdraft agreements") and in
s.82(4) (variation). And note the further exclusions, in relation to each set of regulations mentioned
in the text.

[457]   See CCA 1974 s.189B(3), Sch.2A: in s.55, references to "debtor" in relation to "green deal plans"
(as defined in CCA 1974 s.189(1), see below, para.39-257) are to be read as references to the
"improver", as defined in CCA 1974 s.189B(6). Note also CCA 1974 s.55C (copy of draft credit
agreement available on request), below, para.39-079.

[458]   CCA 1974 s.55(2), as substituted by SI 2010/1010 reg.16. This only applies to the 2004 Regulations (see text) as only these are made under s.55. The 2010 Regulations (see text) are made under
the European Communities Act 1972.

[459]   See above, para.39-011.

regulations in relation to regulated credit (but not hire) agreements: the Consumer Credit (Disclosure of Information) Regulations 2004[460] and (in implementation of the Directive) the Consumer Credit (Disclosure of Information) Regulations 2010.[461] The 2004 Regulations now only apply to agreements outside the scope of the Directive, unless the creditor is able to and has opted into the "Directive" regime.[462] Hence the 2004 Regulations (as well as still applying to regulated hire agreements) only apply to: (a) credit agreements secured on land (except to those to which s.58,[463] applies); (b) agreements for credit in excess of £60,260[464]; (c) "business" credit agreements; and (d) "small" debtor-creditor-supplier agreements for restricted use.[465] The 2010 "Directive" Regulations essentially apply to other regulated credit agreements. They require the pre-contract information to be provided in the exact format set out in the Standard European Consumer Credit Information (SECCI) sheet at Annex 1 of the Directive, reproduced in Sch.1 to the 2010 Regulations.

39-077 **Pre-contract explanations** In consequence of the implementation of the Consumer Credit Directive,[466] a new duty to provide an "adequate explanation" of certain features of the agreement before it is made is imposed on lenders by rules made by the FCA[467] in relation to those regulated credit agreements within the scope of the Directive. Hence the obligation does not apply to agreements for credit in excess of £60,260 or agreements secured on land.[468] However, although "business" credit is not within the scope of the Directive, the duty has been extended to regulated agreements for "business" credit.[469] As the duty is imposed by FCA rules, the usual sanctions for breach of such rules apply.[470] However, the agreement is not, without more, unenforceable.[471]

---

460 SI 2004/1481.

461 SI 2010/1013, as amended by SI 2010/1969 regs 31–40 and SI 2011/11 reg.8.

462 See SI 2004/1483 reg.2, as amended by SI 2010/1010 reg.75 and SI 2010/1969 reg.24. The Regulations also exclude (a) agreements within CCA 1974 s.58 (as an "advance copy" is provided under that section, see below, para.39-535) and (b) "distance contracts", as defined in the Financial Services (Distance Marketing) Regulations 2004 SI 2004/2095 (as (usually, if the contract is made with a "consumer") those regulations will apply, see below, para.39-126).

463 See previous note, above and (for s.58) below, para.39-535.

464 When the Mortgage Credit Directive (see above, para.39-003) was implemented on March 21, 2016, they now also apply to so-called "residential renovation agreements" (as defined in CCA 1974 s.189(1) to mean, essentially, unsecured loans to renovate residential property) above this threshold: see amendments made by SI 2015/910 art.3 and Sch.1 paras 11, 13.

465 See above, para.39-048.

466 See above, para.39-011.

467 In the *FCA Handbook*, see CONC 4.2 (general) and CONC 4.3 (P2P agreements) (previously CCA 1974 s.55A, added by SI 2010/1010 reg.3). Much of the OFT's publication: *Irresponsible lending— OFT guidance for creditors* (OFT 1107, March 2010; updated February 2011) (ILG), Section 3 of which contained extensive guidance on the OFT's interpretation of the requirements of the now repealed CCA 1974 s.55A has been incorporated in CONC.

468 See CONC 4.2.1(3) and (4). It also does not apply to "non-commercial" agreements, see above, para.39-049 (CONC 4.2.5(7)(a)), most overdraft agreements (CONC 4.2.1(5)) or "small" agreements, see above, para.39-048 (CONC 4.2.5(7)(b)).

469 But only "business" credit under £25,000 is "regulated": see above, para.39-046. The duty has also been modified in relation to pawn agreements (see CONC 4.2.5(6), previously CCA 1974 s.55A(7)).

470 See above, para.39-063. Hence breach is actionable under the FSMA 2000 s.138D and could result in the usual FCA disciplinary sanctions. See also ss.140A–140C (unfair relationships), below, paras 39-212 et seq.

471 cf. breach of CCA 1974 ss.55, 61, 61A, 62, 63, 64.

Assessment of creditworthiness   Also in consequence of the implementation of **39-078** the Consumer Credit Directive[472] a new duty to assess the creditworthiness of the borrower before extending credit[473] is imposed on lenders by rules made by the FCA[474] in relation to those regulated credit agreements within the scope of the Directive. Hence the obligation does not apply to agreements secured on land or to pawn agreements.[475] However, although agreements for credit in excess of £60,260 and "business" credit agreements are not within the scope of the Directive, the duty has been extended to such agreements.[476] As the duty is imposed by FCA rules, the usual sanctions for breach of such rules apply.[477] However, the agreement is not, without more, unenforceable.[478]

Copy of draft agreement   In consequence of the implementation of the Consumer **39-079** Credit Directive,[479] a new duty to give the debtor, on request and "without delay", a copy of the prospective agreement (or such of its terms as have at that time been reduced to writing) before a regulated credit agreement is made, is imposed on the creditor by s.55C of the 1974 Act.[480] The obligation does not arise if at the time of the obligation the creditor is unwilling to proceed with the agreement. Moreover, the obligation does not arise[481] in relation to regulated credit agreements that are outside the scope of the Directive, namely: (a) agreements secured on land, (b) pawn agreements, (c) agreements where credit in excess of £60,260 is provided,[482] and (d) "business" credit. Breach of the duty gives rise to a breach of statutory duty action and the normal disciplinary sanctions are available to the FCA.[483] However, failure to provide the copy does not, without more, render the agreement unenforceable.[484]

Form and content of agreement: general   Section 60(1) of the 1974 Act requires **39-080**

significantly increasing credit already available

in the *FCA Handbook*, see CONC 5 (on contracting) and CONC 6 (during agreement) (previously CCA 1974 s.55B, added by SI 2010/1010 reg.5), much of the OFT's publication: *Irresponsible lending—OFT guidance for creditors* (ILG), which contained extensive guidance on the OFT's interpretation of the requirements of CCA 1974 s.55B has been incorporated in CONC.

[475] CONC 5.2.1(4). It also does not apply to "non-commercial" agreements, see above, para.39-049 (CONC 5.2.1(5)(a)), current account overdrawing (CONC 5.2.1(5)(b)) or "small" agreements, see above, para.39-048 (CONC 5.2.1(5)(c)).

[476] But only "business" credit under £25,000 is "regulated": see above, para.39-046.

[477] See above, para.39-063. Hence breach is actionable under the FSMA 2000 s.138D and could result in the usual FCA disciplinary sanctions. See also ss.140A–140C (unfair relationships), below, paras 39-212 et seq.

[478] cf. breach of CCA 1974 ss.55, 61, 61A, 62, 63, 64.

[479] See above, para.39-011.

[480] Added on February 1, 2011 by SI 2010/1010 reg.6 (not repealed and replaced by rules in FCA Handbook, CONC). See CCA 1974 s.189B(3), Sch.2A: in CCA 1974 s.55C, references to "debtor" in relation to "green deal plans" (as defined in CCA 1974 s.189(1), see below, para.39-257) are to be read as references to the "improver"/"first bill payer", as defined in CCA 1974 s.189B(6).

[481] CCA 1974 s.55C also does not apply to the types of agreement listed in (i) s.74(1)(a) ("non-commercial" agreements, see above, para.39-049), (ii) s.74(1)(b) ("authorised business overdrafts", (iii) s.74(1)(d) ("small" agreements, see above, para.39-048). See also s.82(4) (variation).

[482] When the Mortgage Credit Directive (see above, para.39-003) was implemented on March 21, 2016 this exemption ceased to apply to so-called "residential renovation agreements" (as defined in 1974 s.189(1) to mean, essentially, unsecured loans to renovate residential property) above threshold: see amendment to s.55C in SI 2015/910 art.3 and Sch.1 para.2(3).

[483] See above, para.39-063. See also ss.140A–140C (unfair relationships), below, paras 39...

[484] cf. breach of CCA 1974 ss.55, 61, 61A, 62, 63, 64.

the Treasury[485] to make regulations as to the form and content of documents embodying regulated agreements.[486] In consequence of the implementation of the Consumer Credit Directive[487] there are now two sets of regulations made under this section in relation to regulated credit agreements: the Consumer Credit (Agreements) Regulations 1983[488] and (in implementation of the Directive) the Consumer Credit (Agreements) Regulations 2010.[489] The 1983 Regulations now only apply to regulated credit[490] agreements outside the scope of the Directive, unless the creditor is permitted to and has opted into the "Directive" regime.[491] Hence, the 1983 Regulations (as well as still applying to regulated hire agreements) apply to: (a) credit agreements secured on land, (b) agreements for credit in excess of £60,260,[492] and (c) "business" credit agreements.[493] The 2010 "Directive" Regulations apply to other regulated credit agreements.

39-081 **Form and content of agreement: the 1983 Agreements Regulations** These regulations[494] require documents embodying regulated agreements:

(i)   clearly to inform the debtor or hirer that the agreement is regulated Consumer Credit Act 1974;

(ii)   to set out, in a specified order and under specified headings, certain information as to the terms of the agreement, of which the most important items have to be set out together as a whole and not interspersed with other information (a requirement colloquially known as "the holy ground");

(iii)   to contain certain prominent notices advising the debtor or hirer of the protections and remedies available to him under the regime;

(iv)   to contain a box with prescribed wording for the signature of the debtor or hirer to the agreement; and

(v)   in the case of consumer credit agreements, to state the annual percentage rate of charge for credit (APR).

---

485   Before the transfer of regulation to the FCA (see above, para.39-002) the Secretary of State made the regulations.

486   This provision does not apply to the types agreement listed in s.74(1) (see below, para.39-103). See also s.82(4) (variation). See CCA 1974 s.189B(3), Sch.2A: in CCA 1974 s.60, references to "debtor" in relation to "green deal plans" (as defined in CCA 1974 s.189(1), see below, para.39-257) are to be read as references to the "improver" (as defined in CCA 1974 s.189B(6)), including an improver who is not an individual.

487   See above, para.39-011.

488   SI 1983/1553 (brought into force on May 19, 1985) and amended by SI 1984/1600; SI 1985/666; SI 1988/2047; SI 1999/3177; SI 2004/1482; SI 2004/2619; SI 2010/1010. They were completely overhauled by SI 2004/1482 (in force, May 31, 2005).

489   SI 2010/1014, as amended by SI 2010/1969 regs 41–45.

490   As hire agreements are not within the scope of the Directive, the 1983 Regulations also continue to apply to regulated hire agreements.

491   See SI 1983/1553 reg.8(1A), added by SI 2010/1010 reg.53 and amended further by SI 2010/1969 reg.13.

492   But when the Mortgage Credit Directive (see above, para.39-003) was implemented on March 21, 2016, these regulations ceased to apply to so-called "residential renovation agreements" (as defined in CCA 1974 s.189(1) to mean, essentially, unsecured loans to renovate residential property) above this threshold: see amendment to SI 1983/1553 in SI 2015/910 art.3 and Sch.1 para.3.

493   But note that only business credit under £25,000 is "regulated": see above, para.39-046.

494   See above, para.39-080.

495   See CCA 1974 s.20; above, para.39-059. An erroneously calculated APR gave rise to criminal liability under the misleading price indications provisions of the (now repealed by the Consumer Protection from Unfair Trading Regulations 2008 (SI 2008/1277)) Consumer Protection Act 1987

Since these requirements may differ according to the type of agreement entered into, the regulations are of considerable length and complexity.[496] However, on an application made by a person carrying on a consumer credit or consumer hire business, if it appears to the FCA impracticable for the applicant to comply with any requirement of the regulations in a particular case, it may by notice to the applicant direct that the requirement be waived or varied in relation to such agreements, and subject to such conditions (if any) as it may specify.[497] But it can only give such a notice if it is satisfied that to do so would not prejudice the interests of debtors or hirers[498] and few dispensations have in consequence been granted.[499]

Form and content of agreement: the 2010 Agreements Regulations These **39-082** regulations[500] impose similar, but by no means identical, requirements to those imposed by the 1983 Regulations as to the form and content of the regulated credit agreements to which they apply. In particular, the 2010 Regulations are generally less prescriptive as to the manner in which the requisite information[501] needs to be given: it need only be "presented in a clear and concise manner".[502] As the requirements in these regulations (being imposed in implementation of the Consumer Credit Directive) are mandatory, the provision noted above that enables the FCA to relax the requirements in the 1983 Regulations[503] is only available in respect of the 2010 Regulations in so far as they apply (by way of opt-in) to non-Directive agreements.[504]

Signing of agreement[505] A regulated agreement is not properly executed[506] un- **39-083**

---

s.20 in *R. v Kettering Magistrates' Court Ex p. MRB Insurance Brokers Ltd* [2000] 2 All E.R. (Comm) 353, QB. See *Brooks v Northern Rock (Asset Management) Plc* Unreported April 16, 2010, Oldham Cty Ct (on the citation of rates of interest) and *Black Horse Ltd v Speak* [2010] EWHC 1866 (QB).

[496] See Guest and Lloyd *Encyclopedia of Consumer Credit Law* (1975, looseleaf) at paras 3-215 et seq.

[497] CCA 1974 s.60(3)–(6), amended by Sch.25(6) to the Enterprise Act 2002, SI 2013/1881 and SI 2013/1882. See also CCA 1974 s.183 (variation or revocation of directions made under the CCA 1974). Note also that FSMA 2000 ss.55U(4), (5), (7) and (8) apply to an application made under CCA 1974 s.60(3) as if the application were an application made to the FCA under the FSMA 2000 Pt 4A: see the Financial Services and Markets Act 2000 (Regulated Activities) (Amendment) Order 2014 (SI 2014/366) art.4.

[498] CCA 1974 s.60(4).

[499] The FCA stated on March 30, 2015 that this dispensation is available to shared-equity mortgage agreements that provide specified alternative information.

[500] SI 2010/1014, as amended by SI 2010/1969 regs 41–45.

[501] Set out in Sch.1 to the regulations.

[502] SI 2010/1014 reg.3(2).

[503] CCA 1974 s.60(3)–(6), see above, para.39-080.

[504] See CCA 1974 s.60(5)—and note the amendment (as a result of the implementation of the Mortgage Credit Directive (see above, para.39-003) on March 21, 2016) in relation to so-called "residential renovation agreements" (as defined in CCA 1974 s.189(1) to mean, essentially, unsecured loans to renovate residential property) in SI 2015/910 art.3 and Sch.1 para.4.

[505] The Consumer Credit Directive (see above, para.39-011) does not require a signature but is without prejudice to national rules as to the validity of agreements. Hence, the CCA 1974 requirement for a signature has been retained. For a discussion of electronic contracting, see Philpott, "E-Commerce and Consumer Credit" (2001) 3 J.I.F.M. 131; and Guest and Lloyd, *Encyclopedia of Consumer Credit Law* (1975, looseleaf) at para.2-062. See also *Golden Ocean Group Ltd v Salgaocar Mining Industries PVT Ltd* [2012] 2 All E.R. (Comm) 978 at 932 (name typed in an email is a signature); *Bassano v Alfred Toft, Peter Biddulph, Peter Biddulph Ltd, Borro Loan Ltd, Borro Loan 2 Ltd* [2014] EWHC 377 (QB), [2014] C.C.L.R. 8 (clicking "I accept" which generated a PDF document with the debtor's typed name, fulfilled the "signature" requirement in CCA 1974 s.61(1)).

less it satisfies the requirements set out in s.61(1) of the 1974 Act.[507] First, a document in the prescribed form itself[508] containing all the prescribed terms[509] and conforming to regulations under s.60(1)[510] must be signed in the prescribed manner[511] both by the debtor or hirer[512] and by or on behalf of the creditor or owner.[513] Secondly, the document must embody[514] *all the terms of the agreement*,[515] other than implied terms.[516] Thirdly, the document must, when presented or sent to the debtor or hirer for signature, be in such a state that all its terms are readily legible.[517] In addition, where the agreement is one to which s.58(1) of the 1974 Act applies (land mortgage),[518] it is not properly executed[519] unless certain further requirements are satisfied.[520]

39-084 **Supply of copies: general** Sections 61A to 63 of the 1974 Act contain provisions relating to the supply of copies.[521] They use the terms "unexecuted" and "executed" agreement. The latter term is defined[522] to mean the document, signed

---

[506] And hence enforceable on an order of court only, see CCA 1974 s.65 and below, paras 39-093 and 39-094.

[507] CCA 1974 s.61 does not apply to the agreements specified in CCA 1974 s.74(1) (see para.39-103) and note CCA 1974 s.82(4) (variation).

[508] And not by reference to another document.

[509] These prescribed terms are set out in the two sets of Agreement Regulations (see above, paras 39-080 et seq.): (i) SI 1983/1553 Sch.6 and (ii) SI 2010/1014 reg.4(1).

[510] See above, paras 39-080 et seq.

[511] Prescribed in the two sets of Agreement Regulations (see above, paras 39-080 et seq.): (i) SI 1983/1553 (as amended, especially by SI 2004/1482) reg.2(7) and Sch.5 (signature box) and (ii) SI 2010/1014 reg.4(3)–(4).

[512] Signature of a document in blank will be insufficient (*Eastern Distributions Ltd v Goldring* [1957] 2 Q.B. 600; *Campbell Discount Co Ltd v Gall* [1961] 1 Q.B. 431) as will a signature by only one of two joint debtors (*HFC Bank v Grossbard* [2001] C.L.Y. 908). See also CCA 1974 ss.61(4), 185(3), (6), 189(3).

[513] CCA 1974 s.61(1)(a). See also CCA 1974 ss.186, 189(3).

[514] Defined in CCA 1974 s.189(1), (4) (reference to another document). But see *Jerome v Nationwide Building Society* Unreported September 27, 2011, Huddersfield Cty Ct: reference to other document must be accurate (hence loose sheets were not "embodied" in document referring to "attached sheets").

[515] As under s.6(2) of the Moneylenders Act 1927, so that if, e.g. money advanced can be applied in one way only, this must be stated: *Hanyet Securities Ltd v Mallett* [1968] 1 W.L.R. 1265. Contrast *Askinex Ltd v Green* [1969] 1 Q.B. 272. Similarly the case-law under the 1927 Act held that any term to the effect that the loan renews another loan ought to be stated: *Lyle v Chappell* [1932] 1 K.B. 691; *Temperance Loan Fund v Rose* [1932] 2 K.B. 522; *Egan v Langham Investments* [1938] 1 K.B. 667; *Re British Games* [1938] Ch. 240; *Allighan v London and Westminster Loan and Discount Ltd* [1946] 3 All E.R. 530. But see *Holiday Credit v Erol* [1977] 1 W.L.R. 704; *Broadwick Financial Services v Spencer* [2002] EWCA Civ 35 (non-binding concession need not be stated).

[516] CCA 1974 s.61(1)(b). For implied terms, see below, paras 39-382 et seq., 39-457, 39-468.

[517] CCA 1974 s.61(1)(c). See also SI 1983/1553 reg.6(2), as amended by SI 2004/1482 and (to substitute media-neutral wording) by SI 2004/3236.

[518] See below, para.39-535.

[519] And hence enforceable on an order of court only, see CCA 1974 s.65 and below, paras 39-093 and 39-094.

[520] CCA 1974 s.61(2), (3); below, para.39-535.

[521] The provisions do not apply to the agreements specified in CCA 1974 s.74(1) (see para.39-103). See also CCA 1974 s.82(4) (variation) and CCA 1974 ss.180 (form of copies), 185(1)(a) (plurality of debtors or hirers). See CCA 1974 s.189B(3), Sch.2A: in CCA 1974 ss.61A–63, references to "debtor" in relation to "green deal plans" (as defined in CCA 1974 s.189(1), see below, para.39-257) are to be read as references to the "improver" (as defined in CCA 1974 s.189B(6)).

[522] In CCA 1974 s.189(1).

by both parties, embodying the terms of a regulated agreement, whilst the former term apparently refers to such a document not yet signed by both parties.[523]

Supply of copies: two regimes: In consequence of the implementation of the   **39-085**
Consumer Credit Directive[524] there are now two "copy" regimes in relation to regulated credit agreements: the "old" regime under ss.62 and 63 and the "Directive regime" under s.61A.[525] The "old" ss.62–63 regime (as well as continuing to apply to regulated hire agreements[526]) now only applies to so-called "excluded agreements", that is (essentially) credit agreements outside the scope of the Directive, unless the creditor is permitted to and has chosen to opt into the "Directive" regime. Those "excluded agreements" are: (a) credit agreements secured on land,[527] (b) agreements for credit in excess of £60,260[528] and (c) "business" credit agreements.[529] Moreover, ss.62 and 63 continue to apply to "cancellable agreements" within s.67.[530] The "Directive" regime under s.61A applies to all other regulated credit agreements.

Supply of copies: meaning of "copy"   The Consumer Credit (Cancellation   **39-086**
Notices and Copies of Documents) Regulations 1983[531] make provision as to the form and content of the copies to be supplied, and in particular require the copy to be a "true copy"[532] and to be easily legible.[533] The meaning of "true copy" was considered at length in *Carey v HSBC Bank Plc*[534] where it was held that a "true copy" of an executed agreement could be "a reconstituted version of the executed agreement which may be from sources other than the actual signed agreement itself".[535]

Supply of copies: failure to comply   A regulated agreement is not properly   **39-087**
executed if the "copy" requirements are not observed, with the result that it is enforceable on an order of court only.[536]

---

[523] It is defined in CCA 1974 s.189(1) in almost identical terms to those used to define "executed agreement", but with the omission of any reference to signature.

[524] See above, para.39-011.

[525] Added on February 1, 2011 by SI 2010/1010 reg.8. See also CCA 1974 s.61B, added by SI 2010/1010 reg.9: special copy requirements for overdrafts.

[526] As hire agreements are not within the scope of the Directive.

[527] But CCA 1974 ss.62–63 invariably apply to land mortgages to which CCA 1974 s.58 applies, as these cannot opt into the "Directive" regime (see SI 2010/1013 reg.2(2) and (5)).

[528] When the Mortgage Credit Directive (see above, para.39-003) was implemented on March 21, 2016, this exclusion ceased to apply to so-called "residential renovation agreements" (as defined in CCA 1974 s.189(1) to mean, essentially, unsecured loans to renovate residential property) above this threshold: see the new s.61A(6A) inserted by SI 2015/910 art.3 and Sch.1 para.2(5).

[529] But note that only business credit under £25,000 is "regulated": see above, para.39-046.

[530] See below, para.39-102.

[531] SI 1983/1557, as amended by SI 1983/1558; SI 1984/1108; SI 1988/2047; (most extensively) SI 2004/2619; SI 2004/3236. See also, SI 1985/666 and SI 1989/591, made under (inter alia) CCA 1974 s.180.

[532] SI 1983/1557 reg.3(1).

[533] SI 1983/1557 reg.2(1).

[534] [2009] EWHC 3417 (QB), a case on CCA 1974 s.78 (see below, para.39-132). See also *MBNA Europe Bank Ltd v Thorius* Unreported September 21, 2009, South Shields Cty Ct D.D.J. Smart: *original* agreement terms, not terms in force at time of proceedings, need to be provided.

[535] [2009] EWHC 3417, at [54].

[536] CCA 1974 ss.61A(5), 61B(3), 62(3), 63(5), 65; below, paras 39-093 and 39-094. The same consequence follows for breach of CCA 1974 s.64 (see below, para.39-093): s.64(5).

39-088 **Supply of copies: "old" ss.62–63 regime** If the unexecuted agreement is *presented personally* to the debtor or hirer for his signature, and on the occasion when he signs it the creditor or owner signs or has already signed the agreement, then a copy of the executed agreement must there and then be delivered to him, but no further copy is required.[537] If the unexecuted agreement is *sent* to the debtor or hirer for his signature, a copy of it must be sent to him at the same time.[538] But no further copy is required if the unexecuted agreement becomes an executed agreement on the debtor or hirer's signature, i.e. because the creditor or owner has already signed it before it is sent.[539]

39-089 On the other hand, if the unexecuted agreement is *presented personally* to the debtor or hirer for his signature, but on the occasion when he signs it the creditor or owner does not sign and has not already signed the agreement, then (a) a copy of the unexecuted agreement must there and then be delivered to him[540]; and (b) a further copy of the executed agreement must be given to him within seven days[541] of its being made.[542] Likewise, if the unexecuted agreement is *sent* to the debtor or hirer for his signature, a copy of it must be sent to him at the same time,[543] and, if the creditor or owner has not already signed it before it was sent, a further copy of the executed agreement must be given to the debtor or hirer within seven days[544] of its being made.[545] If the agreement is a cancellable agreement, the second copy must be sent by post.[546]

39-090 The copy of the unexecuted or executed agreement must also be accompanied by a copy of "any other document referred to in it".[547] This comprehends not only, e.g. any security referred to in the agreement, but also any document other than a document excepted by regulation.[548]

39-091 **Notice of cancellation rights** In the case of a cancellable agreement, i.e. a regulated agreement which, by virtue of s.67 of the 1974 Act,[549] may be cancelled by the debtor or hirer,[550] s.64 of the Act provides[551] that a notice in the prescribed form indicating the right of the debtor or hirer to cancel the agreement must be included in every copy given to the debtor or hirer under ss.62 or 63.[552] Various forms of notice (differing according to the nature of the agreement) have been prescribed by the Consumer Credit (Cancellation Notices and Copies of Docu-

---

537 CCA 1974 s.63(1), (2)(a). But see CCA 1974 s.64 (cancellable agreements), below, para.39-091.
538 CCA 1974 s.62(1).
539 CCA 1974 s.63(2)(b). But see CCA 1974 s.64 (cancellable agreements), below, para.39-091.
540 CCA 1974 s.62(1).
541 Except in the case of a credit-token agreement: CCA 1974 s.63(4).
542 CCA 1974 s.63(2). So he can check that the terms are the same as those of the document he signed.
543 CCA 1974 s.62(2).
544 Except in the case of a credit-token agreement: CCA 1974 s.63(4).
545 CCA 1974 s.63(2). So he can check that the terms are the same as those of the document he signed.
546 CCA 1974 s.63(3).
547 CCA 1974 ss.62(1), (2), 63(1), (2).
548 See CCA 1974 s.180(1)(b), (3), and (for the relevant regulations) SI 1983/1557 reg.11.
549 See below, para.39-102.
550 See the definition of "cancellable agreement" in CCA 1974 s.189(1).
551 CCA 1974 s.64 does not apply to the agreements excepted under CCA 1974 s.74(1) (see para.39-103) and CCA 1974 s.82(4) (variation). See CCA 1974 s.189B(3), Sch.2A: in s.64, references to "debtor" in relation to "green deal plans" (as defined in CCA 1974 s.189(1), see below, para.39-257) are to be read as references to the "improver" (as defined in CCA 1974 s.189B(6)).
552 See above, para.39-084.

ments) Regulations 1983.[553] These notices indicate how and when the right to cancel the agreement is exercisable, and the name and address of a person to whom notice of cancellation may be given.[554] In those instances where only one copy is required,[555] a notice of cancellation rights must be sent[556] separately to the debtor or hirer within the seven days[557] following the making of the agreement.[558]

Supply of copies: "Directive" s.61A regime   In contrast to the "old" regime, the   **39-092**
Consumer Credit Directive merely (as well as requiring pre-contract informa-
tion[559]) requires a debtor to receive a copy of the final agreement. Hence, for
regulated credit agreements within the scope of the Directive,[560] s.61A[561] requires
the creditor to give the debtor a copy of the executed agreement (and any other
document referred to in it) unless the debtor already has a copy of the unexecuted
agreement and this is in identical terms to the executed agreement. In the latter case,
the creditor must inform the debtor in writing that: (a) the agreement has been made,
(b) the executed agreement is in identical terms to the copy, and (c) the debtor has
14 days to ask for a copy which must be given "without delay". Separate provision is made for overdrafts.[562]

Failure to comply   In the event of non-compliance with ss.60 to 64[563] of the 1974   **39-093**
Act, the agreement is "not properly executed".[564] The consequence of improper
execution is that the agreement is enforceable against the debtor or hirer on an order
of the court only.[565] A retaking of goods or land to which a regulated agreement

---

553   SI 1983/1557, as amended by SI 1983/1558; SI 1984/1108; SI 1988/2047 (and, most extensively)
SI 2004/2619; SI 2004/3236. See also SI 1985/666 and SI 1989/591, made under (inter alia) CCA
1974 s.180. See *Goshawk Dedicated (No.2) Ltd v Bank of Scotland* [2005] EWHC 2906 (Ch), [2006]
C.C.L.R. 1; followed by *Bank of Scotland v Euclidian (No.1) Ltd* [2007] EWHC 1732 (whether the
form of notice of cancellation was correctly drafted).
554   CCA 1974 s.64(1). See also CCA 1974 s.185(1)(a) (plurality of debtors or hirers).
555   See above, para.39-088.
556   The wording of CCA 1974 s.63(3) has been changed from "by post" to "by an appropriate method"
by SI 2004/3236 art.2(4), to allow for electronic communication.
557   Except in the case of a credit-token agreement: CCA 1974 s.64(2).
558   CCA 1974 s.64(1)(b), (2); SI 1983/1557 reg.6 (as amended by SI 2004/3236) and Sch. Pt VI (as
substituted by SI 2004/2619 and subsequently amended by SI 2004/3236). But power is conferred
on the FCA (previously the OFT) to dispense with this requirement in the case of certain mail order
credit agreements pursuant to regulations made by the Treasury (previously the Secretary of State):
CCA 1974 s.64(4), amended by Sch.25(6) to the Enterprise Act 2002; SI 2013/1882. See also CCA
1974 ss.68(b), 183. Regulations may also provide that the separate notice shall be accompanied by
a further copy of the executed agreement, and of any other document referred to in it (CCA 1974
s.64(3)). No regulations have been made.
559   See above, para.39-076.
560   See above, para.39-011.
561   Added on February 1, 2011 by SI 2010/1010 reg.8.
562   CCA 1974 s.61B, added on February 1, 2011 by SI 2010/1010 reg.9.
563   See above, paras 39-080—39-092. Note that CCA 1974 s.55(2) provides for the same consequence
for breach of CCA 1974 s.55: see above, para.39-076.
564   CCA 1974 ss.61(1), (2), 62(3), 63(5), 64(5).
565   CCA 1974 s.65(1). See CCA 1974 s.189B(3), Sch.2A: in CCA 1974 s.65, references to "debtor" in
relation to "green deal plans" (as defined in CCA 1974 s.189(1), see below, para.39-257) are to be
read as references to the "improver"/"current bill payer"/"previous bill payer" (as defined in CCA
1974 s.189B(6)). For case-law on s.65, see *PB Leasing Ltd v Patel (t/a Plankhouse Stores)* [1995]
C.C.L.R. 82, Cty Ct; *Smerdon v Ellis* [1997] C.L.Y. 960, Cty Ct; *Re Dixon-Vincent* [1997] C.L.Y.
958, Cty Ct; *Rendle v Hicks* [1998] C.L.Y. 2504, Cty Ct; *Kemp v Ling* [1998] C.L.Y. 2502, Cty Ct;
Gibbons v Gibbons [1998] C.L.Y. 2500, Cty Ct; *Rahman v Brassil* [1998] C.L.Y. 2503, Cty Ct.;

relates is an enforcement of the agreement.[566] Further, any security[567] provided in relation to the agreement is enforceable (so far as provided in relation to the agreement) where such an order has been made in relation to the agreement, but not otherwise,[568] and if the court dismisses an application for such an order (except on technical grounds only), the security is rendered invalid.[569] No wider restitutionary remedy is available at common law against the debtor or hirer on the basis of unjust enrichment.[570]

39-094 A wide discretion is, however, given to the court as to whether, and, if so, on what terms it will make an enforcement order in situations of infringement.[571] The 1974 Act originally provided that, in three cases, the court was precluded from making an enforcement order at all.[572] However, the Consumer Credit Act 2006[573] repealed the relevant provisions and hence no agreement made after the repeal was brought into force is now "irredeemably unenforceable".[574] Those three cases (which are still relevant to old agreements[575]) were as follows. First,[576] the court could not enforce the agreement unless a document containing all the *prescribed* terms of the agree-

---

Barons Finance Ltd & Reddy Corp Ltd v Makanju [2013] EWHC 153 (QB), [2013] C.C.L.R. 3 (multiple breaches of Agreements Regulations); *Consolidated Finance Ltd v Collins* [2013] EWCA Civ 475. cf. *Eastern Distributors Ltd v Goldring* [1957] 2 Q.B. 600; *North West Securities v Alexander Breckon Ltd* [1981] R.T.R. 518 (enforcement against third parties); *R. v Modupe* [1991] Crim. L.R. 531 (debtor or hirer remains under a liability); *Carlyle Finance Ltd v Pallas Industrial Finance Ltd* [1991] 1 All E.R. (Comm) 659 (offer accepted although agreement not yet signed by creditor); *Hitchens v General Guarantee Corp Ltd* [2001] C.L.Y. 880, CA (valid hire-purchase agreement for purposes of Hire-Purchase Act 1964). No sanction is imposed by the CCA 1974 for enforcing an unenforceable agreement without a court order (CCA 1974 s.170(1)), but the creditor or owner may be subject to liability at common law; see Guest and Lloyd, *Encyclopedia of Consumer Credit Law* (1975, looseleaf) at para.2-066, or to disciplinary action as an FCA authorised person (see above, para.39-063) or (in the case of credit agreements) the relationship may be determined as "unfair" under ss.140A–140C (see below, paras 39-212 et seq.). CPR Pt 7, PD 7B.
566 CCA 1974 s.65(2). But see CCA 1974 s.173(3) (consent); *Wotton v Flagg* [1997] C.L.Y. 959, Cty Ct; *Hatfield v Hiscock* [1998] C.L.Y. 2501, Cty Ct. cf. *Rendle v Hicks* [1998] C.L.Y. 2504, Cty Ct; *Kemp v Ling* [1998] C.L.Y. 2502, Cty Ct; *Gibbons v Gibbons* [1998] C.L.Y. 2500, Cty Ct.
567 Defined in CCA 1974 s.189(1); see below, para.39-180.
568 CCA 1974 s.113(2). See also CCA 1974 s.113(8) (linked transactions) and below, para.39-191.
569 CCA 1974 ss.106, 113(3)(c); below, para.39-193. See also CCA 1974 s.113(8).
570 *Dimond v Lovell* [2002] 1 A.C. 384, 397–398; *Wilson v Secretary of State for Trade and Industry* [2003] UKHL 40, [2003] 3 W.L.R. 568 at [49]–[50].
571 CCA 1974 s.127(1); below, para.39-200. For refusals to enforce, see *PB Leasing Ltd v Patel and Patel (t/a Plankhouse Stores)* [1995] C.C.L.R. 82; *Smerdon v Ellis* [1997] C.L.Y. 960; *Re Dixon-Vincent* [1997] C.L.Y. 958; *Rendle v Hicks* [1998] C.L.Y 2504; *Barons Finance Ltd & Reddy Corp Ltd v Makanju* [2013] EWHC 153 (QB), [2013] C.C.L.R. 3; *Consolidated Finance Ltd v Collins* [2013] EWCA Civ 475. And see below as to the "irredeemably unenforceable" case-law. For enforcement orders made, see *National Guardian Mortgage Corp v Wilkes* [1993] C.C.L.R. 1 (but interest rate reduced); *Rank Xerox v Hepple* [1993] C.C.L.R. 1 (but reduction of amount payable); *Hatfield v Hiscock* [1996] C.C.L.R. 68; *London North Securities Ltd v Meadows* [2005] EWCA Civ 956 (but PPP not payable); *Wilson v Hurstanger Ltd* [2007] EWCA Civ 299 (but some sums not payable).
572 CCA 1974 s.127(3)–(5).
573 Consumer Credit Act 2006 s.15, in force on April 6, 2007 (SI 2007/123).
574 A term coined by Lord Hoffmann in *Dimond v Lovell* [2002] 1 A.C. 384.
575 Those made on or before April 5, 2007.
576 CCA 1974 s.127(3). See also CCA 1974 s.127(5) and s.185(3). For case-law, see *Wilson v First County Trust Ltd (No.1)* [2001] Q.B. 407; *O'Hagan v Wright* [2001] NICA 26, [2003] C.C.L.R. 6; *Dimond v Lovell* [2002] 1 A.C. 384; *McGinn v Grangewood Securities Ltd* [2002] EWCA 522; *Wilson v Robertson (London) Ltd* [2005] EWHC 1425; *London North Securities Ltd v Meadows* [2005] EWCA Civ 956, [2005] C.C.L.R. 7 (distinguished in *Black Horse Ltd v Hanson* [2009] EWCA Civ 73); *Brophy v HFC Bank Ltd* [2011] C.C.L.R. 1; *Napier v HFC Bank Ltd (t/a The GM Card)* [2011] C.C.L.R. 2; *Sternlight v Barclays Bank Plc* [2011] C.C.L.R. 6.

ment,[577] was signed by the debtor or hirer.[578] Secondly, the court could not enforce a "cancellable"[579] agreement if a provision of s.62 or 63 was not complied with,[580] and the creditor or owner did not give a copy of the executed agreement, and of any other document referred to in it, to the debtor or hirer before the commencement of the proceedings in which the order is sought.[581] Thirdly, the court could not enforce a "cancellable"[582] agreement if s.64(1) (notice of cancellation rights)[583] was not complied with.[584] In *Wilson v First County Trust Ltd (No.2)*,[585] the Court of Appeal made a declaration pursuant to s.4(2) of the Human Rights Act 1998 that the absolute bar on enforcement imposed in the first case mentioned above was contrary to the European Convention on Human Rights.[586] This decision was reversed by the House of Lords sub. nom. *Wilson v Secretary of State for Trade and Industry*,[587] although the court queried whether this result would be reached in the absence of the (then £25,000) financial limit. To avoid further challenges once the financial limit was generally removed by the Consumer Credit Act 2006,[588] that Act repealed these "irredeemably unenforceable" provisions in their entirety.

(f) Withdrawal and Cancellation[589]

Offer and acceptance Regulated credit and hire agreements are in principle no **39-095** exception to the general rule[590] that either party is at liberty to withdraw from the intended transaction until such time as an offer has been accepted,[591] and acceptance has been communicated to the offeror.[592] But, in the case of a prospective regulated agreement, the 1974 Act makes certain modifications to the common law rules in respect of the persons to whom notice of withdrawal may be given and the consequences of withdrawal.[593]

Mode of withdrawal The giving to a party of a written or oral notice which, **39-096**

---

577 See above para.39-083. Omission of terms of the agreement other than prescribed terms, did not have this effect: CCA 1974 s.61(1)(b). But see (the now repealed) CCA 1974 s.127(5).

578 See above, para.39-083. The signature did not have to be in the manner prescribed by the Agreements Regulations made under CCA 1974 s.61 (see above, para.39-094).

579 i.e. a regulated agreement which, by virtue of CCA 1974 s.67, could be cancelled by the debtor or hirer (see below, para.39-102).

580 See above, paras 39-088 et seq.

581 CCA 1974 s.127(4)(a). See *VL Skuse & Co v Cooper* [1975] 1 W.L.R. 593. For the commencement of proceedings in the county court, see CPR Pt 7 r.2.

582 See above.

583 See above, para.39-091.

584 s.127(4)(b). *Woodchester Leasing Equipment v Clayton* [1994] C.C.L.R. 87, Cty Ct; *Moorgate Services Ltd v Kabir* [1995] C.C.L.R. 74, CA.

585 [2001] EWCA Civ 633, [2002] Q.B. 74.

586 art.6 and art.1 of the First Protocol.

587 [2003] UKHL 40, [2004] 1 A.C. 816.

588 See above, para.39-005.

589 See Guest and Lloyd, *Encyclopedia of Consumer Credit Law* (1975, looseleaf), paras 2-058, 2-068—2-075; and Goode, *Consumer Credit: Law and Practice* (looseleaf), Pt C, Ch.31.

590 See Vol.I, Ch.2.

591 cf. *Financings Ltd v Stimson* [1962] 1 W.L.R. 1184.

592 cf. *Lowe v Lombank Ltd* [1960] 1 W.L.R. 196, 206; *Robophone Facilities Ltd v Blank* [1966] 1 W.L.R. 1428.

593 CCA 1974 s.57. See CCA 1974 s.189B(3), Sch.2A: in CCA 1974 s.57, references to "debtor" in relation to "green deal plans" (as defined in CCA 1974 s.189(1), see below, para.39-257) are to be read as references to the "improver", as defined in CCA 1974 s.189B(6). Section 57 does not apply to the agreements excepted under CCA 1974 s.74(1) (see para.39-103) and under s.82(4) (variation).

however expressed, indicates the intention of the other party to withdraw from a prospective regulated agreement operates as a withdrawal from it.[594] There can be little doubt that, as at common law,[595] the withdrawal is not normally effective until communicated to the other party, and that a posted withdrawal does not take effect on posting.[596]

39-097 **To whom notice may be given** By s.57(3) of the 1974 Act, each of the following is deemed to be the agent of the creditor or owner for the purpose of receiving a notice of withdrawal—(a) a credit-broker[597] or supplier[598] who is the negotiator[599] in any antecedent negotiations[600]; and (b) any person who, in the course of a business[601] carried on by him, acts on behalf of the debtor or hirer in any negotiations for the agreement. Thus a prospective debtor may, for example, in certain circumstances give notice of withdrawal to the dealer who negotiates the transaction[602] or even to his own broker or solicitor. However, by s.175, where under the 1974 Act a person is deemed to receive a notice as agent of the creditor or owner under a regulated agreement, he is deemed to be under a contractual duty to the creditor or owner to transmit the notice to him forthwith and hence will be liable in contract (to the creditor or owner) if he fails to do so.

39-098 **Consequences of withdrawal** The withdrawal of a party from a prospective regulated agreement operates to apply Pt V of the 1974 Act to the agreement, any linked transaction[603] and any other thing done in anticipation of the making of the agreement as it would apply if the agreement were made and cancelled under s.69.[604] This is so notwithstanding that the agreement, if made, would not be a "cancellable" agreement.[605]

---

[594] CCA 1974 s.57(2). But see the exceptions listed in CCA 1974 s.74(1) (below, para.39-103) and in s.82(4) (variations).

[595] See Vol.I, para.2-094.

[596] *Byrne & Co v Leon Van Tienhoven & Co* (1880) 5 C.P.D. 344. Contrast CCA 1974 s.69(7) (deemed service of notice of cancellation).

[597] Defined in CCA 1974 s.189(1).

[598] Defined in CCA 1974 s.189(1).

[599] Defined in CCA 1974 ss.56(1), 189(1); see above, para.39-073.

[600] Defined in CCA 1974 ss.56(1), 189(1); see above, paras 39-071 et seq.

[601] See CCA 1974 s.189(1), (2).

[602] At common law a dealer who negotiates a transaction is not an agent of the creditor for the purpose of fixing the creditor with knowledge that the offer was made subject to an oral stipulation qualifying the debtor's liability: *Eastern Distributors Ltd v Goldring* [1957] 2 Q.B. 600; *Northgran Finance Ltd v Ashley* [1963] 1 Q.B. 476. But he is the agent of the creditor for the purpose of communicating the withdrawal of the offer: *Financings Ltd v Stimson* [1962] 1 W.L.R. 1184.

[603] See CCA 1974 ss.19(1), 189(1), above, paras 39-055 et seq. But certain linked transactions are excepted by SI 1983/1560 (contracts of insurance, guarantees of goods, and agreements for deposit and current accounts).

[604] CCA 1974 s.57(1). But this is not so in the case of agreements excepted by CCA 1974 ss.74(1) (see below, para.39-103) and 82(4) (variations). For CCA 1974 s.69, see below, para.39-105. See also CCA 1974 s.113(6); below, para.39-189.

[605] CCA 1974 s.57(4).

Prospective land mortgage The 1974 Act contains special "pause" provisions   **39-099**
providing for an opportunity for withdrawal from a prospective land mortgage,[606]
in so far as it is a regulated agreement.[607]

Agreement not to withdraw At common law, a person may bind himself not to   **39-100**
withdraw his offer either absolutely or for a certain time, if his promise to do so is
made by deed or if the promisee furnishes consideration for the promise.[608] But
under s.59(1) of the 1974 Act[609] an agreement is void if, and to the extent that, it
purports to bind a person to enter as a debtor into a prospective regulated agreement.
This provision does not, however, prevent the creditor or owner from being bound
to enter into such an agreement.

14-day "right of withdrawal" In consequence of the implementation of the   **39-101**
Consumer Credit Directive,[610] a new s.66A[611] has been added to the 1974 Act. It
confers an unconditional 14-day "right of withdrawal" (the Directive's term for a
right to cancel an agreement that has already been made) in relation to regulated
credit agreements other than "excluded agreements". "Excluded agreements" are
those for credit exceeding £60,260 (as these are outside the scope of the Directive[612]) and those that are also excluded from the definition of "cancellable" agreement within s.67.[613] Moreover, s.66A does not apply to most overdrafts.[614] Although
"business" credit is outside the scope of the Directive, the new s.66A "right of
withdrawal" has nevertheless been extended to regulated business credit
agreements.[615] In common with all other "Directive" provisions, it has also been
extended to hire-purchase agreements. Section 66A sets out both the mode and timing of withdrawal (the debtor must "give oral or written notice" within 14 days from
(usually) the date the agreement is made) and its effect (hence, as well as the credit
agreement, any "ancillary service" (as defined) contract relating to the agreement,

---

[606] CCA 1974 s.58(1), considered below at para.39-535. But see the exceptions in CCA 1974 ss.58(2), 74(1) (see below, para.39-103) and 82(4) (variations).

[607] Note that many land mortgages are "exempt agreements": see para.30-039.

[608] See Vol.I, Ch.4.

[609] But see the exceptions in CCA 1974 ss.74(1) (see below, para.39-103) and 82(4) (variations). Under CCA 1974 s.59(2) and SI 1983/1552, certain types of agreement are excluded from s.59(1), namely, agreements to enter into prospective hire agreements and agreements to enter into prospective restricted-use agreements for fixed-sum credit, in both cases the goods being used for business purposes. See also *Lakin v Exe Haulage Ltd* [2006] C.L.Y. 705, Cty Ct: s.59 inapplicable to exempt agreement.

[610] See above, para.39-011.

[611] Added on February 1, 2011 by SI 2010/1010 reg.13. See CCA 1974 s.189B(3), Sch.2A: in CCA 1974 s.66A, references to "debtor" in relation to "green deal plans" (as defined in CCA 1974 s.189(1), see below, para.39-257) are to be read as references to the "improver" (as defined in CCA 1974 s.189B(6)).

[612] When the Mortgage Credit Directive (see above, para.39-003) was implemented on March 21, 2016, this exclusion ceased to apply to so-called "residential renovation agreements" (as defined in CCA 1974 s.189(1) to mean, essentially, unsecured loans to renovate residential property) above this threshold: see amendment to s.66A in SI 2015/910 art.3 and Sch.1 para.2(5).

[613] CCA 1974 s.66A(14). For agreements excluded from the definition of "cancellable" agreement, see below, para.39-103: agreements secured on land and various agreements financing the purchase of land.

[614] See CCA 1974 s.74(1)(b) (but see s.74(1D): certain non-business overdrafts). Section 66A also does not apply to "non-commercial" agreements (as to which, see above, para.39-049): s.74(1)(a). See also, in the context of variation (as to which, see below paras 39-148, 39-151), CCA 1974 s.82(4), (6A)–(6B).

[615] But note that only business credit under £25,000 is "regulated", see above, para.39-046.

is treated as if it had never been entered into). Agreements that do not have the benefit of the s.66A right of withdrawal (in particular, credit agreements in excess of £60,260[616] and hire agreements) may be "cancellable" within s.67 of the 1974 Act.[617]

39-102 **"Cancellable" agreements[618]** For agreements not subject to the s.66A "right of withdrawal",[619] s.67 of the 1974 Act sometimes[620] provides for a "cooling off" period within which a debtor or hirer under a regulated agreement, is entitled to cancel the agreement. The section provides that a regulated[621] agreement may be cancelled by the debtor or hirer in accordance with Pt V of the Act if the antecedent negotiations[622] included oral representations[623] made when in the presence of the debtor or hirer by an individual[624] acting as, or on behalf of, the negotiator[625] unless the unexecuted agreement was signed by the debtor or hirer at premises at which any of the following was carrying on any business[626] (whether on a permanent or temporary basis):

    (i)   the creditor or owner[627];

    (ii)   any party to a linked transaction[628] (other than the debtor or hirer or a relative of his);

    (iii)   the negotiator in any antecedent negotiations.[629]

Hence a regulated agreement is not "cancellable" if (broadly) it is signed by the debtor or hirer at trade premises; but it will also not be "cancellable" if, although signed elsewhere, the debtor has not at some stage prior to the making of the agreement been subject to "face-to-face" persuasion. So, for example, if there is no

---

[616] When the Mortgage Credit Directive (see above, para.39-003) was implemented on March 21, 2016, this exclusion ceased to apply to so-called "residential renovation agreements" (as defined in CCA 1974 s.189(1) to mean, essentially, unsecured loans to renovate residential property) above this threshold: see amendment to s.66A in SI 2015/910 art.3 and Sch.1 para.2(5).

[617] See next paragraph. And the *FCA Handbook*, CONC 11.2 confers a "right of withdrawal" (essentially a right to cancel) on borrowers under certain "peer-to-peer" (P2P) credit agreements.

[618] See CCA 1974 Sch.2 Pt II Example 4. The special s.58 "pause" provisions may apply instead in the case of a regulated agreement secured by a land mortgage: see below, para.39-535. For a pre-Directive discussion of the various provisions generally conferring rights of cancellation, see Hellwege (2004) C.L.J. 712.

[619] Viz: regulated credit agreements in excess of £60,260 and regulated hire agreements; see previous paragraph.

[620] See the exceptions noted below, para.39-103. And note that if cancellation rights are conferred by contract on agreements not satisfying s.67, such agreements do not attract the provisions of the Act applicable to "cancellable agreements": *Rankine v MBNA Europe Bank Ltd* [2007] EWCA Civ 1273 (but see the Consumer Credit (Cancellation Notices and Copies of Documents) Regulations 1983 (SI 1983/1557) reg.5(4), added by SI 1984/1108, rendering those *regulations* (only) applicable).

[621] An exempt agreement (above paras 39-038 et seq.) cannot be cancelled under the CCA 1974.

[622] Defined in CCA 1974 ss.56(1), 189(1); above, paras 39-071 et seq.

[623] Defined in CCA 1974 s.189(1). See *Moorgate Services Ltd v Kabir* [1995] C.L.Y. 722.

[624] Defined in CCA 1974 s.189(1).

[625] Defined in CCA 1974 ss.56(1), 189(1); above, para.39-073.

[626] Defined in s.189(1), (2).

[627] e.g. a financier where it is the creditor under a hire-purchase, credit sale or conditional sale agreement.

[628] For linked transactions see CCA 1974 s.19(1); above, para.39-055, et seq. e.g. a dealer selling goods, where a loan is made by a financier on his introduction to purchaser of goods: s.19(1).

[629] e.g. a dealer: see above, para.39-072. But because of the definition of "antecedent negotiations" and "negotiator" in CCA 1974 s.56, a distinction exists between debtor-creditor-supplier agreements on the one hand and debtor-creditor and consumer hire agreements on the other: see Guest and Lloyd, *Encyclopedia of Consumer Credit Law* (1975, looseleaf) at para.2-068.

personal contact at all, as in the case of some types of credit agreement canvassed by "mail shot" or correspondence, or an agreement canvassed by telephone, the agreement is not "cancellable" under the 1974 Act. But, on the other hand, the right to cancel is not confined to the door-to-door context. If negotiations are conducted face to face at a dealer's showroom, and the debtor takes the agreement home for signature, the agreement will be a "cancellable" agreement.

Exceptions   Section 67 itself establishes the following exceptions to its applicability, viz if "the agreement is secured on land, or is a restricted-use[630] credit agreement to finance the purchase of land or is an agreement for a bridging loan in connection with the purchase of land".[631] Further exceptions are established by s.74 of the 1974 Act.[632]   **39-103**

Cooling-off period   The period within which the debtor or hirer is permitted to serve notice of cancellation—sometimes known as the "cooling-off" period—is set out in s.68 of the 1974 Act. Its starting point is always his signing of the unexecuted agreement. The period ends at the end of the fifth day following the day on which he receives the second copy[633] or, if no second copy is required, the notice under s.64(1)(b) of the Act.[634] Thus if he signs the agreement on the 1st, and the second copy (or notice) is received by him on the 7th,[635] he has until midnight on the 12th to serve his notice of cancellation.   **39-104**

Notice of cancellation   A notice of cancellation may be served on: **39-105**

(i)   the creditor or owner[636]; or

(ii)   the person specified in the notice under s.64(1)[637]; or

(iii)   a credit-broker[638] or supplier[639] who is the negotiator[640] in antecedent negotiations[641]; or

---

630   Defined in CCA 1974 ss.11(1), 189(1); see above, para.39-027.

631   CCA 1974 s.67(a). See also CCA 1974 ss.58(1), 61(2).

632   See CCA 1974 s.74(1): (i) non-commercial agreements (as to which, see above, para.39-049); (ii) certain overdrafts; (iii) (in accordance with the OFT's Determination (made on December 21, 1989), see Guest and Lloyd, *Encyclopedia of Consumer Credit Law* (1975, looseleaf) at para.4-4802) a debtor-creditor agreement to finance the making of payments connected with the death of a person as may be prescribed by regulation (see SI 1983/1554) and (iv) small (see above, para.39-048) debtor-creditor-supplier agreements (see above, para.39-030) for restricted use (see above, para.39-027). See also, in the context of variation (as to which, see below paras 39-148—39-150, 39-151), CCA 1974 s.82(4), (6).

633   Of the executed agreement under CCA 1974 s.63(2): see above, para.39-089.

634   See above, para.39-091. If, by virtue of regulations made under s.64(4) (see the regulations made: see SI 1983/1558 (certain mail order consumer credit agreements), s.64(1)(b) does not apply, the period runs to the end of the 14th day following the day on which he signed the unexecuted agreement.

635   The second copy (or notice) must normally be sent by post within the seven days following the making of the agreement: see above, para.39-091.

636   CCA 1974 s.69(1)(a).

637   CCA 1974 s.69(1)(b); see above, para.39-091.

638   Defined in CCA 1974 s.189(1).

639   Defined in CCA 1974 s.189(1).

640   Defined in CCA 1974 ss.56(1), 189(1).

641   CCA 1974 s.69(1)(c), (6)(a). See also CCA 1974 s.175 (contractual duty to the creditor or owner to transmit the notice to him forthwith).

(iv) any person who, in the course of a business[642] carried on by him acts on behalf of the debtor or hirer in any negotiations for the agreement[643]; or

(v) a person who is the agent of the creditor or owner.[644]

It will therefore normally be open to the debtor or hirer to serve the notice on a dealer who negotiated the transaction, and, in certain circumstances, even upon an agent of the debtor or hirer himself.[645] A notice will be an effective notice of cancellation if, however expressed and whether or not conforming to the notice given under s.64(1),[646] it indicates the intention of the debtor or hirer to withdraw from the agreement.[647] A notice of cancellation sent by post to a person is deemed to be served on him at the time of posting whether or not it is actually received by him and an electronic notice[648] is deemed served when it is transmitted.[649]

39-106 **Effect of notice** Service of a notice of cancellation by the debtor or hirer operates, in general, to cancel the agreement and any linked transaction,[650] and to withdraw any offer by the debtor or hirer, or his relative,[651] to enter into a linked transaction.[652] Except so far as is otherwise provided by or under the 1974 Act,[653] an agreement or transaction so cancelled is treated as if it had never been entered into.[654] Thus the cancellation of a regulated agreement will also, for example, operate to cancel any collateral contract for maintenance which is a linked transaction.[655] And if goods are bought from a supplier for cash advanced by a financier as a loan under pre-existing arrangements with the supplier,[656] the cancellation of the loan agreement will operate automatically to cancel the contract of sale.[657] Further, on cancellation, any security provided is rendered invalid.[658]

---

642 Defined in CCA 1974 s.189(1), (2).

643 CCA 1974 s.69(1)(c), (6)(b). See also CCA 1974 s.175 (contractual duty to the creditor or owner to transmit the notice to him forthwith).

644 CCA 1974 s.69(1)(c).

645 And see CCA 1974 s.175 (contractual duty to the creditor or owner to transmit the notice to him forthwith).

646 See above, para.39-091.

647 CCA 1974 s.69(1).

648 In accordance with CCA 1974 s.176A, added by SI 2004/3236 art.2(7).

649 CCA 1974 s.69(7), as amended by SI 2004/3236 art.2(5), adding the reference to electronic communications.

650 Defined in CCA 1974 ss.19(1), 189(1); above, paras 39-055 et seq. But see the linked transactions excepted under CCA 1974 s.69(5) by SI 1983/1560 (contracts of insurance, guarantees of goods and agreements for deposit and current accounts); and note *Goshawk Dedicated (No.2) Ltd v Bank of Scotland* [2005] EWHC 2906 (Ch), [2006] C.C.L.R. 1; *Bank of Scotland v Euclidian (No.1) Ltd* [2007] EWHC 1732.

651 Defined in CCA 1974 ss.184(1), 189(1).

652 CCA 1974 s.69(1). See also CCA 1974 s.142(2). But see above (excepted linked transactions).

653 e.g. by CCA 1974 s.71.

654 CCA 1974 s.69(4); *Colesworthy v Collmain Services Ltd* [1993] C.C.L.R. 4, Cty Ct.

655 See above, paras 39-055 et seq. But see above (excepted linked transactions).

656 CCA 1974 s.19(1)(b). This also applies to services.

657 But see the dictum of Lord Mance in *OFT v Lloyds TSB Bank Plc* [2007] UKHL 48 that s.69(1) is likely only to apply to a "linked transaction which is sufficiently connected with the United Kingdom", although he declined to opine on the nature of the requisite link. Hence he doubted if a foreign supply transaction (financed by a UK credit card agreement) could be cancelled under s.69.

658 CCA 1974 ss.106, 113(3)(a); below, para.39-193. See also CCA 1974 s.113(8).

Special cases Special provision is, however, made for the case of a debtor-   **39-107**
creditor-supplier[659] agreement for restricted-use[660] credit financing—(a) the doing
of work or supply of goods to meet an emergency, or (b) the supply of goods which,
before service of the notice of cancellation, had by the act of the debtor or his relative[661] become incorporated in any land or thing not comprised in the agreement or
any linked transaction.[662] In such a case service of a notice of cancellation operates to cancel only such provisions of the agreement and any linked transaction as
relate to the provision of credit, or require the debtor to pay an item in the total
charge for credit,[663] or subject the debtor to any obligation other than to pay for the
doing of the work, or the supply of the goods.[664] The "credit" obligations of the
debtor under the credit agreement or any linked transaction are therefore released,
but he is still liable for the outstanding balance of the cash price of the goods or
services. Any security provided is, however, rendered invalid.[665]

Repayment to and release of debtor[666] On cancellation,[667] the debtor or hirer is   **39-108**
entitled to be repaid any sum paid by him, or his relative,[668] under or in contemplation of the agreement or transaction,[669] including any item in the total charge for
credit.[670] That sum is repayable by the person to whom it was originally paid.[671] But,
in the case of a debtor-creditor-supplier agreement falling within s.12(b) of the 1974
Act,[672] the creditor and supplier are under a joint and several liability to repay sums
paid by the debtor, or his relative, under the agreement or under a linked transaction falling within s.19(1)(b).[673] However, subject to any agreement between them,
the creditor is entitled to be indemnified by the supplier for loss suffered by the

---

659 Defined in CCA 1974 ss.12, 189(1); see above, para.39-030.
660 Defined in CCA 1974 ss.11(1), 189(1); see above, para.39-027.
661 But not, e.g. by the act of a supplier.
662 CCA 1974 s.69(2). But see CCA 1974 ss.69(3), 70(8), 113(3)(a). "Linked transactions" are defined
    in CCA 1974 ss.19(1), 189(1); see above, paras 39-055 et seq.
663 Defined in CCA 1974 ss.20, 189(1); above, para.39-059.
664 CCA 1974 s.69(2). But see CCA 1974 ss.69(3), 70(8), 72(9), 113(3)(a). See also CCA 1974 s.142(2).
665 CCA 1974 ss.106, 113(3)(a); below, para.39-193. See also CCA 1974 s.113(8).
666 See also the comparable provisions in the Financial Services (Distance Marketing) Regulations 2004
    (SI 2004/2095), below, para.39-126 and the Consumer Contracts (Information, Cancellation and Ad-
    ditional Charges) Regulations 2013 (SI 2013/3134), below, para.39-125. See also (the less elaborate
    provisions in relation to the CCA 1974 s.66A right of withdrawal in) s.66A(9)–(10), above, para.39-
    101.
667 Or withdrawal: see CCA 1974 s.57(1); above, para.39-098. But see the exceptions in CCA 1974 ss.74
    (above, para.39-103) and 82(4) (variations). See also CCA 1974 s.70(5) (credit-tokens).
668 Defined in CCA 1974 ss.184(1), 189(1).
669 i.e. a linked transaction: see CCA 1974 ss.19(1), 189(1); above, paras 39-055 et seq.
670 CCA 1974 s.70(1)(a). For "total charge for credit", see above, para.39-059.
671 CCA 1974 s.70(3). See *Colesworthy v Collmain Services Ltd* [1993] C.C.L.R. 4, Cty Ct (money
    recoverable from collection/management agents of owner under cancelled consumer hire agreement).
    Where a financier supplies goods under a hire-purchase or conditional or credit sale agreement, and
    a deposit is paid by the debtor to the supplier, the deposit is recoverable from the financier at com-
    mon law (*Branwhite v Worcester Works Finance Ltd* [1969] 1 A.C. 552) even though not paid to the
    creditor. For lien of debtor, see CCA 1974 s.70(2); below, para.39-121.
672 See above, para.39-031.
673 CCA 1974 s.70(3). See also above, paras 39-055 et seq. (on s.19(1)). The creditor is entitled, in ac-
    cordance with rules of court, to have the supplier made a party to any proceedings brought against
    the creditor to recover these sums: CPR Pt 20.

creditor in satisfying that liability, including costs reasonably incurred by him in defending proceedings instituted by the debtor.[674]

39-109   If the total charge for credit[675] includes an item in respect of a fee or commission charged by a credit-broker,[676] the amount repayable in respect of that item is the excess of over £5 of the fee or commission[677]; any other sum included in the total charge for credit which is payable or paid by the debtor to a credit-broker is for this purpose treated as if it were such a fee or commission.[678]

A further effect of cancellation[679] is that any sum, including any item in the total charge for credit,[680] which but for the cancellation is, or would or might become, payable by the debtor or hirer, or his relative,[681] under the agreement or transaction ceases to be, or does not become, so payable.[682] The debtor or hirer is thus released (subject to s.71)[683] from liability to pay the sums—including credit charges—payable by him under the cancelled agreement or any linked transaction.[684]

39-110   **Repayment to creditor by supplier**   On cancellation,[685] in the case of a debtor-creditor-supplier agreement falling within s.12(b) of the 1974 Act,[686] any sum paid on the debtor's behalf by the creditor to the supplier[687] becomes repayable to the creditor.[688]

39-111   **Cancellation: repayment of credit[689]**   Money may be advanced to a debtor under a regulated consumer credit agreement in anticipation of the making of the agreement or during the "cooling-off" period, but the debtor may then withdraw from or cancel the agreement. Section 71 of the 1974 Act deals with the repayment of the credit by the debtor in such a situation and is clearly designed to discourage the making of loans before the agreement is executed or, in the case of a cancellable agreement, before the expiration of the period allowed for cancellation.

39-112   In the first place, on cancellation,[690] the loan advanced does not become immediately repayable. Section 71 of the 1974 Act provides that, notwithstanding the

---

[674] CCA 1974 s.70(4).
[675] Defined in CCA 1974 ss.20, 189(1); above, para.39-059.
[676] Defined in CCA 1974 s.189(1); see below, para.39-231.
[677] CCA 1974 s.70(6). The amount was increased from £1 to £3 by SI 1983/1571 and to £5 by SI 1998/997.
[678] CCA 1974 s.70(7).
[679] Or withdrawal: see CCA 1974 s.57(1); above, para.39-098. But see the exceptions in CCA 1974 ss.74(1) (above, para.39-103) and 82(4) (variations).
[680] Defined in CCA 1974 ss.20, 189(1); above, para.39-059.
[681] Defined in CCA 1974 ss.184(1), 189(1).
[682] CCA 1974 s.70(1)(b).
[683] See below, paras 39-111 et seq. See also CCA 1974 s.70(5) (credit-tokens).
[684] Defined in CCA 1974 ss.19(1), 189(1); above, paras 39-055 et seq.
[685] Or withdrawal: see CCA 1974 s.57(1); above, para.39-098. But see the exceptions in CCA 1974 ss.74(1) (above, para.39-103) and 82(4) (variations).
[686] See above, para.39-031.
[687] Defined in CCA 1974 s.189(1).
[688] CCA 1974 s.70(1)(c).
[689] See also the comparable provisions in the Financial Services (Distance Marketing) Regulations 2004 (SI 2004/2095), below, para.39-126 and the Consumer Contracts (Information, Cancellation and Additional Charges) Regulations 2013 (SI 2013/3134), below, para.39-125. See also s.66A(9)–(10).
[690] Or withdrawal: CCA 1974 see s.57(1); above, para.39-098. But see the exceptions in CCA 1974 ss.74 (above, para.39-103) and 82(4) (variation).

cancellation of a regulated consumer credit agreement,[691] other than a debtor-creditor-supplier[692] agreement for restricted-use[693] credit, the agreement is to continue in force so far as it relates to repayment of credit and payment of interest.[694] It is important to realise, however, that all other covenants by the debtor, e.g. for the provision of security or for insurance, become inoperative,[695] and likewise any guarantee or indemnity given in connection with the loan is of no effect.[696] Secondly, if, following the cancellation of the agreement, the debtor repays the whole or a portion of the credit before the expiry of one month following service of the notice of cancellation (or, in the case of a credit repayable by instalments, before the date on which the first instalment is due), no interest is payable on the amount repaid.[697] Thirdly, if the whole of a credit repayable by instalments is not repaid on or before the date mentioned above, the debtor is not liable to repay any of the credit except on receipt of a request in writing in the prescribed form,[698] signed by or on behalf of the creditor.[699] The request must state "the amounts of the remaining instalments (recalculated by the creditor as nearly as may be in accordance with the agreement and without extending the repayment period), but excluding any sum other than principal and interest".[700] So, for example, if a cash loan[701] of £1,000 is made which is repayable with interest of £320 by 24 equal monthly instalments of £55 (APR 32.1 per cent), and the borrower cancels the agreement, he might repay part of the loan, say £400, free of interest before the date on which the first instalment fell due. The remaining £600 would be repayable by him only on the request of the creditor and would be repayable, together with interest at the rate specified in the agreement, over that part of the original repayment period then still unexpired. The debtor is not relieved from paying interest on the £600 not repaid in respect of the period before the request is received. The £600 would, therefore, be repayable with interest at APR 32.1 per cent for 24 months (£192), by (say) 23 monthly instalments of £34.43.[702]

Repayment of credit, and payment of interest, under a cancelled agreement is **39-113** treated as duly made if it is made to any person on whom, under s.69,[703] a notice of cancellation could have been served, other than a person referred to in s.69(6)(b).[704]

---

[691] Defined in CCA 1974 ss.8, 189(1); above, para.39-017.

[692] Defined in CCA 1974 ss.12, 189(1); above, para.39-030.

[693] Defined in CCA 1974 ss.11(1), 189(1); above, para.39-027.

[694] CCA 1974 s.71(1). But see CCA 1974 s.113(5).

[695] CCA 1974 ss.69(1), (4), 106, 113(3).

[696] CCA 1974 ss.69(1), (4), 106, 113(3).

[697] CCA 1974 s.71(2). But there is no relief from interest payable on any amount not so repaid.

[698] For the prescribed form, see SI 1983/1559, as amended by SI 2004/3236 art.7 (electronic communications).

[699] CCA 1974 s.71(3). But see CCA 1974 s.113(5).

[700] CCA 1974 s.71(3).

[701] Which is for "unrestricted-use", above, para.39-029.

[702] For examples of calculations in the case of entire non-repayment or partial repayment, see Guest and Lloyd, *Encyclopedia of Consumer Credit Law* (1975, looseleaf) at para.2-072.

[703] See above, para.39-105. See also CCA 1974 s.175 (duty to remit the notice to the creditor).

[704] CCA 1974 s.71(4). Section 69(6)(b) refers to "any person who, in the course of a business carried on by him, acts on behalf of the *debtor* ... in any negotiations for the agreement". See above, para.39-105.

39-114   **Return of goods**[705]   Section 72 of the 1974 Act deals with the return of goods on cancellation.[706] Where the possession of goods has been acquired by virtue of a cancelled restricted-use[707] debtor-creditor-supplier[708] agreement, consumer hire agreement[709] or linked transaction[710] to which the debtor or hirer under a regulated agreement is a party, or by virtue of a cancelled linked transaction[711] to which a relative[712] of the debtor or hirer under a regulated agreement is a party, the possessor is under a duty[713] to restore the goods to the person from whom he acquired possession.[714] The possessor is, however, not under any duty to deliver the goods except at his own premises,[715] and then only if he is served with a request in writing so to do.[716] The possessor is under a duty from the time when he acquired possession to the date of cancellation ("the pre-cancellation period")[717] to retain possession of the goods and to take reasonable care of them.[718] This duty continues after cancellation,[719] but subject to certain qualifications, viz:

(i)   if no request for delivery of the goods is received by him within 21 days following the cancellation, his duty to take reasonable care of the goods (but not his duty to retain possession of them) ceases at the end of that period; and

(ii)   if he receives a request for delivery of the goods within 21 days following cancellation, but he unreasonably refuses or unreasonably fails to comply with it, his duty to take reasonable care of the goods continues until he does so comply.[720]

39-115   The possessor may deliver the goods, either at his own premises[721] or elsewhere, to any person on whom, under s.69 of the 1974 Act,[722] a notice of cancellation could have been served (other than a person referred to in s.69(6)(b)),[723] or he may send

---

[705] See the comparable provisions in the Financial Services (Distance Marketing) Regulations 2004 (SI 2004/2095), below, para.39-126, and the Consumer Contracts (Information, Cancellation and Additional Charges) Regulations 2013 (SI 2013/3134), below, para.39-125.

[706] Or, by virtue of CCA 1974 s.57, on withdrawal: see above, para.39-098. But see the exceptions listed in CCA 1974 ss.72(9), 74 (above, para.39-103), 82(4).

[707] Defined in CCA 1974 ss.11(1), 189(1); above, para.39-027.

[708] Defined in CCA 1974 ss.12, 189(1); above, para.39-030.

[709] Defined in CCA 1974 ss.15, 189(1); above, para.39-035.

[710] Defined in CCA 1974 ss.19(1), 189(1); above, paras 39-055 et seq.

[711] Defined in CCA 1974 ss.19(1), 189(1); above, paras 39-055 et seq.

[712] Defined in CCA 1974 ss.184(1), 189(1).

[713] Subject to his right of lien under CCA 1974 s.70(2); below, para.39-121. And see CCA 1974 s.113(5).

[714] CCA 1974 s.72(1), (2), (4). For the difficulties confronting a financier which finds itself holding depreciated goods, see Guest and Lloyd, *Encyclopedia of Consumer Credit Law* (1975, looseleaf) at para.2-073.

[715] See CCA 1974 s.72(10).

[716] CCA 1974 s.72(5). The request must be signed by or on behalf of the person from whom he acquired possession and it must be served upon him either before or at the time the goods are collected from those premises: ss.72(2), (5).

[717] CCA 1974 s.72(2)(c).

[718] CCA 1974 s.72(3).

[719] CCA 1974 s.72(4).

[720] CCA 1974 s.72(8). Or until he sends the goods as mentioned in subs.(6).

[721] See CCA 1974 s.72(10).

[722] See above, para.39-105.

[723] CCA 1974 s.72(6)(a). Section 69(6)(b) refers to a person who, in the course of a business carried on by him, acts on behalf of the *debtor or hirer* in any negotiations for the agreement. CCA 1974 s.175, which in terms only imposes a contractual duty on such a person (to the creditor or owner)

the goods at his own expense to such a person.[724] Once he has so delivered or sent the goods, his duty to retain the goods or deliver them to any person, and his duty to take care of them,[725] cease, save that, if he elects to send the goods, he is under a duty to take reasonable care to see that they are received by the person from whom he acquired possession and not damaged in transit.[726]

Breach of a duty imposed by s.72 of the 1974 Act is actionable as a breach of statutory duty.[727]   **39-116**

Exceptions   Certain exceptions are created to s.72. The section does not apply to perishable goods,[728] or to goods which by their nature are consumed by use and which, before cancellation, were so consumed,[729] or to goods supplied to meet an emergency,[730] or to goods which, before the cancellation, had become incorporated in any land or thing not comprised in the cancelled agreement or a linked transaction.[731]   **39-117**

Goods given in part-exchange[732]   Section 73 of the 1974 Act contains provision for the return of goods given in part-exchange where a regulated agreement is cancelled.[733] For the purposes of the section goods are given in part-exchange if, in antecedent negotiations,[734] the negotiator[735] agreed to take goods in part-exchange (the "part-exchange goods") and those goods have been delivered to him.[736] The negotiator is treated as having agreed to take goods in part-exchange if, in pursuance of the antecedent negotiations, he either purchased or agreed to purchase those goods or accepted or agreed to accept them as part of the consideration for the cancelled agreement.[737]   **39-118**

In principle, on cancellation, the part-exchange goods should be returned to the debtor or hirer in a condition substantially as good as when they were delivered to the negotiator.[738] If they are not so delivered before the end of the period of 10 days beginning with the date of cancellation, the debtor or hirer is entitled to recover from the negotiator a sum equal to the "part-exchange allowance", i.e. the sum agreed as the part-exchange allowance in the antecedent negotiations or, if no such agreement was arrived at, such sum as it would have been reasonable to allow in   **39-119**

---

to transmit a "notice or *payment*" (emphasis added) to the creditor or owner forthwith would seem to be inapplicable to the return of goods.

[724] CCA 1974 s.72(6)(b).
[725] CCA 1974 s.72(7).
[726] CCA 1974 s.72(6), (7).
[727] CCA 1974 s.72(11).
[728] CCA 1974 s.72(9)(a).
[729] CCA 1974 s.72(9)(b).
[730] CCA 1974 s.72(9)(c). See also CCA 1974 s.69(2); above, para.39-107.
[731] CCA 1974 s.72(9)(d). "Linked transaction" is defined in CCA 1974 ss.19(1), 189(1); above, paras 39-055 et seq. See also CCA 1974 s.69(2); above, para.39-107.
[732] See the comparable provisions in the Financial Services (Distance Marketing) Regulations 2004 (SI 2004/2095), below, para.39-126, and the Consumer Contracts (Information, Cancellation and Additional Charges) Regulations 2013 (SI 2013/3134), below, para.39-125.
[733] Or, by virtue of CCA 1974 s.57, on withdrawal: see above, para.39-098. But see the exceptions listed in CCA 1974 ss.74 (above, para.39-103) and 82(4) (variations).
[734] Defined in CCA 1974 ss.56, 189(1); above, paras 39-071 et seq.
[735] Defined in CCA 1974 ss.56(1), 189(1).
[736] CCA 1974 s.73(1).
[737] CCA 1974 s.73(7)(a).
[738] CCA 1974 s.73(2).

respect of the part-exchange goods if no notice of cancellation had been served.[739] In the case of a debtor-creditor-supplier agreement within s.12(b) of the 1974 Act,[740] both the negotiator and the creditor are under a joint and several liability to pay that sum to the debtor[741]; but the creditor is given a right (subject to any agreement between them) to be indemnified by the negotiator in satisfying that liability, including costs reasonably incurred by him in reasonably defending proceedings instituted by the debtor.[742]

39-120   Where the debtor or hirer recovers from the negotiator or creditor or both of them jointly a sum equal to the part-exchange allowance, then, if the title of the debtor or hirer to the part-exchange goods has not vested in the negotiator, it vests in the negotiator on the recovery of that sum.[743] Title does not in any circumstances vest in the creditor.

39-121   **Lien**   If, under the terms of a cancelled agreement or transaction, the debtor or hirer, or his relative,[744] is in possession of any goods, he is entitled to a lien on them for any sum repayable to him under s.70(1) of the 1974 Act[745] in respect of that agreement or transaction, or any other linked transaction.[746] Also, during the period of 10 days beginning with the date of cancellation, if the debtor or hirer is in possession of goods to which the cancelled agreement relates, he has a lien on them for delivery of the part-exchange goods[747] in a condition substantially as good as when they were delivered to the negotiator,[748] or a sum equal to the part-exchange allowance,[749] and, if such a lien continues to the end of that period, a lien thereafter for a sum equal to the part-exchange allowance.[750]

39-122   **Agency for receiving notice of rescission**   The right to withdraw from or cancel the agreement conferred by the 1974 Act in no way inhibits the exercise by the debtor or hirer of any other contractual remedy to which he may be entitled and which has the effect of terminating the agreement. Moreover, by s.102(1) of the Act certain persons are deemed to be the agent of the creditor or owner for the purpose of receiving any notice "rescinding" the agreement, which is served by the debtor or hirer. Those persons are:

    (a) a credit-broker[751] or supplier[752] who was the negotiator[753] in antecedent negotiations[754] (e.g. the dealer in an ordinary three-cornered instalment credit transaction); and

---

739 CCA 1974 s.73(2), (7)(b).
740 See above, para.39-031.
741 CCA 1974 s.73(3). The creditor is entitled, in accordance with rules of court to have the negotiator made a party to the proceedings: s.73(8); CPR Pt 20.
742 CCA 1974 s.73(4).
743 CCA 1974 s.73(6).
744 Defined in CCA 1974 ss.184(1), 189(1).
745 See above, para.39-108.
746 CCA 1974 s.70(2). For linked transaction, see ss.19(1), 189(1); above, paras 39-055 et seq.
747 CCA 1974 s.73(1); above, para.39-118.
748 Defined in CCA 1974 ss.56(1), 189(1). See above, para.39-093.
749 CCA 1974 s.73(6); above, para.39-119.
750 CCA 1974 s.73(5).
751 Defined in CCA 1974 s.189(1); below, para.39-231.
752 Defined in CCA 1974 s.189(1).
753 Defined in CCA 1974 ss.56, 189(1); above, para.39-073.
754 See above, paras 39-071 et seq.

(b)   any person who, in the course of a business[755] carried on by him, acted on behalf of the *debtor* or *hirer* in any negotiations for the agreement (e.g. the debtor or hirer's own solicitor or agent).[756]

The word "rescind" is not defined. It does not, however, include service of a notice of cancellation,[757] or termination of an agreement under s.99[758] or 101[759] of the 1974 Act or by the exercise of a right or power in that behalf expressly conferred by the agreement. But it is submitted that "rescind" should not be construed too narrowly so as to comprehend only the equitable remedy of rescission, e.g. for misrepresentation,[760] but should also extend to rescission consequent upon a repudiatory breach of the agreement by the creditor or owner.[761]

Timeshare, Holiday Products, Resale and Exchange Contracts Regulations   **39-123**
2010   These regulations[762] confer on a consumer a 14 day right of cancellation ("withdrawal") from timeshare and other "holiday accommodation" contracts within their scope,[763] that have a requisite connection with the UK or another EEA State.[764] On such cancellation both the obligations under the contract and any "ancillary contract" (i.e. a contract for services provided by the trader or by a third party with whom the trader has arrangements) terminates.[765] Moreover a "related credit contract" is also automatically terminated at no cost to the consumer.[766] A "regulated credit contract" is defined as one that fully or party covers any payment under the holiday accommodation contract and that is made either with the trader or a third party "on the basis of an arrangement" between them.

Package Travel, Package Holidays and Package Tours Regulations   **39-124**
1992   These regulations[767] confer upon a consumer a right of cancellation ("withdrawal") where the organiser is constrained before departure to alter significantly an essential term of a contract for the provision of package travel, etc. services.[768] In the event of withdrawal, the consumer is entitled to have repaid to him as soon as possible all monies paid by him under the contract. The definition of "consumer" in the regulations is not in any way linked to the conceptual framework of the 1974 Act and there is no exception in a case where an associated

---

[755]   Defined in CCA 1974 s.189(1), (2).
[756]   But see CCA 1974 s.175 (duty to transmit the notice to the creditor or owner).
[757]   CCA 1974 s.69(1); above, para.39-106.
[758]   CCA 1974 s.99(1); below, para.39-367.
[759]   CCA 1974 s.101(1); above, para.33-088.
[760]   See Vol.I, Ch.7.
[761]   See Vol.I, Ch.24.
[762]   SI 2010/2960 (implementing the Timeshare etc. Directive 2008/122/EC and repealing the Timeshare Act 1992). See further above, paras 38-148 et seq. See the similar provisions in the Consumer Contracts (Information, Cancellation and Additional Charges) Regulations 2013 (SI 2013/3134), below, para.39-125, which exclude contracts within the 2010 Regulations from their cancellation provisions.
[763]   See SI 2010/2960 regs 3, 4, 6–10.
[764]   See SI 2010/2960 reg.5.
[765]   See SI 2010/2960 reg.22.
[766]   See SI 2010/2960 reg.23.
[767]   SI 1992/3288 (implementing Council Directive 90/314), amended by SIs 1995/1648, 1998/1208, 2003/1376, 2003/1400. See above, paras 38-132 et seq. See also Guest and Lloyd, *Encyclopedia of Consumer Credit Law* (1975, looseleaf) at para.2-068.
[768]   SI 1992/3288 regs 12, 13.

credit agreement is subject to the right of withdrawal under s.66A of the 1974 Act or is a "cancellable" agreement under s.67 of the 1974 Act.

39-125 **Consumer Contracts (Information, Cancellation and Additional Charges) Regulations 2013** Part 3 of these regulations[769] confers a right to cancel without giving any reason or incurring any costs (unless specified) on "consumers" (as defined) in the case of certain "distance" or "off-premises" contracts (as defined) made by "traders" (as defined). The cancellation period is generally 14 days (from the date of conclusion of the contract or the date of delivery), although if the trader does not provide the consumer with the requisite information on cancellation rights,[770] the cancellation period may be extended by up to 12 months. The regulations contain provisions adjusting the position of the parties after cancellation,[771] which are similar to those in ss.70–73 of the 1974 Act.[772] The regulations (including the cancellation right) do not apply to a variety of agreements, including credit agreements.[773] However, a credit agreement may be cancelled if it is a so-called "ancillary contract" in relation to a distance or off-premises contract (the "main contract") that is cancelled by virtue of the regulations.[774] An "ancillary contact" is defined as "a contract by which the consumer acquires goods or services related to the main contract", where those goods or services are provided either by the trader or by a third party (for example a creditor) "on the basis of an arrangement between the third party and the 'trader'". "Arrangement" is not defined in the regulations but it is a word of wide import.[775]

39-126 **Financial Services (Distance Marketing) Regulations 2004** These Regulations[776] extend a right to cancel to certain "distance"[777] consumer financial services contracts, including credit contracts.[778] Credit contracts that are already cancellable as "ancillary contracts" under the Consumer Contracts (Information, Cancel-

---

[769] SI 2013/3134. For a fuller consideration, see above, paras 38-112 et seq. For case-law on the predecessor Cancellation of Contracts made in a Consumer's Home or Place of Work, etc. Regulations 2008 (SI 2008/1816), see *W v Veolia Environmental Services (UK) Plc* [2011] EWHC 2020 (hire contract unenforceable under those regulations as signed at home without the requisite notice); *Salat v Barutis* [2013] EWCA Civ 1499 (lack of cancellation notice in motorcycle hire agreement) and *Allproperty Claims v Tang* [2015] EWHC 2198 (lack of notification of cancellation right rendered agreement unenforceable).

[770] The requisite information is set out in Sch.2 to the regulations.

[771] See regs 34–37.

[772] See above, paras 39-108—39-121.

[773] See reg.6(1)(b).

[774] See reg.38.

[775] See the similar provision in the Timeshare, Holiday Products, Resale and Exchange Contracts Regulations 2010, considered above, para.39-123.

[776] SI 2004/2095 (implementing Directive 2002/65 (the "DMD"—Distance Marketing Directive)). Regs 15 and 22 were amended by the Consumer Protection from Unfair Trading Regulations 2008 (SI 2008/1277) reg.30(1) and Sch.2 para.110 (to remove the criminal offences). For a fuller consideration, see above, paras 38-136 et seq.

[777] The definition is similar to that under the Consumer Contracts (Information, Cancellation and Additional Charges) Regulations 2013 (SI 2013/3134), above, para.39-125, which replaced the Consumer Protection (Distance Selling) Regulations 2000 (SI 2000/2334). However, there is (curiously) no equivalent (either in the 2004 regulations under discussion or in the 2013 Regulations) to the "indicative list" of what constitutes "distance communication" in Sch.1 to the 2000 Regulations.

[778] But not hire contracts. Reg.2(1) defines "credit" in almost identical terms to CCA 1974 s.9(1), see above, para.39-019.

lation and Additional Charges) Regulations 2013[779] or as timeshare credit agreements under the Timeshare, Holiday Products, Resale and Exchange Contracts Regulations 2010[780] are excluded.[781] There is no overlap with s.67 of the 1974 Act[782] in that this section requires "face-to-face" negotiation whereas the regulations require "distance communication". However, if the s.66A right of withdrawal applies,[783] then the right of cancellation conferred by these regulations is excluded.[784] The regulations require the right to cancel to be communicated "in good time" prior to the consumer being bound[785] and the "cooling off" period is generally 14 days from the date the contract is concluded. Provision is also made for the cancellation of an "attached contract", a concept which may include credit contracts.[786]

(g)   Supply of Information[787]

Current account "overrunning": information requirements   In consequence   **39-127** of the implementation of the Consumer Credit Directive[788] there are two new "information" provisions concerning so-called current account "overrunning", a Directive term that has been re-worded in the UK legislation[789] as "overdraw without a pre-arranged overdraft or exceed a pre-arranged overdraft limit". First,[790] where this may be permitted by the creditor, the current account agreement must contain certain information as to the interest rate(s) and any other charges levied for such "overrunning". Moreover, the creditor must also inform the account-holder of this information annually. Second,[791] when "significant" overrunning occurs for more than one month (three months if the excess is secured on land), the creditor must inform the account-holder in writing, within that period or thereafter "without delay", of the rate of interest and any other charges. Overrunning is "significant" if: (a) the account-holder is liable to pay a "charge" for which he would not otherwise be liable, or (b) the overdraft or excess is likely to have an adverse effect on the debtor's ability to receive further credit, or (c) it "otherwise appears significant, having regard to all the circumstances". The provisions applying to variations of agreements[792] do not apply to any debtor-creditor agreement arising as a result of overrunning.

---

[779] See above, para.39-125.

[780] See above, para.39-123.

[781] SI 2004/2095 reg.11(1)(e) (substituted by SI 2013/3134), (f) (substituted by SI 2010/2960).

[782] See above, para.39-102.

[783] See above, para.39-102.

[784] SI 2004/2095 reg.11(1)(h), added by SI 2010/1010 reg.89 and substituted by SI 2013/1881 Sch.1 para.26(b).

[785] SI 2000/2334 reg.7. The right to cancel is exercisable by a "notice of cancellation", with the formal requirements being more flexible than those under the CCA 1974.

[786] SI 2000/2334 reg.12.

[787] See Guest and Lloyd, *Encyclopedia of Consumer Credit Law* (1975, looseleaf), paras 2-078—2-081, 2-087A—2-087E, 2-098, 2-104, 2-108—2-111. See also the Guidance in the *FCA Handbook*, CONC 13.

[788] See above, para.39-011.

[789] The provisions were originally in CCA 1974 ss.74A and 74B (added by SI 2010/1010 regs 21 and 22, as amended by SI 2010/1969 regs 9 and 10) but on the transfer of consumer credit regulation to the FCA (see above, para.39-002) ss.74A and 74B were repealed (see SI 2013/1881 art.20(27)) and replaced by corresponding provisions in the *FCA Handbook* CONC 4.7 and 6.3.3 (old s.74A) and CONC 6.3.3 and 6.3.4 (old s.74B).

[790] *FCA Handbook* CONC 4.7 and 6.3.3 (previously CCA 1974 s.74A, see the previous footnote).

[791] *FCA Handbook* CONC 6.3.4 (previously CCA 1974 s.74A, see above).

[792] Viz (i) CCA 1974 s.82(1) (see s.82(1E), see below, para.39-146) and (ii) (for interest rate varia-

39-128 **Information to debtor under fixed-sum credit agreement on request** Section 77 of the 1974 Act requires[793] the creditor under a regulated agreement for fixed-sum credit[794] (other than a non-commercial agreement[795]) to give[796] the debtor, on request, a copy of the executed agreement (if any)[797] and of any other document referred to in it,[798] together with a statement of the account between them.[799] In order to be valid the request must be in writing, and a fee of £1 must be paid.[800] The statement must be signed by or on behalf of the creditor and must show (according to the information to which it is practicable for him to refer):

(a) the total sum paid under the agreement by the debtor;

(b) the total sum which has become payable under the agreement by the debtor but remains unpaid, and the various amounts comprised in that total sum, with the date on which each became due; and

(c) the total sum which is to become payable under the agreement by the debtor and the various amounts comprised in that total sum, with the date or mode of determining the date, when each becomes due.[801]

If the creditor fails to comply within 12 working days[802] after receiving a request, he is not entitled, while the default continues, to enforce the agreement.[803]

39-129 **Annual information to debtor under fixed-sum credit agreement** Section 77A[804] of the 1974 Act requires the creditor under a regulated agreement for fixed-

---

tions) CCA 1974 s.78A (see s.78A(6)(a), see below, para.39-147).

[793] CCA 1974 s.77(1), except where relieved under s.77(2), below, or s.77(3) (no sums payable and repeated requests).

[794] Defined in CCA 1974 ss.10(1)(b), 189(1); above, para.39-026.

[795] Defined in CCA 1974 s.189(1); above, para.39-049. See CCA 1974 s.77(5).

[796] Defined in CCA 1974 s.189(1) (as amended by SI 2004/3236 art.2(2)) to mean "deliver or send by appropriate method".

[797] See above, para.39-084. See also CCA 1974 s.180.

[798] See above, para.39-090.

[799] See *NRAM Plc v McAdam & Hartley* [2015] EWCA Civ 751, reversing [2014] EWHC 4174 (Comm): (obiter) s.77 does not apply to non-regulated agreements that are documented as regulated agreements. See also CCA 1974 s.189B(3), Sch.2A: in CCA 1974 s.77, references to "debtor" in relation to "green deal plans" (as defined in CCA 1974 s.189(1), see below, para.39-257) are to be read as references to the "current bill payer"/"previous bill payer" (as defined in CCA 1974 s.189B(6)).

[800] CCA 1974 s.77(1). The amount was raised from 15p to 50p by SI 1983/1571 and to £1 by SI 1998/997. See *Carey v HSBC Bank Plc* [2009] EWHC 3417 (QB) (on the similar CCA 1974 s.78 copy (below, para.39-132) requirement). See also the Guidance in the *FCA Handbook* CONC 13.

[801] CCA 1974 s.77(1). But see s.77(2) (modification where creditor possesses insufficient information to comply with (c)). See also CCA 1974 s.172 (statement binding, below, para.39-138), and SI 1983/1557 reg.7. See also CCA 1974 s.86E(3) (if a "default sum" (see CCA 1974 s.187A and below, para.39-135) is payable, the statement may incorporate the notice of default sum required by s.86E) and CCA 1974 s.130A(5) (if post-judgment interest is payable, the statement may incorporate the notice required under s.130A(5)).

[802] Prescribed by SI 1983/1569.

[803] CCA 1974 s.77(4)(a). The court has no discretion to order enforcement. See *McGuffick v Royal Bank of Scotland Plc* [2009] EWHC 2386, [2010] C.C.L.R. 2, on the meaning of "enforcement" (does not cover reporting default to credit reference agency) and for confirmation that the creditor's contractual rights are merely *unenforceable*, not extinguished. Section 77(4)(b) (an offence was committed after one month) was repealed by the Consumer Protection from Unfair Trading Regulations 2008 (SI 2008/1277) reg.30(1) and Sch.2 para.19.

[804] Inserted by the Consumer Credit Act 2006 s.6 from October 1, 2008 (see SI 2007/3300 art.3(3)) but applicable to agreements whenever made. New subss.(1A)–(1E) were substituted and amendments to subss.(5) and (7) made on October 1, 2008 by SI 2008/2826. See also the new subs.(9) (inap-

sum credit[805] (other than a non-commercial agreement[806]) automatically to give[807] the debtor, without charge,[808] annual statements of the account between them[809] in the form and with the contents prescribed.[810] If the creditor fails to comply, he is not entitled to enforce[811] the agreement during the period of non-compliance and the debtor is not liable to pay any interest or default sums referable to that period.[812] It was held in *JP Morgan Chase Bank, National Association v Northern Rock (Asset Management) Plc*[813] that if a s.77A statement that does not comply with the prescribed requirements is served, it is to be treated as if no statement had been served at all (and hence the commencement of the period of non-compliance needs to be calculated accordingly).

Statement of account to debtor under fixed-sum credit agreement on request   39-130 In consequence of the implementation of the Consumer Credit Directive[814] where a fixed-sum regulated credit[815] agreement is of fixed duration and where the credit is repayable in instalments, the new s.77B[816] requires the creditor, at the request of the debtor, to give a written statement of account with a table showing details of the instalments due.[817] The statement must be given "as soon as reasonably practicable" and no charge for it can be made.[818] Breach does not render the agreement unenforceable but is actionable as a breach of statutory duty.[819] Moreover, the normal disciplinary sanctions are available to the FCA for non-compliance, which could also render the agreement an "unfair relationship".[820] As this obligation derives from the Consumer Credit Directive, the obligation does not apply to agreements outside the scope of that Directive, namely: agreements secured

---

plicable to unauthorised overdrawing on current account) inserted by SI 2010/1010 reg.23. See CCA 1974 s.189B(3), Sch 2A: in CCA 1974 s.77A, references to "debtor" in relation to "green deal plans" (as defined in CCA 1974 s.189(1), see below, para.39-257) are to be read as references to the "current bill payer" (as defined in CCA 1974 s.189B(6)).

[805] Defined in CCA 1974 ss.10(1)(b), 189(1); above, para.39-026.

[806] Defined in CCA 1974 s.189(1); above, para.39-049. See s.77A(8).

[807] Defined in CCA 1974 s.189(1) (as amended by SI 2004/3236 art.2(2)) to mean "deliver or send by appropriate method".

[808] CCA 1974 s.77A(3). cf. statements under CCA 1974 ss.77, 78, 79.

[809] CCA 1974 s.77A(1), except where relieved under s.77A(4) (no sums payable).

[810] See SI 2007/1167 regs 3–12 and Sch.1, as amended by SI 2008/1751 and SI 2014/2369. Section 172 (statements binding, below, para.39-143) does *not* apply to s.77A statements. See also CCA 1974 s.86E(3) (if a "default sum" (see s.187A and below, para.39-135) is payable, the statement may incorporate the notice of default sum required by s.86E) and CCA 1974 s.130A(5) (if post-judgment interest is payable, the statement may incorporate the notice required under s.130A(5)).

[811] See *McGuffick v Royal Bank of Scotland Plc* [2009] EWHC 2386 (Comm), [2010] C.C.L.R. 2, (in relation to the similar CCA 1974 s.77) on the meaning of "enforcement", noted above, para.39-128.

[812] CCA 1974 s.77A(5)–(6). "Default sums" (defined in CCA 1974 s.187A, see below, para.39-135) that would have become payable during the period of non-compliance (or would have become payable thereafter in connection with a breach during that period) are irrecoverable.

[813] [2014] EWHC 291 (Ch), [2014] C.C.L.R. 7.

[814] See above, para.39-011.

[815] See above, para.39-026.

[816] Added on February 1, 2011 by SI 2010/1010 reg.26.

[817] See CCA 1974 s.77B(3)–(5).

[818] See CCA 1974 s.77B(7). cf. statements under CCA 1974 ss.77, 78, 79.

[819] See CCA 1974 s.77B(8). This is in contrast to the "unenforceability" sanction for breach of the other "information" provisions: CCA 1974 ss.77(4)(a), 77A(6)(a), 78(6)(a), 79(3)(a).

[820] Within s.140A, see below, paras 39-212 et seq.

on land, pawn agreements, agreements where credit in excess of £60,260[821] is provided and "business" credit agreements.[822]

39-131 **Notices of sums in arrears (NOSIAs)· fixed-sum credit agreements** Further information needs to be given to a debtor under a regulated agreement for fixed-sum credit[823] (other than a non-commercial[824] or small[825] agreement)[826] if they fall into arrears. Section 86B[827] requires the creditor to give,[828] in the form and with the contents prescribed,[829] a "notice of sums in arrears" (a so-called "NOSIA") within 14 days after the debtor becomes two payments (or four payments if made weekly[830]) in arrears[831] and, unless payment is duly made, to continue sending out such a notice at intervals of not more than six months.[832] The notice, which must be free of charge,[833] must also be accompanied by[834] the "arrears information sheet" drafted by the FCA[835] which sets out information as to the legal consequences of falling in arrears and sources of help for debtors. The debtor may make an application to court for a time order after service of the notice but only after giving a counter-notice (a "notice of intent") with a proposal for payment.[836] If the creditor fails to comply with the requirement to give a NOSIA then during the period of non-compliance he is not entitled to enforce the agreement.[837] Moreover, the debtor is not liable to pay any interest that relates to that period or any "default sum" that is incurred or becomes payable during that period.[838]

---

[821] When the Mortgage Credit Directive (see above, para.39-003) was implemented on March 21, 2016, this exclusion ceased to apply to so-called "residential renovation agreements" (as defined in CCA 1974 s.189(1) to mean, essentially, unsecured loans to renovate residential property) above this threshold: see amendment to s.77B in SI 2015/910 art.3 and Sch.1 para.2(8).

[822] See CCA 1974 s.77B(9). Note CCA 1974 s.77B(10): in relation to the business exemption, RAO art.60C(3)–(7), above, para.39-046, apply.

[823] Defined in CCA 1974 ss.10(1)(b), 189(1); above, para.39-026.

[824] Defined in CCA 1974 s.189(1); above, para.39-049. See CCA 1974 s.86B(12)(b).

[825] CCA 1974 s.17, above, para.39-048. See CCA 1974 s.86B(12)(b).

[826] The obligation also arises in relation to regulated hire agreements.

[827] Added by the Consumer Credit Act 2006 s.9 and coming into force on October 1, 2008 (see SI 2007/3300) but see the transitional provisions in the 2006 Act Sch.3 para.6. Section 86B was amended by SI 2008/2826 and to provide for "green deal plans" (see CCA 1974 s.189B) by the Energy Act 2011 and SI 2014/436.

[828] Defined in CCA 1974 s.189(1) (as amended by SI 2004/3236. Art.2(2)) to mean "deliver or send by appropriate method".

[829] CCA 1974 s.86B(8) and see the Consumer Credit (Information Requirements and Duration of Licences and Charges) Regulations 2007 (SI 2007/1167) regs 19–23 and Sch.3, as amended by SI 2008/1751. See also CCA 1974 s.86E(3) (if a "default sum" (see CCA 1974 s.187A and below, para.39-135) is payable, the notice may incorporate the notice of default sum required by s.86E) and CCA 1974 s.130A(5) (if post-judgment interest is payable, the notice may incorporate the notice required under s.130A(5)). Section 172 (statements binding, below, para.39-143) does *not* apply to s.86B notices.

[830] Or lesser interval, CCA 1974 s.86B(9).

[831] CCA 1974 s.86B(1), (2)(a).

[832] CCA 1974 s.86B(2)(b), (4). However a first NOSIA must always be sent, even if the debtor ceases to be in arrears before it is issued: s.86B(3).

[833] CCA 1974 s.86B(7). cf. statements under CCA 1974 ss.77, 78, 79.

[834] CCA 1974 s.86B(6).

[835] CCA 1974 s.86A(1), (2) (added by the Consumer Credit Act 2006 s.8) requires the FCA (previously the OFT) to prepare and publish such a sheet. It is available on the FCA website.

[836] CCA 1974 s.129(1)(ba), see below, para.39-202.

[837] CCA 1974 s.86D(1), (3) (added by the Consumer Credit Act 2006 s.11).

[838] CCA 1974 s.86D(4) (added by the Consumer Credit Act 2006 s.11). For "default sums", see below,

Information to debtor under running-account credit agreement on re-   **39-132**
quest   Section 78[839] contains similar provisions[840] to those in s.77[841] (applicable
to a fixed-sum credit agreement) in relation to a regulated agreement for running-
account credit[842] (other than a non-commercial agreement[843]). But here the statement on request must show:

(a)   the state of the account;
(b)   the amount, if any, currently payable under the agreement by the debtor to
        the creditor; and
(c)   the amounts and dates of payments which, if the debtor does not draw
        further on the account, will later become payable under the agreement by
        the debtor to the creditor.[844]

Again, if the creditor fails to comply within 12 working days[845] after receiving a
request, he is not entitled, while the default continues, to enforce the agreement.[846]

Periodic information to debtor under running-account credit agreement   In   **39-133**
addition, s.78(4) requires the creditor under a regulated agreement for running
account credit[847] (other than a non-commercial agreement[848] or a small agreement),[849] automatically to give[850] the debtor, without charge,[851] periodic statements of the account (according to the information to which it is practicable for the

---

para.39-135.

[839] It was amended by SI 2006/1508 and to provide for "green deal plans" (as defined in CCA 1974
    s.189(1), see below, para.39-257) by the Energy Act 2011. See (i) *McGuffick v Royal Bank of
    Scotland Plc* [2009] EWHC 2386 (Comm), [2010] C.C.L.R. 2, above, para.39-128 (on the similar
    provision in CCA 1974 s.77) (ii) *Carey v HSBC Bank Plc* [2009] EWHC 3417 (QB) and *Phoenix
    Recoveries (UK) Ltd v Kotecha* [2011] EWCA Civ 105 (on the copy requirement under CCA 1974
    s.78). See also FCA's Guidance in its Handbook CONC 13, replacing (in part) the OFT's *Guidance
    on ss.77, 78 and 79 of the Consumer Credit Act 1974* (OFT 1272 Oct 2010).
[840] See also SI 1983/1569 (period of 12 working days prescribed for giving of statement on request);
    SI 1998/997 (fee raised to £1). See also SI 1983/1557, as amended by SI 2004/2619 and SI 2004/
    3236 (copies).
[841] See above, para.39-128. But note s.78(1A): Where a request under s.78(1) also amounts to a request
    under the Payment Services Regulations 2017 (SI 2017/752) reg.49 (information during period of
    contract, see generally, above, para.34-224), no fee is payable under s.78 (as none is payable under
    those regulations).
[842] Defined in CCA 1974 ss.10, 189(1); above, para.39-024.
[843] Defined in CCA 1974 s.189(1); above, para.39-049. See CCA 1974 s.78(7).
[844] CCA 1974 s.78(1). But see s.78(2) (modification if creditor possesses insufficient information to
    comply with (c)) and s.78(3) (exceptions where no sums payable or repeated requests made). See
    also s.172 (statement binding, below, para.39-143), and SI 1983/1557 reg.7. See also s.86E(3) (if a
    "default sum" (see s.187A and below, para.39-135) is payable, the statement may incorporate the
    notice of default sum required by s.86E) and s.130A(5) (if post-judgment interest is payable, the
    statement may incorporate the notice required under s.130A(5)).
[845] Prescribed by SI 1983/1569.
[846] CCA 1974 s.78(6). Originally, if the default continued for one month, an offence was committed
    (s.78(6)(b)) but this provision was repealed by the Consumer Protection from Unfair Trading Regula-
    tions 2008 SI 2008/1277 reg.30(1) and Sch.2 para.20.
[847] Defined in CCA 1974 ss.10(1)(b), 189(1); above, para.39-024.
[848] Defined in CCA 1974 s.189(1); above, para.39-049. See CCA 1974 s.78(7).
[849] Defined in CCA 1974 ss.17, 189(1); above, para.39-048. See CCA 1974 s.78(7).
[850] Defined in CCA 1974 s.189(1) (as amended by SI 2004/3236 art.2(2)) to mean "deliver or send by
    appropriate method".
[851] Although, in contrast to CCA 1974 s.77A(3) (see above, para.39-129) and CCA 1974 s.86B(7) (see
    above, para.39-131), there is no explicit provision to this effect, it seems that one is likely to be
    implied.

creditor to refer) between them in prescribed form.[852] Further, where the agreement provides, in relation to specified periods, for the making of payments by the debtor, or the charging against him of interest or any other sum, the statement must show (according to the information to which it is practicable for the creditor to refer) the state of account at the end of each of those periods during which there is any movement in the account.[853] The terms of s.78(4) differ from those of s.77A (in relation to fixed-sum credit[854]) in referring to statements at "regular intervals of not more than 12 months"[855] and hence if an interval of less than 12 months is initially chosen by the creditor, then this periodicity must be adhered to. Moreover, there is no explicit sanction for failure to comply with s.78(4).[856]

39-134 **Notices of sums in arrears (NOSIAs): running-account credit agreements** Further information needs to be given to a debtor under a regulated agreement for running-account credit[857] (other than a non-commercial[858] or small[859] agreement) if they fall in arrears. Section 86C[860] requires the creditor to give,[861] in the form and with the contents prescribed,[862] a "notice of sums in arrears" (a so-called "NOSIA") after the debtor becomes two payments in arrears.[863] This notice must be given at a time no later than the next periodic statement under s.78(4)[864] and may be incorporated in it.[865] The provisions of s.86C are otherwise similar to those of s.86B. The notice must be free of charge[866] and accompanied by[867] the "arrears

---

852 See SI 1983/1570. And see s.78(4A) (added by the Consumer Credit Act 2006 s.7) which provides for regulations (see SI 2007/1167, as amended) requiring the statement to include prescribed information about the consequences of failing to make payments or of making minimum payments. Section 172 (statements binding, below, para.39-143) does *not* apply to periodic statements under s.78(4) but they may be binding at common law (see *United Overseas Bank v Jiwani* [1976] 1 W.L.R. 694). See also s.86E(3) (if a "default sum" (see s.187A and below, para.39-135) is payable, the statement may incorporate the notice of default sum required by s.86E) and s.130A(5) (if post-judgment interest is payable, the statement may incorporate the notice required under s.130A(5)).

853 s.78(4)(b).

854 See above, para.39-129.

855 s.78(4)(a). But see s.185(2)–(2D) (as substituted (from October 1, 2008) by the Consumer Credit Act 2006 s.7(3) (joint debtors)).

856 However, breach (in common with all breaches of the CCA 1974) is a "domestic infringement" capable of being enforced under the Enterprise Act 2002 Pt 8. Moreover, it could give rise to disciplinary action by the FCA (see above, para.39-063) and possibly render the agreement an "unfair relationship" within CCA 1974 ss.140A–140C, see below, paras 39-212 et seq.

857 Defined in CCA 1974 ss.10(1)(a), 189(1); above, para.39-024.

858 Defined in CCA 1974 s.189(1); above, para.39-049. See CCA 1974 s.86C(7)(b).

859 CCA 1974 s.17, above, para.39-048. See CCA 1974 s.86C(7)(b).

860 Added to the CCA 1974 by the Consumer Credit Act 2006 s.10 and coming into force on October 1, 2008 (see SI 2007/3300) but see the transitional provisions in the 2006 Act Sch.3 para.7. Section 86C was amended by SI 2008/2826.

861 Defined in CCA 1974 s.189(1) (as amended by SI 2004/3236 art.2(2)) to mean "deliver or send by appropriate method".

862 CCA 1974 s.86C(6) and see the Consumer Credit (Information Requirements and Duration of Licences and Charges) Regulations 2007 (SI 2007/1167) regs 24–26 and Sch.3. See also s.86E(3) (if a "default sum" (see s.187A and below, para.39-135) is payable, the notice may incorporate the notice of default sum required by s.86E) and s.130A(5) (if post-judgment interest is payable, the notice may incorporate the notice required under s.130A(5)). Section 172 (statements binding, below, para.39-143) does *not* apply to s.86C notices.

863 CCA 1974 s.86C(1), (2).

864 See above, para.39-133.

865 CCA 1974 s.86C(4).

866 CCA 1974 s.86C(5). cf. statements under ss.77, 78, 79.

information sheet" drafted by the FCA.[868] The debtor may make an application to court for a time order but only after giving a counter-notice (a "notice of intent") with a proposal for payment.[869] The creditor is not entitled during the period of non-compliance to enforce the agreement[870] and the debtor is not liable to pay any interest that relates to that period or any "default sum" that is incurred or becomes payable during that period.[871]

Notice of default sum A "default sum" is defined[872] as a sum (other than a sum **39-135** of interest) payable by a debtor or hirer under a regulated agreement "in connection with a breach of the agreement" but not including a sum which is payable earlier than otherwise required as a consequence of breach. Thus charges (but not interest) imposed for late payment are covered but not amounts payable under acceleration clauses. Section 86E[873] provides that if a "default sum" becomes payable under a regulated agreement (other than a non-commercial[874] or small[875] agreement)[876] the creditor must give[877] the debtor notice in the form and with the contents prescribed[878] within 35 days[879] of the sum becoming payable. The notice must be free of charge[880] and may be incorporated in any other notice or statement given under the Act.[881] If the creditor fails to comply with the requirement to give the notice, then during the period of non-compliance he is not entitled to enforce the agreement.[882] As for interest, the section states that the debtor has no liability to pay interest in connection with the default sum in respect of the period "before the 29th day after the day on which the debtor" is given "notice under this section". Hence

---

867 CCA 1974 s.86C(3).
868 CCA 1974 s.86A(1), (2) (added by the Consumer Credit Act 2006 s.8) requires the FCA to prepare and publish by General Notice such a sheet. It is available on the FCA website.
869 CCA 1974 s.129(1)(ba), see below, para.39-202.
870 CCA 1974 s.86D(2), (3), added by the Consumer Credit Act 2006 s.11.
871 CCA 1974 s.86D(4), added by the Consumer Credit Act 2006 s.11. For "default sums", see below, para.39-135.
872 CCA 1974 s.187A, added by the Consumer Credit Act 2006 s.18.
873 Added to the CCA 1974 by the Consumer Credit Act 2006 s.12 and coming into force on October 1, 2008 (see SI 2007/3300) but see the transitional provisions in the 2006 Act Sch.3 para.8 (applicable to agreements whenever made but only to default sums payable after October 1, 2008). See also CCA 1974 s.189B(3), Sch.2A: in s.86E, references to "debtor" in relation to "green deal plans" (as defined in s.189(1), see below, para.39-257) are to be read as references to the "current bill payer"/"previous bill payer" (as defined in s.189B(6)).
874 Defined in CCA 1974 s.189(1); above, para.39-049. See CCA 1974 s.86C(7)(b).
875 CCA 1974 s.17, above, para.39-048. See CCA 1974 s.86C(7)(b).
876 The obligation arises in relation to both regulated credit and regulated hire agreements.
877 Defined in CCA 1974 s.189(1) (as amended by SI 2004/3236 art.2(2)) to mean "deliver or send by appropriate method".
878 CCA 1974 s.86E(7)(b) and see the Consumer Credit (Information Requirements and Duration of Licences and Charges) Regulations 2007 (SI 2007/1167) regs 27–32 and Sch.4. See also s.130A(5) (if post-judgment interest is payable, the notice may incorporate the notice required under s.130A(5)). Section 172 (statements binding, below, para.39-143) does *not* apply to s.86E notices.
879 The period prescribed by the Consumer Credit (Information Requirements and Duration of Licences and Charges) Regulations 2007 (SI 2007/1167) reg.28.
880 CCA 1974 s.86E(6).
881 CCA 1974 s.86E(3). For example, information statements under CCA 1974 ss.77, 77A or 78, NOSIAs under s.86B or 86C, default notices under s.87. But other communications (not given "by virtue of another provision of [the 1974] Act") cannot incorporate the notice which must therefore be given separately.
882 CCA 1974 s.86E(5).

the creditor cannot charge interest[883] on the default sum until 28 days after the debtor receives[884] the notice.[885]

39-136 Default sums: other provisions   As well as requiring a notice to be given when a default sum has been incurred,[886] the 1974 Act makes other special provision in relation to "default sums". Only simple (and not compound) interest may be charged "in connection with" default sums.[887] Moreover, a debtor is not liable to pay any default sums that are incurred or become payable during a period when the creditor has not complied with his statutory obligation to give a "notice of sums in arrears".[888]

39-137 Information to "surety"   The creditor under a regulated agreement for fixed-sum credit[889] or running-account credit,[890] and the owner under a regulated consumer hire agreement,[891] in relation to which security[892] is provided, is required within 12 working days[893] after receiving a request in writing to that effect from a surety and payment of a fee of £1[894] to give[895] to the surety[896] a statement of the account as between himself and the debtor or hirer in the same terms[897] as the statement to be given to the debtor or hirer.[898] In addition, the creditor or owner is required to give to the surety:

(i)   a copy of the executed agreement (if any) and of any other document referred to in it; and

---

[883]   And only simple interest may be charged on default sums: CCA 1974 s.86F(2).

[884]   As "give" is defined as "deliver or send by appropriate method to" and hence connotes receipt.

[885]   There is no explicit provision as regards the charging of interest where a "late" notice is given after the expiry of the prescribed 35 days (cf. CCA 1974 s.86D(4)(a)) and it may be that such a notice is not a "notice under this section" (in that it is outside the prescribed period) and hence the liability to pay interest in relation to the default sum under s.86E(4) can never arise. (See, in relation to annual statements under s.77A (above, para.39-129) that did not comply with the regulations, *JP Morgan Chase Bank, National Association v Northern Rock (Asset Management) Plc* [2014] EWHC 291(Ch).) However, the terms of s.86E(5) suggest that a "late" notice is a "notice under this section" and hence interest can be charged 28 days after such a late notice is received.

[886]   See above, para.39-135.

[887]   CCA 1974 s.86F(2). And see s.86E(4), above at para.39-135. See CCA 1974 s.189B(3), Sch.2A: in s.86F, references to "debtor" in relation to "green deal plans" (as defined in s.189(1), see below, para.39-257) are to be read as references to the "current bill payer"/"previous bill payer" (as defined in s.189B(6)).

[888]   Under CCA 1974 s.86B (fixed-sum credit and hire), above, para.39-131 or CCA 1974 s.86C (running-account credit), above, para.39-134: see CCA 1974 s.86D(4)(b).

[889]   Defined in CCA 1974 ss.10(1)(b), 189(1); above, para.39-026.

[890]   Defined in CCA 1974 ss.10, 189(1); above, para.39-024.

[891]   Defined in CCA 1974 ss.15, 189(1); above, para.39-035.

[892]   Defined in CCA 1974 s.189(1); see below, para.39-180.

[893]   Prescribed by SI 1983/1569.

[894]   The fee was raised from 15p to 50p by SI 1983/1571 and to £1 by SI 1998/997.

[895]   Defined in CCA 1974 s.189(1) (as amended by SI 2004/3236 art.2(2)) to mean "deliver or send by appropriate method".

[896]   If a different person from the debtor or hirer: see below, para.39-183.

[897]   See above, paras 39-128—39-133 (CCA 1974 ss.77–78).

[898]   CCA 1974 ss.107–109. See also CCA 1974 s.172 (statements binding, below, para.39-143). See CCA 1974 s.189B(3), Sch.2A: in s.107 references to "debtor" in relation to "green deal plans" (as defined in s.189(1), see below, para.39-257) are to be read as references to the "improver" (as defined in s.189B(6)).

(ii)   a copy of the security instrument (if any).[899]

Failure to comply will preclude him, while the default continues, from enforc-   **39-138**
ing the security, so far as provided in relation to the agreement.[900] Non-commercial
agreements are, however, excepted.[901]

Copy of security instrument   The creditor or owner under a regulated agree-   **39-139**
ment (other than a non-commercial agreement)[902] is required, within 12 working
days[903] after receiving a request in writing to that effect from the debtor or hirer and
payment of a fee of £1,[904] to give[905] to the debtor or hirer a copy of any security
instrument[906] executed in relation to the agreement *after* the making of the
agreement.[907] Failure to comply precludes the creditor or owner, while the default
continues, from enforcing the security so far as provided in relation to the
agreement.[908]

Information as to whereabouts of goods   Where a regulated agreement (other   **39-140**
than a non-commercial agreement)[909] requires the debtor or hirer to keep goods to
which the agreement relates in his possession or control, he must, within seven
working days after he has received a request in writing to that effect from the creditor or owner, tell the creditor or owner where the goods are.[910] If he fails to comply
with the request, and the default continues for 14 days, he commits an offence.[911]

---

[899] CCA 1974 ss.107(1)(a), (b), 109(1)(a), (b). See below, para.39-182, for the definition of "security
instrument". See also SI 1983/1557, as amended by SI 2004/2619 and SI 2004/3236.

[900] CCA 1974 ss.107(4)(a), 108(4)(a), 109(3)(a). Originally, if the default continued for one month, an
offence was committed (ss.107(4)(b), 108(4)(b), 109(3)(b)) but these provisions were repealed by
the Consumer Protection from Unfair Trading Regulations 2008 (SI 2008/1277) reg.30(1) and Sch.2
paras 25–27.

[901] CCA 1974 ss.107(5), 108(5), 109(4). See CCA 1974 s.189(1) (definition); above, para.39-049.

[902] Defined in CCA 1974 s.189(1); see above, para.39-049. See CCA 1974 s.110(2)(a).

[903] Prescribed by SI 1983/1569.

[904] The fee was raised from 15p to 50p by SI 1983/1571 and to £1 by SI 1998/997.

[905] Defined in CCA 1974 s.189(1) (as amended by SI 2004/3236 art.2(2)) to mean "deliver or send by
appropriate method".

[906] Defined in CCA 1974 ss.105, 189(1); below, para.39-182.

[907] CCA 1974 s.110(1) (subject to the exceptions listed in s.110(2)(b), (c)). The Consumer Credit
(Agreements) Regulations 1983 SI 1983/1553, as amended (especially by SI 2004/1482) regs 2, 3
and Sch.1 para.21, and Sch.3 para.9, made under ss.60 and 105(9), require any security instrument
executed in relation to the agreement *before* the making thereof to be referred to and so "embodied
in" the regulated agreement itself, so that the debtor or hirer will be entitled to a copy under CCA
1974 ss.77 to 79. See the less prescriptive requirements of the Consumer Credit (Agreements)
Regulations 2010 (SI 2010/1014) reg.3 and Sch.1. See also CCA 1974 ss.180, 181. See CCA 1974
s.189B(3), Sch.2A: in s.110 references to "debtor" in relation to "green deal plans" (as defined in
CCA 1974 s.189(1), see below, para.39-257) are to be read as references to the "improver" (as
defined in CCA 1974 s.189B(6)).

[908] CCA 1974 s.110(3)(a). Originally, if the default continued for one month, an offence was committed (s.110(3)(b)) but this provision was repealed by the Consumer Protection from Unfair Trading
Regulations 2008 (SI 2008/1277) reg.30(1) and Sch.2 para.28.

[909] Defined in CCA 1974 s.189(1); above, para.39-049.

[910] s.80(1). See CCA 1974 s.189B(3), Sch.2A: in s.80, references to "debtor" in relation to "green deal
plans" (as defined in CCA 1974 s.189(1), see below, para.39-257) are to be read as references to the
"improver" (as defined in CCA 1974 s.189B(6)).

[911] CCA 1974 ss.80(2), 167 and Sch.1. Although many of the criminal offences imposed by the CCA
1974 for breaches of notice requirements were repealed by the Consumer Protection from Unfair
Trading Regulations 2008 (SI 2008/1277) reg.30(1) and Sch.2, this one (which exceptionally imposes
criminal liability on the debtor or hirer) has been retained.

39-141 **Information as to settlement figure** The creditor under a regulated consumer credit agreement[912] is required,[913] within seven working days[914] after he has received a request[915] to that effect from the debtor, to give[916] to the debtor a statement in the prescribed form indicating (according to the information to which it is practicable for him to refer), the amount of the payment required to discharge the debtor's indebtedness under the agreement, together with the prescribed particulars showing how the amount is arrived at.[917] If the creditor fails to comply, he is not entitled, while the default continues, to enforce the agreement.[918]

39-142 **Termination statement** Section 103 of the 1974 Act confers upon the debtor or hirer under a regulated agreement (other than a non-commercial agreement)[919] the right to obtain, on request, a termination statement confirming that he has discharged his indebtedness and that the agreement is at an end. In order to obtain a termination statement under this section, the debtor or hirer must serve a notice complying with the requirements of s.103(1). The creditor or owner must then, within 12 working days[920] after receiving the notice, either:

(i) comply with it (by confirming that the statements contained in the notice are correct); or

(ii) serve a counter-notice stating either that he disputes the correctness of the notice or that he asserts that the person serving the notice is not indebted to him under the agreement.[921]

If he disputes the correctness of the notice he must give particulars of the way in which he alleges it to be wrong.[922] A breach of s.103(1) is actionable as a breach

---

[912] Defined in CCA 1974 ss.8, 189(1); above, para.39-017.

[913] Subject to CCA 1974 s.97(2) (repeated request).

[914] Prescribed by SI 1983/1564 and reduced from 12 days by SI 2004/1483 reg.9.

[915] The request need not (since February 1, 2011) be in writing unless the agreement is secured on land: s.97(2A), added by SI 2010/1010 (and note the transitional and "opt-in" provisions in regs 100–101).

[916] Defined in CCA 1974 s.189(1) (as amended by SI 2004/3236 art.2(2)) to mean "deliver or send by appropriate method".

[917] CCA 1974 s.97(1) (as amended by SI 2010/1010 reg.33). The prescribed form and particulars are set out in the Consumer Credit (Settlement Information) Regulations 1983 (SI 1983/1564, as amended by SI 2004/1483 and SI 2004/3236). The settlement figure has to take account of the contractual or statutory rebate on early settlement: see s.95 (below, para.39-158) and SI 2004/1483, as amended by SI 2004/2619; *Home Insulation v Wadsley* [1988] 10 C.L.Y. 419. See also s.172 (statements binding, below, para.39-143); and *Lombard North Central Plc v Stobart*, *The Times*, March 2, 1990, CA (estoppel of creditor at common law). See *NRAM Plc v McAdam & Hartley* [2015] EWCA Civ 751, reversing [2014] EWHC 4174 (Comm): (obiter) s.97 does not apply to non-regulated agreements that are documented as regulated agreements. See also CCA 1974 s.189B(3), Sch.2A: in s.97, references to "debtor" in relation to "green deal plans" (as defined in CCA 1974 s.189(1), see para.39-257) are to be read as references to the "improver"/"current bill payer" (as defined in CCA 1974 s.189B(6)). There is a similar obligation under CCA s.97A to provide a settlement figure after part-payment (see especially s.97A(2)(h), below, para.39-160).

[918] CCA 1974 s.97(3)(a). Section 97(3)(b): (offence was committed after one month) repealed by the Consumer Protection from Unfair Trading Regulations 2008 (SI 2008/1277) reg.30(1) and Sch.2 para.23.

[919] Defined in CCA 1974 s.189(1); above, para.39-049. See CCA 1974 s.103(4).

[920] Prescribed by SI 1983/1569.

[921] CCA 1974 s.103(1). No doubt he would assert that the person serving the notice is not indebted to him under the agreement if he could not trace the agreement or no longer had any record of it. See also CCA 1974 s.172(2) (statements binding, below, para.39-143).

[922] CCA 1974 s.103(2).

of statutory duty.[923] A termination statement is required to be given in pursuance of this provision on one occasion only.[924]

Statements binding on creditor or owner Section 172 renders certain statements given by the creditor or owner binding on him. The section only applies to statements required to be given, on request,[925] to the debtor or hirer under ss.77(1), 78(1) and 79(1) of the Act,[926] the statements required to be given to a surety under ss.107 to 109,[927] and the statement as to the settlement figure required to be given under s.97(1).[928] Further, if, in response to a notice requiring a termination statement under s.103,[929] the creditor or owner by notice confirms that the statements contained in the notice served on him are correct, or if he himself serves a counter-notice asserting that the person serving the notice is not indebted to him under the agreement, the notice of confirmation or counter-notice is binding on him.[930] However, if in proceedings before any court it is sought to rely on any statement or notice given as mentioned above, and the statement or notice is shown to be incorrect, the court may direct such relief (if any) to be given to the creditor or owner as appears to the court to be just.[931] No doubt the court will relieve the creditor or owner if the debtor, hirer or surety was aware that a mistake had been made; and, although negligence on the part of the creditor or owner may be a relevant factor, it is submitted that the fact that he was negligent should not preclude relief.[932] As is the case in relation to estoppel at common law, it would seem that the most important consideration should be whether the person against whom relief is claimed has so changed his position in reliance on the statement that it would be inequitable to allow the creditor or owner to correct the statement.[933]

39-143

Payment Services Regulations 2009[934] These regulations impose additional information requirements[935] in relation to credit agreements within their scope. However, many of these obligations are modified in relation to agreements that are

39-144

---

[923] CCA 1974 s.103(6), added by the Consumer Protection from Unfair Trading Regulations 2008 (SI 2008/1277) reg.30(1) and Sch.2 para.24(b). Section 103(5) (offence committed after one month): repealed by SI 2008/1277 reg.30(1) and Sch.2 para.24(a).

[924] CCA 1974 s.103(3). And note that CCA 1974 s.185 (as amended (from October 1, 2008) by the Consumer Credit Act 2006 s.7(3) (copies to joint debtors/hirers)) does not apply as there is no actual or prospective regulated agreement. See CCA 1974 s.189B(3), Sch.2A: in s.103 references to "debtor" in relation to "green deal plans" (as defined in CCA 1974 s.189(1), see below, para.39-257) are to be read as references to the "improver" (as defined in CCA 1974 s.189B(6)).

[925] But not the automatic periodic statements required by CCA 1974 s.77A (fixed-sum agreement), see above, para.39-120 or s.78(4) (running-account agreement), see above, para.39-133.

[926] Above, paras 39-128, 39-132. Note that s.172 does not apply to statements given under CCA 1974 s.77A, 77B or 78(4) nor to notices under s.86B, 86C or 86E.

[927] Above, para.39-137.

[928] Above, para.39-141.

[929] Above, para.39-142.

[930] s.172(2).

[931] s.172(3).

[932] See *Kelly v Solari* (1841) 9 M. & W. 54; Vol.I, para.29-039.

[933] See, e.g. *Skyring v Greenwood* (1825) 4 B. & C. 281; *Baylis v Bishop of London* [1913] 1 Ch. 127; *Holt v Markham* [1923] 1 K.B. 504; *Larner v LCC* [1949] 2 K.B. 683; *Lloyds Bank Ltd v Brooks* (1950) 6 Legal Decisions Affecting Bankers 161; *United Overseas Bank v Jiwani* [1976] 1 W.L.R. 964; *Avon CC v Howlett* [1983] 1 W.L.R. 605; *Lombard North Central Plc v Stobart, The Times,* March 2, 1990, CA; Vol.I, paras 29-186—29-195.

[934] SI 2017/752. See generally, above, paras 34-223 et seq.

[935] See especially: regs 43–47 ("single payment services contracts"), regs 48–54 ("framework contracts"), reg.66 (charges), regs 67–80 (payment).

"regulated credit agreements" within the 1974 Act and hence subject to the obligations under that Act considered in this section.[936]

(h)   Variation of Agreements[937]

39-145 **Variation and termination**   The parties to a regulated credit or hire agreement are generally[938] free to terminate that agreement by mutual consent and to substitute a new agreement therefor.[939] No particular form is required to effect a termination; but the new agreement must then comply *in all respects* with the provisions of the 1974 Act and regulations made thereunder applicable to original agreements.[940] The parties to a consumer credit or consumer hire agreement are likewise free to vary the agreement by mutual consent.[941] Section 82[942] of the Act, however, contains special provisions relating to the variation of agreements.[943] In principle, the question whether an agreement has merely been varied or whether it has been terminated and a new agreement substituted, depends upon the intention of the parties in each particular case.[944] But, in view of s.82(2), it seems probable that an agreement which "varies or supplements an earlier agreement" will not be construed as a termination and substitution unless such is manifestly the intention of the parties.[945]

39-146 **Unilateral variation under a power in agreement: the general rule**[946]   If the creditor or owner varies a regulated agreement under a power contained in the agreement, by virtue of s.82(1) the variation generally does not take effect before

---

[936] See SI 2017/752 reg.41 (disapplying regs 50–51 and modifying Pt 6) and reg.64 (modifying Pt 7).

[937] See generally, Guest and Lloyd, *Encyclopedia of Consumer Credit Law* (1975, looseleaf), para.2-083; and Goode, *Consumer Credit: Law and Practice*, Pt C, Ch.35.

[938] But see CCA 1974 s.98A (added from February 1, 2011 by SI 2010/1010 reg.38, in implementation of the Consumer Credit Directive (see para.39-011)), below, para.39-173, which makes special provision for the termination of "open-ended" (i.e. of indefinite duration: see s.189(1)) consumer credit agreements, other than overdrafts and agreements secured on land.

[939] See Vol.I, paras 22-025 et seq.

[940] See above, paras 39-080 et seq.

[941] See Vol.I, paras 22-032 et seq. But variation may discharge a guarantor: see below, para.45-104.

[942] As amended by the Financial Services and Markets Act 2000 (Consequential Amendments) Orders 2005 (SI 2005/2967) and 2008 (SI 2008/733). These amendments sought to ensure that a variation under s.82(2) (see below) does not result in dual regulation of a varied mortgage under both the Financial Services and Markets Act 2000 and the Consumer Credit Act 1974. See also the amendment made by SI 2008/2826 in relation to agreements exempt under RAO art.60D (previously CCA 1974 s.16C), above para.39-040. Further amendments were effected in consequence of the Consumer Credit Directive (see above, para.39-011): see SI 2010/1010 regs 15, 28 and 29 (addition of new subss.(6A)–(6B), (1A)–(1E) and (2B), respectively). For amendments consequent on the transfer of regulation to the FCA (see above, para.39-002), see SI 2013/1881 art.20(3). See also CCA 1974 s.189B(3), Sch.2A: in s.82, references to "debtor" in relation to "green deal plans" (as defined in CCA 1974 s.189(1), see below, para.39-257) are to be read as references to the "improver"/ "current bill payer"/"previous bill payer" (as defined in CCA 1974 s.189B(6)).

[943] But CCA 1974 s.82 (see s.82(7)) does not apply to non-commercial agreements (defined in CCA 1974 s.189(1); above, para.39-049). For regulations made: see SI 1977/328 (as amended by SI 1979/661; SI 1979/667; SI 2010/1010).

[944] *Morris v Baron & Co* [1918] A.C. 1, 26; *United Dominions Corp (Jamaica) Ltd v Shoucair* [1969] 1 A.C. 340. See Vol.I, para.22-034.

[945] For CCA 1974 s.82(2), see below, paras 39-148 et seq.

[946] The more complex notice provisions imposed by the Payment Services Regulations 2017 (SI 2017/752) reg.50 in relation to agreements within their scope (as to which, see generally, above, paras 34-224 et seq.), has been disapplied in relation to CCA 1974-regulated agreements: see SI 2017/752 reg.41(2).

notice of it is given to the debtor or hirer in the prescribed[947] form. However, largely as a result of the implementation of the Consumer Credit Directive,[948] there are some special provisions in relation to the variation of interest rates.[949] The general rule requires notice to be served before the variation takes effect, but in certain circumstances notice of a variation in the interest rate (when the special "Directive" provisions do not apply) may be given by public announcement in the press.[950] A typical example where notice is required is where an owner varies the rentals payable under a leasing agreement, in pursuance of a provision in the agreement entitling him so to do. But a provision in the agreement for the *automatic* adjustment of rentals in the event of tax changes, will not attract the requirement of notice.[951] A term in a credit or hire agreement that enables the creditor or owner to alter unilaterally the terms of the agreement or any characteristic of the product or service to be provided may, in certain circumstances, not be binding on the debtor or hirer if successfully challenged under the Consumer Rights Act 2015 Pt 2.[952]

Unilateral variation of interest rate under a power in agreement   Originally, **39-147** unilateral variations in interest rate were covered by the general rule in s.82(1).[953] The implementation of the Consumer Credit Directive[954] has resulted in the addition of a new s.78A,[955] which generally imposes more onerous conditions when the interest rate is varied, although s.82(1) continues to apply to agreements secured on land (which are outside the Directive[956]) unless the agreement secured on land is an overdraft and the rate is reduced.[957] Section 78A generally requires certain information to be given in writing before a change in interest rate under a regulated credit agreement can take effect. The information (set out in s.78A(3)) comprises:

---

[947]   i.e. prescribed by regulation: see SI 1977/328 (as amended by SI 1979/661; SI 1979/667; SI 2010/1010).

[948]   See above, para.39-011.

[949]   See CCA 1974 s.82(1A)–(1D) s.78A and below, para.39-147. Section 82(1) also does not apply (see s.82(1E)) to a so-called current account "overrunning": see the special provisions in the *FCA Handbook* CONC 4.7 and CONC 6.3.3 and 6.3.4 (previously CCA 1974 ss.74A and 74B), above, para.39-127.

[950]   See SI 1977/328 (as amended by SI 1979/661; SI 1979/667; SI 2010/1010).

[951]   Moreover, if the owner reserves the right to determine whether or not to pass on VAT changes (by virtue of the VAT Act 1994 s.89, changes in VAT are automatically incorporated in the consideration *unless* the agreement provides otherwise) the notice requirement is relaxed should the owner decide to pass on the VAT change.

[952]   Replacing (for contracts made on or after October 1, 2015) the Unfair Terms in Consumer Contracts Regulations 1999 (SI 1999/2083) Sch.2 para.1(j) and (k) and para.2(b) (see further, above, paras 38-221 et seq., especially paras 38-233 et seq.). It is submitted that a term which complies with SI 1977/328 (see above) is not for that reason exempted from the Act by s.73. See Guest and Lloyd, *Encyclopedia of Consumer Credit Law* (1975, looseleaf), para.2-083; and above, paras 38-388 et seq. and below, para.39-293.

[953]   See above, para.39-146 and *Lombard Tricity Finance Ltd v Paton* [1989] 1 All E.R. 918; *Paragon Finance Plc v Nash* [2001] EWCA Civ 1466.

[954]   See above, para.39-011.

[955]   With effect from February 1, 2011, by SI 2010/1010 reg.27. See CCA 1974 s.189B(3), Sch.2A: in s.78A, references to "debtor" in relation to "green deal plans" (as defined in CCA 1974 s.189(1), see below, para.39-257) are to be read as references to the "improver"/"current bill payer" (as defined in CCA 1974 s.189B(6)).

[956]   See CCA 1974 s.78A(6)(b). Note also that whilst s.82 does not apply to "non-commercial agreements" (see s.82(7)); for non-commercial agreements see above, para.39-049), s.78A does.

[957]   See CCA 1974 s.82(1B), (1D). There are no special provisions for such reductions (and compare the similar provision in relation to other overdrafts in CCA 1974 s.78A(4), below). Similarly, s.82(1) does not apply to the reduction of *charges* for overdrafts: 82(1C), (1D).

(a) the variation, (b) the new repayment amounts (if changed), and (c) if the number or frequency of payments is to change, the new number or frequency. However, there are some qualifications to this general obligation. First,[958] the obligation does not arise (and hence the rate may be varied without more) where, essentially, the rate varies according to a publicly available reference rate (with information about the reference rate being available on the creditor's premises) and the creditor is contractually obliged to inform the debtor in writing periodically of the information set out in s.78A(3). Second,[959] in the case of overdrafts, the obligation only arises if the rate of interest *increases* and it is only an obligation to inform of the variation (and not the other matters in relation to changes in payments). Third,[960] the obligation does not apply to two categories of agreement (so-called "excluded agreements"): (a) so-called overdraft "overrunning" (a debtor-creditor agreement arising where the a current account holder overdraws on the account without a pre-arranged overdraft or exceeds a pre-arranged overdraft limit)[961]; or (b) agreements secured on land (as these are outside the Directive and governed by s.82(1)).

39-148   **Mutual variation by subsequent agreement: "modifying agreement"**   Section 82(2) deals with the situation where an agreement (a "modifying agreement") "varies or supplements" an earlier agreement.[962] A modifying agreement will arise, for example, where a further advance is made under an existing fixed-sum loan agreement[963]; where additional goods are agreed to be let together with those already let under an existing hire-purchase agreement (an "add-on" agreement); where part of the goods comprised in an existing agreement are released from that agreement, or other goods substituted therefor; where a fixed-term hire agreement is extended by agreement for a further term; and where the security provided in respect of an existing agreement is augmented, changed or released, or where security is now provided for an existing unsecured agreement. The effect of a modifying agreement is:

(i)   to revoke the earlier agreement; and

(ii)   to reproduce the combined effect of the two agreements, so that (inter alia) obligations outstanding in relation to the earlier agreement are treated as outstanding instead in relation to the modifying agreement.[964]

However, so that the effect of s.82(2) does not result in overlap between the two

---

958   See CCA 1974 s.78A(2).

959   See CCA 1974 s.78A(4).

960   See CCA 1974 s.78A(6).

961   Because the special provisions in the *FCA Handbook* CONC 4.7 and CONC 6.3.3 and 6.3.4 (previously CCA 1974 ss.74A and 74B), see above, para.39-127, apply in such a case.

962   See SI 2008/831 art.4: the removal of the financial limit by the Consumer Credit Act 2006 s.2(1) (see above, para.39-005) has no effect for the purposes of the application of s.82(2) where no fresh credit in the form of a "cash loan" is provided or where an *exempt* agreement varies or supplements an existing agreement. The former provision sought to ensure that the removal of the financial limit did not have the unintended consequence of bringing agreements that were originally exempt from regulation, into regulation as a result of a variation that did not increase the cash available. See *Santander UK Plc v Harrison* [2013] EWHC 199 (QB), [2013] C.C.L.R. 4 (noted above at para.39-019): SI 2008/831 art.4 inapplicable as, although new "credit" was provided, it was not in the form of a "cash loan".

963   But see *Swift Advances Plc v McKay* [2013] NICh 3: subsequent extensions of credit held *not* to be modifying agreements varying or supplementing the original regulated agreement but new freestanding separate agreements.

964   CCA 1974 s.82(2). See also CCA 1974 Sch.2 Pt II Example 24.

regulatory regimes presently applicable to mortgages (the one now operated by the FCA under the 1974 Act and the other by the FCA under the Financial Services and Markets Act 2000),[965] it does not apply[966] if the earlier agreement or the modifying agreement is an FCA-regulated exempt agreement under RAO art.60C(2).[967] Similarly, s.82(2) does not apply if the earlier agreement or the modifying agreement is an exempt agreement under RAO art.60D.[968] Moreover, when the statutory right to *part* settle a regulated credit agreement was introduced as a result of the Consumer Credit Directive,[969] s.82(2) was disapplied to any consequent variations of the agreement.[970]

If the earlier agreement is a regulated agreement, but the modifying agreement **39-149** is not, then the modifying agreement is treated as a regulated agreement, unless the modifying agreement is for running-account credit[971] or is an exempt agreement regulated under the Financial Services and Markets Act 2000 or an exempt agreement under RAO art.60D.[972] Thus if the earlier agreement was a loan of £20,000 for a business purposes but that agreement is varied or supplemented by a further advance so that the balance payable is now fixed-sum credit of £30,000, the agreement is still a regulated agreement.[973] If the earlier agreement was not a regulated agreement, but the effect of the variation is such as to make the modifying agreement a regulated agreement, the modifying agreement will be a regulated agreement for the purposes of the Act.[974] For example, if the earlier agreement was for a loan of £26,000 for a business purpose (and so not a regulated credit agreement[975]), but the outstanding balance under that agreement has been reduced to £18,000 and there is a further advance of £5,000, so that the balance payable is now £23,000, the modifying agreement (comprising as it does the combined effect of the

---

[965] See further below, para.39-529.
[966] CCA 1974 s.82(2A), added by SI 2005/2967 and amended by SI 2008/733. See also the new CCA 1974 s.82(3)(b) added by SI 2005/2967, noted below at para.39-149 and SI 2008/831 art.4 (variation of agreements above the financial limit made before it was removed), above.
[967] Previously, CCA 1974 s.16(6C); see above, para.39-039.
[968] Previously, CCA 1974 s.16C; see above, para.39-040. This is provided for in s.82(2A), as amended by SI 2008/2826.
[969] By amendment to CCA 1974 s.94 (see below, para.39-157).
[970] CCA 1974 s.82(2B), added by SI 2010/1010 reg.29.
[971] Defined in ss.10, 189(1); above, para.39-024. See also s.82(4): if by the modifying agreement the creditor allows the credit limit to be exceeded merely temporarily, Pt V of the Act (i.e. ss.55–74 dealing with the formalities etc. of entering into the agreement), apart from s.56, does not apply to the modifying agreement.
[972] Previously, CCA 1974 s.16C, see above, para.39-040. This is provided for in s.82(3), as amended by SI 2005/2967 to add the reference to agreements that are exempt by virtue of s.16(6C) (as to which, see above, para.39-039) and by SI 2008/2826 to add the reference to s.16C agreements (as to which, see above, para.39-040). Hence again (see s.82(2A) and above, para.39-148) by virtue of the first amendment, potential overlap between the two regulatory regimes for mortgages is avoided. See also, SI 2008/831 art.4 (variation of agreements above the financial limit made before it was removed), above. On the transfer of consumer credit regulation to the FCA (see above, para.39-002), further amendments were made by the SI 2013/1881 art.20(31) so as to (essentially) substitute (i) RAO art.60C(2) for s.16(6C) and (ii) RAO art.60D for s.16C.
[973] And not exempted under RAO art.60C(3)–(7) (previously CCA 1974 s.16B) despite providing credit in excess of the financial limit in that article, see above, para.39-046.
[974] Unless the earlier or modifying agreement is an exempt agreement under RAO art.60C(2) (previously CCA 1974 s.16(6C), i.e. regulated by the FCA under the Financial Services and Markets Act 2000) or an exempt agreement under RAO art.60D (previously CCA 1974 s.16C): see s.82(2A) noted above at para.39-148.
[975] Being exempted under RAO art.60C(3)–(7) (previously CCA 1974 s.16B), see above, para.39-046.

earlier agreement and the variation) is a regulated agreement. On the other hand, in this example, if the amount of the further advance exceeded £7,000, so that the total balance now payable under the modifying agreement is in excess of £25,000, the modifying agreement is not regulated.[976]

39-150   A variation may convert one type of agreement mentioned in the 1974 Act into another type of agreement. For example, the taking of a land mortgage as security for a previously unsecured loan agreement will mean that the modifying agreement attracts the "special pause" provisions in ss.58 and 61(2) and (3) of the Act[977] even though the earlier agreement did not do so. And an exempt agreement[978] may become a regulated agreement by reason of the fact that the agreement, as varied, no longer falls within the exemption.[979]

39-151   **Cancellation of modifying agreement**   If the earlier agreement is an agreement to which the s.66A "right of withdrawal"[980] applies or is a "cancellable" agreement[981] and the modifying agreement is made within the period allowed for withdrawal from or cancellation of the earlier agreement, then whether or not the modifying agreement is itself subject to the right of withdrawal or is itself a cancellable agreement, it can be withdrawn from or cancelled within that period,[982] unless the modifying agreement is an exempt agreement under RAO art.60C(2) or RAO art.60D.[983] Otherwise the modifying agreement cannot be withdrawn from or cancelled.[984]

39-152   **Mere indulgence**   It would appear that the word "varies" should be construed in its technical and legal sense, that is to say, an alteration, as a matter of contract, of contractual obligations by mutual agreement of the parties.[985] A mere indulgence by the creditor or owner in allowing the debtor or hirer further time to pay, even at his request, would not constitute a modifying agreement, but take effect as a waiver or equitable forbearance.[986] And if, for example, a creditor, on request, agrees to take

---

[976] This is supported (indirectly) by CCA 1974 Sch.2 Pt II Example 24. For the calculation of the amount of credit under a modifying agreement, see SI 1983/1553 reg.7 (amended by SI 2004/1482 reg.9, SI 2004/2619), and Sch.8 Pt I para.5 (as amended by SI 2004/1482).

[977] See below, para.39-535.

[978] See above, paras 39-038 et seq., unless exempt under (i) RAO art.60C(2) (see CCA 1974 s.82(2A), added by SI 2005/2967 and amended by SI 2008/733 and SI 2013/1881, to ensure that the two regulatory regimes remain mutually exclusive (see above, para.39-148)) or (ii) RAO art.60D (see s.82(2A), as amended by SI 2008/2826 and SI 2013/1881 art.20(31))).

[979] *Bersey v Evans* [2001] C.L.Y. 886, Cty Ct.

[980] See above, para.39-101.

[981] i.e. cancellable under CCA 1974 s.67; above, para.39-102 (see the definition of "cancellable agreement" in CCA 1974 s.189(1)).

[982] CCA 1974 s.82(5), (6A). But see s.82(4): if by the modifying agreement the creditor under an earlier regulated agreement for running-account allows the credit limit to be exceeded merely temporarily, Pt V of the CCA 1974 (which includes CCA 1974 ss.66A and 67) does not apply to the modifying agreement and hence in such a case it will not be subject to the right of withdrawal or cancellation.

[983] s.82(5A), added by SI 2005/2967 and amended (to add the references first to ss.16(6C) and 16C, and then to RAO arts 60C(2) and 60D) by SI 2008/2826 and 2013/1881 art.20(31). For exemption under RAO art.60C(2) see above, para.39-039 and for exemption under RAO art.60D see above, para.39-040.

[984] CCA 1974 s.82(6), (6B).

[985] See Vol.I, para.22-032.

[986] See Vol.I, paras 22-040 et seq.; *Broadwick Financial Services Ltd v Spencer* [2002] EWCA Civ 35, [2002] 1 All E.R. (Comm) 46 ("concession letter" did not contractually vary the repayment terms).

payment by instalments,[987] or to reduce the amount of the instalments payable, or to extend the repayment period, or to grant to the debtor a payment "holiday", this will ordinarily not amount to a variation if the amount payable by the debtor under the agreement remains unchanged, i.e. there is no additional credit charge.[988] On the other hand, there will undoubtedly be situations where, for example, by mutual agreement, accumulated arrears and future instalments are to be discharged in accordance with a new rescheduled payment pattern. In such a case, it seems probable that this will vary the earlier agreement and so give rise to a modifying agreement.

Form, etc. of modifying agreement   A modifying agreement that is a regulated **39-153**
agreement must, as a general rule, comply with all the provisions of Pt V of the 1974 Act, including the special provisions applicable to modifying agreements contained in the Consumer Credit (Agreements) Regulations.[989] Moreover, the other provisions applicable, e.g. to the supply of copies,[990] must also be observed. However, if the earlier agreement is a regulated agreement for running-account credit,[991] and by the modifying agreement the creditor allows the credit limit to be exceeded but intends the excess to be merely temporary, e.g. a temporary excess drawing on a bank overdraft, Pt V of the 1974 Act (except s.56) does not apply to the modifying agreement.[992]

Protected goods   Where an agreement varies or supplements a regulated hire- **39-154**
purchase or conditional sale agreement, provision is made in s.90 of the 1974 Act to safeguard the position of the debtor in relation to so-called "protected goods".[993]

Unilateral or consensual variation?   It is not always easy to draw the line **39-155**
between s.82(1) (variation under a power in the agreement)[994] and s.82(2) (where a subsequent "agreement" varies or supplements the agreement).[995] In particular, it is unclear if s.82(1) applies in all cases where a creditor or owner reserves a contractual power to vary, even though the power can only be (or is in fact) exercised at the request or with the consent of the debtor or hirer, or whether it only applies where the creditor or owner has a *unilateral* power of variation so that any requisite request or consent of the debtor or hirer inevitably gives rise to an "agreement" that engages s.82(2) (and the onerous requirements applicable to "modifying agreements"[996]). It may be that much will depend on the appropriateness of imposing the more onerous requirements when s.82(2) applies.

---

987   *Re Selectmove Ltd* [1995] 1 W.L.R. 474.
988   If interest is charged under the agreement at a fixed or variable rate on the balance outstanding, it is submitted that there will be no modifying agreement if the rate is not increased, even though an extension of the period of the loan will result in the debtor paying more interest (in total) in £p terms.
989   Either SI 2010/1014 reg.5 or SI 1983/1553 reg.7 and Sch.8 (as amended by SIs 2004/1482, 2004/ 2619, 2004/3236); see above, paras 39-082 and 39-081, respectively.
990   SI 1983/1557 (as amended by SIs 1984/1108, 1985/666, 1989/591, 2004/2619, 2004/3236); see above, para.39-086.
991   Defined in CCA 1974 ss.10, 189(1); above, para.39-024.
992   CCA 1974 s.82(4). See also CCA 1974 ss.10(2), 18(5) Sch.2 Pt I Examples 22, 23.
993   See below, para.39-361.
994   See above, paras 39-146 et seq.
995   See above, paras 39-148 et seq.
996   See above, para.39-153.

(i) Appropriation of Payments and Early Settlement[997]

39-156 **Appropriation of payments** Where a debtor or hirer is liable to make payments in respect of two or more regulated agreements, and makes a payment in respect of them which is not sufficient to discharge the total amount then due under all the agreements, he may appropriate the payment in or towards satisfaction of the sum due under any one of the agreements or under any two or more of them in such proportions as he thinks fit.[998] If he fails to appropriate, the ordinary rule of appropriation by a creditor in principle applies.[999] But, in case of such failure to appropriate, where one or more of the agreements is a hire-purchase or conditional sale agreement, a consumer hire agreement, or an agreement in relation to which any security[1000] is provided, the payment must be appropriated towards the satisfaction of the sums due under the several agreements respectively in the proportions which those sums bear to one another.

39-157 **Early settlement** The debtor under a regulated consumer credit agreement enjoys an indefeasible[1001] right at any time, by notice[1002] to the creditor and the payment to the creditor of all amounts payable by the debtor to him under the agreement,[1003] to discharge the debtor's indebtedness under the agreement.[1004] In consequence of the implementation of the Consumer Credit Directive,[1005] debtors (other than those with agreements secured on land as these are outside the scope of the Directive) now also enjoy an indefeasible right at any time by notice[1006] to the creditor, to settle the outstanding amount in *part* by part-payment before the end of the period of 28 days beginning with the day following that on which notice was received by the creditor or such later date as the debtor specifies in the notice.[1007]

---

[997] See Guest and Lloyd, *Encyclopedia of Consumer Credit Law* (1975, looseleaf), paras 2-082, 2-095—2-098; and Goode, *Consumer Credit: Law and Practice*, Pt C, Ch.36.

[998] *FCA Handbook* CONC 6.4.2R (previously CCA 1974 s.81(1)). But he cannot appropriate so as to place one agreement in credit while leaving another in debit. This provision only applies if there is more than one regulated agreement. If there is only one agreement and there has been no appropriation of payments by the debtor or creditor, in the case of a current account the presumption in *Clayton's case* (1816) 1 Mer. 572, 608, will apply so that payments discharge the oldest debts first. However, in *West Bromwich Building Society's Crammer* [2002] EWHC 2618 (Ch) (a mortgage case) it was held that where there is no appropriation in the case of a debt bearing interest, the general presumption is that payments will discharge interest first, before the earliest items of principal.

[999] See Vol.I, para.21-061.

[1000] Defined in RAO art.60L (to include a guarantee or indemnity): see *FCA Handbook*, Glossary.

[1001] See CCA 1974 s.173(1).

[1002] Which need not be in writing unless the agreement is secured on land: s.94(6)(a).

[1003] Including any amount claimed by the creditor under CCA 1974 s.95A(2) or 95B(2) (see below, para.39-160) and less any rebate allowable under CCA 1974 s.95 (see below, para.39-158).

[1004] CCA 1974 s.94(1). See also CCA 1974 s.94(2) (notice may embody the exercise by the debtor of any option to purchase goods conferred by the agreement, etc.) and CCA 1974 s.97 (right to settlement statement, above, para.39-141). See CCA 1974 s.189B(3), Sch.2A: in s.94, references to "debtor" in relation to "green deal plans" (as defined in CCA 1974 s.189(1), see below, para.39-257) are to be read as references to the "improver"/"current bill payer" (as defined in CCA 1974 s.189B(6)).

[1005] See above, para.39-011.

[1006] Which need not be in writing: CCA 1974 s.94(6)(b).

[1007] CCA 1974 s.94(3)–(6), added from February 1, 2011, by SI 2010/1010 reg.30. The indebtedness is discharged by an amount equal to the sum of the payment and any rebate allowable under CCA 1974 s.95 (see below, para.39-158) less any amount claimed by the creditor under CCA 1974 s.95A(2) or 95B(2) (see below, para.39-160). Note CCA 1974 s.82(2B), above, para.39-148: s.82(2) inap-

Rebate on early settlement, etc The Treasury is empowered by s.95 of the 1974 **39-158**
Act to make regulations for the allowance of a rebate of charges for credit to the
debtor under a regulated consumer credit agreement where on the exercise of his
right of early settlement,[1008] on refinancing, on breach of the agreement,[1009] or for
any other reason, his indebtedness is discharged in whole or in part or becomes payable before the time fixed by the agreement,[1010] or any sum becomes payable by him
before the time so fixed.[1011] Pursuant to this power,[1012] the Consumer Credit (Early
Settlement) Regulations 2004[1013] have been made, replacing earlier Regulations.[1014]
Subject to certain exceptions,[1015] an entitlement to rebate arises in the situations
referred to in s.95.[1016] The terms of the regulations, however, have the effect that a
rebate need only be allowed when the debtor actually *pays* any sum.[1017]

The rebate is, of course, a rebate of charges only. Under the old Regulations,[1018] **39-159**
the appropriate formula for calculation of the rebate was a pro rata rule for fixed-
sum credit agreements where the credit was repayable in a single lump sum[1019] and
the "rule of 78" for agreements where the credit was repayable by instalments.[1020]

---

plicable when repayment amounts and/or duration of the agreement are varied as a result of the
discharge of part of the debtor's indebtedness by virtue of s.94(3). For the obligation of the creditor
to provide information to the debtor after part settlement, see CCA 1974 s.97A.

[1008] Under CCA 1974 s.94; above, para.39-157.

[1009] See, e.g. *Overstone Ltd v Shipway* [1962] 1 W.L.R. 117; *Yeoman Credit Ltd v McLean* [1962] 1
W.L.R. 131 (common law).

[1010] e.g. under an acceleration clause.

[1011] s.95(1), as amended by SI 2010/1010 reg.31, to add a reference to part-payment. See CCA 1974
s.189B(3), Sch.2A: in s.95, references to "debtor" in relation to "green deal plans" (as defined in
CCA 1974 s.189(1), see below, para.39-257) are to be read as references to the "improver"/
"current bill payer" (as defined in CCA 1974 s.189B(6)).

[1012] Previously (before the transfer of consumer credit regulation to the FCA, see above, para.39-002)
vested in the Secretary of State.

[1013] SI 2004/1483, amended by SI 2004/2619, in force May 31, 2005. For transitional provisions, see
reg.10 thereof. The regulations were also amended by SI 2010/1010 regs 77–84 (and see SI 2011/
11, amending reg.78) and SI 2010/1969 reg.26, from February 1, 2011 (subject to transitional provisions), in implementation of the Consumer Credit Directive (see above, para.39-011). They were
further amended by the Consumer Credit (Green Deal) Regulations 2012 (SI 2012/2798), implementing the "Green Deal" introduced by the Energy Act 2011 (see below, para.39-257).

[1014] Consumer Credit (Rebate on Early Settlement) Regulations 1983 (SI 1983/1562), which applied to
agreements made before May 19, 1985 if they would have been regulated if made on that date.

[1015] Agreements for running-account credit (see above, para.39-024), agreements "under which no payments of items included in the total charge for credit are required to be made in respect of the period
of time commencing on the settlement date" and certain residential mortgages where no instalments are due whilst the debtor resides on the mortgaged land are excepted by reg.2(2).

[1016] SI 2004/1483 reg.2(1).

[1017] In consequence, a creditor may claim and be given judgment for the balance of instalments due under
an acceleration clause in the agreement without any deduction of rebate (the rebate to be allowed
on actual payment): *Forward Trust Plc v Whymark* [1990] 2 Q.B. 70.

[1018] SI 1983/1562.

[1019] SI 1983/1562 reg.4(1) and Sch.1. See also reg.6.

[1020] SI 1983/1562 reg.4(2) and Sch.2 Pts I and II. See also regs 4(3), 6, 7 and Schs 3, 5. For an explanation of the "rule of 78", see Guest and Lloyd, *Encyclopedia of Consumer Credit Law* (1975,
looseleaf) at para.3-264. It should be noted that "the rule of 78", though prescribed by regulation,
had been criticised, especially when applied to long-term agreements: *OFT Consultation Document* (June 1994), *DTI Consultation Document* (August 1995) and White Paper Cm. 6040 (2003).
Further, the OFT Guidelines concerning "non-status" lenders, provided that lenders inappropriately extracting penalties for early settlement on the basis of "the rule of 78" risked losing their
licences. See also *Grangewood Securities Ltd v Ellis* Unreported November 9, 2000, Milton Keynes
Cty Ct (extortionate credit bargain); but cf. *Broadwick Financial Services Ltd v Spencer* [2002]

However, the 2004 Regulations[1021] provide for an actuarial formula for calculating the rebate.[1022] In order to compensate the creditor for his setting-up costs and other costs involved in early settlement, the regulations permit the settlement date[1023] to be deferred by one month for agreements with a term of more than one year thus making the rebate less than it would have been had that date not been deferred.[1024]

39-160 **Compensatory amount**   In consequence of the implementation of the Consumer Credit Directive,[1025] a new s.95A was added[1026] enabling the creditor, in certain circumstances, to claim compensation that is "fair", "objectively justifiable" and limited in amount, for costs incurred as a result of early repayment of credit (in whole or in part). The circumstances in which this right arises are: (i) that repayment is made during a period where the interest rate is fixed and (ii) the amount of repayment exceeds £8,000 (as long as it is not paid out of the proceeds of payment protection insurance). The right is not available in two categories of agreement: (i) those secured on land (as they are outside the scope of the Directive), and (ii) overdrafts. A new s.95B was added by the Energy Act 2011[1027] as part of the "Green Deal" introduced by that Act.[1028] The new section makes alternative (to s.95A) provision enabling the creditor to claim compensation should the debtor discharge his indebtedness under a "green deal plan" early.[1029]

39-161 **Hire**   The right of early repayment in s.94 is inapplicable to *hire* agreements.[1030]

39-162 **Calculation of rebate: linked transactions**   Subject to certain exceptions,[1031] the rebate is to be calculated by reference to all sums paid or payable by the debtor or

---

EWCA Civ 35, [2002] 1 All E.R. (Comm) 446 at [61]–[78].

[1021] SI 2004/1483, as amended: see above, para.39-158.

[1022] SI 2004/1483 reg.4, as amended by SI 2010/1010 reg.81 from February 1, 2011 (subject to transitional provisions). Note also the new reg.4A (rebate when indebtedness is discharged in part), added from February 1, 2011 (subject to transitional provisions) by SI 2010/1010 reg.81. But see the Home Credit Market Investigation Order 2007, as amended, made by the Competition Commission under the Enterprise Act 2002 ss.161 and 164, which provides for a more generous (to the debtor) rebate in agreements ("home credit loan agreements") subject to that Order.

[1023] SI 2004/1483 reg.5, as amended by SI 2010/1010 reg.83 from February 1, 2011 (subject to transitional provisions), to provide for part-settlement, in implementation of the Consumer Credit Directive (see above, para.39-157).

[1024] SI 2004/1483 reg.6. But the Home Credit Market Investigation Order 2007, as amended, made by the Competition Commission under the Enterprise Act 2002 ss.161 and 164, renders reg.6 inapplicable to agreements ("home credit loan agreements") subject to that Order.

[1025] See above, para.39-011.

[1026] With effect from February 1, 2011 by SI 2010/1010 reg.32 (as amended by SI 2011/11). See CCA 1974 s.189B(3), Sch.2A: in s.95A, references to "debtor" in relation to "green deal plans" (as defined in CCA 1974 s.189(1), see below, para.39-257) are to be read as references to the "improver"/"current bill payer" (as defined in CCA 1974 s.189B(6)).

[1027] s.29(2). It was amended by SI 2014/436.

[1028] See below, para.39-257 and note CCA 1974 s.189B(3), Sch.2A: in s.95B, references to "debtor" in relation to "green deal plans" are to be read as references to the "improver"/"current bill payer" (as defined in CCA 1974 s.189B(6)).

[1029] See also the Consumer Credit (Green Deal) Regulations 2012 (SI 2012/2798) made under CCA 1974 s.95B.

[1030] But see the right of early termination conferred by CCA 1974 s.101, above, para.33-088.

[1031] See SI 2004/1483 reg.3(2), as amended by (i) SI 2004/2619 and (ii) SI 2010/1010 reg.80 from February 1, 2011 (subject to transitional provisions), to provide for part-settlement, in implementation of the Consumer Credit Directive (see above, para.39-157).

a relative[1032] of his under or in connection with the agreement (whether to the creditor or any other person) and included in the total charge for credit.[1033] Sums paid or payable under linked transactions[1034] may therefore be included.[1035]

Effect on linked transactions Where for any reason the indebtedness of the debtor under a regulated consumer credit agreement is discharged before the time fixed by the agreement, he and any relative[1036] of his is at the same time discharged from any liability under a linked transaction,[1037] other than a debt which has already become payable.[1038]   **39-163**

(j) Restrictions on Enforcement or Termination of Agreement[1039]

Enforcement notice (non-default cases) A number of restrictions are imposed upon the power of the creditor or owner to enforce the terms of, or to terminate, a regulated agreement. The first of these restrictions is contained in s.76 of the 1974 Act, which imposes a duty on the creditor or owner to give notice before taking certain action. Section 76(1) provides that a creditor or owner is not entitled to enforce a term of a regulated agreement by: **39-164**

(a) demanding earlier payment of any sum; or

(b) recovering possession of any goods or land; or

(c) treating any right conferred on the debtor or hirer by the agreement as terminated, restricted or deferred,[1040]

except by or after giving the debtor or hirer not less than seven days' notice[1041] of his intention to do so.[1042] The purpose of this provision is not only to give some warning to the debtor or hirer of the action contemplated, but also to allow him to

---

[1032] Defined in CCA 1974 ss.184(1), 189(1).

[1033] CCA 1974 s.95(2). For "total charge for credit", see above, para.39-059. The creditor may thus be compelled to give a rebate on sums payable, not to himself, but to some other person.

[1034] Defined in CCA 1974 ss.19(1), 189(1); above, paras 39-055 et seq.

[1035] Subject to SI 2004/1483 reg.3(2)(b), (c) and SI 1983/1560.

[1036] Defined in ss.184(1), 189(1).

[1037] Defined in CCA 1974 ss.19(1), 189(1); above, paras 39-055 et seq.

[1038] CCA 1974 s.96(1). See CCA 1974 s.189B(3), Sch.2A: in s.96, references to "debtor" in relation to "green deal plans" (as defined in CCA 1974 s.189(1), see below, para.39-257) are to be read as references to the "improver"/"current bill payer" (as defined in CCA 1974 s.189B(6)). See also CCA 1874 s.96(2) (non-application to a linked transaction which is itself an agreement providing the debtor or his relative with credit). But see s.96(3) and SI 1983/1560 (exceptions).

[1039] See Guest and Lloyd, *Encyclopedia of Consumer Credit Law* (1975, looseleaf), paras 2-077, 2-087—2-090, 2-099, 2-112.

[1040] But see s.76(4): s.76(1) does not prevent a creditor from treating the right to *draw* on any credit as restricted or deferred (e.g. by putting a stop to further drawings on the same or another account), and taking such steps as may be necessary to make the restriction or deferment effective. See also the specific requirements as to notice in such cases in CCA 1974 s.98A(4) for certain "open-ended" agreements (i.e. credit agreements of no fixed duration), below para.39-173.

[1041] The notice must be in a form prescribed by the Consumer Credit (Enforcement, Default and Termination Notices) Regulations 1983 (SI 1983/1561, as amended by SI 2004/3237 to require it to be in *paper* form) reg.2(1) and Sch.1. See (i) CCA 1974 s.86E(3) (if a "default sum" (see CCA 1974 s.187A and above, para.39-135) is payable, the notice may incorporate the notice of default sum required by CCA 1974 s.86E) and (ii) CCA 1974 s.130A(5) (if post-judgment interest is payable, the notice may incorporate the notice required under s.130A(5)).

[1042] See CCA 1974 s.189B(3), Sch.2A: in s.76, references to "debtor" in relation to "green deal plans" (as defined in CCA 1974 s.189(1), see below, para.39-257) are to be read as references to the "current bill payer"/"previous bill payer" (as defined in CCA 1974 s.189B(6)). A copy must be served

apply to the court for a "time order" under s.129 of the 1974 Act if he has difficulty in paying any sum owing under the agreement.[1043] Section 76 does not apply to a right of enforcement arising by reason of any *breach* by the debtor or hirer of the regulated agreement, since action by reason of breach is dealt with in o.87 of the Act.[1044] Nor is a s.76 notice required for *termination* of the agreement, since termination otherwise than for breach is dealt with in s.98 of the Act.[1045]

39-165 **Specified duration has not ended** The requirement of notice applies only where a period for the duration of the agreement is specified in the agreement, and that period has not ended when the creditor does an act mentioned above; but it so applies notwithstanding that, under the agreement, any party is entitled to terminate it before the end of the period so specified.[1046] A s.76 notice is therefore required, for example, where an overdraft is granted for 12 months subject to a stipulation that it can be called in at any time, and the overdraft is called in before the 12 months have elapsed. But it is not required where a loan is simply repayable "on demand". Exemption from this section has been granted by regulation to non-commercial agreements[1047] where no security[1048] is provided.[1049]

39-166 **Default notice** Section 87(1) of the 1974 Act requires the service[1050] of a "default notice" on the debtor or hirer before the creditor or owner can be entitled, by reason of any *breach* by the debtor or hirer of a regulated agreement:

(a) to terminate the agreement[1051];
(b) to demand earlier payment of any sum[1052];
(c) to recover possession of any goods or land;
(d) to treat any right conferred on the debtor or hirer by the agreement as restricted or deferred[1053]; or
(e) to enforce any security.[1054]

Exemption has been granted from the need to serve a default notice to non-

---

on any surety: s.111; below, para.39-174.

[1043] CCA 1974 s.129(1)(b)(ii); below, para.39-202. Hence s.76 does not apply once the term of the agreement has expired: *Evans v Finance-U-Ltd* [2013] EWCA Civ 869.

[1044] CCA 1974 s.76(6). For CCA 1974 s.87, see below, para.39-166.

[1045] For CCA 1974 s.98, see below, para.39-172. See also CCA 1974 s.98A, see below, para.39-173.

[1046] CCA 1974 s.76(2).

[1047] Defined in CCA 1974 s.189(1), see above, para.39-049.

[1048] Defined in CCA 1974 s.189(1); see below, para.39-180.

[1049] CCA 1974 s.76(5); SI 1983/1561 reg.2(9). See also CCA 1974 s.130(3).

[1050] Defined in CCA 1974 ss.176, 189(1). See *Lombard North Central v Power-Hines* [1995] C.C.L.R. 24, Cty Ct (notice posted but never received validly served). See also the notice requirements under the Pre-Action Protocol on Debt Claims ("Debt PAP"), in force October 1, 2017.

[1051] For termination in non-breach cases, see CCA 1974 s.98; below, para.39-172. See also CCA 1974 s.98A(3): termination in non-breach cases of certain "open-ended" consumer credit agreements, below para.39-173.

[1052] e.g. under an "acceleration clause" in the agreement.

[1053] See s.87(2): this does not prevent the creditor from treating the right to draw upon any credit as restricted or deferred, and taking such steps as may be necessary to make the restriction or deferment effective. See also s.87(5) (added on February 10, 2011 by SI 2010/1010 reg.37): s.87(1)(d) inapplicable to certain "open-ended" agreements (i.e. credit agreements of no fixed duration) as the specific requirements as to notice in such cases is in CCA 1974 s.98A(4), see below para.39-173.

[1054] s.87(1). See CCA 1974 s.189B(3), Sch.2A: in s.87, references to "debtor" in relation to "green deal plans" (as defined in CCA 1974 s.189(1), see below, para.39-257) are to be read as references to the "current bill payer"/"previous bill payer" (as defined in CCA 1974 s.189B(6)). The doing of an act whereby a floating charge becomes fixed is not an enforcement of a security (see CCA 1974 s.185(5)

commercial agreements[1055] where no security[1056] is provided.[1057]

Form and content of default notice The default notice must be in the form   **39-167**
prescribed by the Consumer Credit (Enforcement, Default and Termination Notices)
Regulations 1983,[1058] must include a copy of the "default information sheet"[1059] and
must specify the nature of the alleged breach.[1060] If the breach is "capable of
remedy", the notice must further specify what action is required to remedy it and
the date before which that action is to be taken.[1061] Where the breach consists of
non-payment of money, the amount of the debt must be accurately stated so that the
debtor can know how much he must pay to remedy the breach.[1062] If the breach is
"not capable of remedy", the notice must further specify the sum (if any)[1063]
required to be paid as compensation[1064] for the breach, and the date before which
it is to be paid.[1065] The date before which remedial action is to be taken or before
which compensation is to be paid must not be less than 14 days[1066] after the date
of service of the default notice, and the creditor must not take the action mentioned
above before the date so specified (if no remedial action or compensation is
required) before those 14 days have elapsed [1067] In addition, the default notice must
contain information in the prescribed terms about the consequences of failure to
comply with it and any other prescribed matters relating to the agreement.[1068]

[(as amended by the Consumer Credit Act 2006 s.5(8))) and the Agricultural Credits Act 1928):
s.87(3). See also CCA 1974 s.111 (service on surety) below, para.39-174.

[1055] Defined in CCA 1974 s.189(1); see above, para.39-049.
[1056] Defined in CCA 1974 s.189(1); see below, para.39-180.
[1057] s.87(4); SI 1983/1561 reg.2(9). See also CCA 1974 s.130(3).
[1058] SI 1983/1561 reg.2(2) and Sch.2, as amended by SI 1984/1109; SI 2004/3237; SI 2007/1167; 2014/2369. The default notice must in *paper* form: see SI 2004/3237.
[1059] Under CCA 1974 s.86A, see above, para.39-131. See s.88(4A), added with effect from October 1, 2008 (see SI 2007/3300), by the Consumer Credit Act 2006 s.14.
[1060] CCA 1974 s.88(1)(a). Although the nature of the breach must be specified, it would seem that a notice is not invalidated by the addition of alleged breaches which are disproved, or of acts which are not in fact breaches of the agreement, or of other useless and irrelevant matter: see (on the similar provision in the Law of Property Act 1925 s.146) *Pannell v City of London Brewery Co* [1900] 1 Ch. 496; *Fox v Jolly* [1916] 1 A.C. 1; *Silvester v Ostrowska* [1959] 1 W.L.R. 1060. Contrast *Guillemard v Silverthorne* (1908) 99 L.T. 584. See *NRAM Plc v McAdam & Hartley* [2015] EWCA Civ 751, reversing [2014] EWHC 4174 (Comm): (obiter) s.88 does not apply to non-regulated agreements that are documented as regulated agreements.
[1061] CCA 1974 s.88(1)(b).
[1062] *Woodchester Lease Management Services Ltd v Swain & Co* [1999] 1 W.L.R. 263 cf. *Rankine (Basil) v Halifax Plc* [2009] C.C.L.R. 3 (de minimis error overlooked).
[1063] The creditor or owner need not claim compensation if he does not desire to do so: *Lock v Pearce* [1893] 2 Ch. 271; *Rugby School (Governors) v Tannahill* [1935] 1 K.B. 87. But he must still serve a default notice.
[1064] See *Duke of Westminster v Swinton* [1948] 1 K.B. 525 (compensation is the amount of the loss or damage sustained by the breach).
[1065] CCA 1974 s.88(1)(c).
[1066] This period was increased (on October 1, 2006, see SI 2006/1508) from 7 days by the Consumer Credit Act 2006 s.14. See *Brandon v American Express Services Europe Ltd* [2011] EWCA Civ 1187: start of 14 day period mis-stated.
[1067] CCA 1974 s.88(2).
[1068] CCA 1974 s.88(4) (as amended by the Consumer Credit Act 2006 s.14 to include "any other prescribed matters relating to the agreement"); SI 1983/1561 Sch.2. See also s.88(5), whereby the default notice may contain a provision for the creditor or owner taking certain action, e.g. recovering possession of goods at the end of the 14-day or other period, provided that it is stated that the provision will be ineffective if the breach is duly remedied or the compensation duly paid. See also

39-168 **"Breach capable of remedy"** The 1974 Act does not define or specify which breaches are and which are not capable of remedy. But some guidance may possibly be obtained from cases decided on the identical expression employed in s.146(1) of the Law of Property Act 1925 (restrictions on and relief against forfeiture of leases). Breach of a covenant to repay the credit or to pay interest is clearly capable of remedy, as is breach of a covenant to pay hire rentals. On the other hand, bankruptcy (if made a breach)[1069] would be an irremediable breach[1070] and the sale of goods let under a hire-purchase or agreed to be sold under a conditional sale agreement would, it is submitted, likewise be an irremediable breach.[1071] If goods are subject to execution or other legal process, or to a lien, whether or not the breach is remediable will depend on the circumstances of the case.[1072] Breach of a covenant to repair will normally be remediable; but breach of a covenant to insure will not necessarily be so. It would seem to be immaterial that the breach is not capable of remedy within the time stipulated in the default notice (not being less than 14 days), provided that it could be remedied within a reasonable time.

39-169 **Cumulative breaches** The default notice must not treat as a breach failure to comply with a provision of the agreement which becomes operative only on breach of some other provision, e.g. a provision whereby the debtor is to pay the whole balance of the credit outstanding in the event of non-payment of a single instalment. But if the breach of that other provision (i.e. the failure to pay the instalment) is not duly remedied or compensation duly paid or (if no remedial action or compensation is required) the 14 days have elapsed, then the creditor may treat the failure (i.e. the failure to pay the balance) as a breach, and the action specified in s.87(1) can be taken without the need for any further default notice.[1073] Otherwise, however, it would appear that the creditor or owner cannot take any action specified in s.87(1) unless that action is specified in the notice.[1074]

39-170 **Application to court** A debtor or hirer on whom a default notice has been served may apply to the court for a "time order" under s.129 of the 1974 Act.[1075]

39-171 **Compliance with default notice** If before the date specified for that purpose in the default notice the debtor or hirer takes the required remedial action or pays the required compensation, the breach is treated as not having occurred.[1076]

(i) CCA 1974 s.86E(3) (if a "default sum" (see CCA 1974 s.187A and above, para.39-135) is payable, the notice may incorporate the notice of default sum required by s.86E) and (ii) CCA 1974 s.130A(5) (if post-judgment interest is payable, the notice may incorporate the notice required under s.130A(5)).

[1069] It is rarely made a breach, so that either s.76 or s.98 would apply: see above, para.39-164; below, para.39-172.

[1070] *Civil Service Co-operative Society Ltd v McGrigor's Trustee* [1923] 2 Ch. 347, 356.

[1071] *Scala House & District Property Co Ltd v Forbes* [1974] Q.B. 575. This, at any rate, would be the case where the purchaser acquired a good title to the goods, and probably also where he did not, for repurchase is too speculative a possibility. See also *Kemp v United Dominions Corp (Australia) Ltd* [1970] Qd.R. 323 (hire-purchase).

[1072] *Hartley v Larkin* (1950) 66 T.L.R. (Pt 1) 896.

[1073] CCA 1974 s.88(5).

[1074] CCA 1974 ss.87, 88(4) and SI 1983/1561 Sch.2.

[1075] CCA 1974 s.129(1)(b)(i); below, para.39-202. See also Vol.I, para.26-255 (relief from forfeiture).

[1076] s.89. Partial compliance is insufficient: *Price v Romilly* [1960] 1 W.L.R. 1360. See *NRAM Plc v*

Notice of termination (non-default cases)[1077]   Section 98(1) of the 1974 Act   **39-172**
provides that the creditor or owner is not entitled to terminate early a regulated
agreement (other than an agreement of indeterminate duration[1078]) except by or after
giving the debtor seven days' notice[1079] of the termination.[1080] The section does not,
however, apply to termination by reason of any breach by the debtor or hirer of the
agreement.[1081] In cases of breach, a default notice[1082] must be served. Bankruptcy
is, for example, not in itself a breach and if made a ground of termination would
require the service of a s.98 notice. No remedial action need be stipulated in the s.98
notice. Nor will any remedial action or payment by the debtor or hirer prevent the
notice from taking effect. The remedy of the debtor or hirer is to apply to the court
for a "time order" under s.129 of the 1974 Act.[1083] The remaining provisions of
s.98,[1084] which limit its application, correspond with those of s.76.[1085] Exemption
has been granted by regulation from the requirements of s.98 in the case of a non-
commercial agreement[1086] where no security[1087] is provided.[1088]

Termination etc. of open-end consumer credit agreements   In consequence of   **39-173**
the implementation of the Consumer Credit Directive[1089] a new s.98A has been
added[1090] to the 1974 Act governing the termination of regulated credit agreements that are "open-ended" (that is, of indefinite duration). However, it does not
apply to overdrafts or to agreements secured on land (mortgages are outside the
scope of the Directive).[1091] First,[1092] it enables a *debtor* by notice and free of charge,
to terminate such an agreement at any time. The agreement may provide for a period
of notice but this must not exceed one month. Moreover, the creditor may require

---

McAdam & Hartley [2015] EWCA Civ 751, reversing [2014] EWHC 4174 (Comm): (obiter) s.89
does not apply to non-regulated agreements that are documented as regulated agreements. See also
CCA 1974 s.189B(3), Sch.2A: in s.89, references to "debtor" in relation to "green deal plans" (as
defined in CCA 1974 s.189(1), see below, para.39-257) are to be read as references to the "current
bill payer"/"previous bill payer" (as defined in CCA 1974 s.189B(6)).

[1077] See CCA 1974 s.189B(3), Sch.2A: in s.98, references to "debtor" in relation to "green deal plans"
(as defined in CCA 1974 s.189(1), see below, para.39-257) are to be read as references to the "current bill payer"/"previous bill payer" (as defined in CCA 1974 s.189B(6)).

[1078] CCA 1974 s.98(2). But see CCA 1974 s.98A(3) (termination of certain "open-ended" agreements,
i.e. agreements of no fixed duration), below para.39-173. And note the Consumer Rights Act 2015
Sch.2 paras 8 and 21, above para.38-391, replacing (for contracts made on or after October 1, 2015)
the Unfair Terms in Consumer Contracts Regulations 1999 (SI 1999/2083) Sch.2 paras 1(g) and 2(a),
above, para.38-309.

[1079] The notice must be in the form prescribed by the Consumer Credit (Enforcement, Default and
Termination Notices) Regulations 1983 (SI 1983/1561, as amended by SI 2004/3237 to require it
to be in *paper* form) reg.2(3) and Sch.3. A copy must be served on any surety: CCA 1974 s.111;
below, para.39-174. See CCA 1974 s.130A(5) (if post-judgment interest is payable, the notice may
incorporate the notice required under s.130A(5)).

[1080] Hence s.98 does not apply once the term of the agreement has expired: *Evans v Finance-U-Ltd*
[2013] EWCA Civ 869.

[1081] CCA 1974 s.98(6).

[1082] See above, para.39-166.

[1083] CCA 1974 s.129(1)(b)(ii); below, para.39-202. See also Vol.I, para.26-255 (relief from forfeiture).

[1084] subss.(2), (4).

[1085] subss.(2), (4). See above, para.39-164.

[1086] Defined in CCA 1974 s.189(1), see above, para.39-049.

[1087] Defined in CCA 1974 s.189(1); see below, para.39-180.

[1088] CCA 1974 s.98(5); SI 1983/1561 reg.2(9). See also CCA 1974 s.130(3).

[1089] See above, para.39-011.

[1090] With effect from February 1, 2011 by SI 2010/1010 reg.38.

[1091] CCA 1974 s.98A(8).

[1092] CCA 1974 s.98A(1).

the notice of termination to be in writing, otherwise it may take any form. But this provision does not affect any right that the debtor has to terminate an agreement for breach of contract in the usual way.[1093] Second,[1094] it limits the exercise of any contractual right that the *creditor* has to terminate such an agreement in that the termination must be effected by notice in writing and may not take effect for two months, or such longer period as the agreement may provide. But again, this does not affect any right that the creditor has to terminate an agreement for breach of contract.[1095] Third,[1096] special provision is made governing the termination or suspension of the debtor's right to draw on credit (whether prompted by the debtor's breach of contract or not, although in the former case the usual default notice provision does not apply[1097]). Generally, the creditor must serve a notice in writing, with objectively justified reasons, on the debtor before the termination or suspension takes effect or, if that is "not practicable", immediately afterwards.

39-174 **Copy of notices to "surety"** When a default notice under s.87(1)[1098] or a notice under ss.76(1)[1099] or 98(1)[1100] is served on a debtor or hirer, a copy of the notice[1101] must be served by the creditor or owner on any surety (if a different person from the debtor or hirer).[1102] A failure to comply means that the security is enforceable against the surety, in respect of the breach or other matter to which the notice relates, on an order of the court only.[1103]

39-175 **Death of debtor or hirer** Section 86 of the 1974 Act is designed to restrict the right of a creditor or owner, e.g. to terminate the agreement or to accelerate payment by reason of the death of the debtor or hirer.[1104] Section 86(1) provides that the creditor or owner under a regulated agreement is not entitled, by reason of the death of the debtor or hirer, to do an act specified in paras (a) to (e) of s.87(1)[1105] if at the death the agreement is "fully secured". And s.86(2) provides that, if at the death, the agreement is only "partly secured" or "unsecured", the creditor or owner is entitled, by reason of the death of the debtor or hirer, to do such an act on an order

---

[1093] CCA 1974 s.98A(7).

[1094] CCA 1974 s.98A(3). Note that CCA 1974 s.129 (time orders, see below, para.39-202) does not apply in relation to a s.98A(3) notice (cf. CCA 1974 ss.76, 87 and 98 notices).

[1095] CCA 1974 s.98A(7). But note that generally a default notice must then be served under CCA 1974 s.87, see above, para.39-166.

[1096] CCA 1974 s.98A(4)–(6). Where the Payment Services Regulations 2017 (SI 2017/752) apply (see generally, above, paras 34-224 et seq.), the provisions in reg.71(2)–(5) as to stopping the use of a "payment instrument" are disapplied in cases covered by s.98A(4)–(6): see SI 2017/752 reg.64(2).

[1097] See CCA 1974 s.87(5), added by SI 2010/1010 reg.37.

[1098] See above, para.39-166.

[1099] See above, para.39-164.

[1100] See above, para.39-172.

[1101] Complying with SI 1983/1557 (as amended by SI 2004/2619 and SI 2004/3236), especially reg.10.

[1102] CCA 1974 s.111(1). For the definition of "surety", see below, para.39-183. Perhaps because of an oversight, s.111 has not been amended to apply also to a s.98A(3) or (4)(b) creditor's notice (see above, para.39-173).

[1103] CCA 1974 ss.111(2), 127(1)(c), 142(1). See also CCA 1974 ss.106, 113(3) (effect on security) and below, para.39-200 (powers of court). See CPR Pt 7 PD 7B.

[1104] See CCA 1974 s.189B(3), Sch.2A: in s.86, references to "debtor" in relation to "green deal plans" (as defined in CCA 1974 s.189(1), see below, para.39-257) are to be read as references to the "current bill payer"/"previous bill payer" (as defined in CCA 1974 s.189B(6)). See also s.185(4) (death of one of two or more hirers or debtors).

[1105] See above, para.39-166.

of the court only.[1106] The terms "fully secured", "partly secured" and "unsecured" are not defined, and difficulties of interpretation arise. In the first place it is uncertain whether "secured" should be construed in its popular sense of supported by real security, or whether personal security,[1107] i.e. a contract of guarantee or indemnity, will suffice. Secondly, it is uncertain whether an agreement is fully secured if it is expressed to be given in respect of the entire debt or whether reference must be made to the actual value of the security. In the latter case it involves a difficult assessment as to the precise value of the security at the death.

For the purposes of the section, an act is done "by reason of" the death of the debtor or hirer if it is done under a power conferred by the agreement which is either exercisable on his death or exercisable at will and exercised at any time after his death.[1108] But the application of the section is otherwise limited[1109] by provisions corresponding to those contained in s.76(2) and (4) of the 1974 Act.[1110] It should be emphasised that nothing in s.86 prevents a creditor or owner from taking action under a power conferred by the agreement which is exercisable on the debtor or hirer's default. **39-176**

Increase of interest rate on default[1111] Section 93 of the 1974 Act prevents a debtor under a regulated consumer credit agreement from being obliged to pay interest on sums which, in breach of the agreement, are unpaid by him at a rate exceeding the rate payable on the principal apart from any default.[1112] And where the charge made for credit is not technically interest but, e.g. a finance charge, then that rate of charge is likewise not to be increased on default.[1113] But the section does not prevent interest being charged on interest due but unpaid at a rate not exceeding the rate payable on the principal apart from any default.[1114] Nor, it is submitted, does the section prevent a creditor (e.g. a bank) stipulating two rates of inter- **39-177**

[1106] For the powers of the court, see CCA 1974 s.128; below, para.39-201. See also CPR Pt 7 r.9, 7PD-003, 3.1(6), 7.4, 9.3. CPR Pt 7 PD7B.

[1107] See the definition of "security" in CCA 1974 s.189(1) and below, para.39-180.

[1108] CCA 1974 s.86(6).

[1109] CCA 1974 s.86(3), (4).

[1110] See above, para.39-165. See also CCA 1974 s.98(2), (4); above, para.39-172. The section does not affect the operation of any agreement providing for payment of sums due under the regulated agreement, or becoming due under it on the death of the debtor or hirer, out of the proceeds of a policy of assurance on his life e.g. under a mortgage protection policy or endowment policy: s.86(5).

[1111] For interest payable on default sums see CCA 1974 s.86F, above, para.39-136 and for interest on judgment debts, see CCA 1974 s.130A, below, para.39-206. See also CCA 1974 s.78A (notification of change of interest, above, para.39-147).

[1112] i.e. "where the total charge for credit includes an item in respect of interest, at a rate exceeding that rate of interest": s.93(a). See *McMullon v Secure the Bridge Ltd* [2015] EWCA Civ 884 (so-called "fee" was clearly "interest"). A similar (but not identical) provision was contained in s.7 of the Moneylenders Act 1927 (see *Mutual Loan Fund Association v Sanderson* [1937] 1 All E.R. 380). This section causes particular difficulty in the case of "interest free" credit, see Guest and Lloyd, *Encyclopedia of Consumer Credit Law* (1975, looseleaf), para.2-094. See CCA 1974 s.189B(3), Sch.2A: in s.93, references to "debtor" in relation to "green deal plans" (as defined in CCA 1974 s.189(1), see below, para.39-257) are to be read as references to the "current bill payer"/"previous bill payer" (as defined in CCA 1974 s.189B(6)).

[1113] s.93(b). In this case, items included in the total charge for credit by virtue of rules made by the FCA under RAO art.60M(2)(d) ("linked transactions" see above, paras 39-055 et seq.) are to be disregarded.

[1114] For the positions at common law, see below, paras 39-285 et seq. Similarly a provision that "on the debtor making default in payment of any instalment, the *whole amount* of principal and interest remaining unpaid shall forthwith become due and payable" would not appear to contravene s.93 since "the whole amount of principal and interest" are not sums which are unpaid in breach of the

est, one for "authorised" overdrafts and the other for overdrafts which are unauthorised.

39-178   The provisions of the Late Payment of Commercial Debts (Interest) Act 1998 do not apply to consumer credit agreements.[1115]

39-179   **Contracting out forbidden**   The restrictions thus placed upon the right of the creditor or owner to enforce the agreement, or to terminate it, are provisions "for the protection of the debtor or hirer or his relative or any surety", and in consequence cannot be abrogated or diminished, whether directly or indirectly, by a term contained in a regulated agreement or linked transaction, or in any other agreement relating to an actual or prospective regulated agreement or linked transaction.[1116]

(k) Security[1117]

39-180   **"Security" defined**   The term "security", in relation to an actual or prospective consumer credit agreement or consumer hire agreement, or any linked transaction[1118] is defined to mean a mortgage, charge, pledge, bond, debenture, indemnity, guarantee, bill, note or other right provided by the debtor or hirer, or at his request (express or implied), to secure the carrying out of the obligations of the debtor or hirer under the agreement.[1119] For the purposes of the 1974 Act,[1120] therefore, security may be either real or personal, and it may be provided by the debtor or hirer, or by a third party (in which case it must be provided at the request, express or implied, of the debtor or hirer). A guarantee or indemnity given by a dealer by way of "recourse" at the request of the financier would not therefore ordinarily constitute security.[1121]

39-181   Difficulty may arise in deciding whether or not certain acts done by the debtor or hirer, or at his request, constitute security.[1122] It has, for example, been suggested[1123] that a "form of consent" given to a mortgagee at the request of the mortgagor by a person in actual occupation of the property to be mortgaged by which that person agrees that his rights in the property under the Land Registra-

---

agreement and thus the interest may be increased on them by virtue of the provision. But see CCA 1974 s.95(1) (rebate on early settlement, above para.39-158). As to whether a clause providing for accelerated payment of principal and interest is a penalty, see below, para.39-272, and *Wadham Stringer Finance Ltd v Meaney* [1981] 1 W.L.R. 39. The provision for a rebate in CCA 1974 s.95 (see above, para.39-158) may prevent it being penal: *Forward Trust Plc v Robinson* [1987] C.C.L.R. 10, Cty Ct.

[1115] See s.2(5)(a) of the 1998 Act.

[1116] CCA 1974 s.173(1), (2).

[1117] See Guest and Lloyd, *Encyclopedia of Consumer Credit Law* (1975, looseleaf), paras 2-106—2-127; and Goode, *Consumer Credit: Law and Practice*, Pt C, Ch.37.

[1118] Defined in CCA 1974 ss.19(1), 189(1); above, paras 39-055 et seq.

[1119] CCA 1974 s.189(1). See the almost identical definition in the RAO art.60L(1) and in the *FCA Handbook* Glossary (for the purpose of CONC).

[1120] And the RAO and the *FCA Handbook* CONC; see the previous footnote.

[1121] cf. *Unity Finance Ltd v Woodcock* [1963] 1 W.L.R. 455. See also *Governor and Company of the Bank of Scotland v Euclidian (No.1) Ltd* [2007] EWHC 1732: indemnity provided in that case not "security" within the CCA 1974 as it neither secured the carrying out of the debtor's obligations nor was it provided at his request. For recourse agreements, see below, para.39-328.

[1122] See Guest and Lloyd, *Encyclopedia of Consumer Credit Law* (1975, looseleaf) at para.2-106.

[1123] Putnam [1983] L.S.Gaz. 219.

tion Act 1925[1124] will be postponed and subject to the rights of the mortgagee, and will not be asserted against the mortgagee, would fall within the definition of "security".[1125] It is thought that the common term in bank loan contracts whereby a bank reserves the right to take missed repayments from other accounts kept by the debtor with the bank, in so far as this confers rights on the bank beyond its common law right to combine *current* accounts,[1126] constitutes "security". Further, it would seem that an insurance policy effected by the debtor or hirer in respect of goods the subject of a hire-purchase, conditional sale or hiring agreement does not fall within the definition, even though the agreement requires such insurance to be effected and provides that, in the event of a total loss, the policy moneys are to be paid to the creditor or owner. The primary purpose of such insurance is to protect the creditor against loss caused by the events insured against, and not to secure, i.e. make more certain, the carrying out of the obligations of the debtor or hirer under the agreement.[1127] On the other hand, an assignment or charge by a debtor of, for instance, a life insurance policy, or moneys standing to his credit in another account, in order to secure a loan, could undoubtedly constitute security.[1128]

"Security instrument"   Any security provided in relation to a regulated agree- **39-182**
ment by a third party[1129] is required by s.105(1) of the 1974 Act to be expressed in writing. A document made in compliance with this requirement is termed a "security instrument".[1130]

"Surety"   The word "surety" is used in the 1974 Act to mean the person by whom **39-183**
any security is provided, or the person to whom his rights and duties in relation to the security have passed by assignment or operation of law.[1131] The expression therefore goes beyond the ordinary legal sense of a guarantor or indemnifier,[1132] and can in appropriate situations even refer to the debtor or hirer himself if he provides security himself.

Form and content of security instrument   The Treasury is empowered to make **39-184**
regulations prescribing the form and content of security instruments.[1133] Regulations have been made, confined to guarantees and indemnities, in the Consumer Credit (Guarantees and Indemnities) Regulations 1983.[1134] These prescribe the form and content of guarantees and indemnities provided in relation to regulated agree-

---

[1124] s.70(1)(g). See *Williams & Glyn's Bank v Boland* [1981] A.C. 487.
[1125] Much may depend on the precise wording of the consent.
[1126] See above, para.34-316 and *Bradford Old Bank Ltd v Sutcliffe* [1918] 2 K.B. 833, CA.
[1127] This submission was reflected in (the now revoked) Advertisements and Quotations Regulations 1989 (SI 1989/1125) Sch.1 Pt III paras 2, 3; and SI 1989/1126 Sch.1 paras 2, 3, where "security" was stated as an alternative to an insurance policy where the proceeds were to be used to repay the loan. However, the subsequent regulations (SI 2004/1481 and SI 1999/2725, respectively, now revoked, see above, para.39-067) were less complex and did not contain corresponding provisions.
[1128] See CCA 1974 Sch.2 Example 11.
[1129] Which, to be "security" (see above, para.39-180), must be provided at the request, express or implied, of the debtor or hirer. Section 105(6) confines s.105(1) to security provided by third parties. For security provided by the debtor or hirer, see below, para.39-188.
[1130] CCA 1974 s.105(2).
[1131] CCA 1974 s.189(1).
[1132] See below, Ch.45.
[1133] CCA 1974 s.105(2), (3). For the meaning of "security instrument", see above, para.39-182.
[1134] SI 1983/1556, as amended by SI 2004/3236 (electronic form). Previously (before the transfer of consumer credit regulation to the FCA, see above, para.39-002) the power to make the regulations was vested in the Secretary of State.

ments at the request (express or implied) of the debtor or hirer, and also provide for the legibility and signing of such guarantees and indemnities. A guarantee or indemnity is not properly executed unless a document in the prescribed form, itself containing all the prescribed terms and conforming to these regulations, is signed in the prescribed manner by or on behalf of the surety.[1135]

39-185   Any security instrument (whether or not a contract of guarantee or indemnity) is not properly executed unless the document embodies all the terms of the security, other than implied terms, and the document, when presented or sent for the purpose of being signed by or on behalf of the surety, is in such a state that its terms are readily legible.[1136]

39-186   **Supply of copies to surety**[1137]   When the document is presented or sent for the purpose of being signed by the surety or on his behalf, there must also be presented or sent a copy of the document.[1138] In addition, the surety is entitled to receive a copy of the executed credit or hire agreement. The precise time at which this copy must be given to him depends on whether the security is provided after or at the time when the regulated agreement is made, or before it is made. In the former case, a copy of the executed agreement, together with a copy of any other document referred to in it, must be given to the surety at the time the security is provided.[1139] In the latter case, a copy of the executed agreement, together with a copy of any other document referred to in it, must be given to the surety within seven days after the regulated agreement is made.[1140] Failure to supply such copies means that the security instrument is not properly executed.

39-187   **Consequence of improper execution**   The consequence of improper execution of a security instrument is that the security, so far as provided in relation to a regulated agreement, is enforceable against the surety on an order of the court only.[1141] The same consequence applies if a security is not expressed in writing in contravention of s.105(1).[1142] If an application for an order is dismissed by the court, except on technical grounds[1143] only, the security, so far as it is provided in relation to a regulated agreement, is rendered invalid.[1144]

39-188   **Security provided by debtor or hirer**   The Consumer Credit (Agreements) Regulations,[1145] include provision governing any security provided in relation to a regulated agreement by the debtor or hirer.[1146] The 1983 Regulations[1147] require

---

[1135] CCA 1974 s.105(4)(a).
[1136] CCA 1974 s.105(4)(b), (c).
[1137] See SI 1983/1557, as amended by SI 2004/2619 and SI 2004/3236 (form of copies). See also above, para.39-137 (supply of information).
[1138] CCA 1974 s.105(4)(d).
[1139] CCA 1974 s.105(5)(a).
[1140] CCA 1974 s.105(5)(b).
[1141] CCA 1974 s.105(7)(a). See also CCA 1974 ss.127, 173(3); below, para.39-200 and CPR Pt 7 PD 7B.
[1142] CCA 1974 s.105(7)(b). CPR Pt 7 PD 7B.
[1143] See CCA 1974 s.189(1), (5).
[1144] CCA 1974 ss.105(8), 106; below, para.39-193.
[1145] Made under CCA 1974 s.60, see above, paras 39-080 et seq.
[1146] CCA 1974 s.105(9).
[1147] Which now generally only apply to agreements outside the scope of the Consumer Credit Directive (see above, para.39-011), unless the creditor has (in effect) opted out by opting in to the "Directive Regime". See SI 1983/1553 (as amended by SI 1984/1600; SI 1985/666; SI 1988/2047; SI 1999/

documents embodying regulated agreements also to embody[1148] the security whilst the 2010 Regulations[1149] impose the less onerous requirement that documents embodying regulated credit agreements need only "contain details of any security" provided.

Withdrawal of security   If security is provided in relation to a prospective agree-   **39-189**
ment or transaction, the security is enforceable in relation to the agreement or transaction only after the time (if any) when the agreement is made. Until that time the person providing the security is entitled, by notice to the creditor or owner, to withdraw the security.[1150]

Enforcement of security   Section 113 of the 1974 Act is designed to ensure that   **39-190**
the creditor or owner cannot, by enforcing security, recover more than they would have been entitled to under the regulated agreement, and so prevents evasion of the Act by the use of security. Where a security is provided in relation to an actual or prospective regulated agreement, the security is not to be enforced so as to benefit the creditor or owner, directly or indirectly, to an extent greater (whether as respects the amount of any payment or the time or manner of its being made) than would be the case if the security were not provided and any obligations of the debtor or hirer, or his relative, under or in relation to the agreement were carried out to the extent (if any) to which they would be enforced under the Act.[1151]

In accordance with this principle, where a regulated agreement is enforceable on   **39-191**
an order of the court[1152] or of the FCA[1153] only, any security provided in relation to the agreement is enforceable (so far as provided in relation to the agreement) where such an order has been made in relation to the agreement, but not otherwise.[1154] The same rules also apply (with appropriate changes of language) where a security is provided in relation to an actual or prospective linked transaction.[1155]

3177; (especially) SI 2004/1482; SI 2004/2619; SI 2004/3236; SI 2010/1010; SI 2010/1969) reg.2(10) (credit) and reg.3(7) (hire).

[1148] Defined in CCA 1974 s.189(1), (4).

[1149] SI 2010/1014, as amended by SI 2010/1969 regs 41–45. See reg.3(5) and Sch.1 para.23.

[1150] CCA 1974 s.113(6). The notice must require "that section 106 shall thereupon apply to the security": see below, para.39-192.

[1151] s.113(1). See CCA 1974 s.189B(3), Sch.2A: in s.113 references to "debtor" in relation to "green deal plans" (as defined in CCA 1974 s.189(1), see below, para.39-257) are to be read as references to the "improver" (as defined in CCA 1974 s.189B(6)). See *Wilson v First County Trust Ltd* [2001] Q.B. 407; *Wilson v Secretary of State for Trade and Industry* [2003] UKHL 40, [2003] 3 W.L.R. 568. But s.113(7) (as amended by the Minors' Contracts Act 1987 s.4) provides in effect that, where the debtor or a hirer is, e.g. a minor, s.113(1) does not produce the result that a contract of guarantee or indemnity becomes unenforceable merely by reason of his minority: see *Yeoman Credit Ltd v Latter* [1961] 1 W.L.R. 828; below, para.45-040; Vol.I, paras 9-005 et seq.

[1152] See CCA 1974 s.65(1) (above, para.39-093) and CCA 1974 s.124(1) (below, para.39-197).

[1153] Previously the OFT. See now the power of the FCA to so order under FSMA 2000 s.28A (above, paras 39-064 and 39-065 and below, paras 39-249 and 39-250).

[1154] CCA 1974 s.113(2).

[1155] CCA 1974 s.113(8). This subsection also applies to s.113(3), see below. For the difficulties with the wording of subs.(8), see Guest and Lloyd, *Encyclopedia of Consumer Credit Law* (1975, looseleaf), para.2-114.

39-192 **Security rendered invalid**   Section 106 provides that where, under any provision of the 1974 Act, that section "is applied" to any security provided in relation to a regulated agreement, then[1156]:

(a) the security, so far as it is so provided, is to be treated as never having effect[1157];

(b) any property lodged with the creditor or owner solely for the purposes of the security as so provided shall be returned by him forthwith;

(c) the creditor or owner shall take any necessary action to remove or cancel an entry in any register, so far as the entry relates to the security as so provided; and

(d) any amount received by the creditor or owner on realisation of the security[1158] shall, so far as it is referable to the agreement, be repaid to the surety.

39-193   Examples of situations where s.106 "is applied" to a security are as follows:

(i)   where a regulated agreement is cancelled under s.69(1)[1159] or becomes subject to s.69(2)[1160];

(ii)   where a regulated agreement is terminated under s.91[1161];

(iii) where the FCA dismisses, except on technical grounds[1162] only, an application for an order[1163] validating agreements made in the context of unauthorised trading[1164];

(iv)   where a court dismisses, except on technical grounds[1165] only, an application for an order under s.65(1) for the enforcement of an improperly executed agreement[1166] or under s.105(8) for enforcement of a security that is not in writing[1167] or improperly executed[1168] or under subs.(1) or (2) of s.124[1169] for enforcement of an agreement or security after contravention of the prohibition on taking or negotiating negotiable instruments[1170];

[1156] Subject to s.177 (saving for registered charges); below, para.39-538.

[1157] Nor can an unpaid vendor's lien be asserted: *Orakpo v Manson Investments Ltd* [1978] A.C. 95.

[1158] On the meaning of "realisation" in s.106 see the contrasting decisions: *Re London Scottish Finance (In Administration)* [2013] EWHC 4047 ("realisation" should be given its conventional meaning of the *creditor* taking steps to release the value of the collateral (cf. "redemption" meaning the repayment by the *debtor* to obtain the return of the collateral)) and *Wilson v Howard (t/a Howard Pawnbrokers)* [2005] EWCA Civ 147, [2005] C.C.L.R. 2 ("realisation" covers repayment by debtor as well as realisation by sale). It is suggested that the former interpretation is to be preferred as otherwise debtors providing security are in a more favourable position than ordinary debtors (who cannot *recover* payments made under unenforceable agreements unless the "unfair relationship" provisions (see below, paras 39-212 et seq.) apply). See also *Wilson v Robertsons (London) Ltd (No.2)* [2006] EWCA Civ 1088, [2007] C.C.L.R. 1 (not "realisation" on the facts).

[1159] CCA 1974 s.113(3)(a); see above, para.39-106. See also s.113(5).

[1160] CCA 1974 s.113(3)(c); see above, para.39-107. See also s.113(5).

[1161] CCA 1974 s.113(3)(b); see below, para.39-365.

[1162] Defined in CCA 1974 s.189(1), (5).

[1163] Under the Financial Services and Markets Act 2000 s.28A.

[1164] CCA 1974 s.113(3)(c). For such orders, see above, paras 39-064 and 39-065 and below, paras 39-249 and 39-250.

[1165] Defined in CCA 1974 s.189(1), (5).

[1166] CCA 1974 s.113(3)(c); see above, para.39-093.

[1167] CCA 1974 s.105(1), (7), (8); above, para.39-187.

[1168] CCA 1974 s.105(4), (5), (7), (8); above, para.39-187.

[1169] See below, para.39-197.

[1170] CCA 1974 ss.113(3)(c), 124(3).

(v)   where a declaration is made by a court under s.142(1) (refusal of an enforcement order)[1171] as respects any regulated agreement[1172]; and

(vi)   where security is provided in relation to a prospective agreement or transaction, and, before the agreement is made, the person providing the security by notice requires that s.106 shall apply to the security.[1173]

Pledges   Sections 114 to 122 of the 1974 Act contain special provisions[1174] relating to articles taken in pawn[1175] under a regulated agreement, other than a non-commercial agreement.[1176] The sections do not apply to a pledge of documents of title[1177] or of bearer bonds[1178]; nor, it is submitted, do they apply to choses in action[1179] or to deeds or certificates of title to land[1180] deposited with a creditor as security.   **39-194**

Pledges: Consumer Credit Directive   The Consumer Credit Directive[1181] does not apply to pawn agreements but, to maintain a coherent regime, the implementing provisions (which made significant changes to the Consumer Credit Act 1974 regime) generally have been extended to pawn agreements, However, the duty to provide pre-contractual explanations[1182] is modified. Moreover, s.55C (copy of draft agreement[1183]) and s.77B (statement of account to be provided on request[1184]) are inapplicable and there is no duty to assess the creditworthiness of the pawnor.[1185]   **39-195**

Negotiable instruments   The 1974 Act also contains provisions[1186] restricting the taking and negotiating of negotiable instruments[1187] in connection with regulated   **39-196**

1171 See below, para.39-210.

1172 CCA 1974 s.113(3)(d). But see s.113(4) (declaration as to part only).

1173 CCA 1974 s.113(6); above, para.39-189.

1174 See above, paras 33-137—33-144. See also CCA 1974 s.130(3). Section 114(3)(a) was amended by the Banking Act 1979 s.38(2). For regulations made, see SI 1983/1553; SI 1983/1565; SI 1983/1566; SI 1983/1568; SI 1998/998; SI 2004/3236.

1175 Defined in CCA 1974 s.189(1); but the definitions of "pawn" and "pledge" contained in that subsection are circular, for "pawn" refers to "pledge" and "pledge" to "pawn".

1176 CCA 1974 s.114(3)(b). "Non-commercial agreement" is defined in CCA 1974 s.189(1); above, para.39-049.

1177 "Documents of title" is not defined and it is submitted does not therefore bear the extended meaning given by s.1(4) of the Factors Act 1889. Credit advanced against the security of documents of title is not otherwise exempted from the regulation of the Act.

1178 Added by the Banking Act 1979: see above, para.33-137.

1179 *Harrold v Plenty* [1901] 2 Ch. 314.

1180 Which create a mortgage or charge. See also *Swanley Coal Co v Denton* [1906] 2 K.B. 873.

1181 See above, para.39-011.

1182 *FCA Handbook* CONC 4.2 (previously in CCA 1974 s.55A), see above, para.39-077.

1183 See above, para.39-079.

1184 See above, para.39-130.

1185 The duty was previously generally imposed by the (now repealed) CCA 1974 s.55B and is now in the *FCA Handbook*; see above, para.39-078.

1186 CCA 1974 ss.123–125. See CCA 1974 s.189B(3), Sch.2A: in ss.123 and 124, references to "debtor" in relation to "green deal plans" (as defined in CCA 1974 s.189(1), see below, para.39-257) are to be read as references to the "current bill payer"/"previous bill payer" (as defined in CCA 1974 s.189B(6)). See also above, paras 34-007, 34-081.

1187 Some doubt exists as to the meaning of "negotiable instrument" in these sections. An instrument is only a negotiable instrument if it can be negotiated: Bills of Exchange Act 1882 s.31(1). An instrument may not be in a state of negotiability: see ss.8(1), 36(1). cf. ss.81, 81A (inserted by s.1 of the Cheques Act 1992). See also *Hibernian Bank Ltd v Gyson and Hanson* [1939] 1 K.B. 483.

agreements, other than non-commercial agreements.[1188] In the first place, a creditor or owner is prohibited from taking a negotiable instrument, other than a banknote or cheque,[1189] in discharge of any sum payable by the debtor or hirer under a regulated agreement, or by any person as surety[1190] in relation to the agreement.[1191] Bills of exchange or promissory notes cannot therefore be taken in payment. Secondly, the creditor or owner is prohibited from negotiating[1192] a cheque taken by him in discharge of a sum payable as mentioned above except to a banker.[1193] Thirdly, the creditor or owner is prohibited from taking a negotiable instrument as security for the discharge of any sum payable as mentioned above.[1194] The old practice of taking, for example, a promissory note as security for payment under an instalment credit agreement has therefore been ruled out.

39-197 **Effect of contravention**   After any contravention of these provisions in relation to a sum payable by the debtor or hirer under a regulated agreement, the agreement under which the sum is payable is enforceable against the debtor or hirer on an order of the court only.[1195] After any contravention of these provisions in relation to a sum payable by any surety, the security[1196] is enforceable on an order of the court only[1197] and, in such case, if an application for an order is dismissed, except on technical grounds[1198] only, the security is rendered invalid.[1199]

39-198   A person who takes a negotiable instrument in contravention of s.123(1) or (3) is not a holder in due course and is not entitled to enforce the instrument.[1200] The 1974 Act does not, however, otherwise seek to undermine the protection of a holder in due course and deals specifically with the effect of contravention on the rights arising under and on the instrument.[1201]

[1188] s.123(5). For the definition of "non-commercial agreement", see CCA 1974 s.189(1); above, para.39-049. See also the exemption by order under s.123(6): SI 1984/435 (certain consumer hire agreements which have a connection with a country outside the UK).

[1189] Not defined in the Act, but see s.73 of the Bills of Exchange Act 1882.

[1190] Defined in CCA 1974 s.189(1); above, para.39-183.

[1191] CCA 1974 s.123(1).

[1192] Not defined in the Act, but see s.31 of the Bills of Exchange Act 1882.

[1193] CCA 1974 s.123(2). To a banker within the meaning of s.1 of the Bills of Exchange Act 1882; see above, para.34-246.

[1194] CCA 1974 s.123(3). As to when a negotiable instrument is considered to have been taken by way of security, see s.123(4).

[1195] CCA 1974 s.124(1). See also CCA 1974 ss.127 (below, para.39-200), 129(1), 142(1). CPR Pt 7 PD 7B.

[1196] Defined in CCA 1974 s.189(1); above, para.39-180.

[1197] CCA 1974 s.124(2). See also CCA 1974 ss.127 (below, para.39-200), 129(1), 142(1). CPR Pt 7 PD 7B.

[1198] Defined in CCA 1974 s.189(1), (5).

[1199] CCA 1974 ss.106, 124(3). See above, para.39-192. The same result ensues if an application to enforce the agreement is dismissed except on technical grounds only: see CCA 1974 ss.106, 113(3)(c).

[1200] CCA 1974 s.125(1).

[1201] CCA 1974 s.125(2)–(4); see above, paras 34-082 and 34-083.

(1) Judicial Control[1202]

Jurisdiction and parties   In England and Wales the county court has *exclusive*[1203] **39-199**
jurisdiction to hear and determine any action by the creditor or owner[1204] to
enforce[1205] a regulated agreement[1206] or any security[1207] relating to the action, and
any action to enforce a linked transaction[1208] against the debtor or hirer or his
relative.[1209] The High Court has no jurisdiction to entertain such an action and it
must be transferred to the county court.[1210] A judgment or order of a county court
for payment of a sum in proceedings arising out of a regulated agreement is enforceable in a county court only.[1211] Except as provided by rules of court,[1212] all the parties to a regulated agreement, and any surety,[1213] must be made parties to any
proceedings relating to the agreement.[1214]

Enforcement orders in cases of infringement   Section 127(1)[1215] of the 1974 Act **39-200**
confers upon the court a wide discretion as to whether, and, if so, on what terms, it

---

[1202] See Guest and Lloyd, *Encyclopedia of Consumer Credit Law* (1975, looseleaf), paras 2-128—2-
145; and Goode, *Consumer Credit: Law and Practice*, Pt C, Ch.46. Note also the requirements of
the Pre-Action Protocol on Debt Claims ("Debt PAP") in force on October 1, 2017.

[1203] In Northern Ireland the jurisdiction of the county court is permissive and not mandatory: CCA 1974
ss.141(4), 143, SR 1981/225 Ord.30 r.3. See (on Northern Irish position): *AIB Group (UK) Plc v
Keenan* [2012] NIQB 16. For transfer from the High Court, see CCA 1974 s.141(2), and below. See
also *Guildprime Specialists Contractors Ltd v Knight* Unreported September 24, 2012, EAT (EAT
has no jurisdiction to consider enforceability of regulated credit agreement (loan to employee)).

[1204] But a debtor or hirer is not so restricted.

[1205] See *Mills v Grove Securities Ltd* [1996] C.C.L.R. 74, CA: service of statutory demand under
Insolvency Act 1986 s.268 and (by concession) presentation of a bankruptcy petition by creditor in
relation to regulated agreement not "action … to enforce a regulated agreement".

[1206] The exclusive jurisdiction does not apply to exempt agreements (see above, para.39-038), but it does
apply to "non-commercial agreements" (as defined in CCA 1974 s.189(1), above, para.39-049). See
CPR Pt 7 r.9 7PD-003. County Courts Act 1984 s.21 (actions for recovery of land and actions where
title is in question) does not apply to a mortgage securing an agreement which is a regulated agreement (s.21(9)). CPR Pt 7PD 7B.

[1207] Defined in CCA 1974 s.189(1); see above, para.39-180.

[1208] Defined in CCA 1974 ss.19(1), 189(1); see above, paras 39-055 et seq.

[1209] CCA 1974 s.141(1). See CCA 1974 s.189B(3), Sch.2A: in s.141(1), (2), (3A), (3B), references to
"debtor" in relation to "green deal plans" (as defined in CCA 1974 s.189(1), see below, para.39-
257) are to be read as references to the "improver"/"current bill payer"/"previous bill payer" (as
defined in CCA 1974 s.189B(6)). See also the Civil Jurisdiction and Judgments Act 1982 Pt II and
Schs 4–7 (and SI 1990/2591) and the Civil Jurisdiction and Judgments Act 1991. For "relative", see
CCA 1974 ss.184(1), 189(1).

[1210] CCA 1974 s.141(2); *Sovereign Leasing Plc v Ali* [1992] C.C.L.R. 1. The High Court must of its own
motion set aside any default judgment entered in such an action: *Automobile Financial Services v
Docherty* Unreported November 10, 1987. Originally it was held that the High Court had no power
to strike out such an action, but only to transfer it: *Sovereign Leasing Plc v Ali*, above. But see now
s.40(1)(b) of the County Courts Act 1984, as substituted by s.2(1) of the Courts and Legal Services
Act 1990 and *Restick v Crickmore, The Times,* December 3, 1993, CA; *Barclays Bank Plc v Brooks*
[1997] C.C.L.R. 60.

[1211] High Court and County Courts (Jurisdiction) Order 1991 (SI 1991/724) art.8(1A) (as amended by
SI 1995/205).

[1212] CPR Pt 7 r.9, 7PD-003 para.9.1. CPR Pt 7 PD7B paras 9.1 and 9.2.

[1213] Defined in CCA 1974 s.189(1); see above, para.39-183.

[1214] CCA 1974 s.141(5).

[1215] See CCA 1974 s.189B(3), Sch.2A: in s.127, references to "debtor" in relation to "green deal plans"
(as defined in CCA 1974 s.189(1), see below, para.39-257) are to be read as references to the
"improver"/"current bill payer"/"previous bill payer" (as defined in CCA 1974 s.189B(6)).

will make an enforcement order[1216] in cases of various infringements of the Act. In the case of an application for an enforcement order under s.55(2) (disclosure of information),[1217] s.61B(3) (duty to supply copy of overdraft agreement),[1218] s.65(1) (improperly executed agreements),[1219] s.105(7)(a) or (b) (improperly executed security instruments),[1220] s.111(2) (failure to serve copy of notice on surety),[1221] or s.124(1) or (2) (taking of a negotiable instrument in contravention of s.123),[1222] the court is to dismiss the application[1223] if, but only if, it considers it just to do so having regard to:

(i)   the prejudice caused to any person by the contravention in question, and the degree of culpability for it[1224]; and

(ii)   the powers conferred on the court by s.127(2) (which permits the court, if it appears just to do so, to reduce or discharge any sum payable by the debtor or hirer, or any surety,[1225] so as to compensate him for prejudice suffered as a result of the contravention in question[1226]), and by ss.135[1227] and 136[1228] of the Act.[1229]

As has already been pointed out,[1230] the provisions providing for "irredeemably unenforceable" agreements,[1231] where the court was precluded altogether from making an enforcement order, have been repealed.[1232]

39-201 Enforcement orders on death of debtor or hirer   The court may make an order under s.86(2) of the 1974 Act enforcing an unsecured or partly secured agreement on the death of a debtor or hirer[1233] if, but only if, the creditor or owner proves that

---

[1216] Defined in CCA 1974 s.189(1). See CPR Pt 7 r.9 7PD–003 para.3.1(6), 7.4, CPR Pt7 PD7B. Given the "multifactorial assessment" that must be made by the court, summary judgment is unlikely to be available: *Newmafruit Farms Ltd v Pither* [2016] EWHC 2205 (QB), [2017] C.C.L.R. 8.

[1217] See above, para.39-076, added on February 10, 2011 by SI 2010/1010 reg.18.

[1218] See above, para.39-092, added on February 10, 2011 by SI 2010/1010 reg.12.

[1219] See above, para.39-093.

[1220] See above, para.39-187.

[1221] See above, para.39-174.

[1222] See above, para.39-197.

[1223] For the effect of dismissal on security, see CCA 1974 ss.106, 113(3); above, para.39-193.

[1224] For cases were no enforcement order was made, see: *PB Leasing Ltd v Patel and Patel (t/a Plankhouse Stores)* [1995] C.C.L.R. 82, Cty Ct; *Smerdon v Ellis* [1997] C.L.Y. 960, Cty Ct; *Re Dixon-Vincent* [1997] C.L.Y. 958; *Rendle v Hicks* [1998] C.L.Y. 2504; *Rahman v Brassil* [1998] C.L.Y. 2503, Cty Ct.

[1225] Defined in CCA 1974 s.189(1); see above, para.39-183.

[1226] See *National Guardian Mortgage Corp v Wilkes* [1993] C.C.L.R. 1, Cty Ct (interest rate reduced); *Rank Xerox Ltd v Hepple* [1994] C.C.L.R. 1, Cty Ct (amount payable reduced); *Hatfield v Hiscock* [1998] C.C.L.R. 68, Cty Ct; *London North Securities Ltd v Meadows* [2005] EWCA Civ 956, [2005] C.C.L.R. 7 (PPP premium not payable); *Wilson v Hurstanger Ltd* 206 WL 2334292, Cty Ct, affirmed [2007] EWCA Civ 299, [2007] C.C.L.R. 2 (administrative and legal costs discharged).

[1227] See below, para.39-208.

[1228] See below, para.39-209.

[1229] See *Nissan Finance UK v Lockhart* [1993] C.C.L.R. 39, CA: Court of Appeal will not normally interfere with the exercise of the discretion conferred by CCA 1974 s.127(1) unless there has been a failure to exercise it on the right principles.

[1230] See above, para.39-094.

[1231] The now repealed CCA 1974 s.127(3)–(5).

[1232] Consumer Credit Act 2006 s.15 (in relation to agreements made on or after April 6, 2007).

[1233] See above, para.39-175; and see CPR Pt 7 r.9 7PD–003 7.4; CCR Ord.49 r.4(9). CPR Pt 7 PD 7B.

he has been unable to satisfy himself that the present and future obligations of the debtor or hirer under the agreement are likely to be discharged.[1234]

Time orders   Section 129 of the 1974 Act empowers the court in certain circumstances to make a "time order".[1235] The four situations where a time order can be made are as follows[1236]: first,[1237] on an application by the creditor or owner for an enforcement order[1238]; second,[1239] on an application made by a debtor or hirer after service on him of a default notice under s.87,[1240] or a notice under s.76(1)[1241] or 98(1)[1242]; third,[1243] on an application made by a debtor or hirer after he has been given a "NOSIA" under s.86B[1244] or 86C[1245]; fourth[1246] in an action brought by a creditor or owner to enforce a regulated agreement or any security,[1247] or recover possession of any goods or land to which a regulated agreement relates.[1248] It will be seen that the court's power to make a time order extends to practically all[1249] applications and actions connected with the enforcement of a regulated agreement or security provided in relation thereto.   **39-202**

Types of order   The time order must provide for one or both of the two following orders, as the court considers just—(1) payment by the debtor or hirer or any surety[1250] of any sum owed[1251] under a regulated agreement or a security[1252] by such   **39-203**

[1234] CCA 1974 s.128. See CCA 1974 s.189B(3), Sch.2A: in s.128, references to "debtor" in relation to "green deal plans" (as defined in CCA 1974 s.189(1), see below, para.39-257) are to be read as references to the "current bill payer"/"previous bill payer" (as defined in CCA 1974 s.189B(6)).

[1235] See CCA 1974 s.189B(3), Sch.2A: in s.129, references to "debtor" in relation to "green deal plans" (as defined in CCA 1974 s.189(1), see below, para.39-257) are to be read as references to the "current bill payer"/"previous bill payer" (as defined in CCA 1974 s.189B(6)). For the content on an application for a time order, see CPR Pt 7 r.9 7PD–003 7,3; CCR Ord.49 r.4(5). CPR Pt 7 PD 7B 3.1; Pt 55 PD 55, 7.1; Form N440. See *Jenkins v Cedar Holdings Ltd* [1988] C.C.L.R. 34, Cty Ct: time order made by Registrar was a final and not interlocutory order (so any appeal subject to (now) CPR Sch.2 CCR Ord.37 r.6). See CCA 1974 s.129(3) in relation to Scotland.

[1236] CCA 1974 s.129(1), as amended (i) by the Debtors (Scotland) Act 1987 s.108(1) and Sch.6 para.17 (to refer to the qualification in subs.(3) in relation to Scotland); and (ii) by the Consumer Credit Act 2006 s.16 (to add subs.(1)(ba), see below).

[1237] CCA 1974 s.129(1)(a).

[1238] Defined in CCA 1974 s.189(1) to mean an order under (i) CCA 1974 s.65(1) (above, para.39-093), (ii) CCA 1974 s.105(7)(a) or (b) (above, para.39-187), (iii) CCA 1974 s.111(2) (above, para.39-174) or (iv) CCA 1974 s.124(1) or (2) (above, para.39-197).

[1239] s.129(1)(b). Note that a notice under CCA 1974 s.98A (see above, para.39-173) is not listed.

[1240] See above, para.39-170.

[1241] See above, para.39-164.

[1242] See above, para.39-172.

[1243] s.129(1)(ba), added (from October 1, 2008, see SI 2007/330) by the Consumer Credit Act 2006 s.16, but regardless of when the agreement was made.

[1244] See above, para.39-131.

[1245] See above, para.39-134. But see CCA 1974 s.129A (inserted by Consumer Credit Act 2006 s.16(2)): debtor or hirer may only make an application for a time order if he has (i) given the creditor or owner a "notice of intent" indicating that he intends to apply for a time order and making proposals as to payment and (ii) waited 14 days.

[1246] s.129(1)(c).

[1247] Defined in CCA 1974 s.189(1); see above, para.39-180.

[1248] See also CCA 1974 ss.90 (below, para.39-361), 92 (below, para.39-366), 126 (below, para.39-537).

[1249] But not after the service of a s.98A(3) or (4)(b) notice (see above, para.39-173). See also *Mills v Grove Securities Ltd* [1996] C.C.L.R. 74 (statutory demand under the Insolvency Act 1986 can be set aside). But see s.130(3) (pledges).

[1250] Defined in CCA 1974 s.189(1); see above, para.39-183.

[1251] See *Cedar Holdings Ltd v Jenkins* [1988] C.C.L.R. 34, Cty Ct; *First National Bank Plc v Syed* [1991]

instalments, payable at such times, as the court, having regard to the means[1253] of the debtor or hirer and any surety, considers reasonable[1254]; (2) the remedying by the debtor or hirer of any breach of a regulated agreement (other than non-payment of money) within such period as the court may specify.[1255] The first type of order is not dissimilar to the type of instalment order that can already be made by the county court under the County Courts Act 1984.[1256] The second type of order, however, has a more far-reaching effect. Without prejudice to anything done[1257] by the creditor or owner before the commencement of the period specified in this type of order ("the relevant period"), he is precluded, while the relevant period subsists, from taking in relation to the agreement any action such as is mentioned in s.87(1)[1258] of the 1974 Act (terminating the agreement, demanding earlier payment of any sum, recovering possession of goods or land, enforcing a security, etc).[1259] Further, if the agreement, for example, provides for the payment of compensation in the event of failure to repair, he cannot treat the provision as to compensation as operative while the relevant period relating to remedying the failure to repair subsists.[1260] During the relevant period the rights and remedies of the creditor or owner are completely suspended. If the breach to which the order relates is remedied within the relevant period, it is treated as not having occurred.[1261] If it is not remedied, at the end of the relevant period, but not before,[1262] the creditor or owner may proceed to enforce his contractual rights.[1263]

39-204   **Discretionary**   The power of the court to make a time order is discretionary. In *First National Bank Plc v Syed*[1264] the Court of Appeal looked to the position of both the creditor and the debtor in deciding whether it was "just" to make a time order. Thus where there was history of default and merely sporadic payments by the debtor and a merely speculative (as opposed to realistic) prospect of an improvement in the debtor's finances, it considered that it was not "just" to require the creditor to

---

2 All E.R. 250; *Ashbroom Facilities v Bodley* [1992] C.C.L.R. 31, Cty Ct; *Cedar Holdings Ltd v Thompson* [1993] C.C.L.R. 7, Cty Ct; Taylor [1993] *Legal Action* (8)14. In *Southern and District Finance Plc v Barnes* [1995] C.L.Y. 726, CA Leggatt L.J. stated that, once a creditor brings possession proceedings, he demands payment of the whole sum outstanding under the charge and so, whether or not the whole loan has actually been called in, that that sum is "owed".

[1252] Defined in CCA 1974 s.189(1); see above, para.39-180.

[1253] Although by CCA 1974 s.130(1) the court is relieved from hearing evidence of means where, in accordance with rules of court, an offer to pay any sum by instalments is made by the debtor or hirer and accepted by the creditor or owner, difficulties can arise where the debtor or hirer makes no such offer, and does not appear, so that there may be no evidence of means.

[1254] CCA 1974 s.129(2)(a). See also CCA 1974 s.136; below, para.39-209.

[1255] CCA 1974 s.129(2)(b).

[1256] County Courts Act 1984 s.71. A time order of this type does not suspend the remedies of the creditor or owner. But see (in relation to hire-purchase, conditional sale and consumer hire agreements) CCA 1974 ss.130(2), 130(4), 133 and also s.135.

[1257] e.g. the creditor or owner may, for example, already have terminated the agreement but not repossessed goods, or both terminated and repossessed, but not recovered arrears of money due.

[1258] See above, para.39-166.

[1259] CCA 1974 s.130(5)(a).

[1260] CCA 1974 s.130(5)(b).

[1261] CCA 1974 s.130(5)(c).

[1262] Unless the order is revoked under CCA 1974 s.130(6).

[1263] Unless a fresh order is made.

[1264] [1991] 2 All E.R. 250. See also *Southern and District Finance Plc v Barnes* [1995] C.L.Y. 726, CA (no time order to be made where debtor unlikely to be able to resume repayment by at least the contractual instalments). cf. *Director General of Fair Trading v First National Bank Plc* [2001] UKHL 52, [2002] 1 A.C. 481 at [28].

accept instalments which were too small even to keep down the accruing interest on the debtor's account.

Variation and revocation   On the application of any person affected by a time order, the court may vary or revoke the order.[1265]

39-205

Interest payable on judgment debts   Section 130A[1266] of the 1974 Act imposes notification requirements in relation to post-judgment interest[1267] arising by virtue of a term in a regulated agreement, as it is not always obvious to judgment debtors that such interest is still payable.[1268] (The section does not apply in relation to post-judgment interest required to be paid under certain statutory provisions.[1269]) The section provides that a creditor or owner under a regulated agreement (other than a "non-commercial"[1270] or "small"[1271] agreement)[1272] cannot recover such interest on a judgment debt until he gives[1273] the debtor or hirer, free of charge,[1274] notice in the prescribed form[1275] after judgment and continues to give such a notice at intervals of not more than six months. Interest can only start running on the day the first notice is given[1276] and ceases to run if the requisite subsequent notice is not given within the six-month period, although it resumes running the day after notice is given.[1277]

39-206

Protection orders   The court on the application of the creditor or owner under a regulated agreement may make such orders as it thinks just for protecting any property of the creditor or owner, or property subject to any security, from dam-

39-207

[1265] CCA 1974 s.130(6). Presumably the court would revoke a time order on the application of the creditor or owner if the debtor or hirer failed to pay the instalments ordered to be paid.

[1266] Inserted by the Consumer Credit Act 2006 s.17 on October 1, 2008 (SI 2007/3300) and applicable to agreements whenever made but only as regards judgments debts arising after commencement (see the 2006 Act Sch.3 para.13). See CCA 1974 s.189B(3), Sch.2A: in s.130A, references to "debtor" in relation to "green deal plans" (as defined in CCA 1974 s.189(1), see below, para.39-257) are to be read as references to the "current bill payer"/"previous bill payer" (as defined in CCA 1974 s.189B(6)).

[1267] CCA 1974 s.130A(9) defines this as interest calculated by reference to the period after the giving of the judgment under which the judgment debt is payable.

[1268] See *Director General of Fair Trading v First National Bank Plc* [2001] UKHL 52, [2002] 1 A.C. 481: such a term, although it took the debtor by surprise, held not to be "unfair" under the Unfair Terms in Consumer Contract Regulations 1999 (SI 1999/2083), above paras 38-246 et seq. As noted above at para.38-220, those regulations are replaced, for contracts made on or after October 1, 2015, by provisions in the Consumer Rights Act 2015 Pt 2.

[1269] viz (a) the AJ (Scotland) Act 1972 s.4; (b) the Judgements Enforcement (NI) Order 1981; and (c) County Courts Act 1984 s.74. The County Court (Interest on Judgments Debts) Order 1991 (SI 1991/1184) (L.12) (made under County Courts Act 1984 s.74) provides that interest shall not be payable under that Order where the relevant judgment debt relates to a CCA 1974-regulated agreement.

[1270] Defined in CCA 1974 s.189(1), see above, para.39-049.

[1271] Defined in CCA 1974 s.17, see above, para.39-048.

[1272] CCA 1974 s.130A(8). And see the further limitation as to interest awarded under statute, noted above.

[1273] Defined in CCA 1974 s.189(1) (as amended by SI 2004/3236 art.2(2)) to mean "deliver or send by appropriate method".

[1274] CCA 1974 s.130A(4).

[1275] CCA 1974 s.130A(6) and see the Consumer Credit (Information Requirements and Duration of Licences and Charges) Regulations 2007 (SI 2007/1167) regs 34–35 and Sch.5 (as amended by SI 2008/1751). The notice may be incorporated in a statement (e.g. a statement under CCA 1974 ss.77–78) or other notice (e.g. under CCA 1974 s.86B, 86C or 87) given under the Act: CCA 1974 s.130A(5).

[1276] CCA 1974 s.130A(2).

[1277] CCA 1974 s.130A(3).

age or depreciation pending the determination of any proceedings under the Act, including orders restricting or prohibiting use of the property or giving directions as to its custody.[1278]

39-208 **Power to impose conditions, or suspend operation of order** If it considers it just to do so, the court may, in an order made by it in relation to a regulated agreement, include provisions making the operation of any term of the order conditional on the doing of specified acts by any party to the proceedings.[1279] In the same circumstances, the court may include provisions suspending the operation of any term of the order either until such time as the court subsequently directs, or until the occurrence of a specified act or omission.[1280] This latter power is used most frequently to suspend an order requiring the debtor under a hire-purchase or conditional sale agreement to deliver up the goods,[1281] or to suspend a possession order in the case of an agreement secured on land,[1282] but it is not confined to those situations. On the application of any person affected by a provision so inserted by the court, the court may vary the provision.[1283]

39-209 **Power to vary agreements and securities** The court may in an order made by it under the 1974 Act include such provision as it considers just for amending any agreement or security in consequence of a term of the order.[1284]

39-210 **Declaratory orders** Section 142 of the 1974 Act confers upon the county court[1285] jurisdiction to make declaratory orders in two situations. First, where under any provision of the Act a thing can be done by a creditor or owner on an enforcement order[1286] only, and either (a) the court dismisses (except on technical grounds only)[1287] an application for an enforcement order, or (b) where no such application has been made or such an application has been dismissed on technical grounds only, an interested party applies specially[1288] to the court for a declaration, the court may if it thinks just make a declaration that the creditor or owner is not entitled to do

---

[1278] CCA 1974 s.131. See also CPR Pt 25; CPR Pt 23.

[1279] CCA 1974 s.135(1)(a). See also CCA 1974 s.136, below, para.39-209.

[1280] CCA 1974 s.135(1)(b), subject to the limitations contained in s.135(2) (goods not in possession or control of a person) and s.135(3) (consumer hire agreements).

[1281] See below, paras 39-375, 39-377 and 39-454. But see CCA 1974 s.135(2).

[1282] See *Southern and District Finance Plc v Barnes* [1995] C.L.Y. 726, CA: possession order suspended so long as terms of time order complied with.

[1283] CCA 1974 s.135(4). Presumably the court is entitled thereby to revoke the provision.

[1284] CCA 1974 s.136. In *Southern and District Finance Ltd v Barnes* [1995] C.L.Y. 726, the Court of Appeal held that the court had jurisdiction in consequence of a time order under CCA 1974 s.129 to reduce the contractual rate of interest in rescheduling the debt. See also *Director General of Fair Trading v First National Bank Plc* [2001] UKHL 52, [2002] 1 A.C. 481 at [28]. See also the power of the court to reopen (and hence vary) agreements in the case of "unfair relationships": CCA 1974 s.140B, below, paras 39-212 et seq.

[1285] CCA 1974 s.189(1).

[1286] Defined in CCA 1974 s.189(1) to mean an order under (i) CCA 1974 s.65(1) (above, para.39-093), (ii) CCA 1974 s.105(7)(a) or (b) (above, para.39-187), (iii) CCA 1974 s.111(2) (above, para.39-174) or (iv) CCA 1974 s.124(1) or (2) (above, para.39-197). See *Carey v HSBC Bank Plc* [2009] EWHC 3417 (QB): no declaration under s.142 where the debtor alleged breach of CCA 1974 s.78 (see above, para.39-132), as the court has no power to make an enforcement order in such a case.

[1287] Defined in CCA 1974 s.189(1), (5).

[1288] i.e. under CCA 1974 s.142(1).

that thing,[1289] and thereafter no application for an enforcement order in respect of it can be entertained.[1290] A debtor or hirer, or a surety, can thus obtain a declaration that the creditor or owner is not entitled to do the thing in question, whether or not the creditor or owner applies to the court for an enforcement order. But this provision does not appear to entitle the creditor or owner to apply for a declaration that he is entitled to do the thing in question.[1291] In *Carey v HSBC Bank Plc*[1292] it was confirmed that s.142 is without prejudice to the general (discretionary) power of the court to grant declarations and that its purpose is to extend this general power so as to, in effect, enable the court (as well as granting the declaration) to bar any further application.

Secondly, where (a) a regulated agreement or linked transaction[1293] is cancelled **39-211** under s.69(1),[1294] or becomes subject to s.69(2),[1295] or (b) a regulated agreement is terminated under s.91,[1296] and an interested party[1297] applies specially[1298] to the court for a declaration, the court may make a declaration to that effect.[1299]

(m)   Unfair Relationships[1300]

Extortionate credit bargains   The Consumer Credit Act 1974[1301] originally **39-212** contained provisions[1302] enabling the court to reopen a credit agreement if it found that the credit bargain was "extortionate".[1303] The threshold for intervention (that payments were "grossly exorbitant" or the bargain otherwise "grossly" contravened

---

[1289] See CCA 1974 s.113(3)(d): effect on security.

[1290] CCA 1974 s.142(1). In *Watson v Progressive Financial Services Ltd* Unreported April 21, 2009, Liverpool Cty Ct it was held that the wording of s.142(1) ("is not entitled"; "and thereafter no application ... shall be entertained") presupposes an extant agreement where the creditor still needs to obtain an enforcement order and hence an order under s.142(1) could no longer be made once the debtor had fulfilled his obligations.

[1291] Nevertheless, it seems the creditor or owner could bring such an action (under the general (discretionary) power of the court to grant declarations) in the High Court (CPR Pt 50 r.2), since this would not be an action to which CCA 1974 s.141 or CCA 1974 s.189(1) applies. On the general (discretionary) power, see *Carey v HSBC Bank Plc*, considered in the text.

[1292] [2009] EWHC 3417 (QB).

[1293] Defined in CCA 1974 ss.19(1), 189(1); above, paras 39-055 et seq.

[1294] See above, para.39-106.

[1295] See above, para.39-108.

[1296] See below, para.39-365.

[1297] This presumably includes the creditor or owner.

[1298] i.e. under CCA 1974 s.142(2).

[1299] CCA 1974 s.142(2). Again, this provision would appear to preclude an application for a declaration that the agreement or transaction has *not* been cancelled or *not* become subject to CCA 1974 s.69(2), or that the agreement has *not* been terminated under CCA 1974 s.91.

[1300] See Guest and Lloyd, *Encyclopedia of Consumer Credit Law* (1975, looseleaf), paras 2-141A—2-141D; and Goode, *Consumer Credit: Law and Practice*, Pt C, Ch.47; Brown [2009] L.M.C.L.Q. 90; Lomnicka [2012] J.B.L. 713; Brown (2016) 36(2) L.S. 230–257.

[1301] See also (on the existing equitable jurisdiction of the Chancery Division in relation to mortgages) *Cityland and Property (Holdings) Ltd v Dabrah* [1968] Ch. 166.

[1302] See the similar provision in the Insolvency Act 1986 s.343 for the reopening of credit transactions of an individual who is adjudged bankrupt. See also Insolvency Act 1986 s.244 (winding-up of companies).

[1303] ss.137–140 came into force on May 16, 1977, SI 1977/325 (c.11). See 29th edn of this work, paras 39-191 and Bentley and Howells [1989] Conv. 234. The OFT reviewed ss.137–140 in *Unjust Credit Transactions* (1991) and recommended the widening of the operation of the sections by the substitution of "unjust credit transaction" for "extortionate credit bargain", but this was never implemented and has been overtaken by the introduction of the new "unfair relationship" provisions.

fair dealing) was very high[1304] and hence very few challenges on this basis were successful.[1305] The Consumer Credit Act 2006 repealed and replaced these provisions[1306] with new ss.140A–140D.[1307] The new provisions essentially lower the threshold to one of a relationship between the creditor and the debtor (taking into account both the credit agreement and "any related agreement") that is "unfair to the debtor".[1308] Such a claim succeeded in the Supreme Court in the context of the sale of PPI in *Plevin v Paragon Personal Finance Ltd*.[1309]

[1304] *Broadwick Financial Services v Spencer* [2002] EWCA Civ 35, [2002] 1 All E.R. (Comm) 446 at [80]. See also *First National Securities Ltd v Bertrand* [1980] C.C.L.R. 1, Cty Ct; *A Ketley Ltd v Scott* [1981] I.C.R. 241; *Wills v Wood* (1984) 128 S.J. 222, CA; *Davies v Directloans Ltd* [1986] 1 W.L.R. 823.

[1305] In *Woodstead Finance v Petrou, The Times,* January 23, 1986, the Court of Appeal did not disturb a mortgage at an APR of 42.5 per cent p.a. as this rate was normal for short-term loans. And see *A Ketley Ltd v Scott* [1981] I.C.R. 241; and *Davies v Directloans Ltd* [1986] 1 W.L.R. 823, where interest rates of 48 per cent and 21.7 per cent (APR), on agreements that were secured by a land mortgage, were upheld. Contrast, however, *Barcabe v Edwards* [1983] C.C.L.R. 11, Cty Ct, interest of 100 per cent p.a. (APR 319 per cent) on unsecured loan reduced to 40 per cent p.a.; *Devogate v Jarvis* Unreported 1987, Cty Ct, interest of APR 39 per cent reduced to 30 per cent where loan was well secured; *Shahabinia v Gyachi* Unreported 1988 interest rates on non-commercial loans of 104 per cent, 78 per cent and 156 per cent reduced to 15 per cent; *Prestonwell Ltd v Capon* Unreported 1988, Cty Ct, interest rate of 42 per cent flat reduced by half, the risk being low; *Castle Phillips & Co v Wilkinson* [1992] C.C.L.R. 83, Cty Ct interest rate of 4 per cent per month (interest being deducted from the loan) on secured "bridging" loan reduced to 20 per cent p.a.; *Batooneh v Asombang* [2003] EWHC 2111 (QB) (interest rate of 100 per cent on informal commercial loan reduced to 25 per cent); *County Leasing Ltd v East* [2007] EWHC 2907 (reopening of business loan of over £370,000).

[1306] Consumer Credit Act 2006 ss.19–22 on April 6, 2007 (SI 2007/123). The new provisions essentially apply to agreements *whenever made*, as long as they have not been paid off (become "completed agreements") by April 6, 2008 (see the (complex) transitional provisions in the 2006 Act Sch.3 para.1(2) (definition of "completed agreement") and para.14). On the application of the transitional provisions, see *Soulsby and Soulsby v FirstPlus Financial Group Plc* Unreported March 5, 2010, QBD, Leeds & District Registry Mercantile Court (old provisions applied) and *Barnes v Black Horse Ltd* [2011] EWHC 1416 (QB) (new provisions applied, see below, para.39-214).

[1307] s.140D (Advice and information from OFT) was repealed on April 1, 2014, by SI 2013/1881 art.20(4), when consumer credit regulation was transferred to the FCA (see above, para.39-002) as the FCA has general power to issue guidance under the Financial Services and Markets Act 2000 s.139A.

[1308] See further, below, para.39-217—39-222.

[1309] [2014] UKSC 61 (see further below, para.39-222) and see *Scotland v British Credit Trust Ltd* [2014] EWCA Civ 790. For previous cases where the claim was successful, see: *Patel v Patel* [2009] EWHC 3264 ("exorbitant" interest and lack of transparency in loans between friends); *Morrison v Betterpace Ltd (t/a Log Book Loans)* Unreported September 1, 2009, Lowestoft Cty Ct (APR of 485.25 of refinancing loan reduced to APR of 343.4 per cent charged on previous loan); *MBNA Europe Ltd v Thorius*, Newcastle Cty Ct [2010] E.C.C. 8 (sale of PPI); *Barons Finance Ltd v Olubisi* Unreported April 26, 2010, Mayor's & City of London Ct (vulnerable consumer "exploited")); *Nelmes v NRAM Plc* [2016] EWCA Civ 491 (in business context, payment by the lender of a "procurement fee" (being half the arrangement fee charged by the lender to the borrower) to the borrower's broker deprived the borrower of the disinterested advice of his broker and hence rendered the credit relationship "unfair"; lender accountable to borrower for all the undisclosed "procurement fee" plus interest from the date of payment); *Townson v FCE Bank Plc (t/a Ford Credit)* Unreported June 23, 2016, Birmingham Cty Ct ("unfair relationship" found where PPI (of which the debtor was unaware and by implication did not want) was sold by car dealer to a debtor under a hire-purchase agreement). For cases where the claim was unsuccessful, see: *Khodari v Tamimi* [2009] EWCA Civ 1109, [2010] C.C.L.R. 3 ("very large" 10 per cent charge for short-term loans to wealthy compulsive gambler, where credit risk was high and "defendant wanted these loans and could well afford to repay them"); *Maple Leaf Macro Volatility Master Fund v Rouvroy* [2009] EWHC 257, [2009] C.C.L.R. 9 ((obiter) funding agreement to assist acquisition of control of company); *McGuffick v RBS Plc* [2009] EWHC 2386 (reporting to credit reference agencies whilst agreement was "temporarily unenforceable" due

Wide application of "unfair relationship" provisions It is important to note **39-213**
four points concerning the application of the "unfair relationship" provisions. First,
the scope of the provisions is wide in generally extending to all consumer credit
agreements with individuals[1310] and hence they apply irrespective of the size of the
loan or purpose of the credit.[1311] The provisions apply not only to regulated credit

---

[1310] to breach of CCA 1974 s.77); *Carey v HSBC Bank Plc* [2009] EWHC 3417 (QB) (breach of CCA 1974 s.78); *Shaw v Nine Regions Ltd* [2009] EWHC 3514 ("log book" loan with high interest rate of 119 per cent per annum); *Black Horse Ltd v Speak* [2010] EWHC 1866 (QB); *Consolidated Finance Ltd v Hunter* [2010] B.P.I.R. 1322 (loan at market rate for similar short-term bridging loans); *Paragon Mortgages Ltd v McEwan-Peters* [2011] EWHC 2491 (Comm); *Rahman v HSBC Bank Plc* [2012] EWHC 11 (Ch); *Deutsche Bank (Suisse) SA v Khan* [2013] EWHC 482 (Comm), noted at [2013] C.C.L.R. 5; *Chubb v Dean* [2013] EWHC 1282 (Ch); *Conlon v Black Horse Ltd* [2013] EWCA Civ 1658, [2014] C.C.L.R. 4; *Gardner v Clydesdale Bank Ltd* [2013] EWHC 4356 (Ch); *Link Financial Ltd v North Wilson* [2014] EWHC 252 (Ch), [2014] C.C.L.R. 6; *Scotland v British Credit Trust Ltd* [2014] EWCA Civ 790 (mis-selling of PPI); *Graves v Capital Home Loans* [2014] EWCA Civ 1297 (buy-to-let loan); *McMullon v Secure the Bridge Ltd* [2015] EWCA Civ 884 (bridging loan); *Barclays Bank Plc v McMillan* [2015] EWHC 1596 (Comm) (loan to finance US law firm's partner's capital subscription on usual terms); *Bluestone Mortgages Ltd v Mumon* [2015] EW Misc B4 (CC) (refusal of permission to appeal the decision of the county court that failure to notify in advance that mortgagee would invoke usual clause in buy-to-let mortgage permitting him to pay outstanding lease charges if mortgagor failed to do so, did not give rise to an unfair relationship), *Commercial First Business Ltd v Pickup* [2017] C.T.L.C. 1, [2017] C.C.L.R. 15 (although only the fact (and not the amount) of commission was disclosed by the brokers, the debtors were experienced property investors and knew all the relevant facts (*Deutsche Bank (Suisse) SA v Khan* applied)); *Clydesdale Bank Plc v Gough (t/a JC Gough & Sons)* [2017] EWHC 2230 (Ch) (in business lending context where debtor and guarantor had independent legal advice, no unfairness found in the way the lender had exercised or enforced its rights against both); *Santander UK Plc v Wells* [2017] EWHC 2413 (Ch) (claimant had delayed too long in making claim); *Ulster Bank I td v Esmulli* [2017] NICh 14; (no unfairness found in business lending context where debtor was experienced property developer); *Holyoake v Candy* [2017] EWHC 3397 (Ch) (permission to appeal refused by Court of Appeal: [2018] C.C.L.R. 8) (Nugee J. rejected an "unfairness" claim in business lending context, applying *Deutsche Bank (Suisse) SA v Khan*, above, where both debtor and creditor were property developers); *Carney v NM Rothschild and Sons Ltd* [2018] EWHC 958 (Comm); (no "unfairness" where the debtors received independent advice and the loan agreement made it clear (via "basis" clauses) that the creditor was not providing advice); *Hodell v Clydesdale Bank Plc* [2018] EWHC 1009 (QB) (no "unfair relationship" in commercial lending to experienced property development partnership).

[1310] "Credit agreement" for these purposes is defined in CCA 1974 s.140C(1) to mean (essentially) a consumer credit agreement (see above, para.39-016). Hence corporate debtors are not covered: *Bank of Ireland (UK) Plc v McLaughlin* [2016] NICA 33, [2017] C.C.L.R. 5 (refusal of appeal from the lower court ([2014] N.I.Q.B. 104) that a guarantor of a corporate debtor could not invoke the unfair relationship provisions); *Newmafruit Farms Ltd v Pither* [2016] EWHC 2205 (QB), [2017] C.C.L.R. 8 (corporate debtor could not invoke the unfair relationship provisions). Moreover, s.140C(2) defines "debtor" and "creditor" for these purpose to cover assignees, in the same way as does CCA 1974 s.189(1) in relation to consumer credit agreements. See the definition of "credit" in CCA 1974 s.9(1): above, para.39-019. The power to reopen does not apply to hiring agreements, but see CCA 1974 s.132 (above, para.33-090). Nor does it apply to a sale and leaseback transaction: *Lavin v Johnson* [2002] EWCA Civ 1138 (not "credit", for the purposes of the previous extortionate credit bargain provisions). See also *Maple Leaf Macro Volatility Master Fund v Rouvroy* [2009] EWHC 257 (funding agreement did not provide "credit"). See s.140C(5)–(6) (adaptation of language). And see CCA 1974 s.189C(1)(a): a "green deal consumer credit agreement" (as defined in CCA 1974 s.189B(8) to mean a green deal plan (as defined in CCA 1974 s.189(1), see below, para.39-257) that is to be treated as a consumer credit agreement for the purpose of this Act by virtue of CCA 1974 s.189B(1) is to be treated as credit agreement for the purposes of s.140A and 140B. And note CCA 1974 s.189B(3), Sch.2A: in s.140A, references to "debtor" in relation to "green deal plans" are to be read as references to the "improver"/"current bill payer"/"previous bill payer" (as defined in CCA 1974 s.189B(6)).

[1311] *Patel v Patel* [2009] EWHC 3264: business loan (albeit between family members) of £200,000 re-

agreements but also to most "exempt agreements",[1312] as well as "non-commercial agreements"[1313] (and even, in theory, "small agreements"[1314]). They do not, however, apply to an agreement that is an exempt agreement by virtue of being a regulated land mortgage or home purchase plan.[1315]

39-214 **"Any related agreement"**   Second, the power of the court is not confined to an examination and reopening of the terms of the credit agreement itself (the "main agreement"[1316]), but extends to an examination and reopening of "any related agreement".[1317] This term is defined[1318] to cover three categories of agreement: (a) any earlier credit agreement(s) consolidated by the main agreement to be reopened[1319]; (b) a "linked transaction"[1320] in relation to the main agreement or any previous agreement consolidated by it[1321]; and (c) any security[1322] provided in relation to the main agreement, any previous credit agreement consolidated by it or a linked transaction within (b).[1323]

39-215 **"Spent" agreements**   Third, even if the relationship between the creditor and debtor has come to an end, most usually if the debtor has repaid the credit, this does

---

opened. And note the "buy-to-let" loans considered (but not re-opened) in *Paragon Mortgages Ltd v McEwan-Peters* [2011] EWHC 2491 (Comm); *Graves v Capital Home Loans Ltd* [2014] EWCA Civ 1297; *Bluestone Mortgages Ltd v Momoh* [2015] EW Misc B4 (CC) and *Nelmes v NRAM Plc* [2016] EWCA Civ 491. See also *Holyoake v Candy* [2017] EWHC 3397 (Ch) (business loan of £12 million—but no "unfairness").

[1312] For exempt agreements, see above, paras 39-038 et seq. There are two exceptions: see below.

[1313] Defined in CCA 1974 s.189(1); above, para.39-049; *Khodari v Tamimi* [2009] EWCA Civ 1109.

[1314] CCA 1974 s.17; above, para.39-048.

[1315] i.e. exempt under RAO art.60C(2) (see above, para.39-039): s.140A(5). See *AIB v Donnelly* [2015] NI Master 13 (Master Hardstaff) (confirmation that unfair relationship provisions do not apply to FSMA 2000 regulated mortgage contracts). Hence when the Mortgage Credit Directive (see above, para.39-003) was implemented on March 21, 2016 and most second charge residential mortgages became "'regulated mortgage contracts" under the 2000 Act regime, this protection was lost for such mortgages.

[1316] As so designated in CCA 1974 s.140C(4).

[1317] CCA 1974 s.140A(1); s.140B.

[1318] CCA 1974 s.140C(4).

[1319] CCA 1974 s.140C(4)(a). See s.140C(7) (meaning of "consolidated" for these purposes) and s.140C(8) (series of consolidated agreement are "related agreements" in relation to final main agreement). See *Barnes v Black Horse Ltd* [2011] EWHC 1416 (QB): "related" agreements that were consolidated into a new agreement were subject to the old "extortionate credit bargain" provisions (see above, para.39-212) and not the new "unfair relationship" regime (because they were "completed" agreements, see the transitional provisions in the Consumer Credit Act 2006 Sch.3 para.14, above, para.39-213), but they were nevertheless held relevant to the application of s.140A to the new agreement (even though no order under s.140B could be made in relation to them).

[1320] CCA 1974 s.19, see above, paras 39-055 et seq. And see CCA 1974 s.140A(5): if main (credit) agreement is not regulated, to be treated as such for purposes of deciding if a transaction is a "linked transaction". Examples are compulsory PPI (CCA 1974 s.19(1)(a)) and optional PPI (CCA 1974 s.19(1)(c)): see *Townson v FCE Bank Plc (t/a Ford Credit)* Unreported June 23, 2016, Birmingham Cty Ct (PPI policy held to be a "linked transaction" within s.19(1)(c) in relation to the credit agreement (and hence a "related transaction") and "unfair relationship" found where that PPI (of which the debtor was unaware and by implication did not want) was sold by car dealer to a debtor under a hire-purchase agreement). See also the linked transactions considered relevant in *Holyoake v Candy* [2017] EWHC 3397 (Ch).

[1321] CCA 1974 s.140C(4)(b).

[1322] CCA 1974 s.189(1) and see above, para.39-180. See CCA 1974 s.140C(6) (if main (credit) agreement is not regulated, to be treated as such for purposes of definition of "security" in CCA 1974 s.189(1) in this context).

[1323] CCA 1974 s.140C(4)(c).

not preclude the court making a determination.[1324] Thus it may reopen credit agreements even if they have ended.[1325]

Discretion   Finally, even if the relationship is found to be "unfair to the debtor", **39-216** the court has a residual discretion whether or not to reopen the credit agreement.[1326] The court might refuse to do so if, for example, the debtor unduly delayed in seeking relief[1327] or the debtor failed to disclose his true financial position[1328] or the debtor obtained the credit by false representations.[1329]

When relationship is "unfair to the debtor"   Section 140A(1) enables a court **39-217** to make an order under s.140B[1330] if it finds that the relationship between the creditor and the debtor arising out of a credit agreement, or that agreement taken with any "related agreement",[1331] is "unfair to the debtor" as a result of one or more of three factors. Those factors[1332] are: (a) any of the terms of the agreement (or any "related agreement"); (b) the way in which the creditor has exercised or enforced any of his rights under the agreement (or any "related agreement"); (c) "any other thing done (or not done) by, or on behalf of, the creditor (whether occurring before or after the making of the agreement or any 'related agreement')". In relation to (b) and (c), the court is required[1333] to look not only to the creditor's actions (or inaction) but also to those of an "associate" or "former associate" of the creditor.[1334]

In determining whether one or more of the three factors in s.140A(1) give rise to an "unfair" relationship, s.140A(2) requires the court to "have regard to all matters it thinks relevant", the subsection making it clear that these may include matters "relating to" the debtor and to the creditor (or an "associate" or "former associate" of the creditor[1335]). This general wording is a departure from the old "extortionate credit bargain" provisions; they listed various "factors" in relation to the debtor and creditor that the court was obliged to have regard to.[1336] It seems clear

---

[1324] CCA 1974 s.140A(4), see below.

[1325] See further, below, para.39-227.

[1326] *Holyoake v Candy* [2017] EWHC 3397 (Ch).

[1327] This would apply especially to a "spent" agreement: see para.39-215 (and, for decisions on "spent" agreements under the old "extortionate credit bargain" provisions, see *First National Securities Ltd v Bertrand* [1980] C.C.L.R. 1, Cty Ct; and *Davies v Directloans Ltd* [1986] 1 W.L.R. 823). See now: *Santander UK Plc v Wells* [2017] EWHC 2413 (Ch) (claimant had delayed too long in making claim).

[1328] *A Ketley Ltd v Scott* [1981] I.C.R. 241 (a decision under the old "extortionate credit bargain" provisions).

[1329] *A Ketley Ltd v Scott*, above (inflated valuation of security given); for further refusals under the old "extortionate credit bargain" provisions, see *First National Securities Ltd v Bertrand* Unreported 1978, Cty Ct; *Premier Finance Co Ltd v Gravesande* [1983] C.C.L.R. 1, Cty Ct. But in *Link Financial Ltd v North Wilson* [2014] EWHC 252 (Ch), [2014] C.C.L.R. 6, misrepresentations by the debtor did not, on the facts, preclude a finding that the relationship was "unfair".

[1330] See below, para.39-225.

[1331] See above, para.39-214.

[1332] CCA 1974 s.140A(1)(a)–(c).

[1333] CCA 1974 s.140A(3).

[1334] "Associate" is defined in CCA 1974 s.184. But, as noted below (para.39-221 and 39-222), the actions (or inaction) of a third party to a *related* agreement (who is not an "associate" or "former associate") is not relevant.

[1335] See previous note.

[1336] The (repealed) s.138(2)(b), (3)–(5), As well as these factors, the court had to have regard to "interest rates prevailing" at the time of contracting and "any other relevant considerations": (repealed) s.138(2)(a), (b).

that this reference to "matters relating to" the debtor or creditor is intended to preserve the relevance of those previously listed factors.[1337]

39-218 **Post-contracting behaviour** Factors (b) and (c) in s.140A(1)[1338] are novel in that they relate to post-contracting behaviour.[1339] Other statutory provisions, for example the Unfair Contract Terms Act 1977[1340] and the Consumer Rights Act 2015 Pt 2[1341] are more limited in focusing on the contractual terms at the time of contracting.[1342]

39-219 **"Terms of the agreement or any related agreement"** The first factor[1343] that can render the relationship "unfair to the debtor" is the actual terms of the credit agreement or any "related agreement".[1344] It should be noted that, unlike the position under the Consumer Rights Act 2015 Pt 2,[1345] the question is not whether the terms themselves are "unfair", but whether the terms render the relationship "unfair to the debtor". Usually, the most relevant terms are likely to be those concerning the charge for credit (especially interest).[1346] However, other terms, for example those requiring the payment of excessive early redemption fees[1347] may, at least if considered in the context of other terms of the credit agreement, be held to render the relationship "unfair to the debtor".[1348] Moreover, the terms of "any related agreement"[1349] are also relevant, for example those in linked transactions that might impose obligations on a debtor[1350] to a third party. Hence in *Link Financial Ltd v North Wilson*[1351] the credit relationship was held to be "unfair" because of the

---

[1337] The (repealed) s.138(3) listed (as factors applicable in relation to the debtor) the debtor's age, experience, business capacity and state of health, and the degree to which he was under financial pressure, and the nature of that pressure. Although there was no specific requirement that these subjective factors should have been known to the creditor, nor that a particular factor should have influenced the terms of the credit bargain, the courts implied such requirements: *Coldunell Ltd v Gallon* [1986] 1 Q.B. 1184, CA and see *Deutsche Bank (Suisse) SA v Khan* [2013] EWHC 482 (Comm), noted at [2013] C.C.L.R. 5, where Hamblen J. adopted a similar approach. The (repealed) s.138(4) listed (as factors applicable in relation to the creditor) the degree of risk accepted by him (having regard to the value of any security provided), his relationship to the debtor and whether a "colourable cash price" was quoted for any goods or services included in the credit bargain.

[1338] See below, paras 39-221 and 39-222.

[1339] CCA 1974 s.140A(1)(c) also covers pre-contracting behaviour: see below, para.39-222.

[1340] See above, Vol.I, paras 15-062 et seq.

[1341] Replacing (for contracts made on or after October 1, 2015) the Unfair Terms in Consumer Contracts Regulations 1999 (SI 1999/2083), see above, paras 38-221 et seq.

[1342] As did the (now repealed) "extortionate credit bargain" provisions themselves.

[1343] CCA 1974 s.140A(1)(a).

[1344] Defined in s.140C(4), see above, para.39-214.

[1345] Replacing (for contracts made on or after October 1, 2015) the Unfair Terms in Consumer Contract Regulations 1999 (SI 1999/2083), see above, paras 38-221 et seq. For the application of the predecessor regulations to a mortgage, see *Falco Finance Ltd v Gough* [1999] C.C.L.R. 16, Cty Ct.

[1346] See below, para.39-220.

[1347] Early redemption payments under *regulated* agreements are controlled by the Act (see above, para.39-158) and it is a moot point whether those protections will, in effect, be extended to non-regulated agreements on the basis that any other approach would be "unfair to the debtor".

[1348] For case-law under the old "extortionate credit bargain" provisions (which required "grossly exorbitant" payments), see *Grangewood Securities Ltd v Ellis* Unreported November 9, 2000, Milton Keynes Cty Ct. But see *Broadwick Financial Services v Spencer* [2002] EWCA Civ 35, [2002] 1 All E.R. (Comm) 446 [61]–[78].

[1349] Defined in s.140C(4), see above, para.39-214.

[1350] Or his relative.

[1351] [2014] EWHC 252 (Ch), [2014] C.C.L.R. 6.

"draconian effect" of a term in the timeshare agreement that was financed by the credit agreement.[1352]

Charge for credit   It is clear that the charge for credit, although normally a "core term" under the Consumer Rights Act 2015[1353] and hence generally not open to challenge under that Act, is very relevant in determining if the relationship is "unfair to the debtor" under the "unfair relationship" provisions.[1354] The previous "extortionate credit bargain" provisions explicitly required the court to have regard to the "interest rates prevailing at the time [the agreement] was made".[1355] The case-law under the "unfair relationship" provisions has so far generally followed[1356] the previous approach under the old "extortionate credit bargain" provisions of judging interest rates against the market rate for that type of loan.[1357] Thus rates charged by banks, building societies and finance houses are of little relevance where money has been borrowed from a moneylender in circumstances that or for a purpose for which such institutions would not have lent money. Further, in relation to the (now repealed) Moneylenders Act, it had been said that "the rate of interest might in certain circumstances be of itself a fallacious test as to whether the transaction was harsh and unconscionable. In many circumstances one shilling interest for a week on £1, or five shillings interest on £1 for a short period, though an enormous rate of interest ought not to be set aside".[1358] However, whilst under the old extortionate credit bargain provisions a subsequent rise or fall in interest rates was irrelevant,[1359] this may now be a relevant "matter",[1360] especially as the third fac-

39-220

[1352] A "related agreement" within s.140C(4)(b): a linked transaction under s.19(1)(b).

[1353] See above, paras 38-363 et seq.

[1354] For successful challenges see: *Patel v Patel* [2009] EWHC 3264 (inter alia, "exorbitant" interest) and some county court decisions (*Morrison v Betterpace Ltd (t/a Log Book Loans)* Unreported September 1, 2009, Lowestoft Cty Ct (APR of 485.25 of refinancing loan reduced to APR of 343.4 per cent charged on previous loan) and *Barons Finance Ltd v Olubisi* Mayor's & City of London Court, April 26, 2010 (vulnerable consumer "exploited")). For unsuccessful challenges see *Khodari v Tamimi* [2009] EWCA Civ 1109, [2010] C.C.L.R. 3 ("very large" 10 per cent charge for short-term loans); *Shaw v Nine Regions Ltd* [2009] EWHC 3514 (APR 341 per cent and interest rate of 119 per cent p.a.); *Consolidated Finance Ltd v Hunter* [2010] B.P.I.R. 1322 (loan at market rate for similar short-term bridging loans); *Chubb v Dean* [2013] EWHC 1282 (Ch) (charges ((i) interest of 1.85 per cent per month compounded monthly and (ii) a 1.25 per cent per month "facility fee") "even in combination" merely represented a "stiff commercial bargain"; an unfair relationship would have required a "very much higher interest rate"); *Holyoake v Candy* [2017] EWHC 3397 (Ch) ("steep" fees, with no explanation of how they had been calculated or whether they were in line with industry norms, for extending credit agreement did not render business credit "unfair").

[1355] (The repealed) s.138(2)(a).

[1356] Implicitly; the case-law under the new provisions has made no reference to the old "extortionate credit bargain" case-law. See the cases cited above (but see *Holyoake v Candy* [2017] EWHC 3397 (Ch) which referred to *A Ketley Ltd v Scott* [1981] I.C.R. 241). For the old case-law on interest rates, see *A Ketley Ltd v Scott* [1981] I.C.R. 241; *Davies v Directloans Ltd* [1986] 1 W.L.R. 823; *Woodstead Finance v Petrou*, The Times, January 23, 1986, CA; *Broadwick Financial Services Ltd v Spencer* [2002] EWCA Civ 35, [2002] 1 All E.R. (Comm) 446.

[1357] The OFT's Guidance under (the now repealed) CCA 1974 s.140D (*Unfair Relationships: Enforcement action under Part 8 of the Enterprise Act 2002* (OFT 854Rev), May 2008, revised August 2011) also accepted that this should be the approach, para.3.21, even requiring the cost to be "much higher" than market rates for an "unfair relationship" to arise.

[1358] *Blair v Buckworth* (1908) 24 T.L.R. 474, 476.

[1359] The wording was: "prevailing at the time [the agreement] was made". See *Paragon Finance Plc v Nash* [2001] EWCA Civ 1466, [2002] 1 W.L.R. 685; *Broadwick Financial Services v Spencer* [2002] EWCA Civ 35, [2002] 1 All E.R. (Comm) 446; *Paragon Finance Plc v Pender* [2005] EWCA Civ 760, [2005] C.C.L.R. 5.

tor[1361] refers to inaction (for example, not lowering interest rates) by the creditor after the making of the agreement.

39-221 **Exercise or enforcement of rights by creditor**   The second factor[1362] that can render a relationship "unfair to the debtor" is "the way in which the creditor has exercised or enforced any of his rights" under either the credit agreement itself of "any related agreement".[1363] Although it is the exercise or enforcement of the *creditor's* rights that are material (and not, for example, the rights of third parties to any "related agreements"), the court must have regard[1364] to activities by or on behalf of an "associate"[1365] or "former associate" of the creditor.[1366] Requiring the court to evaluate how a creditor exercises or enforces his contractual rights is a further novel feature of these provisions. In the business context, the courts have so far not found that the enforcement by creditors of agreements on default have given rise to "unfair relationships",[1367] although there are dicta that "arbitrary" or "exploitative" enforcement could do so.[1368] Similarly, in so far as it was held that the reporting of arrears to a credit reference agency was not an "enforcement" of a temporarily unenforceable agreement (due to a breach of s.77[1369]) it was further held that this did not give rise to an "unfair relationship".[1370] However, in the consumer context there are various regulatory standards requiring creditors to exercise forbearance and consideration towards borrowers experiencing difficulty[1371] and it is likely these will inform decisions on whether enforcement in those contexts has rendered a relationship "unfair". In *Re London Scottish Finance (In Administration)*[1372] it was held that in the case of "irredeemably"[1373] unenforceable credit agreements, the sending of letters demanding payment of arrears and stating that failure could result in the loss of the debtors' home (which was untrue) gave rise to an "unfair relationship" if this threat was a (not necessarily the only) cause of the

---

[1360] CCA 1974 s.140A(2). See *Patel v Patel* [2009] EWHC 3264 (QB).

[1361] CCA 1974 s.140A(1)(c), see below, para.39-222.

[1362] CCA 1974 s.140A(1)(b).

[1363] Defined in CCA 1974 s.140C(4), see above, para.39-214.

[1364] "except to the extent that it is not appropriate to do so".

[1365] Defined in CCA 1974 s.184.

[1366] CCA 1974 s.140A(3).

[1367] *Bluestone Mortgages Ltd v Faith Momoh* [2015] EW Misc B4 (CC) (refusal of permission to appeal the decision of the county court that failure to notify in advance that mortgagee would invoke usual clause in buy-to-let mortgage permitting him to pay outstanding lease charges if mortgagor failed to do so, did not give rise to an unfair relationship); *Clydesdale Bank Plc v R Gough t/t JC Gough & Sons and Anne Michelle Gough* [2017] EWHC 2230 (Ch) (where debtor and guarantor had independent legal advice, no unfairness found in the way the lender had exercised or enforced its rights against both); *Holyoake v Candy* [2017] EWHC 3397 (Ch).

[1368] *Maple Leaf Macro Volatility Master Fund v Rouvroy* [2009] EWHC 257 (Comm); *Paragon Mortgages Ltd v McEwan-Peters* [2011] EWHC 2491 (Comm); *Rahman v HSBC Bank Plc* [2012] EWHC 11 (Ch); *Deutsche Bank (Suisse) SA v Khan* [2013] EWHC 482 (Comm), noted at [2013] C.C.L.R. 5; *Graves v Capital Home Loans* [2014] EWCA Civ 1297.

[1369] See above, para.39-128.

[1370] *McGuffick v RBS Plc* [2009] EWHC 2386 (Comm).

[1371] See the *FCA Handbook* (a) CONC Module, especially CONC 7 and (b) (in relation to regulated mortgages) *MCOB Module*, especially MCOB 13. See also the Standards of Lending Practice (financial difficulties sections), above, para.39-013.

[1372] [2013] EWHC 4047 (Ch).

[1373] By virtue of the now repealed CCA 1974 s.127(3), see above, para.39-094.

debtors' decision to pay. But demanding payment in the case of an unenforceable (but potentially enforceable under s.127) agreement did not.[1374]

Any other action by creditor   The third factor[1375] that can render a relationship   **39-222** "unfair to the debtor" is any other[1376] action or inaction[1377] by, or on behalf of,[1378] the creditor either before or after the making of the credit agreement or "any related agreement".[1379] Again,[1380] the court must have regard[1381] to activities by or on behalf of an "associate"[1382] or "former associate" of the creditor[1383] but not the activities of third parties to any "related agreements" (unless they are agents or associates). This third factor covers pre-contracting behaviour such as (mis)statements[1384] made by the creditor, his agents or "associates" before the credit agreement (or "related" agreement) as well as their post-contracting behaviour. Initially, the courts were generally reluctant to undermine well-established principles of common law[1385] or to augment existing regulatory regimes by imposing novel duties on creditors whether at the time of contracting or thereafter.[1386] However, in *Plevin v Paragon*

[1374] *McGuffick v RBS Plc* [2009] EWHC 2386 (Comm) (above) followed.

[1375] CCA 1974 s.140A(1)(c).

[1376] i.e. other that the exercise or enforcement of rights by the creditor, referred to in CCA 1974 s.140A(1)(b), see above, para.39-221.

[1377] "any other thing done (or not done)".

[1378] It was confirmed in *Plevin v Paragon Personal Finance Ltd* [2014] UKSC 61 (reversing [2013] EWCA Civ 1658 (followed in *Scotland v British Credit Trust Ltd* [2014] EWCA Civ 790)) that these words required an agency relationship and should not be construed more broadly. It would also seem (although this issue was not determined by the Supreme Court) that (if applicable) the "deemed agency" in CCA 1974 s.56(2) (see, above, para.39-075 and below, para.39-302) could also render a creditor liable under s.140A(1)(c) for the acts of a "negotiator" (and see *Scotland v British Credit Trust Ltd* [2014] EWCA Civ 790)).

[1379] Defined in CCA 1974 s.140C(4), see above, para.39-214.

[1380] See the similar position under CCA 1974 s.140A(1)(b), above, para.39-221.

[1381] "except to the extent that it is not appropriate to do so".

[1382] Defined in CCA 1974 s.184.

[1383] CCA 1974 s.140A(3).

[1384] For cases under the Moneylenders Acts jurisdiction reopening loans on this basis, see *Victorian Daylesford Syndicate Ltd v Dott* [1905] 2 Ch. 624; *Carringtons Ltd v Smith* [1906] 1 K.B. 79; and (debtor improperly induced to borrow) *Lewis v Mills* (1914) 30 T.L.R. 438. See also (debtor's vulnerability known to creditor): *Bonnard v Dott* (1906) 21 T.L.R. 491; *Part v Bond* (1906) 22 T.L.R. 253; *Blair v Buckworth* (1908) 24 T.L.R. 474; and (debtor did not understand terms): *Levene v Greenwood* (1904) 20 T.L.R. 389; *Carringtons Ltd v Smith*, above; *Levene v Titchener* (1907) 23 T.L.R. 508; *Harris v Clarson* (1910) 27 T.L.R. 30; *Stirling v Rose* (1913) 30 T.L.R. 67. See *Deutsche Bank (Suisse) SA v Khan* [2013] EWHC 482 (Comm), noted at [2013] C.C.L.R. 5 (misrepresentations alleged but not proved).

[1385] Such as (i) the law on misrepresentation (see Neuberger L.J. in *Harrison v Black Horse Ltd* [2011] EWCA Civ 1128 at [30]–[31], criticising the "open-ended approach" of the judge in *Yates v Nemo Personal Finance* Unreported May 14, 2010, Manchester Cty Ct; (ii) promissory estoppel (see *Paragon Mortgages Ltd v McEwan-Peters* [2011] EWHC 2491 (Comm)); (iii) fiduciary law, breaches of statutory duty and negligence (see *Harrison v Black Horse Ltd* [2010] EWHC 3152 (QB)). But see *Barnes v Black Horse Ltd* [2011] EWHC 1416 (QB), per H.H.J. Waksman Q.C.: "it is not inconceivable that matters that may not be sufficient to generate duties of a fiduciary or tortious nature, or breaches thereof", may be relevant in the unfair relationship context.

[1386] See Lomnicka [2012] J.B.L. 713 at 727 and Lomnicka, "The impact of rule-making by financial services regulators on the common law: the lessons of PPI", in Gullifer and Vogenauer (eds) *English and European Perspectives on Contract and Commercial Law: Essays in Honour of Hugh Beale* (2014), Ch.4. See the views of H.H.J. Waksman Q.C. in *Carey v HSBC Bank Plc* [2009] EWHC 3417 (QB) (refusal to give the "more dramatic remedy" available under the "unfair relationship" provisions when a more limited sanction (temporary unenforceability) was available under the CCA 1974)

Personal Finance Ltd[1387] the sale of (expensive[1388]) PPI (payment protection insurance) in circumstances where neither the large amount nor existence of the commission received by the creditor[1389] was revealed to the debtor, was held by the Supreme Court to give rise to an "unfair relationship" despite the sale having been effected in accordance with the relevant regulatory regime.[1390] Moreover, on the special facts of *Patel v Patel*,[1391] the omission to reduce the interest rate (when the bank base rate reduced) and to provide any elementary periodic documentary evidence of the debtor's (rising) indebtedness over a long period of time (together with an initial "extortionate" interest rate) gave rise to an "unfair relationship". An expansive approach to the jurisdiction was also adopted in *Scotland v British Credit Trust Ltd*.[1392] The limitation period for a claim in misrepresentation had expired but, citing *Patel*,[1393] the Court of Appeal did not regard this as precluding a finding that those misrepresentations rendered the credit relationship "unfair".[1394]

39-223   **Applications**[1395]   An application that the credit or "related agreement" be reopened may be made by the debtor or a surety,[1396] even though no proceedings have been

---

and in *Carney v NM Rothschild and Sons Ltd* [2018] EWHC 958 (Comm); (although it did not matter that the limitation period for the common law claims for bad advice and misrepresentation had expired, "the same elements as are required by the [common law] cause of action should be shown when such matters are raised as constituting an unfair relationship"). But note *Scotland v British Credit Trust Ltd* [2014] EWCA Civ 790 per Kitchen L.J. (the fact that there was an alternative (albeit time-barred) claim under CCA 1974 s.75 (see below, para.39-303) did not preclude application of s.140A).

[1387] [2014] UKSC 61.

[1388] The premium (for a £60,000 loan) was £10,200 for five years; equivalent standalone cover would only have cost £2,083.84.

[1389] 87 per cent of the premium, paid by the insurer, an associated company of the creditor. The FCA has intervened in relation to PPI (see FCA PS 17/3: Payment protection insurance complaints: Feedback on CP16/20 and final rules and guidance (March 2017)) and has set a single 50 per cent commission "tipping point" (with undisclosed profit-share (as defined) being treated in the same way as undisclosed commission) at which it states that firms should presume, for the purposes of handling PPI complaints and making recompense (the excess over 50 per cent together with interest), that the failure to disclose commission gives rise to an unfair relationship under s.140A.

[1390] In the "ICOB" (now ICOBS) Module of the FCA Handbook, issued by the FSA under statutory powers (FSMA 2000 s.138 replaced by new s.137A) after the requisite rigorous consultation which considered at length, and decided against, requiring positive disclosure of the fact and amount of commissions. In the Court of Appeal in *Harrison v Black Horse Ltd* [2011] EWCA Civ 1128, at [58] (overruled by the Supreme Court) Neuberger M.R. had stated that the "touchstone must ... be the standard imposed by the regulatory authorities ... not resort to a visceral instinct that the relevant conduct is beyond the pale".

[1391] [2009] EWHC 3264 (QB). A family elder was advanced a loan of £200,000 in 1992 for his small retail businesses by his younger, but commercially much more sophisticated, former protégé at the "exorbitant" rate of 20 per cent per annum compounded monthly when the bank rate was 7 per cent. With very few repayments demanded, the indebtedness had grown to over £1m.

[1392] [2014] EWCA Civ 790.

[1393] See also below, para.39-228.

[1394] This was so even when the creditor's right of recourse against the misrepresentor (whether statutory (under s.75(2), see below, para.39-303) or common law/contractual (in relation to a s.56 agency claim, see above, para.39-075)) was also time-barred. See also *Carney v NM Rothschild and Sons Ltd* [2018] EWHC 958 (Comm); (unfair relationship claim available even when the limitation period for the common law claims for bad advice and misrepresentation had expired).

[1395] The relevant provisions (CCA 1974 s.140B(1) and s.140B(2)) are similar to the now repealed CCA 1974 s.139(2) and s.139(1) (as amended). See CCA 1974 s.189B(3), Sch.2A: in s.140B, references to "debtor" in relation to "green deal plans" (as defined in CCA 1974 s.189(1), see below, para.39-257) are to be read as references to the "improver"/"current bill payer"/"previous bill payer" (as

instituted by the creditor.[1397] Such an application may, in England and Wales, be brought only in the county court.[1398] Moreover, a credit or "related agreement" may also be reopened at the instance of the debtor or a surety:

(i)   in any proceedings to which the debtor and creditor are parties, being proceedings to enforce the credit agreement or any "related agreement"[1399]; or

(ii) at the instance of a debtor or a surety in other proceedings in any court where the amount paid or payable under the credit agreement is relevant.[1400]

A party to any such proceedings is entitled, in accordance with the rules of court, to have any person who might be the subject of an order under s.140B to be made a party.[1401]

Onus of proof   Section 140B(9)[1402] of the 1974 Act provides that if, in proceedings under s.140B, the debtor or a surety alleges that the relationship between the creditor and debtor is "unfair to the debtor", it is for the creditor to prove the contrary.[1403] Hence it is clear, that the "legal" or persuasive burden of proof rests throughout on the creditor, who must satisfy the court, on the balance of probabilities, that the credit relationship is not "unfair to the debtor". In earlier editions of this work it was submitted that the "evidential burden", that is, the burden of producing sufficient evidence to raise the issue rests initially on the debtor, and that the court need not consider the issue if the debtor does no more than plead that the credit relationship is "unfair" to him without producing any or any sufficient evidence to require the court to consider it.[1404] This approach appears to have been applied in *Carey v HSBC Bank Plc*,[1405] where the claimant debtor adduced no evidence but merely relied on the creditor's failure to supply a s.78 copy in breach of that provision.[1406] It was held that this in itself could not found an "unfair relation-

39-224

---

defined in CCA 1974 s.189B(6)).

[1396] Defined in CCA 1974 s.189(1); see above, para.39-183. See also CCA 1974 s.140C(2).

[1397] CCA 1974 s.140B(2)(a).

[1398] CCA 1974 s.140B(4) For applications in the county court, see CPR Pt 9 7PD–003. For Scotland, see s.140B(4)(b), (5). For Northern Ireland, see s.140B(4)(c), (6), (7). See also the Civil Jurisdiction and Judgments Act 1982 ss.16–19 and Sch.4. CPR Pt 7 PD 7B.

[1399] Defined in CCA 1974 s.140C(4); see above, para.39-214. For case-law under the (now repealed) "extortionate credit bargain" provisions, see *City Mortgage Corp Ltd v Baptiste* [1997] C.C.L.R. 64. See also *Rahman v Sterling Credit Ltd* [2001] 1 W.L.R. 496, CA: an application by way of counterclaim (under (the now repealed) CCA 1974 s.139(1)) could be made in proceedings to enforce a possession order already made, as these were proceedings to enforce any security (and see now the definition of "related agreement" in CCA 1974 s.140C(4) which covers security).

[1400] CCA 1974 s.140B(2)(c).

[1401] CCA 1974 s.140B(8).

[1402] See the (now repealed) provision to similar effect in relation to the "extortionate credit bargain" provisions in CCA 1974 s.171(7).

[1403] cf. the "watershed" of 48 per cent in the (repealed by the Consumer Credit Act 1974) Moneylenders Act 1927 s.10 below, under which the burden of proof rested upon the debtor.

[1404] The position was clearer under the now repealed "extortionate credit bargain" provisions in that CCA 1974 s.138(2) referred to "such evidence as is adduced". In *Coldunell v Gallon* [1986] Q.B. 1184, 1202 Oliver L.J. said that the creditor's burden in relation to the old "extortionate credit bargain" provisions "is sufficiently discharged by showing that the bargain was on its face a proper and not an extortionate credit bargain and that the [creditor] acted in a way that an ordinary commercial lender would be expected to act".

[1405] [2009] EWHC 3417 (QB), [134], [193]–[194].

[1406] On CCA 1974 s.78, see above, para.39-132.

ship" claim and the claim was dismissed.[1407] However, in *Bevin v Datum Finance Ltd*,[1408] where the debtor was seeking to set aside a statutory demand in bankruptcy proceedings and it was not clear that all the relevant evidence was before the court, Peter Smith J. disapproved the suggestion that the evidential burden lay on the debtor and required the creditor to adduce evidence to disprove the mere allegation of "unfair relationship". It is suggested that whilst in principle it is enough for the debtor merely to allege an "unfair relationship" for the issue to be raised, if the debtor is the claimant then in practice he will need to provide supporting evidence if a CPR Pt 18 request for "further information" is served by the creditor. Moreover, even if the debtor is the defendant, it is suggested that if the creditor's evidence provides no suggestion that the relationship is unfair, the court is likely to regard the creditor as having discharged the burden and to dismiss the debtor's claim.[1409]

39-225 **Nature of relief**[1410]   In reopening the agreement, the court may,[1411] make one or more of the seven types of order listed in s.140B(1) of the 1974 Act, viz:

(a)   require the creditor, or any associate[1412] or former associate of his, to repay the whole or part of any sum paid by the debtor or surety[1413] by virtue of the agreement or any related agreement,[1414] whether paid to the creditor or to any other person[1415];

(b)   require the creditor, or any associate[1416] or former associate of his, to do or not to do (or to cease doing) anything specified in the order in connection with the agreement or any related agreement[1417]1410;

[1407] [2009] EWHC 3417 (QB), [134], [193]–[194]. H.H.J. Waksman Q.C. also stated: "It is equally appropriate to strike [the claim] out on the basis of no reasonable grounds".

[1408] [2011] EWHC 3542 (Ch). *Carey v HSBC Bank Plc* was not cited.

[1409] As occurred in *Carey v HSBC Bank Plc* and *Axton v GE Money Mortgages Ltd* [2015] EWHC 1343 (QB) (*Datum Finance Ltd* distinguished and summary judgment given where debtor had no prospects of success). See also *Bluestone Mortgages Ltd v Momoh* [2015] EW Misc B4 (CC) (*Datum Finance Ltd* noted but the Court of Appeal nevertheless refused permission to appeal a summary judgment that the relationship was not unfair even though no evidence was adduced by the creditor to discharge the burden of proof). It is suggested that *Datum Finance* is of doubtful authority in the light of *Axton v GE Money Mortgages Ltd* and *Bluestone Mortgages Ltd v Momoh*. And see *Re M* [2010] EWHC 2324 (Admin): leave to amend to include a s.140A claim on appeal refused, where no supporting evidence provided.

[1410] The relevant provision (CCA 1974 s.140B(1)) is very similar to the (now repealed) CCA 1974 s.139(2), as amended, but note the new provisions in s.140B(1)(b) and (c).

[1411] See above, para.39-216, as to the court's discretion.

[1412] Defined in CCA 1974 s.184.

[1413] Defined in CCA 1974 s.189(1), see above, para.39-183.

[1414] See above, para.39-214.

[1415] CCA 1974 s.140B(1)(a), previously CCA 1974 s.139(2)(c), with the addition of the power to make an order against an associate or former associate as well as the creditor. And see s.140B(3), noted below. For orders to repay premiums of mis-sold PPI policies see *Scotland v British Credit Trust Ltd* [2014] EWCA Civ 790 and *Plevin v Paragon Personal Finance Ltd* [2016] C.C.L.R. 5, March 2, 2015, Manchester Cty Ct (the sequel to *Plevin v Paragon Personal Finance Ltd* [2014] UKSC 61), where the amount of commission received by the PPI seller was, on the facts, regarded as the appropriate remediation. In *Nelmes v NRAM Plc* [2016] EWCA Civ 491 the court ordered the repayment of a secret commission paid by the lender to the borrower's broker, plus interest. But see above, para.39-222: the FCA has suggested that the recompense when complaints are settled by firms should be the excess over 50 per cent of the premium together with interest.

[1416] Defined in CCA 1974 s.184.

[1417] See above, para.39-214. CCA 1974 s.140B(1)(b). There was no corresponding provision in the (now repealed) CCA 1974 s.139(2). See *Link Financial Ltd v North Wilson* [2014] EWHC 252 (Ch) (order

(c) reduce or discharge any sum payable by the debtor or surety[1418] by virtue of the agreement or any related agreement[1419];

(d) direct the return to a surety[1420] of any property provided by him for the purposes of the security[1421];

(e) otherwise set aside the whole or part of any duty imposed on the debtor or a surety[1422] by virtue of the agreement or any related agreement[1423];

(f) alter the terms of the agreement or any related agreement[1424];

(g) direct accounts to be taken[1425] between any persons.[1426]

It is important to note that the court may require the creditor to repay sums paid **39-226** to a person other than himself,[1427] and this is reinforced and extended by a specific provision[1428] to the effect that an order may be made notwithstanding that its effect is to place a burden on the creditor (or any associate or former associate of his) in respect of an advantage unfairly enjoyed by another person.

Compromise of claim In *Holyoake v Candy*[1429] the claimants had entered into an **39-226A** agreement compromising (inter alia) their unfair relationship claim. Nugee J., after referring to *Dimler v Alachouzos*[1430] a case on a compromise of a claim challengeable under the old Moneylenders Act and other case law on the compromising of claims under consumer protection statutes, held that a compromise agreement settling an unfair relationship claim did not in principle act as a jurisdictional bar to the Court considering whether the relationship between the parties was unfair but on the facts he upheld the compromise on the basis of the policy of the Court to encourage good faith compromises. Although the compromise agreement was either a "credit agreement" on the facts or a "related agreement"[1431] he nevertheless declined to decide "whether technically ... the relationship was not unfair because the parties had agreed to compromise that issue; or whether ... that even if unfair, [he declined] to make any order in these respects under s.140B" as "the practical result" was the same: the claims it covered were effectively compromised and hence

---

that no further sum was payable under the credit agreement) and *Scotland v British Credit Trust Ltd* [2014] EWCA Civ 790 (debtor not liable to repay the loan so far as it related to a mis-sold PPI policy).

[1418] Defined in CCA 1974 s.189(1), see above, para.39-183.

[1419] CCA 1974 s.140B(1)(c). See above, para.39-214. There was no corresponding provision in the (now repealed) CCA 1974 s.139(2). See *Patel v Patel* [2009] EWHC 3264 (QB): reduction of amount contractually due by ordering the debtor to repay the amount initially advanced, with such repayments as the debtor had made being regarded as satisfying any entitlement to interest. See also s.140B(3), noted below.

[1420] Defined in CCA 1974 s.189(1), see above, para.39-183.

[1421] CCA 1974 s.140B(1)(d), previously CCA 1974 s.139(2)(d).

[1422] Defined in CCA 1974 s.189(1), see above, para.39-183.

[1423] CCA 1974 s.140B(1)(e), previously s.139(2)(e). See above, para.39-214. See *Pye v Ambrose* [1994] C.L.Y. 594, [1994] N.P.C. 53: jurisdiction in s.139(2)(e) confined to relieving the debtor from payment of a sum of money and did not extend to relieving him from an obligation to convey property.

[1424] CCA 1974 s.140B(1)(f), previously s.139(2)(e). See above, para.39-214.

[1425] Or in Scotland, an accounting to be made.

[1426] CCA 1974 s.140B(1)(g), previously s.139(2)(a).

[1427] CCA 1974 s.140B(1)(a).

[1428] CCA 1974 s.140B(3).

[1429] [2017] EWHC 3397 (Ch); (and see also the comment to refusal of permission to appeal at [2018] C.C.L.R. 8).

[1430] [1972] 2 Q.B. 151.

[1431] As a "linked transaction" under s.19(1)(c)(ii), (2)(a), see above, para 39-214.

dismissed. This issue was considered and the reasoning approved in the permission to appeal hearing[1432] where David Richards L.J. opined[1433] that:

> "This does not open the door to unscrupulous lenders forcing borrowers into compromise agreement. The court will be astute to look as whether an agreement was entered into in good faith or with the benefit of advice."

39-227 **Reopening past or "spent" transactions** Although the old "extortionate credit bargain" provisions[1434] contained no such express words, the courts assumed that they were entitled to reopen an agreement which has been closed and settled,[1435] but exercised their discretion with some reluctance after the lapse of a considerable period of time.[1436] The new "unfair relationship" provisions explicitly state that the court may determine that a relationship is unfair "notwithstanding that the relationship may have ended"[1437] and therefore the court may clearly make an order under s.140B in such a case.

39-228 **Retrospective effect and limitation** The court's powers are not limited to agreements made after the entry into force of the "unfair relationship" provisions but, subject to transitional provisions, extend to agreements and transactions made before that date.[1438] The limitation period for actions under the old "extortionate credit bargain" provisions caused controversy and similar issues arise under the new provisions. First, it seems[1439] that a debtor who invokes the provisions is making a "claim for relief" for the purposes of the Limitation Act 1980 and, hence, that claim (even if raised by way of defence[1440]) is subject to the appropriate limitation period. Second, in principle, the limitation period for an action under the new provisions is 12 years under s.8(1) of the Limitation Act 1980 since the claim is a claim on a specialty.[1441] But in relation to a claim for repayment (as opposed, for example, to a claim for relief from future liability), s.9(1) of the 1980 Act prescribes a limitation period of six years for "an action to recover any sum recoverable by virtue of

---

[1432] See [2018] C.C.L.R. 8.

[1433] At [17].

[1434] The now repealed CCA 1974 ss.137–140, see above, para.39-212. There was express provision in the Moneylenders Act 1900 s.1 allowing past transactions to be reopened and excess payments recovered, although the courts imposed certain limitations on their exercise of this power: see *Meston on Moneylenders*, 5th edn, pp.197–200.

[1435] *Davies v Directloans Ltd* [1986] 1 W.L.R. 823. See also *First National Securities Ltd v Bertrand* [1980] C.C.L.R. 1, Cty Ct. And note Consumer Credit Act 2006 Sch.3 para.15(2) (reopening, under the old provisions, of agreement coming to an end before their repeal).

[1436] See *Santander UK Plc v Clive Roger Wells & Graham Mervyn Wells; Hertford Solutions LLP and Philip Thomas Chave (intervening)* [2017] EWHC 2413 (Ch): claim under new "unfair relationship" provisions rejected as claimant had delayed too long in making it.

[1437] CCA 1974 s.140A(4).

[1438] See *Patel v Patel* [2009] EWHC 3264 (agreement made in 1992). The (complex) transitional provisions are in Consumer Credit Act 2006 Sch.3 paras 14–16. See above, para.39-212.

[1439] It was so held (in relation to the old provisions) in *Nolan v Wright* [2009] EWHC 305, [2009] C.C.L.R. 8.

[1440] In *Nolan v Wright* [2009] EWHC 305 (Ch), [2009] C.C.L.R. 8 the view that the limitation period would not apply if the debtor raised the provisions by way of defence to reduce the amount claimed (put forward by Dobson (1998) 142 S.J. 274, and see, in another context, *Henriksens A/S v Rolimpex* [1974] 1 Q.B. 233, CA, especially 245G, above, para.28-123) was rejected. But see note referring to Limitation Act 1980 s.35(1)(b), below.

[1441] Which covers an obligation imposed by statute: *Collin v Duke of Westminster* [1985] Q.B. 581. See (on the old provisions) *Nolan v Wright* [2009] EWHC 305, [2009] C.C.L.R. 8, relying on dicta in *Rahman v Sterling Credit Ltd* [2001] 1 W.L.R. 498, CA.

any enactment".[1442] The limitation period will run from the date on which the cause of action accrued. It was held in *Patel v Patel*[1443] that the cause of action under the new provisions is a continuing one accruing from day to day until the relationship ends.[1444] This is in contrast to the position under the old extortionate credit bargain provisions where, after much controversy, it was assumed[1445] that the cause of action accrued at the date of the agreement. *Patel* concerned the post-contracting behaviour (and omissions) of the creditor and it may be that if the allegations relate only to the terms and/or the pre-contracting behaviour of the debtor, then the date of the agreement is a more appropriate date from which the limitation period should run. In any event, if the provisions are invoked by way of legal set-off or counterclaim, such a claim is deemed to have been commenced on the date of the original action.[1446]

"Unfair terms"   The terms of a credit agreement where the debtor is a consumer **39-229**
may also be challenged by him as "unfair" and so not binding on him under the
Consumer Rights Act 2015 Pt 2.[1447]

(n)   Ancillary Credit Businesses[1448]

Ancillary credit businesses   The consumer credit regulatory regime applies not **39-230**
only to business concerned with consumer credit and consumer hire agreements
themselves but also extends to what the Consumer Credit Act 1974 terms "ancillary credit businesses" and affects certain agreements made by, with or through a
person who carries on an "ancillary credit business". The categories of "ancillary
credit businesses" were originally defined in s.145 of the 1974 Act, but the definitions are now found in the Financial Services and Markets Act 2000 (Regulated
Activities) Order 2001 ("RAO"),[1449] as amended since the transfer of regulation
from the OFT to the FCA.[1450]

Credit broking: general   The definition of "credit broking" is now in art.36A of **39-231**
the RAO.[1451] There are six categories of "credit broking", the first three[1452] es-

---

[1442] *Rahman v Sterling Credit Ltd* [2001] 1 W.L.R. 496, CA.

[1443] [2009] EWHC 3264 (QB), see above, para.39-222.

[1444] Hence, it accrues at the date of trial in the case of an extant relationship and otherwise at the date when the relationship ended.

[1445] In *Nolan v Wright* [2009] EWHC 305 (Ch), [2009] C.C.L.R. 8 (relying on dicta in *Rahman v Sterling Credit Ltd* [2001] 1 W.L.R. 496, CA). It was so held in *First National Bank Plc v Ann* [1997] C.L.Y. 963, Cty Ct.

[1446] Limitation Act 1980 s.35(1)(b)—although the court has a discretion to order that it be dealt with as a separate action (CPR Pt 20 r.9(1), made under Limitation Act 1980 s.35), in which case the limita-tion period will start when that cause of action accrued (see *Ernst and Young v Butte Mining Plc* [1997] 1 W.L.R. 1485).

[1447] Replacing, for contracts made on or after October 1, 2015, the Unfair Terms in Consumer Contracts Regulations 1999 (SI 1999/2083), as amended by SI 2001/1186. See above, paras 38-221 et seq. and, for a case applying those regulations to a mortgage: *Falco Finance Ltd v Gough* [1999] C.C.L.R. 16 (above, para.39-219).

[1448] See Guest and Lloyd, *Encyclopedia of Consumer Credit Law* (1975, looseleaf), paras 2-146—2-161; and Goode *Consumer Credit: Law and Practice*, Pt C, Ch.48.

[1449] SI 2001/544.

[1450] Especially by the Financial Services and Markets Act 2000 (Regulated Activities) (Amendment) (No.2) Order 2013 (SI 2013/1881) arts 4, 5 and 8. See above, para.39-002.

[1451] With exclusions in RAO arts 36B–36G, see below, para.39-233.

sentially replace (but reword) the old categories of "credit brokerage"[1453] and the last three[1454] are new. It is important to note that the definition extends to cover, not merely brokers in the ordinary sense of that word, but also, in certain circumstances, (i) dealers and providers of services financed by regulated credit agreements, (ii) estate agents and (iii) accountants and lawyers.[1455] Moreover, although termed "*credit* broking", the first three categories also cover brokers of *hire* agreements. Credit broking only arises in relation to an "individual" or "relevant recipient of credit" (which excludes bodies corporate and partnerships with over three partners[1456]) and hence (for example) the effecting of introductions of companies to sources of credit, etc. is not credit broking. However, the agreements need not be "regulated agreements" but only agreements that would be regulated but for the exemptions, other than the "number of payment" exemption in art.60F of the RAO.[1457] The first three categories of credit broking comprise the introduction of individuals, etc. desiring to obtain credit (or to obtain goods on hire) to a source of credit (or hire) or to other credit brokers. The last three (new) categories of credit broking only apply to *credit* and not hire agreements and cover certain activities on behalf of the borrower or lender preparatory to the making of the credit agreement. A person undertaking credit broking is excluded from the definition of "providing credit information services" in art.89A of the RAO.[1458]

39-232   Promotion   Credit broking activity should be distinguished from the preliminary activity of mere *promotion* of credit or hire[1459] in that the first three categories presuppose an individual who (already) "wishes" to obtain credit or hire whilst the last three concern concrete steps taken towards a particular credit agreement.

39-233   Credit broking: exclusions   There are a number of exclusions that apply to the general definition of "credit broking" in art.36A of the RAO. In particular, the old exclusion for individuals who "canvass off trade premises",[1460] "restricted-use credit agreements"[1461] financing a transaction between the lender and the borrower or regulated consumer hire agreements, is maintained.[1462] The old exclusion for members of the legal profession in the context of "contentious business" has been widened.[1463] Other exclusions ensure that if the activity is regulated under another category, it is not also credit broking.[1464]

39-234   Debt-adjusting: general   The definition of "debt-adjusting" is now in art.39D of

---

[1452] RAO art.36A(1)(a)–(c).
[1453] In the now repealed CCA 1974 s.145(2)–(4). Note the change in terminology from "credit broker-age" (in the CCA 1974) to "credit broking" (in the RAO).
[1454] RAO art.36A(1)(d)–(f).
[1455] But note the exclusion for lawyers in the context of contentious business, below, para.39-233.
[1456] As defined in RAO art.60L.
[1457] For these exemptions, see above, paras 39-041 et seq.
[1458] See below, para.39-242.
[1459] See above, para.39-067.
[1460] For example in the context of mail order.
[1461] See above, para.39-027.
[1462] RAO art.36B.
[1463] RAO art.36F (as substituted by SI 2015/853 art.3(2)).
[1464] See (i) RAO art.36(2): activity within RAO art.36H (operating an electronic system in relation to lending, see below, para.39-256); (ii) RAO art.36D (activities within RAO arts 60B(1) and 60L(1): entering into agreements as lender or owner respectively, see above, para.39-061); (iii) RAO art.36E (activities in relation to regulated mortgages and home purchase plans—but note the new version of art.36E inserted on March 21, 2016, by SI 2015/910 art.3 and Sch.1 para.4(7), when the Mortgage

the RAO.[1465] It re-enacts, with some terminological differences, the definition in the now repealed s.145(5) of the 1974 Act. It should be noted that, like all ancillary credit activities in relation to debt,[1466] it applies to debts due under "credit agreements" and "consumer hire agreements", as defined in arts 60B and 60N (respectively) of the RAO[1467] to cover agreements that are not necessarily "regulated" agreements, although the borrower or hirer (as the case may be) must be an individual or "relevant recipient of credit" (which excludes bodies corporate and partnerships with over three partners[1468]). Debt-adjusting is defined to mean, in relation to debts due (whether overdue or not) under such agreements: (a) negotiating with the lender or owner, on behalf of the borrower or hirer, terms for the discharge of a debt; or (b) taking over, in return for payments by the borrower or hirer, his obligation to discharge a debt; or (c) any similar activity concerned with the liquidation of a debt. Examples of debt-adjusters are, or may be, professionals such as solicitors[1469] and accountants as well as dealers who negotiate settlements for their customers, and consumer advice agencies. A person undertaking debt-adjusting is excluded from the definition of "providing credit information services" in art.89A of the RAO.[1470]

Debt-adjusting: exclusions   There are a number of exclusions that apply to "debt-adjusting". First, it is not debt-adjusting for a person to do anything in relation to a debt arising under an agreement if he already has a certain status in relation to the agreement.[1471] Thus (i) the lender or owner under the agreement (this includes an assignee such as a factoring or block-discounting firm) or (ii) the supplier (such as a dealer in relation to loans made by "connected" lenders that finance his sales (but not in relation to hire-purchase, conditional sale or hire agreements made by his customer)) or (iii) the credit-broker who has acquired the business of the person who was the supplier in relation to the agreement, are all excluded from the definition. Second, the old exclusion for members of the legal profession in the context of "contentious business" is widened.[1472] Third, if the activity is in relation to regulated mortgages and home purchase plans (and hence regulated as such), it is excluded from the definition.[1473] Finally there are exclusions for energy suppliers,[1474] local authorities[1475] and insolvency practitioners.[1476]   **39-235**

Debt-counselling: general   The definition of "debt-counselling" is now in art.39E of the RAO.[1477] It re-enacts, with some terminological differences, the definition in the now repealed s.145(6) of the 1974 Act. It should be noted that, like all ancil-   **39-236**

Credit Directive (see above, para.39-003) was implemented.
[1465] With exclusions in RAO arts 39H–39L, see below, para.39-235.
[1466] See below, paras 39-236—39-241.
[1467] See above, paras 39-016 and 39-035.
[1468] As defined in RAO art.60L.
[1469] But note the exclusion for lawyers, below, para.39-235.
[1470] See below, para.39-242.
[1471] RAO art.39H.
[1472] RAO art.39K (as substituted by SI 2015/853 art.3(3)).
[1473] RAO art.39J.
[1474] RAO art.39I.
[1475] RAO arts 39L and 72G.
[1476] RAO arts 39L and 72H.
[1477] With exclusions in arts 39H–39L of the RAO, see below, para.39-237.

lary credit activities in relation to debt,[1478] it applies to debts and payments under "credit agreements" and "consumer hire agreements", as defined in arts 60B and 60N of the RAO (respectively)[1479] to cover agreements that are not necessarily "regulated" agreements, although the borrower or hirer (as the case may be) must be an individual or "relevant recipient of credit" (which excludes bodies corporate and partnerships with over three partners[1480]). The FCA has issued Guidance on the scope of debt-counselling: see the *FCA Handbook*, PERG 17. Essentially it covers the giving of "advice" (which connotes recommendations and not just information) to borrowers or hirers about the liquidation of debts "due" (whether overdue or not) under such agreements. Professionals such as solicitors[1481] and accountants as well as bankers, brokers and consumer advice agencies, may be debt-counsellors. A person undertaking debt-counselling is excluded from the definition of "providing credit information services" in art.89A of the RAO.[1482]

39-237 **Debt-counselling: exclusions**   Essentially the same exclusions as those applicable to debt-adjusting[1483] apply to debt-counselling.

39-238 **Debt-collecting: general**   The definition of "debt-collecting" is now in art.39F of the RAO.[1484] It re-enacts, with some terminological differences (and the addition of the reference to art.39H of the RAO), the definition in the now repealed s.145(7) of the 1974 Act. It should be noted that, like all ancillary credit activities in relation to debt,[1485] it applies to debts and payments under "credit agreements" and "consumer hire agreements", as defined in arts 60B and 60N of the RAO (respectively)[1486] to cover agreements that are not necessarily "regulated" agreements, although the borrower or hirer (as the case may be) must be an individual or "relevant recipient of credit" (which excludes bodies corporate and partnerships with over three partners[1487]). It also applies to debts under a so-called "relevant article 36H agreement".[1488] However an activity does not fall within the definition of "debt-collecting" if the activity *itself* falls within the definition of "operating an electronic system in relation to lending" within art.36H of the RAO.[1489] The definition of "debt-collecting" covers "the taking of steps to procure payment of debts" due under such agreements. This will obviously cover debt-collecting agencies. A person undertaking debt-collecting is excluded from the definition of "providing credit information services" in art.89A of the RAO.[1490]

[1478] See above, para.39-234 and below, paras 39-234 and 39-235, 39-238—39-241.
[1479] See above, para.39-016 and 39-035.
[1480] As defined in RAO art.60L.
[1481] But note the exclusion in the context of contentious business, below, para.39-237.
[1482] Below, para.39-242.
[1483] See above, para.39-235. But see the exclusion from art.39E for pensions guidance in art.39KA, added by SI 2015/489 art.2(4).
[1484] With exclusions in arts 39H–39L of the RAO, see below, para.39-239.
[1485] See above, paras 39-234—39-237 and below, para.39-240.
[1486] See above, para.39-016 and 39-035.
[1487] As defined in RAO art.60L.
[1488] As defined in RAO art.39F(4) and hence art.39H(4)–(6), see below, paras 39-256 and 39-241.
[1489] See below, para.39-256.
[1490] See below, para.39-242.

Debt-collecting: exclusions   Essentially the same exclusions as those applicable   **39-239**
to debt-adjusting[1491] apply to debt-collecting. Hence, for example, if the creditor or
owner (including a factoring or block-discounting firm collecting debts as assignee) merely collects debts due to himself or a "supplier" procures the payment
of debts under an agency discounting agreement, this is not "debt-collecting" within
the definition. Moreover, if the activity falls within art.36H of the RAO (operating
an electronic system in relation to lending)[1492] it is not "debt-collecting" within
art.39F of the RAO.[1493]

Debt administration: general   The definition of "debt administration" is now in   **39-240**
the art.39G of the RAO.[1494] It re-enacts, with some terminological differences (and
the addition of the reference to art.36H of the RAO) the now repealed s.145(7A)
of the 1974 Act.[1495] It should be noted that, like all ancillary credit activities in relation to debt[1496] it applies to rights and duties under "credit agreements" and
"consumer hire agreements", as defined in arts 60B and 60N of the RAO (respectively)[1497] to cover agreements that are not necessarily "regulated" agreements,
although the borrower or hirer (as the case may be) must be an individual or
"relevant recipient of credit" (which excludes bodies corporate and partnerships
with over three partners[1498]). As with debt-collecting, it also applies to debts under
a so-called "relevant article 36H agreement".[1499] However, an activity does not fall
within the definition of "debt administration" if the activity *itself* falls within the
definition of "operating an electronic system in relation to lending" within art.36H
of the RAO.[1500] The definition covers the taking of steps (so far as this is not "debt-
collecting"[1501]) on behalf of the lender or owner, either (a) to perform duties under
such an agreement or (b) to exercise or to enforce rights under such an agreement.
A person undertaking debt-administration is excluded from the definition of
"providing credit information services" in art.89A of the RAO.[1502]

Debt administration: exclusions   Essentially the same exclusions as those ap-   **39-241**
plicable to debt-adjusting[1503] apply to debt administration. Hence, for example, if
the creditor or owner (including a factoring or block-discounting firm collecting
debts as assignee) merely takes those steps that would amount to "debt administration" in relation to agreements with himself or a "supplier", it is not undertaking
"debt administration" within the definition. Moreover, if the activity falls within
art.36H of the RAO (operating an electronic system in relation to lending)[1504] it is
not "debt administration" within art.39G of the RAO.[1505]

Providing credit information services: general   The definition of "providing   **39-242**

1491 See above, para.39-235.
1492 See below, para.39-256.
1493 See RAO art.39F(3).
1494 With exclusions in arts 39H–39L of the RAO, see below, para.39-240.
1495 Added on June 16, 2006 by the Consumer Credit Act 2006 s.24(2).
1496 See above, paras 39-234—39-238.
1497 See above, paras 39-016 and 39-035.
1498 As defined in RAO art.60L.
1499 As defined in RAO art.39F(4) and hence art.39H(4)–(6), see below, para.39-256.
1500 See below, para.39-256.
1501 See above, para.39-238.
1502 See below, para.39-242.
1503 See above, para.39-235.
1504 See below, para.39-256.
1505 See RAO art.39G(3).

credit information services" is now in art.89A of the RAO.[1506] It replaces the old definition in the now repealed s.145(7B)–(7D) of the 1974 Act.[1507] The definition covers two categories of activity. The first is acting on behalf of an "individual" or "relevant recipient of credit" (which excludes bodies corporate and partnerships with over three partners[1508]) so as to discover and correct records "relevant to their financial standing" held by certain business (credit reference agencies and others in the credit and hire industries (collectively referred to as "credit information agencies" and defined in art.89A(6) of the RAO)). It should be noted that the information need not specifically relate to regulated credit agreements. The second is the giving of advice (to an individual or relevant recipient of credit) in relation to the first activity. Hence it is enough to advise the borrower how they might discover and correct records themselves (rather than acting on their behalf).

39-243 **Providing credit information services: exclusions** There are a number of exclusions that apply to this ancillary credit activity. First, there is the usual exclusion for lawyers.[1509] Second, anyone already regulated (as lender or other ancillary credit service provider) does not also fall within art.89A.[1510] Moreover, art.89A(5) of the RAO makes it clear that arts 89A and 36H (operating an electronic system in relation to lending)[1511] are mutually exclusive so if an activity falls within the latter, it cannot also be the provision of credit information services within art.89A. Finally, there are exclusions for local authorities[1512] and insolvency practitioners.[1513]

39-244 **Providing credit references: general** The definition of "providing credit references" is now in art.89B of the RAO.[1514] It replaces and clarifies the old definition of "credit reference agency" in the now repealed s.145(8) of the 1974 Act. The new definition adds the requirement that the business must "primarily consist of" furnishing the information. That "information" must satisfy three conditions. First, it must be information relevant to the financial standing of an "individual" or "relevant recipient of credit" (which excludes bodies corporate and partnerships with over three partners[1515]), although the information need not relate to "regulated" credit agreements. Hence providing financial information about companies is not covered. Second, the information must be "collected", that is to say, assembled or brought together. Third, it must be collected "for that purpose", i.e. for the purpose of furnishing persons with information relevant to the financial standing of individuals, etc. Thus a referee (for example a bank) who habitually furnishes information based on its own accounts as between itself and its customers does not come within the definition since the information arises simply in the course of conducting its own business and is not collected for that purpose. Even more obviously, information about an employee collected by his employer in a personnel file, though it may in some respects be information relevant to the financial standing of the employee, is not collected by the employer for that purpose. In any event, under the new ver-

---

[1506] With the exclusions in arts 89C–89D of the RAO, see below, para.39-243.
[1507] Added on October 1, 2008 by the Consumer Credit Act 2006 s.25.
[1508] As defined in RAO art.60L.
[1509] RAO art.89C (as substituted by SI 2015/853 art.3(7)).
[1510] See RAO art.89A(4).
[1511] See below, para.39-256.
[1512] RAO arts 89D(2) and 72G.
[1513] RAO arts 89D(2) and 72H.
[1514] With the exclusions in arts 89C–89D of the RAO, see below, para.39-245.
[1515] As defined in RAO art.60L.

sion of the definition in art.89B both the bank and the employer would be excluded as their business does not "primarily" consist of furnishing such information. Credit reference agencies are obliged to disclose and correct information.[1516] Moreover, as a result of the implementation of the Consumer Credit Directive,[1517] when a creditor under a prospective regulated agreement refuses credit on the basis of information obtained from a credit reference agency, he is obliged (unless the agreement was to be secured on land), when informing the debtor of the refusal, also to inform the debtor that the refusal is on that basis and to provide the particulars of the agency.[1518] Failure to comply is an offence.[1519]

Providing credit references: exclusions Essentially similar exclusions as those applicable to providing credit information services[1520] apply to providing credit references. They are: (i) the usual exclusion for lawyers[1521]; (ii) if an activity falls within art.36H of the RAO (operating an electronic system in relation to lending)[1522] it cannot also be the provision of credit references within art.89B[1523]; (iii) the usual exclusions for local authorities[1524] and insolvency practitioners.[1525]   **39-245**

Authorisation As noted above[1526] from April 1, 2014, the licensing regime under the 1974 Act (as reformed by the Consumer Credit Act 2006) was replaced by the authorisation regime under the Financial Services and Markets Act 2000 (FSMA 2000), operated by the Financial Conduct Authority (FCA). Section 19 of FSMA 2000 imposes a "general prohibition" on anyone undertaking a "regulated activity" in the United Kingdom unless they are either an "authorised" or "exempt" person. The ancillary credit activities considered above[1527] are "specified" under the RAO. This means that if undertaken "by way of business",[1528] they are "regulated activities"[1529] and hence a person needs authorisation from the FCA in order to undertake them in the United Kingdom unless he is an "exempt person" (under FSMA 2000 s.38 (exemption by Treasury Order) or s.39 ("appointed representatives")).   **39-246**

"Business" Only "specified activities" undertaken "by way of business" are "regulated activities" requiring FCA authorisation.[1530] A special meaning is given to the term "by way of business" in relation to "not-for-profit bodies" (as defined) that carry on debt-adjusting,[1531] debt-counselling[1532] or providing credit informa-   **39-247**

[1516] See CCA 1974 ss.157–160, as amended by the Data Protection Act 1998 s.62 (and for regulations made under ss.157 and 158, see SI 2000/291).
[1517] See above, para.39-011.
[1518] CCA 1974 s.157(A1), added from February 1, 2011 by SI 2010/1010 reg.40.
[1519] See CCA 1974 s.157(3).
[1520] See above, para.39-243.
[1521] RAO art.89C (as substituted by SI 2015/853 art.3(7)).
[1522] See below, para.39-256.
[1523] See RAO art.89B(3).
[1524] RAO arts 89D(2) and 72G.
[1525] RAO arts 89D(2) and 72H.
[1526] See para.39-061.
[1527] See paras 39-230—39-243.
[1528] See below, para.39-247.
[1529] See the FSMA 2000 s.22.
[1530] See FSMA 2000 s.22.
[1531] See above, para.39-234.

tion services,[1533] by Order made under s.419 of the FSMA 2000.[1534] Essentially, as long as such a body does not carry on that activity only on an occasional basis, it is to be regarded as carrying on that activity "by way of business" whether or not it would otherwise be regarded as doing so. Otherwise the phrase "by way of business" is left undefined in the FSMA 2000.[1535]

39-248 **Regulatory control** Authorisation under the FSMA 2000 brings with it all the regulatory control that the FCA may exercise under that Act over "authorised persons".[1536] There are special provisions in relation to ancillary credit businesses in the *FCA Handbook*, CONC Module.[1537]

39-249 **Trading whilst unauthorized** The consequences (criminal and civil) for undertaking regulated activities whilst not authorised or exempt are considered above.[1538]

39-250 **Regulated agreements made on introduction by unauthorised credit-broker** The effect on agreements made on an introduction by an unauthorised person, in particular an unauthorised broker, are considered above.[1539] Essentially, this means, for example, that a bank or other lender must ensure that, where business is introduced by a broker or dealer (whether under pre-existing arrangements or not), that broker or dealer is authorised, otherwise, without an order of the FCA, the consequent agreement and security may be unenforceable and voidable.

39-251 **Seeking business: promotion** The original provisions in the 1974 Act regulating advertisements and quotations in relation to ancillary credit businesses have been replaced[1540] by the provisions of the FSMA 2000 "financial promotion" regime.[1541] The relevant provisions are now the FCA rules in the *FCA Handbook*, CONC 3 (promotion) and 4.1 (quotations). Infringement of these provisions is no longer a criminal offence but (as well as giving rise to the usual consequences for breach of FCA rules[1542]) may also breach the Consumer Protection from Unfair Trading Regulations 2008.[1543]

39-252 **Canvassing certain ancillary credit services off trade premises** Section 154 of the 1974 Act renders it an offence to canvas off trade premises (as defined in s.153 in similar terms to those used in s.48(1)[1544]) certain ancillary credit services, namely,

---

[1532] See above, para.39-236.
[1533] See above, para.39-242.
[1534] See the Financial Services and Markets Act 2000 (Carrying on Regulated Activities by Way of Business) Order 2001 (SI 2001/1177) art.3E, added on April 1, 2014 by SI 2013/1881 art.13.
[1535] See further, above para.39-062.
[1536] See further, above, para.39-063.
[1537] See especially, CONC 2.4–2.6.
[1538] See above, para.39-064.
[1539] See above, para.39-065.
[1540] Since April 1, 2014, following the transfer of consumer credit regulation to the FCA (see above, para.39-002).
[1541] See further, above, para.39-067.
[1542] See above, para.39-063.
[1543] See above, paras 38-165 et seq.
[1544] See above, para.39-068.

credit-broking,[1545] debt-adjusting,[1546] debt-counselling[1547] or the provision of credit information services.[1548]

Right to recover brokerage fees   Section 155 of the 1974 Act confers a right in certain circumstances to recover from the credit-broker brokerage fees paid in advance in the event that an introduction by a credit-broker does not bear fruit within six months.[1549] The section applies[1550] where an individual has sought an introduction for a purpose that would have been fulfilled by his entry into (a) a regulated agreement or (b) an agreement for credit secured on land (in the case of an individual desiring to obtain credit to finance the acquisition or provision of a dwelling) or (c) an exempt agreement[1551] or (d) an agreement which is not a regulated credit agreement or a regulated consumer hire agreement but which would be such an agreement if the law applicable to the agreement were the law of a part of the United Kingdom. However, it does not apply[1552] where the credit-broker is an authorised person (or appointed representative) and the fee relates to a regulated mortgage[1553] or home purchase plan (i.e. the activity is excluded from the definition of "credit broking" by art.36E of the RAO[1554]).

39-253

When s.155 applies, the excess over £5[1555] of a fee or commission for his services charged by a credit-broker to an individual ceases to be payable or, as the case may be, is recoverable by the individual if the introduction does not result in his entering into a "relevant agreement" within the six months following the introduction.[1556] For this purpose, an agreement is a "relevant agreement" in relation to an individual if it is the *type* of agreement sought by that individual.[1557]

Right to recover other payments   In the case of an individual desiring to obtain credit under a consumer credit agreement, any sum payable or paid by him to a credit-broker otherwise than as a fee or commission for the credit-broker's services

39-254

1545 See above, para.39-231.
1546 See above, para.39-234.
1547 See above, para.39-236.
1548 See above, para.39-242.
1549 For a fuller discussion, see Guest and Lloyd, *Encyclopedia of Consumer Credit Law* (1975, looseleaf), para.2-156 and see the guidance in *FCA Handbook*, CONC 2.5.9 and CONC 6.8.3 (more limited than the now revoked OFT's Guidance: *Credit brokers and intermediaries: OFT guidance for brokers, intermediaries and the consumer credit and hire businesses which employ or use their services* (OFT 1288, November 2011), especially Ch.6). There are particular difficulties in deciding what is a "fee or commission" (e.g. sums charged by brokers for "packaging agents") for these purposes. And note s.173 (contracting out not possible). Apart from s.155 there may be rights to recovery at common law (for example on the grounds that the basis for the payment has totally failed, see above paras 29-057 et seq.).
1550 See CCA 1974 s.155(2).
1551 See above, paras 39-038 et seq.
1552 See CCA 1974 s.155(2A).
1553 See below, para.39-529.
1554 See above, para.39-233.
1555 The amount was raised from £1 to £3 by SI 1983/1571 and to £5 by SI 1998/997.
1556 CCA 1974 s.155(1). See also CCA 1974 ss.70(7), 181. If, after making a "relevant agreement", the debtor exercises his right to withdraw (under CCA 1974 s.66A, see above, para.39-101) or cancel (CCA 1974 s.67, see above, para.39-102), it seems s.155 applies as the agreement is (in statutory terms) "treated as if it had never having been entered into".
1557 CCA 1974 s.155(3). The OFT Guidance (see above) stated that the credit-broker's licence was at risk if he did not inform the debtor of (a) the amount of the fee before undertaking the credit brokerage services and (b) the debtor's right under s.155. For similar obligations, see now the *FCA Handbook*, CONC 4.4.1R(2) and (4) and, in relation to (b), see para.39-255, below.

is to be treated as such a fee or commission if it enters, or would enter, into the total charge for credit.[1558] Since the provisions as to the total charge for credit[1559] in certain circumstances embrace sums paid under a linked transaction, e.g. surveyor's or valuer's fees, such fees will become recoverable from the credit-broker notwithstanding that he has paid them over to a third party.

39-255 **"Credit intermediaries"** As a result of the implementation of the Consumer Credit Directive[1560] various obligations are imposed on so-called "credit intermediaries", i.e. persons (other than the creditor) who, in the course of business, carry out, for a fee, various activities preparatory to the conclusion of regulated credit agreements (other than those secured on land as these are outside the scope of the Directive) with or for "individuals". The term "credit intermediaries" covers not only those regulated as credit-brokers[1561] but also certain other persons who escape such regulation.[1562] As regards the former, the *FCA Handbook*, CONC 3.7.3R and CONC 4.4.2R impose the relevant obligations. As regards the latter, the obligations are imposed by the Financial Services and Markets Act 2000 (Regulated Activities) (Amendment) (No.2) Order 2013.[1563] Three obligations are imposed on such persons. First, they must disclose the extent to which they act independently (and in particular whether they work exclusively with a creditor). Second, if they act for a debtor and charge him a fee, they must "ensure" that the fee is disclosed to the debtor and then agreed in writing *before* the agreement is concluded. Third, they must also disclose such a fee to the creditor if he needs it to calculate the APR.[1564]

(o) Operating an Electronic System in Relation to Lending

39-256 **Operating an electronic system in relation to lending** The development of the "peer to peer" (P2P) lending industry required a regulatory response as the borrowers were largely not protected by the 1974 Act (as the relevant agreements were usually "non-commercial agreements"[1565]) and the lenders were largely unprotected because "P2P platforms" were not regulated under the FSMA 2000. Hence on April 1, 2014[1566] a number of new "regulated activities" in relation to P2P lending were introduced by art.36H of the RAO.[1567] Article 36H is a very complex provision and specifies nine activities in total, the main activity being that specified by art.36H(1) (operating an electronic system) whilst the others (in art.36H(3)) cover activities carried on in the course of, or in connection with, the carrying on of that "main" activity. The "main" activity of "operating an electronic system" is defined as enabling the operator ("A") to "facilitate" persons ("B" and "C") becoming the

---

[1558] CCA 1974 s.155(4).

[1559] See above, para.39-059.

[1560] See above, para.39-011.

[1561] See above, para.39-231.

[1562] For example, by virtue of the exclusions in RAO arts 36B(1), 36F and 72G (see above, para.39-233).

[1563] SI 2013/1881 art.12.

[1564] See above, para.39-059.

[1565] See above, para.39-049.

[1566] See above, para.39-002.

[1567] Added by the Financial Services and Markets Act 2000 (Regulated Activities) (Amendment) (No.2) Order 2013 (SI 2013/1881) art.4, as amended by the Financial Services and Markets Act 2000 (Regulated Activities) (Amendment) Order 2014 (SI 2014/366) art.2(9). See the exclusions in arts 36I and 36IA.

lender and borrower under a so-called "article 36H agreement" (as defined), where that system is capable of determining which agreements should be made available to each of B and C. As is the case with the regulated activities of lending under regulated credit agreements[1568] and undertaking ancillary credit businesses,[1569] all the consequences of FCA regulation under the FSMA 2000 follow in relation to this P2P regulated activity. In particular there is the requirement of authorisation from the FCA[1570] and consequent FCA control of that activity.[1571]

(p) Green Deal Plans

Green deal plans   The introduction of "green deal plans" by the Energy Act 2011   **39-257**
has necessitated the amendment[1572] and modification[1573] of the 1974 Act in so far as it applies to the loan component of such plans.[1574] "Green deal plans" are defined by s.1 of the Energy Act 2011, essentially as arrangements that enable owners or occupiers of residential or commercial property to finance energy-saving measures to their property by instalments added to their energy bills (which bills are reduced because of the energy savings). If the property is a domestic property or the occupier or owner of the property is an individual, a "green deal plan" (as so defined) is treated as a "consumer credit agreement" for the purposes of the 1974 Act and is termed a "green deal consumer credit agreement".[1575] It is treated as an agreement for fixed-sum credit within s.10(1)(b) of the 1974 Act[1576] and if a regulated agreement,[1577] it is to be treated as a restricted-use agreement within s.11(1)(a).[1578] It is also treated as credit agreement for the purposes of the "unfair relationship" provisions.[1579] As well as amending various provisions of the 1974 Act in so far as they apply to a "green deal consumer credit agreement" (in particular, ss.77, 77A, 77B, 86B[1580]) and introducing a new s.95B (compensatory amount of early settlement),[1581] the definitions of "debtor" and "creditor" when they occur in the various sections of 1974 Act are given an extended meaning[1582] to cover persons beyond the original parties to the green deal financing agreement. In particular, as the li-

---

[1568] See above, para.39-062.
[1569] See above, para.39-230.
[1570] See, in relation to ordinary lending, above, para.39-062.
[1571] See, in relation to ordinary lending, above, para.39-063. For special P2P regulatory provisions, see *FCA Handbook*, CONC 3.7A (financial promotion); CONC 4.3 (pre-contractual requirements); CONC 5.5 (creditworthiness assessment); CONC 7.17–7.19 (NOSIAs etc.); CONC 11.2 (cancellation). But borrowers are not protected by the Financial Services Compensation Scheme.
[1572] See especially, the Energy Act 2011 ss.25–30 and the Consumer Credit (Green Deal) Regulations 2012 (SI 2012/2798).
[1573] See especially the Consumer Credit Act 1974 (Green Deal) (Amendment) Order 2014 (SI 2014/436) and the Consumer Credit (Information Requirements and Duration of Licences and Charges) (Amendment) Regulations 2014 (SI 2014/2369).
[1574] Note the transitional provisions for green deal plans made between April 1, 2014 and July 14, 2014 in the Financial Services and Markets Act 2000 (Regulated Activities) (Green Deal) (Amendment) Order 2014 (SI 2014/1850) art.12.
[1575] See CCA 1974 s.189B.
[1576] See above, para.39-026 and CCA 1974 s.189C(1)(a).
[1577] See s.8(3), above, para.39-017.
[1578] See above, para.39-027 and CCA 1974 s.189C(2).
[1579] See CCA 1974 s.189C(1)(a))—although CCA 1974 s.140C(2) does not apply (see CCA 1974 s.189C(3)). For these provisions, see above, paras 39-212 et seq.
[1580] See above, paras 39-128—39-131.
[1581] See above, para.39-160.
[1582] By CCA 1974 s.189B and Sch.2A.

ability for repayment attaches to whoever is the "bill payer" from time to time, the definition of "debtor" is modified accordingly.

2. LOANS AND INTEREST

(a) Loans of Money

39-258 **Definition of loan** A contract of loan of money is a contract whereby one person lends or agrees to lend a sum of money to another, in consideration of a promise express or implied to repay that sum on demand, or at a fixed or determinable future time, or conditionally upon an event which is bound to happen, with or without interest.[1583] In many circumstances, the question whether a particular transaction is, in law, a "loan" or not will be immaterial, since the transaction will take effect according to the intention of the parties, however the contract may be classified. But in some circumstances it is necessary to define the nature of a transaction because of particular statutory provisions which may apply to contracts of "loan" but not to other contracts.[1584] In these circumstances the question is, in the last resort, always a question of construction of the particular statutory provision, and it would be unsafe to assume that a transaction which would be classified as a loan for the purposes of one statute will necessarily be so classified for the purposes of other statutory provisions. But subject to this caveat, the authorities on the meaning to be attached to the word "loan" in a particular statutory context are useful in showing the normal commercial definition of a contract of loan.

39-259 **Money paid to third party** Where A pays money to B at the request of C, on the terms that he is to be repaid by C, it is sometimes difficult to say whether the transaction amounts to a loan by A to C. There is no doubt that, in certain contexts, money paid by A to B at the request of C could properly be said to be money paid by A to C,[1585] but that does not necessarily mean that the transaction is a loan for all purposes.[1586] In *Potts Executors v IRC*[1587] a company director had an arrangement with the company whereby the company paid various accounts on behalf of the director, debiting him with the payments in its books, and crediting him with director's fees and sums paid by him to the company. It was held by the House of Lords (in the context of a taxing statute) that the payments by the company were not payments by way of loan to the director. It was said in this case that whether a payment of this kind amounts to a loan must depend on all the circumstances. Thus disbursements by a solicitor on behalf of a client could not be said to be payments by way of loan to the client in the ordinary way because the payments would be made as an incident to a wider relationship than that merely of lender and borrower. "On the other hand, [this] kind of wider relationship ... may provide opportunity for transactions within it which are exceptional and beyond the normal scope of the

---

[1583] It is arguable that a promise to make a loan without interest is, while still executory, unsupported by consideration and therefore unenforceable. There appears to be no authority on the question.

[1584] For an example of a statutory provision that only applied to a "loan" (and hence where the meaning of that term was crucial), see *Belize Bank Ltd v Association of Concerned Belizeans* [2011] UKPC 35. See also *Santander UK Plc v Harrison* [2013] EWHC 199 (QB), [2013] C.C.L.R. 4 on the meaning "cash loan" (see above, para.39-019 and para.39-148).

[1585] *Parsons v Equitable Investment Co Ltd* [1916] 2 Ch. 527; *Law v Coburn* [1972] 1 W.L.R. 1238.

[1586] See, e.g. *Hussey v Palmer* [1972] 1 W.L.R. 1286 (constructive or resulting trust).

[1587] [1951] A.C. 443.

relationship and which may properly be describable as loans and as nothing else".[1588]

Similarly, in *Re HPC Productions Ltd*[1589] it was held that payments made by an **39-260** overseas company at the request of a United Kingdom resident were not loans made to him within the meaning of the Exchange Control Act 1947. In this case it was suggested that an important factor to be considered in deciding whether such a transaction amounts to a loan is whether the recipient of the money is accountable for it to the person at whose request it has been paid. If he is so accountable, this points to the transaction being a loan. On the other hand this is not a decisive consideration, for there is no doubt that in some circumstances the transaction will be a loan even where the recipient is not so accountable. Thus money paid by a banker by means of a cheque drawn on an overdrawn account is undoubtedly money lent to the customer whether the recipient is liable to repay the money to the customer, or whether he is entitled to retain it in settlement of some obligation due to him.[1590] "If a customer draws a cheque for a sum in excess of the amount standing to the credit of his current account, it is really a request for a loan, and if the cheque is honoured the customer has borrowed money".[1591]

Loans distinguished from other forms of debt   The Consumer Credit Act 1974 **39-261** deliberately extends its coverage to embrace forms of financial accommodation other than loans,[1592] as at common law not every form of indebtedness amounts to a loan. A person who buys goods on credit is not borrowing money from the seller.[1593] And a company that issues loan or debenture stock as a consideration for the acquisition of property is not borrowing money.[1594] Even where money passes from one party to the other, this does not necessarily make the transaction one of loan for there are many ways of raising cash besides borrowing money.[1595] The purchase of bills[1596] or book debts[1597] at a discount is not a lending of money, even where the seller gives a collateral security which has the effect of making him personally liable for the amount raised.[1598] Nor does the ordinary hire-purchase transaction amount to a loan of money; although the economic effect of such a transaction may be the same as that of a loan, the legal effect is quite different.[1599]

Borderline cases may, however, arise, and it is difficult to state with any certainty **39-262** whether or not certain types of instalment credit transaction, for example, check and

---

[1588] [1951] A.C. 443 at 465.

[1589] [1962] Ch. 466.

[1590] *Cunliffe Brooks & Co v Blackburn Benefit Society* (1884) 9 App. Cas. 857.

[1591] *Cuthbert v Robarts, Lubbock & Co* [1909] 2 Ch. 226, 233.

[1592] s.9(1); above, para.39-019.

[1593] *Chow Yoong Hong v Choong Fah Rubber Manufactory* [1962] A.C. 209, 216 (for the purposes of money lending control).

[1594] *IRC v Port of London Authority* [1923] A.C. 507 (tax context).

[1595] *Chow Yoong Hong v Choong Fah Rubber Manufactory*, above, at 216.

[1596] *Transport & General Credit Corp Ltd v Morgan* [1939] Ch. 531; *IRC v Rowntree & Co Ltd* [1948] 1 All E.R. 482; *Chow Yoong Hong* case, above.

[1597] *Olds Discount Co Ltd v John Playfair Ltd* [1938] 3 All E.R. 275.

[1598] *Olds Discount Co Ltd v John Playfair*, above; and see *Chow Yoong Hong v Choong Fah Rubber Manufactory* [1962] A.C. 209; *Re Securitibank Ltd* [1978] 1 N.Z.L.R. 97.

[1599] *British Ry Traffic and Electric Co v Kahn* [1921] W.N. 52; *Automobile and General & Finance Corp Ltd v Morris* (1929) 73 S.J. 451; *Olds Discount Co Ltd v Cohen* [1938] 3 All E.R. 281n.; *Trade Promotion Trust Ltd v Young* (1940) 84 S.J. 646; *Premor Ltd v Shaw Bros* [1964] 1 W.L.R. 978. For hire purchase, see below, paras 39-306 et seq.

voucher trading,[1600] revolving shop credit accounts,[1601] and credit cards,[1602] involve loans of money. Further, transactions of the kinds referred to in the preceding paragraph may sometimes amount to contracts of loan, for the real purpose of the parties may be to effect a loan, and the other features of the transaction (such as the purchase of book debts or the making of a hire-purchase agreement) may be merely a front, intended to hide the real nature of the transaction. But it must be stressed that what matters is the real *legal* nature of the transaction and not its economic nature, and the courts will not go behind the actual agreement made unless there is evidence that the parties did not intend the relationship between them to be governed by the ostensible agreement which they have made.[1603] Thus, if a company wishes to acquire property in consideration of the issue of loan stock, a transaction in these terms will not amount to a borrowing of money as mentioned above. If, on the other hand, the parties make a contract which indicates that their intention is that the company should purchase the property at a stated sum, and that the company should then borrow that sum from the seller, and secure the loan by an issue of debenture or loan stock, there will undoubtedly be a loan to the company.[1604]

39-263 Borrower not personally liable   Although a borrower is in the ordinary way personally liable to repay a loan, whatever security he may give for it, it is perfectly possible to have a contract of loan in which the borrower is under no personal liability.[1605] Thus, where property was conveyed to a trustee on trust for the creditors of the settlor, and one of the creditors lent money to the trustee for the purpose of enabling the trustee the better to realise the property, and the money was expressed to be repayable out of the trust property, the court refused to imply any personal obligation on the part of the trustee.[1606] So also, where a trustee advanced money to herself and a co-trustee for the purposes of the trust estate, the transaction was held to be a loan under s.408 of the Income Tax Act 1952 even on the assumption that her only right was to reimbursement in equity out of the trust property.[1607]

39-264 Proof of loan   If money is proved, or admitted, to have been paid by A to B, then in the absence of any circumstances suggesting a presumption of advancement, there is prima facie an obligation to repay the money; accordingly if B claims that the money was intended as a gift, the onus is on him to prove this fact.[1608]

39-265 Breach of executory contract: remedies of borrower[1609]   If a person contracts

---

[1600] *Goldberg v Tait* [1950] N.Z.L.R. 976; *Cash Order Purchases v Brady* [1952] N.Z.L.R. 898; *Premier Clothing Co v Hillcoat* [1969] C.L.Y. 2279a; see below, para.39-481.

[1601] *NG Napier Ltd v Patterson*, 1959 S.C.(J.) 48; *MacDonald v NG Napier Ltd*, 1960 S.L.T. 345; *NG Napier Ltd v Corbett*, 1962 S.L.T. (Sh Ct) 90.

[1602] See below, paras 39-472 et seq.

[1603] On the characterisation of transactions generally, see *Welsh Development Agency v Export Finance Co Ltd* [1992] B.C.C. 270 (sale or security); and *Agnew v Commissioner of Inland Revenue* [2001] UKPC 28, [2001] 2 A.C. 710 (fixed or floating charge).

[1604] *Spargo's Case* (1872-73) L.R. 8 Ch. 407.

[1605] *Levett v Barclays Bank Plc* [1995] 1 W.L.R. 1260, 1271.

[1606] *Mathew v Blackmore* (1857) 1 H. & N. 762.

[1607] *De Vigier v IRC* [1964] 1 W.L.R. 1073.

[1608] *Seldon v Davidson* [1968] 1 W.L.R. 1083.

[1609] For a discussion in the context of the model contract of the Loan Markets Association, Multicurrency Term and Revolving Facilities Agreement (April 2009), see Rawlings (2012) J.B.L. 89.

to lend money,[1610] and then, in breach of contract, refuses or fails to advance the money, the borrower cannot sue for the money agreed to be loaned as a debt, for this would be tantamount to an order of specific enforcement, and such an order will not normally be granted for a contract of loan.[1611] But the borrower can claim damages for the failure to advance the money. The damages will very often be merely nominal,[1612] but if expense has been reasonably incurred in procuring the loan elsewhere, that expense is recoverable as special damage provided it was caused by the breach and was within the contemplation of the parties.[1613] If the borrower can only procure the loan from other sources at a higher rate of interest than that agreed under the contract, and this was reasonably foreseeable at the time when the contract was made, it seems that the borrower can recover the additional interest he will have to pay as damages from the lender.[1614] If the borrower is unable to raise the money from other sources at all, and he is consequently unable to enter into or complete some transaction for which the money is required, the lender may be liable for loss of profit on such a transaction or other consequential loss.[1615] But it would have to be shown that the lender had express notice of the purpose for which the money was required,[1616] and possibly also that the loan was agreed to be made for that purpose and for no other. The same principles will no doubt apply where it is agreed that the borrower shall be entitled to draw down the loan in tranches during a specified period, but the lender, without any breach on the part of the borrower, refuses to allow the borrower to draw down the balance of the loan.[1617]

Breach of executory contract: remedies of lender   An action by a person who **39-266** has agreed to lend money against a borrower who has refused to take the loan would be something of a rarity in practice, but (although specific performance is again unavailable[1618]) there seems no reason in principle why an action for damages should not lie where the lender can prove actual damage as a result of the breach, and the damage was reasonably foreseeable at the time of making the contract.[1619] Damages would presumably be assessed on the same principles as those discussed in the preceding paragraph.

Time for repayment   Where money is lent without any stipulation as to the time **39-267**

1610 Exceptionally, a loan agreement may confer a discretion on the lender whether to make an advance or not: *McKay (t/a Mckay Law Solicitors and Advocates) v Centurion Credit Resources LLC* [2012] EWCA Civ 1941.

1611 *Sichel v Mosenthal* (1862) 30 Beav. 371; *South African Territories v Wallington* [1898] A.C. 309; *Re Smelting Corp* [1915] 1 Ch. 472. But specific performance may now be ordered of a contract to take debentures in a company although such a contract is in law an agreement to make a loan: Companies Act 2006 s.740. cf. also *Beswick v Beswick* [1968] A.C. 58.

1612 *Manchester and Oldham Bank v Cook* (1884) 49 L.T. 674, 678; *Western Wagon & Property Co v West* [1892] 1 Ch. 271, 277; *South African Territories v Wallington* [1897] 1 Q.B. 692 (affirmed [1898] A.C. 309). See Vol.I, para.26-187.

1613 *Prehn v Royal Bank of Liverpool* (1870) L.R. 5 Ex. 92; *Bahamas Sisal Plantation v Griffin* (1897) 14 T.L.R. 139; *Astor Properties Ltd v Tunbridge Wells Equitable Friendly Society* [1936] 1 All E.R. 531.

1614 *South African Territories v Wallington*, above, at 696–697. The damages would doubtless have to be discounted to allow for the fact that the additional interest would have to be paid over a period of time.

1615 *Manchester and Oldham Bank v Cook* (1884) 49 L.T. 674; *Astor Properties Ltd v Tunbridge Wells Equitable Friendly Society*, above; *General Securities Ltd v Don Ingram Ltd* [1940] 3 D.L.R. 641.

1616 *Manchester and Oldham Bank v Cook*, above, at 678, 679.

1617 *Bank Bumiputra Malaysia Bhd v Mae Perkayuan Sdn Bhd* [1993] 1 S.C.R. 385 Malaysia.

1618 *Rogers v Challis* (1859) 27 Beav. 175.

1619 *McGregor on Damages*, 20th edn, para.30-031.

of repayment, a present debt is created which is generally repayable at once without any previous demand.[1620] But it is, of course, open to the parties to fix a time for repayment, or to agree that the loan will only be repayable on demand, and doubtless suitable implications as to such matters would readily be made in appropriate circumstances. In some cases, as, for example, in the case of money in a bank account, it is well settled that the loan is only repayable on demand, either on the ground of an implied term to that effect or on the ground of mercantile custom.[1621] Where the loan is repayable on demand, the making of a valid demand is a precondition of the debt becoming due. In order to constitute a valid demand:

"there must be a clear intimation that payment is required … ; nothing more is necessary, and the word 'demand' need not be used, neither is the validity of a demand lessened by its being clothed in the language of politeness; it must be of a peremptory character and unconditional, but the nature of the language is immaterial provided it has this effect."[1622]

The demand may be for "all monies due" and the amount need not be specified.[1623] Money payable on demand is repayable immediately on demand being made. The borrower is allowed only such time as is necessary to implement the mechanics of payment needed to discharge the debt before being in default; he is not allowed a reasonable time, for example, to muster the resources to pay the debt.[1624]

39-268 Term loans A loan may be made for a specified period (a term loan). In such a case repayment is due at the end of the specified period and, in the absence of any express provision or implication to the contrary, no further demand for repayment is necessary. Sometimes when making a term loan the lender will stipulate, either in the contract of loan or in the security document, that the loan is repayable on demand. Such a provision might be construed simply to mean that the loan is in fact repayable on demand but, if no demand is made, then in any event at the end of the term. However, if the loan is made for a fixed period of time and for a specific purpose, the two provisions will in some cases be inconsistent with each other, since the parties cannot be taken to have agreed both that the borrower is to have the use of the money for the fixed period and that the lender is to have the unqualified right to require repayment on demand at any time. It is submitted that, in the event of an inconsistency, the court is entitled to construe the contract in accordance with its main object and intent[1625]: if the lender makes the loan for a purpose which to his knowledge clearly involves the borrower in incurring expenditure and liabilities

---

[1620] *Norton v Ellam* (1837) 2 M. & W. 461; *Atterbury v Jarvie* (1857) 2 H. & N. 114, 120; *Re George* (1890) 44 Ch. D. 627.

[1621] *Joachimson v Swiss Bank Corp* [1921] 3 K.B. 110; *National Bank of Commerce v National Westminster Bank* [1990] 2 Lloyd's Rep. 514.

[1622] *Re Colonial Finance, Mortgage, Investment and Guarantee Corp Ltd* (1905) 6 S.R.N.S.W. 6, 9; cited with approval in *Re a Company* [1985] B.C.L.C. 37 and in *Bank of Credit and Commerce International SA v Blattner* Unreported November 20, 1986, CA (available on Westlaw).

[1623] *Bunbury Foods Pty Ltd v National Bank of Australia Ltd* (1984) 153 C.L.R. 491; *Bank of Baroda v Panessar* [1987] Ch. 335.

[1624] *Brighty v Norton* (1862) 3 B. & S. 312; *Toms v Wilson* (1862) 4 B. & S. 442, 453; *Moore v Shelley* (1883) 8 App. Cas. 285, 293; *R.A. Cripps & Son Ltd v Wickenden* [1973] 1 W.L.R. 944; *Bank of Baroda v Panessar*, above. But see the Consumer Rights Act 2015 Sch.2 para.8, replacing (for contracts made on or after October 1, 2015) the Unfair Terms in Consumer Contracts Regulations 1999 (SI 1999/2083) Sch.2 para.1(g) above, para.38-309.

[1625] See Vol.I, (generally) paras 13-014 et seq., esp. paras 13-063 and 13-070. Note *Alexander v West Bromwich Mortgage Co Ltd* [2016] EWCA Civ 496.

with a view to ultimate profit, the court may be entitled to read the repayment on demand provision as subject to the provision as to the duration of the loan, or possibly even to ignore it altogether.[1626]

Proof of repayment   Once a debt is proved to have existed, its continuation is presumed[1627]; thus the obligation to repay a loan is presumed to continue to exist unless the borrower proves that the loan has been repaid[1628] or otherwise discharged, or such repayment or discharge can properly be inferred from all the circumstances.[1629] A receipt is not conclusive but only prima facie evidence that a loan has been repaid.[1630]   **39-269**

Breach of contract to repay   Where the borrower fails to repay the loan in accordance with the terms of the contract, the lender has an action against the borrower for the money. It had been held that at common law the lender could not normally recover interest by way of damages for the period between the date when the loan should have been repaid and the date of payment or judgment,[1631] although he could do so where the loan was expressly made to carry interest, even though no express agreement was made for the payment of interest for any period after repayment should have been made.[1632] Moreover, if, by reason of the late payment the lender had actually incurred interest charges in obtaining finance from an alternative source, such loss could be recoverable as special damage, provided that it was in the reasonable contemplation of the parties at the time the contract was made that such charges would be incurred.[1633] Thus in most cases, in the absence of contractual provision, any right of the lender to obtain interest would arise only under statute.[1634] The general common law rule that damages were not recoverable for late payment was heavy criticised over the years and eventually departed from by the House of Lords in *Sempra Metals Ltd v Commissioners of Inland Revenue*.[1635] Hence there is no longer such an exception to the general principles applicable to damages. A creditor receiving late payment may now therefore, in ac-   **39-270**

[1626] *Titford Property Co Ltd v Cannon Street Acceptances* Unreported 1975 (Goff J.), reproduced in Cresswell, *Encyclopedia of Banking Law*, pp.71–72. But see *Lloyds Bank Plc v Lambert* [1999] 1 All E.R. (Comm) 161; *Bank of Ireland AMCD (Property Holdings) Ltd* [2001] 2 All E.R. (Comm) 494.

[1627] *Jackson v Irvin* (1809) 2 Camp. 48, 50; *Penny v Foy* (1828) 8 B. & C. 11.

[1628] This may be proved by any evidence: see Vol.I, para.21-060.

[1629] *Douglass v Lloyds Bank* (1929) 34 Com. Cas. 263.

[1630] See Vol.I, para.21-060.

[1631] *Page v Newman* (1829) 9 B. & C. 378; *London, Chatham & Dover Ry v South Eastern Ry* [1893] A.C. 429; *President of India v La Pintada Compania Navegacion SA* [1985] A.C. 104.

[1632] *Cook v Fowler* (1874) L.R. 7 H.L. 27; *Re Roberts* (1880) 14 Ch. D. 49. Damages for the "detention" of the debt were recoverable, though not necessarily at the contract rate.

[1633] *Trans Trust SPRL v Danubian Trading Co* [1952] 2 Q.B. 297, 306, 307; *Wadsworth v Lydell* [1981] 1 W.L.R. 598. See also *Ozalid Group (Export) Ltd v African Continental Bank Ltd* [1979] 2 Lloyd's Rep. 231; *Bacon v Cooper (Metals) Ltd* [1982] 1 All E.R. 397. cf. *Compania Financiera "Soleada" SA v Hamoor Tanker Corp Inc* [1981] 1 W.L.R. 274. See Vol.I, paras 26-187, 26-274 et seq.

[1634] In particular under the Senior Courts Act 1981 s.35A, the County Courts Act 1984 s.69, and the Arbitration Act 1996 s.49. See Vol.I, paras 26-281 et seq.; below, para.39-295.

[1635] [2007] UKHL 34, [2007] 3 W.L.R. 354. The decision was technically obiter on this point (the claim being for repayment of sums) but their Lordships went out of their way to review the general law on the recovery of interest as damages and the case has since been regarded as authority for that proposition (see e.g. *Mortgage Express v Countrywide Surveyors Ltd* [2016] EWHC 1830 (Ch) ("The law relating to interest as damages was radically altered by this decision of the House of Lords"); *Prudential Assurance Co Ltd v Revenue and Customs Commissioners* [2013] EWHC 3249 (Ch) (reversed on another point, [2016] EWCA Civ 376).

cordance with ordinary principles applicable to damages for breach of contract (including remoteness and mitigation),[1636] recover any lost interest (including compound interest[1637]), provided that the loss is pleaded and proven.

39-271 **"No set-off" clauses** A "no set-off" clause in a loan agreement is not contrary to public policy or to s.49(2) of the Senior Courts Act 1981.[1638] But such a clause might be held to be unenforceable in certain circumstances under the Unfair Contract Terms Act 1977[1639] or the Consumer Rights Act 2015,[1640] although in *Deutsche Bank (Suisse) SA v Khan*[1641] a "conventional 'no set-off' clause" withstood challenge under those provisions. The statutory set-off in a bankruptcy or winding-up is mandatory.[1642]

39-272 **Acceleration clauses** Loan agreements, and in particular those that provide for repayment of the loan by instalments, frequently stipulate that, if the borrower defaults,[1643] the loan and interest are to become immediately due and payable. The question then arises whether such a stipulation imposes a penalty and is therefore unenforceable.[1644] A clause that stipulates for accelerated payment of principal together with accrued interest is not penal.[1645] But if interest is payable on the balance outstanding, then it would seem that a stipulation for payment of future interest is penal and unenforceable.[1646] On the other hand, it has been held that, if the agreement stipulates for repayment of principal together with a certain sum by way of interest on a given date or by (say) monthly instalments of principal and interest, then a stipulation for accelerated payment of the entire sum payable is not penal.[1647]

39-273 **Events of default** Except where the loan agreement expressly or impliedly provides that the loan is repayable on demand,[1648] the right of the lender to accelerate payment will depend upon the occurrence of one or more of a number of "events

---

[1636] See generally, Vol.I, Ch.26.

[1637] See below, para.39-289.

[1638] *Coca-Cola Financial Corp v Finsat International Ltd* [1998] Q.B. 43.

[1639] See Vol.I, para.15-104. But see *Surzur Overseas Ltd v Ocean Reliance Shipping Ltd* [1997] C.L.Y. 906; *Skipskredittforeningen v Emperor Navigation* [1998] 1 Lloyd's Rep. 66; *WRM Group Ltd v Wood* [1998] C.L.C. 189; *FG Wilson (Engineering) Ltd v John Holt & Co (Liverpool) Ltd* [2012] EWHC 2477 (Comm), [2012] 2 Lloyd's Rep 479. See the unsuccessful attempt to invoke that Act in *African Export-Import Bank v Shebah Exploration and Product Co Ltd* [2016] EWHC 311 (Comm) (syndicated loan).

[1640] Replacing (for contracts made on or after October 1, 2015) the Unfair Terms in Consumer Contracts Regulations 1999 (SI 1999/2083). See above, paras 38-221 et seq.

[1641] [2013] EWHC 482 (Comm). It was also held not to give rise to an "unfair relationship" under the CCA 1974 (see above, paras 39-212 et seq.).

[1642] *National Westminster Bank Ltd v Halesowen Presswork & Assemblies Ltd* [1972] A.C. 785; *Stein v Blake* [1996] A.C. 243.

[1643] See below, para.39-273.

[1644] See Vol.I, para.26-232.

[1645] *The Angelic Star* [1988] 1 Lloyd's Rep. 122.

[1646] *The Angelic Star*, above, per Donaldson M.R. at 125.

[1647] *Protector Endowment Loan & Annuity Co v Grice* (1880) 5 Q.B.D. 592; *Wallingford v Mutual Society* (1880) 5 App. Cas. 685. See also *Wadham Stringer Finance Ltd v Meaney* [1981] 1 W.L.R. 39. Contrast *United Dominions Trust Ltd v Patterson* [1973] N.I. 142; *United Dominions Trust v Thomas* [1976] C.L.Y. 1618, Cty Ct. See Vol.I, para.26-232. But see the Consumer Rights Act 2015 Pt 2, replacing (for contracts made on or after October 1, 2015) the Unfair Terms in Consumer Contracts Regulations 1999 (SI 1999/2083) above paras 38-221 et seq.

[1648] A loan may be advanced for a fixed term but nevertheless be repayable at any time on demand, see

of default" specified in the loan agreement. The principal occurrences in respect of which an event of default will be stated to occur are failure to pay interest or an instalment of principal when due, non-compliance with any other covenant in the agreement, and breach of any representation or warranty made or given in respect of the agreement. In addition, the following occurrences are often made events of default: the insolvency of the borrower, the presentation of a petition or the passing of a resolution for the winding-up of the borrower, the appointment of an administrator, the appointment of a receiver of any of the assets of the borrower, the levying of execution or any legal process on any of his property, and (if the borrower is a partnership) the dissolution of the partnership. In some cases it may be required that any breach by the borrower of the loan agreement be "material" or "substantial" before it is to have this effect, or, if the breach is remediable, that the borrower be notified of the breach and allowed a certain period of time within which to remedy it. But, unless otherwise stipulated, there is generally no obligation[1649] on the lender, for example to notify the borrower that he is in arrears or to allow him further time to pay, and the right of the lender to call for immediate repayment of the outstanding balance of the loan may arise automatically upon the occurrence of an event of default.

Defective notice A notice of acceleration purporting to have been given under an **39-274** "events of default" clause when no event of default has arisen will normally be merely ineffective and will not, in the absence of any contractual obligation (express or implied) between the person giving the notice and the borrower, give rise to any liability on the part of that person to the borrower.[1650]

Cross-default clauses The purpose of a cross-default clause is to enable the **39-275** lender to accelerate payment upon default by the borrower in the performance of his obligations under any other agreement with the lender or, in some cases, with any associated company of the lender. The cross-default clause may be drafted even more widely so as to confer a right to accelerate should any indebtedness of the borrower to any other lender not be paid when due for payment or, if payable on demand, should not be paid when demanded. While it may be objected that it is unfair to the borrower that a lender should be entitled to require immediate repayment under a loan agreement when the borrower has fully performed all of his obligations under that agreement, there is no doubt that such a clause will be upheld in a commercial agreement.[1651]

Failure of purposes for which money lent Where money is lent for some **39-276**

---

above, para.39-263.

[1649] Except in the case of a regulated agreement under the Consumer Credit Act 1974, see ss.76, 86B, 86C, 87, 98, 98A(3) (see above, paras 39-131, 39-134, 39-164, 39-166, 39-172, 39-173). See also the "unfair relationship" provisions (above, paras 39-212 et seq., especially *Patel v Patel* [2009] EWHC 3264 (QB), above, para.39-222) and the Consumer Rights Act 2015 Pt 2, replacing (for contracts made on or after October 1, 2015) the Unfair Terms in Consumer Contracts Regulations 1999 (SI 1999/2083) Sch.2 para.1(g); above, para.38-309).

[1650] *Concord Trust v Law Debenture Trust Corp Plc* [2005] UKHL 27, [2005] 1 W.L.R. 1592 at [30]–[45].

[1651] Such a clause survived challenge (in the business context) under the "unfair relationship" provisions (above, paras 39-212 et seq.) in *Rahman v HSBC Bank Plc* [2012] EWHC 11 (Ch). But where the borrower is a consumer, see the Consumer Rights Act 2015 Pt 2, replacing (for contracts made on or after October 1, 2015) Unfair Terms in Consumer Contracts Regulations 1999 (SI 1999/2083) reg.5, above, paras 38-241 et seq.

specific purpose, and the purpose fails for one reason or another, the lender may sometimes have equitable remedies in rem under a so-called "Quistclose Trust" (after the case of that name) for the recovery of his money which are superior to an action in personam on the loan, since they may enable the lender to recover the money even where the borrower is insolvent.[1652] The nature of such a trust and when it arises are of some complexity, but in the loan context it has been said that "the question in every case is whether the parties intended the money to be at the free disposal of the recipient".[1653]

39-277 Secured loans A loan may, and in practice commonly will, be secured in one of a number of different ways. But the existence of security does not mean that the lender is bound to look only to the security for repayment of the debt. Prima facie the borrower's personal obligation remains unaffected by the security, and the lender may either disregard the security and sue the borrower on the loan,[1654] or he may realise the security, and, if it proves insufficient, sue for the balance. But if the lender chooses to sue on the loan he is under an obligation, on payment of the debt, to hand over the security, and if he is unable to do so (e.g. because he has improperly parted with it) he cannot have judgment for the debt.[1655] Acceptance of a negotiable instrument, such as a promissory note, as security for a loan does not suspend the lender's right of action on the loan or extinguish the debt[1656]; but if it is accepted in payment, the lender's right of action on the loan may be suspended during the currency of the instrument, since it normally amounts to conditional payment of the debt.[1657] It is also possible that the lender may agree to look only to the security for repayment, thereby leaving the borrower free of any personal obligation, so that the borrower will not be liable even if the security is insufficient: whether this is so in any particular case depends on the intention of the parties and the construction of any written agreement between them.[1658] But in the absence of special circumstances a court is unlikely to infer that the borrower is under no

---

[1652] *Barclays Bank Ltd v Quistclose Investment Ltd* [1970] A.C. 567; affirming [1968] Ch. 540. See also *Carreras Rothmans Ltd v Freeman Matthews Treasure Ltd* [1985] Ch. 207; *Re EVTR* [1987] B.C.L.C. 646, CA; *Twinsectra Ltd v Yardley* [2002] UKHL 12, [2002] 2 A.C. 164. Contrast *Westdeutsche Landesbank Girozentrale v Islington London BC* [1996] A.C. 669 (loan for ultra vires purpose).

[1653] per Lord Millett in *Twinsectra Ltd v Yardley* [2002] 2 A.C. 164, 185. See discussions (and further references) in the specialist texts, e.g. Beale, Bridge, Gullifer and Lomnicka, *The Law of Security and Title-Based Financing* (2017), paras 8.128 et seq. See also Swadling (ed.) *The Quistclose Trust: Critical Essays* (2004); Chambers, *Resulting Trusts* (1997), Ch.3; Worthington, *Proprietary Interests in Commercial Transactions* (1996), Ch.3; Millett (1985) 101 L.Q.R. 269; Rickett (1991) 107 L.Q.R. 608; Bridge (1992) 12 O.J.L.S. 333; Ho and Smart (2001) 21 O.J.L.S. 267; Glister [2004] L.M.C.L.Q. 460.

[1654] *China and Southsea Bank Ltd v Tan Soon Gin* [1990] 1 A.C. 536, 545; *National Westminster Bank Plc v Kitch* [1996] 1 W.L.R. 1316; *Re Bank of Credit and Commerce International SA (No.8)* [1998] A.C. 214.

[1655] *Ellis & Co's Trustee v Dixon-Johnson* [1925] A.C. 489.

[1656] *Re Rankin and Shiliday* [1927] N.I. 162; *Modern Light Cars Ltd v Seals* [1934] 1 K.B. 32.

[1657] See, e.g. *Bolt & Nut Co (Tipton) Ltd v Rowlands, Nicholls & Co Ltd* [1964] 2 Q.B. 10; Vol.I, para.21-075.

[1658] *Barclays Bank v Beck* [1952] 2 Q.B. 47; *Lloyds Bank v Margolis* [1954] 1 W.L.R. 644; *Levett v Barclays Bank* [1995] 1 W.L.R. 1260, 1271. See also *Tam Wing Chuen v Bank of Credit and Commerce Hong Kong Ltd* [1996] B.C.C. 388; *Re Bank of Credit and Commerce International SA (No.8)* [1998] A.C. 214; *Fairmile Portfolio Management Ltd v Davies Arnold Cooper* [1998] C.L.Y. 2520.

personal liability. Indeed, even in the absence of an express promise to repay the loan, a personal liability may be inferred despite the existence of some security.[1659]

There are, broadly, two kinds of security that may be given for a loan. The first **39-278** is so-called personal security, consisting in a guarantee by a third party of the borrower's indebtedness or an indemnity by a third party against loss sustained by the lender in the event that the borrower fails to repay,[1660] or a negotiable instrument such as a promissory note. The second is so-called real security, consisting in rights in or over property belonging to the borrower (or, sometimes, a third party) which are created in favour of or transferred to the lender and to which the lender can have resort in the event of the borrower's failure to repay and in priority to the claims of other (unsecured) creditors of the borrower. Real security may be taken over land or an interest in land, chattels, documents representing chattels such as bills of lading, sea and air waybills, delivery orders and warehouse receipts,[1661] or over legal rights only, such as stocks and shares, insurance policies,[1662] credit balances,[1663] accounts receivable,[1664] or intellectual or industrial property rights. The lender may take physical possession of the property, as in the case of a pledge.[1665] But more often the security will be non-possessory, and will consist of a mortgage, charge (fixed or floating), bill of sale, hypothecation, assignment or declaration of trust of rights in or over the property. The formalities for the creation or transfer of the security, the remedies available for its enforcement, priorities, the right to the proceeds and the right to trace, and the circumstances in which a third party may acquire an overriding title to the collateral will depend upon the form of security employed and the nature of the collateral. It would be impractical to attempt to discuss such matters in this chapter and reference should therefore be made to specialist works. There is at present no general system for the registration of security interests in property other than land.[1666] But certain security interests may require to be registered (though not necessarily as a condition of their validity), for example, under the Bills of Sale Act (1878) Amendment Act 1882,[1667] the Companies Act 2006,[1668] the Agricultural Credits Act 1928[1669] and the Agricultural Marketing Act 1958,[1670] the Merchant Shipping Act 1995,[1671] the Civil Aviation Act 1982,[1672] the

---

[1659] *Yates v Aston* (1843) 4 Q.B. 182; *Marryat v Marryat* (1860) 28 Beav. 224; *Isaacson v Harwood* (1868) L.R. 3 Ch. App. 225; *Saunders v Milsome* (1866) L.R. 2 Eq. 573; *Jackson v North Eastern Ry* (1877) 7 Ch. D. 573; *MS Fashions Ltd v Bank of Credit and Commerce International SA* [1993] Ch. 425, 431 (but see the observations on this case in *Re Bank of Credit and Commerce International SA (No.8)*, above).

[1660] See below, Ch.45.

[1661] See, e.g. Factors Act 1889 s.1(4).

[1662] See below, Ch.42.

[1663] *Re Bank of Credit and Commerce International SA (No.8)* [1998] A.C. 214; see above, Ch.34.

[1664] See Vol.I, Ch.19.

[1665] See above, para.33-121.

[1666] But see the (Crowther) Report of the Committee on Consumer Credit (1971) Cmnd.4596, *A Review of Security Interests in Property* by Professor A.L. Diamond (DTI Paper, 1989) and the Law Commission's *Company Security Interests* (Law Com No.296, 2005).

[1667] See below, para.39-519.

[1668] s.860. See Vol.I, para.10-046.

[1669] s.9.

[1670] s.15.

[1671] s.16 and Sch.1; see below, para.39-524.

[1672] s.86; see below, para.39-525.

Insolvency Act 1986[1673] and the Co-operative and Community Benefit Societies Act 2014.[1674]

39-279   **Pari passu and negative pledge clauses**   So-called negative pledge clauses take a variety of forms. Their purpose is to protect a first lender should the borrower seek to incur further indebtedness from subsequent lenders. Historically they were included in floating charge agreements and limited the authority of the chargor to deal with the collateral, in particular to create any subsequent security ranking in priority to or pari passu with the charge.[1675] But modern more complex forms of clause can arise in any loan contract[1676] and often preclude the borrower from incurring any further secured debt without the consent of the lender or even (the so-called affirmative negative pledge clause[1677]) requiring the borrower to give parity of position to the first lender[1678] should the borrower incur further secured debt. Whilst such a clause clearly has contractual effect and can be enforced by the lender by injunction should he realise that the borrower is about to breach it,[1679] whether it has any effect on third parties is less clear. Much will depend on the terms of the clause but it seems clear that in some circumstances it will affect subsequent lenders. Ordinary principles of agency will determine if third parties dealing with collateral that is the subject of a floating charge with a negative pledge clause, are bound by it.[1680] Moreover, such a clause is now registrable under the Companies Act 2006.[1681] But beyond this, whether the clause can have any proprietary effect is subject to much dispute and has yet to be authoritatively determined.[1682]

39-280   **Subordination agreements**   A subordination agreement is one by which a creditor agrees that his security or claim to a debt shall be subordinated to the security or claim of another creditor of the borrower. Subordination agreements may take many forms.[1683] The legal problems created by subordination and, in particular,

---

[1673] s.344.

[1674] Pt 5 (Charges over society's assets).

[1675] See *Re Automatic Bottle Makers Ltd* [1926] Ch. 412, CA.

[1676] They are particularly prevalent in international/syndicated loans. See Wood, *International Loans, Bonds Guarantees and Legal Opinions*, 2nd edn (2007), paras 5-008 et seq.; Tennekoon, *The Law and Regulation of International Finance*, 2nd edn (1998); Cranston, *Principles of Banking Law*, 3rd edn (2018), pp.433 et seq. esp. 440.; Boardman & Crosthwaite (1986) 3 J.I.B.L. 162; Maxton [1993] J.B.L. 458; Wo (1999) 14 J.I.B.L. 360; McKnight (2002) 17 J.I.B.L.193, 203.

[1677] Stone (1991) 6 J.I.B.L. 364.

[1678] Either pari passu security over the collateral or security over other collateral of equal value. For the many varieties of such clauses and their possible different consequences, see the texts cited in the footnote above.

[1679] And breach is a "default event", see above, para.39-273.

[1680] In particular, the issue will turn on whether the chargor has ostensible authority to deal with the collateral. See above, Ch.31, esp. para.31-056.

[1681] s.859D(2)(c), added on April 3, 2013 by SI 2013/600.

[1682] For discussions written before the possibility of registering negative pledge clauses under the 2006 Act, see Gough, *Company Charges*, 2nd edn (1996), p.357; *Goode and Gullifer on Legal Problems of Credit and Security*, 5th edn (2017), paras 1.71–1.78; Farrar (1974) 38 Conv. N.S. 315, 319; Beale, Bridge, Gullifer and Lomnicka, *The Law of Security and Title-Based Financing* (2018), paras 8.81 et seq.

[1683] See, e.g. *Cheah v Equiticorp Finance Group Ltd* [1992] 1 A.C. 472 (variation of mortgage priorities); *Banque Financière de la Cité SA v Parc (Battersea) Ltd* [1999] 1 A.C. 221 (letter of postponement); *Re SSSL Realisations (20–02) Ltd* [2004] EWHC 1760 (Ch).

whether it is possible to contract out of pari passu distribution on insolvency,[1684] lie outside the scope of this chapter.[1685]

Unconscionable bargains with expectant heirs   During the eighteenth and nineteenth centuries courts of equity developed a principle that enabled them to set aside loans[1686] at exorbitant rates of interest made to "expectant heirs".[1687] In the *Earl of Aylesford's* case,[1688] the plaintiff, who was 22 years of age, and entitled to large property in the event of his surviving his father, borrowed money at about 60 per cent on bills; the court restrained an action upon the bills and decreed that they should be delivered up on payment of the sums actually advanced and interest at 5 per cent. Since most of these cases were decided, a number of statutes have been passed which make recourse to this equitable principle unnecessary in most circumstances, most recently, the Consumer Credit Act 1974.[1689] In a modern case in which the principle was invoked, the Court of Appeal refused to apply it on the ground that the borrower had renewed bills several times after he had sold his reversion and therefore ceased to be an "expectant heir".[1690] The court also used language which might be understood to mean that they thought the whole principle was obsolete; but there have been a number of cases in which contracts have been set aside as unconscionable.[1691]

39-281

Illegal loans   A loan prohibited by statute is illegal and irrecoverable,[1692] and so is a loan made for the express purpose of accomplishing an illegal object.[1693]

39-282

Student loans   These are governed by Pt II of the Teaching and Higher Education Act 1998 and regulations[1694] made thereunder.

39-283

[1684] See *National Westminster Bank Ltd v Halesowen Presswork and Assemblies Ltd* [1972] A.C. 785; *British Eagle International Airlines Ltd v Air France* [1975] 1 W.L.R. 758; *Re Maxwell Communications Corp Plc (No.3)* [1993] B.C.C. 369.

[1685] See Wood, *Project Finance, Securitisations, Subordinated Debt* (2007), Chs 10–14; Beale, Bridge, Gullifer and Lomnicka, *The Law of Security and Title-Based Financing* (2018), paras 14-108 et seq. ("priority agreements" between secured creditors) and paras 8.104 et seq. ("contractual subordination" between unsecured creditors); Powell [1993] L.M.C.L.Q. 357.

[1686] The principle also applied to the sale of a reversion at an undervalue. By s.174 of the Law of Property Act 1925, a sale of a reversion can no longer be set aside merely because it was at an undervalue, but this does not affect the court's jurisdiction to deal with unconscionable bargains.

[1687] *Earl Chesterfield v Janssen* (1750) 2 Ves. Sen. 125; *Earl of Aylesford v Morris* (1872-73) L.R. 8 Ch. App. 484; *O'Rorke v Bolingbroke* (1877) 2 App. Cas. 814; *Nevill v Snelling* (1880) 15 Ch. D. 679; *Fry v Lane* (1888) 40 Ch. D. 312; *James v Kerr* (1889) 40 Ch. D. 449; *Rees v De Bernardy* [1896] 2 Ch. 437.

[1688] (1872-73) L.R. 8 Ch. App. 484.

[1689] See the "unfair relationship" provisions in ss.140A–140C (above, paras 39-212 et seq.). Previous statutes (repealed by that Act) were the Infants Relief Act 1874 and Betting and Loans (Infants) Act 1892.

[1690] *Levin v Roth* [1950] 1 All E.R. 698n.

[1691] See above, Vol.I, paras 8-132—8-145.

[1692] *Boissevain v Weil* [1950] A.C. 327; see Vol.I, paras 16-175 et seq.

[1693] *Boissevain v Weil*, above; as to money lent for gaming or to pay gaming debts, see below, para.41-035.

[1694] Education (Student Support) Regulations 2011 (SI 2011/1986). See also the Education (Student Loans) (Repayment) Regulations 2009 (SI 2009/470), as amended.

(b) Interest[1695]

39-284   **General rule at common law**   At common law, the general rule was that interest was not payable on a debt or loan in the absence of express agreement or some course of dealing or custom to that effect.[1696] Thus, in the absence of express stipulation, it has been held that interest was not payable on the price of goods sold, although the price was payable on a certain day[1697]; nor for money lent to, or paid for, the defendant[1698]; nor on a claim for money had and received to the plaintiff's use unless fraud was proved[1699]; nor on a guarantee[1700]; nor on money due on a building contract for work done by the contractor, payment for which is in arrears.[1701] This principle differs from the (now abolished) rule already noted,[1702] that interest could not normally be awarded by way of damages for non-payment of money. The former principle means that interest is not payable under the contract itself, in the absence of express agreement or custom; the latter rule meant that interest could not be awarded by way of damages for breach of contract. The former principle remains in force, though its scope has been reduced by both equitable and statutory developments.[1703]

39-285   **Interest payable by agreement, course of dealing or custom**   Contractual interest is, of course, payable wherever there is an express agreement to that effect. Such an agreement may also be inferred from a course of dealing between the parties, e.g. if it has been frequently charged and paid without objection in similar accounts.[1704] Similarly, an obligation to pay interest may arise from the custom or usages of a particular trade or business.[1705]

39-286   A contract to pay interest up to the date of repayment of the debt does not necessarily imply an agreement to pay interest beyond that date in the event of default in repayment[1706] but in this situation interest (though not necessarily at the contract rate) can be awarded by way of damages.[1707]

39-287   **Interest payable in equity**   In certain circumstances, the rule in equity is that interest is payable even in the absence of any agreement or custom to that effect, though subject, of course, to a contrary agreement. Thus, interest is payable on a

---

[1695] See also Vol.I, paras 26-272 et seq.

[1696] *Page v Newman* (1829) 9 B. & C. 378, 381; *Re Gosman* (1881) 17 Ch. D. 771; *London, Chatham & Dover Ry v South Eastern Ry* [1893] A.C. 429; *President of India v La Pintada Compania Navegacion SA* [1985] A.C. 104; *Mathew v TM Sutton Ltd* [1994] 1 W.L.R. 1455.

[1697] *Gordon v Swan* (1810) 12 East 419; *Chalie v Duke of York* (1806) 6 Esp. 45.

[1698] *Calton v Bragg* (1812) 15 East 223; *Carr v Edwards* (1822) 3 Stark. 132.

[1699] *Johnson v The King* [1904] A.C. 817. But see below, para.39-287.

[1700] *Hare v Rickards* (1831) 7 Bing. 254, 256.

[1701] *Hill v South Staffs Ry* (1874) L.R. 18 Eq. 154.

[1702] Above, para.39-270.

[1703] See below, paras 39-287, 39-295.

[1704] *Great Western Insurance Co v Cunliffe* (1874) L.R. 9 Ch. 525; *Re Marquis of Anglesey* [1901] 2 Ch. 548; *Re Duncan & Co* [1905] 1 Ch. 307.

[1705] *Ikin v Bradley* (1818) 8 Taunt. 250; *Lloyds Bank Plc v Voller* [2000] 2 All E.R. (Comm) 987 and *Emerald Meats (London) Ltd v AIB Group (UK) Plc* [2002] EWCA Civ 460 (interest on bank overdrafts). See also below, para.39-289 (compounding of interest).

[1706] *Cook v Fowler* (1874) L.R. 7 H.L. 27, 37.

[1707] Above, para.39-270. In *Chubb v Dean* [2013] EWHC 1282 (Ch) it was confirmed that, in absence of agreement, the High Court only had power to award post-judgment interest pursuant to statute (in particular only at the rate provided for by the Judgments Act 1838, see below, para.39-295).

mortgage debt even though the deed contains no mention of interest.[1708] So also the right of a surety who has paid the creditor, to be indemnified by the principal debtor, carries a right to interest.[1709] Again, where the debtor is in a fiduciary position towards the creditor, and has in his hands moneys due to the creditor, any interest actually earned by the use of the money is recoverable by the creditor,[1710] and, indeed, it seems that interest would be recoverable even if it had not actually been earned.[1711] A trustee or fiduciary may be charged compound interest where he has wrongly profited, or may be presumed to have so profited, from having the use of another person's money.[1712] A claim for compound interest on money obtained or retained by fraud is also maintainable in equity.[1713]

Sale of land   A vendor of land is entitled to require the purchaser to pay interest   **39-288** on his unpaid purchase-money from the date when he takes, or might safely take, possession of the land.[1714] This principle is not confined to the sale of land, but extends to any contract, specific performance of which would be ordered by the court, and in which the defendant has obtained possession of the subject matter before payment of the price.[1715] It also extends to the expropriation of land under statutory powers,[1716] but not to the requisitioning of goods,[1717] though subject, of course, to express statutory provision in both cases.

Compound interest   Compound interest is payable either by agreement or   **39-289** custom, but not otherwise.[1718] By the practice of bankers, interest on a customer's indebtedness is periodically added to the capital sum advanced, so that, in effect, compound interest is achieved.[1719] At one time there was a tendency to look for actual acquiescence by the customer in the practice for holding that it was binding

---

[1708] Re Kerr's Policy (1869) L.R. 8 Eq. 331; Re Drax [1903] 1 Ch. 781; Mcnull v Smith (1943) 112 L.J. Ch. 279; Ezekiel v Orakpo [1997] 1 W.L.R. 340, 346; Al Wazir v Islamic Press Agency Inc [2001] EWCA Civ 1276, [2002] 1 Lloyd's Rep. 410.

[1709] Petre v Duncombe (1851) 20 L.J. Q.B. 242; Re Fox, Walker & Co (1880) 15 Ch. D. 400.

[1710] Brown v IRC [1965] A.C. 244; but as to the particular case of solicitors, see now Solicitors Act 1974 s.33, as amended (from March 31, 2009) by the Legal Services Act 2007 Sch.16 para.33(5).

[1711] Burdick v Garrick (1870) L.R. 5 Ch. App. 233; Harsant v Blaine Macdonald & Co (1887) 56 L.J. Q.B. 511; Dominion Coal Co v Maskinonge S.S. Co [1922] 2 K.B. 132; Mathew v TM Sutton Ltd [1994] 1 W.L.R. 1455; Westdeutsche Landesbank Girozentrale v Islington LBC [1996] A.C. 669. In Barclay v Harris (1915) 85 L.J. K.B. 115 it was held that interest can only be claimed as from the time when payment is requested, even in cases of fiduciary relationships, but where interest has actually been earned this cannot stand with Brown v IRC, above.

[1712] See below, para.39-290.

[1713] Johnson v The King [1904] A.C. 817, 822. But not on damages for deceit at common law: Black v Davies [2005] EWCA Civ 531.

[1714] Birch v Joy (1852) 3 H.L.C. 565; International Ry v Niagara Parks Commission [1941] A.C. 328, 344; Re Priestley's Contract [1947] Ch. 469. See also De Bernales v Wood (1812) 3 Camp. 258; Babacomp Ltd v Rightside Properties Ltd (1975) 234 E.G. 201 (interest payable by vendor on deposit not returned).

[1715] International Ry v Niagara Parks Commission [1941] A.C. 328.

[1716] Inglewood Pulp Co v New Brunswick Electric Power Commission [1928] A.C. 492.

[1717] Swift & Co v Board of Trade [1925] A.C. 520.

[1718] Fergusson v Fyffe (1841) 8 Cl. & F. 121, 140; Williamson v Williamson (1869) L.R. 7 Eq. 542. Re M [2010] EWHC 2324 (Admin) (contractual requirement for compound interest after the indebtedness not repaid); Porter Capital Corp v Masters [2013] EWHC 3929 (agreement expressly provided for payment of compound interest). Note Consumer Credit Act 1974 s.86F(2) (above, para.39-136: debtor or hirer under a regulated agreement under that Act (see paras 39-005 et seq., above) is only liable to pay simple interest in connection with a "default sum" (as defined in s.187A) payable under the agreement).

[1719] But the question arises whether interest can be capitalised, in the absence of express agreement, at

upon him.[1720] But it is now clear that the right to capitalise interest can be implied into the banker-customer relationship by the usage of bankers.[1721] In *National Bank of Greece SA v Pinios Shipping Co (No.1)*,[1722] the House of Lords held that a banker's entitlement to capitalise interest did not, as had previously been suggested,[1723] arise only in respect of "mercantile accounts current for mutual transactions" and that the entitlement continued until payment or judgment, notwithstanding that the banker demanded repayment of the balance due to him from the customer. It may therefore be assumed that earlier authorities to the effect that the banker's entitlement ceases when the customer dies,[1724] becomes bankrupt,[1725] or closes his account[1726] are no longer good law.

39-290   Trustees and fiduciaries   Compound interest has always been awarded in equity against a trustee or other person owing fiduciary duties who is accountable for profits made from his position. The justification for this is that, if he has improperly obtained or retained or misapplied trust money, then he must account for the profit which he made, or ought to or is presumed to have made, from the use of the money.[1727]

39-291   Tender of payment   Where a debt carries interest, and the creditor refuses a proper tender of the full amount of the capital sum and interest, he is not entitled to claim interest for any further period if the money is set aside by the debtor, and is available for repayment at any time thereafter.[1728]

39-292   Rates of interest   Since the Usury Laws Repeal Act 1854 there was, until recently (apart from the discretionary power of the court to alter interest rates conferred by the "unfair relationship" provisions in the Consumer Credit Act 1974[1729] and by the Insolvency Act 1986[1730]) no specific statutory control over the rate of interest that

---

shorter periods than yearly or half-yearly rests. This was discussed in *National Bank of Greece SA v Pinios Shipping Co (No.1)* [1990] 1 A.C. 637 (where quarterly rests were conceded). See also *Kitchen v HSBC Bank Plc* [2000] 1 All E.R. (Comm) 787 (quarterly rests).

[1720] *Lord Clancarty v Latouche* (1810) 1 Ball. & B. 120; *Crosskill v Bower* (1863) 32 Beav. 86, 100; *Deutsche Bank v Banque des Marchands de Moscou* (1931) 4 Legal Decisions Affecting Bankers 293, 295; *IRC v Graham* [1937] 2 K.B. 179, 192.

[1721] *Paris Banking Co Ltd v Yates* [1898] 2 Q.B. 460, 466; *Yourell v Hibernian Bank Ltd* [1918] A.C. 372; *IRC v Holder* [1931] 2 K.B. 81, 96, 98; affirmed on different grounds: *Holder v IRC* [1932] A.C. 624; *Paton v IRC* [1938] A.C. 341, 349, 357, 364; *National Bank of Greece SA v Pinios Shipping Co (No.1)* [1990] 1 A.C. 637.

[1722] [1990] 1 A.C. 637.

[1723] *Fergusson v Fyffe* (1841) 8 Cl. & F. 121; *Deutsche Bank v Banque des Marchands de Moscou* (1931) 4 Legal Decisions Affecting Bankers 293; *National Bank of Greece SA v Pinios Shipping Co (No.1)* [1988] 2 Lloyd's Rep. 126, CA.

[1724] *Fergusson v Fyffe* (1841) 8 Cl. & F. 121, 140; *Williamson v Williamson* (1869) L.R. 7 Eq. 542.

[1725] *Crosskill v Bower* (1863) 32 Beav. 86.

[1726] *Crosskill v Bower*, above.

[1727] *Attorney-General v Alford* (1854) 4 De G.M. & G. 843, 851; *Burdick v Garrick* (1870) L.R. 5 Ch. App. 233; *Wallersteiner v Moir (No.2)* [1975] Q.B. 373; *President of India v La Pintada Compania Navigacion SA* [1985] A.C. 104, 116; *Westdeutsche Landesbank Girozentrale v Islington LBC* [1996] A.C. 669. See also *Guardian Ocean Cargoes Ltd v Banco do Brasil SA* [1994] 2 Lloyd's Rep. 152.

[1728] *Kinnaird v Trollope* (1889) 42 Ch. D. 610; *Bank of NSW v O'Connor* (1889) 14 App. Cas. 273, 282–284; *Edmondson v Copland* [1911] 2 Ch. 301; *Barratt v Gough-Thomas* [1951] Ch. 242.

[1729] ss.140A–140C, see above, paras 39-212 et seq.

[1730] ss.244 and 343.

may be agreed by the parties to a transaction.[1731] But in response to the rise of the "pay-day lending" industry, the Financial Conduct Authority was initially given the power to control the cost of credit and various other terms in certain credit agreements[1732] and now has an *obligation* to make rules controlling the cost of "high-cost short-term credit" (as defined)[1733] and such rules came into force on January 2, 2015.[1734]

Variation of interest rate　The rate of interest stipulated in a loan agreement may be either a fixed rate or a rate that automatically varies, for example, in accordance with movements in a base rate or inter-bank rate or by reference to an index or some other factor specified in the agreement. But some loan agreements provide that the lender has the power to vary the interest rate unilaterally at his discretion.[1735] Such a provision is not unlawful as such at common law, but clear words are required to achieve that result.[1736] The power is, however, even at common law not completely unfettered. In *Paragon Finance Plc v Nash*[1737] the Court of Appeal held that the unilateral power of a mortgagee to set the rate of interest from time-to-time was subject to an implied term that the discretion to vary rates should not be exercised dishonestly, for an improper purpose, capriciously, arbitrarily or in a way in which no reasonable lender, acting reasonably, would do, although on the facts it was held that there was no real prospect of the defendant borrower proving a breach of this implied term at trial.[1738] Some further protection is afforded to a borrower who is a consumer[1739] by Sch.2 to the Consumer Rights Act 2015 Pt 2[1740] which contains an indicative and non-exhaustive list[1741] of the terms which may be regarded as unfair. It includes terms "enabling the trader to alter the terms of the

39-293

[1731] However, there is power under the Credit Unions Act 1979 s.11(5) to limit the interest that can be charged by credit unions: see the Credit Unions (Maximum Interest Rate on Loans) Order 2013 (SI 2013/2589) (3 per cent per month).

[1732] Financial Services and Markets Act 2000 s.137C (added by the Financial Services Act 2012 s.24).

[1733] Financial Services and Markets Act 2000 s.137C, as amended by the Financial Services (Banking Reform) Act 2013 s.131(1).

[1734] They are in the CONC Module of the *FCA Handbook*: see CONC 5A.

[1735] Subject to any statutory notification requirements noted below.

[1736] *Lombard Tricity Finance Ltd v Paton* [1989] 1 All E.R. 918. Applied (in context of raising fees) in: *Amberley UK Ltd v West Sussex CC* [2011] EWCA Civ 11. See *Alexander v West Bromwich Mortgage Co Ltd* [2016] EWCA Civ 496 (power to vary interest inconsistent with mortgage offered as "tracker mortgage").

[1737] [2001] EWCA Civ 1466, [2000] 1 W.L.R. 685 (pet. dis. [2002] 1 W.L.R. 2263) followed in *Broadwick Financial Services Ltd v Spencer* [2002] EWCA Civ 35, [2002] 1 All E.R. (Comm) 446 and applied (in context of raising fees and costs) in *Addison v Esso Petroleum Co Ltd* [2003] EWHC 1730 (Comm) (affirmed, on a different point, [2004] EWCA Civ 1470).

[1738] And see *Sterling Credit Ltd v Rahman (No.2)* [2002] EWHC 3008 (Ch), [2003] C.C.L.R. 13 (no implied obligation to *reduce* interest rate); *Paragon Finance Plc v Plender* [2005] EWCA Civ 760, [2005] C.C.L.R. 5 (lender increased rates due to adverse financial circumstances).

[1739] But in a commercial context see *Myers v Kestrel Acquisitions Ltd (Kestrel)* [2015] EWHC 916 (Ch) (no implied duty to vary in good faith).

[1740] Replacing (for contracts made on or after October 1, 2015) the Unfair Terms in Consumer Contracts Regulations 1999 (SI 1999/2083), as amended; above paras 38-221 et seq.

[1741] s.63, replacing (for contracts made on or after October 1, 2015) the Unfair Terms in Consumer Contracts Regulations 1999 (SI 1999/2083) reg.5(5). See the FCA's consultation paper: GC18/2: *Fairness of variation terms in financial services consumer contracts under the Consumer Rights Act 2015* (May 2018).

contract unilaterally without a valid reason which is specified in the contract",[1742] although this is expressly stated not to include[1743]:

> "… a term by which a supplier of financial services reserves the right to alter the rate of interest payable by or due to the consumer, or the amount of other charges for financial services without notice where there is a valid reason, if (a) the supplier is required to inform the consumer of the alteration at the earliest opportunity, and (b) the consumer is free to dissolve the contract immediately."

How a creditor exercises its powers of variation may also render a credit relationship "unfair" under the "unfair relationship" provisions of the Consumer Credit Act 1974[1744] and hence enable the court to exercise its wide powers to reopen a credit agreement under those provisions. In addition, now that consumer credit is regulated by the Financial Conduct Authority under the Financial Services and Markets Act 2000,[1745] the wide regulatory powers under that Act may be used to control the exercise of such a power.[1746] Moreover, consumers are also protected by various statutory notification requirements[1747] as regards interest rate variations, and the Standards of Lending Practice[1748] also stipulate for the provision by banks and building societies of information as to changes in interest rates.

39-294 **Default interest** A contractual provision for payment of a higher rate of interest after a default in payment by the borrower is open to attack as a penalty.[1749] But a clause that provides for interest to increase on default will not be held to give rise to a penalty if the increase is not retrospective but only prospective from the date of default, if the dominant contractual purpose of the clause is not to deter default, and if the increase is modest and commercially justifiable by reason of the increased

---

[1742] Consumer Rights Act 2015 Sch.2 para.11 (and see also para.12), replacing, with minor changes in wording (for contracts made on or after October 1, 2015) the Unfair Terms in Consumer Contracts Regulations 1999 (SI 1999/2083) Sch.2 para.1(j) and see also SI 1999/2083 Sch.2 para.1(k), above, paras 38-312 et seq.

[1743] Consumer Rights Act 2015 Sch.2 paras 22 (and see also para.23), replacing, with minor changes in wording (for contracts made on or after October 1, 2015) the Unfair Terms in Consumer Contracts Regulations 1999 (SI 1999/2083) Sch.2 para.2(b). See Guest and Lloyd, *Encyclopedia of Consumer Credit Law* (1975, looseleaf), para.2-083.

[1744] See above, paras 39-212 et seq.

[1745] See above, para.39-002.

[1746] Via disciplinary powers, see above, para.39-063. See also, in relation to "regulated mortgage contracts", the FCA's discussion paper, DP14/2: *Variation Terms: Assessing the Fairness of Changes to Mortgage Contracts* (July 2014) and its consultation paper: GC18/2: *Fairness of variation terms in financial services consumer contracts under the Consumer Rights Act 2015* (May 2018).

[1747] Consumer Credit Act 1974 s.82(1) (above, para.39-146) and the *FCA Handbook*, CONC 4.7 (replacing the repealed Consumer Credit Act 1974 s.78A (above, para.39-147) (notice required in the case of regulated agreements); Payment Services Regulations 2017 (SI 2017/752) (above, paras 34-224 et seq.) (notice required in the case of certain "payment services contracts").

[1748] See above, para.39-013.

[1749] *Astley v Weldon* (1801) 2 B. & P. 346, 353; *Wallis v Smith* (1882) 21 Ch. D. 243; *Dunlop Pneumatic Tyre Co Ltd v New Garage and Motor Co Ltd* [1915] A.C. 79, 86; *Cavendish Square Holdings BV v Makdessi* [2015] UKSC 67, see above, paras 26-190 et seq. See also Consumer Credit Act 1974 s.93 (above, para.39-177) and s.86F (above, para.39-136: interest on default sum can only be simple). A reduction in the rate of interest in the event of prompt payment will not make the unreduced interest penal: *Astley v Weldon*, above, at 353; *Herbert v Salisbury and Yeovil Railway Co* (1866) L.R. 2 Eq. 221; *Wallingford v Mutual Society* (1880) 5 App. Cas. 685, 702. See also *Euro London Appointments Ltd v Claessens International Ltd* [2006] EWCA Civ 385, [2006] 2 Lloyd's Rep. 436.

credit risk represented by a debtor in default.[1750] It is submitted that the current practice of banks to charge a certain rate of interest on "authorised" overdrafts, i.e. overdrafts incurred by prior arrangement with the bank, and a higher rate on "unauthorised" overdrafts (incurred without prior arrangement or in excess of the authorised overdraft limit), would not be held to impose a penalty.[1751] However, where the borrower is a consumer, a provision for payment of a higher rate of interest on default is open to challenge as being "unfair", and so not binding on the consumer, under the Consumer Rights Act 2015 Pt 2.[1752] Moreover, the "unfair relationship" provisions of the Consumer Credit Act 1974 may apply to enable the court to reopen the agreement.[1753]

Interest payable by statute　Various statutes provide for the payment of interest **39-295** in special cases. The most important of these enactments is the Late Payment of Commercial Debts (Interest) Act 1998,[1754] which imports an obligation to pay statutory (simple) interest on debts arising under certain contracts for the supply of goods or services[1755] where the purchaser and the supplier are each acting in the course of a business. The rate of interest is that prescribed by order.[1756] Other general statutory provisions are contained in: the Judgments Act 1838 (interest on High Court judgment debts),[1757] the Bills of Exchange Act 1882 (interest on dishonoured bills and notes),[1758] the Partnership Act 1890 (interest on money advanced by partner to firm and on profits made after dissolution),[1759] the Arbitration Act 1996 (power of the arbitral tribunal to award interest),[1760] the Senior Courts Act 1981 (interest on debt or damages in the High Court)[1761] and the County Courts Act 1984 (interest on debt or damages and on judgements in the county court).[1762]

Further provision for the payment of interest is made by a number of miscellane-　**39-296** ous enactments. Thus, after payment of all debts of a bankrupt, interest for the period since the commencement of the bankruptcy is payable under the Insolvency

---

[1750] *Lordsvale Finance Plc v Bank of Zambia* [1996] Q.B. 752 (approved in *Cavendish Square Holdings BV v Makdessi* [2015] UKSC 67 at [26]–[28], [146]–[148], [222] and [239]–[241]); *Lancore Services Ltd v Barclays Bank Plc* [2008] EWHC 1264 (Ch); *Deutsche Bank (Suisse) SA v Khan* [2013] EWHC 482 (Comm), noted at [2013] C.C.L.R. 5. Contrast *Jeancharm Ltd v Barnet Football Club Ltd* [2003] EWCA Civ 58, [2003] 92 Const. L.R. 26 (default interest of 5 per cent per week held penal).

[1751] See also above, para.39-177.

[1752] Replacing, with minor changes in wording, (for contracts made on or after October 1, 2015) the Unfair Terms in Consumer Contracts Regulations 1999, see above, paras 38-221 et seq. and for a case under those regulations: *Falco Finance Ltd v Gough* (1999) 149 N.L.J. 7.

[1753] See below, para.39-301.

[1754] As amended, especially by the Late Payments of Commercial Debts Regulations 2002 (SI 2002/1674). See Vol.I, paras 26-277 et seq.

[1755] s.2 (other than an excepted contract). Consumer credit agreements are excepted (s.2(5)(a)).

[1756] SI 2002/1675 art.4 (presently 8 per cent over the official dealing rate of the Bank of England).

[1757] s.17 (as replaced by SI 1998/2940 art.3). See Vol.I, para.26-291.

[1758] s.57, as amended. See above, para.34-117.

[1759] s.24(3) and 42.

[1760] s.49. See above, para.32-136.

[1761] s.35A, inserted by s.15 and Sch.1 Pt I of the Administration of Justice Act 1982. See Vol.I, para.26-281 (high court).

[1762] s.69, as amended (interest on debt or damages) and s.74, as amended (and County Courts (Interest on Judgment Debts) Order 1991 (SI 1991/1184) (L.12)) (interest on county court judgment debts). See *McMullon v Secure the Bridge Ltd* [2015] EWCA Civ 884 (award of 8 per cent interest in case of CCA 1974-regulated agreement).

Act 1986[1763] if any assets remain, and similar provisions exist in relation to insolvent companies.[1764] There are also a number of rules of court dealing with payment of interest in various circumstances.[1765]

39-297 **Contractual interest after judgment** Often it is agreed that interest at the contractual rate is payable "after as well as before any judgment".[1766] The validity of such a provision depends on "whether the covenant for the payment of interest is an independent covenant or a covenant which is merely ancillary to the payment of the principal money".[1767] If the covenant is merely ancillary, the promise merges in the judgment.[1768] In *Director General of Fair Trading v First National Bank Plc*[1769] the House of Lords held that a term in a consumer contract that the borrower was to continue to pay interest at the contractual rate until the discharge of any judgment obtained by the lender, was not an unfair term under the Unfair Terms in Consumer Contracts Regulations 1994.[1770] However, if an agreement regulated by the Consumer Credit Act 1974 contains such a term, the creditor or owner is now[1771] obliged to notify the debtor or hirer that such post-judgment interest is accruing.[1772]

(c) Effect of Consumer Credit Regulation

39-298 **Moneylenders Acts** The Moneylenders Acts 1900 to 1927 placed severe restrictions upon the conduct of business by persons engaged in money lending. However, the Acts applied only to loans made by moneylenders.[1773] Further, as a general rule, the slightest infringement of the statutory requirements rendered the whole loan irrecoverable and any security unenforceable, with the result that borrowers were encouraged to take technical points which were wholly devoid of merit.[1774] The Acts were entirely repealed by the Consumer Credit Act 1974.[1775]

39-299 **Consumer credit regulation** The consumer credit regulation regime applies to

---

[1763] s.328(4), (5). cf. s.322(2).

[1764] s.189.

[1765] See, e.g. CPR rr.12.6, 14.14, 40.8.

[1766] For a case where there was no such agreement (and hence where the High Court only had power to award post-judgment interest pursuant to statute) see *Chubb v Dean* [2013] EWHC 1282 (Ch).

[1767] *Economic Life Assurance Society v Usborne* [1902] A.C. 147, 152 (no merger). See also *Popple v Sylvester* (1882) 22 Ch. D. 98; *Re Sneyd* (1883) 25 Ch. D. 338; *Ealing London BC v El Isaac* [1980] 1 W.L.R. 932, 936; *Director General of Fair Trading v First National Bank Plc* [2001] UKHL 52, [2002] 1 A.C. 481.

[1768] *Re Sneyd* (1883) 25 Ch. D. 338; see Vol.I, para.25-009.

[1769] [2001] UKHL 52, [2002] 1 A.C. 481.

[1770] SI 1994/3159, subsequently replaced by the Unfair Terms in Consumer Contracts Regulations 1999 (SI 1999/2083), and revoked and replaced, for contracts made on or after October 1, 2015, by the Consumer Rights Act 2015 Pt 2; see above, paras 38-220 et seq.

[1771] From October 1, 2008: see SI 2007/3300 art.3(3) and Sch.3.

[1772] See Consumer Credit Act 1974 s.130A (added by the Consumer Credit Act 2006 s.17), above, para.39-206.

[1773] They did not apply to other forms of credit and certain types of business, e.g. banking was exempted (see Moneylenders Act 1900 s.6(d); Companies Act 1967 s.123). Moreover, (although passed for the protection of the private borrower) the Acts protected large corporations borrowing substantial sums of money.

[1774] See, e.g. *Askinex Ltd v Green* [1969] 1 Q.B. 272; *Congresbury Motors v Anglo-Belge Finance Co* [1971] Ch. 81 (reversed by *Orakpo v Manson Investments Ltd* [1978] A.C. 95).

[1775] s.192(3)(b), (4) and Sch.5. These Acts were repealed in stages, but the final repeal (from May 19, 1985) was effected by SI 1983/1551 (c.44); but see art.6(3).

contracts of loan. Any agreement whereby one person lends or agrees to lend to an individual[1776] (including a sole trader or partnership of three or fewer persons) any amount[1777] is a consumer credit agreement[1778] for the purposes of regulation, and, if the agreement is not an exempt agreement,[1779] it is a "regulated agreement".[1780] The regulatory provisions relating to the authorisation and control of consumer credit businesses,[1781] and the regulation of regulated credit agreements, have been discussed in the first section of the present chapter.

Overdrafts   Special dispensation was originally provided for most overdrafts from   **39-300** the documentation and cancellation provisions in Pt V of the Consumer Credit Act 1974. However, the implementation of the Consumer Credit Directive,[1782] which itself contains special provisions for overdrafts, has resulted in complex modifications (which depend on the type of overdraft) of Pt V in relation to overdrafts.[1783] In particular, there is now an obligation to supply a copy of an overdraft agreement.[1784] Moreover, non-business overdrafts are subject to (special) pre-contract disclosure obligations[1785] and to the new (general) duty to assess creditworthiness.[1786] There are also special information provisions regarding the consequences of "overrunning" (i.e. overdrawing without a pre-arranged overdraft or exceeding a pre-arranged overdraft limit).[1787] The remainder of the 1974 Act generally continues to apply, for example, the provisions of the Act relating to the variation of agreements,[1788] the service of enforcement,[1789] default[1790] or termination[1791] notices (and other requisite notices during the course of the agreement),[1792] security,[1793] the form of guarantees and indemnities given in respect of the overdraft,[1794] and in particular the exclusive jurisdiction of the county court over actions brought by the creditor to enforce the overdraft agreement or any security relating to it.[1795]

Unfair relationships   The provisions of the Consumer Credit Act 1974 relating   **39-301**

[1776] As defined, see above, para.39-016.
[1777] Until April 6, 2007, the Consumer Credit Act 1974 imposed a financial limit, see above, para.39-005.
[1778] See above, para.39-016.
[1779] See above, paras 39-038 et seq.
[1780] See above, para.39-017.
[1781] See above, para.39-063.
[1782] See above, para.39-011.
[1783] See s.74 as amended by SI 2010/1010 reg.17.
[1784] s.61B, added on February 1, 2011 by SI 2010/1010 reg.9, as amended by SI 2010/1969 reg.7.
[1785] See above, para.39-076.
[1786] See above, para.39-078.
[1787] *FCA Handbook*, CONC 4.7 and CONC 6.3.3–6.3.4 (replacing the repealed Consumer Credit Act 1974 Pt VA (ss.74A and 74B), added on February 1, 2011 by SI 2010/1010 regs 21 and 22 (as amended by 2010/1969 regs 9 and 10)), noted above at para.39-127.
[1788] s.82(1); above, para.39-145. But note, in relation to overdrafts, the new s.82(1B)–(1E) (added on February 1, 2011 by SI 2010/1010 reg.28) and the new s.78A(4), the combined effect of which is that only *increases* in charges and interest rate need be notified.
[1789] s.76; above, para.39-164.
[1790] s.87; above, para.39-166.
[1791] s.98; above, para.39-172. But note that s.98A (above, para.39-173) dealing with the termination of agreements of indefinite duration, does not apply to overdrafts: s.98A(8).
[1792] s.78 (above, para.39-132), s.86C (above, para.39-134) and s.86E (above, para.39-135).
[1793] s.113; above, para.39-190.
[1794] SI 1983/1556; above, para.39-184.
[1795] s.141(1); above, para.39-199.

to "unfair relationships" apply to loans to individuals[1796] and they have been invoked in a number of cases concerning loans.[1797] Many cases have concerned business loans and in that context the challenge has invariably been unsuccessful.[1798]

39-302 **Liability of creditor for acts of supplier: antecedent negotiations** Where a creditor lends or agrees to lend money to a debtor under a regulated agreement in order to enable the debtor to obtain goods or services from a supplier, the creditor may in certain circumstances be liable in respect of misrepresentations made or undertakings given or breaches of contract committed by the supplier. In the first place, where negotiations[1799] ("antecedent negotiations") are conducted with the debtor by the supplier[1800] in relation to a transaction[1801] financed or proposed to be financed by a debtor-creditor-supplier agreement[1802] within s.12(b)[1803] or 12(c)[1804] of the Consumer Credit Act 1974, they are deemed to be conducted by the supplier ("the negotiator")[1805] in the capacity of agent of the creditor as well as in his actual capacity.[1806] Thus the creditor will be liable in respect of any misrepresentations made or undertakings given by the negotiator on his behalf.

39-303 **"Connected lender liability": Misrepresentation or breach by supplier** Secondly, under s.75(1) of the Consumer Credit Act 1974,[1807] if the debtor under a debtor-creditor-supplier agreement[1808] falling within s.12(b)[1809] or 12(c)[1810]

[1796] ss.140A–140C, above, paras 39-212 et seq.

[1797] *Plevin v Paragon Personal Finance Ltd* [2014] UKSC 61 (sale of PPI with loan rendered relationship "unfair" on facts); *Patel v Patel* [2009] EWHC 3264 (QB) ("exorbitant" interest "unfair"); cf. *Khodari v Tamimi* [2009] EWCA Civ 1109, [2010] C.C.L.R. 3 ("very large" 10 per cent charge for short-term loans to wealthy compulsive gambler, where credit risk was high and "defendant wanted these loans and could well afford to repay them", not "unfair relationship"); *Consolidated Finance Ltd v Hunter* [2010] B.P.I.R. 1322 (loan at market rate for similar short-term bridging loans not "unfair"); *Carey v HSBC Bank Plc* [2009] EWHC 3417 (QB); *Black Horse Ltd v Speak* [2010] EWHC 1866 (QB); *Link Financial Ltd v North Wilson* [2014] EWHC 252 (Ch), [2014] C.C.L.R. 6; *McMullon v Secure the Bridge Ltd* [2015] EWCA Civ 884. And see cases in next footnote.

[1798] *Paragon Mortgages Ltd v McEwan-Peters* [2011] EWHC 2491 (Comm) (buy to let); *Holyoake & Hotblack Holdings Ltd v Nicholas Candy, Christian Candy, CPC Group Ltd* [2017] EWHC 3397 (Ch). See especially the business bank loan cases: *Rahman v HSBC Bank Plc* [2012] EWHC 11 (Ch); *Deutsche Bank (Suisse) SA v Khan* [2013] EWHC 482 (Comm), noted at [2013] C.C.L.R. 5 and cited in many subsequent "business" cases; *Chubb v Dean* [2013] EWHC 1282 (Ch); *Gardner v Clydesdale Bank Ltd* [2013] EWHC 4356 (Ch); *Barclays Bank Plc v McMillan* [2015] EWHC 1596 (Comm); *Clydesdale Bank Plc v R Gough t/t JC Gough & Sons and Anne Michelle Gough* [2017] EWHC 2230 (Ch); *Santander UK Plc v Clive Roger Wells & Graham Mervyn Wells* [2017] EWHC 2413 (Ch); *Ulster Bank Ltd v Esmaili* [2017] NICh 14; *Holyoake v Candy* [2017] EWHC 3397 (Ch) (permission to appeal refused by Court of Appeal: [2018] C.C.L.R. 8); *Carney v NM Rothschild and Sons Ltd* [2018] EWHC 958 (Comm); *Hodell v Clydesdale Bank Plc* [2018] EWHC 1009 (QB).

[1799] See Consumer Credit Act 1974 (CCA 1974) s.56(1), (4).

[1800] Defined in CCA 1974 s.189(1).

[1801] See above, para.39-027.

[1802] Defined in CCA 1974 ss.12, 189(1); above, para.39-030.

[1803] See above, para.39-031.

[1804] See above, para.39-032.

[1805] CCA 1974 s.56(1); above, para.39-073. See *Scotland v British Credit Trust Ltd* [2014] EWCA Civ 790.

[1806] CCA 1974 s.56(2). See also s.56(3), (4), and above, para.39-075.

[1807] For problems arising under s.75, see Guest and Lloyd, *Encyclopedia of Consumer Credit Law* (1975, looseleaf), para.2-076; Hare [2008] L.M.C.L.Q. 338; Bisping [2011] J.B.L. 457. See also *Rampion v Franfinance SA* (C-429/05) EU:C:2007:575, [2008] C.M.L.R. 8, ECJ (scope of art.11(2) of Consumer Credit Directive (87/102), implemented in the UK by s.75). The Law Commissions' Joint

of that Act has, in relation to a transaction[1811] financed by the agreement, any claim against the supplier[1812] in respect of a misrepresentation[1813] or breach of contract, he has a like claim[1814] against the creditor, who, with the supplier, is accordingly jointly and severally liable to the debtor.[1815] If, therefore, the transaction financed by the loan agreement is a contract of sale of goods, and the quality of the goods is such that the supplier is in breach, say, of the conditions as to satisfactory quality or fitness for purpose of the goods implied by the Sale of Goods Act 1979,[1816] then the creditor is jointly and severally liable with the supplier in damages (including damages for consequential loss) to the debtor, and, in the event that the debtor is entitled to and does reject the goods, is similarly liable with the supplier to repay to the debtor any sums paid by or on behalf of the debtor to the supplier. However, subject to any agreement between them, the creditor is entitled to be indemnified by the supplier for loss suffered by the creditor in satisfying this liability, including costs reasonably incurred by him in defending proceedings instituted by the debtor.[1817] Further, in any action brought against the creditor, he is entitled, in ac-

---

Paper: *Consumer Redress for Misleading and Aggressive Practices* Cm.8323 (March 2012), para.7.139 proposed that a "misleading practice" should qualify as a "misrepresentation" under s.75 but, although originally included in the draft of SI 2014/870, this did not appear in the enacted version.

[1808] Defined in CCA 1974 ss.12, 189(1); above, para.39-030.

[1809] See above, para.39-031.

[1810] See above, para.39-032.

[1811] See above, para.39-027. For liability if the transaction is effected abroad, see *Office of Fair Trading v Lloyds TSB Bank Plc* [2007] UKHL 48 and below, para.39-486. The transaction financed (or to be financed) by the loan will be a "linked transaction" (see CCA 1974 s.19(1)(b), above, para.39-056).

[1812] Defined in CCA 1974 s.189(1).

[1813] See Misrepresentation Act 1967 s.2(5) added by the Consumer Protection (Amendment) Regulations 2014 (SI 2014/870) reg.5: new s.2(4) and (5) (also added by those regulations) do not preclude a CCA 1974 s.75(1) damages claim if one would, but for those provisions, be available. (This is because the new s.2(4) and (5) essentially preclude a claim under s.2(1) of the 1987 Act if a claim for redress under the Consumer Protection from Unfair Trading Regulations 2008 (SI 2008/1277), as amended by SI 2014/870, is available; such a claim under the regulations (as opposed to a claim for "misrepresentation" under the 1967 Act) is not covered by s.75.)

[1814] Whilst the "like claim" does not include a right to rescind the credit agreement on the ground that the debtor is entitled to rescind the supply agreement, it is an implied term of the credit agreement that it is conditional on the survival of the supply agreement and hence the credit agreement may be rescinded on that (implied term) ground: *Durkin v DSG Retail Ltd* [2014] UKSC 21 (disapproving *United Dominions Trust v Taylor*, 1980 S.L.T. 28 Sh Ct). Alternatively (see below) the debtor is entitled to recover from the creditor sums paid to the supplier under the supply agreement when rescinded. For the right of the debtor to set off his monetary claim under s.75(1) against any claim by the creditor under the credit agreement, see *Morgan & Sons Ltd v Martin Johnson & Co Ltd* [1949] 1 K.B. 107; *Hanak v Green* [1958] 2 Q.B. 9 and CPR Pt 16 r.6.

[1815] s.75(1) applies notwithstanding that the debtor, in entering into the transaction, exceeded the credit limit (defined in CCA 1974 ss.10(2), 189(1); above, para.39-024) or otherwise contravened any term of the agreement: s.75(4).

[1816] *Grant v Electro Centre Ltd* [2007] 4 C.L. 66, Cty Ct and see below, paras 44-094 et seq. and for "consumer contracts" made on or after October 1, 2015, the Consumer Rights Act 2015, see generally paras 38-492 et seq.

[1817] s.75(2). See the discussion of the nature and scope of the indemnity in *Office of Fair Trading v Lloyds TSB Bank Plc* [2007] UKHL 48, [2008] 1 A.C. 316. And note *Parker v Black Horse Ltd* Unreported December 17, 2010, Dartford Cty Ct where it was held that a creditor, who could not recover his costs from an unsuccessful "small claims" claimant under CPR r.27.14, could recover those costs from the supplier under s.75(2): "liability" in s.75(2) covered mere "exposure to a claim" and hence there was no need for any actual liability under s.75(1) to the claimant to be established against the

cordance with rules of court,[1818] to have the supplier made a party to the proceedings.[1819]

39-304 **Exceptions**   The liability of the creditor under s.75(1) of the Act does not apply to a claim under a non-commercial agreement.[1820] Nor does it apply so far as the claim relates to any single item to which the supplier has attached a *cash* price not exceeding £100 or more than £30,000.[1821]

39-305 **Additional "connected lender liability"**   A new s.75A was added[1822] to the Consumer Credit Act 1974 in implementation of the Consumer Credit Directive,[1823] which contains additional provisions on creditor liability. The liability is generally[1824] narrower in scope than that imposed by s.75. First, s.75A does not apply to credit agreements outside the scope of the Directive.[1825] Second, it only applies in the case of so-called "linked credit agreements" (a "Directive" concept), defined[1826] to mean regulated consumer credit agreements that: (i) "exclusively" finance an agreement for the supply of specific goods or service; and (ii) where either: (a) the creditor uses the services of the supplier in connection with the preparation or making of the credit agreement, or (b) the specific goods or services are "explicitly specified" in the credit agreement. The section provides that if the debtor under such a "linked credit agreement" has a claim against the supplier in respect of a breach of contract (only), the debtor may pursue that claim against the creditor but only where, essentially, the debtor is unable to obtain satisfaction from the supplier. Thus the section only provides for so-called "second in line" liability on the part of the creditor. Third, the section does not apply if the cash value of the goods or services is £30,000 or less.[1827] Hence, it will apply (to situations otherwise within its scope), where s.75 is unavailable because the cash price exceeds that sum and s.75 will apply (to situations otherwise within its scope) where the cash price is £30,000 or less (as long as it is above £100).

[1818] CPR Pt 20.

[1819] s.75(5).

[1820] s.75(3)(a). For "non-commercial agreement", see above, para.39-049. But no exception exists under CCA 1974 s.56(2) (above, para.39-302) for non-commercial agreements: see s.74(1)(a). See also the exception for charge cards (s.75(3)(c) noted below, para.39-487).

[1821] s.75(3)(b). The lower limit was raised from £30 to £100, and the upper limit from £10,000 to £30,000, by SI 1983/1878. But the limitations in s.75(3)(b) do not apply to the liability of the creditor under CCA 1974 s.56(2) (above, para.39-302).

[1822] On February 1, 2011 by 2010/1010 reg.25 (as amended by SI 2010/1969 reg.11). See CCA 1974 s.189B(3), Sch.2A: in s.75A, references to "debtor" in relation to "green deal plans" (as defined in CCA 1974 s.189(1), see above, para.39-257) are to be read as references to the "improver" (as defined in CCA 1974 s.189B(6)).

[1823] See above, para.39-011. See especially art.15.2 (and 15.3) of the Directive.

[1824] But see below: it (unlike s.75) applies where the cash price is over £30,000.

[1825] s.75A(6)(b)–(c) and (7), viz: (i) credit in excess of £60,260, (ii) "business" credit and (iii) agreements secured on land. Since the Mortgage Credit Directive (see above, para.39-003) was implemented on March 21, 2016, exemption (i) no longer applies to so-called "residential renovation agreements" (as defined in CCA 1974 s.189(1) to mean, essentially, unsecured loans to renovate residential property) above this threshold: see amendment to s.75A in SI 2015/910 art.3 and Sch.1 para.2(7).

[1826] In s.75A(5).

[1827] s.75A(6)(a).

3.   HIRE-PURCHASE AGREEMENTS

(a)   In General[1828]

Nature of hire-purchase   A hire-purchase agreement may be defined as an agreement under which an owner lets chattels of any description out on hire and further agrees that the hirer may either return the goods and terminate the hiring or elect to purchase the goods when the payments for hire have reached a sum equal to the amount of the purchase price stated in the agreement or upon payment of a stated sum.[1829] The essence of the transaction is therefore (i) a bailment of goods by the owner to the hirer; and (ii) an agreement by which the hirer has the option to return or purchase the goods at some time or other.

39-306

Option to purchase goods   One reason for the popularity of hire-purchase as a vehicle of instalment credit lies in the fact that, until the full price is paid, the property in the goods remains in the owner, and in such a way that the hirer is normally unable to pass a good title to a third party during the continuance of the bailment.[1830] If the agreement gives to the hirer a true option to return or purchase the goods, he is under no obligation to purchase them; he is therefore not a person who has "agreed to buy the goods" and so cannot pass a good title to a third party under s.25 of the Sale of Goods Act 1979.[1831]

39-307

Moneylenders Acts   A second reason for the popularity of hire-purchase was that it does not involve any lending of money,[1832] and so fell outside the control of the (now repealed) Moneylenders Acts 1900 to 1927. The normal methods of financing hire-purchase transactions by the "direct collection" method[1833] or by block discounting[1834] or the purchase of bills of exchange at a discount[1835] were not within the Acts. Thus the financier did not have to hold a moneylender's licence; he was

39-308

[1828] The treatises on this subject are Campbell-Salmon, *Hire-Purchase and Credit-Sales Law and Practice* (1962); Goode, *Hire-Purchase Law and Practice*, 2nd edn (1970); Guest, *The Law of Hire-Purchase* (1966) and Supplement (1969); Wild, *The Law of Hire-Purchase*, 2nd edn (1965). For more recent consideration, see Beale, Bridge, Gullifer and Lomnicka, *The Law of Security and Title-Based Financing* (2018), paras 7.34–7.42; 19.23–19.29.

[1829] For the definition of "hire-purchase agreement" in the consumer credit regulatory regime, see below, para.39-356.

[1830] *Helby v Matthews* [1895] A.C. 471; *Payne v Wilson* [1895] 2 Q.B. 537; *Belsize Motor Supply Co v Cox* [1914] 1 K.B. 244; *Lewis v Thomas* [1919] 1 K.B. 319; *Modern Light Cars Ltd v Seals* [1934] 1 K.B. 32; *Staffs Motor Guarantee Ltd v British Wagon Co Ltd* [1934] 2 K.B. 305; *United Dominions Trust (Commercial) Ltd v Parkway Motors Ltd* [1955] 1 W.L.R. 719; *Close Asset Finance Ltd v Care Graphics Machinery Ltd* [2000] C.C.L.R. 43. But see *Forthright Finance Ltd v Carlyle Finance Ltd* [1997] 4 All E.R. 90.

[1831] Re-enacting s.9 of the Factors Act 1889 and replacing s.25(2) of the Sale of Goods Act 1893; see below, paras 44-220 et seq. and 39-399. The option to purchase fee may be nominal even if the hirer is bound to pay all instalments: *Close Asset Finance Ltd v Care Graphics Machinery Ltd* [2000] C.C.L.R. 43.

[1832] *British Ry Traffic and Electric Co Ltd v Kahn* [1921] W.N. 52; *Automobile and General & Finance Corp Ltd v Morris* (1929) 73 S.J. 451; *Old Discount Co Ltd v Cohen* [1938] 3 All E.R. 281n.; *Premor Ltd v Shaw Bros* [1964] 1 W.L.R. 978, 985. Unless the hire-purchase agreement is a refinancing transaction (below, para.39-309) and a sham: *North Central Wagon and Finance Co Ltd v Brailsford* [1962] 1 W.L.R. 1288.

[1833] *Trade Promotion Trust Ltd v Young* (1940) 84 S.J. 646.

[1834] *Olds Discount Co Ltd v John Playfair Ltd* [1938] 3 All E.R. 275.

[1835] *Transport & General Credit Corp Ltd v Morgan* [1939] Ch. 531; *Chow Yoong Hong v Choong Fah Rubber Manufactory* [1962] A.C. 209.

free to employ agents, e.g. dealers, to obtain business; and the hire-purchase agreement itself did not have to meet the highly technical requirements of the Acts. However, as noted above, the Consumer Credit Act 1974 repealed the Moneylenders Acts and brought hire-purchase within its control.[1836]

39-309 **Bills of sale** Yet a third reason for the growth of hire-purchase is that hire-purchase agreements are not bills of sale.[1837] As the property in the chattels remains in the owner, the document by which the hiring is effected does not require to be registered as a bill of sale under the Bills of Sale Acts 1878 and 1882[1838] unless it does not represent the real transaction between the parties, and its intention is merely to create a security for money; in such a case, the courts must disregard the form, and look to the true nature of the transaction.[1839] The most satisfactory way of deciding what is the true nature of the transaction is to see whether the documents set out the deal between the parties as it took place and at the time it took place, or whether the facts, or some of them, therein recorded do not represent that which happened, but were falsified in order to give the transaction an innocent appearance.[1840] A "refinancing" transaction under which the owner of goods sells the goods to a finance company and then immediately enters into a hire-purchase agreement whereby he agrees to hire back the goods is unimpeachable if there is a genuine sale of the goods and a genuine and independent hiring back.[1841] But if the sale and rehiring are, in fact, a sham, the transaction may be invalid and unenforceable by reason of the Bills of Sale Acts.[1842] In order that the transaction should be considered to be a sham, it is not sufficient if one party alone, e.g. the hirer, intends to deceive the other into thinking that the transaction is genuine. There must be a common intention that the acts or documents are not to create the legal rights and obligations that they give the appearance of creating.[1843]

39-310 **Common law and statute** The most important question for the lawyer is whether or not a hire-purchase agreement falls within the statutory control of the consumer credit regulatory regime, in particular the Consumer Credit Act 1974.[1844] However, only certain aspects of hire-purchase are regulated and hence it will often be neces-

---

[1836] See below, paras 39-356 et seq.

[1837] See below, para.39-519.

[1838] *Re Robertson* (1878) 9 Ch. D. 419; *Crawcour v Salter* (1881) 18 Ch. D. 30; *Manchester, Sheffield and Lincolnshire Ry v North Central Wagon Co* (1888) 13 App. Cas. 554; *United Forty Pound Loan Club v Bexton* [1891] 1 Q.B. 28n.; *Modern Light Cars Ltd v Seals* [1934] 1 K.B. 32; *Olds Discount Co Ltd v Krett* [1940] 2 K.B. 117; *Re Apex Supply Co Ltd* [1942] Ch. 108. See Diamond (1960) 23 M.L.R. 399, 516.

[1839] See the cases cited below, and generally below, para.39-519.

[1840] *Polsky v S and A Services* [1951] 1 All E.R. 185, 189.

[1841] *Yorkshire Ry Wagon Co v Maclure* (1882) 21 Ch. D. 309; *British Ry Traffic and Electric Co v Kahn* [1921] W.N. 52; *Staffs Motor Guarantee Ltd v British Wagon Co Ltd* [1934] 2 K.B. 305; *Olds Discount Co Ltd v Krett* [1940] 2 K.B. 117.

[1842] *Re Watson* (1890) 25 Q.B.D. 27; *Madell v Thomas & Co* [1891] 1 Q.B. 230; *Maas v Pepper* [1905] A.C. 102; *Motor Trade Finance Ltd v HE Motors Ltd* Unreported March 26, 1926, HL; *Polsky v S and A Services*, above; *R. v Deller* (1952) 36 Cr. App. R. 184; *North Central Wagon and Finance Co v Brailsford* [1962] 1 W.L.R. 1288; *Bennett v Griffin Finance Ltd* [1967] 2 Q.B. 46. See also the now repealed (and not replaced) Companies Act 1985 s.396(1)(c)) and relevant case-law (*Stoneleigh Finance Ltd v Phillips* [1965] 2 Q.B. 537; *Re Curtain Dream Plc* [1990] B.C.L.C. 925; *Welsh Development Agency v Export Finance Co* [1992] B.C.C. 270).

[1843] *Stoneleigh Finance Ltd v Phillips*, above; *Snook v London and West Riding Investments Ltd* [1967] 2 Q.B. 786. See generally on shams, Vella [2008] L.M.C.L.Q. 488.

[1844] The Act entirely repealed (s.192(3)(b) and Sch.5) the Hire-Purchase Act 1965 as from May 19, 1985:

sary to consider common law principles as laid down by the courts. The implied conditions on the part of the owner relating to title, quality, fitness for purpose, and correspondence with description or sample are those contained in the Supply of Goods (Implied Terms) Act 1973 and for "consumer contracts"[1845] those in the Consumer Rights Act 2015.[1846] The rights and liabilities of third parties relating to the goods let on hire are determined by the Factors Act 1889,[1847] the Sale of Goods Act 1979, the Hire-Purchase Act 1964, and a number of other enactments.[1848]

(b)   At Common Law

The agreement   At common law a hire-purchase agreement may be made in any form, i.e. it may be made under seal, in writing or by word of mouth.[1849] The normal rules of construction apply, and any ambiguity in a written agreement will be construed against the maker of the document.[1850] Capacity to contract is regulated by the general law of contract.[1851]

39-311

Formation   An offer to enter into a contract of hire-purchase is normally constituted by the hirer signing the hire-purchase document, and the acceptance by the owner executing the document that the hirer has signed.[1852] But the acceptance must also be communicated to the hirer, and, until this is done, the hirer is free to withdraw his offer.[1853] At common law,[1854] a dealer who negotiates the transaction is not an agent of the owner for the purpose of fixing the owner with knowledge that the offer was made subject to an oral stipulation qualifying the hirer's liability[1855]; but the dealer is the agent of the owner for the purpose of communicating the withdrawal of the offer.[1856] Where a fraudster assumes the identity of another person whose signature he forges on the hire-purchase agreement, the agreement may be void for mistake.[1857]

39-312

Hirer bound by apparent agreement   Where the hirer signs the document in blank, leaving the dealer to fill in the details in accordance with a collateral

39-313

---

see SI 1983/1551 (c.44); but see art.6(1), (2).

[1845] Made on or after October 1, 2015.

[1846] See below, paras 39-316—39-318.

[1847] See above, paras 31-079 et seq.

[1848] See below, paras 39-398—39-413.

[1849] *Re Fowler* (1883) 23 Ch. D. 261. For the requirements of form and copies under the Consumer Credit Act 1974 ss.60, 61, 61A see above, paras 39-080 et seq.

[1850] *Webster v Higgin* [1948] 2 All E.R. 127; *Abingdon Finance Ltd v Champion* [1961] C.L.Y. 3931. See Vol.I, para.13-095.

[1851] See, e.g. *Mercantile Union Guarantee Corp v Ball* [1937] 2 K.B. 498; *Yeoman Credit Ltd v Latter* [1961] 1 W.L.R. 828; *Stadium Finance Ltd v Helm* (1965) 109 S.J. 471 (minority). See Vol.I, Chs 9–12.

[1852] Contrast *Carlyle Finance Ltd v Pallas Industrial Finance Ltd* [1999] 1 All E.R. (Comm.) 659; *Hitchens v General Guarantee Corp Ltd* [2001] EWCA Civ 359.

[1853] *Financings Ltd v Stimson* [1962] 1 W.L.R. 1184. cf. *Lowe v Lombank Ltd* [1960] 1 W.L.R. 196, 206; *Robophone Facilities Ltd v Blank* [1966] 1 W.L.R. 1428; *Maurice Lee Ltd v Rotheroe and Unipower Ltd* Unreported May 16, 1973, CA. See Vol.I, Ch.2. But the agreement may, and usually does, otherwise provide.

[1854] But see the Consumer Credit Act 1974 s.56, see above, paras 39-071 and 39-302.

[1855] *Eastern Distributors Ltd v Goldring* [1957] 2 Q.B. 600; *Northgran Finance Ltd v Ashley* [1963] 1 Q.B. 476.

[1856] *Financings Ltd v Stimson* [1982] 1 W.L.R. 1184.

[1857] *Shogun Finance Ltd v Hudson* [2003] UKHL 62, [2003] 3 W.L.R. 1371; see Vol.I, paras 3-037 et seq.

understanding between them, and the dealer fills in details that are at variance with this understanding, the hirer will ordinarily be precluded from denying the validity of the ostensible agreement,[1858] unless the circumstances are such that he could successfully plead non est factum.[1859]

39-314 **Effect if contract void**   Where a hire-purchase agreement is void for lack of agreement, any sum paid by the hirer to the dealer by way of deposit, whether in cash or by way of allowance for goods tendered in part-exchange, is recoverable from the owner as money paid on a consideration that has totally failed.[1860]

39-315 **Delivery of goods**   In the absence of any term to the contrary, it is the duty of the owner to deliver the goods to the hirer whose hiring commences when the goods are delivered to him.[1861] If, after entering into the agreement, the owner does not deliver the goods, the hirer cannot as a rule obtain specific performance,[1862] but is entitled to damages for breach of contract.[1863]

39-316 **Title to goods**   Owing to the element of sale in hire-purchase transactions, the common law implied into the agreement a condition that the owner is capable of conferring a good title both at the time when the goods are delivered to the hirer and at the time when the hirer exercises his option to purchase.[1864] But the implied terms as to title are now contained in s.8 of the Supply of Goods (Implied Terms) Act 1973.[1865] The relevant provision for "consumer contracts"[1866] will be in the Consumer Rights Act 2015.[1867] There is a statutory implied condition[1868] on the part of the creditor[1869] that he will have a right to sell the goods at the time when the property is to pass.[1870] Where the breach of this term consists in a failure to pass a good title to the goods, at common law the hirer is entitled to recover all sums paid

---

[1858] *United Dominions Trust Ltd v Western* [1976] Q.B. 513, disapproving *Campbell Discount Co Ltd v Gall* [1961] 1 Q.B. 431. cf. *Unity Finance Ltd v Hammond* (1965) 109 S.J. 70; *Mercantile Credit Co Ltd v Hamblin* [1965] 2 Q.B. 242. See also *British Ry Traffic and Electric Co v Roper* (1939) L.T. 217; *Eastern Distributors Ltd v Goldring* [1957] 2 Q.B. 600; *Spencer v North Country Finance Co Ltd* [1963] C.L.Y. 212; *Hodge Industrial Securities Ltd v Cooper*, The Guardian, December 14, 1961, CA; *Astley Industrial Trust Ltd v Rollinson*, The Guardian, February 19, 1963, CA; *General & Finance Facilities v Hughes* (1966) 116 New L.J. 1474, CA; *P.B. Leasing Ltd v Patel* [1995] C.C.L.R. 82.

[1859] *Mercantile Credit Co Ltd v Hamblin*, above; *Saunders v Anglia Building Society* [1971] A.C. 1004. See Vol.I, para.3-049; but contrast Consumer Credit Act 1974 s.61 (above, paras 39-102 et seq.).

[1860] *Branwhite v Worcester Works Finance Ltd* [1969] 1 A.C. 552.

[1861] *National Cash Register Co Ltd v Stanley* [1921] 3 K.B. 292; *Karsales (Harrow) Ltd v Wallis* [1956] 1 W.L.R. 936. cf. *Bentworth Finance v Lubert* [1968] 1 Q.B. 680 (car log-book not handed over).

[1862] See Vol.I, Ch.27. cf. Sale of Goods Act 1979 s.52; see below, para.44-440.

[1863] The measure of damages is presumably to be calculated on the same principle as in the case of failure to deliver goods sold: see below, paras 44-387 et seq., and Sale of Goods Act 1979 s.51(2).

[1864] *Karflex Ltd v Poole* [1933] 2 K.B. 251, as interpreted in *Mercantile Union Guarantee Corp Ltd v Wheatley* [1938] 1 K.B. 490; and *Warman v Southern Counties Car Finance Corp Ltd* [1949] 2 K.B. 576.

[1865] Amended by (i) s.192 and Sch.4 para.35, of the Consumer Credit Act 1974 and by s.7 and Sch.2 para.4, of the Sale and Supply of Goods Act 1994 and (ii) amended, for contracts made on or after October 1, 2015, by the Consumer Rights Act 2015 s.60 and Sch.1 para.2. Section 8 corresponds closely in language to s.12 of the Sale of Goods Act 1979. See below, para.44-075.

[1866] For contracts made on or after October 1, 2015.

[1867] Consumer Rights Act 2015 s.17. See above, paras 38-508 et seq.

[1868] Supply of Goods (Implied Terms) Act 1973 s.8(3). Except in a case where s.8(2) applies.

[1869] Defined in Supply of Goods (Implied Terms) Act 1973 s.15(1) to mean the owner or his assignee.

[1870] Supply of Goods (Implied Terms) Act 1973 s.8(1)(a). Corresponding terms are "treated as included"

by him as on a total failure of consideration, and it seems that the creditor will not be entitled, either by set-off or counterclaim, to payment by the hirer for the period during which the hirer had use of them.[1871] In consumer contracts the Consumer Rights Act 2015 provides additional remedies.[1872] There are also implied warranties[1873]: that (i) the goods are free, and will remain free until the time when the property is to pass, from any charge or encumbrance not disclosed or known to the hirer before the agreement is made; and (ii) that the hirer will enjoy quiet possession of the goods except so far as it may be disturbed by any person entitled to the benefit of any charge or encumbrance so disclosed or known.[1874]

Limited title In a hire-purchase agreement, in the case of which there appears   **39-317**
from the agreement or is to be inferred from the circumstances of the agreement an intention that the creditor should transfer only such title as he or a third person may have,[1875] there is:

    (a)   an implied warranty[1876] that all charges or encumbrances known to the creditor and not known to the hirer have been disclosed to the hirer before the agreement is made; and

    (b)   an implied warranty[1877] that neither:

        (i)   the creditor; nor

        (ii)   in a case where the parties to the agreement intend that any title which may be transferred shall only be such title as a third person may have, that person; nor

        (iii)   anyone claiming through or under the creditor or that third person otherwise than under a charge or encumbrance disclosed or known to the hirer, before the agreement is made, will disturb the hirer's quiet possession of the goods.[1878]

Liability for breach of the obligations arising from s.8 of the Supply of Goods   **39-318**
(Implied Terms) Act 1973 above cannot be excluded or restricted by reference to any contract term.[1879]

Acceptance of delivery It is the duty of the hirer to accept delivery of the goods   **39-319**
hired; if he refuses to do so, the owner's remedy is not to sue for the rent agreed,

---

in consumer contracts made on or after October 1, 2015 under Consumer Rights Act 2015 s.17(1)(b), see below, para.44-440.

[1871] *Karflex Ltd v Poole* [1933] 2 K.B. 251; *Warman v Southern Counties Car Finance Corp Ltd* [1949] 2 K.B. 576; *Barber v NWS Bank Plc* [1996] 1 W.L.R. 641.

[1872] Consumer Rights Act 2015 ss.19–27. See above, paras 38-512 et seq.

[1873] Supply of Goods (Implied Terms) Act 1973 s.8(3). Except in a case where s.8(2) applies.

[1874] Supply of Goods (Implied Terms) Act 1973 s.8(1)(b); see also below, para.44-078. Corresponding terms are "treated as included" in consumer contracts made on or after October 1, 2015 under Consumer Rights Act 2015 s.17(2)), with the extended statutory rights available in such cases (Consumer Rights Act 2015 ss.19–27 and above, paras 38-512 et seq.).

[1875] See below, para.44-084.

[1876] Supply of Goods (Implied Terms) Act 1973 s.8(3).

[1877] Supply of Goods (Implied Terms) Act 1973 s.8(3).

[1878] Supply of Goods (Implied Terms) Act 1974 s.8(2). Corresponding terms are "treated as included" in consumer contracts made on or after October 1, 2015 ((Consumer Rights Act 2015 s.17(4)–(7)), with the extended statutory rights available in such cases (Consumer Rights Act 2015 ss.19–27 and above, paras 38-512 et seq.).

[1879] Unfair Contract Terms Act 1977 s.6(1) and s.31(4) (repealing Supply of Goods (Implied Terms) Act 1973 s.12(2), (8), (9)). For contracts made on or after October 1, 2015, the relevant provision for "consumer contracts" is the Consumer Rights Act 2015 s.31(1)(i)), above, para.38-531.

but to bring an action for damages.[1880] The measure of damages is prima facie a sum representing the whole of future unpaid instalments, less (i) the value of the goods at the time of refusal to accept; and (ii) a discount in respect of the earlier return to the owner of his capital outlay.[1881]

39-320 Payment of rent The hirer must pay the rent agreed upon. In the absence of a contrary stipulation, he has no right to pay in advance,[1882] nor, if allowed to pay in advance, to deduct a sum by way of rebate of interest.[1883] Failure by the hirer to pay one or two instalments of rent does not necessarily amount to a repudiation of the agreement[1884]; the default must either be a breach of condition[1885] or be such as to evince an intention not to go on with the agreement.[1886] In the absence of a repudiation, the owner's remedy is to sue for arrears of rent alone.[1887]

39-321 Care of goods The hirer is under a duty to take reasonable care of the goods hired,[1888] but he is not responsible for fair wear and tear unless there is an express term of the contract to this effect.[1889] Most hire-purchase agreements, however, require the hirer to keep the goods in good order, repair and condition. In such a case, the hirer's duty is to keep the goods in the condition in which they may reasonably be expected to be if he looks after them properly: he need not put the goods in a better condition than they were when he hired them.[1890]

39-322 Insurance The hirer is under no duty to insure unless there is an express stipulation to this effect in the agreement.[1891]

39-323 Guarantee and indemnity It is common practice for the owners of goods let on hire-purchase to require a third party to guarantee the due performance by the hirer

---

[1880] *National Cash Register Co Ltd v Stanley* [1921] 3 K.B. 292; *Karsales (Harrow) Ltd v Wallis* [1956] 1 W.L.R. 936.

[1881] *Interoffice Telephones v Robert Freeman Co* [1958] 1 Q.B. 190 (overruling *British Stamp and Ticket Automatic Delivery Co Ltd v Haynes* [1921] 1 K.B. 377); *Robophone Facilities Ltd v Blank* [1966] 1 W.L.R. 1428. cf. *Bentworth Finance v Jennings* (1961) 111 L.J. 488; *Bentworth Finance v Reader* (1961) 112 L.J. 208.

[1882] *Aliter* in a credit sale; *Lancashire Waggon Co Ltd v Nuttall* (1879) 42 L.T. 465.

[1883] *Taylor v Wylie Lockhead Ltd*, 1912 S.C. 978; *Higgs v Hodge Industrial Securities Ltd* (1966) 111 S.J. 14. But see the rebate provisions in Consumer Credit Act 1974 ss.94, 95 (above, paras 39-157 et seq.).

[1884] *Financings Ltd v Baldock* [1963] 2 Q.B. 104; *Brady v St Margaret's Trust* [1963] 2 Q.B. 494; *Anglo-Auto Finance Co Ltd v James* [1963] 1 W.L.R. 1042; *Kelly v Sovereign Leasing* [1995] C.L.Y. 720, Cty Ct. Contrast *Cramer v Giles* (1883) Cab. & El. 151.

[1885] *Lombard North Central Plc v Butterworth* [1987] Q.B. 527 (where time of payment was expressly made of the essence of the agreement). But such a term in a consumer contract (a) may be unfair and so not binding on the hirer under the Consumer Rights Act 2015 Pt 2, replacing, for contracts made on or after October 1, 2015, the Unfair Terms in Consumer Contracts Regulations 1999 (SI 1999/2083); above, paras 38-221 et seq., or (b) might give rise to an "unfair relationship" under the Consumer Credit Act 1974 ss.140A–140C, above, paras 39-212 et seq.

[1886] *Yeoman Credit Ltd v Waragowski* [1961] 1 W.L.R. 1124; *Overstone Ltd v Shipway* [1962] 1 W.L.R. 117, 123; *Financings Ltd v Baldock* [1963] 2 Q.B. 104, at 117, 122. See below, para.39-330.

[1887] *Financings Ltd v Baldock* [1963] 2 Q.B. 104.

[1888] See above, para.33-079; below, para.39-370.

[1889] *Blakemore v Bristol & Exeter Ry* (1858) 8 El. & Bl. 1035; *Coupé Co v Maddick* [1891] 2 Q.B. 413; see above, para.33-082.

[1890] *Brady v St Margaret's Trust Ltd* [1963] 2 Q.B. 494. See also *Acceptance Co v Pike* (1961) 111 L.J. 424 (statutory agreement).

[1891] See also *Spruce v Unity Finance* (1961) 105 S.J. 254 (no duty to inform owner of insurance taken out).

of his obligations under the contract.[1892] Such a guarantee, or some memorandum or note thereof, must be in writing and signed by the guarantor or some other person thereunto by him lawfully authorised, otherwise it is unenforceable.[1893] It must also be supported by consideration, and it is usual to state that the guarantee is made in consideration of the owner entering into the hire-purchase agreement or of his letting the goods on hire.[1894] Past consideration, e.g. where the owner has already executed the agreement or let the goods on hire, is insufficient.[1895] There can, in general, be no valid guarantee of a debt or obligation incurred under a hire-purchase agreement which is for some reason void.[1896]

A contract of guarantee must be distinguished from a contract of indemnity.[1897] A contract of indemnity is subject to no requirement of form; if made in connection with a void hire-purchase agreement, it is itself not invalidated[1898]; and the rights and obligations of the parties differ materially from those incurred under a contract of guarantee.[1899]   **39-324**

Rights of guarantor   If sued by the owner on the contract of guarantee, a guarantor is entitled to be credited with any sums paid by the hirer to the owner[1900] and he can also rely on any defence which the hirer possesses against the owner.[1901] When he has paid what is due, he is entitled to be subrogated to the rights of the owner against the hirer and can claim the benefit of any security given to the owner by the hirer,[1902] But he does not succeed to the owner's licence to seize the goods let on hire nor to the owner's right to possession of them, and it is probable that he is not entitled to exercise the hirer's option to purchase the goods.[1903] A guarantor who has paid what is due is also normally entitled to be indemnified by the hirer against all payments properly made by him to the owner.[1904] And, once he becomes compellable to pay the debt, he can claim contribution from any other guarantor who is liable on the same demand.[1905]   **39-325**

[1892] For the position under the Consumer Credit Act 1974, see above, paras 39-180 et seq.

[1893] Statute of Frauds 1677 s.4; see below, paras 45-042 et seq. But see Consumer Credit Act 1974 s.105; above, para.39-184.

[1894] The consideration need not be mentioned in the note or memorandum: Mercantile Law Amendment Act 1856 s.3.

[1895] *Astley Industrial Trust Ltd v Grimston Electric Tools Ltd* (1965) 109 S.J. 149. cf. *Hewison v Ricketts* (1894) 63 L.J. Q.B. 711.

[1896] *Coutts & Co v Browne-Lecky* [1947] K.B. 104; *Stadium Finance Ltd v Helm* (1965) 109 S.J. 471 (minority, under the Infants' Relief Act 1874, now repealed). See also *Brown v Blaine* (1884) 1 T.L.R. 158 (non-compliance with the Bills of Sale Acts), and below, paras 45-027, 45-041.

[1897] See below, para.45-008. But see the position under the Consumer Credit Act 1974, above, para.39-190.

[1898] *Yorkshire Ry Wagon Co v Maclure* (1881) 19 Ch. D. 478; reversed on different grounds (1882) 21 Ch. D. 309; *Yeoman Credit Ltd v Latter* [1961] 1 W.L.R. 828.

[1899] *Sterling Industrial Facilities v Lydiate Textiles* (1962) 106 S.J. 669; *Scottish Midland Guarantee Trust v Woolley* (1964) 114 L.J. 272; *Goulston Discount Co Ltd v Clark* [1967] 2 Q.B. 493. But see *Goulston Discount Co Ltd v Sims* (1967) 111 S.J. 682; *Goulston Discount Co Ltd v Sims* (1968) 112 S.J. 670.

[1900] But not with sums paid by a third party without the authority of the hirer: *Chatterton v Maclean* [1951] 1 All E.R. 761.

[1901] *Bechervaise v Lewis* (1872) L.R. 7 C.P. 372. As to the availability of rights of set-off or counterclaim, see below, para.45-087.

[1902] See below, para.45-144.

[1903] *Chatterton v Maclean* [1951] 1 All E.R. 761.

[1904] See below, para.45-126.

[1905] See below, para.45-136.

39-326 **Discharge of guarantor** Except where it is provided to the contrary,[1906] any variation of the principal agreement by the owner and hirer without his consent will normally discharge the guarantor from his obligations under the contract of guarantee.[1907] The guarantor will also be released if the owner enters into a binding agreement with the hirer to grant him an extension of time for payment, unless the owner at the same time expressly reserves his rights against the guarantor or the extension of time is allowed with the guarantor's consent.[1908] But a mere omission to press the hirer for payment will not have this effect. The termination of the hiring or the hire-purchase agreement, whether upon a repudiation by the hirer accepted by the owner,[1909] or by the owner under the terms of the agreement, or voluntarily by the hirer,[1910] will not discharge the guarantor from liability.[1911]

39-327 Any terms or conditions attached to the enforcement of the contract of guarantee must be strictly complied with[1912]; but a failure by the owner to comply with such terms or conditions will not necessarily render the guarantee unenforceable, but may give rise to a counterclaim for damages only.[1913]

39-328 **Recourse agreements** Many modern hire-purchase transactions are conducted under the "direct collection" system of finance, in which the dealer does not himself let the goods to the hirer, but sells them to a finance company which then lets them to the hirer. In order to safeguard themselves, finance companies occasionally require the dealer to enter into an agreement under which the dealer becomes a surety for the due performance by the hirer of his obligations. This agreement is known as a "recourse agreement".[1914] The dealer may, at the same time, be appointed the company's agent to collect the hire-purchase instalments[1915] or to take possession of the goods on behalf of the company in the event of breach by the hirer.[1916] Recourse agreements normally take the form of a guarantee of the hirer's obligations under the hire-purchase agreement[1917] or of an indemnity against loss caused to the finance company by the hirer's default,[1918] and the dealer's liability will depend upon which form of agreement is entered into.

[1906] *British Motor Trust Co Ltd v Hyams* (1934) 50 T.L.R. 230.

[1907] *Holme v Brunskill* (1877) 3 Q.B.D. 495; see below, para.45-104.

[1908] *Midland Motor Showrooms Ltd v Newman* [1929] 2 K.B. 256. Contrast *Midland Counties Motor Finance Co Ltd v Slade* [1951] 1 K.B. 346 (express provision inserted).

[1909] *Moschi v Lep Air Services Ltd* [1973] A.C. 331; *Hyundai Heavy Industries Co Ltd v Papadoupolos* [1980] 1 W.L.R. 1129, below, paras 45-099 and 45-100.

[1910] Contrast *Western Credit Ltd v Alberry* [1964] 1 W.L.R. 945.

[1911] *Chatterton v Maclean* [1951] 1 All E.R. 761. A lawful seizure of the goods by the owner does not discharge the guarantor's liability: *Brooks v Beirnstein* [1909] 1 K.B. 98. cf. *Hewison v Ricketts* (1894) 63 L.J. Q.B. 711 (conditional sale).

[1912] *Midland Counties Motor Finance Co Ltd v Slade* [1951] 1 K.B. 346. cf. *United Dominions Trust (Commercial) Ltd v Eagle Aircraft* [1968] 1 W.L.R. 74.

[1913] *Bowmaker (Commercial) Ltd v Smith* [1965] 1 W.L.R. 855; *United Dominions Trust (Commercial) Ltd v Eagle Aircraft* [1968] 1 W.L.R. 74.

[1914] It does not constitute "security" for the purposes of the consumer credit regime; see above, para.39-130.

[1915] *Olds Discount Ltd v John Playfair Ltd* [1938] 3 All E.R. 275; *Olds Discount Ltd v Krett* [1940] 2 K.B. 117.

[1916] *Watling Trusts Ltd v Briffault Range Co Ltd* [1938] 1 All E.R. 525; *Reliance Car Facilities Ltd v Roding Motors* [1952] 2 Q.B. 844. A dealer who repossesses goods on the company's behalf cannot pass a good title to a third party under s.24 of the Sale of Goods Act 1979: *Olds Discount Ltd v Krett* [1940] 2 K.B. 117.

[1917] *Midland Counties Motor Finance Co Ltd v Slade* [1951] 1 K.B. 346; *Unity Finance Ltd v Woodcock* [1963] 1 W.L.R. 455.

[1918] *Sterling Industrial Facilities v Lydiate Textiles* (1962) 106 S.J. 669; *Scottish Midland Guarantee*

Termination of agreement by performance   The most usual way in which a hire-   **39-329**
purchase agreement is terminated is by performance, i.e. where the hirer pays all
the instalments and exercises his option to purchase. If payment is made by a third
party, for example, where another finance company or dealer "settles" the balance
outstanding under the agreement, this payment is considered to have been made on
behalf of the hirer and the owner's title to the goods vests in the hirer and not in
the third party.[1919]

Termination of agreement by repudiation   A hire-purchase agreement will also   **39-330**
be terminated if one party repudiates the agreement and the repudiation is accepted by the other. A clear case of repudiation will arise when the hirer renounces
the agreement by refusing to go on with it.[1920] On the other hand, where the hirer
does not renounce the agreement, but is merely guilty of a failure of performance,
the owner will not be entitled to treat the agreement as repudiated unless the hirer's
default is a breach of condition or goes to the root of the contract.[1921] A failure by
the hirer to pay any of the monthly instalments, other than the initial deposit, has
been held to amount to a repudiation where the default continued for six months.[1922]
But a mere failure to pay one or two instalments, even after a warning letter from
the owner, has been held not to amount to a repudiation.[1923] However, the agreement itself may make punctual payment of instalments of the essence of the
contract,[1924] so that any default in payment will entitle the owner to treat the contract
as repudiated.[1925]

Termination of agreement by the hirer   All hire-purchase agreements must   **39-331**
confer upon the hirer an option (as opposed to an obligation) to buy the goods.[1926]
The terms of the agreement must be looked at to ascertain whether and under what
conditions he is entitled to terminate the agreement before it has run its full
course.[1927]

Termination of agreement by the owner   The terms of the hire-purchase agree-   **39-332**

Trust v Woolley (1964) 114 L.J. 272; *Goulston Discount Co Ltd v Clark* [1967] 2 Q.B. 493; *Goulston Discount Co Ltd v Sims* (1967) 111 S.J. 682; *Goulston Discount Co Ltd v Sims* (1968) 112 S.J. 670.

[1919] *Bennett v Griffin Finance Ltd* [1967] 2 Q.B. 46; *Hodge Industrial Securities Ltd v Hynes* Unreported March 22, 1971, CA.

[1920] *Overstone Ltd v Shipway* [1962] 1 W.L.R. 117. Contrast *United Dominions Trust (Commercial) Ltd v Ennis* [1968] 1 Q.B. 54.

[1921] See Vol.I, Ch.24.

[1922] *Yeoman Credit Ltd v Waragowski* [1961] 1 W.L.R. 1124.

[1923] *Financings Ltd v Baldock* [1963] 2 Q.B. 104. See also *Brady v St Margaret's Trust Ltd* [1963] 2 Q.B. 494; *Anglo-Auto Finance Co Ltd v James* [1963] 1 W.L.R. 1042; *Kelly v Sovereign Leasing* [1995] C.L.Y. 720, Cty Ct.

[1924] See Vol.I, para.21-013. cf. *Kelly v Sovereign Leasing* [1995] C.L.Y. 720, Cty Ct.

[1925] *Lombard North Central Plc v Butterworth* [1987] Q.B. 527; *BMW Financial Service (GB) Ltd v Hart* [2012] EWCA Civ 1959. But such a term in a consumer contract (a) may be unfair and so not bind-
ing on the hirer under the Consumer Rights Act 2015 Pt 2, replacing, for contracts made on or after October 1, 2015, the Unfair Terms in Consumer Contracts Regulations 1999 (SI 1999/2083) (see above, paras 38-221 et seq.) or (b) might give rise to an "unfair relationship" under the Consumer Credit Act 1974 ss.140A–140C, above, paras 39-212 et seq.

[1926] See above, para.39-307. For the statutory right of termination under the Consumer Credit Act 1974 s.99, see below, para.39-367.

[1927] In *United Dominions Trust (Commercial) Ltd v Ennis* [1968] 1 Q.B. 54, it was held that the hirer must be aware of any onerous conditions before he will be considered to have exercised his right to terminate.

ment invariably confer upon the owner a power to terminate the agreement, or the bailment thereunder, in the event of any breach by the hirer, even though such a breach does not amount to a repudiation of the contract.[1928] The owner may also reserve the right to terminate upon the happening of an event other than breach, for example, upon the hirer's death, or bankruptcy. It is important to note that it is possible to terminate the hiring (bailment) without terminating the agreement for all purposes.

39-333 **Termination of the hiring** It is well established as a general rule of the law of bailment that any act which is inconsistent with the terms of the bailment, such as a sale,[1929] or pledge,[1930] of the chattel bailed, determines the bailment and the immediate right to possession of the chattel reverts to the bailor.[1931] The fact that the agreement makes specific provision for termination of the hiring, e.g. on notice, in the event of default by the hirer does not ordinarily displace this rule.[1932] But, in other events, the terms of the agreement must be looked at to ascertain what the rights of the owner are in respect of the event which has taken place. Where the agreement states that the hiring is automatically to determine, it will be terminated forthwith if the event occurs. But if the termination is made contingent upon notice being given or a declaration being made, the hiring is not terminated until the notice is given or the declaration is made.[1933]

39-334 A term in the form that the owner "may forthwith and without notice terminate the hiring" does not automatically terminate the hiring upon the happening of the event, and there must be some further unequivocal act on the part of the owner (such as seizure of the goods) which demonstrates his intention to terminate the hiring.[1934] But since the owner can terminate the hiring at any time, he has an immediate right to possession of the goods and this entitles him to retake possession of them from the hirer, or to claim damages from any person who wrongfully interferes with the goods.[1935]

39-335 **Contrasted with termination of the agreement** Although the hiring may have been terminated by the owner, the hire-purchase agreement can nevertheless continue in existence.[1936] In such a case, the hirer may still be entitled in theory to pay the balance of the hire-purchase price and exercise his option to purchase.[1937] The continued existence of the agreement may possibly affect the measure of dam-

---

[1928] But see Consumer Credit Act 1974 ss.86B, 86E, 87, 98 (above, paras 39-131, 39-135, 39-166, 39-172). On the owner's rights on such termination see below, paras 39-339 et seq.

[1929] *Cooper v Willomatt* (1845) 1 C.B. 672; *Fenn v Bittleston* (1851) 7 Ex. 152. Offering goods for sale is enough: *Northern General Wagon & Finance Co Ltd v Graham* [1950] 2 K.B. 7 (instructing auctioneer to sell).

[1930] *Singer Manufacturing Co v Clark* (1879) 5 Ex. D. 37; *Nyberg v Handelaar* [1892] 2 Q.B. 202.

[1931] See above, para.33-014.

[1932] *Union Transport Finance Ltd v British Car Auctions* [1978] 2 All E.R. 385. cf. *North General Wagon & Finance Co Ltd v Graham* [1950] 2 K.B. 7, 11.

[1933] *North General Wagon & Finance Co Ltd v Graham* [1950] 2 K.B. 7, at 13; *Reliance Car Facilities v Roding Motors* [1952] 2 Q.B. 844.

[1934] *North General Wagon & Finance Co Ltd v Graham* [1950] 2 K.B. 7; *Moorgate Mercantile Co Ltd v Finch and Read* [1962] 1 Q.B. 701.

[1935] *Jelks v Hayward* [1905] 2 K.B. 460; *North General Wagon & Finance Co Ltd v Graham* [1950] 2 K.B. 7; *Moorgate Mercantile Co Ltd v Finch and Read*, above; *Union Transport Finance Ltd v British Car Auctions Ltd* [1978] 2 All E.R. 385.

[1936] *Whiteley Ltd v Hilt* [1918] 2 K.B. 808, 822.

[1937] Most hire-purchase agreements, however, make the exercise of the option to purchase dependent

ages recoverable in an action of conversion brought by the owner against the hirer or a third party.[1938]

As in the case of the termination of the bailment, a provision that the agreement **39-336** shall ipso facto determine upon the happening of a certain event will terminate the agreement automatically when the event occurs[1939]; and a provision that the owner may terminate the agreement by notice to the hirer requires the giving of such notice.[1940] Where the agreement provides that the owner "may terminate this agreement", such a term confers upon the owner an option to terminate; but the option has to be exercised, otherwise the agreement continues in force.[1941]

Notice of default   At common law,[1942] it is not necessary for the owner to give the **39-337** hirer notice of his default before terminating the agreement or the hiring, unless there is an express term to this effect.[1943]

Waiver of right to terminate   The owner may be held to have waived his right **39-338** to terminate the agreement upon breach, or to have waived a notice of termination, if he accepts arrears of hire-rent with knowledge of the breach or does some act which unequivocally indicates his intention to allow the agreement to continue.[1944]

Repossession of the goods   Before the owner can lawfully repossess the goods **39-339** let on hire, he must have a right to immediate possession of the goods, and so must prove that the hiring has determined or is terminable at will.[1945] A wrongful repossession by the owner will render him liable in damages to the hirer.[1946]

Retaking without action   In the absence of any statutory restriction,[1947] an owner **39-340** who is entitled to immediate possession may retake his goods either peaceably or

---

upon the due observance by the hirer of the terms of the agreement.

[1938] *Belsize Motor Supply Co v Cox* [1914] 1 K.B. 244; *Whiteley Ltd v Hilt* [1918] 2 K.B. 808. cf. *Wickham Holdings Ltd v Brooke House Motors Ltd* [1967] 1 W.L.R. 295; *Belvoir Finance Co Ltd v Stapleton* [1971] 1 Q.B. 210; *VFS Financial Services (UK) v Euro Auctions (UK) Ltd* [2007] EWHC 1492 and below, para.39-416.

[1939] But see *Hackney Furnishing Co v Watts* [1912] 3 K.B. 225; *Jay's Furnishing Co v Brand* [1915] 1 K.B. 458; see below, para.39-427.

[1940] *Smart v Holt* [1929] 2 K.B. 303; *Drages Ltd v Owen* (1935) 52 T.L.R. 108; *Reliance Car Facilities Ltd v Roding Motors* [1952] 2 Q.B. 844.

[1941] *Belsize Motor Supply Co v Cox* [1914] 1 K.B. 244; *United Dominions Trust (Commercial) Ltd v Marcus* (1951) 101 L.J. 417. See also *BMW Financial Service (GB) Ltd v Hart* [2012] EWCA Civ 1959 (limitation period for recovery of unpaid balance ran from the date the owner gave notice of termination for hirer's breach since, as matter of construction of the contract, the owner's right to claim that amount only arose then (and not earlier, when hirer failed to pay two instalments, see above para.39-330)).

[1942] For the position under the Consumer Credit Act 1974, see above, para.39-166. See also the "unfair relationship" provisions (ss.140A–140C, above, paras 39-212 et seq.), especially s.140A(1)(b), para.39-218.

[1943] But see *Reynolds v General and Finance Facilities* (1963) 107 S.J. 889; *Eshun v Moorgate Mercantile Co Ltd* [1971] 1 W.L.R. 722, 725.

[1944] *Keith, Prowse & Co v National Telephone Co* [1894] 2 Ch. 147; *Reynolds v General and Finance Facilities*, above. See also *Tommey v Finextra* (1962) 106 S.J. 1012 and Vol.I, Ch.24. Waiver of the right to terminate does not necessarily preclude an action for damages for breach: *Stephens v Junior Army and Navy Stores Ltd* [1914] 2 Ch. 516.

[1945] See above, para.39-333.

[1946] For the measure of damages, see *Kelly v Sovereign Leasing* [1995] C.L.Y. 720, Cty. Ct.

[1947] See the Consumer Credit Act 1974 s.90 (below, para.39-363), and the Reserve and Auxiliary Forces

by reasonable force from anyone who is wrongfully detaining them.[1948] But, unless he is given a licence to do so, it seems he may not enter upon the land of the hirer, or of a third party, in order to retake them.[1949] If a licence to seize is granted by the terms of the agreement, it is personal to the licensee and cannot be assigned.[1950] In any event, it is an offence under the Criminal Law Act 1977[1951] to enter by force. By resuming possession of the goods the owner does not abandon his right to sue for arrears of rent[1952]; and where a judgment for arrears of rent is unsatisfied, the owner is not deprived by the judgment of his right to retake the goods.[1953]

39-341   **Recovery by action**[1954]   In most cases where the hirer refuses permission for the retaking of the goods, it will be more prudent for the owner to resort to court action to recover them. In an action for wrongful interference with goods the court may make an order for delivery up of the goods, with or without the option to pay their value,[1955] and for payment of any consequential damages.[1956] Alternatively a claim may be made for damages alone. The measure of damages is normally the value of the goods[1957]; but where the balance of the hire-purchase price outstanding is less than the value of the goods, the measure of damages is the balance of the hire-purchase price outstanding at the date of their conversion.[1958]

39-342   **Retention of sums paid by the hirer**   Upon the termination of the hire-purchase agreement, the owner is prima facie entitled to retain all sums already paid by the hirer whether by way of deposit, initial payment or instalments of hire-rent. If a deposit or initial payment is stated in the agreement to have been made in consideration of the grant of an option to purchase, it can nevertheless not be recovered if the agreement is prematurely determined. It cannot be claimed that the consideration for the deposit has totally failed, since the option to purchase exists from the

---

(Protection of Civil Interests) Act 1951, below, para.39-436.

[1948] *Blades v Higgs* (1861) 10 C.B.(N.S.) 713; (1865) 11 H.L.C. 621; *Devoe v Long* [1951] 1 D.L.R. 203. But the position is far from clear, especially when, as here, the goods have come into the defendant's hands, not by a trespass, but by a consensual delivery. See Branston (1912) 28 L.Q.R. 262; and generally *Clerk & Lindsell on Torts*, 22nd edn (2017), para.30-14. See also the restriction imposed by the Consumer Credit Act 1974 s.92; below, para.39-366.

[1949] Again, the question is disputed; see *Clerk & Lindsell on Torts*, 22nd edn (2017), para.30-14.

[1950] *Brown v Metropolitan Counties Life Assurance Society* (1859) 1 El. & El. 832; *Re Davis & Co* (1888) 22 Q.B.D. 193; *Chatterton v Maclean* [1951] 1 All E.R. 761.

[1951] s.6 (as amended). cf. *Hemmings v Stoke Poges Golf Club* [1920] 1 K.B. 720.

[1952] *Brooks v Beirnstein* [1909] 1 K.B. 98. Compare the position in regard to a conditional sale (below, para.39-440); *Hewison v Ricketts* (1894) 63 L.J. Q.B. 711; *Att-Gen v Pritchard* (1928) 97 L.J. Q.B. 561; *Taylor v Thompson* [1930] W.N. 16.

[1953] *South Bedfordshire Electrical Finance Ltd v Bryant* [1938] 3 All E.R. 580.

[1954] CPR Pt 16, PD 16, para.6.1.

[1955] Torts (Interference with Goods) Act 1977 s.3. Note s.3(8)(a): the section is without prejudice to the remedies afforded by the Consumer Credit Act 1974 s.133 (see below, para.39-374).

[1956] *Strand Electric and Engineering Co Ltd v Brisford Entertainments Ltd* [1952] 2 Q.B. 246; *Hillesden Securities v Ryjack* [1983] 1 W.L.R. 959. See also *BMW Financial Services (GB) Ltd v Taylor* [2006] 1 C.L. 113, Cty Ct (costs of recovery and tracing hirer recoverable under express term).

[1957] *Chubb Cash Ltd v John Crilley & Son* [1983] 1 W.L.R. 599. Consequential damages are recoverable if not too remote: *Hillesden Securities v Ryjack* [1983] 1 W.L.R. 959.

[1958] *Wickham Holdings Ltd v Brooke House Motors Ltd* [1967] 1 W.L.R. 295; *Belvoir Finance Co Ltd v Stapleton* [1971] 1 Q.B. 210; *VFS Financial Services (UK) v Euro Auctions (UK) Lid* [2007] EWHC 1492. See also *Belsize Motor Supply Co v Cox* [1914] 1 K.B. 244; *Whiteley v Hilt* [1918] 2 K.B. 808. cf. *Astley Industrial Trust v Miller* [1968] 2 All E.R. 36 (detinue).

moment of signing the contract even though it may be subject to the condition that the hirer should duly perform the whole of his obligations under the agreement.[1959]

Relief from forfeiture   The court has the power to relieve the hirer from forfeiture of the goods and to reinstate his rights under the contract[1960] by granting him an extension of time to pay off the arrears or to remedy any other breach by him of the agreement.[1961] In exercising its discretion to grant relief, the court will take into account the following factors:

39-343

(i)   whether or not the hirer is in default under the agreement;

(ii)   whether significant prejudice would be caused to the owner by the grant of the relief; and

(iii) whether to refuse relief would give the owner a substantial windfall profit or cause the hirer a disproportionate loss.[1962]

Sums paid by hirer   The view has been advanced[1963] that the court also has power in equity to relieve the hirer from the forfeiture of instalments and other sums already paid. In *Stockloser v Johnson*,[1964] a buyer under a terminated conditional sale agreement[1965] claimed the return of the instalments that he had paid on the ground that the forfeiture clause in the agreement was penal and unconscionable. The Court of Appeal found that it was not in fact penal, but by a majority[1966] they recognised the general power of the court to grant equitable relief against the forfeiture of instalments upon the buyer's breach where the sum forfeited was out

39-344

[1959] *Kelly v Lombard Banking Co Ltd* [1959] 1 W.L.R. 41. See also *Brooks v Beirnstein* [1909] 1 K.B. 98.

[1960] Note that automatic relief, without the need to go to court, is given by the Consumer Credit Act 1974 for hirers under regulated agreements under that Act who remedy a breach after the service of the requisite default notice: see above, paras 39-166 et seq.

[1961] *Goker (Ali) v NWS Bank Queen's* [1990] C.C.L.R. 34 (but, on facts, relief refused); *Transag Haulage Ltd v Leyland Daf Finance Plc* [1994] 2 B.C.L.C. 88. See generally, Vol.I, para.26-255 and *Stockloser v Johnson* [1954] 1 Q.B. 476, at 499, 502; *Re Piggin, Dicker v Lombank* (1962) 112 L.J. 424; *Barton Thompson & Co Ltd v Stapling Machine Co* [1966] Ch. 499, 509; *Shiloh Spinners Ltd v Harding* [1973] A.C. 691, 722, 723; *Starside Properties Ltd v Mustapha* [1974] 1 W.L.R. 816, 822; *BICC Plc v Burndy Corp* [1985] Ch. 232; *On Demand Information Plc v Michael Gerson (Finance) Plc* [2002] UKHL 13, [2003] 1 A.C. 368. Contrast *Hyundai Heavy Industries Co Ltd v Papadoupolos* [1980] 1 W.L.R. 1129, HL; *Scandinavian Trading Co AB v Flota Petrola Ecuatoriana (The Scaptrade)* [1983] Q.B. 529; affirmed [1983] 2 A.C. 694; *Sport International Bussum BV v Inter-Footwear Ltd* [1984] 1 W.L.R. 776, HL; *The Jotunheim* [2004] EWHC 671 (Comm), [2005] 1 Lloyd's Rep. 181; *Celestial Aviation 71 Ltd v Paramount Airways Private Ltd* [2010] EWHC 185 (operating lease).

[1962] *Transag Haulage Ltd v Leyland Daf Finance Plc* [1994] 2 B.C.L.C. 88; cf. *Goker (Ali) v NWS Bank Queen's* [1990] C.C.L.R. 34.

[1963] Diamond (1956) 19 M.L.R. 498; (1958) 21 M.L.R. 199. Contrast Prince (1957) 20 M.L.R. 620. See also Atiyah (1958) 5 B.L.R. 24, 35 and Beatson (1981) 97 L.Q.R. 389. For agreements regulated by the Consumer Credit Act 1974, note (a) the power of the court in relation to "unfair relationships" to re-open agreements and hence order repayment, above, paras 39-223 et seq.; (b) that breach of the "protected goods" provision by the creditor requires him to repay all sums paid by the hirer, below, para.39-361.

[1964] [1954] 1 Q.B. 476.

[1965] The distinction is important: contrast *Brooks v Beirnstein* [1909] 1 K.B. 98; with *Hewison v Ricketts* (1894) 63 L.J. Q.B. 711; *Att-Gen v Pritchard* (1928) 97 L.J. K.B. 561; *Taylor v Thompson* [1930] W.N. 16.

[1966] Somervell and Denning L.JJ. The dissenting judge (Romer L.J.) said that no relief from forfeiture could be given "in the absence of some special circumstances such as fraud, sharp practice or other unconscionable conduct".

of all proportion to the damage suffered and where it would be unconscionable for the seller to retain the money.[1967] But such a principle has not so far been applied to the retention of sums paid by the hirer under a hire-purchase agreement. When *Stockloser v Johnson* was discussed by the Court of Appeal in *Campbell Discount Co Ltd v Bridge*,[1968] the court showed itself disinclined to accept the principle. And when that decision was considered by the House of Lords,[1969] it was reversed on a ground which did not involve consideration of *Stockloser v Johnson*, and only Lord Denning mentioned the ability of equity to restore money already paid by the hirer if it was a penal sum.[1970] Further, in *Galbraith v Mitchenall Estates Ltd*,[1971] Sachs J. refused to apply the principle to the forfeiture of instalments paid under a contract of simple hire even though the terms of the contract were "hideously harsh". This reluctance may be justified in hire and hire-purchase cases as in law the payments are "rent" under a bailment for possession and use of the goods (rather than part-payment for goods, as in the case of conditional sale) and are recoverable as an accrued debt even when the owner subsequently terminates.[1972] In *Cavendish Square Holdings BV v Makdessi*[1973] the Supreme Court declined to opine at length on forfeiture clauses (as the allegation was that the relevant clauses were penalty not forfeiture clauses) and hence only referred to *Stockloser v Johnson* in passing.

39-345 **Recovery of instalments in arrear** The owner is entitled to recover from the hirer as an accrued debt any instalment of hire-rent in arrear at the termination of the hiring[1974] and the right to receive payment of such a debt is a separate cause of action from the right to recover possession of the goods let on hire[1975] and from the right to recover damages for breach of contract.[1976]

39-346 **Damages for breach of contract by hirer** Any breach by the hirer of the terms of the hire-purchase agreement will entitle the owner to sue for damages for breach of contract. But the measure of the damages recoverable depends on whether or not the breach by the hirer amounts to a repudiation[1977] of the agreement.

39-347 **Breach amounting to repudiation** Where a breach by the hirer amounts to a

---

[1967] Following *Steedman v Drinkle* [1916] 1 A.C. 275; see Vol.I, para.26-253.
[1968] [1961] 1 Q.B. 431, 445; below, para.39-351.
[1969] *Bridge v Campbell Discount Co Ltd* [1962] A.C. 600.
[1970] At 631. See also *Cadogan Petroleum Holdings Ltd v Global Process Systems LLC* [2013] 2 Lloyd's Rep. 26: *Stockloser v Johnson* considered when availability of jurisdiction was conceded but not applied in relation to repayments towards acquisition of gas plants.
[1971] [1965] 2 Q.B. 473. And see *UK Housing Alliance (North West) Ltd v Francis* [2010] EWCA Civ 117: no jurisdiction to relieve from forfeiture of 30 per cent of purchase price retained by buyer in sale and leaseback agreement.
[1972] *Brooks v Beirnstein* [1909] 1 K.B. 98: see above.
[1973] [2015] UKSC 67. See above, paras 26-252 et seq. The Supreme Court left open whether the penalty rules apply to forfeiture provisions of this type, so as to render the provision invalid. But it suggested that even if the provision is valid (as a genuine pre-estimate of the innocent party's loss or as a "legitimate deterrent"), in an appropriate case the court may still be able to grant relief against forfeiture.
[1974] *Overstone Ltd v Shipway* [1962] 1 W.L.R. 117; *Anglo-Auto Finance Ltd v Race* Unreported January 28, 1971, CA; *Hyundai Heavy Industries Co Ltd v Papadoupolos*, above. For procedure, see CPR Pt 16 PD 16 6.2. See also CPR Pt 7 PD 7B 3.3, 8.2. For interest on arrears, see *Financings Ltd v Baldock* [1963] 2 Q.B. 104; Senior Courts Act 1981 s.35A; County Courts Act 1984 s.69.
[1975] *South Bedfordshire Electrical Finance Ltd v Bryant* [1938] 3 All E.R. 580.
[1976] *Overstone Ltd v Shipway* [1962] 1 W.L.R. 117.
[1977] See above, para.39-330.

repudiation, with the result that the owner terminates the agreement and recovers possession of the goods, the owner is entitled to recover damages based on his loss of profit unless the right to damages is excluded by the terms of the agreement[1978] or he elects to proceed under an effective minimum payment provision.[1979] In *Yeoman Credit Ltd v Waragowski*,[1980] the Court of Appeal held that, where the hirer repudiates the agreement, the measure of damages recoverable is based on the hire-purchase price of the goods, less:

(i)   the sums already paid or payable[1981] by the hirer at the moment of termination;

(ii)   the value of the goods repossessed, or, if the goods have been sold, the proceeds of their sale[1982];

(iii) the amount (if any) payable on the exercise of the option to purchase[1983]; and

(iv)   a discount in respect of the earlier return to the owner of his capital outlay.[1984]

The owner is, however, under a duty to mitigate his loss[1985] and must, for example, obtain the best price which can reasonably be obtained if he sells the goods repossessed.[1986] If the hire-purchase agreement is subject to the Consumer Credit Act 1974 and hence the debtor has a statutory right to terminate the contract on payment of half the total price,[1987] it would seem that the possibility that the hirer could limit his liability by voluntarily terminating in this way should be taken into account in assessing the amount of damages recoverable by the owner.[1988]

No repudiation   Where, on the other hand, the breach by the hirer does not **39-348** amount to a repudiation by him of the hire-purchase agreement, but the owner terminates the hiring or the agreement by virtue of a right vested in him under the terms of the agreement,[1989] he cannot claim damages for loss of profit as upon a repudiation. He can only recover from the hirer:

[1978] *Overstone Ltd v Shipway* [1962] 1 W.L.R. 117; *Yeoman Credit Ltd v Odgers* [1962] 1 W.L.R. 215.

[1979] See below, para.39-349.

[1980] [1961] 1 W.L.R. 1124.

[1981] Arrears of instalments are in any event recoverable: see above, para.39-345.

[1982] In *Bentworth Finance v Jennings* (1961) 111 L.J. 488, it was said that the owner was under a duty to mitigate his loss by re-letting the goods: sed quaere? See also *Bentworth Finance v Reader* (1961) 112 L.J. 208 (sale permitted). A sale is standard practice.

[1983] This does not refer to any sum already paid by the hirer in consideration of the *grant* of an option to purchase (see above, para.39-307) but to a (usually nominal) sum to be paid by the hirer at the end of the hiring period.

[1984] *Overstone Ltd v Shipway* [1962] 1 W.L.R. 117; *Yeoman Credit Ltd v McLean* [1962] 1 W.L.R. 131.

[1985] In *Yeoman Credit Ltd v Coleman, The Times,* September 28, 1960, Master Jacob held that a finance company was under a duty to mitigate its loss by suing the dealer who negotiated the transaction in respect of defects in the goods before suing the hirer for damages for breach of contract. But see Samuels (1962) 25 M.L.R. 25.

[1986] *Bridge v Campbell Discount Co Ltd* [1962] A.C. 600, 635; *Financings Ltd v Baldock* [1963] 2 Q.B. 104, 107.

[1987] The "voluntary termination right" (VTR) under s.99, see below, para.39-367.

[1988] See above, Vol.I, para.26-083. But see a county court decision to the contrary: *First Response Finance v Donnelly* [2007] C.C.L.R. 4, Cty Ct.

[1989] See above, para.39-332.

(i)   the arrears of instalments (with interest) (if any) up to the time when he terminates the hiring[1990];

(ii) damages for any other breach committed up to the date of such termination, e.g. for failure to repair[1991]; and

(iii) the cost of searching for and repossessing the goods, if this should be specifically provided for in the agreement.[1992]

The reason for this limitation is that the termination is due, not to the hirer's breach of contract, but to the owner's election to determine. He is therefore not entitled to recover damages for his loss of profit, depreciation of the goods, or any breaches committed after the termination.[1993] Where an owner expressly undertakes to sell the goods on termination and to apply the proceeds to reduce the liability of the hirer, a term that he will take reasonable care to obtain the true market value will be implied.[1994]

39-349   **Minimum payment clauses.**[1995]   Where the agreement provides that, on termination of the hiring, the owner shall be entitled to repossess the goods and to claim in addition either a proportion of the outstanding instalments or a further fixed sum by way of depreciation or otherwise, it was at one time considered that the owner was in all cases entitled to rely on the terms of the agreement and that the question of a penalty or liquidated damages could not arise; and this was so whether the agreement was terminated by the owner or by the hirer.[1996] But in *Cooden Engineering Co Ltd v Stanford*[1997] the Court of Appeal, by a majority, held that the question whether a minimum payment clause imposed a penalty or liquidated damages would have to be considered if a breach of the contract was in fact proved. This case was followed by Denning L.J. in *Lamdon Trust v Hurrell*,[1998] where a clause in the agreement bound the hirer, in the event of breach and consequent repossession, to pay such further sum as would bring up his total payments to 75 per cent of the hire-purchase price by way of depreciation of the goods. It was held that this sum was a penalty, since it was imposed as a mere "rule of thumb" and was not a genuine pre-estimate of the damage likely to be suffered.

39-350   **Operative on events other than breach**   In both of these cases, the event relied upon to substantiate the owner's claim was a breach by the hirer in failing to pay

---

[1990] See above, para.39-345.

[1991] *Brady v St Margaret's Trust Ltd* [1963] 2 Q.B. 494.

[1992] *Anglo-Auto Finance Ltd v James* [1963] 1 W.L.R. 1042; *BMW Financial Services (GB) Ltd v Taylor* [2006] 1 C.L. 113 (a breach case).

[1993] *Elsey & Co Ltd v Hyde* (1926), Jones and Proudfoot, Notes on Hire-Purchase Law, 2nd edn, p.113; *Financings Ltd v Baldock* [1963] 2 Q.B. 104; *Brady v St Margaret's Trust Ltd*, above; *Anglo-Auto Finance Ltd v James*, above; *Charterhouse Credit Co Ltd v Tolly* [1963] 2 Q.B. 683; *Eshun v Moorgate Mercantile Co Ltd* [1971] 1 W.L.R. 722; *Capital Finance Co v Donati* (1977) 121 S.J. 270, CA; *Lombard North Central Plc v Butterworth* [1987] Q.B. 527, 540–543. Contrast *Esanda Finance Corp v Plessnig* (1988) 166 C.L.R. 131, HC of Australia.

[1994] *Lombard North Central Plc v Nugent* [2013] EWHC 1588 (QB).

[1995] See generally Atiyah (1958) 5 B.L.R. 24, 31; Goode (1962) 112 L.J. 216, 231; Hughes [1962] J.B.L. 252; Ziegel [1964] C.L.J. 60; Vol.I, paras 26-190 et seq.; below, paras 39-355, 39-368.

[1996] *Elsey & Co Ltd v Hyde* (1926), Jones and Proudfoot at p.107; *Chester & Cole Ltd v Avon* (1926), Jones and Proudfoot at p.115; *Chester & Cole Ltd v Wright* (1930), Jones and Proudfoot at p.124; *Associated Distributors Ltd v Hall* [1938] 2 K.B. 83; *Re Apex Supply Co Ltd* [1942] Ch. 108. cf. *Roadways Transport Development Ltd v Browne and Gray* (1928), Jones and Proudfoot at p.118.

[1997] [1953] 1 Q.B. 86.

[1998] [1955] 1 W.L.R. 391.

the rent by the due date and the question remained open whether a different conclusion would be reached if the right to determine the agreement and to claim payment were based on some event other than breach, such as the death, bankruptcy or liquidation of the hirer.[1999] In the earlier case of *Associated Distributors Ltd v Hall*[2000] the Court of Appeal had held that the question of a penalty or liquidated damages did not arise where the hirer *voluntarily* terminated the agreement: a sum payable upon such a contingency could not be considered a penalty since it was not payable in respect of any breach. This approach has now been approved in by the Supreme Court in *Cavendish Square Holdings BV v Makdessi*[2001] where it declined to follow Australian authority extending the doctrine of penalties to clauses operative on events other than breach.[2002]

Bridge v Campbell Discount Co Ltd   The law relating to minimum payment   **39-351**
clauses in hire-purchase agreements was reviewed, and to some extent clarified, by the House of Lords in *Bridge v Campbell Discount Co Ltd*.[2003] The law on penalties generally has been reconsidered by the Supreme Court decision *Cavendish Square Holdings BV v Makdessi*,[2004] and the old general test of whether the clause was not a genuine pre-estimate of the respondents' loss was replaced with the test of whether it comprised:

> "… a secondary obligation which imposes a detriment on the contract breaker out of all proportion to any legitimate interest of the innocent party in the enforcement of the primary obligation."[2005]

However it seems clear that where the legitimate interest is in performance (and hence compensation) the approach in *Dunlop Pneumatic Tyre Co Ltd v New Garage and Motor Co Ltd* is "usually … perfectly adequate to determine [the clause's] validity".[2006] In *Bridge*, the respondents let to the appellant a van under a hire-purchase agreement. The terms of the agreement provided (i) that the appellant hirer might at any time terminate the agreement by giving notice to the respondents; and (ii) that if for any reason the agreement was terminated before the vehicle became his property, he would pay to the respondents "by way of compensation for depreciation" of the vehicle such further sums as would with those already paid or payable, be equal to two-thirds of the hire-purchase price. Subsequently the appellant wrote to the respondents saying that he would not be able to pay any further instalments, and asking to be informed when and where he would have to return the van. The Court of Appeal[2007] construed the letter as a voluntary termination of the agreement in accordance with the power conferred upon the appellant by its terms; since there had been no breach of the agreement, the law relating to penal-

---

[1999] See *Elsey & Co Ltd v Hyde* (1926), Jones and Proudfoot at p.107; *Re Garrod, Jones and Proudfoot*, above p.167; *Bell Bros (HP) Ltd v Aitken*, 1939 S.C. 577; *Re Apex Supply Co Ltd* [1942] Ch. 108. cf. *Cooden Engineering Co Ltd v Stanford* [1953] 1 Q.B. 86, at 98.
[2000] [1938] 2 K.B. 83. But see below, para.39-354.
[2001] [2015] UKSC 67 at [41]–[43], [129]–[130], [163]–[165].
[2002] See above, para.26-234.
[2003] [1962] A.C. 600.
[2004] [2015] UKSC 67.
[2005] per Lord Neuberger J.S.C. at [32]; see also Lord Mance J.S.C. at [152] and Lord Hodge J.S.C. at [255]).
[2006] per Lord Neuberger J.S.C. at [32])
[2007] [1961] 1 Q.B. 445.

ties did not apply.[2008] The appellant was therefore liable to pay the sum stipulated in the minimum payment clause.

39-352   This decision of the Court of Appeal was reversed by the House of Lords. Their Lordships held that the letter written by the appellant was not an exercise by him of his right to terminate, but a breach of contract.[2009] As a result, the law relating to penalties did apply, and their Lordships unanimously concluded that the minimum payment clause imposed a penalty. It could not, so it was said, be a genuine estimate of the respondents' loss (which was then the test of whether a clause was a penalty or not under *Dunlop Pneumatic Tyre Co Ltd v New Garage and Motor Co Ltd*[2010]) through depreciation of the goods, since the sum payable under it was largest at the commencement of the hiring and grew progressively smaller as time went on.[2011] It was also pointed out that the sum exigible was expressed as a proportion of the hire-purchase price regardless of the fact that this contained a considerable interest element[2012] and also of the fact that the realisable value of the goods repossessed might, in many circumstances, exceed the one-third balance that the owner had not received. The House of Lords therefore ordered the actual damage suffered by the respondents to be assessed.[2013]

39-353   The House of Lords did not specifically strike down every clause designed to compensate the owner for depreciation of the goods let on hire, but it is unlikely that any such clause will now be upheld if it purports to give the owner a sum expressed as a proportion of the hire-purchase price.[2014] Such a clause, it is submitted, will only be valid if:

(i)   it is expressed in some other way, e.g. as a proportion of the cash price of the goods;

(ii)   it increases rather than decreases as the hiring continues[2015];

(iii)   it does not secure to the owner a profit over and above the hire-purchase price when the value of the goods repossessed is taken into account[2016]; and

(iv)   it has regard to the particular nature and condition of the goods in question.[2017]

In view of these difficulties, minimum payment clauses are now invariably formulated, not to compensate the owner for depreciation of the goods, but to compensate him for his loss of profit or as liquidated damages for breach of the agreement. But it must be remembered that the owner can only recover substantial

---

[2008] The court also considered that no other form of "equitable" relief was available to the hirer on the particular facts of the case: see above, para.39-344; below, para.39-354.

[2009] [1962] A.C. 600, 615, 621, 631, 632. cf. at 613. See also *United Dominions Trust Ltd v Ennis* [1968] 1 Q.B. 54.

[2010] [1915] A.C. 79, 86, since reconsidered (but in this context not doubted) in *Cavendish Square Holdings BV v Makdessi* [2015] UKSC 67, see above.

[2011] [1962] A.C. 600 at 614, 616, 623, 628, 634.

[2012] See above, para.39-347.

[2013] The county court judge subsequently assessed the damages as £30, instead of the £206 claimed by the respondents.

[2014] *Lombank Ltd v Excell* [1964] 1 Q.B. 415; *EP Finance Co Ltd v Dooley* [1963] 1 W.L.R. 1313. It would seem from these cases that *Phonographic Equipment Ltd v Muslu* [1961] 1 W.L.R. 1379 is inconsistent with the decision of the House of Lords in *Bridge*, despite the fact that it was followed in *Lombank Ltd v Cook* [1962] 1 W.L.R. 1133; and in *Lombank Ltd v Archbold* [1962] C.L.Y. 1409.

[2015] *Bridge v Campbell Discount Co Ltd* [1962] A.C. 600; *EP Finance Co Ltd v Dooley* [1963] 1 W.L.R. 1313.

[2016] *Bridge v Campbell Discount Co Ltd* [1962] A.C. 600; *Lombank Ltd v Excell* [1964] 1 Q.B. 415.

[2017] *Lombank Ltd v Excell* [1964] 1 Q.B. 415.

damages including his loss of profit if the hirer repudiates the agreement.[2018] So, for example, if a minimum payment clause simply provides for the payment to the owner of the outstanding balance of the hire-purchase price as liquidated damages for breach, it is unlikely that it will be held to do other than impose a penalty.[2019] Damages for loss of future rentals are irrecoverable where there has been no repudiation,[2020] and a clause designed to confer upon the owner a right to such damages in this event will be penal and void.

Since the House of Lords came to the conclusion in *Bridge v Campbell Discount Co Ltd* that the appellant was in breach of the hire-purchase agreement, it was strictly unnecessary for them to decide whether the law relating to penalties, or any form of equitable relief,[2021] was available to a hirer when the hiring was determined by a hirer's option or by an event specified in the contract and not involving breach. But Lord Simonds and Morton thought that there was no possibility of alleviation where the hirer terminated the contract and that the case of *Associated Distributors v Hall*[2022] was rightly decided.[2023] Lord Denning thought that the courts had power to grant relief no matter for what reason the hiring was terminated.[2024] Lord Devlin also considered that a court could intervene, but on the narrower ground that, when (as in this case) the clause falsely stated that a sum was payable as compensation for "depreciation", it was in any event unenforceable.[2025] Lord Radcliffe refused to express an opinion.[2026] In the light of this difference of opinion, the Court of Appeal has subsequently taken the view[2027] that the case of *Associated Distributors v Hall* still stands, so that no question of a penalty can arise if the hirer voluntarily terminates the agreement or the agreement is terminated on some event other than breach[2028] and the Supreme Court has since confirmed that a clause can only be a penalty if it gives rise to a secondary obligation arising upon breach.[2029]

39-354

[2018] See above, para.39-347.

[2019] *Anglo-Auto Finance Co Ltd v James* [1963] 1 W.L.R. 1042. Contrast *Robophone Facilities Ltd v Blank* [1966] 1 W.L.R. 1428 (hire); *JA Leasing v Humphrey* (1971) 46 A.L.J.R. 106.

[2020] *Financings Ltd v Baldock* [1963] 2 Q.B. 104; *Brady v St Margaret's Trust Ltd* [1963] 2 Q.B. 494; *Anglo-Auto Finance Co Ltd v James*, above; *Charterhouse Credit Co Ltd v Tolly* [1963] 2 Q.B. 683; *Capital Finance Co v Donati* (1977) 121 S.J. 270. Contrast *Esanda Finance Corp v Plessnig* (1988) 166 C.L.R. 131, HC of Australia.

[2021] In the Court of Appeal, there was a difference of opinion as to the circumstances (if any) in which a court could intervene by granting the hirer some form of equitable relief: see [1961] 1 Q.B. 445.

[2022] [1938] 2 K.B. 83; above, para.39-350.

[2023] [1962] A.C. 600, 613, 614.

[2024] [1962] A.C. 600 at 631, a view supported by the Law Commission in *Penalty Clauses and Forfeiture of Moneys Paid* (WP No.61, 1975), para.17.26.

[2025] [1962] A.C. 600 at 634.

[2026] [1962] A.C. 600 at 635.

[2027] *Goulston Discount Co Ltd v Harman* (1962) 106 S.J. 369. cf. *United Dominions Trust Ltd v Ennis* [1968] 1 Q.B. 54, 64, 67. See also *Granor Finance Ltd v Liquidator of Fastore Ltd*, 1974 S.L.T. 296 (termination on liquidation); and *Export Credits Guarantee Department v Universal Oil Products Co* [1983] 1 W.L.R. 399; Vol.I, paras 26-230 et seq.

[2028] *Associated Distributors v Hall* was followed (in a swaps agreement context) in *Lomas v JFB Firth Rixson Inc* [2010] EWHC 3372 (Ch) (reversed, on other points: [2012] EWCA Civ 419).

[2029] *Cavendish Square Holdings BV v Makdessi* [2015] UKSC 67, noted above, para.39-351 and see above, para.26–234.

39-355 Challenge under statute A minimum payment clause in an agreement would be open to challenge under the "unfair relationship" provisions of the Consumer Credit Act 1974[2030] and under the Consumer Rights Act 2015 Pt 2.[2031]

(c) Effect of Consumer Credit Regulation

39-356 Definition The consumer credit regulatory regime defines[2032] "hire-purchase agreement" to mean an agreement, other than a conditional sale agreement,[2033] under which (a) goods[2034] are bailed in return for periodical payments by the person to whom they are bailed, and (b) the property in the goods will pass to that person if the terms of the agreement are complied with and one or more of the following occurs—(i) the exercise of an option to purchase by that person, (ii) the doing of any other specified act by any party to the agreement, (iii) the happening of any other specified event.[2035]

39-357 Scope of regulation Hire-purchase agreements are essentially treated in the same way as conditional sale agreements[2036] and hence as *credit*, not hire, agreements. Hence a hire-purchase agreement with an individual[2037] is to be regarded as a fixed-sum credit[2038] agreement where the amount of credit is the balance financed.[2039] A hire-purchase agreement with an individual is therefore a regulated credit agreement unless it is an exempt agreement.[2040] A regulated hire-purchase agreement is a debtor-creditor-supplier agreement[2041] for restricted-use credit.[2042] But it cannot be a "small" agreement.[2043]

39-358 Parties By reason of the fact that a hire-purchase agreement is deemed to be a fixed-sum credit agreement, the owner is referred to as the "creditor" or "lender" and the hirer as the "debtor" or "borrower".[2044] The terms "owner" and "hirer" refer to consumer hire agreements only.[2045]

39-359 Unfair relationships The provisions of the Consumer Credit Act 1974 relating

---

[2030] See above, paras 39-212 et seq. See also below, para.39-368.

[2031] Replacing (for contracts made on or after October 1, 2015) the Unfair Terms in Consumer Contracts Regulations 1999 (SI 1999/2083); see above, paras 38-202 et seq.

[2032] See Consumer Credit Act 1974 ("CCA 1974") s.189(1) and the Financial Services and Markets Act 2000 (Regulated Activities) Order 2001 (SI 2001/544) ("RAO") art.60L(1), as inserted by SI 2013/1881 art.6. See also the almost identical definition in the Consumer Rights Act 2015 s.7.

[2033] Defined in CCA 1974 s.189(1) and RAO art.60L(1); see below, para.39-439.

[2034] Defined in CCA 1974 s.189(1) (but not in the RAO).

[2035] cf. *R. v RW Proffitt Ltd* [1954] 2 Q.B. 35.

[2036] See below, paras 39-439 et seq.

[2037] See above, para.39-016.

[2038] See above, para.39-026.

[2039] See CCA 1974 s.9(3) (and Sch.2 Pt II Example 10) and RAO art.60L(8). The balance financed is therefore equal to the total price (defined in CCA 1974 s.189(1) and RAO art.60L(1)) of the goods less the aggregate of the deposit (also defined in CCA 1974 s.189(1) and RAO art.60L(1)) (if any) and the total charge for credit (see above, para.39-059). Hence the £25,000 ceiling in the "business" exemption (see above, para.39-046) is calculated by taking the total price and deducting any deposit.

[2040] See above, para.39-017.

[2041] See above, para.39-030.

[2042] See above, para.39-027.

[2043] See above, para.39-048.

[2044] See above, para.39-016.

[2045] See above, para.39-037.

to "unfair relationships" apply to hire-purchase agreements where the debtor is an individual.[2046]

Application of the regulatory regime   The provisions of the regime relating to **39-360** the authorisation and control, etc. of consumer credit businesses and the regulation of consumer credit agreements have been dealt with in the first section of this chapter[2047] and they apply to the business of bailing goods on hire-purchase and to hire-purchase agreements. Although the Consumer Credit Directive[2048] does not apply to hire-purchase agreements, in order to maintain a coherent regime (in particular because conditional sales are within the Directive), the consumer credit regime, as amended in implementation of that Directive, has been extended to hire-purchase agreements. But there are a number of specific provisions that apply in particular to regulated hire-purchase (and conditional sale) agreements.[2049]

Protected goods   Restrictions are imposed on the recovery of possession where **39-361** the debtor is in breach of a regulated hire-purchase agreement[2050] and the debtor has paid or tendered[2051] to the creditor one-third or more of the total price[2052] of the goods. The goods then become "protected goods".[2053] Under s.90(1) of the Consumer Credit Act 1974, the creditor is not entitled to recover possession of protected goods from the debtor except on an order of the court.[2054] An exception exists if the debtor has terminated, or terminates, the agreement[2055]; and the restriction does not apply to the recovery of protected goods from a person other than the debtor.[2056] But otherwise the creditor's right to seize the goods is curtailed,[2057] and if the restriction applies to an agreement at the death of the debtor, it continues to apply (in relation to the possessor of the goods) until the grant of probate or administration.[2058]

It is to be noted that goods are not protected goods, even though one-third or **39-362**

[2046] ss.140A–140C, above, paras 39-212 et seq.

[2047] paras 39-001—39-257.

[2048] See above, para.39-011. Art.2(2)(d) of the Directive excludes hire-purchase from its scope.

[2049] See Guest and Lloyd, *Encyclopedia of Consumer Credit Law* (1975, looseleaf), paras 2-091—2-093, 2-100—2-101, 2-130—2-136.

[2050] Or conditional sale agreement: see below, para.39-448.

[2051] See CCA 1974 s.189(1): "payment" includes tender.

[2052] Defined in CCA 1974 s.189(1). For installation charges, see below, para.39-372. The "total price" does not include default interest or other charges payable on default: *Julian Hodge Bank Ltd v Hall* [1998] C.C.L.R. 14.

[2053] CCA 1974 s.90(7).

[2054] CPR Pt 7 PD 7B. *Grace v Black Horse Ltd* [2014] EWCA Civ 1413 ("order of court" can be an oral rather than the usual written order). A similar restriction was imposed by s.33 of the Hire-Purchase Act 1965. Contrast *Bentinck Ltd v Cromwell Engineering Co Ltd* [1971] 1 Q.B. 324 (abandoned goods); *Lombank v Dowdall* (1973) 118 S.J. 96, CA (deteriorating vehicle garaged by creditor to order of debtor); *Black Horse Ltd v Smith* [2002] 5 C.L. 105, Cty Ct (damaged car "released" to garage).

[2055] CCA 1974 s.90(5). cf. *United Dominions Trust (Commercial) Ltd v Ennis* [1968] 1 Q.B. 54; *FC Finance Ltd v Francis* (1970) 114 S.J. 568, CA (termination as a result of repudiation by the debtor is not termination by the debtor); *Chartered Trust Plc v Pitcher* [1988] R.T.R. 72.

[2056] Contrast *Bentinck Ltd v Cromwell Engineering Co Ltd* [1971] 1 Q.B. 324. See also *FC Finance Ltd v Francis* (1970) 114 S.J. 568, CA; *Kassam v Chartered Trust Plc* [1998] R.T.R. 220.

[2057] *Menzies v United Motor Finance Corp* [1940] 1 K.B. 559; *Carr v James Broderick & Co Ltd* [1942] 2 K.B. 275; *Thomas v Varney* (1957) 107 L.J. 412; *United Dominions Trust (Commercial) Ltd v Kesler* (1963) 107 S.J. 15; *Unity Finance Ltd v Woodcock* [1963] 1 W.L.R. 455; *Capital Finance Co Ltd v Bray* [1964] 1 W.L.R. 323.

[2058] CCA 1974 s.90(6). cf. *Peacock v Anglo-Auto Finance Co Ltd* (1968) 112 S.J. 746. After the grant

more of the total price may have been paid, unless the debtor is in breach of the agreement.[2059] Before one-third of the total price has been paid or tendered, or if the debtor is not in breach of the agreement, the creditor may retake possession of the goods,[2060] provided that he is then entitled to immediate possession of them.[2061]

39-363   **Successive agreements**   Section 90 of the 1974 Act also contains provisions designed to ensure that a debtor who has paid one-third or more of the total price under an earlier agreement does not lose the possibility of protection under the section by entering into a new agreement with the creditor whereby the goods comprised in the earlier agreement are transferred to a new agreement, with or without other goods.[2062] Section 90(3) of the Act, in effect, provides that where one-third or more of the total price has been paid under the earlier agreement, any goods comprised in both the earlier and the new agreement will be protected goods if the debtor is in breach of the new agreement, whether or not one-third or more of the total purchase price has been paid under the new agreement. Further, if the new agreement is a modifying agreement, as defined in s.82(2) of the 1974 Act,[2063] it seems that, on breach of the modifying agreement, all the goods in the modifying agreement become protected goods.[2064]

39-364   **Consent to repossession**   There is, however, no contravention of s.90(1) of the 1974 Act if, at the time of recovery of possession, the debtor consents thereto.[2065] But the consent of the debtor must be an "unqualified and informed" consent.[2066]

39-365   **Consequences of contravention**   The consequences of recovery of possession of protected goods in breach of s.90 are severe.[2067] The regulated agreement, if not previously terminated, terminates.[2068] The debtor is further released from all liability under the agreement and is entitled to recover from the creditor all sums paid by the debtor under the agreement.[2069] Any security[2070] provided in relation to the agreement, or to a linked transaction,[2071] is rendered invalid.[2072]

---

of probate or administration, the restriction continues to apply, since the personal representatives become the "debtor": CCA 1974 s.189(1).

[2059] This was a departure from the regime of s.33 of the Hire-Purchase Act 1965.

[2060] But see the need for notices under CCA 1974 ss.76, 86B, 86E, 98 (above, paras 39-164, 39-131, 39-135, 39-172).

[2061] See above, para.39-347.

[2062] This is similar to the position under s.47 of the Hire-Purchase Act 1965.

[2063] See above, para.39-148.

[2064] CCA 1974 s.90(4) and see Guest and Lloyd, *Encyclopedia of Consumer Credit Law* (1975, looseleaf), para.2-091.

[2065] CCA 1974 s.173(3): consent cannot be given earlier. See *McDonald v Bowmaker (Ireland) Ltd* (1950) 84 I.L.T. 64; *Thomas v Varney* (1957) 107 L.J. 412; *Mercantile Credit Co Ltd v Cross* [1965] 2 Q.B. 205; *Hunter v Lex Vehicle Finance Ltd* [2005] EWHC 223, [2005] B.P.I.R. 586. cf. *United Dominions Trust (Commercial) Ltd v Kesler* (1963) 107 S.J. 15.

[2066] *Chartered Trust Plc v Pitcher* [1988] R.T.R. 72.

[2067] CCA 1974 s.91. See also CCA 1974 s.142(2) (declaration) and *Capital Finance Co Ltd v Bray* [1964] 1 W.L.R. 323.

[2068] CCA 1974 s.91(a).

[2069] CCA 1974 s.91(b). But see *Carr v James Broderick & Co Ltd* [1942] 2 K.B. 275.

[2070] As defined in CCA 1974 s.189(1); see above, para.39-180. But see *Unity Finance Ltd v Woodcock* [1963] 1 W.L.R. 455 (guarantor under a recourse agreement also protected).

[2071] CCA 1974 s.113(8). For "linked transaction", see CCA 1974 ss.19(1), 189(1); above, paras 39-055 et seq.

Entry on premises   The creditor is not entitled to enter any premises[2073] to take   **39-366**
possession of goods subject to a regulated hire-purchase agreement[2074] except under
an order of the court.[2075] This restriction applies whether or not the goods are
"protected goods".[2076] Contravention of this prohibition is actionable as a breach of
statutory duty.[2077] A licence to enter and seize the goods conferred by the agreement will be of no effect.[2078] But this does not prevent entry upon premises with the
consent of the occupier given at the time.[2079]

Debtor's right to terminate agreement   Section 99 of the Consumer Credit Act   **39-367**
1974 gives to the debtor an indefeasible[2080] right (VTR—voluntary termination
right) to terminate a regulated hire-purchase agreement[2081] at any time before the
final payment falls due.[2082] The right is exercisable by giving notice to any person
entitled or authorised to receive the sums payable under the agreement, e.g. to a
person deputed by the creditor to collect the instalments.[2083] Termination, however,
does not affect any liability under the agreement which has accrued before the
termination.[2084]

Minimum payment   Upon termination under s.99, the debtor becomes prima   **39-368**
facie liable (unless the agreement provides for a smaller payment,[2085] or does not
provide for any payment) to pay to the creditor the amount (if any) by which one-
half[2086] of the total price[2087] exceeds the aggregate of the sums paid and the sums
due in respect of the total price immediately before the termination.[2088] But if he has

---

[2072] CCA 1974 ss.106, 113(3)(b); above, para.39-193.
[2073] For the meaning of "premises", in other contexts, see, e.g. *Andrews v Andrews and Mears* [1908] 2
K.B. 567, 570; *West Mersea UDC v Fraser* [1950] 2 K.B. 119; *Gardiner v Sevenoaks RDC* [1950]
2 All E.R. 84; *John A Pike (Butchers) ltd v Independent Insurance Co Ltd* [1998] Lloyd's Rep. I.R.
410, CA; *Spring House v Mount Cook Land* [2001] FWCA Civ 1833, [2002] 2 All E.R. 822.
[2074] The provision is applicable also to a regulated conditional sale agreement (below, para.39-443) and
to a regulated consumer hire agreement (above, para.39-036).
[2075] CCA 1974 s.92(1). See CPR Pt 7 PD 7B.
[2076] See above paras 39-361 et seq.
[2077] CCA 1974 s.92(3). Moreover, the usual disciplinary sanctions are available to the FCA, see above
para.39-063. See *Bowmaker Ltd v Tabor* [1914] 2 K.B. 1; *Carr v James Broderick & Co Ltd* [1942]
2 K.B. 275; *Smart Bros Ltd v Ross* [1943] A.C. 84; *Fileman v British Ry Traffic and Electricity Co
Ltd* (1945) 173 L.T. 407; *Harris v Lombard (New Zealand) Ltd* [1974] 2 N.Z.L.R. 161. In many situations, damages may be nominal only.
[2078] CCA 1974 s.173(1).
[2079] CCA 1974 s.173(3).
[2080] See CCA 1974 s.173(1). See also *Acceptance Co v Pike* (1961) 111 L.J. 424.
[2081] The provision applies also to conditional sale agreements, with certain modifications: see below,
para.39-451.
[2082] CCA 1974 s.99(1). cf. *Wadham Stringer Finance Ltd v Meaney* [1981] 1 W.L.R. 39 (acceleration
clause in conditional sale agreement). Despite calls for its abolition, it was decided, after consultation, to retain the VTR, see: *A Consultation on Voluntary Termination of Hire Purchase and
Conditional Sale Agreements under the Consumer Credit Act 1974*, DTI, Sept 2004 and OFT 761.
[2083] CCA 1974 s.99(1).
[2084] CCA 1974 s.99(2).
[2085] See above, paras 39-349—39-354 for the effectiveness of minimum payment clauses at common law.
[2086] For installation charges, see below, para.39-372.
[2087] Defined in CCA 1974 s.189(1).
[2088] CCA 1974 s.100(1). This corresponds to (the now repealed) s.28(1) of the Hire-Purchase Act 1965.
Thus, for example, if the total price is £3,600, and the debtor terminates after he has paid £1,000
and owes £200 in unpaid instalments, he must pay the £200 (s.99(2) and see above, paras 39-345,
39-346) and a further £600 so as to bring his total payments up to one-half of the total price.

paid, or becomes liable to pay, more than one-half of the total price before the termination, he is not entitled to recover, or be relieved from, the excess.

39-369   It is important, however, to note the qualification attached to this "minimum payment" by s.100(3) of the 1974 Act:

> "If in any action the court is satisfied that a sum less than the amount [of one-half the total price] would be equal to the loss sustained[2089] by the creditor in consequence of the termination of the agreement by the debtor, the court may make an order for the payment of that sum in lieu of the amount [of one-half the total price]."

The one-half minimum payment is thus merely the *maximum* amount recoverable by the creditor when the debtor exercises his statutory right of termination.[2090]

39-370   Recompense   If the debtor has contravened an obligation to take reasonable care of the goods, the amount of one-half the total price is to be increased by the sum required to recompense the creditor for that contravention, and the qualification mentioned above likewise has effect accordingly.[2091]

39-371   Wrongful possession   Where the debtor, on his termination of the agreement, wrongfully retains possession of goods to which the agreement relates, then, in any action brought by the creditor to recover possession of the goods from the debtor, the court, unless it is satisfied that having regard to the circumstances it would not be just to do so, must order the goods to be delivered to the creditor without giving the debtor an option to pay the value of the goods.[2092]

39-372   Installation charges   Where under a hire-purchase agreement[2093] the creditor is required to carry out any installation and the agreement specifies, as part of the total price, the amount to be paid in respect of the installation[2094] (the "installation charge") the reference in s.90(1)(b)[2095] of the Act to one-third of the total price and the reference in s.100(1)[2096] of the Act to one-half of the total price are to be construed as references to the aggregate of the installation charge and (as the case may be) to one-third or one-half of the remainder of the total price.[2097] This is best explained by illustration:

> (i)   In a case where the total price is £1,400, of which £200 is specified as an installation charge, if it is sought to discover whether the goods have become protected goods (s.90), the statutory one-third would be £600, arrived at by deducting the installation charge from the total price, taking one-third of the balance, viz £400, and then adding the £200 installation charge.

[2089] For a discussion of the meaning of the "loss sustained", see Goode, *Hire-Purchase Law and Practice*, 2nd edn, pp.406–407; Guest, *The Law of Hire-Purchase* (1966), para.609; *Booth & Phipps Garages Ltd v Milton* [2000] C.L.Y. 2601, Cty Ct.

[2090] See also CCA 1974 s.113(1), (8) (security); above, para.39-190. See above, para.39-347 as to the possible relevance of the VTR in limiting the damages recoverable when the debtor breaches the agreement.

[2091] CCA 1974 s.100(4).

[2092] CCA 1974 s.100(5).

[2093] Or conditional sale agreement: see below, paras 39-448, 39-451.

[2094] Defined in s.189(1).

[2095] See above, para.39-361.

[2096] See above, para.39-369.

[2097] CCA 1974 ss.90(2), 100(2).

(ii) If it is sought to discover the statutory one-half of the total price (s.100) in the above example, the installation charge is first deducted from the total price leaving a balance of £1,200. Take one-half of this, viz £600, and then add back the installation charge in full, making a total of £800.

Time orders In the case of a regulated hire-purchase agreement, as with any **39-373** regulated agreement, the court is empowered to make a "time order" under s.129 of the Consumer Credit Act 1974 in certain circumstances.[2098] But, in the case of a hire-purchase agreement,[2099] the court may, when making a time order under s.129(2)(a) (for payment of any sum owed by instalments), deal with sums which, although not payable by the debtor at the time the order is made, would, if the agreement continued in force, become payable under it subsequently.[2100] Thus the court can, for example, not only order that the debtor be allowed time to pay off arrears and by instalments commensurate with his means, but also that his obligation to pay future instalments of rentals be rescheduled in a similar manner. Also, if the debtor is in possession of the goods following the making of a time order, he is to be treated as a bailee of the goods under the terms of the agreement, notwithstanding that the agreement has been terminated.[2101] His position in this respect may therefore be described as that of a "statutory bailee".[2102]

"Return orders" and "transfer orders" Certain special powers are conferred **39-374** upon the court by s.133 of the Consumer Credit Act 1974 in relation to a regulated hire-purchase agreement[2103] where an application is made for an enforcement order[2104] or for a time order,[2105] or where an action is brought by the creditor to recover possession of goods to which the agreement relates.[2106] These special powers are, if it appears to the court just to do so, to make a return order or a transfer order.[2107]

A return order is an order for the return to the creditor of goods to which the **39-375** agreement relates.[2108] Such an order can be either unconditional or (by virtue of s.135 of the 1974 Act)[2109] suspended. Thus the court can, by combining a time order made under s.129 with a suspended return order, make an order equivalent to the "postponed order" under (the now repealed) s.35(4)(b) of the Hire-Purchase Act 1965, that is to say, to order that the goods be returned to the creditor and suspend the operation of the order on condition that the debtor pays the unpaid balance of the total price by such instalments and at such times as the court provides in the time order. It is this combination of orders that is most extensively used.

A transfer order is an order for the transfer to the debtor of the creditor's title to **39-376**

[2098] See above, para.39-202 and CPR Pt 7 PD 7B; Pt 55 PD 55 7.1 Form N440.

[2099] Or conditional sale agreement.

[2100] CCA 1974 s.130(2).

[2101] CCA 1974 s.130(4). This provision applies also to a regulated consumer hire agreement.

[2102] As was the case under the Hire-Purchase Act 1965 s.38(1) when the goods were protected goods. See also *Bentworth Finance v Jones* (1963) 114 L.J. 140.

[2103] Or conditional sale agreement.

[2104] See above, para.39-200.

[2105] CCA 1974 s.129; above, para.39-202.

[2106] This is not confined to actions to recover protected goods (see above, paras 39-361 et seq.). For the particulars required in the case of such a claim, see CPR Pt 7 PD 7B.

[2107] CCA 1974 s.133(1). See Torts (Interference with Goods) Act 1977 s.3(8)(a): power of court under s.3 is without prejudice to the remedies afforded by CCA 1974 s.133.

[2108] CCA 1974 s.133(1)(i).

[2109] See above, para.39-208.

certain goods to which the agreement relates ("the transferred goods"), and the return to the creditor of the remainder of the goods.[2110] Where a transfer is made, the transferred goods are to be such of the goods to which the agreement relates as the court thinks just; but a transfer order can be made only where "the paid-up sum[2111] exceeds the part of the total price referable to the transferred goods[2112] by an amount equal to at least one-third of the unpaid balance of the total price".[2113]

39-377   Even though a return order or transfer order has been made, the debtor can, before the goods enter the possession of the creditor, on payment of the balance of the total price and fulfilment of any other necessary conditions, claim the goods ordered to be returned to the creditor.[2114] Similarly, if in pursuance of a time order or under s.133, the total price of goods is paid and any other necessary conditions are fulfilled, the creditor's title vests in the debtor.[2115]

39-378   **Monetary judgment on non-compliance**   If, in contravention of a return order or transfer order, any goods to which the order relates are not returned to the creditor, the court, on the application of the creditor, may—(a) revoke so much of the order as relates to those goods; and (b) order the debtor to pay to the creditor the unpaid portion of so much of the total price as is referable to those goods.[2116]

39-379   **Adverse possession**   In an action for the return of goods wrongfully detained a claimant must show that the defendant has wrongfully neglected or refused to deliver up the goods so that the defendant's possession of the goods is adverse.[2117] Since the creditor is, for example, precluded from recovering protected goods otherwise than by action,[2118] and he might in consequence be said to be bound to acquiesce in the debtor's continuing in possession of the goods, difficulties could arise in relation to the creditor's need to prove adverse possession in an action to recover possession of the goods.[2119] Such difficulties are obviated by s.134(1) of the 1974 Act,[2120] which provides that where the creditor brings an action or makes an application to enforce a right to recover possession of goods comprised in a regulated hire-purchase agreement[2121] from the debtor and proves that a demand for delivery of the goods was included in the default notice,[2122] or that, after the right to recover possession of the goods accrued but before the action was begun or the

---

[2110] CCA 1974 s.133(1)(ii). This corresponds to the rarely used "split order" that could be made under s.35(4)(c) of the Hire-Purchase Act 1965.

[2111] See CCA 1974 s.133(2) for the definition of "the paid-up sum" and for its adjustment to take account of a sum owed by the creditor to the debtor, and for the deduction of any sum owed by the debtor in relation to the goods (otherwise than as part of the total price) from the paid-up sum.

[2112] See CCA 1974 s.133(6).

[2113] "Total price" is defined in CCA 1974 s.189(1). As a mathematical formula the maximum value of the goods capable of being transferred (V) can be expressed as: "$V = p - u/3$" where p is the paid up sum and u the unpaid balance of the total price.

[2114] CCA 1974 s.133(4).

[2115] CCA 1974 s.133(5).

[2116] CCA 1974 s.133(6).

[2117] *Clements v Flight* (1846) 16 M. & W. 42.

[2118] See above, para.39-361.

[2119] *Smart Bros Ltd v Pratt* [1940] 2 K.B. 498, 504.

[2120] Similar but narrower provisions appeared in s.10 of the Hire-Purchase Act 1938 and s.48 of the Hire-Purchase Act 1965.

[2121] CCA 1974 s.134(1) also applies to regulated conditional sale and consumer hire agreements.

[2122] Under CCA 1974 s.88(5), see above, para.39-167. It is therefore clear that CCA 1974 s.134(1), unlike (the now repealed) s.48(1) of the Hire-Purchase Act 1965, allows the demand for delivery up of the goods to be included in the default notice.

application was made, he made a request in writing to the debtor to surrender the goods, then, for the purposes of the claim of the creditor to recover possession of the goods, the possession of them by the debtor is to be deemed to be adverse to the owner. However, nothing in s.134(1) is to affect a claim for damages for conversion.[2123]

(d) Defective Goods

Warranties and representations by dealers   In many hire-purchase transac-   **39-380**
tions, the hirer enters into the agreement on the faith of statements made to him by a dealer with whom he is in no direct contractual relationship. The dealer sells the goods to a finance company, and the hire-purchase agreement is made between the hirer and the finance company. At common law the dealer is not normally an agent of the finance company in respect of any statements made by him to the hirer, even though he may decide and state the purchase price, receive the proposal form and initial deposit, and be paid a commission by the finance company.[2124] But the courts have held that, in appropriate circumstances, the hirer may sue the dealer on a col- lateral warranty and recover damages for the breach of it.[2125] The dealer may also be liable in deceit and possibly for negligent misstatement[2126] even if the state- ments do not amount to a warranty.[2127] He can also be sued in tort for negligence if he puts into circulation goods that he knows or ought to know are dangerous or defective and the hirer or some third person is injured as a result.[2128]

However, under the Consumer Credit Act 1974,[2129] any representations (includ-   **39-381**
ing any condition or warranty, and any other statement or undertaking, whether oral or in writing)[2130] made by a dealer who is a negotiator[2131] in antecedent negotia- tions[2132] prior to the making of a regulated hire-purchase agreement are deemed to have been made by him in the capacity of agent of the creditor as well as in his actual capacity.[2133] The finance company will therefore be liable for representa- tions made by the dealer in such circumstances.

[2123] CCA 1974 s.134(2).
[2124] *North Central Wagon and Finance Co Ltd v White and Powell* [1955] C.L.Y. 1204; *Campbell Discount Co Ltd v Gall* [1961] 1 Q.B. 431; *Yeoman Credit Ltd v Apps* [1962] 2 Q.B. 508; *Branwhite v Worcester Works Finance Ltd* [1969] 1 A.C. 552; *Williams (JD) & Co v McCauley Parsons and Jones* [1994] C.C.L.R. 78; *Woodchester Equipment (Leasing) Ltd v British Association of Canned and Preserved Foods Importers and Distributors Ltd* [1995] C.L.Y. 2459; *PB Leasing Ltd v Patel* [1995] C.C.L.R. 82; *Lombard North Central Plc v Gate* [1998] C.C.L.R. 51, Cty Ct; *Brewer v Mann* [2012] EWCA Civ 246. See Guest (1963) 79 L.Q.R. 33; Hughes (1964) 27 M.L.R. 395. Contrast *Purnell Secretarial Services Ltd v Lease Management Services Ltd* [1994] C.C.L.R. 127.
[2125] *Webster v Higgin* [1948] 2 All E.R. 127; *Brown v Sheen and Richmond Car Sales Ltd* [1950] 1 All E.R. 1102; *Andrews v Hopkinson* [1957] 1 Q.B. 229; *Smith v Spurling Motor Bodies Ltd* (1961) 105 S.J. 967; *Yeoman Credit Ltd v Odgers* [1962] 1 W.L.R. 215. See Vol.I, paras 13-004, 13-033. It is possible that a warranty similar to the term implied by s.14(3) of the Sale of Goods Act 1979 might be imported into such a transaction: *Andrews v Hopkinson*, above, at 237. Contrast *Drury v Victor Buckland Ltd* [1941] 1 All E.R. 269.
[2126] See Vol.I, Ch.7. The Misrepresentation Act 1967 s.2(1), would not appear to apply in this situation.
[2127] cf. *Garbett v Rufford Motor Co Ltd*, The Guardian, March 12, 1962.
[2128] *Herschtal v Stewart Ardern Ltd* [1940] 1 K.B. 155; *Andrews v Hopkinson* [1957] 1 Q.B. 229. See also the Consumer Protection Act 1987; below, paras 44-449 et seq.
[2129] See above, para.39-071.
[2130] See CCA 1974 s.189(1): definition of "representation".
[2131] Defined in CCA 1974 s.56(1), see above, para.39-073.
[2132] Defined in CCA 1974 s.56(1), see above, para.39-071.
[2133] CCA 1974 s.56(2).

39-382 Implied terms   Sections 9 to 11 of the Supply of Goods (Implied Terms) Act 1973[2134] import into every hire-purchase agreement certain implied terms as to the quality and fitness for purpose of the goods, and their correspondence with description and sample. These implied terms correspond very closely with the terms implied in contracts of sale of goods by virtue of ss.13 to 15 of the Sale of Goods Act 1979.[2135] The Consumer Rights Act 2015[2136] makes separate provision for "consumer" agreements and treats similar (but more expansive[2137]) terms "as included" in "consumer" hire-purchase agreements (the terms being the same as for sales contracts).[2138] It also confers extensive remedies for their breach.[2139] The exclusion of these implied terms and of the liability of the creditor for the breach of them is ineffective, either absolutely or subject to certain qualifications, the extent depending on whether they are "consumer" contracts or not.[2140]

39-383 Letting by description   By s.9(1) of the 1973 Act, where under a hire-purchase agreement goods are bailed by description, there is implied in the agreement a term[2141] that the goods will correspond with the description[2142]; and if under the agreement the goods are bailed by reference to a sample as well as a description, it is not sufficient that the bulk of the goods corresponds with the sample if the goods do not also correspond with the description.[2143] Goods are not prevented from being bailed by description by reason only that, being exposed for sale or hire, they are selected by the hirer.[2144] The Consumer Rights Act 2015 makes almost identical provision for "consumer" hire-purchase (and sales) agreements.[2145]

39-384 Satisfactory quality   By s.10(2) of the 1973 Act,[2146] where the creditor[2147] bails goods under a hire-purchase agreement in the course of a business[2148] there is an

---

[2134] Re-enacted (as from May 19, 1985: see SI 1983/1551 (c.44)) by s.192 of and Sch.4 para.35, to the Consumer Credit Act 1974 and amended by the Supply of Goods and Services Act 1982 s.17(1), the Sale and Supply of Goods Act 1994 s.7 and Sch.2, and the Sale and Supply of Goods to Consumers Regulations 2002 (SI 2002/3045) reg.13 (revoked, with effect from October 1, 2015, by the Consumer Rights Act 2015 s.60 and Sch.1 para.53).

[2135] See below, paras 44-086—44-115.

[2136] For contracts made on or after October 1, 2015.

[2137] See, in particular, the new terms as to conformity with model seen or examined (s.14, above, para.38-502) and as to incorrect installation (s.15, above, para.38-503).

[2138] And note that certain pre-contract information provided under the Consumer Contract (Information, Cancellation and Additional Charges) Regulations 2013 (SI 2013/3134) are treated as terms of the contract: Consumer Rights Act 2015 s.12 and see above, para.38-500.

[2139] The terms are set out in the Consumer Rights Act 2015 ss.9–15, 18 (see above, paras 38-497 et seq.) and the remedies in ss.19–27 (above, paras 38-512 et seq.).

[2140] See Vol.I, para.15-093; below, para.44-117.

[2141] In England and Wales and Northern Ireland, this term is a condition: s.9(1A).

[2142] Supply of Goods (Implied Terms) Act 1973 s.9(1). See, e.g. *Karsales (Harrow) Ltd v Wallis* [1956] 1 W.L.R. 936; *Astley Industrial Trust Ltd v Grimley* [1963] 1 W.L.R. 584, 597; *Charterhouse Credit Co Ltd v Tolly* [1963] 2 Q.B. 683, 708; *Brewer v Mann* [2012] EWCA Civ 246.

[2143] For the analogous case of sale by description, see below, para.44-086.

[2144] Supply of Goods (Implied Terms) 1973 Act s.9(2).

[2145] For contracts made on or after October 1, 2015. See Consumer Rights Act 2015 s.11 (but note the additional provisions in s.11(4)–(5)). See above, para.38-499.

[2146] As amended by s.17(1) of the Supply of Goods and Services Act 1982 and s.7 of the Sale and Supply of Goods Act 1994. See *Garside v Black Horse Ltd* [2010] EWHC 190 (QB) (not a sale by sample, hence s.10(2) applied).

[2147] Defined in s.15(1) of the 1973 Act to mean the owner or his assignee.

[2148] Defined in s.15(1) of the 1973 Act. See also s.10(5).

implied term[2149] that the goods supplied under the agreement are of satisfactory quality.[2150] But this implied term does not extend to any matter making the quality of goods unsatisfactory (a) which is specifically drawn to the hirer's attention before the agreement is made; or (b) where the hirer examines the goods before the agreement is made, which that examination ought to reveal; or (c) where the goods are bailed by reference to a sample, which would have been apparent on reasonable examination of the sample.[2151] If the hirer deals as consumer[2152] the creditor may be responsible for any public statements on the specific characteristics of the goods made about them by himself, the producer[2153] or his representative particularly in advertising or on labelling.[2154] The Consumer Rights Act 2015 makes almost identical provision for "consumer" hire-purchase (and sales) agreements.[2155]

Fitness for purpose By s.10(3) of the 1973 Act, where the creditor[2156] bails goods under a hire-purchase agreement in the course of a business[2157] and the hirer, expressly or by implication, makes known to the creditor, or to a credit-broker[2158] in the course of negotiations conducted by that broker in relation to goods sold by him to the creditor before forming the subject matter of the hire-purchase agreement, any particular purpose for which the goods are being bailed, there is an implied term[2159] that the goods supplied under the agreement are reasonably fit for that purpose, whether or not that is a purpose for which such goods are commonly supplied,[2160] except where the circumstances show that the hirer does not rely, or that it is unreasonable for him to rely,[2161] on the skill or judgment of the creditor or credit-broker.[2162] The Consumer Rights Act 2015 treats a similar term "as included" in "consumer" hire-purchase (and sales) agreements.[2163] **39-385**

Sample By s.11 of the 1973 Act, where under a hire-purchase agreement goods **39-386**

[2149] In England and Wales and Northern Ireland, this term is a condition: s.10(7).

[2150] Supply of Goods (Implied Terms) 1973 Act s.10(2), as amended by (i) s.17(1) of the Supply of Goods and Services Act 1982; (ii) Sale and Supply of Goods Act 1994, and (iii) Consumer Rights Act 2015 s.60 and Sch.1 para.3. See *Garside v Black Horse Ltd* [2010] EWHC 190 (QB) (not a sale by sample, hence s.10(2) applied). "Satisfactory quality" is defined in s.10(2A), (2B) of the 1973 Act. See below, paras 44-099—44-100. For second hand goods, see, e.g. *Bartlett v Sidney Marcus Ltd* [1965] 1 W.L.R. 1013; *Crowther v Shannon Motor Co* [1975] 1 W.L.R. 30. See also *Lamarra v Capital Bank Plc*, 2006 S.L.T. 1045 (relevance of warranty in determining satisfactory quality): below, para.44-099.

[2151] For the corresponding provision in the Sale of Goods Act 1979, see below, para.44-095.

[2152] This expression is not defined in the 1973 Act. cf. below, para.44-121.

[2153] Defined in s.15(1) of the 1973 Act.

[2154] Supply of Goods (Implied Terms) 1973 Act s.10(2D), (2E), (2F), inserted by the Sale and Supply of Goods to Consumers Regulations 2002 (SI 2002/3045) reg.13. Note the corresponding provisions for "consumer" hire-purchase (and sales) agreements in the Consumer Rights Act s.9(5)–(7), above, para.38-502 and note s.18 (no other implied requirement as to quality), above, para.38-470.

[2155] For contracts made on or after October 1, 2015. See Consumer Rights Act 2015 s.9(5)–(7), above, para.38-502 and note s.18 (no other implied requirement as to quality), above, para.38-505.

[2156] Defined in Supply of Goods (Implied Terms) 1973 Act s.15(1) to mean the owner or his assignee.

[2157] Defined in s.15(1) of the 1973 Act. See also s.10(5).

[2158] Defined in s.10(6) of the 1973 Act.

[2159] In England and Wales and Northern Ireland, this term is a condition: s.10(7).

[2160] *Lowe v Lombank Ltd* [1960] 1 W.L.R. 196; *Unity Finance Ltd v Hammond* (1965) 109 S.J. 70; *Porter v General Guarantee Corp* [1982] R.T.R. 384.

[2161] cf. *Yeoman Credit Co Ltd v Apps* [1962] 2 Q.B. 508; *Astley Industrial Trust Ltd v Grimley* [1963] 1 W.L.R. 584.

[2162] Supply of Goods (Implied Terms) 1973 Act s.10(3). For the corresponding provision in the Sale of Goods Act 1979, see below, para.44-105.

[2163] For contracts made on or after October 1, 2015. See Consumer Rights Act 2015 s.10, above, para.38-

are bailed by reference to a sample, there is an implied term[2164]—(a) that the bulk will correspond with the sample in quality; and (b) that the hirer will have a reasonable opportunity of comparing the bulk with the sample; and (c) that the goods will be free from any defect, making their quality unsatisfactory,[2165] which would not be apparent on reasonable examination of the sample.[2166] The Consumer Rights Act 2015 treats a similar term as included in 'consumer' hire-purchase (and sales) agreements.[2167] Moreover, it includes an additional term that the goods match a model seen or examined.[2168]

39-387 **Remedies for breach** Breach of any of the terms implied by ss.9 to 11 of the Supply of Goods (Implied Terms) 1973 Act normally entitles the hirer to assert the remedies available to him for breach of condition, that is to say, he can reject the goods and treat the agreement as repudiated and sue for damages for any loss or damage (including consequential loss) which he may have suffered as a result of the breach.[2169] The hirer may elect not to treat the breach of condition as a ground for treating the contract as repudiated, but mere acceptance of the goods does not preclude this remedy.[2170] A refusal by the creditor to remedy the defects in the goods bailed constitutes a continuing breach of the agreement and the hirer may refuse to continue with the agreement as the creditor will not honour his obligation.[2171] Alternatively the hirer can affirm the agreement and sue for damages.[2172] However, if the hirer does not deal as consumer,[2173] and the breach is so slight that it would be unreasonable for him to reject them, the breach is not to be treated as a breach of condition but may be treated as a breach of warranty,[2174] i.e. be remediable in damages only. The additional remedies conferred on the consumer by Pt 5A of the Sale of Goods Act 1979[2175] and by Pt 1B of the Supply of Goods and Services Act 1982[2176] do not apply to hire-purchase agreements.[2177] The Consumer Rights Act 2015 repeals those provisions and extends to hirers the much more extensive remedies provided for under that Act.[2178]

39-388 **Total failure of consideration** There is some authority for the view that, where

---

498 and note s.18: no other implied requirement as to quality, above, para.38-505.

[2164] In England and Wales and Northern Ireland, this term is a condition: s.11(2).

[2165] Defined in s.10(2A), (2B), (2D)–(2F) of the 1973 Act.

[2166] Supply of Goods (Implied Terms) 1973 Act s.11. For the corresponding provision in the Sale of Goods Act 1979, see below, para.44-113.

[2167] For contracts made on or after October 1, 2015. See Consumer Rights Act 2015 s.13. See above, para.38-501.

[2168] See Consumer Rights Act 2015 s.14. See above, para.38-502.

[2169] See *Yeoman Credit v Odgers Vospers Motor House (Plymouth) (Third Party)* [1962] 1 W.L.R. 215, CA; *Brewer v Mann* [2012] EWCA Civ 246 (obiter, breach of s.9(1)).

[2170] cf. Sale of Goods Act 1979 s.11(4); below, para.44-068.

[2171] *Yeoman Credit Ltd v Apps* [1962] 2 Q.B. 508; *Ditchburn Equipment Ltd v Crich* (1966) 110 S.J. 266, CA. This sentence was cited with approval in *Garside v Black Horse Ltd* [2010] EWHC 190 (QB) [30].

[2172] See below, para.39-389.

[2173] Defined as in Pt I of the Unfair Contract Terms Act 1977; see Vol.I, para.15-073 and below, para.44-121.

[2174] s.11(A). For the corresponding provision in the Sale of Goods Act 1979, see below, para.44-070.

[2175] Inserted by reg.4 of the Sale and Supply of Goods to Consumers Regulations 2002 (SI 2002/3045); below, paras 38-442 et seq.

[2176] Inserted by reg.9 of the Sale and Supply of Goods to Consumer Regulations 2002 (SI 2002/3045).

[2177] At least until the hirer exercises his option to purchase and buys the goods.

[2178] For contracts made on or after October 1, 2015. See above, paras 38-512 et seq. See especially ss.19–27, in part replacing those now available under Pt 5A (ss.48A to 48F) of the 1979 Act for buyers

the goods are so defective that they are totally unfit for the purpose for which they are let or where they seriously fail to correspond with description, the hirer is entitled at common law to recover all sums which he has paid as upon a total failure of consideration,[2179] provided that he takes immediate steps to rescind the agreement.[2180]

Measure of damages If the hirer elects to treat the contract as repudiated and to sue for damages, there is some doubt as to the measure of damages which he is entitled to recover at common law.[2181] But it would seem that he is entitled to claim the return of all moneys paid by him at the time of the termination of the agreement, together with any sum actually expended on repairing the goods bailed, less a deduction for the use of the goods during the period they were in his possession.[2182] He would also be entitled to recover any additional cost involved in obtaining equivalent goods on hire-purchase elsewhere. If, on the other hand, the breach of the agreement amounts to or is to be treated as a breach of warranty only, or if the hirer elects to affirm the contract and sue for damages, the measure of damages would appear to be the cost of putting the goods into a proper state of repair together with damages for loss of use while they are being put into repair.[2183]

39-389

Exclusion of implied terms: consumer agreements Liability for breach of the obligations arising from ss.9, 10 or 11 of the Supply of Goods (Implied Terms) Act 1973 cannot be excluded or restricted by any contract term as against a person "dealing as consumer" as presently defined in the Unfair Contract Terms Act 1977.[2184] It is important to note that this definition is in no way connected with the concept of a consumer credit agreement in the Consumer Credit Act 1974.[2185] For the purposes of the 1977 Act, the hirer "deals as consumer" if he neither makes the agreement in the course of a business[2186] nor holds himself out as so doing, and if the creditor does make the agreement in the course of a business and (unless the hirer is an individual) the goods[2187] bailed are of a type ordinarily supplied for private use or consumption.[2188] The onus of proving that the hirer did not deal as a

39-390

---

dealing "as consumer" (now defined in Sale of Goods Act 1979 s.61(1) by reference to (now repealed) Unfair Contract Terms Act 1977 s.12) when the goods do not conform to the contract of sale.

[2179] *Karsales (Harrow) Ltd v Wallis* [1956] 1 W.L.R. 936; *Yeoman Credit Ltd v Apps* [1962] 2 Q.B. 508 at 521, 524; *Unity Finance Ltd v Hammond* (1965) 109 S.J. 70.

[2180] cf. *Yeoman Credit Ltd v Apps*, above; *Charterhouse Credit Co Ltd v Tolly* [1963] 2 Q.B. 683.

[2181] Contrast *Yeoman Credit Co Ltd v Apps* [1962] 2 Q.B. 508 with *Charterhouse Credit Co Ltd v Tolly* [1963] 2 Q.B. 683, both considered in *Brewer v Mann* [2012] EWCA Civ 246.

[2182] *Charterhouse Credit Co Ltd v Tolly* [1963] 2 Q.B. 683; *Garside v Black Horse Ltd* [2010] EWHC 190 (QB); *Brewer v Mann* [2012] EWCA Civ 246.

[2183] *Charterhouse Credit Co Ltd v Tolly* [1963] 2 Q.B. 683 at 711–712; *Brewer v Mann* [2012] EWCA Civ 246. See also *Brown v Sheen and Richmond Car Sales Ltd* [1950] 1 All E.R. 1102. Contrast *Doobay v Mohabeer* [1967] 2 A.C. 278.

[2184] s.6(2). See Vol.I, para.15-093. See also *Hughes v Hall & Hall* [1981] R.T.R. 430 DC (offence to include void exclusion term by (now repealed) Consumer Transactions (Restrictions on Statements) Order 1976 (SI 1976/1813)).

[2185] See above, para.39-016.

[2186] Defined in s.14 of the 1977 Act.

[2187] Defined in s.14 of the 1977 Act.

[2188] s.12, as amended by the Sale and Supply of Goods to Consumers Regulations 2002 (SI 2002/3045) reg.14. See Vol.I, para.15-073; below, para.44-121.

consumer lies upon the creditor.[2189] Terms excluding or restricting liability may also be held to be unfair and so not binding the consumer under the Consumer Rights Act 2015 Pt 2.[2190] The Consumer Rights Act 2015 also provides[2191] that liability for breach of the corresponding terms "treated as included" by that Act cannot be excluded or restricted by any contract term as against the consumer.[2192] Terms excluding or restricting liability may also be held to be unfair and so not binding the consumer under the more general provisions on unfair terms in that Act.[2193]

39-391 **Exclusion of implied terms: non-consumer agreements** In the case where the hirer does not "deal as consumer" (as defined above) the liability under ss.9, 10 or 11 of the 1973 Act can be excluded or restricted by reference to a contract term, but only insofar as the term satisfies the requirement of reasonableness.[2194] In order to assist the court to determine whether or not any such term would be reasonable, certain "guidelines" are set out in Sch.2 to the 1977 Act. But the court is also specifically enjoined to have regard in general[2195] to the circumstances which were, or ought reasonably to have been, known to or in the contemplation of the parties when the contract was made.[2196] It might be thought that an exemption clause in a commercial hire-purchase agreement which excluded the terms as to quality and fitness implied by the 1973 Act would be considered reasonable in circumstances where the owner (a finance company) would not see the goods before their delivery to the hirer by the supplying dealer,[2197] but it would appear that this may not be the case.[2198]

39-392 **Construction of clause** A number of cases have arisen where the courts, applying the principle of "fundamental breach"[2199] have held that the exemption clause in question did not cover the breach which occurred.[2200] Such cases must now be considered to have been decided by reference to the true construction of the particular clause, since there is no rule of common law which would prevent an

---

[2189] s.12(3).

[2190] Replacing (for contracts made on or after October 1, 2015) the Unfair Terms in Consumer Contracts Regulations 1999 (SI 1999/2083) as amended; see above, paras 38-202 et seq. See also the "unfair relationship" provisions of the Consumer Credit Act 1974 (above, paras 39-212 et seq.).

[2191] For contracts made on or after October 1, 2015.

[2192] Consumer Rights Act 2015 s.31. See above, para.38-424. See also *Hughes v Hall & Hall* [1981] R.T.R. 430 DC (offence to include void exclusion term by (now revoked) Consumer Transactions (Restrictions on Statements) Order 1976 (SI 1976/1813)).

[2193] i.e. ss.61–76 (and see s.62(8)(a)), see further above, paras 38-389 et seq. See also the "unfair relationship" provisions of the Consumer Credit Act 1974 ss.140A–140C (above, paras 39-212 et seq.).

[2194] 1977 Act s.6(3) (replaced by s.6(1A), by the Consumer Rights Act 2015 s.60 and Sch.4 para.8, when in force). The burden of proving that the contract term satisfies the requirements of reasonableness is on the person claiming that it does: s.11(5) of the 1977 Act. See Vol.I, para.15-100.

[2195] As opposed to the particular guidelines: s.11(2). See Vol.I, para.15-097; below, para.44-122.

[2196] Unfair Contract Terms Act 1977 s.11(1). See Vol.I, para.15-096.

[2197] *R & B Customs Brokers Co Ltd v United Dominions Trust Ltd* [1988] 1 W.L.R. 321, 331–332 (conditional sale); *Abbey National Business Equipment Leasing Ltd v Dora Ife* [2003] 12 C.L. 70, Cty Ct.

[2198] *Sovereign Finance Ltd v Silver Crest Furniture Ltd* [1997] C.C.L.R. 76, following *Purnell Secretarial Services v Lease Management Services* [1994] C.C.L.R. 127 (hire).

[2199] See Vol.I, para.15-023.

[2200] *Karsales (Harrow) Ltd v Wallis* [1956] 1 W.L.R. 936; *Yeoman Credit Co Ltd v Apps* [1962] 2 Q.B. 508; *Charterhouse Credit Co Ltd v Tolly* [1963] 2 Q.B. 683; *Farnworth Finance Facilities v Attryde* [1970] 1 W.L.R. 1053; *Guarantee Trust of Jersey Ltd v Gardner* (1973) 117 S.J. 564. Contrast *Handley v Marston* (1962) 106 S.J. 327; *Astley Industrial Trust Ltd v Grimley* [1963] 1 W.L.R. 584. See Vol.I, para.15-031.

owner, by means of an appropriately drafted exemption clause, from excluding or restricting his liability even for a "fundamental breach".[2201] In any event, such cases are of much less importance since the enactment of the Unfair Contract Terms Act 1977, the Consumer Rights Act 2015 Pt 2[2202] and the "unfair relationship" provisions of the Consumer Credit Act 1974.[2203]

Collateral warranty: acknowledgment by hirer   The protection afforded by an **39-393** otherwise effective exemption clause may prove nugatory where either the owner or his agent has furnished an independent collateral warranty in return for which the hirer has entered into the hire-purchase agreement.[2204] However, it now seems that a properly drafted "acknowledgement" by a contracting party of past or present facts (e.g. that he has not, expressly or by implication, made known any particular purpose for which the goods are being hired) can, contrary to previous authority,[2205] in principle is binding on the basis of the developing doctrine of contractual estoppel.[2206]

(e)   Rights and Liabilities of Third Parties

(i)   Assignment

Assignment by owner   The owner of goods let under a hire-purchase agreement **39-394** can assign two things: his interest in the agreement and his interest in the goods themselves. An assignment by the owner of his entire interest in the agreement will transfer to the assignee all the owner's rights under the agreement except those that are personal to him such as a licence to enter and seize the goods hired. Such an assignment does not have to be registered as a bill of sale[2207] and is governed by the normal rules regarding the assignment of choses in action.[2208]

Where, however, the owner assigns or purports to assign his interest in the goods **39-395** themselves, the document by which the assignment is effected may be registrable as a bill of sale under the Bills of Sale Acts 1878 and 1882. If the assignment is by way of security or if the owner retains the contractual right to possession of the goods,[2209] the assignment is within the provisions of the Acts.[2210] But an assignment that is absolute and made in pursuance of a "block discounting" agreement

---

[2201] *Suisse Atlantique Société d'Armement Maritime SA v NV Rotterdamsche Kolen Centrale* [1967] 1 A.C. 361; *Photo Production Ltd v Securicor Transport Ltd* [1980] A.C. 827; *George Mitchell (Chesterhall) Ltd v Finney Lock Seeds Ltd* [1983] 2 A.C. 803; see Vol.I, paras 15-023—15-027.

[2202] Replacing (for contracts made on or after October 1, 2015) the Unfair Terms in Consumer Contracts Regulations 1999 (SI 1999/2083) as amended; see above, paras 38-221 et seq.

[2203] ss.140A–140C, above, paras 39-212 et seq.

[2204] See above, para.39-380, especially *Webster v Higgin* [1948] 2 All E.R. 127; see generally, Vol.I, para.15-148.

[2205] That this could only operate by way of estoppel by representation: *Lowe v Lombank Ltd* [1960] 1 W.L.R. 196, see Vol.I, para.15-147.

[2206] *Springwell Navigation Corp v JP Morgan Chase Bank* [2010] EWCA Civ 1221, disapproving *Lowe v Lombank Ltd* [1960] 1 W.L.R. 196.

[2207] *Re Davis & Co* (1888) 22 Q.B.D. 193; *Re Isaacson* [1895] 1 Q.B. 333. Nor is it (if absolute) a loan; *Olds Discount Co Ltd v John Playfair Ltd* [1938] 3 All E.R. 275. But see the now repealed (and not replaced) Companies Act 1985 s.396(1)(e), (f) and relevant case-law: *Re George Inglefield Ltd* [1933] Ch. 1; *Illingworth v Houldsworth* [1904] A.C. 355; *Lloyds and Scottish Finance v Cyril Lord Carpet Sales Ltd* (1979) 129 N.L.J. 366, HL.

[2208] See Vol.I, Ch.19.

[2209] *Ancona v Rogers* (1876) 1 Ex. D. 285, 292; *Lincoln Waggon and Engine Co v Mumford* (1880) 41 L.T. 655, 658. This can only happen in the unlikely event of the owner assigning his property inter-

between the owner and a finance company is unlikely to be invalidated as an unregistered bill of sale.

39-396 Charge over rentals Where the owner of goods charges in favour of a bank the rentals payable under hire-purchase agreements but continues to collect them as agent of the bank, he does not receive the rentals in a fiduciary capacity, being free to deal with the money as his own until required by the bank to pay them into a separate account.[2211]

39-397 Assignment by hirer The hirer can legitimately assign only his interest in the agreement since he has no property in the goods themselves.[2212] Most agreements, however, specifically prohibit such assignment.

(ii) Title of Third Parties

39-398 Nemo dat quod non habet The absence of any property in the goods in the hirer means that, as a general rule, he can pass no title to a third party. Any purported conveyance of the goods, as by way of sale,[2213] pledge[2214] or execution of a bill of sale,[2215] will not cause the property in the goods to vest in a third party, for *nemo dat quod non habet*.[2216] In certain exceptional circumstances, however, statute or common law provides that a person who has no right to dispose of goods may nevertheless pass a good title to another. It is therefore necessary to examine these situations and to inquire whether they will affect the owner's title to the goods.

39-399 Buyer in possession Section 25 of the Sale of Goods Act 1979[2217] provides that where a person "having bought or agreed to buy goods obtains, with the consent of the seller, possession of the goods", he may transfer a title to the goods to a third party who receives the same in good faith and without notice of the right of the original seller in respect of the goods. By virtue of this section the hirer of goods under a true hire-purchase agreement, which gives him an option to return or purchase the goods, can pass no title since, until he exercises his option to purchase, he has neither bought nor agreed to buy the goods.[2218]

---

est alone, while retaining a contractual right to recover possession of the goods.

[2210] It was previously within the now repealed (but not replaced) Companies Act 1985 s.396(1)(c).

[2211] *Royal Trust Bank v National Westminster Bank Plc* [1996] 2 B.C.L.C. 699. See also *Re Spectrum Plus Ltd* [2005] UKHL 41, [2005] 2 A.C. 680.

[2212] But see *Belsize Motor Supply Co v Cox* [1914] 1 K.B. 244; *Whiteley Ltd v Hilt* [1918] 2 K.B. 808; *Wickham Holdings Ltd v Brooke House Motors Ltd* [1967] 1 W.L.R. 295 (disapproving *United Dominions Trust (Commercial) Ltd v Parkway Motors Ltd* [1955] 1 W.L.R. 719).

[2213] *Modern Light Cars Ltd v Seals* [1934] 1 K.B. 32; *Staffs Motor Guarantee Ltd v British Wagon Co Ltd* [1934] 2 K.B. 305; *North General Wagon and Finance Co Ltd v Graham* [1950] 2 K.B. 7; *United Dominions Trust (Commercial) Ltd v Parkway Motors Ltd* [1955] 1 W.L.R. 719.

[2214] *Helby v Matthews* [1895] A.C. 471; *Belsize Motor Supply Co v Cox* [1914] 1 K.B. 244.

[2215] *Lewis v Thomas* [1919] 1 K.B. 319.

[2216] Sale of Goods Act 1979 s.21(1); below, para.44-193.

[2217] Re-enacting s.9 of the Factors Act 1889 and replacing s.25(2) of the Sale of Goods Act 1893. See below, para.44-220.

[2218] *Payne v Wilson* [1895] 2 Q.B. 537; *Helby v Matthews* [1895] A.C. 471; *Belsize Motor Supply Co v Cox* [1914] 1 K.B. 244; *Modern Light Cars Ltd v Seals* [1934] 1 K.B. 32; *United Dominions Trust (Commercial) Ltd v Parkway Motors Ltd* [1955] 1 W.L.R. 719; *Close Asset Finance Ltd v Care Graphics Machinery Ltd* [2000] C.C.L.R. 43. But see *Forthright Finance Ltd v Carlyle Finance Ltd* [1997] 4 All E.R. 90.

Seller in possession   Section 24 of the Sale of Goods Act 1979[2219] provides that   **39-400**
where a person, "having sold goods, continues, or is, in possession of the goods",
he is similarly enabled to transfer a good title to a third party who receives the goods
in good faith and without notice of the previous sale. It was at one time thought that
a person who sold goods to a finance company, which then let the goods to him
under a hire-purchase agreement, could pass no title to the goods even though they
had never left his possession. He was considered to be in possession of the goods
as bailee under the agreement, and not as seller under the contract of sale.[2220] But
in *Pacific Motor Auctions (Pty) Ltd v Motor Credits (Hire-Finance) Ltd*[2221] the Privy
Council held that the subsection applied unless there was a break in the continuity
of the physical possession of the seller[2222] and that it was not sufficient for the seller
to attorn to the buyer as bailee.

Mercantile agents   Section 2 of the Factors Act 1889 provides that where a   **39-401**
mercantile agent[2223] is, with the consent of the owner, in possession of goods, any
sale, pledge or other disposition of the goods made by him when acting in the
ordinary course of business as a mercantile agent shall be as valid as if he were
expressly authorised by the owner of the goods to make the same.[2224] Where goods
are let to a mercantile agent under a hire-purchase agreement, this section will not
normally apply, for he is in possession of the goods as hirer and not as mercantile
agent.[2225] But the position is otherwise if the hire-purchase agreement is part of a
"stocking transaction" under which the mercantile agent keeps the goods for display
and sale with the implied authority of the owner to dispose of the goods to his
customers.[2226]

Dispositions of motor vehicles   Part III (ss.27 to 29) of the Hire-Purchase Act   **39-402**
1964[2227] enables a hirer or a conditional buyer of a motor vehicle (referred to as "the
debtor") to pass a good title in certain circumstances to a third party.[2228] It applies
to all hire-purchase agreements,[2229] even if the debtor is a body corporate.[2230] Part

---

[2219] Re-enacting s.8 of the Factors Act 1889 and replacing s.25(1) of the Sale of Goods Act 1893. See
below, para.44-214.

[2220] *Staffs Motor Guarantee Ltd v British Wagon Co Ltd* [1934] 2 K.B. 305; *Eastern Distributors Ltd v
Goldring* [1957] 2 Q.B. 600; *Halfway Garage (Nottingham) v Lepley* The Guardian, February 8,
1964. Contrast *Union Transport Finance Ltd v Ballardie* [1937] 1 K.B. 510 (transaction a complete
sham).

[2221] [1965] A.C. 867, followed in *Worcester Works Finance Ltd v Cooden Engineering Co Ltd* [1972] 1
Q.B. 210, CA.

[2222] *Mitchell v Jones* (1905) 24 N.Z.L.R. 932; *Olds Discount Co Ltd v Krett* [1940] 2 K.B. 117.

[2223] Defined in s.1 of the Act.

[2224] See above, paras 31-079—31-081; below, para.44-204.

[2225] *Staffs Motor Guarantee Ltd v British Wagon Co Ltd* [1934] 2 K.B. 305 at 313; *Astley Industrial Trust
v Miller* [1968] 2 All E.R. 36; *Belvoir Finance Co Ltd v Harold G Cole & Co Ltd* [1969] 1 W.L.R.
1877.

[2226] *St Margaret's Trust v Castle* [1964] C.L.Y. 1685; *Pacific Motor Auctions (Pty) Ltd v Motor Credits
(Hire-Finance) Ltd*, above. cf. *Belvoir Finance Co Ltd v Harold G. Cole & Co Ltd* [1969] 1 W.L.R.
1877.

[2227] As amended (from May 19, 1985: see SI 1983/1551 (c.44)) by s.192 of and Sch.4 para.22 to the
Consumer Credit Act 1974. And note the amendment of s.27(5) (as so re-enacted) by the Sale of
Goods Act 1979 s.63 and Sch.2. See Davies [1995] J.B.L. 36.

[2228] See below, paras 39-404 et seq.

[2229] Even if they fall outside the Consumer Credit Act 1974: see above, para.39-016.

[2230] *Ford Motor Credit Co v Harmack* [1972] C.L.Y. 1649.

III prima facie applies "where a motor-vehicle[2231] has been let under a hire-purchase agreement, and, at a time before the property in the vehicle has become vested in the debtor[2232] he disposes[2233] of the vehicle to another person".[2234] The debtor continues as such whether the agreement has before that time been terminated[2235] or not. This covers the situation where the terms of the agreement provide that, if the debtor disposes of, or attempts to dispose of, the vehicle, the agreement is ipso facto determined. Such a device cannot defeat the operation of the Act.

39-403 **Trade or finance purchasers** The Act draws a distinction between a "trade or finance purchaser" (who does not acquire a good title) and a "private purchaser" (who acquires a good title if bona fide). A "trade or finance purchaser" is a purchaser[2236] who, at the time of the disposition made to him, carries on a business which consists, wholly or partly:

(a) of purchasing motor vehicles for the purpose of offering or exposing them for sale; or

(b) of providing finance by purchasing motor vehicles for the purpose of bailing or (in Scotland) hiring them under hire-purchase agreements or agreeing to sell them under conditional sale agreements.

A "private purchaser" means a purchaser who, at the time of the disposition made to him, does not carry on any such business.[2237] Obvious examples of trade or finance purchasers are motor dealers and finance companies but the definition has been held to cover any financier that uses motor vehicles as security.[2238] No title passes to trade or finance purchasers,[2239] and they can only take advantage indirectly of the Act's provisions, i.e. where they derive title from a bona fide private

---

[2231] Defined in s.29(1).

[2232] Defined in s.29(4) and including the "statutory bailee" following the making of a time order under the Consumer Credit Act 1974 s.130(4). See also *Ford Motor Credit Co v Harmack* [1972] C.L.Y. 1649 (company hirer); *Keeble v Combined Lease Finance Plc* [1996] C.C.L.R. 63, CA (partners); *Majid v TMV Finance* [1999] C.L.Y. 2448, Cty Ct (agent).

[2233] "Disposition" is defined in s.29(1) to mean "sale" or "hire-purchase". In *VFS Financial Services Ltd v JF Plant Tyres Ltd* [2013] EWHC 346 (QB), [2013] 1 Lloyd's Rep. 462 "sale" was given its normal meaning and hence did not cover a transfer in settlement of debts (as opposed to a transfer for money). See also *Dodds v Yorkshire Bank Finance* [1992] C.C.L.R. 92, CA, *Kulkarni v Manor Credit (Davenham) Ltd* [2010] EWCA Civ 69.

[2234] s.27(1). "Person" includes a body corporate: Interpretation Act 1978 s.5 and Sch.1.

[2235] s.29(2). See *Chartered Trust Plc v Conlay* [1998] C.L.Y. 2516, Cty Ct (termination held to include rescission for fraud).

[2236] See s.29(3).

[2237] s.29(2). A trade purchaser who purchases a vehicle for his own use does not thereby become a private purchaser: *Stevenson v Beverley Bentinck Ltd* [1976] 1 W.L.R. 483. But in *GE Capital Bank Ltd v Rushton* [2005] EWCA 1556, [2006] 1 W.L.R. 899 at [39] Moore-Bick L.J. stated that s.29(2) "is intended to direct attention not merely to the business of the purchaser immediately prior to and at the time of the disposition but also the purpose for which the vehicle is bought".

[2238] On the basis that such secured creditors fall within both s.29(2)(a) (in that a secured creditor sells the security on default) and s.29(2)(b) (sed quaere: *Welcome Financial Services Ltd v Nine Regions Ltd (t/a Log Book Loans)* [2010] 2 Lloyd's Rep. 426 (loans secured against the borrower's vehicle by means of a bill of sale).

[2239] They are likely to consult one or more of the databases (HPI, Autocheck) that list outstanding hire-purchase and conditional sale agreements. See, Beale, Bridge, Gullifer and Lomnicka, *The Law of Security and Title-Based Financing* (2018), paras 9.26 et seq.

purchaser.[2240]

Situations covered   The circumstances in which a third party will acquire a good **39-404**
title to the goods are three in number:

First disposition to private purchaser   First, where the disposition is to a private **39-405**
purchaser, and he is a purchaser of the motor vehicle in good faith and without
notice of the hire-purchase agreement, the disposition has effect as if the title of the
owner to the vehicle (the "creditor") had been vested in the debtor immediately
before the disposition.[2241] Thus if a motor vehicle is let under a hire-purchase agreement to A, who wrongfully disposes of it to B, a bona fide private purchaser, B will
acquire a good title to the vehicle.

Subsequent disposition to private purchaser   Secondly, if the first disposition **39-406**
of the vehicle is to a trade or finance purchaser (known as the original purchaser),
then if the person who is the first private purchaser of the vehicle after that disposition is a purchaser in good faith and without notice of the hire-purchase agreement, the disposition to that private purchaser has effect as if the title of the creditor to the vehicle had been vested in the debtor immediately before he disposed of
it to the original purchaser.[2242] Thus if a motor vehicle is let under a hire-purchase
agreement to A, who wrongfully disposes of it to B, a trade or finance purchaser,
who then disposes of it to C, a bona fide private purchaser, C will acquire a good
title to the vehicle. Even if the vehicle has passed through the hands of a number
of trade or finance purchasers, the first bona fide private purchaser is protected. But
if the first private purchaser is mala fide,[2243] this provision does not apply so as to
protect subsequent private purchasers in good faith.

Subsequent disposition to private purchaser under hire purchase agree- **39-407**
ment   Thirdly, if, in the second instance mentioned above, the disposition whereby
the first private purchaser becomes a purchaser of the vehicle in good faith and
without notice of the hire-purchase agreement is itself a letting under a hire-
purchase agreement, and the person who is the creditor in relation to that agreement disposes of the vehicle to the first private purchaser, or a person claiming
under him, by way of transferring to him the property in the vehicle in pursuance
of a provision in the agreement in that behalf, the first private purchaser can acquire
a good title to the vehicle by reason of this transfer of property, whether he is then
bona fide or not.[2244] Suppose, therefore, that a motor vehicle is let under a hire-
purchase agreement to A. A sells the vehicle to a finance company, which then lets
it under a hire-purchase agreement to B. Provided that B was, at the time of the letting, a bona fide private purchaser, the letting under the hire-purchase agreement
is a valid letting; and if, in pursuance of this agreement, the finance company
transfers the property in the vehicle to B, he acquires a good title even though at
the time the property is transferred he had been informed of the original hire-
purchase agreement and so had notice thereof.

Good faith and notice   The expression "in good faith" is not defined in the 1964 **39-408**

[2240] cf. *Soneco Ltd v Barcross Finance Ltd* [1978] R.T.R. 444.
[2241] s.27(2).
[2242] s.27(3).
[2243] For a presumption of good faith, see s.28(4).
[2244] s.27(4).

Act, but generally a purchaser is deemed to be in good faith when he acts honestly, whether he acts negligently or not.[2245] The Act provides that he is to be taken to be a purchaser without notice of a hire purchase agreement if, at the time of the disposition made to him, he has no actual notice that the vehicle is or was the subject of any such agreement.[2246] Constructive notice is therefore insufficient.

39-409 **Presumptions** Once it is proved in any proceedings (whether criminal or civil) relating to a motor vehicle (i) that the vehicle was let under a hire-purchase agreement; and (ii) that a person (whether a party to the proceedings or not) became a private purchaser of the vehicle in good faith and without notice of the hire-purchase agreement; certain *rebuttable* presumptions arise in favour of a litigant who seeks to rely on the protection conferred by Pt III of the 1964 Act.[2247] A litigant might otherwise find it difficult to prove the precise chain of dealings between himself and the debtor, or the state of mind of the parties to these transactions. The presumptions enable him to surmount these difficulties and to connect the links in the chain; but they do not apply where all the transactions are fully known.[2248]

39-410 **Extent of protection** It is important to realise that the only persons who can claim the protection of Pt III of the 1964 Act are the first bona fide private purchaser and those who claim under such a purchaser. An intermediate trade or finance purchaser is not protected, and will be liable for wrongful interference to the true owner of the vehicle.[2249] If the first private purchaser is mala fide, neither he nor any person claiming under him will be protected.[2250] And the liability of the debtor, both civil and criminal, remains.[2251]

39-411 The third party does not obtain a guaranteed title, but only such title as, immediately before the disposition by the debtor, was vested in the person who was then the creditor in relation to the hire-purchase agreement.[2252] But the provisions of the Act operate without prejudice to the provisions of the Factors Acts or of any other enactment enabling the apparent owner of the goods to dispose of them as if he were the true owner.[2253]

39-412 Part III of the 1964 Act leaves few loopholes of which the creditor could take advantage, except, possibly, if the hire-purchase agreement was completely void, e.g. for mistake as to the person.[2254] It is submitted that a bona fide private purchaser would not fail to acquire a good title merely because the agreement was voidable for fraud (even if subsequently avoided),[2255] or "void" for illegality,[2256] or unenforce-

---

[2245] *Dodds v Yorkshire Bank Finance* [1992] C.C.L.R. 92, CA; *GE Capital Bank Ltd v Rushton* [2005] EWCA 1556, [2006] 1 W.L.R. 899; Bills of Exchange Act 1882 s.90; Sale of Goods Act 1979 s.61(3). cf. *Mercantile Credit Co Ltd v Waugh* (1978) 32 Hire Trading 16.

[2246] Hire-Purchase Act 1964 s.29(3). See *Barker v Bell* [1971] 1 W.L.R. 983.

[2247] s.28. See also s.28(5) (admission of facts) and *Ford Motor Credit Co v Harmack* [1972] C.L.Y. 1649.

[2248] *Soneco Ltd v Barcross Finance Ltd* [1978] R.T.R. 444.

[2249] s.27(6).

[2250] *Soneco Ltd v Barcross Finance Ltd*, above.

[2251] *Soneco Ltd v Barcross Finance Ltd*, above; *Barber v NWS Bank Plc* [1996] 1 W.L.R. 641; cf. *Freeman v Walker* [2001] EWCA 923, [2003] C.C.L.R. 4.

[2252] s.29(5).

[2253] s.27(5)(b) as amended by the Sale of Goods Act 1979 s.63 and Sch.2.

[2254] See Vol.I, paras 3-036 et seq.; *Moorgate Mercantile Co Ltd v Bowman* (1974) 28 Hire Trading (No.2), at 25, Cty Ct. *Shogun Finance Ltd v Hudson* [2003] UKHL 62, [2003] 3 W.L.R. 586.

[2255] See Vol.I, Ch.7; *Chartered Trust Plc v Conlay* [1998] C.L.Y. 2516, Cty Ct; *Chartered Trust Plc v Bamford* [1999] C.L.Y. 2512, Cty Ct. Contrast *Morley v Maybray Motors Ltd* (1971) 25 Hire Trad-

able against the hirer by reason of the fact that it failed to satisfy the formal and other requirements laid down by the Consumer Credit Act 1974.[2257]

Sale in market overt Section 22(1) of the Sale of Goods Act 1979, which provided for the acquisition by the buyer of a good title to goods sold in market overt, has been repealed.[2258] **39-413**

Estoppel against owner The owner of goods comprised in a hire-purchase agreement will not be estopped from asserting his title to the goods by the mere fact that he has delivered possession of the goods to the hirer.[2259] And in the case of a motor car let on hire-purchase, the delivery of the registration document to the hirer will raise no estoppel.[2260] Failure by a finance company to notify a central agency[2261] that keeps a record of hire-purchase transactions will not ordinarily give rise to an estoppel.[2262] However, if a finance company alters such an entry so as to represent that the agreement has been settled and that it no longer has title to the goods, this creates an estoppel precluding it from asserting its title in a claim for conversion.[2263] **39-414**

Estoppel against hirer If a person who owns goods enters into an arrangement with a dealer to deceive a finance company, and signs and delivers to the dealer hire-purchase forms which either represent that the goods are the property of the dealer or that the dealer has the owner's authority to sell the goods to the company, the company will acquire a good title to the goods by estoppel.[2264] This title will prevail, not only against the owner of the goods, but also against his privies and assigns.[2265] Further, he will be precluded from denying the validity of the consequent hire-purchase agreement. However, even if the "hirer" is not privy to the representation of title made by the dealer, but merely provides the means for the dealer's fraud (as by signing the hire-purchase agreements in blank without examining them), he may still be bound, unless he can rely on a plea of non est factum.[2266] **39-415**

Recovery from third parties If the goods come into the hands of a third party **39-416**

---

ing (No.3) 15, Cty Ct; *Cawston v Chartered Trust Plc* [2002] C.L.Y. 2602, Cty Ct.

[2256] See Vol.I, Ch.16. But see *Morley v Maybray Motors Ltd*, above.

[2257] See above, paras 39-076—39-094. See *R. v Modupe* [1991] Crim. L.R. 531; *Hitchens v General Guarantee Corp Ltd* [2001] EWCA Civ 359.

[2258] Sale of Goods (Amendment) Act 1994 (as from January 3, 1995); see below, para.44-207.

[2259] *Heap v Motorists Advisory Agency Ltd* [1923] 1 K.B. 577; *Central Newbury Car Auctions Ltd v Unity Finance Ltd* [1957] 1 Q.B. 371, 388; *Astley Industrial Trust v Miller* [1968] 2 All E.R. 36; see below, para.44-197.

[2260] *Central Newbury Car Auctions Ltd v Unity Finance Ltd* [1957] 1 Q.B. 371, 388.

[2261] Such as HPI Ltd or Autocheck; see above, para.39-403.

[2262] *Moorgate Mercantile Co Ltd v Twitchings* [1977] A.C. 890; *United Dominions Trust (Commercial) Ltd v Cartwright* [1961] C.L.Y. 3925, CA. See also *Cadogan Finance Ltd v Lavery and Fox* [1982] Com. L.R. 248 (aircraft).

[2263] *Chatfields-Martin Walter Ltd v Lombard North Central Plc* [2014] EWHC 1222 (QB) (*Moorgate Mercantile Co Ltd v Twitchings* distinguished).

[2264] *Eastern Distributors Ltd v Goldring* [1957] 2 Q.B. 600; *Spencer v North Country Finance Co Ltd* [1963] C.L.Y. 212; *Stoneleigh Finance Ltd v Phillips* [1965] 2 Q.B. 537; *Kingsley v Sterling Industrial Securities Ltd* [1967] 2 Q.B. 747; *Snook v London and West Riding Investments Ltd* [1967] 2 Q.B. 786. See below, para.44-199.

[2265] *Eastern Distributors Ltd v Goldring* [1957] 2 Q.B. 600.

[2266] *United Dominions Trust Ltd v Western* [1976] Q.B. 513. cf. *Mercantile Credit Co Ltd v Hamblin* [1965] 2 Q.B. 242. See also *Saunders v Anglia Building Society* [1971] A.C. 1004 (Vol.I, paras 3-049 et seq.).

from whom the owner wishes to recover them, he must rely upon his rights of action in tort. Although an owner is entitled to retake his goods peaceably from a third party without title who refuses to deliver them up to him,[2267] any licence to enter premises contained in the agreement will not extend to this situation.[2268] In practice, however, an owner will normally sue the third party for wrongful interference with the goods.[2269] In the action, he must probably prove his right to immediate possession of the goods.[2270] The measure of damages is normally the value of the goods converted[2271]; but where the unpaid balance of the hire-purchase price is less than the value of the goods, the measure of damages is limited to the loss which the owner has suffered.[2272]

39-417 Rights of third party Unless the disposition of the goods by the hirer to the third party constitutes an assignment to the third party of the hirer's rights under the contract,[2273] the third party cannot claim to exercise the hirer's option to purchase. His only remedy lies against the person from whom he himself obtained the goods. In the case of a sale of goods, the third party may recover the whole purchase price as money paid upon a consideration which has totally failed.[2274] Yet a sale by the hirer to a third party is not void, but at most voidable for fraud, so that if the "price" paid by the third party consists wholly or in part of chattels, the third party cannot recover the chattels from a person who buys them from the hirer in good faith and for value.[2275]

39-418 Feeding title Where the hirer, having parted with the goods, pays to the owner the balance of the instalments and exercises his option to purchase, the title so acquired may go to feed the previously defective titles of subsequent buyers and enure to their benefit.[2276] Except in the case of claims that are made before the option to purchase is exercised, there will be no total failure of consideration, nor even a breach of condition, but merely a breach of warranty.[2277]

[2267] cf. *Greenwood v Bennett* [1973] 1 Q.B. 195; and *Thomas v Robinson* [1977] 1 N.Z.L.R. 385 (improvements).

[2268] See above, para.39-340. See also *Miller v Strohmenger* (1887) 4 T.L.R. 133; *British Economical Lamp Co Ltd v Empire (Mile End) Ltd* (1913) 29 T.L.R. 386.

[2269] Torts (Interference with Goods) Act 1977 ss.1, 3. See CPR Pt 16 PD 16 6.1.

[2270] *Belsize Motor Supply Co v Cox* [1914] 1 K.B. 244; and see above, para.39-333. cf. *North West Securities v Alexander Breckon* [1981] R.T.R. 518.

[2271] See *Chubb Cash Ltd v John Crilley & Son* [1983] 1 W.L.R. 599. In addition the owner may recover consequential loss: see *Strand Electric and Engineering Co Ltd v Brisford Entertainments Ltd* [1952] 2 Q.B. 246; *Hillesden Securities Ltd v Ryjack* [1983] 1 W.L.R. 959 (hire charges). But see the Torts (Interference with Goods) Act s.6 (improvements).

[2272] *Belsize Motor Supply Co v Cox* [1914] 1 K.B. 244; *Whiteley Ltd v Hilt* [1918] 2 K.B. 808; *Wickham Holdings Ltd v Brooke House Motors Ltd* [1967] 1 W.L.R. 295; *Belvoir Finance Co Ltd v Stapleton* [1971] 1 Q.B. 210. cf. *Astley Industrial Trust v Miller* [1968] 2 All E.R. 36 (detinue). See also Torts (Interference with Goods) Act s.3(6).

[2273] See above, para.39-397.

[2274] *Butterworth v Kingsway Motors* [1954] 1 W.L.R. 1286. See also *Rowland v Divall* [1923] 2 K.B. 500; *Bowmaker (Commercial) Ltd v Day* [1965] 1 W.L.R. 1396; below, para.44-081.

[2275] *Robin and Rambler Coaches Ltd v Turner* [1947] 2 All E.R. 284.

[2276] *Butterworth v Kingsway Motors* [1954] 1 W.L.R. 1286. See also *Blundell-Leigh v Attenborough* [1921] 3 K.B. 235. Contrast *Karflex Ltd v Poole* [1933] 2 K.B. 251; *Mercantile Union Guarantee Corp Ltd v Wheatley* [1938] 1 K.B. 490; *West (HW) Ltd v McBlain* [1950] N.I. 144.

[2277] *Butterworth v Kingsway Motors* [1954] 1 W.L.R. 1286.

(iii) Fixtures and Accession

Fixtures to land[2278] The owner of goods let on hire-purchase may lose the **39-419** property in the goods by reason of the fact that they have been so attached to land as to become a fixture.[2279] The mere fact that the goods attached are let under a hire-purchase agreement does not in itself prevent them from becoming fixtures, nor does an express prohibition in the hire-purchase agreement against attaching the goods to land.[2280] The owner may nevertheless, as against the hirer, validly reserve the right to enter and seize the goods affixed.[2281] Such a right of entry and seizure creates an equitable interest in land.[2282] This interest is important because it may bind third parties such as a mortgagee of the hirer. The respective rights of a mortgagee of the hirer and the owner of the goods will depend on whether the mortgage was created before or after the goods were affixed to the mortgaged land and whether the mortgage is legal or equitable. Prima facie the mortgagee, if he has registered his mortgage, is entitled to the goods as fixtures. But, where the mortgage is a legal mortgage and was created before the goods were affixed, the owner of the goods will have priority if the goods let on hire are trade fixtures, since by leaving the mortgagor (the hirer) in possession a legal[2283] mortgagee impliedly authorises[2284] him to hire and bring and fix goods necessary for his business and to agree with their owner that he shall have the right to remove them at the end of the term for which they were hired.[2285] Where the mortgage is created after the goods are affixed, then the owner of the goods will have priority only if (i) the mortgage is equitable[2286]; or (ii) the mortgage is a legal mortgage of unregistered land[2287]; and the mortgagee took the mortgage with actual notice that the fixtures were the subject of a hire-purchase agreement.[2288]

As against a landlord of the hirer, it would seem that the owner of goods let to a **39-420**

[2278] See generally: Goode, *Hire-Purchase Law and Practice*, 2nd edn, Ch.32; Guest, *The Law of Hire-Purchase* (1966) Ch.18; Guest and Lever (1963) 27 Conv. N.S. 30; Giddings (1993) *Butterworths Journal of International Banking and Financial Law* (June) 263; Bennett and Davis (1994) 110 L.Q.R. 448.

[2279] *Melluish v BMI (No.3) Ltd* [1996] A.C. 454.

[2280] *Hobson v Gorringe* [1897] 1 Ch. 182, 193, 195; *Reynolds v Ashby & Son Ltd* [1903] 1 K.B. 87, 97; affirmed [1904] A.C. 466. See also *Gough v Wood & Co* [1894] 1 Q.B. 713; *Crossley Bros Ltd v Lee* [1908] 1 K.B. 86; *Ellis v Glover & Hobson Ltd* [1908] 1 K.B. 388, 398; *Vaudeville Electric Cinema Ltd v Muriset* [1923] 2 Ch. 74, 87. Contrast *Lyon & Co v London City and Midland Bank* [1903] 2 K.B. 135 (hire).

[2281] But such a right is excluded in the case of CCA 1974-regulated agreements by CCA 1974 ss.92, 173(1), above, para.39-366.

[2282] *Gough v Wood & Co* [1894] 1 Q.B. 713 at 722; *Hobson v Gorringe* [1897] 1 Ch. 182 at 192; *Reynolds v Ashby & Son Ltd* [1903] 1 K.B. 87 at 101; *Re Samuel Allen & Sons Ltd* [1907] 1 Ch. 575; *Re Morrison, Jones & Taylor Ltd* [1914] 1 Ch. 50; *Harmer v London City and Midland Bank Ltd* (1918) 87 L.J. K.B. 973. The interest is not registrable: *Poster v Slough Estates Ltd* [1969] 1 Ch. 495; *Shiloh Spinners Ltd v Harding* [1973] A.C. 691.

[2283] But not an equitable mortgagee, since the mortgagor then remains in possession as of right.

[2284] But the implied authority will be negatived where the mortgage expressly prohibits the removal of fixtures; *Ellis v Glover & Hobson Ltd* [1908] 1 K.B. 388.

[2285] *Gough v Wood & Co* [1894] 1 Q.B. 713 at 720; *Huddersfield Banking Co Ltd v Henry Lister & Son Ltd* [1895] 2 Ch. 273. See also *Ellis v Glover & Hobson Ltd* [1897] 1 Ch. 182 at 396. But the right to enter, sever and remove the fixture ends when the mortgagee takes possession of the mortgaged land: *Hobson v Gorringe* [1897] 1 Ch. 182 at 189; *Reynolds v Ashby & Son Ltd* [1903] 1 K.B. 87.

[2286] See *Meux v Jacobs* (1873) L.R. 7 H.L. 481 (bill of sale).

[2287] Because the right to enter and remove fixtures is not registrable, a mortgagee of registered land will not be bound by it even with express notice.

[2288] *Gough v Wood & Co* [1894] 1 Q.B. 713 at 717, 722; *Hobson v Gorringe* [1897] 1 Ch. 182 at 192;

tenant and which have become tenant's fixtures may enter the premises and remove them if and so long as the hirer would himself as tenant be entitled to sever the fixtures and remove them.[2289]

39-421 **Accession** Goods let on hire-purchase which are attached to, or combined with, goods which are the property of another person may be affected by the common law principles of accession and confusion of chattels.[2290] If livestock let on hire-purchase produce young, in the absence of any contrary agreement, the young belong to the hirer and not to the owner of the dams.[2291]

(iv) Liens

39-422 **Liens** Certain classes of persons, such as innkeepers,[2292] artificers[2293] and common carriers[2294] are entitled to a lien on goods owned by one person until a debt owed to them by another person has been paid.[2295] The hirer of goods let under a hire-purchase agreement may allow the goods to pass into the possession of such persons with the result that the owner of the goods, when he seeks to retake them, may be met by the claim of a lien. Cases concerning hire-purchase agreements have mainly been decided in relation to the lien of artificers for repairs executed to the goods comprised in the agreement.

39-423 **Authority to create lien** A hirer can create a lien binding on the owner of the goods if he has actual or ostensible authority to do so.[2296] He will have actual authority to create a lien if:

(i) the owner specifically authorised him to give possession of the goods to an artificer for repair; or

(ii) the terms of the agreement are such that the owner must have envisaged the possibility of the creation of a lien, for example, by requiring the hirer to keep the goods in repair; or

---

Reynolds v Ashby & Son Ltd [1903] 1 K.B. 87 at 101; *Re Samuel Allen & Sons Ltd* [1907] 1 Ch. 575 at 581; *Re Morrison, Jones & Taylor Ltd* [1914] 1 Ch. 50 at 59.

[2289] *Crossley Bros Ltd v Lee* [1908] 1 K.B. 86; *Becker v Riebold* (1913) 30 T.L.R. 142. See Goode, *Hire-Purchase Law and Practice*, 2nd edn (1975) at p.736; Guest, *The Law of Hire-Purchase* (1966) at p.960. See also the Agricultural Holdings Act 1986 s.10: tenant's right to remove fixtures.

[2290] Guest (1964) 27 M.L.R. 505; Matthews [1981] C.L.J. 340; Matthews [1981] C.L.P 159. See *Thomas v Robinson* [1977] 1 N.Z.L.R. 385.

[2291] *Tucker v Farm and General Investment Trust Ltd* [1966] 2 Q.B. 421.

[2292] An innkeeper has a lien over all goods brought by a guest to his inn even though the goods are the property of a third party: *Threlfall v Borwick* (1875) L.R. 10 Q.B. 210; *Robins & Co v Gray* [1895] 2 Q.B. 501; *Chesham Automobile Supply Ltd v Beresford Hotel (Birchington) Ltd* (1913) 29 T.L.R. 584. See also Hotel Proprietors Act 1956 (extent of lien); Innkeepers Act 1878 s.1 (power of sale). See above, paras 33-101 et seq.

[2293] See below, paras 39-422—39-424.

[2294] *Exeter Carriers' Case*, cited in *Yorke v Grenaugh* (1702) 2 Ld. Raym. 866, 867; see above, para.36-052. cf. *Singer Manufacturing Co v L & SW Ry* [1894] 1 Q.B. 833, where the railway probably held the goods as warehousemen, and not as carriers.

[2295] See *Halsbury's Laws of England*, 4th edn, Vol.28, Title "Lien". See also Beale, Bridge, Gullifer and Lomnicka, *The Law of Security and Title-Based Financing* (2018), Ch.5B (possessory liens).

[2296] *Tappenden v Artus* [1964] 2 Q.B. 185. Contrast *Hiscox v Greenwood* (1802) 4 Especially 174; *Buxton v Baughan* (1834) 6 Car. & P. 674; *Pennington v Reliance Motor Works* [1923] 1 K.B. 127 (no authority).

(iii) it is reasonably incidental to the ordinary use of the goods that the hirer should give possession of them to an artificer for the purpose of repair.[2297]

But even if the actual authority of the hirer to create a lien is excluded by an express term of the agreement, he may still have ostensible authority to do so.[2298] In order, however, to create an artificer's lien, the hirer must be in lawful possession of the goods, so that, if the hiring has come to an end, no lien can arise which is binding on the owner.[2299]

Determination of lien   The existence of the lien is dependent on the repairer continuing in possession of the goods[2300]; but a temporary loss of possession, as where the hirer takes the goods out each day to use them, does not determine the lien.[2301]   **39-424**

Power of sale   At common law, an artificer is not entitled to sell the goods over which he exercises a lien.[2302] But under the Torts (Interference with Goods) Act 1977, a bailee of uncollected goods is empowered to sell the goods upon compliance with certain conditions.[2303] Except where it is authorised by the court,[2304] the sale does not deprive the owner of his property in the goods. But the bailee is placed under a duty to return to the hirer, rather than to the owner, the amount by which the gross proceeds of sale exceed his charges in relation to the goods.[2305]   **39-425**

(v) Execution

Execution   Goods which are in the possession of a hirer under a hire-purchase agreement may be seized in execution against him, and his interest therein sold; but the general property in the goods cannot be disposed of by the person charged with the enforcement of a writ or warrant of execution.[2306] If the hirer has no interest in the goods, or if his interest determines before or upon seizure in execution, the seizure will be unlawful.[2307] Nevertheless, a certain measure of protection is afforded to sheriffs and other officers by the Courts Act 2003.[2308] Where such protection exists, the remedy of the owner is to bring an action against the execution creditor to recover the proceeds of sale.[2309] A purchaser who buys the goods obtains a good title to them unless it is proved that he had notice, or might by making reason-   **39-426**

[2297] *Keene v Thomas* [1905] 1 K.B. 136; *Green v All Motors Ltd* [1917] 1 K.B. 625; *Albemarle Supply Co Ltd v Hind & Co* [1928] 1 K.B. 307; *Tappenden v Artus* [1964] 2 Q.B. 185.

[2298] *Albemarle Supply Co Ltd v Hind & Co* [1928] 1 K.B. 307, where the artificer had knowledge of the hire-purchase agreement, but not of its terms.

[2299] *Bowmaker Ltd v Wycombe Motors Ltd* [1946] K.B. 505. Contrast *Keene v Thomas* [1905] 1 K.B. 136; *Green v All Motors Ltd* [1917] 1 K.B. 625 (mere breach of agreement).

[2300] *Pennington v Reliance Motor Works* [1923] 1 K.B. 127.

[2301] *Albemarle Supply Co Ltd v Hind & Co* [1928] 1 K.B. 307.

[2302] *Thames Iron Works Co v Patent Derrick Co* (1860) 1 J. & H. 93. But see CPR Pt 25.

[2303] s.12. See above, paras 33-095—33-099.

[2304] s.13(2).

[2305] s.12(5).

[2306] *Dean v Whittaker* (1824) 1 Car. & P. 347.

[2307] *Jelks v Hayward* [1905] 2 K.B. 460. But see Consumer Credit Act 1974 s.98, above, para.39-172.

[2308] Sch.7 para.11 (previously the Senior Courts Act 1981 s.138B(1), inserted by s.1(2) of and Sch.2 to the Statute Law (Repeals) Act 1989).

[2309] *Jones Brothers (Holloway) Ltd v Woodhouse* [1923] 2 K.B. 117.

able enquiry have ascertained, that the goods were not the property of the execution debtor.[2310]

39-427 **Distress** A landlord's power at common law to distrain upon all goods found upon the demised premises has now been abolished.[2311] Historically, the position in relation to hire-purchase was complex. Essentially, in order to bring himself within the general protection from distress provided for goods of third parties[2312] the owner had to both (a) provide for the termination of the agreement, either automatically[2313] or by notice to the hirer,[2314] before or upon the levying of distress by the landlord[2315] and (b) effectively notify the hirer, before the landlord levied distress, of the withdrawal of his consent to the hirer's being in possession of the goods.[2316]

(vi)   Insolvency

39-428 **Bankruptcy of hirer** The estate[2317] of a bankrupt hirer vests in the trustee in bankruptcy immediately on his appointment taking effect or, in the case of the official receiver, on his becoming trustee.[2318] Most hire-purchase agreements, however, provide that, if a bankruptcy order is made against the hirer or the hirer petitions for his own bankruptcy, then either the hire-purchase agreement and the hiring are forthwith and automatically to come to an end[2319] or the owner is entitled to terminate the agreement. Once the agreement so terminates, it would seem that the hirer will have no interest in the goods or in the agreement which could pass to his trustee in bankruptcy.[2320]

39-429 There is no longer any "reputed ownership" provision, such as once existed in

---

[2310] Courts Act 2003 Sch.7 para.11(2) (previously Senior Courts Act 1981 s.138B(1), inserted by s.1(2) and Sch.2 of the Statute Law (Repeals) Act 1989). On similar statutory provisions, see *Curtis v Maloney* [1951] 1 K.B. 736; *Singh v Kenyan Insurance* [1954] A.C. 287.

[2311] By the Tribunals Courts and Enforcement Act 2007 s.71 (from April 6, 2014).

[2312] Provided by the (now repealed) Law of Distress Amendment Act 1908 s.4.

[2313] *Times Furnishing Co Ltd v Hutchings* [1938] 1 K.B. 775. But see Consumer Credit Act 1974 s.98, above, para.39-172.

[2314] *Smart Bros Ltd v Holt* [1929] 2 K.B. 303. See also Consumer Credit Act 1974 s.98, above, para.39-172.

[2315] Because "goods bailed under a hire-purchase agreement" where the relevant agreement had not been terminated were excluded from protection by the (now repealed) Law of Distress Amendment Act 1908 s.4A. Hence the owner's rights could be overridden by the landlord: see *Hackney Furnishing Co v Watts* [1912] 3 K.B. 225; *Jay's Furnishing Co v Brand & Co* [1915] 1 K.B. 458 (decided on the previous wording "goods comprised in any hire-purchase agreement made by such tenant" in s.4(1) of the 1908 Act). This was so even if some other person (not the tenant) was the hirer: contrast *Shenstone v Freeman* [1910] 2 K.B. 84; *Rogers, Eungblut & Co v Martin* [1911] K.B. 19 (decided on the previous wording in s.4(1) of the 1908 Act). But where a default notice was required to be served (under the Consumer Credit Act 1974 s.87(1)) before the owner termination (see above, para.39-166) the statutory protection of the 1908 Act was not excluded during the period between the service of the default notice and the date on which the notice expired or was earlier complied with: s.4A(1) of the 1908 Act.

[2316] Because the general protection for third party goods was lost where the tenant was the "reputed owner" of them, even if the agreement was terminated (see *Times Furnishing Co Ltd v Hutchings* [1938] 1 K.B. 775). See *Smart Bros Ltd v Holt* [1929] 2 K.B. 303; *Drages Ltd v Owen* (1935) 52 T.L.R. 108; *Perdana Properties Bhd v United Orient Leasing Co Sdn Bhd* [1981] 1 W.L.R. 1496.

[2317] See Insolvency Act 1986 s.283.

[2318] Insolvency Act 1986 s.306.

[2319] This is not permissible where the agreement is a regulated agreement under the Consumer Credit Act 1974: see CCA 1974 s.98(1), above, para.39-172.

[2320] *Crawcour v Salter* (1881) 18 Ch. D. 30; *McEntire v Crossley Bros Ltd* [1895] A.C. 457; *Re Apex Supply Co Ltd* [1942] Ch. 108. Contrast *Re Piggin, Dicker v Lombank* (1962) 112 L.J. 424.

the Bankruptcy Act 1914,[2321] whereby the trustee was entitled to claim goods in the reputed ownership of the bankrupt. But, if the trustee seizes or disposes of any property which is not comprised in the bankrupt's estate, and at the time of the seizure or disposal the trustee believes and has reasonable grounds for believing that he is entitled to seize or dispose of that property, the trustee is not liable to any person in respect of any loss or damage resulting from the seizure or disposal except insofar as that loss or damage is caused by the negligence of the trustee.[2322]

The trustee may disclaim any unprofitable contract.[2323]

39-430

Winding-up or receivership of hirer   Where the hirer is a company, the hire-purchase agreement again normally provides for its automatic determination or termination by the owner in the event of a winding-up petition being presented against the hirer or the hirer passing a resolution for voluntary winding-up. The hirer company will, after termination, have no interest in the goods which can vest in the liquidator.[2324] The same applies where an administrative receiver is appointed.[2325]

A liquidator may disclaim any unprofitable contract.[2326]

39-431

39-432

Administration[2327]   Where an administration application in respect of a company has been made, no step may be taken to repossess goods in the company's possession under any hire-purchase agreement,[2328] except with permission of the court.[2329] Further, during the period while the company is in administration, no step may be taken to repossess goods in the company's possession under any hire-purchase agreement,[2330] except with the consent of the administrator or the permission of the court.[2331] A moratorium or "freeze" is thus imposed on the owner's right of repossession. On an application by the administrator, the court may, if it is satisfied that the disposal of the goods would be likely to promote the purpose of administration in respect of the company, enable the administrator to dispose of the goods as if all rights of the owner under the agreement were vested in the company.[2332] The administrator may thus overreach the property rights of the owner in the goods. Some protection is, however, afforded to the owner in that the net proceeds of the disposal[2333] are required to be applied towards discharging the sums payable under the hire-purchase agreement.[2334]

39-433

[2321] s.38(c).

[2322] Insolvency Act 1986 s.304(3). And the trustee has a lien on the property or its proceeds of sale for expenses in connection with the seizure or disposal.

[2323] Insolvency Act 1986 s.315.

[2324] Under s.145 of the Insolvency Act 1986 or otherwise.

[2325] But see above, para.39-343 (relief against forfeiture) and *Re Piggin, Dicker v Lombank* (1962) 112 L.J. 424. See also *Lipe Ltd v Leyland DAF Ltd* [1993] B.C.C. 385 (conditional sale agreement).

[2326] Insolvency Act 1986 s.178.

[2327] Sch.B1 to the Insolvency Act 1986 was inserted by s.248 and Sch.16 to the Enterprise Act 2002 and replaces Insolvency Act 1986 Pt II.

[2328] This includes conditional sale agreements and chattel leasing agreements and retention of title agreements: Sch.B1 para.111(1).

[2329] Insolvency Act 1986 Sch.B1 para.44.

[2330] This includes conditional sale agreements and chattel leasing agreements and retention of title agreements: Sch.B1 para.111(1).

[2331] Insolvency Act 1986 Sch.B1 para.43.

[2332] Insolvency Act 1986 Sch.B1 para.72(1).

[2333] In the event of a shortfall in the proceeds below the open market value of the goods, an additional amount may be added to make good the deficiency: Sch.B1 para.72(3).

[2334] Insolvency Act 1986 Sch.B1 para.72.

39-434 Voluntary arrangements A similar moratorium against repossession of goods in a company's possession under a hire-purchase agreement can be obtained by the directors of the company where they propose a voluntary arrangement under Pt I of the Insolvency Act 1986.[2335] This facility is, however, restricted to "eligible companies", that is to say small companies (with certain exceptions).[2336]

(f) Miscellaneous Restrictions

39-435 Control of hire-purchase finance The disposition of goods on hire-purchase terms can be controlled by orders made in pursuance of powers conferred by the Emergency Laws (Re-enactments and Repeals) Act 1964.[2337] Historically, the orders made restricted the credit facilities offered by hire-purchase, conditional sale and credit-sale transactions relating to consumer goods by laying down minimum payments to be made before the contract was entered into and by limiting the time over which the instalments might be spread. All such orders have now been revoked,[2338] but the Act remains in force in this respect.

39-436 Reserve and auxiliary forces By the Reserve and Auxiliary Forces (Protection of Civil Interests) Act 1951[2339] wide discretionary powers are conferred upon the court in respect of hire-purchase and conditional sale agreements entered into by members of the reserve and auxiliary forces. It may be necessary to obtain leave of the court before retaking possession of the goods or before enforcing any judgment against such a hirer.[2340] The court may even make an order restoring the goods to the hirer where the owner has taken possession of them.[2341]

39-437 Consumer protection Part I of the Consumer Protection Act 1987[2342] imposes strict liability in respect of defective (i.e. unsafe) products, and Pt II of the Act[2343] empowers the Secretary of State to make safety regulations,[2344] to serve "prohibition notices", "suspension notices" and "notices to warn" in respect of unsafe goods. References in the Act to supplying goods include entering into a hire-purchase agreement to furnish the goods.[2345]

39-438 Enterprise Act 2002 The provisions of Pt 8 of the Enterprise Act 2002[2346] relating to the enforcement of certain consumer legislation extend to the supply of goods

---

[2335] Insolvency Act 1986 s.1A and Sch.A1, inserted by the Insolvency Act 2000 s.1.

[2336] Insolvency Act 1986 Sch.A1 para.2.

[2337] s.1, as amended by s.192 of and Sch.4 para.23 to the Consumer Credit Act 1974 from May 19, 1985: see SI 1983/1551 (c.44).

[2338] By SI 1982/1034.

[2339] As amended by s.192 of and Sch.4 paras 12, 13, to the Consumer Credit Act 1974 from May 19, 1985: SI 1983/1551 (c.44).

[2340] Reserve and Auxiliary Forces Act 1951 s.2. cf. *Smart Bros Ltd v Ross* [1943] A.C. 84.

[2341] Reserve and Auxiliary Forces Act 1951 s.4.

[2342] Consumer Protection Act 1987 ss.1–9; below, paras 44-449 et seq. Pt III (dealing with misleading price indications) was repealed by the Consumer Protection from Unfair Trading Regulations 2008 (SI 2008/1277) reg.30(1) and Sch.2 para.34.

[2343] ss.11–19; below, para.44-464.

[2344] For details of the regulations made, see Miller, *Product Liability and Safety Encyclopedia* (1991, looseleaf), IV. See also the General Product Safety Regulations 2005 (SI 2005/1803).

[2345] s.46(1)(b). But where a finance company acquires the goods from a dealer in order to finance their acquisition by a consumer, it is the dealer not the finance company that is regarded as supplying the goods for the purposes of liability: s.46(2).

[2346] ss.210–236.

under a hire-purchase agreement, a credit sale agreement or a conditional sale agreement.[2347]

4. CONDITIONAL SALE AGREEMENTS

Conditional sale of goods A contract of sale of goods may be absolute or conditional.[2348] An agreement to sell[2349] goods may therefore be made subject to a condition that the transfer of property from the seller to the buyer is to take place only when the total price of the goods has been paid and that, until that time, although possession of the goods is to be delivered to the buyer, they are to remain the property of the seller. As an instrument of instalment credit, a conditional sale agreement closely resembles a hire-purchase agreement.[2350] But it differs from a hire-purchase agreement in that the buyer is bound under the terms of the agreement to purchase the goods[2351] and does not (as in the case of a hire-purchase agreement) hire the goods with an option to purchase them.[2352]   **39-439**

Remedies of seller Conditional sale agreements invariably contain a provision for termination of the agreement and resumption of possession of the goods by the seller in the event of the buyer's default in the payment of instalments and of other contingencies, e.g. bankruptcy of the buyer.[2353] But it has been held that, in the absence of a stipulation to the contrary, the repossession of the goods by the seller determines the agreement and the seller thereby abandons his right to recover from the buyer or any guarantor[2354] the arrears of instalments remaining unpaid, but accrued due, before he repossessed the goods.[2355] This, of course, is not so in the case of hire-purchase agreements.[2356] But it would seem that the seller could recover an equivalent sum as damages for breach of contract.[2357] Certain conditional sale agreements further provide, as an alternative to termination and repossession, that the seller may elect to pass the property in the goods to the buyer and recover from the buyer the unpaid balance of the purchase price of the goods.   **39-440**

Conditional sale of land A modern phenomenon has been the appearance of conditional sales of land, especially of dwelling-houses, with a provision in the agreement for resumption of possession by the seller in the event of non-payment of instalments of the purchase price.[2358]   **39-441**

Definition A conditional sale agreement is defined in the consumer credit regula-   **39-442**

[2347] See above, paras 38-133 et seq.
[2348] Sale of Goods Act 1979 s.2(3).
[2349] Sale of Goods Act 1979 s.2(5).
[2350] Conditional sale in many cases ousted hire-purchase because it was possible so to draft the agreement as to confer partial exemption from value added tax and to obtain tax relief on finance charges by turning them into interest. But the value added tax exemption was extended to hire-purchase and the tax relief on interest has been (to a great extent) withdrawn.
[2351] But see Consumer Credit Act 1974 s.99, below, para.39-451.
[2352] For the consequences, see below, para.39-461.
[2353] See below, para.39-448.
[2354] *Hewison v Ricketts* (1894) 63 L.J. Q.B. 711.
[2355] *Hewison v Ricketts* (1894) 63 L.J. Q.B. 711; *Att-Gen v Pritchard* (1928) 97 L.J. K.B. 561.
[2356] *Brooks v Beirnstein* [1909] 1 K.B. 98; see above, para.39-340.
[2357] *Att-Gen v Pritchard* (1928) 97 L.J. K.B. 561; *Taylor v Thompson* [1930] W.N. 16.
[2358] No doubt the object has been to avoid both the Rent Acts and the relief traditionally given to mortgagors of land. But see *Starside Properties Ltd v Mustapha* [1974] 1 W.L.R. 816.

tory regime[2359] to mean "an agreement for the sale of goods or land under which the purchase price or part of it is payable by instalments and the property in the goods or land is to remain in the seller (notwithstanding that the buyer is to be in possession of the goods or land) until such conditions as to the payment of instalments or otherwise as may be specified in the agreement are fulfilled". It will be noted that this definition embraces land[2360] as well as goods.

39-443 **Scope of regulation** A conditional sale agreement is a consumer credit agreement, for fixed-sum credit,[2361] if the debtor, i.e. the buyer, is an individual.[2362] The agreement will be a regulated credit agreement unless it is an exempt agreement.[2363] A regulated conditional sale agreement is a debtor-creditor-supplier agreement[2364] for restricted-use credit.[2365]

39-444 Unlike a credit-sale agreement,[2366] a conditional sale agreement under £50 cannot be a "small agreement".[2367]

39-445 Authorisation is required to carry on a business involving consumer credit agreements (other than exempt agreements)[2368] and the general provisions of the regulatory regime apply,[2369] although there are certain provisions that apply in particular to regulated conditional sale agreements.[2370] Most of these provisions are equally applicable to hire-purchase agreements.[2371]

39-446 **Parties** In the regulatory regime, the seller under a conditional sale agreement is referred to as the "creditor" or "lender" and the buyer as the "debtor" or "borrower".[2372]

39-447 **Unfair relationships** The provisions of the Consumer Credit Act 1974 relating to "unfair relationships" apply to conditional sale agreements where the debtor is an individual.[2373]

[2359] See Consumer Credit Act 1974 ("CCA 1974") s.189(1) and the Financial Services and Markets Act 2000 (Regulated Activities) Order 2001 (SI 2001/544) ("RAO") art.60L(1), as inserted by SI 2013/1881 art.6. This definition corresponds to that contained in (the now repealed) s.1(1) of the Hire-Purchase Act 1965, but is extended to land. See the similar definition of "conditional sales contract" (but not covering land) in the Consumer Rights Act 2015 s.5(3) (for the purposes of Pt 1 of that Act), above, para.38-488.

[2360] Defined in CCA 1974 s.189(1).

[2361] See above, para.39-026.

[2362] See above, para.39-016.

[2363] See above, para.39-017. The £25,000 ceiling in the "business purpose" exemption (see above, para.39-046) is calculated by taking the total amount payable under the agreement (less any deposit or initial payment paid), but subtracting any item in the total charge for credit such as credit charges or interest (as these are not "credit": see above, para.39-059).

[2364] See above, para.39-030.

[2365] See above, para.39-027.

[2366] See below, para.39-464.

[2367] CCA 1974 s.17(1)(a). A hire-purchase agreement similarly cannot qualify as a "small agreement", see above, para.39-357.

[2368] See above, para.39-061.

[2369] See above, paras 39-001—39-257.

[2370] Especially CCA 1974 ss.90–92, 99–100, 129–130, 133–135.

[2371] See above, paras 39-356—39-379.

[2372] See above, para.39-018.

[2373] CCA 1974 ss.140A–140C, paras 39-212 et seq.

Protected goods The concept of "protected goods"[2374] applies to a regulated   **39-448**
conditional sale agreement as it does to a regulated hire-purchase agreement,[2375]
provided that the property in the goods remains in the creditor.[2376]

Entry on premises The restriction placed upon entry on premises without an   **39-449**
order of the court applies to a regulated conditional sale agreement as it does to a
regulated hire-purchase agreement.[2377]

Recovery of land At any time when the debtor is in breach of a regulated   **39-450**
conditional sale agreement relating to land, the creditor is entitled to recover possession of the land from the debtor, or any person claiming under him, on an order
of the court only.[2378] Any clause to the contrary contained in the agreement is
void[2379]; but recovery of possession is permissible with the consent of the debtor
given at the time.[2380] An entry in contravention of this prohibition is actionable as
a breach of statutory duty.[2381]

Right to terminate conditional sale agreement The statutory right of the debtor   **39-451**
under s.99 of the Consumer Credit Act 1974 to terminate the agreement (VTR) applies to a regulated conditional sale agreement as it does to a regulated hire-
purchase agreement,[2382] except in the case of an agreement relating to land after the
title to the land has passed to the debtor.[2383] The right to terminate is also taken away
in the case of a conditional sale agreement relating to goods, where the property in
the goods, having become vested in the debtor, is transferred to a person who does
not become the debtor under the agreement.[2384] But otherwise the fact that the
property in the goods has become vested in the debtor does not abrogate his right
of termination. If, however, in those circumstances, the debtor does terminate the
agreement, the property in the goods thereupon revests in the person (the "previous owner") in whom it was vested immediately before it became vested in the
debtor.[2385]

Liability of debtor The liability of the debtor on the exercise of his statutory right   **39-452**
of termination is the same as in the case of a hire-purchase agreement.[2386]

[2374] CCA 1974 s.90(7).
[2375] CCA 1974 ss.90, 91. See above, para.39-361.
[2376] CCA 1974 s.90(1)(c).
[2377] CCA 1974 s.92(1); above, para.39-366.
[2378] CCA 1974 s.92(2). See also CCA 1974 s.113(1), (2), (8).
[2379] CCA 1974 s.173(1).
[2380] CCA 1974 s.173(3).
[2381] CCA 1974 s.92(3). See above, para.39-366.
[2382] See above, para.39-367.
[2383] CCA 1974 s.99(3).
[2384] CCA 1974 s.99(4). See the definition of "debtor" in CCA 1974 s.189(1); above, para.39-018.
[2385] CCA 1974 s.99(5) (i.e. normally in the creditor, and not in the dealer who negotiated the transaction).
  If the previous owner has died, or any other event has occurred whereby the property, if vested in
  him immediately before that event, would thereupon have vested in some other person, the property
  is to be treated as having devolved as if it had been vested in the previous owner immediately before
  that event, as the case may be: s.99(5), proviso.
[2386] CCA 1974 s.100; see above, paras 39-368—39-372.

39-453   **Time orders**   The supplemental provisions relating to time orders in the case of hire-purchase agreements apply also in the case of conditional sale agreements.[2387]

39-454   **Return orders and transfer orders**   The power of the court to make a return order or transfer order in respect of goods applies to a regulated conditional sale agreement.[2388]

39-455   **Adverse possession**   The provisions of s.134 of the Consumer Credit Act 1974 relating to evidence of adverse possession of goods apply to conditional sale agreements.[2389]

39-456   **Title to goods**   The terms about title implied on the part of the seller in any conditional sale agreement are those contained in s.12 of the Sale of Goods Act 1979,[2390] and these cannot be excluded.[2391] The Consumer Rights Act 2015 contains the relevant statutory terms for "consumer" contracts.[2392]

39-457   **Defective goods**   The terms as to quality, fitness for purpose, and correspondence with description and sample implied on the part of the seller in contracts of sale of goods by ss.13 to 15 of the Sale of Goods Act 1979[2393] are implied in every conditional sale agreement. The Consumer Rights Act 2015 treats similar (but more expansive[2394]) terms "as included" in "consumer" conditional sales contracts[2395] (the terms being the same as for hire-purchase agreements)[2396] and will confer extensive remedies for their breach.[2397] The exclusion of such implied terms and of the liability of the creditor for their breach are and will continue to be ineffective, either absolutely or subject to certain qualifications, the extent depending on whether they are "consumer" contracts or not.[2398]

39-458   In relation to the term as to fitness for purpose implied by s.14(3) of the 1979 Act,[2399] since under a conditional sale agreement the purchase price or part of it is payable by instalments, the particular purpose for which the goods are being bought

---

[2387] CCA 1974 s.130(2), (4); see above, para.39-373.

[2388] CCA 1974 s.133; above, paras 39-374—39-377 (including a suspended return order coupled with a time order: above, para.39-375).

[2389] Above, para.39-379.

[2390] Below, para.44-075.

[2391] Unfair Contract Terms Act 1977 s.6(1)(a). See below, para.44-085.

[2392] Made on or after October 1, 2015. See s.17, above, para.38-508. Exclusion will also not be possible: the Consumer Rights Act 2015 s.31(1)(i), above, para.38-531.

[2393] See below, paras 44-086—44-115.

[2394] See, in particular, the more extensive implied term as to quality (s.9, above, para.38-497) and the new terms as to conformity with model seen or examined (s.14, above, para.38-502) and as to incorrect installation (s.15, above, para.38-503).

[2395] Made on or after October 1, 2015.

[2396] And note that certain pre-contract information provided under the Consumer Contract (Information, Cancellation and Additional Charges) Regulations 2013 (SI 2013/3134) are treated as terms of the contract: s.12 and see above, para.38-500.

[2397] The terms are set out in the Consumer Rights Act ss.9–15, 18 (see above, paras 38-497 et seq.) and the remedies in ss.19–27 (above, paras 38-512 et seq.).

[2398] See Vol.I, para.15-093; below, paras 44-117—44-125. See also *Hughes v Hall & Hall* [1981] R.T.R. 430 DC (offence to include void exclusion term by (now repealed) Consumer Transactions (Restrictions on Statements) Order 1976 (SI 1976/1813)).

[2399] See below, para.44-105. The statutory term for consumer contracts made on or after October 1, 2015 is in the Consumer Rights Act 2015 s.10, see above, para.38-498.

may be made known, expressly or by implication, to the credit-broker[2400] (e.g. to a dealer) by whom the goods have been previously sold to the seller, in order to satisfy the requirements of the subsection.[2401] Moreover, in order to displace the implied term, the seller has to prove that the circumstances show that the buyer did not rely, or that it was unreasonable for him to rely, on the skill or judgment both of the seller and of the credit-broker.[2402]

Special provisions as to remedies   Section 11(4) of the Sale of Goods Act 1979   **39-459** (whereby in certain circumstances a breach of condition in a contract of sale is treated only as a breach of warranty)[2403] did not apply to conditional sale agreements[2404] where the buyer dealt as consumer and now generally only applies to non-consumer contracts.[2405] Further, a breach of condition (whether express or implied) to be fulfilled by the seller under any such agreement is to be treated as a breach of warranty, and not as grounds for rejecting the goods and treating the agreement as repudiated, if (but only if) it would have fallen to be so treated had the condition been contained or implied in a corresponding hire-purchase agreement[2406] as a condition to be fulfilled by the owner.[2407]

The Consumer Rights Act 2015 makes special provision for extensive rem-   **39-460** edies[2408] in the case of "consumer 'goods' contracts",[2409] a term that includes both (conditional and credit) sales contracts and hire-purchase agreements.

Title of third parties   One of the most significant differences between a hire-   **39-461** purchase and a conditional sale agreement lies in the fact that a conditional buyer can pass a good title to a third party under s.25(1) of the Sale of Goods Act 1979.[2410] But, where a conditional sale agreement is a consumer credit agreement,[2411] the buyer is deemed not to be a person who has bought or agreed to buy goods[2412] and in consequence cannot pass a good title to a third party by virtue of that

---

[2400] Defined in Sale of Goods Act 1979 s.61(1).

[2401] See below, para.44-106.

[2402] See below, para.44-108.

[2403] See below, para.44-068.

[2404] Defined in s.15(1) of the Supply of Goods (Implied Terms) Act 1973, as amended by s.192 of and Sch.4 para.36 to the Consumer Credit Act 1974.

[2405] See previously, Supply of Goods (Implied Terms) Act 1973 s.14(1), as amended by the Unfair Contract Terms Act 1977 s.31(3) and Sch.3 (and by s.192 of and Sch.4 para.26 to the Consumer Credit Act 1974) but repealed by the Consumer Rights Act 2015 (for contracts made on or after October 1, 2015 (see the 2015 Act s.60 and Sch.1 para.6)). Section 11(4) was simultaneously confined to non-consumer contracts (see new s.11(4A), added by 2015 Act s.60 and Sch.1 para.10).

[2406] Defined in the Supply of Goods (Implied Terms) Act 1973 s.15(1) (amended as above).

[2407] s.14(2) (amended as above).

[2408] Including the additional remedies of repair or replacement of the goods, reduction of the purchase price or rejecting the goods and treating the contract as at an end.

[2409] For contracts made on or after October 1, 2015. See Consumer Rights Act 2015 Act s.3, applying ss.19–27 (as to remedies, see above, paras 38-512 et seq.) to "goods contracts". It repealed (see s.60 and Sch.1 para.27) and replaced the "remedies" provisions in Sale of Goods Act 1979 Pt 5A (ss.48A to 48F), inserted by the Sale and Supply of Goods to Consumers Regulations 2002 (SI 2002/3045).

[2410] Or s.9 of the Factors Act 1889; *Lee v Butler* [1893] 2 Q.B. 318; *Hull Rope Works Co Ltd v Adams* (1895) 73 L.T. 446; *Wylde v Legge* (1901) 84 L.T. 121. But see *Newtons of Wembley Ltd v Williams* [1965] 1 Q.B. 560.

[2411] Within the meaning of s.8(1) of the Consumer Credit Act 1974 (see above, para.39-443).

[2412] Sale of Goods Act 1979 s.25(2), (4), Sch.1 para.9 and Sch.4 para.2; Consumer Credit Act 1974 s.192 and Sch.4 paras 2 and 4.

subsection.[2413] The provisions of Pt III of the Hire-Purchase Act 1964,[2414] which relate to the disposition of motor vehicles, nevertheless apply to motor vehicles that have been agreed to be sold under a conditional sale agreement[2415] as they apply to motor vehicles which have been let under a hire-purchase agreement.[2416] As a result, a conditional sale agreement now confers less security than a hire-purchase agreement vis-à-vis third parties only if the agreement is not a consumer credit agreement and either (i) the goods agreed to be sold do not consist of a motor vehicle; or (ii) they do consist of a motor vehicle, but the vehicle is wrongfully disposed of to a trade or finance purchaser (and not to a private purchaser) within the meaning of the Hire-Purchase Act 1964.[2417] In these situations a third party may acquire a good title from a buyer under a conditional sale agreement where he would not acquire one from a hirer under a hire-purchase agreement, but otherwise the security is identical.

39-462 **Distress**   As noted above, a landlord's power at common law to distrain upon all goods found upon the demised premises has now been abolished.[2418]

39-463 **Miscellaneous restrictions**   The miscellaneous restrictions referred to in paras 39-406 to 39-409 of this chapter also apply to conditional sale agreements.

5.   CREDIT-SALE AGREEMENTS

39-464 **Credit-sale**   A credit-sale agreement may be defined as an absolute[2419] contract of sale of goods in pursuance of an agreement under which payment of the whole or part of the purchase price is deferred. Statutory definitions of a credit-sale have sometimes included conditional sales,[2420] but this is not so in the case of the Consumer Credit Act 1974[2421] where "credit-sale agreement" is defined to mean "an agreement for the sale of goods under which the purchase price or part of it is payable by instalments, but which is not a conditional sale agreement". Unlike a conditional sale agreement, the property in goods sold under a credit-sale agreement is transferred to the buyer when the agreement is made. Since the seller is no longer the owner of the goods he cannot repossess them in the event of default of the buyer in the payment of the instalments or otherwise,[2422] his only remedy being to sue for the unpaid instalments of the price.[2423]

[2413] Or of s.9 of the Factors Act 1889.

[2414] As amended by s.192 of and Sch.4 para.22 to the Consumer Credit Act 1974.

[2415] Defined in s.29(1) of the 1964 Act. These provisions apply regardless of the fact that the debtor is not an individual, i.e. is a body corporate.

[2416] See above, para.39-402.

[2417] See above, para.39-403.

[2418] See above, para.39-427. Historically, the position of goods subject to a conditional sale agreement was similar to that of those subject to a hire-purchase agreement.

[2419] Sale of Goods Act 1979 s.2(1), (3).

[2420] e.g. Advertisements (Hire-Purchase) Act 1967 s.7(2) (now repealed).

[2421] s.189(1). There is no corresponding definition in the Financial Services and Markets Act 2000 (Regulated Activities) Order 2001 (SI 2001/544) ("RAO") art.60L(1),

[2422] A provision to this effect in the agreement would render the agreement void as an unregistered bill of sale: see Bills of Sale Act 1878 s.3; and below, para.39-519.

[2423] Most credit-sale agreements provide that, on default by the buyer, the balance of the purchase price shall immediately become payable. But see the notices required under Consumer Credit Act 1974 ss.76(1)(a), 86D, 87(1)(b), 98(1) (above, paras 39-164, 39-134, 39-166, 39-172) and see also the

Scope of regulation   A credit-sale agreement is a consumer credit agreement[2424]   **39-465**
if the debtor, i.e. the buyer, is an individual[2425] and it is a regulated agreement if it
is not an exempt agreement.[2426] A regulated credit-sale agreement is a debtor-
creditor-supplier agreement[2427] for restricted-use credit.[2428] It is usually, but not
invariably, for fixed-sum credit.[2429] The general provisions of the consumer credit
regulatory regime apply in respect of authorisation and the regulation of the credit
aspect of the agreements.[2430] In the regime, the seller under a credit-sale agreement is referred to as the "creditor" or "lender" and the buyer as the "debtor" or
"borrower".[2431]

Unfair relationships   The provisions of the Consumer Credit Act 1974 relating   **39-466**
to "unfair relationships" apply to credit sale agreements where the debtor is an
individual.[2432]

Under-£50 agreements   Most of Pt V of the Consumer Credit Act 1974, relating   **39-467**
to the making of the agreement, its form and content, signature, and supply of copies to the debtor,[2433] do not apply to "small" (under-£50) restricted-use[2434] (and hence
credit sale agreements) nor can such agreements be "cancellable" agreements.[2435]

Implied terms   The terms as to title, quality, fitness for purpose,[2436] and cor-   **39-468**
respondence with description and sample, implied in any credit-sale agreement are
those contained in ss.12 to 15 of the Sale of Goods Act 1979.[2437] The Consumer
Rights Act 2015 treats similar (but more expansive[2438]) terms "as included" in

---

repayment and rebate provisions in Consumer Credit Act 1974 ss.94, 95 (above, paras 39-143—39-
145).
[2424] CCA 1974 s.8(2); see above, para.39-016. See also Sch.2 Pt II Example 5.
[2425] Defined in CCA 1974 s.189(1); see above, para.39-016.
[2426] See above, para.39-017 and for "exempt agreements", above, paras 39-038 et seq. For the calculation of the ceiling for the "business purpose" exemption in RAO art.60C(3)–(7), see above, para.39-
443 and Sch.2 Pt II Example 5.
[2427] CCA 1974 s.12(a); above, para.39-030.
[2428] CCA 1974 s.11(1)(a); above, para.39-027.
[2429] CCA 1974 s.10(1)(b); above, para.39-026. In certain cases, e.g. shop "option" or "budget" or
"subscription" accounts, a credit-sale agreement can be for running account credit. Also if a credit
card is provided by the retailer, it can also be a credit-token agreement within CCA 1974 s.14 (above,
para.39-034; below, para.39-494). But see CCA 1974 ss.51, 66, 74(2), 78(7), 85(3) on exemptions
for "small" credit-sale agreements.
[2430] See above, paras 39-005—39-255.
[2431] See above, para.39-018.
[2432] ss.140A–140C, above, paras 39-212 et seq.
[2433] CCA 1974 ss.60–65. Sections 59 and 66 also do not apply.
[2434] CCA 1974 s.74(1)(d). For the definition of small agreement, CCA 1974 see ss.17(1), 189(1); above,
para.39-048. The limit was raised from £30 by SI 1983/1878.
[2435] However, the right of withdrawal under CCA 1974 s.66A is available (see above, para.39-101) and
CCA 1974 ss.55 (regulations on disclosure of information, above, para.39-076) and CCA 1974 s.56
(antecedent negotiations, above, para.39-071) do apply: CCA 1974 s.74(2). But see CCA 1974
s.74(2A) (in s.74(2) limit is £42 for agreements within the Consumer Contracts (Information, Cancellation and Additional Charges) Regulations 2013 (SI 2013/3134)).
[2436] The particular purpose for which the goods are bought may be made known to the credit-broker (e.g.
a dealer) who has previously sold the goods to the seller: see above, para.39-458, below and para.44-
106.
[2437] See below, paras 44-075—44-115.
[2438] See, in particular, the more extensive term as to quality (s.9) and the new terms as to conformity with
model seen or examined (s.14, above, para.38-502) and as to incorrect installation (s.15, above,

"consumer" sales contracts, and confers extensive remedies for their breach.[2439] The exclusion of these implied terms and of the liability of the creditor for the breach of them is ineffective, either absolutely or subject to certain qualifications, depending on whether they are "consumer" contracts or not.[2440]

39-469 **Remedies of buyer**   The remedies of the buyer are those conferred by the Sale of Goods Act 1979,[2441] and, for "consumer" sales contracts, those additional remedies conferred by the Consumer Rights Act 2015[2442] including the additional remedies of repair or replacement of the goods, reduction of the purchase price or rejecting the goods and treating the contract as at an end.

39-470 **Title of third parties**   Since the property in the goods passes to the buyer when the agreement is made, he can pass a title to the goods to a third party by virtue of his ownership of them.[2443]

39-471 **Other statutes**   The Consumer Protection Act 1987[2444] and the Enterprise Act 2002[2445] apply to the supply of goods under credit-sale agreements.

6. CREDIT AND OTHER PAYMENT CARDS, AND CHECKS

39-472 **Credit cards**   Credit cards are a relatively modern phenomenon,[2446] but credit card business has grown rapidly in recent years. A credit card transaction may be two-party or three-party or four-party. In a two-party transaction the issuer of the card is itself the supplier of the goods or services bought on credit and the cardholder purchases the goods or services from it. In the United Kingdom two-party credit cards are mainly issued by retail shops and stores. The holder of the card produces the card at the shop or store, or at a branch, and is then permitted to make a purchase on credit. The card will have been issued to the holder in pursuance of an agreement made between himself and the issuer of the card, which agreement will, for example, establish his credit limit and the terms of payment. A two-party transac-

---

para.38-503). And note that certain pre-contract information provided under the Consumer Contract (Information, Cancellation and Additional Charges) Regulations 2013 (SI 2013/3134) are treated as terms of the contract: s.12 and see above, para.38-500.

[2439] For contracts made on or after October 1, 2015. The terms are set out in the Consumer Rights Act ss.9–15, 18 (see above, paras 38-497 et seq.) and the remedies in ss.19–27 (see above, paras 38-512 et seq.).

[2440] See Vol.I, above para.15-093; below, paras 44-117—44-125. See also *Hughes v Hall & Hall* [1981] R.T.R. 430 DC (offence to include void exclusion term by (now repealed) Consumer Transactions (Restrictions on Statements) Order 1976 (SI 1976/1813)).

[2441] See below, Ch.44.

[2442] For contracts made on or after October 1, 2015. See especially Consumer Rights Act 2015 Act s.3, applying ss.19–27 (as to remedies, see above, paras 38-512 et seq.) to "goods contracts". It repealed (see s.60 and Sch.1 para.27) and replaced the "remedies" provisions in Sale of Goods Act 1979 Pt 5A (ss.48A to 48F), inserted by the Sale and Supply of Goods to Consumers Regulations 2002 (SI 2002/3045).

[2443] cf. *Car and Universal Finance Co Ltd v Caldwell* [1965] 1 Q.B. 525; *Newtons of Wembley Ltd v Williams* [1965] 1 Q.B. 560; below, para.44-211.

[2444] See above, para.39-437.

[2445] See above, para.39-438.

[2446] For an excellent historical review, see E. E. Bergsten, "Credit Cards—A Prelude to a Cashless Society" (1967) 8 BC Ind. & Com. L Rev. 485. See also Diamond (ed.) *Instalment Credit* (1970), pp.86 et seq. (R.M. Goode); Stephenson, *Credit, Debit and Cheque Cards* (1993); Smith and Robertson, "Plastic Money", in Brindle and Cox (eds), *Law of Bank Payments*, 5th edn (2017).

tion, at least insofar as it relates to the purchase of goods, would appear to constitute a credit-sale agreement.[2447]

In a three-party transaction, the issuer of the card is not the same person as the **39-473** supplier but a separate entity. The issuer enters into arrangements (usually in the form of a "master" or "merchant" agreement) with approved suppliers who undertake to supply goods or services to the cardholder on production of the card. In a four-party transaction the arrangements are indirect, e.g. through membership of the "Mastercard" or "Visa" scheme so that the issuer is not the person who approves the supplier but both the issuer and supplier are members of a scheme.[2448] Payment for the goods or services is agreed to be made by the issuer of the card (subject to discount) on the rendering of an account by the supplier (in the three-party case) or the operator of the scheme (in the four-party case), usually electronically in the form of or accompanied by a sales document authenticated by the customer. A separate agreement is also entered into between the issuer and the cardholder establishing the holder's credit limit, the terms of payment and the other conditions governing the use of the card.[2449] In some three-party or four-party credit card transactions the documentation may be so formulated as to involve an assignment[2450] by the supplier to the issuer of the cardholder's account with (i.e. his debt to) the supplier created by the purchase.[2451] But in most such transactions there is no such assignment, and the issuer relies directly and solely on the rights created by his agreement with the cardholder.[2452] In *Re Charge Card Services Ltd*,[2453] the Court of Appeal stated that, in a three-party transaction, the underlying contractual scheme was established by two separate bilateral contracts, i.e. between the issuer and the supplier and between the cardholder and the issuer. The actual sale and purchase of the commodity was the subject of a third bilateral contract between the supplier and the cardholder. In that case it was held that, unlike payment by cheque,[2454] payment by credit card was not conditional payment only, but absolute payment. Accordingly, where the issuer company became insolvent and went into liquidation, suppliers had no recourse against the cardholders. The debts incurred by the use of the card were payable to the issuer or (in that case) to a factor to whom they had been assigned by the issuer company.

The term "credit card" is not a term of art. But it has become increasingly com- **39-474** mon for that term to be reserved for a card issued under an agreement by which the cardholder can obtain *extended* credit, as opposed to a "charge card" which provides credit only for a limited period. Credit is provided by a credit card agreement in one

---

[2447] See *NG Napier Ltd v Patterson*, 1959 S.C. (J.) 48; *Napier (NG) Ltd v Corbett*, 1962 S.L.T. 90 Sh Ct. An alternative analysis is that there is a loan made by the issuer to the holder for the purchase of the issuer's goods. See *MacDonald v NG Napier Ltd*, 1960 S.L.T. 345.

[2448] On four-party cards, see *Office of Fair Trading v Lloyds TSB Bank Plc* [2007] UKHL 48. See also *Bank of Scotland v Truman* [2005] EWHC 583, [2005] C.C.L.R. 3.

[2449] *Mekwin v National Westminster Bank Plc* [1998] C.C.L.R. 22 (issuer retains ownership of card).

[2450] Or an agreement to assign.

[2451] The arrangement is then: (a) an immediate debt of the whole amount of the purchase is created between the holder and the supplier; (b) this debt is assigned by the supplier to the issuer; (c) the debt is paid by the holder to the issuer in accordance with the terms of the agreement made between them. But see *Commissioners of Customs and Excise v Diners Club Ltd* [1988] 2 All E.R. 1016.

[2452] This arrangement arguably involves a loan of money by the issuer to the holder; see above, para.39-262.

[2453] [1989] Ch. 497. See also *Commissioners of Customs and Excise v Diners Club Ltd*, above; *Richardson v Worrall* (1985) 58 T.C. 642; *R. v Department of Social Security Ex p. Overdrive Credit Card Ltd* [1991] 1 W.L.R. 635.

[2454] See Vol.I, para.21-076.

of two ways. First, the cardholder may be given the option either to pay off the entire debit balance outstanding on the account, or to pay only a minimum sum, interest being charged on the debit balance remaining unpaid.[2455] This is sometimes referred to as an "option" account. Secondly, the agreement may provide for the making by the cardholder of fixed monthly payments (a "budget" or "subscription" account) and the cardholder's credit limit may be a specified sum or a multiple (say, 24 times) of the fixed monthly payment.[2456] Interest is again charged on the debit balance from time to time outstanding. In either case, payments made by the cardholder will "refresh" the account, that is to say, will enable them to obtain further credit up to their stipulated credit limit.

39-475 Certain credit cards now in use also enable the cardholder to obtain cash on presentation of the card.[2457] Many credit card agreements further provide for the issue of additional cards to relatives, employees, etc. of the principal cardholder or for use on a company account. The principal cardholder (or account holder) is liable for debts incurred by the use of the additional cards by the so-called "authorised users".

39-476 Charge cards The expression "charge card" is usually reserved for a card issued under an agreement that requires the cardholder to settle their account in full within a fixed period after a statement is rendered. If they fail to pay by the due date, there is a breach of the agreement and default interest (or "liquidated damages" for the breach) will be payable. No extended credit is, however, allowed. The cardholder's commitment is to make a single payment to settle their entire indebtedness recorded on the statement by the due date. Like credit cards, a charge card transaction may be two-party[2458] or three-party.[2459] Some charge cards also enable the holder to obtain cash on presentation of the card.

39-477 Debit cards Debit cards[2460] resemble credit cards and charge cards in appearance and similarly enable the cardholder to purchase goods and services from suppliers with whom arrangements have been made for the acceptance of the card. The issuer of the card is usually (but not invariably) a bank or building society with whom the cardholder maintains an ordinary (e.g. current) account. By their agreement with the issuer of the card, the cardholder authorises the issuer to debit that account with the debts incurred by the use of the card. Debits will reach the account within a short period of time, i.e. usually within two or three days. If, for example, the account to be debited is the cardholder's current account with a bank, and the account is in credit, the debits will reduce the credit balance standing on the account. If the account is in overdraft, then the debits will increase the debit balance on the account. The extent of the credit facility afforded by the card depends, therefore, for the most part, on the overdraft arrangements arrived at between the

---

[2455] Most three-party and four-party cards are in this form.

[2456] This type of transaction is usually designed to enable the cardholder to purchase goods or services from a particular store or group of stores.

[2457] An additional charge may be made for the use of this facility, or interest may be charged (sometimes at a higher rate) from the date the cash is withdrawn.

[2458] Issued by a shop or store.

[2459] e.g. Diners' Club and American Express.

[2460] e.g. Visa Debit.

cardholder and the issuer of the card. Debit cards issued by banks and building societies can normally also be used as cash cards[2461] to obtain cash.

Debit cards have become more prevalent with the development of EFTPOS facilities (electronic funds transfer at point of sale). In an EFTPOS transaction, the card is passed through a reader in a terminal installed at the supplier's point of sale and, subject to acceptance, payment is made to the supplier by an electronic transfer of funds from the account of the cardholder to the account of the supplier. Transactions will not be accepted unless the cardholder's account is in credit or within a previously agreed overdraft limit. The customer is required to key in a personal identification number (PIN) or (increasingly rarely in the UK) sign a receipt (his signature being checked against that on the card) as a protection against fraud.

39-478

Cash cards Cash cards, or ATM (automatic teller machine) cards, are again usually, but not invariably, issued by banks and building societies and enable the cardholder to obtain cash by using the card to operate an automatic teller machine. Withdrawals by this means are normally debited by electronic means directly to the account (e.g. a current account) of the customer with the issuer of the card. The machine will be programmed so as to refuse payment unless the cardholder's instruction is accompanied or preceded by his PIN, and unless the cardholder's account is in credit or there is a previously agreed credit facility. However, although most machines are online, thus enabling the withdrawal instruction to be checked against the cardholder's current balance at the time the instruction is received, in other cases the balance is the previous day's balance, and there may even be a "down time" each day during which the cardholder's balance cannot be checked. Many such cards can nowadays be used, not only to obtain cash from the ATMs of the issuer of the card, but also from machines of other banks and building societies with whom arrangements have been made for acceptance of the card. Networks (e.g. "Link") are currently in operation, which provide arrangements for wider or reciprocal acceptance of such cards.

39-479

Electronic purses These are sometimes referred to as "digital cash cards" or "stored value cards". They are cards on which "value" is stored electronically in the form of pre-paid units of money. The card can be used by the cardholder to pay for goods or services supplied, units of value being transferred electronically from buyer to seller. Some cards contain a magnetic strip, but others carry more complex information stored in a microchip. Some cards are reloadable and can be charged with additional value, while others lack this facility and are considered disposable once the entire value has been spent. In some cases, the card can be used by the cardholder to purchase goods or services only from the card issuer or card issuer's organisation. In other cases, however, as in multi-party credit card or charge card transactions, the card may be used to effect purchases from any supplier who has agreed to accept payment in this form and the supplier will be reimbursed in respect of the purchases made by use of the card. Electronic purses are a relatively recent development and the exact relationships between the participants (the scheme originator, participating banks, supplier and cardholder) have yet to be established.[2462]

39-480

Check and voucher trading A check is a document issued by the check trader,

39-481

[2461] See below, para.39-479.
[2462] See Reed and Davies, *Digital Cash—the Legal Implications* (1995); Finlayson-Brown (1997) J.I.B.L. 362; Effros, *Current Law Issues Affecting Central Banks* (1998), Ch.6; Hooley "Payment in a Cash-

and purchased by the customer, which entitles the customer to purchase goods of the face value of the check from retail shops approved by the check trader. The customer may make an initial payment to the check trader, usually of 5 per cent of the face value of the checks purchased, and is then issued with checks of a total value of (say) £100 in smaller denominations. The total face value of the checks so purchased is paid by the customer to the check trader by instalments, the instalments being collected from the customer at their home by a collecting agent (who also supplies fresh checks when required). An agreement is entered into between the check trader and each approved retailer whereby the retailer undertakes to honour checks presented to them by supplying goods to the face value of the check, and the check trader undertakes to reimburse the retailer, but after deduction of a discount, at periodic intervals on receipt of invoices backed by the returned checks. Check trading involves, in relation to each customer, regular, but relatively small, sums. It arguably results in a loan of money by the check trader to the customer,[2463] but an alternative view is that the proper form of action for recovery of instalments unpaid is one for money paid by the check trader to the retailer at the customer's request.[2464]

39-482   Voucher trading, which is now almost obsolete, closely resembles check trading, the voucher taking the place of the check. But the voucher is usually of a much larger face value, and that face value is frequently of the precise value of the goods to be purchased; the repayment period is much longer; there is no initial "poundage", but finance charges are levied and paid together with the instalments; and the voucher may be tenable at only one retail shop or chain of shops.[2465]

39-483   **The consumer credit regulatory regime**   The application of the consumer credit regulatory regime to the various types of card agreement mentioned above is a matter of some complexity,[2466] and, in some cases, not free from doubt. Moreover, with the appearance of "multi-function" cards, each separate function has to be considered in the context of the regime. In broad terms, the position is as set out in the following paragraphs:

39-484   *(i)   Credit card*[2467] *agreements*   (whether two-party, three-party or four-party) made between the issuer (the creditor) and the cardholder (the debtor) under which extended credit is provided to the debtor will almost invariably[2468] be regulated agreements for the purposes of the regime, unless the debtor is not an individual, i.e. is a body corporate or large partnership.[2469] The conduct of its business by the

---

less Society" in *The Realm of Company Law—A Collection of Papers in honour of Professor Leonard Sealy* (1998), p.245; Guest and Lloyd, *Encyclopedia of Consumer Credit Law* (1975, looseleaf), para.2-015.

[2463] *Goldberg v Tait* [1950] N.Z.L.R. 976; *Cash Order Purchases Ltd v Brady* [1952] N.Z.L.R. 898; *Premier Clothing and Supply Co Ltd v Hillcoat* [1969] C.L.Y 2279a, Cty Ct. cf. *Progressive Supply Co Ltd v Dalton* [1942] 2 All E.R. 646, [1943] Ch. 54; *Davies v Customs and Excise Commissioners* [1975] S.T.C. 28.

[2464] See above, para.39-262.

[2465] The voucher trader is very often a wholly-owned subsidiary of the retailing company.

[2466] See, in particular, Guest and Lloyd, *Encyclopedia of Consumer Credit Law* (1975, looseleaf), especially at para.2-015; and Goode, *Consumer Credit: Law and Practice*, Pt C, Ch.39.

[2467] See above, para.39-472.

[2468] Unless exempt as high net worth or business debtors, see above, paras 39-045 and 39-046.

[2469] Neither are "individuals", as defined: see above, para.39-016.

creditor will require FCA authorisation,[2470] but suppliers will not ordinarily require authorisation, unless they introduce customers to the creditor.[2471] Such agreements will be regulated by the general provisions of the regime.

A two-party credit card agreement will normally be for running-account credit.[2472] **39-485** Insofar as the card may be used to obtain goods or services from the creditor, it will be a debtor-creditor-supplier[2473] for restricted-use credit.[2474] The creditor, as supplier of the goods or services, will be liable directly to the debtor if the goods or services are defective.[2475] Insofar as the card may be used to obtain cash, it will be a debtor-creditor[2476] agreement for unrestricted-use credit.[2477]

A three-party or four-party credit card agreement will likewise normally be for **39-486** running-account credit.[2478] Insofar as the card may be used to obtain goods or services, it will be a debtor-creditor-supplier agreement[2479] for restricted-use credit.[2480] The issuer of the card, as creditor, will be liable, under s.75 of the Consumer Credit Act 1974,[2481] jointly and severally with the supplier in respect of any claim that the debtor may have in respect of a misrepresentation or breach of contract in relation to the transaction financed by the agreement, i.e. the supply of the goods or services. Insofar as the card may be used to obtain cash, the agreement is probably a debtor-creditor[2482] agreement for unrestricted-use credit.[2483]

(ii) Charge card[2484] agreements   Although before the implementation of the **39-487** Consumer Credit Directive[2485] these agreements were often "exempt agreements",[2486] this is no longer generally[2487] the case. Hence they are treated no differently from credit card agreements, except in one important respect: their exemption from the "connected lender" liability under s.75 has been preserved.[2488]

[2470] See above, para.39-061.

[2471] In which case they will be "credit brokers"; cf. (mere promotion) *Brookes v Retail Credit Cards Ltd* [1986] Crim. L.R. 327; above, para.39-231.

[2472] See above, para.39-024.

[2473] See above, para.39-030. It will be a category 12(a) agreement.

[2474] See above, para.39-027.

[2475] i.e. under the Sale of Goods Act 1979, or under the Supply of Goods and Services Act 1982, or at common law.

[2476] See above, para.39-033.

[2477] See above, para.39-029.

[2478] See above, para.39-024.

[2479] See above, para.39-030. It will be a category 12(b) agreement, see above, para.39-031.*Office of Fair Trading v Lloyds TSB Bank Plc* [2006] EWCA Civ 268 (affirmed, on another point: [2007] UKHL 48) confirmed that there were the requisite "arrangements" in a four-party credit card transaction. And see *Bank of Scotland v Truman* [2005] EWHC 583, [2005] C.C.L.R. 3 (still "arrangements" between a fifth party with agency relationship with party to four-party credit card).

[2480] See above, para.39-027.

[2481] See above, para.39-303 (subject, in particular, to the £100 minimum cash price referred to in that section). And it was held that the protection applies even where card (issued under a "United Kingdom credit agreement") finances a "foreign transaction": *Office of Fair Trading v Lloyds TSB Bank Plc* [2007] UKHL 48.

[2482] See above, para.39-033.

[2483] See above, para.39-029.

[2484] See above, para.39-476.

[2485] See above, para.39-011.

[2486] Under the (now repealed) original version of art.3(1)(a)(ii) of the Consumer Credit (Exempt Agreements) Order 1989 (SI 1989/869), see above, para.39-041.

[2487] Unless the agreement falls within any of the general exemptions, see above, paras 39-038 et seq.

[2488] CCA 1974 s.75(3)(b), added on February 1, 2011, by SI 2010/1010 reg.24.

39-488 *(iii)   Debit card[2489] agreements*   give rise to greater difficulties.[2490] If the cardholder has an overdraft facility, then it is clear that, insofar as the card may be used to obtain goods or services from suppliers on credit, there will be a debtor-creditor-supplier agreement[2491] for restricted-use credit.[2492] The issuer of the card will therefore be subject to liability under s.75 of the Consumer Credit Act 1974.[2493] If the cardholder does not have an overdraft facility, the position is less clear as a result of s.14(3) of the 1974 Act, which arguably "deems" credit to arise whenever a debit card is used.[2494] However, the preferred view is that s.14(3) merely clarifies, but only in circumstances where the debtor uses a credit facility, *when* and *by whom* credit is provided (on the supply of the goods or services[2495]). In an EFTPOS transaction, it is clear that the EFTPOS arrangements between the suppliers and the card issuers do not themselves give rise to a debtor-creditor-supplier agreement.[2496] The most significant consequence is that the card issuer, as creditor, will not (merely because of those arrangements) be subject to liability under s.75 of the 1974 Act.[2497]

39-489   Insofar as the debit card may be used to obtain cash,[2498] it will be a debtor-creditor agreement[2499] for unrestricted-use credit.[2500] Insofar as the agreement enables the debtor to overdraw on a current account, the Consumer Credit Act 1974 (especially Pt V) will apply, as modified in relation to such overdraft agreements.[2501]

39-490 *(iv)   Cash card (ATM card)[2502] agreements*   also give rise to some uncertainty. Since withdrawals are normally debited directly to the account (e.g. a current account) of the customer with the issuer of the card, it is necessary to ascertain whether the issuer of the card has agreed to provide the customer with credit, for example, an overdraft, in which case there will be a debtor-creditor agreement[2503] for unrestricted-use credit.[2504] But if the automated teller machine is so programmed as to prevent any withdrawal when the customer's account is overdrawn or which would cause a debit balance to arise on the customer's account, or (semble) if the terms of the agreement are such as to prohibit the use of the card except in respect of a credit balance on the account, then there will be no agreement to provide the customer with credit and no regulated agreement. However, different considerations may apply if the customer may use the card to obtain cash from ATMs of

---

[2489] See above, para.39-477.

[2490] See Guest and Lloyd, *Encyclopedia of Consumer Credit Law* (1975, looseleaf), para.2-015.

[2491] See above, para.39-030 (unless debtor is a body corporate or large partnership). It will be a category 12(b) agreement; see above, para.39-031.

[2492] See above, para.39-027.

[2493] See above, para.39-303.

[2494] It states that the card issuer "shall be taken to provide him with credit drawn on whenever a third party supplies him with cash, goods or services". This provision is not replicated in the *FCA Handbook* Glossary definition of "credit token", see below, para.39-494.

[2495] See previous note: "whenever a third party supplies him ...".

[2496] See CCA 1974 s.187(3A) (inserted by the Banking Act 1987 s.89) which states that "arrangements shall ... be disregarded for the purposes of subs.(1) and (2) if they are arrangements for the electronic transfer of funds from a current account at a bank within the meaning of the Bankers' Books Evidence Act 1879". See above, para.39-030.

[2497] See above, para.39-303.

[2498] See above, para.39-488 as to the uncertainty whether the cardholder must use a credit facility.

[2499] See above, para.39-033.

[2500] See above, para.39-029.

[2501] See above, para.39-300.

[2502] See above, para.39-479.

[2503] See above, para.39-033.

[2504] See above, para.39-029.

banks and building societies other than the issuer of the card. It is possible that a deemed extension of credit may then in some cases[2505] arise under s.14(3) of the 1974 Act,[2506] and if that is the case it is immaterial that there is no agreement by the issuer to provide the customer with credit.

Cash cards operated in connection with current accounts with banks[2507] will, in **39-491** so far as they enable the debtor to overdraw on a current account, be subject to the modified provisions of the regulatory regime (especially Consumer Credit Act 1974 Pt V) applicable to overdraft agreements.[2508]

(vi)   Electronic purse[2509] agreements   In principle, since the cardholder pre-pays **39-492** the value loaded electronically on the card, it would seem that no credit is provided and so there will be no consumer credit agreement. But the provision is not free from doubt.[2510] The only credit that would be provided is if the issuer provides credit facilities to the cardholder when issuing the digital cash.

(vi)   Checks[2511] trading agreements   will be debtor-creditor-supplier agree- **39-493** ments[2512] for restricted-use credit.[2513] The credit is fixed-sum credit.[2514]

"Credit-token" and "credit-token agreements"   The definitions of "credit- **39-494** token"[2515] and "credit-token agreement"[2516] have been referred to previously in this chapter.[2517] It should be noted that the definition of "credit-token" is not limited to a regulated agreement, but only a regulated agreement can be a "credit-token agreement". For credit-token agreements that are (exceptionally) not covered by the Consumer Credit (Agreements) Regulations 2010[2518] and hence subject to the "old" regime,[2519] certain special provisions are made for such agreements.[2520] Moreover, for all credit-token agreements there are certain special requirements as to copies.[2521]

Both two-party, three-party and four-party credit cards will be credit-tokens as **39-495**

[2505] Unless, as in many cases, the cash-dispensing bank acts merely as agent for the issuer of the card.
[2506] See above, para.39-488.
[2507] Or building societies.
[2508] See above, para.39-300.
[2509] See above, para.39-480.
[2510] Owing to the provisions of CCA 1974 ss.14(1)(b), 14(3) of the Act; see Guest and Lloyd, *Encyclopedia of Consumer Credit Law* (1975, looseleaf), para.2-015.
[2511] See above, para.39-481.
[2512] See above, para.39-030. They will be a category 12(b) agreements, see above, para.39-031.
[2513] See above, para.39-027.
[2514] See above, para.39-026.
[2515] CCA 1974 s.14(1), (3), (4). The definition in the *FCA Handbook* Glossary is similar (omitting the provisions in s.14(3), considered above, para.39-488).
[2516] CCA 1974 s.14(2).
[2517] See above, para.39-034. And note that the definition of "relevant voucher" in the Home Credit Market Investigation Order 2007, made by the Competition Commission under the Enterprise Act 2002 ss.161, 164 is in almost identical terms to that of "credit-token" in the CCA 1974.
[2518] SI 2010/1014, above, para.39-082.
[2519] See above, para.39-081.
[2520] See CCA 1974 s.63(4): copy of executed agreement required under CCA 1974 s.63(2) (see above, para.39-088) need not be given within the seven days following the making of the agreement if it is given before or at the time when the credit-token is given to the debtor. And see CCA 1974 s.64(2): the notice of cancellation rights under s.64(1)(b) (see above, para.39-091) need not be sent by post within those seven days if either is sent by post to the debtor before the credit-token is given to him, or if it is sent by post to him together with the credit-token.
[2521] Consumer Credit (Cancellation Notices and Copies of Documents) Regulations 1983 (SI 1983/1557) reg.8 (copies under CCA 1974 s.85).

will charge cards[2522] and, since extended credit is granted, the agreement will (if the debtor is an individual and the agreement is not an exempt agreement) be a regulated agreement[2523] and a credit-token agreement.[2524]

39-496 Debit cards will certainly be credit-tokens if the cardholder has an overdraft and may even be credit-tokens if this is not the case.[2525] Whether or not a debit card agreement is a credit-token agreement depends on whether the agreement is a regulated agreement.[2526]

39-497 Cash (ATM) cards will not be credit-tokens if the card can only be used to effect withdrawals from machines operated by the issuer of the card and only when the account is in credit.[2527] But if the card can be used to effect withdrawals from the machines of others than the issuer of the card, the card may be a credit-token[2528] and the card agreement a credit-token agreement.[2529]

39-498 Electronic purses are probably not credit-tokens.[2530]

39-499 Checks are credit-tokens[2531] and the agreements are credit-token agreements.[2532]

39-500 **Prohibition of unsolicited credit-tokens**[2533]   Under the Consumer Credit Act 1974 s.51, it was formally an offence to give a person a credit-token if he had not asked for it and the request had to be contained in a document signed by the person making the request. When consumer credit regulation was transferred to the FCA[2534] that section was repealed[2535] and its provisions essentially replaced by FCA rules in the *FCA Handbook*.[2536] Hence breach of the prohibition now gives rise to the usual sanctions for breach of FCA rules.[2537]

[2522] Under CCA 1974 s.14(1)(a) or (b) and the equivalent provisions in the *FCA Handbook* Glossary definition of "credit token".

[2523] See above, para.39-017.

[2524] CCA 1974 s.14(2).

[2525] Under s.14(1)(b) and the equivalent provisions in the *FCA Handbook* Glossary definition of "credit token". See above, para.39-488 as to whether CCA 1974 s.14(3) operates to "deem" credit to be provided in all s.14(1)(b) cases.

[2526] See above, para.39-017.

[2527] See CCA 1974 s.14(1)(a) and the equivalent provisions in the *FCA Handbook* Glossary definition of "credit token".

[2528] Under CCA 1974 s.14(1)(b), (4) and the equivalent provisions in the *FCA Handbook* Glossary definition of "credit token".

[2529] See CCA 1974 s.14(3) and above, paras 39-488 and 39-490.

[2530] But again (see above, para.39-488) CCA 1974 s.14(3) may "deem" credit to be provided.

[2531] Under CCA 1974 s.14(1)(a) or (b) and the equivalent provisions in the FCA Glossary definition of "credit token".

[2532] CCA 1974 s.14(2); see above, para.39-034.

[2533] There is a more general prohibition of unsolicited credit in the Financial Services (Distance Marketing) Regulations 2004 (SI 2004/2095) reg.15 (as partly revoked by SI 2008/1277). And see the provision in the Payment Services Regulations 2017 (SI 2017/752) reg.73(1)(b) (below, para.39-517) prohibiting unsolicited "payment instruments", noted in para.39-517, below.

[2534] See above, para.39-002.

[2535] On April 1, 2014 by the Financial Services and Markets Act 2000 (Regulated Activities) (Amendment) (No.2) Order 2013 (SI 2013/1881) art.20(15). But see the Financial Services and Markets Act 2000 (Regulated Activities) (Amendment) Order 2014 (SI 2014/366) art.13: notwithstanding the repeal of s.51, it continued to have effect for the purposes of the Payment Services Regulations 2009 reg.52(a) (disapplication of certain regulations in the case of consumer credit agreements) and hence it continued to apply in relation to regulated credit agreements in place of reg.58(1)(b) of those regulations. However, those regulations have been replaced by SI 2017/752, which result in the similar prohibition in reg.73(1)(b) now applying in all cases: see below, para.39-517.

[2536] See CONC 2.9 (prohibiting the giving of unsolicited credit-tokens by FCA-authorised persons).

[2537] See above, para.39-063. Hence breach is no longer criminal. Breach of the Payment Services Regula-

Restrictions on provision of "credit card cheques" In the wake of disquiet **39-501** about the unsolicited sending of "credit card cheques" by credit card issuers to their cardholders, new Consumer Credit Act 1974 ss.51A–51B were enacted prohibiting[2538] the provision of such cheques unless the recipient had "asked for them" or the underlying credit-token agreement was a "business" agreement. When consumer credit regulation was transferred to the FCA[2539] those sections were repealed[2540] and their provisions were replaced by FCA rules in the *FCA Handbook*.[2541] Hence breach of the prohibition now gives rise to the usual sanctions for breach of FCA rules.[2542]

Acceptance of credit-token The debtor accepts a credit-token when it is signed, **39-502** or a receipt for it is signed, or it is first used, either by the debtor himself or by a person who, pursuant to the agreement, is authorised by him to use it.[2543] Unless the debtor has previously accepted the credit-token, or the use constitutes an acceptance of it by him, he is not liable under a credit-token agreement for use made of the credit-token.[2544]

Misuse of credit-token[2545] Section 84 of the Consumer Credit Act 1974 contains **39-503** provisions designed to limit the debtor's liability for misuse of a credit-token. Although, in principle, the debtor under a regulated consumer credit agreement is not liable to the creditor for any loss arising from use of the credit facility by another person not acting, or to be treated as acting,[2546] as the debtor's agent,[2547] this does not prevent the debtor under a credit-token agreement from being made liable to the extent of £50[2548] (or the credit limit[2549] if lower) for loss to the creditor arising from use of the credit-token[2550] by other persons during a period beginning when the credit-token ceases to be in the possession of any authorised person[2551] and ending when the credit-token is once more in the possession of an authorised person. Hence, misuse, for example, of a lost or stolen credit card by an unauthorised person, will involve the debtor in a maximum liability of £50. But this limitation does not extend to a term of the credit-token agreement which makes the debtor liable (to any extent) for loss to the creditor from use of the credit-token by a person

---

[2538] tions 2017 (SI 2017/752) reg.73(1)(b) may also arise with similar consequences: see below, para.39-517.

[2538] The sanction was criminal but the consequent transactions were not affected.

[2539] See above, para.39-002.

[2540] On April 1, 2014 by the Financial Services and Markets Act 2000 (Regulated Activities) (Amendment) (No.2) Order 2013 (SI 2013/1881) art.20(16).

[2541] See CONC 2.3.5R (restricting the provision of credit card cheques by FCA-authorised persons).

[2542] See above, para.39-063. Hence breach is no longer criminal.

[2543] CCA 1974 s.66(2). The burden of proof is on the creditor: CCA 1974 s.171(4)(a).

[2544] CCA 1974 s.66(1).

[2545] Compare the position in relation to the misuse of "payment instruments" under the Payment Services Regulations 2017 (SI 2017/752), noted below, paras 39-512—39-515.

[2546] Presumably by reason of ostensible authority.

[2547] CCA 1974 s.83(1). See *NRAM Plc v McAdam & Hartley* [2015] EWCA Civ 751, reversing [2014] EWHC 4174 (Comm): (obiter) s.83 does not apply to non-regulated agreements that are documented as regulated agreements.

[2548] The amount was raised from £30 by SI 1983/1571. It was not increased by SI 1998/997.

[2549] See above, para.39-025.

[2550] For the position where two or more credit-tokens are given under one agreement, see CCA 1974 s.84(8).

[2551] The debtor, the creditor, and any person authorised by the debtor to use the credit-token are "authorised persons" CCA 1974 s.84(7).

who acquired possession of it with the debtor's consent,[2552] though without his authority to use it.

39-504   The further protection previously conferred on consumers[2553] by the two sets of regulations made in implementation of two EC Directives on "distance contracts"[2554]: the Consumer Protection (Distance Selling) Regulations 2000[2555] and the Financial Services (Distance Marketing) Regulations 2004[2556] has been revoked.[2557]

39-505   In any event, however, no liability can be imposed on the debtor in respect of any use of the credit-token after the creditor has been given notice that the credit-token has been lost or stolen, or is for any other reason liable to misuse.[2558] Notice may be given orally or in writing,[2559] and takes effect when it is received; but where it is given orally, and the agreement so requires, it is to be treated as not taking effect if not confirmed in writing within seven days.[2560] The credit-token agreement must contain, in the prescribed[2561] manner, particulars of the name, address and telephone number of a person stated to be the person to whom notice is to be given. Failure to comply with this requirement results in the release of the debtor from liability for misuse of the credit-token.[2562]

39-506   Where proceedings are brought by the creditor under a credit-token agreement, if the debtor alleges that any use made of the credit-token was not authorised by him, it is for the creditor to prove either (i) that the use was so authorised; or (ii) that the use occurred before the creditor had been given notice as mentioned above.[2563]

39-507   Any sum paid by the debtor for the issue of the credit-token (such as a "membership" or annual fee) is, to the extent (if any) that it has not been previously offset by use made of the credit-token, to be treated as paid towards satisfaction of any liability of the debtor.[2564]

39-508   It is important, however, to appreciate that, under the 1974 Act,[2565] the limitation of the debtor's liability applies only to loss arising from use of the *credit facility* provided by the creditor to the debtor, and there is nothing in the Act[2566] to prevent the debtor from being made fully liable to the creditor for misuse of a credit-

---

[2552] CCA 1974 s.84(2).

[2553] "Consumer" is defined in reg.3(1) of the 2000 Regulations and reg.2(1) of the 2004 Regulations.

[2554] Defined in both sets of Regulations (in regs 3(1) and 2(1), respectively) as contracts "concluded ... under an organised distance sale or service provision scheme run by the supplier who ... makes exclusive use of ... distance communication".

[2555] SI 2000/2334, as amended by SI 2004/2095 and SI 2005/689. These implemented the Distance Contracts Directive 97/7.

[2556] SI 2004/2095. These implement the Distance Marketing Directive (DMD) 2002/65.

[2557] The relevant provisions were repealed by the Payment Services Regulations 2009 (SI 2009/209) Sch.6 Pt 2.

[2558] CCA 1974 s.84(3).

[2559] CCA 1974 s.84(3).

[2560] CCA 1974 s.84(5).

[2561] By the Consumer Credit (Credit-Token Agreements) Regulations 1983 (SI 1983/1555).

[2562] CCA 1974 s.84(4).

[2563] CCA 1974 s.171(4)(b).

[2564] CCA 1974 s.84(6).

[2565] CCA 1974 s.84 is drafted as an exception to CCA 1974 s.83, and CCA 1974 s.83(1) only applies to "loss arising from use of the credit facility".

[2566] But protection may be afforded for misuse of cards when the account is in credit by (a) the Payment Services Regulations 2009 (see below, paras 39-510 et seq., especially para.39-512) or (b) the *"BCOBS" Module of the Financial Conduct Authority's Handbook* (see above, paras 34-218 et seq.), see BCOBS 5.1.11–5.1.12.

token in connection with a credit balance in favour of the debtor. So, for example, where a cash card is a credit-token, the conditions of use of the card could require the debtor fully to indemnify the creditor against any unauthorised withdrawal of cash while the debtor's account is in credit.[2567]

Issue of new credit-tokens Except in the case of a "small" (under-£50)[2568] credit-token agreement,[2569] if a credit-token (other than the first) is given by the creditor to the debtor, a copy of the executed agreement (if any) and of any other document referred to in it must also be given to the debtor.[2570] Non-compliance with this requirement means that, while the default continues, the creditor is not entitled to enforce the agreement.[2571]

39-509

Payment Services Regulations 2017: general The Payment Services Regulations 2017 (PSRs)[2572] are of relevance to payment cards in that all the cards considered in this section[2573] fall within the definition in those Regulations of a "payment instrument" issued under a "payment services" contract. Hence, such cards are subject to the consumer protection provisions in those Regulations concerning information provision and the rights and liabilities of the parties. Part 6 of the Regulations imposes a number of "information" obligations in relation to payment services provided under a "framework contract" and so is prima facie applicable to the contract between the cardholder and the card issuer. Part 7 of the Regulations regulates the rights and obligations of the parties in relation to the provision of payment services and hence again the legal relationship between the cardholder and the issuer. For example, there are elaborate general provisions concerning the imposition of charges,[2574] consent and withdrawal of consent by the cardholder to a payment transaction,[2575] incorrectly executed payment transactions,[2576] unauthorised payment transactions[2577] and the execution of payment

39-510

[2567] Historically, the old "Lending Code" limited the extent to which a subscribing financial institution could make a consumer liable for misuse of a facility in credit but the Standards of Lending Practice (which replace it, see above, para.39-013) do not contain equivalent explicit constraints.

[2568] See CCA 1974 s.17; above, para.39-048.

[2569] CCA 1974 s.85(3).

[2570] CCA 1974 s.85(1). See also SI 1983/1557 reg.8.

[2571] CCA 1974 s.85(2)(a). Originally, if the default continued for one month, an offence was committed (s.85(2)(b)) but this provision was repealed by the Consumer Protection from Unfair Trading Regulations 2008 (SI 2008/1277) reg.30(1) and Sch.2 para.22.

[2572] SI 2017/752, replacing the PSR 2009 (SI 2009/209). See also above, paras 34-224 et seq.

[2573] There is an exclusion for store cards issued by a retailer for use in his store and for cards that can only be used in a limited number of outlets or for a limited range of goods and services and for ATM cards: PSRs Sch.1 paras 2(k) and (o).

[2574] PSRs reg.66. This applies both to agreements regulated under the consumer credit regime and (see PSRs reg.65) to "low value payment instruments" unless disapplied by contract. But see reg.63(5)(a) (contracting out: general).

[2575] PSRs reg.67. This also applies both to agreements regulated under the consumer credit regime and (see PSR reg.65) to "low value payment instruments" unless disapplied by contract. But see reg.63(5)(a) (contracting out: general). Reg.76 requires the card issuer to refund unauthorised transactions, but this does not apply to agreements regulated under the consumer credit regime (see reg.64), which have their own provisions (CCA 1974 ss.83 and 84, see above, para.39-503).

[2576] PSRs reg.74. This is disapplied (reg.64(3)) in relation to agreements regulated under the consumer credit regime (in the light of CCA 1974 ss.66, 83 and 84, see above, paras 39-502- -39-503), but (see PSRs reg.65) it applies to "low value payment instruments" unless disapplied by contract. Contracting out is generally (but see reg.63(5)(b)) not permitted.

[2577] PSRs regs 74–80.

transactions.[2578] Contracting-out of most of these protections[2579] is permitted, unless the "payment services user" is a "consumer", a "micro-enterprise" or a "charity", terms that are all defined in the Regulations.[2580]

39-511 **Relationship with consumer credit regulatory regime** If payment cards are issued under "regulated agreements" within the meaning of the consumer credit regulatory regime,[2581] then the PSRs consumer protection provisions are generally excluded as they would otherwise duplicate the provisions of that regime.[2582] In addition, the PSRs provisions are significantly modified in relation to certain "low-value payment instruments", that is cards that can be used only to execute individual payment transactions of €60 or less,[2583] or have a spending limit of €300 or less[2584] or (in the case of electronic purses) that store funds that do not exceed €500.[2585] Broadly speaking, only minimal information need be provided[2586] and contracting-out of some of the provisions is permitted.[2587]

39-512 **Payment Services Regulations 2017: misuse of cards** The PSRs provide a comprehensive liability framework in relation to the misuse of those payment cards within their scope. First, express obligations are imposed on the cardholder both to "take all reasonable steps" to keep his personalised security credentials (for example, his PIN) safe[2588] and to notify the issuer "in the agreed manner and without undue delay" once he becomes aware of the loss, theft, misappropriation or unauthorised use of the card.[2589] These obligations apply even in relation to "credit tokens" covered by the consumer credit regulatory regime.[2590]

39-513 Except in the case of agreements that are regulated by the consumer credit regime (which has other detailed provisions concerning credit token misuse[2591]), failure to comply with these PSRs obligations "with intent or gross negligence" or acting "fraudulently" renders the cardholder liable for *all* losses incurred in respect of an unauthorised transaction.[2592] Corresponding obligations are imposed on the card issuer to ensure that "appropriate means are available at all times" to so notify of pos-

---

[2578] PSRs regs 81–84, applicable also both to agreements regulated under the consumer credit regime and (see PSRs reg.65) to "low value payment instruments" unless disapplied by contract. But see reg.63(5)(a) (contracting out permitted to some extent).

[2579] Contracting-out is permitted in relation to all of Pt 6 (information provisions, see reg.40(7)) but some provisions in Pt 7 are mandatory (see especially reg.71 (limits on use of cards), reg.72 (obligations of cardholder), reg.73 (obligations of card issuer), reg.74 (notification of errors) and reg.76 (liability of issuer)).

[2580] PSRs reg.2(1). A "consumer" is "an individual … acting for purposes other than a trade, business or profession".

[2581] See above, paras 39-483 et seq.

[2582] PSRs regs 41 and 64.

[2583] If the payment transaction is executed wholly in the UK, otherwise the limit is €30.

[2584] If the payment transaction is executed wholly in the UK, otherwise the limit is €150.

[2585] PSRs regs 42 and 65. There are special provisions in relation to liability for misuse in relation to electronic purses in reg.65(3).

[2586] PSRs reg.42(2)(a).

[2587] PSRs reg.42(2)(b), (c) and reg.65(2). Note also reg.65(3) (electronic money).

[2588] PSRs reg.72(3).

[2589] PSRs reg.72(1).

[2590] See above, para.39-494. Moreover, contracting-out (except in the case of non-consumers) is not permitted (see reg.63(5)) but as regards "low value instruments", contracting out of the second obligation (in reg.72(1)(b) (obligation to notify loss or misuse of instrument)) is permitted (see reg.65(2)(a).

[2591] See above, para.39-503.

[2592] PSRs reg.77(3), see below. The issuer must "must provide supporting evidence" of any fraud or

sible misuse[2593] and to prevent any use once notification has been made.[2594] The issuer is also obliged to ensure that personalised security features "are not accessible" to persons other than the cardholder[2595] and the issuer bears the risk of sending the card or any personalised security features.[2596] If the cardholder disputes a transaction, the onus is on the issuer to prove that the transaction was "authenticated", accurately recorded and "not affected by a technical breakdown or some other deficiency".[2597] And the mere use of the card as recorded by the issuer "is not in itself necessarily sufficient" to prove either that the transaction was authorised by the payer or that the payer acted fraudulently or failed with intent or gross negligence to comply with his notification obligation[2598] so as to make him liable to an unlimited extent.[2599] Again, all these card issuer obligations also apply in relation to regulated agreements covered by the consumer credit regulatory regime.[2600]

Comparison with consumer credit Act regulatory regime   The PSRs liability **39-514** provisions for misuse of cards are similar, but by no means identical, to those applicable to credit tokens issued under "credit-token agreements" in the Consumer Credit Act 1974.[2601] To avoid duplication, if the card is issued under an agreement that is regulated by the consumer credit regulatory regime, the 1974 Act provisions apply instead of those in the PSRs.[2602] The overall result under both liability regimes is similar but there are significant differences in the detail. First, there is a general provision in the PSRs[2603] requiring the card issuer to refund "as soon as practicable"[2604] transactions that are "not authorised" in accordance with the PSRs' provision relating to the giving (and withdrawal) of consent to payment transactions by the cardholder.[2605] This corresponds to the general provision in s.83 of the 1974 Act[2606] but there are clear differences in that s.83 only applies to the use of a "credit facility"[2607] and says nothing about the timing of refunds.

Secondly, as is the case under the 1974 Act, the PSRs provide derogations from **39-515** this general principle so as to impose a degree of liability on the cardholder. However, these PSRs derogations apply as a matter of law and so, unlike the position under the 1974 Act, do not need to be contractually imposed. Moreover, although they are similar in effect to those under the 1974 Act, there are differences in the detail. Thus the cardholder is generally liable up to a maximum of £35

---

failure to comply he alleges: reg.75(4).

[2593] PSRs reg.73(1)(c), and, on request, to provide the cardholder with the means to prove that such notification was made (reg.73(1)(d)).

[2594] PSRs reg.73(1)(f).

[2595] PSRs reg.73(1)(a).

[2596] PSRs reg.73(2).

[2597] PSRs reg.75(1).

[2598] i.e. his obligation to notify on becoming aware of possible misuse imposed by reg.72(1)(b), see above.

[2599] Under PSRs reg.77(2), see below.

[2600] Moreover, contracting-out (except in the case of non-consumers) is not permitted in relation to obligations in reg.73 (although it is allowed for those in reg.75) and, as regards "low value instruments", some contracting out is permitted. See PSRs reg.63(3) and reg.65(2), respectively.

[2601] See above, para.39-503.

[2602] PSRs reg.64(3) and (4).

[2603] PSRs reg.76.

[2604] "… and in any event no later than the end of the business day following the day on which it becomes aware of the unauthorised transaction": reg.76(2). But see the qualifications in reg.76(3)–(5).

[2605] In PSRs reg.67.

[2606] See para.39-503, above.

[2607] See above, para.39-508.

for loss arising from the use of a lost, stolen or misappropriated[2608] card.[2609] Moreover, under the PSRs the cardholder is liable for *all* loss in two cases. The first is where he has acted "fraudulently", a term that is not defined but that clearly connotes knowing that misuse is occurring. The second case where the cardholder is liable for all the loss is where he has "with intent or gross negligence" failed to comply with his obligations[2610] to "take all reasonable steps' to keep his personalised security features safe and to notify the issuer "in the agreed manner and without undue delay" once he becomes aware of the possible misuse of the card.[2611] Where the issuer has not complied with the obligation to ensure that "appropriate means are available at all times" to so notify of possible misuse,[2612] then, unless the cardholder has acted fraudulently, he is not liable for any loss (not even for the first £35).[2613] And again, unless the cardholder has acted fraudulently, his liability terminates (even for the first £35) when he gives the issuer notice "in the agreed manner"[2614] of possible misuse.

39-516   There is no provision in the PSRs that corresponds directly to s.66 of the 1974 Act, which only imposes liability on a cardholder once he has "accepted" the card.[2615] However, the PSRs state that the issuer is to bear the risk of sending the card or any personalised security features[2616] and the burden is on him to prove that any transaction was "authenticated".[2617]

39-517   Payment Services Regulations 2017: unsolicited payment cards   The PSRs forbid the sending of an unsolicited "payment instrument"[2618] except by way of replacement of one already issued.[2619]

39-518   Payment Services Regulations 2017: the card agreement   Card agreements are "framework contracts" for the purposes of the PSRs. Hence the relevant "information" provisions in Pt 6[2620] of those regulations apply. However, again to avoid duplication, where the same information is required to be provided both by Pt 6 and by the consumer credit regime, if it is provided in compliance with the consumer credit regime in a manner that complies with Pt 6, it need not be provided twice.[2621] Hence where the PSRs require "extra" items of information not required by the consumer credit regime, these "extras" must also be given in the case of regulated

---

[2608] "… where the [cardholder] has failed to keep the personalised security features … safe."
[2609] PSRs reg.77(1). The corresponding provision in the 1974 Act, s.84, has been altered from £50 to £35 by PSRs reg.156 Sch.8 para.1(b) but refers to the card not being in the cardholder's "possession".
[2610] Under PSRs reg.72, see above, para.39-512.
[2611] PSRs reg.77(3). The corresponding provision in the 1974 Act refers to losses caused by misuse of the card by a person who acquires possession with the cardholder's consent.
[2612] Imposed by PSRs reg.73(1)(c).
[2613] PSRs reg.77(4)(b).
[2614] "[U]nder" PSRs reg.72(1)(b) which refers to notice "in the agreed manner and without undue delay".
[2615] See above, para.39-502.
[2616] PSRs reg.73(2).
[2617] PSRs reg.75(1).
[2618] See above, para.39-510.
[2619] PSRs reg.73(1)(b). Breach is actionable as a breach of statutory duty by a private person suffering loss (see PSRs reg.148(1)(b)). Compare the prohibition (with the same sanction) in the *FCA Handbook*, CONC replacing the repealed CCA 1974 s.51, noted above, para.39-500.
[2620] See above, para.39-510.
[2621] PSRs reg.41(3). Moreover, reg.50 (changes in contractual information) and reg.51 (termination of framework contract) do not apply: reg.41(2).

agreements.[2622] In outline, the PSRs "information" requirements are as follows. First, pre-contracting information (which may take the form of the draft contract) must usually be provided "in good time" to the cardholder before he is bound by the contract.[2623] Secondly, the cardholder is given the right, during the contract and free of charge,[2624] to obtain certain information and the terms of the contract.[2625] Thirdly, there are elaborate provisions concerning the notification of variations in the contractual information and terms.[2626] Finally, there are provisions concerning information to be provided in relation to each payment transaction[2627] and provisions governing the termination of the contract by either party.[2628] Note also the rights and obligations imposed by Pt 7 of the PSRs, some of which are again excluded or modified in relation to agreements that are "regulated agreements" under the consumer credit regulatory regime.[2629]

7. MORTGAGES OF PERSONAL PROPERTY

Bills of Sale Act 1882[2630]   Credit provided on the security of personal chattels[2631] **39-519** that are retained in the possession of the debtor is likely to fall within the control of the Bills of Sale Act (1878) Amendment Act 1882 if the transaction is contained in, or represented by, a document. Under this Act, a bill of sale given as security for the payment of money by the grantor of the bill must be in the statutory form,[2632] and it must be attested[2633] and registered.[2634] If it is not in the statutory form, it is absolutely void, although the creditor can recover the money lent, with reasonable

---

[2622] For example, any information e.g. as to interest and currency exchange rates in PSRs Sch.4 must be provided under PSRs regs 48 and 49.

[2623] PSRs reg.48 (the requisite information is set out in Sch.4)—unless this cannot be done in the case of a "distance" contract concluded at the user's request, in which case it must be provided immediately after the contract is made. See also reg.55 (communication of information). Reg.48 does not generally apply to CCA 1974 regulated agreements, which have their own requirements as to pre-contract information (see above, para.39-076), but the "extra" PSRs information, e.g. as to details of interest and exchange rates, must be supplied.

[2624] PSRs reg.56(1).

[2625] PSRs reg.49 (the requisite information is set out in Sch.4). Further information may be charged for, at cost: reg.56(2). See also reg.55 (communication of information). Reg.49 does not apply to agreements regulated under the consumer credit regime (reg.41), which have their own information requirements (see above, paras 39-127 et seq.), except in so far as Sch.4 requires "extra" information to be provided.

[2626] PSRs reg.50. Reg.50 does not apply to agreements regulated under the consumer credit regime (reg.41), which have their own provisions as to variation (CCA 1974 s.82, above, paras 39-145 et seq.).

[2627] PSRs regs 52–54. See also reg.55 (communication of information).

[2628] PSRs reg.51. Reg.51 does not apply to agreements regulated under the consumer credit regime which have their own provisions as to termination (CCA 1974 s.87, 98 above, paras 39-166 and 39-172).

[2629] See PSRs reg.64. and above, para.39-511.

[2630] It was expected that the Bills of Sale Acts would be replaced by a new Goods Mortgages Act which was expected to introduce protection measures for borrowers mortgaging their personal property (e.g. their cars under so-called "log-book loans", see below para.39-521) similar to those available under the Consumer Credit Act 1974 in relation to hire purchase and conditional sale (see above, paras 39-356 et seq. and 39-443 et seq.). However, in May 2018 the government announced that it had abandoned this proposal.

[2631] Bills of Sale Act 1878 s.4; Bills of Sale Act 1890.

[2632] Bills of Sale Act (1878) Amendment Act 1882 s.9 and Sch.

[2633] ss.8, 10.

[2634] ss.8, 11.

interest, as money had and received.[2635] If it is in the statutory form, but is not duly attested or not duly registered, it is void as regards the personal chattels comprised in it, that is to say, the security is rendered void, although the creditor remains entitled to enforce the personal covenants contained in the bill, such as those which relate to the repayment of money advanced and the payment of interest.[2636]

39-520   Such a bill of sale cannot, in general, include any reference to after-acquired chattels[2637]; and a bill of sale made or given in consideration of any sum under £30 is void.[2638]

39-521   The 1882 Act has been interpreted with great strictness, and the technicality of this branch of the law is notorious.[2639] While a substantial number of security bills are in fact registered each year, the Act has severely inhibited the use of chattel mortgages as security for credit transactions, although so-called "log-book loans", where a loan is provided on the security of a car, are not uncommon.[2640] But the Act does not apply to mortgages or charges of goods created by companies incorporated under the Companies Acts.[2641]

39-522   **Consumer credit**   The 1882 Act was not repealed by the Consumer Credit Act 1974. Agreements within the control of the consumer credit regulatory regime which are secured by a bill of sale given as security for the payment of money must therefore comply with the requirements (including those relating to security) of that regime as well as those of the Act of 1882. More particularly, however, para.1 of s.7 of the 1882 Act (which entitles a grantee of a bill of sale to take possession of the chattels assigned in the event of default in payment or in performance of any covenant contained in the bill) is, by s.7A(1) of the Act,[2642] made inapplicable to a default relating to a bill of sale given by way of security for the payment of money under a regulated agreement to which s.87(1)[2643] of the Consumer Credit Act 1974 applies—(a) unless the restriction imposed by s.88(2) of that Act (preventing certain action before the expiry of time for remedying the default)[2644] has ceased to apply to the bill of sale; or (b) if, by virtue of s.89 of that Act, the default is to be treated as not having occurred.[2645] Further, where para.1 of s.7 of the 1882 Act does apply, application by the debtor for relief must be made in the case of such a bill of sale to the county court instead of to the High Court as provided in the 1882 Act.[2646]

[2635] *Davies v Rees* (1886) 17 Q.B.D. 408; *North Central Wagon & Finance Co Ltd v Brailsford* [1962] 1 W.L.R. 1288. See also *Bradford Advance Co Ltd v Ayers* [1924] W.N. 152.

[2636] s.8; *Heseltine v Simmons* [1892] 2 Q.B. 547.

[2637] s.5. There will also (semble) be a breach of ss.4 and 9 of the Act, and the bill will be void: *Thomas v Kelly* (1888) 13 App. Cas. 506.

[2638] s.12.

[2639] See Graham S McBain, "Repealing the Bills of Sale Acts", [2011] J.B.L. 475.

[2640] See, for example, *Welcome Financial Services Ltd v Nine Regions Ltd (t/a Log Book Loans)* [2010] 2 Lloyd's Rep. 426; *Evans v Finance-U-Ltd* [2013] EWCA Civ 869.

[2641] *Re Standard Manufacturing Co* [1891] 1 Ch. 627; Bills of Sale Act (1878) Amendment Act 1882 s.17. But a charge created by a company must be registered under Companies Act 2006 s.860 (see the previous more specific provision in Companies Act 2006 s.860(7)(b) (replacing s.396(1)(e) of the Companies Act 1985) cf. *Stoneleigh Finance Ltd v Phillips* [1965] 2 Q.B. 537.

[2642] Added by s.192 of and Sch.4 para.1 to the Consumer Credit Act 1974 from May 19, 1985: SI 1983/1551 (c.44).

[2643] See above, para.39-166.

[2644] See above, para.39-167.

[2645] See above, para.39-171.

[2646] Bills of Sale Act (1878) Amendment Act 1882 s.7A(2) (added by s.192 of and Sch.4 para.1 to the Consumer Credit Act 1974).

Distress As noted above, a landlord's power at common law to distrain upon all **39-523** goods found upon the demised premises has now been abolished.[2647] Historically, goods comprised in a bill of sale were excluded from the protection of the Law of Distress Amendment Act 1908 except during the period between the service of a default notice[2648] under s.87 of the Consumer Credit Act 1974 in respect of the goods and the date on which the notice expired or was earlier complied with.[2649]

Ships or vessels Transfers or assignments of any ship or vessel or any share **39-524** thereof fall outside the Bills of Sale Acts.[2650] A mortgage of a registered ship or a share therein is governed by the Merchant Shipping Act 1995.[2651] A mortgage of an unregistered vessel may be effected at common law.[2652]

Aircraft The mortgaging of aircraft registered in the United Kingdom national- **39-525** ity register is governed by the Civil Aviation Act 1982[2653] and orders made relating thereto.[2654] The Bills of Sale Acts do not apply to such mortgages.[2655]

Agricultural charges An agricultural charge on farming stock and assets is not **39-526** within the Bills of Sale Acts[2656] but must be registered in the register of agricultural charges at the Land Registry.[2657]

Mortgage or charge of choses in action A mortgage or charge of a chose in ac- **39-527** tion,[2658] e.g. a debt, life insurance policy,[2659] a contractual right, share in a company, etc. if made by an individual, is outside the Bills of Sale Act 1882[2660] but may be within the consumer credit regulatory regime.[2661]

Book debts A general assignment of book debts by a trader may in certain **39-528** circumstances require registration as if the assignment were an absolute bill of sale[2662] and a charge on book debts of a company or of certain other intangible

---

[2647] See above, para.39-427.

[2648] See above, para.39-166.

[2649] Law of Distress Amendment Act 1908 s.4A(2) (added by s.192 of and Sch.4 para.5 to the Consumer Credit Act 1974). See also s.4 (as amended by s.192(4) of and Sch.5 to the 1974 Act).

[2650] Bills of Sale Act 1878 s.4.

[2651] s.16 and Sch.1. See also Companies Act 2006 s.860 (previously the more specific s.860(7)(h) (previously Companies Act 1985 s.396(1)(h))).

[2652] The exception in s.4 of the Bills of Sale Act 1878 was not limited to transfers or assignments within the Merchant Shipping Act 1894, nor were the words "ship or vessel" limited to ships registered or registrable under the 1894 Act: *Union Bank of London v Lenanton* (1878) 3 C.P.D. 213; *Gapp v Bond* (1887) 19 Q.B.D. 200.

[2653] s.86.

[2654] Mortgaging of Aircraft Order (SI 1972/1268) as amended by SI 1981/611.

[2655] SI 1972/1268 para.16(1). But see Companies Act 2006 s.860 (previously the more specific s.860(7)(h) (replacing Companies Act 1985 s.396(1)(h)), above.

[2656] Agricultural Credits Act 1928 s.8(1).

[2657] s.9.

[2658] See Vol.I, Ch.19.

[2659] Policies of Assurance Act 1867; see below, para.42-067.

[2660] Bills of Sale Act 1878 s.4; *Re Isaacson* [1895] 1 Q.B. 33.

[2661] But a mortgage or charge of a chose in action is not a pledge: see above, para.39-194.

[2662] Insolvency Act 1986 s.344. See Vol.I, para.19-063.

moveable property vested in a company must be registered under the Companies Act 2006.[2663]

8. MORTGAGES OF LAND

39-529 **Consumer credit regulation** The Consumer Credit Act 1974 (CCA 1974) can apply to an agreement notwithstanding that it is secured by a mortgage or charge on land or relates to an advance for the purchase of land.[2664] But certain land mortgage transactions are "exempt agreements" under the regime.[2665] Most importantly[2666] most residential mortgages[2667] and so-called "regulated home purchase plans",[2668] are "exempt agreements" for the purposes of the regime because they are regulated under a special regime established under the Financial Services and Market Act 2000 (FSMA 2000). Hence there are presently two statutory regimes for the regulation of land mortgages, both now administered by the Financial Conduct Authority.[2669] Other categories of "exempt" land mortgages are considered above.[2670] Moreover, land mortgages may take advantage of the more general exemptions for "high net worth" debtors[2671] and for credit agreements entered into for the debtor's business purposes.[2672] Although otherwise not covered by the CCA 1974 regime, such exempt agreements (apart from those regulated under the FSMA 2000 regime[2673]) are nevertheless not excepted from the "unfair relationship" provisions.[2674]

39-530 **Impact of Consumer Credit Directive** The Consumer Credit Directive[2675] does not apply to land mortgages. Hence, its implementation did not require changes to the old consumer credit regime applicable to mortgages and this generally remained applicable to them. Hence, the new "Directive" provisions, such as the new duties

---

[2663] s.860, previously the more specific s.860(7)(f). See Vol.I, para.19-066.

[2664] See Guest and Lloyd, *Encyclopedia of Consumer Credit Law* (1975, looseleaf), paras 2-059, 2-061, 2-066, 2-068, 2-127; Goode, *Consumer Credit: Law and Practice*, Pt C, Ch.38.

[2665] See above, paras 39-038 et seq.

[2666] See above, para.39-039. The relevant provision is now in the Regulated Activities Order 2001 (SI 2001/544) ("RAO") art.60C(2).

[2667] i.e. "regulated mortgage contracts" within the RAO art.61 as amended by SI 2001/3544 art.8 and SI 2006/2383 art.17.

[2668] Within the RAO art.63F(3)(a) as added (on April 6, 2007) by SI 2006/2383 art.18.

[2669] Since the transfer of consumer credit regulation from the OFT to the FCA: see above, para.39-002.

[2670] para.39-039. There is also a special exemption for so-called "investment mortgages": RAO art.60D, see above, para.39-046.

[2671] See above, para.39-045. The relevant provision is in the RAO art.60H, as amended on March 21, 2016, when the Mortgage Credit Directive (see above, para.39-003) was implemented so as to ensure that the exemption is compatible with it: SI 2015/910 art.3 and Sch.1 para.4(18).

[2672] See above, para.39-047. The relevant provision is in the RAO art.60C(3)–(7) Moreover, second charge business loans are not "regulated mortgage contracts": see new RAO art.61A(1)(c), added by SI 2015/910 art.3 and Sch.1 para.4(22).

[2673] See CCA 1974 s.140A(5). Hence when the Mortgage Credit Directive (see above, para.39-003 and below para.39-428) was implemented on March 21, 2016 and second charge residential loans become regulated under FSMA 2000, they lost the protection of those provisions.

[2674] See above, paras 39-212 et seq. For the application of those provisions to land mortgages, see *Consolidated Finance Ltd v Hunter* [2010] B.P.I.R. 1322, Macclesfield Cty Ct; *Paragon Mortgages Ltd v McEwan-Peters* [2011] EWHC 2491 (Comm). See also McMurtry, "Consumer Credit Act mortgages: unfair terms, time orders and judicial discretion" [2010] J.B.L. 107.

[2675] See above, para.39-011.

of pre-contractual explanation[2676] and of creditworthiness assessment[2677] and the new right to *part* settle a regulated agreement[2678] do not apply to agreements secured on land. However, as will be noted further below, mortgagees may opt into the new Disclosure of Information Regulations 2010[2679] and, hence, into the new Agreements Regulations 2010.[2680] In such a case, the general Total Charge for Credit rules[2681] will then apply to determine the "total charge for credit" and "APR".

The Mortgage Credit Directive   The Mortgage Credit Directive[2682] applies to   **39-531** most consumer residential land mortgages.[2683] As the UK already had a well-developed residential land mortgage regulatory regime under the 2000 Act, it was decided that implementation be achieved by modifying that regime.[2684] Moreover, the opportunity was taken to extend that regime to those (second charge) residential mortgages originally within the CCA 1974 regime. This was achieved by altering the definition of "regulated mortgage contract" under the 2000 regime to cover all mortgages of land in the EEA where at least 40 per cent of the land is used as a dwelling.[2685] Hence such "regulated mortgage contracts" are exempt from the CCA 1974 regime.[2686] In addition, as the Directive permits buy-to-let residential mortgages to be subject to an "appropriate framework" rather than the requirements of the Directive,[2687] the UK decided to introduce a special regime (a modified version of "full" FSMA 2000 regulation requiring registration rather than Pt 4A permission) applicable to businesses lending to consumers for buy-to-let purposes.[2688]

Promotion   Since the transfer of consumer credit regulation to the FCA,[2689] the   **39-532** advertising of residential land mortgages has been regulated as "financial promotion" under the Financial Services and Markets Act 2000.[2690] Hence the implementation on the Mortgage Credit Directive[2691] had little effect in this regard.[2692]

Form, etc   The requirements of the 1974 Act relating to the form and content,   **39-533**

[2676] *FCA Handbook*, CONC 4.2 and 4.3, see above, para.39-077.

[2677] *FCA Handbook*, CONC 5 and 6.2, see above, para.39-078.

[2678] See above, para.39-157.

[2679] SI 2010/1013, as amended by SI 2010/1969 regs 31–40 and SI 2011/11 reg.8 (see above, para.39-076).

[2680] SI 2010/1014, as amended by SI 2010/1969 regs 41–45 (see above, para.39-082).

[2681] Above, para.39-059 and not the Total Charge for Credit Rules applicable to regulated mortgage contracts.

[2682] Directive 2014/17/EU.

[2683] See Directive 2014/17/EU art.3(1) and note the exemptions/qualifications in art.3(2). It was implemented on March 21, 2016: see next note.

[2684] See in particular the legislative amendments in the Mortgage Credit Directive Order 2015 (SI 2015/910). See also the amendments to the *FCA Handbook*.

[2685] See the amendment to be made to RAO art.61(3) by SI 2015/910 art.3 and Sch.1 para.4(21). But note the exclusions in the new RAO art.61A, added by SI 2015/910 art.3 and Sch.1 para.4(22).

[2686] See above, para.39-039.

[2687] Directive 2014/17/EU art. 4.

[2688] See Mortgage Credit Directive Order 2015 (SI 2015/910) Pt 3 and Sch.2 (and the FCA rules made thereunder).

[2689] See above, para.39-002.

[2690] See above, para.39-067.

[2691] Directive 2014/17/EU, see above, para.39-531.

[2692] Although note the amendment to the FPO made by SI 2015/910 art.3 and Sch.1 para.12.

signature, supply of copies, etc. of the agreement and of the security[2693] apply where a regulated agreement is secured by a land mortgage.[2694] As land mortgages are outside the scope of the Consumer Credit Directive,[2695] the old Consumer Credit (Disclosure of Information) Regulations 2004,[2696] the old Consumer Credit (Agreements) Regulations 1983,[2697] and the old copy requirements in ss.61–64[2698] prima facie remain applicable to land mortgages within the 1974 regime. However, lenders under such mortgagees may choose to opt into and comply with the new "Consumer Credit Directive" regime by providing pre-contract information in compliance with the new Consumer Credit (Disclosure of Information) Regulations 2010,[2699] unless the agreement is one to which s.58 applies,[2700] in which case (as the Disclosure of Information Regulations do not apply to such mortgages[2701]) the mortgagee may opt-in by providing a copy of the unexecuted agreement complying with the Agreement Regulations 2010.[2702] If the mortgagee has chosen to opt into the Directive regime, then the new Consumer Credit (Agreements) Regulations 2010,[2703] and the new copy requirement in s.61A[2704] (unless s.58 applies to the agreement) will also become applicable. Finally, the "over-running" information requirements[2705] are modified in relation to overdrafts secured on land.

39-534 **Cancellation** The right to cancel a regulated agreement conferred in certain circumstances by s.67 of the 1974 Act[2706] is removed where the agreement is secured on land, or is a restricted-use credit agreement to finance the purchase of land, or is an agreement for a bridging loan in connection with the purchase of land.[2707] Cancellation of an executed agreement would cause considerable difficulty in relation to mortgages and charges on land. But the right of cancellation is in part replaced by special provisions that give to the debtor an opportunity for withdrawal from a prospective land mortgage.

39-535 **Special "pause" provisions**[2708] These special provisions in principle apply in a case where a prospective regulated agreement is to be secured on land (the

---

[2693] See above, paras 39-184 et seq.

[2694] See also *United Bank of Kuwait Plc v Sahib* [1997] Ch. 107 (equitable mortgage outside the Act made by informal deposit of title deeds void for non-compliance with the requirements of s.2(1) of the Law of Property (Miscellaneous Provisions) Act 1989).

[2695] See above, para.39-011 and below para.39-535.

[2696] SI 2004/1481 (see above, para.39-076).

[2697] SI 1983/1553 (see above, para.39-081). The old Consumer Credit (Total Charge for Credit) Regulations 1980 (SI 1980/51), now replicated in the *FCA Handbook*, also apply (see above, para.39-059.

[2698] Above, paras 39-088—39-090.

[2699] SI 2010/1013 (see above, para.39-076).

[2700] Below, para.39-535.

[2701] But see below, para.39-535.

[2702] SI 2010/1014, as amended by SI 2010/1969 regs 41–45, above, para.39-082.

[2703] As well as the new Consumer Credit (Total Charge for Credit) Regulations 2010 (SI 2010/1011), now replicated in the *FCA Handbook*, see above, para.39-059.

[2704] Above, para.39-092.

[2705] Now in the *FCA Handbook*, CONC 4.7 and CONC 6.3.3 and 6.3.4, see above, para.39-127.

[2706] See above, para.39-102. The new 14-day "right of withdrawal" introduced by CCA 1974 s.66A as a result of the implementation of the Consumer Credit Directive (see above, paras 39-011 and 39-101) does not apply to land mortgages.

[2707] CCA 1974 s.67(a).

[2708] For the problems associated with these provisions, see Guest and Lloyd, *Encyclopedia of Consumer Credit Law* (1975, looseleaf), paras 2-059, 2-062.

"mortgaged land").[2709] The procedure is then as follows: the creditor or owner must give the debtor or hirer an advance copy of the unexecuted agreement which contains notice in the prescribed[2710] form indicating the right of the debtor or hirer to withdraw from the prospective agreement, and how and when the right is exercisable. This copy must be given to him *before* the unexecuted agreement is sent to him for his signature, and it must be accompanied by a copy of any other document[2711] referred to in the unexecuted agreement, e.g. a copy of the deed of mortgage or charge.[2712] Not less than seven days after this copy has been given, the unexecuted agreement must be sent to the debtor or hirer for his signature.[2713] The debtor must be allowed a period ("the consideration period") in which to consider, in isolation, whether or not he wishes to go through with the transaction. The consideration period starts with the giving of the advance copy as mentioned above and ends at the expiry of seven days after the day on which the unexecuted agreement is sent to him for his signature, or on its return after signature by him, whichever first occurs.[2714] During the consideration period the creditor or owner must refrain from approaching the debtor or hirer, whether in person, by telephone or letter, or in any other way, except in response to a specific request made by the debtor or hirer after the beginning of the consideration period,[2715] Further, no notice of withdrawal must have been received by the creditor or owner before the sending of the unexecuted agreement.[2716] This procedure is very elaborate and cumbrous. Since an advance copy, and copies under ss.62 and 63 of the Act, must be sent to each debtor,[2717] no less than six copies may be required where there are joint mortgagors.[2718] The procedure is no doubt designed to ensure that borrowers are not exposed to undue, or, indeed any, pressure; but it also places a considerable period of delay in the path of those who wish to obtain immediate finance. The special pause provisions do not, however, apply to a restricted-use credit agreement to finance the purchase of the mortgaged land, or to an agreement for a bridging loan in connection with the purchase of the mortgaged land or other land.[2719]

Failure to comply A failure to comply with the special pause provisions means that the agreement is not properly executed.[2720] It is enforceable against the debtor or hirer on an order of the court only.[2721] The security,[2722] so far as it is provided in relation to the agreement, is enforceable where such an order has been made, but

39-536

[2709] CCA 1974 s.58(1).

[2710] i.e. prescribed by the Consumer Credit (Cancellation Notices and Copies of Documents) Regulations 1983 (SI 1983/1557), especially reg.4 (as amended by SI 2004/3236 art.6(3)) and Sch. Pt I paras 1, 2.

[2711] See above, para.39-087, and CCA 1974 s.180.

[2712] CCA 1974 s.58(1). The copy must be a "true" copy (SI 1983/1557 reg.3(1)), i.e. complete except for execution, and not merely the form of the mortgage or charge.

[2713] CCA 1974 s.61(2)(b). The unexecuted agreement may now be transmitted in electronic form: SI 2004/3236 art.2(2).

[2714] CCA 1974 s.61(3).

[2715] CCA 1974 s.61(2)(c).

[2716] CCA 1974 s.61(2)(d).

[2717] See CCA 1974 s.185.

[2718] But see the alleviation as to the supply of documents referred to in the agreement by an amendment of the Consumer Credit (Cancellation Notices and Copies of Documents) Regulations 1983 (SI 1983/1557), effected by SI 1989/591.

[2719] CCA 1974 ss.58(2), 61(2)(a).

[2720] CCA 1974 s.61(2).

[2721] CCA 1974 s.65(1). A retaking of land to which a regulated agreement relates is an enforcement of the agreement: s.65(2). See CPR Pt 7 PD 7B 3.2; Pt 55 PD 55; and *National Guardian Mortgage*

not otherwise.[2723] And where an application for an order is dismissed, except on technical grounds only, the security is rendered invalid.[2724]

39-537 **Enforcement** Section 126 of the Consumer Credit Act 1974[2725] renders a land mortgage securing one of three categories of agreement enforceable on an order of the court only. Those three categories are: (a) a regulated agreement[2726]; (b) a regulated mortgage contract[2727]; and (c) a consumer credit agreement which would, but for the "investment mortgage" exemption,[2728] be a "regulated agreement". This does not, however, prevent enforcement at any time with the consent of the mortgagor given at that time.[2729] Breach of s.126 could result in the usual disciplinary consequences[2730] and an injunction could be obtained to restrain enforcement of a mortgage in contravention of the section or to restore possession to the mortgagor.[2731] Moreover, the "unfair relationship" provisions may apply.[2732] Control may be exercised by the court in accordance with Pt IX of the 1974 Act.[2733]

39-538 **Saving for registered charges, etc** Protection is afforded in certain circumstances by the Consumer Credit Act 1974 s.177 to the proprietor of a registered charge (within the meaning of the Land Registration Act).[2734]

Corp v Wilkes [1993] C.C.L.R. 1, Cty Ct.

2722 Defined in CCA 1974 s.189(1); above, para.39-180.

2723 CCA 1974 s.113(2).

2724 CCA 1974 ss.106, 113(3)(c); above, para.39-193.

2725 As substituted on March 30, 2014 by Financial Services and Markets Act 2000 (Consumer Credit) (Miscellaneous Provisions) (No.2) Order 2014 (SI 2014/506) art.5(4).

2726 See above, para.39-017.

2727 See above, paras 39-039 and 39-529.

2728 See RAO art.60D, above, paras 39-040 and 39-529.

2729 CCA 1974 s.173(3).

2730 See above, para.39-063.

2731 CCA 1974 s.170(2).

2732 ss.140A–140C (above, paras 39-212 et seq.), see especially s.140A(1)(b), above, para.39-218. However, they do not apply to "regulated mortgage contracts": s.140A(5).

2733 See above, paras 39-199 et seq. The provisions of Pt IV of the Administration of Justice Act 1970 do not apply to a mortgage securing a regulated agreement: s.38A of the 1970 Act inserted by Consumer Credit Act 1974 s.192 and Sch.4 para.30, from May 19, 1985: SI 1983/1551 (c.44).

2734 CCA 1974 s.177(1) (but see s.177(3), (4)) (as amended by the Land Registration Act 2002 s.133 and Sch.11 para.11). Section 177(3) was extended to debt administration business by the Consumer Credit Act 2006 s.24(5). See also s.104 of the Law of Property Act 1925 and s.177(2) of the 1974 Act. It is doubtful whether breach of s.126 creates a "defect in title", or whether these provisions relate, e.g. to a security rendered void under s.106.

CHAPTER 40

EMPLOYMENT[1]

M. R. Freedland and Jeremias F. B. B. Prassl

---

[1] Freedland (Gen. ed.), *The Contract of Employment* (2016); Freedland, *The Personal Employment Contract* (2003); Gaymer, *The Employment Relationship* (2001); Brodie, *The Employment Contract: Legal Principles, Drafting, and Interpretation* (2008) (on Scottish law, but largely applicable to English law); and, for a comparative perspective, Freedland and Kountouris, *The Legal Construction of Personal Work Relations* (2011).

1. INTRODUCTION

40-001 **Contract law and statute law in relation to employment** The legal regulation of the individual employment relationship is a highly complex body of law which, while it still has at its core the common law of the contract of employment, today consists largely of provisions contained in statutes, statutory regulations and European Union measures. In this chapter, the first aim is to be as complete as space permits in the treatment of the common law of the contract of employment, both as a system of rights and remedies in itself, and as a conceptual system upon which much of the statutory regulation is constructed and depends. The other aim is to indicate in reasonable detail the main areas in which the common law of the contract of employment is overlaid by statute law. It is, however, to be stressed that a complete account of that body of statute law, together with all its interpretative case law, would now occupy much more space than is available for that purpose in this work, and would, moreover, depart further from the law of contract than is consonant with the purpose of this work. For more comprehensive treatments of the statute law of the individual employment relationship, reference should be made to treatises entirely devoted to employment law.[2] Much, though by no means all, of the statute law regulating the individual employment relationship was consolidated first into the Employment Protection (Consolidation) Act 1978, and later into the Employment Rights Act 1996, into which many subsequent amendments have since been integrated, especially though not solely by the Employment Acts 2002 and 2008. Where the relevant statute law is not contained in the latter consolidation, that is specifically indicated in the course of this chapter.

40-002 **The contract of employment or of service and contracts for services** Contracts[3] of employment were known to the law for many years as "master and servant" contracts, but this terminology now has archaic connotations, and is not found in modern legislation. There is no comprehensive definition of such a

---

[2]   See, for instance, Hepple & Fredman, *Labour Law and Industrial Relations in Great Britain*, 2nd edn (1992); Deakin & Morris, *Labour Law*, 6th edn (2012); *Harvey on Industrial Relations and Employment Law* (1972 and updated).

[3]   On the question of whether the employment relationship should be viewed in terms of contract or as a "status" see Rideout [1966] C.L.P. 111; Kahn-Freund (1967) 30 M.L.R. 635; compare Hepple (1986) 15 I.L.J. 83.

contract[4] and the decided cases merely indicate a number of indicia or factors which are relevant to a finding that a particular contract is one of employment, or a "contract of service".[5] The presence or absence of any one such factor is not conclusive, since the decision depends on the combined effect of all the relevant factors, when those pointing towards "employment" are weighed up with those pointing against. A contract of employment or of service is generally contrasted with a contract in which an independent contractor is engaged to perform a particular task, often known as a "contract for services".[6] In order to identify the contract of employment, it is useful first to describe its normal forms and then to indicate the current approach to defining it, which is developed in greater detail in the second section of this chapter.

The normal forms of the contract of employment   It could, at least until recent   **40-003** transformations in the practice of the labour market, be said that in the normal case of employment[7] the employee is selected by his or her employer, works "full-time" as part of the employer's organisation, with regular working hours, at a fixed place of work, with equipment provided by the employer, and under some degree of supervision (arranged by the employer) over his or her method of working; the employee enjoys a fixed wage or salary paid at regular intervals, fixed holidays on full pay, and has some security of employment in that he or she cannot be dismissed without notice (except for misconduct), and until the expiration of his notice of dismissal he or she is entitled to receive his or her full wages or salary, whether or not his or her employer can actually provide him or her with work to do.[8] The instances which come before courts are those where some, but not all, of these normal features of employment are present, and it must be decided whether the departures from the normal patterns of employment are sufficiently important to justify the conclusion that the relationship is not employment for the purpose of the legal rule in question.[9]

However, a large and increasing proportion of the workforce is now employed   **40-004** in "marginal", "atypical" or "flexible" forms of employment, such as part-time, temporary or agency employment, as well as work under so-called "zero-hours contracts".[10] In such cases, it may be even more than usually difficult to decide whether or not a contract of employment exists.[11]

The modern approach to definition of the contract of employment   The   **40-005** traditional statements of what constitutes a contract of service placed most emphasis

---

4 *Montreal Locomotive Works Ltd v Montreal and AG* [1947] 1 D.L.R. 161, 169, PC; *Construction Industry Training Board v Labour Force Ltd* [1970] 3 All E.R. 220, 224; *Maurice Graham Ltd v Brunswick* (1974) 16 K.I.R. 158, 165.
5 *Simmons v Heath Laundry* [1910] 1 K.B. 543, 550; *Short v J & W Henderson Ltd* (1946) 62 T.L.R. 427, 429; *Kilboy v South Eastern Fire Area Joint Committee*, 1952 S.C. 280, 285–286; *Market Investigations Ltd v Minister of Social Security* [1969] 2 Q.B. 173, 184; *Ready-Mixed Concrete (South East) Ltd v Minister of Pensions and National Insurance* [1968] 2 Q.B. 497.
6 See below, para.40-005.
7 *Denham v Midland Employers Mutual Assurance Ltd* [1955] 2 Q.B. 437, 446.
8 All these features are considered in more detail, see below, paras 40-010—40-024.
9 *Short v J & W Henderson Ltd* (1946) 62 T.L.R. 427, 429.
10 See para.40-031, below.
11 See Lewis (ed.), *Labour Law in Britain* (1986), Ch.6 (Leighton) passim; Freedland, *The Personal Employment Contract* (2003), pp.18–22; and see below, paras 40-026—40-027.

tion) Acts also embody a series of rights of "employees" (such as rights in relation to maternity,[38] trade union membership and activities,[39] and insolvency of the employer)[40]; and the procedures for handling redundancies apply to "employees" as defined in s.295 of the Trade Union and Labour Relations (Consolidation) Act 1992.

(5) The Transfer of Undertakings (Protection of Employment) Regulations 2006[41] deal with the rights and obligations relating to employers and employees on certain transfers or mergers of undertakings, businesses or parts of businesses. "Employee" is defined for this purpose as any individual who works for another person whether under a contract of service or apprenticeship or otherwise but so as not to include anyone who provides services under a contract for services.[42]

These and other statutory provisions assume that there is a general legal concept of "a contract of employment" or "a contract of service" by using these terms without any statutory definition.[43] Thus, the trade dispute immunity contained in s.13(1) of the Trade Union and Labour Relations Act 1974[44] referred to the contract of employment. Similarly, the Companies Act 1948 was treated as referring to a contract of employment when it spoke of payments made "on account of wages or salary".[45] (The relevant provision has now been consolidated into the Insolvency Act 1986.[46])

40-008 **Classification for particular purposes** Although, as the foregoing paragraphs show, a uniform concept of the contract of employment or service seems to be assumed in legislation and judge-made law, it is nevertheless true that the court will generally classify a relationship in the light of the particular purpose for which the classification is required, and since there is no single test to determine who is an employee it may be possible for the court to classify a particular relationship as employment for the purpose of one of the foregoing rules, but not for another.[47] Insofar as there is a current trend, it would seem to be towards unity rather than diversity of definition, but for the possible emergence of a greater willingness to

---

[38] See below, para.40-199.
[39] Trade Union and Labour Relations (Consolidation) Act 1992 Pt III. See below, paras 40-115—40-116.
[40] See below, para.40-199.
[41] SI 2006/246. See below, para.40-180.
[42] SI 2006/246 reg.2(1).
[43] Income and Corporation Taxes Act 1988 s.19(1) (Sch.E); and see below, para.40-009, "Contract of service or personally to execute any work or labour".
[44] The corresponding provision, no longer confined to contracts of employment, is now contained in Trade Union and Labour Relations (Consolidation) Act 1992 s.219(1).
[45] s.319(4), dealing with preferential payments on a winding-up. See *Re General Radio Co Ltd* [1929] W.N. 172; *Re CW & AL Hughes Ltd* [1966] 1 W.L.R. 1369; *Redbridge LBC v Dhinsa* [2014] EWCA Civ 178, [2014] I.C.R. 834; and see below, paras 40-182—40-183.
[46] s.386 and Sch.6 paras 9 et seq.
[47] e.g. *Wardell v Kent CC* [1938] 2 K.B. 768; *Hewitt v Bonvin* [1940] 1 K.B. 188, 191–192 (cf. at 194–195); *Denham v Midland Employers Mutual Assurance Ltd* [1955] 2 Q.B. 437; but it has been suggested that where a worker who has elected to be treated as self-employed for tax purposes later claims statutory rights as an employee, the Inland Revenue should take action to recover the fiscal advantage the worker gained from being assessed under Sch.D rather than Sch.E: *Young & Woods Ltd v West* [1980] I.R.L.R. 201, 208, para.34 (per Ackner L.J.).

engage in a different approach to classification in the safety at work field, see the decision of the Court of Appeal in *Lane v Shire Roofing Company (Oxford) Ltd*.[48]

**The contract of service or personally to execute any work or labour: "work-   40-009
ers" and "persons employed"**   In the area of employment legislation, there is one major type of variant upon the contract "of employment" or "service" which is very extensively used and requires distinct consideration. This variant adds to the basic concept of the contract of employment by including any other contract personally to execute any work or labour. This addition brings in some contracts between employers and independent contractors, i.e. some contracts which are not contracts of employment. The conditions for this extension outside the contract of employment are that the contract shall be for personal performance by the worker[49] and probably that it shall be for work alone rather than for work and materials. The extended formula probably includes some labour-only sub-contractors who would be held not to have contracts of employment.[50] Where this kind of formula is used, it is sometimes coupled with the terminology of "workman" or "worker" to distinguish it from the simple concept of "employee", but, as the ensuing examples show, there is a lack of consistency in this respect:

(1)   The provisions, formerly contained in the Industrial Courts Act 1919, for courts of inquiry into industrial disputes, apply in relation to trade disputes defined with reference to "workers" which includes both contracts of employment and any other contract whereby the worker undertakes to do or to perform personally any work or services for another party to the contract who is not a professional client of his.[51] The provisions made by the Employment Relations Act 1999 concerning the recognition of trade unions by employers apply in relation to the same category of "workers".[52]

(2)   Employment Rights Act 1996 Pt II (which deals with protection of workers in relation to the payment of wages, and replaces the Truck Acts 1831–1940) applies to "workers", the worker being defined as an individual who has entered into or works under a contract of service or apprenticeship or any other contract whereby the individual undertakes to do or perform personally any work or services for another party to the contract whose status is not by virtue of the contract that of a client or customer of any profession or business undertaking carried on by the individual.[53] The same formula has been used to identify the scope of a number of major pieces

---

[48]   [1995] I.R.L.R. 493. Comparison should now be made with the decision in *R. (on the application of Health and Safety Executive) v Pola* [2009] EWCA Crim 655, where the Court of Appeal limited the application of the requirement of continuing mutuality of obligation, confirming that in this particular interpretative context there was no requirement of a continuing or overarching obligation between the periods when the workers in question were at work.

[49]   See *Ingram v Barnes* (1857) 7 E. & B. 115; *Broadbent v Crisp* [1974] I.C.R. 248. In *Mirror Group Newspapers Ltd v Gunning* [1986] I.C.R. 145 the Court of Appeal held that the expression referred to a contract the dominant purpose of which was the execution of personal work or labour. See *Wright v Redrow Homes (North West) Ltd* [2004] EWCA Civ 469, [2004] I.C.R. 1126 where the contracts of independent individual bricklaying contractors were construed as intended to require them to work "personally" so as to constitute them as "workers"; compare para.40-022.

[50]   *Stuart v Evans* (1883) 49 L.T. 138; and see below, para.40-026.

[51]   Trade Union and Labour Relations (Consolidation) Act 1992 ss.215, 218.

[52]   See Trade Union and Labour Relations (Consolidation) Act 1992 Sch.A1 para.165, referring to s.296(a) and (b).

[53]   Employment Rights Act 1996 s.230(3). A relatively inclusive approach to the construction of the category of "workers" was taken by the Employment Appeal Tribunal in *James v Redcats (Brands)*

of recent employment legislation, such as the National Minimum Wage Act 1998,[54] the Working Time Regulations 1998,[55] and the Part-time Workers (Prevention of Less Favourable Treatment) Regulations 2000.[56] The Supreme Court, in its decision in *Pimlico Plumbers v Smith*, found that a self-employed plumber was a worker for the purposes of these provisions, emphasising in particular that a limited substitution right in the worker's contract could not defeat a personal service obligation so as to disqualify the claimant from being regarded as a "worker" (or, likewise, from being regarded as an "employee" in "employment" for the purposes of employment equality legislation).[57]

(3) The Equality Act 2010 applies its various provisions concerning employment equality to persons in "employment", defined as "employment under a contract of service or apprenticeship or a contract personally to execute any work or labour".[58] In its decision in *Jivraj v Hashwani*,[59] the Supreme

---

Ltd [2007] I.C.R. 1006. Compare the similarly inclusive approach to the category of "worker" taken by the Court of Appeal in *Hospital Medical Group Ltd v Westwood* [2012] EWCA Civ 1005, [2013] I.C.R. 415 which concerned a doctor engaged on a self-employed basis to carry out cosmetic surgical procedures, and contrast *Suhail v Barking, Havering & Redbridge NHS Trust* Unreported June 11, 2015, EAT, and *Pimlico Plumbers v Smith* [2017] EWCA Civ 51, [2017] I.C.R. 657 which found self-employed plumbers to be workers. A recent string of cases arising from intermittent work arrangements in the so-called "on-demand economy" has similarly found individuals to be workers: see, for example, *Aslam v Uber BV* [2018] I.R.L.R. 97, EAT.

[54] ss.1(2), 54(3). Many of the statutory formulations of categories of "workers" expressly include those working under contracts of apprenticeship. In *Edmonds v Lawson* [2000] I.C.R. 567, it was held that, on the particular facts, a pupil barrister did not have a contract of apprenticeship and hence was not a "worker" within the meaning of s.54 of the National Minimum Wage Act 1998.

[55] SI 1998/1833 regs 3(2), 2(1). In *Byrne Brothers (Formwork) Ltd v Baird* [2002] I.R.L.R. 96, the Employment Appeal Tribunal held that building trade workers working as self-employed labour-only sub-contractors qualified as "workers" within the meaning of the Working Time Regulations 1998 (in which the term is defined in the same way as under s.230(6) of the Employment Rights Act 1996) although they clearly were not employed under contracts of employment and had some power to provide a substitute to carry out their work. Compare para.40-022. Compare *Cotswold Developments Construction Ltd v Williams* [2006] I.R.L.R. 181, which confirms the role of mutuality of obligation in deciding whether the contractual relationship of "worker" and employer exists in a given case. Compare also in this respect *Community Dental Centres Ltd v Sultan-Darmon* [2010] UKEAT/0532/09/1208, [2010] I.R.L.R. 1024 where the Employment Appeal Tribunal held that there was insufficient mutuality of obligation to support the conclusion that there was a contractual relation of "worker" and employer. Compare now also *Conroy v Scottish Football Association Ltd* [2014] UKEATS 0024/13/JW.

[56] SI 2000/1551 regs 3(1), 2, 1(2). See below, para.40-156.

[57] [2018] UKSC 29. A recent string of cases arising from intermittent work arrangements in the so-called "on-demand economy" has similarly found individuals to be workers: see, for example, *Aslam v Uber BV* [2018] I.R.L.R. 97, EAT.

[58] s.83(2). See *Mingeley v Pennock and Ivory* [2004] EWCA Civ 328, [2004] I.C.R. 727, where the relationship between a taxi-driver and the organisation coordinating his work was held not to amount to a contract personally to execute any work or labour. It was expressly recognised in *Quinnen v Hovells* [1984] I.C.R. 525 that this category may include self-employed persons who comply with its requirements. See also *Mirror Group Newspapers Ltd v Gunning* [1986] I.C.R. 145. In *Tanna v Post Office* [1981] I.C.R. 374 it was held that full effect must be given to the word "personally", so that the case was not covered of a sub-postmaster who was responsible for seeing that the work of the Post Office was carried out either by himself or by staff chosen by him. In *Sheehan v Post Office Counters Ltd* [1999] I.C.R. 734, the Employment Appeal Tribunal confirmed the "dominant purpose of personal performance" test as propounded in *Mirror Group Newspapers Ltd v Gunning* [1986] I.C.R. 145, and applied it to hold, much as in *Tanna v Post Office* [1981] I.C.R. 374, that a sub-postmaster was not employed under "a contract personally to do any work". This view of the situation of those persons was confirmed in *Wolstenholme v Post Office Ltd* [2003] I.R.L.R. 546.

Court has adopted a narrow construction of the concept of "employment under a contract personally to execute any work or labour" as that concept is used in the various kinds of employment discrimination legislation detailed under this head of this paragraph, holding that it is in effect limited to work taking place under the direction of the employer.

(4) The Trade Union and Labour Relations (Consolidation) Act 1992 defines "trade disputes" and "trade unions" in terms of "workers" and defines "workers" as in example (2) above.[60]

(5): The concept of "worker"—defined as in example (4) above—is invoked in relation to the duty of employers to disclose information to the representatives of workers for the purposes of collective bargaining.[61]

2. THE FACTORS IDENTIFYING A CONTRACT OF EMPLOYMENT

The factors to be considered   The case law suggests[62] that the factors relevant   **40-010** to the process of identifying a contract of employment may usefully be listed as follows:

(1) the degree of control exercised by the employer;
(2) whether the worker's interest in the relationship involved any prospect of profit or risk of loss;
(3) whether the worker was properly regarded as part of the employer's organisation;
(4) whether the worker was carrying on business on his own account or carrying on the business of the employer;
(5) the provision of equipment;
(6) the incidence of tax and national insurance;
(7) the parties' own view of their relationship;

Comparison should now be made with the decision in *Muschett v HM Prison Service* [2010] EWCA Civ 25, [2010] I.R.L.R. 451, where the Court of Appeal held that there was no contractual obligation between the agency worker and the Prison Service as the end-user of his services such as was necessary to establish a "contract personally to execute any work or labour". In *Burton v Higham* [2003] I.R.L.R. 257 it was held that temporary agency workers came within this definition although not within the definition of "employees" having contracts of employment. See *South East Sheffield Citizens Advice Bureau v Grayson* [2004] I.R.L.R. 353, EAT, where an unpaid volunteer worker was held to fall outside this definition; and the Court of Appeal similarly so decided in *X v Mid-Sussex Citizens Advice Bureau* [2011] EWCA Civ 28. The Supreme Court, [2012] UKSC 59, [2013] 1 All E.R. 1038 confirmed the decision of the Court of Appeal, holding that unpaid volunteer workers were outside the scope of disability discrimination protection afforded by Directive 2000/78/EC. cf. also now *Unite the Union v Nailard* [2016] I.R.L.R. 906.

59   [2011] UKSC 40, [2011] 1 W.L.R. 1872. This continues to cast some doubt, which it will require further litigation to resolve, on the standing and relevance of the authorities cited in the preceding footnote. In *Halawi v WDFG UK Ltd (t/a World Duty Free)* [2014] EWCA Civ 1387, [2015] I.R.L.R. 50, Arden L.J. expressed concern at the resulting exclusionary effects of this approach; though cf. also *Windle v Secretary of State for Justice* [2016] EWCA Civ 459, [2016] I.R.L.R. 628. In the case of personal service companies, another avenue for recourse could be found in *EAD Solicitors LLP v Abrams* [2015] I.R.L.R. 978, EAT.

60   ss.1, 218(1), 244(1), 296(1). Compare *Smith v Carillion (JM) Ltd* [2015] EWCA Civ 209, [2015] I.R.L.R. 467.

61   Trade Union and Labour Relations (Consolidation) Act 1992 s.181.

62   *Addison v London Philharmonic Ltd* [1981] I.C.R. 261, 271. See also *Warner Holidays Ltd v Secretary of State for Social Services* [1983] I.C.R. 440; Collins (1990) 10 O.J.L.S. 353.

(8) the structure of the trade or profession concerned and the arrangements within it.

These and other aspects of the relationship that have been regarded as important to the task of classification are considered in the following paragraphs. Valuable guidance about the way classification should be approached is provided by the judgments of the Privy Council in the case of *Lee Ting Sang v Chung Chi-Keung*[63] and of the Court of Appeal in *Hall (Inspector of Taxes) v Lorimer*.[64]

40-011 **The legal interpretation of the facts** The particular words found in the contract between the parties are not conclusive, since the law is only concerned with the nature or substance of the relationship which the contract has created.[65] Once the relevant facts (which may include the terms of the contract) have been ascertained, the determination whether it is a contract of employment or not is a question of placing the correct legal interpretation upon those facts.[66] "Once the primary facts are found, then it is a pure question of law as to what is the reasonable inference based on the legal interpretation of the contract".[67] But the *answer* to the question involves issues of fact and of degree which it is for the tribunal of first instance to determine.[68] The recent tendency has been for appellate courts to confine their intervention to cases where they find a positive error of law at first instance; to cases, that is, where they find that there was no evidence to support the conclusion reached at first instance or where they find that no reasonable person acting judicially and properly instructed as to the relevant law could reach such a decision.[69]

40-012 **Control and superintendence** An employer normally has the power to direct and control the work of the employee; "but the ultimate question is not what specific orders, or whether any specific orders, were given but who is entitled to give the orders as to how the work should be done".[70] The greater the amount of control exercised over the details of the work to be done, the more likely is the inference that the relationship is one of employment.[71] But the question of control is only one

---

63 [1990] 2 A.C. 374.
64 [1994] I.C.R. 218.
65 *Short v J & W Henderson Ltd* (1946) 62 T.L.R. 427; *Morren v Swinton and Pendlebury BC* [1965] 1 W.L.R. 576, 581; see below, para.40-025.
66 *Benmax v Austin Motor Co Ltd* [1955] A.C. 370.
67 *Morren v Swinton and Pendlebury BC*, see above, at 583. cf. cases decided under the old Workmen's Compensation Acts: *Bobbey v WM Crosbie & Co Ltd* (1915) 114 L.T. 244; *Easdown v Cobb* [1940] 1 All E.R. 49. (This was treated as a matter of law if it depended on the interpretation of a written contract: *Performing Right Society Ltd v Mitchell and Booker (Palais de Danse) Ltd* [1924] 1 K.B. 762.)
68 *O'Kelly v Trusthouse Forte Plc* [1983] I.C.R. 728.
69 *Global Plant Ltd v Secretary of State for Health and Social Security* [1972] 1 Q.B. 139; *Maurice Graham Ltd v Brunswick* (1974) 16 K.I.R. 158. The foregoing passage of text was judicially cited in *Addison v London Philharmonic Ltd* [1981] I.C.R. 261, 268, D–F. This tendency has been confirmed and re-emphasised in *O'Kelly v Trusthouse Forte Plc* [1983] I.C.R. 728; and *Nethermere (St Neots) Ltd v Gardner* [1984] I.C.R. 612.
70 *Mersey Docks and Harbour Board v Coggins and Griffith (Liverpool) Ltd* [1947] A.C. 1, 17. See also *Performing Right Society Ltd v Mitchell and Booker (Palais de Danse) Ltd* [1924] 1 K.B. 762 at 776–779.
71 *Simmons v Heath Laundry* [1910] 1 K.B. 543, 550; *Whittaker v Minister of Pensions and National Insurance* [1967] 1 Q.B. 156.

of the factors to be considered and it is far from conclusive,[72] e.g. a superior employee may exercise control over subordinate employees,[73] and even have the power to appoint and dismiss them, and yet both may be employees of the same employer. The control test must give way, within the same firm or organisation, to another factor, viz that both persons are on the same payroll.[74] Thus the master of a ship,[75] the general manager or director of a company,[76] or even the works foreman in a factory, may have authority to engage or dismiss employees, but this does not make them employers or prevent them from being employees.[77] The same holds for the relationship between senior civil servants and their subordinates.[78] A skilled employee will normally not be subject to actual control over the details of his or her work[79]; but he or she is likely to be an employee if he or she is paid by and can be dismissed by the employer,[80] or if the employer can "give general directions as to the work the other is or is not to do",[81] or as to working hours[82] and working place,[83] or "in incidental or collateral matters".[84] However, it is generally true that the greater the degree of independence from continuous and detailed control enjoyed by the person in question, the more likely the inference that it is not a contract of employment.[85] Moreover, even if an apparent employer does exercise powers of control, discipline, engagement and dismissal over workers, the facts may be such that the workers in question are not working for the apparent employer at

---

[72] In *Ready-Mixed Concrete (South East) Ltd v Minister of Pensions and National Insurance* [1968] 2 Q.B. 497, it was ruled that control by the employer was not sufficient to identify the contract as one of employment and that the other aspects of the contract must not be inconsistent with the relationship of employment; cf. *Hitchcock v Post Office* [1980] I.C.R. 100 (sub-postmaster not employee of Post Office despite their control of him). Compare also *Jennings v Forestry Commission* [2008] EWCA Civ 581, [2008] I.C.R. 988.

[73] This will of necessity be the position when a corporation employs several persons. cf. *Re Church of England Curates* [1912] 2 Ch. 563.

[74] See below, paras 40-016—40-019.

[75] *Hedley v Pinkney & Sons S.S. Co Ltd* [1894] A.C. 222.

[76] *Performing Right Society Ltd v Ciryl Theatrical Syndicates Ltd* [1924] 1 K.B. 1. See also *Folumi v Nigerline (UK) Ltd* [1978] I.C.R. 277; *Eaton v Robert Eaton Ltd* [1988] I.C.R. 302 (managing director).

[77] *Bird v O'Neal* [1960] A.C. 907, 920.

[78] *Bainbridge v Postmaster-General* [1906] 1 K.B. 178; *Fraser v Balfour* (1918) 87 L.J. K.B. 1116, HL.

[79] *Simmons v Heath Laundry* [1910] 1 K.B. 543, 553; *Mersey Docks and Harbour Board v Coggins & Griffith (Liverpool) Ltd* [1947] A.C. 1. (See also the "organisation" test: see below, para.40-016.)

[80] *Morren v Swinton and Pendlebury BC* [1965] 1 W.L.R. 576.

[81] *Stagecraft Ltd v Minister of National Insurance*, 1952 S.C. 288, 302; *Whittaker v Minister of Pensions and National Insurance* [1967] 1 Q.B. 156.

[82] e.g. if the contract provided that the person was to devote the whole of his working time to the employer: *Whittaker v Minister of Pensions and National Insurance*, above, at 167; cf. *Greater London Council v Minister of Social Security* [1971] 1 W.L.R. 641 (school dentist). See below, para.40-021.

[83] *Walker v Crystal Palace Football Club Ltd* [1910] 1 K.B. 87 (professional football player); *Zuijis v Wirth Brothers Pty Ltd* (1955) 93 C.L.R. 561, 572 (acrobat); *Whittaker v Minister of Pensions and National Insurance*, above (trapeze artist). See below, para.40-021.

[84] *Zuijis v Wirth Brothers Pty Ltd*, above, at 571. Doctors employed by a hospital are another illustration: see below, para.40-016.

[85] *Simmons v Heath Laundry* [1910] 1 K.B. 543, 550; cf. *Challinor v Taylor* [1972] I.C.R. 129; *Addison v London Philharmonic Ltd* [1981] I.C.R. 261 (part-time orchestral musicians self-employed where although there was control, it was the minimum necessary to do the work); to like effect is *Midland Sinfonia Concert Society Ltd v Secretary of State for Social Services* [1981] I.C.R. 454 at 466 F–G. Contrast now, however, *White v Troutbeck SA* [2013] EWCA Civ 1171, [2013] I.R.L.R. 949 (low level of day-to-day control not enough to negate employment status).

all, and that the apparent employer is merely licensing them to contract with others.[86]

40-013   **Method of control**   Sometimes the distinction between an employee and an independent contractor depends on the method of control:

"... it is more usual to exercise the control desired through the medium of the contract itself when one is dealing with an independent contractor, and through day-to-day instructions during the performance of the contract when one is dealing with a servant".[87]

But some contracts may prescribe the employee's duties in great detail without ceasing to be contracts of employment, if there are other indications of the relationship of employment, e.g. the power to dispense with the services of the employee if the employer is not satisfied with the manner in which he or she carries them out.[88]

40-014   **Control and the corporate employer**[89]   Company directors with service agreements may be employees of the company, although there is virtually no control exercised over them by superiors[90]; even a managing director of a "one-person" company may be an employee under a contract of service with the company he or she controls.[91] This reflects the legal separation between the company and its directors; it is an assertion of the corporate entity doctrine rather than a conscious departure from the control test. It would seem that there is no rule of law that an individual such as managing director with a controlling beneficial interest in the shares of a company cannot be regarded as an employee of the company for the purposes of employment protection legislation.[92] On the other hand, the members of a cooperative association of workers do not turn themselves into employees merely by adopting a corporate form and electing a board of directors to manage their association.[93] In *Secretary of State for Business, Enterprise and Regulatory Reform v Neufeld*,[94] the Court of Appeal provided guidance on the question of whether and when controlling shareholders and directors can claim to be treated as employees of their insolvent companies so as to enable them to claim payment from

---

[86]   *Cheng Yuen v Royal Hong Kong Golf Club* [1988] I.C.R. 131 (golf caddie not employee of golf club). Compare now *Stringfellow Restaurants Ltd v Quashie* [2012] EWCA Civ 1735, [2013] I.R.L.R. 99; para.40-023 below.

[87]   Atiyah, *Vicarious Liability in the Law of Torts* (1967), p.42.

[88]   *Amalgamated Engineering Union v Minister of Pensions and National Insurance* [1963] 1 W.L.R. 441, 454. See below, para.40-018.

[89]   See J. Prassl, *The Concept of the Employer* (2015) 19ff.

[90]   *Trussed Steel Concrete Co Ltd v Green* [1946] Ch. 115, 121; see *Parsons v AJ Parsons & Sons Ltd* [1978] I.C.R. 456. See now also *Stack v Ajar-Tec Ltd* [2015] EWCA Civ 46, [2015] I.R.L.R. 474.

[91]   *Lee v Lee's Air Farming Ltd* [1961] A.C. 12 (workman's compensation case). See also *Folami v Nigerline (UK) Ltd* [1978] I.C.R. 277; *Eaton v Robert Eaton Ltd* [1988] I.C.R. 302 (managing director). See now also *Secretary of State for Business, Innovation and Skills v Knight* [2014] I.R.L.R. 605, EAT: sole shareholder and managing director can be employee of company so as to claim redundancy payment in insolvency.

[92]   *Bottrill v Secretary of State for Trade and Industry* [2000] 1 All E.R. 915. The compatibility of majority shareholding with employee status was further confirmed by the decision of the Court of Appeal in *Sellars Arenascene Ltd v Connolly (No.2)* [2001] I.R.L.R. 222. Compare also *Nesbitt v Secretary of State for Trade and Industry* [2007] I.R.L.R. 847.

[93]   *Winfield v London Philharmonic Ltd* [1979] I.C.R. 726; contrast *Drym Fabricators Ltd v Johnson* [1981] I.C.R. 274 which was decided on a simple corporate entity basis; sed quaere.

[94]   [2009] EWCA Civ 280, [2007] I.C.R. 1183.

the Secretary of State.[95] While it was confirmed that a controlling shareholder and director can also be an employee, it was also indicated that there may need to be an inquiry as to whether the claimed contract of employment truly represents the character of the relationship, as in cases where an allegation is made that the purported contract is a sham.[96]

Transfer of control An employee may remain in a relationship of employment **40-015** with his or her employer despite the fact that the employer has placed the employee temporarily under the control of another person[97] (e.g. an independent contractor[98]). Thus the temporary transfer of an employee in connection with the hire of equipment—as where a crane driver is provided when a crane is hired out—does not normally result in a transfer of the contract of employment away from the original employer,[99] who may, moreover, be estopped from denying that he or she is the employer where no formal transfer has been agreed with the employee.[100] However, in a case where a company contracted for the provision of drivers for the operation of a private parcel delivery by another company, it was held by the Court of Appeal that the drivers were transferred into the temporary employment of the latter company, because the latter company had a sufficient degree of control over the work of the drivers.[101] The mere fact that a nurse is under the control of a surgeon while an operation is in progress in an operating theatre does not mean that the nurse becomes the surgeon's employee, at least not for the purposes of vicarious liability.[102] If the owner or occupier of premises where work is in progress retains some control over the work in order to maintain some degree of supervision over the activities on his or her premises[103] he or she will not, merely on that account, become an employer of those doing the work.[104] However, special considerations apply where an employment agency arranges for a worker to carry out work under the control of the agency's client. This situation is considered in a later paragraph.[105]

The "organisation" test An employee is usually a regular unit in the complex **40-016** organisation of a business: he or she is an integral part of the firm, not a casual or temporary person engaged only for the purpose of completing a specific task which is accessory to the main business.[106] Thus, doctors and nurses who are paid by a

---

95 Under Pt XII of the Employment Rights Act 1996, see para.40-200.

96 As to which, see below, para.40-025.

97 *Wardell v Kent CC* [1938] 2 K.B. 768, 783. But see now *Construction Industry Training Board v Labour Force Ltd* [1970] 3 All E.R. 220; *Cross v Redpath Dorman Long Ltd* [1978] I.C.R. 730 and see below, para.40-026.

98 *Clelland v Edward Lloyd Ltd* [1938] 1 K.B. 272.

99 *Mersey Docks and Harbour Board v Coggins & Griffith Ltd* [1947] A.C. 1.

100 *Smith v Blandford Gee Cementation Ltd* [1970] 3 All E.R. 154.

101 *Interlink Express Parcels Ltd v Night Trunkers Ltd* [2001] R.T.R. 23. Various passages from the present chapter were quoted with approval by Arden L.J.

102 *Morris v Winsbury-White* [1937] 4 All E.R. 494. See also *Perionowsky v Freeman* (1866) 4 F. & F. 977.

103 Or in order to protect his property: *Doggett v Waterloo Taxi-Cab Co Ltd* [1910] 2 K.B. 336, 341, 343.

104 *Marrow v Flimby and Broughton Moor Coal and Fire Brick Co Ltd* [1898] 2 Q.B. 588; *Fitzpatrick v Evans & Co* [1902] 1 K.B. 505; *Gould v Minister of National Insurance* [1951] 1 K.B. 731.

105 See below, para.40-027; cf. *Road Transport Industry Training Board v Ongaro* [1977] I.C.R. 523.

106 *Stevenson, Jordan and Harrison Ltd v Macdonald and Evans* [1952] 1 T.L.R. 101, 111; *Bank voor Handel en Scheepvaart NV v Slatford* [1953] 1 Q.B. 248, 295; *Roe v Minister of Health* [1954] 2 Q.B. 66, 90.

hospital authority, and are part of the regular staff of the hospital, are employees[107]; but a consultant or anaesthetist selected and employed by the patient themselves may not be an employee of the hospital authority.[108] The organisation test has more recently been reformulated in a negative form as: "Is the person who has engaged himself or herself to perform these services performing them as a person in business on his or her own account?".[109] Expressed in that form, this test has become one of the most significant criteria for identifying the contract of employment.[110] That this is the case was confirmed by the judgment of the Privy Council in the case of *Lee Ting-Sang v Chung Chi-Keung*.[111]

40-017 **Power of selection and appointment** Usually, it is one indication of "employment" that the employer has the power to select and to appoint the employee, but the absence of this power is not conclusive against a contract of employment, e.g. where shipowners accepted dockers on a rota basis.[112] The employer will often delegate the power of selection of employees, sometimes to a superior employee,[113] sometimes even to an independent contractor.[114] Although a statute may give to a specified official the power of making appointments to posts in a public body, the latter will be the employer.[115] The power of a patient to select a surgeon to perform an operation used to be an important factor (especially when the patient pays the surgeon) indicating that the hospital is not the employer of the surgeon in this respect.[116]

40-018 **The power to dismiss or suspend** The power of dismissal[117] or suspension is an important indication of the relationship of employment[118]: although a person may have no right to control the manner in which another does work, if the former can dispense with the services of the latter by giving a certain period of notice, the relationship will normally be one of employment,[119] since an independent contractor cannot be "dismissed". But other factors may outweigh the power to dismiss: thus, although a cloakroom attendant could be suspended or dismissed by restaurant proprietors, she was remunerated only by tips, did not need to keep any fixed work-

---

107 *Cassidy v Ministry of Health* [1951] 2 K.B. 343, 362.
108 *Roe v Minister of Health*, above, at 82; *Higgins v North Western Metropolitan Regional Hospital Board* [1954] 1 W.L.R. 411. See Atiyah at pp.87–89.
109 *Market Investigations Ltd v Minister of Social Security* [1969] 2 Q.B. 173, 187.
110 *Ferguson v John Dawson Ltd* [1976] I.R.L.R. 346, 352; *Young & Woods Ltd v West* [1980] I.R.L.R. 201, 205; *Hitchcock v Post Office* [1980] I.C.R. 100, 105 E–H; *Addison v London Philharmonic Ltd* [1981] I.C.R. 261, 272D–273C.
111 [1990] 2 A.C. 374.
112 *Short v J & W Henderson Ltd* (1946) 62 T.L.R. 427, 429.
113 cf. *Parker v Walker*, 1961 S.L.T. 252.
114 *Morren v Swinton and Pendlebury BC* [1965] 1 W.L.R. 576.
115 *Kilboy v South Eastern Fire Joint Area Committee*, 1952 S.C. 280.
116 *Roe v Minister of Health* [1954] 2 Q.B. 66, 82, see above, para.40-016. cf. *Hall v Lees* [1904] 2 K.B. 602.
117 "Dismissal" is not relevant for this purpose if it merely means that the engagement of a person on a day-to-day basis will not be continued in future: *Doggett v Waterloo Taxi-Cab Co Ltd* [1910] 2 K.B. 336.
118 *Short v J & W Henderson Ltd* (1946) 62 T.L.R. 427, 429; *Mersey Docks and Harbour Board v Coggins and Griffith (Liverpool) Ltd* [1947] A.C. 1, 20.
119 *Binding v Great Yarmouth Port and Haven Commissioners* (1923) 16 B.W.C.C. 28; *Amalgamated Engineering Union v Ministry of Pensions and National Insurance* [1963] 1 W.L.R. 441, 454; *Ferguson v John Dawson Ltd* [1976] I.R.L.R. 346, 349; cf. *Drym Fabricators Ltd v Johnson* [1981] I.C.R. 274, 275, G–H.

ing hours, and was free not to attend whenever she pleased: hence she was held not to be employed under a contract of service.[120] The fact that a public body has only a restricted power of dismissal does not preclude a contract of employment.[121]

Payment of wages or salary   The payment of "wages" or "salary"[122] or of holiday pay[123] is another important pointer to the relationship of employment. Normally a regular, fixed sum is payable to an employee, but it is possible for an employee to be remunerated solely by tips received from others[124] or wholly on a commission basis.[125] Similarly, the manner in which the remuneration is to be calculated may point to a contract of employment; the typical employee is paid according to time worked,[126] but sometimes an employee may be paid by the piece,[127] and sometimes by commission.[128] If, however, payment is "by the job", i.e. in relation to a complete task, this points, though not conclusively, to a contract with an independent contractor.[129]   **40-019**

Supply of equipment and ownership of assets   If one party to the contract supplies the tools, machines or equipment used by the other party, this points to a contract of employment,[130] since an independent contractor normally provides these for herself or himself.[131] In *Ready-Mixed Concrete (South-East) Ltd v Minister of Pensions and National Insurance*[132] an owner-driver of a concrete-mixing lorry was held to be an independent contractor largely by reference to his ownership of the lorry, despite the facts that the lorry was subject to a hire-purchase agreement with an associated company and that the driver was in various senses required to work as part of the company's organisation.   **40-020**

The fixing of times and place of work   The power to fix the hours or times when a person is to work,[133] or when he or she is to take his holidays, is another pointer to a contract of employment; another is the power to direct *where* he or she must work.[134] But these factors are not conclusive. an independent contractor may work   **40-021**

---

[120] *Pauley v Kenaldo Ltd* [1953] 1 W.L.R. 187, 191.

[121] *Barber v Manchester Regional Hospital Board* [1958] 1 W.L.R. 181.

[122] *Short v J & W Henderson Ltd* (1946) 62 T.L.R. 427, 429.

[123] *Hobbs v Royal Arsenal Co-operative Society Ltd* (1930) 23 B.W.C.C. 254; cf. *Wright v Att-Gen for Tasmania* (1954) 94 C.L.R. 409.

[124] *Pauley v Kenaldo Ltd* [1953] 1 W.L.R. 187, 191; *Benjamin v Minister of Pensions and National Insurance* [1960] 2 Q.B. 519.

[125] *Hobbs v Royal Arsenal Co-operative Society Ltd*, above. cf. *Parker v Walker*, 1961 S.L.T. 252. See *Tyne & Clyde Warehouses Ltd v Hamerton* [1978] I.C.R. 661; *102 Social Club v Bickerton* [1977] I.C.R. 911.

[126] But sometimes an independent contractor is paid by time: *Robinson v Scarisbrick* (1939) 32 B.W.C.C. 285.

[127] *Sadler v Henlock* (1855) 4 E. & B. 570.

[128] See above.

[129] See below, para.40-023.

[130] *Binding v Great Yarmouth Port and Haven Commissioners* (1923) 16 B.W.C.C. 28. Compare, for the converse situation, *Jennings v Forestry Commission* [2008] EWCA Civ 581, [2008] I.C.R. 988.

[131] *Humberstone v Northern Timber Mills* (1949) 79 C.L.R. 389; cf. *Hitchcock v Post Office* [1980] I.C.R. 100, 108H.

[132] [1968] 2 Q.B. 497.

[133] *M'Cready v DJ Dunlop & Co* (1900) 2 F. 1027, 1031. cf. *Neale v Atlas Products (Vic) Pty Ltd* (1954) 94 C.L.R. 419.

[134] *Simmons v Heath Laundry Co* [1910] 1 K.B. 543, 550; *Re Ashley and Smith Ltd* [1918] 2 Ch. 378;

regularly on the employer's premises,[135] whilst an employee may have complete freedom as to times of work within the period of a particular task assigned to the employee.[136] These factors are closely linked with the question of the extent of the obligation to work or to employ, which is discussed in a later paragraph.[137]

40-022 **Personal performance** A person cannot normally be an employee if he or she is entitled to delegate the entire performance of his or her work to another person[138]; but a person may possibly be an employee, although he or she personally (with the permission of the employer) employs assistants to help.[139] The Court of Appeal has more recently reasserted the requirement of personal performance,[140] in the form of a holding that the presence of a substitution clause in a lorry driver's work contract deprived that contract of the *mutuality of obligation*[141] of personal performance which would have been necessary to identify it as a contract of employment.[142]

40-023 **The extent of the obligation to work or to employ** If the contract entitles[143] some person to the full-time or exclusive services of the other person, this points to the contract being one of employment.[144] But if it is left entirely to one party to the contract to choose whether to do any work or not (e.g. a travelling salesperson wholly on commission), there is almost certainly not a contract of employment.[145] The courts may exceptionally recognise that there is a short-term contract of

---

Stagecraft Ltd v Minister of National Insurance, 1952 S.C. 288.

[135] *Templeton v William Parkin & Co Ltd* (1929) 140 L.T. 519; *Westall Richardson Ltd v Roulson* [1954] 1 W.L.R. 905.

[136] *Market Investigations v Minister of Social Security* [1969] 2 Q.B. 173.

[137] See below, para.40-012.

[138] *Braddell v Baker* (1911) 104 L.T. 673, 676. cf. *Hill v Beckett* [1915] 1 K.B. 578; *Pauley v Kenaldo Ltd* [1953] 1 W.L.R. 187, 191. See Atiyah, *Vicarious Liability in the Law of Torts* (1967), pp.59–62; cf. *Hitchcock v Post Office* [1980] I.C.R. 100, 109 AC.

[139] This was assumed in *Robinson v Hill* [1910] 1 K.B. 94. In certain cases, the assistants may be employees of the main employer, e.g. if he has delegated to the superior employee the *power* to engage assistants: see *Bobbey v WM Crosbie & Co Ltd* (1915) 114 L.T. 244; cf. above, para.40-017.

[140] In *Express and Echo Publications Ltd v Tanton* [1999] I.C.R. 693. The requirement of personal performance was strictly maintained and applied in *Staffordshire Sentinel Newspapers Ltd v Potter* [2004] I.R.L.R. 752, EAT, so that an express power for the worker to substitute another worker was treated as negating a contract of employment although the power was subject to the approval of the employer. Compare also para.40-009.

[141] As to which see below, para.40-023.

[142] Compare, however, the decision of the Employment Appeal Tribunal in *Macfarlane v Glasgow City Council* [2001] I.R.L.R. 7, to the effect that the worker's capacity to perform via a substitute in exceptional circumstances is not necessarily inconsistent with the existence of a contract of employment.

[143] The mere fact that a person has for a long time worked exclusively for another is not relevant: *Humberstone v Northern Timber Mills* (1949) 79 C.L.R. 389.

[144] *Bauman v Hulton Press Ltd* [1952] 2 All E.R. 1121, 1124. See also *Hobbs v Royal Arsenal Co-operative Society Ltd* (1930) 23 B.W.C.C. 254.

[145] *Egginton v Reader* [1936] 1 All E.R. 7; *Chadwick v Pioneer Private Telephone Co Ltd* [1941] 1 All E.R. 522; *Pauley v Kenaldo Ltd* [1953] 1 W.L.R. 187, 191; *WHPT Association v Social Services Secretary* [1981] I.C.R. 737, 750H–751C; cf. also *Mailway (Southern) Ltd v Willsher* [1978] I.C.R. 511 (part-time packer); but contrast *Airfix Footwear Ltd v Cope* [1978] I.C.R. 1210 (regularly employed outworker held an employee). Compare now *Mingeley v Pennock and Ivory* [2004] EWCA Civ 328, [2004] I.C.R. 727, where the relationship between a taxi-driver and the organisation coordinating his work was held not to amount to a contract personally to execute any work or labour.

employment for each assignment undertaken or performed.[146] However, the more likely analysis in such a case will be that there is no continuous contract in being between the parties, and that the short-term contracts in respect of each task are not contracts of employment.[147] The case law at one stage seemed to suggest that there could be a continuing contract of employment although the employer had a power of indefinite lay-off.[148] It has since been held[149] that for there to be a continuing contract of employment linking up intermittent periods of employment (a so-called "global" contract of employment), there must be some degree of continuing mutual obligation on the employer to offer employment and on the employee to accept employment. The requisite degree of mutuality of obligation cannot be inferred from a "course of dealing" if that amounts to no more than the fact of intermittent employment with one employer, even over a long period of time.[150] Where the employer of a casual worker has clearly disclaimed from the outset any continuing obligation to provide any work at all, it may amount to an error of law to hold that a continuing contract of employment exists with that worker between periods of actual employment.[151] The decision of the House of Lords in *Carmichael v National Power Plc*[152] reinforces the stringency with which the mutuality of obligation requirement is applied in order to decide whether casual workers have continuing contracts of employment. Difficult questions continue to arise with regard to multilateral employment situations, such as those involving service recipients or customers of a proprietor/employer. In *Stringfellow Restaurants Ltd v Quashie*,[153] the Court of Appeal held that an Employment Tribunal had been entitled to conclude that the relation between a lap dancer and the club for which or at which she worked did not consist of a continuing contract of employment, primarily on the basis of

---

[146] *Market Investigations Ltd v Minister for Social Security* [1969] 2 Q.B. 173; but they did not so recognise in *O'Kelly v Trusthouse Forte Plc* [1983] I.C.R. 728; *Nethermere (St Neots) Ltd v Gardiner* [1984] I.C.R. 612.

[147] *Writers Guild of GB v BBC* [1974] I.C.R. 234.

[148] *Puttick v John Wright & Sons (Blackhall) Ltd* [1972] I.C.R. 457; *Airfix Footwear Ltd v Cope* [1978] I.C.R. 1210.

[149] *O'Kelly v Trusthouse Forte Plc* [1983] I.C.R. 728; *Nethermere (St Neots) Ltd v Gardiner* [1984] I.C.R. 612; *Hellyer Bros Ltd v McLeod* [1987] I.C.R. 526.

[150] *Hellyer Bros Ltd v McLeod* [1987] I.C.R. 526.

[151] *Clark v Oxfordshire HA* [1998] I.R.L.R. 125 (staff nurse on "nurse bank", but stated to have no entitlement to guaranteed or continuous work).

[152] [1999] I.C.R. 1226 (power station guides working on casual as required basis held not to have continuing contracts of employment). That decision of the House of Lords was applied by the Court of Appeal in *Stevedoring & Haulage Services Ltd v Fuller* [2001] EWCA Civ 651, [2001] I.R.L.R. 627 to the effect that dock workers working on an "ad hoc and casual basis" were held to have no continuing contracts of employment. Compare, however, *Cornwall CC v Prater* [2006] EWCA Civ 102, [2006] I.C.R. 731, where the Court of Appeal displayed a greater willingness than had previously been shown to regard a sequence of casual work contracts as each consisting of a contract of employment, and as all being linked up into a period of "continuous employment", as to which see para.40-165. But in the rather different context of unpaid voluntary workers, the approach in the *Carmichael* case received a stricter application in *Melhuish v Redbridge Citizens Advice Bureau* [2005] I.R.L.R. 419. Contrast, however, in the context of remunerated employment, *Wilson v Circular Distributors Ltd* [2006] I.R.L.R. 38, where the attempt to argue that the employer was under no clear obligation to provide work and that the claimant accordingly had no contract of employment was unsuccessful. Compare now *Littlewood v Revenue and Customs Commissioners* [2009] S.T.C. (S.C.D.) 243.

[153] [2012] EWCA Civ 1735, [2013] I.R.L.R. 99.

an absence of continuing contractual obligations—thus identifying that worker as self-employed rather than an employee.[154]

40-024 Payment of social security contributions and income tax The deduction by the employer of income tax and employed earner's social security contributions under the PAYE system (and formerly the payment of National Insurance contributions by the employer stamping the employee's national insurance card) are indications that the parties themselves view their relationship as one of employment.[155] But neither this nor the failure to make these payments or deductions is conclusive as to the nature of the relationship in the eyes of the law.[156]

40-025 The intention of the parties A number of decisions have considered the question of whether an express intention to constitute an employment relationship in the form of a contract for services succeeds in excluding the statutory effects accorded to the employment relationship when constituted as a contract of service.[157] The result of those decisions would seem to be as follows. A genuine intention to transform an employment relationship into a situation where the worker is self-employed will be effective, as where the worker becomes an independent commission agent.[158] Moreover, where a situation is in doubt or ambiguous, so that it can be brought under one relationship or the other, it is open to the parties by agreement to stipulate what the legal situation between them shall be.[159] However, while the expression of the parties' intention may be a relevant factor, it is not a conclusive factor in deciding what is the true nature of the contract; and where there is no written contract, the court is entitled to find contractual terms by implication.[160] Hence,

> "It is by now well settled that the label which the parties choose to use to describe their relationship cannot alter or decide their true relationship; but, in deciding what the relationship is, the expression by them of their true intention is relevant but not conclusive. Its importance may vary according to the facts of the case."[161]

Moreover even where a worker has deliberately and openly chosen to be classi-

---

[154] Contrast with that decision, however, *Drake v Ipsos Mori UK Ltd* [2012] I.R.L.R. 973, EAT.

[155] *Short v J & W Henderson Ltd* (1946) 62 T.L.R. 427, 429; *Denham v Midland Employers Mutual Assurance Ltd* [1955] 2 Q.B. 437; cf. *Pauley v Kenaldo Ltd* [1953] 1 W.L.R. 187, 191 (person stamping her own card as a "self-employed person").

[156] *Maurice Graham Ltd v Brunswick* (1974) 16 K.I.R. 158, *pace* the suggestion of Fisher J. in *Construction Industry Training Board v Labour Force Ltd* [1970] 3 All E.R. 220, 226 D–F; *Ferguson v John Dawson Ltd* [1976] I.R.L.R. 346, 349–350; *Thames Television Ltd v Wallis* [1979] I.R.L.R. 136, 137, para.15. cf. *Narich Pty Ltd v Commissioner of Pay-Roll Tax* [1984] I.C.R. 286.

[157] *Ferguson v John Dawson Ltd* [1976] I.R.L.R. 346; *Davis v New England College of Arundel* [1977] I.C.R. 6; *BSM (1257) Ltd v Secretary of State for Social Services* [1978] I.C.R. 894; *Massey v Crown Life Insurance Co* [1978] I.C.R. 590; *Tyne & Clyde Warehouses Ltd v Hamerton* [1978] I.C.R. 661; *Young & Woods Ltd v West* [1980] I.R.L.R. 201; *Addison v London Philharmonic Ltd* [1981] I.C.R. 261.

[158] *Massey v Crown Life Insurance* [1977] I.C.R. 590, 595 E–H.

[159] [1977] I.C.R. 590 at 595C, per Lord Denning M.R.

[160] *Ferguson v John Dawson Ltd* [1976] I.R.L.R. 346.

[161] *Young & Woods Ltd v West* [1980] I.R.L.R. 201, 208, per Ackner L.J. cf. *Warner Holidays Ltd v Secretary of State for Social Services* [1983] I.C.R. 440; *Narich Pty Ltd v Commissioner of Payroll Tax* [1984] I.C.R. 286. In *Smith v Reliance Water Controls Ltd* [2003] EWCA Civ 1153, Arden L.J. stressed the importance, in cases where there was an express change of status from employee to self-employed worker, of nevertheless weighing all the objective factors according to the test laid down in the *Market Investigations* case to assess whether the contract was a contract of employment. Compare also *RNLI v Bushaway* [2005] I.R.L.R. 675, in which a contract of employment was held to arise between the end-user and the worker in a triangular employment situation despite an express

fied as self-employed, he or she may resile from that position where he or she is objectively an employee and would if held to his or her chosen classification be estopped from invoking a statute made for his or her benefit.[162] In *Protectacoat Firthglow Ltd v Szilagyi*[163] the Court of Appeal held that, in determining whether a person, who was working under documents purporting to create a partnership agreement and a service agreement with the partnership, was its employee within the meaning of s.230 of the Employment Rights Act 1996, the employment tribunal was entitled, if the document purporting to retain the services of a person did not represent the true relationship of the parties, to treat it as a sham and to assume jurisdiction on the footing that a contract of employment existed. A similar approach has since been taken both by the Court of Appeal and the Supreme Court in *Autoclenz Ltd v Belcher*.[164] The Supreme Court confirmed that the approach should be to identify the actual legal obligations between the parties by ascertaining what was actually agreed between the parties, either as set out in the written terms, or, if it is alleged that those terms are not accurate, what is proved to be their actual agreement at the time the contract was concluded. The Supreme Court, moreover, agreed with the Court of Appeal's view that:

"... while employment is a matter of contract, the factual matrix in which the contract is cast is not ordinarily the same as that of an arm's length commercial contract" and asserted that "the relative bargaining power of the parties must be taken into account in deciding whether the terms of any written agreement in truth represent what was agreed."[165]

Special cases: (1) labour-only sub-contracting Labour-only sub-contracting is **40-026** the practice by which a main contractor on a project secures the labour required by contracting with one or more sub-contractors. It is normally the intention that there will be no contract of employment involved in this sub-contracting relationship. Labour-only sub-contracting became widespread in the building industry.[166] In relation to that industry, successive Finance Acts have made provision for deduction in respect of income tax to be made by main contractors from any payments to labour-only sub-contractors unless the sub-contractor holds a certificate of exemption.[167] Various different kinds of labour-only sub-contracting arrangement are found in practice, and their legal effects are a matter of difficulty. There are two main types of sub-contracting arrangement: the two-party arrangement where the worker contracts directly with the main contractor, and the three-party arrangement where there is an intermediary, such as a gang-leader or a sub-contracting company, who contracts with the main contractor to provide labour and with the worker to obtain labour. In any given case, there may be room for argument about

---

agreement that the claimant was to be regarded as self-employed, which agreement contained an "entire contract" clause; see also para.13-117.
[162] *Young & Woods Ltd v West* [1980] I.R.L.R. 201 at 207, per Stephenson L.J.
[163] [2009] EWCA Civ 98, [2009] I.C.R. 835.
[164] [2009] EWCA Civ 1046, [2011] UKSC 41, [2011] 4 All E.R. 745. For subsequent instances of this approach, see for example *Boss Projects LLP v Bragg* [2013] UKEAT 0330/13/SM (express term of "in business on own account" disregarded). Compare now also *Farmer v Heart of Birmingham Teaching Primary Care Trust* [2016] I.C.R. 1088, EAT, where the employment judge found that a written agreement identifying a "legal employer" did not reflect the reality of the situation.
[165] [2011] UKSC 41, at [32]–[35], per Lord Clarke.
[166] See the *Report of the Committee of Inquiry under Professor Phelps-Brown into certain matters concerning labour in Building and Civil Engineering*, Cmnd.3714 (1968).
[167] See Finance Act 2004 Pt 3 Ch.3, "Construction Industry Scheme".

whether the arrangement is of the two-party or three-party type. If the arrangement is of the two-party type, the contract will normally purport to be a contract for services and not a contract of employment. The courts have sometimes found that there is indeed no contract of employment in such cases[168]; but the arrangement may be held to fall within statutes dealing with the employment relationship[169] and has even been classified as a true contract of service despite the parties' clear intention that it should be regarded as a contract for services.[170] A variant upon the two-party type of arrangement is that whereby the worker contracts as one of a firm of partners; in this case the existence of a contract of employment is clearly negated. If the labour-only sub-contracting arrangement is held to be of the three-party type, more complex questions arise. The contract between the main contractor and the intermediate sub-contractor will normally not be a contract of employment.[171] The contract between the intermediate sub-contractor and the worker may be a contract of employment,[172] or a contract for services.[173] An important decision in favour of the contract of employment analysis was that of the Privy Council on appeal in *Lee-Ting Sang v Chung Chi-Keung*.[174] It should follow from the three-party classification of the arrangement that there is no contract (of employment or for services) between the main contractor and the worker; but there may be held to be an employment relationship between them for statutory purposes.[175] Some statutes have expressly deemed the worker an employee of the main contractor.[176]

40-027 Special cases: (2) agency workers Where, as now happens in an increasingly wide range of occupations, employment is obtained via an employment agency, radically divergent analyses of the legal relationships may occur. The worker may be held to have contracted with the agency and not with the client under whose control he or she is placed.[177] In other cases, the worker may be held to have contracted with the client and merely to have received an introduction from the agency.[178] On either view, it has then to be decided whether the worker is an employee. It has been suggested that in the case where the worker is under contract with the agency, there is a sui generis type of contract for the provision of services

---

168 *Westall Richardson Ltd v Roulson* [1954] 2 All E.R. 448; *Re CW & AL Hughes Ltd* [1966] 1 W.L.R. 1369.

169 cf. *Rennisson & Son v Ministry of Social Security* [1970] C.L.Y. 1755. The statutory formula, "a contract personally to execute any work or labour" (used, for example, in Equal Pay Act 1970 s.1(6)); Sex Discrimination Act 1975 s.82(1) presumably covers such a contract: see above, para.40-009. In *Byrne Brothers (Formwork) Ltd v Baird* [2002] I.C.R. 667, the Employment Appeal Tribunal held that building trade workers working as self-employed labour-only sub-contractors qualified as "workers" within the meaning of the Working Time Regulations 1998 (in which the term is defined in the same way as under s.230(6) of the Employment Rights Act 1996) although they clearly were not employed under contracts of employment and had some power to provide a substitute to carry out their work.

170 *Ferguson v John Dawson Ltd* [1976] I.R.L.R. 346.

171 *Emerald Construction Co Ltd v Lowthian* [1966] 1 W.L.R. 691.

172 cf. *Maurice Graham Ltd v Brunswick* (1974) 16 K.I.R. 158.

173 *Construction Industry Training Board v Labour Force Ltd* [1970] 3 All E.R. 220; *Jones v Minton Construction Ltd* (1973) 15 K.I.R. 309.

174 [1990] 2 A.C. 374.

175 *Donaghey v Boulton & Paul Ltd* [1968] A.C. 1 (breach of statutory duty).

176 Wages Councils Act 1979 s.21 (now repealed by the Wages Act 1986 which is now spent). cf. Sex Discrimination Act 1975 s.9 (discrimination against contract workers).

177 *O'Sullivan v Thompson-Coon* (1973) 14 K.I.R. 108.

178 *Alderton v Richard Burgon Associates (Manpower) Ltd* [1974] Crim. L.R. 318.

to a third party.[179] It has also been held[180] that where temporaries on the books of an employment agency were under no obligation to accept bookings offered by the employers, who in turn had no obligation to find work for their temporaries, the relationship between the employers and the temporaries lacked the elements of continuity and care associated with the contract of employment. Some labour-only sub-contracting arrangements are comparable to employment via an agency,[181] and both systems can raise problems insofar as they can involve the avoidance of the ordinary legal consequences of employment under contracts of employment.[182] The case law is rather fluctuating on the question whether and when an agency worker has a contract of employment either with the agency or with its client business to which the agency sends the worker. The prevailing trend seemed to have been set by the assertion in the leading case of *McMeechan v Secretary of State for Employment*[183] that there is no rule of law against there being a contract of employment either with the agency or with the client business. However, the Court of Appeal in *Dacas v Brook Street Bureau (UK) Ltd*, held that the temporary agency worker was not an "employee" of the agency, though she might be an employee of the end-user of her services.[104] The approach in the *Dacas* case was applied to similar effect in *Bunce v Postworth Ltd (t/a Skyblue)*.[185] There was at one stage in recent years a readiness to discern an "implied contract of employment" arising between the worker and the client business arising out of an assignment or series of assignments over a long period of time.[186] However, the Court of Appeal ruled in *James v Greenwich BC*[187] that such a contract can be implied only where it is "necessary" to do so,[188] their view being that if this represented a lacuna in the law determining the rights of agency workers, it could be filled only by legislation. The fact that an individual has a contract of employment with one employer does not preclude their being a worker in the extended agency work sense under s.43K of

---

[179] *Construction Industry Training Board v Labour Force Ltd* [1970] 3 All E.R. 220, 225F (Cooke J.). cf. *Ironmonger v Movefield Ltd* [1988] I.R.L.R. 461.
[180] *Wickens v Champion Employment* [1984] I.C.R. 365, 371D.
[181] cf. *Construction Industry Training Board v Labour Force Ltd* [1970] 3 All E.R. 220.
[182] See above, paras 40-025—40-026.
[183] [1997] I.C.R. 549.
[184] *Dacas v Brook Street Bureau (UK) Ltd* [2004] EWCA Civ 217, [2004] I.R.L.R. 358.
[185] [2005] EWCA Civ 490, [2005] I.R.L.R. 557; compare the decision of the Court of Appeal in *Consistent Group Ltd v Kalwak* [2008] EWCA Civ 430, [2008] I.R.L.R. 505.
[186] *Franks v Reuters Ltd* [2003] I.R.L.R. 423; contrast the earlier *Hewlett Packard Ltd v O'Murphy* [2002] I.R.L.R. 4.
[187] [2008] EWCA Civ 35, [2008] I.R.L.R. 302. Comparison should now be made with the decision in *Muschett v HM Prison Service* [2010] EWCA Civ 25, [2010] I.R.L.R. 451, where the Court of Appeal held that there was no contractual obligation between the agency worker and the Prison Service as the end-user of his services such as was necessary to establish a "contract personally to execute any work or labour". (It would follow that there was no contract of employment between them.) Compare also *RSA Consulting Ltd v Evans* [2010] EWCA Civ 866, where the Court of Appeal held that the assessment of whether it was necessary to imply a "worker's" contract between the claimant and an intermediary agency must not be limited to documentary evidence alone and must extend to consideration of the actual relationship between the parties; a further exploration of that position is to be found in the decision of the Court of Appeal in *Evans v Parasol Ltd* [2010] EWCA Civ 866, [2011] I.C.R. 37. The negative tendency against finding a contract of employment between the agency worker and the end-user was further manifested in *Alstom Transport v Tilson* [2010] EWCA Civ 1308.
[188] The test being that laid down by Bingham L.J. in *The Aramis* [1989] 1 Lloyd's Rep. 213 at 224. Compare now also *Smith v Carillion (JM) Ltd* [2015] EWCA Civ 209, [2015] I.R.L.R. 467.

the Employment Rights Act 1996.[189] The conduct of the business of employment agencies is regulated by the Employment Agencies Act 1973,[190] and by regulations made thereunder,[191] The conditions of employment of agency workers are further regulated by the Agency Workers Regulations 2010.[192] The main effect of these Regulations is to provide a right on the part of agency workers, after a qualifying period of 12 weeks' employment, to the same basic terms and conditions of employment as those which they would have been accorded if they had been recruited directly by the hirer of their services from the temporary work agency.[193]

40-028 **Special cases: (3) office-holders**   There is authority to the effect that the fact that a person is the holder of a public ecclesiastical or tenured office does not ipso facto prevent that person from being classified as working under a contract of employment.[194] Those authorities show that the holding of office neither requires nor excludes the conclusion that the holder is an employee, but simply leaves that question to be decided according to the normal criteria.[195] Similarly, in the context of the civil service, "appointment" of a worker may refer either to office holding

---

[189] *Day v Lewisham and Greenwich NHS Trust* [2017] EWCA Civ 329, [2017] I.R.L.R. 623; see also *McTigue v University Hospital Bristol NHS Foundation Trust* [2016] I.R.L.R. 742, EAT.

[190] As amended by Employment Protection Act 1975 s.114 and Sch.13, which transfer the licensing of private employment agencies from local authorities to the Secretary of State for Employment; and further amended by s.31 of and Sch.7 to the Employment Relations Act 1999.

[191] A series of regulations were revised and replaced by the Conduct of Employment Agencies and Employment Businesses Regulations 2003 (SI 2003/3319). Those have since been amended by the Conduct of Employment Agencies and Employment Businesses (Amendment) Regulations 2007 (SI 2007/3575) and by the Conduct of Employment Agencies and Employment Businesses (Amendment) Regulations 2010 (SI 2010/1782) with effect from October 1, 2010. See now also the Conduct of Employment Agencies and Employment Businesses (Amendment) Regulations 2016 (SI 2016/510).

[192] SI 2010/93, in force from October 1, 2010, implementing the EU Temporary Agency Work Directive 2008/104/EC, [2008] O.J. L327/9. (SI 2010/93 was amended by SI 2011/1941 to correct drafting errors.)

[193] reg.5, subject to reg.7 which specifies the qualifying period. Compare, however, *Moran v Ideal Cleaning Services Ltd* [2014] 2 C.M.L.R. 37, EAT: permanent secondees from an agency not within scope of Agency Workers Regulations 2010. In *Coles v Ministry of Defence* [2015] I.R.L.R. 872, EAT the confinement of the equal treatment obligation to basic working and employment conditions was emphasised in the context of recruitment to jobs.

[194] *102 Social Club v Bickerton* [1977] I.C.R. 911; *Barthorpe v Exeter Diocesan Board of Finance* [1979] I.C.R. 900. It was also so held by the Employment Appeal Tribunal in *Johnson v Ryan* [2000] I.C.R. 236, where it was decided that the holding of the statutory office of rent officer was not inconsistent with employee status.

[195] The older cases concerning ecclesiastical office-holders, particularly *Re National Insurance Act 1911—Re Employment of Church of England Curates* [1912] 2 Ch. 563 were doubted in the *Barthorpe* case so far as they suggested an inconsistency between employment and office—see [1979] I.C.R. at 903G–906D, per Slynn J.; though that suggestion had appeared to be reinstated, so far as ecclesiastical office is concerned, by a dictum in *President of the Methodist Conference v Parfitt* [1984] I.C.R. 176, 184H (Dillon L.J.), and when *Re National Insurance Act 1911*, above, was approved and applied, so far as it held that a curate in the Church of England is not employed under a contract of employment, in *Diocese of Southwark v Coker* [1998] I.C.R. 140. However, authority in favour of the approach taken in the *Barthorpe* case, and against the approach taken in the *Parfitt* case, is provided by the decision of the House of Lords in *Percy v Church of Scotland Board of National Mission* [2005] UKHL 73, [2006] 2 A.C. 28, followed in *New Testament Church of God v Stewart* [2007] I.R.L.R. 178, EAT (upheld by CA on its special facts, [2007] EWCA Civ 1004, [2008] I.C.R. 282) and in *President of the Methodist Conference v Preston* [2011] EWCA Civ 1581; taken cumulatively, these decisions effectively negate any presumptions against intention to create legal relations or against the existence of mutuality of obligation in the construction of the relationships between ministers of religion and their churches; see also *JGE v Trustees of Portsmouth Roman*

or to contractual employment.[196] However, in *Gilham v Ministry of Justice*, the Court of Appeal found that judges were office holders, and therefore excluded from statutory whistleblower protection.[197] There is a further, and again quite distinct, question as to whether a contract of employment contains:

"… elements of a public character which would enable the court to extend to the employee the protection flowing from the right to be heard enjoyed by the holders of an office."[198]

Such a "right to be heard" may exist in conjunction with a contract of employment[199] or in the absence of a contract of employment[200]; its presence or absence is in no way conclusive of whether or not the legal relationship takes the form of a contract of employment.

Special cases: (4) Partnerships and Limited Liability Partnerships   The **40-029** traditional assumption that Partnership and Employment status are mutually exclusive categories[201] has come under scrutiny in the Supreme Court's decision in *Bates van Winkelhof v Clyde & Co LLP*.[202] In multi-tiered partnerships, the question as to whether an individual is a genuine "co-adventurer" or an employee under the traditional tests will therefore become increasingly important.[203] In the case of Limited Liability Partnerships,[204] previous decisions denying employee status to salaried LLP partners[205] are similarly likely to come under scrutiny.[206]

Special cases: (5) employee shareholders   The Growth and Infrastructure Act **40-030** 2013 s.31 introduced a new employment status, that of "employee shareholder". Under this provision, if an employee or person entering into employment agrees to

---

Catholic Diocesan Trust [2012] EWCA Civ 938 in which a Roman Catholic priest was held to have been in a relationship sufficiently "akin to employment" to constitute a basis for imposing vicarious liability. In *President of the Methodist Conference v Preston* [2013] UKSC 29, [2013] 2 A.C. 163, however, the Supreme Court, reversing the above-cited decision of the Court of Appeal, held that the relationship between a Methodist minister and the Methodist Church did not, by reason of the particular way in which that relationship had been constituted, take the legal form of a contract of employment, rather consisting of the holding of an office under the constitutional provisions of that Church. Though compare Lady Hale's dissenting opinion, and now also *Sharpe v Worcester Diocesan Board of Finance Ltd* [2015] EWCA Civ 399, [2015] I.R.L.R. 663. See further Ecclesiastical Offices (Terms of Service) Measure 2009 (No.1), as amended.

196 *Secretary of State for Justice v Betts* [2017] I.R.L.R. 804, EAT.
197 [2017] EWCA Civ 2220, [2018] I.R.L.R. 315.
198 *102 Social Club v Bickerton* [1977] I.C.R. 911, 917F, per Phillips J.
199 cf. *Malloch v Aberdeen Corp* [1971] 1 W.L.R. 1578, 1595, per Lord Wilberforce; see below, para.40-192.
200 cf. *Ridge v Baldwin* [1964] A.C. 40, 65, per Lord Reid.
201 Derived from Partnership Act 1890 s.1.
202 [2014] UKSC 32, [2014] 1 W.L.R. 2047 at [29]. The case itself addressed the question of whether an equity partner in a limited liability partnership was a "worker" employed by the LLP within the meaning of s.230(3)(b) of the Employment Rights Act 1996. See also *CVS Solicitors LLP v van der Borgh* [2013] Eq. L.R. 934.
203 In line with the Supreme Court's decision in *Autoclenz Ltd v Belcher* [2011] UKSC 41, [2011] 4 All E.R. 745; and para.40-025, above.
204 "Bodies corporate" under the Limited Liabilities Partnership Act 2000 s.1.
205 *Kovats v TFO Management LLP* [2009] UKEAT 0357/08/2104, [2009] I.C.R. 1140; *Tiffin v Lester Aldridge LLP* [2012] EWCA Civ 35, [2012] 1 W.L.R. 1887.
206 Especially by reason of Limited Liabilities Partnership Act 2000 s.4(4). See further J. Prassl, "Members, Partners, Employees, Workers? Partnership Law and Employment Status revisited" (2014) 43 I.L.J. 495; cf. also the treatment of salaried LLP members as employees for tax purposes: Income Tax (Trading and Other Income) Act 2005 Pt 9 (as amended).

become an "employee shareholder" in consideration of receipt of shares to the value of £2,000 or more in the employing company, he or she becomes subject to a special kind of contract of employment of which the particular incident is that certain statutory rights normally enjoyed by employees under contracts of employment are not applicable—notably, the general right not to be unfairly dismissed, and to a redundancy payment upon dismissal by reason of redundancy. Reference should be made to the detailed legislation in order to ascertain the exact conditions upon which this new status may be conferred and the exact consequences that it will have.[207] As of December 1, 2016, the tax benefits associated with the employee shareholder employment status have no longer been available to new entrants. The government has announced its intention to legislate and close the status itself to new entrants "at the next legislative opportunity".[208]

40-031 **Special cases: (6) zero-hours contracts** There has been considerable recent discussion of so-called zero-hours contracts, that is to say arrangements for employment without any fixed minimum working hours. Such arrangements will be regarded as constituting contracts of employment if the usual tests are met, in particular the requirement of continuing mutual obligation.[209] Following extensive consultation, provision was made in the Small Business, Enterprise and Employment Act 2015 to deal with one of the problems with such arrangements by ensuring that those working under zero-hours contracts cannot be required to work exclusively for the one employer concerned.[210]

3. FORMATION OF THE CONTRACT

40-032 **Formation and variation of the contract** The general principles of the law of contract apply to contracts of employment, which must therefore comply with the rules, such as that requiring consideration, discussed in Vol.I, above. Although these general principles are relevant, there is often no genuine bargaining between the parties to the individual contract of employment, since the terms are typically determined either unilaterally by the employing enterprise itself or by collective agreements[211] and sometimes by statutory regulation.[212] The terms are often not negotiable by the individual employee, and the contract is thus a "contract of adhesion"[213]: the prospective employee must take employment on the proffered terms if he or she wishes to obtain any employment in that section of industry. It has long been recognised that "it is nowadays often impossible to regard the employment of each individual worker as the result of a separate bargain struck

---

[207] s.31 introduced ss.47G, 104G, and 205A into Employment Rights Act 1996. The provisions came into force on September 1, 2013—SI 2013/1766. See J. Prassl, "Employee Shareholder 'Status': Dismantling the Contract of Employment" (2013) 42 I.L.J. 307.

[208] *https://www.gov.uk/guidance/employee-shareholders*.

[209] See for example *St Ives Plymouth Ltd v Haggerty* [2008] UKEAT 0107/08/MAA; cf. para.40-023, above.

[210] Small Business, Enterprise and Employment Act 2015 s.153, inserting a new s.27A into the Employment Rights Act 1996 (in force as of May 26, 2015). See now also the Exclusivity Terms in Zero Hours Contracts (Redress) Regulations 2015 (SI 2015/2021).

[211] See below, paras 40-047 et seq.

[212] See below, paras 40-055 et seq.

[213] Compare Vol.I, para.13-008 "Contracts in standard form".

between master and servant".[214] Similar arguments apply to variations of contractual terms as put forward by employers,[215] or as resulting from collective agreements.[216] In *Sparks v Department for Transport*[217] the High Court held that in the absence of an explicit agreement, the employer could only make unilateral changes to terms and conditions if they were not detrimental to employees. Moreover, any explicit contractual power to vary must be stated in express and clear terms.[218]

The case-law increasingly identifies an important question as to the time at which **40-033** the contract of employment is deemed to have been formed, in the frequent case where there is an interval of time between the acceptance of a job offer and the commencement of actual employment. In *Welton v Deluxe Retail Ltd*[219] Langstaff J. in the Employment Appeal Tribunal lends support to the view that there is a contract of employment in being during that interval, rather than merely a preliminary "contract for employment". There is also an important question as to whether and when the promotion or moving of an employee to a new post or grade with the same employer will involve the formation of a new contract of employment rather than the variation of an existing one; this may be determinative of whether terms and conditions are carried forward from the original contract of employment. In *FW Farnsworth Ltd v Lacy*[220] Hildyard J. held that upon a "step change of grade", the employment relationship obviously and materially changed to such an extent as to imply the making of a new contract. However, it should be noted that in *Pat Systems v Neilly*[221] Underhill J. took the view that the validity of a restrictive covenant in a contract of employment should in any case be assessed as at the moment when it was explicitly entered into by the employee, rather than by considering whether subsequent variations or replacements of the contract of employment might have validated an originally invalid restrictive covenant, for example by promoting the employee into a position to which the covenant was more appropriate.[222]

Capacity   The capacity of persons in special categories to enter contracts of **40-034** employment is discussed in Vol.I, above.[223] The special position of Crown servants is discussed fully in specialised texts,[224] and is mentioned only briefly in this chapter.[225] It is clear that the relationship of employment is not incompatible with that of husband and wife, so that one spouse may enter into a contract of employ-

---

214 *Re Walker* [1944] 1 All E.R. 614, 616.
215 Such as the unilaterally proposed pay rise which was found to be contractually binding in *Hershaw v Sheffield City Council* [2014] I.C.R. 1120, EAT, or the contractual check-off mechanism which was held not to be derogable in *Cavanagh v Secretary of State for Work and Pensions* [2016] EWHC 1136, [2016] I.R.L.R. 591.
216 Compare *Cabinet Office v Beavan* [2014] I.R.L.R. 434, EAT as to the question of whether the employee's acceptance of a pay increase derived from a collective agreement also connotes acceptance of other changes to terms and conditions of employment which would result from that agreement.
217 [2015] EWHC 181 (QB), [2015] I.R.L.R. 641.
218 *Norman v National Audit Office* [2015] I.R.L.R. 634, EAT.
219 [2013] I.R.L.R. 166, EAT.
220 [2012] EWHC 2830 (Ch), [2013] I.R.L.R. 198.
221 [2012] EWHC 2609 (QB), [2012] I.R.L.R. 979.
222 See especially [2012] EWHC 2609 (QB) at [57].
223 Ch.9 (Personal incapacity): e.g. minors: Vol.I, paras 9-030—9-031.
224 See, for example, Watt, Ch.11 of Sunkin and Payne, *The Nature of the Crown* (1999).
225 See below, para.40-035.

ment with the other.[226] Employment legislation tended to assume this, but to exclude some of the statutory consequences of employment in the case of contracts of employment between spouses.[227]

40-035 **Crown employment** Even when the relationship between a Crown employee and the Crown can be regarded as contractual[228] (a conclusion more readily reached in view of recent decisions such as that in *R. v Lord Chancellor's Department Ex p. Nangle*[229]), the relationship may nevertheless be regarded as terminable at the pleasure of the Crown, so that no claim for wrongful dismissal will lie against the Crown.[230] Any agreement providing that the service can only be terminated on a certain procedure being complied with may be held to be a fetter upon the power of the Crown to dismiss at pleasure and therefore unenforceable.[231] Crown employees have been regarded as probably unable to sue for remuneration due to them[232]; furthermore, the redundancy payments legislation[233] does not bind the Crown.[234] However, recent legislation concerning individual employment rights has in several instances been extended to Crown employment,[235] and the Crown employee has thus been placed in a position more akin to that of other employees than was formerly the case.[236]

40-036 **Public policy, restraint of trade, and illegality** The courts will not enforce a contract of employment the terms of which are so stringent that the employee is virtually treated as his employer's "slave or chattel", without any freedom in his or her private life.[237] Such terms might also amount to a contravention of modern

---

226 *Re Kendrew* [1953] Ch. 291.

227 The exclusionary provisions were repealed by the Employment Act 1982.

228 cf. *Att-Gen for Guyana v Nobrega* [1969] 3 All E.R. 1604; *Kodeeswaran v Att-Gen of Ceylon* [1970] A.C. 1111. cf. now, *R. v Civil Service Appeal Board Ex p. Bruce* [1989] I.C.R. 171.

229 [1992] 1 All E.R. 897.

230 cf. *Dunn v R* [1896] 1 Q.B. 116; *Dunn v Macdonald* [1897] 1 Q.B. 401; *Hales v R* (1918) 34 T.L.R. 589; *Denning v Secretary of State for India* (1920) 37 T.L.R. 138; *Shenton v Smith* [1895] A.C. 229 (medical officer employed by Government of Western Australia dismissed at pleasure); *Terrell v Secretary of State for the Colonies* [1953] 2 Q.B. 482 (colonial judge dismissed at pleasure); *IRC v Hambrook* [1956] 2 Q.B. 641, 654. In *Council of Civil Service Unions v Minister for the Civil Service* [1985] I.C.R. 14, Lord Diplock, at 39C, referred to "the rule of terminability of employment in the civil service without notice, of which the existence is beyond doubt". cf. Wade (1985) 101 L.Q.R. 153 et seq. and 180 et seq.

231 *Rodwell v Thomas* [1944] K.B. 596; *Riordan v War Office* [1959] 1 W.L.R. 1046 (upheld by the CA [1961] 1 W.L.R. 210, without reference to this point).

232 *Mitchell v R* (1890) 1 Q.B. 121n; *Leaman v R* [1920] 3 K.B. 663; *Lucas v Lucas and High Commissioner for India* [1943] P. 68; cf. *Dudfield v Ministry of Works, The Times,* January 24, 1964 (printed in Wedderburn, *Cases and Materials on Labour Law* (1967), p.296). See Logan (1945) 61 L.Q.R. 240.

233 Contained in Employment Rights Act 1996 Pt XI.

234 Civil servants are specifically excluded from the redundancy payments legislation by Employment Rights Act 1996 s.159(b).

235 Employment Rights Act 1996 s.191(1), (2) (unfair dismissal) (including members of the military services—s.192(1), and s.191(1), (2)) applying to the Crown some but not all of the rights of individual employees created by the Employment Protection Act 1975 (including members of the military services—Employment Rights Act 1996 s.192(1)), Equality Act 2010 s.83(2)(b). See also now Employment Rights Act 1996 s.193(1), (2) ("national security").

236 cf. *R. v Civil Service Appeal Board Ex p. Bruce* [1989] I.C.R. 171; *R. v Lord Chancellor's Department Ex p. Nangle* [1992] 1 All E.R. 897. For the case of office holders more generally, see *Secretary of State for Justice v Betts* [2017] I.R.L.R. 804, EAT above, para 40-028.

237 *Davies v Davies* (1887) 36 Ch. D. 359, 393; *Horwood v Millar's Trading Co* [1917] 1 K.B. 305. cf.

slavery legislation.[238] Contracts of employment which unduly restrict the employee in the exercise of his or her profession or calling may, in certain circumstances, be subject to the doctrine of restraint of trade[239]; that doctrine will also apply to covenants imposed upon an employee which restrict his freedom of action after the termination of his or her contract of employment. A full discussion of the principles applicable to such covenants can be found in Ch.16 on "Illegality and Public Policy" in Vol.I.[240]

Effect of illegality on statutory rights   An apparent contract of employment may **40-037** be unenforceable by reason of its illegality,[241] with the result that the worker may lack the status of an employee for statutory purposes. This may arise where the purported contract involves, for instance, sexually immoral purposes.[242] It might possibly occur where the worker is an immigrant and the purported contract contravenes restrictions placed upon his or her freedom to work under the legislation controlling immigration. (In this connection, it should be noted that the Asylum and Immigration Act 1996 made it an offence on the part of an employer to employ a person who is in the United Kingdom without valid and subsisting leave to be so).[243] However, it appears from the decision of the Supreme Court in *Hounga v Allen* that there needs to be a sufficiently close connection between the illegality and the claim, and that any such connection may be disregarded in favour of workers who have been "trafficked" into the country or otherwise gravely exploited.[244] The question of illegality has frequently arisen where the purported contract involves a fraud on the Revenue.[245] But while unprepared to offer a forum where tainted contracts can be relied upon,[246] the courts have been reluctant to let employees easily lose their statutory rights by reason of illegalities of which their employers were the prime movers, and have accordingly required that the illegality should be part of the contract or of the employee's purpose in entering into the contract[247] or, if not ex facie part of the contract, then subjectively known to the employee as being

---

Gaumont-British Picture Corp Ltd v Alexander [1936] 2 All E.R. 1686; *Nokes v Doncaster Amalgamated Collieries* [1940] A.C. 1014, see below, para.40-179.

[238] Modern Slavery Act 2015 (c.30).

[239] *Esso Petroleum Co Ltd v Harper's Garage (Stourport) Ltd* [1968] A.C. 269, 294, 307, 328, 336; cf. *Instone v A Schroeder Music Publishing Co Ltd* [1974] 1 W.L.R. 1308; *Greig v Insole* [1978] 1 W.L.R. 302, 325F–326D.

[240] See above, Vol.I, paras 16-135 et seq.

[241] See Vol.I, paras 16-001 et seq.

[242] *Coral Leisure Group Ltd v Barnett* [1981] I.C.R. 503, 506 D–F, per Browne-Wilkinson J.

[243] s.8; and Deakin & Morris, *Labour Law*, 6th edn (2012), para.3.13. See *V v Addey & Stanhope School Governing Body* [2004] EWCA Civ 1065, [2004] 4 All E.R. 1056. That decision was applied in *Blue Chip Trading Ltd v Helbawi* [2008] UKEAT 0397/08/2011, [2009] I.R.L.R. 128, where however the contract of employment was treated as severable and recovery was allowed in respect of the lawful elements. It should be noted that further restrictions upon immigration and obligations in respect of immigration are imposed by the Immigration Asylum and Nationality Act 2006, and the Borders Citizenship and Immigration Act 2009, to which reference should be made.

[244] *Hounga v Allen* [2014] UKSC 47, [2014] 1 W.L.R. 2889.

[245] *Miller v Karlinski* (1945) 62 T.L.R. 85; *Napier v National Business Agency* [1951] 2 All E.R. 264; *Tomlinson v Dick Evans "U" Drive Ltd* [1978] I.C.R. 639; *Davidson v Pillay* [1979] I.R.L.R. 275; *Corby v Morrison* [1980] I.C.R. 564; *Newland v Simons & Willer Ltd* [1981] I.C.R. 521. cf. *Hyland v JH Barker (North West) Ltd* [1985] I.C.R. 861.

[246] A vivid paraphrase received judicial approval in *Tomlinson v Dick Evans "U" Drive Ltd* [1978] I.C.R. 639, 642B, per Bristow J.

[247] *Coral Leisure Group Ltd v Barnett* [1981] I.C.R. 503. cf. *Hyland v JH Barker (North West) Ltd* [1985] I.C.R. 861.

integral to its performance.[248] In *Hewcastle Catering Ltd v Ahmed* it was held that where the employees had not benefited from and were not essential parties to the fraud, it would be contrary to public policy for them to be deprived of compensation for being unfairly dismissed because they had assisted in the investigation of the fraud.[249] It was held, moreover, in *Leighton v Michael*[250] that an employee whose wages were paid without deduction of tax could nevertheless complain of unlawful sex discrimination in employment without enforcing, relying on or founding a claim on the contract of employment. That decision was approved, and applied in circumstances regarded as comparable, in *Hall v Woolston Hall Leisure Ltd*.[251] It was held in *Brigden v American Express Bank Ltd*[252] that an employee may in certain circumstances be able to claim that a term of the contract of employment is void as being unreasonable by virtue of s.3 of the Unfair Contract Terms Act 1977[253]; the Court of Appeal, however, disapproved that decision and held to the contrary in *Keen v Commerzbank AG*.[254]

40-038 **Gangmasters Licensing Act 2004** The Gangmasters Licensing Act 2004, the essential provisions of which were brought into effect from April 1, 2005, requires individuals to be licensed as gangmasters if they are to engage in the supplying of workers for the use of their services in agricultural work and various kinds of gathering, harvesting, processing or packaging of foodstuffs. Sections 12–14 of that Act create a series of criminal offences involving the disregarding of these licensing requirements, including an offence of acting as a gangmaster without a licence, and an offence of entering into arrangements with gangmasters who are not licensed. The principles discussed in this paragraph will apply to determine whether and when contracts of employment will be rendered unenforceable because their formation or performance involves the commission of one or more of those offences.

40-039 **Selection for employment and the terms on which employment may be offered** Statute law imposes various restrictions upon the freedom of employers to select the individuals with whom they may make contracts of employment and the terms on which employment may be offered. These measures are mainly directed against various kinds of discrimination in the selection of employees.

They are as follows:

---

248 *Davidson v Pillay* [1979] I.R.L.R. 275; *Corby v Morrison* [1980] I.C.R. 564. The court in the latter case was however sceptical of the acceptance of the employee's innocence in the former case— [1980] I.C.R. 564 at 570 E–G. Compare *Enfield Technical Services Ltd v Payne, Grace v BF Components Ltd* [2008] EWCA Civ 393, [2008] I.R.L.R. 500.

249 [1992] I.C.R. 626; compare *Annandale Engineering v Samson* [1994] I.R.L.R. 59; but contrast *Salvesen v Simons* [1994] I.R.L.R. 52.

250 [1995] I.C.R. 1091.

251 [2000] I.C.R. 99, CA. The approach in the *Woolston Hall Leisure* case was reiterated and applied in *Colen v Cebrian (UK) Ltd* [2003] EWCA Civ 1676, [2004] I.C.R. 568; and in *Wheeler v Qualitydeep Ltd (t/a Thai Royale Restaurant)* [2004] EWCA Civ 1085, [2005] I.C.R. 265, where the requirement of active participation by the employee in the illegality as to performance was insisted upon; compare now, however, *V v Addey & Stanhope School Governing Body* [2004] EWCA Civ 1065.

252 [2000] I.R.L.R. 94, QBD.

253 As to which, see generally Vol.I, paras 15-066 et seq.

254 [2006] EWCA Civ 1536, [2007] I.C.R. 623.

(1) *Racial discrimination* Under the Equality Act 2010, it is unlawful for an employer to discriminate on racial grounds[255] against an applicant for employment; (a) in the arrangements made for determining who should be offered the employment; or (b) in the terms on which the employment is offered; or (c) by refusing to offer the employment.[256] Enforcement of these requirements is by means of employment tribunal proceedings,[257] which may lead to an order for compensation or other remedies.[258]

(2) *Sex discrimination* Under the Equality Act 2010 it is unlawful for an employer to discriminate[259] as regards the sex[260] of applicants for a job: (a) in the arrangements the employer makes for determining who shall be offered the job; or (b) in the terms on which the job is offered; or (c) by refusal to offer the job.[261] Contravention of these requirements may be the subject of a complaint to an employment tribunal,[262] which may award compensation[263] among other remedies.[264]

(3) *Discrimination against married persons and civil partners* Under the Equality Act 2010, provisions similar to those concerned with sex discrimination apply to discrimination against married persons and civil partners (by comparison with the treatment which a single person would in comparable circumstances receive).[265]

(4) *Pregnancy and maternity discrimination* Provision is made by the Equality Act 2010 against pregnancy and maternity discrimination in "work cases"[266]; the provisions are described more fully in a later paragraph[267] in respect of such discrimination occurring during the period of employment; particular provision is made against such discrimination as to the arrangements which an employer makes for deciding to whom to offer employment, and as to the terms on which employment is offered, or by not offering employment.[268]

(5) *Disability discrimination* The Disability Discrimination Act 1995, which replaced the Disabled Persons (Employment) Act 1944, conferred new rights on disabled persons in respect of access to employment and the terms on which employment may be offered. A number of significant amendments were made with effect from October 2004 by Regulations implementing EC Directive 2000/78.[269] The Disability Discrimination Act 2005 amended and extended in various respects the provisions of the Disability

---

[255] As defined by ss.9, 13(1), (5), 19.
[256] s.39(1), subject to the exception contained in s.83(11) and Sch.9 Pt 1 (occupational requirements).
[257] ss.124–126.
[258] s.124(2)(b), (6).
[259] As defined by ss.9, 13(1), (6), 19.
[260] Or on the grounds of gender reassignment; s.7.
[261] s.39(1), subject to a defined exception where being of a certain gender is an occupational requirement, s.83 and Sch.9 Pt I.
[262] s.120.
[263] s.124(2)(b).
[264] s.124(2)(a), (c), (3)–(7).
[265] s.8.
[266] s.18.
[267] See para.40-132 below.
[268] s.39(1).
[269] The Disability Discrimination Act 1995 (Amendment) Regulations 2003 (SI 2003/1673), implementing Council Directive 2000/78.

Discrimination Act 1995 concerning disability discrimination in employment. Corresponding provisions are now made by the Equality Act 2010; in brief summary, the provisions are as follows. It is unlawful under the 2010 Act for an employer of employed persons[270] to discriminate against a disabled person in the arrangements made for determining who should be offered employment, or in the terms on which employment is offered, or by refusing to offer employment.[271] An employer engages in unlawful discrimination by failing without justification to discharge a duty to make reasonable adjustments to the arrangements under which employment is offered and to any physical feature of the employment premises which are such as to place the disabled person at a substantial disadvantage in comparison with persons who are not disabled.[272] Unlawful disability discrimination may be the subject of complaint to an employment tribunal, which has remedial powers similar to those which it has in relation to sex or race discrimination.[273]

(6) *Religion or belief and sexual orientation* Provisions concerning access to employment very closely comparable to those relating to sex and race discrimination, and victimisation in connection with sex and race discrimination, have been made, with effect from December 2, 2003, with regard to religion or belief and with regard to sexual orientation, by, respectively, the Employment Equality (Religion or Belief) Regulations 2003[274] and the Employment Equality (Sexual Orientation) Regulations 2003.[275] Both of these sets of regulations were enacted in implementation of the requirements of Council Directive 2000/78 establishing a general framework for equal treatment in employment and vocational training.[276] Corresponding provisions are now contained in the Equality Act 2010.[277]

(7) *Age* Provisions concerning access to employment generally comparable to those relating to discrimination on the grounds of sex, race, disability, religion or belief and sexual orientation were made, with effect from October 2006, with regard to age by the Employment Equality (Age) Regulations 2006,[278] and corresponding provisions are now contained in the Equality Act 2010,[279] as since significantly amended by the Employment Equality (Repeal of Retirement Age Provisions) Regulations 2011.[280]

(8) *Victimisation in connection with discrimination* The provisions concerned with discrimination on all these grounds also apply to victimisation, in the

---

[270] For the broad category of workers included, see s.83(2), and for the extension to contract workers, s.41. The 1995 Act s.7 originally restricted the application of the Act to employers of 20 or more employed persons; that exemption for small businesses was removed with effect from October 2004 by reg.7 of the 2003 Regulations.

[271] See ss.6, 15, 39(1).

[272] See ss.20, 39(5).

[273] See ss.120, 124.

[274] SI 2003/1660, in particular reg.6(1).

[275] SI 2003/1661, in particular reg.6(1).

[276] Directive 2000/78.

[277] ss.10, 12, 39 subject to s.83(11) and Sch.9 Pt 1 (occupational requirements).

[278] SI 2006/1031, similarly enacted in implementation of the requirements of Council Directive 2000/78 establishing a general framework for equal treatment in employment and vocational training.

[279] ss.10, 12, 39 subject to s.83(11) and Sch.9 Pt 2 (exceptions relating to age).

[280] SI 2011/1069 which, inter alia, repealed para.9 of Sch.9 Pt 2 (applicants at or approaching retirement age).

sense of discriminatory treatment of persons taking action connected with asserting rights under or alleging contravention of the Equality Act 2010.[281]

(9)   *Rehabilitation of offenders* The Rehabilitation of Offenders Act 1974 provides that a conviction which has become spent or any circumstances auxiliary thereto or any failure to disclose a spent conviction shall not be a proper ground for excluding a person from any office, profession, occupation or employment.[282] However, no enforcement mechanism is provided, so that where the exclusion from employment takes the form of a simple refusal to engage a particular applicant not previously employed by the employer, it is not yet clear whether the applicant can found any claim on that statutory provision or make good any claim by invoking its aid.[283]

(10) *Trade union membership* It is unlawful for an employer to refuse a person employment because he or she is, or is not, a member or is unwilling to accept a requirement to become, or to cease to be, a member of a trade union.[284] Once employed, moreover, an employee acquires certain statutory rights in connection with trade union membership, non-membership, and activities.[285]

Form: written particulars   By statute, the contracts of employment of merchant **40-040** seamen must be in writing.[286] But the common law does not require any particular formalities or form for contracts of employment.[287] However, legislation now imposes on employers the obligation to give to employees written particulars of certain of the terms of their employment. By s.1 of the Employment Rights Act 1996,[288] an employer, subject to certain exceptions, is obliged not later than two months after the beginning of an employment to give to his employee a written statement identifying the parties, specifying the date when the employment began (stating whether any employment with a previous employer counts as part of the employee's continuous period of employment[289] with him and if so specifying the date on which the continuous period of employment began), and giving the following particulars of the terms of employment (as at a specified date not more than one week earlier than the statement):

(a)   the scale or rate of remuneration (or the method of calculation);
(b)   the intervals at which remuneration is paid;

---

281   See ss.27, 39(3).
282   s.4(3)(b). The term "spent conviction" is defined by s.1(1) with reference to s.5. The Data Protection Act 1998 s.56 makes it a criminal offence to require job applicants or existing employees to make subject access requests in lieu of providing a normal criminal record check, which would not disclose spent convictions.
283   Compare, however, para.40-064, see below, where the effect of s.4(3)(a) upon non-disclosure of a conviction, in connection with an application for employment, is discussed.
284   Trade Union and Labour Relations (Consolidation) Act 1992 s.137, originally s.1 of the Employment Act 1990.
285   See below, paras 40-115—40-116.
286   Merchant Shipping Act 1995 s.25 ("crew agreements"); and the requirements for written particulars made by Pt I of the Employment Rights Act 1996 accordingly do not apply to merchant mariners—see Employment Rights Act 1996 s.199(1).
287   Specific requirements of form are, however, made by the Apprenticeships (Form of Apprenticeship Agreement) Regulations 2012 (SI 2012/844). See also Deakin & Morris, *Labour Law*, 6th edn (2012), para.4.13.
288   Employment Rights Act 1996 ss.1–7, 210–219.
289   As assessed under the provisions detailed below, paras 40-165—40-168.

(c) any terms and conditions relating to hours of work including terms relating to normal working hours;

(d) any terms and conditions relating to—

(i) holidays and holiday pay (including entitlement to accrued holiday pay on the termination of employment);

(ii) incapacity for work due to sickness or injury, including any provisions for sick pay;

(iii) pensions and pension schemes[290];

(e) the length of notice which the employee is obliged to give and entitled to receive to determine his contract of employment[291];

(f) the title of the job which the employee is employed to do or a brief description of the work for which the employee is employed;

(g) where the employment is not intended to be permanent, the period for which it is expected to continue or, if it is for a fixed term, the date when it is to end;

(h) either the place of work or an indication that the employee works at various places;

(i) any collective agreements directly affecting the terms and conditions of employment; and

(j) where the employee is required to work abroad for more than one month, various details of that employment abroad.

40-041 Particulars of disciplinary and dismissal procedures The written particulars must in addition specify any disciplinary rules applicable to the employee[292] (except such as relate to health or safety at work which must, under s.2(3) of the Health and Safety at Work, etc. Act 1974, be included in the written statement of health and safety policy required to be issued to employees)[293] or at least refer to a document reasonably accessible to the employee which specifies the rules. There must also be specified a person to whom the employee can apply if dissatisfied with any disciplinary decision relating to him; and a person to whom the employee can apply to seek redress of any employment grievance; the manner of making such applications; and any steps consequent upon any such application.[294] With effect from October 2004, these particulars must also cover the procedure which applies when an employee is disciplined or dismissed.[295] Employers with fewer than 20 employees were exempt from the requirement to include a note about disciplinary rules and procedures in the written statement of main terms and conditions[296]; but that exemption ceased to have effect from October 2004.[297]

---

[290] Subject to the proviso to s.1(4)(d)(iii) of the Employment Rights Act 1996, made by s.1(5) relating to statutory schemes. It must also be stated whether a contracting-out certificate is in force for the employment concerned: s.3(5).

[291] See below, paras 40-163 et seq.

[292] Employment Rights Act 1996 s.3(1)(a).

[293] Employment Rights Act 1996 s.3(2).

[294] Employment Rights Act 1996 s.3(1)(b), (c).

[295] Employment Rights Act 1996 s.3(1)(aa), (b)(i), (2) as inserted or amended by s.35 of the Employment Act 2002 with effect from that date.

[296] Employment Rights Act 1996 s.3(3).

[297] By virtue of s.36 of the Employment Act 2002, implemented with effect from that date.

Statement of initial employment particulars; and use of alternative docu-   **40-042**
ment to give particulars   Formerly, the obligation to provide written particulars
could generally be discharged by referring to other documents, such as collective
agreements, containing the required information; but that facility of reference to
other documents was then restricted to certain particulars only[298]; and most of the
particulars must be gathered together in a single document known as the "statement of initial employment particulars".[299] However, with effect from October 4,
2004, provision was made for particulars to be given in the alternative form of a
written contract of employment or letter of engagement, including such documents given to the employee before his employment begins.[300]

Changes in terms   Any change in the terms of employment to be included in the   **40-043**
statement is likewise to be notified to the employee within one month after the
change.[301] The employer may, for this purpose, refer the employee to some document which is made reasonably accessible to him to the extent, but only to the
extent, that the obligation to give the original particulars may be so discharged.[302]
A change in the name of the employer must be notified to the employee as a change
of terms,[303] as must a change in the identity of the employer which does not break
the employee's continuity of employment,[304] in which case the date must be specified on which the employee's period of continuous service began.[305]

Effect of particulars   If the written statement describes itself as a contract of   **40-044**
employment and if its receipt is acknowledged by the employee, the statement may
be deemed to be the contract of employment itself and not a mere description of
the contract, with the consequent application of the parol evidence rule to exclude
inconsistent evidence of contractual terms verbally agreed.[306] Even where that does
not occur, the written statement may form the basis of an estoppel against the
employer[307]; and the employee's acquiescence in the statement may, exceptionally, have the effect of raising an estoppel against him.[308]

Failure to provide accurate statement or to notify change in terms   If an   **40-045**
employer fails to comply with his obligation to give his employee a written state-

---

[298] Employment Rights Act 1996 s.2(2), (3), and s.6. See further below, para.40-054.
[299] Employment Rights Act 1996. See s.2(4).
[300] By virtue of s.37 of the Employment Act 2002, inserting new ss.7A and 7B of the Employment
Rights Act 1996, to be implemented with effect from that date.
[301] Employment Rights Act 1996 s.4(1), (3).
[302] Employment Rights Act 1996 s.4(2), (3), (4), (5) and s.6.
[303] Employment Rights Act 1996 s.4(6)(a).
[304] Employment Rights Act 1996 s.4(6)(b).
[305] Employment Rights Act 1996 s.4(8).
[306] *Gascol Conversions Ltd v Mercer* [1974] I.C.R. 420.
[307] cf. *Smith v Blandford Gee Cementation Ltd* [1970] 3 All E.R. 154; but contrast *Parkes Classic
Confectionery Ltd v Ashcroft* [1973] I.T.R. 43; and *System Floors Ltd v Daniel* [1981] I.R.L.R. 475,
476—"Nor are the statements of the terms finally conclusive: at most, they place a heavy burden
on the employer to show that the actual forms of contract are different from those which he has set
out in the statutory statement" (Browne-Wilkinson J.).
[308] cf. *Soutar v Fisher* (1975) 10 I.T.R. 38; *Boyce v Torquay Cemetery Co* [1975] I.R.L.R. 80; but see
Jones v Associated Tunnelling Co Ltd [1981] I.R.L.R. 477, 481—"In our view to imply an agreement to vary or to raise an estoppel against the employee on the grounds that he has not objected to
a false record by the employers of the terms actually agreed is a course which should be adopted
with great caution" (Browne-Wilkinson J.). See Deakin & Morris, *Labour Law*, 6th edn (2012),
para.4.25.

ment of the specified terms of employment,[309] the matter may be referred to an employment tribunal which is empowered to determine which particulars ought to have been given.[310] The tribunal is also empowered to "substitute other particulars", as it may determine to be appropriate, when an incomplete or inaccurate statement has been given.[311] If the employer fails to give written particulars of a term, he or she may be unable to sue his employee for breach of that term; but the court might hold that it is not the intention of the Act that such a failure should affect the enforceability of the contract.[312] Failure to notify changes in terms and inaccurate notification of changes are treated in the same way as failure to provide an accurate original statement.[313] It is not fully clear whether or when failure to notify changes in terms and failure to complain of lack of notification of changes appear not to vitiate or create an estoppel against a valid contractual variation.[314]

40-046 **Compensation for failure with respect to the provision of employment particulars** In addition to the powers and remedies described in the previous paragraph, provision is made by s.38 of the Employment Act 2002, with effect from October 4, 2004, for employment tribunals to award compensation to an employee where the lack, incompleteness or inaccuracy of the employment particulars provided by the employer is established in the course of proceedings under specified employment tribunal jurisdictions.[315] In particular, the tribunal must in those circumstances increase any award made against the employer in respect of the claim under the other jurisdiction(s) by a minimum amount of two weeks' pay and may increase any such award by the higher amount of four weeks' pay, or must award a minimum amount of two weeks' pay and may award a higher amount of four weeks' pay where compensation is not a remedy available for the claim in question, or where the tribunal does not award compensation in respect of that claim. There is, however, no duty to make or increase an award in this way "if there are exceptional circumstances which would make an award or increase ... unjust or inequitable".[316]

---

[309] Employment Rights Act 1996 s.1. See above, paras 40-040—40-044.

[310] Employment Rights Act 1996 s.11(1), (2), 12(2); see *Owens v Multilux Ltd* [1974] I.R.L.R. 113; *Leighton v Construction Industry Training Board* [1978] I.C.R. 577; *WPM Retail Ltd v Lang* [1978] I.C.R. 787; and *Mears v Safecar Security Ltd* [1982] I.C.R. 626, for discussion of the scope of this power. cf. *Eagland v British Telecommunications Plc* [1993] I.C.R. 644. It was held by the Court of Appeal in *Southern Cross Healthcare Ltd v Perkins* [2010] EWCA Civ 1442 that this power does not extend to the construction of the terms of the contract of employment themselves save so far as might be necessary in order to assess whether the statutory statement correctly reflected those terms.

[311] Employment Rights Act 1996 s.12(2); see *Mears v Safecar Security Ltd* [1982] I.C.R. 626.

[312] cf. *Anderson v Daniel* [1924] 1 K.B. 138, 149.

[313] Employment Rights Act 1996 s.11(1).

[314] cf. *Chant v Turriff Construction Ltd* (1966) 2 I.T.R. 380; *Parkes Classic Confectionery v Ashcroft* (1973) 8 I.T.R. 43; *System Floors Ltd v Daniel* [1981] I.R.L.R. 475; *Jones v Associated Tunnelling Co Ltd* [1981] I.R.L.R. 477. Note that in *Scally v Southern Health Board* [1991] I.C.R. 771 a failure by the employer to inform the employee of a new pension entitlement was treated as a breach of an implied term of the contract of employment. See below, para.40-040.

[315] The jurisdictions are specified under s.38(1) by Sch.5, subject to the possibility of amendment by ministerial order. The list includes all the major employment tribunal jurisdictions over employment rights.

[316] Employment Act 2002 s.38(5).

4. COLLECTIVE AGREEMENTS AND STATUTORY AWARDS OF TERMS

(a) Collective Agreements as Contracts

Legal enforceability Although there was between 1975 and 1980, and has since **40-047** 1999 been, legal provision which may be used to secure compulsory recognition of trade unions,[317] the tradition and style of British collective bargaining strongly reflects its voluntary and informal development. The leading decision on the legal status of a collective agreement[318] confirmed the majority[319] opinion of those concerned with such agreements that they are not normally intended to create legal relations.[320] This means that they are binding in honour only, and that their enforcement must depend on industrial and political pressure. This view is given statutory force under the Trade Union and Labour Relations (Consolidation) Act 1992[321] and the presumption which it creates against intention to make a legally enforceable contract can be rebutted only where an agreement is in writing stating specifically that a legally enforceable contract is intended[322]; in the latter case it is conclusively presumed that a legally enforceable agreement was intended.[323] The same presumptions apply to the different parts of agreements where an agreement is in writing, and is stated to be intended to be legally enforceable as to part only.[324]

The process by which collective agreements are made is known as "collective **40-048** bargaining" rather than "contract"[325] and the application to them of the ordinary rules of the law of contract could lead to great difficulties. Some collective agreements are vague as to who are the parties (e.g. between "the Workpeople's side and the Employer's side of" the industry) and their language is often not legal language; there would be many difficulties in interpreting them if they were held to be legally enforceable. However, the former statutory obstacle to enforcement of collective agreements,[326] which applied to certain collective agreements even if they could be

---

[317] Employment Protection Act 1975 ss.11–16, repealed by the Employment Act 1980; Trade Union and Labour Relations (Consolidation) Act 1992 Ch.VA and Sch.1 inserted by the Employment Relations Act 1999.

[318] *Ford Motor Co Ltd v AEF* [1969] 2 Q.B. 303.

[319] To the contrary, see Gayler, *Industrial Law* (1955), pp.172–174; and cf. *Edwards v Skyways Ltd* [1964] 1 W.L.R. 349; *East London Bakers' Union v Goldstein, The Times,* June 9, 1904 (printed in Wedderburn at p.272); Selwyn (1969) 32 M.L.R. 377; (1970) 33 M.L.R. 117, 238.

[320] Kahn-Freund in Flanders and Clegg (eds), *The System of Industrial Relations in Great Britain* (1954), p.57, and in (1942) 6 M.L.R. 112, 115–116; Wedderburn, *Cases and Materials on Labour Law,* pp.267–281; Wedderburn, *The Worker and the Law,* 2nd edn, pp.171–180, and in 24 M.L.R. 572, 583–584; *Ardley and Morey v London Electricity Board, The Times,* June 16, 1956; cf. *Spring v National Amalgamated Stevedores and Dockers' Society* [1956] 1 W.L.R. 585, 592; *Ayling v London and India Docks Committee* (1893) 9 T.L.R. 409; Hepple [1970] C.L.J. 122.

[321] Trade Union and Labour Relations (Consolidation) Act 1992 s.179.

[322] Trade Union and Labour Relations (Consolidation) Act 1992 s.179(1); see *National Coal Board v National Union of Mineworkers* [1986] I.C.R. 736. Compare also now *Malone v British Airways Plc* [2010] EWHC 302 (QB), [2010] I.R.L.R. 431 where it was held that there was no sufficient objective intention to give the terms of the collective agreement legal enforceability regarding cabin crew complements at the behest of any individual crew member.

[323] Trade Union and Labour Relations (Consolidation) Act 1992 s.179(2).

[324] Trade Union and Labour Relations (Consolidation) Act 1992 s.179(3).

[325] See Kahn-Freund in Flanders and Clegg (eds), *The System of Industrial Relations in Great Britain* (1954), pp.57 et seq.

[326] Trade Union Act 1871 s.4(4).

shown to be intended to have contractual force, has long since been removed entirely.[327]

(b) Incorporation of Collective Agreements into Individual Contracts of Employment

40-049 **Agency and collective agreements** A collective agreement might, in theory, be made by the negotiating parties as agents for their respective members, but the associations and unions making collective agreements appear to act as principals, and not as agents on behalf of their members[328]; although some dicta[329] suggest that there is agency in this bargaining procedure.[330] Many difficulties would arise if the agency doctrine were accepted, e.g. what would be the position of non-unionists in the industry who were not represented in the collective bargaining? or of members who join the union after the date of the collective agreement? It may, however, be legitimate to employ the agency doctrine when union officials negotiate a settlement of a dispute on behalf of a few employees identified by name.[331] In *Harris v Richard Lawson Autologistics Ltd*[332] the Court of Appeal held that a shop steward had ostensible authority to negotiate an agreement on holiday pay on behalf of the members of the Transport and General Workers' Union employed by the company concerned, and that it was reasonable for the company to conclude that the revised terms had been adopted by the workers concerned although they had not been put to those workers for their approval.

40-050 **Express incorporation** It is clear that the terms of a collective agreement may be *expressly* incorporated by a reference in an individual contract of employment.[333] In 1958, the Court of Appeal held that a provision in a collective agreement between the National Coal Board and a trade union had been incorporated into the individual contracts of employment, so that the employee was liable for breach of the obligation to work "such days or part days in each week as may be reasonably required

---

327 Industrial Relations Act 1971 Sch.9 (itself repealed by Trade Union and Labour Relations Act 1974 s.1).

328 *Holland v London Society of Compositors* (1924) 40 T.L.R. 440.

329 *Rookes v Barnard* [1961] 2 All E.R. 825, 827 (there is no mention of this in [1964] A.C. 1129, but it was doubted in the Court of Appeal [1963] 1 Q.B. 623, 675); *Edwards v Skyways Ltd* [1964] 1 W.L.R. 349, 354, 357 ("representatives": it was conceded in this case that the union was acting as agent; the court also treated the negotiated terms of settlement as a standing offer by the company, which each individual employee could "accept": [1964] 1 W.L.R. 349 at 353); *Chappell v Times Newspapers Ltd* [1975] I.C.R. 145, 172 D, H.

330 Discussed by Kahn-Freund (1942) 6 M.L.R. 112; in Flanders and Clegg (eds), *The System of Industrial Relations in Great Britain* (1954), pp.55 et seq. and in Ginsberg (ed.), *Law and Opinion in England in the 20th Century* (1959), pp.215–263; Wedderburn (1961) 24 M.L.R. 572, 583; (1962) 25 M.L.R. 513, 526–530; and in *The Worker and the Law*, 3rd edn, pp.327–329; cf. *Ford Motor Co Ltd v AEF* [1969] 2 Q.B. 303, 331.

331 *Deane v Craik, The Times,* March 16, 1962 (see Wedderburn, *Cases and Materials on Labour Law* (1967), p.459; sed contra in *The Worker and the Law*, 3rd edn, p.328). cf. *Edwards v Skyways Ltd* [1964] 1 W.L.R. 349; *The Burton Group v Smith* [1977] I.R.L.R. 350.

332 [2002] I.C.R. 765.

333 *Hooker v Lange, Bell & Co* [1937] 4 L.J.N.C.C.R. 199 ("at union rates"); *Young v Canadian Northern Ry* [1931] A.C. 83; *National Coal Board v Galley* [1958] 1 W.L.R. 16. cf. *Hulland v Saunders* [1945] K.B. 78; *Secretary of State for Employment v ASLEF (No.2)* [1972] I.C.R. 19, especially, per Roskill L.J. at 69.

by the management".[334] But express reference in an individual contract of employment to a collective agreement as regulating the employee's wages or other substantive conditions of service will normally be held not to incorporate procedural provisions of the collective agreement.[335] There may be express incorporation of terms from a collective agreement where the employer, for the purpose of complying with the statutory obligation to give written particulars of the terms of employment,[336] issues the employee with a document styling itself a contract of employment, which refers to one or more collective agreements, and which is signed as received by the employee.[337] The express incorporation, into individual contracts, of "no-strike" obligations derived from collective agreements is now subject to certain special statutory conditions which are considered below.[338] Express incorporation can give rise to an enforceable term in the individual contract of employment although, as is frequently the case, the collective agreement is expressed to be binding in honour only as between the parties to it.[339] As to the latitude of construction which is allowed (or denied) in relation to changed industrial relations circumstances, see *Adams v British Airways Plc*.[340] In the absence of any contrary intention, where terms from a collective agreement are specifically incorporated into individual contracts, the relevant terms will be those contained in the current collective agreement, and thus they may be varied from time-to-time.[341] On the other hand, once a term derived from a collective agreement has been incorporated into individual contracts, the termination of the collective agreement does not in itself affect the incorporated terms.[342]

Incorporation by implication   The problem of incorporation is more difficult **40-051** when there is no relevant express term in the individual contract of employment, but it is alleged that the parties have tacitly agreed to incorporate terms of the relevant collective agreement.[343] There is some informative case law from periods when national and local sectoral collective bargaining was more widespread than

---

[334] *National Coal Board v Galley* [1958] 1 W.L.R. 16. cf. *Spring v National Amalgamated Stevedores and Dockers' Society* [1956] 1 W.L.R. 585.

[335] *R. v Industrial Disputes Tribunal Ex p. Portland UDC* [1955] 1 W.L.R. 949; *National Coal Board v National Union of Mineworkers* [1986] I.C.R. 736.

[336] See above, paras 40-040—40-042 and see below, para.40-054.

[337] *Gascol Conversions Ltd v Mercer* [1974] I.C.R. 420; cf. *Secretary of State for Employment v ASLEF (No.2)* [1972] I.C.R. 19, 53H–54A, 69C–70F; *System Floors Ltd v Daniel* [1981] I.R.L.R. 475.

[338] See below, para.40-053; *Bloomfield v Springfield Hosiery Ltd* [1972] I.C.R. 91, 93E.

[339] *Marley v Forward Trust Group Ltd* [1986] I.C.R. 891.

[340] [1995] I.R.L.R. 577.

[341] *National Coal Board v Galley* [1958] 1 W.L.R. 16; see as to the effect of the employer's resignation from the employers' federation that made the agreement, *Burroughs Machines Ltd v Timmoney* [1977] I.R.L.R. 404. Compare, however, *Ackinclose v Gateshead MBC* [2005] I.R.L.R. 79, EAT, where it was held that when a contract of employment only made reference to a national agreement as the relevant collective agreement without any further reference or incorporation, a successor agreement would not thereby be incorporated so as to take effect following transfer of the employment in question from a local authority employer party to the national bargaining structure to a private employer not party to that structure. Contrast, however, *Griffiths v Salisbury DC* [2004] EWCA Civ 162, where an agreement implementing the national agreement was held to be incorporated in the individual contract and where therefore a backdated pay freeze imposed under that agreement was effective.

[342] *Robertson v British Gas Corp* [1983] I.C.R. 351; *Gibbons v Associated British Ports* [1985] I.R.L.R. 376. See also now *Whent v T Cartledge Ltd* [1997] I.R.L.R. 153.

[343] On the doctrine of implied terms, see Vol.I, Ch.14, especially para.14-033.

it is today. When the employee knows[344] of the terms of the collective agreement, it may well be legitimate to infer that it was the presumed common intention of both parties to the contract that these terms should apply when the contract itself was silent on any issue.[345] The terms of a collective agreement accepted by a Joint Council cannot be incorporated by implication if the functions of the Joint Council are not executory but "purely consultative"[346] and not intended to create legally enforceable rights of action.[347] The terms of a national collective agreement may be modified by a local collective agreement between the employers and union representatives, and in these circumstances the appropriate inference should be that it is the local agreement which is incorporated into individual contracts of employment.[348] However, the cases show some tendency to treat the local agreement as not intended to affect the terms of individual contracts, particularly when the local agreement is a less formal one than the national agreement.[349] In determining whether a particular part of a collective agreement has been incorporated into the individual contracts of employment of the employees, it is necessary to look at the content and character of those parts and whether they were apt to be a term of the contracts.[350] A part of a collective agreement may, for instance, be treated as designed to give flexible and informal guidance as to what is expected to happen in given situations, in a way which is inconsistent with contractual rights being created.[351] In the case of *Henry v London General Transport Services Ltd*[352] Lindsay J. in the Employment Appeal Tribunal gave some important indications as to when the terms of individual contracts of employment will be treated as having been varied as the result of a collective agreement negotiated between the employer and a trade union or trade unions. In the instant case, it was held that individual contracts had been so varied by a collective agreement for the reduction of wages which had

---

[344] There is some uncertainty about the extent of the requirement of knowledge. See Hepple, *Employment Law*, 4th edn (1981), para.267. See Deakin & Morris, *Labour Law*, 6th edn (2012), para.4.29, "The 'bridge term'".

[345] *McLea v Essex Lines* (1933) 45 Ll.L. Rep. 254; *Tomlinson v LMS Ry* [1944] 1 All E.R. 537; *Hulland v Saunders* [1945] K.B. 78; *Joel v Cammell Laird (Ship Repairers) Ltd* [1969] I.T.R. 206. cf. incorporation of customary terms: *Sagar v Ridehalgh* [1931] 1 Ch. 310.

[346] *Dudfield v Ministry of Works*; *Faithfull v Admiralty*, *The Times,* January 24, 1964 (printed in Wedderburn, *Cases and Materials on Labour Law* (1967), pp.296–300).

[347] cf. *Grieve v Imperial Tobacco Ltd*, The Guardian, April 30, 1963 (see Wedderburn at p.118).

[348] *Clift v West Riding CC*, *The Times,* April 10, 1964 (see Wedderburn at p.293). The written particulars to be supplied to the employee under the contracts of employment legislation, see above, paras 40-040—40-042, will now usually specify to which agreement reference is made.

[349] *Loman and Henderson v Merseyside Transport Services Ltd* (1967) 3 K.I.R. 726, 732; *Gascol Conversions Ltd v Mercer* [1974] I.C.R. 420, 425 B-C. Compare also the decision of the Court of Appeal in *Keeley v Fosroc International Ltd* [2006] EWCA Civ 1277, [2006] I.R.L.R. 961, and the comments by Auld L.J. on the construction of which terms will be treated as apt for incorporation where a staff handbook or collective agreement is generally incorporated (by express words) into individual contracts of employment.

[350] *Alexander v Standard Telephones and Cables (No.2)* [1991] I.R.L.R 286. Compare now *Anderson v London Fire and Emergency Planning Authority* [2013] EWCA Civ 321, [2013] I.R.L.R. 459 in which Maurice Kay L.J. sets out, at [16], a general approach to the incorporation by implication into contracts of employment of terms from collective agreements which treats the whole issue as one of "giving a fair meaning to the words used in the factual context (known to the parties) which gave rise to the agreement", following the approach which Sir Thomas Bingham M.R. had taken in *Adams v British Airways Plc* [1996] I.R.L.R. 574, CA.

[351] *Wandsworth LBC v D'Silva* [1998] I.R.L.R. 193.

[352] [2001] I.R.L.R. 132; upheld by the Court of Appeal: [2002] I.C.R. 910.

been acted upon for two years; it followed that the employers had not made an unlawful deduction from wages[353] in paying the reduced remuneration.

In most collective agreements there will be many terms not directly applicable **40-052** to the individual employee, e.g. procedural matters between the unions and the employers, and these may be held not appropriate to be incorporated by implication into individual contracts.[354] As the result of a statutory provision which is considered below,[355] "no strike" obligations contained in collective agreements can be incorporated into individual contracts by an implied term only where certain stringent requirements are observed. Also, since an express term in a contract must prevail over any alleged implied term, an express term in an individual contract of employment will displace any term in a collective agreement which would otherwise be incorporated in the contract under the implied-term doctrine.[356]

Incorporation of "no-strike" obligations Section 180 of the Trade Union and **40-053** Labour Relations (Consolidation) Act 1992 imposes special safeguards upon the incorporation, into individual contracts of employment, of "no-strike" obligations derived from collective agreements. Section 180 enacts that provisions in collective agreements placing restrictions upon strikes or other industrial action by workers will not be incorporated into individual contracts of employment unless the collective agreement:

(a)   is in writing; and
(b)   expressly states that its "no-strike" provisions are liable to be incorporated into individual contracts of employment; and
(c)   is reasonably accessible to the workers affected at their place of work and is available to be consulted during working hours.

The union(s) concerned must be independent union(s)[357] and the ordinary rules of express[358] or implied[359] incorporation must be satisfied. It is not clear how wide a range of collectively bargained terms fall within this provision; many clauses relating to dispute procedures could be regarded as terms which "have the effect of restricting the right" to take industrial action. Such clauses might in any event not be appropriate for incorporation into individual contracts, and s.180 should not be seen as altering the doctrine of appropriateness for incorporation.[360]

---

[353]   As to which see below, para.40-099.
[354]   *Barber v Manchester Regional Hospital Board* [1958] 1 W.L.R. 181, 190. cf. *Rodwell v Thomas* [1944] K.B. 596, 601; *British Leyland Ltd v McQuilken* [1978] I.R.L.R. 245 (long-term planning agreement). Compare *Kaur v MG Rover Group Ltd* [2004] EWCA Civ 1507, [2005] I.R.L.R. 40, where a set of provisions concerning job security in a collective agreement were held to be inappropriate for incorporation into individual contracts of employment, as to certain of them because they were aspirational in character, and as to certain others because they were essentially collective undertakings rather than undertakings to individuals. Compare also now *Malone v British Airways Plc* [2010] EWHC 302 (QB), [2010] EWCA Civ 1225 where it was held both at first instance and on appeal to the Court of Appeal that a collective agreement regarding cabin crew complements was intended for planning for the deployment of cabin crew generally and not apt for incorporation into the contract of employment of each individual crew member.
[355]   See below, para.40-053.
[356]   cf. *Simpson v Kodak* [1948] 2 K.B. 184.
[357]   Defined in s.5.
[358]   See above, para.40-050.
[359]   See above, para.40-051.
[360]   See above, para.40-051.

40-054 **Effect of statement of particulars under the contracts of employment legislation** Before 1993, it could be said that the obligation imposed by the contracts of employment legislation[361] on employers to issue a written statement giving certain particulars of the terms of employment had greatly strengthened the likelihood of incorporation, since the written notice was allowed to refer directly to the collective agreement. If the employee accepted the terms of the written statement without demur, the giving and the receipt of the notice would, in the absence of any indication to the contrary, often be treated as having the effect of incorporating the terms of the collective agreement into the individual contract of employment of each employee.[362] However, under the current legislation, the facility of reference to collective agreements is restricted to certain particulars only,[363] and the written particulars are required to specify any collective agreements which directly affect the terms and conditions of the employment in question.[364] Moreover, it should be remembered that the written particulars are merely strong, and not conclusive, *evidence* of the terms of the contract,[365] unless, perhaps, the employee signs a copy of the particulars which is retained by the employer and the document can be regarded as the contract itself.[366] Where the written particulars are regarded merely as evidence of the contract, rather than the contract itself, there should accordingly be no objection to parol evidence tending to add to, vary or contradict the effect of the written particulars; but once the written statement is regarded as an actual contractual instrument, the parol evidence rule does come into effect against evidence of inconsistent verbal agreements.[367]

(c) Statutory Awards of Terms

40-055 **Statutory awards of terms generally** It is appropriate to consider together with collective agreements certain statutory and governmental provisions which have this in common with collective agreements, that they establish terms and conditions of employment which are incorporated into the individual contracts of employment within the sphere of their operation. In these instances, the contract of employment provides the means of giving legal effect to a process by which terms of employment are determined at a collective level.[368]

40-056 **Statutory arbitration awards following non-disclosure** A source of implied terms in individual contracts of employment arises from the provisions of the Employment Protection Act 1975 concerning disclosure of information by employ-

---

[361] See above, paras 40-040 et seq.
[362] *Camden Exhibition and Display Ltd v Lynott* [1966] 1 Q.B. 555, 562–563, 565; Grime (1966) 29 M.L.R. 199; *Tarmac Roadstone Holdings Ltd v Peacock* [1973] I.C.R. 273; *Soutar v Fisher* (1975) 10 I.T.R. 38.
[363] Employment Rights Act 1996 s.2(2), (3) and s.6.
[364] Employment Rights Act 1996 s.1(4)(j).
[365] *Turriff Construction Co Ltd v Bryant* (1967) 2 I.T.R. 292, 294; *Gascol Conversions Ltd v Mercer* [1974] I.C.R. 420, 427; *Jones v Associated Tunnelling Ltd* [1981] I.R.L.R. 477, 481, paras 21–22. See also above, para.40-044.
[366] cf. *Gascol Conversions Ltd v Mercer* [1974] I.C.R. 420; *System Floors Ltd v Daniel* [1981] I.R.L.R. 475, 476, para.10 treats this as applicable only where the employee acknowledges receipt of the document *specifically as a correct contract*.
[367] *Gascol Conversions Ltd v Mercer*, above, at 426F.
[368] The provisions, which fell into this category, of the Employment Protection Act 1975 concerning statutory extension of terms and conditions of employment (Sch.11) and for statutory arbitration awards following non-recognition of unions (s.16), were repealed by the Employment Act 1980 s.19.

ers to trade unions.[369] In these provisions, the sanction upon the employer consists in the right of the aggrieved trade union to apply to the Central Arbitration Committee,[370] complaining of the employer's breach of duty[371] and making a claim for changes in the terms and conditions of employment of the relevant group of employees.[372] If the Committee upholds the complaint of breach of duty, it may make an award[373] as to certain terms and conditions[374] of employment which will form part of the individual contracts of employment[375] of the employees concerned.[376] In this way, the collective procedural duties of the employer (that is, in certain circumstances to disclose information to recognised trade unions for the purposes of collective bargaining) are enforced by the right of the union to obtain a compulsory arbitration by the Central Arbitration Committee whose award will take legal effect via individual contracts of employment.

Provisions for statutory awards of terms and conditions or minimum terms and conditions in particular industries[377]   The Wages Councils system formerly provided awards of minimum terms in particular industries[378]; the most recent provisions to be abolished were for the setting of minimum terms and conditions of employment for agricultural workers by the Agricultural Wages Board.[379] There are some remaining provision for the fixing by the Secretary of State of remuneration and terms and conditions of teachers employed by local education authorities.[380]   **40-057**

5.   Rights and Duties Under and Associated with a Contract of Employment

Introduction   The express terms of the contract of employment will govern any aspect of the relationship between the parties which falls within those terms. But in practice many aspects of the relationship will be left to implied terms which the parties must have intended to be incorporated into the contract.[381] The rights and duties of the respective parties are thus often left to be governed by a set of normally implied terms, and this section will proceed to consider, first, the duties of the employee, and, secondly, the duties of the employer. It is obvious that the duty of the one party in a particular aspect will be a right when viewed from the point of view of the other. It will appear in the course of this discussion that the rights and   **40-058**

---

369   Trade Union and Labour Relations (Consolidation) Act 1992 ss.181–185.

370   Trade Union and Labour Relations (Consolidation) Act 1992 s.183(1).

371   Trade Union and Labour Relations (Consolidation) Act 1992 s.183(1) and s.184(1) (further complaint arising from failure to disclose information).

372   Trade Union and Labour Relations (Consolidation) Act 1992 s.185(1).

373   Trade Union and Labour Relations (Consolidation) Act 1992 s.185(3).

374   Trade Union and Labour Relations (Consolidation) Act 1992. As specified by s.185(3), (4).

375   Trade Union and Labour Relations (Consolidation) Act 1992 s.185(5) (which also limits the subsequent variation of the terms implied into individual contracts to prevent the employer from contracting out of the award with any individual employee).

376   Trade Union and Labour Relations (Consolidation) Act 1992. As specified by s.185(3), (4).

377   Compare now the general minimum wage provisions of and under the National Minimum Wage Act 1998, discussed see below, para.40-080.

378   Until its total abolition by the Trade Union Reform and Employment Rights Act 1993.

379   Enterprise and Regulatory Reform Act 2013 s.72, with effect from June 25, 2013: SI 2013/1455.

380   School Teachers' Pay and Conditions Act 1991, as significantly amended by the Education Act 2002 ss.130, 216 and Sch.22 Pt I.

381   cf. see above, paras 40-049—40-054 on the incorporation of the terms of a collective agreement into the individual contract of each employee.

duties under a contract of employment are in some cases the result of an interaction between common law and statute law and that in many other cases there are rights and duties associated with the contract of employment which are entirely the product of statutes. Whilst it is useful to consider the statutory consequences of a contract of employment alongside the consequences normally implied at common law, it is important to keep the two categories distinct because the statutory consequences will not normally be susceptible of exclusion by express contractual terms in the way that the common law consequences will normally be.[382] The rules about exclusion of statutory provisions by express contracting out are specially mentioned where necessary in the ensuing discussion; in the absence of special reference thereto, it should be assumed that the statutory rights and duties cannot be modified or excluded by contract.[383]

(a) Duties of the Employee

40-059 **Duty to exercise skill** An employee who holds himself out as being skilled to do a certain type of work and is employed on that basis impliedly undertakes that he or she possesses and will exercise reasonable skill or competence in that work; throughout the period of the employment he or she owes a duty to his or her employer to perform his or her work with reasonable skill or competence.[384] In the leading, though now antiquated, case on this point, the defendant advertised for a scene painter, the plaintiff applied for the job and was engaged, and the defendant was held entitled to dismiss him without notice when he showed himself to be incompetent as a scene painter.[385] The employee's implied undertaking that he possesses the necessary skill may include an implied undertaking by the employee to indemnify his employer if the latter is held vicariously liable to a third person in respect of a tort committed by the employee against the third person arising out of a failure to exercise that skill.[386] It has been held that an employee is expected, under the terms of his or her employment, to adapt to new methods and techniques in performing his or her duties, provided that the employer arranges for him or her to receive the necessary instruction in the new skills, and that the nature of the work does not alter so radically as to be no longer the work the employee agreed to perform.[387]

40-060 **Duty to exercise reasonable care** Even where the employee does not profess a particular skill or competence requiring training or experience,[388] there is an implied term in the contract that the employee will exercise reasonable care in the

---

[382] See below, paras 40-087—40-088, 40-095—40-101, 40-109—40-112, 40-115 (statutory consequences).

[383] This is generally the case for the provisions of the Employment Rights Act 1996, see s.203. See also, for example, the Equality Act 2010, see below, para.40-119 and para.40-126.

[384] *Harmer v Cornelius* (1858) 5 C.B.(N.S.) 236. cf. *Jones v Manchester Corp* [1952] 2 Q.B. 852; *Lister v Romford Ice and Cold Storage Co Ltd* [1957] A.C. 555 (lorry driver). The terms of the contract may make the employer sole judge of the employee's competence, provided the employer decides bona fide: *Diggle v Ogston Motor Co* (1915) 112 L.T. 1029.

[385] *Harmer v Cornelius* (1858) 5 C.B.(N.S.) 236. As to summary dismissal, see below, para.40-190. As to unfair dismissal, see below, para.40-225.

[386] See below, para.40-077.

[387] *Cresswell v Board of Inland Revenue* [1984] I.C.R. 508.

[388] See above, para.40-059.

performance of his or her duties.[389] Breach of this duty will not entitle the employer to dismiss the employee summarily unless the breach goes to the root of the contract,[390] but it may give rise to an obligation to indemnify the employer.[391] It would seem that the restrictions placed upon contracting out of liabilities resulting from negligence by s.2 of the Unfair Contract Terms Act 1977 do not apply to provisions in a contract of employment excluding, or restricting liability for breach of, this duty, because the provisions of s.2 do not extend to the contract of employment except in favour of the employee.[392] Under s.7 of the Health and Safety at Work, etc. Act 1974, it is the duty of every employee while at work to take reasonable care for the health and safety of himself or herself and of other persons who may be affected by his or her acts or omissions at work,[393] and, as regards any duty imposed on the employer by any health and safety legislation, to co-operate with the employer as far as necessary to enable the duty to be complied with.[394] This provision may give rise to criminal liability[395] but does not give rise to civil liability.[396]

Obedience to lawful and reasonable orders   The employee impliedly contracts to obey the lawful and reasonable orders of his or her employer (or the employer's delegate) within the scope of the employment he or she contracted to undertake: this obligation is usually discussed in relation to summary dismissal.[397] The scope of the employment undertaken by the employee has been held to include adaptation to new methods and techniques of performing his duties.[398] It is a further implied term that the employer should not require an employee to do anything illegal, such as to drive a vehicle which is not insured against third-party risks as required by the road traffic legislation[399]; the employer will be liable to indemnify an employee if the latter is held liable to a third person as a result of the unlawful act which the employer required the employee to do.[400] **10 061**

Duty of fidelity   It is another implied term in a contract of employment that the employee will serve the employer with fidelity and in good faith.[401] Thus an employee, during his or her period of employment, may not solicit the customers **40-062**

---

389 *Lister v Romford Ice and Cold Storage Co Ltd* [1957] A.C. 555; *Janata Bank v Ahmed* [1981] I.C.R. 791. And see the cases cited sec below, para.40-190.

390 See below, para.40-184.

391 See below, para.40-072. But cf. *Harvey v RG O'Dell Ltd* [1958] 2 Q.B. 78 (storekeeper does not warrant his skill as driver: see below, para.40-072).

392 Unfair Contract Terms Act 1977 s.1(2) and Sch.1 para.4.

393 s.7(a).

394 s.7(b).

395 s.33(1)(a), (3).

396 s.47(1)(a), (4).

397 See below, para.40-189. As to unfair dismissal, see below, paras 40-224 et seq.

398 *Cresswell v Board of Inland Revenue* [1984] I.C.R. 508; see above, para.40-059. However, *Bull v Nottinghamshire Fire and Rescue Authority* [2007] EWCA Civ 240, [2007] B.L.G.R. 439 indicates that the employer cannot unilaterally impose its managerial aspirations without clear evidence of their incorporation into the contracts of employment in question.

399 *Gregory v Ford* [1951] 1 All E.R. 121. cf. *Semtex Ltd v Gladstone* [1954] 1 W.L.R. 945.

400 *Gregory v Ford* [1951] 1 All E.R. 121. See below, para.40-114; cf. Vol.I, para.29-126.

401 *Robb v Green* [1895] 2 Q.B. 315; *Wessex Dairies Ltd v Smith* [1935] 2 K.B. 80; *Hivac Ltd v Park Royal Scientific Instruments Ltd* [1946] Ch. 169; *Sanders v Parry* [1967] 1 W.L.R. 753. See also *Morison v Moat* (1851) 9 Hare 241. It was confirmed in *Lonmar Global Risks Ltd v West* [2010] EWHC 2878 (QB), [2011] I.R.L.R. 138, reiterating the view previously taken in *University of Nottingham v Fishel* [2000] I.C.R. 1462, that the duty of loyalty or good faith is not without more to

of his or her employer to transfer their custom to him or her after he or she has left the employment[402]; nor may the employee solicit orders from the employer's customers or suppliers, or otherwise deal with them, on his or her own behalf rather than the employer's behalf.[403] But in the absence of a special covenant[404] a former employee cannot be restrained from soliciting or doing business with the customers of a former employer.[405] This proposition has been the subject of an important reaffirmation, in the context of a contract of employment between a solicitor-employee and the firm by which he was employed in *Wallace Bogan & Co v Cove*.[406] An employee cannot, however, rid themselves of the duty of fidelity to which the employee is subject during the currency of his or her employment by wrongfully repudiating his or her contract of employment.[407] On the other hand, an employee is not in breach of his or her duty of fidelity at a given moment merely because at that time he or she intends to act subsequently in a way which would be in breach of his or her fiduciary duty.[408]

40-063   **Work for another employer**   Acceptance of employment with one employer implies an obligation not to work for another employer so long as the first employment continues, if the other employment would be inconsistent with the first employment,[409] but there are severe restrictions upon the availability of an order for specific performance, or an injunction to enforce this kind of obligation.[410] In his or her spare time (when the employee is not obliged to work for his employer) an employee is normally entitled to work for a third person.[411] But he or she may not,

---

be equated with a fiduciary obligation; compare the discussion of the "duty to account" in para.40-069. Compare also *Threlfall v ECD Insight Ltd* [2012] EWHC 3543 (QB), [2013] I.R.L.R. 185 where Lang J. reinforces the proposition that a senior employee with a duty of fidelity as to act in good faith vis-à-vis the employer is nevertheless not thereby necessarily or ordinarily under a fiduciary obligation to that employer. The contrast between the duty of fidelity owed by an employee and the fiduciary duty owed by a company director had also been emphasised by the Court of Appeal in *Ranson v Customer Systems Plc* [2012] EWCA Civ 841, [2012] I.R.L.R. 769 and had also been invoked by the Court of Appeal in *Caterpillar Logistics Services (UK) Ltd v Huesca de Crean* [2012] EWCA Civ 156, [2012] 3 All E.R. 129 as a factor in refusing to the employer of barring-out relief against a former employee.

[402] *Wessex Dairies Ltd v Smith* [1935] 2 K.B. 80; *Sanders v Parry* [1967] 1 W.L.R. 753.

[403] *Thomas Marshall Ltd v Guinle* [1978] I.C.R. 905, 922E–H.

[404] *National Provincial Bank of England v Marshall* (1888) 40 Ch. D. 112.

[405] *Re Irish* (1888) 4 Ch. D. 49. cf. *Faccenda Chicken Ltd v Fowler* [1986] I.C.R. 297; *Balston Ltd v Headline Filters Ltd* [1987] F.S.R. 330. But a former employee may be restrained from using trade secrets or confidential information: see below, paras 40-068—40-069. In *Imam-Sadeque v Bluebay Asset Management (Services) Ltd* [2012] EWHC 3511 (QB), [2013] I.R.L.R. 344 it was confirmed that, although the employee was relieved of the obligation of work while on "garden leave", the negative obligations imposed on him by his employment contract remained part of his duties.

[406] [1997] I.R.L.R. 453.

[407] *Thomas Marshall Ltd v Guinle* [1978] I.C.R. 905, 920H–921C. cf. *Evening Standard Ltd v Henderson* [1987] I.C.R. 588.

[408] *Horcal Ltd v Gatland* [1984] I.R.L.R. 288.

[409] cf. the special cases of *Lumley v Wagner* (1852) 1 De G.M. & G. 604; *National Provincial Bank of England v Marshall* (1888) 40 Ch. D. 112.

[410] These remedies are discussed see below, paras 40-208—40-210. cf. *Evening Standard Ltd v Henderson* [1987] I.C.R. 588. Compare also *GFI Group Ltd v Eaglestone* [1994] I.R.L.R. 119.

[411] *Hivac Ltd v Park Royal Scientific Instruments Ltd* [1946] Ch. 169. cf. *Nova Plastics Ltd v Froggatt* [1982] I.R.L.R. 146.

consistently with his or her duty to his or her employer, do in his or her spare time something which would inflict great harm on the employer's business.[412]

Duties to disclose information   A further instance of an employee's duty of fidel-   **40-064**
ity is that, although the employee is under no duty to disclose his or her own previous breaches of duty,[413] the employee may, in the circumstances of a particular case,
be under a duty to disclose the misconduct of fellow-employees[414]; there is,
however, no authority that the latter duty is generally to be implied in a contract of
employment.[415] In one case,[416] an employee was held to be so senior in the managerial hierarchy as to have a duty in the circumstances of the case to report the
misconduct of his superiors or subordinates even though thereby incriminating
himself. The decision in *Tesco Stores Ltd v Pook* suggests that a sufficiently senior
employee may in certain circumstances come under a generally implied duty to
disclose his or her own breaches of trust as well as those of other employees.[417]
Insofar as the employee's duty of fidelity requires disclosure of his or her own or
another's personal circumstances, that duty is now limited by s.4(3)(a) of the
Rehabilitation of Offenders Act 1974, which provides that such a duty shall not
extend to requiring the disclosure of a spent conviction[418] or any circumstances
ancillary to a spent conviction, whether the conviction be one's own or another's.
The section goes on to provide, inter alia, that:

"… any failure to disclose a spent conviction … shall not be a proper ground for dismissing … a person from any … employment, or for prejudicing him in any way in any …
employment."[419]

An employee also owes a duty to convey to his or her employer information of
value to the employer which the employee obtained in the course of his or her
employment; and the employee will be restrained from using the information if he
or she deliberately conceals it, intending to make use of it for his or her own
advantage.[420]

Duty to refrain from disruption   It has also been held that the employee's duty   **40-065**
of fidelity includes a duty to refrain from wilful disruption of the functioning of the
enterprise.[421] Although this duty seems to extend to individual acts,[422] it applies

---

412   *Hivac Ltd v Park Royal Scientific Instruments Ltd* [1946] Ch. 169 at 178 (spare-time work for trade
      rival was restrained by injunction).
413   *Bell v Lever Bros* [1932] A.C. 161.
414   *Swain v West (Butchers) Ltd* [1936] 3 All E.R. 261. Compare also *Dunn v AAH Ltd* [2010] EWCA
      Civ 183, [2010] I.R.L.R. 709, with regard to disclosure by a finance director of fraud in which an
      ex-employee was implicated.
415   *Swain v West (Butchers) Ltd* [1936] 3 All E.R. 261.
416   *Sybron Corp v Rochem Ltd* [1985] Ch. 299.
417   [2003] EWHC 823 (Ch), [2004] I.R.L.R. 618. See also *Thomson Ecology Ltd v Apem Ltd* [2013]
      EWHC 2875 (Ch), [2014] I.R.L.R. 184.
418   Defined by s.1 by reference to a set "rehabilitation period". Data Protection Act 1998 s.56 makes it
      a criminal offence to require job applicants or existing employees to make subject access requests
      in lieu of providing a normal criminal record check, which would not disclose spent convictions.
419   Rehabilitation of Offenders Act 1974 s.4(3)(b). cf. *Property Guards Ltd v Taylor and Kershaw* [1982]
      I.R.L.R. 175.
420   *Cranleigh Precision Engineering Co Ltd v Bryant* [1965] 1 W.L.R. 1293, 1319; *Industrial Develop-
      ment Consultants Ltd v Cooley* [1972] 1 W.L.R. 443.
421   *Secretary of State for Employment v ASLEF (No.2)* [1972] 2 Q.B. 455, 491, 498, 509. See also below,

primarily as a limit upon the employee's right to take certain kinds of industrial action. It is further considered in that context later in this section.[423]

40-066 **Duty not to disclose confidential information**[424] It is an implied term in every contract of employment that the employee will not disclose or make public any professional or trade secret or confidential information which the employee learns by reason of his or her employment.[425] The employee also impliedly undertakes that he or she will not use to the detriment of his or her employer any information which he or she has obtained in confidence in the course of or as a result of his or her employment.[426] This implied duty was reaffirmed and its scope further defined in *Thomas Marshall Ltd v Guinle*[427] where Megarry V.C. suggested that there were four elements in the identifying of confidential information or trade secrets which the courts will protect, namely:

(1) the owner's belief that release of information would be injurious to him or advantageous to rivals;
(2) the owner's belief in confidentiality of the information;
(3) the reasonableness of these beliefs;
(4) the assessment of the information in the light of the usage and practices of the particular industry or trade.

The employee will be restrained by injunction from publishing or using any such confidential information.[428] And a third party who receives[429] information conveyed to him or her in breach of confidence by an employee or former employee may also be restrained from using the information.[430] Moreover, it appears to follow from the decision in *Seager v Copydex Ltd*[431] that the remedy of damages may be available in such cases against both the employee or ex-employee and the third-party

---

para.40-077.

[422] *Secretary of State for Employment v ASLEF (No.2)* [1972] 2 Q.B. 455 at 492, 508.

[423] See below, paras 40-076—40-077.

[424] North [1965] J.B.L. 397, [1966] J.B.L. 31, [1968] J.B.L. 32; (1972) 12 J.S.P.T.L. 149; Gareth Jones (1970) 86 L.Q.R. 463.

[425] *Amber Size and Chemical Co v Menzel* [1913] 2 Ch. 239; *Alperton Rubber Co v Manning* (1917) 86 L.J. Ch. 377; *British Industrial Plastics v Ferguson* [1940] 1 All E.R. 479; *Initial Services Ltd v Putterill* [1968] 1 Q.B. 396. As to particulars in an action for breach of this term, see *Sorbo Rubber Sponge Products v Defries* (1930) 47 R.P.C. 454.

[426] *Merryweather v Moore* [1892] 2 Ch. 518; *Bent's Brewery Co v Hogan* [1945] 2 All E.R. 570; *Cranleigh Precision Engineering Ltd v Bryant* [1965] 1 W.L.R. 1293. cf. as to the supplying of information about fellow-employees to a competitor interested in recruitment, *GD Searle & Co Ltd v Celltech Ltd* [1982] F.S.R. 92.

[427] [1978] I.C.R. 905, 926D–G. The implied duty here served to protect the employer from "use" of the information, whereas the express covenant in question dealt only with "disclosure" thereof.

[428] *Merryweather v Moore* [1892] 2 Ch. 518; *Robb v Green* [1895] 2 Q.B. 315; *Amber Size & Chemical Co v Menzel* [1913] 2 Ch. 239; *Reid and Sigrist Ltd v Moss and Mechanism Ltd* (1932) 49 R.P.C. 461; *Under Water Welders & Repairers Ltd v Street and Longthorne* [1968] R.P.C. 498; *Industrial Furnaces Ltd v Reaves* [1970] R.P.C. 605. But what was previously a trade secret of the employer may cease to be such when a specification for a patent relating to the secret is published by the employer: *Mustad & Son v Dosen* [1964] 1 W.L.R. 109n. (It is otherwise if publication is by a third person: *Cranleigh Precision Engineering Ltd v Bryant*, above, at 1311–1320.)

[429] It is not necessary that the third party should know when he receives the information that it is given to him in breach of confidence: *Printers & Finishers Ltd v Holloway* [1965] 1 W.L.R. 1, 7. See also *Prince Albert v Strange* (1849) 1 Mac. & G. 25.

[430] *Cranleigh Precision Engineering Ltd v Bryant*, above. See also *Saltman Engineering Co Ltd v Campbell Engineering Co Ltd* (1963) 65 R.P.C. 203, 213, 215.

[431] [1967] 1 W.L.R. 923; on the quantum of damages, see *Seager v Copydex Ltd (No.2)* [1969] 1 W.L.R.

recipient. In one case,[432] an employee secretly copied from his employer's order book a list of the names and addresses of customers with the intention of using it for the purpose of soliciting from them orders for himself; when he used it for this purpose he was held liable in damages, and was also restrained by injunction from making further use of the information.

An employee is, however, entitled after the termination of his employment to **40-067** make use of knowledge and experience honestly acquired in the course of the employment, so long as it was not acquired surreptitiously, nor was it detailed information entrusted to the employee expressly or impliedly in confidence.[433] So if a person, after his or her employment has ceased, embodies in a book the product of his knowledge and skill ("know-how") as a professional which was acquired in the course of his or her work, the copyright vests in him or her.[434] In the leading case of *Faccenda Chicken Ltd v Fowler*,[435] the court insisted that the duty not to disclose confidential information becomes confined, once the employee's employment has ceased, to a duty not to disclose the employer's trade secrets, and cannot be more widely invoked to place fetters on the ability of ex-employees to compete. However, the decision and reasoning of the Court of Appeal in *Thomas v Farr Plc*[436] suggest that the difficulty of policing a post-employment confidentiality clause may be adduced in support of the validity of a relatively wide non-competition covenant.

Exceptions to duty of confidence   There are some exceptions to the employee's **40-068** duty not to disclose secrets, although it has been held to be a breach of the contract of employment for the employee to disclose a document which is libellous.[437] In the case of documents which disclose fraud on the part of the employer an injunction will not be granted to prevent their disclosure.[438] The Court of Appeal has said that there is no duty to keep the information secret when it relates to misconduct on the part of the employer of such a nature that it ought in the public interest to be disclosed to those who have a proper interest in receiving it, e.g. an agreement to maintain prices which is not registered as required by restrictive trade practices legislation.[439] It has, however, been argued[440] that some contracts of employment may contain an implied term ousting the rule in *Bent's Brewery Co Ltd v Hogan*[441] (which treats it as a breach of confidence on the employee's part to disclose certain information about his or her employment to trade union representatives). A further set of exceptions to the employee's duty of confidence is provided by the Public

---

809.

[432] *Robb v Green* [1895] 2 Q.B. 315. See also *Louis v Smellie* (1896) 73 L.T. 226; *Baker v Gibbons* [1972] 1 W.L.R. 693.

[433] *Morris v Saxelby* [1915] 2 Ch. 57, 88; affirmed [1916] 1 A.C. 688; *United Indigo Chemical Co v Robinson* (1931) 49 R.P.C. 178; *Wessex Dairies Ltd v Smith* [1935] 2 K.B. 80, 89; *Worsley & Co v Cooper* [1939] 1 All E.R. 290; *Printers & Finishers Ltd v Holloway* [1965] 1 W.L.R. 1; *United Sterling Corp Ltd v Felton & Mannion* [1974] R.P.C. 162. On express covenants relating to trade secrets, see Vol.I, para.16-140.

[434] *Stevenson, Jordan and Harrison v Macdonald and Evans* [1952] 1 T.L.R. 101. On copyright, see below, para.40-071.

[435] [1986] I.C.R. 297; compare also *Balston Ltd v Headline Filters Ltd* [1987] F.S.R. 330.

[436] [2007] EWCA Civ 118, [2007] I.C.R. 932.

[437] *Weld-Blundell v Stephens* [1919] 1 K.B. 520, [1919] A.C. 956; *Bradstreets British Ltd v Harold Mitchell & Carapanayoti Co Ltd* [1933] Ch. 190.

[438] *Gartside v Outram* (1856) 26 L.J. Ch. 113.

[439] *Initial Services Ltd v Putterill* [1968] 1 Q.B. 396.

[440] Hepple, *Employment Law*, 4th edn (1981), para.312.

[441] [1945] 2 All E.R. 570.

Interest Disclosure Act 1998, the provisions of which are described in a later paragraph.[442]

40-069 **Duty to account**   An employee is bound to account to his or her employer for all property entrusted to him or her by the employer, and for all property received by him or her from a third person for or on account of the employer.[443] An employee is also obliged to account to his or her employer for any bribe,[444] secret profit[445] or secret commission which he or she has received in connection with the employer's affairs, or earned by virtue of his or her position as employee.[446] The employer's right to recover the bribe or secret profit received by the employee arises despite the fact that the employee's act in receiving or earning the money was criminal, and despite the fact that the employer suffered no loss.[447] A further illustration of the duty to account occurs where an employee, upon the termination of his or her employment, is obliged to repay to the employer any commission paid to the employee in advance which had not actually been earned by the employee before his or her employment terminated.[448] In the important case of *Nottingham University v Fishel*,[449] Elias J. held that the employment relationship did not give rise in and of itself to a general fiduciary duty to account, so that such a duty arises only where specific terms or aspects of the relationship give rise to it.

40-070 **Inventions and patents**   Sections 39–43 of the Patents Act 1977 deal with employees' inventions.[450] The details of those provisions lie outside the scope of the present work. They deal with the circumstances in which an employee's invention will be taken to belong to the employer[451]; with the compensation of employees for certain inventions[452]; with the amount of such compensation[453]; and with the enforceability of contracts relating to employees' inventions.[454]

40-071 **Copyright and design right**   The law of copyright was restated with amendments by Pt I of the Copyright, Designs and Patents Act 1988, which also conferred

---

[442] See below, para.40-160.

[443] *Biddle v Bond* (1865) 6 B. & S. 225, 231; *Parker v McKenna* (1874) L.R. 10 Ch. App. 96.

[444] *Att-Gen v Goddard* (1929) 98 L.J. K.B. 743.

[445] *Reading v Att-Gen* [1951] A.C. 507.

[446] See Vol.I, para.29-164; see also *Industrial Development Consultants Ltd v Cooley* [1972] 1 W.L.R. 443.

[447] *Reading v Att-Gen* [1951] A.C. 507.

[448] *Bronester Ltd v Priddle* [1961] 1 W.L.R. 1294. (The obligation will depend on the construction of the particular contract of employment.) cf. as to accidental overpayment of wages, *Avon CC v Howlett* [1983] 1 W.L.R. 605; *Att-Gen's Reference No.1 of 1983* [1984] 3 All E.R. 369.

[449] [2000] I.C.R. 1462, QBD. The approach taken in that case was followed and developed by the Court of Appeal in *Helmet Integrated Systems Ltd v Tunnard* [2006] EWCA Civ 1735, [2007] I.R.L.R. 126, to the effect that employees do not automatically owe fiduciary obligations to their employer as a consequence merely of their general duty of loyalty, so that in the instant case the employee owed no fiduciary obligation in respect of activities during employment which were preparatory, but no more than preparatory, to competitive activity in which the employee was planning to engage after leaving his current employment.

[450] Phillips & Hoolahan, *Employees' Inventions in the United Kingdom, Law and Practice* (1982).

[451] s.39.

[452] s.40.

[453] s.41.

[454] s.42.

a design right in original designs.[455] Under that Act,[456] the author of a work is the first owner of any copyright in it[457] subject (inter alia)[458] to the provision that where a literary, dramatic, musical or artistic work or a film is made by an employee in the course of his or her employment, the employer is the first owner of any copyright in the work subject to any agreement to the contrary.[459] So far as the ownership of design right is concerned, the designer is the first owner of any design right in a design which is not created in pursuance of a commission or in the course of employment.[460] However, where a design is created in pursuance of a commission, the person commissioning the design is the first owner of any design right in it[461]; and where, in other cases, a design is created by an employee in the course of his or her employment, the employer is the first owner of any design right in it.[462] The provisions relating to design right are not expressly subject to agreement to the contrary; but design right is transmissible by written and signed assignment,[463] and provision is made for the assignment of prospective ownership of future design right.[464]

Duty to Indemnity the employer[465] If the employee, in breach of his or her duty to an employer to exercise a reasonable degree of competence in a particular skill or to take reasonable care in his or her work,[466] causes damage or injury by negligence to a third person, and the employer pays damages to the third person on account of the employer's vicarious liability for the employee's tort, the employer can recover an indemnity[467] from the employee.[468] It is arguable that the indemnity need not be based on an implied term in the contract of employment to the effect that the employee undertakes to indemnify the employer in these circumstances (although courts have put it on this ground)[469]; it can be based on the breach of the employee's contractual duty to take care, with the measure of damages for that breach being the amount paid to the third person (which is a reasonably foreseeable loss resulting from that breach). So where a man employed to drive a lorry negligently backed it and injured a fellow-employee, the employer was entitled to recover from the driver the full amount of damages payable to the injured employee, together with the costs of defending the action brought by the latter.[470] In another

40-072

---

455 Pt III of the Act.
456 In force, so far as relevant, from August 1, 1989.
457 s.11(1).
458 See s.11(3) (Crown copyright, parliamentary copyright, copyright of international organisations).
459 s.11(2) as amended by SI 1996/2967.
460 s.215(1). (See also s.219.) (Note the special provision of s.220 (qualification by reference to first marketing).)
461 s.215. (See also s.219.)
462 s.215(3).
463 s.222.
464 s.223.
465 See Atiyah, *Vicarious Liability in the Law of Torts* (1967), pp.421–432.
466 See above, paras 40-059—40-060.
467 The employer may, alternatively, be entitled to claim *contribution* from his employee: see below, para.40-074.
468 *Lister v Romford Ice and Cold Storage Co Ltd* [1957] A.C. 555; *Semtex Ltd v Gladstone* [1954] 1 W.L.R. 945.
469 *Lister v Romford Ice and Cold Storage Co Ltd* [1957] A.C. 555; *Harvey v RG O'Dell* [1958] 2 Q.B. 78.
470 *Lister v Romford Ice and Cold Storage Co Ltd* [1957] A.C. 555.

case,[471] the court held that since the employee was engaged as a storekeeper, he did not impliedly agree to indemnify his employers if he negligently injured someone by his negligence in any other capacity; thus, no contractual indemnity could be recovered from him when he injured someone by his negligent driving in the course of his employment.[472] It has been argued that this conclusion is difficult to justify: the only term which need be implied is one that the employee will take reasonable care while about his or her employer's business.[473] Although that argument might be upheld, the enforcement of the employee's duty to indemnify the employer has been considerably restricted by developments described in the next paragraph. On the other hand, it would seem that the enforcement of the implied duty to indemnify is not restricted by s.4 of the Unfair Contract Terms Act 1977 because that applies to unreasonable indemnities arising from express terms, not from implied terms of the kind involved here.[474]

40-073 **No general duty on employer to insure the employee against tortious liability** Even if the employer is insured against his vicarious liability, the employee will not normally be entitled to claim the benefit of the insurance (except in the case of motor insurance)[475] since there is no privity of contract.[476] Nor can the employee maintain that there is an implied term in the contract of employment to the effect that the employer agrees to take out insurance cover on behalf of the employee to protect him or her from liabilities arising from any tortious act committed by him or in the course of his or her employment.[477] This seems contrary to the common expectations of the parties,[478] and although a government committee once investigated the situation,[479] no change in the law has been made by Parliament because there is an agreement[480] among nearly all insurance companies engaged in employers' liability insurance not to make claims for indemnities from employees (using the name of the employer under the doctrine of subrogation)[481] except in cases of collusion or wilful misconduct by the employee, or where the employer consents to the claim being brought.[482] The agreement made by the insurance companies is now reinforced by judicial reluctance to compel an employer to seek

---

[471] *Harvey v RG O'Dell Ltd* [1958] 2 Q.B. 78. (Contribution amounting to a full indemnity under a statute was recovered: see below, para.40-074).

[472] Compare para.40-060.

[473] Jolowicz (1959) 22 M.L.R. 71, 289; Atiyah at p.424.

[474] Compare above, para.38-240. In any event, s.4 protects a person "dealing as consumer"—see above, para.38-242 (which relate to the Unfair Terms in Consumer Contracts Regulations 1999 (SI 1999/2083)); and in its decision in *Keen v Commerzbank AG* [2006] EWCA Civ 1536, [2007] I.C.R. 623 the Court of Appeal makes clear its view that this does not include an employee.

[475] Road Traffic Act 1988 s.148(4). See *Tattersall v Drysdale* [1935] 2 K.B. 174; *Austin v Zurich General Accident Insurance Co Ltd* [1944] 2 All E.R. 243, 248; affirmed on other grounds: [1945] 1 All E.R. 316; *Semtex Ltd v Gladstone* [1954] 1 W.L.R. 945.

[476] See Vol.I, Ch.18.

[477] *Lister v Romford Ice and Cold Storage Co Ltd* [1957] A.C. 555 (a majority decision). *Gregory v Ford* [1951] 1 All E.R. 121 should still be applicable where insurance on behalf of the employee is still compulsory. See Deakin & Morris, *Labour Law*, 6th edn (2012), para.4.108 for an argument about the possible impact of the implied obligation of mutual trust and confidence, as to which compare below, paras 40-151—40-154.

[478] Williams, 20 M.L.R. 220, 437; Jolowicz [1956] C.L.J. 101, [1957] C.L.J. 21; (1959) 22 M.L.R. 71, 189. Compare Deakin & Morris, *Labour Law*, 6th edn (2012), para.4.108.

[479] See Lord Gardiner (1959) 22 M.L.R. 652.

[480] Whitmore, *Employers' Liability Insurance* (1962), p.18, publishes the text.

[481] See below, para.40-090.

[482] For other details of these arrangements, see Atiyah at pp.426–427.

indemnity from his employee at the instance of an insurer of the employer claiming to be subrogated to the employer's right against the employee.[483]

Contribution   Since the employer who is liable under the doctrine of vicarious   **40-074**
liability is a joint tortfeasor with the employee who committed the tort, the employer
is also entitled to contribution (which may, in the court's discretion, amount to a full
indemnity)[484] from the employee under statute.[485] If some blame attaches to the
employer, e.g. for giving a task to the employee for which he or she lacked sufficient experience, the employer may not recover a full indemnity.[486]

Authority of employee to make contracts   The relationship between employer   **40-075**
and employee does not, of itself, confer any authority on the employee to make
contracts binding on the employer. But an employee may, in appropriate
circumstances, be an agent of his or her employer with such authority; the ordinary
principles of agency apply to this situation, and reference should be made to the
chapter on agency.[487]

Duties in relation to industrial action—(1) strikes   It used to be thought clear   **40-076**
that if employees strike without giving the required notice to terminate their
contracts they will be in breach of contract when they withdraw their labour.[488] In
Rookes v Barnard[489] it was conceded that a "no strike" clause in the relevant collective agreement had been incorporated into each employee's contract of employment[490]; hence it was held that it would be a breach of contract for the employees
to strike. Moreover, some dicta in that case[491] made it clear that any strike, even in
the absence of a "no strike" clause, and even if the strikers gave proper notice to
terminate their contracts,[492] would be in breach of contract because there was no
genuine intention to terminate the contracts. As a result of these dicta, the normal
strike notice came to be regarded as a notice of intention to break the contracts of
employment by suspending performance of the employees' duties, and not a notice
of termination, since this would affect pension rights, rights to holidays with pay,
etc.[493] It later appeared, however, from the decision in *Morgan v Fry*[494] that some
contracts of employment may be subject to an implied term conferring a right to
suspend the performance of the contract by way of strike action, provided no less

---

[483]   *Morris v Ford Motor Co* [1973] Q.B. 792.

[484]   *Ryan v Fildes* [1938] 3 All E.R. 517; *Semtex Ltd v Gladstone* [1954] 1 W.L.R. 945.

[485]   Civil Liability (Contribution) Act 1978 s.1. See *Clerk & Lindsell on Torts*, 21st edn (2014), para.4-
        36—4-38; *Ronex Properties Ltd v John Laing Construction Ltd* [1983] Q.B. 398; *Harper v Gray &
        Walker (a firm)* [1985] 1 W.L.R. 1196.

[486]   *Jones v Manchester Corp* [1952] 2 Q.B. 852. See Atiyah at pp.428–432.

[487]   See above, Ch.31.

[488]   e.g. *Parkin v South Hetton Coal Co Ltd* (1907) 97 L.T. 98; affirmed 98 L.T. 162.

[489]   [1964] A.C. 1129.

[490]   See above, paras 40-050—40-054.

[491]   [1964] A.C. 1129, 1204, 1237. cf. in the Court of Appeal [1963] 1 Q.B. 623, 682–683. See Grunfeld,
        Modern Trade Union Law (1966), pp.317–334.

[492]   Under s.86 of the Employment Rights Act 1996, most employees must now give not less than one
        week's notice to terminate their contract, see below, para.40-164.

[493]   *JT Stratford & Son Ltd v Lindley* [1965] A.C. 269, 285. The Contracts of Employment Act 1963 Sch.I
        para.7(2), assumed that some strikes were not in breach of contract since it provided that "continu-
        ity of employment" was not to be interrupted unless a strike was in breach of contract (cf. para.11(1)
        of the Sch.); these words were accordingly repealed: Redundancy Payments Act 1965 s.37 (see now
        Employment Rights Act 1996 s.216).

[494]   [1968] 2 Q.B. 710.

notice of the action is given than would be required for a lawful termination of the contract. Section 147 of the Industrial Relations Act 1971 provided a statutory rule about the effect of strike action upon contracts of employment, but with the repeal of that provision in 1974,[495] the common law again prevailed. The common law position was re-examined in *Simmons v Hoover Ltd*[496] with the conclusion that strike action did not operate to suspend the contract of employment but as a repudiatory breach of the contract which gave the employer the option of accepting the repudiation as a termination of the contract.[497] It was held that:

"... if *Morgan v Fry* has introduced into the law the concept of the suspension of a contract it is only an embryonic form, for none of the consequences has been worked out; and it is difficult to see how this could be done except by legislation."[498]

40-077 **Duties in relation to industrial action—(2) action other than strikes** The question of whether various forms of industrial action other than strikes involve breach of contract on the part of employees has to be considered in relation to the particular kind of act or omission concerned. The "work-to-rule", although designed not to involve breach of contract, may nevertheless be treated as the breach of an implied contractual duty to refrain from disruption of the functioning and purposes of the employing enterprise: such a duty, which can be characterised as a duty of co-operation or an aspect of the duty of fidelity,[499] was recognised in *Secretary of State for Employment v ASLEF (No.2)*.[500] Such an implied term was held, in the case of *British Telecommunications Plc v Ticehurst*[501] to have been breached by a concerted action of withdrawal of goodwill on the part of managerial employees. On the other hand, the duty of co-operation probably does not go to the lengths of requiring the employee to undertake to work normally in response to an ultimatum by the employer.[502] The "go-slow" may be expected to involve breach of contract as a contravention of the employer's implied standing instructions about how work is to be carried out. The "blacking" of particular goods or equipment (in the sense of refusal to handle or use them) may constitute breach on similar reasoning; but may avoid the characterisation of breach if the employer has not specifically required the particular goods or equipment to be handled or used.[503] On the other hand, one case treated refusal by miners to descend in a lift to work with non-union employees

---

[495] Trade Union and Labour Relations Act 1974 s.1.
[496] [1977] I.C.R. 61.
[497] [1977] I.C.R. 61 at 76A–F. cf. *Chappell v Times Newspapers Ltd* [1975] I.C.R. 145, 174H–175A (where Lord Denning M.R. had been clear that a strike was a breach, though less clear that it was a repudiation of the contract); *Haddow v ILEA* [1979] I.C.R. 202. For an argument that the repudiation analysis does not apply where the strike is engineered or provoked by the employer, see Hepple, *Employment Law*, 4th edn (1981), para.491. For the question whether strike action may constitute not just repudiation but also self-dismissal, see below, para.40-193.
[498] [1977] I.C.R. 61, 75H.
[499] See above, paras 40-062—40-065.
[500] [1972] 2 Q.B. 455, 491–492, 498, 508–509. (See Napier (1972) 1 I.L.J. 125.) cf. *Solihull Metropolitan Borough v NUT* [1985] I.R.L.R. 211 (in relation to teachers' lunchtime duties).
[501] [1992] I.C.R. 383.
[502] See *Fisher v York Trailers Ltd* [1979] I.C.R. 834, 838A–C, per Slynn J. cf. *Chappell v Times Newspapers Ltd* [1975] I.C.R. 145 (which indicates, however, that the employee may be unable to enforce the contract against the employer in such a situation: see below, para.40-210); compare also, however, *British Telecommunications Plc v Ticehurst* [1992] I.C.R. 383.
[503] *Thomson & Co Ltd v Deakin* [1952] 1 Ch. 646.

as not merely breach of contract but tantamount to total withdrawal of labour.[504] The contractual status of an overtime ban will depend upon whether the employee can be regarded as having contracted to work such overtime hours as the employer may require him or her to.[505] It is possible for the employee to be under such an obligation although the employer may not correspondingly contract to provide a fixed minimum or maximum of overtime work.[506] In *Ministry of Justice v Prison Officers' Association*[507] it was held on the facts of the case that the implied duty of loyalty or good faith would not be breached by industrial action consisting of refusal to undertake voluntary tasks or roles which were clearly not contractually stipulated ones: earlier authorities pertaining to this question were considered, applied, and distinguished so far as it was necessary to do so. The effect of industrial action other than strikes upon entitlement to remuneration is considered in a later section.[508]

(b)   Duties of the Employer

(i)   Remuneration

Remuneration   The duty of the employer to remunerate an employee for services will normally[509] be found by construing the terms of the contract of employment in the light of the particular circumstances.[510] The remuneration will frequently be specified in a collective agreement,[511] whose terms are incorporated into individual contracts of employment[512]; or the remuneration may be fixed by some special negotiating machinery or statutory authority.[513] Remuneration during illness is discussed in a separate paragraph.[514] Most problems of construction will arise in the case of special terms in individual contracts. Thus, where an employee agreed to look for payment only to some particular fund and not to the employer personally, the employee had no right of action against the latter in the event of failure to recover from the fund.[515] If the contract provides for the employee to receive a sum part of which is stated to be a salary and part to be for expenses, the whole contract will be unenforceable if the provision relating to expenses is intended to evade tax

40-078

---

[504] *Bowes & Partners Ltd v Press* [1894] 1 Q.B. 202.

[505] cf. *Camden Exhibition & Display Ltd v Lynott* [1966] 1 Q.B. 555.

[506] e.g. *Tarmac Roadstone Holdings Ltd v Peacock* [1973] I.C.R. 273.

[507] [2017] EWHC 1839 (QB).

[508] See below, para.40-094.

[509] On the employer's right to make a deduction on account of bad work, see below, para.40-099.

[510] e.g. *Aris-Bainbridge v Turner Manufacturing Co* [1951] 1 K.B. 563 (HC) (commission payable on the annual turnover of an employer's business: lump-sum payments under settlements of wartime contracts held to be included in the turnover). Compare *Judge v Crown Leisure Ltd* [2005] EWCA Civ 571, [2005] I.R.L.R. 823, where the Court of Appeal upheld a decision of an employment tribunal that a verbal promise at a Christmas party eventually to place the claimant on the same salary scale as another employee was too indefinite to have contractual force, rejecting, however, the argument that this was a question of intention to create legal relations. Compare now also *Attrill v Dresdner Kleinwort Ltd* [2013] EWCA Civ 394, [2013] 3 All E.R. 607, where it had been held that an announcement of a "guaranteed" minimum bonus paid could be regarded as "the stuff of contractual obligation" although communicated in a collective informal "town hall forum" to a workforce at large.

[511] See above, paras 40-047 et seq.

[512] See above, paras 40-049 et seq.

[513] See above, paras 40-055—40-057.

[514] See below, paras 40-084—40-085.

[515] *Landman v Entwistle* (1852) 7 Ex. 632; *De Vries v Corner* (1866) 13 L.T. 636.

liabilities.[516] It is a basic principle that an employee is paid for carrying out contractual duties, and must show himself or herself ready and willing to do so if he or she is to claim the corresponding contractual remuneration, so that where, for instance, the employee refuses to work according to new methods which are within his or her terms and conditions of employment, the employer is entitled to withhold payment.[517] Difficult questions of construction arise with regard to the complex compensation and benefit arrangements which are frequently made with managerial or executive employees. In *Mallone v BPB Industries Plc*,[518] the Court of Appeal construed the discretion to cancel mature options under a senior executive share option scheme as being limited by the requirement that it be exercised rationally with regard to the performance of the employee in question; a similar construction was applied with regard to performance bonus in *Clark v Nomura International Plc*.[519]

40-079 **No express or fixed provision for remuneration** If the contract is silent as to remuneration, but the circumstances[520] show that the services of the employee were not to be rendered gratuitously,[521] there is early authority to the effect that the law will imply a term by which the employer undertakes to pay a reasonable sum of money by way of remuneration.[522] In fixing what is a reasonable remuneration the court must look at all the circumstances, including conversations and correspondence between the parties, to see what sum they considered reasonable.[523] The principle that a term specifying a "reasonable" remuneration will be implied when the exact amount has not been fixed extends to additional remuneration as well as to basic remuneration; thus where an employer wrote to his secretary saying that

---

[516] *Napier v National Business Agency Ltd* [1951] 2 All E.R. 264. See above, para.40-037 and cases there cited.

[517] *Cresswell v Board of Inland Revenue* [1984] I.C.R. 508. cf. also below, para.40-094 (effect of industrial action upon entitlement to remuneration).

[518] [2002] I.C.R. 1045.

[519] [2000] I.R.L.R. 766. Compare also *Horkulak v Cantor Fitzgerald International* [2004] EWCA Civ 1287, [2005] I.C.R. 402; the decisions of the High Court in *Takacs v Barclays Services Jersey Ltd* [2006] I.R.L.R. 877, QBD and of the Court of Appeal in *Keen v Commerzbank AG* [2006] EWCA Civ 1536, [2007] I.C.R. 623, below, para.40-153; *Khatri v Cooperatieve Centrale Raiffeisen-Boerenleenbank BA* [2010] EWCA Civ 397, where the requirement of rational exercise of discretions with regard to the awarding of bonuses was reaffirmed. See also *GX Networks Ltd v Greenland* [2010] EWCA Civ 784 where the Court of Appeal was similarly reluctant to treat as unfettered an employer's discretion, expressed to be "by exception only", to cap an employee's commission on sales; *Rutherford v Seymour Pierce Ltd* [2010] EWHC 375 (QB), [2010] I.R.L.R 606 where at first instance an implied term, allegedly customary within the City of London, requiring that the employee must in order to qualify for a bonus be still employed at the time due for payment, was rejected as not being necessary to give business efficacy to the contract, as not being equitable and reasonable, and as not representing a notorious, invariable, or certain custom.

[520] *Way v Latilla Ltd* [1937] 3 All E.R. 759. See also *Higgins v Hopkins* (1848) 3 Exch. 163, 166; *Hulse v Hulse* (1856) 17 C.B. 711; *Lamburn v Cruden* (1841) 2 M. & G. 253; *Reeve v Reeve* (1858) 1 F. & F. 280.

[521] If the services were to be performed gratuitously, there will normally be no valid contract because of the absence of consideration: *Lees v Whitcomb* (1828) 5 Bing. 34; Vol.I, Ch.4.

[522] *Morrison v Baillie* (1855) 2 Macq.H.L. 80; *Price v Hong Kong Tea Co* (1861) 2 F. & F. 466; *Att-Gen v Drapers' Co* (1869) L.R. 9 Eq. 69; *North v Bassett* [1892] 1 Q.B. 333; cf. *Brown v Nairne* (1839) 9 C. & P. 204. Compare *Driver v Air India Ltd* [2011] EWCA Civ 830 where the Court of Appeal rejected the employer's contention that payment for overtime was discretionary as being contrary to the general position that where a contractual payment was not specified, the law implied a reasonable sum. As to implied terms generally, see Vol.I, Ch.14; as to quantum meruit claims generally, see Vol.I, paras 29-004, 29-071—29-073.

[523] *Way v Latilla Ltd* [1937] 3 All E.R. 759, HL.

instead of a rise in salary, he would pay her a bonus on net trading profits of the previous year, the Court of Appeal held that this amounted to an undertaking to pay a reasonable sum as a bonus.[524] Where there is an arrangement for work to be done with remuneration at the discretion of the employer, early authorities seemed to treat the arrangement as creating no contractual right to remuneration.[525] But there are also decisions suggesting that a court would endeavour, if possible, to construe a similar provision as a contract of employment[526] for reasonable remuneration.[527] However, where the articles of association of a company provided that "A managing director shall receive such remuneration ... as the directors may determine", it was held that in the absence of any such determination of an amount the managing director was not entitled to any remuneration, even on the basis of quantum meruit.[528] The situation where an annual hours contract is silent as to payment for overtime working was considered in the case of *Ali v Christian Salvesen Food Services Ltd*.[529] Uncertainties of the kind discussed here may in practice be considerably reduced by the employer's obligation under the contracts of employment legislation to give the employee written particulars of terms relating to remuneration and the intervals at which remuneration is paid,[530] and by the employer's obligation under the employment protection legislation to give the employee an itemised pay statement at the time of each payment of remuneration,[531] which is discussed in a later paragraph.[532] It should, however, be pointed out that some of the difficulties discussed in this paragraph raise the logically prior question of whether the arrangement concerned is a contract of employment at all.[533]

The national minimum wage The National Minimum Wage Act 1998[534] confers   **40-080**
upon workers an entitlement to be paid at least the national minimum wage by their employers. In brief summary, the provisions of the Act are as follows.[535] The category of "workers" is broadly defined[536] (but so as to exclude contracts of apprenticeship)[537] so as to extend beyond those having contracts of employment as such; special provision is also made which applies the Act to agency workers and to home workers who are not otherwise "workers",[538] and power is given to apply

---

[524] *Powell v Braun* [1954] 1 W.L.R. 401; see *WPM Retail Ltd v Lang* [1978] I.C.R. 787; cf. *William Sindall Ltd v North West Thames RHA* [1977] I.C.R. 294.

[525] *Taylor v Brewer* (1813) 1 M. & S. 290; *Roberts v Smith* (1859) 4 Hurl. & N. 315. cf. *Jewry v Busk* (1814) 5 Taunt. 302.

[526] See also see below, para.40-091 for the question of whether a contract of employment must provide the employee with *some* degree of remunerative opportunity.

[527] *Bryant v Flight* (1839) 5 M. & W. 114. But see *Obu v A Strauss & Co Ltd* [1951] A.C. 243, 250.

[528] *Re Richmond Gate Property Co Ltd* [1965] 1 W.L.R. 335, see Vol.I, para.29-082.

[529] [1997] I.C.R. 25.

[530] Employment Rights Act 1996 s.1(4).

[531] Employment Rights Act 1996 ss.8–12.

[532] See below, para.40-097.

[533] See Freedland, *The Personal Employment Contract* (2003), pp.60–64. It was held in *102 Social Club Ltd v Bickerton* [1977] I.C.R. 911 that receipt of an honorarium did not create a contract of employment.

[534] In force at various dates from April 1999 (SI 1998/2574).

[535] The National Minimum Wage Regulations 2015 (SI 2015/621) consolidate and update all previous Regulations enacted under the National Minimum Wage Act 1998.

[536] See s.54.

[537] As to which compare *Chassis & Cab Specialist Ltd v Lee* [2011] UKEAT/0268/10/JOJ.

[538] See ss.34, 35.

the Act to other individuals who are not otherwise "workers".[539] There has been a major question as to whether, and in what circumstances, tips paid by customers to or for workers such as waiters can be counted by employers in fulfilment of their obligation to pay the national minimum wage. In *Revenue and Customs Commissioners v Annabel's (Berkeley Square) Ltd*[540] the Court of Appeal held that money payments made in the form of discretionary service charges by customers to waiters and bar staff by credit or debit card or by cheque, and collected by the proprietor/employer to be transmitted to employees via a "tronc" system, administered by an employee called the "troncmaster", did not count towards the meeting of the requirement of s.1 of the National Minimum Wage Act 1998. Another major issue concerns the qualification of workers' time spent "on-call", in particular where this takes place on the employer's premises. This has now been held to count as "time work".[541] The Act provides for the making of regulations determining the hourly rate of remuneration by referral to the Low Pay Commission, and for excluding certain classes of persons or making modifications in relation to them.[542] In the event of non-compliance by the employer with the minimum wage requirements for any "pay reference period", the worker shall be taken to be entitled under his or her contract to be paid, as additional remuneration in respect of that period, the amount which is the difference between what he or she actually received and what he or she would have received for that period had he or she been remunerated by the employer at a rate equal to the national minimum wage,[543] and officers appointed to enforce the legislation may also sue for that additional remuneration on behalf of the worker.[544] Moreover, workers are given the rights not to suffer detriment, enforceable by complaint to an employment tribunal, nor to be unfairly dismissed by reason of asserting their right to the minimum wage.[545]

40-081 **Holidays and holiday pay** An employee's right to holidays depends usually on the express or implied terms of his or her contract of employment; the terms of a collective agreement[546] frequently provide for holidays and holiday pay, and these terms are likely to be incorporated into individual contracts of employment.[547] It is also a general requirement under the contracts of employment legislation for employees to be given written particulars of any terms and conditions of employment relating to entitlement to holidays, including public holidays, and holiday

---

[539] See s.41. Trainees on Government training schemes are excluded by virtue of the National Minimum Wage Regulations 1999 (Amendment) Regulations 2001 (SI 2001/1108) in force from May 1, 2001.

[540] [2009] EWCA Civ 361, [2007] I.C.R. 1123.

[541] *Whittlestone v BJP Home Support Ltd* [2014] I.C.R. 275, EAT; cf. *Esparon (t/a Middle West Residential Care Home) v Slavikovska* [2014] I.R.L.R. 598, EAT. Different considerations may apply where the worker's home was her place of work: *Shannon v Rampersad (t/a Clifton House Residential Home)* [2015] I.R.L.R. 982, EAT.

[542] See ss.2–8.

[543] See s.17.

[544] See s.20. The Employment Relations Act 2004 ss.44–46 made extensive additions and amendments to the regime for the enforcement of the national minimum wage, with effect from April 6, 2005.

[545] See ss.23–25. The enforcement mechanisms were further reinforced, with effect from July 2003, by the provisions of the National Minimum Wage Enforcement Notices Act 2003. The Employment Act 2008 ss.8–12 made further additions and amendments to the regime for the enforcement of the national minimum wage, with effect from April 2009. Section 152 of the Small Business, Enterprise and Employment Act 2015 modified s.19A of the National Minimum Wage Act 1998 to increase the relevant financial penalties.

[546] See above, paras 40-047 et seq.

[547] See above, paras 40-049 et seq.

pay.[548] The particulars must be sufficient to enable the employee's entitlement, including any entitlement to accrued holiday pay on termination of employment, to be precisely calculated.[549]

Holiday Pay under the Working Time Regulations and Directive   The Working Time Regulations,[550] as described more fully in a later paragraph,[551] now confer an important general entitlement to a minimum period of paid holiday. In *Lock v British Gas Trading Ltd* (C-539/12),[552] the CJEU held that the Working Time Directive required that holiday pay not be limited to basic salary where commission was part of the employee's remuneration. This approach to "normal remuneration" was essentially followed in *Dudley MBC v Willetts*,[553] when the Employment Appeal Tribunal held that voluntary overtime pay could be included for purposes of holiday pay calculation. Moreover, in *King v Sash Window Workshop Ltd*, it was held that EU law prohibits national provisions or practices that prevent a worker from carrying over or accumulating, until the termination of the employment relationship, paid annual leave rights not exercised in respect of several consecutive reference periods because the employer refused to remunerate that leave.[554]   **40-082**

Rolled-up holiday pay   The issue of whether holiday pay entitlements can be discharged by the payment of "rolled-up" holiday pay was referred to the ECJ by the Court of Appeal in *Caulfield v Marshalls Clay Products Ltd*.[555] In the joined cases *Robinson-Steele v RD Retail Services Ltd, Caulfield v Hanson Clay Products*,[556] the ECJ held the practice of payment of "rolled-up holiday pay" to be unlawful, as failing to comply with the paid holiday obligations imposed by the Working Time Directive. However, in *Sumsion v BBC (Scotland)*,[557] the EAT took a wide view of the employer's entitlement to stipulate when leave may be taken. See also *NHS Leeds v Larner*,[558] in which the Court of Appeal held that, in the case of a worker who had been on long-term sick leave, upon the termination of her employment during that sick leave, her entitlement to four weeks' holiday pay representing the four weeks' annual leave required by the Working Time Directive was not forfeited by reason of her never actually having requested any holiday while on sick leave. It was, however, left open whether the same rule applies to the worker's additional holiday entitlement under the Working Time Regulations. Compare furthermore the decision in *Bollacke v Klaas & Kock*, where the CJEU held that the death of worker does not extinguish paid annual leave accrual.[559]   **40-083**

Payment during absence due to sickness: the position at common law   The   **40-084**

---

548 Employment Rights Act 1996 s.1(4)(d)(i).
549 Employment Rights Act 1996 s.1(4)(d)(i). Voluntary overtime cannot automatically be excluded for such purposes: *Patterson v Castlereagh BC* [2015] NICA 47.
550 SI 1998/1833 in force from October 1, 1998. See reg.13 as amended by the Working Time (Amendment) Regulations 2001 (SI 2001/3256).
551 See below, para.40-112.
552 [2014] 3 C.M.L.R. 53, [2014] I.C.R. 813. For the domestic follow-up, see *Lock v British Gas Trading Ltd* [2016] EWCA Civ 983, [2016] I.R.L.R. 946.
553 [2017] I.R.L.R. 870, EAT.
554 C-214/16 EU:C:2017:914 (CJEU), [2018] 2 C.M.L.R. 10.
555 [2004] EWCA Civ 422, [2004] 2 C.M.L.R. 45.
556 C-131/04 and C-257/04 EU:C:2006:177, [2006] I.C.R. 932.
557 [2007] I.R.L.R. 678.
558 [2012] EWCA Civ 1034, [2012] 4 All E.R. 1006.
559 C-118/13 EU:C:2014:1755 (CJEU).

position at common law is that the right of the employee to claim salary or wages during his or her absence from work on account of illness or injury depends entirely on the terms of his or her contract. Particulars of terms relating to incapacity for work due to sickness or injury, including any provisions for sick pay, must be issued to the employee under the Contracts of Employment legislation.[560] There are provisions under that legislation requiring the employer to allow sick pay where absence due to sickness occurs during a statutory period of notice.[561] A large proportion of contracts of employment now include some form of scheme for payment during absence due to sickness. If no express term deals with the matter, the court must attempt to infer an implied term from all the relevant circumstances. In older authorities, the following considerations have been thought relevant in determining such an implied term:

(1) If it is known to the parties that, in practice, the particular employer does not pay wages during illness to employees engaged in a capacity similar to that of the one in question,[562] it is an implied term of the contract that no wages are payable during the employee's illness.[563] On the other hand, if it is known to both parties that wages are usually paid during illness it will be an implied term of the contract that the employee shall be entitled to his wages throughout the period of his employment despite any absence due to illness.[564]

(2) If the employee receives sick pay out of a fund to which both the employer and the employees contribute, the employee is not entitled to wages while he or she receives benefits from the fund.[565] On the other hand, the receipt of social security sickness benefits does not of itself prevent the employee from claiming wages during the time he or she is in receipt of those benefits.[566]

(3) When the employee is paid by time, e.g. by the hour, and is not paid for any time in which he or she does not work, the employee will not normally be entitled to wages in respect of periods of absence through illness.[567] Similarly an employee paid by piecework (without any provision for guaranteed remuneration) is not entitled to wages if, through illness, he or she is unable to work.[568]

(4) Contracts of employment have been said to be of two kinds, one in which the consideration for the wages is actual work, and the other in which it is readiness and willingness to work, if of ability to do so.[569] It has been thought that in the former case, wages are not payable during the employee's

---

[560] Employment Rights Act 1996 s.1(4)(d)(ii).
[561] Employment Rights Act 1996 s.88(1).
[562] e.g. where there was a notice in the place of employment that half-pay up to a total of 21 days a year would be paid *as a matter of grace* during illness: *Petrie v Mac Fisheries Ltd* [1940] 1 K.B. 258; or where the employee had been ill on several previous occasions and had not asked for nor been paid any wages: *O'Grady v Saper Ltd* [1940] 2 K.B. 469.
[563] *Petrie v Mac Fisheries* [1940] 1 K.B. 258; *O'Grady v Saper Ltd* [1940] 2 K.B. 469.
[564] *K v Racchen* (1878) 38 L.T. 38.
[565] *Niblett v Midland Ry* (1907) 23 T.L.R. 240.
[566] cf. *Marrison v Bell* [1939] 2 K.B. 187.
[567] *Hancock v BSA Tools Ltd* [1939] 4 All E.R. 538.
[568] See *Browning v Crumlin Valley Collieries* [1926] 1 K.B. 522.
[569] *Petrie v Mac Fisheries Ltd* [1940] 1 K.B. 258; *O'Grady v M Saper Ltd* [1940] 2 K.B. 469; *Hancock v BSA Tools Ltd* [1939] 4 All E.R. 538. See also Lord Denning (1939) 55 L.Q.R. 353.

illness, whilst in the latter case they are.[570] In *Beveridge v KLM UK Ltd*[571] it was ruled that an employee who offers her services to an employer is entitled, at common law, to be paid unless a specific condition of the contract regulates otherwise. However, that pronouncement has to be related to the specific context in which an employee claimed to be fit and certified to return to work, while the employers required their own medical adviser to confirm.

(5)   It has been held that where there is a contractual obligation to pay sick pay, but no agreed term as to its duration, a term should be implied which is reasonable having regard to the normal practice in the industry.[572]

(6)   It should be noted that the existence of an express sick pay scheme may result in an implied term restricting the employer's power to terminate the contract during the absence of the employee due to sickness.[573]

A common law presumption of entitlement to sick pay?   The decision in *Orman v Saville Sportswear Ltd*[574] suggested that a presumption of entitlement to sick pay should be applied to contracts of employment in general. It was said that: **40-085**

"Where the written terms of the contract of service are silent as to what is to happen in regard to the employee's rights to be paid whilst he is absent from work due to sickness, the employer remains liable to continue paying so long as the contract is not determined by proper notice, except where a condition to the contrary can properly be inferred from all the facts and the evidence in the case. If the employer ... seeks to establish an implied condition that no wages are payable, it is for him to make it out."[575]

In this case no such term could be implied because it was clear on the evidence that the plaintiff would not have agreed to it. The status of the suggested presumption of entitlement to sick pay was hard to assess. The question was re-examined and the authorities were reviewed in *Mears v Safecar Security Ltd*,[576] with the conclusion that it was wrong to apply a general presumption of entitlement to sick pay; the correct approach was to consider the circumstances according to the kind of factors listed above[577]; it was said that:

"It may be, at the end of the day, if there are no factors either way which can properly be relied upon, that the correct inference is that if a man is employed for a period on a wage, then, if nothing else can be found, the presumption will be that the wage is to be paid during the period of employment; but if there are other factors it seems to us that they come in at the beginning of the exercise and not after certain presumptions have been made."[578]

Moreover, the judgment of the Employment Appeal Tribunal, which was upheld by

---

570 *Cuckson v Stones* (1859) 1 E. & E. 248; *Warren v Whittingham* (1902) 18 T.L.R. 508; *Marrison v Bell* [1939] 2 K.B. 187. The headnote is inaccurate: *O'Grady v Saper Ltd* [1940] 2 K.B. 469, 473.
571 [2000] I.R.L.R. 765.
572 *Howman & Son v Blyth* [1983] I.C.R. 416.
573 Compare *Aspden v Webbs Poultry & Meat Group (Holdings) Ltd* [1996] I.R.L.R. 521. (As to the effect on such a scheme of the termination of the insurance policy which supports it, compare *Bainbridge v Circuit Foil (UK) Ltd* [1997] I.C.R. 541).
574 [1960] 1 W.L.R. 1055.
575 [1960] 1 W.L.R. 1055 at 1064–1065.
576 [1981] I.C.R. 409, EAT; upheld by the Court of Appeal [1982] I.R.L.R. 183.
577 See above, para.40-084.
578 [1981] I.C.R. 409, 419C–D, per Slynn J., a passage adopted by the Court of Appeal [1982] I.R.L.R. 183, 189.

the Court of Appeal, in that case suggests that even where there was an implied provision for payment during sickness, it was subject to deduction of social security sickness benefit received by the employee.[579]

40-086 **Statutory sick pay** Part XI of the Social Security Contributions and Benefits Act 1992 provides for the payment of statutory sick pay by employers.[580] The employee[581] is entitled to statutory sick pay for days where three qualifying conditions are satisfied,[582] namely, that the day in question (1) is part of a period of incapacity for work[583]; (2) falls within a period of entitlement[584]; and (3) is a qualifying day.[585] The entitlement derived from these conditions is then subjected to certain limitations.[586] The overall effect[587] is that the employee is entitled to statutory sick pay for certain periods of incapacity up to a limit of 28 weeks' entitlement in any three years.[588] Each period of incapacity must consist of a minimum of four consecutive days; the days in question must be, in effect, working days or their equivalent; and the first three days of any one period[589] of incapacity are excluded.[590] There must be prescribed notification of incapacity for work to the employer.[591] Statutory sick pay is at prescribed rates, set by and under the Act,[592] subject to provisions for periodical review by the Secretary of State.[593] Provision was formerly but is no longer made, except in the case of small employers, for recovery by employers of amounts paid by way of statutory sick pay by setting such sums off against national insurance contributions or reclaiming them from the National Insurance Fund.[594] Provision is also made to ensure that payments of statutory sick pay operate in discharge of liability to contractual remuneration and vice versa.[595] The determination of questions of entitlement to statutory sick pay is to be carried out by the national insurance adjudication system with some modifications.[596] Enforcement of entitlement as so determined is by County Court process.[597] Provision is made to prevent employers from avoiding their liability to statutory sick pay by

---

579 [1981] I.C.R. 409 at 419D–421B, distinguishing *Sun and Sand Ltd v Fitzjohn* [1979] I.C.R. 268 as based upon a concession by counsel for the employers.

580 The Statutory Sick Pay Scheme has been in force since April 6, 1983. For details of its operation, reference should be made to the following regulations: Statutory Sick Pay (General) Regulations 1982 (SI 1982/894); Statutory Sick Pay (Compensation of Employers and Miscellaneous Provisions) Regulations 1983 (SI 1983/376); Statutory Sick Pay (General) Amendment Regulations 1985 (SI 1985/126); Statutory Sick Pay (Additional Compensation of Employers and Consequential Amendments) Regulations 1985 (SI 1985/1411) and successive amending regulations.

581 Defined in s.163(1).

582 s.151(1).

583 As defined by s.152.

584 Defined by s.153.

585 See s.154.

586 By s.155.

587 This is necessarily a simplification, and further reference should be made to the detailed provisions of ss.152–155 and regulations for which provision is made by ss.153(5), 153(10), 155(5), 152(4).

588 See ss.155 as amended by the Social Security (Incapacity for Work) Act 1994 s.8 and SI 1982/894.

589 Periods of incapacity separated by no more than two weeks are consolidated together by s.152(3).

590 See s.152(2), (3), (4), (6), 154, 155(1).

591 s.156 and regulations made under s.156(1).

592 s.157(1), (3).

593 s.157(2).

594 s.159 and regulations made thereunder. The Statutory Sick Pay Act 1994 removed the right of employers, other than small employers, to recover sums paid by them by way of statutory sick pay.

595 s.160 and Sch.2.

596 Statutory Sick Pay Percentage Threshold Order 1995 (SI 1995/512).

597 Statutory Sick Pay Percentage Threshold Order 1995 (SI 1995/512).

contracting out or by obliging an employee to make payments towards his or her statutory sick pay.[598] It is suggested that the provisions for statutory sick pay do not affect the express or implied[599] provisions of the contract of employment for sick pay or the continuance of remuneration during absence due to sickness, save insofar as the statute prevents the avoidance of statutory sick pay by contract,[600] and insofar as it makes provision for mutual discharge of liabilities for statutory and for contractual sick pay.[601]

Remuneration during suspension from work on medical grounds Employees engaged upon certain industrial processes involving potential health hazards may be temporarily suspended from their normal work, usually on the advice of an Employment Medical Adviser, under certain statutory health and safety regulations, or by reason of a recommendation in a code of practice issued or approved under s.16 of the Health and Safety at Work, etc. Act 1974.[602] The employment protection legislation gives the employee a right to be remunerated by their employer during suspension on medical grounds, for a period not exceeding 26 weeks.[603] The employee cannot claim this right in respect of periods during which he or she is incapable of work by reason of disease or bodily or mental disablement[604]; he or she must at such times rely on such entitlement to sick pay or sickness or industrial injuries benefits as he or she may possess. Nor may the employee claim the right to remuneration on suspension on medical grounds, in respect of a time during which the employer has offered suitable alternative work and the employee has unreasonably refused to perform the work.[605] The amount of the entitlement is determined by the statutory concept of a week's pay.[606] The employer may set off any contractual remuneration the employer pays at such times against the statutory entitlement and vice versa.[607] The employee may complain to an employment tribunal of the employer's failure to pay the statutory entitlement and the tribunal may order the employer to pay the amount due.[608]

40-087

Statutory maternity pay Under the provisions of Pt XII of the Social Security Contributions and Benefits Act 1992 as amended or expanded by statutory regulations, a woman who is or has been an employee is entitled to statutory maternity pay for a Maternity Pay Period of up to 52[609] weeks where she satisfies the statutory conditions. A number of the provisions relating to statutory maternity pay either require regulations to be made, or enable other provisions to be defined or modi-

40-088

---

598 s.151(2).
599 See above, paras 40-084—40-085.
600 See s.151(2), (3) of the 1992 Act.
601 See s.160 and Sch.12 para.2 of the 1992 Act.
602 See Employment Rights Act 1996 s.64; and the Employment Protection (Medical Suspension) Order 1980 (SI 1980/1581).
603 Employment Rights Act 1996 s.64; subject to the exclusion in s.199(2) (share fishermen).
604 Employment Rights Act 1996 s.65(3).
605 Employment Rights Act 1996 s.65(4)(a) (see also s.65(4)(b)—compliance with employer's reasonable requirements to ensure the availability of his services).
606 Employment Rights Act 1996 s.69(1) and ss.220–229.
607 Employment Rights Act 1996 s.69(3).
608 Employment Rights Act 1996 s.70.
609 Increased from 26 weeks by s.1 of the Work and Families Act 2006 as from October 1, 2006.

fied by regulations, and reference should be made to the regulations which have been made in accordance with those provisions.[610]

40-089 Statutory paternity pay   Under the provisions of Pt XIIZA of the Social Security Contributions and Benefits Act 1992, inserted by the Employment Act 2002,[611] as expanded by statutory regulations, an employee is entitled to statutory paternity pay for a Paternity Pay Period of up to two weeks where he satisfies the statutory conditions. The right to paternity pay is extended to the partner of an adopting parent, or to the member of an adopting couple who does not take adoption leave and pay.[612] A number of the provisions relating to statutory paternity pay either require regulations to be made, or enable other provisions to be defined or modified by regulations, and reference should be made to the regulations which have been made in accordance with those provisions.[613] The Work and Families Act 2006 conferred a further entitlement in certain circumstances to additional statutory paternity pay in the cases either of birth or adoption of a child.[614]

40-090 Statutory adoption pay   Under the provisions of Pt XIIZB of the Social Security Contributions and Benefits Act 1992, inserted by the Employment Act 2002,[615] as expanded by statutory regulations, an employee is entitled to statutory paternity pay for an Adoption Pay Period normally of 26 weeks where he satisfies the statutory conditions. The right to adoption pay applies to the adopting parent, or to the member of an adopting couple who elects to take it.[616] A number of the provisions relating to statutory adoption pay either require regulations to be made, or enable other provisions to be defined or modified by regulations, and reference should be made to the regulations which have been made in accordance with those provisions.[617]

40-091 Opportunity to earn and the right of lay-off   Where the employee's remuneration is dependent upon the number of hours he works within each week or upon the amount of his or her output (as in piece-work systems or systems of payment by commission) the question arises whether the employer impliedly contracts not only to pay for work done but also to provide a certain minimum remunerative opportunity for the employee and to make good any shortfall below that minimum. There is some older authority to the effect that the courts will imply an obligation on the employer's part to provide the piece-work employee with the opportunity in each week to earn a reasonable average rate of remuneration for the employment

---

[610] Especially the Statutory Maternity Pay (General) Regulations 1986 (SI 1986/1960), as lately amended by the Social Security, Statutory Maternity Pay and Statutory Sick Pay (Miscellaneous Amendments) Regulations 2002 (SI 2002/2690).

[611] s.2, as from December 8, 2002, the entitlement to statutory paternity pay taking effect from April 6, 2003.

[612] See s.171ZB of the Social Security Contributions and Benefits Act 1992 and Pt 3 of the Statutory Paternity Pay and Statutory Adoption Pay (General) Regulations 2002 (SI 2002/2822).

[613] Especially the Statutory Paternity Pay and Statutory Adoption Pay (General) Regulations 2002 (SI 2002/2822).

[614] ss.6–10, inserting new ss.171ZEA–171ZEE to the 1992 Act.

[615] s.4, as from December 2002, the entitlement to statutory adoption pay taking effect from April 2003.

[616] See s.171ZL(2) of the Social Security Contributions and Benefits Act 1992.

[617] Especially the Statutory Paternity Pay and Statutory Adoption Pay (General) Regulations 2002 (SI 2002/2822).

concerned.[618] On the other hand, older authorities suggest that a contract which contains no such obligation at all on the employer's part will be void for want of mutuality where the employee is under some obligation to work.[619] Another approach to the same problem is to consider the extent to which the employer is entitled to lay the employee off work; that is to say, to suspend contractual working (and remuneration accordingly) by reason of lack of available work to be done.[620] There is older authority implying in the employer's favour a wide right of lay-off—the leading case was that of a coal-mining company which successfully asserted the right to lay off underground workers (without remuneration) while the workings underwent maintenance.[621] In *Bond v CAV Ltd*[622] it was said that it is plain that there is no general right to lay off without pay at common law, and that such a right exists only in very limited circumstances. If such an issue were to recur, the employer would probably have to base the claim to a right of lay-off on the existence of a practice of lay-off in the particular employment concerned, and would have to show the practice to have contractual force. It is unlikely that such a claim could be based on a term implied in the contracts of piece-workers generally. It is also thought that an arrangement purporting to give the employer an *unlimited* right of lay-off should not be classified as a continuous contract of employment; or, in other words, that in such a case no contract of employment subsists between periods of contractual working.[623] In *Dakri & Co Ltd v Tiffen*,[624] it was said that "unless a time was specified in the contract, then the law implies that the lay-off is to be for not more than a reasonable time". In practice, the employer's right of lay-off is often curtailed by guaranteed pay provisions, which are considered in the next paragraph.

Provisions for guaranteed remuneration   There are various kinds of provision   **40-092**
by which employees whose remuneration depends upon actual work rather than their availability for work are partly protected from the consequences of being laid off work or put on short-time working by a guarantee of minimum remuneration in those circumstances. In many cases such provision is, or at least used to be, made as a term in individual contracts of employment incorporating the results of collective bargaining.[625] Where the individual contract contains such a term, the unilateral suspension by the employer of the guaranteed pay agreement has been held to constitute a repudiatory breach of contract by the employer.[626] Another source of guaranteed pay provisions used to be wages regulation orders emanating from

---

618 *Devonald v Rosser & Sons* [1906] 2 K.B. 728.
619 *R. v Welch* (1853) 2 El. & Bl. 357; *Whittle v Frankland* (1862) 2 B. & S. 49; *Thomas v Vivian* (1872) 37 J.P. 228. (These cases recognise a *wide* but not *unlimited* right to lay the employee off.)
620 In *Johnson v Cross* [1977] I.C.R. 872, the Employment Appeal Tribunal duly applied *Devonald v Rosser & Sons* as representing a restriction on the employer's power of lay-off, but rather curiously interpreted that restriction as amounting to a duty to provide a reasonable level of work for the one week's minimum period of notice required of the *employee* by the contracts of employment legislation, see below, para.40-164.
621 *Browning v Crumlin Valley Collieries Ltd* [1926] 1 K.B. 522. This was treated, questionably, as a case where the stoppage of work was beyond the employer's control. See also the cases cited in the previous and the next note.
622 [1983] I.R.L.R. 360, 366.
623 The decision to the contrary in *Puttick v John Wright & Sons Ltd* [1972] I.C.R. 457 was necessary for the avoidance of an injustice in the particular circumstances.
624 [1981] I.C.R. 256, 260C. Compare, however, *Craig v Bob Lindfield & Son Ltd* [2016] I.C.R. 527, EAT.
625 Some details are given in Freedland, *The Contract of Employment* (1976), pp.93–95.
626 *Powell Duffryn Ltd v House* [1974] I.C.R. 123.

Wages Councils,[627] which frequently resulted in the incorporation of such provisions as terms in the contracts of employment of employees within the particular industries concerned.[628] A further innovation in this direction was made originally by the Contracts of Employment Act 1963[629] which provided a scheme of guaranteed minimum remuneration during the minimum periods of notice required by that Act.[630] The next development was the creation of a general right of employees to guarantee payments under the Employment Protection Act 1975. Under these provisions, as re-enacted in the Employment Rights Act 1996, an employee is entitled to a guarantee payment from his employer if his or her employer fails to provide him with work on a normal working day.[631] The employee must have been continuously employed by the employer for not less than one month before the day concerned.[632] An employee is not entitled to a guarantee payment if the failure to provide him or her with work is the consequence of industrial action involving any employee of his or her employer or of an associated employer.[633] Nor will an employee be entitled to a guarantee payment if the employer has offered the employee suitable alternative work and he or she has unreasonably refused that offer.[634] The guarantee payment is payable only where the employee has a pattern of normal working hours[635] as statutorily defined.[636] The payment is calculated on a basis which approximates the guarantee payment to the employee's normal week's pay for his or her statutory "normal working hours".[637] The guarantee payment is, however, limited to a prescribed sum,[638] and the entitlement to it is limited to a maximum of five days, or the employee's number of working days in a normal week if that is less than five,[639] in any period of three months.[640] Contractual remuneration paid by the employer may be set off against the obligation to make guarantee payments (and vice versa),[641] so that the employee whose remuneration is not dependent on being provided with work on particular days will automatically receive remuneration satisfying the obligation to make guarantee payments.[642] The employee has a right to complain to an employment tribunal that his or her employer has failed to make a guarantee payment,[643] and the tribunal may order the payment of the amount of guarantee payment due.[644] The Secretary of State for Employment is given extensive powers to vary the limits upon and method of

[627] Wages Councils were abolished by s.35 of Trade Union Reform and Employment Rights Act 1993.
[628] See Freedland at pp.92–93.
[629] First consolidated into the Contracts of Employment Act 1972 and then into the Employment Protection (Consolidation) Act 1978 and then consolidated into the Employment Rights Act 1996.
[630] See now Employment Rights Act 1996 s.87(3) and ss.88–91.
[631] ss.28–35 (excluding share fisherman: s.199). For guidance on the interpretation of s.28, see *Abercrombie v Aga Rangemaster Ltd* [2013] EWCA Civ 1148, [2014] 1 All E.R. 1101.
[632] s.29.
[633] s.29(3).
[634] s.29(4), (5).
[635] s.30(1).
[636] ss.221–229.
[637] s.30(2)–(4).
[638] s.31(1) and regulations made from time to time.
[639] s.31(3)–(5).
[640] s.31(2).
[641] s.32(2).
[642] Employment Rights Act 1996 s.32(3). See *Cartwright v G Clancey Ltd* [1983] I.C.R. 552.
[643] s.34(1) (limitation period—s.34(2)).
[644] s.34(3).

calculation of guarantee payments.[645] The "appropriate Minister" is also empowered to make orders conferring exemption from the statutory scheme in favour of guarantee payments provisions made by collective agreements or by the orders of Agricultural Wages Boards,[646] provided that there is a joint application by all the parties to the collective agreement or by the Agricultural Wages Board concerned,[647] and provided the guarantee pay arrangements concerned provide adequate procedural safeguards for individual employees.[648]

Payment during disciplinary suspension   Since suspension from work is often **40-093** in practice a part of the disciplinary procedures used by employers, it is important to consider the circumstances in which the employee will or will not be entitled to remuneration in respect of a period of disciplinary suspension. There is no generally implied contractual right on the part of employers to suspend employees without pay on disciplinary grounds.[649] It must be shown that there is an express or implied term in the particular contract justifying this inroad upon the employer's normal obligations to the employee; and written particulars of such terms must now be given to employees.[650] It has been held that the contractual provision of a particular procedure for disciplinary suspension will exclude any right of disciplinary suspension outside that procedure,[651] and it seems that disciplinary suspension cannot be justified by reference to the employer's contractual right to *dismiss* for misconduct.[652] An express right to disciplinary suspension has, however, been construed as a right to impose suspension with loss of pay,[653] and such loss of pay may be inherent in the method of calculation of remuneration or otherwise be indicated as the intention of the parties.[654] Although disciplinary suspension without pay results in a kind of deduction from wages, it was held[655] that when the right to suspend was suitably formulated, it fell outside the prohibitions upon deductions then contained in the Truck Acts.[656] Similarly, disciplinary suspension without pay would probably not constitute a deduction from wages contravening s.14 of the Employment Rights Act 1996[657] and in any event would not do so where the disciplinary suspension was authorised by any provision of the contract of employment which had been notified in writing to the worker concerned,[658] or where it was imposed on account of the worker's having taken part in any industrial action.[659]

The effect of industrial action upon entitlement to remuneration   In *Henthorn*   **40-094**

---

[645] s.33.
[646] Employment Rights Act 1996 s.35(1) and (2).
[647] Employment Rights Act 1996 s.35(1) and (2).
[648] Employment Rights Act 1996 s.35(4), (5).
[649] *Hanley v Pease & Partners Ltd* [1915] 1 K.B. 698; *Marshall v English Electric Ltd* [1945] 1 All E.R. 653.
[650] Employment Rights Act 1996 s.3; see above, para.40-041.
[651] *Gorse v Durham CC* [1971] 1 W.L.R. 775.
[652] cf. *Warburton v Taff Vale Ry* (1902) 18 T.L.R. 420.
[653] *Wallwork v Fielding* [1922] 2 K.B. 66.
[654] cf. *Marshall v English Electric Ltd* [1945] 1 All E.R. 653.
[655] *Bird v British Celanese Ltd* [1945] K.B. 336.
[656] See below, para.40-098.
[657] See below, para.40-100.
[658] Employment Rights Act 1996 s.13(1), (2).
[659] Employment Rights Act 1996 s.14(5). See *Norris v London Fire and Emergency Planning Authority* [2013] I.C.R. 819, EAT.

and Taylor v CEGB,[660] the Court of Appeal held that there was a general common law principle that a plaintiff who claims that he or she is entitled to be paid money under a contract which he or she alleges the defendant has broken must prove that he or she was ready and willing to perform the contract; and that this rule meant that an employer sued for wages could plead that employees who had been "working to rule" had not been ready and willing to perform their part of the contract, without thereby assuming the burden of so proving. This doctrine not only serves to explain why an employee is not entitled to remuneration while striking, but also suggests that an employee may readily be found to have disentitled themselves from remuneration not only by taking part in a "go-slow" or a "work-to-rule" but also by associating themselves with threats of future industrial action.[661] It is a doctrine which in effect may give the employer indirectly a power of lock-out which is not directly conceded by the common law of implied terms of the contract of employment.[662] It is arguable that the common law doctrine in question, when properly understood, should disable the employee from claiming to be "ready and willing" only when his or her conduct amounts to a repudiation of his contract or a breach going to the root of it.[663] Several decisions have confirmed the existence of this common law doctrine and its applicability to industrial action.[664] These cases show that if the industrial action consists of a partial or conditional refusal to perform the employee's contractual duties, and if the employer accepts the partial or conditional performance offered by the employee,[665] then the employee is entitled to the appropriate proportion of his ordinary remuneration. It is not yet clear whether and in what circumstances that proportion is arrived at by, on the one hand, applying the principle of equitable set-off,[666] or, on the other hand, calculating remuneration due on a quantum meruit basis.[667] If the employer makes it quite clear that a partial or conditional performance of contractual duties is not acceptable as substantial performance of those duties, then that partial or conditional performance does not entitle the employee to any remuneration; it is as if there has been no performance.[668]

40-095 Remuneration during statutory time off The Employment Protection Act 1975 and the Employment Act 1980 conferred upon employees the right in certain circumstances to time off work for particular purposes. These, as contained in the Trade Union and Labour Relations (Consolidation) Act 1992 and Employment Rights Act 1996 are: for carrying out trade union duties,[669] for taking part in trade

---

660 [1980] I.R.L.R. 361.
661 cf. *Chappell v Times Newspapers Ltd* [1975] I.C.R. 145.
662 cf. *Cummings v Charles Connell & Co Ltd*, 1969 S.L.T. 25.
663 cf. *Secretary of State for Employment v ASLEF (No.2)* [1972] I.C.R. 19.
664 *Royle v Trafford BC* [1984] I.R.L.R. 184; *Sim v Rotherham MBC* [1986] I.C.R. 897; *Miles v Wakefield MDC* [1987] I.C.R. 368; *Wiluszynski v Tower Hamlets LBC* [1989] I.C.R. 493; *McPherson v Lambeth LBC* [1988] I.R.L.R. 470; compare also *Spackman v London Metropolitan University* [2007] I.R.L.R. 74.
665 *Wiluszynski v Tower Hamlets LBC* [1989] I.C.R. 493; *McPherson v Lambeth LBC* [1988] I.R.L.R. 470.
666 *Sim v Rotherham MBC* [1986] I.C.R. 897.
667 *Miles v Wakefield MDC* [1987] I.C.R. 368, per Lords Brightman and Templeman, sed contra Lord Bridge. Compare now *Cooper v Isle of Wight College* [2007] EWHC 2831, [2008] I.R.L.R. 124.
668 *McPherson v Lambeth LBC* [1988] I.R.L.R. 470; *Wiluszynski v Tower Hamlets LBC* [1989] I.C.R. 493.
669 Trade Union and Labour Relations (Consolidation) Act 1992 s.168.

union activities,[670] for performing public duties,[671] to look for work or make arrangements for training in the case of employees declared redundant,[672] or for antenatal care.[673] These rights are described later[674]; reference is made to them here because the employee is in some cases given a statutory right to remuneration during such time off, so that these rights are in those cases also rights to guaranteed *remuneration* during absence from work for the recognised statutory purposes. The statutory rights to time off include a right to guaranteed remuneration in the case of time off for carrying out trade union duties,[675] and in the case of time off to look for work or make arrangements for training.[676] In the case of time off for carrying out trade union duties, the guaranteed remuneration is calculated as the amount the employee would have received for that time spent at work if he or she is paid solely with reference to time.[677] If he or she is paid partly by reference to the amount of work done, the payment is arrived at by applying the employee's average hourly earnings rate to the time spent off work.[678] The amount of contractual remuneration paid in respect of such a period of time off may be set off against this statutory liability and vice versa.[679] The employee may complain to an employment tribunal of failure to make the statutory payment[680] and an employment tribunal finding the complaint substantiated must order the payment to be made.[681] In the case of time off to look for work or to make arrangements for training, the guaranteed remuneration is calculated on the generally more restrictive basis of an "appropriate hourly rate"[682] arrived at by applying the statutory "week's pay"[683] to the statutory "normal working hours"[684] for the employee concerned. The amount is in this case also limited to two-fifths of one week's pay for the employee concerned.[685] The relationship to contractual remuneration and the enforcement mechanism are the same as in relation to remuneration for time off for union duties.[686] In the case of the right to time off for ante-natal care, also, an "appropriate hourly rate" of remuneration is defined,[687] and the usual sort of provisions are made with regard to the relationship with contractual remuneration[688] and to enforcement.[689] In the case of the rights to time off which do not include a statutory right to guaranteed remuneration,[690] it will depend upon the nature and construction of the contract of employment whether the employee loses remunera-

670 Trade Union and Labour Relations (Consolidation) Act 1992 s.170.
671 Employment Rights Act 1996 s.50 s.51(1).
672 Employment Rights Act 1996 ss.52–54.
673 Employment Rights Act 1996 ss.55–57.
674 See below, paras 40-117—40-123.
675 Trade Union and Labour Relations (Consolidation) Act 1992 s.169.
676 Employment Rights Act 1996 s.53.
677 Trade Union and Labour Relations (Consolidation) Act 1992 s.169(2).
678 s.169(3).
679 s.169(4).
680 s.169(5).
681 s.172(1).
682 Employment Rights Act 1996 s.56(1).
683 Employment Rights Act 1996 ss.221–229.
684 Employment Rights Act 1996 s.234.
685 Employment Rights Act 1996 ss.53(5), 54(4).
686 Employment Rights Act 1996 s.53(7).
687 Employment Rights Act 1996 s.56(1)–(4).
688 Employment Rights Act 1996 s.56(5)–(6).
689 Employment Rights Act 1996 s.57(1)–(5).
690 i.e. the rights to time off for trade union activities—s.28, and for public duties—Employment Rights
       Act 1996 s.50; see below, paras 40-119—40-120.

tion in respect of the time spent off work. If the remuneration is normally varied with reference to the time spent at work within each week, the employee will lose remuneration by virtue of the application of that normal pattern, unless a particular agreement to the contrary can be implied.

40-096 **Equality of pay between men and women** Employers were placed by the Equal Pay Act 1970 (as subsequently amended by, in particular, the Equal Pay (Amendment) Regulations 1983[691] and the Sex Discrimination Act 1986 and the Employment Equality (Sex Discrimination) Regulations 2005[692]) under obligations to eliminate certain inequalities of pay between men and women. Despite the title of the Act, however, these obligations were not confined to remuneration but extend to all terms and conditions of employment. Corresponding provisions are now made by the Equality Act 2010 and those provisions of the Equal Pay Act are accordingly considered in later paragraphs under the broader head of equality of terms and conditions of employment between men and women.[693] Inequalities of treatment as between men and women employees (including inequalities in relation to pay) are also now subject to the wider provisions concerning sex discrimination in employment which were originally made by the Sex Discrimination Act 1975, and were then amended by the Sex Discrimination Act 1986. Corresponding provisions are now made by the Equality Act 2010 which are considered in later paragraphs[694] under the general heading of sex discrimination in the treatment of employees.

40-097 **The right to itemised statements of pay and deductions** Under Pt I of the Employment Rights Act 1996, an employer is obliged to give each employee an itemised pay statement at the time of each payment of wages or salary.[695] The statement must give particulars of the gross amount of the remuneration, any deductions and the purpose for which they have been made, of the net amount of the remuneration and the amount and method of any part payment made in a different way[696] (such as in kind to the extent permissible).[697] Fixed deductions may be dealt with by a standing statement of fixed deductions made in writing and particularising the amount, frequency and purpose of each deduction; if such a standing statement is made, it will be effective for 12 months to reduce the employer's duty to particularise fixed deductions in each itemised pay statement so that it becomes a duty simply to give the aggregate amount of the fixed deductions described in the standing statement.[698] The standing statement may be kept up-to-date by written notice to the employee,[699] but there must be a re-issue of the statement in a consolidated form each year.[700] An employee who complains of failure to give him or her an itemised pay statement may refer to an employment tribunal the ques-

---

[691] SI 1983/1794.
[692] SI 2005/2467.
[693] See below, para.40-127.
[694] See below, paras 40-128—40-132.
[695] Employment Rights Act 1996 s.8. (Merchant seamen are excluded: s.199.)
[696] Employment Rights Act 1996 s.8(2)(a)–(d). The statement is not required to include particulars of tips paid to a waiter by customers, nor of an amount deducted by the employer in respect of tips— *Cofone v Spaghetti House Ltd* [1980] I.C.R. 155.
[697] Some very limited restrictions upon payments in kind are imposed by the Employment Rights Act 1996—see below, para.40-097.
[698] Employment Rights Act 1996 s.9(1), (2).
[699] Employment Rights Act 1996 s.9(3).
[700] Employment Rights Act 1996 s.9(4).

tion of what particulars ought to have been given.[701] When a reference is made to a tribunal in these cases, the tribunal shall, where it finds a deficiency, make a declaration to that effect,[702] and may in addition order the employer to repay to the employee any un-notified deductions made during the 13 weeks preceding the application to the tribunal.[703]

The protection of wages legislation Before 1986, a number of restrictions were **40-098** placed upon payment of wages in kind, deductions from wages, and payment of money wages other than in cash, by the Truck Acts 1831–1940 as modified by the Payment of Wages Act 1960. That legislation was repealed[704] and replaced by Pt I of the Wages Act 1986. That Act imposed certain general restrictions on deductions made from workers' wages, or payments received from workers, by their employers[705]; it also imposed restrictions on deductions from wages, or payments by workers, in retail employment, on account of cash shortages or stock deficiencies[706]; and provided for complaint to an employment tribunal in respect of contraventions.[707] The Wages Act 1986 has subsequently been consolidated into the Employment Rights Act 1996. The relevant provisions are described in greater detail in the next two paragraphs. They extend to Crown employment,[708] and there is power to extend them to employment outside the United Kingdom.[709] The remedy for any contravention of them is by way of complaint to an employment tribunal as provided by the statute, and not otherwise[710]; a provision in an agreement is void so far as it purports to limit or exclude them, or to preclude complaint of contravention unless it is a settlement promoted by a conciliation officer.[711] Provision is made to ensure that complaint can also be made that a deduction has not been itemised as required by ss.11 and 12 of the Employment Rights Act 1996,[712] but double recovery is prevented.[713] A complaint to an employment tribunal must be brought within three months of the deficient wage payment or the payment by the worker which is in issue (or of the latest of a series of such) or, if that is not reasonably practicable, within such further period as the tribunal considers to be so.[714] The remedies consist of a declaration and an order to the employer to pay or repay as necessary to repair the contravention.[715]

---

[701] Employment Rights Act 1996 s.11(1).
[702] Employment Rights Act 1996 s.12(3).
[703] Employment Rights Act 1996 s.12(4), (5).
[704] Wages Act 1986 s.11 and Sch.1 which lists the legislation in full.
[705] s.1, since consolidated into Employment Rights Act 1996 ss.13–16.
[706] See now Employment Rights Act 1996 ss.17–22.
[707] See now Employment Rights Act 1996 ss.23–26, 203–205.
[708] Employment Rights Act 1996 s.191(1)–(4) and s.192(1).
[709] Employment Rights Act 1996 s.201.
[710] Employment Rights Act 1996 s.205(2).
[711] Employment Rights Act 1996 s.203(1), (2).
[712] See above, para.40-095.
[713] Employment Rights Act 1996 s.26.
[714] Employment Rights Act 1996 s.23.
[715] Employment Rights Act 1996 ss.24 and 25. The Employment Act 2008 s.7(1) provided, with effect from April 2009, for the insertion of a new s.24(2) into the Employment Rights Act 1996, which enables an Employment Tribunal to award compensation for financial loss which is sustained by the worker and is attributable to unlawful deduction from or unauthorised payment of wages.

40-099 **General restrictions on deductions made, or payments received, by employers** Under ss.13–15 of the Employment Rights Act 1996, an employer shall not make any deduction from any wages of any worker employed by him or her,[716] or receive any payment from any worker employed by him or her,[717] unless the deduction or payment is made by virtue of any statutory provision or any provision of the worker's contract,[718] or the worker has previously agreed to it in writing.[719] A provision in a worker's contract must, in order to sustain a deduction or payment, be comprised in a written term previously copied by the employer to the worker[720] or in a term whose effect the employer has previously notified in writing to the worker.[721] These requirements do not apply to deductions or payments:

(1) by way of reimbursement of the employer in respect of overpayment of wages or in respect of expenses[722];

(2) in consequence of statutory disciplinary proceedings[723];

(3) in pursuance of a duty on the part of the employer to deduct and pay over to a public authority[724];

(4) in pursuance of an arrangement for deduction and payment over to a third person to which the worker has previously agreed in writing[725];

(5) on account of the worker having taken part in a strike or other industrial action[726]; or

(6) in satisfaction of a court or tribunal order for payment by the worker to the employer.[727]

The wages which are protected include:

(1) any fee, bonus, commission, holiday pay or other emolument referable to the employment[728];

(2) any sum payable under a statutory reinstatement or re-engagement order or a statutory order for the continuation of a contract of employment[729];

---

[716] Employment Rights Act 1996 s.13(1).

[717] Employment Rights Act 1996 s.15(1).

[718] Employment Rights Act 1996 s.13(1)(a). On the question of when it is appropriate to imply terms into the contract of employment in order to decide whether a deduction is authorised, see *Luke v Stoke on Trent City Council* [2007] EWCA Civ 761, [2007] I.C.R. 1678. Compare *Bateman v Asda Stores Ltd* [2010] I.R.L.R. 370 where it was held by the EAT that an imposed transfer to a new pay structure, less favourable than the old one for the complainant employee, did not represent an unauthorised deduction from wages because it was sustained by a wide power of variation of terms which the employer had reserved to itself by a provision in the staff handbook which was regarded as having contractual force despite its apparently unrestricted character.

[719] Employment Rights Act 1996 s.13(1)(b).

[720] Employment Rights Act 1996 s.13(2)(a) and s.15(2)(a).

[721] Employment Rights Act 1996 s.13(2)(b) and s.15(2)(b).

[722] Employment Rights Act 1996 s.14(1) and s.16(1).

[723] Employment Rights Act 1996 s.14(2) and s.16(2).

[724] Employment Rights Act 1996 s.14(3).

[725] Employment Rights Act 1996 s.14(4).

[726] Employment Rights Act 1996 s.14(5) and s.16(3). See *Sunderland Polytechnic v Evans* [1993] I.C.R. 392. In *Hartley v King Edward VI College* [2015] EWCA Civ 455, [2015] I.R.L.R. 650 the Court of Appeal held that the appropriate amount to be deducted for a day's strike is 1/260th of a worker's annual salary.

[727] Employment Rights Act 1996 s.14(6) and s.16(4).

[728] Employment Rights Act 1996 s.27(1)(a); it was held in *Ainsworth v IRC* [2009] UKHL 31, [2009] I.C.R. 985 that this includes holiday pay due under the Working Time Regulations 1998.

[729] Employment Rights Act 1996 s.27(1)(g), (h).

(3) a statutory guarantee payment or other statutory payment in lieu of wages, statutory sick pay or maternity, paternity, or adoption pay[730]; and

(4) any payment in the nature of a non-contractual bonus.[731]

Specifically excluded, however, are:

(1) payments by way of advance under a loan agreement by way of advance of wages,[732] or any payment of expenses[733];

(2) any payment by way of a pension, retirement gratuity or compensation for loss of office or redundancy payment[734];

(3) any payment to the worker other than in the capacity of a worker[735]; and

(4) any payment or benefit in kind, unless it is a voucher or stamp with a fixed money value and capable of being exchanged for money, goods or services.[736]

A worker is defined for this purpose as a person who has entered into or works under a contract of service, of apprenticeship, or for the personal performance of any work or services unless for a client or customer of a profession or business undertaking carried on by that person.[737] Any deficiency, in the amount of wages paid on a particular occasion compared with the amount of wages properly payable on that occasion qualifies as a deduction from the wages, except insofar as it is attributable to an error of computation of the gross amount of wages then payable.[738] It was held in *Bruce v Wiggins Teape (Stationery) Ltd*[739] that unilateral reduction of wages by the employer might amount to unauthorised deduction within the meaning of the Act. The complete withholding of a week's wages has been held to constitute a deduction within the meaning of the statute.[740] In *New Century Cleaning Co Ltd v Church*,[741] the reduction of the job rates or piece rates for work which determined the amount of wages under a team-working payment system was held not to amount to an unauthorised deduction from payable wages within the meaning of the Act. Compare also the decision of the Employment Appeal Tribunal in *Davies v Wyatt (Decorators) Ltd*[742] where it was held that a unilateral reduction of wages in order to discharge the employer's liability under the Working Time Regulations[743] to provide for paid leave resulted in an unauthorised and unlawful deduction from wages. In *Delaney v RJ Staples*,[744] the House of Lords held that pay-

---

[730] Employment Rights Act 1996 s.27(1)(b)–(f).
[731] Employment Rights Act 1996 s.27(3). It was held in *Farrell Matthews & Weir v Hansen* [2005] I.C.R. 509, EAT that there was no reason to construe s.27(3) as meaning that non-contractual bonuses could not come within the definition of wages unless they were actually paid.
[732] Employment Rights Act 1996 s.27(2)(a).
[733] Employment Rights Act 1996 s.27(2)(b).
[734] Employment Rights Act 1996 s.27(2)(c), (d).
[735] Employment Rights Act 1996 s.27(2)(e).
[736] Employment Rights Act 1996 s.27(5).
[737] Employment Rights Act 1996 s.230(3).
[738] Employment Rights Act 1996 s.13(3), (4).
[739] [1994] I.R.L.R. 536.
[740] *Pename Ltd v Paterson* [1989] I.C.R. 12. It was reconfirmed in *Elizabeth Claire Care Management Ltd v Francis* [2005] I.R.L.R. 858 that non-payment of remuneration may qualify as "deduction from wages".
[741] [2000] I.R.L.R. 27, CA.
[742] [2000] I.R.L.R. 759.
[743] See below, para.40-112.
[744] [1992] I.C.R. 483.

ment in lieu of notice, being related to the termination of employment, did not come within the definition of wages for this purpose.

40-100 **Deductions from wages of and payments by workers in retail employment** Part II of the Employment Rights Act 1996 also provides for certain additional protection in the case of workers in retail employment,[745] the essence of which is that deductions from the wages of such workers, and payments by such workers to their employers, on account of a cash shortage or stock deficiency, may not in aggregate exceed 10 per cent of the gross wages payable to the worker on the pay day in question[746] (though that requirement does not apply in relation to such deductions from the final instalment of wages, or to such payments made at or after the time of the payment of the final instalment of wages).[747] Moreover, such a payment may only be received by the employer if the employer has previously notified the worker in writing of the worker's total liability to him or her in respect of the shortage or deficiency in question, and has made the demand for the payment in writing on a pay day not before the notification of total liability.[748] Furthermore, such a deduction or the first in a series of such deductions, or a demand for such a payment or the first in a series of demands for such payments, may only be made within 12 months of the employer's establishing the existence of the cash shortage or stock deficiency in question, or of any earlier date when he or she ought reasonably to have established it.[749] "Retail employment" is defined in terms of the carrying out of retail transactions (meaning the sale or supply of goods or supply of services) directly with members of the public or with fellow workers or other individuals in their personal capacities, or the collection of amounts payable in connection therewith.[750]

40-101 **Attachment of earnings** In some instances an employer may lawfully make deductions from remuneration in implementation of judicial orders attaching earnings of the employee in execution of judgment debts and certain other court orders. The wages of "servants, labourers or workmen" were the subject of special legislation excluding attachment orders[751] but this was overridden by subsequent legislation later consolidated into the Attachment of Earnings Act 1971.[752] Under that Act, various courts have power to make an attachment of earnings order to secure payments under a maintenance order, or the payment of certain judgment debts, or payments under an administration order, or the payment of any sum adjudged to be paid by a conviction, or by a legal aid contribution order.[753] An attachment of earnings order requires the employer to make periodical deductions from the debtor's earnings and to pay them to the collecting officer of the court.[754] On each occasion on which the employer makes a deduction from the debtor's earnings in compliance with an attachment order, he or she must give the debtor a statement in writing of

---

[745] Employment Rights Act 1996 ss.17–22.
[746] Employment Rights Act 1996 ss.18(1), 17(1)–(3), (6), 19(1)–(4), 21(1), (2), 20(5), 21(3) and 22(4).
[747] Employment Rights Act 1996 s.22(1)–(3).
[748] Employment Rights Act 1996 s.20(1)–(3)(a) and s.20(4).
[749] Employment Rights Act 1996 ss.18(2) (3), 20(3)(b), 20(5).
[750] Employment Rights Act 1996 s.17(2), (3).
[751] Wages Attachment Abolition Act 1870 s.1.
[752] See Freedland, *Attachment of Earnings* (1971), for a description of the Act's provisions.
[753] s.1.
[754] s.6 (see s.23 for offence of non-compliance with the order on the part of the employer and penalty on summary conviction of a fine).

the total amount of the deduction.[755] He or she may presumably include this in a statutory itemised pay statement,[756] but it will presumably not be sufficient to deal with it by a statutory standing statement of fixed deductions.[757] The employer is authorised to make a small deduction from the remuneration of the employee concerned, at a rate determined under the legislation, towards his administrative expenses while he or she is implementing an attachment order.[758]

(ii) Other Duties

The duty to provide work It has been shown in an earlier paragraph that the **40-102** employer is under some degree of obligation to provide work when such provision of work is necessary to enable the employee to earn remuneration.[759] The further question arises of whether the employer is under a duty to provide work independently of the immediate remunerative opportunity which the work may provide. The assumption has tended to be that in the normal case of employment, the employer is under no obligation to provide the employee with work to do; it is sufficient for the employer to pay the agreed salary or wages regularly.[760] Thus where a commercial traveller[761] or a sales representative[762] is employed at a salary for a fixed period, as long as the salary is paid, there has been thought to be no obligation to provide work "to enable the employee to become *au fait* at [sic] his work".[763] However, it may be legitimate to infer in certain contracts that the employer is to give the employee (e.g. an actor or singer)[764] an opportunity for publicity to advance his or her career and reputation.[765] Moreover, when a man was employed as chief sub-editor of a Sunday newspaper for three years and the paper was sold, it was held that, although his salary was continued, the employers had broken the contract because "by selling the newspaper they destroyed the office to which they had appointed him".[766] A more generalised approach to the right to work has been discussed. In *Langston v AUEW*[767] the Court of Appeal thought it arguable that there was an implied right to work in contracts of employment generally, in the sense of a right to the satisfaction involved in working, earning one's remuneration by work, and having a useful function in the enterprise. Lord Denning M.R. referred, more specifically, to "a right to have the opportunity of doing his work when it is there to be done"[768] while Cairns L.J. spoke of "not merely a right to be paid his agreed wage but a right to come to work to earn it".[769] But the existence of such a right was only there decided to be arguable (and, in the view

---

[755] s.7(4)(b).
[756] See the Employment Rights Act 1996 s.8, and see above, para.40-095.
[757] See Employment Rights Act 1996 s.9 and see above, para.40-095.
[758] Attachment of Earnings Act 1971 s.7(4).
[759] See above, para.40-089.
[760] *Collier v Sunday Referee Publishing Co Ltd* [1940] 2 K.B. 647, 650.
[761] *Lagerwall v Wilkinson, Henderson & Clarke Ltd* (1899) 80 L.T. 55.
[762] *Turner v Sawdon & Co* [1901] 2 K.B. 653.
[763] [1901] 2 K.B. 653 at 657.
[764] *Clayton & Waller v Oliver* [1930] A.C. 209; *Withers v General Theatre Corp Ltd* [1933] 2 K.B. 536.
[765] cf. *Collier v Sunday Referee Publishing Co Ltd* [1940] 2 K.B. 647, 650.
[766] cf. *Collier v Sunday Referee Publishing Co Ltd* [1940] 2 K.B. 647, 650. See also *Driscoll v Australian RMSN Co* (1859) 1 F. & F. 458 (employers sold ship in which the employee served).
[767] [1974] I.C.R. 180, 190B–F (Lord Denning M.R.).
[768] [1974] I.C.R. 180 at 190F–G.
[769] [1974] I.C.R. 180 at 192E–F.

of Cairns and Stephenson L.JJ., very dubiously arguable).[770] In the subsequent proceedings,[771] the National Industrial Relations Court which existed at that period held that the employee concerned, a spot welder, had no such general right to work, but that he did have the right to such allocation of hours and overtime work as would give him the opportunity of earning such premium payments as he could expect to earn in his normal working conditions.[772]

40-103 **The duties of the employer relating to safety, health and welfare of employees**   A full description of the law relating to the safety, health and welfare of employees is outside the scope of the present chapter. A very brief outline is given in the next two paragraphs, which deal with employer's liability and with statutory duties generally. Beyond that, reference should be made to the treatises which concentrate upon this particular aspect of the law of employment.[773]

40-104 **Employer's liability to provide for safety of employee**   It is the common law duty of the employer to each of his or her employees to take reasonable care to see that the plant, tools, equipment, premises and system of work used in his business are safe[774] and to select and engage other employees who are competent.[775]

40-105 **Defective equipment**   The employer is under no absolute duty at common law to warrant the safety of its employee. Therefore, where the employee was injured by a latent defect in a tool which the employer had bought from a reputable retailer who in turn had bought it from reputable manufacturers, it was held that the employer was not liable because the employer had in fact fulfilled his duty to take reasonable care.[776] The law in this particular type of case was altered by the Employer's Liability (Defective Equipment) Act 1969. Under that Act, an employer is liable when:

(a)   an employee suffers personal injury in the course of his employment in consequence of a defect in equipment provided by his or her employer for the purposes of his business; and

(b)   the defect is attributable wholly or partly to the fault of a third party (whether identified or not).[777]

The law on contributory negligence applies to such a claim[778]; but any agreement purporting to exclude or limit the liability of the employer under the Act is void.[779]

40-106 **Action in tort**   In general, the duty to use reasonable care may be enforced either by an action in tort for negligence or by an action for breach of an implied term in

---

[770] [1974] I.C.R. 180 at 192F–G, 193F–G.

[771] *Langston v AUEW (No.2)* [1974] I.C.R. 510, 521D–522F.

[772] [1974] I.C.R. 510 at 522D–H.

[773] Munkman, *Employer's Liability at Common Law*, 15th edn (2009); *Redgrave's Health and Safety*, 7th edn (2010).

[774] *Wilsons & Clyde Coal Co v English* [1938] A.C. 57; *Wilson v Tyneside Window Cleaning Co* [1958] 2 Q.B. 110. Compare now *Jagedo v Smiths Industries Ltd* [1982] I.C.R. 47; *Johnstone v Bloomsbury HA* [1992] 1 Q.B. 333. Note the discussion of s.2(1) of the Unfair Contract Terms Act 1977.

[775] *Black v Fife Coal Co Ltd* [1912] A.C. 149.

[776] *Davie v New Merton Board Mills Ltd* [1959] A.C. 604.

[777] s.1(1). See *Knowles v Liverpool City Council* [1994] I.C.R. 243.

[778] s.1(1).

[779] s.1(2).

the contract of employment[780]; but the action is usually brought in tort. It has been said in the House of Lords that the question whether there has been a breach of the duty is largely a question of fact, in the sense of an appraisal of the particular facts in the light of the broad legal principles which apply.[781] For these reasons a detailed analysis of the cases has been omitted from this work and must be sought in works on the law of torts.[782] It is, however, important to note that it was held in *Walker v Northumberland CC*[783] that the employer was liable in respect of psychiatric illness suffered by the employee as the result of stress associated with his workload, and which the employer had been, in the particular circumstances of the case, negligent in failing to prevent. In *Sutherland v Hatton*,[784] the Court of Appeal reviewed the law concerning the employer's liability to the employee in respect of psychiatric illness caused by stress at work. Guidelines were laid down for determining the incidence and extent of such liability, this liability being the same whether regarded for the tort of negligence or under an implied term in contracts of employment. The guidelines emphasise that the ordinary principles of employer liability apply; they require it to be demonstrated that the risk of injury to health from stress at work should be reasonably foreseeable in relation to the particular employee, that if so the employer is in breach of duty as having failed to take steps which were reasonable in the circumstances, and that if so the particular breach of duty caused or materially contributed to the harm in question. In *Barber v Somerset CC*,[785] the House of Lords broadly endorsed the guidelines laid down in *Sutherland v Hatton*, though applying them to somewhat different outcomes in the particular cases which were under appeal. In *Daw v Intel Corp (UK) Ltd*,[786] the Court of Appeal considered the extent to which employers could discharge this duty of care by the provision of counselling services, making it clear that such provision would not operate as a panacea in all cases.

40-107   Although there may be differences between the relevant rules of tort and contract,[787] it seems to be assumed by the courts and the profession that the rules to be applied when an employee brings an action against an employer for personal injuries suffered by the former in the course of his employment are the rules of tort.[788] This may perhaps be justified on the basis that there is an implied term in the contract of employment to the effect that if the employee suffers personal injury as the result of a breach of a tortious or statutory duty[789] of the employer, the liability of the employer and the remedy of the employee are to depend on the rules of tort.[790]

40-108   **Compulsory employers' liability insurance**   Under the provisions of the

---

[780] *Matthews v Kuwait Bechtel Corp* [1959] 2 Q.B. 57, CA; *Yapp v Foreign and Commonwealth Office* [2014] EWCA Civ 1512, [2015] I.R.L.R. 112.

[781] *Qualcast (Wolverhampton) Ltd v Haynes* [1959] A.C. 743, 755, 757–758, 759, 761. See also *General Cleaning Contractors Ltd v Christmas* [1953] A.C. 180; *Latimer v AEC Ltd* [1953] A.C. 643, 658.

[782] See *Clerk & Lindsell on Torts*, 21st edn (2014), paras 13-23—13-35.

[783] [1995] I.C.R. 702.

[784] [2002] I.C.R. 613.

[785] [2004] UKHL 13, [2004] 1 W.L.R. 1089.

[786] [2007] EWCA Civ 70, [2007] I.R.L.R. 355.

[787] e.g. relating to remoteness of damage: *Koufos v C Czarnikow Ltd* [1969] 1 A.C. 350.

[788] e.g. *Doughty v Turner Manufacturing Co Ltd* [1964] 1 Q.B. 518.

[789] viz a duty which would be owed irrespective of the contract. But the Occupiers' Liability Act 1957 has not been treated as relevant in these cases, and that presumably would also be the case for the Defective Premises Act 1972. cf. as to the employee of a sub-contractor on a building site, *Ferguson v Welsh* [1987] 3 All E.R. 777.

[790] A similar assumption must be made in a case such as *Re Polemis and Furness, Withy & Co Ltd*

Employers' Liability (Compulsory Insurance) Act 1969,[791] an employer carrying on any business in Great Britain is required to maintain insurance under an approved policy with an authorised insurer against liability for bodily injury or disease sustained by his employees and arising out of and in the course of their employment in Great Britain.[792] The term "employee" here means an individual who has entered into or works under a contract of service or apprenticeship.[793] Insurance need not be maintained in respect of certain close relatives of an employer,[794] nor in respect of employees not ordinarily resident in Great Britain.[795] Local authorities, statutory nationalised corporations and certain employers specified by regulation are exempted from the obligation to insure.[796] There is provision for regulations to secure the issue and production for inspection of insurance certificates.[797] Failure to insure is an offence subject to a fine[798]; there is a fixed amount for which insurance must be maintained in respect of claims arising out of any one occurrence.[799]

40-109 **Statutory duties of the employer relating to safety, health and welfare** Apart from the statutory modifications of employers' liability considered in the two previous paragraphs, the statute law relating to the safety, health and welfare of employees can conveniently be considered in three parts:

(1) A wide range of duties is imposed on an employer by a system of statutes and regulations relating to particular types of workplace, industrial process or safety hazard. The statutory framework of this system is contained principally in the Mines and Quarries Act 1954, the Agriculture (Safety, Health and Welfare Provisions) Act 1956, the Factories Act 1961, the Offices, Shops and Railway Premises Act 1963,[800] and in the Management of Health and Safety at Work Regulations 1992.[801] Breaches of the statutes are sanctioned by criminal penalties upon the employer (and sometimes upon the employee), but such breaches may, in the case of certain duties, give an employee injured by the breach a cause of action for damages against his employer.[802] The enumeration of those duties and the detailed description

[1921] 3 K.B. 560, where, although there was a contract between the parties, the Court of Appeal decided the problem of remoteness of damage by reference to the rules of tort.
791 See Simpson (1972) 35 M.L.R. 63; Hasson (1974) 3 I.L.J. 79.
792 s.1 (the terms "approved policy" and "authorised insurer" being defined by s.1(3) as amended by the Financial Services and Markets Act 2000).
793 s.2(1).
794 s.2(2)(a).
795 s.2(2)(b).
796 s.3. See SI 1971/1933, SI 1974/208, SI 1975/1443, SI 1998/2573; and National Health Service and Community Care Act 1990 Sch.8 Pt I para.1.
797 s.4. See Employers' Liability (Compulsory Insurance) General Regulations 1971 (SI 1971/1117) as amended by SI 1974/208 and SI 1975/194. The Employers' Liability (Compulsory Insurance) General Regulations have been amended in various respects by the Employers' Liability (Compulsory Insurance) General (Amendment) Regulations 1994, and, more recently, SI 2004/2882.
798 s.6.
799 See Employers' Liability (Compulsory Insurance) General Regulations 1971 (SI 1971/1117) reg.3.
800 A fuller list of the relevant statutes is contained in Sch.1 to the Health and Safety at Work, etc. Act 1974 as since amended.
801 SI 1992/2051, implementing European Union Council Directive 89/391 (the Framework Directive).
802 *Clerk & Lindsell on Torts*, 21st edn (2014), paras 13-36—13-73.

of the actions for breach of statutory duty are outside the scope of the present work.

(2)   The modern framework of statute law concerning safety, health and welfare at work was established by the Health and Safety at Work, etc. Act 1974.[803]

The principal effects of the Act upon the employment relationship are as follows:

(a)   The Act imposes a set of general duties upon employers, all of which are directed towards making the employer ensure the health, safety and welfare at work of all his employees.[804] The duties extend the employers' common law duty in various directions,[805] but do not create a cause of action on which civil proceedings may be based.[806]

(b)   Included among the general duties is a duty to make to all employees, and to keep up-to-date, a statement of the employers' general policy with respect to the employees' health and safety at work and of the arrangements for carrying out that policy.[807]

(c)   Further included among the general duties is a power of the Secretary of State to make regulations providing for the appointment by recognised trade unions of safety representatives from amongst the employees,[808] and a duty on the part of the employer to consult such representatives with a view to making and maintaining effective arrangements for the health and safety of employees.[809]

(d)   The authorities entrusted by or under the Act with the enforcement of health and safety obligations[810] are empowered to appoint inspectors[811] who are placed under a duty to pass on to employees and their representatives information relating to health and safety, where it is necessary in order to keep them adequately informed about health and safety matters.[812] The information may include that which the inspectors themselves may obtain in exercise of their powers of entry and investigation.[813]

---

[803]   Based upon the Report of the Robens Committee, "Safety and Health at Work", Cmnd.5034 (1972). See Lewis (1975) 38 M.L.R. 442–448; (1975) 4 I.L.J. 34–38.

[804]   s.2 as supplemented by regulations.

[805]   See above, para.40-104, and s.2(2)–(7) of the Act.

[806]   s.47(1)(a). Criminal penalties are provided by s.33 (as extended by ss.36 and 37), and administrative sanctions (which extend to the existing statutory provisions described in the first part of the present paragraph) are provided by ss.21–24 in the form of a power on the part of the inspectorate to issue improvement and prohibition notices.

[807]   s.2(3).

[808]   s.2(4). See the Safety Representatives and Safety Committees Regulations 1977 (SI 1977/500). See also White v Pressed Steel Fisher [1980] I.R.L.R. 176, EAT.

[809]   s.2(6) as amended by Employment Protection Act 1975 s.116 and Sch.15 para.2, to limit this duty to consultation with trade union safety representatives.

[810]   s.18(7) as amended by Employment Protection Act 1975 s.116 and Sch.15 para.8, to extend to agricultural operations. The responsibility devolves primarily upon the Health and Safety Executive established by s.10 of the Act. See the Health and Safety (Enforcing Authority) Regulations 1977 (SI 1977/746) as amended by SI 1980/1744.

[811]   s.19. The provision has been used to establish a combined unified inspectorate under the aegis of the Health and Safety Executive.

[812]   s.28(8). cf. also s.28(3)(b) which can create a privilege for disclosure of information to trade union safety representatives and cf. s.28(9) as amended by Employment Protection Act 1975 s.116 and Sch.15 para.9.

[813]   s.28(8)(a) referring to s.28(7), referring in turn to s.20.

(e) Provision is made for the appropriate Secretary of State to make health and safety regulations, which may replace existing statutory provisions, for any of the general purposes of Pt I of the Act.[814] This provided authority for the gradual replacement of the existing statutory framework and regulations by a completely new structure, to be augmented by codes of practice issued by the Health and Safety Commission.[815]

(f) Provision was made, by Pt III of the Act, from which employees generally have benefited, for extending the scope of the Building Regulations[816] and for including among the purposes for which they may be made, the securing of the health, safety, welfare and convenience of persons in or about buildings and of others who may be affected by buildings or matters connected with buildings.[817]

(3) The Employment Rights Act 1996 makes provision for a right of employees not to suffer detriment in health and safety cases, and for treating certain dismissals as unfair in health and safety cases. These provisions confer protections upon employees who are carrying out health and safety duties as designated by the employer, or are safety representatives or members of safety committees carrying out their functions, or who report safety or health hazards to the employer, or who absent themselves from the workplace in circumstances of danger, or who in those circumstances take protective measures.[818]

40-110 **Hours of work** The employer is required to give the employee written particulars of any terms and conditions relating to hours of work (including any relating to normal working hours).[819] It is often necessary for various statutory purposes to determine whether an employee has normal working hours and if so what those hours are.[820] This frequently involves a decision about the contractual status of overtime working. The prevailing view has been that in order for overtime to form part of "normal working hours" it must be contractually obligatory upon both parties.[821] It also appears that most overtime working arrangements will be classified as not being contractually obligatory upon the employee.[822]

40-111 **Statutory restrictions on hours of work** Various statutory provisions have imposed maxima upon the working hours and employment in certain circumstances

---

[814] s.15 as amended by Employment Protection Act 1975 s.116 and Sch.15 para.6, to extend the new system to agricultural operations.

[815] ss.16–17 as amended by Employment Protection Act 1975 s.116 and Sch.15 para.7, to extend the new system to agricultural operations.

[816] s.61, amending the Public Health Act 1936 ss.61–62 (itself later overtaken by the Building Act 1984).

[817] s.61(2)(a).

[818] Employment Rights Act 1996 ss.44, 48, 49, 98(6), 100, 105(3), 108(3), 117(3), (4), 118, 119(1), 120, 122(3), 125, 128–132, 236(3). See Ewing (1993) 22 I.L.J. 165, 170–171.

[819] Employment Rights Act 1996 s.1(4)(c).

[820] e.g. for the purposes of the Employment Rights Act 1996 ss.162, 135, 155 and 139 (calculation of redundancy payment); Employment Rights Act 1996 ss.87–91 rights of employee during period of notice); Employment Rights Act 1996 s.30 (calculation of guarantee payment). See below, para.40-256.

[821] *Tarmac Roadstone Holdings Ltd v Peacock* [1973] I.C.R. 273; see below, para.40-256.

[822] cf. *Pearson v William Jones Ltd* [1967] 1 W.L.R. 1140; *The Darlington Forge Ltd v Sutton* [1968] I.T.R. 196; *Turriff Construction Co Ltd v Bryant* [1967] 2 I.T.R. 292; *Tarmac Roadstone Holdings Ltd v Peacock* [1973] I.C.R. 273. See below, para.40-256.

of women, young persons and children.[823] Further statutory provisions have imposed limits upon the hours of work of all employees in certain industries.[824] Many of these restrictions were repealed or amended by ss.8 and 9 of the Employment Act 1989, to which reference should now be made. Terms and conditions of employment relating to hours of work may now fall within the provisions concerning equal terms and conditions of employment as between men and women, and the provisions for elimination of various kinds of discrimination in employment, which are considered in subsequent paragraphs of the present section.[825]

The Working Time Regulations   Important controls upon working time, required **40-112** by the EC Working Time Directive[826] and the Young Workers Directive,[827] were introduced by the Working Time Regulations 1998,[828] which have been the subject of various subsequent amending Regulations.[829] The main provisions of these Regulations are, in brief summary, as follows. The Regulations apply to "workers"; the original restriction to those above the minimum school leaving age was revoked in 2003.[830] "Workers" are so defined as not to be confined to those with contracts of employment, though so as to exclude the genuinely self-employed.[831] "Working time" is to be interpreted widely and purposively, including for example travel from a worker's place of residence to customer premises,[832] or the attendance of meetings as a trade union or health and safety representative.[833]

The Regulations set a working time limit of an average of 48 hours per week, with a standard averaging period of 17 weeks which may be extended to up to 52 weeks by a collective agreement between employer(s) and trade union(s), or by a "workforce agreement" between employers and elected workforce representatives, or, in the case of employers of no more than 20 workers, which the workers sign individually.[834] Workers may agree in writing as individuals to disapply the

---

[823] Employment of Women, Young Persons and Children Act 1920; Hours of Employment (Conventions) Act 1936; Shops Act 1950; Young Persons (Employment) Acts 1938 and 1964; Factories Act 1961 Pt VI; Children and Young Persons Act 1933 s.18; Children and Young Persons Act 1963 ss.37–44; Employment of Children Act 1973 s.1. See Hepple and O'Higgins, *Encyclopedia of Labour Relations Law*, paras 1-105, 1-230 and 1-231.

[824] Coal Mines Regulation Act 1908 s.1, as amended by Coal Mines Act 1919 s.1; Mines and Quarries Act 1954 s.189; Transport Act 1968 Pt VI; Factories Act 1961 s.76; Shops Act 1950. See *Encyclopedia of Labour Relations Law*, para.1-232. The Baking Industry (Hours of Work) Act 1954 was repealed by s.8 of the Sex Discrimination Act 1986.

[825] See below, paras 40-125—40-136.

[826] Directive 2003/88.

[827] Directive 94/33.

[828] SI 1998/1833, in force from October 1, 1998.

[829] The Working Time Regulations 1999 (SI 1999/3372), the Working Time (Amendment) Regulations 2001 (SI 2001/3256), the Working Time (Amendment) Regulations 2002 (SI 2002/3128), and the Working Time (Amendment) Regulations 2003 (SI 2003/1684). See also now the Working Time (Amendment) Regulations 2006 (SI 2006/99) and, in relation to agricultural workers, the Working Time (Amendment) (England) Regulations 2013 (SI 2013/2228).

[830] SI 1998/1833 reg.26 was revoked by SI 2003/1684 reg.9.

[831] See regs 3, 36; and see above, para.40-009.

[832] *Federacion de Servicios Privados del sindicato Comisiones obreras (CC OO) v Tyco Integrated Security SL* (C-266/14) EU:C:2015:578, [2016] 1 C.M.L.R. 22.

[833] *Edwards v Encirc Ltd* [2015] I.R.L.R. 528, EAT.

[834] See reg.23 and Sch.1. It was, however, held in *Barber v RJB Mining (UK) Ltd* [1999] I.C.R. 679, QBD that where an employer seeks to require workers to work longer hours than the maximum hours applicable to them under the Regulations, and they are unwilling to agree to do so, they may be granted a declaration that the employer's attempt so to require them to exceed the statutory maximum

weekly working hours limit.[835] Provision is made to protect workers from suffering detriment (such as a denial of promotion or of training opportunities) because they refuse to agree to disapply the limits.[836] There are also measures by which night workers are subject to a working time limit of an average of 8 hours in each 24 hour period, and by which night workers whose work involves special hazard or heavy physical or mental strain are subject to an 8 hour limit for each 24 hour period.[837] Stricter limits upon maximum working time and night work are set for young workers.[838] There are also measures relating to rest breaks and rest periods, whereby workers are entitled to one day off each week and young workers are entitled to two days off each week,[839] whereby workers are entitled to 11 hours consecutive rest per day and young workers are entitled to 12 hours consecutive rest per day,[840] and whereby workers are entitled to a rest break of at least 20 minutes in a working day of longer than 6 hours, and young workers are entitled to a rest break of at least 30 minutes in a working day of longer than 4.5 hours.[841] It is incumbent on the employer proactively to ensure that working arrangements allow for workers to take their due rest breaks.[842] Certain of those provisions are subject to exceptions in respect of collective or "workforce" agreements.[843] The Regulations also confer upon workers within their scope, an entitlement to four weeks paid annual leave.[844] There is provision for the enforcement of the limits on weekly working time and night work by the health and safety enforcing authorities,[845] and for workers to assert in claims or complaints to employment tribunals, their entitlements, such as to rest periods and breaks and paid annual leave, and their rights to be protected from detriment, such as for refusing to agree to disapply limits on working time.[846] The Court of Justice has given a wide interpretation to these provisions: in *Ville de Nivelles v Matzak*, for example, it was held that even standby time spent at home could count as "working time".[847]

40-113 **Employee's belongings** Although an employer is under a duty to take reasonable care for his or her employee's personal safety,[848] the employer has been thought to be under no similar duty to take positive steps to protect employee's personal belongings; thus, the employer of an actor was not liable when the actor's clothing was stolen from a dressing-room.[849] However, a failure on the part of the employer to take reasonable steps to protect the employee's personal belongings

violates an obligation which has become part of their contract of employment.
[835] See reg.5.
[836] See reg.31.
[837] See reg.6.
[838] See new regs 5A, 6A, inserted by the Working Time (Amendment) Regulations 2002 (SI 2002/3128).
[839] See reg.11.
[840] See reg.10.
[841] See reg.12.
[842] *Grange v Abellio London Ltd* [2017] I.R.L.R. 108, EAT.
[843] See reg.23. Compare, as to collective agreements, *Prison Service v Bewley* [2004] I.C.R. 422, EAT.
[844] See reg.13 as amended by the Working Time (Amendment) Regulations 2001 (SI 2001/3256). For details, see above, para 40-081.
[845] See reg.28.
[846] See regs 30–32.
[847] C-518/15 EU:C:2018:82.
[848] See above, para.40-104.
[849] *Deyong v Shenburn* [1964] K.B. 227; cf. *Edwards v West Herts Group Hospital Management Committee* [1957] 1 W.L.R. 415.

might possibly amount to a breach of the implied obligation of mutual trust and confidence.[850]

Duty to indemnify the employee   The relationship of employment imposes a duty on the employer to indemnify or reimburse the employee against all expenses, losses and liabilities incurred by the employee in the execution of his employer's instructions, or within the authority granted to him by the employer, or during the reasonable performance of his employment.[851] Thus an employer who failed to insure his vehicle in respect of third-party risks[852] was obliged to indemnify his employee who drove the vehicle in the course of his employment and who was held liable to a third person injured by his negligent driving.[853] Nor, it was held in *Reid v Rush & Tompkins Group Plc*,[854] is the employer under any implied obligation to advise an employee working overseas to arrange his own insurance cover against accidents. But there is no general duty to keep the employee insured against all third party risks or to indemnify the employee against liability for his or her own negligence.[855] Ancient authority suggests that if the act or omission of the employee was manifestly unlawful, he or she is not entitled to such an indemnity[856]; but he may still be entitled to an indemnity from his employer if the act was apparently lawful[857] or he was ignorant of the facts which made it unlawful[858] and could not be presumed to know that the particular transaction was unlawful.[859]

40-114

The rights of the employee in relation to trade union membership and activities   Under the provisions of ss.146 to 151 of the Trade Union and Labour Relations (Consolidation) Act 1992 as subsequently amended,[860] a worker[861] has a right not to be subjected to any detriment as an individual by any act, or any deliberate failure to act,[862] by his employer if the act or failure takes place for the purpose of preventing or deterring him from becoming a member of an independent trade union, or penalising him for doing so,[863] or from taking part in the activities of an

40-115

---

850   See below, paras 40-151—40-154.
851   *Adamson v Jarvis* (1827) 4 Bing. 66; *Re Famatina Development Corp* [1914] 2 Ch. 271.
852   As required by the Road Traffic Act 1988 s.143.
853   *Gregory v Ford* [1951] 1 All E.R. 121.
854   [1990] 1 W.L.R. 212.
855   *Semtex Ltd v Gladstone* [1954] 1 W.L.R. 945; *Lister v Romford Ice and Cold Storage Ltd* [1957] A.C. 555. See above, paras 40-072—40-073.
856   cf. *Southern v How* (1618) Cro. Jac. 468.
857   *Adamson v Jarvis* (1827) 4 Bing. 66.
858   *Burrows v Rhodes* [1899] 1 Q.B. 816; *Thacker v Hardy* (1878) 4 Q.B.D. 685.
859   *Southern v How* (1618) Cro. Jac. 468; *Adamson v Jarvis*, see above.
860   The most important amendments were made by s.13 of the Trade Union Reform and Employment Rights Act 1993, and by s.2 of and Sch.2 to the Employment Relations Act 1999, and also by ss.29–32 of the Employment Relations Act 2004.
861   Excluded classes of employees are: share fishermen—s.284, work outside Great Britain—s.285. Crown employees are included—s.273. The Employment Act 2004 s.31 amended ss.146–151 of the 1992 Act to extend, to workers who are not employees, the existing protections of employees against detrimental action by their employer for being, or not being, a member of a trade union or for taking part in the activities of their union.
862   The effects of deliberate omission, as well as of positive action, are now included, reversing by statute the decision of the House of Lords on this point in *Associated Newspapers Ltd v Wilson; Associated British Ports Ltd v Palmer* [1995] I.C.R. 406.
863   s.146(1)(a). Compare, in relation to unfair dismissal, see below, para.40-229.

independent trade union at any appropriate time, or penalising him for doing so,[864] or compelling him to be or become a member of any trade union or of a particular trade union or of one of a number of particular trade unions.[865] The Employment Relations Act 2004 established new or enhanced rights for workers not to be offered inducements relating to trade union membership and collective bargaining, and extended their rights not to suffer detrimental action in circumstances relating to trade union membership.[866]

40-116   A worker may complain to an employment tribunal of an alleged infringement of any of these rights,[867] and the employer has to show the purpose of the act or omission in question.[868] A complaint upheld by the tribunal must be the subject of a declaration and may be the subject of an award of compensation.[869]

40-117   Statutory rights of employees to time off   The Trade Union Labour Relations (Consolidation) Act 1992 and the Employment Rights Act 1996 as subsequently amended require employers to allow employees time off for various particular purposes.[870] Special procedures are created for the enforcement of these rights,[871] but they must in addition modify, pro tanto, the ordinary effects of the contract of employment so far as the employee's obligation to attend for work is concerned. The extent to which these rights include the right to *remuneration* during the time off has been considered in an earlier paragraph.[872] Some[873] of the most important rights to time off are as follows:

---

[864] s.146(1)(b). See *Robb v Leon Motor Services Ltd* [1978] I.C.R. 506, EAT: and *Marley Tile Co v Shaw* [1980] I.C.R. 72. See also now *Department of Transport v Gallacher* [1994] I.C.R. 967.

[865] s.146(1)(c).

[866] ss.29–32 of the 2004 Act make a series of additions and amendments to ss.146–151 of the Trade Union and Labour Relations (Consolidation) Act 1992; s.29 of the 2004 Act inserts new ss.145A–F into the 1992 Act.

[867] s.146(5) (limitation period—s.147).

[868] s.148(1) (as amended by the Employment Relations Act 2004) (see also s.148(2)—disregard of industrial pressure).

[869] s.149(1). Compensation is asserted in accordance with the provisions of s.149. See *Brassington v Cauldron Wholesale Ltd* [1978] I.C.R. 405, EAT.

[870] Employment Rights Act 1996 ss.50–63C, Trade Union and Labour Relations (Consolidation) Act 1992 ss.168–173. Employees excluded are: those working abroad, Employment Rights Act 1996 s.196, Trade Union and Labour Relations (Consolidation) Act 1992 s.285. Crown employees are included, Employment Rights Act 1996 ss.191–193, Trade Union and Labour Relations (Consolidation) Act 1992 s.273, subject to a power of exemption on the grounds of national security in s.275.

[871] Employment Rights Act 1996 ss.51, 54, 57 and 60; Trade Union and Labour Relations (Consolidation) Act 1992 ss.168, 170, 171, 172.

[872] See above, para.40-095; and *Corner v Buckinghamshire CC* [1978] I.C.R. 836, EAT.

[873] Other such rights, not described in detail here, are those for occupational pension scheme trustees—Employment Rights Act 1996 ss.58–60; for employee representatives—Employment Rights Act 1996 ss.61–63; for young persons for study or training—Employment Rights Act 1996 ss.63A–63C inserted by the Teaching and Higher Education Act 1998 s.32; and for union learning representatives and consultation by union members with union learning representatives—Trade Union and Labour Relations (Consolidation) Act 1992 s.168A, 170(2A)–(2C) inserted by s.43 of the Employment Act 2002 with effect from April 27, 2003. A new kind of statutory right to time off has been conferred on employees by s.40 of the Employment Relations Act 2004, which by inserting a new s.43M into the Employment Rights Act 1996 protects employees from being subjected to detriment by the employee by reason of being summoned for or being absent from work on jury service, with effect from April 6, 2005.

(1)   Trade union officials; industrial relations duties and training   An employer **40-118** must permit an employee who is an official of an independent trade union[874] recognised[875] by the employer to take time off work to carry out duties concerned with industrial relations between the employer or an associated employer and their employees, or to undergo training in industrial relations of a relevant and ap-proved kind.[876] The amount of time off to be allowed, and the circumstances in which it is to be allowed, are the subject of guidance contained in a Code of Practice issued by the Advisory, Conciliation and Arbitration Service ("the Service").[877] Sec-tion 14 of the Employment Act 1989 amended what was then s.27 of the 1978 Act so that the duties in respect of which an employer is required to allow officials of a trade union time off with pay are limited to duties concerned with matters in respect of which the employer recognises the trade union.

(2)   Trade union activities   An employer must permit an employee who is a **40-119** member of an independent trade union recognised by the employer to take time off work for the purpose of taking part in any trade union activity of a recognised independent trade union of which the employee is a member or of which he is act-ing as a representative, provided that the activities do not themselves consist of industrial action.[878] The amount of such time off and the circumstances in which it must be allowed are to be the subject of guidance contained in a Code of Practice to be issued by the Service.[879]

(3)   Public duties   An employer must permit employees who hold certain public **40-120** offices (such as that of justice of the peace) or who are members of certain public bodies (such as a local authority or statutory tribunal) to take time off work for the performance of their duties in the discharge of their office or of the functions of the public body to which they belong.[880] The amount of time off thus required is the amount which is reasonable having regard to the extent of the public duties concerned, the amount of time off work already permitted under this head or for trade union duties or activities, and the effect of the employees' absence on the run-ning of the employer's business.[881]

(4)   Employees under notice of redundancy; time off to look for work or make ar- **40-121** *rangements for training*   An employee who has been given notice of dismissal by reason of redundancy is entitled during his period of notice to be allowed by his employer reasonable time off work to look for new employment or to make arrange-ments for training for future employment,[882] provided that by the time of expiry of

874 As defined by Trade Union and Labour Relations (Consolidation) Act 1992 s.5 (definition of "independent") and s.1 (definition of "trade union").
875 As defined by s.178(3).
876 Trade Union and Labour Relations (Consolidation) Act 1992 s.168. See *Beal v Beecham Group Ltd* [1982] I.C.R. 460; *Thomas Scott & Sons (Bakers) Ltd v Allen* [1983] I.R.L.R. 329; *Ashley v MOD* [1984] I.C.R. 298.
877 Trade Union and Labour Relations (Consolidation) Act 1992 s.168(3).
878 s.170(1), (2).
879 s.170(3).
880 Employment Rights Act 1996 s.50(1)–(3), (5)–(9). Rights extended to members of police authori-ties by the Time Off for Public Duties Order 1995 (SI 1995/694) with effect from April 1, 1995.
881 Employment Rights Act 1996 s.50(4). See *Corner v Buckinghamshire CC* [1978] I.C.R. 836, EAT.
882 Employment Rights Act 1996 s.52(1). See *Dutton v Hawker Siddeley Aviation Ltd* [1978] I.C.R. 1057, EAT.

his statutory period of notice, or such longer notice as is actually given, the employee has been continuously employed for two years or more.[883]

40-122 *(5) Ante-natal care* An employee who has, on the advice of a doctor, midwife or health visitor, made an appointment for the purpose of ante-natal care has the right not to be unreasonably refused time off during her working hours to enable her to keep the appointment.[884]

40-123 *(6) Time off for domestic reasons relating to dependants* The Employment Relations Act 1999 created a new entitlement for an employee to be allowed a reasonable amount of time off for specified domestic reasons involving incidents befalling the dependants of the employee and requiring action by the employee.[885] The provisions of the newly inserted s.57A of the Employment Rights Act 1996 entitle an employee to be allowed a reasonable amount of time off for specified domestic reasons involving the care of dependants of the employee, and new s.57B enables the employee to complain to an employment tribunal that the employer has unreasonably refused to permit that time off. Further provisions protect the employee from being subjected to detriment, or from being dismissed, by his or her employer by reason of exercising or seeking to exercise this right to time off.[886]

40-124 **Effect of failure to allow time off** An appropriately qualified employee may complain to an employment tribunal of failure to allow him or her time off in accordance with any of the foregoing provisions for time off.[887] If the complaint is upheld, the tribunal must, in the cases of time off for trade union duties, trade union activities and public duties, make a declaration to that effect and may in those cases award compensation assessed with regard to the employer's default, and to any loss sustained by the employee.[888] If a complaint is upheld of failure to allow a redundant employee time off to look for work or make arrangements for training, the tribunal must make a declaration to that effect and must also order the employer to pay to the employee an amount equal to the remuneration to which he or she would have been entitled if he or she had been allowed the time off,[889] the total amount recoverable being limited to two-fifths of a week's pay of the employee concerned.[890] If a complaint is upheld of unreasonable refusal of time off for ante-natal care, or of remuneration due for that time off, the tribunal must make a declaration to that effect and must order the employer to pay the equivalent or due remuneration.[891] (The rights to remuneration during time off in this case and in the case of the other rights to time off have been described in an earlier paragraph).[892]

---

[883] Employment Rights Act 1996 s.52(2).

[884] Employment Rights Act 1996 s.55(1)–(3).

[885] Employment Relations Act 1999 s.8 and Pt II of Sch.4, with effect from December 15, 1999.

[886] See below, paras 40-146, 40-236.

[887] Employment Rights Act 1996 s.51(1), 54(1), 57(1); Trade Union and Labour Relations (Consolidation) Act 1992 ss.168(4), 169(5), 170(4) (limitation periods—Employment Rights Act 1996 ss.51(2), 54(2), 57(2); Trade Union and Labour Relations (Consolidation) Act 1992 s.171).

[888] Employment Rights Act 1996 s.51(3), 54(4) and Trade Union and Labour Relations (Consolidation) Act 1992 s.172.

[889] Employment Rights Act 1996 s.54(3), referring to s.53(3) referring to Employment Rights Act 1996 s.53(4).

[890] Employment Rights Act 1996 s.53(5) and 54(4).

[891] Employment Rights Act 1996 s.57(3)–(5).

[892] See above, para.40-093.

Provisions against sex discrimination during the period of employment The **40-125**
legislation concerning sex discrimination in relation to employment deals with the
three stages of the employment relationship:

(1) formation of the contract under which a person is employed;
(2) during the period of employment; and
(3) the termination of employment.

The provisions concerning sex discrimination in the formation and termination of
the employment relationship are considered elsewhere in the present chapter.[893] The
provisions concerning sex discrimination during the period of employment are
themselves of two kinds:

(1) provisions originally in the Equal Pay Act 1970, known as the "Equal Pay
     Legislation", and now contained in the Equality Act 2010, for an equality
     clause in individual contracts under which a person is employed;
(2) other provisions, formerly in the Sex Discrimination Act 1975 and now in
     the Equality Act 2010 against sex discrimination during the period of
     employment generally (and after the period of employment).

These provisions are described in the ensuing paragraphs.[894]

Equality clauses in contracts of employment (1) gender equality The Equal- **40-126**
ity Act 2010, consolidating provisions previously contained in the Equal Pay Act
1970 as subsequently amended, principally by the Sex Discrimination Act 1975 and
by the Equal Pay (Amendment) Regulations 1983,[895] provides for mandatory
implication of an equality clause into the contracts under which certain persons are
employed.[896] The equality clause requires an individual woman (or man) to be accorded contractual terms not less favourable than those accorded to an employed
person of the opposite sex.[897] The corresponding provisions in the antecedent
legislation were held to require a term-by-term equalisation of the compared
contracts of employment, for the purpose of which different elements of remuneration and benefits are to be regarded as distinct terms.[898] The equality clause applies where a woman and a man are employed on "equal work", a concept which
includes (1) like work, (2) work rated as equivalent in the same employment, or (3)
work which is, in terms of the demands made on the one (for instance under such
headings as effort skill and decision-making), of equal value to that of the other.[899]
"Like work" means work of the same or a broadly similar nature as the other work
in question,[900] whilst "work rated as equivalent" means work accorded a value equal
to that of the other work in question in a job evaluation study (assuming the removal
of differentiations between men's work and women's work in the system of
evaluation).[901] For the purposes of the equality clause, the comparators include but
are limited to those in the employment of the same employer or of an associated

---

[893] See above, para.40-039 and see below, para.40-247.
[894] See below, paras 40-128—40-132.
[895] SI 1983/1794.
[896] Equality Act 2010 ss.64–69. By s.83(2), these provisions extend to employment under contracts of
       service or of apprenticeship or personally to execute any work or labour; see above, para.40-009.
[897] s.66.
[898] *Hayward v Cammell Laird Shipbuilders Ltd (No.2)* [1988] I.C.R. 464.
[899] s.65.
[900] s.65(2).
[901] s.65(4).

employer, working at the same establishment or at another establishment but at which terms of work common to both apply.[902] The equality clause operates to bring less favourable terms in the contract up to the level of their more favourable counterparts, and to bring about the inclusion of terms not included in the contract which are included in the more favourable counterpart contract.[903] The equality clause does not operate upon a variation between the contract and its counterpart if the employer shows that the variation is genuinely due to a material factor which is not the difference of sex; that factor must be a material difference between the woman's case and the man's, reliance on which is a proportionate means of achieving a legitimate aim where like work or work rated as equivalent is in issue.[904] An employed person may present a claim to an employment tribunal in respect of the breach of a contractual term modified or included by the operation of an equality clause.[905] The tribunal may award arrears of remuneration or damages,[906] provided that arrears of remuneration are not awarded in respect of a time before the "arrears day".[907] An employer may apply to an employment tribunal for a declaration to resolve a dispute concerning the effect of an equality clause.[908] Finally, any court may refer to an employment tribunal a question arising in proceedings before the court in respect of the operation of an equality clause.[909] Where, on a complaint or reference to an employment tribunal, a dispute arises as to whether any work is of equal value within the meaning of the statute, the tribunal may determine that question, or may require a member of the panel of independent experts[910] to prepare a report with respect to that question.[911]

40-127 **Equality clauses in contracts of employment (2) maternity equality** Provision was made by the Equality Act 2010 ss.72–74 for the contracts under which women are employed to be treated as including a maternity equality clause. The main effect of the maternity equality clause is to ensure that pay and bonus pay for a woman on maternity leave keep pace with the pay and bonus pay which the

---

902 See s.79(1)–(4). See *British Coal Corp v Smith* [1996] I.C.R. 515, HL. Compare *Allonby v Accrington & Rossendale College* (C-256/01) EU:C:2004:18, [2004] I.R.L.R. 224, ECJ, as to the construction of the "same employment" concept in accordance with art.141(1) of the EC Treaty. Compare also *DEFRA v Robertson* [2005] EWCA Civ 138, [2005] I.C.R. 750, expounding the notion of attributability of differences between terms and conditions of employment to a "single source" which had been articulated by the ECJ in *Lawrence v Regent Office Care Ltd* (C-320/00) EU:C:2002:498, [2002] E.C.R. I-7325. See further *North v Dumfries and Galloway Council* [2013] UKSC 45, [2013] 4 All E.R. 413.

903 s.66(2).

904 See s.69(1)–(3); leading authorities on the interpretation of the corresponding provisions in the antecedent legislation include *Jenkins v Kingsgate (Clothing Productions) Ltd* [1981] I.C.R. 715; *(No.2)* [1981] I.C.R. 592; *Rainey v Greater Glasgow Health Board* [1987] A.C. 224; *Leverton v Clwyd CC* [1989] I.C.R. 33; *Enderby v Frenchay HA* [1994] I.C.R. 112. The decision of the House of Lords in *North Yorkshire CC v Ratcliffe* [1995] I.C.R. 833 placed some restriction upon the scope for treating market forces as a material factor other than the difference of sex. See also *Strathclyde Regional Council v Wallace* [1998] I.C.R. 205; *Glasgow City Council v Marshall* [2000] I.C.R. 196; *Middlesborough Council v Surtees* [2007] I.R.L.R. 869.

905 s.127.

906 s.132(1)–(2).

907 s.132(3)–(4).

908 s.127(3).

909 s.128.

910 See s.131(8).

911 s.131.

woman would have received if she had not been on maternity leave.[912] In order to avoid re-duplication or conflict as between these provisions for a maternity equality clause and the general provisions against pregnancy and maternity discrimination,[913] provision is made to exclude the latter provisions where the maternity equality clause is applicable.[914]

Sex discrimination during and after the period of employment The Sex   **40-128**
Discrimination Act 1975 as amended by the Sex Discrimination Act 1986 and by subsequent legislation made wide provisions concerning sex discrimination against an employed person during and after the period of employment; corresponding provisions are now made by the Equality Act 2010.[915] It is unlawful for an employer to discriminate[916] against an employed person in the way that access is afforded, or by refusing or deliberately omitting to afford access, to opportunities for promotion, transfer or training or to any other benefits, facilities or services.[917] It is also made unlawful for the employer to discriminate against an employed person on the grounds of sex by dismissing the employed person[918] or by subjecting him or her to any other detriment[919] (such as suspension of employment where that is not imposed on employed persons of the opposite sex).

Exceptions to requirement not to discriminate There are some exceptions to   **40-129**
these requirements not to discriminate during employment. The main exception consists in provision that the requirements relating to opportunities for promotion, transfer or training do not apply in respect of an employment for which being of a particular sex is an occupational requirement as statutorily defined.[920] It is also provided that the provision of benefits, facilities or services to employees falls outside these provisions if those benefits, facilities or services are also provided to the public[921] unless their provision to the employed persons differs in a material respect from their provision to the public, or their provision to the employed person is regulated by the contract under which that person is employed or the benefits, facilities or services relate to training.[922]

Complaints procedure An employed person may complain of contravention of   **40-130**
the statutory requirements to an employment tribunal[923] which may if it upholds the complaint award one or more of the following remedies:

---

[912] s.74.
[913] The provisions in question are those of s.18. See above, para.40-132.
[914] s.76.
[915] The provisions concerned apply to employment under a contract of service or of apprenticeship or a contract personally to execute any work or labour—s.83(2) (definition of employment); see above, para.40-009. Corresponding provisions are made for discrimination on the grounds of gender reassignment by s.7. The provisions are extended to discrimination occurring after the employment relationship has come to an end where the discrimination arises out of and is closely connected to the relationship in question—s.108.
[916] "Discrimination" (meaning sex discrimination in this context) is defined by ss.13 (direct discrimination) and 19 (indirect discrimination).
[917] s.39(2)(b).
[918] See below, para.40-247.
[919] s.39(2)(d).
[920] s.83(11) and Sch.9 Pt 1.
[921] In which event the matter is determined under Pt 3 of the Act, and in particular s.29.
[922] s.83(11) and Sch.9 para.19.
[923] s.120.

(a) an order declaring the rights of the parties[924];

(b) an order for compensation[925] assessed on the basis which would apply if the complaint were a tort action in the High Court[926]; or

(c) a recommendation of a particular course of action for the purpose of minimising the detriment complained of, with a sanction of compensation in the event of non-compliance limited as under sub-para.(b) above.[927]

40-131 Relationship to gender equality clauses The relationship between the provisions concerning sex discrimination during the period of employment described in the immediately preceding paragraphs[928] and the provisions concerning gender equality clauses described in an earlier paragraph[929] are as follows. Within their area of application, the gender equality clause provisions automatically remove certain inequalities by the operation of those clauses. The sex discrimination provisions, on the other hand, render unlawful certain acts of discrimination during the period of employment which fall outside the scope of an equality clause in that they do not themselves consisting of the setting of contractual terms. It is provided that the latter provisions do not in general apply where the former provisions do[930]; however, there are certain defined circumstances in which the sex discrimination provisions may nevertheless operate in relation to contractual pay where direct discrimination or combined discrimination are involved.[931] The upshot is that the sex discrimination provisions can apply in respect of matters not included in the contract under which a person is employed, can apply outside the area of comparison existing between workers doing like work or equivalently rated work, and are not limited to comparison between *actual* cases (that is to say, they can extend to comparison with a hypothetical employed person of the opposite sex).[932]

40-132 Pregnancy and maternity discrimination during the period of employment Provision is made by s.18 of the Equality Act 2010 to ensure that it counts as unlawful discrimination for an employer, during the period in which a woman is pregnant or on ordinary or additional maternity leave,[933] to treat her unfavourably because of the pregnancy or because of illness suffered by her as a result of it, or because she is on compulsory maternity leave or because she is seeking to exercise the right to ordinary or additional maternity leave.[934] In particular an employer must not discriminate against a woman in the above-mentioned sense as to her terms of employment,[935] or in the way that access is afforded to her or not afforded to her to opportunities to promotion, transfer, or training, or for receiving any other benefit, facility, or service[936] or by subjecting her to any other detriment.[937] There is a right to complain to an employment tribunal in respect of such

---

[924] s.124(2)(a).
[925] s.124(2)(b).
[926] s.124(6) referring to s.119.
[927] s.124(2)(c), (7).
[928] paras 40-128—40-130.
[929] para.40-126.
[930] See s.70.
[931] See s.71.
[932] See Deakin & Morris, *Labour Law*, 6th edn (2012), para.6.50.
[933] As to which see below para.40-141.
[934] s.18(1)–(4).
[935] s.39(2)(a).
[936] s.39(2)(b).
[937] s.39(2)(d).

discrimination[938]; and the tribunal has power to award remedies including that of compensation.[939]

Discrimination against married persons and civil partners during and after the period of employment   The Sex Discrimination Act 1975 (as amended by the Sex Discrimination Act 1986 and the Civil Partnership Act 2004) made provision concerning direct and indirect discrimination against married persons and civil partners in the employment field which was broadly similar to the provisions relating to sex discrimination during the period of employment described in the previous paragraphs, with this main difference, that the exception where being of a particular gender was a genuine occupational qualification had no application and no counterpart in cases of discrimination against married persons or civil partners. Corresponding provisions are now contained in the Equality Act 2010.[940]   **40-133**

Racial discrimination during the period of employment   Under the provisions of the Race Relations Act 1976 (as amended by subsequent legislation), it was unlawful for an employer or any person concerned with the employment of others to discriminate against any person employed on work of any description by refusing or deliberately omitting to afford or offer him the like terms of employment, the like conditions of work and the like opportunities for training and promotion as the employer makes available for persons of the like qualifications employed in like circumstances on work of that description. This provision afforded a continuing protection during employment, as well as at the stage of the initial offer of employment. Contravention of this provision was subject to the same enforcement mechanism as applies to the corresponding provisions relating to the formation of the employment relationship. Corresponding provisions are now contained in the Equality Act 2010.[941]   **40-134**

Disability discrimination during the period of employment   In a way which is comparable with the protections against sex and race discrimination described in the foregoing paragraphs, the provisions of the Disability Discrimination Act 1995 imposed continuing duties upon employers during the period of employment, making it unlawful for an employer to discriminate against a disabled person whom he or she employs in the terms of employment which he or she affords him or her, in the opportunities which he or she affords him or her for promotion, training, transfer, or receiving any other benefit, or by refusing him or her any such benefit, and in particular requiring the employer to make reasonable adjustment to ensure that the disabled person is not placed at a substantial disadvantage. The Disability Discrimination Act 2005 amended and extended in various respects the provisions of the Disability Discrimination Act 1995 concerning disability discrimination in   **40-135**

---

[938] s.120.

[939] s.124.

[940] ss.8, 12–14, 39. The provisions are extended to discrimination occurring after the employment relationship has come to an end where the discrimination arises out of and is closely connected to the relationship in question—s.108. Provision for complaint to an employment tribunal is made by s.120(1), and for the awarding of remedies by s.124.

[941] ss.9, 12–14, 39 subject to s.83(11) and Sch.9 Pt 1 (occupational requirements). The provisions are extended to discrimination occurring after the employment relationship has come to an end where the discrimination arises out of and is closely connected to the relationship in question—s.108. Provision for complaint to an employment tribunal is made by s.120(1), and for the awarding of remedies by s.124.

employment. Corresponding provisions are now contained in the Equality Act 2010.[942]

40-136 **Equality with regard to religion or belief, sexual orientation, and age during the period of employment** Provisions very closely comparable to those relating to sex and race discrimination, were made, with effect from December 2003, with regard to religion or belief, with regard to sexual orientation, and with regard to age by, respectively, the Employment Equality (Religion or Belief) Regulations 2003,[943] the Employment Equality (Sexual Orientation) Regulations 2003,[944] and the Employment Equality (Age) Regulations 2006,[945] all of these sets of regulations being enacted in implementation of the requirements of Council Directive 2000/78 establishing a general framework for equal treatment in employment and vocational training.[946] Corresponding provisions are now contained in the Equality Act 2010.[947]

40-137 **Victimisation and harassment during and after the period of employment** The various aforementioned provisions of the Equality Act 2010 concerning discrimination during and after the period of employment are reinforced by provision against discrimination by way of victimisation, and against harassment.[948] Such victimisation occurs where a person subjects another person to a detriment by reason of the fact that the person victimised has done, or where it is believed that he or she has done or may do, any of a series of "protected acts" concerned with the claiming of rights under or assertion of contravention of the Act.[949] In such cases, the exception relating to occupational requirement[950] does not apply and has no counterpart. "Harassment" is essentially defined as unwanted conduct, related to the protected characteristics of age, disability, gender reassignment, race, religion or belief, sex, and sexual orientation, which has the purpose or effect of violating a person's dignity or creating an intimidating, hostile, degrading, humiliating or offensive environment for a person.[951] It is provided that employers must not harass

---

[942] ss.6, 12–14, 20 (duty to make adjustments), 39 subject to s.83(11) and Sch.9 Pt 1 (occupational requirements). The provisions are extended to discrimination occurring after the employment relationship has come to an end where the discrimination arises out of and is closely connected to the relationship in question—s.108. Provision for complaint to an employment tribunal is made by s.120(1), and for the awarding of remedies by s.124. Compare also *Hainsworth v Ministry of Defence* [2014] EWCA Civ 763, [2014] I.R.L.R. 728 (employer's reasonable adjustment duty did not extend to an employee's association with a disabled person).

[943] SI 2003/1660; in particular reg.6(2)–(4).

[944] SI 2003/1661; in particular reg.6(2)–(4).

[945] SI 2006/1031.

[946] 2000/78.

[947] ss.5, 10, 12–14, 39 subject to s.83(11) and Sch.9 Pt 1 (occupational requirements) and Pt 2 (exceptions relating to age). The provisions are extended to discrimination occurring after the employment relationship has come to an end where the discrimination arises out of and is closely connected to the relationship in question: s.108. Provision for complaint to an employment tribunal is made by s.120(1), and for the awarding of remedies by s.124.

[948] ss.26–27. The provisions are extended to harassment occurring after the employment relationship has come to an end where the harassment arises out of and is closely connected to the relationship in question—s.108.

[949] s.27(1)–(5).

[950] s.83(11) and Sch.9 Pt 1.

[951] s.26(1), (5); there is a further extension involving unwanted conduct of a sexual nature, as to which see s.26(2).

persons in their employment or who have applied to them for employment[952]; and employers are treated as harassing where in certain circumstances they fail to take reasonably practicable steps to prevent a third party from so doing.[953] The provisions in s.40 holding employers vicariously liable for such third party harassment have however been repealed as of October 1, 2013.[954]

Terms involving unlawful discrimination   Under s.142 of the Equality Act 2010, **40-138** a term of a contract, or in certain circumstances a term of a non-contractual agreement, is unenforceable where it involves unlawful discrimination, in which case provision exists for any person interested in such a contract to apply to a county court for an order removing or modifying such a term.[955] Further provision is made by s.145 of the Act to render void any term of a collective agreement, including an agreement not intended to be a legally enforceable contract, and to render unenforceable any rule of an employing undertaking so far as it constitutes, promotes, or provides for treatment which is unlawful under the Act.[956]

Protection of rehabilitated offenders during the period of employment   Under **40-139** the Rehabilitation of Offenders Act 1974,[957] it is provided that a spent conviction or any circumstances ancillary thereto or any failure to disclose a spent conviction or any such circumstances shall not be a proper ground for prejudicing a person in any way in any occupation or employment.[958] This appears to extend to detriments suffered by an employee during his or her period of employment. However, no machinery of enforcement is provided in relation to this enactment. The ability of this provision to have any specific effect on the rights of the employee during employment therefore depends upon whether it could be used as the basis of a new cause of action based upon breach of statutory duty[959] or upon a notion of the right to work,[960] and upon whether it can serve as a canon of construction of the employee's contractual rights, in relation, for instance, to a disciplinary procedure.

Rights in connection with parenthood and family responsibility   In this and the **40-140** succeeding paragraphs, a brief summary is provided of the rights in connection with parenthood and family responsibility (formerly described as "maternity rights" but now constituting a broader category of rights)[961] for which provision is made by Pt

---

952 s.40(1). Provision for complaint to an employment tribunal is made by s.120(1), and for the awarding of remedies by s.124. This has now been held to extend to post-employment victimisation: *Rowstock Ltd v Jessemey* [2014] EWCA Civ 185, [2014] 1 W.L.R. 3615.

953 s.40(2)–(4).

954 Enterprise and Regulatory Reform Act 2013 (Commencement No.3, Transitional Provisions and Savings) Order 2013 (SI 2013/2227).

955 s.143.

956 In which case provision is made by s.146 for complaint to an employment tribunal, which may make an order declaring such a term to be void or such a rule to be unenforceable.

957 In force from July 31, 1975, subject to the Rehabilitation of Offenders Act 1974 (Exceptions) Order 1975 (SI 1975/1023).

958 s.4(3)(b). "Spent conviction" is defined in s.1, by reference to s.5.

959 See *Clerk & Lindsell on Torts*, 21st edn (2014), paras 13-36—73; 22-75.

960 cf. *Nagle v Feilden* [1966] 2 Q.B. 633; *Edwards v SOGAT* [1971] Ch. 354 and see above, para.40-102.

961 Pt VIII of the Employment Rights Act 1996 still has the heading "Maternity Rights", but that heading no longer describes all the chapters comprising that part of the Act.

VIII of the Employment Rights Act 1996 as amended by subsequent legislation[962] and by Pt 8A of that Act as inserted by the Employment Act 2002. This legislation makes the following sets of provisions for rights in connection with parenthood, which are respectively summarised in the following paragraphs: (1) maternity leave; (2) adoption leave; (3) parental leave; (4) paternity leave; and (5) flexible working. There is also summarised, in this connection, the new legislation which makes provision for: (6) protection from detriment in connection with parenthood. In the cases of maternity leave, adoption leave, and paternity leave, associated provision is made for rights to maternity pay, adoption pay, and paternity pay, and those rights were detailed earlier in this chapter.[963] Other statutory rights in connection with parenthood and family responsibility are also described elsewhere in this chapter[964]; particular note should be taken of the articulation of general notions of pregnancy and maternity equality and pregnancy and maternity discrimination in the Equality Act 2010, as described earlier in this chapter.[965]

40-141   *(1)   Maternity leave*   Part VIII Ch.I of the Employment Rights Act 1996 deals with maternity leave. Section 71 and the associated regulations provide for an "ordinary maternity leave period" of 26 weeks[966] of which the characteristic is that the employee is entitled to return to her own previous job; s.72 and its associated regulations[967] provide for a compulsory maternity leave period of not less than two weeks; new s.73 and its associated regulations provide for an additional maternity leave period of 26 weeks from the beginning of the week of childbirth, of which the characteristic is that the employee is entitled to return to work though not necessarily to her own previous job.

40-142   *(2)   Adoption leave*   Part VIII Ch.IA of the Employment Rights Act 1996, as inserted by the provisions of the Employment Act 2002 deals with adoption leave. Section 75A and the associated regulations provide, in the case of qualified employees who adopt a child individually, or for one partner of a couple who adopt a child jointly, for an "ordinary adoption leave period" of 26 weeks from the beginning of the week of adoption which is normally paid leave; s.75B and its associ-

---

962   The combined provisions of s.7 of and Sch.4 Pt I to the Employment Relations Act 1999, and the Maternity and Parental Leave, etc. Regulations 1999 (SI 1999/3312) replaced (with effect from December 15, 1999) the provisions of Pt VIII of the Employment Rights Act 1996 with a new and more elaborate set of rights to maternity and parental leave, which were such as to implement the provisions of Council Directive 96/34 on the framework agreement on parental leave. Provisions about paternity leave and adoption leave were added by Pt 1 Ch.1 of the Employment Act 2002, and further provisions about maternity leave were made by Pt 1 Ch.2 of that Act. Subsequent changes have been made by the Maternity and Parental Leave (Amendment) Regulations 2001 (SI 2001/4010); the Maternity and Parental Leave (Amendment) Regulations 2002 (SI 2002/2789); the Paternity and Adoption Leave Regulations 2002 (SI 2002/2788); the Paternity and Adoption Leave (Amendment) Regulations 2004 (SI 2004/923); and the Maternity and Parental Leave, etc. and the Paternity and Adoption Leave (Amendment) Regulations 2006 (SI 2006/2014).

963   See above, paras 40-086—40-088.

964   The further rights conferred apart from Employment Rights Act 1996 Pts VIII and 8A are the right to time off for dependants—see above, para.40-123, and certain rights in connection with dismissal—see below, para.40-236.

965   See above, paras 40-127—40-132.

966   This period was increased from 18 weeks with effect from April 6, 2003, under the provisions of Pt 1 Ch.2 of the Employment Act 2002. A new s.71(3) was substituted by s.11(1) of and Sch.1 para.31 to the Work and Families Act 2006, which would enable that period to be further increased by regulations.

967   SI 1999/3312 regs 6, 7.

ated regulations provide for an additional adoption leave period of 26 weeks from the beginning of the week of adoption, in respect of which there is no statutory right to pay.

(3) Parental leave   Part VIII Ch.II of the Employment Rights Act 1996 deals **40-143** with parental leave. Sections 76 to 79 and the regulations made thereunder confer an entitlement, upon employees who satisfy the specified conditions, to be absent from work for up to 13 weeks for the purpose of caring for a child of theirs, before the child's fifth birthday. This is extended to 18 weeks before the child's eighteenth birthday in the case of disabled children. Section 80 provides for an employee to complain to an employment tribunal that his or her employer has unreasonably postponed such leave or prevented or attempted to prevent the employee from taking such leave.

(4) Paternity leave   Part VIII Ch.III of the Employment Rights Act 1996, as **40-144** inserted by Pt 1, Ch.1 of the Employment Act 2002, deals with paternity leave. Sections 80A to 80E and the regulations made thereunder confer an entitlement, upon employees who satisfy the specified conditions, to be absent from work for up to two weeks for the purpose of caring for a newly born child of theirs and to support the child's mother, and also confer a corresponding entitlement in the case of adoption.

(5) Flexible working: the right to request contract variation   The Employment **40-145** Act 2002 makes provision under the title of "flexible working"[968] for parents, who are qualifying employees, of children aged under six or disabled children aged under 18, to have the right to apply to their employer for a contract variation relating to hours or times of work, or location of work as between home and a place of business of the employer, or for such other aspects of terms and conditions of employment as may be specified by regulations. That right imposes duties upon the employer, first to process the application in the manner prescribed by regulations, and secondly to refuse the application only where "he considers" that one or more of a prescribed set of grounds for refusal, such as "the burden of additional costs" applies or apply.[969] Section 12 of the Work and Families Act 2006, amending new s.80F of the Employment Rights Act 1996, extends the category of employees who are entitled to request flexible working by including "carers" within the scheme. The categories of adult relatives in respect of whom such a request may be made are specified by regulations.[970]

---

[968] The provisions are those of s.47, inserting new Pt 8A "Flexible Working" into the Employment Rights Act 1996. See now also the Flexible Working Regulations 2014 (SI 2014/1398), which extend the right to make a flexible working application to all employees who have been continuously employed for a period of at least 26 weeks.

[969] In *Shaw v CCL Ltd* [2008] I.R.L.R. 284, EAT it was held that, although there is no right to return to work on a part time basis, refusal of such request may amount to unlawful direct or indirect sex discrimination, as such amounting to breach of the implied obligation as to mutual trust and confidence, and entitling the employee to resign and claim constructive unfair dismissal.

[970] SIs 2006/3314 and 2007/1184. Moreover, SI 2009/595 extended the category of children in respect of whom such a request may be made so that it extends to children under 17 (with effect from April 2009).

40-146 *(6) Protection from detriment in connection with parenthood and family responsibility* By a succession of enactments beginning with the Employment Relations Act 1999,[971] there have been conferred upon employees a series of protections against detriment in connection with various aspects of parenthood and family responsibility or with the exercise of rights relating to parenthood and family responsibility. As a brief summary of the effect of those enactments, an employee has the right not to suffer detrimental treatment at work (other than dismissal, which is the subject of separate provision)[972] for the reason that:

- she is pregnant or has given birth to a child; or
- she has exercised or has sought to exercise the rights to maternity leave or maternity pay; or
- she or he has exercised or has sought to exercise the rights to parental leave; or
- she or he has exercised or has sought to exercise the rights to time off for domestic reasons (to care for dependants)[973]; or
- he has exercised or has sought to exercise the rights to paternity leave or paternity pay; or
- she or he has exercised or has sought to exercise the rights to adoption leave or adoption pay, or the rights to paternity leave or paternity pay which apply to adoptive parents[974]; or
- she or he has exercised or has sought to exercise the rights which relate to flexible working.[975]

An employee may complain to employment tribunal of subjection to detriment for any of these reasons,[976] and the tribunal may award the remedies of declaration and/or compensation.[977]

40-147 **References and testimonials** Early authorities suggest that an employer need not give his employee a reference or testimonial when the employment ends, nor answer any inquiries from prospective employers of a former employee.[978] It was once said[979] to be an unreasonable custom that, on quitting at the end of the first month by notice given in the first fortnight, a domestic employee was entitled to have the character reference she came with handed to her to enable her to show it to her next employer. If the employer does give a reference or testimonial to an

---

[971] s.9 and Sch.4 Pt III.

[972] See below, para.40-236.

[973] Employment Rights Act 1996 s.47C (as inserted by the Employment Relations Act 1999), as supplemented by reg.19 of the Maternity and Parental Leave, etc. Regulations 1999 (SI 1999/3312).

[974] Employment Rights Act 1996 s.47C (as amended by the Employment Act 2002), as supplemented by reg.28 of the Paternity and Adoption Leave Regulations 2002 (SI 2002/2788).

[975] Employment Rights Act 1996 s.47E (as inserted by s.47(1), (3) of the Employment Act 2002) (originally numbered s.47D, that number being corrected to 47E).

[976] Employment Rights Act 1996 s.48 (as amended by the Employment Relations Act 1999 and by the Employment Act 2002).

[977] Employment Rights Act 1996 s.49.

[978] *Carroll v Bird* (1800) 3 Esp. 201; *Handley v Moffatt* (1872) 21 W.R. 231. Even if the former employer gives some information, he is under no obligation to give all the information he has about the employee: *Wilkin v Reed* (1854) 15 C.B. 192. The employer is now, however, under a statutory obligation to give the employee a written statement of the reasons for his dismissal, see below, para.40-195.

[979] *Moult v Halliday* [1898] 1 Q.B. 125, 129, 130. (On the right to the property in such a reference, see the cases cited below.)

employee, an employer may be guilty of an offence[980] if the employer gives a false character, either orally or in writing[981]; the employer may also be liable in damages to a subsequent employer who suffers loss by engaging the employee in reliance upon the reference if it contains a statement of fact which the employer knows to be untrue,[982] or (possibly) if the employer is negligent in making statements in it.[983] It was held in *Spring v Guardian Assurance Plc*[984] that an employer who gave a reference to an employer of one of his ex-employees did owe a duty of reasonable care to the ex-employee to ensure that the facts stated in the reference were accurate, in accordance with the earlier decision recognising such a duty in the case of *Lawton v BOC Transhield Ltd*.[985] The duty of care which was recognised in *Spring v Guardian Assurance Plc* was later expounded by the Court of Appeal[986] as a duty to provide a true, fair and accurate reference when taken as a whole rather than as a series of discrete statements. It has since been ruled[987] that there is only a duty to take reasonable care not to give misleading information about the worker in question, and not a duty to give a reference that is full and comprehensive. The Court of Appeal has in a later case[988] upheld a decision of the County Court that the employers were negligent in providing a reference in respect of the claimant to subsequent employers which relied upon allegations of dishonest conduct which they had not properly investigated, and has since[989] held that there was no liability for negligent misstatement where the former employing company claimed that the former employee had left owing repayment of an advance commission payment, but where that was not asserted to any third party or in any reference given to a potential employer. The former employee will have an action for libel or slander against the employer for any untrue statement in the reference or testimonial which injures his or her reputation only if he or she can prove malice on the part of the employer,[990] since the occasion is one protected by the defence of qualified privilege.[991] If a written character reference is produced by the employee to the

---

980   Servants' Characters Act 1792 (repealed by the Statute Law (Repeals) Act 2008 Sch.1 Pt 3).
981   See *R. v Costello and Bishop* [1910] 1 K.B. 28.
982   *Foster v Charles* (1830) 7 Bing. 105 (an action for deceit). cf. *Wilkin v Reed* (1854) 15 C.B. 192.
983   *Hedley Byrne & Co Ltd v Heller & Partners Ltd* [1964] A.C. 465. (The principles laid down in this case may be wide enough to justify the courts in holding that a duty of care arises between the employer who gives the reference, and a subsequent employer who acts in reliance on it. See *Clerk & Lindsell on Torts*, 21st edn (2014), paras 8-113 et seq. *Esso Petroleum Co v Mardon* [1976] 1 Q.B. 801).
984   [1995] 2 A.C. 296.
985   [1987] I.C.R. 7.
986   In *Bartholomew v Hackney LBC* [1999] I.R.L.R. 246, CA. Yet further exposition of the requirement of fairness of references for former employees is provided by the Court of Appeal in *Jackson v Liverpool City Council* [2011] EWCA Civ 1068, [2011] I.R.L.R. 1009; the relevance of the public law duty of honesty and integrity was considered *AB v A Chief Constable* [2014] EWHC 1965 (QB), [2014] I.R.L.R. 700.
987   In *Kidd v AXA Equity and Law Life Assurance Society Plc* [2000] I.R.L.R. 301, QBD. Compare now also, to comparably restrictive effect, *Aspin v Metric Group Ltd* [2004] EWHC 1265.
988   *Cox v Sun Alliance Life Ltd* [2001] I.R.L.R. 448.
989   In *Legal & General Assurance Ltd v Kirk* [2002] I.R.L.R. 124.
990   Unless the case can be brought within a duty of care in negligence, see above, or if the employer communicates the reference to a person who has no "proper interest" in receiving it.
991   *Clerk & Lindsell on Torts*, 21st edn (2014), paras 22-105 et seq.; *Gatley on Libel and Slander*, 12th edn (2013), paras 14-11 et seq.

prospective employer, the document will usually belong to the employee, who will be entitled to damages if the prospective employer destroys or defaces it.[992]

40-148 **References and the Rehabilitation of Offenders Act 1974** The writing of references and testimonials may be affected by the provisions of the Rehabilitation of Offenders Act 1974.[993] If a reference is given in answer to questions, the questions are to be treated as not related to spent convictions or their ancillary circumstances and no penalty or liability can attach to failure to disclose these in the answer.[994] If the writer of a reference or testimonial does refer to spent convictions, and is sued for defamation for so doing, the writer cannot rely on the defence of justification (truth) if the statement is shown to have been made with malice.[995] The Act created a new offence of unauthorised disclosure of spent convictions which may be committed by a person who has in the course of his or her official duties had access to any "official record" or the information in it and who discloses a spent conviction other than in the course of his or her duties.[996]

40-149 **Data protection and privacy** The common law of the contract of employment has little to say about data protection and employees' privacy, though the employer's implied duty to deserve the trust and confidence of the employee might be invoked.[997] However, there is an increasingly significant body of statute law in this area, of which the main provisions, in very brief summary, are as follows. The Data Protection Act 1984 imposed requirements of registration, with the Data Protection Registrar (later replaced by the Information Commissioner),[998] upon all data users holding personal data which could be processed automatically and formed part of a collection of data; these requirements therefore extended to many employers.[999] The data user was obliged to comply with the data protection principles derived from the Council of Europe Convention on Data Protection. A more extensive and elaborate regime of data protection was envisaged by the EC Data Protection Directive of 1995.[1000] The Data Protection Act 1998[1001] was enacted to implement the requirements of that Directive; it replaces in a more extended form the provisions of the 1984 Act. The concept of personal data is enlarged to include data within a relevant filing system as well as automatically processed data—that is, it goes beyond data held in computers or on disk.[1002] Under the provisions of the Act, data controllers—which includes employers—are required to abide by the data protection principles of the Act,[1003] and also to give effect to special controls placed upon

---

[992] See *Wennhak v Morgan* (1888) 20 Q.B.D. 635, 638, 640. (But cf. *Taylor v Rowan* (1835) 7 Car. & P. 70.)

[993] In force from July 31, 1975, subject to the Rehabilitation of Offenders Act 1974 (Exceptions) Order 1975 (SI 1975/1023).

[994] s.4(2)—"spent conviction" is defined in s.1 by reference to s.5.

[995] s.8(5).

[996] s.9.

[997] See below, para.40-151.

[998] Under the provisions of the Freedom of Information Act 2000 s.18 and Sch.2.

[999] See now Pt III of the 1998 Act.

[1000] Directive 95/46.

[1001] Referred to in this paragraph as "the 1998 Act". The principal substantive provisions of the Act came into force on March 1, 2000.

[1002] See s.1 of the 1998 Act and Schs 1, 2, 4.

[1003] s.4 and Sch.2.

the use of a category of data designated as "sensitive personal data".[1004] The Act confers important rights upon data subjects, such as employees, in particular the right of access, in and on certain conditions, to personal data,[1005] the right to prevent processing likely to cause damage or distress,[1006] and rights in relation to automated decision-making which place significant restrictions on the way that the appraisal of employees' performance may be conducted.[1007] Provision is made for claims to compensation for failure to comply with certain of these requirements.[1008] There are also important controls placed by the Access to Medical Reports Act 1988 upon the conditions on which an employer or prospective employer may have access to a medical report made on an employee or prospective employee for employment purposes.

Privacy and the Human Rights Act More generally, employees of public **40-150** authorities may be able to invoke against their public authority employers the right to respect for private and family life which is embodied in art.8 of the European Convention on Human Rights and is incorporated into the law of the United Kingdom by virtue of the provisions of the Human Rights Act 1998.[1009] In *Antovic and Mirkovic v Montenegro* the European Court of Human Rights held that art 8 could also be engaged in the context of professional activities in a public university,[1010] and in *Lopez Ribalda v Spain*, the Court was particularly critical of covert electronic surveillance in the workplace.[1011]

Trust and confidence and other associated implied duties The decision of the **40-151** Court of Appeal in *Western Excavating (ECC) Ltd v Sharp*,[1012] that the statutory concept of constructive dismissal[1013] was to be interpreted as requiring either fundamental breach or repudiation of the contract of employment, has proved a fruitful source of case law about the employer's implied duties under the contract of employment and has given rise to the recognition of a number of new general and particular implied duties. The most important of those is a general implied duty to preserve the trust and confidence that an employee should have in his or her employer.[1014] This implied term received the recognition of the House of Lords in *Malik v Bank of Commerce and Credit International SA*,[1015] where it was held that there might be a breach of the implied term of trust and confidence, giving rise to "stigma damages", where the conduct of the employer's business was so

---

[1004] s.2 and Sch.3. The circumstances in which sensitive personal data may be processed are specified by the Data Protection (Processing of Sensitive Personal Data) Order 2000 (SI 2000/417).

[1005] s.7.

[1006] s.10.

[1007] s.12.

[1008] s.13.

[1009] Compare *Halford v United Kingdom* [1997] I.R.L.R. 471 (ECtHR), applied in *Copland v United Kingdom* (2007) 45 E.H.R.R. 37 (ECtHR). See also *Swansea v Gayle* [2013] I.R.L.R. 768, EAT: covert monitoring of employee outside the workplace not in violation of right to respect for private life.

[1010] Application No.70838/13, Judgment of November 28, 2017.

[1011] Applications Nos 1874/13 and 8567/13, Judgment of January 9, 2018.

[1012] [1977] I.C.R. 221.

[1013] See below, para.40-194.

[1014] *Courtaulds Northern Textiles Ltd v Andrew* [1979] I.R.L.R. 84; *Post Office v Roberts* [1980] I.R.L.R. 347; *Woods v WM Car Services Ltd* [1981] I.C.R. 666; *Bliss v South East Thames RHA* [1987] I.C.R. 700.

[1015] [1998] A.C. 20.

disreputable as to damage the employee's prospects of obtaining other employment.[1016] Other implied duties so recognised have been: an implied duty not to behave arbitrarily, capriciously and inequitably in matters concerning remuneration[1017]; an implied duty to investigate a genuine and bona fide safety grievance[1018]; an implied duty to take reasonable steps to maintain an appraisal of a probationer during a trial period, giving guidance by advice or warning where necessary.[1019] This whole development can be seen as the counterpart of the employee's duty of contractual co-operation[1020]; but it stops short of an absolutely general implied term requiring the employer to behave reasonably towards the employee.[1021] Moreover, it has not permitted an argument to succeed that an employer's equal opportunity policy must be regarded as an implied term of the contract of employment capable of overriding an express term in conflict with the policy.[1022]

40-152   Extensions of the implied obligation of trust and confidence   A significant extension of the development occurred (outside the context of constructive dismissal) in *Scally v Southern Health Board*,[1023] where the House of Lords held that where a contract of employment negotiated between employers and a representative body, or otherwise settled on a non-individual basis, contained a term conferring on the employee a valuable right contingent upon his acting as required, of which he could not be expected to be aware unless that term was brought to his attention, there was an implied obligation on the employer to take reasonable steps to bring the term to the employee's attention so as to enable him to enjoy the right in question. The implied obligation has been held to apply in the following situations: the Employment Appeal Tribunal has held that a local authority employer was vicariously liable for a breach of the implied obligation of trust and confidence

---

[1016] A conclusion which the House of Lords ruled was not precluded by their older decision in *Addis v Gramophone Co Ltd* [1909] A.C. 488. However, it should be noted that such "stigma damages" are effectively excluded from the assessment of damages for wrongful dismissal, in particular where the wrongfulness consists in failure to follow contractual dismissal procedures, by the doctrine propounded in *Johnson v Unisys Ltd* [2001] I.C.R. 480 as re-confirmed by the Supreme Court in *Edwards v Chesterfield Royal Hospital NHS Trust* [2011] UKSC 58; see below, paras 40-154, 40-204.

[1017] *FC Gardner Ltd v Beresford* [1978] I.R.L.R. 63.

[1018] *British Aircraft Corp v Austin* [1978] I.R.L.R. 332. See, for authority for the view that the duty of trust and confidence results in a general implied duty to provide an effective grievance procedure, *WA Goold (Pearmark) Ltd v McConnell* [1995] I.R.L.R. 516.

[1019] *White v London Transport Executive* [1982] Q.B. 489.

[1020] Compare above, paras 40-062 (duty of fidelity), 40-065 (duty to refrain from disruption).

[1021] *Post Office v Roberts* [1980] I.R.L.R. 347, 350, para.28. In *Waltham Forest LBC v Omilaju (No.2)* [2004] EWCA Civ 1493, [2005] I.R.L.R. 35 it was reasserted that the test of whether an act was capable of breaching the implied obligation was an objective one, so that the employee's subjective loss of trust and confidence was not sufficient in itself. In *Nottinghamshire CC v Meikle* [2004] EWCA Civ 859, [2004] 4 All E.R. 97, the objectivity of the test had been likewise asserted, but to the contrary effect that it was not necessary for the employee subjectively to have lost confidence in her employer in an overall sense. In *Baldwin v Brighton and Hove City Council* [2007] I.C.R. 680 it was held that it was not necessary to show that the employer's conduct was intended, as well as likely, to destroy the relationship of mutual trust and confidence.

[1022] *Grant v South-West Trains Ltd* [1998] I.R.L.R. 188.

[1023] [1991] I.C.R. 771. Compare however *Crossley v Faithful & Gould Holdings Ltd* [2004] EWCA Civ 293, [2004] I.R.L.R. 377, in which it was held that there is no general obligation upon the employer to take reasonable care for the employee's economic well-being, and that the application of the criteria articulated in the *Scally* case did not require disclosure on the present facts. To similar effect has been *Lennon v Commissioner of Police of the Metropolis* [2004] EWCA Civ 130.

where a councillor subjected the employee to harassment in the course of his work[1024]; the Court of Appeal has held that another local authority employer was in breach of the implied obligation of trust and confidence where the employee was suspended, pending the investigation of an allegation of abuse of a child in her care, without sufficient cause[1025]; the Court of Appeal has also held that an employing company was liable for breach of the implied obligation of trust and confidence in failing to offer a revised contractual package of pay and benefits to one worker which was offered to others in a similar situation.[1026]

Further applications and extensions of the implied obligation of trust and confidence There continue to be cases in which employing enterprises are held to be in breach of specific obligations which are implied in and from the particular circumstances but are derived from or associated with the general implied obligation as to trust and confidence.[1027] The decision of the Court of Appeal in *Horkulak v Cantor Fitzgerald International*[1028] confirmed the application of the implied obligation to the exercise of a contractual discretion as to the level of bonus payment to be awarded. The decisions of the High Court in *Takacs v Barclays Services Jersey Ltd*[1029] and of the Court of Appeal in *Keen v Commerzbank AG*[1030] suggest that the implied controls upon the exercise of contractual discretions with regard

40-153

[1024] *Moores v Bude-Stratton Town Council* [2001] I.C.R. 271.
[1025] *Gogay v Hertfordshire CC* [2000] I.R.L.R. 703.
[1026] *Transco Plc v O'Brien* [2002] EWCA Civ 379, [2002] I.C.R. 721.
[1027] *Jenvey v Australian Broadcasting Corp* [2003] I.C.R. 79; *Glendale Managed Services v Graham* [2003] I.R.L.R. 465. Compare, at one further remove, *Hagen v ICI Chemicals and Polymers Ltd* [2002] I.R.L.R. 31. Compare also now *Bunning v GT Bunning & Sons Ltd* [2005] EWCA Civ 104 where it was held to be arguable that a failure to conduct a proper risk assessment of the continued employment of the employee as a welder, as required by Regulations when she became pregnant, might constitute a serious breach of the implied obligation as to trust and confidence. Compare also *Greenhof v Barnsley MBC* [2006] I.R.L.R. 98, where it was held that a serious failure to make reasonable adjustments in favour of a disabled person, as required by the Disability Discrimination Act 1995, amounted to a breach of the implied obligation as to trust and confidence and a constructive dismissal; and *Deadman v Bristol CC* [2007] EWCA Civ 822, [2007] I.R.L.R. 888, where it was held that, as an aspect of maintaining mutual trust and confidence, the employer was obliged to follow the procedures for the investigation of complaints which it had published and implemented. Compare also now *Shaw v CCL Ltd* [2008] I.R.L.R. 284, EAT where it was held that, although there is no right to return to work on a part time basis, refusal of such request may amount to unlawful direct or indirect sex discrimination, as such amounting to breach of the implied obligation as to mutual trust and confidence and entitling the employee to resign and claim constructive unfair dismissal. A different kind of extension took place in *Tullit Prebon Plc v BGC Brokers LP* [2011] EWCA Civ 131, where the Court of Appeal held that the implied obligation as to mutual trust and confidence applied to and came into operation under a set of "forward contracts" under which a group of brokers employed by TP engaged to join BGCB at future dates, and that BGCB placed itself in repudiatory breach of those "forward contracts" by conspiring to bring about a mass early departure of those brokers whether or not lawful grounds existed for those departures. By contrast, TP were held not to be in breach of their implied obligation as to mutual trust and confidence to those brokers in seeking to persuade them renege on their "forward contracts" with BGCB, the intention being to reinforce rather than to abandon the relations between TP and the brokers. Compare also *IBM United Kingdom Holdings Ltd v Dalgleish* [2014] EWHC 980 (Ch) at [1537]–[1594]: breach of implied contractual duty of trust and confidence through failure to consult on pension changes (especially given previous statements).
[1028] [2004] EWCA Civ 1287, [2005] I.C.R. 402.
[1029] [2006] I.R.L.R. 877 (QB).
[1030] [2006] EWCA Civ 1536, [2007] I.C.R. 623. Compare also now *Khatri v Cooperatieve Centrale Raiffeisen-Boerenleenbank BA* [2010] EWCA Civ 397, where the requirement of rational exercise of discretions with regard to the awarding of bonuses was reaffirmed, and *Patural v DB Services (UK) Ltd* [2015] EWHC 3659 (QB), [2016] I.R.L.R. 286.

to bonus payments are increasingly being envisaged in terms of obligations on the part of the employer to refrain from irrational or perverse exercise or non-exercise of such discretions, and also to refrain from termination of employment for the purpose of avoiding liability to bonus payment. In *Braganza v BP Shipping Ltd*,[1031] the Supreme Court highlighted the extension of the implied term of trust and confidence to the employer's exercise of contractual discretion, holding that "[a]ny decision-making function entrusted to the employer has to be exercised in accordance with the implied obligation of trust and confidence".[1032] The Court opined in *Bradbury v BBC* that an employer's several actions might cumulatively amount to a breach of the implied term.[1033]

40-154 **The limits of the implied obligation of trust and confidence** Although the implied obligation as to trust and confidence has thus continued to be extended in various directions in recent years, limiting decisions and limiting doctrines also present themselves. In *BCCI v Ali (No.2)*,[1034] the Court of Appeal upheld the finding that two former employees had not shown a sufficiently strong causative link between the employer's breach of the implied term of trust and confidence and their difficulty in obtaining subsequent employment; the indications are that claims to stigma damages will in practice be difficult to establish. Most importantly, in *Johnson v Unisys Ltd*[1035] the House of Lords held that the implied obligation of mutual trust and confidence did not apply to limit the manner in which an employer exercised a power of dismissal, so that a claim for "stigma damages" or for damages for distress or injury to feelings could not be made where that would be the basis of the claim. This was said to be for the reason that Parliament when enacting the provisions concerning remedies for unfair dismissal had intended that those provisions should provide the sole source of complaint and compensation for injury caused by the manner of dismissal from employment. That has left a difficulty of deciding whether, when dismissal eventuates from or at the end of a course of conduct on the part of the employing enterprise which would otherwise be regarded as a breach of the implied obligation of trust and confidence, the course of conduct is not to be so regarded by reason of the rule in *Johnson v Unisys*. In *Eastwood v Magnox Electric Plc, McCabe v Cornwall CC*[1036] the House of Lords sought definitively to draw the boundary between the area of exclusion of liability for breach of the implied term of trust and confidence envisaged in the *Johnson* case, and the area of pre-dismissal conduct on the part of the employer, apparently including conduct capable of being treated as constructive dismissal, within which liability for breach of the implied term may arise; their approach was to distinguish those situations in which a cause of action for breach of the implied obligation had arisen before the dismissal took place, and to regard that cause of action as vested

---

[1031] [2015] UKSC 17, [2015] 1 W.L.R. 1661.

[1032] [2015] UKSC 17 at [32]. Compare now also *Hills v Niksun Inc* [2016] EWCA Civ 115, [2016] I.R.L.R. 715, as well as *Stevens v University of Birmingham* [2015] EWHC 2300 (QB), [2015] I.R.L.R. 899 and *Simpkin v Berkeley Group Holdings Plc* [2016] EWHC 1619 (QB), [2017] 1 Costs L.O. 13.

[1033] [2015] EWHC 1368 (Ch), [2015] Pens. L.R. 457.

[1034] [2002] I.C.R. 1258, CA. In *Holladay v East Kent Hospitals NHS Trust* [2003] EWCA Civ 1696, (2004) 76 B.M.L.R. 201 it was held that the breach of the implied obligation must be a material cause of the event (arrest on suspicion of theft) which had caused the employee harm, but that it was not necessary to conclude that the event would not have occurred but for the breach.

[1035] [2001] I.C.R. 480. Compare *Reda v Flag Ltd* [2002] I.R.L.R. 747, PC.

[1036] [2004] UKHL 35, [2005] 1 A.C. 503.

and protected from the *Johnson* exclusion.[1037] The existence of the *"Johnson* exclusion" and the delineation of its scope in the *Eastwood* case were confirmed by the Supreme Court in the case of *Edwards v Chesterfield Royal Hospital NHS Trust*[1038] so that the implied obligation of trust and confidence has effectively been precluded from attaching to the conduct of dismissal proceedings, as also has been the associated liability to damages for loss suffered as a result of a breach of a term (express or implied) in the contract of employment as to the manner of dismissal, unless the loss can be said to precede and be independent of the dismissal.[1039] Moreover, the decision of the Employment Appeal Tribunal in *Claridge v Daler Rowney Ltd*[1040] seemed to confirm the emergence of a doctrine adumbrated in *Abbey National Plc v Fairbrother*[1041] to the effect that, at least in the context of the carrying out of grievance procedures, the employer will not be regarded as having constructively dismissed the employee or as having acted in breach of the obligation of mutual trust and confidence if the employer's conduct lay within the range of reasonable responses which the generality of employers might have made. However, in *Bournemouth University Higher Education Corp v Buckland*,[1042] the Court of Appeal rejected the argument that a "band of reasonable responses" test should apply to determine what constitutes fundamental breach of contract and therefore constructive dismissal on the part of the employer. Moreover, further illustration of the way in which failures in disciplinary or dismissal procedure may nevertheless amount to breach of the implied obligation of trust and confidence is provided by the decision in *Lakshmi v Mid-Cheshire Hospitals NHS Trust*[1043]; and comparison should also be made with the decision in *Lauffer v Barking, Havering and Redbridge University Hospitals NHS Trust*.[1044]

Disclosures of information in the public interest Provision is made by the **40-155** Public Interest Disclosure Act 1998[1045] for the protection of workers who make certain disclosures of information in the public interest, and to allow such individuals to bring action in respect of victimisation.[1046] In brief summary, these provisions are as follows. The protection applies to an especially enlarged category of "workers" which includes, for example, certain persons being provided with work experience or training for employment, although they do not have contracts of employment.[1047] Claims can be brought both against a worker's employer, an end-

---

[1037] Compare also *GAB Robins (UK) Ltd v Triggs* [2008] EWCA Civ 17, [2008] I.R.L.R. 317.

[1038] [2011] UKSC 58.

[1039] See further below, paras 40-194, 40-204.

[1040] [2008] I.R.L.R. 672.

[1041] [2007] I.R.L.R. 320, EAT.

[1042] [2010] EWCA Civ 121, [2010] I.R.L.R. 445.

[1043] [2008] EWHC 878 (QB).

[1044] [2009] EWHC 2360 (QB), [2010] Med. L.R. 68.

[1045] Referred to in this paragraph as the 1998 Act. The Act came into force on July 2, 1999. In *Miklasewicz v Stolt Offshore Ltd* [2002] I.R.L.R. 344, the Court of Session held that its provisions applied to a disclosure before that date giving rise to a dismissal after that date.

[1046] These provisions mainly take the form of sections in a new Pt IVA of the Employment Rights Act 1996, inserted by s.1 of the 1998 Act.

[1047] Employment Rights Act 1996 s.43K. Indeed, this has been held to include a health and safety consultant supplied by an agency and operating via his own service company: *Keppel Seghers UK Ltd v Hinds* [2014] I.R.L.R. 754, EAT. Though cf. *Day v Lewisham and Greenwich NHS Trust* [2016] I.R.L.R. 415, EAT.

user of agency services, or both if the exercise of employer functions is shared.[1048] The protection applies to qualifying disclosures, which are defined by reference to the kind of failure they tend to show—for example, the commission of criminal offences, miscarriages of justice or danger to health and safety,[1049] and by reference to the persons to whom the disclosures are made—for example, to the employer or other responsible person, to a legal adviser, or to a Minister of the Crown—and the circumstances in which they are made—for example disclosure in good faith of exceptionally serious failure which it is reasonable in all the circumstances to make.[1050] It has been held that in a whistle-blower case where the disclosure related to a breach of the worker's own contract of employment, or some other matter under s.43B(1) where the interest was personal in character, there might nevertheless be features of the case making it reasonable to regard disclosure as being in the public interest as well as in the personal interest of the worker.[1051] The Act confers upon workers the right not to suffer detriment on the ground that the worker has made a protected disclosure,[1052] and provides for them to enforce that right by complaint to an employment tribunal,[1053] which may award compensation within prescribed limits.[1054] It is also provided that a dismissal, the reason or principal reason for which is that the employee made a protected disclosure, will be automatically treated as unfair for the purposes of the unfair dismissal legislation.[1055] It is further provided that any provision in any agreement between a worker and his or her employer is void insofar as it purports to preclude the worker from making a protected disclosure—that is, insofar as it seeks to impose a countervailing duty of confidentiality.[1056]

40-156 **Duties to avoid less favourable treatment of part-time work and fixed-term work** Two important measures have been taken in response to EC Directives, conferring (to the extent defined) upon those working under certain specific types of employment contract or arrangement a right to equality of treatment with those employed under the corresponding "standard" type of employment contract or arrangement. The Part-time Workers (Prevention of Less Favourable Treatment) Regulations 2000,[1057] implementing Council Directive 97/81 on part-time work,[1058] require part-time workers[1059] not to be treated less favourably than full-time work-

---

[1048] *McTigue v University Hospital Bristol NHS Foundation Trust* [2016] UKEAT/0354/15/JOJ, [2016] I.R.L.R. 742.

[1049] Employment Rights Act 1996 s.43B. See *Norbrook Laboratories (GB) Ltd v Shaw* [2014] I.C.R. 540, EAT.

[1050] Employment Rights Act 1996 ss.43C–43H.

[1051] *Chesterton Global Ltd (T/A Chestertons) v Nurmohamed* [2017] EWCA Civ 979, [2017] I.R.L.R. 837.

[1052] Employment Rights Act 1996 s.47B as inserted by s.2 of the 1998 Act.

[1053] Employment Rights Act 1996 s.48(1A) as amended by s.3 of the 1998 Act.

[1054] Employment Rights Act 1996 s.49(6) as amended by s.4 of the 1998 Act.

[1055] Employment Rights Act 1996 s.103A as inserted by s.5 of the 1998 Act.

[1056] Employment Rights Act 1996 s.43J.

[1057] SI 2000/1551, in force from July 1, 2000. See also now the Part-time Workers (Prevention of Less Favourable Treatment) Regulations 2001 (SI 2001/1107), in force from May 1, 2001, and the Part-time Workers (Prevention of Less Favourable Treatment) Regulations 2002 (SI 2002/2035), in force from October 1, 2002, which make further consequential provisions.

[1058] Directive 97/81 as extended to the UK by Directive 98/23.

[1059] As defined in reg.1(2), similarly as in Employment Rights Act 1996 s.230(3). Compare *Christie v Department for Constitutional Affairs* [2007] I.C.R. 1553, EAT, where it was held that a part-time tribunal chairman came within the Regulations. In *O'Brien v Department of Constitutional Affairs*

ers of the same employer who work under the same type[1060] of employment contract,[1061] on the ground of being a part-time worker, unless there is objective justification for that less favourable treatment.[1062] A part-time worker may complain to an employment tribunal of the violation of that right.[1063]

Rather similarly, though by no means identically, the Fixed-term Employees **40-157** (Prevention of Less Favourable Treatment) Regulations 2002[1064] implementing[1065] Council Directive 99/70 on fixed-term work,[1066] require fixed-term employees[1067] not to be treated less favourably than comparable permanent employees of the same employer engaged in the same or broadly similar work[1068] on the ground that the worker is part-time, unless that less favourable treatment is justified on objective grounds. The right of no less favourable treatment is conferred by reg.3; it is a right not to be treated less favourably, on the ground of being a fixed-term employee, than the employer treats a comparable permanent employee as regards the terms of contract or by being subjected to any other detriment, if the treatment is not justified on objective grounds.[1069] Regulation 4 provides that less favourable treatment with regard to any contract term is to be regarded as justified on objective grounds if the terms of the fixed-term employee's contract of employment, taken as a whole, are at least as favourable as the terms of the comparable permanent employee's contract of employment. A fixed-term employee may complain to an employment tribunal of the violation of that right.[1070]

6. TERMINATION OF THE CONTRACT

(a) Termination by Notice

Construction of the contract Apart from any relevant statutory provision,[1071] any **40-158** question as to the duration of the employment, its terminability by notice, the length

---

[2008] EWCA Civ 1448, [2009] I.R.L.R. 294 the Court of Appeal held that part-time judicial office holders are not "workers" for the purpose of these Regulations; however, in *O'Brien v Ministry of Justice* (C-393/10) EU:C:2012:110 the ECJ suggested that this decision was non-compliant with the Directive. In *O'Brien v Department of Constitutional Affairs* [2013] UKSC 6, [2013] 1 W.L.R. 522 the Supreme Court duly held that the decision of the ECJ did require a recognition that the part-time Recorder was entitled to be regarded as a "worker" for the purposes of the 2000 Regulations. *O'Brien* was distinguished in *Gilham v Ministry of Justice* [2017] I.R.L.R. 23, EAT, where a narrower interpretation was favoured in the context of purely domestic employment rights.

[1060] See reg.2. See for the judicial construction of this Regulation, and the clarification of the notion of comparable workers which it articulates, *Mathews v Kent and Medway Towns Fire Authority* [2006] UKHL 8, [2006] I.C.R. 365.

[1061] SI 2000/1551.

[1062] See reg.5(2).

[1063] See regs 5(2), 8.

[1064] SI 2002/2023, in force from October 1, 2002.

[1065] But also in certain respects going beyond the scope of the Directive, the whole set of Regulations being made under the authority of ss.45, 51(1) of the Employment Act 2002.

[1066] Directive 97/81 as extended to the UK by Directive 98/23.

[1067] As defined in reg.1(2), "employee" being defined by s.45(6) of the Employment Act 2002 as in Employment Rights Act 1996 s.230(1).

[1068] See reg.2(1).

[1069] In *Department for Work and Pensions v Webley* [2004] EWCA Civ 1745, [2005] I.C.R. 577 it was confirmed that the employer's allowing a fixed-term contract to expire by effluxion of time without renewal does not in itself constitute a detriment, or less favourable treatment of a fixed-term employee than of a permanent employee, within reg.3 of the 2002 Regulations.

[1070] SI 2002/2023 reg.7.

[1071] See below, paras 40-165—40-170.

of the notice required to determine it, or the time at which notice to determine it may be given, will depend on the intention of the parties, either revealed in the express or implied terms of their contract, or to be inferred from all the surrounding circumstances. If there are express terms relevant to these issues, the problem is one of construction. Thus, an early authority held that a contract of employment "for 12 months certain", and to "continue from time to time, until three months' notice in writing be given by either party, to determine the same", could be determined at the expiration of the first year, by giving three months' previous notice.[1072] Where the agreement was "for 12 months certain, *after which time* either party should be at liberty to terminate the agreement, by giving the other a three months' notice", it was held that the engagement could be determined by either party at the end of 12 months, without giving any notice.[1073] But where a similar agreement provided that it was to hold good for 12 months, with six months' notice thereafter to terminate, it was held that notice could not be given until the 12 months had expired.[1074]

40-159   Under the provisions of Pt I of the Employment Rights Act an employer is required to give an employee, not later than two months after employment has begun, written particulars of terms of employment stating inter alia the length of notice which the employee is obliged to give and entitled to receive to determine his or her contract of employment,[1075] or stating if there is no term as to notice,[1076] and, where the employment is not intended to be permanent, stating the period for which it is expected to continue, or, if the contract is for a fixed term, stating the date when the contract expires.[1077] The employee may require a reference to an employment tribunal to have such particulars supplied,[1078] and either party may refer the question of the accuracy of particulars to an employment tribunal.[1079] The particulars given by an employer are not themselves normally contractual documents, but will provide strong presumptive evidence as to the provisions of the contract of which they purport to give details.[1080]

40-160   **Form of notice**   In the absence of express or specifically implied contractual provision dealing with the matter, there is no rule as to the form of notice; it may be oral or in writing, as long as the intention to terminate is clear.[1081] Moreover, even where a written contract of employment requires notice to terminate to be given in writing, the contract may nevertheless be terminated by word of mouth by agreement between the parties.[1082] When an employee is given oral notice terminating his or her employment, the period of notice given is counted as running from the begin-

---

[1072] *Brown v Symons* (1860) 8 C.B.(N.S.) 208; cf. *Costigan v Gray & Bovier Engines* (1925) 41 T.L.R. 372.

[1073] *Langton v Carleton* (1873) L.R. 9 Ex. 57.

[1074] *Jacks v Palmer's Shipbuilding & Iron Co* (1928) 98 L.J. K.B. 366.

[1075] Employment Rights Act 1996 s.1(4)(e). See generally above, para.40-040, and below, paras 40-163—40-164.

[1076] Employment Rights Act 1996 s.2(1).

[1077] Employment Rights Act 1996 s.1(4)(g).

[1078] Employment Rights Act 1996 s.11(1).

[1079] Employment Rights Act 1996 s.11(2).

[1080] See above, para.40-054.

[1081] cf. *Stephenson v London Joint Stock Bank Ltd* (1903) 20 T.L.R. 8. See, as to contingent or equivocal notice, *Rai v Somerfield Stores Ltd* [2004] I.C.R. 656, EAT.

[1082] *Latchford Premier Cinema Ltd v Ennion* [1931] 2 Ch. 409, 410.

ning of the day after that upon which the notice is given.[1083] However, it seems that employers will not be allowed to invoke notions of "constructive notice" where notice has not actually been received by an employee.[1084] Where, moreover, an employee is employed under a fixed-term contract, it is necessary to distinguish between notice to terminate and notification that the contract will terminate by effluxion of time.[1085]

"Permanent" employment   A provision for "permanent employment" or   **40-161**
"pensionable employment" does not normally mean for life or even until the normal age of retirement: apart from a special condition in the contract, such employment can be terminated by reasonable notice.[1086] But since it is a problem of construing the particular contract, words such as "permanent" may in some circumstances mean employment for life.[1087] The mere fact that the employee becomes a member of the endowment and pension scheme for the permanent staff of the employer raises no implied term that the employment cannot be determined on reasonable notice.[1088] However, in *McClelland v Northern Ireland General Health Services Board*,[1089] it was held that a contract of employment based upon an advertisement for "permanent and pensionable" employment, and which contained express provision for termination in the event of "gross misconduct" on the part of the employee, was not impliedly terminable by the employer by reasonable notice in any other event.

Employment for an unspecified period: terminability by reasonable notice   If   **40-162**
a contract of employment makes no express or specifically implied provision for its duration or termination by notice, there is likely to be implied at common law a presumption that the contract is for an indefinite period and terminable by a reasonable notice given by either party.[1090] The older case law, generalising a custom formerly attaching to the employment of agricultural workers, revealed a presumption in such circumstances that the contract of employment was for a fixed term of a year or for a series of such terms.[1091] Although that presumption could still be found at work in later cases,[1092] it now appears to have given way entirely to the

---

[1083] *West v Kneels* [1984] I.C.R. 146.

[1084] *McMaster v Manchester Airport Plc* [1998] I.R.L.R. 112.

[1085] Compare *London Underground Ltd v Fitzgerald* [1997] I.C.R. 271.

[1086] *McClelland v Northern Ireland General Health Services Board* [1957] 1 W.L.R. 594, 601; *Walsh v Dublin HA* (1962) 98 I.L.T.R. 82.

[1087] *Salt v Power Plant Co Ltd* [1936] 3 All E.R. 322, 325. Quaere, whether this should not have been construed as employment until the normal age of retirement. cf. *Ivory v Palmer* [1975] I.C.R. 340. cf. *Duke v Reliance Systems Ltd* [1982] I.C.R. 449.

[1088] *Ward v Barclay Perkins & Co* [1939] 1 All E.R. 287.

[1089] [1957] 1 W.L.R. 594.

[1090] See Freedland, *The Contract of Employment* (1976), pp.151–153 and cases there cited. The principle was established in cases such as *Vibert v Eastern Telegraph Co* (1883) Cab. & E. 17; *Lowe v Walter* (1892) 8 T.L.R. 358, 367; *Creen v Wright* (1876) 1 C.P.D. 591; *Payzu Ltd v Hannaford* [1918] 2 K.B. 348.

[1091] *Bailey v Rimmell* (1836) 1 M. & W. 506; *Beeston v Collyer* (1827) 4 Bing. 309; *Lilley v Elwin* (1848) 11 Q.B. 742; *Turner v Robinson* (1833) 5 B. & Ad. 789; *Fawcett v Cash* (1834) 5 B. & Ad. 904; *Buckingham v Surrey & Hants Canal Co* (1882) 46 L.T. 885; *Taylor v Garnett* (1892) 8 T.L.R. 647; *Cayme v Allan Jones & Co* (1919) 35 T.L.R. 453.

[1092] *Vernon v Findley* [1938] 4 All E.R. 311; reversed on other grounds [1939] 2 All E.R. 716; *Jackson v Hayes Candy & Co* [1938] 4 All E.R. 587; *Mulholland v Bexwell Estates Co* (1950) 66 T.L.R. (Pt 2) 764.

presumption of an indefinite duration and terminability by reasonable notice.[1093] The latter presumption is itself subject to the statutory provisions concerning minimum entitlements to notice.[1094] The statutory provisions may in many cases, especially in relation to manual workers with some seniority of employment, give rise to longer periods of entitlement than the common law would presume as a matter of "reasonable notice" in the particular circumstances; the details of the two sets of rules are considered in the following paragraphs.

40-163 **The length of notice: common law** Although the contracts of employment legislation[1095] prescribes *minimum* periods of notice to terminate a contract of employment, the common law rules on the subject may, in particular cases, require a longer period of notice to terminate a contract. The general rule is that the length of notice depends on the intention of the parties, revealed in their contract, as to what constitutes reasonable notice.[1096] All the circumstances, such as the type of employment, local, trade[1097] or professional[1098] customs on the topic, the intervals at which remuneration is paid, or the period in relation to which the remuneration is stated (e.g. "£450 a year"),[1099] have been regarded as relevant in fixing what amounts to reasonable notice in an individual case. A number of the many older reported decisions on this question are summarised in the footnotes below, but they do not lay down any rule of law and are merely guides to what may in the past have been held to be reasonable in different circumstances. They are summarised under the headings of clerical workers,[1100] managers and directors,[1101] editors and journal-

---

[1093] *De Stempel v Dunkels* [1938] 1 All E.R. 238; *Fisher v WB Dick & Co Ltd* [1938] 4 All E.R. 467; *Adams v Union Cinemas Ltd* [1939] 3 All E.R. 136; *James v Thomas H Kent & Co Ltd* [1951] 1 K.B. 551; *Richardson v Koefod* [1969] 1 W.L.R. 1812.

[1094] See below, para.40-164.

[1095] See below, para.40-164.

[1096] A custom cannot prevail over the express terms of the contract relating to notice or the length of notice required: *Evans v Roe* (1872) L.R. 7 C.P. 138; *Baxter v Nurse* (1844) 6 Man. & G. 935.

[1097] *Foxall v International Land Credit Co* (1867) 16 L.T. 637. Domestic service used to be the subject of a particularly well established custom for a month's notice on either side—see, for the details, *Moult v Halliday* [1898] 1 Q.B. 125; *George v Davies* [1911] 2 K.B. 445.

[1098] A producer or owner of a play has been held to be entitled to terminate the run of the play by giving a fortnight's notice according to the custom of the theatrical profession (*Gubertini v Waller* [1947] 1 All E.R. 746). Musicians not employed for a fixed term have been held to be, by custom, entitled to a fortnight's notice: *Davson v France* (1959) 109 L.J. 526.

[1099] *Cayme v Allan Jones & Co* (1919) 35 T.L.R. 453.

[1100] The length of notice for a clerk has been from one month for a clerk payable fortnightly (*Vibert v Eastern Telegraph Co* (1883) 1 Cab. & E. 17) to three months for those in a superior position (*Fairman v Oakford* (1860) 5 Hurl. & N. 635, 636; *Foxall v International Land Credit Co* (1867) 16 L.T. 637); a person called a general manager (though in fact only a superior clerk) was entitled to three months' notice (*Mulholland v Bexwell Estates Co* (1950) 66 T.L.R. (Pt 2) 764; followed in *SW Strange Ltd v Mann* [1965] 1 W.L.R. 629, 642); clerk to merchant, six weeks held insufficient (*De Stempel v Dunkels* [1938] 1 All E.R. 238). "Month" in this context means a calendar month: *P Phipps & Co (Northampton & Towcester Breweries) Ltd v Rogers* [1925] 1 K.B. 14, 26, 27.

[1101] Marine superintendent of shipping company, 12 months (*Kaukul v Anglo-Soviet Shipping Co Ltd* (1931) 41 Ll.L. Rep. 90); manager of life insurance department of an insurance company, one month held insufficient (*Jupiter General Insurance Co v Shroff* [1937] 3 All E.R. 67); controller of cinemas, six months (*Adams v Union Cinemas Ltd* [1939] 3 All E.R. 136); production manager at a factory one week insufficient (*Orman v Saville Sportswear Ltd* [1960] 1 W.L.R. 1055); a director under an implied general contract of employment was entitled to three months' notice (*James v Thomas H Kent & Co* [1951] 1 K.B. 551); a director and company secretary of a furniture firm, entitled to three months (*HW Smith (Cabinets) Ltd v Brindle* [1973] I.C.R. 12, 21).

ists,[1102] commercial travellers and salespersons,[1103] superior employees in manual occupations[1104] and in non-manual occupations.[1105] At common law,[1106] a period as short as one week might be regarded as reasonable notice for subordinate employees.[1107] The notice need not, in the absence of express provision, be given on a pay day, nor need it expire at the end of any period for which salary or wages are calculated,[1108] but a term of the contract or a custom may require the notice to expire at the end of a particular period of employment.[1109]

Statutory minimum periods of notice   The contracts of employment legisla-   **40-164**
tion[1110] prescribes minimum periods of notice which must be given to terminate contracts of employment of persons who have been continuously employed[1111] for one month or more.[1112] For less than two years' continuous employment, not less than one week's notice must be given by the employer; for two years or more but less than 12 years, not less than one week's notice for each year of service; for 12 years or more, not less than 12 weeks' notice.[1113] An employee who has been continuously employed for one month or more must give not less than one week's notice to terminate his contract of employment.[1114] Contractual provisions for shorter notice take effect subject to the foregoing provisions, but either party may

---

[1102] Newspaper editor, 12 months (*Grundy v Sun Printing Association* (1916) 33 T.L.R. 77; *Brennan v Gilbert-Smith* (1892) 8 T.L.R. 284—a case where a custom appears to have been established), although six months has been found to be reasonable (*Fox-Bourne v Vernon & Co Ltd* (1894) 10 T.L.R. 647) and was apparently treated as an established custom for editors in *McCabe v Pathe, etc. Ltd* (1919) 35 T.L.R. 313, where it was held that the editor of a film newsreel was entitled only to one month's notice; sub-editor of newspaper, six months, evidence of custom (*Chamberlain v Bennett* (1892) 8 T.L.R. 234); foreign correspondent to *The Times*, six months (*Lowe v Walter* (1892) 8 T.L.R. 358); a journalist and photographer, six months (*Bauman v Hulton Press Ltd* [1952] 2 All E.R. 1121); regular contributors to newspaper, one month (*Re Illustrated Newspaper Corp* (1900) 16 T.L.R. 157); advertising agent for a newspaper, one month (*Hiscox v Batchellor* (1867) 15 L.T. 543).

[1103] Commercial traveller, three months (*Metzner v Bolton* (1854) 9 Exch. 518; *Grundon v Master & Co* (1885) 1 T.L.R. 205); one month (*Sellers v London Counties Newspapers* [1951] 1 K.B. 784); one month, pursuant to a custom of the trade (*Parker v Ibbetson* (1858) 4 C.B.(N.S.) 347); salesman, three months (*Fisher v WB Dick & Co Ltd* [1938] 4 All E.R. 467); cf. a commercial agent (analogous to an employee), three months (*Martin-Baker Aircraft Co Ltd v Canadian Flight Equipment Ltd* [1955] 2 Q.B. 556, 581, 583).

[1104] Head gardener, one month (*Nowlan v Ablett* (1835) 2 C.M. & R. 54); farm bailiff, one month (*Johnson v Blenkensopp* (1841) 5 Jur. 870).

[1105] Governess, schoolmistress, three months (*Todd v Kerrich* (1852) 8 Exch. 151); private tutor, three months (*Wilson v Ucelli* (1929) 45 T.L.R. 395); chief officer of a passenger steamer, 12 months (*Savage v British India Steam Navigation Co* (1930) 46 T.L.R. 294); claims assessor in insurance office, 10 weeks (*Constable v Stuartson* (1932) 44 Ll.L. Rep. 91); employed chartered engineer, at least six months, possibly 12 (*Hill v CA Parsons & Co Ltd* [1972] 1 Ch. 305).

[1106] See below, para.40-164 for statutory provisions.

[1107] e.g. for a milk roundsman: *Evans v Ware* [1892] 3 Ch. 502. See also *Evans v Roe* (1872) L.R. 7 C.P. 138 (foreman paid a weekly wage of £2).

[1108] cf. *Ryan v Jenkinson* (1855) 25 L.J. Q.B. 11; *Lowe v Walter* (1892) 8 T.L.R. 358.

[1109] *Metzner v Bolton* (1854) 9 Exch. 518.

[1110] As originally enacted in the Contracts of Employment Act 1963 and later amended and consolidated into in the Employment Rights Act 1996 Pt IX.

[1111] Defined in the Act: see below, paras 40-165—40-169.

[1112] Employment Rights Act 1996 s.86. Various categories of employment are exempted from the application of these provisions of the Act: the master, skipper or seamen on certain ships and fishing boats (s.199(1) Employment Rights Act 1996).

[1113] Employment Rights Act 1996 s.86(1).

[1114] Employment Rights Act 1996 s.86(2). On the effect of notice to strike, see above, para.40-076.

still waive his right to notice, or accept a payment in lieu of notice.[1115] The foregoing provisions apply to a contract for a term certain of one month or less, provided the period of continuous employment has been three months or more.[1116] In general, these provisions do not affect any right of either party to treat the contract as terminable without notice by reason of such conduct by the other party as would have enabled him so to treat it before the passing of the legislation.[1117] If an employer fails to give the required notice,[1118] the rights conferred by the legislation[1119] on the employee during the minimum period of notice applicable to the employee shall be taken into account in assessing the employer's liability for breach of contract.[1120]

40-165 **"Continuous employment"** The legislation[1121] contains detailed rules for ascertaining the length of an employee's period of employment and whether it has been "continuous".[1122] The main provisions are: years are to be computed as aggregated periods making up twelve months[1123]; a week means a week ending with Saturday[1124]; periods of absence from employment will still count as periods of continuous employment, even where there is no contract of employment in force during the absence, if they come within the following descriptions:

(a) when the employee is incapable of work in consequence of sickness or injury for up to 26 weeks[1125];

(b) when the employee is absent on account of a temporary cessation of work[1126]; or

---

[1115] Employment Rights Act 1996 s.86(3). See *Secretary of State for Employment v Rooney* [1977] I.C.R. 440.

[1116] Employment Rights Act 1996 s.86(4).

[1117] Employment Rights Act 1996 s.86(6). This subsection preserves the employer's power to dismiss for misconduct, incompetence, etc.: see below, paras 40-184 et seq.

[1118] Employment Rights Act 1996 s.86.

[1119] Employment Rights Act 1996 ss.87–91(4) (see below, para.40-184).

[1120] Employment Rights Act 1996 s.91(5). Held in *Secretary of State for Employment v Wilson* [1977] I.R.L.R. 483, [1978] I.C.R. 200; and in *Westwood v Secretary of State for Employment* [1985] A.C. 20, to mean that the rights conferred by the legislation took effect as contractual rights and so were subject to common law rules of mitigation; see below, paras 40-201—40-202.

[1121] Employment Rights Act 1996 ss.210–219. The legislation is now to be read subject to the Employment Protection (Continuity of Employment) Regulations 1996 (SI 1996/3417), in force from January 13, 1997, which provide for the preservation of continuity of employment in certain special circumstances relating to the remedy of reinstatement or re-engagement of the employee.

[1122] This term, and "continuously", is used in s.86 of Employment Rights Act 1996.

[1123] Employment Rights Act 1996 s.210(3).

[1124] Employment Rights Act 1996 s.235(1).

[1125] Employment Rights Act 1996 s.212(3)(a).

[1126] Employment Rights Act 1996 s.212(3)(b), see *Fitzgerald v Hall, Russell & Co Ltd* [1970] A.C. 984 (*held*, that the reference is to work for the employee, not to the employer's work); *Hunter v Smith's Dock Co Ltd* [1968] 1 W.L.R. 1865; *Thompson v Bristol Channel Ship Repairers Ltd* [1970] 1 Lloyd's Rep. 105; *Clarke Chapman-John Thompson Ltd v Walters* [1972] 1 W.L.R. 378; *Puttick v John Wright & Sons (Blackwall) Ltd* [1972] I.C.R. 457; *McGarry v Earls Court Stand Fitting Co Ltd* [1973] I.C.R. 100; *Rashid v Inner London Education Authority* [1977] I.C.R. 157; and *Hanson v Fashion Industries* [1981] I.C.R. 35. *Flack v Kodak Ltd* [1986] I.C.R. 775; *Ford v Warwickshire CC* [1983] I.C.R. 273 (a series of consecutive fixed-term contracts, each for an academic year, with a summer break between each contract). Contrast, however *Surrey CC v Lewis* [1987] I.C.R. 982 (concurrent fixed-term contracts of varying length). Compare *Cornwall CC v Prater* [2006] EWCA Civ 102, [2006] I.C.R. 731, where the Court of Appeal displayed a greater willingness than had previously been shown to regard a sequence of casual work contracts as being linked up, by periods

(c) when the employee is absent under an arrangement or custom whereby the employment continues.[1127]

The treatment of part-time employment Formerly, the provisions here referred **40-166** to, by defining "continuous employment" so as to exclude part-time employment below the stated thresholds of weekly hours, have excluded part-time employment as thus defined from the scope of various statutory employment protection rights, most significantly rights to protection against unfair dismissal and to redundancy payments. It was clear from the decision of the House of Lords in *R. v Secretary of State for Employment Ex parte Equal Opportunities Commission*[1128] that some or all of these exclusionary provisions in relation to part-time employment violated EU requirements of equal pay and treatment as between men and women (that is to say, they unlawfully discriminated against women). The exclusionary provisions were, accordingly, removed by the Employment Protection (Part-time Employees) Regulations 1995.[1129]

The treatment of periods of strike or lockout Any week in which the employee **40-167** takes part in a strike will not count towards the period of continuous employment.[1130] On the other hand, continuity of employment is preserved in relation to weeks in which the employee takes part in a strike or is absent from work because of a lockout by the employer, provided those weeks occurred after 1963.[1131] This provision has been held to apply even where the employee was dismissed during the strike and re-engaged after the strike had ended.[1132]

Other provisions concerning continuity The legislation also contains provi- **40-168** sions preserving the continuity of employment in the event of reinstatement after military service[1133] and causing previous employments to count towards the total period of employment where the change from one employment to the next was:

(a) a transfer between associated employers[1134]; or

(b) consequent upon the transfer of the trade, business or undertaking in which the employee was employed[1135]; or

---

of "temporary cessation of work" into a period of "continuous employment". See also para.40-023, and compare *Welton v Deluxe Retail Ltd* [2013] I.R.L.R. 166, EAT.

[1127] Employment Rights Act 1996 s.212(3)(c); see *Wishart v National Coal Board* [1974] I.C.R. 460; and *Corton House v Skipper* [1981] I.C.R. 307. Compare now also *Welton v Deluxe Retail Ltd* [2013] I.R.L.R. 166, EAT, where it was held that the "arrangement" cannot be a retroactive one.

[1128] [1995] 1 A.C. 1.

[1129] SI 1995/31 with effect from February 6, 1995.

[1130] Employment Rights Act 1996 s.216(1).

[1131] Employment Rights Act 1996 s.216(2)–(3).

[1132] *Bloomfield v Springfield Hosiery Finishing Co Ltd* [1972] I.C.R. 91.

[1133] Employment Rights Act 1996 s.217.

[1134] Employment Rights Act 1996 s.218(6). See *Zarb v British and Brazilian Produce Co (Sales) Ltd* [1978] I.R.L.R. 78; *Hillingdon AHA v Kaunders* [1979] I.C.R. 472; and *Merton LBC v Gardiner* [1981] I.C.R. 186, CA. Compare also *Da Silva v Composite Mouldings & Design Ltd* [2009] I.C.R. 416.

[1135] Employment Rights Act 1996 s.218(2). See *Dallow Industrial Properties Ltd v Else* [1967] 2 Q.B. 449; *Kenmir Ltd v Frizzell* [1968] 1 W.L.R. 329; *Woodhouse v Peter Brotherhood Ltd* [1972] 2 Q.B. 520; *Secretary of State for Employment v Rooney* [1977] I.C.R. 440; *Dhami v Top Spot Night Club Ltd* [1977] I.R.L.R. 231; *Young v Daniel Thwaites & Co Ltd* [1977] I.C.R. 877; *Pambakian v Brentford Nylons Ltd* [1978] I.C.R. 665; *Rastill v Automatic Refreshment Services Ltd* [1978] I.C.R.

(c) a transfer from an employer to his or her personal representatives upon his or her death[1136]; or

(d) a consequence of a change in the partners, personal representatives or trustees who employed the employee.[1137]

The legislation does not require that the period of "continuous employment" should be under a single contract: it may be "continuous" under a whole succession of new contracts between the same parties.[1138] It has been held that appointment of a receiver out of court does not normally determine current contracts of employment,[1139] but that if the receiver does make a new contract with the employee, the receiver does so as agent of the company so that continuity of employment is not broken.[1140]

40-169 **The right to guaranteed remuneration during a statutory period of notice** Not only does the contract of employment legislation provide for minimum periods of notice, but it also provides for guaranteed minimum remuneration during such periods. The 1996 Act[1141] prescribes the rights of employees for the period of notice required by the Act[1142]; these rights cannot be excluded or limited by the contract.[1143] If during "the normal working hours"[1144] of the period of notice the employee is ready and willing to work but no work is provided, or the employee is incapable of work because of sickness or injury, or absent from work in accordance with the terms of his or her employment relating to holidays, the employer must pay him or her for the normal working hours he or she has lost at an average hourly rate of remuneration based upon the statutory calculation of a week's pay.[1145] Where there are no "normal working hours" but the employee is ready and willing to work or incapable of work through sickness or injury, or absent on holiday, the employer must, for each week of the period of notice, pay the employee a statutory week's pay.[1146] The liability of the employer under these provisions does not arise if the notice to be given by the employer to terminate the contract exceeds,

---

289. In *Lord Advocate v de Rosa* [1974] 1 W.L.R. 946, it was held that the provision of the 1963 Contracts of Employment Act corresponding to the present s.218(2) was not to be treated as qualified, in a redundancy payments case, by s.3(2) or s.13(2) of the Redundancy Payments Act 1965 s.136(1)–(3) of the 1996 Act. In *Evenden v Guildford City Association Football Club Ltd* [1975] I.C.R. 367, it was held that the limits of para.17(2) could be transcended, in a redundancy payments case, by reference to s.9(2)(a) of the Redundancy Payments Act 1965 (s.210(5) of the 1996 Act) (presumption of continuity); but this was overruled in *Secretary of State for Employment v Globe Elastic Thread Ltd* [1979] I.C.R. 706. The provision of s.218(2) should be considered in conjunction with those of the Transfer of Undertakings (Protection of Employment) Regulations 2006—see below, para.40-180.

[1136] Employment Rights Act 1996 s.218(4). See *Rowley Holmes & Co v Barber* [1977] 1 W.L.R. 371.
[1137] Employment Rights Act 1996 s.218(5). See *Harold Fielding Ltd v Mansi* [1974] I.C.R. 347; and *Allen & Son v Coventry* [1980] I.C.R. 9; and see below, para.40-181.
[1138] *Re Mack Trucks (Britain) Ltd* [1967] 1 W.L.R. 780, 787.
[1139] See below, para.40-183.
[1140] *Re Mack Trucks (Britain) Ltd*, above; cf. *Deaway Trading Ltd v Calverley* [1973] I.C.R. 546.
[1141] Employment Rights Act 1996 ss.87–91.
[1142] Employment Rights Act 1996 s.86(1); see above, para.40-164.
[1143] Employment Rights Act 1996 s.203.
[1144] As defined by s.234 of Employment Rights Act 1996. See below, para.40-256.
[1145] Employment Rights Act 1996 s.88(1). The "week's pay" is calculated by reference to ss.220–229 of Employment Rights Act 1996. See below, para.40-255.
[1146] Employment Rights Act 1996 s.89(1)–(4), the week's pay being calculated as above. See below, para.40-255.

hy one week or more, the minimum period of notice required by the Act.[1147] Payments such as sick pay or holiday pay count towards the employer's liability under the Act.[1148] Moreover, if the employer ordinarily reduces the amount of sick pay in respect of short-term incapacity benefit or industrial injury benefit claimable by the employee, the employer may continue to do so during a statutory period of notice.[1149] If the employee gives notice, the employer's liability does not arise unless and until the employee leaves the service of the employer in pursuance of the notice.[1150] No payment need be made for the employee's absence from work with the leave of the employer granted at the request of the employee[1151]; nor is any payment due if the employee gives notice and then, on or before termination of the contract, takes part in a strike of employees of the employer.[1152] If the employer breaks the contract during the period of notice, payments made thereafter under the Act go towards mitigating damages recoverable by the employee for loss of earnings[1153]; if the employee breaks the contract during the period of notice, and the employer rightfully treats the breach as terminating the contract, the employer need pay nothing for the remaining period of the notice.[1154] It was held in *Secretary of State for Employment v Wilson*[1155] and confirmed in *Westwood v Secretary of State for Employment*[1156] that the rights conferred by those provisions take effect via the contract of employment so that the common law rules as to mitigation of loss[1157] apply when quantifying the loss attributable to denial of these rights.

(b) Termination by Payment in Lieu of Notice

The contractual status of payments in lieu of notice Contracts of employ- **40-170** ment are frequently in practice terminated by payment in lieu of notice. There is some doubt as to the contractual status of a payment in lieu of notice.[1158] One view is that in the absence of express provision to the contrary in the original contract of employment, the payment is normally to be regarded as liquidated damages for a breach of contract consisting in the refusal to allow the employee to work out his notice.[1159] Some payments in lieu of notice can be viewed as an ordinary giving of notice accompanied by a waiver of services by the employer which is accepted by the employee.[1160] Another view might be that a right to terminate by payment in lieu of notice can be viewed as a normally implied corollary of a contractual right on the part of an employer to terminate by notice, unless it is clear that the employee

---

[1147] Employment Rights Act 1996 s.87(4). The better view seems to be that this includes the case where the implied obligation to give reasonable notice see above, paras 40-162—40-163, applies to produce a period exceeding the applicable statutory minimum period by one week or more.
[1148] Employment Rights Act 1996 ss.88(2), 89(4).
[1149] Employment Rights Act 1996 s.90.
[1150] Employment Rights Act 1996 ss.88(3), 89(5).
[1151] Employment Rights Act 1996 s.91(1).
[1152] Employment Rights Act 1996 s.91(2).
[1153] Employment Rights Act 1996 s.91(3).
[1154] Employment Rights Act 1996 s.91(4).
[1155] [1977] I.R.L.R. 483.
[1156] [1985] A.C. 20.
[1157] See below, paras 40-201—40-202.
[1158] See Freedland, *The Personal Employment Contract* (2003), pp.305 et seq.
[1159] *Dixon v Stenor Ltd* [1973] I.C.R. 157, 158G.
[1160] *Lees v Arthur Greaves Ltd* [1974] I.C.R. 501.

has some special interest in being allowed to work out his notice.[1161] In the case of *Delaney v Staples*,[1162] Lord Browne-Wilkinson distinguished four principal categories of payment in lieu of notice, while making it clear that this was not necessarily an exhaustive list.[1163] The categories, and the contractual status of each, were, in effect:

(1) The employer gives proper notice of termination to the employee, tells the employee that he or she need not work until the termination date and gives him or her the wages attributable to the notice period in a lump sum. In this case, commonly called "garden leave", there is no breach of contract by the employer; the employment continues until the expiry of the notice: the lump sum payment is simply advance payment of wages.

(2) The contract of employment provides expressly that the employment may be terminated either by notice or, on payment of a sum in lieu of notice, summarily. In this case, summary dismissal accompanied by payment in lieu of notice is not in breach of contract.

(3) At the end of the employment, the employer and the employee agree that the employment is to terminate forthwith on payment of a sum in lieu of notice. Again, the employer is not in breach of contract.

(4) The employer summarily dismisses the employee without the agreement of the employee and tenders a payment in lieu of notice. In this case, which is the most common one, the employer is in breach of contract, and the payment in lieu of notice is in the nature of liquidated damages.

Subsequent case law suggests that the contractual status of payments in lieu of notice will now be determined by applying these four categories to the particular facts in question.[1164] Difficult issues may nevertheless still arise. The Supreme Court's decision in *Société Générale (London Branch) v Geys*[1165] raised complex issues as to whether the employer had correctly and validly exercised a contractual right to terminate the contract of employment by payment in lieu of notice.[1166] Lady Hale, agreeing with the majority of the Supreme Court, opined that it is an "obviously necessary incident of the employment relationship" that the other party is notified in clear and unambiguous terms that the right to bring the contract to an end is being exercised, and how and when it is intended to operate.[1167] In *Cerberus Software Ltd v Rowley*[1168] it was held that an employee, who had been wrongfully summarily dismissed, but the terms of whose contract were such that the employer could lawfully have terminated by six months' notice or payment in lieu of notice, could claim the payment in lieu only subject to the duty to mitigate his loss. In

---

[1161] cf. *White v Riley* [1921] 1 Ch. 1, 6.

[1162] [1992] I.C.R. 483.

[1163] [1992] I.C.R. 483 at 488–9.

[1164] cf. *Abrahams v Performing Right Society Ltd* [1995] I.C.R. 1028; *Gregory v Wallace* [1998] I.R.L.R. 387. Compare also *Locke v Candy & Candy Ltd* [2010] EWCA Civ 1350, [2011] I.R.L.R. 163, where it was held that the express contractual entitlement to payment in lieu of notice should be construed so as to include compensation equivalent to the annual bonus which would have been payable had the full period of notice been served.

[1165] [2012] UKSC 63, [2013] 1 A.C. 523.

[1166] See also above, para.24-001.

[1167] [2012] UKSC 63, at [57].

[1168] [2001] I.R.L.R. 160, CA.

contrast to that is *HQ Service Children's Education (MOD) v Davitt*[1169] where payment in lieu was made but the contract was deemed to have been terminated by notice which the employee had not been required to work out. As to payments in lieu of notice and "garden leave", comparison may be made with the decision in *Symbian Ltd v Christiansen*,[1170] which deals with the application of the restraint of trade doctrine to contractual arrangements for garden leave.

The statutory and contractual effects of payment in lieu of notice   The view   **40-171**
was at one stage taken[1171] that the provision now contained in s.86(3) of the Employment Rights Act 1996 treats payment in lieu of notice as a derogation from the statutory obligation to give certain minimum periods of notice unless the employee accepts the payment when it is made, though it has more recently been held that if the contract of employment provides for payment in lieu of notice, or if the parties agree upon a payment in lieu of notice no shorter than the period to which the employee is entitled by contract or statute, the last part of s.86(3) applies, and a payment in lieu of notice can properly terminate the contract of employment.[1172] However, in *Hardy v Polk Ltd*[1173] Burton P. held, in effect, that s.86 did not create an entitlement to payment in lieu of notice, or a claim in debt for failure to give the statutory minimum period of notice or payment in lieu thereof. Whether a payment in lieu of notice is regarded as a contractual right of the employer or as liquidated damages (as to which, reference may be made to the previous paragraph), the question of its quantum arises, and early authority suggests that it might not include any allowance for benefits conferred gratuitously, or in kind, during employment.[1174] The question also arises of the time at which the termination of the contract takes effect. The view of such payments as liquidated damages for breach seems to require the view that termination is immediate upon the ending of actual employment.[1175] The view of such arrangements as involving a waiver of the right to the services of the employee may result in an extension of the date of termination to the date at which the notice in lieu of which payment is made would have expired.[1176] Where an arrangement for payment in lieu of notice does result in a continuation of the contract for the duration of the notice period, the question whether the employee forfeits the right to the payment by taking other work depends upon whether that amounts on the facts to a repudiatory breach on the employee's part.[1177]

(c)   Termination by Agreement or by Expiry of Fixed Period

Termination by prior agreement or expiry of fixed period: fixed-term contracts   **40-172**
and limited-term contracts   When we speak of the termination of contracts of employment by agreement, we normally intend to refer to an agreement made

---

[1169] [1999] I.C.R. 978, EAT.

[1170] [2000] I.R.L.R. 879, CA.

[1171] *Chapman, Blair & Atchinson v Executors of WG Leadley* (1966) 1 T.R. 84 (Sir Diarmaid Conroy Q.C.) (commenting on the corresponding provision in the Contracts of Employment Act 1963).

[1172] *Rex Stewart Jeffries Parker Ginsberg Ltd v Parker* [1988] I.R.L.R. 483, 486.

[1173] [2004] I.R.L.R. 420, EAT.

[1174] cf. *Gordon v Potter* [1859] 1 F.& F. 644.

[1175] *Dixon v Stenor* [1973] I.C.R. 157.

[1176] *Lees v Arthur Greaves* [1974] I.C.R. 501; but contrast *Dedman v British Building Appliances Ltd* [1974] I.C.R. 53.

[1177] *Hutchings v Coinseed Ltd* [1998] I.R.L.R. 190.

subsequently to the original formation of the contract of employment in question. We might, however, properly also include within this category the termination of the contract of employment by prior agreement, which is to say by an agreement made when the contract of employment itself is made and as part of that contract. A contract of employment containing such an agreement will normally be referred to as a "fixed-term contract", though the duration of a contract of employment may be limited other than by reference to a period of time (or to a period of notice), for example by reference to the completion of a task,[1178] in which case it may not be appropriate to refer to it as a "fixed-term contract". It should also be noted that the termination of a fixed term contract on completion of the fixed term may be referred to as a termination "by effluxion of time" or "by expiry of the fixed term" rather than as termination by agreement. Moreover, it should also be noted that for the purposes of statutory rights associated with the termination of employment, such as the rights to statutory redundancy payment or not to be unfairly dismissed, the expiry of a fixed-term contract without renewal is treated as a *dismissal*, and is considered under that heading later in this chapter.[1179] Finally, and most important, it should be noted that the Fixed-term Employees Regulations 2002[1180] introduced the new terminology of "limited-term contracts" and substituted that new terminology for the previously used terminology of "contract for a fixed term" in relation to many statutory employment rights.[1181] A statutory definition is provided for the "limited-term contract"[1182] which is very similar to the definition of the previously used terminology of the "contract for a fixed term", and coincides with the conception of the fixed-term contract articulated in the present paragraph: that is to say, it includes contracts limited either by the expiry of a fixed period of time, or by the completion of a defined task, or by the occurrence of another previously specified limiting event. At the same time, the terminology of "fixed-term" contracts is used in the Fixed-term Employees Regulations themselves, and is defined[1183] in almost the identical way, except that the limiting event of the attainment of normal retirement age is excluded. For the avoidance of the confusion which might otherwise result, the terminology of the "fixed-term contract" is retained throughout this chapter except where the particular context specially requires otherwise.

40-173 **The conversion of successive fixed-term contracts into the contracts of employment of "a permanent employee"** The operation and effect of fixed-term contracts of employment has been extensively modified by the Fixed-term Employees Regulations 2002,[1184] which were made under the authority of s.45 of the Employment Act 2002, mainly with the purpose of implementing Council Directive 99/70 on fixed-term work,[1185] and came into force on October 1, 2002. The Regulations make two main sets of new provisions, one conferring a right of no less favourable treatment upon fixed-term employees as compared with permanent employees, and the other converting certain successive fixed-term contracts of

---

[1178] Such a contract may more readily be classified as a contract for services; cf. above, para.40-004.

[1179] See above, para.40-125 (unfair dismissal), and below, 40-250 (redundancy payments).

[1180] SI 2002/2034.

[1181] SI 2002/2034 reg.11 and Sch.2, amending Employment Rights Act 1996 ss.29, 65, 86, 92, 105, 108, 109, 136, 145, 199, 203, 235.

[1182] SI 2002/2034 reg.11 and Sch.2 Pt 1 para.3, inserting new Employment Rights Act 1996 s.235(2A)–(2B).

[1183] SI 2002/2034 reg.1(2).

[1184] SI 2002/2034.

[1185] Directive 97/81 as extended to the UK by Directive 98/23.

employment into the contracts of employment of permanent employees. The right of no less favourable treatment was considered in an earlier section of this chapter[1186]; the conversion of successive fixed-term contracts into the contracts of employment of "a permanent employee" is considered in this paragraph. That conversion is effected by and according to reg.8. It occurs where an employee is employed under a fixed-term contract[1187] which follows successively upon a previous fixed-term contract or has itself previously been renewed, and where the employee has been continuously employed for four years under a renewed fixed-term contract or successive fixed-term contracts; the conversion takes effect either when such a contract is entered into or renewed, or when the employee has been continuously employed for four years, whichever is the later.[1188] There is some need for clarification of what it means to convert a fixed-term contract into the contract of employment of "a permanent employee". It would seem to mean a conversion into a contract of employment which is of indefinite duration, terminable upon reasonable notice[1189] and subject to the statutory minimum periods of notice.[1190] Comparison should be made with the case law, considered in an earlier paragraph,[1191] concerning the construction of provisions for "permanent employment" in contracts of employment.

Termination by subsequent agreement   In accordance with general contractual **40-174** principles, it is open to an employer and employee at any time during the currency of a contract of employment to terminate the contract by agreement.[1192] The agreement will be effective by virtue of the mutual release by the parties of their obligations under the contract of employment.[1193] The agreement may be subject to terms,

---

[1186] See above, para.40-156.

[1187] As defined in reg.1(2).

[1188] Under reg.8(4), any period of continuous employment falling before July 10, 2002 is to be disregarded. It should be noted that, by virtue of reg.8(2)(b), the conversion effect occurs only if the employment of the employee under a fixed-term contract was not justified on objective grounds; as to the assessment of objective justification, compare *Duncombe v Department for Education and Skills* [2011] UKSC 14. Compare now also *Hudson v Department for Work and Pensions* [2012] EWCA Civ 1416, [2013] 1 All E.R. 1370 where the Court of Appeal considers the working of reg.8 and construes the scope of reg.18 as excepting employees currently employed on fixed-term contracts made pursuant to a Government training scheme, but does not exclude such employment under past contracts.

[1189] See above, para.40-161.

[1190] See above, para.40-163.

[1191] See above, para.40-160.

[1192] See Vol.I, paras 22-001 et seq.

[1193] Hence an "accord and satisfaction"—see *Lees v Arthur Greaves Ltd* [1974] I.C.R. 501, 506D. In *Lambert v Croydon College* [1999] I.C.R. 409, the Employment Appeal Tribunal held that a compromise agreement for early retirement on grounds of ill-health could validly fix the "effective date of termination of employment" for statutory purposes, see below, paras 40-219—40-220, even though it fixed it at a date earlier than that on which the agreement was made. In *Bank of Credit and Commerce International SA (In Liquidation) v Ali* [2001] I.C.R. 337, it was held in the House of Lords that the standard settlement agreement which ACAS proposes to parties to employment tribunal proceedings, known as the COT3 agreement, did not extend to the release of future liability from potential claims which could not have been foreseen or in the contemplation of the parties when the agreement was made—such as, in this case, the claim for "stigma damages" which had subsequently been successfully made against the BCCI by some of its former employees, see below, para.40-204. Compare *Solectron Scotland Ltd v Roper* [2004] I.R.L.R. 4, EAT as to the validity of a compromise agreement which could be regarded as limiting the application of the TUPE Regulations.

provided these do not, for instance, constitute an unlawful restraint of trade.[1194] The agreement will be effective to override formal or substantive restrictions placed on the termination of the contract by the original contract itself.[1195] Because a termination by agreement may not be a "dismissal" for statutory purposes, the industrial (now, employment) tribunals and courts have been vigilant in distinguishing between genuinely bilateral termination and ostensible agreements generated solely by the employer.[1196] It used to be thought that there might be a termination by agreement rather than a dismissal where the parties agree in advance that the employee's failure to return to work on a due date will operate to determine the contract,[1197] unless there was simply a unilateral stipulation by the employer to that effect.[1198] However, the Court of Appeal has held that the fact that there is some measure of agreement on the part of the employee to the termination of a contract of employment does not of itself prevent an employee from counting as dismissed for the purposes of the Act of 1978 (now the 1996 Act); and that a provision for automatic termination of a contract of employment for failure to report for work on one specific future date was void by virtue of s.140(1) of that Act, now s.203 of the 1996 Act, as purporting to limit the operation of the statutory right not to be unfairly dismissed, by trying to convert that right into a merely conditional one.[1199] Nevertheless, there may be held in appropriate circumstances to be a "consensual resignation" rather than a dismissal, for example under a genuinely consensual early retirement scheme.[1200] A termination of a contract of employment by agreement occurs also where there is an agreed change in the terms and conditions of employment, for instance by way of promotion, which is sufficiently fundamental to constitute the rescission of the original contract and its replacement by a new contract on different terms.[1201]

40-175 **Retirement** The notion of "retirement" from employment is one which is far from precise either in practical or in legal terms. In practical terms its normal or approximate meaning is the ending of the employment of a worker by reason of his or her having reached the end of his or her normal working life or career. In legal terms this may take various forms, such as termination of the contract of employment by the employing enterprise, perhaps by notice to terminate, or termination by expiry of a fixed-term contract of employment, or it might be regarded as

---

[1194] See Vol.I, paras 16-135 et seq. and cf. *Wyatt v Kreglinger & Fernau* [1933] 1 K.B. 793. In *Fish v Dresdner Kleinwort Ltd* [2009] EWCA Civ 2246, [2009] I.R.L.R. 1035 it was held that the express provisions of termination agreements for the payment of bonus and severance pay could not be cut down by reference to fiduciary obligations or obligations of mutual trust and confidence owed by the employees, who had been senior managers, to the employer, although those payments had been reduced for remaining senior managers by reason of the impact of the banking crisis of 2008.

[1195] e.g. *Latchford Premier Cinema Ltd v Ennion & Paterson* [1931] 2 Ch. 409, see above, para.40-160.

[1196] *East Sussex CC v Walker* (1972) 7 I.T.R. 280; and, in the context of transfer to different work or work on different terms, *Marriott v Oxford & District Co-operative Society Ltd (No.2)* [1970] 1 Q.B. 186; *Sheet Metal Components Ltd v Plumridge* [1974] I.C.R. 373. A further example of this vigilance is provided by the decision of the Court of Appeal in *Hellyer Bros v Atkinson* [1994] I.R.L.R. 88.

[1197] *British Leyland Ltd v Ashraf* [1978] I.C.R. 979.

[1198] *Midland Electric Ltd v Kanji* [1980] I.R.L.R. 185.

[1199] *Igbo v Johnson Mathey Chemicals Ltd* [1985] I.C.R. 505; overruling *British Leyland Ltd v Ashraf* [1978] I.C.R. 979.

[1200] *Birch v University of Liverpool* [1985] I.C.R. 470.

[1201] See Freedland, *The Contract of Employment* (1976), pp.72–76; and cf. *Meek v Port of London Authority* [1918] 2 Ch. 96; *SW Strange Ltd v Mann* [1965] 1 W.L.R. 629; *BBC v Ioannu* [1974] I.R.L.R. 77 at para.17 (decision affirmed [1975] I.C.R. 267).

termination by agreement, whether prior or ad hoc, or it might consist of termination by the worker (the latter especially in the case of so-called "early retirement", itself a notion with further imprecisions).[1202] Without defining the notion of "retirement", the Employment Equality (Age) Regulations 2006[1203] attached very significant new legal incidents to it,[1204] some of which were immediately embodied in the unfair dismissal provisions of the Employment Rights Act 1996 and the rest of which were subsequently transposed into the Equality Act 2010. Many of those provisions, in particular those which had authorised employers to maintain a "default retirement age" of 65 or more, were repealed by the Employment Equality (Repeal of Retirement Age Provisions) 2011.[1205] The result is that if an employer requires an employee to retire from his or her employment, while no breach of the employee's contract of employment may be involved—that is to say, while the retirement may take the form of a contractually lawful termination of employment—the imposition of retirement upon the employee may nevertheless represent an unfair dismissal[1206] and/or a dismissal which amounts to unlawful age discrimination.[1207]

(d) Termination Under the Doctrine of Frustration

Frustration The doctrine of frustration applies to a contract of employment.[1208] **40-176** Death of either party and permanent illness of the employee discussed in the following paragraphs, are instances where the doctrine applies. But other events may frustrate a contract of employment: a contract between a variety artiste and a manager was held to be frustrated by the calling up of the artiste for military service, even though the parties, so far as possible, treated the contract as subsisting throughout the War.[1209] It was held in *Hare v Murphy Bros Ltd*[1210] that a contract of employment may be terminated when the employee is sentenced to a substantial term of imprisonment, and there was some suggestion in the judgments of the Court of Appeal that this could be regarded as a termination under the doctrine of frustration.[1211] In a later case, it was held that a contract of apprenticeship was frustrated when the apprentice received a custodial sentence, and that he could not negate that frustration as being induced by his own fault.[1212]

Death of either party The death of either party terminates the contract of **40-177** employment, unless the contract expressly or implicitly provides otherwise. The contract is terminated only as from the time of death so that any right of action

---

[1202] Compare Freedland, *The Personal Employment Contract* (2003), pp.400–401, 429–431.

[1203] SI 2006/1031.

[1204] See also para.40-226.

[1205] SI 2011/1069 which took full effect on October 1, 2011.

[1206] As to which see para.40-226.

[1207] As to which see para.40-247.

[1208] See Vol.I, paras 23-037 et seq. So also does the distinct doctrine of supervening legal impossibility— *Tarnesby v Kensington Chelsea & Westminster AHA* [1981] I.R.L.R. 369.

[1209] *Morgan v Manser* [1948] 1 K.B. 184.

[1210] [1974] I.C.R. 603.

[1211] [1974] I.C.R. 603 at 607E–F (per Lord Denning M.R.), 607H–608A (Stephenson L.J.), 608E–F (Lawton L.J.); not followed, however, in *Norris v Southampton City Council* [1982] I.C.R. 177. Compare now the restricted approach to frustration of the contract of employment which was taken in *Four Seasons Healthcare Ltd v Maughan* [2005] I.R.L.R. 324.

[1212] *Shepherd & Co Ltd v Jerrom* [1986] I.R.L.R. 358. See Vol.I, para.23-061.

which has accrued to either party before that time remains enforceable[1213]; but no claim lies to enforce rights which would accrue only after that time.[1214] The death of the employer normally operates to terminate the contract of employment just as the death of the employee: the personal representative of the employer is not normally obliged to continue the employment.[1215] On the death of either party, a claim lies for the salary or wages of the employee up to the date of the death which terminates the contract.[1216] Moreover, legislation now protects the position of employees in respect of their statutory rights in the event of the employer's death, and in certain circumstances securing those rights for the estate of the employee in the event of the employee's death.[1217] It is provided, furthermore, that where, upon the death of an employer, an employee takes up employment with the personal representatives, the period of employment with the deceased employer counts as part of the period of continuous employment with the personal representatives for the purposes of statutory rights depending upon length of service or requiring a qualifying period of service.[1218]

40-178 **Illness frustrating the contract** If the illness or injury is of such a nature, or if it appears likely to continue for such a period, as to defeat the purpose or object of the employment, the contract of employment will be frustrated.[1219] The effect of the expected[1220] period of the illness must depend upon the period and nature of the employment. In *Marshall v Harland & Wolff Ltd*,[1221] the test was formulated as follows:

> "Was the employee's incapacity, looked at before the purported dismissal, of such a nature, or did it appear likely to continue for such a period, that further performance of his obligations in the future would either be impossible or would be a thing radically different from that undertaken by him and accepted by the employer under the agreed terms of his employment?"

Although in that case the principle was maintained[1222] that there need be no act of the employer marking the point of time at which the frustration occurred, the current judicial approach to frustration by incapacity of the employee due to illness seems to be on the whole a cautious one which emphasises that frustration must be

---

[1213] *Stubbs v Holywell Ry* (1867) L.R. 2 Ex. 311.

[1214] *Graves v Cohen* (1930) 46 T.L.R. 121; cf. *Harvey v Tivoli (Manchester) Ltd* (1907) 23 T.L.R. 592. Contrast *Phillips v Alhambra Palace Co* [1901] 1 K.B. 59. This is merely an application of the general rule as to frustration.

[1215] *Farrow v Wilson* (1896) L.R. 4 C.P. 744. But cf. *Graves v Cohen* (1930) 46 T.L.R. 121, 123–124.

[1216] Law Reform (Frustrated Contracts) Act 1943, see Vol.I, paras 23-074 et seq., also, possibly, by the Apportionment Act 1870 (see below, para.40-197).

[1217] See ss.136(5), 206, 207 of Employment Rights Act 1996.

[1218] Employment Rights Act 1996 s.218(4); see above, para.40-168.

[1219] *Poussard v Spiers & Pond* (1876) 1 Q.B.D. 410 (opera singer engaged for three months, unable to perform on first night and duration of illness uncertain—contract frustrated); *Storey v Fulham Steel Works* (1907) 24 T.L.R. 89 (engagement for five years as manager—after two years, six months' illness—no frustration); *Warburton v Co-operative Wholesale Society* [1917] 1 K.B. 663. For the question of *payment* during absence due to sickness, see above, paras 40-084—40-086. For the relationship with the reasonable adjustment duty (disability), see now *Warner v Armfield Retail & Leisure Ltd* [2014] I.C.R. 239, EAT.

[1220] cf. the cases on the effect on an ordinary contract of a delay whose duration is uncertain; Vol.I, para.23-035.

[1221] [1972] I.C.R. 101, 105A–B.

[1222] [1972] I.C.R. 101 at 106F.

a conclusion made necessary by the circumstances of the particular employment.[1223] There is even some suggestion that frustration by illness cannot in practice arise at all in relation to contracts of employment terminable by notice as distinct from contracts of employment for a substantial fixed term not terminable by notice,[1224] though the better view seemed to regard the doctrine of frustration as restricted rather than totally excluded where the employer has the power to terminate by notice.[1225] This was confirmed in a more recent case[1226] where it was held that the contract of employment of a skilled workman was, though a periodic contract terminable by relatively short notice, nevertheless terminated by frustration without notice when it became apparent to both parties that the employee had become incapacitated by sickness from ever again performing his contract of employment. If a contract of employment is frustrated, the legal consequences upon the rights and obligations of the parties will be determined by the ordinary legal rules applicable to frustration.[1227] Early authority suggests that if the illness or injury is of a type or of a duration which does not frustrate the contract of employment, it is nevertheless a justification for the employee's failure to work while the illness or injury continues.[1228]

(e) Assignment, Winding-up and Changes in the Employing Enterprise

Transfer of employment: (1) the position at common law   A contract for   **40-179** personal service cannot be assigned by one party without the consent of the other.[1229] Thus where two companies were amalgamated under an order of the court, the employer's rights under a contract of employment could not be assigned to the new company without the consent of the employee.[1230] Similarly, it has been held that the sale by a receiver (appointed by the debenture-holders) of the company's business as a going concern may operate to terminate the contracts of employment of all the company's employees.[1231] Where the identity of the employer is changed in such circumstances that statutory continuity of employment is preserved,[1232] the new employer is not required to issue a complete new set of statutory particulars of terms of employment[1233] unless there is some change in the terms; the change in the identity of the employer can in those circumstances be notified by way of amend-

---

[1223] [1972] I.C.R. 101 at 105B–106A, 106H–107C; *Puttick v John Wright & Sons (Blackwall) Ltd* [1972] I.C.R. 457; *Hebden v Forsey & Son* [1973] I.C.R. 607.

[1224] *Harman v Flexible Lamps Ltd* [1980] I.R.L.R. 418, 419, para.7.

[1225] cf. *Egg Stores Ltd v Leibovici* [1977] I.C.R. 260, 264C–265E; *Hart v AR Marshall Ltd* [1977] I.R.L.R. 61, 62, paras 5–7. The "short-term periodic contract of employment" referred to by Phillips J. in those cases is the ordinary contract of employment of indeterminate duration impliedly terminable by notice, see above, para.40-162.

[1226] *Notcutt v Universal Equipment Co (London) Ltd* [1986] I.C.R. 414.

[1227] See Vol.I, paras 23-070 et seq.

[1228] *Boast v Firth* (1868) L.R. 4 C.P. 1.

[1229] See Vol.I, para.19-055.

[1230] *Nokes v Doncaster Amalgamated Collieries* [1940] A.C. 1014; cf. *Denham v Midland Employers Mutual Assurance Ltd* [1955] 2 Q.B. 437.

[1231] *Re Foster Clark Ltd's Indenture Trusts* [1966] 1 W.L.R. 125 sed quaere; insofar as the decision is founded on *Brace v Calder* [1895] 2 Q.B. 253, it is questionable because sale of the business does not dissolve the employing entity as dissolution of a partnership does, cf. see below, para.40-181. On the appointment of a receiver, see below, para.40-183.

[1232] See above, para.40-168.

[1233] See above, para.40-040.

ment of the existing particulars as if it were simply itself a change of terms.[1234] This should not, however, be seen as overriding the requirement of the employee's consent to the change of employer.[1235]

40-180   Transfer of employment: (2) the effect of the TUPE Regulations The position concerning transfer of employment as described in the previous paragraph was very significantly altered by the Transfer of Undertakings (Protection of Employment) Regulations 1981.[1236] More recently, the existing Transfer of Undertakings (Protection of Employment) Regulations were revised and replaced by the Transfer of Undertakings (Protection of Employment) Regulations 2006 ("the TUPE Regulations").[1237] The Regulations provide that upon a transfer of an undertaking to which the regulations apply,[1238] or upon a "service provision change"[1239]—that is to say, in essence, where services are either outsourced, brought back in house, or assigned by a client to a new contractor—the contract of employment of any person employed immediately before the transfer[1240] by the transferor in the undertaking or part transferred shall not be terminated by the transfer but, if it is a contract which would otherwise have been terminated by the transfer[1241] shall have effect after the transfer as if originally made with the transferee of the undertaking,[1242] unless the employee in questions lodges an objection to being employed by the transferee, in which case the transfer operates to terminate the contract of employment, though this is not to be treated as a dismissal of the employee.[1243] So in such cases, if the employee does not lodge an objection, there is an automatic novation of the contract of employment, which is extended by the regulations to include all the transferor's rights powers duties and liabilities under or connection

---

[1234] Employment Rights Act 1996 s.2(2), (3).

[1235] cf. *Ubsdell v Paterson* [1973] I.C.R. 86, 89C; *Cartin v Botley Garages Ltd* [1973] I.C.R. 144.

[1236] SI 1981/1794, made under the European Communities Act 1972 in implementation of EEC Directive 77/187 of the Council of February 14, 1977, on the approximation of the laws of the Member States relating to the safe-guarding of employees' rights in the event of transfer of undertakings, businesses and parts of businesses; amended by the Transfer of Undertakings (Protection of Employment) (Amendment) Regulations 1987 (SI 1987/442). For recent judicial analyses of the aims and effects of the Directive and the Regulations, see *Unison v Allen* [2007] I.R.L.R. 975; *Computershare Investor Services Plc v Jackson* [2007] EWCA Civ 1065, [2008] I.R.LR. 70; and *Regent Security Services Ltd v Power* [2007] EWCA Civ 1188, [2008] I.R.LR. 66.

[1237] SI 2006/246, implementing amendments to Directive 77/187 which were made by Directive 98/50 and consolidated into the replacement Directive 2001/23. See now also the Collective Redundancies and Transfer of Undertakings (Protection of Employment) (Amendment) Regulations 2014 (SI 2014/16). For a full overview, see J. McMullen, "TUPE: ringing the (wrong) changes" (2014) 43 I.L.J. 149.

[1238] See reg.3(1)(a), 3(2), 3(4)–(6). The key concept is that of the "economic entity", as to which see, most recently, *Wain v Guernsey Ship Management Ltd* [2007] EWCA Civ 294, [2007] I.C.R. 1350. By reg.3(1)(a), the regulations apply to the transfer of an undertaking *from one person to another*—which excludes share takeovers of companies, where, however, a transfer provision is in a sense unnecessary because no change in the identity of the employer is involved; compare, however, *Print Factory (London) 1991 Ltd v Millam* [2007] EWCA Civ 322, [2007] I.C.R. 1331, which shows the difficulty of distinguishing, at the margin, between a share sale and the transfer of an undertaking.

[1239] See reg.3(1)(b), 3(3).

[1240] See reg.4(3) and compare *Secretary of State for Employment v Spence* [1987] Q.B. 179; *Litster v Forth Dry Dock & Engineering Co Ltd* [1989] I.R.L.R. 161.

[1241] See reg.4(1), cf. above, para.40-179, below, paras 40-182—40-184.

[1242] See reg.4(1). See now *Alemo-Herron v Parkwood Leisure Ltd* (C-426/11) EU:C:2013:521, [2014] All E.R. (EC) 400; See J. Prassl, "Freedom of contract as a general principle of EU law? Transfers of undertakings and the protection of employer rights in EU labour law" (2013) 42 I.L.J. 434, and Vol.I, para.1-034, above.

[1243] SI 2006/246 reg.4(1), (7).

with the contract.[1244] This would seem to include accumulated entitlement to statutory employment rights based on the contract of employment insofar as not otherwise transferred by other statutory rules relating to the continuity of employment.[1245] The question of the effectiveness of variations in transferred contracts had proved a very difficult one under the pre-2006 Regulations.[1246] The Regulations now provide that in respect of a contract of employment which is or will be transferred, any purported variation will be void if it is by reason of the transfer itself or for a connected reason which is not an economic technical or organisational reason entailing changes in the workforce,[1247] but that otherwise a variation may validly be agreed.[1248] The Regulations also, however, provide that where a transfer involves or would involve a substantial change in working conditions to the material detriment of the employee in question, that employee may treat the contract of employment as having been terminated, and that the employee shall be treated as having been dismissed by the employer.[1249] Moreover, the Regulations also expressly preserve any independently arising right of an employee "to terminate his contract of employment without notice in acceptance of a repudiatory breach of contract by his employer".[1250]

Dissolution or change in composition of partnership[1251] A dissolution of **40-181** partnership of employers may operate as a wrongful dismissal[1252]; but if the continuing partners offer new employment on the old terms and the employee unreasonably refuses it, he or she is only entitled to nominal damages in an action for such dismissal.[1253] There are provisions whereby statutory continuity of employment is preserved in the event of a change in the membership of a partnership of employers,[1254] and these provisions have been held to extend to the case of a change from employment by a partnership to employment by the sole surviving partner.[1255] It should be noted that, under the provisions of the Limited Liability Partnerships Act 2000, employing partnerships may now be constituted in this new form of corporate entity, in which case different considerations apply.

[1244] SI 2006/246 reg.4(2)(a). But criminal liability is excepted by reg.4(6).

[1245] See above, para.40-165.

[1246] It had been under consideration by the House of Lords in the case of *Wilson v St Helen's BC* [1998] I.C.R. 1141.

[1247] SI 2006/246 reg.4(4), subject to reg.9 which is more permissive towards variations of contract where transferors are subject to insolvency proceedings. See *Kavanagh v Crystal Palace FC 2000 Ltd* [2013] EWCA Civ 1410, [2014] 1 All E.R. 1033, and *Manchester College v Hazel* [2014] EWCA Civ 72, [2014] I.R.L.R. 392.

[1248] SI 2006/246 reg.4(5).

[1249] SI 2006/246 reg.4(9) subject to reg.9 which is more permissive towards variations of contract where transferors are subject to insolvency proceedings. See below, para.40-194 as to the impact of reg.4(9) upon the pre-existing law.

[1250] SI 2006/246 reg.4(11); as to the extent of such a right, compare below, para.40-194 on constructive dismissal.

[1251] See Freedland, *The Personal Employment Contract* (2003), at pp.500–501.

[1252] *Titmus v Rose & Watts* [1940] 1 All E.R. 599; but it may not do so where there is no fundamental disruption to the work of the partnership, as where one partner among a number retires or dies: cf. *Phillips v Alhambra Palace Co* [1901] 1 Q.B. 59; *Tunstall v Condon* [1980] I.C.R. 786, 790F–791F.

[1253] *Brace v Calder* [1895] 2 Q.B. 253. On mitigation, see Vol.I, paras 26-087 et seq.

[1254] Employment Rights Act 1996 s.218(5). See above, para.40-168.

[1255] *Stevens v Bower* [2004] EWCA Civ 496, [2004] I.C.R. 1582 where the approach earlier taken in *Harold Fielding Ltd v Mansi* [1974] I.C.R. 347 was rejected and it was held that the employees in question had continuity of service despite the change in the status of their employer from that of a partnership of solicitors to that of a sole practitioner.

40-182 **Corporate insolvency and restructuring (1)**[1256] As the law of corporate insolvency and restructuring is itself subject to changes over time which cannot be fully detailed here, it is emphasised that the case law which is treated in this and the following paragraph must be understood in the context of its own contemporary company law regime. In the case of a company, the making of a compulsory winding-up order has been thought to operate automatically as notice of (wrongful) discharge to the employees of the company, since it amounts to notice that the company cannot continue to fulfil its obligations under its contracts of employment.[1257] This would seem correct if there is an immediate termination of employment when the winding-up order is made. If, after the making of the order, the employment is continued by the liquidator, various views of the resulting situation are possible. The liquidator may be viewed as continuing the employment as the agent of the company.[1258] In that case the making of the order could be seen as having *no* effect on the continuity of employment,[1259] or as the giving of due notice to terminate, the period of notice to be worked out in the employment of the liquidator.[1260] Alternatively, the order could still be viewed as a wrongful dismissal, but a wrongful dismissal rendered merely technical by the continuance of employment by the liquidator as agent of the company.[1261] If the liquidator is viewed as employing in his or her personal capacity and not as the agent of the company, the winding-up order must then be seen as a wrongful dismissal followed by transfer of employment to the liquidator.[1262] A resolution for voluntary winding-up accompanied by a discontinuance of employment will constitute a wrongful dismissal of the employees.[1263] Where the employment is continued by the liquidator after the resolution, the question of whether the resolution constitutes a wrongful repudiation has been thought to depend upon whether it is clear that the company cannot continue to fulfil its obligations.[1264] The better view would seem to be that the employee can in general in such cases opt to treat the resolution as a wrongful dismissal.[1265]

40-183 **Corporate insolvency and restructuring (2)** The view has been taken that where a receiver and manager is appointed to a company by the court, the receiver does not generally act as the agent of the company,[1266] and it would seem accordingly that

---

[1256] See Freedland, *The Personal Employment Contract* (2003), at pp.501—505.

[1257] See Graham, "The Effect of Liquidation on Contracts of Service" (1952) 15 M.L.R. 48, 52; citing *Re Oriental Bank Corp Ltd* (1886) 32 Ch. D. 366. See *Deaway Trading Ltd v Calverley* [1973] I.C.R. 46, 550H–551D.

[1258] cf. *McEwan v Upper Clyde Shipbuilders Ltd (In Liquidation)* [1972] I.T.R. 296 (Industrial Tribunal).

[1259] *Ex p. Harding* (1868) L.R. 3 Eq. 341.

[1260] This seems to be the correct view of *Re Oriental Bank Corp Ltd* (1886) 32 Ch. D. 366.

[1261] cf. *McEwan v Upper Clyde Shipbuilders Ltd (In Liquidation)* [1972] I.T.R. 296.

[1262] cf. *Golding and Howard v Fire, Auto and Marine Insurance Co Ltd (In Liquidation)* [1968] I.T.R. 372 Industrial Tribunal.

[1263] *Reigate v Union Manufacturing Co Ltd* [1918] 1 K.B. 592; *Fowler v Commercial Timber Co Ltd* [1930] 2 K.B. 1.

[1264] Graham, "The Effect of Liquidation on Contracts of Service" (1952) 15 M.L.R. 48, 54; and see Davies, *Modern Company Law*, 6th edn (1997), pp.833 et seq.

[1265] Contra, *Midland Counties Bank v Attwood* [1905] 1 Ch. 357; but see *Reigate v Union Manufacturing Co Ltd* [1918] 1 K.B. 592, 606 where Scrutton L.J. exposed a fallacy in the earlier case. See also Freedland, *The Contract of Employment* (1976), pp.335–337.

[1266] cf. *Burt Boulton & Hayward Ltd v Bull* [1895] 1 Q.B. 276, 279.

there is a wrongful dismissal of employees of the company[1267] (followed by transfer of employment to the receiver). On the other hand, where a receiver and manager is appointed to a company out of court by the debenture holders, the view has been taken that he or she will normally be empowered to act as the agent of the company in continuing the employment of its employees.[1268] There may nevertheless be held to be a wrongful dismissal of employees upon the appointment of the receiver out of court if (a) the employment of the employee concerned is of such a nature that its continuance was inconsistent with the appointment of a receiver and manager[1269]; or if (b) the receiver is regarded as continuing the employment on behalf of the debenture holders rather than on behalf of the company itself,[1270] though the latter view of the receiver's position pending liquidation of the company was preferred in *Deaway Trading Ltd v Calverley*.[1271] A receiver and administrator was rendered personally liable, by s.44(1) *(b)* of the Insolvency Act 1986 on any contract of employment adopted by him in the carrying out of his function. The circumstances in which a contract of employment would be held to have been so adopted were considered by the Court of Appeal and the House of Lords in *Re Paramount Airways Ltd (No.3)*.[1272]

(f) Summary Dismissal

Summary dismissal generally   The law concerning summary dismissal used to   **40-184**
form a very prominent part of the law of the contract of employment. This was because the common law implied very wide rights of summary dismissal into contracts of employment, and also because the common law duties of the employee were worked out in the context of actions concerning summary dismissals alleged to be wrongful.[1273] The law of summary dismissal has been considerably reduced in its importance for two reasons, first, because the employer's rights of summary dismissal have, since the decision in *Laws v London Chronicle Ltd*,[1274] been regarded as confined to cases of repudiation or fundamental breach of contract by the employee, in accordance with general contractual principles.[1275] Secondly, the justifiability of dismissal is now in practice normally raised as an issue of unfair dismissal,[1276] and the question of whether a summary dismissal was wrongful dismissal at common law has to that extent lost its former significance. The following paragraphs should be read as subject to those general considerations.

Misconduct   Where the employee is guilty of sufficient misconduct in his or her   **40-185**

[1267] *Reid v Explosives Co Ltd* (1887) 19 Q.B.D. 264.
[1268] *Re Foster Clarke Ltd's Indenture Trusts* [1966] 1 W.L.R. 125, 128B-G; *Re Mack Trucks (Great Britain) Ltd* [1967] 1 W.L.R. 780, 786C–E.
[1269] *Re Mack Trucks (Great Britain) Ltd* [1967] 1 W.L.R. 780, 786C; but this doctrine held inapplicable even to a managing director in *Griffiths v Secretary of State for Social Services* [1974] Q.B. 468.
[1270] cf. *Hopley-Dodd v Highfield Motors Ltd* [1969] I.T.R. 289 Industrial Tribunal.
[1271] [1973] I.C.R. 546, 552D–E.
[1272] Sub nom. *Powdrill v Watson* [1994] I.C.R. 395, CA, [1995] 2 A.C. 394, HL. The Insolvency (No. 2) Act 1994 amended s.44 of the 1986 Act to reverse certain of the effects of that decision in respect of contracts of employment adopted on or after March 15, 1994. The resulting position has been stated in detail in an earlier chapter of this work; see Vol.I, para.10-050.
[1273] cf. above, paras 40-059—40-069.
[1274] [1959] 1 W.L.R. 698; see below, para.40-189.
[1275] See Freedland, *The Contract of Employment* (1976), pp.212–219.
[1276] See below, paras 40-215 et seq. A dismissal can be contractually wrongful without being unfair, and vice versa—cf. *Treganowan v Robert Knee & Co Ltd* [1975] I.C.R. 405.

capacity as an employee he or she may be dismissed summarily without notice and before the expiration of a fixed period of employment.[1277] Although the power of dismissal in these circumstances may be by virtue of an implied term in the contract,[1278] it is also possible to view it as a power to rescind the contract upon a repudiatory breach of contract committed by the employee.[1279] There is no rule of law defining the degree of misconduct which will justify dismissal.[1280] The test to be applied must vary with the nature of the business and the position held by the employee,[1281] and reported cases are therefore only a general guide. The general rule is that if the employee does anything which is incompatible with the due or faithful[1282] discharge of his or her duty to his or her employer, he or she may be dismissed without notice[1283]; the employee's conduct need not be dishonest, since it is sufficient if it is "conduct of such a grave and weighty character as to amount to a breach of the confidential relationship"[1284] between employer and employee. So where a manager of a betting shop borrowed money from petty cash to place a bet in another betting shop, knowing that his employer would not have granted permission for this borrowing had he been asked, the employer was justified in dismissing him summarily, even though the manager put an IOU in the till, and was not surreptitious.[1285] On the other hand, even (conceded) gross negligence on the part of a senior social worker was held not to amount to "gross misconduct" meriting summary dismissal within the meaning of her contractual dismissal procedure.[1286]

40-186   Illustrations of misconduct   Many of the decisions on misconduct date from the last century, and may be out of accord with current social conditions. However, courts may endeavour to adapt to modern circumstances the principles derived from

---

[1277] *Spain v Arnott* (1817) 2 Stark. 256; *Atkin v Acton* (1830) 4 C. & P. 208; *Turner v Robinson* (1833) 5 B. & Ad. 789; *Boston Deep Sea Fishing Co v Ansell* (1888) 39 Ch. D. 339. Compare *Cavenagh v William Evans Ltd* [2012] EWCA Civ 697, [2013] 1 W.L.R. 238 in which the *Boston Deep Sea Fishing* case was distinguished on the basis that it did not go so far as to say that after-discovered misconduct provided an employer with a defence to an action for payment of an accrued debt consisting of six months' pay in lieu of notice due upon making the employee redundant.

[1278] Any express disciplinary rules applicable to the employee must be notified to him: Employment Rights Act 1996 s.1(4)(a) (see above, para.40-040).

[1279] See below, para.40-184; Vol.I, paras 24-035 et seq. In *Ministry of Justice v Parry* [2013] I.C.R. 311, EAT, Langstaff J. expounds this approach, holding in particular that the employee's conduct should be seen as a whole, so that an employer would usually be justified in dismissing an employee who committed a further act of misconduct within the period of effect of a warning, even though the act on its own might not merit dismissal.

[1280] *Clouston & Co v Corry* [1906] A.C. 122. Where the plaintiff was required to serve to the satisfaction of the defendants, it was held that a real though unreasonable dissatisfaction justified them in dismissing him: *Diggle v Ogston Motor Co* (1915) 84 L.J. K.B. 2165.

[1281] *Jupiter General Insurance Co Ltd v Shroff* [1937] 3 All E.R. 67, 74, PC.

[1282] The duty of fidelity is discussed see above, para.40-062. It has been held that if the employer produces sufficient evidence to establish a strong prima facie case of infidelity on the part of his employee, the onus of rebutting this inference may shift to the employee: *Federal Supply Co v Angehrn* (1910) 103 L.T. 150.

[1283] *Pearce v Foster* (1886) 17 Q.B.D. 536; *Swale v Ipswich Tannery Ltd* (1906) 11 Com. Cas. 88; *Tomlinson v LMS Ry* [1944] 1 All E.R. 537; *Sinclair v Neighbour* [1967] 2 Q.B. 279.

[1284] *Sinclair v Neighbour* [1967] 2 Q.B. 279 at 289. Compare now *Leach v OFCOM* [2012] EWCA Civ 959, [2012] I.C.R. 1269 where the Court of Appeal held that the claimant had "abused the trust and confidence placed in him to a degree that was sufficiently serious to justify summary dismissal" (at [56]).

[1285] *Sinclair v Neighbour* [1967] 2 Q.B. 279.

[1286] *Dietman v Brent LBC* [1988] I.C.R. 842.

the older cases, and there is scope for judicial innovation when principles have to be applied to novel situations. Insubordination,[1287] breach of confidence in disclosing trade or other secrets,[1288] taking a secret commission[1289] and drunkenness affecting performance of duties[1290] are kinds of misconduct which have, in the circumstances of the case, justified summary dismissal. An employee may obviously be dismissed for dishonesty or fraud in his employment.[1291] But conviction[1292] of a crime is sufficient only if the conduct constituting the crime is inconsistent with the proper performance of his or her duties as an employee.[1293] In the absence of fraud, there is no obligation on a prospective employee to disclose to his or her prospective employer all the facts which might be material to the latter's decision whether or not to employ him or her, nor, during the employment, to disclose his or her own misconduct.[1294] Thus, the mere concealment of a material fact, without fraud, does not entitle the employer to dismiss the employee.[1295] In *Adesokan v Sainsbury's Supermarkets Ltd* the Court of Appeal held that an act of gross negligence might in an appropriate case amount to gross misconduct justifying dismissal where it inflicted grave damage upon the relationship between the parties.[1296]

Misconduct outside hours of employment It has been held that dishonesty committed by the employee outside the hours of his employment will justify summary dismissal where it reveals the employee as "unfit for a position of trust and confidence".[1297] Other forms of misconduct outside the course of employment may justify dismissal if the misconduct is incompatible with the due or faithful discharge of the employee's duty qua employee, as where the confidential clerk to a merchant

40-187

[1287] *The Marina* (1881) 50 L.J. P. 33. cf. on insolence *Shaw v Chairitie* (1850) 3 Car. & K. 21; *Hicks v Thompson* (1857) 28 L.T. (O.S.) 255; *Edwards v Levy* (1860) 2 F. & F. 94; *Wilson v Racher* [1974] I.C.R. 428 (summary dismissal held not justified by the use of obscene language on a solitary occasion); but see *Pepper v Webb* [1969] 1 W.L.R. 514, see below, para.40-189.

[1288] See above, paras 40-066—40-068. *Beeston v Collyer* (1827) 2 Car. & P. 607.

[1289] *Boston Deep Sea Fishing Co v Ansell* (1888) 39 Ch. D. 339; *Federal Supply Co of South Africa v Angehrn* (1910) 103 L.T. 150; *Bell v Lever Bros* [1932] A.C. 161. And see *Reading v Att-Gen* [1951] A.C. 507 for the situation where the employer claims the amount of the secret commission from his employee: Vol.I, para.29-164; see above, para.40-069.

[1290] *Wise v Wilson* (1845) 1 C. & K. 662; *Drysdale v New Era Co* (1936) 55 Ll. L. Rep. 45, 49. cf. *Clouston & Co v Corry* [1906] A.C. 122, 129; *Hands v Simpson Fawcett & Co Ltd* (1928) 44 T.L.R. 295.

[1291] *Brown v Croft* (1828) 6 Car. & P. 16n; *Cunningham v Fonblanque* (1833) 6 Car. & P. 44, 49; *Phillips v Foxall* (1872) L.R. 7 Q.B. 666.

[1292] The employee may show he was wrongly convicted: *Parsons v LCC* (1893) 9 T.L.R. 619. The imposition of a custodial sentence may make the contract impossible of further performance— *Hare v Murphy Bros Ltd* [1974] I.C.R. 603; see above, para.40-176.

[1293] *Hands v Simpson Fawcett & Co Ltd* (1928) 44 T.L.R. 295. See also *Pearce v Foster* (1886) 17 Q.B.D. 536, 539, 540; *Proctor v Bacon* (1886) 2 T.L.R. 845.

[1294] *Bell v Lever Bros* [1932] A.C. 161, especially at 228; *Healey v Soc Anon Française Rubastic* [1917] 1 K.B. 946, 947. Compare above, para.40-064 on duties to disclose information.

[1295] *Fletcher v Krell* (1872) 42 L.J. Q.B. 55 (where a governess, described as a spinster, had in fact been married and divorced); *Hands v Simpson Fawcett & Co Ltd* (1928) 44 T.L.R. 295 (commercial traveller, who by terms of employment was to use motor-car, did not disclose previous driving conviction).

[1296] [2017] EWCA Civ 22, [2017] I.R.L.R. 346.

[1297] *Boston Deep Sea Fishing Co v Ansell* (1888) 39 Ch. D. 339; *Pearce v Foster* (1886) 17 Q.B.D. 536 at 539–540. *Federal Supply, etc. of South Africa v Angehrn & Piel* (1910) 103 L.T. 150. cf. *Sinclair v Neighbour* [1967] 2 Q.B. 279.

was speculating to an enormous amount on the Stock Exchange in "differences".[1298] Again, where the employee presided irregularly at a canteen committee meeting (held outside his ordinary hours of employment) at which he assaulted a fellow employee and was disrespectful to a superior officer, the employer was justified in dismissing him summarily.[1299] The older authorities suggest that it is doubtful whether an employee's immorality unconnected with the employment[1300] can justify dismissal without notice, unless the immorality is such as to show that he or she could not reasonably be trusted in the particular employment concerned.[1301]

40-188 Misconduct of apprentice   Special rules have been held to apply to minors who are employed as apprentices.[1302] It has been held that conduct on the part of an apprentice which might justify the dismissal of an adult, such as words irritating his or her fellow employees and leading to the loss of the employer's time, does not justify the dismissal of the apprentice,[1303] nor does insolence and insubordination.[1304] Nor is it sufficient for the employer to show that the apprentice has repudiated the contract, unless it also appears that the repudiation was for the benefit of the apprentice.[1305] Since the covenants by the employer in an apprenticeship deed were regarded as independent covenants, it has been held to be normally no excuse for the breach of the employer's obligations that the apprentice had broken his obligations.[1306] But where an apprentice by his or her own wilful act prevents an employer from teaching him, the employer could set this up as a defence to an action on the covenant to keep, teach and maintain[1307]; and it has also been held a good defence that the apprentice was an habitual thief.[1308]

40-189 Summary dismissal for disobedience   An employee may be summarily dismissed if he or she wilfully disobeys any lawful and reasonable order of his employer, provided that:

"The disobedience must at least have the quality that it is 'wilful': it does ... connote a deliberate flouting of the essential contractual conditions."[1309]

In circumstances which show that the employee is repudiating one of the essential conditions of the contract of employment, a single act of disobedience will justify dismissal.[1310] But not every order of the employer will be a "lawful order" or a "reasonable order"[1311] for this purpose, since the employee is not bound to obey an

---

[1298] *Pearce v Foster* (1886) 17 Q.B.D. 536.

[1299] *Tomlinson v LMS Ry* [1944] 1 All E.R. 537.

[1300] cf. *Gillet v Bullivant* (1846) 7 L.T. 490.

[1301] *Pearce v Foster* (1886) 17 Q.B.D. 536, 539–540.

[1302] See Vol.I, paras 9-025—9-028. On apprentices in general, see Fridman, *The Modern Law of Employment* (1963), pp.973–978. The present chapter does not deal with the law as between employer and apprentice except where expressly stated.

[1303] *Newell v Gillingham Corp* [1941] 1 All E.R. 552.

[1304] *McDonald v John Twiname Ltd* [1953] 2 Q.B. 304.

[1305] *Waterman v Fryer* [1922] 1 K.B. 499.

[1306] *Winstone v Linn* (1823) 1 B. & C. 460; *Phillips v Clift* (1859) 4 H. & N. 168.

[1307] *Raymond v Minton* (1886) L.R. 1 Ex. 244.

[1308] *Learoyd v Brook* [1891] 1 Q.B. 431.

[1309] *Laws v London Chronicle Ltd* [1959] 1 W.L.R. 698, 701.

[1310] *Laws v London Chronicle Ltd* [1959] 1 W.L.R. 698; cf. *Pepper v Webb* [1969] 1 W.L.R. 514; *Gorse v Durham CC* [1971] 1 W.L.R. 775.

[1311] *Jacquot v Bourra* (1839) 7 Dowl. 348; cf. now *UCATT v Brain* [1981] I.C.R. 542, 548E–G (order

order to do something which is outside the contract of employment,[1312] nor an order which places him or her in danger not reasonably contemplated at the time he or she entered the employment, e.g. an order to remain in a place in which his personal safety is endangered by violence or disease.[1313]

Summary dismissal for incompetence or negligence If an employee was **40-190** engaged on the basis that he or she possessed a particular skill, it has been held that he or she may be dismissed summarily without notice if he fails to display a reasonable degree of competence in that skill.[1314] It has also been held that any employee (whether he or she professes a particular skill or not) is liable to be dismissed summarily if he or she performs his work so negligently that his or her employer's business is likely to be seriously injured.[1315] The view has been taken that an isolated act of forgetfulness or carelessness on the part of an employee will not normally entitle the employer to dismiss him or her without notice[1316]; but this has been said to be a question "of fact and degree in all cases"[1317]; "to forget to do a thing which, if not done, may cause considerable damage to the employer, or to his property, ... may be a serious neglect of duty".[1318] The older cases concerning summary dismissal for incompetence or negligence might well now be held to be restricted in their application by the development of the principle that summary dismissal is justified only by fundamental or repudiatory breach of contract on the part of the employee.[1319]

Grounds for dismissal need not be known at the time nor stated An employer, **40-191** when he or she dismisses his employee, need not allege any specific act of misconduct on the employee's part as the ground for the dismissal; it is sufficient if such a ground did exist, whether or not the employer knew of it at the time of the dismissal.[1320] But if the employer does know of the misconduct in question and thereafter continues the employment, he or she may be taken to have waived his or her right to dismiss the employee on that ground.[1321] The employee now has a

---

to employee to undertake to settle a libel action to which he was defendant was unreasonable).

[1312] *Price v Mouat* (1862) 11 C.B.(N.S.) 508; *Kaukul v Anglo-Soviet Shipping Co Ltd* (1931) 41 Ll.L. Rep. 90; cf. *Secretary of State for Employment v ASLEF (No.2)* [1972] 2 Q.B. 455.

[1313] *Turner v Mason* (1845) 14 M. & W. 112, 117, 118; *Bouzourou v Ottoman Bank* [1930] A.C. 271; *Ottoman Bank v Chakarian* [1930] A.C. 277. cf. *McDonald v Moller Line (UK) Ltd* [1953] 2 Lloyd's Rep. 662, 667. In *Buckoke v GLC* [1970] 1 W.L.R. 1092, it was held not unlawful for the GLC to have a regulation for firemen employed by them which left it to the discretion of the firemen whether to disregard traffic signals.

[1314] *Harmer v Cornelius* (1858) 5 C.B.(N.S.) 236. See above, para.40-059.

[1315] *Callo v Brouncker* (1831) 4 C. & P. 518; *Wise v Wilson* (1845) 1 C. & K. 662; *Edwards v Levy* (1860) 2 F. & F. 94; *Fillieul v Armstrong* (1837) 7 Ad. & El. 557. See above, para.40-060.

[1316] *Baster v London & County Printing Works* [1899] 1 Q.B. 901, 903.

[1317] *Baster v London & County Printing Works* [1899] 1 Q.B. 901.

[1318] *Baster v London & County Printing Works*, above, at 903; *Power v British India Steam Navigation Co Ltd* (1930) 46 T.L.R. 294.

[1319] See above, para.40-184.

[1320] *Mercer v Whall* (1845) 5 Q.B. 447, 466; *Ridgway v Hungerford Market Co* (1835) 3 Ad. & El. 171; *Cussons v Skinner* (1843) 11 M. & W. 161; *Spotswood v Barrow* (1850) 5 Ex. 110; *Boston Deep Sea Fishing Co v Ansell* (1888) 39 Ch. D. 339. cf. *Cyril Leonard & Co v Simo Securities Trust Ltd* [1972] 1 W.L.R. 80 (employment as managing agents). The Irish Supreme Court has not followed the proposition in the text: *Carvill v Irish Industrial Bank Ltd* [1968] I.R. 325.

[1321] *Boston Deep Sea Fishing Co v Ansell*, above, at 358. But the employer does not lose his right of dismissal if he honestly accepts the employee's denial of guilt: *Federal Supply, etc. of South Africa*

statutory right to a written statement of reasons for dismissal.[1322] The existence of that right does not in itself alter this aspect of the law of summary dismissal, unless the employer were held to be estopped from asserting grounds for dismissal which do not form part of a statutory written statement of reasons for dismissal.

40-192 **The right to be heard on dismissal from public employment** Certain employees whose employment is in some sense public employment or involves the tenure of an office are entitled to the benefit of the application of the principles of natural justice before they can be dismissed.[1323] The category of employees so entitled is not yet clearly defined but seems to include employees who are holders of a tenured office[1324] or whose employment takes place under the authority and regulation of a statute or other constituent instrument giving it a public nature.[1325] It seemed that where the employee has this protection, remedies of a public law nature might be available to invalidate a dismissal not carried out in accordance with the principles of natural justice.[1326] The more recent view has been that a person employed under a contract of employment cannot invoke public law remedies to complain of his or her dismissal even if his or her employment is of a public nature,[1327] though an officer or office-holder who does not have a contract of employment may be able to do so.[1328] In *R. (Shoesmith) v OFSTED*,[1329] a senior manager employed by a local authority did succeed in obtaining judicial review of the decision to dismiss her summarily on the footing that she was an office-holder as well as being a contractual employee; on the other hand, it was held in *Christou v Haringey LBC*[1330] that social workers in that senior manager's department, who were regarded as ordinary contractual employees, could not invoke the doctrines of res judicata or abuse of process to complain of having been subjected to a second internal disciplinary process relating to a particular course of conduct on their part. The question whether an employee dismissed for misconduct is entitled to wages or salary up to the date of his dismissal is discussed in a later paragraph.[1331]

(g) Wrongful Dismissal or Repudiation

40-193 **Termination by wrongful dismissal or wrongful repudiation** As a matter of general contract principle, the wrongful repudiation or wrongful purported termination of a contract cannot in itself terminate the contract,[1332] at least unless it renders any continuance of the contract totally impossible by reason of its catastrophic

---

v *Angehrn & Piel* (1910) 103 L.T. 150; and if the alleged misconduct consists, not in a single act, but in a series of acts, the whole course of the employee's conduct must be taken into account. Compare now *Cavenagh v William Evans Ltd* [2012] EWCA Civ 697.

1322 See below, para.40-195.
1323 See Freedland, *The Personal Employment Contract* (2003), pp.70–71. Compare *McLaughlin v Governor of the Cayman Islands* [2007] UKPC 50, [2007] 1 W.L.R. 2839.
1324 cf. *Stevenson v URTU* [1977] I.C.R. 893, 902G–H, per Buckley L.J.
1325 cf. *Malloch v Aberdeen Corp* [1971] 1 W.L.R. 1578, 1596, per Lord Wilberforce. Contrast, however, *Gunton v Richmond LBC* [1980] I.C.R. 755, 764B, 774B–F, 777B.
1326 See below, para.40-027.
1327 *R. v East Berkshire HA Ex p. Walsh* [1985] Q.B. 152.
1328 *R. v Secretary of State for the Home Department Ex p. Benwell* [1985] Q.B. 554.
1329 [2011] EWCA Civ 642, [2011] I.C.R. 1195.
1330 [2013] EWCA Civ 178, [2014] Q.B. 131.
1331 See below, para.40-198.
1332 See above, Vol.I, paras 24-001 et seq.

nature.[1333] There is, however, a body of authority which treats wrongful dismissal as an exception to that general principle, so that the contract of employment is said to be terminated by wrongful dismissal even where the employee refuses to accept the dismissal as a termination of the contract.[1334] That view is a conclusion based on the fact that common law and equitable remedies will not normally be so applied as to keep a contract of employment in being following a wrongful dismissal.[1335] The contrary view is that the contract of employment is not necessarily *in principle* terminated by wrongful dismissal even though no remedy may lie to maintain the contract in being.[1336] That theoretical issue has acquired a new importance because of the statutory consequences now attached to the termination of the contract of employment.[1337] The ultimate answer is that "termination of the contract of employment" is not really a concept with a single clear meaning[1338]; but with that qualification the better view now seems to be in favour of regarding wrongful dismissal as not in principle terminatory of the contract unless accepted as such by the employee. Moreover, the courts now seem prepared to take the same view of a wrongful repudiation consisting in a fundamental change by the employer in the terms of employment which is not accepted by the employee as a termination of his or her contract.[1339] The elective view of termination of the contract of employment was followed in granting a declaration that a wrongful dismissal was ineffective to determine the contract[1340]; in holding that an unaccepted wrongful repudiation could be the subject of injunctive relief to prevent a wrongful dismissal from taking effect until the proper contractual procedures had been followed[1341]; in holding that an employee could not free himself or herself of his or her obligation not to work for a rival employer during his contractual notice period by a wrongful repudiation which was not accepted by the employer[1342]; and in rejecting the view that an employee normally dismisses himself or herself so is not dismissed by his or her employer when he or she commits a repudiatory breach of contract.[1343]

[1333] cf. *Harbutt's "Plasticine" Ltd v Wayne Tank & Pump Co Ltd* [1970] 1 Q.B. 447. cf. also *Hounslow LBC v Twickenham Garden Developments Ltd* [1971] Ch. 233, 251E–254A for discussion of a different kind of exception to the general principle.

[1334] *Ridge v Baldwin* [1964] A.C. 40, 64; *Denmark Productions Ltd v Boscobel Productions Ltd* [1969] 1 Q.B. 699, 737E–F; *Decro-Wall International SA v Practitioners in Marketing Ltd* [1971] 1 W.L.R. 361, 381E; *Hill v CA Parsons & Co Ltd* [1972] 1 Ch. 305, 314B–E "in the ordinary course of things"; *GKN (Cwmbran) Ltd v Lloyd* [1972] I.C.R. 214, 221B–C; *Sanders v Ernest Neale Ltd* [1974] I.C.R. 565.

[1335] See below, para.40-208 (specific performance and injunction); paras 40-211—40-212 (declaration).

[1336] *Denmark Productions Ltd v Boscobel Productions Ltd* [1969] 1 Q.B. 699, 731F–732F; *Decro-Wall International SA v Practitioners in Marketing Ltd* [1971] 1 W.L.R. 361, 376C–D.

[1337] See below, paras 40-215 et seq. (unfair dismissal provisions); paras 40-224 et seq. (redundancy payments legislation); paras 40-247 et seq. (dismissal contravening the Sex Discrimination Act 1975).

[1338] See Freedland, *The Contract of Employment* (1976), pp.299–300.

[1339] *Rigby v Ferodo Ltd* [1988] I.C.R. 29; cf. *Burdett-Coutts v Hertfordshire CC* [1984] I.R.L.R. 91.

[1340] *Gunton v Richmond LBC* [1980] I.C.R. 755, Shaw L.J. dissenting on this point. *Thomas Marshall Ltd v Guinle* [1978] I.C.R. 905, see above, para.40-066 was approved by the majority. Compare *Marsh v National Autistic Society* [1993] I.C.R. 453, where, however, it was held that the claim for remuneration is thereafter a claim in damages and not in debt.

[1341] *Dietman v Brent LBC* [1978] I.C.R. 737 (affirmed by the Court of Appeal on other grounds [1988] I.C.R. 842). The plaintiff was held on the facts not to be entitled to an injunction, because she had accepted the Council's repudiation before the trial of the action, inter alia by accepting employment elsewhere.

[1342] *Evening Standard Co Ltd v Henderson* [1987] I.C.R. 388; cf. *Thomas Marshall Ltd v Guinle* [1978] I.C.R. 905.

[1343] *London Transport Executive v Clarke* [1980] I.C.R. 532, Lord Denning M.R. dissenting on this point.

The Court of Appeal in its decision in *Boyo v Lambeth LBC*[1344] rather doubtingly applied the elective view of wrongful repudiation by the employer. In the case where the employer wrongfully purported to treat the contract of employment as frustrated, the contract was treated, for the purpose of assessing contractual compensation, as not validly terminated until the time that notice to terminate would have expired if given after a disciplinary process had been provided and had been completed within a reasonable period of time. The elective view of the effect of the employer's wrongful and repudiatory purported dismissal was confirmed by the Supreme Court in *Société Générale (London Branch) v Geys*.[1345] In the particular case, the employee having elected to affirm the contract, the contract of employment was deemed to have remained in being until validly terminated by the eventual proper exercise of a payment in lieu of notice clause,[1346] with the effect that the period of service upon which the employee's bonus entitlement was based was extended by some weeks, and the amount of the bonus entitlement was thereby increased by several million pounds. The current view seems to be that the difficulties raised by this approach in relation to the statute law that depends on the concept of dismissal can satisfactorily be resolved by treating a wrongful dismissal as resulting in an effective termination for statutory purposes whatever its theoretical effect as a matter of common law.[1347] It has been held that a threatened breach by an employing company of its continuing obligation to employ the employee as a director was comparable to an anticipatory repudiatory breach of an executory contract, rather than an actual repudiatory breach, which could therefore be withdrawn at any time before its unequivocal acceptance by the employee.[1348]

(h)   Constructive Dismissal

40-194   Termination as the result of constructive dismissal   For the purposes of the various legislative provisions concerning dismissal, such as the unfair dismissal legislation and the redundancy payments legislation, "dismissal" includes the case where the employee terminates the contract of employment with or without notice in circumstances such that he or she is entitled to terminate it without notice by reason of the employer's conduct.[1349] Where these conditions are fulfilled, the employee's resignation is treated as a constructive dismissal by the employer, provided that the employer's conduct is the main operative cause of the resignation.[1350] In *Western Excavating (ECC) Ltd v Sharp*,[1351] it was decided that the test for constructive dismissal as so defined was a contractual one, namely whether the employer's conduct amounted to a fundamental breach or repudiation of the contract of

---

The majority did not follow the cases that had developed a doctrine of "constructive resignation", e.g. *Gannon v JC Firth Ltd* [1976] I.R.L.R. 415 (strike action); *Kallinos v London Electric Wire Ltd* [1980] I.R.L.R. 11.

[1344] [1994] I.C.R. 727.

[1345] [2012] UKSC 63, [2013] 1 A.C. 523.

[1346] As to which see above, para.40-170.

[1347] See *Robert Cort & Son Ltd v Charman* [1981] I.R.L.R. 437 and see below, paras 40-222—40-223.

[1348] *Norwest Holst Group Administration Ltd v Harrison* [1985] I.C.R. 668.

[1349] Employment Rights Act 1996 ss.95(1)(c), 136(1)(c); see below, paras 40-220—40-221, 40-250.

[1350] cf. *Jones v Sirl & Son (Furnishers) Ltd* [1997] I.R.L.R. 493.

[1351] [1978] I.C.R. 221. The decision was applied and reaffirmed in *Bournemouth University Higher Education Corp v Buckland* [2010] EWCA Civ 121, [2010] I.R.L.R. 445, where the Court of Appeal rejected the argument that a "band of reasonable responses" test should apply, and moreover rejected the argument that there was any doctrine of cure of fundamental breach which was special to employment law.

employment. This decision has resulted not only in considerable development of case law on the generally implied duties of the employer such as the duty to preserve trust and confidence[1352] but also in extensive discussion in the case law of what constitutes repudiation on the part of the employer. This frequently involves an inquiry into the implied terms of the particular contract concerning geographical mobility[1353] or into the question of when the employer repudiates the contract by altering the terms and conditions of employment.[1354] It would seem that the question of whether there has been a repudiation by the employer should be viewed as a mixed question of law and fact with the result that a finding by an employment tribunal about repudiation or fundamental breach of an implied term should be disturbed on appeal only where there was no basis of evidence properly to support such a finding.[1355] It would also seem that the notion that a party to a contract does not repudiate it by pursuing a bona fide but mistaken view of its effect[1356] can have only a very limited application in disputes between employer and employee over terms and conditions of employment.[1357] There is no constructive dismissal if the employee affirms the contract after and despite the employer's repudiation.[1358] But delay in accepting the repudiation, and even continuing to work and accept remuneration are not in themselves conclusive of affirmation on the employee's part; there must be a consideration of the whole of the circumstances including factors such as whether the employee acted under protest or not.[1359] It was held by the Employment Appeal Tribunal in *Morrow v Safeway Stores Ltd*[1360] that conduct on the part of the employer which was sufficiently undermining of trust and confidence

---

[1352] See above, para.40-151. Compare now, on the question of breach of the implied term of trust and confidence arising out of the transfer of an undertaking, *Sita (GB) Ltd v Burton* [1998] I.C.R. 17. See also now *Glendale Managed Services v Graham* [2003] I.R.L.R. 465.

[1353] See *Little v Charterhouse Magna Ltd* [1980] I.R.L.R. 19; *Jones v Associated Tunnelling Ltd* [1981] I.R.L.R. 477.

[1354] See, e.g. *Ford v Millthorn Toleman Ltd* [1980] I.R.L.R. 30; *Millbrook Furnishing Ltd v McIntosh* [1981] I.R.L.R. 309; *Pedersen v Camden LBC* [1981] I.C.R. 674n. For attempted imposition of a variation in terms, coupled with the threat of dismissal if variation rejected, as constructive dismissal, see *Greenaway Harrison Ltd v Wiles* [1994] I.R.L.R. 380.

[1355] See *Pedersen v Camden LBC* [1981] I.C.R. 674n.; *Millbrook Furnishing Ltd v McIntosh* [1981] I.R.L.R. 309; *Woods v WM Car Services Ltd* [1981] I.C.R. 666. There is, however, authority for the view that the question is one of law for the appellate tribunal—*Walker v Josiah Wedgwood Sons Ltd* [1978] I.C.R. 744, 750E–H, or that if the question is a mixed one, that nonetheless gives the appellate tribunal primary control over the issue—cf. *O'Brien v Associated Fire Alarms Ltd* [1968] 1 W.L.R. 1916.

[1356] *Sweet & Maxwell Ltd v Universal News Services Ltd* [1964] 3 All E.R. 30; *Woodar Investments v Wimpey Construction Ltd* [1980] 1 All E.R. 571.

[1357] *Financial Techniques Ltd v Hughes* [1981] I.R.L.R. 32, paras 28, 29, per Templeman L.J.; doubting *Frank Wright Ltd v Punch* [1980] I.R.L.R. 217; *Millbrook Furnishing Ltd v McIntosh* [1981] I.R.L.R. 309.

[1358] *Western Excavating (ECC) Ltd v Sharp* [1978] I.C.R. 221, 226; *Bashir v Brillo Manufacturing Co* [1979] I.R.L.R. 295; *Cox Toner International Ltd v Crook* [1981] I.C.R. 823.

[1359] *Bashir v Brillo Manufacturing Co* [1979] I.R.L.R. 295, at paras 15–19; *Cox Toner International Ltd v Crook* [1981] I.C.R. 823, 829C–H. See also *Chindove v Morrisons Supermarket Plc* [2014] UKEAT 0043/14/BA.

[1360] [2002] I.R.L.R. 9. In *Waltham Forest LBC v Omilaju (No.2)* [2004] EWCA Civ 1493, [2005] I.R.L.R. 35 it was held that the final act or "last straw" in a series of actions which cumulatively amounted to constructive dismissal need not itself be a breach of contract or unreasonable; but it had to be more than very trivial and had to be capable of contributing, however slightly, to a breach of the implied obligation as to mutual trust and confidence. Compare also now *Bunning v GT Bunning & Sons Ltd* [2005] EWCA Civ 104, in which the judgment of Wall L.J. adds further support to the notion of the "last straw" as articulated in the *Omilaju* case; compare also *GAB Robins (UK) Ltd v Triggs* [2008] EWCA Civ 17, [2008] I.R.L.R. 317.

to amount to a breach of the implied obligation of trust and confidence was as such repudiatory of the contract of employment and so entitled the employee to resign and claim to have been constructively dismissed. It was held by the Court of Appeal in *Rossiter v Pendragon Plc*[1361] that the test for constructive dismissal in relation to changes of terms and conditions associated with the transfer of an undertaking involved the same requirement of a repudiatory breach of contract as in other situations, this requirement being neither negated nor reduced by the TUPE Regulations.[1362] As has been explained and explored in an earlier paragraph,[1363] the decision of the House of Lords in the leading case of *Johnson v Unisys Ltd*,[1364] that the implied obligation as to trust and confidence does not apply to limit the employer's power of dismissal, has left a difficult question as to when that implied obligation is applicable to conduct on the part of the employer which would, if the obligation applies to it, amount to constructive dismissal. In *Edwards v Chesterfield Royal Hospital NHS Trust*[1365] the Supreme Court confirmed the demarcation of the "*Johnson* exclusion" which had emerged from the *Eastwood* case,[1366] whereby that exclusion applies in respect of "steps on the part of the employer leading to dismissal" unless the loss complained of as resulting from those steps "precedes and is independent of the dismissal process".[1367] According to this demarcation, the mere fact that a step taken by the employer might in itself amount to a *constructive* dismissal, even if it is eventually followed by a distinct act of dismissal on the part of the employer, does not in and of itself place that step within the "*Johnson* exclusion"—so that, for example, the suspension of an employee may still on its facts be held to be in breach of the implied obligation of mutual trust and confidence and may give rise to liability as a contractually wrongful constructive dismissal not caught by the "*Johnson* exclusion".[1368]

[1361] [2002] I.C.R. 1063, CA.

[1362] Compare above, para.40-180, from which it will be seen that reg.4(9) of the 2006 TUPE Regulations apparently provides an alternative statutory form of constructive dismissal in such circumstances.

[1363] See above, para.40-154.

[1364] [2001] I.C.R. 480. In *Kerry Foods Ltd v Lynch* [2005] I.R.L.R. 681, the doctrine in *Johnson v Unisys Ltd* received an important application or extension, in that it was held that where an employing enterprise sought to impose a six-day week on an employee working a five-day week, its conduct amounted not to a repudiatory breach of the obligation as to mutual trust and confidence, but rather to a giving of lawful notice to terminate the contract of employment coupled with an offer of re-engagement on different terms.

[1365] [2011] UKSC 58.

[1366] *Eastwood v Magnox Electric Plc, McCabe v Cornwall CC* [2004] UKHL 35, [2005] 1 A.C. 503.

[1367] Lord Dyson in *Edwards* at [51] quoting from Lord Nicholls in *Eastwood* at [29]. Lord Dyson continued: "In other words 'the court must decide whether earlier events do or do not form part of the dismissal process' " quoting from Lord Steyn in *Eastwood* at [39].

[1368] Hence the possibility that "an employer may be better off dismissing an employee than suspending him", an outcome regarded as "unsatisfactory and anomalous" but "the inevitable consequence of the interrelation between the common law and statute": Lord Dyson in *Edwards* at [51] quoting from Lord Nicholls in *Eastwood* at [15] and [30] to [33].

7. REMEDIES, AND RIGHTS INCIDENTAL TO THE TERMINATION OF EMPLOYMENT

(a) Statement of Reasons for Dismissal

Written statement of reasons for dismissal Under s.92 of the Employment **40-195**
Rights Act 1996 an employee[1369] whose contract of employment is terminated by
his or her employer with or without notice[1370] or, being a limited-term[1371] contract,
expires without renewal,[1372] is entitled to be provided by the employer, on request,
within 14 days of the request, with a written statement giving particulars of the
reason for the dismissal.[1373] It seems, however, that the obligation may be complied
with by unambiguous reference to earlier letters if copies of them are included.[1374]
The employee must for this purpose have completed two years of continuous
employment[1375] by the effective date of termination[1376] of his or her contract. An
employee may complain to an employment tribunal of an unreasonable failure on
the part of his or her employer to provide any, or an adequate and accurate, written statement of reasons.[1377] The tribunal, if it upholds the complaint, must make
an award of two weeks' pay[1378] to the employee [1379] The provisions of s.92 are
important in practice, especially in relation to the unfair dismissal legislation.[1380]
They represent a reversal of the common law position as to dismissal where the rule
is that no reasons need normally be given.[1381] The qualifying period of continuous
employment is one year[1382]; but neither that requirement nor the requirement of a

---

[1369] The following categories of employees are excluded: share fishermen—s.199(2) of Employment
Rights Act 1996; such further categories as may be specified by order—s.209(1) of Employment
Rights Act 1996. The section *does* apply to Crown employment—s.191(1), (2) of Employment
Rights Act 1996.

[1370] Employment Rights Act 1996 s.92(1)(a) and (b). Quaere to what extent this includes "constructive" dismissal; cf. *Sutcliffe v Hawker Siddeley Aviation Ltd* [1973] I.C.R. 560.

[1371] See *British Broadcasting Corp v Ioannu* [1975] I.C.R. 267; and *BBC v Dixon* [1979] I.R.L.R. 114,
CA. See also above, para.40-172. For an explanation of the change of terminology from "fixed-
term" to "limited-term".

[1372] Employment Rights Act 1996 s.92(1)(c).

[1373] Employment Rights Act 1996 s.92(2). It is not clear how specific the particulars have to be.
Particulars are to be express, not by reference: *Horsley Smith & Sherry Ltd v Dutton* [1977] I.C.R.
594.

[1374] *Gilham v Kent CC* [1985] I.C.R. 227.

[1375] Employment Rights Act 1996 s.92(3) as amended by the Unfair Dismissal and Statement of Reasons
for Dismissal (Variation of Qualifying Period) Order 2012 (SI 2012/989) with effect upon periods
of employment beginning from April 6, 2012. For the period of "continuous employment", see s.210
Employment Rights Act 1996 (which includes a presumption of continuity) see above, paras 40-
165—40-168.

[1376] Employment Rights Act 1996 s.92(6).

[1377] Employment Rights Act 1996 s.93(1) (limitation period—s.93(3) of Employment Rights Act 1996).
See *Charles Lang & Sons Ltd v Aubrey* [1978] I.C.R. 168; *Daynecourt Insurance Brokers Ltd v Iles*
[1978] I.R.L.R. 335; and *Brown v Stuart Scott & Co* [1981] I.C.R. 166.

[1378] Employment Rights Act 1996 s.226(2).

[1379] Employment Rights Act 1996 s.93(2)(b). The tribunal also has a power to declare what it finds were
the reasons for dismissal; Employment Rights Act 1996 s.93(2)(a).

[1380] See below, paras 40-215 et seq.

[1381] See above, para.40-184.

[1382] Employment Rights Act 1996 s.92(3), as amended by the Unfair Dismissal and Statement of Reasons
for Dismissal (Variation of Qualifying Period) Order 1999 (SI 1999/1436).

request by the employee apply while the employee is pregnant or on maternity leave.[1383]

(b) Recovery of Remuneration

40-196 **Payment for services actually rendered**   Where the employee is not paid for a period of employment[1384] which the employee has actually served, the employee's claim is not one for damages, but for a debt, viz payment of an agreed sum,[1385] since he or she is entitled to be paid according to the agreed rate.[1386] It has been held that the employee cannot claim, in addition to the sum due, damages for the delay in paying the salary or wages.[1387] It appears that if the contract of employment did not specify a particular amount or rate of salary or wages, the employee who is not paid for a period of employment is entitled to sue upon a quantum meruit for a reasonable remuneration.[1388] An employee may be able to make a claim for non-payment of wages to an employment tribunal under Pt II of the Employment Rights Act 1996 on the basis that it represents an unlawful deduction from his wages.[1389]

40-197 **Apportionment of wages or salary**[1390]   Wages or salary were thought not to be apportionable at common law, and early authority held that failure (for any reason other than breach of contract by the employer) by the employee to complete the entire period in respect of which he or she was to receive a definite sum as remuneration meant that he or she was unable to recover anything at all.[1391] The terms of the contract of employment could nevertheless make the employer liable to pay a proportionate part of the agreed remuneration if the entire period was not completed.[1392] However, the Apportionment Act 1870[1393] provides (inter alia) that:

"... all ... annuities ... and other periodical payments in the nature of income ... shall, like interest on money lent, be considered as accruing from day to day, and shall be apportionable in respect of time accordingly."

[1383] Employment Rights Act 1996 s.92(4), as amended.

[1384] viz a period of employment in respect of which the employee is entitled, by the contract, to be paid a fixed amount.

[1385] See Vol.I, para.26-009.

[1386] See above, paras 40-078 et seq.

[1387] *Harper v Linthorpe Dinsdale Smelting Co* (1909) 101 L.T. 608. Compare, however, Vol.I, para.24-168.

[1388] See above, para.40-079 and Vol.I, para.29-071 for a full discussion of this principle.

[1389] See above, para.40-099, and cf. *Pename Ltd v Paterson* [1989] I.C.R. 12. The employee's claim in respect of "unlawful deduction" may extend to the withholding of part of the employee's remuneration following a purported but wrongful demotion of the employee—see *Morgan v West Glamorgan CC* [1995] I.R.L.R. 68.

[1390] See Williams (1941) 57 L.Q.R. 373, 375–383.

[1391] *Cutter v Powell* (1795) 6 T.R. 320, see Vol.I, para.21-031.

[1392] *Moriarty v Regent's Garage Co Ltd* [1921] 1 K.B. 423; reversed on another ground: [1921] 2 K.B. 766. See also *Swabey v Port Darwin Gold Mining Co* (1889) 1 Megone 385.

[1393] s.2. Though compare *Amey v Peter Symonds College* [2013] EWHC 2788 (QB), [2014] I.R.L.R. 206, where the s.2 presumption was displaced pursuant to s.7. A similar approach was followed in *Hartley v King Edward VI College* [2015] EWCA Civ 455, [2015] I.R.L.R. 650, but that decision was subsequently overturned by the Supreme Court [2017] UKSC 39, [2017] 1 W.L.R. 2110, where the statutory principle of equal daily apportionment was held to apply and not to have been excluded by the particular contract.

It has been held[1394] that this Act applies to "wages" as well as to "salary"[1395] and it seems just that, if it is not due to the employee's fault that the period of employment is not completed, the Act should apply.[1396] It was held in *Thames Water Utilities Plc v Reynolds*[1397] that accrual "day by day" is to be calculated by reference to calendar days rather than working days.

Entitlement to apportioned wages or salary upon summary dismissal for misconduct   It has never been decided whether the Act entitles an employee dismissed for misconduct to claim his salary or wages pro rata for the broken period up to the date of the dismissal.[1398] The older cases[1399] and those decided without reference to the Act[1400] held that the dismissed employee was not entitled to any wages or salary for the broken period of employment immediately preceding his or her dismissal, because his or her entitlement had not accrued due by then. The employee was, however, entitled to recover any arrears which had already accrued due by that time[1401] even although they were in respect of a period after he had been guilty of misconduct.[1402] It has been held that the contract may provide that if the employee is dismissed for misconduct, he or she shall forfeit all wages due to him,[1403] but it is possible that such a provision might now be subject to equitable relief against such forfeiture.[1404]

40-198

(c)   Protection of the Employee's Accrued Rights in the Employer's Insolvency

Preferential claims for wages in bankruptcy, or liquidation   Where an employer becomes bankrupt, or, in the cases of a company is wound up, under the Insolvency Act 1986 any arrears of remuneration (up to a limit laid down by statutory instrument[1405]) payable to an employee or ex-employee in respect of the whole or any part of the four months before the relevant date, becomes a preferential debt ranking with certain debts due to the Inland Revenue, and to Customs and Excise, and with certain social security contributions and contributions to occupational pen-

40-199

[1394] *Moriarty v Regent's Garage Co Ltd*, above. The Court of Appeal in this case held that the question of apportionment should not have been considered by the Divisional Court because the point had not been taken in the county court.

[1395] "Salaries" are, by s.5, expressly included within "annuities".

[1396] The Law Reform (Frustrated Contracts) Act 1943 will sometimes apply to this type of situation, and will enable the court to order payment of a "just" amount when the other party has "obtained a valuable benefit" before the frustrating event: s.1(3); see Vol.I, paras 23-084—23-091.

[1397] [1996] I.R.L.R. 186. Since followed in *Taylor v East Midlands Offender Employment* [2000] I.R.L.R. 760, EAT.

[1398] *Moriarty v Regent's Garage Co Ltd* [1921] 1 K.B 423 at 448–449.

[1399] *Lilley v Elwin* (1848) 11 Q.B. 742; *Ridgway v Hungerford Market Co* (1835) 3 Ad. & El. 171.

[1400] *Boston Deep Sea Fishing Co v Ansell* (1888) 39 Ch. D. 339; *Healey v Soc Anon Française Rubastic* [1917] 1 K.B. 946.

[1401] *Taylor v Laird* (1856) 1 Hurl. & N. 266; *Button v Thompson* (1869) L.R. 4 C.P. 330; *Healey v Soc Anon Française Rubastic*, above.

[1402] *Ramsden v David Sharratt & Sons Ltd* (1930) 35 Com. Cas. 314. (The remedy of the employer is a counterclaim for damages for the employee's breach of duty.)

[1403] *Walsh v Walley* (1874) L.R. 9 Q.B. 367.

[1404] cf. *Stockloser v Johnson* [1954] 1 Q.B. 476 and see Freedland, *The Contract of Employment* (1976), pp.232–233.

[1405] [1954] 1 Q.B. 476 Pt I para.9.

sion schemes and state pension scheme premiums, above other debts.[1406] The same preference extends to arrears of accrued holiday remuneration without limit of time or amount.[1407] Amounts payable by way of remuneration are defined to include certain pecuniary rights which may accrue to the employee, namely amounts owed in respect of statutory guarantee payments,[1408] remuneration on suspension on medical or maternity grounds,[1409] any statutorily guaranteed payment during statutory time off,[1410] or remuneration under a protective award in respect of redundancy dismissal.[1411]

40-200 **Recourse to the National Insurance Fund on insolvency of employer** Under ss.166 and 167 of the Employment Rights Act 1996 the Secretary of State[1412] may, where an employer is insolvent,[1413] pay the unpaid amount of a redundancy payment owed to an employee by the insolvent employer, the payment being made directly out of the National Insurance Fund,[1414] which is subrogated to the rights of the employer.[1415] Under Pt XII of the Employment Rights Act 1996 the same system is extended to a number of other debts owed to the employee by the insolvent[1416] employer, which have accrued due by the time of the employer's insolvency and the termination of the employee's employment.[1417] It should be noted that the list of such debts is in some respects wider than the list of debts due to the employer which are accorded priority in the employer's insolvency.[1418] The list includes[1419]:

(a) arrears of pay[1420] for up to eight weeks;
(b) statutorily guaranteed payments due in respect of statutory minimum notice periods, or compensation due for failure to give statutory minimum notice[1421];

[1406] s.386 and Sch.6 paras 9–15 (to be read with Sch.4 to the Pension Schemes Act 1993. It should be noted that provision has been made, though not yet implemented, for the repeal of these provisions by s.1295 of and Sch.16 to the Companies Act 2006.

[1407] Sch.6 para.10.

[1408] Sch.6 para.13(2)(a).

[1409] Sch.6 para.13(2)(c).

[1410] Sch.6 para.13(2)(b).

[1411] Sch.6 para.13(2)(d).

[1412] Currently the Department for Business, Enterprise and Regulatory Reform.

[1413] Defined by s.166(6), (7) of Employment Rights Act 1996 to include individual bankruptcy or composition with creditors, bankruptcy of estate, liquidation of or appointment of receiver to a company.

[1414] Employment Rights Act 1996 s.167(1).

[1415] Employment Rights Act 1996 s.167(3).

[1416] Defined by s.183 as in s.166(6), (7) of Employment Rights Act 1996. This has been held to include a company trading under a company voluntary arrangement (CVA): *Secretary of State for Business, Innovation and Skills v McDonagh* [2013] I.C.R. 1177, EAT.

[1417] Employment Rights Act 1996 ss.182, 185.

[1418] See above, para.40-199.

[1419] Employment Rights Act 1996 s.184(1).

[1420] Employment Rights Act 1996 s.184(1)(a), (2). The term probably also includes sick pay.

[1421] See above, paras 40-164—40-169. This entitlement has been held to be subject to the rules as to mitigation of loss that would have applied to the employee's own claim for damages for breach of contract—*Secretary of State for Employment v Wilson* [1977] I.R.L.R. 483. On the other hand, the entitlement has been held to be limited by the rules determining the statutory week's pay—see below, para.40-255, and not to include contractual fringe benefits falling outside those rules—*Secretary of State for Employment v Haynes* [1981] I.R.L.R. 270.

(c) arrears of holiday pay, for up to six weeks accruing due in the last 12 months of the employment[1422];

(d) any basic award of compensation for unfair dismissal[1423];

(e) any reasonable sum by way of reimbursement of any fee or premium paid by an apprentice or articled clerk.[1424]

Insofar as these sums accrue due in respect of particular periods of time, they are limited to the fixed maximum statutory week's pay for this purpose.[1425] The employee may complain to an employment tribunal of a failure by the Secretary of State for Employment to make or make in full an amount payable to the employee out of the National Insurance Fund under these provisions,[1426] and the tribunal may make a declaration upholding the complaint and declaring the amount due.[1427] The Secretary of State is subrogated to the rights of the employee in the employer's insolvency,[1428] but, since this recourse to the National Insurance Fund is more widely defined than the employee's rights to priority in the employer's insolvency,[1429] and since the Fund's priority apparently does not extend quite as far as the employee's own priority[1430] (not extending to the priorities set out in s.184(1) of the 1996 Act),[1431] the Fund may possibly find itself subrogated to unsecured and non-preferential rights in the insolvency.

(d) Damages for Wrongful Dismissal

Damages for loss of earnings following wrongful dismissal The remedy of an **40-201** employee who has been wrongfully dismissed is an action for damages. The normal measure of damages is the amount the employee would have earned under the contract for the period until the employer could lawfully have terminated it, less the amount he or she could reasonably be expected to earn in other employment.[1432] The dismissed employee, like any innocent party following a breach of contract by the other party, must take reasonable steps to minimise his or her loss.[1433] In the case of wrongful dismissal these reasonable steps mean that the employee must seek and accept any reasonable offer of other employment[1434]; if he or she fails to take other employment when he or she ought reasonably to have done so, damages will be assessed on the basis of the difference between the salary or wages under the broken contract, and what he or she would have received from the substituted employment. A reasonable offer of alternative employment may come from the defendant himself

---

[1422] Employment Rights Act 1996 s.184(1)(c); see above, para.40-081.

[1423] Employment Rights Act 1996 s.184(1)(d); see below, para.40-241.

[1424] Employment Rights Act 1996 s.184(1)(e).

[1425] Employment Rights Act 1996 s.186(1); and see the current Employment Protection (Variation of Limits) Order.

[1426] Employment Rights Act 1996 s.188(1), (2) (note limitation period).

[1427] Employment Rights Act 1996 s.188(3).

[1428] Employment Rights Act 1996 ss.189(1), (5).

[1429] See above, para.40-199.

[1430] Employment Rights Act 1996 s.189(2).

[1431] Employment Rights Act 1996 s.184—see above, para.40-199.

[1432] For the working out of the details of this measure of damages in relation to the wrongful dismissal of the chief executive of a large public company, see *Clark v BET Plc* [1997] I.R.L.R. 348.

[1433] Vol.I, paras 26-087 et seq.

[1434] *Beckham v Drake* (1847–49) 2 H.L.C. 579; *Reid v Explosives Co* (1887) 19 Q.B.D 264; *Re Newman* [1916] 2 Ch. 309; *Shindler v Northern Raincoat Co Ltd* [1960] 1 W.L.R. 1038; *Yetton v Eastwood Froy Ltd* [1967] 1 W.L.R. 104; see also *Paterson v South-West Scotland Electricity Board*, 1951 S.L.T. 9.

or herself.[1435] A deduction must be made, however, on account of the accelerated receipt of damages for loss of future earnings.[1436]

40-202   The onus of proof is on the defendant employer to produce evidence to show that the dismissed employee ought reasonably to have obtained alternative employment.[1437] If the defendant has a right to terminate the contract before the expiry of the term, damages for the wrongful dismissal should be assessed only up to the earliest time at which the defendant could validly have terminated the contract.[1438] Thus, if the contract expressly provides that it is terminable upon, e.g. a month's notice, the damages will ordinarily be a month's wages.[1439] In *Gunton v Richmond LBC*[1440] it was held that where a dismissal was wrongful by reason of a failure to comply with a contractually binding dismissal procedure,[1441] the damages were to be assessed only up to the expiry of the contractually due notice of one month notionally served on the day when the proper disciplinary procedure, if followed, could have been concluded. (In *Edwards v Chesterfield Royal Hospital NHS Trust*[1442] a body of doctrine was articulated which, by excluding or severely restricting the awarding of damages at common law for the breach of contractual disciplinary procedures,[1443] seemed apt to preclude damages of the kind awarded in the *Gunton* case. However, the Supreme Court declined to overrule *Gunton*, or to declare it to be inapplicable in this respect,[1444] so that the possibility still seems to obtain that damages of that kind may be awarded.) Except in cases of alleged bad faith on the part of the employer, the court is not to analyse the chances that the employee would not have been dismissed had the procedure been followed.[1445] If the employee's claim is on the ground that the employer dismissed him or her with insufficient notice,[1446] in an action for damages the defendant employer is entitled to particulars of the period of time claimed by the plaintiff to constitute reasonable notice.[1447] Similarly, the amount of damages for loss of salary and commission which would have been earned during a period of reasonable notice, had it been given, must be specially pleaded.[1448] The value of the benefits which the employee receives from the substituted employment should be assessed by looking at the

---

[1435] *Brace v Calder* [1895] 2 Q.B. 253; *Barnes v Port of London Authority* [1957] 1 Lloyd's Rep. 486; cf. *Jackson v Hughes* [1938] 4 All E.R. 587.

[1436] *Lavarack v Woods of Colchester Ltd* [1967] 1 Q.B. 278.

[1437] See Vol.I, para.26-089. The defendant is entitled to particulars of other employment obtained by the plaintiff after his dismissal: *Monk v Redwing Aircraft Co Ltd* [1942] 1 K.B. 182.

[1438] *British Guiana Credit Corp v Da Silva* [1965] 1 W.L.R. 248, 259–260. Compare also now *Fosca Services (UK) Ltd v Birkett* [1996] I.R.L.R. 325; and *Wise Group v Mitchell* [2005] I.C.R. 896.

[1439] *Hartley v Harman* (1840) 11 A. & E. 798. See now *Harper v Virgin Net Ltd* [2004] EWCA Civ 271, in which it was held that damages for wrongful dismissal should not include compensation for the chance that, if the employee had not been dismissed with insufficient notice, she would have become time-qualified to make a claim for unfair dismissal. The decision in *Harper v Virgin Net Ltd* was followed and applied in *Wise Group v Mitchell* [2005] I.C.R. 896.

[1440] [1980] I.C.R. 755; cf. *Dietman v Brent LBC* [1987] I.C.R. 787; affirmed on other grounds [1988] I.C.R. 842. Compare also now *Boyo v Lambeth LBC* [1994] I.C.R. 727; see above, para.40-193.

[1441] The judges in the Court of Appeal differed on whether the wrongful dismissal determined the contract in the face of the employee's non-acceptance of it as doing so (see above, para.40-193), but were all agreed that this was correct measure of damages on either footing.

[1442] [2011] UKSC 58.

[1443] This body of doctrine is explained more fully below at para.40-204.

[1444] See, per Lord Dyson at [48] and (rather differently) Lord Mance at [94].

[1445] *Janicuk v Winerite Ltd* [1998] I.R.L.R. 63.

[1446] See above, paras 40-163 et seq.

[1447] *Monk v Redwing Aircraft Co Ltd* [1942] 1 K.B. 182.

[1448] *Hayward v Pullinger & Partners* [1950] 1 All E.R. 581.

whole of his or her new situation, and not merely by reference to his or her nominal salary or wages. Thus, it was held that where, following his wrongful dismissal, the employee made a substantial investment in another firm and took employment in it at a low salary on the basis that he or she hoped to benefit from an increase in the value of his or her investment, account should be taken of the increase in value (during the relevant period) when assessing damages for wrongful dismissal.[1449]

Damages for other lost benefits Damages for wrongful dismissal may also **40-203** include an assessment of other benefits which the dismissed employee would have received from the continuation of his or her employment, e.g. the value of board and lodging or of a rent-free house.[1450] But the employee cannot claim for the loss of expected benefits if these were not benefits which the employer was contractually bound to give.[1451] Thus, where the grant of bonuses was entirely in the employer's discretion, damages for wrongful dismissal should not include any compensation for the loss of expected bonuses in the future.[1452] But if the employee was entitled, by the terms of his or her employment, to receive gratuities given by customers, the estimated value of these gratuities may be taken into account in assessing damages.[1453]

Damages for injury to feelings or reputation If it is a term of the contract, **40-204** express or implied, that the employer should not only pay a salary, but also give the employee an opportunity of publicity, damages may be awarded for loss of publicity, insofar as the employee has lost an opportunity of enhancing his or her reputation.[1454] It used to be considered that in an action for wrongful dismissal (as distinct from one for defamation) the employee is not entitled to damages for the injury caused by the dismissal to his or her existing reputation[1455]; and that damages could not normally be given, in an action for wrongful dismissal, for injury to the employee's feelings, his or her distress, social discredit or loss of reputation[1456]: so where an employee was wrongfully dismissed in a humiliating manner, he or she could not recover damages for these results of the dismissal, nor for the extra difficulty in finding other employment which was caused by the circumstances of his or her dismissal.[1457] The proposition that damages for wrongful dismissal do not include damages for loss of reputation, or for stigma associ-

---

[1449] *Lavarack v Woods of Colchester Ltd* [1967] 1 Q.B. 278.

[1450] *Lindsay v Queen's Hotel Co* [1919] 1 K.B. 212; *Re English Joint Stock Bank* (1867) L.R. 4 Eq. 350; *British Guiana Credit Corp v Da Silva* [1965] 1 W.L.R. 248, 259–260. In *Silvey v Pendragon Plc* [2001] EWCA Civ 784, the Court of Appeal held that an employee wrongfully dismissed 12 days short of his reaching the age at which pension rights would have accrued was entitled to damages for the loss of those rights and was not precluded from that entitlement by his acceptance of a payment in lieu of notice.

[1451] *Lavarack v Woods of Colchester Ltd*, above. It should be noted, however, how the decision in the *Lavarack* case was distinguished by the Court of Appeal in *Horkulak v Cantor Fitzgerald International* [2004] EWCA Civ 1287, [2005] I.C.R. 402.

[1452] See para.40-079, above.

[1453] *Manubens v Leon* [1919] 1 K.B. 209. cf. *Palmanor Ltd v Cedron* [1978] I.C.R. 1008.

[1454] *Marbé v George Edwardes Ltd* [1928] 1 K.B. 269; *Clayton & Waller Ltd v Oliver* [1930] A.C. 209; *Tolnay v Criterion Film Productions Ltd* [1936] 2 All E.R. 1625. cf. *Re Golomb and Porter & Co's Arbitration* (1931) 144 L.T. 583; *Collier v Sunday Referee Publishing Co Ltd* [1940] 2 K.B. 647.

[1455] *Withers v General Theatre Corp Ltd* [1933] 2 K.B. 536.

[1456] *Addis v Gramophone Co Ltd* [1909] A.C. 488; *British Guiana Credit Corp v Da Silva* [1965] 1 W.L.R. 248, 259; *Bliss v South East Thames RHA* [1987] I.C.R. 700.

[1457] *Addis v Gramophone Co Ltd*, above. Contrast the position of the wrongfully dismissed apprentice: see *Dunk v George Waller & Son Ltd* [1970] 2 Q.B. 163.

ated with the employment or the manner of its ending, seemed to have been greatly circumscribed by the decision of the House of Lords in *Malik v Bank of Credit and Commerce International SA*,[1458] which did not itself concern a wrongful dismissal as such, but where, in comparable circumstances, the House of Lords refused to follow, or at least greatly circumscribed, the rule in *Addis v Gramophone Co*[1459] and held that the employees might prove in the employer's liquidation for "stigma damages" reflecting the damage to the employees' prospects of future employment caused by the wrongful and apparently corrupt way in which the employer's business had been run. However, in *Johnson v Unisys Ltd*,[1460] the House of Lords held that the implied obligation of mutual trust and confidence did not apply to limit the exercise by an employer of a power of dismissal, so that a claim for stigma damages could not be made where that would be the basis of the claim. To that extent, the rule in *Addis v Gramophone Co* is reinstated, at least where it is the manner of a dismissal which is the basis for claiming that it is contractually wrongful, so as to preclude a claim for "stigma damages" or for damages for distress or injury to feelings. However, as has been explained earlier,[1461] the decision of the House of Lords in *Eastwood v Magnox Electric Plc, McCabe v Cornwall CC*[1462] limited the scope of that exclusionary rule so that it did not apply to rule out a claim for psychiatric illness alleged to have been caused by a course of harassing conduct associated with disciplinary proceedings against the employee although that course of conduct culminated in his dismissal, on the footing that the course of conduct in question could be regarded as independent of the subsequent dismissal itself. The reinstatement of the doctrine in the *Addis* case has now been effectively completed, and the doctrine itself has even been reinforced, by the Supreme Court in *Edwards v Chesterfield Royal Hospital NHS Trust*.[1463] Not only did the Supreme Court take the approach of the House of Lords in the *Addis* case as the starting point for the modern common law position[1464] and confirm the existence of the "*Johnson* exclusion" (which as has been explained earlier precluded the implied contractual obligation of trust and confidence from applying to dismissal proceedings[1465]), but it also articulated the view that even express contractual obligations to follow specified dismissal procedures should not be treated as giving rise to damages at common law for their breach in the current context where the law of unfair dismissal can be seen as providing for the enforcement of such obligations.[1466] It should be noted, however, that the holding of the Supreme Court as thus summarised was the subject of several dissents,[1467] and that, within the deciding majority, different views were taken as to the basis on which the doctrine in *Addis* survives.[1468] So the controversies surrounding this area of the common law[1469] cannot be regarded as fully resolved.

[1458] [1998] A.C. 20.

[1459] [1909] A.C. 488.

[1460] [2001] I.C.R. 480.

[1461] See above, para.40-154.

[1462] [2004] UKHL 35, [2005] 1 A.C. 503; compare also *GAB Robins (UK) Ltd v Triggs* [2008] EWCA Civ 17, [2008] I.R.L.R. 317.

[1463] [2011] UKSC 58.

[1464] See, in particular Lord Dyson at [21].

[1465] See above, paras 40-154, 40-194.

[1466] This view is most directly put forward by Lord Dyson at [39] adopting the view of Lord Hoffmann in the *Johnson* case at [66].

[1467] On the part of Lady Hale and Lords Kerr and Wilson.

[1468] Lord Phillips, differing in this respect from Lords Dyson, Walker and Mance, regarded it as being

Taxation   In an assessment of damages for loss of wages or salary in an action for   **40-205**
wrongful dismissal, a deduction must be made on account of estimated income tax
which would have been payable in respect of the wages or salary.[1470] If the damages exceed £30,000, however, notional tax should not be taken into account in
respect of the amount by which the total exceeds £30,000, because tax is chargeable on the excess[1471] in the hands of the plaintiff.[1472] (The rule that tax must be
deducted applies only where the earnings would have been subject to tax, and the
damages awarded to the plaintiff are not subject to tax in his hands).[1473] Full details
will be found in Vol.I, above.[1474]

Deductions for social security contributions and benefits   In calculating the   **40-206**
damages to be awarded for loss of wages, a deduction should be made for the
employee's social security contributions which the employer would have been
obliged to deduct from the plaintiff's wages.[1475] Similarly, it has been decided[1476]
that unemployment benefit (now contribution-based Jobseeker's Allowance under
the Jobseekers Act 1995) received by the plaintiff directly mitigates the plaintiff's
loss of earnings and should be taken into account by way of deduction in assessing damages for wrongful dismissal.[1477] But sums received by way of national assistance benefit (now income-based Jobseeker's Allowance under the Jobseekers
Act 1995), being discretionary payments, should not be taken into account.[1478]
Moreover, it was held in *Westwood v Secretary of State for Employment*[1479] that
unemployment benefits were deductible in mitigation of damages only to the extent
that they constituted a net gain to the employee, that net gain being reduced by his
having exhausted his limited entitlement to that benefit earlier than he would have
done if he had not been wrongfully dismissed.

Deductions for redundancy payments and unfair dismissal compensation   It   **40-207**

---

concerned not with the scope of the employer's contractual duty but with the measure and remoteness of damages for breach of that duty at [78]–[81].

[1469] See Freedland, *The Personal Employment Contract* (2003) at pp.356–368.

[1470] *Parsons v BNM Laboratories Ltd* [1964] 1 Q.B. 95 (following *British Transport Commission v
Gourley* [1956] A.C. 185). See *Lyndale Fashion Manufacturers v Rich* [1973] 1 W.L.R. 73. For the
manner of calculating the effect of income tax, see *Shore v Downs Surgical Plc* [1984] I.C.R. 209.

[1471] Income Tax (Earnings and Pensions) Act 2003 ss.403–404.

[1472] *Bold v Brough, Nicholson & Hall Ltd* [1964] 1 W.L.R. 201.

[1473] *British Transport Commission v Gourley* [1956] A.C. 185.

[1474] Vol.I, paras 26-262—26-270.

[1475] *Cooper v Firth Brown Ltd* [1963] 1 W.L.R. 418. (This was a negligence case, but the same rule, it
is submitted, would apply to the assessment of damages in contract for wrongful dismissal.)

[1476] *Parsons v BNM Laboratories Ltd* [1964] 1 Q.B. 95. cf. *Parry v Cleaver* [1968] 1 Q.B. 195
(negligence case, concerning a police pension receivable as of right); *Cheeseman v Bowaters Paper
Mills Ltd* [1971] 1 W.L.R. 1773. It was decided by the Court of Appeal in *Hopkins v Norcross* [1994]
I.C.R. 11 that the employee did not have to give credit for retirement pension payments received fol-
lowing wrongful dismissal, these being exempt collateral benefits within the principle of *Parry v
Cleaver* [1968] 1 Q.B. 195.

[1477] Claims for damages for wrongful dismissal would seem not to be affected by the recoupment provisions either of the Social Security (Recovery of Benefits) Act 1997, which applies to "payments in
consequence of any accident, injury or disease" (s.1(1)(a)) or of the Employment Protection (Recoupment of Benefits) Regulations 1996 (SI 1996/2349), which apply to certain payments awarded by
Employment Tribunals but not to common law damages.

[1478] *Foxley v Olton* [1965] 2 Q.B. 306 (criticised by Ganz (1965) 23 M.L.R. 224). cf. *Eley v Bedford*
[1972] 1 Q.B. 155.

[1479] [1985] I.C.R. 209.

was held at first instance in *Stocks v Magna Merchants Ltd*[1480] that in assessing damages for a wrongful dismissal the court should deduct the amount of a redundancy payment received by the plaintiff employee in respect of that dismissal. It had been thought to follow, although it had not been established by decided cases, that there should also be a deduction of the amount of unfair dismissal compensation received in respect of the dismissal concerned. However, in *O'Laoire v Jackel International Ltd (No.2)*,[1481] it was held that unless the defendants can prove a double recovery for the same loss, there is no basis for setting off an unfair dismissal compensatory award against common law damages for wrongful dismissal.

(e)   Equitable Remedies and Declarations

40-208   Specific performance and injunction against employees (1)   In order to understand the role of the remedies of specific performance and injunction in the law of the contract of employment, it is necessary to distinguish between, on the one hand, a long history of the granting of those remedies against employees, and, on the other hand, a more recent history of the granting of those remedies against employers also. The granting of orders for specific performance or injunctions in enforcement of contracts of employment against employees is the subject both of a statutory provision and of case law authority. The statutory provision is that of s.236 of the Trade Union and Labour Relations (Consolidation) Act 1992, which limits enforcement against employees by providing that no court shall whether by way of an order for specific performance of a contract of employment or an injunction restraining the breach of such a contract compel an employee to do any work or attend any place for the doing of any work. The case law suggests the following rules. The court will not grant specific performance of a contract of employment. Such a contract is one for personal services and comes within the category of contracts whose execution the court cannot supervise and will not, therefore, enforce by an order for specific performance.[1482] Early authority holds that the same rule applies to a contract of apprenticeship.[1483] For the same reason, the court will not usually grant an injunction for the fulfilment of a contract of employment[1484]; it will, however, grant an injunction to enforce an express negative stipulation,[1485] except where the effect of doing so would be to compel the employee to remain in the employment.[1486] When there is a positive undertaking to serve the plaintiff and a negative stipulation not to serve any other person, an injunction may be granted to enforce the negative stipulation if a breach of the positive undertaking would cause damage, even though the plaintiff fails to prove that a breach of the negative stipulation would do so.[1487] The availability of an injunction in such cases would be subject, however, to the applicability thereto of s.236 of the Trade Union and Labour Relations (Consolidation) Act 1992, considered earlier in this paragraph.

[1480] [1973] I.C.R. 530, applying *Parry v Cleaver* [1970] A.C. 1; and *Parsons v BNM Laboratories Ltd* [1964] 1 Q.B. 95. But see *Basnett v J & A Jackson Ltd* [1976] I.C.R. 63.

[1481] [1991] I.C.R. 718.

[1482] See Vol.I, paras 27-036 et seq.

[1483] *Webb v England* (1860) 29 Beav. 44.

[1484] *De Francesco v Barnum* (1889) 45 Ch. D. 430; *Ehrman v Bartholomew* [1898] 1 Ch. 671.

[1485] *Lumley v Wagner* (1852) 1 De G.M. & G. 604 (opera singer); *Warner Bros v Nelson* [1937] 1 K.B. 209 (film actress).

[1486] *Ehrman v Bartholomew* [1898] 1 Ch. 671; *Kirchner v Gruban* [1909] 1 Ch. 413; *Rely-a-Bell Burglar and Fire Alarm Co v Eisler* [1926] Ch. 609.

[1487] *Marco Productions Ltd v Pagola* [1945] K.B. 111.

Specific performance and injunction against employees (2)   In *Thomas* **40-209**
Marshall Ltd v Guinle,[1488] the Vice-Chancellor granted interim injunctions to
restrain an employee from acts of trade competition and disclosure of information
in breach of his implied obligations of fidelity,[1489] holding that the employee's unaccepted wrongful repudiation of his contract of employment had not released him
from the obligations thereof,[1490] and that although the court was powerless to force
the employee to work in accordance with his contract, the court could restrain him
from committing other breaches of his obligations during the period of his contract.
A similar result was reached in *Evening Standard Ltd v Henderson*[1491] where an
employer, seeking to restrain the employee, the production manager of an evening
newspaper, from working for any rival in the newspaper trade for the duration of
the contractual notice period, was prepared to provide the employee with all his
contractual benefits until the contract expired without insisting that he perform any
services under the contract; the employee would not therefore be forced either to
work for the plaintiffs or be reduced to a condition of starvation or idleness, and
the balance of convenience was therefore in favour of granting an interlocutory
injunction. However, it would now seem that in order to obtain an injunction to
enforce the imposition of a period of "garden leave" (that is to say, a period of
enforced idleness during which an employee may be prevented from working for
any other employer during a period of notice, though not being required or even
permitted to work for the original employer), the employer must show that the
employee has no contractual entitlement to be allowed to work, and must justify
the enforcement as if it were of an express covenant against post-employment
competition.[1492]

Specific performance and injunction against employers   Until relatively **40-210**
recently, there was little or no indication of any willingness on the part of the courts
to grant orders for the specific performance of contracts of employment by employers, or injunctions against dismissal, such as would result in the reinstatement of
the employee in an employment from which he or she had been, or was about to
be, dismissed. However, in *Hill v CA Parsons & Co Ltd*[1493] an injunction was
granted to restrain the implementation of an employer's notice to dismiss where the
dismissal would if carried out have been wrongful (by reason of the shortness of
notice).[1494] A majority of the Court of Appeal[1495] regarded the normal rule against
such injunctions as displaced by:

    (a)   the need to preserve the plaintiff's position until the unfair dismissal legisla-
           tion came into force; and

[1488] [1978] I.C.R. 905, applied in *SG & R Valuation Service Co LLC v Boudrais* [2008] EWHC 1340
(QB), [2008] I.R.L.R. 770.
[1489] See above, para.40-062.
[1490] See above, para.40-193.
[1491] [1987] I.C.R. 588.
[1492] *William Hill Organisation Ltd v Tucker* [1999] I.C.R. 291. Compare, however, *SG & R Valuation
Service Co LLC v Boudrais* [2008] EWHC 1340 (QB), [2008] I.R.L.R. 770 where the balance of
convenience was held to favour the granting of interim relief. Compare now *JM Finn & Co Ltd v
Holliday* [2013] EWHC 3450 (QB), [2014] I.R.L.R. 102.
[1493] [1972] 1 Ch. 305.
[1494] See above, para.40-163.
[1495] Lord Denning M.R. and Sachs L.J.; Stamp L.J. dissenting.

(b) the fact that the employer had no lack of confidence in the employee and intended to dismiss him solely because of trade union pressure.[1496]

It appears, on the other hand, from the decision in *Chappell v Times Newspapers Ltd*[1497] that employees would be most unlikely to obtain a similar injunction to restrain a dismissal which was a response to industrial action on the part of the employees, because in that situation the courts' normal objection to intervening once the relationship of mutual confidence has been destroyed will apply.[1498] Moreover, that decision suggests that employees will be unable to show the readiness, ability and willingness to continue to perform their part of the contract, which is necessary if they are to obtain equitable relief, if they are members of a trade union currently engaged in industrial action and are, or are likely to be, a party to that action.[1499] In certain cases, the courts have been willing to issue interlocutory injunctions to restrain breach of the contract of employment by the employer consisting of purporting to dismiss without following contractual dismissal procedure,[1500] purporting to re-advertise the post to which the employee had been validly appointed,[1501] or purporting to reorganise the employees' work inconsistently with their contractual job specification.[1502] It has been a condition of that willingness that the court can find that a basis of mutual trust and confidence survives between the employer and the employee.[1503] The Court of Appeal recently held, in *Mezey v South West London and St George's Mental Health NHS Trust*[1504] that there was no reason of principle why the court should be without power, if in all the circumstances it judged it right to do so, to stay a suspension just as it was able to stay a dismissal. A full discussion of the relevant principles will be found in Vol.I, above.[1505]

40-211 **Declaration and other remedies** The Civil Procedure Rules give the court power to make a declaration even where no other consequential relief is or could be claimed.[1506] A party may obtain a declaration that he or she is not bound by a

---

[1496] See, per Lord Denning M.R. at 315A to 316C, Stamp L.J. at 320E–H.

[1497] [1975] I.C.R. 145.

[1498] See, per Lord Denning M.R. at 173H–174B, Stephenson L.J. at 176B–D, Geoffrey Lane J. at 178H–179B.

[1499] See, per Lord Denning M.R. at 173D–H, Stephenson L.J. at 177A–D and Geoffrey Lane J. at 179C–D.

[1500] *Irani v Southampton & Southwest Hampshire HA* [1985] I.C.R. 590. In *Barros d' Sa v University Hospital Coventry and Warwickshire NHS Trust* [2001] EWCA Civ 983, [2001] I.R.L.R. 691, the Court of Appeal upheld the grant of an injunction preventing the consideration at the appeal stage of a disciplinary procedure of material adverse to the employee which had not been the subject of findings at the original inquiry stage. A further example is provided by *Kircher v Hillingdon Primary Care Trust* [2006] EWHC 21 (QB), [2006] Lloyd's Rep. Med. 215. Comparison should also be made with the decision in *Lauffer v Barking, Havering and Redbridge University Hospitals NHS Trust* [2009] EWHC 2360 (QB), [2010] Med. L.R. 68, and now also with *West London Mental Health NHS Trust v Chhabra* [2013] UKSC 80, [2014] 1 All E.R. 943 at [37] (breach of "implied contractual right to a fair disciplinary process").

[1501] *Powell v Brent LBC* [1988] I.C.R. 176.

[1502] *Hughes v Southwark LBC* [1988] I.R.L.R. 55.

[1503] *Ali v Southwark LBC* [1988] I.C.R. 567. Compare *Lakshmi v Mid-Cheshire Hospitals NHS Trust* [2008] EWHC 878 (QB), [2008] I.R.L.R. 956, and see *Ashworth v Royal National Theatre* [2014] EWHC 1176 (QB), [2014] I.R.L.R. 526 on the question of the employer's right to artistic freedom of expression.

[1504] [2007] EWCA Civ 106, [2007] I.R.L.R. 244.

[1505] Vol.I, paras 27-025 et seq.

[1506] CPR Ord.15 r.16 as re-enacted in Sch.1 to the Civil Procedure Rules 1998. The circumstances in

contract because the other party has repudiated it,[1507] but such a declaration will not lie if the party seeking the declaration continues to perform his or her duties under the contract. Thus an employee who was still working under his or her contract of employment with a company could not claim a declaration that his or her contract had been repudiated because the chairperson of the company interfered with his or her work.[1508] It used to be thought that if one party has purported to terminate a contract of employment, the court would grant a declaration that the contract still subsists, where the employed person enjoys a special "status" or "office" by virtue of a statute.[1509]

In *Malloch v Aberdeen Corp*,[1510] a case decided by the House of Lords applying **40-212** Scottish law, an order for the reduction of a dismissal (which had the effect of nullifying the dismissal) was granted in favour of a teacher who had been dismissed without a hearing. It was held that the legislation controlling the employment of teachers by education authorities in Scotland impliedly conferred a right to be heard before dismissal,[1511] and it was held to follow that the teacher thence derived a special status or office which made it appropriate for his dismissal to be nullified.[1512] It was thought that similar reasoning might be invoked to support the grant of a declaration of nullity of dismissal or an order of certiorari to quash the dismissal in an English case in which the plaintiff was regarded as having an employment similarly subject to the public law principle of natural justice.[1513] The decision in *R. v British Broadcasting Corp Ex p. Lavelle*[1514] seemed to suggest that view. However, the cases now suggest that an applicant for judicial review of a dismissal from employment must show that a public law right of his or hers has been infringed; and the fact that he or she is an employee under a contract of employment will normally mean that he or she does not have such a public law right. Thus

---

which there may be a declaration of continuing breach of a contract of employment were considered in *Birmingham City Council v Wetherill* [2007] EWCA Civ 599, [2007] I.R.L.R. 781.

[1507] *Spettabile Consorzio Veneziano di Armamento e Navitazione v Northumberland Shipbuilding Co* (1919) 121 L.T. 628. Compare *Kaur v MG Rover Group Ltd* [2004] I.R.L.R. 279, QBD, where a declaration was granted of contractual entitlement not to be made redundant. The decision was reversed on appeal on other, substantive, grounds ([2004] EWCA Civ 1507, [2005] I.R.L.R. 40), but remains of interest as to this remedial point.

[1508] *Howard v Pickford Tool Co* [1951] 1 K.B. 417; *Cranleigh Precision Engineering Ltd v Bryant* [1965] 1 W.L.R. 1293, 1304–1305.

[1509] *Francis v Municipal Councillors of Kuala Lumpur* [1962] 1 W.L.R. 1411, 1417–1418; *Vine v National Dock Labour Board* [1957] A.C. 488, 500, 507. See further, Vol.I, para.27-037. In *Gunton v Richmond LBC* [1980] I.C.R. 755, the Court of Appeal upheld a declaration that a contract of employment had not been validly terminated by an unaccepted wrongful repudiation by the employer, despite their unanimous view that this was an ordinary contract of employment not conferring any special status, see above, para.40-192. But Shaw L.J. dissented from the view that the contract had not come to an end, see above, para.40-193, and thought that declaration was an unnecessary and inappropriate form of relief in this sort of case ([1980] I.C.R. 755 at 764A), Buckley L.J. thought that the relationship of employment had been effectively terminated even if the contract had not ([1980] I.C.R. 755 at 778D), and all three judges agreed that the measure of damages should be based not on a total nullification of the purported dismissal but merely on its notional postponement to the date on which it could validly have taken effect, see above, para.40-193 (and also para.40-202 with regard to the relation between the *Gunton* case and the decision in *Edwards v Chesterfield Royal Hospital NHS Trust* [2011] UKSC 58). So the decision scarcely serves to qualify the proposition in the text.

[1510] [1971] 1 W.L.R. 1578. See above, para.40-192.

[1511] See, per Lord Reid at 1581A–1583B.

[1512] See, per Lord Reid at 1584D–E.

[1513] cf. per Lord Wilberforce at 1595E–1597E.

[1514] [1983] I.C.R. 99.

in *R. v East Berkshire HA Ex p. Walsh*[1515] a senior nursing officer failed in such a claim on the ground that he or she was seeking to enforce purely private contractual rights; in *R. v Secretary of State for the Home Department Ex p. Benwell*,[1516] on the other hand, a prison officer succeeded because as a holder of the office of constable he or she had no contract of employment and hence no relevant private law rights.

(f) Employment Tribunal Jurisdiction

40-213 Jurisdiction of employment tribunals in relation to contracts of employment   Under what is now s.3 of the Employment Tribunals Act 1996,[1517] the appropriate Minister was empowered (originally in 1971) to make an order to confer upon employment tribunals a jurisdiction to make pecuniary awards based upon contracts of employment.[1518] The claims concerned include claims for damages for breach of a contract of employment or any other contract connected with employment[1519] (but not damages for personal injuries)[1520] and claims for sums due under such contracts.[1521] The purpose of this provision is chiefly to enable an employment tribunal to deal with contractual claims which often arise incidentally to claims before employment tribunals for redundancy payments[1522] and complaints of unfair dismissal,[1523] and thus to avoid an inconvenient separation of common law and statutory jurisdictions. An Order made[1524] under this provision enables an employee to bring a claim for damages for breach of the contract of employment, or for a sum due under that contract, before an employment tribunal if the claim arises or is outstanding on the termination of his employment.[1525] The Order also enables an employer to make such a claim against an employee where the employee has

---

[1515] [1984] I.C.R. 743.

[1516] [1984] I.C.R. 723. For the position of Crown servants who have a relationship with the Crown analogous to a contract of employment, see *R. v Civil Service Appeal Board Ex p. Bruce* [1989] I.C.R. 171; and compare above, para.40-192.

[1517] Provision was made for industrial tribunals to be known as employment tribunals by s.1 of the Employment Rights (Dispute Resolution) Act 1998 (with effect from August 1, 1998: SI 1998/1658).

[1518] Employment Tribunals Act 1996 (as renamed by the Employment Rights (Dispute Resolution) Act 1998) ss.3(1), 8(1).

[1519] Employment Tribunals Act 1996 (as renamed by the Employment Rights (Dispute Resolution) Act 1998) s.3(2)(a).

[1520] Employment Tribunals Act 1996 (as renamed by the Employment Rights (Dispute Resolution) Act 1998) s.3(3).

[1521] Employment Tribunals Act 1996 (as renamed by the Employment Rights (Dispute Resolution) Act 1998) s.3(2)(b).

[1522] See below, paras 40-248 et seq.

[1523] See below, para.40-245.

[1524] Industrial Tribunals Extension of Jurisdiction (England and Wales) Order 1994 (SI 1994/1623), in force from July 12, 1994.

[1525] SI 1994/1623 art.3. It was held in *Sarker v South Tees Acute Hospitals NHS Trust* [1997] I.C.R. 673 that this extended to the case of the employer's wrongfully resiling from a contract of employment before employment had commenced; and in *Rock-it Cargo Ltd v Green* [1997] I.R.L.R. 581 that it enabled an employee to claim a payment due under a compromise agreement on termination of employment. In *Miller Bros and Butler Ltd v Johnston* [2002] I.R.L.R. 386, the Employment Appeal Tribunal held that this jurisdiction is limited to claims arising or outstanding at the time of the termination of employment, and does not extend to claims arising later even though they arise out of the termination of employment, as, in this case, upon a subsequently finalised compromise agreement. Compare *Peninsula Business Services Ltd v Sweeney* [2004] I.R.L.R. 49, EAT, denying entitlement to commission payments which would normally have accrued due at a date later than that of termination of employment, and where the rules of the commission scheme excluded post-termination accrual.

claimed against him under the Order.[1526] There are exclusions of claims about the provision of living accommodation, intellectual property, obligations of confidence on the employee and covenants in restraint of trade.[1527] An employee's complaint about a contractual claim must normally be presented within a period of three months beginning with the "effective date of termination" of the contract of employment as defined in s.97(1) of the Employment Rights Act 1996[1528]; an employer's complaint about a contractual claim must normally be presented within six weeks of receiving a copy of an originating application relating to the employee's complaint.[1529] The maximum which a tribunal may order to be paid in respect of a contract claim, or a number of claims relating to the same contract, is £25,000.[1530] The contractual claims before employment tribunals may now be subject to the provisions for other methods of dispute resolution for which provision has been made by the Employment Rights (Dispute Resolution) Act 1998.[1531]

(g) Employer's Damages

Damages recoverable by the employer The employee may be held liable in damages for the breach of any term of his or her contract of employment, whether express or implied,[1532] such as by his or her failure to use due care or skill.[1533] Early authority holds that the employer is entitled to damages for those consequences which might reasonably be expected to have been in the contemplation of the parties (at the time when the contract of employment was made) as likely to result from the breach.[1534] Damages for failure or refusal to work will normally be assessed by reference to the value of the work lost[1535] or the cost of procuring a substitute to do the work,[1536] less the wages payable under the contract. But the loss of output suffered by the employer's business cannot be caused by any one employee's failure to work when there was a general stoppage by many employees on the same day.[1537] The suspension of salary when an employee fails to work is not a "penalty".[1538] In

40-214

[1526] SI 1994/1623 art.4.

[1527] SI 1994/1623 art.5.

[1528] SI 1994/1623 art.7. See, for "effective date of termination", below, paras 40-222—40-223.

[1529] SI 1994/1623 art.8.

[1530] SI 1994/1623 art.10.

[1531] See ss.7–8 (arbitration), ss.9–10 (compromise agreements).

[1532] See above, paras 40-058 et seq.

[1533] *Hindley v Haslam* (1878) 3 Q.B.D. 481; *Sagar v Ridehalgh* [1931] 1 Ch. 310, 316; *Stumore, Weston & Co v Breen* (1886) 12 App. Cas. 698; *Baster v London & County Printing Works* [1899] 1 Q.B. 901.

[1534] *Cassaboglou v Gibb* (1883) 11 Q.B.D. 797. For these general principles with regard to damages, see Vol.I, paras 26-117 et seq.

[1535] *Ebbw Vale Steel, etc. Co v Tew* (1935) 79 S.J. 593. cf. *National Coal Board v Galley* [1958] 1 W.L.R. 16.

[1536] *Richards v Hayward* (1841) 2 Man. & G. 574; *National Coal Board v Galley* [1958] 1 W.L.R. 16.

[1537] *National Coal Board v Galley*, above.

[1538] See Vol.I, paras 26-190 et seq. However, in *Giraud UK Ltd v Smith* [2000] I.R.L.R. 763 it was held by the Employment Tribunal that a clause purporting to entitle the employer to make a deduction from the employee's final remuneration payment, which was the equivalent of his pay for the number of days short of the contractually required four weeks' notice to leave given by the employee, was unenforceable as an unlawful penalty clause. The drawing of the distinction between "liquidated damages" and "penalty" clauses, in the context of employers' claims against prospective employees for breach of contract to enter into employment, was further expounded in *Tullett Prebon Group Ltd v El-Hajjali* [2008] EWHC 1924 (QB), [2008] I.R.L.R. 760, where the clause in question was upheld as not being a penalty on the basis that, although the clause had some purpose of deterrence of

Imam-Sadeque v Bluebay Asset Management (Services) Ltd,[1539] it was confirmed that the "penalty" doctrine extended to terms which provided that the contract breaker was to forfeit sums to which he was entitled, or would otherwise have been entitled, from the innocent party; but it was held that it did not apply to a compromise agreement for the termination of a contract of employment insofar as it prevented the employee from acquiring certain fund units in which his contract of employment had given him a contingent future interest.[1540] The employer may, in addition to suspending the salary, be entitled to damages for breach of contract.[1541] An employer who is entitled to dismiss his or her employee cannot, however, on that basis alone elect to treat the contract as continuing and suspend him or her for a period so as to prevent him or her (as a punishment) from earning his wages for that period.[1542] The circumstances in which an employer may claim an indemnity from a tortfeasor employee in respect of the claim of a third person have been considered earlier.[1543]

8. UNFAIR AND DISCRIMINATORY DISMISSAL

(a) Unfair Dismissal

(i) General Considerations

40-215 **Introduction** By s.22 of the Industrial Relations Act 1971 (which came into force on February 28, 1972) in every employment except those excluded by ss.27–31, the employee was given the right not to be unfairly dismissed by his or her employer. That right was made enforceable by a right of complaint to an employment tribunal which was empowered to make a recommendation for re-engagement or reinstatement, or to award compensation. The unfair dismissal provisions of that Act were repealed but re-enacted with only minor amendments by the Trade Union and Labour Relations Act 1974. The Employment Protection Act 1975 made further amendments to those unfair dismissal provisions, and in particular replaced the provisions about remedies with a new and more extensive set of provisions. Hence the present law concerning unfair dismissal is derived from the Trade Union and Labour Relations Act 1974 as amended by the Employment Protection Act 1975. Those provisions were consolidated into Pt V of the Employment Protection (Consolidation) Act 1978 which was subsequently amended by the Employment Acts 1980, 1982, 1988 and 1990. Some relevant provisions were transformed into the Trade Union and Labour Relations (Consolidation) Act 1992, and some further amendments were made by the Trade Union Reform and Employment Rights Act 1993. The present law is mainly contained in the latest consolidation, Pt X of the Employment Rights Act 1996, as subsequently amended.[1544] The case law concerning the interpretation of the unfair dismissal provisions is now very extensive, and

---

breach, that was not its predominant purpose.

[1539] [2012] EWHC 3511 (QB), [2013] I.R.L.R. 344.

[1540] See now also *Cleeve Link Ltd v Bryla* [2014] I.R.L.R. 86, EAT, and compare *Li v First Marine Solutions* [2014] UKEAT 0045/13/BI.

[1541] *Gaumont-British Picture Corp Ltd v Alexander* [1936] 2 All E.R. 1686.

[1542] *Hanley v Pease and Partners Ltd* [1915] 1 K.B. 698. Compare above, para.40-092 which discusses the effect of industrial action upon entitlement to remuneration.

[1543] See above, para.40-072.

[1544] For example, by the Public Interest Disclosure Act 1998—see below, para.40-234.

in the following account of those provisions it is generally only cases which are broadly relevant to the common law of the contract of employment that are cited.

Employments covered, employments specifically excluded　The unfair **40-216** dismissal provisions cover every employee under a contract of employment[1545] subject to certain exclusions and to certain extensions, which are described in the next paragraphs. Certain exclusions arise inherently as a matter of common law. Thus a director, acting only as such, may be held not to be an employee for the purposes of these provisions.[1546] A claimant may be excluded where his or her contract of employment is void for illegality, as where a fraud upon the Revenue is involved.[1547] A series of exclusions are made by express statutory provisions. Those in the police service are excluded from the unfair dismissal provisions,[1548] as are share-fishermen.[1549] However, in *Wandsworth LBC v Vining* the Court of Appeal relied on s.3 of the Human Rights Act 1998 in narrowly construing the statutory exclusion of those in "police service" so as not to apply to parks police officers.[1550]

Qualifying period　There is an exclusion which normally applies, but does not ap- **40-217** ply where the dismissal is for any one or more of a set of specified reasons or in any one or more of a set of specified situations[1551]; that is to say, the employee is normally excluded where he or she has not been continuously employed for the qualifying period at the effective date of termination of his employment.[1552] The qualifying period is two years[1553]; and is one month in relation to dismissal on grounds justifying statutory medical suspension.[1554] There may also be an exclusion on the basis of state immunity, despite the potential conflict with art.6 of the European Convention of Human Rights; the State Immunity Act 1978 cannot,

---

[1545] Employment Rights Act 1996 s.94, taken in conjunction with s.230(1) of Employment Rights Act 1996 (definition of "employee"). See above, paras 40-010—40-025, for definition of the contract of employment. As to the implicit exclusion of employees working abroad, see now *Lawson v Serco Ltd* [2006] UKHL 3, [2006] I.C.R. 250, in which the House of Lords allowed the appeals of certain claimants in a group of joined appeals, remitting their cases to the employment tribunal for rehearing, and further explicated the territorial scope of the right not be unfairly dismissed. Compare now *Dhunna v Creditsights Ltd* [2014] EWCA Civ 1238, [2014] I.C.R. 105.

[1546] See *Margetts v Underwood (Zelah)* [1973] I.T.R. 478. See above, para.40-014.

[1547] cf. *Cole v Fred Stacey Ltd* [1974] I.R.L.R. 73. See above, para.40-036.

[1548] Employment Rights Act 1996 s.200(1).

[1549] Employment Rights Act 1996 s.199(2).

[1550] [2017] EWCA Civ 1092, [2017] I.R.L.R. 1140.

[1551] The reasons are as specified by Employment Rights Act 1996 s.108(3) in relation to the qualifying period of employment.

[1552] Employment Rights Act 1996 s.108(1). For the definition of "effective date of termination", see below, paras 40-222—40-223. It is no longer necessary to distinguish between full-time and part-time employees, by reason of the Employment Protection (Part-time Employees) Regulations 1995 (SI 1995/31). The upper age limit of 65 or normal retirement age, which formerly applied, was abolished with effect from October 1, 2006 by the Employment Equality (Age) Regulations 2006 (SI 2006/1031) Sch.8 para.25. See also paras 40-175, 40-226.

[1553] Employment Rights Act 1996 s.108(1) as amended by the Unfair Dismissal and Statement of Reasons for Dismissal (Variation of Qualifying Period) Order 2012 (SI 2012/989) with effect upon periods of employment beginning from April 6, 2012. For "continuously employed" see s.213 Employment Rights Act 1996; see also above, paras 40-165—40-168.

[1554] Employment Rights Act 1996 s.108(2).

however, operate to defeat claims based on employment rights derived from EU law.[1555]

40-218 **Employments to which the unfair dismissal provisions are specifically extended or applied** There is a significant set of types of employment in the public service to which the unfair dismissal legislation is specifically extended or applied, partly in order to ensure that this legislation applies to such employments despite possible doubts whether the public servants concerned are employed under contracts of employment,[1556] and partly in order to modify the application of the legislation in ways regarded as appropriate to the public service relationships in question.[1557] The unfair dismissal legislation is applied in this way to parliamentary staff, both of the House of Lords[1558] and of the House of Commons.[1559] It is also applied to Crown employment,[1560] in which are included members of the armed forces,[1561] but subject to provision that its application to members of the armed forces may be modified (or withdrawn) by Order in Council,[1562] and that any Crown employment may be excepted from the legislation by a ministerial certificate that such exception is necessary for the purpose of safeguarding national security.[1563]

40-219 **Contracting-out of the unfair dismissal provisions** An agreement for contracting-out of unfair dismissal liability is normally void and of no effect, as is any agreement not to bring unfair dismissal procedures before an employment tribunal.[1564] There are certain limited exceptions to this rule. Formerly, an employer might obtain a waiver of unfair dismissal rights in respect of the expiry without renewal of a fixed-term contract of one year or more,[1565] but that facility was later withdrawn.[1566] A surviving exception consists in the fact that the parties to a dismissal procedure agreement may jointly apply for an order recognising the agreement recognised as a valid substitute for the unfair dismissal provisions.[1567] The Act sets out the matters of which the Secretary of State for Employment must be satisfied before he may give this recognition[1568] and also provides for applications for the revoking of such orders where the agreement has ceased to fulfil the statutory requirements.[1569] A second exception is a provision allowing effect to agreements to refrain from presenting or proceeding with a complaint about a dismissal which

---

[1555] *Benkharbouche v Embassy of Sudan* [2017] UKSC 62, [2017] 3 W.L.R. 957. For diplomatic immunity in the same context, see *Al-Malki v Reyes* [2017] UKSC 61, [2017] 3 W.L.R. 923.
[1556] As to which see above, para.40-035 (Crown employment).
[1557] cf. in addition to the employments specifically mentioned in this paragraph, the provisions of s.134 of the Employment Rights Act 1996 relating to teachers in aided schools. The police service is still, however, outside the scope of the provisions: s.200(1) of Employment Rights Act 1996.
[1558] Employment Rights Act 1996 s.194.
[1559] s.195.
[1560] s.191.
[1561] s.192.
[1562] s.192(3).
[1563] s.193. The reviewability of such a certificate was considered in the case of *Council of Civil Service Unions v Minister of the Civil Service* ("The GCHQ case") [1985] A.C. 374.
[1564] Employment Rights Act 1996 s.203(1). See *Sutherland v Network Appliance Ltd* [2001] I.R.L.R. 12—the compromise agreement remains effective in respect of claims for damages for breach of contract. And contrast this position with the Employee Shareholder status, above, para.40-030.
[1565] Employment Rights Act 1996 s.197(1).
[1566] s.197(1) was repealed by s.18 of the Employment Relations Act 1999.
[1567] Employment Rights Act 1996 s.110(1).
[1568] Employment Rights Act 1996 s.110(3).
[1569] Employment Rights Act 1996 s.110(4), (5).

has actually occurred.[1570] This power to make agreements compromising actions for unfair dismissal is subject to the proviso that some action must first have been taken by a conciliation officer.[1571]

(ii) Dismissal and Effective Date of Termination

The definition of dismissal   Dismissal is defined for the purposes of the unfair **40-220** dismissal provisions so as to extend to certain types of situation, and to no others. The statutory definition is expressed to be exhaustive.[1572] These situations are:

(a)   Where the contract of employment is terminated by the employer, whether it is so terminated by notice or without notice.[1573]

(b)   Where the contract is for a limited term[1574] and that term expires without being renewed "under the same contract".[1575]

(c)   Where the employee terminates the contract, with or without notice, in circumstances such that he or she is entitled to terminate it without notice by reason of the employer's conduct.[1576] There was no corresponding provision in the original unfair dismissal legislation of 1971, but this provision declares the result of case law development.[1577] Reference may be made to case law concerning both unfair dismissal and redundancy payments for indications as to when the employee's entitlement to claim constructive dismissal arises.[1578]

(d)   Where an employee under notice from his or her employer himself or herself gives notice which terminates earlier than the employer's notice is due to expire; and in that event the reason for dismissal is taken to be the reason for which the employer's notice was given.[1579]

The operation of this statutory definition of dismissal is affected at various points **40-221**

[1570] Employment Rights Act 1996 s.203(2)(e).

[1571] Employment Rights Act 1996 s.203(2)(e); see *BCCI v Ali* [2001] I.C.R. 337 as to the effect of such agreements, known as ACAS COT3 compromise agreements. Compare now the alternative dispute resolution provisions of ss.9–10 of the Employment Rights (Dispute Resolution) Act 1998—see also para.40-264.

[1572] Employment Rights Act 1996 s.95(1), the opening words.

[1573] Employment Rights Act 1996 s.95(1)(a). See above, para.40-193, for the question whether the employer can terminate the contract unilaterally in breach of contract. Also see *Chesham Shipping Ltd v Rowe* [1977] I.R.L.R. 391; *Walker v Cotswold Chine Home School* (1977) 12 I.T.R. 342; *Tanner v DT Kean Ltd* [1978] I.R.L.R. 110; *Pambakian v Brentford Nylons Ltd* [1978] I.C.R. 665 (hiving-down agreement); *British Midland Airways Ltd v Lewis* [1978] I.C.R. 782.

[1574] Now styled a limited-term contract—see above, para.40-173; see *Wiltshire CC v NATFHE* [1980] I.C.R. 455; *British Broadcasting Corp v Dixon* [1979] Q.B. 546.

[1575] s.95(1)(b). The concluding words are probably intended to exclude a renewal or re-engagement on different terms and conditions. cf. *British Broadcasting Corp v Kelly-Phillips* [1998] I.C.R. 587. That decision was followed, and the reasoning in it was applied, by the Court of Appeal in *Bhatt v Chelsea and Westminster Healthcare NHS Trust* [2000] C.L. 193.

[1576] Employment Rights Act 1996 s.95(1)(c).

[1577] See *Sutcliffe v Hawker Siddeley Aviation Ltd* [1973] I.C.R. 560.

[1578] See above, para.40-194; and *Western Excavating (ECC) Ltd v Sharpe* [1978] I.C.R. 221; *FC Gardner Ltd v Beresford* [1978] I.R.L.R. 63; *Robinson v Crompton Parkinson Ltd* [1978] I.C.R. 401; *Walker v Josiah Wedgwood Sons Ltd* [1978] I.C.R. 744; *Warner v Barbers Stores* [1978] I.R.L.R. 109; *Simmonds v Dowty Seals Ltd* [1978] I.R.L.R. 211; *Palmanor Ltd v Cedron* [1978] I.C.R. 1008; *Milthorn Toleman Ltd v Ford* [1978] I.R.L.R. 306; *British Aircraft Corp v Austin* [1978] I.R.L.R. 332; *Woods v WM Car Services Ltd* [1981] I.C.R. 666; *Pedersen v Camden LBC* [1981] I.C.R. 674 (note).

[1579] Employment Rights Act 1996 s.95(2).

by the common law concerning the termination of the contract of employment. Events affecting the employer such as liquidation of an employing company, appointment of a receiver or dissolution of partnership will not as such constitute dismissal,[1580] but will often have an effect on the contract of employment which will satisfy the definition of dismissal, or will entitle the employee to terminate his employment and claim constructive dismissal, as involving a unilateral termination of employment, a purported assignment of the contract of employment, or a repudiatory change in the terms and conditions of employment.[1581] Similarly, suspension of employment by the employer by way of disciplinary action or by way of lay-off in adverse economic conditions will not as such constitute dismissal, but may involve a termination of the contract by the employer or a repudiation of it entitling the employee to accept the termination and then claim constructive dismissal.[1582] On the other hand certain cases where there might at first sight appear to be a dismissal by the employer may fail to satisfy the definition of dismissal because the contract has been terminated under the doctrine of frustration by, for instance, the prolonged illness of the employee,[1583] or because the employee has unilaterally terminated the contract[1584] or rendered it impossible of performance,[1585] or because there has been a termination by mutual agreement.[1586] These alternatives to dismissal are firmly established as a matter of principle, but the tribunals and courts will not lightly allow them to operate to defeat claims of unfair dismissal. In *Morton Sundour Fabrics Ltd v Shaw*[1587] it was held that a warning of impending dismissal (for redundancy) at an unspecified future date did not constitute a dismissal for statutory purposes.

40-222   The effective date of termination   The date at which dismissal is deemed to occur, and the date upon which the contract of employment is deemed to terminate are important in the application of the unfair dismissal provisions for the following reasons:

(1)   the "effective date of termination of employment" is used to establish:
    (a)   whether the employee has served the qualifying period[1588];
    (b)   whether the employee presented his complaint in time[1589];

[1580] Contrast here ss.136(5), 139(4), (5) of Employment Rights Act 1996 in connection with redundancy—see below, para.40-253.

[1581] See generally above, paras 40-179—40-183 (changes in the employing enterprise).

[1582] See *Powell Duffryn Wagon Co Ltd v House* [1974] I.C.R. 123.

[1583] See *Marshall v Harland Wolff Ltd* [1972] I.C.R. 101; *Hebden v Forsey & Son* [1973] I.C.R. 607; *Egg Stores (Stamford Hill) Ltd v Leibovici* [1977] I.C.R. 260; *Hart v AR Marshall & Sons (Bulwell) Ltd* [1977] 1 W.L.R. 1067, and see above, para.40-176.

[1584] For the distinction between dismissal by the employer and "resignation" by the employee, see now *Sandhu v Jan de Rijk Transport Ltd* [2007] EWCA Civ 430, [2007] I.C.R. 1137; distinguishing *Sheffield v Oxford Controls Ltd* [1979] I.C.R. 396.

[1585] *Hare v Murphy Bros Ltd* [1974] I.C.R. 603. Contrast *Forgings & Presswork Ltd v McDougall* [1974] I.C.R. 532; and see above, para.40-176.

[1586] See *MacAlwane v Boughton Estates Ltd* [1973] I.C.R. 470; *Lees v Arthur Greaves Ltd* [1974] I.C.R. 501; *British Leyland (UK) Ltd v Ashraf* [1978] I.C.R. 979; *Midland Electric Manufacturing Co Ltd v Kanji* [1980] I.R.L.R. 185; and *Tracy v Zest Equipment Ltd* [1982] I.C.R. 481. See above, para.40-174.

[1587] (1966) 2 K.I.R. 1; see now *Haseltine, Lake & Co v Dowler* [1981] I.R.L.R. 25; *International Computers Ltd v Kennedy* [1981] I.R.L.R. 23.

[1588] Employment Rights Act 1996 s.108(1)—see above, para.40-125.

[1589] Employment Rights Act 1996 s.111(2)—see below, para.40-245.

    (c)   whether the provisions concerning dismissal in connection with a lock-out, strike or other industrial action are applicable[1590];

    (d)   the length of the employee's period of continuous employment[1591] for the purpose of calculating the amount of the basic award[1592] of compensation for unfair dismissal[1593]; and

    (e)   the calculation date of the employee's "week's pay"[1594] for the purpose of calculating the amount of basic award of compensation.[1595]

  (2)   the effective date of termination of employment is defined[1596] as:

    (a)   in relation to an employee whose contract of employment is terminated by notice, the date on which the notice expires;

    (b)   in relation to an employee whose contract is terminated without notice, the date on which termination takes effect;

    (c)   in relation to an employee employed under a limited-term contract which expires without being renewed under the same contract, the date on which the termination takes effect.

40-223

For certain above-mentioned purposes for which the definition applies, namely that of the initial qualifying period and that of the calculation of basic award of compensation, the effective date of termination is postponed[1597] to the date when a duly given statutory minimum period of notice[1598] would have expired. The application of the above statutory definition to termination by payment in lieu of notice depends upon the view taken of the juridical nature of a payment in lieu of notice, a matter considered in an earlier paragraph.[1599] Where a dismissal is expressed in a notice or letter, it has been held that the termination does not take effect until the employee has read that notice or letter or had a reasonable opportunity to do so.[1600] Where an employee is suspended without pay pending a domestic appeal against dismissal, it has been held that where the appeal is unsuccessful, the effective date of termination is that of the original dismissal.[1601] If, however, the employee is contractually entitled to remuneration during such suspension, the effective date of

---

[1590] See s.238(5) of Trade Union and Labour Relations (Consolidation) Act 1992.

[1591] See above, para.40-165.

[1592] See below, para.40-241.

[1593] Employment Rights Act 1996 s.119(1) and (2).

[1594] See below, para.40-255.

[1595] Employment Rights Act 1996 s.226(6).

[1596] Employment Rights Act 1996 s.97(1). See *Hammerton Shipping Co Ltd v Borg* [1977] 12 I.T.R. 54; and *Robert Cort & Son Ltd v Charman* [1981] I.C.R. 816. Compare *Fitzgerald v University of Kent at Canterbury* [2004] EWCA Civ 143, [2004] I.C.R. 737, in which it was held that a retrospective agreement did not validly alter the effective date of termination. But compare also now *Palfrey v Transco Plc* [2004] I.R.L.R. 916, EAT where a later agreement for payment in lieu of notice was held to have advanced the effective date of termination.

[1597] Employment Rights Act 1996 s.97(2)–(5). See *Dhami v Top Spot Night Club* [1977] I.R.L.R. 231.

[1598] See above, para.40-164; *Fox Maintenance Ltd v Jackson* [1978] I.C.R. 110. In *Harper v Virgin Net Ltd* [2004] EWCA Civ 271, [2004] I.R.L.R. 390 it was held that the legislation did not bring about a further postponement of the effective date of termination to the later date at which a contractual notice period, longer than the statutory minimum notice period, would have expired.

[1599] See above, para.40-182.

[1600] *Brown v Southall & Knight* [1980] I.C.R. 617. The decision was followed, and its doctrine was re-vindicated and elaborated, by the Court of Appeal and by the Supreme Court in *Gisda Cyf v Barratt* [2009] EWCA Civ 648, [2010] UKSC 41. See now also *Sandle v Adecco UK Ltd* [2016] I.R.L.R. 941, EAT.

[1601] *Sainsbury Ltd v Savage* [1981] I.C.R. 1.

termination is postponed until notification of the rejection of the appeal.[1602] Where an employer wrongfully repudiates the contract of employment by wrongful dismissal, it has been held that even if the elective theory whereby wrongful repudiation requires acceptance to terminate the contract is applicable,[1603] the effective date of termination for statutory purposes is nevertheless the date of the summary dismissal rather than the later date on which notice duly given on that date would have expired[1604] (subject only to the statutory extension for the statutory minimum period of notice).[1605]

(iii) Unfairness

40-224 Introduction Normally, the fairness or unfairness of a dismissal is, under the statutory provisions[1606] decided as a two-stage process. At the first stage, it is for the employer to show that he or she dismissed the employee for a substantial justificatory reason[1607] and at the second stage it is for the tribunal to decide whether in the circumstances (including the size and administrative resources of the employer's undertaking) he or she acted reasonably in treating the reason as a sufficient reason for dismissing the employee.[1608] In the ensuing paragraphs, these two stages are described in more detail and certain situations are described which are governed by special statutory rules ousting the two-stage test of fairness.[1609] The principal such situations are concerned with:

(1) trade union membership and activity[1610];
(2) dismissal during lock-out, strike or other industrial action[1611];
(3) selection for redundancy[1612];
(4) dismissal on the ground of pregnancy or childbirth or leave for family reasons[1613];
(5) health and safety cases[1614];
(6) jury service[1615]; and

[1602] *Drage v Governors of Greenford High School* [2000] I.R.L.R. 314.

[1603] See above, para.40-193.

[1604] *Robert Cort & Son Ltd v Charman* [1981] I.C.R. 816; compare also *BMK Ltd v Logue* [1993] I.C.R. 601. In *Lambert v Croydon College* [1999] I.C.R. 409, the Employment Appeal Tribunal held that a compromise agreement (see above, para.40-174) for early retirement on grounds of ill-health could validly fix the effective date of termination of employment for statutory purposes, even though it fixed it at a date earlier than that on which the agreement was made.

[1605] See above, para.40-169.

[1606] Employment Rights Act 1996 ss.98–100, 103–105. As to the impact of the Human Rights Act 1998 on the adjudication of unfairness, see *X v Y (Employment: Sex Offender)* [2004] EWCA Civ 662, [2004] I.R.L.R. 625.

[1607] Employment Rights Act 1996 s.98(1), see below, para.40-225.

[1608] Employment Rights Act 1996 s.98(4).

[1609] Compare also s.98(3A) Employment Rights Act 1996, and see below, para.40-226 as to the treatment of retirement under the law of unfair dismissal.

[1610] Trade Union and Labour Relations (Consolidation) Act 1992 s.152; see below, para.40-229.

[1611] Trade Union and Labour Relations (Consolidation) Act 1992 ss.237–239; see below, para.40-229.

[1612] Employment Rights Act 1996 s.105. Trade Union and Labour Relations (Consolidation) Act 1992 s.153, see below, para.40-231.

[1613] Employment Rights Act 1996 s.99 and regulations thereunder. See below, para.40-232.

[1614] Employment Rights Act 1996 s.100. See below, para.40-232.

[1615] A new specially designated ground of unfair dismissal has been created by s.40 of the Employment Relations Act 2004, which, by inserting a new s.98B into the Employment Rights Act 1996, renders it unfair to dismiss an employee by reason of his or her being summoned for or being absent from

(7) dismissal on ground of assertion of statutory right.[1616]

Substantial reasons for dismissal It is provided[1617] that at the first stage[1618] of the **40-225**
determination whether a dismissal was fair or unfair, it is for the employer to show
what was the reason or principal reason for the dismissal,[1619] and that it was a reason
falling within a statutory list[1620] of substantial reasons justifying dismissal.[1621] The
list is as follows:

(1) Reasons related to the capability[1622] or qualifications[1623] of the employee for
performing work of the kind which he or she was employed to do.[1624] This
may include supervening ill-health incapacitating the employee from carrying out his or her former work.[1625]

(2) Reasons related to the conduct of the employee.[1626] These need *not* necessarily be reasons going to the lengths of justifying summary dismissal for
misconduct at common law.[1627]

(3) Redundancy of the employee.[1628] This is defined by reference to the definition of the term used in the redundancy payments legislation.[1629]

---

work on jury service, unless the employer shows the likelihood of substantial injury to the undertaking being caused by the absence on jury service. This provision was effective from April 6, 2005.
[1616] Employment Rights Act 1996 s.104. See below, para.40-233.
[1617] Employment Rights Act 1996 s.98.
[1618] See above, para.40-224.
[1619] Employment Rights Act 1996 s.98(1)(a).
[1620] Employment Rights Act 1996 s.98(2), subject to s.98(2A) with regard to retirement, as to which see
below, para.40-226.
[1621] Employment Rights Act 1996 s.98(1)(b).
[1622] Defined by s.98(3)(a) Employment Rights Act 1996; compare *Abernethy v Mott, Hay & Anderson*
[1974] I.C.R. 323; *Turner v Wadham Stringer Ltd* [1974] I.C.R. 277; *Blackman v Post Office* [1974]
I.C.R. 151; *Kraft Foods Ltd v Fox* [1978] I.C.R. 311; *Miller v Executors of JC Graham* [1978]
I.R.L.R. 309; *Bristol-Meyers Co Ltd v Matlock* [1978] 13 I.T.R. 158; *Sutton & Gates v Boxall* [1979]
I.C.R. 67, EAT.
[1623] Defined by s.98(3)(b) of Employment Rights Act 1996.
[1624] Employment Rights Act 1996 s.98(2)(a).
[1625] cf. *Merseyside and North Wales Electricity Board v Taylor* [1975] I.C.R. 185. See *Patterson v Messrs
Bracketts* [1977] I.R.L.R. 137; *Spencer v Paragon Wallpapers Ltd* [1976] I.R.L.R. 373; *Liverpool
AHA v Edwards* [1977] I.R.L.R. 471; *Finch v Betabake (Anglia) Ltd* [1977] I.R.L.R. 470; *Wil-
liamson v Alcan (UK) Ltd* [1978] I.C.R. 104; *Post Office v Jones* [1977] I.R.L.R. 422; *East Lindsey
DC v Daubney* [1977] I.R.L.R. 181.
[1626] Employment Rights Act 1996 s.98(2)(b). See, among the earlier leading authorities, *Morrish v
Henlys (Folkestone) Ltd* [1973] I.C.R. 482; *Wallace v Guy Ltd* [1973] I.C.R. 119; *St Anne's Board
Mill Co Ltd v Brien* [1973] I.C.R. 444; *Shipside (Ruthin) Ltd v TGWU* [1973] I.C.R. 503; *Hilti (Great
Britain) Ltd v Windridge* [1974] I.C.R. 352; *Atkin v Enfield Group Hospital Management Commit-
tee* [1975] I.R.L.R. 217; *Conway v Matthew Wright & Nephew Ltd* [1977] I.R.L.R. 89; *Singh v
London County Bus Services* [1976] I.R.L.R. 176; *Trust Houses Forte Ltd v Murphy* [1977] I.R.L.R.
186; *Torr v British Railways Board* [1977] I.C.R. 785; *Redbridge LBC v Fishman* [1978] I.C.R. 569;
Horrigan v Lewisham LBC [1978] I.C.R. 15; *West Yorkshire MDC v Platts* [1978] I.C.R. 33;
Mansard Precision Engineering Co Ltd v Taylor [1978] I.C.R. 828; *Nottinghamshire CC v Bowley*
[1978] I.R.L.R. 252; *Johnson Matthey Metals Ltd v Harding* [1978] I.R.L.R. 248; *Tesco Stores Ltd
v Heap* [1978] 13 I.T.R. 17; *Boychuk v H. & J. Symons Holdings Ltd* [1977] I.R.L.R. 395; *Coward
v John Menzies (Holdings) Ltd* [1977] I.R.L.R. 428; *British Labour Pump Co Ltd v Byrne* [1979]
I.C.R. 347; *Monie v Coral Racing* [1981] I.C.R. 109, CA; *Weddell & Co Ltd v Tepper* [1980] I.C.R.
286, CA; *British Home Stores Ltd v Burchell* [1980] I.C.R. 303, EAT; *UCATT v Brain* [1981] I.C.R.
542, CA; *Whitbread & Co Plc v Mills* (1988) I.R.L.R. 501.
[1627] See above, paras 40-226 et seq.
[1628] Employment Rights Act 1996 s.98(2)(c)—see below, paras 40-231—40-252.
[1629] Employment Rights Act 1996 s.235(3).

(4) Contravention of a statutory duty if the employment is continued.[1630] This covers cases such as that where an employee employed as a driver is disqualified from driving or driving a particular type of vehicle by order of a court.

(5) Dismissal of an employee engaged expressly as a statutory replacement employee in order to make it possible for the replaced employee to resume his or her original work.[1631]

(6) Any other substantial reason of a kind such as to justify the dismissal of an employee holding the position which that employee held.[1632] This is a residual catch-all category leaving the whole issue ultimately within the discretion of the tribunals and courts. That discretion has not been limited by decided cases; there is no reason to suppose, for instance, that this category need be construed ejusdem generis with the other, specific, categories.[1633]

Special considerations apply to dismissals taking place because of the transfer of an undertaking within the meaning of the Transfer of Undertakings (Protection of Employment) Regulations. With effect from April 6, 2006, the existing Transfer of Undertakings (Protection of Employment) Regulations were revised and replaced by the Transfer of Undertakings (Protection of Employment) Regulations 2006.[1634] The new Regulations contain provisions which clarify the circumstances under which it is unfair for employers to dismiss employees for reasons connected with a relevant transfer.[1635]

40-226 **Retirement and unfair dismissal** Among the very significant new legal incidents which the Employment Equality (Age) Regulations 2006[1636] attached to the notion of "retirement"[1637] was a special regime for "retirement" within the law of unfair dismissal. This special regime was created by introducing new provisions into the Employment Rights Act 1996; it was known as the "default retirement age" regime because it authorised employers, on certain specified conditions, to maintain a mandatory retirement age for their employees which by default would be that of 65. These provisions were repealed by the Employment Equality (Repeal of Retirement Age Provisions) Regulations 2011,[1638] and the effect of that repeal, when coupled with the abolition of the previously existing age limits on claims for unfair dismissal which had accompanied the introduction of that special regime, is to expose the imposition of retirement upon an employee by an employer to the general law of unfair dismissal at whatever age it takes place. There is some official indication that employers may be able to maintain their own "employer-

---

[1630] Employment Rights Act 1996 s.98(2)(d).

[1631] Employment Rights Act 1996 s.106(2)–(3) (replacement of employee suspended from work on medical grounds—see above, para.40-087—or on maternity grounds or absent by reason of pregnancy or confinement).

[1632] Employment Rights Act 1996 s.98(1)(b).

[1633] cf. *RS Components Ltd v Irwin* [1973] I.C.R. 535; *Hollister v National Farmers Union* [1979] I.C.R. 542.

[1634] SI 2006/246. See above, para.40-180.

[1635] See reg.7.

[1636] SI 2006/1031.

[1637] As to which see also paras 40-039, 40-125.

[1638] SI 2011/1069 which took full effect on October 1, 2011.

justified retirement age" regimes[1639]; but the scope of this facility has yet to be effectively tested in litigation.[1640]

Reasonableness of dismissal   If the employer shows that he or she has a   **40-227**
substantial reason for dismissal within the provisions previously discussed,[1641] that
does not in itself establish the fairness or unfairness of the dismissal. Except in the
special cases which have been enumerated,[1642] it is necessary to the second stage
of adjudication of fairness. At that stage, the issue of fairness depends upon whether
the tribunal is satisfied that in the circumstances the employer acted reasonably in
treating the reason shown to him or her as a sufficient reason for dismissing the
employee.[1643] The tribunals are able to take matters both of substance and procedure
into account when deciding the issue of reasonableness. At the substantive level,
the tribunals can consider the whole sequence of developments leading to a
dismissal[1644] and can, in effect, apply their own standards of good employment
practice in order to evaluate the dismissal.[1645] Moreover, it has long been recognised
that the reasonableness of a dismissal also raises procedural considerations[1646]; the
significance of those procedural considerations is now the subject of special statutory provisions concerning dispute resolution which are detailed in later

---

[1639] ACAS *Working without the default retirement age-guidance for employers* (March 2011).

[1640] Compare, however, *Seldon v Clarkson Wright and Jakes* [2010] UKSC 16 from which some incidental guidance may be derived. The maintaining of a retirement age of 65 was subsequently held to have been proportionate on the facts: *Seldon v Clarkson Wright & Jakes* [2014] I.R.L.R. 748, EAT.

[1641] i.e. ss.98(1), (2) of Employment Rights Act 1996.

[1642] See above, para.40-224.

[1643] Employment Rights Act 1996 s.98(4)–(6).

[1644] See, for instance (a) in capability cases: *Judge International Ltd v Moss* [1975] I.R.L.R. 208; *Abernethy v Mott, Hay & Anderson* [1974] I.C.R. 323; *Luckings v May & Baker Ltd* [1974] I.R.L.R. 151; *Tan v Berry Bros & Rudd Ltd* [1974] I.R.L.R. 244; (b) in conduct cases: *Winterhalter Gastronom Ltd v Webb* [1973] I.C.R. 245; *St Anne's Board Mill Co Ltd v Brien* [1973] I.C.R. 444; *Morrish v Henley's (Folkestone) Ltd* [1973] I.C.R. 482; *Shipside (Ruthin) Ltd v TGWU* [1973] I.C.R. 503; *Tiptools Ltd v Curtis* [1973] I.R.L.R. 276; *Hilti (Great Britain) Ltd v Windridge* [1974] I.C.R. 352; *Forgings & Presswork Ltd v MacDougall* [1974] I.C.R. 532; *Treganowan v Robert Knee & Co Ltd* [1975] I.C.R. 405; *Shortland v Chantrill* [1975] I.R.L.R. 208; *Atkin v Enfield Group Hospital Management Committee* [1975] I.R.L.R. 217; (c) in redundancy cases: *Rigby v British Steel Corp* [1973] I.C.R. 160; *Axe v British Domestic Appliances Ltd* [1973] I.C.R. 133; *Clarkson International Tools Ltd v Short* [1973] I.C.R. 191; *Vokes Ltd v Bear* [1974] I.C.R. 1; *Bessenden Properties Ltd v Corness* [1974] I.R.L.R. 338; *British Olivetti Ltd v Kay* [1975] I.R.L.R. 29; *Beardmore v Westinghouse Brake & Signal Co Ltd* [1976] I.C.R. 49. See *Khanum v Mid-Glamorgan AHA* [1979] I.C.R. 40, EAT; *Bailey v BP Oil (Kent Refinery) Ltd* [1980] I.C.R. 642, CA; *Weddell (W) & Co Ltd v Tepper* [1980] I.C.R. 286, CA; *UCATT v Brain* [1981] I.C.R. 542, CA. The Court of Appeal in *Turner v East Midland Trains Ltd* [2012] EWCA Civ 1470, [2013] 3 All E.R. 375 confirmed that in misconduct cases the "band of reasonable responses test" is to be regarded as the overarching one; and it was held that this test met the requirements of art.8 of the European Convention on Human Rights and hence ensured that the legislative provision in question was compliant with the Human Rights Act 1998.

[1645] It has been held that the fact that tribunals reach opposite conclusions as to fairness on similar facts does not necessarily render either conclusion perverse: *Gilham v Kent CC (No.2)* [1985] I.C.R. 233. Compare now the decisions of the EAT in *Haddon v Van den Bergh Foods Ltd* [1999] I.R.L.R. 672; and of the Court of Appeal in *Foley v Post Office* [2000] I.C.R. 1283.

[1646] Because of their bearing on the substantial issue—*Dunning (Shopfitters) Ltd v Jacomb* [1973] I.C.R. 448, 452F–H. See also *Alidair v Taylor* [1978] I.C.R. 445, CA; and *Bailey v BP Oil (Kent Refinery) Ltd* [1980] I.C.R. 642.

paragraphs.[1647] The statute specifically provides that the size and administrative resources of the employer's undertaking shall be treated as circumstances relevant to the question of reasonableness.[1648]

40-228 **Cases on "reasonableness"** Leading cases have provided important guidance for the application of this notion of "reasonableness". The reasonableness of the dismissal must be judged on the basis of facts and circumstances known to the employer and acted upon by him or her at the time of the dismissal and not circumstances which subsequently come to light,[1649] though those may affect the amount of compensation.[1650] Nevertheless, in judging the reasonableness of a dismissal, an employment tribunal is entitled to have regard to an employer's refusal to entertain the employee's contractual right of appeal, as any evidence given in such an appeal would have been admissible before the tribunal in considering whether the employer's real reason for dismissal could reasonably be treated as sufficient.[1651] Moreover, an employer may be held to have acted unreasonably by failing to take the appropriate procedural steps in deciding to dismiss, although it cannot be said the employee would not have been dismissed but for the procedural defects, unless the employer could reasonably have concluded, when deciding to dismiss, that the procedural steps would have been utterly useless.[1652] (Statutory provision was made that failure by an employer to follow a dismissal procedure should not be regarded by itself as making the employer's action unreasonable if the employer shows that it would have been decided to dismiss the employee even if the procedure had been followed[1653]; but that provision was subsequently repealed,[1654] so that the previously applicable case law is apparently restored to effect.[1655])

40-229 **Dismissal by reason of trade union membership, non-membership or activity** The ordinary rules for determining the fairness of a dismissal[1656] are overridden by a special provision[1657] that a dismissal is to be regarded as unfair if the reason or principal reason for the dismissal was the employee's being or proposing to become a member of an independent trade union[1658] or that he had taken or proposed

---

[1647] See below, para.40-264. The provisions came into force on October 1, 2004.

[1648] Employment Rights Act 1996 s.98(4).

[1649] *Devis & Sons Ltd v Atkins* [1977] I.C.R. 662; contrast the law of summary dismissal: see above, para.40-189.

[1650] *Devis & Sons Ltd v Atkins* [1977] I.C.R. 662 and see below, para.40-241.

[1651] *West Midland Co-operative Society Ltd v Tipton* [1986] I.C.R. 192.

[1652] *Polkey v Dayton Services Ltd* [1988] I.C.R. 142; overruling *British Labour Pump Co Ltd v Byrne* [1979] I.C.R. 347. In *Duffy v Yeomans & Partners Ltd* [1995] I.C.R. 1, the Court of Appeal treated it as permissible for the employer to argue that consultation would have been pointless although the employer had not at or before the time of dismissal taken a decision about the utility of consultation.

[1653] Employment Rights Act 1996 s.98A(2) inserted by s.34 of Employment Act 2002 with effect from October 2004.

[1654] By s.2 of the Employment Act 2008; see below, para.40-264.

[1655] That is the view taken in the Explanatory Notes to the Employment Act 2008 at para.18.

[1656] i.e. s.98(1), (3) and s.106(1) (2); see above, para.40-224.

[1657] Trade Union and Labour Relations (Consolidation) Act 1992 s.152(1). Section 152 of the 1992 Act has been amended by s.32 of the Employment Relations Act 2004 so as to make the dismissal of an employee unfair where it is for making use of the services of his union or refusing to accept certain specified inducements in respect of trade union membership or collective bargaining. This provision was brought into effect on October 1, 2004.

[1658] As defined by ss.1, 5.

to take part at any appropriate time in the activities of an independent trade union[1659] or the employee's non-membership of, or refusal to become or remain a member of a trade union.[1660] Where these reasons obtain, the law of unfair dismissal has a specially wide scope,[1661] extending to employees who have not served a qualifying period.[1662] These provisions provide the counterpart to the rights of employees in respect of trade union membership, non-membership and activity provided during the currency of employment by ss.146–151 of the Trade Union and Labour Relations (Consolidation) Act 1992.[1663] Where they apply, the calculation of the basic award of compensation is subject to a statutory minimum,[1664] and may obtain special interim relief pending determination of his or her complaint of unfair dismissal.[1665] That interim relief may consist of an order for the continuation of his contract of employment.[1666]

Dismissal during lock-out, strike or other industrial action Where the date on **40-230** which an employee is dismissed[1667] falls during or at the institution of a lock-out by the employer[1668] or while the employee was taking part in a strike or other industrial action[1669] the ordinary provisions about the fairness of dismissal[1670] are overridden by special provisions.[1671] The law of unfair dismissal is in those cases totally excluded, there being no determination of fairness or unfairness,[1672] save as follows: the law of unfair dismissal is not excluded if it is shown that one or more relevant employees have not been dismissed,[1673] or have been offered re-engagement within three months of the dismissal complained of whilst the employee concerned had not had such an offer.[1674] The relevant employees are those directly interested in the trade dispute in the contemplation or furtherance of which the lock-out occurred,[1675] or those at the establishment at or from which the complainant was working taking part in the strike or other industrial action at the complainant's date of dismissal.[1676] However, the foregoing proviso relating to selective dismissal or selective non-re-engagement does not operate in relation to the dismissal of those taking part in *unofficial* industrial action as statutorily defined,

---

[1659] s.152(1)(b). "Appropriate time" is defined by s.152(2). See *Chant v Aquaboats Ltd* [1978] I.C.R. 643; *City of Birmingham DC v Beyer* [1977] I.R.L.R. 211; *Marley Tile Co Ltd v Shaw* [1980] I.C.R. 72, CA.

[1660] s.152(1)(c). Employment Protection (Consolidation) Act 1978 s.58(3)–(12), which created an important exception in relation to union membership agreements, were repealed by s.11 of the Employment Act 1988.

[1661] cf. above, para.40-125.

[1662] s.154. See above, para.40-250. See also *Goodwin (H) Ltd v Fitzmaurice* [1977] I.R.L.R. 393; *Smith v Hayle Town Council* [1978] I.R.L.R. 413.

[1663] See above, paras 40-115—40-116.

[1664] s.156.

[1665] ss.161–163 (see below, para.40-243). See *London City Airport Ltd v Chacko* [2013] I.R.L.R. 610, EAT.

[1666] ss.164–166 (see below, para.40-243).

[1667] See above, para.40-222 and *Heath v JF Longman (Meat Salesman) Ltd* [1973] I.C.R. 407.

[1668] The terminology is not statutorily defined. See *Express & Star Ltd v Bunday* [1988] I.C.R. 379.

[1669] There is no statutory definition, for this purpose, of "strike or other industrial action". See *Power Packing Casemakers Ltd v Faust* [1983] I.C.R. 292.

[1670] i.e. Employment Rights Act 1996 ss.98, 104, 105.

[1671] Trade Union and Labour Relations (Consolidation) Act 1992 ss.237–238.

[1672] s.238(1), (2).

[1673] s.238(2)(a).

[1674] s.238(2)(b).

[1675] s.238(3)(a).

[1676] s.238(3)(b).

as employees dismissed while so doing have no right to complain of unfair dismissal.[1677] Where the unfair dismissal provisions are not excluded they apply in the ordinary way, except that in cases of selective failure to re-engage,[1678] the ordinary provisions apply to the failure to re-engage rather than to the original dismissal[1679] (thus bringing into question the selection the employer makes by re-engaging some employees and not others). Where the unfair dismissal provisions are not excluded,[1680] a dismissal or failure to re-engage which has as its reason the employee's trade union membership or activity, or non-membership of a non-independent trade union, will be necessarily unfair as in the ordinary case of a dismissal on those grounds not occurring during a lock-out, strike or other industrial action.[1681] Moreover, the Employment Relations Act 1999[1682] made significant changes to the law relating to unfair dismissal of striking workers. In summary, a new category of "protected industrial action" was created within the existing category of official industrial action, so that in defined situations within this new category, employees are to be regarded as unfairly dismissed if they are dismissed wholly or principally by reason of having taken protected industrial action.[1683]

40-231 **Fairness in redundancy cases**   The fact that an employee is redundant in the statutory sense[1684] is in itself a reason capable of establishing the dismissal as a fair one.[1685] Within that framework the area of overlap between the redundancy payments legislation[1686] and the unfair dismissal provisions is regulated as follows. First, there are provisions rendering certain dismissals for redundancy automatically unfair.[1687] These provisions apply to dismissals for redundancy where there has been selection between employees in a similar position and the selection was made either on the statutorily inadmissible grounds, such as those concerned with health and safety cases, with pregnancy or childbirth, or with assertion of statutory rights,[1688] or on the statutorily defined grounds concerned with trade union member-

---

[1677] s.237(1), subject to s.237(1A) which lifts that exclusion in relation to certain specified grounds of dismissal (or selection for redundancy).

[1678] i.e. in the case referred to in s.238(2)(b) and which fall outside the exclusion relating to unofficial industrial action which is imposed by s.237(1).

[1679] s.239(3).

[1680] i.e. in the cases referred to in s.238(2)(a) and (b).

[1681] See above, para.40-229.

[1682] s.16 and Sch.5.

[1683] s.238A. The provisions of s.238A of the 1992 Act concerning "protected industrial action" have been amended by the Employment Relations Act 2004. The 2004 Act ss.27–28, which, by amending s.238A and adding a new s.238B to the 1992 Act, increase the protections against the dismissal of employees taking official lawfully organised industrial action by extending the "protected period" from 8 to 12 weeks, by exempting days of lock-out from the 12-week protected period, and also defining more closely the actions which employers and unions should undertake by way of recourse to conciliation and mediation with regard to "protected industrial action". These provisions were brought into effect on April 6, 2005.

[1684] As defined by s.139(1), (2) of Employment Rights Act 1996, see below, para.40-252, a definition adopted for the purposes of the unfair dismissal legislation by s.235(3) of Employment Rights Act 1996. See *Elliott v University Computing Co (Great Britain) Ltd* [1977] I.C.R. 147; *Higgs & Hill Ltd v Singh* [1977] I.C.R. 193; *Robinson v British Island Airways Ltd* [1978] I.C.R. 304.

[1685] Employment Rights Act 1996 s.98(2)—see above, para.40-225.

[1686] See below, paras 40-249 et seq.

[1687] Employment Rights Act 1996 s.105, Trade Union and Labour Relations (Consolidation) Act 1992 s.153.

[1688] Employment Rights Act 1996 s.105(1)–(3), (7); see below, paras 40-232—40-238.

ship, non-membership or activity.[1689] Secondly, outside those special provisions, a dismissal for redundancy may also be unfair if the employer's decision to dismiss is judged unreasonable[1690] as in all ordinary unfair dismissal issues. Thirdly, it seems clear that the presumption of redundancy applying for the purposes of the redundancy payments legislation[1691] may operate to permit that a redundancy payment is due to the employee and yet that the dismissal is not a dismissal for redundancy for the purposes of the unfair dismissal legislation.[1692] Fourthly, there is provision for the reduction of the amount of a basic award of compensation for unfair dismissal by the amount of any redundancy payment made by the employer or awarded by the tribunal in respect of the dismissal concerned.[1693] Finally it should be noted that special considerations apply under the Transfer of Undertakings (Protection of Employment) Regulations 2006 where the dismissal is attributable to the transfer of an undertaking.[1694]

Dismissal on grounds of pregnancy or leave for family reasons   Under s.99 of **40-232** the Employment Rights Act 1996 an employee is to be treated as unfairly dismissed if she is dismissed because she is pregnant or for any other reason connected with leave for family reasons as prescribed by regulations. In such cases, the normally applicable provisions concerning the qualifying period for unfair dismissal rights do not apply.[1695]

Dismissal in health and safety cases, or on the ground of assertion of statu- **40-233** **tory right**   Provision has been made and is now contained in the Employment Rights Act 1996 for dismissals to be treated as unfair dismissals in particular health and safety cases and in certain cases of dismissal on the ground of assertion of statutory right, as follows. In such cases, the normally applicable provisions concerning the qualifying period for unfair dismissal rights do not apply.[1696]

(1) *Health and safety cases* A dismissal is to be regarded as unfair if the reason for it was that the employee was involved in health and safety activities, or was performing representative functions with regard to health and safety, or brought health and safety hazards to the employer's attention, or absented himself or herself from work by reason of health and safety hazards, or took

---

[1689] Trade Union and Labour Relations (Consolidation) Act 1992 s.153, referring to s.152(1).
[1690] Employment Rights Act 1996 s.98(4)–(6); see, as to the early and leading authorities, *Axe v British Domestic Appliances Ltd* [1973] I.C.R. 133; *Clarkson International Tools Ltd v Short* [1973] I.C.R. 191; *Rigby v British Steel Corp* [1973] I.C.R. 160; *Vokes Ltd v Bear* [1974] I.C.R. 1; *Bessenden Properties Ltd v Corness* [1977] I.C.R. 821 (Note); *Cruikshank v Hobbs* [1977] I.C.R. 725; *Bristol Channel Ship Repairers Ltd v O'Keefe* [1978] I.C.R. 691; *Vickers Ltd v Smith* [1977] I.R.L.R. 11; *Moon v Homeworthy Furniture (Northern) Ltd* [1977] I.C.R. 117; *Kelly v Upholstery & Cabinet Works (Amesbury) Ltd* [1977] I.R.L.R. 91; *North East Midlands Co-operative Society Ltd v Allen* [1977] I.R.L.R. 212; *Forman Construction v Kelly* [1977] I.R.L.R. 468; *Cox v Wildt Mellor Bromley Ltd* [1978] I.C.R. 736; *Thomas & Betts Manufacturing Co Ltd v Harding* [1978] I.R.L.R. 213; *Jowett v Earl of Bradford (No.2)* [1978] I.C.R. 431; *NC Watling & Co Ltd v Richardson* [1978] I.C.R. 1049; *Clyde Pipeworks Ltd v Foster* [1978] I.R.L.R. 313; *Williams v Compair Maxam Ltd* [1982] I.C.R. 156; *Polkey v Dayton Services Ltd* [1988] I.C.R. 142.
[1691] Employment Rights Act 1996 s.163(2) expressly excluded from unfair dismissal issues by s.7(6) of Employment Tribunals Act 1996.
[1692] *Midland Foot Comfort Centre Ltd v Moppett* [1973] I.C.R. 220.
[1693] Employment Rights Act 1996 s.122.
[1694] Compare above, para.40-177.
[1695] Employment Rights Act 1996 s.108(3) and s.109(2).
[1696] See above, para.40-215.

protective measures in circumstances of danger (in each case, subject to the particular conditions laid down in the statutory provision).[1697]

(2) *Assertion of statutory right* A dismissal is to be regarded as unfair if the reason for it was that the employee brought proceedings against the employer to enforce a relevant statutory right, or alleged that the employer had infringed such a right of his or hers; the statutory rights in question are, in effect, the individual employment protection rights conferred by the Employment Rights Act 1996 and by the provisions of the Trade Union and Labour Relations (Consolidation) Act 1992 concerning deductions from pay, trade union activities and time off.[1698]

40-234 **Dismissal on grounds of public interest disclosure** Under the provisions of the Public Interest Disclosure Act 1998,[1699] a dismissal, for which the sole or principal reason is that the worker concerned made a protected public interest disclosure, may be taken to be an unfair dismissal within the meaning of the unfair dismissals legislation, thus coming within the jurisdiction of an Employment Tribunal as such.[1700]

40-235 **Dismissal on grounds of refusal of Sunday working** It is provided that where an employee who is a "protected shop worker" or "protected betting worker" or an "opted-out shop worker" or "opted-out betting worker" is dismissed, he or she is to be regarded as unfairly dismissed if the reason or principal reason for the dismissal was his or her refusal to do shop work or betting work on Sundays or on a particular Sunday.[1701]

40-236 **Dismissal on grounds connected with parenthood and family responsibility** As with the protections from detriment previously considered,[1702] by a succession of enactments beginning with the Employment Relations Act 1999,[1703] there have been conferred upon employees a series of protections against dismissal or selection for redundancy on grounds connected with various aspects of parenthood and family responsibility or with the exercise of rights relating to parenthood and family responsibility. As a brief summary of the effect of those enactments, an employee will be regarded as having been unfairly dismissed or selected for redundancy if the ground for the dismissal or selection for redundancy was that:

- she is pregnant or has given birth to a child; or
- she has exercised or has sought to exercise the rights to maternity leave or maternity pay; or
- she or he has exercised or has sought to exercise the rights to parental leave; or

---

[1697] Employment Rights Act 1996 s.100.

[1698] Employment Rights Act 1996 s.104(4). See, for the scope of this provision, *Menell v Newell and Wright Transport Contractors Ltd* [1997] I.C.R. 1039.

[1699] See above, para.40-155.

[1700] See Employment Rights Act 1996 s.103A as inserted by s.5 of the 1998 Act.

[1701] See Employment Rights Act 1996 s.101, and, for the provisions identifying protected and opted-out shop and betting workers, Employment Rights Act 1996 s.41. For the effect of opting-out notices upon contracts of employment, see s.42.

[1702] See above, para.40-146.

[1703] s.9 and Sch.4 Pt III.

- she or he has exercised or has sought to exercise the rights to time off for domestic reasons (to care for dependants)[1704]; or
- he has exercised or has sought to exercise the rights to paternity leave or paternity pay; or
- she or he has exercised or has sought to exercise the rights to adoption leave or adoption pay, or the rights to paternity leave or paternity pay which apply to adoptive parents[1705]; or
- she or he has exercised or has sought to exercise the rights which relate to flexible working.[1706]

(iv) Remedies

Introduction   Under the unfair dismissal provisions of the Industrial Relations Act   **40-237**
1971 and of the Trade Union and Labour Relations Act 1974, the normal remedy for unfair dismissal tended to be the award of compensation by an industrial tribunal based upon the pecuniary loss sustained by the employee.[1707] The tribunals were also empowered to recommend reinstatement or re-engagement where they judged it practicable for the employer to do so.[1708] The provisions of the Trade Union and Labour Relations Act 1974 concerning remedies for unfair dismissal were replaced by a new set of provisions in the Employment Protection Act 1975.[1709] Under the new provisions, as re-enacted in the 1978 Act,[1710] and then in the 1996 Act, employment tribunals are empowered to order reinstatement or re-engagement and have extensive ancillary powers in relation to those orders.[1711] The remedy of compensation is to consist of a basic award as well as a compensation award.[1712] Finally, the tribunals are given extensive powers of interim relief in cases concerning trade union membership, non-membership or activity and in certain cases concerning health and safety.[1713]

Orders for reinstatement   Where an employment tribunal upholds a complaint   **40-238**
of unfair dismissal, it must explain to the complainant what orders of reinstatement or re-engagement it can make and must ask the complainant whether he or she wishes for such an order.[1714] An order may be made if (but only if) the complainant expresses that wish,[1715] and may within the discretion of the tribunal be either

---

[1704] Maternity and Parental Leave Etc Regulations 1999 (SI 1999/3312) reg.20.

[1705] Paternity and Adoption Leave Regulations 2002 (SI 2002/2788) reg.29.

[1706] Employment Rights Act 1996 s.104C (as inserted by s.47(1), (4) of the Employment Act 2002) (though no corresponding extension appears to have been made to s.105 with regard to selection for redundancy).

[1707] Trade Union and Labour Relations Act 1974 Sch.1 para.17(3)—see generally *Norton Tool Co Ltd v Tewson* [1972] I.C.R. 501.

[1708] Trade Union and Labour Relations Act 1974 Sch.1 para.17(2).

[1709] ss.71–80.

[1710] ss.68–79.

[1711] Employment Rights Act 1996 ss.112–117: see below, paras 40-238—40-241. See now generally *McBride v Scottish Police Authority* [2016] UKSC 27, [2016] I.R.L.R. 633.

[1712] Employment Rights Act 1996 s.118(2). Further provisions for "special awards" were repealed by the Employment Relations Act 1999 ss.33, 44 and Sch.9.

[1713] See below, para.40-243.

[1714] Employment Rights Act 1996 s.112(1), (2).

[1715] Employment Rights Act 1996 s.112(3).

for reinstatement or re-engagement.[1716] In exercising that discretion, the tribunal must first consider reinstatement,[1717] taking into account the issues of whether the complainant wishes for reinstatement,[1718] whether compliance would be practicable for the employer[1719] and whether an order for reinstatement would be just in view of the employee's contribution to causing the dismissal.[1720] In considering the issue of practicability of compliance, the tribunal must exclude the difficulty caused by the engagement of a permanent replacement for the dismissed employee unless the employer shows that this was the only way he or she could arrange for the work to be done, or that he or she engaged the replacement after the lapse of a reasonable period without having heard from the dismissed employee that he or she wished to be reinstated or re-engaged and that a permanent replacement had become the only reasonable alternative.[1721] The reinstatement order is an order to treat the complainant in all respects as if he or she had not been dismissed[1722]; the order must specify any amount payable by the employer for benefits (including remuneration) the employee would have received in the interim period,[1723] and any rights and privileges, including seniority and pension rights, to be restored to the employee,[1724] and the date by which the order must be complied with.[1725] The order must also require the employee to be treated as if he or she had benefited from an improvement in his or her terms and conditions of employment which he or she would have enjoyed if he or she had not been dismissed.[1726] This will certainly include pay awards occurring between dismissal and reinstatement; it is a matter of interpretation whether it includes the results of a promotion which would have occurred.

40-239 **Orders for re-engagement** Where an employment tribunal, having followed the procedure described in the previous paragraph, decides not to make an order for reinstatement, it must consider whether to make an order for re-engagement and on what terms.[1727] It must take into account any wish of the complainant as to the nature of the order,[1728] whether compliance is practicable for the employer or a successor or associated employer,[1729] and whether an order would be just, and if so on what

---

[1716] Employment Rights Act 1996 s.113. As to the difference between reinstatement and re-engagement, see *British Airways Plc v Valencia* [2014] I.R.L.R. 683, EAT.

[1717] Employment Rights Act 1996 s.116(1).

[1718] Employment Rights Act 1996 s.116(1)(a).

[1719] Employment Rights Act 1996 s.116(1)(b). See, for early authorities on the issue of practicability: *Curtis v James Paterson (Darlington) Ltd* [1973] I.C.R. 496; *Bateman v British Leyland (UK) Ltd* [1974] I.C.R. 403; *Coleman v Magnet Joinery Ltd* [1975] I.C.R. 46. But these decisions on the corresponding provisions of the 1974 Act may be of limited weight in the interpretation of the more recent provisions. See also *Meridian Ltd v Gomersall* [1977] I.C.R. 597.

[1720] Employment Rights Act 1996 s.116(1)(c). cf. below, para.40-242—contribution to compensation.

[1721] Employment Rights Act 1996 s.116(5), (6).

[1722] Employment Rights Act 1996 s.114(1). See *McBride v Scottish Police Authority* [2016] UKSC 27, [2016] I.R.L.R. 633.

[1723] Employment Rights Act 1996 s.114(2)(a), subject to s.114(4) of Employment Rights Act 1996 (reduction of employer's liability by reference to remuneration or payment in lieu of notice or ex gratia payments).

[1724] Employment Rights Act 1996 s.114(2)(b).

[1725] Employment Rights Act 1996 s.114(2)(c).

[1726] Employment Rights Act 1996 s.114(3).

[1727] Employment Rights Act 1996 s.116(2)–(4).

[1728] Employment Rights Act 1996 s.116(3)(a).

[1729] Employment Rights Act 1996 s.116(3)(b), subject to s.116(5) of Employment Rights Act 1996 (effect of engagement of permanent replacement).

terms, in view of any contribution by the complainant to causing the dismissal.[1730] The order for re-engagement is an order for the complainant to be engaged by the employer, or by a successor or by an associated employer in some suitable employment.[1731] The order may be on such terms as the tribunal decides[1732] provided that the re-engagement must be on terms which are, so far is reasonable practicable, as favourable as an order for reinstatement.[1733] The order must specify the identity of the employer,[1734] the nature of and remuneration for the employment,[1735] the amount payable in respect of benefits, including arrears of pay, lost in the interim period,[1736] and any seniority or pension rights to be restored to the employee.[1737] The tribunals are thus given a very flexible power to achieve the effects of reinstatement in a case where reinstatement is not itself possible or appropriate.

Enforcement of orders for reinstatement or re-engagement   If an order is made   **40-240** for reinstatement or re-engagement and the employee is reinstated or re-engaged, but the terms of the order are not fully complied with, an employment tribunal must make an award of compensation for the loss sustained by the employee in consequence of the failure to comply with the order.[1738] If there is no reinstatement or re-engagement in compliance with the order, the tribunal must make an ordinary award of compensation for unfair dismissal.[1739] They may also be under a duty to make an additional award (for the failure to comply with the order).[1740] This award must be between 26 and 52 weeks' pay.[1741] The additional award (normal or higher as the case may be) must be made unless the employer satisfies the tribunal that it was not practicable to comply with the order.[1742] This would seem to enable the employer to show that it has not turned out to be practicable to comply, rather than enabling him or her to reopen the question of whether the order should have been made in the first place. If the complainant himself or herself unreasonably prevents compliance with an order, his or her award of compensation will be reduced by reference to this failure to mitigate his or her loss by allowing the order to be complied with.[1743] In general, then, non-compliance with orders for reinstatement or re-engagement attracts the remedy of compensation which may be enhanced by way of penalty for non-compliance; there is, however, no enforcement by way of general sanctions for contempt of court.

Compensation for unfair dismissal; the basic award   Under the Employment   **40-241**

[1730] Employment Rights Act 1996 s.116(3)(c) (cf. below, para.40-242—contribution to the dismissal as a ground for reducing compensation).

[1731] Employment Rights Act 1996 s.115(1).

[1732] Employment Rights Act 1996 s.115(1).

[1733] Employment Rights Act 1996 s.116(4) (except where the tribunal takes into account contributory fault under s.116(3)(c)).

[1734] Employment Rights Act 1996 s.115(2)(a).

[1735] Employment Rights Act 1996 s.115(2)(b), (c).

[1736] Employment Rights Act 1996 s.115(2)(d) calculated according to s.115(3) of Employment Rights Act 1996.

[1737] Employment Rights Act 1996 s.115(2)(e).

[1738] Employment Rights Act 1996 ss.117(1) and 124(3).

[1739] Employment Rights Act 1996 s.117(3)(a)—see below, paras 40-241—40-243.

[1740] Employment Rights Act 1996 ss.117(3)(b), 117(4)(a).

[1741] Employment Rights Act 1996 s.117(4)(b).

[1742] Employment Rights Act 1996 s.117(3)(b) and s.117(4)(a) as qualified by s.117(7) of Employment Rights Act 1996 in the case where the employer has engaged a permanent replacement.

[1743] Employment Rights Act 1996 s.117(8).

Rights Act 1996, an award of compensation for unfair dismissal must be made in any case where a complaint of unfair dismissal is upheld but no order for reinstatement or re-engagement is made.[1744] The compensation must consist of a basic award and a compensatory award.[1745] The basic award provides a fixed element of compensation for the employee's loss of his accrued rights and protection. It is initially calculated in virtually the same way as a statutory redundancy payment,[1746] that is to say, it allows one and a half weeks' pay for each year of continuous employment over the age of 41, one week's pay for each such year between 22 and 40 and half a week's pay for each such year up to the age of 22.[1747] The calculation is limited to the last 20 years of employment[1748] and to a week's pay not exceeding a stated limit.[1749] The basic award is limited to two weeks' pay in certain redundancy situations where no statutory redundancy payment is payable.[1750] There is also provision for the reduction of the basic award,[1751] whether or by reference to an unreasonable refusal by the employee to accept an offer of reinstatement by the employer[1752]; or by reference to any conduct of the employee before the dismissal making it just and equitable to do so.[1753]

40-242   Compensation for unfair dismissal; the compensatory award   Under the Employment Rights Act 1996, compensation for unfair dismissal must include, in addition to the basic award,[1754] a compensatory award[1755] assessed by reference to the loss sustained by the employee in consequence of the dismissal[1756] and attributable to action taken by the employer.[1757] The loss is ascertained subject to the common law rule concerning the employee's duty to mitigate his or her loss.[1758] The compensatory award is a modified version of the awards of compensation for unfair

---

[1744] Employment Rights Act 1996 s.112(4).

[1745] Employment Rights Act 1996 s.118(1).

[1746] See below, para.40-254.

[1747] Employment Rights Act 1996 s.119(2). The lower age limit, which had previously applied, was, so far as it had continued to be applicable, abolished with effect from October 1, 2006 by the Employment Equality (Age) Regulations 2006 (SI 2006/1031) Sch.8 para.35. See also below, paras 40-175, 40-254. The period of continuous employment is calculated in accordance with ss.210–219 of Employment Rights Act 1996, see above, paras 40-165—40-168 applied subject to s.119(3) of Employment Rights Act 1996. The "week's pay" is calculated in accordance with ss.220–229 of Employment Rights Act 1996. See *Palmanor v Cedron* [1978] I.C.R. 1008.

[1748] Employment Rights Act 1996 s.119(3).

[1749] Employment Rights Act 1996 s.227(1). The stated limit is periodically adjusted by statutory instrument.

[1750] Employment Rights Act 1996 s.121.

[1751] Employment Rights Act 1996 s.122.

[1752] Employment Rights Act 1996 s.122(1).

[1753] Employment Rights Act 1996 s.122(2), in order to overcome a problem of unjust enrichment commented upon by the House of Lords in *Devis & Sons Ltd v Atkins* [1977] I.C.R. 662, 672, 684, 685.

[1754] See above, para.40-241.

[1755] Employment Rights Act 1996 s.118 referring to ss.123, 124, 124A,126, 127 of Employment Rights Act 1996.

[1756] Employment Rights Act 1996 s.123(1) as qualified by s.123(2) of Employment Rights Act 1996. See *W Devis & Sons Ltd v Atkins* [1977] A.C. 931; *Lifeguard Assurance Ltd v Zadrozny* [1977] I.R.L.R. 56; *Trend v Chiltern Hunt Ltd* [1977] I.C.R. 612; *Brittains Arborfield Ltd v Van Uden* [1977] I.C.R. 211; *DG Moncrieff (Farmers) v Macdonald* [1978] I.R.L.R. 112; *Help the Aged Housing Association (Scotland) Ltd v Vidler* [1977] I.R.L.R. 104.

[1757] Employment Rights Act 1996 s.123(1) as qualified by s.123(5) of Employment Rights Act 1996 (exclusion of effect of pressure on employer by the organising of industrial action).

[1758] Employment Rights Act 1996 s.123(4). See *Smith Kline & French Laboratories Ltd v Coates* [1977] I.R.L.R. 220; *Peara v Enderlin Ltd* [1980] I.C.R. 804.

dismissal made under the earlier legislation,[1759] modified by limiting the loss attributable to loss of statutory redundancy rights to the amount by which an immediate or subsequent redundancy payment might have exceeded the basic award[1760]; and on the other hand by reducing the compensation award by the amount by which a redundancy payment made by the employer in fact exceeds the basic award.[1761] These modifications are designed to ensure that the compensatory award will deal only with the marginal differences between the basic award and the employee's actual or potential redundancy rights or redundancy payments received. This suggests that the cases concerning the assessment of compensation under the old law of remedies for unfair dismissal[1762] are still applicable,[1763] except so far as they are concerned with the relationship between unfair dismissal compensation and redundancy rights and payments.[1764] That suggests that compensatory awards will be concerned with loss of future earnings,[1765] loss of pension rights,[1766] loss of rights based on continuity of service,[1767] pecuniary loss attributable to the manner of dismissal,[1768] and possibly also loss of death-in-service benefits.[1769] It is unclear how far a compensatory award is to be reduced by reference to damages for wrongful dismissal[1770] recovered at common law in respect of the same dismissal. An argument based upon the principle of collateral benefits might result in such a reduction.[1771] There was some authority for regarding the employee as having suffered no reckonable loss when the unfairness of the dismissal consisted in a procedural defect and when it is judged that the employee would still have been dismissed had the procedure been fair.[1772] However, the subsequent preference has

---

[1759] See Trade Union and Labour Relations Act 1974 Sch.1 paras 17(3), 19.

[1760] Employment Rights Act 1996 s.123(3).

[1761] Employment Rights Act 1996 s.123(7).

[1762] See above, para.40-215.

[1763] The leading case was *Norton Tool Co Ltd v Tewson* [1972] I.C.R. 501 The principle in the *Norton Tool* case was upheld on the appeal to the House of Lords in *Dunnachie v Kingston-upon-Hull City Council* [2004] UKHL 36.

[1764] A statement of the law in that particular area being found in *Millington v Goodwin Ltd* [1975] I.C.R. 104.

[1765] See *Donnelly v Feniger & Blackburn Ltd* [1973] I.C.R. 68; *York Trailer Co Ltd v Sparkes* [1973] I.C.R. 518; *British Olivetti Ltd v Kay* [1975] I.R.L.R. 29; *Shortland v Chantrill* [1975] I.R.L.R. 208; see also on the effect of payment in lieu of notice: *Cawthorn & Sinclair Ltd v Hedger* [1974] I.C.R. 146; *Everwear Candlewick Ltd v Isaac* [1974] I.C.R. 525; *Mullett v Brush Electrical Machines Ltd* [1977] I.C.R. 829; *Youngs of Gosport Ltd v Kendall* [1977] I.C.R. 907; *Green v J Waterhouse & Sons Ltd* [1977] I.C.R. 759; *Tidman v Aveling Marshall Ltd* [1977] I.C.R. 506; *Brownson v Hire Service Shops Ltd* [1978] I.C.R. 517; *Palmanor Ltd v Cedron* [1978] I.C.R. 1008. Compare also *GAB Robins (UK) Ltd v Triggs* [2008] EWCA Civ 17, [2008] I.R.L.R. 317, deciding that this did not include loss of earnings attributable to incapacity brought about by repudiatory conduct on the part of the employer amounting to, and treated by the employee as, constructive dismissal.

[1766] See *Copson v Eversure Accessories Ltd* [1974] I.C.R. 636; *Smith Kline & French Laboratories Ltd v Coates* [1977] I.R.L.R. 220; *Hill v Sabco Houseware (UK) Ltd* [1977] I.C.R. 888; *Powermatic Ltd v Bull* [1977] I.C.R. 469; *Sweetlove v Redbridge AHA* [1979] I.C.R. 477; *Willment Bros v Oliver* [1979] I.C.R. 378; *Sturdy Finance v Bardsley* [1979] I.C.R. 249; *Manning v Wale (Export) Ltd* [1979] I.C.R. 433; and *Griffin v Plymouth Hospital NHS Trust* [2014] EWCA Civ, [2014] I.R.L.R. 962.

[1767] See *Brook Bros Ltd v Preece* [1974] I.C.R. 231; *Hilti (Great Britain) Ltd v Windridge* [1974] I.C.R. 352. These matters might, however, be regarded as subsumed into the basic award of compensation.

[1768] See *Vaughan v Weighpack Ltd* [1974] I.C.R. 525.

[1769] See *Fox v British Airways Plc* [2013] EWCA Civ 972, [2013] I.C.R. 1257.

[1770] See above, paras 40-201—40-206.

[1771] cf. *Stocks v Magna Merchants Ltd* [1973] I.C.R. 530 (common law)—see above, para.40-206. Contrast *Basnett v J & A Jackson Ltd* [1976] I.C.R. 63.

[1772] *Earl v Slater Wheeler (Airlyne) Ltd* [1972] I.C.R. 508; *British United Shoe Machines Co Ltd v Clarke*

clearly been[1773] to treat such issues as going to the reduction of compensation by reference to the contributory action of the employee, for which provision is made in relation to the compensatory[1774] award. Those provisions are considered in the following paragraph. Provision was also made by s.3 of the Employment Act 2008 for the compensatory award to be reduced or increased by reference to non-compliance with a statutory code of practice concerning disciplinary and grievance procedures.[1775] A compensatory award is normally subject to a stated upper limit,[1776] the limit being applied after any reduction by reference to the fault of the employee.[1777] Section 16 of the Enterprise and Regulatory Reform Act 2013 confers an additional power on employment tribunals to impose financial penalties on employers where the tribunal concludes that the employer has breached a worker's right, and that the breach has one or more aggravating factors.[1778]

40-243   **Reduction of compensation by reference to the contributory action of the employee**   Under the Employment Rights Act 1996 it is provided that where a tribunal finds that a dismissal was to any extent caused or contributed to by any action of the complainant it shall reduce the amount of a compensatory[1779] award by such proportion as it considers just and equitable having regard to that finding. The corresponding provisions in the earlier legislation[1780] gave rise to controversy about their application, especially in cases of procedural unfairness,[1781] but this difficulty seems not to arise under the new provisions, referring as they do to any contribution by the employee to the dismissal itself (and not just to the reasons for its unfairness).[1782] The early case law suggests that this gives tribunals a very wide discretion to consider any relevant conduct on the part of the employee,[1783] and to reduce the compensation by proportions of up to 100 per cent,[1784] though the assessment becomes more questionable as it comes near to 100 per cent.[1785]

[1978] I.C.R. 70; *Barley v Amey Roadstone Corp (No.2)* [1978] I.C.R. 190.

[1773] Compare, for instance, *Smyth v Autocar Transporters Ltd* [1975] I.C.R. 180 and see generally, below, para.40-242.

[1774] Employment Rights Act 1996 s.123(6).

[1775] Amending s.124A of the Employment Rights Act 1996; see below, para.40-264.

[1776] Employment Rights Act 1996 s.124(1), subject to s.124(1A), (3)–(4), and to s.124A as inserted by s.39 of the Employment Act 2002, and as varied by statutory instrument from time to time.

[1777] Employment Rights Act 1996 s.124(5).

[1778] By inserting a new s.12A into the Employment Tribunals Act 1996.

[1779] Employment Rights Act 1996 s.123(6).

[1780] Trade Union and Labour Relations Act 1974 Sch.1 para.19(3), reproducing Industrial Relations Act 1971 s.116(3).

[1781] See, for instance, *Springbank Sand & Gravel Co Ltd v Craig* [1974] I.C.R. 7; *Maris v Rotherham Corp* [1974] I.C.R. 435.

[1782] The earlier legislation, see above, caused the controversy concerned by requiring the employee's contribution to be to "the matters to which the complaint relates". See *Nudds v W & J B Eastwood Ltd* [1978] I.C.R. 171.

[1783] *Shortland v Chantrill* [1975] I.R.L.R. 208; *Jamieson v Aberdeen CC* [1975] I.R.L.R. 348, Ct of Session; *George Wimpey & Co Ltd v Cooper* [1977] I.R.L.R. 205; *Garner v Grange Furnishing Ltd* [1977] I.R.L.R. 206; *Kraft Foods Ltd v Fox* [1978] I.C.R. 311; *Hazells Offset Ltd v Luckett* [1977] I.R.L.R. 430; *Ladbroke Racing Ltd v Mason* [1978] I.C.R. 49; *DG Moncrieff (Farmers) v Macdonald* [1978] I.R.L.R. 112; *Brown's Cycles Ltd v Brindley* [1978] I.C.R. 467; *Moncur v International Paint Co Ltd* [1978] I.R.L.R. 223. Compare now also *Cumbria CC v Bates* [2014] UKEAT 0039/13/JOJ (post-termination conduct).

[1784] *Smyth v Autocar Transporters Ltd* [1975] I.C.R. 180. See also *Courtney v Babcock & Wilcox (Operations) Ltd* [1977] I.R.L.R. 30; contra, *Kemp v Shipton Automation Ltd* [1976] I.R.L.R. 305.

[1785] *Cooper v British Steel Corp* [1975] I.C.R. 454; and *Trend v Chiltern Hunt Ltd* [1977] I.C.R. 612.

Interim relief in cases concerned with trade union rights or health and   **40-244**
safety   An employee who presents a complaint to an employment tribunal that he
or she has been unfairly dismissed on the grounds of his membership of or taking
part in the activities of an independent trade union (or his intention to join or take
part) or of his or her non-membership or refusal to become or remain a member of
a trade union, or in one of the statutorily defined health and safety cases, may apply to the tribunal for interim relief pending the determination of the complaint.[1786]
He or she must complain within seven days of the effective date of termination of
employment[1787] and must, in a claim relating to trade union membership or activity, present a supporting written certificate from an authorised official of the
independent trade union concerned.[1788] If when it hears the application for interim
relief the tribunal finds it likely that the complaint will ultimately be upheld, the
tribunal must make an interim order of reinstatement or re-engagement if the
employer is willing for such an order and, if it is for re-engagement, the employee
is also willing.[1789] If the employer is not willing, the tribunal must make an order
for the continuation of the contract of employment.[1790] This is in effect an order
continuing or reviving the contract of employment pending the hearing of the
complaint, but only for the purpose of maintaining the employee's rights to
remuneration and preserving his or her rights based upon the continuity of his or
her employment.[1791] It is thus not meant to require the employer to keep the
employee actually at work, and is apparently not dependent for its effectiveness
upon the employee's making himself or herself available for work.[1792] An employee
or employer can apply to a tribunal for a variation or revocation of an order for
interim relief where there has been a change of circumstances since the order was
made.[1793] The tribunal must also make an order for compensation if the employer
has failed to comply with the terms of an interim order for reinstatement or re-
engagement, or of an order for the continuation of the contract of employment, and
it must convert the former type of order into the latter type where the former type
of order is not complied with.[1794]

Procedure; time within which complaint must be made   The details of the   **40-245**
procedure relating to complaints to employment tribunals under the unfair dismissal

---

[1786] Trade Union and Labour Relations (Consolidation) Act 1992 s.161; Employment Rights Act 1996
s.128(1). See *Barley v Amey Roadstone Co Ltd (No.2)* [1978] I.C.R. 190.
[1787] Trade Union and Labour Relations (Consolidation) Act 1992 s.161(2); Employment Rights Act 1996
s.128(2). As to the "effective date of termination of employment", see above, paras 40-222—40-
223.
[1788] Trade Union and Labour Relations (Consolidation) Act 1992 s.161(3). See *Stone v Charrington &
Co Ltd* [1977] I.C.R. 248.
[1789] Trade Union and Labour Relations (Consolidation) Act 1992 s.163(4)–(6); Employment Rights Act
1996 s.129(5)–(7).
[1790] Trade Union and Labour Relations (Consolidation) Act 1992 s.163(6); Employment Rights Act 1996
s.129(9).
[1791] Trade Union and Labour Relations (Consolidation) Act 1992 s.164; Employment Rights Act 1996
s.130.
[1792] This appears to be the effect of s.164(2). Employment Rights Act 1996 s.130(2).
[1793] Trade Union and Labour Relations (Consolidation) Act 1992 s.165; Employment Rights Act 1996
s.131.
[1794] Trade Union and Labour Relations (Consolidation) Act 1992 s.166; Employment Rights Act 1996
s.132.

provisions[1795] are outside the scope of the present work, but attention is drawn to the provisions concerning the time within which complaint must be made. It is provided that an employment tribunal shall not consider a complaint of unfair dismissal unless it is presented before the end of the period of three months beginning with the effective date of termination or within such further period as the tribunal considers reasonable in a case where it was satisfied that it was not reasonably practicable for the complaint to be presented before the end of the period of three months.[1796] A body of case law exists concerning the concept of "practicability"[1797] but it is to be borne in mind that the initial cases were concerned with the earlier provision made under the Industrial Relations Act 1971 which took four weeks instead of three months, as the basic period of limitation. Provision was first made by the Employment Protection Act 1975 (and now found in the 1996 Act) to enable a complaint to be brought before a dismissal takes effect, once notice of dismissal has been given,[1798] thus reversing by statute an earlier judicial ruling.[1799]

(b) Discriminatory and Victimising Dismissals

40-246 Introduction Apart from the unfair dismissals legislation, there have been various other sets of legislative provisions dealing with particular kinds of discriminatory and victimising dismissals, major instances of which have been: (1) the Sex Discrimination Acts 1975 and 1986; (2) the Race Relations Act 1976; (3) the Rehabilitation of Offenders Act 1974; (4) the Disability Discrimination Act 1995; (5) the Employment Equality (Religion or Belief) Regulations, the Employment Equality (Sexual Orientation) Regulations 2003, and the Employment Equality (Age) Regulations 2006.[1800] Most of these provisions have been consolidated into the Equality Act 2010; the provisions in question are briefly summarised in the ensuing paragraphs.

40-247 Dismissals unlawful under the Equality Act 2010 Under the relevant provisions of the Equality Act 2010, the dismissal of an employee by an employer is unlawful if it is discriminatory[1801] in the defined sense that it involves direct[1802] or indirect[1803] discrimination by reference to one or a combination of[1804] a specified set of "protected characteristics"[1805] consisting of age,[1806] disability,[1807] gender reas-

---

[1795] The procedural rules are contained in ss.6–15 of Employment Tribunals Act 1996 (As renamed by the Employment Rights (Dispute Resolution) Act 1998) and in the Employment Tribunals (Constitution and Rules of Procedure) Regulations as from time-to-time revised and amended.

[1796] Employment Rights Act 1996 s.111(2).

[1797] See among the earlier cases, *Hammond v Haigh Castle & Co Ltd* [1973] I.C.R. 148; *Singh v Post Office* [1973] I.C.R. 437; *Westward Circuits Ltd v Read* [1973] I.C.R. 301; *Leigh v James Arnold Ltd* [1973] I.T.R. 364; *Dedman v British Building Appliances Ltd* [1974] I.C.R. 53; *Porter v Bandridge Ltd* [1974] I.C.R. 943; *Walls Meat Co Ltd v Khan* [1979] I.C.R. 52; *Riley v Tesco Stores Ltd* [1980] I.C.R. 323. *Palmer v Southend-on-Sea BC* [1984] 1 All E.R. 945.

[1798] Employment Rights Act 1996 s.111(3), (4).

[1799] *Penrose v Fairey Surveys Ltd* [1973] I.C.R. 26.

[1800] Respectively SI 2003/1660, SI 2003/1661 and SI 2006/1031, all of which were enacted in implementation of Directive 2000/78/EC.

[1801] s.39(2)(c).

[1802] s.13.

[1803] s.19.

[1804] s.14.

[1805] s.4.

signment,[1808] marriage or civil partnership,[1809] pregnancy and maternity,[1810] race,[1811] religion or belief,[1812] sex,[1813] and sexual orientation.[1814] Under further provisions of the same Act, the dismissal of an employee by an employer is also unlawful if it constitutes victimisation[1815] in the defined sense that it takes place because the employee does a "protected act", or because the employer believes that the employee has done or may do such an act,[1816] defined as consisting of, inter alia, the bringing of proceedings under the Act or the taking of steps in connection with such proceedings, or otherwise the alleging of contravention of the Act.[1817] A dismissal[1818] which is unlawful under the provisions of the Act may be the subject of a complaint to an employment tribunal[1819] which, if it upholds the complaint, may make an order declaring the rights of the parties,[1820] an order for the payment of compensation,[1821] formerly but no longer limited in the same way as compensation for unfair dismissal, or a recommendation that a particular course of action be taken by the respondent,[1822] presumably including a recommendation for reinstatement or re-engagement.[1823] There are provisions to prevent double compensation under this Act and the unfair dismissal provisions in respect of the same dismissal.[1824] The definition of discrimination rendered unlawful by this Act, and the scope of and exceptions to its employment provisions have been considered in earlier paragraphs[1825] in relation to unlawful discrimination occurring during the period of employment.

Dismissals affected by the Rehabilitation of Offenders Act 1974 It is provided **40-248**
by the Rehabilitation of Offenders Act 1974[1826] that a conviction which has become spent,[1827] or any circumstances ancillary thereto,[1828] or any failure to disclose a spent conviction or any such circumstances shall not be a proper ground for dismissing

---

[1806] s.5; as to which it should specially be noted that it is provided that dismissal because of age is not discriminatory if the employer shows that it is a proportionate means of achieving a legitimate aim: s.13(2).

[1807] s.6.

[1808] ss.7, 16.

[1809] s.8.

[1810] s.18.

[1811] s.9.

[1812] s.10.

[1813] s.11.

[1814] s.12.

[1815] s.39(4)(c) referring to s.27.

[1816] s.27(1).

[1817] s.27(2)–(5).

[1818] The term "dismissal" is not defined in the Act; compare the case law definition of that term under the unfair dismissal provisions—see above, paras 40-220—40-221.

[1819] s.120.

[1820] s.124(2)(a).

[1821] s.124(2)(b).

[1822] s.124(2)(c).

[1823] Compare above, paras 40-238—40-239.

[1824] Employment Rights Act 1996 s.126. See above, para.40-241.

[1825] Above, paras 40-128—40-134.

[1826] Which takes effect subject to the Rehabilitation of Offenders Act 1974 (Exceptions) Order 1975 (SI 1975/1023).

[1827] Defined by s.1 of the Act. The Data Protection Act 1998 s.56 makes it a criminal offence to require job applicants or existing employees to make subject access requests in lieu of providing a normal criminal record check, which would not disclose spent convictions.

[1828] Defined by s.4(5).

a person from any office, profession, occupation or employment.[1829] There is no machinery provided for the enforcement of that provision, so it can have effect only as a qualification upon rights of summary dismissal arising at common law[1830] or as a factor tending to show the unfairness of a dismissal.[1031]

9. REDUNDANCY PAYMENTS AND PROCEDURE

(a) Redundancy Payments[1832]

40-249 Introduction Part XI of the Employment Rights Act 1996, requires[1833] employers to make "redundancy payments" where "an employee who has been continuously employed for the requisite period" (viz two years[1834]) "(*a*) is dismissed by his employer by reason of redundancy, or (*b*) is laid off or kept on short-time" in specified circumstances for four or more consecutive weeks, or for a series of six or more weeks within a period of 13 weeks.[1835] The provisions of the Act are detailed, and the following is merely an outline of the main principles of the Act.[1836] There is, moreover, some significant recent case-law concerning contractual redundancy pay arrangements, in particular addressing the question of whether and when "custom and practice" might give rise to specific contractual obligations.[1837]

40-250 Dismissal The statutory definition of dismissal for the purposes of the redundancy payments legislation is basically the same as that applying for the purposes of the unfair dismissal legislation, considered in an earlier paragraph.[1838] There are, however, some additional elements which are special to this legislation. There are, then, the same basic elements to the definition:

(1) termination of the contract by the employer with or without notice[1839];

(2) expiry of a limited term contract without renewal[1840];

[1829] s.4(3)(b).

[1830] See above, paras 40-183 et seq.

[1831] See above, paras 40-220 et seq. For a case where a conviction is old but not spent, see *Torr v British Railways Board* [1977] I.C.R. 785.

[1832] See, generally, Grunfeld, *The Law and Practice of Redundancy*, 3rd edn (1989); Bourn, *The Law of Redundancy* (1983).

[1833] The Act prevails over any provisions in a contract which are inconsistent with it: s.203 of Employment Rights Act 1996.

[1834] Employment Rights Act 1996 s.155. On the meaning of "continuous employment" see below, para.40-254, and above, para.40-166. The requirement of "continuous employment" formerly excluded part-time employment but no longer does so by reason of SI 1995/31. See above, para.40-166.

[1835] Employment Rights Act 1996 ss.148–152.

[1836] The redundancy payments' legislation formerly made provision for rebates to employers from a Redundancy Fund, but that system of rebates was abolished by the Employment Act 1989.

[1837] *Shumba v Park Cakes Ltd* [2013] EWCA Civ 974, [2013] I.R.L.R. 800; *Allen v TRW Systems Ltd* [2013] EWCA Civ 1388; *Peacock Stores v Peregrine* [2014] UKEAT 0315/13/SM.

[1838] See above, para.40-176.

[1839] Employment Rights Act 1996 s.136(1)(a). See *Burton Group Ltd v Smith* [1977] I.R.L.R. 351 (under receiving notice); *Pambakian v Brentford Nylons Ltd* [1978] I.C.R. 665 (hiving-down agreement). Note here and generally the application of the Transfer of Undertakings (Protection of Employment) Regulations, as amended by the Transfer of Undertakings (Protection of Employment) (Amendment) Regulations 1987 (SI 1987/442).

[1840] Employment Rights Act 1996 s.136(1)(b). See, for the definition of the "limited-term contract", previously "fixed-term contract", *BBC v Ioannu* [1975] I.C.R. 267. cf. *North-East Coast Shiprepair-*

(3) termination by the employee in circumstances where the employer's conduct entitles him or her to terminate without notice[1841]; or

(4) employee giving notice to quit anticipating the expiry of a notice already given by the employer.[1842]

The case law considered in an earlier paragraph is applicable to these basic elements in the definition.[1843]

There are certain modifications to and extensions of this definition which are particular to the redundancy payments legislation: **40-251**

(1) If an employee is re-engaged in pursuance of an offer (which need not be in writing) made by the employer before the ending of the previous employment, and if the re-engagement takes effect within four weeks after the ending of the previous employment, the employee is, subject to the rule concerning trial periods, to be regarded as not having been dismissed.[1844] The rule concerning trial periods is that if the re-engagement is upon different terms, the employee may try the new employment for up to four weeks without foregoing his or her right to rely upon the ending of the previous employment as a dismissal.[1845] The trial period may alternatively be for such longer period as is agreed between the parties, before the new employment commences, for the purpose of retraining the employee.[1846]

(2) It is provided that where an employee terminates his or her contract of employment without notice, being entitled to do so by reason of a lock-out by his employer, the employee's action will not constitute a constructive dismissal on the part of the employer.[1847] By an accident of drafting, it appears that the employee's action will constitute constructive dismissal if accompanied by notice.[1848]

(3) Under s.136 of the 1996 Act, where in accordance with any enactment or rule of law any act on the part of an employer or any event affecting an employer (including his death)[1849] operates to terminate a contract of employment, that act or event is to be treated as a termination of the contract by the employer,[1850] and hence as a dismissal subject to the rules about re-engagement, and trial periods.[1851] This provision would apparently apply, for

---

ers Ltd v Secretary of State for Employment [1978] I.C.R. 755. See British Broadcasting Corp v Dixon [1979] I.C.R. 281.

[1841] Employment Rights Act 1996 s.136(1)(c) (the former requirement that the employee should terminate *without notice* being removed). See *Priestner v Ball* (1977) 12 I.T.R. 451; *Wilson-Undy v Instrument & Control Ltd* [1976] I.C.R. 508.

[1842] Employment Rights Act 1996 s.142 (which qualifies the rule by setting up a special procedure enabling the employer to challenge the employee's action on the merits).

[1843] See above, para.40-220.

[1844] Employment Rights Act 1996 s.138(1).

[1845] Employment Rights Act 1996 s.138(2)–(5).

[1846] Employment Rights Act 1996 s.138(3), (6).

[1847] Employment Rights Act 1996 s.136(2).

[1848] This results from the failure to adapt s.136(2) of Employment Rights Act 1996 to keep it in step with what is now s.136(1) of Employment Rights Act 1996, see above.

[1849] Employment Rights Act 1996 s.174. See *Ranger v Brown* [1978] I.C.R. 603.

[1850] Employment Rights Act 1996 s.136(5).

[1851] Employment Rights Act 1996 s.139(4), (5).

instance, to frustration of the contract of employment by an event affecting the employer.[1852]

40-252 Redundancy   The concept of redundancy is statutorily defined; by s.139(1) of the
1996 Act a dismissal is by reason of redundancy if the dismissal is wholly or mainly
attributable to:

(a) the cessation or intended cessation of the business for which the employee
was employed, either generally or in the place where the employee was so
employed; or to

(b) the diminution or expected diminution of the requirements of that business
for employees to carry out work of a particular kind either generally or in
the place where the employee was employed.

The definition has been held to be exhaustive[1853] (although it is not expressed to be
exhaustive by the statute itself). The attributability of the dismissal to the statutory
grounds for redundancy has been held to be a subjective matter, in the sense that
there is no redundancy if the employer genuinely and without misdirecting himself
or herself believes in the existence of a ground for dismissal falling outside the
statutory definition of redundancy and genuinely acts upon that ground believed to
be present.[1854] This question of attributability is in any case decided in the context
of a presumption of redundancy which arises under and for the purposes of the
redundancy payment legislation once there has been shown to be a dismissal.[1855] For
the purposes of the statutory definition, the "place where the employee was
employed" has been held to include the area within which he or she could be
required to work under his contract of employment[1856]; but the courts will not imply
an obligation of geographical mobility on the part of the employee unless there is
some particular evidence of an implied term to that effect.[1857] The second limb of
the statutory definition, by referring to the need for work of a particular kind,
defined redundancy in terms of the job itself rather than the employee himself or
herself. Hence a marginal shift in the nature of the employer's requirements may
create a situation in which there is no redundancy although the employee remains
available to continue his or her work as originally defined.[1858] Moreover it has been
held that the employer may seek to impose variations in incidental terms and conditions of employment to reduce his labour costs, without thereby creating a
redundancy in relation to an employee who is unwilling to accept such
variations.[1859] There is also a major statutory qualification upon the concept of
redundancy in that an employee is not entitled to a redundancy payment if he

---

[1852] See above, para.40-176.
[1853] *Hindle v Percival Boats Ltd* [1969] 1 W.L.R. 174 (Lord Denning M.R. dissenting on this point). cf.
Delanair Ltd v Mead [1976] I.R.L.R. 340; *Thomas v Jones* [1978] I.C.R. 274; *North-East Coast
Shiprepairers Ltd v Secretary of State for Employment* [1978] I.C.R. 755.
[1854] *Hindle v Percival Boats Ltd* [1969] 1 W.L.R. 174 (Lord Denning M.R. dissenting on this point also).
[1855] Employment Rights Act 1996 s.163(2). See *Express Lift Co Ltd v Bowles* [1977] I.C.R. 474.
[1856] *United Kingdom Atomic Energy Authority v Claydon* [1974] I.C.R. 128.
[1857] *O'Brien v Associated Fire Alarms Ltd* [1968] 1 W.L.R. 1916; *Rowbotham v Arthur Lee & Sons Ltd*
[1975] I.C.R. 109. Contrast *Stevenson v Teesside Bridge and Engineering Ltd* [1971] 1 All E.R. 296.
[1858] Compare *North Riding Garages Ltd v Butterwick* [1967] 2 Q.B. 56; *Vaux & Associated Breweries
Ltd v Ward* (1969) 7 K.I.R. 308; *Robinson v British Island Airways Ltd* [1978] I.C.R. 304; *Ranson
v G & W Collins Ltd* [1975] I.C.R. 765. Compare now *Safeway Stores Plc v Burrell* [1997] I.C.R.
523.
[1859] *Chapman v Goonvean and Rostowrack China Clay Co Ltd* [1973] I.C.R. 310; *Johnson v Nottinghamshire Combined Police Authority* [1974] I.C.R. 170; *Lesney Products Ltd v Nolan* [1977]

unreasonably refuses an offer of renewal of contract or re-engagement which would have taken effect within four weeks of his or her dismissal and was an offer of the same employment as he previously had or of suitable employment in relation to him or her.[1860] The same rule applies where the employee unreasonably terminates his or her employment during a trial period on new terms.[1861] Decided cases give some slight assistance in applying this concept of unreasonable refusal of suitable employment.[1862]

Lay-off and short-time If an employer lays an employee off work or places him   **40-253** or her on short-time in breach of his or her contract,[1863] that is likely to constitute a dismissal for the purposes of the redundancy payments legislation,[1864] or to entitle the employee to terminate his employment and rely on the transaction as a constructive dismissal.[1865] However, special provision was thought necessary to prevent employers from avoiding liability for redundancy payments by repeated or prolonged exercise of rights to lay employees off work or put them on short-time. It is therefore provided that an employee who is laid off or kept on short-time to the specified extent and who complies with the statutory procedure is entitled to a redundancy payment.[1866] The specified extent is four consecutive weeks or six weeks falling within a 13-week period.[1867] An employee is laid off when he or she gets no pay of any kind from his employer for the week concerned because, although he or she is available for work, there is none for him or her to do.[1868] A week counts as a week of short-time if, because of a shortage of work, the employee gets less than half a week's pay for that week.[1869] The statutory procedure consists in the employee first serving on his or her employer a written notice of intention to claim a redundancy payment because of a lay-off or short-time.[1870] The employer has the opportunity to contest liability by serving a written counter-notice asserting that there is a reasonable prospect of resumption of normal working.[1871] The employee must follow up his or her notice of intention to claim by a notice to terminate his or her employment within a time limit which varies according to whether the employer has served a counter-notice or not.[1872] This whole procedure is elaborate and not frequently invoked in practice.

I.C.R. 235.
[1860] Employment Rights Act 1996 ss.141(1)–(3), 146(2). See also s.140(1) of Employment Rights Act 1996 (effect of employee's misconduct). See *Allman v Rowland* [1977] I.C.R. 201.
[1861] Employment Rights Act 1996 s.141(4). *Camela v Sheerlyn Productions Ltd* [1976] I.C.R. 531.
[1862] *Carron Co v Robertson* [1967] I.T.R. 484; *Taylor v Kent CC* [1969] 2 Q.B. 560; *Collier v Smiths Dock Ltd* [1969] 2 Lloyd's Rep. 222; *Ingham v Bristol Piping Co Ltd* [1970] I.T.R. 218; *Morganite Crucible Ltd v Street* [1972] I.C.R. 110; *Kaye v Cooks (Finsbury) Ltd* [1973] 3 All E.R. 434; *Kane v Raine & Co* [1974] I.C.R. 300; *Rowbotham v Arthur Lee & Sons Ltd* [1975] I.C.R. 109; *Kennedy v Werneth Ring Mills Ltd* [1977] I.C.R. 206; *Forrester v Strathclyde Regional Council* [1977] I.T.R. 424. But compare now *Readman v Devon Primary Care Trust* [2013] EWCA Civ 1110, [2013] I.R.L.R. 878.
[1863] See above, para.40-091.
[1864] See above, para.40-250.
[1865] cf. *Powell Duffryn Wagon Co Ltd v House* [1974] I.C.R. 123.
[1866] Employment Rights Act 1996 s.148.
[1867] Employment Rights Act 1996 s.148(2).
[1868] Employment Rights Act 1996 s.147(1).
[1869] Employment Rights Act 1996 s.147(2).
[1870] Employment Rights Act 1996 s.148(1).
[1871] Employment Rights Act 1996 s.151(2).
[1872] Employment Rights Act 1996 s.150(1), (2).

40-254 **Redundancy payments** Statutory redundancy payments are calculated according to the length of the employee's period of continuous employment.[1873] There is a two years' minimum qualifying period of service,[1874] and the payments are calculated according to the following scale:

- for each year of employment at age 41 or over, one-and-a-half weeks' pay;
- for each year of employment at age 22 or over but under 41, one week's pay;
- for each year of employment at under 22, half a week's pay.[1875]

Up to 20 years' past service may be counted for this purpose.[1876]

The *period of continuous employment* is basically[1877] assessed in accordance with the provisions of the contracts of employment legislation, which have been considered in an earlier paragraph.[1878] There are certain provisions which modify that method of assessment for the purposes of the redundancy payments legislation. Periods of employment abroad for which no employer's social security contributions were payable do not count, but do not break the continuity of employment.[1879] A period of employment does not count in respect of which a redundancy payment was made to an employee who was later re-engaged, or whose contract of employment was renewed, by his or her employer or his or her employer's successor where a change of ownership of the business has occurred; moreover, continuity of employment is in such cases broken by the making of the earlier redundancy payment.[1880] The other statutory concepts used in the calculation of redundancy payments, namely those of the "week's pay" and "normal working hours" are considered in the two following paragraphs.

40-255 **The week's pay** The statutory week's pay which forms the basis of the calculation to a redundancy payment[1881] is assessed in accordance with ss.220–229 of the 1996 Act. Under those provisions the calculation varies according to whether the employee has normal working hours.[1882] If he or she does, and his or her pay does not vary within those hours with the amount of work done, his or her week's pay means his or her earnings for his or her normal weekly working hours.[1883] If the employee has normal working hours but his or her pay varies within those with the amount of work done (as where he or she is paid by piece rates or commission[1884]) his or her week's pay means the pay for his or her normal working hours at the aver-

---

[1873] Employment Rights Act 1996 s.162(1). See *Stowe-Woodward Ltd v Beynon* [1978] I.C.R. 609. The rules relating to the computation of "continuous employment" formerly excluded part-time employment but no longer do so by reason of SI 1995/31. See above, para.40-166.

[1874] Employment Rights Act 1996 s.155.

[1875] Employment Rights Act 1996 s.162(1), (2). The upper and lower age limits, which had previously applied, were, so far as they had continued to be applicable, abolished with effect from October 1, 2006 by the Employment Equality (Age) Regulations 2006 (SI 2006/1031) Sch.8 para.35. See also paras 40-175, 40-254.

[1876] Employment Rights Act 1996 s.162(3).

[1877] Employment Rights Act 1996 s.162(1)(a). See *Wood v York City Council* [1978] I.C.R. 840.

[1878] See above, paras 40-165—40-168.

[1879] Employment Rights Act 1996 s.215(2)–(5).

[1880] Employment Rights Act 1996 s.214.

[1881] See above, para.40-254.

[1882] As to "normal working hours", see the following paragraph.

[1883] Employment Rights Act 1996 s.221(2). See *Lake v Essex CC* [1978] I.C.R. 657; *Bullock v Merseyside CC* [1978] I.C.R. 419; *A. & B. Marcusfield v Melhuish* [1978] I.R.L.R. 484 (regular bonus); *Cole v Birmingham City DC* [1978] I.C.R. 1004; *Weevsmay v Kings* [1977] I.C.R. 244.

[1884] Employment Rights Act 1996 s.221(4).

age hourly rate[1885] prevailing during the last 12 weeks of employment.[1886] If the employee has no normal working hours, his or her week's pay means his or her average weekly pay during the last 12 weeks of employment.[1887] There is a limit, which is varied from time-to-time, upon the amount of the week's pay which can be taken into account for the purpose of calculating a redundancy payment.[1888]

Normal working hours   The calculation of the statutory week's pay, considered in the previous paragraph, depends upon whether the employee has normal working hours and, if so, what those hours are.[1889] The question of whether an employee has a pattern of normal working hours is partly[1890] determined by s.234 of the Employment Rights Act 1996[1891] which provides that an employee is deemed to have normal working hours where he or she is entitled to overtime pay when employed for more than a fixed number of hours in a week or other period.[1892] In such a case the basic rule is that the fixed number of hours shall be the normal working hours.[1893] If, however, there is a minimum working week which exceeds the number of hours without overtime, the minimum working week shall be the normal working hours.[1894] This formula is intended to exclude voluntary overtime while including hours which, although paid at premium rates, are in fact part of the obligatory working week. The effect of this formula as judicially interpreted is that overtime working will count towards the normal working week if, but only if, it is obligatory upon the employers to provide it as well as upon the employees to work it.[1895] The decided cases indicate a reluctance to regard overtime working as contractually obligatory upon the employee.[1896]

40-256

Exclusions from the Act   This part of the 1996 Act applies to all[1897] employees[1898] who are not specifically excluded. But in many situations no claim to a statutory redundancy payment arises[1899]: if the contract of employment was terminated by reason of redundancy where the employer was "entitled to terminate [it] without

40-257

[1885] cf. *Adams v John Wright & Sons (Blackwall) Ltd* [1972] I.T.R. 191; *Mole Mining Ltd v Jenkins* [1972] I.C.R. 282.

[1886] Employment Rights Act 1996 s.221(3).

[1887] Employment Rights Act 1996 s.222.

[1888] The limit is fixed by s.227(1)(c) of Employment Rights Act 1996, and is from time-to-time revised by regulations.

[1889] See above, para.40-255.

[1890] There is no exhaustive definition of all the cases where there are normal working hours. Compare *Minister of Labour v Country Bake Ltd* [1968] 5 K.I.R. 332.

[1891] See *Fox v C Wright (Farmers) Ltd* [1978] I.C.R. 98.

[1892] Employment Rights Act 1996 s.234(1), (2).

[1893] Employment Rights Act 1996 s.234(1), (2).

[1894] Employment Rights Act 1996 s.234(3). See *Ogden v Ardphalt Asphalt Ltd* [1977] 1 W.L.R. 1112.

[1895] *Tarmac Roadstone Holdings Ltd v Peacock* [1973] I.C.R. 273. See *ITT Components Group (Europe) v Kolah* [1977] I.C.R. 740.

[1896] *Pearson v William Jones Ltd* [1967] 1 W.L.R. 1140; *Turriff Construction Ltd v Bryant* (1967) 2 K.I.R. 659; *Loman and Henderson v Merseyside Transport Services Ltd* (1967) 3 K.I.R. 726; *The Darlington Forge Ltd v Sutton* [1968] I.T.R. 196; *Lynch v Dartmouth Auto Castings Ltd* [1969] I.T.R. 273; *Redpatch Dorman Long (Contracting) Ltd v Sutton* [1972] I.C.R. 477; *Gascol Conversions Ltd v Mercer* [1974] I.C.R. 420. Contrast *Armstrong Whitworth Rolls Ltd v Mustard* [1971] 1 All E.R. 598.

[1897] Except for certain relatives of the employer, the Act applies to a domestic servant in a private household: s.161(1) of Employment Rights Act 1996. See *Tomlinson v Dick Evans "U" Drive Ltd* [1978] I.R.L.R. 77 (illegal contract).

[1898] The term is defined in s.230(1).

[1899] The upper age limits, which had formerly applied, were, so far as they had continued to be ap-

notice by reason of the employee's conduct"[1900]; or if a collective agreement has been recognised by the Secretary of State for Employment as the basis of an order excluding the statutory provisions.[1901] Other categories excluded from the operation of the Act include: certain employees on fishing vessels,[1902] and public officers and civil servants.[1903] There was formerly provision for waiver of the statutory right in relation to the expiry of certain fixed-term contracts, but that has since been abolished.[1904]

40-258 Settlement of disputes: time within which claims must be made Any question arising under the redundancy payments legislation as to the right of an employee to a redundancy payment, or as to the amount of a redundancy payment, is to be referred to and determined by an employment tribunal.[1905] The description of the procedure relating to such applications is outside the scope of the present work. Suffice it to deal here with the time within which claims must be made. An employee is not entitled to a redundancy payment unless within six months of the ending of his or her employment[1906] the payment has been agreed and paid or the employee has claimed the payment by notice in writing to the employer or has referred a redundancy payments issue to an employment tribunal or presented a complaint of unfair dismissal to an employment tribunal.[1907] However, an employment tribunal may waive the time limits where the employee claims the payment or presents an issue or complaint to an employment tribunal within the following six months and where the employment tribunal thinks it just and equitable that the employee should receive a redundancy payment.[1908]

(b) Redundancy Procedure[1909]

40-259 Introduction Part IV Ch.II of the Trade Union and Labour Relations (Consolidation) Act 1992 imposes procedural requirements upon employers in the handling of redundancies. The procedural obligations are of two types:

(a) the obligation to consult with representatives of recognised trade unions or of employees; and

(b) the obligation to give advance warning to the Department of Trade and Industry.

---

plicable, abolished with effect from October 1, 2006 by the Employment Equality (Age) Regulations 2006 (SI 2006/1031) Sch.8 para.30. See also paras 40-175, 40-254.

[1900] Employment Rights Act 1996 s.140(1).

[1901] Employment Rights Act 1996 s.157.

[1902] Employment Rights Act 1996 s.199(2).

[1903] See s.159 of Employment Rights Act 1996. (See above, para.40-035.)

[1904] Employment Rights Act 1996 s.197, repealed by the Fixed-term Employees Regulations 2002 (SI 2002/2034) reg.11 and Sch.2.

[1905] Employment Rights Act 1996 s.163. The Employment Act 2008 s.7(2) provided, with effect from April 6, 2009 (SI 2008/3232), for the insertion of a new s.163(5) into the Employment Rights Act 1996 which enables an Employment Tribunal to award compensation for financial loss which is sustained by the employee and is attributable to the non-payment of a redundancy payment to which he or she is entitled.

[1906] See s.164(1) of Employment Rights Act 1996 referring to the "relevant date" and hence to s.235(1) of Employment Rights Act 1996 which refers to ss.145, 153 of Employment Rights Act 1996. See *Watts v Rubery Owen Conveyancer Ltd* [1977] I.C.R. 429.

[1907] Employment Rights Act 1996 s.164(1). See *Nash v Ryan Plant International Ltd* [1977] I.C.R. 560.

[1908] Employment Rights Act 1996 s.164(2), (3).

[1909] See Freedland (1976) 5 I.L.J. 24; Ewing (1993) 22 I.L.J. 176–178.

These provisions, described in the next two paragraphs, represent an intention to give effect to the European Union Directive on the Approximation of the Laws of the Member States relating to Collective Redundancies.[1910] They were further amended by the Trade Union Reform and Employment Rights Act 1993 and give effect to an amending Directive of 1992.[1911]

Consultation with the representatives of recognised trade unions or of   **40-260**
employees   Significant changes to these consultation requirements have continued to be made by statutory instruments.[1912] In brief summary,[1913] requirements to consult in relation to proposed redundancies and proposed transfers of undertakings are no longer confined to consultation with the representatives of recognised trade unions; they are now requirements to consult, at the choice of the employer, either with the representatives of recognised trade unions or with elected representatives of the employees who are affected by the proposed redundancies or the proposed transfer. The requirement to consult in relation to proposed redundancies now attaches only where it is proposed to make 20 or more employees redundant within a period of 90 days or less.[1914] The consultation must begin in good time,[1915] and certain minimum periods are laid down: it must begin within 45 days for 100 or more dismissals within a period of 90 days, and otherwise within 30 days.[1916] The obligation to consult requires the employer to disclose prescribed information[1917] about ways of avoiding the dismissals, reducing the numbers to be dismissed, and mitigating the consequences of the dismissals, and requires the employer to undertake that consultation with a view to reaching agreement with the appropriate representatives.[1918] The employer may be held to be released from the provisions as to minimum periods of consultation and as to disclosure, consideration of representations and reply if he or she can show that it was not in the circumstances reasonably practicable for him or her to comply with those obligations.[1919]

[1910] Council Directive 75/129.

[1911] s.34, implementing Council Directive 92/56.

[1912] Beginning with the Collective Redundancies and Transfer of Undertakings (Protection of Employment) (Amendment) Regulations 1995 (SI 1995/2587) with effect from October 26, 1995. See now also the Collective Redundancies and Transfer of Undertakings (Protection of Employment) (Amendment) Regulations 2014 (SI 2014/16).

[1913] The provisions summarised are those of Trade Union and Labour Relations (Consolidation) Act 1992 s.188 as subsequently amended. See also the Collective Redundancies and Transfer of Undertakings (Protection of Employment) (Amendment) Regulations 1999 (SI 1999/1925), and the Trade Union and Labour Relations (Consolidation) Act 1992 (Amendment) Order 2013 (SI 2013/763), in force from April 6, 2013, which shortened the relevant consultation periods and excluded the expiry of fixed term contracts from counting towards the numerical thresholds.

[1914] s.188(1). The restriction to "at one establishment" had been placed in doubt by *USDAW v Ethel Austin Ltd (In Administration)* [2014] EWCA Civ 142, [2014] 2 C.M.L.R. 45, but was subsequently confirmed by the CJEU in *USDAW v Ethel Austin Ltd* (C-80/14) EU:C:2015:291, [2015] 3 C.M.L.R. 32.

[1915] s.188(1A).

[1916] s.188(1A).

[1917] s.188(4); note the new para.(f) as inserted by Trade Union Reform and Employment Rights Act 1993 s.34(2)(a).

[1918] s.188(2).

[1919] s.188(7); and see also s.189(6) (onus of proof on employer). See, among the earlier leading authorities, *Association of Patternmakers and Allied Craftsmen v Kirvin Ltd* [1978] I.R.L.R. 318; *Amalgamated Society of Boilermakers, Shipwrights, Blacksmiths & Structural Workers v George Wimpey (M E & C) Ltd* [1977] I.R.L.R. 95; *Clarks of Hove Ltd v Bakers' Union* [1978] I.C.R. 1076;

40-261   The sanction for failure to comply with the duty to consult is the obtaining of a protective award by complaint to an employment tribunal.[1920] The protective award is an award of entitlement to remuneration to the affected employees for periods up to a maximum of 90 days.[1921] The entitlement to remuneration is subject to safeguards for both parties, in relation for instance to the employee's absence from work or the unavailability of work.[1922] If an employee unreasonably refuses an offer from his or her employer of a new contract or renewal of the old contract, he or she will lose his entitlement to remuneration under the award.[1923] An employee may complain to an employment tribunal that he or she has not been paid the amount due under an award.[1924] The tribunal shall if the complaint is well-founded order the employer to pay the amount due.[1925]

40-262   A similar requirement of consultation with trade union or employee representatives now arises under the Transfer of Undertakings (Protection of Employment) Regulations 2006[1926] in relation to the transfer of an undertaking or service provision change within the meaning of the regulations.[1927] The obligations to inform and consult arise in relation to affected employees both of the transferor and of the transferee employer.[1928] A recognised union, or employee representatives, may complain to an employment tribunal of failure on the part of either employer to inform or consult[1929] and may obtain an award of up to 13 weeks' pay for the affected employees.[1930]

40-263   **Notification of proposed redundancies to the Secretary of State**   Under Pt IV Ch.II of the Trade Union and Labour Relations (Consolidation) Act 1992 as subsequently amended, an employer who proposes to dismiss 100 or more employees[1931] as redundant[1932] at one establishment[1933] within 90 days or less, must give written notification of the proposal to the Secretary of State[1934] at least 90 days before the first of those dismissals takes effect.[1935] If the proposal is to dismiss 20 or more employees within 90 days or less, the notification must be given at least

---

UCATT v H Rooke & Son (Cambridge) Ltd [1978] I.C.R. 818; *Hamish Armour v ASTMS* [1979] I.R.L.R. 24; and *USDAW v Leancut Bacon Ltd* [1981] I.R.L.R. 295.

[1920] See Trade Union and Labour Relations (Consolidation) Act 1992 s.189(1) (limitation period— s.189(5)). See, as to the making of the award, *Susie Radin Ltd v GMB* [2004] EWCA Civ 180, [2004] 2 All E.R. 279.

[1921] Trade Union and Labour Relations (Consolidation) Act 1992 s.189(4). See, as to length of award, *Sir Alfred McAlpine & Son (Northern) Ltd v Foulkes* [1977] I.C.R. 748; *Talke Fashions Ltd v Amalgamated Society of Textile Workers and Kindred Trades* [1977] I.C.R. 833.

[1922] s.190.

[1923] s.191.

[1924] s.192(1), (2).

[1925] s.192(3).

[1926] With effect from April 6, 2006, the existing Transfer of Undertakings (Protection of Employment) Regulations were revised and replaced by the Transfer of Undertakings (Protection of Employment) Regulations 2006 (SI 2006/246).

[1927] SI 2006/246 reg.13. The regulations do not apply to a takeover by transfer of share control: see reg.3(1) and above, para.40-180.

[1928] SI 2006/246 reg.13(1).

[1929] SI 2006/246 reg.15(1).

[1930] SI 2006/246 reg.16(3).

[1931] For the excluded classes of employees, see Trade Union and Labour Relations (Consolidation) Act 1992 ss.284, 285, 282(1).

[1932] See above, para.40-252.

[1933] See, for the meaning of this term, *Kapur v Shields* [1976] I.C.R. 26.

[1934] That is to say, currently, the Department of Business, Innovation and Skills.

[1935] Trade Union and Labour Relations (Consolidation) Act 1992 s.193(1)–(6), subject to s.193(7)

30 days before the first of the dismissals.[1936] The Collective Redundancies (Amendment) Regulations 2006[1937] amend s.193 of the Trade Union and Labour Relations (Consolidation) Act 1992 to provide that, in addition to the existing requirements of that section, an employer proposing collective redundancies must notify the Secretary of State of his or her proposal before he or she gives notice to an employee to terminate an employee's contract of employment in respect of any of those dismissals. In a case where consultation with trade union or employee representatives is statutorily required[1938] the notification must identify the representatives concerned and state the date when consultation began.[1939] Where appropriate, a copy of the notification must go to the recognised union.[1940] The sanction for failure to give the required notification to the Department is that the Secretary of State may institute criminal proceedings against the employer, who will be liable on summary conviction to a fine not exceeding level 5 on the standard scale.[1941] The purpose of the notification procedure was originally stated to be:

"... to enable the manpower services of the Department to take any necessary measures for re-deployment or re-training of the workers involved, to enable the Government to consider any further steps that may be needed to avoid or minimise the effects of the redundancy, and to provide documentary evidence in all but the smallest redundancies of the commencement of consultations."[1942]

10. STATUTORY DISPUTE RESOLUTION PROVISIONS

Statutory dispute resolution provisions The Employment Act 2002, contained, **40-264** inter alia, a set of provisions introducing new statutory dispute resolution procedures (ss.29–34 and Schs 2–4) which had a great potential impact on the law of the contract of employment.[1943] However, the Employment Act 2008 repealed those provisions and replaced them with a set of provisions reflecting a different approach, for the adjustment of a large set of compensatory awards by reference to non-compliance with statutory codes of practice concerned with dispute resolution.[1944] Specific provision was made for such adjustment of compensatory awards for unfair dismissal[1945]; a code of practice on disciplinary and grievance procedures has been issued as the point of reference for that particular purpose.[1946] In connection with the statutory dispute resolution provisions, reference should also be made to the right for workers to be accompanied by certain trade union officials or fellow workers at non-trivial disciplinary and grievance hearings. That right was originally conferred by ss.10–12 of the Employment Relations Act 1999.

(reasonable practicability).

[1936] Trade Union and Labour Relations (Consolidation) Act 1992 s.193(2).

[1937] SI 2006/2387.

[1938] See above, para.40-260.

[1939] s.193(4).

[1940] s.193(6) subject to s.193(7) (reasonable practicability).

[1941] s.194.

[1942] Consultative Document on the Employment Protection Bill (1974), para.66.

[1943] These provisions were implemented and amplified by the Employment Act 2002 (Dispute Resolution) Regulations 2004 (SI 2004/752).

[1944] s.3(1) inserting into the Trade Union and Labour Relations (Consolidation) Act 1992 a new s.207A providing for the statutory codes of practice which may be issued under that Act to be admissible in evidence before and able to be taken into account by employment tribunals.

[1945] s.3(2) amending s.124A of the Employment Rights Act 1996; see above, para.40-242.

[1946] ACAS *Code of Practice 1—Disciplinary and Grievance Procedures* (April 2009).

Section 37 of the Employment Relations Act 2004 amended s.10 of the 1999 Act, with effect from October 2004, in order further to clarify the role of the companion at such disciplinary and grievance hearings. Reference should also be made to the Employment Tribunals (Early Conciliation, Exemptions and Rules of Procedure) Regulations 2014,[1947] which impose a duty to involve ACAS before the issuance of an Employment Tribunal Claim.

[1947] SI 2014/254.

CHAPTER 41

GAMBLING CONTRACTS

Sir Guenter Treitel

1. INTRODUCTION

Three stages of development   The law relating to gaming, wagering and **41-001**
gambling contracts can be said to have developed in three stages. (1) The original
common law position was that, in general, such contracts were valid, though this
position was subject to significant qualifications.[1] (2) This common law position
was reversed by a number of Gaming Acts of 1710, 1835, 1845 and 1892, originally
with the object of restricting credit for gaming[2] and later for the purpose of
invalidating contracts by way of gaming and wagering[3] as well as certain transactions related to such contracts.[4] (3) Part 17 of the Gambling Act 2005 came in to
force on September 1, 2007[5] and fundamentally changed the law with regard to

---

[1]   See below, para.41-010.

[2]   Gaming Acts 1710 and 1835.

[3]   Gaming Act 1845 s.18.

[4]   Gaming Act 1892 s.1.

[5]   By virtue of Gambling Act 2005 (Commencement No.6 and Transitional Provisions) Order 2006 (SI 2006/3272) art.2(4) (subject to certain transitional provisions not relevant to the ensuing discussion).

gaming and wagering contracts as contained in the legislation which had governed it at the second stage of its development, described above. Section 334(1) of the 2005 Act repeals this legislation,[6] though s.334(2) makes it clear that these repeals do not have retrospective effect.[7] Section 356 repeals those repeals, as well as repealing the remaining provisions of the Gaming Acts of 1710 to 1892 which had not been repealed by earlier legislation.[8] Section 356 also repeals (again without retrospective effect) a number of other Acts, including the Gaming Act 1968,[9] s.16 of which had imposed further restrictions (going beyond those imposed by earlier Gaming Acts) on credit for gaming; though the policy of restricting such credit for gambling continues to be reflected in the 2005 Act.[10] As none of the above repeals are retrospective, the legal effects of gambling transactions concluded before September 1, 2007 continue to depend on the now repealed legislation (and on the associated case law) which governed such transactions during the second of the stages of development described above. The passage of time has so much reduced the practical importance of this body of rules that its continued discussion in the present edition of this book can no longer be justified. Any reader who may still need guidance on the law as it stood before the coming into force of the 2005 Act is referred to paras 40–002—40–088 of the 30th edition of this book. Some of the old cases may, however, continue to provide useful illustrations of fact situations that could still give rise to problems under the law as it now stands under the 2005 Act. To this extent, such cases may still merit discussion even though their reasoning is obsolete, and their outcome would be different, under the present law.

41-002 **Change of course**   For the purposes of this Chapter, the most important of the changes made by the Gambling Act 2005 are (apart from the repeals listed in para.41-001 above) contained in its Part 17. This Part deals with the "Legality and Enforceability of Gambling Contracts" and reverses the approach of the law as it had stood at the second of the stages of development described in para.41-001 above. In particular, s.335(1) lays down the general rule that "[t]he fact that a contract relates to gambling shall not prevent its enforcement". This new general rule is, under the 2005 Act, subject to two exceptions discussed in paras 41–016—41–023, below. By way of further introduction to the ensuing discussion of the 2005 Act, a brief account must be given of the main elements of the structure of the Act,

---

Pt 17 comprises ss.334–338 (out of the 362 sections) of the 2005 Act.

[6] ss.334(1)(e) and 356 and Sch.17 also delete the references to s.18 of the Gaming Act 1845 and s.1 of the Gaming Act 1892 from s.412 of the Financial Services and Markets Act 2000 (below, para.41-003).

[7] s.334(2) provides: "The repeals in subsection (1) do not permit the enforcement of a right which is created, or which emanates from an agreement made, before this section comes into force". Strictly speaking, before the repeals effected by subsection (1) came into force, *no* "rights" would be created or emanate from agreements of the kind in question.

[8] s.356 (3)(a), (c), (d) and (e); s.356(4) and Sch.17.

[9] s.356(3)(g); s.356(4) and Sch.17. Section 356 contains no express provision, comparable to that contained in s.334(2), denying it retrospective effect. With regard to the repeals made by s.356, their prospective nature follows from the general presumption against giving legislation retrospective effect. In *Aspinall's Club Ltd v Al Zayat* [2007] EWCA Civ 1001 the present point did not arise since, though the appeal was heard after s.16 of the 1968 Act had been repealed, this point could not affect the outcome (at [11]), presumably because the action had been begun before the repeal had come into force. The transaction which led to the litigation in the *Al Zayat* case had taken place on March 10, 2000.

[10] Gambling Act 2005, ss.81, 177; "credit" is defined in s.81(4).

and of its terminology, so far as these matters relate to the legal effects of gambling contracts under the Act.

General scheme of the Gambling Act 2005   The main purpose of this Act is to **41-003** create a new scheme for the regulation of gambling in Great Britain, supervised by a body (the Gambling Commission) created by the Act.[11] The scheme does not extend to transactions (such as contracts for differences) which are regulated under the Financial Services and Markets Act 2000,[12] or to the National Lottery.[13] The general principle underlying the Act is that commercial gambling which does not fall within either of the above exceptions is unlawful (so that the provision of facilities, or the use of premises, for gambling is an offence) unless a licence has been obtained from the appropriate local authority[14] and the conditions of the licence have been complied with.[15] It is also an offence under the Act to invite, cause or permit a child or young person to take part in commercial gambling[16] and for a young person to engage in such gambling[17] or to provide facilities for such gambling.[18] The licensing requirements described above, and the offences resulting from failure to comply with them do not extend to "private"[19] gaming or betting or to certain other non-commercial gaming or betting.[20]

"Gambling", "gaming" and "betting"   "Gambling" in the 2005 Act means gam- **41-004** ing, betting and participating in a lottery.[21] "Gaming" means playing (i.e. participating in) a game of chance (not including a sport) for a prize.[22] "Betting" is defined in s.9(1) to mean:

> "... making or accepting a bet on (a) the outcome of a race, competition or other event or process, (b) the likelihood of anything occurring or not occurring or (c) whether anything is or is not true."

The "events" (on which the outcome of the bet can depend) in some important respects resemble those which could, before the coming into force of the 2005 Act, be the subject of a wager (an expression which forms no part of the definition of "gambling" "gaming" or "betting" in the 2005 Act) within the definition which had been formulated and elaborated at common law for the purposes of the earlier Gaming Acts which are now repealed. Thus there can be a bet within s.9(1)(c) on the question "whether anything is true or not true": for example, on which horse won

---

[11]   s.20.
[12]   s.10; see Financial Services and Markets Act 2000 s.412, as amended by Gambling Act 2005 s.334(1)(e), 356(4) and Sch.17.
[13]   Gambling Act 2005 s.15, except for the purposes of ss.42 and 335 (below, para.41-011): s.15(2).
[14]   s.2 gives a list of licensing authorities.
[15]   ss.33(1) and (2), 37(1) and (2).
[16]   s.46.
[17]   s.48.
[18]   s.50.
[19]   s.296.
[20]   ss.297–302.
[21]   s.3.
[22]   s.6. For the purposes of the old law relating to gaming and wagering contracts, "gaming" was judicially defined to mean "the playing of any game for money or money's worth" (*Ellesmere v Wallace* [1929] 2 Ch. 1, 55, but see also p.29) and included horse-racing (*Applegarth v Colley* (1842) 10 M. & W. 723) and presumably other kinds of racing and other kinds of contests.

the Derby last year[23]; this point is explicitly made in s.9(2)(a) by which a "transaction that relates to the outcome of a race" (or certain other events) may be a "bet" within s.9(1) despite the fact that the race (etc.) "has already occurred".[24] The words of s.9(1)(c) (quoted above) do not mean that a contract by which A promises B to pay a sum of money to B for proving a particular hypothesis or establishing a specified fact would necessarily be regarded as a "bet" within the Act. It seems unlikely, for example, that a promise to make a payment to a geologist for establishing that oil or some other mineral was present at a particular location would be so regarded; and the same is probably true of a promise to pay a sum of money to any mathematician who succeeded in proving a particular hypothesis. But under the old law it had been decided in *Hampden v Walsh*[25] that a promise by the claimant, who believed that the earth was flat, to pay £500 to any person who could satisfactorily prove the curvature of the earth was a wager, since the claimant's object was not to establish a scientific fact, but "to establish his own view in a marked and triumphant manner".[26] Presumably a transaction of this kind would now be a "bet" within s.9(1)(c) of the 2005 Act. On the other hand, the concept of a "bet" within s.9 is in some respects wider than the concept of a wager under the old law. It seems that there could be a "bet" within s.9 on an occurrence which was not "uncertain" even in the restricted sense of the old law that the parties must "profess" to hold opposite views on it[27]; under s.9 it would suffice that both parties simply professed ignorance on the matter in question. There is also nothing in s.9 to suggest that an event cannot be the subject of a "bet" within the section merely because the occurrence of the event was within the control of one of the parties; under the previous law it was doubtful whether such an event could be the subject of a wager.[28]

41-005 **"Bet", "making a bet" and "betting"** The word "bet" and the phrase "making a bet" are not defined in the 2005 Act, so that the opening words of the definition in s.9(1) (quoted in para.41-004 above) are self-referential and unhelpful. It can be inferred from other provisions of the Act that the person "making" the bet must normally pay (or undertake to pay or deposit) a stake or be required to make a payment in order to participate in the bet[29]; and that a person "accepting" a bet undertakes that he will make a payment to the person "making" the bet if that person's forecast or assertion on one of the events or states of affairs listed in s.9(1) turns out to be correct. In these respects, the concept of "making a bet" under the Act resembles that of a "wager" at common law: i.e. the essential nature of a "bet" is, like that of a "wager",[30] a transaction by which one party promises to make a pay-

---

23 cf. *Pugh v Jenkins* (1841) 1 Q.B. 631; *Rourke v Short* (1856) 5 E. & B. 904.

24 s.9(2)(a) refers back to s.9(1)(a), which uses the same words as s.9(2)(a) to describe the kinds of occurrences which can be the subject of a bet.

25 (1876) 1 Q.B.D. 189.

26 (1876) 1 Q.B.D. 189 at 197.

27 This requirement is derived from the common law definition of a wager given in the judgment of Hawkins J. in *Carlill v Carbolic Smoke Ball Co* [1892] 2 Q.B. 484, 490, affirmed [1893] 1 Q.B. 256.

28 For the suggestion that on such facts there was, under the old law, no wager, see *Ellesmere v Wallace* [1929] 2 Ch. 1, 29; the suggestion was doubted in para.40-003 of the 30th edition of this book (bet between A and B that A will wear a red tie tomorrow).

29 See Gambling Act 2005 s.11(1) ("despite the fact that he does not deposit a stake in the normal way of betting"), 11(1)(b) ("required to pay").

30 For the common law definition of a wagering contract, see *Carlill v Carbolic Smoke Ball Co* [1892] 2 Q.B. 484, 490, affirmed [1893] 1 Q.B. 256.

ment to (or to confer some other benefit on) another in the circumstances described in the words of s.9(1) quoted in para.41-004 above.

"Gambling" and "wagering"   There are, however, also differences between the **41-006** concept of "gambling" under the 2005 Act and that of the earlier concept of a "wager". On the one hand, "gambling" under the Act is narrower than "wagering" under the previous law in that "betting" (and hence "gambling"[31]) under the Act does not include activities regulated under s.22 of the Financial Services and Markets Act 2000[32]; contracts for differences (which could be wagers under the old law[33]) fall into this category,[34] as do so called "spread bets".[35] On the other hand, the concept of "gambling" under the 2005 Act is in a number of respects wider than that of a wager under the judicially formulated definition of a wager under the old law. First, "betting" is defined[36] to mean "making *or* accepting a bet": these are alternative possibilities, so that there appears to be no scope under the Act for the previous rule that a contract could not be a "wager" if one party could not win or if one party cannot lose.[37] Secondly, the concept of gambling under the 2005 Act is wider than that of a wager under the old law in that it includes participating in a lottery[38] and in that the concept of betting includes pool betting.[39] A third, related,

---

[31] See Gambling Act 2005 s.3, defining "gambling" to mean (inter alia) "betting".

[32] Gambling Act 2005 s.10. Regulation 6(1) of the Consumer Contracts (Information, Cancellation and Additional Charges) Regulations 2013 (SI 2013/3134) likewise provides that "These Regulations do not apply to a contract, to the extent that it is (a) for (i) gambling within the meaning of the Gambling Act 2005 …". For these Regulations, see above paras 14-047, 38-061 et seq.

[33] e.g. *Re Gieve* [1899] 1 Q.B. 794; cf. *Philip v Bennett* (1901) 18 T.L.R. 129; *Re The Futures Index* [1985] F.L.R. 147; Chaikin and Moher, [1986] L.M.C.L.Q 390.

[34] Financial Services and Markets Act 2000 (Regulated Activities) Order 2001 (SI 2001/544) art.85. See also the Contracts for Difference (Standard Terms) Regulations 2014 (SI 2014/2012) as amended by the Contracts for Difference (Standard Terms) (Amendment) Regulations 2017 (SI 2017/112).

[35] Marginal note to Gambling Act 2005 s.10. The expression "spread bets" does not occur in the body of s.10. cf. *WW Properties Investments Ltd v National Westminster Bank Plc* [2016] EWCA Civ 1142, [2017] 1 Lloyd's Rep. 87, where an entity which had borrowed money from a bank entered into four "interest rate hedging contracts" with the bank; the first three of these were called "Collars" while the fourth "was a Swap Agreement" ([2016] EWCA Civ 1142 at [2]). The purpose of these agreements was to hedge the borrower's liabilities which, under the contract of loan, could rise in line with increases in the base rate (at [23]). Although these four agreements were "contracts for differences" (at [24]), it was held that they were not wagers: contracts for differences would not be wagers if they were entered into (as these contracts were) "for a commercial purpose such as hedging" (see at [28], citing Leggatt L.J. IN *City Index Ltd v Leslie* [1992] Q.B. 98, which had in turn been cited by Hobhouse J. in *Morgan Grenfell and Co Ltd v Welwyn Hatfield District Council* [1995] 1 All E.R. 1 (a decision that was approved in the *WW Property* case [2016] EWCA Civ 1142 at [42]); and relying on Financial Services Act 1986 s.63 and Sch.1 Pt 1 para.8 note 1). In *Banco Santander Totta SA v Companjia de Carris de Ferro de Lisboa SA* [2016] EWHC 465 (Coo), [2016] 4 W.L.R. 49 interest rate swaps were likewise found not to be void under Portuguese law as "games of chance", though that finding was not strictly necessary to the outcome in that case. The sentence of this paragraph ending with this footnote was quoted with apparent approval by Vos L.J. in *Nextia Properties Ltd v Royal Bank of Scotland Plc* [2014] EWCA Civ 740 at [24] (refusing leave to appeal from the decision of H.H.J. Behrens [2013] EWHC 3167 (QB)).

[36] In s.9(1), above para.41-004.

[37] This was the reason why the contract in *Carlill v Carbolic Smoke Ball Co* [1892] 1 Q.B. 256 had been held not to be a wager within the now repealed legislation referred to in para.41-001 above; cf. *Kloekner & Co AG v Gatoil Overseas Inc* [1990] 1 Lloyd's Rep. 177, 192.

[38] Gambling Act 2005 s.3(c); but participating in a lottery which forms part of the National Lottery is not gambling for the purposes of the Act except for the purposes of ss.42 (below, para.41-019) and 335 (below, paras 41-011 and 41-017).

[39] Gambling Act 2005 s.12(1); contrast the text above at this note and the following note for the view

point is that under the old law there was some support for the view that there could be only two parties to a wager, or that, if there were more than two, they had to be divided into two sides.[40] There is nothing in the 2005 Act to support the view that its concept of gambling is restricted by any such requirement.

41-007 **Prizes** Section 339 of the 2005 Act provides that "participating in a competition or other arrangement under which a person may win a prize is not gambling for the purpose of this Act"[41] unless it is gaming, participating in a lottery or betting within specified other provisions of the Act.[42] Where such "prize competitions"[43] (e.g. between athletes) are governed by s.339, they are not subject to the regulatory regime of the Act and are legally enforceable quite apart from the provisions of its Part 17.[44] They must be distinguished from "prize gaming" which is regulated by Part 13 of the Act.[45] The essential features of prize gaming are that the size of the prize does not depend on the number of participants or on the stakes paid by them.[46]

41-008 **Disguised bets** Under the old law relating to gaming and wagering contracts, attempts were sometimes made to pass off as valid contracts transactions which were in substance wagers; and the courts then had regard to the substance of the transaction, rather than to the form in which it was cast. For example, in *Rourke v Short*[47] parties to an agreement for the sale of rags began, in the course of fixing the price, to argue about the price of a previous lot, the seller maintaining that it was lower than it was alleged to be by the buyer. It was agreed that if the seller was right, then the price of the present lot was to be twice as much as it would be if the buyer was right. This was held to be a wager (and could now be a bet) on the price of the previous lot. The court recognised that there could be a genuine bargain for the price of goods to be fixed by reference to that paid for a previous lot. But that was not the substance of the bargain here, "for the lower the former price was, the higher the present price was to be".[48] The purpose of such attempts to disguise or conceal the fact that a transaction was a wager was to give it the legal enforceability which, as a wager, it formerly lacked. To this extent, the reasoning of the old cases, and the motive for such attempts to disguise the nature of a transaction which is in substance a gambling contract, are obsolete, now that the effect of s.335(1) of the 2005 Act is that contracts relating to gambling are, in general, legally enforceable. But the reasoning of those cases may still be of practical importance when parties to a bet seek to disguise its true nature in order to avoid the power of the Gambling Commission "to void bet"[49] under s.336 of the 2005 Act[50]; and also where it is alleged that the contract is, by virtue of s.335(2) unenforceable by reason of its unlawful-

that pool betting was not "wagering" under the previous law.
40 *Ellesmere v Wallace* [1929] 2 Ch. 1, 50.
41 In this respect, s.339 carries forward the policy of the third limb of the now repealed s.18 of the Gaming Act 1845.
42 i.e. ss.6 (gaming), 14 (lottery) and 9–11 (betting).
43 Marginal note to s.339.
44 Such as, in particular, s.335(1), below, para.41-011.
45 ss.288–294.
46 s.288.
47 (1856) 5 E. & B. 904; cf. *Brogden v Marriott* (1836) 3 Bing. N.C. 88; contrast *Crofton v Colgan* (1859) 10 Ir. C.L.R. 133.
48 (1856) 5 E. & B. 904, 912.
49 These words occur in the marginal note to Gambling Act 2005 s.336.
50 See paras 41-022, 41-023 below.

ness and this unlawfulness consists of failure to comply with provisions of the 2005 Act which apply to "gambling" or "gambling contracts".[51] As under the old law, the question whether a transaction is a bet may also arise in a context that has nothing to do with its legal enforceability, in particular in the context of the rule that "winnings from betting" are not subject to capital gains tax.[52] An attempt by parties for this purpose to disguise as a bet a contract which did not amount to "betting" within s.9 of the 2005 Act would no doubt be struck down by the courts.

Insurance   The concept of "gambling" under the 2005 Act is not in terms   **41-009**
restricted (as it was in the previous law) to cases in which the party to whom money is to be paid on the outcome of the bet has no other "interest" in the contract than the sum or stake that he will win or lose.[53] The existence of such an "interest" was formerly thought to be one reason why contracts of insurance were not wagers where the requirement of the insured's having an "insurable interest" was satisfied. But under the law as it stood before the coming into force of the 2005 Act, a contract of insurance was not a wager merely because the requirement of insurable interest was not satisfied, since insurer and insured did not, for that reason alone, profess to hold "opposite views touching the issue of a future uncertain event"[54] and even where, for this reason, the contract of insurance was not, in spite of lack of insurable interest, a wager, it was (and is) nevertheless void under s.4 of the Marine Insurance Act 1906 and might be illegal under the Marine Insurance (Gambling Policies) Act 1909.[55] Neither of these enactments is repealed or amended by the 2005 Act, in spite of the fact that by s.4 of the 1906 Act a contract of marine insurance is "deemed to be a gaming or wagering contract"[56] where "the assured has not an insurable interest as defined by this Act ..."[57] and "every contract of marine insurance by way of gaming or wagering is void".[58] The invalidity of such a contract, however (even though it is not actually a wagering contract), follows from its being "deemed to be a gaming or wagering contract"[59] (words which might be regarded as a reference to the now repealed legislation which invalidated contracts falling within this general category),[60] and from its being declared to be "void" by

---

51 See paras 41-017—41-021.
52 Taxation of Chargeable Gains Act 1992 s.51(1).
53 For the rule that a contract was a wager (under the law before the 2005 Act came into force) only if neither party had "any other interest in that contract than the sum or stake that he will so win or lose", see *Carlill v Carbolic Smoke Ball Co* [1892] 2 Q.B. 484, 490, affirmed [1893] 1 Q.B. 256. Hence if the requirement of insurable interest (text below, after this note) was satisfied, a contract of insurance was not a wager.
54 For this requirement of a wagering contract (under the law before the coming into force of the 2005 Act), see *Carlill v Carbolic Smoke Ball Co* [1892] 2 Q.B. 484 at 490.
55 This Act imposes criminal penalties on contracts made in violation of the prohibitions imposed by it. It does not specify the civil consequences of such violations but such contracts made in breach of these prohibitions are illegal as contracts prohibited by statute with penal sanctions.
56 Marine Insurance Act 1906 s.4(2). It followed from the use of the word "deemed" in s.4(2) that the contract was void where the insured had no insurable interest even though the contract was not actually a wagering contract since the insurer and insured did not profess to hold opposite views touching the issue of a future uncertain event.
57 Marine Insurance Act 1906 s.4(2)(a); see also s.4(2)(b) ("interest or no interest policy").
58 Marine Insurance Act 1906 s.4(1).
59 Marine Insurance Act 1906 s.4(2).
60 i.e. in particular, Gaming Act 1845 s.18, one of the repealed enactments referred to in para.41-001 above.

s.4 of the 1906 Act. The absence of any reference to this provision[61] in the 2005 Act seems to indicate a legislative intention not (in that Act) to change the law with regard to insurance without interest, at any rate with regard to marine insurance, and probably with regard to insurance generally since the provisions of the 1906 Act are, where appropriate, regarded as applicable to contracts of insurance generally.[62] It follows that insurance, even without interest, is not subject to the regulatory provisions which form the bulk of the 2005 Act. It also follows that the new rules which are laid down by that Act as to the "legality and enforceability of gambling contracts"[63] (and which are discussed in paras 41-011—41-023, below) do not apply to contracts of insurance, even where such a contract is, for want of insurable interest, "deemed to be a gaming or wagering contract" by virtue of s.4(2) of the 1906 Act. The same is, a fortiori, true where the requirement of insurable interest *is* satisfied: for example, where the owner of an orchard insures "next year's apple crop".[64] By parity of reasoning, it seems that the owner of a horse could insure the prize money which the horse might win; but if a person placed a bet on his own horse in a particular race, the contract would have been a wager under the old law[65] and would be a bet within the 2005 Act.

2. ENFORCEABILITY OF GAMBLING CONTRACTS

(a) Enforceability at Common Law

41-010 **Wagers prima facie valid** The common law position was that wagers were valid and could thus be enforced by the winner.[66] This rule was not much liked by the courts, who refused to enforce wagers on many grounds. Some wagers were illegal: these included wagers on unlawful games[67]; wagers that one of the parties would commit a legal wrong or do an immoral act; wagers which affected the interests and feelings of a third person so as to make a breach of the peace likely; and wagers which were "against sound policy".[68] On this last ground, the following wagers were held void: a wager that peace between England and France would be concluded by September 1797[69]; a wager on the life of Napoleon in time of peace[70]; a wager tending to cause public disorder[71]; a wager with voters in a constituency as to the outcome of an election in that constituency—an obvious cloak for bribery[72]; and a wager on the sex of a living person suspected to be masquerading

---

[61] And to those of the 1909 Act, referred to above.

[62] cf. *Locker & Woolf Ltd v W. Australian Insurance Co Ltd* [1936] 1 K.B. 408 at 414.

[63] Heading to Gambling Act 2005 Pt 17.

[64] *Thacker v Hardy* (1878) 4 Q.B.D. 685, 695.

[65] *Carlill v Carbolic Smoke Ball Co* [1892] 2 Q.B. 484, 492; affirmed [1893] 1 Q.B. 256.

[66] *Micklefield v Hipgin* (1760) 1 Anst. 133; *Good v Elliott* (1790) 3 T.R. 693; *Hussey v Crickitt* (1811) 3 Camp. 168; *Khodari v Tamimi* [2010] EWCA Civ 1109 at [18].

[67] At common law, cock-fighting, card games (other than those of mere skill) and (probably) all games of chance were unlawful: *Jenks v Turpin* (1884) 13 Q.B.D. 505, 524.

[68] *Good v Elliott* (1790) 3 T.R. 693, 695.

[69] *Lacaussade v White* (1798) 2 Esp. 629 (as to recovery of money under illegal contracts, overruled in *Vandyck v Hewitt* (1800) 1 East 96).

[70] *Gilbert v Sykes* (1812) 16 East 150; because this might lead to his assassination (which would be "against sound policy" in time of peace) or to his preservation (which would be "against sound policy" in time of war).

[71] *Eltham v Kingsman* (1818) 1 B. & Ald. 683.

[72] *Allen v Hearn* (1785) 1 T.R. 56.

as a man.[73] The courts also sometimes simply refused to enforce a wager on the ground that it was an "idle wager" and that it was a waste of the court's time to entertain an action on it.[74] Thus the courts refused to enforce a wager "on the number of ways of nicking 7 on the dice"[75]; a wager made between persons who had no pecuniary interest in the matter that the next child of an unmarried woman would be a boy,[76] and a wager on an abstract question of law in which the parties had only an academic interest.[77]

(b) Enforceability Under the Gambling Act 2005

Contracts relating to gambling generally enforceable: s.335(1)   The restric- **41-011** tions on the enforceability of wagering contracts which had been imposed by the legislative provisions referred to in para.41-001 above were removed by the repeal of those provisions by the 2005 Act,[78] but these repeals did not, of themselves, restore the common law rule by which wagering contracts were, in general, legally enforceable.[79] It was therefore necessary for the 2005 Act to contain a specific provision to this effect; s.335(1) accordingly provides that "[t]he fact that a contract

---

[73]   *Da Costa v Jones* (1778) 2 Cowp. 729.
[74]   *Robinson v Mearns* (1825) 6 D. & R.K.B. 26, 27.
[75]   *Brown v Leeson* (1792) 2 H. Bl. 43.
[76]   *Ditchburn v Goldsmith* (1815) 4 Camp. 152.
[77]   *Henkin v Gerss* (1810) 2 Camp. 406.
[78]   Above, para.41-001.
[79]   See Interpretation Act 1978 ss.15, 16. For possible continued relevance of the common law rules stated in para.41-010 above to limits on the enforceability under the 2005 Act of contracts relating to gambling, see below, para.41-020. In *WW Properties Investments Ltd v National Westminster Bank Plc* [2016] EWCA Civ 1142, [2017] 1 Lloyd's Rep. 87 the Court of Appeal held that the "Collar" and "Swap" agreements were not wagers; the reasons for this conclusion are stated in para.41-006 above. But the Court went on to consider what the position would have been, if it had held that those agreements *had* been wagers, and in particular whether in that case they would then have been legally enforceable under the general rule of common law stated in para.41-010 above, having regard also to common law exceptions to that general rule. The Court gave a negative answer to this question on the ground that the Collar and Swap Agreements were contracts for differences and that, in the light of the "comprehensive regime established by the Gambling Act [2005] and the FMSA [i.e. the Financial Services and Markets Act 2000] there was in such a case no room for any common law rule" limiting the validity of gambling contracts by way of exception to the common law rule that such contracts were valid: see at [66]; and at [67] referring to the judgment of Vos L.J. in *Nextia Properties Ltd v Royal Bank of Scotland Plc* [2014] EWCA Civ 740, especially at [22], refusing leave to appeal from the decision of H.H.J. Behrens [2013] EWHC 3167 (QB); for earlier proceedings in which Christopher Clarke L.J. had likewise refused leave to appeal from that decision, see the *Nextia* case [2014] EWCA Civ 740 at [1] to [4] and the *WW Property* case [2016] EWCA Civ 1142 at [20]. The judgment in the latter case also refers at [67] to "the Regulations made thereunder", i.e. to the Financial Services and Markets Act 2000 (Regulated Activities) Order 2001 (SI 2001/544), the relevant parts of which are cited in the *WW Property* case at [64] (Sch.1 para.9 of the Act and art.85 of the Order, refer to "Contracts for differences"). It should be noted that this part of the judgment refers only to contracts subject to the "comprehensive regime" established by all this legislation. The same point is also reflected in the use of words such as "financial contracts", "a contract of the kind in question" and "contracts such as the present" (at [66], where "section 35" is a misprint for "section 335"), all of which indicate that this part of the judgment has a restricted scope. It would not, for example, apply to a wager on the outcome of a sporting competition or of an election. In such cases there might still be room for common law rules recognising or limiting the validity of gambling contracts in ways considered in paras 41-011 and 41-020. It remains true that even in such cases the repeal of the Gaming Act 1845 would not "revive the [common law] rule" (at [68]) which had existed before that repeal but it would not preclude the court from developing new rules which, as a matter of common law, restricted the legal validity of gambling contracts.

relates to gambling shall not prevent its enforcement". Three points must here be made about this provision.

41-012 **"Shall not prevent"** The first arises from what is in substance the double negative contained in the phrase "shall not prevent". Section 335(1) does not in terms say that contracts relating to gambling shall be legally enforceable. Instead, it lays down the general rule to this effect by providing that the fact that a contract is so related shall not prevent its enforcement. The reason for formulating the general rule of enforceability in this way is to make allowance for the fact that the enforcement of such a contract may be refused on some ground *other* than the fact that the contract relates to gambling. The significance of this point is further considered in the discussion in paras 41-017 and 41-021 below of one of the exceptions to the general principle of enforceability laid down by the 2005 Act.

41-013 **"Relates to gambling"** Secondly, s.335(1) refers to "the fact that a contract relates to gambling".[80] This phrase is wide enough to cover, not only the gambling contract itself (also referred to in the Act as the, or a, "bet"[81]), but also associated transactions. Under the law as it stood before the 2005 Act, problems used to arise (and may continue to arise) out of associated transactions such as agency arrangements related to gambling, partnerships, stakeholders, securities and loans for gambling. Such transactions would all seem to be covered by the phrase "relates to gambling" and such related transactions will, in general, be enforceable by virtue of s.335(1).[82]

41-014 **Legal effects other than enforceability** Thirdly, the only direct legal effect of s.335(1) is to make the contracts covered by it enforceable; but the enforceability of such contracts also has repercussions on a number of further legal effects which had, in relation to such contracts, given rise to problems under the previous law. Thus if money is paid or property deposited under a gambling (or related[83]) contract there is no longer any question of its being recoverable by the payor or depositor[84] merely because that contract is a gambling contract. The payment or deposit will simply have been made under a valid contract and any right to its return will depend on the terms of the contract, or on other rules of law governing the recoverability of payments or deposits made under a contract. The fact that a payment was made under a gambling contract which is now (by virtue of s.335(1)) enforceable also has repercussions on the law relating to gambling with stolen money.[85] On the other hand, the legal enforceability of contracts related to gambling has not affected the statutory rule that "winnings from betting" are not subject to capital gains tax.[86]

---

[80] cf. Gambling Act 2005 s.337(1).

[81] e.g. in ss.9 (above, paras 41-004, 41-005) and 336 (below, para.41-022).

[82] See below, paras 41-025—41-027.

[83] cf. above, para.41-013.

[84] The above assumption seems to underlie the claim for the return of money paid under the contracts in *WW Property Investments Ltd v National Westminster Bank Plc* [2016] EWCA Civ 1142, [2017] 1 Lloyd's Rep. 87, as described in paras [18] and [19] of the report. That claim was based on the argument that the claim was *invalid* at common law; but the argument that the outcome continued to be governed by the common law as it stood before the legislation that was repealed by the Gambling Act 2005 (see above, paras 41-001, 41-010) was rejected for the reasons given in para.41-011 above.

[85] See below, paras 41-045—41-050.

[86] Taxation of Chargeable Gains Act 1992 s.51(1); above, para.41-008.

Electronic Commerce   The EC Directive on Electronic Commerce[87] provides that it is not to apply to "gambling activities which involve wagering a stake with monetary value in games of chance, including lotteries and betting transactions".[88] The Electronic Commerce (EC Directive) Regulations 2002,[89] which implement most of the Directive, likewise do not apply in respect of "(d) the following activities of information society services—(iii) betting, gaming or lotteries which involve wagering a stake with monetary value".[90] These exceptions appear to refer only to the gambling contract itself, while the references in the Gambling Act 2005 to contracts "related to gambling"[91] and to similar concepts[92] have a wider scope.[93]

41-015

(c)   Exceptions to Enforceability Under the Gambling Act 2005

The general principle of the legal enforceability of contracts relating to gambling[94] is, under the 2005 Act, subject to two significant exceptions. Enforcement may be refused on the ground of "unlawfulness"; and the Gambling Commission is given power to "void" certain bets. These exceptions are discussed in paras 41-017—41-023, below.

41-016

(i)   "Unlawfulness"

Section 335(2)   Section 335(2) of the 2005 Act provides that:

41-017

> "... subsection (1) is without prejudice to any rule of law preventing the enforcement of a contract on the ground of unlawfulness (*other than a rule of law relating specifically to gambling*)."[95]

Failure to comply with other provisions of the Act   The first question that arises from s.335(2) is its effect on cases in which the unlawfulness is due to failure to comply with other provisions of the Act, outlined above, such as its licensing requirements.[96] In one sense, those requirements might be said to consist of rules of law "relating specifically to gambling"[97] and so not to fall within the restriction on the enforceability of contracts contained in s.335(2). But it is submitted that this reasoning would be contrary to the policy of the Act in that it would allow a party to a gambling contract who had failed to comply with the Act (or with secondary legislation made under it) nevertheless to enforce the contract. Such a conclusion can, and should, be avoided by arguing that, in cases of this kind, the "unlawfulness" arises, not "specifically" (within the phrase italicised in para.41-017 above) because the transaction is a gambling contract, but because the making of the

41-018

---

87 2000/31/EC.
88 art.1(5)(d).
89 SI 2002/2013.
90 reg.3(1)(d)(iii).
91 s.335(1).
92 See ss.336(2)(b) ("contract or other arrangement in relation to the bet"); 337(2) ("any part or aspect, of a betting transaction"). For such related transactions, see below, paras 41-026, 41-030—41-035.
93 See above, para.41-013 and the discussion of "related transactions" in paras 41-026 et seq. below.
94 Above, para.41-011.
95 Italics supplied.
96 Above, para.41-003.
97 s.335(2), quoted above, para.41-017.

contract constitutes a form of activity which is prohibited, with penal sanctions, by law (in this case, by other provisions of, or made under, the Act itself). The purpose of the words italicised in para.41-017 above appears to be to exclude the argument that gambling contracts are "unlawful" as such because their enforcement would be contrary to public policy; for if this argument were accepted, s.335(2) would (if it did not contain the italicised words) wholly negate the validating effect on gambling contracts of s.335(1). The purpose of subs.(2) is, in the terms of the Explanatory Notes[98] to the Act, to ensure that subs.(1):

"… does not … override any other rule that prevents enforcement on the ground of unlawfulness. Therefore gambling contracts may be void on the same basis as any other contract (for example, on the basis of lack of intention, mistake or illegality)."

The common law rule that a contract may be void for illegality because it is one to engage in a form of activity that is prohibited by legislation with penal consequences is of general application in that it applies to all contracts, of whatever nature (including gambling contracts). The common law rule is therefore not covered by the words italicised in para.41-017 above, so that it will continue to restrict the enforceability of a contract by virtue of the preceding words of s.335(2), even though the contract in question is a gambling contract and is illegal by reason of its having been made in circumstances giving rise to an offence under the 2005 Act.

41-019   It follows from the reasoning in para.41-018 above that, if a party to a gambling contract had, in making the contract, provided facilities for gambling without the requisite licence, or failed to comply with the terms of a licence which he held, and had so committed an offence under the Act,[99] then the contract would be affected by illegality and it would normally, though not necessarily, follow that, under the law relating to illegal contracts,[100] the person guilty of the illegality would not be able legally to enforce the gambling contract or a related transaction[101]; while the

---

[98]   See para.829 of the Explanatory Notes; for further discussion of this paragraph of the Notes, see below, para.41-021.

[99]   Gambling Act 2005 ss.33(2), 37(2).

[100] See below, para.41-043.

[101] In *Ritz Hotel Casino Ltd v Al Daher* [2014] EWHC 2847 (QB) the question whether a person who had failed to comply with the restrictions on giving credit contained in s.81 of the 2005 Act could enforce the contract was said (at [40]) to depend on whether such enforcement would "contravene the policy and purpose" of these restrictions i.e. "to protect a player from wagering beyond the extent of his immediate ability to pay" (at [40]); it was further there said that the court "would and should be willing to decline to enforce the gaming contract and the cheque there given" if such a refusal would "satisfy that policy and purpose". But if, in that case, there had (contrary to the actual decision: see below) been an unlawful giving of credit by the claimant casino, then the "policy and purpose" of the prohibition in s.81(4)(b) would, because of the special circumstances of that case, *not* "have required the court to dismiss the casino's action upon the cheques" (at [44]). These special circumstances were that the defendant had been a member of, and had gambled at, the casino for 13 years before the occasion in question; that she was a person of "great" (at [43]) or "almost unimaginable" (at [116]) wealth (so that even losses running into of £2 million sustained on that occasion would not be "beyond the extent of [her] immediate ability to pay"; at [40] (quoted above); that she had in fact had an "irreproachable history of paying over 15 years" (at [43(iii)]); that the cheques given by her to the casino in payment of her losses were "always presented promptly" (at [4]), so that, even if the acceptance of the cheques amounted (contrary to the court's conclusion) to the giving of unlawful "credit", the period of such credit would have been short; and that "there was … no deliberate setting out to break the law as to the giving of credit by the … casino" (at [43(iv)]). This combination of circumstances can fairly be described as exceptional, so that it is submitted that, in general, the giving of credit contrary to s.81 would prevent the enforcement of the contract by

other party's rights to enforce such contracts would depend on the degree of his knowledge of, or complicity in, the failure. Conversely, if that other party committed the offence of cheating contrary to s.42[102] of the Act, then that other party would not be entitled to enforce the contract, though the victim of the offence might be able to do so. Where the gambling amounts to an offence because it is between the holder of a licence and a child or young person,[103] any money paid (e.g. by way of stake) by the child or young person must be returned to the child or young person,[104] even (it seems) to a young person who is himself guilty of an offence by gambling[105]; and the provider of the facilities for gambling "may not give a prize to the child or young person".[106] It follows from this last provision that the contract under which the prize was to be given is not enforceable by the child or young person. A further possible ground of unlawfulness under the 2005 Act lies in the provision of credit for gambling. In this respect, the Act maintains the policy of some of the earlier gaming legislation,[107] which it repeals,[108] of restricting the giving of such credit. Reference may here be made to three provisions of the 2005 Act which give effect to this policy. The Act provides, first, that an operating licence may restrict the giving of credit "in connection with the licensed activities"[109]; and secondly, that certain premises licences shall be subject to the condition that the licensee does not "give credit in connection with gambling authorised by the licence".[110] Failure to comply with such a condition would be an offence under the Act.[111] Thirdly, it is an offence under the Act to supply, install or make available for use a gaming machine which is designed or adapted to permit money to be paid by means of a credit card.[112] In the first and second of the above situations, it follows that the licensee could not enforce the terms of the credit against the person to whom it had been granted; and it is arguable that the illegality of the loan would also infect the gambling transaction itself, on the ground that the object of the illegal loan was to

---

the person guilty of the illegality. See also *Ritz Hotel Casino v Al Geabury* [2015] EWHC 2294 (QB), [2015] L.L.R. 860 where an action on a dishonoured cheque given by a gambler in exchange for chips (which he gambled away) succeeded as there had been *no* breach of the casino's licence condition or of the Gambling Commission's Code of Practice, and hence no illegality by reason of any violation of ss.33 or 82 of the Gambling Act 2005.

[102] For the territorial scope of s.42, see *R. v Majeed* [2012] EWCA Crim 1186, [2013] 1 W.L.R. 1041.
[103] See above, para.41-003.
[104] Gambling Act 2005 ss.58, 83(1)(a).
[105] Gambling Act 2005 s.48.
[106] Gambling Act 2005 s.83(1)(b).
[107] Especially Gaming Act 1710 s.1 and Gaming Act 1968 s.16.
[108] Above, para.41-001.
[109] Gambling Act 2005 s.81(2)(a); see also s.81(2)(b). "Credit" in s.81 is stated in subs.(4)(b) to include acceptance by way of payment of "anything other than ... (ii) a cheque which is not post-dated and for which full value is given ...". In *Ritz Hotel Casino Ltd v Al Daher* [2014] EWHC 2847 (QB) the defendant had given the claimants cheques totalling £2 million in payment for chips which she had lost in the course of an evening's gambling at the claimants' casino; these cheques were promptly presented by the claimants but were dishonoured. It was held that the claimants were entitled to recover the balance of £1m remaining unpaid on the cheques as there had been no giving of "credit" (at [39]). The main reason for this conclusion seems to have been that the giving of the cheques had suspended the defendant's liability to pay until the cheques were dishonoured and that at this stage "the debt [would become] immediately due and payable" (at [29]), where the reference in the Official Transcript to "section 16(2) of the 2005 Act" appears to be a misprint—either for s.16(2) of the Gaming Act 1968 or perhaps for s.81(4) of the Gambling Act 2005).
[110] Gambling Act 2005 s.177(2)(a).
[111] Gambling Act 2005 ss.33(1) and (2), 37(1) and (2).
[112] Gambling Act 2005 s.245.

encourage credit betting in circumstances in which it was the policy of the Act to discourage this form of activity. The latter argument could also be available in the third case, though it would not affect the legal relations between the card-holder and the issuer of the card (assuming the issuer to be a person other than the licensee). A premises licence must also be subject to the condition that the premises shall not be used for gambling on Christmas Day.[113] Such gambling would therefore be unlawful and gambling contracts relating to it would be legally unenforceable.

41-020 **"Unlawfulness" on other grounds** Unlawfulness of a contract relating to gambling can also result from rules of law other than those contained in the 2005 Act: e.g. where the gambling was prohibited by such other rules, or where the event on which the outcome of a bet depended involved the commission of an illegal act, whether by one or more of the parties to the bet or by one or more of the participants in the gaming on which the bet was placed. In such cases, the contract would be invalid, not because it related to gambling, but because it could be said to encourage breaches of the law. It is submitted that the same reasoning could apply where the unlawfulness arose because the conduct in question, though not contrary to law, was contrary to public policy on grounds other than the mere fact that it related to gambling. This was the position at common law before the Gaming Acts of 1710, 1738, 1845 and 1892. As explained in para.41-010 above, at common law wagers were generally valid but a wager could not be enforced if enforcement was "against sound policy"[114]: e.g. because it tended to cause public disorder.[115] While the repeal by the Gambling Act 2005 of earlier legislation invalidating wagering contracts (and certain other contracts related to wagers) has not of itself restored the earlier common law rules,[116] it is submitted that the wording of s.335(2) leaves it open to the courts to develop grounds of public policy on which they could refuse to enforce contracts relating to gambling; and, again, the reason for any such refusal would be, not that the contract related to gambling, but that its enforcement would be contrary to public policy on some other ground. In relation to the example given above, of a wager tending to cause public disorder, it should be emphasised that the first of the "licensing objectives" stated in s.1(a) of the 2005 Act is "preventing gambling from being a source of crime or disorder, being associated with crime or disorder or being used to support crime". It is submitted that a contract which tended to subvert any part of this objective should not be enforceable by virtue of s.335(1) but should be denied enforceability by virtue of s.335(2). In the case of most commercial gambling, a contract which had such a tendency would in all probability involve the breach of a condition of the relevant licence and so amount to an offence under the Act. But the scope of s.335 is quite general: it applies not only to commercial gambling, but also to gambling which is not subject to any licensing requirements, such as private and non-commercial gambling.[117] The court may thus not only enforce contracts relating to such gambling,[118] but also refuse to enforce them on the ground of "unlawfulness" (not relating specifically to gambling).[119] In

---

113 Gambling Act 2005 s.183.
114 *Good v Elliott* (1790) 3 T.R. 693 at 695.
115 *Eltham v Kingsman* (1818) 1 B. & Ald. 683.
116 See Interpretation Act 1978 ss.15, 16.
117 See Gambling Act 2005 ss.33(1)(b)(v) and (vi), 37(7).
118 Gambling Act 2005 s.335(1).
119 Gambling Act 2005 s.335(2).

Ivey v Genting Casinos (UK) Ltd[120] it was, for example, held at first instance by Mitting J. that a gambler could not recover from a casino winnings from gambling there which were the result of his having cheated (in breach of an implied term[121] of the gambling contract that neither party to it would cheat) and that, in view of this conclusion it was "not necessary to decide whether or not the statutory offence of cheating under s.42 of the 2005 Act] had been committed". This reasoning was approved by the Supreme Court when it dismissed an appeal from a decision of the Court of Appeal which had affirmed the decision of Mitting J.[122] though it was also said in the Supreme Court that there was:

"... no reason to doubt that cheating carries the same meaning when considering an implied term not to cheat and when applying section 42 of the Act."[123]

Scope of s.335(2) The grounds on which the courts may refuse to enforce a **41-021** contract relating to gambling are by no means exhaustively stated in s.335(2). That subsection states only *one* such ground, i.e. unlawfulness (other than a rule of law relating specifically to gambling). Enforcement may also be refused on other grounds, such as the failure of the parties to reach agreement, lack of contractual intention, invalidating causes such as mistake, misrepresentation or duress and any other ground on which a contract may be void, voidable or unenforceable irrespective of its being a contract relating to gambling.[124] It has, for example, been held that a gambler could not recover winnings which were the result of his having cheated[125] (in breach of an implied term[126] of the contract); and this was so whether

---

120 [2014] EWHC 3394 (QB); affirmed by a majority of the Court of Appeal [2016] EWCA Civ 1093, [2017] 1 W.L.R. 679, where Arden and Tomlinson L.JJ. (Sharp L.J. dissenting) also held that dishonesty was not a requirement of "cheating" for the purpose of s.42 of the Gambling Act 2005: see at [37], [40], [48] and [97]. There was no direct reference to this reasoning when a further appeal to the Supreme Court was dismissed: [2017] UKSC 67, [2017] 3 W.L.R. 1212 but Lord Hughes (with whom all the other members of that Court agreed) said at [75] that, "if contrary to the conclusions arrived at above" (the reference appears to be to [74], and see also [45]) "there were in cheating at gambling an additional legal element of dishonesty, it would be satisfied by the application of the tests as set out above". Those tests required the "fact-finding tribunal ... first [to] ascertain (subjectively) the actual state of the individual's knowledge or belief as to the facts" (at [74]) and then to determine whether that individual's conduct was honest; in determining this (second) question, the fact-finder must apply "the objective standard of ordinary decent people" (at [74]). On this test, the fact that the gambler in the Ivey case "did not regard what he did as cheating" did not amount "to a finding that his behaviour was honest. It was not" (at [75]). Hence "if the question arose" (i.e. if, contrary to the Court's view (see at [45]) cheating involved an element of "dishonesty") then "the better view would be ... that his conduct was, contrary to his own opinion, also dishonest", so that the "legal element of dishonesty" was satisfied (at [75]).

121 The existence of such an implied term was "common ground throughout this litigation": [2017] UKSC 67 at [35].

122 [2014] EWHC 3394 AT [52]. This reasoning was cited with apparent approval by the Supreme Court: [2017] UKSC 67 at [36].

123 [2017] UKSC 67 at [38].

124 One party's right to enforce a contract may also be lost because the other party has rescinded the contract on account of the former party's failure to perform his part. But the application of this principle to gambling contracts can give rise to difficulty because of the aleatory nature of such contracts in which one party's duty to perform depends, generally, not on the other's performance of his undertaking, but on the occurrence of a chance and uncertain event: see further para.41-027 below.

125 *Ivey v Genting Casinos UK Ltd* [2014] EWHC 3394 (QB) at [50], [51].

126 The existence of such an implied term was admitted by the claimant: [2014] EWHC 3394 (QB) at [33].

or not his conduct amounted to the offence of "cheating" contrary to s.42 of the Act.[127] The Explanatory note to s.335 of the Act gives rise to some difficulty in that it includes among its illustrative list of rules that prevent "enforcement on the grounds of unlawfulness" not only "illegality" but also "lack of intention" and "mistake".[128] It is, however, respectfully submitted that to regard "lack of intention" or "mistake" as illustrations of "unlawfulness" is, to say the least, unusual; and that it may be misleading when the exact legal effects of such factors fall to be considered. The possibility that enforcement may be refused on account of these factors, and other factors such as those listed in this paragraph, follows, not from the exception to enforceability (on the ground of "unlawfulness") contained in s.335(2), but from the negative language of s.335(1).[129] Where the contract is affected by some invalidating cause such as those listed above in this paragraph, it simply does not fall within the scope of s.335(1). The same is true where the alleged contract is impugned for lack of contractual intention, e.g. because it contains an "honour" or similar clause, as appears to be common in the case of agreements between football pool promoters and participants in such betting.[130] In such cases there is simply no "contract" which could be made enforceable by virtue of s.335(1).

(ii)   Power "to Void Bet"[131]

41-022   **Power to make orders where bet is "substantially unfair"**   Section 336 of the 2005 Act empowers the Gambling Commission,[132] in the situations described below, to make an order[133] in relation to a bet if (and only if) the Commission is "satisfied that the bet was substantially unfair".[134] The power is exercisable in relation to a bet accepted by or through the holder of (a) a general operating licence, (b) a pool betting licence, or (c) a betting intermediary licence.[135] It is thus restricted to commercial gambling and so does not, for example, extend to private and non-commercial gaming or betting.[136] The effects of an order under s.336 are that (a) "any contract or other arrangement in relation to the bet is void," and that (b) "any money paid in relation to the bet (whether by way of stake, winnings, commission or otherwise) shall be repaid to the person who paid it ...".[137] In deciding whether a bet is "unfair" the Commission is required to take account of a list of factors set

---

[127] See [2014] EWHC 3394 (QB) at [52].
[128] Explanatory Note, para.829.
[129] See above, para.41-011.
[130] See *Appleson v Littlewood* [1939] 1 All E.R. 464; *Guest v Empire Pools* (1964) 108 S.J. 956; contrast in Scotland, *Ferguson v Littlewood Pools Ltd*, 1997 S.L.T. 309; and above, Vol.I, para.2-172.
[131] Marginal note to s.336.
[132] Created by Gambling Act 2005 s.20; above, para.41-003.
[133] Gambling Act 2005 s.336(1).
[134] Gambling Act 2005 s.336(3).
[135] Gambling Act 2005 s.336(1).
[136] Within Pt 14 of the 2005 Act (ss.295–302).
[137] Gambling Act 2005 s.336(2). "Stake" here seems to be intended to refer to the money paid (or "staked") by the person making the bet to the person accepting it: see the definition of "stake" in s.353(1) and the marginal note to s.83 ("return of stakes to children"); see also the use of the word "stake" in the Directive and in the Regulations relating to "Electronic Commerce" which are referred to in para.41-015 above. Quaere whether "stake" in s.336(2) can also refer to the situation described in para.41-031 below in which money is deposited pursuant to a bet with a third party "stakeholder", i.e. with a person who is not a party to the bet.

out in s.336(4). The list is not intended to be exhaustive[138]; it includes "the fact that either party to the bet supplied insufficient, false or misleading information in connection with it;"[139] or was convicted of the offence (created by s.42 of the Act) of cheating.[140] An order under s.336 can, in general, be made only within six months of the beginning of the day on which the bet is determined[141] but this time limit does not apply where the order is made:

"… taking into account the fact that a party to the bet was convicted of an offence under section 42 [i.e. the offence of cheating] in relation to it."[142]

Where the circumstance which makes the bet unfair would also amount to a factor vitiating the contract under general principles of law, a party to the contract could also rely on that circumstance even after the expiry of the six month period by way of defence to an action on the bet under s.335. This follows from the discussion in paras 41-017 and 41-021, above of "unlawfulness" and other grounds on which the court may refuse to enforce a contract relating to gambling. This reasoning would also apply where the contract was one in respect of which no order under s.336(1) could be made: e.g. because the contract related to private gaming or betting. The legal consequences of raising the defence of "unlawfulness" in ordinary legal proceedings would, however, differ from those of an order made by the Gambling Commission under s.336(1): for example, the legal consequences of the former course would not necessarily be either to make the contract "void"[143] (as opposed to voidable) or lead to the repayment to the payor of money paid in pursuance of the contract[144] nor would powers similar to those (described below[145]) exercisable by the Commission apply, even by analogy, where "unlawfulness" was relied on simply as a defence to an action on the contract. The powers in question are conferred on the Commission by s.337, which provides that an order under s.336(1) may relate to the whole or any part or aspect of a betting transaction[146] and may make incidental provision about other parts of a transaction one part or aspect of which is made void by the order,[147] and about related bets.[148] Any order made by the Commission under s.336 is subject to appeal to the Gambling Appeals Tribunal[149] from which a further appeal lies on a point of law to the High Court with leave of the Tribunal or the Court.[150]

Who may claim an order under s.336 An order under s.336 will no doubt **41-023** normally be sought by the party to the contract who is prejudiced by the unfairness of the bet. But nothing in the section limits the power of the Commission to cases in which the order is sought by that person. On the contrary, s.338 suggests

---

[138] See the words "in particular" in the opening phrase of s.336(4).
[139] s.336(4)(a).
[140] s.336(4)(d).
[141] s.336(5).
[142] s.336(6).
[143] s.336(2)(a).
[144] s.336(2)(b).
[145] See also below, para.41-051.
[146] s.337(2).
[147] s.337(3)(a).
[148] s.337(3)(b).
[149] Established by s.140.
[150] s.143.

that the Commission may act on its own initiative in this respect. That section applies "where the Commission has reason to suspect that it may wish to make an order under section 336(1) in respect of a bet"[151] and empowers the Commission in such a case to make an "interim moratorium" order by which an obligation to pay money in relation to the bet ceases to have effect for 14 days.[152] It seems also to be possible for an order under s.336 to be made on the application of a third party who might be prejudiced by the enforcement of a bet under s.335 or by the retention of money paid under the bet on the ground of such enforceability. The view that at least some such third parties should have standing to seek an order under s.336 is supported by s.337(1) which provides that an appeal against an order under s.336(1) may be brought by "a party to a bet or to any contract or other arrangement in relation to the bet". It would be strange if parties who were thus given a right of appeal against the order had no standing to seek the order in the first place. It is further arguable that an order under s.336 could be sought even by a third party who did not fall within the words quoted above from s.337(1).[153]

(d)   Distance and Off-Premises Contracts

41-024   **Distance and off-premises contracts**   The Consumer Protection (Information, Cancellation and Additional Charges) Regulations 2013[154] provide that, where a contract for the supply of goods or services by a "trader" to a "consumer"[155] is a "distance"[156] or an "off-premises"[157] contract, then the consumer has the "right to cancel"[158] the contract within a "cancellation period",[159] the length of which is specified in the Regulations. The Regulations, however, do not extend to certain types of contract, the first of which is a contract "for ... gambling within the meaning of the Gambling Act 2005".[160] One consequence of so excepting such contracts from the scope of the Regulations is that the "right to cancel" does not extend to such contracts. The assumption underlying the present exception is that the contract is *valid* apart from the Regulations. Under the Gambling Act 2005, this would normally be the case by virtue of the general rule, laid down in s.335(1), that the fact that a contract relates to gambling shall not prevent its enforcement.[161] But where that rule does not apply by reason of the "unlawfulness" of the contract[162] or where, by reason of the bet's being "substantially unfair" the contract made in

---

[151]   s.338(1).

[152]   s.338(2), (3); the time can be extended: s.338(4).

[153]   e.g. by the victim of a theft of money used by the thief for gambling: see below, paras 41-050, 41-051.

[154]   SI 2013/3134 ("the 2013 Regulations") as amended by Consumer Protection (Amendment) Regulations 2014 (SI 2014/870) and Consumer Contracts (Amendment) Regulations 2015 (SI 2015/1629), above paras 38-059 et seq.

[155]   "Trader" and "consumer" are defined in reg.4 of the 2013 Regulations.

[156]   "Distance contract" is defined in reg.5 of the 2013 Regulations. A contract made by, for example, exchange of posted letters, faxes or email messages, or in website trading could fall within this definition.

[157]   "Off-premises" contract is defined in reg.5 of the 2013 Regulations. A contract made in the simultaneous presence of the trader and the consumer in a place which is not the business premises of the trader could fall within this definition.

[158]   2013 Regulations reg.29.

[159]   2013 Regulations reg.30.

[160]   2013 Regulations reg.6(1)(a)(i).

[161]   Above, para.41-011.

[162]   Gambling Act 2005 s.335(2); above, para.41-017.

relation to it becomes "void" in consequence of an order made by the Gambling Commission under s.336(1),[163] the consumer does not need to cancel to escape liability under it. Moreover, the restitutionary consequences of his relying on such factors are then not those specified in the Regulations.[164] They are, in the first of the above situations, those laid down by the general rules of law specifying the consequences of the "unlawfulness"[165] and in the second, those specified in ss.336 and 337 of the 2005 Act.[166]

(e) Related Transactions

(i) Introduction

Introduction Before the coming into force[167] of the rules now laid down in Part   **41-025**
17 of the Gambling Act 2005 as to the "legality and enforceability of gambling contracts,"[168] the law as to gaming and wagering was to a considerable extent concerned with the legal effects, not only of the wagering contract itself, but also of a number of related transactions. These included the effects of a promise to pay a lost bet in consideration of the winner's promise not to post the loser as a defaulter, the effects of payments or deposits made under the wagering contract, agency partnership and stakeholder arrangements made in relation to such a contract, loans for gambling and securities given in relation to wagering transactions. The overriding policy which governed the solution of problems of this kind under the legislation and case law which invalidated wagering contracts[169] and related arrangements before the repeal of that legislation on the coming into force of the Gambling Act 2005,[170] was that the rules against the enforcement of wagers or related arrangements should not be undermined by allowing the winner by means of such related transactions to achieve indirectly what he could not achieve directly, i.e. to recover the amount of the lost bet from the loser. That policy is abandoned by the Gambling Act 2005, by s.335(1) of which the gambling contract itself is, as a general rule, legally enforceable. Two matters here call for further discussion. The first concerns the effect of that enforceability on related transactions of the kind described above: this topic will be discussed in paras 41-026, 41-027, 41-030—41-032 and 41-034—41-035, below. The second concerns the effect on such transactions of the power of the Gambling Commission to "void [a] bet": this topic will be discussed in paras 41-036—41-040, below.

(ii) Enforceability

Related transactions in general enforceable It will be recalled[171] that s.335(1)   **41-026**
of the 2005 Act provides that "The fact that a contract relates to gambling shall not prevent its enforcement". The phrase "that a contract relates to gambling" is capable

---

[163] Above, para.41-022.
[164] See reg.33(1)(b), cross-referring to regs 34 to 38.
[165] See Vol.I, paras 16-011 et seq.
[166] See para.41-022 above and paras 41-036—41-040 below.
[167] See above, para.41-001.
[168] Gambling Act 2005, heading to Pt 17.
[169] See above, para.41-001.
[170] See above, para.41-001.
[171] Above, para.41-011.

of referring to a range of contracts wider than the gambling contract itself. It can, for example, refer to a contract such as that considered in *Hill v William Hill (Park Lane) Ltd*,[172] where a fresh promise by the loser of a bet to pay the amount of his losses to the winner in consideration of the winner's promise not to post him as a defaulter was not enforceable by the winner since such enforcement would have contravened s.18 of the Gaming Act 1845. The repeal of that section[173] by the Gambling Act 2005 has subverted the reasoning of *Hill's* case; and the new contract that would now arise by an exchange of promises of the kind there made would be a contract relating to gambling and therefore, as a general rule, legally enforceable by virtue of s.335(1) of the 2005 Act. The same would be true of a fresh promise by the loser of a bet to pay his losses in consideration of the winner's promise not to sue the loser. Formerly, such a promise did not amount to consideration as it was a promise to not enforce a debt which was void (and, it was assumed, known to be so)[174] but this reasoning, too, would be subverted by the 2005 Act, now that the original gambling contract is, as a general rule, legally enforceable. The same reasoning would, mutatis mutandis, apply where the winner made no *promise* to forbear, but simply forbore in fact, in response to the loser's fresh promise. In all these cases, the winner would now prima facie be entitled to enforce either the original gambling contract or the new contract as one that "relate[d] to gambling". Many other contracts that formerly were, or might have been, void or unenforceable under the legislation that governed wagering contracts, would now fall within the description of "contracts relate[d] to gambling" within s.335(1) of the 2005 Act. These would include agency arrangements (such as the appointment of an agent to make or accept a bet),[175] partnerships for betting and loans to enable the borrower either to engage in gambling or to pay lost bets. The fact that such contracts "relate" to gambling no longer prevents their enforcement: this follows from the repeal (by s.334 of the 2005 Act) of the legislation which formerly governed them and from the express provision of s.335(1) (of that Act) that "the fact a contract relates to gambling shall not prevent its enforcement". This provision can, of course, only apply if the transaction relied upon by the person seeking enforcement has contractual force; and this requirement was held not to have been satisfied in *Ritz Hotel Casino v Al Geabury*[176] where a persistent gambler had entered into a "voluntary self-exclusion agreement" (VSE) with the casino by which he had excluded himself for life from gambling at the casino. In an action by the casino against him on a cheque which he had given to the casino in payment for chips,[177] he counterclaimed for damages for breach of the contract alleged to have been contained in the VSE. The claim was rejected by Simler J. on the ground that the VSE did not amount to a contract since the requirement of consideration was not satisfied. Her reason for this conclusion was that "nothing moved from the Defendant to the Claimant" and that it was "difficult to see what consideration flows from the defendant when he enters a self-exclusion agreement

---

[172] [1949] A.C. 530.
[173] Above, para.41-001.
[174] *Hyams v Coombes* (1912) 28 T.L.R. 413; *Burrell & Son v Leven* (1926) 42 T.L.R. 407; *Poteliakhoff v Teakle* [1938] 2 Q.B. 816; *Goodson v Baker* (1908) 98 L.T. 451 (contra) was hard to support. See also above, Vol.I, para.4-051.
[175] For the terminology of "making" and "accepting" a bet, see Gambling Act 2005 s.9 (above, para.41-005).
[176] [2015] EWHC 2294 (QB), [2015] L.L.R. 860.
[177] See above para.41-018.

providing nothing in return".[178] This reasoning, with respect, gives rise to some difficulty since it makes no reference to the generally accepted principle that, though consideration must move from the promisee, it need not move to the promisor.[179] Evidently the gambler was regarded as the promisee and the casino as the promisor, though it is not altogether clear what promise was made to the gambler by the casino; presumably it was one to deny him the gambling facilities from which he had asked to be excluded. The loss of those facilities, even if only for a limited time,[180] can without implausibility be regarded as a detriment to the gambler (just as is the case where a promisee has, in response to the promise, given up smoking or drinking). The doctrine of consideration does not impose any further requirement that anything should "move to the Claimant" (i.e. to the casino). It could perhaps be argued that the gambler's self-exclusion did not amount to consideration because the gambler's signature of the VSE form had not been requested by the casino; but that is not the ground given in the judgment in its short discussion of the consideration point.[181]

"Unlawfulness" It does not, however, follow from the reasoning of para.41-026 above that such related transaction actually would be legally enforceable. Enforcement could, in particular be denied (by virtue of s.335(2) of the 2005 Act) on the ground of "unlawfulness": e.g. where a loan gave the borrower credit in circumstances amounting to an offence under the 2005 Act[182] or where it was illegal under other rules of law[183] or where the purpose of an agency arrangement or of a partnership for betting was to enable a child or young person to become a principal party to a gambling contract in contravention of the restrictions imposed by 2005 Act on their participation in commercial gambling.[184] All these examples serve merely to illustrate the wider principle that, in deciding whether a contract which "relate[d] to gambling" was legally enforceable, the fact of its being so related must simply be ignored. Whether the result of ignoring this fact was to make

41-027

---

[178] [2015] EWHC 2294 (QB) at [137].
[179] See Vol.I, para.4-040.
[180] The self-exclusion form signed by the gambler was expressed to be "for life" but the VSE agreement was in fact revoked by mutual consent (see at [125]) of the parties to it less than a year after it had been made: see at [2(iii)], [3(ii)], [137].
[181] In the passage quoted above, Simler J. relies on statements by Briggs J. in *Calvert v William Hill Credit Ltd* [2008] EWHC 454 (Ch), [2008] L.L.R. 583 AT [175], [178], [180] to the effect that a voluntary self-exclusion agreement was "without consideration"; the decision was affirmed [2008] EWCA Civ 1427 where the same view is stated at [26]. No reason is given for this view either by Briggs J. or by the Court of Appeal but it should be pointed out that the judgments in the *Calvert* case dealt with a transaction concluded before the Gaming Act 2005 had come into force: see [2008] EWCA Civ 1427 at [2], [13] and when the earlier gambling (or gaming and wagering) legislation referred to in para.41-001 above was still in force. The gambler would therefore be excluding himself from making bets that were void in law while in the *Al Geabury* case he had excluded himself from transactions which, in general, were legally enforceable. This difference makes the argument that the gambler had provided consideration in the *Al Geabury* case more plausible (for the reason given in the *Calvert* case). This would not be the only situation in which the change in the law, making gambling contracts enforceable in law, could affect issues of consideration arising from gambling contracts or related transactions: see, for example, the discussions of *Lipkin Gorman v Karpnale Ltd* [1991] 2 A.C. 548 in paras 41-047 and 41-048 below and in Vol.I, para.4-190 above.
[182] Gambling Act 2005 ss.81, 177.
[183] e.g. where a loan was made to enable the borrower to play an illegal game, as in *M'Kinnell v Robinson* (1838) 3 M. & W. 434.
[184] Above, para.41-003.

the related contract legally enforceable would depend on rules of law applicable to contracts generally, that is, irrespective of the type or category to which they belonged. The related contracts might be unenforceable or void because of some defect in their formation or other vitiating factor or because of a failure in performance on the part of the party claiming to enforce the other party's obligation. An objection to enforcement on the last of these grounds would indeed be inappropriate where enforcement was sought of the main wagering contract itself, in view of the aleatory, as opposed to synallagmatic,[185] nature of gambling contracts, under which one party's liability does not depend on the performance by the other of his undertaking. But this reasoning would not apply to other contracts related to gambling, that is, to "related transactions" of the kind here under discussion. Nor would it apply where one party has failed to perform, not a positive duty, such as one to make a payment expressed to have fallen due under the contract, but a negative duty, such as the duty not to cheat arising by virtue of the implied term not to cheat. This possibility is illustrated by *Ivey v Genting Casinos (UK) Ltd.*[186]

41-028 **"Voiding [a] bet"** The enforceability of a contract which "relates" to gambling may also be affected by an order, made under s.336 of the 2005 Act,[187] to "void" a bet. This possibility is discussed, in the context of a number of the contractual relationships listed above,[188] in paras 41-036—41-039 below.

(iii) Recovering Back Money Paid

41-029 **No right to recover back losses** Section 335(1) of the 2005 Act in terms deals only with the enforcement of contracts related to gaming; but it also indirectly affects the situation in which the claim is one, not for enforcing, but one for undoing, the contract, e.g. where it is one for the return to the claimant of money paid by him under the contract. Before s.335 came into force, it was settled that the loser of a bet could not rely on the invalidity of the wagering contract (under the repealed legislation referred to in para.41-001 above) as a ground for recovering back losses which he had paid. This rule was explained on various (with respect, not entirely convincing) grounds, such as that the loser had waived the benefit of the relevant legislation,[189] or that he was regarded in law as having made a gift of the payment to the winner.[190] Money paid under a contract relating to gambling will now

---

185 The expressions "aleatory" and "synallagmatic" are not often found in English law but they do occasionally occur: e.g. *Re Schebsman* [1944] Ch. 83 at 108; *Foskett v McKeown* [2001] 1 A.C. 102 at 135 (aleatory); *Hong Kong Fir Shipping Co Ltd v Kawasaki Kisen Kaisha Ltd* [1962] 2 Q.B. 26 at 65; *United Scientific Holdings Ltd v Burnley B.C.* [1978] A.C. 904, 928 (synallagmatic); *Arnold v Britton* [2015] UKSC 36, [2015] A.C. 1619 at [21] ("Given that a contract is a bilateral, or synallagmatic, arrangement ..."). For the latter expression, see also Vol.I, para.1-114. A contract may be bilateral without being synallagmatic: e.g. where A bargains for B's *promise* rather than B's performance. The point seems to be recognised (in relation, not to enforceability but to failure of consideration) in *Fibrosa Spolka Atacyjna v Fairbairn, Lawson, Combe Barbour Ltd* [1943] A.C. 32 at 48 (see the words "generally speaking").

186 [2017] UKSC 67, discussed above, para.41-021.

187 Above, para.41-022.

188 e.g. agency and partnership (above, para.41-026).

189 *Bridger v Savage* (1884) 15 Q.B.D. 363, 367; cf. *Richards v Starck* [1911] 1 K.B. 296 (losses paid in advance irrecoverable).

190 *Lipkin Gorman v Karpnale Ltd* [1991] 2 A.C. 548, 562, 577 (but see 581, quoted in para.41-047: club under "an obligation which in business terms it had to comply with").

continue to be irrecoverable by the payor, but on the different ground that it was paid pursuant to a valid contract.[191] Where the gambling contract is illegal or defective in some other way, the right to recover back money paid under it will be governed by the rules of law relating to the recovery of money paid under illegal or otherwise defective contracts in general. An overpayment by the loser was also formerly irrecoverable, but the reasoning of the authority which supported this view[192] is undermined by the repeal of earlier legislation by, and the enforceability of contracts related to gambling under, the 2005 Act.[193] There is now no reason why the normal rules relating to the recovery of overpayments under valid contracts (e.g. as a result of a mistake) should not apply to overpayments made under gambling contracts. There is nothing in Part 17 of the 2005 Act to affect the former rule that, where the winner knows when he receives the payment, that it is excessive and decides to keep it, he is guilty of theft.[194] There is also no reason to suppose that the 2005 Act has changed the former rule that, where the winner has cheated, money paid to him by the loser can be recovered back by the loser on the ground of fraud.[195] If the winner were convicted in the first of the above two situations of theft, or in the second of the new offence of cheating (created by s.42 of the 2005 Act), the court by or before which he was convicted could presumably make a compensation order against him.[196]

(iv) Deposits

Recovering back money or property deposited The outcome of claims for the recovery of money deposited (as opposed to paid out and out) and of property deposited as security under a wager by one party to it with the other depended, before the 2005 Act, on a distinction between illegal and legal wagers. This distinction has survived the Act in the sense that an illegal gambling contract is not now, any more than it was before the Act, legally enforceable.[197] Hence claims for the recovery of such deposits will fall under the general rules on the recovery of money paid or property transferred under an illegal contract. The former general rule was that money paid or property transferred under an illegal contract could not be recovered back, but now enforcement of a claim in restitution will be determined by the "factors-based" approach adopted by the Supreme Court in *Patel v Mirza*.[198] The decision (which permitted recovery of money paid to enable an illegal bet that was in fact never placed) indicates that normally claims for the restitution of money paid or property transferred, if such a claim would otherwise be available, should be allowed.[199] Lord Toulson, speaking for the majority, said[200]:

41-030

---

191 The above reasoning would apply to losses paid in advance, no less than to payments made after the determination of the bet. Under the old law, such payments could likewise not be recovered back, but for the different reason given above.

192 *Morgan v Ashcroft* [1938] 1 K.B. 49.

193 Above, para.41-001.

194 *R. v Gilks* [1972] 1 W.L.R. 1341.

195 For the English common law rule to the above effect, see *Dufour v Ackland* (1830) 9 L.J. (O.S.) K.B. 33. For a review of conflicting American decisions, see *Berman v Riverside Casino Corp*, 323 F. 2d 977 (1963), where it was alleged that loaded dice had been used in a Nevada casino.

196 Powers of Criminal Courts (Sentencing) Act 2000 s.130.

197 Gambling Act 2005 s.335(2), above, para.41-017.

198 [2016] UKSC 42, [2017] A.C. 467; see Vol.I, paras 16-016 et seq.

199 See above, Vol.I, paras 16-217 et seq.

"... a person who satisfied the ordinary requirements of a claim in unjust enrichment will not prima facie be debarred from recovering money paid or property transferred by reason of the fact that the consideration which has failed was an unlawful consideration."

Under normal principles money paid or property transferred cannot be recovered unless there has been a total failure of consideration, or there is some other ground for restitution.[201] One such ground is that the illegal purpose has not been put into effect.[202] Thus a deposit will normally be recoverable if the depositor repudiates the gambling contract in time.[203] Where the gambling contract is not illegal (or affected by any other vitiating factor) the reasoning that the deposit was recoverable as it had been made to secure payment of a void debt[204] no longer applies now that such a gambling contract is, as a general rule, legally enforceable by virtue of s.335(1) of the 2005 Act. Any right to recover the deposit would now depend on the terms of the contract and the general law relating to the recoverability of deposits; the fact that the contract related to gambling would, again,[205] simply be ignored.

(v) Stakeholders

41-031 **Stakeholder contracts** In relation to gambling, a stakeholder is a person with whom the parties to a bet deposit their stakes under a "tripartite contract"[206] to the effect that he will deliver the stakes of both of them to the winner on the determination of the bet. He is normally regarded as the agent of both parties to the bet. Each party authorises him to hold his own stake, to receive the other party's and to dispose of the aggregate in accordance with the outcome of the bet. Under the Gambling Act 2005, such a contract would be a "contract relate[d] to gambling" within s.335(1). As such it would, in general, be enforceable by virtue of that subsection and of the repeal by s.334(1)(c) of s.18 of the Gaming Act 1845.[207] The restriction on the enforceability of contracts related to gambling discussed in paras 41-016—41-021 above could affect the stakeholder contract, no less than the gambling contract itself, so that the stakeholder contract could not be enforced if (for example) it were illegal.[208] It is also arguable that illegality of the principal

---

[200] [2016] UKSC 42 at [201]. Note that the minority seemed to consider that an illegal contract could be set aside, and restitutionary remedies would be available, even if the contract had been performed: see [2016] UKSC 42 at [198]–[199] (Lord Mance) and [253]–[254] (Lord Sumption); see further above, Vol.I, paras 16-031 et seq.

[201] cf. Vol.I, paras 16-225 et seq., above.

[202] Vol.I, paras 16-230 et seq. An alternative way to put it is that until the contract has been performed either party may withdraw, and there will then be a failure of consideration.

[203] See also below, para.41-032.

[204] *Universal Stock Exchange v Strachan* [1896] A.C. 166 (securities deposited by loser recoverable); contrast *Strachan v Universal Stock Exchange (No.2)* [1895] 2 Q.B. 696 (money deposited by loser irrecoverable after it had been appropriated by winner in discharge of loser's "indebtedness"; but such a deposit could have been recovered back if claimed by loser before such appropriation: *Re The Futures Index* [1985] F.L.R. 147).

[205] cf. above, para.41-027.

[206] *Rockeagle Ltd v Alsop Wilkinson* [1992] Ch. 47, 50 (where the stakeholder held a deposit under a contract for the sale of land). For stakeholder contracts, see also *Bristol Alliance Nominee No. 1 Ltd v Neil Andrew Bennett* [2013] EWCA Civ 1626, [2014] P. & C.R. DG 15, where an "escrow amount" paid under an agreement to surrender a lease was held by solicitors as stakeholders.

[207] Above, para.41-001.

[208] Gambling Act 2005 s.335(2) ("unlawfulness").

gambling contract could infect the stakeholder contract and so make that contract illegal.[209]

Illegal bets Where the stakeholder contract was illegal, either in itself or because the bet to which it related was illegal, further problems can arise as to the right of the parties to the bet to recover back their stakes from the stakeholder. The starting principle used to be that a stake deposited in pursuance of such a contract was, in general, irrecoverable as money paid under an illegal contract.[210] But this rule was subject to many exceptions, of which the one most likely to be relevant in the present context was that enabling a person who had paid money under an illegal contract to recover it back if he had demanded its return before execution of the illegal purpose. If the bet was illegal because it was a bet on the outcome of an illegal game, or on some other illegal activity, it could thus be recovered back if it was reclaimed by the payor before the game or activity has taken place.[211] Claims to recover stakes will now fall within the "factors-based" approach to the enforcement of claims that involve illegality adopted by the Supreme Court in *Patel v Mirza*.[212] The Supreme Court held that normally claims for restitution should be allowed despite the illegality but, as pointed out earlier,[213] only where such a claim would otherwise be available.[214] Thus, under the new approach it may still be relevant to determine whether the illegal purpose or contract has been performed. According to one old case,[215] the stake could be recovered back so long as the *contract* has not been executed by payment of the stake to the winner of the bet. It is submitted that the decisive question ought to be whether the illegal *purpose* has been carried into effect,[216] that the illegal purpose is the playing of the illegal game (or the accomplishment of the stipulated illegal act) and that the stake should be irrecoverable once the illegal game or activity has taken place. If the bet is illegal because of its intrinsic nature (e.g. because it is made in violation of a prohibition in the 2005 Act[217]), then it could be argued that the illegal purpose was not "executed" until the stake was paid over to the winner, so that, till then, the loser could recover it back from the stakeholder.[218]

41-032

Unfair bets If the bet is "unfair", an order in relation to it may be made under s.336(1) of the Gambling Act 2005. One consequence of such an order is that "any contract or other arrangement in relation to the bet is void".[219] The order can thus affect, not only the bet itself, but also the stakeholder contract. The effects of an

41-033

---

[209] *De Begnis v Armistead* (1833) 10 Bing. 107; *M'Kinnell v Robinson* (1838) 3 M. & W. 434, 435.
[210] Vol.I, para.16-217.
[211] *Martin v Hewson* (1855) 10 Ex. 737.
[212] [2016] UKSC 42, [2017] A.C. 467; see above, Vol.I, paras 16-016 et seq.
[213] See above, para.41-030.
[214] See above, para.41-030 and Vol.I, paras 16-217 et seq.
[215] *Hastelow v Jackson* (1826) 8 B. & C. 221.
[216] Vol.I, para.16-231. The reason for the above submission is that the second of the two views stated above is more likely than the first to promote the policy of the *locus poenitentiae* principle discussed in Vol. I para.16-230. That second view is also favoured in Peel (ed.), *Treitel on The Law of Contract*, 14th edn (2015), paras 11-139, 11-140.
[217] See above, para.41-003.
[218] cf. *Barclay v Pearson* [1893] 2 Ch. 154 (not a betting contract but a lottery; for the distinction between these concepts under the Gambling Act 2005, see ss.3, 9 and 14).
[219] Gambling Act 2005 s.336(2)(a).

order under s.336(1) on "other arrangement[s]" are considered in paras 41-036—41-040 below.

(vi) Securities

41-034 **When enforceable** Before the repeal of the former legislative provisions preventing the enforcement of wagering contracts and certain related transactions,[220] a security (such as a cheque) given in payment of a lost bet had, between the parties to the bet, no greater validity than the principal contract.[221] The position is different now that those provisions have been repealed[222] and gambling contracts are, in general, legally enforceable.[223] Hence if the loser gives the winner a cheque in payment, the winner can bring an action against the loser not only on the gambling contract but who also on the cheque as a contract which "relates to gambling".[224] But if the original debt were incurred in relation to gambling which had been carried on in violation of restrictions on the giving of credit imposed by 2005 Act[225] or by the terms of a licence held by the creditor (the winner of the bet), then the contract by which credit had been given would be illegal and thus unenforceable "on the ground of unlawfulness".[226] The related contract contained in the cheque would on the same ground not be enforceable by the winner against the loser of the bet. Cheques are now usually deprived of the quality of negotiability by being marked "account payee,"[227] so that problems to which the transfer of negotiable securities given in payment of lost bets formerly gave rise[228] are now unlikely to occur. But where the payment was made by a negotiable bill of exchange, that bill, though not enforceable by reason of the illegality by the original payee, could be enforced by a "holder in due course,"[229] i.e. by one who took the bill (provided that it was regular on its face and not overdue) for value, in good faith and without notice of the illegality[230]; it can also be enforced by a holder who derives his title from a holder in due course.[231] However, once it is admitted that the bill is affected by illegality the holder cannot rely on the usual presumption that he is a holder in due course.[232] He must show that, subsequent to the illegality, value has

---

[220] See above, para.41-001.
[221] *Richardson v Moncrieffe* (1926) 43 T.L.R. 32.
[222] Above, para.41-001. Gambling Act 2005 s.334(1)(a) and (b); s.334(2) expressly provides that these repeals are not to have retrospective effect.
[223] Gambling Act 2005 s.335(1); above, para.41-011.
[224] Gambling Act 2005 s.335(1).
[225] Gambling Act 2005 ss.81, 177.
[226] Gambling Act 2005 ss.335(2); above, paras 41-017—41-021.
[227] Bills of Exchange Act 1882 s.81A as inserted by Cheques Act 1992; *Esso Petroleum Ltd v Milton* [1997] 1 W.L.R. 938 at 946, 954.
[228] Most of these problems arose, in the case of non-gaming wagers, by reason of s.18 of the Gaming Act 1845, and in the case of gaming wagers by reason of s.1 of the Gaming Act 1710, s.1 of the Gaming Act 1835 and s.16 of the Gaming Act 1968. For the repeal of all this legislation by the Gambling Act 2005, see above, para.41-001.
[229] Bills of Exchange Act 1882 s.38(2).
[230] Bills of Exchange Act 1882 s.29(1).
[231] Bills of Exchange Act 1882 s.29(3); this subsection does not apply where the holder who derived title through a holder in due course is himself a party to any illegality affecting the bill.
[232] Bills of Exchange Act 1882 s.30(2).

in good faith been given either by him or by a previous holder through whom he derives title.[233] "In good faith" here means "without notice of the illegality".[234]

(vii) Loans

Loans related to gambling   The law with regard to the effects of loans related to   **41-035**
wagering contracts was, before Part 17 of the Gambling Act 2005 came into force, largely concerned with the effects on such loans, and on the giving of securities in respect of them, of the Gaming Acts 1710 and 1835, of s.18 of the Gaming Act 1845, of the Gaming Act 1892 and of s.16 of the Gaming Act 1968. The repeal of all this legislation by the Gambling Act 2005[235] has made most of the discussion of these effects obsolete. Under the 2005 Act, such loans[236] will fall into the category of contracts related to gambling, so that, by virtue of s.335(1) of that Act,[237] the fact that they are so related no longer, as a general rule, prevents their enforcement. This is so whether the loan is made to enable the borrower to gamble or to enable him to pay losses incurred by gambling before the loan was made; it also no longer makes any difference[238] to the issue of enforceability whether the money lent is paid to the loser or directly to the winner, or whether the loan is subject to a stipulation that it is to be used for gambling or paying losses incurred by the borrower in gambling. The general rule that contracts related to gambling are legally enforceable is, however, under s.335(2) of the 2005 Act subject to the exception that enforcement of such contracts may be refused on the ground of "unlawfulness".[239] Thus if the gambling itself is carried on in contravention of the Act and amounts to an offence under it, the common law principle that a loan made to enable a person to play an illegal game may be irrecoverable[240] will continue to apply. The same would be true if the gambling were illegal on some other ground: e.g. because it amounted to a bet on the outcome of a contest that was unlawful (such as dog fighting). It is assumed that, in the above cases, the lender, though not a party to the bet, is complicit in the illegality, at least to the extent of being aware of it.

---

[233] Bills of Exchange Act 1882 s.30(2).

[234] Bills of Exchange Act 1882 s.90 ("in fact done honestly") and cf. *Tatem v Haslar* (1889) 23 Q.B.D. 345, 348 (a case of fraud not of illegality). It is submitted that a person does not act "honestly" if he acts with notice of the illegality.

[235] Above, para.41-001.

[236] In *Carlton Hall Club Ltd v Laurence* [1929] 2 K.B. 153 the claimant Club advanced chips to the defendant to enable him to play at billiards and poker and the defendant at the time of the advance gave the Club a cheque for the amount of the chips. This transaction was treated as a loan of money; and this characterisation of it was accepted in *R. v Knightsbridge Crown Court, Ex p. Marcrest Properties Ltd* [1983] 1 W.L.R. 300, rejecting the view taken in *Cumming v Mackie*, 1973 S.L.T. 242 that there was no "loan" if the cheque was given at the time of the loan. The *Carlton Hall Club* case is obsolete insofar as the outcome there depended on the now repealed Gaming Acts of 1710 and 1835 (see above, para.41-001) but it remains authoritative for the characterisation of the transaction as a loan, which would now be "related to gambling" within s.335(1) of the 2005 Act. See also the characterisation of a similar transaction as a loan to pay bets already lost in *CHT Ltd v Ward* [1965] 2 Q.B. 63, the actual decision in which is obsolete insofar as it depended on the now repealed Gaming Act 1892 (see above, para.41-001).

[237] Above, para.41-011.

[238] As it did before the coming into force of the Gambling Act 2005 (see para.41-001 above).

[239] Above, paras 41-017—41-021.

[240] Formerly the loan was irrecoverable, *M'Kinnell v Robinson* (1838) 3 M. & W. 434. Now its recoverability will depend on the application of the "factors-based" approach adopted by the Supreme Court in *Patel v Mirza* [2016] UKSC 42, [2017] A.C. 467; see above, paras 41-030 and 41-032.

Further possibilities are that *the loan itself* amounted to the giving of credit in contravention of the 2005 Act[241] so as to make the lender guilty of an offence under it, or that the loan amounted to an offence under some other rule of law. The unlawfulness of the loan would then be a ground for refusing to enforce it.

(viii) *"Voiding Bet" and Related Transactions*

41-036 **Effect of order to "void bet"**[242] Our concern here is with the effect on related transactions of the exercise by the Gambling Commission of its power under s.336(1) of the 2005 Act to make an order in relation to a bet on the ground that the bet was "substantially unfair".[243] Section 336(2) states that, where such an order is made

> "(a) any contract or other arrangement in relation to the bet is void and (b) any money paid in relation to the bet (whether by way of stake, winnings, commission or otherwise) shall be repaid to the person who paid it …"

The words here quoted from paragraph (a) of this subsection appear to be wide enough to cover, not only the gambling transaction itself, but also a number of the related transactions discussed above. They would, for example cover (and so make void) fresh promises to pay the amount of a lost bet, agency arrangements related to gambling, partnerships for betting and stakeholder arrangements. All such arrangements could become void by virtue of an order under s.336 even though they were not themselves unfair: the section requires only *the bet* (and not any other contract or arrangement related to it) to be unfair to enable the Commission to make an order under it. A security given in payment of losses could likewise fall within s.336(2)(a) and so become void in consequence an order made under s.336(1).

41-037 In some situations, the consequences described in para.41-036 above are no doubt necessary to give effect to the policy of s.336, to except "unfair" bets from the general principle, stated in s.335(1), of the enforceability of contracts relating to gambling. It would, for example, make no sense if that exception made the bet void but left it open to the winner to enforce a fresh promise (of the kind considered in para.41-026 above) by the loser to pay his losses; or to allow the winner who could not sue the loser on the bet which had become void to sue the loser on a cheque given in payment of his losses (though such a claim might fail, even if s.336 did not apply to the cheque, on the principle that, between the parties, the cheque has no greater validity than the bet itself[244]). The principle of making "unfair" bets void might also be undermined if the victim of the unfairness were not entitled to the repayment of sums paid by him under the unfair bet before the order under s.336 had been made; this possibility accounts for the express provision of s.336(2)(b) (quoted in para.41-036 above), though it can be argued that a claim for such repayment might succeed at common law as one for the return of money paid under a void contract, apart from s.336(2)(b).

41-038 Other possible consequences of the effects of an order under s.336 on related transactions give rise to more difficulty. Some of these result from the breadth, or

---

241 See ss.81, 177.
242 Marginal note to Gambling Act 2005 s.336.
243 Above, para.41-022.
244 See *Richardson v Moncrieffe* (1926) 43 T.L.R. 32, applying this principle under the old law of gaming and wagering contracts (above, para.41-001).

perhaps the obscurity, of the words of s.336(2)(a) which are quoted in para.41-036 above and which provide for the repayment of "any money paid in relation to the bet (whether by way of stake, winnings, commission or otherwise)". The first question that arises is what is here meant by the word "stake". It seems that this word refers, not to a sum of money deposited with, or paid to, a third party as stake-holder,[245] but to the sum paid by the person making, to the person accepting, the bet[246]; and it is normally consistent with the policy of s.336 that a person who makes a bet and pays a stake in pursuance of it should, if the bet is "unfair", be entitled to the return of the payment. But if this is the correct interpretation of "stake" in s.336(2)(a), one has next to ask what is there meant by "winnings". It seems that this word refers to payments made by the *other* party to the bet, i.e. by the party "accepting" it, who will generally be the holder of a licence of the kind specified in s.336(1)(a) to (c). Since that party is more likely than the person "making" the bet to be responsible for the unfairness, it might at first sight seem strange that the former party (i.e. the party accepting the bet) should, as a result of that unfairness, become entitled to the recovery of winnings which he had paid to the other party. But the factors to be taken into account by the Commission in determining whether the bet was unfair refer to the supply of information by, and the state of mind or conduct of, *either* party[247] (e.g. to the fact that either has been convicted of cheating, contrary to s.42 of the 2005 Act[248]). Hence where it is the maker of the bet who is responsible for the factor making the bet unfair, it would be appropriate for the acceptor of the bet to be entitled to the return of winnings that he had paid. Conversely, in such a situation it would not be appropriate for the maker of the bet to recover his "stake". We shall see in para.41-040 below that it is open to the Commission to reach the appropriate result in both of these two situations.

In a number of further situations, the effect of an order under s.336 could give **41-039** rise to inappropriate consequences insofar as the order made not only the gambling contract, but also related transactions, void. Three examples may be given to illustrate the point. (1) A may make and B accept a bet which was "unfair" by reason of factors for which B was responsible and A has, for the purpose of making the bet, used money borrowed from C in circumstances in which no "unfairness" affected the loan. At first sight, an order under s.336 could have the effect, not only of making the bet void, but also of extending this invalidity to the loan as an "arrangement in relation to the bet".[249] But if, as a result of the order so far as it related to the unfair bet, A obtained repayment of the amount that he had lost and paid to B under the bet,[250] then there would be no good reason why A should not repay to C the money that A had borrowed from C to enable A to make the bet or to pay the amount lost under it. (2) Somewhat similar reasoning could apply where C had acted as stakeholder in relation to a bet between A and B which was unfair by reason of factors for which B was responsible; and where, on B's having won the bet, C, who was not complicit in the unfairness, had paid A's stake to B. Section 336(2)(b)

---

[245] Above, para.41-031.
[246] For the distinction between "making or accepting a bet", see Gambling Act 2005 s.9; for the use of the word "stake" to refer to a payment made by the person "making" the bet, see Gambling Act 2005 s.83 ("return of stakes to children") and the definition of "stake" in s.353(1); and cf. the use of the word "stake" in the Directive and Regulations cited in para.41-015 above.
[247] See Gambling Act 2005 s.336(4).
[248] Gambling Act 2005 s.336(4)(c).
[249] Gambling Act 2005 s.336(2)(a).
[250] Gambling Act 2005 s.336(2)(b).

provides that, if the bet becomes void as a result of an order under s.336, then "any money paid in relation to the bet … shall be repaid to the person who paid it …".[251] If these words refer to the payment from A to C then C would have to repay the money to A even though, in previously paying it to B, he had acted in accordance with his instructions from A and was not involved in the unfairness. The better solution would be to interpret the words quoted above as referring to the payment from C to B and to order its repayment to C, who would then be liable to account for it to A. (3) A third situation which could give rise to difficulty under s.336 is that in which the loser of an unfair bet makes a payment under it by a negotiable security; this situation can still arise although it has become uncommon now that cheques are generally marked "account payee" and hence not negotiable.[252] But where payment was made by a negotiable instrument and an order was made under s.336 on the ground that the bet was unfair, the instrument might, by virtue of the order become "void"[253] and such a result could cause prejudice to a third party to whom the instrument was transferred. It was this possibility which formerly gave rise to difficulty under the Gaming Act 1710[254] and was in part resolved by the Gaming Act 1835.[255] Both these Acts are repealed by the Gambling Act 2005[256] but we shall see[257] that it is open to the Gambling Commission to avoid the difficulty by other means when making an order under s.336 of the latter Act.

41-040   **Flexibility of orders under s.336(1)**   A number of the difficulties described in paras 41-038 and 41-039 above can be averted by the Commission's availing itself of powers which are conferred on it by s.337(2) and (3) of the 2005 Act and introduce considerable flexibility into the making of orders under s.336(1). Section 337(2) enables the Commission to make such an order "in relation to the whole, or any part or any aspect of, a betting transaction"; and s.337(3) enables the Commission to:

"… make incidental provision, in particular … about … (b) the consequences of the order [under s.336(1)] for other aspects of a betting transaction one part or aspect of which becomes void under the order."

The expression "betting transaction" in these provisions seems to embrace not only what s.336 calls the "contract"[258] or the "bet"[259] but also what it calls "any … other arrangement in relation to the bet".[260] (i.e. what in para.41-036 above is called a "related transaction"). The Commission's powers under s.337(2) could, for example, be used in the case of an unfair bet between A and B made with money

---

251 Gambling Act 2005.
252 See above, para.41-034.
253 Gambling Act 2005 s.336(2)(a).
254 s.1 of this Act had made the relevant securities "utterly void, frustrate and of none effect".
255 s.1 of this Act provided that securities of the kind referred to in the previous note should no longer be void, but that they should be "deemed and taken to have been given for an illegal consideration". A bill of exchange so taken can be enforced by a holder in due course, i.e. by one who took the bill (provided that it was regular on its face and not overdue) for value, in good faith and without notice of the illegality: Bills of Exchange Act 1882 ss.29(1) and (2), 38(2); it can also be enforced by a holder who derives his title from a holder in due course: Bills of Exchange Act 1882 s.29(3).
256 Above, para.41-001.
257 In para.41-040 below.
258 In s.336(2)(a).
259 In s.336(1) and (3).
260 In s.336(2)(a).

borrowed from C who was not complicit in the unfairness. The Commission would be enabled by s.337(2) to restrict its order under s.336(1) to the principal contract, and by s.337(3)(b) specifically to except the loan from the order. In this way it could avoid what in para.41-039 above was called the inappropriate result that could follow if the Commission simply made an order that the bet was unfair. Similarly, these powers could be used in the stakeholder example given in para.41-039 above: even if the interpretation of s.336(2)(b) there preferred were rejected, the Commission could restrict its order to the principal contract and except the stakeholder transaction from that order. The powers conferred by s.337(2) and (3)(b) could again be used to resolve the problem, described in para.41-039 above, which can arise where payment under an unfair bet was made by a negotiable security. The Commission could declare the principal contract void and the negotiable security unenforceable between the parties, but specify that the security was not to be "void" to the prejudice of third parties, whose rights could then be governed by the law applicable to negotiable securities which suffer from some defect that falls short of making them "void".[261] The same powers could also be used to resolve the difficulty that could arise in the situation described at the end of para.41-038 above in relation to claims for the repayment of money paid under a bet which is "unfair" within s.336 of the 2005 Act. It was there submitted that if the maker of a bet had been convicted of cheating, then the acceptor of the bet should be entitled to repayment of his winnings but it would not be appropriate to allow the maker (the cheat) to recover back his stake. While there may be no warrant in the words of s.336(2)(b)[262] for such a distinction, it is submitted that an order in these terms could be made by the Commission under the powers conferred on it by s.337(2) and (3)(b), quoted above in this paragraph.

It is finally arguable that the results which can be reached under the provisions of s.337(2) and (3)(b) can also be reached, independently of them, by virtue of s.336(2) which provides that where "the Commission makes an order under subs.(1) in relation to a bet (a) any contract or[263] other arrangement in relation to the bet is void ...". But there are difficulties in relation to this argument which, at the very least, leave the point in doubt. In the first place, it is by no means clear whether the words just quoted refer to the *content* of an order under subs.(1) or to its legal *consequences*. The structure of s.336(2) gives some support to the latter view; certainly the provisions in para.(b) of subs.(2), with regard to the repayment of money paid, appear to be of the latter nature. Secondly, the argument appears to place too much reliance on the word "or", especially where it occurs in a sentence that contains what is in substance a negative proposition. An order that a contract "is void" is of this negative nature: it tells us that the contract can *not* be enforced; and if a proposition which is negative (whether in form or in substance) links two objects with the conjunction "or", then the negative prima facie refers to both objects (as in the sentence "I do not like oranges or lemons"). Thus it is arguable that an order under s.336(1) would, by virtue of s.336(2)(a), if that provision stood alone, have the effect of invalidating both "the contract" *and* "any other arrangement". This seems to be the assumption underlying s.337(2) (quoted above) which gives the Commission the choice between making "an order under s.336(1)

---

261 See Bills of Exchange Act 1882 s.29(2).
262 Quoted in para.41-036 above.
263 Italics supplied.

in relation to the whole, or any part or aspect of, a betting transaction". If this choice were inherent in s.336(2)(a), then there would be no need for s.337(2).

(f) Gambling with Chips

41-041 **Before the Gambling Act 2005** Before the coming into force of Part 17 of the Gambling Act 2005, a number of legal problems arose from the common practice of using chips or tokens for the purpose of gambling in casinos and similar gambling establishments. These problems arose mainly under the Acts of Parliament which deprived wagering contracts and certain related transactions of legal validity; the reference to "money" in such legislation was generally extended by the courts so as to cover transactions in which payments under the contracts were made in chips or tokens[264]; and one of the relevant Acts expressly referred to "cash or tokens".[265] It was also held that the supply of chips in a casino to a person making bets there did not amount to "valuable consideration" for the purpose of the rule that a recipient of stolen money was bound to make restitution of it to the victim of the theft unless the recipient had received the money in good faith and for valuable consideration.[266] One reason for this view was that the recipient's promise to allow the acquirer of the chips to gamble in the club and to pay his winnings did not amount to consideration since these promises were void under s.18 of the Gaming Act 1845.[267]

41-042 **After the Gambling Act 2005** The reasoning in para.41-041 above has been made obsolete by the coming into force of Part 17 of the Gambling Act 2005. Section 334 of that Act has repealed the legislation which had previously impaired the validity of wagering contracts and of certain related transactions, and s.335(1) has laid down the general rule that the fact that a contract relates to gambling shall not prevent its enforcement. Hence the purchase of chips to enable the buyer to gamble at (usually) the seller's establishment now stands legally on the same footing as the purchase of tokens from a department store to enable the purchaser of the tokens to exchange them for goods there. There was authority before the coming into force of Part 17 of the 2005 Act that, in a case of the latter kind, "an independent contract is made for the chips when the customer obtains them at the cash desk".[268] The consideration provided by the customer in such a case would be his payment (or promise to pay), while that provided by the store would be its promise to supply goods of the value of the tokens or the performance of that promise. The same reasoning would now apply to the purchase of chips from a casino by a person wishing to make bets there.[269] Now that contracts related to gambling are, as a general

---

[264] e.g. *Lipkin Gorman v Karpnale Ltd* [1991] 2 A.C. 548, 575 (chips treated as a "mechanism for gambling with money"); *Stuart v Stephen* (1940) 56 T.L.R. 571; *Crockfords Club Ltd v Mehta* [1992] 1 W.L.R. 355.

[265] Gaming Act 1968 s.16.

[266] *Lipkin Gorman v Karpnale Ltd* [1991] 2 A.C. 548; for such cases, see now below, paras 41-042, 41-051.

[267] Above, Vol.I, para.4-016.

[268] *Lipkin Gorman v Karpnale Ltd* [1991] 2 A.C. 548 at 576; contrast 562 ("only one contract"). And see Vol.I, para.4-016.

[269] See *Ritz Hotel Casino Ltd v Al Daher* [2014] EWHC 2847 (QB) at [31]–[32], citing *Lipkin Gorman v Karpnale Ltd* [1991] 2 A.C. 548 (above, para.41-041) and other cases on the point here under discussion decided before the coming into force of the Gambling Act 2005.

rule, legally enforceable,[270] there is (in general) no difficulty with respect to the consideration provided by the casino: it takes the form of its promise to allow its customer to gamble and to pay his winnings, or the performance of that promise. The "independent contract"[271] is, moreover, in general, legally enforceable as one that "relates to gambling".[272] Further problems with regard to such an "independent contract" may, however, arise in the two situations in which, under the 2005 Act, contracts related to gambling are not, or cease to be, legally enforceable. These situations are discussed in paras 41-043 and 41-044 below.

Unlawfulness The circumstances in which a contract relating to gambling may **41-043** be unenforceable, by virtue of s.335(2) of the Gambling Act 2005, on the ground of its "unlawfulness" are discussed in paras 41-017—41-021, above. The point to be made here is that the unlawfulness of the principal contract may infect the "independent"[273] or collateral contract which arises when the person who wishes to bet with chips purchases them. If, for example, the bet were illegal by reason of its contravention of the Act or of some other rule of law,[274] then the collateral contract might itself be illegal on the ground that its object was to facilitate the performance of an illegal act.[275] The exact effects of the illegality on the collateral contract would then depend on the "factors-based" approach now applicable to claims arising from illegality.[276] This would, for example, determine whether the contract could, in spite of the illegality, be enforced by a party who was innocent of it,[277] or even by a guilty party where the object of the rule of law giving rise to the illegality was to prohibit conduct rather than to invalidate contracts.[278] They would also determine in what circumstances money paid or property transferred in pursuance of the contract could be recovered back by the party who had made the payment or transfer.[279]

Effect of order "to void bet"[280] on gambling with chips The power of the **41-044** Gambling Commission to make an order under s.336(1) of the Gambling Act 2005 in relation to a bet which is "substantially unfair" has been described in general terms in para.41-022 above, and the effects of such an order on transactions related to the bet is discussed in paras 41-036—41-040 above. Where chips are bought and used for the purpose of gambling, the contract under which they are so bought is such a related transaction. Under s.336(2)(a) of the Act, the effect of an order under s.336(1) is that "any contract *or other arrangement in relation to the bet* is void". The words here italicised are capable of applying to the "independent"[281] or collateral contract under which the chips are bought, so that this contract, no less than the bet itself, becomes void as a result of the order under s.336(1). It is further

---

[270] Gambling Act 2005 s.335(1); above, para.41-011.
[271] *Lipkin Gorman v Karpnale Ltd* [1991] 2 A.C. 548 at 576.
[272] Gambling Act 2005 s.335(1).
[273] Above, para.41-042.
[274] Above, paras 41-017—41-021.
[275] *M'Kinnell v Robinson* (1836) 3 M. & W. 434.
[276] See *Patel v Mirza* [2016] UKSC 42, [2017] A.C. 467, discussed above at paras 41-030 and 41-032.
[277] Contrast *Archbold's (Freightage) Ltd v Spanglett's Ltd* [1961] 1 Q.B. 374 (innocent party's claim upheld) with *Re Mahmoud and Ispahani* [1921] 2 K.B. 716 (innocent party's claim rejected).
[278] e.g. *St. John Shipping Corp v Joseph Rank Ltd* [1957] 1 Q.B. 267. See also *Ritz Hotel Casino Ltd v Al Daher* [2014] EWHC 2847 (QB), discussed above in para.41-019.
[279] See Vol.I, paras 16-225 et seq.
[280] Marginal note to Gambling Act 2005 s.336.
[281] See *Lipkin Gorman v Karpnale Ltd* [1991] 2 A.C. 548 at 576; above, para.41-042.

provided by s.336(2)(b) that "any money paid *in relation to the bet* shall be repaid to the person who paid it". Again the italicised words are wide enough to cover money paid for chips. Further flexibility is given by s.337 to the Commission when making an order under s.336(1). The Commission's discretion in this respect is discussed in para.41-040 above. It will be recalled that under s.337(2) the Commission "may make an order under section 336(1) in relation to the whole, *or any part or aspect of*, a betting transaction". The words here italicised are capable of referring to the contract relating to the purchase or use of chips. Under s.337(3)(b) the Commission may, in an order under s.336(1):

"... make provision about ... the consequences of the order *for other parts or aspects of the betting transaction one part or aspect of which becomes void under the order.*"

It is not entirely clear whether the words here italicised would apply to the situation here under discussion since the effect of the order under s.336(1) would, by virtue of s.336(2)(a), appear to cover more than (in the words of s.337(3)(b)) "*one part or aspect of*" the betting transaction, i.e. both the bet itself and[282] the contract relating to the purchase and use of the chips. The point could, perhaps, be met by arguing that s.337(3)(b) is not restricted to cases in which the order under s.336(1) covered *only* one part of the betting transaction. Alternatively, and perhaps more plausibly, the Commission could, under s.337(2) order that only the main betting transaction was to be void and then rely on s.337(3)(b) to deal with the further consequences of the order on the contract relating to the purchase and use of chips. The Commission might wish to do this where it was the purchaser of the chips who was responsible for the unfairness which formed the basis for making an order under s.336(1). It could then make adjustments which it regarded as appropriate in view of the purchaser's conduct in relation to the betting transaction as a whole.

(g)   Gambling with Stolen Money

41-045 **Loser using stolen money**   Before the coming into force of Part 17 of the Gambling Act 2005[283] (which deals with the "legality and enforceability of gambling contracts"[284]), it was settled that a loser who paid money lost under a wager could not recover back the amount so paid from the winner, in spite of the fact that the contract was void under s.18 of the Gaming Act 1845.[285] That rule continues, in general, to apply after the coming into force of Part 17 of the 2005 Act, though for the different reason that, as a general rule, the gambling contract under which the money was paid is now legally enforceable.[286] But the further question can still arise whether, where the loser uses stolen money to make such a payment, the victim of the theft can recover the amount so paid from the winner. Because of the negotiable quality of money paid and received as currency, the victim cannot recover an equivalent sum from the winner if the winner has received the money in good faith, without notice of the theft, and for valuable consideration. Before the coming into force of Part 17 of the 2005 Act, the view had prevailed that

---

282 See para.41-040 above for the force of the word "or" in s.336(2)(b).

283 Above, para.41-001.

284 Gambling Act 2005, heading to Pt 17.

285 *Bridger v Savage* (184) 15 Q.B.D. 363, 367; *Lipkin Gorman v Karpnale Ltd* [1991] 2 A.C. 548, 562, 577; *Hillside (New Media) Ltd v Baasland* [2010] EWHC 3336 (Comm).

286 Above, para.41-029.

no such valuable consideration had been provided by the winner; the reasons for this view are discussed in Vol.I, paras 4-016 and 4-017 above and 41-047 below. The effects on these reasons of Part 17 of the 2005 Act are discussed in paras 41-046—41-051 below.

Stolen money used to pay losses under illegal wagers   In the eighteenth century   **41-046** case of *Clarke v Shee and Johnson*[287] a clerk stole money from his employer and paid part of the amount so stolen to the defendant under a lottery which had been made illegal and void by the Lotteries Act 1772. Lord Mansfield held that the employer was entitled to recover from the defendant the amount of the stolen money which had been so paid to the defendant because that money was:

> "... his [the employer's] property which has come into the hands of the defendant iniquitously and illegally and in breach of the Act of Parliament."[288]

The word "iniquitously" seems to indicate that the defendant was held liable because he had not received the money in good faith, his lack of good faith resulting either from his awareness of the circumstances in which the money had come into the hands of the thief or from his knowing participation in the violation of the Act of 1772. This reasoning is not affected by the Gambling Act 2005. Later discussion of the case treats it as authority for the view that the defendant had not provided any consideration for the payment in the shape of any promise which he had made to the thief, since that promise was illegal and void under the Act of 1772.[289] This reasoning, too, would not in a similar case be affected by the Gambling Act 2005 since the general principle contained in s.335(1), that contracts related to gambling are legally enforceable, is by s.335(2) stated to be "without prejudice to any rule of law preventing the enforcement of a contract on the ground of unlawfulness". A contract now made in similar circumstances would still be illegal and void so that the defendant's promise would not constitute any consideration for the receipt of the money. But if he had acted in good faith in relation both to the legality of the contract and to the provenance of the money, then he could be said to have provided consideration for the receipt of the money by accepting it in discharge of what he in good faith believed to be his legally enforceable claim against the loser; for this purpose it would be irrelevant that that claim was bad in law.[290] If his good faith extended only to the legality of the contract, but not to the provenance of the money, then he would be liable to restore the money to the victim of the theft even if he could be said to have provided consideration for its receipt. This follows from the fact that the recipient of stolen money can avoid liability to restore it only if he has received it in good faith *and* for valuable consideration.[291]

---

[287] (1774) 1 Cowp. 197.

[288] (1774) 1 Cowp. 197 at 199–200.

[289] *Lipkin Gorman v Karpnale Ltd* [1991] 2 A.C. 548 at 563, 575.

[290] cf. Vol.I, para.4-053.

[291] See *Lipkin Gorman v Karpnale Ltd* [1991] 2 A.C. 548, below, para.41-047, where the defendant was held liable, even though it had received the stolen money in good faith, because it had not provided "valuable" or "full" consideration for it: see at 570 and 560; above, Vol.I, para.4-016. For the effect of the Gambling Act 2005 on the reasoning of this case, see below, para.41-047.

41-047　**Stolen money used to pay losses under lawful wagers**　In *Clarke v Shee and Johnson*[292] the transaction in respect of which the stolen money had been paid was illegal and void and the payment had apparently been received in bad faith. But in *Lipkin Gorman v Karpnale Ltd*[293] the reasoning of the earlier case was held to apply even though the stolen money had been used for the purpose of wagers which were not illegal but only void under s.18 of the Gaming Act 1845 and even though the defendant had received the stolen money in good faith. In that case one Cass, a salaried partner in a firm of solicitors, wrongfully withdrew money from the firm's client account and over a period of 10 months used money so stolen[294] to pay gambling losses incurred by him at the defendant's club. The club had acted in good faith, without notice of the fact that the money used by Cass had been stolen, and it would have been entitled (as against the victim of the theft) to retain the money if it had, in addition, been able to show that it had provided consideration for its receipt of the money. Three arguments were advanced by the Club in support of the view that it had provided such consideration. Its first argument was that it had provided consideration by allowing Cass to gamble and so promising to pay his winnings on bets which he won. This argument was rejected on the ground that the Club's promise was void under s.18 of the Gaming Act 1845; and this reasoning is in accord with the view that, prima facie, a void promise does not constitute consideration.[295] The Club's second argument was that it had provided consideration by actually paying such winnings to Cass. In cases unconnected with gaming, the law did, at least in some cases, regard the *performance* of a defective promise as consideration,[296] even where the mere making of the promise would not be so regarded. But the Club's second argument, too, was rejected on the ground that any such payment to Cass was in law a gift to him.[297] This may not be a very realistic view of the intention with which the Club made such payments[298]; and it may also, with respect, be doubted whether this is really an explanation of the rule, rather than a statement of its legal consequence. The Club's third argument was that it had provided consideration by supplying Cass with gaming chips. This argument was also rejected for reasons discussed in paras 4-016 and 4-017 of Volume I of this book, where a number of difficulties which arise in reconciling this rejection with rules which, in contexts other than that of the use of stolen money for gambling, determine the presence or absence of consideration, are discussed. It is, however, respectfully submitted that the view that the Club had provided no consideration for its receipt of the stolen money was justified by the context in which the question arose in the *Lipkin Gorman* case. The practical result of that view was twofold. The starting point was that, because the Club had provided no consideration for its receipt of the stolen money, it was liable to restore this money to the victims of the theft. But the House of Lords went on to recognise that claims for the restitution of money were subject to the defence of change of position[299]; that the Club had changed its position by allowing Cass to enter into a series of transactions which

---

[292]　(1771) 1 Cowp. 197; above, para.41-046.
[293]　[1991] 2 A.C. 548; see above, Vol.I, paras 4-016 and 4-017.
[294]　For the amounts involved, see below.
[295]　See above, Vol.I, para.4-186.
[296]　See above, Vol.I, para.4-188.
[297]　[1991] 2 A.C. 548, 562, 577.
[298]　See below ("an obligation which in business terms [the club] had to comply with").
[299]　See generally, above, Vol.I, para.29-186.

"by the laws of chance [yielded] the occasional winning bet"[300]; and that, although the Club was not legally liable to pay on bets won by Cass, such bets placed it, as a practical matter, under "an obligation which, in business terms it had to comply with".[301] The Club was therefore held liable to restore only part of the stolen money that Cass had used in gambling there.[302] The loss resulting from the theft was thus split between two innocent parties (the Club, which had received the stolen money in good faith, and the victim of the theft); and it was no doubt the desire of the House of Lords to reach such a loss-splitting conclusion which led to its rejection of the argument that the Club had provided valuable consideration for the payments to it of the stolen money, and to the recognition of the (partial) defence of change of position.

The reasoning of the *Lipkin Gorman* case,[303] on the issue of whether the club had provided consideration for its receipt from Cass of the money that he had stolen, is now subverted by (a) the repeal of s.18 of the Gaming Act 1845 by s.334(1)(c) of the Gambling Act 2005 and (b) the provision of s.335(1) of the 2005 Act that "the fact that a contract relates to gambling shall not prevent its enforcement".[304] The effect of these changes in the law is that, on facts similar to those of the *Lipkin Gorman* case, the club would be bound by its promise to pay his winnings to Cass (unless the promise was defective for some reason other than that it related to gambling[305]). That promise, or its performance, would therefore constitute consideration for the payment of the stolen money to the club which, since it had received the money in good faith, would no longer be liable (as it had been in the *Lipkin Gorman* case) to restore the money to the victim of the theft. Since the club would no longer now be liable in restitution, no issue could arise as to any reduction of such liability on the ground of change of position. Hence the loss-splitting solution adopted by the House of Lords in the *Lipkin Gorman* case[306] would no longer normally be open to the courts. It will be argued in para.41-051 below that it might be open to the Gambling Commission to reach a similar result in the exercise of its power, conferred by s.336 of the Gambling Act 2005 to "void [a] bet"; but this possibility is restricted to cases in which the bet is "substantially unfair".[307]

41-048

Effect of order to "void bet"[308]   The further question arises whether the reasoning of the *Lipkin Gorman*[309] case on the issue of consideration would still apply, after the coming into force of Part 17 of the Gambling Act 2005, in a case in which it was arguable that the bet was "unfair" so that the Gambling Commission could

41-049

---

[300] [1991] 2 A.C. 548, 582.

[301] [1991] 2 A.C. 548, 581.

[302] The total amount of stolen money used by Cass in gambling at the Club was £222,908.98; the decision was that the Club was liable for no more than £154,695, this being the net amount lost by Cass (deducting his winnings from his losses) during the period of his having gambled with the stolen money (making allowance also for £20,050 attributable to his own money).

[303] [1991] 2 A.C. 548, above para.41-047.

[304] Above, para.41-011. The contract for the purchase of chips would also now generally be enforceable as a contract relating to gambling within s.335(1): above, para.41-042.

[305] See Gambling Act 2005 s.335(2), above paras 41-017—41-022.

[306] See above, para.41-047.

[307] Gambling Act 2005 s.336(3); above, para.41-022.

[308] Marginal note to Gambling Act 2005 s.336.

[309] [1991] 2 A.C. 548; above, para.41-047.

make an order in relation to it under s.336(1)[310]; if such an order were made, the contract or any other arrangement relating to the bet would be "void",[311] and any money which had been "paid in relation to the bet" would have to be "repaid to the person who paid it and repayment may be enforced as a debt due to that person".[312] It is submitted that the possibility of the Commission's making such an order would not deprive the club's promise to pay Cass his winnings (or the performance of that promise) of its potential of constituting consideration for the payment. The power to make the order is discretionary[313] so that there can be no certainty of its being exercised. The club's promise may (by reason of the existence of that power) be of doubtful value but this is not sufficient to negative the possibility of its amounting to consideration.[314] Moreover, the power to make an order under s.336 is, in general[315] exercisable only for six months after the determination of the bet[316]; and, if no attempt were made during that time to obtain such an order there would be no doubt that the club's promise (unless it were otherwise defective) would then constitute consideration for the payment to it of the stolen money. Where the bet is indeed unfair, there may, however, be mechanisms under the Act by which the victim of the theft can, directly or indirectly, secure the return of the stolen money, or at least of part of it. These mechanisms are discussed in paras 41-050 and 41-051 below.

41-050   **Application for order under s.336(1) by victim of the theft**   It has been suggested in para.41-023 above that there is nothing in s.336 which expressly restricts the power to apply for an order under the section to the parties of the bet. If this is right, an application for such an order could be made by the victim of the theft. Under s.336(1), the effect of the order (in cases of the present kind) would be that any money paid in relation to the bet "shall be repaid to the person who paid it and repayment may be enforced as a debt by that person".[317] The person entitled to repayment would indeed be the thief, since he would be the person who would have paid the (stolen) money "in relation to the bet (whether by way of ... stake ... or otherwise)"[318] to the winner; but the victim of the theft would then have a civil claim against the thief for the restitution of the stolen money. It is an open question whether such a claim would be a proprietary claim or a personal one (under which the victim of the theft would rank equally with the thief's other creditors[319]). In this

---

[310] Above, paras 41-022, 41-023.
[311] Gambling Act 2005 s.336(2)(a).
[312] Gambling Act 2005 s.336(2)(b).
[313] s.336(1) begins with the words "The Commission *may* make an order ..." (italics supplied).
[314] cf. above, Vol.I, para.4-052.
[315] i.e. subject to s.336(6), above para.41-022 (contract unfair because a party has been convicted of cheating, contrary to s.42 of the 2005 Act).
[316] Gambling Act 2005 s.336(5).
[317] Gambling Act 2005 s.336(2)(b).
[318] Gambling Act 2005.
[319] See *FHR European Ventures LLP v Mankarious* [2014] UKSC 45, [2014] 4 All E.R. 79 where, in the context of a principal's claim against his agent in respect of a bribe or secret profit received by the agent, Lord Neuberger P. at [1] distinguished between a "proprietary" claim and one for "equitable compensation" and said that the two main advantages of a claim of the former kind were that it gave the claimant priority over the debtor's unsecured creditors and a right to "trace and follow" the subject-matter of the claim in equity, whereas neither of these advantages would be available to a person entitled only to "equitable compensation". The claim in this case was held to be a proprietary one: see at [46]. For the distinction between the two kinds of remedies, see generally

respect, the victim's claim against the thief could be less advantageous to the victim than the victim's claim against the club was in the *Lipkin Gorman* case.[320] On the other hand, in a restitution claim by the victim of the theft *against the thief* the partial defence of change of position *by the club*, that prevailed in the *Lipkin Gorman* case,[321] would not be available to the thief since that defence is not available to a defendant who has changed his position in bad faith.[322] Nor would change of position by the club afford it a partial defence to an order to make repayment to the thief (if the bet is unfair) under s.336. Such repayment "may be enforced as a debt due to that person"[323] (who would be the payor of the money to the Club, i.e. the thief); and in actions for the recovery of a debt there is no defence of change of position. In this respect the rights of the victim of the theft might at first sight seem to be more favourable to him, if he could invoke s.336, than the victim's rights against the club were in the *Lipkin Gorman* case; for it is arguable that the victim could, under that section, get an order for the repayment to the thief of all the stolen money lost by the thief, and that the victim could then bring a restitution claim for the return of that money against the thief. But it will be argued in para.41-051 below that the Commission, in making an order under s.336(1) could so formulate the order as to reach a result substantially similar to that reached by the House of Lords in that case.

Flexibility of orders under s.336(1)   It was pointed out in para.41-040 above that **41-051** s.337 of the Gambling Act 2005 gives considerable flexibility to the Gambling Commission when making an order in relation to an unfair bet under the powers conferred on it by s.336(1). In particular, s.337(2) empowers the Commission to make such an order "in relation to the whole, or any part or aspect of, a betting transaction"; and by s.337(3) such an order may make:

"... incidental provision; in particular ... about ... (b) the consequences of the order for other parts or aspects of a betting transaction one part or aspect of which becomes void under the order."

The question here is whether the facts that the bet was made with stolen money, and that the victim has an interest in the recovery of that money, are a "part or aspect" of the betting transaction within these provisions. The circumstance that stolen money was used to make or pay a bet can scarcely be described as a "part" of the betting transaction; and, although it may be an "aspect" of that transaction, even this line of reasoning is not free from difficulty. Section 337(3)(b) seems to regard a "part or aspect" of the transaction as something that has the potential of becoming

---

Vol.I, Ch.29, section 4.

[320] Above, para.41-047. For discussion of the remedy in *Lipkin Gorman v Karpnale Ltd* [1991] 2 A.C. 548, see *Armstrong DLW GmbH v Winnington Networks Ltd* [2012] EWHC 10 (Ch), [2013] Ch. 156 especially at [71]–[75], where the judgment of Mr Stephen Morris Q.C. at [75] accepted counsel's submission that the *Lipkin Gorman* case was "in substance" one "of a 'proprietary restitutionary claim' and not a claim for restitution for unjust enrichment". It is not entirely clear whether this distinction is concerned with the *basis* of the claim as opposed to its legal *nature*, i.e. whether it is intended to make the same points as the distinction drawn by Lord Neuberger P. in *FHR European Ventures LLP v Mankarious* [2014] UKSC 45, [2014] 4 All E.R. 79 at [1], quoted above, or as those drawn in the distinction (similar to Lord Neuberger's) between "proprietary" and "personal" claims.

[321] *Lipkin Gorman v Karpnale Ltd* [1991] 2 A.C. 548.

[322] Above, Vol.I, para.29-191.

[323] Gambling Act 2005 s.336(2)(b).

"void under the order" and the circumstance that stolen money was used by a party to the bet can hardly be something that so "becomes void". The most plausible argument would seem to be that, under s.337(3)(b), the court could order that the *payment* made with stolen money was "void" and that the Commission could then, as one of the "consequences of the order" specify that the stolen money should be returned, not to the thief (as s.336(2)(b) would seem to require), but to the victim of the theft. This might in turn cause hardship to the other party to the bet if he had received the payment in good faith and for valuable consideration. One solution of this problem would be to say that the Commission's discretion under s.337(3)(b) is sufficiently broad to allow it to take this hardship into account by ordering a partial return of the stolen money to the victim of the theft. This would lead to much the same result (though by a different route) as that which the House of Lords had reached in *Lipkin Gorman v Karpnale Ltd*[324] by subjecting the victim's right of recovery to the partial defence of change of position. For this purpose, the Commission might be able to take account of the degree of responsibility which the party to whom the stolen money had been paid pursuant to the debt bore for the circumstances making the bet "unfair".[325] It should be emphasised that the Commission's power here under discussion exists *only* in relation to such "unfair" bets and, in general, only for six months after the result of the bet had been determined.[326]

---

324 [1991] 2 A.C. 548; above, para.41-047.
325 See Gambling Act 2005 s.336(4) given a list of such factors. The list is not exhaustive: see above, para.41-022.
326 See above, para.41-022.

CHAPTER 42

INSURANCE

P. J. S. MacDonald Eggers

1. THE NATURE OF INSURANCE[1]

Definition   A contract of insurance is one whereby one party (the insurer)   **42-001**
undertakes for a consideration to pay money or provide a corresponding benefit[2] to

---

[1] See generally *MacGillivray on Insurance Law*, 14th edn (2018); Clarke, *The Law of Insurance Contracts* (looseleaf); Merkin, Colinvaux and Merkin's Insurance Contract Law (looseleaf).

[2] *Prudential Insurance v Inland Revenue Commissioners* [1904] 2 K.B. 658, 662. Money's worth is a corresponding benefit, as is any service which cannot logically be distinguished from the payment of money: see *DTI v St Christopher Motorists Assn Ltd* [1974] 1 W.L.R. 99, 106; *Medical Defence Union v Department of Trade* [1980] Ch. 82, 94–95. What benefits fall within the latter category of service is not clear, but it is an exceptional category and the right to the proper considera-

or for the benefit of[3] the other party (the assured) upon the happening of an event which is uncertain, either as to whether it has or will occur at all, or as to the time of its occurrence,[4] where the object of the assured is to provide against loss or to compensate for prejudice caused by the event, or to make provision for some identified contingency, such as for the assured's old age (where the event is the reaching of a certain age by the assured) or for the benefit of others upon his death (where the event is the death of the assured).[5] It is these objectives which distinguish insurance from gaming or wagering.[6] When embodied in a document the contract is usually called a policy, but save in the case of marine and possibly life insurance,[7] an oral contract of insurance, though rare, is perfectly valid[8] and may indeed also be described as a policy.[9]

42-002 **Types of insurance contract** There are many ways in which an insurance contract may be classified. The nature and legal implications of an insurance contract may depend on the type of risk, the type of benefit to be paid, and the nature or circumstances of the assured. As regards the type of risk, insurance policies are broadly classified as non-marine and marine insurance. Marine insurance is defined in s.1 of the Marine Insurance Act 1906. Although it follows that non-marine insurance lies outside the scope of a marine insurance contract, a number of policies will include both marine and non-marine components. Within this broad division, policies may be sub-classified by reference to whether the risks insured against are, to take a few examples, death, personal accident, fire, theft, negligence,

---

tion of a claim or of a request for a service does not fall within it: see *CVG Siderurgicia de Orinoco SA v London Mutual Steamship Owners Assn (The Vainqueur José)* [1979] 1 Lloyd's Rep. 557, 580; *Medical Defence Union v Department of Trade*, above. See also *Re Sentinel Securities Plc* [1996] 1 W.L.R. 316, where it was held that a guarantee protection scheme (under which a company undertook to the customers of suppliers that, in the event of a supplier ceasing to trade because of financial failure, it would honour the supplier's guarantee of the goods supplied and installed) constituted insurance business; *Re Digital Satellite Warranty Cover Ltd* [2013] UKSC 7, [2013] 1 W.L.R. 605 at [18]–[19]. The insurer's undertaking is one by which he or she is obliged to provide the benefit to the assured in case the specified event occurs. If the undertaking is not obligatory (e.g. because it is discretionary), it is not an insurance contract (*Medical Defence Union Ltd v Department of Trade* [1980] Ch. 82; *CVG Siderurgicia del Orinoco SA v London Steamship Owners' Mutual Insurance Association Ltd (Vainqueur José)* [1979] 1 Lloyd's Rep. 557, 580).

3   For beneficiaries under life insurance see below, para.42-132.

4   *Prudential Insurance v Inland Revenue Commissioners* [1904] 2 K.B. 658; *Fuji Finance Inc v Aetna Life Insurance Co Ltd* [1997] Ch. 173, 188–189, 198, where it was held that the benefit payable must be contingent on the event uncertain; it is not necessary for the insurer to be exposed to a risk of loss.

5   See *Tyrie v Fletcher* (1777) 2 Cowp. 666; *Wilson v Jones* (1867) L.R. 2 Ex. 139, 150; *Prudential Insurance v Inland Revenue Commissioners* [1904] 2 K.B. 658; *Gould v Curtis* [1913] 3 K.B. 84. cf. *Lucena v Craufurd* (1806) 2 Bos. & P.N.R. 269, 302; *Fuji Finance Inc v Aetna Life Insurance Co Ltd*, above, at 198.

6   *Wilson v Jones*, above; *Macaura v Northern Assurance* [1925] A.C. 619, 627. See also, *Newbury International v Reliance National Insurance Co* [1994] 1 Lloyd's Rep. 83, where a policy of "prize indemnity insurance" was held to be effectively a wager. The definition of insurance may be of great importance, for legislation imposes many requirements as to financial status, incorporation, etc. on persons carrying on insurance business. See below, para.42-064.

7   See Marine Insurance Act 1906 ss.1, 21, 22; Life Assurance Act 1774 s.2. cf. *Eide UK Ltd v Lowndes Lambert Group Ltd* [1999] Q.B. 199, 207–208. There are other statutes which require a written record of specified insurance contracts: see, e.g. Road Traffic Act 1988 s.147.

8   *Murfitt v Royal* (1922) 38 T.L.R. 334.

9   *Re Norwich Equitable Fire* (1887) 57 L.T. 341; *Forsikringsaktieselskabet National v Att-Gen* [1925] A.C. 639.

or motor accidents. As regards the type of benefit, one may characterise insurance contracts as either indemnity or contingency contracts. The nature and effect of an insurance policy may also depend on the position or means of the assured in that the policy may be regarded as a consumer policy or a commercial insurance.[10] The law's approach to construing and determining the operation of such contracts can depend on the nature of the contract itself.[11]

Indemnity insurance   Most contracts of insurance are contracts of indemnity, **42-003** whereby the insurer agrees to compensate the assured for the loss that the latter may sustain through the happening of the event upon which the insurer's liability may arise,[12] but this is not necessarily so. If the object of the contract is indemnification (that is, the insurer's obligation does not arise unless and until the assured has sustained a loss), the contract remains one of indemnity even if it quantifies in advance the value of the potential loss, in which case the insurance is called "valued".[13] The agreed sum is deemed to be an indemnity even if in the particular circumstances it does not represent the true loss,[14] and the insurer can avoid payment on the grounds that the assured is seeking to recover more than an indemnity only if the discrepancy is so great as to make the contract a wager,[15] or unless the assured knew of such discrepancy but failed to disclose it to the insurer or misrepresented the true position to the insurer.[16] The loss which can be indemnified under such an insurance contract may be physical damage to property, financial loss or a legal liability. If a contract is one of indemnity insurance, there are at least three practical consequences in classifying an insurance contract as a contract of indemnity as opposed to a contingency insurance. First, the assured is entitled only to compensation for his loss. He is not entitled to receive or retain any benefits which result in the assured being over-compensated.[17] Secondly, the assured's cause of action against the insurer arises upon the assured suffering the loss in question. Accordingly, once the "loss" has been sustained, subject to the terms of the contract, time then starts running for the purposes of the Limitation Act 1980. Thirdly, if the insurer refuses or fails to pay an indemnity as required by the contract, at common law the insurer is not liable to the assured for any damages above and beyond the

---

[10]   The Financial Conduct Authority's Handbook contains provisions which are specifically aimed at a "*consumer*" as opposed to a "*commercial customer*". See *Insurance: New Conduct of Business Sourcebook* (ICOBS), made pursuant to the Financial Services and Markets Act 2000 s.138, at *http:// fsahandbook.info/FSA/html/handbook/ICOBS*.

[11]   See recently *Tesco Stores Ltd v Constable* [2007] EWHC 2088 (Comm), [2008] Lloyd's Rep. I.R. 302, [2008] EWCA Civ 362, [2008] Lloyd's Rep. I.R. 636.

[12]   *Castellain v Preston* (1883) 11 Q.B.D. 380; *Leppard Excess Insurance Co Ltd* [1979] 2 Lloyd's Rep. 91, 95; see also the Marine Insurance Act 1906 s.1. The indemnity essentially is an undertaking by the insurer that the assured will not suffer loss caused by specified events or perils so that if such loss occurs, the insurer is in breach of his contract and is liable to the assured in unliquidated damages: *Irving v Manning* (1847) 1 H.L. Cas. 287; *Firma C-Trade SA v Newcastle Protection and Indemnity Association* [1991] 2 A.C. 1.

[13]   *Goole Steam Towing Co v Ocean Marine* [1928] 1 K.B. 589, 594.

[14]   *Elcock v Thomson* [1949] 2 K.B. 755.

[15]   *Lewis v Rucker* (1761) 2 Burr. 1167, 1171. For wagers, see above, Ch.41, and see below, paras 42-014—42-016.

[16]   *Thames Mersey Marine v Gunford* [1911] A.C. 529; *Hoff v De Rougemont* (1929) 34 Com. Cas. 291. See also *Visscherrij Maatschappij Nieuwe Onderneming v Scottish Metropolitan Assurance Co Ltd* (1922) 10 Ll.L. Rep. 579. For misrepresentation and non-disclosure, see below, paras 42-034, 42-035, 42-038.

[17]   *Castellain v Preston* (1883) 11 Q.B.D. 380, 386.

amount of the indemnity. This is because the indemnity is itself regarded by the law as damages and the court cannot award damages for the late payment of damages.[18] However, the common law position was modified upon the entry into force of ss.13A and 16A of the Insurance Act 2015 on May 4, 2017.[19] This new legislation introduced into every insurance contract an implied term that the insurer must pay insurance claims within a reasonable time (allowing for investigation and assessment of the claim). If there is a breach of this implied term, the assured will have remedies (e.g. damages) available at common law (and otherwise) in addition to the payment of the claim under the policy and statutory interest.[20]

42-004 **Contingency insurance** Contracts such as life insurance[21] and certain accident insurances providing for the payment of a specified sum upon the happening of an event or accident[22] are not contracts of indemnity; they are often described as "contingency" policies; they do not possess the attributes of contracts of indemnity. The insurer's liability to provide the specified benefit to the assured is generally not dependent on the assured suffering a loss which is the equivalent in value of the specified benefit. Accordingly, the doctrine of indemnity, and related doctrines, such as subrogation, salvage and contribution, will not apply to contingency policies.[23]

2. INSURABLE INTEREST

42-005 **In general** Indemnity insurance obviously requires the assured to have an interest in the subject matter of the insurance other than that created by the contract itself, for otherwise he will incur no loss through the happening of the event insured against, and so if the assured is without a legally recognised interest, the insurer will have a good defence to any claim under such a contract if he chooses to raise it.[24] Contracts which are not contracts of indemnity do not, it would seem, require such an interest at common law to be enforceable as contracts of insurance.[25] However, whether or not the contract is one of indemnity, if it is made without any legally

---

[18]   *Ventouris v Mountain (The Italia Express)* [1992] 2 Lloyd's Rep. 281; *Sprung v Royal Insurance (UK) Ltd* [1999] Lloyd's Rep. I.R. 111; cf. *Callaghan v Dominion Insurance Co Ltd* [1997] 2 Lloyd's Rep. 541. This characterisation of an indemnity has been adhered to of late in deference to precedent, and has been criticised in that it restricts the scope of recoverable damages: Clarke, *The Law of Insurance Contracts* (looseleaf), para.30-9B1; Campbell [2000] L.M.C.L.Q. 42. See also *Pride Valley Foods Ltd v Independent Insurance Co Ltd* [1999] Lloyd's Rep. I.R. 120. See the Law Commission's Consultation Paper: *Insurance Contract Law: Post Contract Duties and other Issues* (LCCP No.201, December 2011). See below, para.42-105. In the award of interest against an insurer, the Court will generally allow interest to run, not from the date of the loss, but from the date by which the insurer should have considered the validity of the claim, taking into account the nature of the loss, the way the claim was presented and the circumstances which required investigation: *Quorum A/S v Schramm (No.2)* [2002] 2 All E.R. (Comm) 179.

[19]   These provisions of the Insurance Act 2015 were introduced by the Enterprise Act 2016 ss.28–30.

[20]   s.13A. See the Explanatory Notes, para.264. See below para.42-112.

[21]   *Dalby v India and London Life* (1854) 15 C.B. 365; *Law v London Indisputable Life Policy Co* (1855) 1 K. & J. 223; *Gould v Curtis* [1913] 3 K.B. 84, 95; *Fuji Finance Inc v Aetna Life Insurance Co Ltd* [1997] Ch. 173.

[22]   *Theobald v Railway Passengers' Assurance* (1854) 10 Exch. 45; *Bradburn v Great Western Ry* (1874) L.R. 10 Ex. 1.

[23]   See below, paras 42-114—42-118.

[24]   *Anderson v Morice* (1876) 1 App. Cas. 713; *Macaura v Northern Assurance* [1925] A.C. 619; *Rogerson v Scottish Automobile and General* (1930) 47 T.L.R. 46, 47.

[25]   "There is nothing in the *common law* of England which prohibits insurance, even if no interest exists": *Williams v Baltic* [1924] 2 K.B. 282, 288.

recognised interest or any expectation of acquiring such an interest, it may well be void or unenforceable.[26] The kind of interest which is legally recognised and required in indemnity insurance and by statute (called "insurable interest"), the persons who have to possess this interest, the provisions of the statutes in question, and the time when such interest is required, all raise difficulties which are considered separately below.[27]

Definition of insurable interest   There is no authoritative definition of insurable interest and it is probably impossible to give a general formula to cover all the recognised types of insurable interest.[28] The insurable interest must be discernible from the assured's relationship with the subject matter of the insurance. That relationship may have a particular nature or certain manifestations which render the assured's interest insurable. For example, the assured may be prejudiced by the loss of or damage to the subject matter of the insurance (or may benefit from its preservation), because he has a legal or equitable right pertaining to the subject matter, or because he will thereby become subject to a liability by reason thereof or because he will thereby be deprived of an opportunity to earn income or a profit in respect of the subject matter.[29] Quite apart from such considerations, it may be that the assured's insurable interest arises out of commercial convenience.[30] There are no fixed criteria which will determine the existence of an insurable interest. Each interest and each case must be analysed on its own. The principles underlying the court's approach to determining an insurable interest in respect of one type of insurance does not necessarily apply in respect of other types of insurance.[31] However, if there has been a genuine attempt to protect an assured against a specified event by means of a particular type of insurance policy, the court will be reluctant to hold that the assured lacks an insurable interest.[32] There need not be a pecuniary element to the assured's relationship with the subject matter of the insurance. **42-006**

The relevance of the risk of financial loss   An assured can insure against the risk of financial loss, whether it be a loss of income or profits or the loss associated with a monetary expense. The risk of financial loss may indicate an insurable interest for **42-007**

---

[26] See below, para.42-013.

[27] On January 14, 2008, the Law Commission published Issues Paper No.4 on insurable interest as part of its larger review of insurance contract law: *http://www.lawcom.gov.uk/insurance_contract.htm*.

[28] The most famous definition is that given in *Lucena v Craufurd* (1806) 2 Bos. & P.N.R. 269, 302, but this was criticised in *Macaura v Northern Assurance* [1925] A.C. 619, 627. See also *Moran Galloway v Uzielli* [1905] 2 K.B. 555, 563; and *Mark Rowlands Ltd v Berni Inns Ltd* [1986] 2 Q.B. 211, 228. For a consideration of the different senses in which "insurable interest" can be used, see *Glengate-KG Properties Ltd v Norwich Union Fire Insurance Society Ltd* [1996] 2 All E.R. 487.

[29] *Deepak Fertilisers and Petrochemicals Corp v ICI Chemicals Polymers Ltd* [1999] 1 Lloyd's Rep. 387 at [65]; *O'Kane v Jones* [2003] EWHC 3470 (Comm), [2004] 1 Lloyd's Rep. 389, at [154]. The nature of the liability is important to determine whether or not the assured has an insurable interest in property or merely intended to insure the liability. If the liability arises out of the assured's care or custody of the subject matter of the insurance, then there may be an insurable interest in the property *(Petrofina (UK) Ltd v Magnaload Ltd* [1984] Q.B. 127, 135; *O'Kane v Jones*, where a ship manager was held to have an insurable interest in the insured vessel); in other cases, the nature of the liability may be appropriate for no more than a liability insurance *(Deepak)*. cf. *Feasey v Sun Life Assurance Co of Canada* [2003] EWCA Civ 885, [2003] Lloyd's Rep. I.R. 693.

[30] *Hepburn v A Tomlinson (Hauliers) Ltd* [1966] A.C. 451, 477, 481–482; *O'Kane v Jones* [2003] EWHC 3470 (Comm), [2004] 1 Lloyd's Rep. 389.

[31] *Feasey v Sun Life Assurance Co of Canada* [2003] EWCA Civ 885, [2003] Lloyd's Rep. I.R. 693.

[32] *Feasey v Sun Life Assurance Co of Canada* [2003] EWCA Civ 885, [2003] Lloyd's Rep. I.R. 693.

the purposes of other types of insurance. It is generally true that a person who would foreseeably suffer financial loss from the occurrence of an event has an insurable interest in the subject matter which it is sought to insure against that event,[33] but this rule of thumb requires qualification. For example, the assured has an insurable interest in his own life, but can hardly be said himself to suffer financial loss by losing his life.[34] The nature of the interest required for the purposes of the insurance will depend on the subject matter of the insurance, the nature of the cover provided and the loss against which the insurance has been obtained.[35] Normally, the event must either cast upon the assured a legally binding liability, or it must affect a right of the assured which is recognised and protected by the courts.[36] Where a person stands to incur a financial loss, the absence of a legal liability or the absence of harm to a legal or equitable right or expectation will militate against the existence of an insurable interest. For example, a father has no insurable interest in his daughter's personal liability in tort,[37] nor does a person have an insurable interest in another's property in respect of which he merely hopes that he will have an interest in the future,[38] or in his debtor's property over which he has no lien or similar right.[39] Further, an assured has no interest entitling him to insure against an event if he does not seek directly to protect the very right to which he is legally entitled. If, for example, the assured is the sole owner of shares in a company, his interest lies in the shares and their value. The assured has no interest recognised by the law in the profits or assets of the company except insofar as they form the basis of the value of the shares,[40] and hence the only way in which he may insure against loss occasioned by the destruction of the company's assets is by insuring against the resultant loss in value of the shares.[41] Similarly, if the assured is owed a debt by a company he may insure against default in paying the debt, but not against a loss of assets by that company, unless the existence of the debt itself created a proprietary interest in the assets.[42]

42-008 **Types of insurable interest** The following instances of insurable interest are supported by authority[43]:

  (i) *Property insurance* Legal,[44] equitable,[45] joint[46] or sole[47] proprietary rights will give rise to an insurable interest; possession whether defeasible or

---

[33] *Stockdale v Dunlop* (1840) 6 M. & W. 224.

[34] cf. *Gould v Curtis* [1913] 3 K.B. 84.

[35] *Glengate-KG Properties Ltd v Norwich Union Fire Insurance Society Ltd* [1996] 2 All E.R. 487.

[36] *Stockdale v Dunlop* (1840) 6 M. & W. 224; *Moran Galloway v Uzielli* [1905] 2 K.B. 555; Marine Insurance Act 1906 s.5(2). The definition in s.5(2) is not exhaustive: *O'Kane v Jones* [2003] EWHC 3470 (Comm), [2004] 1 Lloyd's Rep. 389 at [145].

[37] *Vandepitte v Preferred Accident* [1933] A.C. 70, 80: "natural love and affection does not give such an interest at law".

[38] *Buchanan v Faber* (1899) 4 Com. Cas. 223; aliter, a legal right depending upon an expectancy: *Cook v Field* (1850) 15 Q.B. 460.

[39] *Wolff v Horncastle* (1798) 1 B.P. 316, 323; *Moran Galloway v Uzielli* [1905] 2 K.B. 555, 562, 563. It is, of course, possible to insure against the debtor's insolvency caused by loss of his property: *Waterkeyn v Eagle Star* (1920) 5 Ll.L. Rep. 42, 43.

[40] *Macaura v Northern Assurance* [1925] A.C. 619.

[41] *Paterson v Harris* (1861) 1 B. & S. 336; *Wilson v Jones* (1867) L.R. 2 Ex. 139.

[42] *Moran Galloway v Uzielli* [1905] 2 K.B. 555, 562.

[43] See the "groups of cases" referred to by Waller L.J. in *Feasey v Sun Life Assurance Co of Canada* [2003] EWCA Civ 885, [2003] Lloyd's Rep. I.R. 693.

[44] *Lucena v Craufurd* (1806) 2 Bos. & P.N.R. 269, 324; *Ex p. Houghton* (1810) 17 Ves. Jr. 251; *North*

not[48] provided that the possessor has some liability or obligation to the bailor, owner or consignee will similarly give rise to an insurable interest.[49] If the assured has an insurable interest in goods or property, he may insure against loss of profits consequent upon their loss or damage,[50] or against other consequential loss,[51] provided that this cover is clearly stipulated in the contract.[52] The participation of contractors or sub-contractors in construction works on the construction site is probably sufficient to endow them with an insurable interest in the property comprising the works. Once the contractors or sub-contractors leave the site, they will cease to have an insurable interest in the works themselves. Any liability which might arise prior to their departure from or by virtue of their presence on the works is emblematic of their relationship with the property and could be insured under a property policy or a liability policy. Any liability which arises thereafter is insurable only under a policy of liability insurance.[53]

(ii) *Liability insurance* All legally enforceable liabilities,[54] whether based upon statutory duty,[55] tort[56] or contract, may represent an insurable interest.[57] It is odd, however, to speak of insurable interest in the context of a liability policy. If the assured's liability is insured by the policy, and the assured is liable, it follows that the policy will respond, whether one speaks of an insurable interest or not. Contractual liability constitutes or gives rise to

---

British and Mercantile v London, Liverpool and Globe (1877) 5 Ch. D. 569, 583; Castellain v Preston (1883) 11 Q.B.D. 380; Re Betty [1899] 1 Ch. 821.

[45] Smith v Lascelles (1788) 2 T.R. 187, 188; Lucena v Craufurd (1806) 2 Bos. P.N.R. 269; Provincial Insurance v Leduc (1874) L.R. 6 P.C. 224; Samuel v Dumas [1924] A.C. 431, 443, 444, 450, 460.

[46] Page v Fry (1800) 2 Bos. & P. 240; Robertson v Hamilton (1811) 14 East 522; Robinson v Gleadow (1835) 2 Bing.N.C. 156.

[47] Inglis v Stock (1885) 10 App. Cas. 263, 270.

[48] Boehm v Bell (1799) 8 T.R. 154, 161; Marks v Hamilton (1852) 7 Exch. 323; Goulstone v Royal (1858) 1 F. & F. 276.

[49] North British v Moffat (1871) L.R. 7 C.P. 25, 30, 31; Macaura v Northern Assurance [1925] A.C. 619, 628.

[50] Barclay v Cousins (1802) 2 East 544; Eyre v Glover (1812) 16 East 218; Royal Exchange v M'Swiney (1850) 14 Q.B. 646; Stockdale v Dunlop (1840) 6 M. & W. 224.

[51] Inman SS Co v Bischoff (1882) 7 App. Cas. 670, 676. In order to insure against loss of profits or other consequential loss suffered by virtue of damage to the property, the assured need not have an interest in the property, but only in the profits or the subject matter lost: Glengate-KG Properties Ltd v Norwich Union Fire Insurance Society Ltd [1996] 2 All E.R. 487; cf. Marine Insurance Act 1906 s.5.

[52] Re Sun Fire and Wright (1834) 3 N. & M. 819; Re Wright and Pole (1834) 1 Ad. & El. 621; Mackenzie v Whitworth (1875) L.R. 10 Ex. 142; affirmed on appeal (1875) 1 Ex. D. 36; Dixon v Whitworth (1879) 4 C.P.D. 371, 375.

[53] Deepak Fertilisers and Petrochemicals Corp v ICI Chemicals & Polymers Ltd [1999] 1 Lloyd's Rep. 387 at [65]; cf. National Oilwell (UK) Ltd v Davy Offshore Ltd [1993] 2 Lloyd's Rep. 582, 611. See MacGillivray on Insurance Law, 14th edn (2018), para.1-161.

[54] The policy may dictate that the liability of the assured may arise by virtue of his particular interest, in which case there must be a sufficient connection between the liability and the interest: see C.F. Turner v Manx Line Ltd [1990] 1 Lloyd's Rep. 137, 143; Chrismas v Taylor Woodrow Civil Engineering Ltd [1997] 1 Lloyd's Rep. 407, 410–411. But see below, para.42-023, for considerations of public policy, etc. which may invalidate some such contracts.

[55] British Cash and Parcel Conveyors v Lamson Store Service [1908] 1 K.B. 1006, 1014, 1015.

[56] British Cash v Lamson [1908] 1 K.B. 1006, 1014, 1015.

[57] Miller v Warre (1824) 1 C. & P. 237, 239; Stock v Inglis (1884) 12 Q.B.D. 564; Anderson v Morice (1876) 1 App. Cas. 713.

a reassured's insurable interest for the purposes of reinsurance contracts[58] and gives the purchaser of goods to whom the risk but not the property has passed an insurable interest in them.[59]

(iii) *Life insurance* The assured has an insurable interest in the life of the assured himself[60]; the lives of those who are legally recognised as being of financial benefit to the assured, e.g. spouses[61]; the lives of those who are bound by legally enforceable obligations to the assured, e.g. debtors, to the amount of the debt when the insurance is made[62]; the lives of employers, to the amount of any remuneration, etc. due under the contract of employment[63]; the lives of employees, to the value of the contracted employment[64]; the lives of partners[65]; and the lives of co-sureties[66] as well as the debtor's life[67]; the lives of those to whom the assured is responsible; or the lives of those whose death or injury gives rise to an obligation on the part of the assured to indemnify another against the latter's liability for those lives.[68] Beneficiaries under life insurances are considered later.[69]

42-009 **Interest need not be stated** The nature of the assured's interest in the subject matter need not be stated in the contract of insurance,[70] unless of course this information is required by an express term or the insurance is to be against loss of profits or other consequential loss.[71] If upon a claim being made the insurer does not admit that the assured had a valid insurable interest at the relevant date,[72] it is for the assured to prove his interest at such date.[73] In cases of nicety the courts will lean towards a finding of valid interest.[74]

---

58 *Re Law Guarantee Trust* [1914] 2 Ch. 617, 631. However, the reinsurer may also have thereby an interest in the subject matter of the original or underlying insurance (see Marine Insurance Act 1906 s.9(1)). See also *British Dominion General Insurance Co v Duder* [1915] 2 K.B. 394, 400; *Toomey v Eagle Star Insurance Co Ltd* [1994] 1 Lloyd's Rep. 516, 522–524; *Charter Reinsurance Co Ltd v Fagan* [1997] A.C. 313, 387, 392; see below, para.42-127.

59 *Anderson v Morice* (1876) 1 App. Cas. 713, 724. See Marine Insurance Act 1906 s.7(2).

60 *Wainwright v Bland* (1835) 1 Moo. & Rob. 481; *M'Farlane v Royal London Friendly Society* (1886) 2 T.L.R. 755.

61 *Reed v Royal Exchange* (1795) Peake Add. Cas. 70; *Griffiths v Fleming* [1909] 1 K.B. 805. But not other relatives in the absence of legal rights or obligations: *Halford v Kymer* (1830) 10 B. & C. 724; *Shilling v Accidental Death* (1858) 1 F. & F. 116; *Harse v Pearl Life* [1903] 2 K.B. 92 (mother); *Att-Gen v Murray* [1904] 1 K.B. 165 (son). See, however, *Barnes v London, Edinburgh and Glasgow Life* [1892] 1 Q.B. 864. cf. *Howard v Refuge Friendly Society* (1886) 54 L.T. 644, 646; *Elson v Crookes* (1911) 106 L.T. 462; and *Goldstein v Salvation Army* [1917] 2 K.B. 291.

62 *Dalby v India and London Life* (1854) 15 C.B. 365; *Law v London Indisputable Life* (1855) 1 Kay. & J. 223; *Hebdon v West* (1863) 3 B. & S. 579.

63 *Hebdon v West* (1863) 3 B. & S. 579; *Turnbull v Scottish Provident* (1896) 34 S.L.R. 146.

64 *Simcock v Scottish Imperial* (1902) 10 S.L.T. 286.

65 *Griffiths v Fleming* [1909] 1 K.B. 805, 815.

66 *Branford v Saunders* (1877) 25 W.R. 650. In the same case, a joint debtor has an insurable interest in the life of the other joint debtor.

67 *Lea v Hinton* (1854) 5 De G.M. & G. 823.

68 *Feasey v Sun Life Assurance Co of Canada* [2003] EWCA Civ 885, [2003] Lloyd's Rep. I.R. 693.

69 See below, para.42-132.

70 *Mackenzie v Whitworth* (1875) L.R. 10 Ex. 142, 148; see also *Crowley v Cohen* (1832) 3 B. & Ad. 478, 485; *Inglis v Stock* (1885) 10 App. Cas. 263, 270, 274. See Marine Insurance Act 1906 s.26(2).

71 See below, para.42-129.

72 See below, para.42-017.

73 *Macaura v Northern Assurance* [1925] A.C. 619, 632.

74 *Stock v Inglis* (1884) 12 Q.B.D. 564, 571; affirmed (1885) 10 App. Cas. 263; *Feasey v Sun Life Assurance Co of Canada* [2003] EWCA Civ 885, [2003] Lloyd's Rep. I.R. 693.

Insurance of another's interest   Subject to the ordinary rules of agency,[75] and the   **42-010**
provisions of the Life Assurance Act 1774 (which is not confined to life insur-
ance),[76] an agent without interest may effect an enforceable contract of insurance
on behalf of a principal who has an insurable interest, and it seems that either the
agent[77] or the principal[78] can sue on such a contract. In addition, certainly in cases
of marine insurance[79] and probably non-marine insurance,[80] a principal can, after
a loss, ratify a contract of insurance made by an agent without authority in order
to claim for that loss. Subject again to the Life Assurance Act 1774, a person
without any interest at all can insure provided he holds himself trustee for the person
who does have an insurable interest.[81] Furthermore, an assured with an insurable
interest may insure the interests of others as well as himself.[82] Thus, for example,
a bailee liable only for negligence can fully insure the goods against any loss[83]; a
carrier with a lien over goods may insure them for their full value[84]; a contractor
may insure the entire contract works on site for their full value, so as to cover all
other contractors and sub-contractors for any damage to the works[85]; and an owner
of land subject to a lease may fully insure the property for the benefit of himself
and the lessee.[86] In the case of motor insurance, moreover, the owner of a vehicle
can insure against third-party liability incurred in its use by others as well as

[75]   See above, Ch.31.
[76]   See below, para.42-014.
[77]   *Provincial Insurance v Leduc* (1874) L.R. 6 P.C. 224, 244. An agent may sue on a policy in his own
       name, for his principal's loss, if the policy is issued in his own name, whether or not the principal's
       interest is noted; any recovery is held by the agent on behalf of his principal: *The Transcontinental
       Underwriting Agency SrL v Grand Union Insurance Co Ltd* [1987] 2 Lloyd's Rep. 409. It is open
       to question whether the agent's ability to sue is limited to the situation where the contract is made
       in the agent's name. This principle applicable to insurance law does not obviate the requirement of
       an insurable interest: *Sharp v Sphere Drake Insurance Plc (The Moonacre)* [1992] 2 Lloyd's Rep.
       501, 516.
[78]   *Browning v Provincial Insurance* (1873) L.R. 5 P.C. 263, 272, 273.
[79]   See Marine Insurance Act 1906 s.86.
[80]   *National Oilwell (UK) Ltd v Davy Offshore Ltd* [1993] 2 Lloyd's Rep. 582, 607–608; cf. *Grover v
       Matthews* [1910] 2 K.B. 401; *Ferguson v Aberdeen Parish Council*, 1916 S.C. 715.
[81]   *Prudential Staff Union v Hall* [1947] K.B. 685. Thus a seller in possession of the goods when the
       property and risk have passed may insure his buyer's interest: *North British v Moffat* (1871) L.R. 7
       C.P. 25, 30, 31. The intention is necessary, for otherwise the contract is likely to be a wager:
       Tomlinson (Hauliers) Ltd v Hepburn [1966] A.C. 451, 480.
[82]   *Castellain v Preston* (1883) 11 Q.B.D. 380, 398. Indeed, the assured may insure another as an
       undisclosed principal, provided that the insurer is willing to contract with an undisclosed principal:
       Talbot Underwriting Ltd v Nausch Hogan & Murray (The Jascon 5) [2006] EWCA Civ 889, [2006]
       2 Lloyd's Rep. 195. If an assured does not insure the interest of another, that other person who is
       interested in the subject matter of the insurance may have recourse against the insurer under the
       Contracts (Rights of Third Parties) Act 1999. cf. *Trident General Insurance Co Ltd v McNiece Bros
       Pty Ltd* (1988) 165 C.L.R. 107 High Court of Australia. See also Married Women's Property Act
       1882 s.11 (as to an insurance taken out by a married spouse) and Civil Partnership Act 2004 ss.70,
       253 (as to an insurance taken out by a civil partner).
[83]   *Waters v Monarch Fire and Life Assurance Co* (1856) 5 E. & B. 870.
[84]   *Tomlinson (Hauliers) Ltd v Hepburn* [1966] A.C. 451.
[85]   *Petrofina (UK) Ltd v Magnaload Ltd* [1984] Q.B. 127; *National Oil Well (UK) Ltd v Davy Offshore
       Ltd* [1993] 2 Lloyd's Rep. 582, 608–612. For an application of this principle in the context of a
       shipbuilding contract, see *Stone Vickers Ltd v Appledore Ferguson Shipbuilders Ltd* [1991] 2 Lloyd's
       Rep. 288 (although the actual decision was reversed on appeal, on the basis that, as a matter of
       construction, the sub-contractor was not intended to have the benefit of the insurance: [1992] 2
       Lloyd's Rep. 578). See also *Hopewell Project Management Ltd v Ewbank Preece Ltd* [1998] 1
       Lloyd's Rep. 448.
[86]   *Mark Rowlands Ltd v Berni Inns Ltd* [1986] Q.B. 211; *Lonsdale & Thompson Ltd v Black Arrow
       Group Plc* [1993] 2 W.L.R. 815; cf. *Talbot Underwriting Ltd v Nausch Hogan & Murray (The Jascon*

himself.[87] Whether interests other than those of the assured are covered depends upon the construction of the contract.[88] The wording of the contract may, of course, limit the interests covered,[89] but certainly in the case of an insurance by a bailee in respect of the goods bailed, the insurer must use precise words in order to limit the cover to the bailee's interest alone[90] or else must establish that the bailee never had any intention of covering the bailor's interest.[91] For example, an insurance of the bailee's goods and those held by the bailee "in trust or on commission" covers the interest of the owners as well as the bailee,[92] whereas an insurance on goods held "in trust[93] or on commission for which they (the assured) are responsible" covers only goods for which the assured is liable[94] and only loss or damage for which he is responsible.[95] Where the words in an insurance policy describe the assured by a particular class, and not by name, so that numerous persons might fall within that class, whether or not a particular person is insured under that policy depends on the intention of the named assured or the person who entered into the contract.[96]

42-011   **Joint and composite insurance**   If the interests of all the assureds are such that in the event of an insured loss occurring, their loss is the same because their interests in the subject matter insured is the same, the insurance may be characterised as "joint". The insurance is described as "composite" if the loss affects each of the assureds in different ways, which is often, but not always, manifested in the differing quantum of their losses.[97] A composite policy may be seen as embodying separate contracts for each interest insured.[98] The classic example of a composite

---

5) [2006] EWCA Civ 889, [2006] 2 Lloyd's Rep. 195.

[87] See *Williams v Baltic Insurance Association of London* [1924] 2 K.B. 282; *Tattersall v Drysdale* [1935] 2 K.B. 174; and now Road Traffic Act 1988 s.148(7). See below, para.42-124.

[88] *Waters v Monarch Fire and Life Assurance Co* (1856) 5 El. & Bl. 870; *Tomlinson (Hauliers) Ltd v Hepburn* [1966] A.C. 451. See, for example, *Newcastle Protection and Indemnity Association v V Ships (USA) Inc* [1996] 2 Lloyd's Rep. 515.

[89] *North British v Moffat* (1871) L.R. 7 C.P. 25; *Engel v Lancashire and General* (1925) 41 T.L.R. 408.

[90] *London and North Western Ry v Glyn* (1859) 1 El. & El. 652, 663. cf. *DG Finance Ltd v Scott* [1999] Lloyd's Rep. I.R. 387, 392.

[91] *Tomlinson (Hauliers) Ltd v Hepburn* [1966] A.C. 451, 473, 481.

[92] *Donaldson v Manchester Insurance* (1836) 14 S. 601, Ct of Sess.; *Waters v Monarch Fire and Life Assurance Co* (1856) 5 El. & Bl. 870; *Cochran v Leckie's Trustee* (1906) 8 F. 975, Ct of Sess.

[93] This means "entrusted": *Waters v Monarch Fire and Life*, above; cf. *Lake v Simmons* [1927] A.C. 487; *Rigby (Haulage) v Reliance Marine* [1956] 2 Q.B. 468; *Ramco (UK) Ltd v International Insurance Co of Hannover Ltd* [2004] EWCA Civ 675, [2004] 2 Lloyd's Rep. 595 at [8].

[94] *North British v Moffat* (1871) L.R. 7 C.P. 25; *Ramco (UK) Ltd v International Insurance Co of Hannover Ltd* [2004] EWCA Civ 675, [2004] 2 Lloyd's Rep. 595.

[95] *Engel v Lancashire and General* (1925) 41 T.L.R. 408; *Ramco (UK) Ltd v International Insurance Co of Hannover Ltd* [2004] EWCA Civ 675, [2004] 2 Lloyd's Rep. 595.

[96] *Boston Fruit Co v British & Foreign Marine Insurance Co* [1906] A.C. 336, 340–341; *National Oilwell (UK) Ltd v Davy Offshore Ltd* [1993] 2 Lloyd's Rep. 582, 596–597; *BP Exploration Operating Co Ltd v Kvaerner Oilfield Products Ltd* [2004] EWHC 999 (Comm), [2005] 1 Lloyd's Rep. 307.

[97] *Samuel & Co Ltd v Dumas* [1924] A.C. 431; *General Accident Fire & Life Assurance Corp Ltd v Midland Bank Ltd* [1940] 2 K.B. 388, 404–406; *New Hampshire Insurance Co v MGN Ltd* [1997] L.R.L.R. 24; *The State of the Netherlands v Youell* [1997] 2 Lloyd's Rep. 440; affirmed [1998] 1 Lloyd's Rep. 236; *Arab Bank Plc v Zurich Insurance Co* [1999] 1 Lloyd's Rep. 262. cf. *DSG Ltd v QBE International Insurance Ltd* [1999] Lloyd's Rep. I.R. 283.

[98] *Arab Bank Plc v Zurich Insurance Co* [1999] 1 Lloyd's Rep. 262. See also *Panzera v Simcoe & Erie Insurance Co*, 74 D.L.R. (4th) 197, 200 (1990), SC Canada. As regards the insurance of partnerships or corporate groups, see *Brit Syndicates Ltd v Grant Thornton International* [2008] UKHL 18; cf. *HLB Kidsons v Lloyd's Underwriters* [2007] EWHC 1951 (Comm), [2008] Lloyd's Rep. I.R. 237 at [80]–[97], [2008] EWCA Civ 1206, [2009] 1 Lloyd's Rep. 8, where the court construed a provi-

insurance is that which covers the interests of the landlord and tenant of property.[99] Even if any or all of the assureds (such as a bailor and bailee of property) may recover under the policy in respect of the whole loss sustained by the subject matter insured, because their interest relates to the whole of the subject matter insured, their interests, whilst "pervasive", may differ so as to characterise the insurance as composite.[100] The classification of the insurance as joint or composite is necessary to gauge the effect of a breach of duty or misconduct by one assured as regards his co-assured.[101]

Rights over the insurance money   If an assured voluntarily insures the interests   **42-012**
of others as well as his own interest, he is only obliged to hand over the balance, if any, of the insurance money after meeting the loss for which he insured himself, but if there was any obligation on the assured to cover the other interests, then it would seem that the latter have first call on the insurance money.[102] In any case where the assured receives more than the loss for which he insured himself because he covered interests other than his own, he must account to those interests,[103] but the latter have no rights to proceed against the insurer directly and, it seems, do not have proprietorial rights to any recoveries in the assured's hands; the funds held by the assured are not trust property.[104]

Statutes requiring insurable interest   Certain statutory provisions render   **42-013**
contracts of insurance void or unenforceable for lack of interest, and where such provisions are applicable, the contract will be unenforceable whether or not the insurers raise the defence.[105] The relevant statutes are the Life Assurance Act 1774 and the Marine Insurance Act 1906.[106]

---

sion requiring notification by the "Assured" as not imposing an obligation on each individual insured where the claim was brought by a partnership.

[99]   *General Accident Fire & Life Assurance Corp Ltd v Midland Bank Ltd* [1940] 2 K.B. 388.

[100]   *The State of the Netherlands v Youell*, above. See also *Tomlinson (Hauliers) Ltd v Hepburn* [1966] A.C. 451; *Petrofina (UK) Ltd v Magnaload Ltd* [1983] 2 Lloyd's Rep. 91, 95–96.

[101]   See below, paras 42-022, 42-042.

[102]   *Dalgleish v Buchanan* (1854) 16 D. 332, Ct of Sess.; *Martineau v Kitching* (1872) L.R. 7 Q.B. 436; *Ferguson v Aberdeen*, 1916 S.C. 715. The assured cannot, of course, deduct for losses for which he was not covered: *Maurice v Goldsbrough* [1939] A.C. 452.

[103]   *Holland v Smith* (1806) 6 Esp. 11; *Re Emmett Ex p. Andrews* (1816) 1 Mad. 573; *Sidaways v Todd* (1818) 2 Stark. 400; *Armitage v Winterbottom* (1840) 1 Man. & G. 130; *Lea v Hinton* (1854) 5 De G.M. & G. 823.

[104]   *DG Finance Ltd v Scott* [1999] Lloyd's Rep. I.R. 387, 392. In this case, the Court of Appeal held that the others whose interests were insured had no right to proceed directly against the insurer. However, the position might now be different under the Contracts (Rights of Third Parties) Act 1999. cf. *Cochran v Leckie's Trustee* (1906) 8 F. 975, Ct of Sess.; cf. *Vandepitte v Preferred Accident* [1933] A.C. 70, 79. If the insurance covers only the interest of the assured, others have no rights over the insurance money in law or equity: *Re Law Guarantee Trust* [1915] 1 Ch. 340; *Re Harrington Motor* [1928] Ch. 105. cf. *Foskett v McKeown* [1998] 2 W.L.R. 298 (rights of beneficiaries to policy proceeds where trustee without authority uses trust funds in payment of premium). Statutory provisions now protect third parties in liability and motor insurance cases. See below, paras 42-122—42-124.

[105]   *Anctil v Manufacturer's Life* [1899] A.C. 604; *Gedge v Royal Exchange* [1900] 2 Q.B. 214. cf. *Smith v Ralph* [1963] 2 Lloyd's Rep. 439.

[106]   The Gaming Act 1845, which had been applicable to contracts purportedly of insurance and had rendered contracts entered into by way of gaming or wagering, was repealed by ss.334 and 356 of and Sch.17 to the Gambling Act 2005, which entered into force on September 1, 2007 (SI 2006/3272).

42-014   Life Assurance Act 1774   Although directed primarily to life insurance, the Act covers a considerably wider field than its title suggests. Insurances of marine risks and of goods, however, are specifically excluded from the Act[107]; and, as a matter of construction, all forms of indemnity insurance fall outside its scope.[108] A capital investment bond paying out a benefit on the death of a person has been held to be an insurance on the life of that person even though the same benefit was also payable on early surrender.[109] The Act renders void all the contracts to which it applies which are made by way of gaming or wagering or without insurable interest.[110] It does not follow that merely because the policy is not a gaming or wagering contract, the assured has an insurable interest, although that will be a consideration.[111] The Act refers to "policies" and it may be that if the contract is not reduced to writing the Act has no effect,[112] though the word "policy" has been used to describe even oral contracts.[113] Section 2 renders unlawful any policy to which the Act applies which does not contain the names of all persons interested; or for whose use or benefit, or on whose account, the same is made.[114] Thus, the intended

---

[107] Life Assurance Act 1774 s.4. A motor policy containing, inter alia, third-party liability cover has been held to be an insurance on goods: *Williams v Baltic Insurance Association of London* [1924] 2 K.B. 282; and so has an insurance against loss of money: *Prudential Staff Union v Hall* [1947] K.B. 282.

[108] *Mark Rowlands Ltd v Berni Inns Ltd* [1985] Q.B. 211 (limiting the Act to insurances which provide for the payment of a specified sum upon the happening of an insured event). The view of the Court of Appeal in the *Mark Rowlands* case to the effect that the Act was not intended to apply to indemnity insurance was expressly approved by the Privy Council in *Siu v Eastern Insurance Co Ltd* [1994] 2 A.C. 199. See *Feasey v Sun Life Assurance Co of Canada* [2003] EWCA Civ 885, [2003] Lloyd's Rep. I.R. 693.

[109] *Fuji Finance Inc v Aetna Life Insurance Co Ltd* [1997] Ch. 173, CA, holding that it was enough that a benefit was payable on an event which was sufficiently life or death related (as was the case here, since the policy came to an end on the death of the person, and the right to surrender was related to the continuance of life). Furthermore, even *were* it necessary for the benefit payable upon surrender to be different from the benefit upon death, the Court of Appeal saw no reason why the difference had to arise from the description or formula adopted for the purpose of fixing the benefit payable. It was sufficient that, given market fluctuations, in practice it was almost inevitable that the benefit payable on death would be different from the value payable on surrender (which would, itself, vary according to when surrender occurred).

[110] s.1. For the purposes of s.1, the fact that some of the persons who are the subject of the insurance were not identifiable at the inception of the cover and might change over the period of the cover did not affect the insurable interest of the mutual insurer who had promised to indemnify the shipowner in respect of crew on board his vessels; *Feasey v Sun Life Assurance Co of Canada* [2002] EWHC 868 (Comm), [2002] All E.R. (Comm) 492; affirmed [2003] EWCA Civ 885, [2003] Lloyd's Rep. I.R. 693. For the time when the interest is required, see below, para.42-017. Married Women's Property Act 1882 s.11 provides that a married woman may take out a policy on her own life or on the life of her husband. Civil Partnership Act 2004 s.253 provides that a civil partner has an interest in the life of the other civil partner for the purposes of the Life Assurance Act 1774 s.1. See also Civil Partnership Act 2004 s.70.

[111] *Feasey v Sun Life Assurance Co of Canada* [2003] EWCA Civ 885, [2003] Lloyd's Rep. I.R. 693. *O'Kane v Jones* [2003] EWHC 3470 (Comm), [2004] 1 Lloyd's Rep. 389 at [145].

[112] *Roebuck v Hammerton* (1778) 2 Cowp. 737; *Good v Elliott* (1790) 3 T.R. 693, 706; *Paterson v Powell* (1832) 9 Bing. 320, 328.

[113] See above, para.42-001.

[114] *Hodson v Observer Life* (1857) 8 El. & Bl. 40; *Evans v Bignold* (1869) L.R. 4 Q.B. 622. Insurance Companies Amendment Act 1973 s.50 provides that s.2 of the 1774 Act does not invalidate a policy for the benefit of unnamed persons from time-to-time falling within a specified class if the class is stated with sufficient particularity so that the identity of all persons within the class can be established. In *Feasey v Sun Life Assurance Co of Canada* [2003] EWCA Civ 885, [2003] Lloyd's Rep. I.R. 693, the Court of Appeal applied a similar consideration in holding that the mere fact that the lives insured were identified by a class and not by name did not mean that the policy was

beneficiary must have an interest and be named in the policy.[115] However, it may be that a trustee without interest, who insures for the benefit of someone with interest, can recover the whole amount insured.[116] Section 3 limits the amount recoverable to that representing the assured's own interest[117]; this section appears inapposite to life insurance which is not an indemnity contract, except in cases where an assured's interest is measurable in money's worth.[118]

The Marine Insurance Act 1906   This Act applies to marine insurance, which is **42-015** defined essentially as a contract of indemnity insurance against "marine losses".[119] The Act provides that any claim by an assured without an insurable interest at the relevant time is effectively unenforceable; it further renders void[120] any such contract entered into without either interest and without the expectation of acquiring interest, and any contract of insurance containing a term obviating the requirement that the assured should prove his interest. Section 5 requires the assured to have an insurable interest in the marine adventure insured, in particular by standing in a "legal or equitable relation to the adventure" or any property within the adventure of a nature such that he may benefit by the safety of the subject matter insured or be prejudiced by its adversity. The existence of such a "legal or equitable relation" however is not essential to the existence of an insurable interest for the purposes of the Marine Insurance Act 1906.[121]

Impact of the Gambling Act 2005   On September 1, 2007, the Gambling Act **42-016** 2005 entered into force.[122] The Act makes no express reference to insurance contracts. Although the Act repealed the Gaming Act 1845,[123] which applied to purported contracts of insurance, no express attempt was made by the Act to amend or repeal the Life Assurance Act 1774 or the Marine Insurance Act 1906.[124] Insofar as either Act makes provision for the requirement of an insurable interest, the 2005 Act can have no effect. There is a distinction between the want of an insurable interest and a gaming or wagering policy. The lack of an insurable interest does not of itself render the insurance contract a gaming or wagering contract. A contract purportedly of insurance will be a gaming or wagering contract if the assured lacks an insurable interest at the relevant time and if the assured has no expectation of

---

invalidated by s.1 of the 1774 Act.

[115] *M'Farlane v Royal London Friendly Society* (1886) 2 T.L.R. 755.

[116] *Collett v Morrison* (1851) 9 Hare 162.

[117] *Feasey v Sun Life Assurance Co of Canada* [2003] EWCA Civ 885, [2003] Lloyd's Rep. I.R. 693.

[118] Such as when a creditor takes out a policy on the life of his debtor: Clarke, *The Law of Insurance Contracts* (looseleaf), para.3-2; cf. *Fuji Finance Inc v Aetna Life Insurance Co Ltd* [1997] Ch. 173, CA (investment account policy). The purpose of s.3 is to outlaw gaming: *Feasey v Sun Life Assurance Co of Canada* [2002] EWHC 868 (Comm), [2002] 2 All E.R. (Comm), 492; affirmed [2002] EWCA Civ 885, [2003] Lloyd's Rep. I.R. 693. This purpose may have to be readdressed in light of the Gambling Act 2005. See below, para.42-016.

[119] See s.1.

[120] s.4. The parties to such a contract may be subject to criminal penalties: Marine Insurance (Gambling Policies) Act 1909.

[121] *Feasey v Sun Life Assurance Co of Canada* [2003] EWCA Civ 885, [2003] Lloyd's Rep. I.R. 693; *O'Kane v Jones* [2003] EWHC 3470 (Comm), [2004] 1 Lloyd's Rep. 389 at [145].

[122] SI 2006/3272.

[123] ss.334 and 356 and Sch.17.

[124] Or indeed the Marine Insurance (Gambling Policies) Act 1909.

acquiring such an interest.[125] The question remains what impact the 2005 Act has on the statutory provisions in the 1774 and 1906 Acts rendering gaming policies void. In one sense, this may be an arid issue, given that the lack of an insurable interest of its own is currently sufficient to render the insurance contract unenforceable or void. It may be the case, albeit practically unlikely, that a contract of insurance supported by an insurable interest at the same time is still a gaming contract, although the courts can (erroneously) equate the two concepts.[126] Section 335 of the 2005 Act provides that the fact that a contract relates to gambling shall not prevent its enforcement, but then states that this provision is "without prejudice to any rule of law preventing the enforcement of a contract on the grounds of unlawfulness (other than a rule relating specifically to gambling)". Although there are clearly issues of the true statutory interpretation of this provision, it appears unlikely that the 2005 Act will affect s.1 of the Life Assurance Act 1774 or s.4 of the Marine Insurance Act 1906, given that the 2005 Act makes no express provision in respect of these statutes. Further, it is questionable whether the making of an insurance contract, even a purported insurance contract, is likely to constitute gambling for the purposes of the 2005 Act.[127] Although the general definition of "gambling" and "betting" is potentially applicable to insurance contracts,[128] s.10 of the 2005 Act provides that a "bet" does not include a bet the making or accepting of which is a regulated activity within the meaning of the Financial Services and Markets Act 2000 and the making of an insurance contract is a regulated activity.[129]

42-017 **When interest is required** The interest of the assured in the subject matter of the insurance need not be present throughout the period of the cover. The time at which the interest must be shown to have existed, in order to enable the assured to recover, depends upon the terms and nature of the contract and statutory provisions. Express contractual terms relating to the time of interest are rare, but insurances which are contracts of indemnity,[130] whether valued or unvalued, required the assured to have an interest at the time of loss,[131] whether or not he had an interest previously during the period of cover, save in the case of retrospective insurance "lost or not lost", where the interest may be acquired after the loss.[132] Goods which are appropriated to the assured's sale contract and the insurance contract after they have been damaged may be insured.[133] The Life Assurance Act 1774 has been held to require the

---

[125] See Marine Insurance Act 1906 s.4(2)(a); *MacGillivray on Insurance Law*, 14th edn (2018), para.1-027, 1-039.

[126] cf. *Feasey v Sun Life Assurance Co of Canada* [2003] EWCA Civ 885, [2003] Lloyd's Rep. I.R. 693 at [53].

[127] See also above, para.41-009.

[128] ss.3 and 9.

[129] Financial Services and Markets Act 2000 (Regulated Activities) Order 2001 (SI 2001/544) arts 3, 4, 10, 64, 75 and Sch.1.

[130] See above, para.42-003.

[131] *Anderson v Morice* (1876) 1 App. Cas. 713. Apart from the statutory provision considered below, interest at any other time appears to be unnecessary: *Williams v Baltic* [1924] 2 K.B. 282, 291.

[132] *Sutherland v Pratt* (1943) 11 M. & W. 296. cf. Marine Insurance Act 1906 s.6(1), and see below, para.42-024.

[133] It may be that the loss is sustained by the assured when he acquires his insurable interest by the fortuitous appropriation of damaged goods. See *Wünsche Handelsgesellschaft International mbH v Tai Ping Insurance Co Ltd* [1998] 2 Lloyd's Rep. 8, where it was also held that goods which were missing could not be appropriated to the contract.

assured in contracts to which it applies[134] to have an interest at the time of entering into the contract,[135] so that if a policy governed by the Act is a contract of indemnity the assured may have to establish his interest at the time of the loss and at the time of making the contract. Furthermore, since the Act limits recovery to the amount of the assured's interest[136] and this interest is that existing at the date of the contract,[137] it seems that only in cases where the subject matter of the insurance (as opposed to the interest therein) is by its nature variable can the assured recover the value of his interest at the time of the loss, if that is greater than the earlier value.[138]

3. The Event Insured Against

Event insured against An insurer undertakes to pay money upon the happening of the event[139] or events stipulated in the contract. The nature of the event, the time and place of its occurrence and the nature of the loss suffered (in indemnity insurance) must be within the scope of the contractual definition.

42-018

---

[134] See above, para.42-014.
[135] *Dalby v India and London Life* (1854) 15 C.B. 365. This was a case of life insurance, but there seems to be no reason why the same reasoning should not apply to other policies covered by the Act. See also *Feasey v Sun Life Assurance Co of Canada* [2002] EWHC 868 (Comm), [2002] 2 All E.R. (Comm) 492; affirmed [2003] EWCA Civ 885, [2003] Lloyd's Rep. I.R. 693.
[136] See above, para.42-014.
[137] *Dalby v India and London Life* (1854) 15 C.B. 365. See above, n.135.
[138] *Barnes v London, Edinburgh and Glasgow Life* [1892] 1 Q.B. 864, 867. cf. *Griffiths v Fleming* [1909] 1 K.B. 805, 810.
[139] The word "event" here refers to the "peril" insured against. In many policies, the word "event" may be used to refer to the originating cause of the peril. This, however, is not necessarily so, being a matter of construction of the contract. As to the meaning of the words "event", "occurrence", "cause" and "claim", see *Kuwait Airways Corp v Kuwait Insurance Co SAK* [1996] 1 Lloyd's Rep. 664, 686, QB, [1997] 2 Lloyd's Rep. 687, CA, [1999] 1 Lloyd's Rep. 803, HL. *Caudle v Sharp* [1995] L.R.L.R. 433; *Cox v Bankside Members' Agency Ltd* [1996] 1 Lloyd's Rep. 26; *Axa Reinsurance (UK) Plc v Field* [1996] 1 W.L.R. 1026; *Municipal Mutual Insurance Ltd v Sea Insurance Co* [1998] C.L.C. 957; *Brown v GIO Insurance Ltd* [1998] Lloyd's Rep. I.R. 201; *Roberts Irving & Burns v Stone* [1998] Lloyd's Rep. I.R. 258; *Spire Healthcare Ltd v Royal & Sun Alliance Insurance Plc* [2016] EWHC 3278 (Comm), [2017] Lloyd's Rep. I.R. 118, [2018] EWCA Civ 317, [2018] Lloyd's Rep. I.R. 425. In *Simmonds v Gammell* [2016] EWHC 2515 (Comm), [2016] 2 Lloyd's Rep. 631 at [22]–[27], Sir Jeremy Cooke confirmed that in identifying an aggregating "event", it should be appropriate to the aggregating function, it should be a common factor which could properly be described as an event, and it should be causative of the losses claimed under the policy, which need not be proximate, but must not be too remote. Such words often define the application of monetary limits or excess or deductible clauses and must be construed having regard to the policy as a whole and applied having regard to the degree of unity of time, cause and location: *Mann v Lexington Insurance Co* [2001] 1 Lloyd's Rep. 1. See also *Aioi Nissay Dowa Insurance Co Ltd v Heraldglen Ltd* [2013] EWHC 154 (Comm), [2013] 2 All E.R. 231, where it was held that losses arising on a reinsurance contract in respect of liabilities incurred by reason of the attacks on the World Trade Center in September 2001 arose out of two events, not one. The words "related series of acts or omissions" have been interpreted to embrace several losses having a common causal relationship, meaning that the acts or events together resulted in each of the claims; the fact that claims might have the same underlying cause and were of a very similar nature was not sufficient to constitute a "related series" in *Lloyd's TSB General Insurance Holdings v Lloyds Bank Group Insurance Co Ltd* [2003] UKHL 48, [2003] Lloyd's Rep. I.R. 623 at [27]–[29], [51]. See also *AIG Europe Ltd v Woodman* [2017] UKSC 18, [2017] 1 W.L.R. 1168.

(a) The Nature of the Event

42-019 **Nature of event** In construing contracts of insurance the courts apply four principles which have the effect of excluding the insurer's liability on the occurrence of particular events, even though such events prima facie may appear to fall within the contractual definition. These principles relate to uncertainty, inherent vice, wilful misconduct and public policy.

42-020 **Uncertainty** Contracts of insurance are construed to cover events which are uncertain either as to their occurrence or as to the time of the occurrence.[140] Losses occasioned to the subject matter in the ordinary course of affairs,[141] such as ordinary depreciation and wear and tear, do not therefore entitle the assured to recover unless an express stipulation enables him to do so, and simply to insure against "all risks" is not enough.[142] The courts consider that it is extremely unlikely that an insurance contract will indemnify the assured against a loss or a peril, which is inevitable, that is which is not fortuitous.[143] Fortuity is to be determined at the time of the making of the contract or, possibly, the inception of the risk.

42-021 **Inherent vice** Contracts of insurance are construed to cover losses arising from events that impinge upon the subject matter, and not those that arise from its very nature and condition. Losses arising from such an internal cause, termed "inherent vice", will not be covered[144] unless there is an express stipulation to that effect,[145]

---

[140] The requirement of a fortuity will often be found to exist, even if the language of the policy does not expressly require it: see e.g. *CA Blackwell (Contracts) Ltd v Gerling General Insurance Co* [2007] EWHC 94 (Comm), [2007] Lloyd's Rep. I.R. 511, at [42]–[43]. See above, para.42-001; Bennett [2007] L.M.C.L.Q. 315.

[141] *The Xantho* (1887) 12 App. Cas. 503, 509. See also *Promet Engineering (Singapore) Pte Ltd v Sturge (The Nukila)* [1997] 2 Lloyd's Rep. 146.

[142] *British & Foreign Marine Insurance Co Ltd v Gaunt* [1921] 2 A.C. 41. cf. *Harris v Poland* [1941] 1 K.B. 462. An event may be fortuitous even if it is foreseeable: *CA Blackwell (Contracts) Ltd v Gerling General Insurance Co* [2007] EWHC 94 (Comm), [2007] Lloyd's Rep. I.R. 511 at [44]– [48]; *Marina Offshore Pte Ltd v China Insurance Co (Singapore) Pte Ltd* [2006] SGCA 28, [2007] 1 Lloyd's Rep. 66 at [56] Singapore Court of Appeal. In *Quek Kwee Kee v American International Assurance Co Ltd* [2016] SGHC 47, [2016] Lloyd's Rep. I.R. 660 at [42]–[54], the Singapore High Court confirmed that the unexpected consequences of a voluntary act may constitute an "accident" under an insurance contract, i.e. a fortuity. See also *Leeds Beckett University v Travelers Insurance Co Ltd* [2017] EWHC 558 (TCC), [2017] Lloyd's Rep. I.R. 417, at [199]–[208].

[143] *British & Foreign Marine Insurance Co Ltd v Gaunt*, above, at 52, 57. In *Soya GmbH v White* [1982] 1 Lloyd's Rep. 136, 149; affirmed on other grounds [1983] 1 Lloyd's Rep. 122, Donaldson L.J. stated that it was "highly improbable" that the parties would insure an inevitability, but preferred to use the term "known certainty", rather than "inevitability", because it was commonly the case that inevitabilities were insured. It is suggested that this approach to construction should apply to all inevitabilities, known or unknown. The fundamental nature of insurance contracts is that they insure risks, not certainties. See also *Leeds Beckett University v Travelers Insurance Co Ltd* [2017] EWHC 558 (TCC), [2017] Lloyd's Rep. I.R. 417, at [199]–[208]. Donaldson L.J. referred to the fact that overdue ships or cargoes can be insured, notwithstanding that the loss might already have occurred. However, such marine losses which have already occurred will only be insured if the vessel or cargo is insured "lost or not lost": see s.6(1), r.1, Sch.1 to the Marine Insurance Act 1906.

[144] *Taylor v Dunbar* (1869) L.R. 4 C.P. 206; *Pink v Fleming* (1890) 25 Q.B.D. 396; *Wadsworth Lighterage v Sea Insurance* (1929) 35 Com. Cas. 1; *British & Foreign Marine Insurance Co Ltd v Gaunt* [1921] 2 A.C. 41; Marine Insurance Act 1906 s.55(2)(c).

[145] See the illustrations considered by Sellers J. in *Berk v Style* [1956] 1 Q.B. 180; *Overseas Commodities v Style* [1958] 1 Lloyd's Rep. 546.

and again an insurance against "all risks" is not enough.[146] "Inherent vice" refers to the risk of deterioration of the subject matter insured as a result of its natural behaviour or the inability of the subject matter insured to withstand the ordinary incidents of carriage or ordinary use without the involvement of an external fortuitous event.[147] Of course, certain types of insurance by their nature cover instances of inherent vice, notwithstanding this general principle of construction. Life insurance, for example, covers death from disease and senility as well as from accident.[148] Similarly, an insurance against loss caused by latent defects is regarded as cover for inherent vice.[149]

Wilful misconduct   Contracts of insurance are construed as protecting the as-   **42-022**
sured against misfortune, and not against his own wilful misconduct. If the assured himself intentionally and without justification[150] brings about the event insured against, then in the absence of express provision he will not be entitled to recover.[151] If the assured's deliberate act was itself the product of insanity, so that it could be said that the assured was labouring under such a defect of reason, from disease of the mind, as not to know the nature and quality of the act he was doing or, if he did know it, that he did not know that what he was doing was wrong, the assured would not be disabled from recovering under the policy.[152] The disability from recovering is confined to the assured[153] whose wilful misconduct (or that of a third party procured or connived at by the assured) caused the loss.[154] Another assured with a separate interest in the same subject matter may recover to the extent of his interest,[155] and loss caused by the wilful misconduct of third parties not

---

146 See above, para.42-020.
147 *Soya GmbH v White* [1983] 1 Lloyd's Rep. 122, 126; *Noten BV v Harding* [1990] 2 Lloyd's Rep. 283; *Global Process Systems Inc v Syarikat Takaful Malaysia Berhad* [2009] EWCA Civ 1398, [2010] Lloyd's Rep. I.R. 221, [2011] UKSC 5, [2011] Lloyd's Rep. I.R. 302 (disapproving *Mayban General Insurance BHD v Alstom Power Plants Ltd* [2004] EWHC 1038 (Comm), [2004] 2 Lloyd's Rep. 609). In *Global Process Systems*, the Supreme Court held that a loss will be caused by an inherent vice, where the inherent vice is the sole cause of the loss.
148 Though conversely an accident policy does not cover death by natural disease: *Winspear v Accident Insurance* (1880) 6 Q.B.D. 42; *Isitt v Railway Passengers'* (1889) 22 Q.B.D. 504.
149 *The Caribbean Sea* [1980] 1 Lloyd's Rep. 338, 347.
150 *Gordon v Rimmington* (1807) 1 Camp. 123; *National Oilwell (UK) Ltd v Davy Offshore Ltd* [1993] 2 Lloyd's Rep. 582 at 622 (as to meaning of "misconduct"). cf. *Compania Maritima San Basilio SA v Oceanus Mutual Underwriting Association (Bermuda) Ltd (The Eurysthenes)* [1977] 1 Q.B. 49; *Manifest Shipping & Co Ltd v Uni-Polaris Insurance Co Ltd (The Star Sea)* [2001] UKHL 1, [2001] 2 W.L.R. 170 concerning the assured's "privity" under Marine Insurance Act 1906 s.39(5). See also *Genesisuk.net Ltd v Allianz Insurance Ltd* [2014] EWHC 3676 (QB) at [20]–[21].
151 *Thurtell v Beaumont* (1823) 1 Bing. 339; *Beresford v Royal* [1938] A.C. 586, 595; *Yorkshire Dale SS Co v Minister of War Transport* [1942] A.C. 691, 704. Marine Insurance Act 1906 s.55(2)(a) does not permit the policy to allow an assured to recover in respect of his own wilful misconduct: *The State of the Netherlands v Youell* [1997] 2 Lloyd's Rep. 440; affirmed [1998] 1 Lloyd's Rep. 236.
152 *Porter v Zurich Insurance Co* [2009] EWHC 376 (QB), [2010] Lloyd's Rep. I.R. 373 at [17]–[24].
153 And his assigns. cf. *British Equitable v GWR* (1869) 48 L.J. Ch. 314. As to whose acts are to be attributed to the assured in respect of a clause excluding from cover the assured's deliberate acts, see, *National Oilwell (UK) Ltd v Davy Offshore Ltd* [1993] 2 Lloyd's Rep. 582 at 620–621; *KR v Royal & Sun Alliance Plc* [2006] EWCA Civ 1454, [2007] Lloyd's Rep. I.R. 368.
154 *Midland Insurance v Smith* (1881) 6 Q.B.D. 561; *Samuel v Dumas* [1924] A.C. 431; see also *Rankin v North Waterloo Farmers Mutual Insurance Co* (1979) 25 O.R. (2d) 102 Can.
155 Provided he is innocent and so long as his recovery would not necessarily benefit the wrongdoer: *Samuel v Dumas*, above; *Central Bank of India v Guardian Assurance* (1936) 54 Ll.L. Rep. 247; *Lombard Australia v NRMA Insurance* [1969] 1 Lloyd's Rep. 575. See also *The State of the Netherlands v Youell* [1997] 2 Lloyd's Rep. 440. See above, para.42-011. cf. *Bains v Yorkshire Insur-*

procured or connived at by the assured is not within this rule,[156] though loss through intentional acts of third parties may not be within the scope of the cover granted.[157] Except in the case of marine insurance,[158] losses caused by the wilful misconduct of the assured may be covered by express stipulation or necessary implication. In such cases, the assured or his estate may recover[159] unless the misconduct is of such a kind that it would be contrary to public policy to allow this to happen.[160] Losses caused by the negligence of the assured do not fall within the principles discussed in this paragraph[161]; but the assured's conduct may be so reckless as to be regarded as wilful,[162] or considerations of public policy may arise so as to disentitle recovery even in the absence of any deliberate intention to cause loss.[163]

42-023 **Public policy** The assured will not be entitled to recover upon the occurrence of an event if it would be contrary to public policy to allow him to do so.[164] Considerations of public policy are difficult to define, but it is clear that a person will not normally be permitted to recover, or be indemnified, under an insurance policy if to do so would allow him to benefit, directly or indirectly, from his own deliberate

---

ance, 38 D.L.R. (2d) 417 (1963); and compare the position as regards fraudulent claims. See below, para.42-098.

[156] *Shaw v Robberds* (1837) 6 Ad. & El. 75, 84; *Midland Insurance v Smith* (1881) 6 Q.B.D. 561 (assured's wife); *Letts v Excess Insurance* (1916) 32 T.L.R. 361 (stranger); *Lind v Mitchell* (1928) 45 T.L.R. 54, 56 (assured's servants). See also, *Schiffshypothekenbank zu Luebeck v Compton (The Alexion Hope)* [1988] 1 Lloyd's Rep. 311.

[157] e.g. insurance against "collapse" of a building would not cover intentional demolition: *Allen Billposting v Drysdale* [1939] 4 All E.R. 113.

[158] Marine Insurance Act 1906 s.55(2)(a); *The State of the Netherlands v Youell* [1997] 2 Lloyd's Rep. 440.

[159] *Moore v Woolsey* (1854) 4 E. & B. 243; *Beresford v Royal* [1938] A.C. 586, 600.

[160] See below, para.42-023.

[161] *Austin v Drewe* (1815) 4 Camp. 360, 362; *Busk v Royal Exchange* (1818) 2 B. & Ald. 73; *Cornish v Accident Insurance* (1889) 23 Q.B.D. 453; *Cole v Accident Insurance* (1889) 5 T.L.R. 736; *Trinder v Thames and Mersey Marine* [1898] 2 Q.B. 114; *Harris v Poland* [1914] 1 K.B. 462; *Yorkshire Dale SS Co v Minister of War Transport* [1942] A.C. 691, 704; *Walters v Whessoe and Shell Refining Co* (1960) 6 B.L.R. 23, 30; *Global Tankers Inc v Amercoat Europa NV (The Diane)* [1977] 1 Lloyd's Rep. 61, 66; *Marcel Beller Ltd v Hayden* [1978] 1 Q.B. 694; and see also *Pentagon Construction (1969) Co Ltd v United States Fidelity & Guarantee Co* [1978] 1 Lloyd's Rep. 93. cf. Marine Insurance Act 1906 s.55(2)(a).

[162] See, e.g. *Pipon v Cope* (1808) 1 Camp. 434; as explained in *Trinder v Thames and Mersey Marine* [1898] 2 Q.B. 114, per Collins L.J. at 129. cf. *Mutual of Omaha Insurance Co v Stats*, 87 D.L.R. (3d) 169 (1978) Can; *CNA Assurance Co v MacIsaac*, 102 D.L.R. (3d) 160 (1979) Can; and also the approach in *Gray v Barr* [1971] 2 Q.B. 554, 567, 580 and 587. See also *Dhak v Insurance Co of North America (UK) Ltd* [1996] 1 W.L.R. 936 where it was held, in the context of a personal accident policy which covered bodily injury "caused by accidental means", that bodily injury which was the natural and direct consequence of a course of conduct embarked upon by an assured taking a calculated risk (in this case, excessive alcohol consumption) was not covered by the policy. In *Patrick v Royal London Mutual Insurance Society Ltd* [2006] EWCA Civ 421, [2007] Lloyd's Rep. I.R. 85, the Court of Appeal considered a policy provision which excluded claims arising from "*any wilful, malicious or criminal acts*" and held that the insured will have acted wilfully if he was reckless as to the consequences of his act, i.e. if he does something knowing that it is risky or not caring whether it is risky or not.

[163] See below, para.42-023.

[164] As to illegality and public policy in the context of a marine war risks policy and the payment of ransom to recover detained property, see *Royal Boskalis Westminster NV v Mountain* [1997] 2 All E.R. 929; *Masefield AG v Amlin Corporate Member Ltd* [2011] EWCA Civ 24, [2011] 1 Lloyd's Rep. 630. For the effect of public policy/illegality on contracts in general, see Vol.I, Ch.16.

criminal conduct.[165] Nor may a person enforce an insurance to indemnify him against a fine or other punishment imposed for committing a criminal offence, at least where the offence was committed deliberately or the assured's conduct is sufficiently anti-social.[166] Similarly, a contract to indemnify a person against the consequences of an intentional and manifestly serious civil wrong or tort is void or at least unenforceable.[167] Therefore, an assured who is liable to a third party by reason of his deceit could not recover under a contract of insurance against his legal liability.[168] On the other hand, not all torts, even if committed deliberately, are unindemnifiable. The prohibition will depend on the seriousness of the act, whether it was committed intentionally and the anti-social nature of the act.[169] There must be turpitude and a sufficient degree of causation between the illegality and the claim under the policy before the assured will be disabled from pursuing a claim under an insurance contract by reason of illegality.[170] The position is more difficult where recovery is sought in respect of a loss which has been caused unintentionally in the course of committing a criminal offence, since much may turn upon an assessment of the competing policy considerations at stake, but it is clear that there are at least some circumstances in which an assured will be denied recovery even

---

[165] *Amicable Assurance v Bolland* (1830) 4 Bli.(N.S.) 194; *Beresford v Royal* [1938] A.C. 586; *Euro-Diam Ltd v Bathurst* [1988] 2 W.L.R. 517, 526. Thus, for example, an assured is precluded from recovery under his policy for the theft of his goods if he has evaded paying import duty on them (*Geismar v Sun Alliance & London Ltd* [1978] Q.B. 383); and a beneficiary under a life policy is precluded from benefiting from the policy if he murders the assured (*Cleaver v Mutual Reserve* [1892] 1 Q.B. 147; *Davitt v Titcumb* [1990] Ch. 110). At common law, the same rule probably applies for manslaughter (see *Re Hall* [1914] P. 1); but see now the Forfeiture Act 1982, which gives the court general discretion to permit a person who has unlawfully killed another to receive the benefits of, inter alia, that other's life assurance policy. (*Re K (deceased)* [1986] Ch. 180; *Dunbar v Plant* [1997] 4 All E.R. 289.) The Act, however, does not apply to murder: see s.5. Where the assured is insane within the M'Naghten rules, he may not have the requisite state of mind to debar him from his claim on the grounds of deliberate misconduct: *Porter v Zurich Insurance Co* [2009] EWHC 376 (QB), [2010] Lloyd's Rep. I.R. 373.

[166] See *Askey v Golden Wine Co* [1948] 2 All E.R. 35; cf. *Osman v J Ralph Moss Ltd* [1970] 1 Lloyd's Rep. 313; *Charlton v Fisher* [2001] EWCA Civ 112, [2002] Q.B. 578 at [58], [60]. Such insurances which are contrary to public policy are totally void: *Haseldine v Hosken* [1933] 1 K.B. 822, 837. Public policy is unlikely to defeat a recovery where the insurance is compulsorily required by law (such as motor insurance): *Lancashire CC v Municipal Mutual Insurance Ltd* [1996] 3 All E.R. 545, 554. See *Bristol Alliance Ltd Partnership v Williams* [2011] EWHC 1657 (QB), [2012] R.T.R. 9.

[167] *Burrows v Rhodes* [1899] 1 Q.B. 816, 828; *Haseldine v Hosken* [1933] 1 K.B. 822. A claim for an indemnity under an insurance policy will be defeated where the loss sustained is sufficiently caused by the illegal or tortious conduct: *Delaney v Pickett* [2011] EWCA Civ 1532, [31]–[37], [60], [73].

[168] It is an open question whether a contract to indemnify a person against the consequences of his libelling of another is enforceable at common law (see *MacGillivray on Insurance Law*, 14th edn (2018), para.30–010). However, under the Defamation Act 1952 s.11, such a contract is not "unlawful unless at the time of the publication that person knows that the matter is defamatory and does not reasonably believe there is a good defence to any action brought upon it". The implication is that an intentional defamation cannot be indemnified.

[169] *Hardy v Motor Insurers' Bureau* [1964] 2 Q.B. 745, 767–770. In *Les Laboratoires Servier v Apotex Inc* [2014] UKSC 55, [2015] A.C. 430 at [23]–[29], the Supreme Court said that generally the conduct should be criminal or quasi-criminal before public policy might be engaged.

[170] *Gray v Thames Trains Ltd* [2009] UKHL 33, [2009] A.C. 1339 at [27]–[30], [51]–[54]; *Delaney v Pickett* [2011] EWCA Civ 1532, [2013] Lloyd's Rep I.R. 24 at [34]–[37]; *Les Laboratoires Servier v Apotex Inc* [2012] EWCA Civ 593, [2013] Bus. L.R. 80 at [77]–[78], [2014] UKSC 55, [2015] A.C. 430, at [22]–[29]; *Sea Glory Maritime Co v Al Sagr National Insurance Co* [2013] EWHC 2116 (Comm), [2014] 1 Lloyd's Rep. 14 at [303].

though the loss was not caused on purpose.[171] It is not contrary to public policy for an employer to recover under a contract of insurance in respect of his vicarious liability to pay damages in respect of the oppressive or unlawful acts of his servants or agents.[172] Unlike the first three principles discussed above, moreover, public policy considerations will override even express stipulations providing for cover against the forbidden event.[173] Save where an insurance policy is entirely void, however (as being illegal from the outset, or prohibited by statute), the inability of an original assured to recover under the policy on account of his unlawful conduct will not necessarily prevent third parties from enforcing the policy themselves,[174] provided of course that the loss falls within the scope of the insurance cover. This is because the assured's inability to recover on the grounds of public policy is a personal disability.[175] However, where the third party stands in the shoes of the assured under the Third Parties (Rights against Insurers) Act 1930 or the Third Parties (Rights against Insurers) Act 2010,[176] public policy will defeat any claim made by that third party if the claim arises out of the assured's criminal conduct.[177] The principles of public policy as they apply to insurance contracts have been cast into some doubt by the recent decision of the majority of the Supreme Court in *Patel v Mirza*,[178] where it was held that a claim will not be enforced if it is contrary to the public interest, meaning that it would be harmful to the integrity of the legal system (or, possibly, certain aspects of public morality). The Supreme Court decided not to follow the reliance test adopted by the House of Lords in *Tinsley v Milligan*.[179]

---

[171] See *Gray v Barr* [1971] 2 Q.B. 554, where an insured was denied any indemnity under his third-party "hearth and home" policy because (inter alia) the death he had unintentionally caused arose whilst threatening another with a gun (although acquitted of murder and manslaughter); but cf. *Tinline v White Cross Insurance* [1921] 3 K.B. 327; and *James v British General* [1927] 2 K.B. 311 (both approved in *Gray v Barr*), where assureds were not precluded from recovering under motor policies which included third-party risks, even though convicted of manslaughter in respect of the deaths caused by their driving. See also *Charlton v Fisher* [2001] EWCA Civ 112, [2002] Q.B. 578 at [58], [60].

[172] *Lancashire CC v Municipal Mutual Insurance Ltd* [1996] 3 All E.R. 545, holding that there was nothing contrary to public policy per se in an insurance which, amongst other things, covered the vicarious liability of a chief constable to pay exemplary damages for wrongful arrest, malicious prosecution, and false imprisonment.

[173] *Beresford v Royal* [1938] A.C. 586. The abolition of the crime of suicide in 1961 might well produce a different decision on the same facts today, although in the absence of a stipulation covering suicide, the insurance would still be unenforceable since the event would have resulted from the wilful act of the assured: see above, para.42-022.

[174] Thus, assignees of a life insurance policy may be able to sue on the policy (*Moore v Woolsey* (1854) 4 El. & Bl. 243), at least if they provided valuable consideration for the assignment (see *Beresford v Royal* [1938] A.C. 586, 601, 605); and a person who is deliberately run down or injured by a motorist is not deprived of his statutory right against the motorist's insurer (as to which, see below, para.42-124) by virtue of the motorist's unlawful conduct: see *Hardy v Motor Insurer's Bureau* [1964] 2 Q.B. 745; *Gardner v Moore* [1984] A.C. 548 (both cases arising in the context of the Motor Insurers' Bureau scheme). See also *Total Graphics Ltd v AGF Insurance Ltd* [1997] 1 Lloyd's Rep. 599, 606; cf. *Charlton v Fisher* [2001] EWCA Civ 112, [2002] Q.B. 578; *Bristol Alliance Ltd Partnership v Williams* [2011] EWHC 1657 (QB), [2012] R.T.R. 9.

[175] *Total Graphics Ltd v AGF Insurance Ltd* [1997] 1 Lloyd's Rep. 599, 606.

[176] See, below, para.42-122.

[177] *Charlton v Fisher* [2001] EWCA Civ 112, [2002] Q.B. 578.

[178] [2016] UKSC 42, [2016] 3 W.L.R. 399 at [101], [120], [174], [186].

[179] [1994] 1 A.C. 340. See above, paras 16-018 et seq.

(b) The Time of the Event

The period of cover Contracts of insurance may stipulate the time when the **42-024**
cover begins and ends but difficulties may arise in deciding whether the commencement or the termination dates stated in the contract are included in the period of
cover. In accordance with ordinary rules of construction the courts seek to determine
the intention of the parties from the terms of their contract but it seems that in cases
of doubt the question is likely to be decided in favour of the assured.[180] Certain rules
of construction should be noted. First, unless otherwise stipulated, "month" means
calendar month.[181] Secondly, a person becomes over N years of age on reaching his
Nth birthday.[182] Thirdly, a period "from"[183] or "after"[184] a named day excludes that
day, and a period "until" a named day includes that day.[185] Lastly, in the absence
of provisions to the contrary, an insurance contract does not apply retrospectively.[186]

Event and loss during period of cover Subject to the terms of the policy, the **42-025**
event insured against must happen during the period of the insurance[187] and (in
indemnity insurance[188]) the loss resulting from that event must, it seems, also occur in that period,[189] though it is immaterial that the full extent of the loss is not
known or made manifest until later,[190] and generally, of course, the event and the
loss coincide. Insurances against liabilities to third parties[191] are usually construed
as contracts indemnifying against the incurring of a liability and not the discharge
of that liability, so that only the facts giving rise to a liability[192] or the making of a

---

180 *Re North* [1895] 2 Q.B. 264, 270.
181 Law of Property Act 1925 s.61(a).
182 *Lloyds Bank v Eagle Star* [1951] 1 T.L.R. 803.
183 *South Staffordshire Tramways v Sickness and Accident* [1891] 1 Q.B. 402. cf. *Cartwright v Mac-
Cormack* [1963] 1 W.L.R. 18 (cover note).
184 *Lester v Garland* (1808) 15 Ves. Jr. 248.
185 *Isaacs v Royal* (1870) L.R. 5 Ex. 296; *Hirdes GmbH v Edmund* [1991] 2 Lloyd's Rep. 546. Whether
this third "rule" is inflexible may perhaps be doubted: see *Re North* [1895] 2 Q.B. 264.
186 *Pritchard v Merchants' Life* (1858) 3 C.B.(N.S.) 622; *Oceanic SS Co v Faber* (1907) 23 T.L.R. 673;
Marine Insurance v Grimmer [1944] 2 All E.R. 197; *Reinhart v Joshua Hoyle* [1961] 1 Lloyd's Rep.
346. For a recent example of retrospective cover, see *Wünsche Handelsgesellschaft International
mbH v Tai Ping Insurance Co Ltd* [1998] 2 Lloyd's Rep. 8.
187 *Buchanan v Faber* (1899) 4 Com. Cas. 223; *Oceanic v Faber* (1907) 23 T.L.R. 673; *Hutchins Brothers v Royal Exchange* [1911] 2 K.B. 398; *Reinhart v Joshua Hoyle* [1961] 1 Lloyd's Rep. 346; *Kelly
v Norwich Union Fire Insurance Society Ltd* [1990] 1 W.L.R. 139. cf. *Soole v Royal Insurance Co
Ltd* [1971] 2 Lloyd's Rep. 332.
188 See above, para.42-003.
189 *Hough v Head* (1885) 55 L.J. Q.B. 43; *Moore v Evans* [1918] A.C. 185; *Allis Chalmers Co v Fidelity Deposit* (1916) 32 T.L.R. 263; *Pennsylvania Insurance v Mumford* [1920] 2 K.B. 537. *Promet
Engineering (Singapore) Pte Ltd v Sturge (The Nukila)* [1997] 2 Lloyd's Rep. 146; *Mitsui Marine
and Fire Insurance Co Ltd v Bayview Motors Ltd* [2002] EWCA Civ 1605, [2003] Lloyd's Rep. I.R.
117.
190 *Knight v Faith* (1850) 15 Q.B. 649; *Andersen v Marten* [1908] A.C. 334, 339. cf. *Frewin v Poland*
[1968] 1 Lloyd's Rep. 100; and *Kuwait Airways Corp v Kuwait Insurance Co SAK* [1996] 1 Lloyd's
Rep. 664, 686, QB, [1997] 2 Lloyd's Rep. 687, CA, [1999] 1 Lloyd's Rep. 803, HL.
191 See below, para.42-119.
192 *Hood's Trustees v Southern Union General* [1928] Ch. 793, 800, 801; *Chandris v Argo Insurance*
[1963] 2 Lloyd's Rep. 65. cf. *Ellerbeck Collieries v Cornhill Insurance* [1932] 1 K.B. 401; *Bosma
v Larsen* [1966] 1 Lloyd's Rep. 22; *Soole v Royal Insurance Co Ltd* [1971] 2 Lloyd's Rep. 332;
County and District Property Ltd v Jenner & Sons Ltd [1976] 2 Lloyd's Rep. 728; *Walker v Pennine Insurance Co Ltd* [1979] 2 Lloyd's Rep. 139; affirmed [1980] 2 Lloyd's Rep. 156. In *Bolton
MBC v Municipal Mutual Insurance Ltd* [2006] EWCA Civ 50, [2006] 1 W.L.R. 1492, the Court

claim against the assured[193] need occur during the period. Those facts may be equated with the insured peril.[194] The loss arising from those facts, namely a liability established by judgment, award or agreement, may not arise for a considerable period after the insured peril. Accordingly, in the case of liability insurance, it is the facts underlying the liability or the making of a claim against the assured, or the notification of a circumstance which might give rise to a claim, and not the establishment of that liability, which generally must occur during the relevant period, subject to the terms of the policy.

(c) The Place of the Event

42-026 **Place of event** A contract of insurance may refer to the place where the subject matter of the insurance is, or is to be, situated.[195] In such cases it may be necessary to determine whether the cover extends to all goods at that place when a loss occurs,[196] or only to goods at that place when the contract is made,[197] and difficulties often arise over the definition of the place at which the goods are to be.[198]

(d) The Nature of the Loss or Damage

42-027 **Nature of loss** Contracts of insurance providing cover for loss or damage are construed so as to extend only to loss[199] of or damage to the subject matter of the

---

of Appeal held that in respect of a claim relating to mesothelioma under a public liability policy insuring against "injury" which took place during the policy period, the "injury" took place when the disease first occurred or manifested itself, not when the body was first exposed to asbestos. The position with respect to employees' liability policies was distinguished by the Supreme Court in *BAI (Run Off) Ltd v Durham* [2012] UKSC 14, [2012] Lloyd's Rep. I.R. 371.

[193] Many liability policies will attach to claims made during the policy period or to claims arising after the policy period provided notice of a circumstance which might give rise to a claim is given to the insurer during the policy period: *HLB Kidsons v Lloyd's Underwriters* [2007] EWHC 1951 (Comm), [2008] Lloyd's Rep. I.R. 237 at [23], [2008] EWCA Civ 1206, [2009] 1 Lloyd's Rep. 8; *McManus v European Risk Insurance Co HF* [2013] EWHC 18 (Ch), [2013] Lloyd's Rep. I.R. 533. As to when a claim is made, see *West Wake Price & Co v Ching* [1957] 1 W.L.R. 45; *J Rothschild Assurance Plc v Collyear* [1999] Lloyd's Rep. I.R. 6; *MJ Gleeson Group Plc v Axa Corporate Solutions Assurance SA* [2013] Lloyd's Rep. I.R. 677 at [51]–[59].

[194] cf. *Yorkshire Water Services Ltd v Sun Alliance & London Insurance Plc* [1997] 2 Lloyd's Rep. 21, 28.

[195] *Dawsons v Bonnin* [1922] 2 A.C. 413.

[196] *Crowley v Cohen* (1832) 3 B. & Ad. 478; *Joyce v Kennard* (1871) L.R. 7 Q.B. 78.

[197] *Gorman v Hand-in-Hand* (1877) Ir.R. 11 C.L. 224; *Harrison v Ellis* (1857) 7 El. & Bl. 465.

[198] e.g. *Wulfson v Switzerland General* (1940) 56 T.L.R. 701 (whilst in store at *x*); *Leo Rapp v McClure* [1955] 1 Lloyd's Rep. 292 (in warehouse); *Overseas Commodities v Style* [1958] 1 Lloyd's Rep. 546; *John Martin Ltd v Russell* [1960] 1 Lloyd's Rep. 554 (final warehouse); *Crow's Transport v Phoenix Assurance* [1965] 1 Lloyd's Rep. 139 (in transit); *Firmin and Collins v Allied Shippers* [1967] 1 Lloyd's Rep. 633 (whilst in public warehouse); *SCA (Freight) Ltd v Gibson* [1974] 2 Lloyd's Rep. 533 (whilst in the normal course of transit temporarily housed); *Kuwait Airways Corp v Kuwait Insurance Co SAK* [1998] 1 Lloyd's Rep. 664, QB, [1997] 2 Lloyd's Rep. 687, CA, [1999] 1 Lloyd's Rep. 803, HL (definition of "any one location" in policy limit); *Wünsche Handelsgesellschaft International mbH v Tai Ping Insurance Co Ltd* [1998] 2 Lloyd's Rep. 8 ("ex factory").

[199] The loss must be a real loss and not a notional loss (*Royal Boskalis Westminster NV v Mountain* [1997] 2 All E.R. 929, where the waiver of a contractual claim unenforceable because of illegality or duress did not constitute a damnifiable loss) nor a negligible loss (*Glengate-KG Properties Ltd v Norwich Union Fire Insurance Society Ltd* [1996] 2 All E.R. 487). See also *McMahon v AGF Holdings (UK) Ltd* [1997] L.R.L.R. 159.

insurance itself.[200] Thus loss of profits[201] and other consequential losses, such as loss of rents when a house is burnt down,[202] or loss of salary after an accident[203] or loss in value of uninjured goods due to damage to other goods,[204] are not covered unless expressly stipulated. Furthermore, the word "loss" does not bear so wide a meaning as might be supposed. The fact that the assured is unlikely to recover the goods, as when they are in enemy territory though not seized by the enemy,[205] is not sufficient to establish a loss under cover for "all losses",[206] and the doctrine of constructive total loss in marine insurance has no application to other kinds of insurance.[207] Earlier suggestions that goods are not "lost" within the meaning of that word in a contract of insurance, when the assured intentionally parted with the property in them, although induced to do so by fraud, should be treated with caution.[208]

Damage Contracts of insurance may provide cover in respect of "damage to" the **42-028** subject matter of the insurance. "Damage" is often construed as physical damage.[209] There are two elements to the notion of physical damage. First, there has to have been a physical alteration to the subject matter,[210] This alteration may take place at the molecular level and may not be palpable without testing or analysis.[211] The alteration need not be permanent or irreparable.[212] Secondly, the physical alteration should result in a decrease in the value or in the impairment of the utility of

---

[200] *Mitsui v Mumford* [1915] 2 K.B. 27; *Campbell v Denman* (1915) 21 Com. Cas. 357; *Moore v Evans* [1918] A.C. 185. As to the meaning of damage, see, e.g. *Promet Engineering (Singapore) Pte Ltd v Sturge (The Nukila)* [1997] 2 Lloyd's Rep. 146; *Quorum A/S v Schramm* [2002] 1 Lloyd's Rep. 249 at [90]. See below, para.42-028.

[201] *Maurice v Goldsborough Mort* [1939] A.C. 452, 461; *Horbury Building Systems Ltd v Hampden Insurance NV* [2004] EWCA Civ 418, [2007] Lloyd's Rep. I.R. 237 at [13]–[27].

[202] *Re Wright and Pole* (1834) 1 Ad. & El. 621; *Menzies v North British* (1847) 9 D. 694, Ct of Sess.; *Theobald v Railway Passengers* (1854) 10 Ex. 45; *Westminster Fire v Glasgow Provident* (1888) 13 App. Cas. 699. But see *City Tailors v Evans* (1922) 38 T.L.R. 230.

[203] *Theobald v Railway Passengers*, above.

[204] *Cator v Great Western* (1873) L.R. 8 C.P. 552.

[205] *Moore v Evans* [1918] A.C. 185; *Fooks v Smith* [1942] 2 K.B. 508.

[206] But see *Webster v General Accident* [1953] 1 Q.B. 520.

[207] *Moore v Evans*, above; *Scott v Copenhagen Reinsurance Co (UK) Ltd* [2002] EWHC 1348 (Comm), [2002] Lloyd's Rep. I.R. 775; affirmed [2003] EWCA Civ 688, [2003] Lloyd's Rep. I.R. 752. cf. Marine Insurance Act 1906 ss.60–63. As to the distinction between actual and constructive total loss in marine insurance law, see *Fraser Shipping Ltd v Colton (The Shakir III)* [1997] 1 Lloyd's Rep. 586; *Kastor Navigation Co Ltd v Axa Global Risks (UK) Ltd* [2002] EWHC 2601 (Comm), [2003] Lloyd's Rep. I.R. 262; affirmed [2004] EWCA Civ 277, [2004] Lloyd's Rep. I.R. 481.

[208] cf. *Eisinger v General Accident* [1955] 1 W.L.R. 869. cf. *Webster v General Accident* [1953] 1 Q.B. 520. See *Dobson v General Accident Fire & Life Assurance Corp Plc* [1990] 1 Q.B. 274.

[209] The precise definition will, of course, depend on the construction of the contract: Clarke, *The Law of Insurance Contracts* (looseleaf), para.16–2C. See *James Longly & Co v Forest Giles Ltd* [2001] EWCA Civ 1242, [2002] Lloyd's Rep. I.R. 421 at [22]–[23]. In *Cementation Piling and Foundations Ltd v Aegon Insurance Co Ltd* [1995] 1 Lloyd's Rep. 97, 102, it was held that an insurance against the cost incurred "in respect of physical damage" included the cost of rectifying the defect which caused the physical damage, but was not itself physical damage.

[210] *Promet Engineering (Singapore) Pte Ltd v Sturge (The Nukila)* [1997] 2 Lloyd's Rep. 146, 151.

[211] *Ranicar v Frigmobile Pty Ltd* [1983] Tas. R. 113, 116, Tas SC; *Quorum A/S v Schramm* [2002] 1 Lloyd's Rep. 249 at [90]. cf. the non-insurance decision in *Bacardi-Martini Beverages v Thomas Hardy Packaging* [2002] 1 Lloyd's Rep. 62, 68–69; affirmed [2002] EWCA Civ 549, [2002] 2 Lloyd's Rep. 379 at [10]–[18], and the authorities referred to therein.

[212] *Ranicar v Frigmobile Pty Ltd*, above.

the subject matter insured.[213] It is not sufficient if a decrease in value results from the mere suspicion that there has been a physical alteration.[214]

42-029 **Expenses incurred to prevent loss** If an assured incurs expense, sacrifices property or waives valuable rights[215] in order to avert or minimise loss recoverable under the insurance contract, in the absence of a contractual provision to the contrary the assured may not be able to recover such expense, even though the insurer benefits as a result of such efforts.[216] However, such expenses may be recovered if they may be said to be a loss caused by the event insured against.[217] It is commonplace, particularly in marine policies, to include a provision[218] allowing the assured to recover such expenses from the insurer.

4. UTMOST GOOD FAITH AND FAIR PRESENTATION OF THE RISK

42-030 **Introduction** Insurance contracts have long been regarded as imposing on the parties to the contract obligations based upon what has been described as the "utmost good faith". Such obligations are most commonly manifested by a duty upon the parties prior to the conclusion of the insurance contract, requiring them not only not to misrepresent material circumstances, but also to provide full disclosure of such circumstances. The nature of the obligation of utmost good faith has been such that it has been relied upon as supporting certain post-contractual duties. Such duties were imposed as a matter of the common law. In 1906, Parliament passed the Marine Insurance Act 1906, ss.17–20 of which codified the common law as it then stood, with an emphasis on the assured's pre-contractual duty of disclosure. Even though the duty of disclosure was set out in the Marine Insurance Act 1906, the Courts had long recognised that ss.17–20 represented the common law applicable to non-marine insurance contracts, as well as to marine insurance contracts.[219] However, Parliament has recently enacted two statutes which modify the assured's pre-contractual duty of utmost good faith, namely the

---

[213] *Ranicar v Frigmobile Pty Ltd*, above; *McMullin v ICI Australian Operations Pty Ltd* [1997] FCA 541, (1997) 72 F.C.R. 1, Aust Fed Ct.

[214] *Quorum A/S v Schramm* [2002] 1 Lloyd's Rep. 249.

[215] *Royal Boskalis Westminster NV v Mountain* [1997] 2 All E.R. 929, 940, 951, 973.

[216] *Yorkshire Water Services Ltd v Sun Alliance and London Insurance Plc* [1997] 2 Lloyd's Rep. 21; *Baker v Black Sea and Baltic General Insurance Co Ltd* [1998] 2 All E.R. 833 (reinsurance); *Astrazeneca Insurance Co Ltd v XL Insurance (Bermuda) Ltd* [2013] EWHC 349 (Comm), [2013] Lloyd's Rep. I.R. 290 at [137], affirmed [2013] EWCA Civ 1660, [2014] Lloyd's Rep. I.R. 509. cf. Clarke, *The Law of Insurance Contracts* (looseleaf) para.28-8G. cf. *Jan de Nul (UK) Ltd v Axa Royale Belge SA* [2002] EWCA Civ 209, [2002] 1 Lloyd's Rep. 583, 595.

[217] See, for example, *Berens v Rucker* (1760) 1 Wm. Bl. 313, 315; *Dent v Smith* (1869) L.R. 4 Q.B. 414; *Canada Rice Mills Ltd v Union Marine & General Insurance Co Ltd* [1941] AC 55, 70, 71.

[218] Known as a "sue and labour" clause in marine policies: see *Aitchison v Lohre* (1879) 4 App. Cas. 755; *Royal Boskalis Westminster NV v Mountain* [1999] Q.B. 674. See Marine Insurance Act 1906 s.78. As to where the purpose of the expense is avert or minimise both an insured loss and an uninsured loss, see *Standard Life Assurance Ltd v Ace European Ltd* [2012] EWHC 104 (Comm), affirmed [2012] EWCA Civ 1713, [2013] Lloyd's Rep. I.R. 415; cf. *Royal Boskalis Westminster NV v Mountain* [1999] Q.B. 674. As to when the right to recover under a sue and labour clause comes to an end, see *Atlasnavios-Navegacao Lda v Navigators Insurance Co Ltd* [2014] EWHC 4133 (Comm), [2015] Lloyd's Rep. I.R. 151 at [335]–[344]; reversed on other grounds [2018] UKSC 26, [2018] 2 W.L.R. 1671; *Suez Fortune Investments Ltd v Talbot Underwriting Ltd* [2015] EWHC 42 (Comm), [2015] 1 Lloyd's Rep. 651 at [283]–[305].

[219] *HIH Casualty and General Insurance Ltd v Chase Manhattan Bank* [2003] UKHL 6, [2003] 2 Lloyd's Rep. 61 at [5], [42].

Consumer Insurance (Disclosure and Representations) Act 2012 and the Insurance Act 2015. Although the common law governing the fair presentation of the risk has now been modified by this legislation, the common law will still be relevant to determining disputes relating to insurance contracts agreed before the entry into force of this legislation and to assist in the interpretation of these statutes. Accordingly, the common law will be considered before considering the impact of the 2012 Act and the 2015 Act.

Consumer Insurance (Disclosure and Representations) Act 2012 The 2012 Act **42-031** was passed on March 8, 2012 and entered into force on April 6, 2013.[220] This Act applies to consumer insurance contracts, which are contracts of insurance entered into between an insurer (being a person who carries on the business of insurance) and an individual who enters into the contract wholly or mainly for purposes unrelated to the individual's trade, business or profession. The Act applies to consumer insurance contracts, and variations to consumer insurance contracts, where the contract or the variation was agreed after the Act comes into force.[221] The common law, and ss.17–20 of the Marine Insurance Act 1906, relating to the duties of utmost good faith applicable to consumer insurance contracts have been modified by the 2012 Act.[222]

Insurance Act 2015 The 2015 Act was passed on February 12, 2015 and entered **42-032** into force on August 12, 2016, and applies (insofar as the pre-contractual duty of utmost good faith is concerned) to insurance contracts, and variations to insurance contracts, agreed after the Act entered into force.[223] Part 2 of the Act, which deals with the duty of disclosure on the part of the assured, applies to non-consumer insurance contracts.[224] The common law, and ss.17–20 of the Marine Insurance Act 1906, relating to the duties of utmost good faith applicable to non-consumer insurance contracts have been modified by Pt 2 of the 2015 Act.[225]

(a) The Common Law

Utmost good faith An insurance contract is a contract uberrimae fidei[226]: it is a **42-033** contract based on the utmost good faith and if the utmost good faith is not observed

---

[220] The Consumer Insurance (Disclosure and Representations) Act 2012 (Commencement) Order 2013 (SI 2013/450). The 2012 Act was amended by the Insurance Act 2015 (ss.14(2), 14(4) and 21(6)).

[221] 2012 Act s.12(4). The 2012 Act was amended by the Insurance Act 2015 (ss.14(2), 14(4) and 21(6)).

[222] 2012 Act ss.2(5), 11(1)–(2). Section 2(5) was replaced by s.14(3) of the Insurance Act 2015. Road Traffic Act 1988 s.52 is also modified by this Act: s.11(3). See below, para.42-125.

[223] 2015 Act ss.22, 23(2).

[224] 2015 Act s.2. A "consumer insurance contract" has the same meaning as in the Consumer Insurance (Disclosure and Representations) Act 2012: s.1.

[225] 2015 Act s.21(2)–(3). Road Traffic Act 1988 s.152 is also modified by this Act: s.21(4).

[226] See Vol.I, paras 7-158 et seq., and generally, *MacGillivray on Insurance Law*, 14th edn (2018), Chs 16–17; Clarke, *The Law of Insurance Contracts* (looseleaf), Chs 22–23; MacDonald Eggers and Picken, *Good Faith and Insurance Contracts*, 4th edn (2017); Hasson, "The Doctrine of Uberrima Fides in Insurance Law—A Critical Evaluation" (1969) 32 M.L.R. 615; Bennett [1999] L.M.C.L.Q. 165. For a somewhat looser duty arising when one insurer authorises another to write insurance on its behalf under a "binding authority" (which is not, strictly speaking, a contract uberrimae fidei), see *Pryke v Gibbs Hartley Cooper* [1991] 1 Lloyd's Rep. 602. See, however, *GMA v Storebrand and Kansa* [1995] L.R.L.R. 333, 348–349, where scepticism was expressed as to whether contracts closely analogous to those of insurance could attract the duty of disclosure attached to contracts uberrimae fidei.

by either party the contract may be avoided by the other party.[227] The obligation to observe utmost good faith, moreover, is a continuing one, which does not cease on the conclusion or execution of the insurance contract, although the ambit of the duty in pre-contract and post-contract situations is not the same,[228] The reason for this principle of insurance law is that contracts of insurance are founded on facts which are nearly always in the exclusive knowledge of one party (usually the assured) and, unless this knowledge is shared, the risk insured against may be different from that intended to be covered by the party in ignorance.[229] The duty most commonly manifests itself as a duty to disclose material facts and not to misrepresent material facts at or before the making of the insurance contract. Although there have been suggestions in the past that the pre-contractual duty of disclosure is founded upon an implied term of the contract,[230] the weight of authority is to the effect that the duty to disclose, as well as the duty not to misrepresent, material facts are obligations imposed by law.[231] Although there is a post-contractual aspect of this duty of good faith, the discussion which follows will concentrate on the duty of full disclosure which applies up to the conclusion of the insurance contract for non-consumer assureds.

42-034 **The duty to disclose material circumstances**   Subject to what follows, the duty is upon the assured, and insurer,[232] to disclose every material circumstance to the other party. In the case of the assured, this requires that he disclose every circumstance which would influence the judgment of a prudent insurer in fixing the premium or in determining whether to take the risk.[233] The test of materiality,

---

[227] These are the words used in the Marine Insurance Act 1906 s.17 (as amended by the Insurance Act 2015), which codifies, in relation to marine insurance, a principle applicable to all insurance contracts: *Carter v Boehm* (1766) 3 Burr. 1905, 1909; *Duffell v Wilson* (1808) 1 Camp. 401; *London Assurance v Mansel* (1879) 11 Ch. D. 363, 367; *Re Bradley and Essex Accident* [1912] 1 K.B. 415, 430; *Rozanes v Bowen* (1928) 32 Ll.L. Rep. 98, 102; *Claude R Ogden & Co Pty Ltd v Reliance Fire Sprinkler Co Pty Ltd* [1975] 1 Lloyd's Rep. 52; *HIH Casualty and General Insurance Ltd v Chase Manhattan Bank* [2003] UKHL 6, [2003] 2 Lloyd's Rep. 61 at [5], [42]; *Dalecroft Properties Ltd v Underwriters* [2017] EWHC 1263 (Comm), [2017] Lloyd's Rep. I.R. 511 at [80].

[228] *Royal Boskalis Westminster NV v Mountain* [1997] L.R.L.R. 523; reversed on other grounds by the Court of Appeal: [1999] Q.B. 674; *Manifest Shipping & Co Ltd v Uni-Polaris Shipping Co Ltd (The Star Sea)* [2001] UKHL 1, [2001] 2 W.L.R. 170; *The Mercandian Continent* [2001] EWCA Civ 1275, [2001] 2 Lloyd's Rep. 563; cf. *Agapitos v Agnew (The Aegeon)* [2002] EWCA Civ 247, [2002] 2 Lloyd's Rep. 42. See Soyer [2003] L.M.C.L.Q. 45.

[229] *Carter v Boehm* (1766) 3 Burr. 1905, 1909; *London General Omnibus v Holloway* [1912] 2 K.B. 72, 86.

[230] *Moens v Heyworth* (1842) 10 M. & W. 147, 157; *Blackburn Low & Co v Vigors* (1886) 17 Q.B.D. 553, reversed on other grounds (1887) 12 App Cas. 531, 536–537, 539.

[231] *Bank of Nova Scotia v Hellenic Mutual War Risks Association (Bermuda) Ltd* [1989] 2 Lloyd's Rep. 238, 263.

[232] For consideration of the insurer's duty of good faith, see *Banque Keyser Ullman SA v Skandia (UK) Insurance Co Ltd* [1990] 1 Q.B. 664, 769–773; affirmed by the House of Lords on somewhat different grounds, but see [1991] 2 A.C. 249 at 268, 281–282; *Bank of Nova Scotia v Hellenic Mutual War Risks Association (Bermuda) Ltd (The Good Luck)* [1990] 1 Q.B. 818; reversed by the House of Lords on other grounds at [1992] 1 A.C. 233; *Aldrich v Norwich Union Life Insurance Co Ltd* [2000] Lloyd's Rep. I.R. 1.

[233] These are the words used in the Marine Insurance Act 1906 s.18(2), but the test is the same for all types of insurance: see Road Traffic Act 1988 s.151(9)(b); *Berger v Pollock* [1973] 2 Lloyd's Rep. 442; *Lambert v Co-operative Insurance Society Ltd* [1975] 2 Lloyd's Rep. 485; *Marine Knitting Mills Property Ltd v Greater Pacific & General Insurance Ltd* [1976] 2 Lloyd's Rep. 631, 642, PC; *Reynolds v Phoenix Assurance Co Ltd* [1978] 2 Lloyd's Rep. 440, 461; *Pan Atlantic Insurance Co Ltd v Pine Top Insurance Co Ltd* [1995] 1 A.C. 501. The materiality of a fact will depend on the

therefore, is not what the assured considers material,[234] nor what a reasonable assured would consider material,[235] but whether the circumstance would be taken into account by a prudent insurer when assessing the risk (even if it would not, of itself, have had a decisive effect on his decision whether to accept the risk and, if so, at what premium).[236] The materiality of the circumstances must be assessed by reference to the true facts, whether or not all such facts have been fully and accurately disclosed.[237] Where the insurer asks the assured to answer specific questions, the parties are taken to have agreed that the facts involved in answering the questions are material,[238] but this does not affect the duty to disclose material circumstances not covered by the questions,[239] unless the way they are drafted has this effect,[240] and except insofar as the failure to ask a particular question may make it difficult for the insurers afterwards to assert that the circumstances which would have been elicited were material.[241] Indeed, the assured is not required to disclose every minute detail of every material circumstance, but rather only to disclose sufficient detail to allow the insurer to ask for more information, if he requires further facts on which to evaluate the risk.[242] Materiality is a question of fact, but it has long been the practice to adduce expert evidence on the point from insurers, brokers and the

---

nature of the insurance product: *Johnson v IGI Insurance Co Ltd* [1997] 6 Re L.R. 283.

[234] *Bates v Hewitt* (1867) L.R. 2 Q.B. 595, 607; *Joel v Law Union and Crown Insurance Co* [1908] 2 K.B. 863, 884; *Godfrey v Britannic Insurance* [1963] 2 Lloyd's Rep. 515, 529; *Roselodge v Castle* [1966] 2 Lloyd's Rep. 113.

[235] *Lambert v Co-operative Insurance Society Ltd* [1975] 2 Lloyd's Rep. 485. Though note Longmore [2001] L.M.C.L.Q. 356, 365–368.

[236] *Pan Atlantic Insurance Co Ltd v Pine Top Insurance Co Ltd* [1995] 1 A.C. 501 (rejecting the "decisive influence" test of materiality, but holding that an insurer cannot rely upon a material non-disclosure (or misrepresentation) as a ground for avoiding the contract if the non-disclosure (or misrepresentation) did not actually *induce* the making of the contract), as interpreted by the Court of Appeal in *St Paul Fire & Marine Insurance Co (UK) Ltd v McConnell Dowell Constructors Ltd* [1996] 1 All E.R. 96. On this basis, a circumstance can be "material" even if it actually *decreases* the risk, but this does not mean that such a circumstance would have to be disclosed because, in the absence of inquiry, Marine Insurance Act 1906 s.18(3)(a) specifically exempts the assured from having to disclose any circumstance which diminishes the risk: see *St Paul Fire & Marine Insurance Co (UK) Ltd v McConnell Dowell Constructors Ltd*, above, at 107.

[237] *Drake Insurance Plc v Provident Insurance Plc* [2003] EWCA Civ 1834, [2004] Q.B. 601 at [75], [138]; *Sea Glory Maritime Co v Al Sagr National Insurance Co* [2013] EWHC 2116 (Comm), [2014] 1 Lloyd's Rep. 14 at [163]–[166].

[238] *Anderson v Fitzgerald* (1853) 4 H.L.C. 484, 503; *London Assurance v Mansel* (1879) 11 Ch. D. 363; *Dawsons v Bonnin* [1922] 2 A.C. 413; *Glicksman v Lancashire and General* [1925] 2 K.B. 593, 608; affirmed [1927] A.C. 139, 144; *Kumar v Life Insurance Corp of India* [1974] 1 Lloyd's Rep. 147; *Whitlam v Hazel* [2004] EWCA Civ 1600, [2005] Lloyd's Rep. I.R. 168. As to the position where an agent of the insurer incorrectly fills in the proposal form, see *Stone v Reliance Marine Insurance Co Ltd* [1972] 1 Lloyd's Rep. 469.

[239] *Wainwright v Bland* (1836) 1 M. & W. 32; *Dawsons v Bonnin*, above; *Glicksman v Lancashire and General*, above; *Bond v Commercial Union* (1930) 36 Ll.L. Rep. 107; *Taylor v Eagle Star Insurance* (1940) 67 Ll.L. Rep. 136; *Schoolman v Hall* [1951] 1 Lloyd's Rep. 139; *Lee v British Law Insurance Co Ltd* [1972] 2 Lloyd's Rep. 49; *March Cabaret Club v London Assurance* [1975] 1 Lloyd's Rep. 169.

[240] See below, para.42-035. For the effect of failing to answer a question, see *Marcovitch v Liverpool Victoria* (1912) 28 T.L.R. 188; *Roberts v Avon* [1956] 2 Lloyd's Rep. 240; *Arterial Caravans Ltd v Yorkshire Insurance Co Ltd* [1973] 1 Lloyd's Rep. 169; *Roberts v Plaisted* [1989] 2 Lloyd's Rep. 341, 347–348; *O'Kane v Jones* [2003] EWHC 3470 (Comm), [2004] 1 Lloyd's Rep. 389 at [237]–[239].

[241] *Newsholme Bros v Road Transport and General* [1929] 2 K.B. 356, 362; *McCormick v National Motor Accident* (1934) 40 Com. Cas. 76, 78; *Zurich General v Morrison* [1942] 2 K.B. 53, 64; *Doheny v New India Assurance Co Ltd* [2004] EWCA Civ 1705, [2005] Lloyd's Rep. I.R. 251 at [16]–[20].

[242] *Asfar & Co v Blundell* [1896] 1 Q.B. 123, 129.

like.[243] A circumstance is material for disclosure by the assured if the circumstance relates to the likelihood or the extent of loss which might be sustained by the insurer under the insurance contract,[244] whether the circumstance relates to the likelihood of the operation of an insured peril or renders the subject matter of the insurance more or peculiarly susceptible to a peril to be insured against,[245] or relates to matters of subrogation, or to the "moral hazard" of the assured.[246] Thus, so far as the assured is concerned, circumstances which diminish the risk need not be disclosed.[247] So far as the insurer's duty is concerned, a circumstance is material and must be disclosed to the assured if it is relevant to the nature of the risk sought to be covered, or to the recoverability of a claim under the policy which a prudent assured would take into account in deciding whether or not to place the risk with the proposed insurer.[248]

42-035 **Scope of duty of disclosure** The duty of disclosure extends only to circumstances which are within the knowledge of one party but not within the knowledge of the other. The assured must disclose what he knows, even though he does not appreciate that it is material.[249] An assured is deemed to know every circumstance which in the ordinary course of business ought to be known to him,[250] so that the assured may be liable to disclose circumstances known to someone acting on his behalf of

---

[243] *Ionides v Pender* (1874) L.R. 9 Q.B. 531, 535; *Glasgow Assurance v Symondson* (1911) 16 Com. Cas. 109; *Yorke v Yorkshire Insurance* [1918] 1 K.B. 662, 669; *Roselodge v Castle* [1966] 2 Lloyd's Rep. 113. The Court may well be able to assess materiality without the benefit of expert evidence: *Bate v Aviva Insurance UK Ltd* [2014] EWCA Civ 334, [2014] Lloyd's Rep. I.R. 527 at [35].

[244] *Glasgow Assurance Corp Ltd v William Symondson and Co* (1911) 16 Com. Cas. 109, 119–120; *Société Anonyme d'Intermédiaires Luxembourgeois v Farex Gie* [1995] L.R.L.R. 116, 149; *O'Kane v Jones* [2003] EWHC 3470 (Comm), [2004] 1 Lloyd's Rep. 389 at [222]. See also MacDonald, Eggers and Picken, *Good Faith and Insurance Contracts*, 4th edn (2017), paras 14.62–14.81; *Permanent Trustee Australia Ltd v FAI General Insurance Co Ltd* (2003) 77 A.L.J.R. 1070 at [32]–[33] High Court of Australia.

[245] *Sealion Shipping Ltd v Valiant Insurance Co* [2012] EWHC 50 (Comm), [2012] Lloyd's Rep. I.R. 252.

[246] As to the disclosure of circumstances relating to the moral hazard, see *Strive Shipping Corp v Hellenic Mutual War Risks Association (The Grecia Express)* [2002] EWHC 203 (Comm), [2002] 2 Lloyd's Rep. 88, 131; *Brotherton v Aseguradora Colseguros SA* [2003] EWCA Civ 705, [2003] Lloyd's Rep. I.R. 746; *Sharon's Bakery (Europe) Ltd v AXA Insurance UK Plc* [2011] EWHC 210 (Comm), [2012] Lloyd's Rep. I.R. 164. This may involve an assured having to disclose the fact that he has been dishonest in the past or has been convicted or charged with some offence impugning his honesty or competence or disclose any other fact affecting the "moral hazard": *Inversiones Manria SA v Sphere Drake Insurance Co Plc (The Dora)* [1989] 1 Lloyd's Rep. 69, 93; *Insurance Corp of the Channel Islands Ltd v McHugh* [1998] Lloyd's Rep. I.R. 151; *North Star Shipping Ltd v Sphere Drake Insurance Plc* [2006] EWCA Civ 378, [2006] 2 Lloyd's Rep. 183; *ERC Frankona Reinsurance v American National Insurance Co* [2005] EWHC 1381 (Comm), [2006] Lloyd's Rep. I.R. 157. The assured indeed may be obliged to disclose that he has obtained another insurer's agreement to this or an earlier policy by reason of a breach of the duty of the utmost good faith: *Aneco Reinsurance Underwriting Ltd (In Liquidation) v Johnson & Higgins* [1998] 1 Lloyd's Rep. 565. As regards subrogation, see *Tate & Sons v Hyslop* (1885) 15 Q.B.D. 368.

[247] *Carter v Boehm* (1766) 3 Burr. 1905; Marine Insurance Act 1906 s.18(3)(a).

[248] *Banque Keyser Ullman SA v Skandia (UK) Insurance Co Ltd* [1990] 1 Q.B. 665, 771–772. The decision of the Court of Appeal was subsequently affirmed by the House of Lords on somewhat different grounds, but the statement of the ambit of the duty was not dissented from: [1991] 2 A.C. 249, 268, 269, although Lord Jauncey was prepared to consider a test of materiality which was reciprocal to that applicable to the assured's duty of disclosure (281–282). See also *Aldrich v Norwich Union Life Insurance Co Ltd* [2000] Lloyd's Rep. I.R. 1.

[249] *Joel v Law Union and Crown Insurance Co* [1908] 2 K.B. 863, 883–884; *Zeller v British Caymanian Insurance Co Ltd* [2008] UKPC 4, [2008] Lloyd's Rep. I.R. Plus 16.

[250] Both at common law (*Proudfoot v Montefiore* (1867) L.R. 2 Q.B. 511) and statute: Marine Insur-

which he is unaware. The kinds of situation in which the knowledge of an agent will so affect the position of the assured have been summarised[251] as being: (i) where the agent, although not effecting the insurance on behalf of the assured, is relied upon by the assured for information concerning the subject matter of the insurance (sometimes referred to as an "agent to know")[252]; (ii) where the agent is in such a predominant position in relation to the assured that his knowledge can be regarded as the knowledge of the assured[253]; and (iii) where the agent is used to effect the insurance (in which case the agent is required to disclose not just all material circumstances which the assured is bound to disclose, but also every material circumstance which ought to be known by the agent, or communicated to him, in the ordinary course of business).[254] However, the assured will not be adversely affected by the knowledge of his agent where the information concerns the agent's own fraud on his principal.[255] Where the assured is a private individual, or effects insurance otherwise than "in the course of business",[256] it is his duty to disclose those circumstances which are known to him, not those which ought to be known to him.[257]

Exceptions to the duty of disclosure   There are four traditional exceptions to the   **42-036** duty of disclosure (at least insofar as it rests on the assured's shoulders). First, the assured need not disclose any circumstance which diminishes the risk.[258] Secondly, the assured need not disclose circumstances which are either known to the insurer,

---

ance Act 1906 s.18(1).

[251] See *Simner v New India Assurance Co Ltd* [1995] L.R.L.R. 240; *ERC Frankona Reinsurance v American National Insurance Co* [2005] EWHC 1381 (Comm), [2006] Lloyd's Rep. I.R. 157 at [122]–[124].

[252] See, in particular, *Fitzherbert v Mather* (1785) 1 T.R. 12; *Gladstone v King* (1813) 1 M. & S. 35; *Proudfoot v Montefiore* (1867) L.R. 2 Q.B. 511; *Blackburn Low Co v Vigors* (1887) 12 App. Cas. 531. In order to determine whether a particular person is the assured's agent to know, it is necessary to analyse both the nature of the relationship between that person and the assured and the nature of the information in question: *ERC Frankona Reinsurance v American National Insurance Co* [2005] EWHC 1381 (Comm), [2006] Lloyd's Rep. I.R. 157 at [132].

[253] As to when an agent will be treated as being in such a position that his knowledge is attributed to his principal, see *Simner v New India Assurance Co Ltd* [1995] L.R.L.R. 240; *PCW Syndicates v PCW Reinsurers* [1996] 1 All E.R. 774; *Group Josi Re v Walbrook Insurance Co Ltd* [1996] 1 Lloyd's Rep. 345; and, more generally, *Meridian Global Funds Management Asia Ltd v Securities Commission* [1995] 2 A.C. 500.

[254] See Marine Insurance Act 1906 s.19. The section does not operate by imputing the knowledge of the agent to the assured, but by requiring the agent to disclose the material circumstances, and enabling the insurer to avoid the contract if he does not: *Société Anonyme D'Intermédiaires Luxembourgeois v Farrex Gie* [1995] L.R.L.R. 116; *PCW Syndicates v PCW Reinsurers* [1996] 1 All E.R. 774. The duty on the agent is independent of that on the assured: *HIH Casualty and General Insurance Ltd v Chase Manhattan Bank* [2003] UKHL 6, [2003] 2 Lloyd's Rep. 61 at [7]–[8], [50]–[54]. However, the section applies only to an agent who actually deals with the insurer, and makes the contract in question, and not to "intermediate" agents: *PCW Syndicates v PCW Reinsurers*, above; nor to an agent who earlier had been instructed to effect the insurance, but did not in fact place the insurance: *Blackburn Low Co v Vigors* (1887) 12 App. Cas. 531.

[255] *PCW Syndicates v PCW Reinsurers* [1996] 1 All E.R. 774; *Group Josi Re v Walbrook Insurance Co Ltd*, above. Further, the agent's knowledge of any "irregularity" in the performance of his duty, short of fraud, will not be imputed to the assured, if it cannot be inferred that the agent would have informed the assured of that irregularity in the ordinary course of business: *Kingscroft Insurance Co Ltd v Nissan Fire and Marine Insurance Co Ltd* [1999] Lloyd's Rep. I.R. 371.

[256] Marine Insurance Act 1906 s.18(1).

[257] *Economides v Commercial Union Assurance Co Plc* [1997] 3 W.L.R. 1066; cf. *Group Josi Reinsurance Co Ltd v Walbrook Insurance Co Ltd* [1996] 1 W.L.R. 1152, 1159.

[258] *Carter v Boehm* (1766) 3 Burr. 1905, 1910; *The Dora* [1989] 1 Lloyd's Rep. 69, 89–90; Marine

or presumed to be known to him as matters of common notoriety or knowledge or which an insurer ought to know in the ordinary course of business.[259] Thirdly, the assured is not obliged to disclose circumstances where the insurer has waived disclosure of such circumstances. For example, if the insurer forbears to ask questions after disclosure of circumstances have put him on inquiry, he may be taken to have waived the right to disclosure of the circumstances which such inquiry would have disclosed[260]; but the doctrine is not applicable to circumstances which are so unusual or special that their non-disclosure would distort the presentation of the risk, since the duty to disclose would otherwise be undermined.[261] Similarly, the question which the insurer may ask the assured (usually in a proposal form) may be so framed as to indicate that the insurer does not require further information on the matters in question, thus relieving the assured from doing more than answering the specific questions.[262] Fourthly, an assured is not bound to disclose to the insurer circumstances, disclosure of which is rendered superfluous by the existence of a warranty in the policy.[263] There may be further exceptions to the duty of disclosure, for example where there is an express exemption granted by a statute.

Insurance Act 1906 s.18(3)(a).

[259] *Carter v Boehm* (1766) 3 Burr. 1905; *Foley v Tabor* (1861) 2 F. & F. 663; *Bates v Hewitt* (1867) L.R. 2 Q.B. 595; *London General Insurance Co v General Marine Underwriters' Association* [1921] 1 K.B. 104; Marine Insurance Act 1906 s.18(3)(b). See also *Aldridge Estates Investments Co Ltd v McCarthy* [1996] E.G.C.S. 167; *Marc Rich & Co AG v Portman* [1997] 1 Lloyd's Rep. 225, 231–232; *Hua Tyan Development Ltd v Zurich Insurance Co Ltd (The Ho Feng 7)* [2013] HKCA 414, [2014] Lloyd's Rep. I.R. 1 at [16.14], Hong Kong CA, [2014] HKCFA 72, [2015] Lloyd's Rep. I.R. 14 (Hong Kong Court of Final Appeal). As to whether an insurer will be presumed to know information reasonably available by reason of searches on electronic databases, see *Sea Glory Maritime Co v Al Sagr National Insurance Co* [2013] EWHC 2116 (Comm), [2014] 1 Lloyd's Rep. 14 at [170]–[179].

[260] *Carter v Boehm* (1766) 3 Burr. 1905; Marine Insurance Act 1906 s.18(3)(c); *Ayrey v British Legal* [1918] 1 K.B. 136; *Becker v Marshall* (1922) 12 Ll. L. Rep. 413, 414; *Greenhill v Federal Insurance* [1927] 1 K.B. 65; *WISE (Underwriting Agency) Ltd v Grupo Nacional Provincial SA* [2004] EWCA Civ 962, [2004] 2 Lloyd's Rep. 483; *Doheny v New India Assurance Co Ltd* [2004] EWCA Civ 1705, [2005] Lloyd's Rep. I.R. 251 at [16]–[20]; *Aldridge v Liberty Mutual Insurance Europe Ltd* [2016] EWHC 3037 (Comm) at [33]–[38]. As to the degree of knowledge required by the insurer to waive disclosure, see *New Hampshire Insurance Co v Oil Refineries Ltd* [2002] 2 Lloyd's Rep. 462.

[261] *CTI v Oceanus Mutual* [1984] 1 Lloyd's Rep. 476, 497–498; *Marc Rich & Co AG v Portman*, above at 234.

[262] e.g. "Have you or your driver during the past five years been convicted of any offence?" This would relieve the assured from disclosing older offences: *Jester-Barnes v Licenses and General* (1934) 49 Ll.L. Rep. 231, 237; see also *Joel v Law Union and Crown Insurance Co* [1908] 2 K.B. 863; *Brewtnall v Cornhill* (1931) 40 Ll.L. Rep. 166; *Schoolman v Hall* [1951] 1 Lloyd's Rep. 139; *Bate v Aviva Insurance UK Ltd* [2013] EWHC 1687 (Comm), [2013] Lloyd's Rep. I.R. 492; affirmed [2014] EWCA Civ 334, [2014] Lloyd's Rep. I.R. 527; cf. *McCormick v National Motor Accident* (1934) 40 Com. Cas. 76, 78. See also *Roberts v Plaisted* [1989] 2 Lloyd's Rep. 341; *O'Kane v Jones* [2003] EWHC 3470 (Comm), [2004] 1 Lloyd's Rep. 389 at [237]–[239]; *Noblebright Ltd v Sirius International Corp* [2007] Lloyd's Rep. I.R. 584; cf. *James v CGU Insurance Plc* [2002] Lloyd's Rep. I.R. 206, para.85.

[263] *Cantiere Meccanico Brindisino v Janson* [1912] 2 K.B. 112, 116, [1912] 3 K.B. 452, 462; *Inversiones Manria SA v Sphere Drake Insurance Co Plc (The Dora)* [1989] 1 Lloyd's Rep. 69, 92; *O'Kane v Jones* [2003] EWHC 3470 (Comm) at [240]; s.18(3)(d) of the Marine Insurance Act 1906. It is an open question whether this exception to the duty of disclosure applies to all warranties. It is likely that the notion of superfluity extends only to promissory warranties, rather than to descriptive warranties. It appears that there is no exception to the duty where the relevant circumstance relates to a policy exclusion (cf. *International Lottery Management Ltd v Dumas* [2002] Lloyd's Rep. I.R. 237 at [59]), unless of course disclosure would diminish the risk; see also *Synergy Health (UK) Ltd v CGU Insurance Plc* [2010] EWHC 2583 (Comm), [2011] Lloyd's Rep. I.R. 500, at [183]–

For example, under the provisions of the Rehabilitation of Offenders Act 1974, an assured is specifically dispensed from any obligation to disclose "spent" convictions, or the circumstances ancillary to them, although this is subject to the Court's discretion to admit evidence of the conviction and so render the conviction a material circumstance requiring disclosure.[264] Further, where the assured is possessed of information which is subject to a privilege belonging to another person, the assured may be excused from disclosing such information.[265] If however the information is subject to a privilege belonging to the assured itself, the assured remains obliged to disclose it to the insurer.[266] Given the reciprocal nature of the duty of disclosure, it is likely that comparable exceptions are applicable to the insurer's duty of disclosure.[267] In addition, circumstances relating to a person's race, nationality, religious belief or gender may not be disclosable, because an insurer is not permitted to assess the risk by reference to a person's race, nationality or religious belief after October 1, 2010 or gender after December 21, 2012. As the law currently stands, the insurer is permitted to assess risks by reference to age or disability.[268]

Time of disclosure   Full disclosure must be made and continue to be made up **42-037** until the moment there is a concluded contract of insurance,[269] and where the assent of the insurer is required for renewal, the duty exists for that renewal.[270] Before the contract is made, any material circumstance which comes to light,[271] or any previous immaterial circumstance which becomes material through change of circumstances[272] must be disclosed. It seems that where a contract of insurance is made and then altered, only circumstances material to the alteration need to be disclosed up to the date of the alteration,[273] although whether the whole contract or only the alteration is vitiated by the failure to disclose such circumstances is undecided.[274] The materiality of a circumstance is judged by the circumstances

---

[184].

[264] Rehabilitation of Offenders Act 1974 s.4. See *Reynolds v Phoenix Assurance Co Ltd* [1978] 2 Lloyd's Rep. 440; *Inversiones Manria SA v Sphere Drake Insurance Co Plc (The Dora)* [1989] 1 Lloyd's Rep. 69, 80; *Power v Provincial Insurance Plc* [1998] R.T.R. 60; *Joseph Fielding Properties (Blackpool) Ltd v Aviva Insurance Ltd* [2010] EWHC 2192 (QB), [2011] Lloyd's Rep. I.R. 238.

[265] *Quinn Direct Insurance Ltd v Law Society* [2010] EWCA Civ 805, [2011] 1 W.L.R. 308.

[266] *March Cabaret Club & Casino Ltd v London Assurance* [1975] 1 Lloyd's Rep. 169; *Quinn Direct Insurance Ltd v Law Society* [2010] EWCA Civ 805, [2011] 1 W.L.R. 308, at [11].

[267] cf. *Banque Keyser Ullman SA v Skandia (UK) Insurance Co Ltd* [1990] 1 Q.B. 665; affirmed [1991] 2 A.C. 249; *Aldrich v Norwich Union Life Insurance Co Ltd* [2000] Lloyd's Rep. I.R. 1.

[268] Equality Act 2010 ss.4–13, 28–29, 31 and Sch.3 Pt 5 paras 20–23, as amended by Equality Act 2010 (Amendment) Regulations 2012 (SI 2012/2992). See *MacGillivray on Insurance Law*, 14th edn (2018), paras 17-063—17-067.

[269] *Wake v Atty* (1812) 4 Taunt. 493; *British Equitable v GW Railway* (1869) 20 L.T. 422; *Allis Chalmers v Fidelity Deposit* (1916) 32 T.L.R. 263; *Looker v Law Union* [1928] 1 K.B. 554; *Berger v Pollock* [1973] 2 Lloyd's Rep. 442; *Hadenfayre v British National Insurance Society* [1984] 2 Lloyd's Rep. 393, 398.

[270] *Pim v Reid* (1843) 6 Man. & G. 1, 25; *Re Wilson and Scottish* [1920] 2 Ch. 28.

[271] *British Equitable v GW Railway* (1869) 38 L.J. Ch. 314; *Canning v Farquhar* (1886) 16 Q.B.D. 727; *Allis Chalmers v Fidelity Deposit* (1916) 114 L.T. 433; *Looker v Law Union* [1928] 1 K.B. 554.

[272] *Re Yager and Guardian* (1912) 108 L.T. 38; *Allis Chalmers v Fidelity Deposit*, above; *Looker v Law Union*, above.

[273] *Sawtell v Loudon* (1814) 5 Taunt. 359; *Lishman v Northern Maritime* (1875) L.R. 10 C.P. 179; *Niger v Guardian Assurance* (1922) 13 Ll.L. Rep. 75.

[274] The Court of Appeal has expressed the opinion (obiter) that it is only the alteration which is affected: *Manifest Shipping & Co Ltd v Uni-Polaris Insurance Co Ltd (The Star Sea)* [1997] 1 Lloyd's Rep. 360, 370; affirmed [2001] UKHL 1, [2001] 2 W.L.R. 170 at [54]–[55]. If this is the case, there may

existing at the time when the contract is concluded,[275] so that, for example, failure to disclose a rumour which at the time would have been considered material is not excused by the fact that after the contract is made it proves unfounded.[276] Conversely a circumstance which at the time would not have been considered material does not affect the validity of the contract even if after the contract is made it becomes material or even causes the loss.[277] However, although once the contract is made there is normally no duty to disclose material circumstances which later occur or which previously were neither known nor ought to have been known,[278] the continuing nature of the duty of good faith may impose upon an assured a limited obligation to inform the insurer of subsequently arising material facts where the terms of the insurance itself require the assured to give the insurer further information after inception of the risk.[279]

42-038 **Misrepresentation** Apart from the ordinary rules relating to misrepresentation[280] the principle of utmost good faith imports a duty not to misrepresent facts which are material in the sense discussed above.[281] The misrepresentation may be of fact or of belief, expectation, opinion or intention. A statement of belief, expectation or opinion may be true even if the belief, expectation or opinion is erroneous,[282] for the representation in such cases is only that the belief, expectation or

---

be circumstances where the alteration is of such proportion effectively as to vitiate the whole contract. See also *K/S Merc-Scandia XXXXII v Lloyd's Underwriters* [2001] EWCA Civ 1275, [2001] 2 Lloyd's Rep. 563 at [22(2)].

[275] *Lynch v Dunsford* (1811) 14 East 494; *Watson v Mainwaring* (1813) 4 Taunt. 763; *Seaton v Burnand* [1900] A.C. 135.

[276] *Lynch v Dunsford*, above. It is not open to the assured to disprove materiality by proving at the trial that the rumour is unfounded: *Brotherton v Aseguradora Colseguros SA* [2003] EWCA Civ 705, [2003] Lloyd's Rep. I.R. 746.

[277] *Watson v Mainwaring*, above; *Associated Oil Carriers v Union Insurance* [1917] 2 K.B. 184.

[278] *Benham v United Guarantee* (1852) 7 Ex. 744; *Whitwell v Autocar Fire and Accident* (1927) 27 Ll.L. Rep. 418; but cf. *Berger v Pollock* [1973] 2 Lloyd's Rep. 442. In *New Hampshire Insurance Co v MGN Ltd* [1997] L.R.L.R. 24, it was held that the exercise of the insurer's contractual right of cancellation does not impose on the assured a continuing duty of disclosure. See also *Iron Trades Mutual v Companhia de Seguros Imperio* [1991] 1 Re. L.R. 213. Where, however, the insurer is asked to withdraw the notice of cancellation, with the effect of reinstating or continuing the cover, the duty may be engaged: *Kingscroft Insurance Co Ltd v Nissan Fire & Marine Insurance Co Ltd (No.2)* [1999] Lloyd's Rep. I.R. 603. However, if there is a "held covered" provision whereby the insurer is required to extend cover on agreement of an additional premium, the assured will be subject to a duty of disclosure: *Overseas Commodities Ltd v Style* [1958] 1 Lloyd's Rep. 546, 559; *Liberian Insurance Agency Inc v Mosse* [1977] 2 Lloyd's Rep. 560, 568; *Black King Shipping Corp v Massie (The Litsion Pride)* [1985] 1 Lloyd's Rep. 437, 511–2; *New Hampshire Insurance Co v MGN Ltd*, above.

[279] As to the effect of provisions requiring post-contractual disclosure, see *Hussain v Brown* [1996] 1 Lloyd's Rep. 627, 631; *Kausar v Eagle Star Insurance Co Ltd* [1997] C.L.C. 129; *Swiss Reinsurance Co v United India Insurance Co Ltd* [2005] EWHC 237 (Comm), [2005] Lloyd's Rep. I.R. 341 at [35]–[36]. See *K/S Merc-Scandia XXXXII v Lloyd's Underwriters* [2001] EWCA Civ 1275, [2001] 2 Lloyd's Rep. 563 for a review of those situations where the duty of disclosure may arise after the insurance contract is made.

[280] See Vol.I, Ch.7.

[281] *Everett v Desborough* (1829) 5 Bing. 503, 518; *Wainwright v Bland* (1836) 1 M. & W. 32; *Anderson v Fitzgerald* (1853) 4 H.L.C. 484, 504; *Dawsons v Bonnin* [1922] 2 A.C. 413. Where the representation is made in answer to a question in a proposal form, the question must be construed objectively and any ambiguity will be construed by applying the *contra proferentem* principle: *R&R Developments Ltd v Axa Insurance UK Plc* [2009] EWHC 2429 (Ch), [2010] 2 All E.R. (Comm) 527.

[282] *Wheelton v Hardisty* (1857) 8 El. & Bl. 232; *Anderson v Pacific Fire and Marine* (1871-72) L.R. 7

opinion is then sincerely held.[283] For some reason which has not been adequately explained, the representation of an intention is treated as an ordinary representation of fact and not in the same way as a representation of an opinion or belief.[284] So long as the assured honestly entertains his opinion or belief, there need be no reasonable grounds for the opinion or belief.[285] Changes of belief, opinion or intention after the contract has been made are immaterial, for, like non-disclosure, the duty only exists up to the moment when the contract is concluded[286]: until that time, of course, such changes must be communicated.[287] Where a representation is made a substantial period of time before the conclusion of the insurance contract or during the negotiation of an earlier insurance contract, the assured will either be under a duty to correct the earlier representation if it has become untrue (which would be akin to a duty of disclosure and so would require the assured to be aware of the falsity of the representation),[288] or the representation will be treated as a continuing representation so that if it is untrue at the time of the conclusion of the insurance contract in question, there will have been a misrepresentation.[289] The right analysis awaits an authoritative decision of the Courts. It is clear, however, that not all representations will be treated as continuing.[290]

Partial non-disclosure   A statement, though true in itself, may be a misrepresentation because it does not tell the whole truth, and thereby gives a false impression.[291] An ambiguous statement may be false if it is in fact understood in a false sense, though equally it could have been understood in a sense that was true.[292] However, statements are considered as a whole and will not constitute misrepresentations if

42-039

C.P. 65.

[283] *Bowden v Vaughan* (1809) 10 East 415; *Jones v Provincial Insurance* (1857) 3 C.B. N.S. 65.

[284] *St Paul Fire & Marine Insurance Co (UK) Ltd v McConnell Dowell Constructors Ltd* [1995] 2 Lloyd's Rep. 116, 127; *Limit No.2 Ltd v AXA Versicherung AG* [2007] EWHC 2321 (Comm), [2008] Lloyd's Rep. I.R. 330 at [46], reversed in part [2008] EWCA Civ 1231, [2009] Lloyd's Rep. I.R. 396; cf. *Benham v United Guarantee* (1852) 7 Ex. 744; *Grant v Aetna Insurance* (1862) 15 Moo. P.C. 516; *Weber and Berger v Employers' Liability* (1926) 24 Ll.L. Rep. 321.

[285] *Economides v Commercial Union Assurance Co Plc* [1997] 3 W.L.R. 1066; *Rendall v Combined Insurance Co of America* [2005] EWHC 678 (Comm), [2006] Lloyd's Rep. I.R. 732; see Marine Insurance Act 1906 s.20(5); contra, *Highland Insurance Co v Continental Insurance Co* [1987] 1 Lloyd's Rep. 109. There may be occasions where the opinion is expressed in such a way or such circumstances as to imply that there are reasonable grounds for the belief or opinion: cf. above, Vol.I, paras 7-007—7-013.

[286] *Benham v United Guarantee*, above. cf. *Notman v Anchor Assurance* (1858) 4 C.B.(N.S.) 476, and see above, para.42-037.

[287] *Traill v Baring* (1864) 4 De G.J. & S. 318; *Canning v Farquhar* (1886) 16 Q.B.D. 727; *Re Marshall and Scottish Employers* (1901) 85 L.T. 757. See also *Limit No.2 Ltd v AXA Versicherung AG* [2007] EWHC 2321 (Comm), [2008] Lloyd's Rep. I.R. 330 at [78]–[81], [2008] EWCA Civ 1231, [2009] Lloyd's Rep. I.R. 396 at [22]–[28].

[288] *Traill v Baring* (1864) 4 De G.J. & S. 318 at 330; *With v O'Flanagan* [1936] Ch. 575 at 583–585; *Spice Girls Ltd v Aprilia World Service BV* [2002] EWCA Civ 15, [2002] E.M.L.R. 27 at [51].

[289] *Smith v Kay* (1859) 7 H.L.C. 750 at 769; *Briess v Woolley* [1954] A.C. 333 at 344, 349, 352–353, 358; *Synergy Health (UK) Ltd v CGU Insurance Plc* [2010] EWHC 2583 (Comm), [2011] Lloyd's Rep. I.R. 500 at [159]–[163].

[290] *WPP Group Plc v Reichmann* [2000] All E.R. (D) 1409 (Aug) at [62]–[63]; *Limit No.2 Ltd v AXA Versicherung AG* [2008] EWCA Civ 1231, [2009] Lloyd's Rep. I.R. 396. See Vol.I, paras 7-022—7-023.

[291] *Re General Provincial Life* (1870) 18 W.R. 396; *Dent v Blackmore* (1927) 29 Ll.L. Rep. 9.

[292] *Glicksman v Lancashire and General* [1925] 2 K.B. 593.

inaccurate only in trivial or immaterial particulars which do not colour the whole picture.[293]

42-040 Honesty As a general rule misrepresentation makes the contract voidable however innocent the representor may have been.[294] There is some authority that the misrepresentation has to be fraudulent to have this effect in respect of life insurance policies,[295] but such an exception is to be doubted. Even if this is so, an innocent misrepresentation may well also involve non-disclosure so that the contract may be avoided on the latter ground.[296]

42-041 Inducement The decision of the House of Lords in *Pan Atlantic Insurance Co Ltd v Pine Top Insurance Co Ltd*[297] established that an insurer cannot rely upon the misrepresentation or non-disclosure of a material circumstance to avoid the insurance contract if that misrepresentation or non-disclosure did not in fact induce the making of the contract on the terms accepted (in the sense in which "inducement" is used in the general law of misrepresentation). The insurer has to show that the misrepresentation or non-disclosure was an effective cause of his entering into the contract on the terms in fact agreed; he must show at least that but for the misrepresentation or non-disclosure he would not have entered into the contract on those terms; he does not have to show it was the sole effective cause.[298] Whether the insurer has been induced is a question of fact, not one of degree; therefore, if the non-disclosure or misrepresentation had only a slight or trivial effect on the decision of the insurer (for example, if the insurer would have insisted on only slightly different terms), he will have been induced.[299] However, if the non-disclosed or misrepresented circumstance is deemed trivial by a prudent underwriter, the circumstance may not be material. If the insurer would merely have asked further questions of the assured had full and accurate disclosure been made, that would not be sufficient to constitute inducement.[300] There is said to be a presumption of inducement in the event that a material non-disclosure or misrepresentation is

---

[293] *Re Universal Non-Tariff Fire* (1875) L.R. 19 Eq. 485; *Dawsons v Bonnin* [1922] 2 A.C. 413, 425. See Marine Insurance Act 1906 s.20(4); cf. *Svenska Handelsbanken v Sun Alliance and London Insurance Plc* [1996] 1 Lloyd's Rep. 519, 561–562.

[294] *Golding v Royal London* (1914) 30 T.L.R. 350, 351; *Graham v Western Australian* (1931) 40 Ll.L. Rep. 64, 66; *Merchant's and Manufacturers' Insurance v Hunt* [1941] 1 K.B. 295, 318; *Whitlam v Hazel* [2004] EWCA Civ 1600, [2005] Lloyd's Rep. I.R. 168 at [28]; cf. Marine Insurance Act 1906 s.20. cf. *Economides v Commercial Union Assurance Co Plc* [1997] 3 W.L.R. 1066.

[295] *Anderson v Fitzgerald* (1853) 4 H.L.C. 484, 504; *Wheelton v Hardisty* (1857) 8 El. & Bl. 232, 299; *Thomson v Weems* (1884) 9 App. Cas. 671, 683; *Scottish Provident v Boddam* (1893) 9 T.L.R. 385; *Joel v Law Union* [1908] 2 K.B. 863, 877.

[296] *British Equitable v Great Western Ry* (1869) 38 L.J. Ch. 314; *London Assurance v Mansel* (1879) 11 Ch. D. 363; *British Equitable v Musgrave* (1887) 3 T.L.R. 630.

[297] [1995] 1 A.C. 501.

[298] *Assicurazioni Generali SpA v Arab Insurance Group (BSC)* [2002] EWCA Civ 1642, [2003] Lloyd's Rep. I.R. 131 at [62]; *AXA Versicherung AG v Arab Insurance Group (BSC)* [2017] EWCA Civ 96, [2017] Lloyd's Rep. I.R. 216 at [138]. For cases where the following underwriters were induced to enter into a contract by reason of the decision of the leading underwriter to enter into the contract, see *International Lottery Management Ltd v Dumas* [2002] Lloyd's Rep. I.R. 237 at [72], [78]; *Brotherton v Aseguradora Colseguros SA* [2003] EWHC 1741 (Comm), [2003] Lloyd's Rep. I.R. 762.

[299] *Aldridge Estates Investments Co Ltd v McCarthy* [1996] E.G.C.S. 167.

[300] *O'Kane v Jones* [2003] EWHC 3470 (Comm), [2004] 1 Lloyd's Rep. 389 at [235].

established.[301] If there is such a presumption, it is not one of law, but an inference of fact.[302] It is unlikely that the Court will rely on such a presumption or inference if the underwriter who assessed the risk is called to give evidence.[303] In some cases, the materiality of the circumstance may be so obvious that the Court will readily infer that the insurer was induced to enter into the insurance contract by reason of the circumstance being withheld or misrepresented, but even in such cases the inference may be rebutted by evidence.[304]

Effect of non-disclosure or misrepresentation Non-disclosure or misrepresentation by one party entitles the other party to avoid the contract,[305] and the avoidance takes effect ab initio.[306] Despite misgivings only recently expressed by the courts, an insurer confronted with a fraudulent claim is entitled to avoid the insurance contract.[307] In the event of a breach of the duty of utmost good faith, the innocent party has an unfettered right to avoid the insurance contract. There is no equitable discretion exercisable by the court which could restrain or set aside an otherwise effective avoidance of the contract.[308] In any event, it would appear that a claim paid out by an insurer is recoverable if, after payment is made, a non-

42-042

---

[301] *Pan Atlantic Insurance Co Ltd v Pine Top Insurance Co Ltd* [1995] 1 A.C. 501; *St Paul Fire & Marine Insurance Co (UK) Ltd v McConnell Dowell Contractors Ltd* [1995] 2 Lloyd's Rep. 116, 127; *Svenska Handelsbanken v Sun Alliance and London Insurance Plc* [1996] 1 Lloyd's Rep. 519, 564; *Gunns v Par Insurance Brokers* [1997] 1 Lloyd's Rep. 173, 176. In *Marc Rich & Co AG v Portman* [1996] 1 Lloyd's Rep. 430, 442–442, the court suggested that the presumption should be relied upon where the underwriter cannot be called for good reason to give evidence and no reasonable supposition can be made that he acted imprudently; affirmed [1997] 1 Lloyd's Rep. 225. See also *Laker Vent Engineering Ltd v Templeton Insurance Ltd* [2009] EWCA Civ 62, [2009] Lloyd's Rep. I.R. 704 at [69]–[70].

[302] *Assicurazioni Generali SpA v Arab Insurance Group (BSC)* [2002] EWCA Civ 1642, [2003] Lloyd's Rep. I.R. 131; *Aldridge v Liberty Mutual Insurance Europe Ltd* [2016] EWHC 3037 (Comm) at [28].

[303] *Sea Glory Maritime Co v Al Sagr National Insurance Co (The Nancy)* [2013] EWHC 2116 (Comm), [2014] 1 Lloyd's Rep. 14 at [56], [116].

[304] *Bate v Aviva Insurance UK Ltd* [2014] EWCA Civ 334, [2014] Lloyd's Rep. I.R. 527 at [35]; *Aldridge v Liberty Mutual Insurance Europe Ltd* [2016] EWHC 3037 (Comm) at [29].

[305] *Morrison v Universal Marine* (1872-73) L.R. 8 Ex. 197. See also above, para.42-033, n.227. If the contract is separable into distinct parts such that they represent separate insurances, the insurer's remedy of avoidance is likely to relate to that divisible part rather than the entire contract: *Dalecroft Properties Ltd v Underwriters* [2017] EWHC 1263 (Comm), [2017] Lloyd's Rep. I.R. 511 at [99]–[100]. Misrepresentation Act 1967 s.2(2) provides that the court or arbitrator may declare the contract subsisting where a party would otherwise be entitled to rescind, so it is arguable that the right to avoid a contract of insurance for misrepresentation of a material fact now depends upon the discretion of the tribunal. However, dicta in *Highland Insurance Co v Continental Insurance Co* [1987] 1 Lloyd's Rep. 109, 117 indicate that, in contracts of reinsurance at least, relief from avoidance will be wholly exceptional. It may be that the parties have agreed that the various sections constituting the policy are each separate insurance contracts, in which case a non-disclosure or misrepresentation might result in the avoidance of one section of the policy, as opposed to the entire policy (*James v CGU Insurance Plc* [2002] Lloyd's Rep. I.R. 206). There is, of course, a statutory right to avoid contracts of marine insurance for material misrepresentation: see Marine Insurance Act 1906 s.20.

[306] *Cornhill Insurance Co v Assenheim* (1937) 58 Ll.L. Rep. 27, 31; *Black King Shipping Corp v Massie (The Litsion Pride)* [1985] 1 Lloyd's Rep. 437, 514–516 (where even post-contract breaches of the duty of utmost good faith were held to be capable of entitling avoidance ab initio).

[307] *Galloway v Guardian Royal Exchange (UK) Ltd* [1999] Lloyd's Rep. I.R. 209; *Direct Line Insurance Plc v Khan* [2001] EWCA Civ 1794, [2002] Lloyd's Rep. I.R. 364 at [29]; cf. *Manifest Shipping & Co Ltd v Uni-Polaris Shipping Co Ltd (The Star Sea)* [2001] UKHL 1, [2001] 2 W.L.R. 170; *K/S Merc-Scandia XXXXII v Lloyd's Underwriters* [2001] EWCA Civ 1275, [2001] 2 Lloyd's Rep. 563; *Agapitos v Agnew (The Aegeon)* [2002] EWCA Civ 247, [2002] 2 Lloyd's Rep. 42; Bennett [1999] L.M.C.L.Q. 165.

[308] *Drake Insurance Plc v Provident Insurance Plc* [2003] EWHC 109 (Comm), [2003] 1 All E.R.

disclosure or misrepresentation comes to the notice of the insurer who then avoids the contract.[309] In some cases, moreover, damages may be recoverable. An action for damages in deceit will lie for deliberate misrepresentation and, possibly, for deliberate concealment of material circumstances,[310] provided that there is a duty to speak.[311] Damages will be recoverable if a misrepresentation (as opposed to a non-disclosure) is made negligently in breach of a duty of care[312]; damages will be recoverable under the Misrepresentation Act 1967 if the misrepresentation is made without reasonable grounds.[313] Apart from this, however, no action for damages will lie[314]; so that damages cannot be recovered for breach of the duty to disclose material circumstances.[315] It would seem that non-disclosure or misrepresentation by one joint assured enables the insurer to avoid the contract against the others as well.[316] However, if one co-assured under a composite, as opposed to a joint, insurance fails

(Comm) 759 at [31]–[32]; *Brotherton v Aseguradora Colseguros SA* [2003] EWCA Civ 705; overruling *Strive Shipping Corp v Hellenic Mutual War Risks Association (The Grecia Express)* [2002] EWHC 203 (Comm), [2002] 2 Lloyd's Rep. 88, 129. However, the Court of Appeal has expressed the opinion that the insurer cannot avoid the contract if the insurer acts in bad faith: *Drake Insurance Plc v Provident Insurance Plc* [2003] EWCA Civ 1834, [2004] Q.B. 601. See MacDonald Eggers [2003] L.M.C.L.Q. 249.

309 *Holland v Russell* (1863) 4 B. & S. 14; *Cornhill Insurance Co v Assenheim* (1937) 58 Ll.L. Rep. 27, 31. Moreover, in *Magee v Pennine Insurance Co* [1969] 2 Q.B. 507, a compromise of a claim was set aside on the grounds that the insurance had been procured by a misrepresentation. As to whether a settlement may be avoided if it was procured by a non-disclosure, there is conflicting authority: *Callisher v Bischoffsheim* (1870) L.R. 5 Q.B. 449; *Miles v New Zealand Alford Estate Co* (1886) 32 Ch. D. 266; *Piper v Royal Exchange Assurance* (1932) 44 Ll.L. Rep. 103, 117 (per Roche J.); *Diggens v Sun Alliance and London Insurance Plc* [1994] C.L.C. 1146; *Royal Boskalis Westminster NV v Mountain* [1997] L.R.L.R. 523, 600; reversed on other grounds [1997] 2 All E.R. 929. See also *Direct Line Insurance Plc v Fox* [2009] EWHC 386 (QB), [2009] 1 All E.R. (Comm) 1017.

310 *Dalglish v Jarvie* (1850) 2 Mac. & G. 231, 243. The dishonest concealment of material facts, or the intentional or reckless making of misleading statements, may also amount to a criminal offence: see the Fraud Act 2006 ss.2–3 and ss.89–90, 93 of the Financial Services Act 2012; Financial Services Act 2012 (Misleading Statements and Impressions) Order 2013 (SI 2013/637) art.2. The predecessor to these provisions, s.397 of the Financial Services and Markets Act 2000, did not impose a wider duty of disclosure than that which subsists at common law and does not create an entitlement to damages or other civil relief: *Aldrich v Norwich Union Life Insurance Co Ltd* [2000] Lloyd's Rep. I.R. 1. See also Road Traffic Act 1988 s.174(5). In respect of actions in deceit for fraudulent misrepresentation, see Vol.I, paras 7-048—7-074.

311 It is questionable if the duty of utmost good faith suffices for the purposes of the "duty to speak". See *Brownlie v Campbell* (1880) 5 App. Cas. 925, 950; *Society of Lloyd's v Jaffray* [2002] EWCA Civ 1101, [2002] All E.R. (D) 399 at [29]; *HIH Casualty and General Insurance Ltd v Chase Manhattan Bank* [2003] UKHL 6, [2003] 2 Lloyd's Rep. 61 at [21], [75].

312 The Court of Appeal has recently held that, in the usual case, there is no duty of care not to make negligent misstatements implicit in the relationship between insurer and assured: *HIH Casualty and General Insurance Ltd v Chase Manhattan Bank* [2001] EWCA Civ 1250, [2001] 2 Lloyd's Rep. 483 at [74]; reversed in part on other grounds [2003] UKHL 6, [2003] 2 Lloyd's Rep. 61.

313 *Argo Systems FZE v Liberty Insurance Pte Ltd* [2011] EWHC 301 (Comm), [2011] 2 Lloyd's Rep. 61 at [41]–[45], [2011] EWCA Civ 1572, [2012] 1 Lloyd's Rep. 129 at [35]; cf. *Highlands Insurance Co v Continental Insurance Co* [1987] 1 Lloyd's Rep. 109, 117–118.

314 *Glasgow Assurance v Symondson* (1911) 104 L.T. 254, 258.

315 *Banque Keyser Ullman SA v Skandia (UK) Insurance Co Ltd* [1990] 1 Q.B. 665, 773–805 (affirmed by the House of Lords on somewhat different grounds, though see [1991] 2 A.C. 249, 280); *Bank of Nova Scotia v Hellenic Mutual War Risks Association (Bermuda) Ltd (The Good Luck)* [1990] 1 Q.B. 818, 886–888, 890–902; reversed by the House of Lords on a different point: [1992] 1 A.C. 233. It is possible that interest might be recoverable as damages pursuant to the House of Lords' decision in *Sempra Metals Ltd v Commissioners of Inland Revenue* [2007] UKHL 34, [2007] 3 WLR 354; see Clarke [2008] J.B.L. 291.

316 *General Accident Fire and Life v Midland Bank* [1940] 2 K.B. 388, *Direct Line Insurance Plc v Khan*

to disclose or misrepresents a material circumstance, the insurance contract with each innocent co-assured may not be avoided, unless the latter is implicated in a breach of the duty of the utmost good faith.[317]

Affirmation and waiver by estoppel   Non-disclosure or misrepresentation makes   **42-043** the contract voidable, not void, so that the aggrieved party has an election whether or not to avoid the contract.[318] Once the aggrieved party knows all the facts, he should inform the other party within a reasonable time if he elects to avoid the contract,[319] for otherwise his subsequent conduct may be taken to be either an affirmation of the contract, or as leading the other party to suppose that the contract is being affirmed and causing him to act accordingly.[320] Thus where the aggrieved party does some act which is inconsistent with an intention to avoid the contract, such as paying a claim[321] or accepting further premiums[322] after acquiring the requisite knowledge, the right to avoid the contract will be lost. However, the aggrieved party will not have affirmed the contract and lost his right to avoid[323] unless he has knowledge both of the facts concerning the non-disclosure or misrepresentation and of his resulting right to avoid[324]; constructive knowledge or

---

[2001] EWCA Civ 1794, [2002] Lloyd's Rep. 364 and see below, para.42-098—42-099.

[317] *New Hampshire Insurance Co v MGN Ltd* [1997] L.R.L.R. 24. *Arab Bank Plc v Zurich Insurance Co* [1999] 1 Lloyd's Rep. 262; *First National Commercial Bank Plc v Barnet Devanney (Harrow) Ltd* [1999] 1 Lloyd's Rep. I.R. 43. See above, para.42-011.

[318] *Morrison v Universal Marine* (1872) L.R. 8 Ex. 197; *Mackender v Feldia AG* [1967] 2 Q.B. 590. For a statement of the principles applicable to affirmation, see *Moore Large & Co Ltd v Hermes Credit and Guarantee Plc* [2003] EWHC 26 (Comm), [2003] Lloyd's Rep. I.R. 315.

[319] *McCormick v National Motor* (1934) 40 Com. Cas. 76, 81, 82; *Simon, Haynes v Beer* (1946) 78 Ll.L. Rep. 337; *Svenska Handelsbanken v Sun Alliance and London Insurance Plc* [1996] 1 Lloyd's Rep. 519, 569.

[320] *Hemmings v Sceptre Life* [1905] 1 Ch. 365; *Holdsworth v Lancashire and Yorkshire* (1907) 23 T.L.R. 521; *Ayrey v British Legal* [1918] 1 K.B. 136; *Liberian Insurance v Mosse* [1977] 2 Lloyd's Rep. 560.

[321] *Bilbie v Lumlie* (1802) 2 East 469; *Wing v Harvey* (1854) 5 De G.M. & G. 265.

[322] *Scottish Equitable v Buist* (1877) 4 R. 1076, Ct of Sess.; merely not returning premiums already paid does not amount to waiver: *March Cabaret Club v London Assurance* [1975] 1 Lloyd's Rep. 169. As to whether the issuance of a policy may constitute an affirmation, see *Morrison v The Universal Marine Insurance Co* (1872) L.R. 8 Ex. 40; (1873) L.R. 8 Ex. 197; cf. *Svenska Handelsbanken v Sun Alliance and London Insurance Plc* [1996] 1 Lloyd's Rep. 519, 569. As to the affirmatory effect of a contractual notice of cancellation, see *Mint Security Ltd v Blair* [1982] 1 Lloyd's Rep. 188 at 198; *WISE (Underwriting Agency) Ltd v Grupo Nacional Provincial SA* [2004] EWCA Civ 962, [2004] 2 Lloyd's Rep. 483. See also *Scottish Coal Co Ltd v Royal & Sun Alliance Insurance Plc* [2008] EWHC 880 (Comm), [2008] Lloyd's Rep. I.R. Plus 31.

[323] The aggrieved party alternatively might be estopped from denying his affirmation of the contract: see below, para.42-086. As to when an insurer will be treated as knowing all the relevant facts by reason of the knowledge of an agent being imputed to him, compare *Evans v Employers' Mutual Insurance Association Ltd* [1936] 1 K.B. 505; and *Malhi v Abbey Life Assurance Co Ltd* [1996] L.R.L.R. 237. If the affirming conduct was that of an agent, rather than the aggrieved party himself, that agent himself must have the authority and capacity to affirm the contract: *Tate & Sons v Hyslop* (1885) 15 Q.B.D. 368, 374; *Aldridge Estates Investments Co Ltd v McCarthy* [1996] E.G.C.S. 167. See also *Callaghan v Thompson* [2000] Lloyd's Rep. I.R. 125.

[324] *Insurance Corp of the Channel Islands Ltd v McHugh* [1997] L.R.L.R. 94, [1998] Lloyd's Rep. I.R. 151. In *Sea Glory Maritime Co v Al Sagr National Insurance Co* [2013] EWHC 2116 (Comm), [2014] 1 Lloyd's Rep. 14 at [126], it was held that an insurer is entitled to a reasonable time to conduct its enquiries before making an election to affirm the contract. As to the requirement of knowledge of the legal right to avoid in circumstances where the insurer is being advised by solicitors, see *Moore Large & Co Ltd v Hermes Credit and Guarantee Plc* [2003] EWHC 26 (Comm), [2003] Lloyd's Rep. I.R. 315 at [92]–[100]; *Involnert Management Inc v Aprilgrange Ltd* [2015]

being put on inquiry is not sufficient.[325] Once the aggrieved party has made his election it is irrevocable.[326] The insurer may also lose the right to avoid the insurance contract by estoppel if the insurer promises not to exercise the right to avoid, even if he does not have full knowledge of the circumstances giving rise to his right to avoid (provided that the promise carries with it some apparent awareness of the right to avoid),[327] and if the assured relies on that promise to his detriment, and it would be inequitable to allow the insurer to resile from that promise.[328]

42-044 **Modification of the duty by contract**   The duty to act in good faith in the manner discussed above is often modified by the contract. Thus there may be in the contract a condition precedent based on the accuracy of statements made during the negotiations or a warranty[329] that such statements are true, and in such case it is no defence that the statement was immaterial or did not induce the making of the insurance contract.[330] Conversely, the contract may expressly restrict the duty as, for example, by providing that the insurance is to be indisputable except on the ground of fraud,[331] or that the policy is voidable only if the assured is guilty of a fraudulent non-disclosure or misrepresentation,[332] or by defining the extent of disclosure required from the assured,[333] or by excluding or limiting liability or restricting the remedies available for any breach.[334] In either case the duty becomes pro tanto

---

EWHC 2225 (Comm), [2015] 2 Lloyd's Rep. 289 at [157]–[161].

[325] *Morrison v Universal Marine* (1872) L.R. 8 Ex. 197; *McCormick v National Motor* (1934) 40 Com. Cas. 76; *Simon, Haynes v Beer* (1946) 78 Ll.L. Rep. 337; *CTI v Oceanus Mutual* [1984] 1 Lloyd's Rep. 476; *Hadenfayre v British National Insurance Society* [1984] 2 Lloyd's Rep. 393; *Insurance Corp of the Channel Islands Ltd v McHugh* [1997] L.R.L.R. 94, [1998] Lloyd's Rep. I.R. 151.

[326] *Clough v London & NW Ry* (1871) L.R. 7 Ex. 26, 34, 35.

[327] *IHC v Amtrust Europe Ltd* [2015] EWHC 257 (QB).

[328] See below, para.42-086.

[329] See below, para.42-080. The Consumer Insurance (Disclosure and Representations) Act 2012 s.6, will abolish such warranties. The Law Commission has recommended a similar abolition for other types of insurances, Consultation Paper No.204, paras 15.11–15.12.

[330] *Newcastle Fire v Macmorran* (1815) 3 Dow 225; *Anderson v Fitzgerald* (1853) 4 H.L.C. 484, 503; *Stebbing v Liverpool and London and Globe Insurance Co Ltd* [1917] 2 K.B. 433, 437; *Condogianis v Guardian Assurance* [1921] 2 A.C. 125, 129; *Dawsons v Bonnin* [1922] 2 A.C. 413; *Mackay v London General* (1935) 51 Ll.L. Rep. 201; *Babatsikos v Car Owners' Mutual Insurance Co Ltd* [1970] 2 Lloyd's Rep. 314; see, generally, Hasson (1971) 34 M.L.R. 29; *Svenska Handelsbanken v Sun Alliance and London Insurance Plc* [1996] 1 Lloyd's Rep. 519, 551–553. Such terms are to be interpreted in accordance with established rules of construction and, unless the parties so intended, will not be interpreted as a continuing warranty: *Hussain v Brown* [1996] 1 Lloyd's Rep. 627, 629.

[331] *Hemmings v Sceptre Life* [1905] 1 Ch. 365; *Anstey v British National Premium Life* (1908) 24 T.L.R. 594, 871; *Toomey v Eagle Star (No.2)* [1995] 2 Lloyd's Rep. 88, where it was held that it is possible in principle to include a provision excluding the right to rescind for material misrepresentation or non-disclosure, but that the clause in that case (which provided that the policy was "neither cancellable nor voidable by either party") did not, on its proper construction, preclude rescission for a misrepresentation or non-disclosure made negligently. cf. *Highland Insurance Co v Continental Insurance Co* [1987] 1 Lloyd's Rep. 109, 116–117; *Pan Atlantic Insurance Co Ltd v Pine Top Insurance Co Ltd* [1992] 1 Lloyd's Rep. 101, 108–109, [1993] 1 Lloyd's Rep. 496, 502–503 (both cases concerned an "errors and omissions" clause which purported to excuse inadvertent misrepresentations and non-disclosures). Regard should also be had to s.3 of the Misrepresentation Act 1967, which treats contractual provisions relieving a misrepresentor, from liability as invalid, unless reasonable; it is unlikely that such clauses will be struck down, at least from the assured's perspective, given the harshness of the remedy of avoidance as perceived by the court. See above, paras 7-148 et seq.

[332] *Mutual Energy Ltd v Starr Underwriting Agents Ltd* [2016] EWHC 590 (TCC), [2016] B.L.R. 312.

[333] *Sumitomo Bank Ltd v Banque Bruxelles Lambert SA* [1997] 1 Lloyd's Rep. 487, 495.

[334] *HIH Casualty and General Insurance Ltd v Chase Manhattan Bank* [2003] UKHL 6, [2003] 2

contractual,[335] and stipulations which extend the duty are strictly construed against the party relying on them.[336] However, the law will not permit any attempt to restrict or exclude liability for the assured's own fraud, although excluding or limiting liability for the fraud of the assured's agent is not prohibited as a matter of law.[337]

FCA Insurance Conduct of Business Sourcebook (ICOBS) In the light of the **42-045** harsh consequences which may sometimes be caused by the absolute nature of the obligations to disclose, and not misrepresent, material facts,[338] the Association of British Insurers and Lloyd's of London issued a Statement of General Insurance Practice, to which their members were expected to adhere, with a view to mitigating the severity of the obligations in the case of private policies. There were also statements dealing separately with non-life policies, and long-term life policies.[339] Since January 2005, the self-regulatory Statement of General Insurance Practice was replaced by the Financial Services Regulation, ICOB and in January 2008 by ICOBS,[340] which currently provides that insurers must handle claims promptly and fairly, provide reasonable guidance to policyholders, not unreasonably reject a claim, and pay claims promptly after agreeing to a settlement.[341] The Regulation further provides that the rejection of a consumer policyholder's claim is unreasonable where, in the absence of any evidence of fraud, the ground relied on by the insurer is the non-disclosure of a material fact which the policyholder could not reasonably be expected to disclose or non-negligent misrepresentation.[342]

Lloyd's Rep. 61; *Seashell of Lisson Grove Ltd v Aviva Insurance Ltd* [2011] EWHC 1761 (Comm). As to the effect of innocent non-disclosure clauses, see *Arab Bank Plc v Zurich Insurance Company* [1999] 1 Lloyd's Rep. 262; *Kumar v AGF Insurance Ltd* [1999] 1 W.L.R 1747.

[335] *Anderson v Fitzgerald* (1853) 4 H.L.C. 484, 496; *Joel v Law Union* [1908] 2 K.B. 863, 886; *Stebbing v Liverpool and London Globe* [1917] 2 K.B. 433, 437.

[336] *Thomson v Weems* (1884) 9 App. Cas. 671, 682; *Joel v Law Union*, above.

[337] *HIH Casualty and General Insurance Ltd v Chase Manhattan Bank* [2001] EWCA Civ 1250, [2001] 2 Lloyd's Rep. 483; reversed in part on other grounds [2003] UKHL 6, [2003] 2 Lloyd's Rep. 61.

[338] For consideration of the harsh effects of the absolute obligation to disclose material facts, and recommendations for reform, see the Law Commission's Report No.104, Cmnd.8064 (1980). See also Australian Law Reform Commission Report No.91 (April 2001), *Review of the Marine Insurance Act 1909*; Derrington [2002] L.M.C.L.Q. 214; *Insurance Contract Law Reform*, Recommendations to the Law Commission, A Report of the Sub-Committee of the British Insurance Law Association, September 1, 2002; Law Commission's Consultation Paper No.182 on "*Insurance Contract Law: Misrepresentation, Non-Disclosure and Breach of Warranty by the Insured*" (July 2007); Law Commission's Consultation Paper No.204 on "*The Business Insured's Duty of Disclosure and the Law of Warranties*" (June 2012).

[339] For the texts of the Statement of General Insurance Practice, see *http://www.abi.org.uk*.

[340] See *https://www.handbook.fca.org.uk/handbook/ICOBS* made pursuant to ss.137A to 137F, 137T and 139A of the Financial Services and Markets Act 2000, as amended by s.24 of the Financial Services Act 2012. In *Parker v National Farmers Union Mutual Insurance Society Ltd* [2012] EWHC 2156 (Comm), [2013] Lloyd's Rep. I.R. 253 at [197], it was held that the obligations under ICOBS were not implied terms of the insurance contract. See also *Bate v Aviva Insurance UK Ltd* [2013] EWHC 1687 (Comm), [2013] Lloyd's Rep. I.R. 492 at [33]–[34]; affirmed [2014] EWCA Civ 334, [2014] Lloyd's Rep. I.R. 527. A contravention of such rules by an authorised person may entitle a private person to claim damages for loss sustained pursuant s.138D(2) of the 2000 Act, introduced pursuant to an amendment by s.24 of the Financial Services Act 2012. See *Goodman v Central Capital Ltd* [2012] EWHC 8 (QB), [12].

[341] ICOBS para.8.1.1. See *Parker v National Farmers Union Mutual Insurance Society Ltd* [2012] EWHC 2156 (Comm), [2013] Lloyd's Rep. I.R. 253 at [193]–[202]; *Bate v Aviva Insurance UK Ltd* [2013] EWHC 1687 (Comm), [2013] Lloyd's Rep. I.R. 492, affirmed [2014] EWCA Civ 334, [2014] Lloyd's Rep. I.R. 527.

[342] ICOBS para.8.1.2. In *Bate v Aviva Insurance UK Ltd* [2013] EWHC 1687 (Comm), [2013] Lloyd's

(b) Consumer Insurance Contracts

42-046 **Consumer Insurance (Disclosure and Representations) Act 2012** On March 8, 2012, the Consumer Insurance (Disclosure and Representations) Act 2012 was passed. The 2012 Act applies to consumer Insurance contracts agreed on or after April 6, 2013 or to variations to pre-existing contracts agreed on or after that date.[343] This Act has fundamentally altered the consumer assured's duty of utmost good faith as it applies up to the making of the insurance contract. A consumer is an individual who contracts wholly or mainly for purposes unrelated to the individual's trade, business or profession.[344] The consumer assured's duty of utmost good faith and the insurer's remedies for breach of that duty are exhaustively set out in the Act. The previous law no longer applies to consumer assureds and the common law duty of disclosure no longer applies to such consumer assureds. By s.10, a term of a consumer insurance contract which would put the consumer in a worse position in respect of the disclosure and representations required of the consumer and the insurer's remedies than the consumer would be in by the provisions of the 2012 Act are of no effect.[345]

42-047 **The duty to take reasonable care not to misrepresent** Under s.2(2) of the 2012 Act, it is the duty of the consumer to take reasonable care not to make a misrepresentation to the insurer. Whether or not a consumer has taken reasonable care not to make a misrepresentation is to be determined in the light of all the relevant circumstances, including: the type of consumer insurance contract and its target market, any relevant explanatory material or publicity produced or authorised by the insurer; how clear and how specific the insurer's questions to the assured were; in the case of a failure to respond to the insurer's questions in connection with the renewal or variation of a consumer insurance contract, how clearly the insurer communicated the importance of answering those questions; and whether or not an agent was acting for the consumer.[346] The standard of care required by the assured's duty is that of a reasonable consumer.[347] A misrepresentation made dishonestly is always to be taken as showing a lack of reasonable care.[348]

42-048 **Basis of the contracts clauses** Insurance contracts in many instances contain provisions which warrant the truth of pre-contractual representations, for example contained in a proposal form, or which render the truth of such representations as conditions precedent to the insurer's liability under the insurance contract. Such provisions often take the form of a clause providing that the representations made by the assured form the "basis" of the insurance contract or are incorporated into

---

Rep. I.R. 492, [2014] EWCA Civ 334, [2014] Lloyd's Rep. I.R. 527 at [48]–[49], the Court held that a fraudulent device used in the pursuit of a fraudulent claim was sufficient to attract the fraud exception. See also *Ashfaq v International Insurance Co of Hannover Plc* [2017] EWCA Civ 357, [2017] H.L.R. 29.

[343] 2012 Act s.12(4); The Consumer Insurance (Disclosure and Representations) Act 2012 (Commencement) Order 2013 (SI 2013/450).

[344] 2012 Act s.1. cf. *Ashfaq v International Insurance Co of Hannover Plc* [2017] EWCA Civ 357, [2017] H.L.R. 29 at [45]–[58]. The 2012 Act did not apply to the insurance contract in this case: at [15].

[345] This provision does not apply to settlement contracts in respect of claims made under a consumer insurance contract: s.10(3).

[346] 2012 Act s.3(2).

[347] 2012 Act s.3.

[348] 2012 Act s.3(5).

the insurance contract, without identifying any particular representation. The effect of such a warranty (or condition precedent) is that if a pre-contractual representation coming within the basis of the contract clause is untrue, there is a breach of warranty (or condition precedent) and the insurer is discharged from liability from the date of the breach, which in many cases is the date of the inception of the cover or the conclusion of the contract.[349] The Consumer Insurance (Disclosure and Representations) Act 2012, by s.6, abolishes such warranties with respect to consumer insurance contracts. This prohibition, however, is unlikely to apply to specific warranties, i.e. warranties that specific representations of fact (e.g. that the assured has suffered no losses during the previous 12 months) are true, so that such warranties will remain valid.[350]

The insurer's remedies The insurer will have a remedy for a misrepresentation **42-049** made by the consumer assured where the assured has breached its duty under s.2(2) and where the insurer shows that without the misrepresentation, that insurer would not have entered into the contract (or agreed to the variation) at all, or would have done so only on different terms.[351] The insurer's remedies will depend on whether the misrepresentation is deliberate or reckless (in the sense that the assured knew that, or did not care whether, the representation was untrue or misleading and the representation was relevant to the insurer) or careless. The finding that an assured's breach of duty was deliberate or reckless may be supported by the presumptions allowed under s.5(5), in particular that the consumer knew that a matter about which the insurer asked a clear and specific question was relevant to the insurer.[352] If the misrepresentation was deliberate or reckless, the insurer may avoid the contract and retain the premium. If it was careless (i.e. lacking in reasonable care), and if the insurer would not have entered into the contract had the truth been told, the insurer may avoid the contract but must return the premium. If it was careless, and the insurer would have entered into the same contract had the truth been told but on different terms (other than as to premium), the insurer may require the contract to be treated as if it had been concluded on those terms. If the misrepresentation was careless, and the insurer would have entered into the same contract but at a higher premium, the claims payable under the contract will be proportionately reduced.[353] Contracting out is not permitted under the Act.[354]

FCA Insurance Conduct of Business Sourcebook (ICOBS)[355] Under ICOBS, **42-050** a "consumer" is any natural person who is acting for purposes which are outside his trade or profession.[356] ICOBS provides that insurers must handle claims promptly and fairly, provide reasonable guidance to policyholders, not unreason-

---

[349] See above, para.42-044.
[350] Explanatory Notes to the 2012 Act, paras 41–42. Such warranties, to be valid, would have to be fair within the meaning of the Unfair Terms in Consumer Contracts Regulations 1999 (SI 1999/2083) and, for contracts made on or after October 1, 2015, the Consumer Rights Act 2015 ss.62–66, as to which see paras 38-389—38-426.
[351] 2012 Act s.4.
[352] *Tesco Underwriting Ltd v Achunche* Unreported July 7, 2016.
[353] 2012 Act s.5 and Sch.1.
[354] 2012 Act s.10.
[355] See above, para.42-045.
[356] ICOBS para.2.1.1(3).

ably reject a claim, and pay claims promptly after agreeing to a settlement.[357] Further, ICOBS provides that, in respect of insurance contracts concluded on or before April 5, 2013, the rejection of a consumer policyholder's claim is unreasonable where, in the absence of any evidence of fraud, the ground relied on by the insurer is the non-disclosure of a material fact which the policyholder could not reasonably be expected to disclose or non-negligent misrepresentation.[358] In respect of insurance contracts concluded on or after April 6, 2013, the rejection of a consumer policyholder's claim is unreasonable where, in the absence of fraud, the ground relied on by the insurer is a misrepresentation which is not made in breach of the consumer's duty in s. 2(2) of the Consumer Insurance (Disclosure and Representations) Act 2012 or is such that the insurer would have entered into contract on the same terms even if no misrepresentation had been made.[359] It is worth noting that in consumer cases the approach of the Financial Ombudsman Service (FOS)[360] is to consider, first whether there has been a clear case of misrepresentation or non-disclosure inducing the conclusion of the insurance contract[361] and, secondly, the policyholder's state of mind.[362] The FOS will permit the insurer to avoid the policy in the case of a deliberate or reckless misrepresentation or non-disclosure, will require the insurer to pay the claim in respect of an innocent breach of duty, and in the case of an "inadvertent" breach will require the insurer to handle the claim on the basis of what contract the insurer would have entered into, if any, had full disclosure been made.

(c)   Insurance Act 2015

42-051   **The duty of the utmost good faith**   The Insurance Act 2015 entered into force on August 12, 2016 and applies to contracts of insurance, and variations to contracts of insurance, agreed after the Act entered into force.[363] The 2015 Act makes a number of modifications to the duty of utmost good faith which applies to the contract of insurance at common law and under the Marine Insurance Act 1906. By s.14 of the 2015 Act, any rule of law permitting a party to an insurance contract to avoid the contract on the ground that the utmost good faith has not been observed by the other party is abolished. Section 17 of the 1906 Act (which declares the law applicable to non-marine insurance contracts as well as to marine insurance contracts) is therefore amended to provide that "A contract of marine insurance is a contract based upon the utmost good faith". Accordingly, the concept of utmost

---

[357] ICOBS para.8.1.1. See *Parker v National Farmers Union Mutual Insurance Society Ltd* [2012] EWHC 2156 (Comm), [2013] Lloyd's Rep. I.R. 253 at [193]–[202]; *Bate v Aviva Insurance UK Ltd* [2013] EWHC 1687 (Comm), [2013] Lloyd's Rep. I.R. 492, affirmed [2014] EWCA Civ 334, [2014] Lloyd's Rep. I.R. 527.

[358] ICOBS para.8.1.2(1). In *Bate v Aviva Insurance UK Ltd* [2013] EWHC 1687 (Comm), [2013] Lloyd's Rep. I.R. 492, [2014] EWCA Civ 334, [2014] Lloyd's Rep. I.R. 527, at [48]–[49], the Court held that a fraudulent device used in the pursuit of a fraudulent claim was sufficient to attract the fraud exception.

[359] ICOBS para.8.1.2(2), 8.1.3.

[360] The approach is set out in various of the FOS's publications (see *http://www.financial-ombudsman.org.uk*) and in an appendix to the Law Commission's Consultation Paper No.182 (see *http://www.lawcom.gov.uk*). The FOS may also apply the same approach to small businesses.

[361] The FOS appears to apply a test which is more appropriate for misrepresentations, than non-disclosures, by focusing on the insurer's question and the assured's response.

[362] At various points in its publications, the FOS appears to distinguish between five states of mind: fraudulent, deliberate, reckless, inadvertent and innocent.

[363] 2015 Act ss.22, 23(2).

good faith is retained by the 2015 Act, but any remedy for failing to observe the utmost good faith is abolished and is replaced by remedies provided for by the 2015 Act, which apply only to a breach of the assured's pre-contractual duty of fair presentation. Any duty which applies after the conclusion of the contract (other than in respect of claims) or which applies to the insurer might still exist after the 2015 Act entered into force, but as matters stand there is no obvious remedy available for any such failures. In the Explanatory Notes accompanying the Act, it is said that "good faith will remain an interpretative principle".[364]

The duty of fair presentation By s.3(1) of the 2015 Act, the assured is under a   **42-052**
duty to make a fair presentation of the risk before the insurance contract is entered into. There are four elements of the duty of fair presentation. First, the assured is obliged to disclose to the insurer every material circumstance which the assured knows or ought to know. Failing such full disclosure, the assured is obliged to disclose sufficient information to put a prudent insurer on notice that it needs to make further inquiries to reveal further material circumstances.[365] Secondly, the assured must provide such disclosure in a manner which is reasonably clear and accessible to a prudent insurer.[366] A fair presentation need not be contained in only one document or oral presentation.[367] Thirdly, the assured must ensure that every material representation of fact is substantially correct. A material representation of fact is substantially correct, if a prudent insurer would not consider the difference between what is represented and what is actually correct to be material.[368] Fourthly, the assured must ensure that every material representation of expectation or belief is made in good faith.[369] In many respects, the duty of fair presentation is substantially similar to the requirements of the common law insofar as it governs the assured's pre-contractual duty of full and accurate disclosure. There are however some substantial changes effected by the 2015 Act. The two must substantial changes relate to the concept of knowledge as it applies to the assured and the insurer, and the remedies available to the insurer in the event of a breach of the assured's duty of fair presentation.[370]

Materiality The 2015 Act retains the test of materiality as applied under the com-   **42-053**
mon law, namely that a circumstance or representation is material if it would influence the judgment of a prudent insurer in determining whether to take the risk and, if so, on what terms.[371] This is the same test as is currently applied at common law and under ss.18(2) and 20(2) of the Marine Insurance Act 1906.[372] However, the 2015 Act identifies certain facts which *may* be material, namely special or unusual facts relating to the risk, any particular concerns which led the assured to seek insurance cover for the risk, and anything which those concerned with the class of insurance and the field of insured activity in question would generally understand as be-

---

364 Explanatory Notes, para.117.
365 2015 Act s.3(3)–(4).
366 2015 Act s.3(3)(b).
367 2015 Act s.7(1).
368 2015 Act ss.3(3)(c), 7(5).
369 2015 Act s.3(3)(c). See *Economides v Commercial Union Assurance Co Plc* [1997] 3 W.L.R. 1066.
370 See below, para.42-057.
371 2015 Act s.7(3).
372 See above, para.42-034.

ing something that should be dealt with in a fair presentation of risks of the type in question.[373]

42-054 **Exceptions to the duty of disclosure** The exceptions to the assured's duty of disclosure as required by the duty to make a fair presentation are largely the same as apply under the common law.[374] The assured is not obliged to disclose a circumstance, even if material, if it diminishes the risk, if the insurer knows, ought to know or is presumed to know the circumstance in question, or if the circumstance is something as to which the insurer waives information.[375] There is one exception which applies under the common law, but which has been omitted by the 2015 Act: under the common law, the assured is not obliged to disclose a circumstance if its disclosure is superfluous by reason of the presence in the policy of a promissory warranty. This exception has been removed by reason of the changes introduced by the 2015 Act to the law governing promissory warranties.[376]

42-055 **The assured's knowledge** Pursuant to the duty of fair presentation, the assured is in the first instance obliged to disclose every material circumstance which the assured knows (actual knowledge) or ought to know (constructive knowledge).[377] With respect to the assured's actual knowledge, if the assured is an individual, the assured knows only what is known to that individual or to the individual or individuals who are responsible for the assured's insurance (typically, an insurance broker).[378] If the assured is not an individual (such as a company or an unincorporated association), the assured knows only what is known to one or more individuals who are part of the assured's "senior management" or responsible for the assured's insurance.[379] The Act defines "senior management" to mean those individuals who play significant roles in the making of decisions about how the assured's activities are to be managed or organised.[380] In the Explanatory Notes to the Act, it is said that in a corporate context the senior management is likely to include members of the board of directors but may extend beyond this, depending on the structure and management arrangements of the assured.[381] However, the assured will not be taken to know information known to its insurance agent, where the insurance agent acquired the information in question through a business relationship with a person who is not connected with the contract of insurance.[382] Furthermore, the assured will be taken to know a circumstance which the individual suspected and of which the individual would have had knowledge but for deliberately refraining from confirming or enquiring about such circumstance.[383] With respect to the assured's constructive knowledge, whether the assured is an individual or not, the assured ought to know that which should reasonably have been revealed by a reasonable search of information available to the assured (whether the search is conducted by making enquiries or by any other means) and includes information held within

---

[373] 2015 Act s.7(4).
[374] See above, para.42-036.
[375] 2015 Act s.3(5).
[376] See below, para.42-080.
[377] 2015 Act s.3(4)(a).
[378] 2015 Act s.4(2).
[379] 2015 Act s.4(3).
[380] 2015 Act s.4(8)(c).
[381] Explanatory Notes, para.55.
[382] 2015 Act s.4(4)–(5).
[383] 2015 Act s.6(1).

the assured's organisation or by any other person.[384] In this respect, the assured's constructive knowledge is apparently much broader than the assured's constructive knowledge under the common law, where the assured was deemed to know only that which ought to have been known to the assured "in the ordinary course of business".[385]

The insurer's knowledge   Pursuant to the duty of fair presentation, the assured   **42-056**
is not obliged to disclose to the insurer a circumstance if the insurer knows it, ought to know it, or is presumed to know it.[386] An insurer knows something only if it is known to one or more of the individuals who participate in the decision whether or not to insure the risk on behalf of the insurer, namely the individual underwriters.[387] An insurer ought to know something only if an employee or agent knows it and ought reasonably to have passed on the relevant information to the underwriter in question or if the relevant information is held by the insurer and is readily available to the underwriter in question. In the Explanatory Notes, it is suggested that an insurer ought to know information held by the claims department or reports produced by surveyors or medical experts for the purpose of assessing the risk and information which would be revealed to the underwriter in question by making a reasonable effort to search for such information as is available to the underwriter within the insurer's organisation, such as in the insurer's electronic records.[388] An insurer is presumed to know things which are common knowledge and things which an insurer offering insurance of the class in question to assureds in the field of activity in question would reasonably be expected to know in the ordinary course of business.[389] An insurer's knowledge will include its "blind-eye" knowledge.[390]

The insurer's remedies for unfair presentation of the risk   If there has been a   **42-057**
breach of the duty of fair presentation and if the insurer has been induced by the breach in the sense that but for the breach the insurer would not have entered into the insurance contract at all or would have done so on different terms, the insurer is entitled to a remedy for that breach.[391] By s.14(1), the 2015 Act abolished the avoidance of the insurance contract as the universal remedy for any breach of the duty of utmost good faith. In its place, where there has been a breach of the duty of fair presentation, the 2015 provides different remedies depending on (a) whether the breach was deliberate or reckless and (b), where the breach was not deliberate or reckless, the extent of the inducement.[392] If the breach was deliberate (meaning that the assured knew that it was in breach of the duty) or reckless (meaning that the assured did not care whether or not it was in breach of the duty), the insurer is

---

[384] 2015 Act s.4(6)–(7).
[385] See above, para.42-035.
[386] 2015 Act s.3(5)(b)–(d).
[387] 2015 Act s.5(1).
[388] 2015 Act s.5(2); Explanatory Notes, para.64–65.
[389] 2015 Act s.5(3). See *North British Fishing Boat Insurance Co Ltd v Starr* (1922) 13 Ll.L. Rep. 206, 210; cf. *Greenhill v Federal Insurance Co Ltd* [1927] 1 K.B. 65; *Marc Rich & Co AG v Portman* [1996] 1 Lloyd's Rep. 430, 442; affirmed [1997] 1 Lloyd's Rep. 225.
[390] 2015 Act s.6(1).
[391] 2015 Act s.8(1).
[392] 2015 Act s.8 and Sch.1.

entitled to avoid the insurance contract and to retain the premium.[393] If the breach was neither deliberate nor reckless, and if the insurer would not have entered into the insurance contract at all, but for the breach, the insurer is entitled to avoid the insurance contract, but must also return the premium.[394] If the breach is neither deliberate nor reckless and, but for the breach, the insurer would have entered into the insurance contract on different terms, there are two remedies depending on whether the different terms relate to premium or not; these remedies are cumulative.[395] If they do not relate to premium, the insurer may treat the insurance contract as having been written on those different terms.[396] If the different terms relate to premium, and if the insurer would have charged a higher premium but for the breach, the insurer is entitled to reduce proportionately any amount to be paid on the claim. For example, if the insurer actually charged a premium of £1,000 but would have charged a premium of £2,000 but for the breach, a claim under the insurance contract which ordinarily would be quantified in the sum of £1,000,000 may be reduced by 50 per cent to £500,000.[397] There are similar remedies available where the breach of the duty of fair presentation relates to the agreement of a variation.[398]

42-058   **The insurer's election and waiver**   The 2015 Act does not state in what circumstances the insurer may lose the right to the remedies stipulated by the Act by way of affirmation or estoppel. It is clear however that the remedial rights available to the insurer under the 2015 Act may be exercised if the insurer so chooses. The 2015 Act provides that the insurer "may" avoid or "may" reduce proportionately the amount of the recoverable claim and that the insurance contract will be treated as if written on the different terms the insurer would have agreed but for the breach of duty, "if the insurer so requires".[399] Accordingly, the insurer must elect to exercise any such remedial rights. The insurer may lose such rights by affirmation or estoppel in accordance with the principles explained above.[400]

42-059   **Basis of the contract clauses**   It has been a common feature of many commercial insurance contracts that pre-contractual representations of fact made by the assured to the insurer, often in a proposal form, are warranted to be true or that the policy contains conditions precedent to the liability of the insurer that such pre-contractual representations are true. Such warranties or conditions precedent may be express or may be introduced by provisions stating that the pre-contractual representations are the "basis" of the contract or are incorporated into the contract. The effect of such provisions is that if any pre-contractual representation which is the subject of such a warranty or condition precedent is untrue, the insurer is automatically discharged from all liability under the insurance contract as from the

---

[393] 2015 Act ss.8(2), 8(5) and Sch.1 para.2. As to what constitutes a deliberate non-disclosure, see *Mutual Energy Ltd v Starr Underwriting Agents Ltd* [2016] EWHC 590 (TCC), [2016] B.L.R. 312.
[394] 2015 Act s.8(2) and Sch.1 para.4.
[395] 2015 Act s.8(2) and Sch.1 paras 5–6; para.6 begins with the words "In addition".
[396] 2015 Act s.8(2) and Sch.1 para.5.
[397] 2015 Act s.8(2) and Sch.1 para.6.
[398] 2015 Act s.8(2) and Sch.1 paras 7–11.
[399] 2015 Act Sch.1 paras 2, 4, 5, 6(1). As regards variations, see Sch.1 paras 8, 9(2), 9(3), 10(2), 10(3), 11(1).
[400] See above, para.42-043 and below, para.42-086.

date of the breach of the warranty or condition precedent.[401] The 2015 Act renders such provisions as invalid in that s. 9(2) provides that a representation made by the assured cannot be converted into such a warranty (or presumably conditions precedent) by such means (including by means of a "basis of the contract" clause). This prohibition appears to be aimed at provisions which seek to convert, without discrimination, all or a large number of pre-contractual representations into a warranty by basis of the contract clauses or the like. As recognised in the Explanatory Notes accompanying the Act, it should remain possible for insurers to include specific warranties relating to existing or past facts within their policies.[402]

Contracting out of the 2015 Act   Except in one instance, the 2015 Act recognises **42-060** that the parties to the insurance contract may contract out of the provisions of the 2015 Act, for example providing for different duties of disclosure or different remedies for an unfair presentation of the risk. Where such a term of the insurance contract intends to contract out of the provisions of the 2015 Act and where a term (if valid) would put the assured in a worse position than it would be in under the provisions of the Act, in order to be effective, any such "disadvantageous" term purporting to contract out of the Act must satisfy two conditions (which are described as the "transparency requirements").[403] First, the insurer must take sufficient steps to draw the disadvantageous term to the assured's attention before the insurance contract is agreed (or before the relevant variation is agreed).[404] However, the assured may not rely on any failure to comply with this condition if the assured or its agent had actual knowledge of the disadvantageous term when the contract (or variation) was agreed.[405] Second, the disadvantageous term must be clear and unambiguous as to its effect.[406] In order to assess whether these conditions have been complied with, the characteristics of the assured of the kind in question and the circumstances of the transaction are to be taken into account.[407] The exception referred to at the beginning of this paragraph relates to "basis of the contract" clauses which put the assured in a worse position than allowed by s.9 of the 2015 Act; such provisions are not permitted in any circumstances.[408] The 2015 Act's provisions relating to contracting out do not apply to contracts for the settlement of claims under an insurance contract.[409]

(d) Post-contractual Duty of Utmost Good Faith

The post-contractual duty of utmost good faith: the common law   The preced- **42-061** ing discussion has concentrated on the duty of full disclosure which exists up to the time of the making of the insurance contract. There are, however, other aspects of the duty. For example, there is a "post-contractual" duty of disclosure in cases where the insurance contract is to be amended or renewed; in reality, in such cases, the pre-contractual duty of disclosure revives so that the insurer may exercise his

---

[401] See above, para.42-044.
[402] Explanatory Notes, para.85.
[403] 2015 Act s.16.
[404] 2015 Act s.17(2).
[405] 2015 Act s.17(5).
[406] 2015 Act s.17(3).
[407] 2015 Act s.17(4).
[408] 2015 Act ss.9, 16(1).
[409] 2015 Act s.16(4).

underwriting judgment afresh with the benefit of material information.[410] In other contexts, concerning the insurance contract's performance, the courts have held that there is a duty not to be fraudulent, but no wider duty.[411] Obviously, there is a duty not to present fraudulent claims, although the precise nature and ambit of this duty is presently uncertain; in particular, it is unclear whether it properly falls within the wider duty of utmost good faith. The duty not to make fraudulent claims, which at the least is recognised as a sui generis common law duty, is considered separately in the context of claims in general.[412] In addition, the parties should not perform the insurance contract, in contexts other than claims, fraudulently: for example, where the assured provides information to the insurer during the course of the risk. It may be that the doctrine of utmost good faith has a wider role to play, such as where a liability insurer or a reinsurer assumes a contractual right to act on behalf of the assured or reassured respectively,[413] or possibly influencing the construction to be given to the terms of an insurance contract.[414] There may be circumstances where, having regard to the duty of utmost good faith, the insurer will assume a duty to warn the assured that it is not complying with the relevant terms of the insurance contract in respect of claims.[415]

42-062 **Post-contractual duty of utmost good faith: Insurance Act 2015**   Although the 2015 Act does not remove the general post-contractual duty of utmost good faith insofar as it applies to insurance contracts, it does abolish any rule of law which allows the insurer to avoid the insurance contract for the breach of the duty of utmost good faith.[416] Accordingly there is no remedy available for such failures to observe the utmost good faith, save insofar as the 2015 Act provides for alternative remedies. The only such remedy which the 2015 Act provides for in this post-contractual context are remedies for the assured's presentation of a fraudulent claim.[417] The 2015 Act does not alter the law concerning what constitutes a fraudulent claim and whether or not a fraudulent claim represents a breach of duty; it only makes provision for the remedies for any such offending fraudulent claim.[418]

5. THE PARTIES

42-063 **The assured**   The assured (often referred to as the "insured") is a person who may enter into and bind himself by a contract may effect a valid contract of insurance,

---

[410] For a survey of the post-contractual duty of disclosure, see *K/S Merc-Scandia XXXXII v Lloyd's Underwriters* [2001] EWCA Civ 1275, [2001] 2 Lloyd's Rep. 563. It is now established that there is no general duty of disclosure in respect of claims: *Royal Boskalis Westminster NV v Mountain* [1997] L.R.L.R. 523; reversed on other grounds by the Court of Appeal: [1999] Q.B. 674; *Manifest Shipping & Co Ltd v Uni-Polaris Shipping Co Ltd (The Star Sea)* [2001] UKHL 1, [2001] 2 W.L.R. 170.

[411] *Manifest Shipping & Co Ltd v Uni-Polaris Shipping Co Ltd (The Star Sea)* [2001] UKHL 1, [2001] 2 W.L.R. 170; *K/S Merc-Scandia XXXXII v Lloyd's Underwriters* [2001] EWCA Civ 1275, [2001] 2 Lloyd's Rep. 563; *Agapitos v Agnew (The Aegeon)* [2002] EWCA Civ 247, [2002] 2 Lloyd's Rep. 42.

[412] See below, para.42-098.

[413] *Cox v Bankside Members' Agency Ltd* [1995] 2 Lloyd's Rep. 437, 471–472; cf. *Gan Insurance Co Ltd v Tai Ping Insurance Co Ltd (No 2 and 3)* [2001] 1 Lloyd's Rep. I.R. 667 at [68], [76].

[414] *Harrower v Hutchinson* (1870) LR 5 Q.B. 584, 592.

[415] *Ted Baker Plc v Axa Insurance UK Plc* [2017] EWCA Civ 4097, [2017] Lloyd's Rep. I.R. 682 at [69]–[90].

[416] 2015 Act s.14.

[417] 2015 Act s.12.

[418] See below, paras 42-099—42-100.

provided he has the necessary insurable interest in its subject matter.[419] A minor will not be bound by an insurance contract that is not for his benefit[420]; and in any event a minor is not bound by the assignment of an insurance contract as security for an unenforceable loan.[421] The assured is usually identified in the insurance contract specifically or as a member of a class, although there is no reason why the assured cannot contract as an undisclosed principal, provided that the insurer has not manifested his unwillingness to contract with such principals. In such cases, however, there may be a duty of disclosure to identify the principal to the insurer, if it is material.[422]

The insurer   Persons carrying on business as insurers are required by the Financial   **42-064**
Services and Markets Act 2000[423] to be authorised by the Financial Conduct Authority and to comply with the regulatory regime instituted thereunder.[424] At common law, a contract of insurance with an insurer acting without statutory authorisation was void for illegality and therefore as unenforceable by an innocent assured as by the insurer himself.[425] Sections 26 and 28 of the Financial Services and Markets Act 2000 now provide statutory relief from the consequences of this rule, which

---

[419] See above, paras 42-005 et seq. See *New Hampshire Insurance Co v MGN Ltd* [1997] L.R.L.R. 24, 56; *Sumitomo Bank Ltd v Banque Bruxelles Lambert SA* [1997] 1 Lloyd's Rep. 487, 495. As to the insurance for the benefit of more than one assured, see above, paras 42-010—42-011.

[420] *Clements v London, NW Ry* [1894] 2 Q.B. 482.

[421] *Nottingham Building Society v Thurston* [1903] A.C. 6 (decided under the Infants Relief Act 1874, now repealed by the Minors' Contracts Act 1987); see above, Vol.I, paras 9-005—9-009.

[422] *National Oilwell (UK) Ltd v Davy Offshore Ltd* [1993] 2 Lloyd's Rep. 582, 596–597; *Talbot Underwriting Ltd v Nausch Hogan & Murray (The Jascon 5)* [2006] EWCA Civ 889, [2006] 2 Lloyd's Rep. 195.

[423] As amended by the Financial Services Act 2012. The "effecting" and "carrying out" of a contract of insurance is a regulated activity for the purposes of s.22 of the Act: the Financial Services and Markets Act 2000 (Regulated Activities) Order 2001 (SI 2001/544) art.10. The expressions "effecting" and "carrying out" include the making and performance of insurance contracts (*Bedford Insurance Co Ltd v Institutio de Resseguros do Brasil* [1985] 1 Q.B. 966, 981–982; *Bates v Barrow Ltd* [1995] 1 Lloyd's Rep. 680, 689; *Group Josi Reinsurance Co Ltd v Walbrook Insurance Co Ltd* [1996] 1 Lloyd's Rep. 345, 369) and their negotiation which begins not later than the invitation to treat (*R. v Wilson* [1997] 1 All E.R. 119, 126; *Re Great Western Assurance Co SA* [1999] Lloyd's Rep. I.R. 377). "Contract of insurance" is defined in art.3 of the Order. This probably includes a contract of reinsurance (*Re NRG Victory Reinsurance Ltd* [1995] 1 All E.R. 533; *New Hampshire Insurance Co v Grand Union Insurance Co Ltd* [1996] L.R.L.R. 102, 104, HK CA); note that "a reinsurance contract" is excluded from the definition of "qualifying contract of insurance" in art.3.

[424] See McMeel [2005] L.M.C.L.Q. 186.

[425] *Phoenix General Insurance Co of Greece SA v Halvanon Insurance Co* [1988] Q.B. 216 (where the Court of Appeal expressed an admittedly obiter view after full argument in order to resolve the uncertainty caused by the conflict between *Bedford Insurance Co v Instituto de Ressaguros do Brasil* [1985] Q.B. 966; and *Stewart v Oriental Fire and Marine Insurance Co* [1985] Q.B. 988); *Re Cavalier Insurance Co Ltd* [1989] 2 Lloyd's Rep. 430; *DR Insurance Co v Seguros America Banamex* [1993] 1 Lloyd's Rep. 120. See, however, the observations of Parker L.J. in *Overseas Union Insurance Ltd v Incorporated General Insurance Ltd* [1992] 1 Lloyd's Rep. 439, 444–445; and of the Court of Appeal in *Fuji Finance Inc v Aetna Life Insurance Co Ltd* [1997] Ch. 173. The Insurance Companies Act 1982 prohibited the effecting or carrying out of unauthorised insurance business within the UK, whether or not the proper law of the insurance contract is English law (*DR Insurance Co v Central National Insurance Co* [1996] 1 Lloyd's Rep. 74). The 1982 Act did not prohibit the insurance of UK risks offshore: *Secretary of State for Trade and Industry v Great Western Assurance Co SA* [1997] Re L.R. 197. The fact that the contract of insurance is made outside the jurisdiction does not mean that insurance business is not conducted in the jurisdiction, if for example there is continuity or regularity of services provided within the jurisdiction, which are an integral part of the way in which the insurer conducts business: *Re Great Western Assurance Co SA* [1999] Lloyd's Rep. I.R. 377. See also Financial Services and Markets Act 2000 s.418.

includes a right to compensation and may include, subject to the discretion of the court, the enforcement of the contract.[426]

42-065 **Agents of the insurer** An insurer often employs local agents to solicit business.[427] The extent of the authority of such agents varies widely and depends upon the facts of each case. In general, the authority is limited to issuing and receiving proposal forms,[428] but it may be extended, depending upon the circumstances, either expressly or impliedly,[429] or by holding out,[430] to embrace, for example, the granting of temporary cover,[431] the acceptance of premiums[432] or the receipt of notices.[433] Whether the knowledge of the agent is imputed to the insurer depends upon whether the agent is one to whom the principal looks for information of the kind in question,[434] and often insurers are estopped from denying that an agent has passed on information to them.[435] The insurer's agent is not, by reason of the agency alone, a party to the insurance contract.[436]

42-066 **Broker** Persons seeking insurance frequently engage brokers, whose services are usually remunerated on a commission basis by the insurer,[437] but who are nonetheless agents of the assured,[438] though they may act for the insurer as well,[439] in which

---

[426] See *New Hampshire Insurance Co v Grand Union Insurance Co Ltd* [1996] L.R.L.R. 102. As to the transitional effect of the statutory predecessor to ss.26 and 28 (s.132 of the Financial Services Act 1986, now repealed by the Financial Services and Markets Act 2000 (Consequential Amendments and Repeals) Order 2001 (SI 2001/3649) art.3); see *Bates v Barrow Ltd* [1995] 1 Lloyd's Rep. 680; *Deutsche Ruckversicherung AG v Walbrook Insurance Co Ltd* [1996] 1 All E.R. 791.

[427] As to the regulatory requirements for the authorisation of agents and representatives, see s.39 of the Financial Services and Markets Act 2000 and art.25 of the Financial Services and Markets Act 2000 (Regulated Activities) Order 2001 (SI 2001/544). See *Personal Touch Financial Services Ltd v Simplysure Ltd* [2016] EWCA Civ 461, [2016] Bus. L.R. 1049 (private medical insurance).

[428] *Gale v Lewis* (1846) 9 Q.B. 730: *Linford v Provincial Horse and Cattle* (1864) 34 Beav. 291.

[429] *Murfitt v Royal* (1922) 38 T.L.R. 334. cf. *Mackie v European Assurance* (1869) 21 L.T. 102.

[430] *Willis, Faber v Joyce* (1911) 27 T.L.R. 388. cf. *Rossiter v Trafalgar Life* (1859) 27 Beav. 377.

[431] *Murfitt v Royal*, above.

[432] *Rossiter v Trafalgar Life*, above; *Linford v Provincial Horse and Cattle* (1864) 34 Beav. 291; *London and Lancashire Life v Fleming* [1897] A.C. 499. cf. *British Industry Life v Ward* (1856) 17 C.B. 644.

[433] *Marsden v City and County* (1865) L.R. 1 C.P. 232.

[434] *Blackburn v Vigors* (1887) 12 App. Cas. 531, 537; *Evans v Employers' Mutual Insurance Association Ltd* [1936] 1 K.B. 505; *Malhi v Abbey Life Assurance Co Ltd* [1996] L.R.L.R. 237, 242–243.

[435] *Wing v Harvey* (1854) 5 De. G.M. & G. 265; *Golding v Royal London* (1914) 30 T.L.R. 350; *Lennard's Co v Asiatic Petroleum* [1915] A.C. 705; *Ayrey v British Legal* [1918] 1 K.B. 136; *Houghton v Northard, Lowe* [1928] A.C. 1; *Newsholme v Road Transport* [1929] 2 K.B. 356. cf. *Acey v Fernie* (1840) 7 M. & W. 151; *Bawden v London, Edinburgh and Glasgow* [1892] 2 Q.B. 534; *Biggar v Rock Life* [1902] 1 K.B. 516; *Keeling v Pearl Assurance Co* (1923) 129 L.T. 573; *St Margaret's Trust v Navigation and General* (1949) 82 Ll.L. Rep. 752; *Facer v Vehicle & General* [1965] 1 Lloyd's Rep. 113; *Stone v Reliance Mutual Insurance Co Ltd* [1972] 1 Lloyd's Rep. 469; *Woolcott v Excess Insurance Co Ltd* [1978] 1 Lloyd's Rep. 633, 638; approved on the point of law involved [1979] 1 Lloyd's Rep. 231, 240–241.

[436] *Temple Legal Protection Ltd v QBE Insurance (Europe) Ltd* [2009] EWCA Civ 453, [2009] Lloyd's Rep. I.R. 544; *PM Law Ltd v Motorplus Ltd* [2016] EWHC 193 (QB), [2016] 1 Costs L.R. 143 at [58].

[437] The broker will be entitled to commission if he was effective in achieving the result for the accomplishment of which the principal had promised to pay him: *Harding Maughan Hambly Ltd v Compagnie Européene de Courtage d'Assurances et de Reassurances SA* [2000] 1 Lloyd's Rep. 316. As to the broker's entitlement to claim commission from either the insurer or the assured, see *Carvill America Inc v Camperdown UK Ltd* [2005] EWCA Civ 645, [2005] 2 Lloyd's Rep. 457.

[438] *Empress Assurance v Bowring* (1905) 11 Com. Cas. 107; *Glasgow Assurance v Symondson* (1911) 16 Com. Cas. 109; *Rozanes v Bowen* (1928) 32 Ll.L. Rep. 98; *Anglo African Merchants Ltd v Bayley*

case conflicts of interest may well arise.[440] The broker will remain subject to a duty of care even if he has assumed responsibilities to another principal creating a potential conflict of interests.[441] The broker must act with reasonable care and skill,[442] and if, for example, he fails to arrange a contract of insurance as instructed or fails to make full disclosure, it is no defence that the insurer could have escaped liability if the contract had been made, if as a matter of business the insurer would not have refused payment.[443] Nor can the broker escape liability where his negligence does not in fact prejudice the assured's insurance cover, if by his negligence he has exposed the assured to the uncertainties of a dispute or litiga-

---

[1970] 1 Q.B. 311; *North and South Trust Co v Berkeley* [1971] 1 W.L.R. 470. In the latter two cases the right of the assured to see documents in the possession of the brokers (or the duty of the brokers in relation to such documents) is discussed. See also *Roberts v Plaisted* [1989] 2 Lloyd's Rep. 341, 343; *Pryke v Gibbs Hartley Cooper Ltd* [1991] 1 Lloyd's Rep. 602, 614–615; *Searle v AR Hales & Co Ltd* [1996] L.R.L.R. 68, 71. *Aneco Reinsurance Underwriting Ltd (In Liquidation) v Johnson & Higgins* [1998] 1 Lloyd's Rep. 565. As to the scope of the broker's authority, see *Pacific and General Insurance Co v Hazell* [1997] L.R.L.R. 65. As to the relationship between assureds, producing brokers and placing brokers, see *Prentis Donegan & Partners v Leeds & Leeds Co Inc* [1998] 2 Lloyd's Rep. 326.

439 *Gale v Lewis* (1846) 9 Q.B. 730; *Edwards v Martin* (1865) L.R. 1 Eq. 121; *Equitable Life v General Accident*, 1904 12 S.L.T. 348; *Stockton v Mason* [1978] 2 Lloyd's Rep. 430. See also *Goldschlager v Royal Insurance*, 84 D.L.R. (3d) 355 (1978) Can.

440 *Anglo African Merchants Ltd v Bayley* [1970] 1 Q.B. 311; *North and South Trust Co v Berkeley*, above; *Eagle Star Insurance Co Ltd v Spratt* [1971] 2 Lloyd's Rep. 116; *Excess Life Insurance Co v Fireman's Insurance Co of New York* [1982] 2 Lloyd's Rep. 599, 618–620. If the broker acts as agent for the insurer, he ceases to be the assured's broker and may be in breach of duty to the assured: *Re Great Western Assurance Co SA* [1999] Lloyd's Rep. I.R. 377, 386.

441 *HIH Casualty & General Insurance Ltd v JLT Risk Solutions Ltd* [2007] EWCA Civ 710, [2007] 2 Lloyd's Rep. 278.

442 *Park v Hammond* (1816) 6 Taunt. 495; *Levy v Merchants' Marine* (1885) 52 L.T. 263; *Dickson v Devit* (1916) 86 L.J. K.B. 315; *Sarginson Bros v Keith Moulton* (1943) 73 Ll.L. Rep. 104; *General Accident v Minet* (1943) 74 Ll.L. Rep. 1; *Lyons v Bentley* (1944) 77 Ll. L. Rep. 335; *United Mills v Bray* [1952] 1 T.L.R. 149; *Osman v J Ralph Moss Ltd* [1970] 1 Lloyd's Rep. 313; *London Borough of Bromley v Ellis* [1971] 1 Lloyd's Rep. 97; *O'Connor v BDB Kirby & Co* [1972] 1 Q.B. 90; *Warren v Henry Sutton & Co* [1976] 2 Lloyd's Rep. 276; *McNealy v Pennine Insurance Co Ltd* [1978] 2 Lloyd's Rep. 18; *The Superhulls Cover Case* [1990] 2 Lloyd's Rep. 431, 445; *Harvest Trucking Co Ltd v Davis* [1991] 2 Lloyd's Rep. 638; *Bates v Barrow Ltd* [1995] 1 Lloyd's Rep. 680, 689–691; *Jones v Environcom Ltd* [2010] EWHC 759 (Comm), [2011] EWCA Civ 1152; *Ground Gilbey Ltd v Jardine Lloyd Thompson UK Ltd* [2011] EWHC 124 (Comm), [2012] Lloyd's Rep. I.R. 12; *Eurokey Recycling Ltd v Giles Insurance Brokers Ltd* [2014] EWHC 2989 (Comm), [2015] Lloyd's Rep. I.R. 225, at [86]; *RR Securities Ltd v Towergate Underwriting Group Ltd* [2016] EWHC 2653 (QB); *Jackson & Powell on Professional Negligence*, 7th edn (2012), Ch.16. For an informative discussion of the scope of a broker's duty as to the collection and payment of premiums and claims proceeds, as to the making of claims, and as to the maintenance of records, see *Equitas Ltd v Walsham Bros & Co Ltd* [2013] EWHC 3264 (Comm), [2014] P.N.L.R. 8. As to the assumption of a duty of care, see *European International Reinsurance Co Ltd v Curzon Insurance Ltd* [2003] EWCA Civ 1074, [2003] 1 Lloyd's Rep. 793. For the possibility of contributory negligence by an assured, see *Mint Security Ltd v Blair* [1982] 1 Lloyd's Rep. 188, 200; and by a sub-broker, see *Tudor Jones v Crowley Colosso Ltd* [1996] 2 Lloyd's Rep. 619; *Involnert Management Inc v Aprilgrange Ltd* [2015] EWHC 2225 (Comm), [2015] 2 Lloyd's Rep. 289 at [288]–[292]. As to the scope of damages recoverable from a negligent broker, see *Aneco Reinsurance Underwriting Ltd v Johnson & Higgins Ltd* [2001] UKHL 51, [2002] 1 Lloyd's Rep. 157.

443 *Fraser v Furman (Productions) Ltd* [1967] 1 W.L.R. 898; though damages may be awarded on the basis that a compromise would have been reached with the insurer (*Everett v Hogg, Robinson & Gardner Mountain (Insurance) Ltd* [1973] 2 Lloyd's Rep. 217), or be assessed by reference to the *chance* of recovering on the policy (*Dunbar v A & B Painters Ltd* [1986] 2 Lloyd's Rep. 38).

tion with the insurer.[444] The broker will be responsible for the maintenance of records and accounts.[445] The conduct of the business of insurance brokers is regulated by the Financial Conduct Authority pursuant to the Financial Services and Markets Act 2000.

42-067 **Lloyd's**   The members of Lloyd's who act as insurers, called underwriters, enter into insurance contracts as individual members,[446] though for convenience they group themselves into syndicates, the head of each syndicate usually having authority to bind the other members of that syndicate. The syndicates are composed of individual and corporate members, whose capital provide the security of the policies written at Lloyd's. Lloyd's is an organisation governed by the Corporation of Lloyd's which operates pursuant to the Lloyd's Act 1982. Persons seeking to insure at Lloyd's cannot approach the underwriters directly, but must engage brokers, who are nonetheless agents of the assured, except for the purpose of receiving the premium.[447] Pursuant to Pt XIX of the Financial Services and Markets Act 2000, Lloyd's is an authorised person and has permission to carry on regulated activities, including the arranging of deals in contracts of insurance written at Lloyd's and arranging deals in participation in Lloyd's syndicates.[448] The Council of Lloyd's retains responsibilities under the Lloyd's Act for the governance of Lloyd's. By usage, underwriters and Lloyd's brokers deal with each other as principals, settling quarterly accounts between themselves relating to premiums due and money payable for claims, and this usage may affect the assured as regards the payment of premiums and claims if he has knowledge of it and acquiesces in its adoption.[449] It is also the practice at Lloyd's for Lloyd's brokers to collect claims on behalf of assureds when called upon to do so, and a Lloyd's broker is under a continuing duty to exercise reasonable care and skill to retain the information enabling him to advance the claim for as long as a reasonable broker would regard a claim as possible.[450]

---

[444] *FNCB Ltd v Barnet Devanney (Harrow) Ltd* [1999] Lloyd's Rep. I.R. 459; *Talbot Underwriting Ltd v Nausch Hogan & Murray Inc* [2005] EWHC 2359 (Comm), [2006] 2 Lloyd's Rep. 195 at [103]–[112] (Cooke J.); affirmed [2006] EWCA Civ 889, [2006] 2 Lloyd's Rep. 195.

[445] *Johnston v Leslie & Godwin Financial Services Ltd* [1995] L.R.L.R. 472; *Equitas Ltd v Horace Holman & Co Ltd* [2007] EWHC 903 (Comm), [2007] Lloyd's Rep. I.R. 567.

[446] And they may be able to sue in their own name when the reputation of "Lloyd's" is put at risk: *Scott v Tuff-Kote (Australia) Pty Ltd* [1976] 2 Lloyd's Rep. 103, NSW SC. For a description of the business conducted at Lloyd's, see *Society of Lloyd's v Robinson* [1997] L.R.L.R. 1 at 7.8, [1999] 1 W.L.R. 756, 759–760.

[447] See the cases cited in para.42-066. As to the relationship between the underwriters, brokers and assureds in the context of premium payable under a marine policy, see Marine Insurance Act 1906 s.53, *Prentis Donegan & Partners v Leeds & Leeds Co Inc* [1998] 2 Lloyd's Rep. 326; and *JA Chapman & Co Ltd (In Liquidation) v Kadirga Denizcilik Ve Ticaret AS* [1998] Lloyd's Rep. I.R. 377; *Heath Lambert Ltd v Sociedad de Corretaje de Seguros* [2004] EWCA Civ 792, [2004] 1 W.L.R. 2820. As to the brokers' lien on the policy in respect of unpaid premium see *Eide UK Ltd v Lowndes Lambert Group Ltd* [1999] Q.B. 199; *Heath Lambert Ltd v Sociedad de Corretaje de Seguros* [2006] EWHC 1345 (Comm), [2006] 2 Lloyd's Rep. 551.

[448] As amended by the Financial Services Act 2012 s.40 and the Financial Services and Markets Act 2000 (PRA-regulated Activities) Order 2013 (SI 2013/556) art.2. See also the Financial Services and Markets Act 2000 (Regulated Activities) Order 2001 (SI 2001/544) arts 56–58.

[449] See the discussion in Gilman and Merkin (eds), *Arnould's Law of Marine Insurance and Average*, 18th edn (2013), Ch.4 and *MacGillivray on Insurance Law*, 14th edn (2018), Ch.37.

[450] *Johnstone v Leslie & Godwin* [1995] L.R.L.R. 472, holding also that the broker is under a duty not to destroy a policy held on behalf of his principal (which is the principal's property) or, where there

6. THE CONTRACT OF INSURANCE

Formation of the contract   Apart from the doctrine of uberrima fides,[451] normal   **42-068**
principles of contract law apply to the formation of the contracts of insurance,[452]
though an offer by an insurer to insure may (in the absence of stipulations to the
contrary) be subject to an implied condition that the risk does not materially change
prior to acceptance.[453] There must, of course, be an unconditional acceptance by one
party of the offer made by the other.[454] Thus where an insurer "accepts" a proposal
subject to payment of the premiums, his acceptance is in truth either a counter-
offer to be accepted by tendering that premium, or perhaps only an invitation to the
assured to offer that premium to the insurer for his acceptance of it and the terms
proposed.[455] If an offer is made and accepted on the basis that the insurer will not
be liable unless the premium is paid within a specified time, it appears that a binding contract is made at once, though the insurer will escape liability if the premium
is not paid.[456] As in contract generally, one party may be taken to have contracted
on terms of which he was only constructively aware,[457] and generally the insurer's
proposal form, which the assured uses to give the insurer particulars of the risk,
contains express reference to the insurer's terms and conditions.[458]

---

is no policy, the slip (which belongs to the broker) without the consent of the principal. In *Goshawk
Dedicated Ltd v Tyser & Co Ltd* [2006] EWCA Civ 54, [2006] 1 Lloyd's Rep. 566, the Court of Appeal held that there is an implied term in a contract of insurance between an assured and a Lloyd's
underwriter that the Lloyd's broker will make available to the underwriter documents previously
shown to the underwriter during the placement of the risk or the presentation of a claim; in addition, certain premium accounting documents would be disclosable to the underwriter.

[451] See above, para.42-033.

[452] *Canning v Farquhar* (1886) 16 Q.B.D. 727; *Rust v Abbey Life Assurance Co Ltd* [1979] 2 Lloyd's
Rep. 334. For an example of a contract concluded by exchange of emails, see *Allianz Insurance Co
Egypt v Aigaion Insurance Co SA (No.2)* [2008] EWCA Civ 1455, [2009] Lloyd's Rep. I.R. 3. As
to when a contract is concluded at Lloyd's, see *Jaglom v Excess Insurance Co Ltd* [1971] 2 Lloyd's
Rep. 171. For the application of agency principles of undisclosed principal and ratification where a
named insured takes out insurance cover on behalf of another as well as himself, see *National Oil
Well (UK) Ltd v Davy Offshore Ltd* [1993] 2 Lloyd's Rep. 582, 592–602. See, also, *Siu v Eastern
Insurance Co Ltd* [1994] 2 A.C. 199, PC, holding that the personal nature of an insurance contract
does not, of itself, preclude the application of the doctrine of undisclosed principal to contracts of
indemnity insurance. See also *O'Kane v Jones* [2003] EWHC 3470 (Comm), [2004] 1 Lloyd's Rep.
389; *Talbot Underwriting Ltd v Nausch Hogan & Murray* [2005] EWHC 2359 (Comm), [2006] 2
Lloyd's Rep. 195: [2006] EWCA Civ 889, [2006] 2 Lloyd's Rep. 195. cf. *Haberdashers' Aske's
Federation Trust Ltd v Zurich Insurance Plc* [2018] EWHC 558 (TCC), [2018] Lloyd's Rep. I.R.
382.

[453] *Siu v Eastern Insurance Co Ltd* [1994] 2 A.C. 199, PC.

[454] In *Rust v Abbey Life Assurance Co Ltd*, above, at 340, the Court of Appeal held that it was an
inevitable inference from the assured's retention of the policy document for seven months after
receipt that she had accepted the insurer's offer. See also *Yona International Ltd v La Réunion
Française Société Anonyme d'Assurances et de Réassurances* [1996] 2 Lloyd's Rep. 84, 109–111;
New Hampshire Insurance Co v MGN Ltd [1997] L.R.L.R. 24, 32–34, 54.

[455] *New Hampshire Insurance Co v MGN Ltd* [1997] L.R.L.R. 24, 32–34, 54. See also *Re Yager &
Guardian* (1912) 108 L.T. 38.

[456] *Roberts v Security Co* [1897] 1 Q.B. 111; *Equitable Fire and Accident v Ching Wo Hong* [1907] A.C.
96; *Harrington v Pearl Life* (1914) 30 T.L.R. 613. But see the cases cited in para.42-066, above.

[457] *Adie v Insurance Corp* (1898) 14 T.L.R. 544; *Rust v Abbey Life Assurance Co Ltd* [1979] 2 Lloyd's
Rep. 334.

[458] The contract of insurance is exempt from the stricture upon exemption clauses imposed by the Unfair
Contract Terms Act 1977: see s.1(2), Sch.1 para.1(a). See, however, see below, paras 42-087—42-
088.

42-069 **The slip** In London, brokers commonly submit to underwriters a document called a slip which contains brief particulars of the risk, and each underwriter approached (if willing to accept the risk) initials the slip and puts against his initials the percentage of the risk he is willing to insure. Save for marine and possibly life insurance where, by statute, the contract must be embodied in a policy,[459] the slip itself constitutes a binding contract of insurance on which an underwriter may be sued even if no signed policy is subsequently issued.[460] The writing of a line on the slip by each underwriter gives rise to an independent binding contract with that underwriter (distinct from the contracts with the other underwriters) to the extent of the percentage written, from which neither party can resile even if the slip is never fully subscribed.[461] By custom at Lloyd's, however, the percentage of risk accepted by any particular underwriter may be proportionately "written down" if the slip is oversubscribed on closing.[462] Furthermore, where one or more underwriters are permitted under a "leading underwriter's clause" contained in the slip to make amendments to cover, they have (subject to the particular terms of the clause) actual authority to bind the other underwriters on the same slip, and act as their agents in doing so.[463] One consequence of each line on the slip giving rise to a distinct contract appears to be that a false statement made to a leading underwriter will not, in itself, permit the other (following) underwriters to avoid their own contracts for misrepresentation,[464] although the non-disclosure to the following underwriter of that misrepresentation may allow the following underwriter to avoid their respec-

---

[459] See Marine Insurance Act 1906 s.22; Life Assurance Act 1774 s.2. This is a formal or evidential requirement; the contract of marine insurance is concluded when the proposal is accepted by the insurer, by the signing of his line of the slip: Marine Insurance Act 1906 s.21; *General Accident Fire & Life Assurance Corp v Tanter (The Zephyr)* [1984] 1 Lloyd's Rep. 58, 69. There are other statutes which require a written record of specified insurance contracts: see, e.g. Road Traffic Act 1988 s.147.

[460] *Thompson v Adams* (1889) 23 Q.B.D. 361; *Grover v Mathews* [1910] 15 Com. Cas. 249; *Re Yager and Guardian* (1912) 108 L.T. 38; *Eagle Star Insurance v Spratt* [1971] 2 Lloyd's Rep. 116; *The Zephyr* [1984] 1 Lloyd's Rep. 58. For the position where a policy wording differs from slip, see *HIH Casualty and General Insurance Ltd v New Hampshire Insurance Co* [2001] EWCA Civ 735, [2001] 2 All E.R. (Comm) 39 at [81]–[95], where the Court of Appeal held that there was no rule of law that the policy was conclusive evidence of the insurance contract. Identifying the terms and meaning of the contract depended on a process of construction and analysis of the relationship between the slip and the policy and determining the parties' intention (cf. *Youell v Bland Welch & Co Ltd* [1992] 2 Lloyd's Rep. 127). See *New Hampshire Insurance Co v MGN Ltd* [1997] L.R.L.R. 24, 32–34, 53–54.

[461] *General Reinsurance Corp v Forsakringsaktiebolaget Fennia Patria* [1983] Q.B. 856, where the Court of Appeal held, inter alia, that (at least on the evidence adduced in that case) there was no legally binding custom in the Lloyd's market, nor could a term be implied, giving the assured a right of cancellation prior to full subscription of the slip. See Marine Insurance Act 1906 s.24(2).

[462] *General Reinsurance Corp v Forsakringsaktiebolaget Fennie Patria*, above. For the reasons for oversubscription, and the position which arises if a broker misstates the likely level of "writing down", see *The Zephyr* [1984] 1 Lloyd's Rep. 58, [1985] 2 Lloyd's Rep. 529.

[463] *Roadworks (1952) Ltd v JR Charman* [1994] 2 Lloyd's Rep. 99 (where it was held that the particular leading underwriter's clause under consideration even gave the leading underwriter authority to waive a contingent condition to which the entire cover had been subject); cf. *Mander v Commercial Union Assurance* [1998] Lloyd's Rep. I.R. 93, 143–144. Similar authority may be given to a leading underwriter to settle claims: see *Roar Marine Ltd v Bimeh Iran Insurance Co* [1998] 1 Lloyd's Rep. 423; *Unum Life Insurance Co of America v Israel Phoenix Assurance Co Ltd* [2002] Lloyd's Rep. I.R. 374; *PT Buana Samudra Pratama v Marine Mutual Insurance Association (NZ) Ltd* [2011] EWHC 2413 (Comm), [2011] 2 Lloyd's Rep. 655.

[464] *Bank Leumi Le Israel BM v British National Insurance Co* [1988] 1 Lloyd's Rep. 71, though it was there accepted that following underwriters may well be able to take advantage of misrepresentations or non-disclosures to a lead underwriter if they had subscribed on the basis of trusting the skill and judgment of the leading underwriter, and assumed that he had, himself, subscribed only after

tive contracts,[465] or the presentation of the risk to the following underwriter might have taken place on the assumption that a fair presentation had been made to the leading underwriter.[466]

Open covers and declarations   The contract of insurance may be constituted by **42-070** means of a declaration which is presented to the insurer pursuant to the terms of an open cover.[467] The open cover identifies the terms and conditions of the insurance and the scope of the risk which might be declared thereunder. Upon the presentation and acceptance of the declaration, provided that it falls within the scope of the risk permitted by the open cover, the contract is formed on the terms and conditions set out in the open cover. It may be that the open cover provides that the insurer is obliged to accept the declaration[468] or that the insurer is entitled to refuse or accept the declaration as he pleases. It is often the case that the assured can choose whether or not to declare a particular risk under the open cover.[469] Occasionally, it may be that the open cover provides that the assured is obliged to present all risks falling within the scope of the open cover to the insurer. Whether or not the insurer or the assured is obliged to accept or present the declaration will consequently determine the time at which the contract is made and at which the duty of disclosure of material facts ceases.[470]

Cover notes   The assured may require cover from the moment when he offers to **42-071** enter into a contract with an insurer who is usually willing to provide such preliminary protection.[471] Such an engagement is usually set out in a "cover note"[472]

---

considering full and accurate information about the risk; and cf. *The Zephyr* [1984] 1 Lloyd's Rep. 58, 70.

[465] *Aneco Reinsurance Underwriting Ltd (In Liquidation) v Johnson & Higgins* [1998] 1 Lloyd's Rep. 565.

[466] *Brotherton v Aseguradora Colseguros SA* [2003] EWHC 1741 (Comm), [2003] Lloyd's Rep. I.R. 762.

[467] See *Glencore International AG v Ryan* [2001] EWCA Civ 2051, [2002] 1 Lloyd's Rep. 574.

[468] In the case of an open cover which obliges the insurer to accept declarations under it, the open cover is a standing offer whereby the insurer agrees to accept liability in respect of any declarations made within the terms of the cover; however, the insurer is not bound until the declaration—the acceptance of his offer—has been communicated to him: *BP Plc v GE Frankona Reinsurance Ltd* [2003] EWHC 344 (Comm), [2003] 1 Lloyd's Rep. 537 at [82]–[87]. This is, however, subject to a contrary market practice: *Limit No.2 Ltd v AXA Versicherung AG* [2007] EWHC 2321 (Comm), [2008] Lloyd's Rep. I.R. 330 at [108]–[111], reversed in part [2008] EWCA Civ 1231, [2009] Lloyd's Rep. I.R. 396. Such open covers are to be distinguished from "floating policies" as defined by Marine Insurance Act 1906 s.29, where the making of the declaration is not operative in binding the insurer: *Glencore International AG v Ryan (The Beursgracht)* [2001] EWCA Civ 2051, [2002] Lloyd's Rep. I.R. 335 at [26]–[32]; *Hanwha Non-Life Insurance Co Ltd v Alba Pte Ltd* [2011] SGHC 271, [2012] Lloyd's Rep. I.R. 505 at [48] (Singapore High Court).

[469] Where the assured is able to choose whether or not to declare a risk under an open cover and the insurer is bound to accept such declaration as is made by the assured, there is no obligation upon the assured to exercise care in his selection of the risks he chooses to declare: *BP Plc v GE Frankona Reinsurance Ltd*, above. As regards the insurer's obligations towards his reinsurer in deciding whether or not to accept a risk which would be ceded to the reinsurer, see *Bonner v Cox Dedicated Corporate Member Ltd* [2004] EWHC 2963 (Comm) at [255], [2005] EWCA Civ 1512, [2006] 2 Lloyd's Rep. 152 at [85]–[111].

[470] See *HIH Casualty and General Insurance Ltd v Chase Manhattan Bank* [2001] EWCA Civ 1250, [2001] 2 Lloyd's Rep. 483; reversing in part [2001] 1 Lloyd's Rep. 30; reversed in part [2003] UKHL 6, [2003] 2 Lloyd's Rep. 61. See above, para.42-037.

[471] In the case of motor insurance, the cover note must give the holder immediate protection; see Road Traffic Act 1988 s.143.

(though cover may, of course, be given informally),[473] and constitutes a separate contract.[474] The cover note usually incorporates by reference the terms and conditions of the insurer's ordinary policy, but in the absence of such a reference, or of actual or constructive notice of those terms and conditions, the preliminary cover will not be subject to them.[475] The period of the preliminary cover commonly takes one of two forms: either a fixed length of time; or the period until the insurer indicates his decision whether or not to enter into a more permanent contract.[476] Since promptness may be of importance, an insurer may authorise local agents to grant temporary cover and issue cover notes on his behalf, and such authority has sometimes been implied.[477]

42-072 **Issue of policy**   The contract of insurance may be embodied in a policy, but unless required by statute or contract, the contract may exist and be enforceable without a policy. The policy is the physical incarnation of the contract, but they should not be confused.[478] Where the contract pre-dates the issue of the policy, questions will arise as to whether the parties intended that the policy supersede the pre-existing contract. Even in cases where the policy supersedes the earlier contract, the court may have regard to the earlier contract (which may be in the form of a slip or an insurer's cover note) with a view to construing the policy.[479] There is no longer a requirement that life or any other policies be stamped.[480] The Life Assurance Act 1774[481] makes it unlawful to make a policy without inserting the name of the persons interested in it, but does not specifically enact that a policy shall be made, although such a requirement might be implied. Marine insurance contracts must be embodied in a policy in accordance with the Marine Insurance Act 1906.[482]

42-073 **Renewal**   If the event insured against occurs after the termination of the period of insurance, the assured cannot, of course, recover unless the contract has been renewed. The term "renewal" is used to denote both the extension of the original period of cover by the exercise of a right given to one party (almost invariably the assured) by the contract to extend the period of the cover without the assent of the other, and the making of a new contract through the agreement of both. It is important to distinguish the two types of renewal, since only in the former case will

---

[472] *Thompson v Adams* (1889) 23 Q.B.D. 361, 366; *Re Yager and Guardian* (1912) 108 L.T. 38, 40. Cover notes should be distinguished from brokers' cover notes, which if issued without the authority of the insurer, merely record the terms of the insurance contract agreed between the insurer and broker. Whilst brokers' cover notes might evidence the terms of the insurance contract, it is not itself a contractual document.

[473] *Murfitt v Royal* (1922) 38 T.L.R. 334; *Stockton v Mason* [1978] 2 Lloyd's Rep. 430.

[474] *Mackie v European Assurance* (1869) 21 L.T. 102.

[475] *Re Coleman's Depositories* [1907] 2 K.B. 798; *Symington v Union Insurance (No.2)* (1928) 142 L.T. 48; *Queen Insurance v Parsons* (1881) 7 App. Cas. 96.

[476] See *Mackie v European Assurance*, above; *Levy v Scottish Employers* (1901) 17 T.L.R. 229. cf. *Cartwright v MacCormack* [1963] 1 W.L.R. 18.

[477] *Mackie v European Assurance* (1869) 21 L.T. 102; *Murfitt v Royal* (1922) 38 T.L.R. 334; *Stockton v Mason*, above. See above, para.42-064, for the position of agents in insurance.

[478] *New Hampshire Insurance Co v MGN Ltd* [1997] L.R.L.R. 24, 42 (per Potter J.), 58 (per Staughton L.J.). Note also the use of the words "contract" and "policy" in the Marine Insurance Act 1906. See also M.A. Clarke, *The Law of Insurance Contracts* (looseleaf), para.1-1A.

[479] *HIH Casualty and General Insurance Ltd v New Hampshire Insurance Co* [2001] EWCA Civ 735, [2001] 2 All E.R. (Comm) 39 at [81]–[95].

[480] Finance Act 1970 s.32 and Sch.7 Pt I para.1(2)(b); Finance Act 1989 ss.173, 187 and Sch.17.

[481] See above, para.42-014.

[482] s.22. cf. *Eide UK Ltd v Lowndes Lambert Group Ltd* [1999] Q.B. 199, 207–208.

vitiating elements in the original contract, such as failure to make full disclosure, affect the extension, and conversely only in the latter case will a duty arise to make full disclosure at the time of the renewal.[483] Life insurance usually gives the assured the right to renew automatically on the payment of a further premium at the end of the first period, and such renewal does not constitute a new contract,[484] but contracts which provide for the tender of the renewal premium *and* its acceptance by the insurer,[485] and those which provide for automatic renewal unless one party gives notice to the other,[486] are of the other type.

Days of grace   Often the assured is given a period beyond the end of the original period of insurance during which the renewal premium may be paid. This period, termed "days of grace", may be granted either by an express stipulation in the original contract, or by the terms of a renewal notice sent by the insurer to the assured. Whether the assured may recover for a loss occurring during this period depends upon the nature of the stipulation providing for the days of grace.[487] If the insurer has a right not to accept the renewal premium, then prima facie he will not be liable for such a loss if he chooses not to renew.[488] On the other hand, if the assured can renew as of right, then it seems that the insurer is liable if the premium is tendered before the days of grace expire,[489] but each case must depend upon the provisions used. **42-074**

Payment of premium   The price for which the insurer agrees to insure is called the premium and is usually payable in money.[490] Some contracts contain a term that the insurer shall not be on risk until the premium is paid[491] and such a term is effective,[492] but in its absence the insurer is bound before actual payment.[493] The insurer can maintain an action for the premium if he comes on risk before it is **42-075**

---

483   See above, paras 42-034—42-037 for the duty of disclosure.
484   *Pritchard v Merchant's Life* (1858) 3 C.B.(N.S.) 622, 643; *Phoenix Life v Sheridan* (1860) 8 H.L. Cas. 745, 750; *Stuart v Freeman* [1903] 1 K.B. 47. cf. *MacGillivray on Insurance Law*, 14th edn (2018), paras 7-038—7-039.
485   *Sun Fire v Hart* (1889) 14 App. Cas. 98.
486   *Solvency Mutual v Froane* (1861) 7 Hurl. & N. 5. See *Dalecroft Properties Ltd v Underwriters* [2017] EWHC 1263 (Comm), [2017] Lloyd's Rep. I.R. 511 at [85.2].
487   cf. *Salvin v James* (1805) 6 East 571; *McKenna v City Life* [1919] 2 K.B. 491.
488   *Tarleton v Staniforth* (1794) 5 T.R. 695; *Simpson v Accidental Death* (1857) 2 C.B.(N.S.) 257. Quaere whether the Unfair Terms in Consumer Contracts Regulations 1999 or, for contracts made on or after October 1, 2015, the Consumer Rights Act 2015 (see above, paras 38-389—38-426) might circumscribe the insurer's right of refusal: see below, paras 42-087—42-088.
489   *Stuart v Freeman* [1903] 1 K.B. 47; but see *Pritchard v Merchants' Life* (1858) 3 C.B.(N.S.) 622.
490   *Equitable Fire v Ching Wo Hong* [1907] A.C. 96. The premium need not necessarily be money: *Lion Insurance v Tucker* (1883) 12 Q.B.D. 176, 187; *Great Britain 100 AI v Wyllie* (1889) 22 Q.B.D. 710, 722. If the insurer gives the assured (being an individual) credit for the premium, the Consumer Credit Act 1974 may regulate the transaction; see, further, *MacGillivray on Insurance Law*, 14th edn (2018), paras 7-019—7-021.
491   *Roberts v Security Co* [1897] 1 Q.B. 111; *Equitable Fire v Ching Wo Hong*, above; *Re Yager and Guardian* (1912) 108 L.T. 38; *Looker v Law Union* [1928] 1 K.B. 554. Subject, of course, to days of grace: see above, para.42-074. Premium warranties may be inserted into the contract, whereby the insurer is discharged from liability if the premium is not paid in accordance with the warranty: *JA Chapman & Co Ltd (In Liquidation) v Kadirga Denizcilik Ve Ticaret AS* [1998] Lloyd's Rep. I.R. 377; *Heath Lambert Ltd v Sociedad de Corretaje de Seguros* [2004] EWCA Civ 792, [2004] 1 W.L.R. 2820.
492   *Phoenix Life v Sheridan* (1860) 8 H.L. Cas. 745.
493   *Kelly v London and Staffordshire Fire* (1883) 1 Cab. & El. 47, 48.

paid,[494] and this may be the case even where there is a term that he shall not be on risk until it is paid.[495] Subject to the foregoing the assured is liable to pay the premium as soon as the contract is made[496] and his failure to do so might, depending on the circumstances, amount to a repudiation of the contract open to acceptance by the insurer.[497] The amount, manner and form of payment of the premium are, of course, to be decided by agreement between the parties as may be modified by their conduct,[498] and an insurance "at a premium to be arranged"[499] would, it seems, be a valid and enforceable contract and a reasonable premium would be payable,[500] though in such a case the assured need make no payment by way of premium until the amount of a reasonable premium has been agreed or determined by the court.[501]

42-076 **Return of premium** In some circumstances the assured may be able to recover the premium and generally his right to do so depends upon whether the insurer has ever been on risk.[502] In marine insurance recovery of the premium is governed by the Marine Insurance Act 1906[503] but the wide rights of recovery provided therein have not been applied to non-marine insurance and it is unwise to assume that the same rules will be applied.[504] It seems, however, that the assured can claim a refund of the premium if:

(a) The contract is void for mistake of fact,[505] even if the true facts make it illegal.[506] Thus if a house is insured in the mistaken belief that it is still standing, or a life in the mistaken belief that the life assured is still living,[507] the premium may be recovered.

(b) The contract is void for illegality, provided that the assured was not *in pari*

---

494 *General Accident v Cronk* (1901) 17 T.L.R. 233.
495 *Municipal Mutual v Pontefract* (1917) 116 L.T. 671. cf. *Solvency Mutual v York* (1858) 3 Hurl. & N. 588. But see above, para.42-074 and the cases cited there.
496 *General Accident v Cronk* (1901) 17 T.L.R. 233; *JA Chapman & Co Ltd (In Liquidation) v Kadirga Denizcilik Ve Ticaret AS* [1998] Lloyd's Rep. I.R. 377. As regards the position in respect of marine insurance, see *Heath Lambert Ltd v Sociedad de Corretaje de Seguros* [2004] EWCA Civ 792, [2004] 1 W.L.R. 2820.
497 cf. *Salvin v James* (1805) 6 East 571; *Edge v Duke* (1849) 18 L.J. Ch. 183; *Kirby v Cosindit Societa per Azioni* [1969] 1 Lloyd's Rep. 75. See also, *Fenton Insurance Co Ltd v Gothaer* [1991] 1 Lloyd's Rep. 172, 180, where the view was expressed that one could rarely infer a repudiatory intention by reason merely of non-payment of balances under a reinsurance treaty (as opposed to persistent non-payment in the face of demands or protests). See also *Figre v Mander* [1999] Lloyd's Rep. I.R. 193; cf. *Pacific and General Insurance Co v Hazell* [1997] L.R.L.R. 65.
498 See *London and Lancashire Life v Fleming* [1897] A.C. 499; *Daff v Midland Colliery* (1913) 82 L.J. K.B. 1340.
499 *Gliksten v State Assurance* (1922) 10 Ll.L. Rep. 604.
500 Marine Insurance Act 1906 s.31. cf. *Kirby v Cosindit Societa per Azioni* [1969] 1 Lloyd's Rep. 75. There seems no reason why the rule for marine insurance should not be applied generally, since it accords with the analogous rule for the sale of goods. See, however, *Canning v Farquhar* (1886) 16 Q.B.D. 727; *Re Yager and Guardian* (1912) 108 L.T. 38; *Murfitt v Royal Insurance* (1922) 38 T.L.R. 334. In *American Airlines v Hope* [1973] 1 Lloyd's Rep. 233 the Court of Appeal decided as a matter of construction that the words "at additional premium to be agreed" in the particular context conferred no cover until agreement was reached.
501 *Kirby v Cosindit Societa per Azioni*, above.
502 *Stevenson v Snow* (1761) 3 Burr. 1237, 1240.
503 ss.82–84.
504 *Wolenburg v Royal Co-operative Society* (1915) 84 L.J. K.B. 1316.
505 *Kelly v Solari* (1841) 9 M. & W. 54.
506 *Oom v Bruce* (1810) 12 East 225; *Hentig v Staniforth* (1816) 5 M. & S. 122.
507 *Pritchard v Merchant's Life* (1858) 3 C.B.(N.S.) 622, 645.

delicto,[508] or withdrew before the risk (but for the illegality) would have commenced to run.[509] Where the assured enters into an unenforceable contract of insurance with an insurer acting without statutory authorisation, he has a statutory right to recover his premium.[510]

(c) The insurer avoids the contract for innocent misrepresentation or non-disclosure not amounting to fraudulent concealment.[511] But, even where the assured has acted fraudulently, the insurer, if he seeks to avoid the contract,[512] will be entitled to retain the premium in the case of marine insurance by reason of s.84(3)(a) of the Marine Insurance Act 1906.[513] In the case of non-marine insurance, however, as a matter of principle, there is no reason why the insurer should be entitled to retain the premium because the contract's avoidance is dependent on restitutio in integrum.[514] The policy may provide that premium is not returnable in the event of a misrepresentation or non-disclosure even in the absence of fraud.[515]

(d) The insurer is discharged from liability under the contract for breach of warranty occurring before he came on risk,[516] or before renewal in the case of renewal premiums.[517]

(e) The assured exercises his right of cancellation of a long-term insurance contract under the Financial Conduct Authority's Insurance Conduct of Business Sourcebook.[518]

(f) The insurer exercises a contractual right of cancellation, in which case the assured may depending on the construction of the contract be entitled, or pursuant to an implied term, to a return of the balance of the premium in respect of that part of the risk which has not yet been run.[519]

---

[508] *Howarth v Pioneer Life* (1912) 107 L.T. 155; *British Workman's v Cunliffe* (1902) 18 T.L.R. 502; *Hughes v Liverpool Victoria* [1916] 2 K.B. 482; *Re Cavalier Insurance Co Ltd* [1989] 2 Lloyd's Rep. 430. Contrast *Harse v Pearl Life* [1904] 1 K.B. 558; *Phillips v Royal London Mutual* (1911) 105 L.T. 136.

[509] *Lowry v Bourdieu* (1780) 2 Doug. 468; *Busk v Walsh* (1812) 4 Taunt. 290; *Kearley v Thomson* (1890) 24 Q.B.D. 742.

[510] See Financial Services and Markets Act 2000 ss.26, 28. See above, para.42-063.

[511] *Feise v Parkinson* (1812) 4 Taunt. 640, 641; *Anderson v Thornton* (1853) 8 Exch. 425; *Anderson v Fitzgerald* (1853) 4 H.L.C. 484, 507; *Biggar v Rock Life* [1902] 1 K.B. 516, 526. See above, paras 42-033—42-046.

[512] See above, para.42-042.

[513] *HIH Casualty and General Insurance Ltd v Chase Manhattan Bank* [2003] UKHL 6, [2003] 2 Lloyd's Rep. 61 at [73], [88].

[514] *Clarke v Dickson* (1858) El. Bl. & El. 148; see also Vol.I, paras 7-124—7-131. There are conflicting authorities concerning the return of premium where a contract of non-marine insurance has been avoided: *Whittingham v Thornburgh* (1690) 2 Vern. 206; *Feise v Parkinson* (1812) 4 Taunt. 640, 641; *Anderson v Thornton* (1853) 8 Exch. 425; *Anderson v Fitzgerald* (1853) 4 H.L.C. 484, 507; *Biggar v Rock Life Assurance Co* [1902] 1 K.B. 516, 526; *Joel v Law Union and Crown Insurance Co* [1908] 2 K.B. 431, 440. See *MacGillivray on Insurance Law*, 14th edn (2018), para.8-030.

[515] *Thomson v Weems* (1884) 9 App. Cas. 671; *Kumar v Life Insurance Corp of India* [1974] 1 Lloyd's Rep. 147.

[516] *Thomson v Weems* (1884) 9 App. Cas. 671, 682.

[517] *Sparenborg v Edinburgh Life* [1912] 1 K.B. 195, 204. Contrast *Annen v Woodman* (1810) 3 Taunt. 299; *Langhorn v Cologan* (1812) 4 Taunt. 330.

[518] Rule 7 of *Insurance Conduct of Business Sourcebook* (ICOBS), made pursuant to ss.137A to 137F, 137T and 139A of the Financial Services and Markets Act 2000, as amended by s.24 of the Financial Services Act 2012.

[519] *Re Drake Insurance Plc* [2001] Lloyd's Rep. I.R. 643, 646. In that case, the making of a claim did not vitiate the right to a return of premium at (649). cf. *Swiss Reinsurance Co v United India Insur-*

Subject to the terms of the contract, once the insurer has been on risk, the risk is indivisible. If the assured cancels the contract prior to the expiry of the policy, at common law, the assured is not entitled to a return of premium in respect of that proportion of the risk that has not expired.[520] However, it has recently been held that in the event of the insurer's contractual cancellation of the policy, the assured may be entitled to a return of the premium pursuant to an implied term and the indivisible nature of the risk will not prevent that recovery.[521]

42-077   **Construction of insurance contracts**   Insurance contracts are subject to the same approach to contractual construction as other contracts, namely that the words of the contract will be interpreted to divine their contextual meaning consistently with the sense and purpose of the policy, even if that is at odds with the literal meaning of the contract.[522] The commercial purpose of the insurance contract, however, should not be lightly invoked to undermine the importance of the contractual language which the parties have chosen to embody their agreement.[523] Therefore, where a word is used in an insurance policy which has a technical, legal connotation, the court will not necessarily infer that the parties intended that meaning and will inquire into the ordinary, commercial meaning to be ascribed to the word.[524] On the other hand, if an insurance term has a settled judicially accepted meaning, the courts are loathe to apply a different interpretation.[525] Similarly, the Court will assume that the parties intended to use words which had a special or peculiar meaning in the particular market or trade in that sense.[526] If the insurance contract is based on a standard form of contract to which the parties have added special clauses, greater weight will be given to the special provisions, and, in the event of conflict or inconsistency between the general and special provisions, the latter will prevail.[527] There is one rule of construction applicable to ordinary contracts which applies with particular force in the context of insurance contracts, namely that *verba*

  ance Co Ltd [2005] EWHC 237 (Comm), [2005] Lloyd's Rep. I.R. 341.

[520] *Lynch v Dalzell* (1729) 4 Bro.P.C. 431; *Sadlers Co v Badcock* (1743) 2 Atk. 554; *Tyrie v Fletcher* (1777) 2 Cowp. 666; *Berman v Woodbridge* (1781) 2 Doug.K.B. 781; *Swiss Reinsurance Co v United India Insurance Co Ltd* [2005] EWHC 237 (Comm), [2005] Lloyd's Rep. I.R. 341. Where the payment of premium by instalment during the currency of a marine policy is warranted and premium has not been paid with the effect that the insurer is discharged before the expiry of the policy term, the insurer still is entitled to the entire premium: *JA Chapman & Co Ltd (In Liquidation) v Kadirga Denizcilik Ve Ticaret AS* [1998] Lloyd's Rep. I.R. 377. The Apportionment Act 1870, by s.6, does not apply.

[521] *Re Drake Insurance Plc* [2001] Lloyd's Rep. I.R. 643, 646–647.

[522] *Sirius International Insurance Co (Publ) v FAI General Insurance Ltd* [2004] UKHL 54, [2004] 1 W.L.R. 3251 at [18]–[19]; *Blackburn Rovers Football & Athletic Club Plc v Avon Insurance Plc* [2005] EWCA Civ 423, [2005] Lloyd's Rep. I.R. 447 at [9]. In *AXA Corporate Solutions SA v National Westminster Bank Plc* [2010] EWHC 1915 (Comm), [2011] Lloyd's Rep. I.R. 438, the Court construed the term *"Terrorism exclusion (wording to be agreed)"* to operate as an exclusion and did not require a further clause to be identified.

[523] *Spire Healthcare Ltd v Royal & Sun Alliance Insurance Plc* [2016] EWHC 3278 (Comm), [2017] Lloyd's Rep. I.R. 118 at [11], [2018] EWCA Civ 317, [2018] Lloyd's Rep. I.R. 425.

[524] *Wooldridge v Canelhas Comercio Importacao e Exportacao Ltda* [2004] EWCA Civ 984, [2005] 1 All E.R. (Comm) 43 ("robbery"); cf. *Dobson v General Accident Fire & Life Assurance Corp Plc* [1990] 1 Q.B. 274 ("theft").

[525] See, e.g. *Ramco (UK) Ltd v International Insurance Co of Hannover Ltd* [2004] EWCA Civ 675, [2004] 2 Lloyd's Rep. 595 at [32]; *AIG Europe (Ireland) Ltd v Faraday Capital Ltd* [2006] EWHC 2707, [2007] Lloyd's Rep. I.R. 267 at [24]; reversed on other grounds [2007] EWCA Civ 1208, [2008] Lloyd's Rep. I.R. 454.

[526] *Gard Marine v Tunnicliffe* [2011] EWHC 1658 (Comm), [2012] Lloyd's Rep. I.R. 1.

[527] *Milton Furniture Ltd v Brit Insurance Ltd* [2015] EWCA Civ 671, [2016] Lloyd's Rep. I.R. 192 at

chartarum fortius accipiuntur contra proferentem: i.e. where the contractual provision is ambiguous, the provision will be construed against the person who drafts or puts forward the provision, which in many (but not all) cases will be the insurer.[528] The construction of contractual terms "against the insurer" is not limited to cases where the insurer has produced the wording. If the insurer seeks to rely on a provision, such as a condition precedent or warranty, so as to extinguish or reduce his basic obligations, the court will resist such a construction unless the contractual terms are especially clear.[529] Having regard to the decision of the Supreme Court in *Impact Funding Solutions Ltd v Barrington Support Services Ltd*,[530] the fact that a provision in an insurance contract is expressed as an exception or exclusion does not necessarily mean that it should be approached with a pre-disposition to construe it narrowly or restrictively, at least insofar as it delineates the scope of the insurer's primary obligation of indemnity, as opposed to excluding a liability or a remedy where the primary obligation would otherwise have rendered the insurer liable.

7. THE TERMS OF THE INSURANCE CONTRACT

Classification of terms Insurance contracts nearly always contain a number of terms and conditions which may be classified according to their effect as follows: **42-078**

(i) terms which, if not fulfilled, entitle the insurer to treat himself as discharged from further liability under the contract;

(ii) terms which, if not fulfilled, entitle the insurer to refuse to pay a particular claim under the policy, but which do not affect the continued validity of the policy;

(iii) terms the breach of which gives the insurer the right to claim damages only;

(iv) terms which delimit the scope of the risk covered, failure to comply with which will take the insurer off risk while the breach continues;

(v) innominate terms, which are neither an essential term which discharge the insurer from all liability under the contract or merely a term the breach of which results in damages, but terms which give the insurer different rights depending on the seriousness of the breach.

The most stringent of such terms are conditions precedent and warranties, which shall now be considered. These are to be contrasted with the terms of the policy which identify whether a particular event, loss or damage falls within the scope of cover afforded by the insurance contract.[531]

Conditions precedent The term "condition precedent" often refers to a condition which, if not fulfilled, entitles the insurer to refuse payment under the insurance policy, without necessarily importing the right to treat the entire contract as **42-079**

---

[24].

[528] *Tektrol Ltd v International Insurance Co of Hanover Ltd* [2005] EWCA Civ 845, [2005] 1 All E.R. (Comm) 132.

[529] *Tektrol Ltd v International Insurance Co of Hanover Ltd* [2005] EWCA Civ 845, [2005] 1 All E.R. (Comm) 132; *Royal & Sun Alliance Insurance Plc v Dornoch Ltd* [2005] EWCA Civ 238, [2005] 1 All E.R. (Comm) 590; *Blackburn Rovers Football & Athletic Club Plc v Avon Insurance Plc* [2005] EWCA Civ 423, [2005] Lloyd's Rep. I.R. 447 at [9].

[530] [2016] UKSC 57, [2017] A.C. 73 at [35]. See also *Crowden v QBE Insurance (Europe) Ltd* [2017] EWHC 2597 (Comm), [2018] Lloyd's Rep. I.R. 83.

[531] See below, paras 42-102—42-103.

discharged. So, a term, depending on its context, may be interpreted as a condition precedent to an insurer's liability (actual or contingent) in respect of a particular claim or under the entire policy[532] or may be construed as a condition precedent to the attachment of the risk or the continuance of the insurance cover,[533] The use or absence of the words "condition precedent" are not determinative; nonetheless, the use of the term "condition precedent" to the insurer's liability will often be construed as such unless the term is used indiscriminately.[534] Typically, conditions precedent will be concerned with obligations which an assured must comply with after the loss has occurred,[535] but in principle it should be possible for such conditions to be concerned with obligations imposed upon the assured during the currency of the policy.[536] Moreover, what is described as a condition precedent in a policy may sometimes simply be construed as a collateral promise giving the insurer neither the right to treat the policy as terminated, nor even to refuse payment of the claim, when not complied with.[537] Indeed, a term may be classified as an innominate term and the insurer's rights upon its breach may be determined by the seriousness of that breach.[538] Ambiguities in conditions or warranties will usually be construed against the insurer.[539] Furthermore, conditions will be construed in the context of the commercial purpose of the policy, so that, for example, a condition requiring the assured to take reasonable precautions to prevent an accident, or to take all reasonable steps to safeguard any property insured, will usually be construed as requiring more than mere negligence upon the part of the assured

---

[532] See, e.g. *Kazakstan Wool Processors (Europe) Ltd v Nederlandsche Credietverzekering Maatschappij NV* [2000] Lloyd's Rep. I.R. 371.

[533] See, e.g. *Zeus Tradition Marine Ltd v Bell (The Zeus)* [2000] 2 Lloyd's Rep. 587.

[534] *George Hunt Cranes Ltd v Scottish Boiler and General Insurance Co Ltd* [2001] EWCA Civ 1964, [2002] Lloyd's Rep. I.R. 178; *HLB Kidsons v Lloyd's Underwriters* [2007] EWHC 1951 (Comm), [2008] Lloyd's Rep. I.R. 237 at [51]–[54]. See also *Denso Manufacturing UK Ltd v Great Lakes Reinsurance (UK) Plc* [2017] EWHC 391 (Comm), [2017] Lloyd's Rep. I.R. 240 at [22]–[40].

[535] Such as timely notification. See, generally, below, paras 42-093. As to a claims control clause in a reinsurance policy, see *Eagle Star Insurance Co Ltd v Cresswell* [2004] EWCA Civ 602, [2004] 2 All E.R. (Comm) 244.

[536] See, e.g. *Jones v Provincial Insurance Co Ltd* (1929) 35 Ll.L. Rep. 135; *Brown v Zurich General Accident Co* [1954] 2 Lloyd's Rep. 243; and the observations in *MacGillivray on Insurance Law*, 14th edn (2018), paras 10-010—10-011.

[537] See, e.g. *Stoneham v Ocean Railway and General* (1887) 19 Q.B.D. 237; *Re Bradley and Essex and Suffolk Accident Indemnity Society* [1912] 1 K.B. 415.

[538] *Alfred McAlpine Plc v BAI (Run-off) Ltd* [2000] 1 Lloyd's Rep. 437, where the Court of Appeal held that a breach of an innominate term might result in the entire policy being repudiated or the liability for the claim being defeated or might have other serious consequences. See also *Trans-Pacific Insurance Co (Australia) Ltd v Grand Union Insurance Co Ltd* (1989) 18 N.S.W.L.R. 675; *K/S Merc-Scandia XXXXII v Lloyd's Underwriters* [2001] EWCA Civ 1275, [2001] 2 Lloyd's Rep. 563. That there is a separate class of innominate terms, the breach of which will entitle the insurer to decline the claim as opposed to terminate the contract, is now in doubt, given the Court of Appeal's decision in *Sirius International Insurance Corp v Friends Provident Life & Pensions Ltd* [2005] EWCA Civ 601, [2005] 2 Lloyd's Rep. 517, although (putting aside the good sense of that decision) it must be questioned whether the Court of Appeal was free to overrule the court's decisions in *Alfred McAlpine v BAI* and *K/S Merc-Scandia v Lloyd's Underwriters*.

[539] *Re Bradley and Essex and Suffolk Accident Indemnity Society* [1912] 1 K.B. 415; *S & M Hotels Ltd v Legal and General Assurance Society Ltd* [1972] 1 Lloyd's Rep. 157; *Tektrol Ltd v International Insurance Co of Hanover Ltd* [2005] EWCA Civ 845, [2005] 1 All E.R. (Comm) 132; *Royal & Sun Alliance Insurance Plc v Dornoch Ltd* [2005] EWCA Civ 238, [2005] Lloyd's Rep. I.R. 544. See also Unfair Terms in Consumer Contracts Regulations 1999 reg.7 and the Consumer Rights Act 2015 s.64 (below, paras 42-087—42-088) and *Re Drake Insurance Plc* [2001] Lloyd's Rep. I.R. 643, 649.

before the condition is breached, particularly if the assureds' negligence is an insured peril under the policy in question.[540]

Promissory warranties and their effect: the common law   A warranty is a   **42-080**
promise by the assured that a particular thing shall or shall not be done in the future (a continuing or future warranty) or that a particular state of facts exists or does not exist (an existing fact warranty).[541] Such a promissory warranty may be express in the policy or may be implied (usually as a matter of law).[542] An express warranty should be written in the policy (assuming one exists).[543] In addition to those expressly set out in the policy, warranties may arise from statements made by an assured in a proposal form, the accuracy of which is warranted in a declaration which is said to be "the basis of the contract".[544] All such warranties must be exactly complied with,[545] and it is immaterial that a breach of warranty has no connection with the loss[546] or that it does not affect the risk[547] or has been remedied before the

---

[540] *Fraser v BN Furman (Productions) Ltd* [1967] 1 W.L.R. 898 (where a condition in an employers' liability policy requiring the assured to take reasonable precautions to prevent an accident was construed as applying only where inadequate measures are taken by the assured in the face of a recognised danger, without caring whether or not it was averted); *Sofi v Prudential Insurance Co Ltd* [1993] 2 Lloyd's Rep. 559 (applying a similar approach to a property insurance, where the policy required all reasonable steps to be taken to safeguard the property). In *Gunns v Par Insurance Brokers* [1997] 1 Lloyd's Rep. 173, 177, it was suggested that this approach should apply to all types of insurance policy. It has been held in *Amey Properties Ltd v Cornhill Insurance Plc* [1996] L.R.L.R. 259 that, in the case of motor policies, a condition requiring a vehicle to be kept in good repair will not have been satisfied if the insurer proves the assured simply to have been negligent in the upkeep of his vehicle. See also *Frans Maas (UK) Ltd v Sun Alliance and London Insurance Plc* [2003] EWHC 1803 (Comm), [2004] 1 Lloyd's Rep. 484; *The Board of Trustees of the Tate Gallery v Duffy Construction Ltd (No.2)* [2007] EWHC 912 (TCC), [2008] Lloyd's Rep. I.R. 159; cf. *Milton Furniture Ltd v Brit Insurance Ltd* [2014] EWHC 965 (QB), [2014] Lloyd's Rep. I.R. 540 at [157]–[172], [2015] EWCA Civ 671. It may be that (unless the context or wording compels a contrary conclusion) the word "reasonable" will be interpreted more leniently to the assured in respect of obligations to safeguard the subject matter of the insurance than in respect of obligations to maintain, although the distinction will often be blurred: *Hayward v Norwich Union Insurance Ltd* [2000] Lloyd's Rep. I.R. 382.

[541] Marine Insurance Act 1906 s.33. See *Bank of Nova Scotia v Hellenic Mutual War Risks Association (Bermuda) Ltd (The Good Luck)* [1992] 1 A.C. 233, a marine insurance case. It is generally assumed that the law of warranties is the same for marine and non-marine insurance: see, e.g. *Bank of Nova Scotia v Hellenic Mutual War Risks Association (Bermuda) Ltd (The Good Luck)* [1992] 1 A.C. 233, 262–264; *HIH Casualty and General Insurance Ltd v New Hampshire Insurance Co* [2001] EWCA Civ 735, [2001] 2 All E.R. (Comm) 39 at [122].

[542] For example, certain marine insurance policies have implied into them a warranty of seaworthiness and a warranty of legality (Marine Insurance Act 1906 ss.39–41). There is no equivalent warranty of legality implied into non-marine insurance contracts as a matter of law: *Euro-Diam Ltd v Bathurst* [1988] 2 W.L.R. 517.

[543] *MacGillivray on Insurance Law*, 14th edn (2018), paras 10-026—10-027.

[544] See, e.g. *Thomson v Weems* (1884) 9 App. Cas. 671; *Dawsons Ltd v Bonnin* [1922] 2 A.C. 413; *Provincial Insurance v Morgan* [1993] A.C. 240. The truth of the circumstances warranted may be qualified by that which is known to the assured: *Arab Bank Plc v Zurich Insurance Co* [1999] 1 Lloyd's Rep. 262, 283; *International Lottery Management Ltd v Dumas* [2002] Lloyd's Rep. I.R. 237 at [65]. See also *Zeller v British Caymanian Insurance Co Ltd* [2008] UKPC 4, [2008] Lloyd's Rep. I.R. 545; *Genesis Housing Association Ltd v Liberty Syndicate Management Ltd* [2013] EWCA Civ 1173, [2014] Lloyd's Rep. I.R. 318; *Aldridge v Liberty Mutual Insurance Europe Ltd* [2016] EWHC 3037 (Comm) at [119]; *Ashfaq v International Insurance Co of Hannover Plc* [2017] EWCA Civ 357, [2017] H.L.R. 29 at [58]–[59].

[545] *Pawson v Watson* (1778) 2 Cowp. 785; *De Hahn v Hartley* (1786) 1 T.R. 343.

[546] *Maynard v Rhode* (1824) 1 Car. & P. 360; *Glen v Lewis* (1853) 8 Ex. 607; *Foley v Tabor* (1861) 2 F. & F. 663.

loss[548] or that it occurs without the fault of the assured.[549] In the case of continuing warranties, the insurer is discharged from any further liability under the contract as from the date the warranty is breached (thereby still allowing the assured to claim in respect of any loss occurring before the warranty was breached) and the discharge operates automatically without the insurer having to accept any repudiation or make any election.[550] In the case of existing fact warranties, the contract is effectively, although not technically, vitiated ab initio, since fulfilment of the warranty is a condition precedent to the attachment of the risk.[551] Given the draconian nature of some warranties, such terms will be construed, in the absence of a clearly expressed provision, against being a continuing warranty[552] and any ambiguity will be construed against the insurer,[553] and might be construed to be limited in their scope to a discrete part or section of the policy, rather than to the entire contract.[554] Further, a warranty may be construed to apply subject to implied exceptions.[555] When construing whether a statement in a proposal form gives rise to a continuing warranty or a warranty as to past or existing fact, there is no special principle of insurance law requiring answers to be read as importing promises as to the future.[556] The insurer will not be entitled to rely on a breach of warranty as a defence if non-compliance with the warranty is excused when, by reason of a change of circumstances, the warranty ceases to be applicable to the circumstances of the contract, or when compliance with the warranty is rendered unlawful by any subsequent law.[557] Further, the insurer will not be entitled to rely on a breach of warranty if the breach has been waived by the insurer.[558]

---

547 *Newcastle Fire v Macmorran* (1815) 3 Dow. 255; *Dawsons v Bonnin* [1922] 2 A.C. 413. cf. *HIH Casualty & General Insurance Ltd v New Hampshire Insurance Co* [2001] EWCA Civ 735, [2001] 2 Lloyd's Rep. 161.

548 Marine Insurance Act 1906 s.34(2).

549 *Philips v Baillie* (1784) 3 Doug. K.B. 374; *Worsley v Wood* (1796) 6 T.R. 710. Note, however, that a condition requiring all reasonable precautions to be taken may be construed as applying only to the assured himself, and not to neglects or defaults of his employees: *Fraser v BN Furman (Productions) Ltd* [1967] 2 Lloyd's Rep. 1; *Duncan Logan (Contractors) v Royal Exchange Assurance Group*, 1973 S.L.T. 192.

550 *Bank of Nova Scotia v Hellenic Mutual War Risks Association (Bermuda) Ltd (The Good Luck)* [1992] 1 A.C. 233.

551 *Thomson v Weems* (1884) 9 App. Cas. 671, 683–684.

552 *Hussain v Brown* [1996] 1 Lloyd's Rep. 627. cf. *Cornhill Insurance Plc v DE Stamp Felt Roofing Contractors Ltd* [2002] EWCA Civ 395, [2002] Lloyd's Rep. I.R. 648 at [20].

553 *Pratt v Aigaion Insurance Co SA* [2008] EWCA Civ 1314, [2009] 1 Lloyd's Rep. 225; *AC Ward & Sons Ltd v Catlin (Five) Ltd* [2009] EWCA Civ 1098, [2010] Lloyd's Rep. I.R. 301; *Amlin Corporate Member Ltd v Oriental Assurance Corporation (The Princess of the Stars)* [2013] EWHC 2380 (Comm), [2013] 2 Lloyd's Rep. 523 at [30], [2014] EWCA Civ 1135, [2014] 2 Lloyd's Rep. 561 at [43]–[45].

554 *Printpak v AGF Insurance Ltd* [1999] Lloyd's Rep. I.R. 542. cf. *International Management Group (UK) Ltd v Simmonds* [2003] EWHC 177 (Comm), [2004] Lloyd's Rep. I.R. 247, [118].

555 See, e.g. *GE Frankona Reinsurance Ltd v CMM Trust No 1400 (The Newfoundland Explorer)* [2006] EWHC 429 (Admlty), [2006] Lloyd's Rep. I.R. 704; *Pratt v Aigaion Insurance Co SA* [2008] EWCA Civ 1314, [2009] 1 Lloyd's Rep. 225. Further exceptions are provided for in Marine Insurance Act 1906 s.34(1).

556 *Hussain v Brown* [1996] 1 Lloyd's Rep. 627, where the answer yes to a question "Are the premises fitted with any system of intruder alarm?" was held not to constitute a continuing warranty that the premises would be fitted with such an alarm.

557 Marine Insurance Act 1906 s.34(1). cf. *Agapitos Laiki Bank (Hellas) SA v Agnew (No.2)* [2002] EWHC 1558 (Comm), [2003] Lloyd's Rep. I.R. 54 at [59]; *Sugar Hut Group Ltd v Great Lakes Reinsurance (UK) Plc* [2010] EWHC 2636 (Comm), [2011] Lloyd's Rep. I.R. 198 at [42].

558 Marine Insurance Act 1906 s.34(3). See below, para.42-086.

Suspensive, delimiting or descriptive warranties   In order to evade the harsher   **42-081**
effects of a breach of a promissory warranty, the courts have often resorted to
construing a "warranty" not as a promissory warranty, but rather as a suspensive
(or delimiting or descriptive) warranty. Such a warranty does not impose a promissory obligation on the assured; instead, it purports to delineate the risk being
insured, much like an exclusion clause. A breach of a suspensive warranty does not
entitle the insurer either to terminate the contract or sue for damages if not complied
with[559]; it merely means that the relevant loss or damage is not covered by the insurance policy if the loss or damage is sustained whilst the breach is operating; but the
cover would be reinstated once the breach comes to an end or is remedied. Such a
suspensive warranty is more likely to be found to exist where the term is not
fundamental to the risk and where a breach of the term is not likely to alter or
increase the risk after the breach lapses or has been rectified.[560]

Warranties and the Insurance Act 2015   The 2015 Act applies to all insurance   **42-082**
contracts agreed on or after August 12, 2016.[561] The 2015 Act, by s.10, applies to
"warranties". Although it does not say so expressly, it appears to be aimed at
promissory warranties.[562] The effect of s.10 is to treat promissory warranties in both
consumer and non-consumer insurance contracts in the same way as suspensive
warranties. Thus, any rule of law that a breach of an express or implied warranty
results in the discharge of the insurer's liability under the insurance contract is
abolished.[563] In place of such a rule of law, the 2015 Act provides that where there
has been a breach of warranty, the insurer has no liability under the insurance
contract in respect of any loss occurring, or attributable to something happening,
after the breach of warranty but before the breach has been remedied.[564] Thus, the
insurer will remain liable under the insurance contract where the loss occurred or
was attributable to something happening before the breach of warranty or after the
breach has been remedied.[565] The 2015 Act provides when a breach of warranty will
be regarded as remedied. If the warranty is one which requires something to be done
or not done or a condition to be fulfilled or something to be the case or not the case

---

[559] See, e.g. *CTN Cash and Carry Ltd v General Accident Fire and Life Assurance Corp Plc* [1989] 1
Lloyd's Rep. 299. See also *Farr v Motor Traders Mutual Society* [1920] 3 K.B. 669; *Roberts v
Anglo-Saxon Insurance Co* (1927) 27 Ll.L. Rep. 313; *Morgan v Provincial Insurance Co* [1932] 2
K.B. 70. For an illustration of the expression "warranty" apparently even being used to refer to a
term the breach of which sounds in damages only, see *W. & J. Lane v Spratt* [1970] 2 Q.B. 480, 487,
493.

[560] *De Maurier (Jewels) Ltd v Bastion Insurance Co Ltd* [1967] 2 Lloyd's Rep. 550, 558–559; *Svenska
Handelsbanken v Sun Alliance and London Insurance Plc* [1996] 1 Lloyd's Rep. 519, 551–553. It
appears the court will be inclined to construe a term as a suspensive condition if it purports to impose
a continuing obligation on the assured: *Kler Knitwear Ltd v Lombard General Insurance Co Ltd*
[2000] Lloyd's Rep. I.R. 47. See also *Toomey v Banco Vitalicio de Espana sa de Seguros y
Reaseguros* [2003] EWHC 1102 (Comm); affirmed [2004] EWCA Civ 622, [2004] Lloyd's Rep. I.R.
354 at [40]–[46]; *Sugar Hut Group Ltd v Great Lakes Reinsurance (UK) Plc* [2010] EWHC 2636
(Comm), [2011] Lloyd's Rep. I.R. 198; *Bluebon Ltd (In Liquidation) v Ageas (UK) Ltd* [2017]
EWHC 3301 (Comm), [31]–[67].

[561] 2015 Act s.22(2).

[562] Explanatory Notes, paras 86–87, 92. Further, 2015 Act s.10(7) amends ss.33–34 of the Marine Insurance Act 1906, which applies to promissory warranties.

[563] 2015 Act s.10(1).

[564] 2015 Act s.10(2).

[565] 2015 Act s.10(4).

by an "ascertainable time"[566] and that requirement is not complied with, the breach will be remedied when the risk to which the warranty relates later becomes essentially the same as that originally contemplated by the parties.[567] In any other case, the breach of warranty will be remedied when the assured ceases to be in breach of warranty. The legislation recognises that there are some warranties which cannot be remedied, for example a specific warranty as to a past fact or event (such as a warranty that the assured has suffered no losses during the previous 12 months).[568] The insurer cannot rely on a breach of warranty as a defence where by reason of a change of circumstances the warranty ceases to be applicable to the circumstances of the contract, compliance with the warranty is rendered unlawful by any subsequent law, or the insurer waives the breach of warranty. These exceptions are the same as that provided for under the common law.[569] As discussed above, "basis of the contract" clauses are no longer permitted.[570]

42-083 **Contracting out of the Insurance Act 2015 provisions applicable to warranties** In respect of consumer insurance contracts, it is not open to the parties to contract out of the provisions of the 2015 Act applicable to warranties where the contractual provision would put the consumer in a worse position than the consumer would be in by virtue of the 2015 Act.[571] However, this prohibition does not apply to contracts for the settlement of claims under a consumer insurance contract.[572] "Basis of the contract" clauses cannot be agreed in any circumstances.[573] Similarly, in respect of non-consumer insurance contracts, the parties are not permitted to agree a contractual provision which would put the assured in a worse position than allowed by s.9 (which abolishes "basis of the contract" clauses).[574] Other than the prohibition against "basis of the contract" clauses, it is open to the parties to a non-consumer insurance contract to contract out of the 2015 Act insofar as it is applicable to warranties by a provision in their insurance contract which puts the assured in a worse position by the insurer, provided that the insurer takes sufficient steps to draw the assured's or his agent's attention to the provision in question and the provision is clear and unambiguous as to its effect.[575]

42-084 **Terms not relevant to the actual loss** Section 11 of the Insurance Act 2015 introduces a restriction upon the ability of insurers to rely on certain terms of the insurance contract as a defence to an insurance claim. The terms to which this restriction applies are, subject to one exception, all terms, including warranties,[576] compliance with which would tend to reduce the risk of loss of a particular kind, loss at a particular location or loss at a particular time. The exception is a term which defines the risk as a whole. Presumably, this exception would apply to a

---

[566] Explanatory Notes, para.91, refer to this as a "deadline".
[567] 2015 Act ss.10(5)(a), 10(6).
[568] Explanatory Notes, para.89. See 2015 Act s.10(4)(b).
[569] 2015 Act ss.10(3). See Marine Insurance Act 1906 ss.34(1) and (3). See above, para.42-080 and below, para.42-086.
[570] See above, paras 42-048, 42-059.
[571] 2015 Act s.15(1).
[572] 2015 Act s.15(3).
[573] Consumer Insurance (Disclosure and Representations) Act 2012 ss.6, 10(1)–(2). This prohibition does not apply to contracts for the settlement of claims under a consumer insurance contract: s.10(3). See above, para.42-048.
[574] 2015 Act s.16(1).
[575] 2015 Act ss.16–17. See above, para.42-060.
[576] 2015 Act s.11(4). See Explanatory Notes, paras 95, 98.

policy exclusion which provides that an insurer is not liable for losses caused by certain specified excluded perils; but it may not be so limited. If the contract term is one compliance with which would tend to reduce the risk of loss as described, the insurer may not rely on non-compliance with such a term to exclude, limit or discharge its liability under the insurance contract in answer to a claim under the insurance contract in respect of a loss, if the assured shows that the non-compliance with the term could not have increased the risk of the loss which actually occurred in the circumstances in which it occurred.[577] If for example the insurance contract contains a warranty or condition that the insured property will be secured by a speci-fied type of lock or alarm and if the property was damaged by flood or fire, it is likely that the assured could show that a failure to secure the property with the specified lock could not have increased the risk of loss by flood or fire.[578] It is not open to the parties to a consumer insurance contract to contract out of the effect of s.11 if such a contract would put the assured in a worse position than that allowed under s.11.[579] It is open to the parties to a non-consumer insurance contract to contract out of the effect of s.11 by a provision which puts the assured in a worse position than that allowed under s.11, provided that the transparency requirements of the Act are complied with.[580]

FCA Insurance: Conduct of Business Sourcebook (ICOBS)   In the case of poli-cies taken out by individuals in a private capacity, the harsh effects of these rules[581] were to some extent mitigated by the Statement of General Insurance Practice.[582] Since January 2008, the Financial Services Authority Regulation, ICOBS, provides that insurers must handle claims promptly and fairly, provide reasonable guidance to policyholders, not unreasonably reject a claim, and pay claims promptly after set-tlement,[583] and that it is unreasonable for an insurer to reject a consumer policyholder's claim on the ground of breach of warranty or breach of condition, unless there is evidence of fraud or unless the circumstances of the claim are con-nected to the breach of warranty or condition and the warranty was material to the risk and was drawn to the policyholder's attention before the conclusion of the contract.[584]   **42-085**

Waiver   The insurer may, of course, waive any breach of condition or warranty   **42-086**

---

577   2015 Act ss.11(1)–(3).
578   Explanatory Notes, para.96.
579   2015 Act s.16(1).
580   2015 Act s.17. See above, para.42-060.
581   For criticism of insurers' avoidance of liability in reliance upon the assured's breach of warranty, see Hasson (1971) 34 M.L.R. 29; Law Commission Report, *Non-Disclosure and Breach of War-ranty*, Cmnd.8064 (1980); Merkin (1981) L.M.C.L.Q. 347; Clarke [2007] L.M.C.L.Q. 474.
582   See above, para.42-045.
583   ICOBS para.8.1.1. In *Parker v National Farmers Union Mutual Insurance Society Ltd* [2012] EWHC 2156 (Comm), [2013] Lloyd's Rep. I.R. 253 [196]–[197], it was held that the standards of conduct in ICOBS were not implied terms of the contract but that their breach gave rise to a civil action for damages. See *Goodman v Central Capital Ltd* [2012] EWHC 8 (QB), [12]; *Bate v Aviva Insurance UK Ltd* [2013] EWHC 1687 (Comm), [2013] Lloyd's Rep. I.R. 492, affirmed [2014] EWCA Civ 334, [2014] Lloyd's Rep. I.R. 527; s.138D(2) of the Financial Services and Markets Act 2000.
584   ICOBS para.8.1.2(3). ICOBS may be viewed at the FSA's website: *https://www.handbook.fca.org.uk/handbook/ICOBS*. As to the fraud exception, see *Bate v Aviva Insurance UK Ltd* [2013] EWHC 1687 (Comm), [2013] Lloyd's Rep. I.R. 492; affirmed [2014] EWCA Civ 334, [2014] Lloyd's Rep. I.R. 527. See also *Ashfaq v International Insurance Co of Hannover Plc* [2017] EWCA Civ 357, [2017] H.L.R. 29.

either expressly or by conduct.[585] The insurance contract itself may restrict or exclude the remedies available for a breach of warranty.[586] There are generally said to be two (principal) types of waiver: waiver by election and waiver by estoppel. The former arises where the insurer, with full knowledge of the facts,[587] acts unequivocally in a manner consistent only with an intention to continue with the contract,[588] as, for example, where he accepts premiums,[589] or possibly where he renews the contract.[590] However, waiver by election is inapplicable to cases where the insurer's liability is automatically discharged by a breach of warranty or a condition precedent.[591] It has been held by the Court of Appeal that a breach of warranty or a breach of a condition precedent may be waived only by estoppel. This will be so where the insurer promises to the assured, by words or by conduct, that he will not act upon the assured's breach, and the assured so alters his position in reliance upon this promise as to make it unjust for the insurer to go back upon it. In this situation (unlike a waiver by election), an insurer may lose the right to treat himself as discharged from liability before he has full knowledge of the circumstances and of his right to treat himself as discharged.[592]

42-087 **Unfair Terms in Consumer Contracts Regulations 1999**[593] Although insurance contracts are excluded from the ambit of the Unfair Contract Terms Act 1977,[594] the Unfair Terms in Consumer Contracts Regulations 1999 (which implement Council Directive 93/13 and apply to consumer contracts concluded after October 1, 1999 and before October 1, 2015[595])[596] do embrace insurance contracts. The 1999 Regulations replaced the Unfair Terms in Consumer Contracts Regula-

---

585   For waiver generally, and the different senses in which the word is used, see above, Vol.I, paras 24-007—24-010. See also the discussion in *MacGillivray on Insurance Law*, 14th edn (2018), paras 10-098—10-121.

586   *Seashell of Lisson Grove Ltd v Aviva Insurance Ltd* [2011] EWHC 1761 (Comm).

587   *Ayrey v British Legal* [1918] 1 K.B. 136; *Scottish Equitable v Buist* (1877) 4 R. 1076, Ct of Sess.; *Russell v Thornton* (1860) 6 Hurl. & N. 140; see also *Melik Co Ltd v Norwich Union* [1980] 1 Lloyd's Rep. 523.

588   *Compagnia Tirrena Di Assicuranzione SpA v Grand Union Insurance Co Ltd* [1991] 2 Lloyd's Rep. 143; *Fortisbank SA v Trenwick International Ltd* [2005] EWHC 399 (Comm), [2005] Lloyd's Rep. I.R. 464.

589   *Wing v Harvey* (1854) 5 De G.M. & G. 265; *Ayrey v British Legal*, above; *Compagnia Tirrena Di Assicuranzione SpA v Grand Union Insurance Co Ltd*, above.

590   *Sulphur Pulp v Faber* (1895) 1 Com. Cas. 146; *Handler v Mutual Reserve Fund* (1904) 90 L.T. 192; *Barrett Bros (Taxis) Ltd v Davies* [1966] 1 W.L.R. 1334.

591   *Brownsville Holdings Ltd v Adamjee Insurance Co Ltd (The Milasan)* [2002] 2 Lloyd's Rep. 458, 467; *HIH Casualty and General Insurance Ltd v Axa Corporate Solutions* [2002] Lloyd's Rep. I.R. 325; affirmed [2002] EWCA Civ 1253, [2003] Lloyd's Rep. I.R. 1; *Kosmar Villa Holidays Plc v Trustees of Syndicate 1243* [2008] EWCA Civ 147, [2008] Lloyd's Rep. I.R. 489; *Argo Systems FZE v Liberty Insurance Pte Ltd* [2011] EWCA Civ 1572, [2012] 1 Lloyd's Rep. 129; cf. *Bhopal v Sphere Drake Insurance Plc* [2002] Lloyd's Rep. I.R. 413. See also Soyer [2002] L.M.C.L.Q. 199, 208–209.

592   *Argo Systems FZE v Liberty Insurance Pte Ltd* [2011] EWCA 1572, [2012] 1 Lloyd's Rep. 129. See also above, Vol.I, paras 24-007 et seq. There remains one unexplained aspect of a waiver of a breach of warranty: s.34(3) of the Marine Insurance Act 1906 provides that the insurer may waive a breach of warranty, but when the 1906 Act was passed, there was no concept of a waiver by equitable estoppel. This suggests that the draftsman of the Act had some other species of waiver in mind.

593   SI 1999/2083. For a comprehensive discussion, see above, Ch.38.

594   Unfair Contract Terms Act 1977 Sch.1 para.1.

595   See next paragraph.

596   SI 1999/2083 reg.1.

tions 1994, which applied to consumer contracts concluded after July 1, 1995.[597] The Regulations provide that unfair terms included in a contract with a consumer[598] by a seller or supplier[599] are not binding on the consumer.[600] A contract term which has not been individually negotiated is to be regarded as unfair if, contrary to the requirement of good faith,[601] it causes a significant imbalance in the parties' rights and obligations arising under the contract to the detriment of the consumer.[602] If the contract is capable of continuing in existence without the offending unfair term, it is to continue to bind the parties, albeit that the unfair term is not to be binding upon the consumer.[603] Furthermore, terms reduced to writing must be in plain, intelligible language, and if there is any doubt about the meaning of a term, the interpretation most favourable to the consumer must prevail.[604] Despite the apparent width of these provisions, it is to be borne in mind that many of the severer aspects of insurance law (such as the absolute nature of the obligation to disclose material facts[605]) derive from the general principles of insurance law, rather than specific terms in the insurance contract. The Regulations therefore will not apply to such principles of law.[606] Furthermore, the Regulations specifically provide that assessment of the unfair nature of terms shall not relate to the definition of the main subject matter of the contract, nor to the adequacy of the price and remuneration on the one hand, as against the services or goods supplied in exchange on the other.[607] Thus, terms of the insurance which define or circumscribe the insured risk

---

[597] SI 1994/3159 reg.1.

[598] A "consumer" is any natural person who, in contracts covered by the Regulations, is acting for purposes which are outside his trade, business or profession: reg.3(1), 1999 Regulations; reg.2(1), 1994 Regulations. See *Ashfaq v International Insurance Co of Hannover Plc* [2017] EWCA Civ 357, [2017] H.L.R. 29 at [45]–[58].

[599] A "seller or supplier" is any person (natural or legal) who, in making a contract to which the Regulations apply, is acting for purposes relating to his trade, business or profession, whether publicly or privately owned.

[600] 1999 Regulations reg.8(1); 1994 Regulations reg.5(1). If the term is capable of being both fair and unfair depending on the circumstances, it may be that the term will be binding only to the extent that the term is fair: *Bankers Insurance Co Ltd v South* [2003] EWHC 380 (QB); cf. *The Hollandia* [1983] 1 A.C. 565, 575 (concerning the interpretation of "clause, covenant or agreement" being void under art.III r.8 of the Hague Rules).

[601] *Lacey's Footwear (Wholesale) Ltd v Bowler International Freight Ltd* [1997] 2 Lloyd's Rep. 369, 385.

[602] 1999 Regulations reg.5(1); 1994 Regulations reg.4(1). In *Parker v National Farmers Union Mutual Insurance Society Ltd* [2012] EWHC 2156 (Comm), [2013] Lloyd's Rep. I.R. 278, at [189]–[190], it was held that a condition requiring the provision of information was not unfair.

[603] 1999 Regulations reg.8(2); Regulations reg.5(2).

[604] 1999 Regulations reg.7; 1994 Regulations reg.6. See *Re Drake Insurance Plc* [2001] Lloyd's Rep. I.R. 643, 649. In *AJ Building and Plastering Ltd v Turner* [2013] EWHC 484 (QB), [2013] Lloyd's Rep. I.R. 629, at [53], the Court said that there was no material difference between this principle of construction and the contra proferentem principle. See also art.31 and Annex II of the Third Life Assurance Directive (92/96) which specifies certain information, both about the insurer and about the life assurance policy, which must be communicated to the proposed policy-holder in a clear and accurate manner, and in writing, before the contract is concluded, and further information which must be provided during the term of the contract. This Directive was implemented by the Insurance Companies (Third Insurance Directives) Regulations 1994 (SI 1994/1696).

[605] See above, para.42-034.

[606] *Direct Line Insurance Plc v Khan* [2001] EWCA Civ 1794, [2002] Lloyd's Rep. I.R. 364.

[607] 1999 Regulations reg.6(2); 1994 Regulations reg.3(2). Terms delimiting the scope of cover, such as the description of the insured perils or exceptions to cover, should not (if expressed in plain intelligible language) fall for consideration as fair or unfair: cf. *Bankers Insurance Co Ltd v South* [2003] EWHC 380 (QB).

will not directly be subject to assessment as fair or unfair.[608] However, conditions concerned with, for example, the assured's obligations following the occurrence of a loss should be subject to assessment.

42-088 **Consumer Rights Act 2015** The Consumer Rights Act 2015 entered into force on October 1, 2015 and applies to contract made on or after that date.[609] The Unfair Terms in Consumer Contracts Regulations 1999 are revoked, remaining applicable only to contracts made before October 1, 2015.[610] By s.62(1)–(5) of the 2015 Act, a term of a consumer contract is not binding on the consumer if it is unfair, although the consumer may choose to rely on it. A term of a consumer contract is unfair if, contrary to the requirement of good faith, it causes a significant imbalance in the parties' rights and obligations under the contract to the detriment of the consumer, taking into account the nature and terms of the contract and all of the circumstances existing when the term was agreed.[611] However, a term of a consumer contract will not be assessed for unfairness if it specifies the main subject matter of the contract or if the assessment concerns the appropriateness of the price payable under the contract for the services provided,[612] provided that the term is transparent (meaning it is both legible if in writing and expressed in plain and intelligible language) and prominent (meaning that it is brought to the consumer's attention in such a way that an average—reasonably well-informed, observant and circumspect—consumer would be aware of the term).[613] The Act contains certain restrictions as to a term which purports to exclude or restrict liability for negligence; however, such restrictions do not apply to insurance contracts.[614]

8. ASSIGNMENT

42-089 **Assignment of the policy** In principle, contracts of insurance, whether or not contracts of indemnity, are choses in action[615]; and, as such, the assured has rights which (subject to what follows) may be assigned at law under the provisions of s.136 of the Law of Property Act 1925, or in equity in any of the ways in which contractual rights may be so assigned.[616] Two sorts of restriction, however, upon the assignability of policies must be noted. First: subject to any contrary stipulation, a

---

[608] para.19 of the Preamble, which has not been included in the Regulations, although reg.6(2) of the 1999 Regulations; reg.3(2) of the 1994 Regulations deals with such terms with respect to all contracts.

[609] See Consumer Rights Act 2015 (Commencement) (England) Order 2015 (SI 2015/000) and above, Ch.38. As to the meaning of "consumer", cf. *Ashfaq v International Insurance Co of Hannover Plc* [2017] EWCA Civ 357, [2017] H.L.R. 29 at [45]–[58].

[610] 2015 Act s.75, Sch.4 para.34.

[611] 2015 Act Sch.2 lists a number of terms which may be assessed as unfair: see s.63.

[612] See *Van Hove v CNP Assurances SA* (C-96/14) EU:C:2015:262, [2015] 3 C.M.L.R. 31 at [34]–[35].

[613] 2015 Act s.64.

[614] 2015 Act ss.65, 66(1)(a).

[615] *Re Moore* (1878) 8 Ch. D. 519, 520; *Castellain v Preston* (1883) 11 Q.B.D. 380, 388.

[616] *Raiffeisen Zentralbank Österreich AG v Five Star Trading LLC* [2001] EWCA Civ 68, [2001] 2 W.L.R. 1344. For general principles of assignment, see above, Vol.I, Ch.19. Marine policies are assignable at law merely by indorsement or in any other customary manner: see Marine Insurance Act 1906 s.50. For life insurance policies, see below, para.42-132; *MacGillivray on Insurance Law*, 14th edn (2018), paras 26-070—26-113.

policy cannot normally be assigned without the consent of the insurer[617]; though, if it is assigned without any such consent, it seems that the policy is only voidable, and therefore remains in force until avoided by the insurer.[618] In practice, most policies will contain express provisions dealing with assignment. Secondly: if the contract is one of indemnity, the assignment of the policy must accompany the transfer of an interest in the subject matter of the insurance,[619] since a policy which is assigned after a transfer of the subject matter will have ceased to be in force.[620] There is nothing objectionable in the assured assigning a policy to another person who has an insurable interest in the subject matter insured (such as a mortgagee), but a policy which is assigned prior to the assignment of the subject matter to a person with no insurable interest in the subject matter will thereby become void.[621] A partial equitable assignment of an insurance policy occurs when it is taken out pursuant to a covenant to insure contained in a mortgage. If the policy is effected in the name of the mortgagor, the mortgagee has a charge to secure repayment of the mortgage debt, which takes effect by way of assignment; if it is effected in the name of the mortgagee, the mortgagees' interest remains by way of charge, and he is accountable to subsequent mortgagees or the mortgagor for any surplus.[622]

Position of assignees When a policy is effectively transferred, the assignee takes **42-090** the policy subject to equities, so that the insurer will still be able to rely on any misrepresentation or non-disclosure by the assignor which took place before assignment.[623] Where, however, an assignee has taken an assignment of the policy by way of security, it is unclear whether the insurer can rely upon breaches of duty by the assignor after assignment. There are cases which suggest that the assignee is not affected by an assignor's post-assignment breaches,[624] but recent authority suggests the contrary.[625] If the assignment is absolute, the assignee will be bound by and entitled to observance of the policy conditions so that any conduct on the part of the assignor which otherwise would render the contract voidable, will not affect the contract to the prejudice of the assignee. Where only the benefit of the

---

[617] Special rules govern life assurance policies (see Policies of Assurance Act 1867), and policies of marine insurance (see Marine Insurance Act 1906 s.50(1)).

[618] *Doe d Pitt v Laming* (1814) 4 Camp. 73, 75.

[619] *Lloyd v Fleming* (1872) L.R. 7 Q.B. 299; *North of England Oil and Cake Co v Archangel Marine* (1875) 10 Q.B. 249; though a contemporaneous *agreement* to transfer the subject matter may suffice (*North of England Oil and Cake Co v Archangel Marine*, above, at 253). For a transfer of the subject matter accompanied by an agreement to assign, see *Powles v Innes* (1843) 11 M. & W. 10.

[620] See Marine Insurance Act 1906 s.51. cf. *Dodson v Peter H Dodson Insurance Services* [2001] 1 W.L.R. 1012, where a motor insurance policy was held to continue to provide liability cover even though the car which the policy insured had been sold.

[621] *Lynch v Dalzell* (1729) 4 Bro. P.C. 431.

[622] *Colonial Mutual Insurance Co Ltd v ANZ Banking Group (New Zealand) Ltd* [1995] 1 W.L.R. 1140, PC.

[623] *William Pickersgill & Sons Ltd v London and Provincial Marine and General Insurance Co Ltd* [1912] 3 K.B. 614, 617. The position is otherwise if, as a matter of construction, the third party has an original interest in the subject matter of the policy which has not been derived by assignment: *Samuel & Co v Dumas* [1924] A.C. 431. See Marine Insurance Act 1906 s.50(2).

[624] *Burton v Gore District Mutual Fire Insurance* (1865) 12 Gr. 156; *Central Bank of India v Guardian Assurance Co* (1936) 54 Ll. L. Rep. 247, 259–260.

[625] *Black King Shipping Corp v Massie (The Litsion Pride)* [1985] 1 Lloyd's Rep. 437, 517–519, where mortgagees were affected by the assignor's breach of good faith in making a fraudulent claim after the loss had occurred (although the judgment appears to treat the mortgagees as assignees of the *proceeds* of the policy). For the effect upon assignees of a deliberate act of the assured and of public policy, see above, paras 42-022—42-023.

contract has been assigned, if the assignor acts in breach of the duty of utmost good faith or of a warranty or condition precedent after the assignment, the insurer still may hold the contract as avoided or discharged respectively.[626]

42-091 **Assignment of a right under or the proceeds of the policy** Quite separately from assigning the policy itself, it is possible to assign the right to recover under the policy or the proceeds of the policy either before or after a loss has occurred.[627] Where the loss has already occurred, the assignment can simply operate as an assignment of the existing right to an indemnity or the proceeds[628]; but in the case of an assignment of proceeds prior to any loss arising, it would seem that it operates in equity as an assignment of a future chose in action,[629] and therefore being an agreement to assign requires consideration to be enforceable by the assignee.[630] Since, in either case, the assignment is not of the policy itself, the consent of the insurer is not required,[631] and it is irrelevant that the assignment is not accompanied by the transfer of an interest in the subject matter of the insurance[632]; but the corollary is that the insurer may rely upon breaches of condition or duty by the assignor after as well as before assignment, and even after the loss itself.[633] Whether there has been an assignment of the policy or an assignment of the right to its proceeds may in some cases be a fine question of construction.

9. CLAIMS

42-092 **Contractual provision** In a simple contract of insurance the assured becomes entitled to payment upon the occurrence of the event insured against.[634] The law does not imply any terms requiring the assured to give notice or to furnish details of the event or his loss,[635] save in the case of a constructive total loss in marine insurance, when the assured must give notice of abandonment.[636] It is, however, the general practice for insurance contracts to contain terms stipulating the steps which the assured must take after the occurrence of the event insured against,[637] and it is

---

[626] *Bank of Nova Scotia v Hellenic Mutual War Risks Association (Bermuda) Ltd (The Good Luck)* [1988] 1 Lloyd's Rep. 514, 546–547, [1989] 2 Lloyd's Rep. 238, 264.

[627] *Raiffeisen Zentralbank Österreich AG v Five Star Trading LLC* [2001] EWCA Civ 68, [2001] 2 W.L.R. 1344.

[628] *Lloyd v Fleming* (1872) L.R. 7 Q.B. 299, 302–303.

[629] *Re Turcan* (1889) 40 Ch. D. 5.

[630] *Tailby v Official Receiver* (1888) 13 App. Cas. 523.

[631] *Re Turcan* (1889) 40 Ch. D. 5; *McPhillips v London Mutual Fire Insurance Co* (1896) 23 A.R. 524.

[632] *Lloyd v Fleming* (1872) L.R. 7 Q.B. 299; *McPhillips v London Mutual Fire Insurance Co* (1896) 23 A.R. 524.

[633] *Black King Shipping Corp v Massie (The Litsion Pride)* [1985] 1 Lloyd's Rep. 437, 517–519. *Bank of Nova Scotia v Hellenic Mutual War Risks Association (Bermuda) Ltd (The Good Luck)* [1988] 1 Lloyd's Rep. 514, 546–547, [1989] 2 Lloyd's Rep. 238, 264.

[634] Ordinarily, the sum payable under an insurance contract is payable to the assured himself. However, the contract may provide that the "loss payee", that is the person who is to receive the insurance proceeds, is a person other than the assured (e.g. a bank). At common law, the loss payee, not being privy to the contract, had no right to enforce this contractual provision, relying on the assured to enforce the insurer's contractual undertaking. However, with the passage of the Contracts (Rights of Third Parties) Act 1999, the loss payee is likely to be able to enforce this contractual right directly against the insurer, subject of course to the terms of the policy.

[635] *Rankin v Potter* (1873) L.R. 6 H.L. 83.

[636] Marine Insurance Act 1906 ss.61–62.

[637] *Wilkinson v Car and General* (1913) 110 L.T. 468; *Terry v Trafalgar Insurance Co Ltd* [1970] 1

a matter of construction in each case[638] as to whether such terms are conditions precedent to the liability of the insurer,[639] innominate terms the breach of which (if sufficiently serious) will entitle the insurer to terminate the contract or decline the claim,[640] or only collateral terms not enabling the insurer to escape liability but merely entitling him to recover or set off any damages suffered by the breach.[641] In the absence of clear words, the courts are reluctant to construe provisions as conditions precedent.[642] Where such provisions are included in consumer insurance contracts, assuming they have not been separately negotiated, they may fall foul of the Unfair Terms in Consumer Contracts Regulations 1999 or, for contracts made on or after October 1, 2015, the Consumer Rights Act 2015,[643] if they, contrary to the requirement of good faith, cause an imbalance in the parties' position to the detriment of the consumer.[644]

Notice of loss   Often the contract stipulates the time and manner in which, and the persons to whom, the assured must notify the event or loss.[645] If drafted precisely the provision will enable the insurer to escape liability even if the breach occurred through no fault of the assured,[646] or has not even prejudiced the insurer.[647] This is regularly achieved by the agreement of a notice provision as a condition precedent

42-093

Lloyd's Rep. 524, where it was unsuccessfully argued that a condition prohibiting admissions of liability without the consent of the insurers was contrary to public policy.

[638] *Stoneham v Ocean Accident* (1887) 19 Q.B.D. 237; *Re Coleman's Depositories* [1907] 2 K.B. 798; see above, paras 42-077—42-078.

[639] e.g. *Elliott v Royal Exchange* (1867) L.R. 2 Ex. 237; *Cassel v Lancashire and Yorkshire Accident* (1885) 1 T.L.R. 495; *Cox v Orion Insurance Co Ltd* [1982] R.T.R. 1; *Hamptons Residential Ltd v Field* [1998] 2 Lloyd's Rep. 248.

[640] *Alfred McAlpine Plc v BAI (Run-off) Ltd* [2000] 1 Lloyd's Rep. 437. The possibility of declining a claim for a breach of an innominate term is unlikely since the Court of Appeal's decision in *Sirius International Insurance Corp v Friends Provident Life & Pensions Ltd* [2005] EWCA Civ 601, [2005] 2 Lloyd's Rep. 517.

[641] e.g. *Stoneham v Ocean Accident* (1887) 19 Q.B.D. 237; *Re Bradley and Essex Accident* [1912] 1 K.B 415.

[642] *Jones and James v Provincial* (1929) 46 T.L.R. 71, 73; *Alfred McAlpine Plc v BAI (Run-off) Ltd* [2000] 1 Lloyd's Rep. 437. However, if the condition precedent is express and unequivocal, then the Court will construe it accordingly: *Bass Brewers Ltd v Independent Insurance Co Ltd*, 2002 S.L.T. 512; *AXA Insurance UK Plc v Thermonex* [2012] EWHC B10 (Merc), [2013] Lloyd's Rep. I.R. 323. See above, para.42-078.

[643] See above, paras 38-389—38-426.

[644] See above, paras 42-087—42-088.

[645] *Hamptons Residential Ltd v Field* [1998] 2 Lloyd's Rep. 248; *Layher Ltd v Lowe* [1997] 58 Con. L.R. 42, where it was held that an assured was not obliged, under a clause requiring the assured to notify the insurer of an occurrence "likely" to give rise to a claim, to notify the insurer of the mere possibility of a claim; *Alfred McAlpine Plc v BAI (Run-off) Ltd* [2000] 1 Lloyd's Rep. 437; *J Rothschild Assurance Plc v Collyear* [1999] 1 Lloyd's Rep. I.R. 6; *Zurich Insurance Plc v Maccaferri Ltd* [2016] EWCA Civ 1302, [2017] Lloyd's Rep. I.R. 200. In *Tioxide Europe Ltd v Commercial Union Assurance Co Plc* [2005] EWCA Civ 928, [2006] Lloyd's Rep. I.R. 31, the relevant notice was given to the wrong addressee. For an example of a clause which exercised the court's powers of interpretation, see *Royal & Sun Alliance Insurance Plc v Dornoch Ltd* [2005] EWCA Civ 238, [2005] Lloyd's Rep. I.R. 544; cf. *AIG Europe (Ireland) Ltd v Faraday Capital Ltd* [2007] EWCA Civ 1208, [2008] Lloyd's Rep. I.R. 454. See also *William McIlroy (Swindon) Ltd v Quinn Insurance Ltd* [2011] EWCA Civ 825, [2012] 1 All E.R. (Comm) 241.

[646] *Cassel v Lancashire and Yorkshire Accident* (1885) 1 T.L.R. 495; *Adamson v Liverpool and London* [1953] 2 Lloyd's Rep. 355; *CVG Siderurgicia Orinoco SA v London Steamship Owners Mutual Insurance Assn Ltd (The Vainqueur Jose)* [1979] 1 Lloyd's Rep. 557; *Walker v Pennine Insurance Co Ltd* [1979] 2 Lloyd's Rep. 139; affirmed [1980] 2 Lloyd's Rep. 156.

[647] *Pioneer Concrete (UK) Ltd v National Employers' Mutual General Insurance* [1985] 2 All E.R. 395. The reasoning in the *Pioneer Concrete* case was expressly approved by the Privy Council in *Motor*

to the insurer's liability to pay a claim.[648] Alternatively, the courts may construe the provision as an innominate term, the consequences of the breach of which will depend on the seriousness of that breach.[649] However, it seems that even a provision requiring notice to be given "immediately" will only be construed as meaning within a reasonable time and without unjustifiable delay,[650] and it seems that if the insurer has received the required information from another source, at least an authoritative source, he cannot rely upon the failure of the assured to furnish it.[651] Where notification is required of the possibility or likelihood of a loss, and where the circumstances giving rise to the potential loss are fluid, the assessment of that possibility or likelihood should not be coloured by hindsight.[652] There is no rule of law which relieved an assured of the obligation to comply with policy provisions concerning the notification of a claim or loss where the insurer had earlier repudiated liability under the policy on other grounds.[653]

42-094 **Details of loss** In the absence of fraud, minor inaccuracies in detailing the nature and extent of the loss will not usually prevent the assured from altering the sum claimed or from recovering under the contract,[654] but again, if drafted precisely, a provision requiring these particulars can have this effect (especially by way of a

---

and General Insurance Co Ltd v Pavy [1994] 1 W.L.R. 462, 469 as fully and correctly stating the law. See also Total Graphics Ltd v AGF Insurance Ltd [1997] 1 Lloyd's Rep. 599, 608.

[648] HLB Kidsons v Lloyd's Underwriters [2007] EWHC 1951 (Comm), [2008] Lloyd's Rep. I.R. 237 at [51]–[54], [2008] EWCA Civ 1206, [2009] 1 Lloyd's Rep. 8; Involnert Management Inc v Aprilgrange Ltd [2015] EWHC 2225 (Comm), [2015] 2 Lloyd's Rep. 289 at [225]–[243]. As to the construction of a provision requiring notification of a circumstance "which may give rise to a claim", see also Laker Vent Engineering Ltd v Templeton Insurance Ltd [2009] EWCA Civ 62, [2009] Lloyd's Rep. I.R. 704 at [78]–[81]; AXA Insurance UK Plc v Thermonex [2012] EWHC B10 (Merc), [2013] Lloyd's Rep. I.R. 323.

[649] Alfred McAlpine Plc v BAI (Run-off) Ltd [2000] 1 Lloyd's Rep. 437.

[650] Williams v Lancashire and Yorkshire Accident (1902) 51 W.R. 222. In Zurich Insurance Plc v Maccaferri Ltd [2016] EWCA Civ 1302, [2017] Lloyd's Rep. I.R. 200 at [31]–[32], the Court of Appeal held that "'Immediately' itself does not mean instantaneously but 'with all reasonable speed considering the circumstances of the case'". As to the impact of prejudice in determining what is a reasonable time, see Shinedean Ltd v Alldown Demolition (London) Ltd [2006] EWCA Civ 939, [2006] Lloyd's Rep. I.R. 846. For a recent decision on the meaning of "as soon as practicable", see HLB Kidsons v Lloyd's Underwriters [2007] EWHC 1951 (Comm), [2008] Lloyd's Rep. I.R. 237 at [60], [2008] EWCA Civ 1206, [2009] 1 Lloyd's Rep. 8. In Denso Manufacturing UK Ltd v Great Lakes Reinsurance (UK) Plc [2017] EWHC 391 (Comm), [2017] Lloyd's Rep. I.R. 240 at [55]–[56], the Court considered the meaning of "as soon as" and "without delay" in a different context.

[651] Barrett Bros (Taxis) Ltd v Davies [1966] 1 W.L.R. 1334. cf. The Vainqueur José [1979] 1 Lloyd's Rep. 557; The Mozart [1985] 1 Lloyd's Rep. 239. This decision has been confined and questioned in reinsurance disputes (CNA International Reinsurance Co Ltd v Companhia de Seguros Tranquilidade SA [1999] Lloyd's Rep. I.R. 289, 302–303). Under the Third Parties (Rights against Insurers) Act 2010 s.9(2), it is provided that anything done by the third party which, if done by the insured, would have amounted to or contributed to fulfilment of the condition is to be treated as if done by the insured. This would include notification obligations. However, under ss.9(3) and (4), any condition requiring the insured to provide information or assistance to the insurer—other than notification of the existence of a claim—need not be fulfilled if the insured no longer exists.

[652] Clothing Management Technology Ltd v Beazley Solutions Ltd [2012] EWHC 727 (QB), [2012] 1 Lloyd's Rep. 571, [44].

[653] Nasser Diab v Regent Insurance Co Ltd [2006] UKPC 29, [2007] 1 W.L.R. 797.

[654] Mason v Harvey (1853) 8 Exch. 819. As to the adequacy of particulars provided by the assured, see Super Chem Products Ltd v American Life and General Insurance Co Ltd [2004] UKPC 2, [2004] Lloyd's Rep. I.R. 446 at [28]–[30].

condition precedent).[655] The assured may be required by the contract to give assistance to the insurer in substantiating the loss or dealing with claims made by third parties against the assured.[656]

Arbitration   Insurance contracts often provide for arbitration in the case of **42-095** disputes and such provisions may validly make arbitration a condition precedent to the insurer's liability.[657] The arbitration clause in the policy is treated as separable from the insurance contract[658] so that if the contract is void or avoided ab initio, the arbitration clause will generally survive and bind the parties to resolve their dispute by arbitration, unless the arbitration agreement may be avoided.[659] There is implied into an arbitration agreement a term that the parties will keep confidential the resulting arbitration award, unless it is necessary to disclose the award to a third party in order to enforce or protect the legal rights of one of the parties.[660] Arbitration, if commenced after January 30, 1997, is governed by the Arbitration Act 1996.[661] The 1996 Act[662] extends the Unfair Terms in Consumer Contracts Regulations 1999 to arbitration agreements and provides that a term of the contract which amounts to

---

[655] *Illidile v National Fire of New Zealand* [1896] A.C. 372; *Welch v Royal Exchange* [1939] 1 K.B. 294. The effect of such provisions may be mollified for consumers by the Unfair Terms in Consumer Contracts Regulations 1999 or, for contracts made on or after October 1, 2015, the Consumer Rights Act 2015: see above, paras 42-087—42-088.

[656] *Braunstein v Accidental Death* (1861) 1 B. & S. 782; *Manby v Gresham Life* (1861) 4 L.T. 347; *Gan Insurance Co Ltd v Tai Ping Insurance Co Ltd (Nos 2 and 3)* [2001] 1 Lloyd's Rep. I.R. 667. cf. *All Leisure Holidays Ltd v Europaische Reiseversicherung AG* [2011] EWHC 2629 (Comm), [2012] Lloyd's Rep. I.R. 193, [27]–[29]. See also *Porter v Zurich Insurance Co* [2009] EWHC 376 (QB), [2010] Lloyd's Rep. I.R. 373 at [124]–[130]. See also *Ted Baker Plc v Axa Insurance UK Plc* [2017] EWCA Civ 4097, [2017] Lloyd's Rep. I.R. 682. In *Widefree Ltd v Brit Insurance Ltd* [2009] EWHC 3671 (QB), [2010] 2 All E.R. (Comm) 477, the Court held that a condition precedent requiring the assured to provide such information as the insurers may reasonably require, should be construed to extend only to information which was in the insured's power to provide when the insurer requested the information.

[657] *Scott v Avery* (1856) 5 H.L.C. 811; *Jureidini v National British* [1915] A.C. 499, 504; *Atlantic v Louis Dreyfus* [1922] 2 A.C. 250, 255; *Czarnikow v Roth, Schmidt* [1922] 2 K.B. 478, 488; *Callaghan v Dominion Insurance Co Ltd* [1997] 2 Lloyd's Rep. 541, 545 (where the agreement which required only disputes on quantum to be referred to arbitration, provided that the award would be a condition precedent to a right of action against the insurer). In *William McIlroy Swindon Ltd v Quinn Insurance Ltd* [2011] EWCA Civ 825, [2012] 1 All E.R. (Comm) 241, the Court of Appeal construed a clause in a public liability insurance contract requiring the reference of a dispute "*in respect of a claim*" to arbitration as applying only to claims which can arise only upon or after the public liability in question has been established by the ascertainment of both liability and quantum: see below, para.42-120.

[658] Arbitration Act 1996 s.7.

[659] *Harbour Assurance Co (UK) Ltd v Kansa General International Insurance Co Ltd* [1993] 1 Lloyd's Rep. 455.

[660] *Insurance Co v Lloyd's Syndicate* [1995] 1 Lloyd's Rep. 272. See also *Hassneh Insurance Co v Mew* [1993] 2 Lloyd's Rep. 243; *Ali Shipping Corp v Shipyard Trogir* [1998] 2 All E.R. 136.

[661] Arbitrations commenced before January 30, 1997 are governed by the Arbitration Acts 1950, 1975 and 1979. By the 1996 Act, international insurance arbitration agreements now may exclude the court's jurisdiction in respect of any appeal on a point of law, whereas previously such agreements were ineffective (Arbitration Act 1979 ss.3 and 4). Such exclusion agreements relating to "domestic" arbitrations are effective if agreed after the commencement of proceedings (Arbitration Act 1996 s.87(1)).

[662] ss.89–91. The Regulations apply whatever the applicable law of the contract: s.89(3). The Arbitration Act 1996 was amended to accommodate the Consumer Rights Act 2015, instead of the 1999 Regulations, when the 2015 Act entered into force: s.75, Sch.4 paras 30–33.

an arbitration agreement is unfair for the purposes of the 1999 Regulations to the extent that it relates to a claim for a pecuniary remedy not exceeding £5,000.[663]

42-096 **Jurisdiction** Where a dispute arises between the insurer and the assured, the country in which suit may or must be brought will be determined in accordance with: (i) Regulation (EU) 1215/2012 of the European Parliament and Council which applies in respect of EU Member States and proceedings instituted on or after January 15, 2015[664]; (ii) EC Council Regulation 44/2001 (Brussels I Regulation) which applies in respect of the EU Member States and proceedings instituted before January 15, 2015[665]; (iii) the Civil Jurisdiction and Judgments Act 1991, which applies to the Contracting States to the Lugano Convention[666]; or (iv) in all other cases, in accordance with the non-Regulation and non-Convention rules in each Member or Contracting State.[667] Articles 10 to 16 of Regulation 1215/2012 determine where suit may be brought where the defendant insurer or assured is domiciled in a Member State. These provisions generally allow the assured to sue the insurer in a Member State where the insurer or the assured is domiciled, or where the insurer is a co-insurer in a Member State where the leading insurer is sued.[668] Where the insurance contract insures immovable property or liability, the insurer may additionally be sued in the Member State where the harmful event occurred[669]; in the case of liability insurance, the insurer may also be sued in the Member State by being joined in the proceedings by which the assured is sued by a third party.[670] By contrast, Regulation 1215/2012 requires the insurer to sue the assured only in the Member State where the assured is domiciled.[671] A third party, such as a person to whom the assured is liable, may sue the insurer in the Member States where the insurer or the assured is domiciled in the Member State where the harmful event occurred or as a co-defendant in proceedings instituted by the third party against the assured.[672] The insurance contract may provide that any dispute under the

---

663 This limit was fixed by the Unfair Arbitration Agreements (Specified Amount) Order 1999 (SI 1999/2167).

664 Civil Jurisdiction and Judgments (Amendment) Regulations 2014 (SI 2014/2947) reg.1.

665 By the Civil Jurisdiction and Judgments Order 2001 (SI 2001/3929), the Regulation entered into force on March 1, 2002. Prior to this date, the Civil Jurisdiction and Judgments Act 1982, incorporating the Brussels Convention on Jurisdiction and the Enforcement of Judgments in Civil and Commercial Matters 1968, as amended, and the Civil Jurisdiction and Judgments Act 1991 applied.

666 See the Civil Jurisdiction and Judgments Act 1991, as amended by the Civil Jurisdiction and Judgments Order 2001 (SI 2001/3929). A new Lugano Convention was signed on October 30, 2007, designed to harmonise the rules applicable under the Lugano Convention and Regulation 44/2001: see the Civil Jurisdiction and Judgments Regulations 2009 (SI 2009/3131).

667 In England and Wales, such rules are found in CPR r.6.37 and Practice Direction 6B.

668 Regulation 1215/2012 art.11. See *New Hampshire Insurance Co v Strabag Bau AG* [1992] 1 Lloyd's Rep. 361; *Tradigrain SA v SIAT SpA* [2002] EWHC 106 (Comm), [2002] 2 Lloyd's Rep. 553. See also arts 8 to 11 of the 2007 Lugano Convention.

669 Regulation 1215/2012 art.12.

670 Regulation 1215/2012 art.13(1).

671 Regulation 1215/2012 art.14(1). Under art.14(1) of the Regulation (art.12 of the 2007 Convention), the insurer must sue the assured in the state of domicile of the assured, whether or not the insurer is domiciled in a Member State: *Jordan Grand Prix Ltd v Baltic Insurance Group* [1999] 1 All E.R. 289. As to the scope of art.12, see also *National Justice Compania Naviera SA v Prudential Assurance Co Ltd (The Ikarian Reefer) (No.2)* [2000] 1 W.L.R. 603.

672 Regulation 1215/2012 arts 11–13. See Case 463/06 *FBTO Schadeverzekeringen NV v Odenbreit* [2008] Lloyd's Rep. I.R. 354; *Mapfre Mutualidad Compania de Seguros y Reaseguros SA v Keefe* [2015] EWCA Civ 598.

contract be submitted to the courts of a particular country. By arts 15(5) and 16,[673] such agreements will be enforced in respect of marine and aviation policies and insurance contracts in respect of "large risks",[674] provided that there has been a consensual agreement to the jurisdiction and that the formal requirements are satisfied.[675] Jurisdiction agreements in other types of policy will be enforced in the more limited circumstances set out in art.13.[676] Reinsurance contracts are not governed by arts 8 to 14, but are treated as normal commercial contracts and are dealt with under the general provisions of the Regulation.[677]

Choice of law   Where an English arbitration tribunal or court is properly seised   **42-097** of a dispute, the choice of law is determined by the application of the Contracts (Applicable Law) Act 1990 which incorporates the Rome Convention 1980.[678] Where contracts insure risks in the territories of EEA States and the contracts were concluded before December 17, 2009, the Financial Services and Markets Act 2000 (Law Applicable to Contracts of Insurance) Regulations 2001 apply to determine the applicable law.[679] The law applicable to contracts of insurance concluded on or after December 17, 2009 is determined in accordance with Regulation (EC) 593/2008 on the law applicable to contractual obligations (the Rome I Regulation).[680] Article 7 of the Rome I Regulation makes provision for insurance contracts covering a "large risk" wherever the risk is located and all other insurance contracts covering risks situated within the territory of a Member State.[681]

Fraudulent claims   There appear to be three species of "fraudulent claim",[682]   **42-098** namely: (a) a fraudulent claim for a loss which is non-existent; (b) a fraudulent

---

673 Lugano Convention 2007 arts 13(5) and 14. See *Charman v WOC Offshore BV* [1993] 1 Lloyd's Rep. 378, [1993] 2 Lloyd's Rep. 551; *Tradigrain SA v SIAT SpA* [2002] EWHC (Comm) 106, [2002] 2 Lloyd's Rep. 553.

674 "Large risks" are defined in Directive 2009/138/EC of the European Parliament and Council.

675 See art.23 of the Regulation (art.23 of the 2007 Convention). See *AIG Europe (UK) Ltd v Anonymous Greek Insurance Co of General Insurances (The Ethniki)* [2000] Lloyd's Rep. I.R. 343. As an example of a case where the Court has had to decide whether the parties have chosen a particular jurisdiction from a variety listed in the open cover, see *Tradigrain SA v SIAT SpA* [2002] EWHC (Comm) 106, [2002] 2 Lloyd's Rep. 553.

676 2007 Convention art.13.

677 *Fisher v Unione Italiana de Riassicurazione SpA* [1999] Lloyd's Rep. I.R. 215; *Agnew v Lansförsäkringsbølagens AB* [2000] 1 All E.R. 737; *AIG Europe (UK) Ltd v Anonymous Greek Insurance Co of General Insurances (The Ethniki)* [2000] Lloyd's Rep. I.R. 343; *Group Josi Reinsurance Co SA v Universal General Insurance Co* (C-412/98) EU:C:2000:399, [2001] Lloyd's Rep. I.R. 483.

678 Incorporating the Convention on the Law Applicable to Contractual Obligations 1980. See *Gan Insurance Co Ltd v Tai Ping Insurance Co Ltd* [1999] Lloyd's Rep. I.R. 472. See above, Vol.I, Ch.30.

679 SI 2001/2635. As amended by the Financial Services and Markets Act 2000 (Law Applicable to Contracts of Insurance) (Amendment) Regulations 2001 (SI 2001/3542). See *Crédit Lyonnais v New Hampshire Insurance Co* [1997] 2 Lloyd's Rep. 1; *American Motorists Insurance Co v Cellstar Corp* [2003] EWCA Civ 206, [2003] Lloyd's Rep. I.R. 295 (a case concerning a composite policy); *Travelers Casualty & Surety Co of Europe Ltd v Sun Life Assurance Co of Canada (UK) Ltd* [2004] EWHC 1704 (Comm), [2004] Lloyd's Rep. I.R. 846. The Regulations do not apply to contracts of reinsurance (reg.3(1)). By the Financial Services and Markets Act 2000 (Law Applicable to Contracts of Insurance) Regulations 2009 (SI 2009/3075), the 2001 Regulations do not apply to contracts of insurance concluded on or after December 17, 2009.

680 See above, Vol.I, Ch.30.

681 art.7. See above, Vol.I, paras 30-170—30-194. As to "large risks" and where a risk is situated, see Council Directive 73/239/EEC and Council Directive 88/357/EEC, as amended by Directive 2005/68/EC.

682 In *Agapitos v Agnew (The Aegeon)* [2002] EWCA Civ 247, [2002] 2 Lloyd's Rep. 42 at [15]–[18]

claim for a loss which is itself genuine, but which is excluded or not covered by the insurance policy; (c) a fraudulent claim for a loss which is otherwise genuine and covered by the policy but which is exaggerated.[683] Each of these will attract the same remedy. The precise definition of a fraudulent claim has not been authoritatively stated, although it is likely to require proof of the elements of deceit (other than inducement).[684] In order to be fraudulent, the claim must be substantially fraudulent, that is if the fraudulent element of the claim was de minimis, the assured would not bear the legal consequences of a fraudulent claim.[685] Mere exaggeration is not conclusive evidence of fraud,[686] though it affords strong evidence of fraud if the claim is out of all proportion to the true loss,[687] as does gross negligence.[688] The availability of the remedy for a fraudulent claim does not depend on actual inducement of the insurer, so that the fraud does not have to be successful; the mere making of the fraudulent claim is sufficient to engage the appropriate remedy.[689] In order for the fraudulent claim rule to apply, the fraud must be material to the recoverability of the claim under the insurance policy or, in other words, to the insurer's liability under the policy. That is, if the insurer would be liable to indemnify the assured in respect of the claim, absent any lie, the making of such a lie is necessarily collateral and will not constitute a fraudulent claim in itself. This was the finding of the Supreme Court in *Versloot Dredging BV v HDI Gerling Industrie Versicherung AG*,[690] overriding earlier authorities.[691] The fraud of the assured will preclude his trustee in bankruptcy,[692] and any joint assured, from recover-

---

the Court of Appeal considered that an originally honest claim which was subsequently appreciated as unfounded or exaggerated would be a fraudulent claim and that the deliberate suppression of a valid defence would render a claim fraudulent. See also *Versloot Dredging BV v HDI Gerling Industrie Versicherung AG* [2016] UKSC 45, [2017] A.C. 1 at [96]. A fraud committed in performance of a contract of compromise of an insurance claim will not be a fraudulent claim attracting the remedies discussed in this paragraph: *Direct Line Insurance Plc v Fox* [2009] EWHC 386 (QB), [2009] 1 All E.R. (Comm) 1017.

[683] As to exaggerated claims, see *Versloot Dredging BV v HDI Gerling Industrie Versicherung AG* [2016] UKSC 45, [2017] A.C. 1, at [25]–[26], [36], [51], [92]–[93].

[684] *Lek v Mathews* (1927-28) 29 Ll. L. Rep. 141; *Aviva Insurance Ltd v Brown* [2011] EWHC 362 (QB), [2012] Lloyd's Rep. I.R. 211 at [61]–[73], although in this case it was submitted that there was an additional requirement of dishonesty within the meaning discussed in *Twinsectra Ltd v Yardley* [2002] UKHL 12, [2002] 2 A.C. 164; such an additional requirement would appear to go beyond the bounds of the authorities. There is also a question whether the fraudulent claim can be constituted by a non-disclosure, as well as by a misrepresentation: *Marc Rich Agriculture Trading SA v Fortis Corporate Insurance NV* [2004] EWHC 2632 (Comm), [2005] Lloyd's Rep. I.R. 396; *Aviva Insurance Ltd v Brown* [2011] EWHC 362 (QB), [2012] Lloyd's Rep. I.R. 211 at [64].

[685] *Galloway v Guardian Royal Exchange (UK) Ltd* [1999] Lloyd's Rep. I.R. 209; *Tonkin v UK Insurance Ltd* [2006] EWHC 1120 (TCC), [2007] Lloyd's Rep. I.R. 283 at [176]–[178]; *Aviva Insurance Ltd v Brown* [2011] EWHC 362 (QB), [2012] Lloyd's Rep. I.R. 211 at [76]–[77].

[686] *London Assurance v Clare* (1937) 57 Ll.L. Rep. 254, 268; *Orakpo v Barclays Insurance Services Co Ltd* [1995] L.R.L.R. 443 at 451.

[687] *Chapman v Pole* (1870) 22 L.T. 306; *Herman v Phoenix Assurance Co Ltd* (1924) 18 Ll.L. Rep. 371; *Dome Mining Corp Ltd v Drysdale* (1931) 41 Ll.L. Rep. 109; *Central Bank of India Ltd v Guardian Assurance Co Ltd* (1936) 54 Ll.L. Rep. 247; *Shoot v Hill* (1936) 55 Ll.L. Rep. 29.

[688] *Goodman v Harvey* (1836) 4 Ad. & El. 870.

[689] *Versloot Dredging BV v HDI Gerling Industrie Versicherung AG* [2016] UKSC 45, [2017] A.C. 1 at [28]–[36], although Lord Sumption in that case appeared to curtail the principle underlying the fraudulent claim rule to the fact that inducement was not required.

[690] [2016] UKSC 45, [2017] A.C. 1, at [36], [39], [92]–[93], [100]–[103], [109]. See also *K/S Merc-Scandia XXXXII v Lloyd's Underwriters* [2001] EWCA Civ 1275, [2001] 2 Lloyd's Rep. 563 at [35].

[691] *Agapitos v Agnew (The Aegeon)* [2002] EWCA Civ 247, [2002] 2 Lloyd's Rep. 42 at [38].

[692] *Re Carr and Sun Insurance* (1897) T.L.R. 186.

ing, and the same appears to be true for an assignee of the policy.[693] Where, however, the policy is a composite one (embodying a separate insurance contract for each assured) insuring several parties for their different interests, an innocent assured is not prejudiced by another's fraud.[694] The assured, although himself innocent, may be affected by a claim presented fraudulently by his agent insofar as the latter was acting within the scope of his authority.[695] The duty of utmost good faith does not impose any duty to disclose or not to misrepresent material facts in connection with a claim wider than the duty not to present a fraudulent claim.[696]

Remedy for fraudulent claims: the common law   It is axiomatic that if the as-   **42-099**
sured presents a fraudulent claim, the claim will fail.[697] If, it is the case, albeit it is not entirely clear, that, the duty not to present fraudulent claims is a breach of the duty of utmost good faith, the insurer would be entitled to avoid the insurance contract ab initio.[698] However, the harshness of the remedy of avoidance has led recently to a fundamental reappraisal of the circumstances in which the contract of insurance might be avoided. Lord Hobhouse in *Manifest Shipping Co Ltd v Uni-Polaris Shipping Co Ltd (The Star Sea)*[699] was sceptical as to whether the remedy of avoidance was applicable to a fraudulent claim. In *Versloot Dredging BV v HDI Gerling Industrie Versicherung AG*,[700] Lords Sumption and Hughes were similarly sceptical. Mance L.J. in *Agapitos v Agnew (The Aegeon)*[701] considered that the common law had its own rule for the presentation of fraudulent claims, quite apart from the duty of utmost good faith and held that the remedy appropriate in the event of a fraudulent claim is the forfeiture of benefit under the policy (although the scope of that remedy remains undecided).[702] It has been held by the Court of Appeal that it is an implied term of the contract of insurance that the making of a fraudulent

---

693 *Black King Shipping Corp v Massie (The Litsion Pride)* [1985] 1 Lloyd's Rep. 437, 517–519.
694 *General Accident, Fire and Life Assurance Corp Ltd v Midland Bank Ltd* [1940] 2 K.B. 388; *Lombard Australia v NRMA Insurance* [1969] 1 Lloyd's Rep. 575. See also *Woolcott v Sun Alliance and London Insurance Ltd* [1978] 1 Lloyd's Rep. 629; *New Hampshire Insurance Co v MGN Ltd* [1997] L.R.L.R. 24; *Arab Bank Plc v Zurich Insurance Co* [1999] 1 Lloyd's Rep. 262.
695 *Savash v CIS General Insurance Ltd* [2014] EWHC 375 (TCC), [2014] Lloyd's Rep. I.R. 471 at [55]–[59].
696 *Royal Boskalis Westminster NV v Mountain* [1997] L.R.L.R. 523; reversed on other grounds [1997] 2 All E.R. 929; *Manifest Shipping & Co Ltd v Uni-Polaris Insurance Co Ltd (The Star Sea)* [2001] UKHL 1, [2001] 2 W.L.R. 170. See also *Alfred McAlpine Plc v BAI (Run-off) Ltd* [2000] 1 Lloyd's Rep. 437, where it was held that mere negligence in supplying details of claim pursuant to a notice provision in the policy did not constitute a breach of the obligation of utmost good faith.
697 *Manifest Shipping & Co Ltd v Uni-Polaris Shipping Co Ltd (The Star Sea)* [2001] UKHL 1, [2001] 2 W.L.R. 170 at [62].
698 *Manifest Shipping & Co Ltd v Uni-Polaris Shipping Co Ltd (The Star Sea)*, above; affirming [1997] 1 Lloyd's Rep. 360; *K/S Merc-Scandia XXXXII v Lloyd's Underwriters* [2001] EWCA Civ 1275, [2001] 2 Lloyd's Rep. 563. See above, para.42-042. See also *Goulstone v Royal* (1858) 1 F. & F. 276; *Britton v Royal* (1866) 4 F. & F. 905, 909; *Royal Boskalis Westminster NV v Mountain* [1997] L.R.L.R. 523; reversed on other grounds by the Court of Appeal: [1999] Q.B. 674. The duty not to make a fraudulent claim persists even after the insurer wrongfully repudiates the policy (*Transthene Packaging Co Ltd v Royal Insurance (UK) Ltd* [1996] L.R.L.R. 32, 43) but not after the commencement of litigation (*Agapitos v Agnew (The Aegeon)* [2002] EWCA Civ 247, [2002] 2 Lloyd's Rep. 42 at [52]).
699 [2001] UKHL 1, [2001] 2 W.L.R. 170. Lord Hobhouse does not appear to have come to any conclusion concerning the availability of the remedy of avoidance. Lords Clyde and Scott left the question open.
700 [2016] UKSC 45, [2017] A.C. 1, at [8], [67].
701 [2002] EWCA Civ 247, [2002] 2 Lloyd's Rep. 42 at [45].
702 In *The Aegeon*, at [21], [35] and [45], the Court of Appeal expressed a preference for the forfeiture

claim will result in the assured forfeiting all benefit under the policy,[703] and not just the benefit which attaches to the fraudulent claim or fraudulent part of the claim.[704] Nevertheless, it has been subsequently suggested by the Court of Appeal that forfeiture is limited to the fraudulent claim itself (including the non-fraudulent parts of the claim) or, less likely, only prospective benefit under the policy.[705] In *Versloot Dredging BV v HDI Gerling Industrie Versicherung AG*,[706] the Supreme Court appeared to assume that forfeiture of the insurance claim (including the genuine parts of the claim)—as opposed to the forfeiture of any other benefit under the policy—was the consequence of a fraudulent claim. As is evident from this discussion, the common law was in an uncertain state.[707] If, however, the insurance contract contains a clause permitting the insurer to avoid the contract in the event of a fraudulent claim, avoidance pursuant to the clause is likely to be effective.[708]

42-100 **Remedy for fraudulent claims under the Insurance Act 2015** The Insurance Act 2015 applies to insurance contracts agreed on or after August 12, 2016.[709] The 2015 Act, by s.12, clarifies the uncertain state of the law as explained in the previous paragraph. The 2015 Act does not identify what constitutes a fraudulent claim, leaving such matters to the common law.[710] Under s.12, where there has been a fraudulent claim, the insurer has two distinct remedies, both of which he may exercise. First, the insurer is not liable to pay the claim and the insurer may recover from the assured any sums paid by the insurer to the assured in respect of the claim.[711] Where the insurance claim comprises both fraudulent and honest parts, it is not clear whether this means that the insurer is absolved from paying the entire claim tainted by fraud, even the genuine parts of the claim, or whether the insurer

---

to be prospective applying to all claims or benefits which had not yet accrued at the date of the fraudulent claim. There were earlier dicta that the forfeiture extended to all benefit under the policy, including entitlements which had already accrued (see *Royal Boskalis Westminster NV v Mountain* [1997] L.R.L.R. 523, 592–595). In many cases there is an express provision in the policy that in the event of the presentation of a fraudulent claim "the policy shall become void and all claims hereunder shall be forfeited".

[703] *Diggens v Sun Alliance and London Assurance Plc* [1994] C.L.C. 1146; *Orakpo v Barclays Insurance Services* [1995] L.R.L.R. 443 (disapproved by the Court of Appeal in *K/S Merc-Scandia XXXXII v Lloyd's Underwriters*, in reliance on the judgment of the obiter dicta of Lord Hobhouse in *The Star Sea*). As to forfeiture clauses, see *Insurance Corp of the Channel Islands Ltd v McHugh* [1997] L.R.L.R. 94; cf. *Fargnoli GA Bonus Plc* [1997] C.L.C. 653.

[704] *Orakpo v Barclays Insurance Services*, above; *Royal Boskalis Westminster NV v Mountain*, above; *Galloway v Guardian Royal Exchange (UK) Ltd* [1999] Lloyd's Rep. I.R. 209; *Aviva Insurance Ltd v Brown* [2011] EWHC 362 (QB), [2012] Lloyd's Rep. I.R. 211, at [78], [122].

[705] *Agapitos v Agnew (The Aegeon)* [2002] EWCA Civ 247, [2002] 2 Lloyd's Rep. 42; *Axa General Insurance Ltd v Gottlieb* [2005] EWCA Civ 112, [2005] Lloyd's Rep. I.R. 369; *Churchill Car Insurance v Kelly* [2007] EWHC 18 (QB), [2007] R.T.R. 26.

[706] [2016] UKSC 45, [2017] A.C. 1.

[707] *Interpart Comerciao e Gestao SA v Lexington Insurance Co* [2004] Lloyd's Rep. I.R. 690; *Marc Rich Agriculture Trading SA v Fortis Corporate Insurance NV* [2004] EWHC 2632 (Comm), [2005] Lloyd's Rep. I.R. 396. See the Law Commission's Consultation Paper: *Insurance Contract Law: Post Contract Duties and other Issues* (LCCP No.201, December 2011).

[708] *Joseph Fielding Properties (Blackpool) Ltd v Aviva Insurance Ltd* [2010] EWHC 2192 (QB), [2011] Lloyd's Rep. I.R. 238 at [88]–[99]. In the event of a fraudulent claim, the insurer may also have a remedy for deceit. In *AXA Insurance UK Plc v Financial Claims Solutions Ltd* [2018] EWCA Civ 1330, the Court of Appeal allowed an insurer to recover exemplary damages by reason of a fraudulent claim.

[709] 2015 Act s.22(2).

[710] Explanatory Notes, para.100.

[711] 2015 Act s.12(1)(a)–(b).

is absolved from paying only the fraudulent part of the claim. It seems likely that the insurer will not be liable to pay any part of the claim tainted by fraud, including those parts which are genuine.[712] Second, the insurer may by notice to the assured treat the insurance contract as having been terminated with effect from the time of the fraudulent act. If the insurer does terminate the insurance contract in this way, he may refuse all liability to the assured under the insurance contract in respect of a "relevant event" (namely, the event which gives rise to the insurer's liability under the insurance contract such as the occurrence of a loss, the making of a claim or the notification of a potential claim, depending on the terms of the contract) occurring after the time of the fraudulent act and he may retain all premiums paid under the contract. Nevertheless, in the case of such termination, the insurer's obligations with respect to a "relevant event" before the time of the fraudulent act will remain unaffected.[713] The parties may contract out of the effect of s. 12, but in the case of a consumer insurance contract, any such contracting out is not permitted if it would put the assured in a worse position; in the case of a non-consumer insurance contract, any such contracting out which puts the assured in a worse position would be effective provided that the transparency requirements of the 2015 Act are complied with.[714]

The burden of proof   The burden is upon the assured to prove on the balance of   **42-101** probabilities that his loss or the event was proximately caused by perils insured against.[715] Thus under an "all risks" insurance the assured must establish that the loss was due to a fortuitous event,[716] and similarly where there is a claim for loss by perils of the sea,[717] and though theoretically there is no need to go further and prove the exact nature of the casualty,[718] in practice this generally has to be done.[719] The burden of proving that the assured caused the loss deliberately lies on the insurer,[720] but where the assured has to establish an accident, he will, of course, fail if the evidence is equally consistent with his wilful misconduct.[721]

---

712 See above, para.42-099; *Agapitos v Agnew (The Aegeon)* [2002] EWCA Civ 247, [2002] 2 Lloyd's Rep. 42; *Axa General Insurance Ltd v Gottlieb* [2005] EWCA Civ 112, [2005] Lloyd's Rep. I.R. 369.

713 2015 Act s.12(1)(c), (2)–(4).

714 2015 Act ss.15–17. See above, para.42-060.

715 *British and Foreign Marine v Gaunt* [1921] 2 A.C. 41, 58; *Regina Fur v Bossom* [1958] 2 Lloyd's Rep. 425; *Richard Aubrey Film Productions v Graham* [1960] 2 Lloyd's Rep. 101; see also *Fuerst Day Lawson Ltd v Orion Insurance Co Ltd* [1980] 1 Lloyd's Rep. 656; *Rhesa Shipping Co SA v Edmunds* [1985] 1 W.L.R. 948; *Kastor Navigation Co Ltd v Axa Global Risks (UK) Ltd* [2002] EWHC 2601 (Comm), [2003] Lloyd's Rep. I.R. 262 at [63]; affirmed, [2004] EWCA Civ 277, [2004] Lloyd's Rep. I.R. 481. Where there are a number of insured perils, only one insured peril need be proved: *Kuwait Airways Corp v Kuwait Insurance Co SAK* [1999] 1 Lloyd's Rep. 803.

716 *British and Foreign Marine v Gaunt* [1921] 2 A.C. 41.

717 *The Tropaioforos* [1960] 2 Lloyd's Rep. 469; *The Gold Sky* [1972] 2 Lloyd's Rep. 187; *The Vainqueur* [1973] 2 Lloyd's Rep. 275 (US); affirmed [1974] 2 Lloyd's Rep. 494.

718 *British and Foreign Marine v Gaunt*, above.

719 *Regina Fur v Bossom* [1958] 2 Lloyd's Rep. 425.

720 *London Assurance v Clare* (1937) 57 Ll.L. Rep. 254; *Slattery v Mance* [1962] 1 Q.B. 676; though generally the assured has the right and duty to begin at the trial of his claim, even if the substantial issue is fraud: *Grunther Industrial Developments v Federated Employers Insurance Association Ltd* [1973] 1 Lloyd's Rep. 394; affirmed [1976] 2 Lloyd's Rep. 259; *S and M Carpets (London) Ltd v Cornhill Insurance Co Ltd* [1981] 1 Lloyd's Rep. 667; affirmed [1982] 1 Lloyd's Rep. 423; *Watkins & Davis v Legal General Assurance Co Ltd* [1981] 1 Lloyd's Rep. 674; *Broughton Park Textiles (Salford) Ltd v Commercial Union Assurance* [1987] 1 Lloyd's Rep. 194; *Polvitte v Commercial Union Assurance* [1987] 1 Lloyd's Rep. 379. Where the insurer alleges fraud or wilful misconduct, the standard of proof remains the civil standard, although the difficulty in satisfying the court will

42-102 **Proof of insured and excepted perils** The assured must bring himself within the scope of the perils insured against but when, as is usual, these are expressed in general terms and then made subject to specific exceptions which do not qualify the whole of the general undertaking but merely exclude certain forms of the perils, leaving part of the general undertaking unqualified, it seems that it is sufficient for the assured to adduce evidence to bring the loss or the event within the scope of the general undertaking, and it is then for the insurer to prove on a balance of probabilities that the loss or the event resulted from one of the specific excepted causes.[722] When, however, the whole of the general undertaking is qualified, the assured cannot bring himself within the cover, unless he shows that the loss or the event resulted from the perils so limited.[723] In each case it is a question of construction[724] whether there is a general promise subject, to a degree, to exceptions, or only a limited and qualified promise; and though perhaps illogical, the courts are inclined to treat as cases falling into the former category contracts where the excepted perils are described as such[725] or as conditions precedent[726] or warranties.[727] It is, of course, open to the parties to make provision in the contract as to the incidence of the burden of proof on any issue that may arise between them.[728]

42-103 **Causation** The courts seek the "proximate", "direct",[729] "dominant",[730] "operative and efficient"[731] cause of the loss or an event in order to determine whether it was caused by an insured or an excepted peril, though by the use of apt words in the contract, such as "directly or indirectly",[732] it is, of course, possible to include or exclude losses or events not caused proximately by the perils insured or excepted.

---

be greater in proportion to the seriousness of the insurer's charge: *Hornal v Neuberger Products Ltd* [1957] 1 Q.B. 247, 258; *The Zinovia* [1984] 2 Lloyd's Rep. 264; *Re H* [1996] A.C. 563, 586–587; *Re D* [2008] UKHL 33.

[721] *Regina Fur v Bossom* [1958] 2 Lloyd's Rep. 425 at 434. cf. *Slattery v Mance*, above; with *The Tropaioforos* [1960] 2 Lloyd's Rep. 469.

[722] *Munro Brice v War Risks Association* [1918] 2 K.B. 78; reversed on facts [1920] 3 K.B. 94. cf. *Motor Union v Boggan* (1923) 130 L.T. 588, 591; *Greaves v Drysdale* (1935) 53 Ll.L. Rep. 16; reversed on facts (1936) 55 Ll.L. Rep. 95; *Pan American World Airways v Aetna* [1974] 1 Lloyd's Rep. 207 US; affirmed [1975] 1 Lloyd's Rep. 77; *Leeds Beckett University v Travelers Insurance Co Ltd* [2017] EWHC 558 (TCC), [2017] Lloyd's Rep. I.R. 417 at [199]–[208].

[723] *Munro Brice v War Risks Association*, above. See *Hurst v Evans* [1917] 1 K.B. 352, which can hardly be reconciled with *Greaves v Drysdale*, above. Where the assured and the insurer put forward rival explanations as to the cause of the loss, if the Court is in doubt as to the probable cause, it may reject the assured's claim on the ground that it has failed to discharge the onus of proof: *European Group Ltd v Chartis Insurance UK Ltd* [2012] EWHC 1245 (Comm), [2012] 2 Lloyd's Rep. 117 at [78]–[81]; *Nulty v Milton Keynes Borough Council* [2013] EWCA Civ 15, [2013] Lloyd's Rep. I.R. 243.

[724] *Gorman v Hand-in-Hand* (1877) Ir. R. 11 C.L. 224. In *Kuwait Airways Corp v Kuwait Insurance Co SAK* [1999] 1 Lloyd's Rep. 803 the House of Lords held that an extension of cover by reference to a list of perils "other than" a specified peril was not an exclusion.

[725] *American Tobacco v Guardian* (1925) 69 S.J. 621; *Re National Benefit* (1933) 45 Ll.L. Rep. 147.

[726] *Gorman v Hand-in-Hand* (1877) Ir.R. 11 C.L. 224.

[727] *Macbeth v King* (1916) 115 L.T. 221; *Bond Air Services v Hill* [1955] 2 Q.B. 417.

[728] *Levy v Assicurazioni Generali* [1940] A.C. 791.

[729] *Becker, Gray v London Assurance* [1918] A.C. 101, 114.

[730] *Leyland v Norwich Union* [1918] A.C. 350, 363; *Gray v Barr* [1971] 2 Q.B. 554, 567; *Naviera de Canarias SA v Nacional Hispanica Aseguradera SA* [1978] A.C. 853, 865, 881; *Marcel Beller Ltd v Hayden* [1978] 1 Q.B. 694.

[731] *Leyland v Norwich Union*, above, at 369, 370; *Samuel v Dumas* [1924] A.C. 431, 447. See also *Suez Fortune Investments Ltd v Talbot Underwriting Ltd* [2015] EWHC 42 (Comm), [2015] 1 Lloyd's Rep. 651, at [283]–[297].

[732] *Coxe v Employers Liability* [1916] 2 K.B. 629; *American Tobacco v Guardian* (1925) 69 S.J. 621; *Oei v Foster and Eagle Star Insurance* [1982] 2 Lloyd's Rep. 170; *ARC Capital Partners Ltd v Brit*

The application of this doctrine of proximate cause cannot be reduced to rigid rules and its application is really a matter of common sense rather than logic.[733] The doctrine of causation applied to insurance contracts is the same as that applied in the realm of tort or other breach of duty.[734] The peril insured against or excepted must operate,[735] and the loss or the event must be such as can fairly be attributed to that operation.[736] Thus loss caused by trying to avert a peril which has not yet begun to operate is not a loss caused by that peril,[737] whereas loss caused by trying to minimise the effects of an operating peril is regarded as being proximately caused by that peril.[738] Similarly, death through disease attributable to an accident[739] or through an operation necessitated by an accident[740] is generally regarded as caused by the accident, whereas losses merely facilitated by an insured peril, as where an air raid facilitates theft,[741] are not caused by that peril.

Multiple causes   There may be more than one cause which contributes to a loss.   **42-104**
Where the causes are concurrent and it is their combination which procures the loss,[742] then the loss will be covered by the insurance, if at least one of the causes

---

Syndicates Ltd [2016] EWHC 141 (Comm), [2016] 4 W.L.R. 18; *Crowden v QBE Insurance (Europe) Ltd* [2017] EWHC 2597 (Comm), [2018] Lloyd's Rep. I.R. 83 at [71]. cf. *Smith v Accident Insurance* (1870) L.R. 5 Ex. 302.

[733] *Yorkshire Dale SS Co v Minister of War Transport* [1942] A.C. 691, 706; *Boiler Inspection Co v Sherwin-Williams* [1951] A.C. 319, 333, 334. Many examples of the application of the doctrine are to be found in Ivamy, *General Principles of Insurance Law*, 6th edn (1993), Ch.38.

[734] *Lloyds TSB General Insurance Holdings Ltd v Lloyds Bank Group Insurance Co Ltd* [2001] 1 All E.R. (Comm) 13, 23 Q.B.D., [2001] EWCA Civ 1643, [2002] Lloyd's Rep. I.R. 113 at [42]; reversed on other grounds [2003] UKHL 48, [2003] Lloyd's Rep. I.R. 623.

[735] *Kacianoff v China Traders* [1914] 3 K.B. 1121; *Becker, Gray v London Assurance* [1918] A.C. 101.

[736] *Fitton v Accidental Death* (1864) 17 C.B.(N.S.) 122; *Re Etherington and Lancashire and Yorkshire Accident* [1909] 1 K.B. 591.

[737] *Knight of St Michael* [1898] P. 30; *Yorkshire Water v Sun Alliance & London Insurance* [1997] 2 Lloyd's Rep. 21 (where the assured unsuccessfully sued for the recovery of expenses incurred to prevent the incurring of insured liabilities on the alternative grounds that the event which would result in the insured liability had already occurred, although the insured peril had not yet operated, and that it was an implied term of the policy that such expenses would be indemnified).

[738] *Johnston v West of Scotland* (1828) 7 S. 52, Ct of Sess.; *Stanley v Western Insurance* (1868) L.R. 3 Ex. 71; *Symington v Union Insurance of Canton* (1928) 97 L.J. K.B. 646.

[739] *Isitt v Railway Passengers* (1889) 22 Q.B.D. 504; *Mardorf v Accident Insurance* [1903] 1 K.B. 584; *Re Etherington and Lancashire and Yorkshire Accident* [1909] 1 K.B. 591; *Fidelity and Casualty Co of New York v Mitchell* [1917] A.C. 592. But cf. *Cawley v National Employers' Accident* (1885) 1 T.L.R. 255; and *Jason v Batten (1930) Ltd* [1969] 1 Lloyd's Rep. 281. Indeed, a failure reasonably to attempt to minimise such loss may interfere with the chain of causation and deprive the assured of an indemnity for some or all of his loss: *National Oilwell (UK) Ltd v Davy Offshore Ltd* [1993] 2 Lloyd's Rep. 582, 618–619; *The State of The Netherlands v Youell* [1997] 2 Lloyd's Rep. 440; affirmed [1998] 1 Lloyd's Rep. 236; See also *Strive Shipping Corp v Hellenic Mutual War Risks Association (The Grecia Express)* [2002] EWHC 203 (Comm), [2002] 2 Lloyd's Rep. 88, 159–162.

[740] *Fitton v Accidental Death* (1864) 17 C.B.(N.S.) 122.

[741] *Winicofsky v Army and Navy* (1919) 35 T.L.R. 283. See also *Marsden v City and Country* (1865) L.R. 1 C.P. 232; *Liverpool and London War Risks v Ocean SS Co* [1948] A.C. 243; *Costain-Blankevoort (UK) Dredging Co Ltd v Davenport (The Nassau Bay)* [1979] 1 Lloyd's Rep. 395. cf. *Tappoo Holdings Ltd v Stuchbery* [2006] FJSC 1, [2008] Lloyd's Rep. I.R. 34, where the Supreme Court of the Fiji Islands held that loss and damage caused by looters amidst the breakdown of law and order following the armed seizure of Parliament constituted an "insurrection" which was excluded by the relevant policy.

[742] There must first be a finding that the loss is attributable to concurrent causes: *Handelsbanken Norwegian Branch of Svenska Handelsbanken AB v Dandridge (The Aliza Glacial)* [2002] EWCA

is a peril insured against,[743] unless one of the causes is an excepted peril, in which case there is no cover.[744] Where the loss is caused by a peril which itself inevitably is attributable to another peril, the loss will generally be covered if the peril first in time is insured against, and excluded if the first peril is excepted.[745]

42-105   **The amount recoverable**   A claim under a contract of insurance which is a contract of indemnity is a claim for unliquidated damages even, it seems, when the contract is a valued one.[746] The amount recoverable, or the "measure of indemnity", will depend on the nature (and terms) of the insurance contract. Losses under contingency policies and insurances against financial loss or liability will be readily calculated. As regards property policies, for the purposes of measuring the indemnity under the policy, there are two types of losses, namely a total loss and a partial loss. A total loss generally refers to the irretrievable deprivation of posses-

---

Civ 577, [2002] 2 Lloyd's Rep. 421 at [47]–[48]. If it is possible to attribute a discrete part of the loss to one concurrent cause and another part to the other concurrent cause, then the loss will be recoverable to the extent that it is attributable to a peril insured against. If however, both causes would have independently procured the same loss, the loss will be covered if one of the perils is insured against, unless the other is excepted. See Clarke, *The Law of Insurance Contracts* (looseleaf), para.25-6B.

[743] *Dudgeon v Pembroke* (1877) 2 App. Cas. 284, 297; *Reischer v Bornwick* [1894] 2 Q.B. 548, 551; *Lloyd Instruments Ltd v Northern Star Insurance Co (The Miss Jay Jay)* [1987] 1 Lloyd's Rep. 32. See also *Reynolds v Accidental Insurance* (1870) 22 L.T. 820; *Winspear v Accidental Insurance* (1880) 6 Q.B.D. 42; and *Lawrence v Accident Insurance* (1881) 7 Q.B.D. 216; *Seashore Marine SA v Phoenix Assurance Plc* [2002] Lloyd's Rep. I.R. 51 at [94]–[95]; *Kiriacoulis Lines SA v Compagnie D'Assurances Maritime Aeriennes et Terrestre (Camat) (The Demetra K)* [2002] EWCA Civ 1070, [2002] 2 Lloyd's Rep. 581 at [18].

[744] *Saqui v Stearns* [1911] 1 K.B. 426; *Lawrence v Accident Insurance*, above; *Wayne Tank Co Ltd v Employers' Liability Assurance Corp Ltd* [1974] Q.B. 57; see also *Seddon v Binions* [1978] 1 Lloyd's Rep. 382; *Midland Mainline Ltd v Eagle Star Insurance Co Ltd* [2004] EWCA Civ 1042, [2004] 2 Lloyd's Rep. 604; *Navigators Insurance Company Ltd v Atlasnavios-Navegacao Lda* [2018] UKSC 26, [2018] 2 W.L.R. 1671, [43]. cf. *Kuwait Airways Corp v Kuwait Insurance Co SAK* [1996] 1 Lloyd's Rep. 664, [1997] 2 Lloyd's Rep. 687, [1999] 1 Lloyd's Rep. 803.

[745] It may be too early to say that this is a rule of law, as the inquiry into proximate cause is one concerned with fact; nevertheless there are several decisions of the courts which follow the pattern of this proposition (e.g. *P Samuel & Co Ltd v Dumas* [1924] A.C. 431), but there are those which run counter (e.g. *Cory & Son v Burr* (1883) 8 App. Cas. 393). It is submitted to be a sensible formulation of the doctrine of successive proximate causes, as proposed by Clarke, *The Law of Insurance Contracts* (looseleaf), paras 25-5 and 25-7. In *Atlasnavios-Navegacao Lda v Navigators Insurance Co Ltd* [2014] EWHC 4133 (Comm), [2015] Lloyd's Rep. I.R. 151 at [233]–[247], Flaux, J considered such an approach to be too mechanistic; on appeal, the Supreme Court considered that *Cory v Burr* was a case of concurrent causes: [2018] UKSC 26; [2018] 2 W.L.R. 1671, [49].

[746] *Jabbour v Custodian of Israeli Absentee Property* [1954] 1 W.L.R. 139. Accordingly, the assured may not recover as damages any losses occasioned as a result of the insurer's failure to pay other than that which was to be indemnified under the policy: *Ventouris v Mountain (The Italia Express)* [1992] 2 Lloyd's Rep. 281; *Sprung v Royal Insurance (UK) Ltd* [1999] Lloyd's Rep. I.R. 111; *Callaghan v Dominion Insurance Co Ltd* [1997] 2 Lloyd's Rep. 541; contra *Grant v Co-operative Insurance Society Ltd* (1983) 134 N.L.J. 81; *Transthene Packaging Co Ltd v Royal Insurance (UK) Ltd* [1996] L.R.L.R. 32, 41. The assured's entitlement to damages may be different if the insurer is in breach of other obligations under the insurance contract: *Transthene Packaging Co Ltd v Royal Insurance (UK) Ltd*, above; cf. *Sprung v Royal Insurance (UK) Ltd*, above; *Tonkin v UK Insurance Ltd* [2006] EWHC 1120 (TCC), [2007] Lloyd's Rep. I.R. 283 at [34]–[39]. Upon the entry into force of ss.13A and 16A of the Insurance Act 2015 on May 4, 2017, the assured is entitled to recover damages for the late payment of a claim under an insurance contract in breach of a term implied by s.13A requiring the insurer to pay insurance claims within a reasonable time. In non-consumer insurance contracts, it is open to the parties to agree to a modification of this implied term to the insurer's benefit subject to the restrictions imposed by s.16A of the 2015 Act and the transparency requirements of the Insurance Act 2015. See below, para.42-112.

sion of the property (e.g. theft or confiscation) or to the physical destruction of the property.[747] In the realm of marine insurance, there is an additional category of total loss, namely a "constructive total loss", which applies commercial considerations to establishing the existence of a total loss.[748] A partial loss is any loss other than a total loss. A partial loss is often measured by reference to a depreciation in value or the cost of reinstatement or repair.[749] The measure of damages in the case of valued contracts[750] raises few difficulties. If there is a total loss the assured recovers the agreed value, and if there is a partial loss the assured recovers a proportion (which reflects the depreciation in the actual value) of the agreed value or, where appropriate, the cost of repair or reinstatement.[751] The measure of indemnity under the unvalued contracts is the value[752] at the date[753] and place[754] of the loss, and, if available, the market value will prima facie be the amount recoverable, but otherwise the cost of restoration may provide the basis for the indemnity,[755] and this latter basis is usually used for cases of partial loss.[756] In marine insurance rules have

---

[747] *Scott v Copenhagen Reinsurance Co (UK) Ltd* [2003] EWCA Civ 688, [2003] Lloyd's Rep. I.R. 752 at [22], [34]–[40]. The fact that there is a "mere chance" of recovery of the property does not mean that there has been no loss: at [40].

[748] Marine Insurance Act 1906 s.60. The doctrine of constructive total loss does not apply to non-marine insurance: *Moore v Evans* [1917] 1 K.B. 458; *Scott v Copenhagen Reinsurance Co (UK) Ltd* [2003] EWCA Civ 688, [2003] Lloyd's Rep. I.R. 752.

[749] *Prattley Enterprises Ltd v Vero Insurance New Zealand Ltd* [2016] NZSC 158, [2017] Lloyd's Rep. I.R. 175 at [38]–[43].

[750] The policy may be in part a valued policy and in part an unvalued policy: *Grimaldi Ltd v Sullivan* [1997] C.L.C. 64.

[751] *Elcock v Thomson* [1949] 2 K.B. 755; *Kusel v Atkin* [1997] 2 Lloyd's Rep. 749. As to the relationship between depreciation in value and the reasonable cost of repair, see *Coles v Hetherton* [2012] EWHC 1599 (Comm), [2013] Lloyd's Rep. I.R. 9 at [31].

[752] This value does not include loss of profits or other consequential losses unless specifically insured: see above, para.42-027.

[753] *Hercules Insurance v Hunter* (1835) 14 S. 147, Ct of Sess.; *Chapman v Pole* (1870) 22 L.T. 306; *Re Wilson and Scottish Insurance* [1920] 2 Ch. 28; *Leppard v Excess Insurance Co Ltd* [1979] 2 Lloyd's Rep. 91; *Tonkin v UK Insurance Ltd* [2006] EWHC 1120 (TCC), [2007] Lloyd's Rep. I.R. 283 at [20]–[25].

[754] *Rice v Baxendale* (1861) 7 H. & N. 96, 101.

[755] *Westminster Fire v Glasgow Provident* (1888) 13 App. Cas. 699, 713; *Exchange Theatre Ltd v Iron Trades Mutual Insurance Co* [1983] 1 Lloyd's Rep. 674, 688–689; affirmed [1984] 1 Lloyd's Rep. 149. cf. *Anderson v Commercial Union*, 1998 S.L.T. 826, where it was held that whilst the insurer was bound to indemnify the assured against the costs of repair, he was not obliged (absent a clause) to indemnify the assured *as and when* such costs were incurred. In *Great Lakes Reinsurance (UK) SE v Western Trading Ltd* [2016] EWCA Civ 1003, [2016] Lloyd's Rep. I.R. 643 at [40], the Court of Appeal held that where real property is destroyed the measure of indemnity to which the insured is entitled will depend on: (i) the terms of the policy; (ii) the interest of the insured in, or its obligations in respect of, the property insured; and (iii) the facts of the case including, in particular, the intention of the insured at the time of the loss. If the insured has a limited interest in the property it will be material to consider whether the subject matter of the insurance is the whole interest in the property insured and not solely that of the insured himself and, if it is the whole interest, whether the insured is accountable to others for any sum received in excess of his interest. At [67]–[75], the Court held that where no reinstatement costs had yet been incurred, whether or not the cost of reinstatement was the correct measure of indemnity depended on whether the insured had a fixed, settled and genuine intention to reinstate. See also *Prattley Enterprises Ltd v Vero Insurance New Zealand Ltd* [2016] NZSC 158, [2017] Lloyd's Rep. I.R. 175 at [38]–[43].

[756] *Scottish Amicable v Northern Assurance* (1883) 11 R. 287, Ct of Sess., 295; *Pleasurama v Sun Alliance* [1979] 1 Lloyd's Rep. 389, 393. However, the position may vary depending on the practicability of doing the repairs and the genuineness of the assured's intentions to undertake them or to sell: *Glad Tidings v Wellington Fire Insurance Co*, 46 D.L.R. (2d.) 475 (1964); *Reynolds v Phoenix Assurance Co* [1978] 2 Lloyd's Rep. 440; *Leppard v Excess Insurance Co Ltd* [1979] 2 Lloyd's Rep.

been worked out to make an adjustment for "new for old"[757] but there are no settled rules for this in non-marine insurance.[758] The policy may contain a policy limit,
often referred to as the "the sum insured". This does not represent the sum which
the assured will receive in the event of a loss. The assured will recover the amount
of his loss, subject to the ceiling imposed by the limit.[759] However, subject to the
terms of the policy, it will be presumed that the policy limit will apply to each of
successive losses under the policy and not to the aggregate of those losses, even if
the aggregate exceeds the policy limit.[760] It may be that the policy will provide that
the limit will apply to aggregated losses.[761] In such cases, where the assured has a
number of claims to be presented under the policy, the assured, not the insurer, has
the right to determine the sequence in which the claims are presented against the
insurer.[762] Where two or more assureds, or third parties deriving title to sue, present
claims under the one policy and there is insufficient cover to indemnify all the
claimants, the available cover shall respond to each claim in the order it is
established under the policy[763] and if each of the claims are established at the same
time, the claims must be satisfied on a pro rata basis.[764]

42-106 **Indemnification aliunde** The insurer is liable to pay a claim against him irrespective of any rights which the assured may have against others in respect of the loss[765]

---

91. See also *Gleniffer Finance Corp v Bamar Wood and Products* [1978] 2 Lloyd's Rep. 49.

[757] See Marine Insurance Act 1906 s.69(1). As to claims for partial losses under the Marine Insurance
Act 1906 ss.69 and 77; see *Manifest Shipping & Co Ltd v Uni-Polaris Insurance Co Ltd (The Star
Sea)* [1995] 1 Lloyd's Rep. 651, 664–666, [1997] 1 Lloyd's Rep. 360; affirmed [2001] UKHL 1,
[2001] 2 W.L.R. 170; *Kusel v Atkin* [1997] 2 Lloyd's Rep. 749.

[758] *Prattley Enterprises Ltd v Vero Insurance New Zealand Ltd* [2016] NZSC 158, [2017] Lloyd's Rep.
I.R. 175 at [38]–[43]. cf. *Vance v Forster* (1841) Ir. Circ. Rep. 47; *Castellain v Preston* (1883) 11
Q.B.D. 380, 400.

[759] *Leppard v Excess Insurance Co Ltd* [1979] 2 Lloyd's Rep. 91, 95. See also *Kyzuna Investments Ltd
v Ocean Marine Mutual Insurance Association (Europe)* [2000] 1 Lloyd's Rep. 505, where it was
held that the words "sum insured" did not represent the insured value for the purposes of Marine
Insurance Act 1906 s.27(2). The principles applicable to determining whether a policy of marine
insurance is a valued or unvalued policy are generally applicable to non-marine insurance policies:
Quorum A/S v Schramm [2002] 1 Lloyd's Rep. 249; *Thor Navigation Inc v Ingosstrakh Insurance
Co Ltd* [2005] EWHC 19 (Comm), [2005] 1 Lloyd's Rep. 547.

[760] *South Staffordshire Tramways Co Ltd v Sickness & Accident Assurance Association Ltd* [1891] 1
Q.B. 402; *Re Law Car and General Insurance Corp Ltd* [1913] 2 Ch. 103, 118. See also Marine
Insurance Act 1906 s.77. In *Ridgecrest NZ Ltd v IAG New Zealand Ltd* [2014] NZSC 117, [2015]
Lloyd's Rep. I.R. 34 at [48]–[52] the New Zealand Supreme Court held that the doctrine of merger
(by which the assured is not entitled to recover an indemnity for unrepaired damage amounting to
a partial loss where it is followed by a total loss) did not apply, as a matter of law, to non-marine
insurance.

[761] Where there is a danger of the policy limit being exhausted, it is important to be able to identify to
what event, peril or cause the limit will apply: *Kuwait Airways Corp v Kuwait Insurance Co SAK*
[1996] 1 Lloyd's Rep. 664, 686; affirmed [1997] 2 Lloyd's Rep. 687, [1999] 1 Lloyd's Rep. 803;
Caudle v Sharp [1995] L.R.L.R. 433; *Cox v Bankside Members' Agency Ltd* [1996] 1 Lloyd's Rep.
26; *Axa Reinsurance (UK) Plc v Field* [1996] 1 W.L.R. 1026; *Mann v Lexington Insurance Co* [2001]
1 Lloyd's Rep. 1; *Standard Life Assurance Ltd v Oak Dedicated Ltd* [2008] EWHC 222 (Comm),
[2008] Lloyd's Rep. I.R. 552 ("and/or claimant"); *Aioi Nissay Dowa Insurance Co Ltd v Heraldglen
Ltd* [2013] EWHC 154 (Comm), [2013] 2 All E.R. 231.

[762] *Cox v Deeny* [1996] L.R.L.R. 288, 298–299.

[763] *Cox v Bankside Members' Agency Ltd* [1995] 2 Lloyd's Rep. 437.

[764] *Cox v Deeny* [1996] L.R.L.R. 288, 299.

[765] *Cullen v Butler* (1816) 5 M. & S. 461; *Quebec v St Louis* (1851) 7 Moo. P.C. 286; *Dickenson v
Jardine* (1867-68) L.R. 3 C.P. 639, 644; *North British v London, Liverpool and Globe* (1877) 5 Ch.

and in the absence of stipulation to the contrary, before payment[766] he has no right[767] nor is obliged[768] to call upon the assured to reduce the loss by enforcing such rights. If, however, before payment by the insurer under a contract of indemnity, the loss (which in a valued policy is taken to be the amount of the valuation)[769] is extinguished by the assured enforcing such rights[770] or by a voluntary payment by a third party intended to have this effect,[771] the insurer's liability is extinguished, since there is nothing left to indemnify.[772] Similarly, if the loss is reduced the insurer's liability is limited to the balance of the loss remaining.[773]

Express provisions permitting less than a full indemnity   Contracts of insur-   **42-107** ance which are contracts of indemnity often contain three kinds of provisions which may prevent the assured from recovering more than a certain proportion of the amount insured, viz rateable proportion provisions, those dealing with underinsurance, and excess clauses.

Rateable proportion clauses   These clauses are designed to prevent the assured   **42-108** who has insured with other insurers from recovering his loss in full from one of them, leaving that one to obtain contribution from the others.[774] Such clauses apply only if the same loss is insured by each insurer.[775] They usually provide that where there are other insurances, the assured can only recover a rateable proportion under the insurance in question[776]; but they can go so far as to relieve the insurers from all liability when the assured is entitled to recover under another policy,[777]

D. 569; *Collingridge v Royal Exchange* (1877) 3 Q.B.D. 173, 176, 177. cf. *Royal Boskalis Westminster NV v Mountain* [1997] 2 All E.R. 929, where the Court of Appeal held that the fact that the waiver of contractual claims was ineffective as a matter of law meant that no damnifiable loss was suffered.

766 For the position after payment see below, paras 42-113—42-118.
767 *Dickenson v Jardine*, above; *Collingridge v Royal Exchange*, above; *Darrell v Tibbetts* (1880) 5 Q.B.D. 560.
768 *West of England Fire v Isaacs* [1897] 1 Q.B. 226.
769 *Bruce v Jones* (1863) 1 H. & C. 769; *Goole and Hull Steam Towing Co v Ocean Marine* [1928] 1 K.B. 589. See above, para.42-003.
770 *Bruce v Jones* (1863) 1 H. & C. 769.
771 *Godsall v Boldero* (1807) 9 East 72 (overruled by *Dalby v Indian and London Life* (1854) 15 C.B. 365 on the grounds that the insurance was not one of indemnity so that the principles discussed did not apply). See also *Colonia Versicherung AG v Amoco Oil Co* [1997] 1 Lloyd's Rep. 261, 270–271.
772 *Law v London Indisputable Life* (1855) 1 Kay. & J. 223, 228; *Burnand v Rodocanachi* (1882) 7 App. Cas. 333, 339.
773 *Bruce v Jones* (1863) 1 H.C. 769; *Goole and Hull Steam Towing Co v Ocean Marine* [1928] 1 K.B. 589.
774 *North British v London, Liverpool and Globe* (1877) 5 Ch. D. 569; *Commercial Union Assurance Co Ltd v Hayden* [1977] 1 Lloyd's Rep. 1; *Legal and General Assurance Society Ltd v Drake Insurance Co Ltd* [1992] Q.B. 887; *Drake Insurance Plc v Provident Insurance Plc* [2003] EWHC 109 (Comm), [2003] 1 All E.R. (Comm) 759, [2003] EWCA Civ 1834, [2004] Q.B. 601 and see below, para.42-118.
775 If the loss is divisible over policies covering successive years, the same loss may have been insured by both insurers and the rateable proportion clause might apply: *International Energy Group Ltd v Zurich Insurance Plc* [2015] UKSC 33, [2015] 2 W.L.R. 1411 at [58]–[64]; *Phillips v Gunner* [2003] EWHC 1084, [2004] Lloyd's Rep. I.R. 426 at [22]–[23].
776 *Phillips v Gunner* [2003] EWHC 1084 (Comm), [2004] Lloyd's Rep. I.R. 426 at [22]–[23].
777 See *Gale v Motor Union* [1928] 1 K.B. 359; *Weddell v Road Transport and General* [1932] 2 K.B. 563; *National Employees Mutual General Insurance Assn Ltd v Haydon* [1980] 2 Lloyd's Rep. 149.

though this latter category is construed strictly against the insurers by the courts,[778] and the burden in either case is upon the insurers to show that the assured is in fact so entitled.[779] There has been no authoritative statement as to how a rateable proportion should be calculated.[780]

42-109 **Underinsurance** The assured may not insure the subject matter fully, and by so doing may pay less by way of premium than he would otherwise. In marine insurance the assured is deemed to be his own insurer for the balance uninsured,[781] so that on a partial loss he has to bear his proportion of the loss even if it is less than the amount for which he has insured. This rule does not apply in non-marine insurance,[782] and in order to prevent the assured from receiving a full indemnity on the occurrence of a partial loss, despite not having paid the premium for complete cover, the insurers often insert a provision making this rule applicable.[783] The provision is often known as the "subject to average" or "average" clause.[784]

42-110 **Excess clauses** Often (and notoriously in motor insurance)[785] the insurer stipulates that the assured must bear the amount of any loss up to a specified figure, the insurer only being liable for the excess (if any) over that figure.[786]

42-111 **Reinstatement** The insurer's normal liability is to pay money; but the contract may give him an option either to pay or to reinstate the loss or damaged property.[787] Once the insurer has made his election he is bound by it.[788] If he has elected to reinstate, the contract is treated as if it had always been a contract to reinstate without the option of payment.[789] It follows that the insurer is not bound to expend the sum insured and equally cannot limit his expenditure to that sum, and he will be liable in damages if he fails to restore the damaged property, even though restoration proves more expensive than he expected.[790] The assured must allow the insurer

---

[778] *National Employees Mutual General Insurance Assn Ltd v Hayden* [1980] 2 Lloyd's Rep. 149. cf. *Portavon Cinema v Price* (1939) 161 L.T. 417.

[779] *Jenkins v Deane* (1933) 103 L.J. K.B. 250, 255.

[780] cf. *Weddell v Road Transport and General* [1932] 2 K.B. 563; Marine Insurance Act 1906 s.80(1); *Commercial Union Assurance Co Ltd v Hayden* [1977] 1 Lloyd's Rep. 1; *O'Kane v Jones* [2003] EWHC 3470 (Comm), [2004] 1 Lloyd's Rep. 389. See also *American Surety Co v Wrightson* (1910) 27 T.L.R. 91.

[781] Marine Insurance Act 1906 s.81.

[782] *Sillem v Thornton* (1854) 3 El. & Bl. 868; *Joyce v Kennard* (1871) L.R. 7 Q.B. 78; *Fifth Building Society v Traveller Insurance* (1893) 9 T.L.R. 221; *Newman v Maxwell* (1899) 80 L.T. 681; *Anglo-Californian Bank v London Marine and General* (1904) 10 Com. Cas. 1.

[783] *Carreras v Cunard SS Co* [1918] 1 K.B. 118, 122. cf. *Crowley v Cohen* (1832) 3 B. & Ad. 478.

[784] *Acme Wood Flooring v Marten* (1904) 20 T.L.R. 229.

[785] See below, paras 42-124 et seq.

[786] See *Re Law Guarantee Trust* [1914] 2 Ch. 617, 645; *Beacon Insurance v Langdale* [1939] 4 All E.R. 204. cf. *Trollope & Colls Ltd v Haydon* [1977] 1 Lloyd's Rep. 244. The excess clause is often called a "deductible" in commercial insurances. For the effect of such a clause on the assured's obligations to account to his insurer by way of subrogation, see *Lord Napier and Ettrick v Hunter* [1993] 2 W.L.R. 42, and see below, para.42-115.

[787] *Prattley Enterprises Ltd v Vero Insurance New Zealand Ltd* [2016] NZSC 158, [2017] Lloyd's Rep. I.R. 175 at [38].

[788] *Times Fire v Hawke* (1858) 1 F. & F. 406.

[789] *Brown v Royal* (1859) 1 El. & El. 853, 858. As the clause is for the insurer's benefit, the assured cannot demand reinstatement if the insurer elects to pay: see *Leppard v Excess Insurance Co Ltd* [1979] 2 Lloyd's Rep. 91.

[790] *Brown v Royal*, above, at 860; cf. *Anderson v Commercial Union* (1885) 55 L.J. Q.B. 146.

to take possession of the property to reinstate it,[791] and the insurer must bear any loss or damage to the property while he is in possession.[792] By the Fires Prevention (Metropolis) Act 1774,[793] the insurer under a fire policy may in certain circumstances be obliged to apply the insurance moneys to the reinstatement of the damaged premises.[794] Where the policy provides for reinstatement and if the insurer initially declines the claim, any policy requirement that the reinstatement should be undertaken by the assured with reasonable despatch will be enforced only once the insurer has confirmed that he will provide an indemnity.[795]

Late payment of insurance claims   At common law, if the insurer unreasonably failed to pay an insurance claim within a reasonable time, the assured had no remedy over and above the entitlement to an insurance indemnity and statutory interest.[796] This was the result of a peculiarity of insurance law in that the claim for an indemnity is, as a legal fiction, a claim for unliquidated damages for breach of contract by the insurer (the breach being constituted by the assured's suffering an insured loss),[797] and in that a contracting party is not entitled to recover damages for the late payment of damages.[798] In addition, the Court held that there was no implied term in the insurance contract obliging the insurer to assess and pay an insurance claim with reasonable diligence and due expedition.[799] In order to address the perceived unfairness with this state of the law, the Enterprise Act 2016 ss.28–30 were passed so as to amend the Insurance Act 2015 (by the addition of ss.13A and 16A). This legislation entered into force on May 4, 2017 and introduces into every insurance contract an implied term that the insurer must pay insurance claims within a reasonable time (allowing for investigation and assessment of the claim).[800] If there is a breach of this implied term, the assured will have remedies (e.g. damages) available at common law (and otherwise) in addition to the payment of the claim under the policy and statutory interest.[801] By s.13A(4), if the insurer shows there are reasonable grounds for disputing the claim,[802] there is no breach of the implied term while the dispute is continuing. Insofar as any term of

42-112

---

[791] *Bisset v Royal Exchange* (1821) 1 S. 174, Ct of Sess.

[792] *Waring & Gillow v Doughty, The Times,* February 21, 1922.

[793] s.83.

[794] See below, para.42-131.

[795] *Western Trading Ltd v Great Lakes Reinsurance (UK) Plc* [2015] EWHC 103 (QB) at [127]–[129].

[796] *The Italia Express* [1992] 2 Lloyd's Rep. 281; *Sprung v Royal Insurance (UK) Ltd* [1999] Lloyd's Rep. I.R. 111; *Callaghan v Dominion Insurance Co Ltd* [1997] 2 Lloyd's Rep. 541; *Tonkin v UK Insurance Ltd* [2006] EWHC 1120 (TCC), [2007] Lloyd's Rep. I.R. 283 at [34]–[38]; *Turville Heath Inc v Chartis Insurance UK Ltd* [2012] EWHC 3019 (TCC), (2012) 145 Con L.R. 163 at [36].

[797] *Grant v Royal Exchange Assurance Co* (1816) 5 M. & S. 439, 442; *Swan and Cleland's Graving Dock and Slipway Co v Maritime Insurance Co* [1907] 1 K.B. 116, 123–124; *William Pickersgill & Sons Ltd v London and Provincial Marine & General Insurance Co Ltd* [1912] 3 K.B. 614, 622; *Seele Austria GmbH & Co KG v Tokio Marine Europe Insurance Ltd* [2009] EWHC 2066 (TCC) at [50]–[52].

[798] *President of India v Lips Maritime Corp* [1988] 1 A.C. 395, 424–425.

[799] *Insurance Corp of the Channel Islands Ltd v McHugh* [1997] L.R.L.R. 94, 136–138.

[800] What constitutes a reasonable time depends on all of the circumstances of the case, including the type, size and complexity of the claim, compliance with statutory or regulatory rules or guidance and factors beyond the control of the insurer (s.13A(3)).

[801] Explanatory Notes, para.264. See also s.13A(5) of the 2015 Act. By amendment to the Limitation Act 1980 s.5, introduced by the Enterprise Act 2016 s.30, a claim for breach of the implied term may not be brought after the expiration of one year from the date on which the insurer has paid all the sums due under the insurance contract.

[802] In respect of consumer insurances, ICOBS specifies what constitutes an unreasonable rejection of

the insurance contract puts the assured in a worse position as regards the implied term provided for in s.13A, such term is invalid insofar as consumer insurances are concerned and, as far as non-consumer insurance contracts are concerned, insofar as any breach of the implied term by the insurer is deliberate or reckless. Otherwise, such a term is valid if it satisfies the transparency requirements of the Insurance Act 2015.[803]

10. THE RIGHTS OF THE INSURER UPON PAYMENT

42-113 **Rights of insurer** If the contract of insurance is not one of indemnity,[804] then in the absence of a right to rescind the contract or of express contractual rights the insurer has no right to recoup from the assured or other persons any of the money paid under the contract.[805] On the other hand, if the insurance cover is intended to indemnify the assured, the insurer may be entitled, apart from express contractual provisions, to exercise three distinct rights. These rights are salvage, subrogation, and contribution.

42-114 **Salvage** In both marine and non-marine insurance, if the subject matter is lost[806] or totally destroyed, and the insurer pays to the assured a sum representing an indemnity for the total loss of the subject matter, the assured may be required to abandon his interest in the subject matter to the insurer.[807] If the subject matter is subsequently found or becomes of value, the insurer benefits to the extent of such interest.[808] If the insurer takes the money value of such interest (which may be given as a credit against the claim) rather than the subject matter of the insurance itself, the value will be the market value of the property as at the time of its recovery rather than its insured value (if there is one).[809] In marine insurance these principles apply to circumstances in which the subject matter has not actually been lost or destroyed, but in which it is not commercially worthwhile or not foreseeably likely to recover or restore it.[810] In such circumstances of "constructive total loss", the assured may offer to abandon his interest in the subject matter to the insurer who may

---

a claim under para.8.1.2 (in respect of contracts concluded before August 1, 2017) and paras 8.1.2A–2B (in respect of contracts concluded on or after August 1, 2017).

[803] Insurance Act 2015 s.16A. As to the transparency requirements, see para.42-060.

[804] See above, paras 42-003—42-004.

[805] *Simpson v Thompson* (1877) 3 App. Cas. 279, 284; cf. *Edwards v Motor Union* [1922] 2 K.B. 249, 252.

[806] See above, paras 42-027 and 42-105.

[807] *Rankin v Potter* (1873) L.R. 6 H.L. 83; *Kaltenbach v Mackenzie* (1878) 2 C.P.D. 467, 471; *Dane v Mortgage Insurance* [1894] 1 Q.B. 54; *Holmes v Payne* [1930] 2 K.B. 301. See Marine Insurance Act 1906 s.79(1). But cf. *MacGillivray on Insurance Law*, 14th edn (2018), paras 24-006—24-010. It has been held, with respect to a marine insurance policy, that the insurer's election to take over the insured property will endow him with a beneficial interest under a trust pending the completion of all legal formalities for the transfer of ownership: *Dornoch Ltd v Westminster International BV (The W D Fairway)* [2009] EWHC 889 (Admlty), [2009] 2 Lloyd's Rep. 191.

[808] *Oldfield v Price* (1860) 2 E. & F. 80; *Rankin v Potter*, above; *Kaltenbach v Mackenzie*, above. It may be that this benefit accrues to the insurer as an instance of subrogation.

[809] *Kuwait Airways Corp v Kuwait Insurance Co SAK (No.2)* [2000] 1 Lloyd's Rep. 252.

[810] Marine Insurance Act 1906 ss.60–63. In *Fraser Shipping Ltd v Colton (The Shakir III)* [1997] 1 Lloyd's Rep. 586, 591–593, it was held that if the insured vessel was salvageable even at exorbitant costs, the vessel was constructively, not actually, lost.

accept the abandoned interest and who then pays as for a total loss.[811] The doctrine of constructive total loss applies only to marine insurance.[812]

Subrogation[813]   If the insurer does pay under a valid[814] insurance contract, even   **42-115** if he is under no legal liability to do so,[815] and the assured then receives a payment or benefit in respect of the loss,[816] which together with the insurance money exceeds the loss insured against, again taken to be the valuation in a valued policy,[817] he must (subject to any terms in the contract to the contrary) by the doctrine of subrogation account to the insurer for the excess up to the amount that the insurer has paid.[818] Not only does the insurer have an action in money had and received against the assured to recover the amount payable to the insurer,[819] but the insurer also has an equitable proprietary interest in the money received from the third party by the assured.[820] The proprietary interest takes the form of an equitable lien over the fund of money received by the assured, and it is enforceable against the fund to secure repayment of the amount payable to the insurer so long as the fund is traceable and has not been acquired by a bona fide purchaser for value without notice.[821] The insurer, however, does not have a proprietary interest in the assured's cause of action against a third party in respect of the loss which has been indemnified by the insurer.[822] The assured's obligation to account to his insurer arises once he is indemnified in respect of the particular loss against which he has insured: if, therefore, the assured has agreed to bear a part of a loss himself, the assured may have to account to the insurer before he receives a complete indemnity against his

---

[811] *Royal Boskalis Westminster NV v Mountain* [1997] L.R.L.R. 523, 554–558; *Kastor Navigation Co Ltd v AGF MAT* [2002] EWHC 2601 (Comm), [2003] 1 Lloyd's Rep. 296, [2004] EWCA Civ 277, [2004] 2 Lloyd's Rep. 119.

[812] *Moore v Evans* [1917] 1 K.B. 458; *Scott v Copenhagen Reinsurance Co (UK) Ltd* [2002] EWHC 1348 (Comm), [2002] Lloyd's Rep. I.R. 775; affirmed [2003] EWCA Civ 688, [2003] Lloyd's Rep. I.R. 752.

[813] For a useful monograph on the doctrine, see Mitchell and Watterson, *Subrogation—Law and Practice* (2007), Ch.10.

[814] *Edwards v Motor Union* [1922] 2 K.B. 249.

[815] *King v Victoria Insurance* [1896] A.C. 250; *BUPA Australia Pty Ltd v Shaw* [2013] VSC 507, [2014] Lloyd's Rep. I.R. 151, Victoria SC; *MacGillivray on Insurance Law*, 14th edn (2018), para.24-032; cf. *Scottish Union & National Insurance Co v Davis* [1970] 1 Lloyd's Rep. 1.

[816] *Castellain v Preston* (1883) 11 Q.B.D. 380; *Law, Fire v Oakley* (1888) 4 T.L.R. 309; *Ironfield v Eastern Gas Board* [1964] 1 W.L.R. 1125n. This right of subrogation, however, does not extend to the purchase price received by the assured for the sale of the subject matter insured in circumstances where the insurer chooses not to exercise salvage rights in respect of the subject matter: *Dornoch Ltd v Westminster International BV (The W D Fairway) (No.3)* [2009] EWHC 1782 (Admlty), [2009] 2 Lloyd's Rep. I.R. 191 at [14]–[17].

[817] *Thames and Mersey Marine v British and Chilean SS Co* [1916] 1 K.B. 30.

[818] *Commercial Union v Lister* (1873-74) L.R. 9 Ch. App. 483; *Darrell v Tibbetts* (1880) 5 Q.B.D. 560; *Castellain v Preston*, above; *Thames and Mersey Marine v British and Chilean SS Co*, above; *Yorkshire Insurance v Nisbet* [1962] 2 Q.B. 330. But cf. *The Commonwealth* [1907] P. 216, where a system of apportionment was applied to a marine policy where the sum insured was less than the agreed value; and *L. Lucas Ltd v ECGD* [1974] 1 W.L.R. 909 where a system of apportionment was stipulated in the contract.

[819] *Yorkshire Insurance v Nisbet* [1962] 2 Q.B. 330.

[820] *Lord Napier and Ettrick v Hunter* [1993] 2 W.L.R. 42. See also *Bristol & West Building Society v May May & Merrimans* [1998] 1 W.L.R. 336; *Arab Bank Plc v John D Wood* [2000] Lloyd's Rep. P.N. 173. For the position where the assured is paid by his insurer after having received a payment from a third party, see *Stearns v Village Main Reef Gold Mining Co Ltd* (1905) 10 Com. Cas. 89.

[821] *Lord Napier and Ettrick v Hunter* [1993] 2 W.L.R. 42.

[822] *Re Ballast Plc; St Paul Travellers Insurance Co Ltd v Dargan* [2006] EWHC 3189 (Ch), [2007] Lloyd's Rep. I.R. 4 at [87]–[109].

overall loss.[823] The doctrine of subrogation applies to voluntary payments[824] so long as the gift was not intended to benefit the assured beyond the insurance money.[825]

42-116 **Subrogation: rights of action** Similarly, the insurer, once he has paid under the insurance,[826] is entitled to the benefit of all rights possessed by the assured in respect of the loss insured against.[827] Thus the insurer is entitled to enforce the assured's right of action against tortfeasors who have caused the loss[828] or against persons who are contractually bound to compensate the assured in damages for the loss,[829] and such parties cannot raise as a defence or in mitigation of damages the fact that the assured has been indemnified by the insurer.[830] An insurer, however, is not entitled to sue one co-insured in the name of another co-insured where the former is covered under the policy for the loss,[831] although it may be that this is dependent on any contract between the assured and the co-assured excluding a right of ac-

---

[823] *Re Ballast Plc*, above distinguishing between the part of a loss sustained by an assured above a monetary *limit* in a policy (which the assured can recoup in full before accounting to the insurer) and the loss sustained below an excess in the policy (which the assured can recoup only after fully accounting to the insurer for the money paid under the policy). This is occasionally referred to as the "top-down" principle, namely that any recoveries from third parties are applied to the uppermost layer of the loss first and the bottom-most last.

[824] *Stearns v Village Main Reef Gold Mining Co Ltd* (1905) 10 Com. Cas. 89.

[825] *Burnand v Rodocanachi* (1882) 7 App. Cas. 333. cf. *Merrett v Capitol Indemnity Corp* [1991] 1 Lloyd's Rep. 169. See also *Colonia Versicherung AG v Amoco Oil Co* [1997] 1 Lloyd's Rep. 261, where the Court of Appeal confirmed that the assured need not account for the voluntary payment only if the donor intended to benefit the assured to the exclusion of the insurer and rejected the suggestion that the insurer may be subrogated only if the donor had to intend to benefit the insurer.

[826] *City Tailors v Evans* (1921) 91 L.J. K.B. 379, 385; *Edwards v Motor Union* [1922] 2 K.B. 249. If the parties agree that the insurer can exercise rights of subrogation prior to payment under the policy, such a term will not be given effect: *Rathbone Brothers Plc v Novae Corporate Underwriting* [2013] EWHC 3457 (Comm), [2014] Lloyd's Rep IR 203 at [60]–[61], [2014] EWCA Civ 1464, [2015] Lloyd's Rep IR 95 at [109].

[827] *Castellain v Preston* (1883) 11 Q.B.D. 380, 388. In *Lord Napier and Ettrick v Hunter* [1993] 2 W.L.R. 42, the House of Lords left open for further consideration whether an insurer has an equitable proprietary interest in the assured's cause of action. See also Marine Insurance Act 1906 s.79. See further the Mercantile Law Amendment Act 1856.

[828] *King v Victoria Insurance* [1896] A.C. 250; *Horse, Carriage and General v Petch* (1916) 33 T.L.R. 131. But cf. *Morris v Ford Motor Co Ltd* [1973] Q.B. 792. The assured may maintain an action against the tortfeasor for the full amount of his claim notwithstanding that he has already been paid by his insurers: see *Hobbs v Marlowe* [1978] A.C. 16. See Automated and Electric Vehicles Act 2018 s.5 (not yet in force).

[829] *North British v London, Liverpool and Globe* (1877) 5 Ch. D. 569. The insurer is entitled to enforce by way of subrogation the assured's right to a contractual indemnity, rather than pursuing a right of contribution, because the contractual indemnity is not coordinate with the insurer's secondary liability to indemnify: *Caledonia North Sea Ltd v British Telecommunications Plc* [2002] UKHL 4, [2002] Lloyd's Rep. I.R. 261 at [14]–[16].

[830] *Mason v Sainsbury* (1782) 3 Doug. 61; *Clark v Blything* (1823) 2 B. & C. 254; *Yates v Whyte* (1838) 4 Bing. N.C. 272; *Bradburn v GW Ry* (1874) L.R. 10 Ex. 1; *Nichols v Scottish Union* (1885) 2 T.L.R. 190; *King v Victoria Insurance* [1896] A.C. 250; *Parry v Cleaver* [1970] A.C. 1; *The Yasin* [1979] 2 Lloyd's Rep. 45. *Brown v Albany Construction Co* [1995] N.P.C. 100; *Europe Mortgage Co v Halifax Estate Agencies* [1996] E.G.C.S. 84; *FNCB Ltd v Barnet Devanney (Harrow) Ltd* [1999] Lloyd's Rep. I.R. 43; *Caledonia North Sea Ltd v British Telecommunications Plc* [2002] UKHL 4, [2002] Lloyd's Rep. I.R. 261. As to the award of interest on damages where the assured has been indemnified by the insurer, see *H Cousins & Co Ltd v D. & C. Carriers Ltd* [1971] 2 Q.B. 230.

[831] *Petrofina (UK) Ltd v Magnaload Ltd* [1984] Q.B. 127; *Stone Vickers Ltd v Appledore Ferguson Shipbuilders Ltd* [1991] 2 Lloyd's Rep. 288; reversed on appeal, however, on the basis that, as a matter of construction, the sub-contractor was not intended to be covered by the policy: [1992] 2 Lloyd's Rep. 578; *National Oil Wells (UK) Ltd v Davy Offshore Ltd* [1993] 2 Lloyd's Rep. 582. cf. *Woodside Petroleum Development Pty Ltd v H & R-E & W Pty Ltd* (1999) 20 W.A.R. 380, Full Ct, WA; *Cape*

tion[832]; nor can he sue a person for whose joint benefit the insurance has been effected if it was intended by the assured and that other person that any loss should be recouped solely from the insurance moneys.[833] The rights to which the insurer is subrogated[834] are those of the assured so that they must be exercised in the name of the assured[835] unless they are assigned at law to the insurer,[836] and the assured can be compelled to allow the insurer the use of his name against an indemnity as to costs.[837] Where the contract does not provide for a full indemnity it seems that the insurer (in the absence of provisions to the contrary) cannot prevent the assured from exercising the rights himself so long as he acts in good faith,[838] and he may deduct his reasonable expenses of recovery before accounting to the insurer,[839] but otherwise it seems that the insurer can, if he wishes, restrain the assured from so doing.[840] Where the insurer recovers funds which are in excess of the amount to which the insurer is entitled pursuant to his right of subrogation, the insurer will

---

Distribution Ltd v Cape Intermediate Holdings Plc [2016] EWHC 1786 (QB), [2017] Lloyd's Rep. I.R. 1. The corollary is that the insurer may exercise rights of subrogation against a co-assured where the co-assured is not entitled to cover under the policy, subject to any express or implied terms in the policy and subject to the terms of any contract between the co-assureds: In *Rathbone Brothers Plc v Novae Corporate Underwriting* [2013] EWHC 3457 (Comm), [2014] Lloyd's Rep. I.R. 203, reversed [2014] EWCA Civ 1464, [2015] Lloyd's Rep. I.R. 95. See also *Gard Marine & Energy Ltd v China National Chartering Co Ltd* [2017] UKSC 35, [2017] 1 W.L.R. 1793 at [109]–[126], [131]–[146]; contra at [48]–[57], [89], [99]–[103].

[832] *Tyco Fire & Integrated Solutions (UK) Ltd v Rolls-Royce Motor Cars Ltd* [2008] EWCA Civ 286, [2008] 2 All E.R. (Comm) 584. See, however, Ward, "Joint names insurance and contracts to insure: untangling the threads" [2009] L.M.C.L.Q. 239, 242–245. See also See also *Gard Marine & Energy Ltd v China National Chartering Co Ltd (The Ocean Victory)* [2013] EWHC 2199, [2014] 1 Lloyd's Rep. 59 at [199]–[204], reversed [2015] EWCA Civ 16, [2015] 1 Lloyd's Rep. 381.

[833] *Mark Rowlands Ltd v Berni Inns Ltd* [1986] Q.B. 211; *Fresca-Judd v Golovina* [2016] EWHC 497 (QB), [2016] 4 W.L.R. 107. cf. *Woolwich Building Society v Brown* [1996] C.L.C. 625, where it was held that an insurer who had paid the assured building society under a mortgage indemnity insurance was entitled, by way of subrogation, to sue the defaulting mortgagor in the name of the building society, since the insurance against the mortgagor's non-payment was not for the joint benefit of mortgagee and mortgagor in the relevant sense contemplated in the *Rowlands* case. The Contracts (Rights of Third Parties) Act 1999 may well improve the position of the beneficiary.

[834] If, therefore, an assured has himself sued to recover his uninsured losses from a tortfeasor, the insurer may not thereafter bring a separate action in the name of the assured for the balance of the claim: see *Buckland v Palmer* [1964] 1 W.L.R. 1109. The CA in that case did contemplate circumstances where an insurer might be able to pursue the rest of the claim by resurrecting the assured's original action; but it seems this will rarely be permitted: see *Hayler v Chapman* [1989] 1 Lloyd's Rep. 490, CA.

[835] *Symons v Mulkern* (1882) 46 L.T. 763; *Dickenson v Jardine* (1868) L.R. 3 C.P. 639, 644; cf. *Oriental Fire and General Insurance Co Ltd v American President Lines Ltd* [1968] 2 Lloyd's Rep. 372; *Smith (Plant Hire) Ltd v DL Mainwaring* [1986] 2 Lloyd's Rep. 244.

[836] *Cia Columbiana de Seguros v Pacific Steam Navigation* [1965] 1 Q.B. 101.

[837] *Duus Brown v Binning* (1906) 11 Com. Cas. 190; *Edwards v Motor Union* [1922] 2 K.B. 249, 254. But cf. *Morris v Ford Motor Co Ltd* [1973] Q.B. 792.

[838] *Commercial Union v Lister* (1873-74) L.R. 9 Ch. App 483. cf. *Page v Scottish Insurance* (1929) 140 L.T.R. 571, 576.

[839] *Assicurazioni v Express Assurance* [1907] 2 K.B. 814. Such expenses may be deducted only if the recoveries were made after the insurance proceeds were paid, when the insurer's rights of subrogation crystallise. It does not matter that such expenses were incurred in unsuccessful litigation, provided that they were reasonably spent: *England v Guardian Insurance Ltd* [1999] 2 All E.R. (Comm) 481.

[840] *Law, Fire v Oakley* (1888) 4 T.L.R. 309. Most contracts of insurance contain express provisions giving the insurer the right to conduct proceedings, etc.

hold that excess on trust for the assured so that the assured will have an equitable proprietorial interest in that excess.[841]

42-117 **Duty of assured** The assured is under a duty to do nothing which prejudices the insurer's rights of subrogation,[842] and thus if he releases or compromises with persons who are under a liability to him in respect of the loss insured against, he will be liable to the insurer for the full value of the rights released or compromised.[843] Indeed it may be that even before a loss has occurred the assured is possibly under a similar duty not to contract so as to diminish or exclude rights to which the insurer would otherwise become subrogated upon paying for a loss.[844]

42-118 **Contribution** There is nothing to prevent an assured from taking out as many insurances as he chooses against the same risks, and he may claim payment from his insurers in such order as he chooses,[845] though, once he has received a full indemnity, other insurers will be under no liability (for there will be nothing left to indemnify).[846] If the assured receives more than a full indemnity, he will hold the excess on trust for the insurers.[847] It also seems that, in cases where the Life Assurance Act 1774 applies, once the assured has insured to the full extent of his interest any further insurances will be void and illegal.[848] Although it is no defence to an insurer against whom a claim is made that other insurers are liable in respect of the same loss, such an insurer has, upon payment, an equitable[849] right to require

---

[841] *Lonrho Exports Ltd v Export Credit Guarantee Department* [1996] 2 Lloyd's Rep. 649, 661–663; cf. *Lord Napier and Ettrick v Kershaw* [1993] 1 Lloyd's Rep. 197.

[842] The question whether this duty extends to the insurer's right of contribution was not decided in *O'Kane v Jones* [2003] EWHC 3470 (Comm), [2004] 1 Lloyd's Rep. 389 at [252]–[253].

[843] *West of England v Isaacs* [1897] 1 Q.B. 226; affirming [1896] 2 Q.B. 377; *Phoenix Assurance v Spooner* [1905] 2 K.B. 753; *Horse, Carriage and General v Petch* (1916) 33 T.L.R. 131; *Boag v Standard Marine* [1937] 2 K.B. 113; *Faircharm Investments Ltd v Citibank International Plc* [1998] Lloyd's Rep. Bank 127. In *BUPA Australia Pty Ltd v Shaw* [2013] VSC 507, [2014] Lloyd's Rep. I.R. 151, Victoria SC), the Court ordered equitable compensation to the insurer for breach of the assured's obligation. In the United States it has been held that where the third party knows that the assured has been paid by the insurers, a release of the assured's rights is void as being a fraud on the insurers. See, for example, *Monmouth County Fire v Hutchinson* (1870) 21 N.J.Eq. 107.

[844] See *Boag v Standard Marine* [1937] 2 K.B. 113, 124; *Canadian Transport v Court Line* [1940] A.C. 934. Sed quaere. Failure to disclose that the assured is accustomed to make such contracts may amount to non-disclosure: *Tate v Hyslop* (1885) 15 Q.B.D. 368, 377. cf. *Marc Rich & Co AG v Portman* [1996] 1 Lloyd's Rep. 430, 440; affirmed [1997] 1 Lloyd's Rep. 225.

[845] *Godin v London Assurance* (1758) 1 Burr. 489; *Newby v Reed* (1762) 1 Wm. Bl. 416; *Rogers v Davis* (1777) 2 Park (8th edn) 601; *North British v London, Liverpool and Globe* (1877) 5 Ch. D. 569, 583, 587. In cases of "valued" policies the claims are made may affect the amount finally recoverable: see *Bruce v Jones* (1863) 1 H. & C. 769. See also Marine Insurance Act 1906 s.32.

[846] See above, para.42-106.

[847] Marine Insurance Act 1906 s.32(2)(d).

[848] See above, para.42-014, and *Hebdon v West* (1863) 3 B. & S. 579; *Simcock v Scottish Imperial* (1902) 10 S.L.T. 286.

[849] *American Surety Co v Wrightson* (1910) 27 T.L.R. 91, 93. The right of contribution may also arise under s.80 of the Marine Insurance Act 1906. As to the availability of a contribution under the Civil Liability (Contribution) Act 1978, see *O'Kane v Jones* [2003] EWHC 3470 (Comm), [2004] 1 Lloyd's Rep. 389 at [188]; *Greene Wood & McClean LLP v Templeton Insurance Ltd* [2009] EWCA Civ 65, [2009] Lloyd's Rep. I.R. 505, [2010] EWHC 2679 (Comm), [2011] Lloyd's Rep. I.R. 557; *International Energy Group Ltd v Zurich Insurance Plc* [2015] UKSC 33, [2016] A.C. 509, [181]; cf. *Bovis Construction Ltd v Commercial Union Assurance Co Plc* [2000] 1 Lloyd's Rep. 416.

contribution from the other insurers so that the payment is borne fairly by all.[850] This right exists only between insurers who have covered, by enforceable contracts of insurance,[851] the same interest[852] in the same subject matter[853] and against the same perils.[854] The right to contribution arises as between the insurers upon the occurrence of the loss, because it is at that point that the insurers each become liable to indemnify the assured in respect of the loss.[855] The nature and extent of all the provisions of the cover need not be the same, provided that each contract is alike in covering the actual loss that has occurred.[856] Where both policies in question contain exclusions in respect of losses covered by other insurances, the exclusions will cancel each other out and will be ineffective.[857] Where (as will frequently be the case in practice) the relevant insurance policies contain "rateable proportion" clauses, making each insurer liable only for its rateable proportion of any loss or damage, despite earlier authority, it would seem that the right of contribution will

---

[850] *Newby v Reed* (1762) 1 Wm. Bl. 416; *North British v London, Liverpool and Globe* (1877) 5 Ch. D. 569; *Sickness and Accident v General Accident* (1892) 19 R. 977, Ct of Sess.; *American Surety Co v Wrightson* (1910) 27 T.L.R. 91, 93; *Commercial Union Assurance Co v Hayden* [1977] 1 Lloyd's Rep. 1. See Mitchell, *The Law of Contribution and Reimbursement* (2003). In *International Energy Group Ltd v Zurich Insurance Plc* [2015] UKSC 33, [2015] 2 W.L.R. 1471, the Supreme Court held that there may be rights of contribution between insurers insuring different periods of time, in respect of the same loss ([58]–[64]).

[851] *Woods v Co-operative Insurance*, 1924 S.C. 692; *Jenkins v Deane* (1933) 103 L.J. K.B. 250; *Monksfield v Vehicle and General Insurance Co Ltd* [1971] 1 Lloyd's Rep. 139. In *Legal and General Assurance Society Ltd v Drake Insurance Co Ltd* [1992] Q.B. 887, a majority of the Court of Appeal (Ralph Gibson L.J. dissenting) overruled the *Monksfield* case, expressing the view that, provided the second policy was in force at the time of the loss, an insurer could obtain contribution from the second insurer even if the assured would no longer have been able to claim on that second policy himself (because of a failure to notify the claim in accordance with a condition precedent to liability under the policy). See now, however, *Eagle Star Insurance Co v Provincial Insurance Plc* [1993] 3 All E.R. 1, where the Privy Council (in applying the principle of contribution to a case where both insurers were *statutorily* liable to a third party) disapproved *Legal and General v Drake Insurance*. The decision in *Legal and General* stands as binding precedent, subject to any contrary decision of the House of Lords and, in any event, is to be preferred, because its reasoning rests on an analysis of a right to contribution which is consistent with the liability of the insurer to the assured. See *O'Kane v Jones* [2003] EWHC 3470 (Comm), [2004] 1 Lloyd's Rep. 389 at [196]–[203].

[852] *Scottish Amicable v Northern Assurance* (1883) 11 R. 287, Ct of Sess.; *Nichols v Scottish Union* (1885) 2 T.L.R. 190; *Portavon Cinema v Price* (1939) 161 L.T. 417.

[853] *North British v London Liverpool and Globe* (1877) 5 Ch. D. 569; *American Surety Co v Wrightson* (1910) 27 T.L.R. 91; *Boag v Standard Marine* [1937] 2 K.B. 113.

[854] *American Surety Co v Wrightson*, above.

[855] *Legal and General Assurance Society Ltd v Drake Insurance Co Ltd* [1992] Q.B. 887, 892; *O'Kane v Jones* [2003] EWHC 3470 (Comm), [2004] 1 Lloyd's Rep. 389; contra *Eagle Star Insurance Co Ltd v Provincial Insurance Plc* [1994] 1 A.C. 130. See also Marine Insurance Act 1906 s.80. Accordingly, if after the occurrence of an insured loss, one insurer agreed with the assured that their insurance contract be cancelled, that cancellation would be ineffective to deprive the other insurer of his right of contribution, even though the cancellation would be effective to deprive the assured of any rights against the insurer under the cancelled contract (*O'Kane v Jones* [2003] EWHC 3470 (Comm), [2004] 1 Lloyd's Rep. 389). The position will be different in the event that one of the insurance contracts has been avoided for a breach of the duty of the utmost good faith, in which case the other insurer will have no right of contribution (*Legal and General Assurance Society Ltd v Drake Insurance Co Ltd*, above). cf. *Bolton MBC v Municipal Mutual Insurance Ltd* [2006] EWCA Civ 50, [2007] Lloyd's Rep. I.R. 173, [42].

[856] See *North British v London, Liverpool and Globe* (1877) 5 Ch. D. 569.

[857] *Weddell v Road Transport & General Insurance Co Ltd* [1932] 2 K.B. 563. The position is more complex where one policy contains an "other insurance" exclusion and the other policy contains a rateable proportion clause: *National Farmers Union Mutual Insurance Society Ltd v HSBC Insurance (UK) Ltd* [2010] EWHC 773 (Comm), [2011] Lloyd's Rep. I.R. 86. See above, para.42-108.

still exist as between those insurers, even if one insurer mistakenly pays the entire claim in ignorance of the existence of another policy.[858] The amount of the contribution recoverable will depend on calculating the insurers' respective proportionate shares, although the precise method of calculation has still not been authoritatively determined.[859]

11.   SPECIFIC TYPES OF INSURANCE CONTRACT

42-119   **Introduction**   The principles so far discussed in ss.1–10 above are applicable to contracts of insurance in general. Below are outlined the peculiar features of the specific types of insurance contract most commonly encountered. The reader should consult the specialist books referred to in the footnotes for more detailed consideration of these features and the problems to which they give rise.

(a)   **Liability Insurance**[860]

42-120   **General characteristics**   Under contracts of liability insurance, the insurer undertakes to indemnify the assured against legal liability to third persons. Proof of liability is usually a condition precedent to the assured's right to recover, but proof of payment to the third party is not required in the absence of a stipulation to that effect.[861] Detailed provisions usually give the insurer the right to contest or to compromise the assured's liability,[862] since otherwise the insurer cannot use his ordinary rights of subrogation without first paying the assured the full amount of his estimated loss.[863] The terms of the policy usually indemnify the assured against the costs of his defence.[864] Often liability insurance excludes contractual as opposed to tortious liability, and it may be that even where both exist in respect of the

---

[858]   *Drake Insurance Plc v Provident Insurance Plc* [2003] EWCA Civ 1834, [2004] Q.B. 601, doubting *Legal and General Assurance Society Ltd v Drake Insurance Co Ltd*, above (holding that, because the insurer who pays the entirety of the loss is legally liable to the assured to pay only its due proportion, the payment as to the balance is a voluntary payment made without legal obligation, and therefore outside the scope of the equitable doctrine of contribution).

[859]   The two most acceptable methods are: (a) the independent liability method, which calculates the proportions by reference to the amounts for which each insurer would be liable to the assured under their respective policies for the particular loss; and (b) the maximum liability method, which calculates the proportions by reference to the maximum amounts for which each insurer would be liable to the assured for any loss under their respective policies. See *Commercial Union Assurance Co Ltd v Hayden* [1977] 1 Lloyd's Rep. 1; *O'Kane v Jones* [2003] EWHC 3470 (Comm), [2004] 1 Lloyd's Rep. 389.

[860]   See *MacGillivray on Insurance Law*, 14th edn (2018), Ch.30; Clarke, *The Law of Insurance Contracts* (looseleaf), s.17–4; Simpson (ed.), *Professional Negligence and Liability* (looseleaf).

[861]   *Johnston v Salvage Association* (1887) 19 Q.B.D. 458, 460; *Lancashire Insurance v IRC* [1899] 1 Q.B. 353, 359; *Brice v Wackerbarth* [1974] 2 Lloyd's Rep. 274.

[862]   As to the effect of clauses requiring the insurer's consent to any settlement of the assured's liability and/or prohibiting admissions of liability, see *Gan Insurance Co Ltd v Tai Ping Insurance Co Ltd* [2001] EWCA Civ 1042, [2001] Lloyd's Rep. I.R. 291; *Beazley Underwriting Ltd v Al Ahleia Insurance Co* [2013] EWHC 677 (Comm), [2013] Lloyd's Rep. I.R. 561.

[863]   See above, para.42-116.

[864]   See, e.g. *Forney v Dominion Insurance Co Ltd* [1969] 1 W.L.R. 928. As to cases where defence costs are incurred in respect of both an insured liability and a non-insured liability, see *New Zealand Forest Products Ltd v New Zealand Insurance Co Ltd* [1997] 1 W.L.R. 1237; *John Wyeth & Brothers Ltd v Cigna Insurance Co of Europe SA/NV* [2001] EWCA Civ 175, [2001] Lloyd's Rep. I.R. 420, 454. In the absence of a contractual provision providing such cover, there is no entitlement to defence costs under a liability insurance policy: *Astrazeneca Insurance Co Ltd v XL Insurance (Bermuda) Ltd* [2013] EWCA Civ 1660, [2014] Lloyd's Rep. I.R. 509. Defence costs cover is itself not an

same damage to the same person, the insurer is protected.[865] However, if a policy covers an assured against all sums which he may become liable at law to pay as damages, the natural and ordinary meaning of "liable at law" includes contractual liability.[866] "Liability" for these purposes exists when it has been established by judgment, award or agreement.[867] The establishment of loss by a judgment or settlement does not automatically establish the existence or basis of such legal liability; it is still open to the insurer to challenge that there was an actual legal liability, in which case it is for the assured to prove that there was such an actual legal liability.[868] The actual cause of the liability must be established in order to determine whether the liability falls within the insured perils of the policy; the manner in which the claim is brought against the assured is not determinative.[869] Liability policies place much importance on notification provisions, by which the assured will

instance of liability insurance: *The Cultural Foundation v Beazley Furlonge Ltd* [2018] EWHC 1083 (Comm); contra *Tarbuck v Avon Insurance* [2002] Lloyd's Rep. I.R. 393, 395, which was commented on obiter in *In Re OT Computers* [2004] EWCA Civ 653, [2004] Lloyd's Rep. I.R. 669, [17]–[22].

[865] See *Dominion Bridge Co v Toronto General*, 32 D.L.R. (2d) 374 (1962). See also *Foundation of Canada Engineering Corp Ltd v Canadian Indemnity Co* [1977] 2 W.W.R. 75 Can. In *Cape Distribution Ltd v Cape Intermediate Holdings Plc* [2016] EWHC 1786 (QB), [2017] Lloyd's Rep. I.R. 1, at [161]–[163] the Court held that the contractual liability exclusion applied only to claims which could be made only in contract.

[866] *Aswan Engineering Establishment Co Ltd v Iron Trades Mutual Insurance Co Ltd* [1989] 1 Lloyd's Rep. 289. cf. *Smit Tak Offshore Services v Youell* [1992] 1 Lloyd's Rep. 154; *Tesco Stores Ltd v Constable* [2007] EWHC 2088 (Comm), [2008] Lloyd's Rep. I.R. 302, [26], [30]–[31], [2008] EWCA Civ 362, [2008] Lloyd's Rep. I.R. 636 (where it was held that a public liability policy did not cover contractual liability); *MJ Gleeson Group Plc v Axa Corporate Solutions Assurance SA* [2013] Lloyd's Rep. I.R. 677. If the policy insures against the assured's legal liability to pay "as damages" to third parties, this suggests that compensation must be payable by reason of the assured's wrongdoing: *Bartoline Ltd v Royal & Sun Alliance Insurance Plc* [2007] Lloyd's Rep. I.R. 423; and a claim for restitution may not be covered: *Peninsular and Oriental Steam Navigation Co v Youell* [1997] 2 Lloyd's Rep. 136, 141. Certain types of liability policies may be subject to certain restrictions if not prohibition. As regards "directors and officers" liability insurance, see Companies Act 2006 ss.232–234.

[867] *Post Office v Norwich Union Fire Insurance Society* [1967] 2 Q.B. 363; *Bradley v Eagle Star* [1989] 1 Lloyd's Rep. 465; *Yorkshire Water v Sun Alliance & London Insurance Ltd* [1997] 2 Lloyd's Rep. 21. In *Lumbermens Mutual Casualty Co v Bovis Lend Lease Ltd* [2004] EWHC 2197 (Comm), [2005] Lloyd's Rep. 74, the court held that a liability will not be established by a settlement agreement where that settlement agreement does not identify the specific cost of discharging the liability in question. Accordingly, where under a global settlement agreement, the assured agreed to receive, not pay, a single sum in settlement of all claims and counterclaims, the assured's liability for the counterclaims was held not to have been established and extrinsic evidence could not be adduced for that purpose. This proposition is questionable. The decision in *Lumbermens* was subjected to a disapproving critique in *Enterprise Oil Ltd v Strand Insurance Co Ltd* [2006] EWHC 58 (Comm), [2006] 1 Lloyd's Rep. 500 at [150]–[175]; *AIG Europe (Ireland) Ltd v Faraday Capital Ltd* [2006] EWHC 2707, [2007] Lloyd's Rep. I.R. 267 at [69]–[71]; reversed on other grounds [2007] EWCA Civ 1208, [2008] Lloyd's Rep. I.R. 454. If the assured settles a claim made against him, it may be open to the insurer to defend the claim under the policy on the ground that there had been no legal liability: *Peninsular and Oriental Steam Navigation Co v Youell* [1997] 2 Lloyd's Rep. 136; *Beazley Underwriting Ltd v Travelers Companies Inc* [2011] EWHC 1520 (Comm), [2012] Lloyd's Rep. I.R. 78; cf. *Commercial Union Assurance Co Plc v NRG Victory Reinsurance Ltd* [1998] 2 All E.R. 434 (reinsurance).

[868] *Astrazeneca Insurance Co Ltd v XL Insurance (Bermuda) Ltd* [2013] EWHC 349 (Comm), [2013] Lloyd's Rep. I.R. 290 at [38]–[39], [96]; affirmed [2013] EWCA Civ 1660, [2014] Lloyd's Rep. I.R. 509.

[869] *West Wake Price & Co v Ching* [1957] 1 W.L.R. 45; *Thornton Springer v NEM Insurance Co Ltd* [2000] 1 All E.R. (Comm) 486. This is so, even if the policy uses the word "alleging" in order to describe the insured peril (*MDIS Ltd v Swinbank* [1999] Lloyd's Rep. I.R. 516), although it will

inform the insurer either of a claim or a circumstance which might give rise to a claim. The purpose of such provisions is to give the insurer the opportunity to investigate the claim or require the assured to defend the claim. It also serves as a mechanism to attach the policy under which notice was given to a claim arising subsequently to the expiry of the policy.[870]

42-121 **Employers' liability** The Employers' Liability (Compulsory Insurance) Act 1969 requires employers[871] carrying on business in the United Kingdom to maintain insurance against liability for bodily injury or disease sustained by their employees.[872] The 1969 Act requires employers to take out an "approved policy" against such liability. Regulations[873] made under this Act prescribe the amount of insurance required, make provision for the issue of insurance certificates and their display at places of work and have extended the requirement to insure so as to protect employees who are only temporarily in this country. The Regulations prohibit certain conditions being included in the policy which would otherwise entitle the insurer to be discharged from liability in the event of a breach.[874] The Act does not impose any civil liability upon an employing company or its directors, for the consequences of a failure to insure.[875]

42-122 **Statutory assignment** The Third Parties (Rights against Insurers) Act 1930 enables the third party, in the event of the insolvency of the assured,[876] to claim against the insurer; but the third party cannot proceed directly against the insurer until the existence and extent of the liability of the assured has been ascertained by judgment or agreement.[877] If two or more third party claimants obtain judgments against an insolvent assured, their respective statutory rights to claim directly from

---

always be a question of construction. As to the effect of a judgment obtained by a claimant against the assured, see *Omega Proteins Ltd v Aspen Insurance UK Ltd* [2010] EWHC 2280 (Comm), [2011] Lloyd's Rep. I.R. 183; cf. *London Borough of Redbridge v Municipal Mutual Insurance Ltd* [2001] Lloyd's Rep. I.R. 545, 550–551; cf. *Cheltenham & Gloucester Plc v Sun Alliance and London Insurance Plc* Unreported May 30, 2001, Inner House, Ct of Sess.; cf. *Sun Life Assurance Co of Canada v Lincoln National Life Insurance Co* [2004] EWCA Civ 1660, [2005] 1 Lloyd's Rep. 606.

[870] *HLB Kidsons v Lloyd's Underwriters* [2007] EWHC 1951 (Comm), [2008] Lloyd's Rep. I.R. 237 at [22]–[23], [2008] EWCA Civ 1206, [2009] 1 Lloyd's Rep. 8.

[871] s.3 exempts certain employers such as state corporations and local government authorities.

[872] s.2 excludes from the definition of "employee" persons who are employed by close relatives. As to the boundary between the 1969 Act and the Road Traffic Act 1988 s.145(4A), see *AXA Insurance UK Plc v Norwich Union Insurance Ltd* [2007] EWHC 1046 (Comm), [2008] Lloyd's Rep. I.R. 122. As to the insurance of the employers' liability for exposing an employee to the risk of harm from asbestos, see *International Energy Group Ltd v Zurich Insurance Plc UK* [2013] EWCA Civ 39, [2013] Lloyd's Rep. I.R. 379 reversed in part [2015] UKSC 33, [2015] 2 W.L.R. 1471; *BAI (Run Off) Ltd v Durham* [2012] UKSC 14, [2012] Lloyd's Rep. I.R. 371.

[873] Employers' Liability (Compulsory Insurance) Regulations 1998 (SI 1998/2573, amended SI 2004/2882). As to reg.3, see *R (on the application of Geologistics Ltd) v Financial Services Compensation Scheme* [2003] EWCA Civ 1877, [2004] Lloyd's Rep. I.R. 336 at [20]–[22].

[874] reg.2. See *Amlin UK Ltd v Geo-Rope Ltd* [2016] CSOH 165, [2017] Lloyd's Rep. I.R. 277.

[875] *Richardson v Pitt-Stanley* [1995] Q.B. 123; *Campbell v Gordon* [2016] UKSC 38, [2016] Lloyd's Rep. I.R. 591. The Contracts (Rights of Third Parties) Act 1999 may grant rights of recourse to third parties in so far as they are contemplated by the insurance contract. See *Amlin UK Ltd v Geo-Rope Ltd* [2016] CSOH 165, [2017] Lloyd's Rep. I.R. 277 at [25]–[27].

[876] *Re Compania Merabello San Nicholas SA* [1973] Ch. 75.

[877] *Post Office v Norwich Union Fire* [1967] 2 Q.B. 363. Although doubts have occasionally been expressed about the reason for this requirement (see, e.g. *Poclain SA v SCAC SA* [1986] 1 Lloyd's Rep. 404, 407), it has been affirmed by the House of Lords: see *Bradley v Eagle Star* [1989] 1 Lloyd's Rep. 465. See also *Sea Voyager Maritime Inc v Bielecki* [1999] Lloyd's Rep. I.R. 356; *William McIlroy (Swindon) Ltd v Quinn Insurance Ltd* [2011] EWCA Civ 825, [2012] 1 All E.R.

his insurer take effect in the order in which the extent of the assured's liability to the third parties was ascertained: there is no mechanism, either under the general law or under the Act, to enable rateable division of the proceeds of the insurance policy between the third party claimants, except where their judgments are simultaneous.[878] The third party can have no better right against the insurer than the assured had, and the insurer is entitled to raise against the third party any defence under the contract which he could have raised against the assured.[879] The parties cannot effectively contract out of the Act by purporting, directly or indirectly, to avoid the insurance or to alter the rights of the parties under it on insolvency[880]; nor can the rights of the third party be defeated by an agreement made between the insurer and the insolvent assured after the liability has been incurred to the third party.[881] The cause of action under the Act will become time-barred unless the third party, himself, commences proceedings within six years of the assured's cause of action against the insurer having accrued; and this is so even if the assured has already commenced proceedings against the insurer within the limitation period.[882]

The Third Parties (Rights against Insurers) Act 2010   The 1930 Act has been **42-123** replaced by the Third Parties (Rights against Insurers) Act 2010.[883] The 2010 Act entered into force on August 1, 2016.[884] Under s.1(2) of the 2010 Act, the insured's rights under a contract of liability insurance are transferred to a third party claimant where the insured is insolvent and is liable to that third party, and where either the liability was incurred or the insolvency took place after the Act's commencement. The rights are transferred only up to the limits of the insurance

---

(Comm) 241. As to the nature of the liability to which the Act applies, see *T & N Ltd (in administration) v Royal & Sun Alliance Plc* [2003] EWHC 1016 (Ch), [2004] Lloyd's Rep. I.R. 106; *In the matter of OT Computers Ltd (in administration)* [2004] EWCA Civ 653, [2004] 2 All E.R. (Comm) 331; *Freakley v Centre Reinsurance International Co* [2005] EWCA Civ 115, [2005] Lloyd's Rep. I.R. 303; *The Cultural Foundation v Beazley Furlonge Ltd* [2018] EWHC 1083 (Comm).

878   *Cox v Bankside Members' Agency Ltd* [1995] 2 Lloyd's Rep. 437, *Cox v Deeny* [1996] L.R.L.R. 288, 299; *Teal Assurance Co Ltd v WR Berkley Insurance (Europe) Ltd* [2011] EWCA Civ 1570, [2012] Lloyd's Rep. I.R. 315, [2013] UKSC 57, [2014] Lloyd's Rep. I.R. 56.

879   *Farrell v Federated Employers' Assurance Association* [1970] 1 W.L.R. 1400; *CVG Siderurgicia de Orinoco SA v London Mutual Steamship Owners Assn Ltd (The Vainqueur José)* [1979] 1 Lloyd's Rep. 557; *Socony Mobil Oil Inc v West of England Shipowners Mutual Assurance (The Padré Island)* [1984] 2 Lloyd's Rep. 408; *Pioneer Concrete (UK) Ltd v National Employers' Mutual General Insurance* [1985] 2 All E.R. 395; *Centre Reinsurance International Co v Curzon Insurance Ltd* [2004] EWHC 200 (Ch), [2004] 2 All E.R. (Comm) 28. As to the availability of a set off to the insurer in respect of the insurer's claims against the assured, see the conflicting decisions in *McCormick v National Motor and Accident* (1934) 40 Com. Cas. 76; *Murray v Legal and General Assurance Society* [1970] 2 Q.B. 495; *Cox v Bankside Members' Agency Ltd* [1995] 2 Lloyd's Rep. 437, 451; *Denso Manufacturing UK Ltd v Great Lakes Reinsurance (UK) Plc* [2017] EWHC 391 (Comm), [2017] Lloyd's Rep. I.R. 240 at [142]–[152]. For the position as regards motor insurance (see below, para.42-124) and public policy (see above, para.42-023), see *Charlton v Fisher* [2001] EWCA Civ 112, [2001] 1 All E.R. (Comm) 769.

880   s.1(3). See also s.2(1). An insurance containing a clause requiring the assured to have paid the third party before he becomes entitled to an indemnity under the insurance does not fall foul of s.1(3)—even though its effect is to prevent the third party having a cause of action against the insurer on the assured's insolvency—since such a clause does not avoid the policy or alter the rights of the parties under it: *Firma C-Trade SA v Newcastle Protection and Indemnity Association* [1991] 2 A.C. 1.

881   s.3.

882   *Lefevre v White* [1990] 1 Lloyd's Rep. 569.

883   Amendments have been made to the 2010 Act by the Insurance Act 2015 ss.19–20 and Sch.2.

884   Third Parties (Rights against Insurers) Act 2010 (Commencement) Order 2016 (SI 2016/550). See also Third Parties (Rights against Insurers) Regulations 2016 (SI 2016/570).

contract.[885] The Act applies irrespective of any connection with the United Kingdom.[886] Subject to the insurer's own insolvency, the third party cannot enforce the insured's liability against the insured to the extent that the insured's rights under the insurance contract are transferred to the third party.[887] The insurer is entitled to exercise rights of set off with respect to the insured's liability.[888] By s.9(2), conditions in the insurance policy may be performed by the third party claimant. By s.9(5), the transfer of rights under the policy is not subject to a condition requiring prior discharge by the insured of the insured's liability to the third party claimant.[889] Accordingly, "pay to be paid" clauses cannot be relied on by the insurer in answer to a claim under the 2010 Act. By s.17, provisions which purport to terminate the policy on the insured's insolvency are ineffective. The 2010 Act permits the third party claimant to institute proceedings against the insurer seeking a declaration as to the insurer's liability to the insured or the insured's liability to the third party, before the insured's liability to the third party is established by judgment, award or agreement, even if there is a dispute as to whether the third party claim, if proved and established, falls within the scope of cover afforded by the policy.[890] However, any such declaration cannot be enforced prior to the establishment of the insured's liability. In such proceedings, the insurer can rely on any defence available to the insured.[891] The 2010 Act contains extensive provisions as to the third party claimant's rights to information concerning the insurance policy and claims made thereunder.[892]

(b)   Motor Insurance[893]

42-124   Road Traffic Act 1988   The Road Traffic Act 1988[894] requires persons who control[895] the use[896] of motor vehicles on the road or other public place[897] to maintain

---

[885] s.8.

[886] s.18.

[887] s.14.

[888] s.10. Though note *International Energy Group Ltd v Zurich Insurance Plc* [2015] UKSC 33, [2015] 2 W.L.R. 1471, [93], [97].

[889] Although this is subject to an exception in respect of claims under a marine insurance policy other than in respect of death or personal injury: s.9(6).

[890] *BAE Systems Pension Funds Trustees Ltd v Royal & Sun Alliance Insurance Plc* [2017] EWHC 2082 (TCC), [2018] 1 W.L.R. 1165, at [15]–[24].

[891] s.1(3)–(4), 2(2)–(4). As to time bar defences, see ss.2(5) and 12.

[892] s.11 and Sch.1.

[893] See *MacGillivray on Insurance Law*, 14th edn (2018), Ch.31.

[894] Replacing the Road Traffic Act 1972, as amended by (inter alia) the Motor Vehicle (Compulsory Insurance) (No.2) Regulations 1973 (SI 1973/2143); SI 1974/791 (extending compulsory motor-vehicle insurance to cover liabilities arising out of use in other European Community countries); and the Motor Vehicles (Compulsory Insurance) Regulations 1987 (SI 1987/2171) (extending compulsory insurance to cover liability for damage to the property of a third party); and the Motor Vehicles (Compulsory Insurance) Regulations 1992 (SI 1992/3036) (ensuring that cover extends to the entire Community and affords cover no less than the law required than by the relevant Member States). The 1973, 1987 and 1992 Regulations each seek to implement EC Directives 72/166, 85/5 and 90/232. The 1988 Act came into force (subject to the transitory provisions in Sch.5 to the Road Traffic (Consequential Provisions) Act 1988) on May 15, 1989: see Road Traffic Act 1988 s.197.

[895] See *Monk v Warbey* [1935] 1 K.B. 75, 80; *Lloyd v Singleton* [1953] 1 Q.B. 357; *Kelly v Cornhill Insurance* [1964] 1 Lloyd's Rep. 1; *Newbury v Davis* [1974] R.T.R. 367.

[896] "Use" connotes control, management or operation: *Brown v Roberts* [1965] 1 Q.B. 1; and has been held to include the owner of a parked vehicle which owing to its condition could only be moved and not driven: *Elliott v Grey* [1960] 1 Q.B. 367; but there is no use if the vehicle is completely

insurance[898] against liability for death or injury to third parties (including passengers[899] in the vehicle) arising out of such use[900] and also against the liability (imposed by the Act)[901] to pay for emergency medical treatment for injuries (including fatal injuries) arising out of such use. With effect from December 31, 1988, insurance against liability for damage to the property of a third party has also been compulsory.[902] The Act does not require the personal liability of everyone using the vehicle to be covered so long as the insurance covers the use by the person in question[903]: thus an insurance by an employer which covers his liability for use by his employees is sufficient,[904] though if the insurance specifies the persons or classes of persons who are covered, such persons are given a statutory right to seek indemnity from the insurer, although not strictly parties to the contract of insurance.[905] The Act does not require insurance, inter alia, against contractual liability, against liability for death or injury sustained by persons in the employ-

---

immovable: *Thomas v Hooper* [1986] R.T.R. 1. In *UK Insurance Ltd v Holden* [2017] EWCA Civ 259, [2017] 3 W.L.R. 450 at [68]–[69], the Court of Appeal held that the repair of a car, which the owner was driving but due to disrepair could not be lawfully and safely driven, and which the owner wished to effect as soon as possible in order to be able to drive the car lawfully and safely, was "use" of the car. See also: *Leathley v Tatton* [1980] R.T.R. 21; *B (A Minor) v Knight* [1981] R.T.R. 136, *Stinton v Stinton* [1995] R.T.R. 167; *Hatton v Hall* [1997] R.T.R. 212. In *O'Mahoney v Joliffe* [1999] Lloyd's Rep. I.R. 321, the Court of Appeal held that a pillion passenger on a motorcycle who had agreed on a joint venture to go for a drive was a "user" within the meaning of the 1972 Uninsured Drivers Agreement (see below, para.42-126) and that "user" had the same meaning under the 1988 Act. See *Vnuk v Zavarovalnica Triglav dd* (C-162/13) EU:C:2014:2146, [2015] Lloyd's Rep. I.R. 142. In *Sahin v Havard* [2016] EWCA Civ 1202, [2017] 1 W.L.R. 1853 at [20], the Court of Appeal held that permitting the use of a vehicle is not the same as using the vehicle such that the liability of someone who permits another to use a vehicle without an insurance policy is not a liability which is itself required to be insured under s.145 and is not therefore a liability which an insurer is obliged to satisfy under s.151.

[897] s.192(1); *Lister v Romford Ice and Cold Storage Co* [1957] A.C. 555. The House of Lords held that a car park was not a "road": *Clarke v General Accident Fire and Life Assurance Corp Plc* [1998] 1 W.L.R. 1647. The legislation was amended to extend to "other public place" by the Motor Vehicles (Compulsory Insurance) Regulations 2000 (SI 2000/726). In *UK Insurance Ltd v Holden* [2016] EWHC 264 (QB), [2016] 4 W.L.R. 38, [2017] EWCA Civ 259, [2017] 3 W.L.R. 450 at [44], the Court held that a motor insurance policy might extend beyond roads, if there was no express limitation in the policy to use on roads. The Court also discussed whether "roads" under the Road Traffic Act 1988 s.145(3) meant "public roads".

[898] See ss.144 and 146 for alternative schemes for deposits and securities and for the classes of persons exempted from the provisions of the Act.

[899] See *Farrell v Whitty* (C-356/05) EU:C:2007:229, [2007] Lloyd's Rep. I.R. 525; *Drozdovs v Baltikums AAS* (C-277/12) EU:C:2013:685, [2014] R.T.R. 14; *Haasová v Petrik (Note)* (C-22/12) EU:C:2013:692, [2014] R.T.R. 15.

[900] In *Dunthorne v Bentley* [1996] R.T.R. 428, the Court of Appeal held that the plaintiff's injuries were caused by the defendant who, having run out of petrol had left her car to seek assistance, ran in front of the plaintiff's car, and that the injuries arose out of the defendant's use of her vehicle. In *Dodson v Peter H Dodson Insurance Services* [2001] 1 W.L.R. 1012, a motor insurance policy was construed as continuing to provide an indemnity against the driver's liabilities even though the principal vehicle which had been insured under the policy had been sold. cf. *Slater v Buckinghamshire CC* [2004] Lloyd's Rep. I.R. 432. In *AXN v Worboys* [2012] EWHC 1730 (QB), [2013] Lloyd's Rep. I.R. 207 the Court held that the liability of an insured taxi driver who administered poison and carried out sexual assaults on his passengers did not arise out of the use of a motor vehicle on the road or other public place, because such acts broke the chain of causation.

[901] See ss.157 and 158.

[902] Road Traffic Act 1988 s.145(3)(a).

[903] *Ellis v Hinds* [1947] K.B. 475; see also *Baugh v Crago* [1976] 1 Lloyd's Rep. 563. Nor does it require cover in respect of liability to a person driving the vehicle: *Cooper v MIB* [1985] Q.B. 575.

[904] See n.872, above.

[905] s.148(7); *Tattersal v Drysdale* [1935] 2 K.B. 174; *Austin v Zurich* [1945] 1 K.B. 250, 255.

ment of a person insured in accordance with the foregoing requirements, where the injury arises out of and in the course of that employment, or against damage to the vehicle insured; or cover in excess of £1,000,000 in respect of property damage arising out of any one accident.[906] An insurance is ineffective for the purposes of the Act unless a certificate of insurance in prescribed form is delivered by the insurer to the assured.[907] Failure to insure in accordance with the statutory requirements not only constitutes a criminal offence[908] but also a breach of a statutory duty which may give rise to liability in damages to persons thereby prejudiced.[909] On July 19, 2018, the Automated and Electric Vehicles Act 2018 received Royal Assent. By s.2(1) of that Act, an insurer is liable for any damage (meaning death, personal injury and, subject to exceptions, property damage) sustained by an insured person or any other person which has been caused by an automated vehicle when driving itself on a road or other public place in Great Britain. By s.2(4), unless there has been an unauthorised software alteration or a failure to update software, the insurer's liability for such damage cannot be excluded or limited by a term of the insurance policy or in any other way. This Act has not yet entered into force.

42-125   **Rights of third parties**   The Act entitles the third party to make a direct claim upon the insurer upon obtaining judgment against the person insured,[910] so long as notice[911] of the bringing of proceedings has been given to the insurer before or within seven days after their commencement and there has been no stay of execution pending an appeal.[912] In order that the third party may make a direct claim against the insurer, the assured's liability to the third party must be covered by the terms of the policy.[913] This right is not available, however, if before the event giving rise to the death, injury or damage the insurance was cancelled (and the

---

906 Road Traffic Act 1988 s.145(4), as amended by the Motor Vehicles (Compulsory Insurance) Regulations 2007 (SI 2007/1426). As to the boundary between the Employers Liability (Compulsory Insurance) Act 1969 and the Road Traffic Act 1988 s.145(4A), see *AXA Insurance UK Plc v Norwich Union Insurance Ltd* [2007] EWHC 1046 (Comm), [2008] Lloyd's Rep. I.R. 122.

907 s.147.

908 s.143(2). The offence is an absolute one: *Baugh v Crago* [1976] 1 Lloyd's Rep. 563.

909 *Monk v Warbey* [1935] 1 K.B. 75; *Martin v Dean* [1971] 2 Q.B. 208. In *Norman v Aziz* [2000] Lloyd's Rep. I.R. 52, a civil right to damages for breach of s.143(1)(b) of the 1988 Act was held to exist in favour of a victim against the owner of a vehicle who allowed an uninsured driver to use that vehicle; the existence of the Motor Insurers Bureau uninsured drivers agreement (see below, para.42-125) and the relevant EC Directive had no effect on this cause of action. The defendant to a claim for damages for personal injury is not entitled to counterclaim for a breach of this statutory duty for purely economic losses in connection with the defendant's liability to the claimant, as opposed to the defendant's own injuries: *Bretton v Hancock* [2005] EWCA Civ 404, [2005] Lloyd's Rep. I.R. 454 at [42]–[50].

910 This is so, even if the third party claimant has obtained judgment against the insured as an "unknown" or "unnamed" driver: *Cameron v Hussain* [2017] EWCA Civ 366, [2017] R.T.R. 23; *Farah v Abdullahi* [2018] EWHC 738 (QB).

911 As to the requirements of the notice to be given, see *Wylie v Wake* [2001] P.I.Q.R. P13.

912 ss.151–152. With effect from December 31, 1988, an insurer is bound, subject to certain exceptions, to satisfy a judgment obtained even against a person not insured by the policy if it relates to a liability required to be covered: see Road Traffic Act 1988 s.151(2)(b). In *Churchill Insurance Co Ltd v Fitzgerald* [2012] EWCA Civ 1166, [2013] Lloyd's Rep. I.R. 137 the Court of Appeal considered s.151(8) of the Road Traffic Act 1988, by which the insurer is entitled to recover the amount of the judgment from the assured who caused or permitted the use of the vehicle which gave rise to the liability.

913 s.151(2)(a). In *EUI Ltd v Bristol Alliance Ltd Partnership* [2012] EWCA Civ 1267, [2013] Lloyd's Rep. I.R. 351 the Court of Appeal held that the third party could not recover from the motor insurer in circumstances where the damage to property to which the third party's claim related arose by

certificate dealt with in accordance with the Act)[914] or if the insurer in an action commenced before or within three months[915] of the commencement of the action by this third party has obtained a declaration that he is entitled (apart from any provision in the insurance) to avoid the insurance for non-disclosure or misrepresentation.[916] In addition to the foregoing, the Act renders ineffective any provisions of the insurance restricting the cover by reference to such matters as the characteristics of the vehicle or the driver,[917] though the insurer can recover from the person insured any payments made to third parties which but for the provision he would not have been obliged to make. Similarly provisions relieving the insurer by reason of some act or omission after the event giving rise to a claim under the insurance are ineffective[918] as are other rights to avoid or cancel the insurance unless falling within the qualifications to the rights of the third party outlined above.[919] Finally, it should be noted that the Act also renders ineffective any prior agreement or understanding between the user of a vehicle and a passenger whereby the liability of the user is restricted or excluded or the enforcement of such liability is made subject to conditions.[920] European Council Directives[921] require Member States to ensure that insurance coverage exists for civil liability for personal injuries and property damage arising as a result of the use of motor vehicles. The intention of the Directives is to ensure that the victims of motor accidents are able to prosecute and establish their claims in comparable ways in each Member State.[922] By the European Communities (Rights against Insurers) Regulations 2002,[923] where a person has a cause of action in tort against a person insured under a policy complying with s.145 of the Road Traffic Act 1988 arising out of an accident involving the insured vehicle, the claimant may, without prejudice to his right against the insured person, issue proceedings directly against the insurer immediately and the insurer shall be liable to the claimant to the extent that he is liable to the insured person.

Third parties and uninsured drivers   In 1945 the Motor Insurers' Bureau (MIB)   **42-126**
entered into an agreement with the Minister of Transport under which the MIB undertook (subject to the terms of the agreement) to satisfy any judgment in respect of a liability compulsorily insurable under the Act against any person or persons and whether or not covered by a contract of insurance, where the judgment was not satisfied in full within seven days from the date when it became enforceable. The current agreements are on agreement dated August 13, 1999 which is between the

---

reason of the assured's deliberate act, which was expressly excluded from cover under the motor policy. See also *Stych v Dibble* [2012] EWHC 1606 (QB), [2013] Lloyd's Rep. I.R. 80; *AXN v Worboys* [2012] EWHC 1730 (QB), [2013] Lloyd's Rep. I.R. 207.

[914] s.152(1)(c).
[915] If the insurer starts proceedings after the proceedings by the third party have been started, then to take advantage of this provision, he must give the claimant in the action by the third party notice specifying the non-disclosure or misrepresentation relied upon and (if required) make such claimant a party to his action: s.152(2); *Cross v British Oak Insurance Co Ltd* [1938] 2 K.B. 167; *Zurich v Morrison* [1942] 2 K.B. 53.
[916] s.152(2), as amended by the Insurance Act 2015 s.21(4).
[917] s.148.
[918] s.148.
[919] s.152. cf. *Matadeen v Caribbean Insurance Co Ltd* [2002] UKPC 69, [2003] 1 W.L.R. 670.
[920] s.149.
[921] Directives 72/166, 84/5, 88/357, 90/232, 2000/26 and 2005/14.
[922] *Criminal Proceedings against Ruiz Bernáldez* (C-129/94) EU:C:1996:143, [1996] All E.R. (EC) 741.
[923] SI 2002/3061.

MIB and the Secretary of State for the Environment, Transport and the Regions, and applies to claims arising on or after October 1, 1999 and before August 1, 2015; and there is a further agreement dated July 3, 2015 (as supplemented by a further agreement on January 10, 2017) in respect of accidents on or after August 1, 2015. It is effectively based upon the original 1945 agreement, with subsequent agreements in 1946, 1971, 1972 and 1988. A more complex scheme (first introduced in 1969) covers the position of untraced drivers. This is now governed by the Untraced Drivers Agreement dated February 14, 2003, in respect of accidents occurring before March 1, 2017, and a further agreement dated February 28, 2017 in respect of accidents occurring on or after March 1, 2017.[924] The MIB's liability under the 2003 and 2017 Agreements is dependent on establishing that the untraced driver would have been liable to the victim and that that liability is of a kind required to be covered by compulsory insurance under the Road Traffic Act 1988.[925] It is the publicly declared policy of the MIB not to take the point that there is no privity of contract between the MIB and persons seeking to enforce the undertaking of the MIB.[926] If the claimant knew or "ought to have known" that the driver was uninsured, the MIB will not be liable.[927] Further, the liability of the MIB is subject

---

[924] Applicants for compensation under these agreements cannot rely on the doctrine of direct effect as against the MIB in the event that there is any shortfall in the cover provided by them (including issues of time limitation) as against the cover required to be legislated by the United Kingdom by the EC Directives, because the MIB is not an emanation of the state: *Byrne v Motor Insurers Bureau* [2007] EWHC 1268 (QB), [2007] 3 All E.R. 499 at [48]–[63] affirmed [2008] EWCA Civ 574, [2008] Lloyd's Rep. I.R. Plus 30; cf. *Evans v Motor Insurers' Bureau* [1999] Lloyd's Rep. I.R. 30; *Farrell v Whitty* (C-356/05) EU:C:2007:229, [2007] Lloyd's Rep. I.R. 525, ECJ. However, *Francovich* damages might be recoverable from the Secretary of State for any failure to implement the Directive (*Byrne v Motor Insurers Bureau* [2007] EWHC 1268 (QB), [2007] 3 All E.R. 499 at [78] affirmed [2008] EWCA Civ 574, [2008] Lloyd's Rep. I.R. 705; *Delaney v Secretary of State for Transport* [2014] EWHC 1785 (QB), [2014] R.T.R. 25; cf. *Moore v Secretary of State for Transport* [2007] EWHC 879 (QB), [2007] P.I.Q.R. P24). Further, in *Evans v Secretary of State for the Environment, Transport and the Regions* [2001] EWCA Civ 32, [2002] Lloyd's Rep. I.R. 1 at [4], the Court of Appeal indicated that the victim might have the right to enforce the Agreement pursuant to the Contracts (Rights of Third Parties) Act 1999. Clause 31(5) of the Untraced Drivers Agreement dated February 14, 2003, confirms that the Agreement is intended to benefit the victim. As to the level of compensation obtainable under the agreements, see *Evans v Secretary of State for the Environment, Transport and the Regions* (C-63/01) EU:C:2003:650, [2004] Lloyd's Rep. I.R. 391, ECJ. As to the relationship between the MIB and the Secretary of State, see *Sharp v Pereira* [1999] Lloyd's Rep. I.R. 242.

[925] In *Moreno v Motor Insurers' Bureau* [2016] UKSC 52, [2017] Lloyd's Rep. I.R. 99 at [39] the Supreme Court held that the Motor Vehicles (Compulsory Insurance) (Information Centre and Compensation Body) Regulations 2003 (SI 2003/37) proceed on the basis that a victim's entitlement to compensation will be measured on a consistent basis, by reference to the law of the state of the accident, whichever of the routes to recovery provided by the Directives he invokes. In so doing, the Court overruled *Jacobs v Motor Insurers' Bureau* [2010] EWCA Civ 1208, [2011] 1 All E.R. 844. See also *Wigley-Foster v Wilson* [2016] EWCA Civ 454, [2016] 1 W.L.R. 4769.

[926] *Carswell v Secretary of State for Transport* [2010] EWHC 3230 (QB), [2011] Lloyd's Rep. I.R. 644, at [57]–[63]; cf. *Hardy v Motor Insurers' Bureau* [1964] 2 Q.B. 745; *Gurtner v Circuit* [1968] 2 Q.B. 587; *Albert v Motor Insurers' Bureau* [1972] A.C. 301; *Persson v London Country Buses* [1974] 1 W.L.R. 569; *Porter v Addo* [1978] R.T.R. 503; *Phillips v Rafiq* [2006] EWHC 1461 (QB) at [12]; affirmed [2007] EWCA Civ 74, [2007] 1 W.L.R. 1351.

[927] In *White v White* [2001] UKHL 9, [2001] 1 W.L.R. 481, the House of Lords construed the words "ought to have known" by reference to Directive 84/5 and held that the agreement excused the MIB where the claimant actually knew or deliberately refrained from making inquiries, but not where the claimant's ignorance was occasioned by mere negligence or carelessness. cf. *Delaney v Pickett* [2011] EWCA Civ 1532 at [44]–[49], [67], [75]. In *Pickett v Motor Insurers Bureau* [2004] EWCA Civ 6, [2004] Lloyd's Rep. I.R. 513, the Court of Appeal considered whether the MIB was liable

to the following principal conditions precedent[928]: that notice of bringing, or intention to bring, legal proceedings against an insured person is given to the MIB within specified periods of time[929]; that the MIB is supplied with any information it reasonably requires; that the claimant has demanded relevant information from the relevant driver in accordance with s.154 of the Road Traffic Act 1988; that (if required to do so by the MIB) the claimant take steps to obtain judgment against all responsible tortfeasors; and that any judgments obtained should be assigned to the MIB. The liability of the MIB is not affected by the fact that the uninsured motorist deliberately injured the person seeking recovery.[930]

(c) Reinsurance[931]

General characteristics   An insurer may take out insurance in respect of the risk   **42-127**
covered by the original insurance.[932] Such a contract of reinsurance is quite separate
from the underlying contract of insurance,[933] so that there is no privity of contract
between the insured and the reinsurer,[934] though the contract of reinsurance will
often provide (by the use of general words such as "all terms, clauses and conditions as original") for the terms and conditions of the underlying insurance to be
incorporated into the reinsurance. The fact that the reinsurer and reassured intended
the reinsurance cover to be "back-to-back" with the original direct insurance policy
will be a persuasive aid to construing the scope of cover afforded by the reinsur-

---

under the 1988 Agreement where the claimant, who was also the owner of, but a passenger in, the vehicle, knew that the vehicle was uninsured. The court held that the claimant had not withdrawn her consent to be carried in the vehicle because she had not unambiguously required the vehicle to be stopped so that she could get out, thus permitting the MIB to rely on an exception to liability. The 1999 Agreement provides that the relevant knowledge is that of the claimant as opposed to the person suffering the relevant injury, whereas the 1988 Agreement applied the relevant exception to the knowledge of the person who suffered the injury. This distinction proved to be critical in *Phillips v Rafiq* [2006] EWHC 1461 (QB), [2007] EWCA Civ 74, [2007] 1 W.L.R. 1351, where the deceased's wife brought the proceedings and was entitled to maintain the claim against the MIB even though her husband was aware that the driver was uninsured. Where the third party claimant is himself an insured, see *Churchill Insurance Co Ltd v Wilkinson* [2010] EWCA Civ 556, [2010] Lloyd's Rep. I.R. 591.

[928] See the 1999 Agreement cll.9–5.

[929] Where a policy of insurance actually exists, the claimant should notify the insurer within seven days of having commenced proceedings against the driver.

[930] *Hardy v Motor Insurers' Bureau* [1964] 2 Q.B. 745; *Gardner v Moore* [1984] A.C. 548.

[931] *Butler and Merkin's Reinsurance Law* (looseleaf); O'Neill and Woloniecki, *The Law of Reinsurance in England and Bermuda*, 4th edn (2015), *MacGillivray on Insurance Law*, 14th edn (2018), Ch.35; Edelman and Burns, *The Law of Reinsurance*, 2nd edn (2013).

[932] *Mackenzie v Whitworth* (1875) 45 L.J. Q.B. 233; *Phoenix General Insurance Co v Halvanon Insurance Co* [1985] 2 Lloyd's Rep. 599, 607, [1986] 2 Lloyd's Rep. 552, 563. See, *Toomey v Eagle Star* [1993] 1 Lloyd's Rep. 429, emphasising that reinsurance is the insurance of an insurable interest in the subject matter of the original insurance, and not inherently a form of liability insurance. The reinsurer may himself reinsure, the reinsurance of a contract of reinsurance being commonly, though not universally, known as a retrocession: see *Commonwealth Insurance Co of Vancouver v Sprinks* [1983] 1 Lloyd's Rep. 67, 87–88.

[933] *Re Law Guarantee Trust and Accident Society* [1914] 2 Ch. 617, 647–648; *English Insurance Co v National Benefit Assurance Co* [1929] A.C. 114, 124; *Phoenix General Insurance Co v Halvanon Insurance Co* [1985] 2 Lloyd's Rep. 599, 614.

[934] *British Dominions General Insurance Co Ltd v Duder* [1915] 2 K.B. 394. See also *Excess Insurance Co Ltd v Mander* [1997] 2 Lloyd's Rep. 119; See also *The Federal Mogul Asbestos Personal Injury Trust v Federal-Mogul Ltd* [2014] EWHC 2002 (Comm), [2014] Lloyd's Rep. I.R. 671; Marine Insurance Act 1906 s.9(2).

ance policy,[935] but it will not be sufficient to override a sufficiently explicit term of the reinsurance contract which alters or restricts the scope of cover compared to that afforded by the original policy.[936] In the event of an attempt so to incorporate the general terms and conditions of the underlying insurance, difficult questions may arise as to which of the terms are appropriate for incorporation,[937] and how to construe the terms if the contracts of insurance and reinsurance are governed by the laws of different countries.[938] The contract of reinsurance will also be governed by the same rules as apply to the underlying insurance, so that, for example, the duty of utmost good faith will apply so as to require the reinsured to disclose all material facts to the reinsurer and to make a fair and substantially accurate presentation of the risk,[939] and, if the underlying insurance is a marine policy, the reinsurance contract must itself be embodied in a policy in the form required by the Marine Insurance Act 1906.[940] The restrictions imposed by the Financial Services and Markets Act 2000 (and the statutory instruments made thereunder) on the carrying on of insurance business apply to reinsurance.[941]

42-128 **Liability of the reinsurer** Subject to contrary stipulation, a reinsurer is only obliged to reimburse the reinsured if the latter was legally liable on the underlying insurance,[942] so that the reinsurer may take against the reinsured all the defences

---

[935] *Groupama Navigation et Transports v Catatumbo CA Seguros* [2000] 2 Lloyd's Rep. 350; *WASA International Insurance Co Ltd v Lexington Insurance Co* [2008] EWCA Civ 150, [2008] Lloyd's Rep. I.R. 510, [2009] UKHL 40, [2009] 3 W.L.R. 575.

[936] *GE Reinsurance v New Hampshire* [2003] EWHC 302 (Comm), [2004] 1 Lloyd's Rep. I.R. 404. See also *Metlife Insurance Ltd v RGA Reinsurance Company of Australia Ltd* [2016] NSWSC 980, [2017] Lloyd's Rep. I.R. 160 at [57] (NSWSC).

[937] See, e.g. *Pine Top Insurance Co Ltd v Unione Italiana Anglo-Saxon Reinsurance Co Ltd* [1987] 1 Lloyd's Rep. 476; and *Trygg Hansa Insurance Co Ltd v Equitas Ltd* [1998] 2 Lloyd's Rep. 439 (with respect to Arbitration Act 1996 s.6) where an arbitration clause in the contract of insurance was held not to be incorporated into the reinsurance. See also *AIG Group (UK) Ltd v Ethniki* [1998] 4 All E.R. 301 (jurisdiction clause); *American International Marine Agency of New York Inc v Dandridge* [2005] EWHC 829 (Comm), [2005] Lloyd's Rep. I.R. 643 ("follow the leader" clause). The principles governing the incorporation into the reinsurance contract of provisions found in the original insurance contract were helpfully explained in *HIH Casualty and General Insurance Ltd v New Hampshire Insurance Co* [2001] EWCA Civ 735, [2001] 2 All E.R. (Comm) 39. For a case where the terms of the underlying insurance are summarised in the reinsurance contract itself, see *Toomey v Banco Vitalcio De Espana SA de Seguros y Reaseguros* [2004] EWCA Civ 622, [2005] Lloyd's Rep. I.R. 423.

[938] See, e.g. *Forsikringsaktieselskapet Vesta v Butcher* [1989] A.C. 852, holding in the context of a back to back reinsurance, that the provision there incorporated into a reinsurance governed by English law should, in the absence of any express provision to the contrary, be regarded as having the same effect as it did in the underlying insurance from which it was incorporated, notwithstanding that the latter was governed by Norwegian law. See recently *Amlin Corporate Member Ltd v Oriental Assurance Corp* [2012] EWHC 540 (Comm), affirmed [2012] EWCA Civ 1341, [2013] Lloyd's Rep. I.R. 131.

[939] See, e.g. *CTI v Oceanus Mutual Underwriting Association (Bermuda) Ltd* [1984] 1 Lloyd's Rep. 476; *Highlands Insurance Co v Continental Insurance Co* [1987] 1 Lloyd's Rep. 109; *Mander v Commercial Union Assurance Co Plc* [1998] Lloyd's Rep. I.R. 93.

[940] *Imperial Marine v Fire Insurance Corp* (1879) 4 C.P.D. 166.

[941] *DR Insurance Co v Seguros America Banamex* [1993] 1 Lloyd's Rep. 120. *Re NRG Victory Reinsurance Ltd* [1995] All E.R. 533 (holding, also, that retrocessions are "insurance" business for the purposes of the Insurance Companies Act 1982). See also *New Hampshire Insurance Co v Grand Union Insurance Co Ltd* [1996] L.R.L.R. 102.

[942] *Assicurazioni Generali SpA v CGU International Insurance Plc* [2003] EWHC 1073 (Comm), [2003] Lloyd's Rep. I.R. 725, [2004] EWCA Civ 429, [2004] 2 Lloyd's Rep. I.R. 457. The reinsur-

which were available to the reinsured against the insured.[943] If, however, the reinsured's liability has been established by judgment or award, that judgment or award will be evidence of that liability for the purposes of the reinsurance contract. The ascertainment of loss by a judgment or settlement does not automatically establish such actual legal liability or the basis of such liability; it is still open to the reinsurer to challenge that there was an actual legal liability, in which case it is for the reinsured to prove that there was such an actual legal liability.[944] Because of the impractical restriction which this places on the bona fide settlement of claims by the insured on the underlying policy, it is very common for reinsurance contracts to include a "follow the settlements" clause so as to make strict proof by the reinsured of his legal liability to the insured unnecessary.[945] The effect of such a clause is to bind the reinsurer to indemnify the reinsured in respect of a settlement made with the insured provided the claim as recognised by the reinsured falls within the risks covered by the reinsurance as a matter of law, and provided also the reinsured has acted honestly and taken all proper and business-like steps in making the settlement.[946] Moreover, the burden is upon the reinsurer to prove that one or other exception to its obligation to follow the reinsured's settlements is made

ance contract, however, may not be an insurance of the reinsured's liability; the subject matter of the reinsurance contract may be the same as the insurance contract: *Toomey v Eagle Star Insurance Co Ltd* [1994] 1 Lloyd's Rep. 516, 522–524; *Charter Reinsurance Co Ltd v Fagan* [1997] A.C. 313, 387, 392; Marine Insurance Act 1906 s.9(1); cf. *Commercial Union Assurance Co Plc v NRG Victory Reinsurance Ltd* [1998] 2 All E.R. 434, 448; *Travellers Casualty & Surety Co of Europe Ltd v Commissioners of Customs and Excise* [2006] Lloyd's Rep. I.R. 63 (VAT Tribunal). See the discussion in O'Neill and Woloniecki, *The Law of Reinsurance in England and Bermuda*, 4th edn (2015), Ch.1. In an excess of loss reinsurance, the contract may provide for reimbursement of losses in excess of an ultimate net loss which is to be determined by reference to the sum actually *paid* in settlement of losses. In *Charter Reinsurance Co Ltd v Fagan*, above, however, it was held that, on a proper construction of the policies before the court, this did not mean that payment of the relevant losses by the reassured was a condition precedent to the liability of the reinsurer to reimburse him. Liability under the reinsurance contract is dependent on the establishment of the insurer's liability and not payment by the insurer: *Re Eddystone Marine Insurance Co* [1892] 2 Ch. 423.

[943] *Chipendale v Holt* (1895) 65 L.J. Q.B. 104.

[944] *Astrazeneca Insurance Co Ltd v XL Insurance (Bermuda) Ltd* [2013] EWHC 349 (Comm), [2013] Lloyd's Rep. I.R. 290 at [39], [96]; affirmed [2013] EWCA Civ 1660, [2014] Lloyd's Rep. I.R. 509. It has been suggested that there is an implied term that if the judgment is of a foreign court of competent jurisdiction, the court will treat that as decisive, unless the judgment was manifestly perverse or was obtained in breach of a jurisdiction clause or if the reinsured had failed to take proper defences: *Commercial Union Assurance Co Plc v NRG Victory Reinsurance Ltd* [1998] 2 All E.R. 434. In *Astrazeneca Insurance Co Ltd v XL Insurance (Bermuda) Ltd* [2013] EWHC 349 (Comm), [2013] Lloyd's Rep. I.R. 290 at [62]–[65] Flaux, J. did not follow this obiter suggestion. The Court of Appeal affirmed this decision: [2013] EWCA Civ 1660, [2014] Lloyd's Rep. I.R. 509.

[945] See, e.g. *Excess Liability Insurance Co Ltd v Mathews* (1925) 31 Com. Cas. 43.

[946] *Insurance Co of Africa v SCOR (UK) Reinsurance Ltd* [1985] 1 Lloyd's Rep. 312. However, the clause will not bind the reinsurer where the settlement involves the reassured waiving or failing to consider a policy defence: *Assicurazioni Generali SpA v CGU International Insurance Plc* [2003] EWHC 1073 (Comm), [2003] Lloyd's Rep. I.R. 725; affirmed [2004] EWCA Civ 429, [2004] 2 Lloyd's Rep. I.R. 457. The clause does not bind the reinsurer to judgments: *Amlin Corporate Member Ltd v Oriental Assurance Corp* [2012] EWHC 540 (Comm), affirmed [2012] EWCA Civ 1341, [2013] Lloyd's Rep. I.R. 131. For the scope of the first proviso (that the claim falls within the risks covered by the reinsurance), and its impact upon the second proviso, in a situation where the reinsurance is subject to the same terms and conditions as the underlying insurance, cf. *Insurance Co of the State of Pennsylvania v Grand Union Insurance Co* [1990] 1 Lloyd's Rep. 208; and *Hiscox v Outhwaite (No.3)* [1991] 2 Lloyd's Rep. 524. The clause does not require the reinsurer to indemnify the reinsured in respect of his costs of investigating, settling and defending claims under the underlying insurance nor will a term be implied to such effect: *Baker v Black Sea & Baltic General Insurance Co Ltd* [1998] 2 All E.R. 833. As to the reinsurer's right of inspection of the reinsured's records

out.[947] It seems, however, that the inclusion of a "claims co-operation" clause in the reinsurance contract (providing that the reinsured should cooperate with the reinsurer and not make a settlement without the approval of the reinsurer)[948] will effectively emasculate a "follow the settlements" clause, since it has been held that, as a matter of construction, the combined effect of the clauses is to require the reinsurer to follow only those settlements which the reinsurer has himself approved.[949] In *Hill v Mercantile & General Reinsurance Co Plc*,[950] a "follow settlements" clause which provided for all loss settlements by the reinsured to be binding on its reinsurers:

"... providing such settlements are within the terms and conditions of the original policies and/or contracts ... and within the terms and conditions of this reinsurance"

was held by the House of Lords to contemplate a distinction between the facts generating a particular claim, and the legal extent of the respective covers. Although the reinsurers could be bound by the reassured's honest conclusions as to the former, it would not be bound by its determination of the latter, since this would enable the reinsured to bind its reinsurers to a definition of cover different from that which they had contracted to accept. It should be noted that the Third Parties (Rights against Insurers) Act 1930 and the Third Parties (Rights against Insurers) Act 2010 do not apply to reinsurance contracts.[951]

(d)   Insurance Against Financial Loss[952]

42-129   Types of financial loss insurance   The essential characteristic of an insurance against financial loss is that it indemnifies the assured against his economic loss. Economic loss may take the form of a loss of anticipated profits,[953] the incurring of an expense or additional expense,[954] the loss of an advance,[955] the loss of a source of revenue[956] or the waste of an expense. Such insurance contracts are often referred to as "consequential loss" policies. Tailored policies have been developed to protect the assured against specific types of loss caused by specific perils and include

---

of his settlement of the underlying claim, see *Pacific & General Insurance Co Ltd (In Liquidation) v Baltica Insurance Co (UK) Ltd* [1996] L.R.L.R. 8; *Commercial Union Assurance Co v Mander* [1996] 2 Lloyd's Rep. 640. See also *Aegis Electrical and Gas International Services Ltd v Continental Casualty Co* [2007] EWHC 1762 (Comm), [2008] Lloyd's Rep. I.R. 17. For twin decisions concerning the application of different aspects of the follow settlements clause, see *Tokio Marine Europe Insurance Ltd v Novae Corporate Underwriting Ltd* [2013] EWHC 3362 (Comm), [2014] Lloyd's Rep. I.R. 490 and [2014] EWHC 2105 (Comm), [2014] Lloyd's Rep. I.R. 638.

[947] *Insurance Co of the State of Pennsylvania v Grand Union Insurance Co*, above; *Charman v Guardian Royal Exchange Assurance Plc* [1992] 2 Lloyd's Rep. 607.

[948] On the construction of this provision, see *Gan Insurance Co Ltd v Tai Ping Insurance Co Ltd* [2001] Lloyd's Rep. I.R. 291, [2001] EWCA Civ 1042, [2002] Lloyd's Rep. I.R. 612; *Beazley Underwriting Ltd v Al Ahleia Insurance Co* [2013] EWHC 677 (Comm), [2013] Lloyd's Rep. I.R. 561.

[949] *Insurance Co of Africa v SCOR (UK) Reinsurance Ltd* [1985] 1 Lloyd's Rep. 312.

[950] [1996] 1 W.L.R. 1239.

[951] 1930 Act s.1(5); 2010 Act s.15.

[952] See *MacGillivray on Insurance Law*, 14th edn (2018), Ch.33.

[953] *Maurice v Goldsborough, Mort & Co* [1939] A.C. 452.

[954] *Henry Booth v Commercial Union Assurance Co* (1923) 14 Ll.L. Rep. 114; cf. *Polikoff v North British and Mercantile Insurance Co Ltd* (1936) 55 Ll.L. Rep. 279.

[955] e.g. a mortgagee indemnity policy: *Svenska Handelsbanken v Sun Alliance and London Insurance Plc* [1996] 1 Lloyd's Rep. 519.

[956] *Farmers Co-operative Ltd v National Benefit Assurance Co Ltd* (1922) 13 Ll.L. Rep. 530; *Agra Trading Ltd v McAuslin (The Frio Chile)* [1995] 1 Lloyd's Rep. 182.

guarantee (or credit) insurance, fidelity insurance, business interruption insurance and insurance guaranteeing the assured's warranty of performance. Insurance policies against financial loss often afford an indemnity only if the loss itself arises by reason of damage to property[957]; in some cases, the assured must have an interest in the property.[958] If consequential loss alone is to be insured, and there is no reason in principle why such losses cannot be insured, the draftsmen of the policy should be assiduous in making their intention clear.

Guarantee insurance   Guarantee insurance, whereby the assured is indemnified **42-130** against loss caused by the non-payment of a debt, closely resembles guarantee by way of surety. A fine distinction is drawn between them,[959] but in practice the distinction is probably negligible.[960] Fidelity policies, whereby the assured is indemnified against breaches of his contract of employment by an employee, are also regarded as guarantee policies.[961]

(e)   Fire Insurance[962]

Special features   Insurance against fire is governed by the general principles of **42-131** insurance, but presents certain recurrent problems, in particular that of causation, in that fire may be accompanied by explosion or pilfering, which may be the cause or effect of the fire and may themselves be excepted perils. The law is complex and in some respects archaic, and the reader is referred to the specialised works of reference for guidance.[963] Where premises are damaged by fire, reinstatement may be specifically required by statute. In certain circumstances the insurer may be obliged, by virtue of the Fires Prevention (Metropolis) Act 1774,[964] to apply the insurance moneys to the restoration of the damaged premises. Unlike the case of reinstatement under the contract of insurance,[965] the insurer may limit his expenditure to the sum insured.

(f)   Life Insurance[966]

Life insurance   Everyone has an insurable interest in his own life, and may under **42-132** certain circumstances acquire an insurable interest in the life of another.[967] Suicide of the assured was formerly an exception to the risk under a life policy even where

---

[957] *Agra Trading Ltd v McAuslin (The Frio Chile)* [1995] 1 Lloyd's Rep. 182; cf. *Pilkington United Kingdom Ltd v CGU Insurance Plc* [2004] EWCA Civ 23, [2004] Lloyd's Rep. I.R. 891.

[958] *Glengate-KG Properties Ltd v Norwich Union Fire Insurance Society Ltd* [1996] 2 All E.R. 487.

[959] *Trade Indemnity Co v Workington Harbour Board* [1937] A.C. 1; *Seaton v Heath* [1899] 1 Q.B. 782; reversed on other grounds [1900] A.C. 135; *Re Denton's Estate* [1904] 2 Ch. 178. See also below, Ch.45.

[960] Except for the purposes of the Financial Services and Markets Act 2000, the Financial Services and Markets Act 2000 (Regulated Activities) Order 2001 (SI 2001/544) and associated statutory instruments made under the 2000 Act; see above, para.42-064. See also *Travellers Casualty & Surety Co of Europe Ltd v Commissioners of Customs and Excise* [2006] Lloyd's Rep. I.R. 63 (VAT Tribunal).

[961] The term "Guarantee Insurance" has also been used to describe a policy covering the assured's liability under a guarantee: *Global Tankers Inc v Amercoat Europa NV* [1977] 1 Lloyd's Rep. 61.

[962] See *MacGillivray on Insurance Law*, 14th edn (2018), Ch.28.

[963] See *MacGillivray on Insurance Law*, 14th edn (2018), Ch.28.

[964] s.83.

[965] See above, para.42-111.

[966] See *MacGillivray on Insurance Law*, 14th edn (2018), Ch.26.

[967] See above, para.42-008.

the contract was expressed to extend to suicide.[968] Since the abolition of the crime of suicide[969] the rule no longer applies; however, in certain circumstances suicide may still be a bar to recovery under a life policy.[970] Since the insurer is bound to pay the sum insured at some date, apart from the operation of excepted perils, life policies are frequently treated as securities.[971] The assignment of life policies is therefore a matter of some importance, and most of the cases relating to the assignment of insurance contracts have been decided in this field. The principles of assignment in the context of insurance have been discussed above.[972] In the case of life assurance, the assured also has power to nominate as beneficiary, the spouse, civil partner or children of the assured, pursuant to s.66 of the Friendly Societies Act 1974 or s.11 of the Married Women's Property Act 1882, thus creating a direct right of enforcement against the insurer, by virtue of a trust.[973]

(g)   Marine Insurance

42-133   Marine Insurance Act 1906   Marine insurance is governed by the Marine Insurance Act 1906, the general provisions of which differ in certain respects from the general law applicable to all other forms of insurance contracts. The 1906 Act applies to contracts of marine insurance, which are defined as contracts under which the insurer undertakes to indemnify the assured against "marine losses".[974] Accordingly, a contingency policy cannot be a marine policy for these purposes. Marine losses are property losses, financial losses or liabilities, which occur incidentally to a "marine adventure", namely those situations where insurable property (especially, a ship, offshore rigs or platforms, or cargo) is exposed to maritime perils.[975] As noted in this chapter, although there are many similarities between the law governing marine insurance and non-marine insurance, there are important differences. The reader should consult the standard works on the subject.[976]

---

[968]   *Beresford v Royal* [1938] A.C. 586.

[969]   Suicide Act 1961.

[970]   See above, para.42-023. cf. *Dunbar v Plant* [1997] 4 All E.R. 289 (beneficiary aided and abetted the assured's suicide).

[971]   cf. *Fuji Finance Inc v Aetna Life Insurance Co Ltd* [1997] Ch. 173.

[972]   See above, paras 42-089—42-091.

[973]   See *Rooney v Cardona, The Times,* March 4, 1999. As to civil partners, see Civil Partnership Act 2004 ss.70, 253, 261(1) and Sch.27 para.52.

[974]   Marine Insurance Act 1906 s.1.

[975]   Marine Insurance Act 1906 s.3.

[976]   Gilman and Merkin (eds), *Arnould's Law of Marine Insurance and Average*, 18th edn (2013); Ivamy (ed.), *Chalmers' Marine Insurance Act 1906*, 10th revised edn (2007); Rose, *Marine Insurance: Law and Practice*, 2nd edn (2012); Bennett, *The Law of Marine Insurance*, 2nd edn (2006).

CHAPTER 43

RESTRICTIVE AGREEMENTS AND COMPETITION

R. P. Whish

1. INTRODUCTION

Scope and plan of the chapter The way in which the common law treats agree- **43-001**
ments in restraint of trade is dealt with in Vol.I of this work.[1] The present chapter
considers the ways in which agreements may be affected by the competition law
applicable in the United Kingdom. The chapter first describes Council Regulation
1/2003, which significantly changed the way in which the European Union ("the
EU") competition rules are enforced; it then explains the relationship between the
EU competition rules and the provisions of domestic law. The competition rules of
the EU themselves are described in section 2 of this chapter, and the domestic
system of law contained in the Competition Act 1998 is explained in section 3. Brief
mention will also be made in section 3 of the Enterprise Act 2002, as amended by
the Enterprise and Regulatory Reform Act 2013, which provides for the possibility of "market investigations" by the Competition and Markets Authority and for
criminal sanctions, including imprisonment, to be imposed upon individuals
responsible for cartel activity.

---

[1] Vol.I, paras 16-106 et seq.

43-002   **Council Regulation 1/2003**   The way in which arts 101 and 102[2] of the Treaty on the Functioning of the European Union ("TFEU") are applied in practice was fundamentally changed as a result of the application of Regulation 1/2003 from May 1, 2004.[3] The European Commission has since 1962 been the principal institution charged with the enforcement of the competition provisions of the TFEU as a result of powers conferred upon it by Council Regulation 17.[4] That Regulation provided for the notification of agreements to the Commission which had exclusive competence to grant an "individual exemption" under art.101(3) to an agreement that infringed art.101(1). However, it became increasingly clear that a centralised system of enforcement was no longer appropriate for the effective application of the competition rules, especially with the enlargement of the European Union to 25 Member States on May 1, 2004 (and subsequently to 28). Regulation 1/2003, which also applies from May 1, 2004, introduced significant changes to the enforcement of arts 101 and 102. The system of notification of agreements for individual exemption was abolished and in its place art.101, in its entirety, and art.102 are directly applicable without prior decision of the Commission. The Commission shares the competence to apply arts 101 and 102 with national competition authorities and national courts.[5]

43-003   **Relationship between the EU competition rules and the provisions of domestic law**   One of the main principles behind the reforms leading to the enactment of the Competition Act 1998 in the UK was the desire to harmonise domestic law with the EU competition rules in order to reduce the costs incurred by the business community in complying with the previous domestic regime, which was formulated in very different terms from arts 101 and 102. The extent to which the provisions of the Competition Act must be interpreted consistently with EU law is considered below at paras 43-140 and 43-142. Many agreements which fall within art.101 TFEU will also infringe the Ch.I prohibition in the 1998 Act; similarly conduct which is unlawful under art.102 of the Treaty will also fall within the Ch.II prohibition. There may, however, be a small number of cases where, notwithstanding the modelling of the Ch.I and II prohibitions upon arts 101 and 102, different outcomes would be achieved under the EU and the domestic rules. With effect from May 1, 2004, art.3 of Regulation 1/2003 determines the relationship between the EU competition rules and the provisions of domestic competition law. Where national competition authorities and national courts apply national competition law to agreements and conduct that may affect trade between Member States, they must also apply arts 101 and 102.[6] If an agreement affects trade between Member States but does not fall within art.101(1) or satisfies the conditions in art.101(3), it is not possible to apply stricter domestic competition law to it.[7] However, where conduct affects trade between Member States but does not infringe art.102, Member States are not precluded from imposing stricter national competition laws or sanctions on

---

[2]   Arts 101 and 102 TFEU were previously arts 85 and 86 of the European Economic Community Treaty and subsequently arts 81 and 82 of the European Community Treaty. Much of the relevant case law and literature, of course, refers to the articles by their former numbers; however, the text below will always refer to the current ones.

[3]   [2003] O.J. L1/1.

[4]   [1962] O.J. 204/62, [1962] O.J.Sp.Ed. 87.

[5]   See below, paras 43-065—43-076.

[6]   Regulation 1/2003 art.3(1).

[7]   Regulation 1/2003 art.3(2).

such conduct.[8] It is also possible for a Member State to apply stricter national rules, both in relation to agreements and to conduct, where those rules predominantly pursue an objective different from that pursued by arts 101 and 102 of the Treaty.[9] Clearly the substance of this paragraph may require fundamental change following withdrawal by the United Kingdom from the European Union pursuant to the referendum of June 23, 2016.[10]

2.   COMPETITION RULES UNDER THE TFEU

(a)   In General

Purpose of this section   The purpose of this section is to give a brief outline of the rules on competition law under the TFEU insofar as they may affect contractual rights and obligations. Specialised works should be consulted for a fuller treatment.[11]   **43-004**

Article 101   The principal provision of the TFEU likely to affect contracts is art.101[12] which has been part of the law of the United Kingdom since January 1, 1973.[13] Article 101(1) prohibits all agreements between undertakings, decisions by associations of undertakings and concerted practices which may affect trade between Member States and which have as their object or effect the prevention, restriction or distortion of competition within the internal market. Article 101(2) provides that any agreement or decision prohibited under art.101(1) "shall be automatically void".[14] Article 101(3) provides that, in certain circumstances, the prohibition in art.101(1) "may be declared inapplicable" either to individual agreements on their particular merits[15] or by the application of block exemptions covering certain common types of agreement.[16]   **43-005**

Article 102   Contractual obligations may also be affected by art.102 TFEU which applies to one or more undertakings which hold a dominant position within the internal market and which prohibits any abuse by such an undertaking of its dominant position, in so far as it may affect trade between Member States. Certain terms in agreements between dominant firms and their customers have been held to constitute abusive conduct and are therefore unenforceable by the dominant firm.[17]   **43-006**

Direct effect   Both arts 101 and 102 have direct effect,[18] which means that they create rights which can be enforced in the national courts of the Member States and   **43-007**

---

8   Regulation 1/2003 art.3(3).
9   Regulation 1/2003 art.3(3).
10   For a general note on "Brexit", see Vol.I, paras 1-014—1-018.
11   e.g. Bellamy and Child, *European Union Law of Competition*, 8th edn (2018). For comparative treatment of EU and UK competition law see Whish and Bailey, *Competition Law*, 9th edn (2018).
12   See below, paras 43-011 et seq.
13   European Communities Act 1972 s.2.
14   See below, para.43-068.
15   See below, para.43-032.
16   See below, paras 43-033—43-034.
17   See below, paras 43-061—43-064.
18   *BRT v SABAM* EU:C:1974:6, [1974] E.C.R. 51, 62; European Communities Act 1972 s.2(1).

which those courts must protect.[19] The implications of the direct effect of TFEU provisions are discussed below.[20]

43-008 **Principal sources of law** Apart from the relevant provisions of the Treaty, there is a considerable body of secondary legislation, in particular the block exemptions[21] promulgated by the EU institutions.[22] The European Commission, which, together with the national competition authorities and national courts, is responsible for the enforcement of the competition law provisions of the Treaty, also publishes official notices and announcements giving guidance on matters of interpretation.[23] In addition to this legislation there are the decisions of the European Commission concerning particular agreements and conduct, and the jurisprudence of the General Court (formerly the Court of First Instance of the European Communities) and the European Court of Justice.[24]

43-009 **Supremacy of EU law** Generally EU law takes precedence over the domestic law of the United Kingdom.[25] It follows that in certain circumstances rights which would be valid under domestic law may not be exercised where such exercise would be contrary to the provisions and objectives of the Treaty.[26] In *Irish Sugar v Commission*[27] the General Court stressed that it was immaterial whether the grant of the price rebates in dispute in that case was compatible with Irish law given the supremacy of EU law and the direct effect of art.102. The English courts take judicial notice of the TFEU, the contents of the *Official Journal* of the European Union[28] and the judgments of the General Court and the Court of Justice.[29]

43-010 **European Economic Area** The European Economic Area, first established in 1994, now comprises all the 28 states of the European Union and the EFTA states other than Switzerland (namely Iceland, Norway and Liechtenstein). The aim of the EEA Agreement is, inter alia, to ensure the uniform application of competition law throughout the EEA, and to this end art.53(1), (2) and (3) of the EEA Agreement in effect reproduces art.101(1), (2) and (3) TFEU and art.54 of the EEA Agree-

---

19 For the English courts' analysis of this obligation see *Garden Cottage Foods v Milk Marketing Board* [1984] A.C. 130, HL; *Bourgoin v Ministry of Agriculture* [1986] Q.B. 716, CA; *R. v Secretary of State for Transport Ex p. Factortame Ltd (No.2)* [1991] 1 A.C. 603.

20 See below, paras 43-065—43-071.

21 See below, paras 43-033—43-034.

22 For a description of the EU institutions and of the different forms of secondary legislation see Hartley, *The Foundations of European Union Law*, 8th edn (2014).

23 The relevant legislation, notices, etc. can be found in *Butterworths Competition Law Handbook*, 24th edn (2018). The European Commission also issues an *Annual Report of Competition Policy*, available on its website: *http://europa.eu.int/comm/competition/annual_reports*.

24 The General Court was established in 1988 and hears appeals from Commission decisions in, inter alia, competition cases. Appeals from the General Court on points of law are made to the Court of Justice. Decisions of these courts are binding on the English courts: European Communities Act 1972 s.3(1) (as amended by the European Communities (Amendment) Act 1986).

25 European Communities Act 1972 ss.2(1) and 3(1). For the EU point of view see *Simmenthal* EU:C:1978:49, [1978] E.C.R. 629. For the English courts' approach see *Ex p. Factortame*, above.

26 See below, para.43-054.

27 EU:T:1999:246, [1999] E.C.R. II-2969.

28 Regulations, directives, notices and Commission decisions are generally published in the *Official Journal*.

29 European Communities Act 1972 s.3(2) (as amended by the European Communities (Amendment) Act 1986).

ment reproduces art.102 TFEU. Other provisions of the EEA Agreement contain procedural and substantive rules which mirror the existing EU secondary legislation in the competition field. The EEA Agreement also provides for the establishment of the EFTA Surveillance Authority which has similar powers to the Commission and is subject to review by the EFTA Court of Justice. Article 56 of the EEA Agreement provides complex rules for the allocation of jurisdiction between the Commission and the EFTA Surveillance Authority in competition cases depending on the effect that the conduct under scrutiny has on trade between the EU and EFTA. A full analysis of the scope of the EEA Agreement is beyond the scope of this work[30] but practitioners should bear in mind the possible application of EU competition law to contracts affecting the above-named territories.

(b)   Article 101(1)

Article 101(1)   Article 101(1) provides that: **43-011**
"The following shall be prohibited as incompatible with the internal market: all agreements between undertakings, decisions by associations of undertakings and concerted practices which may affect trade between Member States and which have as their object or effect the prevention, restriction or distortion of competition within the internal market, and in particular those which:
   (a)   directly or indirectly fix purchase or selling prices or any other trading conditions;
   (b)   limit or control production, markets, technical development, or investment;
   (c)   share markets or sources of supply;
   (d)   apply dissimilar conditions to equivalent transactions with other trading parties, thereby placing them at a competitive disadvantage;
   (e)   make the conclusion of contracts subject to acceptance by the other parties of supplementary obligations which, by their nature or according to commercial usage, have no connection with the subject of such contracts."

The elements in the test   In deciding whether a particular transaction falls within   **43-012**
art.101(1) one must consider: (i) whether there exists an "agreement" or "concerted practice" made between, or operated by, "undertakings", or a "decision" by an association of undertakings; (ii) whether competition within the internal market may be prevented, restricted or distorted; and (iii) whether there is an actual or potential effect on trade between Member States. It is also necessary to consider whether the effect on competition and on trade between Member States is appreciable.[31]

Undertaking   A "functional" approach must be taken to the meaning of the term   **43-013**
"undertaking": a legal entity may be acting as an undertaking when performing some functions but not when performing others.[32] The term "undertaking" is a wide one covering almost any legal or natural person engaged in an economic activity, regardless of its legal status and the way in which it is financed.[33] It is capable of

---

[30]   For discussion of the EEA rules see Bellamy and Child, *European Union Law of Competition*, 8th edn (2018), paras 1.077–1.087.
[31]   See below, paras 43-024—43-027.
[32]   See, e.g. *SELEX Sistemi Integrati SpA v Commission* EU:C:2009:191, [2009] E.C.R. I-2207.
[33]   *Höfner & Elser v Macrotron* EU:C:1991:161, [1991] E.C.R. I-1979; *Enichem v Commission* EU:T:1991:74, [1991] E.C.R. II-1623, para.235; *Commission v Italy* EU:C:1998:303, [1998] E.C.R. I-3851 where the Court added that any activity consisting in offering goods or services on a given market is an economic activity.

covering public and private companies, partnerships, trade associations,[34] individuals,[35] professionals,[36] and sole traders.[37] An undertaking need not be a profit-making body.[38] Employees are not undertakings[39]; in *Becu*[40] the Court of Justice confirmed that employees are incorporated into the economic unit of the undertaking they work for and so are not themselves undertakings within the meaning of EU competition law. A commercial agent is capable of acting as an undertaking, though an agreement between a principal and a "genuine" commercial agent will normally fall outside art.101(1).[41] So far as Member States[42] are concerned, a distinction must be drawn between the situation where the State acts in the exercise of its powers as a public authority or carries on non-economic activities (in relation to which it is not to be treated as an undertaking)[43] and where it is engaged in economic activities of an industrial or commercial nature (in relation to which it is covered by art.101).[44]

43-014   **Parents and subsidiaries**   Agreements between a parent company and its subsidiary, or between members of a group of companies under common control ordinarily fall outside art.101(1).[45] But the mere fact of common ownership is not decisive as account must be taken of the actual nature of the relationship between the companies and in particular whether they have economic independence or pursue the same market strategy as determined by the parent company.[46] In *Hydrotherm v Compact*[47] the Court of Justice stated that the term "undertaking" must be understood as "designating an economic unit ... even if in law that economic unit consists of several persons, natural or legal". Therefore, where a number of parties to an agreement have identical interests and are controlled by the same person, who also participates in the agreement, those parties can be treated as a single undertaking.[48]

---

34   *Luttikhuis v Coberco* EU:C:1995:434, [1995] E.C.R. I-4515 (dairy cooperative); *Dansk Pelsdyravlerforening v Commission* EU:T:1992:79, [1992] E.C.R. II-1931 (fur traders association). A body can be both an undertaking and an association of undertakings: *Frubo v Commission* EU:C:1975:61, [1975] E.C.R. 563.

35   See, e.g. *RAI v UNITEL* [1978] O.J. L157/39 (opera singer).

36   See, e.g. *Wouters v Algemene Raad van de Nederlandse Orde van Advocaten* EU:C:2002:98, [2002] E.C.R. I-1577, paras 45–49.

37   *CNSD* [1993] O.J. L203/27 (customs agents); *COAPI* [1995] O.J. L122/37 (industrial property agents).

38   *Van Landewyck v Commission* EU:C:1980:248, [1980] E.C.R. 3125, para.88.

39   *Suiker Unie v Commission* EU:C:1975:174, [1975] E.C.R. 1663, 2007, para.539.

40   EU:C:1999:419, [1999] E.C.R. I-5665.

41   *Suiker Unie*, above, paras 538–540. See below, para.43-059.

42   *Diego Calì & Figli v Servici ecologici Porto di Genova* EU:C:1997:160, [1997] E.C.R. I-1547.

43   See, e.g. *SAT Eurocontrol v Commission* EU:C:1994:7, [1994] E.C.R. I-43 (body set up under international law to levy air traffic control charges not an undertaking); *Poucet* EU:C:1993:63, [1993] E.C.R. I-637 (body administering state sickness benefit not an undertaking); *Diego Calì & Figli*, above (body providing harbour pollution control services not an undertaking); *FENIN v Commission* EU:C:2006:453, [2006] E.C.R. I-6295 (organisations responsible for operation of the Spanish health service not undertakings).

44   See, e.g. *IAZ v Commission* EU:C:1983:310, [1983] E.C.R. 3369 (water supply companies)

45   *Viho Europe BV v Commission* EU:T:1995:3, [1995] E.C.R. II-17 upheld on appeal by the Court of Justice: EU:C:1996:405, [1996] E.C.R. I-5457.

46   *Bodson v Pompes Funèbres* EU:C:1988:225, [1988] E.C.R. 2479, para.20.

47   EU:C:1984:271, [1984] E.C.R. 2999, 3016, para.11.

48   This is important in applying the block exemptions, some of which stipulate that agreements covered must have only two parties.

Agreements The term "agreement" in art.101(1) is not confined to legally bind- **43-015** ing contracts but covers any morally binding commitment[49]: it is sufficient if the undertakings have expressed their joint intention to conduct themselves in the market in a particular way.[50] An agreement may be written or oral or inferred from the circumstances and can consist in a continuing course of business dealings between the parties.[51] The leading case on the consensual nature of the conduct required to infer an agreement is *Bayer v Commission*.[52] The General Court stressed that to support the finding of an agreement for the purposes of art.101, there must be evidence of "the subjective element that characterises the very concept of an agreement, that is to say a concurrence of wills between economic operators on the implementation of a policy, the pursuit of an objective, or the adoption of a given line of conduct on the market". An agreement between undertakings may be made on the undertaking's behalf by an employee acting in the course of his employ- ment despite the ignorance of more senior management.[53] A series of agreements can be read together as one agreement.[54] The incorporation of a particular term in an agreement can be inferred from the surrounding circumstances,[55] but the plac- ing of new orders by a customer does not necessarily indicate acceptance of a new policy introduced by the supplier. In *Bayer*[56] the General Court rejected the Com- mission's argument that the mere continuation of commercial relations with the manufacturer when it had adopted a policy designed to inhibit exports amounted to acquiescence by the wholesalers in that policy so as to create an agreement between them. The evidence showed rather that the wholesalers had actively tried to circumvent the supplier's policy by other means. However, the fact that a sup- plier has not taken steps to enforce a clause imposing an export ban or that a customer is acting contrary to its best interests in agreeing to such a clause is not sufficient to remove the clause from the ambit of art.101.[57]

"Horizontal" and "vertical" agreements The competition affected by prohibited **43-016** conduct may be competition between the parties to the agreement themselves. This will be the case in a "horizontal" agreement where the parties are active at the same level of production or supply, for example where a number of manufacturers agree on the prices they will charge to their respective customers. But art.101(1) is also capable of applying to "vertical" agreements where the parties are at different levels of production or supply and the competition affected is between them and third parties.[58] For example, where a manufacturer concludes an exclusive supply and

---

[49] *Van Landewyck v Commission* EU:C:1980:248, [1980] E.C.R. 3125, 3250. But an agreement concluded in the context of collective negotiations between management and labour falls outside art.101(1): see *Brentjens* EU:C:1999:434, [1999] E.C.R. I-6025.

[50] *Hercules v Commission* EU:T:1991:75, [1991] E.C.R. II-1711, para.256.

[51] *Konica* [1988] 4 C.M.L.R. 848, para.40.

[52] EU:T:2000:242, [2000] E.C.R. II-3383, upheld on appeal, EU:C:2004:2, [2004] E.C.R. I-23. For further examples of cases where the General Court concluded that the evidence did not support the inference of an agreement see *JCB v Commission* EU:T:2004:3, [2004] E.C.R. II-49; *General Motors v Commission* EU:T:2003:275, [2003] E.C.R. II-4491; *Volkswagen v Commission* EU:C:2006:460, [2006] E.C.R. I-6585.

[53] *Musique Diffusion Française v Commission* EU:C:1983:158, [1983] E.C.R. 1825 at 1903.

[54] *ENI/Montedison* [1989] 4 C.M.L.R. 444.

[55] *Sandoz v Commission* EU:C:1990:6, [1990] E.C.R. I-45.

[56] EU:T:2000:242, [2000] E.C.R. II-3383.

[57] *Sandoz*, above.

[58] *Consten and Grundig v Commission* EU:C:1966:41, [1966] E.C.R. 299 (affirmed many times).

purchasing agreement with his dealer, the competition affected is between that manufacturer and other manufacturers who wish to supply that dealer, and between that dealer and other dealers who wish to obtain supplies from that manufacturer.

43-017   Concerted practices   The concept of "concerted practices" is very wide and covers forms of cooperation that fall short of an agreement.[59] It denotes "any form of co-ordination by undertakings which, without having reached the stage where an agreement properly so called has been concluded, knowingly substitutes practical cooperation between them for the risks of competition".[60] A concerted practice does not require a plan to be worked out nor must it have been put into effect for art.101(1) to apply.[61] Parallel conduct by undertakings does not necessarily give rise to a presumption of collusion if another plausible explanation for such parallelism can be found, for example in the characteristics of the market.[62] But where there is parallel conduct and evidence of meetings between the parties then a concerted practice will often be inferred.[63]

43-018   Decisions of associations of undertakings   These include the agreements entered into by and the constitution of, or other rules governing, the association, decisions binding upon the members and non-binding recommendations.[64]

43-019   Prevention, restriction or distortion of competition   The requirement that the conduct must have as its object or effect the prevention, restriction or distortion of competition lies at the heart of art.101. In applying this test one must bear in mind the dual purpose of the competition provisions of the Treaty. First, the Treaty aims to promote competition as the means of bringing about increased efficiency, wider choice, better products, greater innovation and lower prices, thereby ensuring the optimal allocation of resources. The examples set out in art.101(1) of the kinds of agreements likely to be prohibited illustrate the classic forms of anti-competitive behaviour: price fixing, market sharing and agreements to limit production.[65]

43-020   Creation of a single market   Secondly, the competition provisions of the Treaty should help the creation of a single market by eliminating trade barriers between the Member States and encouraging the free movement of goods and services.[66] EU law is therefore particularly concerned to proscribe conduct which has the effect of re-erecting national boundaries or impeding the free flow of goods or services. Any

---

[59]   The leading cases are *ICI v Commission* EU:C:1972:70, [1972] E.C.R. 619; *Suiker Unie v Commission* EU:C:1975:174, [1975] E.C.R. 1663; *Musique Diffusion Française v Commission* EU:C:1983:158, [1983] E.C.R. 1825; *Hercules v Commission* EU:T:1991:75, [1991] E.C.R. II-1711 and the other appeals in the *Polypropylene* proceedings; *T-Mobile Netherlands BV v Raad van bestur van de Nederlandse Mededingsautoriteit* EU:C:2009:343, [2009] E.C.R. I-4529. Conduct can be *both* an agreement *and* a concerted practice: *Hercules*, para.43-015.

[60]   *ICI*, above, at 655, para.64. This formulation was reaffirmed in the *PVC Cartel II* EU:T:1999:80, [1999] E.C.R. II-931, para.720.

[61]   *Suiker Unie v Commission* EU:C:1975:174, [1975] E.C.R. 1663 at 1942.

[62]   *Ahlström Oy v Commission* EU:C:1993:120, [1993] E.C.R. I-1307.

[63]   e.g. *Società Italiano Vetro v Commission* EU:T:1992:38, [1992] E.C.R. II-1403.

[64]   At least if a significant number of the members in fact comply with the recommendation: *Van Landewyck v Commission* EU:C:1980:248, [1980] E.C.R. 3125, 3250.

[65]   The categories of anti-competitive agreements set out in the subparas of art.101(1) are illustrative, not exhaustive.

[66]   See, e.g. *Consten and Grundig v Commission* EU:C:1966:41, [1966] E.C.R. 299, 340.

contractual terms which prevent or limit the export of goods to other Member States should be scrutinised very carefully to ensure that they are compatible with art.101.[67] The enlargement of the European Union on May 1, 2004 and again subsequently, with the possibility of further enlargement to follow, means that single market integration will continue to influence the way in which the EU competition rules are applied.

The test to be applied   The test for determining whether conduct has as its object   **43-021**
or effect[68] the prevention, restriction or distortion of competition has been laid down in a number of leading cases, in particular in *Société Technique Minière*[69]; *Delimitis v Henninger Bräu*[70]; *Wouters*[71]; and *Cartes Bancaires*.[72] Generally speaking, the first step is to determine the object of the agreement. If it is not clear that the object is to restrict competition, one must then analyse the effect of the agreement within its legal and economic context; that is, assess the way in which competition would occur in the absence of the agreement and consider how this is likely to have been affected by the operation of the agreement. Among the many relevant factors for working out whether an agreement has a restrictive effect are the nature and quantity of the products covered by the agreement, the position and importance of the parties in the market for the products concerned, the isolated nature of the agreement or, alternatively, whether it forms part of a network of similar agreements.[73] Other material factors include the existence of any intellectual property rights and the number and size of competing undertakings.

The "object" of the agreement   The purpose of the agreement must be   **43-022**
ascertained objectively and it is not necessary to show that the parties' subjectively intended to restrict competition.[74] Some kinds of agreement have been held by the courts to have "by their very nature" the object of restricting competition. The question to be asked is whether the agreement "reveals in itself a sufficient degree of harm to competition".[75] Such agreements include horizontal agreements[76] to fix prices, to limit production or to partition markets and vertical agreements[77] imposing export bans or requiring the buyer to re-sell the products at fixed or minimum prices. Provided that such agreements have an appreciable effect on competition and affect trade between Member States they will fall within art.101(1).[78]

---

[67]   See below, paras 43-040 et seq.
[68]   The terms "object" or "effect" are disjunctive rather than cumulative, so that the existence of either is sufficient: see *Technique Minière*, below.
[69]   *Société Technique Minière v Maschinenbau Ulm* EU:C:1966:38, [1966] E.C.R. 235.
[70]   *Delimitis v Henninger Bräu* EU:C:1991:91, [1991] E.C.R. I-935. For an analysis of the application of art.101 to a distribution agreement covering non-EEA states see *Javico International v Yves Saint Laurent Parfums* EU:C:1998:173, [1998] E.C.R. I-1983.
[71]   EU:C:2002:98, [2002] E.C.R. I-1577.
[72]   EU:C 2014:2204.
[73]   The *Delimitis* case restated the law on the relevance of the existence of a network of agreements; cf. the earlier case of *Brasserie De Haecht v Wilkin* EU:C:1967:54, [1967] E.C.R. 407.
[74]   e.g. *IAZ v Commission* EU:C:1983:310, [1983] E.C.R. 3369.
[75]   *Cartes Bancaires v Commission* EU:C:2014:2204.
[76]   See below, para.43-035.
[77]   See below, paras 43-038 et seq.
[78]   For "appreciability" see below, paras 43-024—43-026; for effect on trade between Member States see below, paras 43-027—43-030.

43-023 **The "effect" of the agreement** If a simple analysis of the terms of the agreement is not sufficient to determine whether it has or may have an anti-competitive object, one must look at the consequences (or potential consequences)[79] of the operation of the agreement to see whether it has an anti-competitive effect. One must consider how the parties would have been expected to act in the absence of the agreement: has their freedom to determine the terms and conditions on which they supply their goods or services been curtailed in any way; has their choice of potential suppliers or potential customers been narrowed by the agreement; is it more difficult for other manufacturers to start supplying goods or services which compete with those offered by the parties to the agreement? In short, is the agreement likely to alter the commercial decisions of the parties to the agreement or of third parties[80] when they respond to changing market conditions? It should be added that a contractual restriction does not necessarily result in a restriction of competition; account should be taken of the actual conditions in which the agreement operates, the products or services covered by the agreement and the actual structure of the market to properly analyse its effect thereon.[81] The economic analysis required in the application of this test may appear somewhat daunting. In practice, guidelines have been established by the jurisprudence of the Courts of the European Union and the Commission in respect of the application of art.101 to certain categories of agreement and certain contractual terms. In particular valuable guidance can be derived from the Commission's Guidelines on the Application of Article 101(3) of the Treaty[82]; Guidelines on Vertical Restraints[83]; Guidelines on Horizontal Co-operation Agreements[84]; and Guidelines on the Application of Article 101 TFEU to technology transfer agreements[85].

43-024 **Requirement of appreciable effect** In *Völk v Vervaecke*[86] the Court of Justice stated that art.101(1) is not contravened if the agreement has only an insignificant effect on competition. In that case the parties to an agreement for the distribution of washing machines had only a 0.2 per cent share of the market and the agreement escaped the prohibition as the agreement was treated as de minimis. Subsequently in *Expedia Inc v Autorité de la Concurrence*[87] the Court of Justice held that any agreement that has an appreciable effect on trade between Member States and that "restricts competition by object" has an appreciable effect on competition.

43-025 **Notice concerning agreements of minor importance** Following the decision in *Völk*, the Commission published a Notice giving guidance on the thresholds below which an agreement would be considered de minimis. The Commission's current

---

[79] This is especially relevant in joint venture cases; see below, para.43-036. More generally, see, e.g. *Javico International v Yves Saint Laurent Parfums* EU:C:1998:173, [1998] E.C.R. I-1983.

[80] e.g. in exclusive distribution or licensing agreements which foreclose outlets to competing manufacturers' goods.

[81] See, e.g. *European Night Services v Commission* EU:T:1998:198, [1998] E.C.R. II-3141, para.136.

[82] [2004] O.J. C101/97.

[83] [2010] O.J. C130/1.

[84] [2011] O.J. C11/1.

[85] [2014] O.J. C89/3.

[86] EU:C:1969:35, [1969] E.C.R. 295.

[87] EU:C:2012:795.

Notice on Agreements of Minor Importance was adopted in June 2014.[88] It provides that the Commission does not consider horizontal agreements between firms with a market share of 10 per cent or less, or vertical agreements between firms each with a market share of 15 per cent or less, to restrict competition to an appreciable extent. However, consistently with the judgment in *Expedia*, this relaxed approach does not apply to restrictions of competition by object such as horizontal or vertical price fixing, market sharing or the imposition of export bans on distributors. If an agreement falls below the de minimis thresholds, the possibility remains that there might be an infringement of national law.

Relevance of networks of agreements   Generally speaking, when considering   **43-026** whether the effect of an agreement is likely to be appreciable, one must consider whether it is one of a network of similar agreements in operation in the relevant market.[89] For example, when assessing whether an agreement between a manufacturer and one of his distributors in the European Union has an appreciable effect on competition or on trade between Member States, one must look not only at the market share and turnover of the parties to that particular agreement but also of the other dealers in that manufacturer's network who are party to agreements in similar terms. Where the industry in which the agreement operates is characterised by a series of networks of restrictive agreements,[90] account should be taken of the proportion of the market covered by such agreements and their duration when assessing the extent of the effect of an agreement.[91] The Commission's Notice on Agreements of Minor Importance states that agreements between firms with a market share of 5 per cent or less are not generally considered to significantly contribute to a cumulative foreclosure effect; and that such an effect is unlikely to exist if less than 30 per cent of the market is covered by parallel networks of agreements having similar effects.

Effect on trade between Member States   Anti-competitive conduct does not fall   **43-027** within the prohibition in art.101(1) unless it may appreciably affect trade between Member States.[92] However, this requirement has been widely interpreted by the Commission and the Courts of the EU. Thus many agreements between parties in a single Member State which concern the supply of goods within that same state satisfy the test. The Treaty does not require that every restrictive clause in an agreement should be shown to have an effect on trade before it falls within art.101(1), provided that the agreement as a whole satisfies the test.[93] The Commission has published Guidelines on the effect on trade concept in arts 101 and 102 TFEU.[94]

---

88   [2014] O.J. C291/1.
89   *Brasserie De Haecht v Wilkin* EU:C:1967:54, [1967] E.C.R. 407. For two further cases which show how the network effect of agreements should be analysed see the Court of Justice's judgment in *Neste Markkinointi Oy v Yötuuli Ky* EU:C:2000:679, [2000] E.C.R. I-11121 dealing with a network of petrol station exclusive purchasing agreements.
90   e.g. brewery tied house estates, petrol solus agreements, selective distribution of luxury perfumes.
91   *Delimitis v Henninger Bräu* EU:C:1991:91, [1991] E.C.R. I-935; *VGB v Commission* EU:T:1997:70, [1997] E.C.R. II-759.
92   The requirement is satisfied even if the effect is to increase trade since the aim of the Treaty is to maintain undistorted competition: *Consten and Grundig v Commission* EU:C:1966:41, [1966] E.C.R. 299, 341.
93   *Windsurfing International v Commission* EU:C:1986:75, [1986] E.C.R. 611; affirmed in *VGB v Commission* EU:T:1997:70, [1997] E.C.R. II-759.
94   [2014] O.J. C291/1.

43-028 **"Direct or indirect, actual or potential"**   Conduct affects trade between Member States if it is possible to foresee with a sufficient degree of probability that it may have an influence, direct or indirect, actual or potential, on the pattern of trade between Member States.[95] Conduct will also be held to affect trade if it alters or has "repercussions" on the competitive structure of the market.[96] It is not necessary to show that the conduct has *in fact* affected trade; it is enough that it is *capable* of having an effect.[97] Clearly, any agreement which directly or indirectly restricts exports between Member States will satisfy the test. Agreements which cover the whole territory of a single Member State usually have the necessary effect, because they tend to reinforce national boundaries and hinder the economic inter-penetration which the Treaty is designed to realise.[98] There have been some cases in which the Courts of the European Union and the Commission have concluded that an agreement had no appreciable effect on trade between Member States. In *Bagnasco v BPN and Carige*[99] the Court of Justice held that an agreement between banks in Italy setting the terms on which they offered current accounts to custom-ers fell outside art.101(1) because the economic activities in question had very limited impact on trade. This was followed by the decision of the Commission in *Dutch Acceptance Giro System*[100] where it found that the agreement did have an ap-preciable effect on competition but did not appreciably affect trade between Member States because the banking services were concentrated on domestic activity.

43-029 **Undertakings outside the EU**   Agreements between undertakings outside the EU may fall within art.101 if the agreement is implemented within the internal market[101] or if it produces foreseeable, immediate and substantial effects there.[102]

43-030 **Agreements concerning trade outside the EU**   Agreements between undertak-ings concerning trade outside the EU may fall within art.101 if they produce an ap-preciable effect both on competition and on trade between Member States.[103]

(c)   Article 101(3)

43-031 **Criteria of article 101(3)**   If conduct falls within art.101(1), it is always open to the parties to argue that their agreement fulfils the criteria contained in art.101(3).[104] Any agreement which satisfies all the conditions laid down in art.101(3) is covered by that provision. Article 101(3) provides that the prohibition may be "declared inapplicable" to an agreement which:

---

[95]   *Société Technique Minière v Maschinenbau Ulm* EU:C:1966:38, [1966] E.C.R. 235, 249 and 251 and affirmed many times.
[96]   This formulation of the test is sometimes used in cases under art.102, e.g. *Commercial Solvents v Commission* EU:C:1974:18, [1974] E.C.R. 223, 252.
[97]   *Miller v Commission* EU:C:1978:19, [1978] E.C.R. 131, 151.
[98]   See, e.g. *Commission v Italy* EU:C:1998:303, [1998] E.C.R. I-3851.
[99]   EU:C:1999:12, [1999] E.C.R. I-135.
[100]   [1999] O.J. L271/28.
[101]   *Wood Pulp I* EU:C:1988:447, [1988] E.C.R. 5193.
[102]   *Intel Corp Inc v European Commission* (C-413/14 P) EU:C:2017:632, [2017] 5 C.M.L.R. 18.
[103]   *Javico International v Yves Saint Laurent Parfums* EU:C:1998:173, [1998] E.C.R. I-1983.
[104]   *Matra Hachette v Commission* EU:T:1994:89, [1994] E.C.R. II-595, para.85.

"... contributes to improving the production or distribution of goods or to promoting technical or economic progress while allowing consumers a fair share of the benefit, and which does not:

(a) impose upon the undertakings concerned restrictions which are not indispensable to the attainment of these objectives;

(b) afford such undertakings the possibility of eliminating competition in respect of a substantial part of the products in question."

Agreements likely to satisfy article 101(3)   All four criteria must be satisfied in order for art.101(3) to be applicable.[105] The Commission has published Guidelines on the application of art.81(3) of the Treaty (art.101(3) TFEU).[106] Since May 1, 2004 Regulation 1/2003 abolished the system of notification of agreements to the Commission for individual exemption under art.101(3) and the exclusive competence of the Commission to make decisions under that provision in individual cases; instead the parties to agreements and their advisers are expected to assess the application of art.101(3) themselves.   **43-032**

Block exemptions   The Commission is empowered to issue block exemptions in the form of Commission regulations.[107] These regulations identify for certain common types of agreements the contractual obligations which fulfil the criteria set out in art.101(3) and which are therefore entitled to the benefit of exemption. Agreements which do not contain restrictions going beyond the terms permitted by the block exemption may automatically be treated as valid and enforceable.[108] Agreements which contain restrictions beyond those in the block exemption may still satisfy the criteria of art.101(3), but an individual assessment will have to be made by the parties and their legal advisers in each case. The older block exemptions were very specific as to the clauses which could benefit from the block exemption; by contrast the newer block exemptions such as Regulations 330/2010, 1217/2010, 1218/2010 and 316/2014 on vertical agreements, research and development agreements, specialisation agreements and technology transfer agreements respectively adopt a less proscriptive approach, simply setting out what is not covered. Another key feature of these regulations is the use of a market share cap to determine eligibility of agreements for block exemption. The Commission and the national competition authorities have the power to withdraw the benefit of the block exemption from agreements which have effects incompatible with the criteria of art.101(3).   **43-033**

Block exemptions currently in force   At present there are block exemptions[109] covering the following types of agreement: **43-034**

---

[105] See, e.g. *Métropole Télévision SA v Commission* EU:T:1996:99, [1996] E.C.R. II-649.

[106] [2004] O.J. C101/97.

[107] The vires for the main block exemptions are Council Regulation 19/65 (exclusive dealing agreements and bilateral licences of intellectual property, amended by Regulation 1215/99 [1999] O.J. L148/1 to extend the delegated legislative powers of the Commission which enabled it to adopt a wider block exemption on vertical agreements) and Regulation 2821/71 (agreements on uniform standards, specialisation agreements and research and development agreements).

[108] Note that if the agreement falls within an EU block exemption it will automatically enjoy parallel exemption from the Ch.I prohibition in UK competition law by virtue of the Competition Act 1998 s.10: see below, para.43-114.

[109] The texts of the block exemptions, as amended, and the Commission Notices giving guidance on the interpretation of certain regulations, are printed in *Butterworths Competition Law Handbook*,

- vertical agreements[110];
- distribution of motor vehicles[111];
- research and development agreements[112];
- specialisation agreements[113];
- shipping agreements[114];
- technology transfer agreements.[115]

(d)   Application of Art.101 to Specific Agreements

43-035   **Typical horizontal agreements**   The following constitute some of the most frequently encountered kinds of horizontal agreement in relation to which the application of art.101 needs to be carefully considered, in particular because very substantial fines can be imposed on the members of horizontal cartels, who may also be sued by victims of such cartels for damages[116]:

(i)   *Price fixing*   Since price is the main instrument of competition, art.101(1)(a) expressly prohibits agreements which "directly or indirectly fix purchase or selling prices or any other trading conditions". There have been many cases in which horizontal price-fixing agreements have been condemned and in which very substantial fines have been imposed. Price fixing in any form is caught, including, for example, agreements on the level of discounts, prior consultation on price lists, agreements on recommended prices, maximum prices and collective resale price maintenance. Price fixing in the services sector is unlawful as well as in the goods sector. Buyers' cartels can be caught as well as those of sellers.[117]

(ii)   *Market sharing*   Prominent among agreements which fall within art.101(1)(b) and (c) are horizontal agreements between competitors to refrain from supplying into each other's markets. Such agreements frustrate the aims of the TFEU since they often divide up supplies along the lines of national boundaries and thus directly inhibit the free movement of goods and the creation of the single market.[118] Market sharing can be achieved by the sharing of customers as well as by allocating

---

24th edn (2018).

[110]   Regulation 330/2010 [2010] O.J. L102/1. See also the Commission's Guidelines on Vertical Restraints [2010] O.J. C130/1.

[111]   Regulation 461/2010 [2010] O.J. L129/52. See also the Commission's Supplementary Guidelines on Vertical Restraints in Agreements for the Sale and Repair of Motor Vehicles and the Distribution of Spare Parts for Motor Vehicles [2010] O.J. C138/16.

[112]   Regulation 1217/2010 [2010] O.J. L335/36. See also the Commission's Guidelines on Horizontal Cooperation Agreements [2010] O.J. C11/1.

[113]   i.e. where undertakings agree to concentrate their production in different product areas: Regulation 1218/00 [2010] O.J. L335/43. See also the Commission's Guidelines on Horizontal Cooperation Agreements [2010] O.J. C11/1.

[114]   Reference should be made to specialist works for the legislation in these sectors.

[115]   Regulation 316/2014 [2014] O.J. L93/7. See also the Commission's Guidelines on Technology Transfer Agreements [2014] O.J. C89/3.

[116]   See below, paras 43-065—43-076.

[117]   For detailed analysis of horizontal price-fixing agreements see Bellamy and Child, *European Union Law of Competition*, 8th edn (2018), paras 5.041–5.065; Whish and Bailey, *Competition Law*, 9th edn (2018), pp.530–541.

[118]   For detailed analysis of horizontal market-sharing agreements see Bellamy and Child, *European Union Law of Competition*, 8th edn (2018), paras 5.071–5.091; Whish and Bailey, *Competition Law*, 9th edn, pp.541–544.

geographic areas to the parties. A further kind of agreement likely to infringe art.101(1) occurs where manufacturers allocate to each other quotas for the production or supply of products to the market of each participant. Article 101(1) may also be infringed where one manufacturer grants exclusive selling rights to a competitor in respect of a particular territory. A market sharing arrangement confined to the territory of one Member State may still infringe art.101(1) since it is liable to affect the patterns of imports and exports that might otherwise take place.

(iii) *Exchange of information* Whether the exchange of information restricts competition within the meaning of art.101(1) depends inter alia on the nature of the information exchanged and the structure of the market to which the information agreement relates.[119] The exchange of information among competitors is likely to infringe art.101(1) if that information would normally be regarded as a business secret. Information about prices and other trading conditions is usually regarded as commercially sensitive and confidential. There is no objection to the collection by a trade association of statistical information giving an aggregate picture of the output and sales of the industry provided that individual company figures cannot be identified, or provided the information is sufficiently historical that it is unlikely to affect future behaviour.

(iv) *Collusive tendering* The practice of collusive tendering whereby firms agree amongst themselves to collaborate over their response to invitations to tender infringes art.101(1) and may attract large fines.[120]

(v) *Joint selling or purchasing* Joint selling or purchasing agreements may fall within art.101(1) where the parties agree the price they are prepared to charge or to pay or where they agree to buy or sell wholly or mainly through a joint operation such as a subsidiary company or other trade association they have established for this purpose. The Commission has published guidance on the applicability of art.101 to those kinds of benign horizontal agreements which often generate beneficial effects on competition; these include joint purchasing or production, research and development and standardisation agreements.[121]

(vi) *Pay-for-delay agreements* An agreement between the owner of a patent and a manufacturer of generic drugs contemplating entry into the market upon expiry of the patent, whereby the patent owner makes a payment to the generic producer not to enter the market, may amount to an agreement that restricts competition by object.[122]

Joint ventures One category of arrangement which is often considered by the Commission is where two or more undertakings set up a joint venture and pool their resources for the purpose of carrying out joint research and development of a new product or to establish more efficient production, distribution or promotion of their **43-036**

---

[119] For detailed analysis of the exchange of information see Whish and Bailey, *Competition Law*, 9th edn (2018), pp.551–559.

[120] For detailed analysis of collusive tendering agreements see Whish and Bailey, *Competition Law*, 9th edn (2018), pp.547–549.

[121] Commission's Guidelines on Horizontal Cooperation Agreements [2010] O.J. C11/1.

[122] See, e.g. *Lundbeck*, Commission decision of June 19, 2013, upheld on appeal *H. Lundbeck A/S v Commission* (T-472/13) EU:T:2016:449, [2016] 5 C.M.L.R. 18; *Servier/Perindopril*, Commission decision of July 9, 2014.

products. Such arrangements often impose restrictions on the parent companies' ability to compete with each other and/or with the joint venture, the grant by the parents of intellectual property or know-how licences to the joint venture, and restrictions on the use by the parents of the results of the activities of the joint enterprise. The basic principles according to which such arrangements are assessed under art.101(1) are set out in the Commission's Guidelines on Horizontal Cooperation Agreements.[123] Some of these agreements will benefit from the block exemption regulations for research and development agreements and specialisation agreements promulgated by the Commission.[124] Reference should be made to specialist works for the detailed rules to be applied to these kinds of agreements.[125]

43-037 **Mergers** Article 101(1) does not apply to the acquisition of control of one company by another and mergers are governed by a separate legal regime under the EU Merger Regulation, Council Regulation 139/2004[126] and the subsidiary legislation and Commission Notices issued in implementation of the Merger Regulation. Some joint ventures fall to be considered under the Merger Regulation, if they are "full function", that is if they have all the necessary resources in terms of funding, staff and assets to carry out the functions normally carried out by undertakings operating on the same market.[127] Again, reference should be made to specialist works for an analysis of this complex area of the law.[128]

43-038 **Application of article 101(1) to vertical agreements** The prohibition in art.101(1) is capable of applying to vertical agreements between suppliers and wholesalers or retailers as it does to horizontal agreements between undertakings at the same level of production.[129] Generally, vertical agreements are likely to have a detrimental effect on competition only where competition with other firms' products, so-called "inter-brand competition", is restricted; this may be the case either directly as a result of a contractual restraint or due to the power of a supplier over the market in which it operates. It should be borne in mind that in the EU the integration of the single market is also an important consideration when applying art.101 to vertical agreements. However, the law recognises that many vertical agreements, while in one sense restricting competition, have countervailing benefits in terms of improving distribution which satisfy the requirements of art.101(3). This recognition is exemplified by the Commission's block exemption Regulation on vertical agreements, Regulation 330/2010. The Commission has also published comprehensive Guidelines on Vertical Restraints[130] which cover those agreements falling outside art.101(1) as well as discussing issues arising from the application of the block exemption and its enforcement policy in relation to such agreements. There are some clauses which are commonly found in the various categories of

---

123 [2010] O.J. C11/1.
124 Regulation 1217/2010 (research and development agreements) and Regulation 1218/2010 (specialisation agreements); see nn.112 and 113, above.
125 e.g. Bellamy and Child, *European Union Law of Competition*, 8th edn (2018), Ch.6; Whish and Bailey, *Competition Law*, 9th edn (2018), Ch.15.
126 [2004] O.J. L24/1.
127 See *Commission Consolidated Jurisdictional Notice*, July 10, 2007.
128 See, e.g. Levy, *European Merger Control Law: a Guide to the Merger Regulation* (2003); Bellamy and Child, *European Union Law of Competition*, 8th edn (2018), Ch.8; Whish and Bailey, *Competition Law*, 9th edn (2018), Ch.21.
129 *Consten & Grundig v Commission* EU:C:1966:41, [1966] E.C.R. 299.
130 [2010] O.J. C130/1.

vertical agreements which may require particularly careful scrutiny under art.101(1) and these are described in the following paragraphs.

Exclusivity provisions Many vertical agreements contain exclusivity provi-   **43-039**
sions where the supplier appoints a single dealer in a particular territory and
undertakes not to supply any other dealer in that territory[131] and/or where a dealer
undertakes that he will buy all his supplies of a particular product only from a single
supplier.[132] The mere grant of exclusive marketing rights in a particular territory
does not, of itself, have as its object the restriction of competition; it must be
examined in its legal, factual and economic context in order to determine whether
it has such an effect.[133] On balance, the case law indicates that a wide range of factors must be taken into account in deciding whether an exclusive supply contract
falls within art.101(1), such as the novelty or technical complexity of the product
to which the agreement relates, the level of investment and marketing commitment the distributor is expected to undertake,[134] and the strength of the undertakings on the market for the product involved.[135] The block exemption will apply to
agreements containing these kinds of clauses provided the supplier's and the buyer's
market shares are less than 30 per cent and that they are not combined with any
hardcore restrictions proscribed by art.4 of the Regulation.[136] It is therefore only
where the agreement as a whole does not benefit from the block exemption that the
question of the application of art.101(1) to such clauses is an important issue.
Specific guidance on the application of art.101 to individual vertical agreements is
provided by the Commission's Guidelines on Vertical Restraints.[137]

Restrictions on imports or exports If an agreement contains any term which af-   **43-040**
fects the freedom of the distributor to export the goods supplied under the agreement to other Member States or which obstructs the ability of third parties to import
or export those goods, it needs to scrutinised carefully for compatibility with
art.101(1). In the leading case of *Consten and Grundig v Commission*,[138] Grundig
established a network of distributors in the different Member States, including the
French distributor Consten. Grundig assigned the GINT trade mark to its products
in France to Consten and agreed not to deliver Grundig products to anyone in
France except to Consten and Consten agreed not to sell the products outside
France. Grundig further undertook to procure that its distributors in the other
Member States would also be subject to an export ban so that Consten enjoyed what
is termed "absolute territorial protection", i.e. it was protected not only from
competing sales by other French Grundig distributors but from sales in France of
products emanating from distributors in the other Member States. This aspect of the

---

[131] Sometimes the supplier also undertakes that he will not supply end-users himself in the territory.
[132] Sometimes the dealer also undertakes that he will not deal in goods which compete with the goods
supplied under the agreement.
[133] See *Société Technique Minière v Maschinenbau Ulm* EU:C:1966:38, [1966] E.C.R. 235; *Nungesser
v Commission* EU:C:1982:211, [1982] E.C.R. 2015, 2069; *Dansk Pelsdyravlerforening v Commission* EU:T:1992:79, [1992] E.C.R. II-1931 for exclusive supply; and *Delimitis v Henninger Bräu*
EU:C:1991:91, [1991] E.C.R. I-935 for exclusive purchase.
[134] e.g. *Nungesser*, above.
[135] e.g. *Delimitis*, above; *Javico International v Yves Saint Laurent Parfums* EU:C:1998:173, [1998]
E.C.R. I-1983.
[136] See Regulation 330/2010 arts 3 and 4; discussed below, paras 43-048 to 43-050.
[137] See n.110, above.
[138] EU:C:1966:41, [1966] E.C.R. 299.

distribution system was condemned by the Court of Justice. The principle laid down in *Consten and Grundig* has been affirmed many times; any attempt to ban exports or to provide absolute territorial protection for exclusive dealers will normally be prohibited by art.101(1). The finding of the General Court that an indirect export ban in the *GlaxoSmithKline* case[120] did not have the object of restricting competition due to the specific conditions of the pharmaceutical sector in the EU, in which laws and regulations adopted by various Member States have a distortive effect on competition, was overruled by the Court of Justice on appeal.[140] However, the Court of Justice agreed with the General Court that the Commission had insufficiently considered Glaxo's argument that the agreements in question might be justifiable under art.101(3) TFEU. For technical reasons no answer was ever forthcoming from the Commission on the latter point.

43-041   **The distinction between "active" and "passive" sales**   In defining the extent to which exclusivity can legitimately be granted to a dealer in distribution agreements the block exemption, Regulation 330/2010, and the Commission's Guidelines draw a distinction between bans on "active" sales by a dealer outside his contract territory and bans on "passive" sales outside the contract territory.[141] "Active" sales are those which are sought by the dealer, for example by placing advertisements or setting up a branch office or distribution apparatus outside his contract territory and, broadly speaking, a ban on such sales is regarded as legitimate and capable of satisfying art.101(3). "Passive" sales are those made in response to an order or request for products from a customer outside the territory, which is not solicited by the dealer; in general, passive selling includes the advertising or selling of a product via the internet.[142] Generally speaking the dealer must remain free to make passive sales outside his territory, even if the territory from which the request comes has been allocated to a different exclusive dealer in the network; this is explained further in para.43-050, below.

43-042   **Other measures impeding parallel imports**   The freedom of a distributor or third party to import and export the goods supplied by the manufacturer to his dealer may be hindered by more sophisticated measures than a simple export ban. A provision requiring that the dealer supply only to end-users,[143] or preventing him from supplying goods to other dealers in the network,[144] or requiring him to provide information for the purpose of monitoring the destination of products[145] will be prohibited. The refusal to service parallel imported goods or to honour guarantees in relation to such goods[146] will also fall foul of art.101. Suppliers sometimes aim to discourage exports by charging a different price according to the territory into which the goods are to be delivered. An agreement under which different prices are charged

---

[139] EU:T:2006:265, [2006] E.C.R. II-2969.

[140] *GlaxoSmithKline Services Unltd v Commission* EU:C:2009:610, [2009] E.C.R. I-9291.

[141] This distinction is drawn in art.4(b) of Regulation 330/2010 and by the Commission's Guidelines on Vertical Restraints: see below, para.43-050.

[142] *Commission's Guidelines on Vertical Restraints* paras 51-54.

[143] *Société de Vente de Ciments et Bétons v Kerpen & Kerpen* EU:C:1983:374, [1983] E.C.R. 4173.

[144] See, e.g. *Hasselblad v Commission* EU:C:1984:65, [1984] E.C.R. 883.

[145] *Hasselblad v Commission* EU:C:1984:65, [1984] E.C.R. 883. See also *BASF Coatings v Commission* EU:T:1999:99, [1999] E.C.R. II-1581, where the General Court concluded that a clause requiring the wholesaler to pass onto the manufacturer any inquiries from customers outside his contract territory operated as an export ban.

[146] *ETA v DK Investment* EU:C:1985:494, [1985] E.C.R. 3933 (Swatch watches).

to a purchaser merely on the grounds of his nationality or because he intends to export will very often contravene art.101(1).[147] The view of the General Court that this practice may not infringe art.101(1) in the specific circumstances of the pharmaceutical sector was reversed on appeal to the Court of Justice.[148]

Resale price maintenance   A provision which seeks to control the minimum price   **43-043** at which a distributor may resell goods, or to impose a fixed price on the distributor, is likely to contravene art.101(1), at least if it applies to goods which are imported or reimported from, or exported to, another Member State.[149] However, the communication by the supplier to the distributor of the supplier's recommended resale price is not unlawful unless a concerted practice grows up whereby the dealers in fact always charge the recommended price.[150] A clause requiring the joint setting of prices by supplier and reseller is illegal even if it is never enforced.[151]

Typical vertical agreements covered by article 101(1)   The kind of agree-   **43-044** ments most likely to be encountered by the practitioner and which require consideration under art.101(1) include exclusive distribution agreements; exclusive purchasing agreements; brewery tied house agreements; petrol solus agreements, intellectual property licences; franchise agreements; agency agreements; and selective distribution agreements. When considering each of these types of agreements one must consider both which terms of the agreement fall within art.101(1) and whether the agreement benefits from block exemption under Regulation 330/2010 (in the case of vertical agreements) or Regulation 316/2014 (in the case of intellectual property licences or, as they are often called, "technology transfer agreements"). In practice, the latter question—does an agreement benefit from one of the block exemptions—may be tackled first, since it is only if an agreement falls outside the block exemptions that the possible invalidity of the agreement under art.101(1) arises.

Application of the block exemptions   In the following paragraphs each category   **43-045** of agreement is considered in turn dealing both with the application of art.101(1) and the relevant block exemption regulation. It is important to bear in mind that if an agreement contains a clause which takes it outside the block exemption then the agreement as a whole cannot enjoy the benefit of the block exemption in respect of any of the clauses in it. In such a case *all* the clauses that are found to fall within art.101(1) and do not fulfil the conditions in art.101(3) will be invalid and unlawful, not just the clauses which go beyond those permitted by the block exemption.[152] The following paragraphs contain only a summary of the provisions of the block exemptions and reference should be made to the full text of Regulation 330/2010 in any assessment of an agreement.

---

[147] *Distillers v Commission* EU:C:1980:186, [1980] E.C.R. 2229.
[148] *GlaxoSmithKline Services v Commission* EU:C:2009:610, [2009] E.C.R. I-9291.
[149] *Hasselblad v Commission* EU:C:1984:65, [1984] E.C.R. 883; *Publishers' Association v Commission* EU:T:1992:84, [1992] E.C.R. II-1995.
[150] *Pronuptia de Paris v Schillgalis* EU:C:1986:41, [1986] E.C.R. 353.
[151] *Novalliance/Systemform* [1997] O.J. L47/11.
[152] *Delimitis v Henninger Bräu* EU:C:1991:91, [1991] E.C.R. I-935.

43-046 **Block exemption for vertical agreements**   Regulation 330/2010[153] is the block exemption for vertical agreements generally, although Regulation 461/2010 applies to certain agreements in the motor car sector.[154]

43-047 **Meaning of vertical agreement**   Regulation 330/2010 applies to agreements or concerted practices entered into between two or more undertakings, each of which operates, for the purposes of the agreement, at a different level of the production or distribution chain. Typically this will be between a manufacturer and a wholesaler or between a wholesaler and a retailer. However, an agreement for the supply of goods by one manufacturer to another manufacturer will count as a vertical agreement, because they are at different levels of distribution *for the purposes of the agreement*. The application of the Regulation will, however, be different depending on whether the two manufacturers in question are competing in the same market: where they are, their agreement will benefit from block exemption only if the terms of art.2(4) are satisfied.

43-048 **Market share cap**   Where the vertical agreement is between parties who are not in competition with each other, then arts 2 and 3 of Regulation 330/2010 provide that the agreement is block exempted provided that the market share of the supplier does not exceed 30 per cent of the relevant market on which it sells the goods or services and that the market share of the buyer does not exceed 30 per cent of the relevant market on which it purchases the goods or services. Article 8 of the Regulation provides guidance on how to ascertain the market shares of the parties.

43-049 **Prohibited clauses: resale price maintenance**   Article 4(a) of the Regulation provides that it will not apply to an agreement which directly or indirectly restricts the ability of the buyer to set its sale prices. This does not, however, prohibit the supplier from imposing a maximum sales price or from recommending a price provided that there is no pressure or incentive on the buyer to treat this as a fixed price.

43-050 **Prohibited clauses: territorial restrictions**   Article 4(b) of the Regulation sets the limits of the block exemption so far as the imposition of restrictions on the territory into which the buyer can sell the goods or as to the customers to whom he can sell the goods acquired under the contract. The block exemption will apply provided that such restrictions limit only active sales into the territory or to a customer group which has been exclusively allocated by the supplier to a different buyer or reserved to itself. In other words the buyer must be able to sell goods into the exclusive territory of either the supplier or another buyer if the sale is made at the customer's initiative. In the case of a selective distribution network, the agreement may prohibit the buyer from selling to unauthorised distributors outside the network but must not prohibit them from selling to other authorised distributors or to any end users. In the case of an agreement for the supply of components, the agreement may not restrict the supplier to selling the components as spare parts to end users.

43-051 **Non-compete obligations**   Article 5(1)(a) of the Regulation provides that the block exemption will not apply to "any direct or indirect non-compete obligation,

---

[153] [2010] O.J. L102/1.
[154] [2010] O.J. L129/52.

the duration of which is indefinite or exceeds five years". However, art.5(2) permits a longer period where goods or services are sold from premises owned by the supplier, or leased by the supplier from a third party, provided that the obligation does not exceed the period of occupancy of the premises by the buyer. A non-compete obligation is defined broadly by art.1 of the Regulation to include any obligation on the buyer to purchase from the supplier more than 80 per cent of its total purchases. Article 5(1)(b) provides that the block exemption will not apply to post-termination non-compete clauses; however, art.5(3) permits such a clause for up to one year where the supplier makes the premises available to the buyer.

Networks of parallel agreements   Article 29 of Regulation 1/2003 provides that   **43-052**
the Commission or a national competition authority of a Member State may withdraw the benefit of the block exemption from a particular vertical agreement that is incompatible with the conditions laid down in art.101(3); this may be the case where there are parallel networks of similar agreements which seal off access to the market. Where parallel networks of similar vertical agreements cover more than 50 per cent of the relevant market, art.6 of the Regulation authorises the Commission by regulation to disapply the block exemption to vertical agreements containing specific restraints in that market. Any such regulation must not take effect earlier than six months following its adoption.

Transitional provisions   According to art.9 of the Regulation, the exempt status   **43-053**
of existing agreements which benefited from exemption under Regulation 2790/99 continued until June 1, 2011. Otherwise, Regulation 330/2010 took effect from June 1, 2010 and expires on May 31, 2022.

Intellectual property licences   The exercise of intellectual property rights may   **43-054**
be affected not only by the competition provisions of the TFEU but also by the articles[155] which deal with the free movement of goods. There is substantial jurisprudence of the Court of Justice limiting the extent to which the owner or licensee of, say, a UK patent, copyright or registered trade mark can rely on the rights conferred by UK intellectual property law to prevent imports into the UK of goods which have been lawfully placed on the market in another Member State.[156] However, art.101 also affects the validity of certain terms in licences of intellectual property rights. This is a complex area with many detailed rules to be applied and reference should be made to works on competition law and/or intellectual property rights.[157]

Intellectual property licences and article 101(1)   Many intellectual property   **43-055**
licences provide for the exclusive grant of the licence to the licensee in the particular territory covered by the agreement whereby the licensor undertakes that he will not exploit the property himself in the territory and he will not license any other person to do so. Such a restriction may fall outside art.101(1) if the grant of the exclusive licence is the sole means whereby the licensor is able to ensure that the rights will

---

155   arts 34–37 TFEU.
156   See, e.g. *Merck v Primecrown* EU:C:1996:468, [1996] E.C.R. I-6285 (patents); *Phytheron v Bourdon* EU:C:1997:170, [1997] E.C.R. I-1729 (trade marks); *Metronome Musik v Music Point Hokamp* EU:C:1998:172, [1998] E.C.R. I-1953.
157   See e.g. Bellamy and Child, *European Community Law of Competition*, 7th edn (2013), Ch.9; Whish and Bailey, *Competition Law*, 9th edn (2018), Ch.19.

be fully exploited in the territory concerned.[158] This depends on the novelty and complexity of the technology involved and the level of investment and other resources which the licensee will have to devote to launching the product incorporating the rights in the territory concerned [159] Many other terms commonly found in licences may fall within art.101(1), in particular any terms purporting to limit the number of products manufactured using the rights or the export of any such product, "no challenge" clauses, field of use restrictions or tying obligations which are not essential for the proper exploitation of the rights.

43-056 **Technology transfers agreements** The Commission adopted Regulation 316/2014 on March 21 2014.[160] It entered into force on May 1, 2014 and will expire on April 30, 2026.[161] The format of Regulation 316/2014 is similar to Regulation 330/2010 on vertical agreements. Regulation 316/2014 applies to licences of patents, know-how and software copyright, including mixed licences thereof. Article 2 confers block exemption on certain bilateral technology transfer agreements. Article 3 imposes market share caps, which differ depending on whether an agreement is horizontal or vertical, the former being treated more strictly: the cap is 20 per cent for horizontal agreements and 30 per cent for vertical agreements. Article 4 contains a list of hardcore restrictions, the inclusion of which in an agreement will prevent the block exemption from applying: the list is stricter for horizontal than for vertical agreements. Article 5 sets out certain restrictions that are not block exempted, but which do not prevent the application of the Regulation to the rest of the agreement. Articles 6 and 7 provide for the block exemption to be withdrawn from agreements in certain circumstances. Subsequent provisions deal with matters such as the calculation of market share thresholds and transitional arrangements. Regulation 772/04 should be read in conjunction with the Commission's Technology Transfer Guidelines.[162]

43-057 **Franchise agreements** Franchise agreements are those whereby the proprietor of a trade mark, business name or other distinctive marketing presentation (the franchisor) grants one or more parties (the franchisees) the rights to use the mark or other marketing format in the supply of goods or services and to present their premises in accordance with the distinctive layout or format associated with the franchisor. Each franchisee remains an independent trader bearing his own financial risk but he benefits from the goodwill associated with the franchisor's business. To the outside observer the franchisees' premises look uniform and sell products of the same appearance and quality. The franchisee normally undertakes to pay a royalty on sales from his premises and to buy at least part of his stock from the franchisor or from suppliers nominated by the franchisor. The franchisor provides know-how which may include staff training and guidance as well as allowing the franchisee to use the marketing image which usually has proven customer appeal.

---

[158] *Nungesser v Commission* EU:C:1982:211, [1982] E.C.R. 2015; *Louis Erauw-Jacquery v La Hesbignonne Société Co-opérative* EU:C:1988:183, [1988] E.C.R. 1919.

[159] *Louis Erauw-Jacquery v La Hesbignonne Société Co-opérative* EU:C:1988:183, [1988] E.C.R. 1919.

[160] [2014] O.J. L93/7; Regulation 316/2014 replaces the earlier technology transfer regulation, Regulation 772/2004.

[161] Regulation 316/2014 art.11.

[162] [2014] O.J. C89/3.

Franchise agreements and article 101 In the leading case of *Pronuptia*[163] the   **43-058**
Court of Justice considered the terms of a standard form franchise agreement for
the well-known bridal outfitters. The Court held that those clauses which were essential to the proper operation of the franchise system did not fall within art.101(1).
Thus, since it was essential that the franchisor be able to protect the know-how and
other expertise that he provides to the franchisee, art.101(1) is not infringed if the
franchisee is prohibited from opening a shop of the same nature in an area where
he may compete with another member of the network. Similarly, since it is essential that the uniformity of appearance and quality of the outlets in the franchise
network is maintained, obligations on the franchisee to decorate his premises in a
certain way or, in some circumstances, to buy his supplies of product from the
franchisor are permissible. For those franchise agreements which may fall within
art.101(1) such as those that divide the market territorially, Regulation 330/2010
provides block exemption, provided that such agreements do not contain restrictions going beyond those set out in the Regulation. In *Carewatch Care Services Ltd
v Focus Caring Services Ltd*[164] the High Court rejected a claim by the defendants
that a one-year post-termination non-compete clause was contrary to art.101(1) and
therefore unenforceable as the clause was to protect the know-how of the franchisor.

Agency agreements Generally speaking, art.101(1) does not apply to an agree-   **43-059**
ment between a principal and agent under which the latter agrees to procure business or to close transactions in the name and on behalf of the principal, in
circumstances in which the agent is not acting as an independent trader on his own
account.[165] However, the position is different where the agent is in business on his
own account and bears financial or commercial risk in addition to carrying out his
agency duties.[166] In such circumstances, clauses whereby the agent agrees not to act
for suppliers other than the principal or to promote the principal's products in preference to those of other suppliers need to be scrutinised under art.101.[167] In
DaimlerChrysler v Commission[168] the General Court annulled a finding of an
infringement of art.101(1) by the Commission because the Commission had incorrectly concluded that DaimlerChrysler's dealers were not agents. Further guidance on the application of art.101 to agency agreements, in the context of service
stations for the sale of petrol, can be found in the Court of Justice's judgment in
Confederacion Española de Empresarios de Estaciones de Servicio.[169] The Commission's Guidelines on Vertical Restraints provide helpful guidance on the way in
which it considers that art.101 does or does not apply to agency agreements.[170]

Selective distribution systems Sometimes a supplier chooses to distribute his   **43-060**

---

163 EU:C:1986:41, [1986] E.C.R. 353.
164 [2014] EWHC 2313 (Ch).
165 See, e.g. *Sugar* EU:C:1975:174, [1975] E.C.R. 1663, 2007, paras 538–540.
166 *VVR v Sociale Dienst* EU:C:1987:418, [1987] E.C.R. 3801, 3828 (travel agents).
167 Cases on the application of art.101 to agency agreements include *Suiker Unie; Vereniging van
Vlaamse Reisbureaus v Sociale Dienst van de Plaatselijke en Gewestelijke Overheidsdiensten*
EU:C:1987:418, [1987] E.C.R. 3801; *DaimlerChrysler v Commission* EU:T:2005:322, [2005] E.C.R.
II-3319. See also the Council Directive on coordination of the law relating to self-employed commercial agents brought into force as from January 1, 1994 by the Commercial Agents (Council Directive) Regulations 1993 (SI 1993/3053).
168 EU:T:2005:322, [2005] E.C.R. II-3319.
169 *EU:C:2006:784*, [2006] E.C.R. I-11987.
170 Commission's Guidelines on Vertical Restraints paras 12–21.

goods through a limited number of dealers who are able to offer a level of technical expertise or whose premises are in keeping with the luxury image of the goods.
Agreements between the supplier and the approved dealers in these cases will
contain restrictions on the on-sale of the goods to dealers outside the network and
will place obligations on the dealer concerning the training of staff and the extent
and quality of promotional and advertising activity, etc. Article 101(1) will not in
general apply to such agreements, provided that the dealers are selected only on the
basis of non-discriminatory criteria relating to their technical ability to handle the
goods or the suitability of their premises [171] An outright restriction on dealers within
the selective distribution system preventing them from selling the contract goods
online will be held to restrict competition by object and to be ineligible for block
exemption under Regulation 330/2010.[172] However the dealer may be prevented
from selling online through third-party market places over which the brand owner
is unable to exercise control.[173] If there is any limit on the number of dealers whom
the supplier is prepared to approve, or any additional restrictions or obligations
imposed on the reseller, art.101(1) may apply, in which case the selective distribution system would have to satisfy the criteria in art.101(3). In practice, a selective
distribution agreement may benefit from the block exemption conferred by Regulation 330/2010 provided that the supplier's and the buyer's market shares are 30 per
cent or less; that resale prices are not fixed; that there are no restrictions on active
or passive sales to end-users; and that there are no restrictions on cross-supplies
between authorised distributors.

(e)   Article 102

43-061   **Contractual clauses as infringements of article 102**   Article 102 TFEU prohibits
any abuse by one or more undertakings of a dominant position within the internal
market or a substantial part of it insofar as it may affect trade between Member
States.[174] It used to be thought that art.101(1) applied to contracts and that art.102
applied to unilateral conduct on the part of dominant undertakings. However,
increasingly the Commission and the Courts of the European Union have held that
certain contractual provisions constitute an abuse of a dominant position when
entered into by dominant firms.

43-062   **Dominant undertakings**   A detailed description of the test for ascertaining
whether an undertaking enjoys a dominant position is beyond the scope of this
work.[175] Broadly speaking, one must first identify the product sector and the

---

[171]   See *Metro v Commission (No.1)* EU:C:1977:167, [1977] E.C.R. 1875.

[172]   See *Pierre Fabre Dermo-Cosmetique SAS v President de l'Autorite de la Concurrence*
EU:C:2011:649, [2011] 5 C.M.L.R. 31.

[173]   See *Coty Germany GmbH v Parfumerie Akzente GmbH* EU:C:2017:941, [2018] 4 C.M.L.R. 9.

[174]   The requirement of an actual or potential effect on trade between Member States is discussed above,
paras 43-027—43-030.

[175]   See, e.g. Bellamy and Child, *European Union Law of Competition*, 8th edn (2013), Ch.10; Whish
and Bailey, *Competition Law*, 9th edn (2018), pp.25–46 and pp.187–196. Note also that the European
Commission has published "Guidance on the Commission's enforcement priorities in applying
Article [102 TFEU] to abusive exclusionary conduct by dominant undertakings", [2010] O.J. C45/7.
This document is not a formal set of guidelines describing the law of art.102 TFEU; however, it does
provide useful insights into the way in which the Commission regards particular types of behaviour
under art.102, and indicates the circumstances in which it might be inclined to open proceedings in
relation to possibly abusive behaviour.

geographical area in which the undertaking being scrutinised competes[176] and then calculate the market share of that market supplied by the undertaking and the number and size of its competitors.[177] Many other factors are relevant in determining dominance, in particular the ownership of intellectual property rights and the existence of any other barriers to new entry to the market by potential competitors. Dominance of itself is not a contravention of the Treaty, but dominant undertakings have a "special responsibility" not to engage in any conduct which will hinder the maintenance of such competition that still takes place in the market.[178] This responsibility becomes greater, and as a corollary a finding of abuse becomes more likely, the weaker the competitive constraints facing the dominant undertaking in a market are. However, in *Irish Sugar v Commission*[179] the General Court stated that the fact that an undertaking is in a dominant position cannot deprive it of its entitlement to protect its own commercial interests when they are attacked, although such behaviour cannot be allowed if its purpose is to strengthen the dominant position and thereby abuse it. Articles 101 and 102 are not mutually exclusive and conduct which falls within art.101 may also be an abuse.[180]

Examples of abusive contractual provisions   The following contractual clauses   **43-063**
have been held to be capable of amounting to abusive conduct when engaged in by a dominant undertaking[181]:

   (i)   *Loyalty rebates* Special discounts or rebates granted by a dominant firm
           in return for securing all or most of a customer's business may well
           infringe art.102 since it is likely to have the same effect that a contractual
           stipulation to purchase exclusively would have done, making it more dif-
           ficult for competitors to persuade customers to buy otherwise than from
           the dominant undertaking.[182] In *Virgin/British Airways*[183] the Commis-
           sion synthesised the case law on loyalty rebates as follows: a dominant
           supplier can give discounts that relate to efficiencies, for example
           discounts for large orders that allow the supplier to produce large volumes
           of the product; however a dominant undertaking cannot give discounts or

---

[176] The leading cases on definition of the relevant market include *United Brands v Commission* EU:C:1978:22, [1978] E.C.R. 207; *Hoffmann-La Roche v Commission* EU:C:1979:36, [1979] E.C.R. 461; *Michelin v Commission* EU:C:1983:313, [1983] E.C.R. 3461; *Hilti v Commission* EU:T:1991:70, [1991] E.C.R. II-315.

[177] A broad rule of thumb is that a market share of over 40 per cent sustained over a number of years may be an indication of dominance; there has only been one finding of dominance below 40 per cent, in *Virgin/British Airways* [2000] O.J. L30/1, where the Commission considered British Airways held a dominant position with a market share of 39.7 per cent in the market for the procurement of air travel agency services (the case was upheld on appeal to the General Court in *British Airways v Commission* EU:T:2003:343, [2003] E.C.R. II-5917 and on appeal to the Court of Justice in *British Airways v Commission* EU:C:2007:166, [2007] E.C.R. I-2331).

[178] *Michelin v Commission* EU:C:1983:313, [1983] E.C.R. 3461, 3511.

[179] EU:T:1999:246, [1999] E.C.R. II-2969.

[180] On the relationship between arts 101 and 102 see, e.g. *Ahmed Saeed* EU:C:1989:140, [1989] E.C.R. 803; *Tetra Pak I* EU:T:1990:41, [1990] E.C.R. II-309.

[181] Various other clauses were also condemned in *Tetra Pak II* EU:T:1994:246, [1994] E.C.R. II-755.

[182] *Hoffmann-La Roche* EU:C:1979:36, [1979] E.C.R. 461; *BPB Industries* EU:T:1993:31, [1993] E.C.R. II-389 which also stated that the fact that the clause was included in the contract at the request of the customer does not affect its abusive nature.

[183] [2000] O.J. L30/1, [2000] 4 C.M.L.R. 999, upheld on appeal by the General Court in *British Airways v Commission* EU:T:2003:343, [2003] E.C.R. II-5917 and on appeal to the Court of Justice *British Airways v Commission* EU:C:2007:166, [2007] E.C.R. I-2331.

incentives that encourage loyalty on the part of a customer, that is for avoiding purchases from a competitor of the dominant supplier. BA's arrangements with travel agents were condemned as abusive. In *Intel v Commission* the Court of Justice held that rebates offered by a dominant undertaking in return for exclusivity may infringe art.102 where they could have the effect of foreclosing access to the market on the part of competitors as efficient as the dominant undertaking.[184]

(ii) *Turnover related discounts* Similarly, discounts or rebates which are related to the customer achieving a certain value or volume of purchases over a set period may be abusive.[185]

(iii) *Tying clauses* Clauses which require the customer to acquire additional products or services from a supplier when it buys the product in which that supplier is dominant may infringe art.102 unless there is an objective justification for doing so such as making the production or distribution of goods cheaper.[186] One of the abusive practices for which the European Commission fined Microsoft €497 million in March 2004 was that it had "tied" its *Windows Client PC Operating System* with its *Windows Media Player*.[187]

43-064 **Refusal to contract as abusive conduct** The common law doctrine of "freedom of contract"[188] which provides that any company is free to decide not to enter into a contract with a particular company is circumscribed in relation to dominant undertakings. A dominant undertaking may, in exceptional circumstances, be found to have acted abusively where it refuses to supply an established customer, and in some cases a new customer, unless it has a legitimate objective justification for such a refusal.[189] One of the abusive practices for which the European Commission fined Microsoft €497 million in March 2004 was that it had refused to supply interoperability information to competitors wishing to make use of it for the purpose of developing and distributing work group server operating system products.[190]

(f) Enforcement at the National Level

43-065 **Direct applicability of articles 101 and 102** Article 1 of Regulation 1/2003[191] provides that arts 101 and 102 are directly applicable; agreements contrary to those prohibitions are prohibited, "no prior decision to that effect being required".

---

184 EU:C:2017:632.

185 *Michelin v Commission* EU:C:1983:313, [1983] E.C.R. 3461.

186 *Hilti v Commission* EU:T:1991:70, [1991] E.C.R. II-315; *Tetra Pak II* EU:T:1994:246, [1994] E.C.R. II-755.

187 *Microsoft* [2007] O.J. L32/23, upheld on appeal to the General Court *Microsoft v Commission* EU:T:2007:289, [2007] E.C.R. II-3601.

188 Vol.I, paras 1-031—1-040.

189 See, e.g. *Commercial Solvents v Commission* EU:C:1974:18, [1974] E.C.R. 223. Refusal to grant an intellectual property licence can in some circumstances amount to an abuse: *Radio Telefis Eireann v Commission* EU:T:1991:39, [1991] E.C.R. II-485.

190 See n.187 above.

191 [2003] O.J. L1/1; see also *BRT v SABAM* EU:C:1974:6, [1974] E.C.R. 51. For the scope of this doctrine as applied in the UK, see *R. v Secretary of State for Transport Ex p. Factortame Ltd (No.2)* [1991] 1 A.C. 603. See also *Eco Swiss China Time v Benetton* EU:C:1999:269, [1999] E.C.R. I-3055, [2000] 5 C.M.L.R. 816 for the effect on an arbitration award of an allegation made on appeal that the agreement was contrary to art.101(1).

National competition authorities and national courts therefore have the power to apply the EU competition rules in full.

Role of the national courts   The direct effect of arts 101 and 102 means that   **43-066**
contracting parties may rely on those provisions in national courts as a defence to the enforcement of a prohibited restriction and, furthermore, that third parties may in some circumstances plead an infringement of the competition rules as a defence to an action or as creating a cause of action sounding in damages.

Effect of Regulation 1/2003   Regulation 1/2003 art.6 specifically provides that   **43-067**
national courts shall have power to apply arts 101 and 102 in full, and art.3 goes further by stating that they are under an obligation to apply arts 101 and 102 where an agreement or conduct have an effect on trade between Member States. Regulation 1/2003 contains several further provisions on the role of national courts in enforcing the EU competition rules. Article 15 of the Regulation makes provision for the national courts to request the Commission's opinion on the application of the competition rules; requires national courts to submit to the Commission any written judgment deciding on the application of arts 101 and 102; and enables national competition authorities and the Commission to make observations in proceedings before national courts. Article 16 of the Regulation is concerned with preserving the uniform application of EU law and gives effect to the Court of Justice's judgment in *Masterfoods*.[192] In that case the Court of Justice stated that when national courts rule on agreements or conduct which are already the subject of a Commission decision they cannot take a decision running contrary to that of the Commission. Article 16 adds that a national court must avoid giving a decision which would conflict with a decision contemplated by the Commission in parallel proceedings and must consider whether to stay its proceedings. The Commission has published a Notice on the cooperation between the Commission and the courts of the EU Member States in the application of arts 101 and 102 TFEU.[193]

Severance of void terms   Although art.101(2) provides that the prohibited *agree-*   **43-068**
ment is void, the Court of Justice has held that it is in fact only the restrictive clauses in the agreement which are invalidated by art.101(2).[194] If those clauses can be severed from the agreement in accordance with the test usually applied under domestic law, the remainder of the agreement may be enforced.[195] However, in *English Welsh & Scottish Railway Ltd v E.ON Plc* the High Court held that directions by the Office of Rail Regulation, which has concurrent powers with the CMA to enforce the competition rules in the UK, that various terms of a coal carriage agreement between the parties were unlawful and should be removed altered the contract so fundamentally that it became void and unenforceable in its entirety.[196] In *Calor Gas Ltd v Express Fuels (Scotland) Ltd* the Outer House of the Court of Session in Scotland reached the conclusion that an exclusive dealing agreement was

---

[192] EU:C:2000:689, [2000] E.C.R. I-11369.
[193] [2004] O.J. C101/54.
[194] *Société de Vente de Ciments et Bétons v Kerpen & Kerpen* EU:C:1983:374, [1983] E.C.R. 4173, 4184.
[195] See *Richard Cound Ltd v BMW (GB) Ltd* [1997] Eu.L.R. 277, CA; applied in, e.g. *Benford Ltd v Cameron Equipment* [1997] Eu.L.R. 334, Merc Ct; *Parkes v Esso Petroleum* [1999] 1 C.M.L.R. 455. See also *Byrne v Inntrepreneur Beer Supply Co Ltd* [1999] Eu.L.R. 834. For the English law of severance see Vol.I, paras 16-236 et seq.
[196] [2007] EWHC 599 (Comm), [2007] U.K.C.L.R. 1653.

unenforceable by the supplier, Calor Gas, as it infringed art.101.[197] In *Robert Andrew Jones v Ricoh UK Ltd*[198] the Chancery Division of the High Court concluded that cl.7 of a Confidentiality Agreement was void and unenforceable as it was contrary to art.101(1) TFEU; the High Court subsequently held that cl.7 was severable from the remainder of the agreement which remained enforceable.[199] In *Martin Retail Group Ltd v Crawley Borough Council*[200] the Central London County Court held that a Proposed User clause in a letting scheme of retail premises was void and unenforceable under the Competition Act 1998 s.2.

43-069 **Rights of third parties**   In some circumstances a defendant who is not a party to a relevant agreement can plead art.101 or art.102 as a defence. This principally arises in actions brought by the holder of an intellectual property right who sues an alleged infringer of the right and is met by the defence that the licence under which he holds the right, or his conduct in exploiting the right, in some way contravenes the Treaty.[201]

43-070 **Breaches of arts 101 or 102 as a cause of action**   It is clear, following the judgment of the Court of Justice in *Courage Ltd v Crehan*,[202] that a person who suffers economic injury as a result of an infringement of the competition rules may bring an action for damages; such an action should, in principle, be available in order to safeguard the effective application ("effet utile") of the competition rules. The judgment in *Courage Ltd v Crehan* even establishes that one party to an agreement that infringes art.101 may be able to sue the other party for damages where the former does not bear the same responsibility for the infringement as the latter. Further judgments of the Court of Justice confirming the availability of damages for the victims of anti-competitive behaviour are *Manfredi*[203] and *Kone AG v ÖBB Infrastruktur AG*.[204] The private enforcement of EU competition law was given added impetus by the adoption of the EU Damages Directive in November 2014 which entered into force on December 27, 2016.[205] The Damages Directive was implemented in UK law by the Claims in Respect of Loss or Damage Arising from Competition Infringements (Competition Act 1998 and Other Enactments (Amendment)) Regulations 2017.[206]

43-071 **Causes of action in English law**   Even before the judgment of the Court of Justice in *Courage Ltd v Crehan* it had been established as a matter of domestic law that a breach of arts 101 or 102 can give rise to a cause of action on the part of someone injured by the prohibited conduct. In the leading case of *Garden Cottage Foods v*

---

[197] [2008] CSOH 13.

[198] [2010] EWHC 1743 (Ch).

[199] *Robert Andrew Jones v IOS (RUK) Ltd and Ricoh UK Ltd* [2012] EWHC 348 (Ch) at [44].

[200] [2014] L. & T.R. 17.

[201] See *Philips Electronics v Ingman Ltd* [1998] Eu.L.R. 666, Ch D, and the cases cited therein; *Chiron Corp v Murex Diagnostics (No.2)* [1994] 1 C.M.L.R. 410; *Sportswear SpA v Stonestyle Ltd* [2006] EWCA Civ 380, [2006] U.K.C.L.R. 893.

[202] EU:C:2001:465, [2001] E.C.R. I-6297.

[203] EU:C:2006:461, [2006] E.C.R. I-6619.

[204] EU:C:2014:1317.

[205] Directive 2014/14/EU of the European Parliament and of the Council on certain rules governing actions for damages under national law for infringements of the competition law provisions of the Member States and of the European Union, [2014] O.J. L349/1.

[206] SI 2017/385; on the private enforcement of EU (and UK) competition law in national courts see generally Whish and Bailey, *Competition Law*, 9th edn (2018), Ch.8.

Milk Marketing Board[207] the House of Lords held that in the light of the doctrine of direct effect, a breach of art.102 can be categorised in English law as a breach of statutory duty that is imposed not only for the purpose of promoting the general prosperity of the internal market but also for the benefit of private individuals to whom loss or damage is caused by a breach of that duty.[208] *Garden Cottage Foods* was a decision at an interlocutory stage, but it was affirmed obiter by the Court of Appeal and relied upon in later actions. However, the fact that an action may be brought for breach of statutory duty does not preclude the possibility that an infringement of competition law might be tortious in some other way, such as conspiracy.[209] In *Gibbs v Gemmell* the Court of Appeal held that, as a matter of English law, there was no action in damages or restitution at the suit of a party to a contract in respect of loss resulting from his compliance with terms which are in fact invalid because of art.101(2).[210] However, this case must now be read subject to the judgment of the Court of Justice in *Courage Ltd v Crehan*[211] which says quite clearly, as a matter of EU law, that there should not be an absolute bar to a person in the position of a co-contractor bringing an action for damages for loss caused by a contract that is liable to restrict competition; otherwise the effectiveness of art.101 would be put at risk.

Role of national competition authorities Under the regime introduced by **43-072** Regulation 1/2003 national competition authorities share the competence to apply arts 101 and 102 alongside the national courts and the European Commission. National competition authorities have the power to make decisions bringing an infringement to an end, to order interim measures, to accept commitments from the parties in lieu of an adverse decision and to decide that there are no grounds for action on their part. The Regulation contains a number of provisions which are intended to promote cooperation between the Commission and the national competition authorities; a network of competition authorities, the "European Competition Network", has been established which will facilitate the handling of cases between the competition authorities in Europe. The Commission has published a Notice on Cooperation within the Network of Competition Authorities.[212]

(g) Enforcement at the EU Level

Regulation 1/2003 The powers of the European Commission to enforce the **43-073** competition rules were originally laid down in Regulation 17; that Regulation was replaced by Regulation 1/2003 with effect from May 1, 2004.[213]

Commission investigations and adverse decisions A Commission investiga- **43-074**

---

207 [1984] A.C. 130.
208 See, e.g. *Kirklees MBC v Wickes Building Supplies* [1993] A.C. 227; *An Bord Bainne v Milk Marketing Board* [1988] 1 C.M.L.R. 605; *Cutsforth v Mansfield Inns* [1986] 1 W.L.R. 558.
209 *W.H. Newson Ltd v IMI Plc* [2013] EWCA Civ 1377.
210 *Gibbs Mew Plc v Gemmell* [1998] Eu.L.R. 588; *Passmore v Morland* [1999] 1 C.M.L.R. 1129; *Parkes v Esso Petroleum* [1999] 1 C.M.L.R. 455 and the cases cited therein.
211 EU:C:2001:465, [2001] E.C.R. I-6297; when the case reverted to the UK, the court held the agreement did not infringe art.101(1) in *Crehan v Inntrepreneur Pub Co* [2003] EWHC 1510 (Ch), a finding that was upheld by the House of Lords, [2006] UKHL 38.
212 [2004] O.J. C101/43.
213 [2003] O.J. L1/1.

tion into the existence of anti-competitive conduct may be prompted by a complaint made by a competitor or customer, or may result from the Commission's own analysis of a particular market and an ex officio investigation. The Commission has wide powers to seek information and examine documents when carrying out investigations into infringements of the Treaty.[214] The Commission has adopted an implementing regulation to accompany the entry into force of Regulation 1/2003 which explains the circumstances and manner in which the Commission conducts proceedings in art 101 and 102 cases.[215] The implementing regulation lays down provisions on the issue of a Statement of Objections (setting out the Commission's provisional findings of fact, legal analysis and its view on appropriate remedies) and the parties' written and oral rights of defence. Regulation 1/2003 provides that the Commission may adopt decisions requiring termination of an infringement; accepting commitments which bind the parties and conclude the Commission's proceedings; or, where the EU public interest requires, making a finding that art.101 and/or art.102 does not apply to an agreement. A decision of the Commission is binding on the undertakings to which it is addressed but is subject to appeal to the General Court.

43-075 **Interim measures** Article 8 of Regulation 1/2003 gives the Commission the power to order interim measures either on its own initiative or on the application of the complainant in a case; case law had held that such a power also existed under the old Regulation 17, although that instrument did not explicitly say so.[216] The Commission has adopted interim measures on very few occasions; a complainant in need of interim relief may find this easier to obtain on application to a domestic court, which might require an undertaking to pay damages in the event of a failure to establish a claim at the trial of the action. Interim relief was successfully obtained by a claimant in *Adidas-Salomon AG v Roger Draper and Paul Howorth*, in which Adidas was granted an interim injunction against the International Tennis Federation and the "Grand Slam" tennis tournaments in relation to the dress rules for players; a settlement was subsequently reached so that the case did not go to final trial.[217] In *Dahabshiil Transfer Services Ltd v Barclays Bank Plc*[218] Dahabshiil was awarded an interim injunction against Barclays Bank on the basis that the latter may have been guilty of an unlawful refusal to supply contrary to art.102.

43-076 **Fines and other remedies** The Commission may order termination of the infringement and may impose positive obligations such as a duty to provide information periodically to the Commission to enable it to monitor future compliance. The Commission has power to impose a fine where the undertaking has intentionally or negligently infringed arts 101(1) or 102.[219] The maximum fine is 10 per cent of the worldwide turnover of the undertaking concerned in the preceding business year. The Commission has issued guidance on the method it will adopt

---

[214] Regulation 1/2003 arts 18 and 20–21.
[215] Regulation 773/2004 [2004] O.J. L123/18.
[216] For an example of interim measures having been ordered see, e.g. *La Cinq v Commission* EU:T:1992:5, [1992] E.C.R. II-1.
[217] [2006] EWHC 1318 (Ch), [2006] U.K.C.L.R. 823.
[218] [2013] EWHC 3379 (Ch).
[219] Regulation 1/2003 art.23(2).

when calculating the level of a fine.[220] The Commission may reduce the fine imposed on a company that voluntarily approaches it and "blows the whistle" on a cartel of which it is a member.[221]

3. UNITED KINGDOM COMPETITION LAW

(a) Introduction

Reform of the law The domestic competition law of the UK underwent **43-077** fundamental reform with the passing of the Competition Act 1998, which entered into force on March 1, 2000. The Enterprise Act 2002 made further changes to UK competition law including the introduction of a new merger control regime, a new system of market investigation references,[222] the establishment of a criminal cartel offence[223] and the possibility of the disqualification of directors of companies that infringe competition law.[224] Changes were made to the Competition Act 1998 as a result of the application of Regulation 1/2003 by the Competition Act 1998 and Other Enactments (Amendment) Regulations 2004.[225] Further amendments were made to the law by the Enterprise and Regulatory Reform Act 2013. The provisions of the Competition Act 1998 are substantially modelled upon arts 101 and 102 TFEU. Wide powers to request information, conduct on-the-spot investigations and to impose substantial fines are given to the Competition and Markets Authority (CMA)[226] and, concurrently, to sectoral regulators such as the Office of Communications, the Gas and Electricity Markets Authority and the Financial Conduct Authority within their areas of competence. These radical changes to the law will be described in the rest of this chapter. The withdrawal by the UK from the European Union pursuant to the referendum of June 23, 2016 is likely to lead to significant changes to the domestic competition law of the UK in due course.[227]

Structure of the Competition Act 1998 The Competition Act 1998 is a complex **43-078** and technical piece of legislation. It is divided into four parts, as follows:

Pt I—Competition;
Pt II—Investigations in relation to arts 101 and 102[228];
Pt III—Monopolies (these provisions were repealed and replaced by the Enterprise Act 2002);
Pt IV—Supplemental and transitional.

This chapter will analyse the provisions in Pt I of the Act, which introduces the prohibitions modelled upon arts 101 and 102. Where relevant, some of the provisions in Pts II–IV will also be referred to.

---

[220] Guidelines on the method of setting fines imposed pursuant to art.23(2)(a) of Regulation No.1/2003 [2006] O.J. C210/2.

[221] Commission Notice on immunity from fines and reduction of fines in cartel cases [2006] O.J. C298/17.

[222] See below, paras 43-127—43-129.

[223] See below, para.43-135.

[224] See below, para.43-136.

[225] SI 2004/1261.

[226] Unless the text otherwise requires, the expression "CMA" should be taken to include the sectoral regulators who are given concurrent power to apply the provisions of the Act: see s.54 and Sch.10.

[227] For a general note on "Brexit", see Vol.I, paras 1-014 et seq.

[228] The Act refers to arts 85 and 86, but they have since been renumbered as arts 101 and 102 TFEU: see above, para.43-002.

43-079 **Part I of the Competition Act 1998** Part I of the Competition Act 1998 is divided into five Chapters, as follows:

Ch.I—Agreements;
Ch.II—Abuse of dominant position,
Ch.III—Investigation and enforcement;
Ch.IV—The Competition Commission and appeals;
Ch.V—Miscellaneous.

There are also numerous Schedules to the Act, containing much important detail, for example on exclusions, regulators and transitional provisions. The Act requires the CMA and the sectoral regulators to publish guidance as to how they will apply the Act in practice. There are also procedural rules, pursuant to s.51 and Sch.9, on the way in which the competition law proceedings are conducted as well as rules to deal with appeals to the Competition Appeal Tribunal.[229] A number of statutory instruments have been adopted under the Competition Act. Numerous guidelines have been published by the CMA, pursuant to s.52 of the Act, on various aspects of the new legislation. These guidelines are an important, albeit non-binding, source when applying the provisions of the Competition Act 1998.[230]

43-080 **Section 60: the "governing principles" clause** Section 60 is a crucially important provision in the Competition Act 1998, since it entitles and to some extent requires the competition authorities in the UK to apply EU jurisprudence on arts 101 and 102 when applying the Ch.I and Ch.II prohibitions. Section 60 is discussed at paras 43-140—43-142 below.

(b) The Ch.I Prohibition: Agreements

43-081 **Format of the Ch.I prohibition**[231] The Competition Act controls anti-competitive agreements by means of a prohibition modelled upon art.101 TFEU. Section 3 and Schs 1–3 provide for a number of exclusions from the Ch.I prohibition.[232] Sections 4–11 deal with exemptions.[233] The Ch.I prohibition must also be read subject to s.50, which provides for the exclusion, by order, of vertical and land agreements.[234]

43-082 **Section 2(1): the prohibition** Section 2(1) provides as follows:

"Subject to s.3, agreements between undertakings, decisions by associations of undertakings or concerted practices which—
(a) may affect trade within the United Kingdom, and
(b) have as their object or effect the prevention, restriction or distortion of competition within the United Kingdom,
are prohibited unless they are exempt in accordance with the provisions of this Part."

---

[229] See below, para.43-139.
[230] All the materials referred to in the text are listed in Whish and Bailey, *Competition Law*, 9th edn (2018), pp.345–346; the guidelines are available at *http://www.cma.gov.uk*.
[231] s.2(8) of the Act specifically provides that the prohibition imposed by s.2(1) is to be called "the Chapter I Prohibition".
[232] See below, paras 43-094—43-109.
[233] See below, paras 43-111—43-115.
[234] See below, para.43-110.

Section 2(2): illustrative list   Section 2(2) sets out an illustrative list of agree-   **43-083**
ments that could be prohibited under s.2(1):

> "Subsection (1) applies in particular to agreements, decisions or practices which—
>   (a) directly or indirectly fix purchase or selling prices or any other trading condi-
>   tions;
>   (b) limit or control production, markets, technical development or investment;
>   (c) share markets or sources of supply;
>   (d) apply dissimilar conditions to equivalent transactions with other trading par-
>   ties, thereby placing them at a competitive disadvantage;
>   (e) make the conclusion of contracts subject to acceptance by the other parties of
>   supplementary obligations which, by their nature or according to commercial
>   usage, have no connection with the subject of such contracts."

Effect on trade within the United Kingdom[235]   The obvious point about this   **43-084**
expression is that there is no requirement under s.2(1) that trade *between Member
States* may be affected, only that *trade within the United Kingdom* should be
affected. The Competition Appeal Tribunal has held that there is no need for the "effect on trade" within the UK to be appreciable.[236] although doubt has been cast on
the correctness of this in two High Court judgments.[237] Insofar as an agreement affects both trade between Member States and trade within the United Kingdom, it
may be subject both to art.101(1) and to the Ch.I prohibition.

"Undertakings"   This expression will be interpreted as it has been in EU law: **43-085**
should be made to para.43-013, above. The Competition Appeal Tribunal handed
down an important judgment on the meaning of the term "undertaking" in *BetterCare Group Ltd v Director General of Fair Trading*.[238] The Tribunal concluded
that a Northern Irish Health Trust, when procuring facilities for the provision of
residential and nursing care to elderly people, was acting as an undertaking and
therefore fell within the ambit of the Competition Act 1998. It is possible that this
case might have been decided differently if it had been heard after the judgment of
the Court of Justice in *FENIN v Commission*.[239]

Agreements, decisions and concerted practices   These expressions are an exact   **43-086**
replica of the provisions in art.101(1) TFEU: reference should be made to paras 43-
015—43-018, above as to their meaning in EU law and to paras 43-140—43-142,
below on the extent to which the competition authorities in the UK will be obliged
and/or able to follow the jurisprudence of the Courts of the European Union and
the decisional practice of the European Commission in interpreting these
expressions. In its decision in *Hasbro UK Ltd, Argos Ltd and Littlewoods Ltd* the
OFT (the predecessor of the CMA) found that a single, overall agreement and/or
concerted practice existed between Hasbro, a toy manufacturer, and two of its retail-

---

[235] The UK for this purpose includes England, Wales, Scotland plus the subsidiary islands (excluding
       the Isle of Man and the Channel Islands) and Northern Ireland: CMA's Guideline: "*Agreements and
       Concerted Practices*" at para.2.27.
[236] *Aberdeen Journals Ltd v Office of Fair Trading* [2003] C.A.T. 11 at [459]–[462].
[237] *P&S Amusements Ltd v Valley House Leisure Ltd* [2006] EWHC 1510 (Ch) and *Pirtek (UK) Ltd v
       Joinplace Ltd* [2010] EWHC 1641 (Ch).
[238] [2002] C.A.T. 7, [2002] Comp. A.R. 299.
[239] See above, para.43-013 n.43.

ers, Argos and Littlewoods, to fix the resale prices of various toys; this decision was upheld on appeal to the Competition Appeal Tribunal[240] and to the Court of Appeal.[241] An important judgment of the Competition Appeal Tribunal, exploring the application of the concept of a concerted practice to the practice of collusive tendering, is *Apex Asphalt and Paving Co Ltd v OFT*, which concluded that the OFT's finding that there had been an infringement of the Ch.I prohibition was correct.[242] Section 2(5) and (6) of the Act provides that, unless the context otherwise requires, any reference in the Act to an agreement includes a reference to a decision and/or concerted practice.

43-087 **Object or effect of preventing, restricting or distorting competition** The test to be applied in applying the Ch.I prohibition is to determine whether the "object or effect" of the agreement is to prevent, restrict or distort competition. In *Institute of Independent Insurance Brokers v Director General of Fair Trading*[243] the Tribunal stated that the first step is normally to determine the object of the agreement; if it is not plain that the object is to restrict competition, one should then move on to consider the effects. The illustrative list in s.2(2) is obviously of assistance in determining the types of agreement that might be caught. Considerable additional guidance is available in the jurisprudence of the EU on this: reference should be made to paras 43-019—43-026, above on this subject; and to the guidelines of the CMA referred to in para.43-079, above.

43-088 **Establishing an effect on competition** Where an agreement does not have the object of restricting competition it is necessary to examine, within its legal and economic context, whether it might have the effect of doing so. In *The Racecourse Association v OFT* the Competition Appeal Tribunal concluded that the OFT had failed to establish that the collective selling of the right to broadcast horse-racing events had an anti-competitive effect[244]; and in *P&S Amusements Ltd v Valley House Leisure Ltd* the High Court considered that there was no possibility of establishing that a beer tie in a lease of a public house in Blackpool could do so.[245]

43-089 **Appreciability** EU law applies to an agreement only to the extent that any effect on competition (or trade between Member States) is appreciable.[246] The CMA has regard to the European Commission's Notice on Agreements of Minor Importance when considering whether there is an appreciable effect on competition.[247]

43-090 **Section 2(3): territorial scope** Section 2(3) provides as follows:

---

[240] *Argos Ltd v OFT* [2004] C.A.T. 24, [2005] Comp. A.R. 588.
[241] *Argos Ltd v OFT* [2006] EWCA Civ 1318, [2006] U.K.C.L.R. 1135; see similarly the so-called *Football Shirt* case, *JJB Sports Plc v OFT*, which is also the subject of the Court of Appeal judgment in [2006] EWCA Civ 1318.
[242] [2005] C.A.T. 4, [2005] Comp. A.R. 507; see similarly *Makers UK Ltd v OFT* [2007] C.A.T. 11, [2007] Comp A.R. 699.
[243] [2001] C.A.T. 4, [2001] Comp. A.R. 62.
[244] [2005] C.A.T. 29, [2005] Comp. A.R. 99.
[245] [2006] EWHC 1510 (Ch), [2006] U.K.C.L.R. 867.
[246] See above, paras 43-024—43-026.
[247] See the CMA Guideline *Agreements and concerted practices*, OFT 401 para.2.18; on the Commission's de minimis Notice see above, para.43-025.

"Subsection (1) applies only if the agreement, decision or practice is, or is intended to be, implemented in the United Kingdom."

This gives effect to the judgment of the Court of Justice in the so-called *Wood Pulp* case,[248] that an agreement entered into outside the EU but implemented within it can be caught by art.101(1). The judgment stopped short of holding that any agreement that produces *an effect* within the EU could be subject to EU law: the Court specifically required *implementation* there. The UK has traditionally disfavoured the application of an effects doctrine in competition law matters, and has objected to assertions of an effects doctrine by the competition authorities in the US. The insertion of s.2(3) in the Act is intended to bring UK law into line with the position under *Wood Pulp*, and is equally intended to demonstrate a refusal to go further and to adopt the effects doctrine.[249]

Section 2(4): voidness   Section 2(2), which mirrors art.101(2), provides as **43-091** follows:

"Any agreement or decision which is prohibited by subsection (1) is void."

This provision clearly has very serious consequences for agreements that infringe s.2(1) but do not benefit from a parallel exemption under s.10 or satisfy the criteria set out in s.9. For many undertakings, the fact that their agreements may be unenforceable may be of much more significance than that they might be fined. Should an exclusive purchasing term imposed by a supplier on a distributor be prohibited by s.2 and therefore void and enforceable, this may fundamentally undermine the terms of the bargain agreed between the parties. Whilst it is no doubt true that judges will have a preference for enforcing agreements that have been voluntarily entered into and adhering to the maxim *pacta sunt servanda*, and that a dim view might be taken of an attempt to get out of a freely-negotiated contract on the basis of the "technicality" of infringing competition law,[250] nevertheless where there clearly is an infringement s.2(4) and art.101(2) spell out quite clearly what the consequences will be. The High Court has said, in *A Nelson & Co Ltd v Guna SpA*, that an allegation that an agreement violates art.101 is a serious one that needs, in litigation, to be pleaded in detail so that it may be defended but also so that it can be evaluated at an early stage by a court when deciding how far such an extensive and expensive claim should be allowed to go forward.[251] As to the temporal quality of this voidness, the Court of Appeal has held that an agreement that infringes the Ch.I prohibition may, through a change in circumstances, subsequently cease to do so, in which case the voidness would cease; conversely

---

[248] Cases 114/85, etc. *A Ahlstrom Oy v Commission* EU:C:1988:447, [1988] E.C.R. 5193, [1988] 4 C.M.L.R. 901.

[249] See Lord Simon of Highbury, HL Deb November 13, 1997, col.261; the General Court followed the *Wood Pulp* judgment in *Gencor v Commission* EU:T:1999:65, [1999] E.C.R. II-753, while also considering whether the effects (in that case of a concentration that would have taken place in South Africa) would have been sufficiently immediate, substantial and foreseeable within the EU to justify jurisdiction in terms of public international law.

[250] See, e.g. *Panayiotou v Sony Music Entertainment (UK) Ltd* [1994] E.M.L.R. 229 as an example of a case in which the Court appears to have taken an unsympathetic approach to a plea based on art.101(2).

[251] [2011] EWHC 1202 (Comm) at [53].

an agreement that was originally valid could subsequently become void.[252]

43-092 **Severance** Section 2(4) provides that "any agreement" which violates s.2(1) is void. It does not contain on its face any wording to suggest that the voidness might attach only to the provisions in the agreement that violate the Ch.I prohibition, nor does it say anything about the consequences of such voidness on the remaining provisions of the agreement. However, despite the clear wording of both art.101(2) and s.2(4) that "agreements" that infringe are void, it has been established by the Court of Justice as a matter of EU law that it may be possible to sever the offensive parts of the agreement, leaving the remainder enforceable.[253] The Court of Justice regards it as a matter for the court trying the action to consider whether, and by reference to what technique, severance should be effected; this is, presumably, a matter to be determined by reference to the applicable law, rather than the *lex fori*, since the issue goes to the substance of the remaining obligations under the contract.[254] The intention is that the courts in the UK should interpret s.2(4) in the same way as the Court of Justice has interpreted art.101(2): this is to be achieved through the "governing principles" clause in s.60.[255]

43-093 **Void or illegal?** In *Gibbs Mew v Gemmell*[256] the Court of Appeal concluded that an agreement that infringes art.101(1) is not only void and unenforceable, but also illegal. This can have serious consequences: for example, under domestic law a party who has paid money to another under an illegal agreement cannot recover that money unless it can be shown that the parties were not *in pari delicto*.[257] However, in *Crehan v Courage Ltd*[258] the Court of Justice has held that EU law precludes a national law which imposes an absolute bar on an action by one party to an agreement that infringes art.101 against another party to it: see above, para.43-070.

43-094 **Section 3 and Schs 1–4: exclusions** Section 3(1) provides that the Ch.I prohibition does not apply in any of the cases in which it is excluded by or as a result of:

    (a)   Sch.1: mergers and concentrations;
    (b)   Sch.2: competition scrutiny under other enactments;
    (c)   Sch.3: planning obligations and other general exclusions;
    (d)   Sch.4: professional rules: this Schedule has been repealed by s.207 of the Enterprise Act 2002.

Section 3(2)–(5) makes provision for the Secretary of State to amend Schs 1 and 3 in certain circumstances, whether by adding additional exclusions or by amending or removing existing ones.[259] Section 3(6) points out that Sch.3 itself enables the Secretary of State himself in certain circumstances to exclude agreements from the

---

[252] *Passmore v Morland Plc* (decided under art.101(2)) [1999] 1 C.M.L.R. 1129.
[253] *Société de Vente de Ciments et Bétons v Kerpen & Kerpen* EU:C:1983:374, [1983] E.C.R. 4173.
[254] On the applicable law, see Vol.I, paras 30-018 et seq. and on severance in English law, see Vol.I, paras 16-236 et seq.; on severance under art.101(2), see above, para.43-068 and the cases cited therein.
[255] See below, paras 43-140—43-143.
[256] [1998] Eu.L.R. 588, CA.
[257] See Goff and Jones, *The Law of Restitution*, 9th edn (2016), Ch.25.
[258] EU:C:2001:465, [2001] E.C.R. I-6297.
[259] This order-making power is subject to s.71 which requires an "affirmative resolution of each House of Parliament".

Ch.I prohibition.[260]

Schedule 1: mergers and concentrations Mergers and concentrations (the **43-095**
expression adopted in EU law) are, of course, of considerable interest to competition authorities, which will wish to have the opportunity to monitor transactions that
might lead to a serious reduction of competition in the market place. Both the UK,
in the form of the merger provisions in the Enterprise Act 2002, and the EU, in the
form of the EU Merger Regulation, possess specialised systems for the investigation of mergers. These provisions are beyond the scope of this book, and reference
should be made to the specialist texts on them.[261] Where undertakings merge, there
will usually be a complex matrix of contractual documents, some of which effect
the merger itself (in the sense of bringing the assets of different undertakings
together), and others of which may not in themselves bring about the merger but
may be necessary to the broader intentions of the parties and the success of the
transaction. The intention of Sch.1 to the Act, in general terms, is to provide that
agreements that bring about a merger or concentration, and any "ancillary restrictions", should be dealt with under the provisions of UK or EU merger control, and
should not be subject to the Ch.I and Ch.II prohibitions. The provisions work
slightly differently in relation to UK and EU merger control, and a few additional
refinements should be noted. There is a CMA Guideline on mergers and ancillary
restrictions that explains the operation of Sch.1 to the Act.

Schedule 1 Pt I: UK mergers The Ch.I and II prohibitions do not apply to agree- **43-096**
ments which will result in two or more enterprises ceasing to be distinct in the sense
of s.26 of the Enterprise Act; nor do these prohibitions apply to any provision
"directly related and necessary to the implementation of the merger provisions".[262]
A power is given to the CMA to "clawback"—that is to say to withdraw the exclusion from the prohibitions—where it considers that an agreement, if not excluded,
would infringe the Ch.I prohibition, that it would not grant unconditional individual
exemption and that it is not a protected agreement.[263] Protected agreements are
defined to include, for example, an agreement which is connected with a merger that
the CMA or Secretary of State, as the case may be, has decided not to refer to the
Competition Commission.[264]

Schedule 1 Pt II: EU mergers Mergers in relation to which the European Com- **43-097**
mission has exclusive jurisdiction are not subject to the Ch.I and II prohibitions.[265]
This is true as a matter of EU law, as set out in the EU Merger Regulation; there is
no power of clawback in such a case, since this would infringe the exclusive
jurisdiction of the Commission. Schedule 1 does not mention ancillary restraints but
since the European Commission is under an obligation to assess these under the EU
Merger Regulation, it would seem to follow that national competition law cannot
be applied to them as well.

Schedule 2: competition scrutiny under other enactments Several UK statutes **43-098**

---

[260] See below, para.43-106.
[261] On the UK system of merger control see Whish and Bailey, *Competition Law*, 9th edn (2018), Ch.22.
[262] Competition Act 1998 Sch.1 paras 1 and 2.
[263] Sch.1 para.4.
[264] Sch.1 para.5.
[265] Sch.1 para.6.

make provision for certain matters—such as the constitutions of self-regulating organisations or for certain arrangements in the broadcasting sector—to be subjected to "competition scrutiny" prior to their approval. The principle of Sch.2 is that where agreements have been subjected to such scrutiny, they should not require separate assessment for compatibility with the Ch.I prohibition. In consequence, they are given an exclusion from the Ch.I prohibition, though not from the Ch.II prohibition. Various amendments have been made to Sch.2 as a result of subsequent enactments.[266]

43-099   **Schedule 3: "general exclusions"**   Schedule 3 contains a number of "general exclusions", in some cases from the Ch.I prohibition and in some from both Chs I and II.

43-100   **Schedule 3 para.1: planning obligations**   This paragraph provides that the Ch.I prohibition does not apply to certain planning obligations as defined in the Town and Country Planning Act 1990. There is no exclusion from the Ch.II prohibition.

43-101   **Schedule 3 para.2: s.21(2) agreements**   This paragraph provided that the Ch.I prohibition did not apply to an agreement that had received directions under s.21(2) of the Restrictive Trade Practices Act 1976 where those directions were still in force immediately before s.2 of the Competition Act entered into force on March 1, 2000. These were agreements in relation to which the Secretary of State had absolved the now-defunct OFT of its duty to take an agreement to the, now abolished, Restrictive Practices Court because the restrictions in the agreement were not of material significance. The exclusion ceased where a material variation was made to the agreement.[267] The OFT had a power of "clawback", that is to say to withdraw the exclusion, in specified circumstances.[268] There was no exclusion from the Ch.II prohibition. This provision was repealed with effect from May 1, 2007.[269]

43-102   **Schedule 3 para.3: EEA regulated markets**   This paragraph provides that the Ch.I prohibition does not apply to an agreement for the constitution of an "EEA regulated market" to the extent to which the agreement relates to any of the rules made, or guidance issued, by that market[270]; the exclusion extends further to other matters, such as a decision of an EEA regulated market.[271] An EEA regulated market is a market which is listed by an EEA State other than the UK pursuant to art.16 of Council Directive 93/22 on investment services in the securities field and operates without any requirement that a person should have a physical presence in the EEA State from which any trading facilities are provided or any trading floor that the market may have.[272]

43-103   **Schedule 3 para.4: services of general economic interest**   This paragraph provides that neither the Ch.I prohibition, nor the Ch.II prohibition, shall apply to an undertaking:

---

[266] For the current position see Whish and Bailey, *Competition Law*, 9th edn (2018), pp.366–367.
[267] Sch.3 para.2(2).
[268] Sch.3 para.2(3)–(9).
[269] Competition Act 1998 and Other Enactments (Amendment) Regulations 2004 (SI 2004/1261) reg.4, Sch.1.
[270] Sch.3 para.3(1).
[271] Sch.3 para.3(2)–(4).
[272] Sch.3 para.3(5).

"entrusted with the operation of services of general economic interest or having the character of a revenue-producing monopoly in so far as the prohibition would obstruct the performance, in law or in fact, of the particular tasks assigned to that undertaking."

This provision mirrors, albeit not in precisely the same language, art.106(2) of the TFEU. It can be very important where, for example, an undertaking is required to carry out a service in the public interest such as the maintenance of a daily delivery of letters to all addresses at a uniform tariff: such a service may be operable only on the basis of a pricing policy that might otherwise amount to an infringement of the competition rules. In such circumstances the exclusion in this paragraph may be available to the undertaking concerned. The CMA has published guidelines on this provision.[273]

Schedule 3 para.5: compliance with legal requirements   This paragraph   **43-104**
provides that neither the Ch.I prohibition, nor the Ch.II prohibition, shall apply to an agreement or to conduct which is required in order to comply with a legal requirement.[274] An example of the way this exclusion operates arose in *Vodafone*[275] in which that mobile phone operator was required under the terms of its licence under the Telecommunications Act 1984 to print the prices to be charged by retailers on its "pre pay mobile phone vouchers": this behaviour therefore could not infringe the Ch.I prohibition by virtue of this exclusion.

Schedule 3 para.6: avoidance of conflict with international obligations   This   **43-105**
paragraph provides that the Secretary of State may make an order that neither the Ch.I prohibition, nor the Ch.II prohibition, shall apply to an agreement, category of agreements or conduct where this is necessary to avoid a conflict between the Competition Act and an international obligation of the United Kingdom. International arrangements in relation to civil aviation may be treated as "obligations" for this purpose.[276]

Schedule 3 para.7: public policy   This paragraph provides that the Secretary of   **43-106**
State may by order exclude the application of the Ch.I prohibition, and the Ch.II prohibition, to an agreement, category of agreements or conduct where there are "exceptional and compelling reasons of public policy" for doing so. One would expect that this provision will very rarely be invoked: a possible case could be in relation to the defence industry, which is not otherwise excluded or exempted from the Act.

Schedule 3 para.8: coal and steel   This paragraph provides that neither the Ch.I   **43-107**
prohibition, nor the Ch.II prohibition, shall apply to matters within the exclusive jurisdiction of the European Commission under the European Coal and Steel Community: however, this exclusion ceased to have effect when the expired on July 23, 2002.[277]

Schedule 3 para.9: agricultural products   This paragraph provides that the Ch.I   **43-108**
prohibition does not apply to agricultural products: this is to reflect their exclusion

---

[273] Guideline 421 on "*Services of general economic interest exclusion*" December 2004.
[274] "Legal requirement" is defined in para.5(3).
[275] OFTEL Decision, April 5, 2002.
[276] Sch.3 para.6(1).
[277] Sch.3 para.8(2), (4).

from art.101 TFEU. The CMA has a power of clawback.[278] There is no exclusion from the Ch.II prohibition (just as there is no exclusion from art.102).

43-109 **Schedule 4: professional rules**   Schedule 4 provided that "professional rules" regulating certain professional services and the persons providing, or wishing to provide, those services, may be excluded from the Ch.I prohibition. However s.207 of the Enterprise Act 2002 has repealed Sch.4 with effect from April 1, 2003 and professional rules are consequently now subject to the Ch.I prohibition. By virtue of the "governing principles" s.60, it is likely that the Ch.I prohibition will be interpreted in the same way as the Court of Justice has interpreted art.101: professional rules which have a restrictive effect on competition may nevertheless fall outside art.101 TFEU insofar as they are necessary for the proper practice of a profession.[279]

43-110 **Section 50: vertical and land agreements**   As mentioned at para.43-081, above, s.50 makes provision for the exclusion or exemption of vertical and land agreements from the Ch.I, but not the Ch.II, prohibition. Vertical agreements were excluded from the Ch.I prohibition until May 1, 2005, but that exclusion was then repealed.[280] Certain land agreements, for example containing covenants and conditions for the sake of good estate management, were excluded from the Ch.I prohibition as a result of the Competition Act 1998 (Land Agreements Exclusion and Revocation) Order 2004[281]; however, that exclusion has also been repealed.[282] In *Martin Retail Group Ltd v Crawley Borough Council*[283] the Central London County Court held that a restrictive covenant in a lease of retail premises was void and unenforceable under the Competition Act 1998 s.2.

43-111 **Section 9: exemption criteria**   The criteria for exemption under domestic law are set out in s.9. The wording is similar to, though not identical to, art.101(3). Unlike art.101(3), s.9 expressly applies to improvements in the production or distribution of goods *and* services. Section 9 provides as follows:

> "This section applies to any agreement which—
>
> (a)   contributes to—
>
>   (i)   improving production or distribution, or
>
>   (ii)   promoting technical or economic progress, while allowing consumers a fair share of the resulting benefit; but
>
> (b)   does not—
>
>   (i)   impose on the undertakings concerned restrictions which are not indispensable to the attainment of those objectives; or
>
>   (ii)   afford the undertakings concerned the possibility of eliminating competition in respect of a substantial part of the products in question."

In applying s.9(1) the CMA will have regard to the European Commission's

---

[278] Sch.3 para.9(3)–(8).

[279] See *Wouters* EU:C:2002:98, [2002] E.C.R. I-1577.

[280] See the Competition Act 1998 and Other Enactments (Amendment) Regulations Order 2004 (SI 2004/1261).

[281] SI 2004/1260.

[282] See the Competition Act 1998 (Land Agreements Exclusion Revocation) Order 2010 (SI 2010/1709).

[283] [2014] L. & T.R. 17.

Guidelines on the Application of art.101(3) TFEU.[284]

Sections 4 and 5: individual exemption   Sections 4 and 5 of the Competition Act   **43-112**
1998 provided for the OFT to grant individual exemption to agreements that were
notified to it and which satisfied the criteria of s.9 of the Act. However, these provisions were repealed by the Competition Act 1998 and Other Enactments (Amendment) Regulations 2004,[285] which bring the position in the UK into conformity with
the principles of Regulation 1/2003.[286]

Sections 6–8: block exemption   Provision is made in ss.6–8 for the Secretary of   **43-113**
State to make block exemptions. For the reasons given in para.43–114, below, and
in particular the fact that EU exemptions can be invoked in domestic law by virtue
of the provisions in s.10 on "parallel exemptions", it is likely that relatively few
block exemptions will be issued; however one block exemption for public transport
ticketing schemes has been enacted and took effect on March 1, 2001.[287]

Section 10: parallel exemption   Section 10 provides for "parallel exemption".   **43-114**
This is a device whereby an agreement that benefits from an EU individual or block
exemption, or which would so benefit if the agreement were to affect trade between
Member States, automatically is also exempted from the Ch.I prohibition. The same
benefits are available for exemptions obtained under the EEA Agreement.[288] A
controversial aspect of s.10 is that it states that the CMA has power, in certain
circumstances, to impose conditions or obligations subject to which a parallel
exemption is to take effect, to vary it in other ways, or even cancel it.[289] However,
art.3(2) of Regulation 1/2003 provides that it would be unlawful, as a matter of EU
law, for the CMA to impose stricter terms on an agreement that is permitted under
art.101.[290]

Section 11: exemption for other agreements   This section has been repealed.   **43-115**

Sections 12–16: notification   The provisions in the Competition Act 1998 on   **43-116**
notification for guidance and a decision were repealed by the Competition Act and
Other Enactments (Amendment) Regulations 2004.[291]

(c)   The Ch.II Prohibition: Abuse of a Dominant Position

Format of the Ch.II prohibition   The Competition Act controls anti-competitive   **43-117**
agreements entered into by dominant undertakings by means of a prohibition
modelled upon art.102 TFEU.[292] Section 17 repeals the anti-competitive practices
provisions of the Competition Act 1980. Section 18 contains the prohibition of the

---

[284] See the CMA's Guideline *Agreements and Concerted Practices*, OFT 401 para.5.5.
[285] SI 2004/1261.
[286] See para.43-002, above.
[287] Competition Act 1998 (Public Transport Ticketing Schemes Block Exemption) Order 2001 (SI 2001/
319, amended by SI 2005/3347, SI 2011/227 and SI 2016/126); see also *OFT Guideline Public
transport ticketing schemes block exemption*, OFT439.
[288] s.10(11).
[289] s.10(5)–(8).
[290] See above, para.43-067; see also Whish and Bailey, *Competition Law*, 9th edn (2018), pp.75–79.
[291] SI 2004/1261.
[292] See below, paras 43-118 et seq.

abuse of a dominant position. Section 19 and Schs 1 and 3 provide for some exclusions from the Ch.I prohibition, although these are less extensive than in the case of Ch.I. Sections 20–24 contain provisions on notification.

43-118 **Section 18(1): the prohibition**[293]   Section 18(1) provides as follows:

"(1)   Subject to s.19, any conduct on the part of one or more undertakings which amounts to the abuse of a dominant position in a market is prohibited if it may affect trade within the United Kingdom."

43-119 **Section 18(2): illustrative list**   Section 18(2) sets out an illustrative list of conduct that could be prohibited under s.18(1):

"(2)   Conduct may, in particular, constitute such an abuse if it consists in—
(a)   directly or indirectly imposing unfair purchase or selling prices or other unfair trading conditions;
(b)   limiting production, markets or technical development to the prejudice of consumers;
(c)   applying dissimilar conditions to equivalent transactions with other trading parties, thereby placing them at a competitive disadvantage;
(d)   making the conclusion of contracts subject to acceptance by the other parties of supplementary obligations which, by their nature or according to commercial usage, have no connection with the subject of the contracts."

43-120 **Effect on trade within the United Kingdom**[294] **and territorial scope**   As in the case of s.2(1),[295] the obvious point about s.18(1) is that there is no requirement that trade *between Member States* may be affected, only that *trade within the United Kingdom* should be affected; it is not necessary for the effect on trade within the UK to be appreciable. Section 18(3) provides that:

"… 'dominant position' means a dominant position within the United Kingdom; and the 'United Kingdom' means the United Kingdom or any part of it."

Lord Simon, in the House of Lords, explained that there must be dominance within the United Kingdom, although the geographical market in which that dominance is held could be larger than the United Kingdom.[296] The Act does not have a provision in relation to s.18 that resembles s.2(3),[297] so that it is not clear what the territorial scope of the Ch.II prohibition is where the abuse is "committed" outside the UK.

43-121 **"Undertakings"**   This expression will be interpreted as it has been in EU law and useful guidance can be found in *BetterCare*,[298] where the Competition Appeal Tribunal stated that the Ch.II prohibition could apply to a public sector body: reference is made to paras 43-013 and 43-085, see above.

---

[293] Section 18(4) of the Act specifically provides that the prohibition imposed by s.18(1) is to be called "the Chapter II prohibition".
[294] On the meaning of the United Kingdom, see n.235, above.
[295] See above, para.43-084.
[296] HL Deb March 5, 1998, col.1336.
[297] See above, para.43-090.
[298] [2002] C.A.T. 17, [2002] Comp. A.R. 299.

Abuse of a dominant position The meaning of "abuse of a dominant position" **43-122**
has been discussed in relation to art.102 at paras 43-061—43-064, see above, to
which reference should be made. In the UK, the CMA has published guidelines on
market definition and the assessment of market power,[299] which, in addition to the
judgments of the Competition Appeal Tribunal and EU jurisprudence and s.60 of
the Act, are of assistance in interpreting the provisions of the Ch.II prohibition.

Voidness The Act does not refer to voidness in the case of Ch.II explicitly. An **43-123**
agreement that infringes art.102 is most probably void and unenforceable, although
there is no direct authority on this in the Court of Justice, and the same consequence
would presumably follow in the case of the Ch.II prohibition by virtue of s.60.[300]

Section 19 and Schs 1 and 3: exclusions As in the case of the Ch.I prohibition, **43-124**
there are a number of exclusions from the Ch.II prohibition. Not surprisingly these
are less extensive than in the case of Ch.I: the Act is less indulgent to "abuse" than
it is to agreements that "restrict competition". In particular, Sch.2 (other competition scrutiny) is inapplicable in the case of the Ch.II prohibition. As for Schs 1 and
3, the exclusions are available in some cases for the Ch.II prohibition, but they are
not identical. The Ch.II prohibition will also not apply to certain conduct pursuant
to the provisions of the Financial Service and Markets Act 2000. The exclusions are
described at paras 43-094 et seq. see above, where relevant differences as to Chs I
and II are pointed out.

Section 50: vertical and land agreements The exclusions for vertical and land **43-125**
agreements were only from the Ch.I, and not from the Ch.II, prohibition.[301]

Sections 20–24: notification The provisions in the Competition Act 1998 on **43-126**
notification for guidance and a decision were repealed by the Competition Act and
Other Enactments (Amendment) Regulations 2004.[302]

(d) Market Investigations

Market investigation references[303] The market investigation regime contained **43-127**
in the Enterprise Act 2002 entered into force on June 20, 2003 and replaced the
monopoly provisions in the Fair Trading Act 1973. It provides an alternative
mechanism whereby agreements, in particular networks of agreements, might be
scrutinised. However, it is intended that the market investigation provisions will be
used relatively infrequently, since the Competition Act is the main legal instrument for controlling agreements which result, or are likely to result, in an anti-
competitive outcome. The making and determination of market investigation references will be briefly described below; reference should be made to specialised
works for further detail.

---

[299] See above, para.43-079.
[300] See above, para.43-068 on voidness and severance under art.101(2) TFEU and the cases cited therein.
[301] See above, para.43-110.
[302] SI 2004/1261.
[303] On market investigation references under the Enterprise Act generally see Whish and Bailey,
Competition Law, 9th edn (2018), Ch.11.

43-128 **Making of a reference** Under Pt 4 of the Enterprise Act the CMA or, in exceptional cases, the Secretary of State may initiate a market investigation reference when there are reasonable grounds for suspecting that one or more "features" of a market prevent, restrict or distort competition in the supply or acquisition of goods or services in the whole or part of the UK[304], the investigation will be conducted, within a prescribed period, by a group of members of the CMA Panel, appointed by the Chair of that Panel. The Act defines features of a market to include the structure of the market or any characteristic thereof; the conduct of persons supplying or acquiring goods or services who operate in that market; and the conduct of those persons' customers.[305] The CMA has published guidance that explains how it intends to exercise its discretion to make market investigation references[306]; in particular where competition problems arise that are industry-wide and are not capable of being adequately addressed under the Competition Act. This may be the case in sectors of the economy that are oligopolistic in market structure—that is to say a market in which a few firms account for a substantial proportion of the market—and there is a diminution of competition which is not obviously attributable to an agreement or concerted practice subject to the Ch.I prohibition, nor to an abuse of a collective dominant position contrary to the Ch.II prohibition. A reference might also be appropriate to deal with the foreclosure of a market due to the operation of parallel networks of agreements.

43-129 **Determination of a reference** Once a reference has been made, the CMA group conducting the investigation must investigate and then decide whether any feature of the market or combination thereof prevents, restricts or distorts competition in the market or markets that have been referred to it.[307] The CMA has published guidance on its procedures during market investigation references and the way in which it intends to exercise its powers. If it considers there is an adverse effect on competition, it must decide what action, if any, that either it or anyone else should take to remedy the adverse effect on competition or any detrimental effect on customers it has identified.[308] When considering remedial action, the CMA must have regard to the need to obtain as comprehensive a solution as is reasonable and practical to the adverse effect on competition and any detrimental effect on customers[309] as well as any "relevant customer benefits", as defined in the Act.[310] The CMA has a number of remedial powers available to it, including, significantly, the power to order the division of a business.[311]

(e) Investigation and Enforcement

43-130 **Role of the CMA** The CMA has wide powers to obtain information and to adopt decisions to terminate infringements and to impose fines.

---

[304] Enterprise Act 2002 ss.131–132.

[305] s.131(2).

[306] OFT 511 *"Market investigation references: Guidance about the making of references under Pt 4 of the Enterprise Act"*.

[307] s.134(1)–(3).

[308] s.134(4).

[309] s.134(6).

[310] s.134(7)–(8).

[311] The remedial powers of the CMA are set out in Sch.8.

Power to investigate   The CMA is given power to investigate suspected infringe-   **43-131**
ments of the Chs I and II prohibitions (and arts 101 and 102 TFEU),[312] including
the power to request information,[313] to enter premises without a warrant[314] or, in
certain circumstances, with a warrant.[315] However, it is not able to require a person
to produce or disclose a privileged communication[316] and it may not ask for explanations that might elicit admissions of an infringement of the competition rules.

Decisions following an investigation   If, as a result of an investigation, the CMA   **43-132**
proposes to make a decision that there has been an infringement of the Chs I or II
prohibitions, (or of arts 101 or 102) it must give written notice to the person or
persons affected and give an opportunity for representations to be made.[317] When
adopting a decision that there has been an infringement, the CMA may make directions requiring the agreement or conduct to cease or be modified[318]; directions have
been issued by the CMA (or its predecessor, the OFT) in several cases under the
Act.[319] If there is a default in complying with a direction, the CMA may apply to
the court for an appropriate order.[320] The CMA is given power to adopt interim
measures where there is a case of urgency.[321]

Penalties   An important feature of the Act is the possibility of the imposition of   **43-133**
substantial penalties for infringement. The infringement must have been intentional
or negligent.[322] There is limited immunity from fines for "small agreements"[323] and
"conduct of minor significance".[324] Penalties may not exceed 10 per cent of an
undertaking's worldwide turnover.[325] Pursuant to s.38 of the Act, the CMA has
published guidance on its likely approach to the imposition of fines which has been
approved by the Secretary of State.[326] The CMA (or its predecessor, the OFT) has
granted, and will grant, leniency from the fines it would otherwise impose on
companies who "blow the whistle" on a cartel in which it has participated.[327] The
Competition Appeal Tribunal has full jurisdiction to assess the level of penalty
imposed[328] and reduced the fines imposed in *Napp Pharmaceutical Holdings*[329] and

---

[312] Competition Act 1998 s.25.
[313] s.26.
[314] s.27.
[315] s.28.
[316] s.30.
[317] s.31.
[318] ss.32 and 33.
[319] See, e.g. *Directions given by the Director General of Fair Trading under section 33 of the Competition Act 1998 to Napp Pharmaceutical Holdings Ltd and its subsidiaries, May 4, 2001, upheld on
appeal Napp Pharmaceutical Holdings Ltd v Director General of Fair Trading [2002] C.A.T. 1,
[2002] Comp. A.R. 13*, paras 553–562; OFT Decision, *Lladró Comercial*, March 31, 2003, paras
117–118; OFT Decision, *Genzyme*, March 27, 2003; the C.A.T. granted interim relief in *Genzyme
Ltd v Office of Fair Trading* [2003] C.A.T. 8.
[320] Competition Act 1998 s.34.
[321] s.35.
[322] s.36(3).
[323] s.36(4) and s.39.
[324] s.36(5) and s.40.
[325] Competition Act 1998 (Determination of Turnover for Penalties)(Amendment) Order 2004 (SI 2004/
1259).
[326] CMA73 *"CMA's Guidance as to the appropriate amount of a penalty"*.
[327] CMA73, paras 3.1–3.24.
[328] Competition Act 1998 Sch.8 para.3(2).

Aberdeen Journals to a limited extent.[330] Much larger reductions have been made in some subsequent cases.[331] The Tribunal has stated that it may have regard to the CMA's guidance on the level of a penalty and will take into account the severity and duration of any infringement as well as any mitigating factors.[332]

43-134 **Offences under the Competition Act**   Not only does the Act provide for the imposition of penalties for infringing the competition rules; it also provides for a number of offences where there is a failure on the part of any person to comply with a requirement in relation to investigations. These offences are set out in ss.42 44 of the Act. It is important to appreciate that these offences can entail serious consequences for individuals as well as legal persons and that the penalty, for example for destroying or falsifying documents, can include a term of up to two years in prison.[333]

43-135 **Cartel offence**   The Enterprise Act introduced criminal sanctions for commission of the "cartel offence" which, on indictment, can result in the imposition of a term of imprisonment of up to five years and/or an unlimited fine.[334] Under the Enterprise Act an individual was guilty of an offence if he or she dishonestly agrees with one or more other persons that undertakings will engage in one or more of the following cartel activities: direct and indirect price fixing; limitation of supply or production; market sharing; or bid rigging.[335] The law was amended by the Enterprise and Regulatory Reform Act which has eliminated the requirement of dishonesty from the offence. The CMA has been given specific powers of investigation in criminal cases and has published guidance on how it intends to exercise them.[336] Individuals may be granted immunity from prosecution where they have provided information about cartels to the CMA.[337]

43-136 **Company director disqualification**   The Enterprise Act provides for the possibility of company directors being disqualified from office for a period of up to 15 years where they knew, or ought to have known, that their company has transgressed EU or UK competition law.[338] The CMA has published guidance on the situations in which it will apply to court for a disqualification order.[339]

43-137 **Third party actions**   Although the Act does not specifically say so, it is intended that third parties should be able to bring an action for an injunction and/or damages where they suffer harm as a result of an infringement of the Chs I or II

---

[329] [2002] C.A.T. 1, [2002] Comp. A.R. 13.
[330] [2003] C.A.T. 11.
[331] See e.g. Construction Bid-rigging case, in which the fines were reduced from £129.2 million to £63.9 million: Case 1114/1/1/09 etc. *Kier Group Plc v OFT* [2011] C.A.T. 3.
[332] *Napp Pharmaceutical Holdings Ltd v Director General of Fair Trading* [2002] C.A.T. 1, [2002] Comp. A.R. 13, paras 502–538.
[333] Competition Act 1998 s.41.
[334] s.43(2)(b).
[335] Enterprise Act 2002 s.190(1).
[336] OFT Guidelines 513 *"The cartel offence: Guidance on the issue of no-action letters for individuals"* para.2.3; OFT 515 *"Powers for investigating criminal cartels"*.
[337] s.190(4); the OFT has published guidance on the issue of no-action letters, see OFT 513.
[338] s.204.
[339] OFT 510 *"Competition disqualification orders"* and OFT 1340 *"Company directors and competition law"*.

prohibitions.[340] The Court of Justice has clarified the position under EU law in the judgment it handed down in *Courage v Crehan*[341] which, by virtue of s.60, may lead to a greater number of damages actions in the UK. There have been several actions before the UK civil courts. Claims for damages may also be brought under ss.47A and 47B of the Competition Act, as inserted by the Enterprise Act, before the Competition Appeal Tribunal.

(f) The Competition and Markets Authority

The Competition and Markets Authority   The Competition Commission was   **43-138** created by the Competition Act[342] and was responsible for carrying out merger and market investigations under the Enterprise Act 2002. However, the Competition Commission was abolished with effect from April 1, 2013 when its functions, and those of the former Office of Fair trading, were transferred to the newly created Competition and Markets Authority.

(g) The Competition Appeal Tribunal

The Competition Appeal Tribunal   The Competition Appeal Tribunal was cre-   **43-139** ated by the Enterprise Act, is headed by a President, and is seised of appeals from decisions of the CMA and the sectoral regulators under the Competition Act; claims for damages following decisions finding an infringement of either the UK or EU competition law provisions; and applications for judicial review of decisions of the CMA and the Secretary of State in market investigation references. The Competition Appeal Tribunal Rules 2003 (as amended)[343] set out the procedure to be followed in appeals to the Tribunal and apply from June 20, 2003. Appeals may be made by the subjects of such decisions[344] and by third parties.[345] Appeals on points of law may be made with leave from the Competition Appeal Tribunal to the Court of Appeal.[346] It is also now possible for the Competition Appeal Tribunal to hear so-called "standalone" actions for an injunction and/or damages as a result of changes introduced with effect from October 1, 2015; that is to say it can now hear cases where there has been no prior decision by a competition authority in the UK or the EU.

(h) Miscellaneous

Section 60: the "governing principles" clause   A key provision in the Competi-   **43-140** tion Act is s.60. Its purpose is to enable and require the courts and the competition authorities in the UK to take into account and maintain consistency with EU law. The obvious benefits of this are, first, that advantage can be taken of the substantial body of case law that has built up since the provisions of arts 101 and 102 came into effect and, second, that there should be consistency in the application of

---

[340] See Lord Simon, HL Deb, October 30, 1997, col.1 148; also DTI Press Release P/98/552, July 9, 1998.
[341] EU:C:2001:465, [2001] E.C.R. I-6297, [2001] 5 C.M.L.R. 1058.
[342] s.45(1).
[343] SI 2003/1372.
[344] s.46.
[345] s.47.
[346] s.49.

domestic and EU law. However, s.60 is not without its subtleties and requires careful scrutiny.

13 141 Section 60(1) Section 60(1) provides as follows:

"The purpose of this section is to ensure that so far as is possible (having regard to any relevant differences between the provisions concerned), questions arising under this Part in relation to competition within the United Kingdom are dealt with in a manner which is consistent with the treatment of corresponding questions arising in Community law in relation to competition within the Community."

This paragraph states the purpose of s.60, which is the maintenance of consistency with the treatment of corresponding questions in EU law. However, this is to be achieved "so far as is possible (having regard to any relevant differences …)". Thus it is recognised that there may not be total symmetry between the application of domestic and EU law. For example, there are certain respects in which the Act itself contains a provision which differs from a corresponding EU rule: an obvious example of this is s.30, which provides a wider concept of legal professional privilege than EU law.[347] Furthermore, there are certain respects in which EU jurisprudence is inappropriate in the context of domestic competition law as it affects the market within the UK: in particular, that element of EU law which is concerned with the development and protection of the single market would appear to be "relevantly different". This means therefore that there will be circumstances where the case law of the General Court and Court of Justice will not be followed in the UK where it is clear that the EU court was deciding a matter on the basis of single market considerations rather than "orthodox" competition grounds. It hardly needs to be added that it may not always be clear what the motivation of a particular judgment of the EU courts may have been. In *BetterCare*[348] the Competition Appeal Tribunal stated that s.60 required it to approach an issue of competition law:

"… in the manner in which we think the European Court would approach it, as regards the principles and reasoning likely to be followed by that Court."[349]

43-142 Section 60(2) and (3) Section 60(2) establishes the duty which follows from the purpose set out in s.60(1). The duty of the domestic court, the Competition Appeal Tribunal[350] and of the CMA[351] (including the sectoral regulators)[352] is to determine questions with a view to securing that there is no inconsistency between the principles applied and the decision reached domestically and the principles laid down by the Treaty and the Court of Justice's and the General Court's decisions that would be applicable in determining corresponding questions in EU law. Significantly s.60(3) provides that the domestic court or competition authority "must, in addition, have regard to any relevant decision or statement of the Commission". This means that the duty is lesser in the case of the Commission's decisions and

---

[347] On EU law, see Case 155/79 *AM and S Europe v Commission* EU:C:1982:157, [1982] E.C.R. 1575, [1982] 2 C.M.L.R. 264; this judgment was followed by the Court of Justice in *AKZO Nobel Chemicals Ltd v Commission* (C-550/07 P) EU:C:2010:512 [2010] E.C.R. I-8302.

[348] [2002] C.A.T. 7, [2002] Comp. A.R. 299.

[349] [2002] C.A.T. 7, [2002] Comp. A.R. 299, para.32.

[350] s.60(5) provides that court includes any tribunal.

[351] s.60(4).

[352] As to the sectoral regulators, see above, para.43-077.

statements, the obligation being only to "have regard" to them, rather than to "maintain consistency" with them.

Section 60 and Brexit   It is reasonable to assume that s.60 will be amended once   **43-143** the UK exits the EU, as an obligation to maintain consistency with the jurisprudence of the Court of Justice would be regarded as inconsistent with the spirit of Brexit.[353] Precisely how s.60 will be amended, or indeed whether it will be repealed, will be followed in future supplements to this edition of *Chitty*.

Section 73: Crown application   Section 73 specifically provides that the Act   **43-144** binds the Crown, although the Crown is not criminally liable, is not liable to a penalty, and nothing affects Her Majesty in her private capacity.

---

[353] See further Vol.I, paras 1-014 et seq.

CHAPTER 44

SALE OF GOODS

L. Merrett

[1895]

1. IN GENERAL

(a) Introduction

44-001 **Sale of Goods Act 1979** The Sale of Goods Act 1979, which came into force on January 1, 1980, consolidates the law relating to sale of goods. It replaced the Sale of Goods Act 1893 (as amended). Prior to the Consumer Rights Act 2015, the 1979 Act had itself been subject to three amending Acts, viz the Sale of Goods (Amendment) Act 1994, the Sale and Supply of Goods Act 1994 and the Sale of Goods (Amendment) Act 1995, and (in relation to consumers) to the Sale and Supply of Goods to Consumers Regulations 2002[1] as well as a number of minor statutory amendments. The Consumer Rights Act 2015[2] has a major impact on contracts for the sale of goods by businesses to consumers. Many of the rules discussed in this chapter are now limited to business-to-business sales. Consumer contracts are covered in detail in Ch.38. Cases prior to the 1893 Act are of course only relevant in so far as they are consistent with the Act.[3] But they are occasionally cited

---

[1] SI 2002/3045.

[2] The Act has been brought into force so as to apply to contracts made on or after October 1, 2015. See above, para.38-012.

[3] "The object and intent of the statute of 1893 was, no doubt, simply to codify the written law applicable to the sale of goods, but, in so far as there is an express statutory enactment, that alone must be looked at and must govern the rights of the parties, even though the section may to some extent have altered the prior common law": *Bristol Tramways and Carriage Co v Fiat Motors Ltd* [1910]

nevertheless. Cases decided on the 1893 Act are usually relevant but should be approached with caution. They may have been based on a form of words no longer contained in the 1979 Act, either because the 1979 Act consolidated amendments made to the 1893 Act or because of the subsequent amendments to the 1979 Act. But such cases may legitimately be used where the 1979 Act, as often, preserves earlier forms of wording (sometimes in a slightly "modernised" form which it appears was not meant to effect practical changes).

The Act is not exhaustive, and by s.62 it is provided that:　　　　　　　　**44-002**

"(1)　The rules in bankruptcy relating to contracts of sale apply to those contracts, notwithstanding anything in this Act.[4]

(2)　The rules of the common law, including the law merchant,[5] except in so far as they are inconsistent with the provisions of this Act, and in particular the rules relating to the law of principal and agent[6] and the effect of fraud, misrepresentation,[7] duress or coercion,[8] mistake,[9] or other invalidating cause,[10] apply to contracts for the sale of goods.

(3)　Nothing in this Act or the Sale of Goods Act 1893 affects the enactments relating to bills of sale,[11] or any enactment relating to the sale of goods which is not expressly repealed or amended by this Act or that.[12]

(4)　The provisions of this Act about contracts of sale do not apply to a transaction in the form of a contract of sale which is intended to operate by way of mortgage, pledge, charge or other security."[13]

Rights, etc. enforceable by action　By s.60:　　　　　　　　**44-003**

"Where a right, duty or liability is declared by this Act, it may (unless otherwise provided by this Act) be enforced by action."[14]

Consumer Rights Act 2015　The Consumer Rights Act 2015 has a major impact　**44-004**
on contracts for the sale of goods by businesses (referred to as "traders") to consumers made on or after October 1, 2015.[15] The provisions of the Act are discussed in detail in Ch.38.

Legislative background to the Consumer Rights Act 2015[16]　Between the enact-　**44-005**
ment of the Sale of Goods Act 1893 and the amendment in 2002 of its successor,

---

2 K.B. 831, 836, per Cozens-Hardy M.R. See also *Bank of England v Vagliano Brothers* [1891] A.C. 107, 144–145.

4　See Insolvency Act 1986 as amended. See also Vol.I, Ch.20.

5　It seems clear that these include the rules of equity, which have in numerous cases been assumed to be applicable: the prime example is that of rescission for misrepresentation, as to which see below, para.44-058. See in general *Benjamin's Sale of Goods*, 10th edn (2017), paras 1-008, 1-009.

6　See above, Ch.31.

7　See Vol.I, Ch.7; below, para.44-058.

8　See Vol.I, Ch.8.

9　See Vol.I, Ch.6.

10　See Vol.I, Ch.16 (Illegality).

11　See the Bills of Sale Acts 1878 and 1882; above, para.39-519.

12　e.g. Factors Act 1889.

13　See below, paras 44-030, 44-031. New subss.(5) and (6) are added by the Consumer Rights Act 2015 making it clear that certain sections or subsections of the Act no longer apply to consumer sales contracts which are subject to Ch.2 of Pt 1 of the 2015 Act.

14　In Chalmers, *Sale of Goods*, 18th edn (1981), p.261, it is suggested that the purpose of this provision is to exclude the criminal law.

15　See above, n.2.

16　For further detail see above, paras 38-432—38-435.

the Sale of Goods Act 1979,[17] the legislative frameworks governing contracts for the sale of goods did not themselves apply special rules to govern consumer contracts, that is, broadly speaking, contracts between sellers acting in the course of business and buyers *not* acting in the course of business, though they distinguished between sellers acting or not acting in the course of business. On the other hand, from 1973 legislation controlling the validity of contract terms seeking to exclude or to limit the seller's liability under the statutory implied terms in ss.12 to 14 of the Sale of Goods Act 1979 did distinguish according to the position of the buyer, first by reference to "consumer sales"[18] and then, under the Unfair Contract Terms Act 1977, by reference to a buyer "dealing as consumer".[19]

44-006 **Consumer Sales Directive 1999** However, this established pattern of treatment was changed on implementation of the European Consumer Sales Directive of 1999.[20] The main purpose of this directive is to require uniform rules governing certain aspects of contracts of sale of goods by sellers acting in the course of a business to consumer buyers.[21] The Directive has three main requirements to be given effect in national laws. First, it requires that "the seller must deliver goods to the consumer which are in conformity with the contract of sale", defining "conformity" in terms familiar to the English lawyer from the statutory implied terms of s.14 and 15 of the Sale of Goods Act 1979.[22] However, some aspects of the 1999 Directive's requirement of conformity were new to English law, notably, the specified relevance to the quality which a consumer can reasonably expect of goods of "public statements on the specific characteristics of the goods made about them by the seller, the producer or his representative".[23] Secondly, the Directive requires a series of rights for consumer buyers in respect of the "contractual non-conformity" of the goods: at a first level, a right to repair or replacement of the goods[24]; and, if these remedies are unavailable or fail, a right to "an appropriate reduction in the price"[25] and a right to "rescission" of the contract as long as the non-conformity of the goods is not minor.[26] Thirdly, the Directive requires that "guarantees" by sellers or producers to consumers[27] shall be binding.[28]

---

[17] These amendments were effected by the Sale and Supply of Goods to Consumers Regulations 2002 SI 2002/3045 implementing the Directive 1999/44/EEC ("the Consumer Sales Directive 1999").

[18] Supply of Goods (Implied Terms) Act 1973 s.4 creating new Sale of Goods Act 1893 s.55(4) and (7) (repealed by Unfair Contract Terms Act 1977).

[19] Unfair Contract Terms Act 1977 s.6(2)(a) (in relation to the terms implied by the Sale of Goods Act 1979 ss.13–15).

[20] Directive 1999/44/EC on certain aspects of the sale of consumer goods and associated guarantees [1999] O.J. L171/12 ("Consumer Sales Directive" or "1999 Directive"). See above, para.38-433.

[21] 1999 Directive art.2(a) "consumer"; (b) "goods" and (c) "seller".

[22] 1999 Directive art.3(2). The formulations of these requirements are elaborated further in the Directive.

[23] 1999 Directive art.3(3)(d).

[24] 1999 Directive art.3(3).

[25] 1999 Directive art.3(5).

[26] 1999 Directive art.3(5) and (6).

[27] Defined in 1999 Directive art.1(2)(e).

[28] 1999 Directive art.6.

First implementation of 1999 Directive: amendment of existing legisla-   **44-007**
tion   The 1999 Directive was first implemented in the UK by the Sale and Supply of Goods to Consumers Regulations 2002 ("the 2002 Regulations")[29] and took
effect principally by the amendment of existing UK legislation: the Sale of Goods
Act 1979,[30] the Supply of Goods and Services Act 1982,[31] the Supply of Goods
(Implied Terms) Act 1973[32] and the Unfair Contract Terms Act 1977.[33] In particular,
the 2002 Regulations inserted a new Pt 5A into the Sale of Goods Act 1979 providing a bespoke scheme of remedies based on the Directive for those dealing as a
consumer. The 2002 Regulations also made provision for "consumer guarantees"
as required by the 1999 Directive, which was not inserted into any existing primary
legislation.[34] In implementing the Directive in this way, the new English law provisions were extended so as to benefit persons "dealing as consumer" within the
meaning of the Unfair Contract Terms Act 1977[35] and not merely "consumers" as
understood by the 1999 Directive. This law still applies to contracts made before
October 1, 2015[36] and is discussed in detail in Ch.38.[37]

The Consumer Rights Act 2015   The Consumer Rights Act 2015 takes a radi-   **44-008**
cally different approach to implementation of the Consumer Sales Directive 1999
and introduces wider reform to the substantive rights of consumers against traders
in respect of the conformity of goods, digital content or services with the contract.
As described in detail in Ch.38, Pt 1 of the 2015 Act identifies three broad categories
of consumer contract: "contracts for a trader to supply goods to a consumer" or
"goods contracts" (Ch.2)[38]; "contracts for a trader to supply digital content to a
consumer" or "digital content contracts" (Ch.3)[39]; and "contracts for a trader to supply a service to a consumer" or "services contracts" (Ch.4)[40]; providing for each
category a series of terms which are "treated as included" in the contract, these being broadly equivalent to the traditional implied terms of earlier legislation, as
amended and supplemented.[41]

Secondly, in respect of each category of contract, the 2015 Act provides a series   **44-009**
of remedies, referred to as "rights to enforce terms".[42] In the case of "goods

---

[29] SI 2002/3045.
[30] 2002 Regulations regs 3–6, amending Sale of Goods Act 1979 ss.14, 20 and 61(1) and inserting new
Pt 5A.
[31] 2002 Regulations regs 7–12, amending Supply of Goods and Services Act 1982 ss.4, 11D, 11J and
18, and inserting new Pt 1B.
[32] 2002 Regulations reg.13, amending Supply of Goods (Implied Terms) Act 1973 s.10.
[33] 2002 Regulations reg.14, amending Unfair Contract Terms Act 1977 s.12 (for English law).
[34] 2002 Regulations reg.15. The definitions in reg.2 apply only to this provision as the remainder of
the substantive provisions of the 2002 Regulations provide for amendments of other legislation (as
explained in the text) whose terms fall to be interpreted, therefore, by the legislation which these
amendments concern.
[35] The definition in UCTA was amended to include contracts made by an individual buyer for goods
of a kind not normally supplied for private use or consumption.
[36] For the temporal application of the Consumer Rights Act 2015, see above, para.38-012.
[37] See the discussion of the "old law" above, paras 38-438—38-464.
[38] Consumer Rights Act 2015 s.3(1). See above, paras 38-485—38-534.
[39] 2015 Act s.33(1). See above, paras 38-535—38-566.
[40] 2015 Act s.48(1). See above, paras 38-567—38-587.
[41] i.e. the Supply of Goods (Implied Terms Act) 1973, the Sale of Goods Act 1979, and the Supply of
Goods and Services Act 1982.
[42] 2015 Act s.19 (goods contracts), s.42 (digital content contracts) and s.54 (services contracts); and
see above, paras 38-512—38-525, 38-557—38-562 and 38-580—38-584.

contracts" and "digital content contracts", these rights are modelled broadly on the rights in respect of contractual non-conformity of goods provided by the 1999 Directive and earlier implemented by Pt 5A in the Sale of Goods Act 1979,[43] but there are a series of adjustments and differences.[44] Part 1 of the 2015 Act also gives effect to certain aspects of the Consumer Rights Directive 2011, notably its require ment that information provided by the trader about the goods or services as set out by the Directive is to form part of the contract[45] and its rules governing delivery of goods and the passing of risk in goods in consumer sales contracts.[46]

44-010 Thirdly, the 2015 Act provides that a term in a contract to which it applies can not exclude or restrict the trader's liability arising under its substantive provisions.[47]

44-011 In this way, the 2015 Act seeks to set out comprehensively in a single Act all the rules governing the issues arising between the parties to consumer contracts. As a result, the 2015 Act disapplies earlier legislation affecting these categories of contracts (particularly the 1979 Act) so as no longer to apply to them or to apply to them only with qualifications.[48] Thus, as special provision is made in the 2015 Act[49] for the issues formerly (and generally) governed by the 1979 Act's provi sions on statutory implied terms as to title, sale by description, quality or fitness for purpose and sale by sample[50] the 2015 Act disapplies these provisions in the 1979 Act so as no longer apply to "goods contracts" within the meaning of Pt 1 of the 2015 Act.[51] Similarly, the 2015 Act makes special provision for "goods contracts" regarding delivery of goods generally,[52] delivery of wrong quantity,[53] instalment deliveries[54] and the passing of risk[55] and, as a result, it disapplies the equivalent provisions applicable to contracts of sale of goods under the 1979 Act.[56] Finally, because the 2015 Act also provides a new scheme of remedies for the consumer under "goods contracts" it also deletes Pt 5A of the 1979 Act and disapplies other provisions in the 1979 Act.[57] The remainder of this chapter accordingly focuses on rules which are either common to consumer contracts for goods and business sales

[43] 1982 Act Pt 1B.

[44] See above, paras 38-512—38-525, 38-557—38-562 and 38-580—38-584 for the details.

[45] 2011 Directive art.6(5), above para.38-500, 2015 Act ss.11(4)–(6), 12 (goods contracts); above para.38-549; s.36(3)–(4) and 37 (digital content contracts); above para.38-572, ss.50(3)–(4) (services contracts).

[46] 2011 Directive arts 18 and 20; 2015 Act ss.28–29. See above, para.38-527.

[47] 2015 Act s.31 (goods contracts), s.47 (digital content contracts) and s.57 (services contracts) and see above, paras 38-531, 38-564 and 38-585 respectively.

[48] 2015 Act s.60 and Sch.1.

[49] 2015 Act ss.9–18.

[50] 1979 Act ss.11–15.

[51] 2015 Act s.60; Sch.1, paras 8, 10–14.

[52] 2015 Act s.28.

[53] 2015 Act s.25.

[54] 2015 Act s.26.

[55] 2015 Act s.29.

[56] 1979 Act ss.20, 29–33; 35–36; 2015 Act s.60, Sch.1 paras 17–22.

[57] 2015 Act s.60, Sch.1 paras 24–30, 31–32 disapplying 1979 Act s.35 (acceptance), s.35A (right of partial rejection) and s.36 (buyer not bound to return rejected goods) which are inconsistent with the new scheme for consumers. The 2015 Act also disapplies s.51 (damages for non-delivery), s.52 (specific performance), s.53 (remedy for breach of warranty) and s.54 (interest). In consumer contracts for the sale of goods the 2015 Act provides special remedies for buyers. Where there is no direct equivalent to ss.51, 52 and 53 the consumer buyer will have to rely on the common law. The 2015 Act s.60, Sch.1 also makes other minor amendments to the 1979 Act consequential on its enactment of Pt 1.

(summarised in para.44-012 below), or which now only apply to non-consumer sales which are not subject to Ch.2 of Pt 1 of the 2015 Act.

Issues still regulated by the Sale of Goods Act 1979   The 2015 Act leaves unaf-   **44-012**
fected a number of provisions of the 1979 Act, which are therefore potentially applicable to the contracts to which the 2015 Act applies. In particular, the 2015 Act leaves unaffected provisions in the 1979 Act governing capacity to buy and sell,[58] how contracts of sale of goods are made,[59] existing or future goods,[60] perished goods,[61] goods perishing before sale but after agreement to sell,[62] ascertainment of price,[63] agreement to sell at a valuation,[64] stipulations about time,[65] when property passes (though the 2015 Act refers instead to "ownership" rather than "property"),[66] sales by a person other than the owner,[67] duties of sellers and buyers in general,[68] payment and delivery as concurrent conditions,[69] the buyer's liability for not taking delivery of goods,[70] the unpaid seller's rights against goods,[71] the seller's action for the price,[72] and damages for non-acceptance against the buyer.[73]

The Uniform Laws on International Sales Act 1967   This Act implemented two   **44-013**
international conventions signed at The Hague in 1964. It contains, in Schedules, two uniform laws, the Uniform Law on the International Sale of Goods ("ULIS") and the Uniform Law on the Formation of Contracts for the International Sale of Goods ("ULFIS"), both of which differ in important respects from the English domestic law. The Laws received the requisite number of ratifications to be brought into effect in 1972.[74] The Uniform Law on Sales was intended to regulate international sales between parties whose places of business or habitual residence are in the territories of different contracting states,[75] but by virtue of reservations made by the United Kingdom on ratification, under English law the law applied only where chosen by the parties.[76] The Uniform Laws had comparatively little effect, and in the United Kingdom virtually none. They have in effect been superseded by the Vienna Convention, below.

Vienna Convention of 1980   A new Convention on Contracts for the International   **44-014**
Sale of Goods (CISG), prepared by UNCITRAL and intended to supersede ULIS

---

58   1979 Act s.3, on which see Vol.I, Ch.9 and below, para.44-033.
59   Though parallel provision is made for all the types of contract to which Pt 1 of the 2015 Act applies: 2015 Act s.1(2).
60   1979 Act s.5, on which see below, para.44-038.
61   1979 Act s.6, on which see below, para.44-046.
62   1979 Act s.7, on which see below, paras 44-047—44-048.
63   1979 Act s.8, on which see below, paras 44-051—44-052.
64   1979 Act s.9, on which see below, para.44-053.
65   1979 Act s.10, on which see below, para.44-128.
66   2015 Act s.4; 1979 Act ss.16–19, 20A–20B, below, paras 44-130—44-188.
67   1979 Act ss.21–26, below, paras 44-193—44-235.
68   1979 Act s.27, on which see below, para.44-236.
69   1979 Act s.28, on which see below, para.44-237.
70   1979 Act s.37, on which see below, para.44-291.
71   1979 Act ss.41–48, on which see below, paras 44-304 et seq.
72   1979 Act s.49, on which see below, paras 44-359 et seq.
73   1979 Act s.50, on which see below, paras 44-367 et seq.
74   Uniform Laws on International Sales Order 1972 (SI 1972/973).
75   SI 1972/973 art.1.
76   Uniform Law on International Sales Act 1967 s.1(3).

and ULFIS, was approved in Vienna in April 1980.[77] Its scope is similar, and though its rules vary considerably from those of ULIS and ULFIS they are still substantially different from those of English law: they represent, in fact, a compromise between common law and civil law techniques. The Convention came into force on January 1, 1988. It has been ratified or acceded to by over 78 States, including the United States, China, Japan, Australia, New Zealand and most EU countries, but not by the United Kingdom, Brazil, countries in the Indian subcontinent or (with the exception of Singapore) South-East Asia or most African countries. Should the United Kingdom adopt the Convention, its application would (within its own terms) be automatic and not dependent on the positive choice of the parties; and the same is the case in other countries which become parties to it. The contracting parties, however, may exclude the Convention in whole or in part if they wish. Contracts governed by foreign law may well be governed or affected by the Convention. In 2011 the European Commission proposed a Common European Sales Law, a different project from CISG; but that proposal has recently been withdrawn.[78]

(b) Definitions

44-015 **Definitions** By s.61(1), unless the context or subject matter otherwise requires:

"'Action' includes counterclaim and set-off;
'Bulk' means a mass or collection of goods of the same kind which—

(a) is contained in a defined space or area; and
(b) is such that any goods in the bulk are interchangeable with other goods therein of the same number or quality[79];

---

[77] See Nicholas (1989) 105 L.Q.R. 201; Honnold, *Uniform Law for International Sales*, 4th edn (2009); Schlechtriem, *Commentary on the UN Convention on the International Sale of Goods (CISG)*, 3rd edn (2010); Bianca and Bonell (eds), *Commentary on the International Sales Law* (1987); Bridge, *The International Sale of Goods: Law and Practice*, 2nd edn (2007).

[78] See COM(2011) 635 (final) of 11.10.2011. Following a positive opinion from the Legal Affairs (JURI) Committee (Memo/13/792) on February 26, 2014 the proposal received strong backing from the European Parliament (Memo 14/137). However, on December 16, 2014 the EU Commission presented its Work Programme for 2015 to the European Parliament and the existing proposal for a Common European Sales Law was listed as item 60 in the Annex of withdrawn proposals (Com (2014) 910 final). The reason given for the withdrawal was: "Modify proposal in order to fully unleash the potential of e-commerce in the Digital Single Market". In its Digital Single Market Strategy published on May 6, 2015 (Com (2015) 192 final) the Commission referred to the need to modernise and simplify consumer rules for online and digital purchases, but the Digital Single Market agenda also covers a wide range of other issues and the likely substance and form of any new proposal in relation to sales remains very unclear. In December 2015, the Commission proposed a directive on contracts for online and other distance sales of goods (the Online Sale of Goods Directive COM(2015) 635 final). This would partly replace the existing Consumer Sales Directive with regard to distance sales (both online and offline). The proposed Online Sale of Goods Directive is part of the Digital Single Market Strategy and comes alongside several other proposed legal instruments, notably in connection with digital content supply and the portability of digital content. On May 25, 2016 the Commission published an e-commerce package (COM(2016) 320 final) aimed at three particular aspects of ecommerce: unjustified geo-blocking, transparency of parcel delivery prices and enforcement of consumer rights. On October 31, 2017, the Commission published an amended proposal (COM(2017) 637) which would repeal the Consumer Sales Directive 1999 and create a set of rules common to all consumer sales, both online and offline and including face-to-face sales. See further above, paras 38-024 et seq.

[79] Inserted by s.2 of the Sale of Goods (Amendment) Act 1995: see ss.20A, 20B, see below, paras 44-160 et seq. It is probable that this definition does not apply to s.15: see below, para.44-114.

'Business' includes a profession and the activities of any government department (including a Northern Ireland department), or local or public authority;

'Buyer' means a person who buys or agrees to buy goods;

'Contract of sale' includes an agreement to sell as well as a sale;

'Delivery' means voluntary transfer of possession from one person to another[80] except that in relation to ss.20A and 20B … it includes such appropriation of goods to the contract as results in property in the goods being transferred to the buyer[81];

'Document of title to goods' has the same meaning as it has in the Factors Acts[82];

'Factors Acts' means the Factors Act 1889 and any enactment amending or substituted for the same;

'Fault' means wrongful act or default;

'Future goods' means goods to be manufactured or acquired by the seller after the making of the contract of sale[83];

'Goods' includes all personal chattels other than things in action and money.[84] The term includes emblements, industrial growing crops, and things attached to or forming part of

---

[80] But the delivery may be constructive; see below, para.44-241.

[81] Amended by s.2 of the Sale of Goods (Amendment) Act 1995. See below, paras 44-160 et seq.

[82] See ss.24, 25. The expression "document of title" is stated by s.1 of the Factors Act 1889 to include "any bill of lading, dock warrant, warehouse-keeper's certificate, and warrant or order for the delivery of goods, and any other document used in the ordinary course of business as proof of the possession or control of goods, or authorising or purporting to authorise, either by endorsement or by delivery, the possessor of the document to transfer or receive goods thereby represented". This is considerably wider than the common law notion of a document of title, viz a document which is treated as representing the goods, which is effectively confined to bills of lading. See *Benjamin's Sale of Goods*, 10th edn (2017), para.18-007. A motor vehicle registration document is not in England a document of title under the Act: *Joblin v Watkins and Roseveare (Motors) Ltd* (1949) 64 T.L.R. 464; and see *Beverley Acceptances Ltd v Oakley* [1982] R.T.R. 417.

[83] See below, para.44-037.

[84] The term "personal chattels" covers any tangible movable property except money: s.61(1) (but see *Moss v Hancock* [1899] 2 Q.B. 111; coin bought as curiosity, and not received as current coin). It includes ships: *Behnke v Bede Shipping Co* [1927] 1 K.B. 649, 659; but these are largely governed by their own special rules: see Merchant Shipping Act 1995. It does not include things in action, such as shares, insurance policies, negotiable instruments, and industrial property; but it does include a part interest in goods (see s.2(2), below, para.44-020; *Nicol v Hennessy* (1896) 1 Com. Cas. 410). It has been held that a sale of a computer system, including both hardware and software, is a sale of goods: quaere as to software alone: *Toby Constructions Products Pty Ltd v Computa Bar (Sales) Pty Ltd* [1983] 2 N.S.W.L.R. 48; *Rubicon Computer Systems Ltd v United Paints Ltd* (2000) 2 T.C.L.R. 454; and see *St. Albans City and DC v International Computers Ltd* [1996] 4 All E.R. 481; but cf. *Beta Computers (Europe) Ltd v Adobe Systems (Europe) Ltd* 1996 S.L.T. 604. In *Southwark LBC v IBM UK Ltd* [2011] EWHC 549 (TCC), 135 Con. L.R. 136 it was said that compact discs impressed with software can be considered as "goods". The issue does not easily arise as such because matters of quality and suitability for purpose can be disposed of under express contract terms, the implied terms of the Sale and Supply of Goods Act 1982 and the implication of terms by analogy with that statute and the Sale of Goods Act. See also discussions by Green and Saidov [2007] J.B.L. 161; Naranjan [2009] J.B.L. 799; and below, para.44-109. It was decided, after a careful survey of the authorities, that software is not "goods" in *Gammasonics Institute for Medical Research Pty Ltd v Comrad Medical Systems Ltd* [2010] NSWSC 267. In *Software Incubator Ltd v Computer Associates UK Ltd* [2018] EWCA Civ 518 the Court of Appeal held that the concept of a "sale of goods" in the Commercial Agents (Council Directive) Regulations 1993 was limited to a sale of tangible rather than intangible property. Given the judge's finding of fact that the licence to use electronically supplied software was intangible property (see [68]) the Regulations accordingly were not engaged. The Court of Appeal accepted that it might seem superficially illogical that the medium on which software was supplied became determinative ([51]) and that the tangible/intangible construction that excludes software seems artificial in the modern age but given the state of the authorities held that it was not open to the Court of Appeal to adopt what might be seen as a common sense meaning. The Consumer Rights Act 2015 Ch.3 provides statutory terms for contracts for the supply of digital content to consumers and provide the consumer with remedies for breach. See

---

the land which are agreed to be severed before sale or under the contract of sale[85]; and includes an undivided share in goods[86];

'Plaintiff' includes defendant counterclaiming;

'Property' means the general property in goods, and not merely a special property[87];

'Seller' means a person who sells or agrees to sell goods[88];

'Specific goods' means goods identified and agreed on at the time a contract of sale is made and includes an undivided share, specified as a fraction or percentage, of goods identified and agreed on as aforesaid[89];

'Warranty' means an agreement with reference to goods which are the subject of a contract of sale, but collateral to the main purpose of such contract, the breach of which gives rise to a claim for damages, but not to a right to reject the goods and treat the contract as repudiated."[90]

44-016   By s.61(3), a thing is deemed to be done "in good faith" within the meaning of the Act when it is in fact done honestly, whether it is done negligently or not.[91]

By s.61(4), a person is deemed to be insolvent within the meaning of the Act if he has either ceased to pay his debts in the ordinary course of business or he cannot pay his debts as they become due.[92]

By s.61(5), goods are in a "deliverable state" within the meaning of the Act when they are in such a state that the buyer would under the contract be bound to take delivery of them.[93]

44-017   Reasonable time   By s.59:

"Where a reference is made in this Act to a reasonable time the question what is a reasonable time is a question of fact."[94]

44-018   Consumer Rights Act 2015   The Consumer Rights Act 2015 removes from the Sale of Goods Act those definitions that are relevant only to consumer contracts,

---

above, paras 38-535—38-564.

[85]   Slag, cinder tips or other artificially formed mounds of débris may, in the process of time, so accede to the soil as to become incapable of forming the subject matter of a contract of sale within the Sale of Goods Act: *Morgan v Russell* [1909] 1 K.B. 357; *Mills v Stokman* (1967) 116 C.L.R. 61 (abandoned slate); cf. *Kursell v Timber Operators and Contractors Ltd* [1927] 1 K.B. 298 (growing timber). Mineral oil extracted and removed from the soil is in the category of movables: *Anglo-Iranian Oil Co Ltd v Jaffrate* [1953] 1 W.L.R. 246, 260. It has been held in Australia that the sale of a house to be moved on a trailer was a sale of goods: *Symes v Laurie* [1985] 2 Qd.R. 547.

[86]   Amended by s.2 of the Sale of Goods (Amendment) Act 1995; see below, paras 44-160 et seq.

[87]   A special property could arise, for example, by way of pledge. For the distinction, see *Sewell v Burdick* (1884) 10 App. Cas. 74; *The Odessa* [1916] 1 A.C. 145.

[88]   See s.2, below, para.44-020.

[89]   Amended by s.2 of the Sale of Goods (Amendment) Act 1995; see below, paras 44-160 et seq.

[90]   See s.11, below, para.44-056; Vol.I, paras 13-019 et seq.

[91]   See *Jones v Gordon* (1877) 2 App. Cas. 616; *Janesich v Attenborough & Son* (1910) 102 L.T. 605; *Moody v Pall Mall Deposit and Forwarding Co Ltd* (1917) 33 T.L.R. 306; *Heap v Motorist'Advisory Agency Ltd* [1923] 1 K.B. 577, 590, 591; *Davey v Paine Bros (Motors) Ltd* [1954] N.Z.L.R. 1122, 1130; *Barclays Bank Ltd v TOSG Trust Fund Ltd* [1984] B.C.L.C. 1, 18; *GE Capital Bank Ltd v Rushton* [2005] EWCA Civ 1556, [2006] 1 W.L.R. 899. cf. *Bishopsgate Motor Finance Corp Ltd v Transport Brakes Ltd* [1949] 1 K.B. 322, 338; *Pearson v Rose and Young Ltd* [1951] 1 K.B. 275, 289; *Stadium Finance Ltd v Robbins* [1962] 2 Q.B. 664, 672, 675; *Astley Industrial Trust Ltd v Miller* [1968] 2 All E.R. 36 (whether purchase of vehicle without registration document is evidence of bad faith). See ss.23–25, below, paras 44-208 et seq.

[92]   See below, para.44-313.

[93]   See below, paras 44-140—44-141.

[94]   e.g. s.18 r.4, ss.29(3), 35, 37, 48(3).

and provides its own definitions. The principal change is that the concept of "dealing as a consumer"[95] is abolished and the Act applies "where there is an agreement between a trader and a consumer for the trader to supply goods, digital content or services, if the agreement is a contract".[96] "Trader" is defined as "a person acting for purposes relating to that person's trade, business, craft or profession, whether acting personally or through another person acting in the trader's name or on the trader's behalf".[97] "Consumer" is defined as "an individual acting for purposes that are wholly or mainly outside that individual's trade, business, craft or profession".[98] The principal changes of substance is that only an individual can now count as a consumer and that there is now explicit provision for the case in which goods are bought partly for business and partly for non-business purposes: the question will be which was the main purpose.[99]

Overseas sales   Special forms of contract have been developed by traders for overseas sales, and in particular for sales which contemplate that the goods will be carried to their destination by ship or by multimodal transport. The most frequently encountered types of contract are CIF (cost, insurance and freight), where the price is inclusive of insurance and freight to the designated port of destination, and FOB (free on board), where the seller is required at his own expense to deliver the goods to and place them on board a ship at the designated port of shipment. But the standard types of such contract also include: C&F or CFR (cost and freight), FAS (free alongside ship), FCA or FRC (free to carrier at a named place), CIP (carriage and insurance paid to a named place of destination), as well as Ex Works, Ex Ship and Ex Quay. Agreed terminology has been formulated by the International Chamber of Commerce in *Incoterms*,[100] but the incidents of the contracts there defined are sometimes at variance with those implied by English law. A detailed discussion of the law applicable to overseas sales can be found in Pt 7 of *Benjamin's Sale of Goods*.[101]   **44-019**

2.   FORMATION OF THE CONTRACT

(a)   Contract of Sale

Sale and agreement to sell   The terms "sale" and "agreement to sell" are defined as follows by s.2 of the Sale of Goods Act 1979:   **44-020**

> "(1)   A contract of sale of goods is a contract by which the seller transfers or agrees to transfer the property[102] in goods to the buyer for a money consideration, called the price.
> (2)   There may be a contract of sale between one part owner and another.
> (3)   A contract of sale may be absolute or conditional.[103]

---

95   Previously found in Sale of Goods Act 1979 s.61(5A).
96   s.1(1).
97   s.2(2).
98   s.2(3).
99   See further above, para.38-481.
100   *Incoterms* 2010 (ICC Publication 715).
101   10th edn (2017).
102   It is not, of course, essential that any immediate right to possession should be passed by the contract: see *Watts v Seymour* [1967] 2 Q.B. 647. But the title passed must be absolute and not merely possessory: see *Rowland v Divall* [1923] 2 K.B. 500; and the transfer of property must be the essence of the contract: see *PST Energy 7 Shipping LLC v OW Bunker Malta Ltd (The Res Cogitans)*

(4)   Where under a contract of sale the property in the goods is transferred from the seller to the buyer the contract is called a sale.

(5)   Where under a contract of sale the transfer of the property in the goods is to take place at a future time or subject to some condition later to be fulfilled the contract is called an agreement to sell.

(6)   An agreement to sell becomes a sale when the time elapses or the conditions are fulfilled subject to which the property in the goods is to be transferred."[104]

Two points here are to be noted. The first is the distinction between a sale and an agreement to sell. The second is the distinction between a contract of sale, which includes both a sale and an agreement to sell, and other similar contracts.

44-021   **Sales distinguished from agreements to sell**   It is necessary to make this distinction because a sale of goods is both a contract and a conveyance[105]; an agreement to sell, on the other hand, is a contract and nothing more. It follows that if one party to an agreement to sell defaults, the other party is limited to a personal remedy. But if there has been a sale the buyer also may have proprietary remedies in respect of the goods themselves, and the seller can sue for the price. Further, the risk of destruction or deterioration of the goods in a business-to-business transaction normally remains with the owner: thus it usually lies on the seller under an agreement to sell, but if there has been a sale the prima facie rule is that the buyer assumes the risk.[106]

44-022   **Contracts of sale distinguished from other contracts**   Before the repeal of s.4 of the Sale of Goods Act 1893,[107] the distinction between sale and other similar contracts was important, for until then sales, but not other contracts relating to goods, required written evidence. Since that time the matter is of less significance. But it may still be necessary to draw the distinction. For example, the Act lays down implied terms as to title, quality and description[108]; and the Unfair Contract Terms Act 1977 contains special provisions regulating the exclusion of these terms,[109] which are different from those applicable to other contracts for the supply of

---

[2016] UKSC 23. The Supreme Court, upholding the decision of the Court of Appeal ([2015] EWCA Civ 1058; see L. Shmilovits [2016] L.M.C.L.Q. 20 and A. Tettenborn [2016] L.M.C.L.Q. 24 and, in relation to the decision of the Supreme Court, L. Gullifer [2017] L.Q.R 244), held that a contract for the supply of fuel bunkers, which contained a retention of title clause and permitted the purchasing vessel owners to consume the bunkers during the credit period, was not a contract for the sale of goods within the meaning of s.2(1). See below, para.44-174.

[103]   The meaning of the term "conditional" is not clear, but it is submitted that it refers to a contract in which the duties are subject to a suspensive or resolutive condition, of which an example is discussed in connection with future goods: In *Hughes v Pendragon Sabre Ltd (t/a Porsche Centre Bolton)* [2016] EWCA Civ 18 there was a contract to sell if the seller was allocated one of a new model of car by the manufacturer. The contract was construed as an agreement to sell future goods to be acquired by the seller which depended on a contingency: see below, para.44-037. As such it should be distinguished from an option to buy: see *Marten v Whale* [1917] 2 K.B. 480. cf. *Spiro v Glencrown Properties Ltd* [1991] Ch. 537. Difficulties occur because of the use of the term "unconditional" in s.18 r.1 (see below, para.44-028); and because of conditions affecting the passage of property creating a "conditional sale" (see below, para.44-028).

[104]   As to when the property is transferred, see below, paras 44-130 et seq.

[105]   See *Mischeff v Springett* [1942] 2 K.B. 331, 336.

[106]   See below, para.44-189.

[107]   See below, para.44-034.

[108]   1977 Act ss.12–15, see below, paras 44-075 et seq.

[109]   s.6, see below, paras 44-117 et seq.

goods[110] or to contracts in general.[111] Although similar terms are laid down for hire-purchase contracts, they did not apply to contracts of barter, for work and materials, or of pure hire. Thus the section of the Unfair Contract Terms Act 1977, which applied to these contracts,[112] when first passed had little to bite on. However, the courts applied similar rules by analogy[113]; and subsequently the Supply of Goods and Services Act 1982 laid down implied terms for these contracts also[114]; but they are not identical with those for sale or hire-purchase. Again, the Sale of Goods Act contains detailed provisions under which the property in goods passes, in many cases independently of delivery.[115] These rules as such do not apply to contracts which are not contracts of sale.[116] The distinction may also be important in the case of frustration: certain contracts for the sale of goods are governed by s.7 of the Act, but the consequences of frustration when the case falls outside s.7 are governed by the general law and by the Law Reform (Frustrated Contracts) Act 1943.[117] And in general, the other provisions of the Act are intended for contracts of sale and not for other contracts.[118]

Transactions outside the Act   The following transactions are outside the scope of the Act.   44-023

(i) Gift   The provisions of the Act, e.g. those as to quality and as to the passing of property, do not apply to gifts. This can be important in the case of advertising and promotional offers of goods: if there is a sale, the Act will apply, but if there is merely a gift it will not.[119]   44-024

(ii) Exchange or barter[120]   A sale presupposes a price, and if the consideration for the transfer of property is goods and not money, the transaction is one of exchange or barter and not one of sale.[121] For s.61(1) defines goods so as to exclude money.[122] But in order to constitute a sale it is not necessary that the entire consideration should be money, and if it consists partly of the delivery of goods and   44-025

---

110   See s.7; Vol.I, para.15-094.
111   1977 Act ss.2, 3; Vol.I, paras 15-081 et seq.
112   s.7.
113   See below, para.44-026.
114   See ss.1, 2–5, 6–10.
115   See below, paras 44-130 et seq.
116   See *Flynn v Mackin and Mahon* [1974] I.R. 101, noted (1976) 39 M.L.R. 589 (barter).
117   See below, para.44-047 and Vol.I, paras 23-074 et seq.
118   See *Widenmeyer v Burn, Stewart & Co Ltd* 1967 S.C. 85 (pre-1893 rules as to risk applied to contract of barter).
119   The point arose in connection with purchase tax: see *Esso Petroleum Co Ltd v Customs and Excise Commissioners* [1976] 1 W.L.R. 1. See also *Beecham Foods Ltd v North Supplies (Edmonton) Ltd* [1959] 1 W.L.R. 643; *Chappell & Co Ltd v Nestlé Co Ltd* [1960] A.C. 87. Equally, Pt 1 of the Consumer Rights Act 2015 does not apply to gifts of goods. Nor does it apply to gifts of digital content: it applies only where the consumer is to pay a price or the digital content is available "free" but only with goods, services or other digital content for which the consumer must pay. See above, para.38-541.
120   See Law Com. No.95 (1979); Forte (1983) 28 J. Law Soc. Scotland 108, 314; Jacobs (1986) 15 Anglo-Am.L.R. 234.
121   *Harrison v Luke* (1845) 14 M. & W. 139; *Simpson v Connolly* [1953] 1 W.L.R. 911, 915. Contracts of barter or exchange between a consumer and a trader are within the scope of Ch.2 of Pt 1 of the Consumer Rights Act 2015 as far as the trader's obligations are concerned as they constitute "contracts for the transfer of goods" under s.8. See above, para.38-491.
122   See above, para.44-015.

partly of money, the contract is probably one of sale; for such a part-exchange arrangement may be treated as involving reciprocal sales with a set-off of prices,[123] or as a sale where the buyer has the option of satisfying the price in part by delivery of goods.[124] On the latter interpretation the traded-in article would not be the subject of a contract of sale. But implied terms are provided for contracts of barter by the Supply of Goods and Services Act 1982.

44-026 *(iii) Contract for work and materials* The distinction between such contracts and contracts of sale has long given rise to controversy. Where the person for whom the work is done supplies all or the principal materials,[125] or where the work done involves affixing, or installing materials on the land[126] or a chattel[127] of that person, the contract is likely (but not certain)[128] to be treated as one for work and materials. More difficulty occurs where the work done goes into the actual creation of something produced with materials furnished by the creator. In *Lee v Griffin*[129] Blackburn J. stated that the test was whether the contract was intended to pass the property; if so, the contract must be one of sale. But in *Robinson v Graves*[130] the Court of Appeal held that a contract to paint a portrait was one for work and materials and not for the sale of goods, and Greer L.J. stated the law as follows:

> "If the substance of the contract ... is that skill and labour have to be exercised for the production of the article and ... it is only ancillary to that that there will pass from the artist to his client or customer some materials in addition to the skill involved in the production of the portrait, that does not make any difference to the result, because the substance of the contract is the skill and experience of the artist in producing the picture."

The latter dictum, being more recent, presumably carries more weight, but it has been observed that the question is one of choice between two equally arbitrary rules.[131] The tendency in the courts was in any case to construe contracts for work

---

123 See *Sheldon v Cox* (1824) 3 B. & C. 420; *Aldridge v Johnson* (1857) 7 E. & B. 885. But cf. *Chappell & Co Ltd v Nestlé Co Ltd* [1960] A.C. 87.

124 See *GJ Dawson (Clapham) Ltd v H & G Dutfield* [1936] 2 All E.R. 232.

125 See *Dixon v London Small Arms Co* (1876) 1 App. Cas. 632 (manufacture of rifles).

126 *Tripp v Armitage* (1839) 4 M. & W. 687 (building); *Appleby v Myers* (1867) L.R. 2 C.P. 651 (machinery); *Reg Glass Pty Ltd v Rivers Locking Systems Ltd* (1968) 120 C.L.R. 516 (burglarproof door); *Archivent Sales and Development Ltd v Strathclyde RC* (1984) 14 B.L.R. 70 (building).

127 *Stewart v Reavell's Garage* [1952] 2 Q.B. 545 (relining car brakes).

128 See *H Parsons (Livestock) Ltd v Uttley Ingham & Co Ltd* [1978] Q.B. 791, 805, 809 (contract to install bulk food hopper held one of sale: but cf. Lord Denning M.R. at 800).

129 (1861) 1 B. & S. 272.

130 [1935] 1 K.B. 579, 587. Transactions held not to be sales include printing (*Clay v Yates* (1856) 1 H. & N. 73); supply of veterinary medicines (*Dodd and Dodd v Wilson and McWilliam* [1946] 2 All E.R. 691); supply of building materials by builder (*Young and Marten Ltd v McManus Childs Ltd* [1969] 1 A.C. 454); a contract to build, launch, equip and complete a ship (*Hyundai Heavy Industries Co Ltd v Papadopoulos* [1980] 1 W.L.R. 1129; and *Stocznia Gdanska SA v Latvian Shipping Co* [1998] 1 W.L.R. 574); and a contract to build and deliver a transportable house (*Hewett v Court* (1983) 149 C.L.R. 639). Transactions treated as sales include supply of medicine on prescription (*R. v Wood Green Profiteering Committee* (1920) 89 L.J. K.B. 55) (but supply under the National Health Service is not a sale at all: *Pfizer Corp v Ministry of Health* [1965] A.C. 512; *Appleby v Sleep* [1968] 1 W.L.R. 948); supply of meal in a restaurant (*Lockett v A & M Charles Ltd* [1938] 4 All E.R. 170; *Gee v White Spot Ltd* (1986) 32 D.L.R. (4th) 238); manufacture of a ship propeller (*Cammell Laird & Co Ltd v Manganese Bronze and Brass Co Ltd* [1934] A.C. 402); manufacture of jacket to order (*J Marcel (Furriers) Ltd v Tapper* [1953] 1 W.L.R. 49); compounding of mink food to formula specified (*Christopher Hill Ltd v Ashington Piggeries Ltd* [1972] A.C. 441).

131 *Benjamin's Sale of Goods*, 10th edn (2017), para.1-047. The test laid down in *Robinson v Graves*

and materials as though terms analogous to the implied terms of the Sale of Goods Act were applicable to them.[132] But implied terms applicable to contracts for work and materials are now provided by the Supply of Goods and Services Act 1982.[133] The Consumer Rights Act 2015 introduces a new concept of the "mixed contract", i.e. one that involves the trader supplying more than one of the three elements (goods, digital content and services) covered by the three chapters of Pt 1. The 2015 Act also provides that a contract is a sales contract if the goods are to be manufactured or produced, the trader agrees to supply them to the consumer, and the goods will then be owned by the consumer.[134]

(iv) Hire-purchase agreements, conditional sale agreements and credit sale agreements[135] A hire-purchase agreement is an agreement for the bailment of goods for hire with an option to purchase.[136] Such a transaction is not governed by the Sale of Goods Act, and indeed this form of contract was in part devised to avoid its provisions, especially that by which a person who has agreed to buy goods and obtained possession of them with the consent of the seller can in some circumstances pass a good title to a bona fide purchaser though he has no property in the goods.[137] Hire-purchase agreements, however, have since 1938 been controlled by other statutes in the interests of consumer protection. The principal current statute imposing such control[138] is the Consumer Credit Act 1974 (which applies when the hirer is an individual).[139] Terms analogous to those implied by ss.12 to 15 of the Sale of Goods Act are implied in all hire-purchase agreements by the Supply of Goods (Implied Terms) Act 1973.[140] Hire-purchase agreements under which a trader sup-

44-027

---

was rejected by the Supreme Court of Victoria in *Deta Nominees Pty Ltd v Viscount Plastic Products Pty Ltd* [1979] V.R. 167.

[132] See *Harmer v Cornelius* (1858) 5 C.B.(N.S.) 236 (painter); *Myers & Co v Brent Cross Service Co* [1934] 1 K.B. 46 (car repairs); *Watson v Buckley, Osborne, Garrett & Co Ltd* [1940] 1 All E.R. 174 (hair dye); *Samuels v Davis* [1943] K.B. 526 (dentures); *Dodd and Dodd v Wilson and McWilliam* [1946] 2 All E.R. 691 (veterinary medicines); *Stewart v Reavell's Garage* [1952] 2 Q.B. 545 (car repairs); *Ingham v Emes* [1955] 2 Q.B. 366 (hair dye); *Young and Marten Ltd v McManus Childs Ltd* [1968] 1 A.C. 454; cf. *Gloucestershire CC v Richardson* [1969] 1 A.C. 480 (building materials); *Helicopter Sales (Australia) Pty Ltd v Rotor-Work Pty Ltd* (1974) 132 C.L.R. 1 (helicopter replacement part); *Cheeld v Alliott* [2013] EWCA Civ 508 (defective workmanship in metal porch where nothing turned on whether it was a contract for goods or services). See also Vol.I, paras 14-037 et seq.

[133] See ss.2–5.

[134] See above, para.38-028.

[135] See in general above, Ch.39.

[136] For statutory definition, see Consumer Credit Act 1974 s.189(1).

[137] Factors Act 1889 s.9; Sale of Goods Act 1979 s.25; see below, para.44-220; see *Helby v Matthews* [1895] A.C. 471. Such a transaction was not caught by the Bills of Sale Acts: *McEntire v Crossley Bros Ltd* [1895] A.C. 457; nor by the Moneylenders Acts. A limited exception as regards motor vehicles was introduced by the Hire-Purchase Act 1964 Pt III, which is re-enacted by Sch.4 para.22 to the Consumer Credit Act 1974; see above, para.39-402.

[138] The Hire-Purchase Act 1964 was entirely repealed by s.192(3)(b) of and Sch.5 to the Consumer Credit Act 1974 and SI 1983/1551 (c.44), but see art.6(1) (2) of that Order.

[139] ss.8, 9. The general financial limit in the 1974 Act was removed by s.2 of the Consumer Credit Act 2006. For the definition of "individual", see s.189(1) (as amended by the Consumer Credit Act 2006): it includes (a) a partnership consisting of two or three persons not all of whom are bodies corporate; and (b) an unincorporated body of persons which does not consist entirely of bodies corporate and is not a partnership. See also above, paras 39-016, 39-017.

[140] ss.8–11; see above, para.39-316. The 1973 Act is re-enacted by s.192 of and Sch.4 paras 35–36 to the Consumer Credit Act 1974, and was amended by the Sale and Supply of Goods Act 1994 and by the Sale and Supply of Goods to Consumers Regulations 2002 (SI 2002/3045) reg.13.

plies goods to a consumer are within the scope of Ch.2 of Pt 1 of the Consumer Rights Act 2015.[141]

44-028 **Conditional sale agreements** A conditional sale agreement is an agreement for the sale of goods under which the purchase price or part of it is payable by instalments, and the property in the goods is to remain in the seller (notwithstanding that the buyer is to be in possession of the goods) until such conditions as to the payment of instalments or otherwise as may be specified in the agreement are fulfilled.[142] Such a transaction is a contract of sale of goods[143] and is governed by the Sale of Goods Act. But it is also subject to the control of the Consumer Credit Act 1974[144] if the buyer is an individual. Unlike a hirer under a hire-purchase agreement, who has merely an option to purchase the goods, a buyer under a conditional sale agreement will have agreed to buy them, so that if he is in possession of the goods with the consent of the seller he may be able to pass a good title to a bona fide purchaser.[145] But a buyer under a conditional sale agreement which is a consumer credit agreement within the meaning of the Consumer Credit Act 1974 is deemed not to be a person who has bought or agreed to buy goods.[146] Such an agreement is therefore assimilated to a hire-purchase agreement for the purposes of restricting the buyer's ability to pass a good title to the goods. Conditional sale agreements under which a trader supplies goods to a consumer are within the scope of Ch.2 of Pt 1 of the Consumer Rights Act 2015.[147]

44-029 **Credit-sale agreements** The term "credit-sale agreement" is largely of statutory origin: it refers to "an agreement for the sale of goods under which the purchase price or part of it is payable by instalments, but which is not a conditional sale agreement",[148] viz the property passes to the buyer in accordance with normal rules and is not reserved to the seller.[149] Such a transaction is a sale of goods and is therefore governed by the Sale of Goods Act. A credit-sale agreement is a consumer credit agreement if the buyer is an individual[150] and (unless otherwise exempt)[151] the agreement will be a regulated agreement[152] and subject to the control of the

---

[141] See above, para.38-489.

[142] Consumer Credit Act 1974 s.189(1); see above, para.39-464.

[143] Sale of Goods Act 1979 s.2(3). However, if the terms of an agreement mean that property is unlikely ever to pass then the Sale of Goods Act does not apply, see *PST Energy 7 Shipping LLC v OW Bunker Malta Ltd* [2016] UKSC 23 in the context of a bunker supply contract.

[144] ss.8, 9; see above, para.39-461. The general financial limit in the 1974 Act was removed by s.2 of the Consumer Credit Act 2006.

[145] Sale of Goods Act 1979 s.25(1); Factors Act 1889 s.9; *Lee v Butler* [1893] 2 Q.B. 318; *Hull Rope Works Co v Adams* (1895) 73 L.T. 446; *Thompson and Shackell Ltd v Veale* (1896) 74 L.T. 130; *Horton v Gibbins* (1897) 13 T.L.R. 408; *Wylde v Legge* (1901) 84 L.T. 121; *Marten v Whale* [1917] 2 K.B. 480; see below, para.44-220.

[146] Sale of Goods Act 1979 s.25(2) (4), Sch.1 para.9 and Sch.4 para.2; Consumer Credit Act 1974 s.192 and Sch.4 paras 2, 4; SI 1983/1572. But see Pt III of the Hire-Purchase Act 1964 (motor vehicles), see above, para.39-402, which is re-enacted by Sch.4 para.22 to the Consumer Credit Act 1974.

[147] See above, para.38-490.

[148] Consumer Credit Act 1974 s.189(1).

[149] See above, para.39-442.

[150] 1974 Act s.8(2). The general financial limit in the 1974 Act was removed by s.2 of the Consumer Credit Act 2006.

[151] Under ss.16, 16A, 16B, 16C of the 1974 Act (as amended); see above, para.39-038.

[152] s.8(3).

Consumer Credit Act 1974,[153] unless the number of payments to be made by the buyer in respect of credit does not exceed four.[154] A buyer under a credit-sale agreement can pass title to a third party by virtue of the fact that he is the owner of the goods.

(v) Mortgages of goods A legal mortgage of goods consists in the transfer of **44-030** property in the goods in order to secure a debt; the mortgagor retains possession of the goods, subject to the mortgagee's power of taking possession on default in payment. As such, a mortgage of goods bears certain similarities to a contract of sale, since there is a transfer of the property in the goods by the mortgagor to the mortgagee with a proviso for retransfer on redemption. But a transaction in the form of a contract of sale which is intended to operate by way of mortgage, charge or other security is not subject to the provisions of the Sale of Goods Act.[155] If, however, it is reduced to writing, the transaction may fall within the Bills of Sale Acts 1878 and 1882.[156] Considerable difficulty may, however, arise where an owner of goods sells the goods to a purchaser and then immediately enters into a hire-purchase agreement whereby he (the original owner) agrees to hire the goods. The combined effect of the sale and lease back may be that of a loan on security of the goods. A genuine sale and a genuine lease back of the same goods will be upheld as falling outside the Bills of Sale Acts.[157] But circumstances may be present which indicate that such a two-stage transaction is in reality a cloak for a mortgage and so void under the Bills of Sale Act 1882.[158]

(vi) Pledges A pledge consists in the bailment of goods to secure payment of a **44-031** debt.[159] The general property in the goods remains in the pledgor, though the pledgee thereby acquires a special property for securing repayment of the debt. The provisions of the Sale of Goods Act about contracts of sale do not apply to a transac-

---

[153] See above, para.39-465.
[154] Consumer Credit (Exempt Agreements) Order 1989 (SI 1989/869) art.3(1)(a)(i) (provided the payments are to be made within 12 months from the date of the agreement). As a result of the implementation of the Consumer Credit Directive (see para.39-011, above), art.3(1)(a)(i) has been amended by SI 2010/1010 reg.66 (in force from February 1, 2011) and a further condition for exemption has been added: that the credit must be provided without interest or any other charge.
[155] s.62(3), (4): see above, para.44-002; nor the Consumer Rights Act 2015.
[156] Or (in the case of a company) a registrable charge: Companies Act 2006 s.860(7)(b). See also Bills of Sale Act (1878) (Amendment) Act 1882 s.17; *Re Standard Manufacturing Co* [1891] 1 Ch. 627; and see above, para.39-519.
[157] *Yorkshire Ry Wagon Co v Maclure* (1882) 21 Ch. D. 309; *Victoria Dairy Co of Worthing v West* (1895) 11 T.L.R. 233; *British Ry Traffic and Electric Co v Kahn* [1921] W.N. 52; *Staffs Motor Guarantee Ltd v British Wagon Co Ltd* [1934] 2 K.B. 305; *Olds Discount Co Ltd v Krett* [1940] 2 K.B. 117; Diamond (1960) 23 M.L.R. 518.
[158] *Re Watson* (1890) 25 Q.B.D. 27; *Wheatley's Trustee v Wheatley Ltd* (1901) 85 L.T. 491; *Maas v Pepper* [1905] A.C. 102; *Polsky v S and A Services* [1951] 1 All E.R. 185, 1062n.; *North Central Wagon Finance Co Ltd v Brailsford* [1962] 1 W.L.R. 1288. cf. *Kingsley v Sterling Industrial Securities Ltd* [1967] 2 Q.B. 747. See also *Stoneleigh Finance Ltd v Phillips* [1965] 2 Q.B. 537; *Snook v London and West Riding Investments Ltd* [1967] 2 Q.B. 786; *Re Curtain Dream Plc* [1990] B.C.L.C. 925; *Benjamin's Sale of Goods*, 10th edn (2017), para.1-066.
[159] See above, para.33-121.

tion in the form of a contract of sale[160] which is intended to operate by way of pledge.[161]

44-032 *(vii) Agency*   A person who agrees to procure goods for another may be an agent, or he may buy them and resell them to that other. Conversely a person who agrees to sell goods for another may be an agent, or he may be a person buying for resale, whether outright or on a "sale or return" basis.[162] An agent's duties are normally no more than to use his best endeavours and are quite different from those of a seller. The extent to which the person concerned is remunerated by commission is relevant to this distinction: even more relevant is the extent to which he has to account to the other.[163]

(b) Capacity of Parties

44-033 **Capacity of parties**   By s.3[164]:

"(1)   Capacity to buy and sell is regulated by the general law concerning capacity to contract and to transfer and acquire property.

(2)   Where necessaries are sold and delivered to a minor or to a person who by reason of drunkenness is incompetent to contract, he must pay a reasonable price for them.

(3)   In subs.(2) above, 'necessaries' means goods suitable to the condition in life of the minor or other person concerned and to his actual requirements at the time of the sale and delivery."[165]

Section 7 of the Mental Capacity Act 2005, which deals with mental incapacity, is expressed in similar terms. These provisions are considered elsewhere in this work.[166] The liability to pay a reasonable price for necessaries appears to be restitutionary: a person who in law is incompetent to make a contract cannot bind himself to pay for necessaries supplied, but if it is for his benefit that he should have them, he must pay a reasonable price for goods received, though not necessarily the contract price.[167] Hence it is usually thought that a minor would not be liable on an executory contract for necessaries.[168]

(c) Formalities

44-034 **Formalities**   Section 4 of the Sale of Goods Act 1893,[169] which required written evidence or part performance for contracts for the sale of goods of the value of £10

---

[160] For pledge and sale contrasted, see *Burdick v Sewell* (1884) 13 Q.B.D. 159, 175; (1884) 10 App. Cas. 74, 93. For a case where a storage arrangement having some appearance of a bailment was held to be a sale, see *Chapman Bros v Verco Bros & Co Ltd* (1933) 49 C.L.R. 306.

[161] 1974 Act s.62(4): see above, para.44-002.

[162] See below, para.44-146.

[163] For full discussion, see *Benjamin's Sale of Goods*, 10th edn (2017), paras 1-048—1-049; *Bowstead and Reynolds on Agency*, 21st edn (2017), para.1-036. See also above, para.31-129.

[164] As amended by the Mental Capacity Act 2005 Sch.6 para.24.

[165] See *Nash v Inman* [1908] 2 K.B. 1.

[166] Vol.I, Ch.9. See also *Benjamin's Sale of Goods*, 10th edn (2017), paras 2-028 et seq.

[167] *Re Rhodes* (1890) 44 Ch. D. 94, 105; approved in *Nash v Inman* [1908] 2 K.B. 1, 8.

[168] But in *Roberts v Gray* [1913] 1 K.B. 520 a minor was held liable on an executory contract for education. cf. also Treitel, *The Law of Contract*, 14th edn (2015), para.12-008; Goff and Jones, *The Law of Unjust Enrichment*, 9th edn (2016), para.24-018 (liability is contractual).

[169] s.4 re-enacted, with some variations, the Statute of Frauds 1677. See Vol.I, Ch.5.

or upwards, was repealed by the Law Reform (Enforcement of Contracts) Act 1954. The result is that contracts for the sale of goods may be made without formalities.[170]

(d)   Subject Matter

Subject matter of contract   By s.5(1):   44-035

"The goods which form the subject of a contract of sale may be either existing goods, owned or possessed by the seller, or goods to be manufactured or acquired by him after the making of the contract of sale, in this Act called future goods."

Existing goods   These may be specific or unascertained. This distinction, which   44-036
is important as regards the passing of property and as regards the effects of destruction of the goods, is discussed in what follows.

Future goods   This expression covers goods which are not yet in existence and   44-037
existing goods not yet acquired by the seller.[171] Section 5(3) provides: "Where by a contract of sale the seller purports to effect a present sale of future goods, the contract operates as an agreement to sell the goods". Future goods will usually[172] be unascertained: as such property in them cannot pass.[173] Even if they are specific, the passing of property would sometimes be deferred until they were in a deliverable state.[174]

Contracts for the sale of future goods   Such contracts are capable of three   44-038
interpretations. First, the seller may promise that they will come into existence or be acquired, and will be liable if this does not occur.[175] Secondly, there may be a conditional sale on the basis of s.5(2), which provides: "There may be a contract for the sale of goods, the acquisition of which by the seller depends on a contingency which may or may not happen".[176] In such a case (e.g. the sale of a future crop) both seller and buyer may owe subordinate duties to each other not to prevent the occurrence of the condition, and in some cases to facilitate its occurrence[177]; but the buyer only pays for such goods as are supplied and cannot sue for non-delivery of goods that never came into existence or were never acquired.[178] When only part of the goods come into existence or are acquired it is a question of

---

[170] But there are statutory requirements for certain hire-purchase agreements, conditional sale agreements, and credit-sale agreements: see above, paras 39-076 et seq.

[171] 1893 Act s.61(1); see above, para.44-015.

[172] See below, para.44-038.

[173] See s.16, see below, para.44-131. Before the 1893 Act equity held that a beneficial interest passed to the buyer as soon as the goods became present goods and the contract could be implemented by specific performance (see *Holroyd v Marshall* (1862) 10 H.L. Cas. 191). But this doctrine did not survive the Act, at any rate in England and Wales: see *Re Wait* [1927] 1 Ch. 606, 635–636, applied in *Hughes v Pendragon Sabre Ltd (t/a Porsche Centre Bolton)* [2016] EWCA Civ 18 (at [42]).

[174] See s.18 r.2: below, para.44-141.

[175] e.g. *Blackburn Bobbin Co Ltd v TW Allen & Sons Ltd* [1918] 2 K.B. 467 (sale of generic goods).

[176] See also s.2(3) of the Act: above, para.44-020. See *Hughes v Pendragon Sabre Ltd (t/a Porsche Centre Bolton)* [2016] EWCA Civ 18.

[177] e.g. the seller of a future crop must cultivate it. See *Mackay v Dick* (1881) 6 App. Cas. 251 (duty to test machine). See Vol.I, paras 14-023, 14-024.

[178] e.g. *Lovatt v Hamilton* (1839) 5 M. & W. 639 (sale of goods "to arrive").

interpretation whether he can demand, or must take, such goods as there are, and whether he can reject completely.[179]

44-039 **Sale of a chance** The third interpretation is that the buyer agrees to pay whether or not goods are supplied (though there would here again be subordinate duties as to the prevention of the goods coming into existence or being acquired). The subject matter here would be a mere chance. This possibility is not mentioned in the Act, and indeed it is arguable that such a sale of a chance is not a sale of *goods* at all: but there seems little merit in excluding the Act from such a closely assimilated transaction. There is no clear authority, but it is commonly said that an old decision in *Bagueley v Hawley*[180] could be explained on this basis.

44-040 **Specific, ascertained and unascertained goods** Although two possibilities are referred to in s.5 as forming the subject matter of a contract of sale, there is another important distinction to be drawn. This is the distinction between specific, ascertained and unascertained goods, which to some extent cuts across the distinction between existing and future goods.

44-041 **Specific goods; ascertained goods** Specific goods are those "identified and agreed on at the time a contract of sale is made".[181] By an amendment made by the Sale of Goods (Amendment) Act 1995, this definition was extended to include "an undivided share, specified as a fraction or percentage of goods identified and agreed on as aforesaid". Thus a contract for the sale of a quarter-share in a named racehorse, or a contract for the sale of 20 per cent of the existing cargo of a named ship, will be a contract for the sale of specific goods. Ascertained goods are not defined by the Act, although various references are made to such a category.[182] In *Re Wait*[183] Atkin L.J. said that ascertained "probably means identified in accordance with the agreement after the time a contract of sale is made".

44-042 **Unascertained goods** Unascertained goods may be said to fall into three categories:

(i)   future goods, except identified goods to be acquired by the seller;
(ii) generic goods, e.g. "100 tons of wheat";
(iii) the unascertained portion of an ascertained whole, for instance, "100 tons of wheat from the larger quantity which A has in his warehouse".

44-043 **Problem cases** It is clear that existing goods may be either specific or unascertained: if unascertained they may later become ascertained. Future goods will certainly for the most part be unascertained. The clearest example of future goods which seem to be specific is that of identified goods owned by a third party at the time the contract is made.[184] But it can be argued that there is nothing in the Act saying that specific goods must actually be in existence at the time they are identified and agreed upon: on this basis a contract for the entire future crop of a

---

[179] See *HR & S Sainsbury Ltd v Street* [1972] 1 W.L.R. 834 (barley).
[180] (1867) L.R. 2 C.P. 625 (resale of goods seized under distress).
[181] 1893 Act s.61(1); see above, para.44-015.
[182] e.g. ss.16, 17, 52.
[183] [1927] 1 Ch. 606, 630.
[184] This was in the case in *Varley v Whipp* [1900] 1 Q.B. 513, and there is no suggestion in the case that the goods were not specific.

particular piece of land might be argued to be a contract for specific goods.[185] In *Howell v Coupland*[186] it was held before the Act that a contract for the sale of a specified quantity of potatoes to be grown on a designated piece of land was frustrated by failure of the crop, and the contract was said to be one for "what will be and may be called specific things".[187] But in *Re Wait*[188] it was held that a contract for a specified quantity of goods out of a particular mass was not a contract for specific goods, and though the context was one of the availability of specific performance the reasoning seems of general application. Thus the sale of a particular quantity of future goods from a defined source is not a sale of specific goods, and it is submitted that even a sale of the whole crop from that source would not be, for the wording of ss.6 and 7 of the Act, which deal with perishing of the goods,[189] seem clearly to envisage "specific goods" as being in existence at the time of contract, and the wording of s.5(3)[190] points to a similar conclusion. In *HR & S Sainsbury Ltd v Street*[191] it was held that a contract similar to that in *Howell v Coupland* was governed by s.5(2) of the Act[192] and was not a contract for specific goods covered by s.7. Although the case was also one of sale of a specified quantity to be grown at a particular place, it is submitted that the reasoning is again of general application and that, except in the situation indicated at the beginning of the paragraph, future goods cannot be specific.

Importance of distinction   The distinction between specific, ascertained and unascertained goods is of importance in relation to ss.6 and 7 of the Act, as explained below. It is also of importance in relation to the passing of the property and the risk. This is discussed in detail elsewhere.[193]   **44-044**

Sale of goods already perished   By s.6:   **44-045**

> "Where there is a contract for the sale of specific goods, and the goods without the knowledge of the seller have perished[194] at the time when the contract is made, the contract is void."

This section deals with mistake as to the existence of the specific subject matter of the contract.[195] If the terms of the section are satisfied the contract is void, so that no action will lie for breach of contract by either party and the buyer may recover the price if he has already paid it. The section is commonly thought to be intended

---

[185] *Benjamin's Sale of Goods*, 10th edn (2017), paras 1-114, 1-115. See also *Lister v Munro* [1924] N.Z.L.R. 1137, 1140.
[186] (1876) 1 Q.B.D. 258.
[187] At 262.
[188] [1927] 1 Ch. 606.
[189] See below, paras 44-045 et seq.
[190] See above, para.44-037.
[191] [1972] 1 W.L.R. 834.
[192] See above, para.44-038.
[193] See below, paras 44-130 et seq., paras 44-189 et seq.
[194] On the meaning of "perish", see note to s.7: below, para.44-048. Section 6 does not apply if the goods have never been in existence at all, for in that case they have not "perished": *McRae v Commonwealth Disposals Commission* (1951) 84 C.L.R. 377, where sellers were held liable on the basis that they had warranted that the goods (a wrecked oil tanker sold for salvage) existed. The case could also be solved on the basis of a collateral contract or of an action in tort for negligent misrepresentation.
[195] See Vol.I, paras 6-042 et seq.

to represent the effect of the old decision in *Couturier v Hastie*.[196] In that case there was a sale (effectively what is now called CIF) of a specific cargo of corn then believed to be on the high seas but which had in fact, before the sale, become so heated that it had been unloaded and sold at a nominal price by the master of the ship. The sellers had delivered the shipping documents. The House of Lords held that they were not entitled to recover the price from the buyer. The case was regarded as turning on the construction of the contract[197]: it was decided that this was a contract for the sale of a specific cargo rather than the adventure represented by the documents, and so in the circumstances the plaintiffs could not recover. The question whether the contract was void can be said not to have been directly in issue, though had it been void the same result would have ensued. Nevertheless, the case was and is taken to stand for the proposition that such a sale is based on the initial existence of the goods, and hence inoperative if there were none.[198]

44-046 Three points arising from s.6 require brief comment:

(i) *Specific goods:* The section does not cover a sale of unascertained goods. Thus if A contracts to sell to B 1,000 tons of grain, it is normally immaterial that A's intended source of supply has already been destroyed. The case is governed by the maxim *genus nunquam perit*, and A remains liable to procure the grain from another source.[199]

(ii) *Partial destruction:* It seems that the section applies where there is a contract to sell an indivisible parcel of specific goods part only of which has perished when the contract is made. In *Barrow, Lane and Ballard Ltd v Phillip Phillips & Co*,[200] where, at the date of the contract to sell 700 bags, 109 bags had been stolen, it was held that the whole contract was avoided. Had the contract been severable it could perhaps have been void only as to the perished part.

(iii) *Knowledge of the seller:* If at the time of the contract the seller knows that the goods have perished, he is perhaps estopped from pleading that no contract exists.[201] But if the seller is ignorant and the buyer aware, or if both parties are ignorant, it seems that the contract is in each case void. There is however nothing to exclude the application of common law doctrines which might render the contract inoperative for any other reason, e.g. some other type of fundamental mistake, even if this would be rare.[202]

44-047 Goods perish after contract made By s.7:

"Where there is an agreement to sell specific goods and subsequently the goods, without

---

[196] (1856) 5 H.L. Cas. 673; affirming (1853) 9 Ex. 102.

[197] Twigg-Flessner, Canavan and MacQueen (eds), *Atiyah and Adams Sale of Goods*, 13th edn (2016), p.77, concludes, citing s.55(1) (see below, para.44-127) and *McRae's* case (see above, n.194) that s.6 is not mandatory; that is, it will not apply if, on the construction of the contract, the seller has contracted that the goods are in existence, or if the buyer can genuinely be regarded as having bought a chance. See also *Benjamin's Sale of Goods*, 10th edn (2017), paras 1-122—1-135; Vol.I, paras 6-021 et seq. Such an interpretation would only be necessary where a claim in tort or upon a collateral contract would yield damages inadequate to the circumstances.

[198] The question connects with problems of risk in documentary sales. See *Benjamin's Sale of Goods*, 10th edn (2017), para.19-113.

[199] *Re Thornett and Fehr and Yuills Ltd* [1921] 1 K.B. 219.

[200] [1929] 1 K.B. 574. See *Benjamin's Sale of Goods*, 10th edn (2017), para.1-126.

[201] See *Bell v Lever Bros* [1932] A.C. 161, 217.

[202] See Vol.I, Ch.6.

any fault on the part of the seller or buyer, perish before the risk passes to the buyer, the agreement is avoided."

Section 7 relates to a particular case of frustration. The scope of the section is comparatively narrow. First, it is limited to specific goods and does not apply to sales of unascertained goods. This excludes sales of generic goods, sales of an unascertained quantity of an ascertained whole,[203] and most sales of future goods from the operation of the section.[204] Secondly, it is limited to goods which have perished.[205] Perishing covers of course physical destruction, and also the case where the goods are so damaged as no longer to answer to the description under which they were sold.[206] But if the goods retain their commercial identity, and have merely deteriorated in quality, the section does not apply.[207] Further, it probably does not apply where the goods have not perished but are simply unavailable, because for example, of requisition[208] or the outbreak of war,[209] though where they are stolen or otherwise lost irretrievably, it may apply.[210] Thirdly, it is limited to an agreement to sell, that is, a case where the property in the goods has not passed to the buyer.[211] Fourthly, the risk must not yet have passed to buyer: so, for example, s.7 will not apply where the property in the goods remains in the seller; but the goods are nevertheless at the buyer's risk.[212] Fifthly, the section is limited to cases where the goods perish without any fault[213] on the part of the seller or the buyer.

Frustration at common law   There is however nothing to exclude the operation of the common law doctrine of frustration in situations other than that where the goods perish, even if it would rarely apply.[214]

Operation of s.7   The Law Reform (Frustrated Contracts) Act 1943 s.2(5)(c), excepts from the Act's provisions any contract to which s.7 of the Sale of Goods Act applies.[215] Consequently cases falling under s.7 are governed by the common

44-048

44-049

44-050

---

203 e.g. 200 bottles from a larger quantity in an identified bin. But a contract for the sale of a fraction ("one-fifth") or percentage ("20%") of the wine in an identified bin is a contract for the sale of specific goods: s.61(1); see above, para.44-015.

204 See above, para.44-037; *HR & S Sainsbury Ltd v Street* [1972] 1 W.L.R. 834.

205 Including part of an indivisible parcel: see above, para.44-046.

206 *Barr v Gibson* (1838) M. & W. 390; *Asfar & Co Ltd v Blundell* [1896] 1 Q.B. 123. For a recent example see *Oldfield Asphalts Ltd v Grovedale Coolstores (1994) Ltd* [1998] 3 N.Z.L.R. 479.

207 *Horn v Minister of Food* [1948] 2 All E.R. 1036 (rotten potatoes held still to be potatoes). But cf. *Rendell v Turnbull & Co* (1908) 27 N.Z.L.R. 1067 (a case on s.6).

208 See *Re Shipton, Anderson & Co* [1915] 3 K.B. 676, where, however, the contract was held to be frustrated at common law.

209 See *Re Badische Co Ltd* [1921] 2 Ch. 331, where again common law was applied.

210 See *Barrow, Lane & Ballard Ltd v Phillip Phillips & Co Ltd* [1929] 1 K.B. 574 (theft).

211 As in cases falling within s.18 rr.2 and 3 of the Act (below, paras 44-141 et seq.) or where the seller reserves the right of disposal (below, para.44-170).

212 See below, para.44-189. Frustration only starts where risk stops.

213 Defined in s.61(1); see above, para.44-015.

214 See Vol.I, Ch.23; *Blackburn Bobbin Co Ltd v TW Allen & Sons* [1918] 2 K.B. 467; *Re Shipton, Anderson & Co*, above; *Lewis Emanuel & Son Ltd v Sammut* [1955] 2 Lloyd's Rep. 629. Alternatively, the contract may be subject to a condition precedent as to the goods coming into existence as in *Howell v Coupland* (1876) 1 Q.B.D. 258.

215 The second part of s.2(5)(c) excepts from the Law Reform (Frustrated Contracts) Act 1943 "any other contract for the sale or for the sale and delivery of specific goods where the contract is frustrated by reason of the fact that the goods have perished". It is far from clear to what situations this obscure provision applies: see *Benjamin's Sale of Goods*, 10th edn (2017), para.6-052; Twigg-Flesner,

law rules as to the consequences of frustration, and not by the apportionment provisions introduced by the 1943 Act, irrational though this difference may be.[216]

(e) The Price

44-051 **Ascertainment of price** By s.8:

"(1) The price in a contract of sale may be fixed by the contract, or may be left to be fixed in manner agreed by the contract, or may be determined by the course of dealing between the parties.[217]

(2) Where the price is not determined as mentioned in subs.(1) above the buyer must pay a reasonable price.[218]

(3) What is a reasonable price is a question of fact dependent on the circumstances of each particular case."

In the latter case the current market price may or may not be a reasonable price.[219]

44-052 **Price not fixed** The fact that the price is not fixed may be an indication that no binding contract has been concluded at all. The authorities are discussed elsewhere.[220] But briefly it seems that each case must be decided on the construction of the particular contract.[221] If there is nothing that can be regarded as an agreement about the price, this may be evidence that the parties have not in fact completed the making of their contract[222]; if on the other hand it appears that the parties have made a contract, the courts may be able to determine what is the price by resort to provisions for arbitration, trade custom, etc., or will apply s.8 in order to establish a reasonable price.[223]

44-053 **Agreement to sell at a valuation** By s.9:

"(1) Where there is an agreement to sell goods on the terms that the price is to be fixed by the valuation of a third party, and he cannot or does not make the valuation, the

---

Canavan and MacQueen (eds), *Atiyah and Adams' Sale of Goods*, 13th edn (2016), p.290.

[216] See Vol.I, para.23-096; *Benjamin's Sale of Goods*, 10th edn (2017), para.6-052; Twigg-Flesner, Canavan and MacQueen (eds), *Atiyah and Adams' Sale of Goods*, p.293.

[217] The contract may provide that one of the parties may fix the price: see *May and Butcher Ltd v The King* [1934] 2 K.B. 17, 21.

[218] This probably extends to executory contracts and is not restricted to cases where the buyer has taken delivery: see *Acebal v Levy* (1834) 10 Bing. 376; *Haudly v M'Laine* (1834) 10 Bing. 482; *Hall v Busst* (1960) 104 C.L.R. 206, 243–244; cf. at 222, 234.

[219] *Acebal v Levy* (1834) 10 Bing. 383. As to agreements to sell at "market price", see *Charrington & Co Ltd v Wooder* [1914] A.C. 71. See also *Davies v Davies* (1887) 36 Ch. D. 359, 392–393.

[220] Vol.I, paras 2-120 et seq.

[221] See *Foley v Classique Coaches Ltd* [1934] 2 K.B. 1, 10, 12.

[222] See, e.g. *May & Butcher Ltd v The King* [1934] 2 K.B. 17.

[223] See, e.g. *Foley v Classique Coaches Ltd* [1934] 2 K.B. 1; *Hillas & Co Ltd v Arcos Ltd* (1932) 147 L.T. 503. See also *British Bank for Foreign Trade Ltd v Novinex Ltd* [1949] 1 K.B. 623; *R & J Dempster Ltd v Motherwell Bridge and Engineering Co Ltd*, 1964 S.L.T. 353; *F & G Sykes (Wessex) Ltd v Fine Fare Ltd* [1967] 1 Lloyd's Rep. 53; *Smith v Morgan* [1971] 1 W.L.R. 803; *Brown v Gould* [1972] Ch. 53; *Courtney & Fairbairn Ltd v Tolaini Bros (Hotels) Ltd* [1975] 1 W.L.R. 297; *Bushwall Properties Ltd v Vortex Properties Ltd* [1976] 1 W.L.R. 591; *Mallozzi v Carapelli SpA* [1976] 1 All E.R. 407; *Hall v Busst* (1960) 104 C.L.R. 206, 222, 232–235, 241–245; *Att-Gen v Barker Bros* [1976] 2 N.Z.L.R. 445; *Didymi Corp v Atlantic Lines and Navigation Co Inc (The Didymi)* [1988] 2 Lloyd's Rep. 108; *Queensland Electricity Generating Board v New Hope Collieries Pty Ltd* [1989] 1 Lloyd's Rep. 205; *Mamidoil-Jetoil Greek Petroleum SA v Okta Crude Oil Refinery Co* [2001] 2 Lloyd's Rep. 76. See Berg (2003) 119 L.Q.R. 357.

agreement is avoided; but if the goods or any part of them have been delivered to and appropriated by the buyer he must pay a reasonable price for them.

(2) Where the third party is prevented from making the valuation by the fault of the seller or buyer, the party not at fault may maintain an action for damages against the party at fault."[224]

Such a valuer is not an arbitrator so that the Arbitration Act 1996[225] will not apply. He cannot be sued for failure to give a valuation, unless he has contracted to do so. But if he does make a valuation, it seems that he may be liable in tort if he does so fraudulently or negligently.[226] The actual valuation is normally valid unless there is fraud or collusion.[227]

3. TERMS OF THE CONTRACT

(a) Conditions, Warranties, Misrepresentations and Puffs

General Where promises and statements are made in connection with a contract of sale, it may be necessary to determine into what category they should be put, for the consequences of a promise or statement not being made good or being untrue may vary in accordance with the category to which it is attributed. **44-054**

Puffs and statements of opinion A puff is a statement extolling the virtues of goods which by virtue of its vagueness or extravagance would not be expected to and does not ground any form of liability.[228] *Simplex commendatio non obligat.* Difficulties can arise regarding expressions of opinion.[229] Although these may similarly give rise to no liability, they may, especially when made by skilled persons, amount to promises, or to representations that the opinion is honestly held or of the facts upon which they purport to be based.[230] In general, liability on statements is more readily imposed than formerly.[231] **44-055**

---

[224] This section applies to a named valuer. Where the valuer is to be appointed, and the machinery for appointing him breaks down, it has been held that, where on its true construction the agreement was one to sell at a reasonable price to be determined by the valuer, the court will substitute its own machinery for ascertaining a fair and reasonable price: *Sudbrook Trading Estate Ltd v Eggleton* [1983] 1 A.C. 444 (option to purchase land). See also *Wenning v Robinson* (1964) 64 S.R. (N.S.W.) 157 (no mention of particular valuer).

[225] See above, Ch.32.

[226] See *Sutcliffe v Thackrah* [1974] A.C. 727; *Campbell v Edwards* [1976] 1 W.L.R. 403; *Arenson v Arenson* [1977] A.C. 405.

[227] *Campbell v Edwards* [1976] 1 W.L.R. 403; above; and see *Baber v Kenwood Mfg Co Ltd* [1978] 1 Lloyd's Rep. 175. But it may sometimes be possible to impeach the valuation if it can be shown to be based on a wrong principle: *Baber v Kenwood*, above; *Finnegan v Allen* [1943] K.B. 425; *Dean v Prince* [1954] Ch. 409; *Frank H Wright (Constructions) Ltd v Frodoor* [1967] 1 W.L.R. 506; *Smith v Gale* [1974] 1 W.L.R. 9; *Burgess v Purchase & Sons (Farms) Ltd* [1983] Ch. 216; *Jones v Sherwood Computer Services Plc* [1992] 2 All E.R. 170; *Nikko Hotels (UK) v MEPC* (1991) 28 E.G. 86; *Pontsarn Investments v Kasallis-Osake-Pankki* (1992) 22 E.G. 103. See above, para.32-197.

[228] e.g. *Chalmers v Harding* (1868) 17 L.T. 571 ("very good second-hand reaper"); *JJ Savage & Sons Pty Ltd v Blakney* (1970) 119 C.L.R. 435 (speed of boat); *Ross v Allis-Chalmers Australia Pty Ltd* (1981) 55 A.L.J.R. 8 (capacity of harvesting machine).

[229] Vol.I, paras 7-008 et seq.

[230] e.g. *Jendwine v Slade* (1797) 2 Esp. 572; cf. *Power v Barham* (1836) 4 Ad. & El. 473 (cases on pictures); *Hopkins v Tanqueray* (1854) 15 C.B. 130; cf. *Schawel v Reade* (1912) 46 I.L.T. 281; *Holmes v Burgess* [1975] 2 N.Z.L.R. 311 (assertions of soundness of horses). See also *Andrews v Hopkinson* [1957] 1 Q.B. 229 ("It's a good little bus"); *Cremdean Properties Ltd v Nash* [1977]

44-056 **Contractual promises: conditions and warranties**   Other statements may be contractual promises, for which the maker must in general answer strictly, i.e. guarantee their truth.[232] The Sale of Goods Act refers to two types of such promise or term, conditions and warranties. A condition is a promise in respect of which the parties have agreed, whether by express words or by implication, that any failure of performance by one party, irrespective of the gravity of the event that has in fact resulted from the breach, shall entitle the other party not only to damages but also to treat the contract as discharged.[233] A warranty is defined by the Act[234] as "an agreement with reference to goods which are the subject of a contract of sale, but collateral to the main purpose of such contract, the breach of which gives rise to a claim for damages, but not to a right to reject the goods and treat the contract as repudiated". It is thus a minor promise within the contract, for which the promisor still answers strictly, but normally[235] only in damages. It should be distinguished from a genuinely separate or collateral warranty, which is a promise contained in a separate contract with its own consideration, and which may override terms of the main contract or otherwise create liability independently of the main contract.[236] Section 11(3) provides:

> "Whether a stipulation in a contract of sale is a condition, the breach of which may give rise to a right to treat the contract as repudiated, or a warranty, the breach of which may give rise to a claim for damages but not to a right to reject the goods and treat the contract as repudiated, depends in each case on the construction of the contract; and a stipulation may be a condition, though called a warranty in the contract."[237]

The converse of the last proposition is also true: a stipulation designated a condition may be held not to be so.[238] The Consumer Rights Act 2105 does not refer to terms (whether "terms that are to be treated as included" in the contract, or express terms, which the Act often describes as "requirements stated in the contract") as being conditions or warranties. Chapters 2 and 3 of the Act set out the remedies which are available for various breaches of contract by the trader.[239] However, there is nothing in the Act to prevent the parties agreeing that an express term shall be a condition or a warranty, with the normal consequences. Section 11(3) of the 1979 Act is not disapplied from consumer contracts for goods.

44-057 **Dichotomy not exhaustive**   It has subsequently become clear, however, that, whatever the words of the Act, this dichotomy is not exhaustive, and that in sale as in other contracts there may be discharge by virtue of the nature and effect of

---

E.G.D. 63; *Porter v General Guarantee Corp Ltd* [1982] R.T.R. 384.

[231]   See Vol.I, paras 7-004 et seq.

[232]   See below, para.44-060.

[233]   *Photo Production Ltd v Securicor Transport Ltd* [1980] A.C. 827, 849, per Lord Diplock; and see Sale of Goods Act 1979 s.11(3), quoted below; unless the right is lost; see below. As to the history of this use of the word "condition" see Vol.I, paras 13-025 et seq.; *Benjamin's Sale of Goods*, 10th edn (2017), paras 10-024 et seq.

[234]   s.61(1); see also s.11(3), quoted below.

[235]   But see below, para.44-067.

[236]   *Couchman v Hill* [1947] K.B. 554; see Vol.I, paras 13-003, 13-033, 13-110.

[237]   There are leading dicta to the same effect in *Bentsen v Taylor, Sons & Co* [1893] 2 Q.B. 274, 281.

[238]   See *Wickman Machine Tool Sales Ltd v L Schuler AG* [1974] A.C. 235.

[239]   See above, paras 38-481 et seq.

the breach.[240] The operation of these general principles is preserved by s.62(2) of the Act.[241] The normal approach seems to be to treat this as indicating the existence of a third type of term, the "intermediate" or "innominate" term, breach of which may or may not give rise to (in this context) the right to reject, depending on the nature and consequences of the breach,[242] though in truth the technique deployed is a different one.[243]

Misrepresentations external to the contract The law recognises a third **44-058** category, that of a misrepresentation of fact which does not constitute a contractual promise but which nevertheless forms sufficient part of the inducement to contract to justify the granting of a remedy to the representee. Such representations, not being promises, did not originally ground any relief at common law unless they were made fraudulently, in which case there was liability in deceit. From the late nineteenth century however it was established that equity would grant relief by way of rescission and indemnity,[244] and although it was arguable that since the Act made no reference to this jurisdiction it did not apply to sale of goods,[245] it is now clear that it does so.[246] The jurisdiction was much improved by the Misrepresentation Act 1967, which by s.1(b) abolished a possible limit on the right to rescind; by s.2(1) created a statutory action against a party to a contract who made such a misrepresentation negligently[247]; and by s.2(2) empowered the court to grant damages in lieu of rescission.[248] It also made provision for the control of terms excluding liability for misrepresentation.[249] Meanwhile the possibility of a tortious action for a negligent statement leading to pure economic loss was established in *Hedley Byrne & Co Ltd v Heller & Partners Ltd*,[250] and the action on a collateral contract, the use of which had earlier been restricted in this context,[251] also became

---

[240] *Cehave NV v Bremer Handelsgesellschaft mbH (The Hansa Nord)* [1976] Q.B. 44, where the words "shipment to be made in good condition" were held not to be a condition, but to be subject to the general principles of repudiatory breach, following *Hong Kong Fir Shipping Co Ltd v Kawasaki Kisen Kaisha Ltd* [1962] 2 Q.B. 26, in which the test was said to be whether the breach deprived the innocent party of "substantially the whole benefit" of the contract. See also *Reardon Smith Line Ltd v Yngvar Hansen-Tangen (The Diana Prosperity)* [1976] 1 W.L.R. 989, 998. In *RG Grain Trade LLP v Feed Factors International Ltd* [2011] EWHC 1889 (Comm), [2011] 2 Lloyd's Rep. 432 it was said that it was not the law that there was a right of rejection for quality matters unless the contract provides otherwise: at [42]. As to the general principles of discharge by breach, see Vol.I, Ch.24.

[241] *The Hansa Nord* [1976] Q.B. 44.

[242] e.g. *Bunge Corp v Tradax Export SA* [1981] 1 W.L.R. 711, 717, 718, 719. See Vol.I, paras 24-040 et seq.; below, para.44-067.

[243] See *Koompahtoo Local Aboriginal Land Council v Sanpine Pty Ltd* (2007) 82 A.L.J.R. 345, per Kirby J.

[244] *Redgrave v Hurd* (1881) 20 Ch. D. 1. See below, para.44-072; Vol.I, Ch.7.

[245] *Riddiford v Warren* (1901) 20 N.Z.L.R. 572; followed in *Watt v Westhoven* [1933] V.L.R. 458; see *Benjamin's Sale of Goods*, 10th edn (2017), paras 1-008 et seq., 10-008.

[246] For examples, see *Leaf v International Galleries* [1950] 2 K.B. 86 (painter of picture); *Long v Lloyd* [1958] 1 W.L.R. 753 (condition of lorry); *Goldsmith v Rodger* [1962] 2 Lloyd's Rep. 249 (misrepresentation by *buyer* as to condition of boat); *Royscot Trust Ltd v Rogerson* [1991] Q.B. 297 (sale by dealer to finance company). See also as to misrepresentation by buyer *Riddiford v Warren* (1901) 20 N.Z.L.R. 572.

[247] Below, para.44-073.

[248] See Vol.I, paras 7-076 et seq., 7-105 et seq.

[249] s.3 (as amended by Unfair Contract Terms Act 1977 s.8): see Vol.I, paras 7-145 et seq.

[250] [1964] A.C. 465; Vol.I, paras 7-091 et seq.

[251] *Heilbut, Symons & Co v Buckleton* [1913] A.C. 30. See Vol.I, para.13-004.

prominent.[252] Thus there has been a movement from a paucity of remedies to almost an excess.[253]

44-059 **Distinction between terms of the contract and external misrepresentations** The distinction between these two notions can be extremely difficult to make in this context. It is easier to classify a statement as a mere representation where there is a considerable time-gap between negotiation and contract, or where the negotiations are oral and the contract written, e.g. in the sale of land.[254] These conditions less frequently occur in the sale of goods. The test of a contractual promise traditionally asks whether there is "evidence of an intention by both parties that there should be contractual liability in respect of the accuracy of the statement".[255] But it may be that to some extent one should, to determine this intention, consider the consequences of attributing a statement to either category before doing so.[256] There are important differences between those consequences.

44-060 **Standard of liability** First, if the statement is treated as a contractual promise the seller will prima facie answer strictly for it, however carefully or honestly he made it. If (the tort of) negligence is pleaded, he can prove that he was not at fault; and if sued under s.2(1) of the Misrepresentation Act 1967 he has the statutory defence contained in it, that he had reasonable grounds to believe and did believe up to the time the contract was made that the facts represented were true. If it is treated as a mere representation, deliberate or negligent conduct is not required: he will be liable to have the contract rescinded against him, unless it is too late to do so[257] or the court awards damages in lieu of rescission.[258]

44-061 **Measure of damages** Secondly, if the statement is treated as a contractual promise; the damages for which the seller will be liable will be such as to put the buyer in the position in which he would have been had the promise been made good.[259] These will include the difference between the value of the goods as promised and their value as delivered,[260] and the buyer's loss of profit.[261] If the statement is treated as a mere representation, the measure of damages recoverable is that

---

[252] e.g. *Esso Petroleum Co Ltd v Mardon* [1976] Q.B. 801. But cf. *Howard Marine and Dredging Co Ltd v A Ogden & Sons (Excavations) Ltd* [1978] Q.B. 574.

[253] In the case of consumer contracts for the sale of goods which fall within Ch.2 of Pt 1 of the Consumer Rights Act 2015 certain information provided under the Consumer Contracts (Information, Cancellation and Additional Charges) Regulations 2013 is also to be treated as included as a term of the contract (ss.11(4) and 12). The consumer will be entitled to rely on the remedies set out in s.19 of the Act; see above, paras 38-493 et seq.

[254] And, in the nineteenth century, of stocks and shares, on which there are several cases.

[255] *Heilbut, Symons & Co v Buckleton* [1913] A.C. 30, 51; see Vol.I, para.13-004.

[256] See *Dick Bentley (Productions) Ltd v Harold Smith (Motors) Ltd* [1965] 1 W.L.R. 623, 627 (though some of this passage should be viewed with caution); Vol.I, para.13-003. In cases decided before the advent of a remedy in damages for negligent misrepresentation, there perhaps was a tendency to hold that, whereas statements by dealers and others with special means of knowledge were contractual promises (the *Dick Bentley* [1965] 1 W.L.R. 623, 627), statements by private persons were misrepresentations only (*Oscar Chess Ltd v Williams* [1957] 1 W.L.R. 370). cf. *Beale v Taylor* [1967] 1 W.L.R. 1193. But this is less important after the enactment of the Misrepresentation Act 1967.

[257] See below, para.44-073.

[258] Under s.2(2) of the Misrepresentation Act 1967; see below, para.44-072.

[259] See below, paras 44-411 et seq.

[260] Sale of Goods Act 1979 s.53; see below, para.44-411.

[261] See below, paras 44-422 et seq.

in tort, which seeks to put the buyer in the position in which he would have been had the representation not been made.[262] This will prima facie be restricted to his "reliance" or "out-of-pocket" loss,[263] although consequential loss is recoverable.[264]

Unfair commercial practices   The Consumer Protection from Unfair Trading Regulations 2008,[265] which implemented the Unfair Commercial Practices Directive,[266] have recently been amended[267] to provide remedies for individual consumers who have been the victim of certain types of unfair commercial practice, namely misleading actions and aggressive practices.[268]
44-062

Contributory negligence   Thirdly, although contributory negligence will normally be no defence in an action by the buyer for breach of a contractual promise,[269] it may in certain circumstances be raised as a defence where the buyer's claim is for breach of the common law duty of care or under s.2(1) of the Misrepresentation Act 1967.[270]
44-063

Conditions   Which terms in a contract of sale will be held conditions? The implied terms as to title, description and quality are, as regards England and Wales and Northern Ireland, all designated by the Act as implied conditions.[271] This classification has the merit of certainty and facilitates rejection by the buyer where a term is sharply formulated.[272] It may well be reasonable in consumer transactions to uphold strictly the buyer's right to reject. In commercial transactions, however, the right to reject the goods for minor disparities or defects may be abused by the buyer for market reasons.[273] Accordingly, s.15A of the Act seeks to limit the right of rejection in such cases.[274]
44-064

Express terms are most likely to be held conditions if they are designated as
44-065

---

[262] *Sharneyford Supplies Ltd v Edge* [1986] Ch. 128 (actual decision reversed [1987] Ch. 305); *Royscot Trust Ltd v Rogerson* [1991] 2 Q.B. 297. But as to this distinction see *Omak Maritime Ltd v Mamola Challenger Shipping Co Ltd (The Mamola Challenger)* [2010] EWHC 2026 (Comm), [2010] 2 C.L.C. 194; McLauchlan (2011) 127 L.Q.R. 23. See Vol.I, paras 7-080, 7-081.

[263] *Saunders v Edwards* [1987] 1 W.L.R. 1116. cf. *East v Maurer* [1991] 1 W.L.R. 461.

[264] *Davis & Co (Wines) Ltd v Afa Minerva Ltd (EMI) Ltd* [1974] 2 Lloyd's Rep. 27; *Royscot Trust Ltd v Rogerson* [1991] 2 Q.B. 297. In the *Royscot Trust* case, however, the Court of Appeal held that the measure of damages under s.2(1) of the 1967 Act was the same as that in deceit, and hence that even unforeseeable damage was recoverable. This is, however, arguable. The Singapore Court of Appeal doubted the correctness of *Royscot* in *RBC Properties v Defu Furniture Pte Ltd* [2014] SGCA 62, [2015] 1 S.L.R. 997; see Liau [2015] L.M.C.L.Q. 464.
   See Vol.I, para.7-080. For the measure of damages in deceit, see *Doyle v Olby (Ironmongers) Ltd* [1969] 2 Q.B. 158, and Vol.I, paras 7-056 et seq.

[265] SI 2008/1277.

[266] Directive 2005/29/EC of May 11, 2005.

[267] By the Consumer Protection (Amendment) Regulations 2014 (SI 2014/870). The bulk of the Regulation came into force on October 1, 2014 and apply to contracts made on or after that date: reg.1(3). See generally paras 38-172 et seq.

[268] See above, paras 38-172 et seq.

[269] See Vol.I, para.1-207.

[270] cf. *Gran Gelato Ltd v Richcliff Ltd* [1992] Ch. 560; Vol.I, para.7-084.

[271] 1979 Act ss.12(5A), 13(1A), 14(6), 15(3).

[272] e.g. *Arcos Ltd v EA Ronaasen & Son* [1933] A.C. 470 (description): see below, para.44-089. But a looser term such as "satisfactory quality" (below, para.44-099) facilitates flexibility.

[273] e.g. *Cehave NV v Bremer Handelsgesellschaft mbH (The Hansa Nord)* [1976] Q.B. 44.

[274] See below, para.44-070.

such[275]; if they have been held to be conditions in other cases[276]; if they relate to the time of performance in mercantile contracts[277]; if they relate to duties which must be performed by fixed times in sequence with the duties of the other party[278]; or if the circumstances of the particular case indicate that it was contemplated that rejection should follow if the term was not complied with.[279]

44-066 **Effect of breach of condition** Where the term broken is a condition, upon any breach the buyer may treat the contract as discharged, i.e. refuse to perform his own obligations and refuse to accept the goods or further performance.[280] He may also sue for damages[281]; or he may instead elect to recover money he has paid in restitution, if there has been a total failure of consideration.[282] If he has already received part performance which he cannot return he therefore may not be able to recover the price paid.[283] But the courts will allow recovery of part of the price despite the fact that part of the goods have been delivered and retained, if the price is readily apportionable.[284] It is arguable that the mere tender of defective goods is not itself a repudiatory breach of contract, though where it causes loss (for example, by payment for a survey) it may give rise to liability in damages. A small group of cases, mostly concerned with documentary sales with time limits for performance, hold that if there is still time, the seller can withdraw a rejected tender and submit another.[285] But it is uncertain how far this goes: in many cases a faulty tender would be prejudicial to the buyer and entitle him to treat the contract as repudiated and purchase elsewhere.[286]

44-067 **Effect of breach of other terms** It might seem from the wording of the Act that where the term broken is not a condition it must be a warranty, and hence give rise to a right to damages only. However, as stated above,[287] it has been held that the common law principles, whereby a breach which goes to the root of the contract or which deprives the innocent party of the whole benefit of the contract entitles that

---

275 Though this is not conclusive: see above, para.44-056.

276 e.g. *Maredelanto Cia Naviera SA v Bergbau-Handel GmbH (The Mihalis Angelos)* [1971] 1 Q.B. 164.

277 *United Scientific Holdings Ltd v Burnley BC* [1978] A.C. 904, 924, 937, 944, 950, 958; *Bunge Corp v Tradax Export SA* [1981] 1 W.L.R. 711, 716. But see *Compagnie Commerciale Sucres et Denrées v C Czarnikow Ltd* [1990] 1 W.L.R. 1337, 1347 (no presumption or rule of law to that effect). See also below, para.44-128.

278 *Bunge Corp v Tradax Export SA* [1981] 1 W.L.R. 711, 729; *Toepfer v Lenersan-Poortman NV* [1980] 1 Lloyd's Rep. 143.

279 e.g. *Harling v Eddy* [1950] 2 K.B. 739 (promise to take goods back); *Bergerco v Vegoil Ltd* [1984] 1 Lloyd's Rep. 440 ("direct ship"); *Kuwait Rocks Co v AMN Bulkcarriers Inc (The Astra)* [2013] EWHC 865 (Comm), [2013] 2 Lloyd's Rep. 69 (breach of an express obligation to make punctual payment of time charterparty hire). See also Vol.I, para.13-040.

280 See Vol.I, Ch.24.

281 See below, paras 44-387 et seq.

282 *Giles v Edwards* (1797) 7 T.R. 181; *Bragg v Villanova* (1923) 40 T.L.R. 154.

283 See *Yeoman Credit Ltd v Apps* [1962] 2 Q.B. 508; cf. *Charterhouse Credit Co Ltd v Tolly* [1963] 2 Q.B. 683.

284 See Vol.I, para.29-066.

285 Principally *Borrowman, Phillips & Co v Free and Hollis* (1878) 4 Q.B.D. 500; *EE & Brian Smith (1928) Ltd v Wheatsheaf Mills Ltd* [1939] 2 K.B. 392. But if loss was thereby caused to the buyer the seller might be liable in damages.

286 But cf. *McDougall v Aeromarine of Emsworth Ltd* [1958] 1 W.L.R. 1126. Curing of a faulty tender may be easier in the case of delivery of wrong quantity: see below, paras 44-257 et seq. See in general *Benjamin's Sale of Goods*, 10th edn (2017), para.12-032.

287 See above, para.44-057.

party to treat the contract as discharged, are not excluded by the Act.[288] From the reasoning in the case it follows that if the term broken is held not to be a condition, the next stage should be to examine the extent of the breach to see whether it justifies discharge on common law principles, which consider the nature and consequences of the breach[289] and whether there has been a renunciation or repudiation.[290] If it does, the consequences are the same as those of breach of condition: if it does not there will be a right to damages. It might seem that only damages are available for breach of what is clearly a warranty, but it may be that if there was an aggregation of breaches of warranty, or if serious consequences resulted there could be repudiatory conduct on general principles.[291]

Loss of right to reject[292]   The right to reject must be exercised clearly.[293] And even **44-068** though the term broken is a condition, the buyer may lose the right to reject for breach of it. He can do this by waiving the breach completely, or by electing to affirm the contract and sue for damages. Thus s.11(2) of the Sale of Goods Act provides:

"Where a contract of sale is subject to a condition to be fulfilled by the seller, the buyer may waive the condition, or may elect to treat the breach of the condition as a breach of warranty and not as a ground for treating the contract as repudiated."

A waiver in this sense is usually treated by the law as a promise not to sue, and it may be possible to go back on it on giving notice, unless it is supported by consideration or the other party has acted on it in some way making it inequitable to retract.[294] An affirmation on the other hand is an act of election and may not normally be retracted regardless of whether it has been acted on.[295] It requires in principle a manifestation of choice ("election"), communicated to the other party, by a person who knows that he has the right to reject. But affirmation may in this context also be simply implied by law[296] when the goods have been accepted. Sec-

[288] *Cehave NV v Bremer Handelsgesellschaft mbH (The Hansa Nord)* [1976] Q.B. 44.
[289] [1976] Q.B. 44 at 60, 72–73, 84. See Vol.I, paras 13-034 et seq.; below, paras 44-264 et seq.
[290] See *Koompahtoo Local Aboriginal Land Council v Sanpine Pty Ltd* (2007) 82 A.L.J.R. 345 (see per Kirby J. at [114], where however for English law the word "substantial" is too weak). In *Gregg & Co (Knottingley) Ltd v Emherst Glass Ltd* [2005] EWHC 804 (TCC) it was held that continuing malfunctions of computerised machines, despite best efforts at remediation over two years, were repudiatory of an obligation of sale and service though the right to reject had been lost.
[291] See *Rubicon Computer Systems Ltd v United Paints Ltd* (2000) 2 T.C.L.R. 453 (Sale of Goods Act 1979 s.12(2)); but cf. *The Ymnos* [1982] 2 Lloyd's Rep. 574, 583. Such an idea is accepted in the context of an elaborately drafted agreement in *GB Gas Holdings Ltd v Accenture (UK) Ltd* [2010] EWCA Civ 912; but different uses of the word "warranty" make it difficult to generalise further.
[292] The Consumer Rights Act 2015 makes elaborate provisions as regards the different circumstances which give rise to the remedies (often referred to as "rights to enforce") which the Act provides for the consumer. Under the 2015 Act, the buyer will have a so-called "short-term right to reject", which will normally be lost after 30 days from delivery of the goods, and a final right to reject. See above, paras 38-513 et seq.
[293] See *Grimoldby v Wells* (1875) L.R. 10 C.P. 391, 396; *Chapman v Morton* (1843) 11 M. & W. 534.
[294] See *Panoutsos v Raymond Hadley Corp of New York* [1917] 2 K.B. 473; *Charles Rickards Ltd v Oppenhaim* [1950] 1 K.B. 616; *Société Italo-Belge, etc. v Palm and Vegetable Oils (Malaysia) Ltd (The Post Chaser)* [1982] 1 All E.R. 19; Vol.I, paras 22-040 et seq.
[295] *Motor Oil Hellas (Corinth) Refineries SA v Shipping Corp of India (The Kanchenjunga)* [1990] 1 Lloyd's Rep. 391, 397–399. See also Vol.I, para.24-003; *Benjamin's Sale of Goods*, 10th edn (2017), para.12-036.
[296] And there may be situations where a buyer is estopped from alleging that he has affirmed even

tion 11(4) of the Act[297] provides:

> "Subject to s.35A … where a contract of sale is not severable,[298] and the buyer has accepted the goods or part of them, the breach of any condition to be fulfilled by the seller can only be treated as a breach of warranty, and not as a ground for rejecting the goods and treating the contract as repudiated, unless there is an express or implied term of the contract to that effect."

The nation of acceptance is dealt with below.[299] Under this provision the buyer may lose the right to reject before he has discovered a defect in the goods, and without any communication with the seller.

44-069   Rejection in severable contract   In principle, as s.11(4) indicates, acceptance of part of the goods bars rejection of the remainder. But the subsection does not apply where the contract of sale is severable (or divisible), for example, where it provides for the delivery of goods by stated instalments, which are to be separately paid for.[300] Then the buyer's right to treat the contract as discharged depends on the relation of the breach to the total contractual obligation and is regulated by s.31(2) of the Act[301]: acceptance of instalments already delivered does not prevent the buyer from treating the rest of the contract as discharged. Moreover, s.11(4) is subject to s.35A which permits the buyer to accept conforming goods and to reject those that do not conform.[302]

44-070   Limitation of right to reject in non-consumer cases   A further limitation is placed on the right to reject for breach of condition in *non-consumer* cases by s.15A of the 1979 Act:

> "(1)   Where in the case of a contract of sale—
>   (a)   the buyer would, apart from this section, have the right to reject goods by reason of a breach on the part of the seller of a term implied by s.13, 14 or 15 … , but
>   (b)   the breach is so slight that it would be unreasonable for him to reject them, [then, if the buyer does not deal as consumer],[303] the breach is not to be treated as a breach of condition but may be treated as a breach of warranty.
>   (2)   This section applies unless a contrary intention appears in, or is to be implied from, the contract.
>   (3)   It is for the seller to show that the breach does not fall within subs.(1)(b) above."

---

though he did not know he had a right to reject. See *Panchaud Frères SA v Et. General Grain Ltd* [1970] 1 Lloyd's Rep. 53 (documentary sale); *Peyman v Lanjani* [1985] Ch. 457; *Glencore Grain Rotterdam BV v Lebanese Organisation for International Commerce* [1997] 2 Lloyd's Rep. 386.

[297]   The subsection in the 1893 Act originally based rejection of specific goods on the passing of property, creating considerable problems which remain in some other common law jurisdictions. This provision does not apply to consumer contracts for the sale of goods which fall within Ch.2 of Pt 1 of the Consumer Rights Act 2015. In consumer contracts for the sale of goods the 2015 Act provides a corresponding right of partial rejection, see above, para.38-515.

[298]   See below, paras 44-262 et seq.

[299]   See below, paras 44-278 et seq.

[300]   See below, paras 44-263 et seq.

[301]   See below, para.44-263.

[302]   See below, para.44-286. But see s.35(7).

[303]   See s.61(5A). The words in brackets are deleted by the Consumer Rights Act 2015. Special rules in that Act apply to consumer sales. In particular, the implied terms in ss.13, 14 and 15 of the 1979 Act no longer apply in consumer sales contracts.

This section was introduced into the 1979 Act by the Sale and Supply of Goods Act 1994.[304] Its purpose was to prevent a commercial buyer from abusing the right to reject by taking advantage of a trivial breach, for example, when the real reason for rejecting the goods is a fall in the market. But it only applies to a breach of the *implied* terms as to quality, fitness for purpose and correspondence with description or sample set out in ss.13, 14 and 15 of the 1979 Act and not to the breach of any express term. It may also be excluded expressly or by implication. This may give rise to some uncertainty,[305] e.g. as to whether the application of the section is impliedly excluded in the case of the breach of a term as to the date of shipment of goods to be carried by sea (which is treated as part of their description); and there may be other situations where its application is similarly uncertain. No reported decisions on this section have been traced.[306]

Further remedies in consumer cases   The paragraphs above state the common   **44-071** law position as to the buyer's rights to reject the goods, terminate the contract and/or sue for damages. The Sale and Supply of Goods to Consumers Regulations 2002, which came into effect on March 31, 2003 provided (in a new Pt 5A inserted into the 1979 Act) a further range of remedies for consumers based on an EU Directive of 1999 on certain aspects of the sale of consumer goods and associated guarantees. These exist alongside the common law remedies and interact in a way that is not easy to formulate. The Consumer Rights Act 2015 incorporates these Pt 5A remedies, together with new remedies for consumers, into a new comprehensive scheme. Consumer contracts are dealt with in detail in Ch.38.

Rescission for misrepresentation   Where the statement made by the seller ranks   **44-072** as a misrepresentation inducing the contract, and is not a contractual promise, the basic remedy is rescission (with indemnity where appropriate) only,[307] though if it was subsequently incorporated as a term in the contract the remedies for breach of contract will also apply.[308] The buyer may therefore rescind unless his right to do so is barred by affirmation of the contract, the impossibility of restitutio in integrum, the intervention of third-party rights, or lapse of time.[309] However, the court may exercise the power to award damages in lieu of rescission under s.2(2) of the Misrepresentation Act 1967,[310] and it is possible that this power applies also to misrepresentations subsequently incorporated into the contract as conditions.[311]

Remedies in tort   Where the buyer has suffered loss caused by a wilfully false   **44-073** statement by the seller, he may sue the seller in deceit.[312] The damages here will be

---

[304] s.4(2).

[305] *Benjamin's Sale of Goods*, 10th edn (2017), paras 12-024 et seq., 18-332 et seq.

[306] The provision was used in an argument *e contrario* in *Lowe v W Machell Joinery Ltd* [2011] EWCA Civ 794, below, para.44-089.

[307] See Vol.I, paras 7-112 et seq.

[308] Misrepresentation Act 1967 s.1(a); see Vol.I, para.7-114. For practical difficulties of tactics in this connection, see *Benjamin's Sale of Goods*, 10th edn (2017), para.12-074.

[309] See Vol.I, paras 7-124 et seq. A fifth possible limitation, that rescission was barred by performance of the contract, was removed by s.1(b) of the Misrepresentation Act 1967.

[310] See *Atlantic Lines and Navigation Co Inc v Hallam Ltd* [1983] 1 Lloyd's Rep. 188, 202; *William Sindall Plc v Cambridgeshire CC* [1994] 1 W.L.R. 1016; Beale (1995) 111 L.Q.R. 60; and Vol.I, paras 7-105 et seq.

[311] See Vol.I, para.7-113.

[312] *Derry v Peek* (1889) 14 App. Cas. 337; Vol.I, paras 7-048 et seq.

calculated by the rules applicable to that tort, and hence may include consequential loss even if unforeseeable.[313] So also if loss is caused by a negligent statement made by the seller, the buyer may sue in negligence if he can establish the existence of a duty of care.[314] As regards a seller, however, these remedies are of less importance in England than they might be in view of that provided by s.2(1) of the Misrepresentation Act 1967,[315] which provides what appears to be a statutory tort action.[316] Section 2(1) of that Act gives a party to a contract a statutory action for damages against the other party who makes a false representation, unless that other party shows that he had reasonable grounds to believe and did believe that the facts represented were true.[317] Where defective goods cause damage to person or property the seller may be liable in negligence[318] or under Pt I of the Consumer Protection Act 1987.[319]

(b)   Implied Terms

44-074   The Act lays down a number of implied terms as to title, compliance with description and quality or fitness, and these are now discussed. Further new terms were added by the Consumer Contracts (Information, Cancellation and Additional Charges) Regulations 2013[320]; if the trader provides pre-contractual information in compliance with those Regulations, the information "is to be treated as included as a term of the contract" and the contract is to be treated as including a term that the trader has supplied the information required.[321] The Consumer Rights Act 2015 seeks to set out in a comprehensive way all of a consumer buyer's statutory rights under a consumer sale of goods contract. The consumer will have rights directly equivalent to the existing rights under current law and several new rights.[322] The corollary of the 2015 Act's enactment of special and separate provision for

---

[313]   *Doyle v Olby (Ironmongers) Ltd* [1969] 2 Q.B. 158: *Archer v Brown* [1985] Q.B. 401; Vol.I, paras 7-056 et seq.

[314]   See *Esso Petroleum Co Ltd v Mardon* [1976] Q.B. 801; *Capital Motors Ltd v Beecham* [1975] 1 N.Z.L.R. 576; *Sealand of the Pacific Ltd v Ocean Cement Ltd* 33 D.L.R. (3d) 625 (1973); affirmed 51 D.L.R. (3d) 702 (1975); *James McNaughton Paper Group Ltd v Hicks Anderson & Co* [1991] 2 Q.B. 113; *Clerk & Lindsell on Torts*, 22nd edn (2017), paras 8-51 et seq. See Vol.I, paras 7-091 et seq.

[315]   For an example of possible difference, see *Howard Marine and Dredging Co Ltd v A Ogden & Sons (Excavations) Ltd* [1978] Q.B. 574. cf. Vol.I, para.7-099.

[316]   See, e.g. *Royscot Trust Ltd v Rogerson* [1991] 2 Q.B. 297; Vol.I, para.7-080.

[317]   See Vol.I, paras 7-077 et seq. The action does not lie against an agent who induces a contract with his principal by misrepresentation: *Resolute Maritime Inc v Nippon Kaiji Kyokai (The Skopas)* [1983] 1 W.L.R. 857.

[318]   *Clarke v Army and Navy Co-operative Society Ltd* [1903] 1 K.B. 155; *Herschtal v Stewart and Ardern Ltd* [1940] 1 K.B. 155; *Andrews v Hopkinson* [1957] 1 Q.B. 229; *Vacwell Engineering Ltd v BDH Chemicals Ltd* [1971] 1 Q.B. 88, 108; *Rasbora Ltd v JCL Marine Ltd* [1977] 1 Lloyd's Rep. 645; *Bacardi-Martini Beverages Ltd v Thomas Hardy Packaging Ltd* [2002] EWCA Civ 549, [2002] 2 Lloyd's Rep. 379. But the duty can sometimes be discharged by a warning: see *Hurley v Dyke* [1979] R.T.R. 265. Such an action may perhaps lie, on the analogy of building cases, in respect of damage to another part of a complex structure: but not merely because the article is unsatisfactory and involves financial loss to the buyer: see *Benjamin's Sale of Goods*, 10th edn (2017), paras 12-075 et seq. and in general *Clerk & Lindsell on Torts*, 22nd edn (2017), Ch.11.

[319]   See also Pt II of the 1987 Act (breach of statutory duty).

[320]   SI 2013/3134.

[321]   See above, paras 38-058 et seq.

[322]   The new rights granted to consumers by the 2015 Act in the case of consumer sale of goods contracts are described above, paras 38-492 et seq.

consumer contracts in certain respects is that it amends certain provisions of the Sale of Goods Act 1979, including the implied terms in ss.12, 13, 14 and 15, so that the 1979 Act no longer applies to consumer sales contracts or applies to them only with qualifications.

(i)   Implied Terms about Title

Implied terms about title   By s.12 of the Sale of Goods Act 1979[323]:   **44-075**

"(1)   In a contract of sale, other than one to which subs.(3) below applies,[324] there is an implied term on the part of the seller that in the case of sale, he has a right to sell the goods, and in the case of an agreement to sell,[325] he will have a right to sell the goods at the time when the property is to pass.

(2)   In a contract of sale, other than one to which subs.(3) below applies, there is also an implied term that—

(a)   the goods are free, and will remain free until the time when the property is to pass, from any charge or encumbrance not disclosed or known to the buyer before the contract is made, and

(b)   the buyer will enjoy quiet possession of the goods except so far as it may be disturbed by the owner or other person entitled to the benefit of any charge or encumbrance so disclosed or known."

Breaches of s.12   Section 12(1) is clearly broken if the goods belong to a third   **44-076**
party and the seller has at the relevant moment no power to transfer the property in them to the buyer. It requires no knowledge or fault on the part of the seller nor any disturbance of possession, merely absence of the right to sell. Further, in *Niblett v Confectioners' Materials Co Ltd*,[326] where the goods sold bore a label which infringed the trade mark of a third party, it was held that the sellers had no right to sell them because the third party could have obtained an injunction to restrain the sale. Scrutton L.J. said[327]: "If a vendor can be stopped by process of law from selling he has not the right to sell".

The seller need not, however, own the goods at any time: he only promises that   **44-077**
he will be able to create the appropriate rights in the buyer.[328] He can therefore perform by causing transfer direct from a third party. There is no clear decision as

---

[323]   This section does not apply to consumer contracts for the sale of goods which fall within Ch.2 of Pt 1 of the Consumer Rights Act 2015. In consumer contracts for the sale of goods the 2015 Act provides a corresponding term relating to the right to supply which is to be treated as included in the contract, see above, paras 38-507 et seq.

[324]   See below, para.44-084.

[325]   See above, paras 44-020—44-021.

[326]   [1921] 3 K.B. 387, disapproving *Monforts v Marsden* (1895) 12 R.P.C. 266. See also *Egekvist Bakeries v Tizel & Blinick* [1950] 1 D.L.R. 585; affirmed [1950] 2 D.L.R. 592 (goods subject to detention order by pure food administration); *J Barry Winsor & Associates Ltd v Belgo Canadian Mfg Co Ltd* (1976) 76 D.L.R. (3d) 685 (non-compliance with electrical standards). Applied in *Azzurri Communications Ltd v International Telecommunications Equipment Ltd* [2013] EWPCC 17 where it was accepted that there was a breach of s.12(1) and s.12(2) where telephone handsets infringed a registered trademark. The decision of the buyer to return the handsets to the owner constituted reasonable mitigation and the buyer was entitled to damages for buying replacement goods.

[327]   At 398.

[328]   *Karlshamns Oljefabriker v Eastport Navigation Corp (The Elafi)* [1986] 1 All E.R. 208, 215; in the context of retention of title clauses, see *PST Energy 7 Shipping LLC v OW Bunker Malta Ltd* [2015] EWCA Civ 1058 (noted Tettenborn [2016] L.M.C.L.Q. 24), affirmed [2016] UKSC 23 and see L. Gullifer [2017] L.Q.R 244.

to whether the term is broken where a person sells who has no right to sell, but who nevertheless has a power to pass title in a situation where a non-owner can do so by statute.[329] The above dictum of Scrutton L.J. might suggest that it is: but it is submitted that since the goods will not be affected by any third party right after sale, the seller should be regarded as having had the right to sell.[330]

44-078   **Charges and encumbrances: quiet possession**   Section 12(2), dealing with charges and encumbrances and quiet possession, is an amalgamation of what were in the original Act two separate provisions.[331] There has been little authority on the application of their requirements, and both are more reminiscent of the law of land than of sale of goods.[332] It does not however appear that rules from land law should be imported into this area.[333] Thus though the warranty against encumbrances in relation to land is not broken until the buyer's possession is disturbed,[334] the wording of the subsection, at any rate in its present form, appears to envisage breach simply because of the presence of an encumbrance at the relevant time, which is not necessarily (as in the case of s.12(1)) the time at which property is to pass. And though there is authority that the warranty of quiet possession in land law only applies to disturbance by the vendor and not those claiming by title paramount,[335] this is not so in the case of sale of goods.[336]

44-079   The term as to quiet possession seems in fact to have at least three applications where the condition as to title may fail. First, it may apply to interference not related to title. Thus it was held in *Microbeads AG v Vinhurst Road Markings Ltd*[337] that where goods were sold, and after the sale letters patent were granted which enabled third parties to restrain the use of the goods, there was a breach of s.12(2)(b), though s.12(1) was not infringed; and in *The Playa Larga*[338] it was held broken when subsequent to the sale the seller connived at a governmental decision to withdraw goods from a contract after appropriation. But interference by *wrongful* acts of third parties unconnected with the seller would not be covered.[339] Secondly, the term may

---

329 See below, paras 44-193 et seq. But see *Reg v Wheeler* (1991) 92 Cr. App. R. 279 (sale in market overt).

330 Contra, *Benjamin's Sale of Goods*, 10th edn (2017), para.4-004. See *Kolkarni v Manor Credit (Davenham) Ltd* [2010] EWCA Civ 69, [2010] 2 Lloyd's Rep. 431 at [43]. It may, however, be argued that a person who holds title to a vehicle only by virtue of Pt III of the Hire-Purchase Act 1964 (see above, para.39-370) will find the vehicle virtually unsaleable through the motor trade. See also *Barber v NWS Bank Plc* [1996] 1 W.L.R. 641 (express term).

331 1979 Act ss.12(2) and (3).

332 cf. Conveyancing Act 1881 s.7. But encumbrances can certainly be relevant when ships are sold: see *The Barenbels* [1985] 1 Lloyd's Rep. 528 (where the debt in respect of which the ship was arrested did not constitute an encumbrance).

333 See *Mason v Burningham* [1949] 2 K.B. 545, 563.

334 *Nottidge v Dering* [1909] 2 Ch. 647, 656; affirmed [1910] 1 Ch. 297.

335 See *Niblett v Confectioners' Materials Co Ltd* [1921] 3 K.B. 387, 403; *Jones v Lavington* [1903] 1 K.B. 253.

336 *Mason v Burningham* [1949] 2 K.B. 545, 562–563; *Microbeads AG v Vinhurst Road Markings Ltd* [1975] 1 W.L.R. 218.

337 See above. See also *Gencab of Canada Ltd v Murray-Jensen Mfg Ltd* (1980) 114 D.L.R. (3d) 92 (threat of action by patent holder); *Rubicon Computer Systems Ltd v United Paints Ltd* (2000) 2 T.C.L.R. 454 (supplier of computer equipment attached lock to it).

338 *Empresa Exportadora de Azucar v Industria Azucarera Nacional SA (The Playa Larga)* [1983] 2 Lloyd's Rep. 171.

339 In *Great Elephant Corp v Trafigura Beheer BV* [2012] EWHC 1745 [2013] 1 All E.R. (Comm) 415 a Nigerian Government Department had refused to issue cargo documents which prevented the ves-

allow the buyer a longer period of limitation than that which is available to him under s.12(1); for under s.12(2)(b) time will not begin to run until the disturbance of possession has actually taken place.[340] Thirdly, it may provide the buyer with a remedy in a situation where the seller has a right to sell but the goods are subject to the rights of a third party. If, for instance, a debtor sells goods which have been seized by a sheriff but which remain in the debtor's possession, the buyer may have a remedy for breach of the terms as to quiet possession and freedom from encumbrances if he is compelled to surrender the goods.[341]

Effect of breach of s.12[342]   As regards England and Wales and Northern Ireland **44-080** the term implied by s.12(1) is a condition.[343] Hence on its breach the buyer can treat the contract as repudiated and claim damages.[344] He can alternatively affirm the contract and claim damages.[345] The obligations laid down in s.12(2) are, in England and Wales and Northern Ireland, warranties only.[346] They will normally give rise to no more than the right to damages.[347] The rules as to damages are discussed elsewhere,[348] but it may be noted that buyers have been held entitled to recover the cost of improvements done to the goods in the ordinary course of events, if evicted,[349] and of discharging the adverse claim[350] or defending an action brought by the true owner.[351]

Total failure of consideration despite use of goods   A well-known problem **44-081** arises as to whether the buyer, when he treats the contract as repudiated, is entitled to recover the whole purchase price as upon a total failure of consideration in spite of the fact that he has used the thing sold. In *Rowland v Divall*[352] the plaintiff bought a car from a person who, unknown to him, did not own it. He and his sub-purchaser used the car for several months before it was seized by the police and

---

sel carrying the oil which was the subject of the contract of sale from sailing. There was a breach of s.12(2)(b) as although the interference occurred after property had passed it arose out of circumstances which existed at the time of the sale. However, when the Government unlawfully demanded a fine, the breach stopped as the guarantee did not extend to unlawful acts. The judge's decision on s.12(2)(b) was upheld by the Court of Appeal ([2013] EWCA Civ 905) although the appeal was allowed on different grounds.

[340] See *Howell v Richards* (1809) 11 East 633, 642, 643; *Baynes & Co v Lloyd & Sons* [1895] 1 Q.B. 820, 824 (cases on land, however).

[341] See *Lloyds and Scottish Finance Ltd v Modern Cars & Caravans (Kingston) Ltd* [1966] 1 Q.B. 764.

[342] The Consumer Rights Act 2015 introduces a separate scheme of remedies for breaches of the provisions equivalent to those of s.12, but the effect appears to be much the same: if the trader had no right to sell the goods, the consumer may reject the goods and treat the contract as at an end; if the goods are subject to an encumbrance, the consumer will have no right to reject or treat the contract as at an end but will be entitled to damages. See above, para.38-511.

[343] 1979 Act s.12(5A).

[344] See above, para.44-056.

[345] e.g. *Mason v Burningham* [1949] 2 K.B. 545.

[346] 1979 Act s.12(5A).

[347] But see *Rubicon Computer Systems Ltd v United Paints Ltd* (2000) 2 T.C.L.R. 454 (repudiatory breach rules applied).

[348] See below, paras 44-387 et seq. See also *Healing (Sales) Pty Ltd v English Electrix Pty Ltd* (1968) 121 C.L.R. 584.

[349] *Mason v Burningham* [1949] 2 K.B. 545.

[350] *Stock v Urey* [1954] N.I. 71; *Ed Learn Ford Sales Ltd v Giavannone* (1990) 74 D.L.R. (4d) 761.

[351] *Lloyds and Scottish Finance Ltd v Modern Cars and Caravans (Kingston) Ltd* [1966] 1 Q.B. 764. See further *Benjamin's Sale of Goods*, 10th edn (2017), para.4-028.

[352] [1923] 2 K.B. 500.

restored to the true owner; nevertheless, he was allowed to recover the purchase price in full on the ground that there had been a total failure of consideration. This case was followed in *Butterworth v Kingsway Motors Ltd*[353] and *Barber v NWS Bank Plc*[354] and a similar principle has been applied in relation to hire-purchase agreements.[355] As a result, the buyer's use of the goods, their consequent deterioration and any alterations in the conditions of the market are regarded as irrelevant; though where improvements have in good faith been made to the goods, the amount recovered may be reduced to the extent to which the value of the goods is attributable to the improvement.[356] It is arguable that the buyer should be obliged to bring into account any benefit that he has received, although as the law now stands he has the right to recover the entire purchase price paid.[357] It is, however, possible that if the seller's title is made good, or "fed", before the buyer elects to treat the contract as repudiated, the purchase price cannot be recovered.[358] And if the buyer satisfies a judgment against him in conversion, the true owner's title is extinguished[359] and it is arguable that the buyer cannot then treat the contract as repudiated, though he can sue for damages.[360]

44-082   A further difficulty in this connection is that by virtue of s.11(4) of the Act[361] acceptance by the buyer will normally deprive him of his right to treat the contract as repudiated, and confine him to his remedy in damages. In cases such as *Rowland v Divall* it is difficult to see that the buyer had not accepted the goods. Atkin L.J. however held that s.11(4) had no application to a breach of s.12 in that case.[362]

44-083   **Change of position no defence**   Since a claim by the buyer to recover the purchase price paid on the ground of a total failure of consideration is a restitutionary claim, he could in principle be met by a defence of "change of position",[363] that is to say, that the seller had changed his position as a result of the payment so that

---

[353] [1954] 1 W.L.R. 1286.

[354] [1996] 1 W.L.R. 641.

[355] *Karflex Ltd v Poole* [1933] 2 K.B. 251; *Mercantile Union Guarantee Corp v Wheatley* [1938] 1 K.B. 490; *Warman v Southern Counties Car Finance Corp Ltd* [1949] 2 K.B. 576; see above, para.39-285. See also *Rover International Ltd v Cannon Film Sales Ltd* [1989] 1 W.L.R. 912, 925, 938.

[356] Torts (Interference with Goods) Act 1977 s.6(3). The reason is that the damages recoverable by the true owner are under the Act similarly reducible.

[357] See the *Twelfth Report of the Law Reform Committee* (1966) Cmnd.2958, para.36; see also *Benjamin's Sale of Goods*, 10th edn (2017), para.4-006. cf. Law Commission, *Final Report on Sale and Supply of Goods* (1987), Law Com. No.160, paras 6.1–6.5.

[358] *Lucas v Smith* [1926] V.L.R. 400, 403–404; *Butterworth v Kingsway Motors Ltd* [1954] 1 W.L.R. 1286; *Patten v Thomas Motors Pty Ltd* [1965] N.S.W.R. 1457. But cf. *HW West Ltd v McBlain* [1950] N.I. 144. See also *Whitehorn Bros v Davison* [1911] 1 K.B. 463, 475; *Blundell-Leigh v Attenborough* [1921] 3 K.B. 235, 240, 242; *Robin and Rambler Coaches Ltd v Turner* [1947] 2 All E.R. 284; *Bennett v Griffin Finance Ltd* [1967] 2 Q.B. 46, 50; *Benjamin's Sale of Goods*, 10th edn (2017), paras 4-010—4-011.

[359] Torts (Interference with Goods) Act 1977 s.5(1). It is arguable that the title also vests in the buyer. This is the position at common law: *USA v Dollfus Mieg & Cie* [1952] A.C. 582, 622.

[360] *Benjamin's Sale of Goods*, 10th edn (2017), at para.4-012. See also *Ed Learn Ford Sales Ltd v Giavannone* (1990) 74 D.L.R. (4d) 761.

[361] See above, para.44-068.

[362] At 506–507. The provision was then s.11(1)(c). A possible argument is that the subsection does not apply where the breach is fundamental. See Reynolds (1963) 79 L.Q.R. 534, 553–555; Ellinger (1969) 5 Victoria U. of Wellington L.R. 168. But the demise of the notion of fundamental breach makes this now difficult to argue: see Vol.I, paras 15-023 et seq.

[363] *Lipkin Gorman v Karpnale Ltd* [1991] 2 A.C. 548, 558, 562, 567–568, 577. See Vol.I, paras 29-186 et seq.

it would now be inequitable to require him to make restitution in whole or in part.[364] But it is submitted that his defence is not open to a seller since he is, by his breach (even if unwitting) of the contract of sale, a "wrongdoer" to whom the defence is not available.[365]

Sales of limited title   Subsections (3) to (5) of s.12 of the 1979 Act deal with sales **44-084** of limited title:

"(3)   This subsection applies to a contract of sale in the case of which there appears from the contract or is to be inferred from its circumstances an intention that the seller should transfer only such title as he or a third person may have.

(4)   In a contract to which subs.(3) above applies there is an implied term that all charges or encumbrances known to the seller and not known to the buyer have been disclosed to the buyer before the contract is made.

(5)   In a contract to which subs.(3) above applies there is also an implied term that none of the following will disturb the buyer's quiet possession of the goods, namely—

(a)   the seller;

(b)   in a case where the parties to the contract intend that the seller should transfer only such title as a third person may have, that person;

(c)   anyone claiming through or under the seller or that third person otherwise than under a charge or encumbrance disclosed or known to the buyer before the contract is made."

There is at present no authority on the scope of subs.(3).[366] Section 12 of the 1893 Act was expressed to apply "unless the circumstances of the contract are such as to show a different intention". It was accordingly held in connection with that Act that there was no breach of subs.(1) where an auctioneer sold goods known to have been distrained by a bailiff,[367] and Atkin L.J. suggested that the qualification was introduced to exclude sales by a sheriff under an execution, and "other cases where by implication or by express terms there is no warranty of title".[368] Certain cases prior to the Act of 1893 are also sometimes cited,[369] but none of these authorities can be regarded as conclusively indicating the appropriate interpretation of the present wording. In England and Wales and Northern Ireland, these implied terms are warranties.[370]

Exclusion of s.12   By s.6(1) of the Unfair Contract Terms Act 1977, "Liability for **44-085** breach of the obligation arising from s.12 of the Sale of Goods Act 1979 … cannot be excluded or restricted by reference to any contract term". It should be noted that this provision, is not limited to sales made in the ordinary course of business.[371]

---

[364] cf. *Barber v NWS Bank Plc* [1996] 1 W.L.R. 641 (where the defence failed on the facts).

[365] *Lipkin Gorman v Karpnale Ltd*, above, at 579. Contra, *Benjamin's Sale of Goods*, 10th edn (2017), para.4-008.

[366] But see *Reg v Wheeler* (1991) 92 Cr. App. R. 279 (sale in market overt, now abolished).

[367] *Payne v Elsden* (1900) 17 T.L.R. 161.

[368] *Niblett v Confectioners' Materials Co Ltd* [1921] 3 K.B. 387, 401.

[369] See, e.g. *Chapman v Speller* (1850) 14 Q.B. 621 (sheriff); *Baguely v Hawley* (1867) L.R. 2 C.P. 625 (resale of goods seized under distress); *Wood v Baxter* (1883) 49 L.T. 45 (auctioneer); *Morley v Attenborough* (1849) 3 Exch. 500 (pawnbroker); *Page v Cowasjee Eduljee* (1866) L.R. 1 P.C. 127 (shipmaster). See also *Warmings Used Cars Ltd v Tucker* [1956] S.A.S.R. 249 (commission agent).

[370] 1979 Act s.12(5A).

[371] The Consumer Rights Act 2015 Act repeals or disapplies provisions in the Unfair Contract Terms Act 1977 governing the contracts to which Ch.1 applies, and instead makes its own provision control-

Thus the section can only be limited by the techniques which it itself provides in subss.(3) to (5). Evasion of this provision by means of a "choice of law" clause is prevented by s.27(2) of the 1997 Act.[372] However, by s.26 the limits on contracting out imposed by the Act do not apply to international supply contracts.[373] In such a contract therefore the common law principles will apply. There was much controversy over the possibility of contracting out of the provisions of s.12 before the introduction of the present subss.(3) to (5). It seems that it is in principle possible to do so if the true intention of the parties is that the seller should transfer only such title as he or a third person may have within subss.(3) to (5). Otherwise it is submitted that a clause which, in general terms, purported to relieve the seller from his obligation to pass a good title to the buyer would be inconsistent with the notion of sale and would not be upheld,[374] although a clause which merely restricted the seller's liability for breach of that obligation or any right or remedy available to the buyer could well be effective. However, in a consumer contract made before October 1, 2015, any term which purported to exclude or even limit the seller's liability would probably be regarded as improper and "unfair" within the meaning of the Unfair Terms in Consumer Contracts Regulations 1999[375] and hence not be binding on the consumer.[376]

(ii)   Implied Term as to Correspondence with Description

44-086   Sale by description   Section 13 of the Act provides[377]:

> "(1)   Where there is a contract for the sale of goods by description, there is an implied term that the goods will correspond with the description.
> (2)   If the sale is by sample as well as by description it is not sufficient that the bulk of the goods corresponds with the sample if the goods do not also correspond with the description."

The section applies to all sales of unascertained goods,[378] and has been interpreted as applying to many sales of specific goods.[379] As regards the latter, it may be said

---

ling the exclusion of liabilities arising under its provisions.

[372] See Vol.I, para.30-009; Mann (1974) 90 L.Q.R. 42.

[373] See below, para.44-125.

[374] See *Suisse Atlantique Société d'Armement Maritime SA v NV Rotterdamsche Kolen Centrale* [1967] 1 A.C. 361, 398, 432; *Benjamin's Sale of Goods*, 10th edn (2017), para.4–019.

[375] SI 1999/2083 (as amended by SI 2001/1186) reg.5(1), Sch.2 para.1(b); paras 38-220 et seq.

[376] Consumer contracts entered into after October 1, 2015 are now governed by the Consumer Rights Act 2015.

[377] This section does not apply to consumer contracts for the sale of goods which fall within Ch.2 of Pt 1 of the Consumer Rights Act 2015. In consumer contracts for the sale of goods the 2015 Act provides a corresponding requirement that goods be as described which is to be treated as included in the contract, see above, para.38-499. There will be one additional element. Under the Consumer Contracts (Information, Cancellation and Additional Charges) Regulations 2013, traders are required to give various types of information to consumers before or at the time the contract is made, including information about the main characteristics of the goods. The information about the main characteristics that is given will be included as a term of the contract, so that the consumer will have the same remedies as in other cases in which the goods do not comply with the description. Other information that is given by the trader in compliance with the Regulations is to be treated differently: see above, paras 38-499—38-500.

[378] *Kidman v Fisken Bunning & Co* [1907] S.A.L.R. 101, 107; see above, paras 44-040 et seq.

[379] For the historical background, see *Benjamin's Sale of Goods*, 10th edn (2014), paras 11-002, 11-003; *Taylor v Combined Buyers Ltd* [1924] N.Z.L.R. 627. Prior to 1973 the condition as to merchant-

that there is a sale by description in two types of cases. The first occurs where the buyer contracts in reliance on the description of the goods in the contract without having seen them. Thus in *Varley v Whipp*[380] the defendant agreed to buy a reaping machine which he had never seen, and which the plaintiff described as nearly new. In fact it did not correspond with this description, and the defendant was held to be entitled to reject it. It was said that, although the most usual application of this section is to the case of unascertained goods, it "must apply to all cases where the purchaser has not seen the goods but is relying on the description alone", and was therefore applicable to a contract for the sale of specific goods where there was no identification otherwise than by description.[381]

The second goes further: the buyer has seen the goods, but the stated character-   **44-087**
istics of the goods are still intended to form part of the description by which they are sold.[382]

> "It may also be pointed out that there is a sale by description even though the buyer is buying something displayed before him on the counter: a thing is sold by description, though it is specific, so long as it is sold not merely as the specific thing but as a thing corresponding to a description, e.g. woollen undergarments, a hot-water bottle ..."[383]

This is subject to the proviso that the difference between the goods and the description of them was not apparent at the time of the sale.[384] This type of case also extends to situations where the buyer, though he has seen the goods, relies, at least in part, on the description given to them,[385] for example, that table linen is "the authentic property of Charles I"[386] or that a painting is the work of a particular artist.[387] However, if the buyer purchases specific goods, not in reliance on the description, but such as they are,[388] then the goods will not have been sold by description. Thus in *Harlingdon and Leinster Enterprises Ltd v Christopher Hull Fine Art Ltd*[389] a sale between art dealers of a painting attributed to Gabriele Münter was held not to be by description where the seller had disclaimed any knowledge as to the artist and the buyer had, after inspection, relied on his own judgment in buying the painting, even though the attribution had been made in negotiations, in an old auction catalogue, and in an invoice issued after the sale.

---

ability in s.14(2) of the 1893 Act only applied to sales by description, and many of the authorities on the meaning of the phrase arise in connection with that subsection.

[380] [1900] 1 Q.B. 513.

[381] [1900] 1 Q.B. 513, 516.

[382] *Gill & Duffus SA v Berger & Co Inc* [1984] A.C. 382, 394; *Harlingdon and Leinster Enterprises Ltd v Christopher Hull Fine Art Ltd* [1991] 1 Q.B. 564.

[383] *Grant v Australian Knitting Mills Ltd* [1936] A.C. 85, 100 per Lord Wright.

[384] See *Beale v Taylor* [1967] 1 W.L.R. 1193, 1196.

[385] *Benjamin's Sale of Personal Property*, 7th edn (1931), p.641; *Joseph Travers & Son Ltd v Longel Ltd* (1947) 64 T.L.R. 150. See also *Speedway Safety Products Ltd v Hazell & Moore Industries Pty Ltd* [1982] 1 N.S.W.L.R. 225; *Elder Smith Goldsborough Mort Ltd v McBride* [1976] 2 N.S.W.L.R. 631.

[386] *Nicholson and Venn v Smith Marriott* (1947) 177 L.T. 189.

[387] *Leaf v International Galleries* [1950] 2 K.B. 86, 89 (a case of misrepresentation). But see *Harlingdon and Leinster Enterprises Ltd v Christopher Hull Fine Art Ltd* [1991] 1 Q.B. 564.

[388] In *Hughes v Hall* [1981] R.T.R. 430, Donaldson L.J. said that a clause in a contract "sold as seen and inspected" would prima facie negative a sale by description. The case was, however, doubted in *Cavendish-Woodhouse Ltd v Manley* (1984) 82 L.G.R. 376. See also *Speedway Safety Products Ltd v Hazell & Moore Industries Pty Ltd* [1982] 1 N.S.W.L.R. 225 (sale by receiver of stock situated at identified premises).

[389] [1991] 1 Q.B. 564.

44-088 **Goods selected by buyer** Though it was probably already the case, it is made clear by s.13(3) of the Act that a sale where the buyer selects the goods, in, e.g. a self-service shop, can be a sale by description. The subsection provides: "A sale of goods is not prevented from being a sale by description by reason only that, being exposed for sale or hire, they are selected by the buyer".

44-089 **Correspondence with description** The time for correspondence with description is the time of delivery, or if the time of passing of property is earlier, at that time.[390] Once it is established that a given contract of sale is a sale by description, the test applied by the courts to determine whether or not the goods correspond with the description is a strict one. If the goods do not correspond with the description, it is not enough for the seller to show that they were of satisfactory quality, or fit for the particular purpose for which they were required. Some cases are fairly obvious. Thus a contract for common English sainfoin seed is not performed by the delivery of giant sainfoin,[391] a contract for a new car is not performed by delivery of a second-hand car,[392] and a contract for a 1961 Triumph Herald is not performed by delivery of a car made up of two portions from different models welded together.[393] But in commercial cases particularly stringent rules may be applied. In *Arcos Ltd v EA Ronaasen & Son*,[394] a case where timber did not meet specified measurements, Lord Atkin put the point as follows: "If the written contract specifies conditions of weight, measurement and the like, those conditions must be complied with. A ton does not mean about a ton, or a yard about a yard". The same reasoning may apply to packaging: thus in *Re Moore & Co and Landauer & Co*[395] a buyer was held entitled to reject a whole consignment of tinned fruit on the grounds that some of the cases contained 24 tins instead of the stipulated 30, though the total number of tins was correct. In such cases also stipulations as to the time and method of shipment are usually held part of the description.[396] Nevertheless, it has been said that some of these cases are "excessively technical and due for fresh examination" in the House of Lords.[397]

---

[390] See *KG Bominflot Bunkergesellschaft etc. & Co v Petroplus Marketing AG (The Mercini Lady)* [2010] EWCA Civ 1145, [2011] 1 Lloyd's Rep. 442, holding that it will not normally be appropriate to imply a term that the goods hold their specification for a period: if they cease to conform, that is a matter of quality covered by s.14, below, paras 44-094 et seq.

[391] *Wallis, Son and Wells v Pratt and Haynes* [1911] A.C. 394.

[392] *Andrews Bros Ltd v Singer & Co Ltd* [1934] 1 K.B. 17.

[393] *Beale v Taylor* [1967] 1 W.L.R. 1193 (a case very near the line, however). *Brewer v Mann* [2010] EWHC 2444 (QB) (car sold as "1930 Speed Six Bentley" actually contained 1927 reconstructed standard 6.5 litre engine).

[394] [1933] A.C. 470, 479. But contracts frequently stipulate for tolerances: and trade custom may be received in this connection: see *Montague L Meyer Ltd v Vigers Bros Ltd* (1939) 63 Ll.L. Rep. 10.

[395] [1921] 2 K.B. 519, a case on s.30(4) (now repealed).

[396] *Bowes v Shand* (1877) 2 App. Cas. 455; *Macpherson Train & Co Ltd v Howard Ross & Co Ltd* [1955] 1 W.L.R. 640 (date of due arrival). cf. *J Aron & Co Inc v Comptoir Wegimont* [1921] 3 K.B. 435.

[397] *Reardon Smith Line Ltd v Yngvar Hansen-Tangen (The Diana Prosperity)* [1976] 1 W.L.R. 989, 998, per Lord Wilberforce. *Bowes v Shand*, above, was, however, approved by the House of Lords in *Bunge Corp v Tradax Export SA* [1981] 1 W.L.R. 711; and Lord Wilberforce himself reserved the position as to unascertained future goods (e.g. commodities), as to which the date of shipment is often of commercial importance.

Description or quality?   Difficulty may occur in distinguishing between descrip-   **44-090**
tion and quality. In principle the two are clearly different.[398] But indications of quality may in appropriate cases be part of the description of the goods,[399] as may indications of purpose (e.g. "cough mixture", "pet food"), and goods may be of such bad
quality as not to comply with their description for that reason.[400] In commercial
cases much may turn on the form of the contract[401] and on commercial usage.[402]
Where goods contain admixtures of other substances the question is whether the addition is such as to make the basic substance lose its identity, or merely to vary the
quality.[403] "Ultimately the test is whether the buyer could fairly and reasonably
refuse to accept the physical goods proffered to him on the ground that their failure
to correspond with that part of what was said about them in the contract makes them
goods of different kind from those he had agreed to buy".[404]

Identification   Descriptive words may however identify the goods with varying   **44-091**
degrees of preciseness. In a charterparty case[405] the ship chartered was described
as "Japanese flag ... Newbuilding motor tank vessel called Yard No.354 at Osaka
Zosen ... described as per Clause 24 hereof". The vessel tendered had been built
at an associated yard, Oshima, in whose books it was No.004. The words were held
not descriptive of the ship but simply to provide an indication or identification of
the vessel meant.[406]

---

[398] See, e.g. *Arcos Ltd v EA Ronaasen & Son* [1933] A.C. 470, where the goods were found to be merchantable under the contract specification and suitable for their purpose. See also *Proton Energy Group SA v Orien Letuva* [2013] EWHC 2872 (Comm), [2014] 1 Lloyd's Rep. 100 (oil specification went to quality not description).

[399] See *Toepfer v Continental Grain Co* [1974] 1 Lloyd's Rep. 11 ("hard amber durum wheat"); *Toepfer v Warinco AG* [1978] 2 Lloyd's Rep. 569 ("fine-ground"); cf. *Christopher Hill Ltd v Ashington Piggeries Ltd* [1972] A.C. 441, 470 ("fair average quality" not part of description, though in clause headed "Quantity and Description"); *Tradax International SA v Goldschmidt SA* [1977] 2 Lloyd's Rep. 604 (provision as to impurities); *Gill & Duffus SA v Berger & Co Inc* [1984] A.C. 382, 393–394; *Total International Ltd v Addax BV* [1996] 2 Lloyd's Rep. 333 ("usual Dakar refinery quality" not part of description). And see *Montedison SpA v Icroma SpA (The Caspian Sea)* [1980] 1 W.L.R. 48; *NV Bunge v Cie Noga, etc. SA (The Bow Cedar)* [1980] 2 Lloyd's Rep. 601.

[400] *Christopher Hill Ltd v Ashington Piggeries Ltd* [1969] 3 All E.R. 1496, 1516; affirmed on this point [1972] A.C. 441, 470; *Lockhart v Osman* [1981] V.R. 57 (cattle sold at cattle breeders' sale infected with brucellosis).

[401] See, e.g. *Montague L Meyer Ltd v Kivisto* (1929) 35 Ll.L. Rep. 265 (timber: "to be properly seasoned" not part of description); cf. *Tradax Export SA v European Grain & Shipping Ltd* [1983] 2 Lloyd's Rep. 100 ("maximum 7.5 per cent fibre" part of description).

[402] See *Grenfell v EB Meyrowitz Ltd* [1936] 2 All E.R. 1313 ("safety glass"); *Steels & Busks Ltd v Bleecker Bik & Co Ltd* [1956] 1 Lloyd's Rep. 228 ("pale crepe rubber, quality as previously delivered").

[403] See *Pinnock Bros v Lewis and Peat Ltd* [1923] 1 K.B. 690 (copra cake containing castor seed poisonous and not copra cake); *Robert A Munro & Co Ltd v Meyer* [1930] 2 K.B. 312 (adulterated bone meal); cf. *Christopher Hill Ltd v Ashington Piggeries Ltd* [1972] A.C. 441 (contaminated herring meal, toxic to mink but not to other animals, still herring meal); *Gill & Duffus SA v Berger & Co Inc* [1984] A.C. 382. But see Coote (1976) 50 A.L.J. 17, pointing out that exclusion clause cases have used a more generalised approach than the precise correspondence required in some commodity cases on rejection.

[404] *Christopher Hill Ltd v Ashington Piggeries Ltd*, above, at 503–504 per Lord Diplock.

[405] *Reardon Smith Line Ltd v Yngvar Hansen-Tangen (The Diana Prosperity)* [1976] 1 W.L.R. 989; see also *Joseph Travers & Sons Ltd v Longel Ltd* (1947) 64 T.L.R. 50 ("waders").

[406] As to when descriptive words can constitute warranties or external representations, see *Taylor v Combined Buyers Ltd* [1924] N.Z.L.R. 627; *The Diana Prosperity* [1976] 1 W.L.R. 989 at 998; *Howard Marine and Dredging Co Ltd v A Ogden & Sons (Excavations) Ltd* [1978] Q.B. 574;

44-092 **Sale by sample and description** It follows from the wording of s.13(1) that a sale may be by sample as well as by description. In such a case the rule is that the goods must correspond with both sample and description. Thus, in *Nichol v Godts*[407] the sale was for "foreign refined rape oil, warranted only equal to sample". The goods tendered were equal to sample but contained an admixture of hemp oil. It was held that the buyer was entitled to reject because the goods, though corresponding with the sample, did not correspond with the description. But sometimes the sample is given under circumstances making it the only description of the thing to be supplied[408]; and where quality is part of the description,[409] certification as to quality may sometimes be conclusive as to compliance with sample and hence with description.[410]

44-093 **Remedies for breach**[411] As regards England and Wales and Northern Ireland, the term implied by s.13 is a condition.[412] Breach of the term by the seller will therefore entitle the buyer, if he so chooses, to reject the goods and normally treat the contract as repudiated[413] and to recover damages for any loss sustained as a result of the breach. But in the case of a very slight breach in a non-consumer case the right to reject is subject to s.15A.[414]

(iii) Implied Terms about Quality and Fitness for Purpose

44-094 **Preliminary** Section 14(1) of the Sale of Goods Act provides: "Except as provided by this section and s.15 below and subject to any other enactment,[415] there is no implied term about the quality or fitness for any particular purpose of goods supplied under a contract of sale". Subsection (4) however adds that "An implied term about quality or fitness for a particular purpose may be annexed to a contract of sale by usage".[416]

44-095 **Implied term as to satisfactory quality**[417] By subss.(2) to (2F) of s.14 of the 1979 Act:

Benjamin's Sale of Goods, 10th edn (2017), paras 11-012, 11-013.

[407] (1854) 10 Exch. 191. See also *Azémar v Casella* (1867) L.R. 2 C.P. 677; *Wallis, Son and Wells v Pratt and Haynes* [1911] A.C. 394; *ES Ruben & Co Ltd v Faire Bros & Co Ltd* [1949] 1 K.B. 254.

[408] *Boshali v Allied Commercial Exporters Ltd* (1961) 105 S.J. 987.

[409] See above, para.44-090.

[410] e.g. *Toepfer v Continental Grain Co* [1974] 1 Lloyd's Rep. 11; *Gill & Duffus SA v Berger & Co Inc* [1984] A.C. 382, 393–394; cf. *NV Bunge v Cie Naga d'Importation et d'Exportation SA (The Bow Cedar)* [1980] 2 Lloyd's Rep. 601; *Cauwenberghe & Fils SA v Tropical Product Sales SA* [1986] 1 Lloyd's Rep. 535.

[411] The Consumer Rights Act 2015 introduces a separate scheme of remedies for breaches of the provisions equivalent to those of s.13; see above, paras 38-499—38-500.

[412] 1979 Act s.13(1A).

[413] See above, para.44-066.

[414] See above, para.44-070.

[415] Various statutes impose warranties upon sales: see, e.g. Agriculture Act 1970 (as amended) Pt IV (fertilisers and feeding stuffs); Plant Varieties and Seeds Act 1964 (as amended) ss.16, 17.

[416] As to custom or usage, see Vol.I, paras 14-033 et seq. An example is *Jones v Bowden* (1813) 4 Taunt. 847 (warranty against seawater damage).

[417] This section does not apply to consumer contracts for the sale of goods which fall within Ch.2 of Pt 1 of the Consumer Rights Act 2015. In consumer contracts for the sale of goods the 2015 Act provides a corresponding requirement of satisfactory quality which is to be treated as included in the contract, see above, para.38-497. Section 14(2) is amended by removing subss.(2D)–(2F).

"(2)   Where the seller sells goods in the course of a business, there is an implied term that the goods supplied under the contract are of satisfactory quality.

(2A)   For the purposes of this Act, goods are of satisfactory quality if they meet the standard that a reasonable person would regard as satisfactory, taking account of any description of the goods, the price (if relevant) and all the other relevant circumstances.

(2B)   For the purposes of this Act, the quality of goods includes their state and condition and the following (among others) are in appropriate cases aspects of the quality of the goods—

    (a)   fitness for all the purposes for which goods of the kind in question are commonly supplied,

    (b)   appearance and finish,

    (c)   freedom from minor defects,

    (d)   safety, and

    (e)   durability.

(2C)   The term implied by subsection (2) above does not extend to any matter making the quality of goods unsatisfactory—

    (a)   which is specifically drawn to the buyer's attention before the contract is made,

    (b)   where the buyer examines the goods before the contract is made, which that examination ought to reveal, or

    (c)   in the case of a contract for sale by sample, which would have been apparent on a reasonable examination of the sample.[418]"

The concept of "satisfactory quality" and the guidelines were introduced into the 1979 Act by the Sale and Supply of Goods Act 1994[419] and replace that of "merchantable quality" the 1893 Act. As regards England and Wales and Northern Ireland, the term implied by subs.(2) is a condition.[420]

Sale in course of a business   The subsection requires that the seller sells goods **44-096** "in the course of a business" and the Act provides that "'business' includes a profession and the activities of any government department ... or local or public authority".[421] It has been held[422] that these words cover, not only sales by business sellers of the type of goods which they are in the business of selling,[423] but also sales by business and professional sellers who are in the business of selling one thing and sell something else incidentally (e.g. a commercial fisherman selling his fishing vessel,[424] or a coal merchant selling his truck) and business and professional sellers who are not in the business of selling at all but who make a sale in connection with another business (e.g. a television rental company selling one of its vans or a doctor the computer used by his secretary). This is so despite the fact that cases in other contexts, especially with regard to buyers (more likely to be thought of as needing protection), suggest that the words "in the course of a business" require that the transaction is an integral part of the business carried on or, if it is only incidental

---

[418]   subss.(2D) to (2F) are deleted by the Consumer Rights Act 2015. These subsections were inserted by the Sale and Supply of Goods to Consumers Regulations 2002 and are set out above at para.38-440. The provisions of s.14(2) no longer apply to consumer sales contracts.

[419]   s.1(1).

[420]   1979 Act s.14(5A). As to conditions, see above, para.44-093.

[421]   1979 Act s.61(1).

[422]   *Stevenson v Rogers* [1999] Q.B. 1028; *MacDonald v Pollock* [2012] CSIH 12, 2012 G.W.D. 8–162 (sale of a cruise ship).

[423]   As to which see *Christopher Hill Ltd v Ashington Piggeries Ltd* [1972] A.C. 441, 474, 485, 495.

[424]   *Stevenson v Rogers* [1999] Q.B. 1028.

thereto, that there is a sufficient degree of regularity about the transaction in question.[425] It has been held that the final sale of the live and dead stock of a farm was made in the course of a business.[426] Difficult cases may also arise where non-profit making organisations (schools, hospitals) conduct commercial activities such as bookshops and restaurants: authority as to the meaning of the word "business" in other contexts, though relevant, will not be conclusive.[427]

44-097 Sale through an agent   Section 14(5) provides:

> "The preceding provisions of this section apply to a sale by a person who in the course of a business is acting as agent for another as they apply to a sale by a principal in the course of a business, except where that other is not selling in the course a business and either the buyer knows that fact or reasonable steps are taken to bring it to the notice of the buyer before the contract is made."

This subsection applies to any sale by an agent whether the principal is disclosed or undisclosed.[428] Thus a sale will be in the course of a business if it is effected by an agent in the course of a business on behalf of a principal who would, if selling himself, be selling privately, unless the buyer knows that the principal is selling privately or reasonable steps are taken to make him aware of this. This provision is particularly relevant to sales by auction.

44-098 Goods supplied under the contract   These words take account of case law under the 1893 Act, whereby the duty to supply merchantable goods was applied to the containers and other additions in and with which they were supplied.[429]

44-099 Satisfactory quality   The duty to supply goods of satisfactory quality is strict: it is no defence to prove that all care was taken.[430] Section 14(2A) defines satisfactory quality: "For the purposes of this Act, goods are of satisfactory quality if they meet the standard that a reasonable person would regard as satisfactory, taking account of any description of the goods, the price (if relevant) and all the other relevant circumstances". It has been said that the provision is "to establish a general standard of quality which goods are required to reach"[431] and that it is "primarily

---

[425] See *R & B Customs Brokers Co Ltd v United Dominions Trust Ltd* [1988] 1 W.L.R. 321 (buyer); *Feldaroll Foundry Plc v Hermes Leasing (London) Ltd* [2004] EWCA Civ 747 (buyer); *Peter Symmons & Co v Cook* (1981) 131 L.J. 758 (buyer) (Unfair Contract Terms Act 1977); *Davies v Sumner* [1984] 1 W.L.R. 1301 (seller, but in context of criminal offence under Trade Descriptions Act 1968); below, para.44-121.

[426] *Buchanan-Jardine v Hamilink*, 1983 S.L.T. 149 (deplenishing sale to buyer of farm: not actual sale of business). See also *Browning v Brachers* [2005] EWHC 16 (QB), [2004] P.N.L.R. 28 at [47] (sale of items as part of the majority of a business).

[427] See, e.g. Trade Descriptions Act 1968 s.1; Moneylenders Act 1900 ss.2, 6 (now repealed) (see *Litchfield v Dreyfus* [1906] 1 K.B. 584); *Stroud's Judicial Dictionary*, 7th edn (2006), "Business". See also *Stevenson v Beverley Bentinck Ltd* [1976] 1 W.L.R. 483.

[428] *Boyter v Thomson* [1995] 2 A.C. 628.

[429] *Geddling v Marsh* [1920] 1 K.B. 668 (returnable mineral water bottle); *Morelli v Fitch and Gibbons* [1928] 2 K.B. 636 (ginger beer bottle); *Niblett v Confectioners' Materials Ltd* [1921] 3 K.B. 387 (tins of condensed milk); *Chaproniere v Mason* (1905) 21 T.L.R. 633 (stone in Bath bun); *Wilson v Rickett, Cockerell & Co Ltd* [1954] 1 Q.B. 598 (explosive mixed in Coalite).

[430] *Grant v Australian Knitting Mills Ltd* [1936] A.C. 85, 100.

[431] *Jewson Ltd v Boyhan* [2003] EWCA Civ 1030, [2004] 1 Lloyd's Rep. 505 at [68].

directed towards substandard goods".[432] There is as yet a modest amount of case law on the application of this new definition[433] although there are numerous cases on "merchantable quality" in the previous legislation.[434] These are, however, unlikely to be of direct assistance in interpreting the current definition. The reference to "a reasonable person" suggests an objective standard, but presumably must take into account the position of the individual buyer and must necessarily presuppose that the reasonable person is fully acquainted with the condition of the goods (including any hidden defects)[435] and would with that knowledge regard them as being of a satisfactory standard. In determining the appropriate standard, it will obviously be relevant to take account of any description given of the goods[436]: this is particularly the case where the goods are described as having certain characteristics,

---

[432] *Balmoral Group Ltd v Borealis (UK) Ltd* [2006] EWHC 1900 (Comm), [2006] 2 Lloyd's Rep. 629 at [140].

[433] See *Thain v Anniesland Trade Centre*, 1997 S.C.L.R. 991 (second hand car failed after a few weeks: sufficient durability); *Britvic Soft Drinks Ltd v Messer UK Ltd* [2002] 1 Lloyd's Rep. 20; affirmed [2002] EWCA Civ 549, [2002] 2 Lloyd's Rep. 379 (carcinogenic additive to CO2 gas: too little to cause harm but necessitated product recall: quality not satisfactory), contrast *Jewson Ltd v Boyhan* [2003] EWCA Civ 1030, [2004] 1 Lloyd's Rep. 505 (home energy rating of boilers: boilers satisfactory in themselves); *Bramhill v Edwards* [2004] EWCA Civ 403, [2004] 1 Lloyd's Rep. 653 (American mobile home slightly wider than UK regulations permitted: satisfactory quality though use in UK would be illegal: doubted by Twigg-Flesner (2005) 121 L.Q.R. 205); *Balmoral Group Ltd v Borealis (UK) Ltd* [2006] EWHC 1900 (Comm), [2006] 2 Lloyd's Rep. 629 (polymer satisfactory for making storage tanks if properly processed); *Darren Egan v Motor Services (Bath Ltd)* [2007] EWCA Civ 1002, [2008] 1 All E.R. 1156n. (car veered with camber of road: satisfactory); *Webster Thompson Ltd v JG Pears (Newark) Ltd* [2009] EWHC 1070 (Comm), [2009] 2 Lloyd's Rep. 339 (Supply of Goods and Services Act 1982 s.4, as amended) (goods liable to be downgraded under EU animal by-products regulations); *Lowe v W Machell Joinery Ltd* [2011] EWCA Civ 794, [2012] 1 All E.R. (Comm) 153 (staircase supplied as specified but did not comply with Building Regulations, though change to specification required would have been very slight: not satisfactory); *Activa DPS Europe SARL v Pressure Seal Solutions Ltd* [2012] EWCA Civ 943, [2012] 3 C.M.L.R. 33 (goods lacked certification of conformity required by EC Directive—satisfactory quality as no evidence that Directive implemented in country of sale and buyer able to resell goods inside and outside EU); *Ward v MGM Marine Ltd* [2012] EWHC 4093 (QB) (luxury yacht caught fire and exploded 15 minutes after delivery: quality not satisfactory); *Cheeld v Alliott* [2013] EWCA Civ 508 (defective workmanship in metal porch); *KG Bominflot Bunkergesellschaft, etc & Co v Petroplus Marketing AG (The Mercini Lady) (No.2)* [2012] EWHC 3009 (Comm), [2013] 1 Lloyd's Rep. 360 (unstable gasoil: discussion of principles). cf. *United Central Bakeries Ltd v Spooner Industries Ltd* 2013 CSOH 150, 2013 G.W.D. 302–608 (baking equipment of satisfactory quality though part of the cause of fire).

[434] For examples see *Wren v Holt* [1903] 1 K.B. 610 (contaminated beer); *Bristol Tramways, etc. Carriage Co v Fiat Motors Ltd* [1910] 2 K.B. 831 (buses not strong enough for heavy passenger work); *Niblett v Confectioners' Materials Ltd*, above (goods carrying labels infringing trade mark) (cf. *Sumner, Permain & Co v Webb & Co* [1922] 1 K.B. 55 (tonic water unsaleable in Argentina only)); *Buchanan-Jardine v Hamilink*, 1983 S.L.T. 149 (cattle subject to temporary health "stop order" preventing movement); *Rasbora Ltd v JCL Marine Ltd* [1977] 1 Lloyd's Rep. 645 (boat); *Jackson v Chrysler Acceptances* [1978] R.T.R. 474 (car); *Leaves v Wadham Stringer (Cliftons) Ltd* [1980] R.T.R. 308 (car); *Rogers v Parish (Scarborough) Ltd* [1987] Q.B. 933 (car); *M/S Aswan Engineering Establishment Co v Lupdine Ltd* [1987] 1 W.L.R. 1 (plastic pails). For a recent example see *Russo v Belcar Pty Ltd* [2011] SASCFC 151 (car merchantable despite many alleged defects).

[435] *Bristol Tramways, etc. Carriage Co v Fiat Motors Ltd* [1910] 2 K.B. 831 at 841; *Australian Knitting Mills Ltd v Grant* (1933) 50 C.L.R. 387, 418; *Henry Kendall & Sons v William Lillico & Sons Ltd* [1969] 2 A.C. 31, 79, 108, 118.

[436] *Harlingdon and Leinster Enterprises Ltd v Christopher Hull Fine Art Ltd* [1991] 1 Q.B. 564. This passage from the 31st edition of this work (para.43-086) is cited in *Saint Gobain Building Distribution Ltd (t/a International Decorative Surfaces) v Hillmead Joinery (Swindon) Ltd* [2015] B.L.R. 555, QBD, [60].

e.g. "heavy duty" equipment, or are described as second-hand[437] or sub-standard goods. The price may also be relevant in that the buyer may reasonably expect a standard of quality that is not grossly out of line with the price that he has paid.[438] But all other relevant circumstances may be taken into account.[439]

44-100 **Guidelines** Section 14(2B) further provides a non-exhaustive list of features which, in addition to the state and condition of the goods, are "in appropriate cases" to be regarded as "aspects of the quality of the goods".[440] The first is "fitness for all the purposes for which the goods in question are commonly supplied". By including fitness for *all* such purposes this feature appears to go further than the previous law, which held goods to be merchantable if they were fit for a purpose for which goods of that description would normally be used even if they were unfit for another such purpose intended by the buyer.[441] However, the reference to the purposes for which the goods are *commonly* supplied may, in addition to excluding an abnormal or idiosyncratic use of the goods, enable the courts to avoid the extreme position that the goods must be fit for whatever purpose the buyer happens to require them.[442] Moreover, this feature is only to be applied "in appropriate cases". The second and third features ("appearance and finish" and "freedom from minor defects") are especially applicable to consumer sales, where the existence of slight defects may cause a reasonable person to regard the goods as unsatisfactory[443] even if they do not make the goods unfit for their purpose and even if the cost of remedying the defects is small.[444] The fourth feature ("safety") is important in both consumer and non-consumer sales. Goods may be rendered

---

[437] As to second-hand goods, see *Bartlett v Sydney Marcus Ltd* [1965] 1 W.L.R. 1013 (car); *McDonald v Empire Garage (Blackburn)* [1975] 10 C.L. 388 (car); *Feast Contractors Ltd v Ray Vincent Ltd* [1974] 1 N.Z.L.R. 212 (engine); *Lee v York Coach and Marine* [1977] R.T.R. 35 (car); *Kealey v Guy McDonald Ltd* (1984) 134 N.L.J. 706 (car); *Shine v General Guarantee Corp Ltd* [1988] 1 All E.R. 911 (car); *Business Application Specialists Ltd v Nationwide Credit Corp Ltd* [1988] R.T.R. 332 (car); *Brewer v Mann* [2010] EWHC 2444 (QB) (car).

[438] See *BS Brown & Son v Craiks Ltd* [1970] 1 W.L.R. 752. It has been held that the existence of a warranty is not relevant to the issue of satisfactory quality: *Lamarra v Capital Bank Plc*, 2007 S.C. 95, Sh Ct (Range Rover). On the construction of contractual warranties and specifications which apparently contradict see *MT Hojgaard A/S v E.ON Climate and Renewables UK Robin Rigg East Ltd* [2017] UKSC 59, [2017] Bus. L.R. 1610.

[439] Where the seller makes up the goods to the buyer's instructions, the requirement may attach to the ingredients only: *Christopher Hill Ltd v Ashington Piggeries Ltd* [1972] A.C. 441, 494 (mink food); *Bowen v RB Young Products Pty Ltd* [1967] W.A.R. 97, 105 (poultry food).

[440] In the case of consumer contracts for the sale of goods which fall within Ch.2 of Pt 1 of the Consumer Rights Act 2015 the satisfactory quality of goods also depends on other relevant circumstances including public statements made about the goods. See Consumer Rights Act s.9, above para.38-497.

[441] *Henry Kendall & Sons v William Lillico & Sons Ltd* [1969] 2 A.C. 31; *M/S Aswan Engineering Establishment Co v Lupdine Ltd* [1987] 1 W.L.R. 1. See also *Cehave NV v Bremer Handelsgesellschaft mbH (The Hansa Nord)* [1976] Q.B. 44 (part of consignment damaged, still usable for same purpose in lesser concentration).

[442] This is supported by *Jewson Ltd v Boyhan* [2003] EWCA Civ 1030, [2004] 1 Lloyd's Rep. 505 (boilers yielding low home energy ratings and reducing attractiveness of newly converted flats: satisfactory—see at [67] et seq.), cited in *Balmoral Group Ltd v Borealis (UK) Ltd* [2006] EWHC 1900 (Comm), [2006] 2 Lloyd's Rep. 629 at [140].

[443] *Rogers v Parish (Scarborough) Ltd* [1987] Q.B. 933, 944 (car); *Jackson v Rotax Motor and Cycle Co Ltd* [1910] 2 K.B. 937 (motor horns).

[444] cf. *Bernstein v Pamson Motors (Golders Green) Ltd* [1987] 2 All E.R. 220, 227.

unsafe by the absence of appropriate instructions for their use.[445] Conversely, goods may be rendered safe if accompanied by clear and adequate instructions as to their use or by warnings as to the risks involved.[446] The fifth feature ("durability") does not mean that the seller gives a continuing guarantee that the goods will last for any particular period of time. But the inherent durability of the goods at the time of their sale to the buyer is a matter to be taken into account in determining whether the goods are of satisfactory quality.[447] The extent of the durability which it is reasonable to expect will, on the other hand, depend on the nature and description of the goods, their price and the circumstances of the sale.[448]

Provisos The first proviso, relating to defects drawn to the buyer's attention, is particularly relevant to the sale of second-hand and sub-standard goods.[449]   **44-101**

The second proviso, on examination, replaced a similar proviso in the original 1893 Act with one difference of wording: there is no liability for defects which *that* (previously "such") an examination ought to reveal. It seems likely that this change in wording was intended to reverse the effect of the decision in *Thornett and Fehr v Beers & Son*[450] where the buyer made a hasty examination though offered further facilities; it was held that the proviso applied to defects which a proper examination would have revealed. The present wording may be taken to refer to the examination actually conducted.[451] It is to be noted, however, that the term continues to be implied where the buyer is given the opportunity to examine the goods but fails to do so.   **44-102**

The third proviso applies only in the case of a contract for sale by sample.[452] Its effect is that the seller is under no liability in respect of defects which could have   **44-103**

---

445 *Henry Kendall & Sons v William Lillico & Sons Ltd* [1969] 2 A.C. 31 at 119.
446 *Wormell v RHM Agricultural (East) Ltd* [1987] 1 W.L.R. 1091 (herbicine). See in general McLeod (1981) 97 L.Q.R. 550; Brown [1988] L.M.C.L.Q. 502.
447 See *Whitecap Leisure Ltd v John H Rundle Ltd* [2008] EWCA Civ 429, [2008] 2 Lloyd's Rep. 216 at [45] (subsequent deterioration evidence of original quality, not part of a continuing breach); see also *Peebles v Rembrand Builders Merchants Ltd* Unreported April 18, 2017, Sherriff Court (Tayside, Central and Fife) (Dundee) (roof tiles which became patchy and discoloured were not of satisfactory quality).
448 *Priest v Last* [1903] 2 K.B. 148 (hot-water bottle); *MP Evanghelinos v Leslie & Anderson* (1920) 4 Ll.L. Rep. 17 (tinned salmon); *AB Kemp v Tolland* [1956] 2 Lloyd's Rep. 681 (peaches); *Shillingford v Baron* [1959] 2 Lloyd's Rep. 453 (sugar syrup); *Godley v Perry* [1960] 1 W.L.R. 9 (catapult); *Oleificio Zucchi SpA v Northern Sales Ltd* [1965] 2 Lloyd's Rep. 496, 517 (rapeseed screenings); *Crowther v Shannon Motor Co* [1975] 1 W.L.R. 30.
449 See above, n.437. See also *Stephenson v Cookson* [2009] EWCA Civ 1270 (horse: different defect from that to which attention drawn).
450 [1919] 1 K.B. 486 (barrels of glue); cf. *Frank v Grosvenor Auctions Pty Ltd* [1960] V.R. 607 (car). It may be that the proviso is not applicable where the buyer has reason to believe that the defect will be rectified: see *R & B Customs Brokers Co Ltd v United Dominions Trust Ltd* [1988] 1 W.L.R. 321, 326, 333.
451 But this point was ignored by the Court of Appeal in *Bramhill v Edwards* [2004] EWCA Civ 403, [2004] 1 Lloyd's Rep. 653 (mobile home inspected but not measured for conformity with width regulations): see Twigg-Flesner (2005) 121 L.Q.R. 125. It was, however, so decided in *MacDonald v Pollock* [2012] CSIH 12, [2012] 1 Lloyd's Rep. 425. See further *Garside v Black Horse Ltd* [2010] EWHC 190 (QB) (Supply of Goods (Implied Terms) Act 1973) (new car: examination of an allegedly identical item not sufficient).
452 See below, paras 44-113, 44-114.

been detected on reasonable examination of the sample.[453] In this situation it is immaterial whether or not the buyer examines the sample.[454]

44-104 **Time for compliance** In principle the goods must be of satisfactory quality at the time of sale,[455] though in CIF and FOB contracts the duty normally relates to the time when risk passes, viz the time of shipment,[456] and this may be so in most cases where property and risk are separated. But the fact that goods deteriorate soon after purchase may be evidence that they were not of the requisite standard (including in respect of durability) when sold[457]; and in contracts involving transportation of the goods, s.14(2) may be held to require that the goods are on shipment in a fit state to endure normal transit and to be satisfactory in quality on arrival.[458]

44-105 **Implied term as to fitness for purpose**[459] Section 14(3) of the Act[460] provides:

"Where the seller sells goods in the course of a business and the buyer, expressly or by implication, makes known—

(a) to the seller, or
(b) where the purchase price or part of it is payable by instalments and the goods were previously sold by a credit-broker to the seller, to that credit-broker,

any particular purpose for which the goods are being bought, there is an implied term that the goods supplied under the contract are reasonably fit for that purpose, whether or not that is a purpose for which such goods are commonly supplied, except where the circumstances show that the buyer does not rely, or that it is unreasonable for him to rely, on the skill or judgment of the seller or credit-broker."

The meaning of "sells goods in the course of a business" and the rules as to a sale through an agent have already been discussed[461] as has also the meaning of the

---

453 See *Joseph Travers & Sons Ltd v Longel Ltd* (1948) 64 T.L.R. 50 ("waders" not waterproof—apparent on examination). cf. *Godley v Perry* [1960] 1 W.L.R. 9 (catapult dangerous—not apparent).
454 But, if the buyer fails to examine the sample, this might be an indication that the sale is not one by sample. See also Murdoch (1981) 44 M.L.R. 388, 396–399.
455 For the meaning of "sale", see s.2 above, para.44-020. See *AB Kemp Ltd v Tolland* [1956] 2 Lloyd's Rep. 681, 685, 691 (peaches); *Crowther v Shannon Motor Co* [1975] 1 W.L.R. 30, 33 (car). But in *Lambert v Lewis* [1982] A.C. 225, 276; *Viskase Ltd v Paul Kiefel GmbH* [1999] 1 W.L.R. 1305 and *Whitecap Leisure Ltd v John H Rundle Ltd* [2008] EWCA Civ 429, [2008] 2 Lloyd's Rep. 216 at [45] it is said that the duty relates to the time of delivery. See Hudson (1978) 94 L.Q.R. 566.
456 *Oleificio Zucchi SpA v Northern Sales Ltd* [1965] 2 Lloyd's Rep. 496, 518. But see *Cehave NV v Bremer Handelsgesellschaft mbH (The Hansa Nord)* [1976] Q.B. 44, where the discussion concentrates entirely on the condition of the goods on arrival.
457 See above, para.44-100.
458 *Mash and Murrell Ltd v Joseph I Emanuel Ltd* [1961] 1 W.L.R. 862, 867–868 (potatoes); reversed on other grounds [1961] 2 Lloyd's Rep. 326. See also *Cordova Land Co Ltd v Victor Bros Inc* [1966] 1 W.L.R. 793, 796 (skins); discussion in *KG Bominflot Bunkergesellschaft etc. & Co v Petroplus Marketing AG (The Mercini Lady)* [2010] EWCA Civ 1145, [2011] 1 Lloyd's Rep. 442, especially at [18] (rejecting an argument that the goods must hold their specification for such a period); and below, para.44-273. But where any goods of the type would deteriorate in transit, the seller may not be liable: see *Broome v Pardess Co-operative Society of Orange Growers* [1940] 1 All E.R. 603.
459 This section does not apply to consumer contracts for the sale of goods which fall within Ch.2 of Pt 1 of the Consumer Rights Act 2015. In consumer contracts for the sale of goods the 2015 Act provides a corresponding requirement of fitness for purpose which is to be treated as included in the contract, see above, para.38-498.
460 Formerly s.14(1) of the 1893 Act.
461 See above, paras 44-096, 44-097.

phrase "goods supplied under the contract".[462] As regards England and Wales and Northern Ireland, the term implied by s.14(3) is a condition.[463]

Credit-broker   The references to a credit-broker are intended to cover instal-   **44-106**
ment credit transactions where the supplier of the goods, e.g. a retailer, sells the goods to a finance company which then sells them to the buyer on credit terms (under a credit sale[464] or conditional sale[465] agreement). The finance company is not a party to the original negotiations. In this case the purpose for which the goods are being bought is not made known to the seller, the finance company, but to the supplier (the credit-broker) with whom there is no contract of sale. The effect of the amendment is to make the actual seller subject to s.14(3) as well as to s.14(2).[466] A credit-broker is defined by the subsection as:

"… a person acting in the course of a credit brokerage carried on by him, that is a business of effecting introductions of individuals desiring to obtain credit—(i) to persons carrying on any business so far as it relates to the provision of credit, or (ii) to other persons engaged in credit brokerage."[467]

Making known purpose for which goods bought   As the subsequent words   **44-107**
"whether or not that is a purpose for which such goods are commonly supplied" make clear, the subsection is not confined to the ordering of goods for specific purposes. The wording at this point is similar to that of s.14(1) of the 1893 Act, case-law on which had established that the purpose need not be made known expressly. Thus where an article can only be used for one purpose, e.g. a hot-water bottle, it is unnecessary for the buyer to make clear that he wants the article for the purpose of containing hot water without leakage.[468] Where however the goods may be used for any of several purposes, it may be necessary to specify the purpose: but here again knowledge may readily be inferred, e.g. from extraneous communications,[469] the purpose of the contract,[470] or the general background of the particular trade.[471]

Reliance may be rebutted   The 1893 Act required the buyer to allege reliance on   **44-108**
the seller's skill or judgment, though the court would readily infer such reliance.[472] The present wording of s.14(3) dispenses the plaintiff from this requirement, and

---

[462] See above, para.44-098.
[463] 1979 Act s.14(5A). As to conditions, see para.44-093.
[464] See above, para.44-029.
[465] See above, para.44-028.
[466] Provisions as to the agency of the supplier in respect of express statements in negotiations are contained in s.56 of the Consumer Credit Act 1974: see above, para.39-075.
[467] Problems may arise where the buyer is a corporation and so not an "individual": see Dobson [1983] J.B.L. 313.
[468] *Preist v Last* [1903] 2 K.B. 148.
[469] *Bristol Tramways, etc. Carriage Co v Fiat Motors Ltd* [1910] 2 K.B. 831 (buses required for heavy passenger work in Bristol).
[470] *Cammell Laird & Co Ltd v Manganese Bronze & Brass Co Ltd* [1934] A.C. 402 (ship propeller).
[471] e.g. *Henry Kendall & Sons v William Lillico & Sons Ltd* [1969] 2 A.C. 31 (Cattle Food Trade Assn: foreseeable that pig and poultry food might be fed to pheasants); *Christopher Hill Ltd v Ashington Piggeries Ltd* [1972] A.C. 441 (claim against third parties: foreseeable that herring meal might be fed to mink).
[472] See *Henry Kendall & Sons v William Lillico & Sons Ltd* [1969] 2 A.C. 31 at 81–84; *Godley v Perry* [1960] 1 W.L.R. 9 (child buying catapult).

it is for the seller to prove the absence of reliance or that reliance was not in the circumstances reasonable.[473] This could occur for instance where the seller disclaims any knowledge or expertise in relation to the goods, or if the buyer knows more about the conditions in which the goods are to be used than the seller,[474] or selects the goods from stock himself,[475] or where the buyer makes assumptions as to the product which are not justified[476] or takes a commodity as it is.[477] Dealers in established markets may likewise be held to rely on their own judgment when buying, though there is no rule to this effect.[478] Reliance may be partial: for example, where mink farmers asked a compounder of animal foods to make up mink food to a supplied formula it was held that there was reliance as to the suitability of the ingredients only.[479]

44-109   **Reasonably fit for purpose**   The duty to provide goods reasonably fit for the purpose made known is a strict one: it is no defence that all care was taken.[480] There are many cases on this subsection,[481] for s.14(2) of the original 1893 Act applied

---

[473] *Central Regional Council v Uponor*, 1996 S.L.T. 645 (water pipes). For a case on the old wording in which reliance was not proved, see *Hamilton v Papakura DC* [2002] 3 N.Z.L.R. 308, PC (water supply to tomato grower).

[474] *Teheran-Europe Co Ltd v ST Belton (Tractors) Ltd* [1968] 2 Q.B. 545 (air compressors for resale in Iran); *Sumner, Permain & Co v Webb & Co* [1922] 1 K.B. 55 (tonic water for resale in Argentina); *Phoenix Distributors Ltd v LB Clarke (London) Ltd* [1966] 2 Lloyd's Rep. 285, [1967] 1 Lloyd's Rep. 518 (potatoes for export to Poland); *Nikka Traders Ltd v Gizella Pastry Ltd* [2012] BCSC 1412 (cookies for importation into Japan needing to pass customs). As to reliance by an agent, see *Ashford Shire Council v Dependable Motors Pty Ltd* [1961] A.C. 336. See also *Britvic Soft Drinks Ltd v Messer UK Ltd* [2002] 1 Lloyd's Rep. 20 at [93]; affirmed [2002] EWCA Civ 548, [2002] 2 Lloyd's Rep. 368 (sufficient that buyer relies on seller or any person from whom seller acquired the goods). Sed quaere: see *Jewson Ltd v Kelly* Unreported August 2, 2002 Q.B.D. at [88]; reversed without reference to this point [2003] EWCA Civ 1030, [2004] 1 Lloyd's Rep. 505. See Sealy [2003] C.L.J. 260.

[475] *H Beecham & Co Pty Ltd v Francis Howard & Co Pty Ltd* [1921] V.L.R. 428 (timber).

[476] *Balmoral Group Ltd v Borealis (UK) Ltd* [2006] EWHC 1900 (Comm), [2006] 2 Lloyd's Rep. 629 (polymer: different process required).

[477] See *Turner v Mucklow* (1862) 6 L.T. 690; *Ipswich Gaslight Co v WB King & Co* (1886) 3 T.L.R. 100—cases on sale of industrial waste.

[478] See *CEB Draper & Son Ltd v Edward Turner & Son Ltd* [1965] 1 Q.B. 424, 433, 434; but cf. *Henry Kendall & Sons v William Lillico & Sons Ltd* [1969] 2 A.C. 31, 84, 95, 107, 124 (London Cattle Foods Trading Association). See also *Feast Contractors Ltd v Ray Vincent Ltd* [1974] 1 N.Z.L.R. 212 (cartage contractor buying engine from garage); *South Coast Basalt Pty Ltd v RW Miller & Co Pty Ltd* [1981] 1 N.S.W.L.R. 356, PC (reliance though buyer and seller associated companies).

[479] *Christopher Hill Ltd v Ashington Piggeries Ltd* [1972] A.C. 441; see also *Cammell Laird & Co Ltd v Manganese Bronze and Brass Co Ltd* [1934] A.C. 402; cf. *Central Regional Council v Uponor*, 1996 S.L.T. 645. See also *Jewson Ltd v Kelly* [2003] EWCA Civ 1030, [2004] 1 Lloyd's Rep. 505 (boilers for flats); *Medivance Instruments Ltd v Gaslane Pipework Services Ltd* [2002] EWCA Civ 500 (heater: BS compliance relevant to s.14(2) not s.14(3)); *BSS Group Plc v Makers (UK) Ltd* [2011] EWCA Civ 809 (plumbing equipment: made known to seller that parts to be used with Uponor piping: reliance reasonable). On the construction of contractual warranties and specifications which apparently contradict see *MT Hojgaard A/S v E.ON Climate and Renewables UK Robin Rigg East Ltd* [2017] UKSC 59, [2017] Bus. L.R. 1610.

[480] *Bigge v Parkinson* (1862) 7 Hurl. & N. 955, 959 (tinned goods); *Frost v Aylesbury Dairy Co* [1905] 1 K.B. 608 (typhoid germs in milk); *Henry Kendall & Sons v William Lillico & Sons Ltd* [1969] 2 A.C. 31, 84.

[481] e.g. *Wallis v Russell* [1902] 2 I.R. 585 (infected boiled crab); *Bristol Tramways, etc. Carriage Co v Fiat Motors Ltd* [1910] 2 K.B. 831 (buses unsuitable for heavy passenger work); *Henry Kendall & Sons v William Lillico & Sons Ltd* [1969] 2 A.C. 31, 84 (groundnut extractions unsuitable for compounding into poultry food); *Vacwell Engineering Co Ltd v BDH Chemicals Ltd* [1971] 1 Q.B.

only to sales "by description": and difficulties over the meaning of that phrase, and over the meaning of "merchantable quality", seem for a period to have discouraged litigants from relying on that provision. As already stated, "reasonably fit" covers fitness for purposes for which the goods are commonly supplied as well as for specific purposes expressly made known to the seller. It does not however require that the goods are absolutely suitable for their purpose,[482] nor proof against misuse,[483] nor usable for purposes outside the range of purposes foreseeable by the seller,[484] nor proof against an abnormal peculiarity or sensitivity, not known to the seller,[485] in the buyer, or in the circumstances of the use of the goods by the buyer. This is the provision of the Act most likely to be relevant, whether directly or by analogy, to defective consumer software.[486] The analogy would however (unless a service element can be isolated) create strict liability, which may not always be appropriate to a composite transaction.

Patent or trade name   Under the wording in the 1893 Act the order of an article   **44-110**
by its patent or trade name would exclude the condition as to fitness, though the proviso to this effect was restrictively interpreted.[487] Under the present wording the fact that an article is ordered by a patent or trade name is relevant only as a pos-

---

88 (dangerous chemical without warning label); *Christopher Hill Ltd v Ashington Piggeries Ltd* [1972] A.C. 441 (herring meal toxic to mink); *Jackson v Chrysler Acceptances Ltd* [1978] R.T.R. 474; but cf. *Millar's of Falkirk Ltd v Turpie*, 1976 S.L.T. (Notes) 66; *Leaves v Wadham Stringer (Cliftons) Ltd* [1980] R.T.R. 308 (cases on new cars); *Farnworth Finance Facilities Ltd v Attryde* [1970] 1 W.L.R. 1053 (motorcycle); *Finch Motors Ltd v Oris (No.2)* [1980] 2 N.Z.L.R. 519 (car unsuitable for towing boat); *Milne Construction Ltd v Expandite Ltd* [1984] 2 N.Z.L.R. 163 (epoxy resin accompanied by inadequate instructions); *Hazlewood Grocery Ltd v Lion Foods Ltd* [2007] EWHC 1887 (QB) (dye in food: danger of intervention by Food Standards Agency); *Fluor Ltd v Shanghai Zhenhua Heavy Industries Ltd* [2016] EWHC 2062 (TCC) (if a buyer knows of goods' true condition but is unable to discover without lengthy investigation whether or not that condition affects use of the goods, they are not fit for purpose).

482 e.g. *Bartlett v Sidney Marcus Ltd* [1965] 1 W.L.R. 1013 (second-hand car); cf. *Crowther v Shannon Motor Co* [1975] 1 W.L.R. 30; *Lee v Coach and Marine* [1977] R.T.R. 35.

483 *Heil v Hedges* [1951] 1 T.L.R. 512 (pork insufficiently cooked). As to the legal significance of instructions see McLeod (1981) 97 L.Q.R. 550.

484 See *Christopher Hill Ltd v Ashington Piggeries Ltd* [1972] A.C. 441 at 477, 498–499 (applying the test of remoteness laid down in *Koufos v C Czarnikow Ltd (The Heron II)* [1969] 1 A.C. 350).

485 *Slater v Finning Ltd* [1997] A.C. 473 (engine for boat). See also *Griffiths v Peter Conway Ltd* [1939] 1 All E.R. 685 (skin sensitive to tweed): *Ingham v Emes* [1955] 2 Q.B. 366 (hair dye); *Crozier v A & P Canada Inc* (2010) 329 D.L.R. (4th) 565 (peanut butter: claimant had long history of Crohn's disease). cf. *BSS Group Plc v Makers (UK) Ltd* [2011] EWCA Civ 809 (the fact that the plumbing equipment supplied was not compatible was not due to some unknown idiosyncrasy of the buyer).

486 See above, para.44-015 n.84. For examples see *Salvage Assn v CAP Financial Services Ltd* [1995] F.S.R. 654; *St Albans City and DC v International Computers Ltd* [1996] 4 All E.R. 481; *Jonathan Wren & Co Ltd v Microdec Plc* (1999) 65 Con. L.R. 157; *Pegler Ltd v Wang UK Ltd* [2000] B.L.R. 218; *Watford Electronics Ltd v Sanderson CFL Ltd* [2001] EWCA Civ 317, [2001] 1 All E.R. (Comm) 696; *Rubicon Computer Systems Ltd v United Paints Ltd* (2000) 2 T.C.L.R. 454; *SAM Business Systems Ltd v Hadley & Co* [2002] EWHC 2733 (TCC), [2003] 1 All E.R. (Comm) 465; *Brocket v DGS Retail Ltd* [2004] C.L.Y. 3269 (seller should warn about incompatibility of packages). A recent example in the context of defective software (though for commercial use) is *Kingsway Hall Hotel Ltd v Red Sky IT (Hounslow) Ltd* [2010] EWHC 965 (TCC) (reservation system for hotel). See also *Southwark LBC v IBM UK Ltd* [2011] EWHC 549 (TCC), 135 Con. L.R. 136 (no sale involved in supply of third party software and associated services). The Consumer Rights Act 2015 provides new statutory rights in relation to digital content: see above, paras 38-535 et seq.

487 See *Baldry v Marshall* [1925] 1 K.B. 260, 267.

sible indication that the buyer did not rely, or that it was unreasonable for the buyer to rely, on the seller's skill or judgment.

44-111 **Time for compliance** This question has been discussed in connection with s.14(2).[488] There can, however, be a difference of application, in that if a contract contemplates transportation of the goods and the goods are perishable, they must be shipped in a condition to endure normal transit to their destination.[489]

44-112 **Relation between ss.14(2) and (3)** There is a considerable overlap between ss.14(2) and 14(3) and claims under both subsections are frequently made. But three main differences exist.[490] First, s.14(2) requires that the goods be of satisfactory quality whereas s.14(3) requires that they be reasonably fit for the purpose made known. The latter standard will normally be higher than the former if a special purpose is made known; and though "satisfactory quality" includes in appropriate cases fitness for purpose, it can be argued to impose a somewhat lower standard than s.14(3).[491] Secondly, if there is no reliance, or if reliance is unreasonable, s.14(3) is excluded, but s.14(2) may still apply.[492] Thirdly, s.14(2) is excluded as regards defects drawn to the buyer's attention, and defects which ought to have been revealed by an examination made: in connection with s.14(3) either of these factors may be relevant to show lack of reliance, but the lack of reliance may be partial only and not exclude the provision altogether.

(iv)   Sale by Sample

44-113 **Sale by sample**[493]   By s.15(1):

"A contract of sale is a contract for sale by sample where there is an express or implied term to that effect in the contract."

It seems that there is a sale by sample only if the parties intended this and made it a term of their contract that "the goods should answer the description of a small parcel exhibited at the time of sale".[494] Thus the fact that a sample was exhibited

---

[488] See above, para.44-104. See *Lambert v Lewis* [1982] A.C. 225, 276–277; *Viskase Ltd v Paul Kiefel GmbH* [1999] 1 W.L.R. 1305.

[489] See *Mash and Murrell Ltd v Joseph I Emanuel Ltd* [1961] 1 W.L.R. 862, 867–868; reversed on other grounds [1961] 2 Lloyd's Rep. 326 (potatoes), below, para.44-273; cf. *AB Kemp Ltd v Tolland* [1956] 2 Lloyd's Rep. 681, 684–685 (peaches). But this is a matter of quality on shipment: see *KG Bominflot Bunkergesellschaft etc. & Co v Petroplus Marketing AG (The Mercini Lady)* [2010] EWCA Civ 1145, [2011] 1 Lloyd's Rep. 442, especially at [18].

[490] See also (under the 1893 Act), e.g. *Bristol Tramways, etc. Carriage Co Ltd v Fiat Motors Ltd* [1910] 2 K.B. 831; *Lee v York Coach and Marine* [1977] R.T.R. 35. See Franzi (1977) 51 A.L.J. 298; and *Teheran-Europe Co Ltd v ST Belton (Tractors) Ltd* [1968] 2 Q.B. 545, 562–563.

[491] See above, para.44-099.

[492] But see *Harlingdon and Leinster Enterprises Ltd v Christopher Hull Fine Art Ltd* [1991] 1 Q.B. 564, where this was not so.

[493] See Murdoch (1981) 44 M.L.R. 388. This section does not apply to consumer contracts for the sale of goods which fall within Ch.2 of Pt 1 of the Consumer Rights Act 2015. In consumer contracts for the sale of goods the 2015 Act provides corresponding terms requiring goods to match any sample which are to be treated as included in the contract; see above, para.38-501. The 2015 Act also introduces a new requirement that goods must match a model seen or examined; see above, para.38-502.

[494] *Parker v Palmer* (1821) 4 B. & Ald. 387, 391.

during the negotiations for the contract does not of itself render it a sale by sample.[495] But evidence of usage is admissible to show that a sale is by sample even where the written contract is silent on this point.[496] In view of the fact that the term as to satisfactory quality does not apply to defects apparent on reasonable examination of the sample,[497] it may be suggested that private buyers, who usually lack expertise for such examination, will not readily be held to buy by sample, nor private sellers to sell by sample.

Bulk to correspond with sample   By s.15(2) certain terms are implied in the case   **44-114**
of a contract for sale by sample.[498] In England and Wales and Northern Ireland these terms are conditions.[499] Unlike the requirements of s.14, they are not restricted to business sellers, though, as stated above, it may be that private sales by sample are rare. The first is "(a) that the bulk will correspond with the sample in quality".[500] The fact that the bulk, though not in accordance with the sample, could be made to conform by a simple process is irrelevant: correspondence must be precise.[501] It has been held that an exclusion of any implied term as to quality does not exclude the duty of securing that the bulk correspond with the sample.[502] The extent to which there must be conformity—whether it need be visual only, or whether the two must correspond on analysis—depends on the contemplation of the parties and the usage of trade.[503] The word "bulk" is defined in s.61(1) of the Act,[504] but in a way that appears to be inappropriate in the context of the present section,[505] since specific goods,[506] goods manufactured after contract,[507] and further articles supplied on the pattern of that shown as a sample, may all count as "bulk" under it.

Freedom from latent defect   The second term implied by s.15(2) is: **44-115**

> "(c)   that the goods will be free from any defect, making their quality unsatisfactory, which would not be apparent on reasonable examination of the sample."

The effect of this provision is that the seller is liable for latent defects which make

---

[495]   *Gardiner v Gray* (1815) 4 Camp. 144; *Ginner v King* (1894) 7 T.L.R. 140. And in commercial contracts for commodities samples may perform quite different functions: see *John Bowron & Sons Ltd v Rodema Canned Foods Ltd* [1967] 1 Lloyd's Rep. 183 (preliminary shipment); cf. *Wood Components of London v James Webster & Bros Ltd* [1959] 2 Lloyd's Rep. 200.

[496]   See *Syers v Jonas* (1848) 2 Exch. 111.

[497]   See above, para.44-102.

[498]   1979 Act s.15 should be read in conjunction with s.13, see above, paras 44-086 et seq.; a sale is frequently both by sample and by description.

[499]   1979 Act s.15(3).

[500]   "Quality" of goods includes their state or condition and, in appropriate cases, certain other features: s.14(2B); see above, para.44-095.

[501]   *ES Ruben Ltd v Faire Bros & Co Ltd* [1949] 1 K.B. 254, 260; *Aitken, Campbell & Co v Boullen and Gatenby*, 1908 S.C. 490. Unless the de minimis principle applies.

[502]   *Champanhac & Co Ltd v Waller & Co Ltd* [1948] 2 All E.R. 724.

[503]   See *FE Hookway & Co Ltd v Alfred Isaacs & Son* [1954] 1 Lloyd's Rep. 491; *Steels and Busks Ltd v Bleecker Bik & Co Ltd* [1956] 1 Lloyd's Rep. 228. Sometimes there are provisions making certain types of certification or testing conclusive: e.g. *Gill & Duffus SA v Berger & Co Inc* [1984] A.C. 382.

[504]   See above, para.44-015. The definition is plainly directed at ss.20A and 20B, below, paras 44-160 et seq.

[505]   *Benjamin's Sale of Goods*, 10th edn (2014), para.11-073.

[506]   e.g. *Azémar v Casella* (1867) L.R. 2 C.P. 677.

[507]   e.g. *Drummond & Sons v Van Ingen & Co* (1887) 12 App. Cas. 284; *Jones v Padgett* (1890) 24 Q.B.D. 650.

the quality of the goods unsatisfactory.[508] Where, however, the defect could have been detected on reasonable examination of the sample there is no liability.[509] It follows from this provision that, if there is a latent defect of this kind in the goods, the buyer may reject them even though bulk and sample correspond.[510]

(v) Pre-contractual Information to Consumers

44-116 **Pre-contractual information to be included as term of consumer contract** The Consumer Contracts (Information, Cancellation and Additional Charges) Regulations 2013[511] implement the Consumer Rights Directive.[512] They replace the Consumer Protection (Distance Selling) Regulations 2000 and the Cancellation of Contracts made in a Consumer's Home or Place of Work, etc. Regulations 2008 with effect from June 13, 2014, and apply to contracts made on or after that date. The 2013 Regulations impose duties on traders making distance contracts, off-premises contracts and some other ("on-premises") contracts with consumers to give or make available a wide range of information to the consumer before the contract is concluded.[513] The Consumer Rights Act 2015, refers to the information requirements and provides that information provided in accordance with the Regulations becomes a term of the contract. Information about the main characteristics of the goods will be treated as part of the description, and the consumer will have the normal remedies for non-conformity[514]; whereas for other information that is given the trader is in effect, treated as giving a contractual warranty that the information was correct at the time.[515]

(vi) Exclusion of Terms Implied by ss.13, 14, and 15

44-117 **Unfair Contract Terms Act 1977** The Unfair Contract Terms Act 1977 controls, for the contracts to which it applies, attempts to exclude the seller's duties laid down in ss.13, 14 and 15 of the Sale of Goods Act.[516] In addition to the general provisions of the Act, which are dealt with elsewhere in this work,[517] s.6(2) (which in substance re-enacts earlier controls imposed by the Supply of Goods (Implied Terms) Act 1973) provided an absolute bar on exclusions in consumer cases:

> "As against a person dealing as consumer, liability for breach of the obligations arising from—(a) sections 13, 14 or 15 of the 1979 Act … cannot be excluded or restricted by reference to any contract term."[518]

In the case of non-consumer sales, s.6(3) of the 1977 Act provided:

---

[508] *Godley v Perry* [1960] 1 W.L.R. 9 (catapult dangerous—not apparent): "satisfactory quality" is defined in s.14(2A); see above, para.44-099.

[509] *Joseph Travers & Sons Ltd v Longel Ltd* (1948) 64 T.L.R. 150 ("waders" not waterproof—apparent on examination). This is expressly covered for in a proviso to s.14(2) contained in s.14(2C); see above, para.44-103.

[510] *Mody v Gregson* (1868) L.R. 4 Ex. 49; *Drummond & Sons v Van Ingen & Co* (1887) 12 App. Cas. 284, 297.

[511] SI 2013/3134.

[512] 2011/83/EU of October 15, 2011.

[513] See above, paras 38-059 et seq.

[514] See above, para.38-499.

[515] See above, para.38-500.

[516] As to s.12, see above, para.44-085.

[517] Vol.I, paras 15-066 et seq.

[518] The use of terms purporting to exclude such liability was an offence under the Consumer Protec-

"As against a person dealing otherwise than as consumer, the liability specified in subs.(2) above can be excluded or restricted by reference to a contract term, but only in so far as the term satisfies the requirement of reasonableness."[519]

However, for contracts entered into after October 1, 2015, the Consumer Rights Act 2015 repeals or disapplies provisions in the Unfair Contract Terms Act 1977 in relation to consumer contracts. In relation to contracts to which Ch.1 applies, the Act makes its own provision controlling the exclusion of liabilities arising under its provisions,[520] though this follows the pattern of the relevant provisions in the 1977 Act to a considerable extent. As a result, s.31 of the 2015 Act provides that a term of a goods contract[521] is not binding on the consumer to the extent that it would exclude or restrict the trader's liability under the statutory terms which the Act treats as included,[522] in respect of its special provisions governing non-conformity of the goods,[523] delivery of goods and the passing of risk.[524] Section 6 of the Unfair Contract Terms Act 1977 no longer applies to consumer contracts. It should be noted that the new provisions have a different scope of application from that of the 1977 Act, because the test whether the party was "dealing as a consumer"[525] is to be replaced by one of whether the contract for goods was one under which a trader was to supply goods to a consumer, and only a natural person who is buying goods wholly or mainly for purposes outside that individual's trade, business craft or profession as a consumer.[526]

44-118

Thus, control of unfair terms is now divided sharply between terms found in consumer contracts (regulated by the 2015 Act, principally in Pt 2) and terms (principally exemption clauses[527]) in other contracts (regulated by the Unfair Contract Terms Act 1977).

In non-consumer sales, a new s.6(1A) (replacing the previous s.6(2) and (3)) provides that:

44-119

"Liability for breach of the obligations arising from—

---

tion (Restriction on Statements Order) 1976 (SI 1976/1813) as amended by SI 1978/127 (now repealed); as was the supply of statements about consumer rights relating to quality, fitness or description without at the same time notifying the consumer that his statutory rights are unaffected. See *Hughes v Hall* [1981] R.T.R. 430; but cf. *Cavendish-Woodhouse Ltd v Manley* (1984) 82 L.G.R. 376.

[519] The subsection also refers to hire-purchase (see above, para.39-382); and s.7 makes similar, but not identical, provision for other contracts where possession or ownership of goods passes (see Vol.I, para.15-094).

[520] See above, paras 38-365 et seq. On the general strategy of the 2015 Act in relation to the control of unfair contract terms, see above, paras 38-365 et seq.

[521] On s.31 see above, para.38-531.

[522] i.e. 2015 Act s.9 (goods to be of satisfactory quality), s.10 (goods to be fit for particular purpose), s.11 (goods to be as described), s.12 (other pre-contract information included in contract); s.13 (goods to match a sample); s.14 (goods to match a model seen or examined) and s.17 (trader to have right to supply the goods etc): 2015 Act s.31(1)(a)–(f), (i). On these provisions see above, paras 38-492 et seq.

[523] i.e. 2015 Act s.15 (installation as part of conformity of the goods with the contract) and s.16 (goods not conforming to contract if digital content does not conform): 2015 Act s.31(1)(g) and (h). On these provisions see above, paras 38-503 and 38-504 respectively.

[524] 2015 Act ss.28 and 29 respectively: 2015 Act s.31(j) and (k), on which see above, para.38-527.

[525] See below, para.44-121.

[526] See above, para.38-481.

[527] The Unfair Contract Terms Act 1977 as amended by the 2015 Act applies only to exemption clauses (as defined in s.13) and other clauses falling within s.3(2)(b) of the 1977 Act: see Vol.I, paras 15-085 et seq.

(a)   Section 13,14 or 15 of the 1979 Act (seller's implied undertakings as to conformity of goods with description or sample, or as to their quality or fitness for a particular purpose);

(b)   Section 9, 10 or 11 of the 1973 Act (the corresponding things in relation to hire purchase),

Cannot be excluded or restricted by reference to a contract term except in so far as the term satisfies the requirement of reasonableness."

44-120   The provisions are not confined, as is the rest of the 1977 Act,[528] to business liability, but of course the duties created by s.14 are already limited to business sellers.[529] As elsewhere explained,[530] there are possibilities of reducing the operation of the Act by reducing the contractual description, as by providing for tolerances. If the seller points out defects these will not be covered by the provisions as to merchantable quality of s.14(2). And where the seller indicates to the buyer that the buyer should not rely on the seller's skill or judgment, this may make it unreasonable for the buyer to do so under s.14(3). It has however been held that a clause "sold as seen and inspected" was an actual exclusion of s.13.[531]

44-121   **Businesses dealing as consumer[532]**   For contracts entered into before October 1, 2015, s.12(1) of the Unfair Contract Terms Act 1977 provided that:

"(1)   A party to a contract 'deals as consumer' in relation to another party if—
(a)   he neither makes the contract in the course of a business nor holds himself out as doing so; and
(b)   the other party does make the contract in the course of a business; and
(c)   in the case of a contract governed by the law of sale of goods ... the goods passing under or in pursuance of the contract are of a type ordinarily supplied for private use or consumption.[533]

---

[528]   s.1(3); Vol.I, para.15-072.
[529]   See above, paras 44-096, 44-105.
[530]   Vol.I, para.15-070.
[531]   *Hughes v Hall* [1981] R.T.R. 430 (a prosecution under the Consumer Protection (Restriction on Statements) Order 1976 (now repealed)), above, n.518. The decision was however doubted in *Cavendish-Woodhouse Ltd v Manley* (1984) 82 L.G.R. 376. If such a clause is not an exclusion it seems that the operation of the 1977 Act can be fairly easily avoided. But in *Titan Steel Wheels Ltd v Royal Bank of Scotland Plc* [2010] EWHC 211 (Comm), [2010] 2 Lloyd's Rep. 92 several clauses in a sale of derivatives were said merely to define "the basis on which [the contractor] was providing its services". See also *Avrora Fine Arts Investment Ltd v Christie Manson & Woods Ltd* [2012] EWHC 2198 (Ch), [2012] P.N.L.R. 35 (clause purporting to negative reliance on statements at fine art auction "parts company with reality" because it attempted retrospectively to alter the character of what had gone before, so subject to Act: but also held reasonable); *Dalmare SpA v Union Maritime Ltd (The Union Power)* [2012] EWHC 3537 (Comm), [2013] 1 Lloyd's Rep. 509 (sale of ship "as she was" at time of inspection wording held not clear enough to exclude the conditions stated in ss.13 and 14—even if the words "as is where is" could exclude statutory implied terms). On the other hand a "certificate of acceptance" and associated terms in an aircraft lease were assumed valid in principle in *Olympic Airlines SA v ACG Acquisition XX LLC* [2013] EWCA Civ 369, [2013] 1 Lloyd's Rep. 658. This problem links to that of entire agreement clauses and "no-reliance" clauses: see Vol.I, paras 15-147 and 7-146 respectively.
[532]   1977 Act s.5 deals with guarantees of consumer goods: see Vol.I, para.15-091; and see above, paras 38-528 et seq.
[533]   By virtue of the Sale and Supply of Goods to Consumers Regulations 2002 (SI 2002/3045) reg.14 subs.(c) does not apply where the buyer is an individual.

(2)   But on a sale by auction or competitive tender the buyer is not in any circumstances to be regarded as dealing as consumer.[534]

(3)   Subject to this, it is for those claiming that a party does not deal as consumer to show that he does not."

This definition, which is deleted by the Consumer Rights Act 2015, also applied to the same words as used in the Sale of Goods Act 1979,[535] and was amended (for both) by the Sale and Supply of Goods to Consumers Regulations 2002.[536] Under this definition, except in certain situations a corporation can in appropriate cases deal as consumer.[537] The phrase "in the course of a business" is the same as that used in s.14 of the Sale of Goods Act 1979,[538] where it has been held that these words cover, not only a seller selling goods of a type which he is in the business of selling, but a seller in the business of selling one type of goods who incidentally in his business sells another type of goods or even one who sells goods in the course of a business which does not consist of selling goods at all, for example, the sale by a plumber of his van.[539] But it has been held that, in the context of the 1977 Act, for a *buyer*[540] to make the contract in the course of a business the transaction must be an integral part of the business carried on, or, if only incidental thereto, be of a type regularly entered into. Thus the purchase of a second-hand motor car by a firm of surveyors[541] or by a company which carried on the business of freight forwarders and shipping agents[542] was held not to be a contract made in the course of a business. The overall result favours buyers, which seems appropriate, albeit there is some loss of consistency. Problems may also arise (when it applies) as to the phrase "goods ordinarily supplied for private use or consumption". Does this mean that the *majority* of such goods are supplied for private use, or that such goods are *commonly* supplied for such use? The second interpretation is much wider, and it is submitted that it should be adopted: the effect would be that only goods which are not supplied, or only exceptionally supplied, for such use would be excluded (e.g. beer pumps, furniture vans).[543]

---

534   By virtue of the above Regulations, where the buyer is an individual this exception is limited to second-hand goods sold by public auction at which individuals have the opportunity of attending in person.

535   Sale of Goods Act 1979 s.61(5A), added by Sale and Supply of Goods Act 1994: for application see ss.14(2D), 14(2F), 15A, 20(4), 30(2A), 32(4), 35(3), 48A–48F.

536   2002 Regulations reg.14.

537   See *Peter Symmons & Co v Cook* (1981) 131 N.L.J. 758; *R & B Customs Brokers Co Ltd v United Dominions Trust Ltd* [1988] 1 W.L.R. 321; *Air Transworld Ltd v Bombardier Inc* [2012] EWHC 243 (Comm), [2012] 1 Lloyd's Rep. 349 at [108], though in the case itself the corporation did not do so.

538   See above, para.44-096.

539   *Stevenson v Rogers* [1999] Q.B. 1028; *MacDonald v Pollock* [2012] CSIH 12, [2012] 1 Lloyd's Rep. 425.

540   i.e. the party referred to in s.12(1)(a): *R & B Customs Brokers Co Ltd v United Dominions Trust Ltd* [1988] 1 W.L.R. 321 (buyer); following *Davies v Sumner* [1984] 1 W.L.R. 1301 (Trade Descriptions Act 1968: seller); and cf. *Corfield v Sevenways Garage Ltd* [1985] R.T.R. 109.

541   *Peter Symmons & Co v Cook* (1981) 131 N.L.J. 758.

542   *R & B Customs Brokers Co Ltd v United Dominions Trust Ltd* [1988] 1 W.L.R. 321. This case contains a suggestion (at 331) that the corporate veil might sometimes be pierced in such a case. See also *Rasbora Ltd v JCL Marine Ltd* [1977] 1 Lloyd's Rep. 645.

543   An expensive power boat was held to come within the similar terminology laid down by the Supply of Goods (Implied Terms) Act 1973 in *Rasbora Ltd v JCL Marine Ltd* [1977] 1 Lloyd's Rep. 645. In *Air Transworld Ltd v Bombardier Inc* [2012] EWHC 243 (Comm), [2012] 1 Lloyd's Rep. 349 at [122], a Challenger 605 jet aircraft (sold to a corporation) was held to be such an item.

44-122 Non-consumer sales In non-consumer sales, exclusions are enforceable if clearly expressed, but only insofar as the term satisfies the requirement of reasonableness. Schedule 2 lays down guidelines[544] for the exercise of the court's discretion stating that:

> "The matters to which regard is to be had in particular ... are any of the following which appear to be relevant—
>
> (a) the strength of the bargaining positions of the parties relative to each other, taking into account (among other things) alternative means by which the customer's requirements could have been met;
>
> (b) whether the customer received an inducement to agree to the term, or in accepting it had an opportunity of entering into a similar contract with other persons, but without having to accept a similar term[545];
>
> (c) whether the customer knew or ought reasonably to have known of the existence and extent of the term (having regard, among other things, to any custom of the trade and any previous course of dealing between the parties);
>
> (d) where the term excludes or restricts any relevant liability if some condition is not complied with, whether it was reasonable at the time of the contract to expect that compliance with that condition would be practicable[546];
>
> (e) whether the goods were manufactured, processed or adapted to the special order of the customer."

44-123 Reasonableness[547] The Act's more general provision, applicable to non-consumer sales, is that the clause must have been a:

> "... fair and reasonable one to be included having regard to the circumstances which were, or ought reasonably to have been, known to or in the contemplation of the parties when the contract was made."[548]

It has been held that the term must be taken as a whole: if the term as a whole is unreasonable, it is not open to a party to say that the part of the term on which he relies is reasonable, or that a particular application of it is reasonable, or vice versa.[549] The question of reasonableness is obviously a general one and is considered in Vol.I.[550] The same is true of the question to which types of clause the Act applies.[551] As regards sale of goods and closely related transactions, some of the reported authority relates to s.3 of the Misrepresentation Act 1967 and the amendments to the Sale of Goods Act 1893 inserted by the Supply of Goods (Implied Terms) Act 1973, under both of which the test was whether the *reliance* on the term was reasonable in the particular case. In the leading case of *George Mitchell (Chesterhall) Ltd v Finney Lock Seeds Ltd*[552] reliance on a term in a contract for the supply of cabbage seed limiting liability to the price of the seed was

---

[544] See Vol.I, para.15-097, for cases in which these guidelines were considered.

[545] See *Denham Fish Selling Ltd v Anderson*, 1991 S.L.T. (Sh Ct) 24.

[546] See *Rees Hough Ltd v Redland Reinforced Plastics Ltd* (1984) 134 New L.J. 706.

[547] See in general Vol.I, paras 15-104 et seq.

[548] 1977 Act s.11(1). See Vol.I, para.15-096.

[549] *Stewart Gill Ltd v Horatio Myer & Co Ltd* [1992] Q.B. 600; Vol.I, para.15-112; but see doubts expressed in *Bacardi-Martini Beverages Ltd v Thomas Hardy Packaging Ltd* [2002] EWCA Civ 549, [2002] 2 Lloyd's Rep. 379 at [26].

[550] Ch.15, paras 15-104 et seq.

[551] See Ch.15, para.15-069.

[552] [1983] 2 A.C. 803; contrast *RW Green Ltd v Cade Bros Farms* [1978] 1 Lloyd's Rep. 602.

held unreasonable where the term was contained in a standard contract which had not been negotiated between interested parties or trade associations, insurance against liability for supply of the wrong seed was easily obtainable at low cost and the evidence showed that the proponent did not in fact usually rely on the term but sought to negotiate against its background. In cases decided under the 1977 Act, where the test is one of reasonableness of *inclusion*, the following terms have been held to be unreasonable: a term in a contract for the supply of piping which excluded all liability unless the seller was notified of defects in the piping within three months of delivery[553]; a term in a contract for the supply of a drilling rig which limited liability to replacement parts[554]; a term in a contract for the supply of computer software limiting liability to £100,000[555]; a term in a contract for the supply of radar equipment excluding the terms implied by the Sale of Goods Act save for a warranty that the equipment was free of defects caused by faulty materials or bad workmanship[556]; an exclusion and time-bar in a computer software contract inserted by a party who had so misrepresented what was being supplied that breaches of contract were not unlikely[557]; exclusion of all liability for the typical consequences of delivery of impure CO_2 gas, subject to a derisory recovery if complaint was made within an impossibly short period[558]; a term in a contract for the supply of a polymer for making storage tanks limiting liability to replacement or refund of the price was unreasonable as a blanket exclusion of liability[559]; a term in a contract for the supply of O-rings purporting to exclude liability, subject to certain exceptions, unless defects were reported within a very short period[560] and terms in a contract for supply of laminated sheets excluding implied terms, damages for consequential loss and excluding liability where there had been no inspection.[561] On the other hand, it has been stated that it would not be unreasonable for a finance company to exclude its liability with respect to goods sold on credit where it had never had possession of or inspected the goods[562]; and a commercially acceptable warranty in place of the normal implied terms has been held

---

[553] *Rees Hough Ltd v Redland Reinforced Plastics Ltd* (1984) 134 N.L.J. 706 (piping); cf. *Knight Machinery (Holdings) Ltd v Rennie*, 1995 S.L.T. 166 (meaning of similar clause not clear).

[554] *Edmund Murray Ltd v BSP International Foundations Ltd* (1992) 33 Con. L.R. 1; cf. *British Fermentation Products Ltd v Compair Reavell Ltd* (1999) 66 Con. L.R. 1 (air compressor).

[555] *St Albans City and DC v International Computers Ltd* [1995] F.S.R. 686; affirmed [1996] 4 All E.R. 481; but cf. *Bacardi-Martini Beverages Ltd v Thomas Hardy Packaging Ltd* [2002] 1 Lloyd's Rep. 62; affirmed [2002] EWCA Civ 549, [2002] 2 Lloyd's Rep. 379 (CO2 gas for drinks: £500,000 reasonable).

[556] *AEG (UK) Ltd v Logic Resource Ltd* [1996] C.L.C. 265 (noted [1996] L.M.C.L.Q. 334).

[557] *Pegler Ltd v Wang UK Ltd* [2000] B.L.R. 218. cf. *Southwark LBC v IBM UK Ltd* [2011] EWHC 549 (TCC), 135 Con. L.R. 136, where a clause in a software contract excluding implied conditions or warranties of fitness for purpose would have been reasonable had the Act applied.

[558] *Bacardi-Martini Beverages Ltd v Thomas Hardy Packaging Ltd* [2002] EWCA Civ 549, [2002] 2 Lloyd's Rep. 379; see also *Britvic Soft Drinks Ltd v Messer UK Ltd* [2002] EWCA Civ 548, [2002] 2 Lloyd's Rep. 368; and *Rasbora Ltd v JCL Marine Ltd* [1977] 1 Lloyd's Rep. 645. For a recent example in connection with hotel computer software see *Kingsway Hall Hotel Ltd v Red Sky IT (Hounslow) Ltd* [2010] EWHC 965 (TCC).

[559] *Balmoral Group Ltd v Borealis (UK) Ltd* [2006] EWHC 1900 (Comm), [2006] 2 Lloyd's Rep. 629 (some reliance on insurance position and fact that buyer had sometimes settled claims).

[560] *Sterling Hydraulics Ltd v Dichtomatik Ltd* [2006] EWHC 2004 (QB), [2007] 1 Lloyd's Rep. 8.

[561] *Saint Gobain Building Distribution Ltd (t/a International Decorative Surfaces) v Hillmead Joinery (Swindon) Ltd* [2015] B.L.R. 555, QBD.

[562] *R & B Customs Brokers Co Ltd v United Dominions Trust Ltd* [1988] 1 W.L.R. 321, 332. But contrast *Purnell Secretarial Services v Lease Management Services* [1994] C.C.L.R. 127; *Sovereign Finance Ltd v Silver Crest Furniture Ltd* [1997] C.C.L.R. 76.

to make an accompanying exclusion reasonable.[563]

44-124 **Burden of proof** The burden of proof is on the party contending that the clause is reasonable.[564]

44-125 **International sales** Section 26 excludes from the scope of the 1977 Act international supply contracts. An "international supply contract" (a term which of course also covers transactions other than sale) is defined by subs.(3) as having the following characteristics:

"(a) either it is a contract of sale of goods or it is one under or in pursuance of which the possession or ownership of goods passes[565]; and

(b) it is made by parties[566] whose places of business (or, if they have none, habitual residences) are in the territories of different States (the Channel Islands and the Isle of Man being treated for this purpose as different States from the United Kingdom)."

This definition is amplified by subs.(4) which reads:

"A contract falls within subsection (3) above only if either—

(a) the goods in question are, at the time of the conclusion of the contract, in the course of carriage, or will be carried,[567] from the territory of one State to the territory of another; or

(b) the acts constituting the offer and acceptance have been done in the territories of different States; or

(c) the contract provides for the goods to be delivered to the territory of a State other than that within whose territory those acts were done." [568]

---

[563] *Air Transworld Ltd v Bombardier Inc* [2012] EWHC 243 (Comm), [2012] 1 Lloyd's Rep. 349 at [122] et seq.; cf. *KG Bominflot Bunkergesellschaft etc. & Co v Petroplus Marketing AG (The Mercini Lady)* [2010] EWCA Civ 1145, [2011] 1 Lloyd's Rep. 442 at [62]. See also *Avrora Fine Arts Investment Ltd v Christie Manson & Woods Ltd* [2012] EWHC 2198 (Ch), [2012] P.N.L.R. 35 (limited rejection rights at fine art auction reasonable. Important considerations were that there was a remedy to cancel the sale under an express warranty and that this was a rich claimant with no imperative to deal with the defendant); *Allen Fabrications Ltd v ASD Ltd* [2012] EWHC 2213 (TCC) (commercial sale of parts of rigid steel platform: limits of liability for personal injuries reasonable. Both parties were substantial commercial entities, there was insurance in place and such terms were common in the industry).

[564] 1977 Act s.11(5).

[565] The term covers related services which are part of the contract: *Amiri Flight Authority v BAE Systems Plc* [2002] EWHC 2481 (Comm), [2003] 1 Lloyd's Rep. 50; reversed on other grounds [2003] EWCA Civ 1447, [2003] 2 Lloyd's Rep. 767.

[566] Not their agents: *Ocean Chemical Transport Inc v Exnor Craggs Ltd* [2000] 1 Lloyd's Rep. 446, 453. See further *Balmoral Group Ltd v Borealis (UK) Ltd* [2006] EWHC 1900 (Comm), [2006] 2 Lloyd's Rep. 629 at [437]–[439].

[567] There is no requirement under s.26(4)(a) that the carriage of the goods be in the fulfilment of a contractual obligation, though there is under s.26(4)(c). See *Amiri Flight Authority v BAE Systems Plc* [2003] EWCA Civ 1447, [2003] 2 Lloyd's Rep. 767 at [32]; *Trident Turboprop (Dublin) Ltd v First Flight Couriers Ltd* [2009] EWCA Civ 290, [2009] 1 Lloyd's Rep. 702 at [32] (indicating also that carriage includes self-propulsion); *Air Transworld Ltd v Bombardier Inc* [2012] EWHC 243 (Comm) at [87] et seq.; see also *Yuanda (UK) Ltd v WW Gear Construction Ltd* [2010] EWHC 720 (TCC), [2010] 1 C.L.C. 491 (goods to be brought in from third country).

[568] See *Amiri Flight Authority v BAE Systems Plc* [2003] EWCA Civ 1447, [2003] 2 Lloyd's Rep. 767 (goods must be delivered to a different country); *Balmoral Group Ltd v Borealis (UK) Ltd* [2006] EWHC 1900 (Comm), [2006] 2 Lloyd's Rep. 629 at [442], [443].

It should be noted first that the definition is not restricted to commercial transactions, and thus applies to consumer transactions if made before October 1, 2015.[569] It covers liability under s.3 of the Misrepresentation Act 1967.[570] It also causes certain difficulties. It does not indicate how to treat parties who have places of business in more than one State: presumably the place of business from which the transaction is conducted is intended. The reference to "the acts constituting the offer and acceptance" being "done" leaves it in doubt whether it is the physical acts which are referred to or the place where these legally take effect (which under English law may differ, for example, in the case of letters of acceptance). It has been held that these words refer to "the totality of the acts which constitute the offer and acceptance including both the making and receiving of each" without recourse to technicalities of communication. What is excluded is the situation where all elements occur in the same state.[571] For other situations, s.27 provides that the 1977 Act's controls of exclusion or restriction of liability do not apply where the law applicable to the contract is the law of any part of the United Kingdom only by choice of the parties.[572] It also seeks to preserve the effect of the Act despite an evasive choice of a foreign law and in certain consumer situations.[573]

Unfair Terms in Consumer Contracts Regulations 1999[574]   These Regulations   **44-126** are replaced by Pt 2 of the Consumer Rights Act 2015 for contracts made on or after October 1, 2015.[575] The Regulations and the provisions of Pt 2 of the 2015 Act are considered in detail in Ch.38.

Common law   The common law technique of holding that a clause is not part of   **44-127** the contract at all[576] is expressly preserved by s.11(2) of the Unfair Contract Terms Act, and though there is no express reference to other ways of attacking exemption clauses it may be assumed that the cases on collateral warranties,[577] misrepresentation,[578] privity[579] and restrictive interpretation[580] are still valid. Although the scope for the operation of these rules is obviously much cut down by the controls provided by the Act,[581] there are occasions where they will be of use. The common law will still be relevant in the case of international supply contracts[582] and

---

[569] But see below, para.44-126.

[570] *Trident Turboprop (Dublin) Ltd v First Flight Couriers Ltd* [2009] EWCA Civ 290, [2009] 1 Lloyd's Rep. 702.

[571] *Air Transworld Ltd v Bombardier Inc* [2012] EWHC 243 (Comm), [2012] 1 Lloyd's Rep. 349 at [81].

[572] This was so in the *Transworld* case, above. See Vol.I, para.30-009.

[573] See Vol.I, para.30-009.

[574] SI 1999/2083 (with several subsequent amending instruments none involving substance).

[575] See above, paras 38-365 et seq.

[576] See Vol.I, paras 13-009 et seq.; *Benjamin's Sale of Goods*, 10th edn (2017), paras 13-011 et seq. For recent examples of such arguments see *Balmoral Group Ltd v Borealis (UK) Ltd* [2006] EWHC 1900 (Comm), [2006] 2 Lloyd's Rep. 629; *Sterling Hydraulics Ltd v Dichtomatik Ltd* [2006] EWHC 2004 (QB), [2007] 1 Lloyd's Rep. 8; *Baillie Estates Ltd v Du Pont (UK) Ltd* [2009] CSIH 95, 2010 S.C.L.R. 192.

[577] See Vol.I, para.15-148; *Couchman v Hill* [1947] K.B. 554.

[578] See Vol.I, para.15-146; *Curtis v Chemical Cleaning and Dyeing Co* [1951] 1 K.B. 805. But as to this case see *AXA Sun Life Services Plc v Campbell Martin Ltd* [2011] EWCA Civ 133, [2011] 2 Lloyd's Rep. 1 at [99]–[105].

[579] See Vol.I, paras 15-042 et seq.

[580] See Vol.I, paras 15-008 et seq.; *Benjamin's Sale of Goods*, 10th edn (2017), paras 13-019 et seq.

[581] See *Photo Production Ltd v Securicor Transport Ltd* [1980] A.C. 827, 843.

[582] See above, para.44-125.

contracts where English law is applicable only by choice of the parties,[583] and in certain other cases of lesser importance.[584] The common law rules as to exemption clauses are dealt with earlier in this work.[585] In brief, though s.55(1) of the 1979 Act permits exclusion or variation of the Act's provisions, clauses purporting to exclude the central duties of the contract of sale are restrictively construed. Exclusion of warranties does not exclude conditions[586]; exclusion of implied conditions may not cover express conditions[587]; sale "with all faults" may only cover "faults which [the article] may have consistently with being the thing described"[588]; clauses forbidding absolutely or after a period rejection of "the goods herein specified" and the like may not prevent rejection of goods not conforming with the specification[589]; clauses stating that "no warranty is given" need not exclude collateral warranties.[590] Cases of this sort make it difficult to exclude the provisions of s.13, and frequently those of ss.14 and 15 also. There are a few cases appearing to go further, and holding that clauses which on the face might seem to exclude one or more of these provisions were inoperative on the basis of the doctrine of fundamental breach of contract.[591] In view of dicta in the *George Mitchell*[592] case that it is not admissible to reintroduce that doctrine by the back door, these decisions cannot now be justified on that basis; but they have not been overruled and most can probably be regarded as still valid as examples of strict interpretation.[593] It has been said that the principles of interpretation are not applicable in their full rigour to clauses which merely limit liability in monetary terms[594]; but though this may be useful as a commonsense guide, it is difficult to accept it as a clear principle of law, for some monetary limits are so low as to be equivalent to non-liability.[595]

---

583 See above, para.44-125.

584 e.g. certain transactions not caught by s.7.

585 See Vol.I, Ch.15. As to clauses purporting to exclude reliance under s.14(3) see Vol.I, para.15-147.

586 *Baldry v Marshall* [1925] 1 K.B. 260; *Wallis, Son and Wells v Pratt and Haynes* [1911] A.C. 394; *Henry Kendall & Sons v William Lillico & Sons* [1969] 2 A.C. 31, 84, 95–96, 107, 109, 114, 126; *KG Bominflot Bunkergesellschaft etc. & Co v Petroplus Marketing AG (The Mercini Lady)* [2010] EWCA Civ 1145, [2011] 1 Lloyd's Rep. 442 at [61]–[66]; *Dalmare SpA v Union Maritime Ltd (The Union Power)* [2012] EWHC 3537 (Comm), [2013] 1 Lloyd's Rep. 509 (sale of ship "as she was" at time of inspection: wording held not clear enough to exclude the conditions stated in ss.13 and 14 and, in any event, would only have excluded the right to reject whilst leaving the right to claim damages); but cf. *Air Transworld Ltd v Bombardier Inc* [2012] EWHC 243 (Comm), [2012] 1 Lloyd's Rep. 349 at [10] et seq., especially at [30]. See also *Aston FFI (Suisee) SA v Dreyfus* [2015] EWHC 80 (right to reject goods in an FOB contract not excluded by requirement as to certification).

587 *Andrews Bros Ltd v Singer & Co Ltd* [1934] 1 K.B. 17.

588 *Shepherd v Kain* (1821) 5 B. & A. 240, 241; see *Robert A Munro & Co Ltd v Meyer* [1930] 2 K.B. 312; *Champanhac & Co Ltd v Waller & Co Ltd* [1948] 2 All E.R. 724.

589 *Vigers Bros v Sanderson Bros* [1901] 1 K.B. 608; *Beck & Co v Szymonowski & Co* [1924] A.C. 43; cf. *Smeaton, Hanscomb & Co Ltd v Sassoon I Setty, Son & Co* [1953] 1 W.L.R. 1468.

590 *Webster v Higgin* [1948] 2 All E.R. 127; *Harling v Eddy* [1951] 2 K.B. 739.

591 *Yeoman Credit Ltd v Apps* [1962] 2 Q.B. 508; following *Pollock & Co v Macrae*, 1922 S.C. 192, HL. See also *Farnworth Finance Facilities Ltd v Attryde* [1970] 1 W.L.R. 1053. As to this doctrine see in general Vol.I, paras 15-023 et seq.

592 *George Mitchell (Chesterhall) Ltd v Finney Lock Seeds Ltd* [1983] 2 A.C. 803, 813. See above, para.44-123; Vol.I, para.15-026.

593 cf. Vol.I, para.15-027. The proposition that an exclusion clause should be interpreted so as not to cover a deliberate breach is rejected in *Astrazeneca UK Ltd v Albemarle Internatkional Corp* [2011] EWHC 1574 (Comm), [2011] 2 C.L.C. 252.

594 *Ailsa Craig Fishing Co Ltd v Malvern Fishing Co Ltd* [1983] 1 W.L.R. 964, 970, per Lord Fraser of Tullybelton, HL; followed in the *George Mitchell* case [1983] 2 A.C. 803, 813.

595 It was rejected by the High Court of Australia in *Darlington Futures Ltd v Delco Australia Pty Ltd*

(c) Stipulations as to Time

Stipulations as to time Section 10 provides that: **44-128**

"(1)   Unless a different intention appears from the terms of the contract, stipulations as to time of payment are not deemed to be of the essence of a contract of sale.
(2)   Whether any other stipulation as to time is of the essence of the contract or not depends on the terms of the contract."

A contract may always by its terms make prompt or punctual payment a condition,[596] and such an implication may fairly readily be read into a commercial contract.[597] Otherwise, however, the question whether late payment entitles the seller to treat the contract as discharged will be regulated by the rules as to repudiatory breach,[598] though it should be borne in mind that there may sometimes be a right of resale in such a situation.[599] It was long said that an action for damages does not lie for late payment[600]; but it is now the law that a claimant can plead and prove actual interest losses (including compound interest) as well as other loss in the contemplation of the parties incurred by reason of the late payment.[601] Interest on commercial debts may, by statute, also be awarded in certain circumstances.[602] As to delivery,[603] it has been said that "in ordinary commercial contracts for the sale of goods the rule clearly is that time is prima facie of the essence with respect to delivery",[604] although there is no presumption or rule of law to that effect and the question ultimately depends on the terms of the contract and the nature of the goods. Late delivery gives rise to a claim for damages in the usual way.[605]

Late delivery in consumer contracts for goods The Consumer Rights Direc- **44-129**
tive 2011[606] requires Member States to provide that in a consumer sales contract the trader must deliver within certain periods unless the parties have agreed otherwise,

---

(1986) 161 C.L.R. 500.
[596] See, e.g. *Ebbw Vale Steel, Iron and Coal Co v Blaina, etc. Co* (1901) 6 Com. Cas. 33; *Maclaine Galty* [1921] 1 A.C. 376, 389 (loan: "punctual payment"); *The Brimnes* [1975] Q.B. 929 (time charter: "punctual payment"); *Lombard North Central Plc v Butterworth* [1987] Q.B. 527 (hire: "punctual payment to be of essence").
[597] See, e.g. *Ryan v Ridley & Co* (1902) 8 Com. Cas. 105 (CIF contract); *Pavia & Co SpA v Thurmann-Nielsen* [1952] 2 Q.B. 84; *Ian Stach Ltd v Baker Bosley Ltd* [1958] 2 Q.B. 130 (opening of credit in international sale).
[598] See Vol.I, Ch.24; *Mersey Steel and Iron Co v Naylor Benzon & Co* (1884) 9 App. Cas. 434; *Payzu Ltd v Saunders* [1919] 2 K.B. 581; *Decro-Wall International SA v Practitioners in Marketing Ltd* [1971] 1 W.L.R. 361.
[599] Sale of Goods Act 1979 s.48; see below, paras 44-344 et seq.
[600] See Vol.I, para.26-187.
[601] *Sempra Metals Ltd v Inland Revenue Commissioners* [2007] UKHL 34, [2008] 1 A.C. 561; see Vol.I, para.26-187.
[602] Late Payment of Commercial Debts (Interest) Act 1998 (as amended); Vol.I, para.26-277; see below, para.44-300.
[603] See below, paras 44-241 et seq.
[604] *Hartley v Hymans* [1920] 3 K.B. 475, 483–484. See also *Toepfer v Lenersan-Poortman NV* [1980] 1 Lloyd's Rep. 143; *Bunge Corp v Tradax Export SA* [1981] 1 W.L.R. 711; as to a non-commercial contract *McDougall v Aeromarine of Emsworth Ltd* [1958] 1 W.L.R. 1126; and see below, para.44-241. The date of shipment is usually part of the description of the goods: *Bowes v Shand* (1877) 2 App. Cas. 455; see above, para.44-089.
[605] See below, para.44-406.
[606] Directive 2011/83/EU of October 25, 2011.

and to provide the buyer with rights to terminate the contract in the event of late delivery.[607] This provision was initially implemented in the United Kingdom by the Consumer Contracts (Information, Cancellation and Additional Charges) Regulations 2013,[608] which apply to consumer contracts made after June 13, 2014. These provisions are now contained in the Consumer Rights Act 2015.[609]

4. EFFECTS OF THE CONTRACT

(a) Transfer of Property as between Seller and Buyer[610]

44-130 Rules governing transfer of property Sections 16–19 and s.20A of the Act contain the rules which govern the transfer of the property in goods sold from the seller to the buyer.

44-131 Unascertained goods By s.16:

"Subject to s.20A ... where there is a contract for the sale of unascertained goods no property[611] in the goods is transferred to the buyer unless and until the goods are ascertained."

This section states in the clearest terms that, except where s.20A applies,[612] the property in unascertained goods cannot pass.[613] It must be noted that the rule is stated negatively. It does not say that when the goods are ascertained the property will pass, although in very many instances this is what will in fact happen; the intention of the parties is of primary importance in determining when the property is to pass.[614]

44-132 The Act does not define unascertained goods, but for the purpose of the passing of the property they seem to fall into three categories[615]: generic goods,[616] for instance, "100 tons of wheat"; a specified quantity of goods forming part of an identified bulk,[617] for instance, "100 tons of wheat from the larger quantity which A has in his warehouse"; and certain types of future goods.[618]

44-133 Separation of goods from bulk Where there is a contract for the sale of a quantity of unascertained goods forming part of an identified bulk, the goods may become ascertained by "exhaustion", that is to say, if sufficient goods are removed from the bulk that the remaining goods are reduced to (or to less than) the contract

---

607 art.18.

608 SI 2013/3134.

609 See above, paras 38-526 et seq.

610 Lawson (1949) 65 L.Q.R. 352; Battersby and Preston (1972) 35 M.L.R. 268; Ho [1997] C.L.J. 571; Battersby [2001] J.B.L. 1.

611 Defined s.61(1), see above, para.44-015.

612 See below, para.44-160.

613 *Karlshamns Oljefabriker v Eastport Navigation Corp (The Elafi)* [1981] 2 Lloyd's Rep. 679, 683.

614 See s.17, see below, para.44-134.

615 See above, para.44-042.

616 See *Austin v Craven* (1812) 4 Taunt. 644; *Hayward Bros v Daniel* (1904) 91 L.T. 319.

617 See *Hayman v M'Lintock*, 1907 S.C. 936; *Healy v Howlett & Sons* [1917] 1 K.B. 337; *Laurie & Morewood v Dudin & Sons* [1926] 1 K.B. 223; *Kursell v Timber Operators and Contractors Ltd* [1927] 1 K.B. 298; *National Coal Board v Gamble* [1959] 1 Q.B. 11; *Preston v Albuery* [1964] 2 Q.B. 796; *Re Stapylton Fletcher Ltd* [1994] 1 W.L.R. 1181; see below, para.44-160.

618 See above, para.44-042. See also s.18 r.5(1), below, para.44-149.

quantity and there is only one buyer to whom goods are due out of the bulk.[619] The goods may also become ascertained by "consolidation", if all the contracts for the goods which remain in the bulk become vested in a single buyer so that he is then the only buyer to whom goods are due out of the bulk.[620] Otherwise as a general rule[621] the goods must be physically separated from the bulk before they can become ascertained.[622] Previously, since s.16 precluded the passing of property in unascertained goods, a buyer would have no claim at law or in equity[623] to or to a share in unascertained goods while still in bulk, even if he had paid the whole or part of the purchase price, unless the seller was estopped from contending that they buyer was entitled to delivery of the goods.[624] So, for example, if after the buyer had paid for the goods the seller became insolvent or the bulk was seized in execution by a creditor of the seller, the buyer would have no claim to the goods but only a claim as an unsecured creditor for return of the price. However, s.16 was amended by the Sale of Goods (Amendment) Act 1995[625] so as to make the section subject to s.20A (which was also introduced by the 1995 Act). Under s.20A, in certain circumstances property in an undivided share in the bulk will be transferred to the buyer and he will become an owner in common of the bulk.[626]

Intention of the parties By s.17:   **44-134**

"(1)   Where there is a contract for the sale of specific or ascertained goods the property in them is transferred to the buyer at such time as the parties to the contract intend it to be transferred.
(2)   For the purpose of ascertaining the intention of the parties regard shall be had to the terms of the contract, the conduct of the parties, and the circumstances of the case."

It will be noted that this section, which makes the passing of property dependent upon the intention of the parties, applies both to specific goods, viz goods identified and agreed on at the time a contract of sale is made, and also to goods which, though not so identified and agreed on, later become ascertained.

Ascertaining intention By s.18 it is provided that: **44-135**

"Unless a different intention appears, the following are rules for ascertaining the intention of the parties as to the time at which he property in the goods is to pass to the buyer."

---

619 *Wait and James v Midland Bank* (1926) 31 Com. Cas. 172; *Karlshamns Oljefabriker v Eastport Navigation Corp (The Elafi)* [1981] 2 Lloyd's Rep. 679; s.18 r.5(3); see below, para.44-158.
620 *Karlshamns Oljefabriker v Eastport Navigation Corp (The Elafi)*, see above. See also, para. 44-159, below.
621 cf. *Re Stapylton Fletcher Ltd* [1994] 1 W.L.R. 1181.
622 *Gillett v Hill* (1834) 2 C. & M. 530, 535; *R. v Tideswell* [1905] 2 K.B. 273; *Healy v Howlett & Sons* [1917] 1 K.B. 336; *Laurie & Morewood v Dudin & Sons* [1926] 1 K.B. 223; *National Coal Board v Gamble* [1959] 1 Q.B. 11; *Preston v Albuery* [1964] 2 Q.B. 796; *Re London Wine Shippers Ltd* [1986] P.C.C. 121.
623 *Re Wait* [1927] 1 Ch. 606, 623, 634, 636; *Re London Wine Shippers Ltd*, above; *Re Goldcorp Exchange Ltd* [1995] 1 A.C. 74. Contrast *International Finance Corp v DSNL Offshore Ltd* [2005] EWHC 1844 (Comm), [2007] 2 All E.R. (Comm) 305 at [60] (equitable lien).
624 *Stonard v Dunkin* (1810) 2 Camp. 344; *Hawes v Watson* (1824) 2 B. & C. 540; *Gillett v Hill* (1834) 2 C. & M. 530, 535; *Woodley v Coventry* (1863) 2 H. & C. 164; *Knights v Wiffen* (1870) L.R. 5 Q.B. 660; *Simm v Anglo-American Telegraph Co* (1879) 5 Q.B.D. 188, 215; Contrast *Re London Wine Shippers Ltd* (1886) P.C.C. 121; *Re Goldcorp Exchange Ltd* [1995] 1 A.C. 74.
625 s.1(1).
626 See below, para.44-160.

It must be emphasised that these rules are presumptions and nothing more. They are not applied if the parties have agreed when and on what conditions the property is to pass.[627]

44-136   Specific goods in a deliverable state   By r.1:

"Where there is an unconditional contract for the sale of specific goods in a deliverable state the property in the goods passes to the buyer when the contract is made, and it is immaterial whether the time of payment or the time of delivery, or both, be postponed."[628]

44-137   *(i)   Rule 1 applied*   In *Dennant v Skinner*[629] an auctioneer knocked down several motor cars to a bidder who later tendered payment by cheque, representing himself as the son of a well-known car dealer. Before allowing him to drive away a car, the auctioneer made him sign a statement that the ownership in the cars would not pass to him until the proceeds of the cheque were credited to the auctioneer. The bidder was a fraudulent person whose cheque was dishonoured and who sold the car to the defendant. Hallett J. held that the contract was completed on the fall of the hammer and at that time the property passed to the bidder, as the document which purported to delay the passing of the property was signed after the property had in fact passed it was of no effect. The defendant therefore had a good title.

44-138   *(ii)   Unconditional*   It would seem that this word distinguishes cases where the passing of property is subject to a condition later to be fulfilled,[630] e.g. where it is agreed that property is not to pass until the price has been paid.

44-139   *(iii)   Specific goods*[631]   The meaning of the requirement that the goods must be specific is illustrated in relation to r.1 by *Kursell v Timber Operators and Contractors Ltd*.[632] In that case the contract was for the sale of all the timber in a Latvian forest which conformed with certain measurements at a specified date. Shortly afterwards all private rights in relation to the forest were annulled. It was held that the property in the timber had not passed to the buyers because this was not a contract for the sale of specific goods. Scrutton L.J. said: "Specific goods are defined as goods identified and agreed upon at the time a contract of sale is made.

---

627 See *McEntire v Crossley Bros Ltd* [1895] A.C. 457; *Omstein v Alexandra Furnishing Co* (1895) 12 T.L.R. 128; *Re Shipton, Anderson & Co* [1915] 3 K.B. 676; *Re Anchor Line (Henderson Bros) Ltd* [1937] Ch.1; *Karlshamns Oljefabriker v Eastport Navigation Corp (The Elafi)* [1981] 2 Lloyd's Rep. 679 (property passed though no appropriation to specific contracts). Special rules apply where the sale is on CIF, FOB, "ex ship", f.o.r., etc. terms: see *Benjamin's Sale of Goods*, 10th edn (2017), paras 18-259, 19-099, 20-077, 21-003, 21-011, 21-013, 21-021, 21-044, 21-103.
628 *Tarling v Baxter* (1827) 6 B. & C. 360; *Gilmour v Supple* (1858) 11 Moo. P.C. 551, 556; *Seath v Moore* (1886) 11 App. Cas. 350, 370. But see *RV Ward Ltd v Bignall* [1967] 1 Q.B. 534, 545; "in modern times very little is needed to give rise to the inference that the property in specific goods is to pass only on delivery or payment". For such a case, see *Michael Gerson (Leasing) Ltd v Williamson* [2001] Q.B. 514. See also *Orix Australia Corp Ltd v Peter Donnelly Automotive Pty Ltd* [2007] NSWSC 977.
629 [1948] 2 K.B. 164.
630 Sale of Goods Act 1979 s.2(3), (5), 19. The alternative view (based on *Varley v Whipp* [1900] 1 Q.B. 513, 517; *Ollett v Jordan* [1918] 2 K.B. 41, 45; and *Leaf v International Galleries* [1950] 2 K.B. 86, 89–90) that "unconditional" means "subject to no essential undertaking" cannot be supported: see *Benjamin's Sale of Goods*, 10th edn (2017), paras 5-019—5-020. See also *Classic Automobiles of London v Aura Holdings Inc* [1997] EWCA Civ 2834.
631 Defined in s.61(1), see above, para.44-015.
632 [1927] 1 K.B. 298.

It appears to me these goods were neither identified nor agreed upon. Not every tree in the forest passed, but only those complying with a certain measurement not then made".[633] Specific goods also include an undivided share, specified as a fraction or percentage of goods identified and agreed on at the time a contract of sale is made, e.g. a quarter share in a named racehorse.

(iv) Deliverable state The goods must also be in a deliverable state at the time **44-140** the contract is made, that is, "in such a state that the buyer would under the contract be bound to take delivery of them".[634] In *Underwood v Burgh Castle Brick and Cement Syndicate*[635] a fixed condensing engine was sold by the claimants to the defendants; it was to be severed, dismantled and delivered free on rail at a specified price. The main body of the engine was damaged by accident while being loaded on a railway truck and the defendants refused to accept it. It was held that the property had not passed to the defendants under r.1 because the engine was not in a deliverable state at the time the contract was made.

Specific goods to be put into a deliverable state By r.2: **44-141**

"Where there is a contract for the sale of specific goods and the seller is bound to do something to the goods, for the purpose of putting into a deliverable state,[636] the property does not pass until the thing is done, and the buyer has notice that it has been done."[637]

This rule only applies where the obligation to put the goods in a deliverable state rests on the seller. But where a similar obligation is placed on the buyer, the result may be the same: s.18 r.1, will not apply, and the situation will be governed by s.17 of the Act.[638]

It is a question of interpretation in each case whether the thing to be done for the **44-142** purpose of putting the goods into a deliverable state is a condition of the contract of sale so as to suspend the passing of property, or whether the seller's obligation is a supplemental obligation only.[639]

The buyer must have notice that the obligation has been performed. **44-143**

Specific goods to be weighed, etc By r.3: **44-144**

"Where there is a contract for the sale of specific goods in a deliverable state but the seller is bound to weigh, measure, test, or do some other act or thing with reference to the goods for the purpose of ascertaining the price, the property does not pass until the act or thing is done[640] and the buyer has notice that it has been done."

---

633 [1927] 1 K.B. 298 at 311. See also at 314.
634 1987 Act s.61(5). See *Underwood Ltd v Burgh Castle Brick and Cement Syndicate* [1922] 1 K.B. 343, 345; *Pritchett & Gold and Electric Power Storage Co Ltd v Currie* [1916] 1 Ch. 515; *Philip Head & Sons Ltd v Showfronts Ltd* [1970] 1 Lloyd's Rep. 140; *Kulkarni v Manor Credit (Davenham) Ltd* [2010] EWCA Civ 69, [2010] 2 Lloyd's Rep. 431 at [24].
635 [1922] 1 K.B. 243.
636 See above, para.44-140.
637 See (before the 1893 Act) *Rugg v Minett* (1809) 11 East 210; *Acraman v Morice* (1849) 8 C.B. 449. See also *Underwood v Burgh Castle Brick and Cement Syndicate* [1922] 1 K.B. 343.
638 *Kursell v Timber Operators and Contractors Ltd* [1927] 1 K.B. 298; see above, para.44-134.
639 *Pritchett and Gold and Electrical Power Storage Co Ltd v Currie* [1916] 2 Ch. 515; *Jerome v Clements Motor Sales Ltd*, 15 D.L.R. (2d) 689 (1958); *Hartley v Saunders* 33 D.L.R. (2d) 638 (1962); *Anderson v Ryan* [1967] 1 I.R. 34, 37.
640 See *Zagury v Furnell* (1809) 2 Camp. 239, 240: goods to be counted; *Hanson v Meyer* (1805) 6 East

Rule 3 suspends the transfer of property only where the act or thing is to be done by the seller, and not by the buyer or a third party. A mere right on the part of the buyer or a third party to weigh the goods will not suspend the passing of property.[641] Thus in *Nanka-Bruce v Commonwealth Trust Ltd*[642] the appellant sold cocoa to A, who was to resell it to the respondents. The latter were then to weigh the cocoa at their premises and the weight was to be tested there. It was held that the property had passed to A and that accordingly the respondents had a good title. The weighing of the goods was said to be "simply a means to satisfy the purchaser that he had what he had bargained for and that the full price claimed per the contract was therefore due".[643] As in r.2, the buyer must have notice that the seller has done what he is required to do.

44-145 **Different intention** As already indicated, the rules for ascertaining the intention of the parties are of presumptive force only and are open to rebuttal. Thus in a given case the parties may intend the property to pass at once, even though the price has not yet been precisely calculated. The fixing of a provisional estimate of the price is evidence of an intention that the passing of the property is not to depend upon the final weighing.[644]

44-146 **Sale or return** By r.4:

"When goods are delivered to the buyer on approval or on sale or return or other similar terms the property in the goods passes to the buyer:

    (a)   when he signifies his approval or acceptance to the seller or does any other act adopting the transaction;

    (b)   if he does not signify his approval or acceptance to the seller but retains[645] the goods without giving notice of rejection[646] then, if a time has been fixed for the return of the goods, on the expiration of that time, and, if no time has been fixed, on the expiration of a reasonable time.[647]"

What is a reasonable time is a question of fact.[648]

44-147 This states the general rule that where goods are delivered on approval or on sale

---

[641] 614: goods to be weighed; *Logan v Le Mesurier* (1847) 6 Moo. P.C. 116: goods to be measured.

[641] In limiting the rule to acts to be done by the seller, the Act adopted the view taken in *Turley v Bates* (1863) 2 H. & C. 200. There weighing was to be done by the buyer, and it was held that the passing of the property was not suspended. But see s.17.

[642] [1926] A.C. 77 (though not a case of specific goods).

[643] At 79.

[644] See *Martineau v Kitching* (1872) L.R. 7 Q.B. 436, 449; *Anderson v Morice* (1874) L.R. 10 C.P. 58. See also *Howes v Watson* (1842) 2 B. & C. 243; *Kershaw v Ogden* (1865) 3 H. & C. 717; *R. v Tideswell* [1905] 2 K.B. 273, 277.

[645] This rule applies only if it is the buyer who retains. See *Re Ferrier* [1944] Ch. 295 (property did not pass because goods retained by buyer's execution creditors). But cf. *Genn v Winkel* (1912) 107 L.T. 434.

[646] See *Berry v Star Brush Co* (1915) 31 T.L.R. 603. On the contents of the notice, see *Atari Corp (UK) Ltd v Electronic Boutiques Stores (UK) Ltd* [1998] Q.B. 539.

[647] See *Moss v Sweet* (1851) 16 Q.B. 493; *Poole v Smith's Car Sales (Balham) Ltd* [1962] 1 W.L.R. 744. But the transaction does not become a sale if the goods perish in the bailee's possession without his fault: *Elphick v Barnes* (1880) 5 C.P.D. 321. cf. *Poole v Smith's Car Sales (Balham) Ltd*, above. On return of the goods in a damaged condition, see below, para.44-290; cf. *Benjamin's Sale of Goods*, 10th edn (2017), paras 5–055, 5–056.

[648] 1979 Act s.59.

or return the property in them remains with the seller until the buyer adopts the transaction. It is however possible to enter into a transaction which is similar in purpose but under which the property passes immediately subject to the buyer's right to return the goods, as where garments can be exchanged if they are not of the right size: such transactions are not affected by this rule.[649]

Two situations must be contrasted. The first is where the buyer has an option to acquire the property in the goods on the terms set out in r.4; the second is where r.4 is displaced because the contract states that some other event is essential to the passing of the property. With regard to the first situation it is clear that approval of the goods may be signified expressly or it may be implied from the buyer's actions. So in *Kirkham v Attenborough*,[650] where the person to whom the goods were delivered "on sale or return" pledged them with a pawnbroker, it was held that the act of pledging was an act adopting the transaction and operated to transfer the property therein to the buyer. With regard to the second situation, it is established that if the contract states for instance that the property is not to pass until the price is paid, an act of the buyer which purports to adopt the transaction is not, without more, sufficient to pass the property to him. For r.4, like all five rules in s.18, does not operate if a different intention appears. Consequently, third parties are not protected.[651] Thus, where the goods, though delivered "on sale for cash only or return", were to remain the property of the seller till settled for or charged, it was held that, though pawned, they were recoverable by the seller, as the special term took the case out of r.4.[652]

44-148

Appropriation of unascertained or future goods   By r.5:

44-149

"(1)   Where there is a contract for the sale of unascertained or future goods[653] by description,[654] and goods of that description[655] and in a deliverable state[656] are unconditionally[657] appropriated to the contract, either by the seller with the assent of the buyer, or by the buyer with the assent of the seller, the property in the goods then passes to the buyer; and the assent may be express or implied, and may be given either before or after the appropriation is made.

---

[649]   See *Head v Tattersall* (1871) L.R. 7 Ex. 7.

[650]   [1897] 1 Q.B. 291. Followed in *London Jewellers Ltd v Attenborough* [1934] 2 K.B. 206, where an agent to sell was treated as a buyer; see per Scrutton L.J. at 214: the section "appears to contemplate that the person who has goods delivered to him on approval becomes a buyer to whom the property passes". cf. *Genn v Winkel* (1912) 107 L.T. 434.

[651]   Further, a person who takes goods on sale or return is not in possession under an agreement to buy for the purposes of s.25: see *Edwards v Vaughan* (1910) 26 T.L.R. 545, 546. Therefore he cannot pass a good title to a third party. But a third party is protected if the contract is one of mercantile agency within the Factors Act 1889: see *Weiner v Harris* [1910] 1 K.B. 285; *Janesich v Attenborough* (1910) 102 L.T. 605. Contrast *Re Nevill* (1860) L.R. 6 Ch. App. 397; affirmed sub nom. *Towle & Co v White* (1873) 29 L.T. 78, HL. See below, paras 44-204, 44-222.

[652]   *Weiner v Gill* [1906] 2 K.B. 574; see also *Edwards v Vaughan* (1910) 26 T.L.R. 545; *Kempler v Bravingtons Ltd* (1925) 133 L.T. 680 (previous cases reviewed); *R. v Eaton* (1966) 50 Cr. App. R. 189.

[653]   Defined s.61(1), see above, para.44-015, and see s.5(1), see above, paras 44-035 et seq.

[654]   See s.13, see above, paras 44-086 et seq.

[655]   See below, para.44-153.

[656]   Defined, s.61(5), see above, para.44-136.

[657]   See below, para.44-152. Notice of appropriation under a CIF contract does not pass the property because, as the seller retains the documents against the payment of the price, the appropriation is not unconditional: see *Ross T Smyth & Co Ltd v Bailey, Son & Co* [1940] 3 All E.R. 60, 65–66; *Ginzberg v Barrow Haematite Steel Co and McKellar* [1966] 1 Lloyd's Rep. 343; *Benjamin's Sale of Goods*, 10th edn (2017), para.19-101.

(2) Where, in pursuance of the contract, the seller delivers the goods to the buyer or to a carrier or other bailee ... (whether named by the buyer or not) for the purpose of transmission to the buyer, and does not reserve the right of disposal, he is to be taken to have unconditionally appropriated the goods to the contract.[658]

(3) Where there is a contract for the sale of a specified quantity of unascertained goods in a deliverable state[659] forming part of a bulk[660] which is identified either in the contract or by subsequent agreement between the parties and the bulk is reduced to (or to less than) that quantity, then, if the buyer under that contract is the only buyer to whom goods are then due out of the bulk—

  (a) the remaining goods are to be taken as appropriated to that contract at the time when the bulk is so reduced; and

  (b) the property in those goods then passes to that buyer.

(4) Paragraph (3) above applies also (with the necessary modifications) where a bulk is reduced to (or to less than) the aggregate of the quantities due to a single buyer under separate contracts relating to that bulk and he is the only buyer to whom goods are then due out of that bulk."

44-150 **Appropriation by one party with assent of other** Once unascertained goods have become ascertained, the property in them may pass if they are unconditionally appropriated to the contract by one party with the assent of the other party. "Appropriation" will occur only where the contract has become irrevocably attached to the goods in question. Rule 5(1) states that the appropriation may be made either by the buyer or by the seller. In a case where the buyer is to select the goods and take them away, there is normally little difficulty.[661] There is also normally little difficulty if the seller selects the goods, and the buyer subsequently assents to the seller's choice.[662] But when it is the seller who is to select by virtue of the previous assent (express or implied) of the buyer,[663] it may be difficult to point to the act of the seller by which the goods are appropriated so as to pass the property in them to the buyer. This is because it may not be clear whether the seller is exercising irrevocably his right to make an election, or whether, though he intends to appropriate these goods to the contract, he may still change his mind and appropriate others.[664] This is a question of law, and the answer to it is important, not only to the question of risk, but also because if appropriation has taken place the buyer is protected against the insolvency of the seller. Property has been held to pass where goods were placed by the seller in containers provided by the buyer.[665] But in the absence of any such constructive or quasi-delivery, the position is less certain.[666]

---

[658] cf. s.32, see below, para.44-269.

[659] Defined in s.61(5); see above, para.44-140.

[660] Defined in s.61(1); see above, para.44-015.

[661] But cf. *R. v Tideswell* [1905] 2 K.B. 273; *National Coal Board v Gamble* [1959] 1 Q.B. 11.

[662] *Rohde v Thwaites* (1927) 6 B. & C. 388; *Pignataro v Gilroy* [1919] 1 K.B. 459; *Wardar's (Import and Export) Ltd v W Norwood & Sons Ltd* [1968] 2 Q.B. 663.

[663] See below, para.44-151.

[664] See *Blackburn on Sale*, 1st edn, p.128, citing *Heyward's Case* (1595) 2 Co. Rep. 35a. See also *Mucklow v Mangles* (1808) 1 Taunt. 318; *Ridgway v Ward* (1884) 14 Q.B.D. 110, 116; *Cocker v McMullen* (1900) 81 L.T. 784; *Noblett v Hopkinson* [1905] 2 K.B. 214. cf. *Pletts v Beattie* [1896] 1 Q.B. 519; *Furbey v Hoey* [1947] 1 All E.R. 736.

[665] *Aldridge v Johnson* (1857) 7 E. & B. 885; *Langton v Higgins* (1859) 4 Hurl. & N. 402.

[666] But see *Hendy Lennox (Industrial Engines) Ltd v Grahame Puttick Ltd* [1984] 1 W.L.R. 485, 495 (goods invoiced to buyer). See also *Pullman Trailmobile Canada Ltd v Hamilton Refrigeration Ltd* 96 D.L.R. (3d) 322 (1979). Contrast *Carlos Federspiel & Co SA v Charles Twigg & Co Ltd*, below; *Kulkarni v Manor Credit (Davenham) Ltd* [2010] EWCA Civ 69, [2010] 2 Lloyd's Rep. 431.

The principle was thus stated in *Carlos Federspiel & Co SA v Charles Twigg & Co Ltd*[667] by Pearson J.:

> "A mere setting apart or selection of the seller of the goods which he expects to use in performance of the contract is not enough. If that is all, he can change his mind and use those goods in performance of some other contract and use some other goods in performance of this contract. To constitute an appropriation of the goods to the contract, the parties must have had, or be reasonably supposed to have had, an intention to attach the contract irrevocably to those goods, so that those goods and no others are the subject of the sale and become the property of the buyer."

Express or implied assent   Assent to the appropriation may be express or implied.   **44-151**
So in *Pignataro v Gilroy*[668] the defendants sold bags of rice to the claimant who paid for them and received a delivery order identifying the rice agreed to be sold; he delayed for a month before sending for some of the rice. It was held that his subsequent assent to the appropriation must be implied from his conduct. The property had therefore passed to him and the rice was at his risk. If it is alleged that one party assented to an appropriation by the other before it was made, then it must be shown that the latter was authorised, expressly or impliedly, to pass the property in the goods by appropriation[669] and that the appropriation effected was in accordance with the terms of that authority.

Appropriation unconditional   The appropriation must be unconditional, that is   **44-152**
to say, the party appropriating must intend that the property shall pass by the appropriation, if assented to by the other party, and not upon the occurrence of some further event, e.g. payment of the price.[670]

Goods "of that description"   Rule 5(1) also requires that the appropriation be of   **44-153**
goods "of that description", i.e. the description by which the goods are sold. If the goods which are the subject matter of the appropriation are other than those described in the contract of sale, then the property will not pass under the rule.[671] But it may be the intention of the parties that property in such goods shall pass to the buyer, subject to right of the buyer (if he so chooses) to reject them as not being in conformity with the contract.[672] In such a case, property will pass to the buyer under s.17, since r.5(1) establishes only a prima facie rule.

Appropriation by delivery   Appropriation by delivery is dealt with by r.5(2), and   **44-154**
it is probably the commonest example of unconditional appropriation.[673] Four points must be made. The first is that the rule, like all others in s.18, only applies if no dif-

---

[667] [1957] 1 Lloyd's Rep. 240, 255; *Kulkarni v Manor Credit (Davenham) Ltd*, above, at [35].

[668] [1919] 1 K.B. 459.

[669] *Jenner v Smith* (1869) L.R. 4 C.P. 270, 277, 278.

[670] *Godts v Rose* (1854) 17 C.B. 229; *Stein Forbes & Co Ltd v County Tailoring Co Ltd* (1916) 86 L.J. K.B. 448, 449. Notice of appropriation under a CIF contract does not pass the property because, as the seller retains the documents against payment or securing of the price, the appropriation is not unconditional: see *Ross T Smyth & Co Ltd v Bailey Son & Co* [1940] 3 All E.R. 60, 65–66; *Ginzberg v Barrow Haematite Steel Co and McKellar* [1966] 1 Lloyd's Rep. 343; *Benjamin's Sale of Goods*, 10th edn (2017), para.19-101. See also s.19, below, para.44-170.

[671] *Wait v Baker* (1848) 2 Exch. 1, 7; *Vigers v Sanderson* [1901] 1 Q.B. 608; *Hammer & Barrow v Coca-Cola* [1962] N.Z.L.R. 723; *Thornley v Tuckwell Butchers Ltd* [1964] Crim. L.R. 127.

[672] *Kwei Tek Chao v British Traders and Shippers Ltd* [1954] 2 Q.B. 459; *McDougall v Aeromarine of Emsworth Ltd* [1958] 1 W.L.R. 1126.

[673] *Ogle v Atkinson* (1814) 5 Taunt. 759; *Colonial Insurance Co of New Zealand v Adelaide Marine*

ferent intention appears. Thus if the seller reserves the right of disposal until certain conditions are fulfilled, the appropriation is not unconditional and s.19 provides that the property is not to pass until those conditions are fulfilled.[674] Secondly, where goods are delivered to a carrier, the rule only applies if the carrier is or is deemed to be the buyer's agent (and not the agent of the seller) to take delivery.[675] The third point is that if goods are delivered to a carrier, unmarked with other goods of like kind, the property will not pass. In other words, unless the goods become ascertained goods by virtue of their delivery to a carrier, they are not deemed to be unconditionally appropriated. Thus if the contract is for the sale of 20 boxes of mackerel, the delivery to a carrier of 20 boxes amounts to unconditional appropriation; but the delivery of 190 boxes from which 20 are to be taken does not, unless the 20 are marked with the name of the consignee.[676] Fourthly, the delivery to the carrier must be "in pursuance of the contract", that is to say, the contract must provide, expressly or impliedly, for delivery to a carrier and the delivery must be in accordance with its terms.[677]

44-155 **Appropriation of goods to be manufactured by the seller** In cases where goods are to be manufactured by the seller, the general rule is that the property does not pass until the work is completed and the goods are appropriated to the contract with the assent of the buyer.[678] However, the parties may agree that the property is to pass before completion. Whether or not they have done so is a question of construction of the contract.

44-156 **Shipbuilding contracts** This problem has come up for decision on a number of occasions in shipbuilding contracts. In *Re Blyth Shipbuilding and Dry Docks Co*[679] the Blyth Shipbuilding Company contracted to build a ship for an Italian company; the purchase price was to be paid by instalments, and a clause in the contract provided that "from and after payment by the purchasers to the builder of the first instalment ... the vessel and all materials and things appropriated for her should thenceforth ... become and remain the absolute property of the purchasers". After two instalments had been paid, the Blyth Shipbuilding Company went into liquidation. It was held that on the true construction of the contract, the property in the uncompleted ship had passed to the purchasers. In *Sir James Laing & Sons v Barclay, Curle & Co*,[680] on the other hand, it was held that the property in the ship as she lay had not passed because, although the purchase price was to be paid by instalments, the contract showed no intention that the property was to pass before the vessel was completed and tried.

Insurance Co (1887) 12 App. Cas. 128; *Denny v Skelton* (1916) 115 L.T. 305; *Edwards v Dolin* [1976] 1 W.L.R. 942. See also s.29(4) (delivery by attornment of third party) and *Wardar's (Export and Import) Co Ltd v Norwood & Sons Ltd* [1968] 2 Q.B. 663.

[674] See below, para.44-170.

[675] *Wait v Baker* (1849) 2 Exch. 1, 7. See also *Badische Anilin und Soda Fabrik v Basle Chemical Works* [1898] A.C. 200 (despatch by post); *Scottish and Newcastle International Ltd v Othon Ghalanos Ltd* [2008] UKHL 11, [2008] 1 Lloyd's Rep. 462 at [15]–[37] (C&F contract), and s.32(1) below, para.44-269. It is submitted that r.5(2) is not affected by s.32(4) which affects only risk.

[676] *Healy v Howlett & Sons* [1917] 1 K.B. 337.

[677] *Cooke v Ludlow* (1806) 2 B. & P.N.R. 119; *Ullock v Reddelein* (1828) 5 L.J.(O.S.) K.B. 208; *Aron & Co v Comptoir Wegimont* [1921] 3 K.B. 435.

[678] See *Mucklow v Mangles* (1808) 1 Taunt. 318; *Clarke v Spence* (1836) 4 A. & E. 448, 466; *Laidler v Burlinson* (1837) 2 M. & W. 602; *Reid v Macbeth* [1904] A.C. 223.

[679] [1926] Ch. 494; see also *Wood v Bell* (1856) 6 El. & Bl. 355; *Seath v Moore* (1887) 11 App. Cas. 350, 380; *Benjamin's Sale of Goods*, 10th edn (2017), paras 5-090—5-092.

[680] [1908] A.C. 35.

Materials not yet incorporated   It again appears to be a question of construc-   **44-157**
tion whether the property passes in materials provided by the seller and intended
to be used by him in manufacture but not yet incorporated in the product. If, for
instance, there was "some definite agreement between the parties which amounts
to an assent to the property in the materials passing from the builders to the purchasers",[681] it seems that the materials would be regarded as appropriated to the contract
and that the property in them would pass. The courts, however, are disinclined to
hold that the property in the material passes before they become part of the structure
of the product.[682] The point was put as follows by Lord Watson in *Seath & Co v
Moore*[683]: "materials provided by the builder and portions of the fabric, whether
wholly or partially finished, although intended to be used in the execution of the
contract, cannot be regarded as appropriated to the contract or as 'sold' unless they
have been affixed to or in a reasonable sense made part of the *corpus*". And in *Re
Blyth Shipbuilding and Dry Docks Co*,[684] where the clause regulating the passing
of the property referred specifically to the materials, it was held by the Court of Appeal that the materials had not been effectively appropriated to the contract. Warrington L.J. said[685]:

> "the real way of dealing with this question is to read the word 'appropriated', in its proper
> technical sense and as limited to goods which have been so dealt with that the builder
> could not use them except for the purposes of the ship, and that the purchasers could not
> refuse to accept them as part of the ship, ... the mere intention on the part of the builder
> to use them is not enough to transfer the property to the purchasers."

Appropriation of goods forming part of an identified bulk   Rule 5(3) and r.5(4)   **44-158**
deal with the appropriation of goods forming part of an identified bulk.[686] The effect of r.5(3) may be illustrated as follows: a buyer contracts to purchase, and pays
for,[687] 100 tons of wheat part of a larger bulk of 1000 tons lying in a specified
warehouse. Under s.20A of the Act[688] property in an undivided share in the bulk is
transferred to the buyer and the buyer becomes an owner in common of the bulk.
If, because of deliveries to other buyers or other removal of wheat from the
warehouse, the quantity of wheat in the warehouse is reduced to 100 tons or less
and the buyer is the only buyer to whom wheat is due out of the 1000 tons, the
quantity of wheat remaining becomes ascertained goods by process of
"exhaustion".[689] Further, under r.5(3), if that quantity of wheat is in a deliverable

---

[681] *Re Blyth Shipbuilding and Dry Docks Co* [1926] Ch. 494, 518. See also *Sauter Automation Ltd v
Goodman Mechanical Services Ltd* (1986) 34 B.L.R. 81 (building contract). cf. *McDougall v
Aeromarine of Emsworth Ltd* [1958] 1 W.L.R. 1126, 1129 (contra); *Re Cosslett (Contractors) Ltd*
[1998] Ch. 495; *Smith v Bridgend CBC* [2001] UKHL 58, [2002] 1 A.C. 336 (charge).

[682] See *Wood v Bell* (1856) 6 El. & Bl. 355, 263 (overruling *Woods v Russell* (1822) 5 B. & Ald. 942);
Reid v Macbeth [1904] A.C. 223. But see *Petromec Inc v Petroleo Brasileiro SA Petrobras* [2004]
EWHC 1180 (Comm), [2005] 1 Lloyd's Rep. 219 at [36].

[683] (1887) 11 App. Cas. 350, 381.

[684] [1926] Ch. 494; 518.

[685] At 517–518.

[686] "Bulk" is defined in s.61(1); see above, para.44-015. See below, para.44-163.

[687] If the goods are not paid for, in whole or in part, no property in an undivided share passes to the buyer
under s.20A, but r.5(3) can nevertheless still apply to transfer the property in the goods themselves
to the buyer.

[688] See below, para.44-160.

[689] See above, para.44-133.

state,[690] it is taken as appropriated to the buyer's contract and the property in the wheat itself (as opposed to an undivided share in the bulk) passes to the buyer.

44-159   The effect of r.5(4) may be illustrated as follows: if in the above example the seller has agreed to sell the 100 tons to the buyer under two or more separate contracts, the remaining wheat becomes ascertained by "consolidation"[691] and the property can pass under r.5(4) even though no portion of it has been appropriated to any particular contract. The same result ensues even if the contracts have been made with different sellers, or different buyers, but have become vested in a single buyer.

44-160   **Undivided shares in goods forming part of a bulk**   Subsections (1) and (2) of s.20A provide:

> "(1)   This section applies to a contract for the sale of a specified quantity of unascertained goods if the following conditions are met—
>> (a)   the goods or some of them form part of a bulk which is identified either in the contract or by subsequent agreement between the parties; and
>> (b)   the buyer has paid the price for some or all the goods which are the subject of the contract and which form part of the bulk.
>
> (2)   Where this section applies, then (unless the parties agree otherwise), as soon as the conditions specified in paragraphs (a) and (b) of subs.(1) above are met or at such later time as the parties may agree—
>> (a)   property in an undivided share in the bulk is transferred to the buyer, and
>> (b)   the buyer becomes an owner in common of the bulk."

Section 20A was inserted into the Act by the Sale of Goods (Amendment) Act 1995.[692] It qualifies s.16 of the Act[693] which provides that property cannot pass in the case of a contract for the sale of unascertained goods unless and until the goods are ascertained. Previously, if there was a contract for the sale of a quantity of unascertained goods forming part of an identified bulk, no property or interest in the goods would pass to the buyer unless and until the goods were ascertained either by being separated from the bulk or by process of "exhaustion" or "consolidation".[694] In the event of the insolvency of the seller the buyer could assert no proprietary claim to the goods while still in bulk even though the purchase price had been paid. The object of s.20A is (inter alia)[695] to enable a pre-paying buyer to assert such a claim by transferring to him the property in an undivided share of the bulk. The conditions set out in subs.(1) must, however, be satisfied.

44-161   **Requirements for passing of property in undivided share**   The first requirement of subs.(1) is that there should be "a contract for the sale of a specified quantity of unascertained goods". The quantity may be specified by number, weight,

---

[690] Despite the position of the words "in a deliverable state" in r.5(3), it is submitted that the goods need only be in a deliverable state at the time the bulk is reduced and not at the time of the contract of sale. For the meaning of "deliverable state", see s.61(5), see above, para.44-016, and see above, para.44-140.

[691] See above, para.44-133.

[692] s.1(3).

[693] See above, para.44-131.

[694] See above, para.44-133.

[695] See also the other reasons set out in the Report of the English and Scottish Law Commission *Sale of Goods Forming Part of a Bulk* (Law Com. No.215 and Scot. Law Com. No.145) (1993).

measurement or any other means but cannot be wholly indefinite.[696] The goods must be unascertained goods, for example, 100 tons of wheat part of a larger quantity currently lying in a designated warehouse, and not specific goods[697] (as defined in s.61(1) of the Act).

The second requirement is that the goods or some of them form part of a bulk. **44-162** "Bulk" is defined by s.61(1) to mean "a mass or collection of goods of the same kind which—(a) is contained in a defined space or area, and (b) is such that any goods in the bulk are interchangeable with any other goods therein of the same number or quantity". In addition to the obvious examples of a warehouse, store, hopper, hold or tank, the words "in a defined space or area" will include a ship, vehicle or aircraft, or even a discrete stack or pile.[698] It does not seem necessary that the goods in the bulk are interchangeable in the sense of being identical provided that they are regarded as equivalent to each other under the contract or by trade practice.[699] It would appear to be immaterial that the extent of the bulk is unknown[700] or that it is not in existence at the time of the sale or that the goods comprised in the bulk are constantly changing.[701] But, since the goods agreed to be sold, or some of them, must form part of the bulk it is clear that there must be attribution of those goods to the bulk.

The third requirement is that the bulk must be identified either in the contract or **44-163** by agreement of the parties. It must be certain from which bulk the goods are to come and this must be established by agreement: a unilateral designation by one party will not suffice unless it is agreed or assented to by the other.[702]

The fourth requirement is that the buyer must have paid the price for some or all **44-164** of the goods which are the subject of the contract and which form part of the bulk. Presumably any recognised form of payment, e.g. by bill of exchange or cheque, will suffice.[703]

It is open to the parties to agree that no undivided share is to be transferred to **44-165** the buyer, and it may be assumed that they can do so expressly or by implication, for example, by reserving the right of disposal against payment in full of the price.[704] They may also agree that an undivided share is to be transferred to the buyer at some time later than that specified in subs.(2). But, in the absence of any such agreement, the buyer acquires an undivided share in the bulk and becomes an owner in common of the bulk as soon as these conditions are satisfied. It is important, however, to note that what is transferred to the buyer by s.20A is the property in an undivided share in the bulk. The buyer does not become the sole owner of the goods themselves. The goods, while in bulk, remain unascertained and s.16 still governs the transfer of the property in those goods. They must therefore become

---

[696] For a discussion as to whether, e.g. "80 to 100 tons" or "100 tons 5% more or less" are covered, see *Benjamin's Sale of Goods*, 10th edn (2017), para.5-111.

[697] See below, para.44-168.

[698] The word "contained" should be given its larger meaning of being kept within limits rather than enclosed or kept within a container: *Benjamin's Sale of Goods*, 10th edn (2017), at para.5-113.

[699] *Benjamin's Sale of Goods*, 10th edn (2017), at paras 1-120, 5-113.

[700] But see below, para.44-171.

[701] cf. *Mercer v Craven Grain Storage Ltd* [1994] C.L.C. 328, HL.

[702] For the particular problems to which this may give rise, see *Benjamin's Sale of Goods*, 10th edn (2017), at para.5-114.

[703] See Vol.I, paras 21-040—21-084.

[704] See below, para.44-170. For the position in relation to CIF and C&F contracts, see *Benjamin's Sale of Goods*, 10th edn (2017), paras 5-116, 18-346.

ascertained (normally by being physically separated from the bulk)[705] before the property can pass. Once they have become ascertained, the sole property in the goods themselves will pass to the buyer at such time as the parties intend it to be transferred[706] having regard, in appropriate cases, to s.18 r.5.

44-166 **Extent of the undivided share** Subsections (3) to (6) of s.20A deal with the extent of the buyer's undivided share:

"(3) Subject to subs.(4) below, for the purposes of this section, the undivided share of a buyer in a bulk at any time shall be such share as the quantity of goods paid for and due to buyer out of the bulk bears to the quantity of goods in the bulk at that time.

(4) Where the aggregate of the undivided shares of buyers in a bulk determined under subs.(3) above would at any time exceed the whole of the bulk at that time, the undivided share in the bulk of each buyer shall be reduced proportionately so that the aggregate of the undivided shares is equal to the whole bulk.

(5) Where a buyer has paid the price for only some of the goods due to him out of a bulk, any delivery[707] to the buyer out of the bulk shall, for the purposes of this section, be ascribed in the first place to the goods in respect of which payment has been made.

(6) For the purposes of this section payment of part of the price for any goods shall be treated as payment for a corresponding part of the goods."

Although the buyer becomes owner in common with others of the entire bulk, only a proportionate share of the bulk is attributed to him. The basic rule (set out in subs.(3)) is that the extent of his undivided share in the bulk at any time is such share as the quantity of goods paid for and due to him out of the bulk bears to quantity of goods in the bulk at that time, e.g. if he has agreed to buy and has paid for 100 tons out of a bulk consisting of 1000 tons, there is transferred to him the property in an undivided share of one-tenth of the 1000 tons. Subsection (4) deals with the question of what happens if the aggregate of the undivided shares of buyers in the bulk exceeds the bulk at that time, for example, if 100 tons have been sold to each of ten buyers from a bulk believed to contain 1000 tons, but the bulk is subsequently reduced by theft or wastage to 800 tons or the seller or another person wrongfully removes 200 tons from that bulk. In that case, the undivided share of each buyer in the remaining 800 tons is reduced proportionately to one-tenth of 800 tons. Reduction also occurs where a co-owning buyer has taken delivery of the goods due to him under his contract but in excess of his undivided share.[708] It is, however, doubtful whether subs.(4) applies where the seller purports to sell more than the quantity of goods in the bulk, for example, where he sells to each of three buyers consecutively 500 tons from a bulk which consists only of 1000 tons.[709] In such a case, it is probable that the last buyer will get nothing as the seller will by then have nothing left to sell.[710] The section does not deal with the converse case where the aggregate of the undivided shares is less than the whole of the bulk at that time, for instance, where the seller sells 100 tons to each of ten buyers from a

---

[705] But see above, para.44-133 (exhaustion and consolidation).
[706] 1979 Act s.17.
[707] Defined in s.61(1); see above, para.44-015.
[708] 1979 Act s.20B(1)(a); see below, para.44-167.
[709] See *Benjamin's Sale of Goods*, 10th edn (2017), paras 5-123 to 5-125.
[710] 1979 Act s.21(1); see below, para.44-193 (unless the last purchaser can establish a good title under s.24 of the 1979 Act, see below, para.44-214). See *Benjamin's Sale of Goods*, 10th edn (2017), at paras 5-123 to 5-125, 7-067.

bulk believed to consist of 1000 tons but which actually consists of 1100 tons, or where 100 tons are added by the seller to the bulk. In such a case each buyer becomes (together with the seller) a co-owner of the entire 1100 tons and there is transferred to him an undivided share of one-eleventh of the bulk of 1100 tons. The section also does not deal with the case where the quantity of goods in the bulk is unknown: presumably the calculation must then be done on the basis of an estimate.

Deemed consent by owner to dealings in bulk goods Section 20B supplements s.20A and provides that each co-owner of the bulk is deemed to have consented to deliveries to any other co-owner of the quantity due to the latter under his contract[711] and is deemed to have consented to any dealing with or removal, delivery or disposal of the goods in the bulk by another co-owner (including the seller) falling within the latter's undivided share at the time.[712] This is a useful provision[713] having regard to the fact that the relationship between a buyer's undivided share and his contractual entitlement may be uncertain and may vary from time to time. Section 20B may therefore protect third parties who purchase goods from co-owning buyers, and liquidators and receivers who release goods to co-owning buyers in reliance on the deemed consent.[714] The section also contains other savings,[715] and in particular preserves the rights of any buyer under his contract.[716] **44-167**

Situations outside s.20A A contract for the sale of specific goods falls outside s.20A and by s.61(1) "specific goods" includes an undivided share, specified as a fraction or percentage, of a bulk which is identified and agreed on at the time a contract of sale is made. Thus a contract for the sale of a quarter share in a named racehorse, or a contract for the sale of a fraction ("one-half") or percentage ("50 per cent")—as opposed to a specified quantity ("100 tons")—of a larger quantity of wheat currently lying in a designated warehouse, will be not be a contract for the sale of a specified quantity of *unascertained* goods falling within s.20A but one for the sale of specific goods. Nevertheless, while the goods still form part of the bulk, the result at common law is probably the same: property in an undivided share in the bulk is transferred to the buyer and he becomes an owner in common of the bulk.[717] This proprietary interest will pass when the parties intend it to pass,[718] which may be before or at the time or after the price is paid. **44-168**

Where one or more of the other conditions specified in subs.(1) of s.20A is not satisfied, for example, where the buyer had not paid the price for any of the goods comprised in the contract,[719] or where the buyer has paid the price for only some of the goods, then as regards those goods for which no payment has been made, s.20A will not apply. It is also open to the parties to exclude by agreement the ap- **44-169**

---

[711] 1979 Act s.20B(1)(a).
[712] 1979 Act s.20B(1)(b).
[713] For the position at common law and under s.10(1) of the Torts (Interference with Goods) Act 1977, see *Benjamin's Sale of Goods*, 10th edn (2017), para.5-127.
[714] 1979 Act s.20B(2).
[715] 1979 Act s.20B(3).
[716] For the position in respect of risk, see below, para.44-189.
[717] *Benjamin's Sale of Goods*, 10th edn (2017) at para.5-131. But the rules in subss.(4) to (6) of s.20A are peculiar to that section and cannot therefore apply.
[718] 1979 Act s.17.
[719] 1979 Act s.20A(1)(b).

plication of s.20A.[720] In those cases, there may be exceptional situations where property in an undivided share will pass to the buyer while the goods are still in bulk.[721] But, as a normal rule, this will not be so and the seller will remain the sole owner of the goods unless and until they have become ascertained by being separated from the bulk[722] and have been appropriated to the contract in accordance with s.18 r.5.

44-170   Seller's right of disposal   Section 19(1) provides as follows:

"Where there is a contract for the sale of specific goods or where goods are subsequently appropriated to the contract, the seller may, by the terms of the contract or appropriation, reserve the right of disposal of the goods until certain conditions are fulfilled; and in such a case, notwithstanding the delivery of the goods to the buyer, or to a carrier or other bailee ... for the purpose of transmission to the buyer, the property in the goods does not pass to the buyer until the conditions imposed by the seller are fulfilled."

Section 19(1) states the general rule that it is open to the seller to reserve to himself the right of disposal, i.e. retain property in the goods, until a specified condition is fulfilled—usually payment of the price.[723] If he does this, the property does not pass until that condition is fulfilled, even though the goods are delivered to the buyer or to a carrier or other bailee for the purpose of transmission to the buyer; in other words, delivery to a carrier does not, in this instance, amount to an unconditional appropriation so as to pass the property under s.18 r.5. This point may be illustrated by reference to what is the normal rule in CIF contracts.[724] There the property in the goods does not usually pass upon shipment, nor even upon notice of appropriation, but only when the seller transfers the documents against payment or securing of the price.

44-171   The remaining subsections consist of particular applications of the general rule stated in s.19(1) and are as follows:

"(2)   Where goods are shipped, and by the bill of lading the goods are deliverable to the order of the seller or his agent, the seller is prima facie deemed to reserve the right of disposal.[725]
(3)   Where the seller of goods draws on the buyer for the price, and transmits the bill of exchange and bill of lading to the buyer together to secure acceptance or payment of the bill of exchange, the buyer is bound to return the bill of lading if he does not honour the bill of exchange, and if he wrongfully retains the bill of lading the property in the goods does not pass to him."[726]

---

[720] See above, para.44-165.

[721] *Re Stapylton Fletcher Ltd* [1974] 1 W.L.R. 1181. Contrast *Re London Wine Co (Shippers) Ltd* [1986] P.C.C. 121; *Re Goldcorp Exchange Ltd* [1995] 1 A.C. 74.

[722] See above, para.44-133 (but note also ascertainment by exhaustion and consolidation).

[723] See, e.g. *Leigh and Sillivan Ltd v Aliakmon Shipping Co Ltd* [1986] A.C. 785. If a seller makes a unilateral reservation of property in breach of contract, and/or refuses to transfer the property on tender of the price, it is not clear whether the buyer's tender vests the property in him. See *Benjamin's Sale of Goods*, 10th edn (2017), paras 5-134, 18-262; *City Motors (1933) Pty Ltd v Southern Aerial Super Service Pty Ltd* (1961) 106 C.L.R. 477, 485–486, 487–490.

[724] See *Smyth & Co Ltd v Bailey, Son & Co* [1940] 3 All E.R. 60, 67–68; see also *Wait v Baker* (1848) 2 Exch. 1, 7–8 and *Benjamin's Sale of Goods*, 10th edn (2017), paras 19-099 et seq.

[725] See *Ogg v Shuter* (1875) 1 C.P.D. 47; *Mirabita v Imperial Ottoman Bank* (1878) 3 Ex. D. 164, 172; *Benjamin's Sale of Goods*, 10th edn (2017), paras 18-263, 20-084.

[726] The reference is probably to dishonour by non-acceptance rather than by non-payment. See *Shepherd v Harrison* (1871) L.R. 5 H.L. 116; *The Prinz Adalbert* [1917] A.C. 586; *The Orteric* [1920] A.C.

Section 19(2) states that there is a presumption in favour of the reservation of the right of disposal where by the bill of lading the goods are deliverable to the order of the seller or his agent.[727] It must be added that if the bill of lading is made out to the order of the buyer or his agent it does not necessarily follow that the property in the goods is transferred when they are shipped. If, for instance, the seller retains the bill of lading this may be "inconsistent with an intention to pass the property"[728] so as to prevent the property from passing even though the bill of lading is taken in the buyer's name. The result of s.19(2) seems to be that where goods are shipped under a bill of lading the presumption is that the property does not pass until the bill is transferred unconditionally to the buyer.

Section 19(3) in the circumstances to which it applies makes the passing of the **44-172** property by the transfer of the bill of lading conditional on the bill of exchange being honoured by the buyer. As in s.19(1), the protection given to the seller is limited: so that if the buyer, without honouring the bill of exchange, transfers the bill of lading to a bona fide third party, the latter may by statute acquire a good title.[729]

"Romalpa" clauses: retention of title[730]   Reservation of the right of disposal of **44-173** goods greatly increased in importance as the result of the decision in *Aluminium Industrie Vaassen BV v Romalpa Aluminium Ltd*[731] where the Court of Appeal upheld, as against a receiver of the buyer company, a clause by which (inter alia) the seller retained title to the goods sold until all sums owing from the buyer were paid. This case was distinguished in *Re Bond Worth Ltd*,[732] where the clause in question retained merely "equitable and beneficial" (and not legal) ownership; it was held to create a charge on the assets of the buyer company within s.95(2) of the Companies Act 1948[733] and to require registration. However, if the seller retains legal ownership of the goods agreed to be sold until their price is paid, no question of any charge by the buyer company requiring registration under s.860 of the

---

724. See also *Barton, Thompson & Co v Vigers Bros* (1906) 19 Com. Cas. 175; *Ernest Scragg & Sons Ltd v Perseverance Banking and Trust Co Ltd* [1973] 2 Lloyd's Rep. 101; *Benjamin's Sale of Goods*, 10th edn (2017), paras 5-140, 18-272.

727 *Mitsui & Co Ltd v Flota Mercante Grancolombiana SA* [1988] 1 W.L.R. 1145. cf. *The Parchim* [1918] A.C. 157: presumption rebutted in a Prize case.

728 *The Kronprinsessan Margareta* [1921] 1 A.C. 486, 517. Although property usually passes on transfer of the bill of lading this is not necessarily so: *Carlos Soto SAU v AP Moller-Maersk AS (The SFL Hawk)* [2015] EWHC 458 (Comm), [2015] 1 Lloyd's Rep. 537, [19].

729 *Cahn v Pockett's Bristol Channel Steam Packet Co Ltd* [1899] 1 Q.B. 643. See below, para.44-220.

730 See Parris, *Retention of Title on Sale of Goods* (1982); Parris, *Effective Reservation of Title Clauses* (1986); Dickson, *Retention of Title Clauses* (1987); McCormack, *Reservation of Title*, 2nd edn (1995); Davies, *Effective Retention of Title* (1991); Wheeler, *Retention of Title Clauses: Impact and Implications* (1991); *Benjamin's Sale of Goods*, 10th edn (2017), paras 5-143 et seq.; Palmer and McKendrick, *Interests in Goods*, 2nd edn (1998), Ch.28. The periodical literature is voluminous. For the problems involved regarding conflict of laws see *Benjamin's Sale of Goods*, 10th edn (2017), at para.26-151. On European Union requirements, see Directive 2000/35 art.4 ([2000] O.J. L200/35) and Council Regulation 1346/2000 of May 29, 2000 ([2000] O.J. L160/1); *Benjamin's Sale of Goods*, 10th edn (2017), at para.26-150.

731 [1976] 1 W.L.R. 676; noted (1976) 39 M.L.R. 585, [1977] C.L.J. 27.

732 [1980] Ch. 228. See also *Stroud Architectural Systems Ltd v John Laing Construction Ltd* [1994] 2 B.C.L.C. 276.

733 See now Companies Act 2006 s.860, replacing Companies Act 1985 ss.395, 396, from October 2009. The amendments provided for in ss.92–107 of the Companies Act 1989, were not brought into force and are repealed by s.1295 of and Sch.16 of the 2006 Act. On proposals of the Law Commission for reform: see *Law Com. Consultation Paper No.264* (2002); *Law Com. Consultation Paper No.176* (2004); Law Com. Report No.296 (2005).

Companies Act 2006[734] can arise, because a company can create a charge only on its own property, and if it never acquired property in the goods it cannot charge them.[735] The fact that the buyer is expressly or impliedly[736] entitled to consume the goods in manufacture or to resell them in the ordinary course of business will not invalidate the seller's retention of ownership until such time as the goods are so consumed or sold.[737] Nor will the addition of words which entitle the seller to retake possession of the goods in which he retains title upon certain contingencies, e.g. the insolvency of the buyer company, create a registrable charge,[738] since the seller retains property in the goods and his right to recover the seller's right to possession is a right against his own goods.[739] In the *Romalpa* case, it was conceded that, on the wording of the clause, the buyer held the goods until payment as bailee for the seller.[740] But in subsequent cases, the courts have found it unnecessary to decide whether the relationship between seller and buyer in relation to the goods is one of bailor or bailee[741] or whether, if the buyer resells the goods, he does so as agent of the seller.[742] Such considerations are not relevant to the efficacy of the seller's retention of title to the goods, but only (if at all) to the question of accountability of the buyer for the proceeds of sale.[743]

---

[734] See n.733, above.

[735] *Clough Mill Ltd v Martin* [1985] 1 W.L.R. 111, 116, 122, 125. See also *Re Peachdart Ltd* [1984] Ch. 131, 141; *Hendy Lennox (Industrial) Engines Ltd v Grahame Puttick Ltd* [1984] 1 W.L.R. 485, 491; *Re Andrabell Ltd* [1984] 3 All E.R. 407, 410. But see *Re Curtain Dream Plc* [1990] B.C.L.C. 925 (sale and repurchase of goods).

[736] *Aluminium Industrie Vaassen BV v Romalpa Aluminium Ltd* [1976] 1 W.L.R. 676, 680, 687, 689, 692, 694; *Re Bond Worth Ltd* [1980] Ch. 228, 246; *Borden (UK) Ltd v Scottish Timber Products Ltd* [1981] Ch. 25, 34, 44, 46; *Hendy Lennox (Industrial Engines) Ltd v Grahame Puttick Ltd* [1984] 1 W.L.R. 485, 491; *Re Andrabell Ltd* [1984] 3 All E.R. 407 at 411; *Four Point Garage Ltd v Carter* [1985] 3 All E.R. 12. *Fairfax Gerrard Holdings Ltd v Capital Bank Plc* [2007] EWCA Civ 1226, [2008] 1 Lloyd's Rep. 297 at [34].

[737] *Aluminium Industrie Vaassen BV v Romalpa Aluminium Ltd* [1976] 1 W.L.R. 676, 680, 687, 689, 692, 694; *Re Peachdart Ltd* [1984] Ch. 131, 141; *Hendy Lennox (Industrial Engines) Ltd v Grahame Puttick Ltd* [1984] 1 W.L.R. 485, 491; cf. *Borden (UK) Ltd v Scottish Timber Products Ltd* [1981] Ch. 25, 34, 44, 46; *Re Bond Worth Ltd* [1980] Ch. 228, 246. However, where the buyer is at liberty to consume the goods before the price becomes due, such that the transfer of the property in the goods may never happen, the contract may not be a contract of sale at all: see *PST Energy 7 Shipping LLC v OW Bunker Malta Ltd* [2016] UKSC 23 where the Supreme Court characterised a bunker contract with these characteristics as a sui generis supply contract. See below, para.44-174.

[738] Under s.860(7)(b) of the Companies Act 2006, see n.733, above.

[739] *McEntire v Crossley Brothers Ltd* [1895] A.C. 457, 462; *Smart Brothers Ltd v Holt* [1929] 2 K.B. 303, 308.

[740] [1976] 1 W.L.R. 676, 680. Contrast *Borden (UK) Ltd v Scottish Timber Products Ltd* [1981] Ch. 25, 35, 45; *E Pfeiffer Weinkellerei-Weineinkauf GmbH & Co v Arbuthnot Factors Ltd* [1988] 1 W.L.R. 150, 159.

[741] *Re Peachdart Ltd* [1984] Ch. 131, 141, 142; *Hendy Lennox (Industrial Engines) Ltd v Graham Puttick Ltd* [1984] 1 W.L.R. 485, 499–500; *Re Andrabell Ltd* [1984] 3 All E.R. 407, 414. But see *Clough Mill Ltd v Martin* [1985] 1 W.L.R. 111 at 116.

[742] *Aluminium Industrie Vaassen BV v Romalpa Aluminium Ltd* [1976] 1 W.L.R. 676, 690, 693, 694. But see *Caterpillar (NI) Ltd (formerly FG Wilson (Engineering) Ltd) v John Holt & Co (Liverpool) Ltd* [2013] EWCA Civ 1232, [2014] 1 All E.R. (Comm) 393 at [60], [61], [75]–[76] (buyer sells as agent). For a critical analysis of this decision see Gullifer [2014] L.M.C.L.Q. 564.

[743] See below, para.44-179. In *Caterpillar (NI) Ltd (formerly FG Wilson (Engineering) Ltd v John Holt & Co (Liverpool) Ltd* [2013] EWCA Civ 1232, [2014] 1 All E.R. (Comm) 393, the question of whether the buyer resold as agent was relevant to the question of whether property had ever passed to the buyer, or passed directly to the sub-buyer, which, in turn, was relevant to whether there could be an action for the price under s.49 of the Sale of Goods Act 1979 for the purposes of a non set-off clause.

Right to consume before property has passed If the contract provides for pos-   **44-174**
session of goods to be given, coupled with a legal entitlement to consume them
before the property in them is transferred upon payment, then, according to the
Supreme Court in *PST Energy 7 Shipping LLC v OW Bunker Malta Ltd*[744] the
contract is not one of sale but is sui generis as a bailment coupled with a licence to
consume the goods. Since almost all retention of title clauses allow the buyer to use
or resell the goods before property in them has passed, this means that a very large
number of contracts with reservation of title clauses will no longer be contracts of
sale within the meaning of the Sale of Goods Act.

Sui generis supply contracts analogous to contracts for the sale of goods A   **44-175**
consequence of the conclusion in *PST Energy 7 Shipping LLC* is that a body of common law parallel to the Sale of Goods Act will have to be elaborated to deal with
sui generis supply contracts. Although the Court of Appeal was clear that the
incidents of the sui generis contract should track those of a sale of goods contract,[745]
it cannot be assumed that the entire Sale of Goods Act can be applied by analogy
to sui generis contracts.[746] The Supreme Court gave consideration to an obligation
comparable to the right to sell goods that is the equivalent of s.12 of the Act.
However, the judge at first instance saw no need for a warranty of quiet possession akin to the one that exists for sale of goods contracts in s.12(2)(b).[747] The first
reason given was that the recipient of the goods obtained sufficient protection from
the implied term of lawful permission to use or consume. The second reason was
that the warranty of quiet possession in sale of goods contracts was concerned with
events after the passing of property. However, neither reason seems compelling and
there may be a practical need for such a warranty. It is likely that equivalent common law rules should apply to such sui generis contracts in relation to matters such
as delivery (including time and quantity of delivery and delivery by instalments)
payment and quality (although, on a strict view, the statutory provisions which
modify the common law rules on merchantable quality, etc. would not apply). The
potential applicability of the statutory exceptions to the *nemo dat* rule is complex.
The supplier of goods under a sui generis contract is not a "seller" for the purposes
of s.24, nor is the recipient a "buyer" of goods for the purpose of s.25. However, it
is likely that the receipt of goods with a licence to use or consume them should be
regarded as a disposition for the purposes of these sections. The definition of a
mercantile agent in s.1(1) of the Factors Act 1889 may be broad enough to capture
a person who buys and resells under a sui generis supply contract, given that such
contracts are "in commercial terms" regarded as contracts for the sale of goods[748]

---

[744] [2016] UKSC 23, [2016] 2 W.L.R. 1193, [2016] 1 Lloyd's Rep. 589. For a critical review of this
decision see L. Gullifer [2017] L.Q.R 244. The Court of Appeal in *Wood v TUI Travel Plc (t/a First
Choice)* [2017] EWCA Civ 11, [2017] 1 Lloyd's Rep 322 held that *PST Energy 7 Shipping LLC* was
not authority for the proposition that there was no intention that property in any food or drink served
by a hotel to guests would pass to them. The conclusion in *PST Energy 7 Shipping LLC* depended
upon the relationship between a retention of title clause and the liberty to consume fuel in which
property had not already passed and was accordingly distinguishable.
[745] "There is no reason why the incidents of a contract of sale of goods for which the Act provides should
not apply equally to such a contract at common law": Moore-Bick L.J., [2015] EWCA Civ 1058 at
[33].
[746] See L. Gullifer [2017] L.Q.R. 244, 258 and *Benjamin's Sale of Goods*, 10th edn (2017) at 4-001.
[747] [2015] EWHC 2022 (Comm) at [63].
[748] [2015] EWCA Civ 1058 at [33].

and that the Factors Act is not confined to sale of goods contracts as these are defined in the Sale of Goods Act. Thus the provisions of s.2(1) of the Factors Act may apply. By contrast, certain provisions of the Sale of Goods Act are statutory inventions and did not codify existing common law. Such sections cannot apply by analogy at common law. For example, it is possible, though perhaps unlikely, that a bulk may consist of goods supplied to two or more recipients under sui generis supply contracts and that the bulk has not been exhausted by the time that one or more recipients has paid in full. Section 20A, which is not declaratory of the common law, cannot apply to such contracts by analogy. Similarly, ss.15A and 30(2A) cannot apply.

44-176   Although certain retention of title clauses retain ownership only in such goods as have not been paid for by the buyer, others go further and retain ownership until all goods comprised in the same invoice[749] or in the same contract[750] have been paid for, or until all accounts owing by the buyer have been settled.[751] There is no reason, under s.19(1) of the 1979 Act, why the seller should not reserve the right of disposal of the goods on any terms that he thinks fit,[752] although in the case of an "all accounts" clause this may in practice mean that property will never pass between seller and buyer. In *Clough Mill Ltd v Martin*[753] the Court of Appeal upheld the retention of title in a clause which retained ownership until all goods comprised in the same contract were paid for, but the court discussed[754] the problems that would arise if goods that had already been paid for (but in which the property had not yet passed) were repossessed and sold by the seller: whether account must be taken of the part payment already received, and whether the seller would be accountable to the buyer for the proceeds of sale once full payment was achieved. In *Armour v Thyssen Edelstahlwerke AG*[755] (where an "all accounts" clause was upheld) the House of Lords did not find it necessary to form a concluded view as to the solution of these problems.[756]

44-177 **Products**   If goods which are the subject of a retention of title provision are used by the buyer in his manufacturing process to make other products or are incorporated in other goods owned by the buyer, the seller may lose his title to the goods. In *Borden (UK) Ltd v Scottish Timber Products Ltd*[757] resin supplied by the seller was used by the buyer company in the manufacture of chipboard. The Court

---

[749] *Re Peachdart Ltd* [1984] Ch. 131.

[750] *Re Bond Worth Ltd* [1980] Ch. 228, 246; *Clough Mill Ltd v Martin* [1985] 1 W.L.R. 111.

[751] *Aluminium Industrie Vaassen BV v Romalpa Aluminium Ltd* [1976] 1 W.L.R. 676; *Borden (UK) Ltd v Scottish Timber Products Ltd*, above; *John Snow & Co Ltd v DGB Woodcraft Co Ltd* [1985] B.C.L.C. 54; *Armour v Thyssen Edelstahlwerke AG* [1991] 2 A.C. 339; *Peerless Carpets Ltd v Moorhouse Carpet Market Ltd* (1992) 4 N.Z.B.L.C. 102, 747.

[752] *Aluminium Industrie Vaassen BV v Romalpa Aluminium Ltd* [1976] 1 W.L.R. 676; *Re Peachdart Ltd* [1984] Ch. 131; *Clough Mill Ltd v Martin* [1985] 1 W.L.R. 111; *John Snow & Co Ltd v DGB Woodcraft Co Ltd* [1985] B.C.L.C. 541; *Armour v Thyssen Edelstahlwerke AG* [1991] 2 A.C. 339 at 353. Contrast Goodhart and Jones (1980) 43 M.L.R. 489, 508; Goodhart (1986) 49 M.L.R. 86. In Scotland, "all accounts" clauses were once struck down as an attempt to obtain security without possession, and, by virtue of s.62(4), to fall outside the Sale of Goods Act 1979, but they have since been upheld in *Armour v Thyssen Edelstahlwerke AG* [1991] 2 A.C. 339.

[753] [1985] 1 W.L.R. 111.

[754] At 117–118, 124, 125–126.

[755] [1991] 2 A.C. 339.

[756] At 353. See *Benjamin's Sale of Goods*, 10th edn (2017), para.5-148.

[757] [1981] Ch. 25.

of Appeal held that, once the resin had lost its identity in the chipboard, it ceased to exist and with it the seller's title thereto; the resin could not be traced into the chipboard or the proceeds of its sale, nor could the seller claim any interest in or charge over the chipboard. In *Re Peachdart Ltd*,[758] where leather supplied by the seller was used by the buyer company to manufacture handbags, Vinelott J. held that, once a piece of leather had been appropriated to be manufactured into a handbag and work had started on it, it ceased to be the exclusive property of the seller.[759] And in *Clough Mill Ltd v Martin*,[760] Robert Goff L.J. stated[761] that: "where A's material is lawfully used by B to create new goods, whether or not B incorporates other material of his own, the property in the new goods will generally vest in B, at least where the goods are not reducible to the original materials". On the other hand, in *Hendy Lennox (Industrial Engines) Ltd v Grahame Puttick Ltd*[762] diesel engines supplied by the seller were incorporated by the buyer company into diesel generating sets. The incorporation did not alter or destroy the substance or an engine, and it could be removed from the set within several hours, Staughton J. held that the proprietary rights of the seller were not affected by the incorporation. These cases move into very difficult and uncertain areas of law,[763] in particular where the goods remain identifiable but have, to a greater or less extent, been worked upon by the buyer.[764]

"Romalpa" clauses sometimes expressly provide that ownership of products **44-178** manufactured from goods supplied subject to the seller's retention of title are to vest in the seller, or that the seller is to acquire ownership of any articles in which such goods are incorporated. But there is considerable doubt as to the efficacy of such provisions. In the *Borden* case (see above) it was stated[765] that, had any interest been granted to the seller in the chipboard or the proceeds of its sale, such interest would have been agreed to be granted and must have been created by the buyer company as security for debts owed to the seller and be registrable as a charge.[766] In *Re Peachdart Ltd* (see above),[767] a provision that "the relationship of the buyer to the seller shall be fiduciary in respect ... of other goods in which [the contract goods] are incorporated or used" was held to create a charge over completed and

---

[758] [1984] Ch. 131. See also *Modelboard Ltd v Outer Box Ltd* [1993] B.C.L.C. 623 (cardboard made into boxes); *Ian Chisholm Textiles v Griffiths* [1994] B.C.C. 96 (cloth cut and worked on); *Chaigley Farms Ltd v Crawford, Kay & Grayshire Ltd* [1996] B.C.C. 957 (slaughtered cattle); *Re Highway Foods International* [1995] B.C.L.C. 209 (processed meat); *ICI New Zealand v Agnew* [1998] 2 N.Z.L.R. 129 (plastic pellets made into containers). Contrast *Armour v Thyssen Edelstahlwerke AG* [1991] 2 A.C. 339 (cut steel); *New Zealand Forest Products Ltd v Pongakawa Sawmill Ltd* [1992] 3 N.Z.L.R. 304 (sawn timber); *Coleman v Harvey* [1989] 1 N.Z.L.R. 723 (refined silver).

[759] In this case there was an express "products" provision (see below) and it was held that the intention was to create a charge on the handbags in the course of manufacture and on the end products.

[760] [1985] 1 W.L.R. 111.

[761] At 119. See also at 125.

[762] [1984] 1 W.L.R. 485. Contrast *Specialist Plant Services Ltd v Braithwaite Ltd* (1987) 3 B.C.C. 119 (materials for repair).

[763] *Clough Mill Ltd v Martin* [1985] 1 W.L.R. 111, 124; *Coleman v Harvey* [1989] 1 N.Z.L.R. 723. See *Benjamin's Sale of Goods*, 10th edn (2017), paras 1-058—1-059, 5-150—5-151.

[764] As in *Re Peachdart Ltd* [1984] Ch. 131; and the cases cited in n.758, see above. See also *Re Bond Worth Ltd* [1980] Ch. 228; *Clough Mill Ltd v Martin* [1985] 1 W.L.R. 111 (where the manufacturing process went further).

[765] [1981] Ch. 25, at 44, 45. See also at 46, 47; *Re Bond Worth Ltd* [1980] Ch. 228, 246.

[766] Under what is now s.860(7)(b) of the Companies Act 2006. cf. *ICI New Zealand v Agnew* [1998] 2 N.Z.L.R. 129 (floating charge).

[767] [1984] Ch. 131.

uncompleted handbags manufactured by the buyer company from the leather supplied. In *Clough Mill Ltd v Martin*,[768] however, where yarn was supplied to be manufactured by the buyer company into fabric, Robert Goff and Oliver L.JJ.[769] saw no objection in principle to a provision whereby property in any new product created by manufacture should ipso facto vest in the seller,[770] but the Court of Appeal was unanimous in holding[771] that the clause in that case (which vested property in the products in the seller until payment had been made) could not be read literally so as to produce the result of a "windfall" to the seller of the full value of the new product, and so gave rise to a charge in favour of the seller.

44-179 **Proceeds of sale** A mere reservation of title provision would not appear to impose any duty on the buyer to account for the proceeds of sale of the goods in which title is reserved.[772] Even if the clause further provides that the buyer holds the goods until payment as bailee or sells the goods as agent of the seller,[773] he does not necessarily hold or sell them in a fiduciary capacity,[774] since not all bailees or agents are fiduciaries for their bailors or principals.[775] But provision is commonly found in "Romalpa" clauses that the buyer is to hold the proceeds of sale on trust or in a fiduciary capacity for the seller. The object is to enable the seller to trace the proceeds of sale in accordance with the principles in *Re Hallett's Estate*[776] to the exclusion of other creditors of the buyer. In *Re Bond Worth Ltd*,[777] however, it was pointed out that there is high authority[778] for the view that, if the buyer is not bound to keep the proceeds of sale separately, but is entitled to mix them with his own money and deal with them as he pleases, and when called upon to hand over an equivalent sum of money, then he is not a trustee of the proceeds but merely a

---

[768] [1985] 1 W.L.R. 111.

[769] At 119, 124. But see Donaldson M.R. at 125. See also *Glencore International AG v Metro Trading International Inc* [2001] 1 Lloyd's Rep. 284, 322; *Bacardi-Martini Beverages Ltd v Thomas Hardy Packaging Ltd* [2002] 1 Lloyd's Rep. 62, 75; affirmed [2002] EWCA Civ 549, [2002] 2 Lloyd's Rep. 379.

[770] So that the buyer company would not be creating a charge over its own goods.

[771] At 120, 124, 125. See also *Modelboard Ltd v Outer Box Ltd* [1993] B.C.L.C. 623.

[772] *Michelin Tyre Co Ltd v Macfarlane (Glasgow) Ltd* (1917) 55 S.C.L.R. 35, HL; *Hendy Lennox (Industrial Engines) Ltd v Grahame Puttick Ltd* [1984] 1 W.L.R. 485; *Re Andrabell Ltd* [1984] 3 All E.R. 407; *E Pfeiffer Weinkellerei-Weineinkauf GmbH & Co v Arbuthnot Factors Ltd* [1988] 1 W.L.R. 150, 159. Contrast *Len Vidgen Ski & Leisure Ltd v Timaru Marine Supplies (1982) Ltd* [1986] N.Z.L.R. 349. See also *Caterpillar (NI) Ltd (formerly FG Wilson (Engineering) Ltd v John Holt & Co (Liverpool) Ltd* [2013] EWCA Civ 1232, [2014] 1 All E.R. (Comm) 393 at [60], [61], [75]–[76] (buyer sells as agent). For a critical analysis of this decision see Gullifer [2014] L.M.C.L.Q. 564.

[773] See above, para.44-173.

[774] Contrast *Aluminium Industrie Vaassen BV v Romalpa Aluminium Ltd* [1976] 1 W.L.R. 676, 690, 692, 694. See also *Re Hallett's Estate* (1880) 13 Ch. D. 696, 708–711.

[775] *Kirkham v Peel* (1880) 43 L.T. 171; *Re Coomber* [1911] 1 Ch. 723, 728; *Henry v Hammond* [1913] 2 K.B. 515; *Boardman v Phipps* [1967] 2 A.C. 46, 126; *Hendy Lennox (Industrial Engines) Ltd v Grahame Puttick*, above, at 497–499; *Re Andrabell Ltd*, above, at 411–416; *Compaq Computer Ltd v Abercorn Group Ltd* [1991] B.C.C. 484, 496.

[776] (1880) 13 Ch. D. 696 (as in *Aluminium Industrie Vaassen BV v Romalpa Aluminium Industrie Ltd* [1976] 1 W.L.R. 676, 690, 692, 694).

[777] [1980] Ch. 228.

[778] *Re Nevill* (1870) L.R. 6 Ch. App. 397; affirmed sub nom. *Towle & Co v White* (1873) 29 L.T. 78, HL; *Foley v Hill* (1848) 2 H.L. Cas. 28; *South Australian Insurance Co v Randall* (1869) L.R. 3 P.C. 101. See also *Henry v Hammond* [1913] 2 K.B. 515 at 521; *Neste Oy v Lloyd's Bank Plc* [1983] 2 Lloyd's Rep. 658.

debtor. A "Romalpa" clause should therefore provide that the proceeds of sale are to be placed in a separate account so as to be identifiable as being in the beneficial ownership of the seller. Nevertheless, even in such a case, it is arguable that if the parties never intended that the entire proceeds of sale (including the buyer's profit)[779] could be claimed by the seller, but that the true intention was that the proceeds were to be appropriated by the buyer to satisfy pro tanto and to be security for his debt to the seller this is inconsistent with an intention that the buyer sells as agent for the seller.[780] If the intention was that a charge over the proceeds would thus be created[781] by the buyer company,[782] it would fall within s.860(7) of the Companies Act 2006.[783] On the other hand, in *Associated Alloys Pty Ltd v CAN001 452 106 Pty Ltd (In Liquidation)*[784] the High Court of Australia upheld[785] a clause which required the buyer company to hold on trust for the seller such part of the proceeds of sale as were equal to the amount owing by the buyer at the time of receipt of the proceeds. The High Court held that there was an implied term in the contract that, upon receipt of the relevant proceeds, the obligation in debt of the buyer to the seller was discharged. The clause did not therefore, create any "charge" over the proceeds to secure a debt: it was simply an agreement to constitute a trust of after-acquired property, which did not require registration.

Claims against sub-purchasers   A seller may be able to claim title to goods in **44-180** the possession of a sub-purchaser if the sale and sub-sale are both made subject to a retention of title provision.[786] Otherwise title of bona fide purchasers from the buyer of goods subject to a "Romalpa" clause is not ordinarily[787] affected by the

---

[779] For this reason, some clauses provide for the buyer to hold as trustee for the seller only such part of the proceeds as represent or are equivalent to the price at which the goods resold were invoiced to the buyer. The trust of such a part would appear to be effective even though not separated. See *Hunter v Moss* [1994] 1 W.L.R. 452; *Associated Alloys Pty Ltd v CAN001 452 106 Pty Ltd (In Liquidation)*, below.

[780] cf. *Caterpillar (NI) Ltd (formerly FG Wilson (Engineering) Ltd) v John Holt & Co (Liverpool) Ltd* [2013] EWCA Civ 1232, [2014] 1 All E.R. (Comm) 393 where the majority of the Court of Appeal found that on the terms of the particular clause there was a duty to account for the whole proceeds of sale which was consistent with an agency relationship (per Patten L.J. at [60] and Floyd L.J. (at [76]). For a critical analysis of this decision see Gullifer [2014] L.M.C.L.Q. 564.

[781] *Borden (UK) Ltd v Scottish Timber Products Ltd* [1981] Ch. 25, 45; *Re Bond Worth Ltd* [1980] Ch. 228, 248, 259; *Tatung (UK) Ltd v Galex Telesure Ltd* [1989] 5 B.C.C. 325; *Re Weldtech Equipment Ltd* [1991] B.C.C. 16; *Compaq Computer Ltd v Abercorn Group Ltd* [1991] B.C.C. 484; *Modelboard Ltd v OuterBox Ltd* [1993] B.C.L.C. 623.

[782] cf. *Aluminium Industrie Vaassen BV v Romalpa Aluminium Ltd* [1976] 1 W.L.R. 676, 682–683 (at first instance); *Peerless Carpets Ltd v Moorhouse Carpet Market Ltd* (1992) 4 N.Z.B.L.C. 102, 747.

[783] See n.733, above. Such an argument would be even stronger in the case of a trust in respect of the proceeds of sale of products manufactured from the goods supplied: see *Benjamin's Sale of Goods*, 10th edn (2017), para.5-156; and see above, para.44-178.

[784] (2000) A.L.J.R. 862 (Kirby J. dissenting).

[785] But the seller's claim failed, on the facts, since it could not sufficiently relate the proceeds of sale to the goods that it had supplied.

[786] *W Hanson (Harrow) v Rapid Civil and Engineering and Usborne Developments* (1987) 38 B.L.R. 106; *Re Highway Foods International Ltd* [1995] B.C.L.C. 209. cf. *P4 Ltd v Unite Integrated Solutions Plc* [2006] Build. L.R. 150.

[787] But see *Re Interview Ltd* [1975] I.R. 182; *Dawber Williamson Roofing Ltd v Humberside CC* (1979) 14 Build. L.R. 70; *Feuer Leather Corp v Frank Johnstone & Sons* [1981] Com. L.R. 251; *W Hanson (Harrow) v Rapid Civil Engineering and Usborne Developments* (1987) 38 B.L.R. 106; *Forsyth International (UK) Ltd v Silver Shipping Co Ltd* [1993] 2 Lloyd's Rep. 268.

existence of the clause.[788] However, "Romalpa" clauses sometimes contain a provision (which may take various forms) whereby any claim to the purchase price of the goods resold by the buyer to sub-purchasers is to vest in[789] or to be transferred to the seller. Again, however, it is arguable that the parties never intended that the entire resale price should pass to the seller, but that the right is granted as security and so creates a charge on the book debts of the buyer company.[790] In the *Romalpa* case[791] itself, a provision that the buyer company was, if the seller so required, to "hand over" to the seller claims that it had against sub-purchasers was held not to be a present equitable assignment of those claims. But if the clause is construed as an agreement by the buyer company to assign future choses in action, namely, future debts owed by sub-purchasers to the buyer up to the amount of outstanding indebtedness of the buyer to the seller, then (depending on its wording) it may likewise be held to be a charge created by the buyer company on its book debts.[792] In the event that it is to be construed as an absolute assignment,[793] vesting the buyer's claim to the sub-sale price unconditionally in the seller, then it will not create a charge, but problems of priority[794] may arise as between the seller and other assignees, e.g. where the buyer has factored the debts.[795]

44-181   **Building contracts**[796]   Goods may be supplied by a sub-contractor to the main contractor subject to a "Romalpa" clause, and delivered to the building site. Before the goods are affixed to the building,[797] the main contractor becomes insolvent and the sub-contractor seeks to recover the unfixed goods from the employer. In some cases the sub-contractor's claim may fail because the main contractor is a "buyer in possession" and can therefore pass a good title to the employer under s.25 of the 1979 Act.[798] But in other cases it will succeed, either because the contract between the sub-contractor and the main contractor is not one of sale but for work and materials,[799] or because there is no sufficient "sale, pledge or other disposition of the goods" by the main contractor to the employer to enable the latter to rely on

---

[788] *Aluminium Industrie Vaassen BV v Romalpa Aluminium Ltd* [1976] 1 W.L.R. 676, 681; *Re Peachdart Ltd* [1984] Ch. 131, 141; *Hendy Lennox (Industrial Engines) Ltd v Grahame Puttick Ltd* [1984] 1 W.L.R. 485, 495; *Archivent Sales and Developments Ltd v Strathclyde RC* (1984) 27 B.L.R. 98; *Four Point Garage Ltd v Carter* [1985] 3 All E.R. 12; *Fairfax Gerrard Holdings Ltd v Capital Bank Plc* [2007] EWCA Civ 1226, [2008] 1 Lloyd's Rep. 297 at [16].

[789] See Goode [1964] J.B.L. 523, 525.

[790] Companies Act 2006 s.860(7)(f); see n.733, above. Alternatively see *Re Bond Worth Ltd* [1980] Ch. 228 (floating charge).

[791] [1976] 1 W.L.R. 676, 688, 692.

[792] *E Pfeiffer Weinkellerei-Weineinkauf GmbH & Co v Arbuthnot Factors Ltd* [1988] 1 W.L.R. 150; *Re Weldtech Equipment Ltd* [1991] B.C.C. 16; *Compaq Computer Ltd v Abercorn Group Ltd* [1991] B.C.C. 484.

[793] *Hughes v Pump House Hotel Co* [1902] 2 K.B. 190.

[794] See Vol.I, para.19-069.

[795] *E Pfeiffer Weinkellerei-Weineinkauf GmbH & Co v Arbuthnot Factors Ltd* [1988] 1 W.L.R. 150. See also *Re Interview Ltd* [1975] I.R. 182; *Re Peachdart Ltd* [1984] Ch. 131 at 143; *Benjamin's Sale of Goods*, 10th edn (2017), para.5-163.

[796] See Newman (1999) 10 *Construction Law* 25.

[797] cf. *Aircool Installations v British Telecommunications* [1995] C.L.Y. 821, Cty Ct (goods affixed).

[798] *Archivent Sales and Developments Ltd v Strathclyde RC* (1984) 27 B.L.R. 98; see below, para.44-220.

[799] *Dawber Williamson Roofing Ltd v Humberside CC* (1979) 14 Build. L.R. 70; see below, para.44-222.

s.25,[800] or because the employer had notice of the terms of the sub-contract including the "Romalpa" clause.[801]

Fixtures   Where goods sold subject to "Romalpa" clause are so attached to land   **44-182**
as to become fixtures, the seller's retention of title to the goods will normally[802] be
ineffective, for example, against a mortgagee[803] or landlord[804] of the buyer. The
goods, having become part of the realty, are irrecoverable by the seller.[805]

Non-corporate buyers   Where the buyer is not a company, a "Romalpa" clause   **44-183**
cannot be attacked on the ground that it creates a charge which requires to be
registered under s.860 of the Companies Act 2006,[806] since that provision applies
only to companies. But problems relating to the scope and interpretation of the
clause will nevertheless remain. The "reputed ownership" provision of the
Bankruptcy Act 1914 has now been repealed.[807] However, there are certain further
statutes that have to be taken into account where the buyer is unincorporated. First
there are the Bills of Sales Acts 1878 and 1882.[808] A mere reservation of title clause
will not be affected by these Acts,[809] although an extension of the clause to products
manufactured with the goods supplied may come within their scope.[810] Secondly,
a general assignment by the buyer to the seller of debts due to the buyer from sub-
purchasers of the goods may be invalidated by s.344 of the Insolvency Act 1986[811]
unless the assignment has been registered[812] under the Bills of Sale Act 1878.

Disadvantages of "Romalpa" clauses   The presence of a "Romalpa" clause takes   **44-184**
away entitlement to bad debt relief in respect of value added tax[813] and, by reason
of the fact that the property in the goods has not passed to the buyer, unless it is
expressly stipulated to the contrary, the goods will continue to be at the seller's risk
in the hands of the buyer.[814] It had been held[815] that an action for the price would
not be available unless either s.49(1) or s.49(2) were satisfied and that accordingly
the presence of a "Romalpa" clause, which prevented property from passing to the

---

[800] *W. Hanson (Harrow) Ltd v Rapid Civil Engineering Ltd* (1987) 38 B.L.R. 106; see below, para.44-229.
[801] *W. Hanson (Harrow) Ltd v Rapid Civil Engineering Ltd* (1987) 38 B.L.R. 106; see below, para.44-231.
[802] But see above, para.39-419 (goods let on hire-purchase). The same principles apply.
[803] *Trust Bank Central Ltd v Southdown Properties Ltd* [1991] 1 N.Z. Conv. C. 190, 870. But see Guest and Lever (1963) 27 Conv.N.S. 30, and see above, para.39-419.
[804] See above, para.39-419.
[805] *Melluish v BMI (No.3) Ltd* [1996] A.C. 454; *Aircool Installations v British Telecommunications* [1995] C.L.Y. 821, Cty Ct; Bennett and Davis (1994) 110 L.Q.R. 448.
[806] See n.733 above.
[807] s.38(c). See s.235 and Sch.10 Pts III and IV, of the Insolvency Act 1985. The Insolvency Act 1986 contains no "reputed ownership" provision.
[808] Bills of Sale Act 1878; Bills of Sale Act (Amendment) Act 1882.
[809] *McEntire v Crossley Brothers Ltd* [1895] A.C. 457, 462. See above, para.44-173.
[810] Bills of Sale Act 1878 s.3. The clause must be contained in a document.
[811] See Vol.I, para.19-063.
[812] s.344(4).
[813] Value Added Tax Act 1994 s.36(4)(b). But Customs and Excise have conceded entitlement to such relief if title has passed to the insolvent debtor by the time relief is claimed: see C.C.A.B. TR 388 (May 7, 1980); *VAT Leaflet* 700/18/86 (April 1, 1986). See also s.11 of the Finance Act 1990.
[814] See below, para.44-189. cf. (consumer sales) para.38-527.
[815] *Caterpillar (NI) Ltd (formerly FG Wilson (Engineering) Ltd) v John Holt & Co (Liverpool) Ltd* [2013] EWCA Civ 1232, [2014] 1 All E.R. (Comm) 393 at [60], [61] and [75]–[76].

buyer, would ordinarily mean that the seller could not maintain an action for the price. In *PST Energy 7 Shipping LLC v OW Bunker Malta Ltd*[816] the Supreme Court held that the bunker supply contract fell outside the Sale of Goods Act and accordingly it was not necessary to decide whether an action for the price under the Act would have been maintainable in the circumstances. However, the Supreme Court indicated, obiter, that the price would have been recoverable on the date stated by virtue of the contract's express terms providing the goods had been delivered, indicating that they would have overruled the decision of the Court of Appeal in *Caterpillar* on this point.[817]

44-185   A careful assessment of the advantages and disadvantages of such a clause should therefore be made, in particular since the practical difficulties of identifying the goods sold and not paid for—even if still in the possession of the buyer, and of tracing into a mixed fund in the hands of a liquidator or receiver (possibly in competition with other suppliers under "Romalpa" clauses), may be considerable.

44-186   **Administration**[818]   The ability of the seller to enforce a "Romalpa" clause, or indeed any other agreement for the sale of goods to a company by which the right of disposal is reserved until payment of the price,[819] will be affected once an administration application has been made[820] or during the period in which a company is in administration.[821] No step may be taken to repossess the goods except with the consent of the administrator or permission of the court.[822] Moreover, the administrator is empowered, if he obtains an order of the court, to overreach the rights of the seller by disposing of the goods as if ownership were vested in the company[823] and applying the net proceeds of the disposal towards the sums payable under the agreement.[824]

44-187   **Voluntary arrangements**   A similar temporary moratorium is available to a company against repossession of the goods by the seller where the directors propose a voluntary arrangement under Pt I of the Insolvency Act 1986.[825] This facility is, however, restricted to small companies, and certain companies are excluded.[826]

44-188   **Receivership**   Where goods are supplied on credit to a company subject to a retention of title clause, and the company goes into receivership, the court will not grant an injunction to restrain the receivers from dealing with the goods if they give an undertaking to pay for such of the goods as are used or sold.[827] But the power of a

---

[816] [2016] UKSC 23.
[817] See further below, para.44-396.
[818] See Sch.B1 to the Insolvency Act 1986, substituted by s.248 of and Sch.16 to the Enterprise Act 2002.
[819] i.e. a "retention of title agreement", as defined in s.251 of the Insolvency Act 1986, which is included in the definition of "hire purchase" agreement in Sch.B1 para.111(1).
[820] Insolvency Act 1986 Sch.B1 para.44.
[821] Insolvency Act 1986 Sch.B1 para.43.
[822] Insolvency Act 1986 Sch.B1 paras 43, 44.
[823] Insolvency Act 1986 Sch.B1 para.72.
[824] Insolvency Act 1986 Sch.B1 para.72(3).
[825] Insolvency Act 1986 s.1A and Sch.A1, inserted by the Insolvency Act 2000 s.1.
[826] i.e. banks, insurance companies and companies involved in the performance of market contracts: Insolvency Act 1986 Sch.A1 para.2.
[827] *Lipe Ltd v Leyland DAF Ltd* [1993] B.C.C. 385.

floating charge holder to appoint a receiver has been largely taken away by s.72A of the Insolvency Act 1986.[828]

(b) When the Risk Passes

Passing of the risk   By s.20(1)[829]:　　　　　　　　　　　　　　　　　　　　　**44-189**

"Unless otherwise agreed, the goods remain at the seller's risk until the property in them is transferred to the buyer, but when the property in them is transferred to the buyer, the goods are at the buyer's risk whether delivery has been made or not."[830]

Thus the presumption is that the risk and the property pass together. This means that as a general rule the risk of loss, damage or deterioration falls on the owner of the goods. But the property and the risk may be separated by agreement[831] or by usage.[832] Where the buyer deals as consumer this section does not apply and under the Consumer Rights Act 2015, risk passes only on delivery of the goods.[833]

Goods to which risk relates   The goods must be sufficiently identifiable as those **44-190** to which the risk relates. But in some cases, especially of overseas sales, the risk in goods not yet separated from bulk may pass to the buyer even though the property in the goods is still in the seller.[834] And in *Sterns Ltd v Vickers Ltd*[835] the buyers purchased 120,000 gallons of spirit, part of a larger quantity contained in a 200,000-gallon tank belonging to the storage company. They accepted a delivery warrant whereby the company undertook to deliver to them the quantity which had been sold. They indorsed the warrant to a sub-purchaser, who left the spirit in storage and paid the storage company rent. The bulk of the spirit deteriorated in quality before delivery took place, and it was held that upon acceptance of the delivery warrant the risk passed to the buyers. Bankes L.J. left open the question whether the property had passed. Scrutton L.J. held that it had not because there had been no appropriation; but he regarded the acceptance of the delivery warrant as crucial in that it transferred to the buyers an undivided interest in the bulk which carried with it the risk of loss from deterioration.[836] Under s.20A of the Act[837] where there

---

[828]　Inserted by s.250 of the Enterprise Act 2002.

[829]　This section does not apply to consumer contracts for the sale of goods which fall within Ch.2 of Pt 1 of the Consumer Rights Act 2015. In consumer contracts for the sale of goods the 2015 Act provides special rules for the passing of risk, see above para.38-527. Special rules concerning the passing of risk were required by the Consumer Rights Directive 2011. These rules were initially implemented in reg.43 of the Consumer Contracts (Information, Cancellation and Additional Charges) Regulations 2013. These rules are now repeated in the Consumer Rights Act 2015. See above, para.38-527.

[830]　*Healy v Howlett & Sons* [1917] 1 K.B. 337; *Pignataro v Gilroy* [1919] 1 K.B. 459; *Underwood Ltd v Burgh Castle Brick and Cement Syndicate* [1922] 1 K.B. 343; *Wardars (Export and Import) Co Ltd v W Norwood & Sons Ltd* [1968] 2 Q.B. 663; *Stora Enso Oyj v Port of Dundee* [2006] 1 C.L.C. 453.

[831]　*Castle v Playford* (1872) L.R. 7 Ex. 98, *Martineau v Kitching* (1872) L.R. 7 Q.B. 436; *Anderson v Morice* (1876) 1 App. Cas. 713; *Horn v Minister of Food*, 65 T.L.R. 1906.

[832]　*Bevington v Dale* (1902) 7 Com. Cas. 112.

[833]　See above, para.38-527.

[834]　*Stock v Inglis* (1884) 12 Q.B.D. 564; affirmed sub nom. *Inglis v Stock* (1885) 10 App. Cas. 263. See *Benjamin's Sale of Goods*, 10th edn (2017), paras 18-348, 19-111, 20-095, 21-003, 21-011, 21-021, 21-044, 21-105.

[835]　[1923] 1 K.B. 78.

[836]　At 84, 95. But contrast also *Comptoir d'Achat v Luis de Ridder* [1949] A.C. 293, 312, 319 (emphasis-

is a contract for the sale of a specified quantity of ascertained goods forming part of an identified bulk and the buyer has paid the price for some or all of the goods, property in an undivided share in the bulk will be transferred to the buyer and he will become an owner in common of the bulk. In such a case, it is probable that risk passes to the buyer at the same time as the undivided share[838] although it is by no means clear from ss.20, 20A and 20B that this is the result.[839]

44-191 **Overseas trade** The fact that the goods are to be shipped under a CIF or FOB or similar contract is a strong indication that the property and the risk may pass at separate times.[840] Thus in a CIF contract the risk is transferred on shipment or as from shipment, but the presumption is that the property does not pass until the shipping documents are handed over. In a FOB contract, on the other hand, the property and the risk may pass together on shipment. But if the seller reserves the right of disposal of the goods, the risk passes on shipment or as from shipment, but the property remains with the seller until the buyer effects payment or secures the price against tender of the bill of lading; and, further, if the goods are unascertained, the risk again passes on shipment but the property in the goods themselves[841] does not pass until they become ascertained and are unconditionally appropriated.[842]

44-192 **Qualifications** The main rule stated in s.20(1) does not apply where the loss is caused by the fault of either party. It is therefore qualified as follows:

> "(2)   Where delivery has been delayed through the fault[843] of either buyer or seller the goods are at the risk of the party at fault as regards any loss which might not have occurred but for such fault.[844]
>
> (3)   Nothing in this section affects the duties or liabilities of either seller or buyer as a bailee ... of the goods of the other party."

It must be noted that subs.(2), in speaking of delivery, deals with the transfer of possession, not of property; also that the party in fault does not bear the entire risk, but only the risk of loss "which might not have occurred but for such fault". Subsection (3) means that neither subs.(1) nor subs.(2) alters the common law rule that the party in possession of another person's goods remains liable for them qua bailee for negligence.[845]

---

ing the restricted application of the decision in *Sterns Ltd v Vickers Ltd* [1923] 1 K.B. 78). See *Benjamin's Sale of Goods*, 10th edn (2017), paras 6-005, 18-348.

[837] See above, para.44-160.

[838] *Benjamin's Sale of Goods*, 10th edn (2017), at paras 6-006—6-008. The definition of "goods" in s.61(1), see above, para.44-015, includes an undivided share in goods.

[839] In particular, it is arguable that s.20B(3)(c) means that the passing of property under s.20A is to be disregarded in determining risk: *Benjamin's Sale of Goods*, 10th edn (2017), at para.6-006.

[840] See *Benjamin's Sale of Goods*, 10th edn (2017), at paras 6-005, 18-348.

[841] As opposed to property in an undivided share under s.20A; see above, para.44-160.

[842] *Inglis v Stock* (1885) 10 App. Cas. 263.

[843] Defined, s.61(1), see above, para.44-015.

[844] *Demby Hamilton & Co Ltd v Barden* [1949] 1 All E.R. 435. See *Gatoil International Inc v Tradax Petroleum Ltd* [1985] 1 Lloyd's Rep. 350, 351, 362.

[845] See *Benjamin's Sale of Goods*, 10th edn (2017), paras 6-021—6-026. For the duties and liabilities of a bailee, see above, Ch.33.

(c)   Transfer of Title

(i)   Sale by Person not the Owner

Nemo dat quod non habet[846]   The first part of s.21(1) states the general rule that   **44-193**
"no one can transfer a better title than he himself possesses".[847] It provides that:

"Subject to this Act,[848] where goods are sold by a person who is not their owner and who
does not sell them under the authority or with the consent of the owner, the buyer acquires
no better title to the goods than the seller had."

An owner of goods who has an immediate right to possession[849] of them may either
retake them without action[850] or bring an action for delivery up of the goods[851] or
for damages.[852] Further, any person who has wrongfully converted the goods either
to his own use or to the use of another will be liable to an action for wrongful
interference at the suit of the owner provided that, at the time of the conversion, the
owner had a right to immediate possession of the goods.[853] The liability of a person
who has converted goods is a strict liability and is not dependent upon proof of
knowledge or fault on his part.[854]

An allowance may be made for the extent to which, at the time as at which the   **44-194**
goods fall to be valued in assessing the damages recoverable, the value of the goods
is attributable to an improvement effected by the defendant or by a person from
whom the defendant has derived (whether immediately or not) his supposed "title"
to the goods.[855]

Exceptions   Commercial convenience has, however, called for the recognition of   **44-195**
certain exceptions to the general rule.

---

[846] On this see generally the *Twelfth Report of the Law Reform Committee on the Transfer of Title to Chattels*, Cmnd.2958 (1966).

[847] *Whistler v Forster* (1863) 14 C.B.(N.S.) 248, 257.

[848] ss.21, 23–25, see below.

[849] *Iran v Barakat Galleries Ltd* [2007] EWCA Civ 1374. cf. *North West Securities v Alexander Breckon* [1981] R.T.R. 518 (action by non-owner who had entered into binding contract to purchase).

[850] See *Clerk & Lindsell on Torts*, 22nd edn (2017), para.30-14. On improvements, see Torts (Interference with Goods) Act 1977 ss.3(7), 6(1), (2); *Greenwood v Bennett* [1973] 1 Q.B. 195; *Thomas v Robinson* [1977] 1 N.Z.L.R. 385.

[851] Torts (Interference with Goods) Act 1977 s.3(2)(a), (b). The remedy of specific delivery is, however, discretionary: see s.3(3)(b) of the 1977 Act.

[852] 1977 Act s.3(2)(c).

[853] *Union Transport Finance Ltd v British Car Auctions Ltd* [1978] 2 All E.R. 385; *RH Willis & Son v British Car Auctions Ltd* [1978] 1 W.L.R. 438; *J Sargent (Garages) Ltd v Motor Auctions (West Bromwich) Ltd* [1977] R.T.R. 121; *Chubb Cash Ltd v John Crilley & Son* [1983] 1 W.L.R. 599; *Hillesden Securities Ltd v Ryjack Ltd* [1983] 1 W.L.R. 959. For the measure of damages in conversion, see *Kuwait Airways Corp v Iraqi Airways Co (Nos 4 and 5)* [2002] UKHL 19, [2002] 2 A.C. 883. But see above, para.39-416 (measure of damages where goods let under hire-purchase agreement) and *Uzinterimpex JSC v Standard Bank Plc* [2008] EWCA Civ 819, [2008] 2 Lloyd's Rep. 456 (duty to mitigate). Contrast *OBG v Allan* [2007] UKHL 21, [2008] I A.C. 1 (conversion does not extend to choses in action).

[854] *Hollins v Fowler* (1875) L.R. 7 H.L. 757.

[855] Torts (Interference with Goods) Act 1977 s.6; *Reid v Fairbanks* (1853) 13 C.B. 692, 797; *Munro v Willmott* [1949] 1 K.B. 295. See also s.3(7) of the 1977 Act (allowance to be made on order for delivery up of the goods).

(aa) Estoppel[856]

44-196 **Estoppel** By s.21(1) the owner of the goods may by his conduct be "precluded" from denying the seller's authority to sell. It would appear that this provision was intended to give statutory recognition to a particular principle of estoppel in English law in relation to the sale of goods and that the work "precluded" was used to render the principle intelligible in Scots law where the specific term "estoppel" is unknown.[857] Briefly, in order to raise such an estoppel it must be shown either that there was a representation by the owner that the seller was entitled to sell the goods or that the owner was negligent in allowing the seller to appear to be entitled to sell the goods. Each of these categories, that is estoppel by representation and estoppel by negligence, are relatively narrow in scope. Their extent is discussed below.

44-197 **Estoppel by representation** There must have been a voluntary[858] representation by the owner that the seller was entitled to sell the goods. It is clear that the mere parting with possession of goods, or of documents of title to goods, does not without more raise an estoppel.[859] The owner must have so acted as to mislead the buyer into the belief that the seller was entitled to sell the goods. Thus in *Central Newbury Car Auctions Ltd v Unity Finance Ltd*[860] the claimants, owners of a second-hand car, allowed X, who wished to buy it, to take away the car and the registration book before a finance company had accepted their proposal to buy the car and let it to X on hire-purchase terms; X sold the car to a garage, who sold it to the defendants; it was held that the defence of estoppel failed because a motor-car registration book was not proof of ownership, and the claimants had not represented X to be the owner of the car, or to have their authority to sell the car, by allowing him to take possession of it.

44-198 The representation that the seller has a right to sell the goods must be made by the owner or his agent.[861] He will not be estopped by a representation of ownership made by the seller himself,[862] unless he authorised the representation or consented to its being made.[863] The representation must also be clear and unambiguous,[864] and be addressed to the particular buyer who alleges that he relied on it, or

---

[856] On this generally see Pickering (1939) 55 L.Q.R. 400; *Benjamin's Sale of Goods*, 10th edn (2017), para.7-008.

[857] See above, para.31-076.

[858] *Debs v Sibec Developments Ltd* [1990] R.T.R. 91.

[859] *Cole v North Western Bank* (1875) L.R. 10 C.P. 354, 363; *Johnson v Crédit Lyonnais Co* (1877) 3 C.P.D. 32, 36; *Farquharson Bros & Co v King & Co* [1902] A.C. 325, 330; *Mercantile Bank of India Ltd v Central Bank of India Ltd* [1938] A.C. 287; *Jerome v Bentley & Co* [1952] 2 All E.R. 114, 118; *Central Newbury Car Auctions Ltd v Unity Finance Ltd* [1957] 1 Q.B. 371, 394, 396; *Moorgate Mercantile Co Ltd v Twitchings* [1977] A.C. 890; *Beverley Acceptances Ltd v Oakley* [1982] R.T.R. 417.

[860] [1957] 1 Q.B. 371.

[861] *Central Newbury Car Auctions Ltd v Unity Finance Ltd*, above, *J Sargent (Garages) Ltd v Motor Auctions (West Bromwich) Ltd* [1977] R.T.R. 121.

[862] *Farquharson Bros & Co v King & Co* [1902] A.C. 325; *Weiner v Gill* [1905] 2 K.B. 172; affirmed at 719.

[863] *Pickard v Sears* (1837) 6 A. & E. 469; *Rimmer v Webster* [1902] 2 Ch. 163, 173; *Abigail v Lapin* [1934] A.C. 491; *Eastern Distributors Ltd v Goldring* [1957] 2 Q.B. 600.

[864] *Moorgate Mercantile Co Ltd v Twitchings* [1977] A.C. 890.

be made under such circumstances of publicity as to justify the inference that the buyer knew of and relied on it.[865]

It is important to appreciate that the broad principle stated in *Lickbarrow v Mason*[866] by Ashhurst J. that "wherever one of two innocent persons must suffer by the acts of a third, he who has enabled such third person to occasion the loss must sustain it" cannot be regarded as a reliable guide to the solution of problems in this area. This dictum has been heavily criticised,[867] and although it was relied on in *Commonwealth Trust v Akotey*,[868] that case cannot be regarded as good law in view of the decision in *Mercantile Bank of India Ltd v Central Bank of India Ltd*.[869] There are very few reported cases in which a plea of estoppel by representation has in fact succeeded. But in *Henderson v Williams*[870] an estoppel arose where the owner instructed that goods in the possession of a warehouseman be transferred to the order of another, who sold them as owner. And in *Eastern Distributors Ltd v Goldring*[871] it was held that there was an estoppel since, in the words of Devlin J., the owner of a van had armed a dealer "with documents which enabled him to represent to the plaintiffs [a finance company] that he was the owner of the van and had the right to sell it".

44-199

Estoppel by negligent conduct   In order to establish estoppel by negligence it is necessary for the buyer to show, first, the existence of a duty of care owed to him by the owner; secondly, a breach of that duty by negligence on the part of the owner; thirdly, that this negligence was proximate or real cause of the buyer entering into the transaction with the seller which occasioned the loss.[872] It is the first of these requirements that gives rise to the greatest difficulty. Mere carelessness in relation to the goods, or to documents of title to goods, such as failing to take proper precautions to prevent them from being stolen[873] or to report their theft to the police,[874] a

44-200

---

[865] *Dickinson v Valpy* (1829) 10 B. & C. 128, 140; *Farquharson Bros v King & Co* [1902] A.C. 325 at 341.

[866] (1787) 2 T.R. 63, 70.

[867] See *Farquharson Bros v King & Co*, above, at 342; *London Joint Stock Bank v MacMillan* [1918] A.C. 777, 836; *Jones Ltd v Waring & Gillow Ltd* [1926] A.C. 670, 693; *Central Newbury Car Auctions Ltd v Unity Finance Ltd* [1957] 1 Q.B. 371 at 389, 396.

[868] [1926] A.C. 72.

[869] [1938] A.C. 287.

[870] [1895] 1 Q.B. 521 (in this case, the warehouseman also acknowledged to the buyer that he held the goods to the buyer's order subsequent to the contract of sale). See also *Pickering v Busk* (1812) 5 East 38 (agency); *Colonial Bank v Cady* (1890) 15 App. Cas. 267, 278, 283; *Weiner v Gill* [1906] 2 K.B. 574, 582; *Fry v Smellie* [1912] 3 K.B. 282; *Fuller v Glyn, Mills Currie & Co* [1914] 2 K.B. 168 (documents of title); *Chatfields-Martin Walter Ltd v Lombard North Central Plc* [2014] EWHC 1222 (QB) (representation via the Hire Purchase Register that the owner had no legitimate interest in a vehicle).

[871] [1957] 2 Q.B. 600, 614. See also *Spencer v North Country Finance Co Ltd* [1963] C.L.Y. 212, CA; *Stoneleigh Finance Ltd v Phillips* [1965] 2 Q.B. 537; *Snook v London and West Riding Investments Ltd* [1967] 2 Q.B. 786.

[872] *Johnson v Crédit Lyonnais Co* (1877) 3 C.P.D. 32, 42; *Farquharson Bros & Co v King & Co* [1902] A.C. 325, 335–336; *Mercantile Bank of India Ltd v Central Bank of India Ltd* [1938] A.C. 287, 299; *Central Newbury Car Auctions v Unity Finance Ltd* [1957] 1 Q.B. 371, 381, 389, 395; *Mercantile Credit Co Ltd v Hamblin* [1965] 2 Q.B. 242, 271; *Moorgate Mercantile Co Ltd v Twitchings* [1977] A.C. 890, 903, 906, 912, 920, 921, 924, 927, 928; *Beverley Acceptances Ltd v Oakley* [1982] R.T.R. 434, 439.

[873] *Farquharson Bros & Co v King & Co*, above, at 335; *Central Newbury Car Auctions v Unity Finance Ltd* [1957] 1 Q.B. 371, 381, 394.

[874] *Debs v Sibec Developments Ltd* [1990] R.T.R. 91.

culpable credulity in entrusting them to another,[875] or a careless failure to register in a central register the owner's interest in a vehicle let on hire-purchase[876] will be insufficient. The situation or relationship must be such as to bring into being a duty of care, and on this point decided cases give no firm guidance. The fact that the owner could reasonably foresee that his carelessness would lead the buyer to believe that the seller was the owner of the goods, or that the owner had no interest in the goods, does not in itself impose such a duty.[877] But in *Mercantile Credit Co Ltd v Hamblin*,[878] A delivered possession of a car to B and at the same time delivered to B hire-purchase documents signed in blank. A contemplated and contingently intended that the documents should be used to obtain a loan from any person who might be prepared to advance money on the security of the vehicle. B fraudulently completed the documents in a manner not authorised by A and then represented to C that he (B) had a good title to the car. C purchased the car in reliance on the representation. The Court of Appeal held that A owed to C a duty of care,[879] but further held on the facts that A had not been negligent. The Court of Appeal also took the view that the effective cause of C's loss was the fraud of B, and not any negligence on the part of A. In most cases, however, where a duty of care and breach of that duty has been shown to exist, the negligence of the owner should be regarded as an effective cause of the buyer's loss, albeit concurrent with the fraud of the seller.[880]

44-201 **Non est factum** Where the owner of goods has signed a document which transfers title to the goods to another, he will not be permitted—vis-à-vis an innocent purchaser of the goods from that other—to disown his signature simply by asserting that he did not understand that which he signed.[881] But where, by reason of fraud, he is induced to sign a document which purports to be a transaction essentially different in substance or in kind from the transaction intended, he may be able to rely on the defence of non est factum,[882] but only if he proves that he exercised reasonable care.[883]

---

[875] *Johnson v Crédit Lyonnais Co* (1877) 3 C.P.D. 32; *Farquharson Bros & Co v King & Co* [1902] A.C. 325; *Central Newbury Car Auctions v Unity Finance Ltd* [1957] 1 Q.B. 371; *Beverley Acceptances Ltd v Oakley* [1982] R.T.R. 434.

[876] *Moorgate Mercantile Co Ltd v Twitchings* [1977] A.C. 890: See also *Cadogan Finance Ltd v Lavery and Fox* [1982] Com. L.R. 248 (aircraft) and *Industrial and Corporate Finance Ltd v Wyder Group* (2008) 152 S.J.L.B. 31 (motorcycle). However, if the owner of a vehicle changes the register to represent that it no longer has an interest it will be estopped from going back on that representation (*Chatfields-Martin Walter Ltd v Lombard North Central Plc* [2014] EWHC 1222 (QB)).

[877] *Moorgate Mercantile Co Ltd v Twitchings* [1977] A.C. 890: See also *Cadogan Finance Ltd v Lavery and Fox* [1982] Com. L.R. 248 (aircraft).

[878] [1965] 2 Q.B. 242. See also *British Railway Traffic and Electric Co Ltd v Roper* (1939) 162 L.T. 217; *General and Finance Facilities Ltd v Hughes* (1966) 110 S.J. 847; *United Dominions Trust Ltd v Western* [1976] Q.B. 513; *Allcock* (1982) 45 M.L.R. 18.

[879] [1965] 2 Q.B. 242, 275, 275, 278.

[880] *United Dominions Trust Ltd v Western* [1976] Q.B. 513; *Moorgate Mercantile Co Ltd v Twitchings* [1977] A.C. 890 at 912, 928. cf. at 921; *Gator Shipping Corp v Trans-Atlantic Oil Ltd* [1978] 2 Lloyd's Rep. 357, 378; *Cadogan Finance Ltd v Lavery and Fox* [1982] Com. L.R. 248.

[881] *Blay v Pollard & Morris* [1930] 1 K.B. 628; *Muskham Finance Ltd v Howard* [1963] 1 Q.B. 904, 914.

[882] See Vol.I, paras 1-146 et seq.

[883] *Mercantile Credit Co Ltd v Hamblin* [1965] 2 Q.B. 242; *Saunders v Anglia Building Society* [1971] A.C. 1004, 1016, 1019, 1027, 1028.

Estoppel by judgment   Where, in an action between two parties brought to determine the ownership of goods, title to the goods is established by judgment, the unsuccessful party will be estopped *per rem judicatam* from claiming the goods and that estoppel will bind also his privies, i.e. those claiming title from or through him, but only if the title claimed was acquired after (and not before) the date of the judgment.[884]   **44-202**

Nature of title   The effect of an estoppel is to transfer a real title to the buyer.[885]   **44-203**

(bb)   Sales under the Factors Acts

Sales under the Factors Acts   The Factors Act 1889 s.2(1) provides that: **44-204**

"Where a mercantile agent is, with the consent of the owner, in possession of goods or of the documents of title to goods, any sale, pledge, or other disposition of the goods, made by him when acting in the ordinary course of business of a mercantile agent, shall, subject to the provisions of this Act, be as valid as if he were expressly authorised by the owner of the goods to make the same; provided that the person taking under the disposition acts in good faith, and has not at the time of the disposition notice that the person making the disposition has not authority to make the same."

Section 21(2)(a) of the Sale of Goods Act states that: **44-205**

"nothing in this Act affects ... the provisions of the Factors Acts ... enabling the apparent owner of goods to dispose of them as if he were their true owner."

The provision quoted above is therefore an important qualification of the general rule in s.21(1) safeguarding the title of the owner. In order that a bona fide disponee of the goods without notice should be able to claim the benefit of it, five conditions must be satisfied; first, the person disposing of the goods must be a mercantile agent as defined by the Factors Act 1889 s.1(1); secondly, he must be in possession of the goods or of the documents of title to goods; thirdly, he must be in possession with the consent of the owner; fourthly, there must be a sale, pledge or other disposition of the goods by him; fifthly, he must dispose of the goods when acting in the ordinary course of business of a mercantile agent. These conditions are discussed elsewhere.[886]

(cc)   Sales Under Special Powers or Court Orders[887]

Sales under special powers or court orders   Section 21(2)(b) states that: **44-206**

"nothing in this Act affects ... the validity of any contract on sale under any special common law or statutory power of sale or under the order of a court of competent jurisdiction."

---

[884] *Powell v Wiltshire* [2004] EWCA Civ 534, [2005] Q.B. 117.
[885] *Eastern Distributors Ltd v Goldring* [1957] 2 Q.B. 600, 611.
[886] See above, paras 31-079 et seq.
[887] See *Benjamin's Sale of Goods*, 10th edn (2017), paras 7-109—7-114.

(i)   Special common law powers   These may be exercised by pledgees, for a pledge carries with it an implied power of sale.[888] They may also be exercised by agents of necessity.[889]

(ii)   Special statutory powers   There are numerous examples of these. Amongst the most important are those given to pawnees by the Consumer Credit Act 1974[890]; to innkeepers by the Innkeepers Act 1878[891] s.1; to an enforcement officer charged with the enforcement of a warrant of control against goods[892]; to trustees in bankruptcy by the Insolvency Act 1986 s.134 and Sch.5; to liquidators of companies by the Insolvency Act 1986 ss.165–167 and Sch.4; to a criminal court[893]; to the police[894]; to a local authority in respect of abandoned vehicles[895]; to bailees of uncollected goods under the Torts (Interference with Goods) Act 1977 ss.12, 13[896]; to an unpaid seller of goods under the Sale of Goods Act 1979 s.48[897]; to enforcement authorities[898] and to administrators of companies.[899]

(iii)   Court orders   Under the Civil Procedure Rules r.25.1[900] the court has power to order the sale of goods which are of a perishable nature, or which for any other good reason it is desirable to sell quickly.

(dd)   Sale in Market Overt

44-207   Market overt   Section 22(1) of the Sale of Goods Act 1979 gave effect in England[901] to the ancient market overt rule which protected the bona fide purchaser of goods from shops in the City of London and more generally from any open, public and legally constituted market. The rule was replete with artificiality and s.22(1) was repealed as from January 3, 1995, by the Sale of Goods (Amendment) Act 1994.

(ee)   Sale under a Voidable Title

44-208   Sale under a voidable title   By s.23:

> "When the seller of goods has a voidable title to them, but his title has not been avoided at the time of the sale, the buyer acquires a good title to the goods, provided he buys them in good faith and without notice of the seller's defect of title."

---

888   See above, para.33-121.
889   See above, para.31-035; *Bowstead and Reynolds on Agency*, 21st edn (2017), paras 4-001 et seq.
890   ss.120, 121; see above, para.33-144.
891   See above, para.33-118.
892   See para.44-233.
893   Powers of the Criminal Courts (Sentencing) Act 2000 s.143; Proceeds of Crime Act 2002 Pts 2, 5; Police Reform Act 2002 Sch.4 para.10; Serious Organised Crime and Police Act 2005 s.97.
894   Police (Property) Act 1897 ss.2 (as amended), 2A; Police Reform Act 2002 Sch.4 para.10.
895   Road Traffic Regulation Act 1984 s.101 (as amended); Removal and Disposal of Vehicles Regulations 1986 (SI 1986/183) reg.15; *Bulbruin Ltd v Romanyszyn* [1994] R.T.R. 273.
896   See above, para.33-095.
897   See below, para.44-345.
898   Proceeds of Crime Act 2002 s.267 and Sch.7; Serious Crime Act 2007 Sch.8.
899   Insolvency Act 1986 Sch.B1 paras 59, 70–72, inserted by s.248 of and Sch.16 to the Enterprise Act 2002.
900   See also CPR r.61.10, 2D–61 (sale of a ship), County Courts Act 1984 ss.38, 100.
901   The rule did not apply in Scotland or in Wales.

Thus if A, the true owner of goods, is induced by the fraud of B (the seller) to sell goods to B which B resells to C, an innocent buyer, C will acquire a good title to the goods, provided that A had not exercised his right to avoid B's voidable title before the time of the sale by B to C.[902]

However, the transaction between the true owner and the seller must confer upon the seller a voidable title to the goods; so if that transaction is not a sale, but merely an agreement to sell, or a bailment of the goods,[903] then the seller will not have a voidable title to, but merely possession of, the goods, and cannot pass a good title under this section.[904]   **44-209**

Voidable distinguished from void title   A voidable title must be distinguished from a void title. The latter is a nullity, the former may be set aside, but unless and until it has been set aside, is valid.[905] If the fraud practised by the seller is of such a kind as to make the contract between himself and the true owner void for mistake, he will have no title to the goods and can pass none to the bona fide purchaser. A mistake to identity, induced by fraud, may sometimes have this effect.[906] There may be a mistake of identity, induced by fraud, sufficient to render the contract void and thus prevent the property passing, even if the negotiations take place when the parties are in each other's presence.[907]   **44-210**

The meaning of avoidance   The general rule is that in order to avoid the contract the true owner's intention to rescind must be communicated to the seller who has obtained the goods by fraud. But in *Car and Universal Finance Co Ltd v Caldwell*[908] the Court of Appeal held that a contract induced by fraud could be rescinded without communication to the fraudulent party where that party had deliberately absconded but the true owner had nevertheless taken steps to trace him, for instance, by notifying the police and the Automobile Association. This exception to the general rule was justified by Upjohn L.J. as follows[909]: "If one party, by absconding, deliberately puts it out of the power of the other to communicate his intention to rescind which he knows the other will almost certain want to do, I do not think he can any longer insist on his right to be made aware of the election to determine the contract. In these circumstances communication is a useless formality". The effect of this decision has, however, been considerably curtailed by the subsequent decision of the Court of Appeal in *Newtons of Wembley Ltd v Williams*.[910] From this later case it   **44-211**

---

[902] See, e.g. *Lewis v Averay* [1972] 1 Q.B. 198; Vol.I, paras 3-036 et seq., 6-001.

[903] *Truman v Attenborough* (1910) 26 T.L.R. 601. But cf. *Whitehorn Bros v Davidson* [1911] 1 K.B. 463.

[904] But see below, para.44-220 (s.25).

[905] *Whitehorn Bros v Davidson* [1911] 1 K.B. 463 at 481; and see *Robin and Rambler Coaches v Turner* [1947] 2 All E.R. 284.

[906] *Cundy v Lindsay* (1878) 3 App. Cas. 459; Vol.I, para.3-042. The Law Reform Committee, Cmnd.2958 (1966), para.15, recommended that contracts of sale that are void for mistake as to identity should be voidable as against a third party.

[907] *Ingram v Little* [1961] 1 Q.B. 31 (Vol.I, para.3-041). See also *Lake v Simmons* [1927] A.C. 487; *Rigby (Haulage) Ltd v Reliance Marine Insurance Co* [1956] 2 Q.B. 468, where *Lake v Simmons* was distinguished; *Shogun Finance Ltd v Hudson* [2003] UKHL 62, [2004] 1 A.C. 919. But cf. *Lewis v Averay* [1972] 1 Q.B. 198.

[908] [1965] 1 Q.B. 525. See also *Thomas v Heelas*, November 27, 1986 (C.A.T. No.1065); *Colwyn Bay Motorcycles v Poole* [2000] C.L.Y. 4675, Cty Ct. Contrast (Scotland) *Macleod v Kerr*, 1965 S.C. 253; *Young v DS Dalgleish & Son (Hawick)* 1994 S.C.L.R. 696, Sh Ct.

[909] At 555.

[910] [1965] 1 Q.B. 560. See below, paras 44-220, 44-227.

would appear[911] that, notwithstanding that the true owner has avoided the seller's voidable title, the seller may be able to pass a good title under s.25, even if he cannot do so under s.23.

44-212 Sale to buyer Although s.23 applies in its terms only to the situation where the person with a voidable title is a "seller" and the person seeking to establish a good title is a "buyer" of the goods, at common law a similar rule applies to a person with a voidable title who pledges the goods with an innocent pledgee.[912]

44-213 Good faith and notice The burden of proving that the buyer bought with notice[913] or otherwise than in good faith[914] appears to rest upon the true owner.[915]

(ff) Disposition by Seller in Possession[916]

44-214 Seller in possession By s.24 of the Act[917]:

"Where a person having sold goods continues or is in possession of the goods, or of the documents of title[918] to the goods, the delivery or transfer by that person, or by a mercantile agent acting for him,[919] of the goods or documents of title under any sale, pledge, or other disposition thereof, to any person receiving the same in good faith and without notice of the previous sale, has the same effect as if the person making the delivery or transfer were expressly authorised by the owner of the goods to make the same."

The effect of this section is that where a seller in possession wrongfully disposes of the goods, contrary to the terms of the contract, to a person receiving them in good faith,[920] the title acquired by the latter prevails over that of the buyer.

44-215 Possession of seller The seller must be or continue in possession[921] of the goods sold or of the documents of title to the goods. It was at one time regarded as settled law that s.24 would only apply if the seller was in possession or continued in possession as seller, and that the subsection would not apply if, for example, he continued in possession in some other capacity, e.g. as bailee under a separate agreement.[922] But this was not the view taken by the Privy Council in *Pacific Mo-*

---

911 In *Newton's* case, there appears to have been an agreement to sell, and not a sale of the goods. But see below, para.44-221.

912 *Babcock v Lawson* (1880) 5 Q.B.D. 284; *Whitehorn Bros v Davidson* [1911] 1 K.B. 463; *Phillips v Brooks* [1919] 2 K.B. 243.

913 See below, para.44-231.

914 Defined in s.61(3); see above, para.44-016.

915 *Whitehorn Bros v Davidson* [1911] 1 K.B. 463. But see *Thomas v Heelas*, November 27, 1986 (C.A.T. No.1065).

916 See *Benjamin's Sale of Goods*, 10th edn (2017), para.7-055; Merrett [2008] C.L.J. 376.

917 1979 Act s.24 reproduces, with slight modifications, s.8 of the Factors Act 1889.

918 Defined, s.61(1), see above, para.44-016. See also below, para.44-220.

919 As to mercantile agents, see above, para.31-079.

920 See Rutherford and Todd [1979] C.L.J. 346.

921 See s.1(2) of the Factors Act 1889 and *City Fur Manufacturing Co Ltd v Fureenbond (Brokers) London Ltd* [1937] 1 All E.R. 799.

922 *Staffs Motor Guarantee Ltd v British Wagon Co Ltd* [1934] 2 K.B. 305; *Ahrens Ltd v Cohen & Co Ltd* (1934) 50 T.L.R. 411; *Dore v Dore, The Times,* March 18, 1953; *Eastern Distributors Ltd v Goldring* [1957] 2 Q.B. 600; *Halfway Garage (Nottingham) Ltd v Lepley, Guardian,* February 8, 1964. cf. *Union Transport Finance Ltd v Ballardie* [1937] 1 K.B. 510.

tor Auctions Pty Ltd v Motor Credits (Hire Finance) Ltd.[923] In that case, dealers sold cars to the claimants, remaining in possession for display purposes and being authorised to sell as agents for the claimants. This authority was later revoked but the dealers sold to the defendants, who were bona fide purchasers. It was held that the defendants had obtained a good title by virtue of a provision identical to s.24.[924] The Privy Council decided that "continues ... in possession" in s.24 refers to the continuity of physical possession regardless of any private transaction between seller and buyer which might alter the legal title under which possession was held. In order to defeat the operation of s.24, there would have to be a break in the continuity of physical possession of the goods, for instance, by delivery of the goods to the buyer or to some third party.[925] But the subsection would not cease to apply where the seller simply attorned to the buyer as bailee. This decision was followed by the Court of Appeal in *Worcester Works Finance Ltd v Cooden Engineering Co Ltd*.[926]

Consent of buyer Section 24 does not require that the seller should continue or be in possession of the goods or documents of title with the consent of the buyer.[927]   **44-216**

Delivery or transfer he delivery[928] or transfer[929] of the goods or documents of title[930] must be effected "under", i.e. in consequence of, a sale, pledge or other disposition thereof. So in *Nicholson v Harper*[931] where a merchant sold wine stored in a warehouse and later pledged it to the warehouse-keeper to secure an advance made in good faith and without notice of the sale, the pledge was held by North J. to confer no title to the wine as there had been no delivery or transfer to the warehouseman after the sale. It was, however, subsequently held in the context of s.25(1) of the Act[932] that a constructive delivery would suffice[933] and it is now clear that this also applies in the case of s.24.[934]   **44-217**

---

[923] [1965] A.C. 867. For a discussion of this decision, see Thornely [1965] C.L.J. 181.

[924] New South Wales Sale of Goods Act 1923–1953 s.28(1).

[925] *Mitchell v Jones* (1905) 24 N.Z.L.R. 932; *Olds Discount Co Ltd v Krett* [1940] 2 K.B. 117; *Worcester Works Finance Ltd v Cooden Engineering Co Ltd* [1972] 1 Q.B. 210, 217–218.

[926] [1972] 1 Q.B. 210. See also *Astley Industrial Trust Ltd v Miller* [1968] 2 All E.R. 36.

[927] *Worcester Works Finance Ltd v Cooden Engineering Co Ltd* [1972] 1 Q.B. 210, 217–218.

[928] As to whether physical delivery is required, see para.44-229, below (s.25).

[929] In *Benjamin's Sale of Goods*, 10th edn (2017), para.7-062, it is suggested that these words should be read distributively in relation to "goods" and "documents of title to goods". See *Nicholson v Harper* [1895] 2 Ch. 415; *Kitto v Bilbie, Hobson & Co* (1895) 72 L.T. 266, 267; *Ahrens Ltd v Cohen, Sons & Co Ltd* (1934) 30 T.L.R. 411, 412; cf. *Worcester Works Finance Ltd v Cooden Engineering Co Ltd* [1972] 1 Q.B. 210.

[930] cf. *Mount Ltd v Jay and Jay (Provisions) Ltd* [1960] 1 Q.B. 159, 168; see below, para.44-341.

[931] [1895] 2 Ch. 415.

[932] See below, para.44-229.

[933] *Gamers Motor Centre (Newcastle) Pty Ltd v Natwest Wholesale Australia Pty Ltd* (1987) 63 C.L.R. 236; *Forsyth International (UK) Ltd v Silver Shipping Co Ltd* [1993] 2 Lloyd's Rep. 268. See also *Four Point Garage Ltd v Carter* [1985] 2 All E.R. 12, and see below, para.44-229.

[934] *Michael Gerson (Leasing) Ltd v Wilkinson* [2001] Q.B. 514; see below, para.44-229.

44-218   **Disposition**   It has been said that "disposition" extends to all acts by which a new interest (legal or equitable) in the property is effectually created,[935] although there is some doubt whether a purely gratuitous disposition, e.g. a gift, would suffice.[936]

44-219   **Good faith and notice**   The burden of proving good faith[937] and absence of notice[938] appears to rest upon the person receiving the goods.[939]

(gg)   Disposition by Buyer in Possession[940]

44-220   **Buyer in possession**   By subs.(1) of s.25[941]:

> "Where a person having bought or agreed to buy goods obtains, with the consent of the seller, possession of the goods or the documents of title[942] to the goods, the delivery or transfer by that person, or by a mercantile agent[943] acting for him, of the goods or documents of title,[944] under any sale, pledge, or other disposition thereof, to any person receiving the same in good faith and without notice of any lien or other right of the original seller in respect of the goods, has the same effect as if the person making the delivery or transfer were a mercantile agent in possession of the goods or documents of title with the consent of the owner."

The effect of this subsection is, for example, that a seller who agrees to sell goods to a buyer and retains title to them until the price is paid, but who nevertheless allows the buyer to have possession of the goods, may lose his title if the buyer wrongfully sells the goods to an innocent purchaser.

44-221   **"Having bought"**   The inclusion of the words "having bought" has been criticised as superfluous in that it is unnecessary to protect a third party who has bought from a buyer in possession and to whom the property has already passed. But if the buyer has a voidable title (for instance, where he has obtained the goods by fraud) and this has been avoided by the seller, the buyer may yet be a person who has bought within the meaning of s.25(1): in consequence, although the property has reverted to the seller, he may be able to pass a good title to a third party buyer in good faith. In *Newtons of Wembley Ltd v Williams*[945] a buyer obtained goods by fraud. The seller,

---

935 *Worcester Works Finance Ltd v Cooden Engineering Co Ltd* [1972] 1 Q.B. 210, 218. cf. *P4 Ltd v Unite Integrated Systems Plc* [2006] B.L.R. 150 at [18].

936 cf. *Kitto v Bilbie Hobson & Co* (1895) 72 O.T. 266; *Worcester Works Finance Ltd v Cooden Engineering Co Ltd* [1972] 1 Q.B. 210, Preston (1972) 88 L.Q.R. 239.

937 Defined, s.61(3); see above, para.44-016.

938 See below, para.44-231.

939 *Heap v Motorists' Advisory Agency Ltd* [1923] 1 K.B. 577 (Factors Act 1889 s.2).

940 See *Benjamin's Sale of Goods*, 10th edn (2017), para.7-069; Merrett [2008] C.L.J. 376.

941 Re-enacting, with slight modifications, s.9 of the Factors Act 1889.

942 Defined, s.61(1), see above, para.44-015. A vehicle registration document is not a document of title: *Pearson v Rose and Young Ltd* [1951] 1 K.B. 275; *Central Newbury Car Auctions Ltd v Unity Finance Ltd* [1957] 1 Q.B. 371; *J Sargent (Garages) Ltd v Motor Auctions (West Bromwich) Ltd* [1977] R.T.R. 121; *Beverley Acceptances Ltd v Oakley* [1982] R.T.R. 417; *Shaw v Commissioner of Metropolitan Police* [1987] 1 W.L.R. 1322, 1335–1336.

943 As to mercantile agents, see above, para.31-079.

944 See *Mount Ltd v Jay and Jay (Provisions) Co Ltd* [1960] 1 Q.B. 159, see below, para.44-341, where Salmon J. said obiter that the document which is transferred to the sub-purchaser need not be the same document as that which was given to the buyer; and therefore that the requirements of s.25(1) are less rigorous than those of what is now s.47(2).

945 [1965] 1 Q.B. 560; see also below, para.44-227.

having attempted to trace him, rescinded the contract and thus avoided the buyer's title. But it was held that, as the buyer had agreed to buy the goods and obtained possession of them with the seller's consent, such consent was deemed to continue[946] and he could pass a good title under s.25(1) to a third party buyer in good faith.[947] The same reasoning, it is submitted, would apply where the buyer bought and not merely agreed to buy the goods.[948]

"Having ... agreed to buy" With regard to the phrase "agreed to buy", it is **44-222** necessary to distinguish between those situations where the buyer is contractually bound to purchase the goods and those situations where he is not under any such binding obligation. Under a hire-purchase agreement, for example, the hirer is not bound to purchase the goods, but has merely an option to do so: thus until he exercises the option he is not a person who has bought or agreed to buy goods. In consequence he cannot pass a good title to a buyer in good faith by virtue of s.25(1).[949] The same is true where goods are delivered "on sale or return".[950] or under a contract for work and materials.[951] In a conditional sale agreement, on the other hand, the buyer is bound to purchase the goods and, accordingly, at common law, he is a person who has agreed to buy the goods; thus he can pass a good title by s.25(1).[952] However, where the agreement is one which is a consumer credit agreement within the meaning of the Consumer Credit Act 1974,[953] the buyer is to be deemed not to be a person who has bought or agreed to buy goods, and so cannot pass title by virtue of the subsection.[954]

Possession of buyer Having bought or agreed to buy goods the buyer must obtain **44-223** possession of the goods or the documents of title to the goods.[955] By s.1(2) of the

---

[946] Within s.2(2) of the Factors Act 1889; see below, para.44-225.

[947] *Car and Universal Finance Co Ltd v Caldwell* [1965] 1 Q.B. 525 was distinguished on the ground that there the buyer from the seller with a voidable title had notice of the defect and so could not be protected by s.25(1).

[948] Thus the disponee could acquire a good title under s.25(1), even though he could not do so under s.23.

[949] *Helby v Matthews* [1895] A.C. 471; *Payne v Wilson* [1895] 2 Q.B. 537; *Belsize Motor Supply Co v Cox* [1914] 1 K.B. 244; *Modern Light Cars Ltd v Seals* [1934] 1 K.B. 32; *Close Asset Finance Ltd v Care Graphics Machinery Ltd* [2000] E.C.L.R. 43. Contrast *Forthright Finance Ltd v Carlyle Finance Ltd* [1997] 4 All E.R. 90. See above, para.39-307. But see the exception for motor vehicles established by the Hire-Purchase Act 1964; see above, para.39-402.

[950] *Edwards v Vaughan* (1910) 26 T.L.R. 545. But see *London Jewellers Ltd v Attenborough* [1934] 2 K.B. 206, and s.18 r.4 of the Act; see above, para.44-146.

[951] *Dawber Williamson Roofing Ltd v Humberside CC* (1979) 14 Build. L.R. 70.

[952] *Lee v Butler* [1893] 2 Q.B. 318. See above, para.39-464.

[953] ss.8(1), 189(1).

[954] See above, para.39-464. A "conditional sale agreement" means an agreement for the sale of goods which is a consumer credit agreement within the meaning of the Consumer Credit Act 1974 (s.8(2)) under which the purchase price or part of it is payable by instalments, and the property in the goods is to remain in the seller (notwithstanding that the buyer is to be in possession of the goods) until such condition as to payment of instalments or otherwise as may be specified in the agreement are fulfilled: see Sale of Goods Act 1979 s.25(2) (4), Sch.1 para.9 and Sch.4 para.1; Consumer Credit Act 1974 s.192 and Sch.4 paras 2, 4 (SI 1983/1572). A conditional sale agreement is a consumer credit agreement if the buyer is an "individual", as defined in s.189(1) of the 1974 Act, as amended by the Consumer Credit Act 2006: see above, para.39-443. See also for the removal of the general financial limit by the 2006 Act, above, para.39-010.

[955] cf. *Four Point Garage Ltd v Carter* [1985] 3 All E.R. 12 (buyer requests seller to deliver goods direct to a sub-purchaser). See for example *Carlos Soto SAV v AP Moller-Maersk AS* [2015] EWHC 458

Factors Act 1889, a buyer will be deemed to be in possession of goods or of the documents of title to goods, where the goods or documents of title are in his actual custody or are held by any other person subject to his control or for him or on his behalf.[956]

44-224   Meaning of "consent of seller"   The meaning of "consent" in this context was at one time somewhat controversial. But it is now settled that the crucial question is whether the seller *in fact* consented to the buyer's possession. It is immaterial that the goods have been obtained by fraud or in circumstances amounting to theft if the de facto consent of the seller has been given.[957]

44-225   Consent withdrawn   Where possession of goods is in fact obtained with the consent of the seller, s.2(2) of the Factors Act provides that such consent is deemed to continue notwithstanding that it has been withdrawn, provided that the third party had no notice of the withdrawal. Thus in *Newtons of Wembley Ltd v Williams*[958] the fact that the contract had been rescinded by the seller did not mean that he had withdrawn his consent to the buyer continuing in possession; and accordingly the latter was able to pass a good title under s.25(1).

44-226   Burden of proof   The consent of the seller is to be presumed in the absence of evidence to the contrary,[959] so that the burden is on him to prove the lack of consent.

44-227   Mercantile agent   Section 25(1) provides that a delivery or transfer of the goods or documents of title by a buyer in possession is to have:

"... the same effect as if the person making the delivery or transfer were a mercantile agent in possession of the goods or documents of title with the consent of the owner."

This necessitates a reference to s.2 of the Factors Act which applies to the case of a disposition by a mercantile agent, and validates the disposition only where it is made by a mercantile agent when acting in the ordinary course of business as a mercantile agent. Where the buyer is in fact a mercantile agent acting in the course of his business, clearly there is no difficulty and the transaction is validated. And where he is not so acting it seems equally clear that the transaction is not validated.[960] The difficulty arises where the buyer is not a mercantile agent at all, for it is not easy to see how such a person could be said to be acting in the ordinary course of business of a mercantile agent. This problem arose for consideration in *Newtons of Wembley Ltd v Williams*.[961] Pearson L.J. said[962]:

(Comm), where the buyer had obtained a bill of lading in good faith and without notice.

[956] *Capital and Counties Bank Ltd v Warriner* (1896) 12 T.L.R. 216; *Forsythe International (UK) Ltd v Silver Shipping Co Ltd* [1993] 2 Lloyd's Rep. 268. cf. *Fairfax Gerrard Holdings Ltd v Capital Bank Plc* [2006] EWHC 3439, [2007] 1 Lloyd's Rep. 170 (reversed on other grounds, [2007] EWCA Civ 1226, [2008] 1 Lloyd's Rep. 297).

[957] *Du Jardin v Beadman Bros Ltd* [1952] 2 Q.B. 712.

[958] [1965] 1 Q.B. 560; see above, para.44-221.

[959] Factors Act 1889 s.2(4).

[960] See *Newtons of Wembley Ltd v Williams* [1965] 1 Q.B. 560, 579; *Colwyn Bay Motorcycles v Poole* [2000] C.L.Y. 4675, Cty Ct.

[961] [1965] 1 Q.B. 560; see also above, paras 44-221, 44-225. A similar problem was considered in *Lambert v G&C Finance Corp* (1963) 107 S.J. 666. See also *Angara Maritime Ltd v OceanConnect UK Ltd* [2010] EWHC 619 (QB), [2011] 1 Lloyd's Rep. 61.

"It follows that, when applying the hypothesis in s.2, one assumes that he is a mercantile agent: if he has a business it is assumed to be the business of a mercantile agent; or the other way of putting it is that the transaction will be validated if this buyer is doing something which would constitute acting in the ordinary course of business if he were a mercantile agent."

Thus, as the original buyer was not a mercantile agent, it was said that he must act in the way he would have been expected to act if he had been a mercantile agent; and that here he had done so as the sale had taken place in a recognised street market.[963]

A sale of a second-hand vehicle without its registration document is ordinarily not in the ordinary course of business.[964] **44-228**

Delivery or transfer   As in the case of s.24 of the Act,[965] there must be a "delivery or transfer" of the goods or documents of title under any sale, pledge or other disposition thereof.[966] The question, however, arises under both sections whether an actual, as opposed to constructive, delivery of the goods is required.[967] In *Gamer's Motor Centre (Newcastle) Pty Ltd v Natwest Wholesale Australia Pty Ltd*[968] the defendant sellers delivered to car dealers possession of certain vehicles under an agreement for a sale by which they reserved property in the vehicles until the price was paid. The dealers immediately sold the vehicles to the claimants, who bought them in good faith, but allowed the dealers to retain possession of them for the purposes of display though reserving the right to take possession of the vehicles at any time without notice. The High Court of Australia, by a bare majority, held that "delivery" in s.25(1) did not require a physical delivery of the goods to the disponee. There was a sufficient delivery of the vehicles by the dealers to the claimants when the character of the dealers' possession changed and they became bailees of the vehicles for the claimants.[969] The conclusion that a constructive delivery of the goods will suffice was endorsed in relation to s.25(1) by Clarke J. in *Forsyth International (UK) Ltd v Silver Shipping Co Ltd*[970] and adopted in relation to s.24 **44-229**

---

[962] At 579.

[963] The general implications of this decision have been much criticised. See *Benjamin's Sale of Goods*, 10th edn (2017), para.7-081; Cornish (1964) 27 M.L.R. 472; Thornely [1965] C.L.J. 24; *Langmead v Thyer Rubber Co Ltd* [1947] S.A.S.R. 29, 39; *Jeffcott v Andrew Motors Ltd* [1960] N.Z.L.R. 721, 729; *Gamer's Motor Centre (Newcastle) Pty Ltd v Natwest Wholesale Australia Pty Ltd* (1987) 163 C.L.R. 236, 243, 252; *Forsyth International (UK) Ltd v Silver Shipping Co Ltd* [1993] 2 Lloyd's Rep. 268, 280. The Law Reform Committee, Cmnd.2958 (1966), para.23, recommended an amendment to s.25(1) so as to make it unnecessary for the buyer in possession of goods to have acted in disposing of them, as if he were a mercantile agent.

[964] *Stadium Finance Ltd v Robbins* [1962] 2 Q.B. 664; *Lambert v G&C Finance Corp* (1963) 107 S.J. 666. *Dreverton v Regal Garage Ltd* [1998] C.L.Y. 4382. See also *Pearson v Rose and Young Ltd* [1951] 1 K.B. 275; *George v Revis* (1966) 111 S.J. 51 (stolen registration book).

[965] See above, para.44-217.

[966] Or (by virtue of s.9 of the Factors Act 1889) under any agreement for the sale, pledge or other disposition thereof: see *Shenstone & Co v Hilton* [1894] 2 Q.B. 452. For the meaning of "disposition", see para.44-218 above. cf. *W. Hanson (Harrow) Ltd v Rapid Civil Engineering Ltd* (1987) 38 B.L.R. 106; *Re Highway Foods International* [1995] B.C.L.C. 209.

[967] See *Benjamin's Sale of Goods*, 10th edn (2017), para.7-077.

[968] (1987) 63 C.L.R. 236.

[969] *Pacific Motor Auctions Pty Ltd v Motor Credits (Hire Finance) Ltd* [1965] A.C. 867; see above, para.44-215.

[970] [1993] 2 Lloyd's Rep. 268.

by the Court of Appeal in *Michael Gerson (Leasing) Ltd v Wilkinson.*[971] It must therefore now be taken to represent English law.[972] A physical delivery of the goods by the seller to the disponee at the request of the buyer will in any event be a sufficient delivery, since such delivery will be considered to have been effected by him as agent for the buyer.[973] The delivery (whether actual or constructive) must be voluntary.[974]

44-230 **Effect of delivery or transfer** Despite the fact that the subsection states that the delivery or transfer shall have the same effect as if the buyer were a mercantile agent in possession of the goods or documents of title with the consent of the *owner*, a buyer whose possession of the goods derives ultimately from a thief cannot pass title to an innocent purchaser.[975]

44-231 **Good faith and notice** The burden of proving good faith and absence of notice rests upon the person receiving the goods.[976] "Good faith" is defined in s.61(3).[977] "Notice" in this subsection and other similar provisions[978] prima facie means actual notice.[979] The doctrine of constructive notice does not normally apply to commercial transactions, and there is no general duty on a buyer of goods in an ordinary commercial transaction to make inquiries as to the right of the seller to dispose of the goods.[980] However, means of knowledge in his power wilfully disregarded will amount to notice, i.e. "deliberately turning a blind eye".[981] Moreover, the test to be applied is an objective one, that is to say, would the circumstances known to the buyer lead him to conclude, as a reasonable man, that the relevant fact existed.[982]

---

971 [2001] Q.B. 514.

972 Even though it does not appear to accord with the decision of North J. in *Nicholson v Harper* [1895] 2 Ch. 415; see above, para.44-217.

973 *Four Point Garage Ltd v Carter* [1985] 3 All E.R. 12.

974 *Forsyth International (UK) Ltd v Silver Shipping Co Ltd* [1993] 2 Lloyd's Rep. 268; *Angara Maritime Ltd v OceanConnect UK Ltd* [2010] EWHC 619 (QB), [2011] 1 Lloyd's Rep. 61. cf. *Worcester Works Finance Ltd v Cooden Engineering Co Ltd* [1972] 1 Q.B. 210 (voluntary surrender of goods).

975 *National Mutual General Insurance Ltd v Jones* [1990] 1 A.C. 24.

976 *Heap v Motorists' Advisory Agency Ltd* [1923] 1 K.B. 577; *Lambert v G & C Finance Corp* (1963) 107 S.J. 666; *Feuer Leather Corp v Frank Johnstone & Sons* [1981] Com. L.R. 251, 253; *Forsyth International (UK) Ltd v Silver Shipping Co Ltd* [1993] 2 Lloyd's Rep. 268, 279.

977 See above, para.44-016.

978 Sale of Goods Act 1979 ss.22, 23, 24; s.2(1) of the Factors Act 1889; and see s.138(2) of the Senior Courts Act 1981 (now replaced: see para.44-233).

979 *Feuer Leather Corp v Frank Johnstone & Sons* [1981] Com. L.R. 251, 253; *Forsyth International (UK) Ltd v Silver Shipping Co Ltd* [1993] 2 Lloyd's Rep. 268, 279; *P4 Ltd v Unite Integrated Solutions Plc* [2006] B.L.R. 150.

980 *Hambro v Burnand* [1904] 2 K.B. 10, 20; *Dobell, Beckett & Co v Neilson* (1904) 7F. 281, 288; *Reckett v Barnet and Slater Ltd* [1928] 2 K.B. 244, 258, 266; reversed [1929] A.C. 176; *Feuer Leather Corp v Frank Johnstone & Sons*, above, at 253; *Forsythe International (UK) Ltd v Silver Shipping Co Ltd* [1993] 2 Lloyd's Rep. 279; *Carlos Soto SAU v AP Moller-Maersk AS (The SFL Hawk)* [2015] EWHC 458 (Comm), [2015] 1 Lloyd's Rep. 537.

981 *Heap v Motorists' Advisory Agency Ltd* [1923] 1 K.B. 577, 591; *Worcester Works Finance Ltd v Cooden Engineering Co Ltd* [1972] 1 Q.B. 210, 218; *Feuer Leather Corp v Frank Johnstone & Sons*, above, at 253; *Forsyth International (UK) Ltd v Silver Shipping Co Ltd* [1993] 2 Lloyd's Rep. 268, 279; *Summers v Havard* [2011] EWCA Civ 764, [2011] 2 Lloyd's Rep. 283 at [16].

982 *Evans v Trueman* (1830) 1 Moody & R. 10, 12; *Navulshaw v Brownrigg* (1852) 2 De G.M. & G. 441, 451; *Feuer Leather Corp v Frank Johnstone & Sons* [1981] Com. L.R. 251, 253; *Forsythe International (UK) Ltd v Silver Shipping Co Ltd* [1993] 2 Lloyd's Rep. 279; *Ceres Orchard Partnership v Fiatagari Australia Pty Ltd* [1995] N.Z.L.R. 112, 117.

And it has been said that "if by an objective test clear notice was given liability cannot be avoided by proof merely of the absence of actual knowledge".[983]

(hh) Sale of a Motor Vehicle Under the Hire-Purchase Act 1964

Sale of a motor vehicle under the Hire-Purchase Act 1964 The Hire-Purchase **44-232**
Act 1964[984] creates an important further exception to the general rule set out in
s.21(1) of the 1979 Act. This is discussed in detail elsewhere.[985] Briefly, it is
provided that the disposition of a motor vehicle by a hirer under a hire-purchase
agreement or by a buyer under a conditional sale agreement to a private purchaser
in good faith and without notice is effective to vest a good title in such a purchaser.
The operation of this Act is not confined to agreements within the statutory control
of the Consumer Credit Act 1974.

(ii) Effect on Title of Warrants of Control

Effect on title of writs or warrants of execution From April 6, 2014[986] the provi- **44-233**
sions previously contained in para.8(1) of Sch.7 to the Courts Act 2003[987] were
replaced by Pt 3 of Sch.23 to the Tribunals, Courts and Enforcement Act 2007 and
the old "writs of execution" were renamed warrants of control. The property in the
goods of the debtor becomes bound from the time when a writ issued by the High
Court is received.[988] However, subpara.5(2) of para.5 to Sch.2 provides that the
provisions are not to prejudice the title to any goods of the execution debtor
acquired by a person in good faith and for valuable consideration[989] without
notice.[990] Thus, a warrant of control does not prevent the property passing on a sale
of them by the execution debtor, although the buyer, if he has notice or is not in
good faith, takes the goods subject to the rights of the execution creditor.[991] If he
has no notice and is in good faith, the buyer acquires an unencumbered title
provided that the warrant has not been executed. Once, however, the warrant has
been executed by seizure of the goods then the execution debtor cannot pass an
unencumbered title to a buyer, even though the goods have been seized under arrangements which leave the debtor in possession of the goods.[992]

---

[983] *Feuer Leather Corp v Frank Johnstone & Sons* [1981] Com. L.R. 251 at 253; *Forsyth International
(UK) Ltd v Silver Shipping Co Ltd* [1993] 2 Lloyd's Rep. 268 at 279; *Fairfax Gerrard Holdings Ltd
v Capital Bank Plc* [2006] EWHC 3439, [2007] 1 Lloyd's Rep. 170 at [31(e)] (reversed on the
grounds [2007] EWCA Civ 1226, [2008] 1 Lloyd's Rep. 297).

[984] ss.27–29 (as re-enacted from May 19, 1985 (see SI 1983/1551 (C. 44)) by s.192 of and Sch.4 para.22
to the Consumer Credit Act 1974).

[985] See above, paras 39-402 et seq.

[986] Tribunals, Courts and Enforcement Act 2007 (Commencement No.11) Order 2014 (SI 2014/768).

[987] Replacing s.138 of the Senior Courts Act 1981.

[988] Sch.12, 4(2). Where the power is conferred by a warrant to which s.99 of the County Courts Act 1984
(c.28) or s.125ZA of the Magistrates' Courts Act 1980 (c.43) applies, the warrant binds the property
in the goods from the time when it is received by the person who is under a duty to endorse it under
that section (Sch.12, 5(1)).

[989] *Beeber & Co v Turner's Successors* (1931) 48 T.L.R. 61 cf. *Re Cooper* [1958] Ch. 922, 928. See
also *Ellis & Co v Cross* [1915] 2 K.B. 654.

[990] See *Ehlers v Kauffman* (1883) 49 L.T. 806.

[991] *Samuel v Duke* (1838) 3 M. & W. 622; *Woodland v Fuller* (1840) 11 A. & E. 859, 867; *McPherson
Temiskaming Lumber Co Ltd* [1913] A.C. 145, 156.

[992] *Lloyds & Scottish Finance Ltd v Modern Cars & Caravans (Kingston) Ltd* [1966] 1 Q.B. 764.

(iii)   Effect of Limitation

44-234   **Limitation**   Where goods have been converted, the owner of the goods has six years thereafter[993] in which to bring an action in respect of that and all subsequent acts of conversion whether or not committed by the same person.[994] After the expiration of that period, unless he has previously recovered possession, s.3(2) of the Limitation Act 1980 provides that his title to the goods is extinguished. However, these rules are qualified where the goods have been stolen.[995] As against a purchaser in good faith of stolen goods or a person who has converted the goods following such a purchase, the owner's title is extinguished and his right to claim damages barred, after six years from the date of purchase.[996] But otherwise the right of a person from whom goods are stolen to bring an action in respect of the theft or of any conversion following the theft is not barred by limitation, nor is his title to the goods extinguished.[997] And the same applies to cases where the goods are obtained by deception[998] or blackmail.[999] Theft and these allied offences are therefore "imprescriptible" as against the person from whom the goods are stolen, and no subsequent converter (other than a bona fide purchaser or person claiming through such a purchaser) can claim the benefit of limitation.[1000]

44-235   **Actions for the recovery of property obtained through unlawful conduct etc**   By s.27A of the Limitation Act 1980[1001] (inserted by s.288 of the Proceeds of Crime Act 2002) none of the limits given in the preceding provisions of the 1980 Act apply to any proceedings under Ch.2 of Pt 5 of the 2002 Act (civil recovery of proceeds of unlawful conduct) brought by a "relevant person", that is to say, by the Serious Organised Crime Agency, the Director of Public Prosecutions, the Director of Revenue and Customs Prosecutions or the Director of the Serious Fraud Office.[1002] A relevant person has 12 years in which to bring proceedings[1003] for a recovery order from the date on which his cause of action accrued.[1004] Moreover, if proceedings are started by a relevant person for a recovery order in respect of a chattel, s.3(2) of the 1980 Act does not prevent a claimant from asserting on an application under s.281 of the 2002 Act (victims of theft, etc.) that the property belongs to him, or the court making a declaration in his favour under that section. If the court makes such a declaration, his title to the chattel is to be treated as not having been extinguished by s.3(2) of the 1980 Act.

---

[993] Unless he has recovered possession in the meantime.

[994] Limitation Act 1980 ss.2, 3(1). But see s.32 of the 1980 Act.

[995] See the *Twenty-first Report of the Law Reform Committee*, Cmnd.6923 (1977), paras 3.1 et seq.

[996] Limitation Act 1980 s.4(1), (2).

[997] Limitation Act 1980 s.4(1), (2), (3).

[998] Limitation Act 1980 s.4(5)(b); Theft Act 1968 s.15(1).

[999] Limitation Act 1980 s.4(5)(b); Theft Act 1968 s.21.

[1000] By s.4(4) of the 1980 Act, the claimant bears the burden of proving that the goods were stolen from him or anyone through whom he claims, but the defendant bears the burden of proving that he is or claims through a bona fide purchaser. See *Kuwait Airways Corp v Iraqi Airways Co (Nos 4 and 5)* [2002] UKHL 19, [2002] 2 A.C. 883 at [103].

[1001] As amended by the Serious Organised Crime and Police Act 2005 Sch.6 para.2; Serious Crime Act 2007 Sch.8 para.147.

[1002] 1980 Act s.27A(8).

[1003] Defined in s.27A(3).

[1004] Defined in s.27A(4).

5. PERFORMANCE OF THE CONTRACT

(a) Duties of Seller and Buyer

Duties of seller and buyer   By s.27:   **44-236**

"It is the duty of the seller to deliver[1005] the goods, and of the buyer to accept[1006] and pay for them, in accordance with the terms of the contract of sale."

By s.28:   **44-237**

"Unless otherwise agreed,[1007] delivery of the goods and payment of the price are concurrent conditions, that is to say, the seller must be ready and willing to give possession of the goods to the buyer in exchange for the price and the buyer must be ready and willing to pay the price in exchange for possession of the goods."[1008]

In cases to which the section does apply, the rule is that the seller can claim the price only when ready and willing to deliver the goods, and the buyer can claim the goods only when ready and willing to pay the price. The section is, however, satisfied if the party making the claim is in a position to perform his side of the contract; he need not tender.[1009]

The effect of s.28 may be adopted by express terms. Thus if, for instance, it is   **44-238**
provided that payment is to be made against documents, tender of the documents and payment are concurrent conditions.[1010] Section 28 prima facie applies to CIF contracts. It must be noted that here of course documents represent the goods,[1011] so that the duty of the seller is to tender the shipping documents, and the buyer must pay the price on tender of the documents even though the goods are still afloat.[1012]

Export or import licences[1013]   It seems that there is no general rule as to whether,   **44-239**
in the absence of an express provision in the contract, it is the duty of the seller or of the buyer to obtain any necessary export or import licence. The question is one of construction. This was the approach favoured by the House of Lords in *Pound & Co Ltd v Hardy & Co Inc*.[1014] In that case a buyer agreed to buy turpentine from the seller, f.a.s. the buyer's ship at Lisbon; the destination of the turpentine was East Germany, as the seller knew. Turpentine could not be exported from Portugal without a licence, and this was not granted. It was held that on the construction of the contract and in the light of the surrounding circumstances, the obligation to

---

[1005] "Delivery" is defined in s.61(1), see above, para.44-015. But usually it is the duty of the buyer to collect the goods: s.29(2), see below, para.44-244.

[1006] See also ss.20, 37.

[1007] For an example of a contrary implication, see *Amos & Wood Ltd v Kaprow* (1948) 64 T.L.R. 110.

[1008] But payment of price in exchange for possession does not of itself preclude the buyer from subsequently rejecting the goods. See ss.34 and 35, see below, paras 44-277—44-289.

[1009] *Levey & Co Ltd v Goldberg* [1922] 1 K.B. 688, 692.

[1010] *Polenghi Bros v Dried Milk Co Ltd* (1904) 92 L.T. 64.

[1011] By "documents" is meant the bill of lading, the insurance policy and the invoice (unless otherwise agreed).

[1012] See *E Clemens Horst & Co v Biddell Brothers* [1912] A.C. 18: but payment does not deprive the buyer of the right to reject the goods; see s.35, see below, para.44-278.

[1013] See Vol.I, para.14-025, and *Benjamin's Sale of Goods*, 10th edn (2017), paras 18-355.

[1014] [1956] A.C. 588; distinguishing *Brandt & Co v Morris & Co Ltd* [1917] 2 K.B. 784; observations of Scrutton L.J. (which might be read as placing duty primarily on buyer) limited to facts of that case.

obtain the licence lay on the seller; but the House of Lords was clearly of the opinion that each case must depend on its own facts. Once it has been determined upon whom the duty lies, it is then necessary to consider whether that duty is an absolute one.[1015] or whether it is merely a duty to use best endeavours and reasonable diligence to obtain a licence.[1016]

44-240 Letters of credit[1017] In *Ian Stach Ltd v Baker, Bosley Ltd*[1018] Diplock J. said:

> "The commercial purpose of a banker's confirmed credit is more than a mere method of payment: it creates a direct liability on the banker independent of the contract of sale, and is an undertaking by the banker that if the seller presents the required documents in the required time he will receive payment of the contract price."

Where the parties to an export sale arrange for payment under a letter of credit without arranging when the credit shall be opened, the credit has to be opened sufficiently early to enable the seller to be assured of payment during the whole agreed shipment period. This now seems to be the rule with regard both to CIF and FOB contracts. For CIF contracts, it was decided in *Pavia & Co SpA v Thurmann-Nielson*[1019] that the letter of credit must be opened at the latest by the beginning of the shipment period. But a different view was expressed in *Sinason-Teicher Inter-American Grain Corp v Oilcakes and Oilseeds Trading Co Ltd*,[1020] which concerned a bank guarantee for payment to be given to the sellers. Lord Denning stated[1021]: "The correct view is that, if nothing is said about time in the contract, the buyer must provide the letter of credit within a reasonable time before the first date for shipment. The same applies to a bank guarantee". With regard to FOB contracts, it was decided in *Ian Stach Ltd v Baker, Bosley Ltd*[1022] that it was the buyer's duty to open the credit at the latest by the first day of the shipping period, and not a reasonable time before the date nominated by the buyer in the shipping instructions. If a date for opening of the credit is stipulated, the buyer must furnish it by that date.[1023]

(b) Rules Governing Delivery

44-241 Delivery Delivery is defined[1024] to mean "voluntary transfer of possession from one person to another". Delivery may be actual or constructive.[1025] There will be

---

[1015] e.g. *KC Sethia Ltd v Partabmul Rameshwar* [1950] 1 All E.R. 51; affirmed [1951] 2 All E.R. 352n.; *Peter Cassidy Seed Co v Osuustukkukauppa Ltd* [1957] 1 W.L.R. 273. cf. *Pagnan SpA v Tradax Ocean Transportation SA* [1987] 3 All E.R. 565.

[1016] e.g. *Re Anglo-Russian Merchant Traders and John Batt & Co (London) Ltd* [1917] 2 K.B. 679.

[1017] See *Benjamin's Sale of Goods*, 10th edn (2017), Ch.23; see above, Ch.34.

[1018] [1958] 2 Q.B. 130, 139.

[1019] [1952] 2 Q.B. 84.

[1020] [1954] 1 W.L.R. 1394. See also above, para.34-487.

[1021] At 1400.

[1022] [1958] 2 Q.B. 130; see also *Heisler v Anglo-Dal Ltd* [1954] 1 W.L.R. 1273; *Glencore Grain Rotterdam BV v Lebanese Organisation for International Commerce* [1997] 2 Lloyd's Rep. 386; *Kolmar Group AG v Traxpo Enterprises Pvt Ltd* [2010] EWHC 113 (Comm), [2010] 2 Lloyd's Rep. 653.

[1023] *Nichimen Corp v Gatoil Overseas Inc* [1987] 2 Lloyd's Rep. 47; *Vitol SA v Conoil Plc* [2009] EWHC 1144 (Comm), [2009] 2 Lloyd's Rep. 466. But the seller may agree to extend the time or be held to have waived the failure: see Vol.I, paras 22-040—22-047.

[1024] 1979 Act s.61(1); see above, para.44-015.

[1025] But delivery for the purpose of one rule in the Act need not necessarily be delivery for the purpose of another separate rule: see *Benjamin's Sale of Goods*, 10th edn (2017), para.8-002.

actual delivery where possession of goods is transferred from the seller to the buyer, or to a carrier (whether named by the buyer or not) for the purpose of transmission to the buyer.[1026] Delivery is constructive when it is effected without any change in the actual possession of the thing delivered, as in the case of delivery by attornment (i.e. acknowledgement) or symbolic delivery.[1027] Delivery by attornment may take place in three classes of cases.[1028] First, the seller may be in possession of the goods, but after the sale he may attorn to the buyer, and continue to hold the goods as his bailee.[1029] Secondly, the goods may be in the possession of the buyer before sale, but after the sale he may hold them on his own account.[1030] Thirdly, the goods may be in the possession of a third person, as bailee for the seller. After the sale such third person may attorn to the buyer and continue to hold them as bailee.[1031]

The transfer of possession must in all cases be voluntary.[1032] Section 29 contains **44-242** rules relating to the place, time, expense and other details of the delivery; they will be considered in the following paragraphs. It must be emphasised that the rules apply only if the parties have not expressly or impliedly made other arrangements.

The Consumer Rights Directive 2011 required there to be special rules govern- **44-243** ing delivery in consumer contracts. This Directive was initially implemented in reg.42 of the Consumer Contracts (Information, Cancellation and Additional Charges) Regulations 2013[1033] which contained provisions relating to the time for delivery of the goods where the contract of sale is made between a buyer who is a "consumer" and a seller who is a "trader" (as defined in reg.4) and is entered into on or after June 13, 2014. Regulation 42 is now subsumed by the special rules relating to delivery in consumer sales contracts contained in the Consumer Rights Act 2015.[1034]

(i)   Place of Delivery

Place of delivery   By s.29(1):   **44-244**

"Whether it is for the buyer to take possession of the goods or for the seller to send them to the buyer is a question of depending in each case on the contract, express or implied, between the parties."

And by s.29(2):

[1026] See s.32(1); see below, para.44-269.
[1027] *Ellis v Hunt* (1789) 3 T.R. 464, 468; *Chaplin v Rogers* (1800) 1 East 192, 195; *Elmore v Stone* (1809) 1 Taunt. 458, 460; *Ancona v Rogers* (1876) 1 Ex. D. 285, 290; *Hilton v Tucker* (1888) 39 Ch. D. 669, 676; *Lloyd's Bank Ltd v Swiss Bankverein* (1913) 108 L.T. 143, 146; *Wrightson v McArthur and Hutchinson (1919) Ltd* [1921] 2 K.B. 807, 816.
[1028] *Chalmers Sale of Goods Act 1893*, 5th edn, p.118.
[1029] *Dublin City Distillery Ltd v Doherty* [1914] A.C. 823, 843; *Gamers' Motor Centre (Newcastle) Pty Ltd v Natwest Wholesale Australia Pty Ltd* (1987) 163 C.L.R. 236; *Michael Gerson (Leasing) Ltd v Wilkinson* [2001] Q.B. 514.
[1030] *Manton v Moore* (1796) 7 Term Rep. 67; *Eden v Dudfield* (1841) 1 Q.B. 302; *Lillywhite v Devereux* (1846) 15 M. & W. 285; *Forsythe International (UK) Ltd v Silver Shipping Co Ltd* [1993] 2 Lloyd's Rep. 268, 276. cf. *Nicholson v Harper* [1895] 2 Ch. 415; see above, para.44-217.
[1031] See s.29(4); see below, para.44-254.
[1032] *Forsythe International (UK) Ltd v Silver Shipping Co Ltd*, above: cf. *Worcester Works Finance Ltd v Cooden Engineering Co Ltd* [1972] 1 Q.B. 210.
[1033] SI 2013/3134, amended by SI 2014/870. The Regulations are subject to the exceptions set out in reg.6.
[1034] See above, para.38-526.

"Apart from any such contract, express or implied, the place of delivery is the seller's place of business, if he has one, and if not, his residence; except that if the contract is for the sale of specific goods, which to the knowledge of the parties when the contract is made are in some other place, then that place is the place of delivery."[1035]

It follows from this rule that it is basically the duty of the buyer to collect the goods rather than that of the seller to send them. But the rule is frequently displaced, especially in overseas sales.[1036]

44-245 **Delivery at buyer's premises to unauthorised person** Under a contract to deliver at the buyer's premises, the seller discharges his obligation if he makes delivery there without negligence to a person "apparently having authority to receive them", although in fact the person to whom the goods were delivered had no authority to receive them and misappropriated them.[1037]

(ii) Time for Delivery[1038]

44-246 **Express stipulation** The parties are at liberty to stipulate in their contract that time is to be of the essence in relation to the seller's obligation to deliver within an agreed time. If no such stipulation is inserted, but a time for delivery is nevertheless fixed, the question whether time is of the essence depends on the terms of the contract.[1039] There is no presumption or rule of law that stipulations as to time of delivery are of the essence of the contract[1040] but, in commercial contracts, they are frequently so construed.[1041]

44-247 **No time fixed** By s.29(3)[1042]:

[1035] See also *Benjamin's Sale of Goods*, 10th edn (2017), paras 8-018—8-024.

[1036] See *Benjamin's Sale of Goods* at Chs 18–21; *Scottish & Newcastle International Ltd v Othon Ghalanos Ltd* [2008] UKHL 11, [2008] 1 Lloyd's Rep. 462. Different rules apply to contracts which are subject to Ch.2 of Pt 1 of the Consumer Rights Act 2015. In consumer sales, unless the trader and consumer have agreed otherwise, the contract is to be treated as including a term that the trader must deliver the goods to the consumer. See above, para.38-526.

[1037] *Galbraith & Grant Ltd v Block* [1922] 2 K.B. 155; *Computer 2000 Distribution Ltd v ICM Computer Solutions Plc* [2004] EWCA Civ 16345, [2005] Info. T.L.R. 147. cf. *E & D Thomas v HS Alper & Sons* [1953] C.L.Y. 3277, CA. Contrast *Linden Tricotagefabrik v White and Meacham* [1975] 1 Lloyd's Rep. 384.

[1038] As to damages for delayed delivery, see below, para.44-406.

[1039] 1979 Act s.10(1); see above, para.44-128. cf. *Hartley v Hymans* [1920] 3 K.B. 475, 483. See also *ERG Raffinerie Mediterranee SpA v Chevron USA Inc* [2007] EWCA Civ 494, [2007] 2 Lloyd's Rep. 542 (lay can shipment term in FOB contract).

[1040] *Compagnie Commerciale Sucres et Denrées v C Czarnikow Ltd* [1990] 1 W.L.R. 1337, 1347.

[1041] *Wimshurst v Deeley* (1845) 2 C.B. 253; *Bowes v Shand* (1877) 2 App. Cas. 455, 463; *Reuter v Sala* (1879) 4 C.P.D. 239, 246, 249; *Hartley v Hymans* [1920] 3 K.B. 475, 484; *Brooke Tool Manufacturing Ltd v Hydraulic Gears Co Ltd* (1920) 89 L.J. K.B. 263; *Finagrain SA v P Kruse Hamburg* [1976] 2 Lloyd's Rep. 508; *United Scientific Holdings Ltd v Burnley BC* [1978] A.C. 904, 924, 937, 944, 950, 958; *Bunge Corp v Tradax Export SA* [1981] 1 W.L.R. 711; *Scandinavian Trading Co A/B v Zodiac Petroleum SA* [1981] 1 Lloyd's Rep. 81; *Cerealmangimi SpA v Toepfer* [1981] 1 Lloyd's Rep. 337; *Tradax Export SA v Italgrani Francesco Ambrosio* [1986] 1 Lloyd's Rep. 112; *Gill & Duffus SA v Société pour l'Exportation des Sucres SA* [1986] 1 Lloyd's Rep. 322; *Compagnie Commerciale Sucres et Denrées v C Czarnikow Ltd* [1990] 1 W.L.R. 1337, 1347.

[1042] This provision does not apply to consumer contracts for the sale of goods which fall within Ch.2 of Pt 1 of the Consumer Rights Act 2015. In consumer contracts for the sale of goods the 2015 Act provides special rules in relation to delivery in consumer sales contracts, see above, para.38-526.

"Where under the contract of sale the seller is bound to send the goods to the buyer, but no time for sending them is fixed, the seller is bound to send them within a reasonable time."

This is but one aspect of a more general rule that, if the contract is silent as to the time of delivery, the seller is bound to deliver the goods within a reasonable time.[1043] What is a reasonable time is a question of fact,[1044] but may be affected by the usage of trade.[1045]

Goods to be delivered "as required"   Where the goods are to be delivered as required, the rule is as follows: the seller is not bound to deliver any goods until the buyer requires him to do so; once the buyer has made his request, the seller must deliver within a reasonable time; if the buyer fails to make known his requirements within a reasonable time, the seller may not rescind the contract for delay without giving notice to the buyer,[1046] but extreme delay in requiring delivery may support the inference that there is a mutual intention to abandon the contract.[1047]   **44-248**

"Reasonable hour"   By s.29(5):   **44-249**

"Demand or tender of delivery may be treated as ineffectual unless made at a reasonable hour; and what is a reasonable hour is a question of fact."

Variation of delivery time   The buyer may agree to an extension of the time fixed for delivery and such an agreement will constitute an effective variation of the contract of sale provided that sufficient consideration to support the variation moves from the promisee.[1048]   **44-250**

Waiver of delivery time   Although the contract fixes a time for delivery, the buyer's right to require delivery within that period may be waived even after the expiry of that period. So in *Hartley v Hymans*,[1049] where the buyer continued to   **44-251**

[1043] *Ellis v Thompson* (1838) 3 M. & W. 445, 456; *Jones v Gibbons* (1853) 8 Ex. 920, 923; *Hick v Raymond and Reid* [1893] A.C. 22, 29; *Thomas Borthwick (Glasgow) Ltd v Bunge & Co Ltd* [1969] 1 Lloyd's Rep. 17, 28; *SHV Gas Supply and Trading SAS v Naftomar Shipping & Trading Co Ltd Inc* [2005] EWHC 2528 (Comm), [2006] 1 Lloyd's Rep. 163. Contrast *ERG Raffinerie Mediterranee SpA v Chevron USA Inc* [2006] EWHC 1322 (Comm), [2006] 2 Lloyd's Rep. 543 at [56] (affirmed [2007] EWCA Civ 494, [2007] 2 Lloyd's Rep. 542) (FOB contract: ship provided by buyer).
[1044] 1979 Act s.59.
[1045] *Bradley & Sons v Colonial Continental Trading* (1964) 108 S.J. 599.
[1046] *Jones v Gibbons* (1853) 8 Ex. 920, 923.
[1047] *Pearl Mill Co v Ivy Tannery Co* [1919] 1 K.B. 78. See also *Honck v Muller* (1881) 7 Q.B.D. 92. But see Vol.I, para.22-027.
[1048] *South Caribbean Trading Ltd v Trafigura Beheer BV* [2004] EWHC 2676 (Comm), [2005] 1 Lloyd's Rep. 128; see Vol.I, para.4-080.
[1049] [1920] 3 K.B. 475. See also *Ogle v Earl Vane* (1868) L.R. 3 Q.B. 272; *Besseler Waechter Glover & Co v South Derwent Coal Co* [1938] 1 K.B. 408; *Charles Rickards Ltd v Oppenhaim* [1950] 1 K.B. 616; *Woodhouse v Nigerian Produce Marketing Co Ltd* [1972] A.C. 741, 755; *Finagrain SA Geneva v P Kruse Hamburg* [1976] 2 Lloyd's Rep. 508; *Bremer Handelsgesellschaft mbH v Vanden Avenne-Izegem PVBA* [1978] 2 Lloyd's Rep. 109, 116, 120, 126, 130, 131; *Cerealmangimi SpA v Toepfer* [1981] 1 Lloyd's Rep. 337; *Cook Industries v Meunerie Liegeois* [1981] 1 Lloyd's Rep. 359; *Cremer v Granaria BV* [1981] 2 Lloyd's Rep. 583; *Société Italo Belge pour le Commerce et l'Industrie v Palm and Vegetable Oils (Malaysia) Sdn Bhd* [1982] 1 All E.R. 19; *Bremer Handelsgesellschaft mbH v Raiffeissen* [1985] 1 Lloyd's Rep. 355; *Bremer Handelsgesellschaft mbH v Deutsche Conti-Handelsgesellschaft mbH* [1983] 2 Lloyd's Rep. 45; *Motor Oil (Hellas) (Corinth) Refineries SA v*

demand and accept deliveries long after the fixed date and then alleged that the contract had been broken by failure to deliver punctually, the court held that the buyer, by his demands after the fixed date, had waived his right to insist that the period of delivery terminated on that date. He was also by his conduct estopped from alleging that the period for delivery terminated on the date originally fixed by the contract.

44-252 **Affirmation** The parties may be found to have mutually affirmed the contract on the same terms, after the contractual date for delivery has passed.[1050]

44-253 **Force majeure** By a clause in the contract the seller may be entitled to suspend delivery or extend the time for delivery or even cancel the contract on the happening of a specified event or events beyond his control.[1051] Such clauses are very common in commercial contracts of sale; but force majeure clauses may assume a variety of forms and must be construed in the light of their precise wording, and with regard to the nature and general terms of the contract.[1052]

(iii)   Goods in Possession of Third Person

44-254 **Goods in possession of third person** By s.29(4):

"Where the goods at the time of sale are in possession of a third person, there is no delivery by seller or buyer unless and until the third person acknowledges to the buyer that he holds the goods on his behalf; but nothing in this section affects the operation of the issue or transfer of any document of title[1053] to goods."[1054]

This subsection states that where goods are possessed by a third person, there is no delivery to the buyer unless there is an attornment.[1055] The qualification of the rule is merely negative in nature. The issue or transfer of a document of title[1056] does not necessarily dispense with an attornment.[1057] As between seller and buyer[1058] a bill of lading would appear to be the only document of title which will have this

---

Shipping Corp of India [1990] 1 Lloyd's Rep. 391, 399; *Fleming & Wendeln GmbH & Co v Sanofi SA/AG* [2003] EWHC 561 (QB), [2003] 2 Lloyd's Rep. 473; *Westbrook Resources Ltd v Metallurgical Inc* [2009] EWCA Civ 310, [2009] 2 Lloyd's Rep. 224. See also Vol.I, paras 22-040 et seq. Contrast *South Caribbean Trading Ltd v Trafigura Beheer BV*, above (estoppel cannot be invoked where unconscionable to do so): see Vol.I, para.4-096.

[1050] *Glencore Energy UK Ltd v Transworld Oil Ltd* [2010] EWHC 141 (Comm), [2010] 1 C.L.C. 284.

[1051] See *Benjamin's Sale of Goods*, 10th edn (2017), para.8-074.

[1052] See Vol.I, para.15-152.

[1053] Defined, s.61(1), see above, para.44-015.

[1054] See also ss.24, 25 and 47, see above, paras 44-214 et seq., see below, paras 44-340 et seq.

[1055] *Farina v Home* (1846) 16 M. & W. 119; *Dublin City Distillery Ltd v Doherty* [1914] A.C. 823, 847–848, 864–865; *Laurie and Morewood v Dudin & Sons* [1926] 1 K.B. 223, 237; *Peter Dumenil & Co Ltd v James Ruddin Ltd* [1953] 1 W.L.R. 815; *Wardar's (Import and Export) Co Ltd v Norwood and Sons Ltd* [1968] 2 Q.B. 663; *Mercuria Energy Trading PTE Ltd v Citibank NA* [2015] EWHC 1481 (Comm); see also above, para.44-133.

[1056] As defined in s.61(1) of the Sale of Goods Act (see above, para.44-015) and s.1(4) of the Factors Act 1889.

[1057] See the cases cited in n.1055, see above; and *Mordaunt Bros v British Oil and Cake Mills Ltd* [1910] 2 K.B. 502; *Comptoir d'Achat et de Vente du Baerenbond Belge SA v Luis de Ridder Ltd* [1949] A.C. 293; *Margarine Union GmbH v Cambay Prince Steamship Co Ltd* [1969] 1 Q.B. 219.

[1058] Contrast ss.9, 10 of the Factors Act 1889 and ss.25(1), 47 of the Sale of Goods Act 1979.

effect.[1059] The issue or transfer of other documents, for example, a delivery order, does not constitute delivery without an attornment by the bailee.

The seller and buyer must do what is necessary to obtain the attornment. If the third person then refuses to acknowledge the buyer's right, the latter is entitled to treat the contract as discharged.[1060]

44-255

(iv)   Expenses in Connection with Delivery

Expenses of delivery   By s.29(6): "Unless otherwise agreed, the expenses of and incidental to putting the goods into a deliverable state[1061] must be borne by the seller". This subsection does not deal with the expenses of the actual delivery. Here the rule is that, unless otherwise agreed, the expenses of and incidental to making delivery of the goods must be borne by the seller, but those of and incidental to receiving delivery must be borne by the buyer.[1062] So where buyers of oil undertook to receive it from the sellers' ship through the buyers' pipe-lines at the discharging berth, it was held that on the construction of the contract the buyers had undertaken to procure for the sellers the right to have the steamer at the berth for the purpose of discharging there, and that the buyers must bear the cost of the dredging operations, which proved necessary.[1063] Special rules have, however, been elaborated where the sale is on CIF or FOB, etc. terms.[1064]

44-256

(v)   Delivery of the Wrong Quantity[1065]

Defective delivery   Section 30 deals with the delivery of the wrong quantity.[1066]
It is submitted that a delivery which is defective under the section does not ipso facto entitle the buyer to treat the contract as repudiated, but it is open to the seller to withdraw the rejected tender, and substitute a tender of goods in conformity with the contract, provided he does so within the time limited for delivery.[1067]

44-257

Insufficient delivery   By s.30(1):

44-258

[1059] See *Benjamin's Sale of Goods*, 10th edn (2017), paras 8-013, 18-089, 18-237.

[1060] *Pattison v Robinson* (1816) 5 M. & S. 105, 110; cf. *Peter Dumenil & Co Ltd v James Ruddin Ltd* [1953] 1 W.L.R. 815.

[1061] Defined, s.61(5), see above, para.44-016.

[1062] cf. *Neill v Whitworth* (1866) L.R. 1 CP 684; *Playford v Mercer* (1870) 22 L.T. 41; *Acme Wood Flooring Co v Sutherland Innes Co* (1904) 9 Com. Cas. 170; *White v Williams* [1912] A.C. 814.

[1063] *Re Shell Transport Co & Consolidated Petroleum Co* (1904) 20 T.L.R. 517.

[1064] See *Benjamin's Sale of Goods*, 10th edn (2017), paras 19-009, 19-011, 20-008, 20-012, 21-002, 21-010, 21-012, 21-014.

[1065] It is a matter of speculation whether, if the buyer deals as consumer, the additional remedies conferred by Pt 5A of the 1979 Act (see above, para.38-442) would be available to him on the ground of non-conformity of the goods due to the breach of an express term: see *Benjamin's Sale of Goods*, 10th edn (2017), para.8-041 n.241. For contracts made on or after October 1, 2015, the Consumer Rights Act 2015 repeals and replaces those provisions.

[1066] The section is subject to s.31(2), where the contract is one for the sale of goods by instalments: *Regent OHG Aisenstadt und Barig v Francesco of Jermyn Street Ltd* [1981] 3 All E.R. 327. This section does not apply to consumer contracts for the sale of goods which fall within Ch.2 of Pt 1 of the Consumer Rights Act 2015. In consumer contracts for the sale of goods the 2015 Act provides special rules in relation to delivery of the wrong quantity in consumer sales contracts, see above, para.38-526.

[1067] *Borrowman, Phillips & Co v Free & Hollis* (1878) 4 Q.B.D. 500; see *Benjamin's Sale of Goods*, 10th edn (2017), paras 8-045, 12-032.

"Where the seller delivers to the buyer a quantity of goods less than he contracted to sell, the buyer may reject them, but if the buyer accepts the goods so delivered he must pay for them at the contract rate."

Two alternatives are therefore open to the buyer: (i) to reject the insufficient quantity delivered, recover the price (if paid) and sue for any loss occasioned by the seller's breach[1068]; or (ii) to accept the quantity delivered, paying for this at the contract rate, and recovering such part of the price as has been paid for the undelivered balance[1069]; he can also claim damages for breach.[1070] In *Behrend & Co v Produce Brokers Co*[1071] the claimants had sold certain seed to the defendants to be delivered in London, and the claimants' ship, after discharging part only of the seed, left with the remainder to discharge other cargo elsewhere. She returned a fortnight later to complete the delivery to the defendants, who rejected it. It was held that once the delivery had begun the buyers were entitled to receive the whole quantity before the ship left port, and that in the circumstances they were entitled to keep the part actually delivered and to reject the balance.

Unless the seller consents, the subsection does not allow the buyer to accept part only of the goods tendered in attempted performance of the contract and to reject the rest.[1072]

The seller cannot protect himself from the consequences of a short delivery by promising a completed delivery in due course, because s.31(1) provides that "Unless otherwise agreed, the buyer of goods is not bound to accept delivery by instalments".[1073]

44-259 Excessive delivery   By s.30(2):

"Where the seller delivers to the buyer a quantity of goods larger than he contracted to sell, the buyer may accept the goods included in the contract and reject the rest, or he may reject the whole."

And by s.30(3):

"Where the seller delivers to the buyer a quantity of goods larger than he contracted to sell and the buyer accepts the whole of the goods so delivered he must pay for them at the contract rate."

The buyer therefore has three options: first, to reject the whole of the goods delivered[1074]; secondly, to select the correct quantity and to reject the rest[1075]; thirdly,

---

1068 *Harland & Wolff Ltd v Burstall & Co* (1901) 84 L.T. 324.

1069 *Oxendale v Wetherell* (1829) 9 B. & C. 386; *Biggerstaff v Rowatt's Wharf Ltd* [1896] 2 Ch.93; *Behrend & Co v Produce Brokers Co* [1920] 3 K.B. 530.

1070 *Household Machines Ltd v Cosmos Exporters Ltd* [1947] K.B. 217.

1071 [1920] 3 K.B. 530.

1072 *Champion v Short* (1807) 1 Camp. 53; *Tarling v O'Riordan* (1878) 2 L.R.Ir. 82. cf. Hudson (1976) 92 L.Q.R. 506.

1073 See *Reuter v Sala* (1879) 4 C.P.D. 239; *Cobec Brazilian Trading and Warehousing Corp v Toepfer* [1983] 2 Lloyd's Rep. 386 and see below, para.44-262.

1074 *Cunliffe v Harrison* (1851) 6 Exch. 903, 906. But there is some doubt whether the buyer is so entitled if the seller does not seek to charge the buyer with the excess and the excess quantity is not otherwise a burden to the buyer: *Levy v Green* (1857) 8 E. & B. 575, 587; (1859) 1 E. & E. 969, 975; *Rylands v Kreitman* (1865) 19 C.B.(N.S.) 351; *Shipton Anderson & Co v Weil Bros & Co* [1912] 1 K.B. 574, 577.

1075 But not part of the correct quantity or part of the excess. cf. Hudson (1976) 92 L.Q.R. 506.

to accept the whole delivery, paying for the excess at the contract rate.[1076]

Limitation of right to reject   The right to reject the goods for failure to deliver   **44-260**
the exact quantity of goods contracted for is nevertheless alleviated in non-
consumer cases by subs.(2A) of s.30:

"A buyer[1077] may not—

(a)   where the seller delivers a quantity of goods less than he contracted to sell, reject
the goods under subs.(1) above, or

(b)   where the seller delivers a quantity of goods larger than he contracted to sell,
reject the goods under subs.(2) above.

if the shortfall or, as the case may be, excess is so slight that it would be unreasonable for
him to do so."

It is for the seller to show that a shortfall or excess falls within this subsection. At
common law, whether or not the buyer deals as consumer, the right to reject is
subject to the principle *de minimis non curat lex*: a trifling or minute departure from
the exact quantity stipulated does not entitle the buyer to reject the goods.[1078] But
it would appear that subs.(2A), despite its reference to the shortfall or excess being "slight", goes further than this and that a departure which is more than de
minimis could fall within its scope. It might be unreasonable for the buyer to reject
if, for example, a shortfall could be adequately compensated for by damages or, in
the case of an excessive delivery, if it was commercially practical for the buyer to
separate out the correct quantity and return the excess or if he did not have to pay
for the excess.

Derogation from s.30   The whole of s.30 (including subs.(2A)) is subject to any   **44-261**
usage of trade, special agreement, or course of dealing between the parties.[1079] The
most common way for the parties to derogate from its provisions is to stipulate for
a margin by using terms such as "about" or "more or less", but then the seller must
not deliver a quantity outside the margin.[1080] The parties may also include in their
contract a "non-rejection" clause which limits the remedy of the buyer to damages
only.

[1076] *Hart v Mills* (1846) 15 M. & W. 85; *Cunliffe v Harrison*, above; *Gabriel Wade and English Ltd v Arcos Ltd* (1929) 34 Ll. L. Rep. 306.

[1077] The former reference to consumers is deleted by the Consumer Rights Act 2015. Contracts for the sale of goods which fall within Ch.2 of Pt 1 of the 2015 Act are subject to special rules in relation to delivery, see above, para.38-526.

[1078] See *Harland and Wolff Ltd v Burstall & Co* (1901) 6 Com. Cas. 113, 116; *Shipton Anderson & Co v Weil Brothers* [1912] 1 K.B. 574; *EA Ronaasen & Son v Arcos Ltd* (1932) 48 T.L.R. 356; affirmed sub nom. *Arcos Ltd v EA Ronaasen & Son* [1933] A.C. 470; *Margaronis Navigation Agency Ltd v Peabody & Co Ltd* [1965] 1 Q.B. 300. cf. *Jackson v Rotax Motor and Cycle Co* [1910] 2 K.B. 937, 948; *Payne & Routh v Lillico & Sons* (1920) 36 T.L.R. 569; *Wilensko Slaski v Fenwick & Co Ltd* [1938] 3 All E.R. 429; *Rapalli v KL Take Ltd* [1958] 2 Lloyd's Rep. 469.

[1079] 1979 Act s.30(5).

[1080] *Payne & Routh v Lillico & Sons* (1920) 36 T.L.R. 569. See also *Cross v Eglin* (1831) 2 B. & Ad. 106; *Reuter v Sala* (1974) 4 C.P.D. 239; *Harland and Wolff Ltd v Burstall & Co* (1901) 6 Com. Cas. 113 (reasonable latitude exceeded).

(vi)   Instalment Deliveries

44-262   **Instalment deliveries**   By s.31(1)[1081]: "Unless otherwise agreed, the buyer of goods is not bound to accept delivery of them by instalments".[1082] Nor can he demand delivery by instalments.[1083] But the parties may provide, expressly or impliedly,[1084] for delivery by instalments, and in *Howell v Evans*[1085] a contract for the sale of 13 engravings "to be sent to me as published" was held, by its very terms, to be an instalments contract.

44-263   **Stated instalments**[1086]   By s.31(2):

> "Where there is a contract for the sale of goods to be delivered by stated instalments,[1087] which are to be separately paid for, and the seller makes defective deliveries in respect of one or more instalments, or the buyer neglects or refuses to take delivery of or pay for one or more instalments, it is a question in each case depending on the terms of the contract and the circumstances of the case whether the breach of contract is a repudiation of the whole contract or whether it is a severable breach giving rise to a claim for compensation but not to a right to treat the whole contract as repudiated."[1088]

By its express terms s.31(2) applies only if the goods are to be delivered by stated instalments and if the instalments are to be separately paid for, but the common law applies the same principle to other severable contracts for the delivery of goods by instalments.[1089] However, the rule set out in the subsection does not apply to entire contracts, that is, where full and complete delivery of the entire quantity is a condition precedent to the liability of the buyer to pay any part of the price, though the delivery may be made by instalments. In these cases a partial breach is treated as a total breach.[1090]

44-264   **Repudiation of whole contract**   Failure of performance by one party may entitle the other party to treat an instalment contract as repudiated, but only if the breach goes "to the root or essence of the contract"[1091] or deprives the other party of substantially the whole benefit which it was intended that he should receive from

---

[1081] This section does not apply to consumer contracts for the sale of goods which fall within Ch.2 of Pt 1 of the Consumer Rights Act 2015. In consumer contracts for the sale of goods the 2015 Act provides special rules in relation to instalment deliveries in consumer sales contracts, see above, para.38-525.

[1082] *Reuter v Sala* (1879) 4 C.P.D. 239; *Behrend & Co v Produce Brokers Co* [1920] 3 K.B. 530, 534–535; *Cobec Brazilian Trading and Warehousing Corp v Toepfer* [1983] 2 Lloyd's Rep. 386.

[1083] *Reuter v Sala* (1879) 4 C.P.D. 239, 247.

[1084] *Brandt v Lawrence* (1876) 1 Q.B.D. 344; *Colonial Insurance Co of New Zealand v Adelaide Marine Insurance Co* (1886) 12 App. Cas. 128, 138; *Jackson v Rotax Motor and Cycle Co* [1910] 2 K.B. 937.

[1085] (1926) 134 L.T. 570.

[1086] It is probable that s.31(2) applies also by analogy where the buyer deals as consumer and so has the additional remedies conferred by Pt 5A of the Act: see above, n.1065.

[1087] Semble the same principle applies if the instalments are not stated: *Calaminus v Dowlais Iron Co* (1878) 47 L.J. Q.B. 5757 and *Benjamin's Sale of Goods*, 10th edn (2017), para.8-065.

[1088] See also Vol.I, para.24-046.

[1089] See below, para.44-264, and *Benjamin's Sale of Goods*, 10th edn (2017), para.8-065.

[1090] *Longbottom & Co Ltd v Bass, Walker & Co* [1922] W.N. 245.

[1091] *Mersey Steel and Iron Co v Naylor Benzon & Co* (1884) 9 App. Cas. 434, 443–444. See also *Foxholes Nursing Home Ltd v Accora Ltd* [2013] EWHC 3712 (Ch).

the contract.[1092] In *Maple Flock Co Ltd v Universal Furniture Products (Wembley) Ltd*[1093] the test to be considered in applying the subsection was stated by Lord Hewart C.J. to be: "First, the ratio quantitatively which the breach bears to the contract as a whole, and secondly, the degree of probability or improbability that such a breach will be repeated". In that case the contract was for the sale of 100 tons of rag flock, the flock to conform to government standards and to be delivered in separate loads. The sixteenth load was found not to conform to government standards, and the buyers refused to accept further deliveries. The Court of Appeal held that the seller's breach of contract with regard to one delivery was not a repudiation of the whole contract, for the character of the breach was said to be isolated and limited and there was also an "extreme improbability of the breach being repeated".[1094] By contrast in *Robert A Munro & Co Ltd v Meyer*[1095] the contract was for the sale of 1,500 tons of meat and bone meal of a specified quality, to be shipped in equal weekly quantities. After more than half of the whole had been delivered it was found that the meal was adulterated, and the buyer claimed to treat the contract as repudiated. Wright J. came to the following conclusion: "Where the breach is substantial and so serious as the breach in this case and has continued so persistently, the buyer is entitled to say that he has the right to treat the whole contract as repudiated".[1096]

Renunciation of obligations   One party may also be entitled to treat an instalment contract as repudiated if the other party renounces his obligations under it in some fundamental respect.[1097] In *Freeth v Burr*[1098] Lord Coleridge C.J. stated the test to be "whether the acts and conduct of the party evince an intention no longer to be bound by the contract". So in *Mersey Steel and Iron Co v Naylor*,[1099] where the buyer's failure to pay was due to his thinking in error that there was no one to whom payment could safely be made, the vendor company having gone into liquidation, it was held that this was not to be treated as a repudiation of the whole contract.

Disablement from performing   Where one party has, by his own act or default, finally and completely disabled himself from performing an obligation undertaken

44-265

44-266

[1092] See Vol.I, paras 24-041, 24-046.
[1093] [1934] 1 K.B. 148, 157. See also *Cornwall v Henson* [1900] 2 Ch. 298, 304; *Millar's Karri & Jarrah Co v Weddel, Turner & Co* (1909) 100 L.T. 128, 129.
[1094] See also *Simpson v Crippin* (1872) L.R. 8 Q.B. 14; *Payzu Ltd v Saunders* [1919] 2 K.B. 581; *Taylor v Oakes Roncoroni & Co* (1922) 127 L.T. 267; *Ross T Smyth & Co Ltd v TD Bailey Son & Co* [1940] 3 All E.R. 60; *Amos & Wood Ltd v Kaprow* (1948) 64 T.L.R. 110; *Regent OHG Aisenstadt und Barig v Francesco of Jermyn Street Ltd* [1981] 3 All E.R. 327.
[1095] [1930] 2 K.B. 312. See also *Hoare v Rennie* (1859) 5 H. & N. 19; *Honck v Muller* (1881) 7 Q.B.D. 92; *Millar's Karri & Jarrah Co v Weddel, Turner & Co* (1909) 100 L.T. 128, 129.
[1096] At 331.
[1097] See Vol.I, para.24-018.
[1098] (1874) L.R. 9 C.P. 208, 213.
[1099] (1884) 9 App. Cas. 434. See also *Kent v Godts* (1855) 26 L.T.(O.S.) 88; *Freeth v Burr* (1874) L.R. 9 C.P. 208, 213; *Dominion Coal Co Ltd v Dominion Iron and Steel Co Ltd* [1909] A.C. 293; *Household Machines v Cosmos Exports* [1947] K.B. 217; *Shaffer Ltd v Findlay Durham & Brodie* [1953] 1 W.L.R. 106; *Peter Dumenil & Co Ltd v James Ruddin Ltd* [1953] 1 W.L.R. 815; *Bunge GmbH v CCV Landbouwbelang GA* [1980] 1 Lloyd's Rep. 458. Contrast (renunciation); *Withers v Reynolds* (1831) 2 B. & Ad. 882; *Morgan v Bain* (1874) L.R. 10 C.P. 15; *Bloomer v Bernstein* (1874) L.R. 9 C.P. 588; *Berk & Co Ltd v Day and White* (1897) 13 T.L.R. 475; *Warinco AG v Samor SpA* [1979] 1 Lloyd's Rep. 450; *Metro Meat Ltd v Fares Rural Co Pty Ltd* [1985] 2 Lloyd's Rep. 13.

by him, the other party will be entitled to treat an instalment contract as repudiated,[1100] provided that the resulting non-performance would amount to a fundamental breach.[1101]

44-267 **Anticipatory breach: repudiation accepted**[1102] If one party commits a repudiatory breach of the contract of sale, and the repudiation is accepted by the other party, this brings to an end all primary obligations of both parties which have not yet been performed.[1103] The seller is not bound to deliver, nor is the buyer bound to accept and pay for, any further instalments of the goods.[1104] Further, the repudiating party cannot raise as a defence to liability any plea that, had he not repudiated the contract, there would have been no performance by the other party at the time fixed for performance or that the performance would have been defective.[1105] However, when assessing damages for breach, the compensatory principle requires the court to undertake a hypothetical assessment of what would have occurred if there had been no repudiatory breach. The burden would accordingly fall on the innocent party to prove that, had there been no breach, it would have been in a position to fulfil its own obligations under the contract, thereby entitling it to earn whatever consideration was due to it under the contract.[1106] Exceptionally, if, at the time of the repudiation, the other party has (unknown to the repudiating party) committed a breach which would have justified the repudiation[1107] or (semble) if it is clear that the other party was at that time finally and completely disabled from performing,[1108] then he may raise this as a defence to any action for damages brought against him by the other party based on the repudiation. Although he repudiated the contract for the wrong reason or for no reason at all, he may yet justify his action if there were at the time facts in existence which would have provided a good reason.[1109]

44-268 **Repudiation not accepted** On the other hand, if one party commits a repudiatory breach of the contract of sale, but the repudiation is not accepted by the other

---

[1100] See Vol.I, para.24-029.

[1101] *Afovos Shipping Co SA v R Pagnan & Filli* [1984] 1 W.L.R. 195, 203.

[1102] See *Benjamin's Sale of Goods*, 10th edn (2017), paras 9-010—9-017.

[1103] See Vol.I, para.24-049.

[1104] *Cort v Ambergate Ry* (1851) 17 Q.B. 127; *Bank of China, Japan and the Straits v American Trading Co* [1894] A.C. 266, 274; *Braithwaite v Foreign Hardwood Co Ltd* [1905] 2 K.B. 543, 552; *Cooper Ewing & Co v Hamel & Horley Ltd* (1922) 13 Ll.L. Rep. 590, 592; *British and Beningtons Ltd v North Western Cachar Tea Co Ltd* [1923] A.C. 48, 63–66; *Gill & Duffus SA v Berger & Co Inc* [1984] A.C. 382, 395–396.

[1105] *Cooper Ewing & Co v Hamel & Horley Ltd* (1922) 13 Ll.L. Rep. 590, 593; *Taylor v Oakes Roncoroni & Co* (1922) 38 T.L.R. 349, 517; *British and Beningtons Ltd v North Western Cachar Tea Co Ltd* [1923] A.C. 48, 72; *Gill & Duffus SA v Berger & Co Inc* [1984] A.C. 382, 392, 396.

[1106] *Braithwaite v Foreign Hardwood Co Ltd* (1905) 92 L.T. 637 (cf. at [1905] 2 K.B. 543); *British and Beningtons Ltd v North Western Cachar Tea Co Ltd* [1923] A.C. 48, 71, 72; *Esmail v Rosenthal & Sons* [1964] 2 Lloyd's Rep. 447, 466; *Gill & Duffus SA v Berger & Co Inc* [1984] A.C. 382, 392, 396; *Golden Strait Corp v Nippon Yusen Kubishika Kaisha (The Golden Victory)* [2007] UKHL 12, [2007] 2 A.C. 253; *Flame SA v Glory Wealth Shipping PTE Ltd* [2013] EWHC 3153, [2014] 1 All E.R. (Comm) 1043. Contrast *Taylor v Oakes Roncoroni & Co* (1922) 38 T.L.R. 349, 517. On whether damages should be assessed in a different way in commodity sales see P. Todd [2017] L.M.C.L.Q 122.

[1107] *Taylor v Oakes Roncoroni & Co* (1922) 38 T.L.R. 349, 351; affirmed at 517; *Esmail v Rosenthal & Sons Ltd* [1964] 2 Lloyd's Rep. 447, 466.

[1108] *Cooper Ewing & Co v Hamel & Horley Ltd* (1922) 13 Ll.L. Rep. 590; *British and Beningtons Ltd v North Western Cachar Tea Co Ltd* [1923] A.C. 48 at 72. See Vol.I, para.24-029.

[1109] See Vol.I, para.24-014.

party who continues to require performance, then the contract remains alive for the benefit of both parties.[1110] It might therefore be expected that each party would continue to be bound to carry out those of his obligations under the contract which remain unperformed and that it would be a defence for the repudiating party to show that, notwithstanding his repudiation, the other party had failed to perform the contract in accordance with its terms. In *Braithwaite v Foreign Hardwood Co Ltd*,[1111] however, where buyers under a CIF contract wrongfully repudiated the contract by refusing to accept any goods under it, the Court of Appeal held that they thereby waived the performance by the seller of the conditions precedent which would otherwise have been necessary to the enforcement by him of the contract and that the buyers could not raise as a defence to liability the fact that two instalments of the goods subsequently tendered[1112] by the seller were not of the quality required by the contract. The facts of *Braithwaite*'s case are, however, open to interpretation and the case has been explained as one in which the buyer's repudiation was in fact accepted by the seller and at a time at which he had committed no breach of contract which would have justified the repudiation.[1113] In any event, the House of Lords has now held[1114] that, if a repudiation is not accepted, the repudiating party can rely upon a term of the contract which entitles him to terminate the contract upon the other party's subsequent breach. Since the contract remains alive for the benefit of both parties, it would seem that the repudiating party could also take advantage of any subsequent non-performance by the other party which would entitle him to be discharged,[1115] unless he is estopped from so doing by representing to the other party that he will no longer require performance of that obligation[1116] or unless the other party can prove that his breach was caused by or due to the repudiation.[1117]

(vii)   Delivery to a Carrier

Delivery to a carrier   By s.32(1)[1118]:   **44-269**

"Where, in pursuance of a contract of sale, the seller is authorised or required to send the goods to the buyer, delivery of the goods to a carrier (whether named by the buyer or not) for the purpose of transmission to the buyer is prima facie deemed to be a delivery of the goods to the buyer."[1119]

[1110] See Vol.I, paras 24-003, 24-011—24-012.

[1111] [1905] 2 K.B. 543. See also *Cerealmangimi SpA v Toepfer* [1981] 1 Lloyd's Rep. 337; *Bunge Corp v Vegetable Vitamin Foods (Private) Ltd* [1985] 1 Lloyd's Rep. 613.

[1112] Or offered to be tendered.

[1113] *Taylor v Oakes Roncoroni & Co* (1922) 38 T.L.R. 349, 351; affirmed at 517; *Esmail v J Rosenthal & Sons Ltd* [1964] 2 Lloyd's Rep. 447, 466 (not discussed on appeal to the House of Lords [1965] 1 W.L.R. 1117).

[1114] *Fercometal SARL v Mediterranean Shipping Co SA* [1989] A.C. 788 (Vol.I, paras 24-011, 24-026). See also *Segap Garages Ltd v Gulf Oil (Great Britain) Ltd, The Times,* October 24, 1988. (Vol.I, para.24-026). But see *Foran v Wight* (1989) 168 C.L.R. 385, 421–422.

[1115] See Vol.I, para.24-025.

[1116] *Fercometal SARL v Mediterranean Shipping Co SA* [1989] A.C. 788, 805.

[1117] *Segap Garages Ltd v Gulf Oil (Great Britain) Ltd, The Times,* October 24, 1988.

[1118] This section does not apply to consumer contracts for the sale of goods which fall within Ch.2 of Pt 1 of the Consumer Rights Act 2015. In consumer contracts for the sale of goods the 2015 Act provides special rules in relation to delivery in consumer sales contracts, see above, para.38-526.

[1119] *Scottish & Newcastle International Ltd v Othon Ghalanos Ltd* [2008] UKHL 11, [2008] 1 Lloyd's Rep. 462; see *Benjamin's Sale of Goods*, 10th edn (2017), paras 8-014, 19-011, 20-014, 21-073.

The effect of delivery to a carrier for the purpose of transmission to the buyer is prima facie to pass possession to the buyer. It must also be noted that although delivery to a carrier normally terminates the unpaid seller's lien,[1120] the goods may still be stopped in transit[1121]; further, delivery to a carrier does not amount to acceptance by the buyer within the meaning of s.35.[1122]

44-270 Reasonable contract with carrier By s.32(2):

"Unless otherwise authorised by the buyer, the seller must make such contract with the carrier on behalf of the buyer as may be reasonable having regard to the nature of the goods and the other circumstances of the case; and if the seller omits to do so, and the goods are lost or damaged in course of transit, the buyer may decline to treat the delivery to the carrier as a delivery to himself or may hold the seller responsible in damages."

The question which arises here is whether the contract made by the seller with the carrier on the buyer's behalf is a reasonable one. It was considered in *Thomas Young & Sons v Hobson & Partners*.[1123] In that case engines sold and sent to the buyers by railway "at owner's risk" were damaged in the course of transit because they were improperly secured. If the sellers had arranged for the goods to be sent "at company's risk" the railway would have made an inspection to see that the goods were suitably secured. There was no difference in rates at owner's risk and at company's risk. It was held that the sellers had failed to make a reasonable contract with the carrier and the buyers were therefore entitled to refuse to treat the delivery to the carrier as delivery to themselves.

44-271 Notice to enable insurance By s.32(3):

"Unless otherwise agreed, where goods are sent by the seller to the buyer by a route involving sea transit, under circumstances in which it is usual to insure, the seller must give such notice to the buyer as may enable him to insure them during their sea transit; and, if the seller fails to do so, the goods are at his risk during such sea transit."

This provision does not normally apply to CIF contracts because in such contracts it is the seller's duty to insure[1124]; but it does apply to FOB contracts unless the buyer has sufficient information to enable him to insure or has waived notice.[1125] Thus in

---

Contrast *Dunlop v Lambert* (1839) 6 Cl. & F. 600, 620; *Badische Anilin und Soda Fabrik v Basle Chemical Works* [1898] A.C. 200, 207; *Galbraith and Grant Ltd v Block* [1922] 2 K.B. 155, 156; *Scottish & Newcastle International Ltd v Othon Galanos Ltd* [2008] UKHL 11, 39 (carrier employee or agent of seller).

[1120] 1979 Act s.43(1), see below, para.44-321.

[1121] 1979 Act s.45(1), see below, para.44-326.

[1122] See below, paras 44-278—44-289. The presumption is that the carrier is the buyer's agent to take delivery, but is not his agent to accept the goods in performance of the contract.

[1123] (1949) 65 T.L.R. 365. See also *Wimble, Sons & Co Ltd v Rosenberg & Sons* [1913] 3 K.B. 743; *Gatoil International Inc v Tradax Petroleum Ltd* [1985] 1 Lloyd's Rep. 350; *Benjamin's Sale of Goods*, 10th edn (2017), paras 8-015, 18-296.

[1124] *Law and Bonar Ltd v British American Tobacco Co Ltd* [1916] 2 K.B. 605. See *Benjamin's Sale of Goods*, 10th edn (2017), paras 18-297, 19-118, 20-044, 21-106.

[1125] It does not apply to FOB contracts if the seller has undertaken to arrange for shipment and insurance. For a discussion of this point, see *Pyrene Co Ltd v Scindia Navigation Co Ltd* [1954] 2 Q.B. 402, 424; *Benjamin's Sale of Goods*, 10th edn (2017), paras 18-290, 20-043. See also (C&F) *Benjamin's Sale of Goods*, 10th edn (2017), para.21-013. cf. *ERG Raffinerie Mediterranee SpA v Chevron USA Inc* [2006] EWHC 1322 (Comm), [2006] 2 Lloyd's Rep. 543 at [56] (affirmed [2007] EWCA Civ

Wimble Sons & Co v Rosenberg & Sons[1126] goods were sold FOB Antwerp to be shipped as required, payment by cash against bills of lading; the sellers were left to select the ship. The sellers shipped the goods, without having insured them, and both goods and ship were lost at sea. When the bills were presented for payment, the buyers refused to pay on the ground that the sellers had not given them such notice as was required by s.32(3) and they had consequently not insured the goods. It was held that, before the goods were shipped, the buyers had all the information necessary to enable them to make a particular insurance, and that therefore there was no obligation upon the sellers to give notice of the shipment on a particular ship. It is a moot point whether this rule could be extended by analogy to other forms of transport.

Deterioration   By s.33[1127]:   **44-272**

"Where the seller of goods agrees to deliver them at his own risk at a place other than that where they are when sold, the buyer must nevertheless (unless otherwise agreed) take any risk of deterioration in the goods necessarily incident to the course of transit."

The rule only applies where the seller has agreed (expressly or impliedly) to assume the risk during transit. The buyer is bound to accept the goods if only deteriorated to the extent that they are necessarily subject to in the course of transit from one place to another.[1128] The rule is excludable by contrary agreement and it is quite possible for the seller to agree to bear the whole risk.

Seller's responsibilities at point of delivery   In *Mash & Murrell Ltd v Emanuel* **44-273**
Ltd,[1129] Diplock J. said that, where goods are sold under a contract which involves transit before use, there is an implied term in the contract of sale that the goods should be dispatched in such a condition that they can endure the normal journey and upon arrival at their destination be suitable for the ordinary purpose for which such goods are intended to be used and be of merchantable quality. This dictum appears to be good law,[1130] at least so far as perishable goods are concerned.[1131] In the

---

[1126] 494, [2007] 2 Lloyd's Rep. 542).

[1126] [1913] 3 K.B. 743. Buckley L.J., however, pointed out at 754 that the fact that the buyer could protect himself by a general covering policy would not prevent the application of s.32(3): if this were so, the subsection would be meaningless.

[1127] This section does not apply to consumer contracts for the sale of goods which fall within Ch.2 of Pt 1 of the Consumer Rights Act 2015. In consumer contracts for the sale of goods the 2015 Act provides special rules in relation to delivery and risk in consumer sales contracts, see above paras 38-526 and 38-490.

[1128] *Bull v Robison* (1854) 10 Exch. 342, 346. See *Benjamin's Sale of Goods*, 10th edn (2017), paras 6-018, 18-295, 19-119, 20-099.

[1129] [1961] 1 W.L.R. 862.

[1130] *Beer & Walker* (1877) 46 L.J. Q.B. 677; *Ollett v Jordan* [1918] 2 K.B. 41; *Broome v Pardess Co-operative Society* [1939] 3 All E.R. 978; reversed on other grounds [1940] 1 All E.R. 603; *AB Kemp Ltd v Tolland* [1956] 2 Lloyd's Rep. 681, 685; *H Glynn (Covent Garden) Ltd v Wittleder* [1959] 2 Lloyd's Rep. 409; *Gardano and Giampieri v Greek Petroleum, etc. Co* [1962] 1 W.L.R. 40, 53; *Gatoil International Inc v Tradax Petroleum Ltd* [1985] 1 Lloyd's Rep. 350, 358; *Benjamin's Sale of Goods*, 10th edn (2017), paras 6-020, 11-067, 18-322, 20-042. Contrast *KG Bominflot Bunkersgesellschaft etc. & Co v Petroplus Marketing AG* [2010] EWCA Civ 1145, [2011] 1 Lloyd's Rep. 442 at [45], where Rix L.J. suggested that the implied term was precluded by s.14(1) of the 1979 Act.

[1131] On non-perishable goods, see *Oleificio Zucchi SpA v Northern Sales Ltd* [1965] 2 Lloyd's Rep. 496; *Cordova Land Co Ltd v Victor Brothers Inc* [1966] 1 W.L.R. 793.

case itself, Cyprus potatoes were sold C&F Liverpool. They were in good condition when shipped but were rotten on arrival. If the cause of the rotting had been, for example, a fungus infection, or wetting before or at the time of shipment, the seller would have been liable for breach of the implied term stated by Diplock J. But the cause of the rotting was found by the Court of Appeal[1132] to be poor ventilation occurring after shipment, so that the seller was not liable for the deterioration. As a result, where the warranty applies "an extraordinary deterioration of the goods due to abnormal conditions experienced during transit [is one] for which the buyer takes the risk. A necessary and inevitable deterioration during transit which will render them unmerchantable on arrival is normally one for which the seller is liable".[1133] On the other hand the terms of the contract may be such as to show that the goods are to meet their specification at the time they are delivered on board the vessel but that thereafter the buyer should assume the risk of any deterioration of or changes in the goods.[1134]

44-274   At first sight, this rule appears to be the precise opposite to that stated in s.33. However, it must be noted that s.33 applies only where the seller agrees to deliver the goods at his own risk at a place other than that where they are when sold, and does not apply to a case where (as under a C&F, CIF or FOB contract) the goods are effectively at the buyer's risk after shipment. But in situations to which s.33 applies, it would seem that the words "necessarily incident to the course of transit" should not be taken to extend to cases where perishable goods are dispatched by the seller in such a state as to be unable to withstand normal transit, but only to cover deterioration which all goods of that kind would necessarily suffer during transit.[1135]

(c)   Examination and Acceptance

44-275   **Buyer's right of examining the goods**   By s.34[1136]:

> "Unless otherwise agreed, when the seller tenders delivery of goods to the buyer, he is bound on request to afford the buyer a reasonable opportunity of examining the goods for the purpose of ascertaining whether they are in conformity with the contract and, in the case of a contract for sale by sample, of comparing the bulk with the sample."

Thus where the buyer has not been given an opportunity to examine the goods, he is not in breach of contract by not accepting them: though conversely if he refuses to examine, the seller may not be in breach if he does not deliver.[1137]

44-276   **Place for examination**   The prima facie rule is that the place of delivery is the place for examination.[1138] This presumption is, however, displaced if the terms of

---

[1132] [1962] 1 W.L.R. 16.

[1133] *Mash & Murrell Ltd v Joseph I Emanuel Ltd* [1961] 1 W.L.R. 862, 871.

[1134] *KG Bominflot Bunkersgesellschaft etc. & Co v Petroplus Marketing AG* [2010] EWCA Civ 1145, [2011] 1 Lloyd's Rep. 442; see para.44-111, above.

[1135] See Sassoon (1965) 28 M.L.R. 189.

[1136] Nothing in this section affects the operation of the time limit for the consumer's short-term right to reject under the Consumer Rights Act 2015. On the consumer buyer's right to reject under the 2015 Act see above, paras 38-513—38-521.

[1137] *Walter W Potts & Co Ltd v Brown, Macfarlane & Co Ltd* (1924) 30 Com. Cas. 64.

[1138] *Perkins v Bell* [1893] 1 Q.B. 193.

the contract[1139] or the circumstances of the case (e.g. that the place is inconvenient[1140] or the goods are packed in such a way that examination before final destination would be difficult[1141]) indicate a different intention. Such will frequently be the case in overseas sales.[1142]

Waiver   On general principle the buyer may waive his right to examine the goods, for instance, where he expressly accepts them without troubling to examine them. This is, however, not so if the buyer deals as consumer and has had no opportunity to examine.[1143] Subject to this, the right may also be excluded by the terms of the contract express or implied: thus in a CIF sale the buyer must pay against the documents without having examined the goods,[1144] and in auctions examination after sale is only relevant for the purpose of ascertaining that the goods received are those bought.[1145]

44-277

Acceptance   Section 35 of the 1979 Act[1146] provides:

44-278

"(1)   The buyer is deemed to have accepted the goods subject to subs.(2) below—
(a)   when he intimates to the seller that he has accepted them, or
(b)   when the goods have been delivered to him and he does any act in relation to them which is inconsistent with the ownership of the seller.
(2)   Where goods are delivered to the buyer, and he has not previously examined them, he is not deemed to have accepted them under subs.(1) above until he has had a reasonable opportunity of examining them for the purpose—
(a)   of ascertaining whether they are in conformity with the contract, and
(b)   in the case of a contract for sale by sample, of comparing the bulk with the sample.
(3)   Where the buyer deals as consumer ... the buyer cannot lose his right to rely on subs.(2) above by agreement, waiver or otherwise."[1147]

This section relates to the loss of the right to reject the goods by acceptance under s.11(4).[1148] It should be noted that as a matter of principle the party entitled to insist that goods have been accepted may waive his rights in this respect and take them

---

[1139] See *Heilbutt v Hickson* (1872) L.R. 7 C.P. 438.

[1140] See *Grimoldby v Wells* (1875) L.R. 10 C.P. 391 (transfer from one vehicle to another).

[1141] See *Molling & Co v Dean & Son Ltd* (1901) 18 T.L.R. 217 (books); *Van den Hurk v R Martens & Co Ltd* [1920] 1 K.B. 850 (sodium sulphate); cf. *Saunt v Belcher and Gibbons Ltd* (1920) 90 L.J. K.B. 541 (coke).

[1142] See *Benjamin's Sale of Goods*, 10th edn (2017), paras 12-045, 19-166, 20-115, 20-116, 21-107.

[1143] On the consumer buyer's right to reject under the 2015 Act see above, paras 38-513—38-521.

[1144] *E Clemens Horst & Co v Biddell Bros* [1912] A.C. 18 (though he may reject later). See also *Polenghi Bros v Dried Milk Co Ltd* (1904) 92 L.T. 64 (sale by sample).

[1145] *Pettitt v Mitchell* (1842) 4 Man. & G. 819; *Isherwood v Whitmore* (1843) 11 M. & W. 347.

[1146] This section does not apply to consumer contracts for the sale of goods which fall within Ch.2 of Pt 1 of the Consumer Rights Act 2015. In consumer contracts for the sale of goods the 2015 Act provides special rules in relation to the right to reject in consumer sales contracts, see above paras 38-513—38-521.

[1147] subs.(3) only applies to acceptance under subs.(2). General principles of waiver are however presumably relevant. This subsection is deleted by the Consumer Rights Act 2015. In consumer contracts for the sale of goods the 2015 Act provides special rules in relation to the right to reject in consumer sales contracts, see above, paras 38-513—38-521. In consumer sales contracts the buyer has a so-called "early right to reject", which is normally lost after 30 days from delivery of the goods.

[1148] See above, para.44-068.

back.[1149]

44-279 Intimation of acceptance   The intimation may presumably be express or implied. Signature by or on behalf of the buyer of a delivery note acknowledging that he had taken delivery of the goods would not of itself amount to an intimation of acceptance unless it could reasonably be inferred from the wording of the note and the surrounding circumstances that the buyer had accepted the goods. An acknowledgment that the buyer had inspected goods when he had not would only be effective in favour of a seller who relied on it.[1150] And by virtue of subs.(3), none of these would affect a buyer dealing as consumer and seeking to reject at common law who had not had the opportunity to examine. Asking for information or discussing remedial measures, so keeping the matter open, need not be an intimation of acceptance.[1151]

44-280 Act inconsistent with the ownership of the seller   The second instance of acceptance listed in subs.(1) gives rise to some problems of interpretation. In many situations where the goods have been delivered to the buyer, the property in the goods will have passed to the buyer, so that the seller has no ownership of the goods with which the buyer can inconsistently deal. It is, however, said that the fact that the buyer has a right to reject makes the property conditional only and leaves a reversionary interest in the seller, and it is with that reversionary interest that the buyer must not act inconsistently.[1152]

44-281   The policy which lies behind this provision is also not clear. Some, perhaps the majority, of cases concern situations where the goods cannot in fact be returned, because, for example, they have been incorporated into a structure[1153] or consumed, or more of them used than is necessary for testing or fitting.[1154] In such cases it is not difficult to see why the goods should be held to have been accepted, and the right to reject consequently lost, because restitutio in integrum is no longer possible. The wording of the provision is, however, in wider terms and a second group of cases brings within the concept of "any act in relation to [the goods] which is inconsistent with the ownership of the seller" acts done in relation to the goods, most clearly resale and forwarding to a sub-buyer.[1155] This line of reasoning has been extended still further, on an uncertain basis, to cover putting goods up for sale in one's own name and buying them in,[1156] mortgaging them[1157] and reselling them[1158] (but not unloading them,[1159] rebagging them,[1160] insuring them,[1161] claim-

---

[1149] *Whitecap Leisure Ltd v John H Rundle Ltd* [2008] EWCA Civ 429, [2008] 2 Lloyd's Rep. 216.

[1150] cf. "acknowledgment" clauses: see Vol.I, para.15-147.

[1151] *Clegg v Anderson* [2003] EWCA Civ 320, [2003] 2 Lloyd's Rep. 32; as explained in *Jones v Gallagher* [2004] EWCA Civ 10, [2005] 1 Lloyd's Rep. 377.

[1152] *Kwei Tek Chao v British Traders & Shippers Ltd* [1954] 2 Q.B. 459, 487; *J Rosenthal & Sons Ltd v Esmail* [1965] 1 W.L.R. 1117, 1131.

[1153] *Mechan & Sons v Bow, M'Lachlan & Co Ltd*, 1910 S.C. 758 (ship).

[1154] See a case before the Act, *Harnor v Groves* (1855) 15 C.B. 667.

[1155] *Hardy & Co v Hillerns & Fowler* [1923] 2 K.B. 490; *E & S Ruben Ltd v Faire Bros & Co Ltd* [1949] 1 K.B. 254; *Pelhams (Materials) Ltd v Mercantile Commodities Syndicate* [1953] 2 Lloyd's Rep. 281. But contrast (dealings with documents) *Kwei Tek Chao v British Traders & Shippers Ltd* [1954] 2 Q.B. 459, 485–488.

[1156] *Parker v Palmer* (1821) 4 B. & A. 387, also before the Act.

[1157] *Metals Ltd v Diamond* [1930] 4 D.L.R. 886.

[1158] *Chapman v Morton* (1843) 11 M. & W. 534; *Vargas Pena Apezteguia y Cia SAIC v Peter Cremer GmbH* [1987] 1 Lloyd's Rep. 394; cf. *J & J Cunningham Ltd v Robert A Munro & Co Ltd* (1922)

ing on insurance relating to them[1162] or making inquiries about resale[1163]). It may be argued that the reason why, in these cases, the buyer is deemed to have accepted the goods and so lost his right of rejection is because the acts in question show that he has thereby elected to affirm the contract, and he should not be permitted to resile from that election. But, if this is so, then it is difficult to see how there is any true election to "affirm" the contract in situations where the buyer has no knowledge that the goods are defective or of his right to reject; yet rejection in such a situation may be barred. It would be preferable if s.35(1)(b) were confined to cases where the goods simply cannot be returned. Hence if the buyer has resold the goods but can recover the goods from the sub-buyer (i.e. because the sub-buyer has himself rejected them) he should be able to reject them.[1164] He should also be able to reject them if he delivers the goods to a third party for repair.[1165] This approach is to some extent supported by s.35(6)(b) which provides that the buyer is not by virtue of s.35 deemed to have accepted the goods "merely because the goods are delivered to another under a sub-sale or other disposition".

Opportunity to examine   The acts which are stated in s.35(1)(a) and (b) to   **44-282**
constitute acceptance are both subject to s.35(2). The effect of this subsection is that, where goods are delivered to the buyer, he will not be deemed to have accepted them unless he has previously examined the goods or has had a reasonable opportunity of examining them. A commercial buyer could nevertheless agree to forego or waive his right of examination.[1166] But if the buyer deals as consumer he cannot so lose his right to rely on s.35(2).

Lapse of reasonable time   Section 35 provides yet a third way in which accept-   **44-283**
ance will take place and the right to reject become barred:

> "(4)   The buyer is also deemed to have accepted the goods when after the lapse of a reasonable time he retains the goods without intimating to the seller that he has rejected them.
> (5)   The questions that are material in determining for the purposes of subs.(4) above whether a reasonable time has elapsed include whether the buyer has had a reasonable opportunity of examining the goods for the purpose mentioned in subs.(2) above."

What is a "reasonable time" for rejection is a question of fact.[1167] In general the   **44-284**
buyer is entitled to a reasonable time in which to assess the defects and decide what to do[1168]; but if his delay is unnecessarily prejudicial to the seller, it may be held unreasonable.[1169] There was a tendency to assume that in the interests of finality the

---

28 Com. Cas. 42.
[1159] *Libar Wood Co v H Smith & Sons Ltd* (1930) 37 Ll.L. Rep. 296.
[1160] *Dower & Co v Corrie, Maccoll & Son Ltd* (1925) 23 Ll. L. Rep. 100.
[1161] *Clegg v Anderson* [2003] EWCA Civ 320, [2003] 2 Lloyd's Rep. 32.
[1162] *JS Robertson (Aust) Pty Ltd v Martin* (1956) 94 C.L.R. 30.
[1163] *Fisher Reeves & Co Ltd v Armour & Co Ltd* [1920] 3 K.B. 614.
[1164] But see *Jordeson & Co v Stora Kopparbergs Bergslags Aktiebolag* (1931) 41 Ll.L. Rep. 201.
[1165] cf. s.35(6) (repair by or under an arrangement with the seller).
[1166] See above, para.44-277.
[1167] 1979 Act s.59. See *Fisher, Reeves & Co Ltd v Armour & Co Ltd* [1920] 3 K.B. 614, 624; *Leaf v International Galleries* [1950] 2 K.B. 86; *Long v Lloyd* [1958] 1 W.L.R. 753.
[1168] *Fisher, Reeves & Co Ltd v Armour & Co Ltd*, above; *Manifatture Tessile Laniera Wooltex v J B Ashley Ltd* [1979] 2 Lloyd's Rep. 28; *Patient* (1980) 43 M.L.R. 463.
[1169] *Morrison and Mason Ltd v Clarkson Bros* (1898) 25 R. 427 (goods subjected to rough usage).

time should not be long: and there is certainly no requirement that the time be sufficiently long to enable a defect of the type concerned to manifest itself, for this may in the case of some products not be for several years. In 1987 an approach was adopted at first instance that the time should not be related to special circumstances of the buyer, but should be more generally "a reasonable practical interval in commercial terms".[1170] It has more recently, however, been held in the Court of Appeal that, since the amendments of 1994, this no longer represents the law, and time taken to ascertain what repairs or changes are needed and implement them is not necessarily to be counted.[1171] The question whether the buyer has had a reasonable opportunity for examination is relevant to the determination whether a reasonable time has elapsed.[1172] Where goods are sold for resale, a reasonable time to intimate rejection will usually be the time actually taken to resell the goods together with an additional period in which they can be inspected and tried out by the sub-purchaser.[1173] In determining what is a reasonable time the seller's conduct also may be relevant; as where he has acquiesced in an extension of time,[1174] or by means of a misrepresentation has caused the buyer to prolong the trial of the goods.[1175] Custom may also be considered, and in one old case a custom that only one day should be allowed for rejection was upheld.[1176]

44-285   **Attempts at repair**   Where the buyer allows the seller to attempt to repair defects in the goods, there might be a risk that the buyer would in consequence lose his right to reject, whether because this was an implied indication of acceptance or because the attempts cause a reasonable time to elapse. Section 35(6) seeks to meet this problem by providing that the buyer is not deemed to have accepted the goods "merely because he asks for, or agrees to, their repair by or under an arrangement with the seller". The House of Lords has recently considered the question whether a buyer must accept goods which have been repaired to the appropriate standard, but where no information is given as to what was or had been wrong with them. It was held that he need not; and it would seem that even if an explanation is given, sometimes (as in this case) the indication of the nature of the repair would be

---

[1170] *Bernstein v Pamsons Motors (Golders Green) Ltd* [1987] 2 All E.R. 220 (decided before s.35 was amended and replaced by the Sale and Supply of Goods Act 1994 s.2(1)): the right to reject a defective new car was held to have been lost after 21 days, though the buyer had been ill for part of the time and had only driven 120 miles. cf. *M & J Hurst Consultants Ltd v Grange Motors (Brentwood) Ltd* (Russell J.), Manchester, October 1981 (about four months): see (1988) 104 L.Q.R. 16; *Fiat Auto Financial Services v Connelly*, 2007 S.L.T. (Sh Ct) 111 (attempts to rectify: car used as taxi over 40,000 miles over more than eight months: rejectable); *Kingsway Hall Hotel Ltd v Red Sky IT (Hounslow) Ltd* [2010] EWHC 965 (TCC) (computer program: five months).

[1171] *Clegg v Andersson* [2003] EWCA Civ 320, [2003] 2 Lloyd's Rep. 32 (yacht: eight months); as explained in *Jones v Gallagher* [2004] EWCA Civ 10, [2005] 1 Lloyd's Rep. 377 (fitted kitchen: too late to reject after four month's negotiation). See also *Douglas v Genvarigill Co Ltd* [2010] CSOH 14 (car not rejectable after 15 months); *Russo v Belcar Pty Ltd* [2011] SASCFC 151 (acceptance by acquiescence in performance of warranty work and lack of unequivocal rejection).

[1172] 1979 Act s.35(5).

[1173] *Truk (UK) Ltd v Tokmakidis GmbH* [2000] 1 Lloyd's Rep. 543, 551.

[1174] *Lucy v Mouflet* (1860) 5 H. & N. 229 (failure to answer letter of complaint). And see *Farnworth Finance Facilities Ltd v Attryde* [1970] 1 W.L.R. 1053.

[1175] *Munro & Co v Bennet & Son*, 1911 S.C. 337; *Cork v Greavette Boats Ltd* [1940] 4 D.L.R. 202; but cf. *Long v Lloyd* [1958] 1 W.L.R. 753, 760. And if the buyer negotiates for a reduction in price this may indicate acceptance: see *Canterbury Seed Co Ltd v J G Ward Farmers' Association Ltd* (1895) 13 N.Z.L.R. 96.

[1176] *Sanders v Jameson* (1848) 2 Car. & K. 557.

enough to justify continued rejection. The basis of the reasoning cannot be that there is a *right* to retender, nor that the retender of goods so repaired of itself puts the seller in compliance under the main contract, for either of these (unless perhaps the view is taken that the returned goods would not have been of satisfactory quality unless accompanied by an explanation) would have led to a different result. It is rather that the arrangement for repair was a separate transaction suspending the right to reject. It seems that this may have been by way of a separate contract, unilateral or even bilateral, or by way of a conditional waiver; and the implied terms of that arrangement in the situation in issue (though not necessarily always) required the seller to state what had been wrong, or even sometimes to specify this before commencing on repair.[1177]

Acceptance of part In principle acceptance of part of the goods is acceptance of the whole and thus bars the right to reject.[1178] But this rule is subject to two exceptions. In the first place it does not apply where the contract is severable. One example of a severable (or divisible) contract is a contract for the sale of goods to be delivered by stated instalments which are to be separately paid for,[1179] though there can be other cases.[1180] Where the contract is severable, a buyer may treat it as discharged if there is a renunciation or repudiatory failure of performance by the seller, despite the fact that he has accepted instalments of the goods previously delivered to him.[1181] He must of course pay for any deliveries accepted.[1182]

44-286

The second exception is set out in s.35A(1) of the Act[1183]:

44-287

"If the buyer—

    (a)   has the right to reject the goods by reason of a breach on the part of the seller that affects some or all of them, but

    (b)   accepts some of the goods, including, where there are any goods unaffected by the breach, all such goods,

he does not by accepting them lose his right to reject the rest."

Goods are "affected by a breach" if by reason of a breach they are not in conformity with the contract.[1184] Where the sale is by instalments, the provision applies to

---

[1177] *J & H Ritchie Ltd v Lloyd Ltd* [2007] UKHL 9, [2007] 1 W.L.R. 670. See Bridge [2007] J.B.L. 814; Loi [2007] J.B.L. 807; Low (2007) 123 L.Q.R. 536. In *Gregg & Co (Knottingley) Ltd v Emherst Glass Ltd* [2005] EWHC 804 (TCC) it was held that continuing malfunctions of computerised machines, despite best efforts at remediation over two years, were repudiatory of "the contract for sale and after sales services" though the right to reject had been lost.

[1178] 1979 Act s.11(4); see above, para.44-068.

[1179] 1979 Act s.31(2); see above, para.44-263.

[1180] See *Longbottom & Co Ltd v Bass, Walker & Co* [1927] W.N. 245 (delivery in instalments, price payable by monthly account); *Jackson v Rotax Motor & Cycle Co* [1910] 2 K.B. 937 (deliveries "as required"); *Molling & Co v Dean & Son Ltd* (1901) 18 T.L.R. 217; *Regent OHG Aisenstadt und Barig v Francesco of Jermyn St Ltd* [1981] 3 All E.R. 327.

[1181] 1979 Act s.31(2); see above, paras 44-263 et seq.

[1182] *Jackson v Rotax Motor & Cycle Co*, above; *Cehave NV v Bremer Handelsgesellschaft mbH (The Hansa Nord)* [1974] 2 Lloyd's Rep. 216, 226; decision reversed [1976] Q.B. 44. See also *Tarling v O'Riordan* (1878) 2 L.R. Ir. 82.

[1183] This section does not apply to consumer contracts for the sale of goods which fall within Ch.2 of Pt 1 of the Consumer Rights Act 2015. In consumer contracts for the sale of goods the 2015 Act provides special rules in relation to partial rejection in consumer sales contracts, see above, para.38-515.

[1184] 1979 Act s.35A(3).

each instalment.[1185] The section applies unless a contrary intention appears in, or is to be implied, from the contract.[1186]

44-288 It will be noted that, in order to take advantage of s.35A(1), the buyer must accept *all* the conforming goods; he cannot accept part of them only. But he is permitted to choose how much of the *non*-conforming goods he will accept or reject. The subsection does not, however, impose on the buyer any obligation to accept those goods which are in conformity with the contract: he can always reject the whole. Presumably the buyer must pay for the goods accepted at the contract rate or, if the price has been paid, can recover the price of the goods rejected.

44-289 Section 35A(1) is nevertheless qualified where the goods sold can be divided into "commercial units". Section 35(7) provides:

> "Where the contract is for the sale of goods making one or more commercial units, a buyer accepting any goods included in a unit is deemed to have accepted all the goods making the unit; and in this subsection 'commercial unit' means a unit division of which would materially impair the value of the goods or the character of the unit."

Standard examples are one of a pair of shoes or a volume of a multi-volume encyclopedia. Although part acceptance of goods within a unit amounts to total acceptance of that unit, a buyer could nevertheless accept a unit or units which conform with the contract while rejecting those that do not conform.

44-290 **Return to seller** By s.36[1187]:

> "Unless otherwise agreed, where goods are delivered to the buyer, and he refuses to accept them, having the right to do so, he is not bound to return them to the seller, but it is sufficient if he intimates to the seller that he refuses to accept them."

The property in the goods is by rejection revested in the seller and they become at his risk[1188] if they were not so already. If they have been damaged or destroyed without the buyer's fault it is not clear whether they may still be rejected. Cases suggest that they may[1189]; but it is arguable that unless the damage or destruction arises from the very defect complained of, the risk should be on the buyer.[1190] It is certainly true that the fact that goods have deteriorated has been taken into account in the assessment of what is a "reasonable time" under what is now s.35(4).[1191] A buyer who rejects cannot exercise a lien over the goods against repayment of the price.[1192]

[1185] 1979 Act s.35A(2).

[1186] 1979 Act s.35A(4).

[1187] This section does not apply to consumer contracts for the sale of goods which fall within Ch.2 of Pt 1 of the Consumer Rights Act 2015. In consumer contracts for the sale of goods the 2015 Act provides special rules in relation to the right to reject in consumer sales contracts, see above, paras 38-513—38-521.

[1188] See *Grimoldby v Wells* (1875) L.R. 10 C.P. 391; *Lucy v Mouflet* (1860) 5 H. & N. 229. A buyer was awarded damages for storing rejected goods in *Kolfor Plant Ltd v Tilbury Plant Ltd* (1977) 121 S.J. 390. As to the effect of acts by a buyer after rejection see *Tradax Export SA v European Grain and Shipping Ltd* [1983] 2 Lloyd's Rep. 100; *Whitecap Leisure Ltd v John H Rundle Ltd* [2008] EWCA Civ 429, [2008] 2 Lloyd's Rep. 216.

[1189] *Head v Tattersall* (1871) L.R. 7 Ex. 7; *Chapman v Withers* (1888) 20 Q.B.D. 824; *Kinnear v Brodie* (1902) 3 F. 540, 544, 545; *Boyd & Forrest v Glasgow and South-Western Ry Co*, 1915 S.C. (H.L.) 20, 29; *Vitol SA v Esso Australia Ltd* [1989] 1 Lloyd's Rep. 96.

[1190] See *Benjamin's Sale of Goods*, 10th edn (2017), paras 12-059—12-061.

[1191] *Morrison and Mason Ltd v Clarkson Bros* (1898) 25 R. 427.

[1192] *J L Lyons & Co Ltd v May & Baker Ltd* [1923] 1 K.B. 685.

Refusal to take delivery   By s.37:   **44-291**

"(1)   When the seller is ready and willing to deliver the goods, and requests the buyer to take delivery,[1193] and the buyer does not within a reasonable time[1194] after such request take delivery of the goods, he is liable to the seller for any loss occasioned by his neglect or refusal to take delivery,[1195] and also for a reasonable charge for the care and custody of the goods.[1196]

(2)   Nothing in this section affects the rights of the seller where the neglect or refusal of the buyer to take delivery amounts to a repudiation of the contract."

Where the property has passed but the buyer does not take delivery, the seller's   **44-292** principal remedy is an action for the price under s.49.[1197] He may also claim damages under s.37. Where the property has not passed his remedy normally lies in damages.[1198] In such a case failure to take delivery would normally indicate wrongful repudiation and would often be difficult to distinguish from non-acceptance; but cases could arise where the two were distinguishable.[1199]

(d)   Payment

Payment by buyer   It is the duty of the buyer to pay for the goods in accordance   **44-293** with the terms of the contract of sale.[1200] The method, place and time of payment are, therefore, in the first instance to be determined by reference to the terms of the contract of sale.[1201] The duty of the buyer to pay the price does not, however, necessarily connote a right on the part of the seller to sue for the price[1202] and a wrongful neglect or refusal by the buyer to pay the price may give rise only to an action for damages for non-acceptance.[1203]

Amount of payment   The buyer is bound to pay to the seller the full price of the   **44-294** goods unless by their contract the parties have agreed that a discount shall be allowed. If a discount is stipulated for a particular period, the full price is payable should the reduced price not be paid before the end of the period.[1204]

Payment in cash   Unless otherwise agreed the seller is entitled to payment in cash   **44-295** and in legal currency.[1205] But the parties may expressly or impliedly agree that payment may be made in some other manner, e.g. by cheque or by credit or charge card

---

[1193] Defined, s.61(1), see above, para.44-015.

[1194] This is a question of fact: s.59.

[1195] But the seller may claim only if he himself is ready and willing to deliver: see *Forrest & Son Ltd v Aramayo* (1900) 83 L.T. 335.

[1196] See *Greaves v Ashlin* (1813) 3 Camp. 426. See also *Penarth Dock Engineering Co v Pounds* [1963] 1 Lloyd's Rep. 359 (benefit of free storage given as damages for trespass).

[1197] See below, para.44-359.

[1198] Unless the price is payable on a day certain irrespective of delivery: s.49(2): see below, para.44-364.

[1199] e.g. where in an overseas sale the buyer accepts documents but not goods; or accepts goods after delay. See *Benjamin's Sale of Goods*, 10th edn (2017), paras 19-235, 20-147.

[1200] Sale of Goods Act 1979 s.29.

[1201] Otherwise, see s.28 of the Act; see above, para.44-237.

[1202] See below, para.44-359.

[1203] See below, para.44-367.

[1204] *Amos and Wood Ltd v Kaprow* (1948) 64 T.L.R. 110. *Aliter* if the discount is a "trade" discount.

[1205] See Vol.I, para.21-040.

or by credit transfer,[1206] and such an implication may be made by course of dealing between the parties or by trade custom.

44-296 **Conditional and absolute payment** Payment by negotiable instrument[1207] or by letter of credit[1208] is normally regarded as conditional payment only: the seller's remedy to sue for the price is suspended, but revives if the instrument is dishonoured on presentation[1209] or if payment of the letter of credit is wrongfully refused. However, payment by means of a credit or charge card[1210] and probably by cheque supported by a cheque guarantee card[1211] is absolute payment and a discharge of the buyer's obligation to pay.

44-297 **Place of payment** Where a place of payment is specified in the contract of sale, payment must be made at that place. Otherwise payment is to be made at the seller's place of business, if he has one, or if not, his residence.[1212] The place of payment may be a condition of the contract and not merely an intermediate term.[1213]

44-298 **Time of payment** The time of payment may be stipulated in the contract, or, if not expressly so stipulated, be determined by reference to the course of dealing between the parties or by trade custom. Where no time of payment can thus be implied, payment will prima facie be due when the seller informs the buyer that he is ready and willing to deliver the goods, since by virtue of s.28 of the 1979 Act delivery of the goods and payment of the price are, unless otherwise agreed, concurrent conditions.[1214]

44-299 **Whether time for payment of essence** Unless a different intention appears from the terms of the contract,[1215] stipulations as to time of payment are not deemed to be of the essence of a contract of sale.[1216] But the seller may expressly reserve the right of re-sale in the event of default[1217] and by s.48(3) of the Act the seller has in certain circumstances a statutory right of resale.[1218]

44-300 **Late payment of commercial debts** Statutory interest may be payable under the Late Payment of Commercial Debts (Interest) Act 1998 on a debt created by virtue of an obligation to pay the whole or part of the contract price.[1219] Such interest starts to run on the day after the relevant day for the debt determined in accordance with

---

[1206] See Vol.I, paras 21-046, 21-076, 21-084.

[1207] See Vol.I, paras 21-075—21-083.

[1208] See above, para.34-441.

[1209] See also below, para.44-311 (when seller is "unpaid").

[1210] *Re Charge Card Services Ltd* [1989] Ch. 497; see Vol.I, para.21-084.

[1211] [1987] Ch. 150, 166 (Millett J.). This question was left open by the Court of Appeal [1989] Ch. 497, 517.

[1212] See Vol.I, para.21-056.

[1213] *PT Berlian Laju Tanker TBK v Nuse Shipping Ltd* [2008] EWHC 1330 (Comm), [2008] 2 Lloyd's Rep. 246.

[1214] See above, para.44-236.

[1215] See above, para.44-128.

[1216] Sale of Goods Act 1979 s.10(1); see above, para.44-128 and generally Vol.I, paras 21-011, 21-055.

[1217] Sale of Goods Act 1979 s.48(4); see below, para.44-355.

[1218] See below, para.44-346.

[1219] See Vol.I, para.26-289.

s.4 of the 1998 Act. This will not necessarily be the same as the time of payment referred to above.[1220]

Advance payment   The question whether the time for payment of a deposit or other advance payment is of the essence depends on the intention of the parties to be ascertained by construing the contract.[1221] A term which stipulates for payment of a deposit is not usually a condition precedent to the formation of the contract,[1222] but it may be construed as a fundamental term of the contract entitling the seller to treat the contract as repudiated if the deposit is not duly paid.[1223] The Late Payment of Commercial Debts (Interest) Act 1998 contains specific provisions for the calculation of the date from which statutory interest starts to run in a case where the debt relates to an obligation to make an advance payment.[1224]   **44-301**

Credit   Where goods are sold on credit, payment is not due until the period of credit has expired.[1225] Before that time the seller is not entitled to withhold delivery until payment or tender of the price, unless the buyer becomes insolvent,[1226] in the absence of an express stipulation in the contract to the contrary.[1227]   **44-302**

A contract for the sale of goods on credit, where the buyer is to pay the price of the goods by instalments, may be regulated by the Consumer Credit Act 1974 if the buyer is an individual.[1228]   **44-303**

6.   REMEDIES OF THE SELLER

(a)   Rights of Unpaid Seller against the Goods

Summary of remedies against the goods   It is provided by s.39(1) of the Act that: **44-304**

"Subject to this[1229] and any other[1230] Act, notwithstanding that the property[1231] in the goods may have passed to the buyer, the unpaid seller of goods, as such, has by implication of

---

[1220] See, e.g. s.4(5).

[1221] *Portaria Shipping Co v Gulf Pacific Navigation Co Ltd* [1981] 2 Lloyd's Rep. 180.

[1222] *Damon Compañía Naviera SA v Hapag-Lloyd International SA* [1985] 1 W.L.R. 435. See also *Millichamp v Jones* [1982] 1 W.L.R. 1422. cf. *Myton Ltd v Schwab-Morris* [1974] 1 W.L.R. 331.

[1223] *Myton Ltd v Schwab-Morris*, above, at 337; *Millichamp v Jones*, above, at 1430; *Portaria Shipping Co v Gulf Pacific Navigation Co Ltd*, above; *Damon Compañía Naviera SA v Hapag-Lloyd International SA* [1985] 1 W.L.R. 435.

[1224] ss.4(4), 11; see Vol.I, para.26-289. In *Griffon Shipping LLC v Firodi Shipping Ltd (The Griffon)* [2013] EWCA Civ 1567, [2014] 1 All E.R. (Comm) 593, there was an express contractual right to cancel in the event that a deposit was not paid. If the right to receive the deposit had accrued it could survive termination of the agreement.

[1225] *Price v Nixon* (1813) 5 Taunt. 338.

[1226] Sale of Goods Act 1979 ss.39(1) (2), 41(1); see below, paras 44-304, 44-314.

[1227] cf. *BV Oliehandel Jongland v Coastal International Ltd* [1983] 2 Lloyd's Rep. 463.

[1228] Consumer Credit Act 1974 s.8; see above, paras 39-016 et seq. But credit sale agreements of four instalments or less are not regulated agreements provided that the payments are to be made within a period not exceeding 12 months beginning with the date of the agreement: Consumer Credit (Exempt Agreements) Order 1989 (SI 1989/869) art.3(1)(a)(i). This exemption does not apply to conditional sale agreements where the seller retains the property in the goods.

[1229] The provisions of the Act which are directly relevant are ss.24, 25 and 41–48.

[1230] e.g. Factors Act 1889 ss.8, 9, 10 (cf. ss.24, 25, 47(2) of the Sale of Goods Act 1979); Carriage of Goods by Sea Act 1992; Bills of Sale Act 1878.

[1231] Defined, s.61(1): see above, para.44-015.

law[1232]—

    (a)   a lien on the goods or right to retain[1233] them for the price while he is in posses-
           sion of them;

    (b)   in case of the insolvency[1234] of the buyer, a right[1235] of stopping the goods in transit
           after he has parted with the possession of them;

    (c)   a right of re-sale as limited by this Act." [1236]

Although the unpaid seller's normal remedy is to sue the buyer for the price[1237] or
for damages for non-acceptance, the law gives him certain remedies in respect of
the goods themselves, analogous to a form of "security" for payment of the price.[1238]
By exercising these remedies, the unpaid seller in effect secures a form of preference over the general creditors of a bankrupt buyer.[1239] They are known as "real"
remedies, since they depend on, and are directed against, the res, the goods
themselves.[1240] The remedies of lien and stoppage in transit are designed to give
protection to an unpaid seller so long as the goods have not reached the actual possession of the buyer or his agent. Until then, the buyer's right to possession is
defeasible upon certain conditions: the main one[1241] is where the buyer becomes
insolvent while the goods are still subject to the control of the unpaid seller or his
agent; the seller[1242] is then, by virtue of his right of lien, entitled to retain possession of them until the price is paid. If the buyer becomes insolvent while the goods
are still in the control of a carrier and before the buyer or his agent obtains delivery
of them, the seller may, by giving notice to the carrier, prevent delivery to the buyer
and direct redelivery to himself or his agent: this is the right of stoppage in transit,
which enables the unpaid seller to resume possession of the goods and to retain
them until the price is paid.[1243] The unpaid seller who has exercised either of the
rights of lien or of stoppage is given the power to pass to a new buyer a good title
to the goods, so that the resale will divest the original buyer of the title which he
may have had.[1244] In practice, the unpaid seller will need to be in possession of the

---

[1232] These remedies may therefore be excluded or varied by the parties: s.55.

[1233] The "right to retain" is a term of Scots law.

[1234] On the definition of "insolvent", see s.61(4); see below, para.44-313.

[1235] It is a right not only against the buyer, but also against the carrier: see below, para.44-337. In the
1893 Act, and in most of the common law cases on the topic, the Latin phrase "stoppage *in transitu*"
is used. The 1979 Act uses the English version "in transit".

[1236] The provision referred to is s.48(3): *RV Ward Ltd v Bignall* [1967] 1 Q.B. 534, 549. The "right" of
resale includes the "power" to confer a good title on the new buyer (as against the original buyer).

[1237] The right of the seller to sue for the price is independent of his remedies against the goods: see e.g.
s.43(2).

[1238] The creation of a *security* recognised at law requires the debtor to have both ownership and possession (actual or constructive) of the goods: *Armour v Thyssen Edelstahlwerke AG* [1991] 2 A.C. 339,
353.

[1239] cf. the use of retention of title clauses under which the seller retains the property in the goods until
he has been fully paid: see above, paras 44-173—44-188.

[1240] These remedies are historically derived from the law merchant.

[1241] For other conditions in the case of liens, see s.41(1) (see below, para.44-315).

[1242] An agent who has actual or apparent authority from the unpaid seller may exercise on his behalf the
seller's remedies against the goods: *Whitehead v Anderson* (1842) 9 M. & W. 518 (stoppage in
transit). Similarly, the doctrine of ratification may apply: *Hutchings v Nunes* (1863) 1 Moo. P.C. N.S.
243; *Bird v Brown* (1850) 4 Ex. 786 (see above, paras 31-027 et seq.; below, para.44-327).

[1243] See below, paras 44-326—44-348.

[1244] See below, para.44-345.

goods before he can effectively exercise his right to resell them.[1245]

Effect on third parties   The real remedies exercisable by the unpaid seller **44-305**
normally prevail over the rights of a sub-buyer or pledgee,[1246] and may affect third
parties in that remedies for wrongful interference with the goods (e.g. trespass or
conversion) will depend on who is in possession of them or entitled to possession
of them.[1247]

Remedies of seller who retains the property in the goods   Section 39(2) **44-306**
provides:

"Where the property in goods has not passed to the buyer, the unpaid seller has (in addition to his other remedies)[1248] a right[1249] of withholding delivery similar to and co-
extensive with his rights of lien or retention and stoppage in transit where the property
has passed to the buyer."[1250]

The purpose of this subsection is to bring into line the law on the seller's right to
retain the goods pending payment of the price in the two possible situations which
could arise in respect of the property in the goods. A lien is a right to retain possession of goods owned by another person, and the unpaid seller's "lien" is therefore
an appropriate term when the property in the goods has already passed to the buyer
before the seller claims to retain possession of the goods.[1251] When, however, the
property in the goods is not to pass until a future event[1252] (e.g. upon payment[1253]),
the seller is claiming to retain, pending payment of the price, goods in which he still
has the property.[1254] One result of s.39(2) is that in an instalment contract[1255] the
seller may usually[1256] "withhold delivery" of future instalments until he is paid for
instalments already delivered to the buyer.[1257]

Retention of title   A special contractual clause (a *Romalpa* or retention of title **44-307**
clause) may reserve to the seller the property in the goods supplied to the buyer,
until the full price has been paid; such a clause may also purport to entitle the unpaid

---

[1245] See below, paras 44-344—44-358.
[1246] 1979 Act s.47 (see below, paras 44-339–44-343).
[1247] *Clerk & Lindsell on Torts*, 22nd edn (2017), paras 17-43, 17-059 et seq., 17-135.
[1248] e.g. s.49 (see below, para.44-359); s.50 (see below, para.44-367).
[1249] A "right" as against the buyer: as owner of the goods, the seller has the legal "power" to withhold
delivery.
[1250] The omission of a reference in s.39(2) to a *right* of resale (as against the original buyer) does not
mean that the unpaid seller in these circumstances lacks the right to resell, since s.48(3) (see below,
para.44-351) can be interpreted as applicable to cases where the property has not passed to the buyer
as well as to those where it has: *RV Ward Ltd v Bignall* [1967] 1 Q.B. 534, 545. See also *Benjamin's
Sale of Goods*, 10th edn (2017), para.15-011.
[1251] *Lickbarrow v Mason* (1793) 6 East 21, 24n. ("… it is a contradiction in terms to say a man has a
lien upon his own goods …").
[1252] See above, paras 44-170 et seq.
[1253] Or in a contract to deliver unascertained goods by instalments, when the goods are "unconditionally appropriated" to that instalment: s.18 r.5(1) (see above, paras 44-149 et seq.).
[1254] This was the position before the Act: e.g. *Bellamy v Davey* [1891] 3 Ch. 540; *Ex p. Chalmers* (1873)
L.R. 8 Ch. App. 289, 293 (following *Griffiths v Perry* (1859) 1 E. E. 680, 688).
[1255] See above, para.44-306 n.1253.
[1256] The contract may, however, be "severable" into separate contracts: see below, para.44-320.
[1257] *Longbottom Co Ltd v Bass, Walker Co* [1922] W.N. 245, 246 (see below, para.44-320).

seller to claim any product manufactured by the buyer from the goods, or the proceeds of resale of the goods, or of the manufactured product.[1258]

44-308 **Future and unascertained goods** If, under an agreement to sell[1259] "future goods"[1260] or "unascertained goods"[1261] the seller has not yet obliged himself to deliver any particular goods to the buyer (e.g. by a notice of appropriation), he is obviously under no contractual obligation towards the buyer in regard to any goods subject to his control which happen to fit the contractual description, or which he has in mind to use in order to perform his obligations to the buyer.[1262] Since such goods have not been attached to the particular contract, the seller's right and power over them are in no way restricted by the contract, and his rights over them are therefore wider than rights arising under s.39(2), see above (which should not be interpreted so as to *restrict* any of his rights arising under common law rules).[1263]

44-309 **Extended meaning of "seller"** Section 38(2) extends[1264] the meaning of "seller" as follows:

> "In this part of this Act 'seller' includes any person who is in the position of a seller, as, for instance, an agent of the seller to whom the bill of lading has been indorsed,[1265] or a consignor or agent who has himself paid (or is directly responsible for) the price."

Thus, a wider group of persons are given the opportunity of protecting their interests when they have not been paid. The main illustration is that of the agent who has himself paid the price to the seller,[1266] as in the decisions before the Act on the position of a commission agent who accepted an order to obtain goods for his principal on the understanding that the agent would buy the goods in his own name and then consign them to the principal. By buying in his own name, the commission agent pledged his own credit when buying the goods, and not the credit of his principal[1267]: he was thus treated (for this purpose) as a seller of the goods to his principal and was held to be entitled to exercise the right of stoppage in transit when his principal became insolvent during the course of transit of the goods.[1268] It is submitted that a surety for the buyer is, when he has paid the seller, a "person who is in the posi-

---

[1258] On these clauses, see above, paras 44-173—44-188.

[1259] s.2(5) (see above, paras 44-020—44-022).

[1260] s.61(1) (see above, paras 44-015, 44-037, 44-042).

[1261] s.16 (see above, paras 44-040 et seq., para.44-131). cf. s.18 r.5(1) (see above, para.44-149).

[1262] cf. *Carlos Federspiel Co SA v Charles Twigg Co Ltd* [1957] 1 Lloyd's Rep. 240.

[1263] See the saving provisions of s.62(2) (see above, para.44-002).

[1264] The main definition of "seller" is in s.61(1): it includes a person who "agrees to sell", e.g. a buyer who resells the goods before the property in the goods has passed to him: *Jenkyns v Usborne* (1844) 7 M. & G. 678, 698–699 (buyer who resold is entitled, as against the insolvent sub-buyer, to stop the goods in transit).

[1265] See the early decision of *Morison v Gray* (1824) 2 Bing. 260. (This was an action of trover, on which point reference should now be made to *Burgos v Nascimento* (1908) 100 L.T. 71 and to the Torts (Interference with Goods) Act 1977 (see below, paras 44-447—44-448)); see above, paras 33-010 et seq.

[1266] *Imperial Bank v London and St. Katharine Docks Co* (1877) 5 Ch. D. 195.

[1267] *Feise v Wray* (1802) 3 East 93; *Ex p. Miles* (1885) 15 Q.B.D. 39, 42.

[1268] *Ireland v Livingston* (1872) L.R. 5 H.L. 395, 408–409; *Cassaboglou v Gibb* (1883) 11 Q.B.D. 797, 804, 806–807 (following *Feise v Wray* (1802) 3 East 93). (By s.38(2), such an agent could exercise any of the real remedies.) See also above, para.31-165.

tion of a seller" within the meaning of subs.(2) above.[1269] Before the buyer has defaulted in paying the price, the surety has only a contingent liability to pay the price,[1270] but after payment by him he is subrogated to the rights of the seller against the defaulting buyer.[1271]

Claim for repayment   The term "seller" in s.38(2) does not extend to a buyer who   **44-310** has a claim against the seller for repayment of the price.[1272] So where the buyer paid the price to the seller, but later, and justifiably, rejected the goods, he could not claim a lien to retain the goods until the seller repaid him the price.[1273] If the buyer who has paid the price wishes to reject the goods on the ground that they are not in accordance with the contractual description, he is dependent on the solvency of the seller for his recovery of the price[1274]: the buyer's rejection of the goods revests the property in the seller and leaves the buyer with only a personal claim against the seller.

Definition of unpaid seller   Section 38(1) provides: **44-311**

"The seller of goods is an unpaid seller within the meaning of this Act—

(a)   when the whole[1275] of the price has not been paid or tendered,

(b)   when a bill of exchange or other negotiable instrument has been received as conditional[1276] payment, and the condition on which it was received has not been fulfilled by reason of the dishonour of the instrument or otherwise." [1277]

The buyer's obligation to pay the price depends on construction of the contract.[1278] The meaning of s.38(1)(a) is that the whole of the price has not in fact been paid or tendered to the seller, whether or not payment is due according to the contract.[1279] During a period of credit, or during the currency of a negotiable instrument taken for the price, the seller is taken to have waived his right to a lien, but he is nevertheless an unpaid seller, whose right to exercise the real remedies revives[1280] if the buyer becomes insolvent.[1281] The same position obtains where by the contract the

---

[1269] The Mercantile Law Amendment Act 1856 s.5, may also lead to the same result: *Imperial Bank v London and St Katharine Docks Co* (1877) 5 Ch. D. 195. (See below, para.45-147.)

[1270] See below, paras 45-001 et seq.

[1271] See below, para.45-144.

[1272] *JL Lyons Co Ltd v May and Baker Ltd* [1923] 1 K.B. 685.

[1273] *JL Lyons Co Ltd v May and Baker Ltd* [1923] 1 K.B. 685.

[1274] This is the reason given in *Kwei Tek Chao v British Traders and Shippers Ltd* [1954] 2 Q.B. 459, 483, for the buyer not rejecting the goods after he had paid the price.

[1275] Before the Act, payment of part of the price did not prevent exercise of the right of stoppage in transit: this rule now applies to all the real remedies (even the right of resale). The price may, however, be apportioned where separate deliveries are to be paid for separately: see above, para.44-262.

[1276] For the circumstances in which a negotiable instrument is taken as absolute payment, see Vol.I, para.21-079. In this situation, the seller's only remedy is to sue on the instrument.

[1277] *Gunn v Bolckow, Vaughan Co* (1875) L.R. 10 Ch. App. 491, 501 (dishonour by non-payment: a fortiori in the case of non-acceptance of the draft). See also above, paras 34-103—34-108 ("or otherwise" at the end of s.38(1)(b) refers to the buyer's insolvency).

[1278] See Vol.I, paras 13-041 et seq.; see above, paras 44-051—44-053.

[1279] This is implied by ss.41(1)(b) and 43(2).

[1280] If the other conditions of entitlement are satisfied, e.g. s.44 (see below, para.44-326); *Gunn v Bolckow, Vaughan Co* (1875) L.R. 10 Ch. App. 491 at 501.

[1281] The fact that the seller, who has taken a bill of exchange as conditional payment, has negotiated the

buyer is obliged to pay the price by arranging for a banker's commercial credit to be opened in favour of the seller: the opening of the credit is normally only conditional payment,[1282] and if the banker defaults in honouring the credit, the seller may claim payment of the price directly from the buyer,[1283] and the seller's remedies against the goods revive.

44-312 **Tender of price** For entitlement to exercise the real remedies, tender of the price is equated with payment.[1284] The general principles of the law on tender of money to pay a debt are discussed in Vol.I.[1285] If the seller waives[1286] tender of the price by the buyer, he will be estopped from claiming subsequently that he is an "unpaid seller" for the purpose of exercising the real remedies.[1287]

44-313 **Definition of insolvency**[1288] Section 61(4) provides a definition of insolvency[1289]:

> "A person is deemed to be insolvent within the meaning of this Act if he has either ceased to pay his debts in the ordinary course of business[1290] or he cannot pay his debts as they become due."[1291]

This definition is of crucial importance for two of the remedies against the goods: the right of stoppage in transit arises only upon the buyer's insolvency,[1292] while in the case of the unpaid seller's lien, it is one of the three alternative situations which justify the seller's retention of the goods.[1293] The word "insolvent" has been interpreted in other contexts, from which analogies may cautiously be sought.[1294]

---

bill to a third person, does not alter the rule that there has been only a conditional payment of the price, because the seller may have to take up the bill: if such a bill is dishonoured while it is in the hands of a third person, the seller's remedies revive: *Gunn v Bolckow, Vaughan Co* (1875) L.R. 10 Ch. App. 503. cf. *Bunney v Poyntz* (1833) 2 L.J. K.B. 55.

[1282] *WJ Alan Co Ltd v El Nasr Export and Import Co* [1972] 2 Q.B. 189, 209–212, 221; *Maran Road Saw Mill v Austin Taylor Co Ltd* [1975] 1 Lloyd's Rep. 156; *ED F Man Ltd v Nigerian Sweets and Confectionery Co Ltd* [1977] 2 Lloyd's Rep. 50.

[1283] *Newman Industries Ltd v Indo-British Industries Ltd* [1956] 2 Lloyd's Rep. 219, 236; reversed on another ground: [1957] 1 Lloyd's Rep. 211; *Soproma SpA v Marine and Animal By-products Corp* [1966] 1 Lloyd's Rep. 367, 386. See also above, para.34-490.

[1284] s.38(1)(a) above; ss.41(1) (see below, para.44-315), 44 (see below, para.44-326), and 48(3) (see below, para.44-351). A valid tender does not discharge the buyer's obligation to pay the price.

[1285] Vol.I, paras 21-085 et seq.

[1286] Vol.I, paras 22-040—22-047.

[1287] *Cohen v Roche* [1927] 1 K.B. 169 ("waiver of tender will produce the same result as actual tender in divesting a [seller] of his right to assert a vendor's lien": at 180).

[1288] On bankruptcy, see Vol.I, paras 20-015 et seq.

[1289] This definition is required by ss.41 and 44 (in addition to s.39).

[1290] A special reason for a failure to pay debts may prevent the debtor being held to be "insolvent" within the definition, e.g. if an alien enemy failed to meet an acceptance because of the outbreak of war: *The Feliciana* (1915) 59 S.J. 546, 547 (obiter: the goods were seized as prize before the seller purported to give notice of stoppage).

[1291] The words omitted from subs.(4) were repealed by the Insolvency Act 1985 s.235(3), Sch.10 Pt III (and by corresponding legislation for Scotland).

[1292] Sales Goods Act 1979 s.44 (see below, para.44-326). The time when the buyer became insolvent may be important for this remedy: at common law, the stoppage was held to be valid if the buyer became insolvent before the expected termination of the transit, even where it later appeared that he was not insolvent at the time of the stoppage: *The Constantia* (1807) 6 C.Rob.Adm.R. 321, 326. (Section 44 could possibly be interpreted so as to enable such a retroactive justification of a premature stoppage.)

[1293] s.41(1) (see below, para.44-315).

[1294] cf. the grounds on which a bankruptcy order may be made: Insolvency Act 1986 ss.267(2), 271(1);

Thus, the word has often been construed, "both in private instruments and upon the construction of a statute, to apply to a person labouring under a general disability to pay his just debts in the ordinary course of trade and business".[1295] When a clause in a contract is to take effect upon the "insolvency" of a party, the ordinary meaning of the word has been held to be "an incapability of paying the party's just debts",[1296] or "a general inability to pay debts".[1297] The buyer's own statements in documents or correspondence may be strong evidence against him.[1298] Some cases have dealt with the effect of the buyer's alleged insolvency upon the contract of sale. If the buyer declares that he is insolvent this does not of itself terminate the contract[1299]: but he may make the declaration in such circumstances as to show that he cannot, or does not intend to, perform his side of the contract, in which case the seller may treat the declaration as a repudiation and terminate the contract.[1300] In this context, the mere fact that a debtor calls a meeting of his creditors, or some of them, need not necessarily imply that he is insolvent: the debtor may merely be discussing his need for more capital or for more credit, or the possibility that he may have to wind up an unprofitable business.[1301]

Effect of bankruptcy   The rules on bankruptcy apply notwithstanding the Act.[1302]   **44-314**
The fact that the buyer has become bankrupt does not of itself terminate the contract, but the buyer's trustee in bankruptcy may exercise his power to disclaim onerous property, including any unprofitable contract.[1303] The buyer's trustee in bankruptcy (and, probably, a sub-buyer of the same goods bought from the buyer) is entitled to choose to fulfil the original contract by paying the price in cash to the seller within a reasonable time of the buyer's default in payment.[1304] If, however, the goods are still in transit because a bankrupt or insolvent buyer refused to take delivery of the goods from the seller or the carrier, the seller may still have the opportunity of exercising his rights of lien or of stoppage in transit, and thus of gaining priority over the general creditors of the buyer.[1305]

(i)   Unpaid Seller's Lien[1306]

Seller's right to retain possession   Section 41(1) provides: **44-315**

---

also s.268.

[1295] *R. v Saddlers' Co* (1863) 10 H.L. Cas. 404, 425.

[1296] *Parker v Gossage* (1835) 2 C.M. R. 617, 620.

[1297] *Biddlecombe v Bond* (1835) 4 Ad. & El. 332, 337. (It is not restricted to a person who actually becomes "bankrupt" within the meaning of the Insolvency Act 1986 (referring to the Insolvent Debtors' Act 1820).)

[1298] *Billson v Crofts* (1873) L.R. 15 Eq. 314.

[1299] *Ex p. Chalmers* (1873) L.R. 8 Ch. App. 289, 293–294; *Mess v Duffus* (1901) 6 Com. Cas. 165, 167.

[1300] *Mess v Duffus* (1901) 6 Com. Cas. 165, 167. On this point, see Vol.I, para.24-018.

[1301] *Re Phoenix Bessemer Steel Co* (1876) 4 Ch. D. 108, 120. (Nor is mere suspicion of the buyer's insolvency sufficient.)

[1302] 1979 Act s.62(1).

[1303] Insolvency Act 1986 s.315.

[1304] *Ex p. Stapleton* (1879) 10 Ch. D. 586, 590. cf. Insolvency Act 1986 ss.311(5), 314; *Kemp v Falk* (1882) L.R. 7 App. Cas. 573, 578.

[1305] *Ex p. Cooper* (1879) 11 Ch. D. 68, 73. See below, paras 44-330, 44-335.

[1306] On the general law of lien, see Silvertown, *The Law of Lien* (1988). The seller's lien should be distinguished from the equitable lien that a party may have over goods in the possession of another if he has paid for them: see *International Finance Corp v DSNL Offshore Ltd* [2005] EWHC 1844 (Comm), [2007] 2 All E.R. (Comm) 305.

"Subject to this Act, the unpaid seller[1307] of goods who is in possession of them is entitled to retain possession of them until payment or tender of the price in the following cases—

    (a)   where the goods have been sold without any stipulation as to credit[1308];

    (b)   where the goods have been sold on credit but the term of credit has expired;

    (c)   where the buyer becomes insolvent."

Apart from an express term in the contract of sale,[1309] the seller's only right of lien arises under the Act and the seller cannot rely on the equitable principle of a vendor's lien.[1310] The gist of the unpaid seller's lien is his entitlement to retain the goods until the buyer has paid or tendered[1311] the whole[1312] of the price[1313]; his lien is therefore a qualification on his duty to deliver the goods to the buyer,[1314] and the seller will in practice exercise his right of lien as a first step towards exercising a right of resale.[1315] The lien arises whether the contract is a sale of specific goods or an executory contract to supply unascertained goods, e.g. by instalments over a future period[1316]; in the case of unascertained goods, the lien will arise when the goods have been ascertained.[1317] The extent of the lien is limited to the price: it does not cover the expenses of keeping the goods, since the seller is detaining them for his own benefit.[1318]

44-316   **Effect of grant of credit**   Where the seller grants credit to the buyer, he waives his lien for the agreed period of credit,[1319] but the lien will revive after that period

---

[1307] s.38 (see above, para.44-311). The unpaid seller who retains the property in the goods has a similar right of withholding delivery: s.39(2) (see above, para.44-306). But a right to a lien, *stricto sensu*, can arise only when the property held belongs to another: *Nippon Yusen Kaisha v Ramjiban Serowgee* [1938] A.C. 429, 444.

[1308] s.28 (see above, para.44-237) applies. This was the common law position: *Bloxam v Sanders* (1825) 4 B. & C. 941, 948; *Miles v Gorton* (1834) 2 Cr. & M. 504, 511.

[1309] s.55. Express terms creating a lien or security for the price will prevail over the statutory implication of a lien: *Re Leith's Estate* (1866) L.R. 1 P.C. 296. See also above, paras 44-173—44-188 (on retention of title clauses).

[1310] *Transport and General Credit Corp Ltd v Morgan* [1939] 2 All E.R. 17, 25.

[1311] See above, para.44-311.

[1312] s.38(1)(a) (see above, para.44-311).

[1313] The contract of sale is not rescinded (terminated) by exercise of the lien: s.48(1) (see below, para.44-344). The right to be paid is independent of the existence of the lien: *The Eider* [1893] P. 119, 131. For a discussion of the nature of a lien, see Fletcher Moulton L.J.'s dissenting judgment in *Lord's Trustee v GE Ry* [1908] 2 K.B. 54, 61–73. (The House of Lords allowed the appeal: *GE Ry v Lord's Trustee* [1909] A.C. 109.)

[1314] s.27 (see above, para.44-236).

[1315] For the seller's power to resell, see below, para.44-345. If the unpaid seller resells while exercising his right of lien, the second buyer acquires a good title to the goods as against the original buyer: s.48(2). During the exercise of the lien the seller's possession of the goods will support an action for wrongful interference with the goods: *Nippon Yusen Kaisha v Ramjiban Serowgee* [1938] A.C. 429, 445.

[1316] *Griffiths v Perry* (1859) 1 E. & E. 680; *Ex p. Chalmers* (1873) L.R. 8 Ch. App. 289. See also s.39(2) (see above, para.44-306).

[1317] See above, paras 44-149 et seq.

[1318] *Somes v British Empire Shipping Co* (1860) 8 H.L. Cas. 338 (a case on a repairer's lien: see above, para.33-093). A claim for damages may lie for such expenses: *Bloxam v Sanders* (1825) 4 B. & C. 941, 950 (cf. s.37).

[1319] *Spartali v Benecke* (1850) 10 C.B. 212, 223; *Poulton and Son v Anglo-American Oil Co Ltd* (1910) 27 T.L.R. 38, 39; on appeal (1911) 27 T.L.R. 216. The normal implication of granting credit is that the buyer is immediately entitled to delivery without making payment: (1910) 27 T.L.R. 38, 39. But the parties may agree that, despite the granting of credit, delivery is to take place concurrently with

has expired,[1320] whether or not the buyer is then insolvent. Where the buyer is given credit for the period of a negotiable instrument given by him to the seller in payment of the price, the seller's lien is waived for that period, since acceptance of a negotiable instrument is normally treated as conditional[1321] payment.[1322] But if, before the goods are delivered to the buyer, the negotiable instrument is dishonoured, or the buyer becomes insolvent,[1323] the seller's lien[1324] will revive, so that he may retain the goods until he is paid.[1325] The lien revives upon dishonour despite the fact that the dishonour occurred after the seller had, during the period of the buyer's solvency, committed a breach of his obligations under the contract (e.g. by failure to deliver part of the goods[1326]). In these circumstances, the buyer has a cause of action, but the seller has his lien for payment of the whole of the price, which will be taken into account in assessing the buyer's damages for the seller's breach.[1327]

Buyer insolvent   Where the buyer becomes insolvent,[1328] the seller may retain the   **44-317**
goods[1329] until the buyer, or his trustee in bankruptcy,[1330] pays the whole price. Thus, unless full payment is made, the seller's power of retention enables him to avoid the alternative of proving in the bankruptcy for the price.[1331] The buyer's trustee in bankruptcy may elect to fulfil the contract by paying the price in cash within a reasonable time[1332]; dicta also suggest that a sub-buyer might have the same election.[1333]

The seller's possession   The unpaid seller must be in "possession" of the goods   **44-318**
in order to exercise his right of lien,[1334] and what amounts to possession for this purpose may be different from that required for other types of lien[1335] or for other

---

payment: *Bloxam v Sanders*, above, at 948; *Miles v Gorton* (1834) 2 Cr. & M. 504, 511; *Benjamin's Sale of Goods*, 10th edn (2017), para.15-034. cf. *Field v Lelean* (1861) 6 H. & N. 617.

[1320] *Poulton and Son v Anglo-American Oil Co Ltd* (1910) 27 T.L.R. 38, 39.

[1321] The seller may convert it into an absolute payment by negotiating the instrument without recourse: *Bunney v Poyntz* (1833) 2 L.J. K.B. 55. (See all the reports: 1 N. & M. 229; 4 B. & Ad. 568.) cf. *Re J Defries Sons Ltd* [1909] 2 Ch. 423, 429.

[1322] s.38(1)(b). cf. *Horncastle v Farran* (1820) 3 B. & Ald. 497 (carrier's lien); *Hewison v Guthrie* (1836) 2 Bing. N.C. 755, 759 (broker's lien).

[1323] *Miles v Gorton* (1834) 2 Cr. & M. 504 at 512, 514; *Gunn v Bolckow Vaughan Co* (1875) L.R. 10 Ch. App. 491, 501.

[1324] It may be that it is not a right to a lien *stricto sensu* because the lien had been waived by the granting of credit; but it is a right of withholding delivery analogous to a lien: *Griffiths v Perry* (1859) 1 E. & E. 680, 688.

[1325] *Valpy v Oakeley* (1851) 20 L.J. Q.B. 380; *Griffiths v Perry* (1859) 1 E. & E. 680, 688.

[1326] *Valpy v Oakeley* (1851) 20 L.J. Q.B. 380; *Griffiths v Perry* (1859) 1 E. & E. 680, 688.

[1327] *Valpy v Oakeley* (1851) 20 L.J. Q.B. 380; *Griffiths v Perry* (1859) 1 E. & E. 680, 688.

[1328] On insolvency, see above, para.44-313.

[1329] *Grice v Richardson* (1877) L.R. 3 App. Cas. 319.

[1330] *Ex p. Stapleton* (1879) 10 Ch. D. 586, 590; *Ex p. Chalmers* (1873) L.R. 8 Ch. App. 289, 294.

[1331] *Gunn v Bolckow Vaughan Co* (1875) L.R. 10 Ch. App. 491 at 501.

[1332] *Ex p. Stapleton* (1879) 10 Ch. D. 586, 590.

[1333] *Ex p. Stapleton* (1879) 10 Ch. D. 586, 590. cf. *Kemp v Falk* (1882) L.R. 7 App. Cas. 573, 578.

[1334] *Benjamin's Sale of Goods*, 10th edn (2017), paras 15-038—15-039. The seller's lien does not entitle him to regain possession of the goods after he has given it up: *Jeffcott v Andrew Motors Ltd* [1960] N.Z.L.R. 721, CA. cf. stoppage in transit (see below, paras 44-326 et seq.).

[1335] *GE Ry v Lord's Trustee* [1909] A.C. 109, 115 (carrier's lien: see also the dissenting judgment of Fletcher Moulton L.J. in the court below: *Lord's Trustee v GE Ry* [1908] 2 K.B. 54, 71).

rules of law.[1336] Provided he retains general control over the goods,[1337] the seller's possession for the purpose of maintaining his lien may continue despite the fact that the buyer has been given a measure of control over them or temporary possession of them for a limited and specific purpose,[1338] e.g. to allow the buyer to mark them[1339] or to pack them in his (the buyer's) own containers.[1340] The seller may act in the dual role of seller and warehouseman for the buyer, but he retains his lien[1341]: s.41(2) of the Act provides that: "The seller may exercise his lien or right of retention notwithstanding that he is in possession of the goods as agent or bailee ... for the buyer".[1342] Thus, the seller does not lose his lien by attorning[1343] to the buyer, viz by acknowledging to the buyer that he holds the goods on the buyer's account.[1344]

44-319   **Wrongful refusal to deliver on credit**   If the buyer is entitled to delivery of the goods without paying the price, because the goods are sold on credit terms,[1345] a wrongful refusal by the unpaid seller to deliver the goods to the buyer should, it is submitted, debar the seller from exercising his lien if the buyer should later become insolvent.[1346]

44-320   **Part delivery and instalment contracts**   By s.42:

"Where an unpaid seller has made part delivery of the goods, he may exercise his lien or right of retention on the remainder, unless such part delivery has been made under such circumstances as to show an agreement to waive[1347] the lien or right of retention."[1348]

The onus is on the buyer, who claims that the seller has lost his lien, to show that it was the intention of the parties that the part delivery should constitute a delivery

---

[1336] See Harris in Guest (ed.), *Oxford Essays in Jurisprudence* (1961), p.69.

[1337] *Milgate v Kebble* (1841) 3 M. & G. 100 (retention of key to premises): cf. *Wrightson v McArthur and Hutchisons (1919) Ltd* [1921] 2 K.B. 807.

[1338] *Paton's Trustees v Finlayson*, 1923 S.C. 872; *GE Ry v Lord's Trustee* [1909] A.C. 109; *Milgate v Kebble* (1841) 3 M. & G. 100. See further *Benjamin's Sale of Goods*, 10th edn (2017), at paras 15-038—15-039, and (on trust receipts) *Benjamin* at paras 18-286 et seq.

[1339] *Dixon v Yates* (1833) 5 B. & Ad. 313. cf. *Cooper v Bill* (1865) 3 H. & C. 722. See also *Tansley v Turner* (1835) 2 Bing. N.C. 151.

[1340] *Goodall v Skelton* (1794) 2 H.Bl. 316; *Boulter v Arnott* (1833) 1 Cr. & M. 333. See also *Milgate v Kebble* (1841) 3 M. & G. 100; and cf. *Holderness v Shackels* (1828) 8 B. & C. 612.

[1341] *Miles v Gorton* (1834) 2 Cr. & M. 504, 513, 514; *Grice v Richardson* (1877) L.R. 3 App. Cas. 319, 323, 323–324 (the buyer's agreement to pay warehousing charges to the seller does not prevent continuance of the lien).

[1342] In *United Plastics Ltd v Reliance Electric (NZ) Ltd* [1977] 2 N.Z.L.R. 125 it was held that the corresponding section in the New Zealand Act applied only where the seller had never parted with possession of the goods.

[1343] On attornment, see above, para.33-030.

[1344] *Poulton Son v Anglo-American Oil Co Ltd* (1911) 27 T.L.R. 216. (Under the common law before the Act, the seller lost his lien in these circumstances: *Cusack v Robinson* (1860) 1 B. & S. 299, 308.) The seller's conduct may, however, be evidence of waiver: see s.43(1)(c) (see below, paras 44-321, 44-324); and the delivery of a document of title to the goods may bring s.47(2) into operation (see below, para.44-341).

[1345] See above, para.44-311.

[1346] cf. the analogous case in s.45(6) (see below, para.44-335).

[1347] On waiver, see s.43(1)(c) (see below, para.44-324). cf. s.45(7) (see below, para.44-335).

[1348] This section sets out what was the position at common law: *Dixon v Yates* (1833) 5 B. & Ad. 313, 341–342; *Bunney v Poyntz* (1833) 4 B. & Ad. 568; *Miles v Gorton* (1834) 2 Cr. & M. 504 at 513; *Kemp v Falk* (1882) L.R. 7 App. Cas. 573, 586.

of the whole.[1349] Where there is a contract for the sale of a specified quantity of goods by instalments, the presumption is that it is an indivisible or entire contract, so that the seller may exercise his lien over any part of the goods not yet delivered, if any part[1350] of the total price is unpaid.[1351] But if the contract is severable, in the sense that there are to be separate deliveries of specified instalments, with a separate payment to be made for each delivery, each delivery will be treated for the purposes of the seller's lien as if it were a separate contract[1352]; in these circumstances, no lien can be exercised by the seller in regard to a particular instalment of the goods for which payment has been made,[1353] and the lien can be exercised only over goods forming part of an instalment which has not been paid for.[1354]

Termination of the lien   By s.43 of the Act it is provided that: **44-321**

> "(1)   The unpaid seller of goods loses his lien or right of retention in respect of them—
>
>   (a)   when he delivers the goods to a carrier or other bailee ... for the purpose of transmission to the buyer without reserving the right of disposal[1355] of the goods;
>
>   (b)   when the buyer or his agent lawfully obtains possession of the goods;
>
>   (c)   by waiver of the lien or right of retention."

The lien may also be lost in other circumstances, e.g. the seller will lose his lien if the whole of the price is paid or tendered to him, since he then ceases to be an "unpaid" seller within the meaning of s.38(1).[1356]

Delivery to carrier ends lien   The delivery of the goods to a carrier[1357] will   **44-322**
terminate the lien[1358] unless there are special circumstances; e.g. where the seller contracts to deliver the goods to the buyer at a particular destination, the carrier may be treated as the seller's agent.[1359] Where the goods are shipped under a bill of lading, possession of the goods is treated as having been transferred to the buyer or

---

[1349] *Kemp v Falk* (1882) L.R. 7 App. Cas. 573, 586; *Ex p. Cooper* (1879) 11 Ch. D. 68, 73 (both cases of stoppage in transit: see below, para.44-335). Section 42 does not apply where the seller's bailee attorns to the buyer: *Miles v Gorton*, above, at 509–510; *Hammond v Anderson* (1803) 1 Bos. & P. N.R. 69 (as explained in *Ex p. Cooper* above, at 74–75).

[1350] See s.38(1)(a) (see above, para.44-311).

[1351] *Ex p. Chalmers* (1873) L.R. 8 Ch. App. 289; *Longbottom Co Ltd v Bass, Walker Co* [1922] W.N. 245; *Re Grainex Canada Ltd*, 34 D.L.R. (4th) 646 (1987).

[1352] *Longbottom Co Ltd v Bass, Walker Co* [1922] W.N. 246.

[1353] *Merchant Banking Co of London v Phoenix Bessemer Steel Co* (1877) 5 Ch. D. 205, 219–220; *Longbottom Co Ltd v Bass, Walker Co* [1922] W.N. 246.

[1354] An express term in the contract itself, however, may entitle the seller to exercise a general lien over any goods of the buyer in the seller's possession.

[1355] For this right, see s.19 (see above, paras 44-170—44-172). See also *Benjamin's Sale of Goods*, 10th edn (2017), paras 5-133 et seq., 18-259 et seq., 20-077 et seq. cf. the retention of title under *Romalpa* clauses: see above, paras 44-173—44-188.

[1356] See above, para.44-312.

[1357] 1979 Act s.32 (see above, paras 44-269—44-271). By s.32(1), delivery to a carrier is prima facie deemed to be delivery to the buyer.

[1358] *Bolton v Lancs and Yorks Ry* (1866) L.R. 1 C.P. 431, 439; *Badische Anilin und Soda Fabrik v Basle Chemical Works* [1898] A.C. 200 (for this purpose "the post office is simply a carrier of parcels like any other carrier": at 204); but cf. *Postmaster-General v WH Jones Co (London) Ltd* [1957] N.Z.L.R. 829.

[1359] This was the rule at common law, and it is not altered by the Act: *Dunlop v Lambert* (1839) 6 Cl. & F. 600; *Badische case* [1898] A.C. 200, 207, 209.

his agent when the bill has been indorsed and delivered to him.[1360] But while the goods are in transit, the unpaid seller may exercise the separate right of stoppage in transit.[1361]

44-323 **Delivery to buyer ends lien** Possession[1362] of the goods passes to the buyer or his agent (s.43(1)(b) above) only[1363] upon delivery,[1364] whereupon the seller loses his lien.[1365] Analogies relevant to the buyer's obtaining possession may be found in the decisions on the termination of transit for the purpose of the right of stoppage in transit,[1366] and in the decisions on what constituted an actual receipt by the buyer within the (now repealed) provision of the Statute of Frauds.[1367] The seller's lien is not lost by the buyer's wrongful taking of the goods,[1368] but once the lien is lost by delivery to the buyer or his agent, it does not revive when the goods are handed back to the seller for a different purpose (e.g. repacking).[1369] The seller will lose possession, and thus his lien as unpaid seller, whenever a third person (such as a warehouseman) who is in possession of the goods as the seller's bailee, attorns to the buyer,[1370] or sub-buyer.[1371] But the fact that a delivery note or order for goods stored in a warehouse is handed to the buyer does not normally give the buyer possession until the warehouseman attorns to the buyer[1372]: until then the seller's lien continues. The delivery of part only of the goods sold does not normally preclude the unpaid seller from exercising his right of lien over the remainder of the goods which continue in his possession.[1373]

[1360] *Sanders Bros v Maclean* (1883) 11 Q.B.D. 327, 341; *The Prinz Adalbert* [1917] A.C. 586, 589. There is no need for an attornment by the carrier to the buyer.

[1361] See below, paras 44-326 et seq.

[1362] See above, para.44-318.

[1363] The buyer may, however, have previously been in possession as bailee, and the seller may assent to the buyer's holding for himself as from the date of the contract. cf. s.41(2) (see above, para.44-318). cf. also a symbolic or constructive delivery in a sale and leaseback transaction: *Michael Gerson (Leasing) Ltd v Wilkinson* [2000] Q.B. 514.

[1364] See above, paras 44-239 et seq. (The definition of "delivery" in s.61(1) reads: "voluntary transfer of possession from one person to another".) Where delivery and payment of the price are to be contemporaneous, the seller will intend to retain his lien (and so intend not to complete delivery) until payment: *Kidman v Patterson* (1887) 8 N.S.W.L.R. (L.) 290.

[1365] s.43(1)(b), see above. Even in this situation, the contract itself may create a special right in the seller which is analogous to a lien: *Dodsley v Varley* (1840) 12 A. & E. 632 (goods delivered to warehouse employed by buyer, but the course of dealing (s.55(1)) was that they were to remain there until they were paid for). In New Zealand, an express power for the seller to retake possession upon the buyer's default has been interpreted to allow the unpaid seller's lien to revive: *Bines v Sankey* [1958] N.Z.L.R. 886, 895–896. (But cf. *United Plastics Ltd v Reliance Electric (NZ) Ltd* [1997] 2 N.Z.L.R. 125). cf. also *Howes v Ball* (1827) 7 B. & C. 481 (commented on in *Sewell v Burdick* (1884) 10 App. Cas. 74, 96); *Re Hamilton Young Co* [1905] 2 K.B. 772.

[1366] s.45(1) and (2) (see below, paras 44-328—44-332).

[1367] *Cusack v Robinson* (1861) 1 B. & S. 299, 308; *Baldey v Parker* (1823) 2 B. & C. 37, 44. See above, para.44-034; *Benjamin's Sale of Goods*, 10th edn (2017), para.15-050.

[1368] *Wallace v Woodgate* (1824) Ry. Moo. 193 (followed in *Jeffcott v Andrew Motors Ltd* [1960] N.Z.L.R. 721, 730, CA); *Mason v Morley* (1865) 11 Jur.(N.S.) 459, 461. See *Benjamin* at para.15-055.

[1369] *Valpy v Gibson* (1847) 4 C.B. 836; *United Plastics Ltd v Reliance Electric (NZ) Ltd* [1997] 2 N.Z.L.R. 125.

[1370] s.29(4). See *Harman v Anderson* (1809) 2 Camp. 243; *Capital and Counties Bank Ltd v Warriner* (1896) 12 T.L.R. 216. See also s.45(3) (see below, para.44-333).

[1371] *Hawes v Watson* (1824) 2 B. & C. 540.

[1372] *M'Ewan and Sons v Smith* (1849) 2 H.L.C. 309.

[1373] See s.42 (see above, para.44-320).

Waiver of lien   The seller may waive his lien by assenting to a sub-sale,[1374] or by **44-324** dealing with the goods in a manner inconsistent with the lien,[1375] or by making a new arrangement with the buyer which is inconsistent with the continuance of his lien.[1376] A lien may be lost if the seller refuses to deliver the goods on some ground other than the buyer's failure to pay or tender the price, or on some ground other than his right of lien.[1377] Where the seller obtains judgment for the price he does not waive his lien: by s.43(2) of the Act, "An unpaid seller of goods who has a lien or right of retention in respect of them does not lose his lien or right of retention by reason only that he has obtained judgment or decree for the price of the goods".[1378] Only full satisfaction[1379] of a judgment[1380] for the price can amount to payment so as to defeat the seller's lien.[1381]

Effect of sub-sales and other dispositions   The fact that the buyer has resold the **44-325** goods to a sub-buyer, or agreed to pledge them or disposed of them in some other way, will not deprive the unpaid seller of his lien,[1382] even where he knows of the sub-sale or other disposition, or knows that the sub-buyer has paid the buyer.[1383] There are, however, a number of special circumstances in which the unpaid seller's right of lien will be lost or adversely affected by a sub-sale or other disposition of the goods.[1384]

(ii)   Stoppage in Transit[1385]

Right of stoppage in transit   Section 44 of the Act provides: **44-326**

"Subject to this Act, when the buyer of goods becomes insolvent[1386] the unpaid seller[1387] who has parted with the possession of the goods has the right of stopping them in transit,

---

[1374] See s.47(1) (see below, para.44-339).

[1375] e.g. by wrongfully reselling (*Chinery v Viall* (1860) 5 H. & N. 288) or consuming the goods (*Gurr v Cuthbert* (1843) 12 L.J. Ex. 309). See *Benjamin's Sale of Goods*, 10th edn (2017), para.15-057.

[1376] *Bank of Africa Ltd v Salisbury Gold Mining Co Ltd* [1892] A.C. 281, 284 (lien on a member's shares in a company). cf. *Clifford Harris & Co v Solland International Ltd* [2005] EWHC 141 (Ch), [2005] 2 All E.R. 334.

[1377] *Boardman v Sill* (1808) 1 Camp. 410(n) (a claim for a lien for warehouse charges: approved (obiter) in *Yungmann v Briesemann* (1892) 67 L.T. 642, 644); *Weeks v Goode* (1859) 6 C.B.(N.S.) 367. cf. *White v Gainer* (1824) 2 Bing. 23 (no waiver of lien for work done on chattels).

[1378] *Benjamin* submits at para.15-059 that s.43(2) also applies when the seller has resumed possession of the goods by exercising his right of stoppage in transit.

[1379] cf. *Jacobs v Latour* (1828) 5 Bing. 130 (a stable-keeper's lien lost when creditor caused sheriff to take the goods in execution).

[1380] It is not clear whether the lien would cover the costs of the judgment as well as the judgment debt itself (the price).

[1381] The position was the same before the Act: *Houlditch v Desanges* (1818) 2 Stark. 337; *Scrivener v GN Ry* (1871) 19 W.R. 388.

[1382] s.47(1) (see below, para.44-339).

[1383] *M'Ewan Sons v Smith* (1849) 2 H.L.C. 309. Nor can the fact that the unpaid seller has knowledge of a sub-sale be used to found an estoppel, so as to prevent him from setting up his lien: *Poulton and Sons v Anglo-American Oil Co Ltd* (1910) 27 T.L.R. 38, 39.

[1384] See s.47(1) and (2) (see below, paras 44-339—44-342); *Benjamin's Sale of Goods*, 10th edn (2017), paras 15-092—15-100; attornment by bailee to the buyer (*M'Ewan and Sons v Smith*, above); and s.25 (see above, paras 44-220—44-231).

[1385] In the 1893 Act, and in the common law cases before that Act, the Latin phrase *in transitu* was used. The 1979 Act uses the English phrase "in transit".

[1386] s.61(4): see above, para.44-313.

[1387] s.38: see above, para.44-311. (The seller is "unpaid" where only part of the price has been paid.)

that is to say, he may resume possession of the goods as long as they are in course of transit,[1388] and may retain them until payment or tender of the price."[1389]

The main purpose of the right of stoppage is to enable the unpaid seller, by resuming his lien,[1390] to gain priority (in regard to the goods) over the general creditors of an insolvent buyer who becomes bankrupt.[1391] By stopping the goods in the course of their transit, the seller puts the carrier under an obligation to redeliver the goods to him,[1392] and thereby reacquires the right to possession of the goods.[1393] But the exercise of the right of stoppage does not of itself terminate the contract of sale[1394]: it merely prevents the buyer from obtaining possession of the goods, and puts the seller in a position in which he can effectively exercise his statutory power of resale.[1395] The practical importance of the right of stoppage in transit has greatly diminished with the development of more sophisticated methods of payment, particularly the use of bankers' commercial credits[1396] when the parties carry on business in different countries: where a bank is in possession of the documents of title to the goods until payment it is in a position to protect both the seller and itself if the buyer becomes insolvent. The right of stoppage in transit may be exercised despite the fact that property in the goods has passed to the buyer[1397]; where the property remains in the seller,[1398] he may withhold delivery by virtue of his ownership.[1399]

44-327   **Who is entitled to exercise the right**   The definition of seller in the Act[1400] includes one who agrees to sell: thus a buyer who resells the goods before the property in the goods has passed to him may exercise the right of stoppage as against the sub-buyer.[1401] The right of stoppage has also been extended to some quasi-sellers[1402]; and it is submitted that a surety of the buyer who has paid the seller would be entitled to exercise it.[1403] A commission agent may accept an order to obtain goods for his principal by buying them in his own name[1404] and consigning

---

[1388] s.45 (see below, paras 44-328—44-330).

[1389] The right of stoppage may be negatived or varied by agreement: s.55.

[1390] Which he would normally have lost by delivery of the goods to the carrier: s.43(1)(a) (see above, para.44-322). But the right under s.44 does not depend on the seller having previously enjoyed a right of lien under s.41.

[1391] For the justification of the doctrine, see *Benjamin's Sale of Goods*, 10th edn (2017), para.15-064.

[1392] s.46(4) (see below, para.44-337).

[1393] *Booth S.S. Co Ltd v Cargo Fleet Iron Co* [1916] 2 K.B. 570, 581.

[1394] s.48(1) (see below, para.44-344).

[1395] s.48(3) (see below, para.44-351). cf. a retention of title clause: see above, paras 44-171—44-188.

[1396] See above, paras 34-441 et seq.

[1397] s.39(1) (see above, para.44-304); *Bloxam v Sanders* (1825) 4 B. & C. 941, 948 (cited with approval in *Ex p. Chalmers* (1873) L.R. 8 Ch. App. 289, 291–292). The effect of the property passing is that the goods are then at the risk of the buyer: see above, paras 44-189—44-192.

[1398] This may include the situation when the seller has retained a right of disposal over the goods, in accordance with s.19 (see above, paras 44-170—44-172).

[1399] s.39(2) (see above, para.44-306). See also *Bolton v Lancs. and Yorks Ry* (1866) L.R. 1 C.P. 431, 439; *Ex p. Chalmers*, see above, at 292.

[1400] s.61(1) (see above, para.44-015).

[1401] *Jenkyns v Usborne* (1844) 7 M. & G. 678, 698–699.

[1402] See above, para.44-309; *Imperial Bank v London and St Katharine Docks Co* (1877) 5 Ch. D. 195.

[1403] See above, para.44-309.

[1404] This means that the agent pledges his own (and not his principal's) credit when buying the goods: *Feise v Wray* (1802) 3 East 93; *Ex p. Miles* (1885) 15 Q.B.D. 39, 42.

them to him: such an agent is treated as a seller[1405] of the goods to his principal and may exercise the right of stoppage in transit if the principal becomes insolvent.[1406] Obviously, the seller's agent may exercise the right of stoppage on his behalf.[1407] Where the right was exercised by a purported agent who lacked actual authority to do so, the seller may subsequently ratify the agent's act, provided the ratification is before the transit terminates.[1408]

Duration of transit Section 45 contains seven subsections setting out various **44-328** rules on the duration of transit[1409] for the purposes of the unpaid seller's right of stoppage. These rules reflect the following principle: "The essential feature of a stoppage in transit ... is, that the goods should be at the time in the possession of a middleman, or of some person intervening between the vendor who has parted with and the purchaser who has not yet received them".[1410] The whole of s.45 indicates that the carrier "middleman" must be independent of both the seller and the buyer, in the sense that he is not acting exclusively as the agent of one of them, even though he may have been appointed by only one of them.[1411]

"In course of transit" By s.45(1): **44-329**

"Goods are deemed to be in course of transit from the time when they are delivered to a carrier or other bailee[1412] or custodier[1413] for the purpose of transmission to the buyer, until the buyer or his agent[1414] in that behalf takes delivery[1415] of them from the carrier or other bailee or custodier."[1416]

The duration or extent of the transit will normally depend on the interpretation of the particular words used in the contract or in the directions of the buyer to the

---

[1405] At least for the purpose of the remedy of stoppage in transit: *Cassaboglou v Gibb* (1883) 11 Q.B.D. 797; cf. above, para.31-165. (By virtue of s.38(2), his remedies under the Act will now include the three "real" remedies in s.39(1).)

[1406] *Ireland v Livingston* (1872) L.R. 5 H.L. 395, 408–409; *Cassaboglou v Gibb* (1883) 11 Q.B.D. 797, 804, 806–807 (following *Feise v Wray* (1802) 3 East 93).

[1407] *Whitehead v Anderson* (1842) 9 M. & W. 518.

[1408] *Hutchings v Nunes* (1863) 1 Moo. P.C. N.S. 243; *Bird v Brown* (1850) 4 Ex. 786. (Under the general law of agency, the principal may ratify only if he was competent at the time of the ratification to do the act in question: see above, para.31-031; *Bowstead and Reynolds on Agency*, 21st edn (2017), paras 2-047 et seq.)

[1409] "Transit" does not mean that the goods must be actually moving at the relevant time: they must, however, be still in the possession of the carrier. The duration of transit is a question which is entirely distinct from the passing of property: *Bethell v Clark* (1888) 20 Q.B.D. 615, 617.

[1410] *Schotsmans v Lancs Yorks Ry* (1867) L.R. 2 Ch. App. 332, 338.

[1411] Thus the mere fact that the carrier was appointed by the buyer does not mean that transit ended when the delivery was made to the carrier: *Bethell v Clark*, above, at 617. See also *Ex p. Rosevear China Clay Co* (1879) 11 Ch. D. 560.

[1412] These words would include a carrier by air: see McNair, *Law of the Air*, 3rd edn, pp.161–163. (s.45(1) of the 1893 Act read "... a carrier by land or water or other bailee ...").

[1413] The Scottish term for bailee.

[1414] *Bethell v Clark* (1888) 20 Q.B.D. 615 at 620. It is immaterial that the buyer has instructed his agents to forward the goods to another destination: *Kendal v Marshall Stevens Co* (1883) 11 Q.B.D. 356; *Jobson v Eppenheim Co* (1905) 21 T.L.R. 468. See also *Dixon v Baldwen* (1804) 5 East 175.

[1415] Defined in s.61(1): see above, para.44-015. Although the buyer may have taken delivery of the goods, the seller may still, through the reservation of the right of disposal, have rights over them: see above, paras 44-170—44-172.

[1416] See Todd [1978] J.B.L. 39.

seller.[1417] If the ultimate destination is specified by the buyer,[1418] and no fresh directions by the buyer are needed,[1419] transit will continue until the goods reach that ultimate destination. So long as the seller knows he is delivering to a carrier, who receives them in that capacity,[1420] the right of stoppage arises despite the fact that the buyer had not informed the seller of the ultimate destination of the goods.[1421]

44-330   Delivery   The question whether delivery has taken place may depend on the buyer's intention to take delivery[1422] or the carrier's intention not to deliver until the freight has been paid.[1423] The buyer will not obtain possession of the goods merely by marking them or by taking samples while they remain in the carrier's possession.[1424] A bankrupt buyer[1425] (or his trustee in bankruptcy)[1426] may terminate the transit by accepting delivery; but the seller's right of stoppage will be preserved by the bankrupt buyer's refusal to accept delivery.[1427]

44-331   Shipment on buyer's ship: transfer of bill of lading   Transit prima facie comes to an end[1428] when goods are shipped by the seller on a ship belonging to the buyer[1429]; but the seller may continue the transit by taking in his name a bill of lading for the goods to be delivered "unto order or assigns".[1430] Similarly, a seller may preserve his right of stoppage in the case of a delivery to a ship under a FOB contract, if pending the issue of the bill of lading, he takes a mate's receipt acknowledging that the goods are shipped on account of the seller.[1431] The transfer of a bill of lading by the seller to the buyer (or his agent) does not in itself terminate

---

[1417] For illustrations, see *Jackson v Nichol* (1839) 5 Bing. N.C. 508; *Ex p. Watson* (1877) 5 Ch. D. 35 (as explained in *Ex p. Miles* (1885) 15 Q.B.D. 39, 46, 47); *Kemp v Ismay, Imrie Co* (1909) 100 L.T. 996.

[1418] *Bethell v Clark* (1888) 20 Q.B.D. 615. See also *Coates v Railton* (1827) 6 B. & C. 422.

[1419] cf. *Valpy v Gibson* (1847) 4 C.B. 836, 865 (goods received by buyer's shipping agents who had no authority to forward the goods until they received the buyer's order to do so).

[1420] Delivery to a ship (unless it is the buyer's ship: see below, n.1429) is "an indication that the goods were to go on a voyage": *Kendal v Marshall Stevens Co* (1883) 11 Q.B.D. 356, 367.

[1421] *Ex p. Rosevear China Clay Co* (1879) 11 Ch. D. 560 (FOB contract).

[1422] *James v Griffin* (1837) 2 M. & W. 623 (wharf not intended to be "place of final deposit"). See also s.45(4) and *Bolton v Lancs and Yorks Ry* (1866) L.R. 1 C.P. 431. cf. *Fairfax v Illawarra Steam Navigation Co* (1872) 11 S.C.R. (N.S.W.) 103. cf. also symbolic or constructive delivery in a sale and leaseback transaction: *Michael Gerson (Leasing) Ltd v Wilkinson* [2000] Q.B. 514.

[1423] *Edwards v Brewer* (1837) 2 M. & W. 375. cf. *Allan v Gripper* (1832) 2 Cr. & J. 218; *Crawshay v Eades* (1823) 1 B. & C. 181.

[1424] *Whitehead v Anderson* (1842) 9 M. & W. 518, 535.

[1425] *Scott v Pettit* (1803) 3 Bos. & P. 469. On bankruptcy, see above, para.44-314.

[1426] *Ellis v Hunt* (1789) 3 T.R. 464.

[1427] *Ex p. Cooper* (1879) 11 Ch. D. 68, 73. (See above, para.44-314.)

[1428] This proposition may have to give way to the parties' intention: *Merchant Banking Co v Phoenix Bessemer Steel Co* (1877) 5 Ch. D. 205, 219.

[1429] *Van Casteel v Booker* (1848) 2 Exch. 691, 699, 708; *Berndston v Strang* (1867) 4 Eq. 481, 488–489; (on appeal) (1868) L.R. 3 Ch. App. 588; *Ex p. Francis Co Ltd* (1887) 56 L.T. 577; *Schotsmans v Lancs and Yorks Ry* (1867) L.R. 2 Ch. App. 332 (buyer's ship employed as general trader). cf. s.45(5) (see below, para.44-334).

[1430] *Van Casteel v Booker* (1848) 2 Exch. 691, 699, 708–709; *Berndston v Strang* (1867) 4 Eq. 481, 488–489. On such a reservation of a right of disposal, see s.19(2) (see above, para.44-171) and *Benjamin's Sale of Goods*, 10th edn (2017), para.18-262.

[1431] *Craven v Ryder* (1816) 6 Taunt. 433; *Ruck v Hatfield* (1822) 5 B. & Ald. 632. cf. *Cowasjee v Thompson* (1845) 5 Moo. P.C. 165. On mate's receipts in general, see *Benjamin* at paras 18-206 et seq.

the transit for the purposes of stoppage in transit[1432]: provided that possession of the goods was intended by the parties to pass directly from the seller to the carrier, and to be received by him as carrier (i.e. purely in his capacity as such and not as agent of the buyer), the transit as between the seller and the buyer will continue.[1433]

Buyer obtains delivery before arrival Section 45(2) provides: **44-332**

"If the buyer or his agent in that behalf[1434] obtains delivery of the goods before their arrival at the appointed destination, the transit is at an end."[1435]

In many circumstances of inland transport the consignee may, in the absence of special terms in the contract of carriage, demand the goods from the carrier at a place en route to the designated destination[1436]; similarly, circumstances may arise in which the carrier attorns[1437] to the buyer in the course of the transit, and thus terminates the transit.[1438]

Acknowledgment to the buyer Section 45(3) provides: **44-333**

"If, after the arrival of the goods at the appointed destination,[1439] the carrier or other bailee or custodier acknowledges to the buyer or his agent that he holds the goods on his behalf and continues in possession of them as bailee or custodier for the buyer or his agent, the transit is at an end, and it is immaterial that a further destination[1440] for the goods may have been indicated by the buyer."

Such an acknowledgment is an illustration of the doctrine of attornment[1441]: a bailee who acknowledges to the claimant that the claimant now has title to a chattel,

---

[1432] *Schotsmans v Lancs and Yorks Ry* (1867) L.R. 2 Ch. App. 332 at 337.

[1433] *Lyons v Hoffnung* (1890) 15 App. Cas. 391; *The Tigress* (1863) 32 L.J.Adm. 97; *Ex p. Golding Davis Co Ltd* (1880) 13 Ch. D. 628, 633. (But if the buyer transfers the bill of lading to a sub-buyer or pledgee, s.47(?) will apply: see below, paras 44-341—44-342).

[1434] This means an agent with authority to take delivery at a place other than the appointed destination: *Mechan Sons Ltd v NE Ry*, 1911 S.C. 1348, 1357–1358.

[1435] *Johann Plischke and Sohne GmbH v Allison Bros Ltd* [1936] 2 All E.R. 1009. The common law before the Act was to the same effect: *Whitehead v Anderson* (1842) 9 M. & W. 518, 534.

[1436] *Cork Distilleries Co v GS and W Ry* (1874) L.R. 7 H.L. 269. See also *L and NW Ry v Bartlett* (1861) 7 Hurl. & N. 400, 407–408. However, in modern conditions it may often be impossible or impracticable for the carrier to deliver the goods to the consignee at any place en route to the appointed destination. The terms of the contract of carriage may expressly or by implication deny the consignee the right to demand the goods before arrival at that destination. (On container transport, see *Benjamin's Sale of Goods*, 10th edn (2017), paras 21-073 et seq.) The buyer's tortious acquisition of possession without the carrier's consent should not terminate the transit: *Benjamin's Sale of Goods*, para.15-074; and see Todd [1978] J.B.L. 39, 43–44.

[1437] See above, para.33-030; cf. see below, para.44-333.

[1438] *Reddall v Union Castle Mail S.S. Co Ltd* (1914) 84 L.J. K.B. 360. The carrier is not obliged to attorn to the buyer in the course of transit: *Jackson v Nichol* (1839) 5 Bing. N.C. 508.

[1439] This depends on the provisions of the contract for sale: *Mechan Sons Ltd v NE Ry*, 1911 S.C. 1348, 1356, 1358. The name of the person to whom the goods are sent, as well as the place, is implied in "destination": *Ex p. Miles* (1885) 15 Q.B.D. 39, 45.

[1440] *Kendall v Marshall, Stevens Co* (1883) 11 Q.B.D. 356; *Bethell v Clark* (1888) 20 Q.B.D. 615, 617; *Ex p. Miles* (1885) 15 Q.B.D. 47 (referring to *Ex p. Watson* (1877) 5 Ch. D. 35). See also *Rodger v Comptoir D'Escompte de Paris* (1869) L.R. 2 P.C. 393.

[1441] See above, para.33-030. Attornment cannot be inferred from the mere fact that the carrier has notified the buyer that he is ready to deliver the goods: *Mechan Sons Ltd v NE Ry*, 1911 S.C. 1348 at 1359.

becomes the bailee of the claimant.[1442] The assent of both parties (the carrier[1443] and the buyer)[1444] is required to the change from the carrier holding the goods as carrier to holding them as warehouseman or agent for the buyer.[1445] The buyer's request to the carrier to hold the goods in the carrier's warehouse pending further instructions from the buyer, is strong evidence that the carrier thereupon becomes the buyer's agent so that transit ends.[1446]

44-334   **Other provisions as to transit**   Section 45 further provides:

> "(4)   If the goods are rejected by the buyer, and the carrier or other bailee or custodier continues in possession of them, the transit is not deemed to be at an end, even if the seller has refused to receive them back.[1447]
>
> (5)   When goods are delivered to a ship chartered by the buyer it is a question depending on the circumstances of the particular case[1448] whether they are in the possession of the master as a carrier or as agent to the buyer."

Under subs.(5) the proper test to apply[1449] is whether the master of the ship is an employee of the shipowner[1450] or of the buyer as demise charterer[1451]: in the latter situation, the seller loses his right of stoppage upon delivery to the ship, unless he takes a bill of lading in a form under which he retains control over the goods[1452]; in the former situation, transit is not terminated by delivery to the ship.

44-335   Section 45 continues:

[1442] *Henderson Co v Williams* [1895] 1 Q.B. 521; *Dublin City Distillery Ltd v Doherty* [1914] A.C. 823, 847–848. See also *Bolton v Lancs and Yorks Ry* (1866) L.R. 1 C.P. 431, 438; *Ex p. Cooper* (1879) 11 Ch. D. 68, 78. At common law, the bailee was also estopped (by the attornment) from denying the claimant's title to the chattel, but by s.8(1) of the Torts (Interference with Goods) Act 1977 the bailee may now set up the title of a third person in reply to the claimant's demand for the chattel: see above, paras 33-015—33-017, 33-030.

[1443] *Whitehead v Anderson* (1842) 9 M. & W. 518 (silence on the part of the carrier is insufficient to show assent); *Coventry v Gladstone* (1868) L.R. 6 Eq. 44.

[1444] *Bolton v Lancs and Yorks Ry* (1866) L.R. 1 C.P. 431, 438; *Ex p. Barrow* (1877) 6 Ch. D. 783, 789. Silence and delay on the part of the buyer may lead to an inference of assent, e.g. after the carrier sends the buyer a notice that he will hold the goods as warehouseman and charge rent to the buyer: *Taylor v GE Ry* (1901) 17 T.L.R. 394; *Ex p. Catling* (1873) 29 L.T. 431.

[1445] The parties may agree that the change is made despite the fact that the carrier insists on his lien until freight has been paid: *Kemp v Falk* (1882) 7 App. Cas. 573, 584; *Crawshay v Eades* (1823) 1 B. & C. 181; *Ex p. Barrow* (1877) 6 Ch. D. 783, 789; *Ex p. Cooper* (1879) 11 Ch. D. 68, 72–73, 74, 76 (delivery of part after payment of part of the freight). cf. *Whitehead v Anderson* (1842) 9 M. & W. 518, 535–536.

[1446] *Johann Plischke and Sohne GmbH v Allison Bros Ltd* [1936] 2 All E.R. 1009.

[1447] *Bolton v Lancs and Yorks Ry* (1866) L.R. 1 C.P. 431. (The buyer's consent is needed for "delivery": see above, paras 44-241 et seq.). A bankrupt buyer, by refusing to take delivery, preserves the seller's right of stoppage: see above, para.44-314.

[1448] cf. delivery to the buyer's ship: see above, para.44-331.

[1449] The question depends on the intention of the parties as shown by the terms of the charterparty and particularly by the form of the bill of lading: in whose name and to whose order was it made out? See *Benjamin's Sale of Goods*, 10th edn (2017), paras 15-082, 20-077 et seq.

[1450] As in the case of a charterparty which is not by demise (see below, n.1451).

[1451] *Berndtson v Strang* (1868) L.R. 3 Ch. App. 588. In a charter by demise (a type of "lease" of a ship: see *Scrutton on Charterparties and Bills of Lading*, 23rd edn (2015), para.1.103 et seq.) the charterer is in possession of the ship and the master is his employee.

[1452] *Berndtson v Strang*, above (bill of lading for the goods to be delivered to the seller's "order or assigns"). In *Ex p. Rosevear China Clay Co* (1879) 11 Ch. D. 560, although delivery had been made to a ship chartered by the buyer, the stoppage was made before any bill of lading had been signed.

"(6) Where the carrier or other bailee or custodier wrongfully[1453] refuses to deliver the goods to the buyer or his agent in that behalf, the transit is deemed to be at an end.[1454]

(7) Where part delivery of the goods has been made to the buyer or his agent in that behalf, the remainder of the goods may be stopped in transit, unless such part delivery has been made under such circumstances as to show an agreement[1455] to give up possession of the whole of the goods.[1456]"

Subsection (7) implies that normally part delivery is not to be treated as delivery of the whole.[1457] But circumstances may indicate constructive delivery of the whole; thus where the goods constitute one entire machine, and the consignee is permitted to take an essential part of it, that transfer might amount to transfer of the whole machine.[1458]

Methods of exercising right of stoppage It is provided by s.46: **44-336**

"(1) The unpaid seller may[1459] exercise his right of stoppage in transit either by taking actual possession of the goods or by giving notice[1460] of his claim to the carrier or other bailee or custodier in whose possession the goods are.

(2) The notice may be given either to the person in actual possession of the goods[1461] or to his principal.[1462]

(3) If given to the principal, the notice is ineffective unless given at such time and under such circumstances that the principal, by the exercise of reasonable diligence, may communicate it to his servant or agent in time to prevent a delivery to the buyer.[1463]"

The seller takes the risk of the stoppage being unjustified[1464] so that the carrier is not concerned to investigate the facts to see whether the seller is justified in stopping the goods[1465]; the carrier must give effect to the stoppage as soon as he is satis-

---

[1453] "Wrongfully" implies that the carrier has no legal justification for refusing to deliver, e.g. no lien for unpaid freight or demurrage (see below, para.44-337). But the carrier need not attorn to the buyer in the course of transit: see above, para.44-332.

[1454] *Bird v Brown* (1850) 4 Ex. 786. cf. s.45(1) (see above, para.44-329).

[1455] On the part of *both* parties: *Kemp v Falk* (1882) 7 App. Cas. 573, 586.

[1456] *Jones v Jones* (1841) 8 M. & W. 431; *Tanner v Scovell* (1845) 14 M. & W. 28; *Bolton v Lancs and Yorks Ry* (1866) L.R. 1 C.P. 431, 440; *Ex p. Cooper* (1879) 11 Ch. D. 68; *Kemp v Falk* (1882) 7 App. Cas. 579, 586. cf. s.42 (see above, para.44-320).

[1457] *Mechan Sons Ltd v NE Ry*, 1911 S.C. 1348, 1358. Unpaid freight charges indicate that delivery of part is not constructive delivery of the whole: *Ex p. Cooper* (1879) 11 Ch. D. 68.

[1458] *Ex p. Cooper* (1879) 11 Ch. D. 68, 75–76. cf. s.45(3) (attornment, see above, para.44-333).

[1459] At common law, no particular formality was needed: *Snee v Prescot* (1753) 1 Atk. 245, 250; *Litt v Cowley* (1816) 7 Taunt. 169. The seller's notice may be given with the full agreement of the buyer: *Nicholls v Le Feuvre* (1835) 2 Bing. N.C. 81.

[1460] The notice may tell the carrier not to deliver to the buyer (e.g. *Booth S.S. Co Ltd v Cargo Fleet Iron Co Ltd* [1916] 2 K.B. 570, 592) or to hold the goods to the seller's orders.

[1461] *Whitehead v Anderson* (1842) 9 M. & W. 518, 534.

[1462] Notice to the consignee is probably not sufficient: *Phelps, Stokes Co v Comber* (1885) 29 Ch. D. 813, 822, 826.

[1463] e.g. a shipowner who receives notice is under a duty to communicate it with reasonable diligence to the master of the ship carrying the goods: *Kemp v Falk* (1882) 7 App. Cas. 573, 585–586 (failure in this duty would render the shipowner liable to the seller, either in conversion, or under s.60).

[1464] *The Tigress* (1863) 32 L.J.Adm. 97, 101. Thus, a shipowner need not require the seller to show that the bill of lading has not been transferred by the buyer to a third person: see below, paras 44-336, 44-337.

[1465] *The Tigress* (1863) 32 L.J.Adm. 97. (See also s.46(4).) If the seller acts without justification, e.g. if the buyer is not insolvent, the buyer's remedy is a claim for damages against the seller: *The Constantia* (1807) 6 C.Rob.Adm.R. 321, 326. (The seller is still bound to deliver to the buyer, who

fied that it is the seller who claims the goods.[1466]

44-337 **Duties of the parties after notice is given** By s.46(4):

"When notice of stoppage in transit is given by the seller to the carrier or other bailee or custodier in possession of the goods, he must re-deliver the goods to, or according to the directions of, the seller; and the expenses of the re-delivery must be borne by the seller."[1467]

The stoppage does not entitle the seller to direct the carrier to deliver the goods to him except at the contractual destination.[1468] The only effect on the contract of carriage is to prevent delivery to the consignee at the destination, and to entitle the seller to direct delivery there[1469] to himself or to his order.[1470] The exercise of the seller's power places the seller[1471] under a direct obligation to the carrier either to take delivery or to give him directions for delivery.[1472] In order to regain actual possession of the goods, the seller must pay any unpaid freight due to the carrier[1473] and if he fails to do so, he must pay damages to the carrier for the amount of the freight.[1474] Similarly, if the seller fails to give directions to the carrier after the stoppage, he will be liable to the carrier in damages for expenses, such as demurrage or landing charges.[1475] If the carrier disregards a valid notice, and delivers the goods to the consignee, e.g. by mistake,[1476] he is liable to the seller for conversion,[1477] since by the notice the seller resumes the right to possession of the goods.[1478]

---

apparently has no claim against the carrier.)

[1466] *The Tigress* (1863) 32 L.J.Adm. 97, at 101. If the carrier is aware of a legal defect in the seller's claim, he need not give effect to the stoppage; if the carrier is uncertain as to his position, he can interplead: above at 102; *Bethell v Clark* (1888) 20 Q.B.D. 615. On interpleader proceedings, see CPR Pts 17 and 33.

[1467] *The Tigress* (1863) 32 L.J.Adm. 97.

[1468] *Booth SS Co Ltd v Cargo Fleet Iron Co Ltd* [1916] 2 K.B. 570, 600–601. The carrier may redeliver to the seller before the goods are carried to the contractual destination, but it is prudent for the carrier to do so only under an indemnity from the seller.

[1469] *Booth SS Co Ltd v Cargo Fleet Iron Co Ltd* [1916] 2 K.B. 570.

[1470] 1979 Act s.46(4), see above. See also *United States Steel Products Co v GW Ry* [1916] 1 A.C. 189, 203.

[1471] Even where he is not a party to the contract of affreightment: *Booth S.S. Co Ltd v Cargo Fleet Iron Co Ltd* [1916] 2 K.B. 570.

[1472] *Booth SS Co Ltd v Cargo Fleet Iron Co Ltd* [1916] 2 K.B. 570.

[1473] *Booth SS Co Ltd v Cargo Fleet Iron Co Ltd* [1916] 2 K.B. 570, 583, 588. The carrier's lien on the goods for the freight takes priority over the seller's right of stoppage (which in turn takes priority over any general lien on the goods which the consignment contract may give the carrier in respect of sums owing to him from the consignee under other transactions): *United States Steel Products Co v GW Ry*, above; *Oppenheim v Russell* (1802) 3 Bos. P. 42; *Nicholls v Le Feuvre* (1835) 2 Bing. N.C. 81 (shipping agent's general lien).

[1474] *Booth SS Co Ltd v Cargo Fleet Iron Co Ltd* [1916] 2 K.B. 570, 583.

[1475] *Booth SS Co Ltd v Cargo Fleet Iron Co Ltd* [1916] 2 K.B. 570, 583. (See the last clause of s.46(4) above.)

[1476] *Litt v Cowley* (1816) 7 Taunt. 169. (This case is no longer authority on the question of revesting of title: see now s.48(1) (see below, para.44-344).)

[1477] *The Tigress* (1863) 32 L.J. Adm. 97; *Mechan Sons Ltd v NE Ry*, 1911 S.C. 1348. The action will fall under s.60 and is classified as an action in tort, not in contract: *Pontifex v Midland Ry* (1877) 3 Q.B.D. 23: it will be governed by the Torts (Interference with Goods) Act 1977. Refusal of the carrier to deliver upon demand being made by the seller would also be evidence of conversion: *Wilson v Anderton* (1830) 1 B. & A. 450, 456; *The Tigress* (1863) 32 L.J. Adm. 102.

[1478] Sales of Goods Act s.44 (see above, para.44-326). Other remedies of the seller may include an injunction: *Schotsmans v Lancs and Yorks Ry* (1867) L.R. 2 Ch. App. 332, 340; or Admiralty proceedings if the goods are in the possession of a shipowner: *The Tigress*, above (a proceeding by

Stoppage limited to the goods themselves   Since the right of stoppage is a right   **44-338**
exercisable only against the goods themselves, the unpaid seller has no right against
money paid or payable to the buyer under a policy of insurance for damage suffered by the goods in the course of transit.[1479] (The same principle prevents the
unpaid seller from using his right of stoppage, after the actual transit has ended, to
intercept the price due to be paid to the buyer under a sub-sale of the same
goods.[1480])

(iii)   Sub-sales and Other Subsequent Transactions

Sub-sale by buyer   Section 47(1) of the Act provides: **44-339**

"Subject to this Act,[1481] the unpaid seller's right of lien or retention or stoppage in transit
is not affected by any sale or other disposition of the goods[1482] which the buyer may have
made, unless the seller has assented to it."

Thus, the fact that the seller knows of a sub-sale, or knows that the sub-buyer has
paid the buyer, will not deprive the seller of his lien,[1483] nor can such knowledge
be used to found an estoppel, so as to prevent the seller from setting up his lien [1484]
(The important exception to subs.(1) is found in subs.(2), which concerns the
transfer of a document of title [1485]) But the "assent" of the seller to the sub-sale will
prevent his remedy by way of lien or stoppage.[1486] In one case before the 1893
Act,[1487] the sellers were held to have assented to the buyers dealing with the goods,
because the sellers had issued to the buyers a warrant which was (by custom) treated
as a representation that the goods were free from any seller's lien. But in a case[1488]
interpreting s.47 of the 1893 Act, it was held that:

"... the assent which affects the unpaid seller's right of lien must be such an assent as in
the circumstances shews that the seller intends to renounce his rights against the goods.[1489]
It is not enough to shew that the fact of a sub-contract has been brought to his notice and
that he has assented to it merely in the sense of acknowledging the receipt of the information ..."

---

the seller to recover, by arrest of the ship, damages for refusal to deliver goods to him).
[1479] *Berndtson v Strang* (1868) L.R. 3 Ch. App. 588, 591. See also *Latham v Chartered Bank of India*
(1873) 17 Eq. 205, 216. cf. *Phelps, Stokes Co v Comber* (1885) 29 Ch. D. 813. cf. also *Northern
Grain Co v Wiffler* (1918) 223 N.Y. 169 (where the carrier has sold the goods to meet his freight
charges, the unpaid seller's right of stoppage can attach to the balance of the proceeds of the sale).
[1480] See below, para.44-343.
[1481] s.25 (see above, paras 44-220—44-231); s.47(2).
[1482] A sale of unascertained goods is within the section: *DF Mount Ltd v Jay and Jay (Provisions) Co
Ltd* [1960] 1 Q.B. 159, 167–168.
[1483] *McEwan and Sons v Smith* (1849) 2 H.L. Cas. 309.
[1484] *Poulton and Sons v Anglo-American Oil Co Ltd* (1910) 27 T.L.R. 38, 39.
[1485] See below, paras 44-341—44-342. In the 1893 Act, the provision now contained in s.47(2) was the
proviso to s.47, and is referred to as such in the cases.
[1486] The previous law was to the same effect: Blackburn, *Sale*, 1st edn, p.271; *Stoveld v Hughes* (1811)
14 East 308; *Pearson v Dawson* (1858) El. Bl. & El. 448; *Merchant Banking Co v Phoenix Bessemer
Steel Co* (1877) 5 Ch. D. 205.
[1487] *Merchant Banking Co v Phoenix Bessemer Steel Co* (1877) 5 Ch. D. 205.
[1488] *Mordaunt Bros v British Oil and Cake Mills Ltd* [1910] 2 K.B. 502, 507.
[1489] Or an intention "that the sub-contract shall be carried out irrespective of the terms of the original
contract": [1910] 2 K.B. 502, 507.

In another case,[1490] the sellers were held to have "assented" to the sub-sale, and thus to have lost their lien: the sellers sold cartons in the possession of a wharfinger to the buyer for resale to two of the buyer's customers and agreed with the buyer that the price should be paid by the buyer out of the money received from the sub-sales. The sellers made out delivery orders in favour of the buyer, who sold some of the cartons to a sub-buyer and gave him a delivery order. The sub-buyer paid the buyer but the buyer failed to pay the original sellers. The court held that the sellers had "assented" to the sub-sale "in the sense that they intended to renounce their rights against the goods and to take the risk of [the buyer's] honesty".[1491]

44-340   Attornment   Attornment[1492] obviously comes within "assent", as where the unpaid seller who retains possession of the goods attorns to the sub-buyer, by acknowledging to the sub-buyer that he holds the goods on behalf of the sub-buyer, or to his order.[1493] The same principle applies where the seller accepts a delivery order in favour of a sub-buyer in respect of a certain quantity of goods held in bulk in his warehouse: the seller is estopped from denying the sub-buyer's title (vis-à-vis himself[1494]) despite the fact that a specific part of the bulk has not been appropriated to the sub-buyer.[1495]

44-341   Transfer of document of title   It is provided by s.47(2):

"Where a document of title[1496] to goods has been lawfully transferred[1497] to any person as buyer or owner of the goods, and that person transfers the document to a person who takes it in good faith[1498] and for valuable consideration, then—

(a)   if the last-mentioned transfer was by way of sale the unpaid seller's right of lien or retention or stoppage in transit is defeated; and

(b)   if the last-mentioned transfer was made by way of pledge[1499] or other disposition for value, the unpaid seller's right of lien or retention or stoppage in transit can only be exercised subject to the rights of the transferee." [1500]

The person who transfers the document of title to the buyer may himself create the document (e.g. a delivery order); it is therefore unnecessary that he should have received it from a third person before he can "transfer" it within the meaning of

---

[1490] *DF Mount Ltd v Jay and Jay (Provisions) Co Ltd* [1960] 1 Q.B. 159.

[1491] [1960] 1 Q.B. 159 at 167. (The assent was given in anticipation of the sub-sale.)

[1492] See above, para.33-030.

[1493] And without notice to the sub-buyer of his claim to a lien (or to a contingent lien) over the goods in respect of the unpaid price: *Pearson v Dawson* (1858) El. Bl. & El. 448. cf. *Hawes v Watson* (1824) 2 B. & C. 540 (attornment by seller's warehouseman).

[1494] The seller may, however, defend a claim by reference to a third party who has a better title than himself: see s.8 of the Torts (Interference with Goods) Act 1977 (see above, paras 33-015—33-018).

[1495] *Woodley v Coventry* (1863) 2 H. & C. 164; *Knights v Wiffen* (1870) L.R. 5 Q.B. 660. (On the passing of property in part of a larger bulk, see above, paras 44-160 et seq.)

[1496] See above, para.44-015.

[1497] On the meaning of "lawfully transferred", see s.61(1) ("delivery") (see above, paras 44-015, 44-236 et seq.) and s.11 of the Factors Act 1889. (These two provisions must be read together: *Cahn and Mayer v Pockett's Bristol Channel Steam Packet Co Ltd* [1899] 1 Q.B. 643, 665.)

[1498] On the meaning of "good faith" see s.61(3), above, para.44-016.

[1499] See above, paras 33-121 et seq.

[1500] The corresponding provision in the 1893 Act was "the proviso to section 47", and is referred to as such in the reported cases (s.10 of the Factors Act 1889 has a similar effect).

subs.(2).[1501] So when sellers gave a delivery order to a buyer for part of a consignment of seed, and the buyer indorsed the order to sub-buyers who took in good faith and for value, it was held that the order was a document of title whose transfer terminated the seller's right to a lien.[1502] It has been said obiter that the words of subs.(2) confine it to cases where a document of title is transferred to the buyer and the same document is then transferred to the sub-buyer or transferee.[1503] Thus, where the original seller gave delivery orders to the buyer, who (instead of indorsing them over to the sub-buyer) sent them to the warehouseman and gave fresh delivery orders to the sub-buyer, the latter was not protected by the subsection.[1504]

Section 47(2) expressly covers pledges of a document of title. Before the 1893 Act, it was held that where a bill of lading for goods in transit had been indorsed by the buyer to a third person to secure a loan to the buyer, the unpaid seller had a claim in equity to stop the goods, subject to the mortgage: subject to repayment of the loan, the seller had a right to the surplus of the proceeds of the goods in preference to the general creditors of the buyer.[1505] **44-342**

> "The unpaid vendor's right, except so far as the interest had passed by the pledging of the bill of lading to the pledgee ... enabled the unpaid vendor in equity to stop in transit everything which was not covered by that pledge."[1506]

Stoppage in respect of price payable under sub-sale A principle similar to that applied in the pledge cases has been applied in *Ex p. Golding Davis Co Ltd*,[1507] where a buyer resold the goods while the transit continued, but the sub-buyer had not yet paid the price under the sub-sale. On the ground that the seller has an equitable right to stop the goods in transit "except in so far as it is necessary to give effect to interests which other persons have acquired for value",[1508] the Court of Appeal allowed the seller (who had given notice of stoppage before the transit ended) to intercept the unpaid purchase price due from the sub-buyer and to take from it the full price due to him as original seller, leaving only the balance to the buyer.[1509] It is very doubtful whether this remedy should be allowed after the transit has ended, but before the price due under the sub-sale has been actually paid by the sub-buyer to the buyer.[1510] A special term in the contract may, however, purport to entitle the seller to "trace" and recover the proceeds of sub-sales made by the buyer.[1511] **44-343**

[1501] *Ant Jurgens Margarinefabrieken v Louis Dreyfus Co* [1914] 3 K.B. 40.

[1502] *Ant Jurgens Margarinefabrieken v Louis Dreyfus Co* [1914] 3 K.B. 40. The document of title need not be one in respect of specific goods: [1914] 3 K.B. 40, 45; *Capital and Counties Bank Ltd v Warriner* (1896) 1 Com. Cas. 314. (But on this point, see Nicol (1979) 42 M.L.R. 129.)

[1503] *DF Mount Ltd v Jay and Jay (Provisions) Co Ltd* [1960] 1 Q.B. 159, 168.

[1504] *DF Mount Ltd v Jay and Jay (Provisions) Co Ltd* [1960] 1 Q.B. 159, 168. But s.25 overlaps with s.47(2), and is not limited to cases where the buyer transfers the same document as that which is in his possession with the consent of the seller: [1960] 1 Q.B. 159, 169. (See above, paras 44-218 et seq.) For a critical review of this decision, see Borrie (1960) 23 M.L.R. 100.

[1505] *Kemp v Falk* (1882) 7 App. Cas. 573, 576–577 (upholding *Re Westzinthus* (1833) 5 B. & Ad. 817; and *Spalding v Ruding* (1843) 6 Beav. 376; affirmed (1846) 15 L.J. Ch. 375).

[1506] *Kemp v Falk*, above, at 582.

[1507] (1880) 13 Ch. D. 628.

[1508] (1880) 13 Ch. D. 628 at 638.

[1509] This could simply be a novel way of implementing a valid stoppage: *Benjamin's Sale of Goods*, 10th edn (2017), para.15-100.

[1510] The Court of Appeal was ready to allow it in *Ex p. Falk* (1880) 14 Ch. D. 446, but it was seriously doubted in the House of Lords in the same case: *Kemp v Falk* (1882) 7 App. Cas. 573, 577–578 (the appeal turned on a different point). See *Benjamin's Sale of Goods*, para.15-100, and cf. see above,

(iv) Resale by the Seller

44-344 Contract not rescinded by exercise of lien or stoppage Section 48(1) provides[1512]:

> "Subject to this section, a contract of sale is not rescinded by the mere exercise by an unpaid seller[1513] of his right of lien or retention or stoppage in transit,"

The seller may terminate[1514] further performance of the contract only by taking further steps.[1515] The important effect of s.48(1) is that where the property in the goods has passed to the buyer, the exercise of the lien or of the right of stoppage does not in itself revest the property in the seller; the property is revested in the seller only when he validly terminates the contract, by reselling or otherwise.[1516]

44-345 Power of the seller to pass a good title to a second buyer The seller has the power to transfer a good title to the goods to a second buyer in several situations, in some of which he does not have, as against the original buyer, the right to resell the goods.[1517] In a resale, the seller has such a power to pass to a second buyer a good title to the goods:

(1) when, at the time of the resale, he has the property in the goods[1518]: as owner, the seller can transfer a good title to a new buyer under a second contract of sale[1519];

(2) under s.24, discussed above[1520];

(3) even where the property in the goods has passed to the original buyer, the seller has power, by reselling, to pass a good title to a second buyer where he has exercised his right of lien or of stoppage in transit. This is provided by s.48(2): "Where an unpaid seller who has exercised his right of lien or retention or stoppage in transit resells the goods, the buyer acquires a good title to them as against the original buyer". The effect of the subsection[1521] is that the title of the second buyer is good as against the original buyer,[1522]

---

para.44-339.

[1511] On such retention of title clauses, see above, paras 44-173 et seq. (On tracing orders, see Vol.I, paras 29-166 et seq.)

[1512] For a suggestion as to the purpose of s.48(1), see *RV Ward Ltd v Bignall* [1967] 1 Q.B. 534, 549.

[1513] See above, para.44-311.

[1514] s.48(1) uses the term "rescinded" (as does s.48(4)) but the more usual terms now are "terminate" or "treat the contract as discharged".

[1515] e.g. reselling under s.48(3) (see below, para.44-346).

[1516] See below, paras 44-346—44-349.

[1517] The seller will be liable in damages to the original buyer for breach of contract (and in tort, if the property in the goods has passed to the original buyer).

[1518] This situation is not mentioned in s.48, but it is implicit in it: Benjamin at para.15-102; *RV Ward Ltd v Bignall* [1967] 1 Q.B. 534, 545.

[1519] *Lickbarrow v Mason* (1793) 6 East 21, 24, 25; *Wait v Baker* (1848) 2 Exch. 1.

[1520] See above, paras 44-214 et seq. For a comparison of the statutory powers of resale (s.24 and s.48(2), see below) see *Benjamin's Sale of Goods*, 10th edn (2017), para.15-103.

[1521] The subsection assumes that the seller who has, in the past, validly exercised his right of lien or stoppage, continues in possession, with the right to possession as against the original buyer, up to the time of the resale: see Benjamin at para.15-102.

[1522] Who therefore could not sue the second buyer for trespass, or conversion. The limitation in the subsection "as against the original buyer" is included because the original seller's own title to the goods may be inferior to that of a third party. cf. see above, paras 33-015—33-017.

whether or not the seller, as against the original buyer, has a right of resale.

Right to resell   The seller has the right to resell (viz the power to transfer a good **44-346** title in the goods to a second buyer, but without committing any breach of his contract with, or any tort against the original buyer) in the following situations[1524]:

(1)   where he has in the original contract expressly reserved a right to do so[1525];
(2)   in the two situations specified in s.48(3)[1526];
(3)   where the buyer repudiates his obligations under the contract or commits a fundamental breach. The seller is entitled at common law to terminate the contract and to deal with the goods as their owner[1527];
(4)   (possibly) where the seller can act as an "agent of necessity" on behalf of the buyer.[1528]

Repudiation or fundamental breach by the buyer   If the buyer repudiates his **44-347** obligations under the contract,[1529] the seller is entitled[1530] to accept the repudiation, viz to treat the contract as terminated and to deal with the goods as their owner.[1531] The buyer will be treated as having repudiated the contract if he becomes insolvent, and informs the seller of his insolvency in circumstances which show that he is unable or unwilling to pay the price of the goods.[1532] But a mere declaration of insolvency by a party to a contract will not, on its own,[1533] amount to a repudiation of his obligations, since he may still intend to perform and have a reasonable expectation of his ability in the future to do so.[1534] On similar principles the seller is entitled[1535] to terminate the contract where the buyer has committed a fundamental

---

[1523] *R. v Ward Ltd v Bignall* [1967] 1 Q.B. 534, 549. The seller will be liable in damages to the original buyer if he had no right to resell: *Bloxam v Sanders* (1825) 4 B. & C. 941, 949. (On the possibility of the original buyer claiming the difference between the higher resale price and the original price, on a principle analogous to "waiver of tort", see Benjamin at para.15-104.)

[1524] Where there is a contract to sell unascertained or future goods by description, but the seller has not yet assumed any obligation to deliver particular goods, he is entitled to deal as owner with any goods of his which happen to meet the description.

[1525] 1979 Act s.48(4): (see below, para.44-355).

[1526] See below, para.44-351.

[1527] See below, paras 44-347—44-349.

[1528] See above, para.31-035, Vol.I, para.29-136; *Benjamin's Sale of Goods*, 10th edn (2017), para.15-106. cf. *Prager v Blatspiel, Stamp and Heacock Ltd* [1924] 1 K.B. 566.

[1529] See Vol.I, para.24-018. The buyer must show by his actions, or his failure to fulfil his obligations, that he intended to abandon the contract, e.g. *Bloomer v Bernstein* (1874) L.R. 9 C.P. 588. cf. s.31(2) (see above, paras 44-262—44-265).

[1530] But not obliged: he has the option of either affirming the contract, or of treating it as discharged in the sense of refusing further performance: *Mersey Steel and Iron Co Ltd v Naylor, Benson Co* (1884) 9 App. Cas. 434, 440; *Michael v Hart Co* [1902] 1 K.B. 482, 490. On the general principle, see *White and Carter (Councils) Ltd v McGregor* [1962] A.C. 413; Vol.I, paras 24-018 et seq.

[1531] *Cornwall v Henson* [1900] 2 Ch. 298 (a contract for the sale of land). See below, paras 44-348, 44-349, 44-350.

[1532] *Re Phoenix Bessemer Steel Co* (1876) 4 Ch. D. 108; *Ex p. Stapleton* (1879) 10 Ch. D. 586; *Morgan v Bain* (1874) L.R. 10 C.P. 15; *Mess v Duffus* (1901) 6 Com. Cas. 165. See above, para.44-313.

[1533] A special term in the contract may entitle the other party to rescind or terminate the contract upon the occurrence of such an event, e.g. suspension of payment: *Shipton, Anderson Co (1927) Ltd v Micks, Lambert Co* [1936] 2 All E.R. 1032.

[1534] *Mess v Duffus* (1901) 6 Com. Cas. 165.

[1535] But not obliged: see n.1530, above.

breach of his contractual obligations.[1536] In a contract in which the buyer undertakes other important obligations in addition to payment of the price, the seller may terminate the contract on the ground of the buyer's breach of one of these obligations, despite the fact that the buyer has paid the price.[1537] The result is that, as from the time of the termination, he is released from any obligation to perform his remaining contractual duties.[1538] The seller can no longer sue the buyer for the price,[1539] but the contract remains alive for the purpose of assessing the seller's right of action for damages for the buyer's breach,[1540] and for purposes incidental thereto.[1541]

44-348 **Seller's remedies after termination** A New Zealand case[1542] deals with the common law rights of the seller of goods to resell following his termination of the contract on the ground of the buyer's repudiation or fundamental breach.[1543] Where a contract for the sale of land is validly terminated by the vendor on account of the purchaser's repudiation or default in completion, the vendor is entitled to deal with the property as owner and to resell[1544]; he may retain the whole of the proceeds of the resale (even when he sells at a higher price[1545]) and either: (a) claim from the original purchaser any difference between the original price and that under the resale,[1546] after giving credit for any deposit paid; or (b) keep the deposit.[1547] The New Zealand case[1548] holds that exactly the same principles apply to the seller's termination of a contract for the sale of goods: that at common law the seller's acceptance of the buyer's repudiation revests the property in the seller[1549] so that he can resell as owner,[1550] keep the whole proceeds of the resale and either forfeit the

---

[1536] See Vol.I, paras 24-001 et seq. See s.10(1) and (2) (see above, para.44-128) and cf. s.11 (see above, para.44-056) and s.53(1) (see below, para.44-411). The power to terminate is implied by s.50(3) (see below, para.44-015) see *Benjamin's Sale of Goods*, 10th edn (2017), para.15-109.

[1537] If the price has been paid, s.48(3) (see below, para.44-351) is not applicable.

[1538] *Honck v Muller* (1881) 7 Q.B.D. 92; *Boston Deep Sea Fishing and Ice Co v Ansell* (1888) 39 Ch. D. 339, 364–365; *Heyman v Darwins Ltd* [1942] A.C. 356, 399. See Vol.I, paras 24-001 et seq.

[1539] *Chinery v Viall* (1860) 5 H. & N. 288. See below, paras 44-354 et seq.

[1540] *Michael v Hart Co* [1902] 1 K.B. 482 at 490; *Johnstone v Milling* (1886) 16 Q.B.D. 460, 467; *Moschi v Lep Air Services Ltd* [1973] A.C. 331; *Photo Production Ltd v Securicor Transport Ltd* [1980] A.C. 827; cf. *Johnson v Agnew* [1980] A.C. 367.

[1541] e.g. an arbitration clause: *Heyman v Darwins Ltd* [1942] A.C. 356. See Vol.I, para.24-049.

[1542] *Commission Car Sales (Hastings) Ltd v Saul* [1957] N.Z.L.R. 144.

[1543] It is submitted that it would be too late for the seller to purport to terminate the original contract if the buyer had already transferred the property in the goods to a third person. cf. s.23 (see above, paras 44-208—44-213).

[1544] *Cornwall v Henson* [1900] 2 Ch. 298 (vendor held not entitled to terminate the contract).

[1545] *Ex p. Hunter* (1801) 6 Ves. Jr. 94, 97.

[1546] *Noble v Edwards* (1877) 5 Ch. D. 378, 385 (appeal allowed on a different point: (1877) 5 Ch. D. at 393–394).

[1547] *Howe v Smith* (1884) 27 Ch. D. 89, 104–105 (vendor remained in possession). On the forfeiture of deposits, see below, para.44-358; Vol.I, paras 26-245—26-256.

[1548] *Commission Car Sales (Hastings) Ltd v Saul* [1957] N.Z.L.R. 144 (following *Howe v Smith* (1884) 27 Ch. D. 89).

[1549] See *Benjamin's Sale of Goods*, 10th edn (2017), para.15-113.

[1550] This position is accepted (without discussion) by the judge in *Compagnie de Renflouement, etc. v W Seymour Plant Sales Hire Ltd* [1981] 2 Lloyd's Rep. 466, 482. As owner the unpaid seller may, of course, keep the goods for his own use instead of reselling.

deposit[1551] paid by the buyer or sue for damages for any net deficiency after giving credit for the deposit paid.[1552]

Where the seller retains property in the goods If the seller is to exercise his   **44-349** common law power to resell, in terms of the preceding paragraphs, he will usually need to obtain possession of the goods. In two English cases where the goods had been delivered to the buyer but the property in them remained with the unpaid seller, it was held that a seizure of them by the seller operated as a "rescission" or termination of the contract and that this applied even where the seizure was made under an express power in the contract to do so upon the buyer's default.[1553] Where the contract confers no power to retake the goods, the unpaid seller who retains the property may be entitled to retake them from the buyer, by analogy with the position on contracts for the sale of land[1554]: where the purchaser has been let into possession of land pending completion, and he commits a breach of contract entitling the vendor to terminate the contract, the vendor who chooses to terminate is entitled[1555] to be reinstated in possession of the land[1556]; the vendor resumes his position as full owner, and may therefore resell.[1557] Where the seller cannot himself retake the goods he may seek specific restitution of the goods by bringing proceedings for wrongful interference with them.[1558]

Where the buyer has property in the goods However, it is submitted that the   **44-350** seller cannot lawfully retake (or obtain an order for specific restitution of) the goods, where, following the contract of sale, the buyer has both possession of, and the property in, the goods[1559]; any retaking of the goods by the seller in these circumstances would (except in cases of fraud or misrepresentation) be a conversion against the buyer.[1560] In the cases which support this proposition, the seller did not purport, prior to the retaking, to terminate the contract of sale on the ground of

---

[1551] On the difference between a deposit and a part payment of the price, see *Reid Motors Ltd v Wood* [1978] 1 N.Z.L.R. 319, 325, 329.

[1552] *Commission Car Sales (Hastings) Ltd v Saul* [1957] N.Z.L.R. 144 at 146. An earlier Canadian case is to the same effect: *McCowan v Bowles* [1923] 3 D.L.R. 756. cf. *Clough Mill Ltd v Martin* [1985] 1 W.L.R. 111, 118–119, 122 (retention of title clause on which see above, paras 44-173—44-188). cf. also *Armour v Thyssen Edelstahlwerke AG* [1991] 2 A.C. 339, 353.

[1553] *Hewison v Rickets* (1894) 63 L.J. Q.B. 711; *Att-Gen v Pritchard* (1928) 97 L.J. K.B. 561. The situation is different in the case of a contract to let out goods on hire, with only an option to purchase: *Brooks v Beirnstein* [1909] 1 K.B. 98.

[1554] See Benjamin at para.15-115. cf. *Clough Mill Ltd v Martin* [1985] 1 W.L.R. 111. But in *Keetley v Quinton Pty Ltd* (1991) 4 W.A.R. 133 it was held that the seller was not entitled to retake the goods in these circumstances (unless there was express power to do so conferred by the contract).

[1555] In equity (see the cases in the following footnote) or at law: *Williams on Vendor and Purchaser*, 4th edn, pp.1004–1005.

[1556] *Clark v Wallis* (1866) 35 Beav. 460. cf. *King v King* (1833) 1 My. K. 442; *Hope v Hope* (1856) 22 Beav. 351, 365. See Williams at pp.1004-1005, 1009. cf. also Misrepresentation Act 1967 s.1(b) (see Vol.I, para.7-144).

[1557] cf. *Howe v Smith* (1884) 27 Ch. D. 89, 105 (vendor remained in possession).

[1558] Under s.3(2)(a) of the Torts (Interference with Goods) Act 1977 the court may make an order for delivery of the goods which does not give the defendant the alternative of retaining them on payment of their value as assessed by the court. See Benjamin at para.15-116. See CPR Pt 45 para.4(1). cf. s.52 (see below, paras 44-440—44-444).

[1559] Benjamin at para.15-117. cf. retention of title clauses (n.1552, above).

[1560] *Page v Cowasjee Eduljee* (1866) L.R. 1 P.C. 127 (see below, para.44-448). See also *Stephens v Wilkinson* (1831) 2 B. A. 320, 327; *Gillard v Brittan* (1841) 8 M. & W. 575; *Re Humbertson* (1846) De G. 262. The seller's seizure may also be a breach of s.12(2)(b) (see above, para.44-076): *Healing (Sales) Pty Ltd v Inglis Electrix Pty Ltd* (1968) 42 A.L.J.R. 280.

the buyer's repudiation or fundamental breach, but it is submitted that this would not have altered the position[1561]: the assumption behind these cases is that, once the seller has lost both his possession and his right to stoppage in transit, and has transferred the property in the goods to the buyer, he has no remedy against the goods themselves[1562] and his only remedy is a claim for the price or for damages under the contract.[1563] This submission is made despite[1564] the fact that, in two other apparently similar situations, the property in the goods will revest in the seller, namely, when the buyer validly rejects the goods,[1565] or the seller or buyer "rescinds"[1566] the contract on the ground that the other's misrepresentation induced him to enter the contract.[1567] Where a contract of sale of goods is voidable by the seller for the fraud of the buyer, a retaking of the goods by the seller without the knowledge of the buyer (but before a resale to an innocent sub-buyer) rescinds the contract and revests the property in the goods in the seller[1568]: the retaking is treated as an unequivocal act of election to rescind the contract.[1569]

44-351 Statutory right of resale   Section 48(3) provides that:

> "Where the goods are of a perishable nature, or where the unpaid seller[1570] gives notice to the buyer of his intention to re-sell, and the buyer does not within a reasonable time pay or tender the price, the unpaid seller may re-sell the goods and recover from the original buyer damages for any loss occasioned by his breach of contract."[1571]

Under his common law rights[1572] the seller may terminate the contract and keep the goods for his own use; he may also be entitled to terminate for a breach other than a failure to pay the price. The assumption behind the part of s.48(3) dealing with perishable goods is that the seller retains possession of the perishable goods and is

---

[1561] See the dicta in *Page v Cowasjee Eduljee* (1866) L.R. 1 P.C. 127, 145. cf. *Worcester Works Finance Ltd v Cooden Engineering Co Ltd* [1972] 1 Q.B. 210 (voluntary transfer of title back to the seller).

[1562] It is implicit in the decision in *Healing (Sales) Pty Ltd v Inglis Electrix Pty Ltd* (1968) 42 A.L.J.R. 280, that the seller cannot enforce his right to the price by seizing the goods from a buyer who has both the property in, and possession of the goods.

[1563] Otherwise the statutory restrictions on the real remedies of lien and stoppage could easily be evaded. cf. s.11(4) which might provide an analogy (see above, para.44-068). An express power in the contract might entitle the seller to retake or to resell in these circumstances: *Bines v Sankey* [1958] N.Z.L.R. 886 (but the Bills of Sale Act 1878 might then apply).

[1564] See *Benjamin's Sale of Goods*, 10th edn (2017), para.15-118.

[1565] *Kwei Tek Chao v British Traders and Shippers Ltd* [1954] 2 Q.B. 459, 487; *McDougall v Aeromarine of Emsworth Ltd* [1958] 1 W.L.R. 1126, 1130. See above, para.44-280. It could be argued, however, that rejection is a voluntary and deliberate act by the then owner (the buyer).

[1566] This use of this word has different consequences in the context of misrepresentation from those when the contract is "rescinded" in the sense of terminated by the innocent party upon the other party's repudiation or fundamental breach.

[1567] See Vol.I, paras 7-112 et seq. See especially s.1(b) of the Misrepresentation Act 1967 (see Vol.I, para.7-144).

[1568] *Car and Universal Finance Co Ltd v Caldwell* [1965] 1 Q.B. 525, 551, 554, 558 (the analogy with termination for breach ("repudiation") was not accepted by the Lords Justices in another respect: at 550, 556, 559); *Newtons of Wembley Ltd v Williams* [1965] 1 Q.B. 560, 571. The difference is discussed by Beale, *Remedies for Breach of Contract* (1980), pp.117–118.

[1569] *Car and Universal Finance Co Ltd v Caldwell* [1965] 1 Q.B. 525.

[1570] For definition, see above, para.44-311. (The seller is "unpaid" when only part of the price has been paid. cf. on severable contracts: see above, paras 44-262, 44-286; Vol.I, paras 21-028, 21-038, 24-046.)

[1571] This subsection confers a *right* (as against the original buyer) to resell, whereas s.48(2) conferred a *power* to confer a good title. cf. s.12(1) (see above, paras 44-075 et seq.).

[1572] See above, paras 44-347—44-350.

only willing (and contractually obliged) to deliver the goods to the buyer in return for contemporaneous payment.[1573] Goods will be "perishable" within the meaning of the subsection when they are likely to deteriorate physically as time elapses,[1574] and also, it is submitted, when they are likely to change in a commercial sense,[1575] viz when "it is not dealt with by business people as the thing which it originally was".[1576] Although it has been argued[1577] that for the resale of perishable goods the further condition set out in s.48(3) applies, viz "and the buyer does not within a reasonable time pay or tender the price", it is submitted that the better view is that this condition is inapplicable. Benjamin submits[1578] that it could be the purpose of the subsection, in the case of a contract relating to perishable goods, to make time of the essence of the contract,[1579] at least when payment and delivery were concurrent conditions,[1580] so that, upon the buyer's failure to pay on the stipulated date, the seller is immediately entitled to resell.[1581]

Resale upon giving notice to the buyer   The second aspect of s.48(3) applies irrespective of the nature of the goods: it enables the unpaid seller, by giving notice, to make payment within a reasonable time[1582] thereafter to be of the essence of the contract,[1583] so that failure to pay within a reasonable time after notice will entitle the seller to treat the contract as repudiated: he can then terminate the original contract and resell the goods.[1584]   **44-352**

The seller's power of resale when he is out of possession   There are a number of judicial statements which assume that the unpaid seller's statutory power of resale under s.48(3) may be validly exercised only where the seller is in possession of the goods at the time of the resale.[1585] But it is submitted that a seller has the right and the power to pass a good title to a second buyer under a resale, not   **44-353**

[1573] See s.28 (see above, para.44-237).

[1574] e.g. potatoes are "a perishable commodity" in the sense that if they are held too long they become rotten: *Sharp v Christmas* (1892) 8 T.L.R. 687, 688. cf. the discussion of the meaning of the word "perish" in ss.6 and 7 (see above, paras 44-045—44-050).

[1575] cf. on the concept of the goods having changed in nature in a commercial sense: *Asfar Co v Blundell* [1896] 1 Q.B. 123; *Duthie v Hilton* (1868) L.R. 4 C.P. 138 (cement, after being submerged, had ceased to be "cement"); *Dakin v Oxley* (1864) 15 C.B.(N.S.) 646 (entitlement of carrier to freight when goods are delivered in a damaged state).

[1576] *Asfar & Co v Blundell*, above, at 128. An example would be a souvenir designed for sale on one specific occasion.

[1577] Sutton, *Sales and Consumer Law*, 4th edn, p.620.

[1578] *Benjamin's Sale of Goods*, 10th edn (2017), para.15-122.

[1579] See Vol.I, paras 21-011—21-019. cf. a case before the Act: *Sharp v Christmas* (1892) 8 T.L.R. 687, 688, where the time for the buyer to take delivery of potatoes ("a perishable commodity") was held to be of the essence of the contract.

[1580] See s.28 (see above, para.44-237).

[1581] cf. the power to sell any perishable goods in a bankrupt's estate: Insolvency Act 1986 s.287(2)(b).

[1582] This is a question of fact: s.59. The calculation of the time runs from the date the notice is given, and the reasonableness of any time fixed by the notice will be judged as at that time: *Charles Rickards Ltd v Oppenhaim* [1950] 1 K.B. 616, 624–625 (not a case on s.48(3), but on a similar common law rule). The court will also take into account any previous delay on the buyer's part: above.

[1583] Apart from s.48(3), a stipulation as to time of payment would not normally be of the essence: s.10(1) (see above, para.44-128).

[1584] This is in accord with the common law: see Vol.I, paras 21-011—21-017.

[1585] *RV Ward Ltd v Bignall* [1967] 1 Q.B. 534, 545; *Commission Car Sales (Hastings) Ltd v Saul* [1957] N.Z.L.R. 144, 146.

only at common law,[1586] but also under s.48(3) where, at the time of the resale, he has: (a) the property in the goods[1587]; or (b) possession of the goods[1588]; or (c) the immediate right to possession as against the original buyer.[1589]

44-354 **Resale terminates the original contract**   Although s.48(3) does not expressly provide that the original contract is terminated by the resale,[1590] the Court of Appeal has decided that, by exercising the statutory right of resale under the subsection, the seller thereby "rescinds" or terminates the original contract but may sue the original buyer for damages.[1591] The result[1592] of this interpretation of subs.(3) is that the seller who resells under s.48 cannot thereafter sue the buyer for the original price (even though he is willing to give the buyer credit against the price for the net proceeds of the resale); the seller is relegated by the subsection to his claim for damages for non-acceptance under s.50.[1593] The practical result is that the seller is not accountable to the buyer for any profit above the original contract price which he makes on the resale; nor has the buyer a right of action against a seller who does not act with reasonable care in making the resale.[1594]

44-355 **Express reservation of the right of resale**   Section 48(4) of the Act provides:

> "Where the seller expressly[1595] reserves the right of resale in case the buyer should make default,[1596] and on the buyer making default resells the goods, the original contract of sale is rescinded[1597] but without prejudice to any claim the seller may have for damages."[1598]

Since the original contract is terminated, the seller is entitled to retain any profit which he may make on the resale above the price in the original contract. If, however, the seller can resell only at a loss, the original buyer is, by this subsection, liable to pay damages, viz the amount by which the contract price exceeds the

---

[1586] See above, paras 44-347—44-350.

[1587] See above, para.44-345. The seller may be able to retake the goods, or recover possession by bringing proceedings for wrongful interference with the goods in which he seeks an order for specific delivery of the goods.

[1588] This is what the draftsman of s.48(3) had mainly in mind: cf. s.48(2) immediately preceding. The remedies of lien and stoppage (see above, paras 44-315 et seq., 44-326 et seq.) are aimed at giving the seller an entitlement to possession.

[1589] There are a number of grounds on which the seller who is out of possession may be entitled to resume the right to possess them: see *Benjamin's Sale of Goods*, 10th edn (2017), para.15-125. So long as the buyer continues in possession of the goods, there is a risk that the buyer may transfer a good title to a third party: s.25 (see above, paras 44-220—44-231).

[1590] cf. s.48(4).

[1591] *RV Ward Ltd v Bignall* [1967] 1 Q.B. 534. (A resale of part of the goods has the same effect: at 550.)

[1592] A further implication is that the termination of the contract divests the original buyer of his property in the goods if the property had passed to him before the termination: *RV Ward Ltd v Bignall*, above.

[1593] *RV Ward Ltd v Bignall* [1967] 1 Q.B. 534. Forfeiture of any deposit paid by the buyer is a separate question: see below, para.44-358.

[1594] But if the *seller* sues for damages, it is submitted that a resale at a lower price than the seller ought reasonably to have obtained on the resale will constitute a failure to mitigate: see Vol.I, paras 26-089 et seq.; see below, paras 44-368 et seq.

[1595] Similar rules apply where a relevant usage of trade confers a right of resale upon the seller: *Re Tait* (1841) 2 Mont.D. De G. 170.

[1596] It is submitted in *Benjamin's Sale of Goods*, 10th edn (2017), para.15-129, that it would be possible for the parties to agree to an express right which arose upon an occurrence not involving the buyer's "default"; and that an express right to resell could be wider than s.48(4) in other ways.

[1597] Thus the seller resells as owner, not as agent for the original buyer: *RV Ward Ltd v Bignall* [1967] 1 Q.B. 534, 551. cf. s.48(3), see above.

[1598] The subsection follows the common law: *Lamond v Davall* (1847) 9 Q.B. 1030.

resale price, and the expenses of the resale.[1599]

Express reservation not exclusive remedy   Where the contract confers an   **44-356**
express right of resale or of repurchase on the innocent party, following a default
by the other party, the former may pursue his ordinary remedies at common law
without complying with the terms of the special remedy conferred by the
contract.[1600] It is submitted that, in the same way, the seller could exercise his statutory right of resale under s.48(3) without relying on his contractual right to resell.[1601]

The method of reselling   Neither the Act nor the common law provides author-   **44-357**
ity on the question of the method of exercising the seller's right to resell. It therefore
seems that the seller is free to sell to anyone he chooses and that he is under no
restriction as to the price he obtains, or whether the sale is by public auction or made
privately, without advertisement. He is under no obligation to the buyer to act
reasonably in deciding whether or not to resell; but if he acts unreasonably the rules
of mitigation may limit the damages which he can recover from the original buyer
following the resale.

Forfeiture of deposits   Whether the seller resells under his common law rights,   **44-358**
under his statutory right, or under an express power, it is submitted that the same
rules apply to the forfeiture of deposits[1602] or other prepayments made by the buyer.
The seller is bound to bring the deposit into account if he sues the buyer for damages, since he cannot allege a net deficiency without taking the deposit into
account.[1603] If, however, the seller makes no claim for damages under the original
contract, he is entitled to keep all the proceeds of the resale and to forfeit the
deposit[1604] paid by the defaulting original buyer.[1605] (The rules applicable to a clause
"forfeiting" sums already paid by the buyer under a contract for payment of the
price by instalments are discussed elsewhere.[1606])

[1599] See below, paras 44-382—44-383. The buyer is not liable to be sued for the whole of the agreed
price: *Lamond v Davall*, above, at 1032. See also *Hore v Milner* (1797) Peake 58n.
[1600] *Shipton, Anderson Co (1927) Ltd v Micks, Lambert Co* [1936] 2 All E.R. 1032. cf. the same rule for
contracts for the sale of land: *Howe v Smith* (1884) 27 Ch. D. 89, 105.
[1601] Unless the terms of the contract indicated that the contractual remedy was to be the exclusive remedy.
[1602] "A deposit is ... a security for completion of the purchase": *Howe v Smith*, above, at 98. See Vol.I,
paras 26-245—26-256. A "trade-in" of goods may be intended to be treated in the same way as a
deposit: *Commission Car Sales (Hastings) Ltd v Saul* [1957] N.Z.L.R. 144, 145.
[1603] [1957] N.Z.L.R. 144 at 146.
[1604] The Privy Council has held, in a case on the sale of land, that a deposit must be "reasonable" in
amount for the forfeiture rule to apply: *Workers Trust Merchant Bank Ltd v Dojap Investments Ltd*
[1993] A.C. 573 (above, para.26-249). cf. *Reid Motors Ltd v Wood* [1978] 1 N.Z.L.R. 319, 325–
329. The Unfair Terms in Consumer Contract Regulations 1999 or for contracts entered into on or
after October 1, 2015, the Consumer Rights Act 2015 may now also apply: see above, paras 38-
211 et seq.
[1605] *Commission Car Sales (Hastings) Ltd v Saul*, above, at 146 (following the principles laid down in
cases on contracts for the sale of land: *Ockenden v Henly* (1858) E.B. & E. 485; *Howe v Smith* (1884)
27 Ch. D. 89 at 104–105; *Shuttleworth v Clews* [1910] 1 Ch. 176). cf. *Damon Compania Naviera
SA v Hapag-Lloyd International SA* [1985] 1 W.L.R. 435 (recovery of damages measured at the
amount of unpaid deposit). See *Benjamin's Sale of Goods*, 10th edn (2017), paras 15-132—15-
133. (It is submitted that *Gallagher v Shilcock* [1949] 2 K.B. 765, having been overruled on another
(but relevant) point (see *RV Ward Ltd v Bignall* [1967] 1 Q.B. 534 (see above, para.44-354)) should
not be followed in regard to the recovery of deposits.)
[1606] Vol.I, paras 26-254—26-256. cf. see above, paras 39-342—39-344.

(b)　Action for the Price

44-359　**Action for price when property has passed**　Section 49(1) provides[1607] that:

"Where, under a contract of sale,[1608] the property in the goods has passed to the buyer and he wrongfully neglects or refuses[1609] to pay for the goods according to the terms of the contract, the seller may maintain an action against him for the price of the goods."[1610]

The claim for the price is a claim for a debt, as distinct from a claim for damages.[1611] The property may pass to the buyer before delivery of the goods to him, and before his acceptance of the goods[1612]; hence, the price may sometimes be claimed under s.49(1) even where the buyer refuses to accept the goods.[1613] The passing of the property will depend on the terms of the contract; e.g. since under a FOB contract property does not pass before shipment,[1614] the seller may sue for the price only after he has put the goods on board.[1615]

44-360　Where the property in the goods has not passed to the buyer, no action for the price can be brought under s.49(1),[1616] despite the fact that it is a wrongful act of the buyer which prevents the passing of the property.[1617] Thus, where the buyer

---

[1607] This section follows the previous common law: *Scott v England* (1844) 14 L.J. Q.B. 43. See also *Studdy v Sanders* (1826) 5 B. & C. 628.

[1608] It is submitted that any express provision of the contract should prevail over s.49 to the extent of any inconsistency: see Benjamin at para.16-002; cf. s.55, and see below, para.44-365.

[1609] See below, para.44-361.

[1610] Many cases before the Act illustrate the proposition that, where there is no specific term of the contract dealing with the time when the price is to be paid, the seller cannot sue for the price until the property in the goods has passed to the buyer: *Atkinson v Bell* (1828) 8 B. & C. 277; *Boswell v Kilborn and Morrill* (1862) 15 Moo. P.C. 309. The seller may, however, obtain a declaratory judgment to the effect that the buyer is bound to pay the price upon the seller's fulfilling his obligations: see below, para.44-386. The seller cannot sue for the price if he has terminated the contract following the buyer's repudiation or fundamental breach: *Chinery v Viall* (1860) 5 H. & N. 288; *Att-Gen v Pritchard* (1928) 97 L.J. K.B. 561. See above, paras 44-347—44-350.

[1611] For the importance of this distinction, see Vol.I, para.26-009. Where the seller claims the price, he may be awarded damages if they are his correct remedy: *Mediterranean and Eastern Export Co Ltd v Fortress Fabrics (Manchester) Ltd* [1948] 2 All E.R. 186.

[1612] On the passing of property, see above, paras 44-130 et seq. In special circumstances, the doctrine of estoppel by conduct may operate to prevent the buyer from disputing the fact that property has passed to him: *Colley v Overseas Exporters* [1921] 3 K.B. 302, 311–312. cf. *Knights v Wiffen* (1870) L.R. 5 Q.B. 660.

[1613] Alternatively, the seller could claim damages under s.50(1) (see below, para.44-367). To claim the price the seller must show that he continues to be able and willing to deliver the goods: *Maclean v Dunn and Watkins* (1828) 6 L.J. (O.S.) C.P. 184, 190.

[1614] *Benjamin's Sale of Goods*, 10th edn (2017), para.20-078.

[1615] *Green v Sichel* (1860) 7 C.B.(N.S.) 747; *Henderson and Glass v Radmore Co* (1922) 10 Ll.L. Rep. 727. Even after shipment, however, the seller may have reserved a right of disposal, in which case he may sue for the price only if he has waived his right of disposal (where this is possible): *Benjamin* at para.20-133.

[1616] See, however, s.49(2) (see below, para.44-364).

[1617] *Stein, Forbes Co v County Tailoring Co* (1916) 86 L.J. K.B. 448; *Colley v Overseas Exporters* [1921] 3 K.B. 302. See also *Nortier Co v Wm Maclean Sons Co* (1921) 9 Ll.L. Rep. 192. The decision of the House of Lords in *White and Carter (Councils) Ltd v McGregor* [1962] A.C. 413 (see Vol.I, paras 24-010, 26-100) may affect the rule on wrongful prevention of the passing of property: see *Benjamin* at paras 16-021—16-022, 16-059, 20-140; *White and Carter's* case was distinguished in *Attica Sea Carriers Corp v Ferrostaal Poseidon Bulk Reederei GmbH (The Puerto Buitrago)* [1976] 1 Lloyd's Rep. 250, CA (charterparty case); and cf. *Anglo-African Shipping Co of New York Inc v J Mortner Ltd* [1962] 1 Lloyd's Rep. 81, 94; on appeal, [1962] 1 Lloyd's Rep. 610. But see *Gator Shipping Corp v Trans-Asiatic Oil Ltd SA (The Odenfeld)* [1978] 2 Lloyd's Rep. 357, 372–373.

under a FOB contract failed (in breach of his contractual obligation) to designate an effective ship, the seller's remedy was not a claim for the price but a claim for damages for non-acceptance, because the property in the goods could not pass until the goods were actually put on board a ship.[1618] There is a contrasting decision of the House of Lords in a Scottish appeal, where a machine had been delivered to the buyer, who was bound to keep and pay for it, unless it failed on a stipulated test to do specified work. The buyer neglected to put the machine to this test, but it was held that the seller could recover the price: the buyer's own failure to give it a fair test according to the contract relieved the seller of having to prove that the condition did not apply.[1619]

Wrongful neglect or refusal to pay   The question whether the buyer has wrong- **44-361**
fully[1620] neglected or refused to pay the price[1621] depends on his duty to pay,[1622] and this is not the same question as whether the seller is entitled to bring an action for the price, because other conditions must also be satisfied for such an action to lie in terms of either ss.49(1) or (2). Since the terms of the contract will specify when payment is due, the meaning of "wrongful" must be gathered from those terms[1623]; thus, where the contract entitles the buyer to a period of credit, he will not be liable to an action for the price until that period has expired.[1624] The buyer may similarly show that his failure to pay the price is not "wrongful" where the seller has waived[1625] the time for payment fixed by the contract.

Payment to be made in special way   Where payment is to be made in a special **44-362**
way the seller cannot sue for the price as an ordinary debt.[1626] Thus, if it is agreed that the price of the goods should be an item in settlements of accounts between the parties at stated intervals, the seller can sue only by showing a settlement of accounts on which the balance is in his favour.[1627]

Justification for refusal to pay   The buyer's failure to pay the price may be justi- **44-363**
fied on the ground that the seller had previously broken his contractual obligation in such a way as to disentitle him to the price, e.g. by failure to deliver, or by delivering defective goods[1628] or the wrong quantity. Similarly, the seller cannot claim the price from the buyer if it turns out that the seller has no title to the

---

[1618] *Colley v Overseas Exporters*, above.
[1619] *Mackay v Dick* (1881) L.R. 6 App. Cas. 251 (distinguished in *Colley v Overseas Exporters*, above, at 307–308, on the ground that *Mackay v Dick* concerned a condition subsequent, a "resolutive condition" after the property had passed to the buyer).
[1620] It is normally the duty of a debtor to tender the amount due to his creditor without waiting for a demand: see Vol.I, para.21-010. On the effect of tender of the price to the seller, see Vol.I, paras 21-085 et seq.
[1621] Both s.49(1) and (2) contain this phrase. (The definition of the price is found in ss.2(1), 8 and 9.)
[1622] 1979 Act ss.27 and 28 (see above, paras 44-236—44-237).
[1623] See s.10(1) (above, para.44-128).
[1624] *Ferguson v Carrington* (1829) 9 B. & C. 59; *Strutt v Smith* (1834) 1 Cr. M. R. 312.
[1625] See Vol.I, paras 22-040 et seq.
[1626] *Garey v Pyke* (1839) 10 A. & E. 512. cf. *Smith v Winter* (1852) 12 C.B. 487. On payment by negotiable instrument, see Vol.I, paras 21-075—21-083; on payment by banker's commercial credit, see above, paras 34-441 et seq.
[1627] *Garey v Pyke* (1839) 10 A. & E. 512.
[1628] *Wayne's Merthyr Steam Coal and Iron Co v Morewood* (1877) 46 L.J. Q.B. 746; *Underwood Ltd v Burgh Castle Brick and Cement Syndicate* [1922] 1 K.B. 343 (goods damaged in process of loading before property passed to the buyer).

goods.[1629] But the buyer may be liable to pay the price if, before the goods were delivered to him, they perished while the risk was on him.[1630] A previous breach of contract by the seller may not, however, be sufficiently serious to relieve the buyer of his entire obligation to pay the price: in these circumstances the buyer may rely on a set-off against the seller,[1631] or may bring a counterclaim for damages.

44-364   Claim for price due on "a day certain"   Section 49(2) provides that:

"Where, under a contract of sale, the price is payable on a day certain irrespective of delivery and the buyer wrongfully neglects or refuses[1632] to pay such price, the seller may maintain an action for the price, although the property in the goods has not passed and the goods have not been appropriated to the contract."[1633]

Where the goods have not been delivered to the buyer, the seller's entitlement to sue for the price depends on his continuing ability and willingness to deliver the goods to the buyer in accordance with the contract.[1634] The meaning of "a day certain" in this provision has been held to be "a time specified in the contract not depending on a future or contingent event".[1635] Thus, where the price was payable against delivery of the shipping documents,[1636] the case did not fall within s.49(2).[1637] It is submitted[1638] that the better view is that a day can be "certain" under s.49(2) only if it is fixed in advance by the contract in such a way that it can be determined independently of the action of either party or of any third person. If, for example, an instalment of the price becomes due when the seller has reached a specified stage in the construction of the goods, it is submitted that the instalment should not be held to be "payable on a day certain" within the meaning of this subsection.[1639] It has been said that the section does not apply if the date for payment was initially fixed but subsequently has been varied to so that the payment is

---

[1629] *Dickenson v Naul* (1833) 4 B. & Ad. 638; *Allen v Hopkins* (1844) 13 M. & W. 94. (Although this decision is based also on the fact that the buyer had had to pay the value of the goods to the true owner, it is submitted that the principle need not be so limited.)

[1630] See above, paras 44-189—44-192.

[1631] See s.53(1)(a) (see below, paras 44-411 et seq.). See also s.53(4) (see below, para.44-411). cf. *Berger Co Inc v Gill Duffus SA* [1984] A.C. 382, 392 (see below, para.44-367).

[1632] See above, paras 44-361—44-363.

[1633] The subsection is based on *Dunlop v Grote* (1845) 2 Car. & K. 153 ("if the delivery of the said iron should not be required before ... April 30", payment was to be made on that date).

[1634] *Maclean v Dunn and Watkins* (1828) 6 L.J. (O.S.) C.P. 184, 190.

[1635] *Shell-Mex Ltd v Elton Cop Dyeing Co Ltd* (1928) 34 Com. Cas. 39, 43 (sellers were entitled "at any time to invoice the buyers ...").

[1636] Similarly, where the goods were sold on terms of "prompt cash against invoice": *Henderson and Keay Ltd v AM Carmichael Ltd*, 1956 S.L.T. (Notes) 58.

[1637] *Stein, Forbes Co v County Tailoring Co* (1916) 86 L.J. K.B. 448. (An earlier case, *Polenghi v Dried Milk Co Ltd* (1904) 10 Com. Cas. 42, is inconsistent with this view: see *Benjamin's Sale of Goods*, 10th edn (2017), paras 19-239—19-240.) For other cases on overseas sales, see *Muller, Maclean Co v Leslie and Anderson* (1921) 8 Ll. L. Rep. 328, 330–331; *Nortier Co v Wm Maclean Sons Co* (1921) 8 Ll.L. Rep. 192, 194; *Colley v Overseas Exporters* [1921] 3 K.B. 302, 311; *Tradax Internacional SA v Goldschmidt SA* [1977] 2 Lloyd's Rep. 604, 614.

[1638] On the basis of the decisions in nn.1636–1637, above; see *Benjamin* at paras 16-027, 19-239—19-240.

[1639] *Benjamin's Sale of Goods*, 10th edn (2017), para.16-027. Some dicta in the Court of Appeal cast doubt on this submission: *Workman, Clark Co v Lloyd Brazileno* [1908] 1 K.B. 968, 977, 978, 981; see Benjamin at paras 16-026, 19-239—19-240, 19-223 (s.50(1) also assumes that the normal remedy when the property has not passed is a claim for damages for non-acceptance).

no longer due on "a day certain".[1640] However, the price must also be due "irrespective of delivery". This may not cover a case in which the price is due so many days or months after delivery, as is commonly provided in retention of title cases.[1641]

Action for the price outside s.49   There are a number of judicial statements which **44-365** assume that s.49, above, provides an exhaustive statement of the circumstances in which the seller may sue for the price.[1642] However, it is submitted that the seller should be entitled to sue for the price whenever the terms[1643] of the contract expressly or impliedly so provide[1644]; and that by the terms of the contract, the time fixed for payment need not be related either to delivery or to the passing of property.[1645] The contract may provide that the price is to be paid before delivery is made (e.g. "net cash before delivery") and that property is to pass only upon delivery.[1646] The implication of these provisions is that the price must be paid on demand or within a reasonable time,[1647] and thus it has been held in Australia that the seller may sue for the price, although neither subsection of s.49 applied.[1648] But in *Caterpillar (NI) Ltd (formerly FG Wilson (Engineering) Ltd) v John Holt & Co*

[1640] *Caterpillar (NI) Ltd (formerly FG Wilson (Engineering) Ltd) v John Holt & Co (Liverpool) Ltd* [2013] EWCA Civ 1232, [2014] 1 W.L.R. 2365 at [44]). The sellers did not rely on s.49(2) (at [23]).

[1641] cf. *PST Energy 7 Shipping LLC v OW Bunker Malta Ltd* [2015] EWHC 2022 (Comm) although held that the Sale of Goods Act did not apply to the bunker supply contract, the judge would have held that s.49(2) applies where payment is to be within a fixed period after delivery. This point was not considered in detail by the Court of Appeal [2015] EWCA Civ 1058 or Supreme Court [2016] UKSC 23. In *Caterpillar (NI) Ltd (formerly FG Wilson (Engineering) Ltd) v John Holt & Co (Liverpool) Ltd* [2013] EWCA Civ 1232, [2014] 1 All E.R. (Comm) 393 Longmore L.J. (at [44]) indicated that a term for payment 30 days after invoice would have fallen within s.49(2), but as the sending of an invoice itself depended on delivery, it seems questionable whether this is a term for payment on a day certain "irrespective of delivery". See below, para.44-365.

[1642] *Stein Forbes Co v County Tailoring Co* (1916) 86 L.J. K.B. 448; *Colley v Overseas Exporters* [1921] 3 K.B. 302 at 310; *Muller, Maclean Co v Leslie and Anderson* (1921) 8 Ll. L. Rep. 328 at 330–331; *Plaimar Ltd v Waters Trading Co Ltd* (1945) 72 C.L.R. 304, 318; cf. *Martin v Hogan* (1917) 24 C.L.R. 234; *White and Carter (Councils) Ltd v McGregor* [1962] A.C. 413, 437; *Otis Vehicle Rentals Ltd v Ciceley Commercials Ltd* [2002] EWCA Civ 1064 at [12].

[1643] The terms must permit the seller to recover the price by action, and not merely specify when the price is payable; the buyer's duty to pay the price is not identical with the seller's entitlement to sue for the price. Retention of title clauses (see above, paras 44-173 et seq.) often provide that the seller may maintain an action for the price, notwithstanding that the property in the goods will not pass until full payment of the price has been made. See also *Armour v Thyssen Edelstahlwerke AG* [1991] 2 A.C. 339. However, in the light of the decisions in *Caterpillar (NI) Ltd (formerly FG Wilson (Engineering) Ltd) v John Holt & Co (Liverpool) Ltd* [2013] EWCA Civ 1232, [2014] 1 W.L.R. 2365, below, and of dicta in that case about when an action may be brought under s.49(2) (see above, para.44-364), there must now be doubt whether such a provision will be effective. Longmore L.J. found himself "in the somewhat unsatisfactory position of concluding that, if property never passed to Holt Liverpool, FG Wilson have no claim for the price nor even a claim to damages. That is just an inherent result of a retention of title clause and shows that it has dangers as well as benefits" (at [56]). That conclusion does indeed seem unsatisfactory.

[1644] *Benjamin's Sale of Goods*, 10th edn (2017), at paras 16-028—16-029. It is, however, arguable that to increase the scope of the action for the price has the undesirable effect of limiting the scope of the mitigation rules.

[1645] cf. s.28 (see above, para.44-237). The wide freedom of the parties to fix their own terms is supported by *White and Carter (Councils) Ltd v McGregor* [1962] A.C. 413 (see Vol.I, paras 24-010, 26-100).

[1646] *Minister for Supply and Development v Servicemen's Co-op Joinery Manufacturers Ltd* (1951) 82 C.L.R. 621, 636.

[1647] *Minister for Supply and Development v Servicemen's Co-op Joinery Manufacturers Ltd* (1951) 82 C.L.R. 621, 636, 642 (cf. the view of the dissenting judge at 644).

[1648] *Minister for Supply and Development v Servicemen's Co-op Joinery Manufacturers Ltd* (1951) 82

(Liverpool) Ltd[1649] Popplewell J. held that, despite the arguments made in this paragraph, the seller can bring an action for the price only in the circumstances set out in s.49; and this was affirmed by unanimously by the Court of Appeal.[1650] In *PST Energy 7 Shipping LLC v OW Bunker Malta Ltd*[1651] the Supreme Court held that the bunker supply contract fell outside the Sale of Goods Act and accordingly it was not necessary to decide whether an action for the price under the Act would have been maintainable in the circumstances. However, Lord Mance, delivering the unanimous judgment of the Court, said that he would have overruled the decision of the Court of Appeal in *Caterpillar* on this point. Section 49 was not a complete code of situations in which the price may be recoverable under a contract of sale. There was room for claims for the price in other circumstances, including the present case, where the bunkers remained the seller's property but were at the buyer's risk and where under the contract the buyer was permitted to use the goods before payment.

In most cases there would in any event be a claim for damages for non-acceptance, but even if such a claim were not available, there is no reason why an inability to bring an action for the price under s.49 should prevent the seller from claiming damages for breach of the terms of the contract concerning payment.[1652]

44-366 **Claim for consequential loss in addition to the price**   The seller may wish to claim damages in addition to his claim for the agreed price, on the ground that the buyer's failure to pay the price at the agreed time caused consequential loss to the seller. The traditional common law rule that interest cannot be awarded by way of general damages for delay in payment of a debt has recently been abandoned and (subject to the normal rules of remoteness and mitigation) damages for loss of interest may be recovered provided the loss is pleaded and proved.[1653] The contract itself may provide for interest to be payable; and interest can also be claimed under statute or statutory powers.[1654] The seller may also be entitled to claim damages for

---

C.L.R. 621, 636, 642.

[1649] [2012] EWHC 2477 (Comm), [2012] 2 Lloyd's Rep. 479 at [53]. In the previous edition of this work (at [43]–[402]) it was suggested that where it is agreed that until all the instalments are paid, the goods remain the property of the seller, and that upon default in payment of an instalment or upon the occurrence of a certain event (e.g. the bankruptcy of the buyer) the total amount is to become payable that the seller should be able to sue for the price even though the claim would be outside the scope of s.49. Reliance was placed in particular on *McEntire v Crossley Bros Ltd* [1895] A.C. 457, 465. The decision in *Caterpillar (NI) Ltd (formerly FG Wilson (Engineering) Ltd) v John Holt & Co (Liverpool) Ltd* [2013] EWCA Civ 1232, [2014] 1 W.L.R. 2365 that an action for the price can only be brought in accordance with the terms of s.49 seems to preclude such an argument.

[1650] [2013] EWCA Civ 1232, [2014] 1 W.L.R. 2365. Section 49 is not just a default rule that can be negative or varied by agreement in accordance with s.55 of the Act: see at [53].

[1651] [2016] UKSC 23 at [40]–[58].

[1652] cf. Longmore L.J. in *Caterpillar (NI) Ltd (formerly FG Wilson (Engineering) Ltd) v John Holt & Co (Liverpool) Ltd* [2013] EWCA Civ 1232, [2014] 1 W.L.R. 2365, [54]–[56]. While noting the artificiality, Lord Mance, delivering the unanimous judgment of the Supreme Court in *PST Energy 7 Shipping LLC v OW Bunker Malta Ltd* [2016] UKSC 23, saw no reason why a claim for damages for non-payment should not in principle be available (at [48]–[49]).

[1653] *Sempra Metals Ltd v Commissioners of Inland Revenue* [2007] UKHL 34, [2008] 1 A.C. 561. See Vol.I, para.26-275.

[1654] See Vol.I, paras 26-277 et seq. Note especially the Late Payment of Commercial Debts (Interest) Act 1998.

expenses incurred by him,[1655] e.g. for storage during the buyer's delay in taking delivery, or for his own "care and custody of the goods" during such delay.[1656]

(c) Action for Damages[1657]

Damages for non-acceptance Where the property in the goods has not passed **44-367** to the buyer, the seller's remedy in most circumstances[1658] is an action for damages: for damages for non-acceptance under s.50(1), for consequential losses or expenses under s.54,[1659] or for losses or expenses under s.37.[1660] Section 50 provides:

> "(1) Where the buyer wrongfully neglects or refuses to accept and pay for the goods, the seller may maintain an action against him for damages for non-acceptance.[1661]
>
> (2) The measure of damages is the estimated loss directly and naturally resulting, in the ordinary course of events, from the buyer's breach of contract.[1662]
>
> (3) Where there is an available market for the goods in question the measure of damages is prima facie to be ascertained by the difference between the contract price and the market or current price at the time or times when the goods ought to have been accepted or (if no time was fixed for acceptance) at the time of the refusal to accept."

Section 50(1) is based on wrongful neglect or refusal by the buyer to pay the price,[1663] and on wrongful neglect or refusal to accept the goods.[1664] Where the buyer has not taken delivery of the goods and there is some doubt as to whether the property in the goods has passed to the buyer, the seller who sues for the price[1665] runs the risk that the court may hold that property had not passed to the buyer: in this event, it follows that the seller's only remedy is a claim for damages for non-acceptance, and that the seller was subject to the rules on mitigating his loss (e.g. by reselling) as from the date when the buyer should have accepted the goods. The seller's damages (for the buyer's refusal to accept the goods, or the documents representing the goods) may be reduced "by any sum which the buyers could establish they would have been entitled to set up in diminution of the contract price"

[1655] See below, paras 44-382—44-383.

[1656] s.37 (see above, paras 44-291—44-292).

[1657] The general rules on damages are examined in Vol.I, Ch.26.

[1658] Except where s.49(2) applies or there is a special term in the contract: see above, paras 44-364, 44-365. The seller may only be able to bring an action for damages if it is or would have been willing and able to deliver the goods; see above, paras 44-237 and 44-266. If it is shown that on the balance of probabilities the seller would have been able to do so, the damages should not be discounted for the chance that it would not have been able to do so: *AerCap Partners 1 Ltd v Avia Asset Management AB* [2010] EWHC 2431 (Comm), [2010] 2 C.L.C. 578 at [76].

[1659] See below, paras 44-382—44-383.

[1660] See above, paras 44-291—44-292.

[1661] This subsection is wide enough to cover non-acceptance when the property has already passed to the buyer, in which case it allows damages for non-acceptance as an alternative remedy to a claim for the price. But a claim in debt for the price is more advantageous to the seller (see above, para.44-359, Vol.I, paras 21-040 and 26-009).

[1662] Subs.(2) uses the language of the first rule in *Hadley v Baxendale* (1854) 9 Exch. 341 (see above, Vol.I, para.26-119). It is submitted that the common law developments (since the date of the 1893 Act) in the rules for remoteness of damage may be used to aid the interpretation of the subsection (see Vol.I, paras 26-117 et seq.).

[1663] See above, paras 44-361—44-363.

[1664] See above, para.44-236 (s.27). cf. see above, para.44-291 (s.37).

[1665] So long as the seller is claiming the price, he must hold the goods available for delivery to the buyer when the buyer pays the price.

as a result of any *previous* breach by the sellers.[1666] Section 50(2) comes into operation either where there is no available market (within the meaning of s.50(3))[1667] or
where the "prima facie" rule in s.50(3) is deemed to be inapplicable for some special
reason.[1668]

44-368 **An available market** The rule in s.50(3) is that when the buyer fails both to pay
the price and to accept the goods, the seller's damages are calculated by deducting
from the contract price the market price at the time and place fixed by the contract
for acceptance.[1669] The doctrine of mitigation[1670] is one of the bases of this principle:
it is assumed that with this additional amount of money the seller could, by selling
in the market at the current price, put himself into the same financial position he
would have been in had the contract been performed according to its terms.[1671]
There have been different views as to the meaning of an "available market".[1672] An
early view was that an available market is some place (e.g. an exchange) where the
goods in question can be sold[1673]; a later view was that it "means a particular level
of trade"[1674] in a particular locality; another that it refers to a sufficient demand for
the goods "to absorb readily all the goods that were thrust on it"[1675]; yet another that
it means a situation where the current price for the goods may fluctuate according
to supply and demand[1676] (which rules out the situation "where the goods can only
be sold at a fixed retail price"[1677]). It is submitted that the courts are likely to eschew
formal limitations on the meaning of an "available market",[1678] especially in the
light of the fact that the concept provides only a prima facie measure of damages

[1666] *Berger Co Inc v Gill Duffus SA* [1984] A.C. 382, 392.
[1667] See below, para.44-368.
[1668] See below, para.44-379. The Court of Appeal may now be more willing to depart from the prima
facie rules on the Act: see *Bence Graphics International Ltd v Fasson UK Ltd* [1998] Q.B. 87 (see
below, paras 44-413, 44-415). See also *Bern Dis A Turk Ticaret SA TR v International Agri Trade
Co Ltd* [1999] 1 All E.R. (Comm) 619, CA.
[1669] A claim under s.50(3) will not be affected by a clause excluding liability for loss of profit: *Glencore
Energy UK Ltd v Cirrus Oil Services Ltd* [2014] EWHC 87 (Comm) ("The contract price/market
price differential is not a computation of lost profit. Lost profit is the difference between the total
net cost to the seller of acquiring the goods and bringing them to market on the one hand and the
net sale price that would have been achieved on the other" (at [98])). For a discussion of the market
price rule generally and how it interacts with the compensation principle, see M. Bridge [2016]
L.Q.R. 405.
[1670] See Vol.I, paras 26-087 et seq.
[1671] But if s.50(3) applies, the plaintiff need not satisfy the requirements of reasonable mitigation:
Shearson Lehman Hutton Inc v Maclaine Watson Co Ltd (No.2) [1990] 3 All E.R. 723, 726.
[1672] See Waters (1958) 36 Can. Bar Rev. 360; Lawson (1969) 43 A.L.J. 52, 106.
[1673] *Dunkirk Colliery Co Ltd v Lever* (1878) 9 Ch. D. 20, 25 (an obiter dictum made prior to the 1893
Act, which was not expressly accepted by the other Lords Justices; followed in *Thompson Ltd v
Robinson (Gunmakers) Ltd* [1955] Ch. 177).
[1674] *Heskell v Continental Express Ltd* [1950] 1 All E.R. 1033, 1056. See also *The Arpad* [1934] P. 189,
191 ("Market means buyers and sellers"; at 202).
[1675] *Thompson Ltd v Robinson (Gunmakers) Ltd* [1955] Ch. 177, 187. (See on this case see below,
para.44-371).
[1676] *Charter v Sullivan* [1957] 2 Q.B. 117, 128 (see below, para.44-372). To the same effect, see *Eclipse
Motors Pty Ltd v Nixon* [1940] V.L.R. 49. cf. *Marshall Co v Nicoll Son*, 1919 S.C. 244, 253.
[1677] *Charter v Sullivan* [1957] 2 Q.B. 117, 128.
[1678] *Charrington Co Ltd v Wooder* [1914] A.C. 71, 82 ("Market" is "a term of no fixed legal
significance": per Lord Dunedin). See also *Charter v Sullivan* above at 128; and *ABD (Metals and
Waste) Ltd v Anglo-Chemical Ore Company Ltd* [1955] 2 Lloyd's Rep. 456, 466. ("… there must
be sufficient traders who are in touch with each other …") (followed in the *Shearson Lehman (No.2)*
case [1990] 3 All E.R. 723, 730). The existence or absence of an available market need not be specifically contemplated by the parties: *Coastal (Bermuda) Petroleum Ltd v VTT Vulcan Petroleum SA*

which need not be applied when there is some justification for not doing so. The availability of buyers and sellers, and their ready capacity to supply or to absorb the relevant goods[1679] is the basic concept of an "available market": it is submitted that there is no need to add to this the test of a price liable to fluctuations in accordance with supply and demand, as occurs in official exchanges or certain commodity markets. A fixed market price may render s.50(3) ineffective as a ground for substantial damages, but it should not make the term "available market" inapplicable.[1680] A fluctuating market price indicates the existence of an available market, but it should not be a necessary test. In order to establish that there was a market for the goods at a particular price it is not necessary to identify a willing buyer at a specified price. The judge is entitled to infer the existence of a market from any sufficient evidence relevant to that issue. He is entitled to infer the value of goods from any sufficient relevant evidence of value.[1681]

The temporal test implied in the "ready" or "immediate" accessibility to **44-369** substitute buyers or sellers should, it is submitted,[1682] be a test of a reasonable time after the breach, given the nature of the goods in question[1683] (e.g. whether they are perishable or durable goods) and the business situation of the claimant.[1684] With many types of goods there would need to be the possibility of an immediate resale or new purchase before the test would be satisfied; but this test permits some flex-

---

(No.2) (The Marine Star) [1994] 2 Lloyd's Rep. 629. "The best evidence of market value is constituted by arm's length deals actually made in the market. The last transaction effected effectively sets the benchmark": Glencore Energy UK Ltd v Cirrus Oil Services Ltd [2014] EWHC 87 (Comm) at [70].

[1679] Marshall Co v Nicoll Son, 1919 S.C. 244, 253; affirmed 1919 S.C.(H.L.) 129; Thompson Ltd v Robinson (Gunmakers) Ltd [1955] Ch. 177, 187. There is no "available market" for a unique article like a second-hand car: Lazenby Garages Ltd v Wright [1976] 1 W.L.R. 459, CA; nor is such a market likely in a "command economy": Derby Resources AG v Blue Corinth Marine Co Ltd (The Athenian Harmony) [1998] 2 Lloyd's Rep. 410, 416. In Air Studios (Lyndhurst) Ltd v Lombard North Central Plc [2012] EWHC 3162 (QB), [2013] 1 Lloyd's Rep. 63, a case of non-delivery by a seller, it was said that there may be a market for used goods even if the precise model or brand sold was not available: "the availability of equivalent second-hand goods capable of performing the same functions in much the same way would constitute an available market for 'the goods in question'. A buyer of such equivalent goods would be in the same financial position as if the contract had been performed" (at [93]). In Hughes v Pendragon Sabre Ltd (t/a Porsche Centre Bolton) [2016] EWCA Civ 18 a rare new limited edition Porsche was sufficiently specialised for there to be insufficient activity to evidence a market.

[1680] Waters (1958) 36 Can. Bar Rev. 360, 371; Lawson (1969) 43 A.L.J. 106, 110; see below, paras 44-371. cf. McGregor on Damages, 19th edn (2015), paras 23-118 et seq.

[1681] Bulkhaul Ltd v Rhodia Organique Fine Ltd [2008] EWCA Civ 1452, [2009] 1 Lloyd's Rep. 353 at [29].

[1682] This submission is "consistent with the effect of the Garnac Grain case" (see below, para.44-370 n.1692) but it is not based on any express reference to "a reasonable time after breach" in any case: the Shearson Lehman case (No.2) [1990] 3 All E.R. 723 at 730.

[1683] It is most unlikely that there will be an available market where the goods have been specially manufactured to suit the particular requirements of the buyer: Elbinger Aktien Gesellschaft v Armstrong (1874) 9 Q.B. 473, 476–477; Hinde v Liddell (1875) 10 Q.B. 265, 269. cf. Borries v Hutchison (1865) 18 C.B.(N.S.) 445, 447; Re Vic Mill Ltd [1913] 1 Ch. 183, 187; on appeal, above at 465, 472-473.

[1684] It is submitted that the opinion of Sellers L.J. on this point in Charter v Sullivan [1957] 2 Q.B. 117, 133–134 is not correct. cf. Lesters Leather and Skin Co v Home and Overseas Brokers Ltd (1948) 64 T.L.R. 569 (eight or nine months' delay in obtaining substitute goods: see below, para.44-389). In Air Studios (Lyndhurst) Ltd v Lombard North Central Plc [2012] EWHC 3162 (QB), [2013] 1 Lloyd's Rep. 63, a case of non-delivery by a seller, there was held to be no relevant market when there was only a possibility that equivalent goods would become available within about three months (at [95]).

ibility in the particular circumstances. With some types (or quantities) of goods, negotiations with potential buyers would take several days to achieve a sale: in these circumstances, the market price should be fixed on the assumption that the hypothetical seller had begun to negotiate sufficiently far ahead to enable a sale to be made on the day in question.[1685] The question also arises whether the concept of "market" extends to places other than the place of delivery.[1686] It has been assumed by one judge that the seller might have to send the goods elsewhere,[1687] and, in another case where the seller's business area was the East Riding of Yorkshire, it was assumed that was the area in which he should seek a substitute buyer.[1688] It is submitted that the test is one of reasonableness,[1689] in the light of the time, expense and trouble involved.[1690]

44-370   The size of the market is also relevant: thus, a few sales of small quantities of the relevant goods will not constitute an available market.[1691] The House of Lords (in a case of a seller's breach) has been willing to accept that there could be a market in which to buy 15,000 tons of lard where the only purchases which could be made were of smaller quantities (up to 2,000 tons at a time) and spread over a period.[1692] Thus, a seller who cannot find a substitute buyer for a large quantity of goods may have to mitigate by dividing it into separate sales of quantities which are readily saleable.[1693] A very high or a very low price may[1694] indicate that there is either a scarcity or glut[1695] of the relevant goods,[1696] and so no available market. But the fact that the market price is seriously affected by a governmental intervention (e.g. the sudden imposition of import restrictions) does not prevent there being an available market.[1697] A "black" market, where the goods are bought and sold surreptitiously to evade contractual restrictions (e.g. restrictions on price or supplies) may also be an available market.[1698]

[1685] The *Shearson Lehman (No.2)* case [1990] 3 All E.R. 723, 731.

[1686] It is submitted that *Wertheim v Chicoutimi Pulp Co* [1911] A.C. 301 (see below, para.44-407: delayed delivery) which is often cited in this connection, really concerns the question of reaching a market *value* in one place by basing the calculation on the market price elsewhere; it did not decide that the latter place constituted an available market. cf. however, the approval of *Wertheim's* case by Auld L.J. in *Bence Graphics International Ltd v Fasson UK Ltd* [1998] Q.B. 87, 103–105 (see below, paras 44-413, 44-415).

[1687] *Dunkirk Colliery Co v Lever* (1878) 9 Ch. D. 20, 25.

[1688] *Thompson Ltd v Robinson (Gunmakers) Ltd* [1955] Ch. 177. cf. *Lesters Leather and Skin Co v Home and Overseas Brokers Ltd* (1948) 64 T.L.R. 569 (seller's breach: see below, para.44-389).

[1689] *Kwei Tek Chao v British Traders and Shippers Ltd* [1954] 2 Q.B. 459, 499; *Lesters Leather and Skin Co v Home and Overseas Brokers Ltd* (1948) 64 T.L.R. 569 (seller's breach).

[1690] cf. *Ströms Brucks Aktie Bolag v Hutchinson* [1905] A.C. 515 (breach of charterparty: plaintiffs recovered cost of transporting the substitute goods to the contractual place of delivery).

[1691] *Kwei Tek Chao v British Traders and Shippers Ltd* [1954] 2 Q.B. 459, 498.

[1692] *Garnac Grain Co Inc v HMF Faure Fairclough Ltd* [1968] A.C. 1130, 1138 (see below, para.44-389); cf. (in the Court of Appeal) [1966] 1 Q.B. 650, 687.

[1693] *Tredegar Iron and Coal Co v Gielgud* (1883) 1 Cab. El. 27. In the case of the sale of 10,000 tonnes of gasoline it was held that there could be an available market where the seller could have disposed of the gasoline in smaller cargo loads of 1,000 to 3,000 tonnes over a period of about two weeks from the buyer's breach: *Petrotrade Inc v Stinnes Handel GmbH* [1995] 1 Lloyd's Rep. 142.

[1694] But not necessarily: *Bradley Sons Ltd v Colonial and Continental Trading Ltd* [1964] 2 Lloyd's Rep. 52, 64.

[1695] *Kwei Tek Chao v British Traders and Shippers Ltd* [1954] 2 Q.B. 459 at 498; *Campbell Mostyn (Provisions) Ltd v Barnett Trading Co* [1954] 1 Lloyd's Rep. 65, 69.

[1696] cf. *O'Hanlan v GW Ry* (1865) 6 B. S. 484, 494.

[1697] *Campbell Mostyn (Provisions) Ltd v Barnett Trading Co* [1954] 1 Lloyd's Rep. 65, 69.

[1698] *Mouat v Betts Motors Ltd* [1959] A.C. 71; *British Motor Trade Association v Gilbert* [1951] 2 T.L.R.

Fixed retail price   A problem has arisen when the relevant goods can be sold only   **44-371**
at a fixed retail price. It has been considered in two cases[1699] where, after the buyer
defaulted, the seller was able to resell only at the same fixed price: in both cases
the court held that the same result would follow whether or not there was an available market, so that a definite decision on the meaning of the term was not
necessary. The result of the two decisions is that if the seller had the ability and the
opportunity to make a profit for every buyer he could find (because the supply of
the goods exceeded the demand) he is entitled to the loss of profits on the sale to
the defaulting buyer.[1700] But if the demand for the goods exceeded the supply, so
that the seller could readily sell every item he could obtain from the manufacturers, he is not entitled to loss of profits on the first sale when he made the same profit
on a substituted sale following the first buyer's default.[1701] The former situation is
illustrated by *Thompson Ltd v Robinson (Gunmakers) Ltd*.[1702] The plaintiffs, car
dealers, agreed to sell a new Vanguard car to the defendants, at the retail price fixed
by the manufacturers. On the defendants' refusal to accept the car, the plaintiffs
persuaded the wholesale suppliers to take the car back. Although there was no difference between the current retail price and the contract price, Upjohn J. awarded
damages for the loss of profit on the sale. There was no shortage of Vanguard cars
to meet all immediate demands in the locality: since a substitute buyer could not
be found readily, the judge thought that there was not an available market.[1703] If the
second buyer was an additional customer of the seller, and not merely a substituted
customer, and the seller had the ability and the opportunity of making two profits
on the two transactions, he is entitled to damages for his loss of the first profit when
the first buyer defaults.[1704]

The second situation, where the demand for the goods in question exceeds the   **44-372**
supply, occurred in *Charter v Sullivan*.[1705] The defendant refused to accept delivery
of a Hillman Minx car which he had agreed to buy from the plaintiff, a car dealer,
at the fixed retail price. Within 10 days the plaintiff resold the car to another buyer
at the same price. As the evidence showed that the plaintiff could find a buyer for
every Hillman Minx car he could get from the manufacturers, the Court of Appeal
refused to allow him to recover more than nominal damages: he made the same
number of sales (and therefore the same number of fixed profits) as he would have
done if the defendant had performed his contractual obligation; hence it was a

---

514. (These decisions imply that the sellers were entitled to mitigate by themselves going into the
black market to buy a substitute. It is, however, doubtful whether a black market where the goods
are available in breach of statutory controls would be treated similarly.)

[1699] *Thompson Ltd v Robinson (Gunmakers) Ltd* [1955] Ch. 177; *Charter v Sullivan* [1957] 2 Q.B. 117.

[1700] *Thompson Ltd v Robinson (Gunmakers) Ltd* [1955] Ch. 177 (following *Re Vic Mill Ltd* [1913] 1 Ch.
465).

[1701] *Charter v Sullivan* [1957] 2 Q.B. 117.

[1702] See above. In *Lazenby Garages Ltd v Wright* [1976] 1 W.L.R. 459, the Court of Appeal distinguished
the sale of a second-hand car, a "unique article" for which there is no "available market", from that
of a new car.

[1703] [1955] Ch. 177, 187. See above, paras 44-368—44-370. Moreover, since the market price rule in
s.50(3) was only a "prima facie" rule, the judge held that it did not apply where it was clearly foreseeable by the parties that the rule would not compensate the seller for his loss of profit if the buyer
defaulted: [1955] Ch. 177 at 188.

[1704] *Re Vic Mill Ltd* [1913] 1 Ch. 465. cf. *Interoffice Telephones Ltd v Robert Freeman* [1958] 1 Q.B.
190 (hire of telephone equipment). cf. above, para.26-146.

[1705] [1957] 2 Q.B. 117.

substituted, not an additional sale, because the seller had the ability to make only one sale and one profit.[1706]

44-373 **The relevant "market"** Normally, the concept of "available market" should be the same, whether the defaulting party is the buyer or the seller.[1707] But the claimant's position could be crucial: if he is a seller, the issue is the availability of alternative buyers; whereas, if he is a buyer, it is the availability of alternative sellers.[1708] The selling, not the buying, price is relevant in one situation, but not necessarily the other, and vice versa.[1709] Thus, the relevant available market is that available to the innocent party in the circumstances in which he is placed by the breach.[1710] But there are other types of market relationships which may be relevant,[1711] e.g. between wholesaler and retailer, retailer and private buyer, as the prices for the goods in question may vary according to the particular relationship in which the claimant and defendant are involved.[1712]

44-374 **The relevant time** Section 50(3) provides that "the market or current price" is to be taken "at the time or times when the goods ought to have been accepted or (if no time was fixed for acceptance) at the time of the refusal to accept". The contract itself will normally fix the exact time for acceptance.[1713] Where the goods are to be delivered within a stipulated period of time, the time when the goods ought to have been accepted is the time, within the period, when the goods were actually tendered to the buyer by the seller.[1714] Where the contract provides that delivery is to be made by separate deliveries of part of the goods at stated times or intervals, the damages in respect of the buyer's failure to accept an instalment must be calculated by refer-

---

[1706] The court considered it immaterial whether or not there was an "available market": for tests for this, see above, paras 44-368—44-370.

[1707] Lawson (1969) 43 A.L.J. 106, 113. The parties may in their contract agree which market is to be the relevant one for fixing market value: *Orchard v Simpson* (1857) 2 C.B.(N.S.) 299.

[1708] *Kwei Tek Chao v British Traders and Shippers Ltd* [1954] 2 Q.B. 459, 497; *C Czarnikow Ltd v Bunge Co Ltd* [1987] 1 Lloyd's Rep. 202, 205. The difference is referred to in *The Arpad* [1934] P. 189, 211; and in *Dominion Motors Ltd v Grieves* [1936] N.Z.L.R. 766, 771.

[1709] *Kwei Tek Chao v British Traders and Shippers Ltd*, above at 497–498.

[1710] But the individual characteristics of the claimant (e.g. his personal skill in negotiating) are not relevant: *Shearson Lehman Hutton Inc v Maclaine Watson Co Ltd (No.2)* [1990] 3 All E.R. 723, 726.

[1711] FOB contracts raise problems as to the relevant market: see *Benjamin's Sale of Goods*, 10th edn (2017), paras 20-141 et seq. (cf. also at para.19-224).

[1712] *Heskell v Continental Express Ltd* [1950] 1 All E.R. 1033. See also *Rice v Baxendale* (1861) 7 H. & N. 96, 100. cf. *Charrington and Co Ltd v Wooder* [1914] A.C. 71, where the House of Lords held that a contractual provision for the "fair market price" for beer meant, in the circumstances, the market for tied public houses and not that for free houses; cf. also *James Buchanan Co Ltd v Babco Forwarding and Shipping (UK) Ltd* [1978] A.C. 141 (there may be different market prices for the same type of goods, depending on whether the goods are intended for export or not). If the claimant cannot find a relevant market for the goods, he may try any reasonable alternative market relationship: *O'Hanlan v GW Ry* (1865) 6 B. & S. 484, 494.

[1713] See above, paras 44-236, 44-237, 44-246 et seq. The time may be fixed by reference to the happening of an event, e.g. the arrival of a ship: *Melachrino v Nickoll Knight* [1920] 1 K.B. 693, 696 (on s.51(3)). Since the seller will normally know of the buyer's refusal to accept on the day he tenders delivery of the goods, he will in most cases (where there is an available market for the goods) be able to find a substitute buyer on the same day. cf. *Kaines (UK) Ltd v Osterreichische Warrenhandelsgesellschaft, etc* [1993] 2 Lloyd's Rep. 1 (seller's breach: buyer should have repurchased on the next day: at pp.11, 12). cf. see below, para.44-390.

[1714] cf. the rule in cases of non-delivery: see below, para.44-390.

ence to the market price prevailing at the time fixed for delivery of that instalment.[1715]

No time fixed for acceptance   The final provision in s.50(3) deals with cases of   **44-375**
the buyer's refusal to accept delivery of the goods when tendered by the seller under
a contract which did not fix a time for acceptance: in these circumstances, the prima
facie rule for the assessment of damages is based on the market price "at the time
of the refusal to accept". But the calculation of the market price at the time of the
buyer's "refusal to accept" in terms of s.50(3) does not apply to an anticipatory
breach by the buyer.[1716] A Divisional Court has held[1717] that a contract for delivery
within a reasonable time is not a contract with a fixed time for acceptance of the
goods within the scope of the analogous s.51(3).[1718]

Postponement of time fixed for delivery   Where the buyer requests and obtains   **44-376**
the seller's consent to postpone[1719] the time for delivery fixed by the contract, but
fails to accept the goods when the seller tenders them at the substituted time (or
within the extended period), the calculation of the seller's damages will be made
on the basis of the market price at the substituted time (or at the last day of the
extended period)[1720]; if the seller agreed to postpone the original delivery date but
no definite date or period was substituted by agreement, the calculation of damages will be made at the market price at a reasonable time after the last request by
the buyer for postponement of delivery, or at the date when the seller refused to give
any further time.[1721] Where the request for postponement of the agreed delivery date
came from the seller, and at first the buyer agreed to waive delivery at that date but
later repudiated his obligations in breach of the contract, the damages should be
calculated on the basis of the market price at the time of the buyer's repudiation.[1722]

Proof of the market price   If there is proof of the market price at the date of the   **44-377**
buyer's breach,[1723] the actual price obtained by the seller upon his reselling the
goods at a later date is irrelevant to the assessment of damages, whether the resale

---

[1715] 1979 Act s.50(3) above. There appear to be no reported cases directly in point, but the cases on the
buyer's damages for non-delivery under an instalment contract are analogous: *Brown v Muller* (1872)
L.R. 7 Ex. 319; *Roper v Johnson* (1873) L.R. 8 C.P. 167 (see below, para.44-390).

[1716] See below, paras 44-380—44-381.

[1717] *Millett v Van Heek Co* [1920] 3 K.B. 535; *Melachrino v Nickoll and Knight* [1920] 1 K.B. 693, 696.
In the Court of Appeal, opinions on the point were reserved: [1921] 2 K.B. 369; Atkin L.J. thought
that there were arguments against the view taken by the Divisional Court: above at 378. The Privy
Council, in a case on a seller's breach, doubted whether any meaning could be given to the similar
concluding words of the corresponding provision (s.51(3)): *Tai Hing Cotton Mill Ltd v Kamsing Knitting Factory* [1979] A.C. 91, 104 (see below, para.44-393).

[1718] See below, para.44-391.

[1719] On waiver, see Vol.I, paras 4-082 et seq., paras 22-040 et seq.

[1720] *Hickman v Haynes* (1875) 10 C.P. 598, 607 (following the similar rule in the case of the seller's
failure to deliver: *Ogle v Earl Vane* (1868) L.R. 3 Q.B. 272 (see below, para.44-392)).

[1721] *Hickman v Haynes* (1875) 10 C.P. 598. (This case was mentioned with approval by the HL in
Johnson v Agnew [1980] A.C. 367, 401.)

[1722] *Hartley v Hymans* [1920] 3 K.B. 475, 496 (following the similar rule in the case of the seller's failure
to deliver: *Tyers v Rosedale and Ferryhill Co* (1875) L.R. 10 Ex. 195 (see below, para.44-392)). In
Hartley v Hymans, above, the market price had fallen heavily between the contractual date for
delivery and the date of the buyer's repudiation; but the judgment is very brief on the question of
the assessment of damages.

[1723] The court may infer the approximate market price on a given date from evidence that there was a
steady decline in that price between an earlier and a later date: *Tai Hing Cotton Mill Ltd v Kamsing*

price is higher or lower than the market price.[1724] But where normal proof of the market price of the goods is not available (viz by reference to published or recorded prices of deals at the relevant date) the court may accept other evidence, e.g. proof of the price at which the seller in fact resold the goods to a new buyer,[1725] or of an offer for the goods received by the seller,[1726] or proof of compromises in other disputes relating to the market value of similar goods at the same time.[1727]

44-378   If the seller has, at the date of the buyer's breach, only the one set of the relevant goods, viz the set left on his hands following the buyer's breach, the price (higher[1728] than the market price) which he actually receives by reselling *immediately* is a direct consequence of the buyer's breach, and should be taken into account in assessing the seller's damages.[1729] The seller should recover only his actual loss, viz the difference between the contract price and the actual resale price, since, but for the breach, he would not have had the opportunity of reselling.[1730] If, on the other hand, the seller had, at the date of the breach, further supplies of the relevant goods, a resale of only some of his stock at a higher than market or current price could not necessarily be attributed to the buyer's breach and, in these circumstances, the seller should be entitled to the normal measure of damages under s.50(3).[1731] Although there is no authority directly in point to support the submissions just made, inferences may be drawn from cases where the seller chooses to retain the goods for a period, instead of reselling them in the market immediately following the buyer's breach. The Court of Appeal has held[1732] that if the seller subsequently resells the goods at a gain because the market price rises after the date of the breach, the enhanced price received by the seller does not reduce his damages, which are still to be determined by the difference between the contract price and the market price on the date of the breach. By retaining the goods after that date the seller is taking on himself the risk of fluctuations in the market price: if the price later fell, the buyer would not be liable for the seller's additional loss, and, correspondingly, the seller is entitled to the gain if the price later rises.[1733] There should be symmetry of risk. From this reasoning it may be inferred that if the seller does not take a chance on later fluctuations in the market price, but chooses to sell the one set of goods im-

---

Knitting Factory [1979] A.C. 91, 106, PC.

[1724] *Campbell Mostyn (Provisions) Ltd v Barnett Trading Co* [1954] 1 Lloyd's Rep. 658.

[1725] *Maclean v Dunn* (1828) 4 Bing. 722, 729; *Ex p. Stapleton* (1879) 10 Ch. D. 586, 590. (*Aliter* if the resale was on significantly different terms: *Macklin v Newbury Sanitary Laundry* (1919) 63 S.J. 337.) cf. *Aryeh v Lawrence Kostoris Son Ltd* [1967] 1 Lloyd's Rep. 63, 73.

[1726] The seller may be able to establish the "current price" by seeking several offers for the goods from prospective buyers, with a view to accepting the best price obtainable.

[1727] *Hong Guan Co Ltd v R Jumabhoy Sons Ltd* [1960] A.C. 684, 703–704.

[1728] If the seller resells at *lower* than the market price, he cannot recover the difference between the contract price and the actual resale price: s.50(3).

[1729] See the second rule of mitigation: Vol.I, para.26-103; *British Westinghouse Electric and Manufacturing Co Ltd v Underground Electric Rys* [1912] A.C. 673, 689.

[1730] *Benjamin's Sale of Goods*, 10th edn (2017), paras 16-077—16-077. cf. *R Pagnan and Fratelli v Corbisa Industrial Agropacuaria* [1970] 1 W.L.R. 1306 (see below, para.44-396).

[1731] cf. the similar problem in *Charter v Sullivan* [1957] 2 Q.B. 117 (see above, para.44-372); *In Re Vic Mill Ltd* [1913] 1 Ch. 465.

[1732] *Campbell Mostyn (Provisions) Ltd v Barnett Trading Co* [1954] 1 Lloyd's Rep. 65.

[1733] The court followed the reasoning of the Privy Council in *Jamal v Moolla Dawood* [1916] 1 A.C. 175, 179. See also *Koch Marine Inc v D'Amica Societa di Navigazione ARL (The Elena D'Amica)* [1980] 1 Lloyd's Rep. 75, 87–90.

mediately upon the breach and happens to obtain a price higher than the market price at that time, his damages should be limited to his actual loss.[1734]

Damages where there is no available market If s.50(3) does not apply, because **44-379** there is no available market, the court is thrown back on the general principle enunciated in s.50(2), see above. The seller's loss is the difference between the contract price and the value of the goods to the seller at the time and place of the breach,[1735] and any relevant evidence may be admissible to prove this value.[1736] The seller's damages will be assessed on the basis that he should have acted reasonably in mitigating his loss.[1737] He is entitled to deal with the goods "in any reasonable way",[1738] e.g. by adapting them to suit another customer, and his damages will then include the cost of the adaptation, as well as the loss of profit on the first sale.[1739] Although the seller need not incur speculative expenditure,[1740] there may be circumstances in which it would be reasonable for the seller, under the rules of mitigation, to incur a limited amount of expenditure to adapt the goods in such a way as to make them readily saleable.[1741] If the seller has been able to resell, he may claim the loss of profits on the abortive sale on the ground that the second buyer was an additional, not a substituted, buyer. The test is whether the seller had the ability and the opportunity to make the two separate profits[1742]: if the seller had fulfilled the first contract, would he have been able to fulfil the second contract as well? If so, he is entitled to recover from the defaulting buyer his loss of profit on the first contract.[1743]

Anticipatory breach by the buyer: repudiation accepted[1744] Where the buyer **44-380** commits an anticipatory breach by repudiating, before the date fixed for delivery,

---

[1734] cf. below, para.44-396.

[1735] *Harlow and Jones Ltd v Panex (International) Ltd* [1967] 2 Lloyd's Rep. 509, 530.

[1736] *Harlow and Jones Ltd v Panex (International) Ltd* [1967] 2 Lloyd's Rep. 509 (seller able to find a substitute buyer: resale price evidence of seller's loss); *Derby Resources AG v Blue Corinth Marine Co Ltd (The Athenian Harmony)* [1998] 2 Lloyd's Rep. 410, 416 (evidence of the market price of the goods at a different place and even at a different time may be the only available means of quantification.) See also *Robbins of Putney Ltd v Meek* [1971] R.T.R. 345.

[1737] *Gebruder Metelmann GmbH Co KG v NBR (London) Ltd* [1984] 1 Lloyd's Rep. 614 (where the physical goods cannot be immediately resold, it may be reasonable for the seller (e.g. when prices are falling) to resell in a "terminal" or "futures" market, which is a mechanism by which he can insulate himself from future changes in market values); Vol.I, paras 26-087 et seq.; *Harlow and Jones Ltd v Panex (International) Ltd* [1967] 2 Lloyd's Rep. 509, 530, 531.

[1738] *Re Vic Mill Ltd* [1913] 1 Ch. 465, 473.

[1739] [1913] 1 Ch. 465 at 473, 474. cf. see below, para.44-397.

[1740] cf. *Jewelowski v Propp* [1944] K.B. 510.

[1741] cf. below, para.44-396.

[1742] *Re Vic Mill Ltd* [1913] 1 Ch. 465; *Hill Sons v Edwin Showell Sons Ltd* (1918) 87 L.J. K.B. 1106, HL.

[1743] *Re Vic Mill Ltd* [1913] 1 Ch. 465, 472, 474. cf. *Charter v Sullivan* [1957] 2 Q.B. 117, 130 (see above, para.44-372, and also paras 26-099 and 26-104). The burden of proof lies on the defaulting buyer to show that the seller could have earned only one profit: *Hill Sons v Edwin Showell Sons Ltd* (1918) 87 L.J. K.B. 1108, 1114. See *Thompson Ltd v Robinson (Gunmakers) Ltd* [1955] Ch. 177 (see above, para.44-372) (distinguished in *Lazenby Garages Ltd v Wright* [1976] 1 W.L.R. 459 (seller able to find a substitute buyer for a second-hand car at a higher price: no damages awarded) (see above, para.44-371)). See also *Sony Computer Entertainment UK Ltd v Cinram Logistics UK Ltd* [2008] EWCA Civ 955, [2009] Bus. L.R. 529.

[1744] See Vol.I, paras 24-022 et seq.; George [1971] J.B.L. 109. cf. see below, para.44-389.

his obligation to take delivery of the goods the seller has an option[1745]: he may either accept the repudiation and so treat it forthwith as a breach, or he may continue to treat the contract as binding and thus not accept the repudiation as a breach.[1746] If the seller accepts the buyer's anticipatory repudiation, he may sue immediately for damages for breach of contract: but in those situations in which there is an available market for the goods,[1747] the relevant date for ascertaining the market price remains prima facie (and subject to any requirement of mitigation) the date fixed for delivery,[1748] since that is when the contract ought to be performed.[1749] If the action is heard before the date for delivery arrives, the court should attempt to estimate what the market price is likely to be at that future date.[1750] But if the seller does accept the buyer's anticipatory repudiation, he is forthwith subject to the rules on mitigation and must take reasonable steps to minimise his loss.[1751] Where the seller should have mitigated by reselling,[1752] the relevant market price is that existing at the date he ought reasonably to have resold,[1753] not that at the date of the repudiation, nor that at the date when the repudiation is accepted.[1754]

44-381 **Repudiation not accepted** If the seller does not accept the buyer's anticipatory repudiation, he may continue to treat the contract as binding on both himself and the buyer, and wait until the date fixed for delivery before he tenders the goods: if the buyer then fails to accept the goods, the seller thereupon should mitigate his loss by taking reasonable steps (viz in normal circumstances by reselling forthwith).[1755] Where there is an available market for the goods, the relevant market price will be that at the date fixed for delivery: if the seller did not accept the buyer's anticipa-

---

[1745] The seller is not obliged to act "reasonably" in exercising this choice: *Tredegar Iron and Coal Co Ltd v Hawthorn Bros Co* (1902) 18 T.L.R. 716, 716–717; *White and Carter (Councils) Ltd v McGregor* [1962] A.C. 413. See Vol.I, para.26-114.

[1746] *Fercometal SARL v Mediterranean Shipping Co SA* [1989] A.C. 788.

[1747] See above, paras 44-368 et seq.

[1748] It is submitted that the provision in s.50(3) that, when no time is fixed for acceptance, damages should be assessed by reference to the market price "at the time of the refusal to accept" should not apply to an anticipatory breach by the buyer. cf. see below, paras 44-393—44-394.

[1749] *Frost v Knight* (1872) L.R. 7 Ex. 111, 113; approved by the House of Lords in *Fercometal SARL v Mediterranean Shipping Co SA* [1989] A.C. 788; *Melachrino v Nickoll and Knight* [1920] 1 K.B. 693 (seller's anticipatory repudiation); *Millett v Van Heek* [1920] 3 K.B. 535, [1921] 2 K.B. 369, CA. It is submitted that the contrary statement in *Tredegar Iron and Coal Co (Ltd) v Hawthorn Bros Co* (1902) 18 T.L.R. 717, is incorrect. (On the question of discounting any sum not due until a future date, see below, para.44-393; Vol.I, para.26-009.)

[1750] See the cases cited in the preceding note.

[1751] *Roth Co v Taysen Townsend Co* (1895) 73 L.T. 628, 629–630; affirmed on appeal (1896) 12 T.L.R. 211, 212; *Tredegar Iron and Coal Co (Ltd) v Hawthorn Bros Co*, above; *Sudan Import and Export Co (Khartoum) v Société Générale de Compensation* [1958] 1 Lloyd's Rep. 310, 316. cf. below, paras 44-393—44-394.

[1752] The onus of proof is on the buyer. cf. the analogous cases where the seller is in default: *Roper v Johnson* (1873) L.R. 8 C.P. 167; *Garnac Grain Co Inc v HMF Faure and Fairclough Ltd* [1968] A.C. 1130.

[1753] *Melachrino v Nickoll and Knight* [1920] 1 K.B. 693, 697, 699; *Sudan Import and Export Co (Khartoum) Ltd v Société Générale de Compensation* [1958] 1 Lloyd's Rep. 310, 316. The same rule applies to the analogous case of the seller's anticipatory breach which is accepted by the buyer: *Kaines (UK) Ltd v Osterreichische Warrenhandelsgesellschaft, etc.* [1993] 2 Lloyd's Rep. 1.

[1754] Although the date of the seller's acceptance of the repudiation may be the date when he ought to have resold (e.g. if there was an available market), it will not always be the same date: *Kaines (UK) Ltd v Osterreichische etc.* [1993] 2 Lloyd's Rep. 1 (seller's breach). Incorrect statements are found in earlier cases to the effect that the relevant date is the date of the seller's acceptance of the repudiation.

[1755] For an illustration, see *Tredegar Iron and Coal Co (Ltd) v Hawthorn Bros Co* (1902) 18 T.L.R. 716.

tory repudiation, a higher or a lower market price at the date of the repudiation, or at any date during the period up to the date fixed for delivery, is irrelevant, because the rules of mitigation do not apply until the date of the actual breach.[1756] Of course, during the interval the contract is kept alive for the benefit of *both* parties[1757]: the buyer may change his mind and accept the goods when tendered[1758]; or the seller may decide to accept the repudiation (before it has been retracted by the buyer) whereupon the rules of mitigation will forthwith apply to the seller; or the obligations of the parties may be determined by the occurrence of a frustrating event[1759]; or the buyer may exercise a right under the contract to cancel it.[1760]

Special cases of seller's damages[1761]   If the unpaid seller resells under his statutory powers (s.48(3) and (4)),[1762] he may claim damages, which will be:

44-382

(a)   the difference between the original contract price (less any deposit[1763] paid) and the price obtained on the resale (provided that it was not less than either the market price[1764] or a reasonable price[1765]); and

(b)   any expenses reasonably incurred by the seller as a result of the buyer's breach of contract or in connection with the resale (e.g. reasonable advertising expenses[1766] or storage charges).[1767]

Similarly, where there is a market, and the seller resells at the market price immediately upon the buyer's failure to accept the goods, he will (in addition to damages under s.50)[1768] be entitled to damages for any expenses reasonably incurred in effecting the resale.[1769]

"Special damages"   Section 54 preserves the right of both the buyer and the seller to recover "special damages".[1770] Consequential losses and expenses are often

44-383

[1756] *White and Carter (Councils) Ltd v McGregor; Tredegar Iron and Coal Co (Ltd) v Hawthorn Bros Co*, above cf. *Tai Hing Cotton Mill Ltd v Kamsing Knitting Factory* [1979] A.C. 91, 102, 105 (see below, paras 44-393—44-394).

[1757] *Fercometal SARL v Mediterranean Shipping Co SA* [1989] A.C. 788, 805.

[1758] In which case, the buyer is not in breach of his contractual obligations, since his earlier repudiation is a "mere nullity" when not accepted by the seller: *Phillpotts v Evans* (1839) 5 M. & W. 475, 477; *White and Carter (Councils) Ltd v McGregor* [1962] A.C. 413, 444.

[1759] *Fercometal SARL v Mediterranean Shipping Co SA* [1989] A.C. 788 at 805. See Vol.I, Ch.23.

[1760] The *Fercometal* case, above, at 805–806.

[1761] Where the buyer fails to pay the agreed deposit, and the seller later accepts the buyer's repudiation of the contract, the seller may recover damages measured at the amount of the deposit: *Damon Compania Naviera SA v Hapag-Lloyd International SA* [1985] 1 W.L.R. 435; *Griffon Shipping LLC v Firodi Shipping Ltd (The Griffon)* [2013] EWCA Civ 1567, [2014] 1 All E.R. (Comm) 593.

[1762] See above, paras 44-351, 44-355.

[1763] On the position in regard to the deposit if the seller does not claim damages, see above, para.44-358.

[1764] If there was an available market: s.50(3) (see above, paras 44-367 et seq.).

[1765] See above, para.44-379.

[1766] *RV Ward Ltd v Bignall* [1967] 1 Q.B. 534.

[1767] s.37 (see above, paras 44–291—44–292). See *Vitol SA v Phibro Energy AG (The Mathraki)* [1990] 2 Lloyd's Rep. 84 (buyer's breach caused seller to become liable in damages to the carrier).

[1768] See above, paras 44-367 et seq.

[1769] See the doctrine of mitigation: Vol.I, paras 26-087 et seq.

[1770] See below, paras 44-387, 44-419—44-420. This section does not apply to consumer contracts for the sale of goods which fall within Ch.2 of Pt 1 of the Consumer Rights Act 2015. In consumer contracts for the sale of goods the 2015 Act provides special remedies for buyers in consumer sales contracts, see above paras 38-512 et seq.

claimed by the buyer,[1771] but seldom by the seller, who normally has not made other arrangements which both depend on the fulfilment of the contract and also involve losses or expenses which fall within the tests for remoteness.[1772] The seller's normal loss when the buyer fails to pay the price on the agreed date is the loss of the use of the money: for this type of loss, the seller may claim interest[1773] and, in some circumstances, damages,[1774] provided that it was not unreasonable to think that the buyer was assuming responsibility for such a loss.[1775]

(d)   Other Remedies of the Seller

44-384   **Miscellaneous remedies of the seller**[1776]   When the buyer has possession of the goods but not the property in them, he is the bailee of the seller who may be entitled, either under the terms of the contract[1777] or under the ordinary law of contract, to determine the bailment and demand the immediate return of the goods, if the buyer commits a breach of his obligations under the contract.[1778] The appropriate remedies are the proprietary ones for chattels under the law of torts,[1779] viz proceedings for wrongful interference with the goods[1780] in which the claimant seeks an order for the specific delivery of the goods,[1781] or damages for conversion when the buyer has dealt with the goods in a manner which denies the seller's title to them.[1782] In appropriate cases the seller may also be able to obtain an injunction against the buyer to prevent him from breaking his contractual obligation, e.g. under an exclusive purchasing agreement.[1783]

44-385   Remedies for mistake, fraud and misrepresentation are considered in Vol.I,[1784] as

---

[1771] e.g. below, paras 44-400, 44-408.

[1772] Vol.I, paras 26-117 et seq. The seller may claim expenses on resale, storage charges when the buyer delays in taking delivery, or cancellation expenses (*Bem Dis Turk Ticaret SA TR v International Agri Trade Co Ltd* [1999] 1 All E.R. (Comm) 619).

[1773] See Vol.I, paras 26-272 et seq. (s.54 preserves the right "... to recover interest ...").

[1774] See Vol.I, para.26-273; and see above, para.44-366.

[1775] See *Transfield Shipping Inc v Mercator Shipping Inc (The Achilleas)* [2008] UKHL 48, [2009] 1 A.C. 61, discussed above, Vol.I, paras 26-137 et seq.

[1776] s.52 (specific performance) applies in practice only to claims by the buyer (see below, paras 44-440—44-444): *Shell-Mex Ltd v Elton Cop Dyeing Co Ltd* (1928) 34 Com. Cas. 39, 46. (On the wording of the section, it is just possible to argue that the section could apply to the seller's claim to recover the goods.) See also *Elliott v Pierson* [1948] 1 All E.R. 939, 942; Treitel [1966] J.B.L. 211, 229–230.

[1777] *McEntire v Crossley Bros* [1895] A.C. 457, 464; and see above, paras 44-347—44-350.

[1778] On repudiatory breach, see Vol.I, paras 24-001 et seq. Under the terms of the contract, the seller may also be entitled to "trace" and recover the proceeds of sub-sales made by the buyer: *Aluminium Industrie Vaassen BV v Romalpa Aluminium Ltd* [1976] 1 W.L.R. 676 (see above, paras 44-173—44-188).

[1779] e.g. *Bishop v Shillito* (1818) 2 B. & A. 329n. (conversion); *Rew v Payne, Douthwaite Co* (1885) 53 L.T. 932. For these actions in general, see *Salmond and Heuston, on the Law of Torts*, 21st edn (1996), paras 6.1 et seq. cf. below, paras 44-447—44-448.

[1780] Under the Torts (Interference with Goods) Act 1977.

[1781] See above, para.44-349; see below, para.44-440.

[1782] The seller who is entitled to immediate possession may also have these proceedings against *strangers* who interfere with the possession of the buyer. cf. s.46(4) (see above, para.44-337).

[1783] *Metropolitan Electric Supply Co Ltd v Ginder* [1901] 2 Ch. 799. See Vol.I, paras 27-077 et seq.; Sharpe, *Injunctions and Specific Performance*, looseleaf edition, paras 9-130 to 9-200. cf. below, para.44-445.

[1784] Vol.I, Chs 6 and 7.

is forfeiture of deposits and prepayments.[1785] The seller may have special remedies where he has taken a negotiable instrument[1786] or a documentary credit[1787] for the price, or an export credit guarantee[1788]; or where the contract contains an arbitration clause.[1789] The provisions of s.60 should also be noted.

Declarations   The seller may in appropriate circumstances obtain a declaration setting out his legal rights against the buyer.[1790] For instance, although the seller who retains the property in the goods cannot normally sue for the price,[1791] he may obtain a declaration that the buyer is bound to pay the price upon the seller's fulfilling his obligations, e.g. upon tender of the shipping documents.[1792] But the Court of Appeal[1793] has decided that a declaration of indemnity should not be made where, as a result of the buyer's breach of contract, a third party (e.g. the supplier to the seller) has a potential claim against the seller: if that liability is not too remote a head of loss in the seller's action against the buyer, the proper course is for the court to reserve that head of damages.[1794]   **44-386**

7.   REMEDIES OF THE BUYER

(a)   Damages for Non-Delivery

Introduction[1795]   Section 51 of the Act[1796] lays down the following rules: **44-387**

[1785] Vol.I, paras 26-245 et seq. and 29-068. See also above, para.44-358.

[1786] See above, paras 34-001 et seq.

[1787] See above, paras 34-445 et seq.

[1788] See *Benjamin's Sale of Goods*, 10th edn (2017), Ch.24.

[1789] Above, Ch.32.

[1790] e.g. *Household Machines Ltd v Cosmos Exporters Ltd* [1947] K.B. 217; *Trans Trust SPRL v Danubian Trading Co Ltd* [1952] 2 Q.B. 297 (see below). See Zamir and Woolf, *The Declaratory Judgment*, 4th edn, and see below, para.44–446 (buyer's claim).

[1791] s.49(1) (see above, para.44-359); but he may be entitled to do so under s.49(2) (see above, para.44-364) or an express term in the contract (see above, para.44-365).

[1792] *Polenghi Brothers v Dried Milk Co Ltd* (1904) 10 Com. Cas. 42. The court has a discretion to make a negative declaration e.g. to the effect that the claimant is not liable to the defendant in respect of a certain matter: *Messier-Dowty Ltd v Sabena SA* [2000] 1 W.L.R. 2040, CA.

[1793] *Trans Trust SPRL v Danubian Trading Co Ltd* [1952] 2 Q.B. 297.

[1794] [1952] 2 Q.B. 297. cf. *Deeny v Gooda Walker Ltd (No.3)* [1995] 4 All E.R. 289 (not a sale of goods case).

[1795] General principles on the law of damages are discussed in Vol.I, Ch.26. The rules to be discussed in this section are "default rules" in the sense that the parties are free to fashion their own compensatory scheme, subject to the rules on penalties (see Vol.I, paras 26-190 et seq.) and legislative controls such as the Unfair Contract Terms Act 1977 (see Vol.I, Ch.15). In *Bunge SA v Nidera BV* [2013] EWHC 84 (Comm), [2013] 1 Lloyd's Rep. 621 Hamblen J. said, in relation to the Default Clause in a GAFTA sale contract, that: "There is nothing unusual about the parties seeking to set out the measure of damages in advance and being confined, for good or bad, to that measure even if it does not reflect the measure that would be available at common law" (at [51]). The penalty rules do not appear to have been argued. However, the judge thought that the measure applied by the Default Clause did not depart from the rules of common law. cf. the Supreme Court held that the clause was not intended to be a complete code for the assessment of damages but covered some of the same field [2015] UKSC 43, [32], [61]. In *Novasen SA v Alimenta SA* [2013] EWHC 345 (Comm), [2013] 1 Lloyd's Rep. 648, at [18], Popplewell J. said that the Default Clause did not constitute a penalty clause, applying his dicta in *Imam-Sadeque v Bluebay Asset Management (Services) Ltd* [2012] EWHC 3511 (QB); see above, para.26-235.

[1796] This section does not apply to consumer contracts for the sale of goods which fall within Ch.2 of Pt 1 of the Consumer Rights Act 2015. In consumer contracts for the sale of goods the 2015 Act

"(1)   Where the seller wrongfully neglects or refuses to deliver the goods to the buyer, the buyer may maintain an action against the seller for damages for non-delivery.[1797]

(2)   The measure of damages is the estimated loss directly and naturally-resulting, in the ordinary course of events, from the seller's breach of contract.[1798]

(3)   Where there is an available market for the goods in question the measure of damages is prima facie to be ascertained by the difference between the contract price and the market or current price of the goods at the time or times when they ought to have been delivered or (if no time was fixed) at the time of the refusal to deliver."

In addition to this section, the buyer may by s.54 also recover interest[1799] and special damages, e.g. for expenses or for unusual loss resulting from special circumstances known to the seller,[1800] or, in certain circumstances, loss of profits under a resale.[1801] A clause in the contract may permit the buyer, upon the seller's default, to repurchase elsewhere, and to claim any loss from the seller.[1802] The minimum legal obligation[1803] of the seller is the basis for assessing damages against him for failure to deliver the goods.[1804] Thus, where the contract was for "200 tons, 5 per cent. more or less", the margin was held to be at the seller's option and the damages were assessed on the basis of failure to deliver 190 tons.[1805]

44-388   **Damages where there is an available market**   Section 51(3) spells out the normal application of the rule in s.51(2) to the situation where there is "an available market" for the goods. The normal measure of damages when the seller[1806] fails to deliver the goods is the difference between: (a) the market price of the relevant goods at the time fixed for delivery and at the place fixed for delivery; and (b) the

---

provides special rules in relation to buyer's remedies in consumer sales contracts; see above, paras 38-442 et seq.

[1797] The buyer may claim damages for non-delivery even where the property in the goods has passed to the buyer; but, whether or not the property in the goods has passed to the buyer, his damages for the seller's failure to deliver should be assessed on the same basis.

[1798] This subsection is in terms of the first rule in *Hadley v Baxendale* (1854) 9 Exch. 341 (see Vol.I, para.26-117). It does not refer to the further limitation that there will not be liability if it was unreasonable to think that the buyer was assuming responsibility for such a loss: see *Transfield Shipping Inc v Mercator Shipping Inc (The Achilleas)* [2008] UKHL 48, [2009] 1 A.C. 61, discussed above, Vol.I, paras 26-137 et seq. It may be argued that that the question of assumption of responsibility is merely an aspect of the remoteness rule, in which case s.51(2) might prevent it applying in sale of goods contracts, but s.51(2) is probably best viewed as a "default rule" which applies only when the circumstances do not indicate otherwise. If on the facts it was not reasonable for the buyer to think that the seller was assuming responsibility for a particular loss, the loss will not be recoverable even though it would otherwise fall under s.51(2). See above, Vol.I, para.26-137.

[1799] Vol.I, paras 26-272 et seq.

[1800] See below, paras 44-397, 44-405.

[1801] See below, paras 44-400—44-405.

[1802] It was held in *Simmonds v Millar Co* (1898) 15 T.L.R. 100 that, in making such a repurchase, the buyer is not acting as the seller's agent: hence, the seller cannot claim any profit arising from the fact that the buyer was able to repurchase at a price lower than the contract price.

[1803] See Vol.I, paras 26-001, 26-083.

[1804] *Cockburn v Alexander* (1848) 6 C.B. 791, 814.

[1805] *Re Thornett and Fehr and Yuills Ltd* [1921] 1 K.B. 219, 229–230. cf. *Bunge Corp New York v Tradax Export SA, Panama* [1981] 1 W.L.R. 711; *Paula Lee Ltd v Robert Zehil Co Ltd* [1983] 2 All E.R. 390 (not a sale of goods case).

[1806] By analogy, the same measure of damages has been used when an auctioneer at an auction expressed to be "without reserve" is liable to the highest bidder under a collateral contract that he would sell to that bidder: *Barry v Davies (trading as Heathcote Ball Co)* [2000] 1 W.L.R. 1962, CA. (the goods were new).

contract price.[1807] One of the grounds for this measure of damages is the doctrine of mitigation[1808] since s.51(3) assumes that the reasonable buyer should have gone into the market, immediately following the seller's breach of contract, and bought substitute goods.[1809] Section 51(3) is only a "prima facie" rule, and will not apply when the parties ought, at the time of making the contract, to have contemplated as reasonable men that the rule would not compensate the buyer for his loss, should the seller fail to deliver.[1810] Nor will it apply if it is inappropriate in special circumstances.[1811]

An available market   The meaning of "available market" has already been considered,[1812] which is in general as applicable to the buyer's claim as it is to the seller's.[1813] The buyer is naturally concerned with an available market in the sense of his ability to *buy* substitute goods, i.e. the ready capacity of willing sellers to supply quickly goods of the relevant category.[1814] Thus if the demand for the goods   **44-389**

[1807] When s.51(3) applies, and the market price at the time of the breach is the same as, or less than, the contract price, the buyer is still entitled to nominal damages: *Erie County Natural Gas and Fuel Co Ltd v Carroll* [1911] A.C. 105, 117–118, PC (citing *Valpy v Oakeley* (1851) 16 Q.B. 941; and *Griffiths v Perry* (1859) 1 E. & E. 680). cf. *Charter v Sullivan* [1957] 2 Q.B. 117. See also Vol.I, para.26-010. "The contract price/market price differential is not a computation of lost profit": *Glencore Energy UK Ltd v Cirrus Oil Services Ltd* [2014] EWHC 87 (Comm) at [98], see above, para.44-368.

[1808] See Vol.I, paras 26-087 et seq.

[1809] The injured party should ordinarily go out into the market to make a substitute contract to mitigate his loss: *Golden Strait Corp v Nippon Yusen Kubishika Kaisha* [2007] UKHL 12, [2007] 2 A.C. 353 at [79]; *Deutsche Bank AG v Total Global Steel Ltd* [2012] EWHC 1201 (Comm) at [160]. The purpose for which the buyer wanted the goods is normally irrelevant: hence, where the buyer is a non-profit-making organisation the ordinary rule still applies: *Diamond Cutting-Works Federation Ltd v Triefus Co Ltd* [1956] 1 Lloyd's Rep. 216, 227. On the possible relevance of the buyer's lack of financial resources, see above paras 26-091—26-094.

[1810] *Bence Graphics International Ltd v Fasson UK Ltd* [1998] Q.B. 87 (see below, paras 44-413, 44-415) cf. on the analogous s.50(3): *Thompson Ltd v Robinson (Gunmakers) Ltd* [1955] Ch. 177 (see above, para.44-371).

[1811] See below, paras 44-400, 44-405. *Carbopego-Abastecimento de Combustives SA v Amci Export Corp* [2006] EWHC 72 (Comm), [2006] 1 Lloyd's Rep. 736 (date of breach assessment need not be followed if it would give rise to injustice). cf. *Golden Strait Corp v Nippon Yusen Kubishika Kaisha (The Golden Victory)* [2007] UKHL 12, [2007] 2 A.C. 353; in *Bunge SA v Nidera BV* [2013] EWHC 84 (Comm), [2013] 1 Lloyd's Rep. 621 at [55] the judge questioned whether the *Golden Victory* should apply to one-off sales contracts. An appeal was dismissed by the Court of Appeal on other grounds [203] EWCA Civ 1628, [2014] 1 Lloyd's Rep. 404 (see above, para.26-082). The Supreme Court confirmed that the market price rule should be applied at the date of delivery. But disagreeing with the judge and Court of Appeal applied the principle in *The Golden Victory* which allows contingencies other than a change in the market price to be taken into account if subsequent events show that they would have reduced the value of performance even without the defaulter's renunciation [2015] UKSC 43, [16], [18], [85]. As to the question whether the subsection is appropriate when the buyer has paid the price to the seller in advance of the time fixed for delivery, and the market price rises between the time when the seller fails to deliver and the judgment in favour of the buyer, see *Benjamin's Sale of Goods*, 10th edn (2017), para.17-009; Peel [2016] L.Q.R. 177 and Yip and Goh [2016] J.B.L. 335. On the possible relevance of the buyer's lack of financial resources, see above paras 26-091—26-094.

[1812] See above, paras 44-368—44-378.

[1813] Lawson (1969) 43 A.L.J. 106, 113.

[1814] cf. see above, paras 44-368—44-378. Where goods are in short supply, so that retail sellers have agreed to a fixed price for selling the goods, a "black market" operating in defiance of contractual obligations has been treated as relevant to fix the market price when that is the only source of substitute goods available to the disappointed buyer: *Mouatt v Betts Motors Ltd* [1959] A.C. 71; *British Motor Trade Association v Gilbert* [1951] 2 T.L.R. 514. In *Air Studios (Lyndhurst) Ltd v Lombard*

exceeds the supply, so that some prospective buyers are unable to obtain the goods they wish, the rule in s.51(3) will not apply.[1815] An excessive price may show that the supply of the goods is insufficient to constitute an "available market".[1816] The willing sellers should be immediately accessible to the buyer, and within a reasonable distance of the place fixed by the contract for delivery.[1817] But the question of the time within which the substitute goods are available may depend on the nature of the goods in question and the business situation of the buyer.[1818] Where the buyer needed to obtain 15,000 tons of lard for immediate delivery in the United Kingdom, the House of Lords apparently accepted[1819] that there could be an available market from the buyer's point of view when he could buy in the United States of America, for delivery to ports for shipment to the United Kingdom, smaller quantities separately (up to 2,000 tons at a time) and spread over a period. In another case, where the sellers failed to deliver goods of merchantable quality at a United Kingdom port, the Court of Appeal held[1820] that the fact that there was a market for the purchase of similar goods in India did not require the buyers to mitigate by ordering substitute goods from India.

44-390 **The relevant time for taking the market price**   Section 51(3) specifies "the time or times when [the goods] ought to have been delivered or (if no time was fixed)[1821] at the time of the refusal to deliver". The terms of the contract will normally fix the relevant time.[1822] When the contract specifies that delivery is to be made by separate instalments at different times, the market price for each instalment is taken separately at the date when the particular instalment should have been delivered.[1823] Where the contract fixes a period within which the seller is to make delivery of the goods, the time for fixing the market price in the event of non-delivery is the last possible time within that period.[1824] If the contract requires the seller to deliver the

---

North Central Plc [2012] EWHC 3162 (QB), [2013] 1 Lloyd's Rep. 63, it was said that there may be a market for used goods even if the precise model or brand sold was not available: "the availability of equivalent second-hand goods capable of performing the same functions in much the same way would constitute an available market for 'the goods in question'. A buyer of such equivalent goods would be in the same financial position as if the contract had been performed" (at [93]). However, it was held there was no relevant market when there was only a possibility that equivalent goods would become available within about three months (at [95]).

[1815] cf. *Charter v Sullivan* [1957] 2 Q.B. 117 (the opposite case, where the buyer defaulted in this situation: see above, para.44–372).

[1816] cf. *O'Hanlan v GW Ry* (1865) 6 B. S. 484, 494.

[1817] Reasonableness is judged from the buyer's point of view: *Garnac Grain Co Inc v HMF Faure and Fairclough Ltd* [1968] A.C. 1130; *Lesters Leather and Skin Co Ltd v Home and Overseas Brokers Ltd* (1948) 64 T.L.R. 569. See above, paras 44–373—44–374, and cf. *Hasell v Bagot, Shakes and Lewis Ltd* (1911) 13 C.L.R. 374.

[1818] cf. *Charter v Sullivan* [1957] 2 Q.B. 117 at 133–134 (see above, para.44–372).

[1819] *Garnac Grain Co Inc v HMF Faure and Fairclough Ltd*, above, at 1138. cf. the different opinion in the same case in the Court of Appeal: [1966] 1 Q.B. 650, 687. cf. also *Petrotrade Inc v Stinnes Handel GmbH* [1995] 1 Lloyd's Rep. 142 (see above, para.44–370).

[1820] *Lesters Leather and Skin Co Ltd v Home and Overseas Brokers Ltd* (1948) 64 T.L.R. 569 (snake skins).

[1821] Time may be fixed by reference to the happening of a future event, e.g. the arrival of a ship at a certain destination: *Melachrino v Nickoll and Knight* [1920] 1 K.B. 693, 696 ("if no time was fixed" does not apply to anticipatory repudiation by the seller: see below, paras 44–393—44–394).

[1822] See above, paras 44–236, 44–237, 44–236 et seq.

[1823] *Brown v Muller* (1872) L.R. 7 Ex. 319; *Roper v Johnson* (1873) L.R. 8 C.P. 167; *Re Voss* (1873) L.R. 16 Eq. 155.

[1824] *Leigh v Paterson* (1818) 8 Taunt. 540, 541. cf. see above, para.44–374.

goods after transporting them to a specified destination, it is the normal[1825] rule that the time and place of the final destination are the time and place which are relevant for fixing the relevant market price.[1826] If the obligation imposed on the seller is to deliver the goods on a fixed date, it may be assumed that he has the whole of the usual business hours of that day in which to make delivery.[1827] In these circumstances the relevant time for taking the market price under s.51(3) should be the first practical opportunity which the buyer reasonably[1828] had to buy in the market, e.g. normally on the next business day.[1829]

No time fixed for delivery[1830]   A Divisional Court has decided[1831] that a contract **44-391** for delivery of the goods within a reasonable time is not a contract with a fixed time for delivery within s.51(3); but the Court of Appeal in the same case expressly reserved its opinion[1832] on this point.[1833] It is submitted that the natural application of the concluding words of s.51(3) would be to a contract where the seller was to deliver at the request of the buyer.[1834] Where delivery is to be made within a reasonable time of the making of the contract,[1835] the relevant market price should not necessarily be that prevailing at the date of the seller's refusal to deliver but at the time, perhaps later than the refusal, when it would have been reasonable for the seller to deliver.[1836]

Postponement of time fixed for delivery   If the time fixed for delivery was **44-392**

[1825] cf. *Van den Hurk v R Martens Co Ltd* [1920] 1 K.B. 850 (the parties knew that the goods could not be examined until the time they finally reached the sub-buyer: see below, para.44-410).

[1826] *Melachrino v Nickoll and Knight* [1920] 1 K.B. 693; *ABD (Metals and Waste) Ltd v Anglo Chemical and Ore Co Ltd* [1955] 2 Lloyd's Rep. 456, 466. On the relevant time in FOB and CIF contracts, see *Benjamin's Sale of Goods*, 10th edn (2017), paras 19-192—19-203, 20-121 et seq., 21-032.

[1827] cf. *Leigh v Paterson* (1818) 8 Taunt. 540. cf. also s.29(5) (see above, para.44-249).

[1828] See Vol.I, para.26-090. In *Bear Stearns Bank Plc v Forum Global Equity Ltd* [2007] EWHC 1576 (Comm) (a case involving shares rather than goods) Andrew Smith J. held that the question is whether the buyer was reasonable in delaying making a purchase (at [214]).

[1829] *Kaines (UK) Ltd v Osterreichische Warrenhandelsgesellschaft, etc.* [1993] 2 Lloyd's Rep. 1, 11, 12. cf. *Gainsford v Carroll* (1824) 2 B. & C. 624, 625 (the buyer "might have purchased" similar goods "the very day after the contract was broken"); *Roper v Johnson* (1873) L.R. 8 C.P. 167 at 179 ("... there is no breach until that day has passed"); *Gelmini v Moriggia* [1913] 2 K.B. 549 (duty to pay on a certain day: the cause of action is complete on the following day). It is submitted that the (obiter) view of Lord Wilberforce in *Bremer Handelsgesellschaft mbH v Vanden Avenne-Izegem PVBA* [1978] 2 Lloyd's Rep. 109, 117, that s.51 provides "for damages to be ascertained by reference to the price as on the last day for performance" should not be followed. (The case concerned a special clause in the contract, referring to "the date of default" which was construed to mean the day immediately following the last day for performance, on the ground that this accorded "with commercial reality and business sense": [1978] 2 Lloyd's Rep. 109 at 117, 129, 131.) See also *C Czarnikow Ltd v Bunge Co Ltd* [1987] 1 Lloyd's Rep, 202, 205; *Benjamin's Sale of Goods*, para.17-008. cf. the *Golden Strait* case [2007] UKHL 12, [2007] 2 A.C. 353 at [79]–[80] (see above, para.26-082).

[1830] On anticipatory repudiation, see below, paras 44-393—44-394.

[1831] *Millett v Van Heek Co* [1920] 3 K.B. 535. cf. see above, para.44-375.

[1832] [1921] 2 K.B. 369.

[1833] In *Tai Hing Cotton Mill Ltd v Kamsing Knitting Factory* [1979] A.C. 91, 104, the Privy Council doubted whether the second limb of s.51(3) had any meaning at all.

[1834] See the dictum of Atkin L.J. [1921] 2 K.B. 369 at 378. But see *Tai Hing Cotton Mill Ltd v Kamsing Knitting Factory* [1979] A.C. 91, 104.

[1835] Or from some other fixed point of time.

[1836] *Tai Hing Cotton Mill Ltd v Kamsing Knitting Factory* [1971] A.C. 91. cf. *Melachrino v Nickoll and Knight* [1920] 1 K.B. 693, 696.

postponed at the seller's request,[1837] but he fails to deliver the goods at or before the postponed date of delivery, the breach occurs at the latter date[1838] and the damages should be assessed on the basis of the market price at that date.[1839] If the request for postponement of the delivery date was made by the buyer, and the seller agreed to the postponement but later repudiated his obligation to deliver,[1840] this repudiation will constitute a breach by the seller,[1841] so that the damages should be calculated by reference to the market price at the date of the seller's repudiation.[1842]

44-393 **The seller's anticipatory repudiation: repudiation accepted**[1843] Where the seller, before the date fixed for delivery of the goods, repudiates his liability under the contract, the buyer has a choice.[1844] If he treats the repudiation as an immediate breach of contract, the relevant date for taking the market price is, prima facie, and subject to the rules on mitigation, the due date for delivery—not the date of the repudiation[1845] nor the date of the buyer's acceptance of the repudiation.[1846] If the buyer's claim is heard before the date for delivery arrives, the court must attempt to estimate what the market price is likely to be at that date,[1847] e.g. by taking into

---

[1837] But a mere *forbearance* by the buyer from insisting upon delivery upon the original contractual date for delivery will not entitle him to claim damages on the basis of a higher market price at a later date: *Re Voss* (1873) L.R. 16 Eq. 155 (distinguishing *Ogle v Earl Vane* (1868) L.R. 3 Q.B. 272).

[1838] If a period was fixed within which the postponed delivery was to take place, the last day of the period should be taken: *Ogle v Earl Vane* (1868) L.R. 3 Q.B. 272. cf. *Leigh v Paterson* (1818) 8 Taunt. 540, 541. If there was a simple waiver by the buyer of the date fixed for delivery, without a specific date being substituted, a reasonable time (presumably calculated from the due date) is taken as the new date for delivery: *Sheik Mohammad Habib Ullah v Bird Co* (1921) 37 T.L.R. 405, 406; *Johnson Matthey Bankers Ltd v The State Trading Corp of India Ltd* [1984] 1 Lloyd's Rep. 427, 436–437.

[1839] *Ogle v Earl Vane* (1868) L.R. 3 Q.B. 272 (this decision was mentioned with approval by the House of Lords in *Johnson v Agnew* [1980] A.C. 367, 401); *Blackburn Bobbin Co Ltd v TW Allen Sons Ltd* [1918] 1 K.B. 540, 553–554; affirmed on another ground: [1918] 2 K.B. 467; *Sheik Mohammad Habib Ullah v Bird Co* (1921) 37 T.L.R. 405, 406, PC (accepting the principles in *Tyers v Rosedale and Ferryhill Iron Co Ltd* (1875) L.R. 10 Ex. 195, where the buyer requested postponement) (see below); the *Johnson Matthey case* [1984] 1 Lloyd's Rep. 427. cf. above, para.44-376.

[1840] Unless there was a binding variation (viz supported by consideration), the seller may by giving reasonable notice to the buyer that he retracts his agreement to the postponement, oblige the buyer to accept the goods upon the expiry of that notice: see Vol.I, paras 4-082, 22-040 et seq.

[1841] *Tyers v Rosedale and Ferryhill Iron Co Ltd*, above. cf. *Hartley v Hymans* [1920] 3 K.B. 475 (see above, para.44-376).

[1842] *Tyers v Rosedale and Ferryhill Iron Co Ltd* (1875) L.R. 10 Ex. 195. If at the request of the buyer, the delivery date was postponed indefinitely, the buyer may give notice fixing the date for delivery a reasonable time thereafter: (1875) L.R. 10 Ex. 195 at 199. (As to postponement of delivery by instalments over a period, see also at 199.)

[1843] cf. above, para.44-380. See George [1971] J.B.L. 109.

[1844] *Fercometal SARL v Mediterranean Shipping Co SA* [1989] A.C. 788; *Kaines (UK) Ltd v Osterreichische Warrenhandelsgesellschaft, etc.* [1993] 2 Lloyd's Rep. 1. See Vol.I, para.24-022. The buyer is not bound to act "reasonably" in choosing between his alternative courses of action: see Vol.I, para.26-090.

[1845] The last part of s.51(3), see above ("if no time was fixed ...") does not apply to an anticipatory breach by the seller: *Tai Hing Cotton Mill Ltd v Kamsing Knitting Factory* [1979] A.C. 91, following *Millett v Van Heek Co* [1921] 2 K.B. 369 (Court of Appeal affirmed [1920] 3 K.B. 535). See also *Bunge SA v Nidera BV* [2015] UKSC 43.

[1846] *Garnac Grain Co Inc v HMF Faure and Fairclough Ltd* [1968] A.C. 1130, 1140; *Tai Hing Cotton Mill Ltd v Kamsing Knitting Factory* [1979] A.C. 91 at 102. (But in this case, the PC was not asked to consider whether the rules on mitigation applied.) See Note (1978) 41 M.L.R. 486. The earlier authorities were *Roper v Johnson* (1873) L.R. 8 C.P. 167; and *Melachrino v Nickoll and Knight* [1920] 1 K.B. 693, 699.

[1847] *Melachrino v Nickoll and Knight* [1920] 1 K.B. 693, 699; *Millett v Van Heek Co* [1921] 2 K.B. 369;

account the current trend of the market. However, under the rules of mitigation[1848] the buyer must, following his acceptance of the repudiation, take reasonable steps to reduce his loss, e.g. by buying substitute goods in the market.[1849] If the seller[1850] fails to produce evidence to show that the buyer ought reasonably to have bought substitute goods at a time earlier than the date fixed for delivery under the contract, the buyer's damages should be calculated with reference to the market price at that date.[1851] But where the seller can prove that the buyer should have mitigated his loss by repurchasing before the due date, the relevant market price is that existing at the date the buyer ought reasonably[1852] to have bought the substitute goods.[1853] However, if the buyer accepts the anticipatory repudiation but does not in fact mitigate by repurchasing in the market when he ought reasonably to have done so, the market price may fall between that date and the date fixed for delivery: it has been held that in these circumstances the buyer's damages will be assessed by reference to the lower price at the later date.[1854]

Repudiation not accepted If the buyer chooses not to accept the seller's anticipatory repudiation, it is treated as a "nullity"[1855] and the contract continues to bind both parties[1856]: the buyer will then await the date fixed for delivery, and the seller will commit a breach of contract only if he then fails to deliver. Thus, the seller may change his mind before the due date and (without breach of contract) fulfil his contractual obligation by delivering on that date[1857]; or the contract may be terminated without a breach by the seller, e.g. by the seller exercising a right under

44-394

Roper v Johnson (1873) L.R. 8 C.P. 167. cf. *The Mihalis Angelos* [1971] 1 Q.B. 164. A discount should be made in respect of any accelerated receipt (through the damages award) of any sum due in the future: cf. *Lavarack v Woods of Colchester Ltd* [1967] 1 Q.B. 278; and see Vol.I, para.26-009.

[1848] See Vol.I, paras 26-087 et seq. It is not strictly a "duty" to mitigate: the buyer's damages are assessed on the basis that he should have acted reasonably so as to mitigate his loss.

[1849] *Kaines (UK) Ltd v Osterreichische, etc.* [1993] 2 Lloyd's Rep. 1; *Melachrino v Nickoll and Knight* [1920] 1 K.B. 693, 697; *Garnac Grain Co Inc v HMF Faure and Fairclough Ltd* [1966] 1 Q.B. 650, 687 (on appeal [1968] A.C. 1130, 1140). If the buyer reasonably attempts to mitigate by buying substitute goods in the market, he is entitled to have his damages assessed by reference to the market price at the date of the repurchase, despite the fact that the market price happened to be lower by the time the due date for delivery arrived: *Melachrino v Nickoll and Knight* [1920] 1 K.B. 693 at 697, 699. cf. *Roth Co v Taysen Townsend Co* (1896) 12 T.L.R. 211 (buyer's anticipatory refusal: see above, para.44-380). See also Vol.I, para.26-112.

[1850] The onus of proof is on the contract-breaker: *Roper v Johnson* (1873) L.R. 8 C.P. 167; *Garnac Grain Co Inc v HMF Faure and Fairclough Ltd* [1968] A.C. 1130.

[1851] *Roper v Johnson*, above; *Garnac Grain Co Inc v HMF Faure and Fairclough Ltd*, above, at 1140; *Tai Hing Cotton Mill Ltd v Kamsing Knitting Factory* [1979] A.C. 91 at 105. (The seller in this case did not argue that the buyer should have mitigated by buying in the market between the date he accepted the seller's repudiation and the date when delivery could have been required under the contract: the market price was falling between the two dates.)

[1852] The buyer is allowed a "reasonable time" after his acceptance of the seller's breach before he must repurchase: *Kaines (UK) Ltd v Osterreichische, etc.* [1993] 2 Lloyd's Rep. 1 at 11, 12 (buyer should have repurchased on the next day). cf. *Tredegar Iron and Coal Co Ltd v Hawthorn Bros Co* (1902) 18 T.L.R. 716.

[1853] *Kaines (UK) Ltd v Osterreichische, etc.* [1993] 2 Lloyd's Rep. 1; *Melachrino v Nickoll and Knight* [1920] 1 K.B. 693 at 697, 699. cf. above, para.44-380.

[1854] This was the actual decision in *Melachrino v Nickoll and Knight* [1920] 1 K.B. 693, 698 (although the judgment contains many other propositions cited in this paragraph).

[1855] *Phillpotts v Evans* (1839) 5 M. & W. 475, 477; *White and Carter (Councils) Ltd v McGregor* [1962] A.C. 413, 444.

[1856] *Fercometal SARL v Mediterranean Shipping Co SA* [1989] A.C. 788.

[1857] *Leigh v Paterson* (1818) 8 Taunt. 540.

the contract to cancel it,[1858] or be discharged by frustration.[1859] The rules on mitigation[1860] do not apply to the buyer until the seller commits an actual breach, and thus the buyer's damages are assessed with reference to the market price at the date of the breach.[1861]

44-395 **The market price** The methods of ascertaining the market price in a buyer's claim are the same as in a seller's claim[1862]; but when the buyer is claiming under s.51(3), the relevant price is the *buying* price at which the buyer could obtain equivalent goods.[1863] In *Williams Bros v Ed T Agius Ltd*,[1864] the House of Lords held that where there is evidence of the market price at the date of the seller's breach, the buyer's damages for non-delivery cannot be reduced by reference to the fact that he had actually resold goods of the same description at a price lower than what happened to be the market price at the time fixed for delivery. In these circumstances, the buyer is entitled to fulfil his obligations under the sub-contract by buying equivalent goods in the market at the price current at the time of non-delivery.[1865] Where normal proof of the market price at the date of the seller's breach is not available, other evidence may be relied upon, e.g. the price at which a sub-buyer had agreed to take the goods from the buyer,[1866] or the price in an offer to buy from a

---

[1858] cf. the *Fercometal* case [1989] A.C. 788.

[1859] *Avery v Bowden* (1855) 5 E. & B. 714; affirmed (1856) 6 E. & B. 953.

[1860] During the interval, the buyer may at any time decide to accept the seller's repudiation (provided it has not been retracted by the seller), whereupon the rules on mitigation will apply.

[1861] *Leigh v Paterson*, above (damages assessed by reference to the market price on the last day of the period fixed for delivery); *Brown v Muller* (1872) L.R. 7 Ex. 319; *Tai Hing Cotton Mill Ltd v Kamsing Knitting Factory* [1979] A.C. 91, 104. See also the explanation of *C Sharpe Co Ltd v Nosawa* [1917] 2 K.B. 814 in *Benjamin's Sale of Goods*, 10th edn (2017), paras 19-195—19-197. The buyer's damages cannot be reduced because the market price was lower at the date of the repudiation (or at any date between the repudiation and the due date for delivery): *Tredegar Iron and Coal Co Ltd v Hawthorn Bros Co* (1902) 18 T.L.R. 716 (buyer's breach).

[1862] See above, paras 44-377—44-378 (also paras 44-368—44-375).

[1863] See above, para.44-373. In *Air Studios (Lyndhurst) Ltd v Lombard North Central Plc* [2012] EWHC 3162 (QB), [2013] 1 Lloyd's Rep. 63 it was said that there may be a market for used goods even if the precise model or brand sold was not available: "the availability of equivalent second-hand goods capable of performing the same functions in much the same way would constitute an available market for 'the goods in question'. A buyer of such equivalent goods would be in the same financial position as if the contract had been performed" (at [93]). "The best evidence of market value is constituted by arm's length deals actually made in the market. The last transaction effected effectively sets the benchmark": *Glencore Energy UK Ltd v Cirrus Oil Services Ltd* [2014] EWHC 87 (Comm) at [70]. The relevant market price may also depend on the relevant market relationship, e.g. whether between wholesaler and retailer, or between retailer and private buyer, or any other relationship. But the individual characteristics of the claimant (e.g. his personal skill in negotiating) are not relevant: *Shearson Lehman Hutton Inc v Maclaine Watson Co Ltd (No.2)* [1990] 3 All E.R. 723, 726.

[1864] [1914] A.C. 510 (see below, para.44-401).

[1865] Even if the sub-sale was of the identical goods bought by the buyer from the defaulting seller, the buyer's damages are nevertheless assessed with reference to the market price, since the buyer's liability in damages to the sub-buyer might easily exceed the price in the sub-sale: [1914] A.C. 510 at 523. But cf. *Bence Graphics International Ltd v Fasson UK Ltd* [1998] Q.B. 87 (see below, paras 44-413, 44-415).

[1866] cf. *Williams Bros v Ed T Agius Ltd*, above. But a sub-sale with a different place of delivery, or under different terms, may not be relevant: *Ayreh v Lawrence Kostoris Son Ltd* [1967] 1 Lloyd's Rep. 63, 72–73. cf. *Macklin v Newbury Sanitary Laundry* (1919) 63 S.J. 337 (buyer's breach: see above, para.44-377).

third party, or the amount paid by the buyer in compromising disputes relating to the market value of similar goods at the relevant time.[1867]

Substitute goods obtained at below market price Where there is normal proof **44-396** of the market price at the place and date fixed for delivery, damages for non-delivery should be calculated by reference to that price despite the fact that the buyer had succeeded in obtaining substitute goods at a price lower than that price, or even at no cost to himself (e.g. by gift).[1868] If the buyer does not buy substitute goods in the market immediately following the seller's failure to deliver, his damages should be assessed by reference to the market price at that date despite the fact that the buyer later bought substitute goods at a lower price.[1869] The position may be different if the buyer later bought the *same* goods from the seller at a price lower than the market price. In one case,[1870] the buyer justifiably rejected the goods on the ground of their defective quality. There were continuous negotiations[1871] between the parties following this rejection, leading to the buyer finally accepting the same goods from the seller at a reduced price. The Court of Appeal held that the market price rule in s.51(3) did not apply: the buyer had suffered no loss since the price at which he obtained the goods was less than the market price for similar goods at the date of the seller's breach of contract.

Damages for non-delivery in the absence of an available market If there was **44-397** no available market for goods of the contractual description at the time and place of the seller's failure to deliver (e.g. because the goods were to be specially manufactured[1872]) the buyer's damages must be assessed under the general rule of s.51(2), see above.[1873] The assessment must be made on the basis of the value[1874]

[1867] *Hong Guan Co Ltd v R Jumabhoy Sons Ltd* [1960] A.C. 684, 703–704. The court may also infer the approximate market price on a given date from evidence that there was a steady decline in that price between an earlier and a later date: *Tai Hing Cotton Mill Ltd v Kamsing Knitting Factory* [1979] A.C. 91, 106.

[1868] The buyer's opportunity to buy at the lower price did not arise only because of the seller's breach: see *Joyner v Weeks* [1891] 2 Q.B. 31, 34; and cf. *Campbell Mostyn (Provisions) Ltd v Barnett Trading Co* [1954] 1 Lloyd's Rep. 65. cf. also above, para.44-377; *Erie County Natural Gas and Fuel Co Ltd v Carroll* [1911] A.C. 105 (see below, para.44-398).

[1869] This reasoning is supported by the analogous case of the buyer's breach: *Campbell Mostyn (Provisions) Ltd v Barnett Trading Co*, above; *Jamal v Moolla Dawood* [1916] 1 A.C. 175, 179 (on which cases, see above, paras 44-373—44-374).

[1870] *R Pagnan Fratelli v Corbisa Industrial Agropacuaria* [1970] 1 W.L.R. 1306 (distinguished in *Mobil North Sea Ltd v PJ Pipe Valve Co* [2001] 2 All E.R. (Comm) 289). cf. *Bence Graphics International Ltd v Fasson UK Ltd* [1998] Q.B. 87 (see below, paras 44-413, 44-415). cf. also *Nimmo v Habton Farms* [2003] 1 All E.R. 1136 (breach of warranty of authority).

[1871] The final purchase was not "an independent or disconnected transaction": [1970] 1 W.L.R. 1306 at 1315. The decision in *Pagnan* would not preclude a claim for any consequential loss caused by the delay between the date fixed for delivery in the original contract and the date of actual delivery under the new arrangements.

[1872] *Hinde v Liddell* (1875) L.R. 10 Q.B. 265. The effect of governmental regulation of the market may also mean that there is no available market in which the buyer can obtain substitute goods: *J Leavey Co Ltd v Geo H Hirst Co Ltd* [1944] K.B. 24, 28.

[1873] The fact that there is no available market in which the buyer can purchase the goods does not mean that the buyer's loss should be measured by the profit the buyer might have made from the goods: *Air Studios (Lyndhurst) Ltd v Lombard North Central Plc* [2012] EWHC 3162 (QB), [2013] 1 Lloyd's Rep. 63 at [100]. Nor does the fact that the buyer has not purchased a substitute mean that it has suffered no loss (at [102]). The buyer's damages should be assessed by reference to the cost of procuring the nearest equivalent goods (at [103]).

of the contract goods at the time and place of the breach,[1875] which may be ascertained by any relevant evidence, such as the cost of the nearest equivalent,[1876] or a resale price, or the profits which the buyer would have made had he acquired the goods and manufactured them into other articles, as the seller knew that he intended to do.[1877] The price under a resale may be put in evidence in order to show "the real value of the goods", despite the fact that the seller did not know of the resale[1878]; but a resale price fixed some months earlier is not satisfactory evidence of the value of the goods at the time of the breach of contract.[1879] The buyer must mitigate if reasonable steps are open to him, but what is reasonable is a question of fact.[1880] Thus, where the seller tendered to the buyer a bill of lading which was not accurately dated, but the buyer could nevertheless have legally compelled his sub-buyers to accept the goods, the Court of Appeal held that the buyer had not failed to mitigate when he refused to enforce the sub-contracts because to do so in the circumstances would have injured his commercial reputation by giving him a bad name in the trade.[1881]

44-398 **Purchase of near equivalent** The buyer may[1882] be able to buy substitute goods from another source: in these circumstances, the price at which he reasonably[1883] bought them will be the basis for assessing his damages under the general principle of s.51(2).[1884] Provided that the buyer's mitigating action was reasonable in all the circumstances,[1885] he may recover as damages the reasonable cost of obtaining goods which are the nearest available equivalent in quality and price to goods of the contractual description[1886]; he may also claim the extra expense of adapting the substitute goods to suit his requirements, to the extent that goods of the contractual

---

[1874] The "value" of goods for which no substitutes are available may, in appropriate circumstances, include an element of subjective or idiosyncratic value: Harris, Ogus and Phillips (1979) 95 L.Q.R. 581 (applied, but not in the context of a sale of goods, in *Ruxley Electronics and Construction Ltd v Forsyth* [1996] A.C. 344 at 360; and in *Farley v Skinner* [2001] UKHL 49, [2002] 2 A.C. 732 at [21]) (see Vol.I, paras 26-151 et seq.).

[1875] *Borries v Hutchinson* (1865) 18 C.B.(N.S.) 445, 465; *Elbinger Actien-Gesellschaft v Armstrong* (1874) L.R. 9 Q.B. 473, 476; *Hinde v Liddell* (1875) L.R. 10 Q.B. 265.

[1876] *Hughes v Pendragon Sabre Ltd (t/a Porsche Centre Bolton)* [2016] EWCA Civ 18.

[1877] *J Leavey Co Ltd v George H Hirst Co Ltd* [1944] K.B. 24 at 29.

[1878] *Grébert-Borgnis v J and W Nugent* (1885) 15 Q.B.D. 85, 89–90; *The Arpad* [1934] P. 189, 210, 219–221, 230 (breach of contract of carriage treated as analogous to seller's failure to deliver: at 223, 233).

[1879] *The Arpad* [1934] P. 189, 210 (five months earlier).

[1880] *Payzu Ltd v Saunders* [1919] 2 K.B. 581 at 588, 589. cf. *The Solholt* [1983] 1 Lloyd's Rep. 605 (see below, para.44-399). See Vol.I, para.26-102.

[1881] *James Finlay Co Ltd v NV Kwik Hoo Tong HM* [1929] 1 K.B. 400, 410, 415, 418. Compare the case in which the victim of a breach pays compensation to a sub-purchaser though not legally obliged to do so: above, para.26-036.

[1882] It is submitted that (despite the assumption to the contrary in *C Sharpe Co Ltd v Nosawa* [1917] 2 K.B. 814, 820) the buyer is not *obliged* to buy the nearest equivalent in mitigation of his loss: see *Benjamin's Sale of Goods*, 10th edn (2017), para.17-025.

[1883] The buyer has a reasonable time to decide whether or not to buy substitute goods: *C Sharpe Co Ltd v Nosawa* [1917] 2 K.B. 814, 820.

[1884] cf. the similar rule in the case of a seller's claim for damages (see above, para.44-379).

[1885] *Hinde v Liddell* (1875) L.R. 10 Q.B. 265, 268, 270; *Erie County Natural Gas and Fuel Co Ltd v Carroll* [1911] A.C. 105, 117. cf. *Le Blanche v LNW Ry* (1876) 1 C.P.D. 286, 302. It will normally be unreasonable for the buyer to order the manufacture of substitute goods, where none are readily available: *Elbinger Actien-Gesellschaft v Armstrong* (1874) L.R. 9 Q.B. 473; *Sealace Shipping Co Ltd v Oceanvoice Ltd (The Alecos M)* [1991] 1 Lloyd's Rep. 120 (criticised by Treitel (1991) 107 L.Q.R. 364) ("spare propeller" not included in sale of ship).

[1886] *Hinde v Liddell* (1875) L.R. 10 Q.B. 265. See also *Blackburn Bobbin Co Ltd v TW Allen Sons Ltd* [1918] 1 K.B. 540, 554 (the appeal was decided on another ground: [1918] 2 K.B. 467). The near-

description would suit these requirements.[1887] However, the courts are anxious to prevent the buyer from receiving an extra benefit at the seller's expense. If the substitute goods bought by the buyer were later resold by him at an extra profit because they were of better quality or higher value than goods of the contractual description, the extra profit must be set off against the cost of buying the substitute goods which the buyer claims from the defaulting seller.[1888] But if the buyer acts reasonably in buying "near equivalent" goods for his own use (and not for resale nor for the purpose of making a profit through using them),[1889] it is submitted that he should not be compelled, by a reduction in his damages for their cost, to "pay for" an extra benefit to himself because of some advantage which the substitute goods have over those of the contractual description.[1890]

Offers by the seller to mitigate his breach   The rules of mitigation do not oblige **44-399** the buyer to accept from the seller goods which do not conform with the contractual standard and which he is therefore entitled to reject.[1891] Thus, where the buyer properly rejects goods on the ground of their defective quality, he is not obliged to accept them when the seller offers them in mitigation of his breach of contract.[1892] However, the buyer may be bound to accept a reasonable offer by the seller to mitigate his breach by supplying goods which are in fact up to the contractual standard, but are to be delivered on different terms so far as the timing and method of payment are concerned.[1893] Thus, where sellers in breach offered to continue deliveries in accordance with the contract if the buyers would pay cash against each delivery in lieu of the agreed credit terms, the Court of Appeal held that it would have been reasonable for the buyers to have accepted the seller's bona fide offer and thus to have mitigated their loss.[1894] Even where the seller fails to take the initia-

---

est equivalent may be of superior quality and so higher in price than the contract goods: *Hinde v Liddell*, above; *Diamond Cutting Works v Treifus* [1956] 1 Lloyd's Rep. 216. cf. *Intertradex SA v Lesieur-Tourteaux SARL* [1978] 2 Lloyd's Rep. 509, 519. cf. also *Le Blanche v LNW Ry* (1876) 1 C.P.D. 286.

[1887] *Blackburn Bobbin Co Ltd v TW Allen Sons Ltd* [1918] 1 K.B. 540, 554.

[1888] *Hinde v Liddell* (1875) L.R. 10 Q.B. at 270; *Erie County Natural Gas and Fuel Co Ltd v Carroll*, above (see *Benjamin's Sale of Goods*, 10th edn (2017), para.17-024).

[1889] cf. *British Westinghouse Electric and Manufacturing Co Ltd v Underground Electric Rys* [1912] A.C. 673 (see below, para.44-414).

[1890] cf. *Harbutt's "Plasticine" Ltd v Wayne Tank and Pump Co Ltd* [1970] 1 Q.B. 447. (This decision has been overruled on another point: *Photo Production Ltd v Securicor Transport Ltd* [1980] A.C. 827.)

[1891] See above, para.44-066.

[1892] *Heaven and Kesterton Ltd v Etablissements Francois Albiac Cie* [1956] 2 Lloyd's Rep. 316, 321. cf. *R Pagnan Fratelli v Corbisa Industrial Agropacuaria* [1970] 1 W.L.R. 1306 (see above, para.44-396). The buyer may also be required to act reasonably in considering an offer by the seller to modify defective goods: *Manton Hire and Sales Ltd v Ash Manor Cheese Co Ltd* [2013] EWCA Civ 548 (on the facts the buyer had not acted unreasonably).

[1893] *Payzu Ltd v Saunders* [1919] 2 K.B. 581; *Heaven and Kesterton Ltd v Etablissements Francois Albiac Cie* [1956] 2 Lloyd's Rep. 316, 321. cf. *Houndsditch Warehouse Co Ltd v Waltex Ltd* [1944] K.B. 579 (genuine offer by seller to accept return of goods which buyer alleged not to correspond with sample).

[1894] *Payzu Ltd v Saunders* [1919] 2 K.B. 581. (The goods could not be obtained from any other source; nor was there any doubt about the seller's ability and willingness to fulfil his offer.) cf. above, para.26-102 and the criticism of Bridge (1989) 105 L.Q.R. 398. cf. where the seller refused to "guarantee" a substituted delivery date: *ABD (Metals and Waste) Ltd v Anglo-Chemical Ore Co Ltd* [1955] 2 Lloyd's Rep. 456.

tive, it may be reasonable for the buyer to minimise his loss by offering to repurchase the goods at a later date but at the original price.[1895]

44-400 **Loss of profits under sub-sale** Where a market price at the date of the seller's breach is ascertainable, a higher or lower price at which the buyer has resold the goods to a sub-buyer is generally irrelevant to the assessment of damages for the seller's failure to deliver.[1896] Thus, the seller cannot take advantage of the fact that the buyer, following the seller's failure to deliver, fulfilled his obligations under a resale by using other goods, and thereby made a greater profit on the resale than he would have done if the seller had not broken the contract.[1897] In the exceptional cases where the seller is liable for loss of profits or expenses under the sub-sale, his liability is based on the parties' reasonable contemplation of the consequences of a breach of the contract,[1898] and now, presumably, the limitation that there will not be liability if it was unreasonable to think that the buyer was assuming responsibility for such a loss.[1899] The buyer may have contracted to sell to his sub-buyer the very same goods as he bought from the seller,[1900] or he may have fixed the same delivery date in the contract of resale as in the original contract.[1901] In these two situations, when the seller fails to deliver on the due date, the buyer cannot, despite the presence of an available market, avoid loss under the contract of resale: but the buyer can recover damages for that loss only where the seller should have contemplated, at the time the original contract was made, both that the buyer was, or was probably,[1902] buying for resale,[1903] and that the buyer could perform his obligations under a contract of resale only by delivering the same goods.[1904] Thus,

---

[1895] *Sotiros Shipping Inc and Aeco Maritime SA v Sameiet Solholt (The Solholt)* [1983] 1 Lloyd's Rep. 605 (the buyer had cancelled the original contract on the ground of the seller's failure to deliver by the agreed date. The hypothetical offer by the buyer would have been without prejudice to his claim for damages for the delay).

[1896] *Williams Bros Ltd v Ed T Agius Ltd* [1914] A.C. 510; *James Finlay Co Ltd v NV Kwik Hoo Tong HM* [1929] 1 K.B. 400, 411; *The Arpad* [1934] P. 189, 214, 223, 230; *Kwei Tek Chao v British Traders and Shippers Ltd* [1954] 2 Q.B. 459, 489–490. Where the buyer is a trader, most sellers would be able to contemplate the possibility of resale: *The Arpad* [1934] P. 189, 230; *Kwei Tek Chao v British Traders and Shippers Ltd* [1954] 2 Q.B. 489. cf. however, *Bence Graphics International Ltd v Fasson UK Ltd* [1998] Q.B. 87 (see below, paras 44-413, 44-415). But the *Bence Graphics* case was distinguished in *Bear Stearns Bank Plc v Forum Global Equity Ltd* [2007] EWHC 1576 (Comm) (a case involving shares rather than goods) on the grounds that the Bear Stearns case was a case of non-delivery rather than of delivery of defective goods (at [208]).

[1897] *Sheik Mohammad Habib Ullah v Bird Co* (1921) 37 T.L.R. 405, PC.

[1898] *Biggin & Co Ltd v Permanite Ltd* [1951] 1 K.B. 422, 435–436. (Such contemplation depends on the knowledge, actual or imputed, of the seller at the time of the contract: see Vol.I, paras 26-117 et seq.)

[1899] *Transfield Shipping Inc v Mercator Shipping Inc (The Achilleas)* [2008] UKHL 48, [2009] 1 A.C. 61; see below, para.44-402.

[1900] *Williams Bros v Ed T Agius Ltd* [1914] A.C. 510 at 523; *The Arpad* [1934] P. 189 at 215.

[1901] *Patrick v Russo-British Grain Export Co Ltd* [1927] 2 K.B. 535, 541; *Kwei Tek Chao v British Traders and Shippers Ltd* [1954] 2 Q.B. 459 at 489–490.

[1902] *Re R and H Hall Ltd and WH Pim (Junior) Co's Arbitration* [1928] All E.R. Rep. 763, 766, 767, 769; *Patrick v Russo-British Grain Export Co Ltd* [1927] 2 K.B. 535, 540.

[1903] e.g. *Frank Mott Co Ltd v Muller Co (London) Ltd* (1922) 13 Ll.L. Rep. 492; *Household Machines Ltd v Cosmos Exporters Ltd* [1947] K.B. 217, 219. The seller may even know that the buyer has already entered into an existing sub-contract and was buying in order to fulfil that particular contract: *Aryeh v Lawrence Kostoris Son Ltd* [1967] 1 Lloyd's Rep. 63, 68.

[1904] *Re R and H Hall Ltd and WH Pim (Junior) Co's Arbitration* [1928] All E.R. Rep. 763; *Kwei Tek Chao v British Traders and Shippers Ltd* [1954] 2 Q.B. 459 at 489–490; *Aryeh v Lawrence Kostoris Son Ltd* [1967] 1 Lloyd's Rep. 63, 67–68, 72. cf. *Biggin & Co Ltd v Permanite Ltd* [1951] 1 K.B. 422 at 436; *Euro-Asian Oil SA (formerly Euro-Asian Oil AG) v Credit Suisse AG* [2018] EWCA Civ

in the leading case of *Hall v Pim*,[1905] the buyers bought a cargo under a CIF contract, which expressly contemplated that the buyer might resell during the voyage,[1906] and that any resale would be of the identifiable or named cargo, which meant that the buyers would necessarily be in default under the sub-contract if the sellers failed to deliver under the original contract.[1907] The buyers were able to recover the difference between the contract price and the resale price since "the seller in such a case contracted to put the buyer in a position to fulfil his sub-contracts if he entered into them".[1908] But the actual loss of profits on a resale will be awarded only if the terms of the resale were reasonable and usual.[1909]

Although the decision in *Hall v Pim* has been criticised,[1910] it is submitted that it **44-401** is sound in principle.[1911] It can be distinguished[1912] from another House of Lords' decision, *Williams v Agius*,[1913] on the ground[1914] that the original contract of sale in *Hall v Pim* contemplated that the buyer might resell the identical cargo, so that he would necessarily be in default under the sub-sale if the seller failed to deliver under the original sale; whereas in *Williams v Agius* the buyer could reasonably, under the rules of mitigation, have gone into the market to procure a substitute. Since the resale was not "for the identical article which was the subject of the principal sale",[1915] the buyers were entitled to fulfil their contract of resale by buying in the market at the date of the breach.[1916]

1720, [71]–[72] (see below, para.44-435).

[1905] *Re R and H Hall Ltd and WH Pim (Junior) Arbitration* [1928] All E.R. Rep. 763. See *Benjamin's Sale of Goods*, 10th edn (2017), paras 17-030—17-033.

[1906] [1928] All E.R. Rep. 763 at 765, 766, 768. This type of contract might, depending on the circumstances, be one where the sub-buyers are "identified" as third parties intended to have an enforceable claim against the seller under the Contracts (Rights of Third Parties) Act 1999: see above, Vol.I, para.18-090; see below, paras 44-428, 44-437.

[1907] [1928] All E.R. Rep. 763 at 766, 768, 769, 771.

[1908] [1928] All E.R. Rep. 763 at 765.

[1909] [1928] All E.R. Rep. 763 at 767, 768, 773. In *Household Machines Ltd v Cosmos Exporters Ltd* [1947] K.B. 217, where there was no available market for the goods, the damages were less than the actual profit, which was held to be "too high" (at 219). (This was applied in *Coastal International Trading Ltd v Maroil AG* [1988] 1 Lloyd's Rep. 92, 96.) cf. *Horne v Midland Ry* (1872) L.R. 7 C.P. 583; (1873) L.R. 8 C.P. 131 (delayed delivery under contract of carriage); *Victoria Laundry (Windsor) Ltd v Newman Industries Ltd* [1949] 2 K.B. 528 (delayed delivery under contract of sale: see below, para.44-408); *The Arpad* [1934] P. 189, 201.

[1910] In the Court of Appeal the decision has been said to be dependent on the special fact that the contract expressly provided for resale: *James Finlay Co Ltd v NV Kwik Hoo Tong HM* [1929] 1 K.B. 400, 410–412, 417–418. (cf. at 415, where Greer L.J. approved the decision.)

[1911] See *Benjamin's Sale of Goods*, 10th edn (2017), at paras 17-032—17-033. It is also significant that in *Koufos v C Czarnikow Ltd* [1969] 1 A.C. 350, the House of Lords frequently referred to statements made in *Hall v Pim* on the general question of remoteness of damage in contract, without any suggestion of disapproval of the actual decision in the case: above at 387–388, 405–406, 410, 414, 424. (See Vol.I, paras 26-125—26-127).

[1912] This was considered to be a difficulty in *James Finlay Co Ltd v NV Kwik Hoo Tong HM* [1929] 1 K.B. 400, 410, 415, 417.

[1913] *Williams Bros v Ed T Agius Ltd* [1914] A.C. 510 (see Benjamin at paras 17-032—17-033).

[1914] A further distinction is that in *Hall v Pim* the buyer, by reference to a higher resale price, claimed as damages a *larger* sum than "the market price at the breach" test would have given him; whereas in *Williams v Agius* the innocent buyer claimed damages on the basis of this, the normal test, but the defaulting seller argued that the buyer was entitled only to a reduced sum because the resale price happened to be *lower* than the market price at breach. But cf. *Bence Graphics International Ltd v Fasson UK Ltd* [1998] Q.B. 87 (see below, paras 44-413, 44-415).

[1915] [1914] A.C. 510, 523; *The Arpad* [1934] P. 189, 214, 215.

[1916] Their Lordships followed *Rodocanachi v Milburn* (1886) 18 Q.B.D. 67 ("That case rests on the

44-402 **Assumption of responsibility** Following the recent decision of the House of Lords in *Transfield Shipping Inc v Mercator Shipping Inc (The Achilleas)*[1917] it now seems that a claimant will not recover, even for losses that were not unlikely to occur in the usual course of things, if the defendant cannot reasonably be regarded as having assumed responsibility for losses of the particular kind suffered. In that case, time-charterers of a vessel that was re-delivered late were held not liable to the owners for loss of the following fixture; their liability was merely to pay the difference between the charter rate and the market rate for the period of delay. One of the principal reasons, at least by Lord Hoffmann (with whom the other members of the majority agreed), was that there was a general understanding in the industry that the charterer would be liable only for the lower amount.[1918] Since *Hall v Pim*[1919] is said to be a decision that "astonished the Temple and surprised St Mary Axe",[1920] it might seem to be open to the same criticism as the majority of the House of Lords made of the decision of the lower courts in *The Achilleas*. In that case only Lord Walker referred to *Hall v Pim* and he said that "[it] is now generally regarded as a sound decision on its special facts". However, care must be taken in arguing by analogy to *Hall v Pim*, and when the facts are not on all fours with that case it must also be asked whether it was reasonable to think that the seller was assuming responsibility for the loss. That applies even if the loss was not unlikely to occur on the ordinary course of things or its likelihood been brought to the seller's attention.

44-403 **Loss of future business** Where, at the time they made their contract, it was within the reasonable contemplation of the parties that defects in the goods supplied by the seller (in breach of his warranty as to their quality) might lead to sub-buyers (customers of the buyer) withdrawing their custom from the buyer, damages have been awarded for loss of profits on "repeat orders" from the sub-buyers.[1921] It is submitted that a similar principle should apply where the seller's failure to deliver causes the buyer a general loss of custom which was within the reasonable contemplation of the parties at the time of contracting, subject again to whether it was reasonable to think that the seller was assuming responsibility for the loss.[1922]

44-404 **Loss of profits on resale: no available market** If there was no market for the goods in question but the seller knew,[1923] or ought to have known,[1924] that the buyer bought the goods with a view to resale, the buyer is entitled to his loss of profit on

---

sound ground that it is immaterial what the buyer is intending to do with the purchased goods": [1914] A.C. 510, 530–531).

[1917] [2008] UKHL 48, [2009] 1 A.C. 61, discussed above, Vol.I, paras 26-137 et seq.

[1918] See above, Vol.I, para.26-139.

[1919] *Re R and Hall Ltd and WH Pim (Junior) Co's Arbitration* [1928] All E.R. Rep. 763.

[1920] *James Finlay & Co Ltd v Kwik Hoo Tong HM* [1929] 1 K.B. 400, 417, per Sankey L.J. (echoing a submission of counsel); quoted by Lord Walker in *Transfield Shipping Inc v Mercator Shipping Inc (The Achilleas)* [2008] UKHL 48 at [64].

[1921] *GKN Centrax Gears Ltd v Matbro Ltd* [1976] 2 Lloyd's Rep. 555, 573–574, 579–580 (not following *Simon v Pawsons and Leafs Ltd* (1933) 38 Com. Cas. 151, 158). See below, para.44-425. cf. *Jackson v Royal Bank of Scotland* [2005] UKHL 3, [2005] 1 W.L.R. 377 (loss of repeat orders caused by breach of obligation to maintain confidence; see Vol.I, para.26-149).

[1922] See previous paragraph.

[1923] e.g. *Frank Mott Co Ltd v Muller Co (London) Ltd* (1922) 13 Ll.L. Rep. 492. See also *Grébert-Borgnis v J and W Nugent* (1885) 15 Q.B.D. 85, 89.

[1924] *Patrick v Russo-British Grain Export Co Ltd* [1927] 2 K.B. 535, 541. See also above, para.44-400.

the resale[1925] when the seller fails to deliver the goods.[1926] Thus, if the goods were to be specially manufactured for the buyer, and the seller knew that they were to be resold by him, the buyer's loss of profit is the measure of damages when the seller fails to deliver.[1927]

Damages payable by the buyer to the sub-buyer Wherever the buyer can recover loss of profits on a resale,[1928] he is also entitled to recover the loss which he incurred as a result of being made liable in damages to his sub-buyer for breach of the terms of the contract of resale,[1929] subject again to whether it was reasonable to think that the seller was assuming responsibility for the loss.[1930] In *Grébert-Borgnis v J and W Nugent*[1931] the seller had actual knowledge, at the time of contracting, that the buyer had already sold the goods on the same terms (except as to price) to a sub-buyer in France, and that the buyer was purchasing the goods in order to fulfil that contract. The Court of Appeal awarded the buyer damages[1932] in respect of the compensation which the buyer had been compelled to pay to the sub-buyer in proceedings in France.[1933] Where the buyer can recover damages in respect of compensation paid to his sub-buyer, he may also recover costs reasonably incurred by him in defending a claim made by his sub-buyer.[1934] The buyer may be entitled to substantial damages from the seller even before he has discharged his liability to the sub-buyer by payment.[1935] If the sub-buyer has not claimed damages from the buyer by the time the buyer's claim against the original seller is being decided by the court, the buyer may be entitled to a declaration of indemnity in respect of the sub-buyer's potential claim[1936]; or the court may reserve this item of the buyer's claim for assessment of damages if and when the sub-buyer's claim is met by the buyer.[1937]

44-405

[1925] The sub-contract must be of a usual type, and the profit must be reasonable in amount: see above, para.44-400.

[1926] *Patrick v Russo-British Grain Export Co Ltd* [1927] 2 K.B. 535, 541; *Household Machines Ltd v Cosmos Exports Ltd* [1947] K.B. 217, 219; *J Leavey Co Ltd v George H Hirst Co Ltd* [1944] K.B. 24. See also *Satef-Huttenes Albertus SpA v Paloma Tercera Shipping Co SA (The Pegase)* [1981] 1 Lloyd's Rep. 175, 183–184; *Coastal (Bermuda) Petroleum Ltd v VTT Vulcan Petroleum SA (No.2) (The Marine Star)* [1994] 2 Lloyd's Rep. 629.

[1927] *Kwei Tek Chao v British Traders and Shippers Ltd* [1954] 2 Q.B. 459, 489.

[1928] See above, para.44-400.

[1929] *Re R and H Hall Ltd and WH Pim (Junior) Co's Arbitration* [1928] All E.R. Rep. 763 at 767, 769 HL, following *Grébert-Borgnis v J and W Nugent* (1885) 15 Q.B.D. 85. The breach of the original contract must have been the cause of the breach of the contract of resale.

[1930] See above, para.44-402 and, more generally, Vol.I, paras 26-137 et seq.

[1931] See above, following *Elbinger Actien-Gesellschaft v Armstrong* (1874) L.R. 9 Q.B. 473: see below, para.44-410.

[1932] In addition to the buyer's loss of profit under the contract of resale.

[1933] The French award was not "necessarily" the sum to be awarded: (1885) 15 Q.B.D. 85, 93. The seller would not be liable in respect of unusual clauses in the contract of resale, of which he had no knowledge, e.g. a penalty clause: (1885) 15 Q.B.D. 85 at 90. It is submitted that the *Grébert-Borgnis* decision is to be preferred to that in *Borries v Hutchinson* (1865) 18 C.B.(N.S.) 445.

[1934] cf. *Agius v Great Western Colliery Co* [1899] 1 Q.B. 413, 420 (analogous case where seller delayed delivery: see below, para.44-408); see also the analogous cases where the goods were defective in quality (see below, paras 44-411—44-435).

[1935] *Total Liban SA v Vitol Energy SA* [2001] Q.B. 643 (referring to various techniques available to prevent any "windfall" recovery by the buyer).

[1936] *Household Machines Ltd v Cosmos Exporters Ltd* [1947] 1 K.B. 217. (But see above, para.44-386.)

[1937] *Trans Trust SPRL v Danubian Trading Co* [1952] 2 Q.B. 297, 303, 307; *Total Liban SA v Vitol*

(b) Damages for Delay in Delivery

44-406 Delay in delivery The Act contains no provision which expressly provides for the assessment of the buyer's damages when the seller fails to deliver on the date fixed for delivery, but the buyer accepts delivery of the goods from the seller at a later date.[1938] Where there is an available market[1939] for the goods, the usual measure of the buyer's damages[1940] is the difference between (a) their market value at the time and place[1941] fixed by the terms of the contract for delivery; and (b) their market value at the time when (and the place where)[1942] the goods were in fact delivered to the buyer.[1943] Apart from consequential losses, such as extra or wasted expenses[1944] or loss of profits,[1945] this sum should put the buyer into the financial position he would have been in if the seller had fulfilled his contractual obligation. Where there is no available market for the goods, the court may use any relevant test to arrive at the "value" of the goods at the time fixed for delivery and at the actual date of delivery. Thus, when the goods were to be delivered at Hull, whence the buyer (to the seller's knowledge) intended to send them to a sub-buyer on the Continent, the value was said to be dependent on the relative cost of freight and insurance on the transport to the Russian destination at the different times.[1946]

44-407 Resale prices are irrelevant The market prices at the due date for delivery and at the actual date of delivery cannot be proved (except in the absence of other evidence of market value) by either the contract price or by the price under a resale of the goods to a sub-buyer. Whether the resale price is higher or lower than the market price at the date of actual delivery, the buyer's damages must be calculated exclusively by reference to the market prices at the due date and at the actual date, since the buyer could have bought other goods to fulfil his obligations under the

---

Energy SA [2001] Q.B. 643. cf. *Deeny v Gooda Walker Ltd (No.3)* [1995] 4 All E.R. 289 (not a sale of goods case). In another context it has been held that reasonable payments made when there was no obligation to make them may be recovered.

[1938] The case probably falls under the general provisions of s.53(2). See *Taylor & Sons Ltd v Bank of Athens* (1922) 91 L.J. K.B. 776, 778. cf. s.54 (see above, para.44-383).

[1939] On the meaning of this term, and the evidence to prove the market price, see above, paras 44-368—44-378.

[1940] This is the same as in cases of delay in the carriage of goods by sea: see *Koufos v C Czarnikow Ltd (The Heron II)* [1969] 1 A.C. 350, especially at 400, 407, 417–418 (cf. at 392, 393, 427).

[1941] *Aryeh v Lawrence Kostoris Son Ltd* [1967] 1 Lloyd's Rep. 63, 73.

[1942] In the cases cited in the next footnote, the place is assumed to be the same place as in (a).

[1943] *Addax Ltd v Arcadia Petroleum Ltd* [2000] 1 Lloyd's Rep. 493. See also *Borries v Hutchinson* (1865) 18 C.B.(N.S.) 445, 465; *Elbinger Actien-Gesellschaft v Armstrong* (1874) L.R. 9 Q.B. 473, 477; *Koufos v C Czarnikow Ltd* [1969] 1 A.C. 350 at 417–418; *Taylor & Sons Ltd v Bank of Athens* (1922) 91 L.J. K.B. 776. It could be argued that the seller, by tendering the goods late, has estopped himself from relying on s.51(3). In *Galaxy Energy International Ltd v Murco Petroleum Ltd* [2013] EWHC 3720 (Comm), [2013] C.L.C. 1007 a spread of prices provided by Platts gave the best evidence of market value.

[1944] e.g. extra freight and insurance incurred by the buyer: *Borries v Hutchinson*, above. See also *Smeed v Foord* (1859) 1 E. & E. 602; *Hydraulic Engineering Co Ltd v McHaffie Goslett Co* (1878) 4 Q.B.D. 670; *Watson v Gray* (1900) 16 T.L.R. 308; *Steam Herring Fleet Ltd v VS Richards Co Ltd* (1901) 17 T.L.R. 731; *John M Henderson Co Ltd v Montague L Meyer Ltd* (1941) 46 Com. Cas. 209; *Aruna Mills Ltd v Dhanrajmal Gobindram* [1968] 1 Q.B. 655. See Vol.I, paras 26-025 et seq.

[1945] See below, paras 44-408—44-410.

[1946] *Borries v Hutchinson* (1865) 18 C.B.(N.S.) 445. See also *Fletcher v Tayleur* (1855) 17 C.B. 21.

sub-contract and the market price of the goods delivered late by the seller would then be relevant to those goods left on his hands at that date.[1947]

Loss of profit caused by delay in delivery   Where the seller makes a late delivery **44-408** of a profit-earning chattel,[1948] the buyer may (in the absence of an available market for such a chattel[1949]) recover damages for loss of use, based on the normal use made of such a chattel, not on an exceptional use unknown to the seller.[1950] The buyer's claim is for "user profits", viz the loss of profits which he would have made from use of the goods during the period after the goods should have been delivered until the actual date of delivery.[1951] In *Victoria Laundry (Windsor) Ltd v Newman Industries Ltd*[1952] the plaintiffs were launderers and dyers who wished to expand their business by installing a larger boiler. The defendants were engineers who agreed to sell them a large boiler, and a delivery date was fixed. While the boiler was being dismantled for delivery it was damaged, and delivery to the plaintiffs was not made until five months after the delivery date. The plaintiffs sued for damages for delay in delivery[1953] and claimed loss of profits in respect of:

(1)   the large number of new customers they could have taken on had the boiler been installed on the due date; and

(2)   the amount which they could have earned under special, "highly lucrative", dyeing contracts with the Ministry of Supply.

The defendants knew that the plaintiffs were launderers and that they wanted the boiler for immediate use; the Court of Appeal held that with such knowledge the

---

[1947] *Slater v Hoyle Smith Ltd* [1920] 2 K.B. 11, 23–24, per Scrutton L.J., whose criticism of the inconsistent decision of the Privy Council in *Wertheim v Chicoutimi Pulp Co* [1911] A.C. 301 should, it is submitted, be accepted. But cf. *Bence Graphics International Ltd v Fasson UK Ltd* [1998] Q.B. 87 (see below, paras 44-413, 44-415). (See *Benjamin's Sale of Goods*, 10th edn (2017), para.17-039.) In *Wertheim* the Privy Council assessed the damages as the difference between: (a) the market value at the port of delivery at the due date for delivery; and (b) the actual price obtained on their resale. But the buyer was not bound to fulfil the sub-contracts by delivering the specific goods which he received under the original contract (cf. above, para.44-401). It is submitted that the choice of the buyer not to repurchase in the market on the date of the breach should not benefit the defaulting seller any more than it should harm him by increasing the damages payable by him if the resale price is below the market price at that date. cf. the analogous position in *Campbell Mostyn (Provisions) Ltd v Barnett Trading Co Ltd* [1954] 1 Lloyd's Rep. 65 (see above, para.44-378).

[1948] Or part of a profit-earning chattel: *Victoria Laundry (Windsor) Ltd v Newman Industries Ltd* [1949] 2 K.B. 528, 543–544; *Elbinger Actien-Gesellschaft v Armstrong* (1874) L.R. 9 Q.B. 473, 477.

[1949] Where there is an available market, the buyer should normally be able to avoid loss of profits by immediately purchasing or hiring a substitute. cf. *Smeed v Foord* (1859) 1 E. & E. 602.

[1950] *Victoria Laundry (Windsor) Ltd v Newman Industries Ltd* [1949] 2 K.B. 528. See also *Cory v Thames Ironworks and Shipbuilding Co Ltd* (1868) L.R. 3 Q.B. 181 (see below, para.44-409). cf. *Re Trent and Humber Co* (1868) L.R. 4 Ch. App. 112, 117; *Fletcher v Tayleur* (1855) 17 C.B. 21; *Watson v Gray* (1900) 16 T.L.R. 308; *Satef-Huttenes Albertus SpA v Paloma Tercera Shipping Co SA (The Pegase)* [1981] 1 Lloyd's Rep. 175 (carrier's delay).

[1951] The earlier cases concerned delay in delivery of ships or vessels which clearly were intended to earn profits for their owners, e.g. *Cory v Thames Ironworks Co*, above, *Re Trent and Humber Co*, above; *Steam Herring Fleet Ltd v VS Richards Co Ltd* (1901) 17 T.L.R. 731; or some essential part of a ship, e.g. *Wilson v General Screw Colliery Co* (1877) 37 L.T. 789 (propeller shaft); *Saint Line Ltd v Richardsons Westgarth Co Ltd* [1940] 2 K.B. 99, 104–105 (engines).

[1952] [1949] 2 K.B. 528. (The language in which the judgment was expressed may need to be modified in the light of *Koufos v C Czarnikow Ltd (The Heron II)* [1969] 1 A.C. 350, but their Lordships appear to have accepted that the *Victoria Laundry* case was correctly decided even on the basis of their slightly different formulation of the remoteness test: [1969] 1 A.C. 350 at 389, 399, 414, 415. See Vol.I, paras 26-117 et seq.)

[1953] A similar boiler was not readily available on the market.

reasonable man could have foreseen that delay in delivery would lead to some loss of business (and therefore loss of profits) though he would not have foreseen the loss of profits under the special contracts with the Ministry, since these were special circumstances not within the defendant's actual knowledge. Hence, the plaintiffs could not recover the actual loss they had incurred under these contracts, but only the normal loss of business[1954] in respect of dyeing and laundering contracts to be reasonably expected.[1955]

44-409 **Contemplated loss as limit on liability** In *Cory v Thames Ironworks and Shipbuilding Co Ltd*[1956] coal merchants bought the hull of a floating boom derrick from the sellers, who finally delivered it six months late. The normal use of the hull would have been as a coal store, but the buyers (unknown to the sellers) intended to use it for a new method of transferring coal from colliers to barges. Some loss of profits from delay was within the reasonable contemplation of the parties at the time the contract was made, and the buyers actually lost profits through the delay; but their recovery was limited to the extent of the profits which would have been made through the method of using the hull which the seller could reasonably have contemplated. The court did not hold that no loss of the reasonably contemplated type in fact occurred merely because the buyers did not intend to earn profits by the normal use of the hull; the buyers intended to earn profits by its use, and they had actually lost greater profits than they claimed.

44-410 **Loss on resale** Normally, the buyer cannot recover his loss of profits under a resale when the seller makes a late delivery under the original contract.[1957] Where, however, the seller actually[1958] contemplated a resale by the buyer, he will be liable for the buyer's loss of profits under the resale caused by the seller's failure to deliver on time[1959]; in these circumstances, the seller may be liable to the buyer in respect of the latter's liability in damages to his sub-buyer caused by the seller's delay.[1960]

Again, there will now be liability only if it was reasonable to think that the seller was assuming responsibility for the loss.[1961]

[1954] On the loss of custom in general, viz loss of business or custom resulting from the fact that the buyer was forced to default in fulfilling his sub-contract, see above, para.44-403, see below, para.44-425.

[1955] cf. cases on delayed delivery of part of a machine in a contract of carriage (Vol.I, paras 26-119, 26-148); and cases concerning the buyer's loss of profit on a resale (see below, para.44-410).

[1956] (1868) L.R. 3 Q.B. 181. See the analysis of the case in *Victoria Laundry (Windsor) Ltd v Newman Industries Ltd* [1949] 2 K.B. 528 at 538.

[1957] cf. above, paras 44-400—44-405; and *Portman v Middleton* (1858) 4 C.B.(N.S.) 322.

[1958] Or where he "ought" to have contemplated a resale as "probable": see above, paras 44-400.

[1959] *Hydraulic Engineering Co Ltd v McHaffie Goslett Co* (1878) 4 Q.B.D. 670. It is submitted that the buyer should not be allowed to recover his *gross* profit (viz gross receipts) as well as his wasted expenses: cf. below, para.44-423.

[1960] *Elbinger Actien-Gesellschaft v Armstrong* (1874) L.R. 9 Q.B. 473, 479; *Hydraulic Engineering Co Ltd v McHaffie Goslett Co* (1878) 4 Q.B.D. 670, 674, 677; *Agius v Great Western Colliery Co* [1899] 1 Q.B. 413 (where the buyer reasonably defends the claim brought against him by his sub-buyer, he may also recover from the seller his reasonable costs: above; cf. below, paras 44-431—44-435; see above, para.44-405). The situation where the seller knew that the buyers were already contracted to deliver to a sub-buyer might, depending on the circumstances, in future give the sub-buyer a claim against the seller under the Contracts (Rights of Third Parties) Act 1999. See above, paras 18-090 et seq.; see below, paras 44-428, 44-437.

[1961] See above, para.44-402 and, more generally, Vol.I, paras 26-137 et seq.

(c)   Damages for Defective Quality

(i)   Diminution in Value

Breach of warranty   Section 53 of the Act[1962] prescribes the measure of damages for breach of warranty, viz a contractual undertaking which is not, or cannot be, treated by the buyer as a ground for rejecting the goods[1963]:

44-411

"(1)   Where there is a breach of warranty by the seller, or where the buyer elects (or is compelled) to treat any breach of a condition on the part of the seller as a breach of warranty, the buyer is not by reason only of such breach of warranty entitled to reject the goods; but he may—

(a)   set up[1964] against the seller the breach of warranty in diminution or extinction of the price,[1965] or

(b)   maintain an action against the seller for damages for the breach of warranty.

(2)   The measure of damages for breach of warranty is the estimated loss directly and naturally resulting, in the ordinary course of events, from the breach of warranty.[1966]

(3)   In the case of breach of warranty of quality[1967] such loss is prima facie the difference between the value of the goods at the time of delivery to the buyer and the value they would have had if they had fulfilled the warranty.

[1962] s.53(5) relates only to Scots law and is therefore not reproduced here. Section 53 does not apply to consumer contracts for the sale of goods which fall within Ch.2 of Pt 1 of the Consumer Rights Act 2015. In consumer contracts for the sale of goods the 2015 Act provides special remedies for buyers in consumer sales contracts, see above, paras 38-442 et seq.

[1963] If the buyer is entitled to, and does reject the goods his damages are assessed on the basis of the seller's failure to deliver (s.51: see above, paras 44-387 et seq.). Completely different principles from those in s.53 may apply in the case of incorrect documents being supplied under overseas sales: see *Benjamin's Sale of Goods*, 10th edn (2017), paras 19-204 et seq., 20-115.

[1964] The meaning of set-off is examined in *BICC Plc v Burndy Corp* [1985] Ch. 232, 247–251, 254–259 (not a sale of goods case); and in *Axel Johnson Petroleum AB v MG Mineral Group AG* [1992] 1 W.L.R. 270. By a term in the contract, the buyer may agree to waive his right to a set-off against the price: see *Caterpillar (NI) Ltd (formerly FG Wilson (Engineering) Ltd) v John Holt & Co (Liverpool) Ltd* [2013] EWCA Civ 1232, [2014] 1 W.L.R. 2365. cf. also *Hong Kong and Shanghai Banking Corp v Kloeckner Co AG* [1990] 2 Q.B. 514 and *Connaught Restaurants Ltd v Indoor Leisure Ltd* [1994] 4 All E.R. 834 (not sale of goods cases). But such a term may be invalid under Unfair Contract Terms Act 1977 or under the Unfair Terms in Consumer Contract Regulations 1999, or for contracts entered into on or after October 1, 2015, the Consumer Rights Act 2015, see above paras 38-211 et seq.

[1965] s.53(1)(a) and (4) follow the law in *Mondel v Steel* (1841) 8 M.W. 858. The buyer may also have a set-off (in respect of the seller's *previous* breach of warranty) when the seller claims damages for non-acceptance: see above, para.44-367. The buyer need not set up his defence: the fact that the buyer has paid the full price, or that the seller has recovered the full price by action against the buyer, does not prevent the buyer from subsequently bringing a separate action against the seller for breach of warranty: cf. the analogous case of a building contract: *Davis v Hedges* (1871) L.R. 6 Q.B. 687 (the sale of goods case is expressly said to be the same: at 690). The buyer cannot defend by way of set-off if the seller sues to enforce a negotiable instrument (*Cebora SNC v SIP (Industrial Products) Ltd* [1976] 1 Lloyd's Rep. 271; cf. *Nova (Jersey) Knit Ltd v Kammgarn Spinnerei GmbH* [1977] 1 W.L.R. 713) or a different contract (*Bow, McLachlan Co Ltd v Ship (Camosun)* [1909] A.C. 597, 610–613 (mortgage back to the seller)). On the question of an equitable set-off against a claim in debt, see *British Anzani (Felixstowe) Ltd v International Marine Management (UK) Ltd* [1980] Q.B. 137 (a landlord and tenant case).

[1966] This subsection is in terms of *Hadley v Baxendale* (1854) 9 Exch. 341 (see Vol.I, para.26-119); *H Parsons (Livestock) Ltd v Uttley Ingham Co Ltd* [1978] Q.B. 791, 800, 807. Consequential damages can be claimed under s.53(2) if they arise directly and naturally from the breach: *Saipol SA v Inerco Trade SA* [2014] EWHC 2211 (Comm). In addition, special damages may be claimed under

(4)   The fact that the buyer has set up the breach of warranty in diminution or extinction of the price does not prevent him from maintaining an action for the same breach of warranty if he has suffered further damage."[1968]

The succeeding paragraphs in this part of the chapter cover all breaches of ss.13, 14 and 15 of the Act and any other breach of a contractual undertaking about the condition or attributes of the goods to be delivered.[1969]

44-412 **Damages for diminution in market value**   As is illustrated by s.53(3) the usual measure of damages for breach of the seller's contractual undertaking as to the quality or condition of the goods is the difference[1970] between: (a) the value of the goods if they had complied with the undertaking, measured at the time[1971] and place[1972] of delivery; and (b) the actual value of the goods, in their actual condition, at the same time and place.[1973] This is the "prima facie" measure of damages, which will be superseded where the buyer claims loss of profits or other consequential losses.[1974] Where there is a market price[1975] for goods of the contractual description and quality, this will fix their "value"; in the absence of an available market, any relevant[1976] evidence should be admitted, e.g. the price at which a sub-buyer had agreed to buy the goods from the buyer before the defect was discovered may be some evidence of their value,[1977] as may the price at which an offer for the goods was made by a third person.[1978] The value of the defective goods actually delivered by the seller

---

s.54 (see below, para.44-416—44-435).

[1967] It is submitted that a similar measure would apply to breaches of other undertakings, such as those relating to the fitness of the goods for a particular purpose (s.14(3)), or to the description of the goods (s.13).

[1968] It is not clear whether the word "further" relates to fresh damage suffered after the first action was disposed of, or to damage which was not taken account of in assessing the extent of the reduction in the price in the first action. *Mondel v Steel* (1841) 8 M.W. 858, suggests the latter interpretation, but the former is probably the more normal meaning of the word "further". (Another possible meaning could be that "further" refers to a sum "over and above" the price (at least in cases where the breach of warranty had been set up in "extinction" of the price).)

[1969] Where the buyer is a consumer he has new remedies under Pt 5A of the Act or the Consumer Rights Act 2015 where the goods delivered to him do not conform to the contract: these remedies are likely to be more advantageous to him than those under s.53. See above, paras 38-442 et seq.

[1970] s.53(3) assumes that the buyer has paid the full price for the goods (cf. s.53(1)(a)). The fact that the buyer has paid the price to the seller makes no difference to the measure of damages: *Loder v Kekule* (1857) 3 C.B.(N.S.) 128.

[1971] The buyer is entitled to any rise in the market price between the date of the contract and the date of delivery: *Jones v Just* (1868) L.R. 3 Q.B. 197 (the court treated as irrelevant the actual resale price obtained by the buyer at a date later than the date of delivery).

[1972] cf. the similar situation in assessing the market price: see above, paras 44-368—44-370.

[1973] If the goods were to be delivered by separate instalments, the measure of damages in s.53(3) should be applied separately to each delivery: *Slater v Hoyle and Smith Ltd* [1920] 2 K.B. 11, 19. See, applying the market price rule, *Amira G Foods Ltd v RS Foods Ltd* [2016] EWHC 76 (QB).

[1974] *Saipol SA v Inerco Trade SA* [2014] EWHC 2211 (Comm). See below, paras 44-419 et seq.

[1975] See above, paras 44-368 et seq.

[1976] The contract price should not be taken: *Loder v Kekule* (1857) 3 C.B.(N.S.) 128; *Slater v Hoyle and Smith Ltd* [1920] 2 K.B. 11 at 17, 18. (cf. *Dingle v Hare* (1859) 29 L.J. C.P. 143; *Minster Trust Ltd v Traps Tractors Ltd* [1954] 1 W.L.R. 963, 988–989.)

[1977] As suggested in *Clare v Maynard* (1837) 6 A. & E. 519. The sub-sale price is normally irrelevant: *Slater v Hoyle and Smith Ltd* [1920] 2 K.B. 11 cf. *Bence Graphics International Ltd v Fasson UK Ltd* [1998] Q.B. 87 (see below, paras 44-413, 44-415). (cf. see above, paras 44-400—44-402, 44-407.)

[1978] *Cox v Walker* (1835) 6 A. & E. 523n.

may be fixed by any relevant evidence,[1979] e.g. the price at which the buyer has been able to resell the goods to a sub-buyer who has knowledge of their defective condition.[1980] The courts may follow the commercial practice of fixing a "price allowance" for damaged goods.[1981]

Prima facie rule only   Section 53(3) lays down only a "prima facie" rule, from **44-413** which the court may depart in appropriate circumstances. For instance, the time when the actual value of the goods in their defective state is assessed may be postponed until the defect is discovered.[1982] Similarly, when the seller knows that the buyer intends to resell the goods to a sub-buyer at another place, and that the goods will not be examined until they reach the sub-buyer (e.g. because they are packaged), the date at which the latter examines the goods may be the date at which the market price should be taken to assess the buyer's damages for the defective condition of the goods.[1983] Again, a warranty as to quality may relate to the future (e.g. that seed will produce a certain crop) so that there can be no question of the buyer's opportunity to resell the defective goods until the defect becomes apparent at a later date. The market value test should not be applied until the future event is known.[1984] In *Bence Graphics International Ltd v Fasson UK Ltd*[1985] the Court of Appeal held that s.53(3) provided only a "prima facie" rule, which should not be applied if it would give the buyer "more than his true loss".[1986] Section 53(2) should be the "starting point".[1987]

Damages for the cost of adaptations, or of substitute goods[1988]   If there is no **44-414** market, damages may be awarded on the basis of the cost of bringing the defective goods up to the contractual standard which would make them saleable.[1989] In

---

[1979] There is normally no market in the ordinary sense for damaged or defective goods: *Biggin & Co Ltd v Permanite Ltd* [1951] 1 K.B. 422, 438. (The appeal was allowed, but on a different ground: [1951] 2 K.B. 314.) As to damages in respect of goods not of merchantable quality, see *Jackson v Chrysler Acceptances* [1978] R.T.R. 474.

[1980] *Cox v Walker*, above; *Biggin & Co Ltd v Permanite Ltd* [1951] 1 K.B. 422, 438. (But the evidence of "hypothetical buyers" may be weak: at 439.)

[1981] [1951] 1 K.B. 422 at 439–440 (allowance of 15 per cent on the price); *Cehave NV v Bremer Handelsgesellschaft mbH (The Hansa Nord)* [1976] Q.B. 44, 63. cf. the remedy of a reduction in price where the buyer is a consumer: above, para.38-442.

[1982] *Naughton v O'Callaghan* [1990] 3 All E.R. 191; *Bominflot Bunkergesellschaft fur Mineralole mbH & Co v Petroplus Marketing AG (The Mercini Lady)* [2012] EWHC 3009 (Comm), [2013] 1 Lloyd's Rep. 360 at [60]–[61]; *Saipol SA v Inerco Trade SA* [2014] EWHC 2211 (Comm) (approving arbitrators' assessment of damages on that basis).

[1983] *Van den Hurk v Martens Co Ltd* [1920] 1 K.B. 850. See above, para.44-376. cf. the similar ruling in *Kwei Tek Chao v British Traders Ltd* [1954] 2 Q.B. 459. Normally, the place of delivery is the place for examination of the goods under s.34.

[1984] *Ashworth v Wells* (1898) 14 T.L.R. 227. cf. *Loder v Kekule* (1857) 3 C.B.(N.S.) 128, 140 (seller's negotiations with the buyer delayed the resale of the defective goods).

[1985] [1998] Q.B. 87 (see below, para.44-415) (applied in *Bern Dis A Turk Ticaret S/A v International Agri Trade Co Ltd* [1999] 1 All E.R. (Comm) 619, CA).

[1986] [1998] Q.B. 87 at 102. See also *Louis Dreyfus Trading Ltd v Reliance Trading Ltd* [2004] EWHC 525 (Comm), [2004] 2 Lloyd's Rep. 243; *Choil Trading SA v Sahara Energy Resources Ltd* [2010] EWHC 374 (Comm) at [124]–[139].

[1987] [1998] Q.B. 87, 102.

[1988] The consumer may now have the further remedies of repair or replacement: see above para.38-442.

[1989] *Minster Trust Ltd v Traps Tractors Ltd* [1954] 1 W.L.R. 963, 988–989. The cost of repairs to the goods was also accepted as a basis for damages in *Mondel v Steel* (1841) 8 M. & W. 858, 872. cf.

some circumstances the buyer may be entitled to claim, as damages for defective quality, the cost of buying substitute goods to perform the function intended to be performed by the contractual goods.[1990] The House of Lords has been willing to award damages on this basis when machines were bought to perform in a specified way: but the House also held that the damages for the cost of the substitute machines should take account of any extra profit to the buyer resulting from the replacement of the defective machines. The evidence showed that the new machines bought by the buyer to replace the defective machines were so superior in efficiency and in economy of working expenses that it would have been to the buyer's pecuniary advantage to have replaced the seller's machines by them even if the seller's machines had complied with all the contractual specifications. The House held that, even though the buyers may not have been under a "duty" to mitigate their loss in this way,[1991] when their action had in fact diminished their loss, their claim for damages for the cost of installing the newer machines must take account of the extra profit[1992] (including the saving of expenses) resulting from this action.[1993] Similarly, where the buyer claims damages for his loss of profit or other consequential losses caused by the defective quality of the goods delivered by the seller, the seller may show that the buyer ought reasonably to have mitigated his loss by acquiring substitute goods.[1994]

44-415   **Buyer performing sub-contract despite seller's breach**   It was held by the Court of Appeal in *Slater v Hoyle and Smith Ltd*[1995] that where the seller delivers defective goods, but the buyer is nevertheless able to perform a sub-contract by delivering the goods to his sub-buyer, the buyer's damages against the seller should not be reduced by taking this into account; the buyer is entitled to rely on the normal measure of damages under s.53(3) viz the difference between (a) the market price, at the time and place of delivery, of goods up to the contractual quality; and (b) the market price, at the time and place of delivery, of the goods actually delivered.[1996]

---

buying the nearest equivalent goods and adapting them: see above, para.44-398. However, in *Peebles v Rembrand Builders Merchants Ltd* Unreported April 18, 2017, Sherriff Court (Tayside, Central and Fife) (Dundee), the court refused to award the full cost of replacing defective roof tiles because the expense was unreasonable and the claimant had failed to mitigate its loss.

[1990] *British Westinghouse Electric and Manufacturing Co Ltd v Underground Electric Rys Co of London Ltd* [1912] A.C. 673.

[1991] If the buyers had claimed the normal measure of damages under s.53(3) see above, there would have been no need to mitigate at a later date: see *Benjamin's Sale of Goods*, 10th edn (2017), para.17-055. But cf. *Bence Graphics International Ltd v Fasson UK Ltd* [1998] Q.B. 87 (see above, para.44-413, see below, para.44-415).

[1992] The extra profit in fact exceeded the cost of the substitute.

[1993] cf. *Erie County Natural Gas and Fuel Co Ltd v Carroll* [1911] A.C. 105 (see above, para.44-398); *Nadreph Ltd v Willmett Co* [1978] 1 W.L.R. 1537 (not a sale of goods case). cf. also *Hussey v Eels* [1990] 2 Q.B. 227 (not a sale of goods case).

[1994] *British Westinghouse Electric and Manufacturing Co Ltd v Underground Electric Railways Co of London Ltd* [1912] A.C. 673.

[1995] [1920] 2 K.B. 11.

[1996] The buyers were not obliged to deliver to the sub-buyer the goods which they bought from the original seller, and in fact some of the goods which they delivered to the sub-buyer came from a different source. It is submitted that the decision in this case is to be preferred to the reasoning of the Privy Council in the analogous case of *Wertheim v Chicoutimi Pulp Co* [1918] A.C. 301 (late delivery), which is criticised see above, para.44-408 n.1947, and in Benjamin at paras 17-039, 17-057—17-058. However, in *Bence Graphics International Ltd v Fasson UK Ltd* [1998] Q.B. 87 at 103–105, Auld L.J. approved the decision in *Wertheim's* case (see below (this paragraph) and see above, paras26-043, 26-166 and 26-170).

However, the authority of *Slater v Hoyle and Smith Ltd* has been severely undermined by the decision of the Court of Appeal in *Bence Graphics International Ltd v Fasson UK Ltd*.[1997] The seller knew that the buyer would sell on to others (after manufacturing the goods into another product); the Court of Appeal held that the parties contemplated that the measure of damages for defects in the goods should be the extent of the buyer's liability (if any) to those others resulting from the defect. In *Bence's* case the decision in *Slater's* case was doubted, on the ground that s.53(3) laid down only a prima facie rule, which should not be applied if it would give the buyer "more than his true loss".[1998] The *Bence* case has been the subject of trenchant criticism on the grounds that remoteness is relevant only to claims for consequential loss, not to the difference in value between the goods delivered and the goods as they should have been; and that the effect of the sub-sale should be taken into account only when the buyer was legally obliged to supply the same specific goods under the sub-sale, in which case it is arguable that if the buyer received the full sub-sale price, it suffered no loss at all.[1999] Nonetheless, in *Euro-Asian Oil SA (formerly Euro-Asian Oil AG) v Credit Suisse AG*[2000] the Court of Appeal approved the trial judge's decision to limit the claimant's to the loss on the sub-sale, rather than the higher difference between the contract price and the market price at the date for delivery, even though the buyer could have fulfilled the sub-sale using other goods, on the ground that the parties contemplated a sub-sale. It is submitted that these cases should not be followed and that the buyers should have recovered the difference in value. First, remoteness is not relevant when the claim is simply for the difference in value between what was contracted for and what was delivered. The sub-sale is relevant only if the buyer was bound to deliver the same specific goods under the sub-sale. If the buyer was not so obliged, it might have fulfilled the sub-sale by purchasing and processing other goods, or have used other goods from stock and then have re-sold the contract goods at the current price; in either case the buyer should be entitled to the difference between the contract price and market price.[2001] The fact that they were able to pass on the defective goods without incurring liability again seems to be their own good fortune.[2002] Moreover, it can be argued that even when the sub-sale requires delivery of the same goods, the buyer should always be entitled to the difference between the

---

[1997] [1998] Q.B. 87. See *Louis Dreyfus Trading Ltd v Reliance Trading Ltd* [2004] EWHC 525 (Comm), [2004] 2 Lloyd's Rep. 243 (parties contemplated sale of the same goods to the sub-buyer under a specific contract); *Choil Trading SA v Sahara Energy Resources Ltd* [2010] EWHC 374 (Comm) at [124]–[139].

[1998] [1998] Q.B. 87 at 102 (see above, para.44-413). The *Bence Graphics* case was distinguished in *Bear Stearns Bank Plc v Forum Global Equity Ltd* [2007] EWHC 1576 (Comm) (a case involving shares rather than goods) on the grounds that in the *Bear Stearns* case the parties had not contemplated that the buyers would resell precisely the same shares (at [204]–[207]); and that it was a case of non-delivery rather than of delivery of defective goods (at [208]).

[1999] See Treitel (1997) 113 L.Q.R. 188 and Peel (ed.), *Treitel on The Law of Contract*, 14th edn (2015), para.20-051. See also *Benjamin's Sale of Goods*, 10th edn (2017), paras 17-057—17-082. Contrast *McGregor on Damages*, 20th edn (2017), paras 25-068—25-069.

[2000] [2018] EWCA Civ 1720.

[2001] See above, para.26-043; and Peel (ed.), *Treitel on The Law of Contract*, 14th edn (2015), para.20-048.

[2002] See the powerful criticism of Treitel (1997) 113 L.Q.R. 188, and Peel (ed.), *Treitel on The Law of Contract*, 14th edn (2015), para.20–051. In *OMV Petrom SA v Glencore International AG* [2016] EWCA Civ 778, [2016] 2 Lloyd's Rep. 432 Christopher Clarke L.J. seemed to think that the *Bence Graphics* case could not stand with *Slater v Hoyle Smith Ltd*, but left the matter open (at [45]–[46]).

contract price and the market price, by analogy to the decisions on failures to provide services which do not result in any further loss to the claimant.[2003] The *Bence* case seems to be a further example of the court concentrating on the end-result rather than the buyer's performance interest.[2004] It is true that in cases in which the buyer has reached a reasonable settlement with the sub-buyer, who has retained the goods, the amount paid under the settlement has been treated as the most that the buyer can recover, even if the settlement was at an undervalue, but the point seems to have been assumed rather than argued.[2005]

(ii) Losses other than Diminution in Value

44-416 **The buyer's actual or imputed knowledge of the defect** Where the seller delivers goods which fail to meet the contractual description or standard, the buyer may not immediately discover the defect or the failure of the goods to satisfy the description. As soon as the buyer knows of the defect, he will be unable to recover damages for any further or consequential loss which he ought reasonably to have avoided by taking remedial or precautionary steps.[2006] The buyer is not justified in continuing to rely on the seller's warranty after he knows that the goods are defective in that respect.[2007] After the buyer knew of the defect, he cannot, by reselling the goods to a third person, increase the original seller's liability by holding him liable for the buyer's own responsibility towards his sub-buyer.[2008] If the buyer acquired knowledge of the defect at a time when the goods were already in the hands of the sub-buyer, he ought to have notified the sub-buyer if the latter could take reasonable steps to avoid further loss or injury.[2009]

44-417 **The buyer's failure to discover the defect** It is not yet established, however, whether the same principle applies where the buyer ought reasonably to have discovered a defect which was not obvious.[2010] The buyer is not debarred from claiming damages merely because he did not make a thorough examination of the goods delivered by the seller to see whether they complied with the contract. Where the defect is not patent or obvious, he may rely on the seller's contractual undertaking as to quality or description. But in the cases[2011] supporting this proposition, there is an underlying assumption that the buyer acted reasonably in not examining the goods, or in not discovering the defect in question. The language used in the judg-

---

[2003] See above, para.26-043.
[2004] See above, paras 26-042—26-046.
[2005] *Biggin v Permanite* [1951] 2 K.B. 314; *Fluor v Shanghai Zhenhua Heavy Industry Co Ltd* [2018] EWHC 1 (TCC) at [465].
[2006] This principle is implicit in the decision of the House of Lords in *Lambert v Lewis* [1982] A.C. 225. (See below, para.44-432.) See also *British Oil and Cake Co Ltd v Burstall Co* (1923) 39 T.L.R. 406, 407; *Hammond Co v Bussey* (1887) 20 Q.B.D. 79, 86.
[2007] *Lambert v Lewis* [1982] A.C. 225. The rules of mitigation apply to this situation.
[2008] *Biggin & Co Ltd v Permanite Ltd* [1951] 1 K.B. 422, 435 (the appeal was decided on another point). See also *GC Dobell Co Ltd v Barber and Garratt* [1931] 1 K.B. 219, 238, 246–247.
[2009] *Biggin & Co Ltd v Permanite Ltd* [1951] 1 K.B. 422, 435.
[2010] *Biggin & Co Ltd v Permanite Ltd* [1951] 1 K.B. 422, 435. See also *Smith v Johnson* (1899) 15 T.L.R. 179, 180.
[2011] *Pinnock Bros v Lewis and Peat Ltd* [1923] 1 K.B. 690, 698; *British Oil and Cake Co Ltd v Burstall Co* (1923) 39 T.L.R. 406 at 407. cf. *GC Dobell Co Ltd v Barber and Garratt* [1931] 1 K.B. 219. cf. also the analogous cases of *Mowbray v Merryweather* [1895] 2 Q.B. 640, 644, 646, 647; *Scott v Foley, Aikman Co* (1899) 16 T.L.R. 55.

ments, however, suggests that when the circumstances ought to have put the buyer on inquiry, so that as a reasonable man he ought then to have discovered the defect, he should not be able to recover damages in respect of further loss caused by the defect which he should reasonably have been able to avoid after the date when he ought to have discovered it.[2012] The first question will be whether the buyer's actions or omissions broke the chain of causation between the breach and any subsequent loss or damage. The buyer's knowledge is highly relevant to this. Reckless conduct on the buyer's part is likely to break the chain of causation, whereas merely unreasonable conduct will not necessarily do so.[2013] The second question is, if the buyer was aware of the breach, or possibly if he should have been aware of it,[2014] whether he took reasonable steps to mitigate the loss.[2015]

Sometimes the seller knows that there are some possible defects in the goods **44-418** which can be discovered only by the buyer, or the ultimate buyer, actually using them.[2016] Thus, the presence of a deleterious substance in a fur skin collar could not be discovered until it was worn and the defect shown by the injury to the skin of the wearer.[2017] And where seed of inferior quality is delivered to a farmer, the fact of the inferior quality may not become apparent until the crop has been grown.[2018] In these circumstances there can be no question of the buyer failing to discover the defect before the use of the goods reveals it.[2019]

Additional or wasted expenses[2020]   If it was within the reasonable contempla- **44-419** tion of the parties, at the time of making the contract, that the buyer was not unlikely to incur additional expenses if the seller delivered defective goods in breach of his undertaking as to their description or quality, the buyer may recover from the seller the reasonable amount of any expenses which he has reasonably incurred as the result of the seller's breach.[2021] Thus, where defective steam turbines were delivered it was not disputed that the buyers could recover damages for the extra coal consumption and labour due to the defects in the machines during the period of their

---

[2012] *Lambert v Lewis* [1982] A.C. 225 was based partly on the buyer's actual knowledge and partly on his imputed knowledge: see *Benjamin's Sale of Goods*, 10th edn (2017), para.17-059. cf. Vol.I, para.26-095. It is submitted that the speech of Lord Diplock indicates that he would treat imputed knowledge of the defect as actual knowledge for the purpose of the legal principle in question. See also *Smith v Johnson* (1899) 15 T.L.R. 180; *Wagstaff v Shorthorn Dairy Co* (1884) Cab. Ell. 324.

[2013] The authorities on when the claimant's intervening act or omission will break the chain of causation are helpfully reviewed in *Borealis AB v Geogas Trading SA* [2010] EWHC 2789 (Comm), [2011] 1 Lloyd's Rep. 482 at [42]–[47]. See above, para.26-071. Applied in *Stacey (t/a The New Gailey Caravan/Motorhomes Centre) v Autosleeper Group Ltd* [2014] EWCA Civ 1551.

[2014] See para.44-417.

[2015] See paras 26-087 et seq.; *Borealis AB v Geogas Trading SA* [2010] EWHC 2789 (Comm), [2011] 1 Lloyd's Rep. 482 at [49]–[50].

[2016] *Kasler and Cohen v Slavouski* [1928] 1 K.B. 78, 85–86.

[2017] *Kasler and Cohen v Slavouski*, above, at 84. See also *Hammond Co v Bussey* (1887) 20 Q.B.D. 79, 86.

[2018] *Wagstaff v Shorthorn Dairy Co* (1884) Cab. Ell. 324.

[2019] See also the facts of *George Mitchell (Chesterhall) Ltd v Finney Lock Seeds Ltd* [1983] 2 A.C. 803, where the House of Lords' decision was based on the assumption that the farmer was entitled to recover all his costs wasted in cultivating the worthless crop, as well as the net profit he would have made from a successful crop: see below, para.44-423.

[2020] See Vol.I, paras 26-025 et seq. This heading may even cover pre-contract expenditure if it was in the reasonable contemplation of the parties as not unlikely to be wasted in the event of a breach: *Anglia Television Ltd v Reed* [1972] 1 Q.B. 60; *Lloyd v Stanbury* [1971] 1 W.L.R. 535 (neither case is on the sale of goods). See Vol.I, para.26-033.

[2021] *Smith v Johnson* (1899) 15 T.L.R. 179.

use.[2022] Similarly, the buyer may be able to recover expenses incurred by him in reliance on the seller's undertaking as to the quality of the goods, where the breach of the undertaking made the expenditure futile.[2023]

44-420 **Limits on recovery of reliance loss** But the buyer may recover his wasted expenditure only to the extent that it would have been covered by the gross return which he would have made from his use of the goods if the seller had fully performed the contract.[2024] This proposition refers only to expenditure which the buyer intended to recoup from his gross return, not to additional expenditure incurred by the buyer after, and as a result of, the breach. It is unsettled how far the buyer can recover damages in respect of both his "expectation interest" (the profit or gain which he expected to receive from performance of the contract but which was prevented by the seller's breach of contract) and his "reliance interest" (wasted expenditure).[2025]

44-421 **Fines paid by the buyer** If it was within the reasonable contemplation[2026] of the parties at the time of making the contract that the buyer might be prosecuted if the goods supplied by the seller were defective, e.g. food unfit for human consumption,[2027] the buyer (in the absence of fault on his part) has been held entitled to recover from the seller both the fine and the costs of his defence.[2028] If, however, the buyer's own negligence led, at least partly, to the imposition of the fine, it has been said that the buyer is not entitled to recover damages in respect of it.[2029] However, a number of later cases[2030] have raised the issue of public policy.[2031] In these it has been said that if the punishment inflicted by a criminal court is personal to the offender, the civil courts should not entertain an action by the offender to

---

[2022] *British Westinghouse Electric and Manufacturing Co Ltd v Underground Electric Railways Co of London Ltd* [1912] A.C. 673, 683. (In fact, the buyers later replaced the defective turbines with a newer, more efficient, model: see above, para.44-414.) See also *Molling Co v Dean Son Ltd* (1901) 18 T.L.R. 217 (wasted freight and customs duty; on avoidance of double recovery in such cases, see *Benjamin's Sale of Goods*, 10th edn (2017), para.17-061).

[2023] Illustrations of this type of recovery are *Cullinane v British "Rema" Manufacturing Co Ltd* [1954] 1 Q.B. 292 (see below, para.44-422); *Molling Co v Dean Son Ltd*, above; *Richard Holden Ltd v Bostock Co Ltd* (1902) 18 T.L.R. 317; *Bostock Co Ltd v Nicholson Sons Ltd* [1904] 1 K.B. 725. If s.53(3) applies, so that the buyer could buy substitute goods in the market, he will not be able to claim for wasted expenditure. See also Stoljar (1975) 91 L.Q.R. 68.

[2024] See Vol.I, paras 26-027, 26-031. (The onus of proof is on the seller to show that the buyer would not have recouped all of his expenditure if the contract had been fully performed by the seller: para.26-027.)

[2025] See below, para.44-423; Vol.I, para.26-032.

[2026] And if it was reasonable to think that the seller was assuming responsibility for the loss: see above, para.44-402 and, more generally, Vol.I, paras 26-137 et seq.

[2027] But see s.21 of the Food Safety Act 1990 (defence of due diligence).

[2028] *Cointat v Myham & Son* [1913] 2 K.B. 220 (reversed on question of warranty: (1914) 30 T.L.R. 282). cf. *Crage v Fry* (1903) 67 J.P. 240 (no evidence as to what influenced the court in imposing the fine); *Marles v Philip Trant Sons Ltd* [1954] 1 Q.B. 29, 39–40. cf. also *Osman v J Ralph Moss Ltd* [1970] 1 Lloyd's Rep. 313.

[2029] *Cointat v Myham Son* [1913] 2 K.B. 220, 222.

[2030] *R Leslie Ltd v Reliable Advertising and Addressing Agency Ltd* [1915] 1 K.B. 652; *Proops v WH Chaplin Co* (1920) 37 T.L.R. 112, 114; *Askey v Golden Wine Co Ltd* (1948) 64 T.L.R. 379 (only the third case concerned the sale of goods).

[2031] If the buyer is acquitted, he may recover his costs in defending a prosecution resulting from the seller's breach of warranty, since public policy is not in question: *Proops v WH Chaplin Co* (1920) 37 T.L.R. 112.

recover an indemnity against the consequences of that punishment.[2032] It is submitted that the issue should turn on whether or not the buyer had mens rea[2033]: if he had not, the court should be willing to award him damages in respect of a fine imposed on him.

The buyer's loss of profit[2034]   Where, at the time of making the contract, the seller **44-422** knew, or ought reasonably to have contemplated, that the buyer intended to use the goods to produce a profit,[2035] and that a breach of the seller's undertaking as to description or quality of the goods would impede that profit-making, the buyer may recover damages for his loss of profits caused by the breach.[2036] Where the goods sold were a profit-earning machine,[2037] which the seller undertook would perform in a specified manner or at a specified rate, the buyer may claim (subject to his taking reasonable steps to mitigate his loss) his loss of profits caused by the failure of the machine to perform as warranted. Thus, in *Cullinane v British "Rema" Manufacturing Co Ltd*[2038] where the seller warranted that a clay-pulverising machine had a certain productive capacity, but the machine failed to achieve this, the Court of Appeal held that the buyer was entitled to recover his net[2039] loss of profits during the normal commercial life of the machine.[2040] But any claim for loss of profits must be considered in the light of the requirement to mitigate: for a period after delivery it may be reasonable for the buyer to use the machine to see if it meets the warranty, but as soon as a reasonable buyer would have replaced the defective machine with one which functioned properly or efficiently,[2041] the buyer should not be entitled to claim for any further loss of profits.[2042] Only if no suitable replacement can reasonably be found should the buyer's claim for loss of profits extend over the full period of the original machine's expected life.[2043]

[2032] See also *Payne v Ministry of Food* (1953) 103 L.J. 141.

[2033] There was mens rea in the plaintiff in both *R Leslie Ltd v Reliable Advertising and Addressing Agency Ltd* [1915] 1 K.B. 652; and *Askey v Golden Wine Co Ltd* (1948) 64 T.L.R. 379.

[2034] For loss of profits under a sub-sale, see below, paras 44-424—44-425.

[2035] The seller must have actual or imputed knowledge of the category of use intended by the buyer: *Bunting v Tory* (1948) 64 T.L.R. 353 (seller did not know that buyer intended to use a bull for breeding): see the discussion in *Benjamin's Sale of Goods*, 10th edn (2017), paras 17-065; and cf. see above, paras 44-400, 44-413.

[2036] *Richard Holden Ltd v Bostock Co Ltd* (1902) 18 T.L.R. 317. See also *Wagstaff v Shorthorn Dairy Co* (1884) Cab. Ell. 324; *Ashworth v Wells* (1898) 14 T.L.R. 227; *Randall v Raper* (1858) E.B. & E. 84; and the facts of *Wallis, Son and Wells v Pratt and Haynes* [1910] 2 K.B. 1003; on appeal [1911] A.C. 394 where the sub-buyer had grown inferior seeds, and his damages appear to have been assessed on the above basis.

[2037] Or part thereof: cf. see above, para.44-408 for authority in an analogous situation.

[2038] [1954] 1 Q.B. 292.

[2039] viz after deducting from his expected gross profits (or gross receipts) the necessary expenditure in earning it.

[2040] [1954] 1 Q.B. 292, 303, 308 (at 315, Morris L.J., dissenting, accepted this proposition).

[2041] In the *Cullinane* case [1954] 1 Q.B. 292 it was held that the buyer did not act unreasonably in continuing to use the machine after he knew that its performance was defective: [1954] 1 Q.B. 292, 314, 316. But cf. *Lambert v Lewis* [1982] A.C. 225 (see above, para.44-417 and below, para.44-432).

[2042] *British Westinghouse Electric and Manufacturing Co Ltd v Underground Electric Railways Co of London Ltd* [1912] A.C. 673 (see above, para.44-414); *Cullinane v British "Rema" Manufacturing Co Ltd* [1954] 1 Q.B. 292, 314, 316. cf. *Lambert v Lewis* above (see below, para.44-432). If the substitute machine made extra profits, these will be taken into account in assessing damages for the cost of the substitute: *British Westinghouse* case, above (see above, para.44-414).

[2043] Macleod [1970] J.B.L. 19, 26; Stoljar (1975) 91 L.Q.R. 68, 77–78.

44-423 **Claims for both wasted expenses and loss of profits**[2044] Difficult problems arise
from a split claim for damages which is based partly on the expenses incurred by
the claimant which the breach renders useless, and partly on the loss of profits
caused by the breach. In *Cullinane v British "Rema" Manufacturing Co Ltd*[2045]
(discussed in the preceding paragraph), the majority of the Court of Appeal held that
the plaintiff could not claim both his capital loss (expenditure incurred) and his loss
of profits[2046]: in their opinion, the plaintiff must elect[2047] between these two claims,
and either seek to be put back into the position he would have been in if the contract
had not been made (viz recover his net outlay, his "reliance expenditure") or,
alternatively, claim what he would have received if the contract had been fully
performed (viz the gross profit he would have received if the machine had
functioned in accordance with the contractual warranty). It is submitted that the
position taken by the majority in this case is confusing: their concern to avoid
double recovery led them to overlook the fact that a *net* loss of profit can be
calculated in such a way as to avoid overlapping with the wasted capital
expenditure. As Morris L.J. pointed out in his dissent,[2048] the plaintiff was claiming only his net profit calculated after a deduction of depreciation, which
represented the return to the buyer of the capital element; therefore, his claim for
his net capital outlay did not overlap with his claim for loss of net profits.[2049] It is
submitted that the view of Morris L.J. is to be preferred, and that a split claim should
be permitted so long as the calculations show that no overlapping occurs in the different heads of claim.[2050]

44-424 **Loss of profits under a sub-sale** Where the seller knew that the buyer intended
to resell the goods, and ought reasonably to have contemplated that a breach of his
contractual undertaking as to the description or condition of the goods would be not
unlikely to cause the buyer to lose the profit he hoped to make under the sub-
sale,[2051] the buyer may recover damages in respect of such a loss of profits caused
by a breach of the seller's undertaking,[2052] provided it was reasonable to think that
the seller was assuming responsibility for the loss.[2053]

44-425 **Loss of future business** Where, at the time they made their contract, it was within
the reasonable contemplation of the parties that defects in the goods supplied by the

---

[2044] The question would also arise of a ceiling on recovery imposed by the gross return expected by the
buyer: see Vol.I, paras 26-027, 26-031.

[2045] [1954] 1 Q.B. 292 (criticised by Macleod [1970] J.B.L. 19; Stoljar (1975) 91 L.Q.R. 68; and Street,
Principles of the Law of Damages (1962), pp.242–245).

[2046] [1954] 1 Q.B. 292, 302, 303, 308, 311, 312.

[2047] The Court of Appeal took the same position in cases not concerned with the sale of goods: *Anglia
Television Ltd v Reed* [1972] 1 Q.B. 60, 63–64; *CCC Films Ltd v Impact Quadrant Films Ltd* [1985]
Q.B. 16. cf. *George Mitchell (Chesterhall) Ltd v Finney Lock Seeds Ltd* [1983] 2 A.C. 803, 812 (the
leading speech approved damages which included both wasted costs and loss of profit).

[2048] [1954] 1 Q.B. 292, 315, 317–318.

[2049] Macleod [1970] J.B.L. 19. The distinction between gross and net profits is recognised (in relation
to recoupment of expenditure) in the *CCC Films* case [1985] Q.B. 16, 32.

[2050] See *TC Industrial Plant Pty Ltd v Robert's Queensland Pty Ltd* [1964] A.L.R. 1083. See also Vol.I,
para.26-032. Split claims were allowed in two earlier cases at first instance (neither of which was
referred to in the *Cullinane* case [1954] 1 Q.B. 292, 314): *Foaminol Laboratories v British Artid
Plastics* [1941] 2 All E.R. 393; and *Molling Co v Dean Son Ltd* (1901) 18 T.L.R. 217.

[2051] Or under potential sub-sales: see *Richard Holden Ltd v Bostock Co Ltd* (1902) 18 T.L.R. 317.

[2052] *Molling Co v Dean Son Ltd*, above, at 218. cf. above, paras 44-400, 44-404, 44-422.

[2053] See above, para.44-402 and, more generally, Vol.I, paras 26-137 et seq.

seller (in breach of his warranty as to their quality) might lead to sub-buyers (customers of the buyer) withdrawing their custom from the buyer, damages may be awarded for loss of profits on "repeat orders" from the sub-buyers[2054] and for expenses reasonably incurred by the buyer in attempting to minimise a possible loss of business.[2055]

Loss of amenity   In the chapter on Damages in Vol.I[2056] there is an examination   **44-426**
of the recent authorities on damages for "loss of amenity". In no reported cases has such an award been made to a buyer of goods, but it is possible that an analogy might be drawn from the cases on the purchase of land or building construction.

Physical injury to the buyer   If it was in the reasonable contemplation of the par-   **44-427**
ties, at the time of making the contract, that the seller's breach of his contractual undertaking as to quality or description was not unlikely to cause physical injury to the buyer's person[2057] or property, the buyer may recover damages for such injury.[2058] Thus, where the buyer of woollen underwear contracted dermatitis through the defective condition of the garment, he recovered substantial damages from the retailers for breach of the statutory condition imposed by s.14 of the Act.[2059] (There may often be concurrent liability in tort,[2060] but the advantage of suing in contract is that the claimant may not have to prove the negligence of the defendant.)

Loss through injury to others   Where it was within the reasonable contempla-   **44-428**
tion of the parties that the goods sold to the buyer would be used by members of the buyer's family, and that a defect in them was not unlikely to cause injury to them, the buyer is entitled to recover damages (in contract) for any pecuniary loss (such as expenses) caused to him by such injury.[2061] So where food for human consumption was sold to the buyer and eaten by his wife who died as a result, the buyer recovered damages for the medical and funeral expenses he had paid, and for

---

[2054] *GKN Centrax Gears Ltd v Matbro Ltd* [1976] 2 Lloyd's Rep. 555, 573–574, 577, 579–580 (not following *Simon v Pawsons and Leafs Ltd* (1933) 38 Com. Cas. 151, 158). See also *Aerial Advertising v Batchelor's Peas* [1938] 2 All E.R. 788. cf. *Cointat v Myham Son* [1913] 2 K.B. 220 reversed on another point (1914) 30 T.L.R. 282. cf. also *Amstrad Plc v Seagate Technology Inc* (1998) 86 B.L.R. 34. cf. also *Jackson v Bank of Scotland* [2005] UKHL 3, [2005] 1 W.L.R. 377 (see Vol.I, para.26-149).

[2055] *Richard Holden Ltd v Bostock Co Ltd* (1902) 18 T.L.R. 317.

[2056] See Vol.I, paras 26-152 et seq.

[2057] *Grant v Australian Knitting Mills Ltd* [1936] A.C. 85. See also *Wren v Holt* [1903] 1 K.B. 610; *Geddling v Marsh* [1920] 1 K.B. 668; *Morelli v Fitch Gibbons* [1928] 2 K.B. 636; *Andrews v Hopkinson* [1957] 1 Q.B. 229; *Godley v Perry* [1960] 1 W.L.R. 9. (The damages may include the normal heads of damages in the assessment in tort for personal injuries or death: [1960] 1 W.L.R. 9 at 13.) Special rules apply to the award of interest on such damages: see Vol.I, para.26-281.

[2058] *Grant v Australian Knitting Mills Ltd* [1936] A.C. 85. The buyer will not be able to continue to rely on the undertaking after he knew (or ought reasonably to have known) that the goods were defective: cf. *Lambert v Lewis* [1982] A.C. 225 (see below, para.44-432).

[2059] *Grant v Australian Knitting Mills Ltd* [1936] A.C. 85. (The relevant provision was s.14 of the South Australian Act, which was identical with s.14 of the 1893 United Kingdom Act before the 1973 amendment.)

[2060] See above, Vol.I, paras 1-172 et seq.

[2061] *Priest v Last* [1903] 2 K.B. 148; *Frost v Aylesbury Dairy Co Ltd* [1905] 1 K.B. 608; *Jackson v Watson Sons* [1909] 2 K.B. 193; *Square v Model Farm Dairies (Bournemouth) Ltd* [1939] 2 K.B. 365, 374. On the recovery of damages in respect of loss suffered by third parties, see Vol.I, paras 18-051 et seq.

the loss of his wife's services which led to his employing extra staff.[2062] But it should be noted that under the Contracts (Rights of Third Parties) Act 1999 members of the buyer's family may be sufficiently "identified" as third parties intended to have conferred on them the benefit of a term of the contract, so as to be entitled to enforce that term directly against the seller[2063]

44-429 **Damage to other property of the buyer**[2064] Where it was within the reasonable contemplation of the parties that a defect in the goods bought by the buyer was not unlikely to cause loss of, or damage to, other property belonging to the buyer, his damages may include compensation for this loss or injury.[2065] So where game farmers bought compounded meal for feeding to their pheasants and many chicks died and others grew up stunted because the meal contained a toxic substance, the farmers recovered damages for the loss of the birds and the reduced value of the survivors.[2066] If the other property was damaged in the course of the use made of the goods by the buyer, the category of use in question must be one which was within the reasonable contemplation of the parties as a not unlikely use of the goods. If there are several categories of ordinary or common use, the buyer may recover if his use of the goods was within one of these categories,[2067] even though it may not have been the main type of use.[2068]

44-430 **Disruption to buyer's business** Where defective performance of a contract causes disruption to a business, for example because its staff have to spend time dealing with the ensuing problems, the reasonable costs can be recovered.[2069]

44-431 **Compensation paid to a stranger (other than a sub-buyer)**[2070] It may have been within the reasonable contemplation of the parties at the time of making the contract that: (a) if the goods were defective, a third person (or his property) was not unlikely to be injured as a result of the defect; and (b) as a result the buyer was not unlikely to be held legally liable to compensate the third party for his injury or loss. In these circumstances, if such an injury occurs, and the defect was in breach of the seller's contractual obligations to the buyer, the latter may recover as damages from the

---

[2062] *Jackson v Watson Sons* [1909] 2 K.B. 193, CA.

[2063] See Vol.I, paras 18-090 et seq.

[2064] cf. above, para.44-428, last sentence.

[2065] *Borradaile v Brunton* (1818) 8 Taunt. 535 (defective anchor cable caused loss of the anchor); *Randall v Newson* (1877) 2 Q.B.D. 102 (pole for a carriage broke in use, frightening the horses, which were injured); *Bostock Co Ltd v Nicholson Sons Ltd* [1904] 1 K.B. 725 (impure acid caused waste of other ingredients mixed with it); *Wilson v Rickett Cockerell Co Ltd* [1954] 1 Q.B. 598 (coalite exploded when burning in grate causing damage to the room and furniture); *H Parsons (Livestock) Ltd v Uttley Ingham Co Ltd* [1978] Q.B. 791. See above, para.44-427 n.2050 and Vol.I, para.26-128.

[2066] *Hardwick Game Farm Ltd v SAPPA* [1969] 2 A.C. 31. (The decision of the House of Lords assumes that the game farmers were entitled to recover damages for these losses.) See also *Smith v Green* (1875) 1 C.P.D. 92 (cow with infection infected others); *H Parsons (Livestock) Ltd v Uttley Ingham Co Ltd* [1978] Q.B. 791 (defective hopper caused mouldy food, which was fed to pigs).

[2067] *Bostock Co Ltd v Nicholson Sons Ltd* [1904] 1 K.B. 725.

[2068] *Hardwick Game Farm Ltd v SAPPA* [1969] 2 A.C. 31. cf. *Bunting v Tory* (1948) 64 T.L.R. 353. cf. also *Christopher Hill Ltd v Ashington Piggeries Ltd* [1972] A.C. 441 (claim against the third party under s.14).

[2069] See above, para.26-184. *Azzurri Communications Ltd v International Telecommunications Equipment Ltd* [2013] EWPCC 17 (the exercise of pulling out and replacing handsets caused significant disruption to business but investigation of faults was part of the normal support function: at [93]).

[2070] Compare below, para.44-433.

seller the damages[2071] and costs paid to the third party,[2072] and the buyer's own costs incurred in reasonably defending the third party's claim.[2073] The legal basis of the buyer's liability towards the stranger is normally under the law of torts,[2074] but it could be under a contract, e.g. a contract of employment.

Buyer must not act unreasonably   The buyer is not justified in continuing to rely   **44-432** on the seller's warranty after he knows that the goods are defective in that respect.[2075] Where a buyer bought a trailer coupling, the House of Lords held that the warranty[2076] that it was reasonably fit for towing trailers would continue in effect for a reasonable time after delivery, so long as it remained in the same apparent state as that in which it was delivered (apart from normal wear and tear). But as soon as the buyer learned[2077] that the handle of the locking mechanism of the coupling was missing, he could no longer rely on the seller's warranty to excuse him from making his own examination to see if it was still safe to use. The buyer was held liable[2078] to third parties injured when the trailer broke away, but he could not recover from the seller the damages paid to them, because his reliance on the warranty was no longer justified. The buyer's actions or omissions may break the chain of causation between the breach and any subsequent loss or damage. The buyer's knowledge is highly relevant to this. Reckless conduct on the buyer's part is likely to break the chain of causation, whereas merely unreasonable conduct will not necessarily do so.[2079] If the buyer was aware of the breach, and possibly if he should have been aware of it,[2080] he will not be able to recover for losses he could have avoided by taking reasonable steps to mitigate the loss.[2081]

[2071] A reasonable settlement out of court would be included: see the analogous situation, see below, para.44-433, and *Mowbray v Merryweather* [1895] 2 Q.B. 640.

[2072] This principle is implicit in the decision of the House of Lords in *Lambert v Lewis* [1982] A.C. 225. The previous cases were not on sale of goods but on contracts where chattels were to be supplied for the use of the plaintiff and others: *Mowbray v Merryweather* [1895] 2 Q.B. 640 (approved by the House of Lords in *Lambert v Lewis*, above); *Scott v Foley, Aikman Co* (1899) 16 T.L.R. 55 (breach of a warranty as to the condition of appliances on a ship). cf. *Hadley v Droitwich Construction Co Ltd* [1968] 1 W.L.R. 37.

[2073] *Scott v Foley, Aikman Co* (1899) 16 T.L.R. 55 at 56. On reasonableness in appealing, cf. *Vogan v Oulton* (1899) 81 L.T. 435 (a case of hire). The buyer may also recover the costs incurred by him in successfully defending a claim brought against him by a stranger as a result of the seller's breach of contract: see the analogous case where the plaintiff's lorry was negligently repaired by the defendants: *Britannia Hygienic Laundry Co Ltd v John I Thorneycroft Co Ltd* (1925) 41 T.L.R. 667 (reversed by the Court of Appeal on a different view of the facts: (1926) 42 T.L.R. 198). On the basis for the assessment of costs, see below, para.44-433 n.2082.

[2074] *Mowbray v Merryweather* [1895] 2 Q.B. 640; *Scott v Foley, Aikman Co* (1899) 16 T.L.R. 55.

[2075] *Lambert v Lewis* [1982] A.C. 225 (cf. see above, para.44-416).

[2076] Under s.14(1) of the 1893 Act. (See now s.14(3) of the 1979 Act.)

[2077] Although the House of Lords did not advert to the situation where the buyer *ought* reasonably to have known of the missing handle, it is submitted that the same legal consequences should apply in the case of imputed knowledge (see above, para.44-417).

[2078] On the ground of his negligence in continuing to use the coupling without having it examined.

[2079] The authorities on when the claimant's intervening act or omission will break the chain of causation are helpfully reviewed in *Borealis AB v Geogas Trading SA* [2010] EWHC 2789 (Comm), [2011] 1 Lloyd's Rep. 482 at [42]–[47] and applied in *Stacey (t/a The New Gailey Caravan/ Motorhomes Centre) v Autosleeper Group Ltd* [2014] EWCA Civ 1551. See above, para.26-071.

[2080] See para.44-417.

[2081] See paras 26-087 et seq.; *Borealis AB v Geogas Trading SA* [2010] EWHC 2789 (Comm), [2011] 1 Lloyd's Rep. 482 at [49]–[50].

44-433 **Compensation paid by the buyer to a sub-buyer**[2082]   This paragraph is concerned with the situation where the seller was in breach of his contractual undertaking as to the description or condition of the goods and (1) it was within the reasonable contemplation of the parties, at the time of making the contract, that[2083] (a) the buyer would, or probably[2084] would, resell the goods to a sub-buyer; and (b) that the contract of sub-sale would, or probably would, contain the same,[2085] or a similar,[2086] contractual undertaking as to the description or condition of the goods; and (c) that it was not unlikely[2087] that a breach of the seller's undertaking would cause the buyer to be in breach of his undertaking to the sub-buyer who would claim damages from the buyer for the loss or damage he suffered; and (2) it was reasonable to think that the seller was assuming responsibility for the loss.[2088] If loss or injury occurs in these circumstances, the buyer who has paid damages and costs[2089] to his sub-buyer for breach of the undertaking in the sub-sale may recover this amount from the seller, together with his own costs[2090] in reasonably defending the sub-buyer's claim, as damages for the seller's breach of the original contract.[2091] A reasonable settlement with the sub-buyer out of court may be the basis of the buyer's claim for damages[2092]; but the seller may attempt to show that the buyer was not liable to pay anything to the sub-buyer[2093] or may produce new evidence or new factors to show

---

[2082] The sub-buyer may possibly have a direct claim against the seller: see below, para.44-437.

[2083] The composite propositions in the first two sentences of this paragraph are supported by the cases cited in the following footnotes. In particular, the propositions are supported by the judgment of Bowen L.J. in *Hammond Co v Bussey* (1887) 20 Q.B.D. 79, 94–95 (a passage cited with approval by the Court of Appeal in *Biggin & Co Ltd v Permanite Ltd* [1951] 2 K.B. 314, 318–319). The cases on a chain of sub-sales (see below, para.44-434) also support these propositions. In one case, *Bostock Co Ltd v Nicholson Sons Ltd* [1904] 1 K.B. 725, the buyer's claim failed, but it is submitted in *Benjamin's Sale of Goods*, 10th edn (2017), para.17-076, that the case is no longer authoritative.

[2084] *Hammond Co v Bussey* (1887) 20 Q.B.D. 79, 88, 89.

[2085] As in *Hammond Co v Bussey* (1887) 20 Q.B.D. 79, 88, 89.

[2086] The possibility of a "similar" warranty leading to recovery of damages by the buyer was mentioned (obiter) in *Hammond Co v Bussey* (1887) 20 Q.B.D. 79, 89, 96. See further the discussion, see below, para.44-436.

[2087] In *Hammond Co v Bussey* (1887) 20 Q.B.D. 79, 89, 96, reference was made at 93 to the parties' reasonable contemplation that "the highly probable result of a breach" of the original undertaking would be a lawsuit between the buyers and their sub-buyers. But it is submitted that the "not unlikely" test is now the correct one (see Vol.I, para.26-132).

[2088] *Transfield Shipping Inc v Mercator Shipping Inc (The Achilleas)* [2008] UKHL 48, [2009] 1 A.C. 61, described as exceptional in *Saipol SA v Inerco Trade SA* [2014] EWHC 2211 (Comm). See above, para.44-402 and, more generally, Vol.I, paras 26-137 et seq.

[2089] The costs must be reasonably incurred (and will be assessed on the standard basis): *Hammond Co v Bussey*, above; *Pinnock Bros v Peat and Lewis Ltd* [1923] 1 K.B. 690, 698; *Sidney Bennett Ltd v Kreeger* (1925) 41 T.L.R. 609. See Benjamin at para.17-077, and cf. above, para.44-400; see below, para.44-436.

[2090] The buyer's own reasonable (see para.44-431 n.2066, above) costs will be assessed on the standard basis which is now the proper basis for the recovery of the claimant's costs incurred in litigation with a third party: *British Racing Drivers' Club Ltd v Hextall Erskine Co* [1996] 3 All E.R. 667 (not a sale of goods case). cf. the analogous case in delayed delivery: *Agius v Great Western Colliery Co* [1899] 1 Q.B. 413.

[2091] In some situations, the buyer's damages may be *restricted* by reference to the extent of the buyer's liability towards his sub-buyer (see below, para.44-435).

[2092] *Biggin & Co Ltd v Permanite Ltd* [1951] 2 K.B. 314 (applied in *Meadowbank Vac Alloys Ltd v Eurokey Recycling Ltd* Unreported May 16, 2016, QBD Manchester District Registry). (It is also implicit in this case that it may be reasonable for the buyer to submit his dispute with the sub-buyer to arbitration.) cf. *Grébert-Borgnis v J and W Nugent* (1885) 15 Q.B.D. 85.

[2093] *Biggin & Co Ltd v Permanite Ltd* [1951] 2 K.B. 314, 320 (citing *Kiddle v Lovett* (1885) 16 Q.B.D. 605). The principle in *Biggin's* case covers compromises of issues of liability as well as of quantum:

that the sum paid was not reasonable.[2094] As soon as the buyer, whether before or after reselling the goods, has discovered[2095] the defect in their description or condition, he is unable to pass on to his seller any liability which he thereafter incurred towards his sub-buyer (but which he could reasonably have avoided) in respect of that defect,[2096] e.g. where he could, by passing on the knowledge to his sub-buyer, reduce his liability towards the sub-buyer.[2097]

Compensation paid to sub-buyers in a series of "string contracts"[2098] This **44-434** paragraph is concerned with the situation where the seller was in breach of his contractual undertaking as to the description or condition of the goods, and it was within the reasonable contemplation of the parties, at the time of making the contract, that:

(a) the buyer intended[2099] to resell, or probably[2100] would do so, and that his sub-buyer would probably resell, and so on, so that there would be a series of sub-sales or "string contracts" of the same goods; and

(b) that each contract in the series would, or probably would, contain the same,[2101] or a similar,[2102] contractual undertaking as to the description or condition of the goods; and

(c) that it was not unlikely that a breach of the seller's undertaking would cause the buyer and each sub-buyer in the series to be in breach of his undertaking to his own buyer[2103]; and

(d) that it was not unlikely that, in the case of such a breach, the ultimate buyers would recover damages from their sellers, so that liability would in turn be passed up the chain of sellers and buyers.[2104]

In these circumstances, the buyer who has paid to his sub-buyer damages and costs[2105] for breach of the undertaking in the first contract of sub-sale (which the

---

Royal Brompton Hospital NHS Trust v Hammond (1999) 149 N.L.J. 89.

[2094] *Biggin & Co Ltd v Permanite Ltd* [1951] 2 K.B. 314, 321, 325. No matter how reasonable a settlement may appear to the parties, it does not determine the liability of a third party: *PO Developments Ltd v Guy's and St Thomas' NHS Trust* (1998) 62 Con. L.R. 38 (not a sale of goods case). The reasonableness of a settlement must be judged in the light of the facts available at the time it was made: *General Feeds Inc Panama v Slobodna Plovidba Yugoslavia* [1999] 1 Lloyd's Rep. 688.

[2095] On the question of *imputed* knowledge, see above, paras 44-416—44-428.

[2096] *British Oil and Cake Co Ltd v Burstall Co* (1923) 39 T.L.R. 406, 407; *GC Dobell Co Ltd v Barber and Garratt* [1931] 1 K.B. 219, 238 (cf. at 246–247); *Biggin & Co Ltd v Permanite Ltd* [1951] 2 K.B. 314 at 435. cf. *Lambert v Lewis* [1982] A.C. 225 (see above, para.44-432).

[2097] The sub-buyer would thereupon come under a duty towards the buyer to take reasonable steps to mitigate his loss caused by the defect.

[2098] This paragraph was cited in *Louis Dreyfus Trading Ltd v Reliance Trading Ltd* [2004] EWHC 525 (Comm), [2004] 2 Lloyd's Rep. 243 at [24].

[2099] e.g. *GC Dobell Co v Barber and Garratt* [1931] 1 K.B. 219 at 231; *Biggin & Co Ltd v Permanite Ltd* [1951] 1 K.B. 422, 431; reversed by the Court of Appeal on another ground: [1951] 2 K.B. 314.

[2100] cf. *Hammond Co v Bussey* (1887) 20 Q.B.D. 79, 88, 89.

[2101] e.g. *Kasler and Cohen v Slavouski* [1928] 1 K.B. 78, 85; *GC Dobell Co v Barber and Garratt* [1931] 1 K.B. 219 (warranty as to quality implied by statute).

[2102] See below, para.44-436.

[2103] But consider the question of a buyer's knowledge (actual or implied) at a date after the contract was made: see above, para.44-432.

[2104] *Biggin & Co Ltd v Permanite Ltd* [1951] 1 K.B. 422 at 431–432. See also *Kasler and Cohen v Slavouski* [1928] 1 K.B. 78 at 85, 87.

[2105] The total costs may include both those incurred by the buyer and also by sub-buyers lower in the chain, provided each acted reasonably in incurring the costs: *Kasler and Cohen v Slavouski* [1928]

sub-buyer claimed from the buyer, as the result of similar payments of compensation between successive sub-buyers down the chain) may recover the amount paid by him to the sub-buyer,[2106] together with his own reasonable costs[2107] in reasonably defending the sub-buyer's claim against him; the damages and costs paid or incurred by the buyer are taken as the measure of damages for the seller's breach of the original contract.[2108]

44-435   In a chain of sales, the buyer may sometimes be precluded from relying on the normal rule for the assessment of damages laid down by s.53(3). In *Biggin & Co Ltd v Permanite Ltd* Devlin J. held that where the sub-sale was within the contemplation of the parties, the original buyer's damages must be assessed by reference to it, whether he likes it or not: if it is the original buyer's "liability to the ultimate user that is contemplated as the measure of damage and if in fact it is used without injurious results so that no such liability arises, the [original buyer] could not claim the difference in market value, and say that the sub-sale must be disregarded".[2109]

44-436 **Variations in descriptions or undertakings** The question whether the contractual undertakings as to the description or condition of the goods in the string contracts must be the same as in the original contract caused difficulty in the earlier cases.[2110] In *Biggin & Co Ltd v Permanite Ltd*,[2111] Devlin J. said:

> "If the variation to a description is such that it is impossible to say whether the injury that ultimately results would have flowed from the breach of the original warranty, the parties must as reasonable men be presumed to have put the liability for the injury outside their contemplation as a measure of compensation. If this is, as I believe, the nature of the principle, it must be applied very differently according to whether the injury for which the defendant is being asked to pay is a market loss or physical damage. In the former case[2112] ... any variation that is more than a matter of words is likely to be fatal, because there is no way of telling its effect on the market value. In the latter case the nature of the physical damage will show whether the variation was material or not."

It is submitted that this passage states the correct principle. If one of the buyers in

---

1 K.B. 78; *Godley v Perry* [1960] 1 W.L.R. 9, 16–17. See also *Pinnock Bros v Lewis and Peat Ltd* [1923] 1 K.B. 690. (cf. above, para.44-433.) The costs will be each party's own reasonable costs assessed on the standard basis (see above, para.44-433 n.2082) and the assessed costs paid to the next person in the chain. cf. the similar situation where there is a breach of the implied condition as to title in a chain of sub-sales: *Butterworth v Kingsway Motors* [1954] 1 W.L.R. 1286, 1297–1300; *Bowmaker (Commercial) Ltd v Day* [1965] 1 W.L.R. 1396.

[2106] *Pinnock Bros v Lewis and Peat Ltd* [1923] 1 K.B. 690; *GC Dobell Co v Barber and Garratt* [1931] 1 K.B. 219; *Biggin & Co Ltd v Permanite Ltd* [1951] 1 K.B. 422.

[2107] *Kasler and Cohen v Slavouski* [1928] 1 K.B. 78. cf. see above, para.44-433.

[2108] See also the limitation in the last sentence of para.44-433, see above.

[2109] [1951] 1 K.B. 422 at 436. The principle stated in the text was followed in *Bence Graphics International Ltd v Fasson UK Ltd* [1998] Q.B. 87 (see above, paras 44-413, 44-415); but see the criticism of Treitel (1997) 113 L.Q.R. 188, who argues that *Biggin & Co Ltd v Permanite Ltd* [1951] 1 K.B. 422, was a "consequential loss" case where the remoteness rules were relevant. See also *Louis Dreyfus Trading Ltd v Reliance Trading Ltd* [2004] EWHC 525 (Comm), [2004] 2 Lloyd's Rep. 243.

[2110] In *Dexters Ltd v Hill Crest Oil Co (Bradford) Ltd* [1926] 1 K.B. 348, 359, it was held to be "essential" that the contractual description should be the same; but recovery was allowed in *British Oil and Cake Co Ltd v Burstall Co* (1923) 39 T.L.R. 406 despite some differences in the wording of the contracts.

[2111] [1951] 1 K.B. 422, 433–434; reversed by the Court of Appeal on a different point: [1951] 2 K.B. 314.

[2112] As illustrated by *Dexters Ltd v Hill Crest Oil Co (Bradford) Ltd*, above.

the chain added to the description of the goods sold to him, or varied the undertaking as to their condition, the original seller should still be liable for the loss or injury suffered by the ultimate buyer if it was caused by a defect in the goods covered both by the original seller's description or undertaking and also by the descriptions or undertakings in all the intervening contracts.[2113]

A direct claim by the sub-buyer against the seller Under the Contracts (Rights **44-437** of Third Parties) Act 1999[2114] a sub-buyer as a "third party" may be able to enforce[2115] a term in the main contract between the seller and the buyer if *either* the contract expressly provides that he may; *or* the term purports to confer a benefit on him and he is sufficiently "identified" (e.g. as a sub-buyer, an agent or employee of the buyer). But the contract may show that the third party was not intended to be entitled to enforce the term. Where the buyer has already agreed to sell the goods to the sub-buyer, the 1999 Act will not apply merely if the seller knows that the buyer is buying the goods in order to fulfil that contract; the contract must purport to benefit the third party which seems to require at a minimum that it refers to the third party.[2116] It is conceivable that the contract between the buyer and the seller might expressly entitle the sub-buyer to enforce an obligation on the seller (e.g. an obligation to deliver to the sub-buyer's premises) or it might "purport to confer" such a benefit on the sub-buyer so as to bring the case within the Act.

(d) Other Remedies of the Buyer[2117]

Rejection of the goods: termination of the contract Where the seller repudi- **44-438** ates his obligations under the contract, or commits a fundamental breach of contract or a breach of condition, the buyer may choose to treat the contract as terminated, reject the goods,[2118] and sue for damages. Where the buyer justifiably rejects the goods, he can treat the seller's failure to deliver goods in conformity with the contract as a simple case of failure to deliver, and the buyer's damages will be assessed in accordance with s.51.[2119]

Restitution: recovery of money paid to the seller Section 54 of the Act[2120] **44-439** provides that:

[2113] cf. *Pinnock Bros v Lewis and Peat Ltd* [1923] 1 K.B. 690, at 696–697, 698–699; cf. also *Lambert v Lewis* [1982] A.C. 225, 275–278 (see above, para.44-432).

[2114] See above, Vol.I, paras 18-090 et seq.

[2115] As far as remedies are concerned, the third party is treated as a party to the contract: s.5(1).

[2116] See above, paras 18-093—18-096.

[2117] Remedies in cases of illegality, mistake, misrepresentation, frustration and other invalidating causes, are examined in Vol.I.

[2118] See above, para.44-056.

[2119] See above, paras 44-387 et seq. Under Pt 5A of the Act and now the Consumer Rights Act 2015, the consumer's remedies where the goods do not conform to the contract include "rescission". The traditional remedy of rejection is also available to the consumer, who must therefore compare the relative advantages in pursuing either remedy. See above, paras 38-442 et seq.

[2120] This section does not apply to consumer contracts for the sale of goods which fall within Ch.2 of Pt 1 of the Consumer Rights Act 2015. In consumer contracts for the sale of goods the 2015 Act provides special rules in relation to rejection in consumer sales contracts and provides that in principle the trader has a duty to give the consumer a refund; see above, paras 38-451, 38-453, 38-454.

"Nothing in this Act affects the right of the buyer or the seller ... to recover money paid where the consideration for the payment of it has failed."[2121]

The claim referred to in this provision is one in restitution where the claimant has failed to receive the benefit of the other party's performance.[2122] For instance, the buyer has a claim in restitution to recover the price he has paid to the seller if the seller, in breach of his obligation under s.12(1), failed to pass a good title to the goods sold.[2123] Similarly, if the seller failed to deliver the goods[2124] or delivered goods which the buyer was entitled to and did reject, the buyer may recover the deposit[2125] or prepayment of the price[2126] (or part of the price) which he paid to the seller.[2127] Even where the buyer himself is in default as to his obligations, he may be entitled to claim restitution of advance payments made to the seller.[2128]

44-440   **Specific performance[2129]**   Section 52[2130] provides:

"(1)   In any action for breach of contract to deliver specific or ascertained goods[2131] the court may, if it thinks fit, on the plaintiff's[2132] application, by its judgment or decree

---

[2121] Other aspects of s.54 are mentioned see above, paras 44-387, 44-419, 44-421.

[2122] See Vol.I, paras 29-057 et seq. Goff and Jones, *Law of Unjust Enrichment*, 9th edn (2016), Chs 12–16.

[2123] *Rowland v Divall* [1923] 2 K.B. 500 (see Vol.I, para.29-060; see above, para.44-083; and *Benjamin's Sale of Goods*, 10th edn (2017), paras 4-002 et seq.); *Barber v NWS Bank Plc* [1996] 1 W.L.R. 641. cf. *Yeoman Credit Ltd v Apps* [1962] 2 Q.B. 508. See the Law Commission's Report No.160 (1987), paras 6.1–6.5.

[2124] If the contract was divisible, the buyer could recover only the part of the money paid which was apportioned to that part of the contract which the seller had failed to perform: *Fibrosa Spolka Akcyjna v Fairbairn Lawson Combe Barbour Ltd* [1943] A.C. 32, 77; *Devaux v Conolly* (1849) 8 C.B. 640. See also *Biggerstaff v Rowatt's Wharf Ltd* [1896] 2 Ch. 93; *Behrend Co Ltd v Produce Brokers Co Ltd* [1920] 3 K.B. 530; *Ebrahim Dawood Ltd v Heath Ltd* [1961] 2 Lloyd's Rep. 512.

[2125] *Fitt v Cassanet* (1842) 4 M. G. 898.

[2126] e.g. *Comptoir D'Achat et De Vente du Boerenbond Belge SA v Luis de Ridder Limitada (The Julia)* [1949] A.C. 293; the *Fibrosa* case [1943] A.C. 32.

[2127] The claim in restitution can avoid the rules on damages: see Vol.I, para.29-062. (The buyer could, alternatively, sue for damages—which would include the amount paid to the seller—but he would then have to prove his loss and would be subject to all the rules on damages.)

[2128] Vol.I, paras 26-253—26-256.

[2129] Treitel [1966] J.B.L. 211; Sharpe, *Injunctions and Specific Performance* (looseleaf), paras 8-230—8-510; Jones and Goodhart, *Specific Performance*, 2nd edn, pp.143–154; Spry, *The Principles of Equitable Remedies*, 9th edn (2012), Ch.3; and Vol.I, Ch.27, especially paras 27-022—27-028.

[2130] This section does not apply to consumer contracts for the sale of goods which fall within Ch.2 of Pt 1 of the Consumer Rights Act 2015. Under Pt 5A of the Act and the Consumer Rights Act 2015, the remedy of specific performance is available to a consumer-buyer to enforce his requirement of the repair or replacement of non-conforming goods. See Harris (2003) 119 L.Q.R. 541. However, the use of specific performance under those provisions is subject to different rules from those governing its use under s.52. See above, para.38-521 on the discretion to order specific performance of the trader's obligations under the Act and para.38-512 in relation to consumer's other remedies generally.

[2131] See above, paras 44-040 et seq. Provided that the goods are specific or ascertained, s.52 applies whether or not the property in the goods has passed to the buyer: *James Jones Sons Ltd v Tankerville* [1909] 2 Ch. 440, 445; *Re Wait* [1927] 1 Ch. 606, 617; *Cohen v Roche* [1927] 1 K.B. 169, 180. Goods are not ascertained for the purposes of s.52 if they are yet to be manufactured and even then will form an unidentifiable part of the seller's output: *TTK LIG Ltd* [2011] EWCA Civ 1170, [2012] 1 All E.R. (Comm) 429 at [89].

[2132] If a third party is entitled to enforce a term of the contract under the Contracts (Rights of Third Parties) Act 1999, he may claim any remedy which would be available to him if he were a party: see above, Vol.I, para.18-100.

direct that the contract shall be performed specifically, without giving the defendant the option of retaining the goods on payment of damages.

(2) The plaintiff's application may be made at any time before judgment or decree.

(3) The judgment or decree may be unconditional, or on such terms and conditions as to damages, payment of the price and otherwise as seem just to the court."[2133]

Before the 1893 Act, the remedy of specific performance was an equitable one,[2134] and the courts have used the cases in equity to guide their use of s.52.[2135]

Specific or ascertained goods "Specific goods" are defined by s.61(1) as "goods **44-441** identified and agreed on at the time a contract of sale is made[2136] and includes an undivided share, specified as a fraction or percentage, of goods identified and agreed on as aforesaid".[2137] "Ascertained goods", according to Atkin L.J. in *Re Wait*,[2138] "probably means identified in accordance with the agreement after the time a contract of sale is made", i.e. goods which were unascertained[2139] at the time the contract was made.[2140] The 1995 extension of the definition[2141] means that if a bulk (such as the cargo of a ship) was identified and agreed upon when the contract was made, an order of specific performance may be made under s.52 in respect of a fraction or percentage of the bulk. But where the part sold is a specified quantity to be taken from an identified bulk it appears that no order can be made, because the goods are not "specific" in terms of the new definition, and they remain unascertained. In *Re Wait*,[2142] the majority of the Court of Appeal held that no order for specific performance should be made of a sub-contract to sell 500 tons out of a consignment of 1,000 tons of wheat bought by the seller, because the 500 tons were neither specific nor ascertained goods.[2143] (This decision preceded the new definition, but the facts fall outside it, because no "fraction or percentage" was specified).

[2133] The last subsection, which refers to Scots law, is omitted. The implementation of s.52 is covered by a procedural rule, which provides that a judgment or order for the delivery of goods which does not give the defendant the alternative of paying the assessed value of the goods may be enforced by a "writ of specific delivery" without alternative provision for recovery of the assessed value of the goods: CPR r.83.14.

[2134] Details must be sought in standard works on equity: Fry, *Specific Performance of Contracts*, 6th edn, especially pp.36–41; McGhee (ed) *Snell's Equity*, 33rd edn (2015), Ch.17; *Ashburner's Principles of Equity*, 2nd edn, pp.382–408. See also Vol.I, Ch.27.

[2135] e.g. *Re Wait* [1927] 1 Ch. 606, CA.

[2136] Thus, an order for specific performance could not be made where the seller agreed to supply all the coal that might be required for the buyer's steel works: *Dominion Coal Co Ltd v Dominion Iron and Steel Co Ltd* [1909] A.C. 293, 311. For an examination of the problems of enforcing long-term supply contracts, see Sharpe at paras 8-390—8-510, 9-130—9-200. Jones and Goodhart at pp.148–149, argue that English courts should follow US practice in being willing to grant specific performance of contracts to sell all the seller's output or to satisfy all the buyer's requirements.

[2137] The words "and includes … as aforesaid" were added by s.2(d) of the Sale of Goods (Amendment) Act 1995. The effect of this change on the availability of specific performance is examined see above, para.27-024; paras 44-160 et seq.

[2138] [1927] 1 Ch. 606 at 630.

[2139] See above, paras 44-040 et seq., para.44-131. cf. see above, para.44-149.

[2140] *Thames Sack and Bag Co Ltd v Knowles Co Ltd* (1918) 88 L.J. K.B. 585, 588 ("'ascertained' means that the individuality of the goods must in some way be found out"); cf. *Laurie and Morewood v Dudin Sons* [1926] 1 K.B. 223, CA (no appropriation by a warehouseman of 200 quarters of maize out of a bulk of 618 quarters). cf. also ss.16, 17 (see above, paras 44-131, 44-134).

[2141] See above, n.2130.

[2142] [1927] 1 Ch. 606. (The dissenting judge, at 656, held that s.52 included "the enforcement of a specific equitable assignment or lien".)

[2143] See also *Re London Wine Co (Shippers)* [1986] P.C.C. 121. On the facts of *Re Wait* an order of specific performance would have given the buyer priority over the general creditors in the seller's

44-442 **Order for specific delivery** Instead of asking for an order under s.52, the buyer who has the property in the goods may, in proceedings for wrongful interference with the goods, seek an order for specific delivery of the goods which does not give the seller the alternative of retaining them on payment of their value as assessed by the court.[2144] But in such proceedings the court has a discretion whether or not to make such an order.[2145]

44-443 **Discretion of the court** Section 52 confers a wide discretion on the court, similar to the discretionary nature of the equitable remedy of specific performance.[2146] No order should be made if the goods sold were "of a very ordinary description"[2147] and were not alleged to be "peculiar" in the sense that similar goods could not be obtained elsewhere.[2148] (The award of damages is considered to be an "adequate" remedy in such cases.) An order has been made in respect of a ship, which "was of peculiar and practically unique value to" the buyer, who wanted it for immediate use[2149]; another order was made for the specific delivery of an ornamental door designed by the famous architect Adam.[2150] Similarly, before the 1893 Act, specific performance could be granted to compel sellers to transfer rare or unique articles such as a jewel,[2151] china vases,[2152] particular stones from Old Westminster Bridge,[2153] and, in some cases, chattels which (although not unique) possessed a special value to the plaintiff.[2154]

44-444 In addition to considering the type of goods in question, the court is entitled to

---

bankruptcy.

[2144] Under s.3(2)(a) of the Torts (Interference with Goods) Act 1977: see above, para.44-440. (By s.2(1) of this Act, the old action of detinue was abolished.) See *Cohen v Roche* [1927] 1 K.B. 169, 179–180.

[2145] 1977 Act s.3(3)(b), (4) and (6). See *Howard E Perry Co Ltd v British Railways Board* [1980] 1 W.L.R. 1375, 1382–1383; *Cohen v Roche*, see above, at 180–181; above, para.33-013; see below, paras 44-443—44-444.

[2146] See Fry, *Specific Performance of Contracts*, 6th edn, pp.36–41. In view of this discretion, the buyer should always ask for damages in the alternative. The buyer may be estopped from seeking an order for specific performance after he has elected to accept damages in lieu thereof: *Meng Leong Development Pte Ltd v Jip Hong Trading Co Pte Ltd* [1985] A.C. 511 (sale of land).

[2147] Where damages would be an adequate remedy: *Re Wait* [1927] 1 Ch. 606, 630 ("Possibly the statutory remedy [s.52] was intended to be available even in those cases"). See Treitel [1966] J.B.L. 211; and Vol.I, paras 27-015 et seq. The wider use of specific performance in the sale of goods is discussed in *Butler v Countrywide Finance Ltd* [1993] 3 N.Z.L.R. 623. See also Vol.I, paras 27-022—27-025.

[2148] *Fothergill v Rowland* (1873) L.R. 17 Eq. 132, 139; *Cohen v Roche* [1927] 1 K.B. 169 at 179–181 ("ordinary Hepplewhite furniture" which "possessed no special features at all"). See also *Re Clarke* (1887) 36 Ch. D. 348, 352; and *Whiteley Ltd v Hilt* [1918] 2 K.B. 808, 819 (a hire-purchase case); *Société des Industries Metallurgiques SA v The Bronx Engineering Co Ltd* [1975] 1 Lloyd's Rep. 465, CA. cf. *Lingen v Simpson* (1824) 1 Sim. & St. 600; *Sky Petroleum Ltd v VIP Petroleum Ltd* [1974] 1 W.L.R. 576 (interlocutory injunction granted to protect the plaintiff's supply of scarce goods).

[2149] *Behnke v Bede Shipping Co Ltd* [1927] 1 K.B. 649, 661. See also *Allseas International Management Ltd v Panroy Bulk Transport SA* [1985] 1 Lloyd's Rep. 370; *CN Marine Inc v Stena Line A/B (The Stena Nautica) (No.2)* [1982] 2 Lloyd's Rep. 336, 341, 348–349; *Eximenco Handels AG v Partrederiet Oro Chief (The Oro Chief)* [1983] 2 Lloyd's Rep. 509, 521. cf. a case where the buyer merely intended to resell at a profit: *Cohen v Roche*, above, at 179–181.

[2150] *Phillips v Lamdin* [1949] 2 K.B. 33, 41–42. In Australia, an order has been made in respect of a taxi-cab to which a taxi-cab licence was attached: *Dougan v Ley* (1946) 71 C.L.R. 142.

[2151] *Pearne v Lisle* (1749) Amb. 75, 77.

[2152] *Falcke v Gray* (1859) 4 Drew. 651, 658.

[2153] *Thorn v Commissioners of Public Works* (1863) 32 Beav. 490.

[2154] Fry at p.39, citing *North v Great Northern Ry* (1860) 2 Giff. 64, 69 (an injunction case). See also

look at all the circumstances of the case,[2155] including the conduct of both the buyer[2156] and the seller,[2157] and to consider the hardship which an order would inflict on the seller.[2158] If the seller becomes insolvent after he has received the price from the buyer but before he has delivered the goods and before the property in them has passed to the buyer, an order for specific performance will give the buyer priority over other creditors of the seller by taking the goods out of the seller's estate: for this reason an order is unlikely to be made in these circumstances.[2159] Conversely, if the property has passed to the buyer before the seller becomes insolvent, an order will normally be made.[2160] By subs.(3) of s.52, the court, when making an order for specific performance, also has a wide discretion to impose conditions: thus, the buyer may be ordered to pay the price into court as a condition of the order being made against the seller.[2161] In another case, a court of first instance made an order in favour of sub-buyers upon payment of their share in the freight of the consignment.[2162]

Injunction This is the appropriate remedy when the buyer seeks an order of the   **44-445** court restraining the breach of a purely negative promise by the seller.[2163] Like specific performance, an injunction is an equitable[2164] and discretionary[2165] remedy, but, unlike specific performance, it is not expressly referred to in the Act.[2166] An order for specific delivery of the chattel sold may be supported by an injunction restraining the seller from parting with the chattel to anyone but the buyer.[2167] Similarly, the court has power by injunction to prevent a specific chattel from be-

---

Harris, Ogus and Phillips (1979) 95 L.Q.R. 581 and cf. the assessment of damages for a personal and subjective "loss of amenity" in *Ruxley Electronics and Construction Ltd v Forsyth* [1996] A.C. 344; and in *Farley v Skinner* [2001] UKHL 49, [2002] 2 A.C. 732 (see Vol.I, paras 26-151 et seq.).

[2155] Fry at Pt III. It is submitted that inadequacy of the price should not be a ground for refusing an order: cf. cases on the sale of land: *Coles v Trecothick* (1804) 9 Ves. 234, 246; *Sullivan v Jacob* (1828) 1 Moll. 472, 477. cf. also *Falcke v Gray* (1859) 4 Drew. 651 at 664–665 (specific performance denied when parties had not been on an equal footing). The defence of set-off is available in a claim for non-money relief (such as specific performance) which itself arises upon non-payment of money: *BICC Plc v Burndy Corp* [1985] Ch. 232.

[2156] e.g. *Snell's Equity*, 33rd edn (2015), paras 17-038, 17-039; Vol.I, paras 27-050, 27-053.

[2157] e.g. whether the seller had entered into the contract as the result of a mistake.

[2158] The authorities for the latter part of this proposition are not sale of goods cases: *Tamplin v James* (1880) 15 Ch. D. 215, 221; *Stewart v Kennedy* (1890) 15 App. Cas. 75, 105; *Patel v Ali* [1984] Ch. 283.

[2159] See *Re Wait* [1927] 1 Ch. 606, 640. See Jones and Goodhart at pp.150–152. cf. *Anders Utkilens Rederi A/S v O/Y Louisa Stevedoring Co A/B (The Golfstraum)* [1985] 2 All E.R. 669, 674.

[2160] *Re BA Peters* [2008] EWHC 2205 (Ch), [2008] B.P.I.R. 1180 at [65]–[66].

[2161] *Hart v Herwig* (1873) L.R. 8 Ch. App. 860, 864 (a similar injunction case). cf. *Langen and Wind Ltd v Bell* [1972] Ch. 685. cf. also *Harvela Investments Ltd v Royal Trust Co of Canada (CI) Ltd* [1986] A.C. 207 (sale of shares: buyer to pay interest on purchase price retained until order made).

[2162] *Re Wait* [1926] Ch. 962, 972. The Court of Appeal, however, did not consider this, as it held that no order should have been made: [1927] 1 Ch. 606.

[2163] e.g. the seller's express undertaking not to sell similar goods during the two-year period of the contract to any other manufacturer than the buyer: *Donnell v Bennet* (1883) 22 Ch. D. 835.

[2164] Sharpe, *Injunctions and Specific Performance*, 3rd edn, Pt I; Kerr, *Injunctions*, 6th edn, pp.409 et seq.; *Ashburner's Principles of Equity*, 2nd edn, pp.384–387; *Snell's Equity*, 33rd edn (2015), Ch.18; Spry, *The Principles of Equitable Remedies*, 8th edn (2010), Chs 4 and 5; *Doherty v Allman* (1878) 3 App. Cas. 709, 719–721. See also Vol.I, paras 27-077 et seq.

[2165] Snell at para.18-36; *James Jones Sons Ltd v Tankerville* [1909] 2 Ch. 440, 445–446. (But see Snell at para.18-35 (quoting *Doherty v Allman*, above, at 720).)

[2166] See, however, s.62(2) preserving "the rules of common law", which might include the rules of equity: *Benjamin's Sale of Goods*, 10th edn (2017), paras 1-007—1-011.

[2167] *Behnke v Bede Shipping Co Ltd* [1927] 1 K.B. 649. cf. *Dominion Coal Co Ltd v Dominion Iron and*

ing removed out of the jurisdiction until a question relating to it has been decided by the court,[2168] or to restrain the seller from preventing the due execution of the contract where the goods sold to the buyer are on the land of the seller, and the contract gives the buyer a right to enter the land to remove the goods.[2169] But an affirmative obligation will not be enforced by injunction merely because it implies a negative obligation: where a colliery agreed to sell to the buyer all the coal produced for five years, an injunction was not granted to prevent the colliery from being sold to third parties within the five years.[2170]

44-446 **Declaration**[2171]   In appropriate circumstances, the buyer may obtain a declaration setting out his legal rights against the seller.[2172] A declaration may be made before any breach of contract has occurred, and may thus guide the parties in the implementation of a contract whose performance is spread over a long period.[2173] Even where the defendant is liable to pay damages, the claimant may claim only a declaration that the defendant was in breach of contract and that the damages for the loss caused by the breach amounted to a stated sum.[2174] In one case,[2175] the buyers obtained against the sellers, who had committed a breach of their obligation to deliver, a declaration of indemnity that the buyers were entitled to recover from the sellers such damages as the buyers might be held liable to pay (as a result of the seller's breach) in respect of their legal liability to a sub-buyer.[2176] However, the Court of Appeal, in another case,[2177] has said that the proper course in this situation is for the court to reserve that head of damages.

44-447 **Claims for possession or damages for conversion**   Where the property in the

---

Steel Co Ltd [1909] A.C. 293, 310.

[2168] *Hart v Herwig* (1873) L.R. 8 Ch. App. 860. cf. *North v Great Northern Ry* (1860) 2 Giff. 64 (plaintiff hired coal wagons of special value to him: railway company could be restrained from selling them).

[2169] *James Jones Sons Ltd v Tankerville*, above (timber growing on the seller's land). cf. *Astro Exito Navegacion SA v Chase Manhattan Bank NA* [1983] 2 A.C. 787 (injunction to buyers to sign document needed by sellers to comply with letter of credit: Master of Supreme Court to sign if buyers failed to do so). cf. also an injunction to enforce a buyer's agreement to obtain all his supplies from the seller: *Metropolitan Electric Supply Co Ltd v Ginder* [1901] 2 Ch. 799; and an injunction to enforce a "solus agreement": *Esso Petroleum Co Ltd v Harper's Garage (Stourport) Ltd* [1968] A.C. 269 (see Vol.I, paras 16-155, 27-086).

[2170] *Fothergill v Rowland* (1873) L.R. 17 Eq. 132. (Such an injunction would have amounted to specific performance "by a roundabout method": at 140.) cf. *Sky Petroleum Ltd v VIP Petroleum Ltd* [1974] 1 W.L.R. 576 (interlocutory injunction).

[2171] See Zamir and Woolf, *The Declaratory Judgment*, 3rd edn. cf. above, para.44-386.

[2172] Declaratory proceedings in the Commercial Court are often quicker and cheaper than arbitration: *JH Vantol Ltd v Fairclough Dodd Jones Ltd* [1955] 1 W.L.R. 642, 648 (approved by the House of Lords in the same case: [1957] 1 W.L.R. 136, 137, 138, 144).

[2173] *Spettabile Consorzio Veneziano di Armamento e Navigazione v Northumberland Shipbuilding Co Ltd* (1919) 121 L.T. 628, 635.

[2174] *Louis Dreyfus Co v Parnaso Cia Naviera SA* [1959] 1 Q.B. 498, [1960] 2 Q.B. 49. If it would serve a useful purpose, the court may use its discretion to make a negative declaration e.g. to the effect that the claimant is not liable to the defendant in respect of a certain matter: *Messier-Dowty Ltd v Sabena SA* [2000] 1 W.L.R. 2040, CA.

[2175] *Household Machines Ltd v Cosmos Exporters Ltd* [1947] K.B. 217.

[2176] The amount of this liability was not ascertained at the time of the hearing between the buyer and seller. On this type of liability, see above, para.44-405. cf. *Total Liban SA v Vitol Energy SA* [2001] Q.B. 643.

[2177] *Trans Trust SPRL v Danubian Trading Co Ltd* [1952] 2 Q.B. 297. But see the uncertainty which this decision has created: *British Electrical and Associated Industries (Cardiff) Ltd v Patley Pressings Ltd* [1953] 1 W.L.R. 280, 284. cf. *Deeny v Gooda Walker Ltd (No.3)* [1995] 4 All E.R. 289 (not a sale of goods case).

goods and the immediate right to possession[2178] of them has passed to the buyer, he may bring against the seller[2179] a proprietary action for chattels under the law of torts, viz proceedings for wrongful interference with the goods seeking an order for specific delivery of the goods,[2180] or damages for conversion when the seller's detention of the goods amounts to a denial of the buyer's title to them.[2181] In *Chinery v Viall*,[2182] where the unpaid seller, without a right to resell, wrongfully resold the goods at a time when the original buyer was entitled to possession of them (the sale being on credit terms),[2183] the seller was held liable to the original buyer for damages for non-delivery,[2184] or for conversion.[2185]

Wrongful re-taking by seller   Where the property in the goods has passed to the **44-448** buyer, and the seller has delivered them to him, but the price remains unpaid, the contract of sale is not terminated by the act of the seller in tortiously retaking the goods and reselling them.[2186] In these circumstances, the seller still has his action for the price, while the buyer (even where his failure to pay the price is a breach of contract) has an independent claim[2187] for conversion for the full value of the goods at the time of the retaking[2188]: these are separate claims and neither is a defence to the other.[2189]

8. CONSUMER PROTECTION ACT 1987[2190]

Part I of the 1987 Act   Part I of the Consumer Protection Act 1987[2191] is intended **44-449** to implement Council Directive 85/374[2192] on the approximation of the laws, regula-

---

[2178] cf. the seller's right to a lien: see above, paras 44-315 et seq.

[2179] Such an action may also lie against strangers: *Chinery v Viall* (1860) 5 H. & N. 288 (stranger taking goods out of seller's possession); cf. *Lord v Price* (1874) L.R. 9 Ex. 54 (buyer did not have immediate right to possession); *Langton v Higgins* (1859) 4 H. & N. 402 (wrongful second sale by seller to second buyer); *Denny v Skelton* (1916) 115 L.T. 305 (part of a cargo taken mistakenly in the name of the wrong sub-buyer). Quaere whether the buyer could bring an action on the case for injury to his reversionary interest in the goods: cf. *Mears v L and SW Ry* (1862) 11 C.B.(N.S.) 850; and see *Bloxam v Sanders* (1825) 4 B. & C. 941, 949.

[2180] See above, para.33-013. cf. s.52 (see above, para.44-440). In proceedings for wrongful interference, the court has a discretion not to order specific delivery of the goods: see above, paras 33-013, 44-443, 44-444.

[2181] cf. see above, para.44-384.

[2182] (1860) 5 H. & N. 288.

[2183] Even where the buyer had failed to pay the price on the date fixed by the contract, he would be entitled to possession of the goods if he tendered the price to the seller within a reasonable time and before the seller had justifiably resold or terminated the contract: *Martindale v Smith* (1841) 1 Q.B. 389. See also *Bloxam v Sanders* (1825) 4 B. & C. 941.

[2184] *Fitt v Cassanet* (1842) 4 M. & G. 898.

[2185] *Bloxam v Sanders*, above, at 949. The damages for conversion are assessed on the basis of the buyer's actual loss, which is the difference between the market price of the goods at the time of the conversion and the contract price: *Chinery v Viall* (1860) 5 H. & N. 288. See also above, paras 33-017, 33-018. cf. *Johnson v Stear* (1863) 15 C.B.(N.S.) 330; *Brierly v Kendall* (1852) 17 Q.B. 937 (wrongful sale by pledgee); *Wickham Holdings Ltd v Brooke House Motors Ltd* [1967] 1 W.L.R. 295 (wrongful sale of goods held on hire-purchase terms; distinguished in *Chubb Cash Ltd v John Crilley Son* [1983] 1 W.L.R. 599).

[2186] *Page v Cowasjee Eduljee* (1866) L.R. 1 P.C. 127.

[2187] Proceedings for wrongful interference under the Torts (Interference with Goods) Act 1977.

[2188] *Stephens v Wilkinson* (1831) 2 B. & Ad. 320, 327; *Page v Cowasjee Eduljee*, above, at 147.

[2189] *Page v Cowasjee Eduljee* (1866) L.R. 1 P.C. 127; *Stephens v Wilkinson* (1831) 2 B. & Ad. 320, 327; *Gillard v Brittan* (1841) 8 M. & W. 575; *Re Humberston* (1846) De & G. 262.

[2190] See Miller, *Product Liability and Safety Encyclopaedia* (1979–date), Div. V; Miller and Goldberg,

tions and administrative provisions of the Member States concerning liability for defective products. Very broadly the effect of the Directive is to impose liability on manufacturers and certain other persons for death, personal injury and physical damage to property caused by defective, i.e. unsafe, products. The liability imposed is (subject to certain defences) a strict liability and does not depend upon proof of negligence. The claimant still bears the burden of proving that the injury or damage complained of was caused by the product and that the product was defective.[2193] But, where Pt I of the 1987 Act applies, he is relieved from the necessity of proving—as would be the case at common law—either that he was in a contractual relationship with the defendant or that the defendant was negligent. The Act is therefore of particular significance (inter alia) in relation to pharmaceutical products, chemical compounds, foodstuffs, machinery, vehicles and building materials, where a claimant might otherwise encounter difficulty in proving fault on the part of the producer.

44-450 Products covered by Pt I All goods are covered,[2194] including component parts and raw materials.[2195]

44-451 Meaning of "defect" The definition of "defect" in s.3 is closely related to the type of damage which is remediable. There is a defect in a product for the purposes of Pt I if "the safety of the product is not such as persons generally are entitled to expect"; and for those purposes "safety" in relation to a product includes safety with respect to products comprised in that product and safety in the context of risks of damage to property, as well as in the context of risks of death or personal injury.[2196] By s.3(2) all the circumstances are to be taken into account in determining that standard.[2197] But three circumstances are specifically mentioned. First:

> "the manner in which, and purposes for which, the product has been marketed, its get-up, the use of any mark in relation to the product and any instructions for, or warnings with respect to, doing or refraining from doing anything with or in relation to the product."[2198]

Secondly, "what might reasonably be expected to be done with or in relation to the

---

Product Liability (2004); Stapleton, *Product Liability* (1994); Whittaker, *Liability for Products* (2005); *Benjamin's Sale of Goods*, 10th edn (2017), paras 14-227 et seq.

[2191] 1987 Act ss.1–9.

[2192] [1985] O.J. L210/29.

[2193] See paras 44-451, 44-453, below.

[2194] "Product" is defined in s.1(2) to mean any goods or electricity. "Goods" are defined in s.45(1) to include substances, growing crops and things comprised in land by virtue of being attached to it and any ship, aircraft or vehicle.

[2195] 1987 Act s.1(2). But see ss.1(3), 4(1)(f). The exception for game and primary agricultural produce was removed by SI 2000/2771, implementing Directive 1999/34 ([1999] O.J. L141/20).

[2196] 1987 Act s.3(1).

[2197] See *Richardson v LRC Products* [2000] Lloyd's Rep. Med. 280 (burst condom leading to pregnancy); *A v National Blood Authority* [2001] 3 All E.R. 289 (blood infected with hepatitis C); *Abouzaid v Mothercare (UK) Ltd, The Times,* February 20, 2001 (cover attachment to child's pushchair snaps back); *Foster v Biosil* (2001) 59 B.M.L.R. 178 (breast implants); *B v McDonald's Restaurants Ltd* [2002] EWHC 490 (QB) (scalding coffee); *Palmer v Estate of Palmer* [2006] EWHC 1284 (QB) (seat belt); *Ide v ATB Sales Ltd* [2008] EWCA Civ 424, [2009] R.T.R. 8 (handlebar of bicycle); *Wilkes v DePuy International Ltd* [2016] EWHC 3096 (QB), [2018] 2 W.L.R. 531 (failed replacement hip not defective).

[2198] 1987 Act s.3(2)(a).

product".[2199] Thirdly, "the time when the product was supplied[2200] by its producer to another".[2201] However, the subsection recognises that improvements over time may render a product progressively more safe, since it provides that a defect is not necessarily to be inferred from the fact alone that the safety of a product which is supplied after that time is greater than the safety of the product in question.[2202] It will nevertheless be appreciated that the safety standard embodied in this provision is one which is extremely difficult to apply: the product does not have to be absolutely safe and the degree of safety which persons generally are entitled to expect may well depend upon the practicability, and cost, of rendering the product more safe.

Damage giving rise to liability By s.5(1), "damage" means death or personal injury[2203] or any loss of or damage to property (including land). It should be noted that no claim can be made for economic loss incurred by the fact that the product cannot be used or that its use is impaired, or for expenses incurred in replacing or repairing the product or rendering it safe for use. Further s.5 proceeds to impose important restrictions in the case of loss of or damage to property.   **44-452**

Causation The claimant must prove that the defect in the product caused the damage.[2204]   **44-453**

Damage to product itself First, there is no liability under Pt I where a defect in the product causes loss of or damage to the product itself; nor can the producer of a component or materials be liable for loss of or damage to the product of which the component or materials form part. Section 5(2) provides: **44-454**

"A person shall not be liable ... for the loss of or any damage to the product itself or for the loss of or damage to the whole or any part of any product which has been supplied with the product in question comprised in it."

Property not for private use Secondly, by s.5(3), liability will not be incurred for: **44-455**

"any loss of or damage to property which, at the time it is lost or damaged, is not–

(a) of a description of property ordinarily intended for private use, occupation or consumption; and

(b) intended by the person suffering the loss or damage mainly for his own private use, occupation or consumption." [2205]

[2199] 1987 Act s.3(2)(b).

[2200] 1987 Act s.46.

[2201] 1987 Act s.3(2)(c).

[2202] 1987 Act s.3(2).

[2203] Defined in s.45(1). See also s.6(3) (congenital disabilities).

[2204] But see *Ide v ATB Sales Ltd* [2008] EWCA Civ 424, [2009] R.T.R. 8 (where various possible explanations exist); *Lexus Financial Services T/A Toyota Financial Services UK Plc v Russell* [2008] EWCA Civ 424, [2008] P.I.Q.R.P. 13 (probability).

[2205] Despite the clumsy double negative, and the use of the word "and" in subs.(3), it is clear that for damage to property to be compensatable the property must fall within both (a) and (b) of this subsection.

44-456 **Damage not exceeding £275** Thirdly, by s.5(4), no claim can be made by a person for loss of or damage to property if the amount which would fall to be awarded to that person does not exceed £275.

44-457 **Who can sue** The right of action conferred by Pt I is not expressly limited to "consumers". Any person can sue. An action may be brought in respect of death or personal injury even though the product was acquired by a person for the purposes of his business. However, in respect of loss of or damage to property, the restriction imposed by s.5(3) (see above) virtually limits the right of action to consumers.

44-458 **Upon whom liability is imposed** Section 2(2) of the Act lists the persons upon whom liability for any damage is imposed. The first such person is "the producer of the product".[2206] In this context it is necessary to bear in mind that both the producer of a defective component or defective materials and the producer of the finished product which is rendered defective by the inclusion of the defective component or materials may be liable.[2207] The second is "any person who, by putting his name on the product or using a trade mark or other distinguishing mark in relation to the product, has held himself out to be the producer of the product".[2208] The third is "any person who has imported the product into a Member State from outside the Member States in order, in the course of a business of his, to supply it to another".[2209] No doubt the person upon whom liability will most frequently be sought to be imposed will be the producer, e.g. the manufacturer of the product. But the second case mentioned is important for "own brand" products and the third is a novel imposition of liability in tort upon traders who are merely importers. Where two or more persons are liable by virtue of Pt I for the same damage, their liability is joint and several.[2210]

44-459 **Supplier** By a somewhat complicated provision, s.2(3) further extends liability in certain circumstances to any supplier of the product, i.e. "any person who supplied the product (whether to the person who suffered the damage, to the producer of any product in which the product in question is comprised or to any other person)".[2211] One purpose of this provision is to enable the person who has suffered the damage, e.g. a retail customer, to trace back the chain of supply to a person or persons who will be liable to him in situations where the identification of those persons is not reasonably practicable, for example, where the product does not bear the manufacturer's name. A supplier will be liable if he fails to comply with a request made by the person who has suffered the damage to identify one or more of the persons mentioned in s.2(2) (para.44-458, above). However, a supplier may avoid such liability if, on receiving the request, he identifies the person who supplied the product to him. So, for example, a retail customer who is injured by a defective product may first make such a request to the retailer, who can avoid liability by identifying the wholesaler who supplied him with the product. Subsequent requests may then be made to the prior wholesaler, etc. up the chain of supply until

---

[2206] 1987 Act s.2(2)(a). "Producer" is defined in s.1(2).
[2207] But see s.4(1)(f).
[2208] 1987 Act s.2(2)(b). cf. *Tesco Stores Ltd v Pollard* [2006] EWCA Civ 393.
[2209] 1987 Act s.2(2)(c). "Supply" is defined in s.46. See also *Ide v ATB Sales Ltd* [2008] EWCA Civ 424, [2009] R.T.R. 8.
[2210] 1987 Act s.2(5).
[2211] See s.1(3). See also s.46 ("supply").

the retail customer has identified the persons referred to in s.2(2) upon whom liability is imposed.

Defences   Section 4(1) of the Act sets out six defences that are available   **44-460**
notwithstanding the strict liability imposed. It is a defence for the person proceeded
against to show:

"(a)   that the defect is attributable to compliance with any requirement imposed by or
under any enactment or with any Community obligation; or
(b)   that the person proceeded against did not at any time supply[2212] the product to
another; or
(c)   that the following conditions are satisfied, that is to say—
(i)   that the only supply[2213] of the product to another by the person proceeded
against was otherwise than in the course of a business of that person's; and
(ii)   that s.2(2) does not apply to that person or applies to him by virtue only of
things done otherwise than with a view to profit; or
(d)   that the defect did not exist in the product at the relevant time[2214]; or
(e)   that the state of technical and scientific knowledge at the relevant time[2215] was not
such that a producer of products of the same description as the product in question
might be expected to have discovered the defect if it had existed in his products
while they were under his control; or
(f)   that the defect—
(i)   constituted a defect in a product ('the subsequent product') in which the
product in question had been comprised; and
(ii)   was wholly attributable to the design of the subsequent product or to compliance by the producer of the product in question with instructions given by the
producer of the subsequent product."

Only two of these defences require comment. The defence set out in s.4(1)(d),
enables a person to escape liability if he can prove that the defect arose after the
time when he supplied the product to another, for example, because of subsequent
contamination, or improper treatment, storage, installation or maintenance.[2216] The
defence set out in s.4(1)(e), sometimes referred to as "the state of the art" or
"development risks" defence, is controversial. The Directive allowed Member
States, if they so wished, to adopt such a defence, and the United Kingdom
exercised this option.[2217] It is of particular importance in relation to pharmaceutical and medical products, to which the thalidomide cases bear witness.

Contributory negligence   Contributory negligence on the part of the person suf-   **44-461**
fering the damage is also a defence.[2218]

[2212] Defined in s.46.

[2213] 1987 Act s.46.

[2214] "The relevant time" is defined in s.4(2). In essence, it is the time of supply to another. See *Piper v
JRI Manufacturing Ltd* [2006] EWCA Civ 1344, [2006] All E.R. (D) 181 (Oct).

[2215] 1987 Act s.4(2).

[2216] *Piper v JRI Manufacturing Ltd* [2006] EWCA Civ 1344, [2006] 92 B.JM.L.R. 141 (hip prosthesis).

[2217] In *Commission of the EC v UK* (C300/95) [1997] All E.R. (EC) 481, it was held that s.4(1)(e) had
fully implemented art.7 of the Directive. For a discussion of the defence, see Newdick (1988) 47
C.L.J. 55, (1992) 20 Anglo-Am L.R. 309; Hodge (1998) 61 M.L.R. 560. The defence was not made
out in *A v National Blood Authority* [2001] 3 All E.R. 289; and in *Abouzaid v Mothercare (UK) Ltd*,
The Times, February 20, 2001.

[2218] 1987 Act s.6(4) (5).

44-462   Limitation   The Act establishes[2219] a three-year limitation period in which to commence proceedings.[2220] Actions are also subject to an overriding 10-year cut-off period.[2221]

44-463   Liability in contract[2222]   Part I of the Act in no way affects the remedies of a buyer of goods against his immediate seller for breach of the express or implied terms of the contract of sale.

44-464   Consumer safety   Part II of the 1987 Act[2223] deals with consumer safety. Section 11 of the Act enables the Secretary of State to make regulations for the purposes of securing that goods are safe, that unsafe goods are not made available to persons generally or to persons of a particular description, and as to information provided in respect of goods. A considerable number of regulations has been made.[2224] Contravention of the regulations constitutes a criminal offence.[2225] But a failure to perform an obligation imposed by the regulations is also actionable as a breach of statutory duty owed to any person who may be affected by the failure.[2226]

44-465   The Secretary of State is also empowered to issue prohibition notices[2227] and notices to warn[2228] in respect of goods which he considers are unsafe, and the enforcement authority[2229] may issue a notice (a suspension notice) prohibiting a person for a limited period from supplying goods if it has reasonable grounds for suspecting that a safety provision has been contravened in relation to the goods in question.[2230] Goods which contravene a safety provision may be the subject of a forfeiture order.[2231]

44-466   The General Product Safety Regulations 2005[2232]   These regulations implement Directive 2001/95 of the European Parliament and Council on general product safety. They apply to nearly all products,[2233] including second-hand or reconditioned goods, intended for consumers or likely to be used by consumers. The central obligation in the Regulations is imposed by reg.5(1): "No producer shall place a product on the market unless it is a safe product". But "producer" is widely

---

[2219] Through s.6 and Sch.1, inserting s.11A into the Limitation Act 1980.
[2220] See Vol.I, para.28-009. For substitution under the general provisions of the Limitation Act 1980 s.35, see *OB v Aventis Pasteur SA* [2008] UKHL 34, [2008] 4 All E.R. 881; *O'Byrne v Aventis Pasteur SA* (C-358/08) EU:C:2009:744, ECJ.
[2221] Limitation Act 1980 s.11A(3); Vol.I, para.28-009.
[2222] Liability under Pt I is a liability in tort: s.6(7).
[2223] ss.10–19.
[2224] Or under the Consumer Safety Act 1978. See Miller, *Product Liability and Safety Encyclopedia* (1979–date), Div.IV; *Benjamin's Sale of Goods*, 10th edn (2017), para.14-261.
[2225] 1987 Act s.12.
[2226] 1987 Act s.41.
[2227] 1987 Act s.13(1)(a). But see the limit imposed by s.13(7), added by SI 2005/1803 reg.46(4).
[2228] 1987 Act s.13(1)(b), i.e. to warn consumers.
[2229] Defined in s.45(1) and by reference to s.27. For enforcement, see Pt IV of the Act (ss.27–35).
[2230] 1987 Act ss.14, 15.
[2231] 1987 Act s.16.
[2232] SI 2005/1803. See Miller, *Product Liability and Safety Encyclopedia* (1979–date), Div.IV; *Benjamin's Sale of Goods*, 10th edn (2017), para.14-264.
[2233] Defined in reg.2(1).

defined[2234] and a person may also be liable as a "distributor" of a product.[2235] The Regulations contain detailed enforcement provisions.

Misleading price indications   Part III of the 1987 Act[2236] rendered it an offence   **44-467** to give, in the course of a business, a misleading price indication to consumers.[2237] This was intended to deal (inter alia) with the abuses that can arise from the making of so-called "bargain offers". Part III ceased to have effect as a result of the Consumer Protection from Unfair Trading Regulations 2008[2238] which impose a more general prohibition on misleading commercial practices.

[2234] SI 2005/1803 reg.2(1).
[2235] SI 2005/1803 reg.2(1).
[2236] ss.20–26.
[2237] s.20(1). See *R. v Warwickshire CC Ex p. Johnson* [1993] A.C. 583.
[2238] SI 2008/1277. These Regulations were amended in 2014 (see SI 2014/870 above, para.38-008 and Vol.I, paras 28-055 et seq.).

CHAPTER 45

SURETYSHIP

Simon Whittaker

1. In General

General nature of the contract A contract of suretyship is in essence a contract **45-001**
by which one person (the surety) agrees to answer for some liability of another (the
principal debtor) to a third person (the creditor). The contract may be constituted
by a personal engagement on the part of the surety, or by a charge on property
without any personal liability, or by both.[1] Prima facie a surety does not merely
undertake to perform if the principal debtor fails to do so; he undertakes to see that
the principal debtor will perform.[2] Important results flow from this prima facie rule

---

[1] *Smith v Wood* [1929] 1 Ch. 14; *Re Conley* [1938] 2 All E.R. 127.
[2] *Moschi v Lep Air Services Ltd* [1973] A.C. 331. cf. *Trafalgar House Construction (Regions) Ltd v General Surety & Guarantee Co Ltd* [1996] 1 A.C. 199; *Sunbird Plaza Pty Ltd v Maloney* (1988) 166 C.L.R. 245, HC Aus.

of construction. In particular it means that a surety is normally liable to the same extent as the principal debtor for damages for breach of the latter's obligations even though he has not in terms guaranteed the payment of damages.[3]

45-002 **Parties to the contract** In *Duncan Fox & Co v North & South Wales Bank*[4] it was pointed out by Lord Selborne that there are three possible variations in the parties to a contract of suretyship. The first and simplest case is that in which all three parties concerned are parties to the contract in the sense that both the principal debtor and the creditor agree that the surety's liability is a secondary liability only, and that the principal debtor is primarily liable for the obligations guaranteed. But it also is possible that the contract of suretyship may be recognised only as between the principal debtor and the surety, or as between the creditor and the surety, in which event the rights and duties arising out of the contract of suretyship only affect those parties.

45-003 **Contract of suretyship as against principal debtor alone**[5] It is by no means unusual for a party to a contract to be a principal debtor as against the creditor, but a surety as against another debtor. Such an arrangement is commonly entered into where the creditor wishes to avoid the technical rules relating to contracts of suretyship under which the surety may become discharged from liability in various circumstances.[6] In this event, the transaction takes effect according to its terms,[7] that is to say, there will be a contract of suretyship between the principal debtor and the surety, but there will be no contract of suretyship between the surety and the creditor. The creditor is accordingly entitled to treat the surety as a principal debtor in every respect.[8]

45-004 **Creditor knows or later discovers that not principal but surety** However, the mere fact that two parties have, on the face of some written document or instrument, apparently contracted as joint (or joint and several) debtors does not preclude the possibility that one of the debtors is in fact a surety: it is still open to one of the debtors to prove by parol evidence that the creditor knew that the intention of the debtors was that one should be a surety and not a principal debtor.[9] Thus, it has been held that an agreement expressly declaring a party to be liable "as a primary obligor and not merely as a surety" does not prevent that party being a surety for the purpose of determining the effect of the voidness of the main agreement.[10] Furthermore, even if the creditor does not know that one of the debtors intends to

---

3   *Moschi v Lep Air Services Ltd* [1973] A.C. 331. For other consequences of this rule of construction, see paras 45-040, 45-086.
4   (1880) 6 App. Cas. 1, 11–12. See also *Selous Street Properties Ltd v Oronel Fabrics Ltd* (1984) 270 E.G. 643.
5   This paragraph was quoted by Rix L.J. (with whom Sir Anthony Clarke M.R. and Arden L.J. agreed) with apparent approval in *Berghoff Trading Ltd v Swinbrook Developments Ltd* [2009] EWCA Civ 413, [2009] 2 Lloyd's Rep. 233 at [25].
6   See below, paras 45-085 et seq.
7   *Duncan Fox & Co v North and South Wales Bank*, above, at 11–12; *Nicholas v Ridley* [1904] 1 Ch. 192.
8   See footnote above. See also *Esso Petroleum Co Ltd v Alstonbridge Properties Ltd* [1975] 1 W.L.R. 1474.
9   *Mutual Loan Fund Association v Sudlow* (1858) 5 C.B.(N.S.) 449.
10   *Heald v O'Connor* [1971] 1 W.L.R. 497; cf. *General Produce Co v United Bank Ltd* [1979] 2 Lloyd's Rep. 255.

contract only as surety at the time of making the contract, but subsequently has notice of this fact, he will thereafter have to treat that debtor as a surety, with the consequence that any variation by the creditor and principal debtor will discharge the surety.[11] And if two parties contract as joint principals in the first instance, but they subsequently agree between themselves that one of them is to assume primary liability, the creditor will, on acquiring notice of this fact, be obliged to treat the other as a surety only.[12]

Contract of suretyship as against creditor alone   It is also perfectly possible for   **45-005** a surety to guarantee the liability of a third person in such circumstances that a contract of suretyship is created as against the creditor, but not as against the principal debtor. Normally a guarantee is entered into at the request, express or implied, of the principal debtor, and this suffices to create a contract of suretyship as against him, but the contract may not be entered into at his request at all. For example, a "recourse agreement"[13] entered into by a dealer at the request of a finance company, whereby the dealer guarantees the due performance of a hire-purchase agreement, may be a contract of suretyship as against the creditor (the finance company) but there will not be a contract of suretyship as against the debtor (the hirer). Similarly, it often happens that a surety guarantees a loan made to a company at the request of the company's parent or holding company, and the company-debtor may not itself be in a contractual relationship with the surety.[14] In practice, however, this will usually make little difference to the rights and duties of the parties. The principal right of a surety as against the debtor is his right to be indemnified by him if called on to meet the liability,[15] and even if there is no contract of suretyship as against the debtor, there will still be a right to an indemnity, though in this case it will arise only by way of subrogation or by way of a right to restitution.[16] Such a right may be less extensive than a contractual right to an indemnity in some cases. For example, a surety has a right that the principal debtor should meet his obligations and this right may be enforceable to some extent even before the surety has been called upon to pay[17]; but a guarantor who has no contract of suretyship as against the debtor probably has no right to require the debtor to meet his obligations, and subrogation and restitution probably give no remedy until actual payment.[18] There is also a danger that subrogation rights may be lost by a technical "payment" of the debt, even though the money is provided by the surety.[19]

---

[11]   *Oakeley v Pasheller* (1836) 4 Cl. & Fin. 207; *Overend Gurney & Co v Oriental Financial Corp* (1874) L.R. 7 H.L. 348; *Goldfarb v Bartlett* [1920] 1 K.B. 639 and see below, para.45-104.

[12]   *Rouse v Bradford Banking Co Ltd* [1894] A.C. 586.

[13]   As to these, see above, para.39-180. Recourse agreements will usually be drafted as indemnities and not guarantees (see below, paras 45-006 et seq., 45-044 as to this distinction) but there is nothing to prevent such an agreement being drafted as a guarantee, though it will not be a security within the meaning of s.189(1) of the Consumer Credit Act 1974, for it is not entered into at the request (express or implied) of the debtor or hirer.

[14]   See, e.g. *Brown Shipley & Co Ltd v Amalgamated Investment (Europe) BV* [1979] 2 Lloyd's Rep. 488.

[15]   See below, para.45-126.

[16]   See below, para.45-127.

[17]   See below, para.45-134.

[18]   See also below, paras 45-132, 45-133. And see above, para.45-115, as to subrogation.

[19]   *Brown Shipley & Co Ltd v Amalgamated Investment (Europe) BV* [1979] 2 Lloyd's Rep. 488.

45-006 **Indemnities** The term "indemnity" is used in the law in several different senses. In its widest sense it means recompense for any loss or liability which one person has incurred, whether the duty to indemnify comes from an agreement or not.[20] For example, where a breach of contract gives rise to a claim for damages, that claim may include a claim to be indemnified against some loss or liability.[21] So also, on rescission of a contract for misrepresentation, the representee may be entitled to an indemnity against liabilities incurred under the contract even where there is no claim to damages.[22] In cases of this nature the claim to an indemnity arises by operation of law, not out of a contract of indemnity.[23] A person who breaks a contract or makes a misrepresentation is not agreeing to indemnify the other party against the loss he may suffer. Indemnities of this nature fall outside the scope of this chapter. But an obligation to indemnify another may also arise out of a contract of indemnity, and the term "contract of indemnity" is also used in more than one sense. In its widest sense a contract of indemnity includes all contracts of guarantee and many contracts of insurance; in its narrow sense, a contract of indemnity is used in contrast to a contract of guarantee, and it is in this narrow sense that the term is generally used in this chapter.

45-007 **Guarantees and indemnities: the significance of the distinction** The distinction between a contract of indemnity and a contract of guarantee was originally evolved by the courts in the process of construing s.4 of the Statute of Frauds 1677 which required writing for certain classes of contracts including contracts of guarantee, and it is therefore dealt with in detail in the consideration of that section.[24] But the distinction has also come to have a more general importance throughout the law of suretyship and it is therefore necessary to explain it briefly here. Thus, apart from the fact that contracts of guarantee but not of indemnity must be evidenced by a note or memorandum in writing under the Statute of Frauds, the distinction is of importance in at least three other situations. First, the question whether a surety is liable where the main contract is void because of the principal debtor's incapacity, has been said to depend on the distinction between guarantees and indemnities,[25] and the same may also be true of other invalidating causes. Secondly, the liability of a guarantor is normally co-extensive with the liability of the principal debtor, so that if the debtor is discharged the surety will also be discharged, whereas if the contract is one of indemnity, the surety is not necessarily discharged.[26] Thirdly, certain other rules of law apply to guarantees (where only a secondary liability is undertaken) but not to indemnities (where a primary liability is undertaken), for example, the rule that any material variation of the

---

20 *Pitts v Jones* [2007] EWCA Civ 1301, [2008] 2 W.L.R. 1289 at [21]. cf. Vol.I, paras 15-018 and 15-088—15-090 (indemnity clauses).

21 See, e.g. *Lister v Romford Ice & Cold Storage Co Ltd* [1957] A.C. 555 (employer's right to indemnity in respect of vicarious liability arising from employee's negligence); cf. *Morris v Ford Motor Co Ltd* [1973] Q.B. 792.

22 See Vol.I, paras 7-130—7-131.

23 There are some cases in which it is hard to say whether the liability arises by operation of law or from an implied contract of indemnity; see, e.g. *Secretary of State v Bank of India* [1938] 2 All E.R. 797, 800.

24 See below, paras 45-042 et seq.

25 See below, para.45-040.

26 See below, paras 45-086 et seq.

contract between the debtor and the creditor will in principle discharge a guarantor but not a person undertaking a primary liability.[27]

Guarantees and indemnities: the distinction itself The distinction between the **45-008** two contracts is, in brief, that in a contract of guarantee the surety assumes a secondary liability to answer for the debtor who remains primarily liable; whereas in a contract of indemnity the surety assumes a primary liability, either alone or jointly with the principal debtor.[28] Whether a contract falls into one class or the other, and whether the normal incidents of a contract of that class are modified, are ordinary questions of construction.[29] In this respect, while the presence or absence of the language of "guarantee" in the document is not conclusive, outside the context of documents issued by banks,[30] the absence of language appropriate to provide for the creditor "the additional security of a demand bond" creates a strong presumption in favour of a merely secondary liability.[31] Moreover:

> "... with the parties free to agree whatever terms they choose, there is in this field of law
> a spectrum of contractual possibilities ranging from the classic contract of guarantee,
> properly so called, at the one end, where liability of the guarantor is exclusively second-
> ary and will be discharged if, for example, there is any material variation to the underly-
> ing contract between principal and creditor, to the performance or demand bond (or
> demand guarantee)[32] at the other end, where liability in the giver of the bond may be trig-
> gered by mere demand and without proof of default by the principal (and indeed where
> it may be apparent that the principal is not in default)."[33]

However, as has been explained, the nature of the relationship between the creditor and the surety may differ from the nature of the relationship between the debtor and the surety. It is therefore possible that even where the relationship between the surety and the creditor is that of a contract of indemnity, the debtor may still be primarily liable as between himself and the surety.[34] Thus although a contract of indemnity cannot itself *be* a contract of suretyship, the party liable under such a contract may be a surety as against the debtor and it is common and convenient to speak of him as such, even though he has assumed a primary liability towards the creditor. On the other hand, it is of course perfectly possible to have a contract of indemnity in which there is no suretyship at all, because, for example, the party li-

---

27 *Holme v Brunskill* (1877) 3 Q.B.D. 495 (on which see below, paras 45-104 et seq.); *Marubeni Hong Kong and South China Ltd v The Mongolian Government* [2005] EWCA Civ 395, [2005] 1 W.L.R. 2497.

28 This sentence was quoted by the Court of Appeal with apparent approval in *Marubeni Hong Kong and South China Ltd v The Mongolian Government* [2005] EWCA Civ 395, [2005] 1 W.L.R. 2497 at [20]. See also *Vossloh Aktiengesellschaft v Alpha Trains (UK) Ltd* [2010] EWHC 2443 (Ch), [2010] All E.R. (D) 86 (Oct) at [23]–[25].

29 *Moschi v Lep Air Services Ltd* [1973] A.C. 331; *Associated British Ports v Ferryways NV* [2009] EWCA Civ 189, [2009] 1 Lloyd's Rep. 595; *Multiplex Construction Europe Ltd v Dunne* [2017] EWHC 3073 (TCC), [2018] B.L.R. 36.

30 See below, para.45-009 (performance guarantees).

31 *Marubeni Hong Kong and South China Ltd v The Mongolian Government* [2005] EWCA Civ 395, [2005] 1 W.L.R. 2497 at [30].

32 On which see below, para.45-009.

33 *Vossloh Aktiengesellschaft v Alpha Trains (UK) Ltd* [2010] EWHC 2443 (Ch), [2010] All E.R. (D) 86 (Oct) at [34], per Sir William Blackburne.

34 But the "common form" provision stating that the guarantor is liable as a principal debtor does not convert every guarantee into an indemnity: *General Produce Co v United Bank Ltd* [1979] 2 Lloyd's Rep. 255.

able under the indemnity has not contracted at the request of another debtor. Thus a dealer who agrees by a "recourse agreement" to indemnify a finance company against any loss under a hire-purchase transaction is not a surety either against the creditor or against the debtor. And even where, as between two debtors, one is primarily liable and the other only secondarily liable, there is not necessarily a contract of suretyship. For instance, where a tenant assigns his interest under a lease and the assignee covenants to indemnify the assignor against liability for breach of covenants in the lease, the assignee is, as between himself and the assignor, primarily liable, but there is no contract of suretyship between them.[35] And similarly, where property is sold subject to a mortgage, the mortgagor is not surety for the purchaser.[36]

45-009   **Performance guarantees**[37]   A number of cases have involved discussion of the nature of "performance guarantees" which are, in essence, exceptionally stringent contracts of indemnity.[38] They are contractual undertakings, normally granted by banks, to pay or repay, a specified sum in the event of any default in performance by the principal debtor of some other contract with a third party, the creditor. Sometimes the bank's liability arises on mere demand by the creditor, notwithstanding that it may appear on the evidence that the principal debtor is not in any way in default, or even that the creditor himself is in default under the principal contract.[39] Such guarantees are sometimes called "first demand guarantees"[40] or "demand bonds".[41] It has been held that performance guarantees of this nature are analogous to a bank's letter of credit, and that the bank's liability is of a primary nature which is unaffected by allegations that the creditor is in breach of the main

---

[35]   *Baynton v Morgan* (1888) 22 Q.B.D. 74 and see *Allied London Investments Ltd v Hambro Life Assurance Ltd* (1983) 269 E.G. 41; and *Selous Street Properties Ltd v Oronel Fabrics Ltd* (1984) 270 E.G. 643 and 743. On the effect of the Landlord and Tenant (Covenants) Act 1995 on tenant's covenants on assignment see below, paras 45-015—45-017.

[36]   *Re Errington* [1894] 1 Q.B. 11.

[37]   See further above, paras 37-126 et seq.

[38]   *Edward Owen Engineering Ltd v Barclays Bank International Ltd* [1978] Q.B. 159; *RD Harbottle (Mercantile) Ltd v National Westminster Bank Ltd* [1978] Q.B. 146; *Howe Richardson Scale Co Ltd v Polimex-Cekop* [1978] 1 Lloyd's Rep. 161; *Bolivinter Oil SA v Chase Manhattan Bank NA* [1984] 1 W.L.R. 392; *Attaleia Marine Co Ltd v Bimeh Iran (Iran Insurance Co) (The Zeus)* [1993] 2 Lloyd's Rep. 497. cf. *Trafalgar House Construction (Regions) Ltd v General Surety & Guarantee Co Ltd* [1996] 1 A.C. 199; *Frans Maas (UK) Ltd v Habib Bank AG Zurich* [2001] Lloyd's Rep. Bank 14; *Solo Industries UK Ltd v Canara Bank* [2001] EWCA Civ 1059, [2001] 1 W.L.R. 1800; *Banque Saudi Fransi v Lear Siegler Services Inc* [2005] EWHC 2395, [2006] 1 Lloyd's Rep. 273; *Wuhan Guoyu Logistics Group Co Ltd v Emporiki Bank of Greece SA* [2012] EWCA Civ 1629, [2012] 2 C.L.C. 986.

[39]   See cases cited in previous note; cf. *General Surety & Guarantee Co Ltd v Francis Parker Ltd* (1977) 6 Build. L.R. 16. This does not mean, though, that a bank must always pay when asked: "a Bank is not obliged to accept without investigation a demand which is ambiguous, or potentially misleading": *Frans Maas (UK) Ltd v Habib Bank AG Zurich*, above, at [27].

[40]   See further on the nature and variety of such guarantees, *Benjamin's Sale of Goods*, 10th edn (2017), Ch.24 especially at paras 24-003—24-006, contrasting "orthodox guarantees" and "autonomous guarantees". *Benjamin's Sale of Goods*, paras 24-007—24-010 explains the various international uniform rules which may be incorporated into an "autonomous guarantee", notably the I.C.C. Uniform Rules on Demand Guarantees (URDG 458) whose revised version URDG 758 applies, subject to contrary intention, to any guarantee incorporating the URDG issued on or after July 1, 2010. For an example of the application of the URDG 458 see *Meritz Fire & Marine Insurance Co Ltd v Jan de Nul NV* [2011] EWCA Civ 827, [2011] 2 Lloyd's Rep. 379.

[41]   *Marubeni Hong Kong and South China Ltd v The Mongolian Government* [2005] EWCA Civ 395, [2005] 1 W.L.R. 2497 at [30].

contract between him and the principal debtor.[42] The question whether a particular instrument (such as a "refund guarantee") takes the form of an independent performance bond (or stand-by letter of credit) or a true "see to it" guarantee is one of construction of the instrument in its factual and contractual context having regard to its commercial purpose.[43] While there may be a number of indications in an instrument which argue in favour of it being a "true guarantee" or, conversely, an "on-demand bond",

"... [w]here an instrument (i) relates to an underlying transaction between the parties in different jurisdictions, (ii) is issued by a bank, (iii) contains an undertaking to pay 'on demand' (with or without the words 'first' and/or 'written') and (iv) does not contain clauses excluding or limiting the defences available to a guarantor, it will almost always be construed as a demand guarantee."[44]

On the other hand, there is a "strong presumption" that a "guarantee" concluded other than by a bank is not a demand or independent performance bond,[45] although this presumption may be rebutted.[46] In the event of fraud the court may be able to intervene to protect the surety; but the court has refused to imply a term to the ef-

---

[42] See cases cited above, second note in the present paragraph. As to bankers' letters of credit, see above, paras 34-441 et seq.

[43] *Gold Coast Ltd v Caja de Ahorros del Mediterraneo* [2002] 1 Lloyd's Rep. 617, 620; *Marubeni Hong Kong and South China Ltd v The Mongolian Government* [2005] EWCA Civ 395, [2005] 1 W.L.R. 2497 at [28].

[44] *Paget's Law of Banking*, 11th edn (1996), quoted with approval by the Court of Appeal in *Caja de Ahorros v Gold Coast Ltd* [2002] 1 Lloyd's Rep. 617 at [16]; *Wuhan Guoyu Logistics Group Co Ltd v Emporiki Bank of Greece SA* [2012] EWCA Civ 1629, [2012] 2 C.L.C. 986 at [26]–[27]; *Caja de Ahorros v Gold Coast Ltd* [2001] EWCA Civ 1806, [2002] 1 Lloyd's Rep. 617 at [16]; *Caterpillar Motoren GmbH & Co KG v Mutual Benefits Assurance Co* [2015] EWHC 2304 (Comm), [2015] 2 Lloyd's Rep. 261 at [13]–[15], [19]–[22] and [25]–[27]; *Spliethoff's Bevrachtingskantoor BV v Bank of China Ltd* [2015] EWHC 999 (Comm), [2015] 2 Lloyd's Rep. 123 at [69]–[85]; *Autoridad del Canal de Panama v Sacyr SA* [2017] EWHC 2228 (Comm), [2017] 2 Lloyd's Rep. 351 at [81]–[103]. But where a contract contains a clause as is mentioned in (iv) of "Paget's presumption" (quoted in the text) this may be explicable as inserted so as to put beyond doubt that the rule applicable to true guarantees does not apply: [2015] EWHC 2304 (Comm) at [21], referring to *Caja de Ahorros v Gold Coast Ltd del Mediterraneo* [2001] EWCA Civ 1806, [2002] 1 Lloyd's Rep. 617 at [25]. The passage quoted in the text appears in almost identical words in *Paget's Law of Banking*, 14th edn (2014), para.34.8.

[45] *Marubeni Hong Kong and South China Ltd v The Mongolian Government* [2005] EWCA Civ 395, [2005] 1 W.L.R. 2497 at [30]; *IIG Capital LLC v Van Der Merwe* [2008] EWCA Civ 542, [2008] 2 Lloyd's Rep. 187 at [8]; cf. *Caterpillar Motoren GmbH & Co KG v Mutual Benefits Assurance Co* [2015] EWHC 2304 (Comm), [2015] 2 Lloyd's Rep. 261 at [20] (no material distinction between bank and other financial institution, such as an insurance company engaged in the business of providing bonds to its customers).

[46] *IIG Capital LLC v Van Der Merwe* [2008] EWCA Civ 542, [2008] EWCA Civ 542 at [33], per Waller L.J. (with whom Lawrence Collins and Rimer L.JJ. agreed). cf. *Carey Value Added SL v Grupo Urvasco SA* [2010] EWHC 1905 (Comm), [2011] 2 All E.R. (Comm) 140 at [38]–[43]; *Vossloh Aktiengesellschaft v Alpha Trains (UK) Ltd* [2010] EWHC 2443 (Ch), [2010] All E.R. (D) 86 (Oct) at [53]; *North Shore Ventures Ltd v Anstead Holdings Inc* [2011] EWCA Civ 230, [2011] 2 Lloyd's Rep. 45 at [46]–[47]; *Ultrabulk A/S v Jagatramka* [2017] EWHC 2792 (Comm), [2018] 1 Lloyd's Rep. 384 at [16]. Where the principal contract is in the nature of a financing transaction (even though in the form of a sale and demise charter with a "deed of guarantee" as part of it), any presumption generally applicable to non-banking cases will more readily give way to language to the contrary: *Bitumen Invest AS v Richmond Mercantile Ltd FZC* [2016] EWHC 2957 (Comm), [2017] 1 Lloyd's Rep. 219 at [17] (where the fact that the trigger for payment was the issue of a demand for an amount certified by the beneficiary of the guarantee provided the key feature in finding it to be an "on demand guarantee" ([2016] EWHC 2957 (Comm) esp. at [21]–[26])).

fect that the beneficiary of such a guarantee will give notice of a claim only if there is reasonable cause.[47] Clear evidence is needed that the beneficiary's demand is fraudulent to the knowledge of the bank if the bank is to be restrained from paying under such a guarantee or bond, but this does not mean that all possible explanations other than fraud must be totally ruled out. It means that fraud must be the "only realistic inference".[48]

45-010 Performance guarantees: counter-guarantee or indemnity   The bank or other financial institution which grants a performance guarantee will, of course, demand a counter-guarantee or indemnity from the customer at whose request the guarantee is granted.[49] As the customer will be liable to reimburse the bank on their payment under the guarantee, and as he will be unable to prevent the bank from paying (except in cases of fraud) when demand is made on the bank, his position is clearly perilous: "these performance guarantees are virtually promissory notes payable on demand".[50] Such a counter-indemnity by a customer in favour of a guaranteeing bank takes effect according to its terms. For example, where the customer agrees to indemnify the bank in respect of claims made "under or *in connection with* the issue of the guarantee" and the guarantee obligations are expressed not to be "in any way discharged or diminished" by the guarantee's total or partial invalidity, then the bank may claim on the indemnity in respect of payments made by it under or in connection with the guarantee even if the latter was at no time legally valid.[51] Of course, the party at whose request a performance guarantee is issued, may have his remedy on the contract in the event of his being wrongfully called upon to pay, as the result of his bank's being similarly called upon. But where the other contracting party is abroad, and the contract is governed by the law of a foreign country, this remedy may in practice be of small value.

45-011 Performance guarantees: injunction to restrain creditor   It may, however, be somewhat easier to obtain an injunction to restrain the creditor himself from receiving payment from the bank, particularly where an interim remedy is being sought; but even in this sort of procedure, it has been held that an interim remedy should not normally be given unless the validity of the bond or guarantee is itself being challenged, or unless the circumstances are such that they would justify the grant of a freezing injunction.[52]

---

[47] *State Trading Corp of India Ltd v ED & F Man (Sugar) Ltd* [1981] Com. L.R. 235.

[48] *United Trading Corp SA v Allied Arab Bank Ltd* [1985] 2 Lloyd's Rep. 554; *TTI Team Telecom International Ltd v Hutchison 3G UK Ltd* [2003] EWHC 762, [2003] 1 All E.R. (Comm) 914 at [29] et seq.; *Korea Industry Co v Andoll* [1990] 2 Lloyd's Rep. 183, CA Sing. cf. *Themehelp Ltd v West* [1995] 3 W.L.R. 751 which concerned a claim by the principal debtor for an injunction to restrain the beneficiary of the bond from serving notice under the guarantee.

[49] cf. *Wahda Bank v Arab Bank Plc* [1996] 1 Lloyd's Rep. 470 in which the Court of Appeal held that such a counter-guarantee was intimately connected with such a performance bond with the result that, in the absence of any express choice, it felt entitled to find that the parties intended the counter-guarantee to be governed by the same law as governed the guarantees.

[50] *Edward Owen Engineering Ltd v Barclays Bank International Ltd* [1978] Q.B. 159 at 170, per Lord Denning M.R.

[51] *Gulf Bank KSC v Mitsubishi Heavy Industries (No.2)* [1994] 2 Lloyd's Rep. 145.

[52] *Bolivinter Oil SA v Chase Manhattan Bank SA* [1984] 1 W.L.R. 392; *Potton Homes Ltd v Coleman (Contractors) Overseas Ltd* (1984) 28 Build. L.R. 19.

Performance guarantees: implied term for repayment In *Cargill International* **45-012**
SA v Bangladesh Sugar and Food Industries Corp[53] the Court of Appeal held that
a party to a contract who has paid money under a performance bond to the other
party may recover it, provided that the latter has suffered no damage in consequence
of the first party's breach. According to Potter L.J., in view of the very considerable commercial advantages which a performance bond gives to its beneficiary, "the
obligation to account later to the seller, in respect of what turns out to be an
overpayment, is a necessary corrective if a balance of commercial fairness is to be
maintained between the parties".[54] Furthermore, the court construed a clause of the
contract between the parties which referred to the bond being "forfeited" as referring to the bond (i.e. the exercise of party's right to call on the bond as against the
bank), not to the moneys paid under the bond, a result which, according to the
learned Lord Justice, "accords more with reason, fairness and commercial good
sense" as to exclude the obligation to account "would be to provide the defendant
with a substantial windfall in any case where it had suffered no loss or relatively
nominal loss, and would run counter to the general proposition that compensation
for breach of contract depends on proof of loss".[55] On the other hand, in *Uzinterimpex JSC v Standard Bank Plc*[56] a demand guarantee was given by a seller's bank
to a buyer's bank (which financed the transaction) in respect of advance payments
of the purchase price of goods not delivered. In these circumstances, the Court of
Appeal refused to imply a term that, if any demand made under it should exceed
the loss sustained by the buyer of goods or the buyer's bank, or should otherwise
be excessive, the buyer's bank would repay the excess to the seller's bank/
guarantor on the basis that if such a term were not implied, the buyer's bank would
obtain a windfall.[57] According to Moore-Bick L.J.,

> "The guarantee stands as an independent contract between [the seller's bank] and the
> [buyer's bank] and is capable of operating effectively without the need for such a term.
> If a demand under the guarantee resulted in the wrongful refund of part of the price due
> to the seller, the seller would have a remedy against [the buyer] under the contract of sale
> ... That provides the answer to the 'windfall' argument, despite the fact that in this case
> the remedy may be of little practical value because [the buyer] is insolvent."[58]

Moreover, in the learned Lord Justice's view, there are:

> "... other, and perhaps even stronger, reasons why [the argument for an implied term] must
> be rejected. It is essential to the maintenance of international commerce, much of which
> is supported by undertakings of this kind given by banks and other financial institutions,
> that the documents by which those undertakings are given should operate in accordance
> with the terms which appear on their face ... [Banks] cannot be expected to be aware of,
> or to implement, terms that do not appear on the face of the documents. The implied term
> for which [the seller's bank] contends would have the potential effect of imposing on [the

---

53 [1998] 1 W.L.R. 461 applied by *Tradigrain SA v State Trading Corp of India* [2005] EWHC 2206
(Comm), [2006] 1 Lloyd's Rep. 216.
54 [1998] 1 W.L.R. 461 at 469.
55 [1998] 1 W.L.R. 461 at 469.
56 [2008] EWCA Civ 819, [2008] Bus. L.R. 1762.
57 [2008] EWCA Civ 819 at [19].
58 [2008] EWCA Civ 819 at [20], per Moore-Bick L.J.

buyer's bank] a liability which could not be identified from the face of the document and which would be very uncertain in its effect."[59]

And in *Wuhan Guoyu Logistics Group Co Ltd v Emporiki Bank of Greece SA*[60] the Court of Appeal rejected an analogous claim by a bank based on constructive trust. There the bank had paid under an on-demand performance guarantee in respect of a buyer's obligations to a seller, but it was later established by arbitration that the sums paid had not fallen due by the buyer. According to Christopher Clarke L.J. (with whom Rimer and Longmore L.JJ. agreed), the principles according to which such a guarantee is independent of disputes between the seller and the buyer:

"... are completely inimical to the implication of a trust impressed upon the monies in the Seller's hands by reason of circumstances arising after accrual of the Seller's completed cause of action under the guarantee. It is critical to the efficacy of these financial arrangements that as between beneficiary and bank the position crystallises as at presentation of documents or demand as the case may be, and that it is only in the case of fraudulent presentation or demand by the beneficiary that the bank can resist payment against an apparently conforming presentation or demand."[61]

Nor is there anything unconscionable in the seller retaining sums paid by the bank in these circumstances.[62]

45-013 **"Charge-back transactions"** In *Tam Wing Chuen v Bank of Credit & Commerce Hong Kong Ltd*[63] the Privy Council considered the legal effect of a deposit of funds by A to B to be used to secure a loan by B to C, a transaction known as a "charge-back". It held that the question whether A (the depositor) should be considered *personally liable* to B in respect of the loan (and therefore a guarantor) is a question of construction of the contract under which he made the deposit. In this respect, Lord Mustill observed that the mere "[c]onsistency with [such a personal] liability [in the depositor] which could have been expressed is no ground for imposing a liability which was not expressed".[64]

45-014 **Assignment by creditor of benefit of contract guaranteed** In *Kumar v Dunning*, the Court of Appeal held that an assignment of the reversion of a lease may pass the benefit of a covenant by a surety which guaranteed the tenant's covenants, even in the absence of an express assignment of such benefit.[65] The court was satis-

---

59   [2008] EWCA Civ 819 at [23], per Moore-Bick L.J.
60   [2013] EWCA Civ 1679, [2014] 1 Lloyd's Rep. 273. cf. *Wuhan Guoyu Logistics Group Co Ltd v Emporiki Bank of Greece SA* [2012] EWCA Civ 1629, [2012] 2 C.L.C. 986 (where the Court of Appeal decided that the instrument was an on-demand performance guarantee); above, para.45-009.
61   [2013] EWCA Civ 1679 at [22] and see similarly at [25], relying on *Uzinterimpex JSC v Standard Bank Plc* [2008] EWCA Civ 819, [2008] Bus. L.R. 1762. Moore-Bick L.J. held, in the alternative, that if it were relevant to have regard to matters arising after the accrual of the seller's cause of action against the bank (which he considered it was not) then the seller's contractual obligation to account to the buyer for any sums paid by the bank to the seller which were not owed to the seller would be "diametrically inconsistent with the notion of the Seller holding the money on trust for the Bank": [2013] EWCA Civ 1679 at [27].
62   [2013] EWCA Civ 1679 at [23].
63   [1996] B.C.C. 388.
64   [1996] B.C.C. 388 at 393.
65   [1989] 1 Q.B. 193; Harpum [1988] 47 C.L.J. 180; not following the decisions at first instance in *Pinemain Ltd v Welbeck International Ltd* (1984) 272 E.G. 1166; *Re Distributors and Warehousing Ltd* [1986] B.C.L.C. 129; and *Coastplace Ltd v Hartley* [1987] 1 Q.B. 948. The Landlord and Ten-

fied that such a covenant by the surety "touches and concerns the land" so as to come within the general rules as to the running of positive covenants with land[66] and that this result accorded with "the commercial common sense and justice of the case".[67] However, the court[68] distinguished the position in an Australian case, in which it was held that an assignment of a mortgage did not operate to transfer the benefit of a covenant by a surety that the borrower would repay the principal debt on the basis that neither the borrower's nor the surety's covenant to pay the principal could "touch and concern" the land.[69] This approach was followed by the House of Lords in *P & A Swift Investments v Combined English Stores Group Plc*[70]: as Lord Templeman observed, "[a] covenant by a surety that a tenant's covenant which touches and concerns the land shall be performed and observed must itself be a covenant which touches and concerns the land".[71] However, this position at common law was changed as regards "new tenancies" (notably, those which were entered on or after January 1, 1996)[72] by s.3(1) of the Landlord and Tenant (Covenants) Act 1995, which provides that:

"... the benefit and burden of all landlord and tenant covenants of a tenancy—

(a)   shall be annexed and incident to the whole, and to each and every part, of the premises demised by the tenancy and of the reversion in them, and

(b)   shall in accordance with this section pass on an assignment of the whole or any part of those premises or of the reversion in them."

Thus, with the qualifications which appear in s.3(3) of this Act, the benefit of a covenant by a surety guaranteeing the tenant's covenants will pass on assignment by the landlord whether or not it "touches and concerns the land".

Guarantees of tenancy covenants on assignment: common law   At common law, a tenant remains liable on assignment of his interest under the lease for the payment of rent and due performance of other tenants' covenants, this being the result of privity of contract remaining between the landlord and original tenant, even though assignment creates privity of estate between the landlord and tenant's assignee.[73] Furthermore, any guarantee of a tenant's covenants in principle also remains enforceable by the landlord (and, as we have seen, often by the landlord's assignees)[74] notwithstanding assignment by the tenant.

45-015

---

ant (Covenants) Act 1995 ss.17–19 restrict the liability of former tenants and their guarantors in various respects, these provisions applying to tenancies made before as well as after this Act: s.1(2) and see below, paras 45-016 et seq.

[66]   *Mayor of Congleton v Pattison* (1808) 10 East 130, 138; *Vernon v Smith* (1821) 5 B. & Ald. 1.

[67]   *Kumar v Dunning* [1989] 1 Q.B. 193, 201, per Sir Nicolas Browne-Wilkinson V.C.

[68]   [1989] 1 Q.B. 193 at 206–207.

[69]   *Consolidated Trust Co Ltd v Naylar* (1936) 55 C.L.R. 423.

[70]   [1989] 1. A.C. 632 and see *Coronation Street Industrial Properties Ltd v Ingall Industries Plc* [1989] 1 W.L.R. 304.

[71]   [1989] 1 A.C. 632, 637.

[72]   Landlord and Tenant (Covenants) Act 1995 s.1(3); Landlord and Tenant (Covenants) Act 1995 (Commencement) Order 1995 (SI 1995/2963).

[73]   *City of London Corp v Fell* [1994] 1 A.C. 458, 465.

[74]   See above, para.45-014.

45-016 **"New tenancies": breaking privity of contract** However, this position was radically altered by the provisions of the Landlord and Tenant (Covenants) Act 1995.[75] First, the key purposes of this Act were to "break privity of contract" after assignment by the tenant and, on the fulfilment of certain conditions, by the landlord, terminating their contractual obligations *inter se*, but to preserve and extend the effectiveness of tenancy obligations for those within privity of estate.[76] However, this "breaking of privity" does not rule out the creation of liability in a former tenant for the performance of the tenant's covenants by his assignee as s.16(1) of the 1995 Act provides that "where on an assignment a tenant is to any extent released from a tenant covenant of a tenancy by virtue of this Act ... nothing in this Act ... shall preclude him from entering into an authorised guarantee agreement with respect to the performance of that covenant by the assignee", s.16(8) expressly declaring that "the rules of law relating to guarantees (and in particular those relating to the release of sureties) are, subject to its terms, applicable in relation to any authorised guarantee agreement as in relation to any other guarantee agreement".[77] It is clearly important to note that s.16 applies only to "*new* tenancies" as defined by s.1 of the Act, which include, notably, those made on or after January 1, 1996[78] and is carefully restricted by subss.3 and 4 of s.16, to which further reference should be made. On the other hand, a landlord is not *automatically* entitled to require as a condition for his consent to an assignment under the terms of a lease granted before the coming into force of the Landlord and Tenant (Covenants) Act 1995 the entering by the assigning tenant of an "authorised guarantee agreement" under s.16 of that Act, for by s.19(1) of the Landlord and Tenant Act 1927 such a consent to assignment can be refused only if it is reasonable for him to do so[79] and any unreasonable refusal would prevent a landlord's requirement of such a guarantee from being "lawfully imposed" as the 1995 Act requires.[80] Moreover, where the renewal of a tenancy granted before the coming into force of the 1995 Act is to be ordered under Pt 2 of the Landlord and Tenant Act 1954,[81] the landlord may not as a condition of his consent to renewal of the lease require a clause in the new lease to allow him automatically to require an "authorised guarantee agreement" be entered by the tenant on the latter's assignment.[82] Given that the 1995 Act prevents a landlord from enjoying the rights on assignment of the term of the lease which he had enjoyed under the old law, the 1954 Act does not entitle the landlord to say that on renewal under that Act, he should be given as generous terms as the 1995 Act provides:

---

[75] See generally Megarry & Wade, *The Law of Real Property*, 7th edn (2008) by Harpum, paras 20-064 et seq.

[76] Landlord and Tenant (Covenants) Act 1995 especially ss.3–8. For analysis of these and other provisions of the Landlord and Tenant (Covenants) Act 1995, see Bridge (1996) 55 C.L.J. 313.

[77] cf. *Prudential Assurance Co Ltd v Ayres* [2008] EWCA Civ 52, [2008] L. & T.R. 30 at [46] where the "ordinary rules of law relating to guarantees (in particular those relating to the discharge of sureties)" were excluded by the terms of the guarantee.

[78] Landlord and Tenant (Covenants) Act 1995 s.1(1) and (3); Landlord and Tenant (Covenants) Act 1995 (Commencement) Order 1995 (SI 1995/2963).

[79] *Wallis Fashion Group Ltd v CGU Life Assurance Ltd* [2000] L. & T.R. 520, 526, (2001) 81 P. & C.R. 28.

[80] Landlord and Tenant (Covenants) Act 1995 s.16(3)(b).

[81] Landlord and Tenant Act 1954 s.35.

[82] *Wallis Fashion Group Ltd v CGU Life Assurance Ltd* [2000] L. & T.R. 520, 528–529.

"The 1995 Act represents a sea change in the law relating to the tenant's liability after he assigns the lease, and it also alters the law relating to the landlord's power to impose terms on assigning the lease. It does not merely represent a sea change in what had been common practice, but in what a landlord can lawfully require, both in terms of what is to be included in the lease initially and what he can demand on assignment."[83]

Instead, at least in some circumstances, a clause allowing a landlord to require such a guarantee by the tenant only if reasonable represents a fair balance between the interests of the landlord and of the tenant.[84] If, prior to assignment, performance of the tenant's covenants is guaranteed by a third party, that person will be released on assignment to the same extent as the tenant.[85] And if the landlord purports to require such a third party surety to guarantee performance by the assignee, that agreement will not count as an "authorised guarantee agreement" (as not being made with the tenant[86]) and may be void as frustrating the operation of the Act for his release.[87] The Court of Appeal has held that a clause in a contract of guarantee of a tenant's obligations under a lease which requires the guarantor to give a *further* guarantee in respect of an assignee of a lease is not enforceable, as this would frustrate the operation of the Act.[88]

---

[83] [2000] L. & T.R. 520 at 529, per Neuberger J.

[84] [2000] L. & T.R. 520 at 531. cf. *Legends Surf Shops Plc v Sun Life Assurance Society Plc* [2005] EWHC 1438 (Ch), [2006] 1 P. & C.R. D. G1.

[85] Landlord and Tenant (Covenants) Act 1995 ss.16(4), 24(2). An assignment by a tenant of the lease to the guarantor of that tenant's covenants (the guarantee being expressed as imposing the same liability as if principal debtor) has been held void under the 1995 Act: *EMI Group Ltd v O & H Q1 Ltd* [2016] EWHC 529 (Ch), [2016] Ch. 586 at [77]–[91]. This is because on such an assignment the provisions of the Act would apply as follows: (i) the original tenant (T1) is released from the tenant covenants (s.5(2)(a)); (ii) the guarantor is released from the tenant covenants as from T1's release (s.24(2)); (iii) the effect of s.24(2) is that as from the release of T1 (i.e. as from the assignment to the guarantor/second tenant (T2)), the guarantor should be released from its liabilities as guarantor; however, (iv) as from the assignment to T2/the guarantor, T2 becomes bound by the tenant covenants (s.3(2)(a)). As a result, the assignment releases the guarantor from the tenant covenants but at the same moment binds the guarantor to them as T2, the liability under the guarantee being the same or essentially the same as the liability of T1. Such an assignment "frustrates" the operation of s.24(2)(b) and is therefore rendered void by s.25(1)(a): [2016] EWHC 529 (Ch) at [79]–[80]. Given that the assignment is void, the lease remains vested in the original tenant and the purported assignee remains bound as guarantor of that tenant's covenants: [2016] EWHC 529 (Ch) at [89]–[91].

[86] Landlord and Tenant (Covenants) Act 1995 ss.16(4), 16(1), above.

[87] Landlord and Tenant (Covenants) Act 1995 ss.16(4), 25(1).

[88] *K/S Victoria Street (A Danish Partnership) v House of Fraser (Stores Management) Ltd* [2011] EWCA Civ 904, [2012] 2 W.L.R. 470 at [21]–[24], [34], [44], [46], [51], [53], considering that (i) "any agreement which involves a guarantor of the assignor guaranteeing that assignor's assignee" is invalidated under s.25(1) except to the extent that such an agreement requires a guarantor to guarantee a liability undertaken by a tenant under an "authorised guarantee agreement"; but that (ii) a guarantor of an assignor can validly guarantee the liability of an assignee on a further assignment (largely approving *Good Harvest Partnership LLP v Centaur Services Ltd* [2010] EWHC 330 (Ch), [2010] Ch. 426 especially at [22]–[23]). The question whether a clause comes within s.25(1) depends on ordinary rules of construction and the maxim *verba intelligenda ut res magis valeat quam pereat* (on which see Vol.I, para.13-078) should not be used simply as a means to avoid the consequences of s.25 being applied to the contract which the parties have made: *Tindall Cobham 1 Ltd v Adda Hotels* [2014] EWCA Civ 1215, [2015] 1 P. & C.R. 5 at [29]–[32] (where the proper meaning of a condition of consent by landlord to assignment by tenant required tenant to procure a continuing guarantee from an existing guarantor, and therefore fell within s.25). cf. *Pavilion Property Trustees Ltd v Permira Advisers LLP* [2014] EWHC 145 (Ch), [2014] 1 P. & C.R. 21 at [15]–[20] (not discussed by the Court of Appeal in *Tindall Cobham 1 Ltd v Adda Hotels* [2014] EWCA Civ. 1215)

45-017 **All tenancies: former tenants and guarantors**   Secondly, s.17 of the Landlord and Tenant (Covenants) Act 1995, which applies to *all tenancies* whether new or otherwise,[89] subjects the liability of a former tenant *or his guarantor* for rent, service charge or liquidated damages for breach of covenant, to a condition of service by the landlord within six months of the charge becoming due of a notice informing either the tenant, or the guarantor as the case may be, "that the charge is now due; and that in respect of the charge the landlord intends to recover from the former tenant [or guarantor] such amount as is specified in the notice and (where payable) interest calculated on such basis as is so specified".[90] Where such a notice has been served, the former tenant or guarantor's liability is in principle restricted to the amount specified in it.[91] Moreover, s.19(1) of the same Act provides that where any person makes full payment as he has been duly required to under s.17, then he "shall be entitled ... to have the landlord under that tenancy grant him an overriding lease of the premises demised by the tenancy". The purpose of such a legally imposed lease is to give the claimant some control over the defaulting tenant and in this respect s.19(8)(a) provides that where two or more requests for such an overriding lease are made on the same day, then a request by a former tenant shall be treated as made before a request made by a guarantor.

45-018 **All tenancies: new variations**   Thirdly, s.18(1) and (2) provide that a former tenant "shall not be liable ... to pay any amount in respect of the covenant to the extent that the amount is referable to any relevant variation of the tenant covenants of the tenancy effected after the assignment", "relevant variation" being defined by s.18(4). Similarly, s.18(3) provides that a *guarantor* of a former tenant's covenants "(where his liability ... is not wholly discharged by any such variation of the tenant covenants of the tenancy) shall not be liable under the agreement to pay any amount in respect of the covenant to the extent that the amount is referable to any such variation". It is to be noted that s.18 applies to *all tenancies* whether new or

---

where the court found that the language of a guarantee was "open to interpretation" and felt able to avoid the illegality required by s.25 by construction under the maxim. It has also been held that a court can sever parts of a contract which cannot have effect under s.25 (*Pavilion Property Trustees Ltd v Permira Advisers LLP* [2014] EWHC 145 (Ch) at [21]–[22]), though the Court of Appeal in *Tindall Cobham 1 Ltd v Adda Hotels* [2014] EWCA Civ 1215 at [46] considered that the principle of severance would not be applied for this purpose unless the unenforceable provision is capable of being removed without the necessity of adding to or modifying the wording that remains, the remaining terms are supported by consideration and the removal of the unenforceable provisions does not alter the character of the contract: *Sadler v Imperial Life Assurance Co of Canada* [1988] I.R.L.R. 388, 393 and see generally Vol.I, paras 16-236 et seq. See also *UK Leasing Brighton Ltd v Topland Neptune* [2015] EWHC 53 (Ch), [2015] 2 P. & C.R. 2 (assignment by tenant in breach of covenant; re-assignment back and fresh guarantee).

[89] Landlord and Tenant (Covenants) Act 1995 s.1(2).

[90] Landlord and Tenant (Covenants) Act 1995 s.17(2), (3); *Scottish & Newcastle Plc v Raguz* [2007] EWCA Civ 150, [2007] 1 Bus. L.R. 851. Notice sent to the intended recipient at last residential address is effective notice: *Commercial Union Life Assurance Co Ltd v Moustafa* [1999] L. & T.R. 489. There is no requirement that a landlord must, in enforcing a guarantee, also serve the former tenant with the notice required under s.17(2) of the 1995 Act: *Cheverell Estates Ltd v Harris* [1998] 1 E.G.L.R. 27. The requirements contained in s.17 do not apply to a claim by a tenant sued by its landlord for an indemnity or contribution "in quasi contract" from an assignee or its guarantor (*Fresh (Retail) Ltd v Emsden* [1999] C.L.Y. 3693) nor to such a claim under an express indemnity contained in the assignment, the latter on the basis that it is not a "tenant covenant" for these purposes: *MW Kellogg Ltd v Tobin* [1999] L. & T.R. 513.

[91] Landlord and Tenant (Covenants) Act 1995 s.17(4).

otherwise,[92] but *only to new variations* of tenant covenants (i.e. those effected on or after January 1, 1996).[93]

2. FORMATION OF THE CONTRACT

(a) Agreement

Offer and acceptance: revocation of offers   A contract of suretyship is formed, like any other contract, by offer and acceptance, supported by consideration. But difficulty has been encountered in applying the ordinary principles to contracts of this nature, particularly with regard to the revocation of guarantees. The difficulty stems largely from the fact that it is frequently hard to say whether the contract is intended to be unilateral or bilateral.[94] If the guarantee is given in return for a *promise* by the creditor that he will enter into some transaction with the principal debtor, then the guarantee will constitute a binding bilateral contract as soon as it is given and accepted, and it cannot then be revoked.[95] But if (as is more usually the case) the guarantee is given in return for an act or forbearance on the part of the creditor, the contract will not be made until the act is done or the forbearance is given, and until then, the guarantee remains revocable.[96]

45-019

Continuing guarantees   Where the guarantee is a continuing one, the question whether it can be revoked after the consideration has been partly performed depends on whether the consideration is divisible or entire. In the former situation the guarantee is treated rather like a standing offer which is accepted pro tanto by part performance of the consideration, but remains revocable at all times as to future liabilities.[97] Therefore, in the case of a continuing guarantee to secure the balance of a running account at a bank, a surety may at any moment revoke his guarantee in respect of future advances.[98] But it is common practice to require a specified period of notice to be given before such a guarantee can be revoked and this is thought to be binding on the surety.[99] But this would not be so if the guarantee were in all respects treated as a standing offer,[100] and it is therefore uncertain whether the surety would be liable for advances made by the creditor after receipt of notice of termination of the guarantee, but before its expiry.[101] However, in *National Westminster Bank Plc v Hardman*,[102] a surety guaranteed payment on demand to a creditor of the continuing liability of a principal debtor, subject to a condition that the guarantee be terminable by three months' notice. The surety gave such notice, but no demand was made before the expiry of the three months. The Court of Ap-

45-020

---

92 Landlord and Tenant (Covenants) Act 1995 s.1(2).
93 Landlord and Tenant (Covenants) Act 1995 s.18(6); Landlord and Tenant (Covenants) Act 1995 (Commencement) Order 1995 (SI 1995/2963).
94 As to this distinction, see Vol.I, paras 1-114, 2-083 et seq.
95 But a guarantee of a future consumer credit agreement generally remains revocable until the credit agreement is made, see Consumer Credit Act 1974 s.113(6).
96 See Vol.I, paras 2-085—2-087; *Offord v Davies* (1862) 12 C.B.(N.S.) 748.
97 Vol.I, para.2-087.
98 *Coulthart v Clementson* (1879) 5 Q.B.D. 42; *Lloyd's v Harper* (1880) 16 Ch. D. 290; and see *Hamilton's Executor v Bank of Scotland*, 1913 S.C. 743.
99 *Paget's Law of Banking*, 14th edn (2014) by Malek and Odgers, para.18-30.
100 See Vol.I, para.2-087.
101 But see Consumer Credit Act 1974 s.113(6), noted above in this paragraph.
102 [1988] F.L.R. 302.

peal held the surety not liable on the guarantee, even in respect of advances made until the date of expiry. As a matter of construction, no sums fell due on the guarantee until demand was made and after the period of notice, the guarantee terminated. Where, on the other hand, the consideration for the guarantee is entire and indivisible, the surety has no right to revoke his guarantee unless such a right is expressly conferred by the agreement.[103] Thus the guarantor of rent payable under a lease for 14 years could not revoke his guarantee before the expiry of the lease, though the guarantor of rent under a weekly tenancy can do so.[104] It has been held that a surety cannot revoke a fidelity bond given to secure the due performance of some office by the debtor, on the ground that the appointment of the debtor is an indivisible consideration[105]; but if the appointment can be terminated by notice there seems no reason why the consideration should not be treated as divisible. The principle underlying these cases seems to be that if, in reliance on the guarantee, the creditor has entered into an irrevocable transaction with the debtor, he should not be deprived of his security by revocation of the guarantee. But where the transaction entered into by the creditor is itself terminable, he would not be prejudiced if the guarantee were revoked as to the future, for the creditor could then decide whether or not to terminate the main transaction.

45-021 **Revocation by death** Death of the surety does not by itself operate to revoke a guarantee,[106] but notice of his death will do so provided that the guarantee was itself revocable,[107] and that there is nothing to the contrary in the terms of the guarantee.[108] Where specified notice is required to be given to revoke a guarantee, the executors of the surety will normally have to give the required notice after his death.[109] But where the executor of a deceased surety was himself the principal debtor, and he failed to give notice of revocation, it was held that knowledge of the facts by the creditor was sufficient to bring the guarantee to an end.[110] Where a guarantee is continuing, it has been held that the supervening insanity of the guarantor revokes the guarantee as from notice to the creditor.[111]

(b) Consideration

45-022 **General** A contract of suretyship, like any other contract, must be supported by consideration if it is not contained in a deed.[112] Where the surety guarantees some

---

[103] *Lloyd's v Harper* (1880) 16 Ch. D. 290.

[104] *Wingfield v De St Croix* (1919) 35 T.L.R. 432.

[105] *Re Crace* [1902] 1 Ch. 733.

[106] *Bradbury v Morgan* (1862) 1 H. & C. 249.

[107] *Coulthart v Clementson* (1879) 5 Q.B.D. 42.

[108] *Re Silvester* [1895] 1 Ch. 573; *Basch v Stekel* [2001] L. & T.R. 1, 7–8, CA applying the general rule stated in Vol.I, para.20-005.

[109] *Re Silvester*, above.

[110] *Harriss v Fawcett* (1873) L.R. 8 Ch. App. 866.

[111] *Bradford Old Bank Ltd v Sutcliffe* [1918] 2 K.B. 833.

[112] For the requirements for deeds, see Vol.I, paras 1-120 et seq. It was suggested in *Amalgamated Investment & Pty Co Ltd v Texas Commerce International Bank Ltd* [1982] Q.B. 84 that promissory estoppel could operate in the case of a representation that a transaction (there a guarantee) had legal effect even if the transaction was not binding (notably for want of consideration). The possibility of a guarantee being enforceable by way of estoppel in the absence of consideration is an example of the wider question of the relationship between the defensive nature of promissory estoppel and the doctrine of consideration which is discussed in Vol.I at para.4-099.

future debt or transaction, the consideration may be a promise on the part of the creditor to grant the credit or enter into the transaction, or the actual act of doing so.[113] Even if the surety derives no benefit from the transaction, the creditor suffers a detriment which is sufficient consideration. More difficulty arises where the surety guarantees some past debt or transaction. Prima facie such a guarantee is given merely for past consideration and is void.[114] So where a surety guaranteed payments under a hire-purchase agreement entered into four days previously, it was held that the guarantee was given for past consideration only and was void.[115] However, if the consideration is expressed so as to be ambiguous whether it is past or not, it is open to the creditor to show that the consideration was not past. Thus where a guarantee was expressed to be given "in consideration of your having this day advanced to" the principal debtor some £750, it was held that parol evidence was admissible to prove that the money was advanced simultaneously with the giving of the guarantee, and that there was therefore good consideration.[116] Moreover, in accordance with the position as regards contracts in general, consideration to support a promise of guarantee may be found in an act done before it is made, provided that the act is done at the guarantor's request, that the parties understood that the act was to be remunerated in some way and that the conferment of a benefit would have been legally enforceable had it been promised in advance.[117]

Forbearance as consideration for past debt or transaction A guarantee even **45-023** of a past debt or transaction will be valid if the creditor promises to forbear from suing, or to give time to, the principal debtor, or if he actually does so at the request of the surety. The mere fact of forbearance, however, is not enough: there must be an actual promise to do so, or the forbearance must be at the request (express or implied) of the surety.[118] It is unnecessary that the forbearance should be for any specific length of time; forbearance for a reasonable time will suffice, and a promise or request to forbear will (if no time is stipulated for) normally be construed as referring to forbearance for a reasonable time.[119] Actual withdrawal of proceedings against the principal debtor at the request of the surety will be a good consideration even if there is no promise that new proceedings will not be started.[120]

Guarantee of past and future transactions If the surety guarantees past transac- **45-024** tions in return for an undertaking by the creditor to continue to deal with the debtor, or to grant him further credit, there will be good consideration. In practice the surety frequently guarantees both past and future transactions in return for such an

---

113 cf. *Pitts v Jones* [2007] EWCA Civ 1301, [2008] 2 W.L.R. 1289 (consideration for promise of guarantee found in promisors' cooperation in making other transactions).
114 *French v French* (1841) 2 M. & G. 644. As to a guarantee of past *and* future transactions, see below, paras 45-024—45-026.
115 *Astley Industrial Trust Ltd v Grimston Electric Tools* (1965) 109 S.J. 149.
116 *Goldshede v Swan* (1847) 1 Ex. 154.
117 *Pau On v Lau Liu Long* [1980] A.C. 614, 629 and see Vol.I, para.4-031.
118 *Crears v Hunter* (1887) 19 Q.B.D. 341; *Miles v New Zealand Alford Estate Co* (1886) 32 Ch. D. 266; *Provincial Bank of Ireland v Donnell* [1934] N.I. 33. cf. *Flying Music Co Ltd v Theater Entertainment SA* [2017] EWHC 3192 (QB) at [71]–[73] (forbearance to cancel performance of theatrical production which was the subject of contract with a company for non-payment held to be consideration for guarantee of that company's debts by its directors).
119 *Oldershaw v King* (1857) 2 H. & N. 517; *Crears v Hunter*, above.
120 See footnote above. See also *Clarke & Walker Pty v Thew* (1967) 116 C.L.R. 465.

undertaking, and such a guarantee is good as to both sets of transactions,[121] for consideration to be executed on the one side is at all events prima facie consideration for all that is done on the other, and all the promises are to be referred to all the considerations.[122]

45-025　Difficult questions of construction may arise in these cases, since guarantees may be expressed in terms which leave it doubtful whether the surety is guaranteeing past and future transactions, or past ones only.[123] In these circumstances extrinsic evidence is admissible to show that the parties contemplated future transactions as falling within the guarantee, and that the whole guarantee is therefore valid.[124] But if it is evident that the guarantee was intended to be limited to past transactions alone, for example, because the surety knew that the principal debtor was already indebted to the creditor in an amount exceeding the limit of the surety's guarantee, the guarantee will be void as being given without consideration.[125] On the other hand, a guarantee to a bank in consideration of the bank's agreeing to advance £750 to the principal debtor was held to be good although in fact the debtor already owed the bank more than £750 and the new advance was merely used to pay off the existing debt without any money actually passing.[126]

45-026　Where a guarantee is given in respect of both past and future transactions it is sometimes important to distinguish between cases where the consideration consists of a promise by the creditor to enter into the future transactions and cases where the consideration is the creditor's act of entering into those transactions. In the former event the guarantee will be binding as to the past transactions as soon as the contract is made; in the latter case the guarantee will not be binding unless in fact the creditor does enter into future transactions.[127] So where A guaranteed past debts owed by B to C in consideration of C "recommencing to supply" B, and in fact C never did recommence to supply B because B never asked him to, it was held that the guarantee was void as lacking consideration.[128] So also where the surety guaranteed past debts in consideration of the creditor agreeing to supply such goods as he might think fit to the debtor, it was held that the guarantee was not binding in the absence of evidence that goods had in fact been supplied[129]; although the creditor had apparently promised to supply the debtor, the promise was illusory

---

121　*Johnston v Nicholls* (1845) 1 C.B. 251; *Boyd v Moyle* (1846) 2 C.B. 644; *White v Woodward* (1848) 5 C.B. 810. cf. *Tailby v HSBC Bank Plc* [2015] B.P.I.R. 143, Ch D (earlier provision of a continuing facility to principal debtor was a "real commercial benefit" to the guarantor and this constituted consideration).

122　*Harris v Venables* (1872) L.R. 7 Ex. 235, 240.

123　See, e.g. *Chapman v Sutton* (1846) 2 C.B. 634; *Morrell v Cowan* (1877) 7 Ch. D. 151.

124　*Butcher v Steuart* (1843) 11 M. & W. 857; *Goldshede v Swan* (1847) 1 Ex. 154; *Steele v Hoe* (1849) 14 Q.B. 431; *Edwards v Jevons* (1849) 8 C.B. 436; *Colbourn v Dawson* (1851) 10 C.B. 765; *Broom v Batchelor* (1856) 1 H. & N. 255.

125　*Bell v Welch* (1850) 9 C.B. 154.

126　*Hamilton v Watson* (1845) 12 Cl. & F. 109; cf. *Glyn v Hertel* (1818) 8 Taunt. 208 and, as to the meaning of an "advance", *Burnes v Trade Credits Ltd* [1981] 1 W.L.R. 805.

127　Unless, of course, there is a separate consideration in respect of the past transactions, i.e. a requested forbearance or promise to forbear, see above, para.45-023. If the guarantee is expressed to be in consideration *both* of a forbearance in respect of past transactions, *and* entry into future transactions, it is presumably a question of construction whether the guarantee is conditional on the future transactions.

128　*Greenham Ready Mixed Concrete v CAS (Industrial Developments)* (1965) 109 S.J. 209.

129　*Westhead v Sproson* (1861) 6 H. & N. 728.

since the creditor was not obliged to supply unless he wished, and the consideration had therefore to be found in an actual supply.

(c) Grounds of Vitiation of the Contract

Introduction   In general, a contract of suretyship may be vitiated on the same   **45-027**
grounds as other contracts, for example, it may be voidable on the ground of the
creditor's fraud or undue influence. However, contracts of suretyship give rise to
three particular questions which relate to possible vitiating elements: the first is
under what circumstances the contract may be vitiated by the pre-contractual
conduct not of the creditor but of a third party, notably, the principal debtor; the
second is whether the nature of the contract demands a duty of disclosure on the
part of the creditor by way of exception to the rule for contracts generally[130]; and
the third is whether the consumer's new rights to redress in relation to certain unfair
commercial practices in traders are available to a guarantor acting other than in the
course of business against a creditor acting in the course of a business. The answer
to this third question (which is in the negative) will be discussed in the wider
context of the legislative protection of sureties.[131]

Vitiation of the contract and third party behaviour   As regards the first of these   **45-028**
questions, a distinction can be drawn between those cases in which the ground on
which the surety is seeking to avoid the contract depends on an action or omission
on the part of the creditor or on the existence of a particular relationship between
the creditor and himself, and those where it does not.

Mistake   In the case of vitiation on the ground of common fundamental mistake,   **45-029**
the conditions for relief do not include any requirement as to the action or omission of the other party to the contract, nor do they rest on any special relationship
between the parties, as does vitiation on the ground of presumed undue influence.
Thus, where a surety seeks to avoid the contract on the grounds of common
fundamental mistake by way of application of the doctrine in *Bell v Lever Bros
Ltd*,[132] it is irrelevant whether his mistake was caused by any (equally mistaken) action or omission of the creditor or whether it was caused by a third party. In *Associated Japanese Bank (International) Ltd v Crédit du Nord SA*[133] a bank, A, entered
a sale and leaseback agreement with B in relation to four specified engineering
machines and under which B received a sum of money from the bank. As a condition of the transaction, another bank, C, agreed to guarantee B's obligations under
it. It was later discovered that the leaseback transaction was a fraud by B who had
deceived both banks, there being no machines in fact in existence. In an action by
A against C under the guarantee, C's defence of common fundamental mistake was
upheld: for both banks, the non-existence of the machines made the contract of
guarantee essentially different from the one which they had believed they entered

---

130   For the general position, see Vol.I, para.7-018 and see below, paras 45-036—45-039.
131   Below, paras 45-148—45-149.
132   [1932] A.C. 161. See also *Great Peace Shipping Ltd v Tsavliris Salvage Ltd* [2002] EWCA Civ 1407,
[2003] Q.B. 679 where the existence of a distinct equitable jurisdiction for mistake was denied on
the ground of its being irreconcilable with *Bell v Lever Bros Ltd*, on which see Vol.I, paras 6-055—
6-060.
133   [1989] 1 W.L.R. 255.

at contract.[134] The fact that the mistake of the guarantor was induced by the fraud of a third party is relevant only in that it provides a reasonable ground for the guarantor's belief, in the absence of which relief on this ground may be denied.

45-030 **Non est factum** The position is similar in relation to non est factum. This ground of vitiation of a contract arises where a person who suffers from a disability, for example, blindness or illiteracy, signs or otherwise executes a document believing it to be essentially different from that which he has in fact signed, as long as he commits no negligence in so doing.[135] Although such a belief is often brought about by fraud or misrepresentation by the other party to the document, it appears that this is not necessary for the defence to apply.[136] In principle, therefore, a guarantor may rely on the defence of non est factum even where his mistake is induced by a third party (notably by the fraud of the principal debtor). For example, in *Lloyds Bank Plc v Waterhouse*[137] an illiterate farmer had signed a guarantee of a loan by a bank to his son, allegedly on the basis of a misrepresentation by the latter as to its effect. However, the Court of Appeal did not rely on this misrepresentation, by which the bank could also be said to be affected, as the basis for refusing to enforce the guarantee for the benefit of the bank,[138] but instead did so by upholding his defence of non est factum.

45-031 **Fraud, misrepresentation or undue influence by the creditor** It is clear that a surety who has been induced to enter the contract by the fraud or misrepresentation of the creditor can avoid the contract, whether or not the latter has acted on the contract by granting credit to the principal debtor.[139] Similarly, a contract of suretyship may be avoided by the surety where the creditor has exercised actual undue influence on him in relation to the contract[140] or where the relationship between them gives rise to a presumption of undue influence.[141] It is clear, however, that the relationship between a bank and its customer is not one which ordinarily gives rise to a presumption of undue influence,[142] although on the facts actual undue influence may be proved.[143]

45-032 **Fraud, misrepresentation or undue influence by a third party** For a party to a contract to avoid it on the ground of fraud, misrepresentation or actual undue influence, he must show some action or conduct by the other party to the contract,

---

[134] The court also held that as a matter of construction the guarantee contained an implied condition that the machines in fact existed.

[135] See, e.g. *O'Brien v Australia and New Zealand Bank Ltd* (1971) 5 S.A.S.R. 347 (difference between a guarantee of future indebtedness and a guarantee and indemnity of future indebtedness not sufficiently fundamental to sustain a plea of non est factum).

[136] See *Saunders v Anglia Building Society* [1971] A.C. 1004 and Vol.I, paras 3-049 et seq.

[137] [1991] Fam. Law 23. cf. *Barclays Bank Plc v Schwartz, The Times,* August 2, 1995.

[138] This defence had been pleaded at first instance but was abandoned on appeal.

[139] *Mackenzie v Royal Bank of Canada* [1934] A.C. 468; and see s.1(b) of the Misrepresentation Act 1967 and Vol.I, para.7-144. An "entire agreement clause" in a contract of suretyship may, depending on its terms, exclude liability in the creditor based on collateral warranty or misrepresentation, subject to applicable legislative controls: *Pananicola v Sandhu* [2011] EWHC 1431 (QB), [2011] 2 B.C.L.C. 811, [41], [44], [46] and cf. Vol.I, paras 7-145, 7-151 and 13-117.

[140] *Lloyds Bank Ltd v Bundy* [1975] Q.B. 326.

[141] See Vol.I, paras 8-058 et seq.

[142] *National Westminster Bank Plc v Morgan* [1985] A.C. 686, 708–709; *Goldsworthy v Brickell* [1987] Ch. 378.

[143] *Lloyds Bank Ltd v Bundy* [1975] Q.B. 326.

whether this is a misrepresentation of fact or wrongful conduct amounting to undue influence.[144] In the case of presumed undue influence, a party must show the existence of a relationship which gives rise to that presumption between himself and the other party.[145] More difficult, therefore, is the question whether a creditor may be affected by the fraud, misrepresentation or actual undue influence of a third party, often the principal debtor, on the surety and whether he will be affected by the existence of a relationship which gives rise to a presumption of undue influence between such a third party and the surety.[146] Older authorities give clear support for three propositions. First, a creditor is responsible for the actions and is imputed with the knowledge of any agent whom he chooses to employ in the transaction.[147] For example, in *Lloyds Bank Ltd v Bundy*,[148] a transaction entered by a bank with the defendant as a result of the actual undue influence of its bank manager was set aside, the manager acting for the bank in the transaction. Secondly, where the creditor knows of or is otherwise a direct party to the misrepresentation or undue influence by the principal debtor to the surety, then the contract of suretyship is voidable at the latter's option.[149] Similarly, where a creditor knows of the existence of a relationship giving rise to a presumption of undue influence between a third party and the surety, then the contract of suretyship is voidable at the surety's option (though this proposition has been qualified by the decision of the House of Lords in *Etridge's* case as described below[150]).[151] Thirdly, as Lord Cranworth L.C. stated in *Owen v Homan*,[152] where:

"... the dealings are such as fairly to lead a reasonable man to believe that fraud must have been used in order to obtain [the surety's] concurrence, [the creditor] is bound to make inquiry, and cannot shelter himself under the plea that he was not called on to ask, and did not ask, any questions on the subject. In some cases wilful ignorance is not to be distinguished in its equitable consequences from knowledge."[153]

In the modern law, a not infrequent problem has arisen in which a bank (the creditor) agrees to lend money to a husband (the principal debtor)[154] if his wife agrees to stand surety or to a charge on the matrimonial home. The husband often **45-033**

---

[144] See *Barclays Bank Plc v O'Brien* [1994] 1 A.C. 180; and see *CIBC Mortgages Plc v Pitt* [1994] 1 A.C. 200, 209, in which Lord Browne-Wilkinson expressed the view that actual undue influence is a species of fraud.

[145] See Vol.I, para.8-062 where the important decision of the HL on the proper categorisation of undue influence in *Royal Bank of Scotland v Etridge (No.2)* [2001] UKHL 44, [2002] 2 A.C. 773 is discussed.

[146] See generally Vol.I, paras 8-110 et seq.

[147] *Barwick v English Joint Stock Bank* (1867) 2 L.R.Ex. 259, 265; *Bank of Montreal v Stuart* [1911] A.C. 120; and see *UBAF v European American Banking Corp* [1984] Q.B. 713 (company liable for misrepresentation by duly authorised agent); *O'Sullivan v Management Agency and Music Ltd* [1985] 1 Q.B. 428, 470 (company affected by undue influence of share-holding directors).

[148] [1975] Q.B. 326.

[149] *Spencer v Handley* (1842) 4 M. & G. 414; *O'Sullivan v Management Agency and Music Ltd*, above, at 447–448 and 464.

[150] See para.45-035.

[151] cf. *O'Sullivan v Management Agency and Music Ltd* [1985] 1 Q.B. 428 at 464.

[152] (1853) IV H.L.C. 997.

[153] (1853) IV H.L.C. 997 at 1035.

[154] In some cases, the husband is not the principal debtor but, for example, a director of a limited company which is the principal debtor. As long as the surety has no direct financial interest in the company, this situation is treated no differently from where it is the principal debtor himself who defrauds the surety: see *Barclays Bank Plc v O'Brien* [1994] 1 A.C. 180, 199.

undertakes to obtain his wife's agreement to the transaction and in order to do so he may resort to misrepresentation or the exercise of actual undue influence (there being no presumption of undue influence between a husband and wife).[155] The courts have used various analyses to determine whether the creditor bank is to be affected by this wrongful conduct in the principal debtor. While older authority recognised that in some circumstances the creditor could be affected by the wrongful act of the husband,[156] after 1985 the courts distinguished two types of situation. Where the bank was able to be said to have entrusted to the principal debtor the task of obtaining the execution of the document, then the latter is constituted the creditor's agent for this purpose so as to infect the creditor with any undue influence he may have exercised or misrepresentation which he may have made.[157] On the other hand, where the bank had not so entrusted the principal debtor, it was unaffected by any undue influence or misrepresentation of the principal debtor, nor is it under an obligation to see that the surety is separately advised.[158]

45-034   Creditor on constructive notice: Barclays Bank Plc v O'Brien[159]   However, in *Barclays Bank Plc v O'Brien*,[160] the House of Lords rejected this resort to the notion of agency to analyse the relationships of the parties in this type of case, stigmatising it as artificial.[161] The House of Lords preferred to rely instead on the ordinary equitable doctrine of notice.[162] Thus, according to Lord Browne-Wilkinson, with whom the rest of their Lordships agreed:

"A wife who has been induced to stand as a surety for her husband's debts by his undue influence, misrepresentation or some other legal wrong has an equity as against him to set aside that transaction. Under the ordinary principles of equity, her right to set aside that transaction will be enforceable against third parties (e.g. against a creditor) if either the husband was acting as the third party's agent[163] or the third party had actual or constructive notice of the facts giving rise to her equity."[164]

Lord Browne-Wilkinson indicated that constructive notice would be found by the courts where the creditor knew of certain facts which put him on inquiry as to the possible existence of the rights of the other and he failed to make such inquiry or

---

155   *Mackenzie v Royal Bank of Canada* [1934] A.C. 468; *Kings North Trust Ltd v Bell* [1986] 1 W.L.R. 119; *Midland Bank Plc v Sheppard* [1988] 2 All E.R. 17. See further *Royal Bank of Scotland v Etridge (No.2)* [2001] UKHL 44, [2002] 2 A.C. 773 at [32]–[33], [36]; *Thompson v Foy* [2009] EWHC 1076 (Ch) at [100]–[101]; *Hewett v First Plus Financial Group Plc* [2010] EWCA Civ 312, [2010] 2 F.L.R. 177 at [29]–[30] (relating the parties' relationship of trust and confidence to a duty of disclosure in the husband); *Royal Bank of Scotland v Chandra* [2011] EWCA Civ 192, [2011] Bus. L.R. D149 especially at [31]–[32]; *Annulment Funding Co Ltd v Cowey* [2010] EWCA Civ 771, [2010] B.P.I.R. 1304 and Vol.I, para.8-091.
156   *Turnbull & Co v Duval* [1902] A.C. 429. The basis of this decision was considered "obscure" by Lord Browne-Wilkinson in *Barclays Bank Plc v O'Brien* [1994] 1 A.C. 180 at 191.
157   *Kings North Trust Ltd v Bell*, above; *Coldunell Ltd v Gallon* [1986] Q.B. 1184; *Avon Finance Co Ltd v Bridger* (1979) reported [1985] 2 All E.R. 281 (both cases of adult children obtaining elderly parents' agreements).
158   *Coldunell v Gallon* [1986] Q.B. 1184; *Bank of Baroda v Shah* [1988] 3 All E.R. 24.
159   For more detailed discussion of this topic, see Vol.I, paras 8-112—8-126.
160   [1994] 1 A.C. 180.
161   [1994] 1 A.C. 180 at 195. cf. [1993] Q.B. 109, 113, 144, CA.
162   [1994] 1 A.C. 180, 195.
163   Lord Browne-Wilkinson made clear that the term agent here was to be understood in a real sense and that such cases will be rare: [1994] 1 A.C. 180 at 195.
164   [1994] 1 A.C. 180 at 195.

take such other steps as were reasonable to verify whether such earlier right did or did not exist.[165] In the present context, this would be the case where the transaction to be guaranteed is on its face of no financial advantage to the wife and, secondly, where the relationship between the parties is such that there is a substantial risk that the husband has committed some legal or equitable wrong in obtaining her consent which would allow the wife to set it aside.[166] His Lordship noted that in the ordinary case:

"... a creditor will have satisfied these requirements if it insists that the wife attend a private meeting (in the absence of the husband) with a representative of the creditor at which she is told of the extent of her liability as surety, warned of the risk she is running and urged to take independent legal advice."[167]

It was further observed that this doctrine of notice could apply wherever there is an emotional relationship of cohabitation between the principal debtor and the would-be surety or where otherwise the creditor is aware that the surety reposes trust and confidence in the principal debtor in relation to his or her financial affairs.[168] Finally, it is clear that this approach based on notice of an equitable right can also apply to cases where a third party is in a relationship with the surety which gives rise to a presumption of undue influence, as long as the creditor has notice of the circumstances from which the court derives the presumption.[169] So, for example, where a bank is aware that the principal debtor is the surety's solicitor, it would be put on notice as to the presumption of undue influence which arises between a solicitor and his client.[170]

Etridge's case *Barclays Bank Plc v O'Brien*[171] was later followed by the House of Lords in *Royal Bank of Scotland v Etridge (No.2)*,[172] where the foundation and implications of the doctrine of constructive notice were explained and refined.[173] In *Etridge (No.2)*, the House of Lords made clear that this doctrine was to be confined to cases of suretyship where the relationship between the principal debtor and the surety is non-commercial[174] and where the transaction between the lender and the surety is on its face to the disadvantage of the latter.[175] Where this is the case, the lender is said to be "put on inquiry" as to the circumstances in which the surety-   **45-035**

---

165 [1994] 1 A.C. 180 at 195–196.
166 In *CIBC Mortgages Plc v Pitt* [1994] 1 A.C. 200, the House of Lords followed this approach based on notice, but held that on the facts there was nothing in the nature of the transaction to put the lender on notice of the risk of either undue influence or fraud by a husband to his wife.
167 [1994] 1 A.C. 180 at 196.
168 [1994] 1 A.C. 180 at 198.
169 This was assumed by the House of Lords in *CIBC Mortgages Plc v Pitt* [1994] 1 A.C. 200 at 211 and cf. *Bainbrigge v Browne* (1881) 18 Ch. D. 188, 197.
170 See Vol.I, para.8-082. In *Barclays Bank Plc v O'Brien*, Scott L.J. noted that none of the decided cases of the previous decade had concerned a case of presumed undue influence by the principal debtor over the surety: [1993] Q.B. 109, 113.
171 [1994] 1 A.C. 180.
172 [2001] UKHL 44, [2002] 2 A.C. 773.
173 See further Vol.I, paras 8-116—8-126.
174 *Moody v Condor Insurance Ltd* [2006] EWHC 100 (Ch), [2006] 1 All E.R. 934 (fraud in the principal debtor practised on a commercial guarantee corporation and unknown to the creditor does not affect the validity of the guarantee).
175 [2001] UKHL 44 at [41], [44]–[49] and see *Mahon v FBN Bank (UK)* [2011] EWHC 1432 (Ch) [2011] B.P.I.R. 1029 at [51], [59]; Vol.I, para.8-119.

ship contract was made. As to past cases, the lender will escape being fixed with constructive notice if it took:

"... steps to bring home to the wife the risk she is running by standing as surety and to advise her to take independent advice ... For the future a bank satisfies these requirements if it insists that the wife attend a private meeting with a representative of the bank at which she is told of the extent of her liability as surety, warned of the risk she is running and urged to take independent legal advice. In exceptional cases the bank, to be safe, has to insist that the wife is separately advised."[176]

Where a lender entrusts this task to an independent legal adviser, the House of Lords indicated the steps which such an adviser ought to take.[177]

45-036 **Non-disclosure** Some early nineteenth century authority suggests that a creditor owes a duty of disclosure to a would-be surety as to those facts which are material to the risk which the surety would run if he enters the contract. In *Railton v Mathews*,[178] a case which concerned the situation of a person standing surety for the fidelity of a person who is the servant or agent of the creditor, Lord Campbell stated that "if the [creditors] had facts within their knowledge which it was material the surety should be acquainted with, and which [they] did not disclose ... the undue concealment of those facts discharges the surety".[179] However, in *Hamilton v Watson* the House of Lords held that a bank which knew of the existence of a debt already owed by the debtor did not have to disclose this fact to the guarantor of a further loan, which was used to repay the first.[180] Lord Campbell rejected the guarantor's argument that "it is essentially necessary that every thing should be disclosed by the creditor that is material for the surety to know".[181] In his view:

"If such was the rule, it would be indispensably necessary for the bankers to whom the security is to be given, to state how the account has been kept: whether the debtor was in the habit of overdrawing; whether he was punctual in his dealings; whether he performed his promises in an honourable manner—for all these things are extremely material for the surety to know. But unless questions be particularly put by the surety to gain this information, I hold that it is quite unnecessary for the creditor, to whom the suretyship is to be given, to make any such disclosure."[182]

However, Lord Campbell considered the following to be:

"... the criterion whether the disclosure ought to be made voluntarily, namely, whether there is anything that might not naturally be expected to take place between the parties who are concerned in the transaction, that is, whether there be a contract between the debtor and the creditor, to the effect that his position shall be different from that which the surety might naturally expect."[183]

For this purpose, the courts distinguished clearly between contracts of guarantee and

---

[176] [2001] UKHL 44 at [50] and see Vol.I, paras 8-120—8-121.
[177] [2001] UKHL 44 at [56], [64]–[67]. See Vol.I, para.8-122.
[178] (1844) 10 Cl. & Fin. 934.
[179] (1844) 10 Cl. & Fin. 934 at 943. cf. *Owen v Homan* (1851) 3 Mac. & G. 378, 396, where Lord Truro stated that the rule as to disclosure is the same for contracts of suretyship and of insurance.
[180] (1845) 12 Cl. & Fin. 109, 118.
[181] (1845) 12 Cl. & Fin. 109 at 119.
[182] (1845) 12 Cl. & Fin. 109 at 119.
[183] (1845) 12 Cl. & Fin. 109 at 119.

contracts of insurance, which at common law require disclosure of all material facts.[184] However, in *London General Omnibus Company Ltd v Holloway*,[185] the Court of Appeal allowed a surety for the fidelity of a servant to avoid the contract on the ground of the creditor's failure to disclose previous known dishonesty of the servant by treating this failure as a misrepresentation:

"Not to disclose such dishonesty is a misrepresentation ... because by non-disclosure the master must be assumed to be contracting on the assumption ... that the suretyship relates to a servant whom the master at the time of taking the security does not know to have been guilty of dishonesty in such service."[186]

This approach clearly seeks to assimilate the position governing contracts of suretyship to the rule applicable to contracts generally which, while denying the existence of a duty of disclosure, allows a partial disclosure of facts to be treated as misrepresentation.[187] On the other hand, it has been held that there is no duty on a banker to disclose to a surety the fact that the principal debtor's husband is an undischarged bankrupt and has authority to draw on her account.[188] And it has been held that the scope for non-disclosure or incomplete disclosure amounting to implied misrepresentation is considerably reduced where the contract is made in the context of an elaborate regime of disclosure undertaken by the parties in response to specific requests for information by the would-be surety: here there is "essentially the environment of caveat emptor".[189]

The question of the existence or extent of a duty of disclosure in contracts of **45-037** suretyship was the subject of comment by their Lordships in *Royal Bank of Scotland Plc v Etridge (No.2)*.[190] While it was accepted that a suretyship contract is not a contract uberrimae fidei and that there is no general duty of disclosure,[191] Lord Scott quoted with approval Vaughan Williams L.J.'s statement in *London General Omnibus Co Ltd v Holloway* to the effect that there is a "general proposition that a creditor must reveal to the surety every fact which under the circumstances the surety would expect not to exist, for the omission to mention that such a fact does exist is an implied representation that it does not".[192] He referred to a dictum of King C.J. in the Supreme Court of South Australia, according to whom the duty of

---

[184] *The North British Insurance Co v Lloyd* (1854) 10 Ex. 523, 533. See further *Seaton v Heath* [1899] 1 Q.B. 782, 792 and see above, paras 42-033 et seq. The position at common law as regards insurance was radically reformed by the Consumer Insurance (Disclosure and Representations) Act 2012 and the Insurance Act 2015, as explained above, paras 42-046 et seq.

[185] [1912] 2 K.B. 72.

[186] [1912] 2 K.B. 72 at 77, per Vaughan Williams L.J. cf. *Smith v Bank of Scotland* (1813) 1 Dow. 272, 292; and *Lee v Jones* (1864) 17 C.B.(N.S.) 482, 503. In the case of a continuing guarantee this limited duty of disclosure will continue to operate as regards the future liability of the surety. If, therefore, the surety engages for the honesty of an employee, and the employer discovers that the employee has been dishonest, but instead of dismissing him, continues him in his employment without notifying the surety of the facts, the surety will not be liable for subsequent defaults by the employee: *Phillips v Foxall* (1872) L.R. 7 Q.B. 666; *Sanderson v Aston* (1873) L.R. 8 Ex. 73.

[187] See Vol.I, paras 7-018, 7-021.

[188] *Cooper v National Provincial Bank* [1946] K.B. 1; and see *National Provincial Bank v Glanusk* [1913] 3 K.B. 335; *Westpac Securities Ltd v Dickie* [1991] 1 N.Z.L.R. 657.

[189] *Geest Plc v Fyffes Plc* [1999] 1 All E.R. (Comm) 672, 685.

[190] [2001] UKHL 44, [2002] 3 W.L.R. 1021.

[191] [2001] UKHL 44, [2002] 3 W.L.R. 1021 at [112], per Lord Hobhouse of Woodborough; at [185], per Lord Scott of Foscote.

[192] [1912] 2 K.B. 72, 78.

disclosure extends to:

"unusual features surrounding the transaction between the creditor and the surety: (1) of which the creditor is or ought to be aware; (2) of which the surety is unaware and (3) which the creditor appreciates, or ought in the circumstances to appreciate might be unknown to the surety and might affect his decision to enter into the guarantee."[193]

In Lord Scott's view:

"this statement of the extent of the disclosure obligation may be too wide. But at least, in my opinion, the obligation should extend to unusual features of the contractual relationship between the creditor and the principal debtor, or between the creditor and other creditors of the principal debtor, that would or might affect the rights of the surety."[194]

Moreover, Lord Nicholls regarded it as "a well-established principle that ... a creditor is obliged to disclose to a guarantor any unusual feature of the contract between the creditor and the debtor which makes it materially different in a potentially disadvantageous respect from what the guarantor might naturally expect".[195] However, "[t]he precise ambit of this disclosure obligation remains unclear".[196]

45-038   However, further light was cast on the creditor's duty of disclosure by *North Shore Ventures Ltd v Anstead Holdings Inc*,[197] where the Court of Appeal reviewed earlier authorities.[198] The court concluded that the instrument before it was:

"... not a contract uberrimae fidei but a loan guarantee. The authorities are clear that in such a case the duty of disclosure does not go further than the limit set by Lord Campbell in *Hamilton v Watson* and by Lord Scott of Foscote in *Royal Bank of Scotland Plc v Etridge (No. 2)*.[199] Accordingly there is no duty to disclose facts or matters which are not unusual features of the contractual relationship between the creditor and the debtor, or between the creditor and other creditors of the debtor."[200]

The Court of Appeal therefore held the contract of guarantee binding on the surety, even though the creditor had failed to disclose that the principal debtors were being investigated for embezzlement and that their bank accounts had been frozen as these were not "unusual features of the contractual relationship between the creditor and the debtor".[201] Although it was not therefore necessary for its decision, the Court of Appeal also expressed the view that where a duty of disclosure does arise the creditor is not absolved from it because he reasonably believes that the surety

---

193 *Pooraka Holdings Pty Ltd v Participation Nominees Pty Ltd* (1991) 58 S.A.S.R. 184.
194 [2001] UKHL 44 at [188].
195 [2001] UKHL 44 at [81]. cf. *Levett v Barclays Bank Plc* [1995] 1 W.L.R. 1260 at 1273 and *Crédit Lyonnais Bank Nederland v Export Credit Guarantee Department* [1996] 1 Lloyd's Rep. 200, 227 (affirmed on other grounds [2000] 1 A.C. 486) in which it was accepted that a creditor must disclose any unusual features in the transaction, but that this did not extend to unusual features of the risk.
196 [2001] UKHL 44 at [81].
197 [2011] EWCA Civ 230, [2012] Ch. 31.
198 Notably, *Hamilton v Watson* (1845) 12 Cl. & Fin. 109; *National Provincial Bank v Glanusk* [1913] 3 K.B. 335; *Smith v Bank of Scotland* 1997 S.C. (H.L.) 111, especially at 118; *London General Omnibus Company Ltd v Holloway* [1912] 1 K.B. 72; *Royal Bank of Scotland Plc v Etridge (No.2)* [2001] UKHL 44, [2002] 3 W.L.R. 102.
199 [2001] UKHL 44 at [188], above, para.45-037.
200 [2011] EWCA Civ 230 at [31], per Sir Andrew Morritt C. (with whom Smith L.J. agreed).
201 [2011] EWCA Civ 230 at [32]. The CA did not express a view on the question whether a suitably drafted term of the guarantee could exclude the effect of an otherwise operative non-disclosure on the validity of the contract of guarantee: [2011] EWCA Civ 230.

knows of it already: "[i]f the belief of the creditor turns out to be not well founded then … he should suffer the consequences not the surety".[202]

Liability in damages for misrepresentation and non-disclosure A creditor who **45-039** induces a surety to enter the contract by fraud[203] or misrepresentation of fact[204] may clearly be liable in damages in tort in accordance with the general position. More difficult is the extent of a creditor's liability in damages in the tort of negligence. In *Perry v Midland Bank Plc*,[205] it was held that once a bank had undertaken the task of explaining the nature and effect of a transaction, then its failure to do so adequately would entail liability in damages by way of application of *Hedley Byrne & Co Ltd v Heller & Partners Ltd*.[206] Moreover, in *Cornish v Midland Bank Plc*, Kerr L.J. expressed the view that a bank is under a duty at least to its own customers to proffer some adequate explanation of the nature and effect of the document which is executed between them.[207] In *Barclays Bank Plc v O'Brien*,[208] as a result of which in certain circumstances a creditor would find it necessary to proffer such an explanation,[209] Scott L.J. accepted that "if the surety is a customer[210] or if the creditor assumes the role of advisor, it may be that the creditor will be found to have owed a contractual or a tortious duty of care to the surety".[211] But he added that:

> "… if there is no more than that the creditor, in an attempt to satisfy itself that the surety properly understands the proposed transaction and that the transaction will not subsequently be impeachable, offers an explanation of the transaction and of the security document, I do not think that the creditor should be taken to have assumed a tortious duty of care. If the explanation was inadequate, the security might not be enforceable but it would not follow that liability in damages would attach."[212]

(d) Effect on Surety of Vitiation of the Transaction Guaranteed

Incapacity of principal debtor: minors Formerly, the question whether a surety **45-040** who had undertaken to meet a liability which was void as against the principal

---

202 [2011] EWCA Civ 230 at [37], per Sir Andrew Morritt C.

203 See Vol.I, para.7-048.

204 Misrepresentation Act 1967 s.2(1). See further Vol.I, para.7-076. This would apparently apply also to misrepresentations of law: Vol.I, para.7-017. As will be seen (below, paras 45-148—45-149), a "consumer surety" cannot have a "right to redress" under Pt 4A of the Consumer Protection from Unfair Trading Regulations 2008 (SI 2008/1277) and this means that such a person does not lose any right to damages under s.2 of the 1967 Act by way of application of s.2(4): see above, para.38-208.

205 [1987] F.L.R. 237 (decision at first instance not challenged on appeal).

206 [1964] A.C. 465. It is unclear how the interpretation of *Hedley Byrne* on the basis of "assumption of responsibility" taken by the House of Lords in *Henderson v Merrett Syndicates Ltd* [1995] 2 A.C. 145; *White v Jones* [1995] 2 A.C. 207; and *Williams v Natural Life Health Foods Ltd And Mistlin* [1998] 1 W.L.R. 830 will affect the approach of the courts to liability in the tort for negligent non-disclosure, but the tendency of these decisions has been to extend liability for pure economic loss: see further Vol.I, paras 1-220 et seq.

207 [1985] 3 All E.R. 513, 522–523.

208 [1993] Q.B. 109 (affirmed on different grounds [1994] 1 A.C. 180).

209 [1993] Q.B. 109, 140 and see above, para.45-034.

210 Purchas L.J. expressed the view that the duty of care in *Perry v Midland Bank Plc* [1987] F.L.R. 237 arose purely from the fact that the surety was also the bank's customer: [1993] Q.B. 109, 147.

211 [1993] Q.B. 109, 140–141.

212 [1993] Q.B. 109 at 140–141. No view was expressed on this issue in the House of Lords: [1994] 1 A.C. 180.

debtor on account of the latter's minority, was himself liable was said to depend on whether the contract was a guarantee or an indemnity. If he had merely guaranteed the liability, it was held that he could not be liable because there was no default by the minor in not meeting the liability, and the surety could not be called upon to meet his liability unless there was such default.[213] Where, on the other hand, the surety had assumed a primary liability to indemnify the creditor in any event, the minority of the debtor provided no defence to the surety.[214] The significance of this distinction here, which had been the subject of criticism, was removed by s.2 of the Minors' Contracts Act 1987 which provides that where a guarantee is given in respect of an obligation of a party to a contract which is itself unenforceable against that party because he was a minor, then the guarantee shall not for that reason alone be unenforceable against the guarantor.[215]

It is uncertain whether the distinction drawn formerly between guarantees and indemnities in relation to a minor's obligations applies to a surety who engages to answer for the ultra vires liability of a company (though the impact of the ultra vires doctrine has been considerably attenuated[216]). In *Garrard v James*[217] it was held that the question was one of construction. If the surety intends to assume the risk of non-payment by the debtor on the grounds of financial inability only, he will not be liable if the reason for the non-payment is legal incapacity rather than financial inability; if, on the other hand, the surety intends to assume the risk of non-payment for any reason, then he is liable even if the reason for non-payment is legal incapacity.[218] It is thought that this is a better approach than that adopted in the cases concerned with minors, but in *Yeoman Credit Ltd v Latter*[219] (itself such a case) it seems to have been assumed that the distinction between a guarantee and an indemnity governs the company cases in the same way as it did the minority cases.

45-041 **Other invalidating cause**   Where the transaction guaranteed by the surety is affected by some other invalidating cause, e.g. fraud or misrepresentation, the question whether the surety is liable may again depend on the distinction between a contract of guarantee and a contract of indemnity. If the contract is one of guarantee the surety cannot be liable if the principal debtor is not liable.[220] But there is no reason why a contract of indemnity should not be so drafted as to extend to losses incurred by the creditor even under a void transaction, though clear words would probably be needed to produce such a result.[221] On the other hand, where a contract

---

213   *Coutts & Co v Browne-Lecky* [1947] K.B. 104; *Stadium Finance Co Ltd v Helm* (1965) 109 S.J. 471. The correctness of *Coutts & Co v Browne-Lecky*, above, was reserved in *Argo Caribbean Group Ltd v Lewis* [1976] 2 Lloyd's Rep. 289.

214   *Wauthier v Wilson* (1912) 28 T.L.R. 239; *Yeoman Credit Ltd v Latter* [1961] 1 W.L.R. 828.

215   The Minors' Contracts Act 1987 also repealed s.1 of the Infants' Relief Act 1874 whose provisions were the basis for the distinction definitively removed by s.2 of the 1987 Act in relation to minors.

216   See above, Vol.I, paras 10-020 et seq.

217   [1925] Ch. 616; see also *Heald v O'Connor* [1971] 1 W.L.R. 497, 506. The ultra vires doctrine was largely, though not wholly, abrogated by s.9 of the European Communities Act 1972: see Vol.I, paras 10-027 et seq. and *TCB Ltd v Gray* [1985] Ch. 621 (affirmed [1987] Ch. 458).

218   [1925] Ch. 616 at 622.

219   See above, in which *Yorks Ry Wagon Co v Maclure* (1881) 19 Ch. D. 478, another company case, was explained in this way.

220   *Swan v Bank of Scotland* (1836) 10 Bligh.(N.S.) 627; *Brown v Blaine* (1884) 1 T.L.R. 158; *Temperance Loan Fund Ltd v Rose* [1932] 2 K.B. 522; *Barclays v Prospect Mortgages Ltd* [1974] 1 W.L.R. 837. But cf. Vol.I, para.8-052, as to duress.

221   cf. *Bentworth Finance Ltd v Lubert* [1968] 1 Q.B. 680, 686; *Gulf Bank KSC v Mitsubishi Heavy*

of suretyship guarantees the payment of a certain sum, this sum having been agreed by the parties to represent the amounts payable under a contract for services rendered to the principal debtor, the surety cannot avoid liability by pointing to a "manifest error" as regards the computation of the liabilities of the principal debtor.[222]

3.   FORMALITIES

Statute of Frauds 1677 s.4.[223]   This section provides that: **45-042**

"… no action shall be brought … whereby to charge the defendant upon any special promise to answer for the debt default or miscarriage of another person … unless the agreement upon which such action shall be brought or some memorandum or note thereof shall be in writing and signed by the party to be charged therewith or some other person thereunto by him lawfully authorised."

"Debt, default or miscarriage"   These words appear to cover any form of legal   **45-043**
liability, so that a promise by A to pay compensation to B for a tort committed by C against B in consideration of B not suing C, is within the statute and must be evidenced in writing.[224] Moreover, they have been held to cover an agreement to give a guarantee, as well as an actual guarantee.[225] On the other hand, it has been said that:

"… since a contract of guarantee is a contract to answer for the debt, default or miscarriage of another who is primarily liable to the creditor, it follows that if, or at any rate in so far as, a contract covers loss to the creditor which does not involve a liability of the other to him, that contract cannot be a contract of guarantee."[226]

Thus, a contract under which a person stands "surety" for a building contractor's due *performance* of a contract and which is subject to a condition of automatic termination on that contractor's voluntary liquidation is not a contract of guarantee since it imposes responsibility on the "surety" on the mere *non-performance* of the contractor's obligations and not only on their breach, there being no breach on operation of the condition.[227] The requirements of the section do not apply to an agreement which varies a guarantee and which is relied on by a guarantor as a defence to an action on the guarantee,[228] but they do apply to any subsequent agreement between the guarantor and the creditor which creates a new contract of guarantee.[229]

Industries (No.2) [1994] 2 Lloyd's Rep. 145.
[222] *Try Build Ltd v Blue Star Garages Ltd* [1999] 66 Con. L.R. 90.
[223] See generally, *Actionstrength Ltd v International Glass Engineering INGLEN SpA* [2003] UKHL 17, [2003] 2 A.C. 541. On satisfying the statutory requirements of form as regards contracts concluded by electronic means, see Vol.I, paras 5-006—5-009.
[224] *Kirkham v Marter* (1819) 2 B. & Ald. 613.
[225] *Compagnie Generale d'Industrie v Myson Group Ltd* (1984) 134 New L.J. 788.
[226] *Northwood Development Co Ltd v Aegon Insurance Co (UK) Ltd* (1994) 10 Const. L.J. 157, 163, per HH Judge Harvey Q.C.
[227] *Northwood Development Co Ltd v Aegon Insurance Co (UK) Ltd*, above.
[228] *Re a Debtor (No.517 of 1991)*, *The Times*, November 25, 1991.
[229] *Samuels Finance Group Plc v Beechmanor Ltd* (1994) 67 P. & C.R. 282, 284–285.

45-044 **Guarantees and indemnities distinguished** It has been established from a very early date that the words "debt, default or miscarriage *of another person*" mean that the section only applies where there is some person other than the surety who is primarily liable.[230] The section therefore applies when the surety assumes a secondary liability and agrees to be answerable if the principal debtor fails to meet his liability, but it does not apply where the surety assumes a primary liability. This is the origin of the distinction between contracts of guarantee and contracts of indemnity, the former falling within the section, and the latter outside it.

45-045 **A question of substance rather than of form** The question whether or not a person agrees "to answer for the debt ... of another person" is one of substance rather than of form.[231] So, where a chairman of a company (the principal debtor) told a creditor that he would make sure that the money owed would be forthcoming, it was held that in substance the chairman had promised to answer for payment by the debtor so as to come within s.4 of the Statute of Frauds.[232] In *Actionstrength Ltd v International Glass Engineering INGLEN SpA*,[233] the claimant was a building sub-contractor which, fearing non-payment by the main contractor, obtained a promise from the employer that the latter "would ensure that the claimant would receive any amount due to it from [the main contractor] ... if necessary by redirecting to the claimant payments due by [the employer] to the [main contractor]".[234] The main contractor was not party to this agreement nor had it accepted that money due to it could be paid to the claimant. The employer applied to the court to strike out the sub-contractor's claim as possessing no reasonable prospect of success on the ground, inter alia, that even on the assumption that the factual allegations of the sub-contractor were true, the agreement constituted a guarantee and failed for lack of the requisite formalities under the Statute of Frauds. The Court of Appeal agreed, holding that the agreement as alleged was a guarantee. According to Simon-Brown L.J.:

> "If payment to the creditor (of an assumed contingent liability) is to be made only from funds which the promisor would otherwise have to pay the debtor, that is one thing and understandably outside the Statute. The payment claimed here seems to me quite another thing. It is, indeed, on analysis quite inaccurate to describe it as a payment out of funds otherwise due to the [main contractor]. Rather it would be a payment out of the [employer's] own funds since the [main contractor] would still remain entitled to be paid."[235]

---

230 *Birkmyr v Darnell* (1705) 1 Salk. 27; and see cases cited in 1 Sm.L.C., 13th edn, 331.
231 *Motemtronic Ltd v Autocar Equipment Ltd* Unreported June 20, 1996, CA (Civ) transcript No.656 of 1996, referred to by CA in *Actionstrength Ltd v International Glass Engineering INGLEN SpA* [2001] EWCA Civ 1477, [2002] 1 W.L.R. 566 (affirmed on other grounds [2003] UKHL 17, [2003] 2 A.C 541) both citing with approval the dictum to this effect of Vaughan Williams L.J. in *Harburg India Rubber Comb Co v Martin* [1902] 1 K.B. 778, 784–785; *Quest 4 Finance Ltd v Maxfield* [2007] EWHC 2313 (QB), [2007] 2 C.L.C. 706.
232 *Motemtronic Ltd v Autocar Equipment Ltd*, above. See also *Erith Holdings Ltd v Murphy* [2017] EWHC 1364 (TCC) at [88] and [90].
233 [2001] EWCA Civ 1477, [2002] 1 W.L.R. 566. The decision of the Court of Appeal on this point was not appealed to the House of Lords, on whose decision on a defence of estoppel; see [2003] UKHL 17, [2003] 2 A.C. 541 and below, para.45-060.
234 [2001] EWCA Civ 1477, [2002] 1 W.L.R. 566 at [17].
235 [2001] EWCA Civ 1477, [2002] 1 W.L.R. 566 at [35]. The CA rejected the contention that there is a rule of law according to which there is no guarantee within the Statute of Frauds where the promisor does not undertake to be liable generally but only in respect of specific funds or sources within

Thus, the absence of the agreement of the main contractor to the redirection of the funds by the employer (and therefore the potential for discharge of the debt owed to it by the employer by the latter's payment of the sub-contractor) was crucial to determining whether it was a guarantee. If agreement by the main contractor had been forthcoming, the agreement would have created a primary liability in the employer (the agreement being "tantamount to, if not in strict law, a novation or assignment of liability"), but in its absence it was clear that the employer had agreed to accept a secondary liability in respect of the main contractor's liabilities.[236]

A question of construction   According to Lord Diplock in *Moschi v Lep Air*   **45-046**
Services Ltd, in distinguishing between guarantees and indemnities, "every case must depend upon the true construction of the actual words in which the promise is expressed".[237] However, it has been said that:

> "The fact that the parties have used the word 'guarantee' is not itself conclusive, but in doubtful cases it may provide some guide, especially if the word is repeated a number of times in the document ... Another guide is whether the creditor's rights against the principal debtor and against the guarantor, or indemnifier, are co-extensive. If the person liable under the contract may be liable for a greater amount than the principal debtor, the contract is probably one of indemnity."[238]

On the other hand, it has been held that the absence of usual provisions included in contracts of guarantee (for example, to permit variation of the obligations or giving of time without discharge of the surety) is "at best neutral" in construing a promise as a guarantee or an indemnity.[239] In common with the general position, this process of construction should bear in mind the factual matrix in which the words were used by the parties.[240]

Examples   Given that s.4 applies only where there is some person other than the   **45-047**
surety who is primarily liable, it does not apply where there has never been any party liable other than the defendant.[241] So, if A orders goods and instructs them to be delivered to B, and the intention of the parties is that A alone is to be liable for the price, this does not fall within the section.[242] This is not indeed a contract of suretyship at all but a mere contract for the sale of the goods to A. But if the intention of the parties is that the recipient of the goods is to be primarily liable, and the other party is only to be liable if the recipient does not pay, this is a contract of

---

[236] his control: at [47]–[51], not following in this respect *Harvey v Edwards Dunlop & Co Ltd* (1927) 39 C.L.R. 302, 311, per Higgins J.

[236] [2001] EWCA Civ 1477 at [34]–[35].

[237] [1973] A.C. 331, 349. See also *Vossloh Aktiengesellschaft v Alpha Trains (UK) Ltd* [2010] EWHC 2443 (Ch), [2010] All E.R. (D) 86 (Oct) at [19]–[27]; *Multiplex Construction Europe Ltd v Dunne* [2017] EWHC 3073 (TCC), [2018] B.L.R. 36 at [40]–[42] (referring to the significance of the commercial purpose of the provision contained in a wider transaction).

[238] *Clement v Clement* (1996) 71 P. & C.R. D19, CA, per Warner J., quoted with approval by Peter Gibson L.J. in the CA.

[239] *Associated British Ports v Ferryways NV* [2008] EWHC 1265 (Comm), [2008] 2 Lloyd's Rep. 353 at [61], per Field J., quoted with approval by Maurice Kay L.J. (with whom Sir Anthony Clarke M.R. and Jacob L.J. agreed) [2009] EWCA Civ 189, [2009] 1 Lloyd's Rep. 595 at [12].

[240] *Clement v Clement*, above and see below, paras 45-064 et seq. and Vol.I, paras 13-041 et seq.

[241] *Lakeman v Mountstephen* (1874) L.R. 7 H.L. 17.

[242] *Birkmyr v Darnell* (1705) 1 Salk. 27.

guarantee within the section.[243] Similarly, the section does not apply where there was originally another party liable to the creditor but his liability has been discharged. So if A agrees to pay B a debt owed to B by C, and B agrees to discharge C, this is a novation and not within the section.[244] A is not agreeing to meet C's liability, for that liability has gone; he is agreeing to meet a new liability which is his alone, and the section does not apply.[245] The same is true where C owes a debt to B and B agrees to discharge C in return for a new joint obligation undertaken by A and C together; A is not undertaking to answer for C's old debt (for that has gone) but for the new joint debt on which he is primarily liable.[246] It has also been held that a promise by A to B that A will pay to C a debt due from B to C is not within the section; if the promise were made by A to C it would be a promise to answer for the debt "of another", but where the promise is made to B himself, it is a promise to answer for the promisee's own debt and not for the debt "of another".[247] So also a promise by a principal debtor to indemnify another if he will act as surety for him is not within the section for the debtor is undertaking to answer for his own debt or default and not for that "of another".[248] Moreover, a clause according to which the promisor agrees to be "bound by any acknowledgment or admission by the [first debtor] and by any judgment" in favour of the creditor against the first debtor provides, when coupled with language of indemnification, "a compelling indication that the [promisor's] liability under the deed of indemnity is primary rather than secondary".[249] Finally, there may be a third possibility beyond the distinction between a guarantee and an indemnity, that is, that an alleged guarantor or surety has not taken on any personal obligation (primary or secondary) but has merely acted as an agent for a third party primarily liable, by doing no more than, for example, communicating what that third party is itself to do to satisfy the primary liability, as in the case where a company director says that he will see to it that the company performs a given task, which is not necessarily to be construed as that director taking any obligation on himself personally.[250]

45-048   Even where there is another debtor it does not necessarily follow that the contract is one of guarantee within the section. Thus if two debtors contract jointly (or jointly and severally) each is answerable for his own debt, and not for the debt of the other, and the case is not within the section. And where the liability assumed by the defendant is different from the liability assumed by the other debtor the case will not be within the section, for it cannot be said here that the defendant has promised to answer for the debt or default of another. Thus where a person acts as surety for a debtor under a consumer credit agreement, but the surety's liability extends to situations in which the debtor himself is not liable, this is a contract of indemnity not within the section, for the surety has clearly assumed a separate and distinct obligation, and is not merely guaranteeing the debtor's obligations.[251] On the other hand,

[243] *Simpson v Penton* (1834) 2 Cr. & M. 430.
[244] As to novation, see Vol.I, para.19-087.
[245] *Goodman v Chase* (1818) 1 B. & Ald. 297; *Butcher v Steuart* (1843) 11 M. & W. 857.
[246] *Ex p. Lane* (1846) 1 De G. 300.
[247] *Eastwood v Kenyon* (1840) 11 A. & E. 438; *Guild & Co v Conrad* [1894] 2 Q.B. 885.
[248] *Thomas v Cook* (1828) 8 B. & C. 728.
[249] *ABM AMRO Commercial Finance Plc v McGinn* [2014] EWHC 1674 (Comm), [2014] 2 Lloyd's Rep. 333 at [36], per Flaux J.
[250] *MyBarrister Ltd v Hewetson* [2017] EWHC 2624 (Ch), [2018] Bus. L.R. 752 at [62]–[63].
[251] *Yeoman Credit Ltd v Latter* [1961] 1 W.L.R. 828; *Unity Finance Ltd v Woodcock* [1963] 1 W.L.R. 455; *Goulston Discount Co Ltd v Clark* [1967] 2 Q.B. 493. See also Consumer Credit Act 1974

where A agrees to "assume full responsibility for ensuring" that B "has and will at all times have sufficient funds and other resources to fulfil and meet all duties, commitments and liabilities" to C, then this promise gives rise to a "'see to it' obligation": B's liability is primary, A's is secondary and A's agreement constitutes a guarantee.[252]

Guarantee only if secondary liability as against creditor   In considering   **45-049** whether the surety has undertaken a primary or a secondary liability, it must be recalled that the position as between the creditor and the surety may differ from the position as between the surety and another debtor.[253] If two joint debtors agree as between themselves that one is to be primarily liable and the other to bear a secondary liability only, this will create the relationship of principal debtor and surety as between them. But if they both assume a joint primary liability as against the creditor there will be no contract of guarantee within the section.[254]

Guarantee as incident to wider transaction   Even where a person clearly does   **45-050** promise to answer for the debt, default or miscarriage of another, the promise will not be within the section where it is merely an incident to a wider transaction. The question is whether the main object of the parties is that one should guarantee the liability of another or whether the promise arose as an incident to a wider transaction with a different object (where the promise is to be seen as one of indemnity).[255] So, for example, where a person contracts to buy goods as agent for a principal on the terms that he is to be liable for the price if the principal fails to pay, this does not fall within s.4 even though the agent is in a sense promising to answer for the debt of the principal, for the object of the parties is to effect a sale of goods, not to enter into a contract of guarantee.[256] Similarly, where a person promises to pay off an encumbrance on property in which he has an interest in order to secure its release, the mere fact that the encumbrance arose out of another's debt does not bring the case within the section.[257] On the other hand, where a company director guarantees the debts of a company, this falls squarely within the section[258] even

---

s.113(7).

[252] *Associated British Ports v Ferryways NV* [2008] EWHC 1265 (Comm), [2008] 2 Lloyd's Rep. 353 at [60], per Field J., quoted with approval by Maurice Kay L.J. (with whom Sir Anthony Clarke M.R. and Jacob L.J. agreed) [2009] EWCA Civ 189, [2009] 1 Lloyd's Rep. 595 at [11] (not in the context of the Statute of Frauds).

[253] See above, paras 45-003—45-005.

[254] But it has been held that there may still be a contract of guarantee for other purposes: *Heald v O'Connor* [1971] 1 W.L.R. 497. cf. the position in relation to bills of exchange. While the position of a person liable as drawer or indorser of a bill of exchange is in some respects similar to that of a surety for the acceptor (*Duncan Fox & Co v North & South Wales Bank* (1880) 6 App. Cas. 1, 19), he cannot set up the Statute of Frauds as a defence to an action on the bill: *McCall Brothers Ltd v Hargreaves* [1932] 2 K.B. 423. But he can do so if it is sought to impose on him a liability under a parol agreement, and the liability does not arise simply from his position as drawer or indorser under the Bills of Exchange Act 1882: *Steele v M'Kinlay* (1880) 5 App. Cas. 754; *Jenkins & Sons v Coomber* [1898] 2 Q.B. 168. But contrast *Lombard Banking Ltd v Central Garage & Engineering Co* [1963] 1 Q.B. 220; *Yeoman Credit v Gregory* [1963] 1 W.L.R. 343.

[255] *Sutton v Grey* [1894] 1 Q.B. 285; *Harburg India Rubber Co v Martin* [1902] 1 K.B. 778, 786; *Pitt v Jones* [2007] EWCA Civ 1301, [2008] 2 W.L.R. 1289 at [32].

[256] *Couturier v Hastie* (1852) 8 Exch. 40; reversed on other grounds (1856) 5 H.L.C. 673; *Sutton v Grey*, above.

[257] *Fitzgerald v Dressler* (1859) 7 C.B.(N.S.) 374; *Marginson v Ian Potter & Co* (1976) 136 C.L.R. 161.

[258] *Harburg India Rubber Co v Martin* [1902] 1 K.B. 778.

though the director may himself have a charge on the company's assets.[259] And the mere fact that the promise is related to one or more other transactions does not take the promise outside s.4. So, in *Pitt v Jones*, the managing director and major shareholder in Company A wished to sell his shares to Company B (which was to finance the purchase by borrowing the money from Company A).[260] In order to effect the sale, the director persuaded the minor shareholders (and employees) of Company A not to exercise their right of pre-emption over his own shares and to agree to the loan by Company A; he also arranged that the minority shareholders should enjoy an option to sell their own shares to Company B and agreed with them that if Company B could not pay for their shares on exercise of this option, he would do so. In these circumstances, the Court of Appeal held that while these transactions were linked, they were not one identical transaction: the director had no interest in the contract between the minority shareholders and Company B "in the sense that he could not possibly benefit" from the share-options, though the latter were a way of persuading the minority shareholders to cooperate with the sale of his own shares.[261] As a result, the director's promise to pay for their shares if Company B did not do so fell within s.4 and was unenforceable for want of formality.

45-051 **"Implied guarantees"** In *Silverburn Finance (UK) Ltd v Salt*,[262] continuing written personal guarantees by a company's directors had been terminated by guarantors at the same time as the termination by the company of the main contract in respect of which the guarantees had been made. About a month later, a new main contract was concluded by the company on the same terms as previously and the question arose as to the position of the guarantors. Although it had not been pleaded, the question was raised by the Court of Appeal as to whether the guarantees could be implied on the renewal of the earlier main agreement. In Mummery L.J.'s opinion:

"... any implication of an agreement to supply a guarantee would face the difficulty of non-compliance with the statutory requirement of writing. That requirement cannot be satisfied by reference back to the guarantees [earlier supplied in writing], as they had been revoked. They are only written evidence of guarantees that have since ceased to exist."[263]

Rix L.J. agreed at least in the absence of an express agreement that the old guarantees would stand as a sufficient note or memorandum of the new or revived guarantees.[264]

45-052 **Requirements of the section**[265] The section requires that the agreement or a note or memorandum thereof should be in writing, and this has been held to mean that

---

[259] *Davys v Buswell* [1913] 2 K.B. 47.

[260] *Pitt v Jones* [2007] EWCA Civ 1301, [2008] 2 W.L.R. 1289.

[261] [2007] EWCA Civ 1301 at [36]–[38], per Smith L.J.

[262] [2001] EWCA Civ 279, [2001] 2 All E.R. (Comm) 438.

[263] [2001] EWCA Civ 279, [2001] 2 All E.R. (Comm) 438 at [32].

[264] [2001] EWCA Civ 279, [2001] 2 All E.R. (Comm) 438 at [40].

[265] There is authority on earlier provisions governing contracts for the sale or other disposition of an interest in land under the Statute of Frauds s.4 and s.40 of the Law of Property Act 1925 for the view that if a material term has been omitted from the memorandum, a claimant may waive such a term where it is solely for his benefit and not of a major importance, and enforce the contract without the term in question: *Morrell v Studd and Millington* [1913] 2 Ch. 648, 660; *North v Loomes* [1919] 1 Ch. 378, 385-386; *Ram Narayan s/o Shankar v Rishad Hussain Shah s/o Tusaduq Hussain Shah*

all the material terms of the contract must be stated in the writing.[266] It was formerly held that the writing should also include a statement of the consideration but this gave rise to many difficulties, and it was eventually provided by s.3 of the Mercantile Law Amendment Act 1856 that this should no longer be necessary in the case of contracts of guarantee.

Written agreement or note or memorandum As Lord Brandon observed in **45-053** *Elpis Maritime Co Ltd v Marti Chartering Inc Co (The Maria D)*,[267] s.4 provides two ways in which a guarantee may be enforceable: the first is by having a written agreement signed by the party to be charged or by his agent and the second is by having a note or memorandum of the agreement similarly signed.[268] Where, therefore, A has previously made an oral agreement with B to guarantee C's liabilities to B, it is immaterial whether A's subsequent signature of a document incorporating the terms of such a guarantee was made on its own behalf or only as agent for C. For if A signed on its own behalf as a contracting party, then the oral agreement became subsumed in the written one and is enforceable in the first way which s.4 provides. On the other hand, if A signed as agent for C, the oral agreement of guarantee between A and B does not become subsumed in the written one, but the written one duly signed is nevertheless a memorandum of the oral agreement so as to satisfy the second way which s.4 provides.[269] The memorandum need not be prepared for the purpose of satisfying the statutory requirement of written evidence. Any writing which contains the requisite particulars will suffice so long as it comes into existence before an action is brought on the contract.[270]

Written agreement The Court of Appeal has held that the written agreement for **45-054** the purposes of the Statute can be contained in "a sequence of negotiating emails or other documents of the sort which is commonplace in ship chartering and ship sale and purchase", although it reserved the question whether "the pattern of contract negotiation and formation habitually adopted in other areas of commercial life" would present difficulty for the adoption of the same approach.[271]

[1979] 1 W.L.R. 1349, 1351. Conversely, a party may cure the omission of a term to his detriment by consenting to perform it: *Martin v Pycroft* (1852) 2 De G.M. & G. 785; *Scott v Bradley* [1971] Ch. 850. Contrast *Burgess v Cox* [1951] Ch. 383, 391. The formal requirements governing contracts for the sale or other disposition of land are now contained in s.2 of the Law of Property (Miscellaneous Provisions) Act 1989, on which see Vol.I, paras 5-010 et seq.

[266] *Holmes v Mitchell* (1859) 7 C.B.(N.S.) 361; *State Bank of India v Kaur* [1996] 5 Bank L.R. 158; *MP Services Ltd v Lawyer* (1996) 72 P. & C.R. D49.

[267] [1992] 1 A.C. 21; and see Baughen (1992) Conv. 330. There is no requirement that any note or memorandum must always postdate the "main contract", i.e. the contract whose obligations are guaranteed or be contemporaneous with it: *Golden Ocean Group Ltd v Salgaocar Mining Industries PVT Ltd* [2011] EWHC 56 (Comm), [2011] 2 All E.R. (Comm) 95 at [77], per Christopher Clarke J. (affirmed without reference to this point [2012] EWCA Civ 265, [2012] 1 Lloyd's Rep. 542).

[268] [1992] 1 A.C. 21 at 27.

[269] [1992] 1 A.C. 21 at 33; and see below, para.45-057.

[270] See *Lucas v Dixon* (1889) 22 Q.B.D. 357 (sale of goods); cf. *Farr, Smith & Co Ltd v Messers Ltd* [1928] 1 K.B. 397 (sale of goods); *Daniels v Trefusis* [1914] 1 K.B. 788 (contracts for the sale of an interest in land).

[271] *Golden Ocean Group Ltd v Salgaocar Mining Industries Pvt Ltd* [2012] EWCA Civ 265, [2012] 1 Lloyd's Rep. 542 at [22], per Tomlinson L.J. and see further at [29] (with whom Rix L.J. and Sir Mark Waller agreed).

45-055 **Note or memorandum** In order to satisfy the Statute the document which is relied on as a note or memorandum of the agreement must itself acknowledge or recognise the existence of a contract and this cannot be the case where it is expressed as "subject to contract".[272] It must also contain a statement of its material terms.[273] On the other hand, it has been held that:

> "... where ... there is an offer in writing made by the party to be bound which contains the essential terms of what is offered *and* the party to be bound accepts that his offer has been accepted unconditionally, albeit orally, there is a sufficient note or memorandum to satisfy section 4."[274]

It is sometimes possible for two documents to be read together so as to find a note or memorandum satisfying the section, but in order for this to be done it is necessary that the document containing the defendant's signature should contain some reference, express or implied, to the other document which it is sought to read with the first.[275]

45-056 **Rectification and the Statute** Where as a result of a shared mistake a guarantee instrument does not record the common intention of the parties, and the creditor is entitled to invoke the court's equitable jurisdiction to rectify the instrument so as to accord with their common intention, the creditor's claim under the instrument as so rectified does not offend s.4 of the Statute of Frauds.[276]

45-057 **Signature to agreement or memorandum**[277] The note or memorandum of the guarantee must be "signed by the party to be charged" or by his agent.[278] It is not necessary that it should be signed by the other party to the transaction.[279] Nor for this purpose need it be a "signature" in the popular sense for it suffices if the defendant's name is written or printed by himself or even by an agent[280]; and it may appear anywhere in the document so long as it is intended to authenticate the whole

---

[272] *Carlton Communications Plc v Football League* [2002] EWHC 1650 at [78] applying *Tiverton Ltd v Wearwell Ltd* [1975] Ch. 146 (Law of Property Act 1925 s.40); *Motemtronic Ltd v Autocar Equipment Ltd* Unreported June 20, 1996, CA, transcript No.656 of 1996, per Aldous L.J.; *Fairstate Ltd v General Enterprise & Management Ltd* [2010] EWHC 3072 (QB), [2010] All E.R. (D) 301 (Nov) at [58] and [88] (identification of principal debtor and duration of guarantee both material).

[273] [2002] EWHC 1650 at [79] and cf. above, para.45-052 (note) referring to the possibility of permitting a claimant to waive a material term omitted from a memorandum where it is solely for his benefit and not of a major importance.

[274] *J Pereira Fernandes SA v Mehta* [2006] EWHC 813 (Ch) at [16], [2006] 2 All E.R. 881, per Judge Pelling Q.C.

[275] *Timmins v Morland Street Property Ltd* [1958] Ch. 110 (a case on s.40 of the Law of Property Act 1925); *Golden Ocean Group Ltd v Salgaocar Mining Industries Pvt Ltd* [2012] EWCA Civ 265, [2012] Lloyd's Rep. 542 at [24].

[276] *GMAC Commercial Credit Development Ltd v Sandhu* [2004] EWHC 716 (Comm), [2006] 1 All E.R. (Comm) 268, especially at [58]; following *USA v Motor Trucks Ltd* [1924] A.C. 196, PC (land contract) and see Vol.I, paras 3-057 et seq. on rectification more generally.

[277] cf. the contrasting position under s.2 of the Law of Property (Miscellaneous Provisions) Act 1989, on which see Vol.I, para.5-037.

[278] Where the original signed guarantee document cannot be found, signature may be established by other evidence: *Bank of Scotland v Mazamal Hussain* [2011] EWHC 1934 (QB) at [42]–[44]; *Mitsui OSK Lines Ltd v Salgaocar Mining Ltd* [2015] EWHC 565 (Comm) at [41].

[279] *Laythoarp v Bryant* (1836) 2 Bing. N.C. 735.

[280] *Leeman v Stocks* [1951] Ch. 941. And see Vol.I, para.5-008 on the status of "electronic signatures" for this purpose.

document.[281] Where the defendant wrote and signed a guarantee which contained a mistake, and on the mistake being discovered, he wrote a memorandum across the original guarantee correcting the mistake, but did not sign it afresh, it was held that his original signature was a signature of the whole and satisfied the section.[282] And where the director of a company agreed orally to guarantee the company's liabilities and signed a contract on behalf of the company, but omitted to sign a guarantee form in the same document, it being orally agreed that his one signature should be sufficient to deal also with his personal capacity, it was held that the requirements of the statute had been satisfied.[283] Moreover, as has been indicated, where an agent has orally agreed to a personal guarantee, but signs a document which includes such a guarantee only on behalf of his principal, he is bound personally: "[t]he question is not what is the intention of the person signing the memorandum, but is one of fact, viz is there a note or memorandum of the promise signed by the party to be charged?".[284] On the other hand, it has been held that where an alleged guarantee was contained in an email sent with the would-be guarantor's authority, the automatic insertion of an email address in the message by an internet service provider did not constitute a signature by its writer within the meaning of s.4 as it did not represent any intention to authenticate the message by the writer.[285] However, the court accepted that:

"... if a party or a party's agent sending an e-mail types his or her or his or her principal's name to the extent required or permitted by existing case law in the body of an e-mail, then ... that would be sufficient signature of the purposes of section 4 [of the Statute of Frauds]."[286]

Alteration in memorandum   Where a memorandum is altered after it has been signed either in order to correct a mistake in the written statement of an existing contract[287] or before the parties are contractually bound at all,[288] parol evidence is admissible to show that the signature was intended to apply to the memorandum as altered.[289] But such signature cannot authenticate subsequent alterations which

45-058

---

281 *Caton v Caton* (1867) L.R. 2 H.L. 127.

282 *Bluck v Gompertz* (1852) 7 Ex. 862.

283 *VSH Ltd v BKS Air Transport Ltd* [1964] 1 Lloyd's Rep. 460.

284 *Re Hoyle* [1893] 1 Ch. 84, 100, per Smith L.J., quoted with approval by Lord Brandon in *Elpis Maritime Co Ltd v Marti Chartering Co Ltd (The Maria D)* [1992] 1 A.C. 21 at 32–33; *Golden Ocean Group Ltd v Salgaocar Mining Industries Pvt Ltd* [2012] EWCA Civ 265, [2012] 1 Lloyd's Rep. 542 at [37].

285 *J Pereira Fernandes SA v Mehta* [2006] EWHC 813 (Ch), [2006] 2 All E.R. 881 at [25]–[30], per Judge Pelling Q.C.

286 *J Pereira Fernandes SA v Mehta*, above, at [31]. It was common ground before (and accepted by) the CA that an electronic signature is sufficient and that a first name, initials or perhaps a nickname will suffice, as long as it was done in a manner which indicates that it is intended to authenticate the document: *Golden Ocean Group Ltd v Salgaocar Mining Industries Pvt Ltd* [2012] EWCA Civ 265, [2012] 1 Lloyd's Rep. 542 at [32].

287 *Bluck v Gompertz* (1852) 7 Ex. 862.

288 *Stewart v Eddowes* (1874) L.R. 9 C.P. 311 (sale of goods); *Koenigsblatt v Sweet* [1923] 2 Ch. 314 (sale of land).

289 *New Hart Builders Ltd v Brindley* [1975] Ch. 342 (sale of land). On the effect of alteration of the instrument of guarantee in any material particular without the knowledge or consent of the surety while in the hands of the party to whom it was given see below, para.45-115.

effect a variation of a contract concluded and binding on the parties at some time previous to the alterations.[290]

45-059 **Effect of non-compliance with the section** It is well settled that a failure to comply with the section renders the contract unenforceable rather than void.[291] So far as contracts of guarantee are concerned, the principal consequence of this is that the section may be satisfied by a written document which is made or signed only after the contract was originally created. Thus a recital in a will confirming a guarantee previously given orally has been held to satisfy the section.[292]

45-060 **Estoppel** In *Actionstrength Ltd v International Glass Engineering IN GL EN SpA*[293] the House of Lords considered how, if at all, a person could be estopped from relying on the invalidity of a guarantee owing to its failure to fulfil the requirements of s.4 of the Statute of Frauds. There a sub-contractor entered into an agreement with the main contractor to supply labour to enable the latter to build a factory for an employer. When arrears built up on the sums due to it from the contractor, the sub-contractor threatened to withdraw its labour and, it alleged, concluded a contract with the employer by which the latter promised to ensure that the sub-contractor received any amount due to it from the main contractor. The sub-contractor then continued to supply labour for the project, allegedly in reliance on this contract. The Court of Appeal had held that the alleged agreement fell within s.4 of the Statute[294] and before the House of Lords the sub-contractor did not challenge this decision, but argued either as a matter of estoppel or otherwise, more generally, that it would be unconscionable for the employer to rely on the Statute and to go back on its promise on which it had relied.[295] However, the House of Lords rejected these arguments. For Lord Hoffmann,

> "The terms of the Statute of Frauds ... show that Parliament, although obviously conscious that it would allow some people to break their promises, thought that this injustice was outweighed by the need to protect people from being held liable on the basis of oral utterances which were ill-considered, ambiguous or completely fictitious. This means that while normally one would approach the construction of a statute on the basis that Parliament was unlikely to have intended to cause injustice by allowing people to break promises which had been relied upon, no such assumption can be made about the Statute of Frauds. Although the scope of the Statute of Frauds must be tested on the assumption that the facts alleged by [the sub-contractor] are true, it must not be construed in a way which would undermine its purpose."[296]

None of the facts before the House distinguished the case from those which attend the giving of every guarantee: the only assurance given to the sub-contractor was the promise of guarantee itself.[297] On these facts, therefore, the purpose of the

---

[290] *New Hart Builders Ltd v Brindley* [1975] Ch. 342 although the court considered that there was no logical ground for this distinction, 352.
[291] *Leroux v Brown* (1852) 12 C.B. 801; *Maddison v Alderson* (1883) 8 App. Cas. 467, 474.
[292] *Re Hoyle* [1893] 1 Ch. 84.
[293] [2003] UKHL 17, [2003] 2 All E.R. 615.
[294] [2001] EWCA 1477, [2002] 1 W.L.R. 566, see above, para.45-045.
[295] [2003] UKHL 17 at [16], [42].
[296] [2003] UKHL 17 at [20].
[297] [2003] UKHL 17 at [9], [28], [35], [53]–[54].

Statute should not be subverted by the acceptance of an estoppel.[298] On the other hand, two of their Lordships indicated the circumstances in which an estoppel could apply so as to prevent reliance on the Statute.[299] So, Lord Clyde suggested that what is required is "some additional encouragement, inducement or assurance" and "some influence exerted by [the employer] on [the sub-contractor] to lead it to assume that the promise would be honoured".[300] For Lord Walker of Gestingthorpe, an example of when estoppel may arise in this context would be where there was some "unambiguous representation that there was an enforceable contract, or that [the employer] would not take any point on s.4 of the Statute of Frauds".[301]

Consumer credit agreements Contracts of guarantee (which for this purpose **45-061** include certain contracts of indemnity) relating to consumer credit agreements and to consumer hire agreements may also be affected by the special requirements of the Consumer Credit Act 1974, for the details of which reference should be made to Ch.39.[302]

4. CONSTRUCTION OF THE CONTRACT

General Difficult questions frequently arise as to the extent of the liability which **45-062** the surety has undertaken. These are essentially questions as to the true construction of the contract in each particular case, and it is sufficient here to indicate the general approach of the courts to these questions and to draw attention to some of the principal types of difficulty which have arisen.[303] Despite some contradictory dicta in the cases,[304] the traditional general approach seems to be that contracts of this kind must be strictly construed in favour of the surety and that no liability is to be imposed on him which is not clearly and distinctly covered by the contract.[305] The strict approach applies also to attempts to exclude rules of common law or equity incidental to the contract of suretyship. As Lord Jauncey of Tullichettle observed:

"... there is no doubt that in a modern contract of guarantee parties may, if so minded, exclude any one or more of the normal incidents of suretyship. However if they choose to do so clear and unambiguous language must be used."[306]

One reason for this strict construction may be that, in principle, the surety need receive no benefit from the contract which is, so far as he is concerned, gratuitous;

---

[298] [2003] UKHL 17 at [9], [53]. See similarly *Bank of Scotland v Wright* [1990] B.C.C. 663, see below, para.45-082 (no estoppel so as to extend guarantor's liability beyond that to which it applies as a matter of construction of the document which satisfies the Statute of Frauds s.4).

[299] Lord Hoffmann explicitly reserved this question: [2003] UKHL 17 at [29]. Lord Bingham implicitly agreed with the position taken by Lord Walker of Gestingthorpe noted in the text: [2003] UKHL 17 at [9].

[300] [2003] UKHL 17 at [35].

[301] [2003] UKHL 17 at [51] referring to *Shah v Shah* [2001] EWCA Civ 527, [2002] Q.B. 35 (in the context of deeds) on which see Vol.I, para.1-139.

[302] Above, paras 39-180 et seq.

[303] See Vol.I, paras 13-041 et seq. on the modern approach of the courts to construction of contracts generally.

[304] See *Eshelby v Federated European Bank Ltd* [1932] 1 K.B. 254, 266.

[305] *Blest v Brown* (1862) 4 De G.F. & J. 367, 376.

[306] *Trafalgar House Construction (Regions) Ltd v General Surety & Guarantee Co Ltd* [1996] 1 A.C. 199, 208.

this may not, however, be the case, for example, where the guarantor has a commercial interest in keeping the principal debtor afloat.[307] Secondly, in most cases contracts of guarantee are drafted by the creditor and therefore, in cases of ambiguity, are traditionally to be construed *contra proferentem*, that is, against the creditor and in favour of the surety.[308] However, it appears that the role of this traditional maxim of construction is less prominent than formerly and that, particularly in commercial cases between parties of equal bargaining power, the courts seek to resolve ambiguities in a contract term by reference to its context in the wider contract, its factual matrix and commercial common sense rather than by reference to this traditional maxim.[309]

45-063   The principle of strict construction does not mean that the court should not look beyond the terms of the written instrument. As in all cases of construction, the court is entitled to look at the surrounding circumstances in order to see what was the subject matter which the parties had in contemplation at the time the contract was made, and to determine the scope and object of the guarantee.[310] A guarantee of a tenant's obligations under a lease may extend, on its true construction, to the liabilities of the tenant under a statutory continuation of the lease,[311] but prima facie it seems that a guarantee of the covenants of a tenant on a lease do not so extend.[312] On the other hand, the court should not "disregard the clear wording of a document simply on the basis of an abstract expectation as to the bargain the parties might have struck".[313] Instead, there should be an indication in the document itself that general words were not intended to cover a particular circumstance. So, for example, the stipulation of a particular rate of interest on amounts owed under a secured guarantee indicated that an "all moneys and liabilities" clause should not include liability for assigned debts, since the opposite construction would allow the creditor to change the debtor's unsecured debts into secured ones and to alter the rate of interest without any consent on the part of the debtors, still less on the part of the guarantor.[314]

45-064   **Modern approach to construction**   Some of the cases decided on the construction of guarantees and indemnities upholding a strict construction were decided at a time before the modern approach to the construction of contracts in general had

---

307   See *Multiplex Construction Europe Ltd v Dunne* [2017] EWHC 3073 (TCC), [2018] B.L.R. 36 at [26]–[28].

308   *Eastern Counties Building Society v Russell* [1947] 1 All E.R. 500, 503; affirmed [1947] 2 All E.R. 734; *West Horndon Industrial Park Ltd v Phoenix Timber Group Plc* [1995] 1 E.G.L.R. 77. Construction of a written instrument against the person who made it has been termed the "classic form" of the rule of construction contra proferentem: *Nobahar-Cookson v Hut Group Ltd* [2016] EWCA Civ 128, [2016] 1 C.L.C. 573 at [14] and is to be distinguished from the traditionally strict approach to the construction of exclusion clauses: see Vol.I, para.15-012.

309   See *Multiplex Construction Europe Ltd v Dunne* [2017] EWHC 3073 (TCC), [2018] B.L.R. 36 at [26]–[34]. See further Vol.I, para.15-012 (in relation to the construction of exclusion clauses). See also below, para.45-064 on the modern approach to construction.

310   *Heffield v Meadows* (1869) L.R. 4 C.P. 595; *Leathley v Spyer* (1870) L.R. 5 C.P. 595; *Nottingham, etc. Hide Co Ltd v Bottrill* (1873) L.R. 8 C.P. 694; *Bank of Scotland v Wright* [1990] B.C.C. 663, 675; *Grovewood (LE) v Lundy Properties* (1995) 69 P. & C.R. 507.

311   *Associated Dairies Ltd v Pierce* (1982) 265 E.G. 127; *Capital and City Holdings Ltd v Dean Warburg Ltd* (1989) 58 P. & C.R. 346, CA.

312   *A Plesser & Co Ltd v Davis* (1983) 267 E.G. 1039.

313   *Kova Establishment v Sasco Investments* [1998] 2 B.C.L.C. 83, 88, per John Martin Q.C.

314   *Kova Establishment v Sasco Investments* [1998] 2 B.C.L.C. 83, 89.

become firmly established and it may be questioned whether they are compatible with it. According to the modern approach to construction:

"... against the background of the admissible matrix of facts known to or at least reasonably available to the parties, the meaning sought is that of the language in question would convey to the reasonable man. In that context, the language used is to be given its natural and ordinary meaning, unless the reasonable man would conclude that something has gone wrong in expressing the parties' intentions."[315]

Viewed in this way, the reasonable man might conclude that the parties must, for whatever reason, have used wrong words or syntax.[316]

Application by courts to contracts of guarantee   This approach to construc-   **45-065**
tion has been applied by the courts to contracts of guarantee[317] and in *Kookmin Bank v Rainy Sky SA* was applied by the Supreme Court to an "advance payment bond", a form of refund guarantee.[318] So, it has been held that where a promise of guarantee is ambiguous on its face as to who is to benefit from the guarantor's undertaking, the court may look at extrinsic evidence to ascertain the proper meaning which the guarantee would convey to a reasonable person having all the background knowledge which would reasonably have been available to the parties at the time it was given.[319] Moreover, a contract of guarantee has also been construed so as to correct a clear mistake in its drafting. In *Vodafone Ltd v GNT Holdings (UK)*[320] a director of a company, company A, had signed on its notepaper a guarantee of the obligations of its subsidiary, company B, and this was expressed to be for the benefit of company C. However, company B had entered an agreement not with company C but with company D, which was in the same group of companies as company C: company C was merely a holding company and no company in the group other than

---

315 *Liberty Mutual Insurance Co (UK) Ltd v HSBC Bank Plc* [2002] EWCA Civ 691 at [54], per Rix L.J. The modern approach can be seen very clearly in the speech of Lord Wilberforce in *Prenn v Simmonds* [1971] 1 W.L.R. 1381 at 1385 but is now particularly associated with the "principles of construction" set out by Lord Hoffmann in *The Investors Compensation Scheme Ltd v West Bromwich Building Society* [1998] 1 W.L.R. 896, especially 912–913, per Lord Hoffmann. See also *Bank of Credit and Commerce International SA v Ali* [2001] UKHL 8, [2002] 1 A.C. 251 at [9]–[11]; *Chartbrook Ltd Persimmon Homes Ltd* [2009] UKHL 38, [2009] 1 A.C. 1101 and Vol.I, paras 13-041 et seq.

316 *The Investors Compensation Scheme Ltd v West Bromwich Building Society* [1998] 1 W.L.R. 896 at 913; *Prudential Assurance Co Ltd v Ayres* [2008] EWCA Civ 52, [2008] L. & T. R. 30 at [22] and see below, para.45-068.

317 *Liberty Mutual Insurance Co (UK) Ltd v HSBC Bank Plc* [2002] EWCA Civ 691 at [19]; *Static Control Components (Europe) Ltd v Egan* [2004] EWCA Civ 392, [2004] 2 Lloyd's Rep. 429 especially at [13] and [15]; *Dumford Trading AG v OAO Atlantrybflot* [2005] EWCA Civ 24, [2005] 1 Lloyd's Rep. 289 at [34]; *Fairstate Ltd v General Enterprise & Management Ltd* [2010] EWHC 3072 (QB), [2011] 2 All E.R. 497 (Comm) at [75]; *Cattles Plc v Welcome Financial Services Ltd* [2010] EWCA Civ 599, [2010] 2 Lloyd's Rep. 514 at [34]–[35], [43]; *National Merchant Buying Society Ltd v Bellamy* [2013] EWCA Civ 452, [2013] 2 All E.R. (Comm) 674 at [40]; *Harvey v Dunbar Assets Plc* [2013] EWCA Civ 952, [2013] B.P.I.R. 722 at [28]–[30]; *Ziggurat (Claremont Place) LLP v HCC International Insurance Co Plc* [2017] EWHC 3286 (TCC), [2018] B.L.R. 98 at [22].

318 [2011] UKSC 50, [2011] 1 W.L.R. 2900 and see above, para.45-009.

319 *Gastronome (UK) Ltd v Anglo Dutch Meats (UK) Ltd* [2006] EWCA Civ 1233, [2006] 2 Lloyd's Rep. 587 at [14], [18]–[19]; cf. *Amalgamated Investment & Property Co Ltd (In Liquidation) v Texas Commerce International Bank Ltd* [1982] Q.B. 84 (guarantee expressed on its terms to cover loan by bank held in the "factual matrix" of the contract also to cover loan by bank's subsidiary).

320 [2004] EWHC 1526 (QB), [2004] All E.R. (D) 194 (Mar).

company D had entered such an agreement. In these circumstances, it was held that the guarantee was given by company A in respect of company B's liabilities to *company D*: "something went wrong with the drafting of the [guarantee] letter ... To construe it literally would be a commercial nonsense."[321]

45-066   However, courts have at times sounded more cautious notes as to the implications of the modern approach to construction in the context of guarantees. In *Fairstate Ltd v General Enterprise & Management Ltd*[322] the High Court followed the modern approach to construction, considering that these principles meant that, in a suitable case "extrinsic evidence may be relied upon to identify the guarantor, the creditor, the principal debtor or the obligation to be guaranteed, where any of these have been inadequately or ambiguously described in the relevant document". But "the Court will be slow to deprive the defendant of a legitimate statutory defence [under the Statute of Frauds] on the basis of contested oral evidence alone".[323] In particular, as earlier noted, where a mistake has led to the omission of a material term from any writing, the contract may be unenforceable under the Statute of Frauds, unless the court is able to rectify the written instrument under normal rules.[324] In *Fairstate* itself, "the sheer length of the catalogue of corrections and additions that [the court] should have to make to the Guarantee Form in order to turn it into an effective guarantee for this transaction" preventing it from so doing: to do so would "be writing a new and different contract for the parties".[325] Moreover, in *Dumford Trading AG v OAO Atlantrybflot*[326] the Court of Appeal considered that (apart from the doctrines of rectification or misnomer[327]), where an existing person is named as guarantor in the guarantee document, there is a danger that extrinsic evidence from the surrounding matrix of facts could create an ambiguity otherwise not present.[328] Where, therefore, company A in a group of companies was identified as guarantor by the document of guarantee, the court should not look at extrinsic evidence (such as the postal address given for this company) so as to construe this unambiguous reference as being to company B, a very similarly-named company in the same group.[329]

45-067   **"Clear words" and "strict construction"**   It has been suggested that "it may be that the concept that a guarantee should be 'strictly construed' now adds nothing" to the modern approach to interpretation,[330] but in *Liberty Mutual Insurance Co (UK) Ltd v HSBC Bank Plc*[331] the Court of Appeal took the view that the modern

---

321 [2004] EWHC 1526 (QB) at [74], per Christopher Moger Q.C. sitting as a deputy judge of the High Court; cf. *Fairstate Ltd v General Enterprise & Management Ltd* [2010] EWHC 3072 (QB), [2011] 2 All E.R. 497 (Comm) at [75] (number of corrections and additions prevented court from so construing it).

322 [2010] EWHC 3072 (QB), [2011] 2 All E.R. 497 (Comm).

323 [2010] EWHC 3072 (QB) at [76].

324 Above, paras 45-055—45-056 and see above, Vol.I, paras 3-057 et seq. especially at para.3-060 for the relationship between the modern approach to construction and rectification.

325 [2010] EWHC 3072 (QB) at [82].

326 [2005] EWCA Civ 24, [2005] 1 Lloyd's Rep. 289 (application for summary judgment under Pt 24 CPR).

327 On which see Vol.I, paras 3-057 et seq. and 13-092 respectively.

328 [2005] EWCA Civ 24, [2005] 1 Lloyd's Rep. 289 at [36].

329 [2005] EWCA Civ 24, [2005] 1 Lloyd's Rep. 289 at [36].

330 *Static Control Components (Europe) Ltd v Egan* [2004] EWCA Civ 392, [2004] 2 Lloyd's Rep. 429 at [19], per Holman J.

331 [2002] EWCA Civ 691.

approach is not inconsistent with a maxim of construction which requires "clear words" to exclude or limit prevailing rules,[332] since "the reasonable man does not expect fundamental principles of law, equity and justice, such as rights of set-off or of subrogation to be excluded unless the contract clearly says so".[333]

The role of "business common sense" In *Kookmin Bank v Rainy Sky SA*[334] Lord **45-068**
Clarke of Stone-cum-Ebony (with whom Lord Phillips of Worth Matravers, Lords Mance, Kerr of Tonaghmore, and Wilson agreed) agreed with Lord Neuberger M.R. in *Pink Floyd Music Ltd v EMI Records Ltd*[335] in considering that the *Investors Compensation* case and *Chartbrook Ltd v Persimmon Homes Ltd*[336] show that:

"… the ultimate aim of interpreting a provision in a contract, especially a commercial contract, is to determine what the parties meant by the language used, which involves ascertaining what a reasonable person would have understood the parties to have meant … [T]he relevant reasonable person is one who has all the background knowledge which would have reasonably have been available to the parties in the situation in which they were at the time of the contract."[337]

The particular issue before the Supreme Court was "the role to be played by considerations of business common sense in determining what the parties meant",[338] there being a contrast of approach in the Court of Appeal below.[339] In Lord Clarke's view, it is not necessary:

"… to conclude that, unless the most natural meaning of the words produces a result so extreme as to suggest that it was unintended, the court must give effect to that meaning."[340]

Rather:

"… [i]f there are two possible constructions, the court is entitled to prefer the construction which is consistent with business common sense and to reject the other;"[341]

but "[w]here the parties have used unambiguous language, the court must apply it".[342] The Supreme Court applied this approach to the construction of the advance payment bonds before it, with the result that, in the context, in the bank's "promise to pay … on your first written demand, all such sums due to [the buyer] under the [ship-building] Contract" the words "such sums" referred to refunds to which the buyer was entitled in the case of any insolvency event and not merely to "pre-

---

[332] *Trafalgar House Construction (Regions) Ltd v General Surety & Guarantee Co Ltd* [1996] 1 A.C. 199, 208.

[333] [2002] EWCA Civ 691 at [56], per Rix L.J., relying in particular on *Bank of Credit and Commerce International SA v Ali* [2001] UKHL 8, [2002] 1 A.C. 251 at [10] (Lord Bingham).

[334] [2011] UKSC 50, [2011] 1 W.L.R. 2900.

[335] [2010] EWCA Civ 1429, [2011] 1 W.L.R. 770 at [17].

[336] [2009] UKHL 38, [2009] 1 A.C. 1101, [21]–[26].

[337] [2011] UKSC 50 at [14], per the Lord Clarke of Stone-cum-Ebony.

[338] [2011] UKSC 50 at [15], per the Lord Clarke of Stone-cum-Ebony.

[339] cf. [2010] EWCA Civ 582 at [19] (Sir Simon Tuckey) and [35]–[44] (Patten L.J.).

[340] [2011] UKSC 50 at [20].

[341] [2011] UKSC 50 at [21].

[342] [2011] UKSC 50 at [23] quoting with approval *Society of Lloyd's v Robinson* [1999] 1 W.L.R. 756, 763, per Lord Steyn. See also (though not in the context of suretyship) *Arnold v Britton* [2015] UKSC 36, [2015] A.C. 1619 at [15]–[23], [66] and [76]–[77]; *Wood v Capita Insurance Services Ltd* [2017] UKSC 24, [2017] 2 W.L.R. 1095 at [8]–[15].

delivery instalments" (as the banks had argued). For this purpose, the Court took into account the view of the experienced commercial judge at trial that the bank's construction would have "the surprising and uncommercial result that the Buyers would not be able to call on the Bonds on the happening of the event, namely the insolvency of the Builder, which would be most likely to require first class security".[343]

45-069 **Construction so as to "validate if possible"** In *Pavilion Property Trustees Ltd v Permira Advisers LLP*[344] a contract of guarantee was concluded between a landlord of premises and the assignee of the tenant of those premises, but its terms were ambiguous as to whether the guarantor's obligation related only to the obligations of the assignee or also to those of the "next assignee". The effect of the Landlord and Tenant (Covenants) Act 1995 s.25(1)[345] was held to be that:

> "if the guarantee is held to extend to the obligations of the Assignee and the Next Assignee, then the guarantee is either void in its entirety or void as to some part, if one can sever the provisions which impose a liability in relation to the obligations of the Next Assignee."[346]

Given this effect, Morgan J. considered that it was proper "to recall the Latin maxim *verba ita sunt intelligenda ut res magis valeat quam pereat* or, in English, 'validate if possible'"[347] and, as a result, to construe the guarantee in a way which avoided the illegality by holding that it extended only to the obligations of the assignee.[348] On the other hand, in *Tindall Cobham 1 Ltd v Adda Hotels*[349] (which concerned a clause in a lease which allowed the landlord to give consent to an assignment on the condition that the "tenant shall procure that the guarantor and any other guarantor of the tenant shall covenant by deed with the landlord" on certain terms), the Court of Appeal noted that the maxim *ut res magis valeat* originated in a concern in the courts to choose a meaning which will "produce the most commercial workable version of the contract" and "was not devised as a means of avoiding the consequences of legislation being applied to the contract which the parties had made".[350] The maxim should therefore not be used "to create an interpretation of the contract or other instrument which on ordinary principles of construction cannot be justified".[351] And as a matter of ordinary language the clause in the lease imposed a condition on the tenant that he should procure a new guarantee from the guarantors and such a clause falls within s.25 of the 1995 Act.[352]

---

[343] [2011] UKSC 50 at [21] at [41], per the Lord Clarke of Stone-cum-Ebony and see also at [45].
[344] *Pavilion Property Trustees Ltd v Permira Advisers LLP* [2014] EWHC 145 (Ch), [2014] 1 P. & C.R. 21.
[345] ss.5, 24 and 25. See above, para.45-016.
[346] [2014] EWHC 145 (Ch), [2014] 1 P. & C.R. 21 at [19], per Morgan J.
[347] [2014] EWHC 145 (Ch) at [20], referring to Lewison, *The Interpretation of Contracts*, 5th edn (2011), para.7.16. And see Vol.I, para.13-078.
[348] [2014] EWHC 145 (Ch) at [20]. Morgan J. held, in the alternative, that if the guarantee were to be construed so as to extend to the obligations of the next assignee, he could sever "the good from the bad" so as to leave a guarantee extending only to the assignee: [2014] EWHC 145 (Ch) at [21]–[22].
[349] [2014] EWCA Civ 1215, [2015] 1 P. & C.R.
[350] [2014] EWCA Civ 1215 at [30], per Patten L.J. (with whom Ryder and Longmore L.JJ. agreed).
[351] [2014] EWCA Civ 1215 at [31], per Patten L.J.
[352] [2014] EWCA Civ 1215 at [33], [36] and [43].

Co-extensiveness principle   In contracts of guarantee there has traditionally been   **45-070**
a strong prima facie rule of construction that the surety's obligations are co-
extensive with those of the principal debtor.[353] Indeed as has been noted above, if
the surety's obligations are not co-extensive with, but greater than those of the
principal debtor, the contract is normally thought to be an indemnity and not a
guarantee.[354] Many consequences flow from the principle of co- extensiveness; in
particular many of the rules relating to the discharge of the surety are often treated
as dependent on this principle.[355] But there is also a tendency to decide new questions by reference to the principle.[356] For example, it has been held that where a
surety has guaranteed fulfilment of a party's obligations under a contract containing an arbitration clause and expressly extending to any award made under it, the
surety will be liable in full for an award made under the clause including interest
and costs.[357] In another case, it was held that the guarantor of a tenant's obligations under the lease had undertaken a primary liability, and was therefore liable not
only for rent payable under the lease, but also for damages in tort (for mesne profits)
where the tenant had wrongfully retained possession after expiry of the lease.[358]
Similarly, where a surety agreed to pay interest as a secondary rather than a primary
liability this "can only … mean that he guaranteed to pay interest on the loan at the
contractual rate payable by the principal debtor" [359] On the other hand, the House
of Lords sanctioned what appears to be a major breach of the co-extensiveness
principle by holding that a guarantor may be liable for instalments accrued due even
though the debtor's primary obligation to pay these instalments has been transmuted
into a secondary obligation to pay damages for breach.[360] But no reference was
made to the co-extensiveness principle in the speeches in this case, so the present
status of this principle remains somewhat uncertain.

Certification of amounts due to creditor   In *North Shore Ventures Ltd v Anstead*   **45-071**
Holdings Inc,[361] the Court of Appeal was prepared to accept that a "conclusive
evidence clause" by which "[a] certificate signed by [the creditor] of the amount
for the time being of the Indebtedness and/or the amounts due to [the creditor] shall
be conclusive evidence for all purposes against the guarantors unless manifestly
incorrect" could take effect on its terms, though it was to be strictly construed so
that any ambiguity is resolved in favour of the guarantor.[362] The Court of Appeal
held that, in its contractual context, the proper construction of the clause before it
was that the guarantors "did not agree to pay the indebtedness as certified, rather
the entitlement to certify was limited to the indebtedness for the time being",[363]

---

[353] *Moschi v Lep Air Services Ltd* [1973] A.C. 331. See Steyn (1974) 90 L.Q.R. 246.
[354] See above, paras 45-007—45-008, 45-044.
[355] See below, paras 45-085 et seq.
[356] See also the significance of the "co-extensiveness principle" in the context of statutory demands
under the Insolvency Act 1986 in *Octagon Assets Ltd v Remblance* [2009] EWCA Civ 581, [2010]
Bus. L.R. 119; *White v Davenham Trust Ltd* [2011] EWCA Civ 747, [2011] Bus. L.R. 1443, below,
para.45-123.
[357] *Compañia Sudamericana De Fletes SA v African Continental Bank Ltd* [1973] 1 Lloyd's Rep. 21.
[358] *Associated Dairies Ltd v Pierce* (1982) 265 E.G. 127.
[359] *MP Services Ltd v Lawyer* (1996) 72 P. & C.R. D49 at D50, per Millett L.J.
[360] *Hyundai Heavy Industries Co Ltd v Papadopoulos* [1980] 1 W.L.R. 1129, see below, para.45-100.
[361] [2011] EWCA Civ 230, [2012] Ch. 31.
[362] [2011] EWCA Civ 230 at [46] citing *British Linen Asset Finance Ltd v Ridgeway* [1999] G.W.D.
2-78 (Sheriff Principal).
[363] [2011] EWCA Civ 230 at [46], per Sir Andrew Morritt (with whom Smith L.J. agreed at [56]).

distinguishing for this purpose the position in *IIG Capital LLC v Van der Merwe*[364] where the definition of "guaranteed moneys" which the guarantors there agreed to pay included those "expressed to be due, owing or payable, to the Lender from or by the Borrower", which showed that the guarantors "were undertaking more than a secondary obligation, thereby approximating to a performance bond".[365] The Court of Appeal further held that there had been an enforceable variation between the creditor and the principal debtor and that this meant that the certification (which related to the amount due under the unvaried principal agreement) was subject to a manifest error on the face of the certificate, even though this error was not manifest at the time of the certification.[366]

45-072 **Arbitration awards** Another possible departure from the co-extensiveness principle is to be found in the well-established rule that general words in a guarantee, by which a surety guarantees all the obligations of a principal debtor, do not of themselves have the effect of making the surety bound by an arbitration award, even though the guaranteed contract contained an arbitration clause out of which the arbitration arose.[367]

45-073 **Liability under a guarantee and entitlement to petition in bankruptcy** As has been noted,[368] prima facie a surety does not merely undertake to perform if the principal fails to do so; he undertakes to see that the principal debtor will perform and this means that a guarantor is liable in damages to the creditor for loss caused by the principal debtor's failure to perform and not merely to any sum owed by the principal debtor to the creditor. Under the Insolvency Act 1986 a creditor's ability to present a bankruptcy petition exists only where the liability is "for a liquidated sum".[369] In *McGuiness v Norwich and Peterborough Building Society*[370] the question arose as to the circumstances in which a creditor benefiting from a guarantee could petition for bankruptcy of the guarantor. Having reviewed the development of the bankruptcy legislation and earlier authorities, the Court of Appeal held that for these purposes

"a debt for a liquidated sum must be a pre-ascertained liability under the agreement which gives rise to it. This can include a contractual liability where the amount due is to be

---

[364] [2008] EWCA Civ 542, [2008] 2 Lloyd's Rep. 187 at [31] and cf. above, para.45-009.

[365] [2011] EWCA Civ 230 at [46], per Sir Andrew Morritt C.

[366] [2011] EWCA Civ 230 at [50]–[53], [58]–[61] cf. [68] (Tomlinson L.J.). While a majority of the Court of Appeal in *North Shore Ventures Ltd* [2011] EWCA Civ 230 considered that the error in the certificate need not be manifest at the time of certification, in *ABM AMRO Commercial Finance Plc v McGinn* [2014] EWHC 1674 (Comm), [2014] 2 Lloyd's Rep. 333 at [51] Flaux J. held that these observations were obiter to the Court of Appeal's decision (which rested on the fact that there was a manifest error on the face of the certificate) and needed to be "viewed with some circumspection". In his view, the possibility of establishing manifest error later (notably, at "a full blown trial as to which debts might or might not have led to recovery") "would render the conclusive evidence clause nugatory": [2014] EWHC 1674 (Comm) at [52].

[367] *Re Kitchin* (1881) 17 Ch. D. 668; *Bruns v Colocotronis* [1979] 2 Lloyd's Rep. 412; *Ards BC v Northern Bank Ltd* [1994] N.I. 121, CA NI; *Sabah Shipyard (Pakistan) Ltd v Pakistan* [2007] EWHC 2602 (Comm), [2008] 1 Lloyd's Rep. 210.

[368] Above, para.45-001.

[369] Insolvency Act 1986 s.267(2)(b).

[370] [2011] EWCA Civ 1286, [2012] 2 All E.R. (Comm) 265; applied in *Dunbar Assets Plc v Fowler* [2013] B.P.I.R. 46, [2013] All E.R. (D) 02 (Jan); *Agarwal v ABN AMRO Bank NN* [2017] B.P.I.R. 816 at [72]–[76].

ascertained in accordance with a contractual formula or contractual machinery which, when operated, will produce a figure."[371]

"The issue therefore in relation to guarantees is whether the liability of the guarantor can be treated as one which is reduced to a specified and agreed sum by the guarantee itself."[372]

In the court's view, this causes no difficulty where the guarantee is construed as containing a promise by the guarantor to pay the principal sum due and interest in the event of the debtor failing to pay, but where a guarantee is of the "see to it" type liability under it would not constitute a debt for a liquidated sum.[373] The Court of Appeal accepted that a guarantee can be drafted so as to create liabilities both in debt and for damages.[374] As regards the contract before the court, a clause which made the sums due under the guarantee payable on demand was to be read as a direct promise to pay the principal debtor's liabilities when they fell due and this meant that the guarantor's liabilities were for a liquidated sum.[375] While expressly obiter, the Court of Appeal considered that in its context a second clause in the contract under which the guarantor undertook "obligations ... [as] principal, not just as surety" confirmed that the "on demand clause" created a liability in debt.[376]

Guarantee and penalty clause in main contract In *Azimut-Bonetti SpA (Benetti* **45-074**
Division) v Healey[377] the question arose whether a guarantor's liability could include liability for a sum agreed as payable on breach by the principal debtor which fell foul of the common law rule against penalty clauses. Blair J. concluded (though obiter given that the relevant clause in the main contract was held not to be a penalty[378]) that while "by clear drafting a guarantor's liability may be other than co-extensive with that of the principal debtor", the standard clause in the guarantee before him by which the liability of the guarantor was not to be "impaired, diminished, discharged or released by reason or in consequence of ... the irregularity, illegality, unenforceability or invalidity in whole or in part" of the main contract made by the principal debtor was not apt to impose on the guarantor a liability for a sum irrecoverable against the principal debtor as a penalty.[379] This was so on its terms, because the invalidity of the clause in the main contract meant that there was no relevant "liability" in the principal debtor but there was a more general reason in the fact that the rule against penalties is based on public policy and "it would be contrary to principle to allow the indirect enforcement of a claim for a penalty in this manner".[380]

---

371 [2011] EWCA Civ 1286 at [36], per Patten L.J. (with whom Moses and Ward L.JJ. agreed) and see at [39].
372 [2011] EWCA Civ 1286 at [42], per Patten L.J.
373 [2011] EWCA Civ 1286 at [42]–[43].
374 [2011] EWCA Civ 1286 at [58].
375 [2011] EWCA Civ 1286 at [61].
376 [2011] EWCA Civ 1286 at [67].
377 [2010] EWHC 2234 (Comm), [2011] 1 Lloyd's Rep. 473.
378 [2010] EWHC 2234 (Comm) at [29]. On the general common law governing penalty clauses, see Vol.I, paras 26-190 et seq.
379 [2010] EWHC 2234 (Comm) at [23] and [24], per Blair J.
380 [2010] EWHC 2234 (Comm) at [24] approving *Citicorp Australia Ltd v Hendry* (1985) 4 N.S.W.L.R. 1 at 21D, CA NSW.

45-075 **Conditional guarantees**[381] A guarantee may, on its true construction, be conditional.[382] So, for example, where a person executed a guarantee on the faith of a representation that it would also be executed by another person as co-surety, the liability of the former was held to be conditional on the execution of the guarantee by the latter.[383] Similarly, if a loan is guaranteed and the loan is expressed to be secured, the guarantee may be conditional on the existence of the security. So in *Greer v Kettle* where a person guaranteed a loan which was expressed to be secured by a charge on certain shares, and the shares had not been validly issued, it was held that the surety was not liable.[384] In order to establish such a condition, the guarantor must show that the giving of some other valid security formed part of the contract of guarantee: it must have been brought home to and accepted by the lender.[385] A guarantee which shows on its face that it was intended to be a joint guarantee, executed by several parties, is not binding on a party who has properly signed it, if it transpires that the signatures of other intended guarantors have been forged, and it is immaterial that the other party is unaware of the forgery.[386] While a guarantee may also be held to be conditional on the execution of a second guarantee on identical terms contained in a different document, the fact that the documents formed part of some larger transaction is not by itself sufficient.[387] On the other hand, the Privy Council distinguished *Greer v Kettle* in *Australia & New Zealand Banking Group Ltd v Beneficial Finance Corp Ltd*[388] where a letter of guarantee contained a recital stating that the debt to be guaranteed was secured by a floating charge, and the floating charge, though in existence, was not executed for some eight months. It was held that the recital could not have been literally intended to mean that the charge had already been granted because the loan was not being provided (or the charge given) until after the letter of guarantee was signed. It was therefore sufficient that the floating charge should be in existence and available to be assigned to the guarantors, if and when they were called upon to meet their liability.

---

[381] In *Harvey v Dunbar Assets Plc* [2013] EWCA Civ 952, [2013] B.P.I.R. 722 at [21]–[22] the Court of Appeal quoted with approval the text of this paragraph up to "not by itself sufficient".

[382] English law does not recognise any wider relief in equity based on a mere expectation on the part of a guarantor that a further guarantee will be executed by a third person: *Capital Bank Cashflow Finance Ltd v Southall* [2004] EWCA Civ 817, [2004] 2 All E.R. (Comm) 675 at [16], discussing *Bleyer v NevilleJefferson Advertising Pty Ltd* Unreported 1987 NSW.

[383] *Evans v Bremridge* (1855) 25 L.J. Ch. 102, 334; but the position is otherwise if another person fails to execute a guarantee for a different liability for there would then be no right to contribution (see below, para.45-136) and the surety who has executed would not be prejudiced: *Coope v Twynham* (1823) 1 T. & R. 426. If A (a bank) requires B (the director of C Co) to provide both real security and his own personal guarantee for a loan to C Co, but executes only the guarantee, A may enforce the guarantee against B as A may waive the condition designed to protect its position: *Barclays Bank Plc v Sutton* [2015] EWHC 3192 (QB) at [21] and [26].

[384] [1938] A.C. 156.

[385] *Byblos Bank SAL v Al-Khudhairy* [1987] B.C.L.C. 232; *Gray v TCB Ltd* [1988] F.L.R. 116. cf. *Barclays Bank Plc v Quincecare* (1988) reported [1992] 4 All E.R. 363.

[386] *James Graham & Co (Timber) Ltd v Southgate Sands* [1985] 2 All E.R. 344; *Harvey v Dunbar Assets Plc* [2013] EWCA Civ 952, [2013] B.P.I.R. 722 at [23], [25]–[26], [32]–[33], [44] where the Court of Appeal emphasised that the prima facie position described in the text to which this note refers may be displaced as a matter of construction of the contract (though it was not so displaced in the terms of the contract before it).

[387] *Capital Bank Cashflow Finance Ltd v Southall* [2004] EWCA Civ 817, [2004] 2 All E.R. (Comm) 675 at [17].

[388] (1982) 44 A.L.R. 241.

Guarantees to, or for, a firm   Prima facie, a surety who engages to be answer-   **45-076**
able for a particular person is not to be understood as engaging himself to answer
for that person's partners.[389] But if in the light of the surrounding circumstances it
is evident that the surety intended to guarantee the liabilities of a person as a partner
in a firm, the mere fact that the guarantee is expressed in terms to relate only to the
one partner, will not protect the surety from liability for the firm's debts.[390] By s.18
of the Partnership Act 1890, a continuing guarantee given either to a firm, or to a
third person in respect of the transactions of a firm, is, in the absence of agreement
to the contrary, revoked as to future transactions by any change in the constitution
of the firm in question. Any change in the identity of the creditor will discharge the
surety unless the contract otherwise provides.[391]

Continuing guarantees   It is often a difficult question whether a guarantee, for   **45-077**
example, of the price of goods to be supplied, or money to be lent up to a specified
amount, is intended to extend to a single or definite number of transactions, or
whether it is intended to be continuing.[392] In the former event, payment by the
principal debtor for the goods sold, or repayment of the money lent, brings the
surety's liability to an end; in the latter event, the surety remains liable if further
goods are supplied or money lent up to the limit of the guarantee. Whether the
guarantee is continuing in any given case is a question of construction; no hard and
fast rule can be laid down, and the construction of one document affords little or
no guidance to the construction of another.[393] Each case depends entirely on the
language used, and the document must be looked at with reference to the
circumstances under which it was given.[394] A guarantee which was expressed to
cover "further advances" has been held not to extend to the situation where, on the
date for repayment, a fresh loan is arranged at an enhanced rate of interest, but no
money actually passes.[395] On the other hand, a contract of guarantee may be
construed as having been given in respect of obligations arising out of a
contemplated course of dealing rather than under a specific contract; where this is
the case:

> "provided the course of dealing remains within the scope of that contemplated by the
> guarantee, the details of the manner of dealing as between principal and creditor are no
> concern of the guarantor; and any variations in them will not affect the continuing nature
> of his liability."[396]

A typical example of this may be found in the "freestanding 'all moneys' guarantee"
in respect of present and future indebtedness commonly given by directors to banks
in respect of their company's liabilities.[397] Where the guarantee is a continuing one,
in the absence of any express provision in the contract providing for termination
of the guarantee by the giving of a prescribed period or form of notice, a guarantor

---

[389]   *Montefiore v Lloyd* (1863) 15 C.B.(N.S.) 203.
[390]   *Leathley v Spyer* (1870) L.R. 5 C.P. 595.
[391]   *First National Finance Corp Ltd v Goodman* (1983) Com. L.R. 184.
[392]   *Silverburn Finance (UK) Ltd v Salt* [2001] EWCA Civ 279, [2001] 2 All E.R. (Comm) 438.
[393]   *Coles v Pack* (1869) L.R. 5 C.P. 65, 70.
[394]   *Nottingham Hide Co v Bottrill* (1873) L.R. 8 C.P. 694.
[395]   *Burnes v Trade Credits Ltd* [1981] 1 W.L.R. 805.
[396]   *National Merchant Buying Society Ltd v Bellamy* [2013] EWCA Civ 452, [2013] 2 All E.R. (Comm)
674 at [33], per Rimer L.J. (with whom Kitchin and Longmore L.JJ. agreed).
[397]   [2013] EWCA Civ 452 at [33].

is entitled at any time to revoke the guarantees in respect of the future liabilities, but the guarantor remains responsible for any sums incurred by the principal debtor which are the subject of the guarantee up to the time of revocation.[398] Even where the guarantee is a continuing one, a further question of construction may sometimes arise which may determine the running of time for the purpose of the Limitation Act 1980. This is discussed elsewhere.[399]

45-078 **Limited guarantee** Where a guarantee, whether continuing or for a particular transaction, is given subject to a limit on the amount for which the surety may be held liable, one important question of construction often causes difficulty. This is whether the surety has guaranteed the whole liability or debt, though his own liability is for the limited amount, or whether he has guaranteed only part of the liability or debt. The distinction is important principally where the debtor or the surety becomes bankrupt. If the surety has guaranteed only part of the debt, and he pays the creditor the amount for which he is liable, then, in the event of the debtor's bankruptcy, the creditor can only prove against the bankrupt's trustee for the balance of the debt, while the surety can prove against the bankrupt's trustee for the amount he has paid.[400] Similarly, where it is the surety himself who becomes bankrupt, the creditor can only prove against his trustee for the part of the debt which he has guaranteed. On the other hand, where the surety has guaranteed the whole debt, though subject to a limit on his liability, the position is different. In this event, the creditor can prove for the whole debt against the bankrupt debtor even though the surety has paid under his guarantee, and the surety has no right of proof of his own, at least until the creditor has recovered 100 pence in the pound.[401] Similarly, if the surety is bankrupt, and has guaranteed the whole debt, the creditor can prove against his trustee for the whole amount though he cannot of course recover more than 100 pence in the pound.[402] Even where no bankruptcy is involved, the distinction may sometimes be important, for it seems that the creditor can recover judgment against the debtor for the whole debt even though the surety has paid under his guarantee, unless the guarantee is for part of the debt alone, though if the creditor recovers more than the balance remaining unpaid, he must account for the surplus to the surety.[403]

45-079 The principle of construction which has been laid down for determining, in the absence of express agreement, whether the surety has undertaken to answer for the whole debt or only a part of it, is as follows.[404] Where the surety has given a continuing guarantee, limited in amount, to secure the floating balance which may from time to time be due from the principal debtor to the creditor, the guarantee is prima facie to be construed as being of part only of the debt. This is because in such a case the creditor can increase the total debt without reference to the surety, and if the

---

[398] *Silverburn Finance (UK) Ltd v Salt* [2001] EWCA Civ 279, [2001] 2 All E.R. (Comm) 438 at [28].

[399] Vol.I, paras 28-046—28-048.

[400] *Re Sass* [1896] 2 Q.B. 12.

[401] *Re Sass* [1896] 2 Q.B. 12.

[402] *Re Houlder* [1929] 1 Ch. 205; see also *Commercial Bank of Australia Ltd v Official Assignee* [1893] A.C. 181. Similarly, if one co-surety pays part of what is due, the creditor can prove against another for the whole debt where it is the whole debt which has been guaranteed; but payment by the *debtor* of part of the debt before proof discharges the debt pro tanto and the creditor can then only prove against a surety for the balance in any event.

[403] *Ulster Bank Ltd v Lambe* [1966] N.I. 161.

[404] *Ellis v Emmanuel* (1876) 1 Ex. D. 157.

surety was to be understood as guaranteeing the whole debt his rights could be gravely prejudiced in the event of the debtor's bankruptcy. On the other hand, where the surety has given a guarantee limited in amount for a debt already ascertained which exceeds that limit, the guarantee is prima facie to be construed as a guarantee of the whole debt, though subject to the limit specified.

Variation between guarantee and transaction guaranteed Where a surety guarantees performance of a transaction subsequently to be entered into between the principal debtor and the creditor, the surety will not be liable if the transaction as entered into is different in terms from that guaranteed, and this principle is very strictly applied.405 For example, a guarantee of a loan to be repayable in instalments was held not enforceable when the loan agreement provided that the whole loan was to be repayable if default was made in the payment of one instalment.406 So also where a surety guaranteed the floating balance on a current account up to a specified amount, she was held not liable when the bank simply credited the debtor with the whole amount guaranteed instead of advancing it as and when required.407 And where the surety guaranteed repayment of a loan to be repayable in three months' time, and the loan was made so as to be immediately repayable, the surety was not liable even though repayment was not in fact sought for over three months.408 On the other hand, where a surety guaranteed a loan to be made by a bank, and in fact the loan was provided through a subsidiary of the bank with the knowledge of all parties concerned, the guarantee was held enforceable at the suit of the bank.409

45-080

Conditions precedent to liability of surety Prima facie the surety may be proceeded against without demand against him, and without first proceeding against the principal debtor.410 But the contract may, of course, lay down conditions precedent to the surety's liability. It may, for instance, provide that the creditor is first to take proceedings (civil411 or criminal412) against the debtor; it may provide that the surety is to be liable only where the debtor repudiates his obligations and the repudiation has been accepted by the creditor413; or that the surety is to be liable only after previous demand against him,414 or after notice of the debtor's default has been given.415

45-081

---

405 Cases of this nature are often treated on the same principle as cases in which there is a subsequent variation of the contract between the creditor and the principal debtor (as to which see below, paras 45-104 et seq.) but although the questions are clearly analogous, the cases here discussed concern the question whether the surety is ever bound at all, not whether the surety is discharged.

406 *Clarke v Green* (1849) 3 Ex. 619; and see *Pickles v Thornton* (1876) 33 L.T. 658.

407 *Archer v Hudson* (1844) 7 Beav. 551.

408 *Bonser v Cox* (1844) 6 Beav. 110, 117.

409 *Amalgamated Investment & Pty Co Ltd v Texas Commerce International Bank Ltd* [1982] Q.B. 84.

410 *Moschi v Lep Air Services Ltd* [1973] A.C. 331, 348; and see *DFC Financial Services Ltd v Coffey* [1991] B.C.C. 218; cf. *Esso Petroleum Co Ltd v Alstonbridge Properties Ltd* [1975] 1 W.L.R. 1474, 1483.

411 *Holl v Hadley* (1835) 2 A. & E. 758; *Lawrence v Walmsley* (1862) 12 C.B.(N.S.) 799.

412 cf. *London Guarantee Co v Fearnley* (1880) 5 App. Cas. 911 (prosecution of employee required expressly by contract of insurance against employee's dishonesty).

413 *Reliance Car Facilities Ltd v Roding Motors* [1952] 2 Q.B. 844.

414 *Re Brown's Estate* [1893] 2 Ch. 300; *Bradford Old Bank Ltd v Sutcliffe* [1918] 2 K.B. 833; *Bank of Adelaide v Lorden* (1970) 127 C.L.R. 185; *General Surety & Guarantee Co Ltd v Francis Parker Ltd* (1977) 6 Build. L.R. 18; *Duchess Theatre Co v Lord* [1993] N.P.C. 163; *Hampton v Minns* [2002]

45-082 **Estoppel by convention** Estoppel by convention may arise where the parties to a transaction have acted on the agreed assumption that a state of facts can, for the purpose of that transaction, be regarded as true, and where this is the case, the parties are precluded from denying the truth of those assumed facts if it would be unjust to allow them or only one of them to do so.[416] Estoppel by convention may apply in the context of the enforcement of contracts of guarantee.[417] For example, in *Bank of Scotland v Wright*,[418] the defendant guarantor argued that his liability did not extend to the liability of one of the two companies of which he was a director. While Brooke J. rejected this argument as a matter of construction, he considered the question whether in any event the defendant was estopped by convention from asserting that the guarantee did not extend to the liability of the second company. However, in this respect he held that one of the conditions for the application of the doctrine was not present as he was not satisfied that the defendant had behaved in any way towards the creditor which would make it unconscionable for him to deny that his guarantee covered the liability in question or to rely on the Statute of Frauds.[419] For, according to Brooke J., while estoppel by convention may apply to the enforcement of a guarantee, for the court to allow it to do so in order to extend the guarantor's liability beyond that to which it applies as a matter of construction, "would deprive the Statute of Frauds of much of its effectiveness".[420]

5. DISCHARGE OF DEBTOR

45-083 **General** No special rules apply to the discharge of a debtor whose debt is guaranteed where this results either from payment of the debt or release by deed. As to the effect of part payment of the debt by the debtor or an agreement to accept part payment of a debt, reference should be made to the relevant passages of Vol.I.[421]

45-084 **Discharge of debtor by payment by surety** Where a surety enters the contract at the request of the principal debtor, it is clear that payment of the debt by the surety

---

1 W.L.R. 1. Where the surety's obligation is primary rather than secondary (as with a true guarantee), a requirement of payment on demand will not import a contingency, so that the cause of action accrues when the debt falls due rather than only on demand, but this does not apply where payment is promised within a period after demand: *Re Brown's Estate* [1893] 2 Ch. 300; *M & S Fashions Ltd v Bank of Credit and Commerce International SA* [1993] Ch. 425, 435–436, 447; *Levin v Tannenbaum* [2013] EWHC 4457 (Ch) at [25]–[37].

[415] cf. *United Dominions Trust (Commercial) Ltd v Eagle Aircraft Services Ltd* [1968] 1 W.L.R. 74. See also *Bache & Co (London) Ltd v Banque Vernes et Commerciales de Paris* [1973] 2 Lloyd's Rep. 437 (notice of default conclusive evidence of guarantor's liability).

[416] See generally, Vol.I, paras 4-108—4-115.

[417] *Amalgamated Investment & Property Co Ltd v Texas Commerce International Bank Ltd* [1982] Q.B. 84; *Bank of Scotland v Wright* [1990] B.C.C. 663; *Actionstrength Ltd v International Glass Engineering INGLEN SpA* [2003] UKHL 17, [2003] 2 A.C. 541 and see above, para.45-060.

[418] *Bank of Scotland v Wright* [1990] B.C.C. 663. See similarly *Ing Lease (UK) Ltd v Harwood* [2008] EWCA Civ 786, [2009] 1 All E.R. (Comm) 1055 where such a common understanding was held not established on the facts.

[419] [1990] B.C.C. 663 at 679 and 681.

[420] [1990] B.C.C. 663 at 680. And see similarly *Actionstrength Ltd v International Glass Engineering INGLEN SpA* [2003] UKHL 17, [2003] 2 A.C. 541 on estoppel and the Statute of Frauds more generally, see above, para.45-060.

[421] See paras 4-117 et seq.

discharges that debt as between the creditor and principal debtor.[422] Indeed, "[a] creditor cannot sue the principal debtor for an amount of the debt which the creditor has already received from a guarantor".[423] In *Milverton Group Ltd v Warner World Ltd*,[424] the Court of Appeal held that part payment of a debt by a surety would discharge the principal debtor by the amount of the payment. That case concerned the liabilities of an original tenant under a lease whose assignees' sureties had paid monies to the landlord's assignee in consideration of their release by deed. The landlord's assignee argued that these payments did not affect the original tenant's liability to pay rent under the lease: but the Court of Appeal rejected this argument. According to Hoffmann L.J.:

"... for the purpose of deciding whether money owed by more than one person has been paid, I do not think that it is possible for the creditor and one of the debtors to characterise a payment in return for a release as anything other than a part performance of the obligation. If this were possible, a creditor could pick off his debtors one by one and recover in total more than the whole debt. For the payment to count as part discharge of the common obligation, it is sufficient for the payment to be referable to the guarantee."[425]

6. DISCHARGE OF SURETY

(a) Discharge of Surety by Payment or Set-off

General Clearly, payment by a surety of amounts owed under the guarantee discharges the surety either wholly or pro tanto. More difficult, however, is the question whether on the insolvency of the creditor a surety may set-off sums owed to it by the creditor against its liability on the guarantee. Where the creditor's claim against the surety has already accrued at the date of the insolvency, then the surety is entitled to set-off against it any claim against the insolvent's estate.[426] Moreover, where a guarantee is expressed so that the liability of the surety is immediate as opposed, for example, to being contingent on a demand by the creditor, then the surety may also set-off its own claim against the creditor.[427] In the case of companies it is now provided that this rule also applies to a case where the contingency accrues due after the date of the commencement of the insolvency; under the revised rule:

45-085

---

[422] More controversial is the question whether payment of the debt by an *unrequested* surety discharges the debt as between the creditor and principal debtor, this question being linked to the question of recovery of an indemnity by that surety against the principal debtor: see Birks and Beatson (1976) 92 L.Q.R. 188; Friedmann (1983) 99 L.Q.R. 534; Burrows, *The Law of Restitution*, 3rd edn (2010), pp.460–468. On the question of restitutionary recovery, see below, para.45-127.

[423] *M & S Fashions Ltd v Bank of Credit and Commerce International SA (In Liquidation)* [1993] 3 W.L.R. 220, 239, per Dillon L.J.

[424] [1995] 2 E.G.L.R. 28.

[425] [1995] 2 E.G.L.R. 28 at 31.

[426] Insolvency Act 1986 s.323 (individuals); Insolvency (England and Wales) Rules (SI 2016/1024) rr.14.25 and 14.26 (in force April 6, 2017) replacing Insolvency Rules 1986 (SI 1986/1925) r.4.90 (companies). See *Stein v Blake* [1996] 1 A.C. 243; *Re Bank of Credit and Commerce International SA (No.8)* [1998] A.C. 214.

[427] *M & S Fashions Ltd v Bank of Credit and Commerce International SA* [1993] Ch. 425 (in relation to the Insolvency Rules 1986 r.4.90). cf. *Re Bank of Credit and Commerce International SA (No.8)* [1998] A.C. 214 at 224–225 (referring to the contract in *M & S Fashions* as "a very unusual document").

"… debts owed to the company that are contingent or payable at a future time are to be included in the set-off account, and liquidators and administrators will be able to put a value on such debts."[428]

(b) Discharge of Surety through Discharge of Principal Debtor

45-086 **Discharge of principal debtor by performance** If the contract is one of guarantee, then performance by the principal debtor which discharges him will necessarily also discharge the guarantor. So, for instance, where the surety guaranteed the due performance by the debtor of his obligations under a hire-purchase agreement, and the hirer terminated the agreement in accordance with its terms and paid the full amounts due under the agreement, the surety was held to be discharged, even though the hire-purchase company did not receive the full amounts it might have expected to receive had the agreement run its full course.[429] So also, partial performance by the debtor (e.g. part payment of the debt guaranteed) will discharge the surety pro tanto.[430] On the other hand, if the contract on its true construction is a contract of indemnity under which the surety assumes a greater liability than the principal debtor,[431] he will not necessarily be discharged merely because the debtor is discharged. So in another hire-purchase case where the surety agreed to indemnify the hire-purchase company against any loss which it might suffer from premature termination of the agreement, it was held that the surety was liable despite the discharge of the hirer.[432]

45-087 **Set-off by principal debtor to be enjoyed by surety** The general rule is that on being sued by the creditor for payment of the debt guaranteed, a surety may avail himself of any right to set-off or counterclaim which the principal debtor possesses against the creditor.[433] However, parties to a contract of suretyship may contract out of this general rule either expressly or impliedly, the contract requiring to be interpreted in its factual matrix.[434] A number of factors have been discerned by the courts in determining whether the parties have intended that the surety should be liable to the creditor "whatever the state of play" between the creditor and the principal debtor:

"… the inclusion in the guarantees of a conditional agreement to pay; the accruing of the guarantors' liability to pay at a time when the principal debtors did not yet have any arguable right of set-off (because the default preceded the termination of the [principal]

---

[428] Sealy & Milman, *Annotated Guide to Insolvency Legislation* 2017, Vol.I, r.14.25 note; Insolvency (England and Wales) Rules 2016 r.14.24(5) and 14.25(5). On the position in personal insolvency under s.323 of the Insolvency Act 1986 see *Muir Hunter on Personal Insolvency* (2018) para.3-2101.

[429] *Western Credit Ltd v Alberry* [1964] 1 W.L.R. 945.

[430] *Perry v National Provincial Bank* [1910] 1 Ch. 464.

[431] See above, paras 45-007—45-008.

[432] *Goulston Discount Co Ltd v Clark* [1967] 2 Q.B. 493; cf. *Bentworth Finance Ltd v Lubert* [1968] 1 Q.B. 680. Contrast Consumer Credit Act 1974 s.113 on which see above, para.39-190.

[433] *Hyundai Shipbuilding and Heavy Industries Co Ltd v Pournaras* [1978] 2 Lloyd's Rep. 502, 508; *BOC Group Plc v Centeon LLC* [1999] 1 All E.R. (Comm) 53; *Lombard North Central Plc v Nugent* [2013] EWHC 1588 (QB) at [90].

[434] *Hyundai Shipbuilding and Heavy Industries Co Ltd v Pournaras* [1978] 2 Lloyd's Rep. 502, 506 and 508; *BOC Group Plc v Centeon LLC* [1999] 1 All E.R. (Comm) 53, 64 and see above, paras 45-064—45-068.

contracts); the guarantors' obligation to pay 'forthwith'; and the overall context (factual matrix) of the contractual arrangements."[435]

Rules of appropriation not affected   Difficulty sometimes arises in deciding whether a performance by the debtor discharges him in respect of the guaranteed liability or in respect of a separate obligation which is not subject to the guarantee. If, for example, the debtor owes two distinct debts to the creditor, only one of which is guaranteed by the surety, and the debtor pays part of the money to the creditor, the question may arise as to which debt is discharged. In these circumstances the general rule is that the contract of suretyship does not affect the normal rights which the debtor and the creditor have of appropriating the payment to a particular debt.[436] Thus if the debtor pays without making any appropriation the creditor is entitled to appropriate the money to the debt which is not guaranteed.[437] Where, however, the surety guarantees a running account the rule in *Clayton*'s case[438] normally applies so that payments in must normally be treated as discharging the earliest debits.[439] But where a surety guaranteed a running account with a bank and the account was closed, and a new one opened which was not guaranteed, it was held that the bank was entitled to appropriate payments to the new account as the debtor had not appropriated them to the current account.[440]

45-088

Discharge other than by performance   If the debtor is discharged not so much because the agreement is fully performed, but rather because, in point of law, he is not liable to the creditor under his agreement in the events which have happened, as, e.g. where a bailee is discharged because the goods are stolen from him without any negligence on his part, a guarantor will also be discharged.[441] Here again, there could, of course, be a liability on the part of the surety if he were made answerable for loss of the goods by any means, and not merely for default by the bailee in his obligations, i.e. if the contract were an indemnity and not a guarantee.

45-089

Discharge of debtor must be effective   In order to discharge a surety, payment by the debtor must be an effective discharge for him. So where, after making such a payment, the debtor became bankrupt and the payment was avoided as a fraudulent preference, the surety was not discharged.[442] Hence, where it is sought to challenge a payment as a fraudulent preference, a surety for that payment should be joined as a party.[443]

45-090

Discharge of debtor by agreement with creditor   The traditional approach to the question whether an agreement by a creditor not to enforce his right against his debtor has the effect of discharging a surety has been to distinguish between cases of a binding release of the debtor and cases in which the creditor merely agrees not to sue the debtor.

45-091

---

[435] *BOC Group Plc v Centeon LLC* [1999] 1 All E.R. (Comm) 53, per Rix J.
[436] See Vol.I, paras 21-061 et seq.
[437] *Re Sherry* (1884) 25 Ch. D. 692.
[438] (1816) 1 Mer. 529.
[439] *Re Sherry* (1884) 25 Ch. D. 692.
[440] *Re Sherry* (1884) 25 Ch. D. 692.
[441] *Walker v British Guarantee Association* (1852) 18 Q.B. 277.
[442] *Petty v Cooke* (1871) L.R. 6 Q.B. 790.
[443] *Re Idenden* [1970] 1 W.L.R. 1015.

45-092 **Release of debtor** According to this traditional approach, the release of the principal debtor discharges the surety,[444] a rule which reflects the more general effect of release of one of two or more joint (or joint and several) debtors on his co-debtors.[445] There are two reasons which may be advanced to support the argument that this general approach should be applied to the suretyship context. First, there is a logical argument, linked to the co-extensiveness principle[446]: for if the principal debtor is discharged, then so should the surety whose liability is secondary to the principal debtor. Secondly, it may be argued that any other rule would lead to one or other of two strange results, having regard to the surety's normal right to an indemnity from the debtor.[447] If the surety were compelled to meet the liability, any attempt by him to sue the debtor for an indemnity might be met by the defence that the debt had gone and that the debtor was no longer liable. But if this were a defence, the surety would be deprived by the act of the creditor of a right which he would have expected to have.[448] On the other hand, if the debtor remained liable to indemnify the surety despite his own discharge, the effect would be to render the discharge largely nugatory.[449] Sometimes this is put another way, so that it is said that to release the principal debtor without releasing the surety would deprive the latter of his right to pay off the creditor and sue the principal in the creditor's name by way of subrogation.[450] However, there are three qualifications to this general rule of discharge of the surety on release of the principal debtor. First, it does not apply where the original contract of suretyship itself provides for the preservation of the surety's liability[451]; secondly, where there is a reservation of the creditor's rights against the surety at the time of discharging the debtor[452] and, thirdly, where the surety agrees to the continuation of his liability with the creditor before the release of the debtor by the creditor.[453] In at least some of these circumstances, some of the arguments in favour of discharge of the surety no longer hold good. As to the "logical argument", it may be countered that where a contract of suretyship contains a clause preserving the surety's liability on release of the debtor, it may no longer count as an "ordinary contract of suretyship", but it may nonetheless take effect on its terms.[454] Where the agreement of release provides for the preservation of the surety's liabilities, then the principal debtor is on notice of the possible and eventual recourse of the surety against him.[455] As to the preservation of the surety's liability

---

[444] *Commercial Bank of Tasmania v Jones* [1893] A.C. 313. This rule does not apply to an "on-demand guarantee", where questions whether the debtor is liable under the underlying contract are irrelevant: see *Meritz Fire & Marine Insurance Co Ltd v Jan de Nul NV* [2011] EWCA Civ 827 [2011] 2 Lloyd's Rep. 379 at [27] and above, para.45-009.

[445] See Vol.I, paras 17-017 et seq.

[446] See above, para.45-070.

[447] See below, para.45-126.

[448] cf. *Polak v Everett* (1876) 1 Q.B.D. 669, 673–674 (in the context of giving the principal debtor time).

[449] *Oriental Financial Corp v Overend, Gurney & Co* [1871] 7 Ch. App. 142, 150.

[450] *Mahant Singh v U Ba Yi* [1939] A.C. 601, 606, per Lord Porter.

[451] *Cowper v Smith* (1838) 4 M. & W. 519; *Perry v National Provincial Bank* [1910] 1 Ch. 464.

[452] *Kearsley v Cole* (1846) 16 M. & W. 128, 135; *Bateson v Gosling* (1871) L.R. 7 C.P. 9; *Cole v Lynn* [1942] 1 K.B. 142; *Greene King Plc v Stanley* [2001] EWCA Civ 1966, [2001] B.P.I.R. 491 at [67], [74] and [81] (where the proposition in the text was expressly approved).

[453] *Davidson v McGregor* (1841) 8 M. & W. 755.

[454] *Perry v National Provincial Bank* [1910] 1 Ch. 464, especially at 471 and 476.

[455] *Kearsley v Cole* (1846) 16 M. & W. 128, 135, per Parke B.

in the contract of suretyship, this can be supported simply on the basis of the need to preserve the binding force of contracts.[456]

Agreement not to sue By contrast, the effect of a mere agreement by a creditor **45-093** not to sue the debtor as regards discharge of the surety (in the absence of any reservation of rights by the creditor) is less clear. For while the established rule as regards the case of an agreement not to sue an ordinary joint (or joint and several debtor) is that it does not discharge the other debtors,[457] in view of the well-settled rule that a binding agreement to give time to the debtor will discharge a surety, it may be thought anomalous if an agreement not to sue at all were not to have the same effect.[458] What is clear, though, is that where an agreement not to sue a principal debtor provides that the surety's liability will be preserved, then the surety will not be discharged.[459] Indeed, for some courts, the presence of such a provision is inconsistent with the interpretation of the contract as one of release[460] and has therefore encouraged them to interpret the words of release as a promise not to sue.[461]

Release with implied reservation However, the force of this traditional distinc- **45-094** tion between agreements to release and agreements not to sue a debtor has itself been challenged by the Court of Appeal in two more recent decisions and while these cases both concerned the position of co-debtors, the approach of the judges in them may apply also to the context of suretyship. In *Watts v Aldington, Tolstoy v Aldington* A had gained judgment for £1.5 million plus costs against W and T in respect of libels made against him.[462] T was adjudicated bankrupt on his own application, whereas W was adjudicated bankrupt on A's petition. Subsequently, A agreed with W (with whom he had four outstanding proceedings) to accept £10,000 from W's family "in full and final settlement of judgment and orders and any liability however arising" (cl.6) and in return for not opposing W's appeal from his bankruptcy order. W also made various undertakings not to repeat the libels made about A. A and W's contract further stipulated (by cl.9) that breach of any term by W would give rise to a right in A "to treat the contract as at an end and to proceed for the full entirety under those judgments as though the agreement had never been entered into". The question arose whether this contract discharged T from his liabilities to A under the judgment debt. At first instance, Morritt J. construed A's promise under the contract as one not to sue W rather than one to release him, principally on the basis that, as cl.9 made clear, its terms were conditional on performance by W of his side of the bargain: this meant that T was not discharged by A's agreement with W. While the Court of Appeal ultimately affirmed this result, all its members (Neill, Steyn and Simon Brown L.JJ.) disapproved the approach

---

[456] *Perry v National Provincial Bank* [1910] 1 Ch. 464, especially at 476.
[457] See Vol.I, para.17-017.
[458] *Bailey v Edwards* (1864) 4 B. & S. 761, 771 where Blackburn J. based the rule discharging a surety on the giving of time to the debtor by the creditor on the fact that otherwise surety would be prevented from exercising his right to call upon the creditor to enforce the debt in equity, even though this right was termed by him "of very little practical value, and is seldom, if ever, exercised". See further, below, para.45-107.
[459] *Bateson v Gosling* (1871) L.R. 7 C.P. 9.
[460] *Commercial Bank of Tasmania v Jones* [1893] A.C. 313.
[461] e.g. *Solley v Forbes* (1820) 2 Br. & B. 38; *Duck v Mayeu* [1892] 2 Q.B. 511.
[462] [1999] L. & T.R. 578.

taken by Morritt J., even though they saw that it enjoyed support in the authorities. For Simon Brown L.J., the difficulty of applying to the contract before the court the distinction between agreements to release and not to sue illustrated "the technicality and intrinsic artificiality of the conventional approach to this rule"[463] as to discharge of co-debtors. In the leading judgment, Neill L.J. described how historically the purpose of this distinction was to carve out an exception to the established rule that release of one joint tortfeasor released them all,[464] which was founded on the unity of the cause of action against them, but he noted how this rule, while still formally valid, had itself been much qualified.[465] Given these changes, Neill L.J. considered that "it will often be more satisfactory to consider whether the relevant document is an absolute release or a release with a reservation rather than to consider whether the document can be fitted into the strait jacket of a covenant or agreement not to sue".[466] Moreover, for the Court of Appeal, this question should be resolved by construing the contract as a whole in its factual matrix and implying any terms in it which were necessary.[467] According to Neill L.J.:

> "In the cases there is much emphasis on an express reservation of rights. But there is apparently no authority holding that an implied reservation is insufficient. That is not surprising because a rule that an implied term, complying with the stringent tests applicable to the implication of terms, cannot render the same service as an express term in this corner of the law would be a curiosity."[468]

On the facts before it, the Court of Appeal held that there was clearly an implied reservation by A of his rights against T.

45-095 In *Johnson v Davies*[469] a differently constituted Court of Appeal[470] adopted the approach taken in *Watts v Aldington, Tolstoy v Aldington*[471] and extended it so as to apply to a joint (but not joint and several) debt.[472] In *Johnson v Davies* the plaintiffs were sureties for the debts of a company, the majority of whose shares they owned and which was a tenant under a lease. Under a contract of sale of its shares to the defendants and one Hopkins ("H"), the purchasers agreed, inter alia, to indemnify the plaintiffs against claims brought under the lease. Subsequently, H entered an individual voluntary arrangement with his creditors under Pt VIII of the Insolvency Act 1986, under which he was to pay to the supervisor 75 per cent of his net income for five years and any "windfall" assets he may receive within that period. The arrangement further provided that when all moneys to be made available had been distributed to the creditors, he would be released. The plaintiffs were given notice of the creditors' meeting (as required by statute) and were therefore deemed parties to the arrangement following the provisions of the 1986 Act. Later,

---

[463] [1999] L. & T.R. 578 at 598.

[464] [1999] L. & T.R. 578 at 589; *Clayton v Kynaston* (1701) 2 Salk. 573.

[465] Notably, by s.6(1) of the Law Reform (Married Women and Tortfeasors) Act 1935, re-enacted by s.3 of the Civil Liability (Contribution) Act 1978.

[466] [1999] L. & T.R. 578, 590.

[467] cf. above, paras 45-064 et seq.

[468] [1999] L. & T.R. 578 at 595.

[469] [1999] Ch. 117.

[470] Chadwick, Ward and Kennedy L.JJ.

[471] See above, para.45-094.

[472] [1999] Ch. 117, 127. See also *Sun Life Assurance Society Plc v Tantofex (Engineers) Ltd* [1999] L. & T.R. 568; *Chelsea Building Society v Nash* [2010] EWCA Civ 1247, [2011] B.P.I.R. 381 at [33]–[38].

they were required to pay as sureties for the company under its lease and so claimed to be indemnified for these sums by the defendants, but the defendants countered that they had been released from their obligations under the sale by the release of their co-debtor, H, by the voluntary arrangement. On the facts, the court found that the contract did not on its express or implied terms intend to discharge all the co-debtors on the (conditional) release of one of their number under a "voluntary arrangement".[473] Indeed, while it was necessary to imply a term in the contract that the creditors bound by the proposals would take no steps to enforce their debts against the debtor while the debtor complied with his obligations under it, it was not necessary, even if it would be a "convenient and tidy result" that the creditors should take no steps to enforce their debts against any co-debtors.[474] The Court of Appeal has held that the burden of proof as to implied reservation of rights by creditor against co-debtor is on the creditor.[475]

Application to surety   *Johnson v Davies* concerned the case of an agreement by   **45-096**
a creditor and one of several jointly liable persons: it is to be noted that while H and the defendants in that case were liable under a contract of indemnity, this was not a contract of indemnity in the sense of a contract which, while imposing a primary liability on a debtor vis-à-vis the creditor, created a relationship of surety-ship with some other person.[476] *Johnson v Davies* is not, therefore, direct authority for the proposition that the question whether an agreement between a creditor and a *principal debtor* as to the latter's future obligations (whether put in terms of "release" or "agreement to sue") will operate to discharge a *surety*, whether the suretyship is a contract of guarantee or one of indemnity. However, it is submitted that the same approach as was taken by the Court of Appeal in that case should be extended to these particular examples of joint obligation, with the result that the question of discharge of the surety would be determined as a matter of the construction of the agreement between the creditor and principal debtor and that, following ordinary principles, this should take into account any implied as well as any express terms. This approach was approved by Richards J. in *Finley v Connell Associates (Application to Strike Out)* in the context of considering the effect on a surety of an agreement between the creditor and principal debtor which was expressed as an agreement not to sue the principal debtor.[477] The learned judge noted that the traditional distinction between releases and covenants not to sue had been criticised by the Court of Appeal in the context of joint debtors in *Watts v Aldington*,[478] in particular on the basis that the traditional approach emphasised the significance of an express reservation of rights in order to retain the liability of a joint debtor, whereas such a reservation may, in accordance with the general legal position, be implied. Richards J. observed:

> "The authorities on sureties often refer in general terms to the distinction between an agreement whereby the creditor releases the debtor (which also discharges the surety) and an agreement whereby the creditor covenants not to sue the debtor (which does not

---

[473] See below, para.45-098 on the status of a "voluntary arrangement" for these purposes.
[474] [1999] Ch. 117, 128.
[475] *Chelsea Building Society v Nash* [2010] EWCA Civ 1247, [2011] B.P.I.R. 381 at [38].
[476] See above, paras 45-002 et seq. See further Andrews and Millett, *The Law of Guarantees*, 7th edn (2015), para.9-011.
[477] [1999] Lloyd's Rep. P.N. 895, *The Times*, June 23, 1999.
[478] [1999] L. & T.R. 578 and see above, para.45-094.

discharge the surety). But it does appear that … the existence of a reservation of rights against the surety is an essential ingredient in the categorisation of an agreement not to sue. The mere use of the language of a covenant not to sue is not decisive."[479]

In his view, moreover, there is no reason why a reservation of rights against a surety should not be implied as well as express: "the reasoning in [*Watts v Aldington* is] compelling and [it is] right to follow it even if it is not strictly binding in relation to the effect of an agreement on sureties".[480]

45-097   If this approach were more generally followed, then, as under the traditional approach, effect would be given to an express reservation of rights against the surety by the creditor, but the absence of such a reservation would not be taken necessarily to imply an intention that the surety should be discharged: a court could hold a principal debtor released, but the surety's liability and right of indemnity against the principal debtor would be preserved. For in answer to the concern that such a construction of the contract would impose a liability on the principal debtor after his release, it may be countered that it would substitute a possible claim by the surety for a claim by the creditor. While this is an unlikely construction in the context of suretyship, it is by no means impossible: to adapt Chadwick L.J.'s words in *Johnson v Davies*, to give a principal debtor a complete protection against all claimants may be a "convenient and tidy result" but may not be a necessary implication of the agreement between the creditor and principal.[481] A possible remaining difficulty with such an approach might be seen to lie in the disharmony created with the rule according to which an agreement to give time to the principal debtor discharges the surety, but this disharmony is only apparent for the latter rule does not apply where the creditor reserves his rights against the surety by notifying the debtor when time is given to him.[482]

45-098   **Discharge of debtor by bankruptcy**   It is expressly provided by s.281(7) of the Insolvency Act 1986, which substantially re-enacted the earlier law,[483] that: "[d]ischarge does not release any person … from any liability as surety for the bankrupt or as a person in the nature of such a surety". But a surety who guarantees the payment of interest on a principal sum so long as it remains due, is not liable to the creditor in respect of interest which would have accrued if the debtor had not become bankrupt and been discharged,[484] as the principal is no longer due.[485] The question of the effect on a co-debtor of a "voluntary arrangement" made between a debtor and his creditors under Pt VIII of the Insolvency Act 1986 was considered by the Court of Appeal in *Johnson v Davies*.[486] There, as has been seen,[487] creditors had entered an "individual voluntary arrangement" under Pt VIII of the Insolvency Act 1986 with H, one of their joint debtors, under which he was to pay to the supervisor 75 per cent of his net income for five years and any "windfall" as-

---

[479] [1999] Lloyd's Rep. P.N. 895, 906–907.
[480] [1999] Lloyd's Rep. P.N. 895, 906–907.
[481] [1999] Ch. 117, 128.
[482] See below, para.45-114.
[483] Insolvency Act 1986 s.281(7) (which since 2016 has moved to Pt IX Ch.1A of the Act), itself replacing Bankruptcy Act 1914 s.28(4).
[484] *Re Moss* [1905] 2 K.B. 307.
[485] See Insolvency Act 1986 s.281(1).
[486] [1999] Ch. 117; cf. *IRC v Adam & Partners* [1999] 2 B.C.L.C. 730, 737 (corporate insolvency).
[487] See above, para.45-095.

sets he may receive within that period and according to which when all moneys to be made available had been distributed to the creditors, he would be released. The creditors were given notice of the creditors' meeting (as required by statute) and were therefore deemed parties to the arrangement following the provisions of the 1986 Act. Later, when the creditors made claims against the joint debtors other than H, those joint debtors countered that they had been released from their obligations by the release of H, their co-debtor, by the voluntary arrangement. The Court of Appeal was able to dispose of this argument and hold for the creditors on the ground that the agreement before them did not on its terms intend to discharge the co-debtors,[488] but Chadwick L.J. (with whom Ward and Kennedy L.JJ. agreed) went on to consider whether, as had been argued, a debtor's voluntary arrangement with his creditors under the 1986 Act necessarily discharges his co-debtors.[489] In this respect, he noted that s.260(2)(b) of the Insolvency Act 1986 provides that such voluntary arrangements:

"... bind every person who in accordance with the rules had notice of, and was entitled to vote at, the meeting ... as if he were a party to the arrangement",

but that, unlike the Bankruptcy Act 1914, the 1986 Act makes no express provision for the effect of these arrangements on sureties.[490] In Chadwick L.J.'s view, the legislature's failure to adopt the earlier statutory precedents gave rise to a strong inference of its deliberate decision that voluntary arrangements should take effect in the same way as did consensual deeds.[491] Finally, the 1986 Act's provision that a voluntary arrangement "binds every person ... as if he were a party" to it requires the creditor to be treated as if he had consented to the arrangement and so a voluntary arrangement made under the Act does not discharge a co-debtor or surety unless it is to be so construed on its terms, express or implied.[492] This consensual nature of individual voluntary arrangements suggests that the rule according to which they discharge the surety attracts the same qualifications as apply to voluntary deeds of release and this has been held to be the case as regards the position where an individual voluntary arrangement is agreed on the basis that a creditor reserves his rights against the surety.[493] Moreover, such a reservation may be made clear to the principal debtor in all the circumstances, including the dealings of the parties before the arrangement is made, and need not be included as a term of the arrange-

---

488 [1999] Ch. 117 at 124–129.
489 [1999] Ch. 117 at 129 et seq. and see *Prudential Assurance Co Ltd v PRG Powerhouse Ltd* [2007] EWHC 1002 (Ch), [2007] Bus. L.R. 1771.
490 [1999] Ch.117 at 129–130. (The wording of s.260(2) of the 1986 Act has been amended, but without relevant substantive change.)
491 [1999] Ch. 117 at 131. Chadwick L.J. considered that *Megrath v Gray, Gray v Megrath* (1874) L.R. 9 C.P. 216; *Ellis v Wilmot* (1874) L.R. 10 Ex. 10; *Ex p. Jacobs* (1875) 10 Ch. App. 211 which held that arrangements between debtors and creditors made under the Bankruptcy Act 1869 by their nature discharged a surety were inapplicable to voluntary arrangements under the Insolvency Act 1986 because under the latter the discharge of the debtor depends entirely on the terms of the arrangement rather than by operation of law (as under the 1869 Act): [1999] Ch. 117, 137–138. The Court of Appeal therefore disapproved the views of Jacobs J. expressed in the case below at [1997] 1 All E.R. 921, 927; and in *RA Securities Ltd v Mercantile Credit Co Ltd* [1995] 3 All E.R. 581, 586–587.
492 [1999] Ch. 117, 137–138.
493 *Greene King Plc v Stanley* [2001] EWCA Civ 1966, [2002] B.P.I.R. 491 at [82]; *Koutrouzas v Lombard Natwest Factors Ltd* [2002] EWHC 1084 (QB).

ment itself.[494]

45-099 **Discharge of debtor through creditor's breach of contract** Where a person guarantees payment of a sum due from the debtor under an entire contract and the creditor cannot sue the debtor because there has been no complete performance,[495] the surety is also not liable.[496] Similarly, if the creditor is guilty of a breach of contract as against the debtor, and as a result the debtor is discharged, a guarantor cannot be liable any more than the debtor.[497] While, therefore, a repudiatory breach of contract by the creditor once accepted by the debtor discharges both the latter and the guarantor, a non-repudiatory breach will not discharge the guarantor, unless it involves a "not unsubstantial" departure from a term of the principal contract which has been itself "embodied" into the guarantee.[498] If such a departure is established, then discharge occurs on the ground of variation of the surety's obligations.[499] If there is a breach of contract by the creditor which does not discharge the debtor but gives him a right to counterclaim for damages, the surety may be able to avail himself of this right by way of set-off, but he can normally only do this if the principal debtor is joined as a party to the proceedings.[500] Similarly, if the debtor has some other valid defence to a claim by the creditor, for example, that the creditor has already elected to exercise a remedy inconsistent with a claim for damages[501] or that the sum claimed is a penalty,[502] or that the creditor has failed to mitigate the damage resulting from the debtor's breach of contract,[503] a guarantor can take advantage of the defence available to the debtor. But in all these cases the position is different where the contract is one of indemnity and not guarantee. If, on the true construction of the contract, the surety has undertaken to pay a given

---

[494] *Greene King Plc v Stanley* [2001] EWCA Civ 1966, [2002] B.P.I.R. 491 at [83].

[495] See Vol.I, paras 21-028 et seq.

[496] *Eshelby v Federated European Bank Ltd* [1932] 1 K.B. 423, 431. See also *Blest v Brown* (1862) 4 De G.F. & J. 367.

[497] *Watts v Shuttleworth* (1861) 7 H. & N. 353.

[498] *National Westminster Bank Plc v Riley* [1986] B.C.L.C. 268, 275-276, explaining *Vavasseur Trust Co Ltd v Ashmore* Unreported 1976; *Spliethoff's Bevrachtingskantoor BV v Bank of China Ltd* [2015] EWHC 999 (Comm), [2015] 2 Lloyd's Rep. 123 at [183]–[199].

[499] *National Westminster Bank Plc v Riley* [1986] B.C.L.C. 268, 275–276 (referring to *Holme v Brunskill* (1878) 3 Q.B.D. 495 (on which see below, para.45-104), cf. *Spliethoff's Bevrachtingskantoor BV v Bank of China Ltd* [2015] EWHC 999 (Comm), [2015] 2 Lloyd's Rep. 123 at [185]–[186], which distinguished between discharge of the guarantor on the ground of not unsubstantial non-repudiatory breach by the creditor and on the ground of variation by reference to *Wardens and Commonality of the Mystery of the Mercers of the City of London v New Hampshire Insurance Co* [1992] 2 Lloyd's Rep. 365 (though the contract there was held not to be a guarantee at least in the ordinary sense (at 369, 371, 374 and 375) and the distinction between discharge by variation and discharge by breach by the creditor reflected a concession by counsel (at 367)).

[500] *Bechervaise v Lewis* (1872) L.R. C.P. 372; but cf. *Trafalgar House Construction (Regions) Ltd v General Surety & Guarantee Co Ltd* [1996] 1 A.C. 199; *Wilson v Mitchell* [1939] 2 K.B. 869. There is an exhaustive discussion of this question in *Cellulose Products Pty Ltd v Truda* (1971) 92 W.N. (N.S.W.) 561; and see *Indrisie v General Credits Ltd* (1985) V.R. 251 in which the Supreme Court of Victoria held that a surety cannot take advantage of any equitable right of set-off which the principal debtor may have against the creditor. cf. *Ashley Guarantee Plc v Zacaria* [1993] 1 W.L.R. 62 (equitable set-off not a ground for refusing creditor's right to possession as mortgagee).

[501] *Hewison v Ricketts* (1894) 63 L.J. Q.B. 711. But contrast *Hyundai Heavy Industries Co Ltd v Papadopoulos* [1980] 1 W.L.R. 1129, see below, para.45-101.

[502] *Cellulose Products Pty Ltd v Truda*, above, at 565. *Sterling Industrial Facilities Ltd v Lydiate Textiles Ltd* (1962) 106 S.J. 669 is inconclusive on this point.

[503] cf. *Scottish Midland Guarantee Trust v Wooley* (1964) 114 L.J. 272.

sum on a given event, then he is liable to pay it on that event, and it is immaterial that the principal debtor could not be sued for it by the creditor.[504]

Discharge of debtor through debtor's breach of contract   Where the debtor **45-100** himself is guilty of a breach of contract in consequence of which the creditor elects to treat the contract as discharged, the possibility of the surety being discharged gives rise to considerable difficulty. It must first be seen whether the surety has guaranteed complete performance of the contract by the principal debtor. Prima facie the surety is treated as guaranteeing that the debtor will perform his contract; consequently, if the debtor is in breach so that the creditor exercises his rights to cancel the whole contract the debtor's liability is transmuted into a liability for damages, but the surety remains liable for the performance of that duty, as he is liable for the performance of the original duty.[505] As has been observed,

"A repudiatory breach [by the debtor] will in the normal course of events lead to the termination of the repudiated contract (although of course it may not do so). It would be extraordinary if a performance guarantee was intended to cease to operate in exactly the situation in which its beneficiary most needs it—when the contract has failed because the principal has repudiated it."[506]

It is possible, though, that the surety may be held to have guaranteed only the debtor's primary obligations under the contract and not his secondary obligation (to pay damages) in the event of breach; in this event it seems that the surety would remain liable for his accrued liability in respect of the primary obligations.[507]

Guarantees of payment by instalments   More problems arise with contracts **45-101** involving payment in instalments, where payment is guaranteed by the surety. The creditor's right to claim payment of instalments, whether from the debtor or the surety, prima facie arises only where the events specified in the contract have occurred; thus; where the contract is prematurely terminated (whether for breach or any other reason) the debtor may never become liable for instalments thereafter due. In this event, the surety cannot be liable either. But the position is different as regards instalments which have accrued due. So where instalments under a shipbuilding contract have accrued due, the fact (if it is a fact) that the buyer's obligation to pay the instalments has been replaced by a general claim for damages as a result of the shipbuilder's exercise of his right to rescind or cancel the contract, will not deprive the shipbuilder of his accrued rights against the guarantor.[508] It is immaterial whether the shipbuilder issues proceedings against the guarantor before[509] or after[510] he has rescinded or cancelled the contract. In fact it

---

504   *Trafalgar House Construction (Regions) Ltd v General Surety & Guarantee Co Ltd* [1996] 1 A.C. 199. cf. *Spliethoff's Bevrachtingskantoor BV v Bank of China Ltd* [2015] EWHC 999 (Comm), [2015] 2 Lloyd's Rep. 123 at [172]–[181] (a term in a contract (assumed to be a true guarantee for this purpose, though held to be a performance bond) whereby the guarantor's obligations "shall not be affected or prejudiced by any dispute" between the creditor and principal debtor held to cover disputes involving an allegation of fraud in the creditor so that guarantor is not discharged).
505   *Moschi v Lep Air Services Ltd* [1973] A.C. 331.
506   *Manx Electricity Authority v JP Morgan Chase Bank* [2003] EWCA Civ 1324, (2003) 147 S.J.L.B. 1205 at [37], per Rix L.J. See similarly at [47], per Chadwick L.J.
507   *Hyundai Heavy Industries Co Ltd v Papadopoulos* [1980] 1 W.L.R. 1129.
508   *Hyundai Heavy Industries Co Ltd v Papadopoulos* [1980] 1 W.L.R. 1129.
509   *Hyundai Heavy Industries Co Ltd v Pournaras* [1978] 2 Lloyd's Rep. 502.

will be unusual for rescission or cancellation of the contract in such circumstances to deprive the shipbuilder of accrued rights to instalments from the principal debtor,[511] but it may do so in some circumstances,[512] and where this occurs there will now, it seems, be a major breach in the co-extensiveness principle.[513] The surety will remain liable for instalments, while the principal debtor's liability will be a liability for damages—which may, of course, in particular circumstances, be for sums significantly less. The surety's right to an indemnity from the principal debtor[514] will presumably remain unaffected by this breach of the co-extensiveness principle which means only that the suretyship contract will be treated as an indemnity rather than a guarantee for some limited purposes.

45-102 **Discharge of debtor as a result of surety's breach of contract** Where a surety has given an undertaking to ensure that something occurs on which the debtor's liability is contingent, but fails to do so, any resulting lack of liability in the debtor does not prevent liability arising in the surety. Thus, in *Cerium Investments Ltd v Evans*,[515] a landlord had granted licences to the defendants to assign a lease and an underlease, the defendants covenanting as surety that the assignees would pay the rents and perform the covenants in the leases. The licences further provided that they should become "null and void" if the assignments were not registered with the landlords within a month. Assignments were made but not registered within this time by the assignees. The Court of Appeal upheld a claim by the landlords against the defendants as sureties in respect of arrears of rent not paid by the assignees, holding that the licences were initially effective and that on assignment the defendants as sureties became immediately contractually liable to the landlords in respect of any breach of covenant in the assignees, including their failure to register their assignments. Thus, the defendants could not rely on the subsequent nullity of the licence as a defence to a claim against them as sureties as this nullity was the consequence of their own wrongdoing in failing to ensure that the assignments were registered.

45-103 **Discharge of debtor by operation of law** A guarantor is generally discharged if the debtor is discharged by operation of law. Thus, where a mortgagee forecloses and thereafter sells the mortgaged property, a guarantor of the mortgage debt is discharged by operation of law because the mortgage debt itself is discharged in these circumstances.[516] And where a finance company retook the goods from the hirer in breach of the provisions of the Hire-Purchase Act so that the hirer was discharged under that Act, the guarantor was also discharged.[517] On the other hand,

---

510 *Papadopoulos* case [1980] 1 W.L.R. 1129.

511 Rescission ab initio may have this effect, but cancellation will normally only operate prospectively: *Johnson v Agnew* [1980] A.C. 367, 393.

512 See *Dies v British International Mining & Finance Corp* [1939] 1 K.B. 724, the correctness of which was assumed but not decided in the *Papadopoulos* case, see above. For some of the difficulties arising out of these cases, see Beatson (1981) 97 L.Q.R. 389.

513 For the co-extensiveness principle, see above, para.45-070.

514 See below, paras 45-126 et seq.

515 (1991) 62 P. & C.R. 203.

516 *Lloyds & Scottish Trust Ltd v Britten* (1982) 44 P. & C.R. 249.

517 *Unity Finance Ltd v Woodcock* [1963] 1 W.L.R. 455. The Consumer Credit Act 1974 ss.91 and 113 (replacing Hire-Purchase Act 1965 s.34(2)) indeed expressly provide for this result in the case of a guarantee or indemnity which is a "security" as defined by s.189(1), but this definition does not include "recourse agreements": see above, paras 39-130 and 39-328.

the House of Lords has held that a disclaimer of a lease by a corporate tenant debtor's liquidator does not discharge the liability of a guarantor of the tenant's liabilities.[518] The reason for this failure to discharge the tenant's guarantors is to be found in s.178(4)(b) of the Insolvency Act 1986, which provides that such a disclaimer "does not, except so far as is necessary for the purpose of releasing the company from any liability, affect the rights or liabilities of any other person". A surety liable under a contract of indemnity is not necessarily discharged if the debtor is discharged by operation of law; but if the creditor is tainted with any illegality this may protect the surety under a contract of indemnity as much as under a contract of guarantee.[519] Where a guarantee is expressed to render the guarantor liable even if the principal debtor's liability is discharged, the liability which began as a guarantee is in effect transmuted into a liability under an indemnity.[520]

(c) Discharge of Surety through Variation of Contract between Debtor and Creditor

Variation of contract between creditor and debtor   It is a well established and **45-104** strictly applied principle that any variation in the terms of the agreement between the creditor and the debtor which could prejudice the surety will, unless he consents thereto, discharge him from liability,[521] unless the contract of suretyship provides to the contrary.[522] It is immaterial that the variation has not in fact prejudiced the surety, or that the likelihood that it may do so is remote.[523] If the variation could prejudice the surety it alters the nature of the risk which he has undertaken and he is entitled to decide whether he wishes to continue bound or not. But if it is self-evident that the variation is unsubstantial or could not prejudice the surety he will not be discharged.[524] The principle is applied very strictly so that even the most

---

[518] *Hindcastle Ltd v Barbara Attenborough Associates Ltd* [1997] A.C. 70 applied in *Scottish Widows Plc v Tripipatkal* [2003] EWHC 1874 (Ch), [2003] B.P.I.R. 1413.

[519] See *Unity Finance Ltd v Woodcock* [1963] 1 W.L.R. 455 as explained in *Goulston Discount Co Ltd v Clark* [1967] 2 Q.B. 493. On the modern law of illegality, see Vol.I, Ch.16.

[520] *General Produce Co v United Bank Ltd* [1979] 2 Lloyd's Rep. 255; cf. *Heald v O'Connor* [1971] 1 W.L.R. 497, 503.

[521] *Whitcher v Hall* (1826) 5 B. & C. 269; *Holme v Brunskill* (1877) 3 Q.B.D. 495; *National Bank of Nigeria Ltd v Awolesi* [1964] 1 W.L.R. 1311; *West Hordon Industrial Park Ltd v Phoenix Timber Group Plc* [1995] 1 E.G.L.R. 77; *Howard de Walden Estates Ltd v Pasta Place Ltd* [1995] 1 E.G.L.R. 79; *Marubeni Hong Kong and South China Ltd v Government of Mongolia* [2004] EWHC 471 (Comm), [2004] 2 Lloyd's Rep. 198 at [58]–[60]; affirmed [2005] EWCA Civ 395, [2005] 1 W.L.R. 2497; *Associated British Ports v Ferryways NV* [2009] EWCA Civ 189, [2009] 1 Lloyd's Rep. 595 at [12]; *Aviva Insurance Ltd v Hackney Empire Ltd* [2012] EWCA Civ 1716, [2013] B.L.R. 57 at [56]–[79]; *Maxted v Investec Bank Plc* [2017] EWHC 1997 (Ch) at [12] and [20]–[22] (guarantor's consent found in their agreement to variation in their capacity as directors of the principal debtor company). For the effect of the Landlord and Tenant (Covenants) Act 1995 s.18 on the effectiveness of some variations of a tenant's covenants on guarantees by either a former tenant or his guarantor, see above, para.45-018.

[522] cf. below, para.45-158, concerning the possible effect of the Unfair Terms in Consumer Contracts Regulations 1999 (SI 1999/2083) or Consumer Rights Act 2015 Pt 2 on such an exclusion.

[523] *Bonar v Macdonald* (1850) 3 H.L.C. 226; *Holme v Brunskill* (1877) 3 Q.B.D. 495.

[524] *Holme v Brunskill* (1877) 3 Q.B.D. 495 at 505; and see *National Westminster Bank Plc v Riley* [1986] B.C.L.C. 268, 276–277; *Howard de Walden Estates Ltd v Pasta Place Ltd* [1995] 1 E.G.L.R. 79; *De Montfort Insurance Co Plc v Lafferty* (1997) G.W.D. 4–140, [1997] C.L.Y. 5722, Outer House of Ct of Sess.; *Barclays Bank Plc v Kingston* [2006] EWHC 533, [2006] 1 All E.R. (Comm) 519. In *Topland Portfolio No.1 Ltd v Smiths News Trading Ltd* [2014] EWCA Civ 18, [2014] 1 P. & C.R. 17 at [20] it was noted (with apparent approval but expressly obiter) that the H.C. of Australia in

trifling variation may discharge the surety. In the leading case of *Holme v Brunskill*[525] the defendant joined in a bond to guarantee that the tenant of a farm would deliver up the farm and a flock of sheep thereon at the expiration of the lease. The lease was later varied without the knowledge of the surety by the surrender of a small field by the tenant in return for a reduction in the rent. It was held that the surety was discharged since it was possible that the surrender of the field might have affected the tenant's ability to pasture the sheep and so to return them in good condition, and the surety might therefore have been prejudiced by the variation. On the other hand, a guarantor who has entered into a fidelity bond to answer for the conduct of a servant has been held not discharged by trifling variations in the contract of employment, such as an increase in salary,[526] or an alteration of the length of notice required to terminate the employment,[527] since it was held that such variations could not have prejudiced the surety. So also a purported variation of the agreement between the creditor and debtor which is, for some reason, ineffective in law will not discharge the surety since he cannot be prejudiced thereby.[528] At common law a deed could not be varied by a parol agreement, and therefore such a variation did not affect the surety,[529] but the position was different in equity[530] and the rules of equity now prevail.

45-105 Effect of breach of contract by debtor The acceptance by the creditor of a fundamental breach or a wrongful repudiation by the principal debtor, with consequential discharge of the principal contract, is not such a variation or discharge of the contract as will discharge the guarantor.[531]

45-106 Agreement by debtor to pay earlier Where the creditor and principal debtor enter a binding agreement under which the debtor is bound to pay earlier than originally agreed, the surety will be discharged on the ground that this agreement varies the principal contract, unless such an agreement is on the facts obviously incapable of prejudicing him.[532] On the other hand, the surety is not discharged if the principal debtor merely chooses to pay before the expiry of any period of credit allowed, even if the early payment is made at the creditor's request, since such a payment is not inconsistent with the contract guaranteed and involves no variation of it.[533] Moreover, where a payment is made by the principal debtor to the creditor under a separate agreement rather than under the original contract guaranteed (and so as not to take effect as a variation of that original contract, save in immaterial

---

Ankar Pty Ltd v National Westminster Finance (Australia) Ltd (1987) 162 C.L.R. 549 at 559 (Mason A.C.J, Wilson, Brennan and Dawson JJ.) considered that the burden of proof is on the creditor to show that the nature of the alteration can only be beneficial to the surety or that by its nature it cannot in any circumstances increase the surety's risk.

[525] (1877) 3 Q.B.D. 495.

[526] *Frank v Edwards* (1852) 8 Exch. 214.

[527] *Sanderson v Aston* (1873) L.R. 8 Exch. 73.

[528] *Egbert v National Crown Bank* [1918] A.C. 903, 909–910 (increase in rate of interest forbidden by statute).

[529] *Davey v Prendergrass* (1821) 5 B. & Ald. 187.

[530] *Prendergast v Devey* (1821) 6 Madd. 124.

[531] *Moschi v Lep Air Services Ltd* [1973] A.C. 331. See above, para.45-100.

[532] *St Microelectronics NV v Condor Insurance Ltd* [2006] EWHC 977 (Comm), [2006] 2 Lloyd's Rep. 525 at [36], [38].

[533] [2006] EWHC 977 at [37].

respects), the surety will not be discharged.[534] Here, "[t]he surety remains liable in respect of the original contract, but not of course in respect of the separate payments or loans which have been made".[535]

Agreement by creditor to give time to the debtor   A binding agreement by the **45-107** creditor to give time to the debtor is, in effect, one instance of variation, and also discharges the surety[536]:

> "It has been established for a very long time, beginning with *Rees v Berrington*[537] to the present day, without a single case going to the contrary, that on the principles of equity a surety is discharged when the creditor, without his assent, gives time to the principal debtor, because by so doing he deprives the surety of part of the right he would have had from the mere fact of entering into the suretyship, namely, to use the name of the creditor to sue the principal debtor, and if this right be suspended for a day or an hour, not injuring the surety to the value of one farthing, and even positively benefiting him, nevertheless, by the principles of equity, it is established that this discharges the surety altogether."[538]

This rule has been said to be based on "highly technical reasoning",[539] for, as appears from the above quotation, it is justified by the theoretical possibility that the surety may at any time choose to pay off the creditor and sue the principal debtor for an indemnity.[540] This right would be prejudiced where time has been given to the debtor, if the surety could not then sue him until the time had expired; while if the surety could sue at once the agreement to give time would be deprived of all effect.[541] But in practice the surety would rarely think of exercising this right in any event, and indeed Blackburn J. once said[542] that he was "not aware of any instance in which a surety ever in practice exercised this right".[543] But he also admitted that the rule itself was firmly established.

Binding agreement   It is not the mere giving of time which discharges the surety: **45-108** there must be a binding agreement to give time.[544] An agreement by a bank to allow a customer to increase his overdraft is not a binding agreement not to sue for the original debt forthwith.[545] Where the principal debtor gives the creditor additional security after the contract of suretyship has been made, such as a promissory note payable in some months' time, the surety will be discharged if the credi-

---

[534] *Aviva Insurance Ltd v Hackney Empire Ltd* [2012] EWCA Civ 1716, [2013] B.L.R. 57 at [67]–[80], [86]–[89], following *Trade Indemnity Co Ltd v Workington Harbour and Dock Board* [1937] A.C. 1, 21–22.

[535] [2012] EWCA Civ 1716 at [78], per Jackson L.J.

[536] *Polak v Everett* (1876) 1 Q.B.D. 669; *Overend Gurney & Co v Oriental Financial Corp* (1874) 7 H.L. 348; *Mahant Singh v U Ba Yi* [1939] A.C. 601.

[537] (1795) 2 Ves. 540.

[538] *Polak v Everett* (1876) 1 Q.B.D. at 669, 673–674.

[539] *Petty v Cooke* (1871) L.R. 6 Q.B. 790, 795.

[540] See below, para.45-126.

[541] *Oriental Financial Corp v Overend Gurney & Co* (1871) L.R. 7 Ch. App. 142, 150.

[542] *Swire v Redman* (1876) 1 Q.B.D. 536, 541. The actual decision in this case was in part overruled in *Rouse v Bradford Banking Co Ltd* [1894] A.C. 586.

[543] But this happened in *Drager v Allison*, 19 D.L.R. (2d) 431 (1959).

[544] *Overend Gurney & Co Ltd v Oriental Financial Corp Ltd* (1874) L.R. 7 H.L. 348.

[545] *Rouse v Bradford Banking Co Ltd* [1894] A.C. 586, 594 et seq.

tor has thereby agreed to waive his rights on the original debt and to give time.[546] But it is otherwise if the promissory note is merely a collateral security not affecting the creditor's rights on the original debt.

45-109   The granting of time does not release the surety where the agreement is made with someone other than the principal debtor, as, for example, where the agreement to give time is made with another surety.[547] Nor does an agreement to give time release the surety where the creditor has already obtained judgment against both debtor and surety; for after judgment both are equally liable to the creditor even though as between themselves the surety's liability remains a secondary one.[548]

45-110   **Security given by surety also released**   The principle that the variation of the contract between creditor and debtor, or the giving of time, discharges the surety, also has the effect of releasing any securities given by the surety to the creditor.[549]

45-111   **Distinct obligations not discharged**   Where the surety has guaranteed several distinct obligations, whether they arise under separate contracts or one contract,[550] a variation or a giving of time in respect of one obligation will discharge the surety as to that obligation, but not as to the others.[551] So where a surety guarantees payment of the price of any goods supplied by the creditor to the debtor, the giving of time in respect of the price of one lot of goods will not discharge the surety with respect to the price of another lot.[552] But where the obligations are indivisible, as, for example, with regard to the payments of instalments under a hire-purchase agreement, the giving of time with respect to one instalment will discharge the surety with respect to all.[553]

45-112   **Agreement to allow variation or giving of time**   The effect of the rules discussed in the preceding paragraphs is so technical and inconvenient that in practice any well-drawn contract of suretyship will nowadays expressly permit variation of the obligations or the giving of time, without discharging the surety.[554] At common law, such an agreement takes effect according to its terms,[555] but in cases of doubt or uncertainty will be construed in favour of the surety.[556] So, for example, where a

---

[546] See *Wyke v Rogers* (1852) 21 L.J. Ch. 611; cf. *Mercantile Bank of Sydney v Taylor* [1893] A.C. 317.

[547] *Frazer v Jordan* (1858) 8 E. & B. 303; *Clarke v Birley* (1889) 41 Ch. D. 422.

[548] *Re a Debtor* [1913] 3 K.B. 11.

[549] *Bolton v Salmon* [1891] 2 Ch. 48; *Smith v Wood* [1929] 1 Ch. 14.

[550] *Harrison v Seymour* (1866) L.R. 1 C.P. 518.

[551] *Croydon Commercial Gas Co v Dickinson* (1876) 2 C.P.D. 46; *WR Simmonds Ltd v Meek* [1939] 2 All E.R. 645.

[552] *WR Simmonds Ltd v Meek* [1939] 2 All E.R. 645.

[553] *Midland Motor Showrooms Ltd v Newman* [1929] 2 K.B. 256.

[554] Having noted the observation in the text, the CA has held that the *absence* of such a usual express term is neutral as to the question whether the agreement constitutes a guarantee or an indemnity: *Associated British Ports v Ferryways NV* [2009] EWCA Civ 189, [2009] 1 Lloyd's Rep. 595 at [12].

[555] *British Motor Trust Co Ltd v Hyams* (1934) 50 T.L.R. 230; *Perry v National Provincial Bank* [1910] 1 Ch. 464; *Trade Indemnity Co v Workington Harbour, etc.* [1937] A.C. 1, 21. cf. *Trafalgar House Construction (Regions) Ltd v General Surety & Guarantee Co Ltd* [1996] A.C. 199, 205; *Aviva Insurance Ltd v Hackney Empire Ltd* [2012] EWCA Civ 1716, [2013] B.L.R. 57 at [71]. For discussion of the possibility that such a term is not effective to retain the surety's liability by reason of the effect of the Consumer Rights Act 2015 Pt 2 (formerly the Unfair Terms in Consumer Contracts Regulations 1999 (SI 1999/2083)) see below, paras 45-155 et seq.

[556] See *West Hordon Industrial Park Ltd v Phoenix Timber Group Plc* [1995] 1 E.G.L.R. 77. cf. *Samuels Finance Group Plc v Beechmanor Ltd* (1994) 67 P. & C.R. 282, 285 and see above, paras 45-062 et

contract of guarantee provided that the guarantor's liability "under or pursuant" to the loan agreement was not to be affected by an arrangement which the creditor may make with the principal debtor and that the creditor could "agree to any amendment, variation, waiver or release ... in respect of an obligation of the [principal debtor] under the Loan Agreement", the question remained whether subsequent contracts of loan between the principal debtor and the creditor which "replaced" the loans guaranteed were indeed "amendments" or "variations" of the guarantor's liability "under or pursuant to" the loans guaranteed or whether they were "substantially different", whether in purpose, amount or terms, so as to fall outside the permitted variation provision in the guarantee contract.[557] In so holding, the Court of Appeal approved the statement of the law found in *Rowlatt on the Law of Principal and Surety* (1898), according to which "assent, whether previous or subsequent to a variation, only renders the surety liable for the contract as varied, where it remains a contract within the general purview of the original guarantee ... If a new contract is to be secured there must be a new guarantee".[558] On the other hand, where a clause in a contract of guarantee allows the creditor to vary the loan with the principal debtor but the creditor later agrees in writing with the guarantor not to renegotiate the loan without the latter's consent, then this subsequent agreement in effect reinstates the rule in *Holme v Brunskill*,[559] with the result that any variation of the loan to the potential detriment or disadvantage of the guarantor discharges him.[560] And a clause in a contract of guarantee of a lessee's obligations to its lessor which preserved the guarantor's liability "notwithstanding any neglect or forbearance on the part of the Lessor" to enforce the lessee's covenants has been held not to extend to a license by the lessor to allow the lessee to perform its covenants, as it concerned instead decisions by the lessor not to enforce the performance of a covenant against the lessee when in breach of that covenant: as a result, on the grant of such a license, the clause did not protect the lessor/creditor from the effect of the rule in *Holme v Brunskill*.[561] Finally, a change in the obligations of the principal debtor (for example, as to the rate of interest payable) under a term of the main contract which provides an option in the creditor to do so is not a variation in the contract at all, but the performance of it on its terms and so will not discharge the surety.[562]

Guarantee of liability after variation   Even where there is no express agreement to allow variation it is sometimes possible for a court to hold that a variation does not discharge the surety because on the true construction of the contract he has guaranteed the liability as varied. Thus where the surety guaranteed the liability of a commission agent up to a specified amount, but nothing was said as to the mode   **45-113**

---

seq.

[557] *Triodosbank NV v Dobbs* [2005] EWCA Civ 630, [2005] 2 Lloyd's Rep. 588 at [11]–[13], [19], per Longmore L.J., with whom Neuberger and Chadwick L.JJ. at [27] and [29] respectively agreed; *CIMC Raffles Offshore (Singapore) Ltd v Schahin Holdings SA* [2013] EWCA Civ 644, [2013] 2 Lloyd's Rep. 575 especially at [41]–[53], [61]–[63].

[558] [2005] EWCA Civ 630 at [14]; applied in *Maxted v Investec Bank Plc* [2017] EWHC 1997 (Ch) at [16]–[19].See further Salter (2017) 8 J.I.B.F.L. 459.

[559] (1877) 3 Q.B.D. 495, on which see above, para.45-104.

[560] *Lloyds TSB Bank Plc v Hayward* [2005] EWCA Civ 466.

[561] *Topland Portfolio No.1 Ltd v Smiths News Trading Ltd* [2014] EWCA Civ 18, [2014] 1 P. & C.R. 17 at [34]–[37].

[562] *Nationwide Building Society v Christie* [2013] EWHC 127 (Ch) at [15].

of accounting between the agent and the creditor, it was held that a variation in the mode did not discharge the surety, because he had guaranteed the liability irrespective of changes in the mode of accounting.[563] Similarly, where a guarantee is expressed as being in respect of "all sums which are now or may hereafter become owing" to the creditor by the principal debtor, the surety will remain liable for sums so owing even if they were not foreseen by the original contract guaranteed.[564]

45-114 Reservation of rights against surety   Even if the contract of suretyship itself does not permit variations or the giving of time, the surety will not be released by an agreement to give time if the creditor reserves his rights against the surety by notifying the debtor when time is given to him.[565] The consent of the surety is not necessary in this event,[566] though it would doubtless be sufficient, but the position is different where there is a variation of the terms of the contract other than a giving of time. In this event a reservation of the creditor's rights will be ineffective unless the surety consents to it.[567] If the surety is informed and consents, he will remain bound in any event, and no further consideration need be provided,[568] but mere knowledge of the creditor's intention to give time or vary the contract is not equivalent to consent unless some estoppel arises.[569]

(d)   Discharge of Surety on Other Grounds

45-115 Altering the terms of guarantee   If, while the instrument of guarantee is in the hands of the party to whom it was given, it is altered in any material particular without the knowledge or consent of the surety, it will become void and the surety will be discharged.[570] The test of materiality for this purpose has been held to be whether there is an alteration which affects "the very nature and character of the instrument" or "one which ... is potentially prejudicial to [the non-consenting party's] legal rights and obligations under the instrument".[571] On the other hand, where a guarantee document is altered in good faith by a third party in circumstances where the guarantee would have been enforceable without the alteration, then the guarantee is valid.[572] Furthermore, it has been held that where a guarantee document consists otherwise of print, type and ink writing, the most natural inference to draw of an amendment to that document *in pencil* is that it is not, and is not intended to be, an operative and final alteration with the result that it does not count

---

563 *Stewart v M'Kean* (1855) 10 Exch. 675.
564 *National Merchant Buying Society Ltd v Bellamy* [2013] EWCA Civ 452, [2013] 2 All E.R. (Comm) 674 at [30]–[33].
565 *Overend Gurney & Co v Oriental Financial Corp* (1874) L.R. 7 H.L. 348; *Mahant Singh v U Ba Yi* [1939] A.C. 601.
566 *Kearsley v Cole* (1846) 16 M. & W. 128, 135; *Bateson v Gosling* (1871) L.R. 7 C.P. 9. cf. *Greene King Plc v Stanley* [2001] EWCA Civ 1966, [2002] B.P.I.R. 491 at [74]–[81] (release of debtor subject to reservation of rights against surety), see above, para.45-092.
567 This seems implicit in *Holme v Brunskill* (1877) 3 Q.B.D. 495.
568 *Yates v Evans* (1892) 61 L.J. Q.B. 446, 449.
569 *Polak v Everett* (1876) 1 Q.B.D. 669.
570 *Davidson v Cooper* (1844) 13 M. & W. 343; and see Vol.I, paras 25-020 et seq.
571 *Raiffeisen Zentralbank Osterreich AG v Crossseas Shipping Ltd* [2000] 1 W.L.R. 1135 at 1146–1148, per Potter L.J. cf. *Bank of Scotland v Henry Butcher & Co* [2003] EWCA Civ 67, [2003] 2 All E.R. (Comm) 557 at [72]–[74] where an alteration by some co-guarantors was held to be plainly beneficial to the others who were not as a result discharged.
572 *Lombard Finance Ltd v Brookplain Trading Ltd* [1991] 1 W.L.R. 271.

as an alteration of the document so as to discharge the guarantor.[573] This decision was explained by the court on the basis that the rule as to alteration of a guarantee leading to discharge rests on a policy of deterrence or punishment of attempted fraud, a policy which cannot apply where, as with a pencilled alteration to a document of this kind, there is no chance of committing a fraud.[574]

Breach by creditor of terms of contract of suretyship.[575] If the creditor is guilty   **45-116**
of a breach of the terms of the contract of suretyship, the question whether the surety is wholly discharged depends on whether the breach goes to the root of the contract, or evinces an intention to repudiate the contract.[576] If it does so, the breach will, in accordance with normal principles, discharge the surety entirely. If, on the other hand, the breach is of a less serious character, the surety will merely have a counterclaim for damages, so that he will, in effect, be discharged to the extent that he has been prejudiced by the breach, but not wholly. It is often difficult to say whether breach by the creditor of a term in a contract of suretyship goes to the root of the contract or not, as may be seen from a number of hire-purchase cases. For example, where the finance company was unable to deliver the goods to the surety this was held in one case to discharge the surety completely,[577] and in another case merely to give rise to a counterclaim in damages.[578] If the creditor fails to perform some act required by the contract (e.g. to give notice to the surety of the debtor's default), this may be construed as the failure of a condition precedent and the surety cannot then be liable.[579] Similarly, breach of a proviso to a term in the contract of surety which allows the creditor to give the debtor time may take the creditor outside the permission of the term, so as to allow the operation of the rules as to discharge by reason of variation.[580]

Release of co-surety   As will be seen below, one surety has in some circumstances   **45-117**
a right of contribution from other co-sureties,[581] so that the release of a surety by the creditor could prejudice this right of contribution if the release were effective against co-sureties. Accordingly, such a release may also discharge the surety, though here again it is sometimes difficult to say whether he is discharged wholly or only to the extent that he has in fact been prejudiced. If the sureties are jointly or jointly and severally liable it seems that the liability of all the sureties will be treated as an essential part of the contract and a release of one without the consent of the others will therefore discharge all.[582] But where they are only severally li-

---

[573] *Co-operative Bank v Tipper* [1996] 4 All E.R. 366, 372 per Roger Cooke J.
[574] *Co-operative Bank v Tipper* [1996] 4 All E.R. 366, 372 per Roger Cooke J.
[575] *Skipton Building Society v Stott* [2001] Q.B. 261, 269–170 where this paragraph was cited with apparent approval.
[576] See Vol.I, paras 24-035 et seq.
[577] *Watling Trust Ltd v Briffault Range Co Ltd* [1938] 1 All E.R. 525.
[578] *Bowmaker (Commercial) Ltd v Smith* [1965] 1 W.L.R. 855.
[579] *United Dominions Trust (Commercial) Ltd v Eagle Aircraft Services Ltd* [1968] 1 W.L.R. 74; cf. *Australia & New Zealand Banking Group Ltd v Beneficial Finance Corp Ltd* (1983) 44 A.L.R. 241 and *Barclays Bank Plc v Quincecare Ltd* (1988) reported [1992] 4 All E.R. 363, 381–382. See also *Greene King Plc v Quisine Restaurants Ltd* [2012] EWCA Civ 698, [2012] 2 E.G.L.R. 64 (notice of arrears held neither a condition nor its breach going to root of contract).
[580] *Midland Counties Motor Finance Co Ltd v Slade* [1951] 1 K.B. 346.
[581] See below, para.45-136.
[582] *Mercantile Bank of Sydney v Taylor* [1893] A.C. 317; *Smith v Wood* [1929] 1 Ch. 14; *Liverpool Corn Trade Association v Hurst* [1936] 2 All E.R. 309; cf. *Commercial Bank of Australia Ltd v Official*

able the position seems to be different.[583] Even in this case a right to contribution would arise between the sureties so that the release of one may discharge the others to the extent (if any) that they have been prejudiced thereby, i.e. to the extent that they are unable to recover contribution which they could otherwise have recovered.[584] It has been held that an appropriately drafted clause in a contract of guarantee may oust the normal rule by which the release of one jointly and severally liable surety discharges the others.[585]

45-118 **Release or surrender of securities** The release or surrender of securities held by the creditor could operate to the prejudice of the surety in the same way as the release of a co-surety, so that this also may discharge the surety. The principle to be applied in determining whether the surety is wholly discharged or is only discharged pro tanto seems to be the same as in the case of a release of a co-surety. That is to say, if the existence of the security was an essential part of the contract of suretyship, then release of the security will discharge the surety entirely,[586] but if it was not an essential part of the bargain (for example, because it was supplied by the debtor after the contract of suretyship was made)[587] the surety will only be discharged to the extent that he has been prejudiced.[588] And if he has not been prejudiced at all, for example, because the security was worthless,[589] or because the security was not one to which the surety was entitled,[590] he remains liable in full. A similar principle operates where a surety is entitled to the benefit of an insurance policy. So, for example, where a car which was let under a hire-purchase agreement was destroyed in an accident, and the finance company settled the claim against the insurers for less than they should have done, the surety was not liable for the amount which the finance company had failed to claim.[591]

45-119 But the contract of suretyship may, expressly or impliedly, give the creditor the right to release securities without thereby prejudicing his rights against the surety. So, for example, where the debtor had mortgaged his farm and stock to a bank for a liability guaranteed by the surety, it was held that the consent of the bank to a sale of some of the stock by the debtor did not discharge the surety, for such normal dealings must have been contemplated by the parties.[592] And if the surety has engaged to answer for the debtor's fraud, he will not be discharged if the debtor fraudulently secures the release of some security.[593] Where the debtor becomes

---

Assignee [1893] A.C. 181; *Canadian Imperial Bank of Commerce v Vopni*, 86 D.L.R. (3d) 383 (1978). cf. the approach to the release of one of joint debtors (and joint and several debtors) in *Watts v Aldington, Tolstoy v Aldington* [1999] L. & T.R. 578; and *Johnson v Davies* [1999] Ch. 117 above, paras 45-091—45-097.

583 *Ward v National Bank of New Zealand Ltd* (1883) 8 App. Cas. 755.
584 *Ward v National Bank of New Zealand Ltd* (1883) 8 App. Cas. 766.
585 *Bank of Montreal v Dobbin and Dobbin* [1996] 5 Bank. L.R. 190 Court of Queen's Bench of New Brunswick.
586 *Smith v Wood* [1929] 1 Ch.14; *Re Darwen & Pearce* [1927] 1 Ch. 176.
587 *Polak v Everett* (1876) 1 Q.B.D. 669, 676.
588 *Carter v White* (1883) 25 Ch. D. 666, 670.
589 *Rainbow v Juggins* (1880) 5 Q.B.D. 422; *Musket v Rogers* (1839) 5 Bing. N.C. 728, 732.
590 *Chatterton v Maclean* [1951] 1 All E.R. 761, 766.
591 *Goulston Discount Co Ltd v Sims* (1967) 111 S.J. 682 (contract of indemnity; a fortiori for contracts of guarantee).
592 *Taylor v Bank of New South Wales* (1886) 11 App. Cas. 596; cf. *Dowling v Ditanda, The Times*, April 15, 1975.
593 *Hull Corp v Harding* [1892] 2 Q.B. 494.

bankrupt, a secured creditor who exercises his statutory right under the Insolvency Act 1986[594] to surrender his security and prove for the total liability does not thereby prejudice his rights against a surety.[595]

Neglect of creditor in relation to securities   It is clear that in some cases equity   **45-120** will intervene so as to discharge a surety where the creditor has failed to deal with the security for the debt as he ought.[596] For example, in *The Mutual Loan Association v Sudlow*,[597] A had obtained a loan from B upon the security of a bill of sale of A's furniture and of C standing surety for him. On A falling into arrears, the agents of B, his creditor, seized the goods and sold them, apparently at a considerable undervalue. The Court of Common Pleas held that the jury was entitled to hold that C, the surety, was discharged as it was through the misconduct of B's agents that the proceeds of sale were not enough to cover the debt. Secondly, it is also clear that in principle the effect of this equitable relief is to reduce or to extinguish the liability of the surety to the extent to which the security would have satisfied the debt, rather than absolutely.[598] In *Skipton Building Society v Stott*[599] the Court of Appeal held that where the liability of a surety is reduced on account of the negligent realisation of security, the basis of this reduction is the difference in value between the amount realised and the market value of the security at the relevant time (although it is to be noted that this case concerned the breach of an implied term in the contract of guarantee). This effect on the liability of a guarantor of neglect of a creditor in relation to securities may be excluded by the terms of the guarantee, and it has been said that the proper approach to such an alleged exclusion "should seek to interpret the guarantee as a whole as a commercial document and to give it a sensible meaning", rather than treat it "with the traditional hostility shown to exemption clauses".[600] Nevertheless, where such an alleged exclusion was contained in the creditor's standard document in circumstances where the guarantor had been encouraged to give the guarantee on the basis that the principal debtor had given valuable security and that, if need be, the creditor would realise the market value of that security properly, then it was held that neglect would reduce the guarantor's

---

[594] Insolvency Act 1986 s.322, Sch.9 para.17; Insolvency (England and Wales) Rules 2016 (SI 2016/ 1024) r.14.19(2) (in force April 6, 2017).

[595] *Rainbow v Juggins* (1880) 5 Q.B.D. 422. cf. *Re Hallett* [1894] 2 Q.B. 256.

[596] *The Mutual Loan Association v Sudlow* (1858) 5 C.B.(N.S.) 449; *Strange v Fooks* (1863) 4 Giff. 408; *Wulff v Jay* (1872) L.R. 7 Q.B. 756.

[597] (1858) 5 C.B.(N.S.) 449.

[598] *Watts v Shuttleworth* (1861) 7 H. & N. 353, 354; *Taylor v Bank of New South Wales* (1886) 11 App. Cas. 596, 603. cf. the position where the release or other dealing constitutes a variation of the principal obligation, in which case the surety is entirely discharged: see *Polak v Everett* (1876) 1 Q.B.D. 669, 676–677, and see above, paras 45-104 et seq.

[599] *Skipton Building Society v Stott* [2001] Q.B. 261, 270–271; *Alpstream AG v PK Airfinance Sarl* [2015] EWCA Civ 1318, [2016] 2 P. & C.R. 2 at [115]–[118].

[600] *Barclays Bank Plc v Kingston* [2006] EWHC 533, [2006] 2 Lloyd's Rep. at [29], per Stanley Burton J. cf. *American Express International Banking Corp v Hurley* [1985] 3 All E.R. 564 at 571 where Mann J. treated such an exclusion as "exclusion of liability for negligence" and *Continental Illinois National Bank & Trust Co of Chicago v Papanicolaou (The Fedora)* [1986] 2 Lloyd's Rep. 441 at 444, where a clause which ruled out any "deductions or withholdings" by the guarantor was not treated as an exclusion of liability by the creditor as it did not prevent the guarantor later claiming independently against the creditor. Moreover, the "traditional hostility shown to exemption clauses" has recently been considerably reduced where the contract is concluded between commercial parties: see Vol.I, paras 15-001 and 15-012.

liability "unless the terms of the guarantor clearly indicate otherwise".[601] It is submitted with respect that this approach to the construction of such an exclusion is to be approved: a contract term excluding the *reduction* of a guarantor's liability is not an exclusion clause properly so-called as it seeks to preserve the guarantor's liability where equity would reduce or extinguish it; and the approach just described reflects both the modern approach to construction of commercial contracts which sets them in their factual matrix and at the same time preserves a certain force to the traditional requirement of "clear words" to exclude this equitable protection for guarantors.[602]

45-121   Creditor free to decide whether to realise security   In *Standard Chartered Bank v Walker*[603] relief on the ground of neglect of creditor in relation to securities was expressed by Lord Denning M.R. very broadly, linking it to the existence of a duty of care owed by the creditor to the surety in the tort of negligence and suggesting that it may apply even to a case of the failure by the creditor to realise the security at an advantageous time, although he acknowledged that "the creditor can choose the time of sale within a considerable margin".[604] Such a broad approach was firmly rejected by the Privy Council in *China and South Sea Bank Ltd v Tan Soon Gin*,[605] in which Lord Templeman observed that while older authority justified the intervention of equity where the security is surrendered, lost,[606] not properly perfected[607] or altered in its condition by reason of what has been done by the creditor, where none of these are the case, the creditor is entitled freely to decide whether to sue the principal debtor, the surety, or to realise the security, or to do none of these.[608] Thus, while the negligent sale at an undervalue of the property discharges the surety,[609] the failure to realise the security at all while it declines in value does not, unless the creditor was personally responsible for that decline.[610] Moreover, it has been held that where a guarantee was given on terms that "all amounts payable by the Guarantor ... shall be paid in full free of set-off or counterclaim", this was effective to prevent resistance of the creditor's claim for summary judgment by the guarantor on the ground of the creditor's negligent realisation of the security for the loan.[611] "Guarantees such as these are the equivalent of letters of credit and only in

---

[601] *Barclays Bank Plc v Kingston* [2006] EWHC 533 at [29].

[602] See above, paras 45-064—45-068 and especially *Liberty Mutual Insurance Co (UK) Ltd v HSBC Bank Plc* [2002] EWCA Civ 691 at [56], above, para.45-067.

[603] [1982] 1 W.L.R. 1410; and see also *American Express International Banking Corp v Hurley* [1985] 3 All E.R. 564.

[604] [1982] 1 W.L.R. 1410, 1416, per Lord Denning M.R.

[605] [1990] 1 A.C. 536 and see *Alpstream AG v PK Airfinance Sarl* [2015] EWCA Civ 1318, [2016] 2 P. & C.R. 2 at [121]–[124].

[606] *Strange v Fooks* (1863) 4 Giff. 408 (security lost by neglect of creditor to give notice of assignment of mortgage to trustees of settlement in which the debtor had an equitable interest); *Wulff v Jay* (1872) L.R. 7 Q.B. 756 (failure to enter and take possession of property under a mortgage when interest became due).

[607] *Wulff v Jay* (1872) L.R. 7 Q.B. 756 (failure of creditor to register bill of sale).

[608] *China and South Sea Bank Ltd v Tan Soon Gin* [1990] 1 A.C. 536, 545 and see *White v Davenham Trust Ltd* [2011] EWCA Civ 747, [2011] Bus. L.R. 1443 at [38].

[609] *The Mutual Loan Association v Sudlow* (1858) 5 C.B.(N.S.) 449; *Standard Chartered Bank v Walker* [1982] 1 W.L.R. 1410; *American Express International Banking Corp v Hurley* [1985] 3 All E.R. 564; cf. *Taylor v Bank of New South Wales* (1886) 11 App. Cas. 596.

[610] [1990] 1 A.C. 536, 545; *Mahomed v Morris (No.2)* [2001] B.C.C. 233 (no duty in secured creditor to consult debtor or surety before realising the charged assets).

[611] *Continental Illinois National Bank, etc. v Papanicolaou* [1986] 2 Lloyd's Rep. 441.

exceptional circumstances should the Court exercise its power to stay execution".[612] Finally, the Privy Council in *China and South Sea Bank Ltd v Tan Soon Gin*[613] also rejected the idea that the creditor could be liable in damages in the tort of negligence to the surety for failing to exercise reasonable care in the realisation of securities[614]: "the tort of negligence has not yet subsumed all torts and does not supplant the principles of equity or contradict contractual promises".[615]

Implied term On the other hand, in *Skipton Building Society v Stott*[616] the County   **45-122** Court below had apparently accepted an implied term in a contract of guarantee on a building society lender towards a guarantor "to take reasonable care to ensure that the price at which the land [the security] is sold is the best price that can reasonably be obtained"[617] on the basis that this "implied term reflects the statutory duty of the building society under para.1(1)(a) of Sch.4 to the Building Societies Act 1986".[618] While the legal basis of the lender's duty to take care of the security was not in issue before the Court of Appeal, no adverse comment was directed to the decision below in this respect. Clearly, however, if the legal basis for the duty is an implied term in the contract of suretyship, a lender's breach would give rise to damages for consequential loss and not merely to the reduction or extinction of the surety's liability. While such an implied term may be justified in the special circumstances of lending by a building society (owing to the influence of the statutory duty noted above), more generally such a term would be unlikely to pass the traditional test of necessity for the implication of terms in general.[619] In this respect, the courts' rejection of a duty of care in the tort of negligence in relation to the realisation of securities suggests an unwillingness to extend the protection which equity has traditionally given to sureties.[620] On the other hand, where a lease purchase agreement (the principal contract) contains an express obligation in the creditor on its termination to sell the goods, a court may imply a term that the lessor/creditor will take reasonable care to obtain the true value of the goods; if the creditor breaches such an implied obligation, the surety may take advantage of the right of set-off or counterclaim of the lessee/principal debtor.[621] Such a guarantee may properly be construed as being given in respect of obligations arising out of a

---

[612] *Continental Illinois National Bank, etc. v Papanicolaou* [1986] 2 Lloyd's Rep. 441, at 445, per Parker L.J.

[613] [1990] 1 A.C. 536.

[614] *Standard Chartered Bank Ltd v Walker* [1982] 1 W.L.R. 1410 at 1415; *American Express International Banking Corp v Hurley* [1985] 3 All E.R. 564; and cf. *Cuckmere Brick Co Ltd v Mutual Finance Ltd* [1971] Ch. 949, 966.

[615] [1990] 1 A.C. 536, 543–544, per Lord Templeman; cf. *Parker-Tweedale v Dunbar Bank Plc (No.1)* [1991] Ch. 12; and *AIB Finance v Debtors* [1998] 2 All E.R. 929, 937 and Vol.I, para.1-185.

[616] [2001] Q.B. 261.

[617] [2001] Q.B. 261 at 265.

[618] [2001] Q.B. 261 at 265.

[619] On the general approach to the implication of terms, see Vol.I, Ch.14. See also *General Mediterranean Holding SA.SPF (aka General Mediterranean Holding SA) v Qucomhaps Holdings Ltd* [2017] EWHC 1409 (QB) (no implied term in principal contract that creditor should take a particular step in foreign court proceedings to protect security).

[620] See especially, *China and South Sea Bank Ltd v Tan Soon Gin* [1990] 1 A.C. 536. cf. the rejection by the CA of implied term as the legal basis of the duty of disclosure in contracts of insurance in *Banque Keyser Ullman SA v Skandia (UK) Insurance Co* [1990] 1 Q.B. 665 (affirmed [1991] 2 A.C. 249) and see above, para.42-040.

[621] *Lombard North Central Plc v Nugent* [2013] EWHC 1588 (QB) at [95]–[98] (no such breach on the facts). The general rule is stated in para.45-087.

contemplated course of dealing rather than a specific contract, with the result that any variation in the obligations of the principal debtor under a specific contract will not discharge the surety.[622]

45-123 **Statutory demands under Insolvency Act against guarantor** The questions have arisen as to whether the existence of a set-off as between the principal debtor and creditor, or of security provided by a principal debtor to the creditor, provide grounds under the Insolvency Rules 1986 r.6.5.(4) for setting aside a statutory demand against a guarantor under the Insolvency Act 1986.[623] In *Octagon Assets Ltd v Remblance*[624] a majority of the Court of Appeal held that, since r.6.5.(4)(a) provides for the setting aside of such a demand against a debtor where he enjoys a "counter-claim, set-off or cross-demand which equals or exceeds the amount of the debt … specified in the statutory demand", then, where a principal debtor enjoys a counter-claim etc. such a statutory demand against a *guarantor* should be set aside under the discretion under r.6.5(4)(d) for cases "where the court is satisfied, on other grounds, that the demand ought to be set aside": "[h]aving regard to the principle of co-extensiveness, it is equally unjust in such circumstances to require the guarantor to face the consequences of bankruptcy" as it is for the debtor.[625] However, in *White v Davenham Trust Ltd*[626] the Court of Appeal distinguished this situation from the position where a creditor enjoys security provided by the principal debtor (and cannot therefore serve a statutory demand against him by reason of r.6.5(4)(c)) and brings a statutory demand against a guarantor. Given that a creditor who has several remedies can choose which remedy is enforced, at what time, in which order and in what way,[627] "it is not open to a guarantor to argue that the creditor should pursue the principal debtor first or should realise security given by the principal debtor first".[628] The "co-extensiveness principle" as between principal debtor and guarantor does not apply so as to create a proper analogy between the position of a creditor bringing a statutory demand against the principal debtor who has provided security under r.6.5.(4)(c) and a creditor bringing a statutory demand against a surety where the principal debtor has provided security for the purposes of the discretion under r.6.5.(4)(d).[629] With effect from April 6, 2017, the Insolvency Rules 1986 were replaced by the Insolvency (England and Wales) Rules 2016,[630] but the provisions formerly contained in the 1986 Rules r.6.5(4) which are the subject of the cases discussed in this paragraph were re-enacted without substantive change in r.10.5(5) of the 2016 Rules.[631]

45-124 **Other conduct of creditor prejudicial to surety** In certain types of transaction, and in particular where a surety engages to answer for the honesty of an

---

[622] [2013] EWHC 1588 (QB) at [53] and cf. above, para.45-077.

[623] s.267–268. See also *Re Salt* [2011] EWHC 2105 (Ch) (no good reason in the circumstances for construing guarantee as implying that a statutory demand could not be made against a guarantor).

[624] [2009] EWCA Civ 581, [2010] Bus. L.R. 119.

[625] [2009] EWCA Civ 581 at [46], per Nicholls L.J., and see at [72] (Ward L.J.).

[626] [2011] EWCA Civ 747, [2011] Bus. L.R. 1443; applied in *Inbakumar v United Trust Bank Ltd* [2012] EWHC 845 (Ch), [2012] B.P.I.R. 758.

[627] *China and South Sea Bank Ltd v Tan Soon Gin* [1990] 1 A.C. 536, 545 above, para.45-121.

[628] [2011] EWCA Civ 747 at [39], per Lloyd L.J.

[629] [2011] EWCA Civ 747 at [40] and see at [44].

[630] SI 2016/1024.

[631] The equivalent provisions are: 2016 Rules rr.10.5(5)(a), 10.5(5)(c) and 10.5(5)(d) replacing 1986 Rules rr.6.5(4)(a), 6.5(4)(c) and 6.5(4)(d) respectively.

employee, the wilful connivance of the creditor in the default of the principal debtor may discharge the surety. In *Dawson v Lawes*,[632] where a surety had signed a fidelity bond for an employee who was from time to time entrusted with money by his employer, the creditor, it was said that there must be:

"... such an act of connivance as enabled the party [sc. the debtor] to get the fund in his hands, or such an act of gross negligence as to amount to a wilful shutting of the person's eyes to the fraud which the party was about to commit, or something approximating to it, to discharge the surety."

But mere negligence on the part of the creditor will not normally discharge the surety except, as seen in the preceding paragraph, where the neglect affects some security which would otherwise have accrued to the benefit of the surety. So the negligence of a creditor in not demanding accounts from an employee whose conduct and honesty have been guaranteed will not discharge the surety,[633] nor will acquiescence by the creditor in an irregular mode of accounting,[634] nor will the failure to demand payment of a debt as soon as it is due.[635] Moreover, the Court of Appeal has affirmed[636] that there is no general principle that "irregular" conduct on the part of the creditor, even if prejudicial to the interests of the surety, will discharge him.[637] Short of bad faith, misrepresentation or concealment amounting to misrepresentation, connivance with the default of the principal debtor, or variation of the terms of the contract to the possible prejudice of the surety, the creditor can act as he chooses. Finally, as has been seen,[638] the courts have clearly set their face against imposing a duty of care in the tort of negligence on a creditor to the

---

[632] (1854) 23 L.J. Ch. 434, 441.

[633] *Mansfield Union v Wright* (1882) 9 Q.B.D. 683, 688.

[634] *Durham Corp v Fowler* (1888) 22 Q.B.D. 394.

[635] *Black v Ottoman Bank* (1862) 15 Moo. P.C. 472.

[636] *Bank of India v Trans Continental Commodity Merchants Ltd* [1983] 2 Lloyd's Rep. 298; *Westpac Securities Ltd v Dickie* [1991] 1 N.Z.L.R. 657; *Socomex Ltd v Banque Bruxelles Lambert SA* [1996] 1 Lloyd's Rep. 156, 197–199; *Dubai Islamic Bank PJSC v PSI Energy Holding Co BSC* [2011] EWHC 2718 (Comm) at [37]–[43] and see Phillips (1990) J.B.L. 325.

[637] cf. *Hackney Empire Ltd v Aviva Insurance UK Ltd* [2011] EWHC 2378 (TCC), [2011] B.L.R. 726 especially at [92] and [124] where the court "tentatively" recognised "the rule, if it is a rule" in *General Steam Navigation Co v Rolt* (1858) 6 C.B.(N.S.) 556 especially at 604–605 that where a creditor acts in a manner in relation to the principal contract which, whilst not amounting to an alteration of its terms, is prima facie prejudicial to the surety who has guaranteed the principal debtor's obligations under the contract, the surety will be discharged (absent any relevant indulgence clause), while holding that on the facts there was no such prima facie prejudicial conduct and so the guarantor was not discharged: [2011] EWHC 2378 (TCC) at [131] and [142]. On appeal, the Court of Appeal affirmed the decision below, but did not treat *General Steam Navigation Co v Rolt* as authority for a general proposition that creditor conduct prejudicial to the surety will discharge the surety, although it recognised a "common principle" underlying the categories of case where the surety will be discharged to the effect "that the creditor must not transact the surety's affairs without consulting him": [2012] EWCA Civ 1716, [2013] B.L.R. 57 at [70], per Jackson L.J. It is submitted that *Rolt's* case itself can be seen as an example of early payment of instalments being treated as analogous to release of security ("the withdrawal of a fund which is a security for the thing in respect of the not doing of which [the surety] is now called upon to pay damages": (1858) 6 C.B.(N.S.) 556 especially 604–605, per Pollock C.B.), on which see above, para.45-118), or as a case of variation of the principal contract (as per its head-note and (1858) 6 C.B.(N.S.) 556 especially at 595, Cockburn C.J. referring to "the alteration of the contract for the performance of which he consented to be bound").

[638] See above, para.45-121.

surety to safeguard the economic welfare of the latter's position.[639] Thus, in *Barclays Bank Plc v Quincecare Ltd*,[640] it was held that a creditor owes no duty to a guarantor of a loan to act reasonably to ensure that the loan is applied for the purposes for which it is given, whether that duty is put by way of an implied term in the contract or of the tort of negligence.

45-125 **Creditor estopped from enforcing guarantee** In principle, a creditor may be estopped from enforcing a guarantee under the doctrine of promissory estoppel (sometimes known as forbearance in equity).[641] However, where, for example, a creditor promises not to enforce a guarantee "indefinitely" while the guarantor works (unpaid) for the principal debtor, such a promise to postpone enforcement is likely to be interpreted as applying only where the creditor agrees to the continuation of the work rather than so as to allow the guarantor unilaterally to prevent the enforcement of the guarantee by continuing to undertake the work.[642]

7. Surety's Right to Indemnity and Contribution

45-126 **Surety's right to indemnity against principal debtor**[643] A surety who has actually met the liability which he has undertaken to answer for is entitled to be indemnified by the principal debtor; and if he alone is sued by the creditor he can bring in the debtor by a Pt 20 claim (the third-party procedure).[644] Where the surety has undertaken his liability at the request, express or implied, of the debtor, this right to an indemnity may be said to arise in one of two ways[645]; that is, either from an implied actual contract between surety and debtor,[646] or it may be said to be a restitutionary remedy arising from the fact that the surety has been compelled by law to discharge a debt for which the debtor is ultimately liable.[647]

45-127 **Payment without request** Where the surety's liability does not arise from any request by the debtor[648] his right to an indemnity must, it seems, be placed on the law of restitution or unjust enrichment. However, in *Owen v Tate*[649] it was held that a right of indemnity is not normally available to a person who has assumed or discharged the liability of another, without any antecedent request of that other. Such a right may arise exceptionally where the claimant has assumed (or paid) the

---

[639] *Hull Corp v Harding* [1892] 2 Q.B. 494; *Barclays Bank Ltd v Thienel* (1980) 247 E.G. 385; *Latchford v Beiren* [1981] 3 All E.R. 705; *China and South Sea Bank Ltd v Tan Soon Gin* [1990] 1 A.C. 536.
[640] (1988) reported [1992] 4 All E.R. 363.
[641] *Dunbar Assets Plc v Butler* [2015] EWHC 2546 (Ch), [2015] B.P.I.R. 1358. On this doctrine generally see Vol.I, paras 4-130 et seq.
[642] *Dunbar Assets Plc v Butler* [2015] EWHC 2546 (Ch) at [49]–[50].
[643] See Goff and Jones, *The Law of Unjust Enrichment*, 9th edn (2016), paras 19-16—19-21.
[644] CPR Pt 20 r.5.
[645] See *Anson v Anson* [1953] 1 Q.B. 636, 641–643.
[646] *Re a Debtor* [1937] Ch. 156.
[647] *Moule v Garrett* (1872) L.R. 7 Ex. 101, 104; *Brook's Wharf v Goodman Brothers* [1937] 1 K.B. 534. A third possibility is to treat the right as arising by way of subrogation, but this would require proceedings to be brought in the name of the creditor. At times it may be important to distinguish between a surety's right to an indemnity and any right of the creditor against the principal debtor which the surety may enjoy by way of subrogation: e.g. *Re Empire Paper Ltd (In Liquidation)* [1999] B.C.C. 406 (compromise agreement preserved "any subrogated claims").
[648] See Vol.I, para.29-119.
[649] [1976] Q.B. 402; *The Zuhal K* [1987] 1 Lloyd's Rep. 151; and see Birks and Beatson in Beatson, *The Use and Abuse of Unjust Enrichment* (1991), Ch.7.

debtor's obligation under some practical necessity, and it is in all the circumstances just and reasonable that he should be indemnified. But it is not clear if the debtor can take the benefit of the payment by the third party without coming under a liability to him.[650] It is also not entirely clear whether *Owen v Tate* can be reconciled with the general principle that, wherever two persons are liable for the same debt, and as between them, one of them is primarily liable, that party is liable to indemnify the other if the other meets the liability. This broad principle, which is known as the principle of *Moule v Garrett*,[651] is apparently that which underlies the third case referred to by Lord Selborne in *Duncan Fox & Co v North & South Wales Bank*[652] and has been applied in two decisions at first instance to give an indemnity to a lessee who had assigned the lease, not only against the assignee, but also against a surety for the assignee.[653] One possible reconciliation of these decisions with *Owen v Tate*[654] may be made by reference to the purpose of its requirement of a request, which is to exclude from restitutionary relief a person who has officiously exposed himself to the liability to make payment.[655] It has been convincingly argued that the requirement of a request has been more broadly interpreted than is necessary to effect this purpose.[656] In the case of a lessee's rights against a guarantor of the assignee of the lease, the payer (lessee) has not officiously exposed himself to liability to pay the rent and, even though he cannot be said to have paid at the guarantor's request, he should not on that ground alone be excluded from recovery: both the transaction of assignment and guarantee took as their assumption the existence of the lessee's obligations and also assumed that, to use the expression in *Moule v Garrett*,[657] as between the lessee and the guarantor, the latter's would be the primary or ultimate liability.[658]

Payment under unenforceable guarantee   The surety's right to an indemnity is   **45-128**
not affected by the fact that the liability which he has discharged was not enforceable against him because of the absence of a written note or memorandum,[659] nor that the liability was not enforceable against the debtor because of an infringement of the Consumer Credit Act.[660] This result has been supported on the ground that the prima facie construction of the debtor's request for an indemnity is: "'Pay if I do not,' and [not]: 'Pay if I do not and if I am legally compellable to pay".'[661]

---

[650] See generally Birks and Beatson in *The Use and Abuse of Unjust Enrichment* (1991).

[651] (1872) L.R. 7 Ex. 101 and See Vol.I, paras 29-105 et seq.

[652] (1880) 6 App. Cas. 1, 11, 12.

[653] *Selous Street Properties Ltd v Oronel Fabrics Ltd* (1984) 270 E.G. 643; *Becton Dickinson Ltd v Zwebner* [1989] Q.B. 208.

[654] [1976] Q.B. 402.

[655] Goff and Jones, *The Law of Restitution*, 7th edn (2007), pp.430–432 et seq. (this point not being addressed by the 9th edition), cf. Burrows, *The Law of Restitution*, 3rd edn (2010), pp.449–452.

[656] Goff and Jones *The Law of Restitution*, 7th edn (2007) p.431. cf. Goff and Jones, *The Law of Unjust Enrichment*, 9th edn (2016), para.20-02 which states that it is not "automatically fatal that [a claimant's] liability to the third party was voluntarily assumed without any prior request from the defendant: this is merely one factor which may bear on the court's decision whether to allow a claim".

[657] (1872) L.R. 7 Ex. 101.

[658] *Becton Dickinson Ltd v Zwebner* [1989] Q.B. 208 at 217–218; and see *Kumar v Dunning* [1989] Q.B. 193, 201.

[659] *Alexander v Vane* (1836) 1 M. & W. 511.

[660] *Re Chetwynd's Estate* [1938] Ch. 13 (decided under the Moneylenders Acts, which were repealed from May 19, 1985, by the Consumer Credit Act 1974).

[661] *Argo Caribbean Group Ltd v Lewis* [1976] 2 Lloyd's Rep. 289, 295, per curiam. But it was sug-

On the other hand, it has been held that if the surety pays a statute-barred debt he has no right to an indemnity.[662]

45-129 Presumption of advancement inapplicable A surety may, of course, agree that he is not to have any right to be indemnified by the debtor, but a husband who has guaranteed his wife's overdraft will not generally be prevented from recovering an indemnity by an application of the presumption of advancement.[663]

45-130 When right to indemnity arises Prima facie the surety's right to an indemnity arises only on actual payment by him,[664] though if he pays before the principal debt becomes due he will have no right to be indemnified until the debtor could have been sued by the creditor.[665] Thus until actual payment by the surety, no debt is due to him from the debtor.[666] Similarly, it has been held that a right to an indemnity (at least a general indemnity, for example, an indemnity against legal liability arising from specified events) does not arise until the person entitled to the indemnity is called upon to pay the principal claim and it is ascertained. Hence the limitation period under such an indemnity agreement does not begin to run until that time.[667] This has also been applied to an implied general indemnity, as where charterers are liable to indemnify shipowners for liability on bills of lading signed by the ship's master.[668] But it seems that the position is different where the indemnity arises out of an express contract which creates a right to an indemnity on a liability "arising". In such a case the time for limitation purposes will run from the date when the right to an indemnity arises.[669] So also, it seems that where the right to an indemnity arises by way of a claim to damages for breach of contract, the limitation period would run from the date of the breach, and not later.

45-131 Amount of indemnity A surety is in principle entitled to be indemnified for monies paid to the creditor in respect of the principal debtor's liabilities. The question arises, though, whether such an indemnity may include recovery in respect of expenses (notably, legal expenses) incurred by a surety as a result of his liability to the creditor under the contract of suretyship. In this respect, it has been stated that in order to be recoverable from the principal debtor the legal costs in question must have been caused by the default of the principal debtor.[670] Therefore, a "surety is entitled to be reimbursed as to the costs reasonably incurred by him in investigat-

---

gested (at 295–296) that if the debtor cancels the indemnitor's instructions to pay the debt, there will no longer be a right of indemnity. This presumably would only be so if the indemnitor is not contractually bound to the creditor.

662 *Coneys v Morris* [1922] 1 Ir.R. 81.
663 *Re Salisbury-Jones* [1938] 3 All E.R. 459; *Anson v Anson* [1953] 1 Q.B. 636.
664 *Re Richardson* [1911] 2 K.B. 705; *Re Beavan* [1913] 2 Ch. 595.
665 *Drager v Allison*, 19 D.L.R. (2d) 31 (1959).
666 *Re Mitchell* [1913] 1 Ch. 201; *Re Fenton* [1931] Ch. 85; *Re a Debtor* [1956] 1 W.L.R. 1226.
667 *R & H Green & Silley Weir Ltd v British Rys Board* (1980) reported [1985] 1 W.L.R. 570.
668 *Telfair Shipping Corp v Inersea Carriers SA* [1985] 1 W.L.R. 553.
669 *Bosma v Larsen* [1966] 1 Lloyd's Rep. 22; followed in *National House-Building Council v Fraser* [1983] 1 All E.R. 1090. cf. *City of London v Reeve & Co Ltd* [2000] C.P. Rep. 73 at [30] (question when cause of action on a contractual indemnity arises an issue of construction) and see Vol.I, para.28-049.
670 *Re Empire Paper Ltd (In Liquidation)* [1999] B.C.C. 406, 412; citing *Howard v Lovegrove* (1870) 6 Exch. 43; and *Pierce v Williams* (1854) 23 L.J. Ex. 322, 323.

ing the validity and quantum of the creditor's claim against the principal debtor",[671] but any entitlement to the costs of investigating the enforceability of the guarantee is "more doubtful", as they appear to be incurred for the benefit of the surety alone.[672]

Surety's right to indemnity in cases of contracts of indemnity   There does not **45-132** appear to be any explicit authority on the surety's right to an indemnity where he is himself liable to the creditor under a contract of indemnity as opposed to a contract of guarantee, but equally there does not appear to be any reason to doubt that such a right usually exists. Prima facie, if the contract of indemnity were entered into at the request of the debtor, there seems no reason why the surety should not be entitled to an indemnity from the debtor on the normal principle that any person who does something involving him in legal liability at the request of another is entitled to be indemnified by that other.[673] And this would presumably remain the case even where the surety's liability is wider than that imposed on the debtor under the principal transaction. But special considerations would obviously apply where the principal debtor was a minor.[674] If, on the other hand, the contract of indemnity was entered into without any request by the debtor, then (as seen above)[675] there would be no relationship of principal and surety at all between the debtor and the party liable under the indemnity. In such circumstances the party liable under the indemnity could only claim subrogation or restitutionary rights against the debtor, and the debtor's liability would probably be limited by the terms of the original transaction.

Arrangements between principal debtor and guarantor incompatible with **45-133 guarantor's right of indemnity**   A guarantor is not entitled to an indemnity by way of restitution from a principal debtor where these same parties contemplated that, as between themselves, only the guarantor would bear a primary liability to the creditor. In *Berghoff Trading Ltd v Swinbrook Developments Ltd*[676] the partners (A) in a Scottish partnership (B) entered a contract as "guarantors" and "obligors" of the partnership which had been lent money by a bank (C) as part of a wider arrangement under which the partners had sold their interests. The interests were later sold to third parties under a "forced sale" by the bank under a power of attorney, and the loan paid out of the proceeds of sale directly to the bank.[677] According to Rix L.J. (with whom Sir Anthony Clarke M.R. and Arden L.J. agreed):

> "From beginning to end of the arrangement ... it was always contemplated and expressly provided for that the loan ... would be paid out of the proceeds of sale, directly to the bank's own account. Since the proceeds would come from the sale of [A's] partnership interest in [B], it would follow that the loan would be repaid by [A], not by [B]. This therefore is not the normal situation where a guarantor's right of indemnification or reimbursement from the principal debtor is designed to ensure that the guarantor does not

---

[671] *Re Empire Paper Ltd (In Liquidation)* [1999] B.C.C. 406, 412, per Stanley Burnton Q.C. (the report adds "and himself" but this is belied by what follows).

[672] *Re Empire Paper Ltd (In Liquidation)* [1999] B.C.C. 406.

[673] *Sheffield Corp v Barclay* [1905] A.C. 392.

[674] Thus the defendant in *Yeoman Credit Ltd v Latter* [1961] 1 W.L.R. 828 could hardly have obtained an indemnity from the minor hire-purchaser.

[675] See above, para.45-005.

[676] [2009] EWCA Civ 413.

[677] [2009] EWCA Civ 413 at [34].

lose out merely from the choice of the creditor as to the source of his payment. This is not the normal situation where as between a principal debtor and his guarantor it is agreed or understood that the debt is only that of the former and that if the guarantor is called upon to pay, he will be reimbursed. This is an entirely special case where, from beginning to end the funds with which to repay the loan were to come from [A]."[678]

In these circumstances, the Court of Appeal held that, in the absence of express agreement between A and B to the contrary, A (as guarantor) had no reasonable prospect of success in establishing a claim to an indemnity in respect of its discharge of the debt owed by B (the principal debtor) to C (as creditor).[679]

45-134 **Surety's rights before payment** Even before he makes payment the surety has certain potential or inchoate rights against the principal debtor which may have important practical consequences. Thus it has already been seen that if the creditor prejudices these rights, the surety may be discharged from liability.[680] And in exceptional circumstances these potential rights may justify the principal debtor in taking appropriate steps to prevent the creditor from enforcing the guarantee against the surety.[681] Moreover, as soon as the surety's liability to the creditor arises in the sense that it is currently enforceable, the surety has a right that the debtor should meet the liability. The surety can enforce this right by suing in a *quia timet* action for a declaration that he is entitled to be exonerated and an order that the debtor pay whatever is due to the creditor.[682] The court cannot order the debtor to pay the money to the surety for this would not discharge the debtor's liability to the creditor, but it can order him to pay the money to the creditor.[683] Such a *quia timet* action can be brought even if there is no particular fund which can be protected by the court's order.[684] It is immaterial that the creditor has not yet demanded payment, or indeed, that he is unlikely to do so in the immediate future,[685] even though the surety's liability is expressly conditioned on a demand[686]; but the amount must be due in the sense that the creditor could proceed against the surety forthwith.[687] It is uncertain whether the surety can proceed in this way before payment where there is no contract of suretyship as against the debtor, i.e. where the surety has guaranteed the debt at the request of the creditor and not at the request of the debtor. On principle it would seem not, for in this event the surety's rights arise only by way of subrogation or by way of a claim to restitution, either of which would seem to require actual payment by the surety. These inchoate rights of a party entitled to

---

[678] [2009] EWCA Civ 413 at [34].

[679] [2009] EWCA Civ 413 at [35].

[680] See above, paras 45-117—45-124.

[681] *Elian and Rabbath v Matsas and Matsas* [1966] 2 Lloyd's Rep. 495. In this case an injunction was granted to prevent the creditor going to arbitration. Presumably, if he sues, the debtor could ask for a stay of proceedings under s.49(3) of the Senior Courts Act 1981. The exceptional nature of the *Elian* case was stressed in *Howe Richardson Scale Co Ltd v Polimex-Cekop* [1978] 1 Lloyd's Rep. 161, 165.

[682] *Wolmershausen v Gullick* [1893] 2 Ch. 514, 528; *Ascherson v Tredegar Dock, etc. Co Ltd* [1909] 2 Ch. 401.

[683] *Wolmershausen v Gullick* [1893] 2 Ch. 514, 528; *Ascherson v Tredegar Dock, etc. Co Ltd* [1909] 2 Ch. 401.

[684] *Watt v Mortlock* [1964] Ch. 84.

[685] *Re Anderson-Berry* [1928] Ch. 290.

[686] *Thomas v Notts Incorporated Football Club Ltd* [1972] Ch. 596.

[687] *Tate v Crewdon* [1938] Ch. 869; *Morrison v Barking Chemicals Co* [1919] 2 Ch. 325.

an indemnity do not generally result in time commencing to run under the Limitation Act.[688]

Surety's rights against bankrupt debtor Complex problems sometimes arise in connection with the surety's right to indemnity when the debtor has been adjudicated bankrupt. The Supreme Court has held that, so long as a creditor had not been paid in full, a surety could not compete with the creditor either directly, by proving against the principal debtor for an indemnity, or indirectly, by setting off his right to an indemnity against any separate debt owed by the surety to the principal debtor.[689] This position reflects the well-established principle in bankruptcy that there cannot be double proof in respect of the same liability in the same estate.[690] If the surety discharges the whole liability the creditor has no further interest, and the surety is entitled to prove in the debtor's bankruptcy. It has already been seen that if the surety discharges part of the liability, his right to prove against the bankrupt debtor depends on whether he has guaranteed the whole debt, or whether he has only guaranteed part.[691]

45-135

Surety's right to contribution from co-sureties[692] It is an old rule of equity that a surety is entitled to contribution from his co-sureties so that none of them should be required, as between themselves, to pay more than his due share.[693] The rules of equity continue to apply to claims for contribution between co-debtors; but they have been superseded by the Civil Liability (Contribution) Act 1978 in respect of claims between sureties arising out of a liability for *damage* as opposed to *debt*. An example of where a surety would be liable for damage may be found in a case where he guaranteed a seller's liability in respect of goods sold, but where the goods caused damage to the buyer's other property. Similarly, where (as is prima facie the case)[694] a contract of suretyship guarantees performance by the principal debtor of its payment obligations, the surety is liable in damages rather than in debt to the creditor; whereas, where a surety agrees to pay to the creditor whatever the principal debtor owes to the creditor, then the surety is liable in debt rather than in damages.[695] This means that in the former, but not the latter circumstances, a claim by a surety for contribution from a co-surety will be governed by the two-year limitation period imposed by s.10 of the Limitation Act 1980.[696] The main features of the statutory

45-136

---

[688] cf. above, para.45-130.

[689] *In Re Kaupthing Singer & Friedlander Ltd (In Administration) (No.2)* [2011] UKSC 48, [2011] 3 W.L.R. 939 especially at [12], [53]–[54], [55]. As a result, the SC held that the "rule in *Cherry v Boultbee*" which was described as "a simple technique of netting-off reciprocal monetary obligations" (at [8], per Lord Walker of Gestingtthorpe) as well as statutory set-off were ousted by the policy of the law underlying the rule against double proof: [2011] UKSC 48 at [48], [53] and [55].

[690] *In Re Kaupthing Singer & Friedlander Ltd (In Administration) (No.2)* [2011] UKSC 48 at [11]–[12]; *Re Oriental Commercial Bank* (1871) L.R. 7 Ch. App. 99; *Re Fenton* [1931] 1 Ch. 85; *Re Glen Express Ltd* [2000] B.P.I.R. 456.

[691] See above, para.45-078.

[692] See Goff and Jones, *The Law of Unjust Enrichment*, 9th edn (2016), paras 19-9—19.13.

[693] *Dering v Earl of Winchelsea* (1787) 2 B. & P. 270.

[694] *Moschi v Lep Air Services* [1973] A.C. 331.

[695] *Hampton v Minns* [2002] 1 W.L.R. 1. cf. the position under the Insolvency Act 1986 as regards a principal debtor's liability for a "liquidated sum" as explained in *McGuiness v Norwich and Peterborough Building Society* [2011] EWCA Civ 1286, [2012] B.P.I.R. 145 above, para.45-073.

[696] *Hampton v Minns* [2002] 1 W.L.R. 1 at 28. Where the claim is for debt the appropriate period has been said to be six years by analogy with the Limitation Act 1980 s.5: [2002] 1 W.L.R. 1 at 33.

right to contribution have been dealt with in an earlier chapter.[697] The equitable right to contribution arises whether the sureties are joint, joint and several, or several; and whether they are liable on the same or different instruments.[698] And one surety has a right to contribution from another even though he did not know of the other's existence at the time he gave his guarantee. The one essential is that the sureties must all be liable in respect of the same debt or liability.[699] There will, however, be no right of contribution where one surety is a guarantor for another surety.[700] In this event the second surety is only liable to the extent that the first surety does not pay, so that on payment by the first the second is discharged; conversely if the second surety is called upon to pay he will have a right of indemnity (and not merely contribution) against the first surety, for the first surety is in the position of a principal debtor in this case. The right to contribution may, of course, be excluded or modified by express contract.[701] For example, if a third party guarantees a bill of exchange for the benefit of a bank which discounts it, the normal understanding will be that the surety guarantees that payment will be made by one or other of the parties to the bill who are liable on it, whether as acceptor, or drawer or indorser. It will not be the normal understanding that the surety intends to place himself on a level with the drawer. So where bills were guaranteed and, on default by the acceptor, were paid by the drawer, it was held that the drawer had no claim for contribution against the surety.[702]

45-137   **Right of contribution in cases of contracts of indemnity**   It is uncertain how far equitable rights of contribution exist between parties liable under contracts of indemnity, as opposed to contracts of guarantee, or where one is liable under a contract of guarantee and another is liable under a contract of indemnity.[703] Where all are liable under contracts of indemnity there seems no reason why contribution should not be ordered on similar principles to those governing contribution between insurers.[704] But where one person is liable under a guarantee and another under a contract of indemnity it is difficult to see how contribution could be ordered if only because the latter may be a more extensive liability than the former. However, if the liability of the sureties is a liability for damage as opposed to debt, then contribution will always be recoverable in principle under the Civil Liability (Contribution) Act 1978 s.1.

---

697 See Vol.I, paras 17-029 et seq.
698 *Re Ennis* [1893] 3 Ch. 238.
699 *Coope v Twynam* (1823) 1 T. & R. 426; *Ellis v Emmanuel* (1876) 1 Ex. D. 157, 162; and see *Frydman Properties v Bejam* (1987) C.L.Y. 1841; *Stimpson v Smith* [1999] Ch. 340.
700 *Craythorne v Swinburne* (1807) 14 Ves. 160; *Re Denton's Estate* [1904] 2 Ch. 178.
701 *Pendlebury v Walker* (1841) 4 Y. & C. Ex. 424; *Re Ennis* [1893] 3 Ch. 238; *Arcedeckne v Howard* (1875) 45 L.J. Ch. 622; *Stimpson v Smith*, above at 348. It has been assumed that such a modification may be made by implied term: *Hampton v Minns* [2002] 1 W.L.R. 1 at 16–17; *Marsden v Elston* [2001] EWCA Civ 1746. To the extent that such an exclusion affects a "business liability", the exclusion may be subject to a test of reasonableness under the Unfair Contract Terms Act 1977 s.3 (on which, see Vol.I, paras 15-084—15-087). It may also be affected by the Consumer Rights Act 2015 Pt 2 (formerly, the Unfair Terms in Consumer Contracts Regulations 1999 (SI 1999/2083)), on which see generally above, paras 38-220 et seq. and see below, paras 45-155 et seq.
702 *Scholefield Goodman & Sons Ltd v Zyngier* [1986] A.C. 562; *Caledonia North Sea Ltd v British Telecommunications Plc* [2002] 1 Lloyd's Rep. 553, 566–567.
703 This situation could well arise where a hire-purchase contract is guaranteed by a surety, and the dealer also enters into a "recourse agreement" under which he agrees to indemnify the finance company against any loss.
704 See above, para.42-118.

Amount of contribution The equitable rule is that prima facie all sureties are   **45-138**
required as between themselves to contribute to the liability equally and if one of
them receives any security from the creditor on discharging his liability, the security
must, as between the sureties, be brought into account.[705] If the security is worth
more than the amount paid by the one surety, but less than the amount paid by all
the sureties together, it must be apportioned equally between them.[706]

Effect of insolvency of one co-surety At common law, the amount of contribu-   **45-139**
tion to which a co-surety was entitled depended on the number of sureties originally
liable. So that if there were three sureties and one of them paid the whole debt, he
could not recover more than a third from a second surety even though the third
surety was insolvent.[707] But in equity the amount of contribution depends on the
number of solvent sureties at the time when contribution is sought,[708] so that in the
above case contribution of half the debt could be ordered, and the equitable rule now
prevails.[709]

Sureties liable for different amounts If the sureties are not liable for the whole   **45-140**
of the amount due from the principal debtor, and they are liable for different
amounts, then the equitable rule is that contribution will be ordered so that in the
result they will pay in proportion to the maximum liability which each assumed.
Thus if one surety is liable up to a maximum of £50 and another up to a maximum
of £25, contribution will be ordered between them so as to leave the liability in the
proportion of two to one.[710]

Set-off between sureties If the co-sureties run accounts together, the general rule   **45-141**
is that a surety may set-off any monies owing against a claim for contribution by
his co-surety. However, if the creditor's claim against the sureties is secured by a
charge, then the surety's subrogated claim to contribution is also secured and not
subject to set-off.[711]

Contribution where liable for same damage The right of contribution under the   **45-142**
Civil Liability (Contribution) Act 1978 s.1 is entirely dependent on the discretion
of the court to order such contribution as "may be found by the court to be just and
equitable having regard to the extent of that person's responsibility for the damage in question".[712] Consequently, contribution under the Act need not be based on
the principle of equality of treatment among the sureties but may have regard to
wider considerations.

Enforcement of right to contribution Prima facie the equitable right to contribu-   **45-143**
tion arises only when one surety has actually paid more than his due share. So, for

---

[705] *Steel v Dixon* (1881) 17 Ch. D. 825. cf. *Official Trustee in Bankruptcy v Citibank Savings Ltd* [1999]
   B.P.I.R. 754, SC NSW (wider equitable considerations relevant to amount of contribution between
   co-sureties).
[706] *Berridge v Berridge* (1890) 44 Ch. D. 168.
[707] *Browne v Lee* (1827) 6 B. & C. 689.
[708] *Peter v Rich* (1830) 1 Ch. Cas. 19, 34.
[709] *Lowe v Dixon* (1885) 16 Q.B.D. 455.
[710] *Ellesmere Brewery Co v Cooper* [1896] 1 Q.B. 75; *Re Denton's Estate* [1903] 2 Ch. 670.
[711] *Brown v Cork* (1986) P.C.C. 78.
[712] Civil Liability (Contribution) Act 1978 s.2(1).

example, where there are two sureties equally liable, and one paid half the debt, but the other was not called on to pay anything by the creditor, the former was held not to be entitled to contribution.[713] But where the liability guaranteed is a debt payable in instalments, one surety cannot claim contribution from another merely because he has paid more than his share of some of the instalments; he must wait until all the instalments have been paid.[714] The position might be different if separate debts were involved, or even if each instalment created a separate and distinct liability.[715] As with the surety's right to an indemnity,[716] the surety may be able to take steps to enforce his potential right to contribution even before he has paid anything. Thus a surety who has had judgment given against him for the full amount of the liability may obtain a prospective order directing a co-surety on payment by the surety of his own share, to indemnify him against further liability and if the principal creditor is a party to the proceedings, the surety can obtain an order directing the co-surety to pay his share directly to the creditor.[717] The principal debtor should normally be made a party to any proceedings for contribution unless it is plain that no useful purpose would be served by doing so, for example, because he is manifestly insolvent.[718] The statutory right to contribution does not appear to be limited in the same way as the equitable right,[719] so contribution in respect of liability for damage may be sought even prior to payment but no doubt the court will protect the position of the paying surety by appropriate orders.

45-144   **Surety's right to securities held by creditor**   A surety who pays the creditor is subrogated to the creditor's rights against the debtor.[720] This means, inter alia, that he is entitled to the benefit of all securities belonging to the debtor and charged with the liability which the surety has been called upon to meet.[721] This right extends to securities given to the creditor after the contract of suretyship was entered into.[722] As in the case of the right to indemnity and contribution, this right does not arise until actual payment by the surety; but (also as in those cases) the surety's potential right to the securities is recognised and protected even before payment. Thus, as already seen, any release of securities by the creditor may discharge the surety.[723] Furthermore, if the creditor makes further advances to the debtor (for which the surety is not liable) on the same security as the original guaranteed loan, the creditor will be postponed, in respect of these advances, to the surety.[724] Thus, the surety may, on paying off the original debt, require the securities to be transferred to him to satisfy his right to an indemnity in priority to the creditor's later rights.[725] But

---

713   *Davies v Humphreys* (1840) 6 M. & W. 153; see also *Ex p. Snowdon* (1881) 17 Ch. D. 44.
714   *Stirling v Burdett* [1911] 2 Ch. 418.
715   *Stirling v Burdett*, above, at 429.
716   See above, para.45-126.
717   *Wolmershausen v Gullick* [1893] 2 Ch. 514. For form of order, see *Kent v Abrahams* [1928] W.N. 266.
718   *Hay v Carter* [1935] Ch. 397.
719   See s.1(1) of the Civil Liability (Contribution) Act 1978.
720   *Hodgson v Shaw* (1834) 3 My. & K. 183, 190–191.
721   It is uncertain whether *Quennell v Maltby* [1979] 1 W.L.R. 318 illustrates any general principle limiting rights of subrogation where a debt is discharged for some ulterior purpose.
722   *Forbes v Jackson* (1882) 19 Ch. D. 615.
723   See above, para.45-118.
724   *Forbes v Jackson* (1882) 19 Ch. D. 615.
725   *Forbes v Jackson* (1882) 19 Ch. D. 615; *Craythorne v Swinburne* (1807) 14 Ves. 160, 162, 169; *Liberty Mutual Insurance Co (UK) Ltd v HSBC Bank Plc* [2002] EWCA Civ 691 at [43].

where the debtor became bankrupt and the creditor released a security to the trustee in bankruptcy who sold it, it was held that a surety had no equitable charge on the property before payment such as might have justified complaint on the ground that the sale had been made at an undervalue.[726] Prima facie it is not to be expected that the surety should be entitled to recover more than an indemnity by claiming securities or pursuing other subrogation rights, and any surplus must be paid over to the principal debtor.[727] Very clear words would be required to exclude or modify the principal debtor's rights in this respect.[728] As has been seen,[729] if the creditor's claim against the surety is secured by a charge, then the surety's subrogated claim to contribution is also secured and not subject to set-off.[730]

Mercantile Law Amendment Act 1856 s.5   The surety's right to securities is   **45-145**
reinforced by s.5 of the Mercantile Law Amendment Act 1856 which declares that the surety is entitled to have assigned to him "every judgment, specialty or other security which shall be held by the creditor" in respect of the debt.[731] Under this section it has been held that it is unnecessary that the surety should actually take an assignment of a judgment against the debtor,[732] but he cannot enforce such a judgment without permission of the court.[733] The section in effect gives a surety who has paid the guaranteed debt an additional right (both against the debtor and against the co-sureties) to be treated as a statutory assignee of the creditor, and in some respects this right may be wider than his right to indemnity and contribution. For example, a surety who has paid a debt can prove in the bankruptcy of a co-surety for the whole debt though he cannot actually recover more than his due share.[734]

Surety who has paid in same position as creditor   The effect of the equitable   **45-146**
principles discussed above and of s.5 of the Mercantile Law Amendment Act 1856 is that in general the surety is, on payment of the debt, in the same position as the creditor himself. Thus, a surety who has paid a Crown debt is entitled to the Crown rights of priority in the bankruptcy of the principal debtor.[735] And a surety paying a debt which has preference under s.386 of the Insolvency Act 1986 is also entitled to the same priority as the original creditor.[736] But there may be some rights of the principal creditor which are so personal that they do not pass to the surety. It has been held, for example, that the right of a finance company to seize goods let on hire-purchase does not pass to the surety on the ground that it is a "personal right".[737] But this decision is hard to understand for the right to seize the goods is merely an incident of the title to the goods and this would seem plainly to pass to

---

[726] *Pratt's Trustee v Pratt* [1936] 3 All E.R. 901.
[727] *L Lucas Ltd v Export Credits Guarantee Department* [1974] 1 W.L.R. 909.
[728] *L Lucas Ltd v Export Credits Guarantee Department* [1974] 1 W.L.R. 909, at 922.
[729] See above, para.45-141.
[730] *Brown v Cork* (1986) P.C.C. 78.
[731] This provision was introduced to overcome the logical problem that on payment by the surety, the principal debtor's debt was discharged and the creditor's rights thereby extinguished: for this effect, see *Hodgson v Shaw* (1834) 3 My. K. 183 at 191.
[732] *Re M'Myn* (1886) 33 Ch. D. 575; *Batchellor v Lawrence* (1861) 9 C.B.(N.S.) 543.
[733] CPR Pt 50.1, Sch.1 r.46.2; and see *Kayley v Hothersall* [1925] 1 K.B. 607.
[734] *Re Parker* [1894] 3 Ch. 400; and see *Brown v Cork* (1986) P.C.C. 78.
[735] *Re Lord Churchill* (1888) 39 Ch. D. 174; and see *R. v Fay* (1878) 4 L.R.Ir. 606.
[736] *Re Lamplugh Iron Ore Co Ltd* [1927] 1 Ch. 308; cf. *Re Walters' Deed of Guarantee* [1933] Ch. 321 (both decided under earlier legislation).
[737] *Chatterton v Maclean* [1951] 1 All E.R. 761, 766.

the surety under s.5 of the Mercantile Law Amendment Act, though no mention of the section was made in this case.[738]

8. LEGISLATIVE PROTECTION OF SURETIES

45-147 **Introduction** Contracts of guarantee and indemnity have not been the object of general legislative intervention, unlike, for example, contracts of sale of goods[739] or of consumer credit,[740] but they have been subject to more general legislative controls on the parties' freedom of contract, such as those created by the Misrepresentation Act 1967 and the Unfair Contract Terms Act 1977 as regards exemption clauses. Moreover, most clauses in consumer contracts of suretyship are subject to the general test of unfairness contained in Pt 2 of the Consumer Rights Act 2015.[741] And as has been noted, contracts of guarantee (which for this purpose include certain contracts of indemnity) relating to consumer credit agreements and to consumer hire agreements may be affected by the special requirements of the Consumer Credit Act 1974.[742] Finally, a "consumer surety" may be protected by the preventive measures against unfair commercial practices put in place by the Consumer Protection from Unfair Trading Regulations 2008, but will not benefit from the new rights to redress for consumers introduced by amendment of these regulations in 2014.[743]

---

[738] However, the case was cited without disapproval in the decision of the House of Lords in *Moschi v Lep Air Services Ltd* [1973] A.C. 331.

[739] Sale of Goods Act 1979; and see above, paras 44-001 et seq. See also the special provisions governing consumer sales contracts in Pt 1 of the Consumer Rights Act 2015, above, paras 39-002 et seq.

[740] Consumer Credit Act 1974; and see above, paras 39-366 et seq.

[741] Pt 2 of the 2015 Act came into force on October 1, 2015 in respect of contracts entered into on or after that date: see further on the temporal application of the Consumer Rights Act 2015, above, para.38-366. As regards contracts made before that date, the Unfair Terms in Consumer Contracts Regulations 1999 continue to apply: see above, paras 38-220 et seq. Under earlier law, EU and UK legislation governing "off-premises contracts" could apply to contracts of suretyship: see *Bayerische Hypotheken- und Wechselbank AG v Dietzinger* (C-45/96) EU:C:1998:111, [1998] E.C.R. I-1199, so interpreting Directive 85/577 of December 20, 1985 to protect the consumer in respect of contracts negotiated away from business premises [1985] O.J. L372/31, which was implemented in UK law by the Cancellation of Contracts made in a Consumer's Home or Place of Work, etc. Regulations 2008 (SI 2008/1816). However, Directive 85/577 was repealed and replaced by Directive 2011/83/EU on consumer rights O.J. L304/64, art.3(3)(d) of which excludes from its scope "contracts for financial services" and this exclusion was reflected on the directive's implementation in the Consumer Contracts (Information, Cancellation and Additional Charges) Regulations 2013 (SI 2013/3134) reg.6(1)(b) (excluding from their scope "services of a banking, credit, insurance, personal pension, investment or payment nature"). The question whether a contract of suretyship made by a consumer surety would fall within this exclusion and therefore outside the requirements of the 2013 Regulations is considered above, paras 38-079, 38-083 and 38-088.

[742] See above, paras 39-180 et seq. On the other hand, the ECJ held that contracts of suretyship do not themselves fall within Directive 87/102 of December 12, 1986 concerning consumer credit even where neither the principal debtor nor the surety are acting in the course of their trade, business or profession: *Berliner Kindl Brauerei AG v Andreas Siepert* (C-208/98) EU:C:2000:152, [2000] E.C.R. I-1741.

[743] Consumer Protection from Unfair Trading Regulations 2008 (SI 2008/1277) ("2008 Regulations"). The amendments were made by the Consumer Protection from Unfair Trading Regulations 2014 (SI 2014/870).

(a)   Consumer Protection From Unfair Trading Regulations 2008

Unfair Commercial Practices by creditors against consumer sureties   As   **45-148**
explained generally in Ch.38,[744] the Consumer Protection from Unfair Trading
Regulations 2008 (which implement the Unfair Commercial Practices Directive
2005) prohibit "unfair commercial practices" by traders[745] against consumers.[746] For
this purpose, "commercial practices" are unfair if they fail a general test (that a commercial practice "contravenes the requirements of professional diligence" and
"materially distorts, or is likely, to materially distort the economic behaviour of the
average consumer with regard to the product"[747]); if they constitute misleading actions,[748] misleading omissions[749] or aggressive commercial practices[750]; or if they
are included in a list of "commercial practices which are in all circumstances
considered unfair".[751] Under the 2008 Regulations, a "commercial practice" is
defined as:

> "... any act, omission, course of conduct, representation or commercial communication
> (including advertising and marketing) by a trader, which is directly connected with the
> promotion, sale or supply of a product to or from consumers, whether occurring before,
> during or after a commercial transaction (if any) in relation to a product."[752]

Furthermore, "consumer" means "any individual who in relation to a commercial
practice is acting for purposes that are wholly or mainly outside that individual's
business"[753] and "product" includes goods, a service, digital content, immoveable
property, and rights or obligations.[754] It will be seen, therefore, that the prohibitions (and consequential enforcement measures[755]) in the 2008 Regulations may apply to the relationship between a commercial lender (the "trader") and a "consumer
surety" (i.e. an individual who concludes a contract of suretyship for purposes
which are wholly or mainly outside that individual's business), for in this situation, the consumer surety may be said to supply a "product" (the financial service
of undertaking to be answerable for the principal debtor's debts[756]) to the com

---

[744] Above, paras 38-157 et seq.

[745] For the definition of "trader" see 2008 Regulations reg.2(1) "trader" and "business", and above,
para.38-168.

[746] Consumer Protection from Unfair Trading Regulations 2008 (SI 2008/1277); Directive 2005/29 on
unfair commercial practices [2005] O.J. L149/22.

[747] 2008 Regulations reg.3(3).

[748] 2008 Regulations regs 3(4)(a) and 5.

[749] 2008 Regulations regs 3(4)(b) and 6.

[750] 2008 Regulations regs 3(4)(c) and 7.

[751] 2008 Regulations regs 3(4)(d) and Sch.1.

[752] 2008 Regulations reg.2(1) "commercial practice". On this definition and the question whether an
isolated event may constitute a commercial practice for this purpose, see above, paras 38-166—38-
167.

[753] 2008 Regulations reg.2(1) "consumer" (as amended by the Consumer Protection from Unfair Trading Regulations 2014 (SI 2014/870) reg.2(3).

[754] 2008 Regulations reg.2(1) "product" (as amended by 2014 Regulations reg.2(6)).

[755] Notably, criminal offences and the possibility of injunctions brought by designated enforcement
authorities: 2008 Regulations Pts 3 and 4 respectively and see above, paras 38-170—38-171, which
also explain the possible availability of enforcement orders under Pt 8 of the Enterprise Act 2002.

[756] "Financial services" are clearly generally included within "product" as the 2005 Directive (which
the 2008 Regulations implement) makes special provision for "financial services" on this premise:
2005 Directive art.3(9), which refers to the definition of "financial service" in Directive 2002/
65/EC of the European Parliament and of the Council of September 23, 2002 concerning the distance

mercial lender, it being expressly stated by the Regulations that a "commercial practice" by a trader may be "directly connected with the promotion, sale or supply of a product to *or from* consumers".[757]

45-149 **No "rights of redress" for consumer sureties** The Unfair Commercial Practices Directive states that it is "without prejudice to contract law"[750] and as originally issued the 2008 Regulations did not provide a remedy to a consumer who had been affected by any unfair commercial practice by a trader.[759] However, on the recommendation of the Law Commissions,[760] in 2014 the 2008 Regulations were amended by the Consumer Protection (Amendment) Regulations 2014[761] so as to create new "rights to redress" in consumers against traders in respect of *certain* unfair commercial practices prohibited by the 2008 Regulations. The details of these rights are explained above in Ch.38,[762] but here it should be noted that they are generally available to consumers who are victims of only two forms of unfair commercial practice—"misleading actions" and "aggressive practices" and who have entered a contract with or made a payment to the trader as a result.[763] For present purposes, however, it is to be noted that a consumer surety cannot enjoy any of the "rights to redress" created by the 2014 Regulations, as the first condition for the existence of these rights is that:

"(a) the consumer enters into a contract with a trader for the sale or supply of a product by the trader (a 'business to consumer contract'),

(b) the consumer enters into a contract with a trader for the sale of goods to the trader (a 'consumer to business contract'), or

(c) the consumer makes a payment to a trader for the supply of a product (a 'consumer payment')."[764]

It will be seen that a consumer surety will not be in a position to satisfy any one of these conditions, given that he or she is not supplied with "a product" by the trader (so as to fall under (a)), does not contract to sell goods to the trader (so as to fall under (b)), nor makes any payment to a trader *for the supply of a product* (so as to fall under (c)): as a result, the new rights to redress arise in "consumer to business contracts" only in the case of contracts of sale of goods.[765] This absence of any rights to redress in a consumer surety against a trader/lender under the 2008 Regulations means that a consumer surety will continue to enjoy any right to damages to which he or she is entitled under the Misrepresentation Act 1967 s.2.[766]

---

marketing of consumer financial services [2002] O.J. L271/16, art.2(b), being "any service of a banking, credit, insurance, personal pension, investment or payment nature".

[757] 2008 Regulations reg.2(1) "commercial practice" (emphasis added).

[758] 2005 Directive art.3(2).

[759] 2008 Regulations reg.29 in its original form. See above, para.38-157.

[760] Law Commission, Scottish Law Commission, *Consumer Redress for Misleading and Aggressive Practices* (2012) Law Com No.332, Scot Law Com No.226.

[761] SI 2014/870.

[762] Above, paras 38-172—38-210.

[763] 2008 Regulations reg.27A(4) (as inserted by the 2014 Regulations).

[764] 2008 Regulations reg.27A(2) (as inserted by the 2014 Regulations).

[765] Moreover, the definition of "product" for the purposes of Pt 4A rights to redress is restricted by 2008 Regulations reg.27D so as to restrict its application to financial services: see above, paras 38-176. The Law Commissions' Report, *Consumer Redress for Misleading and Aggressive Practices* (noted above) did not discuss the position of consumer sureties.

[766] Where a consumer enjoys a right of redress under Pt 4A of the 2008 Regulations (as inserted by the

(b) Misrepresentation Act 1967

Misrepresentation Act 1967 and Consumer Rights Act 2015 Until the coming into force of the Consumer Rights Act 2015 on October 1, 2015,[767] any attempted exclusion by the creditor of his liability for misrepresentation which induces the surety to contract was subject to a test of reasonableness under s.3 of the Misrepresentation Act 1967,[768] whether or not the surety "dealt as consumer" in entering the contract[769] and this control affects attempts to exclude the creditor's liability in damages or to have the contract of suretyship rescinded by the surety.[770] However, s.3 of the 1967 Act no longer applies to contracts entered on or after October 1, 2015 where they are "consumer contracts" within the meaning of Pt 2 of the 2015 Act,[771] and so where a trader/creditor seeks to exclude or restrict its liabilities for misrepresentation under a contract of suretyship with a consumer/surety, this exclusion or restriction will fall under the general requirements of fairness and transparency which Pt 2 of the 2015 Act contains.[772]   **45-150**

(c) Unfair Contract Terms Act 1977

Unfair Contract Terms Act 1977 and Consumer Rights Act 2015 Until the coming into force of the Consumer Rights Act 2015 on October 1, 2015,[773] the Unfair Contract Terms Act 1977 ss.2 and 3 provided controls on exemption clauses which sought to exclude a person's business liability for negligence or for breach of contract respectively, in the latter case being restricted to cases where a party contracts on the other's "written terms of business" or "deals as consumer".[774] However, on the coming into force of the 2015 Act, the references in the 1977 Act to "dealing as consumer" were deleted[775] and s.2 and s.3 no longer apply to "consumer contracts" within the meaning of Pt 2 of the 2015 Act entered into on or after October 1, 2015, the terms in these contracts instead falling under the controls on the fairness and transparency of terms which Pt 2 of the Act itself provides.[776]   **45-151**

2014 Regulations) the consumer no longer possesses any right to damages under the Misrepresentation Act 1967 s.2: Misrepresentation Act 1967 s.2(4) as inserted by 2014 Regulations reg.5 and see above, para.38-208.

[767] See further above, para.38-216.

[768] See Unfair Contract Terms Act 1977 s.11 and generally, Vol.I, paras 15-062 et seq., 38-130—38-131 where it is explained that the reference to persons "dealing as consumer" was deleted by the 2015 Act.

[769] Misrepresentation Act 1967 s.3 (as amended by Unfair Contract Terms Act 1977 s.8).

[770] Misrepresentation Act 1967 s.3(b) (as amended by Unfair Contract Terms Act 1977 s.8). This law still applies to contracts made before October 1, 2015.

[771] 2015 Act s.75, Sch.4 para.1, creating new subs.(2) to s.3 of the 1967 Act.

[772] 2015 Act ss.62 and 68–69, on which see above, paras 38-365 et seq.

[773] Pt 2 of the Consumer Rights Act 2015 came into force on October 1, 2015 so as to apply to contracts made on or after that date: see above, para.38-216 (noting the qualifications on this position).

[774] Unfair Contract Terms Act 1977 ss.2 and 3 and see Vol.I, paras 15-081—15-087.

[775] 2015 Act s.75 Sch.4 paras 5(2) and 11 and see Vol.I, para.15-079.

[776] 2015 Act s.75, Sch.4 paras 4 and 5 inserted new s.2(4) and 3(3) in the 1977 Act. On these changes see generally Vol.I, paras 15-083 and 15-087.

45-152 **Application of 1977 Act to contracts of suretyship** Exemption clauses in contracts of suretyship may be caught by ss.2 or 3 of the 1977 Act (as amended).[777] Thus, any attempt by a creditor acting in the course of business to exclude his liability in the tort of negligence, for example, as a result of explaining inadequately the effect of a guarantee,[778] is subject to a test of reasonableness.[779] Again, as against a surety dealing on the written standard terms of business[780] of the creditor who enters the contract in the course of a business,[781] any exclusion of a surety's right of set-off against the creditor would also be subject to a test of reasonableness.[782]

45-153 **Exclusion of surety's rights to be discharged** On the other hand, the Unfair Contract Terms Act 1977 does not affect any exclusion in the contract of suretyship of the surety's various rights to be discharged. These rights include a right of a guarantor at common law to be discharged if the principal debtor is discharged,[783] a right which can clearly be excluded as this is one of the important distinguishing features between contracts of guarantee and contracts of indemnity, where the surety undertakes a primary liability to the creditor, independent of any liability to him in the principal debtor.[784] Moreover, it has also become not infrequent for creditors to exclude a surety's "equitable rights" against the creditor, such as his right to be discharged if the creditor agrees to discharge the principal debtor[785] or if the creditor varies the terms of the contract with the principal debtor to his prejudice.[786] At common law, it is clear that these rights in the surety can be excluded by the contract of suretyship.[787] These clauses are not caught by the Unfair Contract Terms Act 1977 because, despite common use of the terminology of exclusion, they are not "exemption clauses" within the meaning of s.13 of that Act, for this section ties their effect to the exclusion or restriction of any liability, whether by way of subjecting its enforcement to restrictive conditions[788] or excluding any right or remedy in respect of the liability.[789] By contrast, a clause in a contract of suretyship which excludes the discharge of the surety as a result, for example, of the creditor's variation of the contract, does not exclude any right of the surety in respect of a liability in the creditor: rather, it prevents the discharge of the surety from liability to the creditor.

45-154 However, the position is different if the circumstances which give rise to the right

---

[777] See above, para.45-151.
[778] *Perry v Midland Bank Plc* [1987] F.L.R. 237; and see above, para.45-039 for the ambit of such a liability in the tort of negligence.
[779] Unfair Contract Terms Act 1977 s.2(2); and cf. *Smith v Eric S Bush* [1990] 1 A.C. 831.
[780] But see para.45-151 on the effect of the Consumer Rights Act 2015 in this respect.
[781] Unfair Contract Terms Act 1977 ss.1(3) and 3(1). As regards contracts made before October 1, 2015 the protections in s.2 apply more general and in s.3 apply also to a surety "dealing as consumer".
[782] Unfair Contract Terms Act 1977 s.3(2)(a) and cf. *WRM Group Ltd v Wood* [1998] C.L.C. 189.
[783] See above, para.45-086, where it is noted that this rule does not apply to contracts of indemnity.
[784] See above, paras 45-008, 45-044.
[785] See above, para.45-091.
[786] See above, paras 45-104 et seq.
[787] See above, paras 45-092, 45-112.
[788] Unfair Contract Terms Act 1977 s.13(1)(a). This definition applies to the controls found in ss.2(2) and 3(1) of this Act. While not concerned with exemption clauses in this sense, s.3(2)(b) of the same Act (on which see Vol.I, para.15-085) is not likely to come to the aid of the surety in these circumstances. For it is difficult to see how an exclusion by a creditor of the surety's rights to be discharged would constitute as against the surety an attempt "(i) to render a contractual performance substantially different from that which was reasonably expected of him, or (ii) in respect of the whole or any part of his contractual obligation, to render no performance at all".
[789] 1977 Act s.13(1)(b).

in the surety to be discharged also give rise to liability in the creditor, for example, where the latter has undertaken by its contract the validity of a security provided by the principal debtor.[790] In these circumstances, where the surety contracted on the creditor's written standard terms of business any exclusion of liability in the creditor in respect of the validity of the security would be subject to a reasonableness test under s.3(1) of the Unfair Contract Terms Act 1977.[791] Similarly, in principle if the creditor's conduct were to give rise to a liability in tort for negligence, then any exclusion of such a liability would be subject to a test of reasonableness where the contract of suretyship was made in the course of the creditor's business.[792] Formerly an example of such a liability in tort could be found in the case of the creditor's neglect in relation to securities,[793] but the existence of such a tortious liability has been disapproved by the Privy Council.[794] Finally, if the creditor has undertaken under the contract of guarantee to extend credit to the principal debtor, but has failed to do so in conformity with the contract, then any term of the contract purporting to exclude liability in the creditor for any loss which this causes to the *guarantor* would be caught by s.3(1) of the Unfair Contract Terms Act 1977 if the creditor acted in the course of business and on his written standard terms of business.[795] However, while a "no set-off" clause in a contract of guarantee (which intends to prevent a guarantor from setting off any claims against the creditor's claim for payment under the contract) has been held capable of falling within s.3,[796] in the circumstances of the case (which included the guarantor's access to legal advice at the time of signing the contract) the clause was held reasonable for the purposes of s.11 of the 1977 Act.[797]

(d)   Unfair Terms in Consumer Contracts

Introduction   As explained in Ch.38, the EU Directive on unfair terms in   **45-155**
consumer contracts of 1993[798] was formerly implemented in UK law by the Unfair

---

[790] *TCB Ltd v Gray* [1987] Ch. 458n (in which the court rejected the contention that there was such an undertaking). As regards contracts made before October 1, 2015, the protection in s.3 applies also for persons "dealing as consumer": above, para.45-151.

[791] Unfair Contract Terms Act 1977 s.3(1). It would appear that if such a clause failed the reasonableness test, it could nevertheless still be effective to prevent the surety from being discharged from his liability, as the effect of s.3 is to prevent the creditor from "excluding or restricting any liability of his in respect of breach ... except in so far as ... the contract term satisfies the requirement of reasonableness". cf. Peel (ed.), *Treitel on The Law of Contract*, 14th edn (2015), paras 7-074—7-075.

[792] Unfair Contract Terms Act 1977 ss.1(3) and 2(2). As earlier noted, these provisions do not apply to "consumer contracts" made on or after October 1, 2015: above, para.45-151.

[793] *Standard Chartered Bank v Walker* [1982] 1 W.L.R. 1410, 1416.

[794] *China and South Seas Bank v Tan Soon Gin* [1990] 1 A.C. 536, 543–544; and see above, para.45-121.

[795] Again, this protection also applies as regards contracts made before October 1, 2015 to persons "dealing as consumer", but does not apply to consumer contracts made on or after that date: above, para.45-151.

[796] *Governor and Co of the Bank of Scotland v Singh* Unreported June 17, 2005, QB Mercantile Ct, Manchester at [71]–[75] (although the decision of HH Judge Kershaw Q.C. on this point is not free from doubt given the points which he makes at [75]). On the application of s.3 of the 1977 Act to exclusions of rights of set off more generally see Vol.I, para.15-069.

[797] *Governor and Co of the Bank of Scotland v Singh* Unreported June 17, 2005, QB Mercantile Ct, Manchester at [80]–[81], [84].

[798] Directive 93/13 of April 5, 1993 on unfair terms in consumer contracts [1993] O.J. L95/29. The fol-

Terms in Consumer Regulations 1999[799] but, for contracts made on or after October 1, 2015 the Consumer Rights Act 2015 revoked the 1999 Regulations and created its own controls on unfair terms in consumer contracts, implementing the 1993 Directive and in certain respects going beyond its requirements. These legislative controls and their differences have been discussed generally earlier in the present volume,[800] but here some account will be made of their possible effects on contracts of suretyship.

45-156   **Application of these controls to contracts of suretyship**   The question whether the 1999 Regulations and, for contracts made on or after October 1, 2015, the Consumer Rights Act 2015 Pt 2 apply to contracts of suretyship received no definitive answer until the recent Order of the Court of Justice of the EU in *Tarcău v Banca Comercială Intesa Sanpaolo România SA*.[801] The 1999 Regulations did not specify the types of contract to which they applied beyond defining their parties; and these parties were referred to as the "seller and supplier" (the person contracting in the course of business) and "consumer" (the individual not contracting in the course of business), this reflecting closely the terminology used by the English language version of the 1993 Directive.[802] This terminology suggested that the business sells goods (or other property) or supplies services (including financial services) *to* the consumer,[803] and this in turn suggested that the 1993 Directive (and therefore also the 1999 Regulations) applies to contracts of suretyship only in the rare situation where the *creditor* is a consumer, and the surety the person acting in the course of business.[804] However, other language versions of the 1993 Directive instead refer more openly to a "professional" or "tradesman" defined in a similar manner,[805] and, noting this, the Court of Justice of the EU clarified that the 1993 Directive applies to *all types* of consumer contract, defined merely by reference to their parties: persons contracting in the course of business on the one hand, and consumers, viz, natural persons contracting other than in the course of business, on the other.[806] According to the Court of Justice, this interpretation gives effect to the purpose of the Directive in the protection of consumers as "weaker parties" as

---

lowing notes refer to the 1999 Regulations.

[799] Unfair Terms in Consumer Contracts Regulations 1999 (SI 1999/2083).

[800] Above, paras 38-220 et seq.

[801] C-74/15, EU:C:2015:772, Order of CJEU November 19, 2015 ("Tarčau (C-74/15)") (an "order" is made by the CJEU where it considers that the question for a preliminary ruling admits of no reasonable doubt). In the 32nd edition (2015) of the present work, Vol.II, para.45-156 (and corresponding paragraphs in earlier editions) it was argued that the 1993 Directive (and, therefore, its UK implementing legislation, the 1999 Regulations) applies to contracts of suretyship where the surety is a "consumer" by reference to the same textual and teleological grounds as those which formed the basis of the reasoning of the CJEU in *Brusse v Jahani BV* (C-488/11) EU:C:2013:341, May 30, 2013 and *Šiba v Devėnas* (C-537/13) EU:C:2015:14, January 15, 2015 [2015] Bus. L.R. 291 on which its order in *Tarčau* was based: see above, para.38-222.

[802] Above, para.38-226.

[803] Above, para.38-226.

[804] An example of a contract covered in this way would be a loan by a private individual to another person, whether for that person's business or not, which is guaranteed by a bank or other financial institution. Here, the guarantor (the bank) would be acting in the course of a business and the creditor (the lender of the money) could fall within the definition of a "consumer".

[805] The non-consumer party to the contract is termed *professionnel* in the French and *Gewerbetreibender* in the German versions of Directive 93/13/EEC art.2(c).

[806] *Brusse v Jahani BV* (C-488/11) EU:C:2013:341, May 30, 2013; *Šiba v Devėnas* (C-537/13) EU:C:2015:14, January 15, 2015 [2015] Bus. L.R. 291 on which see above, para.38-222.

regards both their bargaining power and their level of knowledge.[807] This general view was then applied to the context of contracts of suretyship by the Court of Justice in *Tarcău*.[808] There, the parents of the director and sole shareholder of a commercial company had guaranteed and provided real security for the payment of sums owed by that company to a bank. The national court making the preliminary reference considered that the 1993 Directive (and therefore its national implementing legislation) applied only to contracts for the supply of goods or services *to* consumers,[809] but the Court of Justice confirmed that the Directive applies to "all contracts" between consumers and sellers or suppliers and that:

> "... [t]he purpose of the contract is thus, subject to the exceptions listed in the recital 10 of the Directive ... irrelevant in determining the scope of the directive."[810]

As a result, the 1993 Directive could apply to a contract of guarantee undertaken by a "consumer" or to another contract under which a "consumer" provides security for the performance of an obligation by another person, even if that other person is a commercial company rather than another consumer.[811] Indeed, in the view of the Court of Justice, the protection provided by the 1993 Directive for consumers as "weaker parties":

> "... is particularly important in the case of a contract providing security or a contract of guarantee concluded between a banking institution and a consumer. Such a contract is based on a personal commitment of the surety or guarantor to pay a contractual debt owed by a third party. That commitment involves onerous obligations for the person entering into it, the effect of which is to subject that person's own property to a financial risk which is often difficult to quantify."[812]

For this purpose, "consumer" is an "objective" concept (and therefore does not depend on the knowledge or bargaining power of the individual) and is to be assessed by reference to the "functional criterion" of whether the contract arose in the course of activities outside his trade, business or profession.[813] The question whether a particular person is to be categorised as a "consumer" in this way remains for the national court to determine taking into account of all the circumstances,[814] but in the case of security being provided for performance of the obligations of a commercial company, this would turn on whether he "... acted for purposes relating to his trade, business or profession or because of functional links he has with that company, such as a directorship or non-negligible shareholding" or whether instead

---

[807] *Brusse v Jahani BV* (C-488/11) at para.31.

[808] C-74/15 (Order of CJEU) November 19, 2015.

[809] *Tarcău* (C-74/15) at para.14.

[810] *Tarcău* (C-74/15) at para.22. On these "exceptions" see above para.38-222 (note) referring to recital 10 of the 1993 Directive. The CJEU contrasted the position under the former Council Directive 87/102/EEC of 22 December 1986 concerning consumer credit (itself repealed by Directive 2008/48/EC of the European Parliament and of the Council of 23 April 2008 on credit agreements for consumers) which applied only to "contracts whereby a creditor grants or promises to grant a consumer a credit" which has led the Court to exclude contracts of guarantee from its scope: *Tarcău* (C-74/15) at para.22, citing *Berliner Kindl Brauerie AG v Siepert* (C-208/98) EU:C:2000:152, [2000] E.C.R. I-1741 at paras 17–23.

[811] *Tarcău* (C-74/15) at paras 24–25.

[812] *Tarcău* (C-74/15) at para.25.

[813] *Tarcău* (C-74/15) at para.27 citing *Costea v SC Volksbank Romania SA* (C-110/14) EU:C:2015:538, April 23, 2015 para.21, on which see above, para.38-034.

[814] *Tarcău* (C-74/15) at para.28.

"he acted for purposes of a private nature".[815] It is submitted that, given the reasoning of the Court of Justice, the 1993 Directive applies to all types of suretyship contracts and that no distinction is to be made for this purpose between contracts of guarantee and contracts of indemnity as this distinction is understood by English law.[816] Indeed, in its earlier decision in *Ducura v SC Bancpost SA*, the Court of Justice held that the 1993 Directive could apply to a contract under which the alleged "consumer" contracted as "co-debtor" to a person concluding a contract of consumer credit.[817]

45-157 **Consumer Rights Act 2015** It is submitted, therefore, that earlier English decisions on the application of the 1999 Regulations to contracts of suretyship must be read subject to the very clear ruling by the Court of Justice in *Tarčau* on the application of the 1993 Directive.[818] Similarly, the provisions of the Consumer Rights Act 2015 which replaced the 1999 Regulations and which now implement the 1993 Directive in UK law by subjecting the terms of a consumer contract to requirements of unfairness and transparency must also be interpreted as applying to contracts by which a "consumer" guarantees the debt or other obligation of a third party, whether or not that third party is itself a "consumer".[819] In this respect, the terminology used by the 2015 Act to designate the parties to "consumer contracts" fits more naturally the context of suretyship, as it refers to the business party as the "trader" rather than the "seller or supplier".[820] It should also be noted that the 2015 Act extends (or appears to extend) the definition of "consumer" to an individual contracting "wholly or *mainly*" for purposes outside that individual's trade, etc.[821] As a result, the explanation of the situations in which an individual concluding a contract of suretyship with a trader (for example, a bank) set out by the Court of Justice in *Tarčau* and its surrounding case-law may need to be adjusted so as to include persons acting *mainly* and not merely *wholly* outside their "trade, business, craft or profession". In *Harvey v Dunbar Assets Plc*[822] the Court of Appeal was prepared to assume (without deciding) that the decision in *Tarčau* had the effect that an individual who guarantees a company debt *can* be a consumer, provided that he is not connected to the company and has been acting outside his business, trader

---

[815] *Tarčau* (C-74/15) at para.29.

[816] Above, para.45-007.

[817] C-348/14, EU:C:2015:447 July 9, 2015 (available in French) at paras 35–38. See also *Dumitraş v BRD Groupe Société Générale* (C-534/15) EU:C:2016:700, Order of the CJEU of September 14, 2016 (contract of guarantee by individual in context of group of companies); *Bachman v FAER IFN SA* (C-535/16) EU:C:2017:321 (Order of the Court of April 27, 2017, available in French) (contract of novation under which individual undertook obligations arising under earlier commercial contract of loan).

[818] *Governor and Co of the Bank of Scotland v Singh* Unreported June 17, 2005, QB, Mercantile Ct, Manchester; *Manches LLP v Freer* [2006] EWHC 991 (QB) at [25]; *Williamson v Governor of the Bank of Scotland* [2006] EWHC 1289 (Ch) (1999 Regulations cannot apply to contracts of guarantee undertaken by a natural person acting other than in the course of business). cf. *Barclays Bank Plc v Kufner; Royal Bank of Scotland v Chandra* [2010] EWHC 105 (Ch), [2010] 1 Lloyd's Rep. 677 at [102] (affirmed [2011] EWCA Civ 192, [2011] Bus. L.R. D149 on other grounds); *United Trust Bank Ltd v Dohil* [2011] EWHC 3302 (QB) at [73] (1999 Regulations can apply to contracts of guarantee undertaken by a natural person acting other than in the course of business).

[819] It is to be noted that in *Tarčau* itself the principal debtor was a commercial company: above, para.45-156. The general provisions implementing the 1993 Directive are contained in the 2015 Act ss.61–64, 67–71, 73–74: see above, paras 38-382 et seq.

[820] Consumer Rights Act 2015 s.2(2), above, para.38-383.

[821] 2015 Act s.2(3); s.76(2), above, para.38-323.

[822] [2017] EWCA Civ 60, [2017] Bus. L.R. 784 at [68]–[70].

or profession, though the Court of Appeal held that the individual before them did not satisfy those conditions.

Vulnerable types of clause   Where a court holds that a contract of suretyship **45-158** counts as a "consumer contract" (under which a "consumer" undertakes an obligation or liability towards a business creditor, such as a bank), there are a number of possible types of term where the 2015 Act's controls on their fairness and transparency may be significant. The interpretation of these controls by the Court of Justice of the EU has been demanding, particularly in relation to the requirements of transparency (which stands as an independent requirement and also plays a significant role in the fairness of a contract term).[823] In this respect, it is submitted that those clauses under which the creditor excludes the various rights of the surety to be discharged would be particularly vulnerable to the charge of unfairness, given that the average consumer/guarantor may well not "be able to assess the potentially significant economic consequences for him resulting from" such an exclusion.[824] Perhaps most difficult in this respect is the application of the controls on unfair terms to clauses in a contract of suretyship which retain the liability of the surety even where the principal debtor is discharged. In the case of a contract of guarantee, such a clause excludes a right in the surety against the creditor,[825] and could well be seen as causing a "significant imbalance in the parties' rights and obligations under the contract to the detriment of the consumer".[826] However, it is of the very nature of a contract of *indemnity* that liability in the surety exists irrespective of the liability (and therefore of the discharge) of the principal debtor. It could, therefore, be argued that a clause or clauses which merely create this result thereby define the main subject matter of the contract so as to fall within the first limb of the "core exclusion" from the test of unfairness under s.64 of the 2015 Act.[827]

At first sight, more straightforward is the impact of Pt 2 of the 2015 Act[828] on **45-159** clauses in a contract of guarantee which on their terms exclude the right of the surety to be discharged by reason of the variation by the creditor of the contract with the principal debtor,[829] including making a binding agreement to give the latter time,[830] by reason of the release of any co-surety,[831] or by dealing negligently with any security for the debt,[832] or excluding the suretyship's right to set-off or counterclaim.[833] Again, such clauses could well be regarded as creating, contrary to the requirement of good faith, a "significant imbalance in the parties' rights and obligations under the contract to the detriment of the consumer".[834] In the case of a clause in a contract of suretyship which allows the creditor to vary the interest rate

---

[823] Above, paras 38-299—38-414.
[824] See *Kásler v OTP Jelzálogbank Zrt* (C-26/13) EU:C:2014:282, April 30, 2014 at para.74 (in relation to the proviso of transparency in art.4(2) of the Directive). See generally above, paras. 38-261 et seq.
[825] See above, paras 45-086 et seq. as to the nature of this right.
[826] 1999 Regulations reg.5(1); 2015 Act s.62(4).
[827] This exclusion was formerly contained in the 1999 Regulations reg.6(2). See further above, paras 38-245—38-264 and 38-394—38-400.
[828] See above, para.45-157.
[829] See above, para.45-104.
[830] See above, paras 45-108—45-109.
[831] See above, para.45-117.
[832] See above, para.45-120.
[833] Above, para.45-085 and see Andrews and Millett, *The Law of Guarantees*, 7th edn (2015), para.3-038.
[834] 2015 Act s.62(4); formerly 1999 Regulations reg.5(1).

which the principal debtor must pay and for which the surety will therefore in principle also be liable, one of the terms listed in Sch.2 Pt 1 of the 2015 Act which "may be regarded as unfair"[835] appears relevant, as para.11 of this Schedule contains a:

> "term which has the object or effect of enabling the trader to alter the terms of the contract unilaterally without a valid reason which is specified in the contract."[836]

However, in Pt 2 of the Schedule the scope of this example is limited as para.11 is stated as not including:

> "a term by which a supplier of financial services reserves the right to alter the rate of interest payable by or due to the consumer … without notice where there is a valid reason, if—
>
> (a)   the supplier is required to inform the consumer of the alteration at the earliest opportunity, and
>
> (b)   the consumer is free to dissolve the contract immediately." [837]

This limitation is clearly intended to deal with terms which allow for a variable interest rate in contracts of loan to consumers, but it could be used by a creditor (the "trader") to argue that what is fair as regards a (consumer) principal debtor should also be regarded as fair for a (consumer) guarantor. Moreover, Pt 2 of Sch.2 further qualifies the possible unfairness of clauses which reserve a right to unilateral variations,[838] stating that para.11 does not apply:

> "… to a term under which a trader reserves the right to alter unilaterally the conditions of a contract of indeterminate duration if—
>
> (a)   the trader is required to inform the consumer with reasonable notice, and
>
> (b)   the consumer is free to dissolve the contract." [839]

This qualification could well apply by analogy to a "continuing guarantee"[840] made by a consumer which is of indefinite duration. It will be seen, though, that in either case, the conditions for the application of the qualifications on the example in para.11 are that the consumer is given notice of the variation and also a right to dissolve the contract.

45-160   Perhaps the strongest candidate to be regarded as unfair in a contract of suretyship is where the creditor excludes a consumer surety's right to be discharged on the ground of the creditor's neglect in relation to security.[841] Such a clause, which is aimed at defeating the clear policy of protection which equity established for sureties and which is conditional on some negligence in the creditor,[842] may well be held to be unfair.[843]

---

835   2015 Act s.63(1); formerly 1999 Regulations reg.5(5).
836   The equivalent provision in the 1999 Regulations is found in Sch.2 para.1(j).
837   2015 Act Sch.2 para.22; formerly 1999 Regulations Sch.2 para.2(b).
838   2015 Act is found in Sch.2 Pt 2 para.23; formerly 1999 Regulations Sch.2 para.2(b).
839   2015 Act Sch.2 Pt 2 para.23; formerly 1999 Regulations Sch.2 para.2(b).
840   See above, para.45-077.
841   See above, para.45-120.
842   See above, para.45-124 as to the significance of the term negligence in this context.
843   2015 Act s.62(4); formerly 1999 Regulations reg.5(1).

INDEX

FROM SWEET & MAXWELL

This index has been prepared using Sweet and Maxwell's Legal Taxonomy. Main index entries conform to keywords provided by the Legal Taxonomy except where references to specific documents or non-standard terms (denoted by quotation marks) have been included. These keywords provide a means of identifying similar concepts in other Sweet & Maxwell publications and online services to which keywords from the Legal Taxonomy have been applied. Readers may find some minor differences between terms used in the text and those which appear in the index. Suggestions to *sweetandmaxwell.taxonomy@tr.com*.

Location references are to chapters and paragraphs. Chapters 1 to 30 are in Volume I and Chapters 31 to 45 in Volume II.